A Concordance to the Poems of

W. B. YEATS

THE CORNELL CONCORDANCES

Supervisory Committee

M. H. Abrams

Ephim G. Fogel

William R. Keast

James A. Painter, *Computer Programmer*

S. M. Parrish, *General Editor*

POEMS OF MATTHEW ARNOLD
Edited by S. M. Parrish

POEMS OF W. B. YEATS
Edited by S. M. Parrish

A Concordance to the Poems of
W. B. YEATS

Edited by

STEPHEN MAXFIELD PARRISH

Programmed by

JAMES ALLAN PAINTER

Cornell University Press

ITHACA, NEW YORK

CORNELL UNIVERSITY PRESS

First published 1963

Library of Congress Catalog Card Number: 63–11493

PRINTED IN THE UNITED STATES OF AMERICA

EDITOR'S PREFACE

TO invoke the aid of an electronic computer in mapping Yeats's private worlds of myth and symbol and Irish legend may well arouse disquiet. What humanist can remain undisturbed at the cold prospect of tabulating cones (1 occurrence), cubes (2), and gyres (14, in its various forms)— those magical designs which, Yeats tells us, "Robartes describes the Judwali Arabs as making upon the sand for the instruction of their young people, and which, according to tradition, were drawn as described in sleep by the wife of Kusta-Ben-Luka"? But the reader of Yeats who can learn to tolerate these ironies will find in this concordance (produced on an IBM 704 Electronic Data Processing Machine) information never before readily accessible. For this is, I believe, the first concordance of a symbolist poet ever undertaken. Apart from the ordinary uses of such an index, the reader has available here the means of tracing surely and in intricate detail the language patterns of a symbolist imagination.

Consider, to take an elementary instance, the advantages of cataloguing the extraordinary birds that beat, wheel, cry, hover, and keen through Yeats's poems. Birds, to be sure, warble outrageously through all English poetry; in some peculiar way they express the national genius. But a full inventory of this Irish poet's birds overwhelms the mind. I count, for a beginning, some 8 hawks, 21 owls, 6 bats, 2 kites, 6 falcons, 15 eagles, 8 ospreys, and 5 kingfishers—all birds of prey—as well as 2 robins, 2 partridges, 2 gannets, 9 swallows, 3 water-hens, 2 water-fowls, 4 moor-hens, 2 peahens, 3 moorfowl, 10 herons, 12 curlews, 3 bitterns, 6 gulls, 2 seagulls, 1 sea-mew, 10 doves, 1 ringdove, 4 pigeons, 1 crane, 2 night-ingales, 5 sparrows, 4 parrots, 2 crows, 11 cocks, 4 hens, 13 peacocks, 1 daw, 2 rooks, 1 stare, 1 nightjar, 2 lapwings, 1 jay, 1 cormorant, 1 grouse, 2 ducks, 16 swans, 6 ravens, 2 woodpeckers, 3 flamingos, 4 linnets, 2 snipes, 4 peewits, 8 geese, 1 barnacle-goose, 1 turkey, and 6 cuckoos— not to speak of the halcyon (3), the phoenix (8), or the bird that Grecian goldsmiths make. "Bird," incidentally, has 163 occurrences in all its forms, not counting such compounds as "gamebird" (2), "cattle-birds" (1), "sea-

bird" (2), and "song-bird" (2). To carry on a study of bird imagery one would, of course, have not only to complete the inventory, but also to move out through such associated words as "bill," "wing," "feather," "claw," "pinion," "perch," "nest," "cage," and "flutter." And one might appropriately hunt down Yeats's other winged creatures—wasps (1), bees (39), moths (18), grasshoppers (7), flies (27), and the like, ending perhaps with vampire (1) and muse (11).

The symbolic importance of Yeats's birds has been recognized by critics and scholars. Yeats's landscape world of images, we all agree, is a forest of trees (each with a mask hanging on the trunk), their branches alive with birds—a forest running along the edge of the sea, broken by an occasional house with a tower and a rose garden, and overhead (though not all at once) the sun, the moon, and the stars. But one might wonder whether (save for the rough beast that slouches toward Bethlehem) the animals that thickly populate this forest have aroused the interest they deserve. As the concordance reveals, savage or noxious animals (analogous, perhaps, to the birds of prey) abound: 3 leopards, 3 bears, 6 panthers, 9 wolves, 20 lions, 7 weasels, 12 foxes, 1 rat, 1 rhinoceros, 5 boars, 3 adders, 3 lynxes, 4 spiders, 4 serpents, 18 worms, 1 polecat, and 1 mole. But animals of every sort—wild and domestic, large and small, four-legged and aquatic—throng the poems. I count, loosely, 72 horses (also 2 stallions, 5 mares), 23 hares, 3 asses, 1 jackass, 2 antelopes, 33 deer (plus 17 stags, 4 roes, 2 roebucks, and 5 does), 4 badgers, 4 crickets, 18 mice, 1 haymouse, 6 oxen, 6 lambs, 17 sheep, 2 gazelles, 2 pigs, 11 otters, 9 cattle, 3 kine, 7 calves, 1 steer, 4 bulls (excluding of course, John Bull, who shows up 3 times), 10 squirrels, 5 rabbits, 1 coney, 1 lev'ret, 14 cats, 24 dogs (one, at least, is a great Dane), 3 camels, 2 stoats, 8 goats, 2 ponies, 1 monkey, 1 mackerel, 3 herring, 7 trout, 1 eel, 7 salmon, 5 dolphins, 2 goldfish, and a minnow, together with twenty-odd fish, 9 animals, and 26 just plain beasts. (Should we add dragon [11], mermaid [3], and sphinx [1]?) The profusion of animals here—both on the hoof, as it were, and in the vehicle of a metaphor—may give new force to Yeats's complaint of desertion at the waning of his inventive power:

> I sought a theme and sought for it in vain,
> I sought it daily for six weeks or so.
> Maybe at last, being but a broken man,
> I must be satisfied with my heart, although
> Winter and summer till old age began
> My circus animals were all on show.

Although these homely catalogues represent a fairly unsophisticated approach to Yeats's poetry, they will perhaps suggest the kinds of dis-

covery that are now made easier and surer. Ultimately, we hope that this concordance and others to follow (the Blake in particular) will stimulate exploration of the strange, dazzling, highly organized but often ill-charted worlds created by symbolist and mythopoeic genius.

Basic Text and Format

With the permission of The Macmillan Company and Colonel Russell K. Alspach, this concordance is based upon the superb *Variorum Edition of the Poems of W. B. Yeats,* edited by Peter Allt and Colonel Alspach (New York, 1957). The technique of preparing the text for the computer was about the same as that developed for the first volume in this series, *A Concordance to the Poems of Matthew Arnold* (Ithaca, 1959). The lines of Yeats's verse were punched on IBM cards (one line per card) and "verified"; speaker identifications, stage directions, dedications, and all like material not bearing line numbers were omitted. Page numbers and line numbers as shown in the variorum edition were added to the cards by a semiautomatic process. Lines too long for a single card were divided and punched on two (or more) cards with the same line number; the first portion of the line was followed and the last portion preceded by three spaced periods. Variant lines, with certain exceptions as noted below (see "Variants," p. ix), were put together from the Allt and Alspach collations and punched, each with a "v" preceding the line number, then interfiled by page in the main deck. A single title card for each poem, containing an abbreviated title designed to serve as identifying information (for the full list of abbreviations see pp. xv–xxvi) was placed at the head of the cards representing the poem. There was one important departure from the Arnold procedure: complete titles and variant titles of all poems, less subtitles and other prefatory matter, were punched in the same way as lines of verse, but with "т" in the line-number position, so that they could be indexed. Where digits occurred in titles, they were spelled out within brackets.

After proofreading, the material on the cards was transferred to magnetic tape. The 704 was then programmed to search the tape and index alphabetically every word on it, with some exceptions (see "Omitted Words," p. xi), by listing all lines of verse in which the word occurred, together with the identifying information: page number, abbreviated title, and line number (or т) preceded by v for variant lines or titles. The order in which the lines of verse fall under each of the index words is the order in which the cards were fed onto tape—that is, page and line order in the variorum edition. As with the Arnold concordance, the final IBM list, spaced into pages, was reproduced for publication by

an offset process, and a table of index words in order of frequency was provided in an appendix.

Several features of this volume represent sophistications of the techniques developed for Arnold (a twentieth-century poet deserves more help from modern technology than a nineteenth). Particulars of these are given in the Programmer's Preface (p. xxix), but three brief statements must be made here. First, a new print-wheel design made it possible to include punctuation symbols on the text cards and to show them on the concordance page. It might be noted that since apostrophes and single quotation marks would be indistinguishable, all quotation marks are double, even those within quotations. Second, a cross-reference routine was devised whereby the hyphen was treated in the indexing as a letter, not as a space (the computer recognizes only these two categories). Each hyphenated word thus appears as an index entry, and a cross reference is provided from the second (third, fourth, and so on) part of the word to the whole entry, under which the lines of text appear. An occasional word not hyphenated has been held together, for obvious reasons, as though it were (e.g., FOL DE ROL). Finally, the new program made it possible to exercise a certain amount of editorial judgment on an unpaged listing of the concordance text, then to incorporate changes in the final paged list. Thus partial listings of certain homographs have been provided (ART, MIGHT, and WILL) by the simple device of dropping the unimportant meanings. Conceivably, a hardier editor might in much the same way discriminate all homographs, to the limit of his discernment and endurance. But, as with nearly all other concordances, the user can make his own discriminations here (and they might not always be the same as an editor's) by looking through the quoted lines of text. For an illustration of what can be achieved with our elegant new techniques, see the ROSE entries where I have disentangled one of Yeats's important symbols from the occurrences of ROSE as a verb.

In the Appendix to this volume will be found, listed in order of frequency, the 10,666 words of Yeats's poetic vocabulary which are indexed in the concordance. The total of 10,666 (10,465 indexed, 3 partially indexed, 198 wholly omitted), like the total of 10,097 for Arnold, is somewhat inflated by the way in which hyphenated and apostrophized words have been handled, and individual frequencies are swollen by the presence of variant lines. Moreover, it may be useful to repeat here a caution set down in the Arnold Preface: since the Appendix shows raw frequencies, transcribed from the indexing tapes—MAN (456 occurrences), MAN's (54), MEN (263), and MEN's (23) are separate entries— the list cannot be compared directly with other lists of high-frequency words made up by combining variant forms.

Yet these figures should offer a number of suggestive facts even to the casual reader. Among the dozen highest frequencies perhaps OLD (575) is the one surprise; the appearance of LOVE (353) and HEART (272) could have been foretold. In a lower range, parts of the body are unexpectedly prominent. BODY itself has 104 occurrences, BODIES 34, EYES 244, EYE 86, FACE 131, HAIR 138, FEET 108, FOOT 34, BREAST 76, ARMS 58, LIPS 88, and MOUTH 39. (Here, of course, the figures are occasionally padded by homographs.) At the lowest range one is struck by the abundance of nonce words in some of Yeats's most brilliant lyrics. Consider, for an example, the opening stanza of "Byzantium":

> The *unpurged* images of day *recede;*
> The *Emperor's* drunken soldiery are abed;
> Night *resonance recedes, night-walkers'* song
> After great *cathedral* gong;
> A starlit or a moonlit dome *disdains*
> All that man is,
> All mere *complexities,*
> The fury and the mire of human veins.

The italicized forms occur nowhere in Yeats outside this poem; moreover, "abed," "soldiery," "gong," "starlit," and "dome" show up elsewhere only once or twice. It is almost as though on these occasions Yeats rose to a fresh level of poetic discourse.

Variants

> The friends that have it I do wrong
> When ever I remake a song,
> Should know what issue is at stake;
> It is myself that I remake.

So sang Yeats relatively early in his career as maker and remaker of songs. The record of his lifelong struggle for perfection of the work and of the self may be read in the thousands of collations printed by Allt and Alspach. In putting together variant lines from these collations, I have followed the numbering scrupulously, with one exception: variants of a refrain line were punched once only, with REF in the line-number position (refrain lines in the main text were all given proper line numbers).

While I have striven not to leave out any important part of Yeats's self, and have thus swelled this volume and padded the frequency lists with numerous minor variants—some, alas, probably introduced by editors or

printers, not by the poet—certain omissions have seemed desirable, if only to confine the work to a volume. The following variants listed in Allt and Alspach have therefore *not* been recorded:

1) Variants involving punctuation, capitalization, italics, or accents only (for these could not be shown in the IBM print).

2) Variants involving only material not given a line number in the main text (and therefore not punched): speaker identifications, stage directions, subtitles, and the like.

3) Variants involving simply the renumbering or transposition of identical lines or portions of lines that are relatively close together—that is, on the same page of Allt and Alspach (e.g., p. 4, line 34 and var. line 35). Lines moved from one location to another, or from one poem to another, were punched in both.

4) Variants involving only the apostrophization, abbreviation, contraction, or expansion of single words (e.g., "altho'" for "although," "St." for "Saint," "Ha'pence" for "halfpence," and "H——'s" for "Horton's").

5) Variants involving the separation or joining of two words where no word concerned is "significant"—that is, included in the index. Thus "I'll" for "I will," "what's" for "what is," "he's" for "he has," and the like, were not punched ("will" as a verb is nonsignificant, as are all the other words above). But "a while" for "awhile" was punched, since both "while" and "awhile" are significant words.

6) Most variants produced by obvious misprints in one or another edition of Yeats (e.g., "beech-hole" for "beech-bole," p. 278, line 36). Identification of misprints has been conservative, with the result that some unlikely but possible readings are included. I have also thought it best to keep a few apparent misprints that have acquired currency by surviving many printings (see, for example, p. 39, var. line 158 and p. 121, var. line 6). The following misprints, however, appearing in lines which had to be punched, have been corrected silently: "hundrd" for "hundred," p. 8, var. line 85a; "unwieldly" for "unwieldy," p. 18, var. line 268; "lounging" for "lunging," p. 41, var. line 181; "langour" for "languor," p. 44, line 223; "dread-dimmed" for "dream-dimmed," p. 164, var. line 1; "Drumhair" for "Drumahair," p. 207, var. line 11; "Any" for "And," p. 273, line 64; "their" for "there," p. 279, var. line 53; "clanguor" for "clangour," p. 382, line 9; "at" for "a," p. 392, var. line 17; "An" for "And," p. 392, var. line 25; "wndow" for "window," p. 694, line 95; "howewards" for "homewards," p. 757, line 202; and "comortable" for "comfortable," p. 780, line 6.

7) Variant titles to groups of poems after the *first* listing in Allt and Alspach. Thus "Momentary Thoughts" has been punched once only, as a variant title to poem No. 105, p. 260.

8) Variant titles which are simply first lines of poems.

9) Variants involving spelling only. To introduce these would not only have required extensive cross-referencing of a kind the computer could not accomplish unaided, but might also have masked the consistency of spelling in Yeats's final text. I have, however, preserved a few variants that seemed for one reason or another to be of interest or to offer difficulties (e.g., "phantasy" for "fantasy," "faery" for "fairy," and "chaunt" for "chant"). Proper names, of course, are a special case. Most variant names vary only slightly and should give little trouble (e.g., "Hoolihan" for "Houlihan," and "Kyle-na-gno" for "Kyle-na-no"); most of those that might give trouble (e.g., "Usheen" for "Oisin") are listed helpfully on pages 1 and 105 of Allt and Alspach. The connoisseur of Irish spellings will be sorry to have lost "Coulte" and "Moharabuiee" (which occur only as variants) but will perhaps be satisfied with "Shee," "Cu," "Cann," and "Cola," which survive (a number of variant names, "Usheen" among them, show up in the concordance by reason of their occurrence in lines that contain other, significant variants).

Besides the types listed above, a very small number of miscellaneous variants have been omitted for what seemed compelling reasons. These include an occasional line all of whose variants were incorporated separately in variant lines or half-lines already punched, and an occasional curiosity such as var. line 418, p. 242: "O! O! O! But no, that is not it" for "O! O! O! O! But no, that is not it." (Actually, no matter how hard we might punch this particular line, we could not get it to show up anywhere, all words in it being nonsignificant.)

It might be worth remarking, finally, that the omissions do not include any variants of hyphenation (save for a handful of proper names). As a consequence, the user must realize, three forms of a substantial number of terms are to be found in the concordance (e.g., HARPSTRING, HARP STRING, and HARP-STRING).

Omitted Words

Our computer routines have made it possible not only to offer selective listings of the most troublesome homographs, but also to provide frequencies of the omitted words. Words in the first list, below, are indexed only in the forms shown; words in the second list are omitted from the index altogether. DOES, MAY, and WILT were listed for editing, then dropped, since neither of the first two occurs as a noun, nor does the last occur in the sense of "droop"; TILL, which has only two occurrences as a noun, none as a verb, might have been dropped or edited, but the 145 occurrences as a preposition or conjunction were thought to be of sufficient interest to warrant retaining them.

PARTIALLY LISTED

ART	(noun)	12	(12 occurrences as verb omitted)
MIGHT	(noun)	12	(74 occurrences as verb omitted)
WILL	(noun)	32	(262 occurrences as verb omitted)

OMITTED ENTIRELY

A	2841	HADST	3	ME	464	THEIR	633
AGAIN	99	HAS	364	MUST	131	THEIRS	5
AH	88	HAST	17	MY	1118	THEM	219
ALSO	11	HATH	26	MYSEL'	1	THEMSELVES	12
ALTHOUGH	48	HAVE	850	MYSELF	18	THEN	168
AM	165	HE	789	NEITHER	31	THERE	468
AN	300	HE'D	12	NO	526	THERE'S	46
AND	6023	HE'LL	5	NOR	209	THEREFORE	21
ANOTHER	51	HER	737	NOT	540	THERE'LL	5
ANOTHER'S	10	HERE	77	NOW	337	THESE	166
ARE	589	HERE'S	11	O	318	THEY	567
AT	469	HERS	10	O'	3	THEY'D	6
BE	485	HERSELF	13	OF	3320	THEY'LL	5
BECAUSE	158	HE'S	9	OH	64	THEY'RE	10
BEEN	111	HIM	289	ON	992	THEY'VE	2
BOTH	29	HIMSELF	22	OR	799	THINE	23
BUT	974	HIS	1081	OTHER	82	THIS	306
BY	514	HOW	183	OTHER'LL	1	THOSE	229
CAN	267	I	2132	OTHERS	19	THOU	107
CANNOT	65	II	1	OTHER'S	9	THOUGH	218
CANST	1	III	1	OTHERS'	1	THOUL'T	1
COULD	165	IV	2	OUR	318	THOU'RT	1
D	1	I'	2	OURS	4	THRO'	2
DE	9	I'D	57	OURSELVES	2	THROUGH	161
DID	95	IF	281	P	1	THUS	30
DIDST	1	I'LL	42	'S	1	THY	123
DID'ST	1	I'M	13	SHALL	158	THYSELF	2
DO	138	IN	2088	SHALT	14	'TIS	24
DOES	20	IN'T	2	SHE	361	TO	1751
DON'T	1	INTO	179	SHE'D	7	TOO	88
DOST	4	IS	922	SHE'LL	2	T'OTHER	3
DOTH	4	IS'T	1	SHOULD	123	T'OTHER'S	1
EACH	79	IT	713	SO	339	'TWAS	16
EITHER	10	ITS	188	'TH	3	'TWERE	12
'EM	3	IT'S	24	THAT	2357	'TWILL	2
FOR	1007	ITSELF	17	THAT'S	40	'TWOULD	3
FROM	665	I'VE	20	THE	8436	UPON	508
HAD	610	MAY	245	THEE	68	US	174

V	2	WE'VE	5	WHICH	10	WOULDST	1
WAS	344	WHAT	503	WHO	293	YE	65
WAST	1	WHAT'S	31	WHO'D	4	YOU	716
WAS'T	1	WHATE'ER	2	WHOM	32	YOU'D	5
WE	446	WHATEVER	21	WHO'S	2	YOU'LL	10
WE'D	6	WHATEVER'S	2	WHOSE	69	YOUR	362
WE'LL	11	WHEN	590	WHY	95	YOU'RE	8
WERE	330	WHERE	459	WILT	9	YOURS	4
WE'RE	4	WHERE'S	1	WITH	1079	YOURSELF	5
WERE'T	2	WHEREVER	4	WON'T	1	YOU'VE	6
WERT	4	WHETHER	27	WOULD	238		

The presence here of low-frequency words may be explained by a desire for consistency. For example, with HE (789), HIS (1,081), and HIM (289) out for obvious reasons it seemed logical to drop HIMSELF, with only 22 occurrences (regrettable as that omission may seem from the work of an Irish poet). But endless controversy might be waged over my selections. Consider the lowly preposition OF. Having observed that Yeats liked to form metaphors by connecting vehicle and tenor with "of," I listed and examined all 3,320 occurrences of the word (the computer can provide a list of any given word in about 30 minutes). Scattered through the chaff were the following images, which could not, I suppose, have been collected in any other way:

	Page		Line
THE PALE BLOSSOM OF THE MOON	20		288
THE OSPREY OF SORROW	27	V	415D
THE ANVIL OF THE WORLD	42		204
THE FIRE OF SADNESS	73		49
THE GULPH OF SLEEP	83		22
THE ROOD OF TIME	100		title
THE BOUGHS OF LOVE AND HATE	101		10
GREAT WEBS OF SORROW	104		39
THE WHARVES OF SORROW	115		27
FLAMING FOUNTS OF DUTY	124		5
THE GLASS OF OUTER WEARINESS	135		31
THE FLAMING CIRCLE OF OUR LIFE	135	V	16
THE RAVENS OF UNRESTING THOUGHT	136		34
THE NETS OF WRONG AND RIGHT	147		2
THE SHADOWY BLOSSOM OF MY HAIR	152		7
THE HORSES OF DISASTER	154		8
THE PALE FIRE OF TIME	157		6
LILIES OF DEATH-PALE HOPE, ROSES OF PASSIONATE DREAM	172		8
THE NETS OF DAY AND NIGHT	175		12

	Page	Line
THE PALE CUP OF THE SEA	175	14
THE WATERS OF SLEEP	218	25
THE BURNISHED MIRROR OF THE WORLD	228	132
THE SHIVERING CASTING-NET OF THE STARS	237	329
THE LABYRINTH OF HER DAYS	260	13
THE DIM / IMAGINATIONS OF THEIR EYES	272	27/28
THE GOLDEN TOP OF CARE	309	20
THE WICK OF YOUTH	334 V	3
THE PESTLE OF THE MOON	346	30
YELLOW-EYED HAWK OF THE MIND	349	14
THE BALLOON OF THE MIND	358	2
THE CAT-O'-NINE-TAILS OF THE MIND	374	42
THE BASIN OF THE MIND	478	34
THE HONEY-POT OF HIS MIND	481	21
THIS PRAGMATICAL, PREPOSTEROUS PIG OF A WORLD	481	26
THOSE BRANCHES OF THE NIGHT AND DAY	502	68
THE MARE OF TIME	529	5
THE FOAL OF THE WORLD	529	6
THE MATERNAL MIDNIGHT OF MY BREAST	535	7
THE MILL OF THE MIND	575	10
THE CAVERN OF THE MIND	600	2
THE FOUL RAG-AND-BONE SHOP OF THE HEART	630	40
THE BOUGHS OF TIME	756	178
THE LABYRINTH OF THE MIND	785	24

Other insignificant words in Yeats, arbitrarily omitted from this index to economize space, may be of like interest to scholars and critics. To prevent any word from being lost forever, we expect to keep on file the magnetic tapes of all texts in the Cornell series.

Abbreviated Titles

In assigning title abbreviations—as in all things—I have followed the numbering of lines in the variorum edition. Wherever a poem breaks into parts or scenes with separate sequences of numbers, separate titles have been assigned; where numbering is continuous from one section to the next, one title carries over. Yeats's longer titles have not been easy to reduce to fourteen columns of an IBM card, and I have followed no very consistent principle. I have occasionally taken the opening words; more often, I have tried to devise a catch title from words which seemed likely to have lodged in a reader's memory.

Abbreviations are listed below exactly as they appear in the concordance text. Following each abbreviation the reader will find the full title of the poem and the number of the page on which the poem begins in the variorum edition.

Abbreviation	Title	Page
ABBEY THEATRE	At the Abbey Theatre (Imitated from Ronsard)	264
ACCURSED WHO	'Accursed who brings to light of day'	779
ACRE OF GRASS	An Acre of Grass	575
ADAMS CURSE	Adam's Curse	204
AGAINST WITCH	Against Witchcraft	775
ALF POLLEXFEN	In Memory of Alfred Pollexfen	360
ALL SOUL NIGHT	All Souls' Night: Epilogue to 'A Vision'	470
ALL TEMPT ME	All Things can Tempt me	267
AM OF IRELAND	Words for Music Perhaps XX. 'I Am of Ireland'	526
ANASHU VIJAYA	Anashuya and Vijaya	71
ANCEST HOUSES	Meditations in Time of Civil War I. Ancestral Houses	417
ANNE GREGORY	For Anne Gregory	492
APPARITIONS	The Apparitions	624
APPOINTMENT	An Appointment	624
ARROW	The Arrow	199
ASKS FORGIVE	The Lover asks Forgiveness because of his Many Moods	162
AT ALGECIRAS	At Algeciras — A Meditation upon Death	493
BAILE AILLINN	Baile and Aillinn	189
BALLOON MIND	The Balloon of the Mind	358
BEFORE WORLD	A Woman Young and Old II. Before the World was Made	531
BEGGAR CRIED	Beggar to Beggar Cried	299
BELOVED DEAD	He wishes his Beloved were Dead	175
BELOVED PEACE	He bids his Beloved be at Peace	154
BELOVED RHYMES	He gives his Beloved certain Rhymes	157
BEN BULBEN	Under Ben Bulben	636
BLACK CENTAUR	On a Picture of a Black Centaur by Edmund Dulac	442
BLACK PIG	The Valley of the Black Pig	161
BLACK TOWER	The Black Tower	635
BLESS PSALTER	The Players ask for a Blessing on the Psalteries and on Themselves	212
BLESSED	The Blessed	166
BLOOD AND MOON	Blood and the Moon	480
BLOOD BOND	The Blood Bond: from the play 'Grania' by George Moore and W. B. Yeats	769
BONE OF A HARE	The Collar-Bone of a Hare	330

BOOK STORIES	The Dedication to a Book of Stories selected from The Irish Novelists	129
BRAVEST ASK	'The bravest from the gods but ask:'	788
BREAK OF DAY	Towards Break of Day	398
BROKEN DREAMS	Broken Dreams	355
BRONZE HEAD	A Bronze Head	618
BROWN PENNY	Brown Penny	268
BYZANTIUM	Byzantium	497
CAP AND BELLS	The Cap and Bells	159
CARVED STONE	To be Carved on a Stone at Thoor Ballylee	406
CAT AND MOON	The Cat and the Moon	378
CATHLEEN PARA	The Countess Cathleen in Paradise	124
CHANGE BELOVED	He mourns for the Change that has come upon him and his Beloved, and longs for the End of the World	153
CHILD DANCING	I. To a Child Dancing in the Wind	312
CHOICE	The Choice	495
CHOSEN	A Woman Young and Old VI. Chosen	534
CHURCH STATE	Church and State	553
CIRCUS ANIMALS	The Circus Animals' Desertion	629
CLOAK BOAT	The Cloak, the Boat, and the Shoes	69
CLOTHS HEAVEN	He wishes for the Cloths of Heaven	176
COAT	A Coat	320
COLD HEAVEN	The Cold Heaven	316
COLONEL MARTIN	Colonel Martin	594
COLONUS PRAISE	Colonus' Praise (from 'Oedipus at Colonus')	446
COME RIDE	'Come ride and ride to the garden' [from the play 'The Travelling Man,' by Lady Gregory]	773
COMING WISDOM	The Coming of Wisdom with Time	261
CONJUNCTIONS	Supernatural Songs X. Conjunctions	562
CONSOLATION	A Woman Young and Old V. Consolation	534
COOLE BALLYLEE	Coole Park and Ballylee, 1931	490
COOLE PARK 29	Coole Park, 1929	488
CRADLE SONG	A Cradle Song	118
CRAZED GIRL	A Crazed Girl	578
CRAZED MOON	The Crazed Moon	487
CRY OF SEDGE	He hears the Cry of the Sedge	165
CUCHULAIN COMF	Cuchulain Comforted	634
CUCHULAIN SEA	Cuchulain's Fight with the Sea	105
CURSE CROMWELL	The Curse of Cromwell	580
DANAAN QUICK	The Danaan Quicken Tree	742
DANCER CRUACH	Words for Music Perhaps XXI. The Dancer at Cruachan and Cro-Patrick	528
DANCING DAYS	Words for Music Perhaps XIX. Those Dancing Days are Gone	524

DAWN	The Dawn	344
DAWN-SONG	A Dawn-Song	705
DEATH	Death	476
DEATH OF HARE	A Man Young and Old IV. The Death of the Hare	453
DEDICATION	Dedication	790
DEEP-SWORN VOW	A Deep-sworn Vow	357
DEJECTION	Lines Written in Dejection	343
DELPHIC ORACLE	Words for Music Perhaps XXV. The Delphic Oracle upon Plotinus	530
DEMON BEAST	Demon and Beast	399
DOLLS	The Dolls	319
DOLLS DRAWINGS	Upon a Dying Lady II. Certain Artists bring her Dolls and Drawings	362
DOLLS FACES	Upon a Dying Lady III. She turns the Dolls' Faces to the Wall	363
DOR WELLESLEY	To Dorothy Wellesley	579
DRAWING-ROOM	In a Drawing-Room	685
DREAM OF DEATH	A Dream of Death	123
DREAM OF FAERY	The Man who Dreamed of Faeryland	126
DRINKING SONG	A Drinking Song	261
DRUNK SOBRIETY	A Drunken Man's Praise of Sobriety	591
DWELT SYCAMORE	She Who Dwelt among the Sycamores. A Fancy.	715
EARL PAUL	The Ballad of Earl Paul	739
EASTER 1916	Easter 1916	391
EGO DOMINUS	Ego Dominus Tuus	367
ELEMENT POWERS	The Poet-pleads with the Elemental Powers	174
EMPTY CUP	A Man Young and Old V. The Empty Cup	454
END OF DAY	Upon a Dying Lady IV. The End of Day	364
EPHEMERA	Ephemera	79
EVA GORE-BOOTH	In Memory of Eva Gore-Booth and Con Markiewicz	475
EVERLAST VOICE	The Everlasting Voices	141
EVIL OF BELOV	He thinks of those who have Spoken Evil of his Beloved	166
FAERY SONG	A Faery Song	116
FAIRY DOCTOR	The Fairy Doctor	716
FAIRY PEDANT	The Fairy Pedant	706
FALLEN MAJESTY	Fallen Majesty	314
FALLING LEAVES	The Falling of the Leaves	79
FASC DIFFICULT	The Fascination of What's Difficult	260
FATHER CHILD	A Woman Young and Old I. Father and Child	531
FATHER OHART	The Ballad of Father O'Hart	91
FERENCZ RENYI	How Ferencz Renyi Kept Silent. Hungary, 1848.	709
FERGUS DRUID	Fergus and the Druid	102
FIDDLER DOONEY	The Fiddler of Dooney	178
FIRST CONFESS	A Woman Young and Old III. A First Confession	532

FIRST LOVE	A Man Young and Old I. First Love	451
FISH	The Fish	146
FISHERMAN	The Fisherman	347
FOLLY COMFORT	The Folly of Being Comforted	199
FOR DAUGHTER	A Prayer for my Daughter	403
FOR MY SON	A Prayer for my Son	435
FORGOT BEAUTY	He remembers Forgotten Beauty	155
FOUR AGES MAN	Supernatural Songs IX. The Four Ages of Man	561
FOXHUNTER	The Ballad of the Foxhunter	97
FR GILLIGAN	The Ballad of Father Gilligan	132
FRAGMENTS	Fragments	439
FRIEND ILLNESS	A Friend's Illness	267
FRIENDS	Friends	315
FRIENDS WRONG	'The friends that have it I do wrong'	778
FRIENDS YOUTH	A Man Young and Old VII. The Friends of his Youth	455
FROM ANTIGONE	A Woman Young and Old XI. From the 'Antigone'	540
FROM JAPANESE	Imitated from the Japanese	567
FROM OEDIPUS	A Man Young and Old XI. From 'Oedipus at Colonus'	459
GALLERY REVIS	The Municipal Gallery Revisited	601
GALWAY RACES	At Galway Races	266
GARRET CELLAR	'To Garret or Cellar a wheel I send,'	787
GEORGE MOORE	'Moore once had visits from the muse'	792
GHOST ROG CASE	The Ghost of Roger Casement	583
GIRLS SONG A	Girl's Song	723
GIRLS SONG B	Words for Music Perhaps VIII. Girl's Song	515
GLOVE CLOAK	The Glove and the Cloak	744
GOES FERGUS	Who Goes with Fergus?	125
GOING THE ROAD	'I was going the road one day'	779
GRAT INSTRUCT	Gratitude to the Unknown Instructors	505
GREAT DAY	The Great Day	590
GREY ROCK	The Grey Rock	270
GREY ROUND	At the Grey Round of the Hill	782
GYRES	The Gyres	564
HANRAHANS SONG	Red Hanrahan's Song about Ireland	206
HAPPY SHEPHERD	The Song of the Happy Shepherd	64
HAPPY TOWNLAND	The Happy Townland	213
HARP OF AENGUS	The Harp of Aengus [prefixed to 1906 version of 'The Shadowy Waters: A Dramatic Poem']	219
HARUN RASHID	The Gift of Harun Al-Rashid	460
HATED PLAYBOY	On those that hated 'The Playboy of the Western World,' 1907	294
HAWK	The Hawk	349

xviii

HAWTHORN TREE	The Wicked Hawthorn Tree	788
HE AND SHE	Supernatural Songs VI. He and She	559
HEART FRIGHT	Why should the Heart take Fright?	781
HEART OF WOMAN	The Heart of the Woman	151
HEART SLEEVE	'The heart well worn upon the sleeve. . .'	790
HELEN LIVED	When Helen Lived	293
HER ANXIETY	Words for Music Perhaps X. Her Anxiety	517
HER CHRIS TREE	Upon a Dying Lady VII. Her Friends bring her a Christmas Tree	366
HER COURAGE	Upon a Dying Lady VI. Her Courage	365
HER COURTESY	Upon a Dying Lady I. Her Courtesy	362
HER DREAM	Words for Music Perhaps XIII. Her Dream	519
HER PRAISE	Her Praise	350
HER RACE	Upon a Dying Lady V. Her Race	365
HER TRIUMPH	A Woman Young and Old IV. Her Triumph	533
HER VISION	A Woman Young and Old VIII. Her Vision in the Wood	536
HERO GIRL FOOL	The Hero, The Girl, and the Fool	447
HIGH TALK	High Talk	622
HIS BARGAIN	Words for Music Perhaps XIV. His Bargain	520
HIS CONFIDENCE	Words for Music Perhaps XI. His Confidence	517
HIS DREAM	His Dream	253
HIS MEMORIES	A Man Young and Old VI. His Memories	454
HIS PHOENIX	His Phoenix	353
HIS WILDNESS	A Man Young and Old X. His Wildness	458
HOST OF AIR	The Host of the Air	143
HOSTING SIDHE	The Hosting of the Sidhe	140
HOUND VOICE	Hound Voice	621
HOUR DAWN	The Hour before Dawn	302
HOUSE SHAKEN	Upon a House shaken by the Land Agitation	264
HUDDON DUDDON	'Huddon, Duddon and Daniel O'Leary'	787
HUMAN DIGNITY	A Man Young and Old II. Human Dignity	452
IMAGE PAST	An Image from a Past Life	389
IN CHURCH	In Church	735
IN FIRELIGHT	In the Firelight	737
IN TARAS HALLS	In Tara's Halls	609
IN TIME OF WAR	A Meditation in Time of War	406
INDIAN ON GOD	The Indian upon God	76
INDIAN TO LOVE	The Indian to His Love	77
INTO TWILIGHT	Into the Twilight	147
IRISH AIRMAN	An Irish Airman Foresees his Death	328
ISLE IN WATER	To an Isle in the Water	89
ISLE INNISFREE	The Lake Isle of Innisfree	117
ISLE STAT I 1	The Island of Statues (Act I, Scene 1)	645
ISLE STAT I 2	The Island of Statues (Act I, Scene 2)	651

ISLE STAT I 3	The Island of Statues (Act I, Scene 3)	655
ISLE STAT II 1	The Island of Statues (Act II, Scene 1)	658
ISLE STAT II 2	The Island of Statues (Act II, Scene 2)	662
ISLE STAT II 3	The Island of Statues (Act II, Scene 3)	666
JANE AND JACK	Words for Music Perhaps IV. Crazy Jane and Jack the Journeyman	511
JANE BISHOP	Words for Music Perhaps I. Crazy Jane and the Bishop	507
JANE GROWN OLD	Words for Music Perhaps VIII. Crazy Jane grown old looks at the Dancers	514
JANE JUDGMENT	Words for Music Perhaps III. Crazy Jane on the Day of Judgment	510
JANE MOUNTAIN	Crazy Jane on the Mountain	628
JANE ON GOD	Words for Music Perhaps V. Crazy Jane on God	512
JANE REPROVED	Words for Music Perhaps II. Crazy Jane Reproved	509
JANE TALK BISH	Words for Music Perhaps VI. Crazy Jane talks with the Bishop	513
JOHN KINSELLA	John Kinsella's Lament for Mrs. Mary Moore	620
KANVA ON SELF	Kanva on Himself	723
KING NO KING	King and No King	258
LADYS 1ST SONG	The Lady's First Song	572
LADYS 2ND SONG	The Lady's Second Song	572
LADYS 3RD SONG	The Lady's Third Song	573
LAPIS LAZULI	Lapis Lazuli (For Harry Clifton)	565
LAST CONFESS	A Woman Young and Old IX. A Last Confession	538
LEADERS CROWD	The Leaders of the Crowd	398
LEDA AND SWAN	Leda and the Swan	441
LEGEND	A Legend. A drowned city is supposed to lie under the waters of Lough Gill.	724
LIFE	Life	686
LIVING BEAUTY	The Living Beauty	333
LOFTY THINGS	Beautiful Lofty Things	577
LONG-LEG FLY	Long-Legged Fly	617
LONG SILENCE	Words for Music Perhaps XVII. After Long Silence	523
LOSS OF LOVE	The Lover mourns for the Loss of Love	152
LOVE AND DEATH	Love and Death	680
LOVE SONG	Love Song. From the Gaelic.	717
LOVERS QUARREL	A Lover's Quarrel among the Fairies	726
LOVERS SONG	The Lover's Song	574
LOVES LONENESS	Words for Music Perhaps XII. Love's Loneliness	518
LULLABY	Words for Music Perhaps XVI. Lullaby	522
MAD AS MIST	Words for Music Perhaps XVIII. Mad as the Mist and Snow	523
MAD KING GOLL	The Madness of King Goll	81

MAGI	The Magi	318
MAGIC DRUM	Supernatural Songs VII. What Magic Drum?	559
MAID QUIET	Maid Quiet	171
MAIDS 1ST SONG	The Chambermaid's First Song	574
MAIDS 2ND SONG	The Chambermaid's Second Song	575
MAN AND ECHO	The Man and the Echo	632
MANS SONG	Words for Music Perhaps IX. Young Man's Song	516
MARCH SONGS 1	Three Marching Songs (I)	613
MARCH SONGS 2	Three Marching Songs (II)	614
MARCH SONGS 3	Three Marching Songs (III)	615
MASK	The Mask	263
MEETING	A Woman Young and Old X. Meeting	539
MEMORY	Memory	350
MEMORY YOUTH	A Memory of Youth	313
MEN IMPROVE	Men Improve with the Years	329
MERMAID	A Man Young and Old III. The Mermaid	452
MERU	Supernatural Songs XII. Meru	563
MODEL LAUREATE	A Model for the Laureate	597
MOHINI CHATTER	Mohini Chatterjee	495
MOLL MAGEE	The Ballad of Moll Magee	94
MOODS	The Moods	142
MOSADA 1	Mosada (Scene I)	690
MOSADA 2	Mosada (Scene II)	695
MOSADA 3	Mosada (Scene III)	699
MOTHER OF GOD	The Mother of God	499
MOUNTAIN TOMB	The Mountain Tomb	311
MOURN THEN ON	Mourn—and Then Onward!	737
MY DESCENDANTS	Meditations in Time of Civil War IV. My Descendants	422
MY HEART BEAT	Why does my Heart beat so?	781
MY HOUSE	Meditations in Time of Civil War II. My House	419
MY TABLE	Meditations in Time of Civil War III. My Table	421
NATIVITY	A Nativity	625
NEEDLES EYE	Supernatural Songs XI. A Needle's Eye	562
NETTLESHIP	On Mr. Nettleship's Picture at the Royal Hibernian Academy	688
NEVER GIVE ALL	Never Give all the Heart	202
NEW FACES	The New Faces	435
NEWS ORACLE	News for the Delphic Oracle	611
NIGHT COME	That the Night Come	317
NINETEEN 19	Nineteen Hundred and Nineteen	428
NINETEENTH CEN	The Nineteenth Century and After	485
NO SECOND TROY	No Second Troy	256
O DO NOT LOVE	O Do Not Love Too Long	211
OIL AND BLOOD	Oil and Blood	483

xxi

OISIN 1	The Wanderings of Oisin (Book I)	2
OISIN 2	The Wanderings of Oisin (Book II)	29
OISIN 3	The Wanderings of Oisin (Book III)	47
OLD FISHERMAN	The Meditation of the Old Fisherman	90
OLD MEMORY	Old Memory	201
OLD MEN ADMIRE	The Old Men Admiring Themselves in the Water	208
OLD MEN BE MAD	Why should not Old Men be Mad?	625
OLD MOTHER	The Song of the Old Mother	150
OLD PENSIONER	The Lamentation of the Old Pensioner	131
OLD TOM AGAIN	Words for Music Perhaps XXIV. Old Tom Again	530
OLD WICKED MAN	The Wild Old Wicked Man	587
ON GOING HOUSE	A Prayer on going into my House	371
ON WOMAN	On Woman	345
ORAHILLY	The O'Rahilly	584
OWEN AHERNE	Owen Aherne and his Dancers	449
PARDON FATHERS	Pardon, Old Fathers	269
PARN FUNERAL 1	Parnell's Funeral I	541
PARN FUNERAL 2	Parnell's Funeral II	542
PARNELL	Parnell	590
PARNELLITES	Come Gather Round Me, Parnellites	586
PARTING	A Woman Young and Old VII. Parting	535
PAST GREATNESS	He thinks of his Past Greatness when a Part of the Constellations of Heaven	177
PAUDEEN	Paudeen	291
PEACE	Peace	258
PEACOCK	II. The Peacock	310
PEOPLE	The People	351
PERFECT BEAUTY	He tells of the Perfect Beauty	164
PHANTOM HATRED	Meditations in Time of Civil War VII. I see Phantoms of Hatred and of the Heart's Fullness and of the Coming Emptiness	425
PHANTOM SHIP	The Phantom Ship	718
PHASES OF MOON	The Phases of the Moon	372
PILGRIM	The Pilgrim	592
PITY OF LOVE	The Pity of Love	119
PLAYER QUEEN	A Song from 'The Player Queen'	308
PLEADS FRIEND	The Lover pleads with his Friend for Old Friends	172
POET BELOVED	A Poet to his Beloved	157
POLIT PRISONER	On a Political Prisoner	397
POLITICS	Politics	631
PRAYER OLD AGE	A Prayer for Old Age	553
PRESENCES	Presences	358
PRIEST FAIRY	The Priest and the Fairy	728
PROPERTIUS	A Thought from Propertius	355
QUARREL IN AGE	Quarrel in Old Age	503

xxii

QUATRAIN APHOR	Quatrains and Aphorisms	734
QUEEN MAEVE	The Old Age of Queen Maeve	180
RAGGED WOOD	The Ragged Wood	210
REALISTS	The Realists	309
RECONCILIATION	Reconciliation	257
REED WHISPERER	While I, from that reed-throated whisperer	320
REMEMBRANCE	Remembrance	704
REMORSE SPEECH	Remorse for Intemperate Speech	506
REPRISALS	Reprisals	791
REPROVE CURLEW	He reproves the Curlew	155
RESULT THOUGHT	The Results of Thought	504
RIBH AT TOMB	Supernatural Songs I. Ribh at the Tomb of Baile and Aillinn	554
RIBH CHRISTIAN	Supernatural Songs V. Ribh Considers Christian Love Insufficient	558
RIBH ECSTASY	Supernatural Songs III. Ribh in Ecstasy	557
RIBH PATRICK	Supernatural Songs II. Ribh denounces Patrick	556
ROAD AT DOOR	Meditations in Time of Civil War V. The Road at my Door	423
ROBARTES DANCE	Michael Robartes and the Dancer	385
ROBERT GREGORY	In Memory of Major Robert Gregory	323
ROGER CASEMENT	Roger Casement (After Reading 'The Forged Casement Diaries' by Dr. Maloney)	581
ROSE IN HEART	The Lover tells of the Rose in his Heart	142
ROSE OF BATTLE	The Rose of Battle	113
ROSE OF PEACE	The Rose of Peace	112
ROSE OF WORLD	The Rose of the World	111
ROSE TREE	The Rose Tree	396
ROSE UPON ROOD	To the Rose upon the Rood of Time	100
ROSY CROSS	A Song of the Rosy Cross	744
ROUND TOWER	Under the Round Tower	331
RUN PARADISE	Running to Paradise	300
SAD SHEPHERD	The Sad Shepherd	67
SAIL BYZANTIUM	Sailing to Byzantium	407
SAINT HUNCH	The Saint and the Hunchback	379
SALLEY GARDENS	Down by the Salley Gardens	90
SCHOLARS	The Scholars	337
SCHOOL CHILDR	Among School Children	443
SECOND COMING	The Second Coming	401
SECRET ROSE	The Secret Rose	169
SECRETS OF OLD	A Man Young and Old IX. The Secrets of the Old	457
SEEKER	The Seeker. A Dramatic Poem—in Two Scenes.	681
SELF AND SOUL	A Dialogue of Self and Soul	477
SEPTEMBER 1913	September 1913	289
SEVEN SAGES	The Seven Sages	486

SEVEN WOODS	In the Seven Woods	198
SEVERED HEAD	Alternative Song for the Severed Head in 'The King of the Great Clock Tower'	549
SHADOW WATER A	The Shadowy Waters [first version, 1900]	747
SHADOW WATER B	The Shadowy Waters [second version, 1906]	221
SHEP GOATHERD	Shepherd and Goatherd	338
SINGING HEAD	The Singing Head and the Lady	789
SIXTEEN DEAD	Sixteen Dead Men	395
SOLOMON SHEBA	Solomon to Sheba	332
SOLOMON WITCH	Solomon and the Witch	387
SONG	A Song	334
SONG DEIRDRE 1	Queen Edaine [Songs from Deirdre I]	771
SONG DEIRDRE 2	Songs from Deirdre II	777
SONG DEIRDRE 3	Songs from Deirdre III	777
SONG FAERIES	Song of the Faeries	643
SONG OF FOOL	Another Song of a Fool	381
SONGS BURDEN 1	Three Songs to the One Burden (I)	605
SONGS BURDEN 2	Three Songs to the One Burden (II)	606
SONGS BURDEN 3	Three Songs to the One Burden (III)	608
SONGS FOOL 1	Two Songs of a Fool (I)	380
SONGS FOOL 2	Two Songs of a Fool (II)	381
SONGS PLAY 1	Two Songs from a Play (I)	437
SONGS PLAY 2	Two Songs from a Play (II)	438
SONGS REWRIT 1	Two Songs Rewritten for the Tune's Sake (I)	550
SONGS REWRIT 2	Two Songs Rewritten for the Tune's Sake (II)	552
SORROW OF LOVE	The Sorrow of Love	119
SPEAKS HEARERS	The Lover speaks to the Hearers of his Songs in Coming Days	173
SPILT MILK	Spilt Milk	484
SPINNING SONG	Spinning Song	770
SPIRIT MEDIUM	The Spirit Medium	599
SPUR	The Spur	591
STARES NEST	Meditations in Time of Civil War VI. The Stare's Nest by my Window	424
STATES HOLIDAY	The Statesman's Holiday	626
STATISTICS	Statistics	485
STATUES	The Statues	610
STICK INCENSE	A Stick of Incense	619
STOLEN CHILD	The Stolen Child	86
STONE CROSS	The Old Stone Cross	598
STREAM AND SUN	Stream and Sun at Glendalough	506
STREET DANCERS	Street Dancers	731
STUDENTS AGIT	On hearing that the Students of our New University have joined the Agitation against Immoral Literature	262

SUMMER EVENING	A Summer Evening	736
SUMMER SPRING	A Man Young and Old VIII. Summer and Spring	456
SWANS AT COOLE	The Wild Swans at Coole	322
SWEET DANCER	Sweet Dancer	568
SWIFTS EPITAPH	Swift's Epitaph	493
SYMBOLS	Symbols	484
THERE	Supernatural Songs IV. There	557
THESE CLOUDS	These are the Clouds	265
THOSE IMAGES	Those Images	600
THREE BEGGARS	The Three Beggars	294
THREE BUSHES	The Three Bushes (An Incident from the 'Historia Mei Temporis' of the Abbé Michel de Bourdeille)	569
THREE HERMITS	The Three Hermits	298
THREE MONUMENT	The Three Monuments	460
THREE MOVEMENT	The Three Movements	485
THREE THINGS	Words for Music Perhaps XV. Three Things	521
TO A FRIEND	To a Friend whose Work has come to Nothing	290
TO A POET	To a Poet, who would have me Praise certain Bad Poets, Imitators of His and Mine	262
TO A SHADE	To a Shade	292
TO A SQUIRREL	To a Squirrel at Kyle-na-no	359
TO HIS HEART	To his Heart, bidding it have no Fear	158
TO IRELAND	To Ireland in the Coming Times	137
TO SAME TUNE 1	Three Songs to the Same Tune (I)	544
TO SAME TUNE 2	Three Songs to the Same Tune (II)	545
TO SAME TUNE 3	Three Songs to the Same Tune (III)	547
TO SOME I TALK	To Some I have Talked with by the Fire	136
TO WEALTHY MAN	To a Wealthy Man who promised a Second Subscription to the Dublin Municipal Gallery if it were proved the People wanted Pictures	287
TOM CRUACHAN	Words for Music Perhaps XXIII. Tom at Cruachan	529
TOM LUNATIC	Words for Music Perhaps XXII. Tom the Lunatic	528
TOM OROUGHLEY	Tom O'Roughley	337
TOWER	The Tower	409
TRAV PASSION	The Travail of Passion	172
TWO KINGS	The Two Kings	276
TWO TITANS	The Two Titans. A Political Poem.	687
TWO TREES	The Two Trees	134
TWO YEAR LATER	II. Two Years Later	312
UNAPPEAS HOST	The Unappeasable Host	146
UNDER SATURN	Under Saturn	390
UNDER THE MOON	Under the Moon	209
UNWORTH PRAISE	Against Unworthy Praise	259

VACILLATION	Vacillation	499
VALLEY LOVERS	He tells of a Valley full of Lovers	163
VERONIC NAPKIN	Veronica's Napkin	483
VISION ROBART	The Double Vision of Michael Robartes	382
WANDER AENGUS	The Song of Wandering Aengus	149
WAR POEM	On being asked for a War Poem	359
WELL AND TREE	The Well and the Tree	780
WHAT THEN	What Then?	576
WHAT WAS LOST	What Was Lost	591
WHEEL	The Wheel	434
WHENCE COME	Supernatural Songs VIII. Whence Had They Come?	560
WHERE BOOKS GO	Where My Books Go	739
WHITE BIRDS	The White Birds	121
WISDOM	Wisdom	440
WISDOM DREAMS	Wisdom and Dreams	743
WITCH	I. The Witch	310
WITCH VIVIEN	Time and the Witch Vivien	720
WITHER BOUGHS	The Withering of the Boughs	203
WOMAN HOMER	A Woman Homer Sung	254
WOMANS BEAUTY	A Woman's Beauty is like a white frail Bird	784
WOODS OF COOLE	I walked among the Seven Woods of Coole [prefixed to 'The Shadowy Waters: A Dramatic Poem']	217
WORDS	Words	255
YOU ARE OLD	When You are Old	120
YOU ARE SAD	When you are Sad	738
YOU CONTENT	Are You Content?	604
YOUNG BEAUTY	To a Young Beauty	335
YOUNG GIRL	To a Young Girl	336
YOUR HEART	Why does your Heart beat thus?	785
YOUTH AND AGE	Youth and Age	434

Acknowledgments

The beginning of work on this volume was made possible by a grant-in-aid from the American Council of Learned Societies; at a later stage support was given from the grant-in-aid program of the Cornell Department of English; throughout, we have been dependent upon services provided by the International Business Machines Corporation, the Cornell Computing Center in Ithaca, and the Cornell Aeronautical Research Laboratory in Buffalo, New York.

These formal announcements scarcely reveal the warm sense of obligation I feel to the individuals who placed their confidence in this venture and gave it their help: William Andrus, now Director of Standards for IBM (who gave the Arnold concordance its start and nursed this one

along at a critical time); J. A. Kearns, University and Research Institute Representative of IBM; Robert Hoopes, formerly Vice President of the A.C.L.S. and now Dean of the Faculty at Michigan State University—Oakland; John Hastie, Coordinator of Research at Cornell University; Richard Lesser, Director of the Cornell Computing Center; and Theodore P. Wright, Chairman of the Board of Directors, Ira G. Ross, President, and John J. O'Neil, Vice President, of the Cornell Aeronautical Laboratory. The generous support given us by the Laboratory deserves particular mention: it included not only the arrangement of time on the computer together with operating services, but the purchase of print wheels for our exclusive use. This significant investment in the humanities on the part of a corporation committed to scientific research is most gratefully appreciated.

I am further indebted to Miss Laura Franklin, Associate Professor of English at Nebraska State Teachers College, Wayne, who gallantly surrendered her prior claim to the variorum text; to Colonel Alspach, first for passing the rights to me, then for continuing kindly advice; and to Marshall Cohen and George Rice at the Aeronautical Laboratory, who patiently and expertly guided our use of facilities there. In Ithaca, Samuel Miles Weber, Mrs. Marilyn Paul, and Mrs. Elizabeth Savage cheerfully undertook proofreading and editorial chores. The supervisory committee (including the late Stephen E. Whicher) stood loyally ready with counsel of many kinds. Again, I must particularly thank Professor William R. Keast, whose lively interest and encouragement made all difficulties manageable. But this time it is gratifying not to have to thank James Painter, who appears in this volume in his rightful place.

Ithaca, New York   S. M. PARRISH
September 1962

PROGRAMMER'S PREFACE

THE invitation to write this preface was rather unsettling, for my experience with the concordance project had made it clear to me that a language gap exists between the humanities and the sciences. There are in fact several languages here, some highly technical—the language of Arnold and Yeats, the language of the computer, and the language of programming—and one of them was always giving trouble either to the editor or to me. It was further clear that I would probably be an interloper in this volume, since its readers would be likely to be more interested in poetic vocabulary than in computer techniques. However, it seemed that an account of the techniques could be of interest, and I agreed to write it, taking courage from the thought that not all of my readers could have programmed the concordance for the computer.

The Computer

The computer in question was an IBM 704 Data Processing Machine (IBM stands for the International Business Machines Corporation, the manufacturer of the computer; 704 is a number arbitrarily assigned as a means of identifying the type of computer and has no other significance). The IBM 704 can do only a few (about 90) things, but it can do them very rapidly (up to speeds of 42,000 operations per second). The things which the computer can do fall under five functions: input, output, storage, arithmetic, and control.

These terms—which represent our first problem of language—can be simply explained. To begin with, the computer can receive information from the outside world and transmit information back. These functions are called, respectively, "input" and "output," or more familiarly (and anthropocentrically) reading and writing. Input or output to the 704 can make use of magnetic tape, punched cards, printed matter, or lights on the control panel which can be interpreted by the operator. Magnetic tape is usually used for reading and writing because it can be handled much faster than the other input-output media. Computer tape, which is very similar to that used in a tape recorder, is magnetized as data are

inscribed upon it. The tape can be read or written upon very rapidly (15,000 characters per second), but in one direction only. This means that when all the data have been written the reel of tape must be returned to the beginning to be read. This process, called "rewinding," is very slow, usually requiring more than a minute. "Storage" is the function of the section of the machine where data and instructions are stored or preserved for later use in the other sections. For instance, when data are read they must be entered into storage before the arithmetic section can process them. In the 704, the storage unit (or "memory" as it is often called) consists of magnetized cores. These cores are small doughnut-shaped magnets whose magnetism can be changed to represent different numbers. The 704 "memory" has 32,768 "words" of storage, a "word" being either six alphabetic characters or one instruction. The "arithmetic" section does all the addition, subtraction, multiplication, and division; moreover, it can make simple tests (e.g., to discover whether this number is larger than that number). Finally, the "control" section of the computer has the function of supervising the activities of the other four sections.

Information is furnished to a computer in the form of numbers only. It is the outside world that interprets the numbers as actual numbers, or as alphabetic information, or even as computer instructions. Where we see an "A" the computer sees "01"; where we see a "B" the computer sees "02." (This is not the actual code used, but it is analogous.) Thus the question of which comes first in sorting, "APPLE" or "ASPEN," is considered by the 704 to be the question of whether 0116161205 or 0119160514 is smaller. It follows that the 704 could add APPLE to ASPEN and get an answer. In fact this is often done as a check on the machine. A "check sum" is the result of adding certain data together, treating each piece of data only as a number. During sorting, for instance, it is apparent that no matter how the data are rearranged, their sum will be constant. The check here consists of adding all the data before and after a sort and comparing the sums. Of course, all problems do not admit of this error-detection technique. Hence another type of check commonly used on magnetic tape is called "parity" or "redundancy" checking. For this process, each number as it is written has another number added to it, and written automatically on the magnetic tape, such that the sum of the two numbers is odd. This check number is read automatically during reading operations. If the check number plus the read data does not form an odd sum, an error has occurred. Since this type of checking is built into the computer, it is called a "machine" check. The check sum must be programmed, and it is therefore called a "program" check. Both types of check were liberally used in our routines.

The Arnold Concordance Programs

Although I wish to present primarily a description of the program used for the Yeats concordance, I shall begin with a description of the Arnold program so that the changes in the Arnold routines and their motivation can be explained.

Input for the Arnold concordance consisted of magnetic tape prepared from punched cards. The program operated in three phases. The first phase scanned the input cards, each of which contained one line of poetry. It broke the line into its component words and appended an identification of the source line to each word. After all the lines of text had been scanned, the words were sorted into alphabetical order. This was phase two. Phase three retrieved the source lines, edited them, and prepared the printed output. In addition, two auxiliary programs, to be described later, were written.

Because a line of poetry together with its source identification was ordinarily too long to put on one card, two types of cards were used to carry the input information. One type was a title card which identified the following cards as being lines belonging to a specific poem. The title card contained an abbreviation of the title of the poem and a code symbol to indicate that it was a title card. The line cards contained the actual text line of poetry, the page number and line number, and information as to whether or not this was a variant line. During the first phase of the program the appropriate title was appended to the text line; the resultant line was then stored as a record in a "line directory" on a magnetic tape. (A magnetic-tape record is a collection of characters separated physically by blank tape from other similar collections.) The text line was then scanned character by character until all the words on it had been recognized and collected. As each word was collected it was checked against a table of "common" words (that is, words to be omitted from the concordance index). If the word was not "common," a record number or line number was appended to it. This record number "referenced" the corresponding tape record in the line directory. The word and its associated line number were then entered into a section of storage. When this section was filled, its contents were sorted (a very rapid and simple process) and stored on an intermediate magnetic tape in the form of "word blocks." A word block contained 625 words in sorted order, each word with its line number attached. After all words in a line card had been processed—that is, either identified as "common" or prepared for sorting—another input card was read in. This process continued until all the input tape had been exhausted. To sum it up, the first phase of the program read the data tape and produced a line-directory tape and a word-block tape.

The second phase, which was the most time-consuming, consolidated the contents of the word-block tape. The consolidation was accomplished by a series of merges. The data on the word-block tape were written string by string alternately upon two intermediate tapes. (A string is a collection of data in strictly sorted order; for example, each word block produced in the first phase is a string.) The data from two strings, one taken from each of the two tapes, were then merged, producing a single string which was written upon one of a pair of output tapes. Then the data from two more strings, one from each of the two input tapes, were merged and written as a string upon the other output tape. This process of merging two strings into one continued until all the data had been read. The result was to reduce the number of strings to one-half the previous total. The tapes were then rewound, and the merging process was resumed, the old input tapes now becoming output tapes and the old output tapes being used as input. This procedure was repeated, each time reducing the number of strings, until after the final merge only one string remained. At this point all the data had been sorted.

The third phase of the program was the retrieval and editing phase. The word-block tape having been sorted, the words from this tape comprised the index entries for the concordance; the object of this phase was to retrieve the original context of each index word. Two schemes were tried for this retrieval process. The first involved making four copies of the line directory. A count was kept for each tape to specify where the tape was positioned at any given moment. When a new line of context was required, its location as specified by the line number was compared with the present position of each tape. The nearest tape was then moved forward or backward to the proper record; this record was then prepared for printing. This scheme required a lot of useless tape passing; hence it was very slow. It had the advantage that four copies of the line directory were available to the computer at all times, so that an error on one tape could be corrected from another. It was, on the whole, a practical scheme for small volumes of data, but it became impractical at about 10,000 lines of input.

The second scheme was the one used in the actual production of the Arnold concordance. A number of items from the word-block tape were read into core storage. The line numbers associated with these items were then sorted there, and the appropriate lines were looked up in the line directory. Each line requested was read into core storage when found until the table of line numbers was exhausted. The line-directory tape was then rewound. During the time required to rewind the tape, the words from the word block were processed for output. Their context lines were available in core storage; they too were found and prepared for out-

put. The line directory was rewound by the time the editing and output of each group of items were finished. The cycle would then be restarted by bringing in a new group of items from the word-block tape. The third phase was finished when all words from the word-block tape had been processed. Output from the editing process consisted of tapes ready to be printed on the peripheral equipment associated with the computer.

The auxiliary routines mentioned above operated upon either the sorted word-block tape or the line directory. The first routine used the word-block tape to make a frequency table. It counted the number of occurrences of each word and sorted this information according to the frequency. The output from this program was thus a listing of the index words in order of frequency of occurrence. The second auxiliary routine would read the line directory and print in edited form every line containing an occurrence of a specified word. The routine was used to spot-check the main program and to examine homographs. A further, unexpected use of this routine was to prepare printed lines for correction purposes. Imperfections of several sorts occurred during the final printing, the most common arising from ink blots on the paper or from a faulty printing cycle in which an erroneous character was printed. Passes were made to collect single correctly printed lines which could be cut apart and inserted in the proper places before the output page was photographed.

I have already mentioned the system of checks which was written into the programs in an effort to eliminate processing errors in the output. The original input tape was parity-checked. From that point on all core-to-tape information transfers were accompanied by a record check sum, except for the preparation of the final output tape. At every convenient point (at an average of every ten minutes in running the program) the console switches used for program control were examined to see whether the program was running correctly. At the same time a check sum of the program itself was recomputed. If it was not correct, the program "rolled back" to the last check point; that is, the last ten minutes were run again. If the check sum was correct, the program continued.

A harder problem was the checking of data operations and transfers of information from section to section of the computer. This was accomplished both by the built-in parity checks and by the programmed check sums. The line directory was written during the first phase and read during the third. Little tape movement was involved in these operations, and the checks worked very well. During sorting, as has already been explained, the word-block tape was split onto two intermediate tapes and then these two tapes were written upon two more. This process by which two tapes produced two other tapes, continuing until the data were

sorted, involved a very large amount of tape manipulation. To ensure accuracy several precautions were taken. In addition to the record check sum carried with each record, a file check sum was generated by the first phase while the word-block tape was first being written. (A file is simply a collection of records, such as two boxes of cards or one reel of tape.) Before the internal sorting of the word-block tape was begun, a block check sum was generated. It was checked after the sorting of the block and again after the writing of the block on tape. This check sum was then added to the file check sum. During every pass upon the complete file, whether on one tape (first and last passes only) or two tapes, this check sum was recomputed and checked.

Moreover, during the last phase and before printing, a rescanning of the selected line was made to ensure that the line really contained the index word. Despite the fact that all line numbers were check-summed from the time the block was sorted until the line was selected for printing, nine instances were found where the selected line did not contain the specified word. (These nine were from the same section of input text, though not all index words from these lines were in error.) A run was made on the auxiliary selection program to prepare and print replacement lines. It is worth remarking that these nine errors were the only ones found in processing about 17,000 lines, containing over 65,000 indexed words. So far as I know, no machine or programming errors produced errors which survive in the printed Arnold volume. The same is true of the Yeats concordance.

The Yeats Concordance Programs

A critique of the Arnold programs disclosed several problem areas. First, and easiest to correct, the tape merge used during phase two was very inefficient, though it actually was improved during the late stages of production for the Arnold concordance. A second correction introduced a much-improved sorting method for use in phase one. These were, of course, technical changes only, not changes in fundamental method. The fundamental changes from a programmer's viewpoint were based upon two general conclusions. The first was that error detection and correction procedures had to be made an integral part of the entire process, instead of a controlling superstructure. The second was that the context-retrieval problem in phase three would become intolerable with a very moderate increase in the amount of text. An entirely new approach was needed here. Other modifications were also desirable from an editorial viewpoint. The improved print wheels, the cross-reference feature, and the desire for easy editorial control were the main factors to be taken account of here. These matters were negotiated with the editor on a "what is

needed—what is practical" basis, and our common experience with the Arnold procedure made agreements relatively easy to reach.

From a user's point of view, the most impressive change in the Yeats volume is the addition of punctuation to the print. Though this required a new set of type wheels, it involved relatively little programming. From the producer's viewpoint the most impressive change has been the tremendous increase in speed. The Arnold volume was produced in 38 hours of machine time, while the Yeats with one-third more text required only 12 hours. This total could have been reduced even further if the checking for errors had not been so rigorous. These figures, which purport to be the time required to produce the final text, are not all that they seem to be, for they really represent the minimum computer time that would be required if everything ran perfectly. They do not include program-testing time, nor rerun time required by errors (human and machine), nor time used by the auxiliary routines. The figures are thus more nearly indicative of a rate of speed than of a span of actual time. The improvement in speed in Yeats was brought about by improvements in sorting and merging techniques in phases one and two and by one major change in strategy. In the Arnold program, the context of each word was coded as a line number and appended to the text-word entry. This was done to reduce the volume of data sorted in phase two, but it produced a very bad retrieval problem in phase three. In Yeats, the source line itself was appended to the text-word entry and carried through the sort. This meant that the sort processed much more data, but also that the retrieval problem in phase three disappeared. What we were dealing with here was a general problem that always occurs in sorting. For small amounts of data, it is usually more effective to code the context and retrieve it after sorting. For large amounts of data, it is usually more effective to append the context and eliminate the retrieval problem, even though this means that the sort must process more data.

Based upon the Arnold experience, a completely new set of programs was written, checked out, and used to prepare the present volume. They operated in four phases, rather than the three used for Arnold. The first phase operated upon magnetic tape produced from line and title cards very similar to those of Arnold. There were relatively few changes in the input. Output from the first phase consisted of three tapes—the line directory, the word-block tape, and a cross-reference tape. The line directory was identical, except for format, to that of Arnold. The word-block tape contained both index words and their associated context lines. The cross-reference tape was analogous to the word-block tape except that it contained only portions of hyphenated words together with their complete form.

The second phase sorted the word-block tape and the cross-reference tape independently. Once again this phase took the longest time, but it was still quite an improvement over the Arnold program. The third phase merged the word-block and cross-reference tapes and produced "un-paged" printing (i.e., a listing of each line in edited form, but with no attempt made to divide the lines into pages). In addition to the edited line, a unique line number was produced for each line. This line number was used to control the desired editorial changes for the final printing. The last phase made all the changes requested by the editor that could be accomplished by the operations of "insert," "delete," and "replace" any line or lines. It also put the lines into page format, that is, reprinted the index word with (CONTINUED) if needed at the top of a page, titled the identification columns, and adjusted the number of lines per page. In addition to the four basic phases, the same two auxiliary routines (designed to print selected lines and to prepare the frequency data) were written. These were identical in function to those of the Arnold program except that, besides the frequencies of the printed words, frequencies of omitted words were also shown.

The Arnold experience, in which errors had occurred despite the check sums, prompted us to devise a more stringent system of checks for Yeats. To begin with, the first phase of the Yeats was run twice, using the same input data. Between the first and second phases a checking pass was made upon the output tapes produced by the two runs of phase one to make sure that these tapes were identical (machine errors would have produced discrepancies between them). At the end of the check pass, a check sum was punched into cards. This check sum was used as an independent check upon the tape sorting; it guaranteed that the tapes used as input to the merge were correct. The record and file check sums were used as a control during the merge. The third phase used record check sums and parity checks for its control.

With all the checking machine errors were much less troublesome for this volume than for the Arnold one. There are three things that would account for this fact. First, the 704 itself is better, since it has been in operation long enough to become a proven computer. Second, the programmed error procedures were better. Third, the machine time was much shorter, so that the 704 simply had less opportunity to fail.

Conclusion

Based upon our experiences with Arnold and Yeats, minor changes are being incorporated in the programs for future volumes—so minor as to represent my desire to change things for change's sake, rather than any significant improvement. Future volumes should be produced more and

more rapidly as this work becomes more routine. It is axiomatic that a computer should not be used for a problem unless the problem must be solved many times. Thus the preparation of one or two concordances is not efficient, but the preparation of many volumes becomes a valid application of computers. The start we have made should now make it possible to produce basic information of this sort for a whole series of authors.

My motives for participating in the project have been twofold. First, and most important, is the fact that concordances represent a technical problem which I find interesting. Secondly, I am convinced that data of this type should be available, just as data in scientific and mathematical tables are available. I probably will never need to know Yeats's uses of PAINTER. I doubt if I will ever need to know the heat of fusion of acetic acid, though I might need to know what the sine of 78° 15′ is. In any event, I am certain that a good reference library ought to have all this data available. This volume represents my attempt to help compile some of the data.

Poughkeepsie, New York   JAMES A. PAINTER
September 1962

A Concordance to the Poems of

W. B. YEATS

                                                          PAGE   TITLE   LINE

ABASHED
    I WAS ABASHED, AND NOW THEY COME TO MIND . . . .   353 PEOPLE   36
    AFTER NINE YEARS, I SINK MY HEAD ABASHED. . . . .   353 PEOPLE   37
    TIMID, ENTANGLED, EMPTY AND ABASHED, ...   368 EGO DOMINUS   16
    ABASHED BY THAT REPORT, ...   516 MANS SONG   13
ABBEY
    AT THE ABBEY THEATRE . . . .   264 ABBEY THEATRE   T
    MY FATHER UPON THE ABBEY STAGE, BEFORE HIM A RAGING CROWD: 577 LOFTY THINGS   2
    THEN THAT OLD ABBEY ACTOR, DUDLEY DIGGES, ...   790 DEDICATION   7
ABBOT
    AN ABBOT OR ARCHBISHOP WITH AN UPRAISED HAND . . . . .   601 GALLERY REVIS   9
ABD
    TO ABD AL-RABBAN: FELLOW-ROYSTERER ONCE, ...   460 HARUN RASHID   2
ABD-AL-RABBAN
    TO ABD-AL-RABBAN: FELLOW ROYSTERER ONCE . . . .   460 HARUN RASHID   V   2
ABEAT
    ANGERS THAT ARE LIKE NOISY CLOUDS HAVE SET OUR HEARTS   207 HANRAHANS SONG   8
        ABEAT:
    ANGERS THAT ARE LIKE BUNDLED CLOUDS HAVE SET OUR HEARTS   207 HANRAHANS SONG V   8
        ABEAT:
ABED
    THE EMPEROR'S DRUNKEN SOLDIERY ARE ABED: . . . .   497 BYZANTIUM   2
    BUT SHE IS STILL ABED, ...   595 COLONEL MARTIN   31
A-BED
    THE EMPEROR'S DRUNKEN SOLDIERY ARE A-BED: . . . . . .   497 BYZANTIUM   V   2
    BUT SHE IS STILL A-BED . . . .   595 COLONEL MARTIN V   31
ABIDE
    WASHES THE SHORES WHERE YE ABIDE, ...   5 OISIN 1   V 47
    BUT WE IN A LONELY LAND ABIDE . . . .   22 OISIN 1   337
    YOUTH, HERE WILL WE ABIDE, AND BE THOU KING . . . . .   679 ISLE STAT II 3   314
ABIDES
    A TOSSING LAUGH BETWEEN THEIR RED ABIDES: . . . . . .   735 QUATRAIN APHOR   22
ABLE
    I'LL HAVE ASSURANCE THAT YOU ARE ABLE . . . .   304 HOUR DAWN   51
    "I'LL HAVE MY SAY, TILL I AM ABLE . . . .   304 HOUR DAWN   V 51
    "I'D HAVE ASSURANCE THAT YOU ARE ABLE . . . .   304 HOUR DAWN   V 51
ABLOW
    FOR DREAMS ARE THE FLOWERS ABLOW, ...   743 WISDOM DREAMS   6
A-BLOWIN'
    A-BLOWIN' OF HER MORNIN' FIRE, ...   95 MOLL MAGEE   V 35
ABOARD
    WHEN SHE FINDS OUT WE HAVE BETTER MEN ABOARD . . . . .   232 SHADOW WATER B   231
    I SAW A FLAGON OF BROWN ALE ABOARD HER. . . . .   240 SHADOW WATER B   388
    WHEN YOU ARE ABOARD THE LOCHLANN GALLEY, LASH . . . .   752 SHADOW WATER A   128
ABODE
    BOW DOWN, ARCHANGELS, IN YOUR DIM ABODE: . . . . . .   112 ROSE OF WORLD   11
    ABODE, AS BANDED ADDERS IN MY BREAST. . . . .   683 SEEKER   50
ABOLISHED
    ABOLISHED BY A MIRE OF LITTLE THINGS, ...   711 FERENCZ RENYI   36
ABOUNDING
    THE ABOUNDING GUTTER HAD BEEN HELICON . . . .   398 LEADERS CROWD   6
    THE ABOUNDING GLITTERING JET: THOUGH NOW IT SEEMS . . .   417 ANCEST HOUSES   12
    AND WHEN ABOUNDING HEDGES RING . . . .   434 WHEEL   3
    AND WHEN ABOUNDING HEDGES SING . . . .   434 WHEEL   V   3
    WHO FINDS ABOUNDING CEPHISUS . . . .   447 COLONUS PRAISE   23
    ABOUNDING FOLIAGE MOISTENED WITH THE DEW: . . . . . .   500 VACILLATION   13
ABOUT
    ABOUT HIS FADING CRIMSON BALL: . . . .   12 OISIN 1   155
    ABOUT THEM: AND THE HORSE OF FAERY SCREAMED . . . . .   30 OISIN 2   24
    JABBER AND SCREAM ABOUT HIM IN THE NIGHT: . . . . . .   34 OISIN 2   82
    MAKING A WORLD ABOUT HER IN THE AIR, ...   37 OISIN 2   122
    MAKING A WORLD ABOUT HER, PASSED FROM SIGHT . . . . .   37 OISIN 2   V   123
    SHOUTED. WITH FIRE OF HAIR ABOUT HER SWIRLED, . . .   38 OISIN 2   V   134
    COULD SLEEP ON A COUCH OF RUSHES--ROUND AND ABOUT THEM   49 OISIN 3   V   32
        LAID.
    AND LONELY AND LONGING FOR NIAMH, I SHIVERED AND TURNED   60 OISIN 3   181
        ME ABOUT,
    AND SHIVERING AND LONELY, AND LONGING FOR NIAM, I TURNED   60 OISIN 3   V   181
        ME ABOUT,
    TO THOSE ABOUT, "BEAT HIM WITH THONGS OF HIDE . . . .   106 CUCHULAIN SEA V 17A
    WHILE YOUNG STARS ABOUT HER DANCE. . . . .   125 CATHLEEN PARA V   16
    DID NOT THE WORMS THAT SPIRED ABOUT HIS BONES . . . .   128 DREAM OF FAERY   41
    WERE NOT THE WORMS THAT SPIRED ABOUT HIS BONES . . .   128 DREAM OF FAERY V   41
    MY HEART WOULD BRIM WITH DREAMS ABOUT THE TIMES . . .   136 TO SOME I TALK   2
    TRAILS ALL ABOUT THE WRITTEN PAGE. . . . .   138 TO IRELAND   9
    ABOUT MY TABLE TO AND FRO, ...   138 TO IRELAND   24
    FOR ROUND ABOUT MY TABLE GO . . . .   138 TO IRELAND   V   23
    ABOUT MY TABLE TO AND FRO, ...   139 TO IRELAND   40
    THE DANCERS CROWDED ABOUT HIM . . . .   144 HOST OF AIR   17
    ABOUT THE CASTING OUT OF MY NET, ...   146 FISH   4
    OVER MY HEART, AND YOUR HAIR FALL ABOUT MY BREAST . .   154 BELOVED PEACE V   10
    OF UNKNOWN PERISHING ARMIES BEAT ABOUT MY EARS. . . .   161 BLACK PIG   4
    AND DREAM ABOUT THE GREAT AND THEIR PRIDE: . . . . .   166 EVIL OF BELOV   2
    ARE SINGING ABOUT THE WOOD?" . . . .   167 BLESSED   24
    WHEN SHALL THE STARS BE BLOWN ABOUT THE SKY, ...   170 SECRET ROSE   29
    BUT THINK ABOUT OLD FRIENDS THE MOST: . . . .   173 PLEADS FRIEND   5
    ABOUT THE STARS AND MOON AND SUN: . . . .   176 BELOVED DEAD   10
    ABOUT MY THRESHOLD TO COUNSEL AND TO HELP?" . . . .   183 QUEEN MAEVE   82
    ABOUT MY DOOR TO COUNSEL AND TO HELP." . . . . . .   183 QUEEN MAEVE   V   82
    FOR THERE IS NO HIGH STORY ABOUT QUEENS . . . . . .   186 QUEEN MAEVE   134
    ABOUT WHOSE FACE BIRDS WAGGED THEIR FIERY WINGS, . .   187 QUEEN MAEVE   145

1

	PAGE	TITLE		LINE

ABOUT   (CONTINUED)
```
    ABOUT THE TIME WHEN CHRIST WAS BORN, . . . . . . .   189 BAILE AILLINN       13
    BEING TUMBLED AND BLOWN ABOUT . . . . . . . . . .   191 BAILE AILLINN       66
    ABOUT THE WINDY WATER-SIDE, . . . . . . . . . . .   192 BAILE AILLINN       93
    ABOUT THE WINDY WATER SIDE  . . . . . . . . . . .   192 BAILE AILLINN     V 93
    GATHERING HIS CLOAK ABOUT HIM, RUN  . . . . . . .   193 BAILE AILLINN      101
    WHO PEERED ABOUT ON EVERY SIDE, . . . . . . . . .   193 BAILE AILLINN     V 112
    UPON THE THRONE AND CRYING ABOUT THE STREETS  . .   198 SEVEN WOODS          7
    AND LITTLE SHADOWS COME ABOUT HER EYES, . . . . .   199 FOLLY COMFORT        3
    AND THERE ARE LITTLE CREASES ABOUT HER EYES, . .    199 FOLLY COMFORT     V 3
    THE FIRE THAT STIRS ABOUT HER, WHEN SHE STIRS, .    200 FOLLY COMFORT       10
    ABOUT THE STARS AND BROKE IN DAYS AND YEARS, . .    206 ADAMS CURSE         33
    ABOUT THE STARN AND BROKE IN DAYS AND YEARS, . .    206 ADAMS CURSE       V 33
    RED HANRAHAN'S SONG ABOUT IRELAND . . . . . . . .   206 HANRAHANS SONG       T
    AND DO YOU GATHER ABOUT US WHEN PALE LIGHT  . . .   218 WOODS OF COOLE      37
    OR CRY ABOUT ONE'S EARS.  NOTHING TO FEAR, . . .    222 SHADOW WATER B      19
    OR FUMBLING IN A DREAM ABOUT THE HOUSE?   . . . .   230 SHADOW WATER B     174
    CARE MORE ABOUT THE KEGS OF SILVER AND GOLD . . .   232 SHADOW WATER B     234
    AND THAT IS WHY THE WORLD TOTTERS ABOUT. . . . .    233 SHADOW WATER B     238
    OF THE GREAT GOLDEN NET THAT IS ABOUT US, . . . .   238 SHADOW WATER B     352
    BELOVED, HAVING DRAGGED THE NET ABOUT US, . . . .   252 SHADOW WATER B     615
    NOTHING TO MAKE A SONG ABOUT BUT KINGS, . . . . .   257 RECONCILIATION       5
    THESE ARE THE CLOUDS ABOUT THE FALLEN SUN, . . .    265 THESE CLOUDS         1
    THESE ARE THE CLOUDS ABOUT THE FALLEN SUN, . . .    265 THESE CLOUDS        11
    THEY HAVE GONE ABOUT THE WORLD LIKE WIND, . . . .   289 SEPTEMBER 1913      11
    WHEN GREY GULLS FLIT ABOUT INSTEAD OF MEN, . . .    292 TO A SHADE           6
    WHEN GREY GULLS FLY ABOUT INSTEAD OF MEN, . . . .   292 TO A SHADE        V 6
    ABOUT YOUR HEAD TILL THE DUST STOPS YOUR EAR, . .   293 TO A SHADE          20
    ROUND ABOUT HELL'S GATE TO STARE  . . . . . . . .   294 HATED PLAYBOY     V 3
    ABOUT A FARM," THE SECOND CRIED. . . . . . . . .    296 THREE BEGGARS     V 38
    AND SEEN THE RUBBISH RUN ABOUT, . . . . . . . . .   297 THREE BEGGARS       65
    AS THOUGH DRIED STRAW, AND IF WE TURN ABOUT . . .   327 ROBERT GREGORY      83
    SHE GOES ABOUT HER HOUSE ERECT AND CALM . . . . .   340 SHEP GOATHERD       35
    I HAVE GONE ABOUT THE HOUSE, GONE UP AND DOWN . .   350 HER PRAISE           2
    IT IS ABOUT TO DIE. . . . . . . . . . . . . . .     367 HER CHRIS TREE      12
    I LAY ABOUT ME WITH THE TAWS  . . . . . . . . . .   379 SAINT HUNCH          8
    IS MOVING ITS SLOW THIGHS, WHILE ALL ABOUT IT . .   402 SECOND COMING       16
    THAT PITCHES COMMON THINGS ABOUT.  THERE STOOD  .   428 NINETEEN 19          4
    BUT TROD THE ROAD, OR SPLASHED ABOUT THE SHORE, .   447 COLONUS PRAISE      27
    AND A CLOAK WRAPPED ABOUT THE STONE,  . . . . . .   456 FRIENDS YOUTH        7
    AND PAUSE AT LAST, I WAS ABOUT TO SAY, . . . . .    461 HARUN RASHID        11
    AND ASKED ABOUT THE PICTURES OR THE TEXT, . . . .   466 HARUN RASHID       121
    AND ASKED ABOUT THESE PICTURES OR THOSE OTHERS, .   466 HARUN RASHID      V 121
    AND SWEPT THE HOUSE AND SANG ABOUT HER WORK . . .   468 HARUN RASHID       148
    ON THE SOUL'S JOURNEY.  HOW IT IS WHIRLED ABOUT, .  472 ALL SOUL NIGHT      54
    FIVE HUNDRED YEARS AGO, ABOUT IT LIE  . . . . . .   478 SELF AND SOUL       26
    I TURNED ABOUT AND LOOKED WHERE BRANCHES BREAK  .   490 COOLE BALLYLEE      15
    I TURNED ABOUT AND LOOKED WHERE BRANCHES BROKE  .   490 COOLE BALLYLEE    V 15
    WE SHIFT ABOUT--ALL THAT GREAT GLORY SPENT-- . .    491 COOLE BALLYLEE      39
    MAN SHIFTS ABOUT--ALL THAT GREAT GLORY SPENT-- .    491 COOLE BALLYLEE    V 39
    WINGS BEATING ABOUT THE ROOM; . . . . . . . . . .   499 MOTHER OF GOD        3
    CHANGE THEIR LOVES ABOUT. . . . . . . . . . . . .   520 HIS BARGAIN          6
    ABOUT THE SKY, WHERE THAT IS CLEAR OF CLOUD . . .   541 PARN FUNERAL 1       3
    EMPEDOCLES HAS THROWN ALL THINGS ABOUT; . . . . .   564 GYRES                6
    THE GREAT STAGE CURTAIN ABOUT TO DROP, . . . . .    565 LAPIS LAZULI        13
    POETS AND WITS ABOUT HIM DREW; . . . . . . . . .    577 WHAT THEN           14
    AND THERE'S NO LUCK ABOUT A HOUSE . . . . . . . .   584 GHOST ROG CASE      27
    I POKED ABOUT A VILLAGE CHURCH  . . . . . . . . .   584 GHOST ROG CASE      31
    WHAT REMAINS TO SING ABOUT  . . . . . . . . . . .   585 ORAHILLY            28
    "BECAUSE I AM MAD ABOUT WOMEN . . . . . . . . . .   587 OLD WICKED MAN       1
    I AM MAD ABOUT THE HILLS," . . . . . . . . . . .    587 OLD WICKED MAN       2
    ALL KNOW THAT ALL THE DEAD IN THE WORLD ABOUT THAT PLACE  593 PILGRIM        11
       ARE STUCK,
    BOUND A THONG ABOUT HIS HAND, . . . . . . . . . .   595 COLONEL MARTIN      25
    CARRY THE GOLD ABOUT THE TOWN, . . . . . . . . .    596 COLONEL MARTIN      52
    I KNOCK THEIR HEADS ABOUT. . . . . . . . . . . .    605 SONGS BURDEN 1       8
    THAT SOMETHING IS ABOUT TO HAPPEN, I THINK . . .    609 IN TARAS HALLS       4
    PLOTINUS CAME AND LOOKED ABOUT. . . . . . . . . .   611 NEWS ORACLE          9
    I TALKED ABOUT AN APPARITION, . . . . . . . . . .   624 APPARITIONS          2
    WITH BOYS AND GIRLS ABOUT HIM, . . . . . . . . .    627 STATES HOLIDAY      27
    WHAT HE TALKS ABOUT, . . . . . . . . . . . . . .    631 POLITICS             6
    ABOUT THE SEA.  BEFORE HER LIES THAT YOUTH, . . .   687 TWO TITANS          22
    ABOUT A SUN-FLUSHED DOVE-COT, COOING, CLING . . .   710 FERENCZ RENYI       20
    I KEEP SUCH THINGS ABOUT ME; THEY ARE FOOD, . . .   721 WITCH VIVIEN        37
    WHAT SHALLOW THOUGHTS ABOUT DEEP THINGS! . . . .    725 LEGEND              11
    WHEN HUNDREDS STOOD ABOUT TO SEE  . . . . . . . .   740 EARL PAUL           27
    AND PLUMED HEADS ABOUT HIM, . . . . . . . . . . .   740 EARL PAUL           31
    HOW ALL THAT DIE ARE BORNE ABOUT THE WORLD  . . .   750 SHADOW WATER A      84
    AND TURN HIS GALLEY ABOUT AND BRING ME HOME. . .    751 SHADOW WATER A     108
    THE GODS HOLD WATCH ABOUT THE WORDS OF A QUEEN. .   756 SHADOW WATER A     191
    GATHER ABOUT HIM, THAT THE GODS MAY NOT KNOW  . .   758 SHADOW WATER A     231
    THERE'S SO MUCH TO THINK ABOUT  . . . . . . . . .   772 SONG DEIRDRE 1       7
ABOVE
    WE RODE IN SADNESS ABOVE LOUGH LAEN, . . . . . .     2 OISIN 1           V 7H
    AND 'TWEEN HIS EARS, ABOVE HIS MANE, . . . . . .     2 OISIN 1           V 7AA
    AND SET YOUR NAME ALL NAMES ABOVE, . . . . . . .     7 OISIN 1             76
    SHE SAID: "FOR HE IS FAIR ABOVE  . . . . . . . .     7 OISIN 1           V 62A
    BY ROOTS THAT JOINED ABOVE OUR PLUMES-- . . . .     16 OISIN 1           V 224C
    BENT DOWN ABOVE EACH HOOKED KNEE, . . . . . . . .   26 OISIN 1            392
    HE HEARS THE STORM IN THE CHIMNEY ABOVE, . . . .    26 OISIN 1            404
    BENT LOW ABOVE EACH HOOKED KNEE, . . . . . . . .    26 OISIN 1           V 392
```

	PAGE	TITLE		LINE
ABOVE (CONTINUED)				
FOG-DRIPPING, PEDESTALLED ABOVE THE TIDE,	31	OISIN 2	V	36
FROM HIGH ABOVE, LIKE FEATHERS OF YOUNG BIRDS	32	OISIN 2	V	50
WAITED. ABOVE, IN ENDLESS CARVEN JAGS,	38	OISIN 2	V	144
AND THE STARS WERE BLOTTED ABOVE US,	48	OISIN 3		24
THE WOOD WAS SO SPACIOUS ABOVE THEM,	49	OISIN 3		37
SO SPACIOUS THE WOOD WAS ABOVE THEM,	49	OISIN 3	V	37
HIS LANGUID TAIL ABOVE US, LIT WITH MYRIAD SPOTS OF LIGHT,	77	INDIAN ON GOD		20
YELLOW THE LEAVES OF THE ROWAN ABOVE US,	79	FALLING LEAVES		3
I STOOD; KEEN STARS ABOVE ME SHONE,	83	MAD KING GOLL		29
I PAUSED--THE STARS ABOVE ME FLASHED,	83	MAD KING GOLL	V	29
I PAUSED--THE STARS ABOVE ME SHONE	83	MAD KING GOLL	V	29
FROM THE HILLS ABOVE GLEN-CAR,	88	STOLEN CHILD		29
AND THE WAVES FLOWED ABOVE HIM AND HE DIED,	111	CUCHULAIN SEA	V	86
ABOVE THE TIDE OF HOURS, TROUBLE THE AIR,	114	ROSE OF BATTLE		3
ABOVE THE TIDE OF HOURS, RISE ON THE AIR,	114	ROSE OF BATTLE	V	3
AND THE STARS ABOVE:	116	FAERY SONG		8
ABOVE YOUR BED:	118	CRADLE SONG		2
ABOVE YOUR WHITE BED,	118	CRADLE SONG	V	2
THE CLOUDS ON THEIR JOURNEY ABOVE,	119	PITY OF LOVE		4
HE PACED UPON THE MOUNTAINS FAR ABOVE,	121	YOU ARE OLD	V	11
AND THEY HAD NAILED THE BOARDS ABOVE HER FACE,	123	DREAM OF DEATH		3
AND RAISED ABOVE HER MOUND	123	DREAM OF DEATH		6
AND LEFT HER TO THE INDIFFERENT STARS ABOVE	123	DREAM OF DEATH		9
AND GAZED UPON THE MOURNFUL STARS ABOVE,	123	DREAM OF DEATH	V	11
AND ABOVE THE DEEP OF HEAVEN,	125	CATHLEEN PARA	V	15
WHEN WE BENT DOWN ABOVE THE FADING COALS	136	TO SOME I TALK		3
WHILE THE NIGHT GREW, ABOVE THE FADING COALS,	136	TO SOME I TALK	V	3
WHO RISE, WING ABOVE WING, FLAME ABOVE FLAME,	137	TO SOME I TALK		11
WHO RISE, WING ABOVE WING, FLAME ABOVE FLAME,	137	TO SOME I TALK		11
WHAT MEASURER TIME HAS LIT ABOVE,	139	TO IRELAND		38
THE MARINERS OF NIGHT ABOVE,	139	TO IRELAND	V	38
THE NORTH UNFOLDS ABOVE THEM CLINGING, CREEPING NIGHT,	154	BELOVED PEACE		3
THE NORTH UNROLLS ABOVE THEM CLINGING, CREEPING NIGHT,	154	BELOVED PEACE	V	3
ABOVE THE WANDERING TIDE:	162	ASKS FORGIVE		14
AND WRAPPED THE FLAMES ABOVE HIS HOLY HEAD,	162	ASKS FORGIVE		17
AND GATHERED THE FLAMES ABOVE HIS HOLY HEAD,	162	ASKS FORGIVE	V	17
ABOVE ITS CLOUDY RIM:	175	ELEMENT POWERS		16
ABOVE THE STARS AND MOON AND SUN:	176	BELOVED DEAD	V	10
THEY HAVE HEAPED THE STONES ABOVE HIS GRAVE	193	BAILE AILLINN		115
WHAT ARE YOU CALLING OUT ABOVE THE MAST?	243	SHADOW WATER B		437
I WEEP--I WEEP BECAUSE BARE NIGHT'S ABOVE,	246	SHADOW WATER B		499
AND KNELT ABOVE IT WITH DRAWN KNIFE. ON THE INSTANT	278	TWO KINGS		37
ABOVE A WINDY PRECIPICE?" THEN HE:	285	TWO KINGS		195
THE BELL-BEAT OF THEIR WINGS ABOVE MY HEAD,	323	SWANS AT COOLE		17
SOMEWHERE AMONG THE CLOUDS ABOVE:	328	IRISH AIRMAN		2
ABOVE THE CLOUDY SHOULDERS OF THE HORSES:	344	DAWN		12
A LAMP BURNS ON ABOVE THE OPEN BOOK	367	EGO DOMINUS	V	3
NOW SHE HAS THROWN HER ARMS ABOVE HER HEAD:	390	IMAGE PAST		36
IN THE ELMS ABOVE THE FLOODED STREAM:	403	FOR DAUGHTER		12
ABOVE THE MURDEROUS TREACHERY OF THE MOON,	428	NINETEEN 19	V	3
ABOVE THE STAGGERING GIRL, HER THIGHS CARESSED	441	LEDA AND SWAN		2
ABOVE A SINKING FIRE, A TALE THAT SHE	443	SCHOOL CHILDR		10
ABOVE A SINKING FIRE, SOME TALE THAT SHE	443	SCHOOL CHILDR	V	10
GREAT NATIONS BLOSSOM ABOVE:	547	TO SAME TUNE 3		5
FROM ABOVE TO BELOW,	547	TO SAME TUNE 3	V	6
HERE IN THE PITCH-DARK ATMOSPHERE ABOVE	555	RIBH AT TOMB		17
HERE IN THE PITCH DARK ATMOSPHERE ABOVE	555	RIBH AT TOMB	V	17
THE DOOR ABOVE HIS HEAD	585	ORAHILLY		33
ARE SUNG ABOVE THE GLASS,	587	PARNELLITES		30
ARE SUNG ABOVE A GLASS,	587	PARNELLITES	V	30
GREAT NATIONS BLOSSOM ABOVE:	614	MARCH SONGS 2		5
TO PROVE WHAT CAN YE DO? WHAT THINGS ABOVE	650	ISLE STAT I 1		146
ABOVE THESE MEN WHOSE MOUTHS WERE SEALED	656	ISLE STAT I 3		27
FROM YONDER PINNACLE ABOVE THE LAKE	657	ISLE STAT I 3		63
CAN ENTER THERE. SEE! SEE! ABOVE YON BROW	659	ISLE STAT II 1		27
THE AIR IS STILL ABOVE, AND STILL EACH LEAF,	662	ISLE STAT II 2		7
WHERE RISE THE WALLS MAJESTICAL ABOVE	679	ISLE STAT II 3		311
AND THE FLOWING AIR ABOVE,	680	LOVE AND DEATH		14
DROPT DOWN THE VELVET DARKNESS FROM ABOVE,	688	TWO TITANS		37
ABOVE, SALIVA DRIPPING FROM HIS JAWS,	689	NETTLESHIP		4
(SWALLOWS WERE FLASHING THEIR WHITE BREASTS ABOVE	690	MOSADA 1		7
ABOVE THE ALPUJARRAS ON THEIR THRONES:	691	MOSADA 1		27
ABOVE THE FARM-HOUSE BY THE LITTLE LAKE	699	MOSADA 3		3
SOON WILL THE CHURCHMEN NOD ABOVE THE CROWD,	699	MOSADA 3		19
BEFORE WE TAKE OUR SEATS ABOVE THE CROWD,	704	MOSADA 3		134
ABOVE, THE WOODS WHERE WITH THE SOFT MILD EYE	710	FERENCZ RENYI		26
AND EVERY FLOWER ABOVE ITS SHADOW SITS,	712	FERENCZ RENYI		73
AND EVERY FLOWER ABOVE A SHADOW SITS,	712	FERENCZ RENYI	V	73
WHEN WE ROWED NORTH, SINGING ABOVE THE OARS,	749	SHADOW WATER A		39
HE HOVERS ABOVE THE MAST AND WAITS HIS KIND:	753	SHADOW WATER A		135
ABROAD				
RISES, AND SHOWERS ABROAD HIS FRAGRANT ARROWS,	72	ANASHU VIJAYA		27
ABSENT				
I'LL HAVE. OH, ABSENT ONE 'TIS NOT FOR DEARTH	664	ISLE STAT II 2		50
ABSOLVO				
AND HAS NOT HEARD ABSOLVO TE.	656	ISLE STAT I 3		19
ABSTINENCE				
I AM SO LECHEROUS WITH ABSTINENCE	222	SHADOW WATER B	V	8
ABSTRACT				
THEY DO NOT EVEN FEEL, SO ABSTRACT ARE THEY,	382	VISION ROBART		14

3

	PAGE	TITLE		LINE
ABSTRACT (CONTINUED)				
BECAME A BITTER, AN ABSTRACT THING,	397	POLIT PRISONER		9
IN ABSTRACT THINGS; OR BE DERIDED BY	409	TOWER		15
IT HAD BUT MADE US PINE THE MORE. THE ABSTRACT JOY,	427	PHANTOM HATRED		38
IN THE MAD ABSTRACT DARK AND GROUND IT GRAIN BY GRAIN	442	BLACK CENTAUR		8
OR OUT OF ABSTRACT HATRED, AND SHED BLOOD,	482	BLOOD AND MOON		38
AN ABSTRACT GREEK ABSURDITY HAS CRAZED THE MAN--	556	RIBH PATRICK		1
ABSTRACTIONS				
ALL THOSE ABSTRACTIONS THAT YOU FANCIED WERE	469	HARUN RASHID		182
AND THOSE ABSTRACTIONS THAT YOU FANCIED WERE	469	HARUN RASHID	V	182
ABSTRACTIONS OF THE GREEK PHILOSOPHY HAVE CRAZED THE MAN,	556	RIBH PATRICK	V	1
ABSURD				
HE SPLASHED WHERE AN ABSURD	400	DEMON BEAST		27
ABSURDITY				
WHAT SHALL I DO WITH THIS ABSURDITY--	409	TOWER		1
AN ABSTRACT GREEK ABSURDITY HAS CRAZED THE MAN--	556	RIBH PATRICK		1
ABU				
DOWN TO THE TUNE OF O'DONNELL ABU.	544	TO SAME TUNE 1		10
DOWN TO THE TUNE OF O'DONNELL ABU.	545	TO SAME TUNE 1		20
DOWN TO THE TUNE OF O'DONNELL ABU.	545	TO SAME TUNE 1		30
DOWN TO THE TUNE OF O'DONNELL ABU.	546	TO SAME TUNE 2	V	REF
DOWN TO THE TUNE OF O'DONNELL ABU.	548	TO SAME TUNE 3	V	REF
ABUNDANCE				
KING ABUNDANCE GOT HIM ON	440	WISDOM		16
UPON THE ABUNDANCE OF MY BREAST"!	521	THREE THINGS		5
ABYSS				
UPON HIS WINGS. THRO' YONDER GREEN ABYSS	649	ISLE STAT I 1		114
ACACIA				
TO SCATTER THE ACACIA SPRAY	360	ALF POLLEXFEN		10
ACADEMY				
ON MR. NETTLESHIP'S PICTURE AT THE ROYAL HIBERNIAN ACADEMY.	688	NETTLESHIP		T
ACCEPT				
ACCEPT THE MIRACLES OF THE SAINTS AND HONOUR SANCTITY?	503	VACILLATION		79
ACCEPTED				
WHO HAVE ACCEPTED THE BYZANTINE FAITH,	464	HARUN RASHID		78
ACCIDENT				
IT WAS AN ACCIDENT."	319	DOLLS		20
NOR ACCIDENT OF PEACE NOR WAR	446	COLONUS PRAISE		14
ACCIDENTAL				
EVERY ACCIDENTAL CRACK OR DENT,	567	LAPIS LAZULI		44
ACCIDENTS				
THOSE UNDREAMT ACCIDENTS THAT HAVE MADE ME	321	REED WHISPERER		10
ACCLAIMING				
ACCLAIMING, PROCLAIMING, DECLAIMING HIM.	528	DANCER CRUACH		8
ACCOMPLISH				
BEFORE HE CAN ACCOMPLISH FATE,	638	BEN BULBEN		35
ACCOMPLISHED				
MIGHT BE ACCOMPLISHED. BUNCHING THE CURTAIN UP	183	QUEEN MAEVE		68
ALL WAS ACCOMPLISHED. "WHEN THIS DAY	273	GREY ROCK		70
ACCOMPLISHED HIS PREDESTINED WILL,	522	LULLABY		16
ACCOMPLISHED FINGERS BEGIN TO PLAY.	567	LAPIS LAZULI		54
ACCOMPLISHMENT				
YOUTH CAN EXCEL THEM IN ACCOMPLISHMENT,	340	SHEP GOATHERD		47
A MARVELLOUS ACCOMPLISHMENT,	421	MY TABLE		17
ACCORDING				
ACCORDING TO A DIFFERENT PLAN.	379	SAINT HUNCH		6
ACCORDING TO THE WIND, FOR ALL ARE BLIND.	433	NINETEEN 19		124
"ACCORDING TO MY BOYISH PLAN!	577	WHAT THEN		17
"GREATEST SINCE REMBRANDT," ACCORDING TO JOHN SYNGE!	602	GALLERY REVIS		26
ACCOUNT				
AND WE AND ALL THE MUSES ARE THINGS OF NO ACCOUNT.	580	CURSE CROMWELL		12
ACCOUNTED				
KNOW, THAT I WOULD ACCOUNTED BE	137	TO IRELAND		1
ACCURSED SEE MOON-ACCURSED				
MAYBE THE WEATHER WAS ACCURSED	305	HOUR DAWN		65
SO LET HER THINK OPINIONS ARE ACCURSED.	405	FOR DAUGHTER		58
IMAGINING MOON ACCURSED,	454	EMPTY CUP	V	4
OR THE FIDDLE-STRING ACCURSED,	527	AM OF IRELAND		20
OR THE FIDDLE STRING ACCURSED,	527	AM OF IRELAND	V	20
ACCURSED WHO BRINGS TO LIGHT OF DAY	779	ACCURSED WHO		1
ACCURST				
COMPANIONS LONG ACCURST AND DEAD,	11	OISIN 1		130
FOR I AND ALL MY PEOPLE WERE ACCURST	690	MOSADA 1		15
IN EVERY DANCE, BY CHILDREN SOUGHT. "ACCURST,	709	FERENCZ RENYI		12
ACCUSATION				
I THIRST FOR ACCUSATION. ALL THAT WAS SUNG,	542	PARN FUNERAL 1		25
ACCUSE				
THEY MUST TO KEEP THEIR CERTAINTY ACCUSE	398	LEADERS CROWD		1
ACCUSED SEE SELF-ACCUSED				
ACCUSING				
EVEN ACCUSING HEAVEN BECAUSE	399	BREAK OF DAY		15
COME, FIX UPON ME THAT ACCUSING EYE.	542	PARN FUNERAL 1		24
ACCUSTOMED				
NEAR NO ACCUSTOMED HAND!	123	DREAM OF DEATH		2
THAN THIS ACCUSTOMED TOIL. WHEN I WAS YOUNG,	267	ALL TEMPT ME		5
I AM ACCUSTOMED TO THEIR LACK OF BREATH,	325	ROBERT GREGORY		45
HAD SCARCELY ACCUSTOMED OUR EARS	341	SHEP GOATHERD		67
HAD SCARCELY ACCUSTOMED OUR EYES	341	SHEP GOATHERD		69
WHERE ALL'S ACCUSTOMED, CEREMONIOUS!	405	FOR DAUGHTER		74
ACH				
ACH, CALL ME WHAT YOU PLEASE!	627	STATES HOLIDAY		21

4

ACHAIANS'
   ARE STILL THE ACHAIANS' TENTED CHIEFS AT BAY? . . . . . 679 ISLE STAT II 3   910
ACHE
   FOR YOUR SOLE SAKE--THAT ALL HEART'S ACHE HAVE KNOWN, . . 355 BROKEN DREAMS   7
   AND GIVEN TO OTHERS ALL HEART'S ACHE, ... 355 BROKEN DREAMS   8
   BUT FOR YOUR SAKE--THAT ALL HEART'S ACHE HAVE KNOWN, . . 355 BROKEN DREAMS V 7
ACHILLES
   AYE, AND ACHILLES, TIMOR, BABAR, BARHAIM, ALL . . . . . 366 HER COURAGE   9
   ATHENE TAKES ACHILLES BY THE HAIR, ... 374 PHASES OF MOON 45
ACHING
   PITY, AN ACHING HEAD, ... 346 ON WOMAN   38
   NO MOON, ONLY AN ACHING HEART . . . . 421 MY TABLE   13
   HAD SUCH AN ACHING HEART . . . . 422 MY TABLE   28
   THEY FIXED OLD ACHING EYES, ... 432 NINETEEN 19   100
ACKNOWLEDGE
   YOUR COMING BROUGHT; THOUGH I ACKNOWLEDGE I HAVE GONE . . 391 UNDER SATURN V 5
ACORNS
   ACORNS GREEN, WITH EYES AWAKE. . . . . 655 ISLE STAT I 3   5
ACQUAINTANCE
   ACQUAINTANCE; COMPANION; . . . . 504 RESULT THOUGHT 1
ACRE
   AN ACRE OF STONY GROUND, ... 419 MY HOUSE   3
   AN ACRE OF GRASS . . . . 575 ACRE OF GRASS T
   AN ACRE OF GREEN GRASS . . . . 575 ACRE OF GRASS 2
ACROPOLIS
   TO BURN THAT STUMP ON THE ACROPOLIS, ... 430 NINETEEN 19   46
ACROSS
   THY WANDERING STEPS ACROSS THE SEA? . . . . 5 OISIN 1   V 51
   ACROSS THE GLOSSY SEA." "OH, WILD . . . . . . 6 OISIN 1   V 58
   WE RODE ACROSS THE OILY SEA . . . . 10 OISIN 1   V 114
   ACROSS YOUR WANDERING RUBY CARS . . . . 22 OISIN 1   330
   I MOUNTED, AND WE RODE ACROSS THE LONE . . . . . 45 OISIN 2   V 231
   ACROSS THE BARE BOREEN. . . . . 95 MOLL MAGEE   32
   WHEN THE WIND COMES BLOWING ACROSS THE HILLY LAND; . . 207 HANRAHANS SONG V 7
   ACROSS THE BITTER SEA." . . . . 396 ROSE TREE   6
   THE POPLARS GAZE ACROSS THE WATERS GREY, ... 653 ISLE STAT I 2   34
   HE PASSED ACROSS THE LAKE. WHEN WE TWO CAME . . . . 658 ISLE STAT II 1   5
   HALF LIT, SO FLAPT THE WINGS ACROSS THE LAKE-- . . . 659 ISLE STAT II 1   17
   ONE HAND BROW-SHADING, FAR ACROSS THE NIGHT, ... 663 ISLE STAT II 2   27
   HOLD FESTIVAL ACROSS THE LAND, ... 671 ISLE STAT II 3   128
   I FEEL A FINGER DRAWN ACROSS MY CHEEK! . . . . . . 694 MOSADA 1   96
   A FEARFUL PALENESS CREEPS ACROSS HER BREAST . . . . . 701 MOSADA 3   69
   FLAMES THE SHUTTLE OF THE LIGHTNING ACROSS THE DRIVING 718 PHANTOM SHIP   1
      SLEET,
   AN OLD HORSE LOOKED ACROSS A FENCE, ... 725 LEGEND   27
   TRAVELLED TO AND FRO ACROSS THE ATLANTIC, ... 790 DEDICATION   3
A-CROW
   SPOKE AND SET THE COCKS A-CROW. . . . . 637 BEN BULBEN   4
   THE STRONG MARCH BIRDS A-CROW. . . . . 783 GREY ROUND   26
ACTION
   FOR THOSE THAT LOVE THE WORLD SERVE IT IN ACTION, . . . 369 EGO DOMINUS   42
   AND SHOULD THEY PAINT OR WRITE, STILL IT IS ACTION; . . 369 EGO DOMINUS   44
   AND SHOULD THEY PAINT OR WRITE STILL IS IT ACTION, . . 369 EGO DOMINUS   V 44
   EVERY EVENT IN ACTION OR IN THOUGHT; . . . . . . 479 SELF AND SOUL 66
   COUNT EVERY SIN OF ACTION OR OF THOUGHT; . . . . . 479 SELF AND SOUL V 66
   BUT COPY SOME ONE ACTION, ... 600 SPIRIT MEDIUM 13
   "WITH ACTION ALL THE WORLD IS VEXED," . . . . . . 728 PRIEST FAIRY   15
ACTION'S
   AND EVIL STILL IS ACTION'S CHILD. . . . . 728 PRIEST FAIRY   14
ACTOR
   THEN THAT OLD ABBEY ACTOR, DUDLEY DIGGES, ... 790 DEDICATION   7
ACTORS
   BUT ACTORS LACKING MUSIC . . . . 599 STONE CROSS   17
ACTUAL
   BUT ACTUAL SHELLS OF ROSSES' LEVEL SHORE. . . . . . 494 AT ALGECIRAS   12
A-CURSED
   BECAUSE THE WEATHER WAS A-CURSED . . . . 305 HOUR DAWN   V 65
ADAM
   THE FIRST ADAM IN THEIR THOUGHT, ... 617 LONG-LEG FLY   22
   WHERE BUT HALF-AWAKENED ADAM . . . . 638 BEN BULBEN   47
ADAM'S
   ADAM'S CURSE . . . . 204 ADAMS CURSE   T
   SINCE ADAM'S FALL BUT NEEDS MUCH LABOURING, ... 205 ADAMS CURSE   22
   BUT FOR ADAM'S SIN . . . . 621 JOHN KINSELLA 26
ADD
   AND ADD THE HALFPENCE TO THE PENCE . . . . 289 SEPTEMBER 1913 3
   AND FURTHER ADD TO THAT . . . . 415 TOWER   153
   I ADD IN COMMENTARY, ... 496 MOHINI CHATTER 16
ADDER'S
   UNTIL THIS MORN. AS ADDER'S BACK . . . . 667 ISLE STAT II 3   22
   WAS BANDED AS AN ADDER'S BACK, ... 667 ISLE STAT II 3 V 23
ADDERS
   ABODE, AS BANDED ADDERS IN MY BREAST. . . . . . . 683 SEEKER   50
ADDING
   ADDING FEATHER TO FEATHER . . . . 311 PEACOCK   10
ADDRESSED
   APOLOGIA ADDRESSED TO IRELAND IN THE COMING DAYS . . . 137 TO IRELAND   V T
ADMIRED
   ADMIRED AND BEAUTIFUL, ... 472 ALL SOUL NIGHT 43
ADMIRING
   THE OLD MEN ADMIRING THEMSELVES IN THE WATER . . . . 208 OLD MEN ADMIRE T

	PAGE	TITLE	LINE
ADMIT			
IF ON THE LOST, ADMIT YOU TURNED ASIDE	413	TOWER	115
NONE DARED ADMIT, IF SUCH A THOUGHT WERE HIS,	430	NINETEEN 19	44
I ADMIT THE BRIAR	532	FIRST CONFESS	1
ADMONISH			
ADMONISH US TO CLING TO THAT	460	THREE MONUMENT	8
ADOLESCENCE			
SLIM ADOLESCENCE THAT A NYMPH HAS STRIPPED,	612	NEWS ORACLE	25
ADORE			
THAT I DO MUCH ADORE!	592	DRUNK SOBRIETY	6
ADORED			
SOUL'S BEAUTY BEING MOST ADORED,	421	MY TABLE	22
TROY BACKED ITS HELEN, TROY DIED AND ADORED!	547	TO SAME TUNE 3	4
TROY LOOKED ON HELEN, IT DIED AND ADORED!	547	TO SAME TUNE 3 V	4
TROY BACKED ITS HELEN, TROY DIED AND ADORED!	614	MARCH SONGS 2	4
ADORES			
MY SOUL ADORES,	572	LADYS 1ST SONG	10
ADORN			
CAN, TATTERED, STILL PROTECT, FADED ADORN.	477	SELF AND SOUL	16
THAT MIGHT ADORN OLD SONGS OR COURTLY SHOWS!	629	CIRCUS ANIMALS	14
STRANGE DRAPERIES DID ALL THE SIDES ADORN,	657	ISLE STAT I 3	55
ADORNING			
LIKE A BRIDE BENDING OVER HER MIRROR ADORNING,	28	OISIN 1	V 423E
ADORNING EVERY SECRET TRACK	509	JANE REPROVED	9
SOME TAKE DELIGHT IN ADORNING A WOMAN.	547	TO SAME TUNE 3 V	3
ADRIFT			
AND BOTH ADRIFT ON THE MIRACULOUS STREAM	535	CHOSEN	16
ADRIP			
AND SHE WITH GOBAN'S WINE ADRIP,	276	GREY ROCK	121
ADVANCE			
SHOULD STARVE GOOD MEN AND BAD ADVANCE,	626	OLD MEN BE MAD	10
ADVENTURE			
BUT SUMMONS TO ADVENTURE AND THE MAN	373	PHASES OF MOON	37
THAT THE ADVENTURE OF OLD AGE BEGINS.	609	IN TARAS HALLS	5
ADVERSITY			
BEFITTING EMBLEMS OF ADVERSITY.	420	MY HOUSE	30
AEDH			
HEARING AEDH TOUCH THE MOURNFUL STRINGS OF GOLD."	35	OISIN 2	87
AEDH TELLS OF THE ROSE IN HIS HEART	142	ROSE IN HEART V	T
AEDH LAMENTS THE LOSS OF LOVE	152	LOSS OF LOVE V	T
AEDH GIVES HIS BELOVED CERTAIN RHYMES	157	BELOVED RHYMES V	T
AEDH TELLS OF A VALLEY FULL OF LOVERS	163	VALLEY LOVERS V	T
AEDH TELLS OF THE PERFECT BEAUTY	164	PERFECT BEAUTY V	T
AEDH HEARS THE CRY OF THE SEDGE	165	CRY OF SEDGE V	T
AEDH THINKS OF THOSE WHO HAVE SPOKEN EVIL OF HIS BELOVED	166	EVIL OF BELOV V	T
AEDH WISHES HIS BELOVED WERE DEAD	175	BELOVED DEAD V	T
AEDH WISHES FOR THE CLOTHS OF HEAVEN	176	CLOTHS HEAVEN V	T
AENGUS			
AENGUS AND EDAIN, MY OWN NAME	5	OISIN 1	47
AENGUS AND EDAIN, AND MY NAME	5	OISIN 1 V	47
FROM WHERE THE BIRDS OF AENGUS WING?"	6	OISIN 1	53
WHERE AENGUS DREAMS, FROM SUN TO SUN,	16	OISIN 1	218
THE SONG OF WANDERING AENGUS	149	WANDER AENGUS	T
FOR I AM AENGUS, AND I AM CROSSED IN LOVE."	183	QUEEN MAEVE	84
FOR YOU HAVE BEEN, O AENGUS OF THE BIRDS,	185	QUEEN MAEVE	101
SAID, "AENGUS AND HIS SWEETHEART GIVE THEIR THANKS	187	QUEEN MAEVE	146
THEN MAEVE! "O AENGUS, MASTER OF ALL LOVERS,	187	QUEEN MAEVE	149
WHILE OVER THEM BIRDS OF AENGUS FLY,	197	BAILE AILLINN	182
LAND-OF-THE-TOWER, WHERE AENGUS HAS THROWN THE GATES APART,	209	UNDER THE MOON	8
LAND OF THE TOWER, WHEN AENGUS HAS THROWN THE GATES APART,	209	UNDER THE MOON V	8
THE HARP OF AENGUS	219	HARP OF AENGUS	T
BESIDE YOUNG AENGUS IN HIS TOWER OF GLASS,	219	HARP OF AENGUS	2
'TWAS AENGUS AND EDAIN, THE WANDERING LOVERS,	224	SHADOW WATER B	42
AS THAT WILD AENGUS. LONG BEFORE HER DAY	224	SHADOW WATER B	47
AENGUS AND EDAIN, THOSE PASSIONATE WANDERERS,	228	SHADOW WATER B	138
AENGUS AND EDAIN RAN UP OUT OF THE WAVE—	231	SHADOW WATER B	196
IN ISLANDS WHERE THE CHILDREN OF AENGUS WIND	245	SHADOW WATER B	469
WHEN AENGUS AND HIS EDAINE WAKE FROM SLEEP	749	SHADOW WATER A	57
AENGUS LOOKS ON YOU WHEN I LOOK! HE AWAITS	757	SHADOW WATER A	209
AENGUS LOOKS ON YOU WHEN I LOOK! HE WAITS	757	SHADOW WATER A V	209
AS THE AGELESS BIRDS OF AENGUS, OR THE BIRDS	761	SHADOW WATER A	260
O, AENGUS OF THE HERDS, WATCH OVER ME!	762	SHADOW WATER A	291
BESIDE YOUNG AENGUS IN HIS TOWER OF GLASS,	762	SHADOW WATER A	297
AND BRING ME WHERE THE CHILDREN OF AENGUS WIND	763	SHADOW WATER A	317
IN ONE ANOTHER'S ARMS. AENGUS HAS SEEN	763	SHADOW WATER A	321
AENGUS'			
OF AENGUS' BIRDS GLEAM IN THEIR APPLE BOUGHS.	751	SHADOW WATER A	103
FOR HE WHO GAVE IT CALLED IT AENGUS' HARP	762	SHADOW WATER A	288
AEROPLANE			
AEROPLANE AND ZEPPELIN WILL COME OUT,	565	LAPIS LAZULI	6
AERY			
OF BIRDS EVEN, LONGINGS FOR AERY	708	FAIRY PEDANT	26
AFAR			
"THE SOUL IS A DROP OF JOY AFAR,	19	OISIN 1	V 276
AFAR FROM WHERE THE YEARS ARE FLYING	22	OISIN 1	V 340A
WHITENED AFAR WITH SURGE, FAN-FORMED AND WIDE,	31	OISIN 2	28
WHITENING THE SURGE AFAR, FAN-FORMED AND WIDE,	31	OISIN 2	V 28
AFAR IN ANCIENT ERI	32	OISIN 2	V 50E
BY LAKES AND MEADOW LANDS AND LAWNS AFAR,	32	OISIN 2	V 50F
IT DIED AFAR. GREY SLEET THOSE TOWERS HID	46	OISIN 2	V 245
YOU HUNTER OF THE FIELDS AFAR!	75	ANASHU VIJAYA	79

6

AFAR   (CONTINUED)
    SHE MOTIONED HIM AFAR, AND ROSE AND SPOKE: . . . . . .   280 TWO KINGS   68
    ALL DREAD AFAR TILL MORNING'S BACK. . . . .   435 FOR MY SON   6
    MARK AND DIGEST MY TALE, CARRY IT AFAR . . . .   554 RIBH AT TOMB   3
    WE PICKED EACH OTHER FROM AFAR AND KNEW . . . .   622 HOUND VOICE   10
    AFAR, CLEAR-SHINING ON THE HERALD HILLS. . . . . . .   645 ISLE STAT I 1   14
    UNTIL AFAR APPEAR THE GLEAMING DRAGON-SCALES: . . . .   651 ISLE STAT I 1   160
    WHITE LILIES, AND HER SONG FLEW FORTH AFAR . . . . . .   693 MOSADA 1   85
    AWAKE, AWAKE, AND WE WILL SAIL AFAR, ...   702 MOSADA 3   78
    AFAR ALONG THE FLEET WHITE RIVER'S FACE— . . . . . .   702 MOSADA 3   79
    AFAR FROM OUR LAWN AND OUR LEVEE: . . . .   706 FAIRY PEDANT   1
    THE CALLING AFAR OF THE DOE AND THE DEER. . . . . . .   717 LOVE SONG   5
    IN THE BOSOM AFAR OF THE FRAGRANT WOOD. . . . .   717 LOVE SONG   9
    AS THERE FLOATS FROM FIELDS AFAR . . . .   732 STREET DANCERS   20
AFFABLE
    AN AFFABLE IRREGULAR, ...   423 ROAD AT DOOR   1
AFFAIR
    FOR SOME TRIVIAL AFFAIR . . . .   293 HELEN LIVED   3
    IMAGINED SUCH A FINE AFFAIR: . . . .   791 REPRISALS   14
AFFAIRS
    AND PETER THAT HAD GREAT AFFAIRS . . . .   456 FRIENDS YOUTH   13
    THE RICH MAN AND HIS AFFAIRS, ...   540 FROM ANTIGONE   3
AFFECTION
    THAT PASSION, PIETY OR AFFECTION KNOWS, ...   445 SCHOOL CHILDR   54
AFFECTIONS
    IN THE AFFECTIONS OF OUR HEART, ...   324 ROBERT GREGORY   12
AFFIRMS
    SOME PLATONIST AFFIRMS THAT IN THE STATION . . . . .   431 NINETEEN 19   72
AFFLICT
    TO AFFLICT MANKIND, BUT NOW . . . .   431 NINETEEN 19   86
AFFRIGHTING   SEE SELF-AFFRIGHTING
A-FISHING
    WE WENT A-FISHING IN LONG BOATS . . . .   23 OISIN 1   352
AFLAME
    I WENT TO BLOW THE FIRE AFLAME, ...   149 WANDER AENGUS   10
    I BENT TO BLOW THE FIRE AFLAME: . . . .   149 WANDER AENGUS   V 10
    I STOOPED TO BLOW THE FIRE AFLAME, ...   149 WANDER AENGUS   V 10
A-FLAME
    I WENT TO BLOW THE FIRE A-FLAME, ...   149 WANDER AENGUS   V 10
AFLASH
    YOUR EYES ARE ALL AFLASH. SHE IS NOT HERE. . . . . .   669 ISLE STAT II 3 V 68
A-FLASH
    YOUR EYES ARE ALL A-FLASH. SHE IS NOT HERE. . . . . .   669 ISLE STAT II 3   68
A-FLICKER
    OF BEAMS A-FLICKER ON YON LONELY FIR, ...   661 ISLE STAT II 1   72
AFLOAT
    WHO WHEN NIGHT THICKENS ARE AFLOAT . . . .   196 BAILE AILLINN   179
A-FLUTTER
    THEY WILL NOT HUSH, THE LEAVES A-FLUTTER ROUND ME, . . .   82 MAD KING GOLL   12
    THEY WILL NOT HUSH, THE LEAVES A-FLUTTER ROUND ME, . . .   83 MAD KING GOLL   24
    THEY WILL NOT HUSH, THE LEAVES A-FLUTTER ROUND ME, . . .   84 MAD KING GOLL   36
    THEY WILL NOT HUSH, THE LEAVES A-FLUTTER ROUND ME, . . .   84 MAD KING GOLL   48
    THEY WILL NOT HUSH, THE LEAVES A-FLUTTER ROUND ME, . . .   85 MAD KING GOLL   60
    THEY WILL NOT HUSH, THE LEAVES A-FLUTTER ROUND ME, . . .   86 MAD KING GOLL   72
    WHY ARE THEY ALL A-FLUTTER OF A SUDDEN? . . . . . .   243 SHADOW WATER B   436
A-FLUTTERING
    A-FLUTTERING THE PAINTED POPULACE OF LAKE . . . . . .   675 ISLE STAT II 3   224
AFOOT
    WHAT MATTERS WERE AFOOT AMONG THE SIDHE, ...   182 QUEEN MAEVE   61
AFORETIME
    AFORETIME, AND SHALL NOT GROW SAD . . . .   22 OISIN 1   V 340E
AFRAID
    AND DEMONS AFRAID IN THEIR DARKNESS: . . . .   62 OISIN 3   205
    AFRAID, THEIR EARS ON THE EARTH LAID. . . . .   62 OISIN 3   206
    BELOVED, I AM NOT AFRAID OF HER. . . . .   197 BAILE AILLINN   200
    BUT WERE YOU NOT AFRAID? WHY SHOULD I FEAR? . . . . .   224 SHADOW WATER B   41
    BUT THAT I AM AFRAID THEY MAY HAVE PASSED. . . . . .   226 SHADOW WATER B   84
    YOUR SOUL SHALL GIVE THE KISS. I AM NOT AFRAID, . . .   238 SHADOW WATER B   346
    AND THAT IS WHY THEIR LOVERS ARE AFRAID . . . . . .   245 SHADOW WATER B   481
    AND I AM AFRAID THAT YOU WILL RUN . . . .   356 BROKEN DREAMS   30
    I AM AFRAID THAT YOU WILL RUN . . . .   356 BROKEN DREAMS   V 30
    HE WERE AFRAID THE BIRDS, WHO CRY ALOUD . . . . . .   371 EGO DOMINUS   77
    BUT WHY SHOULD YOU GROW SUDDENLY AFRAID . . . . . .   390 IMAGE PAST   29
    I DO NOT KNOW, THAT KNOW I AM AFRAID . . . .   390 IMAGE PAST   41
    THE WEST WIND MADE IT PITIFUL, AND THE NORTH WIND AFRAID.   449 OWEN AHERNE   6
    AFRAID THEY MIGHT BE BEATEN . . . .   582 ROGER CASEMENT   5
    THE RATTLE OF THOSE ARMS MAKES US AFRAID. . . . . . .   634 CUCHULAIN COMF   15
    BE NOT AFRAID, YOU'LL SEE NO FEARFUL THING. . . . . .   693 MOSADA 1   74
    I SAW A GIRL AFRAID TO BE TOO NEAR. . . . .   712 FERENCZ RENYI   68
    AFRAID TO BE TOO FAR." "AY, BRING HER HERE!" . . . .   712 FERENCZ RENYI   69
    I AM AFRAID OF THE HARP. O! WINGS ON WINGS! . . . . .   759 SHADOW WATER A   236
    I AM AFRAID OF HIS LOW-LAUGHING HARP. . . . .   759 SHADOW WATER A   239
    I AM AFRAID OF HIS LOW LAUGHING HARP. . . . .   759 SHADOW WATER A V 239
AFRICA
    IN AFRICA ON MOUNTAIN OF THE MOON. . . . .   277 TWO KINGS   V 20
AFRICAN
    AMONG THE AFRICAN MOUNTAINS OF THE MOON. . . . . . .   277 TWO KINGS   20
AFTER
    THE OSPREY OF SORROW GOES AFTER AND CLUTCHES, ...   27 OISIN 1   V 415D
    GREENISH AND SLIPPERY. TIME AFTER TIME . . . . . .   37 OISIN 2   V 114
    HOUR AFTER HOUR I WAITED, AND THE DOME . . . .   39 OISIN 2   V 147

AFTER   (CONTINUED)
    AND MANANNAN'S DARK TOWER, STONE AFTER STONE, ...   45 OISIN 2   236
    AND THEY HAVE FALLEN OR FLED, AGE AFTER AGE, ...   45 OISIN 2   242
    "AGE AFTER AGE I FEEL MY SOUL DECAY . . . .   45 OISIN 2   V 235
    CAME TO MY TOWER AS AGE DRAGGED AFTER AGE . . . . . .   45 OISIN 2   V 242
    AND NOW THE WARMTH OF SIGHS, AND AFTER THE QUIVER OF LIPS.   47 OISIN 3   8
    . . . AND YEARS AFTER YEARS 'GAN FLOW! . . . . . .   52 OISIN 3   75
    . . . AND YEARS AFTER YEARS 'GAN THEIR FLOW! . . . . .   52 OISIN 3   V 75
    NO MORE TO CRAWL ON THE SEAS WITH LONG OARS MILE AFTER   55 OISIN 3   119
        MILE.
    CAME AFTER THE HARD GAZE OF YOUTH, OR AN OLD MAN LIFTED   59 OISIN 3   170
        HIS HEAD!
    TO HUNGER FIERCELY AFTER TRUTH. . . . .   66 HAPPY SHEPHERD   24
    FAR, FAR AWAY. I NAMED HIM AFTER YOU. . . . .   72 ANASHU VIJAYA   35
    FAR, FAR AWAY. I'VE NAMED HIM AFTER YOU. . . . . . .   72 ANASHU VIJAYA   V 35
    AFTER SHORT FIGHTING IN THE LEAFY SHADE, ...   109 CUCHULAIN SEA   57
    AND AFTER CRIED HE, "GOD FORGIVE! . . . .   132 FR GILLIGAN   11
    AFTER THE RED-ROSE-BORDERED HEM. . . . .   139 TO IRELAND   30
    AFTER THE RED-ROSE-BORDERED HEM. . . . .   139 TO IRELAND   48
    AFTER THE RED ROSE BORDERED HEM. . . . .   139 TO IRELAND   V 30
    AFTER THE RED ROSE BORDERED HEM. . . . .   139 TO IRELAND   V 48
    AFTER THE DEATHS OF MANY MEN, ...   197 BAILE AILLINN   193
    AND AFTER CIRCLING WITH STRANGE CRIES AWHILE . . . . .   223 SHADOW WATER B   26
    BUT HE THAT GETS THEIR LOVE AFTER THE FASHION . . . . .   228 SHADOW WATER B   145
    THAT FOLLOWS AFTER. I UNDERSTAND YOU NOW. . . . . . .   237 SHADOW WATER B   341
    AND AFTER RUNNING AT THE BRIM . . . .   254 HIS DREAM   9
    THE NO KING CRIED WHO AFTER THAT WAS KING. . . . . . .   258 KING NO KING   2
    AND AFTER SET YOUR HEART TO BEAT. . . . .   263 MASK   9
    THE GIFTS THAT GOVERN MEN, AND AFTER THESE . . . . . .   264 HOUSE SHAKEN   10
    AFTER A RAGGED HAT IN BISCAY BAY! . . . .   270 PARDON FATHERS   14
    AND AFTER, WHEN HER BLOOD RAN WILD, ...   272 GREY ROCK   44
    FOOT AFTER FOOT WAS GIVING WAY, ...   274 GREY ROCK   72
    OUTRODE HIS TROOP THAT AFTER TWELVE MONTHS' WAR . . . .   276 TWO KINGS   V 1
    "DAY AFTER DAY YOU QUESTION ME, AND I, ...   281 TWO KINGS   99
    AND AFTER HEAPED UP STONE ON STONE. . . . .   307 HOUR DAWN   116
    AND AFTER HEAPED THE STONES AGAIN . . . .   307 HOUR DAWN   V 116
    AND AFTER, DRAINED DRY, ...   310 WITCH   4
    AFTER NINE YEARS, I SINK MY HEAD ABASHED. . . . . . .   353 PEOPLE   37
    AND AFTER TWENTY YEARS THEY LAID . . . .   360 ALF POLLEXFEN   6
    HE HAS FOUND, AFTER THE MANNER OF HIS KIND, ...   373 PHASES OF MOON   12
    THERE IS NO MUSCLE IN THE ARM! AND AFTER, ...   374 PHASES OF MOON   52
    AND AFTER THAT THE CRUMBLING OF THE MOON. . . . . . .   375 PHASES OF MOON   87
    HE WOULD NEVER KNOW ME AFTER ALL THESE YEARS . . . . .   377 PHASES OF MOON   129
    DAY AFTER DAY, YET NEVER FIND THE MEANING. . . . . . .   377 PHASES OF MOON   135
    AUGUSTUS CAESAR, AND AFTER THESE . . . .   379 SAINT HUNCH   11
    AND AFTER KISSED A STONE, ...   384 VISION ROBART   64
    AND AFTER THAT ARRANGED IT IN A SONG . . . .   384 VISION ROBART   65
    AND SURELY AFTER TWENTY YEARS IT WAS TIME TO COME." . .   391 UNDER SATURN   14
    WAS IT NEEDLESS DEATH AFTER ALL? . . . .   394 EASTER 1916   67
    AND I, THAT AFTER ME . . . .   420 MY HOUSE   27
    AND THERE'S BUT COMMON GREENNESS AFTER THAT. . . . . .   422 MY DESCENDANTS   8
    MOCK MOCKERS AFTER THAT . . . .   432 NINETEEN 19   108
    A SUDDEN BLAST OF DUSTY WIND AND AFTER . . . .   433 NINETEEN 19   119
    AND AFTER THAT THERE'S NOTHING GOOD . . . .   434 WHEEL   5
    AND AFTER BAKED IT SLOWLY IN AN OVEN! BUT NOW . . . . .   442 BLACK CENTAUR   9
    AND AFTER, SWEPT FROM THERE, ...   453 DEATH OF HARE   10
    AND AFTER KEPT IT FROM DECAY! . . . .   460 THREE MONUMENT   7
    IN AFTER TIME THEY WILL SPEAK MUCH OF ME . . . . . .   462 HARUN RASHID   29
    EVEN TO-DAY, AFTER SOME SEVEN YEARS . . . .   468 HARUN RASHID   161
    EVEN TODAY, AFTER SOME SEVEN YEARS . . . .   468 HARUN RASHID   V 161
    . . . CENTURY AFTER CENTURY, ...   481 BLOOD AND MOON   23
    THE NINETEENTH CENTURY AND AFTER . . . .   485 NINETEENTH CEN   T
    FOR SCHOLARS AND FOR POETS AFTER US, ...   488 COOLE PARK 29   6
    AFTER GREAT CATHEDRAL GONG! . . . .   497 BYZANTIUM   4
    SPIRIT AFTER SPIRIT! THE SMITHIES BREAK THE FLOOD, . . .   498 BYZANTIUM   34
    AND AFTER NAILED UPON THE NIGHT . . . .   519 HER DREAM   7
    AND DID AFTER STRETCH AND YAWN"! . . . .   521 THREE THINGS   17
    AFTER LONG SILENCE . . . .   523 LONG SILENCE   T
    SPEECH AFTER LONG SILENCE! IT IS RIGHT, ...   523 LONG SILENCE   1
    FROM MIRROR AFTER MIRROR, ...   532 BEFORE WORLD   5
    AND AFTER THAT I HELD MY FINGERS UP, ...   537 HER VISION   9
    THOSE THAT COME AFTER SHALL MOCK AT O'DONNELL, ...   546 TO SAME TUNE 2   23
    THOSE THAT COME AFTER SHALL MOCK O'DONNELL, ...   546 TO SAME TUNE 2 V 23
    RAVENING THROUGH CENTURY AFTER CENTURY, ...   563 MERU   5
    AFTER CERTAIN YEARS HE WON . . . .   577 WHAT THEN   7
    AND AFTER THAT BETRAYED! . . . .   587 PARNELLITES   28
    THOSE THAT COME AFTER SHALL MOCK AT O'DONNELL, ...   614 MARCH SONGS 1   23
    GROWS MORE DEEP DAY AFTER DAY, ...   624 APPARITIONS   18
    IRELAND AFTER THE REVOLUTION IV . . . .   628 JANE MOUNTAIN   V T
    I LIE AWAKE NIGHT AFTER NIGHT . . . .   632 MAN AND ECHO   9
    PALMER'S PHRASE, BUT AFTER THAT . . . .   639 BEN BULBEN   66
    THE HOLINESS OF MONKS, AND AFTER . . . .   640 BEN BULBEN   76
    THE HOLINESS OF THE MONKS, AND AFTER . . . .   640 BEN BULBEN   V 76
    NAMES AFTER ME. LADY---I COME. FORGIVE, ...   695 MOSADA 1   117
    "WATCHER, WHEREFORE HAVE YE CALLED US?" EYES GO AFTER   718 PHANTOM SHIP   10
        HIS LEAN HAND,
    WHILE THEY MURMUR, "AFTER THIS . . . .   776 AGAINST WITCH   30
    FOR THE THINGS COME AFTER DEATH? . . . .   777 SONG DEIRDRE 2   12
    AT DAYBREAK AFTER STORMY NIGHT . . . .   784 WOMANS BEAUTY   3
AFTERNOON
    WHEN EVERY SUNDAY AFTERNOON . . . .   607 SONGS BURDEN 2   19

8

		PAGE	TITLE		LINE

AFTERNOON   (CONTINUED)
IS STONE: OLD SLEEPER: THIS SAME AFTERNOON . . . . . .   657 ISLE STAT I 3   74
AFTERWARDS
IT SOUGHT ITSELF AND AFTERWARDS THE WORLD. . . . . . .   376 PHASES OF MOON   95
AGAINST
AND SUNKEN SHAPE, AGAINST MY FACE AND BREAST, ...   40 OISIN 2   V 179
SIDLED THEIR BODIES AGAINST HIM, FILLING THE SHADE WITH
  THEIR EYES.   50 OISIN 3   48
THEY HAVE SPOKEN AGAINST YOU EVERYWHERE, ...   166 EVIL OF BELOV   3
THAT MAKES ME FEAR TO RAISE A HAND AGAINST HIM, ...   222 SHADOW WATER B V 16A
THIS LONG WHILE NOW: WE HAD NOT TURNED AGAINST HIM . .   225 SHADOW WATER B V 68B
THAT I WILL NEVER LIFT A HAND AGAINST YOU. . . . . .   227 SHADOW WATER B   108
TOO MANY YEARS TO LIFT A HAND AGAINST YOU. . . . . .   227 SHADOW WATER B   111
THAT RAISED THEIR HANDS AGAINST HIM. THERE ARE SOME . .   235 SHADOW WATER B   291
WOULD RISE AGAINST ME. NO, I AM NOT MAD-- . . . . . .   236 SHADOW WATER B   318
BUT NO, NO: YOUR CRY IS NOT AGAINST ME. . . . . . .   244 SHADOW WATER B   449
BUT I HAVE DONE SO GREAT A WRONG AGAINST YOU. . . . .   245 SHADOW WATER B   483
AGAINST UNWORTHY PRAISE . . . .   259 UNWORTH PRAISE   T
. . . HAVE JOINED THE AGITATION AGAINST IMMORAL LITERATURE   262 STUDENTS AGIT   T
. . . AGITATION AGAINST IMMORAL LITERATURE . . . . . .   262 STUDENTS AGIT V   T
AGAINST A SOUL? . . . .   267 FRIEND ILLNESS   7
AGAINST THE STAG. WHEN HORN AND STEEL WERE MET . . . .   277 TWO KINGS   15
AGAINST A BEECH-BOLE, HE THREW DOWN THE BEAST . . . . .   278 TWO KINGS   36
AGAINST A BEECH BOLE, HE THREW DOWN THE BEAST . . . . .   278 TWO KINGS   V   36
BECAUSE THAT WERE A GUILT AGAINST HER KING, ...   280 TWO KINGS   V 74A
AND THAT WOULD BE AGAINST GOD'S PROVIDENCE. . . . . .   339 SHEP GOATHERD   5
MATCHING OUR BROKEN-HEARTED WIT AGAINST HER WIT, . . .   362 HER COURTESY   7
AS I DO NOW AGAINST OLD AGE? . . . .   413 TOWER   100
FOR EMBLEMS OF THE DAY AGAINST THE TOWER . . . . . .   478 SELF AND SOUL   29
BUT WE OLD MEN ARE MASSED AGAINST THE WORLD. . . . . .   486 SEVEN SAGES   14
BUT WE OLD MEN ARE OUT AGAINST THE WORLD. . . . . .   486 SEVEN SAGES   V   14
HARRIED, AND BURKE'S GREAT MELODY AGAINST IT. . . . .   487 SEVEN SAGES   16
THE AVENGING LEAF THOSE FIELDS RAISED UP AGAINST IT. . .   487 SEVEN SAGES   20
NOW I AM IN THE TAVERN AND LEAN AGAINST THE WALL, . . .   593 PILGRIM   V   21
THOU'RT WELCOME. LIE THERE CLOSE AGAINST MY FINGERS. . .   700 MOSADA 3   44
AND MORE, IF YOU WILL WAR AGAINST THE DANES . . . . .   756 SHADOW WATER A V 190
AGAINST MY FACE AND EYES. MINE TOO ARE BEATEN. . . . .   759 SHADOW WATER A V 233
AGAINST WITCHCRAFT . . . .   775 AGAINST WITCH V   T
AGAMEMNON
AND AGAMEMNON DEAD. BEING SO CAUGHT UP, ...   441 LEDA AND SWAN   11
AGATE
OR MAYBE AN AGATE CUP. . . . .   781 MY HEART BEAT   16
AGE   SEE MIDDLE-AGE
AND FLOWING STRENGTH, WITH AGE IS SUBTLE-SOULED. . . . .   35 OISIN 2   V   83
AND THEY HAVE FALLEN OR FLED, AGE AFTER AGE. . . . . .   45 OISIN 2   242
AND THEY HAVE FALLEN OR FLED, AGE AFTER AGE. . . . . .   45 OISIN 2   242
"AGE AFTER AGE I FEEL MY SOUL DECAY . . . . . .   45 OISIN 2   V 235
"AGE AFTER AGE I FEEL MY SOUL DECAY . . . . . .   45 OISIN 2   V 235
CAME TO MY TOWER AS AGE DRAGGED AFTER AGE . . . . .   45 OISIN 2   V 242
CAME TO MY TOWER AS AGE DRAGGED AFTER AGE . . . . .   45 OISIN 2   V 242
. . . I MURMURED, "IN OLD AGE THEY CEASED": . . . . .   59 OISIN 3   177
. . . AND ITS GODLESS AND PASSIONATE AGE. . . . . .   63 OISIN 3   216
AH ME: TO BE SHAKEN WITH COUGHING AND BROKEN WITH OLD AGE   63 OISIN 3   217
  AND PAIN.
. . . AND THE GODLESS FIRES OF THINE AGE. . . . . .   63 OISIN 3   216
"HE BRINGS THE PEACEFUL AGE OF GOLD"-- . . . . . .   82 MAD KING GOLL V   11
"THIS YOUNG MAN BRINGS THE AGE OF GOLD." . . . . . .   82 MAD KING GOLL V   11
FOR IN THE WORLD'S FIRST BLOSSOMING AGE . . . . . .   138 TO IRELAND   V   10
THE OLD AGE OF QUEEN MAEVE . . . .   180 QUEEN MAEVE   T
THOUGH NOW IN HER OLD AGE, IN HER YOUNG AGE . . . . .   180 QUEEN MAEVE   18
THOUGH NOW IN HER OLD AGE, IN HER YOUNG AGE . . . . .   180 QUEEN MAEVE   18
OF THOSE THAT, IT MAY BE, CAN NEVER AGE. . . . . .   183 QUEEN MAEVE   76
IT MIGHT CALL UP A NEW AGE, CALLING TO MIND . . . . .   201 OLD MEMORY   4
WHERE OLD AGE CANNOT FIND THEM: PAIRC-NA-LEE, ...   217 WOODS OF COOLE   7
THAT IS NOT NATURAL IN AN AGE LIKE THIS, ...   257 NO SECOND TROY   9
THAT COULD SHOW WHAT HOMER'S AGE . . . . . .   258 PEACE   2
YOUTH AND AGE . . . .   261 COMING WISDOM V   T
MOST COURTEOUS TO SLOW AGE AND HASTY YOUTH, ...   339 SHEP GOATHERD   19
WHEN AGE MIGHT WELL HAVE CHILLED HIS BLOOD." . . . . .   356 BROKEN DREAMS   19
DECREPIT AGE THAT HAS BEEN TIED TO ME . . . . . .   409 TOWER   3
DECREPIT AGE THAT HAS BEEN TIED UPON ME . . . . .   409 TOWER   V   3
AS I DO NOW AGAINST OLD AGE? . . . .   413 TOWER   100
AND BUILDINGS THAT A HAUGHTIER AGE DESIGNED, ...   418 ANCEST HOUSES   34
YOUTH AND AGE . . . .   434 YOUTH AND AGE   T
AND WONDER IF SHE STOOD SO AT THAT AGE-- . . . . .   444 SCHOOL CHILDR   19
THAT IS TO AGE WHAT MILK IS TO A CHILD? . . . . .   469 HARUN RASHID   174
QUARREL IN OLD AGE . . . .   503 QUARREL IN AGE   T
THAT HAD FORGIVEN OLD AGE. . . . .   504 QUARREL IN AGE   8
HIDDEN BY OLD AGE AWHILE . . . .   539 MEETING   1
AN AGE IS THE REVERSAL OF AN AGE: . . . . . .   541 PARN FUNERAL 1   16
AN AGE IS THE REVERSAL OF AN AGE: . . . . . .   541 PARN FUNERAL 1   16
A PRAYER FOR OLD AGE . . . .   553 PRAYER OLD AGE   T
OLD AGE . . . .   553 PRAYER OLD AGE V   T
MATTER FOR OLD AGE MEET: . . . .   553 CHURCH STATE   2
SHOULD DANCE ATTENTION UPON MY OLD AGE: . . . . . .   591 SPUR   2
SHOULD DANCE ATTENDANCE UPON MY OLD AGE: . . . . .   591 SPUR   V   2
BECAUSE THIS AGE AND THE NEXT AGE . . . . . .   598 STONE CROSS   9
BECAUSE THIS AGE AND THE NEXT AGE . . . . . .   598 STONE CROSS   9
COULD CRAZY JANE PUT OFF OLD AGE . . . . .   606 SONGS BURDEN 1   19
THAT THE ADVENTURE OF OLD AGE BEGINS. . . . . . .   609 IN TARAS HALLS   5
BANISH AGE AND CARE, ...   620 JOHN KINSELLA   20

9

AGE   (CONTINUED)
        WINTER AND SUMMER TILL OLD AGE BEGAN . . . .   629 CIRCUS ANIMALS   5
        THOU WILT NOT SPEAK, AND I WITH AGE AM NEAR . .   .   .   .   684 SEEKER   62
        WHO, DREAMING TO A WONDROUS AGE, LIVED ON, ...   692 MOSADA 1   52
        OF MIDDLE AGE. "HIS SISTER HERE AND MOTHER." .   .   .   .   711 FERENCZ RENYI   53
        OWLS THERE BE WHOM AGE MAKES NUMB: . . . .   727 LOVERS QUARREL   35
        PEACE OF YOUTH AND PEACE OF AGE, ...   733 STREET DANCERS   46
AGED
        THE WARRIOR DREAMS IN AN AGED LEISURE . . . .   26 OISIN 1   V 401
        SHE LIMPS ALONG IN AN AGED WHITENESS: . . . .   27 OISIN 1   V 415
        SHE LIMPS ALONG IN AN AGED WHITENESS. . . . .   28 OISIN 1   V 423
        AGED AND WISE, THEY SEEK THEIR WONTED PERCHES   .   .   .   72 ANASHU VIJAYA   31
        FOR LEADING AGED HOUNDS AND YOUNG . . . .   98 FOXHUNTER   23
        AND NOW WITH AGED HOUNDS AND YOUNG . . . .   98 FOXHUNTER   V   21
        AGED HOUNDS AND YOUNG. . . . .   99 FOXHUNTER   40
        BOTH AGED HOUNDS AND YOUNG. . . . .   99 FOXHUNTER   V   40
        MY FATHER STANDS." "AGED, WORN OUT WITH WARS   .   .   .   107 CUCHULAIN SEA   29
        AND THEREUPON WITH AGED, HIGH-PITCHED VOICE .   .   .   .   375 PHASES OF MOON   84
        AN AGED MAN IS BUT A PALTRY THING, ...   407 SAIL BYZANTIUM   9
        CEASE TO REMEMBER THE DELIGHTS OF YOUTH, TRAVEL-WEARIED   459 FROM OEDIPUS   2
            AGED MAN:
        UPON AN AGED WOMAN AND HER HOUSE, ...   488 COOLE PARK 29   2
        STRAIGHTEN AGED KNEES. . . . .   505 RESULT THOUGHT   16
        INFIRM AND AGED I MIGHT STAY . . . .   605 YOU CONTENT   17
AGEING
        SUFFICE THE AGEING MAN AS ONCE THE GROWING BOY.   .   .   .   427 PHANTOM HATRED   40
        TILL IT DIP AN AGEING WING . . . .   777 SONG DEIRDRE 2   3
AGELESS
        THE AGELESS SENTINELS WHO HOLD THEIR WATCH . .   .   .   .   664 ISLE STAT II 2   1
        AS THE AGELESS BIRDS OF AENGUS, OR THE BIRDS   .   .   .   761 SHADOW WATER A   260
AGE'S
        BY AGE'S WEARINESS ARE SLAIN, ...   27 OISIN 1   V 415A
AGES   SEE MIDDLE-AGES
        THE FOUR AGES OF MAN . . . .   561 FOUR AGES MAN   T
        DREAMER OF THE MIDDLE AGES. EMPTY EYEBALLS KNEW   .   .   .   610 STATUES   20
        AND WHEN THOU HAST THESE THINGS FOR MANY AGES FELT,   .   .   674 ISLE STAT II 3   214
        AND WHEN THOU HAST THESE THINGS FOR AGES FELT,   .   .   .   674 ISLE STAT II 3 V   214
        SHE IS LONG AGES DUST. AH, WOE IS ME! . . . .   679 ISLE STAT II 3   313
AGHAST
        BACK THE SHADOWS CREEP AGHAST—— . . . .   648 ISLE STAT I 1   98
AGILE
        THE STRONG THIGH AND THE AGILE THIGH WERE MET,   .   .   .   278 TWO KINGS   28
AGIN
        AND FETCH ME HOME AGIN: . . . .   96 MOLL MAGEE   42
AGITATION
        . . . HAVE JOINED THE AGITATION AGAINST IMMORAL LITERATURE   262 STUDENTS AGIT   T
        . . . AGITATION AGAINST IMMORAL LITERATURE . .   .   .   .   262 STUDENTS AGIT V   T
        UPON A HOUSE SHAKEN BY THE LAND AGITATION . .   .   .   .   264 HOUSE SHAKEN   T
AGLEAM
        OUR BREASTS ARE HEAVING, OUR EYES ARE AGLEAM,   .   .   .   140 HOSTING SIDHE   8
A-GLEAM
        FOR BREASTS ARE HEAVING AND EYES A-GLEAM, ...   140 HOSTING SIDHE V   7
        OUR BREASTS ARE HEAVING, OUR EYES ARE A-GLEAM,   .   .   .   140 HOSTING SIDHE V   8
A-GLITTER
        BEFORE THE WIND. SAW YOU HIS EYES A-GLITTER?   .   .   .   683 SEEKER   35
AGO
        LOOSED LONG AGO FROM HEAVEN'S GATE, ...   24 OISIN 1   362
        FROM MACE AND SWORD AND POLE-AXE, LONG AGO . .   .   .   .   31 OISIN 2   30
        "HE DIED AN HOUR AGO." . . . .   133 FR GILLIGAN   34
        A THOUSAND YEARS AGO YOU HELD HIGH TALK . . .   .   .   .   187 QUEEN MAEVE   150
        AWOKE THE HARP-STRINGS LONG AGO. . . . .   190 BAILE AILLINN   37
        AWOKE THE HARP STRINGS LONG AGO. . . . .   190 BAILE AILLINN V   37
        BUT THE GODS LONG AGO DECREED . . . .   194 BAILE AILLINN   119
        THE QUEENS THAT WERE IMAGINED LONG AGO, ...   201 OLD MEMORY   5
        I KNOW THAT HE DIED A THOUSAND YEARS AGO, ...   241 SHADOW WATER B   392
        AND THAT HE DIED A THOUSAND YEARS AGO. . . . .   242 SHADOW WATER B   417
        THAT YOU WERE BORN A THOUSAND YEARS AGO, ...   245 SHADOW WATER B   468
        I HAD THIS THOUGHT A WHILE AGO, ...   255 WORDS   1
        I HAD THIS THOUGHT AWHILE AGO. . . . .   255 WORDS   V   1
        WE'LL OUT, FOR THE WORLD LIVES AS LONG AGO: .   .   .   257 RECONCILIATION   8
        IN MOMENTARY ANGER LONG AGO: . . . .   258 KING NO KING   10
        HE HAD COUNTED, WHERE LONG YEARS AGO . . . .   302 HOUR DAWN   7
        HE COUNTED, WHERE LONG YEARS AGO . . . .   302 HOUR DAWN   V   7
        WITH THE HOT BLOOD OF YOUTH, OF LOVE CROSSED LONG AGO: .   316 COLD HEAVEN   6
        WHEN LONG AGO I SAW HER RIDE . . . .   397 POLIT PRISONER   13
        I THOUGHT IT ALL OUT TWENTY YEARS AGO: . . . .   411 TOWER   64
        WE, WHO SEVEN YEARS AGO . . . .   431 NINETEEN 19   89
        FIVE HUNDRED YEARS AGO, ABOUT IT LIE . . . .   478 SELF AND SOUL   26
        THINGS SAID OR DONE LONG YEARS AGO, ...   501 VACILLATION   51
        HOW MANY YEARS AGO . . . .   524 MAD AS MIST   10
        A YEAR AGO FOR THE FIRST TIME . . . .   570 THREE BUSHES   38
        I MET HER ALL BUT FIFTY YEARS AGO . . . .   602 GALLERY REVIS   15
        IF HE DIED LONG AGO . . . .   635 BLACK TOWER   15
        LONG YEARS AGO, A CHURCH STANDS NEAR, ...   640 BEN BULBEN   87
        LONG YEARS AGO, AND UNTO STONE CONGEALED. . .   .   .   .   656 ISLE STAT I 3   28
        HE WILL BE TALLER NOW——'TWAS LONG AGO. . . . .   699 MOSADA 3   15
        BELOVED, HOW TWO LITTLE YEARS AGO . . . .   713 FERENCZ RENYI   89
        GOD PLANTED HIM LONG AGO. . . . .   743 WISDOM DREAMS   8
        I HAD KILLED HIM LONG AGO, BUT THAT THE FOOL   .   .   .   748 SHADOW WATER A   17
        HE HAS HEARD ME AND NOT YOU. NINE DAYS AGO .   .   .   .   752 SHADOW WATER A   113
        IT PASSED BUT A MOMENT AGO. . . . .   781 MY HEART BEAT   3

```
                                                      PAGE      TITLE             LINE
AGO   (CONTINUED)
      IT PASSED BY A MOMENT AGO. . . . . . . . . . .  781 MY HEART BEAT   V    3
AGONY
      MY HEART'S AGONY . . . . . . . . . . . . . .    452 HUMAN DIGNITY       10
      AN AGONY OF TRANCE. . . . . . . . . . . . . .   498 BYZANTIUM           31
      AN AGONY OF FLAME THAT CANNOT SINGE A SLEEVE. . 498 BYZANTIUM           32
AGREE
      BUT I, BEING YOUNG AND FOOLISH, WITH HER WOULD NOT AGREE.  90 SALLEY GARDENS   4
AGREED
      AGREED THEIR CLOTHES TO SWOP. . . . . . . . .   595 COLONEL MARTIN      20
A-HAWKING
      GOES HIS POPPIES NOW A-HAWKING! . . . . . . .   705 DAWN-SONG            4
AHEAD
      HE RAN ON AHEAD. . . . . . . . . . . . . . .    595 COLONEL MARTIN      42
AHERNE
      AHERNE LAUGHED, THINKING OF THE MAN WITHIN, . . 375 PHASES OF MOON      85
      OWEN AHERNE AND HIS DANCERS . . . . . . . . .   449 OWEN AHERNE          T
AI
      HE SAID, "HIGH QUEEN OF CRUACHAN AND MAGH AI,   183 QUEEN MAEVE         77
AIBHLIN
      A FRUITFUL LAND UNDER THE AIBHLIN HILLS? . . .  748 SHADOW WATER A V    33
AIBRIC
      I'VE THOUGHT OF THAT.  WE MUST HAVE AIBRIC WITH US,  225 SHADOW WATER B  62
      BECOME OUR CAPTAIN, AIBRIC.  I AM RESOLVED . .  225 SHADOW WATER B      64
      BE OF YOUR TROOP! AIBRIC BE ONE OF YOU . . . .  225 SHADOW WATER B      75
      THAT NEVER DID A HAND'S TURN?  AIBRIC! AIBRIC!  228 SHADOW WATER B     130
      THAT NEVER DID A HAND'S TURN?  AIBRIC! AIBRIC!  228 SHADOW WATER B     130
      FOR EVERYTHING IS GONE.  COME HITHER, AIBRIC, . 241 SHADOW WATER B     402
      AND YOU, MY AIBRIC, WHO HAVE BEEN A KING . . .  748 SHADOW WATER A      27
      DO YOU REMEMBER, AIBRIC, HOW YOU BORE . . . .   749 SHADOW WATER A      48
      I HAVE GOOD PILOTS, AIBRIC.  WHEN MEN DIE . .   750 SHADOW WATER A      81
      GIVE HER TO AIBRIC, IF HE WILL.  I WAIT . . .   755 SHADOW WATER A     172
      AND I SHALL LAUGH WITH JOY.  COME HITHER, AIBRIC, 760 SHADOW WATER A   249
      AND WE GO HOME.  COME, AIBRIC! END YOUR TALE .  766 SHADOW WATER A     374
      SEEK AIBRIC ON THE LOCHLANN GALLEY, AND TELL HIM . 767 SHADOW WATER A  401
      LIVING OR DYING.  BID AIBRIC TO YOUR COUNTRY, . 768 SHADOW WATER A     413
AIBRIC'S
      I THINK THAT THERE IS LOVE IN AIBRIC'S EYES. .  768 SHADOW WATER A     407
AID
      THUS BECKON TO OUR AID A PHANTOM FAIR . . . .   693 MOSADA 1            76
AILED
      AND WONDER WHAT HAS AILED HIM THESE TWELVE MONTHS." 284 TWO KINGS      163
      SOME KNEW WHAT AILED THE WORLD . . . . . . .    627 STATES HOLIDAY       9
AILELL
      SHE SAW HER HUSBAND AILELL SLEEPING THERE, . .  183 QUEEN MAEVE         69
      SUDDENLY AILELL SPOKE OUT OF HIS SLEEP, . . .   183 QUEEN MAEVE         73
AILING
      AND MADE--BEING POOR, AILING AND IGNORANT, . .  370 EGO DOMINUS         59
AILLINN
      BAILE AND AILLINN . . . . . . . . . . . . .     188 BAILE AILLINN        T
      AILLINN, WHO WAS KING LUGAIDH'S HEIR. . . . .   189 BAILE AILLINN        7
      BAILE AND AILLINN WOULD BE WED. . . . . . . .   190 BAILE AILLINN       24
      TO TELL HIM HOW THE GIRL AILLINN . . . . . .    191 BAILE AILLINN       49
      WHERE AILLINN RODE WITH WAITING-MAIDS . . . .   193 BAILE AILLINN      102
      WHERE AILLINN RODE WITH WAITING MAIDS . . . .   193 BAILE AILLINN V    102
      RIBH AT THE TOMB OF BAILE AND AILLINN . . . .   554 RIBH AT TOMB         T
      OF BAILE AND AILLINN YOU NEED NOT SPEAK, . . .  555 RIBH AT TOMB         6
AILLINN'S
      BAILE AND AILLINN'S MARRIAGE-BED, . . . . . .   194 BAILE AILLINN      121
      BAILE AND AILLINN'S MARRIAGE BED, . . . . . .   194 BAILE AILLINN V    121
AILS
      OUT OF MY HEART.  THERE'S SOMETHING AILS OUR COLT . . 260 FASC DIFFICULT  4
      FOR HURTS AND AILS AND LOVER'S MOAN-- . . . .   717 FAIRY DOCTOR        18
AIMED
      AIMED AT THE COMMONEST EAR, . . . . . . . . .   347 FISHERMAN           20
      ALL MEN HAVE AIMED AT, FOUND AND LOST! . . .    566 LAPIS LAZULI        18
AIMLESS
      AN AIMLESS JOY IS A PURE JOY," . . . . . . .    338 TOM OROUGHLEY        4
      IN AIMLESS ARGUMENT! . . . . . . . . . . . .    392 EASTER 1916 V       18
      FOR AIMLESS JOY HAD MADE ME STOP . . . . . .    400 DEMON BEAST         22
      AND AIMLESS WANDERINGS THE WOODLANDS LONE, . .  674 ISLE STAT II 3     209
AIMLESSNESS
      MY DAYS OUT OF THEIR AIMLESSNESS. . . . . . .   421 MY TABLE             5
AIR
      BUT THE TALE, THOUGH WORDS BE LIGHTER THAN AIR, . .  3 OISIN 1          11
      CLOSED IN THE MISTY AIR PROFOUND. . . . . . .    10 OISIN 1        V 114D
      AND HOUNDS FOR CENTURIES DUST AND AIR. . . .     11 OISIN 1           131
      OR HAVE THEY BREATHED THE MORTAL AIR?" . . .     12 OISIN 1           147
      OF DANCERS LEAPING IN THE AIR! . . . . . . .     18 OISIN 1           254
      LIKE TULIPS IN THE AIR A-WINGING, . . . . . .    27 OISIN 1           417
      FANNED THE DELIGHTED AIR LIKE WINGS OF BIRDS! .  32 OISIN 2            50
      AND WHEN THE DEW-DROWNED STARS HANG IN THE AIR   32 OISIN 2            54
      THAT FAN THE PULSES OF DELIGHTED AIR, . . . .    32 OISIN 2        V  50A
      MAKING A WORLD ABOUT HER IN THE AIR, . . . .     37 OISIN 2           122
      AND THICKENED ALL THE WHIRLING AIR.  THEN DID .  46 OISIN 2        V 245A
      CAME NOW THE SLIDING OF TEARS AND SWEEPING OF MIST-COLD  47 OISIN 3  V   7
         AIR.
      . . . FROM HIS MILES IN THE MIDST OF THE AIR, . . 54 OISIN 3          103
      . . . WITH ITS BELFRY IN AIR! . . . . . . . .    61 OISIN 3           193
      THE WILD FOWL OF THE AIR INCREASED! . . . . .    82 MAD KING GOLL       8
      AND SHEDS FAINT ODOURS THROUGH THE AIR! . . .    85 MAD KING GOLL      64
```

11

AIR   (CONTINUED)

	PAGE	TITLE		LINE
AND SHEDS FAINT ODOUR THROUGH THE AIR;	85	MAD KING GOLL	V	64
TO THE BIRDS IN THE WHITE OF THE AIR.	92	FATHER OHART		16
OVER THE DOOR-STEP INTO THE AIR,	97	FOXHUNTER	V	3
ABOVE THE TIDE OF HOURS, TROUBLE THE AIR,	114	ROSE OF BATTLE		3
A SONG INTO THE AIR, AND SINGING PASSED	114	ROSE OF BATTLE		14
ABOVE THE TIDE OF HOURS, RISE ON THE AIR,	114	ROSE OF BATTLE	V	3
A SONG INTO THE AIR, AND SINGING PAST	114	ROSE OF BATTLE	V	14
THE HOST OF THE AIR	143	HOST OF AIR		T
THE FOLK OF THE AIR	143	HOST OF AIR	V	T
FOR THESE WERE THE HOST OF THE AIR;	144	HOST OF AIR		26
FOR THESE WERE THE FOLK OF THE AIR;	144	HOST OF AIR	V	26
BUT HE HEARD HIGH UP IN THE AIR	145	HOST OF AIR		41
HE KNEW NOW THE FOLK OF THE AIR,	145	HOST OF AIR	V	40A
AND FADED THROUGH THE BRIGHTENING AIR.	150	WANDER AENGUS		16
O CURLEW, CRY NO MORE IN THE AIR,	155	REPROVE CURLEW		1
AND WAVED IT OFF ON THE AIR.	160	CAP AND BELLS		20
TILL STARS GREW OUT OF THE AIR.	160	CAP AND BELLS		28
AND WAVED IT OUT ON THE AIR.	160	CAP AND BELLS	V	20
THE STARS GREW OUT OF THE AIR.	160	CAP AND BELLS	V	28
WITH WORDS LIGHTER THAN AIR,	162	ASKS FORGIVE		2
I MADE IT OUT OF A MOUTHFUL OF AIR,	166	EVIL OF BELOV		5
AND SMOKE FROM THIS DEAD HEART DRIFTS THROUGH THE VIOLET AIR	173	SPEAKS HEARERS		3
O BEAST OF THE WILDERNESS, BIRD OF THE AIR,	177	PAST GREATNESS		11
ALTHOUGH THE RUSHES AND THE FOWL OF THE AIR	177	PAST GREATNESS	V	11
WAS THAT, THE AIR BEING HEAVY AND THE DOGS	182	QUEEN MAEVE		53
WITH LONG WHITE BODIES CAME OUT OF THE AIR	185	QUEEN MAEVE		118
UNTIL TWO LOVERS CAME OUT OF THE AIR	187	QUEEN MAEVE		143
BUT OUT OF THE DARK AIR OVER HER HEAD THERE CAME	187	QUEEN MAEVE		153
IN OLD TIMES AMONG THE CLOUDS OF THE AIR.	194	BAILE AILLINN		133
AWAKEN WANDERINGS OF LIGHT AIR	197	BAILE AILLINN		185
FOR THE WET WINDS ARE BLOWING OUT OF THE CLINGING AIR;	207	HANRAHANS SONG		12
WHEN THE RAIN IS PELTING OUT OF THE WINTRY AIR;	207	HANRAHANS SONG	V	12
THEIR SUDDEN FRAGRANCES ON THE GREEN AIR;	217	WOODS OF COOLE		10
TO THE OTHER SIDE, AND HIGHER IN THE AIR.	234	SHADOW WATER B		259
I HAVE FLED TO MY BELOVED IN THE AIR,	234	SHADOW WATER B		262
IN THE WASTE OF THE HIGH AIR, THAT WE MAY WANDER	234	SHADOW WATER B		263
BEING TOO BUSY IN THE AIR AND THE HIGH AIR,	234	SHADOW WATER B		274
BEING TOO BUSY IN THE AIR AND THE HIGH AIR,	234	SHADOW WATER B		274
HE HAS FLUNG A DRUID SPELL UPON THE AIR,	240	SHADOW WATER B		385
THEY HAVE BEEN CIRCLING OVER OUR HEADS IN THE AIR,	247	SHADOW WATER B		525
DID NOT THE POET CARRY HIM WITH AN AIR	267	ALL TEMPT ME	V	7
"WHO IS THE FRIEND THAT SEEMS BUT AIR	274	GREY ROCK		83
AMID THE ELABORATE WILDERNESS OF THE AIR.	278	TWO KINGS		31
AND CLIMBED INTO THE AIR, CRUMBLING AWAY,	278	TWO KINGS		42
I WAS YOUR HUSBAND WHEN YOU RODE THE AIR,	284	TWO KINGS		166
OUR SUDDEN PALACES IN THE STILL AIR	284	TWO KINGS		180
ONCE, WHEN MIDNIGHT SMOTE THE AIR,	294	HATED PLAYBOY		1
THREE OLD HERMITS TOOK THE AIR	298	THREE HERMITS		1
AND FIND MY HEALTH AGAIN IN THE SEA AIR,"	299	BEGGAR CRIED		2
THREW UP IN THE AIR HIS MARVELLOUS MOON.	314	MEMORY YOUTH	V	21
A CLEAR ARTICULATION IN THE AIR,	320	REED WHISPERER		3
COMPANIONABLE STREAMS OR CLIMB THE AIR;	323	SWANS AT COOLE		21
"CALL DOWN THE HAWK FROM THE AIR;	349	HAWK		1
IN RAMBLING TALK WITH AN IMAGE OF AIR;	357	BROKEN DREAMS		40
SEA-BORNE, OR BALANCED ON THE AIR	397	POLIT PRISONER		19
A BIT OF BREAD THROWN UP INTO THE AIR;	400	DEMON BEAST		25
IT SEEMED THAT A DRAGON OF AIR	430	NINETEEN 19		51
SO MASTERED BY THE BRUTE BLOOD OF THE AIR?	441	LEDA AND SWAN		12
BY HER DISTRACTED AIR	453	DEATH OF HARE		8
ONE AMONG THE BIRDS OF THE AIR,	460	THREE MONUMENT		3
AS AIR UNDER A WING, CAN GIVE BIRDS' WIT.	462	HARUN RASHID		28
AS AIR UNDER A WING, CAN GIVE BIRD'S WIT.	462	HARUN RASHID	V	28
UPON THE BREATHLESS STARLIT AIR,	477	SELF AND SOUL		4
SYMBOLICAL GLORY OF THE EARTH AND AIR;	483	VERONIC NAPKIN		3
FOUND CERTAINTY UPON THE DREAMING AIR,	489	COOLE PARK 29		22
AN EVENING CHILL UPON THE AIR,	494	AT ALGECIRAS		14
IN A GREAT TUMULT OF THE AIR,	519	HER DREAM		6
BUT ALL THAT RUN IN COUPLES, ON EARTH, IN FLOOD OR AIR,	556	RIBH PATRICK		11
BIRD SIGHS FOR THE AIR,	574	LOVERS SONG		1
FOR AIR AND EXERCISE,	575	ACRE OF GRASS		3
FIND IN MIDDLE AIR	601	THOSE IMAGES		13
THAT AIR IN IMMORTALITY	637	BEN BULBEN		8
AND THRO' THE ODOROUS AIR LOVE-DREAMS ARE WINGING--	645	ISLE STAT I 1		5
OF THIS WIDE VALE, EMBOSOMED IN THE AIR,	652	ISLE STAT I 2		19
OUT OF THE AIR. AND WHEN? WHEN THE SUN GOES DOWN	652	ISLE STAT I 2		29
THE AIR IS STILL ABOVE, AND STILL EACH LEAF,	662	ISLE STAT II 2		7
TO DIE FOR HER IN AIR OR GROUND.	668	ISLE STAT II 3		52
AND THE FLOWING AIR ABOVE,	680	LOVE AND DEATH		14
TO BUILD THE CIRCLING SEATS, WHERE HIGH IN AIR	699	MOSADA 3		18
IN THE BOSOM OF THE AIR--	706	DAWN-SONG		30
HANG THE MIST-THREADS FOR A LITTLE WHILE LIKE COBWEBS IN THE AIR;	719	PHANTOM SHIP		29
HANG THE MIST THREADS FOR A LITTLE WHILE LIKE COBWEBS IN THE AIR,	719	PHANTOM SHIP	V	29
ONE WHOSE BREATHING SHAKES THE AIR,	727	LOVERS QUARREL		31
THE SUNLIGHT IN THE AIR.	736	IN CHURCH		10
AND SHAKE THEIR BIRDS UPON THE AIR;	736	SUMMER EVENING		3
AND SHAKE THEIR BIRDS UPON THE AIR;	737	SUMMER EVENING		19

12

AIR   (CONTINUED)
   LEAPED UP INTO THE AIR. . . . . 741 EARL PAUL 36
   UPON CLEAR NIGHTS THEY LEAVE THE UPPER AIR . . . . . . 750 SHADOW WATER A 87
   TO THE OTHER SIDE AND HIGHER IN THE AIR. . . . . . . 753 SHADOW WATER A 149
   IN THE WASTE AIR. I WILL WANDER BY HIS SIDE . . . . . 754 SHADOW WATER A 152
   HE HAS THROWN A DRUID DREAM UPON THE AIR. . . . . . . 759 SHADOW WATER A 237
   I HAVE HEARD IN THE NIGHT AIR . . . . 783 GREY ROUND 6
   O, WHAT IS LIFE BUT A MOUTHFUL OF AIR? . . . . . . 788 HAWTHORN TREE 9
AIR-BREATH
   FOR THERE CAME AN AIR-BREATH COOL . . . . 667 ISLE STAT II 3 27
AIRMAN
   AN IRISH AIRMAN FORESEES HIS DEATH . . . . 328 IRISH AIRMAN T
AIRS
   DID NOT THE POET SING IT WITH SUCH AIRS . . . . . . 267 ALL TEMPT ME 7
   THAT AIRS IN IMMORTALITY . . . . 637 BEN BULBEN V 8
   THAT AIRS AN IMMORTALITY . . . . 637 BEN BULBEN V 8
AIRY
   WHEN WE ARE HIGH AND AIRY HUNDREDS SAY . . . . . . 265 ABBEY THEATRE 2
   THAT IS AN AIRY SPOT, ... 614 MARCH SONGS 2 9
   THAT IS AN AIRY SPOT, ... 615 MARCH SONGS 2 19
   THAT IS AN AIRY SPOT, ... 615 MARCH SONGS 2 29
   A WANDERING AIRY MUSIC, ... 783 GREY ROUND 7
   A WANDERING AIRY MUSIC, ... 783 GREY ROUND 17
AKIN
   THAT MAKE THE HEART AKIN TO THE DUMB STONE." . . . . 281 TWO KINGS 94
AL   SEE ABD-AL-RABBAN
ALARM
   RAISE THE DOOR-PIN WITH ALARM, ... 727 LOVERS QUARREL 52
ALARMED
   WHAT CAN HAVE SUDDENLY ALARMED YOU . . . . 389 IMAGE PAST 16
ALARMS
   WHERE THROUGH LONG WARS AND SUDDEN NIGHT ALARMS . . . 420 MY HOUSE 24
   WHAT WERE ALL THE WORLD'S ALARMS . . . . 522 LULLABY 3
   WHAT ARE ALL THE WORLD'S ALARMS? . . . . 522 LULLABY V 3
   OF WAR AND WAR'S ALARMS, ... 631 POLITICS 10
ALARUMS
   WHERE THROUGH LONG WARS AND SUDDEN NIGHT ALARUMS . . . 420 MY HOUSE V 24
ALAS
   AND SHAKE THEIR RAGGED WINGS; ALAS! . . . . . . 136 TWO TREES 38
   AND WHEN THEY SHAKE THEIR WINGS--ALAS! . . . . . 136 TWO TREES V 38
   ALAS! I MAKE YOU SADDER, SHEPHERDESS. . . . . . . 659 ISLE STAT II 1 18
ALBAN
   AND HARRIED ALBAN TOWNS, AND OVERTHREW . . . . . . 749 SHADOW WATER A 40
ALCIBIADES
   THAT GREAT ROGUE ALCIBIADES. . . . . 379 SAINT HUNCH 12
   BUT MOST TO ALCIBIADES. . . . . 380 SAINT HUNCH 16
ALCOVE'S
   IN THE DEEP ALCOVE'S DIMNESS SMILES AND HIDES." . . . 735 QUATRAIN APHOR 24
ALCOVES
   IN THE DEEP ALCOVES DIMNESS SMILES AND HIDES. . . . . 685 DRAWING-ROOM 4
   IN THE DEEP ALCOVES DIMNESS SMILES AND HIDES. . . . . 735 QUATRAIN APHOR V 24
ALDER
   TALL WANDS OF ALDER AND WHITE QUICKEN WANDS. . . . . 111 CUCHULAIN SEA V 82A
   AN OWL, WHO IN AN ALDER TREE . . . . 670 ISLE STAT II 3 115
   FORTH FROM THE HOLLOW ALDER TRUNK . . . . 670 ISLE STAT II 3 120
ALE
   I HAVE DRUNK ALE FROM THE COUNTRY OF THE YOUNG . . . 177 PAST GREATNESS 1
   SHOOK THE ALE HORNS AND SHIELDS UPON THEIR HOOKS! . . 181 QUEEN MAEVE V 38
   AND ALL THE ALE RAN OUT AT THE NEW MOON, ... 222 SHADOW WATER B V 11
   THE ALE CUP IS MY FATHER AND MY MOTHER. . . . . . 222 SHADOW WATER B V 11B
   WHEN WE HAVE NEITHER BROWN NOR YELLOW ALE? . . . . 240 SHADOW WATER B 387
   I SAW A FLAGON OF BROWN ALE ABOARD HER. . . . . . 240 SHADOW WATER B 388
   WHO SAID WE HAD A SKIN OF YELLOW ALE? . . . . . . 759 SHADOW WATER A 243
   I SAID THE ALE WAS BROWN. I HAVE FOUND THE ALE, . . 759 SHADOW WATER A 244
   I SAID THE ALE WAS BROWN. I HAVE FOUND THE ALE, . . 759 SHADOW WATER A 244
   FORGAEL CAN DIE TO-MORROW. COME TO THE ALE. . . . 759 SHADOW WATER A 246
   COME TO THE ALE! FOR HE CAN DIE TO-MORROW. . . . . 760 SHADOW WATER A 247
   ALE SETS THEM QUARRELLING. GIVE ME YOUR SWORDS. . . 766 SHADOW WATER A 372
   WHEN THE DARK HOUNDS WERE LOOSED. COME TO THE ALE. . 766 SHADOW WATER A 379
   IT IS THE BROWN ALE DOES IT. GIVE ME YOUR SWORDS. . 766 SHADOW WATER A V 372
   HAVE FOUND IT LIKE THE FROTH UPON THE ALE. . . . . 767 SHADOW WATER A 387
   AND TELL ITS STORY OVER THEIR BROWN ALE. . . . . . 767 SHADOW WATER A 393
ALEEL
   "I AM ALEEL, THE SWINEHERD, WHOM YOU BID . . . . . 105 CUCHULAIN SEA V 3A
   LOOKING ON HER, ALEEL, THE SWINEHERD, SAID: . . . . 106 CUCHULAIN SEA V 9
   ALEEL, THE SWINEHERD, WEPT AND CAST HIM DOWN . . . . 106 CUCHULAIN SEA V 14
   ALEEL, HIS COUNTESS! HANRAHAN . . . . 550 SEVERED HEAD 15
ALE-HORNS
   SHOOK THE ALE-HORNS AND SHIELDS UPON THEIR HOOKS! . . 181 QUEEN MAEVE 38
ALEXANDER
   GREEK ALEXANDER FROM MY FLESH, ... 379 SAINT HUNCH 10
ALEXANDER'S
   WHEN ALEXANDER'S EMPIRE PASSED, THEY SLEPT SO SOUND. . 442 BLACK CENTAUR 12
   WHEN ALEXANDER'S EMPIRE PAST, THEY SLEPT SO SOUND. . 442 BLACK CENTAUR V 12
ALEXANDRIA'S
   ALEXANDRIA'S WAS A BEACON TOWER, AND BABYLON'S . . . 480 BLOOD AND MOON 13
ALFRED
   IN MEMORY OF ALFRED POLLEXFEN . . . . 360 ALF POLLEXFEN T
   AND "MR. ALFRED" BE AGAIN . . . . 361 ALF POLLEXFEN 32
   COME ALFRED NOYES AND ALL THE TROUP . . . . . . 582 ROGER CASEMENT V 17

13

			PAGE	TITLE		LINE
ALGECIRAS						
AT ALGECIRAS--A MEDITATION UPON DEATH			493	AT ALGECIRAS		T
A MEDITATION WRITTEN DURING SICKNESS AT ALGECIRAS . . .			493	AT ALGECIRAS	V	T
IN ALGECIRAS GARDENS, AND THERE REST			494	AT ALGECIRAS	V	5
ALHAMBRA						
OF THE ALHAMBRA BLACK ATHWART HIS DISK:			691	MOSADA 1	V	37
ALIEN						
UNDER AN ALIEN EYELID, FOR IT WAS MY CRAFT			284	TWO KINGS	V	156
AS ALIEN AS A CUCKOO IN A ROBIN'S NEST, ...			671	ISLE STAT II 3		138
ALIEN AS CUCKOO IN A ROBIN'S NEST, ...			671	ISLE STAT II 3	V	138
ALIENS						
EARTH'S ALIENS. WHY SO SORROWFUL? OUR SOULS			80	EPHEMERA	V	12A
ALIGHIERI						
DANTE ALIGHIERI, SO UTTERLY FOUND HIMSELF			368	EGO DOMINUS		19
ALIGHT						
AND ALIGHT AT THE COMELY TREES AND THE LAWN, ...			330	BONE OF A HARE		4
NOR A CAGE, NOR ALIGHT UPON WRIST, ...			349	HAWK		8
ITS OPEN LIGHTED DOORWAY AND ITS WINDOWS ALL ALIGHT, . .			581	CURSE CROMWELL		26
ALIGHTED						
ALIGHTED ON THE WINDY GRASS.			195	BAILE AILLINN		138
ALIKE						
MUST WE PART, VON HUEGEL, THOUGH MUCH ALIKE, FOR WE . . .			503	VACILLATION		78
ALIT						
DOWN TO HER CELL AND THERE ALIT.			397	POLIT PRISONER		4
THE HEAVENS ALL STAR-THROBBING ARE ALIT.			671	ISLE STAT II 3	V	143
A-LIT						
THE HEAVENS ALL STAR-THROBBING ARE A-LIT.			671	ISLE STAT II 3		143
ALIVE						
HAVE FACES ALIVE WITH SUCH BEAUTY BEEN KNOWN TO THE SALT EYE OF MAN,			50	OISIN 3		51
ARE FACES ALIVE WITH SUCH BEAUTY MADE KNOWN TO THE SALT EYE OF MAN,			50	OISIN 3	V	51
ARE FACES ALIVE WITH SUCH BEAUTY MADE KNOWN TO THE SOFT EYE OF MAN,			50	OISIN 3	V	51
FOR THERE MOVES ALIVE IN YOUR FINGERS			55	OISIN 3		124
FOR MOVETH ALIVE IN THY FINGERS THE FLUTTERING SADNESS OF EARTH.			55	OISIN 3	V	124
"NO MAN ALIVE, NO MAN AMONG THE DEAD, ...			106	CUCHULAIN SEA		10
"NOT ANY GOD ALIVE NOR MORTAL DEAD, ...			106	CUCHULAIN SEA	V	10
LIKE THEM THAT ARE NO MORE ALIVE			197	BAILE AILLINN		207
OF THOSE THAT ARE ALIVE FOR EVER AND EVER.			223	SHADOW WATER B		35
WHERE NO SHIP SAILS, WHERE NOTHING THAT'S ALIVE . . .			226	SHADOW WATER B		98
HAD DROWNED ME ALSO. BUT, BEING YET ALIVE, ...			235	SHADOW WATER B		289
FOR NONE ALIVE TO-DAY			458	SECRETS OF OLD		10
FOR NONE ALIVE TODAY			458	SECRETS OF OLD	V	10
WHEN MY BODY WAS ALIVE			521	THREE THINGS		10
TO KEEP THE SOUL OF MAN ALIVE, ...			620	JOHN KINSELLA		19
TO SNATCH ALIVE OUT OF THE STREAMS ALL LOVERS			765	SHADOW WATER A		347
ALL						
YET WILL I MAKE ALL PLAIN FOR THEE.			2	OISIN 1	V	78
THAT YOU THROUGH ALL THAT FOAM SHOULD RUN?"			6	OISIN 1		61
OF ALL THAT WISDOM AND THE FAME			7	OISIN 1		66
AND SET YOUR NAME ALL NAMES ABOVE, ...			7	OISIN 1		76
ALL MEN, AND STRONGER OF HIS HANDS, ...			7	OISIN 1	V	63
BEFORE THY FEET SHALL KNEEL DOWN ALL			7	OISIN 1	V	77
AND THE FENIANS ALL HAD WEPT WITH ME, ...			10	OISIN 1	V	113
ALL PEARLY WHITE, SAVE ONE RED EAR!			12	OISIN 1		141
AS THOUGH THEY ALL WERE BEATING TIME, ...			13	OISIN 1		174
AND SINGING, SINGING ALL TOGETHER:			15	OISIN 1		203
THEIR ROBES WERE ALL OF YELLOW SILK			15	OISIN 1	V	205
FROM ALL THEIR LIPS, AND ONCE THEY SANG			16	OISIN 1		226
AND MADE IN ALL THEIR DISTANT PARTS, ...			16	OISIN 1		228
AND ROSE FROM ALL THEIR DISTANT PARTS, ...			16	OISIN 1	V	228
"O SADDEST HARP IN ALL THE WORLD, ...			17	OISIN 1		245
"THE SADDEST HARP IN ALL THE WORLD!"			17	OISIN 1	V	246
A FIRWOOD HOUSE, ALL COVERED OVER			17	OISIN 1	V	248
AROUND A SCEPTRE OF ALL LIGHTS, ...			18	OISIN 1	V	254
TO ALL THINGS CRIED: "I AM A SLAVE!			19	OISIN 1	V	280
BENT ALL OUR SWAYING BODIES DOWN, ...			20	OISIN 1		297
AND ALL LISTLESS HOURS FEAR US, ...			21	OISIN 1		317
THAT HIDES US FROM ALL HUMAN SPYING, ...			22	OISIN 1	V	338A
FOR LOVE THEY FOLLOWED ONE AND ALL!			23	OISIN 1	V	345G
THE THINGS THAT MOST OF ALL I HATE:			24	OISIN 1		359
TWO THINGS THAT 'FORE ALL ELSE I HATE, ...			24	OISIN 1	V	359
WITH ALL THE ANCIENT SORROW OF MEN":			25	OISIN 1		381
FLOATED IN ALL HER SINGING. HALF ENTRANCED			30	OISIN 2	V	19
THE SADDEST OF ALL MEN."			33	OISIN 2		68
HER FACE SEEMED FASHIONED ALL OF MOONLIT VAPOURS, . .			33	OISIN 2	V	70
JABBER AND SCREAM. YET HE, FOR ALL HIS BOLD . . .			34	OISIN 2	V	82
"FOR ALL MEN FLEE THE DEMONS": BUT MOVED NOT . . .			36	OISIN 2		93
ROOTED IN FOAM AND CLOUDS, AND CRIED TO ALL			38	OISIN 2		132
AND WHEN THE SUN IN ALL HIS FLAGRANT SAFFRON STEPT, .			41	OISIN 2	V	192
AND ALL THE EXULTANT LABOURS OF THE STRONG.			42	OISIN 2		195
FOR ALL YOUR CROZIERS, THEY HAVE LEFT THE PATH . . .			42	OISIN 2		200
ALL IS DONE NOW--I SEE THE RAVENS FLOCK--			43	OISIN 2	V	212
THAT ALL BE OVERTHROWN.			45	OISIN 2		239
"BUT TILL THE MOON HAS TAKEN ALL, I WAGE			45	OISIN 2		240
"WITH ALL IN ALL THE WORLD I BATTLE WAGE.			45	OISIN 2		240
"WITH ALL IN ALL THE WORLD I BATTLE WAGE.			45	OISIN 2	V	240
ARE EMPTY OF ALL POWER." "AND WHICH OF THESE . . .			46	OISIN 2		248
AND THICKENED ALL THE WHIRLING AIR. THEN DID . . .			46	OISIN 2	V	245A

14

	PAGE	TITLE		LINE
ALL (CONTINUED)				
COULD SLEEP ON A COUCH OF RUSHES, AND ALL INWROUGHT AND INLAID,	49	OISIN 3		31
COULD SLEEP ON A BED OF RUSHES, AND ALL INWROUGHT AND INLAID,	49	OISIN 3	V	31
MOVED ROUND ME, OF SEAMEN OR LANDSMEN, ALL WHO ARE WINTER TALES;	53	OISIN 3		86
IN A REVERIE FORGETFUL OF ALL THINGS, OVER THE BUBBLING GROUND.	56	OISIN 3		140
. . . WHERE ALL IS BARREN AND GREY, ...	56	OISIN 3		141
IN REVERIE FORGETFUL OF ALL THINGS, OVER THE BUBBLING GROUND.	56	OISIN 3	V	140
MUCH WONDERING TO SEE UPON ALL HANDS, OF WATTLES AND WOODWORK MADE,	58	OISIN 3		162
MUCH WONDERING TO SEE UPON ALL HANDS, OF WATTLES AND WOOD-WORK MADE,	58	OISIN 3	V	162
AND DEMONS, ALL BROKEN IN PIECES, BE TRAMPLED BENEATH THEM IN DEATH.	61	OISIN 3	V	204
ALL EMPTIED OF PURPLE HOURS AS A BEGGAR'S CLOAK IN THE RAIN,	63	OISIN 3		219
OF ALL THE MANY CHANGING THINGS	65	HAPPY SHEPHERD		7
LEST ALL THY TOILING ONLY BREEDS	66	HAPPY SHEPHERD		25
AND DEAD IS ALL THEIR HUMAN TRUTH.	66	HAPPY SHEPHERD		34
THROUGH ALL THE WELL-BELOVED GLADE.	67	HAPPY SHEPHERD	V	46C
CRIED ALL HIS STORY TO THE DEWDROPS GLISTENING.	68	SAD SHEPHERD		14
HE CALLED ALOUD TO ALL THE STARS TO LEND	68	SAD SHEPHERD	V	5
CHANGED ALL HE SANG TO INARTICULATE MOAN	69	SAD SHEPHERD		27
CHANGED ALL HIS WORDS TO INARTICULATE MOAN	69	SAD SHEPHERD	V	27
O LOVELY TO SEE IN ALL MEN'S SIGHT	69	CLOAK BOAT		3
IN ALL MEN'S SIGHT."	69	CLOAK BOAT		5
O SWIFT ON THE SEAS ALL DAY AND NIGHT	70	CLOAK BOAT		8
ALL DAY AND NIGHT."	70	CLOAK BOAT		10
IN ALL MEN'S EARS OF SORROW, ...	70	CLOAK BOAT		14
SEND PEACE ON ALL THE LANDS AND FLICKERING CORN.— . . .	71	ANASHU VIJAYA		1
WHO IS AMRITA? SORROW OF ALL SORROWS!	71	ANASHU VIJAYA		15
WEARY, WITH ALL HIS POPPIES GATHERED ROUND HIM.	72	ANASHU VIJAYA		25
PAINTING WITH SHADOW ALL THE MARBLE STEPS!	72	ANASHU VIJAYA		30
WITH ALL YOUR WHIRLING HAIR, AND DROP MANY AN AZURE TEAR.	73	ANASHU VIJAYA		46
THEIR FACES ARE ALL WORN, AND IN THEIR EYES	73	ANASHU VIJAYA		48
THE ICICLES THAT FAMISH ALL THE NORTH, ...	73	ANASHU VIJAYA		50
AND LIONESS, WITH ALL THEIR WHIMPERING CUBS!	73	ANASHU VIJAYA		53
WITH ALL YOUR WHIRLING HAIR, AND DROP THROUGH SPACE AN AZURE TEAR.	73	ANASHU VIJAYA	V	46
WITH ALL YOUR WHIRLING HAIR, AND DROP TEAR UPON AZURE TEAR.	73	ANASHU VIJAYA	V	46
WITH ALL OUR WHIRLING HAIR, AND DROP MANY AN AZURE TEAR.	73	ANASHU VIJAYA	V	46
IN THE TREE ROOTS, AND ALL THE SACRED FLOCKS	75	ANASHU VIJAYA	V	88
THE MERRY LAMBS AND ALL THE KINE COMPLACENT, ...	75	ANASHU VIJAYA	V	86
IN THE TREE ROOTS, AND ALL THY SACRED FLOCKS	75	ANASHU VIJAYA	V	88
ALL DRIPPING ON A GRASSY SLOPE, AND SAW THEM CEASE TO CHASE	76	INDIAN ON GOD		4
FOR I AM IN HIS IMAGE MADE, AND ALL THIS TINKLING TIDE . .	76	INDIAN ON GOD		11
HE IS A MONSTROUS PEACOCK, AND HE WAVETH ALL THE NIGHT . .	77	INDIAN ON GOD		19
AND ALL IS OVER SAVE THE MURMUR AND THE SWEETNESS. . . .	77	INDIAN TO LOVE	V	5E
MURMURING HOW FAR AWAY ARE ALL EARTH'S FEVERISH LANDS. . .	78	INDIAN TO LOVE	V	10
I RULED O'ER ALL MY FAIR DOMINIONS, ...	82	MAD KING GOLL	V	7
WITH ALL HIS COLOURS JOURNEY-DULL, ...	82	MAD KING GOLL	V	13
SPLASHED ALL WITH CLAY AND JOURNEY DULL, ...	82	MAD KING GOLL	V	13
I SAW THIS HARP ALL SONGLESS LIE, ...	85	MAD KING GOLL	V	55
IN ALL HIS EVENING VAPOURS ROLLED—	86	MAD KING GOLL	V	71
WE FOOT IT ALL THE NIGHT, ...	87	STOLEN CHILD		16
SLEIVEENS WERE ALL HIS RACE!	92	FATHER OHART		6
ALL LOVED HIM, ONLY THE SHONEEN, ...	92	FATHER OHART		13
THIS WAY WERE ALL REPROVED	93	FATHER OHART		39
MY MONEY'S ALL USED UP, ...	96	MOLL MAGEE		38
THE SUN UPON ALL THINGS THAT GROW	98	FOXHUNTER		15
RED ROSE, PROUD ROSE, SAD ROSE OF ALL MY DAYS!	100	ROSE UPON ROOD		1
IN ALL POOR FOOLISH THINGS THAT LIVE A DAY, ...	101	ROSE UPON ROOD		11
RED ROSE, PROUD ROSE, SAD ROSE OF ALL MY DAYS!	101	ROSE UPON ROOD		24
AND ALL THESE THINGS WERE WONDERFUL AND GREAT!	104	FERGUS DRUID		37
BUT NOW I HAVE GROWN NOTHING, KNOWING ALL.	104	FERGUS DRUID		38
BUT NOW I HAVE GROWN NOTHING, BEING ALL!	104	FERGUS DRUID	V	38
AND RAISING ARMS ALL RADDLED WITH THE DYE, ...	105	CUCHULAIN SEA		7
AND ALL AROUND THE HARP-STRING TOLD HIS PRAISE.	109	CUCHULAIN SEA		44
"HE BADE ME LET ALL KNOW HE GIVES HIS NAME	109	CUCHULAIN SEA		52
OF ALL THIS HOST SO BOUND FROM CHILDHOOD ON."	109	CUCHULAIN SEA		56
AND ALL AROUND THE HARPSTRING TOLD HIS PRAISE, ...	109	CUCHULAIN SEA	V	44
AND ALL AROUND THE HARP STRING TOLD HIS PRAISE, ...	109	CUCHULAIN SEA	V	44
THEN CONCHUBAR, THE SUBTLEST OF ALL MEN, ...	110	CUCHULAIN SEA		75
AND THEN ARISE, AND RAVING SLAY US ALL.	110	CUCHULAIN SEA		79
FOR THESE RED LIPS, WITH ALL THEIR MOURNFUL PRIDE, . . .	111	ROSE OF WORLD		2
AND ALL FOLK SEEING HIM BOW DOWN, ...	113	ROSE OF PEACE		9
SAYING ALL THINGS WERE WELL!	113	ROSE OF PEACE		14
ROSE OF ALL ROSES, ROSE OF ALL THE WORLD!	113	ROSE OF BATTLE		1
ROSE OF ALL ROSES, ROSE OF ALL THE WORLD!	113	ROSE OF BATTLE		1
BUT GATHER ALL FOR WHOM NO LOVE HATH MADE	114	ROSE OF BATTLE		12
TO THESE OLD NIGHT SHALL ALL HER MYSTERY TELL!	114	ROSE OF BATTLE		22
ROSE OF ALL ROSES, ROSE OF ALL THE WORLD!	115	ROSE OF BATTLE		25
ROSE OF ALL ROSES, ROSE OF ALL THE WORLD!	115	ROSE OF BATTLE		25
IF ALL WERE TOLD!	116	FAERY SONG		4
IF ALL WERE TOLD.	116	FAERY SONG		16
THERE MIDNIGHT'S ALL A GLIMMER, AND NOON A PURPLE GLOW,	117	ISLE INNISFREE		7
A PITY BEYOND ALL TELLING	119	PITY OF LOVE		1

15

ALL (CONTINUED)

	PAGE	TITLE		LINE
ALL THREATEN THE HEAD THAT I LOVE.	119	PITY OF LOVE	V	8
THE BRILLIANT MOON AND ALL THE MILKY SKY,	119	SORROW OF LOVE		2
AND ALL THAT FAMOUS HARMONY OF LEAVES,	120	SORROW OF LOVE		3
AND ALL THAT LAMENTATION OF THE LEAVES,	120	SORROW OF LOVE		11
AND ALL THE SORROWS OF HER LABOURING SHIPS,	120	SORROW OF LOVE	V	7
AND ALL THE TROUBLE OF HER LABOURING SHIPS,	120	SORROW OF LOVE	V	7
AND ALL THE BURDEN OF HER MYRIAD YEARS.	120	SORROW OF LOVE	V	8
AND ALL THE TROUBLE OF HER MYRIAD YEARS.	120	SORROW OF LOVE	V	8
ALL THE HEAVY DAYS ARE OVER:	124	CATHLEEN PARA		1
CARRY ALL THAT MOURNFUL BEAUTY	124	CATHLEEN PARA		7
ALL THE HEAVENS BOW DOWN TO HEAVEN,	125	CATHLEEN PARA		15
AND ALL DISHEVELLED WANDERING STARS.	126	GOES FERGUS		12
HIS HEART HUNG ALL UPON A SILKEN DRESS,	126	DREAM OF FAERY		2
HIS MIND RAN ALL ON MONEY CARES AND FEARS,	127	DREAM OF FAERY		14
NOW THAT THE EARTH HAD TAKEN MAN AND ALL:	128	DREAM OF FAERY		40
AND ALL THEIR TROUBLE DIES INTO ITS PEACE:--	128	DREAM OF FAERY	V	35
NOW THAT OLD EARTH HAD TAKEN MAN AND ALL:	128	DREAM OF FAERY	V	40
A DRUID KINDNESS, ON ALL HEARERS FELL.	129	BOOK STORIES		4
AND ALL GREW FRIENDLY FOR A LITTLE WHILE.	129	BOOK STORIES		8
FOR ALL WHO HEARD IT DREAMED A LITTLE WHILE.	129	BOOK STORIES	V	8
AND ALL WHO HEARD GREW FRIENDLY FOR A WHILE.	129	BOOK STORIES	V	8
SPINNING AT ALL TIMES ERI'S GOOD TO-MORROW,	129	BOOK STORIES		10
THE WELL-KNOWN FACES ARE ALL GONE,	132	OLD PENSIONER	V	17
AND ALL THE TREMBLING FLOWERS THEY BEAR.	134	TWO TREES		4
REMEMBERING ALL THAT SHAKEN HAIR	135	TWO TREES		17
FOR ALL THINGS TURN TO BARRENNESS	135	TWO TREES		29
ALL THINGS TURN TO BARRENNESS	135	TWO TREES	V	29
THY TENDER EYES GROW ALL UNKIND!	136	TWO TREES		39
AND THE WHITE HUSH END ALL BUT THE LOUD BEAT	137	TO SOME I TALK		15
AND THE WHITE HUSH END ALL THINGS BUT THE BEAT	137	TO SOME I TALK	V	15
TRAILS ALL ABOUT THE WRITTEN PAGE.	138	TO IRELAND		9
AND TIME BADE ALL HIS CANDLES FLARE	138	TO IRELAND		13
AND ALL BENIGHTED THINGS THAT GO	139	TO IRELAND		39
NO PLACE FOR LOVE AND DREAM AT ALL:	139	TO IRELAND		43
AND ALL THE WIZARD THINGS THAT GO	139	TO IRELAND	V	39
ALL THINGS UNCOMELY AND BROKEN, ALL THINGS WORN OUT AND OLD,	142	ROSE IN HEART		1
ALL THINGS UNCOMELY AND BROKEN, ALL THINGS WORN OUT AND OLD,	142	ROSE IN HEART		1
ALL THINGS UNCOMELY AND BROKEN, ALL THINGS WORN AND OLD,	142	ROSE IN HEART	V	1
ALL THINGS UNCOMELY AND BROKEN, ALL THINGS WORN AND OLD,	142	ROSE IN HEART	V	1
THE EAST TELLS ALL HER SECRET JOY BEFORE DAYBREAK,	154	BELOVED PEACE	V	4
FOR HOURS WHEN ALL MUST FADE LIKE DEW,	156	FORGOT BEAUTY		20
ALL BUT THE FLAMES, AND DEEP ON DEEP,	156	FORGOT BEAUTY		21
AND ALL MEN'S HEARTS MUST BURN AND BEAT;	158	BELOVED RHYMES		9
AND TROUBLE WITH A SIGH FOR ALL THINGS LONGING FOR REST	163	ASKS FORGIVE		23
AND TROUBLE WITH SIGHS FOR ALL HEARTS WITHOUT REST	163	ASKS FORGIVE		23
TILL ALL THE VALLEYS OF THE WORLD HAVE BEEN WITHERED AWAY.	163	VALLEY LOVERS		8
THE POETS LABOURING ALL THEIR DAYS	164	PERFECT BEAUTY		2
WE POETS LABOUR ALL OUR DAYS,	164	PERFECT BEAUTY	V	2
ALL MANNER OF BLESSED SOULS,	167	BLESSED		14
"WHERE ALL ARE COMELY AND GOOD?	167	BLESSED		22
ALL MANNER OF BLESSEDEST SOULS,	167	BLESSED	V	14
FOR ALL EYES BUT THESE EYES.	173	PLEADS FRIEND		8
BEND DOWN AND PRAY FOR ALL THAT SIN I WOVE IN SONG,	173	SPEAKS HEARERS		5
AND SHE FORGET THE WANDERING AND ALL THE CRIMSON GLOOM	175	ELEMENT POWERS	V	11
AND WEEP BECAUSE I KNOW ALL THINGS NOW:	177	PAST GREATNESS		2
KNOWING ONE, OUT OF ALL THINGS, ALONE: THAT HIS HEAD	177	PAST GREATNESS		8
THEY WILL ALL COME UP TO ME,	179	FIDDLER DOONEY		18
WILL ALL COME UP TO ME.	179	FIDDLER DOONEY	V	18
IN COMFORTABLE SLEEP; ALL LIVING SLEPT	180	QUEEN MAEVE		15
THAT'S ALL BUT GONE: FOR THE PROUD HEART IS GONE,	181	QUEEN MAEVE		20
AND THE FOOL HEART OF THE COUNTING-HOUSE FEARS ALL	181	QUEEN MAEVE		21
HAD TROUBLED HIS SLEEP. BUT ALL HE HAD TO SAY	182	QUEEN MAEVE		52
FOR ALL THEIR BEAUTY'S LIKE A HOLLOW DREAM,	184	QUEEN MAEVE		88
FOR ALL THEIR BEAUTY, LIKE A HOLLOW DREAM?	184	QUEEN MAEVE	V	89
AND ALL THAT NIGHT, AND ALL THROUGH THE NEXT DAY	185	QUEEN MAEVE		113
AND ALL THAT NIGHT, AND ALL THROUGH THE NEXT DAY	185	QUEEN MAEVE		113
HAVE ALL THAT GREATNESS, AND NOT HERS ALONE,	186	QUEEN MAEVE		133
TO MAEVE AND TO MAEVE'S HOUSEHOLD, OWING ALL	187	QUEEN MAEVE		147
THEN MAEVE: "O AENGUS, MASTER OF ALL LOVERS,	187	QUEEN MAEVE		149
THAT ALL THINGS FELL OUT HAPPILY,	189	BAILE AILLINN		22
AND THERE, FOR ALL THAT FOOLS HAD SAID,	190	BAILE AILLINN		23
WITH ALL THIS CRYING IN THE WIND,	190	BAILE AILLINN		33
YET THEY THAT KNOW ALL THINGS BUT KNOW	190	BAILE AILLINN		38
THAT ALL THIS LIFE CAN GIVE US IS	190	BAILE AILLINN		39
THAT ALL LIFE HAS TO GIVE US IS	190	BAILE AILLINN	V	39
THAT ALL LIFE HAD TO GIVE US IS	190	BAILE AILLINN		39
FOR ALL THAT COUNTRY HAD BEEN ASTIR	191	BAILE AILLINN		52
OF THE EBB OF ALL THINGS TO MAKE LOVE	193	BAILE AILLINN	V	109
THEY KNOW ALL WONDERS, FOR THEY PASS	196	BAILE AILLINN		160
ALL THE LOVE STORIES THAT THEY KNEW.	197	BAILE AILLINN		197
FOR ALL HER WANDERINGS OVER-SEA:	197	BAILE AILLINN		203
BECAUSE IT IS ALONE OF ALL THINGS HAPPY.	198	SEVEN WOODS		9
ALL THAT YOU NEED IS PATIENCE." HEART CRIES, "NO,	200	FOLLY COMFORT		6
WHEN ALL THE WILD SUMMER WAS IN HER GAZE,"	200	FOLLY COMFORT		12
PATIENCE IS ALL THAT YOU HAVE NEED OF." NO,	200	FOLLY COMFORT	V	6
IT ALL, AND MORE THAN IT ALL, WOULD COME TO NAUGHT,	201	OLD MEMORY		8
IT ALL, AND MORE THAN IT ALL, WOULD COME TO NAUGHT,	201	OLD MEMORY		8
IT ALL, MORE THAN IT ALL, WOULD COME TO NAUGHT,	201	OLD MEMORY	V	8

16

```
                                                             PAGE    TITLE            LINE
ALL   (CONTINUED)
    IT ALL, MORE THAN IT ALL, WOULD COME TO NAUGHT,   . . . .  201  OLD MEMORY      V    8
    NEVER GIVE ALL THE HEART . . . . .  . . . . . . . .        202  NEVER GIVE ALL       T
    NEVER GIVE ALL THE HEART, FOR LOVE  . . . . . . . .        202  NEVER GIVE ALL       1
    FOR THEY, FOR ALL SMOOTH LIPS CAN SAY,  . . . . . .        202  NEVER GIVE ALL       9
    HE THAT MADE THIS KNOWS ALL THE COST,  . . . . . .         202  NEVER GIVE ALL      13
    FOR HE GAVE ALL HIS HEART AND LOST,  . . . . . . .         202  NEVER GIVE ALL      14
    WITH WISDOM, THEY WANDER TILL ALL THE YEARS HAVE GONE BY,  204  WITHER BOUGHS       21
    LIKE AN OLD PAUPER, IN ALL KINDS OF WEATHER;  . . . . .    205  ADAMS CURSE          9
    IS TO WORK HARDER THAN ALL THESE, AND YET   . . . .       205  ADAMS CURSE         11
    THERE'S MANY A ONE SHALL FIND OUT ALL HEARTACHE  . . .     205  ADAMS CURSE         16
    "THERE IS ONE THING THAT ALL WE WOMEN KNOW  . . . . .      205  ADAMS CURSE     V   18
    THAT IT HAD ALL SEEMED HAPPY, AND YET WE'D GROWN  . . .    206  ADAMS CURSE         37
    AND THROWN THE THUNDER ON THE STONES FOR ALL THAT MAEVE    207  HANRAHANS SONG       7
        CAN SAY.
    BUT WE HAD ALL BENT LOW AND LOW AND KISSED THE QUIET FEET  207  HANRAHANS SONG       9
    "ALL THAT'S BEAUTIFUL DRIFTS AWAY . . . . . . . . .        208  OLD MEN ADMIRE       8
    I WILL DRIVE ALL THOSE LOVERS OUT AND CRY--   . . . .      211  RAGGED WOOD         10
    I'LL HOLLO ALL THOSE LOVERS OUT AND CRY-- . . . . .        211  RAGGED WOOD     V   10
    ALL THROUGH THE YEARS OF OUR YOUTH  . . . . . . . .        211  O DO NOT LOVE        5
    WHEN ALL THIS HEAVY HISTORY'S DONE;  . . . . . . .         213  BLESS PSALTER       17
    AT ALL TIMES OF THE YEAR;  . . . . . . . . . . . .        214  HAPPY TOWNLAND       6
    BUT ALL THAT ARE KILLED IN BATTLE  . . . . . . . .        215  HAPPY TOWNLAND      25
    I ONLY KNOW THAT ALL WE KNOW COMES FROM YOU,  . . .       218  WOODS OF COOLE      28
    SWEET WITH ALL MUSIC, OUT OF HIS LONG HAIR,  . . .        219  HARP OF AENGUS       8
    I COULD GIVE ALL MY HEART TO THAT RED MOLL  . . . .       222  SHADOW WATER B       9
    AND ALL THE ALE RAN OUT AT THE NEW MOON;  . . . . .       222  SHADOW WATER B  V   11
    AT THE FULL MOON? HE PLAYED ALL THROUGH THE NIGHT.  . .   223  SHADOW WATER B      21
    MY COURAGE CAME AGAIN.  BUT THAT'S NOT ALL.  . . . .     223  SHADOW WATER B      31
    TO WHOM ALL LOVERS PRAY.  BUT WHAT OF THAT?  . . . .     224  SHADOW WATER B      43
    THE FLAGSTONE UNDER ALL, THE FIRE OF FIRES,  . . . .     227  SHADOW WATER B     103
    IF YOU WILL GIVE ME ALL YOUR MIND AWHILE--  . . . .     227  SHADOW WATER B     117
    ALL, ALL, THE VERY BOTTOM OF THE BOWL--  . . . . .      227  SHADOW WATER B     118
    ALL, ALL, THE VERY BOTTOM OF THE BOWL--  . . . . .      227  SHADOW WATER B     118
    "YOU WILL HAVE ALL YOU HAVE WISHED FOR WHEN YOU HAVE EARNED  228  SHADOW WATER B   124
    OR CREAKY SHOES.  AND AT THE END OF ALL  . . . . .      228  SHADOW WATER B     128
    FOR THAT IS WHAT THEY SAY--ALL, ALL THE SHADOWS--       228  SHADOW WATER B     137
    FOR THAT IS WHAT THEY SAY--ALL, ALL THE SHADOWS--       228  SHADOW WATER B     137
    AND ALL THE OTHERS; BUT IT MUST BE LOVE  . . . . .      228  SHADOW WATER B     139
    HAD SEEMED TO BE THE GIVER OF ALL PEACE,  . . . . .     228  SHADOW WATER B     149
    AND AS SOON FINISHED.  ALL THAT EVER LOVED  . . . .     229  SHADOW WATER B     151
    THAT HE HAS BEEN ALL NIGHT UPON THE HILLS,  . . . .     229  SHADOW WATER B     168
    THAT SET HIM TO THE FANCY.  ALL WOULD BE WELL  . . .    230  SHADOW WATER B     177
    WAKE ALL BELOW!  WHY HAVE YOU BROKEN OUR SLEEP?  . .    233  SHADOW WATER B     242
    AND NOW THEY ALL WHEEL SUDDENLY AND FLY  . . . . .     234  SHADOW WATER B     258
    I ASK A FITTING PUNISHMENT FOR ALL  . . . . . . .     235  SHADOW WATER B     290
    THAT WEIGH AND MEASURE ALL IN THESE WASTE SEAS--      235  SHADOW WATER B     292
    THEY THAT HAVE ALL THE WISDOM THAT'S IN LIFE,  . .    235  SHADOW WATER B     293
    AND ALL THAT PROPHESYING IMAGES   . . . . . . .      235  SHADOW WATER B     294
    BUT ALL THAT'S RAVING.  WHO IS THERE CAN COMPEL       237  SHADOW WATER B     333
    FOR ALL HIS SPELLS WILL VANISH WHEN HE DIES,  . .     240  SHADOW WATER B     376
    AND ALL THE BIRDS ARE SCATTERED.  O! O! O! O!  . .    241  SHADOW WATER B     395
    THROUGH WICKED SPELLS.  THAT IS NOT ALL THE TALE,     242  SHADOW WATER B     408
    I WILL END ALL YOUR MAGIC ON THE INSTANT,  . . .      242  SHADOW WATER B     411
    IT WAS IN ALL HIS BATTLES.  I WILL SPREAD MY HAIR,    242  SHADOW WATER B     413
    WHY ARE THEY ALL A-FLUTTER OF A SUDDEN?  . . . .      243  SHADOW WATER B     436
    AND ALL THAT TOSSING OF YOUR WINGS IS JOY,  . . .     244  SHADOW WATER B     451
    AND ALL THAT MURMURING'S BUT A MARRIAGE-SONG;  . .    244  SHADOW WATER B     452
    BUT IT WAS ALL DECEIT, AND FLATTERY  . . . . .       244  SHADOW WATER B     457
    OUT OF ALL RECKONING.  IS IT NOT TRUE  . . . . .      244  SHADOW WATER B     467
    AND ALL THAT MURMURING IS BUT A MARRIAGE SONG;        244  SHADOW WATER B  V   452
    I WILL CONFESS IT ALL.  WHAT DO I CARE,  . . . .      245  SHADOW WATER B     485
    AND ALL THAT IS AND ALL THAT IS TO BE,  . . . .      246  SHADOW WATER B     505
    AND ALL THAT IS AND ALL THAT IS TO BE,  . . . .      246  SHADOW WATER B     505
    ALL THAT IS NOT THE MEETING OF OUR LIPS,  . . .      246  SHADOW WATER B     506
    LEAPS UPWARD, AS IF ALL THE STREAMS O' THE WORLD     249  SHADOW WATER B     560
    WITH ALL THOSE SIGHTS AND ALL THAT CRYING OUT?  . .   249  SHADOW WATER B     573
    WITH ALL THOSE SIGHTS AND ALL THAT CRYING OUT?  . .   249  SHADOW WATER B     573
    AND ALL THE BIRDS ARE SCATTERED--O! O! O!  . . .     251  SHADOW WATER B     594
    MY DARLING UNDERSTANDS IT ALL,  . . . . . . .       256  WORDS               10
    "WERE NOT ALL HER LIFE BUT STORM,  . . . . . .       259  PEACE                4
    ALL THAT STERNNESS AMID CHARM,  . . . . . . .       259  PEACE                8
    ALL THAT SWEETNESS AMID STRENGTH?"  . . . . .       259  PEACE                9
    THAT'S ALL WE SHALL KNOW FOR TRUTH  . . . . .       261  DRINKING SONG        3
    THROUGH ALL THE LYING DAYS OF MY YOUTH  . . . .      261  COMING WISDOM        2
    "O NO, MY DEAR, LET ALL THAT BE;  . . . . . .       263  MASK                13
    WHERE WINGS HAVE MEMORY OF WINGS, AND ALL  . . .     264  HOUSE SHAKEN         6
    ALL THEIR LIVES THROUGH SOME DRIFT OF WINGS.  . .    265  ABBEY THEATRE        7
    AND ALL THINGS AT ONE COMMON LEVEL LIE.  . . .      265  THESE CLOUDS         6
    DELIGHT MAKES ALL OF THE ONE MIND,  . . . . .       266  GALWAY RACES         2
    ALL THINGS CAN TEMPT ME  . . . . . . . . .          267  ALL TEMPT ME         T
    ALL THINGS CAN TEMPT ME FROM THIS CRAFT OF VERSE;    267  ALL TEMPT ME         1
    TO FIND OUT ALL THAT IS IN IT,  . . . . . .        268  BROWN PENNY         11
    YOU MOST OF ALL, SILENT AND FIERCE OLD MAN,  . .     270  PARDON FATHERS      15
    TILL YOUR BAD MASTER BLENCHED AND ALL WAS LOST;      270  PARDON FATHERS  V   12
    FOR ALL WERE FULL OF WINE AND MEAT.  . . . .        271  GREY ROCK           17
    ALL THOSE HAD LIFTED UP THE DIM  . . . . . .        272  GREY ROCK           27
    FOR HE IS THE WORST OF ALL DEAD MEN."  . . . .      272  GREY ROCK           36
    THAT EMPTIED ALL OUR DAYS TO COME.  . . . . .       272  GREY ROCK           40
    ALL WAS ACCOMPLISHED.  "WHEN THIS DAY  . . . .       273  GREY ROCK           70
    AND WHEN FOR ALL I'D DONE OR SAID--  . . . . .       275  GREY ROCK           99
```

17

ALL (CONTINUED)

	PAGE	TITLE	LINE
TILL ALL THE PLACE WAS BEATEN INTO MIRE.	278	TWO KINGS	27
TILL ALL HAD SEEMED A SHADOW OR A VISION	278	TWO KINGS	43
THAN MOUND AND STONE THAT KEEP ALL VIRTUE IN.	281	TWO KINGS	106
I BADE HIM GO WHEN ALL HIS HOUSEHOLD SLEPT	282	TWO KINGS	133
TOLD HIM, THAT WHEN ORION ROSE, AND ALL	282	TWO KINGS	V 132A
ALONE WITH ALL THIS USELESS HAPPINESS?"	285	TWO KINGS	200
AND BADE ALL WELCOME, BEING IGNORANT.	286	TWO KINGS	218
FOR THIS THAT ALL THAT BLOOD WAS SHED,	290	SEPTEMBER 1913	19
ALL THAT DELIRIUM OF THE BRAVE?	290	SEPTEMBER 1913	22
IN ALL THEIR LONELINESS AND PAIN.	290	SEPTEMBER 1913	27
NOW ALL THE TRUTH IS OUT,	290	TO A FRIEND	1
BECAUSE OF ALL THINGS KNOWN	291	TO A FRIEND	15
THAT ON THE LONELY HEIGHT WHERE ALL ARE IN GOD'S EYE,	291	PAUDEEN	6
"FOR ALL MY PAINS ON LEBEEN—LONE?"	295	THREE BEGGARS	7
AND LAY IT ALL UPON A HORSE";	296	THREE BEGGARS	35
ALL SHOUTED TILL THEIR ANGER GREW	297	THREE BEGGARS	46
THEY MAULED AND BIT THROUGH ALL THAT DAY	297	THREE BEGGARS	50
"TIME'S UP," HE CRIED, AND ALL THE THREE	297	THREE BEGGARS	57
"TIME'S UP," HE CRIED, AND ALL THE THREE	297	THREE BEGGARS	59
WHEN ALL THOUGHTS AND DEEDS ARE RECKONED,	298	THREE HERMITS	15
AND ALL THAT I NEED DO IS TO WISH	300	RUN PARADISE	4
AND STUFFED WITH ALL THAT'S OLD AND BAD:	303	HOUR DAWN	V 25
THAT'S STUFFED WITH ALL THAT'S OLD AND BAD:	303	HOUR DAWN	25
THE BEGGAR DEAF TO ALL BUT HOPE	304	HOUR DAWN	V 44
I'LL SLEEP AWAY ALL TIME WITHIN IT:	306	HOUR DAWN	74
FOR ALL LIFE LONGS FOR THE LAST DAY	306	HOUR DAWN	98
AND SLEEP AWAY ALL TIME WITHIN IT.	306	HOUR DAWN	V 74
FOR ALL THE SLEEPER KNEW OR CARED:	307	HOUR DAWN	115
FROM MAEVE AND ALL THAT JUGGLING PLAIN,	307	HOUR DAWN	120
AND ALL THE WHILE HER NEEDLE PULLED	308	PLAYER QUEEN	7
ALL WISDOM SHUT INTO HIS ONYX EYES,	311	MOUNTAIN TOMB	11
ALL WISDOM SHUT INTO ITS ONYX EYES.	311	MOUNTAIN TOMB	V 11
AND ALL THE SHEAVES TO BIND.	312	CHILD DANCING	10
AND DREAM THAT ALL THE WORLD'S A FRIEND,	313	TWO YEAR LATER	8
AND YET FOR ALL THAT I COULD SAY.	313	MEMORY YOUTH	4
YET WE, FOR ALL THAT PRAISE, COULD FIND .	314	MEMORY YOUTH	13
ALL TILL MY YOUTH WAS GONE	315	FRIENDS	18
AND I TOOK ALL THE BLAME OUT OF ALL SENSE AND REASON,	316	COLD HEAVEN	7
AND I TOOK ALL THE BLAME OUT OF ALL SENSE AND REASON,	316	COLD HEAVEN	7
NOW AS AT ALL TIMES I CAN SEE IN THE MIND'S EYE.	318	MAGI	1
WITH ALL THEIR ANCIENT FACES LIKE RAIN—BEATEN STONES,	318	MAGI	4
AND ALL THEIR HELMS OF SILVER HOVERING SIDE BY SIDE,	318	MAGI	5
AND ALL THEIR EYES STILL FIXED, HOPING TO FIND ONCE MORE,	318	MAGI	6
BUT THE OLDEST OF ALL THE DOLLS,	319	DOLLS	4
NOTORIOUS, TILL ALL MY PRICELESS THINGS	321	REED WHISPERER	13
ALL SUDDENLY MOUNT	322	SWANS AT COOLE	10
ALL, ALL ARE IN MY THOUGHTS TO—NIGHT BEING DEAD.	324	ROBERT GREGORY	8
ALL, ALL ARE IN MY THOUGHTS TO—NIGHT BEING DEAD.	324	ROBERT GREGORY	8
FOR ALL THAT COME INTO MY MIND ARE DEAD.	324	ROBERT GREGORY	16
TILL ALL HIS GREEK AND LATIN LEARNING SEEMED	324	ROBERT GREGORY	21
AND SOLID MEN, FOR ALL THEIR PASSION, LIVE	325	ROBERT GREGORY	37
FOR ALL THINGS THE DELIGHTED EYE NOW SEES	326	ROBERT GREGORY	49
TO HAVE PUBLISHED ALL TO BE A WORLD'S DELIGHT.	327	ROBERT GREGORY	72
IN ALL LOVELY INTRICACIES OF A HOUSE	327	ROBERT GREGORY	74
ALL WORK IN METAL OR IN WOOD,	327	ROBERT GREGORY	76
AND ALL HE DID DONE PERFECTLY	327	ROBERT GREGORY	79
AS 'TWERE ALL LIFE'S EPITOME.	327	ROBERT GREGORY	87
ALL THOSE THAT MANHOOD TRIED, OR CHILDHOOD LOVED	327	ROBERT GREGORY	91
ALL THE COMBUSTIBLE WORLD IN ONE SMALL ROOM	327	ROBERT GREGORY V	82
OF THAT LATE DEATH TOOK ALL MY HEART FOR SPEECH.	328	ROBERT GREGORY	96
I BALANCED ALL, BROUGHT ALL TO MIND,	328	IRISH AIRMAN	13
I BALANCED ALL, BROUGHT ALL TO MIND,	328	IRISH AIRMAN	13
AND ALL DAY LONG I LOOK	329	MEN IMPROVE	4
AT ALL WHO MARRY IN CHURCHES,	330	BONE OF A HARE	15
"ALL DAY LONG FROM MID-DAY	332	SOLOMON SHEBA	3
ALL DAY LONG FROM SHADOWLESS NOON	332	SOLOMON SHEBA	5
"ALL DAY LONG FROM MIDDAY	332	SOLOMON SHEBA V	3
AND ALL DAY LONG WE HAVE FOUND .	333	SOLOMON SHEBA	22
SET ALL HER BLOOD ASTIR	336	YOUNG GIRL	10
ALL SHUFFLE THERE: ALL COUGH IN INK:	337	SCHOLARS	7
ALL SHUFFLE THERE: ALL COUGH IN INK:	337	SCHOLARS	7
ALL WEAR THE CARPET WITH THEIR SHOES:	337	SCHOLARS	8
ALL THINK WHAT OTHER PEOPLE THINK:	337	SCHOLARS	9
ALL KNOW THE MAN THEIR NEIGHBOUR KNOWS.	337	SCHOLARS	10
AND EVERY COUNTRY CRAFT, AND OF US ALL .	339	SHEP GOATHERD	18
OLD GOATHERDS AND OLD GOATS, IF IN ALL ELSE	340	SHEP GOATHERD	46
YOU HAVE PUT THE THOUGHT IN RHYME. I WORKED ALL DAY,	341	SHEP GOATHERD	58
SEED—PODS AND FLOWERS THAT ARE NOT ALL WILD POPPY.	342	SHEP GOATHERD	88
THAT WERE ALL HIS BIRTHDAYS RECKONED	342	SHEP GOATHERD	90
OF ALL 'TWAS PAIN OR JOY TO LEARN,	342	SHEP GOATHERD	98
OF ALL THAT HE HAD MADE.	342	SHEP GOATHERD	99
SEED PODS AND FLOWERS THAT ARE NOT ALL WILD POPPY.	342	SHEP GOATHERD V	88
ALL KNOWLEDGE LOST IN TRANCE	343	SHEP GOATHERD	111
ALL THE WILD WITCHES, THOSE MOST NOBLE LADIES,	343	DEJECTION	4
FOR ALL THEIR BROOM-STICKS AND THEIR TEARS,	343	DEJECTION	5
THAT GIVES UP ALL HER MIND,	345	ON WOMAN	2
THAT COVERS ALL HE HAS BROUGHT	345	ON WOMAN	5
COUNT ALL THE PRAISES DUE	345	ON WOMAN	15
THAT POUNDS UP ALL ANEW	346	ON WOMAN	31
AND ALL BECAUSE OF SOME ONE .	346	ON WOMAN	40

18

ALL   (CONTINUED)

	PAGE	TITLE		LINE
ALL DAY I'D LOOKED IN THE FACE	347	FISHERMAN		9
"WHAT HAVE I EARNED FOR ALL THAT WORK," I SAID,	351	PEOPLE		1
"FOR ALL THAT I HAVE DONE AT MY OWN CHARGE?	351	PEOPLE		2
ALL THE DISHONEST CROWD I HAD DRIVEN AWAY,	352	PEOPLE		24
COMPLAINED OF THE PEOPLE." ALL I COULD REPLY	352	PEOPLE		29
WITH ALL A WOMAN'S PASSION, A CHILD'S IMPERIOUS WAY,	354	HIS PHOENIX		14
THEY CAN SPREAD OUT WHAT SAIL THEY PLEASE FOR ALL I HAVE TO SAY.	354	HIS PHOENIX		22
. . . THROUGH ALL THE CENTURIES,	354	HIS PHOENIX		25
AND ALL THE SHAPELY BODY NO TITTLE GONE ASTRAY,	354	HIS PHOENIX		30
THERE'LL BE THAT CROWD TO MAKE MEN WILD THROUGH ALL THE CENTURIES,	354	HIS PHOENIX	V	25
FOR YOUR SOLE SAKE—THAT ALL HEART'S ACHE HAVE KNOWN,	355	BROKEN DREAMS		7
AND GIVEN TO OTHERS ALL HEART'S ACHE,	355	BROKEN DREAMS		8
BUT FOR YOUR SAKE—THAT ALL HEART'S ACHE HAVE KNOWN,	355	BROKEN DREAMS	V	7
BUT IN THE GRAVE ALL, ALL, SHALL BE RENEWED.	356	BROKEN DREAMS		21
BUT IN THE GRAVE ALL, ALL, SHALL BE RENEWED.	356	BROKEN DREAMS		21
ALL DAY IN THE ONE CHAIR	357	BROKEN DREAMS		38
ALL I HAD RHYMED OF THAT MONSTROUS THING	358	PRESENCES		7
ALL I HAVE RHYMED OF THAT MONSTROUS THING	358	PRESENCES	V	7
WHEN ALL I WOULD DO	359	TO A SQUIRREL		6
AT ALL THESE DEATH-BEDS WOMEN HEARD	361	ALF POLLEXFEN		36
AT ALL THESE DEATHBEDS WOMEN HEARD	361	ALF POLLEXFEN	V	36
THE MEDITATIVE CRITIC: ALL ARE ON THEIR TOES,	363	DOLLS FACES		8
OR KEEP US ALL AWAKE WITH BAYING AT THE MOON,	364	DOLLS FACES		11
ALL BUT THE TERRORS OF THE WOODLAND FLIGHT FORGOT	366	HER COURAGE		5
AYE, AND ACHILLES, TIMOR, BABAR, BARHAIM, ALL ,	366	HER COURAGE		9
ALL BUT THE PERILS OF THE WOODLAND FLIGHT FORGOT,	366	HER COURAGE	V	5
TILL ALL THE BOUGHS ARE GAY,	366	HER CHRIS TREE		5
I CALL TO MY OWN OPPOSITE, SUMMON ALL	367	EGO DOMINUS		8
SHUT OUT FROM ALL THE LUXURY OF THE WORLD,	370	EGO DOMINUS		60
AND PROVE OF ALL IMAGINABLE THINGS	371	EGO DOMINUS		73
ALL THAT I SEEK; AND WHISPER IT AS THOUGH	371	EGO DOMINUS		76
AND PROVE IF ALL IMAGINABLE THINGS	371	EGO DOMINUS	V	73
AND ON MY HEIRS, IF ALL REMAIN UNSPOILED,	371	ON GOING HOUSE		2
WHO KNOW IT ALL RING AT HIS DOOR, AND SPEAK	373	PHASES OF MOON		21
OF ALL THOSE TRUTHS THAT ARE YOUR DAILY BREAD:	373	PHASES OF MOON		24
THE FULL AND THE MOON'S DARK AND ALL THE CRESCENTS,	373	PHASES OF MOON		32
THE STRANGE REWARD OF ALL THAT DISCIPLINE.	374	PHASES OF MOON		57
ALL THOUGHT BECOMES AN IMAGE AND THE SOUL	374	PHASES OF MOON		58
BEYOND THE VISIBLE WORLD. ALL DREAMS OF THE SOUL	374	PHASES OF MOON		63
WHEN ALL IS FED WITH LIGHT AND HEAVEN IS BARE,	375	PHASES OF MOON		74
SHUDDERS IN MANY CRADLES: ALL IS CHANGED,	375	PHASES OF MOON		89
CRADLE UPON CRADLE, AND ALL IN FLIGHT AND ALL	376	PHASES OF MOON		100
CRADLE UPON CRADLE, AND ALL IN FLIGHT AND ALL	376	PHASES OF MOON		100
BECAUSE ALL DARK, LIKE THOSE THAT ARE ALL LIGHT,	376	PHASES OF MOON		104
BECAUSE ALL DARK, LIKE THOSE THAT ARE ALL LIGHT,	376	PHASES OF MOON		104
WHEN ALL THE DOUGH HAS BEEN SO KNEADED UP	377	PHASES OF MOON		114
BESIDE THE CASTLE DOOR, WHERE ALL IS STARK	377	PHASES OF MOON		126
HE WOULD NEVER KNOW ME AFTER ALL THESE YEARS	377	PHASES OF MOON		129
TO ALL THAT IN YOUR FLESH HAVE STOOD	380	SAINT HUNCH		13
HONOURED BY ALL IN THEIR DEGREES,	380	SAINT HUNCH		15
MEN THAT DO ALL BY RULE,	380	SONGS FOOL 1		14
ALTHOUGH I SAW IT ALL IN THE MIND'S EYE	383	VISION ROBART		25
GAZED UPON ALL THINGS KNOWN, ALL THINGS UNKNOWN,	383	VISION ROBART		30
GAZED UPON ALL THINGS KNOWN, ALL THINGS UNKNOWN,	383	VISION ROBART		30
BEING FIXED ON ALL THINGS LOVED, ALL THINGS UNLOVED,	383	VISION ROBART		34
BEING FIXED ON ALL THINGS LOVED, ALL THINGS UNLOVED,	383	VISION ROBART		34
AT ALL THAT IS NOT PICTURED THERE.	385	ROBARTES DANCE		17
AND ALL HIS SACRED COMPANY	386	ROBARTES DANCE		27
IMAGINED BODIES ALL THEIR DAYS	386	ROBARTES DANCE		28
THAT ALL MUST COME TO SIGHT AND TOUCH:	386	ROBARTES DANCE		31
AND THAT ALL BEAUTIFUL WOMEN MAY	387	ROBARTES DANCE		45
ALL SOUNDS BY BIRD OR ANGEL SUNG	387	SOLOMON WITCH	V	7
ALL THAT THE BRIGAND APPLE BROUGHT	388	SOLOMON WITCH		15
AYE, THOUGH ALL PASSION'S IN THE GLANCE—	388	SOLOMON WITCH		21
TILL ALL THE EDDIES GLEAM;	389	IMAGE PAST		4
OUT OF ALL LIKELIHOOD, OR REASON,	389	IMAGE PAST		9
I HAD THOUGHT THAT ALL MY DAYS WERE CAST	389	IMAGE PAST		12
ALL THAT TO THIS MOMENT CHARMED YOU?	390	IMAGE PAST		21
ALL CHANGED, CHANGED UTTERLY:	392	EASTER 1916		15
ALL THAT SHE GOT SHE SPENT,	392	EASTER 1916	V	20
THE STONE'S IN THE MIDST OF ALL.	393	EASTER 1916		56
WAS IT NEEDLESS DEATH AFTER ALL?	394	EASTER 1916		67
FOR ALL THAT IS DONE AND SAID.	394	EASTER 1916		69
FOR ALL SHE HAD DONE AND SAID.	394	EASTER 1916	V	69
"WHEN ALL THE WELLS ARE PARCHED AWAY?	396	ROSE TREE		15
WITH ALL YOUTH'S LONELY WILDNESS STIRRED,	397	POLIT PRISONER		16
ALL THAT ARE DIFFERENT OF A BASE INTENT:	398	LEADERS CROWD		2
THAT ALL MY CHILDHOOD COUNTED DEAR:	398	BREAK OF DAY		7
AND ALL LAUGH IN THE SUN.	400	DEMON BEAST		8
WELCOME, AND THE ORMONDES ALL	400	DEMON BEAST		11
FOR ALL MEN'S THOUGHTS GREW CLEAR	400	DEMON BEAST		19
FOR ALL MEN'S THOUGHT GREW CLEAR	400	DEMON BEAST	V	19
THE BEST LACK ALL CONVICTION, WHILE THE WORST	402	SECOND COMING		7
IS MOVING ITS SLOW THIGHS, WHILE ALL ABOUT IT	402	SECOND COMING		16
THAT ALL HER THOUGHTS MAY LIKE THE LINNET BE,	404	FOR DAUGHTER		42
MAY WELL BE OF ALL EVIL CHANCES CHIEF,	405	FOR DAUGHTER		53
CONSIDERING THAT, ALL HATRED DRIVEN HENCE,	405	FOR DAUGHTER		65
WHEN ALL IS RUIN ONCE AGAIN.	406	CARVED STONE		6

19

		PAGE	TITLE	LINE

ALL   (CONTINUED)

	PAGE	TITLE		LINE
FISH, FLESH, OR FOWL, COMMEND ALL SUMMER LONG	407	SAIL BYZANTIUM		5
CAUGHT IN THAT SENSUAL MUSIC ALL NEGLECT	407	SAIL BYZANTIUM		7
FOR I WOULD ASK A QUESTION OF THEM ALL.	410	TOWER		24
AND HELEN HAS ALL LIVING HEARTS BETRAYED.	411	TOWER		53
I THOUGHT IT ALL OUT TWENTY YEARS AGO:	411	TOWER		64
THAT ALL BUT THE ONE CARD BECAME	411	TOWER		68
AS I WOULD QUESTION ALL, COME ALL WHO CAN:	412	TOWER		89
AS I WOULD QUESTION ALL, COME ALL WHO CAN:	412	TOWER		89
DID ALL OLD MEN AND WOMEN, RICH AND POOR,	413	TOWER		97
FOR I NEED ALL HIS MIGHTY MEMORIES.	413	TOWER		104
ALL THAT YOU HAVE DISCOVERED IN THE GRAVE,	413	TOWER		107
WHEN ALL STREAMS ARE DRY,	414	TOWER		138
AYE, SUN AND MOON AND STAR, ALL,	415	TOWER		152
ALL THOSE THINGS WHEREOF	415	TOWER		163
THE SWEETNESS THAT ALL LONGED FOR NIGHT AND DAY,	418	ANCEST HOUSES		20
FOR ALL ITS BRONZE AND MARBLE, 'S BUT A MOUSE.	418	ANCEST HOUSES		24
OR ELSE ALL JUNO FROM AN URN DISPLAYS	418	ANCEST HOUSES		27
A MIST THAT IS LIKE BLOWN SNOW IS SWEEPING OVER ALL,	425	PHANTOM HATRED		2
BECAUSE OF ALL THAT SENSELESS TUMULT, ALL BUT CRIED	426	PHANTOM HATRED		15
BECAUSE OF ALL THAT SENSELESS TUMULT, ALL BUT CRIED	426	PHANTOM HATRED		15
IN SOMETHING THAT ALL OTHERS UNDERSTAND OR SHARE:	427	PHANTOM HATRED		35
AND ALL THE GOLDEN GRASSHOPPERS AND BEES.	428	NINETEEN 19		8
WE THOUGHT IT WOULD OUTLIVE ALL FUTURE DAYS.	428	NINETEEN 19		14
OR ALL THAT WAYWARD EBB AND FLOW. THERE STOOD	428	NINETEEN 19	V	4
ON ALL THAT WAYWARD EBB AND FLOW. THERE STOOD	428	NINETEEN 19	V	4
AND ALL HIS GOLDEN GRASSHOPPERS AND BEES.	428	NINETEEN 19	V	8
ALL TEETH WERE DRAWN, ALL ANCIENT TRICKS UNLEARNED,	429	NINETEEN 19		17
ALL TEETH WERE DRAWN, ALL ANCIENT TRICKS UNLEARNED,	429	NINETEEN 19		17
AND YET IT LACK ALL GLORY: AND PERCHANCE	429	NINETEEN 19		23
HAS BUT ONE COMFORT LEFT: ALL TRIUMPH WOULD	429	NINETEEN 19		39
ALL MEN ARE DANCERS AND THEIR TREAD	430	NINETEEN 19		57
GREEKS WERE BUT LOVERS: ALL THAT COUNTRY ROUND	430	NINETEEN 19	V	43
TO END ALL THINGS, TO END	431	NINETEEN 19		81
WITH ALL THOSE CALENDARS WHEREON	432	NINETEEN 19		99
ALL BREAK AND VANISH, AND EVIL GATHERS HEAD:	433	NINETEEN 19		117
ALL TURN WITH AMOROUS CRIES, OR ANGRY CRIES,	433	NINETEEN 19		123
ACCORDING TO THE WIND, FOR ALL ARE BLIND.	433	NINETEEN 19		124
DECLARE THAT WINTER'S BEST OF ALL:	434	WHEEL		4
ALL DREAD AFAR TILL MORNING'S BACK,	435	FOR MY SON		6
ALL OF THAT WORST IGNOMINY	436	FOR MY SON		23
AND WHEN THROUGH ALL THE TOWN THERE RAN	436	FOR MY SON		25
AND THEN DID ALL THE MUSES SING	437	SONGS PLAY 1		6
MADE ALL PLATONIC TOLERANCE VAIN	438	SONGS PLAY 2		7
AND VAIN ALL DORIC DISCIPLINE.	438	SONGS PLAY 2		8
STRAIGHTENED ALL THAT WENT AWRY	440	WISDOM	V	4
BY THE WEBBED TOES, AND THAT ALL POWERFUL BILL	441	LEDA AND SWAN	V	3
ALL THE STRETCHED BODY'S LAID ON THE WHITE RUSH	441	LEDA AND SWAN	V	7
MY WORKS ARE ALL STAMPED DOWN INTO THE SULTRY MUD.	442	BLACK CENTAUR		3
I HAVE LOVED YOU BETTER THAN MY SOUL FOR ALL MY WORDS,	442	BLACK CENTAUR		14
BETTER TO SMILE ON ALL THAT SMILE, AND SHOW	444	SCHOOL CHILDR		31
AND THAT ALL HEAVENLY GLORY SYMBOLISE--	445	SCHOOL CHILDR		55
AND SO REMEMBERS THAT WHEN ALL MANKIND	447	COLONUS PRAISE		26
FOR ALL MEN LOVE YOUR WORTH: AND I MUST RAGE	447	HERO GIRL FOOL	V	8
A NUN AT LEAST HAS ALL MEN'S REVERENCE	448	HERO GIRL FOOL		12
ALL MEN HAVE PRAISED MY STRENGTH BUT NOT MY WORTH.	448	HERO GIRL FOOL	V	9
FOR THEY AT LEAST HAVE ALL MEN'S REVERENCE.	448	HERO GIRL FOOL	V	12
WHEN ALL WORKS THAT HAVE	449	HERO GIRL FOOL		18
IT FEARED TO GIVE ITS LOVE A HURT WITH ALL THE TEMPEST THERE:	450	OWEN AHERNE		7
"YOU BUT IMAGINE LIES ALL DAY, O MURDERER," I REPLIED.	450	OWEN AHERNE		17
"AND ALL THOSE LIES HAVE BUT ONE END, POOR WRETCHES TO BETRAY:	450	OWEN AHERNE		18
"SPEAK ALL YOUR MIND," MY HEART SANG OUT,	450	OWEN AHERNE		21
. . . "SPEAK ALL YOUR MIND: WHO CARES,	450	OWEN AHERNE		21
O LET HER CHOOSE A YOUNG MAN NOW AND ALL FOR HIS WILD SAKE."	450	OWEN AHERNE		24
BUT IS THE SAME FOR ALL	452	HUMAN DIGNITY		4
WHEN ALL BUT DEAD OF THIRST,	454	EMPTY CUP		2
WHEN ALL BUT DEAD WITH THIRST,	454	EMPTY CUP	V	2
THE FIRST OF ALL THE TRIBE LAY THERE	455	HIS MEMORIES		13
AND PUT ALL TROY TO WRECK--	455	HIS MEMORIES		16
AND PUT ALL TROY TO WRACK--	455	HIS MEMORIES	V	16
TOLD ALL THAT HAD BEEN SAID OR DONE	456	SUMMER SPRING		3
WHEN WE HAD ALL THE SUMMER-TIME	457	SUMMER SPRING		15
AND SHE HAD ALL THE SPRING:	457	SUMMER SPRING		16
WHEN WE HAD ALL THE SUMMER TIME	457	SUMMER SPRING	V	15
OF ALL THAT ARE GONE,	458	SECRETS OF OLD		14
BEING ALL ALONE I'D NURSE A STONE	459	HIS WILDNESS		11
DELIGHT BECOMES DEATH-LONGING IF ALL LONGING ELSE BE VAIN.	459	FROM OEDIPUS		3
. . . ALL ENTANGLEMENTS OF MANKIND GROW,	459	FROM OEDIPUS		5
. . . AT ALL NOR LOOKED INTO THE EYE OF DAY,	459	FROM OEDIPUS	V	11
AND ALL THE POPULAR STATESMEN SAY	460	THREE MONUMENT		5
AND LET ALL BASE AMBITION BE,	460	THREE MONUMENT		9
THAT SPEECH WAS ALL THAT THE TOWN KNEW, BUT HE	462	HARUN RASHID		35
THAT SPEECH WAS ALL THAT THE COURT KNOW, BUT HE	462	HARUN RASHID	V	35
THAT I COMMEND TO ALL THE CHRONICLERS	463	HARUN RASHID		46
BEING ALL BRIMMED WITH LIFE?" "WERE IT BUT TRUE	465	HARUN RASHID		90
THAN ALL MY BURSTING SPRINGTIME KNEW. A GIRL	466	HARUN RASHID		105
OF ALL THE UNCOUNTED BOOKS THAT I HAVE READ,	467	HARUN RASHID		139
IN CHILDISH IGNORANCE OF ALL THAT PASSED.	468	HARUN RASHID		149

20

ALL   (CONTINUED)

	PAGE	TITLE		LINE
IN CHILDISH IGNORANCE OF ALL THAT PASSED.	468	HARUN RASHID		160
HEARD ALL THE ANXIETY OF MY PASSIONATE YOUTH,	468	HARUN RASHID		168
ITS FIRST SIMPLICITY, LOVE, VOICE AND ALL,	469	HARUN RASHID		177
ALL MY FINE FEATHERS WOULD BE PLUCKED AWAY	469	HARUN RASHID		178
ALL THOSE ABSTRACTIONS THAT YOU FANCIED WERE	469	HARUN RASHID		182
ALL, ALL THOSE GYRES AND CUBES AND MIDNIGHT THINGS	469	HARUN RASHID		184
ALL, ALL THOSE GYRES AND CUBES AND MIDNIGHT THINGS	469	HARUN RASHID		184
ITS FIRST SIMPLICITY, LOVE AND ALL,	469	HARUN RASHID	V	177
OF ALL ARABIA'S LOVERS I ALONE--	470	HARUN RASHID		190
ALL SOULS' NIGHT	470	ALL SOUL NIGHT		T
AND IT IS ALL SOULS' NIGHT,	470	ALL SOUL NIGHT		3
IT IS ALL SOULS' NIGHT AND THE GREAT CHRIST CHURCH BELL	470	ALL SOUL NIGHT	V	1
IT MAY BE ALL THAT HEAR	471	ALL SOUL NIGHT		19
FOR MAYBE ALL THAT HEAR	474	ALL SOUL NIGHT		89
TILL MEDITATION MASTER ALL ITS PARTS,	474	ALL SOUL NIGHT		92
DEAR SHADOWS, NOW YOU KNOW IT ALL,	476	EVA GORE-BOOTH		21
ALL THE FOLLY OF A FIGHT	476	EVA GORE-BOOTH		22
RUN TILL ALL THE SAGES KNOW.	476	EVA GORE-BOOTH		29
DREADING AND HOPING ALL:	476	DEATH		4
SET ALL YOUR MIND UPON THE STEEP ASCENT,	477	SELF AND SOUL		2
THAT QUARTER WHERE ALL THOUGHT IS DONE:	477	SELF AND SOUL		7
HEART'S PURPLE--AND ALL THESE I SET	478	SELF AND SOUL		28
WHAT MATTER IF I LIVE IT ALL ONCE MORE?	478	SELF AND SOUL		43
I AM CONTENT TO LIVE IT ALL AGAIN	479	SELF AND SOUL		57
OR INTO THAT MOST FECUND DITCH OF ALL,	479	SELF AND SOUL		61
AND GOD-APPOINTED BERKELEY THAT PROVED ALL THINGS A DREAM,	481	BLOOD AND MOON		25
WHAT ARE ALL THOSE FISH THAT LIE GASPING ON THE STRAND?	485	THREE MOVEMENT		3
ALL HATED WHIGGERY: BUT WHAT IS WHIGGERY?	486	SEVEN SAGES		10
WHEN SHE IN ALL HER VIRGINAL PRIDE	488	CRAZED MOON		8
FOR ALL HIS TIMID HEART, THERE THAT SLOW MAN,	489	COOLE PARK 29		12
WHEN ALL THOSE ROOMS AND PASSAGES ARE GONE,	489	COOLE PARK 29		26
AND ALL THE SENSUALITY OF THE SHADE--	489	COOLE PARK 29		31
NOW ALL DRY STICKS UNDER A WINTRY SUN	490	COOLE BALLYLEE		10
AND ALL THE RANT'S A MIRROR OF MY MOOD:	490	COOLE BALLYLEE		13
AND ALL THE RANT A MIRROR OF MY MOOD:	490	COOLE BALLYLEE	V	13
WE SHIFT ABOUT--ALL THAT GREAT GLORY SPENT--	491	COOLE BALLYLEE		39
MAN SHIFTS ABOUT--ALL THAT GREAT GLORY SPENT--	491	COOLE BALLYLEE		39
BUT ALL IS CHANGED, THAT HIGH HORSE RIDERLESS,	492	COOLE BALLYLEE		46
ALL THAT IS WRITTEN IN WHAT POETS NAME	492	COOLE BALLYLEE	V	43
WHEN ALL THAT STORY'S FINISHED, WHAT'S THE NEWS?	495	CHOICE		5
ALL THAT TIME DENIED--	496	MOHINI CHATTER		18
ALL THAT MAN IS,	497	BYZANTIUM		6
ALL MERE COMPLEXITIES,	497	BYZANTIUM		7
AND ALL COMPLEXITIES OF MIRE OR BLOOD.	498	BYZANTIUM		24
AND ALL COMPLEXITIES OF FURY LEAVE,	498	BYZANTIUM		29
THE TERROR OF ALL TERRORS THAT I BORE	499	MOTHER OF GOD		4
AND GATHER ALL THE TALK?	499	MOTHER OF GOD		10
ALL THOSE ANTINOMIES	500	VACILLATION		5
IS HALF ALL GLITTERING FLAME AND HALF ALL GREEN	500	VACILLATION		12
IS HALF ALL GLITTERING FLAME AND HALF ALL GREEN	500	VACILLATION		12
AND HALF IS HALF AND YET IS ALL THE SCENE:	500	VACILLATION		14
GET ALL THE GOLD AND SILVER THAT YOU CAN,	500	VACILLATION		19
ALL WOMEN DOTE UPON AN IDLE MAN	500	VACILLATION		23
IS HALF ALL GLITTERING FLAME AND HALF A GREEN	500	VACILLATION	V	12
"LET ALL THINGS PASS AWAY."	502	VACILLATION		61
"LET ALL THINGS PASS AWAY."	502	VACILLATION		66
WHAT'S THE MEANING OF ALL SONG?	502	VACILLATION		70
"LET ALL THINGS PASS AWAY."	502	VACILLATION		71
ALL LIVES THAT HAS LIVED:	504	QUARREL IN AGE		9
ALL BY THEIR YOUTH UNDONE,	504	RESULT THOUGHT		4
ALL, ALL, BY THAT INHUMAN	504	RESULT THOUGHT		5
ALL, ALL, BY THAT INHUMAN	504	RESULT THOUGHT		5
ALL THEIR WHOLESOME STRENGTH.	505	RESULT THOUGHT		12
ALL THE WRECK AND WRACK:	505	RESULT THOUGHT	V	8
ALL THINGS HANG LIKE A DROP OF DEW	505	GRAT INSTRUCT		3
AND ALL MY HEART SEEMED GAY.	507	STREAM AND SUN		3
(ALL FIND SAFETY IN THE TOMB.)	508	JANE BISHOP		3
(ALL FIND SAFETY IN THE TOMB.)	508	JANE BISHOP		10
(ALL FIND SAFETY IN THE TOMB.)	508	JANE BISHOP		17
(ALL FIND SAFETY IN THE TOMB.)	508	JANE BISHOP		24
ALL THOSE DREADFUL THUNDER-STONES,	509	JANE REPROVED		2
ALL THAT STORM THAT BLOTS THE DAY	509	JANE REPROVED		3
ALL THOSE DREADFUL THUNDERSTONES,	509	JANE REPROVED	V	2
ALL THOSE STORMS THAT BLOT THE DAY	509	JANE REPROVED	V	3
"LOVE IS ALL	510	JANE JUDGMENT		1
ALL COULD BE KNOWN OR SHOWN	510	JANE JUDGMENT		18
ALL THINGS REMAIN IN GOD.	512	JANE ON GOD		6
ALL THINGS REMAIN IN GOD.	512	JANE ON GOD		12
ALL THINGS REMAIN IN GOD.	512	JANE ON GOD		18
ALL THINGS REMAIN IN GOD.	512	JANE ON GOD		24
THEY HAD ALL THAT HAD THEIR HATE:	514	JANE GROWN OLD		13
AND THAT WAS ALL MY SONG--	515	GIRLS SONG B		9
DID ALL THE FABRIC FADE:	516	MANS SONG		10
AND ALL SHALL BEND THE KNEE	516	MANS SONG		16
ALL TRUE LOVE MUST DIE,	517	HER ANXIETY		3
ALL WRONGS DONE.	518	HIS CONFIDENCE		4
ALL NIGHT'S FATHOMLESS WISDOM COME,	519	HER DREAM		2
AND ALL THE WINDINGS THERE.	520	HIS BARGAIN		12
"A CHILD FOUND ALL A CHILD CAN LACK,	521	THREE THINGS		3
FOUND ALL THE PLEASURE THAT LIFE GAVE":	521	THREE THINGS		11

21

ALL   (CONTINUED)

	PAGE	TITLE		LINE
WHAT WERE ALL THE WORLD'S ALARMS	522	LULLABY		3
WHAT ARE ALL THE WORLD'S ALARMS?	522	LULLABY	V	3
ALL OTHER LOVERS BEING ESTRANGED OR DEAD, ...	523	LONG SILENCE		2
ALL THAT SILK AND SATIN GEAR, ...	525	DANCING DAYS		3
OF ALL THAT RAMBLED THERE	526	AM OF IRELAND		9
"THE FIDDLERS ARE ALL THUMBS, ...	527	AM OF IRELAND		19
AND THE TRUMPETS ALL ARE BURST, ...	527	AM OF IRELAND		22
ALL THAT COULD RUN OR LEAP OR SWIM	528	DANCER CRUACH		6
ALL THAT RUN OR LEAP OR SWIM	528	DANCER CRUACH	V	6
IN ALL THE VIGOUR OF ITS BLOOD, ...	529	TOM LUNATIC		17
AND ALL THEIR SWELLING CANVAS WEAR, ...	530	OLD TOM AGAIN		2
AND ALL THEIR YELLOW CANVAS WEAR, ...	530	OLD TOM AGAIN	V	2
AND ALL THE CHOIR OF LOVE.	531	DELPHIC ORACLE		10
OF ALL GOOD MEN AND WOMEN, ...	531	FATHER CHILD		3
THAT HAS THE WORST OF ALL BAD NAMES:	531	FATHER CHILD		5
OR ASK IF ALL BE RIGHT	532	BEFORE WORLD		4
BLACKENS ALL OUR LOT?	534	CONSOLATION		10
BIDS ALL TRUE LOVERS REST, ...	536	PARTING		6
ALL STATELY WOMEN MOVING TO A SONG	537	HER VISION		17
THAT THING ALL BLOOD AND MIRE, THAT BEAST-TORN WRECK, . .	537	HER VISION		25
AND, THOUGH LOVE'S BITTER-SWEET HAD ALL COME BACK, . .	537	HER VISION		27
OF ALL THAT WITH ME LAY?	538	LAST CONFESS		2
WHAT SHUDDERS RUN THROUGH ALL THAT ANIMAL BLOOD? . . .	541	PARN FUNERAL 1		5
I THIRST FOR ACCUSATION. ALL THAT WAS SUNG, ...	542	PARN FUNERAL 1		25
ALL THAT WAS SAID IN IRELAND IS A LIE	542	PARN FUNERAL 1		26
TO THIS BARE SOUL, LET ALL MEN JUDGE THAT CAN . . .	542	PARN FUNERAL 1		30
"HEAR, GENTLEMEN, LADIES, AND ALL MANKIND:	544	TO SAME TUNE 1		2
THOSE FANATICS ALL THAT WE DO WOULD UNDO:	544	TO SAME TUNE 1		7
ALL THERE CAUGHT UP THE TUNE:	545	TO SAME TUNE 1		15
THOSE FANATICS ALL THAT WE DO WOULD UNDO:	545	TO SAME TUNE 1		17
THOSE FANATICS ALL THAT WE DO WOULD UNDO:	545	TO SAME TUNE 1		27
JUSTIFY ALL THOSE RENOWNED GENERATIONS:	545	TO SAME TUNE 2		1
"DROWN ALL THE DOGS," SAID THE FIERCE YOUNG WOMAN, . .	546	TO SAME TUNE 2		7
DROWN ALL THE DOGS," SAID THE FIERCE YOUNG WOMAN. . .	546	TO SAME TUNE 2		10
JUSTIFY ALL THOSE RENOWNED GENERATIONS, ...	546	TO SAME TUNE 2		11
JUSTIFY ALL THAT HAVE SUNK IN THEIR BLOOD, ...	546	TO SAME TUNE 2		12
JUSTIFY ALL THAT HAVE DIED ON THE SCAFFOLD, ...	546	TO SAME TUNE 2		13
JUSTIFY ALL THAT HAVE FLED, THAT HAVE STOOD, ...	546	TO SAME TUNE 2		14
"DROWN ALL THE DOGS," SAID THE FIERCE YOUNG WOMAN, . .	546	TO SAME TUNE 2		17
DROWN ALL THE DOGS," SAID THE FIERCE YOUNG WOMAN. . .	546	TO SAME TUNE 2		20
ALL THAT GREAT PAST TO A TROUBLE OF FOOLS:	546	TO SAME TUNE 2		22
THOSE FANATICS ALL THAT WE DO WOULD UNDO:	546	TO SAME TUNE 2	V	REF
JUSTIFY ALL THAT HAVE FLED OR HAVE STOOD, ...	546	TO SAME TUNE 2	V	14
ALL THE RENOWN THAT FELL.	547	TO SAME TUNE 2		26
"DROWN ALL THE DOGS," SAID THE FIERCE YOUNG WOMAN, . .	547	TO SAME TUNE 2		27
DROWN ALL THE DOGS," SAID THE FIERCE YOUNG WOMAN. . .	547	TO SAME TUNE 2		30
TIME FOR US ALL TO PICK OUT A GOOD TUNE, ...	548	TO SAME TUNE 3		13
THOSE FANATICS ALL THAT WE DO WOULD UNDO:	548	TO SAME TUNE 3	V	REF
TIME FOR US ALL BOYS, TO HIT ON A TUNE BOYS, . . .	548	TO SAME TUNE 3	V	13
ALL THOSE TRAGIC CHARACTERS RIDE	549	SEVERED HEAD		4
AND ALL ALONE COMES RIDING THERE	550	SEVERED HEAD		18
FOR ALL MY HEART HAS HAD FOR ITS HIRE	551	SONGS REWRIT 1		3
FOR ALL MY TOIL HAS HAD FOR ITS HIRE	551	SONGS REWRIT 1		3
FOR ALL THAT MY HEART HAS HAD FOR ITS HIRE	551	SONGS REWRIT 1	V	3
I CRIED AND WHISTLED BUT VAIN, ALL VAIN.	551	SONGS REWRIT 1	V	16
FROM ALL THAT MAKES A WISE OLD MAN	553	PRAYER OLD AGE		5
THAT CAN BE PRAISED OF ALL:	553	PRAYER OLD AGE		6
ALL KNOW THEIR TALE, ALL KNOW WHAT LEAF AND TWIG, . .	555	RIBH AT TOMB		7
ALL KNOW THEIR TALE, ALL KNOW WHAT LEAF AND TWIG, . .	555	RIBH AT TOMB		7
THAT'S HOW ALL NATURAL OR SUPERNATURAL STORIES RUN. . .	556	RIBH PATRICK		3
YET ALL MUST COPY COPIES, ALL INCREASE THEIR KIND: . .	556	RIBH PATRICK		7
YET ALL MUST COPY COPIES, ALL INCREASE THEIR KIND: . .	556	RIBH PATRICK		7
BUT ALL THAT RUN IN COUPLES, ON EARTH, IN FLOOD OR AIR, .	556	RIBH PATRICK		11
. . .				
ALL HAPPINESS IN ITS OWN CAUSE OR GROUND.	557	RIBH ECSTASY		4
THERE ALL THE BARREL-HOOPS ARE KNIT, ...	557	THERE		1
THERE ALL THE SERPENT-TAILS ARE BIT, ...	557	THERE		2
THERE ALL THE GYRES CONVERGE IN ONE, ...	557	THERE		3
THERE ALL THE PLANETS DROP IN THE SUN.	557	THERE		4
HOW SOUL MAY WALK WHEN ALL SUCH THINGS ARE PAST, . .	558	RIBH CHRISTIAN		11
ALL CREATION SHIVERS	559	HE AND SHE		11
HE HOLDS HIM FROM DESIRE, ALL BUT STOPS HIS BREATHING LEST	559	MAGIC DRUM		1
ALL THE STREAM THAT'S ROARING BY	562	NEEDLES EYE		1
EMPEDOCLES HAS THROWN ALL THINGS ABOUT:	564	GYRES		6
AND ALL IT KNOWS IS THAT ONE WORD "REJOICE:"	564	GYRES		16
THE WORKMAN, NOBLE AND SAINT, AND ALL THINGS RUN . .	565	GYRES		23
ALL PERFORM THEIR TRAGIC PLAY, ...	565	LAPIS LAZULI		9
GAIETY TRANSFIGURING ALL THAT DREAD.	565	LAPIS LAZULI		17
ALL MEN HAVE AIMED AT, FOUND AND LOST:	566	LAPIS LAZULI		18
AND ALL THE DROP-SCENES DROP AT ONCE	566	LAPIS LAZULI		22
ALL THINGS FALL AND ARE BUILT AGAIN, ...	566	LAPIS LAZULI		35
AND ALL THE DROP SCENES DROP AT ONCE	566	LAPIS LAZULI	V	22
ON ALL THE TRAGIC SCENE THEY STARE.	567	LAPIS LAZULI		52
AND MAYBE WE ARE ALL THE SAME	570	THREE BUSHES		24
AND MAYBE WE ARE ALL THE SAME	570	THREE BUSHES		26
LOOKED HALF ASLEEP ALL DAY.	570	THREE BUSHES		34
HIS LADY SAW IT ALL	571	THREE BUSHES		53
UPON ALL FOURS.	572	LADYS 1ST SONG		12
BODY WERE NOT AT ALL, ...	572	LADYS 2ND SONG		9
ALL THE LABOURING HEAVENS SIGH.	573	LADYS 3RD SONG		12

22

ALL   (CONTINUED),

	PAGE	TITLE	LINE
OUT OF ALL HARM,	574	MAIDS 1ST SONG	8
ALL HIS TWENTIES CRAMMED WITH TOIL;	576	WHAT THEN	4
ALL HIS HAPPIER DREAMS CAME TRUE--	577	WHAT THEN	11
ALL THE OLYMPIANS; A THING NEVER KNOWN AGAIN.	578	LOFTY THINGS	12
ALL NEIGHBOURLY CONTENT AND EASY TALK ARE GONE,	580	CURSE CROMWELL	9
AND WE AND ALL THE MUSES ARE THINGS OF NO ACCOUNT.	580	CURSE CROMWELL	12
THAT I AM STILL THEIR SERVANT THOUGH ALL ARE UNDERGROUND.	581	CURSE CROMWELL	22
ITS OPEN LIGHTED DOORWAY AND ITS WINDOWS ALL ALIGHT,	581	CURSE CROMWELL	26
AND ALL MY FRIENDS WERE THERE AND MADE ME WELCOME TOO;	581	CURSE CROMWELL	27
THEY GAVE IT OUT TO ALL THE WORLD,	582	ROGER CASEMENT	11
COME TOM AND DICK, COME ALL THE TROOP	582	ROGER CASEMENT	17
COME ALFRED NOYES AND ALL THE TROUP	582	ROGER CASEMENT V	17
THAT ALL MUST HANG THEIR TRUST	583	GHOST ROG CASE	16
AND ALL MUST PAY HIM HEED,	583	GHOST ROG CASE	22
ALL THOSE LEARNED HISTORIANS,	584	ORAHILLY	5
KEEPING ALL THE KERRY MEN	585	ORAHILLY	14
COME FILL UP ALL THOSE GLASSES	586	PARNELLITES	7
HE BROUGHT IT ALL TO PASS;	586	PARNELLITES	14
THAT IS ALL I ASK, MY DEAR,	587	OLD WICKED MAN	7
"KIND ARE ALL YOUR WORDS, MY DEAR,	588	OLD WICKED MAN	10
I GAVE IT ALL TO AN OLDER MAN:	588	OLD WICKED MAN	23
HID FROM ALL THOSE WARTY LADS	589	OLD WICKED MAN	43
"ALL MEN LIVE IN SUFFERING,	589	OLD WICKED MAN	46
I FORGET IT ALL AWHILE	590	OLD WICKED MAN	61
AND ALL DEAD MEN ARE DRUNK.	592	DRUNK SOBRIETY	16
AND WHAT'S THE GOOD OF WOMEN, FOR ALL THAT THEY CAN SAY	592	PILGRIM	4
I PRAYED AT ALL THE STATIONS UPON MY MARROW-BONES,	593	PILGRIM	7
AND THERE I FOUND AN OLD MAN, AND THOUGH I PRAYED ALL DAY	593	PILGRIM	8
ALL KNOW THAT ALL THE DEAD IN THE WORLD ABOUT THAT PLACE ARE STUCK,	593	PILGRIM	11
ALL KNOW THAT ALL THE DEAD IN THE WORLD ABOUT THAT PLACE ARE STUCK,	593	PILGRIM	11
I SWEAR TO GOD I QUESTIONED THEM, AND ALL THEY HAD TO SAY	593	PILGRIM	14
FOR I CAN PUT THE WHOLE LOT DOWN, AND ALL I HAVE TO SAY	593	PILGRIM	24
I PRAYED AT ALL THE STATIONS UPON MY MARROW BONES,	593	PILGRIM V	7
I SWEAR TO GOD I QUESTIONED THEM ALL AND ALL THEY HAD TO SAY	593	PILGRIM V	14
I SWEAR TO GOD I QUESTIONED THEM ALL AND ALL THEY HAD TO SAY	593	PILGRIM V	14
FOR ALL TONGUES HE KNEW.	594	COLONEL MARTIN	4
SHE MAY BE ALL ALONE THERE;	594	COLONEL MARTIN	14
"TAKE ALL TO YOUR MISTRESS,"	595	COLONEL MARTIN	34
AND THERE AT ALL STREET-CORNERS	596	COLONEL MARTIN	55
AND ALL MEN HEARD THEM SWEAR	596	COLONEL MARTIN	60
DID ALL THAT FOR THE POOR.	596	COLONEL MARTIN	62
AND THERE AT ALL STREET CORNERS	596	COLONEL MARTIN V	55
ALL SORTS OF KINGS HAVE SAT	597	MODEL LAUREATE	2
THAT MEN AND WOMEN OF ALL SORTS	597	MODEL LAUREATE	3
PUTS ALL MEN IN A FRIGHT,	597	MODEL LAUREATE	12
I MET HER ALL BUT FIFTY YEARS AGO	602	GALLERY REVIS	15
HUGH LANE, "ONLIE BEGETTER" OF ALL THESE;	602	GALLERY REVIS	22
AS THOUGH SOME BALLAD-SINGER HAD SUNG IT ALL;	602	GALLERY REVIS	24
OF ALL THAT PRIDE AND THAT HUMILITY?	602	GALLERY REVIS	29
AS THOUGH SOME BALLAD SINGER HAD SUNG IT ALL.	602	GALLERY REVIS V	24
HONOUR HAD LIVED SO LONG, ALL LACKING FOUND.	603	GALLERY REVIS	35
ALL THAT WE DID, ALL THAT WE SAID OR SANG	603	GALLERY REVIS	42
ALL THAT WE DID, ALL THAT WE SAID OR SANG	603	GALLERY REVIS	42
OF ALL THAT SCHOLARLY GENERATIONS HAD HELD DEAR;	603	GALLERY REVIS V	37A
CONTACT ALL THINGS ANTAEUS-LIKE GREW STRONG;	603	GALLERY REVIS V	44
ALL THINGS DOWN TO THAT COMMON TEST AGAIN,	603	GALLERY REVIS V	46
ALL MANNIONS COME FROM MANANNAN,	606	SONGS BURDEN 1	10
I PITY ALL THE YOUNG,	607	SONGS BURDEN 2	11
COME GATHER ROUND ME, PLAYERS ALL!	608	SONGS BURDEN 3	1
THAT ALL ATTENDANTS AND THE CASUAL CROWD MIGHT HEAR.	609	IN TARAS HALLS	13
ALL ASIATIC VAGUE IMMENSITIES,	610	STATUES	12
MIRROR ON MIRROR MIRRORED IS ALL THE SHOW.	610	STATUES	22
THERE ALL THE GOLDEN CODGERS LAY,	611	NEWS ORACLE	1
REMEMBER ALL THOSE RENOWNED GENERATIONS,	613	MARCH SONGS 1	1
ALL THAT IS FINISHED, LET IT FADE.	613	MARCH SONGS 1	10
REMEMBER ALL THOSE RENOWNED GENERATIONS,	613	MARCH SONGS 1	11
REMEMBER ALL THAT HAVE SUNK IN THEIR BLOOD,	613	MARCH SONGS 1	12
REMEMBER ALL THAT HAVE DIED ON THE SCAFFOLD,	613	MARCH SONGS 1	13
REMEMBER ALL THAT HAVE FLED, THAT HAVE STOOD,	613	MARCH SONGS 1	14
AND ALL THAT'S FINISHED, LET IT FADE.	613	MARCH SONGS 1	20
REMEMBER ALL THESE RENOWNED GENERATIONS,	613	MARCH SONGS 1 V	11
ALL THAT GREAT PAST TO A TROUBLE OF FOOLS;	614	MARCH SONGS 1	22
ALL THE RENOWN THAT FELL.	614	MARCH SONGS 1	26
AND ALL THAT'S FINISHED, LET IT FADE.	614	MARCH SONGS 1	30
"HEAR, GENTLEMEN, LADIES, AND ALL MANKIND!	615	MARCH SONGS 3	2
ALL THERE CAUGHT UP THE TUNE.	616	MARCH SONGS 3	15
(SOMETHING MAY LINGER THERE THOUGH ALL ELSE DIE!)	618	BRONZE HEAD	5
NO DARK TOMB-HAUNTER ONCE! HER FORM ALL FULL	618	BRONZE HEAD	8
BUT EVEN AT THE STARTING-POST, ALL SLEEK AND NEW,	619	BRONZE HEAD	15
ALL THAT IS NOT ITSELF; I HAD GROWN WILD	619	BRONZE HEAD	20
ANCESTRAL PEARLS ALL PITCHED INTO A STY,	619	BRONZE HEAD	26
WHENCE DID ALL THAT FURY COME?	619	STICK INCENSE	1
AND YET GAVE TONGUE, "HOUND VOICES" WERE THEY ALL.	622	HOUND VOICE	9
ALL METAPHOR, MALACHI, STILTS AND ALL. A BARNACLE GOOSE	623	HIGH TALK	11
ALL METAPHOR, MALACHI, STILTS AND ALL. A BARNACLE GOOSE	623	HIGH TALK	11
BUT HE HAS NEED OF ALL THAT STRENGTH	624	APPARITIONS	20

23

ALL   (CONTINUED)

	PAGE	TITLE	LINE
A GIRL THAT KNEW ALL DANTE ONCE	626	OLD MEN BE MAD	5
MY CIRCUS ANIMALS WERE ALL ON SHOW, ...	629	CIRCUS ANIMALS	6
THIS DREAM ITSELF HAD ALL MY THOUGHT AND LOVE. . . .	630	CIRCUS ANIMALS	24
HEART-MYSTERIES THERE, AND YET WHEN ALL IS SAID . . .	630	CIRCUS ANIMALS	27
PLAYERS AND PAINTED STAGE TOOK ALL MY LOVE, ...	630	CIRCUS ANIMALS	31
I MUST LIE DOWN WHERE ALL THE LADDERS START, ...	630	CIRCUS ANIMALS	39
HEART MYSTERIES THERE, AND YET WHEN ALL IS SAID . . .	630	CIRCUS ANIMALS V	27
ALL THAT I HAVE SAID AND DONE, ...	632	MAN AND ECHO	6
AND ALL SEEMS EVIL UNTIL I	632	MAN AND ECHO	17
AND, ALL WORK DONE, DISMISSES ALL	633	MAN AND ECHO	34
AND, ALL WORK DONE, DISMISSES ALL	633	MAN AND ECHO	34
"WE THREAD THE NEEDLES' EYES, AND ALL WE DO	634	CUCHULAIN COMF	16
ALL MUST TOGETHER DO." THAT DONE, THE MAN	634	CUCHULAIN COMF	17
CONVICTED COWARDS ALL, BY KINDRED SLAIN	634	CUCHULAIN COMF	21
THOUGH ALL WAS DONE IN COMMON AS BEFORE;	635	CUCHULAIN COMF	24
THAT ALL ARE OATH-BOUND MEN:	635	BLACK TOWER	5
AND ANCIENT IRELAND KNEW IT ALL.	637	BEN BULBEN	16
KNOW THAT WHEN ALL WORDS ARE SAID	638	BEN BULBEN	27
ALL OUT OF SHAPE FROM TOE TO TOP, ...	639	BEN BULBEN	71
NOW HER SHEEP ALL BROWSING MEET	646	ISLE STAT I 1	22
TILL ALL ELSE IS EMPTY CHAFF, ...	647	ISLE STAT I 1	60
WEEPING WHEN ALL OTHERS LAUGH.	647	ISLE STAT I 1	62
ALL THE WORLD IS RINGING, RINGING:	648	ISLE STAT I 1	93
ALL THE WORLD IS SINGING, SINGING, ...	648	ISLE STAT I 1	94
STRICKEN ALL THE NIGHT IS PAST--	648	ISLE STAT I 1	96
ALL CLAMOUR-CLOTHED--WAS'T CLAMOUR WHEN I SUNG, . .	649	ISLE STAT I 1	108
OF FLIGHT ARE DONE. MOST FAIR OF ALL WHO GRAZE . .	649	ISLE STAT I 1	118
NASCHINA, HAIL! MOST FAIR OF ALL WHO GRAZE	649	ISLE STAT I 1	120
WHERE ALL NIGHT LONG THE HEAVENS WEEP AND WEEP, . .	649	ISLE STAT I 1	124
WHERE ALL NIGHT LONG THE LONELY MOON, THE WHITE . .	650	ISLE STAT I 1	126
ALL FLAME-LIKE GUSHING FROM THE HOLLOW STONES, . .	650	ISLE STAT I 1	129
OF ALL ON WHOM ARCADIAN SUNS HAVE SHONE	650	ISLE STAT I 1	143
THE PALE ANEMONES. WE'VE SOUGHT ALL DAY, ...	651	ISLE STAT I 2	5
ALL RHAPSODY HATH SORROW FOR ITS SOUL.	652	ISLE STAT I 2	17
SOME SAY THAT ALL WHO TOUCH THE ISLAND LONE . . .	653	ISLE STAT I 2	42
TELLS ALL HIS SINNING IN THEIR EARS.	655	ISLE STAT I 3	14
TELLS ALL HER SINNING IN THEIR EARS.	655	ISLE STAT I 3 V	14
AND THEY ARE ALL NOW STONE, AS I SHALL BE, ...	656	ISLE STAT I 3	35
ALL CHOICE, AND GIVE TO CHANCE FOR GUIDING CHANCE .	656	ISLE STAT I 3	39
MOCKING WITH PATIENT LAUGHTER ALL THE NIGHT . . .	657	ISLE STAT I 3	52
STRANGE DRAPERIES DID ALL THE SIDES ADORN, ...	657	ISLE STAT I 3	55
THE WINGED WONDER OF ALL FAERY LAND.	657	ISLE STAT I 3	57
OF THE FORESTS ALL THE PRIDE, ...	658	ISLE STAT I 3	84
IN ALL SUCH THINGS, PRAY LET THINE EARS BE TURNED,	660	ISLE STAT II 1	39
AND ONLY SHEEP HE LOVED OF ALL THE TROOP.	661	ISLE STAT II 1	61
ALL THINGS ARE QUIET IN THE EVE'S WIDE EYE. . . .	662	ISLE STAT II 2	6
ALL SWIM WITH TEARS. THE FAERY BOAT'S AT HAND! . .	663	ISLE STAT II 2	33
OH, LOVELY TO SEE IN ALL MEN'S SIGHT	666	ISLE STAT II 3	3
IN ALL MEN'S SIGHT.	666	ISLE STAT II 3 V	5
O SWIFT ON THE SEAS ALL DAY AND NIGHT	666	ISLE STAT II 3	8
ALL DAY AND NIGHT, ...	666	ISLE STAT II 3	10
OF MY SAD HUNTER-FRIEND WILL ALL DEPART	668	ISLE STAT II 3	45
YOUR EYES ARE ALL A-FLASH. SHE IS NOT HERE. . . .	669	ISLE STAT II 3	68
WITH YOU I AM ALL GENTLENESS: IN TRUTH, ...	669	ISLE STAT II 3	70
MY WORDS WERE ALL: "HERE NO LOVES WANE AND WITHER,	669	ISLE STAT II 3	84
MY WORDS WERE ALL: "O WHITHER, WHITHER, WHITHER .	669	ISLE STAT II 3	87
YOUR EYES ARE ALL AFLASH. SHE IS NOT HERE. . . .	669	ISLE STAT II 3 V	68
AND THOU WILT STAY. ALL THOUGHT OF WHAT THEY FIND	670	ISLE STAT II 3	92
HAS FENCED US ROUND FOR ALL ETERNITY.	670	ISLE STAT II 3	95
AND ALL WAS QUIET ROUND ME SPREAD, ...	670	ISLE STAT II 3	112
AND ALL HIS VEINS HAD NEAR RUN DRY, ...	670	ISLE STAT II 3	119
AND ONE ALONE OF ALL WOULD HARK, ...	671	ISLE STAT II 3	123
FOR EACH WITHIN HIMSELF HATH ALL	671	ISLE STAT II 3	132
THE HEAVENS ALL STAR-THROBBING ARE A-LIT.	671	ISLE STAT II 3	143
THE HEAVENS ALL STAR-THROBBING ARE ALIT.	671	ISLE STAT II 3 V	143
AH! YOU ARE WEEPING! HERE SHOULD ALL GRIEF CEASE.	672	ISLE STAT II 3	149
AND FADED NOW IS ALL THY WONDROUS ART.	673	ISLE STAT II 3	194
YET EVER MORE, THROUGH ALL THY DAYS OF RUTH, . .	674	ISLE STAT II 3	206
YET EVERMORE, THROUGH ALL THY DAYS OF RUTH, . . .	674	ISLE STAT II 3 V	206
I HURL AWAY THESE ALL UNFAERY FEARS.	675	ISLE STAT II 3	228
DOTH STILL THE WANDERER ROVE? WITH ALL HIS SHIPS	677	ISLE STAT II 3	287
IT IS THE VOICE OF ALL OUR HEARTS THAT LAUGH. . .	681	SEEKER	7
A CREEPING HORROR IS ALL OVER ME.	681	SEEKER	12
ARE ALL THINGS WELL WITH YOU AND WITH YOUR SHEEP?	682	SEEKER	13
YES, ALL IS VERY WELL. WHENCE COMEST THOU? . . .	682	SEEKER	14
A COWARD IN THE FIELD: AND ALL MEN CRIED:	684	SEEKER	53
WERE ALL MY WANDERING DAYS OF NO AVAIL.	684	SEEKER	64
MINE HEART-STRINGS ARE ALL BROKEN SAVING ONE, . .	684	SEEKER V	69B
FOR ALL I GAVE THE VOICE, FOR ALL MY YOUTH, . . .	685	SEEKER	78
FOR ALL I GAVE THE VOICE, FOR ALL MY YOUTH, . . .	685	SEEKER	78
FOR ALL MY JOY--AH, WOE!	685	SEEKER	79
TO LIGHTEST OF LIGHT THINGS ALL SANCTITY.	686	DRAWING-ROOM	8
ALL THESE ARE SOULS THAT FLY FROM THEIR DREAD SELVES.	686	LIFE	4
CRAMM'D ALL HER YOUTH: AND HATES HAVE BOUGHT AND SOLD	687	TWO TITANS	13
MAKING ALL ONE O'ER ROCK AND SEA AND SKIES: . . .	687	TWO TITANS	28
THAT ALL MEN EVERMORE MAY HUMBLY BOW	688	TWO TITANS	49
WHERE THEY ALL SUMMER FEED THEIR WANDERING FLOCKS,	690	MOSADA 1	5
FOR I AND ALL MY PEOPLE WERE ACCURST	690	MOSADA 1	15
AND ALL WAS DIMNESS, TILL A DYING LEAF	690	MOSADA 1	20
WE MEET--WE TWO. HOW MERRY ALL THESE ARE	691	MOSADA 1	31

ALL   (CONTINUED)

	PAGE	TITLE		LINE
AWAY FROM ALL THE OTHERS. NOW THE SUN	691	MOSADA 1		33
IN COIL ON COIL OF AZURE. ALL IS READY.	691	MOSADA 1		41
THEY SAY I AM ALL UGLINESS! LAME-FOOTED	692	MOSADA 1		60
AND ALL THE ELDERS SITTING IN THE SUN	693	MOSADA 1		69
AND CALM, ROBED ALL IN RAIMENT MOONY WHITE,	693	MOSADA 1		77
THEM ALL, AND LET THEM FIND YOU IN THE VAPOUR,	694	MOSADA 1	V	108A
TO THEIR FARM WORK! HOW SILENT ALL WILL BE!	699	MOSADA 3		8
TO THEIR FARM-WORK! HOW SILENT ALL WILL BE.	699	MOSADA 3	V	8
FOR IT ALONE OF ALL THE WORLD WILL DO	700	MOSADA 3		28
DAY'S DEAD, ALL FLAME-BEWILDERED, AND THE HILLS	702	MOSADA 3		86
ALL HEAVEN'S FLOOR, WITH VAPOURS BEDDED--	705	DAWN-SONG		11
THOUGH YOUNGEST OF ALL IN OUR GOOD BAND,	707	FAIRY PEDANT		11
THOUGH YOUNGEST OF ALL IN OUR GOOD BAND,	708	FAIRY PEDANT		39
OFTEN HE HAD BENT DOWN SOME BOUGH ALL BRIGHT	710	FERENCZ RENYI		28
OFTEN HE HAD BENT DOWN SOME BOUGH ALL BRIGHT WITH BERRIES!	710	FERENCZ RENYI	V	28
AS THOUGH THEY'D VOWED TO MEASURE ALL ITS WAYS.	711	FERENCZ RENYI		48
THERE FAR AWAY FROM ALL WE TWO WILL GO,	714	FERENCZ RENYI		99
FOR ALL SAVE HIM WHO PINING FELL,	717	FAIRY DOCTOR		19
FOR ALL SAVE HE WHO PINING FELL,	717	FAIRY DOCTOR	V	19
NOW A SCREAM FROM ALL THOSE FISHERS, FOR THERE ON DECK THERE BE	719	PHANTOM SHIP		19
ALL THE DROWNED THAT EVER WERE DROWNED FROM THAT VILLAGE BY THE SEA!	719	PHANTOM SHIP		20
AND THE GHASTLY GHOST-FLAMES GLIMMER ALL ALONG THE TAFFRAIL RAILS	719	PHANTOM SHIP		21
ALL THOSE LONG FORGOTTEN FISHERS, TILL IN THE EASTERN SKIES	719	PHANTOM SHIP	V	32
I AM DULL TO-DAY, OR YOU WERE NOW ALL LOST.	722	WITCH VIVIEN		59
ILL WORDS FOR ALL THINGS SOFT AND FAIR,	723	GIRLS SONG A		6
HAST THOU NOT KNOWN ALL SORROW AND DELIGHT	723	KANVA ON SELF		2
ALL THEIR JEALOUSY DISPLAY,	726	LOVERS QUARREL		22
"WITH ACTION ALL THE WORLD IS VEXED,"	728	PRIEST FAIRY		15
AND ALL THE SAD FAY CHIVALRY	730	PRIEST FAIRY		71
REMOTE FROM ALL THE HARD EARTH TROUBLES,	731	PRIEST FAIRY		80
HANGS O'ER ALL THE WOODED EARTH.	731	STREET DANCERS		8
ALL THE HEALING EARTH MAY-TREASURE,	733	STREET DANCERS		63
ALL THE HEALING EARTH MAY TREASURE,	733	STREET DANCERS	V	63
ALL THESE ARE SOULS WHO FLY FROM THEIR DREAD SELVES.	734	QUATRAIN APHOR		4
TO LIGHTEST OF ALL LIGHT THINGS SANCTITY.	734	QUATRAIN APHOR		8
ALL THESE ARE SOULS THAT FLY FROM THEIR DREAD SELVES.	734	QUATRAIN APHOR	V	4
TO LIGHTEST OF LIGHT THINGS ALL SANCTITY.	734	QUATRAIN APHOR	V	8
FOR ALL GOOD MEN NOW FALLEN ILL,	736	IN CHURCH		5
IN ALL ITS HONEY-THICKENED TUNE	736	SUMMER EVENING		7
MOURN ALL THE NIGHT AND DAY,	737	MOURN THEN ON		2
AND ALL HER STARLIGHT IS WITH SORROW MAD,	738	YOU ARE SAD		3
ALL THE WORDS THAT I GATHER,	739	WHERE BOOKS GO		1
AND ALL THE WORDS THAT I WRITE,	739	WHERE BOOKS GO		2
"AND ALL DOWN FROM NORTHUMBERLAND	740	EARL PAUL		9
TILL ALL THINGS ARE AT REST.	741	EARL PAUL		52
"I ASK THAT I AND ALL MY RACE,"	742	EARL PAUL		61
THAT ARE A POISON TO ALL MEN	743	DANAAN QUICK		16
OR LEAVE SOME SERVICE ALL UNDONE,	743	DANAAN QUICK		21
CAST OUT ALL HOPE, CAST OUT ALL FEAR,	743	DANAAN QUICK		25
CAST OUT ALL HOPE, CAST OUT ALL FEAR,	743	DANAAN QUICK		25
AND NOW THEY ARE ALL GONE, I FOLLOW STILL.	749	SHADOW WATER A		37
TIME AND THE WORLD AND ALL THINGS DWINDLE OUT.	749	SHADOW WATER A		47
AND WERE ALL DREAMS, IT WOULD NOT WEIGH IN THE HAND.	750	SHADOW WATER A		77
HOW ALL THAT DIE ARE BORNE ABOUT THE WORLD	750	SHADOW WATER A		84
NONE SHOULD ESCAPE MY SWORD! I WOULD SEND ALL	752	SHADOW WATER A		111
HE HAS HEARD ME BECAUSE I PROMISED ALL.	752	SHADOW WATER A		116
WAKE ALL BELOW. WHY HAVE YOU BROKEN OUR SLEEP?	753	SHADOW WATER A		132
WHEN ALL GATHER THEY WILL FLY UPON THEIR WAY.	753	SHADOW WATER A		136
AND NOW THEY ALL WHEEL SUDDENLY AND FLY	753	SHADOW WATER A		148
ENDS ALL THINGS. I HAVE SLAIN THE LOCHLANN KING.	754	SHADOW WATER A		163
YOUR HEART'S DESIRE AND THE END OF ALL OUR TROUBLE!	755	SHADOW WATER A		175
BUT NOW I WILL KILL HER. ALL COMES TO AN END.	755	SHADOW WATER A		176
FOR I HAVE ALL HIS GARDEN WISDOM. O SPEAK!	756	SHADOW WATER A		180
I WILL SWEAR BY SUN AND MOON TO PARDON ALL	756	SHADOW WATER A		183
AND TO GIVE WEALTH OF OXEN AND SHEEP TO ALL!	756	SHADOW WATER A		184
ALL THAT TIME KNOWS. SPEAK TO ME, QUEEN. O SPEAK!	756	SHADOW WATER A	V	180
BECAUSE THESE WATERS MAKE ALL WOMEN ONE.	757	SHADOW WATER A		194
THAT HAVE BUILT ALL ARE DUST ON A MOTH'S WING.	757	SHADOW WATER A		205
AND A STRONG GALLEY. I GIVE YOU ALL AS MUCH.	758	SHADOW WATER A		222
I HAVE FORGOT IT ALL. HOW SOON DREAMS FADE!	761	SHADOW WATER A		272
SWEET WITH ALL MUSIC, OUT OF HIS LONG HAIR.	762	SHADOW WATER A		303
ALL DIES AMONG THOSE STREAMS. THE FOOL HAS MADE	764	SHADOW WATER A		335
AND ALL THE WISDOM THAT OLD IMAGES,	764	SHADOW WATER A		344
AND ALL THAT PROPHESYING IMAGES	764	SHADOW WATER A	V	344
TO SNATCH ALIVE OUT OF THE STREAMS ALL LOVERS	765	SHADOW WATER A		347
THE LOVE OF ALL UNDER THE LIGHT OF THE SUN	765	SHADOW WATER A		353
WE WILL NOT QUARREL, NOW THAT ALL IS WELL.	766	SHADOW WATER A		373
ALL THAT KNOW LOVE AMONG THE WINDS OF THE WORLD	767	SHADOW WATER A		386
AMID THE DARKNESS, NOW THAT ALL MY STARS	767	SHADOW WATER A	V	404
PUT ALL YOUR POWER ON THE THREAD	771	SPINNING SONG		12
HAD NOT ALL HIS LIMBS A STIR	772	SONG DEIRDRE 1		11
WHAT IS ALL OUR PRAISE TO THEM	773	SONG DEIRDRE 1		23
AND ALL THE GARDEN BLESS,	774	COME RIDE		10
UNTIL ALL BE RUINOUS.	775	AGAINST WITCH		4
ALL THEIR BODIES, JOINT BY JOINT,	776	AGAINST WITCH		22
ALL HIS BODY CAN BUT SHOVE	776	AGAINST WITCH		33
ALL THAT MINGLING OF OUR BREATH,	777	SONG DEIRDRE 2		10

	PAGE	TITLE	LINE
ALL (CONTINUED)			
"LIVES ALL HIS DAYS	780	WELL AND TREE	3
THAT ALL THE VALLEY FILLS	781	MY HEART BEAT	10
FOR ALL OUR TALKING.	785	YOUR HEART	7
AND ALL SEEM WELL ENOUGH,	786	YOUR HEART	15
I MOCK AT ALL SO BURNING OUT.	787	HUDDON DUDDON	15
CASTLE DARGAN'S RUIN ALL LIT,	788	HAWTHORN TREE	3
YET ALL THE LOVELY THINGS THAT WERE	788	HAWTHORN TREE	11
MAYBE I SHALL NOT DIE AT ALL.	788	HAWTHORN TREE	16
MAY BE I SHALL NOT DIE AT ALL.	788	HAWTHORN TREE V	16
AND ALL MEN LIE THAT SAY THAT I	789	SINGING HEAD	3
OF ALL THAT LOVERS SAID,	789	SINGING HEAD	10
GAVE ALL THE LOVE THAT WOMEN KNOW!	789	SINGING HEAD	21
OUTWEIGHED ALL OTHER YEARS, YOU SAID,	791	REPRISALS	6
ALLAH			
OH, ALLAH! IT WAS THUS THEY SHONE THAT NIGHT	701	MOSADA 3	50
ALLAH'S			
I HERE ARREST THEE. IT WAS ALLAH'S WILL.	694	MOSADA 1	105
I HERE ARREST THEE. IT IS ALLAH'S WILL.	694	MOSADA 1 V	105
FORGIVE ME! IT WAS ALLAH'S WILL. THE CORDS.	695	MOSADA 1	109
FORGIVE, OR I WILL DIE. 'TWAS ALLAH'S WILL.	695	MOSADA 1	118
FORGIVE ME! IT WAS ALLAH'S WILL. NOW CORDS.	695	MOSADA 1 V	109
ALL-DESTROYING			
ALL-DESTROYING SWORD-BLADE STILL	484	SYMBOLS	3
ALLEGORICAL			
THROUGH THREE ENCHANTED ISLANDS, ALLEGORICAL DREAMS,	629	CIRCUS ANIMALS	11
ALLEN'S			
THE FLOOR OF ALLEN'S HOSTING HALL	13	OISIN 1 V	156
ALLEYS			
OR DOWN THE DEWY FOREST ALLEYS,	10	OISIN 1	120
AND DOWN THE DEWY FOREST ALLEYS,	10	OISIN 1 V	120
ALLIANCES			
MARRIAGES, ALLIANCES AND FAMILIES,	491	COOLE BALLYLEE	36
ALL-LABOURING			
AND BY THE HEAVEN'S ALL-LABOURING BROODS!	164	PERFECT BEAUTY V	5
ALLOW			
ALLOW THAT HE, DESPITE	584	ORAHILLY	4
NOT TO ALLOW HIS LOOKS TO TELL	624	APPARITIONS	13
ALLOWS			
MY TRADE ALLOWS! CHOSEN MY COMPANY,	352	PEOPLE	20
ALL-POWERFUL			
BY THE WEBBED TOES, AND THAT ALL-POWERFUL BILL	441	LEDA AND SWAN V	3
ALL'S			
ALL'S CHANGED SINCE I, HEARING AT TWILIGHT,	322	SWANS AT COOLE	15
WHERE ALL'S ACCUSTOMED, CEREMONIOUS!	405	FOR DAUGHTER	74
OR OUT OF DRUNKARD'S EYE. ALL'S WHIGGERY NOW,	486	SEVEN SAGES	13
OR DRUNKARD'S EYE. ALL'S WHIGGERY NOW,	486	SEVEN SAGES V	13
OR OUT OF A DRUNKARD'S EYE. ALL'S WHIGGERY NOW,	486	SEVEN SAGES V	13
THAT ALL'S ARRANGED IN ONE CLEAR VIEW,	633	MAN AND ECHO	31
BE ONE? I THINK ALL'S FINISHED NOW AND SEALED.	701	MOSADA 3	62
ALL-UNNEEDED			
TOLD WHERE--AH, LITTLE, ALL-UNNEEDED VOICE!--	127	DREAM OF FAERY V	30
ALMANACS			
REMEMBERED OUT OF BABYLONIAN ALMANACS,	426	PHANTOM HATRED	20
ALMHUIN			
UNDER A BEECH AT ALMHUIN AND HEARD THE THIN	44	OISIN 2	228
ALMHUIN'S			
THE FLOOR OF ALMHUIN'S HOSTING HALL	13	OISIN 1	156
ALMINTOR			
NAY, NAY, ALMINTOR, YONDER SONG IS GLAD.	652	ISLE STAT I 2	23
ALMINTOR, THOU HAST GROWN SO FULL OF RUTH,	652	ISLE STAT I 2	26
ALMINTOR WITH HER LOVE. WHO ART THOU?--SPEAK,	660	ISLE STAT II 1	50
O, MY ALMINTOR, NOBLE WAS THY QUEST!	679	ISLE STAT II 3	319
ALMINTOR'S			
YON IS THE HUNTER'S, SIR ALMINTOR'S, PAGE!	660	ISLE STAT II 1	35
SIR PAGE, ALMINTOR'S FRIEND, AND THEREFORE LEARNED	660	ISLE STAT II 1	38
BEING ALMINTOR'S PAGE. NOW JUDGE YOU HERE.	660	ISLE STAT II 1	47
ASIDE!--THE WILD HORNS TOLD ALMINTOR'S END,	665	ISLE STAT II 2	68
ALMOST			
AND ALMOST WEPT BECAUSE THEY COULD NOT FIND IT.	229	SHADOW WATER B	155
AND WE ARE ALMOST ON HER! WE HAD NOT KNOWN	232	SHADOW WATER B	220
I ALMOST LONG THAT IT WERE POSSIBLE!	236	SHADOW WATER B	306
NOW THAT WE'RE ALMOST SETTLED IN OUR HOUSE	323	ROBERT GREGORY	1
NOW THAT WE'VE ALMOST SETTLED IN OUR HOUSE	323	ROBERT GREGORY V	1
ALONE			
AND SURGING PHOSPHORUS ALONE GAVE LIGHT	31	OISIN 2	33
OF SURGING PHOSPHORUS ALONE GAVE LIGHT.	31	OISIN 2 V	33
HOPELESS FOR EVER, THEY ALONE SHALL SEEK	42	OISIN 2 V	200
"LAST OF MY RACE, THREE THINGS I RULE ALONE--	45	OISIN 2 V	239A
. . . REMEMBERING ALONE THAT DELIGHT	54	OISIN 3	111
. . . ALONE WITH REMEMBRANCE AND FEAR!	63	OISIN 3	218
WITHOUT LAUGHTER, A COUGHING, ALONE WITH REMEMBRANCE AND FEAR!	63	OISIN 3 V	218
WORDS ALONE ARE CERTAIN GOOD.	65	HAPPY SHEPHERD	10
FOR WORDS ALONE ARE CERTAIN GOOD,	66	HAPPY SHEPHERD	43
AND WORDS ALONE ARE CERTAIN GOOD,	66	HAPPY SHEPHERD V	43
WHILE WE ALONE HAVE ROUND US WOVEN WOODS,	73	ANASHU VIJAYA	56
HOW WE ALONE OF MORTALS ARE	78	INDIAN TO LOVE	11
BUT SEEK ALONE TO HEAR THE STRANGE THINGS SAID	101	ROSE UPON ROOD	19
BUT TELL ALONE YOUR NAME AND HOUSE TO HIM	108	CUCHULAIN SEA V	36
AND WENT DOWN TO THE LONG SANDS ALONE,	111	CUCHULAIN SEA V	84

26

	PAGE	TITLE		LINE

ALONE   (CONTINUED)

AND HE WENT DOWN TO THE LONG SANDS ALONE,	111	CUCHULAIN SEA	V	84
STOOD UP, AND CAME TO THE LONG SANDS ALONE!	111	CUCHULAIN SEA	V	84
AND LIVE ALONE IN THE BEE-LOUD GLADE.	117	ISLE INNISFREE		4
OF SERAPHS, BROODING, EACH ALONE,	156	FORGOT BEAUTY	V	22
NODDING ALONE AND APART,	171	MAID QUIET	V	6
KNOWING ONE, OUT OF ALL THINGS, ALONE, THAT HIS HEAD	177	PAST GREATNESS		8
HAVE ALL THAT GREATNESS, AND NOT HERS ALONE,	186	QUEEN MAEVE		133
BECAUSE IT IS ALONE OF ALL THINGS HAPPY,	198	SEVEN WOODS		9
ALONE AND WINGED. OUR LOVE SHALL BE LIKE THEIRS	250	SHADOW WATER B		581
AND I AM LEFT ALONE WITH MY BELOVED,	251	SHADOW WATER B		600
WE ARE ALONE FOR EVER, AND I LAUGH,	251	SHADOW WATER B		602
SHALL BE ALONE FOR EVER. WE TWO--THIS CROWN--	251	SHADOW WATER B		605
PALE-FACED, ALONE UPON A BENCH, EDAIN	279	TWO KINGS		61
PALE-FACED, ALONE UPON A BENCH, HIS WIFE	279	TWO KINGS	V	61
WHERE I MAY SPEAK TO YOU ALONE, MY CRAFT	284	TWO KINGS		159
ALONE WITH ALL THIS USELESS HAPPINESS?"	285	TWO KINGS		200
BUT I ALONE BEING BLESSED KEEP	307	HOUR DAWN		104
AND EVEN OLD MEN'S EYES GREW DIM, THIS HAND ALONE,	314	FALLEN MAJESTY		2
AS THOUGH HE HAD BUT THAT ONE TRADE ALONE,	327	ROBERT GREGORY		80
BEING OLD, BUT THAT THE OLD ALONE MIGHT DIE,	339	SHEP GOATHERD		4
I LET THEM STRAY. I THOUGHT OF RHYME ALONE,	339	SHEP GOATHERD		11
THAT HE ALONE HAD GATHERED UP NO GEAR,	340	SHEP GOATHERD		49
BURNING ALONE BESIDE AN OPEN BOOK,	370	EGO DOMINUS		63
ALONE, IMPORTANT AND WISE,	379	CAT AND MOON		26
AND BOTH LOOK UP TO ME ALONE	380	SONGS FOOL 1		4
HEARTS WITH ONE PURPOSE ALONE	393	EASTER 1916		41
THAT HAVE AN EAR ALONE	395	SIXTEEN DEAD		14
AND THERE ALONE, THAT HAVE NO SOLITUDE?	398	LEADERS CROWD		9
AND THAT ALONE! YET I, BEING DRIVEN HALF INSANE	442	BLACK CENTAUR		6
BEING ALL ALONE I'D NURSE A STONE	459	HIS WILDNESS		11
UNDER IT WISDOM STANDS, AND I ALONE--	469	HARUN RASHID		189
OF ALL ARABIA'S LOVERS I ALONE--	470	HARUN RASHID		190
AND I ALONE, ONE IN TEN THOUSAND YEARS,	470	HARUN RASHID	V	190
OUT OF TEN THOUSAND WINTERS, I ALONE--	470	HARUN RASHID	V	190
LOVE YOU FOR YOURSELF ALONE	492	ANNE GREGORY		5
MAY LOVE ME FOR MYSELF ALONE	492	ANNE GREGORY		11
COULD LOVE YOU FOR YOURSELF ALONE	492	ANNE GREGORY		17
BUT WERE I LEFT TO LIE ALONE	511	JANE AND JACK		13
I WENT OUT ALONE	515	GIRLS SONG B		1
ONE MAN, ONE MAN ALONE	526	AM OF IRELAND		6
ONE MAN, AND ONE MAN ALONE	526	AM OF IRELAND	V	6
AND ALL ALONE COMES RIDING THERE	550	SEVERED HEAD		18
IS WHAT I CAN WHISTLE ALONE AND ALONE,	551	SONGS REWRIT 1		4
IS WHAT I CAN WHISTLE ALONE AND ALONE?	551	SONGS REWRIT 1		4
ALONE AND ALONE, WITH A SPECKLED SHIN?	551	SONGS REWRIT 1		8
ALONE AND ALONE, WITH A SPECKLED SHIN?	551	SONGS REWRIT 1		8
ALONE AND ALONE NINE NIGHTS I LAY	551	SONGS REWRIT 1		13
ALONE AND ALONE NINE NIGHTS I LAY	551	SONGS REWRIT 1		13
IS DRINKING HER HEALTH WHEN LONE, ALONE--	551	SONGS REWRIT 1	V	4
DRINKING ALONE WITH A SPECKLED SHIN?	551	SONGS REWRIT 1	V	8
LIVE LONE, ALONE WITH A SPECKLED SHIN?	551	SONGS REWRIT 1	V	8
HE RHYMING ALONE IN HIS BED.	552	SONGS REWRIT 2		12
LYING ALONE ON A BED	552	SONGS REWRIT 2	V	10
ALONE WITH A CRAZY HEAD.	552	SONGS REWRIT 2	V	12
IN THE MIND ALONE!	553	PRAYER OLD AGE		2
AND SHE WAS MUCH ALONE,	594	COLONEL MARTIN		11
SHE MAY BE ALL ALONE THERE,	594	COLONEL MARTIN		14
WE THREE ALONE IN MODERN TIMES HAD BROUGHT	603	GALLERY REVIS		45
YOU THAT WOULD JUDGE ME, DO NOT JUDGE ALONE	603	GALLERY REVIS		50
THE POST AND GARDEN-BOY ALONE	607	SONGS BURDEN 2		7
SHE ALONE, MY LADY, LINGERETH	646	ISLE STAT I 1		28
I'D BE ALONE. WE TWO, BY THAT PALE FOUNT,	650	ISLE STAT I 1		132
THAT NESTLES ALONE IN THE WHISTLING WIND,	657	ISLE STAT I 3		68
DOWN TO THEIR FEET THE STARS THAT SHINE ALONE,	662	ISLE STAT II 1		80
LAUGHS NOT. IT DWELLS ALONE ON MORTAL LIPS!	670	ISLE STAT II 3		100
AND ONE ALONE OF ALL WOULD HARK.	671	ISLE STAT II 3		123
I SPEAK ALONE WITH SERVANTS OF THE CROSS	698	MOSADA 2		48
FOR IT ALONE OF ALL THE WORLD WILL DO	700	MOSADA 3		28
ALONE WITH OUR OWN WHISPERS AND REPLIES--	702	MOSADA 3		80
ALONE AMONG THE MURMURS OF THE DAWN.	702	MOSADA 3		81
WHO WANDER AND WHISPER ALONE,	707	FAIRY PEDANT		8
AH! CRUEL ONES, LEAVE ME ALONE NOW	707	FAIRY PEDANT		13
AH! CRUEL ONES, LEAVE ME ALONE	707	FAIRY PEDANT	V	13
GAVE TO ME ALONE THE CROSS!	744	ROSY CROSS		3
GAVE TO ME ALONE THE CROSS,	744	ROSY CROSS		11
THAT FORGAEL HAS FOLLOWED THE GREY BIRDS ALONE,	767	SHADOW WATER A		402
FRAIL BIRD, LIKE A WHITE SEA-BIRD ALONE	784	WOMANS BEAUTY		2

ALONG

NEIGHING ALONG THE LIFELESS WASTE!	13	OISIN 1		170
AND ROLLS ALONG THE UNWIELDY SUN,	18	OISIN 1		267
TRICKLING ALONG THE EARTH, I RAVE!	19	OISIN 1	V	281
ALONG THE BLOOD-BEDABBLED PLAINS,	24	OISIN 1		371
REMEMBERING HOW ALONG THE PLAINS,	24	OISIN 1	V	370
SHE LIMPS ALONG IN AN AGED WHITENESS!	27	OISIN 1		415
HIS SHADOW ALONG IN THE EVENING BLAZE,	27	OISIN 1	V	409
SHE LIMPS ALONG IN AN AGED WHITENESS,	28	OISIN 1	V	423
FLUTTER ALONG THE FROTH LIPS OF THE SEA,	33	OISIN 2		58
FLUTTER ALONG THE FROTH LIPS OF THE SEA.	33	OISIN 2		64
FLUTTER ALONG THE FROTH-LIPS OF THE SEA,	33	OISIN 2	V	58
HIS HAND ALONG THE RUNNEL'S SIDE, AS THOUGH	39	OISIN 2		162

27

ALONG   (CONTINUED)
                                                            PAGE   TITLE   LINE

    BARKING. ALONG THE HERBLESS PLAIN, WITH BLOWS   . . . . .   40 OISIN 2   V   170
    . . . FLUNG LOOSELY ALONG THE DIM GROUND;   . . . .   50 OISIN 3   45
    WENT WALKING WITH SLOW STEPS ALONG THE GLEAMING . . . . .   68 SAD SHEPHERD   3
    ROLLING ALONG IN DREAMS FROM HILL TO HILL.   . . . .   68 SAD SHEPHERD   11
    THEIR HAIR ALONG THE MOUNTAINS ROLLED AND FILLED   . . . .   74 ANASHU VIJAYA   71
    I PASSED ALONG THE WATER'S EDGE BELOW THE HUMID TREES,   .   76 INDIAN ON GOD   1
    ALONG THE GRASS, ALONG THE SANDS.   . . . .   78 INDIAN TO LOVE   9
    ALONG THE GRASS, ALONG THE SANDS.   . . . .   78 INDIAN TO LOVE   9
    PENSIVE THEY PACED ALONG THE FADED LEAVES, ...   80 EPHEMERA   10
    OR WHEN ALONG THE WINTRY STRANDS   . . . .   84 MAD KING GOLL   41
    I LEAD ALONG THE WOODLAND DEER;   . . . .   84 MAD KING GOLL   46
    OR WHERE ALONG THE WINTRY STRANDS   . . . .   84 MAD KING GOLL   V   41
    ALONG THE PEBBLY STREET. . . . .   94 MOLL MAGEE   12
    DRIVING THE DEER ALONG THE WOODY WAYS. . . . .   109 CUCHULAIN SEA   V   48
    AND WHEN THE UPROAR RAN ALONG THE GRASS   . . . .   186 QUEEN MAEVE   127
    SWINGING, SWINGING ALONG.   . . . .   544 TO SAME TUNE 1   V REF
    TAKE TO THE ROADS AND GO MARCHING ALONG.   . . . .   548 TO SAME TUNE 3   14
    MARCHING, MARCHING ALONG.   . . . .   549 TO SAME TUNE 3   25
    AND LAUGH'D, SO, SO ALONG THE BUBBLING RILLS   . . . . .   645 ISLE STAT I 1   18
    ALONG THE WOOD WITH SUBTLE TREAD AND BENDED BOWS.   . . .   649 ISLE STAT I 1   111
    IF SO I MIGHT, ALONG A DEWY VALE, ...   649 ISLE STAT I 1   123
    THAT CALLS. O EVIL STARRED! IT COMES ALONG   . . . . .   653 ISLE STAT I 2   49
    ALONG THE LAKE. THE CRANE HAS HOMEWARD FLED.   . . . .   656 ISLE STAT I 3   23
    TO EASE THEIR WORLD-OLD THIRST ALONG THE BRINK   . . . .   663 ISLE STAT II 2   41
    FAIR YOUTH, ALONG A WANDERING WAY   . . . .   667 ISLE STAT II 3   38
    OF THE DREAD WOODS; ALONG THEIR RUSSET FLOOR   . . . . .   675 ISLE STAT II 3   243
    ALONG THE VELVET VALE I SAW HIM COME--   . . . .   690 MOSADA 1   10
    ALONG THE SEA! AND MANY A MAN GREW HUSHED   . . . . . .   693 MOSADA 1   86
    ALONG THE CORNFIELD, WHERE THE POPPIES GROW, ...   699 MOSADA 3   V   7
    I CANNOT EVEN CRAWL ALONG THE FLAGS   . . . .   701 MOSADA 3   58
    AFAR ALONG THE FLEET WHITE RIVER'S FACE--   . . . . . .   702 MOSADA 3   79
    FROM HERE, ALONG THE SHADOWY WAY THAT WINDS   . . . . .   703 MOSADA 3   111
    AND ALONG THE MOUNTAINS PASS, ...   705 DAWN-SONG   12
    ALONG THE TENTS, THE FIELDS, THE VILLAGE WALLS.   . . .   712 FERENCZ RENYI   71
    ALONG THE TENTS, FIELD, THE VILLAGE WALLS.   . . . . . .   712 FERENCZ RENYI   V   71
    CREEPING ALONG THE HEAVENS' PURPLE CUP, ...   714 FERENCZ RENYI   112
    AY, AND SHAKES IN SEA-GREEN WAVERINGS ALONG THE FISHERS'   718 PHANTOM SHIP   2
        STREET;
    AYE AND SHAKES IN SEA GREEN WAVERINGS, ALONG THE FISHERS'   718 PHANTOM SHIP   V   2
        STREET.
    AND THE GHASTLY GHOST-FLAMES GLIMMER ALL ALONG THE TAFFRAIL   719 PHANTOM SHIP   21
        RAILS
    AND THE GHASTLY GHOST FLAMES GLIMMER ALONG THE TAFFREL   719 PHANTOM SHIP   V   21
        RAILS,
    WHISPERING ALONG THE SUNNY PATH;   . . . .   725 LEGEND   18
    AND RUBBED ALONG THE RAIL HIS NOSE.   . . . .   725 LEGEND   28
    ROLLS ALONG THE SEA SANDS WHITE.   . . . .   732 STREET DANCERS   34
    ROLLS ALONG THE SEA-SANDS WHITE.   . . . .   732 STREET DANCERS   V   34
ALOUD
    HE CALLED ALOUD TO ALL THE STARS TO LEND   . . . . . .   68 SAD SHEPHERD   V   5
    I LAUGHED ALOUD AND HURRIED ON . . . .   83 MAD KING GOLL   31
    WHERE HER GRANDCHILDREN SLEPT, AND CRIED ALOUD,   . . .   185 QUEEN MAEVE   109
    WHERE HER GRAND-CHILDREN SLEPT, AND CRIED ALOUD   . . .   185 QUEEN MAEVE   V 109
    TO CRY ALOUD TO THE GREY BIRDS, AND DREAMS, ...   252 SHADOW WATER B   618
    TILL THE WILDERNESS CRIED ALOUD, ...   259 UNWORTH PRAISE   8
    CRYING ALOUD AS THE RACECOURSE IS, ...   266 GALWAY RACES   14
    CRYING ALOUD AS THE RACE COURSE IS, ...   266 GALWAY RACES   V   14
    CRYING ALOUD AS THE RACE-COURSE IS, ...   266 GALWAY RACES   V   14
    FOR MEDICINE." THEREON HE CRIED ALOUD, ...   281 TWO KINGS   98
    "YOU CRY ALOUD, O WOULD 'TWERE SPRING   . . . .   306 HOUR DAWN   91
    HE WERE AFRAID THE BIRDS, WHO CRY ALOUD   . . . .   371 EGO DOMINUS   77
    THE THREE OLD RASCALS LAUGH ALOUD.   . . . .   460 THREE MONUMENT   12
    OR, BY THE MOON EMBITTERED, SCORN ALOUD   . . . .   498 BYZANTIUM   21
    UPON CRO-PATRICK SANG ALOUD;   . . . .   528 DANCER CRUACH   5
    THE GOLDEN PLOUGH AND HARROW AND SPOKE ALOUD   . . . . .   609 IN TARAS HALLS   12
    LAUGHS ALOUD, HIS HEART AT PEACE.   . . . .   638 BEN BULBEN   32
ALPUJARRAS
    ABOVE THE ALPUJARRAS ON THEIR THRONES!   . . . .   691 MOSADA 1   27
AL-RABBAN
    TO ABD AL-RABBAN; FELLOW-ROYSTERER ONCE, ...   460 HARUN RASHID   2
AL-RASCHID
    DESERT GEOMETRY OR THE GIFT OF HARUN AL-RASCHID   . . .   460 HARUN RASHID   V   T
AL-RASHID
    THE GIFT OF HARUN AL-RASHID   . . . .   460 HARUN RASHID   T
    WHAT GREAT HARUN AL-RASHID, OCCUPIED . . . .   462 HARUN RASHID   24
ALREADY
    DAYLIGHT ALREADY FLIES . . . .   536 PARTING   9
    AMONG THE WHIMPERING GHOSTS, MATE THUS, ALREADY?   . .   722 WITCH VIVIEN   68
    THERE! THERE! THEY HAVE GONE QUICKLY, FOR ALREADY   . .   764 SHADOW WATER A   326
    SHE IS ALREADY FADING, AS THOUGH THE GODS   . . . . .   768 SHADOW WATER A   V 422
ALT
    IN A CLEFT THAT'S CHRISTENED ALT   . . . .   632 MAN AND ECHO   1
ALTAR
    O COLLEENS, KNEELING BY YOUR ALTAR RAILS LONG HENCE,   .   173 SPEAKS HEARERS   V   1
    O, WOMEN, KNEELING BY YOUR ALTAR RAILS LONG HENCE,   . .   173 SPEAKS HEARERS   V   1
    HAVE WALKED TO THE ALTAR . . . .   355 PROPERTIUS   4
ALTAR-PIECE
    IN THIS ALTAR-PIECE THE KNIGHT, ...   385 ROBARTES DANCE   2
ALTAR-RAILS
    O WOMEN, KNEELING BY YOUR ALTAR-RAILS LONG HENCE,   . . .   173 SPEAKS HEARERS   1

28

PAGE   TITLE   LINE

ALTER
   OR ELSE, TO ALTER PLATO'S PARABLE, ... 443 SCHOOL CHILDR   15
   ALTER AT THE BEST . . . . 517 HER ANXIETY   4
ALTERED
   AND THE WORLD'S ALTERED SINCE YOU DIED, ... 276 GREY ROCK   126
   AND DECKED AND ALTERED IT FOR A GIRL'S LOVE, ... 423 MY DESCENDANTS   22
ALTERNATIVE
   ALTERNATIVE SONG FOR THE SEVERED HEAD IN . . . . . 549 SEVERED HEAD   T
ALTERS
   "EVERYTHING ALTERS, ... 208 OLD MEN ADMIRE   2
ALTOGETHER
   AND SINGING, SINGING ALTOGETHER! . . . . 15 OISIN 1   V 203
ALWAY
   AMONG THEMSELVES LAUGH ON AND SING ALWAY! . . . . . 68 SAD SHEPHERD   7
   OF YONDER LAKE, FROM WHOSE GREEN BANKS ALWAY . . . 653 ISLE STAT I 2   33
   WE TURNED AROUND THE PLACE ALWAY, ... 667 ISLE STAT II 3   40
ALWAYS
   AND FEARED ALWAYS THE BOW-STRING'S TWANGING, ... 3 OISIN 1   V 7GG
   AND ALWAYS NEVER-ANXIOUS SLEEP! . . . . 8 OISIN 1   93
   BUT NAUGHT THEY HEARD, FOR THEY ARE ALWAYS LISTENING, . 68 SAD SHEPHERD   15
   I'D ALWAYS BEEN BUT WEAKLY, ... 94 MOLL MAGEE   13
   BUT ALWAYS, AS I'M MOVIN' ROUND, ... 96 MOLL MAGEE   43
   THEY WENT FORTH TO THE BATTLE, BUT THEY ALWAYS FELL . . 113 ROSE OF BATTLE V   T
   I WILL ARISE AND GO NOW, FOR ALWAYS NIGHT AND DAY . . 117 ISLE INNISFREE   9
   AND PLANNING, PLOTTING ALWAYS THAT SOME MORROW . . . 129 BOOK STORIES   10
   AH, WORLD-WIDE NATION, ALWAYS GROWING SORROW, . . . 130 BOOK STORIES   V 11
   AH, WORLDWIDE NATION, ALWAYS GROWING SORROW! . . . . 130 BOOK STORIES   V 11
   GREEN BOUGHS OF TOSSING ALWAYS, WEARY, WEARY, . . . 130 BOOK STORIES   V 14
   YOUR MOTHER EIRE IS ALWAYS YOUNG, ... 148 INTO TWILIGHT   5
   THY MOTHER ERI IS ALWAYS YOUNG, ... 148 INTO TWILIGHT   V 5
   FOR THE GOOD ARE ALWAYS THE MERRY, ... 178 FIDDLER DOONEY   13
   HE ALWAYS WEPT THEM ON THAT DAY, ... 192 BAILE AILLINN   78
   ALWAYS IN HIS ONE SEAT, AND BID ME CARE HIM . . . . 280 TWO KINGS   80
   THOUGH ALWAYS AT MY WORDS HIS TROUBLE GREW! . . . . 281 TWO KINGS   91
   ALWAYS WE'D HAVE THE NEW FRIEND MEET THE OLD . . . . 324 ROBERT GREGORY   9
   YOU SING AS ALWAYS OF THE NATURAL LIFE, ... 342 SHEP GOATHERD   75
   IN THAT MYSTERIOUS, ALWAYS BRIMMING LAKE . . . . . 356 BROKEN DREAMS   32
   YET ALWAYS WHEN I LOOK DEATH IN THE FACE, ... 357 DEEP-SWORN VOW   3
   IS ALWAYS HAPPY LIKE A BIRD OR A BEAST! . . . . . 373 PHASES OF MOON   38
   HAVE YOU NOT ALWAYS KNOWN IT? THE SONG WILL HAVE IT . 374 PHASES OF MOON   65
   OF POETS THAT ARE ALWAYS GAY, ... 565 LAPIS LAZULI   3
   THEY ALWAYS BEAT ON THE SAME SMALL STONE. . . . . . 591 WHAT WAS LOST   5
   I WHO HAVE ALWAYS HATED WORK, ... 605 YOU CONTENT   19
   I ALWAYS SAID YOU COULD NOT TRUST THESE MOORS. . . . 704 MOSADA 3   V 134A
   WHY DO YOU LAUGH? I LAUGH THE LAST ALWAYS. . . . . 721 WITCH VIVIEN   25
   I LOSE! THEY'RE LOADED DICE. TIME ALWAYS PLAYS . . . 721 WITCH VIVIEN   44
   THEY ARE ALWAYS QUARRELLING. GIVE ME YOUR SWORDS. . . 766 SHADOW WATER A   370
   EOCHA AND MAINE ARE ALWAYS QUARRELLING. . . . . . 766 SHADOW WATER A   371
   GIVE ME YOUR SWORDS. THEY ARE ALWAYS QUARRELLING. . . 766 SHADOW WATER A V 370
AMAZED
   HE SAT WITH TIGHTENED REIN AMAZED, HIS HORSE . . . . 277 TWO KINGS   V 10
AMBASSADOR
   BEING THEIR AMBASSADOR, ... 582 ROGER CASEMENT   14
AMBASSADORS
   WITH PERSIAN WARS OR GREEK AMBASSADORS . . . . . . 462 HARUN RASHID V 25
AMBER
   AMONG THE GOLD, THE AMBER, AND THE RED." . . . . . 712 FERENCZ RENYI   76
   AMONG THE BLUE, THE AMBER AND THE RED." . . . . . 712 FERENCZ RENYI V 76
   MY FINGERS FEEL HIS AMBER HAIR. . . . . 723 GIRLS SONG A   8
AMBERGRIS
   BUT FOR THE AMBERGRIS AND SANDALWOOD. . . . . . . 232 SHADOW WATER B   221
AMBERS
   HER GOLDS, HER AMBERS, AND HER BLUES, ... 13 OISIN 1   163
AMBITION
   AND LET ALL BASE AMBITION BE, ... 460 THREE MONUMENT   9
   AND EVERY BRIDE'S AMBITION SATISFIED. . . . . . . 491 COOLE BALLYLEE   37
   SATISFY AMBITION, ANIMATE . . . . 500 VACILLATION   20
   SATISFY AMBITION, OR ANIMATE . . . . 500 VACILLATION V 20
AMBITIONS
   OR THE AMBITIONS THAT HE SERVED, ... 342 SHEP GOATHERD   93
AMBITIOUS
   LIFE OVERFLOWS WITHOUT AMBITIOUS PAINS! . . . . . 417 ANCEST HOUSES   3
   BUT O! AMBITIOUS HEART, HAD SUCH A PROOF DRAWN FORTH . 427 PHANTOM HATRED   36
AMBLING
   WHEN AMBLING DOWN THE VALE WE MET . . . . 2 OISIN 1 V 7U
AMBUSCADE
   AND DOWNY BEES HAVE AMBUSCADE, ... 67 HAPPY SHEPHERD V 46A
AMBUSH
   AN AMBUSH! PILGRIMS AT THE WATER-SIDE! . . . . . 601 GALLERY REVIS   2
   AN AMBUSH! PILGRIMS AT THE WATER SIDE! . . . . . 601 GALLERY REVIS V 2
AMEND
   COULD NOT AMEND. I HAVE GOOD SPIRITS ENOUGH. . . . 227 SHADOW WATER B   116
   THAT NOTHING CAN AMEND IT BUT THESE WATERS, ... 227 SHADOW WATER B   120
AMENDED
   AMENDED WHAT WAS TOLD AWRY . . . . 440 WISDOM   4
AMENDS
   THAT SOME AMENDS BE MADE . . . . 582 ROGER CASEMENT   22
   BUT TIME AMENDS OLD WRONG, ... 613 MARCH SONGS 1   9
   BUT TIME AMENDS OLD WRONG, ... 613 MARCH SONGS 1   19
   BUT TIME AMENDS OLD WRONG, ... 614 MARCH SONGS 1   29

29

	PAGE	TITLE		LINE
AMERGIN				
AND SHOOK AT INVER AMERGIN	81	MAD KING GOLL		3
AMERICAN				
AMERICAN COLONIES, IRELAND, FRANCE AND INDIA	487	SEVEN SAGES		15
AMETHYST				
IVORY IMAGES WITH AMETHYST EYES.	248	SHADOW WATER B		534
THERE'S SOMEBODY I'D GIVE THE AMETHYST EYES TO.	248	SHADOW WATER B		538
AMID				
AMID THE SHADES OF NIGHT, HE CHANGED AND RAN	40	OISIN 2		174
SAINT, DO YOU WEEP? I HEAR AMID THE THUNDER	43	OISIN 2		209
SAINT, DOST THOU WEEP? I HEAR AMID THE THUNDER	43	OISIN 2	V	209
BUT TO BE AMID SHOOTING OF FLIES AND FLOWERING OF RUSHES AND FLAGS."	55	OISIN 3		120
I FEAST AMID MY PEOPLE ON THE HILL,	103	FERGUS DRUID		17
MY FATHER STANDS AMID HIS BATTLE-CARS."	107	CUCHULAIN SEA		26
"STILL TREADS THE WORLD AMID HIS ARMED MEN."	107	CUCHULAIN SEA	V	26
MY FATHER STANDS AMID HIS BATTLE CARS."	107	CUCHULAIN SEA	V	26
HIS EVENING FIRE AMID THE LEAFY SHADE.	109	CUCHULAIN SEA		48
AMID MEN'S SOULS, THAT WAVER AND GIVE PLACE	112	ROSE OF WORLD		7
AMID MEN'S SOULS THAT DAY BY DAY GIVE PLACE,	112	ROSE OF WORLD	V	7
OR SIGHS AMID THE WANDERING, STARRY MIRTH,	114	ROSE OF BATTLE		18
AND HID HIS FACE AMID A CROWD OF STARS.	121	YOU ARE OLD		12
I DREAMED THAT I STOOD IN A VALLEY, AND AMID SIGHS,	163	VALLEY LOVERS		1
AMID THE HOVERING, PITEOUS, PENITENTIAL THRONG."	173	SPEAKS HEARERS		8
AND HURLED IT FROM ITS PLACE AMID THE PEARLY LIGHT	174	ELEMENT POWERS	V	3
WHO STOOD AMID A SILENCE BY THE THORN	187	QUEEN MAEVE		142
WHO AMID LEAFY LIGHTS AND SHADES	193	BAILE AILLINN		103
AND AMID LEAFY LIGHT HE CRIED,	193	BAILE AILLINN	V	113
O HURRY TO THE WATER AMID THE TREES,	210	RAGGED WOOD	V	1
O HURRY TO THE WATER AMID THE TREES,	211	RAGGED WOOD	V	5
CRYING AMID THE GLITTERING SEA,	254	HIS DREAM		17
ALL THAT STERNNESS AMID CHARM,	259	PEACE		8
ALL THAT SWEETNESS AMID STRENGTH?"	259	PEACE		9
AMID THE ELABORATE WILDERNESS OF THE AIR.	278	TWO KINGS		31
BECAUSE THERE IS SUCH A STORM AMID MY THOUGHTS	281	TWO KINGS		100
AMID A PLACE OF STONE,	291	TO A FRIEND		13
KING GUAIRE WALKED AMID HIS COURT	295	THREE BEGGARS		8
AND HEAR AMID THE GARDEN'S NIGHTLY PEACE,"	300	BEGGAR CRIED		18
AMID WET ROCKS AND HEATHER,	311	PEACOCK		8
SHE LIES, HER LOVELY PITEOUS HEAD AMID DULL RED HAIR	362	HER COURTESY		2
AMID THE DREAMS OF YOUTH) LET HER COME FACE TO FACE,	366	HER COURAGE		3
AMID THAT FIRST ASTONISHMENT, WITH GRANIA'S SHADE,	366	HER COURAGE		4
ESTRANGED AMID THE STRANGENESS OF THEMSELVES,	375	PHASES OF MOON		78
AMID MOST LOVELY PLACES; SMITTEN AS THOUGH	389	IMAGE PAST		13
AMID THE RUSTLE OF HIS PLANTED HILLS,	417	ANCEST HOUSES		2
AMID GREAT CHAMBERS AND LONG GALLERIES, LINED	418	ANCEST HOUSES		36
AMID THE ORNAMENTAL BRONZE AND STONE	428	NINETEEN 19		5
IS LOST AMID THE LABYRINTH THAT HE HAS MADE	431	NINETEEN 19		70
AMID THE CLOUDY WRACK,	458	HIS WILDNESS		2
ONE HAND AMID THE GOLDFISH IN THE POOL;	463	HARUN RASHID		44
LIKE THIS PURE JET, NOW LOST AMID BLUE SKY,	464	HARUN RASHID		64
HIDING AMID THE CARGO OF A STEAMSHIP,	578	CRAZED GIRL		5
THERE SIGHED AMID HIS CHOIR OF LOVE	611	NEWS ORACLE		7
AND CHANTS OF VICTORY AMID THE ENCIRCLING HOUNDS.	622	HOUND VOICE		21
THIS HEARD I WHERE, AMID THE APPLE TREES,	735	QUATRAIN APHOR		17
AMID A CLOUD OF BANNERS,	741	EARL PAUL		39
AMID THE DARKNESS, NOW THAT ALL MY STARS	767	SHADOW WATER A	V	404
AMID THE DARK BEFORE DAY HAD BROKEN.	784	WOMANS BEAUTY		20
AMONG				
AMONG THE FIELDS OF WAVING FERN.	2	OISIN 1	V	7N
AMONG THE LEAVES OF THE LAUREL WALL,	3	OISIN 1	V	7FF
YOU ARE STILL WRECKED AMONG HEATHEN DREAMS.	4	OISIN 1		31
AMONG THE WAVING FIELDS OF FERN;	4	OISIN 1		38
AMONG UNDYING PEOPLE HAS RUN	6	OISIN 1	V	60
AMONG THEM 'LIGHTING FROM OUR STEED,	14	OISIN 1	V	193
AMONG THE WOODLAND GRASSES SWEET,	15	OISIN 1	V	199
FROM BEES AMONG THEIR HONEY MARTS,	16	OISIN 1	V	229
AMONG THE FOAMDROPS OF THE SEA,	20	OISIN 1		294
AMONG THE RINGING HALLS A SHOUT	20	OISIN 1	V	288
THEN ON AMONG THE WINDLESS WOODS,	21	OISIN 1	V	320
WRESTLED AMONG THE ISLAND BANDS.	23	OISIN 1		350
THE IMMORTALS MOVED AMONG THE FOUNTAINS	25	OISIN 1		386
THE FAIRIES MOVED AMONG THE FOUNTAINS,	25	OISIN 1	V	386
SHONE MANY TIMES AMONG THE GLIMMERING FLOWERS	30	OISIN 2		21
A JUBILANT LIFE AMONG THE LEAVES, RETURN,	35	OISIN 2	V	89A
AMONG THEMSELVES LAUGH ON AND SING ALWAY;	68	SAD SHEPHERD		7
AMONG HER WILDERING WHIRLS, FORGETTING HIM.	69	SAD SHEPHERD		28
AMONG THE MOULDERING OF ANCIENT WOODS	74	ANASHU VIJAYA		61
WITH VAPOURY FOOTSOLE AMONG THE WATER'S DROWSY BLAZE.	78	INDIAN TO LOVE	V	20
IN POOLS AMONG THE RUSHES	88	STOLEN CHILD		30
"NO MAN ALIVE, NO MAN AMONG THE DEAD,	106	CUCHULAIN SEA		10
"MY FATHER DWELLS AMONG THE SEA-WORN BANDS,	107	CUCHULAIN SEA	V	25
AMONG THOSE FEASTING MEN CUCHULAIN DWELT,	108	CUCHULAIN SEA		39
AMONG THOSE FEASTING KINGS CUCHULAIN DWELT,	108	CUCHULAIN SEA	V	39
HE STOOD AMONG A CROWD AT DROMAHAIR;	126	DREAM OF FAERY		1
AND BRIDGET HIS BRIDE AMONG THEM,	144	HOST OF AIR		15
AND WALK AMONG LONG DAPPLED GRASS,	150	WANDER AENGUS		21
AMONG PALE EYELIDS, HEAVY WITH THE SLEEP	169	SECRET ROSE		6
WHO MET FAND WALKING AMONG FLAMING DEW	169	SECRET ROSE		13
DWELT AMONG WINE-STAINED WANDERERS IN DEEP WOODS;	170	SECRET ROSE		21
VOICES AMONG THE CROWD	172	PLEADS FRIEND		2

AMONG   (CONTINUED)

	PAGE	TITLE		LINE
AMONG MY LEAVES IN TIMES OUT OF MIND:	177	PAST GREATNESS		5
WHAT MATTERS WERE AFOOT AMONG THE SIDHE,	182	QUEEN MAEVE		61
AND PINCHES AMONG HAIL AND SNOW?	191	BAILE AILLINN		46
IN OLD TIMES AMONG THE CLOUDS OF THE AIR,	194	BAILE AILLINN		133
AMONG THE GIANT KINGS WHOSE HOARD,	196	BAILE AILLINN		164
AMONG PIGEONS AND BEES, WHILE THAT GREAT ARCHER,	198	SEVEN WOODS		12
O HURRY WHERE BY WATER AMONG THE TREES	210	RAGGED WOOD		1
O HURRY WHERE BY WATER AMONG TREES,	210	RAGGED WOOD	V	1
IS NOT KNOWN AMONG MEN,	215	HAPPY TOWNLAND		28
I WALKED AMONG THE SEVEN WOODS OF COOLE:	217	WOODS OF COOLE		1
SHINING ON WATER AND FALLEN AMONG LEAVES,	218	WOODS OF COOLE		38
THAT SHE AMONG HER WINDS MIGHT KNOW HE WEPT:	220	HARP OF AENGUS		12
THAT SHE AMONG HER WOODS MIGHT KNOW HE WEPT:	220	HARP OF AENGUS	V	12
AND HID HER AMONG FRUITS OF JEWEL-STONE .	224	SHADOW WATER B		49
IF HE HAD BROUGHT US AMONG PEOPLED SEAS,	225	SHADOW WATER B	V	68C
AMONG SUBSTANTIAL THINGS: FOR IT IS DREAMS	230	SHADOW WATER B		181
AMONG THE WINDY MEADOWS OF THE DAWN."	234	SHADOW WATER B		264
IT HAD WASHED AMONG THE STARS AND PUT THEM OUT,	236	SHADOW WATER B		311
THERE IS NOT ONE AMONG YOU THAT MADE LOVE	244	SHADOW WATER B		454
O FLOWER OF THE BRANCH, O BIRD AMONG THE LEAVES,	251	SHADOW WATER B		608
AND WE FIND HEARTENERS AMONG MEN	266	GALWAY RACES		15
AND FIND HEARTENERS AMONG MEN	266	GALWAY RACES	V	15
AMONG THE AFRICAN MOUNTAINS OF THE MOON,	277	TWO KINGS		20
"I HAVE SENT AMONG THE FIELDS OR TO THE WOODS	280	TWO KINGS		69
WESTWARD OF TARA, AMONG THE HAZEL-TREES--	283	TWO KINGS		135
WENT OUT. AMONG THE IVY-COVERED ROCKS,	283	TWO KINGS		147
WESTWARD OF TARA, AMONG THE HAZEL TREES--	283	TWO KINGS	V	135
AMONG THOSE MOUTHS THAT SING THEIR SWEETHEARTS' PRAISE,	285	TWO KINGS		185
AMONG THE STONES AND THORN-TREES, UNDER MORNING LIGHT:	291	PAUDEEN		3
AMONG THE STONES AND THORN TREES, UNDER MORNING LIGHT,	291	PAUDEEN	V	3
AMONG THE OTHER GENTLEMEN,	296	THREE BEGGARS		34
AMONG THE KINGS OF GREECE AND FRANCE."	296	THREE BEGGARS	V	32A
UPON THE BRIMMING WATER AMONG THE STONES	322	SWANS AT COOLE		5
AMONG WHAT RUSHES WILL THEY BUILD,	323	SWANS AT COOLE		27
SOMEWHERE AMONG THE CLOUDS ABOVE:	328	IRISH AIRMAN		2
AMONG THE STREAMS:	329	MEN IMPROVE		3
BUT I GROW OLD AMONG DREAMS,	329	MEN IMPROVE		16
AMONG THE STREAMS,	329	MEN IMPROVE		18
HE HAD OFTEN PLAYED HIS PIPES AMONG MY HILLS,	339	SHEP GOATHERD		23
AMONG THE EVENING SHADOWS,	341	SHEP GOATHERD		71
AMONG THE POOR BOTH OLD AND YOUNG GAVE HER PRAISE.	351	HER PRAISE		18
OR CLIMBED AMONG THE IMAGES OF THE PAST--	352	PEOPLE		10
YOUR BEAUTY CAN BUT LEAVE AMONG US	356	BROKEN DREAMS		14
AMONG THE COARSE GRASS AND THE CAMEL-DUNG.	369	EGO DOMINUS		31
AMONG THE COARSE GRASS AND THE CAMEL DUNG.	369	EGO DOMINUS	V	31
AMONG WHIMS NOT IMPOSSIBLE, AND THOUGH SCARRED,	374	PHASES OF MOON		41
AMONG TASKS NOT IMPOSSIBLE, IT TAKES	376	PHASES OF MOON		92
AMONG THE STARRY EDDIES OF HER HAIR	390	IMAGE PAST		27
FROM COUNTER OR DESK AMONG GREY	392	EASTER 1916		3
IT HAD SET DOWN AMONG ITS LAWS:	399	BREAK OF DAY		16
AMONG THE DEEPENING SHADES.	416	TOWER		195
SURELY AMONG A RICH MAN'S FLOWERING LAWNS,	417	ANCEST HOUSES		1
HAD FALLEN AMONG DANCERS, HAD WHIRLED THEM ROUND	430	NINETEEN 19		52
AMONG SCHOOL CHILDREN	443	SCHOOL CHILDR		T
AMONG SCHOOLCHILDREN	443	SCHOOL CHILDR	V	T
GLITTERING AMONG GREY-LEAVED OLIVE-TREES,	447	COLONUS PRAISE		21
GLITTERING AMONG GREY-LEAVED OLIVE TREES,	447	COLONUS PRAISE	V	21
AND LIVE AMONG THE ANCIENT HOLY MEN,	448	HERO GIRL FOOL	V	11A
ONE AMONG THE BIRDS OF THE AIR,	460	THREE MONUMENT		3
AMONG DARK SKINS, AND THERE	472	ALL SOUL NIGHT		48
CONSPIRING AMONG THE IGNORANT,	475	EVA GORE-BOOTH		9
THE FINISHED MAN AMONG HIS ENEMIES?--	479	SELF AND SOUL		49
AND SAPLINGS ROOT AMONG THE BROKEN STONE,	489	COOLE PARK 29		28
HAD I NOT FOUND CONTENT AMONG THE SHOWS	499	MOTHER OF GOD		6
AMONG BIRDS OR BEASTS OR MEN	528	DANCER CRUACH		2
AND THEN YOU STOOD AMONG THE DRAGON-RINGS,	533	HER TRIUMPH		7
AND THEN YOU STOOD AMONG THE DRAGON RINGS,	533	HER TRIUMPH	V	7
AMONG THE DOGS AND HORSES THAT UNDERSTAND MY TALK,	581	CURSE CROMWELL		30
FROM THOSE THEY LIVE AMONG;	607	SONGS BURDEN 2		13
I LIVED AMONG GREAT HOUSES,	626	STATES HOLIDAY		1
VIOLENT AND FAMOUS, STRODE AMONG THE DEAD:	634	CUCHULAIN COMF		2
AMONG THOSE BIRD-LIKE THINGS CAME, AND LET FALL	634	CUCHULAIN COMF		8
AMONG THE BOUGHS, BLUE AS THE HALCYON'S WING,	683	SEEKER		38
THIS HEARD I WHERE AMONG THE APPLE TREES,	686	LIFE		19
OF HIS SAD GOD: AND DOWN AMONG THE GRASS	690	MOSADA 1		16
AROUND MY HEAD AND DANCED AMONG THE GRASS:	690	MOSADA 1		19
AMONG THE FRUIT: BUT THERE, LAME COLA CROUCHES	691	MOSADA 1		32
AMONG THE FRUIT. BUT YON, LAME COLA CROUCHES	691	MOSADA 1	V	32
AMONG THE PLANTS: THE FLOWERY SILENCE FELL	692	MOSADA 1		55
ALONE AMONG THE MURMURS OF THE DAWN.	702	MOSADA 3		81
AMONG THY NATION NONE SHALL KNOW THAT I	702	MOSADA 3	V	82
HE FADES AMONG THE MISTS: HOW FAST THEY COME,	703	MOSADA 3		117
AMONG THE GOLD, THE AMBER, AND THE RED."	712	FERENCZ RENYI		76
AMONG THE BLUE, THE AMBER AND THE RED."	712	FERENCZ RENYI	V	76
SHE WHO DWELT AMONG THE SYCAMORES,	715	DWELT SYCAMORE		T
SHE DWELT AMONG THE SYCAMORES.	715	DWELT SYCAMORE	V	T
AMONG THE WHIMPERING GHOSTS. MATE THUS. ALREADY?	722	WITCH VIVIEN		68
HAST THOU NOT RULED AMONG THE GILDED WALLS?	724	KANVA ON SELF		7
A LOVER'S QUARREL AMONG THE FAIRIES.	726	LOVERS QUARREL		T
HE'D SLEPT AMONG THE SINGING TREES,	728	PRIEST FAIRY		17

AMONG   (CONTINUED)

	PAGE	TITLE	LINE
AMONG THE MURMURS OF THE BEES.	728	PRIEST FAIRY	18
AMONG THE HAUNTS OF BEE AND BIRD.	729	PRIEST FAIRY	42
THIS HEARD I WHERE AMONG THE APPLE TREES.	735	QUATRAIN APHOR V	19
A PATH AMONG THESE WAVES AND WEIGH THE WIND?	748	SHADOW WATER A	21
OF PASTURE-LAND AND PLOUGH-LAND AMONG THE HILLS?	748	SHADOW WATER A	33
AND PRAISED YOUR WAR AMONG THE ENDLESS SEAS.	749	SHADOW WATER A	35
AND PRAISE A WAR AMONG THE ENDLESS SEAS.	749	SHADOW WATER A V	35
AMONG THOSE STREAMS. OR ON THEIR CLOUDY EDGE.	750	SHADOW WATER A	63
AND FALLS AMONG THE DREAMS THE DROWSY GODS.	750	SHADOW WATER A	68
AMONG THE WATERS THAT NO PILOT KNOWS.	750	SHADOW WATER A	80
AND FLY AMONG THE FOAM. THRUST DOWN THE HELM.	750	SHADOW WATER A	88
A WOMAN LIES AMONG EMBROIDERIES.	752	SHADOW WATER A	120
AMONG THESE MISTY WATERS. TWO! NOW FOUR!	753	SHADOW WATER A	138
AMONG THE WINDY MEADOWS OF THE DAWN."	754	SHADOW WATER A	153
HAVE THE WINDS BLOWN YOU AMONG THESE EMPTY WATERS?	756	SHADOW WATER A	192
TO CONQUER AMONG THE COUNTRIES OF THE NORTH.	757	SHADOW WATER A	200
AMONG THE WINDS, LOOKS UNDER YOUR PALE EYELIDS.	757	SHADOW WATER A	211
AMONG THE QUEENS, AND CHOSE THE MIGHTIEST	757	SHADOW WATER A	213
FOR THOSE AMONG YOUR PEOPLE THAT ARE DEAD?	758	SHADOW WATER A	224
AMONG THE HEBRIDES. WHEN SHE AWAKENS.	760	SHADOW WATER A V	255
THE STARS WOULD HURL THEIR CROWNS AMONG THE FOAM	761	SHADOW WATER A	265
AMONG GREAT TREES, AND IN THE WINGS OF OWLS.	762	SHADOW WATER A	285
THAT SHE AMONG HER WINDS MIGHT KNOW HE WEPT!	763	SHADOW WATER A	307
AND SHE, NO LONGER BLOWN AMONG THE WINDS.	763	SHADOW WATER A	323
AMONG THE WINDS AND WATERS! AND WHEN THEY PASS	764	SHADOW WATER A	331
ALL DIES AMONG THOSE STREAMS. THE FOOL HAS MADE	764	SHADOW WATER A	335
WHERE TRUE-LOVE WANDERS AMONG THE HOLY WOODS.	764	SHADOW WATER A	337
WHAT WERE TRUE-LOVE AMONG THE RUSH OF HIS STREAMS?	764	SHADOW WATER A	338
WHERE TRUE LOVE WANDERS AMONG THE HOLY WOODS.	764	SHADOW WATER A V	337
WHAT WERE TRUE LOVE AMONG THE RUSH OF HIS STREAMS?	764	SHADOW WATER A V	338
THAT LIVES AMONG THE WOODS OF THE DARK HOUNDS.	766	SHADOW WATER A	376
ALL THAT KNOW LOVE AMONG THE WINDS OF THE WORLD	767	SHADOW WATER A	386
BUT I AM NEW TO LOVE. GO AMONG THESE	767	SHADOW WATER A	391
THAT HAVE KNOWN LOVE AMONG THE WINDS OF THE WORLD	767	SHADOW WATER A	392
AMONG HIGH MOUNTAINS, AND THE MOUNTAIN ROBBERS	768	SHADOW WATER A	411
SO WORTHY AMONG MEN. I FOLLOW YOU.	768	SHADOW WATER A V	412
WHETHER AMONG THE COLD WINDS OF THE DEAD.	768	SHADOW WATER A V	413
OR AMONG WINDS THAT MOVE IN THE MEADOWS AND WOODS.	768	SHADOW WATER A V	413
O FLOWER OF THE BRANCH, O BIRD AMONG THE LEAVES.	769	SHADOW WATER A	424
AMONG HIS CHILDREN, GRANDCHILDREN AND GREAT-GRANDCHILDREN!	790	DEDICATION	6
AMONG THE OTHER CHEATED DEAD.	791	REPRISALS	24

AMOROUS

	PAGE	TITLE	LINE
TRAPPED OF AN AMOROUS DEMON THING.	2	OISIN 1 V	4
MUST I ENDURE YOUR AMOROUS CRIES?	177	PAST GREATNESS	12
ALL TURN WITH AMOROUS CRIES, OR ANGRY CRIES.	433	NINETEEN 19	123
THOSE AMOROUS CRIES THAT OUT OF QUIET COME	557	RIBH ECSTASY	7
THOU SHALT OUTLIVE THINE AMOROUS HAPPY TIME.	674	ISLE STAT II 3	203

AMPLE

	PAGE	TITLE	LINE
TWO MEN WHO LOVE ONE MAID HAVE AMPLE CAUSE	659	ISLE STAT II 1	30

AMRITA

	PAGE	TITLE	LINE
PRAYERS FOR THE LAND. I WILL WAIT HERE, AMRITA.	71	ANASHU VIJAYA	• 13
WHO IS AMRITA? SORROW OF ALL SORROWS!	71	ANASHU VIJAYA	15
AMRITA. DRAW YOU NEAR, AND 'NEATH YON PILLAR	71	ANASHU VIJAYA V	13A
WHO IS AMRITA? WOE! AH, WOE IS ME!	71	ANASHU VIJAYA V	15
AMRITA, WHILE--AH ME! YOU LOVE ANOTHER.	74	ANASHU VIJAYA	58
AMRITA. THIS SAME EVE SHE WATCHED ME PASS.	74	ANASHU VIJAYA V	64

A-MURMUR

	PAGE	TITLE	LINE
A-MURMUR LIKE YOUNG PARTRIDGE! WITH LOUD HORN	32	OISIN 2	52

ANALYTIC

	PAGE	TITLE	LINE
OF THE ANALYTIC MIND, CAN NEITHER CLOSE	353	PEOPLE	33

ANARCHY

	PAGE	TITLE	LINE
MERE ANARCHY IS LOOSED UPON THE WORLD,	402	SECOND COMING	4

ANASHUYA

	PAGE	TITLE	LINE
ANASHUYA AND VIJAYA	70	ANASHU VIJAYA	T
HA!L! HAIL, MY ANASHUYA. NO! BE STILL.	71	ANASHU VIJAYA	11
HAIL! HAIL, MY ANASHUYA. NAY; BE STILL.	71	ANASHU VIJAYA V	11

ANBUAL'S

	PAGE	TITLE	LINE
AND SET THEM DIGGING INTO ANBUAL'S HILL.	184	QUEEN MAEVE V	93

ANCESTOR

	PAGE	TITLE	LINE
AN ANCESTOR WAS RECTOR THERE	640	BEN BULBEN	86

ANCESTORS

	PAGE	TITLE	LINE
WITH FAMOUS PORTRAITS OF OUR ANCESTORS!	418	ANCEST HOUSES	37

ANCESTRAL

	PAGE	TITLE	LINE
MAY SET A STONE UPON ANCESTRAL SORROW!	130	BOOK STORIES	11
OF THEIR RETURN TO THAT ANCESTRAL HOUSE.	286	TWO KINGS V	218C
ANCESTRAL HOUSES	417	ANCEST HOUSES	T
MEDITATIONS IN TIME OF CIVIL WAR ANCESTRAL HOUSES	417	ANCEST HOUSES V	T
THINK OF ANCESTRAL NIGHT THAT CAN.	478	SELF AND SOUL	20
. . . IS MY ANCESTRAL STAIR!	480	BLOOD AND MOON	17
ODOUR OF BLOOD ON THE ANCESTRAL STAIR!	482	BLOOD AND MOON	40
SEEMED ONCE MORE DEAR THAN LIFE! ANCESTRAL TREES.	491	COOLE BALLYLEE	34
THROUGH THEIR ANCESTRAL PATTERNS DANCE.	612	NEWS ORACLE	19
ANCESTRAL PEARLS ALL PITCHED INTO A STY,	619	BRONZE HEAD	26

ANCIENT

	PAGE	TITLE	LINE
FOR THESE WERE ANCIENT OISIN'S FATE	24	OISIN 1	361
WITH ALL THE ANCIENT SORROW OF MEN"!	25	OISIN 1	381
AFAR IN ANCIENT ERI.	32	OISIN 2	50E
TO TWO OLD EAGLES, FULL OF ANCIENT PRIDE.	34	OISIN 2 V	74
FOR THEIR DIM MINDS WERE WITH THE ANCIENT THINGS.	34	OISIN 2	77
TO EAGLES TWAIN THAT, FULL OF ANCIENT PRIDE,	34	OISIN 2 V	73

32

ANCIENT   (CONTINUED)

Text	Page	Title	V	Line
IN SOME DIM MEMORY OR ANCIENT MOOD,	36	OISIN 2		99
MY SOUL, ONCE GLORY OF ITS ANCIENT LINE,	36	OISIN 2	V	95
HOPELESS FOR EVER! ANCIENT OISIN KNOWS,	42	OISIN 2		202
OF ANCIENT WARRIORS, THE LABOURS OF THE STRONG.	42	OISIN 2	V	195
THAT ONCE MORE MOVED IN MY BOSOM THE ANCIENT SADNESS OF MAN,	54	OISIN 3		107
AND LO! MY ANCIENT BURDEN MAY DEPART.	69	SAD SHEPHERD		24
AMONG THE MOULDERING OF ANCIENT WOODS	74	ANASHU VIJAYA		61
AND EVERY ANCIENT OLLAVE SAID,	82	MAD KING GOLL		9
FILLED FULL OF ANCIENT CHEER."	97	FOXHUNTER	V	12
COME NEAR ME, WHILE I SING THE ANCIENT WAYS!	100	ROSE UPON ROOD		2
SING OF OLD EIRE AND THE ANCIENT WAYS!	101	ROSE UPON ROOD		23
FIRST AS A RAVEN ON WHOSE ANCIENT WINGS	102	FERGUS DRUID		3
EVEN AS SPRING UPON THE ANCIENT SKIES,	108	CUCHULAIN SEA		42
STARED LIKE THE SPRING UPON THE ANCIENT SKIES,	108	CUCHULAIN SEA	V	41
THAT YOU COME HERE TO MEET THIS ANCIENT SWORD?"	109	CUCHULAIN SEA	V	61
MAY SURELY MEET THEIR ANCIENT GAZE.	139	TO IRELAND	V	28
WITH A TWINKLING OF ANCIENT HANDS.	144	HOST OF AIR		24
THE ANCIENT BEARDS, THE HELMS OF RUBY AND GOLD	169	SECRET ROSE		8
IN ANY ANCIENT BOOK BUT TELLS OF YOU!	186	QUEEN MAEVE		135
IT WHIRLS INTO THE FOAM. O ANCIENT WORM,	251	SHADOW WATER B		597
. . . HAVE JOINED THE ANCIENT ORDER OF HIBERNIANS AND THE . . .	262	STUDENTS AGIT	V	T
BY THE ANCIENT HOLY HANDS THAT BROUGHT THEM	271	GREY ROCK	V	21
NOR ON THE ANCIENT BEATEN PATHS, THAT WOUND	279	TWO KINGS		52
BECAUSE AN ANCIENT HISTORY SAID	303	HOUR DAWN		24
WITH ALL THEIR ANCIENT FACES LIKE RAIN-BEATEN STONES,	318	MAGI		4
AT KYLE-NA-NO UNDER THAT ANCIENT ROOF	321	REED WHISPERER		7
BEING BUT A PART OF ANCIENT CEREMONY--	321	REED WHISPERER		12
TO KYLE-NA-INO AND TO THAT ANCIENT ROOF	321	REED WHISPERER	V	7
BESIDE A FIRE OF TURF IN TH' ANCIENT TOWER,	324	ROBERT GREGORY		3
FROM RUIN OR FROM ANCIENT TREES,	410	TOWER		23
AND WHEN THAT ANCIENT RUFFIAN'S TURN WAS ON	411	TOWER		66
AN ANCIENT BANKRUPT MASTER OF THIS HOUSE,	412	TOWER		80
AN ANCIENT BRIDGE, AND A MORE ANCIENT TOWER,	419	MY HOUSE		1
AN ANCIENT BRIDGE, AND A MORE ANCIENT TOWER,	419	MY HOUSE		1
AN ANCIENT IMAGE MADE OF OLIVE WOOD--	428	NINETEEN 19		6
ALL TEETH WERE DRAWN, ALL ANCIENT TRICKS UNLEARNED,	429	NINETEEN 19		17
THE ANCIENT HABIT STICKS,	431	NINETEEN 19		74
AND LIVE AMONG THE ANCIENT HOLY MEN,	448	HERO GIRL FOOL	V	11A
NEVER TO HAVE LIVED IS BEST, ANCIENT WRITERS SAY!	459	FROM OEDIPUS		10
I SUMMON TO THE WINDING ANCIENT STAIR!	477	SELF AND SOUL		1
IS SATO'S ANCIENT BLADE, STILL AS IT WAS,	477	SELF AND SOUL		10
I SUMMON TO THE WINDY ANCIENT STAIR!	477	SELF AND SOUL	V	1
IS SATO'S ANCIENT SWORD, STILL AS IT WAS,	477	SELF AND SOUL	V	10
AND ANCIENT LINEAMENTS ARE BLOTTED OUT.	564	GYRES		4
IN ANCIENT TOMBS I SIGHED, BUT NOT AGAIN!	564	GYRES		14
THEIR ANCIENT, GLITTERING EYES, ARE GAY.	567	LAPIS LAZULI		56
SOME ANCIENT FAMOUS AUTHORS MISREPRESENT,	579	DOR WELLESLEY		15
WE IRISH, BORN INTO THAT ANCIENT SECT	611	STATUES		28
AND FIND OUR ANCIENT HOUNDS BEFORE THE DOOR,	622	HOUND VOICE		16
"OBEY OUR ANCIENT RULE AND MAKE A SHROUD!	634	CUCHULAIN COMF		13
AND ANCIENT IRELAND KNEW IT ALL.	637	BEN BULBEN		16
BY THE ROAD AN ANCIENT CROSS.	640	BEN BULBEN		88
HE WAS OUR ANCIENT GOD. IF I SPEAK LOW,	658	ISLE STAT I 3		78
THAT ANCIENT MOTHER CRIES, "SPEAK NOT, MY SON,	711	FERENCZ RENYI		56
OF ANCIENT PASSIONS AND OF ANCIENT FEARS?	724	KANVA ON SELF		16
OF ANCIENT PASSIONS AND OF ANCIENT FEARS?	724	KANVA ON SELF		16
THEREFORE IN THIS ANCIENT CUP	776	AGAINST WITCH		36
THEREFORE FROM THIS ANCIENT CUP	776	AGAINST WITCH	V	36
AN ANCIENT LECHER TOOK TO GEESE	792	GEORGE MOORE		3

ANEMONES

Text	Page	Title	V	Line
THE PALE ANEMONES. WE'VE SOUGHT ALL DAY,	651	ISLE STAT I 2		5

ANEW

Text	Page	Title	V	Line
FLOWED ON ANEW, AND OFT, ANEW DECLINING,	33	OISIN 2	V	68D
FLOWED ON ANEW, AND OFT, ANEW DECLINING,	33	OISIN 2	V	68D
I HUNGER TO BUILD THEM ANEW AND SIT ON A GREEN KNOLL APART,	143	ROSE IN HEART		6
AND THEREFORE MY HEART BOWS DOWN ANEW,	164	PERFECT BEAUTY	V	6
AND WHEN I'D WRITE IT OUT ANEW, THE WORDS,	186	QUEEN MAEVE		139
FOR WHOM THE CAIRN'S BUT HEAPED ANEW,	192	BAILE AILLINN		84
DRAW THE GLASNEVIN COVERLET ANEW	293	TO A SHADE	V	19
THAT POUNDS UP ALL ANEW	346	ON WOMAN		31
SELF-BORN, BORN ANEW?	507	STREAM AND SUN		15
NOW THE HUNT BEGINS ANEW?	773	SONG DEIRDRE 1		18

ANGEL

Text	Page	Title	V	Line
ALL SOUNDS BY BIRD OR ANGEL SUNG	387	SOLOMON WITCH	V	7
GO ASK THE YOUNGEST ANGEL,	680	LOVE AND DEATH		29
THE ARCHANGEL AXEL, VICTOR THE ANGEL	774	COME RIDE		11

ANGELIC

Text	Page	Title	V	Line
BEFORE GOD MADE THE ANGELIC CLAN,	138	TO IRELAND		8
WHEN THE FLAMING LUTE-THRONGED ANGELIC DOOR IS WIDE!	172	TRAV PASSION		1
YOU GREAT ANGELIC POWERS OF WIND, AND WAVE, AND FIRE,	174	ELEMENT POWERS	V	7
THE FATHER AND HIS ANGELIC HIERARCHY	483	VERONIC NAPKIN		4

ANGELO

Text	Page	Title	V	Line
A MIND MICHAEL ANGELO KNEW	576	ACRE OF GRASS		19
MICHAEL ANGELO,	618	LONG-LEG FLY		26
MICHAEL ANGELO LEFT A PROOF	638	BEN BULBEN		45

ANGELO'S

Text	Page	Title	V	Line
WHILE MICHAEL ANGELO'S SISTINE ROOF,	386	ROBARTES DANCE		32

	PAGE	TITLE		LINE

ANGELS
BETWEEN THEM A GATEWAY OF BRASS, AND THE HOWL OF THE ANGELS ... 61 OISIN 3 — 200
   WHO FELL.
THE ANGELS ARE STOOPING ... 118 CRADLE SONG — 1
THE ANGELS ARE RENDING ... 118 CRADLE SONG V 1
'MONG THE FEET OF ANGELS SEVEN ... 125 CATHLEEN PARA — 13
WITH WHITE FEET OF ANGELS SEVEN ... 125 CATHLEEN PARA V 13
AND HER GUIDES ARE ANGELS SEVEN, ... 125 CATHLEEN PARA V 15
SENT ONE OF HIS GREAT ANGELS DOWN ... 134 FR GILLIGAN — 43
FOR THE INTERCOURSE OF ANGELS IS A LIGHT ... 555 RIBH AT TOMB — 15

ANGER
THE SPACIOUS LOVES, THE ANGER WITHOUT SLEEP ... 42 OISIN 2 V 194
IN MOMENTARY ANGER LONG AGO; ... 258 KING NO KING — 10
ALL SHOUTED TILL THEIR ANGER GREW ... 297 THREE BEGGARS — 46
AND THEREUPON THEIR ANGER GREW, ... 297 THREE BEGGARS V 46

ANGERS
WE SANG THE LOVES AND ANGERS WITHOUT SLEEP, ... 42 OISIN 2 — 194
ANGERS THAT ARE LIKE NOISY CLOUDS HAVE SET OUR HEARTS ... 207 HANRAHANS SONG — 8
   ABEAT;
VEERING, FLEETING, FICKLE, OUR LOVES AND ANGERS MEET; ... 207 HANRAHANS SONG V 3
ANGERS THAT ARE LIKE BUNDLED CLOUDS HAVE SET OUR HEARTS ... 207 HANRAHANS SONG V 8
   ABEAT;

ANGRY
MY ANGRY KING-REMEMBERING SOUL ONE JOT. ... 36 OISIN 2 — 94
MY ANGRY, KING REMEMBERING SOUL ONE JOT; ... 36 OISIN 2 V 94
FOR GOD HAS HEARD, AND SPEAKS HIS ANGRY MIND; ... 42 OISIN 2 — 206
DARKEN! HEAVEN IS ANGRY. CEASE! UNTO MY MIND, ... 42 OISIN 2 V 205
AND CRIED WITH ANGRY VOICE, "IT IS NOT MEET ... 107 CUCHULAIN SEA — 20
THE TALE DROVE HIS FINE ANGRY MOOD AWAY. ... 128 DREAM OF FAERY — 36
CUMHAL THE KING, BEING ANGRY AND SAD, ... 166 BLESSED — 1
NOR PUBLIC MAN, NOR ANGRY CROWDS, ... 328 IRISH AIRMAN V 10
THEIR ANGRY TEARS, ARE GONE. ... 344 DEJECTION — 6
WITHOUT AN ANGRY THOUGHT ... 366 HER CHRIS TREE — 2
FOR AN OLD BELLOWS FULL OF ANGRY WIND? ... 405 FOR DAUGHTER — 64
ALL TURN WITH AMOROUS CRIES, OR ANGRY CRIES, ... 433 NINETEEN 19 — 123

ANIGH
"SAY AND THRICE ANIGH THY DOOR ... 730 PRIEST FAIRY — 54

ANIMAL
TROUBLED HIS ANIMAL BLOOD. ... 378 CAT AND MOON — 8
AND FASTENED TO A DYING ANIMAL ... 408 SAIL BYZANTIUM — 22
AND FASTENED TO THIS DYING ANIMAL ... 408 SAIL BYZANTIUM V 22
A DYING ANIMAL; ... 476 DEATH — 2
WHAT SHUDDERS RUN THROUGH ALL THAT ANIMAL BLOOD? ... 541 PARN FUNERAL 1 — 5
WHETHER IT BE AN ANIMAL OR A MAN. ... 542 PARN FUNERAL 1 — 31

ANIMAL'S
THE CIRCUS ANIMAL'S DESERTION ... 629 CIRCUS ANIMALS V T

ANIMALS
MY CIRCUS ANIMALS WERE ALL ON SHOW, ... 629 CIRCUS ANIMALS — 6

ANIMALS'
THE CIRCUS ANIMALS' DESERTION ... 629 CIRCUS ANIMALS — T

ANIMATE
I KNEW THAT ONE IS ANIMATE, ... 406 IN TIME OF WAR — 4
THAT ANIMATE A MOTHER'S REVERIES, ... 445 SCHOOL CHILDR — 51
SATISFY AMBITION, ANIMATE ... 500 VACILLATION — 20
SATISFY AMBITION, OR ANIMATE ... 500 VACILLATION V 20

ANKLES
AND BROKE THE CHAIN AND SET MY ANKLES FREE, ... 533 HER TRIUMPH — 9

ANNE
FOR ANNE GREGORY ... 492 ANNE GREGORY — T
ANNE GREGORY ... 492 ANNE GREGORY V T

ANNIVERSARY
HERE ON THE ANNIVERSARY OF THEIR DEATH, ... 555 RIBH AT TOMB — 19
THE ANNIVERSARY OF THEIR FIRST EMBRACE, ... 555 RIBH AT TOMB — 20

ANNOTATE
EDIT AND ANNOTATE THE LINES ... 337 SCHOLARS — 3

ANNOUNCES
THAT SONG ANNOUNCES DAWN. ... 536 PARTING — 4

ANNUS
OF MAGNUS ANNUS AT THE SPRING, ... 437 SONGS PLAY 1 — 7

ANODYNE
ANODYNE FOR HIS LOVE. ... 471 ALL SOUL NIGHT — 26

ANOINT
WHERE A SHELL THE SEAS ANOINT, ... 732 STREET DANCERS — 32
OR GROW KIND, FOR THEY ANOINT ... 776 AGAINST WITCH — 21

ANOINTING
ANOINTING, TORCH JAMMED DOWN BETWEEN THE FLAGS, ... 38 OISIN 2 V 143

ANON
MY SHEPHERD GARMENTS, AND RETURN ANON. ... 659 ISLE STAT II 1 — 29

ANSWER
THEN DID YOU ANSWER, PEARL-PALE ONE, ... 6 OISIN 1 V 53
HIS LIPS MOVED SLOWLY IN ANSWER, NO ANSWER OUT OF THEM ... 51 OISIN 3 — 66
   CAME!
HIS LIPS MOVED SLOWLY IN ANSWER, NO ANSWER OUT OF THEM ... 51 OISIN 3 — 66
   CAME!
"MY FATHER," MADE HE, SMILING, ANSWER THEN, ... 107 CUCHULAIN SEA V 25
CASTS UP A SHOW AND THE WINDS ANSWER IT ... 186 QUEEN MAEVE — 125
I'LL GIVE MY ANSWER. YOU HAVE AWAKENED HIM. ... 225 SHADOW WATER B — 79
I'LL GIVE MY ANSWER. YOU HAVE AWAKED HIM, ... 225 SHADOW WATER B V 79
BY MAGIC STRINGS, I'LL MAKE THIS ANSWER TO IT; ... 243 SHADOW WATER B — 440
MY MAGIC STRINGS, I'LL MAKE THIS ANSWER TO IT; ... 243 SHADOW WATER B V 440
BUT IF IT BE REPROACH, I ANSWER THIS; ... 244 SHADOW WATER B — 453

	PAGE	TITLE	LINE

ANSWER   (CONTINUED)
"WHAT IS THIS TROUBLE?" HE WOULD ANSWER NOTHING, . . .   281 TWO KINGS   90
BUT I HAVE FOUND AN ANSWER IN THOSE EYES . . . . . .   413 TOWER   101
I ANSWER THAT I GAVE MY SOUL . . . .   538 LAST CONFESS   3
AND THEY'LL ANSWER DEATH AND LOVE. . . . .   680 LOVE AND DEATH   16
"NOW ANSWER, IF THIS LIFE BE DEAR TO THEE, ...   713 FERENCZ RENYI V   83
SHE WILL ANSWER NOW LIKE ANY WAITING WOMAN . . . . .   757 SHADOW WATER A   193
ANSWERED
"O PLEASANT WOMAN," ANSWERED FINN, ...   5 OISIN 1   40
"O PLEASANT MAIDEN," ANSWERED FINN, ...   5 OISIN 1   V   40
YOUNG WARRIOR." "NAY," I ANSWERED: "MY HANDS BURN . . .   35 OISIN 2   V   89B
WHILE SLOWLY ANSWERED HE WHOSE HAND HELD HERS-- . . . .   80 EPHEMERA   V   11
AND WITH GLAD VOICE MAEVE ANSWERED HIM, "WHAT KING . . .   183 QUEEN MAEVE   79
AND WITH GLAD VOICE MAEVE ANSWERED "MANY A TIME . . . .   183 QUEEN MAEVE   V   79
YET ANSWERED HIM, "I AM KING EOCHAID'S WIFE . . . . .   284 TWO KINGS   173
YOUR EMPTY BED." "HOW SHOULD I LOVE," I ANSWERED, . . .   285 TWO KINGS   186
A CURLEW ANSWERED: AND SUDDENLY THEREUPON I THOUGHT . .   291 PAUDEEN   5
A CURLEW ANSWERED, AND I WAS STARTLED BY THE THOUGHT . .   291 PAUDEEN   V   5
THEREON MY PHOENIX ANSWERED IN REPROOF, ...   352 PEOPLE   22
ANSWERED: "A CRESTED COCKEREL CREW . . . .   387 SOLOMON WITCH   V   9
ANSWERED PETER: "ENTER IN, ...   697 MOSADA 2   30
AND ANSWERED UNTO HIM: . . . .   740 EARL PAUL   18
BUT HER GOODMAN ANSWERED HER, ...   772 SONG DEIRDRE 1   9
BUT HER GOOD MAN ANSWERED HER . . . .   772 SONG DEIRDRE 1 V   9
ANSWERING
AND THEN AN ANSWERING WHISPERING FLEW . . . .   15 OISIN 1   197
ERE LONG AN ANSWERING WHISPER FLEW, ...   15 OISIN 1   V 197
AND THEN AN ANSWERING WHISPER FLEW . . . .   15 OISIN 1   V 197
NOW OLD AND MOUSELIKE. FOR AN ANSWERING SIGN . . . .   36 OISIN 2   V   96
EACH OTHER ANSWERING. THEN BETWEEN EACH WING . . . .   659 ISLE STAT II 1   14
ANSWERS
ANOTHER ANSWERS, "MAYBE WE SHALL FIND . . . .   233 SHADOW WATER B   254
AND NEVER GET THE ANSWERS RIGHT. . . . .   632 MAN AND ECHO   10
A SOLDIER ANSWERS: "BY THE CAMP'S FAR END . . . . .   712 FERENCZ RENYI   67
AND THE OTHER ANSWERS, "MAYBE WE SHALL FIND . . . . .   753 SHADOW WATER A   144
ANTAEUS-LIKE
CONTACT EVERYTHING ANTAEUS-LIKE GREW STRONG. . . . .   603 GALLERY REVIS   44
CONTACT ALL THINGS ANTAEUS-LIKE GREW STRONG: . . . .   603 GALLERY REVIS   V   44
ANTELOPE
THE JOYOUS FLOCKS OF DEER AND ANTELOPE, ...   75 ANASHU VIJAYA   74
ANTELOPES
THE JOYOUS FLOCKS OF DEER AND ANTELOPES, ...   75 ANASHU VIJAYA   V   74
ANTHONY
WHEN THAT EXULTANT ANTHONY . . . .   401 DEMON BEAST   46
ANTIGONE
FROM THE "ANTIGONE" . . . .   540 FROM ANTIGONE   T
ANTINOMIES
ALL THOSE ANTINOMIES . . . .   500 VACILLATION   5
ANTIQUARIAN
FOR ANTIQUARIAN MEDITATION. AY, ...   721 WITCH VIVIEN   38
ANTIQUE
AND OVER IS THEIR ANTIQUE JOY: . . . .   64 HAPPY SHEPHERD   2
BY WOOD ANTIQUE, BY WAVE AND WASTE, ...   670 ISLE STAT II 3   109
AWAY IN THE HEART OF THE ANTIQUE WOOD: . . . .   730 PRIEST FAIRY   64
ANTI-SELF
THE MOST UNLIKE, BEING MY ANTI-SELF, ...   371 EGO DOMINUS   74
ANTLERS
WITH ANTLERS AND THE SHAGGY SKIN . . . .   17 OISIN 1   V 249
ANTONIO
AYE, FIGHT WE MUST. TELL ME, ANTONIO, MIGHT . . . .   662 ISLE STAT II 1   77
ANTONIO, IF I RETURN NO MORE, ...   663 ISLE STAT II 2   17
OF GRIEF. AND IF THEY SAY, "ANTONIO LAUGHED," . . . .   664 ISLE STAT II 2   51
ANTONIO! WE HAVE RESOLVED TO FIGHT . . . .   664 ISLE STAT II 2   55
ANVIL
ON THE ANVIL OF THE WORLD. BE STILL: THE SKIES . . . .   42 OISIN 2   204
UPON THE ANVIL OF THE WORLD. THE SKIES . . . . . .   42 OISIN 2   V 204
HOW THE HAMMERS SPRING ON THE ANVIL, ON THE SPEARHEAD'S   52 OISIN 3   83
    BURNING SPOT:
ANXIETY
HEARD ALL THE ANXIETY OF MY PASSIONATE YOUTH, ...   468 HARUN RASHID   168
HER ANXIETY . . . .   517 HER ANXIETY   T
ANXIOUS   SEE NEVER-ANXIOUS
AND IS ANXIOUS IN ITS SLEEP. . . . .   87 STOLEN CHILD   23
ANY
SLEEK AS ANY GRANARY MOUSE . . . .   2 OISIN 1   V   7M
MORE SLEEK THAN ANY GRANARY MOUSE, ...   4 OISIN 1   36
SLEEK AS ANY GRANARY MOUSE, ...   4 OISIN 1   V   37
BEEN SPOKEN OF WITH ANY MAN: . . . .   6 OISIN 1   56
BEEN SPOKEN OF WITH ANY ONE, ...   6 OISIN 1   V   56
I NE'ER LOVED ANY TILL SONG BROUGHT ME . . . .   7 OISIN 1   V   69
OR TIRED ON ANY DAWNING MORROW, ...   23 OISIN 1   V 341
AS ANY RUDDY MOTH, LOOKED DOWN ON US: . . . .   34 OISIN 2   72
. . . FOR NOWHERE IN ANY CLANN . . . .   50 OISIN 3   49
BUT IF WHEN ANY ONE DIED, ...   92 FATHER OHART   V   21
"NOT ANY GOD ALIVE NOR MORTAL DEAD, ...   106 CUCHULAIN SEA   V   10
BEFORE YOU WERE, OR ANY HEARTS TO BEAT, ...   112 ROSE OF WORLD   12
BEFORE YE WERE, OR ANY HEARTS TO BEAT, ...   112 ROSE OF WORLD   V   12
AND NO ONE ANY LEAF-CROWNED DANCER MISS . . . . . .   128 DREAM OF FAERY V   46
NOR BE I ANY LESS OF THEM, ...   137 TO IRELAND   5
AND IF ANY GAZE ON OUR RUSHING BAND, ...   141 HOSTING SIDHE   10
IN ANY ANCIENT BOOK BUT TELLS OF YOU: . . . .   186 QUEEN MAEVE   135

35

ANY   (CONTINUED)   PAGE   TITLE   LINE

        THAN ANY WHOSE UNHAPPINESS . . . .   190 BAILE AILLINN   36
        FOR ANY GENTLE THING SHE SPAKE, ...   191 BAILE AILLINN   63
        ALTHOUGH YOU ARE MORE BEAUTIFUL THAN ANY, ...   236 SHADOW WATER B   305
        BY ANY OTHER MEANS. YOU CALL IT PASSION, ...   244 SHADOW WATER B   455
        FOR NEITHER I NOR ANY LIVING MAN . . . .   250 SHADOW WATER B   588
        IF ANY MAN DREW NEAR . . . .   254 WOMAN HOMER   1
        THAT HAS NOT PASSED THROUGH ANY HUCKSTER'S LOIN, . .   269 PARDON FATHERS   8
        MORE HANDS IN HEIGHT THAN ANY STAG IN THE WORLD . . .   277 TWO KINGS   9
        SHE WOULD NOT LOOK IN ANY KNOWN MAN'S FACE . . . . .   280 TWO KINGS   73
        DEARER THAN ANY THAT THE DUMB STONE HIDES, ...   281 TWO KINGS   V   96
        "NEVER WILL I BELIEVE THERE IS ANY CHANGE . . . . . .   285 TWO KINGS   203
        FROM ANY BRAZEN THROAT, ...   291 TO A FRIEND   3
        YET NEVER HAVE I, NOW NOR ANY TIME, ...   352 PEOPLE   28
        YOU ARE MORE BEAUTIFUL THAN ANY ONE, ...   356 BROKEN DREAMS   27
        YOU WERE MORE BEAUTIFUL THAN ANY ONE, ...   356 BROKEN DREAMS V   27
        MORE PLAIN TO THE MIND'S EYE THAN ANY FACE . . . . .   368 EGO DOMINUS   21
        NOR ANY HUMAN SIGHT WITHIN IT . . . .   389 SOLOMON WITCH   41
        THAT ANY NIGHT COULD BRING . . . .   390 IMAGE PAST   32
        LIKE ANY ROCK-BRED, SEA-BORNE BIRD: . . . .   397 POLIT PRISONER   18
        MY BODILY FORM FROM ANY NATURAL THING, ...   408 SAIL BYZANTIUM   26
        BUT IS THERE ANY COMFORT TO BE FOUND? . . . .   429 NINETEEN 19   41
        I CAN EXCHANGE OPINION WITH ANY NEIGHBOURING MIND, .   450 OWEN AHERNE   9
        I HAVE AS HEALTHY FLESH AND BLOOD AS ANY RHYMER'S HAD,   450 OWEN AHERNE   10
        I DID NOT FIND IN ANY CAGE THE WOMAN AT MY SIDE. . .   450 OWEN AHERNE   19
        O ANY OLD WORDS TO A TUNE. . . . .   548 TO SAME TUNE 3   16
        OR ANY RICH, DARK NOTHING DISINTER . . . .   565 GYRES   22
        FROM ANY PASSING WRETCH: . . . .   598 STONE CROSS   12
        MARCH WIND, AND ANY OLD TUNE, ...   615 MARCH SONGS 2   25
        WITH ANY SORT OF CLOTHES, ...   627 STATES HOLIDAY   28
        AS FAIR AS ANY THAT ON IDA'S MOUNT? . . . .   650 ISLE STAT I 1   134
        IS SORROW IN HIS SONG, OR ANY CARE? . . . .   652 ISLE STAT I 2   20
        AND NEVER ANY MORE THE WIDE-EYED BANDS . . . .   674 ISLE STAT II 3   218
        WOULD HE TEACH ANY SIN? GAZE IN THE CLOUD . . . . .   692 MOSADA 1   58
        OF ANY UNBLESSED EARTHLY BIRD." . . . .   697 MOSADA 2   33
        "NOW HATH HE KITH OR KIN, OR ANY FRIEND?" . . . . . .   712 FERENCZ RENYI   66
        WHERE MOVES THERE ANY BEAUTIFUL AS I. . . . .   720 WITCH VIVIEN   1
        THAN OLD MEN'S ANY DAY, AS MERLIN FOUND. . . . . . .   721 WITCH VIVIEN   47
        ANY THAT LIVED, AND I HAVE BROUGHT MY GALLEY . . . .   756 SHADOW WATER A V 191A
        SHE WILL ANSWER NOW LIKE ANY WAITING WOMAN . . . . .   757 SHADOW WATER A   193
ANYBODY
        IF ANYBODY HALF AS FAIR . . . .   191 BAILE AILLINN   53
ANYONE
        BEEN SPOKEN OF WITH ANYONE: . . . .   6 OISIN 1   V   56
        BUT IF WHEN ANYONE DIED . . . .   92 FATHER OHART   21
        YOU ARE MORE BEAUTIFUL THAN ANYONE . . . .   356 BROKEN DREAMS V   27
ANYTHING
        IS ANYTHING BETTER, ANYTHING BETTER? . . . .   116 FAERY SONG   11
        IS ANYTHING BETTER, ANYTHING BETTER? . . . .   116 FAERY SONG   11
        AND WILL BELIEVE THAT ANYTHING . . . .   191 BAILE AILLINN   68
        "WOULD IT WERE ANYTHING BUT MERELY VOICE!" . . . . .   258 KING NO KING   1
        BECAUSE HE HAD NOT HEARD OF ANYTHING . . . .   258 KING NO KING   3
        "THEY ARE NOT CHANGED TO ANYTHING, ...   299 THREE HERMITS   25
        FOR ANYTHING YOU DID OR SAID . . . .   306 HOUR DAWN   89
        COULD MAKE ME WISH FOR ANYTHING THIS DAY, ...   338 SHEP GOATHERD   3
        AN IMAGE UP, OR ANYTHING . . . .   390 IMAGE PAST   33
        OR ANYTHING CALLED CONSCIENCE ONCE: . . . .   413 TOWER   118
        NOR IS THERE ANYTHING, ...   496 MOHINI CHATTER   7
        OR ANYTHING ELSE BUT A RHYMER . . . .   552 SONGS REWRIT 2   9
        OR ANYTHING ELSE BUT A MAN . . . .   552 SONGS REWRIT 2 V   9
        BUT WHERE IS THE BRUSH THAT COULD SHOW ANYTHING . . .   602 GALLERY REVIS   28
        'TIS BUT TO SEE IF ANYTHING WILL STIR . . . .   669 ISLE STAT II 3   75
        WERE HE ANYTHING BY HALF, ...   772 SONG DEIRDRE 1   13
ANYWHERE
        HAD CHOSEN A HUSBAND ANYWHERE . . . .   191 BAILE AILLINN   54
AODH
        AODH TO DECTORA   THREE SONGS . . . .   152 LOSS OF LOVE   V   T
        AODH PLEADS WITH THE ELEMENTAL POWERS . . . .   174 ELEMENT POWERS V   T
        AODH TO DECTORA . . . .   175 BELOVED DEAD   V   T
AOIBHIN
        DEAR CRAOIBHIN AOIBHIN, LOOK INTO OUR CASE. . . . . .   264 ABBEY THEATRE   1
AOIFE
        ROCK-NURTURED AOIFE TOOK A PIN, ...   274 GREY ROCK   88
AOLAN
        OF GOLDEN ARMED AOLAN AND THE QUEEN . . . .   766 SHADOW WATER A V   375
APART
        "BUT WE ARE APART IN THE GRASSY PLACES, ...   27 OISIN 1   408
        THE STREAM CHURNED, CHURNED, AND CHURNED---HIS LIPS APART,   31 OISIN 2   43
        . . . AND CHURNED. HIS LIPS WERE ROLLED APART, . .   31 OISIN 2   V   43
        SNATCHING THE BIRD IN SECRET: NOR KNEW I, EMBOSOMED APART,   57 OISIN 3   150
        . . . THE SOUND OF TWO STUMBLING APART. . . . .   60 OISIN 3   V   184
        A LITTLE FROM THE OTHER SHADES APART, ...   71 ANASHU VIJAYA   9
        HID UNDER QUIET BOUGHS APART, ...   78 INDIAN TO LOVE   12
        HID UNDER QUIET BOWS APART, ...   78 INDIAN TO LOVE V   12
        PENSIVELY APART, ...   89 ISLE IN WATER   4
        IS HEARD ON THE WATER, AS THEY WERE, THE PROUD AND APART,   91 OLD FISHERMAN   10
        ONE BLIND HOUND ONLY LIES APART . . . .   99 FOXHUNTER   41
        OUR ARMS ARE WAVING, OUR LIPS ARE APART: . . . . . .   140 HOSTING SIDHE   9
        "ARMS ARE A-WAVING AND LIPS APART . . . .   140 HOSTING SIDHE V   9
        OUR ARMS ARE WEAVING, OUR LIPS ARE APART: . . . . . .   140 HOSTING SIDHE V   9
        I HUNGER TO BUILD THEM ANEW AND SIT ON A GREEN KNOLL APART,   143 ROSE IN HEART   6

36

	PAGE	TITLE		LINE

APART   (CONTINUED)
  NODDING ALONE AND APART. . . . . 171 MAID QUIET   V   6
  LAND-OF-THE-TOWER, WHERE AENGUS HAS THROWN THE GATES APART, 209 UNDER THE MOON   8
  LAND OF THE TOWER, WHEN AENGUS HAS THROWN THE GATES APART, 209 UNDER THE MOON V   8
  TOWARDS NIGHTFALL UPON CERTAIN SET APART . . . . . 325 ROBERT GREGORY   29
  THINGS FALL APART! THE CENTRE CANNOT HOLD! . . . . . 402 SECOND COMING   3
  THINGS FALL APART! THE CENTRE CAN NOT HOLD. . . . . 402 SECOND COMING V   3
  NO CIVIL RANCOUR TORN THE LAND APART. . . . . . . 542 PARN FUNERAL 2   4
  AND THEN THE FAY QUEEN SOBBED APART. . . . . . . 730 PRIEST FAIRY   70
  THE GHOSTS WENT BY ME WITH THEIR LIPS APART . . . . 734 QUATRAIN APHOR   13
  AND STOOD IN MY SORROW APART. . . . . 744 GLOVE CLOAK   2
APHORISMS
  QUATRAINS AND APHORISMS. . . . . 734 QUATRAIN APHOR   T
A-PILIN'
  A-PILIN' WOOD OR PILIN' TURF. . . . . 96 MOLL MAGEE   V   45
APOLOGIA
  APOLOGIA ADDRESSED TO IRELAND IN THE COMING DAYS . . . . 137 TO IRELAND   V   T
APPALLED
  THE ROMAN EMPIRE STOOD APPALLED! . . . . 437 SONGS PLAY 1   13
  MY CONSCIENCE OR MY VANITY APPALLED. . . . . 501 VACILLATION   56
APPAREL
  SIGH, O YOU LITTLE STARS! O SIGH AND SHAKE YOUR   72 ANASHU VIJAYA   18
    BLUE APPAREL!
  SIGH, OH YE LITTLE STARS! OH, SIGH AND SHAKE YOUR BLUE   72 ANASHU VIJAYA V   18
    APPAREL!
APPARITION
  THAN 'TWERE AN APPARITION. O HEART, WE ARE OLD! . . . 334 LIVING BEAUTY   8
  I TALKED ABOUT AN APPARITION, ... 624 APPARITIONS   2
APPARITIONS
  THAT YOU HAVE TALKED WITH APPARITIONS. INDEED . . . 342 SHEP GOATHERD   82
  THE APPARITIONS . . . . 624 APPARITIONS   T
  FIFTEEN APPARITIONS HAVE I SEEN! . . . . 624 APPARITIONS   7
  FIFTEEN APPARITIONS HAVE I SEEN! . . . . 624 APPARITIONS   15
  FIFTEEN APPARITIONS HAVE I SEEN! . . . . 624 APPARITIONS   23
APPEAR
  APPEAR AND DISAPPEAR IN THE BLUE DEPTH OF THE SKY . . 318 MAGI   3
  APPEAR AND DISAPPEAR IN THE BLUE DEPTHS OF THE SKY . . 318 MAGI   V   3
  FOUL GOAT-HEAD, BRUTAL ARM APPEAR. . . . . . . 612 NEWS ORACLE   33
  UNTIL AFAR APPEAR THE GLEAMING DRAGON-SCALES! . . . 651 ISLE STAT I 1   160
APPEARED
  A GREAT BLACK RAGGED BIRD APPEARED WHEN I WAS IN THE BOAT! 593 PILGRIM   16
  A GREAT BLACK BIRD APPEARED WHEN I WAS IN THE BOAT, . . 593 PILGRIM   V   16
APPEARS
  IN BRONZE, OR THAT IN DAZZLING MARBLE APPEARS, . . . 334 LIVING BEAUTY   5
  APPEARS, BUT WHEN WE HAVE GONE IS GONE AGAIN, . . . 334 LIVING BEAUTY   6
  APPEARS, AND WHEN WE HAVE GONE IS GONE AGAIN, . . . 334 LIVING BEAUTY V   6
  YET IF NO CHANGE APPEARS . . . . 421 MY TABLE   12
APPEASING   SEE SELF-APPEASING
APPLAUD
  THE YOUNG MEN EVERY NIGHT APPLAUD THEIR GABY'S LAUGHING   353 HIS PHOENIX   9
    EYE,
  APPLAUD A MODERN THRONE! . . . . 597 MODEL LAUREATE   18
APPLAUSE
  WHAT'S NOT FOR THEIR APPLAUSE, ... 259 UNWORTH PRAISE   3
  "THIS LAND OF SAINTS," AND THEN AS THE APPLAUSE DIED OUT, 577 LOFTY THINGS   3
APPLE
  WITH AN APPLE OF GOLD IN HER TOSSING HAND! . . . . 12 OISIN 1   143
  AN APPLE OF GOLD IN HER TOSSING HAND, ... 12 OISIN 1   V   143
  WITH APPLE BLOSSOM IN HER HAIR . . . . 150 WANDER AENGUS   14
  WITH APPLE BLOSSOMS IN HER HAIR, ... 150 WANDER AENGUS V   14
  OR TWO SWEET BLOSSOMING APPLE BOUGHS . . . . . . 195 BAILE AILLINN V   153
  BUT A WILD APPLE HID THE GRASS . . . . 197 BAILE AILLINN   189
  MADE OF THE APPLE AND THE YEW, ... 197 BAILE AILLINN   196
  DELICATE IN COLOUR AS APPLE BLOSSOM. . . . . . . 199 ARROW   6
  AND OF APPLE ISLANDS WHERE THE DANAAN KIND . . . . 203 WITHER BOUGHS V   12
  HE MADE A HARP WITH DRUID APPLE WOOD . . . . . . 220 HARP OF AENGUS V   11
  A HUNGER FOR THE APPLE ON THE BOUGH . . . . . . 368 EGO DOMINUS   24
  CREW FROM A BLOSSOMING APPLE BOUGH . . . . . . 387 SOLOMON WITCH   10
  UPON A BLOSSOMING APPLE BOUGH . . . . 387 SOLOMON WITCH V   10
  CRIED FROM A BLOSSOMING APPLE BOUGH . . . . . . 387 SOLOMON WITCH V   10
  ALL THAT THE BRIGAND APPLE BROUGHT . . . . . . 388 SOLOMON WITCH   15
  WHAT JUNCTURE OF THE APPLE AND THE YEW, ... 555 RIBH AT TOMB   8
  THE TREMBLING OF THE APPLE AND THE YEW, ... 555 RIBH AT TOMB   18
  THIS HEARD I WHERE AMONG THE APPLE TREES, ... 686 LIFE   19
  OF APPLE BLOSSOM CIRCLES IN THE GLOOM, ... 700 MOSADA 3   V   42
  AN APPLE BLOSSOM CIRCLES IN THE GLOOM, ... 700 MOSADA 3   V   42
  WHERE SHADOW OF CHERRY, AND SHADOW OF APPLE TREES, . . 710 FERENCZ RENYI   23
  THIS HEARD I WHERE, AMID THE APPLE TREES, ... 735 QUATRAIN APHOR   17
  THIS HEARD I WHERE AMONG THE APPLE TREES, ... 735 QUATRAIN APHOR V   19
  THAT DRUIDS WRITE ON YEW AND APPLE WOOD, ... 748 SHADOW WATER A   29
  OF AENGUS' BIRDS GLEAM IN THEIR APPLE BOUGHS. . . . 751 SHADOW WATER A   103
  SHOOK THE PALE APPLE BLOSSOM OVER IT! . . . . . 761 SHADOW WATER A V   275
  HE MADE A HARP WITH DRUID APPLE WOOD . . . . . . 763 SHADOW WATER A   306
  UPON THIN BOARDS OF YEW AND APPLE WOOD, ... 764 SHADOW WATER A   343
  OF THE GOLDEN APPLE TREE! . . . . 771 SPINNING SONG   9
  PRAISE THE BLOSSOMING APPLE STEM! . . . . 773 SONG DEIRDRE 1 V   21
APPLE-BLOSSOM
  WITH APPLE-BLOSSOM IN HER HAIR, ... 150 WANDER AENGUS V   14
  OF APPLE-BLOSSOM CIRCLES IN THE GLOOM, ... 700 MOSADA 3   42
  SHOOK THE PALE APPLE-BLOSSOM OVER IT! . . . . . 761 SHADOW WATER A   275

37

```
                                                    PAGE      TITLE            LINE
APPLE-BOUGHS
    OR TWO SWEET BLOSSOMING APPLE-BOUGHS  . . . . . . . .  195 BAILE AILLINN      153
APPLED      SEE O'ER-APPLED
APPLES
    THE SILVER APPLES OF THE MOON,  . . . . . . . . .      150 WANDER AENGUS       23
    THE GOLDEN APPLES OF THE SUN.  . . . . . . . . .       150 WANDER AENGUS       24
    OR APPLES OF THE SUN AND MOON.  . . . . . . . .        196 BAILE AILLINN      176
    AND SLEEPY BOUGHS, AND BOUGHS WHERE APPLES MADE  . . . 219 HARP OF AENGUS       5
    LIKE CHARMED APPLES MADE OF CHRYSOPRASE,  . . . . .    231 SHADOW WATER B     214
    AND SLEEPY BOUGHS, AND BOUGHS WHERE APPLES MADE  . . . 762 SHADOW WATER A     300
    O SCENT OF THE BROKEN APPLES!  . . . . . . . . .       774 COME RIDE           14
APPLE-STEM
    PRAISE THE BLOSSOMING APPLE-STEM.  . . . . . . . .     773 SONG DEIRDRE 1      21
APPLE-WOOD
    HE MADE A HARP WITH DRUID APPLE-WOOD  . . . . . . .    220 HARP OF AENGUS      11
    HE MADE A HARP WITH DRUID APPLE-WOOD  . . . . . . .    763 SHADOW WATER A V   306
    UPON THIN BOARDS OF YEW AND APPLE-WOOD,  . . . . . .   764 SHADOW WATER A V   343
APPOINTED      SEE GOD-APPOINTED
    NO GOVERNMENT APPOINTED HIM.  . . . . . . . . . .      318 APPOINTMENT         12
APPOINTMENT
    AN APPOINTMENT  . . . . . . . . . . . . . .           317 APPOINTMENT          T
    ON A RECENT GOVERNMENT APPOINTMENT IN IRELAND  . . . . 317 APPOINTMENT     V    T
APPROACHING
    THOSE WINDS THAT CLAMOUR OF APPROACHING NIGHT.  . . .  431 NINETEEN 19         68
    HER EIGHTIETH WINTER APPROACHING!  "YESTERDAY HE THREATENED  578 LOFTY THINGS   8
        MY LIFE.
APPROPRIATE
    WITH SOME APPROPRIATE COMMENTARY ON EACH!  . . . . .   328 ROBERT GREGORY      93
    APPROPRIATE TO THAT BEATING BREAST,  . . . . . . .     386 ROBARTES DANCE      22
    TO FIND OUT SOME APPROPRIATE PAIN--  . . . . . . .     388 SOLOMON WITCH       20
    WILL FIND OUT SOME APPROPRIATE PAIN,  . . . . . . .    388 SOLOMON WITCH   V   20
APPROVE
    BUT THE WILD BEDOUIN.  THOUGH I APPROVE  . . . . . .   462 HARUN RASHID        22
APPROVED
    OR BOYISH INTELLECT APPROVED,  . . . . . . . .        328 ROBERT GREGORY      92
    THE SORT OF BEAUTY THAT I HAVE APPROVED,  . . . . .    405 FOR DAUGHTER        50
    APPROVED PATTERNS OF WOMEN OR OF MEN.  . . . . . .     602 GALLERY REVIS       31
APRIL
    SOFTER THAN SNOW-FLAKES IN APRIL AND PIERCING THE MARROW   51 OISIN 3          68
        LIKE FLAME.
    SOFTER THAN SNOWFLAKES IN APRIL, AND PIERCING THE MARROW   51 OISIN 3      V   68
        LIKE FLAME.
APRIL'S
    HE STOOD A MESSENGER.  IN APRIL'S PRIME  . . . . . .   690 MOSADA 1             6
A-QUAKE
    PEACE, PEACE, THE EARTH'S A-QUAKE.  I HEAR  . . . .    656 ISLE STAT I 3       20
AQUAMARINE
    THEIR LEGS LONG, DELICATE AND SLENDER, AQUAMARINE THEIR   426 PHANTOM HATRED   17
        EYES,
    THE CLOUD-PALE UNICORNS, THE EYES OF AQUAMARINE,  . .  427 PHANTOM HATRED      25
    THE CLOUD PALE UNICORNS, THE EYES OF AQUAMARINE.  . .  427 PHANTOM HATRED V    25
AQUILINE
    MADE AQUILINE, ARE OPEN TO THAT LIGHT.  . . . . . .    555 RIBH AT TOMB        24
ARAB
    AND KISSED HER ARAB EYES,  . . . . . . . . . .        333 SOLOMON SHEBA       18
    AND THUS DECLARED THAT ARAB LADY!  . . . . . . .       387 SOLOMON WITCH        1
    LIKE SOME POOR ARAB TRIBESMAN AND HIS TENT.  . . . .   491 COOLE BALLYLEE      40
ARABIAN
    THAT SEEMS UNNATURAL TO ARABIAN MINDS,  . . . . . .    464 HARUN RASHID        79
    MUST DRIVE THE ARABIAN HOST.  THE VOICE GREW STILL,  . 467 HARUN RASHID       145
    MADE DRIVE THE ARABIAN HOST.  THE VOICE GREW STILL,  . 467 HARUN RASHID   V   145
ARABIA'S
    OF ALL ARABIA'S LOVERS I ALONE--  . . . . . . . .     470 HARUN RASHID       190
ARABS
    BUT WANDERING ARABS.  I COMMEND THE ARABS  . . . . .   462 HARUN RASHID   V    22
    BUT WANDERING ARABS.  I COMMEND THE ARABS  . . . . .   462 HARUN RASHID   V    22
ARBITER
    THINKING OF SAINTS AND OF PETRONIUS ARBITER.  . . . .  362 HER COURTESY         8
ARCADIA
    OF GREEN ARCADIA DO NOT HIDE, I TROW,  . . . . . .     651 ISLE STAT I 1      166
ARCADIAN
    SONG OF THE LAST ARCADIAN  . . . . . . . . . .         64 HAPPY SHEPHERD V      T
    OF ALL ON WHOM ARCADIAN SUNS HAVE SHONE  . . . . .     650 ISLE STAT I 1      143
    CLEAR-BROWED ARCADIAN, THOU SHALT BE OUR KING!  . . .  679 ISLE STAT II 3     318
    CLEAR-BROWED ARCADIAN, THOU SHALT BE OUR KING!  . . .  679 ISLE STAT II 3     321
ARCADIANS
    THE ARCADIANS BRING, AND BID THE STONE BE RAISED  . .  663 ISLE STAT II 2      25
    AND ONCE A-YEAR LET THE ARCADIANS COME,  . . . . . .   663 ISLE STAT II 2      29
ARCADIA'S
    WHOM MEN HAVE NAMED ARCADIA'S SWEETEST TONGUE.  . . .  649 ISLE STAT I 1      109
ARCADY
    THE WOODS OF ARCADY ARE DEAD,  . . . . . . . . .       64 HAPPY SHEPHERD        1
    THEIR SHEEP IN ARCADY, NASCHINA, HAIL!  . . . . .      649 ISLE STAT I 1      119
    THEIR SHEEP IN ARCADY, NASCHINA, HAIL!  . . . . .      649 ISLE STAT I 1      121
    POOR RACE OF LEAFY ARCADY, YOUR LOVE  . . . . . .      650 ISLE STAT I 1      145
    O ARCADY, O ARCADY, THIS DAY  . . . . . . . .          676 ISLE STAT II 3     272
    O ARCADY, O ARCADY, THIS DAY  . . . . . . . .          676 ISLE STAT II 3     272
ARCHANGEL
    THE ARCHANGEL AXEL, VICTOR THE ANGEL  . . . . . . .    774 COME RIDE           11
ARCHANGELS
    BOW DOWN, ARCHANGELS, IN YOUR DIM ABODE!  . . . . .    112 ROSE OF WORLD       11
```

38

	PAGE	TITLE	LINE
ARCHANGELS (CONTINUED)			
THE ARCHANGELS STAND IN A ROW THERE	774	COME RIDE	9
ARCHBISHOP			
AN ABBOT OR ARCHBISHOP WITH AN UPRAISED HAND	601	GALLERY REVIS	9
ARCHED			
A WINDING STAIR, A CHAMBER ARCHED WITH STONE, ...	419	MY HOUSE	11
ARCHER			
AMONG PIGEONS AND BEES, WHILE THAT GREAT ARCHER, ...	198	SEVEN WOODS	12
YON ARCHER, HE WHO HATH THE HALCYON'S WING	679	ISLE STAT II 3	316
ARCHERY			
SLEEPING LORD OF ARCHERY, ...	658	ISLE STAT I 3	81
SLEEPING LORD OF ARCHERY.	658	ISLE STAT I 3	96
ARCHES			
AND UNDER THE ARCHES OF THE BRIDGE, AND SCREAM	403	FOR DAUGHTER	11
ARCHIMEDES'			
OR ARCHIMEDES' GUESS, ...	784	WOMANS BEAUTY	12
ARCHITECT			
CALLED ARCHITECT AND ARTIST IN, THAT THEY, ...	418	ANCEST HOUSES	18
ARDAN			
"YOU BROUGHT ME WHERE YOUR BROTHER ARDAN SAT	280	TWO KINGS	79
ARDAN, AND THOUGH I CALLED TO HIM AND TRIED	283	TWO KINGS	142
ARGIVE			
AS ARGIVE CLYTEMNESTRA SAW OUT-BURN	645	ISLE STAT I 1	12
ARGO'S			
ANOTHER ARGO'S PAINTED PROW	437	SONGS PLAY 1	11
ARGOSY			
AND MANNED AN ARGOSY AND SAILING DIED.	693	MOSADA 1	89
ARGUE			
BUT WHO IS THERE TO ARGUE THAT	395	SIXTEEN DEAD	9
ARGUED			
YOU MEAN THEY ARGUED. PUT IT SO!	385	ROBARTES DANCE	13
ARGUMENT			
AND LEFT THEM TO THEIR ARGUMENT.	296	THREE BEGGARS	28
HER NIGHTS IN ARGUMENT	392	EASTER 1916	19
IN AIMLESS ARGUMENT!	392	EASTER 1916 V	18
CAN BE CONTENT WITH ARGUMENT AND DEAL	409	TOWER	14
BUT HEAVY FRUIT. HOW SWIFT THE ARGUMENT	665	ISLE STAT II 2	66
ARISE			
AND THE STARS SHALL ARISE AND SAY IN THE MORNING, . . .	28	OISIN 1 V	423G
ARISE THE LEOPARD-COLOURED TREES!	84	MAD KING GOLL	40
AND THEN ARISE, AND RAVING SLAY US ALL.	110	CUCHULAIN SEA	79
I WILL ARISE AND GO NOW, AND GO TO INNISFREE, ...	117	ISLE INNISFREE	1
I WILL ARISE AND GO NOW, FOR ALWAYS NIGHT AND DAY . . .	117	ISLE INNISFREE	9
ARISE AND BID ME STRIKE A MATCH	476	EVA GORE-BOOTH	26
ARISE THOU AND FOLLOW!	654	ISLE STAT I 2	57
ARISE FROM THE HOLLOW, ...	654	ISLE STAT I 2	68
I SAW HER AS YOU NOW ARISE!	654	ISLE STAT I 2	73
ARISE, WORM, AND FOLLOW!	655	ISLE STAT I 2	83
THAT SHEPHERDESS! ARISE, AND BRING TO ME, ...	673	ISLE STAT II 3	191
ARISEN			
A STRANGER NEW ARISEN WAIT	696	MOSADA 2 V	22
ARISTOTLE			
SOLIDER ARISTOTLE PLAYED THE TAWS	445	SCHOOL CHILDR	43
ARM			
STRETCHED HIS LONG ARM TO WHERE, A MISTY SMOTHER, . . .	31	OISIN 2	42
YOU HAVE THE HEAVIEST ARM UNDER THE SKY."	107	CUCHULAIN SEA	24
AND STRETCHING FORTH HIS ARM AND CUP	275	GREY ROCK	118
AND CROUCHED BY THE ARM OF HIS CHAIR.	319	DOLLS	16
THERE IS NO MUSCLE IN THE ARM! AND AFTER, ...	374	PHASES OF MOON	52
TROOPER BELABOURING TROOPER, BITING AT ARM OR AT FACE, .	426	PHANTOM HATRED	12
THAT RULE BECAUSE A STRONG RIGHT ARM	597	MODEL LAUREATE	11
FOUL GOAT-HEAD, BRUTAL ARM APPEAR	612	NEWS ORACLE	33
AND ONE ARM POINTING THUS, IN MARBLE WHITE.	663	ISLE STAT II 2	28
I STOOD WITH HER CLOAK ON MY ARM	744	GLOVE CLOAK	5
ARMCHAIR			
AND TO THE ARMCHAIR GOES, ...	98	FOXHUNTER	18
ARMED SEE ONE-ARMED LONG-ARMED GOLDEN-ARMED			
. . . WHEN THERE ENTERS THE STRONGLY ARMED GUEST! . .	62	OISIN 3	210
"STILL TREADS THE WORLD AMID HIS ARMED MEN."	107	CUCHULAIN SEA V	26
ARMED MEN HAVE COME UPON US! O I AM SLAIN!	233	SHADOW WATER B	241
ARMED MEN HAVE COME UPON US! O I AM SLAIN!	233	SHADOW WATER B	243
AND TAKE HER IN THE MIDDLE OF ARMED MEN, ...	282	TWO KINGS	114
UNDER IT ARMED WISDOM STANDS, A SEPARATE WISDOM . . .	469	HARUN RASHID V	189
CAN HEAR THE ARMED MAN SPEAK.	470	HARUN RASHID	193
THAT STORMS ARE SHAKING, HEAR THE ARMED MAN SPEAK, . .	470	HARUN RASHID V	193
BEST PLEASES YOU. ARMED MEN HAVE COME UPON US. . . .	752	SHADOW WATER A	131
ARMED MEN HAVE COME UPON US. O! I AM SLAIN!	753	SHADOW WATER A	133
OF GOLDEN ARMED AOLAN AND THE QUEEN	766	SHADOW WATER A V	375
AND SUCKLE CHILDREN NOW? ARMED MEN	791	REPRISALS	20
ARMIES			
LAUGHTER AND CRIES. THE ARMIES CLASH AND SHOCK, . . .	43	OISIN 2	211
HAS SLAIN SO MIGHTY ARMIES, SO GREAT KINGS, ...	106	CUCHULAIN SEA V	10A
IN SHADOWY POOLS, WHEN ARMIES FLED!	155	FORGOT BEAUTY	5
OF UNKNOWN PERISHING ARMIES BEAT ABOUT MY EARS. . . .	161	BLACK PIG	4
WAR-LADEN GALLEYS, AND ARMIES ON WHITE ROADS, ...	757	SHADOW WATER A	203
WAR LADEN GALLEYS, AND ARMIES ON WHITE ROADS, ...	757	SHADOW WATER A V	203
ARMIES'			
OF ARMOUR--LAUGHTER AND CRIES--THE ARMIES' SHOCK. . . .	43	OISIN 2 V	211
ARMLETS			
ARMLETS OF GOLD OR SHIELDS WITH GOLDEN NAILS	749	SHADOW WATER A	43

39

ARMOUR
THE FENIAN HORSES; ARMOUR TORN ASUNDER; . . . . 43 OISIN 2 210
OF ARMOUR--LAUGHTER AND CRIES--THE ARMIES' SHOCK. . . . 43 OISIN 2 V 211
. . . MADE ARMOUR FOR CONOR THE OLD. . . . . 52 OISIN 3 V 80
. . . MADE ARMOUR FOR CONHOR OF OLD. . . . . 52 OISIN 3 V 80
. . . MADE ARMOUR FOR MIDHIR OF OLD . . . . 52 OISIN 3 V 80
WHEN THEY FROZE THE CLOTH ON MY BODY LIKE ARMOUR RIVETED 57 OISIN 3 151
FAST,
"GO BRING ME MY OLD ARMOUR . . . . 740 EARL PAUL 19
GO BRING ME MY OWN ARMOUR . . . . 740 EARL PAUL V 19
AND STOOD IN HIS DIM ARMOUR, ... 741 EARL PAUL 33
WITH SHIELD AND ARMOUR WROUGHT WITH GOLD, ... 741 EARL PAUL 37
I FOUGHT TWELVE BATTLES DRESSED IN GOLDEN ARMOUR. . . . 761 SHADOW WATER A 271
ARMOURED
ARMOURED HORSES NEIGH . . . . 512 JANE ON GOD 9
ARM'S
AT ARM'S LENGTH, THUS TILL DUMB ETERNITY . . . . 671 ISLE STAT II 3 145
ARMS   SEE MAN-AT-ARMS MEN-AT-ARMS
WITH HER TRIUMPHING ARMS AROUND ME, ... 9 OISIN 1 107
IN TRIUMPH WITH HER ARMS AROUND ME. . . . . 9 OISIN 1 V 107
MY HUMAN SORROW HER WHITE ARMS WOUND. . . . . 11 OISIN 1 138
MY HUMAN SADNESS FAY ARMS WOUND. . . . . 11 OISIN 1 V 138
AND WAVERING ARMS AND WANDERING DANCES. . . . . 19 OISIN 1 275
AND WAVING ARMS AND WANDERING DANCES. . . . . 19 OISIN 1 V 275
UNTIL THE TOSSING ARMS GREW STILL . . . . 21 OISIN 1 322
WITH ME IN HER WHITE ARMS A HUNDRED YEARS . . . . . . 30 OISIN 2 17
ONCE HELD BETWEEN MY ARMS, WITH LIVID CHOP . . . . . . 40 OISIN 2 V 178
BLIND AND NIGH DEAF, WITH WITHERED ARMS HE LIES . . . . 42 OISIN 2 V 203
AND RAISING ARMS ALL RADDLED WITH THE DYE, ... 105 CUCHULAIN SEA 7
AND STRETCHING OUT HER ARMS, RED WITH THE DYE, ... 105 CUCHULAIN SEA V 7
WHO LOVES YOU, NO WHITE ARMS TO WRAP YOU ROUND, ... 109 CUCHULAIN SEA 59
IN VAIN HER ARMS, IN VAIN HER SOFT WHITE BREAST. . . . 110 CUCHULAIN SEA 74
MY ARMS ROUND MY OWN; . . . . 118 CRADLE SONG V 10
WITH ARMS ROUND MY OWN, ... 118 CRADLE SONG V 10
OUR ARMS ARE WAVING, OUR LIPS ARE APART; . . . . . . 140 HOSTING SIDHE 9
"ARMS ARE A-WAVING AND LIPS APART . . . . 140 HOSTING SIDHE V 9
OUR ARMS ARE WEAVING, OUR LIPS ARE APART; . . . . . . 140 HOSTING SIDHE V 9
HE BORE HER AWAY IN HIS ARMS, ... 145 HOST OF AIR 33
AND HIS NECK AND HIS BREAST AND HIS ARMS . . . . 145 HOST OF AIR 35
WHEN MY ARMS WRAP YOU ROUND I PRESS . . . . 155 FORGOT BEAUTY 1
WITH SHOUTING AND THE CLANG OF UNHOOKED ARMS. . . . . . 185 QUEEN MAEVE 111
HAVE BURIED NOTHING BUT MY GOLDEN ARMS. . . . . 243 SHADOW WATER B 431
BUT WHEN HE THOUGHT TO TAKE HER IN HIS ARMS . . . . . . 280 TWO KINGS 67
THAT WHEN HE HAS FALLEN ASLEEP WITHIN MY ARMS, ... 285 TWO KINGS 191
THEREON HE SEIZED ME IN HIS ARMS, BUT I . . . . 285 TWO KINGS 201
WITHIN MY ARMS GREAT SOLOMON, ... 387 SOLOMON WITCH 4
NOW SHE HAS THROWN HER ARMS ABOVE HER HEAD; . . . . . . 390 IMAGE PAST 36
IN ONE ANOTHER'S ARMS, BIRDS IN THE TREES . . . . . . 407 SAIL BYZANTIUM 2
ROUGH MEN AT ARMS, CROSS-GARTERED TO THE KNEES . . . . 412 TOWER V 82
AND CERTAIN MEN AT ARMS THERE WERE . . . . 412 TOWER V 84
PLUNGES TOWARDS NOTHING, ARMS AND FINGERS SPREADING WIDE 426 PHANTOM HATRED 13
OR EYES THAT RAGE HAS BRIGHTENED, ARMS IT HAS MADE LEAN, 427 PHANTOM HATRED 27
OF EYES THAT RAGE HAS BRIGHTENED, ARMS IT HAS MADE LEAN. 427 PHANTOM HATRED V 27
MY ARMS ARE LIKE THE TWISTED THORN . . . . 455 HIS MEMORIES 11
AND FELL THE ONE IN T'OTHER'S ARMS . . . . 457 SUMMER SPRING 7
THAT FIRST DAWN IN HELEN'S ARMS? . . . . 522 LULLABY 6
THAT FIRST NIGHT IN HELEN'S ARMS . . . . 522 LULLABY V 6
FLINGING FROM HIS ARMS I LAUGHED . . . . 538 LAST CONFESS 7
HURRY INTO EACH OTHER'S ARMS; THESE EYES, ... 555 RIBH AT TOMB 22
AND HELD HER IN MY ARMS! . . . . 631 POLITICS 12
THE RATTLE OF THOSE ARMS MAKES US AFRAID. . . . . . . 634 CUCHULAIN COMF 15
SINGING OF ARMS AND BATTLES SOME OLD STAVE. . . . . . 650 ISLE STAT I 1 137
OH, HEART! HER DIRGE! WITH RUSHING ARMS THE WAVES . . 665 ISLE STAT II 2 70
THE SHEPHERD RAISED HIS ARMS AND SANK. . . . . 673 ISLE STAT II 3 187
THE YOUTH HAD FLUNG HIS ARMS AROUND THE ROCKS, ... 688 TWO TITANS 40
STAY, STAY, OR I WILL HOLD YOUR WHITE ARMS DOWN, . . . 694 MOSADA 1 92
AND, WHILE THEY GATHER ROUND MY BECKONING ARMS, ... 694 MOSADA 1 100
WHEN MY LOST LOVER LEFT THESE ARMS. MY GOMEZ . . . . . 701 MOSADA 3 51
I TRY TO LIFT MINE ARMS--THEY FALL AGAIN. . . . . . . 701 MOSADA 3 56
AND OUT-SPREAD ARMS. BE NOT SO PALE, DEAR LOVE. . . . 701 MOSADA 3 70
WHEN MY LOST LOVER LEFT THESE ARMS. MY VALLENCE. . . . 701 MOSADA 3 V 51
WHY DO YOU HANG SO HEAVY IN MY ARMS? . . . . 703 MOSADA 3 108
POOR LOVE AND SORROW, WITH THEIR ARMS THROWN ROUND . . . 703 MOSADA 3 119
HER ARMS AROUND HIS FEET. THE SIGNAL GOES . . . . . . 714 FERENCZ RENYI 103
A WOMAN IN MY ARMS, SHE SINKS AWAY . . . . 749 SHADOW WATER A 54
IN ONE ANOTHER'S ARMS. AENGUS HAS SEEN . . . . 763 SHADOW WATER A 321
ARMSTRONG
A BUTLER OR AN ARMSTRONG THAT WITHSTOOD . . . . 270 PARDON FATHERS 10
ARMY
LIKE AN ARMY OF OLD MEN LONGING FOR REST FROM THE MOAN 48 OISIN 3 16
OF THE SEAS.
LIKE AN ARMY OF OLD MEN LONGING FOR REST FROM THE MOAN 57 OISIN 3 144
OF THE SEAS.
LIKE AN ARMY OF OLD MEN LOUNGING FOR REST FROM THE FOAM 57 OISIN 3 V 144
OF THE SEAS.
HE MADE FOR HER AN ARMY CEASE TO BE." . . . . 106 CUCHULAIN SEA V 168
AND A GREAT ARMY BUT A SHOWY THING! . . . . 429 NINETEEN 19 18
AROSE
AROSE FROM EVERY MAID AND BOY, ... 20 OISIN 1 V 289
AS THUS OUR SONG AROSE! "YOU STARS, ... 22 OISIN 1 329
AS THUS OUR SONG AROSE! "YE STARS, ... 22 OISIN 1 V 329

AROSE (CONTINUED)
    LIKE WINGS OF KINGFISHERS! AND HE AROSE . . . .   40 OISIN 2   169
    LONG SIGHS AROSE IN OUR SPIRITS, BENEATH US BUBBLED THE   48 OISIN 3   20
        GROUND.
    A GIRL AROSE THAT HAD RED MOURNFUL LIPS . . . .   120 SORROW OF LOVE   5
    AROSE, AND ON THE INSTANT CLAMOROUS EAVES. . . . . . .   120 SORROW OF LOVE   9
    NEVER STORM AROSE SO SWIFTLY; SCARCE THE CHILDREN WERE   718 PHANTOM SHIP   4
        IN BED,
    THE STORM AROSE AND SUDDENLY FELL . . . .   784 WOMANS BEAUTY   19
AROUND
    WITH HER TRIUMPHING ARMS AROUND ME,   9 OISIN 1   107
    IN TRIUMPH WITH HER ARMS AROUND ME, ...   9 OISIN 1   V   107
    AROUND A SCEPTRE OF ALL LIGHTS, ...   18 OISIN 1   V   254
    AND GAZES AROUND HER WITH EYES OF BRIGHTNESS! . . . .   27 OISIN 1   413
    AND GAZES AROUND HER WITH EYES OF BRIGHTNESS! . . . .   28 OISIN 1   V   421
    NOW, MAN OF CROSIERS, PHANTOMS DREW AROUND . . . .   29 OISIN 2   V   1
    SPRANG FROM A GATEWAY WALLED AROUND WITH BLACK . . .   31 OISIN 2   V   29
    FEEDING WHITE MOTHS AROUND SOME EASTERN SHRINE, . . .   41 OISIN 2   V   186
    FLED FOAM UNDERNEATH US, AND AROUND US, A WANDERING AND   47 OISIN 3   V   1
        MILKY SMOKE,
    IN MIDST OF AN OLD MAN'S BOSOM: OWLS RUFFLING AND PACING   50 OISIN 3   47
        AROUND
    IN THE MIDST OF AN OLD MAN'S BOSOM; OWLS RUFFLING   50 OISIN 3   V   47
        AND PACING AROUND
    LONG FLED THE FOAM-FLAKES AROUND ME, THE WINDS FLED OUT   57 OISIN 3   149
        OF THE VAST,
    AROUND ME SHONE KEEN EYES OF MEN! . . . .   83 MAD KING GOLL   30
    AND SHONE AROUND THE EYES OF MEN! . . . .   83 MAD KING GOLL   V   30
    AND ALL AROUND THE HARP-STRING TOLD HIS PRAISE, . . .   109 CUCHULAIN SEA   44
    AND ALL AROUND THE HARPSTRING TOLD HIS PRAISE, . . .   109 CUCHULAIN SEA   V   44
    AND ALL AROUND THE HARP STRING TOLD HIS PRAISE, . . .   109 CUCHULAIN SEA   V   44
    AROUND THE FIRE AT THE CLUB, ...   392 EASTER 1916   12
    COME SWISH AROUND, MY PRETTY PUNK, ...   591 DRUNK SOBRIETY   1
    AROUND ME THE IMAGES OF THIRTY YEARS! . . . .   601 GALLERY REVIS   1
    AND FLOWERS AROUND IN CLUSTERING THOUSANDS ARE, . . .   656 ISLE STAT I 3   24
    AROUND THE FEATHERY TIP, UNTO THE SHAFT . . . . . .   657 ISLE STAT I 3   71
    WE TURNED AROUND THE PLACE ALWAY, ...   667 ISLE STAT II 3   40
    LONG CITRON COILS THAT HANG AROUND THEE, BLOWN . . .   670 ISLE STAT II 3   105
    BEHOLD, I BEND! AROUND MY BEARD IN DRIFTS . . . . .   684 SEEKER   68
    BEHOLD I BOW! AROUND MY BEARD IN DRIFTS . . . . .   684 SEEKER   V   68
    AROUND THE TWITTER OF THE LIPS OF DUST . . . . . .   685 DRAWING-ROOM   1
    THE YOUTH HAD FLUNG HIS ARMS AROUND THE ROCKS, . . .   688 TWO TITANS   40
    AND THRICE THE CORN AROUND THE SICKLES FLAMED, . . .   690 MOSADA 1   3
    AROUND MY HEAD AND DANCED AMONG THE GRASS! . . . . .   690 MOSADA 1   19
    AND IN HER SINGING WOVE AROUND HER HEAD . . . . . .   693 MOSADA 1   84
    'TIS THOU, FOR THEY'VE GROWN BLUE AROUND THE NAILS. .   700 MOSADA 3   46
    I'LL DRAW MY CLOAK AROUND ME! IT IS COLD. . . . . .   704 MOSADA 3   123
    HER ARMS AROUND HIS FEET. THE SIGNAL GOES . . . . .   714 FERENCZ RENYI   103
    "AROUND, THE TWITTER OF THE LIPS OF DUST   735 QUATRAIN APHOR   21
A-ROVING
    NO MORE A-ROVING SHALT THOU SEE . . . .   658 ISLE STAT I 3   82
ARRAIGNED
    CONSTRAINED, ARRAIGNED, BAFFLED, BENT AND UNBENT . . .   382 VISION ROBART   9
ARRANGED
    AND AFTER THAT ARRANGED IT IN A SONG . . . .   384 VISION ROBART   65
    THAT ALL'S ARRANGED IN ONE CLEAR VIEW, ...   633 MAN AND ECHO   31
ARRAYED
    AND CLOUDS ARRAYED THEIR RANK ON RANK . . . . . .   12 OISIN 1   154
    THE CLOUDS ARRAYED THEM RANK ON RANK . . . .   12 OISIN 1   V   154
ARREST
    I HERE ARREST THEE. IT WAS ALLAH'S WILL. . . . . .   694 MOSADA 1   105
    I HERE ARREST THEE. IT IS ALLAH'S WILL. . . . . .   694 MOSADA 1   V   105
ARROGANCE
    FOR ARROGANCE AND HATRED ARE THE WARES . . . . . .   406 FOR DAUGHTER   75
ARROGANT
    OR ARROGANT LOVELINESS, ...   390 IMAGE PAST   25
    AND MAY HAVE GROWN MORE ARROGANT BEING A GHOST. . . .   473 ALL SOUL NIGHT   80
    A BLOODY, ARROGANT POWER . . . .   480 BLOOD AND MOON   3
    PALLAS ATHENE IN THAT STRAIGHT BACK AND ARROGANT HEAD! .   578 LOFTY THINGS   11
ARROGANTLY
    SO ARROGANTLY PURE, A CHILD MIGHT THINK . . . . . .   491 COOLE BALLYLEE   23
ARROW
    AND BY THEM WERE ARROW AND WAR-AXE, ARROW AND SHIELD AND   49 OISIN 3   29
        BLADE!
    AND BY THEM WERE ARROW AND WAR-AXE, ARROW AND SHIELD AND   49 OISIN 3   29
        BLADE!
    WERE ARROW AND SHIELD AND WAR-AXE, ARROW AND SPEAR AND   49 OISIN 3   V   30
        BLADE!
    WERE ARROW AND SHIELD AND WAR-AXE, ARROW AND SPEAR AND   49 OISIN 3   V   30
        BLADE,
    THE ARROW   199 ARROW   T
    I THOUGHT OF YOUR BEAUTY, AND THIS ARROW, ...   199 ARROW   1
    THE BURNING BOW THAT ONCE COULD SHOOT AN ARROW . . . .   377 PHASES OF MOON   119
    A WOMAN, AND AN ARROW ON A STRING! . . . .   541 PARN FUNERAL 1   11
    I SENT AN ARROW. AND I SAW YOU MISS! . . . .   649 ISLE STAT I 1   115
    LONG ERE AN ARROW WHIZZED OR SWORD LEFT SHEATH . . . .   650 ISLE STAT I 1   135
    SOME CAST OF DIE, OR LET SOME ARROW GLANCE . . . . .   656 ISLE STAT I 3   40
    I'LL SEND MINE ARROW, NOW MY ONE RESOURCE! . . . . .   657 ISLE STAT I 3   64
    FICKLE THE GUIDING HIS ARROW SHALL FIND! . . . . .   657 ISLE STAT I 3   66
    'TIS HERE THE ARROW FELL! THE BREEZES LAUGHED . . . .   657 ISLE STAT I 3   70
    A RED HOUND RUNNING FROM A SILVER ARROW. . . . . .   747 SHADOW WATER A   6

41

```
                                                          PAGE    TITLE            LINE
ARROW   (CONTINUED)
        FOR THESE NINE YEARS?  O ARROW UPON ARROW! . . . . . .   761 SHADOW WATER A    268
        FOR THESE NINE YEARS?  O ARROW UPON ARROW! . . . . . .   761 SHADOW WATER A    268
ARROW'S
        UPON THE WIND, AND GUIDE MINE ARROW'S COURSE. . . . .    657 ISLE STAT I 3      62
        GO PILOT THE COURSE OF HIS ARROW'S DECEIT! . . . . .     657 ISLE STAT I 3      69
ARROWS
        RISES, AND SHOWERS ABROAD HIS FRAGRANT ARROWS. . . . .    72 ANASHU VIJAYA      27
        AH, YOU WILL KNOW MY LOVED ONE BY HIS HUNTER'S ARROWS     75 ANASHU VIJAYA      80
          TRULY.
        MY EYES ARE TROUBLED BY THE SILVER ARROWS! . . . . .     761 SHADOW WATER A    269
ARROWY
        HAS FLUNG ITS ARROWY SHAFT UPON THE FLOOR, . . . . .     482 BLOOD AND MOON     32
        HAD FLUNG ITS ARROWY SHAFT UPON THE FLOOR, . . . . .     482 BLOOD AND MOON V   32
ART
        BECAUSE WE HAVE MADE OUR ART OF COMMON THINGS, . . .     265 ABBEY THEATRE       5
        DELIGHT IN ART WHOSE END IS PEACE, . . . . . . . .       288 TO WEALTHY MAN     26
        AND GREAT ART BEATEN DOWN. . . . . . . . . . . .         348 FISHERMAN          24
        YET SURELY THERE ARE MEN WHO HAVE MADE THEIR ART . .     369 EGO DOMINUS        38
        THE SENTIMENTALIST HIMSELF! WHILE ART . . . . . . .      369 EGO DOMINUS        47
        HIS ART IS HAPPY, BUT WHO KNOWS HIS MIND? . . . . .      370 EGO DOMINUS        54
        CONCEIVES A CHANGELESS WORK OF ART. . . . . . . .        421 MY TABLE           14
        THAT LOVED INFERIOR ART, . . . . . . . . . . . .         422 MY TABLE           27
        HAVE LOVED INFERIOR ART, . . . . . . . . . . . .         422 MY TABLE        V  27
        IN ART OR POLITICS! . . . . . . . . . . . . .            431 NINETEEN 19        71
        UPON THE SUPREME THEME OF ART AND SONG! . . . . . .      523 LONG SILENCE        6
        AND FADED NOW IS ALL THY WONDROUS ART. . . . . . .       673 ISLE STAT II 3    194
ARTERY
        FOR ONE THROB OF THE ARTERY, . . . . . . . . . .         406 IN TIME OF WAR      1
ARTHUR
        WHAT NAME HAD THAT DEAD KING?  ARTHUR OF BRITAIN? . .     242 SHADOW WATER B    404
        NO, NO--NOT ARTHUR.  I REMEMBER NOW. . . . . . .         242 SHADOW WATER B    405
        THE MARVELLOUS STAG OF ARTHUR, . . . . . . . . .         399 BREAK OF DAY       23
        THE AUSTERE ARTHUR, RULE FROM UTHER'S CHAIR? . . . .     678 ISLE STAT II 3    296
ARTICULATE
        FOR TO ARTICULATE SWEET SOUNDS TOGETHER . . . . . .      205 ADAMS CURSE        10
        YOU HAVE LACKED ARTICULATE SPEECH . . . . . . . .        436 FOR MY SON         20
ARTICULATION
        A CLEAR ARTICULATION IN THE AIR, . . . . . . . .         320 REED WHISPERER      3
ARTIFICE
        INTO THE ARTIFICE OF ETERNITY. . . . . . . . . .         408 SAIL BYZANTIUM     24
ARTISSON
        THAT INSOLENT FIEND ROBERT ARTISSON . . . . . . .        433 NINETEEN 19       128
ARTIST       SEE FELLOW-ARTIST
        DEAR FELLOW ARTIST WHY SO FREE . . . . . . . . .         335 YOUNG BEAUTY    V   1
        WHAT PORTION IN THE WORLD CAN THE ARTIST HAVE . . .      369 EGO DOMINUS        49
        CALLED ARCHITECT AND ARTIST IN, THAT THEY, . . . .       418 ANCEST HOUSES      18
ARTIST'S
        A MIMICRY OF YOUTH.  AN ARTIST'S THOUGHT, . . . . .      463 HARUN RASHID    V  62
ARTISTS
        CERTAIN ARTISTS BRING HER DOLLS AND DRAWINGS . . . .     362 DOLLS DRAWINGS      T
AS
        SLEEK AS ANY GRANARY MOUSE . . . . . . . . .               2 OISIN 1         V  7M
        AS THOUGH HE HELD AN EARTHLY MEAD . . . . . .              2 OISIN 1         V  7X
        HER EYES WERE SOFT AS DEWDROPS HANGING . . . .            3 OISIN 1         V  7HH
        AS HER SOFT BOSOM ROSE AND FELL. . . . . . .              4 OISIN 1            30
        "WHY, AS YE RIDE, DROOPS LOW EACH HEAD?" . . . .          4 OISIN 1         V  32
        SLEEK AS ANY GRANARY MOUSE, . . . . . . . .               4 OISIN 1         V  37
        AND GLORIOUS AS ASIAN BIRDS . . . . . . . .               7 OISIN 1         V  65
        AND A HUNDRED LADIES, MERRY AS BIRDS, . . . .             9 OISIN 1            96
        AND A HUNDRED MAIDENS, MERRY AS BIRDS, . . . .            9 OISIN 1         V  96
        AND I BE WITH THEE AS THY WIFE." . . . . . .              9 OISIN 1         V  101
        OR ARE YOU PHANTOMS WHITE AS SNOW, . . . . .             10 OISIN 1            117
        OR ARE YE PHANTOMS WHITE AS SNOW, . . . . .              10 OISIN 1         V  117
        SAID NIAM, AS SHE LAID THE TIP . . . . . .               12 OISIN 1         V  150
        AS, FULL OF LOVING FANTASY, . . . . . . .                13 OISIN 1            158
        AS THOUGH THEY ALL WERE BEATING TIME, . . .              13 OISIN 1            174
        AND, AS THE SUN SANK EVER LOWER. . . . . .               13 OISIN 1         V 170A
        OR CLUNG AS CLOSE AS SWARMS OF BEES, . . . .             14 OISIN 1         V  181
        OR CLUNG AS CLOSE AS SWARMS OF BEES, . . . .             14 OISIN 1         V  181
        THEIR BROWS WERE WHITE AS FRAGRANT MILK . . .            15 OISIN 1            204
        THEIR BROWS WERE WHITE AS THE FRAGRANT MILK . .          15 OISIN 1         V  204
        AND KISSED, AS THEY WOULD NEVER CEASE, . . . .           16 OISIN 1            215
        AS WE KISSED EACH ROSE'S HEAD! . . . . . .               21 OISIN 1         V  307
        AS THUS OUR SONG AROSE! "YOU STARS, . . . .              22 OISIN 1            329
        UNCHAINABLE AS THE DIM TIDE, . . . . . .                 22 OISIN 1            338
        AS THUS OUR SONG AROSE! "YE STARS, . . . .               22 OISIN 1         V  329
        AND, AS THEY SANG, THE PAINTED BIRDS . . .               26 OISIN 1            396
        THE HARE GROWS OLD AS SHE PLAYS IN THE SUN . .           27 OISIN 1            412
        STROKED THE YOUNG WINDS AS THEY ROLLED ON THE PLAIN,     27 OISIN 1         V 415C
        "OLD GROWS THE HARE AS SHE PLAYS IN THE SUN, . .         28 OISIN 1         V  420
        AS THEY GAZE AT EACH OTHER, "OH, WHERE IS THAT GREAT ONE?" 28 OISIN 1       V 423H
        YET SANG NO MORE AS WHEN, LIKE A BROWN BEE . .           30 OISIN 2            15
        HAPPY AS CHILDREN WITH UNWITHERING LIPS, . . .           30 OISIN 2         V 14B
        UNLANGUID AS THE BIRDS, IN PROUD COMPANIONSHIPS!         30 OISIN 2         V 14C
        BUT SANG NO MORE, AS WHEN, LIKE A BROWN BEE . .          30 OISIN 2         V  15
        NO LONGER GLAD AS ON THAT MORNING, SPED . . .            30 OISIN 2         V  16
        I LAY, AS OVER SEA THE LIGHT HOOVES GLANCED . .          30 OISIN 2         V 19A
        AS THOUGH HE TOLD HIS NEVER-SLUMBERING HEART             32 OISIN 2            44
        AS THOUGH UNTO HIS NEVER SLUMBERING HEART . .            32 OISIN 2         V  44
        AS THOUGH HE TOLD HIS NEVER SLUMBERING HEART . .         32 OISIN 2         V  44
```

42

AS   (CONTINUED)

OUR TREAD, AS ROSE AND FELL THE LIQUID TONES . . . . . .   33 OISIN 2   V 68B
AS ANY RUDDY MOTH, LOOKED DOWN ON US; . . . .   34 OISIN 2   72
AS LIKE A RUDDY MOTH THEY WAVED AND FLUTTERED. . . . . .   34 OISIN 2   V 72
WITH HOPE, MINE ENEMY. AS HE BY NIGHT . . . .   34 OISIN 2   V 81
FOR HE IS STRONG AND CRAFTY AS THE SEAS . . . .   35 OISIN 2   83
AS THOUGH HIS HOUR WERE COME. WE SOUGHT THE PART . . . .   37 OISIN 2   112
AS THOUGH HIS HOUR WERE ON HIM. TO THE PART . . . . . .   37 OISIN 2   V 112
A DUSKY DEMON DRY AS A WITHERED SEDGE . . . .   39 OISIN 2   158
HIS HAND ALONG THE RUNNEL'S SIDE, AS THOUGH . . . . . .   39 OISIN 2   162
A DUSK DEMON, DRY AS A WITHERED SEDGE. . . . .   39 OISIN 2   V 158
A HUSKY DEMON, DRY AS A WITHERED SEDGE . . . .   39 OISIN 2   V 158
A DEMON'S LEISURE. EYES FIRST WHITE AS SNOW. . . . . . .   40 OISIN 2   V 168
CAME TO MY TOWER AS AGE DRAGGED AFTER AGE . . . .   45 OISIN 2   V 242
HIGH AS THE SADDLE-GIRTH, COVERING AWAY FROM OUR GLANCES   47 OISIN 3   2
   THE TIDE;
HIGH AS THE SADDLE GIRTH, COVERING AWAY FROM OUR GLANCES   47 OISIN 3   V 2
   THE TIDE;
DRIPPING AND DOUBLING LANDWARD, AS THOUGH THEY WOULD HASTEN   48 OISIN 3   15
   AWAY,
FOR, AS DRIFT FROM A SAILOR SLOW DROWNING . . . .   48 OISIN 3   22
IN THE ROOTS OF THE GRASSES, THE SORRELS, I LAID MY BODY   52 OISIN 3   73
   AS LOW;
OR MOVED AS THEY MOVED ONCE, ...   53 OISIN 3   88
DARK BALOR, AS OLD AS A FOREST, CAR-BORNE, HIS MIGHTY HEAD   53 OISIN 3   91
   SUNK
DARK BALOR, AS OLD AS A FOREST, CAR-BORNE, HIS MIGHTY HEAD   53 OISIN 3   91
   SUNK
IN A LONG IRON SLEEP, AS A FISH IN THE WATER GOES DUMB   53 OISIN 3   96
   AS A STONE.
IN A LONG IRON SLEEP, AS A FISH IN THE WATER GOES DUMB   53 OISIN 3   96
   AS A STONE.
CAME CAR-BORNE BALOR, AS OLD AS A FOREST, HIS VAST FACE   53 OISIN 3   V 91
   SUNK
CAME CAR-BORNE BALOR, AS OLD AS A FOREST, HIS VAST FACE   53 OISIN 3   V 91
   SUNK
CAME BALOR, AS OLD AS A FOREST, CAR BORNE, HIS MIGHTY HEAD   53 OISIN 3   V 91
   SUNK
CAME BALOR, AS OLD AS A FOREST, CAR BORNE, HIS MIGHTY HEAD   53 OISIN 3   V 91
   SUNK
. . . WAKING WHITE AS A SHELL . . . .   54 OISIN 3   103
O HAD YOU SEEN BEAUTIFUL NIAMH GROW WHITE AS THE WATERS   54 OISIN 3   109
   ARE WHITE,
AS SHE MURMURED, "O WANDERING OISIN, ...   55 OISIN 3   123
BRUSH LIGHTLY AS HAYMOUSE EARTH'S PEBBLES, ...   56 OISIN 3   128
BRUSH LIGHTLY AS HAY MOUSE EARTH'S PEBBLES. . . . . . .   56 OISIN 3   V 128
DRIPPING AND DOUBLING LANDWARD, AS THOUGH THEY WOULD HASTEN   57 OISIN 3   143
   AWAY,
AS MY MIND MADE THE NAMES OF THE FENIANS. . . . .   57 OISIN 3   146
I RODE AWAY ON THE SURGES, WHERE, HIGH AS THE SADDLE-BOW,   57 OISIN 3   147
I RODE AWAY ON THE SURGES, WHERE HIGH AS THE SADDLE BOW   57 OISIN 3   V 147
I RODE AWAY ON THE SURGES, WHERE, HIGH AS THE SADDLEBOW,   57 OISIN 3   V 147
IF I WERE AS I ONCE WAS, ...   58 OISIN 3   157
COMING OUT OF THE SEA AS THE DAWN COMES, A CHAUNT OF LOVE   58 OISIN 3   158
   ON MY LIPS,
. . . THE FLESH OF HIS FACE AS DRIED GRASS, ...   59 OISIN 3   173
. . . HE SAD AS A CHILD WITHOUT MILK; . . . .   59 OISIN 3   174
. . . AND THEIR YOUTH, AND THEIR EYES SOFT AS SILK. . . .   59 OISIN 3   V 176
HEARING HELL LOUD WITH A MURMUR, AS SHOUTING AND MOCKING   62 OISIN 3   208
   WE SWEEP.
MAKE CLEAN AS A BROOM CLEANS, ...   62 OISIN 3   211
. . . AND MARCH ON AS OXEN MOVE OVER YOUNG GRASS; . . . .   62 OISIN 3   211
ALL EMPTIED OF PURPLE HOURS AS A BEGGAR'S CLOAK IN THE   63 OISIN 3   219
   RAIN,
AS A HAY-COCK OUT ON THE FLOOD, OR A WOLF SUCKED UNDER   63 OISIN 3   220
   A WEIR.
AS A GRASS SEED CRUSHED BY A PEBBLE, AS A WOLF SUCKED UNDER   63 OISIN 3   V 220
   A WEIR.
AS A GRASS SEED CRUSHED BY A PEBBLE, AS A WOLF SUCKED UNDER   63 OISIN 3   V 220
   A WEIR.
AS IN THE WOODS HE WANDERS, IF HE LOVE . . . .   71 ANASHU VIJAYA V 3
TO MIGHTY BRAHMA, HE WHO MADE YOU MANY AS THE SANDS, . .   72 ANASHU VIJAYA   21
TO MIGHTY BRAHMA--HE WHO MADE YE MANY AS THE SANDS, . .   72 ANASHU VIJAYA V 21
TO MIGHTY BRAHMA, WHO HAS MADE YOU MANY AS THE SANDS. . .   72 ANASHU VIJAYA V 21
GATHERED IN SILENCE, DEWY AS HER EYES, ...   80 EPHEMERA   19
AND AH, THEY KNOW NOT, AS THEY PINE AND CEASE, ...   81 EPHEMERA   V 241
BUT SLOWLY, AS I SHOUTING SLEW . . . .   83 MAD KING GOLL   25
AS ONCE WITHIN A LITTLE TOWN . . . .   85 MAD KING GOLL V 49
TIME WAS, AS IN A LITTLE TOWN, ...   85 MAD KING GOLL   49
AND AS I SANG MY SOUL WAS FREE . . . .   86 MAD KING GOLL   65
AND SHY AS A RABBIT, ...   89 ISLE IN WATER   13
SHE BID ME TAKE LOVE EASY, AS THE LEAVES GROW ON THE TREE;   90 SALLEY GARDENS   3
SHE BID ME TAKE LIFE EASY, AS THE GRASS GROWS ON THE WEIRS;   90 SALLEY GARDENS   7
SHE BID ME TAKE LOVE EASY, AS THE LEAVES GROW ON THE TREES;   90 SALLEY GARDENS V 3
THE HERRING ARE NOT IN THE TIDES AS THEY WERE OF OLD; . .   91 OLD FISHERMAN   5
IS HEARD ON THE WATER, AS THEY WERE, THE PROUD AND APART,   91 OLD FISHERMAN   10
AND HE GAVE THEM AS DOWERS TO HIS DAUGHTERS, ...   92 FATHER OHART   7
AS HE WENT UP AND DOWN; . . . .   92 FATHER OHART   18
BECAUSE I MUTTER AS I GO; . . . .   94 MOLL MAGEE   3
BUT ALWAYS, AS I'M MOVIN' ROUND, ...   96 MOLL MAGEE   43
FIRST AS A RAVEN ON WHOSE ANCIENT WINGS . . . .   102 FERGUS DRUID   3

43

```
AS    (CONTINUED)                                         PAGE    TITLE          LINE
      WITH THONGS OF LEATHER." AS SHE SPAKE IT WAS:  . . . . 106  CUCHULAIN SEA  V   17B
      EVEN AS SPRING UPON THE ANCIENT SKIES, . . . . . . .   108  CUCHULAIN SEA      42
      I CALL, AS THEY GO BY ME ONE BY ONE, . . . . . . . .   114  ROSE OF BATTLE      8
      AND PROUD AS PRIAM MURDERED WITH HIS PEERS: . . . . .  120  SORROW OF LOVE      8
      SHINING BRIGHT AS A NEW LANCE: . . . . . . . . . . .   125  CATHLEEN PARA  V   14
      AS HE WENT BY THE SANDS OF LISADILL . . . . . . . .    127  DREAM OF FAERY V   13
      AND AS IT FALLS AWAKENS LEAFY TUNES:-- . . . . . . .   127  DREAM OF FAERY V   23
      AS IN THE OLD DAYS LONG GONE BY, . . . . . . . . . .   131  OLD PENSIONER  V   15
      HE RODE NOW AS HE NEVER RODE, . . . . . . . . . . .    133  FR GILLIGAN        29
      AS MERRY AS A BIRD." . . . . . . . . . . . . . . .     133  FR GILLIGAN        38
      AS MERRY AS A BIRD." . . . . . . . . . . . . . . .     133  FR GILLIGAN        38
      LIFT UP BEFORE US AS THEY PASS, . . . . . . . . . .    135  TWO TREES      V   23
      AND WHERE IS THERE HOPE OR DEED AS FAIR? . . . . . .   141  HOSTING SIDHE      14
      AS A CLOUD FADED INTO THE SKY. . . . . . . . . . .     145  HOST OF AIR    V   40
      AS THE TIDE WEARS THE DOVE-GREY SANDS, . . . . . . .   157  POET BELOVED        4
      AS THE TIDE HAS THE DOVE-GREY SANDS, . . . . . . . .   157  POET BELOVED   V    4
      AND AS SOON AS THE MORN HAD WHITENED, . . . . . . .    160  CAP AND BELLS  V   23
      AND AS SOON AS THE MORN HAD WHITENED, . . . . . . .    160  CAP AND BELLS  V   23
      AS THE LIGHT ON THE SEA. . . . . . . . . . . . . .     175  ELEMENT POWERS V   14
      OR AS THE CHANGING SPEARS FLUNG BY THE GOLDEN STARS .  175  ELEMENT POWERS V   15
      AS THOUGH ONE LISTENED THERE, AND HIS VOICE SANK . .   180  QUEEN MAEVE         7
      AS IF THERE WERE NO TALE BUT YOUR OWN TALE . . . . .   181  QUEEN MAEVE        32
      BUT THE HORSE-BOYS SLEPT ON, AS THOUGH SOME POWER . . 181  QUEEN MAEVE        39
      HAD COME AS IN THE OLD TIMES TO COUNSEL HER, . . . .   181  QUEEN MAEVE        42
      HAD COME, AS IN OLD TIMES, TO COUNSEL HER, . . . . .   181  QUEEN MAEVE    V   42
      AS IN THE OLD DAYS WHEN THEY WOULD COME AND GO . . .   183  QUEEN MAEVE        81
      AND WITH A GROAN, AS IF THE MORTAL BREATH . . . . .    185  QUEEN MAEVE       103
      AS MIDDLE NIGHT GREAT CATS WITH SILVER CLAWS, . . . . 185  QUEEN MAEVE       115
      IMAGINED, AS THEY STRUCK THE WAY . . . . . . . . .     189  BAILE AILLINN      20
      IF ANYBODY HALF AS FAIR . . . . . . . . . . . . .     191  BAILE AILLINN      53
      AS THOUGH THEIR MUSIC WERE ENOUGH . . . . . . . . .    193  BAILE AILLINN     108
      AS WHEN NEWLY GROWN TO BE A WOMAN, . . . . . . . .     199  ARROW               4
      DELICATE IN COLOUR AS APPLE BLOSSOM. . . . . . . .     199  ARROW               6
      COUPLED WITH GOLDEN CHAINS, AND SING AS THEY FLY. . . 204  WITHER BOUGHS      18
      A MOON, WORN AS IF IT HAD BEEN A SHELL . . . . . .     206  ADAMS CURSE        31
      WASHED BY TIME'S WATERS AS THEY ROSE AND FELL . . .    206  ADAMS CURSE        32
      AS WEARY-HEARTED AS THAT HOLLOW MOON. . . . . . . .    206  ADAMS CURSE        38
      AS WEARY-HEARTED AS THAT HOLLOW MOON. . . . . . . .    206  ADAMS CURSE        38
      A MOON--MOON WORN AS IF IT HAD BEEN A SHELL . . . .    206  ADAMS CURSE    V   31
      AS WEARY HEARTED AS THAT HOLLOW MOON. . . . . . . .    206  ADAMS CURSE    V   38
      AS WEARY HEARTED AS THAT HOLLOW MOON. . . . . . . .    206  ADAMS CURSE    V   38
      BUT PURE AS A TALL CANDLE BEFORE THE TRINITY . . . .   208  HANRAHANS SONG V   14
      WHERE MANY HUNDRED SQUIRRELS ARE AS HAPPY . . . . .    217  WOODS OF COOLE      5
      AS THOUGH THEY HAD BEEN HIDDEN BY GREEN BOUGHS . . .   217  WOODS OF COOLE      6
      FROM HUMAN THOUGHT, AS HARES AND MICE AND CONEYS . .   218  WOODS OF COOLE     31
      AS MEN IN THE OLD TIMES, BEFORE THE HARPS BEGAN, . .   219  WOODS OF COOLE     43
      AS MEN IN THE OLD TIMES, BEFORE THE HARP BEGAN, . .    219  WOODS OF COOLE V   43
      I SAW THEM ON THAT NIGHT AS WELL AS YOU. . . . . .     223  SHADOW WATER B     29
      I SAW THEM ON THAT NIGHT AS WELL AS YOU. . . . . .     223  SHADOW WATER B     29
      AS THAT WILD AENGUS. LONG BEFORE HER DAY . . . . .     224  SHADOW WATER B     47
      HE DOES NOT HATE SEAFARERS AS HE HATES . . . . . .     224  SHADOW WATER B     53
      FOR HE CAN JUDGE THE STARS AS WELL AS FORGAEL. . .     225  SHADOW WATER B     63
      FOR HE CAN JUDGE THE STARS AS WELL AS FORGAEL. . .     225  SHADOW WATER B     63
      YOU'LL BE AS GOOD A LEADER. BE OF YOUR TROOP! . . .    225  SHADOW WATER B V   73
      BEING AS DOUBTFUL? I HAVE CALLED YOU MASTER . . . .    227  SHADOW WATER B    110
      AS THEY HAVE KNOWN IT. NOW THE SECRET'S OUT: . . .     228  SHADOW WATER B    140
      AND AS SOON FINISHED. ALL THAT EVER LOVED . . . .     229  SHADOW WATER B    151
      AS A LAMP SHADOW--NO--NO LAMP, THE SUN. . . . . .     229  SHADOW WATER B    160
      MUTTER SUCH THINGS AS THEY AWAKE FROM TRANCE. . . .    229  SHADOW WATER B    163
      THEY ARE BESETTING YOU AS THEY BESET . . . . . . .     229  SHADOW WATER B    166
      AS THOSE THAT CAN OUTLIVE THE MOON HAVE KNOWN IT, . . 230  SHADOW WATER B    193
      AS THOSE THAT CAN OUTLIVE THE MOON HAVE SHOWN IT, . . 230  SHADOW WATER B V  193
      HAD YOU LOOKED ON THEM FACE TO FACE AS I DID, . . .    231  SHADOW WATER B    198
      ONE OF THE EVER-LIVING, AS I THINK-- . . . . . . .     231  SHADOW WATER B    210
      AS NOW. DOES WANDERING IN THESE DESOLATE SEAS . . .    236  SHADOW WATER B    314
      I CAN PUT FEAR AWAY AS A QUEEN SHOULD. . . . . . .     238  SHADOW WATER B    355
      AS I AM DOING NOW. WHY DO YOU WEEP? . . . . . . .     246  SHADOW WATER B    495
      THAT I MIGHT LAY IT ON YOUR HEAD AS A CROWN. . . .     246  SHADOW WATER B    511
      FLASHES AS IF IT WERE A NET OF HERRINGS. . . . . .     248  SHADOW WATER B    536
      AS FOR THIS WOMAN, I THINK SHE IS COMING WITH ME. .    248  SHADOW WATER B    545
      LEAPS UPWARD, AS IF ALL THE STREAMS O' THE WORLD . .   249  SHADOW WATER B    560
      AS 'TWERE UPON A CLOUD. . . . . . . . . . . . . .     255  WOMAN HOMER        18
      THAT NOBLENESS MADE SIMPLE AS A FIRE. . . . . . . .    256  NO SECOND TROY     7
      WE'LL OUT, FOR THE WORLD LIVES AS LONG AGO: . . . .    257  RECONCILIATION      8
      TO HAVE LIT UPON AS CLEAN AND SWEET A TALE . . . .     258  KING NO KING        8
      WE'LL FIND SO GOOD A THING AS THAT WE HAVE LOST? . .   258  KING NO KING       13
      THAT MUST, AS IF IT HAD NOT HOLY BLOOD . . . . . .     260  FASC DIFFICULT      5
      AS THOUGH IT DRAGGED ROAD-METAL. MY CURSE ON PLAYS .   260  FASC DIFFICULT      8
      AS THOUGH IT DRAGGED ROAD-METAL. MY CURSE ON PLAYS .   260  FASC DIFFICULT V    8
      YOU SAY, AS I HAVE OFTEN GIVEN TONGUE . . . . . . .    262  TO A POET           1
      CRYING ALOUD AS THE RACECOURSE IS, . . . . . . . .     266  GALWAY RACES       14
      CRYING ALOUD AS THE RACE COURSE IS, . . . . . . . .    266  GALWAY RACES       14
      CRYING ALOUD AS THE RACE-COURSE IS, . . . . . . . .    266  GALWAY RACES   V   14
      WORLD, AS IT WERE A COAL, . . . . . . . . . . . .     267  FRIEND ILLNESS      5
      AS THOUGH TO SAY "IT IS THE SWORD ELSEWHERE," . . .    267  ALL TEMPT ME   V    8
      BEFORE THAT ROOMFUL OR AS GOOD. . . . . . . . . .     273  GREY ROCK          52
      THE HORN RESOUNDED AS THOUGH IT HAD BEEN SILVER, . .   277  TWO KINGS          16
      AS THOUGH A STAG AND UNICORN WERE MET . . . . . . .    277  TWO KINGS          19
      AND CAME INTO A WOOD AS THE SUN SET . . . . . . . .    277  TWO KINGS      V    3
      AND RAN AT HIM, AND PASSED, AND AS IT PASSED . . . .   277  TWO KINGS      V  12A
```

44

		PAGE	TITLE	LINE

AS   (CONTINUED)

AND THEN, AS TERROR-STRICKEN AS A CHILD . . . . 279 TWO KINGS V 45A
AND THEN, AS TERROR-STRICKEN AS A CHILD . . . . 279 TWO KINGS V 45A
HER BEAUTY AS THE CONSTELLATIONS POUR . . . . 279 TWO KINGS V 62B
AND AT THESE WORDS HE PALED, AS SHE HAD PALED, . . . 280 TWO KINGS 76
AS ON THE BLUE LIGHT OF A SWORD, A MAN . . . . . . 283 TWO KINGS 148
THAT COULD, AS HE HAD TOLD HER, WORK HIS CURE, . . . 283 TWO KINGS V 137
THAT I MAY CLAIM YOU AS MY WIFE AGAIN." . . . . . 284 TWO KINGS 170
THAT MADE THE BODY SEEM AS IT WERE A STRING . . . . 284 TWO KINGS 176
AND CALL THOSE EXILES AS THEY WERE . . . . 290 SEPTEMBER 1913 26
HAD GIVEN BUT AS THE REST . . . . 293 HELEN LIVED 10
"IF THAT BE TRUE AS IT SEEMS TRUE, ... 295 THREE BEGGARS 20
AND THEREON, MERRY AS A BIRD . . . . 296 THREE BEGGARS 25
I'VE STOOD AS I WERE MADE OF STONE . . . . 297 THREE BEGGARS 64
ARE DRIVEN BY WEALTH AS BEGGARS BY THE ITCH," . . . 300 BEGGAR CRIED 14
AS I CAME OVER WINDY GAP . . . . 300 RUN PARADISE 1
AND THERE THE KING IS BUT AS THE BEGGAR, ... 301 RUN PARADISE 7
AND THERE THE KING IS BUT AS THE BEGGAR, ... 301 RUN PARADISE 14
AND THERE THE KING IS BUT AS THE BEGGAR, ... 301 RUN PARADISE 21
AND THERE THE KING IS BUT AS THE BEGGAR, ... 301 RUN PARADISE 28
CALLED CRUACHAN, AND IT WAS AS MUCH . . . . 302 HOUR DAWN 4
AS THE ONE STURDY LEG COULD DO . . . . 302 HOUR DAWN 5
CURSING THE WIND. IT WAS AS MUCH . . . . 302 HOUR DAWN V 4
AS WHEN I ALSO PLAYED THE FOOL." . . . . 306 HOUR DAWN 79
AS IF IT WERE NOT WORTH THE DOING, ... 306 HOUR DAWN 84
AND SOULS AS IF THEY WERE BUT SIGHS, ... 307 HOUR DAWN 102
LOVE LOST AS SOON AS WON, ... 312 CHILD DANCING 8
LOVE LOST AS SOON AS WON, ... 312 CHILD DANCING 8
SUFFER AS YOUR MOTHER SUFFERED, ... 313 TWO YEAR LATER 9
BE AS BROKEN IN THE END. . . . . 313 TWO YEAR LATER 10
THE MOMENTS PASSED AS AT A PLAY; . . . . 313 MEMORY YOUTH 1
AND SHE SEEMED HAPPY AS A KING, ... 313 MEMORY YOUTH V 6
WE SAT AS SILENT AS A STONE, ... 314 MEMORY YOUTH 15
WE SAT AS SILENT AS A STONE, ... 314 MEMORY YOUTH 15
I SAT AS SILENT AS A STONE . . . . 314 MEMORY YOUTH V 15
I SAT AS SILENT AS A STONE . . . . 314 MEMORY YOUTH V 15
ONCE WALKED A THING THAT SEEMED, AS IT WERE, A BURNING 315 FALLEN MAJESTY V 8
  CLOUD.
THAT SEEMED AS THOUGH ICE BURNED AND WAS BUT THE MORE ICE, 316 COLD HEAVEN 2
OUT NAKED ON THE ROADS, AS THE BOOKS SAY, AND STRICKEN . . 316 COLD HEAVEN 11
BUT LIVED AS 'TWERE A KING . . . . 317 NIGHT COME 6
NOW AS AT ALL TIMES I CAN SEE IN THE MIND'S EYE, . . . 318 MAGI 1
AS THOUGH THEY'D WROUGHT IT. . . . . 320 COAT 7
WHO COMES AT NEED, ALTHOUGH NOT NOW AS ONCE . . . . 320 REED WHISPERER 2
BUT AS THE OUTRAGEOUS STARS INCLINE . . . . . . 325 ROBERT GREGORY 38
A PORTION OF MY MIND AND LIFE, AS IT WERE, ... 325 ROBERT GREGORY 42
AS HE THAT PRACTISED OR THAT UNDERSTOOD . . . . . 327 ROBERT GREGORY 75
AS THOUGH HE HAD BUT THAT ONE TRADE ALONE. . . . . 327 ROBERT GREGORY 80
AS THOUGH DRIED STRAW, AND IF WE TURN ABOUT . . . . 327 ROBERT GREGORY 83
AS 'TWERE ALL LIFE'S EPITOME. . . . . 327 ROBERT GREGORY 87
AS THOUGH I HAD FOUND IN A BOOK . . . . 329 MEN IMPROVE 6
AS THOUGH I HAD FOUND IN BOOK . . . . 329 MEN IMPROVE V 6
IF I SHOULD LIVE AS LIVE THE NEIGHBOURS," . . . . 331 ROUND TOWER 3
IF I SHOULD LIVE AS LIVES THE NEIGHBOURS' . . . . 331 ROUND TOWER V 3
AS COMMON BEAUTIES MAY, ... 336 YOUNG BEAUTY 9
CAN KNOW IT AS I KNOW, ... 336 YOUNG GIRL 4
HER LABOURING MEN, AS THOUGH HER DARLING LIVED, . . . 340 SHEP GOATHERD 38
BUT SUCH AS I HAVE SEEN UPON HER FACE . . . . . 340 SHEP GOATHERD 40
AS OTHERS WILL, WHEN FIRST THEY TAKE POSSESSION, . . 341 SHEP GOATHERD 52
BUT LEFT THE HOUSE AS IN HIS FATHER'S TIME . . . . 341 SHEP GOATHERD 53
AS THOUGH HE KNEW HIMSELF, AS IT WERE, A CUCKOO, . . 341 SHEP GOATHERD 54
AS THOUGH HE KNEW HIMSELF, AS IT WERE, A CUCKOO, . . 341 SHEP GOATHERD 54
YOU SING AS ALWAYS OF THE NATURAL LIFE, ... 342 SHEP GOATHERD 75
I WOULD BE IGNORANT AS THE DAWN . . . . 344 DAWN 1
I WOULD BE IGNORANT AS THE DAWN . . . . 344 DAWN 10
IGNORANT AND WANTON AS THE DAWN. . . . . 344 DAWN 14
I WOULD BE AS IGNORANT AS THE DAWN, ... 344 DAWN V 1
I WOULD BE AS IGNORANT AS THE DAWN, ... 344 DAWN V 1
AS WITH HER FLESH AND BONE, ... 345 ON WOMAN 6
POEM MAYBE AS COLD . . . . 348 FISHERMAN 39
AND PASSIONATE AS THE DAWN." . . . . 348 FISHERMAN 40
POEM MAY BE AS COLD . . . . 348 FISHERMAN V 39
AS A MAN DOES WHO HAS PUBLISHED A NEW BOOK, . . . 350 HER PRAISE 3
AS THOUGH SOME OTHER NAME RAN IN HIS HEAD. . . . . 351 HER PRAISE 9
AND THAT PROUD LOOK AS THOUGH SHE HAD GAZED INTO . . 354 HIS PHOENIX 29
  THE BURNING SUN,
AS IF THE HAIR STOOD UP ON MY HEAD. . . . . . . 358 PRESENCES 2
AS THOUGH I'D A GUN . . . . 359 TO A SQUIRREL 4
AS NARROW NATURES WOULD . . . . 365 HER RACE 2
ALL THAT I SEEK; AND WHISPER IT AS THOUGH . . . . 371 EGO DOMINUS 76
THEY HAD KEPT A STEADY PACE AS THOUGH THEIR BEDS, . . 372 PHASES OF MOON 5
AS WITH THE CAT-O'-NINE-TAILS OF THE MIND, ... 374 PHASES OF MOON 42
BEFORE THE FULL MOON, HELPLESS AS A WORM. . . . . 374 PHASES OF MOON 49
IT WOULD BE THE WORLD'S SERVANT, AND AS IT SERVES, . 376 PHASES OF MOON 90
INSIPID AS THE DOUGH BEFORE IT IS BAKED, ... 376 PHASES OF MOON 112
FOR, WANDER AND WAIL AS HE WOULD, ... 378 CAT AND MOON 6
AS I LOOK UP TO PROVIDENCE. . . . . 380 SONGS FOOL 1 6
AS 'TWERE A SPINNING-TOP, ... 384 VISION ROBART 44
AS THOUGH I HAD BEEN UNDONE . . . . 384 VISION ROBART 55
AMID MOST LOVELY PLACES; SMITTEN AS THOUGH . . . . 389 IMAGE PAST 13
AS THOUGH SHE HAD BEEN FORCED TO LINGER . . . . . 390 IMAGE PAST 23

		PAGE	TITLE	LINE
AS	(CONTINUED)			
AS A MOTHER NAMES HER CHILD		394	EASTER 1916	62
O PLAIN AS PLAIN CAN BE		396	ROSE TREE	16
AND MURMUR IT WITH BATED BREATH, AS THOUGH		398	LEADERS CROWD	5
AND EVEN STRAFFORD SMILED AS THOUGH		400	DEMON BEAST	13
BEING DEAR AS MINE ARE DEAR.		400	DEMON BEAST	20
AND EVEN STAFFORD SMILED AS THOUGH		400	DEMON BEAST V	13
YET I AM CERTAIN AS CAN BE		401	DEMON BEAST	33
A GAZE BLANK AND PITILESS AS THE SUN,		402	SECOND COMING	15
HEARTS ARE NOT HAD AS A GIFT BUT HEARTS ARE EARNED		404	FOR DAUGHTER	34
AS IN THE GOLD MOSAIC OF A WALL,		408	SAIL BYZANTIUM	18
BUT SUCH A FORM AS GRECIAN GOLDSMITHS MAKE		408	SAIL BYZANTIUM	27
AS TO A DOG'S TAIL? NEVER HAD I MORE		409	TOWER	4
AS UPON A DOG'S TAIL. NEVER HAD I MORE		409	TOWER V	4
AS I WOULD QUESTION ALL, COME ALL WHO CAN?		412	TOWER	89
AS I DO NOW AGAINST OLD AGE?		413	TOWER	100
AS AT THE LOOPHOLE THERE		415	TOWER	166
AS THOUGH TO CHOOSE WHATEVER SHAPE IT WILLS		417	ANCEST HOUSES	6
AS IF SOME MARVELLOUS EMPTY SEA-SHELL FLUNG		417	ANCEST HOUSES	13
AS VIGOROUS OF MIND, AND YET IT SEEMS		422	MY DESCENDANTS	4
AS THOUGH TO DIE BY GUNSHOT WERE		424	ROAD AT DOOR	4
SUFFICE THE AGEING MAN AS ONCE THE GROWING BOY,		427	PHANTOM HATRED	40
MELT DOWN, AS IT WERE WAX IN THE SUN'S RAYS;		428	NINETEEN 19	12
THE NIGHT CAN SWEAT WITH TERROR AS BEFORE		429	NINETEEN 19	29
AS THOUGH GOD'S DEATH WERE BUT A PLAY.		437	SONGS PLAY 1	8
SHE STANDS BEFORE ME AS A LIVING CHILD.		444	SCHOOL CHILDR	24
HOLLOW OF CHEEK AS THOUGH IT DRANK THE WIND		444	SCHOOL CHILDR	27
AS RECOLLECTION OR THE DRUG DECIDE,		444	SCHOOL CHILDR	36
BUT THOSE THE CANDLES LIGHT ARE NOT AS THOSE		445	SCHOOL CHILDR	50
IT IS AS THOUGH YOU PRAISED ANOTHER, OR EVEN		448	HERO GIRL FOOL	3
IT IS AS THOUGH YOU PRAISE ANOTHER, OR EVEN		448	HERO GIRL FOOL V	3
I HAVE AS HEALTHY FLESH AND BLOOD AS ANY RHYMER'S HAD,		450	OWEN AHERNE	10
I HAVE AS HEALTHY FLESH AND BLOOD AS ANY RHYMER'S HAD,		450	OWEN AHERNE	10
AS THOUGH MY SORROW WERE A SCENE		452	HUMAN DIGNITY	5
REJOICE AS LOVER SHOULD.		453	DEATH OF HARE	4
BUT FOUND IT DRY AS BONE,		454	EMPTY CUP	8
AND BARREN AS A BREAKING WAVE		456	FRIENDS YOUTH	11
AS THAT OLD WANDERING BEGGAR AND THESE GOD-HATED CHILDREN KNOW.		459	FROM OEDIPUS	6
BUT BRILLIANT AS THE NIGHT'S EMBROIDERY.		461	HARUN RASHID	7
MUST KEEP THAT PERFECT, AS THEY KEEP HER SONG,		461	HARUN RASHID	18
AS AIR UNDER A WING, CAN GIVE BIRDS' WIT.		462	HARUN RASHID	28
AS AIR UNDER A WING, CAN GIVE BIRD'S WIT.		462	HARUN RASHID V	28
"BUT SUCH AS YOU AND I DO NOT SEEM OLD		463	HARUN RASHID	55
AS IF THAT WRITING OR THE FIGURED PAGE		466	HARUN RASHID	126
SHE MOVED HER LIMBS CONFUSEDLY AS THOUGH		466	HARUN RASHID V	125A
AS THOUGH THE WRITTEN OR THE PICTURED PAGE		466	HARUN RASHID V	126
AS MUMMIES IN THE MUMMY-CLOTH ARE WOUND;		471	ALL SOUL NIGHT	14
AS MUMMIES IN THE MUMMY CLOTH ARE WOUND;		471	ALL SOUL NIGHT V	14
AS MUMMIES IN THE MUMMY-CLOTH ARE WOUND.		474	ALL SOUL NIGHT	100
AS MUMMIES IN THE MUMMY CLOTH ARE WOUND.		474	ALL SOUL NIGHT V	100
IS SATO'S ANCIENT BLADE, STILL AS IT WAS,		477	SELF AND SOUL	10
IS SATO'S ANCIENT SWORD, STILL AS IT WAS,		477	SELF AND SOUL V	10
AND CLAIM AS BY A SOLDIER'S RIGHT		478	SELF AND SOUL	31
WHEN SUCH AS I CAST OUT REMORSE		479	SELF AND SOUL	68
SOFT AS THE RUSTLE OF A REED FROM CLOYNE		487	SEVEN SAGES	22
MIMICKING WHAT THEY HEARD, AS CHILDREN MIMIC;		487	SEVEN SAGES	25
NOT SUCH AS ARE IN NEWTON'S METAPHOR,		494	AT ALGECIRAS	11
UNTIL THE MORNING BREAK AS ON A DARK BREAST.		494	AT ALGECIRAS V	6
OR, AS GREAT SAGES SAY,		496	MOHINI CHATTER	27
THAT ARE NOT SUITED FOR SUCH MEN AS COME		501	VACILLATION	33
NOR SO MUCH AS PARISH PRIEST,		508	JANE BISHOP	11
NONE SO OLD AS HE AND I!		508	JANE BISHOP V	6
AS THOUGH TO STRANGLE HER, NO SCREAM		514	JANE GROWN OLD	4
SUCH A DANCE AS THERE WAS DANCED--		515	JANE GROWN OLD	20
SHE WOULD AS BRAVELY SHOW		516	MANS SONG	9
RISE AS KINDRED SHOULD.		518	LOVES LONENESS	2
I DREAMED AS IN MY BED I LAY,		519	HER DREAM	1
AS DID THAT WILD TRISTRAM KNOW		522	LULLABY	8
SUCH A SLEEP AND SOUND AS FELL		522	LULLABY	13
BELOVED SUCH A SLEEP AS FELL		522	LULLABY V	13
MAD AS THE MIST AND SNOW		523	MAD AS MIST	T
MAD AS THE MIST AND SNOW.		523	MAD AS MIST	6
MAD AS THE MIST AND SNOW?		524	MAD AS MIST	12
MAD AS THE MIST AND SNOW.		524	MAD AS MIST	18
IN AS FOUL A RAG!		525	DANCING DAYS	6
CURSE AS YOU MAY I SING IT THROUGH;		525	DANCING DAYS	9
COLD AS THE MARCH WIND HIS EYES.		531	FATHER CHILD	8
AS THOUGH ON MY BELOVED,		532	BEFORE WORLD	10
NOR KNEW, DRUNKEN WITH SINGING AS WITH WINE,		537	HER VISION	30
BEAST GAVE BEAST AS MUCH.		538	LAST CONFESS	12
THAT SUCH AS I HAD SUCH A MAN		539	MEETING	9
BUT SUCH AS HE FOR SUCH AS ME--		539	MEETING	15
BUT SUCH AS HE FOR SUCH AS ME--		539	MEETING	15
AS MAN, AS BEAST, AS AN EPHEMERAL FLY BEGETS, GODHEAD BEGETS GODHEAD,		556	RIBH PATRICK	5
AS MAN, AS BEAST, AS AN EPHEMERAL FLY BEGETS, GODHEAD BEGETS GODHEAD,		556	RIBH PATRICK	5
AS MAN, AS BEAST, AS AN EPHEMERAL FLY BEGETS, GODHEAD BEGETS GODHEAD,		556	RIBH PATRICK	5

46

AS   (CONTINUED)
AND COULD BEGET OR BEAR THEMSELVES COULD THEY BUT LOVE   556 RIBH PATRICK   12
   AS HE.
AS THE MOON SIDLES UP . . . .   559 HE AND SHE   1
AS TRIPS THE SCARED MOON . . . .   559 HE AND SHE   3
SHE SINGS AS THE MOON SINGS! . . . .   559 HE AND SHE   7
AS TRIPS THE SACRED MOON . . . .   559 HE AND SHE   V   3
DRINKING JOY AS IT WERE MILK UPON HIS BREAST. . . . .   559 MAGIC DRUM   3
WHO HANDLED MARBLE AS IF IT WERE BRONZE, ...   566 LAPIS LAZULI   30
HE SHALL LOVE MY SOUL AS THOUGH . . . .   572 LADYS 2ND SONG   8
WEAK AS A WORM. . . . .   574 MAIDS 1ST SONG   10
DULL AS A WORM, ...   575 MAIDS 2ND SONG   2
LIMP AS A WORM, ...   575 MAIDS 2ND SONG   4
BLIND AS A WORM. . . . .   575 MAIDS 2ND SONG   6
"THIS LAND OF SAINTS," AND THEN AS THE APPLAUSE DIED OUT,   577 LOFTY THINGS   3
AS THOUGH THAT HAND COULD REACH TO WHERE THEY STAND, . .   579 DOR WELLESLEY   2
AS THOUGH TO DRAW THEM CLOSER YET. RAMMED FULL . . . .   579 DOR WELLESLEY   5
AS THE FOX IN THE OLD FABLE DESTROYED THE SPARTAN BOY'S,   580 CURSE CROMWELL   18
OR SUCKED SUCH MILK AS HE. . . . .   584 GHOST ROG CASE   26
I KNOW AS FEW CAN KNOW. . . . .   589 OLD WICKED MAN   47
AND WHAT'S THE ODDS IF SUCH AS THESE . . . .   597 MODEL LAUREATE   5
AS THOUGH SOME BALLAD-SINGER HAD SUNG IT ALL' . . . .   602 GALLERY REVIS   24
AS THOUGH SOME BALLAD SINGER HAD SUNG IT ALL. . . . .   602 GALLERY REVIS V   24
HER LIMBS ARE DELICATE AS AN EYELID, ...   612 NEWS ORACLE   27
AS THOUGH WITH MAGNANIMITY OF LIGHT, ...   618 BRONZE HEAD   9
AS THOUGH A STERNER EYE LOOKED THROUGH HER EYE . . .   619 BRONZE HEAD   23
AS MY LONG-PLANNED HALF SOLITUDE, ...   624 APPARITIONS   10
AS MY LONG PLANNED HALF SOLITUDE, ...   624 APPARITIONS   V   10
AS THOUGH UPON A LIGHTED SCREEN, ...   626 OLD MEN BE MAD   12
AS THAT WHICH CLEANS MAN'S DIRTY SLATE. . . . . . .   633 MAN AND ECHO   24
AS THOUGH TO MEDITATE ON WOUNDS AND BLOOD. . . . .   634 CUCHULAIN COMF   6
THOUGH ALL WAS DONE IN COMMON AS BEFORE! . . . . .   635 CUCHULAIN COMF   24
THOUGH THEY BUT FEED AS THE GOATHERD FEEDS, ...   635 BLACK TOWER   2
AS A LEAF THAT IS OLD, AND WITHERED, AND COLD, . . .   643 SONG FAERIES   3
AS A LEAF THAT IS OLD, AND WITHERED, AND COLD, . . .   644 SONG FAERIES   15
COME FORTH! THE MORN IS FAIR! AS FROM THE PYRE . . .   645 ISLE STAT I 1   8
UNTO THE WANDERER'S SHIPS, OR AS DAY FILLS . . . .   645 ISLE STAT I 1   10
AS ARGIVE CLYTEMNESTRA SAW OUT-BURN . . . .   645 ISLE STAT I 1   12
AS WHEN UPON HER CLOUD-O'ER-MUFFLED STEEP . . . . .   645 ISLE STAT I 1   16
AS WITHIN A CELLAR CHILLY . . . .   647 ISLE STAT I 1   57
AS A TOKEN AND A SIGN, ...   648 ISLE STAT I 1   78
AS THE LEAVES IN AUTUMN SCATTER. . . . .   648 ISLE STAT I 1   90
WITH SINGING SWEET AS E'ER ROUND LAKE-LULLED ISLE   649 ISLE STAT I 1   106
AS FAIR AS ANY THAT ON IDA'S MOUNT . . . .   650 ISLE STAT I 1   134
AS FAIR AS ANY THAT ON IDA'S MOUNT . . . . . .   650 ISLE STAT I 1   134
AS LIES DARK WATER IN A MURMUROUS GLADE. . . . .   650 ISLE STAT I 1   138
SUCH QUESTS AS THESE, I TROW, NEED LITTLE WIT. . . .   650 ISLE STAT I 1   150
AS SOME DEAD MAIDEN'S SINGING IN A DREAM. . . . .   654 ISLE STAT I 2   59
AS I SING NOW TO THEE! . . . .   654 ISLE STAT I 2   67
AS I WANDERED UNSEEN! . . . .   654 ISLE STAT I 2   71
I SAW HER AS YOU NOW ARISE! . . . .   654 ISLE STAT I 2   73
AS I SING NOW TO THEE! . . . .   654 ISLE STAT I 2   77
AS I SING NOW TO THEE! . . . .   655 ISLE STAT I 2   81
AS, CLOTHED IN CEREMONIAL GLOOM, ...   655 ISLE STAT I 3   10
EACH SHINING CLEAR AS SOME UNBAFFLED STAR! . . . .   656 ISLE STAT I 3   25
AS I, TO CHOOSE BENEATH DAY'S DYING FLAMES! . . .   656 ISLE STAT I 3   34
AND THEY ARE ALL NOW STONE, AS I SHALL BE, ...   656 ISLE STAT I 3   35
BINDS, AS WITHIN A GIRDLE OR A RING, ...   657 ISLE STAT I 3   59
IF WRONG MY CHOICE, AS SILENT AS THOU ART. . . . .   657 ISLE STAT I 3   76
IF WRONG MY CHOICE, AS SILENT AS THOU ART. . . . .   657 ISLE STAT I 3   76
AS I MY WATCHING LEST YOU WAKE, ...   658 ISLE STAT I 3   95
I, AS A SHEPHERD DRESSED, WILL SEEK AND SEEK . . .   658 ISLE STAT II 1   1
CURVING BENEATH THE PROW! AS SOME WILD DRAKE . . .   659 ISLE STAT II 1   16
AS THE SEA'S FURROWS ON A SEA-TOST SHELL, ...   660 ISLE STAT II 1   51
AS I AM STANDING NOW--AS THOUGH I GAZED, ...   663 ISLE STAT II 2   26
AS I AM STANDING NOW--AS THOUGH I GAZED, ...   663 ISLE STAT II 2   26
WITH STREAMING HAIR AS WANDERING LIGHTS . . . . .   667 ISLE STAT II 3   19
UNTIL THIS MORN. AS ADDER'S BACK . . . .   667 ISLE STAT II 3   22
FILLED THEM AS THEY SAT TOGETHER! . . . .   667 ISLE STAT II 3   31
AS THEY GO WITH DROOPING FEATHER. . . . .   667 ISLE STAT II 3   33
IS ROLLED AS VERDANT SMOKE! O THOU WHOSE FACE . .   667 ISLE STAT II 3   35
IS WORN AS THOUGH WITH FIRE. OH, GOBLIN QUEEN, . .   667 ISLE STAT II 3   36
I'VE LED THEE HERE, AND AS A WHEEL . . . .   667 ISLE STAT II 3   39
AS ON THOSE OTHER HEARTS WERE LAID. . . . . . .   667 ISLE STAT II 3   42
WAS BANDED AS AN ADDER'S BACK, ...   667 ISLE STAT II 3 V   23
I, AS MUSIC THAT GROWS MUTE, ...   668 ISLE STAT II 3   65
AS THOUGH SHE WHOM YOU FEAR HAD CROSSED THE WIDE . .   669 ISLE STAT II 3   77
MY LIPS, FAIR YOUTH. IT SHALL BE AS YOU ASK. . . .   669 ISLE STAT II 3   80
FAIR SHEPHERD, AS WE WANDERED HITHER, ...   669 ISLE STAT II 3   83
IN SHADOWY DIMNESS. TO BE FAIR AS THEE . . . .   670 ISLE STAT II 3   106
AS QUIET AS THE CLAY-COLD DEAD. . . . .   670 ISLE STAT II 3   113
AS QUIET AS THE CLAY-COLD DEAD. . . . .   670 ISLE STAT II 3   113
HE HOOTED AS I WANDERED BY. . . . .   670 ISLE STAT II 3   121
AS BLOSSOMS, WHEN THE WINDS OF MARCH . . . . .   671 ISLE STAT II 3   127
AS ALIEN AS A CUCKOO IN A ROBIN'S NEST. . . . .   671 ISLE STAT II 3   138
AS ALIEN AS A CUCKOO IN A ROBIN'S NEST, ...   671 ISLE STAT II 3   138
AS MOTHS WITH BROKEN WINGS, AND AS WE SIT . . .   671 ISLE STAT II 3   142
AS MOTHS WITH BROKEN WINGS, AND AS WE SIT . . .   671 ISLE STAT II 3   142
ALIEN AS CUCKOO IN A ROBIN'S NEST, ...   671 ISLE STAT II 3 V   138
AS THE CANKER-WORM ON A MILK-WHITE ROSE! . . . .   673 ISLE STAT II 3   177
AND DOWN I CAME AS A FALCON SWOOPS . . . . . .   673 ISLE STAT II 3   178

		PAGE	TITLE		LINE
AS	(CONTINUED)				
	AS LIGHT OF TRIUMPH IN THY GOBLIN EYES--	674	ISLE STAT II 3		199
	AND DEAD AS ARE THE LOVERS OF OLD RIME	674	ISLE STAT II 3		204
	AS AN HURT LEOPARD FILLS WITH CEASELESS MOAN,	674	ISLE STAT II 3		208
	AND DEAD AS ARE THE LOVERS OF OLD RHYME	674	ISLE STAT II 3	V	204
	AS A HURT LEOPARD FILLS WITH CEASELESS MOAN	674	ISLE STAT II 3	V	208
	AS A LEAF THAT IS OLD, AND WITHERED, AND COLD,	676	ISLE STAT II 3		250
	AS A LEAF THAT IS OLD, AND WITHERED, AND COLD,	676	ISLE STAT II 3		262
	AS FIGURES MOVING MIRRORED IN A GLASS,	676	ISLE STAT II 3		270
	O WAKE! WAKE! WAKE! FOR SOFT AS A BEE SIPS	677	ISLE STAT II 3		276
	OLD WARRIOR, WAKE! FOR SOFT AS A BEE SIPS,	677	ISLE STAT II 3		284
	THOSE TWAIN ARE DUST. WAKE! LIGHT AS A BEE SIPS	678	ISLE STAT II 3		290
	HE IS LONG DEAD. WAKE! SOFT AS A BEE SIPS	678	ISLE STAT II 3		297
	AS HERE I CAME I SAW GOD PAN. HE PLAYED	678	ISLE STAT II 3		300
	NAY, HE IS GONE. WAKE! WAKE! AS A BEE SIPS	678	ISLE STAT II 3		305
	AS FLAMING MINSTREL-WORD UPON HIS CREST.	679	ISLE STAT II 3		317
	MY DREAMS ROUND THOUGHTS OF PLENTY, AS IN GLOOM	681	SEEKER		3
	MY DREAMS O'ER THOUGHTS OF PLENTY, AS THE RED-	681	SEEKER	V	3
	HIS BODY SHAKE? AY, QUIVERING AS YON SMOKE	683	SEEKER		36
	AMONG THE ROUGHS, BLUE AS THE HALCYON'S WING,	683	SEEKER		38
	TO MAKE US GLAD WITH WONDER AS WE SAT	683	SEEKER		41
	AS WORDS OF THINE THROUGH FOURSCORE YEARS HAVE FILLED	683	SEEKER		46
	ABODE, AS BANDED ADDERS IN MY BREAST.	683	SEEKER		50
	WITHIN THE WOODWAYS, BLUE AS THE HALCYON'S WING,	683	SEEKER	V	38
	I GO AS SOFT AS FOLLY! I AM FATE."	686	LIFE		18
	I GO AS SOFT AS FOLLY! I AM FATE."	686	LIFE		18
	A SIBYL, WITH FIERCE FACE AS OF A HOUND	687	TWO TITANS		9
	HER SPIRIT. AS SHE MOVES, THE FOAM-GLOBES BURST	687	TWO TITANS		14
	AS ROUND HER, SLOW ON FEET THAT HAVE NO BLOOD,	687	TWO TITANS		18
	NOT AS HE SHAKES THE FOREST! BUT A CRY	689	NETTLESHIP		8
	AS SLOWLY AUTUMN CLIMBED THE GOLDEN THRONE	690	MOSADA 1	V	1A
	WITH DEW, AS THOUGH 'TWERE SEALING THEM FOR DEATH.	691	MOSADA 1		22
	DRAW STAR TO STAR, AS ON THAT EVE HE PASSED	691	MOSADA 1		29
	AS WITH AN AUREOLE. MY SUIT TO YOU--	697	MOSADA 2		38
	AS QUIET AS THE LITTLE RIVULETS	698	MOSADA 2		57
	AS QUIET AS THE LITTLE RIVULETS	698	MOSADA 2		57
	SOFT AS THE WHISPERING OF A LONG-LOST FOOTSTEP	699	MOSADA 3		5
	WILL BE THE FAINT FAR THUNDER-SOUND, AS THOUGH	699	MOSADA 3		10
	I HEAR THE MURMUR AS THEY RAISE THE BEAMS	699	MOSADA 3		17
	SOFT AS A LONG DEAD FOOTSTEP WHISPERING THROUGH	699	MOSADA 3	V	5
	SOFT AS THE WHISPERING OF A LOST FOOTSTEP	699	MOSADA 3	V	5
	WILL MOVE THE FAINT FAR THUNDER-SOUND, AS THOUGH	699	MOSADA 3	V	10
	EACH OTHER'S NECKS, AND WHISPERING AS THEY GO,	703	MOSADA 3		120
	TREMBLES AS A BELL OF GLASS.	705	DAWN-SONG		10
	STRAYING AS THE HERON STRAYETH,	706	DAWN-SONG		27
	AS THE MOORFOWL AND THE HARE,	706	DAWN-SONG		28
	WITH BERRIES. PLACID AS A HOMEWARD BEE,	710	FERENCZ RENYI		29
	AS THOUGH THEY'D VOWED TO MEASURE ALL ITS WAYS.	711	FERENCZ RENYI		48
	SO LITTLE. AS THE MONTHS PASSED BY WE GREW	713	FERENCZ RENYI		93
	AH! IT DWELT WITHIN THE TWILIGHT AS THE WORM WITHIN THE NUT.	718	PHANTOM SHIP		6
	SLOW THE CHAPEL BELL IS TOLLING AS THOUGH THE DEAD PASSED BY.	718	PHANTOM SHIP		16
	WHERE MOVES THERE ANY BEAUTIFUL AS I,	720	WITCH VIVIEN		1
	THAN OLD MEN'S ANY DAY, AS MERLIN FOUND.	721	WITCH VIVIEN		47
	AND AS A SLAVE BEEN WAKEFUL IN THE HALLS	724	KANVA ON SELF		5
	FOR AS THINGS WERE SO SHALL THINGS EVER BE,	724	KANVA ON SELF		20
	AND OUR SLAVES BE AS OF OLD.	727	LOVERS QUARREL		56
	AS THE SUMMER VOICE OF THE DAYTIME CEASED,	728	PRIEST FAIRY		4
	AND AS THE TIME TO DARKNESS PLODDED	728	PRIEST FAIRY		11
	HE THOUGHT WISE THINGS AS HIS GREY HEAD NODDED.	728	PRIEST FAIRY		12
	THREE SPANS HIGH AS HE ROSE TO HIS FEET,	729	PRIEST FAIRY		25
	AND HIS HAIR WAS AS YELLOW AS WAVING WHEAT.	729	PRIEST FAIRY		26
	AND HIS HAIR WAS AS YELLOW AS WAVING WHEAT.	729	PRIEST FAIRY		26
	AND HIS HAIR WAS AS DARK AS A PLOVER'S EYE,	729	PRIEST FAIRY		46
	AND HIS HAIR WAS AS DARK AS A PLOVER'S EYE.	729	PRIEST FAIRY		46
	AS A WREATH OF SMOKE IN WIND-BLOWN FLIGHT	730	PRIEST FAIRY		61
	AS THOUGH HIS DAYS WERE FULL OF RUTH.	731	PRIEST FAIRY		76
	"IF I WERE FREE TO DO AS LITTLE	731	PRIEST FAIRY		77
	AS DANCE UPON THE SPEAR-GRASS BRITTLE,	731	PRIEST FAIRY		78
	AS THERE FLOATS FROM FIELDS AFAR	732	STREET DANCERS		20
	FROM DEATH'S LATE LANGUOR AS THESE LINES I READ	734	QUATRAIN APHOR		14
	I GO AS SOFT AS FOLLY! I AM FATE."	735	QUATRAIN APHOR		20
	I GO AS SOFT AS FOLLY! I AM FATE."	735	QUATRAIN APHOR		20
	AS THOUGH THEIR SEASON HAD NO DATE,	736	SUMMER EVENING		10
	PLAYED ON HIS HARP. AND I WOULD BE AS SAD	747	SHADOW WATER A		3
	AS THOUGH THE WATERS HAD FLOWED UP BETWEEN;	749	SHADOW WATER A		55
	THEY ARE CHANGED AS GREY BIRDS FLY OUT TO SEA,	750	SHADOW WATER A		82
	AND A STRING MURMURS AS THOUGH TIME WERE DEAD	752	SHADOW WATER A		124
	FOR AN IMMORTAL WOMAN, AS I THINK,	755	SHADOW WATER A		173
	HAS BLOSSOMED, AND I GROW AS OLD AS TIME.	756	SHADOW WATER A		179
	HAS BLOSSOMED, AND I GROW AS OLD AS TIME.	756	SHADOW WATER A		179
	I AWAIT YOUR WORDS AS THE BLIND GRASS AWAITS	756	SHADOW WATER A		181
	BY SUN AND MOON AND A HUNDRED GODS AS WELL,	756	SHADOW WATER A		189
	AND I AM OLD AS TIME, BECAUSE I KNOW	756	SHADOW WATER A	V	179
	I WAIT YOUR WORDS AS THE DEAD WAIT THE LIVING.	756	SHADOW WATER A	V	182
	IF YOU WOULD SERVE ME, AS YOUR WORD AND VOICE	756	SHADOW WATER A	V	183
	SO MUCH OF WEALTH AS MAY BEFIT THEIR RANK;	756	SHADOW WATER A	V	186
	BECAUSE I HAD HOPED TO COME, AS DREAMS FORETOLD,	757	SHADOW WATER A		197
	AND A STRONG GALLEY. I GIVE YOU ALL AS MUCH.	758	SHADOW WATER A		222
	I GREW AS OLD AS TIME, AND SHE GROWS YOUNG	761	SHADOW WATER A		259

48

```
                                            PAGE    TITLE             LINE
AS   (CONTINUED)
     I GREW AS OLD AS TIME, AND SHE GROWS YOUNG  . . . . .    761 SHADOW WATER A     259
     AS THE AGELESS BIRDS OF AENGUS, OR THE BIRDS  . . . . .  761 SHADOW WATER A     260
     SHE IS ALREADY FADING, AS THOUGH THE GODS  . . . . .     768 SHADOW WATER A V   422
     DELIGHTED ME AS A CHILD!  . . . . . . . . . . .          787 HUDDON DUDDON        2
     DELIGHTED ME AS A CHILD. . . . . . . . . . . .           787 HUDDON DUDDON        7
     DELIGHTED ME AS A CHILD. . . . . . . . . . . .           787 HUDDON DUDDON       12
     HE, DISGUISED AS A SAILOR BEFORE THE MAST,  . . . . .    790 DEDICATION           2
ASCENDS
     THAT IS TO SAY, ASCENDS TO HEAVEN!  . . . . . . .        478 SELF AND SOUL       38
ASCENT
     SET ALL YOUR MIND UPON THE STEEP ASCENT,  . . . . .      477 SELF AND SOUL        2
ASH
     FLICKERING WITH ASH AND HAZEL, BUT HALF SHOWED  . . .    180 QUEEN MAEVE         12
     WHERE HAZEL AND ASH AND PRIVET BLIND THE PATHS!  . .     217 WOODS OF COOLE       8
     AND THOUGH THEY'RE BUT THE COLOUR OF GREY ASH,  . . .    247 SHADOW WATER B     528
     DESTROY THE VIEW BY CUTTING DOWN AN ASH . . . . . .      372 ON GOING HOUSE      13
A-SHAKE
     I HEAR THE SHADOWY HORSES, THEIR LONG MANES A-SHAKE,  . . 154 BELOVED PEACE        1
ASHEN
     AN ASHEN HUNTING SPEAR. . . . . . . . . . . . . .         32 OISIN 2             56
ASHES
     SHEPHERDS, FAREWELL!  HE SOON WILL BE--ASHES  . . . .    682 SEEKER              34
     THE SOUL UPON THE ASHES OF THE HEART."  . . . . . .      735 QUATRAIN APHOR      16
ASH-GREY
     WHAT IS THERE BUT A TROOP OF ASH-GREY BIRDS  . . . .     247 SHADOW WATER B     517
     SAW ON THE WOOD'S EDGE GLEAM AN ASH-GREY FEATHER!. .     715 DWELT SYCAMORE       2
     FOLLOWED A RINGDOVE'S ASH-GREY GLEAM OF FEATHER. . .     715 DWELT SYCAMORE       6
     FOLLOWED THE RING-DOVE'S ASH-GREY GLEAM OF FEATHER. . .  715 DWELT SYCAMORE V     6
A-SHINING
     OR WEEDING OR PLOUGHING WITH FACES A-SHINING WITH MUCH-TOIL  58 OISIN 3          165
         WET!
     A-SHINING ON THE LITTLE CRUCIFIX  . . . . . . . .        691 MOSADA 1         V  34
ASHORE
     HE NEVER FOUND HIS REST ASHORE,  . . . . . . . .         361 ALF POLLEXFEN       21
ASH-TREES'
     AND 'MONG THE STUNTED ASH-TREES' DROOPING RINGS,  . . .  650 ISLE STAT I 1      128
ASHWOOD
     THAT THE SPEAR-SHAFT IS MADE OUT OF ASHWOOD, . . . .      52 OISIN 3             82
     THAT THE SPEARSHAFT IS MADE OUT OF ASHWOOD, . . . .       52 OISIN 3          V  82
ASH-WOOD
     AN ASH-WOOD HUNTING SPEAR. . . . . . . . . . . . .        32 OISIN 2          V  56
ASIAN
     THAT ARE LIKE COLOURED ASIAN BIRDS  . . . . . . .          7 OISIN 1             69
     AND GLORIOUS AS ASIAN BIRDS . . . . . . . . . . .          7 OISIN 1          V  65
     A STORM OF BIRDS IN THE ASIAN TREES . . . . . . .         27 OISIN 1            416
     OF ASIAN RIVERS, ROLLING ON IN LIGHT. . . . . . .        682 SEEKER              20
ASIATIC
     ALL ASIATIC VAGUE IMMENSITIES, . . . . . . . . .         610 STATUES             12
ASIDE
     AND SAID, CASTING ASIDE HIS DRAGGLED HAIR, . . . . .     105 CUCHULAIN SEA V      3
     AND NO MORE TURN ASIDE AND BROOD . . . . . . . .         125 GOES FERGUS          7
     MERE BONE AND MUSCLE THROWN ASIDE, . . . . . . .         273 GREY ROCK           51
     BUT THE OTHER PUSHED HIS HAND ASIDE, . . . . . .         304 HOUR DAWN     V     48
     IF ON THE LOST, ADMIT YOU TURNED ASIDE  . . . . . .      413 TOWER              115
     WHAT BRUSHES FLY AND MOTH ASIDE?  . . . . . . . .        625 NATIVITY             7
     MAYHAP 'TWERE BETTER THAT ASIDE I THROW . . . . .        656 ISLE STAT I 3       38
     ASIDE!--THE WILD HORNS TOLD ALMINTOR'S END,  . . . .     665 ISLE STAT II 2      68
ASK
     "I ONLY ASK WHAT WAY MY JOURNEY LIES,  . . . . . .       108 CUCHULAIN SEA       31
     SHE'LL NOT ASK A HAUGHTY DRESS!  . . . . . . . . .       124 CATHLEEN PARA        6
     THE PLAYERS ASK FOR A BLESSING ON THE PSALTERIES AND ON  212 BLESS PSALTER        T
         THEMSELVES
     THE PLAYERS ASK FOR A BLESSING ON THE PSALTERIES  . .    212 BLESS PSALTER V      T
         AND THEMSELVES
     AND ASK FOR SATISFACTION UPON THESE  . . . . . . .       235 SHADOW WATER B     281
     I ASK A FITTING PUNISHMENT FOR ALL  . . . . . . .        235 SHADOW WATER B     290
     FOR I WOULD ASK A QUESTION OF THEM ALL. . . . . .        410 TOWER               24
     ENDURE WHAT LIFE GOD GIVES AND ASK NO LONGER SPAN!  . .  459 FROM OEDIPUS         1
     YOU ASK WHAT MAKES ME SIGH, OLD FRIEND, . . . . .        524 MAD AS MIST         13
     OR ASK IF ALL BE RIGHT . . . . . . . . . . . . .         532 BEFORE WORLD         4
     WITH OPEN BOOK YOU ASK ME WHAT I DO. . . . . . . .       554 RIBH AT TOMB         2
     YOU ASK WHAT I HAVE FOUND, AND FAR AND WIDE I GO!  . .   580 CURSE CROMWELL       1
     THAT IS ALL I ASK, MY DEAR. . . . . . . . . . .          587 OLD WICKED MAN       7
     BUT NEVER ASKED FOR LOVE! SHOULD I ASK THAT, . . .       609 IN TARAS HALLS       9
     "GOD I HAVE LOVED, BUT SHOULD I ASK RETURN . . . .       609 IN TARAS HALLS      14
     THIS THING WE ASK! MUST WE TWO FIGHT?--JUDGE THOU. . .   660 ISLE STAT II 1      41
     MY LIPS, FAIR YOUTH. IT SHALL BE AS YOU ASK. . . .       669 ISLE STAT II 3      80
     GO ASK THE SPRINGING FLOWERS, . . . . . . . . . .        680 LOVE AND DEATH      13
     GO ASK THE YOUNGEST ANGEL, . . . . . . . . . . .         680 LOVE AND DEATH      29
     IF PETER WOULD BUT ASK HER LIFE--WHO KNOWS? . . . .      696 MOSADA 2            17
     "I BID HIM ASK WHAT GIFT HE WILL, . . . . . . . .        741 EARL PAUL           57
     "I ASK THAT I AND ALL MY RACE." . . . . . . . . .        742 EARL PAUL           61
     THE BRAVEST FROM THE GODS BUT ASK! . . . . . . .         788 BRAVEST ASK          1
ASKED
     AND I BUT ASKED THE MORE, TILL HE CRIED OUT, . . .       281 TWO KINGS           92
     BUT ASKED THE MORE UNTIL HE SPOKE THESE WORDS, . .       281 TWO KINGS        V 92A
     ON BEING ASKED FOR A WAR POEM . . . . . . . . . .        359 WAR POEM             T
     AND ASKED ABOUT THE PICTURES OR THE TEXT!  . . . .       466 HARUN RASHID       121
     AND ASKED ABOUT THESE PICTURES OR THOSE OTHERS! . .      466 HARUN RASHID  V    121
     I ASKED IF I SHOULD PRAY, . . . . . . . . . . .          495 MOHINI CHATTER       1
```

49

		PAGE	TITLE		LINE

ASKED (CONTINUED)
　　BUT NEVER ASKED FOR LOVE: SHOULD I ASK THAT, ... 609 IN TARAS HALLS 9
ASKS
　　THE LOVER ASKS FORGIVENESS BECAUSE OF HIS MANY MOODS . . 162 ASKS FORGIVE T
　　MICHAEL ROBARTES ASKS FORGIVENESS BECAUSE OF HIS MANY MOODS 162 ASKS FORGIVE V T
　　AND THEN ONE ASKS ANOTHER HOW HE DIED, ... 234 SHADOW WATER B 256
　　ONE ASKS FOR MOURNFUL MELODIES: . . . . 567 LAPIS LAZULI 53
　　AND THEN ONE ASKS ANOTHER HOW HE DIED, ... 753 SHADOW WATER A 146
ASLAUGA
　　AND MEAT TO THE ASLAUGA SHEE. . . . . 743 DANAAN QUICK 17
ASLEEP
　　UNTIL THE GODS AND DEMONS DROP ASLEEP, ... 35 OISIN 2 86
　　WHEN THE POOR TIRED CHILD, PASSION, FALLS ASLEEP. . . . . 80 EPHEMERA 7
　　HE PRAYED AND FELL ASLEEP: . . . . 132 FR GILLIGAN 14
　　HE KNELT, PRAYED, FELL ASLEEP: . . . . 132 FR GILLIGAN V 14
　　ASLEEP UPON A CHAIR." . . . . 134 FR GILLIGAN 48
　　WHERE ONLY BODY'S LAID ASLEEP. . . . . 138 TO IRELAND 22
　　HE HAD FALLEN ASLEEP, AND, THOUGH HE HAD DREAMED NOTHING, 182 QUEEN MAEVE 55
　　AND I FELL ASLEEP UPON LONELY ECHTGE OF STREAMS. . . . . 203 WITHER BOUGHS 6
　　TILL HE HAS FALLEN ASLEEP . . . . 216 HAPPY TOWNLAND 51
　　BUT WHEN I HAD EATEN AND DRUNK MYSELF ASLEEP . . . . . . 223 SHADOW WATER B 30
　　AND OVERPOWER THE CREW WHILE YET ASLEEP: . . . . 233 SHADOW WATER B 240
　　THE WOMEN OF HIS HOUSEHOLD WERE ASLEEP, ... 282 TWO KINGS V 133
　　THAT WHEN HE HAS FALLEN ASLEEP WITHIN MY ARMS, ... 285 TWO KINGS 191
　　WHO IS FIRST ASLEEP, IF BUT HE CAN . . . . 295 THREE BEGGARS 23
　　FALL ASLEEP WHEN I SHOULD PRAY." . . . . 298 THREE HERMITS 12
　　WITH HER WHITE FINGER. I LED HER HOME ASLEEP . . . . . . 468 HARUN RASHID 158
　　LOOKED HALF ASLEEP ALL DAY. . . . . 570 THREE BUSHES 34
　　SEER OF VISIONS! NOW EVE FALLS ASLEEP. . . . . 691 MOSADA 1 36
　　IN THE FAR ISLE SHE SANG HERSELF ASLEEP. . . . . 694 MOSADA 1 90
　　HALF ASLEEP THE OLD COW CROPS, ... 706 DAWN-SONG 20
　　THE HARE HATH LAID ASLEEP HER FROLIC WITS, ... 712 FERENCZ RENYI 72
　　GAVE HIM HIS HARP. NOW THAT HE IS ASLEEP, ... 748 SHADOW WATER A 18
　　SO THESE WOULD HAVE KILLED FORGAEL WHILE ASLEEP . . . . . 748 SHADOW WATER A 25
　　BEFORE I DROPPED ASLEEP, A KINGFISHER . . . . 761 SHADOW WATER A 274
　　I HAVE WET THIS BRAID OF HAIR WITH TEARS WHILE ASLEEP. . . 762 SHADOW WATER A 294
ASS
　　"HARNESS AN ASS AND CART, ... 596 COLONEL MARTIN 51
ASSAILS
　　OF SOME FORGOTTEN FIEND. NOW NONE ASSAILS . . . . . . 31 OISIN 2 V 30B
ASSASSIN
　　SOLDIER, ASSASSIN, EXECUTIONER, ... 482 BLOOD AND MOON 36
　　"ASSASSIN, MY ASSASSIN! THOU WHO LET'ST ME DIE, ... 714 FERENCZ RENYI 106
　　"ASSASSIN, MY ASSASSIN! THOU WHO LET'ST ME DIE, ... 714 FERENCZ RENYI 106
ASSAULT
　　ASSAULT AND BATTERY OF THE WIND . . . . 405 FOR DAUGHTER 55
ASS-BACK
　　CAMEL-BACK, HORSE-BACK, ASS-BACK, MULE-BACK, ... 566 LAPIS LAZULI 26
ASSES
　　WHEELS BY MILK-WHITE ASSES DRAWN . . . . 502 VACILLATION 62
ASSIZE
　　THE JUDGE AT THE ASSIZE COURT, ... 596 COLONEL MARTIN 46
ASS'S
　　BEYOND THE FLING OF THE DULL ASS'S HOOF . . . . 321 REED WHISPERER 5
ASSUAGE
　　A GREATER WITH A LESSER PANG ASSUAGE . . . . 537 HER VISION 5
ASSURANCE
　　I'LL HAVE ASSURANCE THAT YOU ARE ABLE . . . . 304 HOUR DAWN 51
　　"I'D HAVE ASSURANCE THAT YOU ARE ABLE . . . . 304 HOUR DAWN V 51
ASTIR
　　FOR ALL THAT COUNTRY HAD BEEN ASTIR . . . . 191 BAILE AILLINN 52
　　SET ALL HER BLOOD ASTIR . . . . 336 YOUNG GIRL 10
　　NOR FAERIES IN THE HONEY-HEART OF JUNE ASTIR. . . . . . 661 ISLE STAT II 1 73
ASTONISHED
　　SO PERILOUS THAT HALF THE ASTONISHED MEET . . . . . . 326 ROBERT GREGORY 61
　　AND NOW WE STARE ASTONISHED AT THE SEA, ... 534 HER TRIUMPH 11
　　AND WE THOUGH ASTONISHED ARE DUMB . . . . 785 YOUR HEART 11
　　AND WE THOUGH ASTONISHED ARE DUMB . . . . 786 YOUR HEART 24
　　AND WE THOUGH ASTONISHED ARE DUMB . . . . 786 YOUR HEART 37
ASTONISHING
　　A MOST ASTONISHING THING-- . . . . 567 FROM JAPANESE 1
ASTONISHMENT
　　AMID THAT FIRST ASTONISHMENT, WITH GRANIA'S SHADE, . . . 366 HER COURAGE 4
ASTRADDLE
　　ASTRADDLE ON THE DOLPHIN'S MIRE AND BLOOD, ... 498 BYZANTIUM 33
ASTRAY
　　AND ALL THE SHAPELY BODY NO TITTLE GONE ASTRAY. . . . . 354 HIS PHOENIX 30
　　MUSIC HAD DRIVEN THEIR WITS ASTRAY-- . . . . 411 TOWER 47
　　FOR THE EMBRACE OF NOTHING: AND I, MY WITS ASTRAY . . . 426 PHANTOM HATRED 14
　　"WHAT CHANGE HAS PUT MY THOUGHTS ASTRAY . . . . 529 TOM LUNATIC 3
　　LEAD THEM GENTLY ASTRAY! . . . . 568 SWEET DANCER 11
　　IN COUNTRY SHAWL OR PARIS CLOAK, HAD PUT MY WITS ASTRAY, 592 PILGRIM 3
ASTROLOGER
　　HIS SON GEORGE, THE ASTROLOGER; . . . . 360 ALF POLLEXFEN 8
　　WAS BURIED NEAR THE ASTROLOGER. . . . . 361 ALF POLLEXFEN 26
　　WHERE--WROTE A LEARNED ASTROLOGER-- . . . . 535 CHOSEN 17
ASUNDER
　　THE FENIAN HORSES: ARMOUR TORN ASUNDER: . . . . 43 OISIN 2 210
　　THE HORSES OF THE FENIANS--TEARING ASUNDER . . . . . . 43 OISIN 2 V 210
ATE
　　AND FROM HER FINGERS ATE ITS BIT. . . . . 397 POLIT PRISONER 6

	PAGE	TITLE	LINE

ATE   (CONTINUED)
  THEY ATE SPREAD WIDE THAT EACH . . . .   488 CRAZED MOON   V   17
  BECAUSE THE FIRES OF PURGATORY HAVE ATE THEIR SHAPES AWAY: 593 PILGRIM   13
A-TELLING
  A-TELLING WITH THEIR LOW AND REEDY CRY . . . .   128 DREAM OF FAERY V   42
ATHEIST
  THE BISHOP MURMURED, "ATHEIST! . . . .   725 LEGEND   21
ATHENE
  ATHENE TAKES ACHILLES BY THE HAIR, ...   374 PHASES OF MOON   45
  GO PLUCK ATHENE BY THE HAIR! . . . .   386 ROBARTES DANCE   19
  THE GREAT GREY-EYED ATHENE STARES THEREON. . . . . . .   447 COLONUS PRAISE   16
  PALLAS ATHENE IN THAT STRAIGHT BACK AND ARROGANT HEAD! . .   578 LOFTY THINGS   11
ATHENE'S
  AT PALLAS ATHENE'S SIDE, ...   355 PROPERTIUS   6
ATHENIAN
  ATHENIAN INTELLECT ITS MASTERY, ...   446 COLONUS PRAISE   11
ATHWART
  THE FAERY SHIP THAT SWIMS ATHWART THE SKY. . . . . .   663 ISLE STAT II 2   16
  OF THE ALHAMBRA BLACK ATHWART HIS DISK! . . . .   691 MOSADA 1   V   37
A-TIPTOE
  PASSED A-TIPTOE UP AND DOWN . . . .   20 OISIN 1   V   294
  AND PASSED A-TIPTOE UP AND DOWN, ...   85 MAD KING GOLL   51
  I PASSED A-TIPTOE UP AND DOWN, ...   85 MAD KING GOLL   51
  THEY PASSED A-TIP-TOE EVERYWHERE, ...   667 ISLE STAT II 3   20
  THEY PASSED A-TIPTOE EVERYWHERE, ...   667 ISLE STAT II 3 V   20
  THE HOUR OF INCANTATION COMES A-TIPTOE, ...   691 MOSADA 1   37
ATLANTIC
  BRED ON THE ATLANTIC, CAN BE STAYED! . . . .   403 FOR DAUGHTER   6
  TRAVELLED TO AND FRO ACROSS THE ATLANTIC, ...   790 DEDICATION   3
ATLAS
  THAT THE WITCH OF ATLAS KNEW, ...   637 BEN BULBEN   3
ATMOSPHERE
  HERE IN THE PITCH-DARK ATMOSPHERE ABOVE . . . . . .   555 RIBH AT TOMB   17
  HERE IN THE PITCH DARK ATMOSPHERE ABOVE . . . .   555 RIBH AT TOMB   V   17
A-TREMBLE
  LIKE SMALL BROWN MOTHS, A-TREMBLE. "RENYI SAY . . . .   713 FERENCZ RENYI   82
  LIKE SMALL BROWN MOTHS, A-TREMBLE CEASELESSLY. . . . .   713 FERENCZ RENYI V   82
ATTACK
  STRICKEN WITH PANIC FROM THE ATTACK, ...   274 GREY ROCK   75
  THE ATTACK ON THE "PLAY BOY" . . . .   294 HATED PLAYBOY V   T
  THE ATTACK ON "THE PLAYBOY OF THE WESTERN WORLD" . . .   294 HATED PLAYBOY V   T
ATTEMPTED
  I HAVE ATTEMPTED MANY THINGS . . . .   451 FIRST LOVE   9
ATTEND
  ATTEND UPON THEM STILL. . . . .   323 SWANS AT COOLE   24
  NOR DREAD NOR HOPE ATTEND . . . .   476 DEATH   1
ATTENDANCE
  WE, TOO, HAD GOOD ATTENDANCE ONCE, ...   266 GALWAY RACES   5
  SHOULD DANCE ATTENDANCE UPON MY OLD AGE! . . . . . .   591 SPUR   V   2
ATTENDANT
  IT IS MY WHIM! BID SOME ATTENDANT SPRITE . . . . . .   669 ISLE STAT II 3   72
ATTENDANTS
  THAT ALL ATTENDANTS AND THE CASUAL CROWD MIGHT HEAR. . .   609 IN TARAS HALLS   13
ATTENTION
  MADE MY ATTENTION STRAY. . . . .   507 STREAM AND SUN   5
  FOR A MAN'S ATTENTION . . . .   533 FIRST CONFESS   10
  AND WHEN I PAY ATTENTION I MUST OUT AND WALK . . . . .   581 CURSE CROMWELL   29
  SHOULD DANCE ATTENTION UPON MY OLD AGE! . . . .   591 SPUR   2
  MY ATTENTION FIX . . . .   631 POLITICS   2
ATTIC
  IN THE VERSE OF ATTIC STORY . . . .   65 HAPPY SHEPHERD V   16
  WITH PATIENT BEAUTY YONDER ATTIC BUST . . . .   685 DRAWING-ROOM   3
  WITH PATIENT BEAUTY YONDER ATTIC BUST . . . .   735 QUATRAIN APHOR   23
ATTIS'
  AND HE THAT ATTIS' IMAGE HANGS BETWEEN . . . .   500 VACILLATION   16
ATTORNEY
  TILL THE ATTORNEY FOR LOST SOULS CRY HER SWEET CRY, . . .   173 SPEAKS HEARERS   6
AUDIENCE
  IN SCORN OF THIS AUDIENCE, ...   348 FISHERMAN   27
  FIT AUDIENCE FOUND, BUT CANNOT RULE . . . .   506 REMORSE SPEECH   4
  SPEAKING TO A DRUNKEN AUDIENCE HIGH NONSENSICAL WORDS! . .   577 LOFTY THINGS   6
AUGHT
  OR AUGHT REMOTE! OR HAST THOU NEVER HEARD . . . . . .   672 ISLE STAT II 3   153
AUGUSTA
  AUGUSTA GREGORY SEATED AT HER GREAT ORMOLU TABLE, . . .   577 LOFTY THINGS   7
  AUGUSTA GREGORY'S SON! HER SISTER'S SON, ...   602 GALLERY REVIS   21
  MANCINI'S PORTRAIT OF AUGUSTA GREGORY, ...   602 GALLERY REVIS   25
  JOHN SYNGE, I AND AUGUSTA GREGORY, THOUGHT . . . . . .   603 GALLERY REVIS   41
AUGUSTUS
  AUGUSTUS CAESAR, AND AFTER THESE . . . .   379 SAINT HUNCH   11
AUNTS   SEE GREAT-AUNTS
  ON UNCLES, AUNTS, GREAT-UNCLES OR GREAT-AUNTS, ...   604 YOU CONTENT   3
AUREOLE
  AS WITH AN AUREOLE. MY SUIT TO YOU-- . . . .   697 MOSADA 2   38
AUSTERE
  YET HE WHO TREADS IN AUSTERE WAYS . . . .   138 TO IRELAND   V   27
  OF SORROWFUL, AUSTERE, SWEET, LOFTY PIPE TUNES. . . . .   341 SHEP GOATHERD   57
  THE AUSTERE ARTHUR, RULE FROM UTHER'S CHAIR . . . . .   678 ISLE STAT II 3   296
AUSTERITY
  AUSTERITY, A PLACE SET OUT FOR WISDOM . . . .   377 PHASES OF MOON   127

	PAGE	TITLE	LINE
AUSTRIAN			
THE AUSTRIAN HAYNAU HE, IN MANY LANDS	709	FERENCZ RENYI	8
AUTHOR			
TRUE SONG, THOUGH SPEECH: "MINE AUTHOR SUNG IT ME." . . .	373	PHASES OF MOON	30
AUTHORITY			
A SHROUD THAT SEEMED TO HAVE AUTHORITY	634	CUCHULAIN COMF	7
AUTHORS			
SOME ANCIENT FAMOUS AUTHORS MISREPRESENT, ...	579	DOR WELLESLEY	15
AUTUMN			
"I WOULD DIE LIKE A SMALL WITHERED LEAF IN THE AUTUMN, . . .	56	OISIN 3	131
AUTUMN IS OVER THE LONG LEAVES THAT LOVE US, ...	79	FALLING LEAVES	1
AUTUMN WAS OVER HIM: AND NOW THEY STOOD	80	EPHEMERA	16
OR IN THE AUTUMN SOLITUDES	84	MAD KING GOLL V	39
THE TREES ARE IN THEIR AUTUMN BEAUTY, ...	322	SWANS AT COOLE	1
THE NINETEENTH AUTUMN HAS COME UPON ME	322	SWANS AT COOLE	7
BUT A RAVING AUTUMN SHEARS	475	EVA GORE-BOOTH	5
AS THE LEAVES IN AUTUMN SCATTER.	648	ISLE STAT I 1	90
IN AUTUMN, WHEN FAR DOWN THE MOUNTAIN SLOPES	690	MOSADA 1	12
AS SLOWLY AUTUMN CLIMBED THE GOLDEN THRONE	690	MOSADA 1 V	1A
AUTUMNAL			
OR IN AUTUMNAL SOLITUDES	84	MAD KING GOLL	39
CAN SHAKE MORE BLOSSOM FROM AUTUMNAL CHILL	465	HARUN RASHID	104
THAT BRINGS MORE BLOSSOM TO AUTUMNAL CHILL	465	HARUN RASHID V	104
AUTUMN'S			
THEIR DREAD OF AUTUMN'S MORTAL WING	736	SUMMER EVENING	2
AND DREAD NO MORE FOUL AUTUMN'S WING, ...	737	SUMMER EVENING	18
AVAIL			
WERE ALL MY WANDERING DAYS OF NO AVAIL, ...	684	SEEKER	64
AVAILS			
OLD AND REMEMBERING, WHAT AVAILS THE WIND	42	OISIN 2 V	206
AVALANCHE			
SEEMS A WATER-COURSE OR AN AVALANCHE, ...	567	LAPIS LAZULI	45
AVALLON			
OR AVALLON THE GRASS GREEN HOLLOW, OR JOYOUS ISLE . . .	209	UNDER THE MOON V	2
AVALON			
NOR AVALON THE GRASS-GREEN HOLLOW, NOR JOYOUS ISLE, . . .	209	UNDER THE MOON	2
TALL DAMES GO WALKING IN GRASS-GREEN AVALON.	627	STATES HOLIDAY	13
TALL DAMES GO WALKING IN GRASS-GREEN AVALON.	627	STATES HOLIDAY	26
TALL DAMES GO WALKING IN GRASS-GREEN AVALON.	627	STATES HOLIDAY	39
TALL DAMES GO WALKING IN GRASS GREEN AVALON.	627	STATES HOLIDAY V	REF
AVE			
"AVE MARIE," MUTTERED HE	730	PRIEST FAIRY	51
AVENGED			
AND WILL YOU SWEAR NEVER TO BE AVENGED	758	SHADOW WATER A	223
AVENGING			
THE AVENGING LEAF THOSE FIELDS RAISED UP AGAINST IT. . .	487	SEVEN SAGES	20
AVOW			
SOME THERE ARE, FOR I AVOW	435	FOR MY SON	10
AWAIT			
MUSIC AND LOVE AND SLEEP AWAIT, ...	9	OISIN 1	103
"THAT WE ARE TIRED, FOR OTHER LOVES AWAIT US:	80	EPHEMERA	21
A LITTLE STOLEN TRESS. I, TOO, AWAIT	170	SECRET ROSE	27
FOR HOPE WOULD GIVE HIS LIMBS THE POWER--AND AWAIT . .	283	TWO KINGS	136
WESTWARD OF TARA, THERE TO AWAIT A FRIEND	283	TWO KINGS V	136
AWAIT THE HOUR OF WAR, ENTER THE SMALL, ...	461	HARUN RASHID V	8
I AWAIT YOUR WORDS AS THE BLIND GRASS AWAITS	756	SHADOW WATER A	181
AWAITING			
AWAITING IN PATIENCE THE STRAW-DEATH, ...	58	OISIN 3	167
AWAITS			
OUR ISLE AWAITS US, ON EACH LEA	77	INDIAN TO LOVE V	2
WHO BUT AWAITS HIS HOUR TO SHOOT, STILL HANGS	198	SEVEN WOODS	13
A MAN AWAITS HIS END	476	DEATH	3
AWAITS RETURNING SPRING.	517	HER ANXIETY	2
I AWAIT YOUR WORDS AS THE BLIND GRASS AWAITS	756	SHADOW WATER A	181
AENGUS LOOKS ON YOU WHEN I LOOK: HE AWAITS	757	SHADOW WATER A	209
AWAKE			
WHEN THEY AWAKE UPSPRINGING: WITH LOUD HORN	32	OISIN 2 V	52
"OH, SIGH, AWAKE AND GO YOU FORTH FOR ME:	33	OISIN 2 V	57
AND SHOOK HIM WIDE AWAKE, AND BID HIM SAY	182	QUEEN MAEVE	50
AWAKE UNSLEEPING FIRES: AND WOVE SEVEN STRINGS, . . .	219	HARP OF AENGUS	7
MUTTER SUCH THINGS AS THEY AWAKE FROM TRANCE. . . .	229	SHADOW WATER B	163
IT WAS THEIR HANDS THAT PLUCKED THE WINDS AWAKE . . .	237	SHADOW WATER B	324
AND THEN AT LAST BEING WIDE AWAKE	304	HOUR DAWN V	40
DO: BUT AWAKE A HOPE TO LIVE	309	REALISTS	6
DELIGHT MEN'S EYES WHEN I AWAKE SOME DAY	323	SWANS AT COOLE	29
OR KEEP US ALL AWAKE WITH BAYING AT THE MOON, ...	364	DOLLS FACES	11
TO KEEP A DROWSY EMPEROR AWAKE!	408	SAIL BYZANTIUM	29
AND THAT SHE DREAMED AWAKE CONTENT TO TOUCH	466	HARUN RASHID V	125C
"FOR EVER AND FOR EVER": THEN AWAKE	560	WHENCE COME	3
AND WIDE AWAKE KNOW THAT THE HUNT IS ON:	622	HOUND VOICE	17
I LIE AWAKE NIGHT AFTER NIGHT	632	MAN AND ECHO	9
ACORNS GREEN, WITH EYES AWAKE.	655	ISLE STAT I 3	5
BUT WIDE AWAKE HIS TWO EYES WERE.	655	ISLE STAT I 3	7
SLEEPER, AWAKE! HOW LONG MY SLEEP? UNNUMBERED . . .	678	ISLE STAT II 3	307
OH, GOD!--AWAKE! THOU SHALT NOT DIE. SHE SLEEPS, . .	701	MOSADA 3	66
AWAKE, AWAKE, AND WE WILL SAIL AFAR, ...	702	MOSADA 3	78
AWAKE, AWAKE, AND WE WILL SAIL AFAR, ...	702	MOSADA 3	78
HER DREAMS ARE TALKING WITH OLD YEARS. AWAKE, . . .	702	MOSADA 3	89
SHALL AWAKE WITH LONELY BLEAT, ...	726	LOVERS QUARREL	6
AWAKE UNSLEEPING FIRES: AND WOVE SEVEN STRINGS, . . .	762	SHADOW WATER A	302

AWAKE   (CONTINUED)
    AND LANGUORS THAT AWAKE IN MINGLING HANDS • • • • • • 765 SHADOW WATER A   367
AWAKED
    HAS AWAKED IN OUR HEARTS, MY BELOVED, A SADNESS THAT MAY 122 WHITE BIRDS   4
        NOT DIE.
    HAS AWAKED IN OUR HEARTS, MY BELOVED, A SADNESS THAT NEVER 122 WHITE BIRDS   V 4
        MAY DIE.
    I'LL GIVE MY ANSWER. YOU HAVE AWAKED HIM. • • • • • • 225 SHADOW WATER B V   79
AWAKEN
    THE WINDS AWAKEN, THE LEAVES WHIRL ROUND, • • • • • • 140 HOSTING SIDHE   6
    COULD BUT AWAKEN SADLY UPON LIPS • • • • • • • • • 185 QUEEN MAEVE   104
    AWAKEN WANDERINGS OF LIGHT AIR • • • • • • • • • 197 BAILE AILLINN   185
    AWAKEN TO LIFE AGAIN. • • • • • • • • • • • • 215 HAPPY TOWNLAND   26
    AWAKEN, AWAKEN TO NEW-BORN LUSTRE! • • • • • • • 646 ISLE STAT I 1   43
    AWAKEN, AWAKEN TO NEW-BORN LUSTRE! • • • • • • • 646 ISLE STAT I 1   43
AWAKENED   SEE DREAM-AWAKENED HALF-AWAKENED
    THE WINDS THAT AWAKENED THE STARS • • • • • • • 171 MAID QUIET   3
    FOR THE WINDS THAT AWAKENED THE STAR • • • • • • 171 MAID QUIET   V 3
    FOR THE WINDS THAT AWAKENED THE STARS • • • • • • 171 MAID QUIET   V 3
    I'LL GIVE MY ANSWER. YOU HAVE AWAKENED HIM. • • • • 225 SHADOW WATER B   79
    BECAUSE I HAVE AWAKENED HER TO LOVE • • • • • • 243 SHADOW WATER B   439
    HAD HALF AWAKENED SOME OLD MEMORY-- • • • • • • 284 TWO KINGS   172
    WHO HAS AWAKENED FROM THE COMMON DREAM • • • • • • 369 EGO DOMINUS   50
    HAD I BUT AWAKENED FROM SLEEP • • • • • • • • 381 SONGS FOOL 2   10
AWAKENS
    AND AS IT FALLS AWAKENS LEAFY TUNES!-- • • • • • 127 DREAM OF FAERY V   23
    AWAKENS AN OLD MEMORY, AND SAY. • • • • • • • 201 OLD MEMORY   2
    AND THAT OLD HARP AWAKENS OF ITSELF • • • • • • 252 SHADOW WATER B   617
    AMONG THE HEBRIDES. WHEN SHE AWAKENS, • • • • • 760 SHADOW WATER A V   255
AWAKES
    HOW LITTLE AND REEDY A SOUND AWAKES A GOD • • • • 760 SHADOW WATER A   252
    ARE WISER WITCHCRAFT, FOR OUR PEACE AWAKES • • • • 763 SHADOW WATER A   320
AWARDED
    AWARDED HIM FOR DAMAGES • • • • • • • • • • 596 COLONEL MARTIN   48
AWARE
    THE DOLL-MAKER'S WIFE IS AWARE • • • • • • • • 319 DOLLS   14
A-WAVING
    "ARMS ARE A-WAVING AND LIPS APART • • • • • • • 140 HOSTING SIDHE V   9
AWAY   SEE FAR-AWAY
    DID YOUR COMPANION WANDER AWAY • • • • • • • • 6 OISIN 1   52
    "OISIN, THOU MUST AWAY WITH ME • • • • • • • • 8 OISIN 1   V 80
    AWAY, AWAY WITH ME," SHE CRIED, • • • • • • • 8 OISIN 1   V 80B
    AWAY, AWAY WITH ME," SHE CRIED, • • • • • • • 8 OISIN 1   V 80B
    HURRIED AWAY, AND OVER HER RAISED • • • • • • • 12 OISIN 1   V 142B
    BID THEM AWAY AND HOLD THEIR PEACE! • • • • • • 15 OISIN 1   212
    NOW IN THE WOODS, AWAY WITH THEM • • • • • • • 16 OISIN 1   V 216A
    ON IN THE WOODS, AWAY WITH THEM, • • • • • • • 16 OISIN 1   V 222A
    AND CAUGHT THE SILVER HARP AWAY, • • • • • • • 17 OISIN 1   240
    THE HARP AWAY. A DOLOROUS POOL • • • • • • • 17 OISIN 1   V 240
    EAT AWAY THE SLOPING SOD, • • • • • • 20 OISIN 1   V 299
    IT PASSETH AWAY, AND IS HEARD OF NO LONGER. • • • • 26 OISIN 1   V 399B
    AND THE MOON LIKE A PALE ROSE WITHER AWAY." • • • • 28 OISIN 1   427
    AND THEN AWAY, AWAY, LIKE WHIRLING FLAMES! • • • • 29 OISIN 2   2
    AND THEN AWAY, AWAY, LIKE WHIRLING FLAMES! • • • • 29 OISIN 2   2
    YET LOVE AND KISS ON DIM SHORES FAR AWAY • • • • 29 OISIN 2   13
    AND THEN AWAY, AWAY, LIKE SPIRAL FLAMES! • • • • 29 OISIN 2   V 2
    AND THEN AWAY, AWAY, LIKE SPIRAL FLAMES! • • • • 29 OISIN 2   V 2
    THEY LOVE AND KISS IN ISLANDS FAR AWAY, • • • • 29 OISIN 2   V 13
    BUT LOVE AND KISS ON DIM SHORES FAR AWAY • • • • 29 OISIN 2   V 13
    "I BRING THEE A DELIVERER FROM FAR AWAY, • • • • 34 OISIN 2   V 78A
    HIS PURPOSE DRIFTS AWAY." • • • • • • • 45 OISIN 2   V 244
    HIGH AS THE SADDLE-GIRTH, COVERING AWAY FROM OUR GLANCES 47 OISIN 3   2
        THE TIDE!
    HIGH AS THE SADDLE GIRTH, COVERING AWAY FROM OUR GLANCES 47 OISIN 3   V 2
        THE TIDE!
    DRIPPING AND DOUBLING LANDWARD, AS THOUGH THEY WOULD HASTEN 48 OISIN 3   15
        AWAY,
    AND THE EARS OF THE HORSE WENT SINKING AWAY IN THE HOLLOW 48 OISIN 3   21
        NIGHT,
    OF HOLLIES, AND HAZELS, AND OAK TREES, A VALLEY WAS SLOPING 48 OISIN 3   V 26
        AWAY
    DRIPPING AND DOUBLING LANDWARD, AS THOUGH THEY WOULD HASTEN 57 OISIN 3   143
        AWAY,
    I RODE AWAY ON THE SURGES, WHERE, HIGH AS THE SADDLE-BOW, 57 OISIN 3   147
    LATER A SOUND CAME, HALF LOST IN THE SOUND OF A SHORE FAR 57 OISIN 3   155
        AWAY,
    I RODE AWAY ON THE SURGES, WHERE HIGH AS THE SADDLE BOW 57 OISIN 3   V 147
    I RODE AWAY ON THE SURGES, WHERE, HIGH AS THE SADDLEBOW, 57 OISIN 3   V 147
    I FELL ON THE PATH, AND THE HORSE WENT AWAY LIKE A SUMMER 60 OISIN 3   190
        FLY!
    YON TALL ONE EYES MY SUPPER! CHASE HIM AWAY, • • • • 72 ANASHU VIJAYA   34
    FAR, FAR AWAY. I NAMED HIM AFTER YOU. • • • • 72 ANASHU VIJAYA   35
    FAR, FAR AWAY. I'VE NAMED HIM AFTER YOU. • • • 72 ANASHU VIJAYA V   35
    MURMURING HOW FAR AWAY ARE THE UNQUIET LANDS! • • • • 78 INDIAN TO LOVE   10
    MURMURING HOW FAR AWAY ARE ALL EARTH'S FEVERISH LANDS. • • 78 INDIAN TO LOVE V   10
    HOW FAR AWAY THE STARS SEEM, AND HOW FAR • • • • 80 EPHEMERA   8
    THEY PINE AWAY AND YELLOW AND WEAR OUT, • • • • 81 EPHEMERA   V 24H
    AND DROVE TUMULT AND WAR AWAY • • • • • • • 82 MAD KING GOLL   5
    "HE DRIVES AWAY THE NORTHERN COLD." • • • • • • 82 MAD KING GOLL   11
    I PAUSED--AND FAR AWAY I DASHED • • • • • • • 83 MAD KING GOLL V   31
    I PAUSED--AND FAR AWAY RUSHED ON, • • • • • • • 83 MAD KING GOLL V   31

53

AWAY   (CONTINUED)
THAT HIDES AWAY THE DYING SUN . . . .   85 MAD KING GOLL   63
I MUST AWAY BY WOOD AND SEA . . . .   86 MAD KING GOLL   V   67
COME AWAY, O HUMAN CHILD! . . . .   87 STOLEN CHILD   9
COME AWAY, O HUMAN CHILD! . . . .   87 STOLEN CHILD   24
COME AWAY, O HUMAN CHILD! . . . .   88 STOLEN CHILD   38
AWAY WITH US HE'S GOING, ...   88 STOLEN CHILD   42
I WENT AWAY IN SILENCE, ...   95 MOLL MAGEE   27
I WENT AWAY IN SILENCE! . . . .   95 MOLL MAGEE   33
UPON HIS HEAD TO CAST AWAY MY SORROW. . . . . 102 FERGUS DRUID   14
UPON HIS HEAD TO CAST AWAY MY CARE. . . . . 102 FERGUS DRUID   V   14
I'D PUT AWAY THE FOOLISH MIGHT OF A KING, ... 103 FERGUS DRUID   V 21A
TO IDLE LIFE AWAY, A COMMON HERD." . . . .   107 CUCHULAIN SEA   21
TO IDLE LIFE AWAY WITH FLOCKS AND HERDS." . . . . 107 CUCHULAIN SEA   V   21
TROY PASSED AWAY IN ONE HIGH FUNERAL GLEAM, ... 111 ROSE OF WORLD   4
HAD HID AWAY EARTH'S OLD AND WEARY CRY. . . . . 120 SORROW OF LOVE   4
THE TALE DROVE HIS FINE ANGRY MOOD AWAY. . . . . 128 DREAM OF FAERY   36
IT CHARMED AWAY THE MERCHANT FROM HIS GUILE, ... 129 BOOK STORIES   5
AND NIAMH CALLING AWAY, COME AWAY! . . . . 140 HOSTING SIDHE   4
AND NIAMH CALLING AWAY, COME AWAY! . . . . 140 HOSTING SIDHE   4
AWAY, COME AWAY, TO THE DIM TWILIGHT. . . . . 140 HOSTING SIDHE   V   8
AWAY, COME AWAY, TO THE DIM TWILIGHT. . . . . 140 HOSTING SIDHE   V   8
AND NIAMH CALLING AWAY, COME AWAY. . . . . 141 HOSTING SIDHE   16
AND NIAMH CALLING AWAY, COME AWAY. . . . . 141 HOSTING SIDHE   16
HAS FALLEN AWAY? . . . .   142 MOODS   7
YOU PASS NOT AWAY. . . . .   142 MOODS   V   7
A PIPER PIPING AWAY, ...   144 HOST OF AIR   10
AWAY FROM THE MERRY BANDS. . . . .   144 HOST OF AIR   22
AWAY FROM THE MERRY DANCE. . . . .   145 HOST OF AIR   32
HE BORE HER AWAY IN HIS ARMS, ... 145 HOST OF AIR   33
A PIPER PIPING AWAY, ...   145 HOST OF AIR   42
SHE HAS GONE WEEPING AWAY. . . . .   152 LOSS OF LOVE   7
THE WEST WEEPS IN PALE DEW AND SIGHS PASSING AWAY, . . . 154 BELOVED PEACE   5
TILL ALL THE VALLEYS OF THE WORLD HAVE BEEN WITHERED AWAY. 163 VALLEY LOVERS   8
TILL THE VALLEYS OF THE WORLD HAVE BEEN WITHERED AWAY." 163 VALLEY LOVERS   V   8
WHILE TIME AND THE WORLD ARE EBBING AWAY . . . .   168 BLESSED   39
UNTIL TIME AND THE WORLD HAVE EBBED AWAY . . . .   168 BLESSED   V   39
AND SORROW AWAY, AND CALLING BARD AND CLOWN . . . . . . 170 SECRET ROSE   20
AND TRAMPLED THE MOUNTAINS AWAY, ...   171 MAID QUIET   V   4C
AND TRAMPLED THE MOUNTAIN AWAY, ... 171 MAID QUIET   4C
AND COVERS AWAY THE SMOKE OF MYRRH AND FRANKINCENSE! . . 173 SPEAKS HEARERS   4
NOR WOULD YOU RISE AND HASTEN AWAY, ... 176 BELOVED DEAD   7
SHE TURNED AWAY; HE TURNED AGAIN TO SLEEP . . . . 182 QUEEN MAEVE   59
FOR ALTHOUGH YEARS HAD PASSED AWAY . . . .   192 BAILE AILLINN   77
WANDER WHERE EARTH WITHERS AWAY. . . . .   196 BAILE AILLINN   171
HUM IN THE LIME-TREE FLOWERS! AND PUT AWAY . . . . . .   198 SEVEN WOODS   3
HUM IN THE LIME TREE FLOWERS! AND PUT AWAY . . . . . .   198 SEVEN WOODS   V   3
AND ONE BY ONE WE DROP AWAY." . . . .   208 OLD MEN ADMIRE   3
"ALL THAT'S BEAUTIFUL DRIFTS AWAY. . . . .   208 OLD MEN ADMIRE   8
OUR HANDS, OUR HANDS MUST EBB AWAY. . . . . 213 BLESS PSALTER   18
BUT BLESS OUR HANDS THAT EBB AWAY. . . . .   213 BLESS PSALTER   20
IS EDEN FAR AWAY, OR DO YOU HIDE . . . .   218 WOODS OF COOLE   30
PEACEABLE MEN THAT SHUT THE WIND AWAY. . . . .   224 SHADOW WATER B   54
I CAN PUT FEAR AWAY AS A QUEEN SHOULD. . . . .   238 SHADOW WATER B   355
TO CAST HIS DREAMS AWAY. NO OTHER'LL DO IT. . . . . . . 239 SHADOW WATER B   366
WHY DO YOU TURN AWAY AND HIDE YOUR FACE. . . . .   244 SHADOW WATER B   461
YOU TURN AWAY. WHY DO YOU TURN AWAY? . . . .   246 SHADOW WATER B   507
YOU TURN AWAY. WHY DO YOU TURN AWAY? . . . .   246 SHADOW WATER B   507
BUT NOW IT IS YOUR THOUGHTS THAT WANDER AWAY, ... 246 SHADOW WATER B   512
I TOO, I TOO. WHY DO YOU LOOK AWAY? . . . .   246 SHADOW WATER B V   507
YOU ARE BROKEN, YOU ARE BROKEN. THE WORLD DRIFTS AWAY, 251 SHADOW WATER B   599
I MIGHT HAVE THROWN POOR WORDS AWAY . . . . 256 WORDS   15
SOME MAY HAVE BLAMED YOU THAT YOU TOOK AWAY . . . . . . 257 RECONCILIATION   1
TILL THE STARS HAD RUN AWAY . . . .   268 BROWN PENNY   13
NOT DOUBTING TO HAVE SHOULDERED IT AWAY. . . . .   277 TWO KINGS   V 11A
AND CLIMBED INTO THE AIR, CRUMBLING AWAY, ...   278 TWO KINGS   42
"YOUR STRENGTH AND NOBLENESS WILL PASS AWAY"? . . . . . 285 TWO KINGS   189
THRUST HIM AWAY WITH BOTH MY HANDS AND CRIED, ... 285 TWO KINGS   202
THAN TRIUMPH, TURN AWAY . . . .   291 TO A FRIEND   10
AWAY, AWAY! YOU ARE SAFER IN THE TOMB. . . . .   293 TO A SHADE   24
AWAY, AWAY! YOU ARE SAFER IN THE TOMB. . . . .   293 TO A SHADE   24
HAD TUCKED HIMSELF AWAY BESIDE . . . .   303 HOUR DAWN   28
I'LL SLEEP AWAY ALL TIME WITHIN IT! . . . . 306 HOUR DAWN   74
BUT THE HOUR WHEN YOU SHALL PASS AWAY . . . .   306 HOUR DAWN   96
AND SLEEP AWAY ALL TIME WITHIN IT. . . . .   306 HOUR DAWN   V   74
"HE WENT AWAY," MY MOTHER SANG, ...   308 PLAYER QUEEN   5
SUDDENLY HID LOVE'S MOON AWAY. . . . .   313 MEMORY YOUTH   7
LOVE'S MOON WAS WITHERING AWAY. . . . . 313 MEMORY YOUTH   V   7
TO BUNDLE TIME AWAY . . . .   317 NIGHT COME   11
TO FIND THEY HAVE FLOWN AWAY? . . . .   323 SWANS AT COOLE   30
BROUGHT THE BARE NEWS. HE HAD THROWN THE CROOK AWAY . . 339 SHEP GOATHERD   21
ALL THE DISHONEST CROWD I HAD DRIVEN AWAY, ...   352 PEOPLE   24
HEAVEN HAS PUT AWAY THE STROKE OF HER DOOM, ... 356 BROKEN DREAMS   11
AND MASONS DROVE FROM MILES AWAY . . . .   360 ALF POLLEXFEN   9
WE AND OUR DOLLS BEING BUT THE WORLD WERE BEST AWAY. . . 364 DOLLS FACES   12
WOULD CARRY IT AWAY TO BLASPHEMOUS MEN . . . .   371 EGO DOMINUS   79
BODY AND SOUL CAST OUT AND CAST AWAY . . . .   374 PHASES OF MOON   62
THAT, IT MAY BE, HAD DANCED HER LIFE AWAY, ...   383 VISION ROBART   22
THAT IT MAYBE HAD DANCED HER LIFE AWAY. . . . . 383 VISION ROBART   V   22
"WHEN ALL THE WELLS ARE PARCHED AWAY? . . . .   396 ROSE TREE   15
CONSUME MY HEART AWAY; SICK WITH DESIRE . . . . 408 SAIL BYZANTIUM   21

AWAY   (CONTINUED)

Text	Page	Title	Line
I TURN AWAY AND SHUT THE DOOR, AND ON THE STAIR	427	PHANTOM HATRED	33
AND BEAR THAT BEATING HEART AWAY!	437	SONGS PLAY 1	5
LOVE'S PLEASURE DRIVES HIS LOVE AWAY,	438	SONGS PLAY 2	11
"BECAUSE I MADE YOU TURN AWAY AND RUN FROM THAT YOUNG CHILD!	450	OWEN AHERNE	14
O BUT HER HEART WOULD BREAK TO LEARN MY THOUGHTS ARE FAR AWAY."	450	OWEN AHERNE	20
AND TALKED AWAY THE NIGHT,	456	SUMMER SPRING	2
ARE GONE AWAY, AND SOME THAT STAY	458	HIS WILDNESS	5
THE SECOND BEST'S A GAY GOODNIGHT AND QUICKLY TURN AWAY.	459	FROM OEDIPUS	12
ALL MY FINE FEATHERS WOULD BE PLUCKED AWAY	469	HARUN RASHID	178
AWAY FROM NEIGHBOUR OR FRIEND,	472	ALL SOUL NIGHT	47
TO WHERE THE DAMNED HAVE HOWLED AWAY THEIR HEARTS,	474	ALL SOUL NIGHT	95
SHAKESPEAREAN FISH SWAM THE SEA, FAR AWAY FROM LAND!	485	THREE MOVEMENT	1
THE TOMB OF SWIFT WEARS IT AWAY. A VOICE	487	SEVEN SAGES	21
MAY THUNDER TIME AWAY,	496	MOHINI CHATTER	25
"LET ALL THINGS PASS AWAY."	502	VACILLATION	61
"LET ALL THINGS PASS AWAY."	502	VACILLATION	66
"LET ALL THINGS PASS AWAY."	502	VACILLATION	71
THAT TURN DULL-EYED AWAY,	505	RESULT THOUGHT	14
NAKED AND HIDDEN AWAY,	510	JANE JUDGMENT	13
THAT I HAD SHORN MY LOCKS AWAY	519	HER DREAM	3
A MAN MAY PUT PRETENCE AWAY	525	DANCING DAYS	19
AWAY MUST SHE TRIP!	559	HE AND SHE	4
TO LEAD HER AWAY, DO NOT SAY	568	SWEET DANCER	9
FROM TIME LONG PASSED AWAY,	589	OLD WICKED MAN	42
BECAUSE THE FIRES OF PURGATORY HAVE ATE THEIR SHAPES AWAY!	593	PILGRIM	13
SHE, PITY-CRAZED, HAD GIVEN HER SOUL AWAY,	629	CIRCUS ANIMALS	19
AND FAR AWAY THE HERON SAILS, I WIS.	649	ISLE STAT I 1	116
AWAY IN THE GREEN PARADISE,	654	ISLE STAT I 2	70
BLEW MY CRIMSON CAP AWAY.	656	ISLE STAT I 3	16
I WOULD HAVE GONE ALSO; BUT FAR AWAY	663	ISLE STAT II 2	37
AWAY FROM ME WHERE MISTS OF EVENING DRINK	663	ISLE STAT II 2	40
PASS AWAY--	668	ISLE STAT II 3	67
WILT ROAM AWAY FROM THIS RICH ISLAND REST?	669	ISLE STAT II 3	88
HAS ROLLED AWAY THE STARS AND DRIED THE SEA	671	ISLE STAT II 3	146
I HURL AWAY THESE ALL UNFAERY FEARS.	675	ISLE STAT II 3	228
THE SINGING SHEPHERDS, TOO, HAVE PASSED AWAY.	676	ISLE STAT II 3	271
I WILL DISSOLVE AWAY THE FAERIES' GUILE!	677	ISLE STAT II 3	282
HOW HAVE THE YEARS IN TROIA FLOWN AWAY?	679	ISLE STAT II 3	309
WANDER AWAY FROM MINE?	686	LIFE	8
AND LAUGH OUR LOVE AWAY.	686	LIFE	16
HIDING AWAY THE OCEAN'S YELPING FLOCKS.	688	TWO TITANS	38
I SAW HIM SIGH AND TURN AND PASS AWAY!	690	MOSADA 1	14
AWAY FROM ALL THE OTHERS. NOW THE SUN	691	MOSADA 1	33
THIS HEATHEN HORDE AWAY. YOU NEED NOT HOPE!	696	MOSADA 2	5
NO USE. AWAY! HEAR, THOU ENDURING GOD,	698	MOSADA 2	50
NO USE. AWAY! HEAR OH! THOU ENDURING GOD,	698	MOSADA 2 V	50
AND FREE--'TWILL THIEVE AWAY WITH SLEEPY MOOD	700	MOSADA 3	30
SHOWERED AWAY THE KEEN DEW DROPS!	705	DAWN-SONG	18
COME AWAY WHILE THE MOON'S IN THE WOODLAND,	707	FAIRY PEDANT	9
YOU ARE WASTING AWAY, LITTLE FAIRY.	707	FAIRY PEDANT	12
THEN AWAY AND AWAY WILL I WANDER,	707	FAIRY PEDANT	16
THEN AWAY AND AWAY WILL I WANDER,	707	FAIRY PEDANT	16
YOU ARE WASTING AWAY, LITTLE FAIRY.	707	FAIRY PEDANT	20
YOU ARE WASTING AWAY, LITTLE FAIRY.	708	FAIRY PEDANT	28
COME AWAY WHILE THE MOON'S IN THE WOODLAND,	708	FAIRY PEDANT	37
SHE IS WASTING AWAY, LITTLE FAIRY.	708	FAIRY PEDANT	40
SERENE. THEY'RE LED AWAY, AND WHERE A BAND	712	FERENCZ RENYI	63
THERE FAR AWAY FROM ALL WE TWO WILL GO,	714	FERENCZ RENYI	99
AWAY HER CLINGING HANDS, AND TURNS. SHE THROWS	714	FERENCZ RENYI	102
HIS BONDS AWAY, SORE STRUGGLING. NOW AT LAST	714	FERENCZ RENYI	116
HER OFF AND TURNS AWAY. SHE THROWS	714	FERENCZ RENYI V	102
AND AWAY IN THE WOODS WE WILL SCATTER THE DEW!	717	LOVE SONG	2
. . . GONE AND PUFFED AWAY AND DEAD.	718	PHANTOM SHIP	3
AND THE WINDS COME DOWN AND BLOW THEM WITH THE VAPOURS FAR AWAY.	719	PHANTOM SHIP	28
LIFT THEIR CHINS AND TURN AWAY.	726	LOVERS QUARREL	24
COME I KNOW WHERE, FAR AWAY.	727	LOVERS QUARREL	34
AWAY IN THE HEART OF THE ANTIQUE WOOD!	730	PRIEST FAIRY	64
FAR AWAY THE STARRY MIRTH	731	STREET DANCERS	7
I FLING AWAY MY SWORD, BLOOD DIM,	743	DANAAN QUICK	20
A WOMAN IN MY ARMS, SHE SINKS AWAY	749	SHADOW WATER A	54
THAT SHALL BURN TIME WHEN TIMES HAVE EBBED AWAY,	750	SHADOW WATER A	61
THEY HAVE FLOWN AWAY TOGETHER. WE ARE NEARLY	754	SHADOW WATER A	154
BREATHED OUT A DRUID VAPOUR, AND CRUMBLED AWAY	761	SHADOW WATER A	279
HAVE COVERED THEM. WHERE DID THEY VANISH AWAY?	764	SHADOW WATER A	328
AND WHILE SHE FADES AND LIFE WITHERS AWAY,	768	SHADOW WATER A	422
THE WRITINGS I HAVE CAST AWAY!	779	ACCURSED WHO	2
OUR LUCK IS WITHERED AWAY,	783	GREY ROUND	18
AND THE WIND BLOWS IT AWAY.	783	GREY ROUND	20
IT CHASES OTHER THOUGHT AWAY,	791	REPRISALS	9

A-WEARY

Text	Page	Title	Line
OR PERCHING ON THE TENTS, A-WEARY STILL	690	MOSADA 1	8

A-WEAVING

Text	Page	Title	Line
FOR LOVE IS A-WEAVING WHEN A WOMAN'S HEART	761	SHADOW WATER A	262

AWLESS

Text	Page	Title	Line
OF AWLESS BIRDS, AND ROUND THEIR STIRLESS FEET	74	ANASHU VIJAYA	73

AWFUL

Text	Page	Title	Line
WATCHING O'ER HER AWFUL YOUNG,	658	ISLE STAT I 3	87

PAGE   TITLE   LINE

AWHILE
    AWHILE, AND CAME AGAIN, A SECOND LIGHT . . . . 37 OISIN 2   V 124
    THAT EMPTY THE HEART. I HAVE FORGOT AWHILE . . . . . . 198 SEVEN WOODS   5
    WHERE ONE FOUND LANCELOT CRAZED, AND HID HIM FOR AWHILE, 209 UNDER THE MOON V 3
    AND AFTER CIRCLING WITH STRANGE CRIES AWHILE . . . . . 223 SHADOW WATER B 26
    AND LISTEN TO ME FOR AWHILE. THE SAILORS . . . . . . 226 SHADOW WATER B 92
    IF YOU WILL GIVE ME ALL YOUR MIND AWHILE-- . . . . . . 227 SHADOW WATER B 117
    THEY HOVER OVER THE MASTHEAD AWHILE . . . . 233 SHADOW WATER B 246
    I HAD THIS THOUGHT AWHILE AGO, ... 255 WORDS   V 1
    OR HAVE LINGERED AWHILE AND SAID . . . . 392 EASTER 1916   7
    SHE WALKED AWHILE AND BLUSHED AWHILE . . . . 451 FIRST LOVE   3
    SHE WALKED AWHILE AND BLUSHED AWHILE . . . . 451 FIRST LOVE   3
    HIDDEN BY OLD AGE AWHILE . . . . 539 MEETING   1
    STAND UPRIGHT ON YOUR LEGS AWHILE, ... 586 PARNELLITES   3
    I FORGET IT ALL AWHILE . . . . 590 OLD WICKED MAN 61
    AND HAVING STRETCHED AND YAWNED AWHILE . . . . 612 NEWS ORACLE   11
    BE PATIENT YET AWHILE; FOR THIS NINTH MOON, ... 748 SHADOW WATER A V 23
A-WHISPERING
    AND ON TIPTOE THE WINDS A-WHISPERING STOOD. . . . . . 715 DWELT SYCAMORE   8
    AND ON TIP-TOE THE WINDS A-WHISPERING STOOD. . . . . . 715 DWELT SYCAMORE V 8
A-WINGING
    LIKE TULIPS IN THE AIR A-WINGING, ... 27 OISIN 1   417
AWOKE
    I AWOKE! THE STRANGE HORSE WITHOUT SUMMONS OUT OF   54 OISIN 3   105
       THE DISTANCE RAN,
    AND OUT OF HIS DREAM AWOKE! . . . . 145 HOST OF AIR   38
    TILL VAIN FRENZY AWOKE AND HE DIED! AND HIM . . . . . 169 SECRET ROSE   12
    AWOKE THE HARP-STRINGS LONG AGO. . . . . 190 BAILE AILLINN   37
    AWOKE THE HARP STRINGS LONG AGO. . . . . 190 BAILE AILLINN V 37
    THE SLEEPER AWOKE WITH A SUDDEN START, ... 729 PRIEST FAIRY   31
AWRY
    AMENDED WHAT WAS TOLD AWRY . . . . 440 WISDOM   4
    STRAIGHTENED ALL THAT WENT AWRY . . . . 440 WISDOM   V 4
    WHAT KNOWLEDGE OR ITS LACK HAD SET AWRY, ... 490 COOLE BALLYLEE   22
    WHAT KNOWLEDGE OR ITS LACK HAS SET AWRY, ... 490 COOLE BALLYLEE V 22
    I AM! ONE SHOULDER TURNED AWRY--WHY THEN . . . . . . 692 MOSADA 1   61
AXE   SEE POLE-AXE WAR-AXE BATTLE-AXE
AXEL
    THE ARCHANGEL AXEL, VICTOR THE ANGEL . . . . 774 COME RIDE   11
AXES   SEE BATTLE-AXES
    BEND LOWER LEST YOUR BATTLE AXES GLIMMER. . . . . . . 752 SHADOW WATER A V 117
AXLE
    UNTIL THE AXLE BREAK . . . . 165 CRY OF SEDGE   4
AY
    FASTING AND PRAYERS. TELL ON. AY, AY! . . . . 24 OISIN 1   V 360
    FASTING AND PRAYERS. TELL ON. AY, AY! . . . . 24 OISIN 1   V 360
    SAID NIAM. "AY, AND HUGE. WHEN YE HAVE LED . . . . . 35 OISIN 2   V 89
    AY, OISIN KNOWS, FOR HE IS OF THE WEAK, ... 42 OISIN 2   V 202
    AY, AY. SWEAR BY THE PARENTS OF THE GODS, ... 74 ANASHU VIJAYA   66
    AY, AY. SWEAR BY THE PARENTS OF THE GODS, ... 74 ANASHU VIJAYA   66
    AY, BOY. LET'S SEE IF THAT SAME HERON'S DEAD. . . . . 651 ISLE STAT I 1 169
    THE OTTERS DREAMING LAY. NASCHINA! AY! . . . . 677 ISLE STAT II 3 V 280
    HIS BODY SHAKE? AY, QUIVERING AS YON SMOKE . . . . . 683 SEEKER   36
    AFRAID TO BE TOO FAR." "AY, BRING HER HERE!" . . . . . 712 FERENCZ RENYI   69
    AY, AND SHAKES IN SEA-GREEN WAVERINGS ALONG THE FISHERS' 718 PHANTOM SHIP   2
       STREET!
    FOR ANTIQUARIAN MEDITATION. AY, ... 721 WITCH VIVIEN   38
AYE
    SMOTE ON THEIR BRAINS THAT DWELT REMEMBERING AYE. . . . 34 OISIN 2   V 77A
    FOR LONG ENOUGH? AYE, LONG AND LONG ENOUGH. . . . . . 221 SHADOW WATER B   2
    AYE, AND WORSE WRONG THAN THESE. . . . . 260 UNWORTH PRAISE 18
    AYE, HORSEMEN FOR COMPANIONS, ... 266 GALWAY RACES   7
    AYE, AND ACHILLES, TIMOR, BABAR, BARHAIM, ALL . . . . . 366 HER COURAGE   9
    AYE, THOUGH ALL PASSION'S IN THE GLANCE-- . . . . . . 388 SOLOMON WITCH   21
    AYE, SUN AND MOON AND STAR, ALL, ... 415 TOWER   152
    OF EVENING AND GLAD SILENCE DWELLETH AYE, ... 653 ISLE STAT I 2   37
    AYE, VERY LATELY, SORROW CAME TO WEEP . . . . 659 ISLE STAT II 1   25
    IF HER YE LOVE. AYE, COLIN, WE MUST FIGHT. . . . . . 662 ISLE STAT II 1   76
    AYE, FIGHT WE MUST. TELL ME, ANTONIO, MIGHT . . . . . 662 ISLE STAT II 1   77
    EACH ONE AT GAZE FOR AYE UPON HIS WHIRLING THRONE. . . . 662 ISLE STAT II 1   81
    THE OTTERS DREAMING LAY. AYE! . . . . 677 ISLE STAT II 3 280
    THE LIGHTNINGS PULSE--BEHOLD HER, AYE BEHOLD-- . . . . . 687 TWO TITANS   11
    AYE AND SHAKES IN SEA GREEN WAVERINGS, ALONG THE FISHERS' 718 PHANTOM SHIP V 2
       STREET.
A-YEAR
    AND ONCE A-YEAR LET THE ARCADIANS COME, ... 663 ISLE STAT II 2   29
AZOLAR
    WE TWO, BEFORE WE DIE; FOR AZOLAR, ... 691 MOSADA 1   24
AZURE
    WITH ALL YOUR WHIRLING HAIR, AND DROP MANY AN AZURE TEAR. 73 ANASHU VIJAYA   46
    WITH ALL YOUR WHIRLING HAIR, AND DROP THROUGH SPACE AN   73 ANASHU VIJAYA V 46
       AZURE TEAR.
    WITH ALL YOUR WHIRLING HAIR, AND DROP TEAR UPON AZURE TEAR. 73 ANASHU VIJAYA V 46
    WITH ALL OUR WHIRLING HAIR, AND DROP MANY AN AZURE TEAR. 73 ANASHU VIJAYA V 46
    IN COIL ON COIL OF AZURE. ALL IS READY. . . . . . . 691 MOSADA 1   41
    NO SIN TO SEE IN COIL ON COIL OF AZURE . . . . 692 MOSADA 1   43
    IN THE SOUTH SEA'S AZURE MILES, ... 732 STREET DANCERS 28
    IN THE SOUTH SEAS' AZURE MILES, ... 732 STREET DANCERS V 28
AZURES
    HER GOLDS, HER AZURES, AND HER BLUES, ... 13 OISIN 1   V 163

                                         PAGE   TITLE   LINE

BABAR
    AYE, AND ACHILLES, TIMOR, BABAR, BARHAIM, ALL • • • • •   366 HER COURAGE   9
BABBLING
    BABBLING OF FALLEN MAJESTY, RECORDS WHAT'S GONE. • • • •   314 FALLEN MAJESTY   4
    MID BABBLING LEAVES A WANDERING SONG-RAPT BIRD   • • • •   672 ISLE STAT II 3 V   154
    AND SEDGY STREAM, AND IN EACH BABBLING BRAKE • • • • • •   675 ISLE STAT II 3   225
BABY
    AND MY BABY WAS JUST BORN! • • • • • • • • • • • •   94 MOLL MAGEE   14
    I LAY UPON MY BABY! • • • • • • • • • • • • • • •   95 MOLL MAGEE   17
    I LOOKED ON MY COLD BABY • • • • • • • • • • • • •   95 MOLL MAGEE   19
    I'M THINKIN' OF MY BABY • • • • • • • • • • • • •   96 MOLL MAGEE   47
BABYLON
    FROM THEIR PEDANTIC BABYLON • • • • • • • • • • • •   344 DAWN   6
    IN STARRY TOWERS OF BABYLON • • • • • • • • • • • •   440 WISDOM   14
    WHERE BABYLON OR NINEVEH • • • • • • • • • • • • •   502 VACILLATION   63
BABYLONIAN
    WHAT MEDIAN, PERSIAN, BABYLONIAN, • • • • • • • •   420 MY HOUSE   V 20D
    REMEMBERED OUT OF BABYLONIAN ALMANACS, • • • • • •   426 PHANTOM HATRED   20
    THE BABYLONIAN STARLIGHT BROUGHT • • • • • • • • •   438 SONGS PLAY 2   4
    THE BABYLONIAN STAR-LIGHT BROUGHT • • • • • • • • •   438 SONGS PLAY 2   V 4
BABYLON'S
    ALEXANDRIA'S WAS A BEACON TOWER, AND BABYLON'S • • • •   480 BLOOD AND MOON   13
BACCHANT
    BACCHANT AND MOURNFUL, PASSING TO AND FRO • • • • • •   39 OISIN 2   161
BACHELOR
    I AM SO TIRED OF BEING BACHELOR • • • • • • • • • •   222 SHADOW WATER B   8
BACK   SEE HORSE-BACK CAMEL-BACK MULE-BACK ASS-BACK
    A WALL BEHIND HIS BACK, OVER HIS HEAD • • • • • • •   180 QUEEN MAEVE   5
    HE AND HIS BEST TROOPS BACK TO BACK • • • • • • • •   274 GREY ROCK   73
    HE AND HIS BEST TROOPS BACK TO BACK • • • • • • • •   274 GREY ROCK   73
    I COWERED BACK UPON THE WALL IN TERROR, • • • • • •   284 TWO KINGS   164
    SHOOK OFF THE WATER FROM HIS BACK! • • • • • • • •   400 DEMON BEAST   29
    OR THE HUMBLER WORM, I CLIMBED BEN BULBEN'S BACK • •   409 TOWER   9
    ALL DREAD AFAR TILL MORNING'S BACK, • • • • • • • •   435 FOR MY SON   6
    THAT HAD SO STRAIGHT A BACK, • • • • • • • • • •   458 HIS WILDNESS   4
    OR CARRY THE RINGED MAIL UPON MY BACK, • • • • • •   463 HARUN RASHID   58
    BACK TURNED UPON THE BRIGHTNESS OF THE SUN • • • •   489 COOLE PARK 29   30
    I CAN SUMMON BACK • • • • • • • • • • • • •   505 RESULT THOUGHT   11
    I COULD SUMMON BACK • • • • • • • • • • • • •   505 RESULT THOUGHT V   11
    THE HERON'S HUNCH UPON HIS BACK, • • • • • • • •   508 JANE BISHOP   19
    "O CRUEL DEATH, GIVE THREE THINGS BACK," • • • • •   521 THREE THINGS   1
    BRIGHTNESS THAT I PULL BACK • • • • • • • • • •   533 FIRST CONFESS   13
    AND, THOUGH LOVE'S BITTER-SWEET HAD ALL COME BACK, • •   537 HER VISION   27
    SOME BACK A MARE THROWN FROM A THOROUGHBRED, • • •   547 TO SAME TUNE 3   3
    SOME BACK A MARE THROWN FROM A THOROUGH-BRED, • • •   547 TO SAME TUNE 3 V   3
    "OF PLASTER SAINTS" HIS BEAUTIFUL MISCHIEVOUS HEAD THROWN 577 LOFTY THINGS   4
        BACK.
    PALLAS ATHENE IN THAT STRAIGHT BACK AND ARROGANT HEAD! • • 578 LOFTY THINGS   11
    HITCHED IT ON HIS BACK. • • • • • • • • • • • •   595 COLONEL MARTIN   26
    THE SMUGGLER MIDDLETON, BUTLERS FAR BACK, • • • • •   605 YOU CONTENT   15
    STRADDLING EACH A DOLPHIN'S BACK • • • • • • • •   612 NEWS ORACLE   13
    SOME BACK A MARE THROWN FROM A THOROUGHBRED, • • •   614 MARCH SONGS 2   3
    THE KHAKI FROM HIS BACK? • • • • • • • • • • • •   627 STATES HOLIDAY   17
    WITH A STIFF STRAIGHT BACK, • • • • • • • • • •   627 STATES HOLIDAY   33
    BACK IN THE HUMAN MIND AGAIN. • • • • • • • • •   637 BEN BULBEN   24
    BACK THE SHADOWS CREEP AGHAST—— • • • • • • • •   648 ISLE STAT I 1   98
    UNTIL THIS MORN. AS ADDER'S BACK • • • • • • • •   667 ISLE STAT II 3   22
    WAS BANDED AS AN ADDER'S BACK, • • • • • • • • •   667 ISLE STAT II 3 V   23
    BRUSHING BACK HIS YELLOW HAIR! • • • • • • • • •   729 PRIEST FAIRY   38
BACKED
    TROY BACKED ITS HELEN; TROY DIED AND ADORED! • • • •   547 TO SAME TUNE 3   4
    TROY BACKED ITS HELEN; TROY DIED AND ADORED! • • • •   614 MARCH SONGS 2   4
BACKGROUNDS
    ON BACKGROUNDS FOR A GOD OR SAINT • • • • • • • •   639 BEN BULBEN   54
BACKS
    MAGICAL UNICORNS BEAR LADIES ON THEIR BACKS. • • • •   426 PHANTOM HATRED   18
BACKWARD
    UNTIL AT LAST THE DOUBLE HORNS, DRAWN BACKWARD, • • •   278 TWO KINGS   21
    HER HEAD CAST BACKWARD IN HER UNLOOSED HAIR. • • • •   701 MOSADA 3   67
BACKWARDS
    I PLUCKED HER BACKWARDS BY HER DRESS OF GREEN. • • •   676 ISLE STAT II 3   264
BAD
    THE BAD OLD DAYS. THOU WERT, MEN SING, • • • • •   2 OISIN 1   V 3
    THAT IS BAD ENOUGH TO BE TRUE, IS TRUE, • • • • •   191 BAILE AILLINN   69
    • • • CERTAIN BAD POETS, IMITATORS OF HIS AND MINE • •   262 TO A POET   T
    • • • CERTAIN BAD POETS, IMITATORS OF HIS AND OF MINE • • 262 TO A POET   V T
    TILL YOUR BAD MASTER BLENCHED AND ALL WAS LOST! • •   270 PARDON FATHERS V   12
    AND STUFFED WITH ALL THAT'S OLD AND BAD! • • • • •   303 HOUR DAWN   V 25
    THAT'S STUFFED WITH ALL THAT'S OLD AND BAD! • • • •   303 HOUR DAWN   V 25
    IN THE BAD HOUR BEFORE THE DAWN." • • • • • • •   304 HOUR DAWN   55
    AND THOUGH THE WINTER WIND IS BAD • • • • • • •   306 HOUR DAWN   87
    I COUNT MY GOOD AND BAD, • • • • • • • • • • •   316 FRIENDS   22
    WHAT'S GOOD OR BAD, OR WHAT IT IS TO TRIUMPH • • •   376 PHASES OF MOON   108
    THAT HAS THE WORST OF ALL BAD NAMES! • • • • • •   531 FATHER CHILD   5
    SHOULD STARVE GOOD MEN AND BAD ADVANCE, • • • •   626 OLD MEN BE MAD   10
BADE
    SHE BADE THEM BRING US TO THE HALL • • • • • • •   16 OISIN 1   217
    GAVE ME A HARP, AND BADE ME SING, • • • • • • •   16 OISIN 1   V 232
    AND BADE ME SING OF EARTHLY LANDS! • • • • • • •   17 OISIN 1   V 233
    HAD NEITHER HOPE NOR FEAR. I BADE THEM HIDE • • •   38 OISIN 2   139
    OF FEAR, I BADE THEM GO! AND FOR THE FIGHT • • • •   38 OISIN 2   V 142

57

		PAGE	TITLE	LINE
BADE	**(CONTINUED)**			
	HE BADE THEM GIVE OVER THEIR KEENING;	93	FATHER OHART	23
	AND GAVE ME MONEY, AND BADE ME GO	95	MOLL MAGEE	23
	"WHO BADE YOU TELL THESE THINGS UPON MY FLOOR?"	106	CUCHULAIN SEA V	17
	"WHO BADE YOU TELL THESE THINGS?" AND THEN SHE CRIED	106	CUCHULAIN SEA V	17
	"HE BADE ME LET ALL KNOW HE GIVES HIS NAME	109	CUCHULAIN SEA	52
	AT THE SWORD POINT, AND BADE ME BRING HIM ONE	109	CUCHULAIN SEA V	53
	AND TIME BADE ALL HIS CANDLES FLARE	138	TO IRELAND	13
	HE BADE ME OUT INTO THE GLOOM,	151	HEART OF WOMAN	3
	I BADE MY HEART BUILD THESE POOR RHYMES;	158	BELOVED RHYMES	3
	HE BADE HIS SOUL RISE UPWARD	159	CAP AND BELLS	3
	HE BADE HIS HEART GO TO HER.	159	CAP AND BELLS	13
	THEY HAVE BADE YOU FOLLOW THE MAN-HEADED BIRDS,	231	SHADOW WATER B V	204
	I BADE HIM GO WHEN ALL HIS HOUSEHOLD SLEPT	282	TWO KINGS	133
	AND BADE ALL WELCOME, BEING IGNORANT,	286	TWO KINGS	218
	NOR LAW, NOR DUTY BADE ME FIGHT,	328	IRISH AIRMAN	9
	I BADE, BECAUSE THE WICK AND OIL ARE SPENT	333	LIVING BEAUTY	1
	HE BADE THEM TAKE AND BURY HER	571	THREE BUSHES	71
	WHAT IF I BADE YOU LEAVE	600	THOSE IMAGES	1
	I NEVER BADE YOU GO	600	THOSE IMAGES	5
	HE BADE, HIS HUNDRED AND FIRST YEAR AT END,	609	IN TARAS HALLS	16
	I CRIED THE THING YOU BADE ME CRY,	670	ISLE STAT II 3	114
	BADE THAT SWORDSMAN TAKE	789	SINGING HEAD	4
	I BADE THEM FETCH HIS HEAD.	789	SINGING HEAD	12
BADGER				
	THE DEER, THE BADGER, AND THE BOAR,	23	OISIN 1	345
	AND SLEW THE BADGER AND THE DEER.	23	OISIN 1 V	345
	DIM INCHY WOOD, THAT HIDES BADGER AND FOX	218	WOODS OF COOLE	13
	NO FOX CAN FOUL THE LAIR THE BADGER SWEPT—	603	GALLERY REVIS	39
BADGERED				
	CAN BE SO BATTERED, BADGERED AND DESTROYED	130	BOOK STORIES	17
BAFFLED				
	CONSTRAINED, ARRAIGNED, BAFFLED, BENT AND UNBENT	382	VISION ROBART	9
BAG				
	TAKE, IF YOU MUST, THIS LITTLE BAG OF DREAMS;	104	FERGUS DRUID	29
	TAKE THEN THIS SMALL SLATE-COLOURED BAG OF DREAMS;	104	FERGUS DRUID V	29
	LAY HIDDEN IN THE SMALL SLATE-COLOURED BAG;	104	FERGUS DRUID V	40
	AND WITHERED TO A BAG OF BONES!	401	DEMON BEAST	49
	THE MOON IN A SILVER BAG.	525	DANCING DAYS	8
	THE MOON IN A SILVER BAG.	525	DANCING DAYS	16
	THE MOON IN A SILVER BAG.	525	DANCING DAYS	24
	WITH A BAG FULL OF PENNIES,	627	STATES HOLIDAY	35
	WELL THEN, TO BUSINESS; WHAT IS IN YOUR BAG?	720	WITCH VIVIEN	19
BAGPIPES				
	AN OLD MAN PLAYS THE BAGPIPES	214	HAPPY TOWNLAND	9
BAILE				
	BAILE AND AILLINN	188	BAILE AILLINN	T
	BAILE, WHO HAD THE HONEY MOUTH!	189	BAILE AILLINN	5
	YOUNG BAILE HONEY-MOUTH, WHOM SOME	189	BAILE AILLINN	16
	CALLED RATHER BAILE LITTLE-LAND,	189	BAILE AILLINN	17
	YOUNG BAILE HONEY MOUTH, WHOM SOME	189	BAILE AILLINN V	16
	CALLED RATHER BAILE LITTLE LAND,	189	BAILE AILLINN V	17
	BAILE AND AILLINN WOULD BE WED.	190	BAILE AILLINN	24
	I RUN TO BAILE HONEY-MOUTH,	191	BAILE AILLINN	48
	I RUN TO BAILE HONEY MOUTH	191	BAILE AILLINN V	48
	BAILE, THAT WAS OF RURY'S SEED,	194	BAILE AILLINN	118
	BAILE AND AILLINN'S MARRIAGE-BED,	194	BAILE AILLINN	121
	BAILE AND AILLINN'S MARRIAGE BED,	194	BAILE AILLINN V	121
	RIBH AT THE TOMB OF BAILE AND AILLINN	554	RIBH AT TOMB	T
	OF BAILE AND AILLINN YOU NEED NOT SPEAK,	555	RIBH AT TOMB	6
BAILE'S				
	BAILE'S HEART WAS BROKEN IN TWO;	192	BAILE AILLINN	70
BAKE				
	AND THEN I MUST SCRUB AND BAKE AND SWEEP	150	OLD MOTHER	3
	AND THEN I MUST MEND AND BAKE AND SWEEP	150	OLD MOTHER V	3
BAKED				
	INSIPID AS THE DOUGH BEFORE IT IS BAKED,	376	PHASES OF MOON	112
	AND AFTER BAKED IT SLOWLY IN AN OVEN; BUT NOW	442	BLACK CENTAUR	9
BALANCE				
	IN BALANCE WITH THIS LIFE, THIS DEATH.	328	IRISH AIRMAN	16
BALANCED				
	THAT BALANCED WITH A WORD IS MORE THAN NOISE;	258	KING NO KING	4
	I BALANCED ALL, BROUGHT ALL TO MIND,	328	IRISH AIRMAN	13
	SEA-BORNE, OR BALANCED ON THE AIR	397	POLIT PRISONER	19
BALD				
	YOU WHO ARE BENT, AND BALD, AND BLIND,	2	OISIN 1	1
	AH, SWEET TO ME NOW WERE EVEN BALD CONAN'S SLANDEROUS TONGUE!	55	OISIN 3	116
	BALD HEADS FORGETFUL OF THEIR SINS	337	SCHOLARS	1
	OLD, LEARNED, RESPECTABLE BALD HEADS	337	SCHOLARS	2
BALES				
	WHERE THE BALES AND THE BASKETS LAY	578	CRAZED GIRL	12
BALL	**SEE THUNDER-BALL**			
	ABOUT HIS FADING CRIMSON BALL;	12	OISIN 1	155
	IN SILENCE ROUND HIS CRIMSON BALL,	12	OISIN 1 V	155
	AND THE KINGFISHER TURNS TO A BALL OF DUST,	27	OISIN 1 V	418
	AND THE KINGFISHER TURNS TO A BALL OF DUST,	28	OISIN 1	422
BALLAD				
	THE BALLAD OF FATHER O'HART	91	FATHER OHART	T
	THE BALLAD OF MOLL MAGEE	94	MOLL MAGEE	T
	THE BALLAD OF THE FOXHUNTER	97	FOXHUNTER	T

58

BALLAD   (CONTINUED)
      THE BALLAD OF THE OLD FOX-HUNTER . . . .   97 FOXHUNTER   V   T
      THE BALLAD OF THE OLD FOXHUNTER . . . .   97 FOXHUNTER   V   T
      THE BALLAD OF FATHER GILLIGAN . . . . 132 FR GILLIGAN   T
      BALLAD AND STORY, RANN AND SONG: . . . . 137 TO IRELAND   4
      AS THOUGH SOME BALLAD SINGER HAD SUNG IT ALL . . . . 602 GALLERY REVIS V   24
      THE BALLAD OF EARL PAUL . . . . 739 EARL PAUL   T
BALLAD-SINGER
      AS THOUGH SOME BALLAD-SINGER HAD SUNG IT ALL: . . . . 602 GALLERY REVIS   24
BALLINAFAD
      KEENING FROM BALLINAFAD: . . . .   93 FATHER OHART   36
BALLOON
      THE BALLOON OF THE MIND . . . . 358 BALLOON MIND   T
      BRING THE BALLOON OF THE MIND . . . . 358 BALLOON MIND   2
BALLS   SEE PUFF-BALLS BOMB-BALLS EYE-BALLS
      I COUNT THOSE FEATHERED BALLS OF SOOT . . . . 424 ROAD AT DOOR   11
BALLYLEE
      TO BE CARVED ON A STONE AT THOOR BALLYLEE . . . . . 406 CARVED STONE   T
      TO BE CARVED ON A STONE AT BALLYLEE . . . . 406 CARVED STONE   V   T
      COOLE PARK AND BALLYLEE, [NINETEEN-THIRTY-ONE] . . . 490 COOLE BALLYLEE   T
      COOLE PARK AND BALLYLEE [NINETEEN-THIRTY-TWO] . . . 490 COOLE BALLYLEE V   T
      COOLE AND BALLYLEE, [NINETEEN-THIRTY-ONE] . . . . . 490 COOLE BALLYLEE V   T
BALOR
      DARK BALOR, AS OLD AS A FOREST, CAR-BORNE, HIS MIGHTY HEAD   53 OISIN 3   91
        SUNK
      CAME CAR-BORNE BALOR, AS OLD AS A FOREST, HIS VAST FACE   53 OISIN 3   V   91
        SUNK
      CAME BALOR, AS OLD AS A FOREST, CAR BORNE, HIS MIGHTY HEAD   53 OISIN 3 V 91
        SUNK
BAN
      NOR WAS HE BISHOP WHEN HIS BAN . . . . 508 JANE BISHOP   8
      THAT SHE IS UNDER BAN . . . . 531 FATHER CHILD   2
BAND
      AND FROM THE WOODS RUSHED OUT A BAND . . . .   15 OISIN 1   201
      AND FROM THE WOODS THERE RUSHED A BAND . . . . . .   15 OISIN 1   201
      AND, GATHERED IN A PANTING BAND, ...   22 OISIN 1   324
      WHILE HUSHED FROM FEAR, OR LOUD WITH HOPE, A BAND . . 114 ROSE OF BATTLE   5
      AND IF ANY GAZE ON OUR RUSHING BAND, ... 141 HOSTING SIDHE   10
      RODE OUT OF EMAIN WITH A BAND . . . . 189 BAILE AILLINN   18
      PERNING IN A BAND: . . . . 599 SPIRIT MEDIUM   6
      THOUGH YOUNGEST OF ALL IN OUR GOOD BAND, ... 707 FAIRY PEDANT   11
      THOUGH YOUNGEST OF ALL IN OUR GOOD BAND, ... 708 FAIRY PEDANT   39
      SERENE. THEY'RE LED AWAY, AND WHERE A BAND . . . . 712 FERENCZ RENYI   63
      HALF DIZZY WITH THE LIGHTNING THERE RUNS A GATHERING BAND-- 718 PHANTOM SHIP   9
      NOW HALF DIZZY WITH THE LIGHTNING THERE RUNS A GATHERING 718 PHANTOM SHIP V 9
        BAND:
BANDAGING
      THEN CLEANING OUT AND BANDAGING OF WOUNDS, ... 622 HOUND VOICE   20
BANDED
      THE SKY WAS BANDED O'ER WITH WRACK. . . . . 667 ISLE STAT II 3   23
      WAS BANDED AS AN ADDER'S BACK, ... 667 ISLE STAT II 3 V   23
      ABODE: AS BANDED ADDERS IN MY BREAST. . . . . 683 SEEKER   50
BANDIT
      WITH A RAGGED BANDIT CLOAK, ... 627 STATES HOLIDAY   31
BANDS
      WRESTLED AMONG THE ISLAND BANDS. . . . .   23 OISIN 1   350
      "MY FATHER DWELLS AMONG THE SEA-WORN BANDS, ... 107 CUCHULAIN SEA V   25
      AWAY FROM THE MERRY BANDS. . . . . 144 HOST OF AIR   22
      AND NEVER ANY MORE THE WIDE-EYED BANDS . . . . . . 674 ISLE STAT II 3   218
      AND SHE IS DRAGGED TO WHERE THE WILLOW BANDS . . . . 714 FERENCZ RENYI   108
BANDY
      UPON ITS BANDY LEGS, RUN AT THEM NOW, ... 233 SHADOW WATER B   239
BANDY-LEGGED
      YET CHOSE A BANDY-LEGGED SMITH FOR MAN, ... 404 FOR DAUGHTER   29
BANE   SEE STAR-BANE
      "O WHAT OF THE WORLD'S BANE?" . . . . 214 HAPPY TOWNLAND   14
      THAT IS THE WORLD'S BANE." . . . . 214 HAPPY TOWNLAND   20
      O WHAT IS THE WORLD'S BANE?, ... 214 HAPPY TOWNLAND V REF
      "O WHAT OF THE WORLD'S BANE?" . . . . 215 HAPPY TOWNLAND   34
      THAT IS THE WORLD'S BANE." . . . . 215 HAPPY TOWNLAND   40
      "O WHAT OF THE WORLD'S BANE?" . . . . 216 HAPPY TOWNLAND   54
      THAT IS THE WORLD'S BANE." . . . . 216 HAPPY TOWNLAND   60
BANISH
      WILL BANISH EVERY THOUGHT, UNLESS . . . . 387 ROBARTES DANCE   48
      BANISH AGE AND CARE, ... 620 JOHN KINSELLA   20
BANISHED
      BANISHED HEROIC MOTHER MOON AND VANISHED, ... 344 DEJECTION   9
      THE HOLY CENTAURS OF THE HILLS ARE BANISHED: . . . . 344 DEJECTION   V   7
      BANISHED JACK THE JOURNEYMAN, ... 508 JANE BISHOP   9
      POETRY AND MUSIC I HAVE BANISHED, ... 600 SPIRIT MEDIUM   19
BANK
      UPON EUROTAS' GRASSY BANK . . . . 522 LULLABY   14
      BEFORE A DEATH. O'ER WAVE AND BANK . . . . 673 ISLE STAT II 3   185
BANKERS
      OF BANKERS, SCHOOLMASTERS, AND CLERGYMEN . . . . . . 205 ADAMS CURSE   13
BANKRUPT
      AN ANCIENT BANKRUPT MASTER OF THIS HOUSE, ... 412 TOWER   80
BANKS
      AND NOT THE BANKS OF OARS THAT SWAM UPON . . . . . 610 STATUES   13
      OF YONDER LAKE, FROM WHOSE GREEN BANKS ALWAY . . . . 653 ISLE STAT I 2   33
      FROM WHOSE GREEN BANKS NO LIVING THING MAY ROVE, . . . 664 ISLE STAT II 2   57

BANKS   (CONTINUED)
    THE BANKS ARE WORN FOR EVER . . . . 680 LOVE AND DEATH   9
BANNER
    A WOMAN'S BEAUTY IS A STORM-TOSSED BANNER: . . . . . 469 HARUN RASHID   188
    IS BUT A HEAVY, GOLD EMBROIDERED BANNER, ... 469 HARUN RASHID V 188
BANNERET
    WITH BANNERET AND PENNON, ... 317 NIGHT COME   8
BANNERS   SEE BATTLE-BANNERS
    FROM BATTLE BANNERS FOLD UPON PURPLE FOLD, ... 162 ASKS FORGIVE V 11
    THE BANNERS OF EAST AND WEST, ... 165 CRY OF SEDGE   7
    WHERE BANNERS OF THE CALIPHS HANG, NIGHT-COLOURED . . 461 HARUN RASHID   6
    WHERE GOLD-EMBROIDERED BANNERS OF THE CALIF'S . . . . 461 HARUN RASHID V   6
    BANNERS CHOKE THE SKY: . . . . 512 JANE ON GOD   7
    THOSE BANNERS COME NOT IN. . . . . 635 BLACK TOWER   6
    THOSE BANNERS COME TO BRIBE OR THREATEN, ... 635 BLACK TOWER   11
    AMID A CLOUD OF BANNERS, ... 741 EARL PAUL   39
BANQUET
    "THE RED BRANCH KINGS A TIRELESS BANQUET KEEP, . . . 108 CUCHULAIN SEA V 33
    AT A BEANFEAST OR A BANQUET, ... 583 GHOST ROG CASE   15
    AT A BEANFEAST OR A BANQUET, ... 583 GHOST ROG CASE V 15
    HIS TEMPLE AND HIS BANQUET HALL; . . . . 671 ISLE STAT II 3 134
BANSHEE
    YOU WILL WITH THE BANSHEE CHAT, ... 726 LOVERS QUARREL   9
BAR
    TO BAR THAT FOUL STORM OUT, FOR WE . . . . 432 NINETEEN 19   111
    BOLT AND BAR THE SHUTTER, ... 523 MAD AS MIST   1
BARACH
    COOK BARACH, THE TRAITOR: AND WARWARD. . . . . . .   53 OISIN 3   90
BARB
    RECALL THE CRETAN BARB THAT PIERCED A STAR? . . . . 541 PARN FUNERAL 1   7
BARBAROUS
    AND I SPEAK A BARBAROUS TONGUE. . . . . 313 TWO YEAR LATER   12
    THERE'LL BE THAT CROWD, THAT BARBAROUS CROWD, ... 354 HIS PHOENIX   25
    GOES TO THE BARBAROUS CLANGOUR OF A GONG. . . . . . 430 NINETEEN 19   58
    GOES TO THE BARBAROUS CLANGOUR OF GONG. . . . . . . 430 NINETEEN 19 V 58
    SOME BARBAROUS, UN-FAERY THING DRAW NEAR. . . . . . 656 ISLE STAT I 3   21
BARBS
    PIERCING THE TWILIGHT WITH THEIR MURMURING BARBS. . .   72 ANASHU VIJAYA   28
BARCELONA
    AT BARCELONA . . . . 578 CRAZED GIRL V   T
BARD
    BARD OISIN, BOAST NOT OF THY DEEDS . . . .   11 OISIN 1   V 129
    THAN THIS STRANGE HUMAN BARD," HE CRIED: . . . . .   17 OISIN 1   239
    THAN THIS STRANGE BARD," HE CRIED, AND CAUGHT . . . .   17 OISIN 1   V 239
    AND SORROW AWAY, AND CALLING BARD AND CLOWN . . . . 170 SECRET ROSE   20
BARE   SEE THREAD-BARE CLOOTH-NA-BARE
    OVER THE BARE AND WOODY LAND, ...   15 OISIN 1   198
    AND ON THE RUNNEL'S STONY AND BARE EDGE . . . . . .   39 OISIN 2   157
    ACROSS THE BARE BOREEN. . . . .   95 MOLL MAGEE   32
    BLUE-EYED, AND A QUICK RUNNER ON BARE FEET, ... 242 SHADOW WATER B 416
    I WEEP--I WEEP BECAUSE BARE NIGHT'S ABOVE, ... 246 SHADOW WATER B 499
    "AND MAKE MY SOUL BEFORE MY PATE IS BARE." . . . . . 299 BEGGAR CRIED   4
    THAT TOSSED A BARE HEEL WHEN AT SCHOOL, ... 301 RUN PARADISE   19
    THE BARE CHIMNEY IS GONE BLACK OUT . . . . 327 ROBERT GREGORY 84
    BROUGHT THE BARE NEWS. HE HAD THROWN THE CROOK AWAY 339 SHEP GOATHERD   21
    FOR LARDER AND SPIT ARE BARE, ... 349 HAWK   4
    WHEN ALL IS FED WITH LIGHT AND HEAVEN IS BARE. . . . 375 PHASES OF MOON 74
    BUT GREGORY'S WOOD AND ONE BARE HILL . . . . 403 FOR DAUGHTER   4
    BUT GREGORY'S WOODS AND ONE BARE HILL . . . . . . 403 FOR DAUGHTER V   4
    TO THIS BARE SOUL, LET ALL MEN JUDGE THAT CAN . . . 542 PARN FUNERAL 1 30
    THAT STRIP THE BODY BARE." . . . . 570 THREE BUSHES   27
    BECAUSE WE LOVE BARE HILLS AND STUNTED TREES . . . . 621 HOUND VOICE   1
    THOSE GREAT SEA-HORSES BARE THEIR TEETH AND LAUGH AT THE 623 HIGH TALK   14
      DAWN.
    UNDER BARE BEN BULBEN'S HEAD . . . . 640 BEN BULBEN   84
BARGAIN
    YOU HAVE TAKEN PAY AND MADE YOUR BARGAIN FOR IT. . . . 225 SHADOW WATER B 68
    FOR THAT WAS IN THE BARGAIN WHEN WE STRUCK IT. . . . 225 SHADOW WATER B V 68D
    THE EVER-LIVING HAVE KEPT MY BARGAIN FOR ME, ... 232 SHADOW WATER B 223
    HIS BARGAIN . . . . 520 HIS BARGAIN   T
    A BARGAIN WITH THAT HAIR . . . . 520 HIS BARGAIN   11
    THOUGH STIFF TO STRIKE A BARGAIN, ... 620 JOHN KINSELLA 13
    HER BARGAIN STRUCK WE LAUGHED AND TALKED . . . . . . 620 JOHN KINSELLA 15
BARHAIM
    AYE, AND ACHILLES, TIMOR, BABAR, BARHAIM, ALL . . . . 366 HER COURAGE   9
BARK
    . . . IMMENSE IN THEIR WRINKLING BARK: . . . . . .   48 OISIN 3   17
    THE WAILING GREW DISTANT: I RODE BY THE WOODS OF . .   56 OISIN 3   137
      THE WRINKLING BARK,
    CUT OUT OUR RHYMES ON STRIPS OF NEW-TORN BARK . . . . 343 SHEP GOATHERD 115
BARKED
    HOWLED, MIAU-D, BARKED, BRAYED, BELLED, YELLED, CRIED, 387 SOLOMON WITCH   8
      CROWED,
    BUT NO DOGS BARKED, AND MIDNIGHTS CHIMED, ... 570 THREE BUSHES   29
    AND NO DOGS BARKED THROUGH MIDNIGHTS CHIMED . . . . . 570 THREE BUSHES V 29
BARKING
    BARKING. WE TRAMPLED UP AND DOWN WITH BLOWS . . . .   40 OISIN 2   170
    BARKING. ALONG THE HERBLESS PLAIN, WITH BLOWS . . .   40 OISIN 2   V 170
BARLEY
    AND BOWLS OF BARLEY, HONEY, AND WINE, ...   3 OISIN 1   8
    AND OVER THE MICE IN THE BARLEY SHEAVES: . . . . .   79 FALLING LEAVES   2

BARLEY   (CONTINUED)
    IN THE LAST RIDGE OF THE BARLEY? DO OUR WOODS   218 WOODS OF COOLE   33
    OF THE BARLEY SHOOTS IN THE SUN.   643 SONG FAERIES   8
    OF THE BARLEY SHOOTS IN THE SUN.   676 ISLE STAT II 3   255
    THERE'S BARLEY THERE, AND WATER THERE,   774 COME RIDE   7
BARNACLE   SEE GRASS-BARNACLE
    ALL METAPHOR, MALACHI, STILTS AND ALL. A BARNACLE GOOSE   623 HIGH TALK   11
BARNACLE-GEESE
    "THE WIND-BLOWN CLAMOUR OF THE BARNACLE-GEESE."   300 BEGGAR CRIED   20
BARRED
    THE BARRED WOODPECKER'S MANSION IS AND DEEP,   659 ISLE STAT II 1   23
    FLOATING FROM YON BARRED WINDOW. SMALL NEW-COMER,   700 MOSADA 3   43
    FLOATING FROM YON BARRED WINDOW. NEW COMER,   700 MOSADA 3   V   43
BARREL
    MADE LOCK, STOCK AND BARREL   415 TOWER   150
    I BRING FULL-FLAVOURED WINE OUT OF A BARREL FOUND   442 BLACK CENTAUR   10
    I BRING FULL FLAVOURED WINE OUT OF A BARREL FOUND   442 BLACK CENTAUR V 10
BARREL-HOOPS
    THERE ALL THE BARREL-HOOPS ARE KNIT,   557 THERE   1
BARRELS
    BETWEEN TWO BARRELS AT THE INN.   551 SONGS REWRIT 1   10
BARREN
    WITH BARREN WORDS AND FLATTERIES OF THE WEAK.   42 OISIN 2   197
    . . . THE SEA'S EDGE BARREN AND GREY,   48 OISIN 3   13
    . . . WHERE ALL IS BARREN AND GREY,   56 OISIN 3   141
    I TORE IT FROM THE BARREN BOUGHS OF EIRE,   130 BOOK STORIES   15
    IN BARREN HILLS AND MARSHY LAND,   150 WANDER AENGUS V 18
    MY BARREN THOUGHTS HAVE CHILLED ME TO THE BONE,   257 RECONCILIATION   12
    PARDON THAT FOR A BARREN PASSION'S SAKE,   270 PARDON FATHERS   19
    THEY SAY THAT ON YOUR BARREN MOUNTAIN RIDGE   342 SHEP GOATHERD   79
    THROUGH BARREN THEBAID,   401 DEMON BEAST   44
    AND BARREN AS A BREAKING WAVE   456 FRIENDS YOUTH   11
    WEARY OF REAPING THE BARREN NIGHT   648 ISLE STAT I 1   84
BARRENNESS
    FOR ALL THINGS TURN TO BARRENNESS   135 TWO TREES   29
    ALL THINGS TURN TO BARRENNESS   135 TWO TREES   V 29
BARRICADE
    A BARRICADE OF STONE OR OF WOOD!   425 STARES NEST   11
BARROW
    AND IN SOME GLOOMY BARROW LIE   19 OISIN 1   272
BARROWS
    FEASTED, AND WEPT THE BARROWS OF HIS DEAD!   170 SECRET ROSE   18
BARS
    AND BENDING DOWN BESIDE THE GLOWING BARS,   121 YOU ARE OLD   9
    CASEMENT UPON TRIAL, HALF HIDDEN BY THE BARS,   601 GALLERY REVIS   3
    WITH THREE BARS CROSSED, AND THESE FOUR WALLS MY WORLD,   700 MOSADA 3   32
    COOKING CHESTNUTS ON THE BARS--   737 IN FIRELIGHT   2
    COOKING CHESTNUTS ON THE BARS.   737 IN FIRELIGHT   12
BARTER
    MAY SURELY BARTER GAZE FOR GAZE.   139 TO IRELAND   28
    BARTER THAT HORN AND EVERY GOOD   405 FOR DAUGHTER   62
BARTERED
    TO SEE MEN'S SOULS BARTERED AND BOUGHT.   136 TWO TREES   V 36
BASALT
    A HUNDRED HORSEMEN ON THE BASALT FLOOR   36 OISIN 2   102
BASALTIC
    BASALTIC PILLARS MARRED WITH HEW AND HACK   31 OISIN 2   V   30
    BASALTIC, MIGHT HAVE PACED. WE HELD OUR WAY   36 OISIN 2   V 103
BASE
    ALL THAT ARE DIFFERENT OF A BASE INTENT!   398 LEADERS CROWD   2
    AND LET ALL BASE AMBITION BE,   460 THREE MONUMENT   9
    BASE DROVE OUT THE BETTER BLOOD,   626 STATES HOLIDAY   3
    BASE-BORN PRODUCTS OF BASE BEDS.   639 BEN BULBEN   73
BASE-BORN
    BASE-BORN PRODUCTS OF BASE BEDS.   639 BEN BULBEN   73
BASIN
    AND RAINS DOWN LIFE UNTIL THE BASIN SPILLS,   417 ANCEST HOUSES   4
    AND FALLS INTO THE BASIN OF THE MIND .   478 SELF AND SOUL   34
BASKETS
    WHERE THE BALES AND THE BASKETS LAY   578 CRAZED GIRL   12
BAT
    SHOULD BE SO SIMPLE--A BAT ROSE FROM THE HAZELS   377 PHASES OF MOON   137
BATED
    AND MURMUR IT WITH BATED BREATH, AS THOUGH   398 LEADERS CROWD   5
    SHE WILL SAY WITH BATED BREATH,   680 LOVE AND DEATH   30
BATHE
    THAT SCARCE COULD BATHE A STAR,   88 STOLEN CHILD   31
BATHED
    BATHED IN FLAMING FOUNTS OF DUTY   124 CATHLEEN PARA   5
    BATHED IN MIRACULOUS OIL, SWEET ODOURS FROM IT COME,   503 VACILLATION   81
BATHING
    NOW BATHING LILY LEAF AND FISH'S SCALE,   464 HARUN RASHID   65
    NOW BATHING LILY LEAF AND FISHES' SCALE,   464 HARUN RASHID   V 65
BATS
    OUTCRY OF BATS. AND THEN YOUNG NIAMH CAME   44 OISIN 2   229
    OF PASSIONATE MEN, LIKE BATS IN THE DEAD TREES!   136 TO SOME I TALK   5
    WHEN THE BATS CRIED OUT NO MORE!   159 CAP AND BELLS V 14
    CRYING TO ONE ANOTHER LIKE THE BATS!   376 PHASES OF MOON   106
    I CANNOT SEE. THE BEETLES, AND THE BATS,   693 MOSADA 1   63
BATTER
    WE WILL TEAR OUT THE FLAMING STONES, AND BATTER THE GATEWAY   62 OISIN 3   209
    OF BRASS

61

| | PAGE | TITLE | LINE |

BATTER (CONTINUED)
. . . AND WILL BATTER THE GATEWAY OF BRASS . . . . 62 OISIN 3 V 209
BATTERED
"THIS DEMON SHALL BE BATTERED TILL HE DIE, ... 35 OISIN 2 90
CAN BE SO BATTERED, BADGERED AND DESTROYED . . . . . 130 BOOK STORIES 17
BUT DESOLATE WATERS AND A BATTERED SHIP. . . . . . 246 SHADOW WATER B 497
ON GREAT-GRANDFATHER'S BATTERED TOMB." . . . . . . 331 ROUND TOWER 6
UPON A GREY OLD BATTERED TOMBSTONE . . . . 331 ROUND TOWER 7
UPON THE GREY OLD BATTERED TOMBSTONE . . . . 331 ROUND TOWER V 7
ON GREAT-GRANDFATHER'S BATTERED TOMB." . . . . . . 332 ROUND TOWER 30
ON GREAT GRANDFATHER'S BATTERED TOMB." . . . . . . 332 ROUND TOWER V 30
A SORT OF BATTERED KETTLE AT THE HEEL. . . . . . . 409 TOWER 16
BATTERED TO DEATH IN A CELLAR, ... 628 JANE MOUNTAIN 9
BATTERING
A BLIND MAN BATTERING BLIND MEN; . . . . 479 SELF AND SOUL 60
BATTERY
ASSAULT AND BATTERY OF THE WIND . . . . 405 FOR DAUGHTER 55
BATTLE
AND BROKE THE HEAVING RANKS OF BATTLE! . . . . . . 10 OISIN 1 124
WHILE HIS HEART STILL DREAMS OF BATTLE AND LOVE . . . . 27 OISIN 1 406
FOR BATTLE." "FLY YE FROM A THING SO DREAD. . . . . 35 OISIN 2 V 90
AND ONCE MORE TO A DAY-LONG BATTLE FELL. . . . . . 43 OISIN 2 218
"WITH ALL IN ALL THE WORLD I BATTLE WAGE. . . . . . 45 OISIN 2 V 240
HOW THE FETLOCKS DRIP BLOOD IN THE BATTLE. . . . . . 52 OISIN 3 78
WAGE AN ETERNAL BATTLE, AND I FEEL . . . . 104 FERGUS DRUID V 38C
HAS WON THE GOLD HIS CARS OF BATTLE BRING." . . . . 106 CUCHULAIN SEA 11
"AND BREAKS THE RIDGE OF BATTLE WITH HIS HANDS." . . . . 107 CUCHULAIN SEA 26
MY FATHER STANDS AMID HIS BATTLE CARS . . . . 107 CUCHULAIN SEA V 26
AND WEARY OF THE CRASH OF BATTLE CARS." . . . . . . 107 CUCHULAIN SEA V 30
THE CARS OF BATTLE AND HIS OWN NAME CRIED; . . . . . 111 CUCHULAIN SEA 85
THE ROSE OF BATTLE . . . . 113 ROSE OF BATTLE T
THEY WENT FORTH TO THE BATTLE, BUT THEY ALWAYS FELL . . . 113 ROSE OF BATTLE V T
AND HUSHED IN SLEEP THE ROARING RANKS OF BATTLE; . . . . 129 BOOK STORIES 7
FROM BATTLE BANNERS FOLD UPON PURPLE FOLD, ... 162 ASKS FORGIVE V 11
BUT ALL THAT ARE KILLED IN BATTLE . . . . 215 HAPPY TOWNLAND 25
A LUCKY BATTLE, OR A WOMAN'S KISS . . . . 227 SHADOW WATER B 115
WHERE THE GREAT BATTLE WAS . . . . 512 JANE ON GOD 10
I WALK IN A BATTLE FOUGHT OVER AGAIN, ... 591 WHAT WAS LOST 2
ITS GREAT BATTLE LOST. . . . . 617 LONG-LEG FLY 2
VAIN GAIETY, VAIN BATTLE, VAIN REPOSE, ... 629 CIRCUS ANIMALS 12
IF WHEN THE BATTLE IS HALF WON, ... 743 DANAAN QUICK 19
IN DAY OUT-LIVING BATTLE, ON THE BREAST . . . . . . 750 SHADOW WATER A 73
BEND LOWER LEST YOUR BATTLE AXES GLIMMER. . . . . . 752 SHADOW WATER A V 117
THOUGH BATTLE JOY MAY BE SO DEAR . . . . 791 REPRISALS 7
BATTLE-AXE
OF SWORD AND BRAZEN BATTLE-AXE, WHILE DAY . . . . . . 40 OISIN 2 171
BATTLE-AXES
BEND LOWER LEST YOUR BATTLE-AXES GLIMMER. . . . . . 752 SHADOW WATER A 117
BATTLE-BANNERS
FROM BATTLE-BANNERS, FOLD UPON PURPLE FOLD, ... 162 ASKS FORGIVE 11
BATTLE-BREAKING
I CALLED MY BATTLE-BREAKING MEN . . . . 83 MAD KING GOLL 17
BATTLE-CARS
AND MY LOUD BRAZEN BATTLE-CARS . . . . 83 MAD KING GOLL 18
MY FATHER STANDS AMID HIS BATTLE-CARS." . . . . . . 107 CUCHULAIN SEA 26
ON FOOT, ON HORSEBACK OR IN BATTLE-CARS." . . . . . 107 CUCHULAIN SEA 30
BATTLE-HOST
RIDING TO HURLEY, OR IN THE BATTLE-HOST . . . . . . 229 SHADOW WATER B 169
BATTLEMENT
UPON THE BROKEN, CRUMBLING BATTLEMENT, ... 477 SELF AND SOUL 3
BATTLEMENTS
I PACE UPON THE BATTLEMENTS AND STARE . . . . . . 409 TOWER 17
BATTLES
OF BATTLES BROKEN BY HIS HANDS. . . . . 7 OISIN 1 67
THAT WE MAY MUSE IN THE STARLIGHT AND TALK OF THE BATTLES . 51 OISIN 3 63
OF OLD;
TURN IF YOU MAY FROM BATTLES NEVER DONE, ... 114 ROSE OF BATTLE 7
AND WAGE GOD'S BATTLES IN THE LONG GREY SHIPS. . . . . 114 ROSE OF BATTLE 20
"FROM THE GREY SHIPS AND BATTLES NEVER WON. . . . . . 114 ROSE OF BATTLE V 8
OUT OF THE BATTLES OF OLD TIMES. . . . . 158 BELOVED RHYMES 6
IT WAS IN ALL HIS BATTLES. I WILL SPREAD MY HAIR . . . 242 SHADOW WATER B 413
SINGING OF ARMS AND BATTLES SOME OLD STAVE, ... 650 ISLE STAT I 1 137
I FOUGHT TWELVE BATTLES DRESSED IN GOLDEN ARMOUR. . . . 761 SHADOW WATER A 271
BATTLE-WEARY
AND CRIED TO BATTLE-WEARY MEN, ... 502 VACILLATION 65
BATTLING
CUCHULAIN BATTLING WITH THE BITTER TIDE; . . . . . . 100 ROSE UPON ROOD 3
BAUBLE
DRIVE TO A FLASHIER BAUBLE YET. . . . . 437 SONGS PLAY 1 12
YON BAUBLE OF THE HEAVENS, HE LIFTS HIS HANDS, ... 715 FERENCZ RENYI 119
BAWD
NOW MY OLD BAWD IS DEAD? . . . . 620 JOHN KINSELLA 12
NOW MY OLD BAWD IS DEAD? . . . . 621 JOHN KINSELLA 24
NOW MY OLD BAWD IS DEAD? . . . . 621 JOHN KINSELLA 36
BAWDY
BAWDY TALK FOR THE FISHERMEN; . . . . 588 OLD WICKED MAN 32
BAWLS
LOOKS AT THE CRADLE AND BAWLS; . . . . 319 DOLLS 2
BAWN
GOOD FELLOWS SHUFFLED CARDS IN AN OLD BAWN; . . . . . 411 TOWER 65

PAGE TITLE LINE

BAY
NO MIGHTIER CREATURES BAY AT THE MOON: . . . . . . 8 OISIN 1 87
AFTER A RAGGED HAT IN BISCAY BAY: . . . . 270 PARDON FATHERS 14
BUT A GREAT DANE THAT CANNOT BAY THE MOON . . . . . 579 DOR WELLESLEY 10
UNTIL, IN SOME CLIFF-SHELTERED BAY . . . . 612 NEWS ORACLE 21
ARE STILL THE ACHAIANS' TENTED CHIEFS AT BAY? . . . 679 ISLE STAT II 3 310

BAYING
WHEN WE FOLLOWED A DEER WITH OUR BAYING HOUNDS, . . 3 OISIN 1 14
OR KEEP US ALL AWAKE WITH BAYING AT THE MOON, . . . 364 DOLLS FACES 11
AND FOLLOWED UP THOSE BAYING CREATURES TOWARDS-- . . 412 TOWER 72

BAYS
DROPPING AT EVE IN CORAL BAYS . . . . 78 INDIAN TO LOVE V 19
AND WOULD THROUGH HATRED OF THE BAYS . . . . 436 FOR MY SON 15

BEACON
ALEXANDRIA'S WAS A BEACON TOWER, AND BABYLON'S . . . 480 BLOOD AND MOON 13

BEADS
HANDS THAT ARE BUSY WITH HIS BEADS . . . . 588 OLD WICKED MAN 25
OVER THE BEADS OF HIS ROSARY. . . . . 730 PRIEST FAIRY 52

BEAK
IN WHAT LAND DO THE POWERLESS TURN THE BEAK . . . . 42 OISIN 2 198
BEFORE THE INDIFFERENT BEAK COULD LET HER DROP? . . 441 LEDA AND SWAN 14

BEAKED SEE DARK-BEAKED

BEAM
UNDER THE DAY'S DECLINING BEAM, AND CALL . . . . . 410 TOWER 21
ONE INEXTRICABLE BEAM, ... 411 TOWER 55
WHERE THE SHAKING LEAF WITH THE BEAM WAS PLAYING, . 728 PRIEST FAIRY 2
A HURTING BEAM OF LIGHT, ... 741 EARL PAUL 38

BEAMS
SCARCE SPREAD A GLORY TO THE MORNING BEAMS, ... 422 MY DESCENDANTS 6
OF BEAMS A-FLICKER ON YON LONELY FIR. . . . . . . 661 ISLE STAT II 1 72
THROUGH THIS NIGHT-VESTED PLACE THE RED BEAMS BREAK. 662 ISLE STAT II 2 4
O'ER GRIEF. THE WORLD DRINKS SORROW FROM THE BEAMS 664 ISLE STAT II 2 46
I HEAR THE MURMUR AS THEY RAISE THE BEAMS . . . . . 699 MOSADA 3 17

BEAN
NINE BEAN ROWS WILL I HAVE THERE, A HIVE FOR THE HONEY BEE, 117 ISLE INNISFREE V 3

BEANFEAST
AT A BEANFEAST OR A BANQUET, ... 583 GHOST ROG CASE 15

BEANFEST
AT A BEANFEST OR A BANQUET, ... 583 GHOST ROG CASE V 15

BEAN-ROWS
NINE BEAN-ROWS WILL I HAVE THERE, A HIVE FOR THE HONEY-BEE, 117 ISLE INNISFREE 3

BEAR
THE SERVANTS BEAR THE BODY IN: . . . . 99 FOXHUNTER 47
BEAR THE GOLD-EMBROIDERED DRESS-- . . . . 124 CATHLEEN PARA V 6
BEAR THE GOLD EMBROIDERED DRESS-- . . . . 124 CATHLEEN PARA V 6
I ALSO BEAR A BELL-BRANCH FULL OF EASE. . . . . . 130 BOOK STORIES 12
I ALSO BEAR A BELL BRANCH FULL OF EASE. . . . . . 130 BOOK STORIES V 12
AND ALL THE TREMBLING FLOWERS THEY BEAR. . . . . . 134 TWO TREES 4
FOR WINDS WILL BEAR THEM GENTLY WHEN THE EAGLE FLIES, 146 UNAPPEAS HOST V 3
HOW DOES SHE BEAR HER GRIEF? THERE IS NOT A SHEPHERD 340 SHEP GOATHERD 28
I BEAR A BURDEN THAT MIGHT WELL TRY . . . . 380 SONGS FOOL 1 13
BUT BEAR IN MIND YOUR LOVER'S WAGE . . . . 385 ROBARTES DANCE 14
MAGICAL UNICORNS BEAR LADIES ON THEIR BACKS. . . . 426 PHANTOM HATRED 18
AND BEAR THAT BEATING HEART AWAY: . . . . 437 SONGS PLAY 1 5
IT COULD NOT BEAR THAT BURDEN AND THEREFORE IT WENT MAD. 449 OWEN AHERNE 4
BUT O! MY HEART COULD BEAR NO MORE WHEN THE UPLAND CAUGHT 450 OWEN AHERNE 11
   THE WIND:
THAT IF THE SPRING BEAR OFF WHAT THE SPRING GAVE . 464 HARUN RASHID 76
AND COULD BEGET OR BEAR THEMSELVES COULD THEY BUT LOVE 556 RIBH PATRICK 12
   AS HE.
LIVE TO BEAR CHILDREN TO A DUNCE: . . . . 626 OLD MEN BE MAD 6
LET THE SEA BEAR WITNESS, ... 770 BLOOD BOND 7
LET THE WIND BEAR WITNESS, ... 770 BLOOD BOND 8
LET THE EARTH BEAR WITNESS, ... 770 BLOOD BOND 9
LET THE FIRE BEAR WITNESS, ... 770 BLOOD BOND 10
LET THE DEW BEAR WITNESS, ... 770 BLOOD BOND 11
LET THE STARS BEAR WITNESS: . . . . 770 BLOOD BOND 12

BEARD
AND, PATRICK: BY YOUR BEARD, THEY WEPT, ... 17 OISIN 1 236
OH, PATRICK: BY THY BEARD, THEY WEPT, ... 17 OISIN 1 V 236
. . . THE SPITTLE ON HIS BEARD NEVER DRY, ... 53 OISIN 3 90
I MUST GAZE ON THE BEARD OF FINN. . . . . 55 OISIN 3 114
. . . WITH THE SPITTLE ON HIS BEARD NEVER DRY, . . 60 OISIN 3 192
WHOSE BEARD A MOONLIGHT RIVER IS, WHOSE BROW . . . 657 ISLE STAT I 3 73
UNTIL MY BEARD IS IN THE TWISTED LEAVES . . . . . 683 SEEKER 44
BEHOLD, I BEND: AROUND MY BEARD IN DRIFTS . . . . 684 SEEKER 68
BEHOLD I BOW: AROUND MY BEARD IN DRIFTS . . . . . 684 SEEKER V 68
YET WHITER BEARD HAVE YOU THAN MERLIN HAD. . . . . 721 WITCH VIVIEN 30

BEARDED
A BEARDED WITCH, HER SLUGGISH HEAD LOW BENT . . . 685 SEEKER 72
WHEN SOMETHING THAT WAS BEARDED LIKE A GOAT . . . 747 SHADOW WATER A 11

BEARDLESS
ONE HAND UPHELD HIS BEARDLESS CHIN, ... 17 OISIN 1 250
ONE HAND BENEATH HIS BEARDLESS CHIN, ... 17 OISIN 1 V 251

BEARDS
THE ANCIENT BEARDS, THE HELMS OF RUBY AND GOLD . . 169 SECRET ROSE 8

BEARING SEE CHILD-BEARING

BEARS
OF WOLVES, OF BOREAL BEARS, WE QUAFFED THE WINE . . 41 OISIN 2 V 188
AND ON THE SKINS OF WOLVES AND BEARS WE SLEPT: . . 41 OISIN 2 191

63

	PAGE	TITLE		LINE

BEARS   (CONTINUED)
BECAUSE PIEBALD PONIES, LED BEARS, CAGED LIONS, MAKE BUT   623 HIGH TALK   5
   POOR SHOWS,
BEAST
FROM GIRL AND BOY AND MAN AND BEAST! . . . .   82 MAD KING GOLL   6
O BEAST OF THE WILDERNESS, BIRD OF THE AIR, ...   177 PAST GREATNESS   11
AGAINST A BEECH-BOLE, HE THREW DOWN THE BEAST . . . .   278 TWO KINGS   36
AGAINST A BEECH BOLE, HE THREW DOWN THE BEAST . . . .   278 TWO KINGS   V   36
I WISHED BEFORE IT CEASED. NOR BIRD NOR BEAST . . .   338 SHEP GOATHERD   2
YEAR. I WISHED BEFORE IT CEASED. NOR BIRD NOR BEAST   338 SHEP GOATHERD V   2
IS ALWAYS HAPPY LIKE A BIRD OR A BEAST! . . . . . .   373 PHASES OF MOON   38
FROM TERRIFIED, INVISIBLE BEAST OR BIRD! . . . . . .   389 IMAGE PAST   6
DEMON AND BEAST . . . .   399 DEMON BEAST   T
THAT CRAFTY DEMON AND THAT LOUD BEAST . . . . . .   399 DEMON BEAST   2
NOW THAT THE LOUD BEAST RAN . . . .   400 DEMON BEAST   16
BELONGS TO BEAST OR DEMON. . . . .   401 DEMON BEAST   35
AND WHAT ROUGH BEAST, ITS HOUR COME ROUND AT LAST, . .   402 SECOND COMING   21
CRIED THAT WE LIVED LIKE BEAST AND BEAST! . . . . .   508 JANE BISHOP   13
CRIED THAT WE LIVED LIKE BEAST AND BEAST! . . . . .   508 JANE BISHOP   13
BIRD, BEAST, FISH OR MAN. . . . .   529 TOM LUNATIC   14
SANG OF THE BEAST THAT GAVE THE FATAL WOUND. . . . .   537 HER VISION   16
BEAST GAVE BEAST AS MUCH. . . . .   538 LAST CONFESS   12
BEAST GAVE BEAST AS MUCH. . . . .   538 LAST CONFESS   12
AS MAN, AS BEAST, AS AN EPHEMERAL FLY BEGETS, GODHEAD   556 RIBH PATRICK   5
   BEGETS GODHEAD,
WHAT FROM THE FOREST CAME? WHAT BEAST HAS LICKED   560 MAGIC DRUM   6
   ITS YOUNG?
LIKE A DUMB BEAST IN A SHOW, ...   572 LADYS 1ST SONG   2
NO BETTER THAN A BEAST . . . .   572 LADYS 1ST SONG   11
WITH EVERY NOBLE BEAST. . . . .   573 LADYS 2ND SONG   18
OR SOME SMALL BEAST MOST WONDERFULLY FURR'D, ...   650 ISLE STAT I 1   148
BEASTS
AMONG BIRDS OR BEASTS OR MEN . . . .   528 DANCER CRUACH   2
BEAST-TORN
THAT THING ALL BLOOD AND MIRE, THAT BEAST-TORN WRECK, . .   537 HER VISION   25
BEAT   SEE BELL-BEAT
BEAT TIME WITH THEIR BRIGHT WINGS AND FEET. . . . .   26 OISIN 1   V 397
UPLIFTED GATEWAY. WITH THE FLASHING BEAT . . . . .   31 OISIN 2   V 30D
THEN TO HER SERVANTS, "BEAT HIM FROM THE DOOR . . .   106 CUCHULAIN SEA   V 17A
TO THOSE ABOUT, "BEAT HIM WITH THONGS OF HIDE . . .   106 CUCHULAIN SEA   V 17A
BEFORE YOU WERE, OR ANY HEARTS TO BEAT, ...   112 ROSE OF WORLD   12
BEFORE YE WERE, OR ANY HEARTS TO BEAT, ...   112 ROSE OF WORLD   V 12
AND THE WHITE HUSH END ALL BUT THE LOUD BEAT . . . .   137 TO SOME I TALK   15
AND THE WHITE HUSH END ALL THINGS BUT THE BEAT . . .   137 TO SOME I TALK V 15
MADE IRELAND'S HEART BEGIN TO BEAT! . . . .   138 TO IRELAND   12
DESOLATE WINDS THAT BEAT THE DOORS OF HEAVEN, AND BEAT   147 UNAPPEAS HOST   9
DESOLATE WINDS THAT BEAT THE DOORS OF HEAVEN, AND BEAT .   147 UNAPPEAS HOST   9
BELOVED, LET YOUR EYES HALF CLOSE, AND YOUR HEART BEAT   154 BELOVED PEACE   9
AND ALL MEN'S HEARTS MUST BURN AND BEAT! . . . . .   158 BELOVED RHYMES   9
OF UNKNOWN PERISHING ARMIES BEAT ABOUT MY EARS. . . .   161 BLACK PIG   4
LIKE TATTERED CLOUDS OF THE WORLD, PASSIONS CALL AND OUR   207 HANRAHANS SONG V   8
   HEARTS BEAT:
AND BEAT THE BULWARK OF YOUR SHIP ON MINE. . . . . .   236 SHADOW WATER B   312
AND BEAT THE GOLDEN HELMET WITH THEIR SWORDS? . . . .   243 SHADOW WATER B   425
AND AFTER SET YOUR HEART TO BEAT. . . . .   263 MASK   9
WHAT MAKES YOUR HEART BEAT SO! . . . .   336 YOUNG GIRL   3
FOR RHYME CAN BEAT A MEASURE OUT OF TROUBLE . . . .   339 SHEP GOATHERD   12
A CRAZY JUICE THAT MAKES THE PULSES BEAT . . . . .   384 VISION ROBART   54
WHILE THEIR GREAT WOODEN DICE BEAT ON THE BOARD. . . .   412 TOWER   88
AND BEAT UPON THE BONE! . . . .   516 MANS SONG   6
THE HAND AND LASH THAT BEAT DOWN FRIGID ROME? . . . .   560 WHENCE COME   10
BEAT DOWN UPON THEIR NAKED BODIES, KNOW . . . . . .   563 MERU   12
WHO BEAT UPON THE WALL . . . .   576 ACRE OF GRASS   17
THEY ALWAYS BEAT ON THE SAME SMALL STONE. . . . . .   591 WHAT WAS LOST   5
AND I BEAT UP THE COMMON SORT . . . .   605 SONGS BURDEN 1   3
BEAT OUT THEIR LIVES LAMENTING O'ER THE SAND! . . . .   652 ISLE STAT I 2   14
BEAT ON IT WITH THEIR HAMMERS DAY AND NIGHT. . . . .   687 TWO TITANS   4
WHY DOES MY HEART BEAT SO? . . . .   781 MY HEART BEAT   1
WHY DOES YOUR HEART BEAT THUS? . . . .   785 YOUR HEART   1
WHAT MAKES HER HEART BEAT THUS, ...   785 YOUR HEART   V   1
WHAT MAKES YOUR HEART SO BEAT? . . . .   786 YOUR HEART   27
BEATEN   SEE WIND-BEATEN STORM-BEATEN RAIN-BEATEN
BETWEEN THE WALLS COVERED WITH BEATEN BRONZE, ...   180 QUEEN MAEVE   10
TILL ALL THE PLACE WAS BEATEN INTO MIRE. . . . . .   278 TWO KINGS   27
NOR ON THE ANCIENT BEATEN PATHS, THAT WOUND . . . .   279 TWO KINGS   52
AND GREAT ART BEATEN DOWN. . . . .   348 FISHERMAN   24
THERE HYDE BEFORE HE HAD BEATEN INTO PROSE . . . . .   489 COOLE PARK 29   9
UNTIL THE TOWN LIE BEATEN FLAT. . . . .   565 LAPIS LAZULI   8
MY LANGUAGE BEATEN . . . .   572 LADYS 1ST SONG   5
THE LOVERS AND THE DANCERS ARE BEATEN INTO THE CLAY, . .   580 CURSE CROMWELL   3
AFRAID THEY MIGHT BE BEATEN . . . .   582 ROGER CASEMENT   5
THAT WERE BEATEN INTO THE CLAY . . . .   640 BEN BULBEN   79
AND UNDER HER HOOFS THE MARIGOLDS BEATEN. . . . . .   729 PRIEST FAIRY   36
AGAINST MY FACE AND EYES. MINE TOO ARE BEATEN. . . .   759 SHADOW WATER A V   233
BEATING
AS THOUGH THEY ALL WERE BEATING TIME, ...   13 OISIN 1   174
BETWEEN THE PILLARS WITH A BEATING HEART . . . . .   279 TWO KINGS   59
THE BEATING DOWN OF THE WISE . . . .   348 FISHERMAN   23
TILL I COULD HEAR THEIR HEARTS BEATING! . . . . . .   358 PRESENCES   11
APPROPRIATE TO THAT BEATING BREAST . . . .   386 ROBARTES DANCE   22
AND BEAR THAT BEATING HEART AWAY! . . . .   437 SONGS PLAY 1   5

BEATING   (CONTINUED)
    A SUDDEN BLOW! THE GREAT WINGS BEATING STILL . . . . .   441 LEDA AND SWAN   1
    BUT FEEL THE STRANGE HEART BEATING WHERE IT LIES?   . . .   441 LEDA AND SWAN   8
    AND FEELS THE STRANGE HEART BEATING WHERE IT LIES! . .   441 LEDA AND SWAN   V   8
    AND HIS BEATING HEART WOULD BURST. . . . .   454 EMPTY CUP   6
    SWIFT BEATING ON HIS BREAST IN SIBYLLINE FRENZY BLIND . .   481 BLOOD AND MOON   19
    WINGS BEATING ABOUT THE ROOM! . . . .   499 MOTHER OF GOD   3
    IS BEATING ON THE DOOR. . . . .   583 GHOST ROG CASE   10
    IS BEATING ON THE DOOR. . . . .   583 GHOST ROG CASE   20
    IS BEATING ON THE DOOR. . . . .   584 GHOST ROG CASE   30
    IS BEATING ON THE DOOR. . . . .   584 GHOST ROG CASE   40
    WITH OPEN MOUTH AND BEATING HEART. . . . .   729 PRIEST FAIRY   32
    THE BEATING OF A LEV'RET'S HEART! . . . .   730 PRIEST FAIRY   69
    WHAT SETS IT BEATING SO? . . . .   781 HEART FRIGHT   2
    ITS STRANGE HEART BEATING FAST . . . .   785 YOUR HEART   6
BEATS
    THE HAND THAT WOUNDS. A WHITE BIRD BEATS HIS WINGS . .   758 SHADOW WATER A V 232
    A WHITE BIRD BEATS HIS WINGS UPON MY FACE. . . . . .   759 SHADOW WATER A   233
BEAUJOLET
    BUT THOSE OF BEAUJOLET. . . . .   336 YOUNG BEAUTY   V   12
BEAUTIES
    AND YET THE BEAUTIES THAT I LOVED . . . .   131 OLD PENSIONER   15
    AS COMMON BEAUTIES MAY, ...   336 YOUNG BEAUTY   9
    SEE, I TELL THY BEAUTIES O'ER, ...   647 ISLE STAT I 1   56
BEAUTIFUL
    AND A BEAUTIFUL YOUNG MAN FOLLOWED BEHIND . . . . . .   12 OISIN 1   144
    WAS A BEAUTIFUL YOUTH FROM AN UNKNOWN LAND. . . . . .   12 OISIN 1   V   145
    A BEAUTIFUL YOUNG MAN FOLLOWED BEHIND. . . . .   12 OISIN 1   V   145
    A BEAUTIFUL YOUNG MAN DREAMED WITHIN . . . .   17 OISIN 1   248
    O HAD YOU SEEN BEAUTIFUL NIAMH GROW WHITE AS THE WATERS   54 OISIN 3   109
        ARE WHITE,
    OH, HADST THOU SEEN BEAUTIFUL NIAM WAIL TO HERSELF AND   54 OISIN 3   V   109
        BLANCH,
    O, HAD YOU SEEN BEAUTIFUL NEAVE WAIL TO HERSELF AND BLANCH,   54 OISIN 3   V   109
    SHE WAS MORE BEAUTIFUL THAN THY FIRST LOVE, ...   123 DREAM OF DEATH   11
    I HAD A BEAUTIFUL FRIEND . . . .   152 LOSS OF LOVE   2
    SHE HAD BEEN BEAUTIFUL IN THAT OLD WAY . . . .   180 QUEEN MAEVE   19
    AT NEED, AND MADE HER BEAUTIFUL AND FIERCE, ...   181 QUEEN MAEVE   29
    THAT BEAUTIFUL MILD WOMAN, YOUR CLOSE FRIEND, ...   204 ADAMS CURSE   2
    THAT BEAUTIFUL MILD WOMAN FOR WHOSE SAKE . . . . . .   205 ADAMS CURSE   15
    THAT WE MUST LABOUR TO BE BEAUTIFUL." . . . .   205 ADAMS CURSE   20
    PRECEDENTS OUT OF BEAUTIFUL OLD BOOKS! . . . .   205 ADAMS CURSE   26
    THAT YOU WERE BEAUTIFUL, AND THAT I STROVE . . . . .   206 ADAMS CURSE   35
    "ALL THAT'S BEAUTIFUL DRIFTS AWAY . . . .   208 OLD MEN ADMIRE   8
    A BEAUTIFUL YOUNG MAN AND GIRL CAME UP . . . .   223 SHADOW WATER B   33
    BUT OF A BEAUTIFUL, UNHEARD-OF KIND . . . .   228 SHADOW WATER B   142
    HAS BEAUTIFUL WOMEN TO PLEASE EVERY MAN. . . . . . .   228 SHADOW WATER B   144
    ALTHOUGH YOU ARE MORE BEAUTIFUL THAN ANY, ...   236 SHADOW WATER B   305
    MYSTERIOUS, BEAUTIFUL! . . . .   323 SWANS AT COOLE   26
    YOU ARE MORE BEAUTIFUL THAN ANY ONE, ...   356 BROKEN DREAMS   27
    YOUR SMALL HANDS WERE NOT BEAUTIFUL, ...   356 BROKEN DREAMS   29
    YOU WERE MORE BEAUTIFUL THAN ANY ONE, ...   356 BROKEN DREAMS   V   27
    YOU ARE MORE BEAUTIFUL THAN ANYONE, ...   356 BROKEN DREAMS   V   27
    END IN A BEAUTIFUL MAN'S OR WOMAN'S BODY. . . . . . .   374 PHASES OF MOON   64
    AND MUST NO BEAUTIFUL WOMAN BE . . . .   386 ROBARTES DANCE   25
    AND THAT ALL BEAUTIFUL WOMEN MAY . . . .   387 ROBARTES DANCE   45
    WHEN, YOUNG AND BEAUTIFUL, ...   392 EASTER 1916   22
    SWEET VOICED AND BEAUTIFUL, ...   392 EASTER 1916   V   22
    BEING MADE BEAUTIFUL OVERMUCH, ...   403 FOR DAUGHTER   20
    BY THOSE THAT ARE NOT ENTIRELY BEAUTIFUL! . . . . . .   404 FOR DAUGHTER   35
    ADMIRED AND BEAUTIFUL, ...   472 ALL SOUL NIGHT   43
    BEAUTIFUL, ONE A GAZELLE. . . . .   475 EVA GORE-BOOTH   4
    BEAUTIFUL, ONE A GAZELLE. . . . .   475 EVA GORE-BOOTH   20
    THE INNOCENT AND THE BEAUTIFUL . . . .   476 EVA GORE-BOOTH   24
    THAT HIS HAIR IS BEAUTIFUL, ...   531 FATHER CHILD   7
    A BEAUTIFUL SEATED BOY! A SACRED BOW! . . . .   541 PARN FUNERAL 1   10
    BUT RHYMES FOR A BEAUTIFUL LADY, ...   552 SONGS REWRIT 2   11
    BEAUTIFUL LOFTY THINGS . . . .   577 LOFTY THINGS   T
    BEAUTIFUL LOFTY THINGS! O'LEARY'S NOBLE HEAD! . . . .   577 LOFTY THINGS   1
    "OF PLASTER SAINTS"! HIS BEAUTIFUL MISCHIEVOUS HEAD THROWN   577 LOFTY THINGS   4
        BACK.
    A BEAUTIFUL LOFTY THING, OR A THING . . . .   578 CRAZED GIRL   7
    BEAUTIFUL AND GENTLE IN HER VENETIAN WAY. . . . . . .   602 GALLERY REVIS   14
    BEAUTIFUL, GRACIOUS, IN HER VENETIAN WAY, ...   602 GALLERY REVIS   V   14
    A KING HAD SOME BEAUTIFUL COUSINS, ...   628 JANE MOUNTAIN   7
    'TIS BEAUTIFUL, AND THEREFORE IT IS SAD. . . . . . .   652 ISLE STAT I 2   24
    SHOULD I BE GOOD? BUT YOU ARE BEAUTIFUL. . . . . . .   692 MOSADA 1   62
    UNPRUNED IS YOUR BEAUTIFUL PINION . . . .   707 FAIRY PEDANT   7
    WHERE MOVES THERE ANY BEAUTIFUL AS I, ...   720 WITCH VIVIEN   1
    MY IMAGE YONDER? AH, MY BEAUTIFUL, ...   720 WITCH VIVIEN   4
    I DREAMT SOME GREAT ONE. AH, MY BEAUTIFUL, ...   720 WITCH VIVIEN   14
    A STREAM HAS TOLD ME THEY ARE BEAUTIFUL. . . . . . .   767 SHADOW WATER A   398
    PRAISE THE BEAUTIFUL AND STRONG! . . . .   773 SONG DEIRDRE 1   19
BEAUTY
    HAVE FACES ALIVE WITH SUCH BEAUTY BEEN KNOWN TO THE SALT   50 OISIN 3   51
        EYE OF MAN,
    ARE FACES ALIVE WITH SUCH BEAUTY MADE KNOWN TO THE SALT   50 OISIN 3   V   51
        EYE OF MAN,
    ARE FACES ALIVE WITH SUCH BEAUTY MADE KNOWN TO THE SOFT   50 OISIN 3   V   51
        EYE OF MAN,
    THE PHANTOM, BEAUTY, IN A MIST OF TEARS! . . . . . .   73 ANASHU VIJAYA   55

	PAGE	TITLE		LINE

BEAUTY (CONTINUED)

	PAGE	TITLE		LINE
ETERNAL BEAUTY WANDERING ON HER WAY.	101	ROSE UPON ROOD		12
WHO DREAMED THAT BEAUTY PASSES LIKE A DREAM?	111	ROSE OF WORLD		11
BEAUTY GROWN SAD WITH ITS ETERNITY	115	ROSE OF BATTLE		29
AND LOVED YOUR BEAUTY WITH LOVE FALSE OR TRUE,	121	YOU ARE OLD		6
AND LOVED YOUR BEAUTY WILL LOVE FALSE OR TRUE!	121	YOU ARE OLD	V	6
CARRY ALL THAT MOURNFUL BEAUTY	124	CATHLEEN PARA		7
FOR SHE NEEDS NOT HER SAD BEAUTY--	124	CATHLEEN PARA	V	7
HE REMEMBERS FORGOTTEN BEAUTY	155	FORGOT BEAUTY		T
MICHAEL ROBARTES REMEMBERS FORGOTTEN BEAUTY	155	FORGOT BEAUTY	V	T
I HEAR WHITE BEAUTY SIGHING, TOO,	156	FORGOT BEAUTY		19
I HEAR PALE BEAUTY SIGHING TOO,	156	FORGOT BEAUTY	V	19
HE TELLS OF THE PERFECT BEAUTY	164	PERFECT BEAUTY		T
AEDH TELLS OF THE PERFECT BEAUTY	164	PERFECT BEAUTY	V	T
TO BUILD A PERFECT BEAUTY IN RHYME	164	PERFECT BEAUTY		3
TO BUILD THE PERFECT BEAUTY IN RHYME,	164	PERFECT BEAUTY	V	3
MEN HAVE NAMED BEAUTY. THY GREAT LEAVES ENFOLD	169	SECRET ROSE		7
MEN HAVE NAMED BEAUTY. YOUR HEAVY LEAVES ENFOLD	169	SECRET ROSE	V	7
MEN HAVE NAMED BEAUTY. YOUR GREAT LEAVES ENFOLD	169	SECRET ROSE	V	7
YOUR BEAUTY PERISH AND BE LOST	173	PLEADS FRIEND		7
AND YOUR HIGH BEAUTY FALL AND BE LOST	173	PLEADS FRIEND	V	7
WITH BEAUTY HAND IN HAND?	174	ELEMENT POWERS	V	6
BUT SOFT BEAUTY AND INDOLENT DESIRE,	181	QUEEN MAEVE		22
FOR ALL THEIR BEAUTY, LIKE A HOLLOW DREAM?"	184	QUEEN MAEVE	V	89
I THOUGHT OF YOUR BEAUTY, AND THIS ARROW,	199	ARROW		1
TIME CAN BUT MAKE HER BEAUTY OVER AGAIN:	200	FOLLY COMFORT		8
TO DREAM OF WOMEN WHOSE BEAUTY WAS FOLDED IN DISMAY,	210	UNDER THE MOON		19
WITH BEAUTY LIKE A TIGHTENED BOW, A KIND	256	NO SECOND TROY		8
HER BEAUTY AS THE CONSTELLATIONS POUR	279	TWO KINGS	V	628
WHERE WIT AND BEAUTY LEARNED THEIR TRADE	288	TO WEALTHY MAN		16
BEAUTY THAT WE HAVE WON	293	HELEN LIVED		5
THE TREES ARE IN THEIR AUTUMN BEAUTY,	322	SWANS AT COOLE		1
UPON THIS LADY'S BEAUTY	329	MEN IMPROVE		5
A PICTURED BEAUTY.	329	MEN IMPROVE		7
THE LIVING BEAUTY	333	LIVING BEAUTY		T
FROM BEAUTY THAT IS CAST OUT OF A MOULD	334	LIVING BEAUTY		4
THE LIVING BEAUTY IS FOR YOUNGER MEN:	334	LIVING BEAUTY		9
TO A YOUNG BEAUTY	335	YOUNG BEAUTY		T
I KNOW WHAT WAGES BEAUTY GIVES,	336	YOUNG BEAUTY		13
IF HEAD AND LIMB HAVE BEAUTY AND THE INSTEP'S HIGH AND LIGHT	354	HIS PHOENIX		21
BURDENSOME BEAUTY--FOR YOUR SOLE SAKE	356	BROKEN DREAMS		10
YOUR BEAUTY CAN BUT LEAVE AMONG US	356	BROKEN DREAMS		14
BURDENSOME BEAUTY--BUT FOR YOUR SAKE	356	BROKEN DREAMS	V	10
AND YET YOUR BEAUTY HAD A FLAW:	356	BROKEN DREAMS	V	28
BRING WHERE OUR BEAUTY LIES	362	DOLLS DRAWINGS		1
EVEN OUR BEAUTY WITH HER TURKISH TROUSERS ON.	364	DOLLS FACES		9
THEIR BEAUTY DROPPED OUT OF THE LONELINESS	375	PHASES OF MOON		70
EVEN TO EYES THAT BEAUTY HAD DRIVEN MAD,	390	IMAGE PAST		34
A TERRIBLE BEAUTY IS BORN.	392	EASTER 1916		16
A TERRIBLE BEAUTY IS BORN.	393	EASTER 1916		40
A TERRIBLE BEAUTY IS BORN.	394	EASTER 1916		80
THE BEAUTY OF HER COUNTRY-SIDE	397	POLIT PRISONER		15
MAY SHE BE GRANTED BEAUTY AND YET NOT	403	FOR DAUGHTER		17
BEAUTY TO MAKE A STRANGER'S EYE DISTRAUGHT,	403	FOR DAUGHTER		18
CONSIDER BEAUTY A SUFFICIENT END,	403	FOR DAUGHTER		21
THE SORT OF BEAUTY THAT I HAVE APPROVED,	405	FOR DAUGHTER		50
ARE INNOCENCE AND BEAUTY BORN?	406	FOR DAUGHTER		78
SOUL'S BEAUTY BEING MOST ADORED,	421	MY TABLE		22
NOR BEAUTY BORN OUT OF ITS OWN DESPAIR,	445	SCHOOL CHILDR		59
IF YOU ARE NO MORE STRENGTH THAN I AM BEAUTY	448	HERO GIRL FOOL		10
AND YET THERE BEAUTY LAY:	455	HIS MEMORIES		12
A WOMAN'S BEAUTY IS A STORM-TOSSED BANNER:	469	HARUN RASHID		188
THE BEAUTY OF A WOMAN'S MIND OR BODY	469	HARUN RASHID	V	187
WITH 'MINISHED BEAUTY, MULTIPLIED COMMONPLACE,	472	ALL SOUL NIGHT		45
DIMINISHED BEAUTY, MULTIPLIED COMMONPLACE:	472	ALL SOUL NIGHT	V	45
BEAUTY AND FOOL TOGETHER LAID.	484	SYMBOLS		6
EARTH IN BEAUTY DRESSED	517	HER ANXIETY		1
REMEMBERING A WOMAN'S BEAUTY.	552	SONGS REWRIT 2	V	11
FOR BEAUTY DIES OF BEAUTY, WORTH OF WORTH,	564	GYRES		3
FOR BEAUTY DIES OF BEAUTY, WORTH OF WORTH,	564	GYRES		3
SHALL GROW THY BEAUTY AND THY DREAMLESS TRUTH,	674	ISLE STAT II 3		207
WITH PATIENT BEAUTY YONDER ATTIC BUST	685	DRAWING-ROOM		3
WITH PATIENT BEAUTY YONDER ATTIC BUST	735	QUATRAIN APHOR		23
A WOMAN'S BEAUTY IS LIKE A WHITE	784	WOMANS BEAUTY		1
WHEN BEAUTY IS COMPLETE	786	YOUR HEART		29
HE SWORE TO SING MY BEAUTY	789	SINGING HEAD		7

BEAUTY-DRUNKEN

	PAGE	TITLE		LINE
AND BEAUTY-DRUNKEN BY THE WATER	447	COLONUS PRAISE		20

BEAUTY'S

	PAGE	TITLE		LINE
FOR ALL THEIR BEAUTY'S LIKE A HOLLOW DREAM,	184	QUEEN MAEVE		88
ALTHOUGH THEIR BEAUTY'S LIKE A HOLLOW DREAM"	184	QUEEN MAEVE	V	89
THIS BEAUTY'S KINDER, YET FOR A REASON	199	ARROW		7
TO FLATTER BEAUTY'S IGNORANT EAR.	337	SCHOLARS		6
WHO IS MY BEAUTY'S EQUAL, THOUGH THAT MY HEART DENIES,	354	HIS PHOENIX		27
OF BEAUTY'S CRUELTY AND WISDOM'S CHATTER--	377	PHASES OF MOON		121
FOR BEAUTY'S VERY SELF, HAS CHARM MADE WISE,	404	FOR DAUGHTER		37
AND BRING BEAUTY'S BLIND RAMBLING CELEBRANT:	412	TOWER		91
IN BEAUTY'S MURDEROUS BROOD,	451	FIRST LOVE		2

BEAUVARLET

	PAGE	TITLE		LINE
BUT THOSE OF BEAUVARLET.	336	YOUNG BEAUTY		12

		PAGE	TITLE	LINE

BECAME
I BECAME A RUSH THAT HORSES TREAD, ... 177 PAST GREATNESS 6
I BECAME A MAN, A HATER OF THE WIND, ... 177 PAST GREATNESS 7
TIME OUT OF MIND, BECAME TOO RUINOUS . . . . 264 HOUSE SHAKEN 3
BECAME A BITTER, AN ABSTRACT THING, ... 397 POLIT PRISONER 9
THAT ALL BUT THE ONE CARD BECAME . . . . 411 TOWER 68

BECK
OR SERVILE SHAPE, AT OTHERS' BECK AND CALL. . . . . . 417 ANCEST HOUSES 8

BECKON
THUS, THUS I BECKON FROM HER VIEWLESS FIELDS-- . . . 693 MOSADA 1 75
THUS BECKON TO OUR AID A PHANTOM FAIR . . . . 693 MOSADA 1 76

BECKONED
BUT BECKONED TO SWEET COMPANY, ... 400 DEMON BEAST 18

BECKONING
AND, WHILE THEY GATHER ROUND MY BECKONING ARMS, . . . 694 MOSADA 1 100

BECKONS
BLAND RHADAMANTHUS BECKONS HIM, ... 530 DELPHIC ORACLE 3

BECOME
IT HAD BECOME A GLIMMERING GIRL . . . . 149 WANDER AENGUS 13
IT HAD BECOME A LAUGHING GIRL, ... 149 WANDER AENGUS V 13
BECOME OUR CAPTAIN, AIBRIC. I AM RESOLVED . . . . . 225 SHADOW WATER B 64
BECOME ONE MOVEMENT, ENERGY, DELIGHT, ... 231 SHADOW WATER B 217
MAY SHE BECOME A FLOURISHING HIDDEN TREE . . . . . . 404 FOR DAUGHTER 41
BECOME A ROOFLESS RUIN THAT THE OWL . . . . 423 MY DESCENDANTS 14
DID I BECOME A CHRISTIAN MAN AND CHOOSE FOR MY BELIEF . . 503 VACILLATION 85
BECOME A STRANGER'S LEMAN, AND THAT YOU, ... 757 SHADOW WATER A 215

BECOMES
WITHIN THE . . . . . .
ALL THOUGHT BECOMES AN IMAGE AND THE SOUL . . . . . 374 PHASES OF MOON 58
BECOMES A BODY, THAT BODY AND THAT SOUL . . . . . . 374 PHASES OF MOON 59
DELIGHT BECOMES DEATH-LONGING IF ALL LONGING ELSE BE VAIN. 459 FROM OEDIPUS 3

BED SEE DEATH-BED BRIDE-BED FEATHER-BED MARRIAGE-BED A-BED
COULD SLEEP ON A BED OF RUSHES, AND ALL INWROUGHT . . . 49 OISIN 3 V 31
AND INLAID,
ABOVE YOUR BED, ... 118 CRADLE SONG 2
ABOVE YOUR WHITE BED, ... 118 CRADLE SONG V 2
AND THE YOUNG LIE LONG AND DREAM IN THEIR BED . . . . 150 OLD MOTHER 5
WHILE THE YOUNG LIE LONG AND DREAM IN THEIR BED . . . 150 OLD MOTHER V 5
BUT THE YOUNG LIE LONG AND DREAM IN THEIR BED . . . . 150 OLD MOTHER V 5
WHEN THEY HAD COME TO THE MARRIAGE BED, ... 193 BAILE AILLINN V 106
BAILE AND AILLINN'S MARRIAGE BED, ... 194 BAILE AILLINN V 121
AND KEEP TO THE ONE WEARY MARRIAGE BED, ... 224 SHADOW WATER B V 55
THE BED OF LOVE, THAT IN THE IMAGINATION . . . . . . 228 SHADOW WATER B 148
UPON A GAUDY BED?" . . . . 253 HIS DREAM 8
UPON A PAINTED BED?" . . . . 253 HIS DREAM V 8
"I BID THEM MAKE HIS BED UNDER THIS ROOF . . . . . . 280 TWO KINGS 87
YOUR EMPTY BED." "HOW SHOULD I LOVE," I ANSWERED, . . 285 TWO KINGS 186
"WERE IT NOT THAT WHEN THE DAWN HAS LIT MY BED . . . . 285 TWO KINGS 187
A PRETTY GIRL TO SHARE MY BED," . . . . 296 THREE BEGGARS 31
"WHEN I WAS BROUGHT TO BED," . . . . 308 PLAYER QUEEN 6
CLIMB UP THE NARROW WINDING STAIR TO BED, ... 324 ROBERT GREGORY 5
AND SNUG IT IN A FEATHER BED . . . . 332 ROUND TOWER 28
LAID ON THE DEATH BED. . . . . 335 SONG V 16
SLEEP DRIVEN FROM MY BED, ... 346 ON WOMAN 36
RECOVERED HIM UPON THE BED OF DEATH, ... 355 BROKEN DREAMS 6
AND SHE MAY LOOK FROM THE BED . . . . 366 HER CHRIS TREE 6
NOR CRY, NOR TURN IN THE BED . . . . 435 FOR MY SON 3
STORIES OF THE BED OF STRAW . . . . 458 SECRETS OF OLD 17
OR THE BED OF DOWN. . . . . 458 SECRETS OF OLD 18
AND SAW HER SITTING UPRIGHT ON THE BED, ... 467 HARUN RASHID 134
AND SHE LAY DOWN UPON HER BED AND SLEPT, ... 467 HARUN RASHID 146
I SAW HER SITTING UPRIGHT ON THE BED, ... 467 HARUN RASHID V 134
EVERY NIGHT IN BED, ... 495 MOHINI CHATTER 4
THE GRASS MY BED, ... 510 JANE JUDGMENT 12
IN AN EMPTY BED, ... 511 JANE AND JACK 14
NOR GRAVE NOR BED DENIED, ... 513 JANE TALK BISH 10
I DREAMED AS IN MY BED I LAY, ... 519 HER DREAM 1
SLEEP UPON A GOLDEN BED . . . . 522 LULLABY 5
AND SEEMED TO STAND ALTHOUGH IN BED I LAY. . . . . . 535 CHOSEN 9
HE RHYMING ALONE IN HIS BED. . . . . 552 SONGS REWRIT 2 12
LYING ALONE ON A BED . . . . 552 SONGS REWRIT 2 V 10
MAY CREEP INTO YOUR BED, ... 569 THREE BUSHES 11
FROM PLEASURE OF THE BED, ... 575 MAIDS 2ND SONG 1
IN A YOUNG MAN'S BED." . . . . 594 COLONEL MARTIN 17
IN THE COMFORT OF A BED. . . . . 596 COLONEL MARTIN 44
CONFUSION OF THE BED, ... 599 SPIRIT MEDIUM 4
THROW LIKELY COUPLES INTO BED . . . . 606 SONGS BURDEN 1 25
I SCRUB ITS FLOORS AND MAKE MY BED, ... 607 SONGS BURDEN 2 5
AT TABLE OR IN BED. . . . . 620 JOHN KINSELLA 10
WHETHER MAN DIE IN HIS BED . . . . 637 BEN BULBEN 17
WITH ONLY BED AND BEDSTEAD THERE, ... 639 BEN BULBEN 61
NEVER STORM AROSE SO SWIFTLY, SCARCE THE CHILDREN WERE . 718 PHANTOM SHIP 4
IN BED,
"AND HALF FORGET THIS BED OF STRAW . . . . 739 EARL PAUL 5
EARL PAUL STOOD ON THE BED OF STRAW, ... 740 EARL PAUL 17
EAGLES HAVE GONE INTO THEIR CLOUDY BED. . . . . . . 778 SONG DEIRDRE 3 6

BEDABBLED SEE BLOOD-BEDABBLED
BEDDED
ALL HEAVEN'S FLOOR, WITH VAPOURS BEDDED-- . . . . . 705 DAWN-SONG 11
HAVE BEDDED WITH THEIR FANCY-MAN . . . . 789 SINGING HEAD 17

BEDFELLOW
TO BE HIS BEDFELLOW? UNTIL YOUR LIPS . . . . 237 SHADOW WATER B 335

67

		PAGE	TITLE	LINE
BEDOUIN				
BUT THE WILD BEDOUIN. THOUGH I APPROVE		462	HARUN RASHID	22
BEDOUIN'S				
STARING UPON A BEDOUIN'S HORSE-HAIR ROOF		368	EGO DOMINUS	29
MAYBE NOW A BEDOUIN'S BROOD.		732	STREET DANCERS	40
BOWS THE BEDOUIN'S WHITENING HAIR--		733	STREET DANCERS	45
BEDROWNED SEE DEW-BEDROWNED				
BEDS SEE DEATH-BEDS				
"MY BROTHERS SPRING OUT OF THEIR BEDS AT MORN,		32	OISIN 2	51
FOR HALF HIS FLOCK WERE IN THEIR BEDS,		132	FR GILLIGAN	3
FOR HALF HIS FLOCK LAY IN THEIR BEDS		132	FR GILLIGAN	V 3
O WANDERING BIRDS AND RUSHY BEDS.		190	BAILE AILLINN	31
THAT YOUNG MEN, TOSSING ON THEIR BEDS,		337	SCHOLARS	4
THEY HAD KEPT A STEADY PACE AS THOUGH THEIR BEDS,		372	PHASES OF MOON	5
WERE NOT OUR BEDS FAR OFF I'D RING THE BELL,		377	PHASES OF MOON	124
THEY TURN DOWN THEIR BEDS.		589	OLD WICKED MAN	35
OF SOLITARY BEDS, KNEW WHAT THEY WERE,		610	STATUES	5
BASE-BORN PRODUCTS OF BASE BEDS.		639	BEN BULBEN	73
ENCLOSE A QUIET PLACE OF BEDS BOX-BORDERED, BEES,		710	FERENCZ RENYI	24
BEDSTEAD				
WITH ONLY BED AND BEDSTEAD THERE,		639	BEN BULBEN	61
BEE SEE HONEY-BEE				
YET SANG NO MORE AS WHEN, LIKE A BROWN BEE		30	OISIN 2	15
BUT SANG NO MORE, AS WHEN, LIKE A BROWN BEE		30	OISIN 2	V 15
AND CHASE THE WILD BEE HOMEWARD TO HIS HIVE		32	OISIN 2	V 50D
NINE BEAN ROWS WILL I HAVE THERE, A HIVE FOR THE HONEY BEE		117	ISLE INNISFREE	V 3
WITHIN THE DROWSY BLOSSOM HANGS THE BEE;		645	ISLE STAT I 1	2
A NEW DAY'S TROOP OF WASP AND BEE		646	ISLE STAT I 1	44
BY BOSKY JUNE I SWEAR, AND BY THE BEE, HER MINISTER.		661	ISLE STAT II 1	74
O WAKE! WAKE! WAKE! FOR SOFT AS A BEE SIPS		677	ISLE STAT II 3	276
OLD WARRIOR, WAKE! FOR SOFT AS A BEE SIPS,		677	ISLE STAT II 3	284
THOSE TWAIN ARE DUST. WAKE! LIGHT AS A BEE SIPS		678	ISLE STAT II 3	290
HE IS LONG DEAD. WAKE! SOFT AS A BEE SIPS --		678	ISLE STAT II 3	297
NAY, HE IS GONE. WAKE! WAKE! AS A BEE SIPS		678	ISLE STAT II 3	305
WITH BERRIES. PLACID AS A HOMEWARD BEE		710	FERENCZ RENYI	29
LAPPED IN THE LEMON DAFFODILS; A BEE		716	DWELT SYCAMORE	10
AMONG THE HAUNTS OF BEE AND BIRD.		729	PRIEST FAIRY	42
BEECH				
UNDER A BEECH AT ALMHUIN AND HEARD THE THIN		44	OISIN 2	228
A BEECH BOUGH TO ME, AND MY HEART GREW SORE,		44	OISIN 2	V 226
AT EMAN, 'NEATH THE BEECH TREES, ON EACH SIDE,		44	OISIN 2	V 228
. . . THE BEECH LEAVES OLD.		82	MAD KING GOLL	12
. . . THE BEECH LEAVES OLD.		83	MAD KING GOLL	24
. . . THE BEECH LEAVES OLD.		84	MAD KING GOLL	36
. . . THE BEECH LEAVES OLD.		84	MAD KING GOLL	48
. . . THE BEECH LEAVES OLD.		85	MAD KING GOLL	60
. . . THE BEECH LEAVES OLD.		86	MAD KING GOLL	72
A CLUMP OF BEECH TREES MADE AN EMPTY SPACE		277	TWO KINGS	V 4A
BETWEEN THE PALE GREEN LIGHT OF THE BEECH LEAVES		277	TWO KINGS	V 5
AND WHERE BEECH TREES HAD MIXED A PALE GREEN LIGHT		277	TWO KINGS	V 5
AGAINST A BEECH BOLE, HE THREW DOWN THE BEAST		278	TWO KINGS	V 36
I GROPED MY WAY FROM BEECH TO HAZEL WOOD,		283	TWO KINGS	139
CLOSE TO A CLUMP OF BEECH TREES IN THE WOOD		283	TWO KINGS	V 135
TILL OAK AND HAZEL CEASED AND BEECH BEGAN,		283	TWO KINGS	V 139A
I STAGGERED, BUT A BEECH TREE STAYED MY FALL,		286	TWO KINGS	V 209
BEECH-BOLE				
AGAINST A BEECH-BOLE, HE THREW DOWN THE BEAST		278	TWO KINGS	36
BEECH-BOUGH				
A BEECH-BOUGH TO ME, AND MY HEART GREW SORE,		44	OISIN 2	226
BEECHEN				
UNDER OAK AND BEECHEN BOUGH,		522	LULLABY	11
BEECHES				
WHERE CERTAIN BEECHES MIXED A PALE GREEN LIGHT		277	TWO KINGS	V 5
AND IN A COPSE OF BEECHES THERE I STOOD,		490	COOLE BALLYLEE	11
UNDER OAK AND BEECHES BOUGH,		522	LULLABY	V 11
BEECH-LEAVES				
. . . THE BEECH-LEAVES OLD.		82	MAD KING GOLL	V REF
BEECH-TREE				
I STAGGERED, BUT A BEECH-TREE STAYED MY FALL,		286	TWO KINGS	209
BEECH-TREES				
AND WHERE BEECH-TREES HAD MIXED A PALE GREEN LIGHT		277	TWO KINGS	5
BEE-LOUD				
AND LIVE ALONE IN THE BEE-LOUD GLADE.		117	ISLE INNISFREE	4
BEER				
WITH RED BEER AND BROWN BEER.		214	HAPPY TOWNLAND	8
WITH RED BEER AND BROWN BEER.		214	HAPPY TOWNLAND	8
A LADLE AND A TUB OF BEER,		303	HOUR DAWN	29
INTO THE SLEEPER'S TUB OF BEER		304	HOUR DAWN	47
"BEFORE YOU HAVE DIPPED IT IN THE BEER		304	HOUR DAWN	49
TO VALUE BEER; NO HALF-LEGGED FOOL		304	HOUR DAWN	52
AND WOULD HAVE DIPPED IT IN THE BEER		304	HOUR DAWN	V 47
TO VALUE BEER--I WILL HAVE NO FOOL		304	HOUR DAWN	V 52
"WHY, BEER IS ONLY BEER." "BUT SAY		305	HOUR DAWN	56
"WHY, BEER IS ONLY BEER." "BUT SAY		305	HOUR DAWN	56
YOU'VE BUT TO DRINK THE BEER AND SAY		305	HOUR DAWN	V 56
IF YOU BUT DRINK THAT BEER AND SAY		305	HOUR DAWN	V 56
SO STAY AT HOME AND DRINK YOUR BEER		598	STONE CROSS	5
(O THE BROWN AND THE YELLOW BEER!)		779	GOING THE ROAD	2
(O THE BROWN AND THE YELLOW BEER!)		779	GOING THE ROAD	6
(O THE BROWN AND THE YELLOW BEER!)		779	GOING THE ROAD	10

68

BEERY
   A GREAT LAD WITH A BEERY FACE • • • • • • • • • • • 303 HOUR DAWN 27
BEE'S
   THE GIDDY BEE'S COMPLACENT CROON, • • • • • • • • • • 736 SUMMER EVENING 5
BEES   SEE HONEY-BEES
   AND IN THE BLOSSOMS HUNG THE BEES, • • • • • • • 2 OISIN 1 V 7G
   OR CLUNG THEREON LIKE SWARMING BEES! • • • • • • 14 OISIN 1 181
   OR CLUNG AS CLOSE AS SWARMS OF BEES. • • • • • • 14 OISIN 1 V 181
   WITH BOOM OF BEES IN HONEY-MARTS, • • • • • • • 16 OISIN 1 229
   FROM BEES AMONG THEIR HONEY MARTS • • • • • • • 16 OISIN 1 V 229
   WITH BOOM OF BEES IN HONEY MARTS, • • • • • • • 16 OISIN 1 V 229
   AND DOWNY BEES HAVE AMBUSCADE, • • • • • • • • 67 HAPPY SHEPHERD V 46A
   LIKE SWARMING BEES, ONE WITH THE DOVE • • • • • 78 INDIAN TO LOVE V 16
   WHEN SUMMER GLUTS THE GOLDEN BEES, • • • • • • 84 MAD KING GOLL 38
   WHERE SUMMER GLUTS THE GOLDEN BEES, • • • • • • 84 MAD KING GOLL V 38
   WHERE WILD BEES HIVE ON THE GREAT PLAIN. • • • • 194 BAILE AILLINN 123
   MAKE THEIR FAINT THUNDER, AND THE GARDEN BEES • • 198 SEVEN WOODS 2
   AMONG PIGEONS AND BEES, WHILE THAT GREAT ARCHER, • • 198 SEVEN WOODS 12
   DIM PAIRC-NA-CARRAIG, WHERE THE WILD BEES FLING • • 217 WOODS OF COOLE 9
   THE BEES BUILD IN THE CREVICES • • • • • • • 424 STARES NEST 1
   MY WALL IS LOOSENING, HONEY BEES • • • • • • • 424 STARES NEST V 4
   AND ALL THE GOLDEN GRASSHOPPERS AND BEES. • • • • 428 NINETEEN 19 8
   AND ALL HIS GOLDEN GRASSHOPPERS AND BEES. • • • • 428 NINETEEN 19 V 8
   OR TRAFFIC IN THE GRASSHOPPERS OR BEES. • • • • • 430 NINETEEN 19 48
   OR TRAFFIC IN THE GRASSHOPPERS AND BEES? • • • • • 430 NINETEEN 19 V 48
   FOR, LOOK YOU, SAD'S THE MURMUR OF THE BEES, • • • 652 ISLE STAT I 2 9
   BEHOLD, HOW LIKE A SWARM OF FIERY BEES • • • • • 662 ISLE STAT II 2 1
   ENCLOSE A QUIET PLACE OF BEDS BOX-BORDERED, BEES, • 710 FERENCZ RENYI 24
   AMONG THE MURMURS OF THE BEES, • • • • • • • • 728 PRIEST FAIRY 18
BEES'
   WILD BEES' HONEY LAID FOR THEE." • • • • • • • 730 PRIEST FAIRY 56
BEETLES
   I CANNOT SEE. THE BEETLES, AND THE BATS, • • • • • 693 MOSADA 1 63
BEFALL
   AND MAY SOME SUDDEN DREADFUL ILL BEFALL HER! • • • 74 ANASHU VIJAYA 59
   AND MAY SOME DREADFUL ILL BEFALL HER QUICK! • • • • 74 ANASHU VIJAYA V 59
   NOBODY KNOWS WHAT MAY BEFALL, • • • • • • • • 788 HAWTHORN TREE 13
BEFIT
   SO MUCH OF WEALTH AS MAY BEFIT THEIR RANK! • • • • 756 SHADOW WATER A V 186
BEFITTING
   BEFITTING EMBLEMS OF ADVERSITY. • • • • • • • • 420 MY HOUSE 30
BEFORE
   BEFORE THY FEET SHALL KNEEL DOWN ALL • • • • • • 7 OISIN 1 V 77
   BEFORE THE SWIFT THINGS THAT SHE DREAMED OF WERE DONE • • 27 OISIN 1 414
   BEFORE GOD WAS OR MY OLD LINE BEGAN! • • • • • • 29 OISIN 2 8
   BEFORE THIS DAY! FOR NOW THE FALL OF TEARS • • • • 30 OISIN 2 18
   WOVEN INTO HER HAIR, BEFORE DARK TOWERS • • • • • 30 OISIN 2 22
   WOVE IN HER FLOWER-LIKE HAIR, BEFORE DARK TOWERS • • • 30 OISIN 2 V 22
   PATRICK, BEFORE THY CRAFT DIES EACH OLD SONG. • • • 42 OISIN 2 V 196
   AN ISLE LAY LEVEL BEFORE US, WITH DRIPPING HAZEL AND OAK? 47 OISIN 3 10
   AN ISLE LAY LEVEL BEFORE US, DRIPPING WITH HAZEL AND OAK? 47 OISIN 3 V 10
   AND BEFORE I WENT BY THEM SO HUGE AND SO SPEEDY WITH EYES 59 OISIN 3 V 169
     SO BRIGHT,
   WITH MIRTHFUL SONGS BEFORE THE DAWN. • • • • • • 67 HAPPY SHEPHERD 49
   BEFORE US LIES ETERNITY! OUR SOULS • • • • • • • 81 EPHEMERA 23
   COME NEAR! I WOULD, BEFORE MY TIME TO GO, • • • • 101 ROSE UPON ROOD 22
   AND PIERCED HIM. "SPEAK BEFORE YOUR BREATH IS DONE." • 110 CUCHULAIN SEA 67
   BEFORE YOU WERE, OR ANY HEARTS TO BEAT, • • • • • 112 ROSE OF WORLD 12
   BEFORE HER WANDERING FEET. • • • • • • • • • 112 ROSE OF WORLD 15
   BEFORE YE WERE, OR ANY HEARTS TO BEAT, • • • • • 112 ROSE OF WORLD V 12
   WE TIRE OF THE FLAME OF THE METEOR, BEFORE IT CAN FADE 122 WHITE BIRDS 2
     AND FLEE!
   FOR WE TIRE OF THE FLAME OF THE METEOR BEFORE IT CAN PASS 122 WHITE BIRDS V 2
     BY AND FLEE
   WE TIRE OF THE FLAME OF THE METEOR, BEFORE IT CAN PASS 122 WHITE BIRDS V 2
     BY AND FLEE!
   BEFORE EARTH TOOK HIM TO HER STONY CARE! • • • • • 126 DREAM OF FAERY 4
   BEFORE EARTH MADE OF HIM HER SLEEPY CARE! • • • • • 126 DREAM OF FAERY V 4
   BEFORE THEY HEAPED HIS GRAVE UNDER THE HILL! • • • • 127 DREAM OF FAERY 16
   BUT WHILE HE PASSED BEFORE A PLASHY PLACE, • • • • 127 DREAM OF FAERY 17
   LIFT UP BEFORE US WHEN THEY PASS, • • • • • • • 135 TWO TREES 23
   LIFT UP BEFORE US AS THEY PASS, • • • • • • • • 135 TWO TREES V 23
   BEFORE GOD MADE THE ANGELIC CLAN, • • • • • • • 138 TO IRELAND 8
   IS COMELIER THAN CANDLES BEFORE MAURYA'S FEET. • • • 147 UNAPPEAS HOST V 12
   THE EAST HER HIDDEN JOY BEFORE THE MORNING BREAK, • • 154 BELOVED PEACE 4
   THE EAST TELLS ALL HER SECRET JOY BEFORE DAYBREAK, • • 154 BELOVED PEACE V 4
   BEFORE THEY DROWNED THEIR LOVERS' EYES • • • • • 156 FORGOT BEAUTY V 10A
   HIM WHO TREMBLES BEFORE THE FLAME AND THE FLOOD, • • 158 TO HIS HEART 3
   WHO TREMBLES BEFORE THE FLAME AND THE FLOOD, • • • 158 TO HIS HEART V 3
   IT TALKED BEFORE MORN WAS WHITE, • • • • • • • 159 CAP AND BELLS V 6
   SUDDENLY HURTLE BEFORE MY DREAM-AWAKENED EYES, • • 161 BLACK PIG 2
   BEFORE THE UNLABOURING STARS AND YOU. • • • • • • 164 PERFECT BEAUTY 8
   BEFORE UNLABOURING STARS AND YOU. • • • • • • • 164 PERFECT BEAUTY V 8
   AND HURLED IT FROM ITS PLACE BEFORE HIS FOOTSTOOL WHITE, 174 ELEMENT POWERS V 3
   IT WAS BEFORE THE TIME OF THE GREAT WAR • • • • • 182 QUEEN MAEVE 57
   BEFORE MY THOUGHTS BEGIN TO RUN • • • • • • • • 189 BAILE AILLINN 4
   WHERE THE HOUND OF ULADH SAT BEFORE • • • • • • 192 BAILE AILLINN 73
   BEFORE HIS EYES, HE HAS TEARS FOR NONE, • • • • • 192 BAILE AILLINN 82
   BEFORE HER LOVE-WORN HEART HAD BROKE, • • • • • 194 BAILE AILLINN 127
   WAS ROBBED BEFORE EARTH GAVE THE WHEAT! • • • • • 196 BAILE AILLINN 166
   BUT PURER THAN A TALL CANDLE BEFORE THE HOLY ROOD • • 208 HANRAHANS SONG 14

BEFORE   (CONTINUED)

	PAGE	TITLE	LINE
BUT PURE AS A TALL CANDLE BEFORE THE TRINITY	208	HANRAHANS SONG V	14
BUT PURER THAN A TALL CANDLE BEFORE THE BLESSED ROOD	208	HANRAHANS SONG V	14
THAT RUN BEFORE THE REAPING-HOOK AND LIE	218	WOODS OF COOLE	32
THAT RUN BEFORE THE REAPING HOOK AND LIE	218	WOODS OF COOLE V	32
BEFORE THEY READ OF FORGAEL AND DECTORA,	219	WOODS OF COOLE	42
AS MEN IN THE OLD TIMES, BEFORE THE HARPS BEGAN,	219	WOODS OF COOLE	43
AS MEN IN THE OLD TIMES, BEFORE THE HARP BEGAN,	219	WOODS OF COOLE V	43
STRANGE CREATURES FLUTTER UP BEFORE ONE'S EYES,	222	SHADOW WATER B	18
AS THAT WILD AENGUS. LONG BEFORE HER DAY	224	SHADOW WATER B	47
THE ROOTS OF THE WORLD. SHADOWS BEFORE NOW	227	SHADOW WATER B	104
UNTIL YOU STOOD BEFORE ME ON THE DECK--	236	SHADOW WATER B	313
BEFORE A HAND CAN TOUCH ME. MY HANDS ARE STILL,	238	SHADOW WATER B	358
OR CALLED BEFORE HIS EYES. O CARRY ME	249	SHADOW WATER B	568
I SWEAR BEFORE THE DAWN COMES ROUND AGAIN	260	FASC DIFFICULT	12
BEFORE WE GROW OLD AND DIE.	261	DRINKING SONG	4
BEFORE THE MERCHANT AND THE CLERK	266	GALWAY RACES	8
BEFORE THEIR SLEEPY EYELIDS RAN	272	GREY ROCK	30
BEFORE THAT ROOMFUL OR AS GOOD.	273	GREY ROCK	52
AND HALF THE KINGS, BEFORE SUNDOWN	273	GREY ROCK	69
AND HALF HIS KINGS, BEFORE SUNDOWN	273	GREY ROCK V	69
WITH THE LOUD HOST BEFORE THE SEA,	276	GREY ROCK	128
UNTIL HE CAME BEFORE THE PAINTED WALL,	279	TWO KINGS	47
BEFORE HIM OR BEHIND, BUT THAT FAR OFF	279	TWO KINGS	55
SAT UPRIGHT WITH A SWORD BEFORE HER FEET,	279	TWO KINGS	62
BEFORE HIM OR BEHIND, BUT THAT FAR-OFF	279	TWO KINGS V	55
BEFORE HIS CHAIR AND BENDING DOWN MY HEAD	282	TWO KINGS	132
BEFORE YOU'LL PUT YOUR GUINEAS DOWN,	287	TO WEALTHY MAN	5
BEFORE YOU'VE PUT YOUR GUINEAS DOWN,	287	TO WEALTHY MAN V	5
YOU HAD ENOUGH OF SORROW BEFORE DEATH--	293	TO A SHADE	23
SLEEP BEFORE THE THIRD NOON SOUNDS."	295	THREE BEGGARS	24
BEFORE THE THREE TO END THIS TALE,	297	THREE BEGGARS	55
"AND MAKE MY SOUL BEFORE MY PATE IS BARE."	299	BEGGAR CRIED	4
THE HOUR BEFORE DAWN	302	HOUR DAWN	T
BEFORE HIS EYES, WHERE STONES HAD BEEN,	302	HOUR DAWN	20
"AND I WILL TALK BEFORE I SLEEP	304	HOUR DAWN	44
AND DRINK BEFORE I TALK." AND HE	304	HOUR DAWN	45
"BEFORE YOU HAVE DIPPED IT IN THE BEER	304	HOUR DAWN	49
IN THE BAD HOUR BEFORE THE DAWN."	304	HOUR DAWN	55
I SAW, BEFORE I HAD WELL FINISHED,	322	SWANS AT COOLE	9
OR LEAVE THEM HAPPIER THAN BEFORE.	328	IRISH AIRMAN	8
"BEFORE NIGHTFALL I'LL PICK A POCKET	332	ROUND TOWER	27
YOU HAD BEFORE THE SUN HAD THROWN	333	SOLOMON SHEBA	13
I WISHED BEFORE IT CEASED. NOR BIRD NOR BEAST	338	SHEP GOATHERD	2
YEAR. I WISHED BEFORE IT CEASED. NOR BIRD NOR BEAST	338	SHEP GOATHERD V	2
EVEN BEFORE HIS CHILDREN AND HIS WIFE?	340	SHEP GOATHERD	34
AND CRIED, "BEFORE I AM OLD	348	FISHERMAN	37
DUMBFOUNDED BEFORE A KNAVE.	349	HAWK	16
THEIR MOMENTARY CRIES BEFORE IT IS DAWN,	371	EGO DOMINUS	78
BEFORE THE FULL MOON, HELPLESS AS A WORM,	374	PHASES OF MOON	49
THE COARSENESS OF THE DRUDGE. BEFORE THE FULL	376	PHASES OF MOON	94
INSIPID AS THE DOUGH BEFORE IT IS BAKED,	376	PHASES OF MOON	112
BEFORE SHE HAD SETTLED HER MIND	381	SONGS FOOL 2	8
THREE HUNDRED YEARS BEFORE THE FALL,	388	SOLOMON WITCH	11
BEFORE MY TIME, SEEM LIKE A VIVID MEMORY.	391	UNDER SATURN	10
AND THOUGHT BEFORE I HAD DONE	392	EASTER 1916	9
O BUT WE TALKED AT LARGE BEFORE	395	SIXTEEN DEAD	1
RECALL THE YEARS BEFORE HER MIND	397	POLIT PRISONER	8
OR HERS BEFORE A LOOKING-GLASS, FOR SUCH,	403	FOR DAUGHTER	19
BEFORE THAT RUIN CAME, FOR CENTURIES,	412	TOWER	81
BEFORE THE INDIFFERENT GARDEN DEITIES;	418	ANCEST HOUSES	28
THE NIGHT CAN SWEAT WITH TERROR AS BEFORE	429	NINETEEN 19	29
BEFORE THAT BRIEF GLEAM OF ITS LIFE BE GONE,	430	NINETEEN 19	63
BEFORE THE INDIFFERENT BEAK COULD LET HER DROP?	441	LEDA AND SWAN	14
SHE STANDS BEFORE ME AS A LIVING CHILD.	444	SCHOOL CHILDR	24
BEFORE SHE HAD SPREAD A BOOK UPON HER KNEES	466	HARUN RASHID	120
BEFORE THAT END MUCH HAD SHE RAVELLED OUT	472	ALL SOUL NIGHT	51
MUCH BOISTEROUS COURAGE, BEFORE LONELINESS	473	ALL SOUL NIGHT	72
THERE HYDE BEFORE HE HAD BEATEN INTO PROSE	489	COOLE PARK 29	9
BEFORE ME FLOATS AN IMAGE, MAN OR SHADE,	497	BYZANTIUM	9
THAT SHONE BEFORE THESE EYES	504	QUARREL IN AGE	15
BEFORE THEIR EYES A HOUSE	512	JANE ON GOD	13
BEFORE THE WORLD WAS MADE."	516	MANS SONG	12
BEFORE THE THREAD BEGAN.	520	HIS BARGAIN	8
BEFORE THE WORLD WAS MADE.	531	BEFORE WORLD	T
BEFORE THE WORLD WAS MADE.	532	BEFORE WORLD	8
BEFORE THE WORLD WAS MADE.	532	BEFORE WORLD	16
BEFORE I HAD MARKED HIM ON HIS NORTHERN WAY,	535	CHOSEN	13
SAVING THE RHYME RATS HEAR BEFORE THEY DIE.	542	PARN FUNERAL 1	28
BUT HE KICKED BEFORE HE DIED,	545	TO SAME TUNE 1	25
HOW SOUL COULD WALK BEFORE SUCH THINGS BEGAN	558	RIBH CHRISTIAN	12
HOW SOUL HAS WALKED BEFORE SUCH THINGS BEGAN.	558	RIBH CHRISTIAN V	12
THAT DAY BRINGS ROUND THE NIGHT, THAT BEFORE DAWN	563	MERU	13
MY FATHER UPON THE ABBEY STAGE, BEFORE HIM A RAGING CROWD:	577	LOFTY THINGS	2
HIS FATHERS SERVED THEIR FATHERS BEFORE CHRIST WAS CRUCIFIED.	580	CURSE CROMWELL	6
BEFORE THE BENCH OF TIME,	582	ROGER CASEMENT	6
SING A "THE" BEFORE HIS NAME:	584	ORAHILLY	3
"THEN WANT BEFORE YOU DIE."	596	COLONEL MARTIN	67
BEFORE A WOMAN'S PORTRAIT. SUDDENLY I STAND,	602	GALLERY REVIS	13
BEFORE THE PAINTED SCENE.	608	SONGS BURDEN 3	17

BEFORE   (CONTINUED)
BUT HE KICKED BEFORE HE DIED, ...   616 MARCH SONGS 3   25
SOME DAY WE SHALL GET UP BEFORE THE DAWN   .   .   .   .   .   622 HOUND VOICE   15
AND FIND OUR ANCIENT HOUNDS BEFORE THE DOOR, ...   622 HOUND VOICE   16
THOUGH ALL WAS DONE IN COMMON AS BEFORE!   .   .   .   .   .   635 CUCHULAIN COMF   24
BEFORE HE CAN ACCOMPLISH FATE, ...   638 BEN BULBEN   35
BEFORE THE SECRET WORKING MIND!   .   .   .   .   639 BEN BULBEN   51
BEFORE HER I TROD   .   .   .   .   654 ISLE STAT I 2   74
AND THE WAVES BOWED BEFORE IT LIKE MOWN CORN, ...   657 ISLE STAT I 3   56
SAY THEN,---"A POPINJAY BEFORE GRIEF'S SHAFT   .   .   .   .   664 ISLE STAT II 2   52
E'EN THEN, BEFORE HER SHEPHERD HAIR   .   .   .   .   .   .   668 ISLE STAT II 3   54
HE SHRANK BEFORE MY VOICE, AND STOOD   .   .   .   .   .   .   671 ISLE STAT II 3   129
BEFORE A DEATH, O'ER WAVE AND BANK   .   .   .   .   .   .   673 ISLE STAT II 3   185
BEFORE I AM TOO WEAK, FIERCE MORTAL, LET ME FLY,   .   .   .   675 ISLE STAT II 3   245
BEFORE I AM TOO WEAK, OH LET ME FLY, ...   675 ISLE STAT II 3 V   245
BEFORE THE WIND, SAW YOU HIS EYES A-GLITTER?   .   .   .   .   683 SEEKER   35
BEHOLD, I BEND BEFORE THEE TO THE GROUND   .   .   .   .   .   683 SEEKER   43
BEHOLD, I BEND BEFORE THEE TO THE GROUND!   .   .   .   .   .   684 SEEKER   61
THEN LET ME SEE THY FACE BEFORE I DIE.   .   .   .   .   .   .   684 SEEKER   66
BEHOLD, I BEND BEFORE THEE TO THE GROUND!   .   .   .   .   .   684 SEEKER   67
BEHOLD I BOW BEFORE THEE TO THE GROUND!   .   .   .   .   .   684 SEEKER   V   67
WHAT, LOVER, DIE BEFORE OUR LIPS HAVE MET?   .   .   .   .   685 SEEKER   80
ABOUT THE SEA, BEFORE HER LIES THAT YOUTH, ...   687 TWO TITANS   22
AND HE IS DRAGGED AGAIN BEFORE HER FEET, ...   688 TWO TITANS   43
WE TWO, BEFORE WE DIE! FOR AZOLAR, ...   691 MOSADA 3   24
WE'LL FLY FROM THIS BEFORE THE MORNING STAR, ...   702 MOSADA 3   74
SO YOU MUST GO! KISS ME BEFORE YOU GO.   .   .   .   .   .   702 MOSADA 3   96
BEFORE WE TAKE OUR SEATS ABOVE THE CROWD, ...   704 MOSADA 3   134
BEFORE HIS TENT THE GENERAL SIPS HIS WINE, ...   709 FERENCZ RENYI   6
BEFORE HIM ONE WELL GUARDED, WITH BOUND HANDS!   .   .   709 FERENCZ RENYI   10
FLINGS HER BEFORE HIM, "SAVE THYSELF AND ME,   .   .   .   713 FERENCZ RENYI   86
ROUND SHE COMES IN STAYS BEFORE THEM .   .   .   .   .   719 PHANTOM SHIP   17
WHEN WERE YOU BORN? BEFORE YOUR GRANDAM EVE.   .   .   721 WITCH VIVIEN   32
LONG BEFORE THE MORNING FIRE   .   .   .   .   727 LOVERS QUARREL   45
AND STRAIGHT BEFORE THE SLEEPING PRIEST   .   .   .   .   .   729 PRIEST FAIRY   23
BEFORE US IN THE GLOOM!   .   .   .   .   738 MOURN THEN ON   16
WANDERS AND WAILS BEFORE MY HEART MOST TRUE   .   .   .   738 YOU ARE SAD   8
BEFORE A SANDED PLACE!   .   .   .   .   740 EARL PAUL   32
"MAY STAND BEFORE THY RACE AND THEE   .   .   .   .   .   .   742 EARL PAUL   63
IT MAY BE, BEFORE THE WINDS OF BIRTH HAVE WAKED.   .   .   750 SHADOW WATER A   86
FROM ITS FIRST SIGHS AND LAUGHTER, BEFORE THE SLEEP,   .   754 SHADOW WATER A   161
AND THAT DREAM ONLY SHINE BEFORE HER FEET.   .   .   .   761 SHADOW WATER A   258
BEFORE I DROPPED ASLEEP, A KINGFISHER   .   .   .   .   .   761 SHADOW WATER A   274
WHERE THE DEW IS MADE BEFORE DAWN!   .   .   .   .   .   .   771 SPINNING SONG   5
THAT DIES OUT BEFORE 'TIS DAY, ...   777 SONG DEIRDRE 2   8
THE CURLEW CRY BEFORE DAWN   .   .   .   .   783 GREY ROUND   22
TO THE LOUD SANDS BEFORE DAY HAS BROKEN.   .   .   .   .   784 WOMANS BEAUTY   18
AMID THE DARK BEFORE DAY HAD BROKEN.   .   .   .   .   .   784 WOMANS BEAUTY   20
BUT NEVER STOOD BEFORE A STAKE .   .   .   .   790 SINGING HEAD   23
HE, DISGUISED AS A SAILOR BEFORE THE MAST, ...   790 DEDICATION   2
YOU HAD BROUGHT DOWN BEFORE YOU DIED.   .   .   .   .   791 REPRISALS   2
BEG
AH! LEAVE ME, I PRAY YOU AND BEG.   .   .   .   .   .   .   708 FAIRY PEDANT   22
BEGAN
BEFORE GOD WAS OR MY OLD LINE BEGAN!   .   .   .   .   .   29 OISIN 2   8
THINGS DONE ERE GOD FIRST WAS OR MY OLD LINE BEGAN!   .   29 OISIN 2   V   8
. . . NO, NOT SINCE THE WORLD BEGAN.   .   .   .   .   .   50 OISIN 3   49
AND HE BEGAN TO GRIEVE.   .   .   .   .   132 FR GILLIGAN   8
AND STARS BEGAN TO PEEP.   .   .   .   .   133 FR GILLIGAN   16
OF HER, WHOSE HISTORY BEGAN   .   .   .   .   137 TO IRELAND   7
WHEN TIME BEGAN TO RANT AND RAGE   .   .   .   .   .   .   138 TO IRELAND   10
WHEN OWLS BEGAN TO CALL!   .   .   .   .   159 CAP AND BELLS   6
UNTIL THE PILLARED DARK BEGAN TO STIR   .   .   .   .   .   185 QUEEN MAEVE   110
AS MEN IN THE OLD TIMES, BEFORE THE HARPS BEGAN,   .   .   219 WOODS OF COOLE   43
AS MEN IN THE OLD TIMES, BEFORE THE HARP BEGAN,   .   .   219 WOODS OF COOLE V   43
TILL OAK AND HAZEL CEASED AND BEECH BEGAN,   .   .   .   283 TWO KINGS   V 139A
THE BEGGAR IN A RAGE BEGAN   .   .   .   .   306 HOUR DAWN   80
SANG TILL STARS BEGAN TO FADE, ...   332 ROUND TOWER   20
IT'S LONG SINCE I BEGAN   .   .   .   .   347 FISHERMAN   6
SUDDENLY I BEGAN, ...   348 FISHERMAN   26
WHO HAD ENDED WHERE HIS BREATH BEGAN.   .   .   .   .   .   360 ALF POLLEXFEN   12
O NOT SINCE LIFE BEGAN.   .   .   .   .   382 VISION ROBART   8
THAT NOTHING STRANGE! THE TRAGEDY BEGAN   .   .   .   .   411 TOWER   51
BEFORE THE THREAD BEGAN   .   .   .   .   520 HIS BARGAIN   8
HOW SOUL COULD WALK BEFORE SUCH THINGS BEGAN.   .   .   558 RIBH CHRISTIAN   12
HOW SOUL HAS WALKED BEFORE SUCH THINGS BEGAN.   .   .   558 RIBH CHRISTIAN V   12
KNOW WHERE ITS ROOTS BEGAN.   .   .   .   .   571 THREE BUSHES   76
WINTER AND SUMMER TILL OLD AGE BEGAN .   .   .   .   .   629 CIRCUS ANIMALS   5
GREW IN PURE MIND, BUT OUT OF WHAT BEGAN?   .   .   .   630 CIRCUS ANIMALS   34
TOOK UP THE NEAREST AND BEGAN TO SEW.   .   .   .   .   .   634 CUCHULAIN COMF   18
MEASUREMENT BEGAN OUR MIGHT!   .   .   .   .   638 BEN BULBEN   42
WHAT FINGER FIRST BEGAN   .   .   .   .   783 GREY ROUND   11
BEGET
FRESH IMAGES BEGET, ...   498 BYZANTIUM   39
AND COULD BEGET OR BEAR THEMSELVES COULD THEY BUT LOVE   556 RIBH PATRICK   12
    AS HE.
BEGETS
AS MAN, AS BEAST, AS AN EPHEMERAL FLY BEGETS, GODHEAD   556 RIBH PATRICK   5
    BEGETS GODHEAD,
AS MAN, AS BEAST, AS AN EPHEMERAL FLY BEGETS, GODHEAD   556 RIBH PATRICK   5
    BEGETS GODHEAD,

		PAGE	TITLE	LINE
BEGETS (CONTINUED)				
A LOUT BEGETS A LOUT,	• • • • • • • • • • • • •	605	SONGS BURDEN 1	6
BEGETTER				
HUGH LANE, "ONLIE BEGETTER" OF ALL THESE:	• • • • • •	602	GALLERY REVIS	22
BEGGAR				
A BEGGAR SAID, "THEY GET THE MOST	• • • • •	295	THREE BEGGARS	15
"AND IF I WIN," ONE BEGGAR SAID,	• • • • •	296	THREE BEGGARS	29
ONE BEGGAR CRIED: "YOU'RE SHAMMING SLEEP,"	• • •	297	THREE BEGGARS V	45
BEGGAR TO BEGGAR CRIED	• • • • • • • •	299	BEGGAR CRIED	T
BEGGAR TO BEGGAR CRIED	• • • • • • • •	299	BEGGAR CRIED	T
BEGGAR TO BEGGAR CRIED, BEING FRENZY-STRUCK,	• • •	299	BEGGAR CRIED	3
BEGGAR TO BEGGAR CRIED, BEING FRENZY-STRUCK,	• • •	299	BEGGAR CRIED	3
BEGGAR TO BEGGAR CRIED, BEING FRENZY-STRUCK,	• • •	300	BEGGAR CRIED	7
BEGGAR TO BEGGAR CRIED, BEING FRENZY-STRUCK,	• • •	300	BEGGAR CRIED	7
BEGGAR TO BEGGAR CRIED, BEING FRENZY-STRUCK,	• • •	300	BEGGAR CRIED	11
BEGGAR TO BEGGAR CRIED, BEING FRENZY-STRUCK,	• • •	300	BEGGAR CRIED	11
BEGGAR TO BEGGAR CRIED, BEING FRENZY-STRUCK,	• • •	300	BEGGAR CRIED	15
BEGGAR TO BEGGAR CRIED, BEING FRENZY-STRUCK,	• • •	300	BEGGAR CRIED	15
BEGGAR TO BEGGAR CRIED, BEING FRENZY-STRUCK,	• • •	300	BEGGAR CRIED	19
BEGGAR TO BEGGAR CRIED, BEING FRENZY-STRUCK,	• • •	300	BEGGAR CRIED	19
AND THERE THE KING IS BUT AS THE BEGGAR.	• • • •	301	RUN PARADISE	7
AND THERE THE KING IS BUT AS THE BEGGAR.	• • • •	301	RUN PARADISE	14
AND THERE THE KING IS BUT AS THE BEGGAR.	• • • •	301	RUN PARADISE	21
AND THERE THE KING IS BUT AS THE BEGGAR.	• • • •	301	RUN PARADISE	28
I HAD BEEN HURT," THE OLD BEGGAR THOUGHT	• • •	302	HOUR DAWN V	19
THE BEGGAR DEAF TO ALL BUT HOPE	• • • • •	304	HOUR DAWN V	44
THE BEGGAR IN A RAGE BEGAN	• • • • • •	306	HOUR DAWN	80
CRIED THE BEGGAR, BILLY BYRNE:	• • • • •	331	ROUND TOWER	4
SOME BEGGAR SHELTERING FROM THE WIND, AND THERE	• • • •	351	HER PRAISE	13
AS THAT OLD WANDERING BEGGAR AND THESE GOD-HATED CHILDREN KNOW.		459	FROM OEDIPUS	6
I WOULD THAT I WERE AN OLD BEGGAR	• • • • •	552	SONGS REWRIT 2	1
A DREARY, DREEPY BEGGAR	• • • • • • • •	552	SONGS REWRIT 2	5
O A BEGGAR BLIND FROM HIS BIRTH:	• • • • •	552	SONGS REWRIT 2	8
O WOULD THAT I WERE AN OLD BEGGAR	• • • • •	552	SONGS REWRIT 2 V	1
A BEGGAR BLIND FROM HIS BIRTH:	• • • • • •	552	SONGS REWRIT 2 V	8
NO RAGGED BEGGAR MAN,	• • • • • • • •	567	FROM JAPANESE V	6
AND THERE IS AN OLD BEGGAR WANDERING IN HIS PRIDE--	• • •	580	CURSE CROMWELL	5
A BEGGAR UPON HORSEBACK LASHES A BEGGAR ON FOOT.	• • • • •	590	GREAT DAY	2
A BEGGAR UPON HORSEBACK LASHES A BEGGAR ON FOOT.	• • • • •	590	GREAT DAY	2
A BEGGAR UPON HORSEBACK LASHES A BEGGAR UPON FOOT:	• • •	590	GREAT DAY V	2
A BEGGAR UPON HORSEBACK LASHES A BEGGAR UPON FOOT:	• • •	590	GREAT DAY V	2
BEGGAR-KINGS				
SOME BOAST OF BEGGAR-KINGS AND KINGS	• • • • • • •	597	MODEL LAUREATE	9
BEGGARLY				
THIS BEGGARLY HABILIMENT--	• • • • • • •	539	MEETING	17
BEGGARMAN				
DREAM OF THE NOBLE AND THE BEGGARMAN.	• • • • • •	603	GALLERY REVIS V	47
BEGGAR-MAN				
HOLY JOE, THE BEGGAR-MAN,	• • • • • • • •	529	TOM LUNATIC	8
NO RAGGED BEGGAR-MAN,	• • • • • • • •	567	FROM JAPANESE	6
DREAM OF THE NOBLE AND THE BEGGAR-MAN.	• • • • • •	603	GALLERY REVIS	47
BEGGAR'S				
ALL EMPTIED OF PURPLE HOURS AS A BEGGAR'S CLOAK IN THE RAIN,		63	OISIN 3	219
THE FRENZY OF THE BEGGAR'S MOON	• • • • • • • •	296	THREE BEGGARS V	43
BEGGARS				
THE THREE BEGGARS	• • • • • • • • •	294	THREE BEGGARS	T
AND THERE TO THREE OLD BEGGARS SAID,	• • • • •	295	THREE BEGGARS	10
ARE DRIVEN BY WEALTH AS BEGGARS BY THE ITCH,"	• • •	300	BEGGAR CRIED	14
ROADS FULL OF BEGGARS, CATTLE IN THE FIELDS,	• • • •	487	SEVEN SAGES	18
THE BEGGARS HAVE CHANGED PLACES, BUT THE LASH GOES ON.	• • •	590	GREAT DAY	4
BEGGARS'				
THE FRENZY OF THE BEGGARS' MOON	• • • • • • •	296	THREE BEGGARS	43
BEGGARY				
THE EXORBITANT DREAMS OF BEGGARY,	• • • • •	296	THREE BEGGARS	39
THEY UNDERSTOOD THAT WISDOM COMES OF BEGGARY.	• • • • •	487	SEVEN SAGES	26
BEGIN				
MADE IRELAND'S HEART BEGIN TO BEAT:	• • • • •	138	TO IRELAND	12
BEFORE MY THOUGHTS BEGIN TO RUN	• • • • • •	189	BAILE AILLINN	3
ONE CANNOT BEGIN IT TOO SOON.	• • • • • •	268	BROWN PENNY	16
NOR BUT IN MERRIMENT BEGIN A CHASE,	• • • • •	405	FOR DAUGHTER	45
BEGIN THE PREPARATION FOR YOUR DEATH	• • • • •	500	VACILLATION	28
NOW HIS WARS ON GOD BEGIN:	• • • • •	561	FOUR AGES MAN	7
ACCOMPLISHED FINGERS BEGIN TO PLAY.	• • • • •	567	LAPIS LAZULI	54
RED BIRD OF MARCH, BEGIN TO CROW!	• • • • •	782	HEART FRIGHT	5
RED BIRD OF MARCH, BEGIN TO CROW!	• • • • •	782	HEART FRIGHT	12
RED BIRD OF MARCH, BEGIN TO CROW!	• • • • •	782	HEART FRIGHT	19
BEGINNING				
TILL STARS ARE BEGINNING TO BLINK AND PEEP:	• • • •	150	OLD MOTHER	4
AND THAT WAS THE BEGINNING OF A JOY	• • • • •	465	HARUN RASHID V	103
BEGINS				
WHEN DAY BEGINS TO BREAK	• • • • • • • •	316	FRIENDS	21
RIDDLED WITH LIGHT. AH! WHEN THE GHOST BEGINS TO QUICKEN,		316	COLD HEAVEN	9
THE SOUL BEGINS TO TREMBLE INTO STILLNESS,	• • • •	374	PHASES OF MOON	54
WHEN THE CLOCK BEGINS TO CHIME."	• • • • •	570	THREE BUSHES	41
THINK WHERE MAN'S GLORY MOST BEGINS AND ENDS,	• • •	604	GALLERY REVIS	54
THAT THE ADVENTURE OF OLD AGE BEGINS.	• • • • •	609	IN TARAS HALLS	5
NOW THE HUNT BEGINS ANEW?	• • • • • • •	773	SONG DEIRDRE 1	18
BEGONE SEE WOE-BEGONE				
MY CRUELTY MUST KEEP: AND SO BEGONE	• • • • •	448	HERO GIRL FOOL V	7

72

		PAGE	TITLE		LINE

BEGOT
NOR THOUGHT OUT OF HER MIND OR MINE BEGOT, ... 467 HARUN RASHID 140
BEGOT: SELF-BORN, HIGH-BORN, AND SOLITARY, ... 467 HARUN RASHID V 141
A DANCE-LIKE GLORY THAT THOSE WALLS BEGOT. . . . . . 488 COOLE PARK 29 8
GODHEAD ON GODHEAD IN SEXUAL SPASM BEGOT . . . . . . 557 RIBH ECSTASY 5
A FASHION WITH US MOORISH MAIDS, BEGOT . . . . . 700 MOSADA 3 25
BEGOTTEN SEE SELF-BEGOTTEN BLOOD-BEGOTTEN
WHATEVER IS BEGOTTEN, BORN, AND DIES. . . . . . . 407 SAIL BYZANTIUM 6
WHATEVER IS BEGOTTEN BORN OR DIES, ... 407 SAIL BYZANTIUM V 6
NOR STORM DISTURBS, FLAMES BEGOTTEN OF FLAME, . . . 498 BYZANTIUM 27
WHERE BLOOD BEGOTTEN SPIRITS COME . . . . 498 BYZANTIUM V 28
OR THOSE BEGOTTEN OR UNBEGOTTEN . . . . 599 SPIRIT MEDIUM 5
OR THOSE BEGOTTEN OR UNBEGOTTEN, ... 599 SPIRIT MEDIUM 9
BEGUILE
NONE MAY BEGUILE HIM, AND HIS PASSIONS COLD . . . . . 35 OISIN 2 V 83A
YON SHEPHERD--CAME YOUR SPIRIT TO BEGUILE . . . . . 648 ISLE STAT I 1 105
BEGUILED
YOUNG PRINCESS, WHY WERT THOU BEGUILED . . . . . . 6 OISIN 1 V 59
YOUNG PRINCESS, WHEN WERE YOU BEGUILED . . . . . . 6 OISIN 1 V 59
"AND HOW AND WHERE WERE YOU BEGUILED, ... 6 OISIN 1 V 60
BEGUN
NOW THAT MY BODY HAS BEGUN TO DREAM, ... 245 SHADOW WATER B 486
IN ITS OWN BEING, AND WHEN THAT WAR'S BEGUN . . . . 374 PHASES OF MOON 51
SHE HAS BEGUN FORGETTING. WHEN SHE WAKES, ... 760 SHADOW WATER A 255
I HAVE BEGUN REMEMBERING MY DREAMS. . . . . . . 766 SHADOW WATER A 380
THE HARP-STRINGS HAVE BEGUN TO CRY OUT TO THE EAGLES. . 769 SHADOW WATER A 431
IT HAS BEGUN TO CRY OUT TO THE EAGLES. . . . . . 769 SHADOW WATER A V 431
BEHIND
AND FAR BEHIND US, SLOWLY ROUND . . . . . 10 OISIN 1 V 114B
AND A BEAUTIFUL YOUNG MAN FOLLOWED BEHIND . . . . 12 OISIN 1 144
A BEAUTIFUL YOUNG MAN FOLLOWED BEHIND. . . . . 12 OISIN 1 V 145
OF MURMURING OCEAN, AND BEHIND US . . . . . . 25 OISIN 1 V 384
A WALL BEHIND HIS BACK, OVER HIS HEAD . . . . . 180 QUEEN MAEVE 5
NOT WHAT'S BEHIND." . . . . 263 MASK 10
THE CROWD THAT CLOSES IN BEHIND! . . . . . 266 GALWAY RACES 4
THE FIELD THAT CLOSES IN BEHIND. . . . . . 266 GALWAY RACES V 4
BEFORE HIM OR BEHIND, BUT THAT FAR OFF . . . . . 279 TWO KINGS 55
BEFORE HIM OR BEHIND, BUT THAT FAR-OFF . . . . . 279 TWO KINGS V 55
AND WHAT WAITS BEHIND THE DOOR, ... 298 THREE HERMITS 9
AND LEAVE NO SMOKING WICK BEHIND . . . . . . 306 HOUR DAWN 97
A WASTE OF BREATH THE YEARS BEHIND . . . . . . 328 IRISH AIRMAN 15
AND LEAVE A WOMAN AND A MAN BEHIND . . . . . 422 MY DESCENDANTS 3
TO LEAVE A WOMAN AND A MAN BEHIND . . . . . 422 MY DESCENDANTS V 3
TO LEAVE SOME MONUMENT BEHIND, ... 432 NINETEEN 19 96
THE HEART BEHIND ITS RIB LAUGHED OUT. . . . . 450 OWEN AHERNE 13
HIS PROUD HEART HE LEFT BEHIND. . . . . . . 561 FOUR AGES MAN 6
TWO CHINAMEN, BEHIND THEM A THIRD, ... 566 LAPIS LAZULI 37
HE NEVER LAY BEHIND FOUR WALLS . . . . . . 606 SONGS BURDEN 1 12
OR CROWD BEHIND THE BULWARK, THAT WE SEEM . . . . 751 SHADOW WATER A 94
I HAD THROWN IT DOWN BEHIND THIS COIL OF ROPE. . . . 759 SHADOW WATER A 245
BEHOLD
BEHOLD THAT GREAT PLOTINUS SWIM, ... 530 DELPHIC ORACLE 1
BEHOLD, HOW LIKE A SWARM OF FIERY BEES . . . . . 662 ISLE STAT II 2 1
BEHOLD THE BRAZEN-GATED GLADE! . . . . . . 667 ISLE STAT II 3 43
BEHOLD THE LOVING LOVELESS FLOWER OF LONE WAYS, . . . 674 ISLE STAT II 3 201
BEHOLD THE HAPLESS SLEEPERS STANDING BY. . . . . 677 ISLE STAT II 3 281
BEHOLD THE FLASHING WATERS. . . . . 680 LOVE AND DEATH 1
BEHOLD, I BEND BEFORE THEE TO THE GROUND . . . . 683 SEEKER 43
"BEHOLD THE KNIGHT OF THE WATERFALL, WHOSE HEART . . . 684 SEEKER 54
BEHOLD, I BEND BEFORE THEE TO THE GROUND! . . . . 684 SEEKER 61
BEHOLD, I BEND BEFORE THEE TO THE GROUND! . . . . 684 SEEKER 67
BEHOLD, I BEND! AROUND MY BEARD IN DRIFTS . . . . 684 SEEKER 68
BEHOLD I BOW BEFORE THEE TO THE GROUND! . . . . 684 SEEKER V 67
BEHOLD I BOW! AROUND MY BEARD IN DRIFTS . . . . 684 SEEKER V 68
THE LIGHTNING PULSE--BEHOLD HER, AYE BEHOLD-- . . . 687 TWO TITANS 11
THE LIGHTNINGS PULSE--BEHOLD HER, AYE BEHOLD-- . . . 687 TWO TITANS 11
AND THE SALMON BEHOLD, AND THE OUSEL TOO, ... 717 LOVE SONG 3
BEING
BUT I, BEING YOUNG AND FOOLISH, WITH HER WOULD NOT AGREE. 90 SALLEY GARDENS 4
BUT NOW I HAVE GROWN NOTHING, BEING ALL: . . . . 104 FERGUS DRUID V 38
BEING WEARY OF THE WORLD'S EMPIRES, BOW DOWN TO YOU, . 161 BLACK PIG 7
CUMHAL THE KING, BEING ANGRY AND SAD, ... 166 BLESSED V 1
BUT I, BEING POOR, HAVE ONLY MY DREAMS: . . . . 176 CLOTHS HEAVEN 6
MAEVE WALKED, YET WITH SLOW FOOTFALL, BEING OLD, . . . 181 QUEEN MAEVE 43
WAS THAT, THE AIR BEING HEAVY AND THE DOGS . . . . 182 QUEEN MAEVE 53
BEING FORBID TO MARRY ON EARTH, ... 189 BAILE AILLINN 11
BEING TUMBLED AND BLOWN ABOUT . . . . . . 191 BAILE AILLINN 66
AND HE, BEING LAID UPON GREEN BOUGHS, ... 192 BAILE AILLINN 71
WHO BEING LOVELY WAS SO WISE-- . . . . . . 193 BAILE AILLINN 98
IN THE HID PLACE, BEING CRAZED BY LOVE. . . . . 195 BAILE AILLINN 143
AND BEING IN GOOD HEART, BECAUSE . . . . . . 197 BAILE AILLINN 191
THE FOLLY OF BEING COMFORTED. . . . . . . 199 FOLLY COMFORT T
YOU'D KNOW THE FOLLY OF BEING COMFORTED. . . . . 200 FOLLY COMFORT 14
HEAVY LIKE STONE, THEIR WISDOM BEING HALF SILENCE. . . 218 WOODS OF COOLE 26
I AM SO TIRED OF BEING BACHELOR . . . . . . 222 SHADOW WATER B 8
FROM EARLIEST CHILDHOOD, BUT THAT BEING SO, ... 225 SHADOW WATER B V 77
BEING AS DOUBTFUL? I HAVE CALLED YOU MASTER . . . 227 SHADOW WATER B 110
BEING TOO BUSY IN THE AIR AND THE HIGH AIR, . . . 234 SHADOW WATER B 274
HAD DROWNED ME ALSO. BUT, BEING YET ALIVE, . . . 235 SHADOW WATER B 289
BEING DRIVEN ON BY VOICES AND BY DREAMS . . . . 243 SHADOW WATER B 441
THEIR HEADS BEING TURNED WITH PRAISE AND FLATTERY! . . 245 SHADOW WATER B 480

73

	PAGE	TITLE	LINE

BEING (CONTINUED)

	PAGE	TITLE	LINE
THAT HE IS BEING DRIVEN TO HIS DEATH.	248	SHADOW WATER B	551
BEING TOO HIGH, THEIR HEADY PROPHECIES	250	SHADOW WATER B	578
AND NOW, BEING GREY,	255	WOMAN HOMER	9
BEING HIGH AND SOLITARY AND MOST STERN?	257	NO SECOND TROY	10
WHY, WHAT COULD SHE HAVE DONE, BEING WHAT SHE IS?	257	NO SECOND TROY	11
WHEN, THE EARS BEING DEAFENED, THE SIGHT OF THE EYES BLIND	257	RECONCILIATION	3
YET OLD ROMANCE BEING KIND, LET HIM PREVAIL	258	KING NO KING	9
BEING FOR A WOMAN'S SAKE.	259	UNWORTH PRAISE	5
ITS FLESH BEING WILD, AND IT AGAIN	266	GALWAY RACES	13
AND BEING THANKFUL MURROUGH FOUND,	274	GREY ROCK	77
BEING BETRAYED INTO A CRADLE, AND I COME	284	TWO KINGS	169
BEING WEARIED OUT, I LOVE IN MAN THE CHILD?	285	TWO KINGS	192
AND BADE ALL WELCOME, BEING IGNORANT.	286	TWO KINGS	218
AND RIDDEN TOWARDS IT, BEING IGNORANT.	286	TWO KINGS V	218
WHAT NEED YOU, BEING COME TO SENSE,	289	SEPTEMBER 1913	1
BEING HONOUR BRED, WITH ONE	291	TO A FRIEND	5
WHO HAVE FAILED, BEING WEAK OF WILL,	298	THREE HERMITS	18
BEGGAR TO BEGGAR CRIED, BEING FRENZY-STRUCK,	299	BEGGAR CRIED	3
BEGGAR TO BEGGAR CRIED, BEING FRENZY-STRUCK,	300	BEGGAR CRIED	7
BEGGAR TO BEGGAR CRIED, BEING FRENZY-STRUCK,	300	BEGGAR CRIED	11
BEGGAR TO BEGGAR CRIED, BEING FRENZY-STRUCK,	300	BEGGAR CRIED	15
BEGGAR TO BEGGAR CRIED, BEING FRENZY-STRUCK,	300	BEGGAR CRIED	19
BEING CERTAIN IT WAS NO RIGHT ROCK	303	HOUR DAWN	23
BEING CERTAIN IT WAS NO RIGHT PLACE	303	HOUR DAWN V	23
AND THEN AT LAST BEING WIDE AWAKE	304	HOUR DAWN V	40
BUT I ALONE BEING BLESSED KEEP	307	HOUR DAWN	104
BEING YOUNG YOU HAVE NOT KNOWN	312	CHILD DANCING	6
BEING WAKEFUL FOR HER SAKE,	316	FRIENDS	23
BEING OUT OF HEART WITH GOVERNMENT	317	APPOINTMENT	1
BEING OUT OF HEART AT GOVERNMENT	317	APPOINTMENT V	1
BEING BY CALVARY'S TURBULENCE UNSATISFIED,	318	MAGI	7
WHO HAD SEEN, BEING KEPT FOR SHOW	319	DOLLS	5
BEING BUT A PART OF ANCIENT CEREMONY—	321	REED WHISPERER	12
ALL, ALL ARE IN MY THOUGHTS TO-NIGHT BEING DEAD.	324	ROBERT GREGORY	8
BEING MORE INDIFFERENT TO OUR SOLITUDE	334	LIVING BEAUTY	7
THE WICK OF YOUTH BEING BURNED AND THE OIL SPENT,	334	LIVING BEAUTY V	3
BEING OLD, BUT THAT THE OLD ALONE MIGHT DIE,	339	SHEP GOATHERD	4
ON BEING ASKED FOR A WAR POEM	359	WAR POEM	T
WE AND OUR DOLLS BEING BUT THE WORLD WERE BEST AWAY.	364	DOLLS FACES	12
BEING MOCKED BY GUIDO FOR HIS LECHEROUS LIFE,	369	EGO DOMINUS	33
AND MADE—BEING POOR, AILING AND IGNORANT,	370	EGO DOMINUS	59
AND LOOK MOST LIKE ME, BEING INDEED MY DOUBLE,	371	EGO DOMINUS	72
THE MOST UNLIKE, BEING MY ANTI-SELF,	371	EGO DOMINUS	74
IN ITS OWN BEING, AND WHEN THAT WAR'S BEGUN	374	PHASES OF MOON	51
FOR NOW BEING DEAD IT SEEMED	383	VISION ROBART	23
BEING FIXED ON ALL THINGS LOVED, ALL THINGS UNLOVED,	383	VISION ROBART	34
BEING CAUGHT BETWEEN THE PULL	384	VISION ROBART	59
CHANCE BEING AT ONE WITH CHOICE AT LAST,	388	SOLOMON WITCH	14
YOUTH'S BITTERNESS BEING PAST,	389	IMAGE PAST	11
BEING A PORTION OF MY YOUTH, CAN MAKE ME PINE	391	UNDER SATURN V	3
BEING CERTAIN THAT THEY AND I	392	EASTER 1916	13
BEING DEAR AS MINE ARE DEAR.	400	DEMON BEAST	20
BEING NO MORE DEMONIAC	400	DEMON BEAST	30
BEING MADE BEAUTIFUL OVERMUCH,	403	FOR DAUGHTER	20
HELEN BEING CHOSEN FOUND LIFE FLAT AND DULL	404	FOR DAUGHTER	25
BEING FATHERLESS COULD HAVE HER WAY	404	FOR DAUGHTER	28
AND CERTAIN MEN, BEING MADDENED BY THOSE RHYMES,	410	TOWER	41
INTO THE LABYRINTH OF ANOTHER'S BEING,	413	TOWER	112
THAT, BEING DEAD, WE RISE,	415	TOWER	154
BEING OF THAT METAL MADE	416	TOWER	178
SOUL'S BEAUTY BEING MOST ADORED,	421	MY TABLE	22
BEING BY THE WORLD OPPRESSED,	434	YOUTH AND AGE	2
AND AGAMEMNON DEAD. BEING SO CAUGHT UP,	441	LEDA AND SWAN	11
AND THAT ALONE, YET I, BEING DRIVEN HALF INSANE,	442	BLACK CENTAUR	6
BEING BUT HOLY SHOWS	454	HIS MEMORIES	2
BEING ALL ALONE I'D NURSE A STONE .	459	HIS WILDNESS	11
AND SHE AND I, BEING SUNK IN HAPPINESS,	463	HARUN RASHID	51
BEING BRIMMED WITH LIFE?" "WERE IT BUT TRUE	465	HARUN RASHID	90
BUT I BEING NONE CAN PRAISE ITS OPPOSITE.	465	HARUN RASHID	98
BEING SO BRIMMED WITH LIFE. "IF THAT COULD BE	465	HARUN RASHID V	90
BEING SHARPENED BY HIS DEATH,	471	ALL SOUL NIGHT	8
BEING BOTH CHANCE AND CHOICE,	472	ALL SOUL NIGHT	58
AND MAY HAVE GROWN MORE ARROGANT BEING A GHOST.	473	ALL SOUL NIGHT	80
MINE WOULD WALK, BEING DEAD.	511	JANE AND JACK V	18
WHEN, THE POTION'S WORK BEING DONE,	522	LULLABY	9
ALL OTHER LOVERS BEING ESTRANGED OR DEAD,	523	LONG SILENCE	2
BEING MENTIONED WITH A MAN	531	FATHER CHILD	4
I MOCKED, BEING CRAZY, BUT YOU MASTERED IT.	533	HER TRIUMPH	8
THAT THE CRIME OF BEING BORN	534	CONSOLATION	5
THAT SHE IS HAPPY BEING CRAZY!	568	SWEET DANCER	10
BEING THEIR AMBASSADOR,	582	ROGER CASEMENT	14
SOME THAT BEING UNBEGOTTEN	600	SPIRIT MEDIUM	11
AND BEING OLD SHE PUT A SKIN	621	JOHN KINSELLA	21
MAYBE AT LAST, BEING BUT A BROKEN MAN,	629	CIRCUS ANIMALS	3
BEING ALMINTOR'S PAGE. NOW JUDGE YOU HERE.	660	ISLE STAT II 1	47
WILL HE HAVE HAPPINESS? GREAT SOBS HER BEING SHAKE.	676	ISLE STAT II 3	247
BEING THE MOON OF BIRTH, MAY END OUR DOUBT.	748	SHADOW WATER A	24
I CEASED TO BE A WOMAN, BEING A QUEEN.	758	SHADOW WATER A	228
TO RAISE INTO BEING	784	WOMANS BEAUTY	13
BEING IMAGINED WITHIN	785	WOMANS BEAUTY	23

74

		PAGE	TITLE		LINE
BEING (CONTINUED)					
DRAGGED INTO BEING		785	WOMANS BEAUTY		27
BEINGS					
FOR THE ELEMENTAL BEINGS GO		138	TO IRELAND	V	23
YET DREAMED THAT BEINGS HAPPIER THAN MEN		218	WOODS OF COOLE		18
BELABOURING					
TROOPER BELABOURING TROOPER, BITING AT ARM OR AT FACE. . .		426	PHANTOM HATRED		12
BELFRY					
. . . WITH ITS BELFRY IN AIR!		61	OISIN 3		193
SAY WHAT RINGER RINGS AT MIDNIGHT! FOR, IN THE BELFRY HIGH,		718	PHANTOM SHIP		15
BELIEF					
DID I BECOME A CHRISTIAN MAN AND CHOOSE FOR MY BELIEF . .		503	VACILLATION		85
BELIEVE					
AND WILL BELIEVE THAT ANYTHING		191	BAILE AILLINN		68
"NEVER WILL I BELIEVE THERE IS ANY CHANGE		285	TWO KINGS		203
SWEETENED BY DEATH, BUT IF I COULD BELIEVE.		285	TWO KINGS		205
BELIEVE THAT GOLD AND WOMEN TAKEN IN WAR		754	SHADOW WATER A		159
BELIEVED					
BELIEVED THERE WAS SOME OTHER NEAR AT HAND, ...		229	SHADOW WATER B		154
THAT ONE BELIEVED HE HAD A SWORD UPSTAIRS!		267	ALL TEMPT ME		8
BELIEVING					
BELIEVING EVERY WORD I SAID, ...		314	MEMORY YOUTH		8
BELL SEE DUMB-BELL					
O PATRICK, BY YOUR BRAZEN BELL, ...		7	OISIN 1		71
AND GOD'S BELL BUOYED TO BE THE WATER'S CARE! . . .		114	ROSE OF BATTLE		4
GOD'S BELL HAS CLAIMED THEM BY THE LITTLE CRY . . .		114	ROSE OF BATTLE		23
THE BELL THAT CALLS US ON! THE SWEET FAR THING. . . .		115	ROSE OF BATTLE		28
THERE WAS A GREEN BRANCH HUNG WITH MANY A BELL . .		129	BOOK STORIES		1
I ALSO BEAR A BELL BRANCH FULL OF EASE.		130	BOOK STORIES	V	12
MY BELL BRANCH MURMURS! THE GAY BELLS BRING LAUGHTER, . .		130	BOOK STORIES	V	18
CAP AND BELL		159	CAP AND BELLS	V	T
"I'VE CAP AND BELL," HE PONDERED, ...		160	CAP AND BELLS	V	21
THAN DUMB BELL AND FOIL		334	SONG		3
WERE NOT OUR BEDS FAR OFF I'D RING THE BELL, . . .		377	PHASES OF MOON		124
LIKE THE CLANGOUR OF A BELL, ...		382	SONG OF FOOL		9
MIDNIGHT HAS COME, AND THE GREAT CHRIST CHURCH BELL . .		470	ALL SOUL NIGHT		1
AND MANY A LESSER BELL SOUND THROUGH THE ROOM! . .		470	ALL SOUL NIGHT		2
IT IS ALL SOULS' NIGHT AND THE GREAT CHRIST CHURCH BELL		470	ALL SOUL NIGHT	V	1
A SLOW LOW NOTE AND AN IRON BELL.		549	SEVERED HEAD		7
A SLOW LOW NOTE AND AN IRON BELL.		550	SEVERED HEAD		14
A SLOW LOW NOTE AND AN IRON BELL.		550	SEVERED HEAD		21
TREMBLES AS A BELL OF GLASS		705	DAWN-SONG		10
SLOW, THE CHAPEL BELL IS TOLLING AS THOUGH THE DEAD PASSED BY.		718	PHANTOM SHIP		16
WHERE A HAND ON THE BELL		780	WELL AND TREE		4
BELL-BEAT					
THE BELL-BEAT OF THEIR WINGS ABOVE MY HEAD, ...		323	SWANS AT COOLE		17
BELL-BRANCH					
AND I GAZED ON THE BELL-BRANCH, SLEEP'S FOREBEAR, . . .		50	OISIN 3		53
LAID HANDS ON THE BELL-BRANCH AND SWAYED IT, ...		51	OISIN 3		56
THEN HE SWAYED IN HIS FINGERS THE BELL-BRANCH, . . .		51	OISIN 3		67
. . . THE STRENGTH OF THE BELL-BRANCH IS NAUGHT, . .		55	OISIN 3		123
I ALSO BEAR A BELL-BRANCH FULL OF EASE.		130	BOOK STORIES		12
BELLE					
AND WHO CAN SAY BUT SOME YOUNG BELLE MAY WALK AND TALK MEN WILD		354	HIS PHOENIX		26
AND MAY BE THERE'LL BE SOME YOUNG BELLE WALK OUT TO MAKE MEN WILD		354	HIS PHOENIX	V	26
AND MAYBE THERE'LL BE SOME YOUNG BELLE WALK OUT TO MAKE MEN WILD		354	HIS PHOENIX	V	26
BELLED					
HOWLED, MIAU-D, BARKED, BRAYED, BELLED, YELLED, CRIED, CROWED,		387	SOLOMON WITCH		8
BELLIED SEE POT-BELLIED					
BELLIES					
THAT BELLIES AND DRAGS IN THE WIND		358	BALLOON MIND		3
BELL-MOUNTED					
YOUR BELL-MOUNTED CHURCHES, ...		58	OISIN 3		163
THY BELL-MOUNTED CHURCHES, ...		58	OISIN 3	V	163
BELL-NOTES					
. . . AH! WHAT BELL-NOTES DO THEY HEAR?		718	PHANTOM SHIP		14
BELLOW					
I BELLOW TO THE WINDS WHEN STORMS MAKE MOAN, . . .		45	OISIN 2	V	239D
BELLOWED					
ON THE HORIZON EDGE BELLOWED THE HERDS.		279	TWO KINGS		56
BELLOWED AND PRANCED IN THE ROUND TOWER!		331	ROUND TOWER		12
BELLOWING					
THEREON THE BELLOWING OF THE EMPOUNDED HERDS . . .		286	TWO KINGS		214
BELLOWING UP AND BELLOWING ROUND, ...		331	ROUND TOWER		14
BELLOWING UP AND BELLOWING ROUND.		331	ROUND TOWER		14
BELLOWS					
FOR AN OLD BELLOWS FULL OF ANGRY WIND?		405	FOR DAUGHTER		64
OR EVERY BELLOWS BURST, BE HAPPY STILL.		405	FOR DAUGHTER		72
BELLS					
IN ONE WAS A BRANCH SOFT-SHINING WITH BELLS MORE MANY THAN SIGHS		50	OISIN 3		46
. . . AND PRAYING, AND WROTH WITH THE BELLS, . . .		58	OISIN 3		159
THAT HE'S A LOVELESS MAN! GAY BELLS BRING LAUGHTER . .		130	BOOK STORIES		18
GAY BELLS OR SAD, THEY BRING YOU MEMORIES		130	BOOK STORIES		21
MY BELL BRANCH MURMURS! THE GAY BELLS BRING LAUGHTER, . .		130	BOOK STORIES	V	18
THE SAD BELLS BOW THE FOREHEAD ON THE HANDS. . . .		130	BOOK STORIES	V	20

75

		PAGE	TITLE		LINE
BELLS	(CONTINUED)				
	THE CAP AND BELLS	159	CAP AND BELLS		T
	"I HAVE CAP AND BELLS," HE PONDERED, ...	160	CAP AND BELLS		21
BELLY					
	DOWN LIMB AND BREAST OR DOWN THAT GLIMMERING BELLY . . .	560	MAGIC DRUM		5
	BUT THETIS' BELLY LISTENS.	612	NEWS ORACLE		29
	BELLY, SHOULDER, BUM, ...	612	NEWS ORACLE		34
	WHERE MEN FORGIVE IF THE BELLY GAIN?	615	MARCH SONGS 2		14
BELLYFUL					
	BUT WHEN I HAD EATEN AND DRUNK A BELLYFUL	223	SHADOW WATER B	V	30
BELONG					
	LEAVE NOTHING BUT THE NOTHINGS THAT BELONG	542	PARN FUNERAL 1		29
BELONGS					
	BELONGS TO BEAST OR DEMON, ...	401	DEMON BEAST		35
BELOVED	SEE WELL-BELOVED				
	BELOVED IN A THOUSAND SONGS.	7	OISIN 1	V	76
	I WOULD THAT WE WERE, MY BELOVED, WHITE BIRDS ON THE FOAM OF THE SEA!	121	WHITE BIRDS		1
	O WOULD THAT WE WERE, MY BELOVED, WHITE BIRDS ON THE FOAM OF THE SEA,	121	WHITE BIRDS	V	1
	HAS AWAKED IN OUR HEARTS, MY BELOVED, A SADNESS THAT MAY NOT DIE.	122	WHITE BIRDS		4
	AH, DREAM NOT OF THEM, MY BELOVED, THE FLAME OF THE METEOR THAT GOES,	122	WHITE BIRDS		6
	WERE WE ONLY WHITE BIRDS, MY BELOVED, ...	122	WHITE BIRDS		12
	HAS AWAKED IN OUR HEARTS, MY BELOVED, A SADNESS THAT NEVER MAY DIE.	122	WHITE BIRDS	V	4
	BELOVED, GAZE IN THINE OWN HEART, ...	134	TWO TREES		1
	BELOVED, GAZE IN THINE OWN HEART.	135	TWO TREES		20
	. . . AND HIS BELOVED, AND LONGS FOR THE END OF THE WORLD	153	CHANGE BELOVED		T
	MONGAN LAMENTS THE CHANGE THAT HAS COME UPON HIM AND HIS BELOVED	153	CHANGE BELOVED	V	T
	HE BIDS HIS BELOVED BE AT PEACE	154	BELOVED PEACE		T
	MICHAEL ROBARTES BIDS HIS BELOVED BE AT PEACE	154	BELOVED PEACE	V	T
	BELOVED, LET YOUR EYES HALF CLOSE, AND YOUR HEART BEAT .	154	BELOVED PEACE		9
	A POET TO HIS BELOVED	157	POET BELOVED		T
	HE GIVES HIS BELOVED CERTAIN RHYMES	157	BELOVED RHYMES		T
	AEDH GIVES HIS BELOVED CERTAIN RHYMES	157	BELOVED RHYMES	V	T
	A QUEEN WAS BELOVED BY A JESTER, ...	159	CAP AND BELLS	V	1
	OF YOUR BELOVED IN SLEEP.	165	CRY OF SEDGE		10
	HE THINKS OF THOSE WHO HAVE SPOKEN EVIL OF HIS BELOVED .	166	EVIL OF BELOV		T
	AEDH THINKS OF THOSE WHO HAVE SPOKEN EVIL OF HIS BELOVED	166	EVIL OF BELOV	V	T
	WHEN SONGS I WOVE FOR MY BELOVED HIDE THE PRAYER, . . .	173	SPEAKS HEARERS		2
	AND CALL TO MY BELOVED AND ME: "NO LONGER FLY	173	SPEAKS HEARERS		7
	WHEN SONG I WOVE FOR MY BELOVED HIDES THE PRAYER, . . .	173	SPEAKS HEARERS	V	2
	HE WISHES HIS BELOVED WERE DEAD	175	BELOVED DEAD		T
	AEDH WISHES HIS BELOVED WERE DEAD	175	BELOVED DEAD	V	T
	O WOULD, BELOVED, THAT YOU LAY	176	BELOVED DEAD		11
	BELOVED, I AM NOT AFRAID OF HER.	197	BAILE AILLINN		200
	I HAVE FLED TO MY BELOVED IN THE AIR, ...	234	SHADOW WATER B		262
	HAVE CALLED ME THEIR BELOVED, I'LL NOT KISS THEM. . . .	237	SHADOW WATER B		336
	BUT MY BELOVED--THAT NIGHT AND DAY HAD PERISHED, . . .	246	SHADOW WATER B		504
	AND I AM LEFT ALONE WITH MY BELOVED, ...	251	SHADOW WATER B		600
	BELOVED, HAVING DRAGGED THE NET ABOUT US, ...	252	SHADOW WATER B		615
	LOVED AND THOUGHT HIMSELF BELOVED, ...	404	FOR DAUGHTER		39
	BELOVED HAROUN EL RASHID, OCCUPIED	462	HARUN RASHID	V	24
	WHEN OUR BELOVED CALIPH PUT TO DEATH	462	HARUN RASHID		31
	BELOVED BOOKS THAT FAMOUS HANDS HAVE BOUND, ...	491	COOLE BALLYLEE		27
	BELOVED, MAY YOUR SLEEP BE SOUND	522	LULLABY		1
	SLEEP, BELOVED, SUCH A SLEEP	522	LULLABY		7
	BELOVED SUCH A SLEEP AS FELL	522	LULLABY	V	13
	AS THOUGH ON MY BELOVED, ...	532	BEFORE WORLD		10
	DRAW ROUND, BELOVED AND BITTER MEN, ...	584	GHOST ROG CASE		37
	PICTURED, WHERE WANDER THE BELOVED FEET	692	MOSADA 1		44
	BELOVED, HOW TWO LITTLE YEARS AGO	713	FERENCZ RENYI		89
	BELOVED, HEAR MY BITTER TALE!--	742	DANAAN QUICK		1
	BELOVED, BLAME THE DANAAN WHIM, ...	743	DANAAN QUICK		22
	AND SHE CRIES OUT, "I HAVE FLED TO MY BELOVED	754	SHADOW WATER A		151
	AND CRYING, "I HAVE FLED TO MY BELOVED	754	SHADOW WATER A	V	151
	I HAVE COMMANDED MEN IN DREAMS. BELOVED, ...	766	SHADOW WATER A		381
	OUT OF THEIR HATRED. MY BELOVED, FAREWELL.	767	SHADOW WATER A		400
BELOVED'S	SEE WELL-BELOVED'S				
	"YOUR WELL BELOVED'S HAIR HAS THREADS OF GREY, ...	199	FOLLY COMFORT	V	2
BELOVEDS					
	OF MYRIADS OF BELOVEDS, AND ON THINE	724	KANVA ON SELF		10
BELOW					
	THE FLIES BELOW THE LEAVES, AND THE YOUNG MICE	75	ANASHU VIJAYA		87
	I PASSED ALONG THE WATER'S EDGE BELOW THE HUMID TREES, .	76	INDIAN ON GOD		1
	WAKE ALL BELOW! WHY HAVE YOU BROKEN OUR SLEEP?	233	SHADOW WATER B		242
	BUTTED BELOW THE SINGLE AND SO PIERCED	278	TWO KINGS		22
	ONE HEARS THE RUMBLE OF IT FAR BELOW	420	MY HOUSE	V	20B
	OTTERS BELOW AND MOOR-HENS ON THE TOP, ...	490	COOLE BALLYLEE		2
	OTTERS BELOW AND MOOR HENS ON THE TOP, ...	490	COOLE BALLYLEE	V	2
	A RIVERY FIELD SPREAD OUT BELOW, ...	502	VACILLATION		57
	PLATO STANDS BELOW, ...	524	MAD AS MIST		8
	FROM ABOVE TO BELOW.	547	TO SAME TUNE 3	V	6
	FOR THINGS BELOW ARE COPIES, THE GREAT SMARAGDINE TABLET SAID.	556	RIBH PATRICK		6
	'TIS LATE, WAIT ONE MORE DAY! BELOW THE HILLS	702	MOSADA 3		91
	HAVE NOT A MYRIAD SWAYED BELOW STRANGE TREES	724	KANVA ON SELF		11
	WAKE ALL BELOW. WHY HAVE YOU BROKEN OUR SLEEP? . . .	753	SHADOW WATER A		132

76

BELOW   (CONTINUED)
    I HAVE HEARD FROM FAR BELOW . . . .   783 GREY ROUND   25
BELT
    SHE CAUGHT THIS BLADE OUT OF MY BELT AND DIED. . . . .   755 SHADOW WATER A V   168
BEMOCKERS
    WORD BEMOCKERS?--BY THE ROOD . . . .   65 HAPPY SHEPHERD V   12
BE-MOCKERS
    WORD BE-MOCKERS?--BY THE ROOD, ...   65 HAPPY SHEPHERD   12
BEN
    --BEN JONSON'S PHRASE--AND FIND WHEN JUNE IS COME . .   321 REED WHISPERER   6
    BEN JONSON'S PHRASE--AND STILL MAY TURN MY FEET . .   321 REED WHISPERER V   6
    UNDER BEN BULBEN TO THE MEET, ...   397 POLIT PRISONER   14
    UPON BEN BULBEN SIDE . . . .   398 BREAK OF DAY   6
    OR THE HUMBLER WORM, I CLIMBED BEN BULBEN'S BACK . .   409 TOWER   9
    KUSTA BEN LUKA IS MY NAME, I WRITE . . . .   460 HARUN RASHID   1
    OUT OF BEN BULBEN AND KNOCKNAREA, ...   549 SEVERED HEAD   2
    UNDER BEN BULBEN . . . .   636 BEN BULBEN   T
    WHERE BEN BULBEN SETS THE SCENE. . . . .   637 BEN BULBEN   11
    UNDER BARE BEN BULBEN'S HEAD . . . .   640 BEN BULBEN   84
BENCH
    PALE-FACED, ALONE UPON A BENCH, EDAIN . . . .   279 TWO KINGS   61
    HER HANDS ON EITHER SIDE HAD GRIPPED THE BENCH, . . .   279 TWO KINGS   63
    PALE-FACED, ALONE UPON A BENCH, HIS WIFE . . . . .   279 TWO KINGS   V   61
    ON NO LONG BENCH NOR LOFTY MILKING-SHED . . . . . .   341 SHEP GOATHERD   51
    ON NO LONG BENCH NOR LOFTY MILKING SHED . . . . . .   341 SHEP GOATHERD   V   51
    A POT-HOUSE BENCH WITH OLIVER GOLDSMITH ONCE. . . . .   486 SEVEN SAGES   3
    BEFORE THE BENCH OF TIME, ...   582 ROGER CASEMENT   6
BENCHES
    OR ON THE BENCHES UNDERNEATH THE WALLS, ...   180 QUEEN MAEVE   14
    UPON THE ROWERS' BENCHES UNDERNEATH, ...   751 SHADOW WATER A   92
BEND
    AND HE CALLED LOUDLY TO THE STARS TO BEND . . . . .   68 SAD SHEPHERD   5
    WE WILL BEND DOWN AND LOOSEN OUR HAIR OVER YOU, . . .   172 TRAV PASSION   6
    BEND DOWN AND PRAY FOR ALL THAT SIN I WOVE IN SONG, .   173 SPEAKS HEARERS   5
    BEND DOWN AND PRAY FOR THE GREAT SIN I WOVE IN SONG, .   173 SPEAKS HEARERS V   5
    YOU WOULD COME HITHER, AND BEND YOUR HEAD, ...   175 BELOVED DEAD   3
    O TUFTED REEDS, BEND LOW AND LOW IN POOLS ON THE GREEN   206 HANRAHANS SONG V   1
        LAND,
    BUT WE BEND TOGETHER AND KISS THE QUIET FEET . . . .   207 HANRAHANS SONG V   4
    BEND LOWER, O KING, THAT I MAY CROWN YOU WITH IT. . .   251 SHADOW WATER B   607
    BEND LOWER, THAT I MAY COVER YOU WITH MY HAIR, . . .   251 SHADOW WATER B   613
    AND ALL SHALL BEND THE KNEE . . . .   516 MANS SONG   16
    I BEND MY BODY TO THE SPADE . . . .   599 SPIRIT MEDIUM   7
    I BEND MY BODY TO THE SPADE . . . .   600 SPIRIT MEDIUM   15
    I BEND MY BODY TO THE SPADE . . . .   600 SPIRIT MEDIUM   23
    MY MEDIAEVAL KNEES LACK HEALTH UNTIL THEY BEND, . . .   603 GALLERY REVIS   33
    BEHOLD, I BEND BEFORE THEE TO THE GROUND . . . . .   683 SEEKER   43
    BEHOLD, I BEND BEFORE THEE TO THE GROUND! . . . . .   684 SEEKER   61
    BEHOLD, I BEND BEFORE THEE TO THE GROUND! . . . . .   684 SEEKER   67
    BEHOLD, I BEND! AROUND MY BEARD IN DRIFTS . . . . .   684 SEEKER   68
    AND THOU SHALT BEND, ENDURING GOD, THE KNEES . . . .   698 MOSADA 2   59
    AND THOU SHALT BEND, ENDURING GOD, THE KNEES . . . .   698 MOSADA 2   V   59
    WHERE LONG GREY GRASSES BOW AND BEND, ...   736 SUMMER EVENING   6
    AND MADE THE BRIGHT SPEAR BEND, ...   741 EARL PAUL   46
    BEND LOWER LEST YOUR BATTLE-AXES GLIMMER. . . . . .   752 SHADOW WATER A   117
    BEND LOWER LEST YOUR BATTLE AXES GLIMMER. . . . . .   752 SHADOW WATER A V   117
    AND UNDER LOVERS' EYELIDS. BEND YOUR HEAD . . . . .   762 SHADOW WATER A   286
    I CROWN YOU WITH THIS CROWN. BEND LOWER, O KING, . .   768 SHADOW WATER A   423
    BEND LOWER, THAT I MAY COVER YOU WITH MY HAIR, . . .   769 SHADOW WATER A   429
BENDED
    ALONG THE WOOD WITH SUBTLE TREAD AND BENDED BOWS. . .   649 ISLE STAT I 1   111
BENDING
    UPON THE GRASS-BLADES' BENDING TIPS, ...   3 OISIN 1   V   7II
    WITH BENDING STERNS AND BENDING BOWS, ...   14 OISIN 1   189
    WITH BENDING STERNS AND BENDING BOWS, ...   14 OISIN 1   189
    AND BENDING OVER THEM SOFTLY SAID, ...   21 OISIN 1   307
    BENDING OVER THEM IN THE DANCE, ...   21 OISIN 1   308
    WITH BENDING STERNS AND BENDING BOWS, ...   23 OISIN 1   353
    WITH BENDING STERNS AND BENDING BOWS, ...   23 OISIN 1   353
    LIKE A BRIDE BENDING OVER HER MIRROR ADORNING, . . .   28 OISIN 1   V   423E
    BENDING LOW HIS PIOUS HEAD, ...   82 MAD KING GOLL   V   10
    BENDING LOW HIS FADING HEAD, ...   82 MAD KING GOLL   V   10
    THE ANGELS ARE BENDING . . . .   118 CRADLE SONG   V   1
    AND BENDING DOWN BESIDE THE GLOWING BARS, ...   121 YOU ARE OLD   9
    CUMHAL CALLED OUT, BENDING HIS HEAD, ...   166 BLESSED   1
    AND CUMHAL SAID, BENDING HIS KNEES, ...   167 BLESSED   5
    BEFORE HIS CHAIR AND BENDING DOWN MY HEAD . . . . .   282 TWO KINGS   132
    BENDING HER FACE O'ER HIS, SHE WATCHES MEET . . . .   688 TWO TITANS   45
    BENDING HUMBLY EVERY KNEE, ...   726 LOVERS QUARREL   14
BENDS
    AND BENDS TO THE FIRE AND SHAKES WITH THE COLD . . .   26 OISIN 1   405
    THE LION, THE WORLD'S GREAT SOLITARY, BENDS . . . .   689 NETTLESHIP   5
BENEATH
    ONE HAND BENEATH HIS BEARDLESS CHIN, ...   17 OISIN 1   V   251
    BENEATH HAD PACED CONTENT! WE HELD OUR WAY . . . . .   36 OISIN 2   103
    LONG SIGHS AROSE IN OUR SPIRITS, BENEATH US BUBBLED THE   48 OISIN 3   20
        GROUND.
    . . . BENEATH ME THE HOOVES IMPATIENTLY STEPT. . . . .   54 OISIN 3   V   112
    AND DEMONS BE BROKEN IN PIECES, AND TRAMPLED BENEATH THEM 61 OISIN 3   204
        IN DEATH.

77

	PAGE	TITLE	LINE

BENEATH (CONTINUED)

	PAGE	TITLE		LINE
AND DEMONS, ALL BROKEN IN PIECES, BE TRAMPLED BENEATH THEM IN DEATH.	61	OISIN 3	V	204
AND HOW BENEATH THOSE THREE TIMES BLESSED SKIES	127	DREAM OF FAERY	V	21
CRIED OUT UPON THAT THING BENEATH	254	HIS DREAM		10
TREMBLING BENEATH HIM, AND THEN DROVE THE SPUR	277	TWO KINGS	V	11
AS I, TO CHOOSE BENEATH DAY'S DYING FLAMES.	656	ISLE STAT I	3	34
CURVING BENEATH THE PROW. AS SOME WILD DRAKE	659	ISLE STAT II	1	16
BENEATH THE WEIGHT OF GREATER GRIEF THAN I.	661	ISLE STAT II	1	63
BUT LOUD THE GRASSHOPPER THAT SITS BENEATH.	662	ISLE STAT II	2	8
BENEATH THE BURTHEN OF THE INFINITE,	674	ISLE STAT II	3	212
BENEATH THE BURDEN OF THE INFINITE,	674	ISLE STAT II	3	212
MORE DARK BENEATH THE POPLARS, WHERE YON OWL	675	ISLE STAT II	3	233
ON HER BROAD BREAST. BENEATH HER WITHERED BROWS	685	SEEKER		73
BENEATH THE SHELTERING SHADOW OF THY CHURCH.	698	MOSADA 2		58
NOW STEPS DRAW CLOSE, HE HIDES BENEATH A DRUM.	713	FERENCZ RENYI		78
BENEATH THE WILLOW--NAY, TO YONDER STAR,	715	FERENCZ RENYI	V	118
BENEATH THE FLAMING EYEBALLS OF THE NIGHT,	723	KANVA ON SELF		4
BENEATH A POINTED CAP OF GREEN.	728	PRIEST FAIRY		22

BENIGHTED

	PAGE	TITLE		LINE
AND ALL BENIGHTED THINGS THAT GO	139	TO IRELAND		39
BENIGHTED TRAVELLERS	419	MY HOUSE		18

BENT

	PAGE	TITLE		LINE
YOU WHO ARE BENT, AND BALD, AND BLIND,	2	OISIN 1		1
BENT ALL OUR SWAYING BODIES DOWN,	20	OISIN 1		297
BENT DOWN ABOVE EACH HOOKED KNEE,	26	OISIN 1		392
BENT LOW ABOVE EACH HOOKED KNEE,	26	OISIN 1	V	392
WHILE HE BENT DOWN HIS FADING HEAD,	82	MAD KING GOLL		10
WHEN WE BENT DOWN ABOVE THE FADING COALS	136	TO SOME I TALK		3
BECAUSE THEIR BLOSSOMING DREAMS HAVE NEVER BENT	136	TO SOME I TALK		8
I BENT TO BLOW THE FIRE AFLAME.	149	WANDER AENGUS	V	10
BUT WE HAVE ALL BENT LOW AND LOW AND KISSED THE QUIET FEET	207	HANRAHANS SONG		9
CONSTRAINED, ARRAIGNED, BAFFLED, BENT AND UNBENT	382	VISION ROBART		9
I DREAM OF A LEDAEAN BODY, BENT	443	SCHOOL CHILDREN		9
AND DEDICATE--EYES BENT UPON THE GROUND,	489	COOLE PARK 29		29
ROWER BENT IN HIS ROW-BOAT	589	OLD WICKED MAN		50
OR WEAVER BENT AT HIS LOOM,	589	OLD WICKED MAN		51
ROWER BENT IN HIS ROWBOAT	589	OLD WICKED MAN	V	50
OF THOSE STEEL TONGUES. CRASH, SWORDS. WELL THRUST. WELL BENT	665	ISLE STAT II	2	67
A BEARDED WITCH, HER SLUGGISH HEAD LOW BENT	685	SEEKER		72
OFTEN HE HAD BENT DOWN SOME BOUGH ALL BRIGHT	710	FERENCZ RENYI		28
OFTEN HE HAD BENT DOWN SOME BOUGH ALL BRIGHT WITH BERRIES.	710	FERENCZ RENYI	V	28
BENT LOW WITH TOIL AND HOARIEST YEARS. THE OTHER	711	FERENCZ RENYI		52

BERA

	PAGE	TITLE		LINE
. . . FROM RACHLIN TO BERA OF SHIPS.	58	OISIN 3		160

BEREFT

	PAGE	TITLE		LINE
NIGH OF HIS WITS BY FEAR BEREFT.	730	PRIEST FAIRY		50

BERENICE'S

	PAGE	TITLE		LINE
THE HEAVENLY CIRCUIT. BERENICE'S HAIR.	483	VERONIC NAPKIN		1
BERENICE'S BURNING HAIR.	519	HER DREAM		8

BERKELEY

	PAGE	TITLE		LINE
. . . BERKELEY AND BURKE HAVE TRAVELLED THERE.	481	BLOOD AND MOON		18
AND GOD-APPOINTED BERKELEY THAT PROVED ALL THINGS A DREAM,	481	BLOOD AND MOON		25

BERRIES   SEE SLOE-BERRIES

	PAGE	TITLE		LINE
CAME, AND MY FOREHEAD FELL LOW, AND MY TEARS LIKE BERRIES FELL DOWN.	57	OISIN 3		154
AND MY TEARS WERE LARGER THAN BERRIES, AND I MURMURED,	59	OISIN 3		178
AND MY TEARS WERE LARGE LIKE TO BERRIES, AND I MURMURED,	59	OISIN 3	V	178
FULL OF BERRIES	87	STOLEN CHILD		7
WITH BERRIES. PLACID AS A HOMEWARD BEE,	710	FERENCZ RENYI		29
OFTEN HE HAD BENT DOWN SOME BOUGH ALL BRIGHT WITH BERRIES.	710	FERENCZ RENYI	V	28
ROASTING BERRIES STEAM AND SHAKE--	727	LOVERS QUARREL		43
DARK JOAN CALL THE BERRIES SWEET,	743	DANAAN QUICK		28

BERRY

	PAGE	TITLE		LINE
AND HOOKED A BERRY TO A THREAD.	149	WANDER AENGUS		4
I DROPPED THE BERRY IN A STREAM	149	WANDER AENGUS		7
AND PUT A BERRY ON A THREAD.	149	WANDER AENGUS	V	4
A BERRY THREW FOR ME--OR THEE.	743	DANAAN QUICK		11

BERYL

	PAGE	TITLE		LINE
OR CHRYSOBERYL, OR BERYL, OR CHRYSOLITE.	231	SHADOW WATER B		215
OF CHRYSOBERYL, OR BERYL, OR CHRYSOLITE.	231	SHADOW WATER B	V	215
OF CHRYSOBERYL AND BERYL AND CHRYSOLITE,	765	SHADOW WATER A		357

BESEECH

	PAGE	TITLE		LINE
FORBID, BESEECH AND WASTE MY BREATH." THEN I.	281	TWO KINGS		102

BESEECHING

	PAGE	TITLE		LINE
THOUGH FROM BESEECHING THEY DESISTED NOT,	36	OISIN 2	V	93
I KNOW YOU NOW, BESEECHING HANDS AND EYES.	763	SHADOW WATER A		312
BESEECHING HANDS AND MORE BESEECHING EYES?	763	SHADOW WATER A		312
BESEECHING HANDS AND MORE BESEECHING EYES?	763	SHADOW WATER A	V	312

BESET

	PAGE	TITLE		LINE
THE HOUR OF THE WANING OF LOVE HAS BESET US,	79	FALLING LEAVES		5

BESIDE

	PAGE	TITLE		LINE
AND STOOD BESIDE THE SEA TOGETHER.	9	OISIN 1	V	101B
BESIDE THE SEA, WHERE, HUSHED AND SLOW,	20	OISIN 1	V	292
HEAPED BESIDE THE GLIMMERING WAVES,	21	OISIN 1		314
HEAVED BESIDE THE GLIMMERING WAVES,	21	OISIN 1	V	314
BESIDE THE PILED-UP HUNTING SPEARS,	23	OISIN 1		348
BESIDE THE PILED-UP HUNTING-SPEARS,	23	OISIN 1	V	349

BESIDE (CONTINUED)
    WHEN ONCE BESIDE THE SHORE I STOOD,   24 OISIN 1   V 364
    AND RODE AND STOOD BESIDE THE SHORE,   25 OISIN 1   V 379A
    ROLLING HIS WHEEL, WE SANG BESIDE THE DEEP   42 OISIN 2   V 193
    OH, MAY TRANQUILLITY BESIDE HIM GO,   71 ANASHU VIJAYA V   2
    AND I MUST WAIL BESIDE THE SEA   86 MAD KING GOLL V   67
    AND HIS YOUNG SWEETHEART CLOSE BESIDE HIM KNELT,   108 CUCHULAIN SEA   40
    AND HIS YOUNG DEAR ONE CLOSE BESIDE HIM KNELT,   108 CUCHULAIN SEA   40
    WEARY AND KIND ONE STOOD BESIDE HIS SEAT,   112 ROSE OF WORLD V   13
    BESIDE HER CLEAN-SWEPT HEARTH, HER QUIET SHADE!   114 ROSE OF BATTLE   11
    AND BENDING DOWN BESIDE THE GLOWING BARS,   121 YOU ARE OLD   9
    WHERE PEOPLE LOVE BESIDE THE RAVELLED SEAS!   126 DREAM OF FAERY   9
    WHERE PEOPLE LOVE BESIDE STAR-LADEN SEAS!   126 DREAM OF FAERY V   9
    HE MUSED BESIDE THE WELL OF SCANAVIN,   127 DREAM OF FAERY   25
    BESIDE YOUNG AENGUS IN HIS TOWER OF GLASS,   219 HARP OF AENGUS   2
    THIS SWORD IS TO LIE BESIDE HIM IN THE GRAVE.   242 SHADOW WATER B 412
    BESIDE THE BRACKISH WATERS OF THE BOYNE   270 PARDON FATHERS   11
    HAD TUCKED HIMSELF AWAY BESIDE   303 HOUR DAWN   28
    IN SOME OUTLANDISH COAT BESIDE   303 HOUR DAWN   V 28
    BESIDE A FIRE OF TURF IN TH' ANCIENT TOWER,   324 ROBERT GREGORY   3
    IN GLENDALOUGH BESIDE THE STREAM,   331 ROUND TOWER   8
    AND THERE ARE--BUT NO MATTER IF THERE ARE SCORES BESIDE!   354 HIS PHOENIX   15
    ON THE GREY SAND BESIDE THE SHALLOW STREAM   367 EGO DOMINUS   1
    A LAMP BURNS ON BESIDE THE OPEN BOOK   367 EGO DOMINUS   3
    BURNING ALONE BESIDE AN OPEN BOOK,   370 EGO DOMINUS   63
    BESIDE THE CASTLE DOOR, WHERE ALL IS STARK   377 PHASES OF MOON   126
    BUT SHE THAT BESIDE ME LAY   399 BREAK OF DAY   21
    BESIDE THE LITTLE LAKE   400 DEMON BEAST   23
    "SO YOU MUST LIE BESIDE HIM   570 THREE BUSHES   22
    BESIDE HER LADY'S MAN,   571 THREE BUSHES   72
    AND THAT OLD MAN BESIDE ME, NOTHING WOULD HE SAY   593 PILGRIM   9
    THEN STUMBLING TO THE KILL BESIDE THE SHORE!   622 HOUND VOICE   19
    THAT STUMBLING TO THE KILL BESIDE THE SHORE;   622 HOUND VOICE   V 19
    FIERCE MORTAL, AND CROUCHED LOW BESIDE THE LAKE   675 ISLE STAT II 3 V 245A
    IF ONE SHOULD RISE BESIDE THEE,   680 LOVE AND DEATH   27
    THAT WAS BESIDE THE WATERFALL, THY WORDS   683 SEEKER   49
    UNDER A LEMON TREE BESIDE YOUR DOOR!   693 MOSADA 1   68
    BESIDE THE DOOR OF PETER'S GATE.   696 MOSADA 2   V 23
    GRIEVE NOT, FOR GOMEZ KNEELS BESIDE THEE--GOMEZ,   702 MOSADA 3   90
    GRIEVE NOT, FOR VALLENCE KNEELS BESIDE THEE--VALLENCE,   702 MOSADA 3   V 90
    I SAT ME DOWN BESIDE THEE, AND I KNEW   713 FERENCZ RENYI   92
    BESIDE THE WILLOW. NAY, TO YONDER STAR,   715 FERENCZ RENYI   118
    WHERE LIES THE COW AT PEACE BESIDE HER CALF,   715 FERENCZ RENYI   121
    TROTTED BESIDE HIM IN A PLAYFUL MOOD.   715 DWELT SYCAMORE   4
    CRIES A VOICE AT ROARING MIDNIGHT BESIDE THE MOONLESS DEEP. 718 PHANTOM SHIP   8
    PRAYED BESIDE THE OCEAN, THE OLD MUMBLING MOTHER OF THE   719 PHANTOM SHIP   V 34
      DEAD.
    COME, BESIDE A SANDY LAKE,   727 LOVERS QUARREL   41
    OR STAY WITH ME BESIDE THE THAMES,   741 EARL PAUL   59
    BESIDE A LOCHLANN WHARF, AND THOUGH SHE HAD SWORN   756 SHADOW WATER A   188
    I SAT BESIDE MY FOSTER-MOTHER, AND NOW   762 SHADOW WATER A   292
    BESIDE YOUNG AENGUS IN HIS TOWER OF GLASS,   762 SHADOW WATER A   297
    I SAT BESIDE MY FOSTER MOTHER, AND NOW   762 SHADOW WATER A V 292
    OR GO BESIDE HIM TO HIS MOUNTAIN WARS.   768 SHADOW WATER A   414
BESIDES
    BESIDES HER CLEAN SWEPT HEARTH, HER QUIET SHADE!   114 ROSE OF BATTLE V   11
    AND TO GIVE YOU BESIDES A HUNDRED SHIELDS,   756 SHADOW WATER A   185
BESOM
    A SORT OF BESOM THAT CAN CLEAR THE SOUL   558 RIBH CHRISTIAN   5
BESOT
    THEY ARE BESOTTING YOU AS THEY BESOT   229 SHADOW WATER B   166
BESOTTED   SEE WORLD-BESOTTED
    WORLD BESOTTED TRAVELLER! HE   493 SWIFTS EPITAPH V   5
BESOTTING
    THEY ARE BESOTTING YOU AS THEY BESOT   229 SHADOW WATER B   166
BESOUGHT
    "I LOVED NO MAN, THOUGH KINGS BESOUGHT,   7 OISIN 1   62
    "I LOVED NO MAN, THOUGH CANNS BESOUGHT,   7 OISIN 1   V 62
    FULL MANY BOWING KINGS BESOUGHT ME,   7 OISIN 1   V 67
BEST   SEE SECOND-BEST
    FOR OUR BEST WERE DEAD ON GAVRA'S GREEN.   2 OISIN 1   V 71
    . . . OF BEST ONES A SAD THING WERE--   63 OISIN 3   V 222
    AND YET THE SADDEST CHIMES ARE BEST ENJOYED.   130 BOOK STORIES   20
    THAT I HAVE THE BEST OF PILOTS. SHADOWS, ILLUSIONS,   249 SHADOW WATER B   565
    REMEMBERING THAT THE BEST I HAVE DONE   256 WORDS   7
    THAT COMES OF THE BEST KNIT TO THE BEST? ALTHOUGH   264 HOUSE SHAKEN   7
    THAT COMES OF THE BEST KNIT TO THE BEST? ALTHOUGH   264 HOUSE SHAKEN   7
    HE AND HIS BEST TROOPS BACK TO BACK   274 GREY ROCK   73
    IMAGINES BEST TO MAKE IT THRIVE.   287 TO WEALTHY MAN   8
    THAT SOME NEW DAY MAY BREED THE BEST   288 TO WEALTHY MAN   34
    NOR THE BEST LABOURER DEAD   312 CHILD DANCING   9
    AND HE, THE BEST WARRIOR, DEAD   312 CHILD DANCING   V   9
    THAT EVEN THE BEST OF LOVE MUST DIE,   314 MEMORY YOUTH   17
    AND LEARN THAT THE BEST THING IS   330 BONE OF A HARE   6
    CHOOSE YOUR COMPANIONS FROM THE BEST!   335 YOUNG BEAUTY   4
    HE THAT WAS BEST IN EVERY COUNTRY SPORT   339 SHEP GOATHERD   17
    AND CHOSEN WHAT SCENERY HAD PLEASED ME BEST."   352 PEOPLE   21
    WE AND OUR DOLLS BEING BUT THE WORLD WERE BEST AWAY.   364 DOLLS FACES   12
    AND, THOUGH YOU HAVE PASSED THE BEST OF LIFE, STILL TRACE,   367 EGO DOMINUS   5
    WHEREON 'TWERE BEST   389 IMAGE PAST   17
    THE BEST LACK ALL CONVICTION, WHILE THE WORST   402 SECOND COMING   7

BEST   (CONTINUED)
```
    THE BEST LACK CONVICTION, WHILE THE WORST  . . . . .   402 SECOND COMING  V    7
    DECLARE THAT WINTER'S BEST OF ALL,  . . . . . . . .    434 WHEEL               4
    THAT COGNOMEN SOUNDED BEST  . . . . . . . . . . .      440 WISDOM             18
    IN THE BEST MODERN WAY--THE CHILDREN'S EYES  . . .     443 SCHOOL CHILDR       6
    NEVER TO HAVE LIVED IS BEST, ANCIENT WRITERS SAY, . .  459 FROM OEDIPUS       10
    I WOULD HAVE FOUND THE BEST THAT LIFE CAN GIVE, . . .  465 HARUN RASHID       91
    ALTER AT THE BEST  . . . . . . . . . . . . . .        517 HER ANXIETY         4
    OUR MINDS ARE AT THEIR BEST THIS NIGHT, . . . . . .    523 MAD AS MIST         3
    THOSE DEEDS WERE BEST THAT GAVE THE MINUTE WINGS . .   533 HER TRIUMPH         5
    BEST PLEASE A WANDERING MAN. . . . . . . . . . .       606 SONGS BURDEN 1     17
    "NOW MUST WE SING AND SING THE BEST WE CAN, . . . .    634 CUCHULAIN COMF     19
    WE LOVE NASCHINA BOTH.  WHOM LOVES SHE BEST? . . .     660 ISLE STAT II 1     48
    WE, TOO, HAVE SEEN OUR BRAVEST AND OUR BEST  . . .     709 FERENCZ RENYI       1
    THREE MOONS.  IT WERE BEST TO KILL HIM, AND CHOOSE OUT 748 SHADOW WATER A     15
    BEST PLEASES YOU.  ARMED MEN HAVE COME UPON US. . .    752 SHADOW WATER A    131
    HE THAT HAS LOVED THE BEST . . . . . . . . . . .       786 YOUR HEART         19
    THE HEART WELL WORN UPON THE SLEEVE MAY BE THE BEST OF 790 HEART SLEEVE        1
        SIGHTS,
BEST-ENDOWED
    THE BEST-ENDOWED, THE ELECT, . . . . . . . . . .       504 RESULT THOUGHT      3
BESTIAL
    THE UNCONTROLLABLE MYSTERY ON THE BESTIAL FLOOR. . . . 318 MAGI                8
BESTIR
    I MUST BESTIR MYSELF.  BOTH DEAD FOR ME! . . . . .     673 ISLE STAT II 3    189
BEST'S
    THE SECOND BEST'S A GAY GOODNIGHT AND QUICKLY TURN AWAY. 459 FROM OEDIPUS      12
BETAKE
    TO HIS OWN HOUSE DID HIM BETAKE, . . . . . . . . .     725 LEGEND             30
BETHLEHEM
    SLOUCHES TOWARDS BETHLEHEM TO BE BORN? . . . . . .     402 SECOND COMING      22
BETIDE
    MOURNFUL THAT NO NEW WONDER MAY BETIDE, . . . . . .    111 ROSE OF WORLD       3
    OF MY DEAD CHILDREN SOON, WHATE'ER BETIDE, . . . . .   712 FERENCZ RENYI      58
BETRAY
    "AND ALL THOSE LIES HAVE BUT ONE END, POOR WRETCHES TO 450 OWEN AHERNE        18
        BETRAY,
BETRAYED
    FOR ON THAT DAY THEY HAD BEEN BETRAYED, . . . . . .    192 BAILE AILLINN      79
    HE HAD BETRAYED ME TO HIS GRAVE, . . . . . . . . .     275 GREY ROCK          96
    WHY ARE THE GODS BY MEN BETRAYED?" . . . . . . . .     275 GREY ROCK         115
    BEING BETRAYED INTO A CRADLE, AND I COME  . . . .      284 TWO KINGS         169
    AND HELEN HAS ALL LIVING HEARTS BETRAYED. . . . .      411 TOWER              53
    HONEY OF GENERATION HAD BETRAYED, . . . . . . . .      444 SCHOOL CHILDR      34
    OR THAT HE IS BETRAYED? . . . . . . . . . . . .        532 BEFORE WORLD       14
    AND AFTER THAT BETRAYED) . . . . . . . . . . . .       587 PARNELLITES        28
BETTER
    "WERE THERE NO BETTER THAN MY SON  . . . . . . .         6 OISIN 1            60
    IS ANYTHING BETTER, ANYTHING BETTER? . . . . . .      116 FAERY SONG         11
    IS ANYTHING BETTER, ANYTHING BETTER? . . . . . .      116 FAERY SONG         11
    A BETTER TIME HAD COME AGAIN  . . . . . . . .         197 BAILE AILLINN     192
    BETTER GO DOWN UPON YOUR MARROW-BONES  . . . . .      204 ADAMS CURSE         7
    BETTER GO DOWN UPON YOUR MARROW BONES  . . . . .      204 ADAMS CURSE    V    7
    THAT I MAY DROWN MYSELF?  BETTER STEER HOME, . . .    222 SHADOW WATER B     12
    WHETHER HE WILL OR NO, AND BETTER STILL . . . . .     222 SHADOW WATER B     13
    IT WOULD BE BETTER TO TURN HOME AGAIN, . . . . .      222 SHADOW WATER B  V  12
    WE'D BETTER GO, FOR WE HAVE LOST THIS CHANCE. . .     226 SHADOW WATER B     80
    HOW ARE WE BETTER OFF THAN SEAGHAN THE FOOL, . . .    228 SHADOW WATER B    129
    WE HAVE BEEN NO BETTER OFF THAN SEAGHAN THE FOOL, . . 228 SHADOW WATER B  V 129
    OF THAT MORE POWERFUL LIFE?  HIS WIFE KNOWS BETTER. . 230 SHADOW WATER B    172
    WHEN SHE FINDS OUT WE HAVE BETTER MEN ABOARD  . . .   232 SHADOW WATER B    231
    BETTER THAN MY OWN HANDS.  I HAVE DECEIVED YOU  . .   244 SHADOW WATER B    466
    IMAGINING 'TWOULD BETTER PLEASE  . . . . . . .        271 GREY ROCK           4
    THAT THINK SWORD-STROKES WERE BETTER MEANT . . .      276 GREY ROCK         129
    THAT THINK SWORD STROKES WERE BETTER MEANT . . .      276 GREY ROCK      V  129
    FOR HE KNEW BETTER HOW TO LIVE. . . . . . . .         288 TO WEALTHY MAN     30
    "I HAD NO BETTER PLAN AT FIRST. . . . . . . .         305 HOUR DAWN          63
    THAT LOVED HIS LEARNING BETTER THAN MANKIND, . . .    324 ROBERT GREGORY     18
    HAD SOUNDED BETTER TO YOUR MOUNTAIN FANCY. . . .      341 SHEP GOATHERD      61
    I THINK IT BETTER THAT IN TIMES LIKE THESE . . . .    359 WAR POEM            1
    I THINK IT BETTER THAT AT TIMES LIKE THESE . . . .    359 WAR POEM       V    1
    WHAT BETTER THAN CALL A DANCE? . . . . . . . .        378 CAT AND MOON       13
    I HAVE LOVED YOU BETTER THAN MY SOUL FOR ALL MY WORDS, 442 BLACK CENTAUR      14
    BETTER TO SMILE ON ALL THAT SMILE, AND SHOW . . .     444 SCHOOL CHILDR      31
    I HAD BETTER FIND A CONVENT AND TURN NUN, . . . .     448 HERO GIRL FOOL     11
    BETTER CONDUCT MYSELF OR HAVE MORE . . . . . .        507 STREAM AND SUN      9
    MY BETTER SELF DISOWNS, . . . . . . . . . . .         533 FIRST CONFESS       9
    MONEY IS GOOD AND A GIRL MIGHT BE BETTER, . . . .     544 TO SAME TUNE 1      3
    "MONEY IS GOOD AND A GIRL MIGHT BE BETTER, . . . .    545 TO SAME TUNE 1     21
    NO BETTER THAN A BEAST . . . . . . . . . . . .        572 LADYS 1ST SONG     11
    THERE'S BETTER EXERCISE . . . . . . . . . . .         600 THOSE IMAGES        3
    MONEY IS GOOD AND A GIRL MIGHT BE BETTER, . . . .     616 MARCH SONGS 3       3
    "MONEY IS GOOD AND A GIRL MIGHT BE BETTER, . . . .    616 MARCH SONGS 3      21
    AND THAT NO BETTER CAN BE HAD, . . . . . . . .        626 OLD MEN BE MAD     19
    BASE DROVE OUT THE BETTER BLOOD, . . . . . . .        626 STATES HOLIDAY      3
    THAT KNOWING BETTER TALK HAD GONE . . . . . . .       627 STATES HOLIDAY      7
    SO I HAVE PICKED A BETTER TRADE . . . . . . . .       627 STATES HOLIDAY     11
    MAYHAP 'TWERE BETTER THAT ASIDE I THROW  . . . .      656 ISLE STAT I 3      38
    COME TO THE CHESS, FOR YOUNG GIRLS' WITS ARE BETTER . 721 WITCH VIVIEN       46
    IT WERE BETTER TO PASS BY, BECAUSE THE GODS  . . .    751 SHADOW WATER A    104
    ARE BETTER THAN THE WOODS WHERE NO LOVE FADES . . .   754 SHADOW WATER A    160
```

	PAGE	TITLE		LINE
BETTERS				
I SOUGHT MY BETTERS! THOUGH IN EACH • • • • • • • •	506	REMORSE SPEECH.		6
BETWEEN				
WHEN GODS AND GIANTS WARRED. WE RODE BETWEEN • • • •	31	OISIN 2		31
UPON DARK THRONES. BETWEEN THE LIDS OF ONE • • • •	31	OISIN 2		37
OF DANAAN HOOVES WE URGED OUR WAY BETWEEN • • •	31	OISIN 2	V	31
HUGE FORMS OF STONE! BETWEEN THE LIDS OF ONE • • • •	31	OISIN 2	V	37
BURNING BETWEEN HER FINGERS, AND IN MINE • • • • • •	37	OISIN 2		125
AND THRUST THE TORCH BETWEEN THE SLIMY FLAGS. • • •	38	OISIN 2		143
ANOINTING, TORCH JAMMED DOWN BETWEEN THE FLAGS, • • • •	38	OISIN 2	V	143
ONCE HELD BETWEEN MY ARMS, WITH LIVID CHOP • • • • • •	40	OISIN 2	V	178
BETWEEN THEM A GATEWAY OF BRASS, AND THE HOWL OF THE ANGELS WHO FELL.	61	OISIN 3		200
WHO HOLDS THE WORLD BETWEEN HIS BILL AND MADE US STRONG OR WEAK	76	INDIAN ON GOD		6
IS BUT A SLIDING DROP OF RAIN BETWEEN HIS PETALS WIDE. • •	76	INDIAN ON GOD		12
WHO HOLDS THE WORLD BETWEEN HIS BILL AND MAKES US STRONG OR WEAK	76	INDIAN ON GOD	V	6
AND BROKE BETWEEN MY HANDS THE STAFF • • • • • • •	84	MAD KING GOLL	V	33
GO WATCH THE ROAD BETWEEN THE WOOD AND TIDE. • • • • •	105	CUCHULAIN SEA		4
BETWEEN WOOD'S RIM AND THE HORSES OF THE SEA. • • • • •	108	CUCHULAIN SEA		34
BETWEEN THE GAME AND THE HORSES OF THE SEA. • • • • •	108	CUCHULAIN SEA	V	34
BETWEEN THE LAVISH SHELTER OF A WOOD • • • • • • • •	108	CUCHULAIN SEA	V	38A
WE COME BETWEEN HIM AND THE DEED OF HIS HAND. • • • •	141	HOSTING SIDHE		11
WE COME BETWEEN HIM AND THE HOPE OF HIS HEART. • • • •	141	HOSTING SIDHE		12
BETWEEN THE WIND AND THE WOOD. • • • • • • • • •	166	BLESSED		4
BETWEEN THE WIND AND THE WOOD. • • • • • • • • •	167	BLESSED	V	4D
BETWEEN THE WALLS COVERED WITH BEATEN BRONZE, • • • • • •	180	QUEEN MAEVE		10
OF THE HUNTER'S MOON, THAT HUNG BETWEEN THE NIGHT AND THE DAY,	210	UNDER THE MOON		18
OF THE THIRD MOON, THAT HUNG BETWEEN THE NIGHT AND THE DAY,	210	UNDER THE MOON	V	18
AND CARRIES IT BETWEEN US. HOLY FIRE • • • • • • •	239	SHADOW WATER B		371
THAT HE IS HOLDING UP BETWEEN US THERE, • • • • • •	240	SHADOW WATER B		378
A SECRET BETWEEN YOU TWO, • • • • • • • • • •	259	UNWORTH PRAISE		9
BETWEEN THE PROUD AND THE PROUD. • • • • • • • •	259	UNWORTH PRAISE		10
BETWEEN THE DAWN AND DUSK." SHE SAID: • • • • • •	273	GREY ROCK		66
BETWEEN THE WOOD OF DURAS AND MAGAI • • • • • • •	276	TWO KINGS	V	G
BETWEEN THE PALE GREEN LIGHT OF THE BEECH LEAVES • • • •	277	TWO KINGS	V	5
WANDERED BETWEEN THE BLUE AND THE GREEN LEAF • • • • •	278	TWO KINGS		41
BETWEEN THE PILLARS WITH A BEATING HEART • • • • • •	279	TWO KINGS		59
"AND THE WORSE DEVIL THAT IS BETWEEN MY THIGHS." • • • •	300	BEGGAR CRIED		8
BETWEEN ROCK AND WET HEATHER, • • • • • • • •	311	PEACOCK	V	8
COULD EVER COME BETWEEN • • • • • • • • • • •	315	FRIENDS		8
BETWEEN THE PANTRY AND THE LINEN-CHEST, • • • • • •	340	SHEP GOATHERD		36
BETWEEN THE PANTRY AND THE LINEN CHEST, • • • • • •	340	SHEP GOATHERD	V	36
BETWEEN THE NIGHT AND MORNING. I MIGHT HAVE LIVED, • • •	351	PEOPLE		6
THEY STOOD IN THE DOOR AND STOOD BETWEEN • • • • • •	358	PRESENCES		9
AND RIGHT BETWEEN THESE TWO A GIRL AT PLAY • • • • • •	383	VISION ROBART		21
O LITTLE DID THEY CARE WHO DANCED BETWEEN, • • • • •	383	VISION ROBART		37
BEING CAUGHT BETWEEN THE PULL • • • • • • • • •	384	VISION ROBART		59
BETWEEN MY HATRED AND DESIRE, • • • • • • • • •	400	DEMON BEAST		6
BETWEEN EXTREMITIES • • • • • • • • • • •	499	VACILLATION		1
AND HE THAT ATTIS' IMAGE HANGS BETWEEN • • • • • •	500	VACILLATION		16
BETWEEN THE DARK AND DAWN. • • • • • • • • •	511	JANE AND JACK		6
BETWEEN TWO BARRELS AT THE INN. • • • • • • • •	551	SONGS REWRIT 1		10
BETWEEN TWO BUSHES UNDER THE RAIN: • • • • • • •	551	SONGS REWRIT 1		14
AND I MUST LIE BETWEEN THE SHEETS • • • • • • • •	570	THREE BUSHES		40
TO LIE BETWEEN YOUR FEET? • • • • • • • • • •	572	LADYS 2ND SONG		2
AND HE PLAYS TUNES BETWEEN YOUR FEET, • • • • • •	573	LADYS 3RD SONG		2
STANDISH O'GRADY SUPPORTING HIMSELF BETWEEN THE TABLES • •	577	LOFTY THINGS		5
WENT TO THE SACRED HOUSE AND STOOD BETWEEN • • • • •	609	IN TARAS HALLS		11
BETWEEN HIS TWO ETERNITIES • • • • • • • • •	637	BEN BULBEN		14
EACH OTHER ANSWERING. THEN BETWEEN EACH WING • • • •	659	ISLE STAT II 1		14
LET HIM BETWEEN US JUDGE, FOR HE CAN GAUGE • • • • •	660	ISLE STAT II 1		36
BETWEEN THE LONELY FOREST AND THE SAND. • • • • • •	663	ISLE STAT II 2		22
BETWEEN THE HORNED HILLS—SHEPHERDS, FAREWELL! • • • •	682	SEEKER		27
A TOSSING LAUGH BETWEEN THEIR REDNESS 'BIDES— • • • •	685	DRAWING-ROOM		2
A TOSSING LAUGH BETWEEN THEIR RED ABIDES! • • • • •	735	QUATRAIN APHOR		22
A TOSSING LAUGH BETWEEN THEIR REDNESS 'BIDES! • • • •	735	QUATRAIN APHOR	V	22
AS THOUGH THE WATERS HAD FLOWED UP BETWEEN; • • • • •	749	SHADOW WATER A		55
THE TIDE NARROWS BETWEEN, AND ONE OLD MAN • • • • •	752	SHADOW WATER A		118
BETWEEN TWO FURROWS UPON THE PLOUGHED LAND! • • • •	784	WOMANS BEAUTY		4
BETWEEN DARK FURROWS UPON THE PLOUGHED LAND. • • • •	784	WOMANS BEAUTY		6
BETWIXT				
OUT OF THAT RAVING TIDE—IS DRAWN BETWIXT • • • • • •	377	PHASES OF MOON		122
OR DARK BETWIXT THE POLECAT AND THE OWL, • • • • • •	565	GYRES		21
BEWILDER				
FRENZIES BEWILDER, REVERIES PERTURB THE MIND; • • • •	426	PHANTOM HATRED		7
BEWILDERED SEE MORN-BEWILDERED FLAME-BEWILDERED				
THERE, THROUGH BEWILDERED BRANCHES, GO • • • • • •	135	TWO TREES	V	13
GAZING UPON HER WITH BEWILDERED EYES! • • • • • •	280	TWO KINGS	V	84
BEWILDERED THEM TILL THEY DIED? • • • • • • • •	394	EASTER 1916		73
BEWILDERMENT				
THROUGH SHEER BEWILDERMENT? SHE HAD NOT PACED • • • •	466	HARUN RASHID		118
BEWITCHED				
HE SO BEWITCHED THE CARDS UNDER HIS THUMB • • • • •	411	TOWER		67
BEWITCHMENT				
THAT HAD BUT THE ONE EYE. CAN NO BEWITCHMENT • • • •	222	SHADOW WATER B		10
BEYOND				
BEYOND THE TUMBLING OF THIS TIDE." • • • • • • •	5	OISIN 1		49
WE RODE BEYOND THE FURZE AND HEATHER, • • • • • •	9	OISIN 1	V	101A

BEYOND (CONTINUED)
    THE LEAST OF DOORS: BEYOND ON A DIM PLAIN . . . . 39 OISIN 2   155
    THE LEAST OF DOORS: BEYOND THE DOOR A PLAIN, ... 39 OISIN 2   V 155
    THE FLOWERS STILL GREW THERE. MOVED BEYOND HIM THE SEA'S . 39 OISIN 2   V 163
        WASTE:
    WHEN WE ARE DEAD, BEYOND THE SETTING SUNS. . . . . 71 ANASHU VIJAYA   8
    IS AN UNDYING MOORFOWL, AND HE LIVES BEYOND THE SKY. . . . 76 INDIAN ON GOD   7
    AND THEY MARRIED BEYOND THEIR PLACE. . . . . 92 FATHER OHART   8
    BEYOND OLD MARTIN'S BYRE . . . . 95 MOLL MAGEE   34
    BEYOND OLD MARTIN'S WOOD, ... 95 MOLL MAGEE   V 34
    A PITY BEYOND ALL TELLING . . . . 119 PITY OF LOVE   1
    OR IN THE WINE-VAT, DWELL BEYOND THE STIR . . . . 169 SECRET ROSE   4
    OR IN THE WINE VAT, DWELL BEYOND THE STIR . . . . 169 SECRET ROSE V 4
    AND THEY WERE LISTENING THERE BEYOND THE SAIL. . . . . . . 223 SHADOW WATER B 37
    BUT DREAMS THAT HURRY FROM BEYOND THE WORLD . . . . 230 SHADOW WATER B 185
    THAT IN THE BLINDING LIGHT BEYOND THE GRAVE . . . . 258 KING NO KING   12
    THEN HE, DRIVEN BY HIS THOUGHT BEYOND HIS THOUGHT. . . . . 282 TWO KINGS   122
    THAT THE IMMEDICABLE MOUND'S BEYOND . . . . 282 TWO KINGS   129
    OUR QUESTIONING, BEYOND OUR PITY EVEN. . . . . 282 TWO KINGS   130
    THEN HE, DRIVEN BY THIS THOUGHT BEYOND HIS THOUGHT, ... 282 TWO KINGS   V 122
    THAT THE IMMEDICABLE WOUND'S BEYOND . . . . 282 TWO KINGS   V 129
    QUESTION OF OURS, BEYOND OUR PITY EVEN. . . . . 282 TWO KINGS   V 130
    BEYOND THE FLING OF THE DULL ASS'S HOOF . . . . 321 REED WHISPERER 5
    AND DIED IN THE GREAT WAR BEYOND THE SEA. . . . . 339 SHEP GOATHERD 22
    OR IMAGE, FROM BEYOND THE LOADSTONE MOUNTAIN, ... 371 ON GOING HOUSE 11
    BEYOND THE VISIBLE WORLD. ALL DREAMS OF THE SOUL . . . . . 374 PHASES OF MOON 63
    THEY ARE CAST BEYOND THE VERGE, AND IN A CLOUD, ... 376 PHASES OF MOON 105
    DEFORMED BEYOND DEFORMITY, UNFORMED, ... 376 PHASES OF MOON 111
    SO DEAD BEYOND OUR DEATH, ... 382 VISION ROBART 15
    BEYOND THAT RIDGE LIVED MRS. FRENCH, AND ONCE . . . . 410 TOWER   25
    HAD HE NOT FOUND IT CERTAIN BEYOND DREAMS . . . . 417 ANCEST HOUSES 10
    SO STRAINS TO LOOK BEYOND OUR LIFE, AN EYE . . . . 465 HARUN RASHID   87
    SO LONGS TO LOOK BEYOND OUR LIFE, AN EYE . . . . 465 HARUN RASHID V 87
    SOMEWHERE BEYOND THE CURTAIN . . . . 504 QUARREL IN AGE 12
    BEYOND A MORTAL'S YEARS. I WAIT THE SONG . . . . 653 ISLE STAT I 2 48
    BEYOND THE LAKE, WHOSE SMALLEST WAVE WAS BURDENED . . . . . 656 ISLE STAT I 3 31
    WITH ROLLING FIRE, BEYOND THE HIGH TREES TURBANED . . . . . 656 ISLE STAT I 3 32
    CARVED! HERE, BEYOND THE LAKE'S SLOW-MUFFLED TREAD, ... 662 ISLE STAT II 2 11
    BEYOND THE GATEWAY—BY THE SENTRIES NOW— . . . . 720 WITCH VIVIEN   10
    OF RAJAS AND MAHRAJAS BEYOND NUMBER? . . . . 724 KANVA ON SELF   6
    CARE NOT IF BEYOND THE SHADOWS . . . . 737 IN FIRELIGHT   7
    BEYOND WHERE THE WATERS ARE MOVING, ... 739 WHERE BOOKS GO 7
    BEYOND THE SAIL A MAN WITH A RED CROWN . . . . 752 SHADOW WATER A 126
    BEYOND A HILL AND A HILL. . . . . 774 COME RIDE   4
    BEYOND A HILL AND A HILL THERE . . . . 774 COME RIDE   16
    BEYOND EAGLE OR MOLE, ... 784 WOMANS BEAUTY 10
    BEYOND HEARING OR SEEING. . . . . 784 WOMANS BEAUTY 11
BIBLE
    IT'S PLAIN THE BIBLE MEANS . . . . 345 ON WOMAN   10
    THE BIBLE PROMISED US, ... 472 ALL SOUL NIGHT 39
BID
    AND BID ME STAY, WITH MANY A TEAR: . . . . 10 OISIN 1   113
    BID THEM AWAY AND HOLD THEIR PEACE: . . . . 15 OISIN 1   212
    GAVE ME A HARP, AND BID ME SING, ... 16 OISIN 1   232
    AND BID THE STARS DROP DOWN FROM THE SKY, ... 28 OISIN 1   426
    AND STAY A LITTLE WHILE, AND BID THEM WEEP: . . . . 33 OISIN 2   60
    SHE BID ME TAKE LOVE EASY, AS THE LEAVES GROW ON THE TREE: 90 SALLEY GARDENS 3
    SHE BID ME TAKE LIFE EASY, AS THE GRASS GROWS ON THE WEIRS: 90 SALLEY GARDENS 7
    SHE BID ME TAKE LOVE EASY, AS THE LEAVES GROW ON THE TREES: 90 SALLEY GARDENS V 3
    AND SAID, "I AM THAT SWINEHERD WHOM YOU BID . . . . 105 CUCHULAIN SEA   3
    "I AM ALEEL, THE SWINEHERD, WHOM YOU BID . . . . 105 CUCHULAIN SEA V 3A
    WHOSE BLADE COMPELS, AND BID THEM SEND YOU ONE . . . . . . 108 CUCHULAIN SEA V 37
    AND GOD WOULD BID HIS WARFARE CEASE. . . . . 113 ROSE OF PEACE 13
    AND GOD WOULD BID MAN'S WARFARE CEASE. . . . . 113 ROSE OF PEACE V 13
    FOR GOD HAS BID THEM SHARE AN EQUAL FATE! . . . . 115 ROSE OF BATTLE 32
    AND BID THEM WANDER OBEYING YOUR WILL, ... 141 EVERLAST VOICE 3
    I CRIED IN MY DREAM, O WOMEN, BID THE YOUNG MEN LAY . . . . 163 VALLEY LOVERS   5
    AND I CRIED IN MY DREAM "O WOMEN, BID THE YOUNG MEN LAY . . 163 VALLEY LOVERS V 5
    HAVE I NOT BID YOU TELL OF THAT GREAT QUEEN . . . . 181 QUEEN MAEVE   34
    AND SHOOK HIM WIDE AWAKE, AND BID HIM SAY . . . . 182 QUEEN MAEVE   50
    "I AM FROM THOSE RIVERS AND I BID YOU CALL . . . . 184 QUEEN MAEVE   91
    "I COME FROM THE UNDIMMED RIVERS TO BID YOU CALL . . . . . 184 QUEEN MAEVE V 91
    "I AM FROM THE UNDIMMED RIVERS. I BID YOU CALL . . . . . . 184 QUEEN MAEVE V 91
    AND DID THOSE WATCHERS BID YOU TAKE ME CAPTIVE? . . . . . . 236 SHADOW WATER B 322
    ALWAYS IN HIS ONE SEAT, AND BID ME CARE HIM . . . . 280 TWO KINGS   80
    "I BID THEM MAKE HIS BED UNDER THIS ROOF . . . . 280 TWO KINGS   87
    WHAT CARED DUKE ERCOLE, THAT BID . . . . 287 TO WEALTHY MAN 9
    HANDS: DO WHAT YOU'RE BID: . . . . 358 BALLOON MIND   1
    IT SEEMS THAT I MUST BID THE MUSE GO PACK, ... 409 TOWER   11
    BID A STRONG GHOST STAND AT THE HEAD . . . . 435 FOR MY SON   1
    BID THE GHOST HAVE SWORD IN FIST! . . . . 435 FOR MY SON   9
    BID THE GHOST HAVE SWORD IN HAND! . . . . 435 FOR MY SON   V 9
    O BID ME MOUNT AND SAIL UP THERE . . . . 458 HIS WILDNESS   1
    ARISE AND BID ME STRIKE A MATCH . . . . 476 EVA GORE-BOOTH 26
    BID ME STRIKE A MATCH AND BLOW. . . . . 476 EVA GORE-BOOTH 32
    BID IMAGINATION RUN . . . . 494 AT ALGECIRAS   15
    WHAT CAN SHE KNOW UNTIL HE BID HER KNOW! . . . . 558 RIBH CHRISTIAN 23
    THEN BID THEM RAISE MY STATUE ON THE SHORE! . . . . 663 ISLE STAT II 2 18
    THE ARCADIANS BRING, AND BID THE STONE BE RAISED . . . . . 663 ISLE STAT II 2 25
    IT IS MY WHIM! BID SOME ATTENDANT SPRITE . . . . 669 ISLE STAT II 3 72
    I BID THEE STAY, RENOUNCING THY MAD QUEST." . . . . 669 ISLE STAT II 3 89

BID   (CONTINUED)
  I CRIED THE WORDS YOU BID ME CRY. . . . .   673 ISLE STAT II 3   186
  "I BID HIM ASK WHAT GIFT HE WILL. . . . .   741 EARL PAUL   57
  WALKED ON THE WATERS AND BID FORGAEL SEEK . . . . . .   747 SHADOW WATER A   12
  AND BID THEM HIDE IN SHADOW OF THE SAIL. . . . .   751 SHADOW WATER A   93
  HAVE BID ME HOPE, SAIL TO THE LOCHLANN SHORE . . . . .   756 SHADOW WATER A V 184
  THAT I WOULD BID MY PEOPLE PUT TO DEATH. . . . .   760 SHADOW WATER A V 254
  AND BID HIM TO YOUR COUNTRY. I SHOULD WANDER . . . . .   767 SHADOW WATER A   403
  LIVING OR DYING. BID AIBRIC TO YOUR COUNTRY. . . . . .   768 SHADOW WATER A   413
BIDDEN
  THOUGH WE WERE BIDDEN TO SING, CRY NOTHING LOUD. . . .   778 SONG DEIRDRE 3   2
BIDDING
  TO HIS HEART, BIDDING IT HAVE NO FEAR . . . .   158 TO HIS HEART   T
  TO MY HEART, BIDDING IT HAVE NO FEAR . . . .   158 TO HIS HEART   V T
  MY BIDDING. NOW 'TIS DONE, AND I AM GLAD . . . .   700 MOSADA 3   29
BIDDY
  WISE BIDDY EARLY CALLED THE WICKED WOOD. . . . .   218 WOODS OF COOLE   15
BIDDY'S
  BY BIDDY'S HALFPENNIES HAVE LAIN . . . .   287 TO WEALTHY MAN   3
  BY BIDDY'S HALF-PENNIES HAVE LAIN . . . .   287 TO WEALTHY MAN V 3
'BIDES
  A TOSSING LAUGH BETWEEN THEIR REDNESS 'BIDES-- . . .   685 DRAWING-ROOM   2
  A TOSSING LAUGH BETWEEN THEIR REDNESS 'BIDES-- . . .   735 QUATRAIN APHOR V 22
BIDS
  OLD SILENCE BIDS ITS CHOSEN RACE REJOICE, ...   127 DREAM OF FAERY   31
  OLD SILENCE BIDS A LONELY FOLK REJOICE . . . .   127 DREAM OF FAERY V 31
  HE BIDS HIS BELOVED BE AT PEACE . . . .   154 BELOVED PEACE   T
  MICHAEL ROBARTES BIDS HIS BELOVED BE AT PEACE . . . .   154 BELOVED PEACE V T
  AND BIDS MY HAIR STAND UP? . . . .   499 MOTHER OF GOD   15
  WHAT BIDS ME LIVE LIKE THESE THAT SEEM . . . .   507 STREAM AND SUN V 14
  AND BIDS ME TO THE OAK, FOR HE . . . .   508 JANE BISHOP   23
  AND BIDS ME TO THAT OAK, FOR HE, ...   508 JANE BISHOP   V 23
  BIDS ALL TRUE LOVERS REST, ...   536 PARTING   6
  AND HER DIM WAVE BIDS MAN BE NO MORE GLAD, ...   738 YOU ARE SAD   11
  SHE BIDS US FOLLOW HER. I HAVE GROWN WEARY . . . . . .   758 SHADOW WATER A 218
BIER
  TO FIND IT WHEN NIGHT FALLS LAID ON A GOLDEN BIER. . .   209 UNDER THE MOON   10
BIG
  WITH SKELPING HIS BIG BRAWLING LOUT, ...   301 RUN PARADISE   9
  AH! IT IS SO VERY BIG, ...   726 LOVERS QUARREL   17
BIGOT
  INCENDIARY OR BIGOT COULD BE FOUND . . . .   430 NINETEEN 19   45
BILL
  HE RUFFLES WITH HIS BILL THE MINNOWED STREAMS. . . . .   73 ANASHU VIJAYA   37
  WHO HOLDS THE WORLD BETWEEN HIS BILL AND MADE US STRONG   76 INDIAN ON GOD   6
    OR WEAK
  WHO HOLDS THE WORLD BETWEEN HIS BILL AND MAKES US STRONG 76 INDIAN ON GOD V 6
    OR WEAK
  AND THE GREY BIRD WITH CROOKED BILL . . . .   192 BAILE AILLINN   89
  BY THE DARK WEBS, HER NAPE CAUGHT IN HIS BILL, ...   441 LEDA AND SWAN   3
  BY THE WEBBED TOES, AND THAT ALL-POWERFUL BILL . . . .   441 LEDA AND SWAN V 3
  BY THE WEBBED TOES, AND THAT ALL POWERFUL BILL . . . .   441 LEDA AND SWAN V 3
BILLED   SEE HERON-BILLED
BILLOWS
  TRANSFORM THESE RASCAL BILLOWS INTO WOMEN . . . . . .   222 SHADOW WATER B   11
BILLY
  CRIED THE BEGGAR, BILLY BYRNE: . . . .   331 ROUND TOWER   4
  THAT RAMBLING JAILBIRD BILLY SAID: . . . .   332 ROUND TOWER   26
  PITCH LIKE KING BILLY BOMB-BALLS IN . . . .   565 LAPIS LAZULI   7
BIND
  AND BIND UP EVERY WANDERING TRESS: . . . .   157 BELOVED RHYMES   2
  AND BIND UP YOUR LONG HAIR AND SIGH: . . . .   158 BELOVED RHYMES   8
  THAT NOBODY CAN BUY OR BIND: . . . .   301 RUN PARADISE   27
  AND ALL THE SHEAVES TO BIND. . . . .   312 CHILD DANCING   10
  NOW THAT NO FINGERS BIND, ...   390 IMAGE PAST   39
  NO NEED TO BIND MY HANDS. WHERE ARE YE, SIRS? . . . .   695 MOSADA 1   110
BINDING
  SQUARE LEAVES OF THE IVY MOVED OVER US, BINDING US DOWN   52 OISIN 3   76
    TO OUR REST.
  HAVE WITNESSED THE BINDING. . . . .   770 BLOOD BOND   15
BINDS
  BINDS, AS WITHIN A GIRDLE OR A RING, ...   657 ISLE STAT I 3   59
BIRCH
  OF HIS GREAT BIRCH AND HIS GREAT BOOK. . . . .   381 SONG OF FOOL   8
  BUT A BIRCH TREE STOOD MY JACK: . . . .   508 JANE BISHOP   V 20
BIRCH-TREE
  BUT A BIRCH-TREE STOOD MY JACK: . . . .   508 JANE BISHOP   20
BIRD   SEE SEA-BIRD GAME-BIRD
  IN MURMURS, LIKE A FRIGHTED BIRD. . . . .   25 OISIN 1   376
  BUT, THE BIRD IN MY FINGERS, I MOUNTED, ...   54 OISIN 3   111
  BUT, THE BIRD IN MY FINGERS, I MOUNTED, MINDFUL ONLY TO   54 OISIN 3   V 111
    LAUNCH
  SNATCHING THE BIRD IN SECRET; NOR KNEW I, EMBOSOMED APART, 57 OISIN 3   150
  "WITH HIM IS ONE SWEET-THROATED LIKE A BIRD." . . . .   106 CUCHULAIN SEA   16
  "WITH HIM IS ONE SWEET THROATED LIKE A BIRD, ...   106 CUCHULAIN SEA V 16
  AS MERRY AS A BIRD." . . . .   133 FR GILLIGAN   38
  O BEAST OF THE WILDERNESS, BIRD OF THE AIR, ...   177 PAST GREATNESS   11
  AND THE GREY BIRD WITH CROOKED BILL . . . .   192 BAILE AILLINN   89
  LET RUSH AND BIRD CRY OUT THEIR FILL . . . .   197 BAILE AILLINN   198
  BUT I'D HAVE BIRD AND RUSH FORGET . . . .   197 BAILE AILLINN   204
  WHERE THE DEAD DRIFTED, I COULD SEE A BIRD . . . . . .   223 SHADOW WATER B   23

                                                           PAGE   TITLE   LINE
BIRD   (CONTINUED)
     O FLOWER OF THE BRANCH, O BIRD AMONG THE LEAVES, ...   251 SHADOW WATER B   608
     A SQUIRREL WHINNIED AND A BIRD SCREAMED OUT! . . . .   278 TWO KINGS   34
     AND THEREON, MERRY AS A BIRD . . . .   296 THREE BEGGARS   25
     SANG UNNOTICED LIKE A BIRD! . . . .   298 THREE HERMITS   7
     SANG UNNOTICED LIKE A BIRD. . . . .   299 THREE HERMITS   32
     LOVE AND THE BIRD . . . .   313 MEMORY YOUTH   V   T
     OF A MOST RIDICULOUS LITTLE BIRD . . . .   314 MEMORY YOUTH   20
     AND NOT A GLOOMY BIRD OF PREY. . . . .   338 TOM OROUGHLEY   8
     I WISHED BEFORE IT CEASED. NOR BIRD NOR BEAST . . . . .   338 SHEP GOATHERD   2
     YEAR. I WISHED BEFORE IT CEASED.   NOR BIRD NOR BEAST . .   338 SHEP GOATHERD   V   2
     "LIKE THE SPECKLED BIRD THAT STEERS . . . .   341 SHEP GOATHERD   62
     THAT SHE MIGHT BE THAT SPRIGHTLY GIRL TRODDEN BY A BIRD!   353 HIS PHOENIX   4
     THAT SHE MIGHT BE THAT SPRIGHTLY GIRL WHO HAD MARRIED WITH   353 HIS PHOENIX   V   4
        A BIRD!
     THAT SHE MIGHT BE THAT SPRIGHTLY GIRL WHO WAS TRODDEN BY   353 HIS PHOENIX   V   4
        A BIRD!
     A VISIONARY WHITE SEA BIRD . . . .   361 ALF POLLEXFEN   V   37
     IS ALWAYS HAPPY LIKE A BIRD OR A BEAST! . . . .   373 PHASES OF MOON   38
     ALL SOUNDS BY BIRD OR ANGEL SUNG . . . .   387 SOLOMON WITCH   V   7
     FROM TERRIFIED, INVISIBLE BEAST OR BIRD! . . . .   389 IMAGE PAST   6
     LIKE ANY ROCK-BRED, SEA-BORNE BIRD! . . . .   397 POLIT PRISONER   18
     PORTLY GREEN-PATED BIRD . . . .   400 DEMON BEAST   28
     THE MOTHER BIRD WILL REST . . . .   415 TOWER   170
     THE BIRD DESCENDS, AND HER FRAIL THIGHS ARE PRESSED . . .   441 LEDA AND SWAN   V   2
     OLD CLOTHES UPON OLD STICKS TO SCARE A BIRD. . . . . . .   445 SCHOOL CHILDR   48
     LET THE CAGE BIRD AND THE CAGE BIRD MATE . . . .   450 OWEN AHERNE   16
     LET THE CAGE BIRD AND THE CAGE BIRD MATE . . . .   450 OWEN AHERNE   16
     . . . AND THE WILD BIRD MATE IN THE WILD." . . . . . .   450 OWEN AHERNE   16
     TO PASSING BIRD, BUT I AM DUMB . . . .   452 HUMAN DIGNITY   11
     GAME BIRD, OR WOMAN DOES THE SAME THING TWICE! . . . . .   463 HARUN RASHID   V   60
     THE HERON-BILLED PALE CATTLE BIRD, ...   493 AT ALGECIRAS   V   1
     MIRACLE, BIRD OR GOLDEN HANDIWORK, ...   497 BYZANTIUM   17
     MORE MIRACLE THAN BIRD OR HANDIWORK, ...   497 BYZANTIUM   18
     MIRACLE, BIRD OR GOLDEN HANDY-WORK . . . .   497 BYZANTIUM   V   17
     MORE MIRACLE THAN BIRD OR HANDY-WORK . . . .   497 BYZANTIUM   V   18
     COMMON BIRD OR PETAL . . . .   498 BYZANTIUM   23
     WHEN THE HOLY BIRD, THAT THERE . . . .   522 LULLABY   15
     BIRD, BEAST, FISH OR MAN, ...   529 TOM LUNATIC   14
     AND A MIRACULOUS STRANGE BIRD SHRIEKS AT US. . . . . . .   534 HER TRIUMPH   12
     NO, NIGHT'S BIRD AND LOVE'S . . . .   536 PARTING   5
     THAT BIRD . . LET HIM SING ON. . . . .   536 PARTING   12
     THERE'S NOT A BIRD OF DAY THAT DARE . . . .   538 LAST CONFESS   23
     OVER THEM FLIES A LONG-LEGGED BIRD, ...   566 LAPIS LAZULI   39
     BIRD SIGHS FOR THE AIR. . . . .   574 LOVERS SONG   1
     A GREAT BLACK RAGGED BIRD APPEARED WHEN I WAS IN THE BOAT!   593 PILGRIM   16
     A GREAT BLACK BIRD APPEARED WHEN I WAS IN THE BOAT, . . .   593 PILGRIM   V   16
     SHEEP-GUIDING, OR THE BRINGING SOME STRANGE BIRD, ...   650 ISLE STAT I 1   147
     DOTH NOT YON BIRD, YON QUIVERING BIRD, REJOICE? . . . .   652 ISLE STAT I 2   21
     DOTH NOT YON BIRD, YON QUIVERING BIRD, REJOICE? . . . .   652 ISLE STAT I 2   21
     NO OTHER BIRD MAY ENTER IN. WELL? LATE-- . . . . . .   659 ISLE STAT II 1   24
     MID BUBBLING LEAVES A WANDERING SONG-RAPT BIRD . . . . .   672 ISLE STAT II 3   154
     MID BABBLING LEAVES A WANDERING SONG-RAPT BIRD . . . . .   672 ISLE STAT II 3 V   154
     OF ANY UNBLESSED EARTHLY BIRD." . . . .   697 MOSADA 2   33
     REITERANT. A BIRD GOES BY THE TENT, ...   711 FERENCZ RENYI   46
     AND THE BIRD IN THE BRANCHES WILL CRY FOR US CLEAR, . . .   717 LOVE SONG   6
     A BIRD WALK ON THE DOORSTEP. CHECK ONCE MORE. . . . . .   722 WITCH VIVIEN   64
     AMONG THE HAUNTS OF BEE AND BIRD. . . . .   729 PRIEST FAIRY   42
     THE BREATHING OF THE SMALLEST BIRD, ...   730 PRIEST FAIRY   68
     A GREY BIRD HAS FLOWN BY. HE HAS FLOWN UPWARD. . . . .   753 SHADOW WATER A   134
     THE HAND THAT WOUNDS. A WHITE BIRD BEATS HIS WINGS . . .   758 SHADOW WATER A V   232
     A WHITE BIRD BEATS HIS WINGS UPON MY FACE. . . . . . .   759 SHADOW WATER A   233
     A WHITE BIRD HAS TORN ME WITH HIS SILVER CLAWS, ...   759 SHADOW WATER A   234
     O FLOWER OF THE BRANCH, O BIRD AMONG THE LEAVES, ...   769 SHADOW WATER A   424
     RED BIRD OF MARCH, BEGIN TO CROW! . . . .   782 HEART FRIGHT   5
     RED BIRD OF MARCH, BEGIN TO CROW! . . . .   782 HEART FRIGHT   12
     RED BIRD OF MARCH, BEGIN TO CROW! . . . .   782 HEART FRIGHT   19
     AND THE EDDYING CAT-HEADED BIRD. . . . .   783 GREY ROUND   23
     FRAIL BIRD, LIKE A WHITE SEA-BIRD ALONE . . . .   784 WOMANS BEAUTY   2
BIRD-CLAWS
     GOLDEN THE NAILS OF HIS BIRD-CLAWS, ...   50 OISIN 3   45
BIRD-LIKE
     AMONG THOSE BIRD-LIKE THINGS CAME, AND LET FALL . . . .   634 CUCHULAIN COMF   8
BIRDLY
     AND BIRDLY ITERATION IS . . . .   67 HAPPY SHEPHERD V   46B
BIRD'S
     OR A BIRD'S SLEEPY CRY . . . .   416 TOWER   194
     AS AIR UNDER A WING, CAN GIVE BIRD'S WIT. . . . .   462 HARUN RASHID   V   28
     HUMAN, SUPERHUMAN, A BIRD'S ROUND EYE, ...   618 BRONZE HEAD   2
     HUMAN, SUPER-HUMAN, A BIRD'S ROUND EYE, ...   618 BRONZE HEAD   V   2
BIRDS   SEE SONG-BIRDS CATTLE-BIRDS
     AND BIRDS THAT ON THE SEVEN SEAS RANGE. . . . .   4 OISIN 1   V 27A
     FROM WHERE THE BIRDS OF AENGUS WING?" . . . .   6 OISIN 1   53
     THAT ARE LIKE COLOURED ASIAN BIRDS . . . .   7 OISIN 1   69
     AND GLORIOUS AS ASIAN BIRDS . . . .   7 OISIN 1   V   65
     AND A HUNDRED LADIES, MERRY AS BIRDS, ...   9 OISIN 1   96
     AND SWEETER OF VOICE THAN THE PLEASANT BIRDS, ...   9 OISIN 1   V   95
     AND A HUNDRED MAIDENS, MERRY AS BIRDS, ...   9 OISIN 1   V   96
     SUNG OF THE BIRDS. OUR TOIL WAS DONE! . . . .   14 OISIN 1   V   177
     THE MURMURING BIRDS IN SOLEMN POMP . . . .   20 OISIN 1   V   293
     AND, AS THEY SANG, THE PAINTED BIRDS . . . .   26 OISIN 1   396

		PAGE	TITLE		LINE
BIRDS (CONTINUED)					
A STORM OF BIRDS IN THE ASIAN TREES		27	OISIN 1		416
UNLANGUID AS THE BIRDS, IN PROUD COMPANIONSHIPS;		30	OISIN 2	V	14C
FANNED THE DELIGHTED AIR LIKE WINGS OF BIRDS;		32	OISIN 2		50
FROM HIGH ABOVE, LIKE FEATHERS OF YOUNG BIRDS, ...		32	OISIN 2	V	50
. . . THEIR HANDS WERE THE CLAWS OF BIRDS, ...		49	OISIN 3		34
OF AWELESS BIRDS, AND ROUND THEIR STIRLESS FEET		74	ANASHU VIJAYA		73
I LAUGHED BECAUSE BIRDS FLUTTERED BY, ...		84	MAD KING GOLL		33
TO THE BIRDS IN THE WHITE OF THE AIR.		92	FATHER OHART		16
THE BIRDS, FOR HE OPENED THEIR CAGES		92	FATHER OHART		17
THE BIRDS FROM KNOCKNAREA		93	FATHER OHART		30
THE YOUNG BIRDS AND OLD BIRDS		93	FATHER OHART		33
THE YOUNG BIRDS AND OLD BIRDS		93	FATHER OHART		33
THE WHITE BIRDS		121	WHITE BIRDS		T
I WOULD THAT WE WERE, MY BELOVED, WHITE BIRDS ON THE FOAM OF THE SEA!		121	WHITE BIRDS		1
O WOULD THAT WE WERE, MY BELOVED, WHITE BIRDS ON THE FOAM OF THE SEA,		121	WHITE BIRDS	V	1
FOR I WOULD WE WERE CHANGED TO WHITE BIRDS		122	WHITE BIRDS		8
WERE WE ONLY WHITE BIRDS, MY BELOVED, ...		122	WHITE BIRDS		12
THAT YOU CALL IN BIRDS, IN WIND ON THE HILL, ...		141	EVERLAST VOICE		6
THOUGH YOU HAVE THE WILL OF THE WILD BIRDS, ...		176	BELOVED DEAD		8
WHILE BIRDS GREW SILENT ONE BY ONE.		176	BELOVED DEAD	V	13
FOR YOU HAVE BEEN, O AENGUS OF THE BIRDS, ...		185	QUEEN MAEVE		101
ABOUT WHOSE FACE BIRDS WAGGED THEIR FIERY WINGS, ...		187	QUEEN MAEVE		145
O WANDERING BIRDS AND RUSHY BEDS, ...		190	BAILE AILLINN		31
AND IN THE LIGHT BODIES OF BIRDS		190	BAILE AILLINN		44
OR BIRDS LOST IN THE ONE CLEAR SPACE		195	BAILE AILLINN		149
OR BIRDS LOST IN ONE CLEAR SPACE		195	BAILE AILLINN	V	149
WHILE OVER THEM BIRDS OF AENGUS FLY, ...		197	BAILE AILLINN		182
BUT I'D HAVE BIRDS AND RUSH FORGET		197	BAILE AILLINN	V	204
I CRIED WHEN THE MOON WAS MURMURING TO THE BIRDS; . . .		203	WITHER BOUGHS		1
HAVE THE BIRDS PASSED US? I COULD HEAR YOUR VOICE, ...		226	SHADOW WATER B		81
HAS EVER COME BUT THOSE MAN-HEADED BIRDS, ...		226	SHADOW WATER B		99
THEY HAVE MADE YOU FOLLOW THE MAN-HEADED BIRDS, ...		231	SHADOW WATER B		204
THEY HAVE BADE YOU FOLLOW THE MAN-HEADED BIRDS, ...		231	SHADOW WATER B	V	204
"HOW LIGHT WE ARE, NOW WE ARE CHANGED TO BIRDS!"		233	SHADOW WATER B		253
THAT CANNOT BE THE MEANING OF THE BIRDS.		235	SHADOW WATER B		278
AND ALL THE BIRDS ARE SCATTERED. O! O! O!		241	SHADOW WATER B		395
THESE THOUSAND YEARS. WHAT ARE THE BIRDS AT THERE? . . .		243	SHADOW WATER B		435
WHAT IS THERE BUT A TROOP OF ASH-GREY BIRDS		247	SHADOW WATER B		517
WHAT IS THERE BUT THE CRYING OF THE BIRDS?		247	SHADOW WATER B		519
THAT YOU MAY NEVER HEAR THE CRY OF THE BIRDS, ...		250	SHADOW WATER B		575
LET THE BIRDS SCATTER, FOR THE TREE IS BROKEN, ...		250	SHADOW WATER B		584
AND ALL THE BIRDS ARE SCATTERED--O! O! O!		251	SHADOW WATER B		594
TO CRY ALOUD TO THE GREY BIRDS, AND DREAMS, ...		252	SHADOW WATER B		618
HE WERE AFRAID THE BIRDS, WHO CRY ALOUD		371	EGO DOMINUS		77
THE RIDER, THE BIRDS THAT RANGE		393	EASTER 1916		46
REEL SHADOWS OF THE INDIGNANT DESERT BIRDS.		402	SECOND COMING		17
WIND SHADOWS OF THE INDIGNANT DESERT BIRDS.		402	SECOND COMING	V	17
IN ONE ANOTHER'S ARMS, BIRDS IN THE TREES		407	SAIL BYZANTIUM		2
THE MOTHER BIRDS BRING GRUBS AND FLIES.		424	STARES NEST		3
UNWEARIED EYES UPON THOSE HORRIBLE GREEN BIRDS. . . .		442	BLACK CENTAUR		16
ONE AMONG THE BIRDS OF THE AIR, ...		460	THREE MONUMENT		3
THAT THIS UNCONQUERABLE LABYRINTH OF THE BIRDS, . . .		481	BLOOD AND MOON		23
THE HERON-BILLED PALE CATTLE BIRDS, ...		493	AT ALGECIRAS	V	1
AMONG BIRDS OR BEASTS OR MEN		528	DANCER CRUACH		2
THEY HAD CHANGED THEIR THROATS AND HAD THE THROATS OF BIRDS.		635	CUCHULAIN COMF		25
CATCHING SMALL BIRDS IN THE DEW OF THE MORN		636	BLACK TOWER		22
THE BIRDS THAT NESTLE IN THE LEAVES ARE SAD, ...		652	ISLE STAT I 2		15
LIES TORN AND ROTTING. THE FIERCE KESTREL BIRDS		675	ISLE STAT II 3		234
WHERE TO THEMSELVES INNUMERABLE BIRDS		682	SEEKER		25
OF BIRDS EVEN, LONGINGS FOR AERY		708	FAIRY PEDANT		26
AND SHAKE THEIR BIRDS UPON THE AIR		736	SUMMER EVENING		3
AND SHAKE THEIR BIRDS UPON THE AIR		737	SUMMER EVENING		19
THEY ARE CHANGED AND AS GREY BIRDS FLY OUT TO SEA, . . .		750	SHADOW WATER A		82
OF AENGUS' BIRDS GLEAM IN THEIR APPLE BOUGHS. . . .		751	SHADOW WATER A		103
"HOW LIGHT WE ARE NOW WE ARE CHANGED TO BIRDS!" . . .		753	SHADOW WATER A		143
I LINGER WHILE THE BIRDS ARE ON THE WING, ...		754	SHADOW WATER A	V	157
AS THE AGELESS BIRDS OF AENGUS, OR THE BIRDS		761	SHADOW WATER A		260
AS THE AGELESS BIRDS OF AENGUS, OR THE BIRDS		761	SHADOW WATER A		260
THAT FORGAEL HAS FOLLOWED THE GREY BIRDS ALONE, ...		767	SHADOW WATER A		402
THE STRONG MARCH BIRDS A-CROW.		783	GREY ROUND		26
BIRDS'					
AS AIR UNDER A WING, CAN GIVE BIRDS' WIT.		462	HARUN RASHID		28
BIRTH					
THERE WERE AN END OF CHANGE AND BIRTH, ...		18	OISIN 1		270
AND TIME AND BIRTH AND CHANGE ARE HURRYING BY.		153	CHANGE BELOVED		9
PASS THE DOOR OF BIRTH AGAIN, ...		298	THREE HERMITS		19
BRINGS ME TO BIRTH AGAIN--		346	ON WOMAN		32
A COMPENSATION FOR THE PANG OF HIS BIRTH, ...		444	SCHOOL CHILDR		39
DELIVER FROM THE CRIME OF DEATH AND BIRTH.		478	SELF AND SOUL		24
BIRTH IS HEAPED ON BIRTH		496	MOHINI CHATTER		23
BIRTH IS HEAPED ON BIRTH		496	MOHINI CHATTER		23
O A BEGGAR BLIND FROM HIS BIRTH!		552	SONGS REWRIT 2		8
A BEGGAR BLIND FROM HIS BIRTH!		552	SONGS REWRIT 2	V	8
BEING THE MOON OF BIRTH, MAY END OUR DOUBT.		748	SHADOW WATER A		24
IT MAY BE, BEFORE THE WINDS OF BIRTH HAVE WAKED; . . .		750	SHADOW WATER A		86
BIRTHDAY					
FROM OUR BIRTHDAY, UNTIL WE DIE, ...		139	TO IRELAND		35

			PAGE	TITLE	LINE

BIRTHDAYS
THAT WERE ALL HIS BIRTHDAYS RECKONED . . . . 342 SHEP GOATHERD 90
AND BIRTHDAYS AND HOLIDAYS SUCH PRAISES CAN BE HEARD . 353 HIS PHOENIX 2
BIRTH-HOUR
BIRTH-HOUR AND DEATH-HOUR MEET, ... 496 MOHINI CHATTER 26
BISCAY
AFTER A RAGGED HAT IN BISCAY BAY! . . . . 270 PARDON FATHERS 14
BISHOP
DRANK TAR-WATER WITH THE BISHOP OF CLOYNE . . . . . 486 SEVEN SAGES 5
GOLDSMITH AND BURKE, SWIFT AND THE BISHOP OF CLOYNE . . 486 SEVEN SAGES 9
CRAZY JANE AND THE BISHOP . . . . 507 JANE BISHOP T
FOUR POEMS CRACKED MARY AND THE BISHOP . . . . . . 507 JANE BISHOP V T
EIGHT POEMS CRAZY JANE AND THE BISHOP . . . . 507 JANE BISHOP V T
NOR WAS HE BISHOP WHEN HIS BAN . . . . 508 JANE BISHOP 8
THE BISHOP HAS A SKIN, GOD KNOWS, ... 508 JANE BISHOP 15
CRAZY JANE TALKS WITH THE BISHOP . . . . 513 JANE TALK BISH T
I MET THE BISHOP ON THE ROAD . . . . 513 JANE TALK BISH 1
I AM TIRED OF CURSING THE BISHOP, ... 628 JANE MOUNTAIN 1
THE BISHOP CAME WITH OPEN BOOK, ... 725 LEGEND 17
THE BISHOP MURMURED, "ATHEIST! . . . . 725 LEGEND 21
BISHOPS
THE BISHOPS AND THE PARTY . . . . 587 PARNELLITES 25
BIT
THEY MAULED AND BIT THE WHOLE NIGHT THROUGH! . . . . 297 THREE BEGGARS 48
THEY MAULED AND BIT TILL THE DAY SHONE! . . . . . . 297 THREE BEGGARS 49
THEY MAULED AND BIT THROUGH ALL THAT DAY . . . . . . 297 THREE BEGGARS 50
TO THROW ME A BIT OF SALTED FISH! . . . . 301 RUN PARADISE 6
SHE PULLED THE THREAD AND BIT THE THREAD . . . . . . 308 PLAYER QUEEN 9
HE RODE A RACE WITHOUT A BIT? . . . . 326 ROBERT GREGORY 63
AND FROM HER FINGERS ATE ITS BIT. . . . . 397 POLIT PRISONER 6
A BIT OF BREAD THROWN UP INTO THE AIR! . . . . . . 400 DEMON BEAST 25
A BIT OF AN EMBROIDERED DRESS . . . . 421 MY TABLE 6
POSEIDON GAVE IT BIT AND OAR, ... 447 COLONUS PRAISE 28
OF THAT OAR AND OF THAT BIT! . . . . 447 COLONUS PRAISE 30
SO LIKE A BIT OF STONE I LIE . . . . 452 HUMAN DIGNITY 7
THERE ALL THE SERPENT-TAILS ARE BIT, ... 557 THERE 2
COME SPEAK YOUR BIT IN PUBLIC . . . . 582 ROGER CASEMENT 21
ARE BLOWN COLD DUST OR A BIT OF BONE. . . . . 788 HAWTHORN TREE 8
BITE
NOR STAYED FOR BITE OR SUP! . . . . 93 FATHER OHART 38
SHE GIVES ME BITE AND SUP. . . . . 96 MOLL MAGEE 40
BITING
TROOPER BELABOURING TROOPER, BITING AT ARM OR AT FACE, . 426 PHANTOM HATRED 12
BITS
A CROSS THEY HAD MADE OUT OF TWO BITS OF WOOD; . . . 123 DREAM OF DEATH 7
OR BREAK IN BITS THE FAMOUS IVORIES . . . . 430 NINETEEN 19 47
BITTEN   SEE STORM-BITTEN
BUT HAVE NOT BITTEN YET. I AM A QUEEN, ... 235 SHADOW WATER B 280
THEY'D MAULED AND BITTEN THE NIGHT THROUGH, ... 297 THREE BEGGARS V 48
BITTER
THROUGH BITTER TIDE ON FOAM-WET FEET? . . . . 5 OISIN 1 51
CUCHULAIN BATTLING WITH THE BITTER TIDE! . . . . . . 100 ROSE UPON ROOD 3
FOR HE WHO MADE YOU BITTER MADE YOU WISE." . . . . . 108 CUCHULAIN SEA 32
FOR GOD WHO MADE YOU BITTER MADE YOU WISE." . . . . . 108 CUCHULAIN SEA V 32
FOR FOUR DAYS WARRED HE WITH THE BITTER TIDE, ... 111 CUCHULAIN SEA V 85
UPON LOVE'S BITTER MYSTERY . . . . 125 GOES FERGUS 8
GAZE NO MORE IN THE BITTER GLASS . . . . 135 TWO TREES 21
GAZE NO MORE IN THE BITTER GLASS. . . . . 136 TWO TREES V 40
AND BLAME YOU WITH MANY BITTER WORDS. . . . . 146 FISH 8
WILL HIDE US FROM THE BITTER STORM. . . . . 152 HEART OF WOMAN 8
SHALL HIDE US FROM THE BITTER STORM. . . . . 152 HEART OF WOMAN V 8
CROWDED WITH BITTER FACES, THE WOUNDS IN PALM AND SIDE, . 172 TRAV PASSION 4
TIME'S BITTER FLOOD WILL RISE, ... 173 PLEADS FRIEND 6
UNDER A BITTER BLACK WIND THAT BLOWS FROM THE LEFT HAND! . 206 HANRAHANS SONG 2
UNDER THE BITTER BLACK WINDS BLOWING OUT OF THE LEFT HAND! 206 HANRAHANS SONG V 2
BUT O! 'TWAS BITTER WRONG . . . . 255 WOMAN HOMER 5
IN THIS BLIND BITTER LAND." . . . . 256 WORDS 4
THE BITTER SWEETNESS OF FALSE FACES? . . . . 275 GREY ROCK 113
I HAD THOUGHT, SEEING HOW BITTER IS THAT WIND . . . . 327 ROBERT GREGORY 89
AT THE OLD BITTER WORLD WHERE THEY MARRY IN CHURCHES, . 330 BONE OF A HARE 13
LESS BITTER. THEY HAVE BROUGHT ME FROM THAT RIDGE . . 342 SHEP GOATHERD 87
TO CLIMB THAT STAIR AND EAT THAT BITTER BREAD, ... 369 EGO DOMINUS 35
HE HAD DONE MOST BITTER WRONG . . . . 393 EASTER 1916 33
ACROSS THE BITTER SEA." . . . . 396 ROSE TREE 6
BECAME A BITTER, AN ABSTRACT THING, ... 397 POLIT PRISONER 9
OUT OF HIS BITTER SOUL, ... 415 TOWER 151
SOME VIOLENT BITTER MAN, SOME POWERFUL MAN . . . . . 418 ANCEST HOUSES 17
BITTER AND VIOLENT MEN, MIGHT REAR IN STONE . . . . . 418 ANCEST HOUSES 19
AND OTHER COMFORT WERE A BITTER WOUND. . . . . 429 NINETEEN 19 41
DRUNK WITH THE BITTER SWEETNESS OF HER YOUTH. . . . . 469 HARUN RASHID 186
BREAK BITTER FURIES OF COMPLEXITY, ... 498 BYZANTIUM 37
IN THIS BLIND BITTER TOWN, ... 504 QUARREL IN AGE 3
BITTER GLORY WRECKED. . . . . 504 RESULT THOUGHT 6
OVERCOME—O BITTER SWEETNESS, ... 540 FROM ANTIGONE 1
PLUCKED BITTER WISDOM THAT ENRICHED HIS BLOOD. . . . . 543 PARN FUNERAL 2 12
ESCAPED FROM BITTER YOUTH, ... 568 SWEET DANCER 4
DRAW ROUND, BELOVED AND BITTER MEN, ... 584 GHOST ROG CASE 37
HE FIXED A BITTER LOOK! . . . . 585 ORAHILLY 24
I NEVER KNEW A NIGHT SO BITTER COLD. . . . . 704 MOSADA 3 124
THROUGH THE LONG BITTER WAY. . . . . 738 MOURN THEN ON 4
BELOVED, HEAR MY BITTER TALE!— . . . . 742 DANAAN QUICK 1

BITTER   (CONTINUED)
    THE BITTER SWEETNESS OF THE NIGHT . . . .   781 HEART FRIGHT   3
    DRY BONES THAT DREAM ARE BITTER, ...   783 GREY ROUND   14
    O BITTER REWARD . . . .   785 YOUR HEART   9
    O BITTER REWARD . . . .   786 YOUR HEART   22
    O BITTER REWARD . . . .   786 YOUR HEART   35
BITTERER
    HAD WATCHED IN BITTERER SLEEP . . . .   399 BREAK OF DAY   22
BITTEREST
    FROM BITTEREST HOURS! . . . .   293 HELEN LIVED   6
BITTERLY
    AND WRING MY HANDS, AND WAIL HIM BITTERLY. . . . . .   242 SHADOW WATER B   414
    SO BITTERLY, YOU'D DREAM THEY LONGED TO LOOK . . . .   265 ABBEY THEATRE   6
    HIDING MY FACE, I CRIED LONG, BITTERLY. . . . . . .   690 MOSADA 1   17
    UPRAISED THEIR VOICES BITTERLY. . . . .   730 PRIEST FAIRY   72
BITTERN
    AND SAID, "YON BITTERN CRIES, IN TRUTH, ...   731 PRIEST FAIRY   75
BITTERNESS
    WE AND OUR BITTERNESS HAVE LEFT NO TRACES . . . . .   130 BOOK STORIES   23
    THE UNAVAILING OUTCRIES AND THE OLD BITTERNESS . . .   198 SEVEN WOODS   4
    A MAN THAT FINDS GREAT BITTERNESS . . . .   379 SAINT HUNCH   2
    YOUTH'S BITTERNESS BEING PAST, ...   389 IMAGE PAST   11
    BUT TAKE OUR GREATNESS WITH OUR BITTERNESS? . . . .   418 ANCEST HOUSES   40
    THEIR BITTERNESS AND FIND THE HONEYCOMB. . . . . .   463 HARUN RASHID   48
BITTERNS
    OF BITTERNS, AND FISH-EATING STOATS. . . . .   14 OISIN 1   191
    OF BITTERNS AND FISH-EATING STOATS. . . . .   23 OISIN 1   355
BITTER-SWEET
    AND, THOUGH LOVE'S BITTER-SWEET HAD ALL COME BACK, . . 537 HER VISION   27
BITTER-SWEETNESS
    DRUNK WITH THE BITTER-SWEETNESS OF HER YOUTH. . . .   469 HARUN RASHID   V 186
BLACK   SEE COAL-BLACK
    SPRANG FROM A GATEWAY WALLED AROUND WITH BLACK . . .   31 OISIN 2   V   29
    THE VALLEY OF THE BLACK PIG . . . .   161 BLACK PIG   T
    UNDER A BITTER BLACK WIND THAT BLOWS FROM THE LEFT HAND! 206 HANRAHANS SONG   2
    UNDER THE BITTER BLACK WINDS BLOWING OUT OF THE LEFT HAND! 206 HANRAHANS SONG V 2
    OUR COURAGE BREAKS LIKE AN OLD TREE IN A BLACK WIND AND 207 HANRAHANS SONG   3
        DIES.
    LIKE TUFTED REEDS OUR COURAGE DROOPS IN A BLACK WIND AND 207 HANRAHANS SONG V   3
        DIES.
    THE BARE CHIMNEY IS GONE BLACK OUT . . . .   327 ROBERT GREGORY   84
    BLACK MINNALOUSHE STARED AT THE MOON, ...   378 CAT AND MOON   5
    ON A PICTURE OF A BLACK CENTAUR BY EDMUND DULAC . . .   442 BLACK CENTAUR   T
    SUGGESTED BY A PICTURE OF A BLACK CENTAUR . . . . .   442 BLACK CENTAUR V   T
    YOUR HOOVES HAVE STAMPED AT THE BLACK MARGIN OF THE WOOD, 442 BLACK CENTAUR   1
    BROWN, OR BLACK, OR CARROT, ...   492 ANNE GREGORY   9
    NOR CAN HE HIDE IN HOLY BLACK . . . .   508 JANE BISHOP   18
    THAT BLACK DAY" . . . .   510 JANE JUDGMENT   14
    BLACK OUT! HEAVEN BLAZING INTO THE HEAD! . . . . .   566 LAPIS LAZULI   19
    OR OUT OF HER BLACK CLOUD. . . . .   568 SWEET DANCER   6
    A GREAT BLACK RAGGED BIRD APPEARED WHEN I WAS IN THE BOAT! 593 PILGRIM   16
    A GREAT BLACK BIRD APPEARED WHEN I WAS IN THE BOAT, . . 593 PILGRIM   V   16
    OF RASCALS BLACK AND WHITE . . . .   597 MODEL LAUREATE   10
    THE BLACK TOWER . . . .   635 BLACK TOWER   T
    SAY THAT THE MEN OF THE OLD BLACK TOWER, ...   635 BLACK TOWER   1
    AND FIGHT FOR THE BLACK SLOE-BERRIES, ...   644 SONG FAERIES   13
    AND FIGHT FOR THE BLACK SLOE-BERRIES, ...   676 ISLE STAT II 3   260
    TWO FIGURES CROUCHING ON THE BLACK ROCK, BOUND . . .   687 TWO TITANS   5
    OF THE ALHAMBRA BLACK ATHWART HIS DISK! . . . . . .   691 MOSADA 1   V   37
BLACKBIRDS
    COULD LIKE A BRACE OF BLACKBIRDS SING. . . . . . .   332 ROUND TOWER   24
BLACKENED
    BROKEN BOUGHS AND BLACKENED LEAVES. . . . .   135 TWO TREES   28
    WITH BROKEN BOUGHS AND BLACKENED LEAVES. . . . . .   135 TWO TREES   V   26
    AND HIS HEART WAS BLACKENED BY DREAD, ...   145 HOST OF AIR   V 40B
    OVER THE BLACKENED EARTH . . . .   496 MOHINI CHATTER   21
    AND BLACKENED HIS GOOD NAME. . . . .   582 ROGER CASEMENT   8
BLACKENS
    BLACKENS ALL OUR LOT? . . . .   534 CONSOLATION   10
BLACKER
    THERE IN THE TOMB THE DARK GROWS BLACKER, ...   636 BLACK TOWER   27
BLACKNESS
    AND BLACKNESS IN THE DARK. THE SEA ROLLED ROUND, . .   30 OISIN 2   V   23
    AND WHEN THE WHITE STEED SAW WHAT BLACKNESS GLEAMED, .   30 OISIN 2   V   24
    AND YONDER HUDDLING BLACKNESS DRAWETH NIGH— . . . .   663 ISLE STAT II 2   15
BLADDERED   SEE GREAT-BLADDERED
    GREAT BLADDERED EMER SAT, ...   628 JANE MOUNTAIN V   15
BLADE   SEE SWORD-BLADE
    WITH BOWED HEAD, TREMBLING WHEN THE WHITE BLADE SHONE, . 38 OISIN 2   137
    AND BY THEM WERE ARROW AND WAR-AXE, ARROW AND SHIELD AND 49 OISIN 3   29
        BLADE!
    WERE ARROW AND SHIELD AND WAR-AXE, ARROW AND SPEAR AND   49 OISIN 3   V   30
        BLADE!
    WHOSE BLADE COMPELS, AND WAIT TILL THEY HAVE FOUND . . 108 CUCHULAIN SEA   37
    WHOSE BLADE COMPELS, AND BID THEM SEND YOU ONE . . .   108 CUCHULAIN SEA V   37
    AND THROUGH THAT NEW BLADE'S GUARD THE OLD BLADE BROKE, 110 CUCHULAIN SEA   66
    AND THROUGH THE OTHER'S SHIELD HIS LONG BLADE BROKE, . 110 CUCHULAIN SEA V   66
    AND SAYS, "A SWORD BLADE PIERCED ME IN MY SLEEP." . . 234 SHADOW WATER B V   257
    THE CONSECRATED BLADE UPON MY KNEES . . . .   477 SELF AND SOUL   9
    IS SATO'S ANCIENT BLADE, STILL AS IT WAS, ...   477 SELF AND SOUL   10
    GOLD-SOWN SILK ON THE SWORD BLADE! . . . .   484 SYMBOLS   V   5

BLADE   (CONTINUED)
 THAT NOBLE BLADE THE MUSES BUCKLED ON, ... 489 COOLE PARK 29 10
 UPON A BLADE OF GRASS. . . . . 505 GRAT INSTRUCT 4
 HO! HO! HO! THE MERRY BLADE!—— . . . . 727 LOVERS QUARREL 26
 AND SAYS, "A SWORD BLADE PIERCED ME IN MY SLEEP." . . . 753 SHADOW WATER A V 147
 THIS BLADE OUT OF MY HAND AND DIED OF A SUDDEN. . . . 755 SHADOW WATER A 168
 SHE CAUGHT THIS BLADE OUT OF MY BELT AND DIED. . . . . 755 SHADOW WATER A V 168
BLADE'S
 DEEP SUNKEN ON THE BLADE'S LENGTH, "MANANAN!" . . . . . 38 OISIN 2 V 128
 AND THROUGH THAT NEW BLADE'S GUARD THE OLD BLADE BROKE, 110 CUCHULAIN SEA 66
 BRIGHT ON A GRASS BLADE'S UNDER SIDE, MIGHT HEAR, . . . 689 NETTLESHIP 10
BLADES   SEE GRASS-BLADES' SWORD-BLADES
 AND WITH THE CLASHING OF THEIR SWORD BLADES MAKE . . . 137 TO SOME I TALK V 13
 ON THEIR SWAYING BLADES OF GRASS, ... 705 DAWN-SONG 14
 MAY THE SWORD BLADES DRINK THEIR FILL . . . . 776 AGAINST WITCH V 37
BLAKE
 OR THAT WILLIAM BLAKE . . . . 576 ACRE OF GRASS 16
 CALVERT AND WILSON, BLAKE AND CLAUDE, ... 639 BEN BULBEN 64
 AND WILSON, BLAKE AND CALVERT, CLAUDE, ... 639 BEN BULBEN V 64
BLAME
 AND BLAME YOU WITH MANY BITTER WORDS. . . . . 146 FISH 8
 FOR WHEN WE HAVE BLAMED THE WIND WE CAN BLAME LOVE: . . 201 OLD MEMORY 10
 WHY SHOULD I BLAME HER THAT SHE FILLED MY DAYS . . . . 256 NO SECOND TROY 1
 AND I TOOK ALL THE BLAME OUT OF ALL SENSE AND REASON, 316 COLD HEAVEN 7
 THOUGH SHE HAD YOUNG MEN'S PRAISE AND OLD MEN'S BLAME, 351 HER PRAISE 17
 A LAW INDIFFERENT TO BLAME OR PRAISE, ... 428 NINETEEN 19 10
 BELOVED, BLAME THE DANAAN WHIM, ... 743 DANAAN QUICK 22
 AND BLAME THE SNARE THEY SET FOR ME. . . . . 743 DANAAN QUICK 23
BLAMED
 FOR WHEN WE HAVE BLAMED THE WIND WE CAN BLAME LOVE: 201 OLD MEMORY 10
 SOME MAY HAVE BLAMED YOU THAT YOU TOOK AWAY . . . . . 257 RECONCILIATION 1
 I SHOULD BE BLAMED, YOUNG MAN. . . . . 569 THREE BUSHES 6
 FOR WHILE I BLAMED THEM I COULD HEAR . . . . 743 DANAAN QUICK 27
BLANAID
 CAME BLANAID, MAC NESSA, TALL FERGUS WHO FEASTWARD OF OLD 53 OISIN 3 89
  TIME SLUNK,
BLANCH
 OH, HADST THOU SEEN BEAUTIFUL NIAM WAIL TO HERSELF AND 54 OISIN 3 V 109
  BLANCH,
 O, HAD YOU SEEN BEAUTIFUL NEAVE WAIL TO HERSELF AND BLANCH, 54 OISIN 3 V 109
BLANCHED   SEE DEW-BLANCHED LILY-BLANCHED
 A LILY BLANCHED PLACE, SHE SAT AND SANG, ... 693 MOSADA 1 V 83
BLAND
 BLAND RHADAMANTHUS BECKONS HIM, ... 530 DELPHIC ORACLE 3
BLANID
 CAME BLANID, MAC NESSA, CUCHULIN: . . . . 53 OISIN 3 V 89
 CAME BLANID, MAC NESSA, AND FERGUS WHO FEASTWARD OF OLD 53 OISIN 3 V 89
  TIME SLUNK,
BLANK
 UNDER BLANK EYES AND FINGERS NEVER STILL . . . . . . 382 VISION ROBART 5
 A GAZE BLANK AND PITILESS AS THE SUN, ... 402 SECOND COMING 15
BLASPHEMOUS
 WOULD CARRY IT AWAY TO BLASPHEMOUS MEN. . . . . 371 EGO DOMINUS 79
BLAST
 THIS BLAST HAS CHILLED ME TO THE BONE." . . . . 305 HOUR DAWN 62
 A LONG BLAST UPON THE HORN THAT BROUGHT . . . . 324 ROBERT GREGORY 22
 A SUDDEN BLAST OF DUSTY WIND AND AFTER . . . . 433 NINETEEN 19 119
 IF HONOUR FIND HIM IN THE WINTRY BLAST? . . . . 479 SELF AND SOUL 56
 O MARCHING WIND, O A BLAST OF THE WIND, ... 548 TO SAME TUNE 3 24
 OR WHERE THAT SNOW AND WINTER'S DREADFUL BLAST . . . . 563 MERU 11
 A BLAST OF THE WIND, O A MARCHING WIND, ... 615 MARCH SONGS 2 24
 A BLAST OF WIND, O A MARCHING WIND, ... 615 MARCH SONGS 2 V 24
BLASTED
 BRING ME TO THE BLASTED OAK . . . . 507 JANE BISHOP 1
BLASTS
 TILL WINTER BLASTS WERE GONE, BUT SPEAK OF HER . . . . 340 SHEP GOATHERD 33
BLAZE
 WATCHED WHERE THE SUN IN A SAFFRON BLAZE . . . . . . 26 OISIN 1 394
 "AN OLD MAN STIRS THE FIRE TO A BLAZE, ... 26 OISIN 1 400
 HALF SLUMBERED WITH HIS SAFFRON BLAZE! . . . . 26 OISIN 1 V 395
 AND BLOWS ON HIS HANDS IN THE FIRE'S WARM BLAZE! . . . 26 OISIN 1 V 404
 HIS SHADOW ALONG IN THE EVENING BLAZE, ... 27 OISIN 1 V 409
 WITH VAPOURY FOOTSOLE BY THE WATER'S DROWSY BLAZE. . . 78 INDIAN TO LOVE 20
 A VAPOURY FOOTFALL ON THE OCEAN'S SLEEPY BLAZE. . . . 78 INDIAN TO LOVE V 20
 AND DROP A VAPOURY FOOTFALL IN THE WATER'S DROWSY BLAZE. 78 INDIAN TO LOVE V 20
 WITH VAPOURY FOOTSOLE AMONG THE WATER'S DROWSY BLAZE. . 78 INDIAN TO LOVE V 20
 DROPPING A VAPOURY FOOTSOLE ON THE TIDE'S DROWSY BLAZE. 78 INDIAN TO LOVE V 20
 THE BRAZEN SKY, SO BLAZE THE DAFFODILLS: . . . . . . 645 ISLE STAT I 1 11
 IN VALE AND DELL SO BLAZE THE DAFFODILLS: . . . . . . 645 ISLE STAT I 1 15
 IN LEMON-TINTED LINES, SO BLAZE THE DAFFODILLS. . . . 645 ISLE STAT I 1 19
BLAZED
 MY BODY OF A SUDDEN BLAZED: . . . . 501 VACILLATION 41
BLAZING
 BLACK OUT: HEAVEN BLAZING INTO THE HEAD! . . . . . . 566 LAPIS LAZULI 19
 THAT FILL THE BLAZING HOLLOWS OF MY HEART. . . . . . 684 SEEKER V 69D
BLEAK
 WHEREON THE BLEAK NORTH BLOWS, ... 454 HIS MEMORIES 4
BLEAR-EYED
 NOR BLEAR-EYED WISDOM OUT OF MIDNIGHT OIL. . . . . . 446 SCHOOL CHILDR 60
BLEAT
 BUT FAINTER THAN A YOUNG LAMB'S BLEAT. . . . . 26 OISIN 1 399

		PAGE	TITLE		LINE

BLEAT (CONTINUED)
    AND FAINTER THAN A YOUNG LAMB'S BLEAT. . . . .   26 OISIN 1   V   399
    SHALL AWAKE WITH LONELY BLEAT, ...   726 LOVERS QUARREL   6
BLEATING
    AND THE SHEEP BLEATING AT THE WIND   . . . .   306 HOUR DAWN   78
BLEED
    FOR SOULS WHO TIRE AND BLEED. . . . .   134 FR GILLIGAN   42
BLEEDING
    WAS MOVING. BLEEDING NOW, HIS GRASP UNLOCKS, ...   688 TWO TITANS   42
    THEREFORE, O NATION OF THE BLEEDING BREAST, ...   709 FERENCZ RENYI   4
BLEMISH
    AND SMOOTH OUT STAIN AND BLEMISH WITH THE ELEGANCE OF HIS   353 HIS PHOENIX   7
        MIND!
BLENCH
    WHY MUST YOU BLENCH AND SHAKE FROM FOOT TO CROWN?" . . .   106 CUCHULAIN SEA   13
BLENCHED
    TILL YOUR BAD MASTER BLENCHED AND ALL WAS LOST! . . . .   270 PARDON FATHERS V   12
    OUR HANDS ARE BLENCHED, OUR FINGERS SEEM . . . .   488 CRAZED MOON   14
    BLENCHED BY THAT MALICIOUS DREAM . . . .   488 CRAZED MOON   16
BLENCHING
    MY BLENCHING AND TREMBLING, ...   532 FIRST CONFESS   4
    BLENCHING ON HIGH THE DULL STARS SICKEN . . . .   646 ISLE STAT I 1   46
BLENDING
    O'ER HER NEST THE LIGHTS ARE BLENDING! . . . .   646 ISLE STAT I 1   36
BLENT
    TOLD, AND IT SEEMED THAT OUR TWO NATURES BLENT   . . .   443 SCHOOL CHILDR   13
BLESS
    TO BLESS THAT ISLE WITH HONEY IN HIS TONES, ...   128 DREAM OF FAERY V   44
    HURRY TO BLESS THE HANDS THAT PLAY, ...   212 BLESS PSALTER   1
    O KINSMEN, BLESS THE HANDS THAT PLAY. . . . .   213 BLESS PSALTER   15
    BUT BLESS OUR HANDS THAT EBB AWAY. . . . .   213 BLESS PSALTER   20
    STAND UP AND LIFT YOUR HAND AND BLESS . . . .   379 SAINT HUNCH   1
    I SHALL NOT CEASE TO BLESS BECAUSE . . . .   379 SAINT HUNCH   7
    CONSIDER MOST TO MAGNIFY, OR TO BLESS, ...   418 ANCEST HOUSES   39
    THE BOOK OF THE PEOPLE! WHATEVER MOST CAN BLESS . . . .   492 COOLE BALLYLEE   44
    THAT I WAS BLESSED AND COULD BLESS. . . . .   501 VACILLATION   44
    WHEN GONG AND CONCH DECLARE THE HOUR TO BLESS . . . . .   611 STATUES   23
    AND ALL THE GARDEN BLESS. . . . .   774 COME RIDE   10
BLESSED
    WATCHING THE BLESSED ONES MOVE FAR OFF, AND THE SMILE ON   61 OISIN 3   199
        GOD'S FACE,
    IT WERE SAD TO GAZE ON THE BLESSED AND NO MAN I LOVED OF   63 OISIN 3   221
        OLD THERE!
    IT WAS SAD TO GAZE ON THE BLESSED AND NO MAN I LOVED OF   63 OISIN 3   V   221
        OLD THERE!
    UNDER THE BLESSED MOONLIGHT, ...   94 MOLL MAGEE   11
    HOME IN THE BLESSED MOONLIGHT . . . .   94 MOLL MAGEE   V   11
    A DREAM OF A BLESSED SPIRIT . . . .   124 CATHLEEN PARA   V   T
    AND HOW BENEATH THOSE THREE TIMES BLESSED SKIES . . . .   127 DREAM OF FAERY V   21
    THE BLESSED . . . .   166 BLESSED   T
    TO THE CAVE, WHERE DATHI THE BLESSED HAD GONE, ...   166 BLESSED   V   3
    ALL MANNER OF BLESSED SOULS, ...   167 BLESSED   14
    BUT PURER THAN A TALL CANDLE BEFORE THE BLESSED ROOD . .   208 HANRAHANS SONG V   14
    BUT I ALONE BEING BLESSED KEEP . . . .   307 HOUR DAWN   104
    AND BLESSED, I GIVE MY GRATITUDE, ...   380 SAINT HUNCH   14
    THEREFORE A BLESSED MOON LAST NIGHT . . . .   388 SOLOMON WITCH   31
    AND WHERE THE BLESSED DANCE! . . . .   474 ALL SOUL NIGHT   96
    BLESSED BE THIS PLACE, ...   480 BLOOD AND MOON   1
    MORE BLESSED STILL THIS TOWER! . . . .   480 BLOOD AND MOON   2
    THAT I WAS BLESSED AND COULD BLESS. . . . .   501 VACILLATION   44
    A REVOLUTIONARY SOLDIER KNEELING TO BE BLESSED! . . . .   601 GALLERY REVIS   8
    THE BLESSED GOD WAS GOOD TO SEND US SUCH, ...   683 SEEKER   40
    BUT BLESSED HE THAT STIRS THEM NOT . . . .   779 ACCURSED WHO   3
BLESSEDEST
    THE BLESSEDEST SOULS THAT WALK IN THE WORLD   . . . .   167 BLESSED   19
    "AND WHICH IS THE BLESSEDEST," CUMHAL SAID, ...   167 BLESSED   21
    ALL MANNER OF BLESSEDEST SOULS, ...   167 BLESSED   V   14
    "AND WHO IS THE BLESSEDEST," CUMHAL SAID, ...   167 BLESSED   V   21
    I SEE THE BLESSEDEST SOUL IN THE WORLD . . . .   168 BLESSED   31
    AND HAVE SEEN THE BLESSEDEST SOUL IN THE WORLD, ...   168 BLESSED   V   31
BLESSEDNESS
    TO GATHER THE HALF OF YOUR BLESSEDNESS . . . .   167 BLESSED   7
    "AND BLESSEDNESS GOES WHERE THE WIND GOES, ...   168 BLESSED   29
    "O BLESSEDNESS COMES IN THE NIGHT AND THE DAY . . . . .   168 BLESSED   33
    LIVE IN UNCOMPOSITE BLESSEDNESS, ...   387 ROBARTES DANCE   46
BLESSING
    THE PLAYERS ASK FOR A BLESSING ON THE PSALTERIES AND ON   212 BLESS PSALTER   T
        THEMSELVES
    THE PLAYERS ASK FOR A BLESSING ON THE PSALTERIES   212 BLESS PSALTER   V   T
        AND THEMSELVES
    BUT MAYBE SOME OLD GAFFER MUTTERS A BLESSING . . . . .   355 BROKEN DREAMS   4
    GOD GRANT A BLESSING ON THIS TOWER AND COTTAGE . . . .   371 ON GOING HOUSE   1
    BLESSING THE TRICOLOUR. "THIS IS NOT," I SAY, ...   601 GALLERY REVIS   10
BLESSINGS
    SO GET YOU GONE, VON HUEGEL, THOUGH WITH BLESSINGS ON YOUR   503 VACILLATION   89
        HEAD.
BLEST
    HAND LIFTED UP THAT BLEST! . . . .   383 VISION ROBART   20
    THAT BLEST SOULS ARE NOT COMPOSITE, ...   387 ROBARTES DANCE   44
    WE ARE BLEST BY EVERYTHING, ...   479 SELF AND SOUL   71
    EVERYTHING WE LOOK UPON IS BLEST. . . . .   479 SELF AND SOUL   72

	PAGE	TITLE		LINE

BLEST   (CONTINUED)
```
   WHICH IS THE MORE BLEST?  . . . . . . . . .      573 LADYS 2ND SONG      20
   SHE CARES NO WHIT FOR EITHER, BUT HAS BLEST  . . . . .   660 ISLE STAT II 1     49
```
BLEW
```
   AND NIAMH BLEW THREE MERRY NOTES . . . . . . . . .    14 OISIN 1          195
   BLEW ONE LONG NOTE. FROM OVER REED . . . . . . .     14 OISIN 1        V 195
   SNATCHING THE HORN OF NIAMH, I BLEW A LONG LINGERING NOTE.    51 OISIN 3         57
   SNATCHING THE HORN OF NIAM, I BLEW FORTH A LINGERING NOTE!   51 OISIN 3       V  57
   SNATCHING THE HORN OF NIAM, I BLEW A LINGERING NOTE!   . .   51 OISIN 3       V  57
   BY A GREY SHORE WHERE THE WIND NEVER BLEW, . . . . .    170 SECRET ROSE        14
   AND BLEW ME HITHER TO MY LASTING SORROW, . . . . .     235 SHADOW WATER B    288
   AND BLEW YOU HITHER; AND THEIR MOUTHS HAVE PROMISED  . .   237 SHADOW WATER B    325
   BLEW MY CRIMSON CAP AWAY . . . . . . . . . . .      656 ISLE STAT I 3      16
```
BLIND
```
   YOU WHO ARE BENT, AND BALD, AND BLIND, . . . . . .      2 OISIN 1            1
   WHY THOU OUTLIVEST, BLIND AND HOARY, . . . . . . .      2 OISIN 1        V   2
   HAVE BORNE ME WHERE THE TEMPESTS BLIND . . . . . .      6 OISIN 1        V  58
   I BURST THE CHAIN: STILL EARLESS, NERVELESS, BLIND, . .    36 OISIN 2           97
   STILL EARLESS, NERVELESS, BLIND, THE EAGLES STOOD. . .    36 OISIN 2          100
   STILL EARLESS, NERVELESS, BLIND, THE EAGLES DREAMED. . .   36 OISIN 2        V 100
   FOR HE IS WEAK AND POOR AND BLIND, AND LIES  . . . .    42 OISIN 2          203
   BLIND AND NIGH DEAF, WITH WITHERED ARMS HE LIES  . . .    42 OISIN 2        V 203
   WITH HER OLD FATHER THE BLIND WOOD-CUTTER, . . . .     74 ANASHU VIJAYA      63
   ONE BLIND HOUND ONLY LIES APART  . . . . . . . .      99 FOXHUNTER          41
   THE BLIND HOUND WITH A MOURNFUL DIN  . . . . . . .     99 FOXHUNTER          45
   "WITH THE SECRETS OF GOD HALF BLIND . . . . . . .     168 BLESSED            26
   BODIES OF SHADOW AND BLIND EYES LIKE PEARLS, . . . .    185 QUEEN MAEVE       116
   BY ITS OWN BLIND IMAGINING, . . . . . . . . . .     191 BAILE AILLINN      67
   IF DEAF AND DUMB AND BLIND WITH LOVE? . . . . . .     202 NEVER GIVE ALL     12
   HAS MADE THEM SO HAPPY AND HOPELESS, SO DEAF AND SO BLIND   204 WITHER BOUGHS      20
   WHERE HAZEL AND ASH AND PRIVET BLIND THE PATHS; . . .    217 WOODS OF COOLE      8
   IN THIS BLIND BITTER LAND." . . . . . . . . . .     256 WORDS               4
   WHEN, THE EARS BEING DEAFENED, THE SIGHT OF THE EYES BLIND   257 RECONCILIATION     3
   ARE WHAT THE BLIND AND IGNORANT TOWN . . . . . . .    287 TO WEALTHY MAN      7
   OF OUR OLD PAUDEEN IN HIS SHOP, I STUMBLED BLIND  . . .   291 PAUDEEN             2
   OWN NOTHING BUT THEIR BLIND, STUPEFIED HEARTS. . . .    370 EGO DOMINUS        69
   BLIND AND LEADER OF THE BLIND . . . . . . . . .     397 POLIT PRISONER     11
   BLIND AND LEADER OF THE BLIND . . . . . . . . .     397 POLIT PRISONER     11
   STRANGE, BUT THE MAN WHO MADE THE SONG WAS BLIND; . .    411 TOWER              49
   WITH HOMER THAT WAS A BLIND MAN, . . . . . . . .     411 TOWER              52
   AND BRING BEAUTY'S BLIND RAMBLING CELEBRANT; . . . .    412 TOWER              91
   ACCORDING TO THE WIND, FOR ALL ARE BLIND. . . . . .    433 NINETEEN 19       124
   NOT BLIND WITH GOLD, NOR DAZZLED BY THE GOLD . . . .    470 HARUN RASHID    V 191
   AND I GROW HALF CONTENTED TO BE BLIND! . . . . . .    473 ALL SOUL NIGHT     70
   THAT MAN IS STRICKEN DEAF AND DUMB AND BLIND, . . . .    478 SELF AND SOUL      35
   A LIVING MAN IS BLIND AND DRINKS HIS DROP. . . . .     478 SELF AND SOUL      41
   THAT MAN IS DEAF AND DRUNK AND BLIND . . . . . . .    478 SELF AND SOUL   V  35
   WHAT MATTER IF A BLIND MAN DRINK HIS DROP? . . . .     478 SELF AND SOUL   V  41
   INTO THE FROG-SPAWN OF A BLIND MAN'S DITCH. . . . .    479 SELF AND SOUL      59
   A BLIND MAN BATTERING BLIND MEN; . . . . . . . .     479 SELF AND SOUL      60
   A BLIND MAN BATTERING BLIND MEN; . . . . . . . .     479 SELF AND SOUL      60
   SWIFT BEATING ON HIS BREAST IN SIBYLLINE FRENZY BLIND  .   481 BLOOD AND MOON     19
   WHETHER FOR DAILY PITTANCE OR IN BLIND FEAR  . . . .    482 BLOOD AND MOON     37
   A BLIND HERMIT RINGS THE HOUR. . . . . . . . . .     484 SYMBOLS             2
   THAT STARING FURY AND THE BLIND LUSH LEAF  . . . .     500 VACILLATION        17
   IN THIS BLIND BITTER TOWN, . . . . . . . . . . .     504 QUARREL IN AGE      3
   ROLLING A BLIND PEARL EYE, . . . . . . . . . . .     552 SONGS REWRIT 2      2
   O A BEGGAR BLIND FROM HIS BIRTH; . . . . . . . .     552 SONGS REWRIT 2      8
   A BEGGAR BLIND FROM HIS BIRTH; . . . . . . . . .     552 SONGS REWRIT 2 V    8
   "HIS LIGHT HAD STRUCK ME BLIND . . . . . . . . .     559 HE AND SHE          5
   BLIND AS A WORM. . . . . . . . . . . . . . .      575 MAIDS 2ND SONG      6
   AND WHEN THE FOOL AND BLIND MAN STOLE THE BREAD  . .     630 CIRCUS ANIMALS     25
   SOMETHING DROPS FROM EYES LONG BLIND, . . . . . .     638 BEN BULBEN         29
   SEE THE DARKNESS SLOW DISGORGING A VESSEL BLIND WITH      718 PHANTOM SHIP       12
        SQUALL.
   I AWAIT YOUR WORDS AS THE BLIND GRASS AWAITS . . . .    756 SHADOW WATER A    181
   I AM BLIND AND DEAF BECAUSE OF THE WHITE WINGS. . . .    759 SHADOW WATER A    235
```
BLINDED
```
   COME NEAR, THAT NO MORE BLINDED BY MAN'S FATE, . . .    101 ROSE UPON ROOD      9
   LOVE HAS BLINDED HIM WITH TEARS; . . . . . . . .     612 NEWS ORACLE        28
   I AM HALF BLINDED.  I AM HALF BLINDED, TOO. . . . .     759 SHADOW WATER A V  235
   I AM HALF BLINDED.  I AM HALF BLINDED, TOO. . . . .     759 SHADOW WATER A V  235
   HAS MADE MY FEET UNSTEADY, AND BLINDED ME. . . . .     767 SHADOW WATER A    406
```
BLINDER
```
   BLINDER SORROWS, HARDER WAGE-- . . . . . . . . .     733 STREET DANCERS     58
```
BLINDING
```
   INTO THE BLINDING NIGHT.-- . . . . . . . . . .     174 ELEMENT POWERS V    4
   THAT IN THE BLINDING LIGHT BEYOND THE GRAVE  . . . .    258 KING NO KING       12
```
BLINDS
```
   PULL DOWN THE BLINDS, BRING FIDDLE AND CLARIONET  . . .   311 MOUNTAIN TOMB       5
   THE BLINDS DRAWN UP": MAUD GONNE AT HOWTH STATION WAITING   578 LOFTY THINGS       10
        A TRAIN;
```
BLINK
```
   AND UNDER THE BLINK O' THE MORNING STAR, . . . . .     83 MAD KING GOLL   V  20
   TILL STARS ARE BEGINNING TO BLINK AND PEEP; . . . .    150 OLD MOTHER          4
   WITH A BLINK IN HIS EYES, AT THE CAVE-MOUTH, . . . .    166 BLESSED             3
   WITH A BLINK IN HIS EYES AT THE CAVE MOUTH, . . . .    166 BLESSED         V   3
   OF SWORD-BLUE WAVES OF CALM; WHILE O'ER HEAD BLINK  . .   663 ISLE STAT II 2     42
```
BLINKED
```
   THAT BLINKED AND SAW THEM IN A SHROUD. . . . . . .    529 TOM LUNATIC        12
   HE BLINKED AND BLINKED HIS EYES . . . . . . . .     740 EARL PAUL          22
```

90

BLINKED   (CONTINUED)
     HE BLINKED AND BLINKED HIS EYES . . . .   740 EARL PAUL   22
BLINKING
     AND UNDER THE BLINKING OF THE STARS . . . .   83 MAD KING GOLL   20
     WITH BLINKING EYES, AT THE CAVE'S EDGE, ...   167 BLESSED   V   4C
     "MY EYES ARE BLINKING," DATHI SAID, ...   168 BLESSED   25
BLITHER
     I'D GLAD FOLKS' HEARTS WITH BLITHER SONG." . . . . . 731 PRIEST FAIRY   82
BLOCKS
     SALT BLOOD BLOCKS HIS EYES. . . . .   530 DELPHIC ORACLE   5
BLONDE
     THAT BLONDE GIRL THERE IS MY HEART'S DESIRE, ... 550 SONGS REWRIT 1 V   1
BLOOD
     UNDER A CROWN OF THORNS AND DARK WITH BLOOD, ...   38 OISIN 2   135
     HOW THE FETLOCKS DRIP BLOOD IN THE BATTLE, ...   52 OISIN 3   78
     WHO WASTES HIS BLOOD TO BE ANOTHER'S DREAM. . . . .   103 FERGUS DRUID   28
     ARE BLOWING THROUGH MY BLOOD. . . . .   171 MAID QUIET   4
     LIKE HEAVY FLOODED WATERS OUR BODIES AND OUR BLOOD; . 208 HANRAHANS SONG   13
     LIKE HEAVY SWOLLEN WATERS ARE OUR BODIES AND OUR BLOOD; 208 HANRAHANS SONG V   13
     AND NOW THAT TIME PUTS WATER IN MY BLOOD, ...   222 SHADOW WATER B V   11A
     FOR SHE HAD FIERY BLOOD . . . .   255 WOMAN HOMER   15
     THAT MUST, AS IF IT HAD NOT HOLY BLOOD . . . . 260 FASC DIFFICULT   5
     MERCHANT AND SCHOLAR WHO HAVE LEFT ME BLOOD . . . .   269 PARDON FATHERS   7
     TRADERS OR SOLDIERS WHO HAVE LEFT ME BLOOD . . . . . 269 PARDON FATHERS V   7
     NOTHING BUT THAT TO PROVE YOUR BLOOD AND MINE. . . . 270 PARDON FATHERS   22
     AND AFTER, WHEN HER BLOOD RAN WILD, ...   272 GREY ROCK   44
     LED BY A FOOTSOLE DIPPED IN BLOOD . . . .   274 GREY ROCK   78
     LED BY A FOOT-SOLE DIPPED IN BLOOD . . . .   274 GREY ROCK   V   78
     BUT FOR THE TRODDEN MIRE, THE POOL OF BLOOD, ... 278 TWO KINGS   44
     FOR THIS THAT ALL THAT BLOOD WAS SHED, ...   290 SEPTEMBER 1913   19
     LIKE GENTLE BLOOD, HAS BEEN DRIVEN FROM THE PLACE, . 292 TO A SHADE   14
     THEY WERE COMMINGLING LICE AND BLOOD. . . . .   297 THREE BEGGARS   56
     WITH THE HOT BLOOD OF YOUTH, OF LOVE CROSSED LONG AGO; 316 COLD HEAVEN   6
     AND FROZEN ARE THE CHANNELS OF THE BLOOD, ...   333 LIVING BEAUTY   2
     SEEING THAT TIME HAS FROZEN UP THE BLOOD . . . . .   333 LIVING BEAUTY V   2
     SET ALL HER BLOOD ASTIR . . . .   336 YOUNG GIRL   10
     WHEN AGE MIGHT WELL HAVE CHILLED HIS BLOOD." . . . . 356 BROKEN DREAMS   19
     TROUBLED HIS ANIMAL BLOOD. . . . .   378 CAT AND MOON   8
     THERE'S NOTHING BUT OUR OWN RED BLOOD . . . .   396 ROSE TREE   17
     CHILLED BLOOD, THIS SWEETNESS BROUGHT; . . . . . .   401 DEMON BEAST   39
     SLOW DECAY OF BLOOD, ...   416 TOWER   185
     THAT DEAD YOUNG SOLDIER IN HIS BLOOD; . . . .   425 STARES NEST   14
     TO CRAWL IN HER OWN BLOOD, AND GO SCOT-FREE; . . .   429 NINETEEN 19   28
     NOR KNOW THAT WHAT DISTURBS OUR BLOOD . . . .   434 WHEEL   7
     ODOUR OF BLOOD WHEN CHRIST WAS SLAIN . . . .   438 SONGS PLAY 2   6
     SO MASTERED BY THE BRUTE BLOOD OF THE AIR, ...   441 LEDA AND SWAN   12
     I HAVE AS HEALTHY FLESH AND BLOOD AS ANY RHYMER'S HAD, 450 OWEN AHERNE   10
     A HEART OF FLESH AND BLOOD. . . . .   451 FIRST LOVE   6
     AT THE MANTLING OF THE BLOOD. . . . .   453 DEATH OF HARE   6
     OR MANTLING OF THE BLOOD. . . . .   453 DEATH OF HARE V   6
     WHEN MY BLOOD WAS STRONG, ...   457 SECRETS OF OLD   4
     "AND YET THE JASMINE SEASON WARMS OUR BLOOD." . . .   464 HARUN RASHID   73
     BLOOD AND THE MOON . . . .   480 BLOOD AND MOON   T
     THE STRENGTH THAT GIVES OUR BLOOD AND STATE MAGNANIMITY 481 BLOOD AND MOON   29
       . . .
     THE BLOOD OF INNOCENCE HAS LEFT NO STAIN. . . . . .   482 BLOOD AND MOON   34
     OR OUT OF ABSTRACT HATRED, AND SHED BLOOD, ...   482 BLOOD AND MOON   38
     ODOUR OF BLOOD ON THE ANCESTRAL STAIR; . . . . . .   482 BLOOD AND MOON   40
     LIKE EVERYTHING THAT HAS THE STAIN OF BLOOD, . . .   482 BLOOD AND MOON   51
     THERE, ON BLOOD SATURATED GROUND, HAVE STOOD . . .   482 BLOOD AND MOON V   35
     OIL AND BLOOD . . . .   483 OIL AND BLOOD   T
     LIE BODIES OF THE VAMPIRES FULL OF BLOOD; . . . .   483 OIL AND BLOOD   5
     A PATTERN ON A NAPKIN DIPPED IN BLOOD. . . . . . .   483 VERONIC NAPKIN   8
     BUT NEVER SAW THE TREFOIL STAINED WITH BLOOD, . . .   487 SEVEN SAGES   19
     AND ALL COMPLEXITIES OF MIRE OR BLOOD. . . . . . .   498 BYZANTIUM   24
     ASTRADDLE ON THE DOLPHIN'S MIRE AND BLOOD, ...   498 BYZANTIUM   33
     WHERE BLOOD BEGOTTEN SPIRITS COME . . . .   498 BYZANTIUM   V   28
     A STRADDLE ON THE DOLPHIN'S MIRE AND BLOOD . . . .   498 BYZANTIUM   V   33
     THIS LOVE THAT MAKES MY HEART'S BLOOD STOP . . . .   499 MOTHER OF GOD   13
     THAT PROTECT YOUR BLOOD. . . . .   518 LOVES LONENESS   6
     IN ALL THE VIGOUR OF ITS BLOOD; . . . .   529 TOM LUNATIC   17
     SALT BLOOD BLOCKS HIS EYES. . . . .   530 DELPHIC ORACLE   5
     AND MY BLOOD BE COLD THE WHILE . . . .   532 BEFORE WORLD   11
     OR BUT TO FIND IF WITHERED VEIN RAN BLOOD, ...   537 HER VISION   6
     THAT THING ALL BLOOD AND MIRE, THAT BEAST-TORN WRECK, 537 HER VISION   25
     WHAT SHUDDERS RUN THROUGH ALL THAT ANIMAL BLOOD? . . 541 PARN FUNERAL 1   5
     PLUCKED BITTER WISDOM THAT ENRICHED HIS BLOOD. . . . 543 PARN FUNERAL 2   12
     JUSTIFY ALL THAT HAVE SUNK IN THEIR BLOOD, ...   546 TO SAME TUNE 2   12
     HOW CAN SHE LIVE TILL IN HER BLOOD HE LIVE! . . . .   558 RIBH CHRISTIAN   24
     IRRATIONAL STREAMS OF BLOOD ARE STAINING EARTH; . .   564 GYRES   5
     AND BLOOD AND MIRE THE SENSITIVE BODY STAIN? . . .   564 GYRES   10
     HE CHRISTENED HIMSELF WITH BLOOD. . . . .   585 ORAHILLY   8
     R.I.P." WRIT IN BLOOD. . . . .   585 ORAHILLY   35
     WHEN AN OLD MAN'S BLOOD GROWS COLD? . . . .   588 OLD WICKED MAN   13
     MUST IRELAND'S BLOOD BE SHED. . . . .   608 SONGS BURDEN 3   26
     REMEMBER ALL THAT HAVE SUNK IN THEIR BLOOD, ...   613 MARCH SONGS 1   12
     THOSE IMAGES THAT WAKEN IN THE BLOOD. . . . .   622 HOUND VOICE   14
     BASE DROVE OUT THE BETTER BLOOD, ...   626 STATES HOLIDAY   3
     AS THOUGH TO MEDITATE ON WOUNDS AND BLOOD. . . . .   634 CUCHULAIN COMF   6
     AS ROUND HER, SLOW ON FEET THAT HAVE NO BLOOD, . .   687 TWO TITANS   18
     I FLING AWAY MY SWORD, BLOOD DIM, ...   743 DANAAN QUICK   20

BLOOD   (CONTINUED)
    THE BLOOD BOND • • • • • • • • • • • • • • • • •   769 BLOOD BOND   T
BLOOD-BEDABBLED
    ALONG THE BLOOD-BEDABBLED PLAINS, • • • • • • • •   24 OISIN 1   371
    I STARED UPON HIS BLOOD-BEDABBLED BREAST • • • • •   537 HER VISION   23
    I STARED UPON MY BLOOD-BEDABBLED BREAST • • • • • •   537 HER VISION   V 23
BLOOD-BEGOTTEN
    WHERE BLOOD-BEGOTTEN SPIRITS COME • • • • • • • • •   498 BYZANTIUM   28
BLOOD-DARK
    STUMBLING UPON THE BLOOD-DARK TRACK ONCE MORE, • • • 622 HOUND VOICE   18
    A STAR-LIT RAPIER, HALF BLOOD-DARK, • • • • • • • • 671 ISLE STAT II 3   125
BLOOD-DIMMED
    THE BLOOD-DIMMED TIDE IS LOOSED, AND EVERYWHERE • • • 402 SECOND COMING   5
BLOODLESS
    I CANNOT GO INTO THE BLOODLESS LAND • • • • • • •   722 WITCH VIVIEN   67
BLOOD-RED
    WHERE THE BLOOD-RED BLOSSOM BLOWS • • • • • • • • • 744 ROSY CROSS   4
BLOOD-SATURATED
    THERE, ON BLOOD-SATURATED GROUND, HAVE STOOD • • • • 482 BLOOD AND MOON   35
BLOOD-SHOT
    NONE CLOSED HIS BLOOD-SHOT EYES BUT SOUGHT • • • • • 296 THREE BEGGARS   44
    THEY CLOSED THEIR BLOOD-SHOT EYES FOR NAUGHT, • • • • 296 THREE BEGGARS   V 44
    WITH BLOOD-SHOT EYES UPON HIM STARED. • • • • • • • 297 THREE BEGGARS   58
BLOOD-SODDEN
    BECAUSE THE HEART IN HIS BLOOD-SODDEN BREAST • • • • 481 BLOOD AND MOON   20
    FROM MAN'S BLOOD-SODDEN HEART ARE SPRUNG • • • • • • 502 VACILLATION   67
BLOODY
    OR FROM SOME BLOODY WHIP IN THEIR OWN HANDS. • • • • 375 PHASES OF MOON   68
    A BLOODY, ARROGANT POWER • • • • • • • • • • • • • 480 BLOOD AND MOON   3
    THEIR SHROUDS ARE BLOODY AND THEIR LIPS ARE WET. • • • 483 OIL AND BLOOD   6
    A BLOODY AND A SUDDEN END, • • • • • • • • • • • • 620 JOHN KINSELLA   1
    WHAT WOUNDS, WHAT BLOODY PRESS, • • • • • • • • • • 785 WOMANS BEAUTY   26
BLOOM
    THE DAMASK ROSES, BLOOM ON BLOOM, • • • • • • • • •   21 OISIN 1   305
    THE DAMASK ROSES, BLOOM ON BLOOM, • • • • • • • • •   21 OISIN 1   305
    AND SANG WE LIGHTLY TO EACH BLOOM • • • • • • • • •   21 OISIN 1   V 306B
    BRING ROSES IF THE ROSE BE YET IN BLOOM; • • • • • • 311 MOUNTAIN TOMB   2
    WHERE GOLDEN CROCUS AND NARCISSUS BLOOM, • • • • • • 447 COLONUS PRAISE   18
    HER LOVE: TO HER WHO WEARS THAT BLOOM COMES TRUTH. • • 653 ISLE STAT I 2   46
    AND FULL OF WISDOM IS EACH BLOOM, • • • • • • • • • 655 ISLE STAT I 3   9
    FOR GUIDING OF THE GODS. THE SACRED BLOOM • • • • • 656 ISLE STAT I 3   41
    A SCARLET BLOOM. WHY RAISEST THOU, PALE ONE, • • • • 673 ISLE STAT II 3   196
    THE FALLING HAWTHORN BLOOM. BY MERE AND BROOK • • • 677 ISLE STAT II 3   279
BLOSSOM   SEE APPLE-BLOSSOM
    BLOSSOM IN SOME NEW CRIMSON FLOWER, • • • • • • • •   16 OISIN 1   224
    AND THE PALE BLOSSOM OF THE MOON, • • • • • • • • •   20 OISIN 1   288
    WITH APPLE BLOSSOM IN HER HAIR • • • • • • • • • • 150 WANDER AENGUS   14
    THE SHADOWY BLOSSOM OF MY HAIR • • • • • • • • • • 152 HEART OF WOMAN   7
    THEN COVER THE PALE BLOSSOM OF YOUR BREAST • • • • • 163 ASKS FORGIVE   V 21
    WITH ITS SWEET BLOSSOM WHERE HERS WAS: • • • • • • • 197 BAILE AILLINN   190
    DELICATE IN COLOUR AS APPLE BLOSSOM. • • • • • • • • 199 ARROW   6
    BLOSSOM PALE, SHE PULLED DOWN THE PALE BLOSSOM • • • • 199 ARROW   V 5
    BLOSSOM PALE, SHE PULLED DOWN THE PALE BLOSSOM • • • • 199 ARROW   V 5
    BOUGHS HAVE THEIR FRUIT AND BLOSSOM • • • • • • • • 214 HAPPY TOWNLAND   5
    WHERE BOUGHS HAVE FRUIT AND BLOSSOM • • • • • • • • 214 HAPPY TOWNLAND V 5
    AND SHAKE THE BLOSSOM FROM THE BUD • • • • • • • • 396 ROSE TREE   11
    ARE YOU THE LEAF, THE BLOSSOM OR THE BOLE? • • • • • 446 SCHOOL CHILDR   62
    CAN SHAKE MORE BLOSSOM FROM AUTUMNAL CHILL • • • • • 465 HARUN RASHID   104
    THAT BRINGS MORE BLOSSOM TO AUTUMNAL CHILL • • • • • 465 HARUN RASHID   V 104
    BLOSSOM FROM THE SUMMER'S WREATH: • • • • • • • • • 475 EVA GORE-BOOTH   6
    GREAT NATIONS BLOSSOM ABOVE: • • • • • • • • • • • 547 TO SAME TUNE 3   5
    OF ROOT, SHOOT, BLOSSOM OR CLAY • • • • • • • • • • 600 SPIRIT MEDIUM   21
    GREAT NATIONS BLOSSOM ABOVE: • • • • • • • • • • • 614 MARCH SONGS 2   5
    WITHIN THE DROWSY BLOSSOM HANGS THE BEE: • • • • • • 645 ISLE STAT I 1   2
    THE NIGHEST BLOSSOM WHERE IT FALLS I'LL TAKE. • • • • 657 ISLE STAT I 3   65
    THIS BLOSSOM IS MOST NEAR. STATUE: OH, THOU • • • • 657 ISLE STAT I 3   72
    FIERCE THRUST: A TARDY BLOSSOM HAD THE SEED, • • • • 665 ISLE STAT II 2   65
    THE FAERY BLOSSOM LIES UPON THY LIPS. • • • • • • • 677 ISLE STAT II 3   285
    THE FAERY BLOSSOM LIES UPON THY LIPS: • • • • • • • 678 ISLE STAT II 3   291
    THE FAERY BLOSSOM BROODS UPON THY LIPS. • • • • • • 678 ISLE STAT II 3   306
    MY BLOSSOM, I AM DYING, AND THE STARS • • • • • • • 700 MOSADA 3   47
    OF APPLE BLOSSOM CIRCLES IN THE GLOOM, • • • • • • • 700 MOSADA 3   V 42
    AN APPLE BLOSSOM CIRCLES IN THE GLOOM, • • • • • • • 700 MOSADA 3   V 42
    WHERE THE BLOOD-RED BLOSSOM BLOWS • • • • • • • • • 744 ROSY CROSS   4
    THE TOPMOST BLOSSOM ON THE BOUGHS OF TIME • • • • • 756 SHADOW WATER A   178
    AND THE PALE BLOSSOM: BUT I WOKE INSTEAD • • • • • • 761 SHADOW WATER A   281
    SHOOK THE PALE APPLE BLOSSOM OVER IT: • • • • • • • 761 SHADOW WATER A V 275
BLOSSOMED
    THEY BLOSSOMED TO IMMORTAL MIRTH. • • • • • • • • • 189 BAILE AILLINN   12
    HAS BLOSSOMED, AND I GROW AS OLD AS TIME. • • • • • • 756 SHADOW WATER A   179
BLOSSOMER
    O CHESTNUT-TREE, GREAT-ROOTED BLOSSOMER, • • • • • • 446 SCHOOL CHILDR   61
    O CHESTNUT TREE, GREAT ROOTED BLOSSOMER, • • • • • • 446 SCHOOL CHILDR V 61
BLOSSOMING
    BECAUSE THEIR BLOSSOMING DREAMS HAVE NEVER BENT • • • 136 TO SOME I TALK   8
    FOR IN THE WORLD'S FIRST BLOSSOMING AGE • • • • • • 138 TO IRELAND   V 10
    OR TWO SWEET BLOSSOMING APPLE-BOUGHS • • • • • • • • 195 BAILE AILLINN   153
    OR TWO SWEET BLOSSOMING APPLE BOUGHS • • • • • • • • 195 BAILE AILLINN V 153
    CREW FROM A BLOSSOMING APPLE BOUGH • • • • • • • • • 387 SOLOMON WITCH   10
    UPON A BLOSSOMING APPLE BOUGH • • • • • • • • • • • 387 SOLOMON WITCH V 10
    CRIED FROM A BLOSSOMING APPLE BOUGH • • • • • • • • 387 SOLOMON WITCH V 10

BLOSSOMING   (CONTINUED)
    LABOUR IS BLOSSOMING OR DANCING WHERE   • • • • •   445 SCHOOL CHILDR   57
    AND WHAT A BLOSSOMING, • • • • • • • •   457 SUMMER SPRING   14
    PRAISE THE BLOSSOMING APPLE-STEM. • • • • • •   773 SONG DEIRDRE 1   21
    PRAISE THE BLOSSOMING APPLE STEM! • • • • • •   773 SONG DEIRDRE 1 V 21
BLOSSOMS
    AND IN THE BLOSSOMS HUNG THE BEES. • • • • •   2 OISIN 1   V 7G
    ARE WRONGING YOUR IMAGE THAT BLOSSOMS A ROSE • • •   143 ROSE IN HEART   4
    FOR MY DREAMS OF YOUR IMAGE THAT BLOSSOMS A ROSE • • •   143 ROSE IN HEART   8
    WITH APPLE BLOSSOMS IN HER HAIR. • • • • •   150 WANDER AENGUS V 14
    AND COVER THE PALE BLOSSOMS OF YOUR BREAST • • •   163 ASKS FORGIVE   21
    BLOSSOMS OPEN DEWY LIPS! • • • • • • •   647 ISLE STAT I 1   65
    AS BLOSSOMS, WHEN THE WINDS OF MARCH • • • •   671 ISLE STAT II 3 127
    THE FALLING BLOSSOMS, AND THE DEAD THE LIVING. • •   756 SHADOW WATER A 182
BLOT
    TILL THE FAR DOORWAY GREW A BURNING BLOT • • •   39 OISIN 2   V 152
    CAN BLOT OUT OF MY MEMORY THIS LIFE • • • •   285 TWO KINGS   204
    ALL THOSE STORMS THAT BLOT THE DAY • • • • •   509 JANE REPROVED V 3
    NOISE! AND A FLASH, A MOMENTARY BLOT. • • •   714 FERENCZ RENYI   110
    NOISE! UPROAR! AND A MOMENTARY BLOT. • • •   714 FERENCZ RENYI V 110
    AND HEAVEN'S A CLOUDY BLOT. • • • • • •   782 HEART FRIGHT   17
BLOTCH
    AND PENETRATION OF THEIR EYES. WHERE YONDER BLOTCH • •   664 ISLE STAT II 2   47
BLOTS
    ALL THAT STORM THAT BLOTS THE DAY • • • • •   509 JANE REPROVED   3
BLOTTED
    AND THE STARS WERE BLOTTED ABOVE US. • • • •   48 OISIN 3   24
    HAD BLOTTED OUT MAN'S IMAGE AND HIS CRY. • • •   120 SORROW OF LOVE   4
    THIS HUMAN LIFE BLOTTED FROM MEMORY. • • •   285 TWO KINGS   198
    UNDER ECLIPSE AND THE DAY BLOTTED OUT. • • •   414 TOWER   120
    AND ANCIENT LINEAMENTS ARE BLOTTED OUT. • • •   564 GYRES   4
BLOW
    IT SEEMED TO BLOW FROM THE DYING FLAME, • • •   13 OISIN 1   167
    SHALL BLOW INTO RUIN OUR MUSICAL DAYS. • • •   28 OISIN 1   V 425
    BURST FROM A GREAT DOOR MARRED BY MANY A BLOW • •   31 OISIN 2   29
    "HUNTSMAN RODY, BLOW THE HORN, • • • •   98 FOXHUNTER   25
    "NOW HUNTSMAN RODY, BLOW THY HORN, • • •   98 FOXHUNTER V REF
    "MY HUNTSMAN RODY, BLOW THE HORN, • • •   98 FOXHUNTER V REF
    "HUNTSMAN RODY, BLOW THE HORN, • • • •   99 FOXHUNTER   33
    "I CANNOT BLOW UPON MY HORN, • • • • •   99 FOXHUNTER   35
    THE DOORS OF HELL AND BLOW THERE MANY A WHIMPERING GHOST! 147 UNAPPEAS HOST   10
    I WENT TO BLOW THE FIRE AFLAME. • • • •   149 WANDER AENGUS   10
    I BENT TO BLOW THE FIRE AFLAME! • • • •   149 WANDER AENGUS V 10
    I WENT TO BLOW THE FIRE A-FLAME, • • •   149 WANDER AENGUS V 10
    I STOOPED TO BLOW THE FIRE AFLAME, • • •   149 WANDER AENGUS V 10
    I RISE IN THE DAWN, AND I KNEEL AND BLOW • •   150 OLD MOTHER   1
    I RISE AT THE DAWN, AND I KNEEL AND BLOW • •   150 OLD MOTHER V 1
    AND THE WINDS THAT BLOW THROUGH THE STARRY WAYS. •   158 TO HIS HEART   10
    AND BLOW A LITTLE NOISE • • • • • • •   215 HAPPY TOWNLAND   43
    I'LL STRIKE A BLOW FOR HIM TO GIVE HIM TIME • •   239 SHADOW WATER B 365
    THAT WINDS OF WINTER BLOW • • • • • •   431 NINETEEN 19   87
    A SUDDEN BLOW! THE GREAT WINGS BEATING STILL • •   441 LEDA AND SWAN   1
    BID ME STRIKE A MATCH AND BLOW. • • • •   476 EVA GORE-BOOTH   32
    FOR THE FOUL WINDS BLOW! • • • • • •   523 MAD AS MIST   2
    WHERE THE MEADOW-SAFFRONS BLOW, • • • •   680 LOVE AND DEATH   6
    AND THE WINDS COME DOWN AND BLOW THEM WITH THE VAPOURS   719 PHANTOM SHIP   28
        FAR AWAY.
    I AND THAT MIGHTY KING A SUDDEN BLOW • • •   757 SHADOW WATER A 195
    THAT BLOW WHEN HEAVEN AND EARTH ARE WITHERING, •   767 SHADOW WATER A 395
    BECAUSE THE NIGHT WINDS BLOW • • • • •   782 HEART FRIGHT   16
BLOWIN'   SEE A-BLOWIN'
    BLOWIN' HER MORNIN' FIRE. • • • • • • •   95 MOLL MAGEE   36
BLOWING
    THE COLD WET WINDS EVER BLOWING, • • • •   119 PITY OF LOVE   5
    AND THE COLD WET WINDS EVER BLOWING, • • •   119 PITY OF LOVE V 7
    AND THE WINDS BLOWING THROUGH THE STARRY WAYS, •   158 TO HIS HEART V 4
    AND BLOWING US EVIL AND GOOD! • • • • •   158 TO HIS HEART V 4A
    ARE BLOWING THROUGH MY BLOOD. • • • • •   171 MAID QUIET   4
    UNDER THE BITTER BLACK WINDS BLOWING OUT OF THE LEFT HAND! 206 HANRAHANS SONG V 2
    FOR THE WET WINDS ARE BLOWING OUT OF THE CLINGING AIR! •   207 HANRAHANS SONG   12
    WHEN THE WIND COMES BLOWING ACROSS THE HILLY LAND! • •   207 HANRAHANS SONG V 7
    FOR THE GREY WINDS ARE BLOWING UP, OUT OF THE CLINGING   207 HANRAHANS SONG V 12
        SEAS!
    AND WINDS BLOWING FROM FLOWERS, AND WHIRR OF FEATHERS • •   219 WOODS OF COOLE   39
    IF A GOOD EASTER WIND WERE BLOWING, • • • •   306 HOUR DAWN   86
    AND A COLD WIND IS BLOWING IN MY HAIR. • • •   761 SHADOW WATER A 277
BLOWN   SEE WIND-BLOWN
    WITH BLOWN, SPRAY-DABBLED HAIR GATHER AT HAND. • •   114 ROSE OF BATTLE   6
    THE THRONGS WITH BLOWN WET HAIR ARE GATHERING NEAR. • •   114 ROSE OF BATTLE V 6
    WHEN SHALL THE STARS BE BLOWN ABOUT THE SKY! • • •   170 SECRET ROSE   29
    LIKE THE SPARKS BLOWN OUT OF A SMITHY, AND DIE? • •   170 SECRET ROSE   30
    BEING TUMBLED AND BLOWN ABOUT • • • • •   191 BAILE AILLINN   66
    A CLOUD BLOWN FROM THE CUT-THROAT NORTH • • •   313 MEMORY YOUTH   6
    AND QUARRELS ARE BLOWN UP UPON THAT HEAD! • •   324 ROBERT GREGORY   13
    AND YET THEY SPEAK WHAT'S BLOWN INTO THE MIND! • •   376 PHASES OF MOON 110
    THE COLD BLOWN SPRAY IN MY NOSTRIL. • • • •   399 BREAK OF DAY   20
    A MIST THAT IS LIKE BLOWN SNOW IS SWEEPING OVER ALL, •   425 PHANTOM HATRED   2
    A BUNDLE OF TEMPESTUOUS CLOUD IS BLOWN • • •   541 PARN FUNERAL 1   2
    LONG CITRON COILS THAT HANG AROUND THEE, BLOWN •   670 ISLE STAT II 3 105
    AND NO MAN KILL ME! FOR SOME WIND HAS BLOWN • •   751 SHADOW WATER A 97
    HAVE THE WINDS BLOWN YOU AMONG THESE EMPTY WATERS? • •   756 SHADOW WATER A 192

		PAGE	TITLE	LINE
BLOWN (CONTINUED)				
AND SHE, NO LONGER BLOWN AMONG THE WINDS,		763	SHADOW WATER A	323
ARE BLOWN COLD DUST OR A BIT OF BONE.		788	HAWTHORN TREE	8
BLOWS				
AND BLOWS ON HIS HANDS IN THE FIRE'S WARM BLAZE;		26	OISIN 1 V	404
BARKING, WE TRAMPLED UP AND DOWN WITH BLOWS		40	OISIN 2	170
BARKING, ALONG THE HERBLESS PLAIN, WITH BLOWS		40	OISIN 2 V	170
SURELY THINE HOUR HAS COME, THY GREAT WIND BLOWS,		170	SECRET ROSE	31
THE POWERS, NOT KIND LIKE YOU, CAME WHERE GOD'S GARDEN BLOWS,		174	ELEMENT POWERS V	1
UNDER A BITTER BLACK WIND THAT BLOWS FROM THE LEFT HAND;		206	HANRAHANS SONG	2
THAT THEY WOULD COME TO BLOWS		214	HAPPY TOWNLAND	22
THAT THEY MUST COME TO BLOWS		214	HAPPY TOWNLAND V	22
OR MAYBE BUT A WIND THAT BLOWS		396	ROSE TREE	5
OF EVERY WIND THAT BLOWS;		419	MY HOUSE	7
WHEREON THE BLEAK NORTH BLOWS,		454	HIS MEMORIES	4
BUT GOOD STRONG BLOWS ARE DELIGHTS TO THE MIND."		544	TO SAME TUNE 1	4
BUT A GOOD STRONG CAUSE AND BLOWS ARE DELIGHT."		545	TO SAME TUNE 1 V	14
BUT A GOOD STRONG CAUSE AND THE BLOWS ARE DELIGHT."		545	TO SAME TUNE 1 V	14
BUT GOOD STRONG BLOWS ARE DELIGHTS TO THE MIND."		616	MARCH SONGS 3	4
BUT A GOOD STRONG CAUSE AND BLOWS ARE DELIGHT."		616	MARCH SONGS 3	14
THE LONG LILY BLOWS,		672	ISLE STAT II 3	165
WHERE THE BLOOD-RED BLOSSOM BLOWS		744	ROSY CROSS	4
AND THE WIND BLOWS IT AWAY.		783	GREY ROUND	20
BLUE SEE STEEL-BLUE SWORD-BLUE				
WILD FLAMES OF RED AND GOLD AND BLUE,		18	OISIN 1	252
IF THEY STILL SLUMBER, TOUCH THEIR EYELIDS BLUE,		33	OISIN 2 V	61
AH, TOUCH THEIR BLUE VEINED EYELIDS IF THEY SLEEP,		33	OISIN 2 V	61
SIGH, O YOU LITTLE STARS! O SIGH AND SHAKE YOUR BLUE APPAREL!		72	ANASHU VIJAYA	18
SIGH, OH YE LITTLE STARS! OH, SIGH AND SHAKE YOUR BLUE APPAREL!		72	ANASHU VIJAYA V	18
AND THE FLAME OF THE BLUE STAR OF TWILIGHT,		122	WHITE BIRDS	3
OR THE FLAME OF THE BLUE STAR THAT LINGERS		122	WHITE BIRDS	7
OF THE MATCHING OF RIBBONS THE BLUE AND THE RED,		151	OLD MOTHER V	6
IT ROSE IN A STRAIGHT BLUE GARMENT.		159	CAP AND BELLS	5
IN A LONG AND STRAIGHT BLUE GARMENT		159	CAP AND BELLS V	5
TO HER LEFT HAND CAME THE BLUE.		160	CAP AND BELLS	32
THE BLUE AND THE DIM AND THE DARK CLOTHS		176	CLOTHS HEAVEN	3
CAER, HIS BLUE EYED DAUGHTER THAT I LOVE.		184	QUEEN MAEVE V	96
QUEENS, THEIR EYES BLUE LIKE THE ICE,		214	HAPPY TOWNLAND	11
TREMBLING IN THE BLUE HEAVENS LIKE A WHITE FAWN		251	SHADOW WATER B	611
WITH THE GROUND-IVY'S BLUE, HE SAW A STAG		277	TWO KINGS	6
WANDERED BETWEEN THE BLUE AND THE GREEN LEAF		278	TWO KINGS	41
AS ON THE BLUE LIGHT OF A SWORD, A MAN		283	TWO KINGS	148
APPEAR AND DISAPPEAR IN THE BLUE DEPTH OF THE SKY		318	MAGI	3
APPEAR AND DISAPPEAR IN THE BLUE DEPTHS OF THE SKY		318	MAGI V	3
LIKE THIS PURE JET, NOW LOST AMID BLUE SKY,		464	HARUN RASHID	64
THE MOBS OF STARS IN GOLD AND GREEN AND BLUE,		663	ISLE STAT II 2	43
AMONG THE BOUGHS, BLUE AS THE HALCYON'S WING,		683	SEEKER	38
WITHIN THE WOODWAYS, BLUE AS THE HALCYON'S WING,		683	SEEKER V	38
'TIS THOU, FOR THEY'VE GROWN BLUE AROUND THE NAILS.		700	MOSADA 3	46
AMONG THE BLUE, THE AMBER AND THE RED."		712	FERENCZ RENYI V	76
THE GRASS AND THE BLUE SHADOW ON THE STREAM		761	SHADOW WATER A	280
TREMBLING IN THE BLUE HEAVENS LIKE A WHITE FAWN		769	SHADOW WATER A	427
BLUE-EYED				
HOW THE SLOW, BLUE-EYED OXEN OF FINN LOW SADLY AT EVENING TIDE.		52	OISIN 3	84
CAER, HIS BLUE-EYED DAUGHTER THAT I LOVE.		184	QUEEN MAEVE	96
AND THE WOOD-WOMAN, WHOSE LOVER WAS CHANGED TO A BLUE-EYED HAWK;		209	UNDER THE MOON	13
AND THE WOOD WOMAN, WHOSE LOVER WAS CHANGED TO A BLUE-EYED HAWK;		209	UNDER THE MOON V	13
BLUE-EYED, AND A QUICK RUNNER ON BARE FEET,		242	SHADOW WATER B	416
BLUE-GREEN				
AND IN THE TREMBLING BLUE-GREEN OF THE SKY		206	ADAMS CURSE	30
BLUER				
AND THE GROUND IVY'S BLUER LIGHT, A STAG		277	TWO KINGS V	6
BLUES				
HER GOLDS, HER AMBERS, AND HER BLUES,		13	OISIN 1	163
HER GOLDS, HER AZURES, AND HER BLUES,		13	OISIN 1 V	163
BLUE-VEINED				
AH, TOUCH THEIR BLUE-VEINED EYELIDS IF THEY SLEEP,		33	OISIN 2	61
BLUSHED				
SHE WALKED AWHILE AND BLUSHED AWHILE		451	FIRST LOVE	3
BLUSHES				
AND THE BLUSHES OF FIRST LOVE NEVER HAVE FLOWN;		8	OISIN 1	85
BOAR				
THE DEER, THE BADGER, AND THE BOAR.		23	OISIN 1	345
A HUNDRED YEARS I CHASED THE BOAR.		23	OISIN 1 V	344
THE WILD BOAR KNOWS ME, BY ONE EAR		84	MAD KING GOLL V	45
I WOULD THAT THE BOAR WITHOUT BRISTLES HAD COME FROM THE WEST		153	CHANGE BELOVED	10
AND SO WITH WOLF, AND BOAR, AND STEER.		671	ISLE STAT II 3	122
BOARD				
THEY WROTE ON TABLETS OF THIN BOARD,		197	BAILE AILLINN	195
THE GODS WERE SITTING AT THE BOARD		271	GREY ROCK	14
WHILE THEIR GREAT WOODEN DICE BEAT ON THE BOARD.		412	TOWER	88
TWO HEAVY TRESTLES, AND A BOARD		421	MY TABLE	1
SHE HEARS ME STRIKE THE BOARD AND SAY		531	FATHER CHILD	1
WHEN ONE HAS LEAPT ON BOARD. NO, FOR I HAVE HOPE		751	SHADOW WATER A	106

94

BOARD   (CONTINUED)
    FORGAEL MAY FIND HIS HEART'S DESIRE ON BOARD . . . . . 751 SHADOW WATER A   107
BOARDED   SEE CEDAR-BOARDED
    CHRYSELEPHANTINE, CEDAR BOARDED, ... 440 WISDOM   V 10
BOARDS
    AND THEY HAD NAILED THE BOARDS ABOVE HER FACE, ... 123 DREAM OF DEATH   3
    BUT NOW LIES UNDER BOARDS. . . . . 123 DREAM OF DEATH   12
    WITH OLD MILL BOARDS AND SEA-GREEN SLATES, ... 406 CARVED STONE   2
    UPON THIN BOARDS OF YEW AND APPLE WOOD, ... 764 SHADOW WATER A   343
    UPON THIN BOARDS OF YEW AND APPLE-WOOD, ... 764 SHADOW WATER A V 343
BOAST
    BOAST NOT, NOR MOURN WITH DROOPING HEAD . . . . . . 11 OISIN 1   129
    BARD OISIN, BOAST NOT OF THY DEEDS . . . . 11 OISIN 1   V 129
    "LET OTHERS BOAST THEIR FILL," SAID I, ... 539 MEETING   7
    "BUT NEVER DARE TO BOAST • . . . . 539 MEETING   8
    "A LOONY'D BOAST OF SUCH A LOVE," . . . . 539 MEETING   13
    SOME BOAST OF BEGGAR-KINGS AND KINGS . . . . 597 MODEL LAUREATE   9
BOASTING
    HELD TO THE TOWERS WITH BOASTING SONGS AND GAY. . . . 41 OISIN 2   V 184C
BOASTS
    ANOTHER BOASTS, "I PICK AND CHOOSE AND HAVE BUT TWO OR 354 HIS PHOENIX   20
      THREE."
BOAT   SEE ROW-BOAT
    THE CLOAK, THE BOAT, AND THE SHOES . . . . 69 CLOAK BOAT   T
    "I BUILD A BOAT FOR SORROW! . . . . 70 CLOAK BOAT   7
    A BOAT I BUILD FOR SORROW! . . . . 70 CLOAK BOAT   V 7
    ON DAPPLED SKINS IN A GLASS BOAT, ... 196 BAILE AILLINN   180
    A GREAT BLACK RAGGED BIRD APPEARED WHEN I WAS IN THE BOAT! 593 PILGRIM   16
    A GREAT BLACK BIRD APPEARED WHEN I WAS IN THE BOAT, . . 593 PILGRIM   V 16
    OF THOSE VAST WOODS! AND THEN I SAW THE BOAT. . . . . 657 ISLE STAT I 3   53
    THE BOAT DRAWS NEAR AND NEAR. YOU HEED ME NOT! . . . 663 ISLE STAT II 2   23
    SLOW WATERS, AND THE BOAT AND MAIDEN SINK . . . . . 663 ISLE STAT II 2   39
    A BOAT I BUILD FOR SORROW. . . . . 666 ISLE STAT II 3   7
BOATMAN
    BUT I NEVER STOPPED TO QUESTION, WHAT COULD THE BOATMAN SAY 593 PILGRIM   19
BOAT'S
    THE BOAT'S PROW GRATED ON THE SHALLOW SAND, ... 659 ISLE STAT II 1   11
    ALL SWIM WITH TEARS. THE FAERY BOAT'S AT HAND! . . . 663 ISLE STAT II 2   33
BOATS
    AND ON THE SHORES WERE MANY BOATS . . . . 14 OISIN 1   188
    WE WENT A-FISHING IN LONG BOATS . . . . 23 OISIN 1   352
BOB
    OR SEE THE BROWN MICE BOB . . . . 88 STOLEN CHILD   48
BOBBIN
    FOR HADES' BOBBIN BOUND IN MUMMY-CLOTH . . . . . . 497 BYZANTIUM   11
    FOR HADES' BOBBIN BOUND IN MUMMY CLOTH . . . . . . 497 BYZANTIUM   V 11
BODES
    "BODES ME LITTLE GOOD." . . . . 539 MEETING   6
BODICES
    THEIR BODICES IN SOME DIM PLACE . . . . 193 BAILE AILLINN   105
BODIED   SEE GREAT-BODIED
    AND YET HAD BEEN GREAT BODIED AND GREAT LIMBED, . . . 181 QUEEN MAEVE   V 25
BODIES
    BENT ALL OUR SWAYING BODIES DOWN, ... 20 OISIN 1   297
    THEIR NAKED AND GLEAMING BODIES POURED OUT AND HEAPED IN 48 OISIN 3   28
      THE WAY.
    THEIR MIGHTY AND NAKED AND GLEAMING BODIES . . . . . 48 OISIN 3   V 28
    THE BREATHING CAME FROM THOSE BODIES. . . . . . . 49 OISIN 3   36
    SIDLED THEIR BODIES AGAINST HIM, FILLING THE SHADE WITH 50 OISIN 3   48
      THEIR EYES.
    . . . WITH BODIES UNGLORIOUS, THEIR CHIEFTAINS STOOD, . 58 OISIN 3   166
    BODIES OF SHADOW AND BLIND EYES LIKE PEARLS, ... 185 QUEEN MAEVE   116
    WITH LONG WHITE BODIES CAME OUT OF THE AIR, ... 185 QUEEN MAEVE   118
    WITH BODIES MADE OUT OF SOFT FIRE. THE ONE, ... 187 QUEEN MAEVE   144
    BECAUSE THEIR BODIES HAD GROWN OLD. . . . . 189 BAILE AILLINN   10
    AND IN THE LIGHT BODIES OF BIRDS . . . . 190 BAILE AILLINN   44
    LIKE HEAVY FLOODED WATERS OUR BODIES AND OUR BLOOD! . . 208 HANRAHANS SONG   13
    DARK AND DULL AND EARTHY OUR SOULS AND BODIES BE! . . 208 HANRAHANS SONG V 13
    LIKE HEAVY SWOLLEN WATERS ARE OUR BODIES AND OUR BLOOD! 208 HANRAHANS SONG V 13
    ARE YOU NOT HAPPY WINGED BODIES NOW? . . . . 234 SHADOW WATER B   273
    NOW THAT YOU HAVE HAPPY WINGED BODIES? . . . . . . 234 SHADOW WATER B V 273
    THE ROUND GREEN EYES AND THE LONG WAVERING BODIES . . 343 DEJECTION   2
    THEY CHANGE THEIR BODIES AT A WORD. AND THEN? . . . 376 PHASES OF MOON   113
    IMAGINED BODIES ALL THEIR DAYS . . . . 386 ROBARTES DANCE   28
    OF THEIR OWN SWEETNESS, BODIES OF THEIR LOVELINESS. . . 426 PHANTOM HATRED   24
    AND BODIES BROKEN LIKE A THORN . . . . 454 HIS MEMORIES   3
    BODIES OF HOLY MEN AND WOMEN EXUDE . . . . 483 OIL AND BLOOD   2
    LIE BODIES OF THE VAMPIRES FULL OF BLOOD! . . . . . 483 OIL AND BLOOD   5
    THOSE BODIES FROM A PICTURE OR A COIN . . . . 537 HER VISION   28
    DID BUT OUR BODIES TOUCH. . . . . 538 LAST CONFESS   10
    THEY LEFT THEIR BODIES TO FATTEN THE WOLVES, ... 545 TO SAME TUNE 2   2
    BEEN BONE AND SINEW! WHEN SUCH BODIES JOIN . . . . . 555 RIBH AT TOMB   12
    BEAT DOWN UPON THEIR NAKED BODIES! KNOW . . . . . . 563 MERU   12
    THAT BY THEIR BODIES LAY. . . . . 589 OLD WICKED MAN   44
    THEY LEFT THEIR BODIES TO FATTEN THE WOLVES, ... 613 MARCH SONGS 1   2
    BODIES THAT CAN NEVER TIRE . . . . 776 AGAINST WITCH   20
    ALL THEIR BODIES, JOINT BY JOINT, ... 776 AGAINST WITCH   22
    BURN THEIR BODIES UP FOR NOUGHT! . . . . 787 HUDDON DUDDON   14
    GAVE THEIR BODIES, EMPTIED PURSES . . . . 789 SINGING HEAD   19
BODILY
    AND BODILY TENDERNESS, AND FINDS THAT EVEN . . . . . 228 SHADOW WATER B   147

95

		PAGE	TITLE	LINE

BODILY (CONTINUED)

	PAGE	TITLE	LINE
MY BODILY FORM FROM ANY NATURAL THING,	408	SAIL BYZANTIUM	26
MY BODILY HEIRS MAY FIND,	420	MY HOUSE	28
LEARNED IN BODILY LOWLINESS	513	JANE TALK BISH	11
OR BODILY MOVEMENT DID I DARE,	514	JANE GROWN OLD	5
BODILY DECREPITUDE IS WISDOM: YOUNG	523	LONG SILENCE	7
THAT I LOVED BODILY.	538	LAST CONFESS	6
A BODILY OR MENTAL FURNITURE.	558	RIBH CHRISTIAN	20
AND BODILY TENDERNESS TO THE SOFT FIRE	750	SHADOW WATER A	60
AND BODILY TENDERNESS: AND HE WHO LONGS	750	SHADOW WATER A	66
AND BODILY TENDERNESS: BUT LOVE IS MADE	765	SHADOW WATER A	355

BODKIN

	PAGE	TITLE	LINE
IN A BODKIN OR DISEASE,	632	MAN AND ECHO	22

BODY

	PAGE	TITLE	LINE
AND THE WHITE BODY THAT LAY BY MINE:	3	OISIN 1	10
AND HER BRIGHT BODY, SANG OF FAERY AND MAN	29	OISIN 2	7
AND HER BRIGHT BODY—NOW OF FAY AND MAN:	29	OISIN 2 V	7
OF A DROWNED DRIPPING BODY TO MY BREAST:	40	OISIN 2	179
GO CAST YOUR BODY ON THE STONES AND PRAY,	42	OISIN 2	207
IN THE ROOTS OF THE GRASSES: THE SORRELS, I LAID MY BODY AS LOW:	52	OISIN 3	73
WHEN THEY FROZE THE CLOTH ON MY BODY LIKE ARMOUR RIVETED FAST,	57	OISIN 3	151
I WOULD LEAVE NO SAINT'S HEAD ON HIS BODY	58	OISIN 3	160
. . . WHEN LIFE IN MY BODY HAS CEASED,	63	OISIN 3	222
THE SERVANTS BEAR THE BODY IN:	99	FOXHUNTER	47
THIS BODY TREMBLING LIKE A WIND-BLOWN REED.	103	FERGUS DRUID	25
WHEN EARTHY NIGHT HAD DRUNK HIS BODY IN:	127	DREAM OF FAERY	28
NOW THAT DEEP EARTH HAS DRUNK HIS BODY IN:	127	DREAM OF FAERY V	28
MY BODY SPAKE, NOT I!"	132	FR GILLIGAN	12
AND THOUGHT OF DAYS WHEN HE'D HAD A STRAIGHT BODY,	183	QUEEN MAEVE	70
THEY KNEW HIM: HIS CHANGED BODY WAS	195	BAILE AILLINN	139
A YEW-TREE WHERE HIS BODY LAY.	197	BAILE AILLINN	188
A YEW TREE WHERE HIS BODY LAY,	197	BAILE AILLINN V	188
WE'RE IN THE BODY THAT'S IMPOSSIBLE.	230	SHADOW WATER B	190
THAN A STRONG BODY AND A READY HAND.	232	SHADOW WATER B	236
UNTIL MY BODY GIVE YOU KISS FOR KISS.	238	SHADOW WATER B	345
NOW THAT MY BODY HAS BEGUN TO DREAM,	245	SHADOW WATER B	486
WHAT THING HER BODY WAS."	255	WOMAN HOMER	14
WHEN NEITHER SOUL NOR BODY HAS BEEN CROSSED.	258	KING NO KING	16
THAT MADE THE BODY SEEM AS IT WERE A STRING	284	TWO KINGS	176
I PRAISED HER BODY AND HER MIND	314	MEMORY YOUTH	9
TO KEEP THE BODY YOUNG.	334	SONG	4
I THOUGHT 'TWOULD BURN MY BODY	335	SONG	15
AND ALL THE SHAPELY BODY NO TITTLE GONE ASTRAY.	354	HIS PHOENIX	30
AND YET YOUR BODY HAD A FLAW.	356	BROKEN DREAMS	28
HIS BODY MOULDED FROM WITHIN HIS BODY	374	PHASES OF MOON	43
HIS BODY MOULDED FROM WITHIN HIS BODY	374	PHASES OF MOON	43
BECOMES A BODY: THAT BODY AND THAT SOUL	374	PHASES OF MOON	59
BECOMES A BODY: THAT BODY AND THAT SOUL	374	PHASES OF MOON	59
BODY AND SOUL CAST OUT AND CAST AWAY	374	PHASES OF MOON	62
END IN A BEAUTIFUL MAN'S OR WOMAN'S BODY.	374	PHASES OF MOON	64
OF BODY AND SOUL. THE LOVER'S HEART KNOWS THAT.	375	PHASES OF MOON	71
WHO SHUDDER AND HURRY BY: BODY AND SOUL	375	PHASES OF MOON	77
UPON THE BODY AND UPON THE SOUL	376	PHASES OF MOON	93
DEFORMITY OF BODY AND OF MIND.	377	PHASES OF MOON	123
BODY PERFECTION BROUGHT,	383	VISION ROBART	40
THERE IS GREAT DANGER IN THE BODY.	386	ROBARTES DANCE	38
GIVE MAN HIS THOUGHT OR HIS MERE BODY?	386	ROBARTES DANCE	40
A SHAPE WITH LION BODY AND THE HEAD OF A MAN,	402	SECOND COMING	14
TILL THE WRECK OF BODY,	416	TOWER	184
WHERE WE SHOULD CAST OFF BODY AND TRADE.	431	NINETEEN 19	73
AND HOW CAN BODY, LAID IN THAT WHITE RUSH,	441	LEDA AND SWAN	7
I DREAM OF A LEDAEAN BODY, BENT	443	SCHOOL CHILDR	9
THE BODY IS NOT BRUISED TO PLEASURE SOUL,	445	SCHOOL CHILDR	58
O BODY SWAYED TO MUSIC, O BRIGHTENING GLANCE,	446	SCHOOL CHILDR	63
O BODY SWAYED TO MUSIC BRIGHTENING GLANCE	446	SCHOOL CHILDR V	63
UNTIL I THOUGHT HER BODY BORE	451	FIRST LOVE	5
PRESSED HER BODY TO HIS BODY,	453	MERMAID	3
PRESSED HER BODY TO HIS BODY,	453	MERMAID	3
"IF BUT THE SHIRT UPON MY BODY KNEW IT	462	HARUN RASHID	33
THAT SPRINGS FROM BODY AND IN BODY FALLS	463	HARUN RASHID	63
THAT SPRINGS FROM BODY AND IN BODY FALLS	463	HARUN RASHID	63
ARE NEARER TO THE SURFACE OF THE BODY	464	HARUN RASHID	67
ARE BUT A NEW EXPRESSION OF HER BODY	469	HARUN RASHID	185
THE BEAUTY OF A WOMAN'S MIND OR BODY	469	HARUN RASHID V	187
THE BODY CALLS IT DEATH:	500	VACILLATION	7
MY BODY OF A SUDDEN BLAZED:	501	VACILLATION	41
THE BODY OF SAINT TERESA LIES UNDECAYED IN TOMB,	503	VACILLATION	80
ETERNALISED- THE BODY OF A MODERN SAINT THAT ONCE	503	VACILLATION	83
THAT PIERCED MY BODY THROUGH?	507	STREAM AND SUN	13
BODY AND SOUL":	510	JANE JUDGMENT	4
MY BODY IN THE TOMB—	511	JANE AND JACK	10
MY BODY MAKES NO MOAN	512	JANE ON GOD	22
MY BODY HAS NOT MOANED	512	JANE ON GOD V	22
SUCH BODY LOVERS HAVE,	517	HER ANXIETY	7
WHEN MY BODY WAS ALIVE	521	THREE THINGS	10
WRAPPING THAT FOUL BODY UP	525	DANCING DAYS	5
BUT STRETCH THAT BODY FOR A WHILE	534	CONSOLATION	3
SCARCE DID HE MY BODY TOUCH,	535	CHOSEN	4
I TORE MY BODY THAT ITS WINE MIGHT COVER	537	HER VISION	7

96

BODY   (CONTINUED)
  NOR SAW MY BODY FALL NOR HEARD IT SHRIEK,   • • • • • • •   537 HER VISION   29
  BUT WHEN THIS SOUL, ITS BODY OFF, • • • •   •   •   •   •   538 LAST CONFESS   15
  • • • DAMPED BY THE BODY OR THE MIND, • •   •   •   •   •   556 RIBH PATRICK   8
  WHAT SACRED DRAMA THROUGH HER BODY HEAVED   •   •   •   •   •   560 WHENCE COME   11
  HE WITH BODY WAGED A FIGHT, • • • • • • •   •   •   •   561 FOUR AGES MAN   1
  BUT BODY WON: IT WALKS UPRIGHT. • • • • •   •   •   •   •   561 FOUR AGES MAN   2
  AND BLOOD AND MIRE THE SENSITIVE BODY STAIN? • •   •   •   •   564 GYRES   10
  THAT STRIP THE BODY BARE." • • • • • • •   •   •   •   570 THREE BUSHES   27
  WASH: MAKE YOUR BODY SWEET: • • • • • •   •   •   •   •   572 LADYS 2ND SONG   4
  BODY WERE NOT AT ALL. • • • • • •   •   •   •   •   572 LADYS 2ND SONG   9
  HE SHALL LOVE YOUR BODY • • • • • • •   •   •   •   572 LADYS 2ND SONG   10
  IF SOUL MAY LOOK AND BODY TOUCH, • • • •   •   •   •   •   572 LADYS 2ND SONG   19
  NOR THINK THAT BODY IS THE WHOLE, • • • •   •   •   •   •   573 LADYS 3RD SONG   4
  KNOW WORSE EVIL OF THE BODY: • • • • • •   •   •   •   •   573 LADYS 3RD SONG   6
  NOW STRENGTH OF BODY GOES: • • • • • •   •   •   •   •   575 ACRE OF GRASS   4
  I BEND MY BODY TO THE SPADE • • • • • •   •   •   •   •   599 SPIRIT MEDIUM   7
  I BEND MY BODY TO THE SPADE • • • • • •   •   •   •   •   600 SPIRIT MEDIUM   15
  I BEND MY BODY TO THE SPADE • • • • • •   •   •   •   •   600 SPIRIT MEDIUM   23
  AND MIND AND BODY SHRANK. • • • • • •   •   •   •   •   626 STATES HOLIDAY   4
  WHILE MAN CAN STILL HIS BODY KEEP • • • •   •   •   •   •   633 MAN AND ECHO   25
  HAS BODY AND ITS STUPIDITY, • • • • • •   •   •   •   •   633 MAN AND ECHO   28
  BUT BODY GONE HE SLEEPS NO MORE, • • • •   •   •   •   •   633 MAN AND ECHO   29
  HIS BODY SHAKE? AY, QUIVERING AS YON SMOKE   •   •   •   •   683 SEEKER   36
  CLOSELY ROUND US, BODY AND MIND-- • • • •   •   •   •   •   717 FAIRY DOCTOR   23
  IS NOT THY BODY BUT THE GARNERED RUST   • • •   •   •   •   724 KANVA ON SELF   15
  IS THIS POOR BODY THAT REDDENS AND GROWS PALE. • •   •   •   764 SHADOW WATER A   341
  LOOK ON THIS BODY AND THIS HEAVY HAIR: • • •   •   •   •   767 SHADOW WATER A   397
  ALL HIS BODY CAN BUT SHOVE   • • • • • •   •   •   •   •   776 AGAINST WITCH   33
  HIS HEAD FROM OFF HIS BODY • • • • • •   •   •   •   •   789 SINGING HEAD   5
BODY'S
  LEAVE THE BODY'S COLOURED PRIDE • • • • •   •   •   •   •   124 CATHLEEN PARA   2
  WHERE ONLY BODY'S LAID ASLEEP. • • • • •   •   •   •   •   138 TO IRELAND   22
  ALL THE STRETCHED BODY'S LAID ON THE WHITE RUSH • •   •   441 LEDA AND SWAN   V   7
  THE SOUL'S OWN YOUTH AND NOT THE BODY'S YOUTH • •   •   •   464 HARUN RASHID   69
BOG
  AND ONE WAS DROWNED IN THE GREAT BOG OF CLOONE. •   •   •   411 TOWER   48
BOG'S
  THE MAN DROWNED IN A BOG'S MIRE, • • • • • • •   •   •   413 TOWER   95
BOILED
  AND THAT IS CURED BY A BOILED LIQUORICE ROOT. • • •   •   227 SHADOW WATER B V 116B
BOILING
  TO STIR THE BOILING POT? • • • • • • •   •   •   •   395 SIXTEEN DEAD   6
BOISTEROUS
  MUCH BOISTEROUS COURAGE, BEFORE LONELINESS • •   •   •   •   473 ALL SOUL NIGHT   72
BOLD   SEE OVER-BOLD
  JABBER AND SCREAM. YET HE, FOR ALL HIS BOLD •   •   •   •   34 OISIN 2   V   82
  "IS HE SO DREADFUL?" "BE NOT OVER BOLD, • • •   •   •   •   35 OISIN 2   V   88
  THESE HANDS SLEW MANY WARRIORS BOLD-- • • •   •   •   •   83 MAD KING GOLL   V   23
  THESE HANDS SLEW MANY ROBBERS BOLD-- • • •   •   •   •   83 MAD KING GOLL   V   23
  THESE HANDS SLEW MANY A SEAMAN BOLD. • • •   •   •   •   83 MAD KING GOLL   V   23
  THE HARES RUN BY ME GROWING BOLD. • • • • •   •   •   •   84 MAD KING GOLL   V   47
  THE HARE RUNS BY ME GROWING BOLD-- • • • •   •   •   •   84 MAD KING GOLL   V   47
  AND HARES RUN NEAR ME GROWING BOLD. • • • •   •   •   •   84 MAD KING GOLL   V   47
  "O NO, MY DEAR, YOU MAKE SO BOLD   • • • • •   •   •   •   263 MASK   3
  FOR I AM NOT SO BOLD • • • • • • •   •   •   •   346 ON WOMAN   26
  WHETHER IT BE BOLD OR SLY. • • • • • •   •   •   •   •   624 APPARITIONS   6
BOLE   SEE BEECH-BOLE
  AGAINST A BEECH BOLE, HE THREW DOWN THE BEAST • •   •   •   278 TWO KINGS   V   36
  ARE YOU THE LEAF, THE BLOSSOM OR THE BOLE? • •   •   •   •   446 SCHOOL CHILDR   62
BOLT
  AND PUSHED THE BRASS BOLT DOWN.   • • • • •   •   •   •   159 CAP AND BELLS   V   12
  I'LL FIND THE STABLE AND PULL OUT THE BOLT. • •   •   •   •   260 FASC DIFFICULT   13
  BOLT AND BAR THE SHUTTER, • • • • • • •   •   •   •   523 MAD AS MIST   1
BOLTS
  SHE SNICKED THE BRASS BOLTS DOWN. • • • • • • •   •   •   159 CAP AND BELLS   V   12
BOMB-BALLS
  PITCH LIKE KING BILLY BOMB-BALLS IN • • • •   •   •   •   565 LAPIS LAZULI   7
BOND
  HE HOLDS YOU WITH AN IRON BOND, • • • • •   •   •   •   •   22 OISIN 1   333
  THE BLOOD BOND • • • •   • •   •   •   •   •   769 BLOOD BOND   T
  THIS BOND HAS BOUND US • • • • • • •   •   •   •   769 BLOOD BOND   V   1
BONDS
  HIS BONDS AWAY, SORE STRUGGLING. NOW AT LAST •   •   •   •   714 FERENCZ RENYI   116
  YOUNG FERENCZ RENYI BURSTS HIS BONDS--AT LAST, •   •   •   •   714 FERENCZ RENYI   V 116
  WHAT BONDS NO MAN COULD UNBIND, • • • • •   •   •   •   •   785 WOMANS BEAUTY   22
BONE   SEE COLLAR-BONE MARROW-BONE RAG-AND-BONE
  • • • AND FILLED ME FULL TO THE BONE. • • • •   •   •   52 OISIN 3   72
  AND GRANIA, WALKING AND SMILING, SEWED WITH HER NEEDLE
     OF BONE. •   •   •   •   53 OISIN 3   94
  MY BARREN THOUGHTS HAVE CHILLED ME TO THE BONE. • •   •   •   257 RECONCILIATION   12
  AND KNOW THEM TO THE BONE: IMPART TO US-- • • •   •   •   265 ABBEY THEATRE   9
  MERE BONE AND MUSCLE THROWN ASIDE, • • • • •   •   •   •   273 GREY ROCK   51
  YOU HAVE DRIED THE MARROW FROM THE BONE? • • •   •   •   289 SEPTEMBER 1913   5
  THIS BLAST HAS CHILLED ME TO THE BONE." • • • •   •   •   305 HOUR DAWN   62
  THAT FLESH AND BONE MAY DISAPPEAR, • • • • •   •   •   •   307 HOUR DAWN   101
  THROUGH THE WHITE THIN BONE OF A HARE. • • • •   •   •   330 BONE OF A HARE   16
  AS WITH HER FLESH AND BONE, • • • • • • •   •   •   •   345 ON WOMAN   6
  WERE DEAD YET FLESH AND BONE. • • • • • •   •   •   •   384 VISION ROBART   48
  THAT CONVERSE BONE TO BONE? • • • • • • •   •   •   •   395 SIXTEEN DEAD   18
  THAT CONVERSE BONE TO BONE? • • • • • • •   •   •   •   395 SIXTEEN DEAD   18

	PAGE	TITLE	LINE

BONE   (CONTINUED)
OF FLESH AND BONE: . . . .   436 FOR MY SON   24
BUT FOUND IT DRY AS BONE, ...   454 EMPTY CUP   8
HE KNOWS DEATH TO THE BONE-- . . . .   476 DEATH   11
BUT SLENDER NEEDLES OF BONE: . . . .   488 CRAZED MOON   15
I TREMBLE TO THE BONE, ...   511 JANE AND JACK   2
AND BEAT UPON THE BONE: . . . .   516 MANS SONG   6
SANG A BONE UPON THE SHORE: . . . .   521 THREE THINGS   2
A BONE WAVE-WHITENED AND DRIED IN THE WIND. . .   521 THREE THINGS   6
SANG A BONE UPON THE SHORE: . . . .   521 THREE THINGS   8
A BONE WAVE-WHITENED AND DRIED IN THE WIND. . .   521 THREE THINGS   12
SANG A BONE UPON THE SHORE, ...   521 THREE THINGS   14
A BONE WAVE-WHITENED AND DRIED IN THE WIND. . .   521 THREE THINGS   18
AND I AM SHRUNKEN TO SKIN AND BONE, ...   550 SONGS REWRIT 1   2
YET I AM SHRUNKEN TO SKIN AND BONE . . . . . .   550 SONGS REWRIT 1 V   2
YET AM I SHRUNKEN TO SKIN AND BONE, ...   550 SONGS REWRIT 1 V   2
BUT I AM SHRUNKEN TO SKIN AND BONE, ...   550 SONGS REWRIT 1 V   2
THOUGH I AM SHRUNKEN TO BONE AND SKIN, ...   551 SONGS REWRIT 1 V   8
THINKS IN A MARROW BONE . . . .   553 PRAYER OLD AGE V   4
BEEN BONE, AND SINEW: WHEN SUCH BODIES JOIN . .   555 RIBH AT TOMB   12
CONSUMING ITS RAG AND BONE . . . .   575 ACRE OF GRASS   11
IN THE FOUL RAG AND BONE SHOP OF THE HEART. . .   630 CIRCUS ANIMALS V   40
ARE BLOWN COLD DUST OR A BIT OF BONE. . . . . .   788 HAWTHORN TREE   8
BONES   SEE MARROW-BONES
DID NOT THE WORMS THAT SPIRED ABOUT HIS BONES .   128 DREAM OF FAERY   41
WERE NOT THE WORMS THAT SPIRED ABOUT HIS BONES   128 DREAM OF FAERY   41
BETTER GO DOWN UPON YOUR MARROW BONES . . . . .   204 ADAMS CURSE   V   7
"STRETCH BONES TILL THE DAYLIGHT COME . . . . .   331 ROUND TOWER   5
HE STRETCHED HIS BONES AND FELL IN A DREAM . .   331 ROUND TOWER   10
LAID HIS STRONG BONES DOWN IN DEATH . . . . . .   360 ALF POLLEXFEN   3
LAID HIS STRONG BONES IN DEATH . . . .   360 ALF POLLEXFEN   V   3
AND WITHERED TO A BAG OF BONES: . . . .   401 DEMON BEAST   49
EVEN THOSE TRUTHS THAT WHEN MY BONES ARE DUST .   467 HARUN RASHID   144
TRUTHS THAT WHEN MY VERY BONES ARE DUST . . . .   467 HARUN RASHID   V   144
OR STRIKES A SUDDEN CHILL INTO MY BONES . . . .   499 MOTHER OF GOD   14
TO THE CRAVING IN MY BONES. . . . .   533 FIRST CONFESS   12
SURMOUNT THEIR BONES: BUT SPEAK WHAT NONE HAVE HEARD.   555 RIBH AT TOMB   9
SURMOUNTS THEIR BONES: BUT SPEAK WHAT NONE HAVE HEARD.   555 RIBH AT TOMB V   9
THINGS HID IN THEIR MARROW BONES . . . .   589 OLD WICKED MAN V   41
I PRAYED AT ALL THE STATIONS UPON MY MARROW BONES,   593 PILGRIM   V   7
OLD IRON, OLD BONES, OLD RAGS, THAT RAVING SLUT   630 CIRCUS ANIMALS   37
OLD BONES UPON THE MOUNTAIN SHAKE. . . . . . .   635 BLACK TOWER   10
OLD BONES UPON THE MOUNTAIN SHAKE. . . . . . .   636 BLACK TOWER   20
OLD BONES UPON THE MOUNTAIN SHAKE. . . . . . .   636 BLACK TOWER   30
WOULD END THIS PEACEFUL LIFE THAT ROTS THE BONES,   752 SHADOW WATER A   110
FROM THE DRY BONES OF THE DEAD? . . . .   781 MY HEART BEAT   8
THE DREAMING BONES CRY OUT . . . .   782 HEART FRIGHT   15
DRY BONES THAT DREAM ARE BITTER, ...   783 GREY ROUND   14
BONY
O DEATH'S OLD BONY FINGER . . . .   213 HAPPY TOWNLAND V   1
MACDONAGH'S BONY THUMB? . . . .   395 SIXTEEN DEAD   12
BOOK   SEE PICTURE-BOOK PRAYER-BOOK LOG-BOOK
FROM THE BOOK OF KAURI THE INDIAN-- SECTION V. ON THE   76 INDIAN ON GOD V   T
   NATURE OF GOD
AND NODDING BY THE FIRE, TAKE DOWN THIS BOOK, ...   120 YOU ARE OLD   2
THE DEDICATION TO A BOOK OF STORIES SELECTED FROM THE IRISH   129 BOOK STORIES   T
   NOVELISTS
I READ IN MY BOOK OF SONGS . . . .   178 FIDDLER DOONEY   7
THEY READ IN A BOOK OF PRAYER, ...   178 FIDDLER DOONEY V   6
I READ IN A BOOK OF SONGS . . . .   178 FIDDLER DOONEY V   7
IN ANY ANCIENT BOOK BUT TELLS OF YOU: . . . . .   186 QUEEN MAEVE   135
YOU'VE DANDLED THEM AND FED THEM FROM THE BOOK   265 ABBEY THEATRE   8
I HAVE NO CHILD, I HAVE NOTHING BUT A BOOK, . .   270 PARDON FATHERS   21
OUT OF SOME OLD PICTURE BOOK: . . . .   325 ROBERT GREGORY V   44
AS THOUGH I HAD FOUND IN A BOOK . . . .   329 MEN IMPROVE   6
AS THOUGH I HAD FOUND IN BOOK . . . .   329 MEN IMPROVE   V   6
AND NO KNAVE BROUGHT TO BOOK . . . .   347 FISHERMAN   17
AS A MAN DOES WHO HAS PUBLISHED A NEW BOOK, . .   350 HER PRAISE   3
A LAMP BURNS ON BESIDE THE OPEN BOOK . . . . .   367 EGO DOMINUS   3
A LAMP BURNS ON ABOVE THE OPEN BOOK . . . . . .   367 EGO DOMINUS   V   3
BURNING ALONE BESIDE AN OPEN BOOK, ...   370 EGO DOMINUS   63
BECAUSE I SEEK AN IMAGE, NOT A BOOK. . . . . .   370 EGO DOMINUS   67
BOOK I   WHAT THE CALIPH PARTLY LEARNED . . .   372 PHASES OF MOON V   T
AND NOW HE SEEKS IN BOOK OR MANUSCRIPT . . . .   373 PHASES OF MOON   19
AND NEVER WROTE A BOOK, YOUR THOUGHT IS CLEAR.   376 PHASES OF MOON   97
OF HIS GREAT BIRCH AND HIS GREAT BOOK. . . . .   381 SONG OF FOOL   8
FOR WHAT MERE BOOK CAN GRANT A KNOWLEDGE . . .   386 ROBARTES DANCE   20
BOOK III DOVE OR SWAN I. LEDA . . . .   441 LEDA AND SWAN   V   T
BOOK V: DOVE OR SWAN I LEDA . . . .   441 LEDA AND SWAN   V   T
BOOK IV   THE GATES OF PLUTO I. THE FOOL BY THE ROADSIDE.   447 HERO GIRL FOOL V T
BOOK II   WHAT THE CALIPH REFUSED TO LEARN . .   460 HARUN RASHID   V   T
AT THE GREAT BOOK OF SAPPHO'S SONG: BUT NO, . .   461 HARUN RASHID   12
IF YOU SHOULD HIDE MY PARCHMENT IN THAT BOOK .   461 HARUN RASHID   13
BEFORE SHE HAD SPREAD A BOOK UPON HER KNEES . .   466 HARUN RASHID   120
TRUTHS WITHOUT FATHER CAME, TRUTHS THAT NO BOOK   467 HARUN RASHID   138
. . . A LOG BOOK OF THE SUN'S JOURNEY AND THE MOON'S,   480 BLOOD AND MOON V   44
THE BOOK OF THE PEOPLE: WHATEVER MOST CAN BLESS   492 COOLE BALLYLEE   44
AN OPEN BOOK AND EMPTY CUP . . . .   501 VACILLATION   38
YET HE, AN OLD BOOK IN HIS FIST, ...   508 JANE BISHOP   12
WITH OPEN BOOK YOU ASK ME WHAT I DO. . . . . .   554 RIBH AT TOMB   2
I TURN THE PAGES OF MY HOLY BOOK. . . . .   555 RIBH AT TOMB   27

```
                                                   PAGE    TITLE           LINE
BOOK   (CONTINUED)
      PICTURE AND BOOK REMAIN,  . . . . . . . . . .   575  ACRE OF GRASS        1
      THIS BOOK OR THAT, COME TO THIS HALLOWED PLACE   604  GALLERY REVIS      51
      THE PRIESTS HAVE GOT A BOOK THAT SAYS  . . . .   621  JOHN KINSELLA      25
      TO LOVE EACH OTHER.  IN MY PRAYER BOOK STILL .   713  FERENCZ RENYI   V  94
      THE BISHOP CAME WITH OPEN BOOK,  . . . . . . .   725  LEGEND             17
BOOKS      SEE READING-BOOKS
      FOR HE WAS A MAN OF BOOKS. . . . . . . . . . .    93  FATHER OHART       24
      THE BOOKS OF MY NUMBERLESS DREAMS,  . . . . . .  157  POET BELOVED        2
      WOMEN AND CHILDREN, YOUNG MEN WITH BOOKS,  . . .  167  BLESSED            15
      THEY READ IN THEIR BOOKS OF PRAYER:  . . . . . .  178  FIDDLER DOONEY      6
      PRECEDENTS OUT OF BEAUTIFUL OLD BOOKS:  . . . .   205  ADAMS CURSE        26
      IF BOOKS SPEAK TRUTH, IN SLIEVENAMON--  . . . .   271  GREY ROCK       V  15
      WHAT CAN BOOKS OF MEN THAT WIVE  . . . . . . .    309  REALISTS            2
      OUT NAKED ON THE ROADS, AS THE BOOKS SAY, AND STRICKEN .  316  COLD HEAVEN   11
      I WILL TALK NO MORE OF BOOKS OR THE LONG WAR . .  351  HER PRAISE         11
      TO STUDY READING BOOKS AND HISTORY  . . . . . .  443  SCHOOL CHILDR   V   4
      TO STUDY READING BOOKS AND HISTORIES,  . . . . .  443  SCHOOL CHILDR   V   4
      PASS BOOKS OF LEARNING FROM BYZANTIUM  . . . . .  461  HARUN RASHID        9
      OF ALL THE UNCOUNTED BOOKS THAT I HAVE READ, . .  467  HARUN RASHID      139
      THAT FIRST UNNATURAL INTEREST IN MY BOOKS. . . .  468  HARUN RASHID      165
      THAT FIRST STRANGE INTEREST IN MY BOOKS AND STUDIES.  468  HARUN RASHID  V 165
      BELOVED BOOKS THAT FAMOUS HANDS HAVE BOUND,  . .  491  COOLE BALLYLEE     27
      CLIMB TO YOUR CHAMBER FULL OF BOOKS AND WAIT, . .  579  DOR WELLESLEY      8
      NO BOOKS UPON THE KNEE, AND NO ONE THERE  . . .   579  DOR WELLESLEY      9
      AND WHEN THEY KNOW WHAT OLD BOOKS TELL,  . . . .  626  OLD MEN BE MAD     18
      NINE BOOKS OR NINE HATS  . . . . . . . . . . .    628  JANE MOUNTAIN       3
      WHERE MY BOOKS GO. . . . . . . . . . . . . . .    739  WHERE BOOKS GO      T
BOOM
      WITH BOOM OF BEES IN HONEY-MARTS,  . . . . . . .   16  OISIN 1           229
      WITH BOOM OF BEES IN HONEY MARTS,  . . . . . . .   16  OISIN 1         V 229
BOOTH      SEE GORE-BOOTH
BOOTS
      HAD TROD THE UNEVEN ROAD.  THEIR BOOTS WERE SOILED, . .  372  PHASES OF MOON  3
BORDA
      TO EMER OF BORDA, IN HER CLAY-PILED DUN,  . . . .  105  CUCHULAIN SEA   V   2
BORDER
      AND SHAKES O'ER THE WIDTH OF THE SEA-WORLD BORDER . .  28  OISIN 1     V 423C
      YOU LIVE, AND ON THE VILLAGE BORDER SHE,  . . . .   74  ANASHU VIJAYA      62
      YOU LIVE, AND ON THE BORDER OF THE VILLAGE SHE, .   74  ANASHU VIJAYA   V  62
      BY THE LONE BORDER OF THE LAKE ONCE MORE,  . . .    79  EPHEMERA            5
      STAND BY THE BORDER OF THE LAKE ONCE MORE,  . . .   79  EPHEMERA        V   5
      ON THE LONE BORDER OF THE LAKE ONCE MORE:  . . .    80  EPHEMERA           17
      ON THE LONE BORDER OF THE SULLEN LAKE.  . . . . .   80  EPHEMERA        V  17
      IN THE WHITE BORDER OF THE MURMURING SEA:  . . .   103  FERGUS DRUID       19
      UPON THE MISTY BORDER OF THE WOOD,  . . . . . . .  251  SHADOW WATER B    612
      UPON THE BORDER OF THAT LAKE'S A WOOD  . . . . .   490  COOLE BALLYLEE      9
      UNTO THE DOLOROUS BORDER OF THE FAIRY LAKE.  . .   655  ISLE STAT I 2      85
      UPON THE MISTY BORDER OF THE WOOD;--  . . . . . .  769  SHADOW WATER A    428
BORDERED      SEE WILLOW-BORDERED RED-ROSE-BORDERED BOX-BORDERED
      BECAUSE THE RED ROSE BORDERED HEM  . . . . . . .   137  TO IRELAND      V   6
      AFTER THE RED ROSE BORDERED HEM.  . . . . . . . .  139  TO IRELAND      V  30
      AFTER THE RED ROSE BORDERED HEM.  . . . . . . . .  139  TO IRELAND      V  48
      SHANWALLA, WHERE A WILLOW BORDERED POND  . . . .   217  WOODS OF COOLE      2
BORDERS
      AND MARTEN-CAT, AND BORDERS THAT OLD WOOD  . . .   218  WOODS OF COOLE     14
      AND MARTIN CAT, AND BORDERS THAT OLD WOOD  . . .   218  WOODS OF COOLE  V  14
BORE
      I STOOD UPON THE STAIR: THE SURGES BORE  . . . .    44  OISIN 2           225
      THEY BORE IT WITH STAGGERING AND SWEATING,  . . .   60  OISIN 3           186
      AND BORE IT TO THE WOODS WITH ME:  . . . . . . .    85  MAD KING GOLL      57
      WHILE DAY ITS BURDEN ON TO EVENING BORE,  . . . .  110  CUCHULAIN SEA      70
      UNTIL ONE BORE BRIDGET HIS BRIDE  . . . . . . . .  145  HOST OF AIR        31
      HE BORE HER AWAY IN HIS ARMS,  . . . . . . . . .   145  HOST OF AIR        33
      THE DEW-COLD LILIES LADIES BORE  . . . . . . . .   156  FORGOT BEAUTY      11
      KING EOCHAID SAID, AND HE THAT BORE HIS SHIELD .   276  TWO KINGS       V   8
      UNTIL I THOUGHT HER BODY BORE  . . . . . . . . .   451  FIRST LOVE          5
      THE TERROR OF ALL TERRORS THAT I BORE  . . . . .   499  MOTHER OF GOD       4
      BUT SOMETHING BORE THEM OUT OF SIGHT  . . . . . .  519  HER DREAM           5
      IT BORE ME SOFTLY WHERE THE SHALLOW SAND  . . . .  657  ISLE STAT I 3      58
      DO YOU REMEMBER, AIBRIC, HOW YOU BORE  . . . . .   749  SHADOW WATER A     48
BOREAL
      OF WOLVES, OF BOREAL BEARS, WE QUAFFED THE WINE .   41  OISIN 2         V 188
BOREDOM
      ITS BOREDOM OF THE DESK OR OF THE SPADE, BECAUSE .  621  HOUND VOICE        3
BOREEN
      ACROSS THE BARE BOREEN. . . . . . . . . . . . .    95  MOLL MAGEE         32
BORN      SEE SELF-BORN HIGH-BORN SEA-BORN FIRE-BORN ROCK-BORN TWIN-BORN NEW-BORN BASE-BORN
      A SWIFTER CREATURE NEVER WAS BORN,  . . . . . . .    2  OISIN 1         V  7Q
      AND WAS BORN WHERE THE SUN DROPS DOWN IN THE TIDE, .  5  OISIN 1       V  49
      "WERE THESE TWO BORN IN THE DANAAN LAND,  . . . .   12  OISIN 1           146
      AND MY BABY WAS JUST BORN:  . . . . . . . . . . .   94  MOLL MAGEE         14
      ABOUT THE TIME WHEN CHRIST WAS BORN,  . . . . . .  189  BAILE AILLINN      13
      REPLIED: "TO BE BORN WOMAN IS TO KNOW--  . . . .   205  ADAMS CURSE        18
      THAT YOU WERE BORN A THOUSAND YEARS AGO,  . . . .  245  SHADOW WATER B    468
      WHERE NO CHILD'S BORN BUT TO OUTLIVE THE MOON."     247  SHADOW WATER B    531
      FOR MEN WERE BORN TO PRAY AND SAVE:  . . . . . .   289  SEPTEMBER 1913      6
      WAS BORN TO WEAR A CROWN.  . . . . . . . . . . .   308  PLAYER QUEEN       12
      WE DREAMED THAT A GREAT PAINTER HAD BEEN BORN .    326  ROBERT GREGORY     65
      BORN UNDER THE SKIES  . . . . . . . . . . . . .   333  SOLOMON SHEBA      20
      WHO WERE NOT BORN TO KEEP IN TRIM  . . . . . . .   336  YOUNG BEAUTY       10
```

99

		PAGE	TITLE	LINE

BORN   (CONTINUED)
HECTOR IS IN THE DUST, NIETZSCHE IS BORN, ...   374 PHASES OF MOON   46
AND YET, TWICE BORN, TWICE BURIED, GROW HE MUST, ...   374 PHASES OF MOON   48
HAS CALLED UP THE COLD SPIRITS THAT ARE BORN . . . . . .   382 VISION ROBART   2
A TERRIBLE BEAUTY IS BORN. . . . .   392 EASTER 1916   16
A TERRIBLE BEAUTY IS BORN. . . . .   393 EASTER 1916   40
A TERRIBLE BEAUTY IS BORN. . . . .   394 EASTER 1916   80
SLOUCHES TOWARDS BETHLEHEM TO BE BORN? . . . .   402 SECOND COMING   22
HAVE I NOT SEEN THE LOVELIEST WOMAN BORN . . . .   405 FOR DAUGHTER   59
ARE INNOCENCE AND BEAUTY BORN? . . . .   406 FOR DAUGHTER   78
WHATEVER IS BEGOTTEN, BORN, AND DIES. . . . .   407 SAIL BYZANTIUM   6
WHATEVER IS BEGOTTEN BORN OR DIES, ...   407 SAIL BYZANTIUM V   6
NOR BEAUTY BORN OUT OF ITS OWN DESPAIR, ...   445 SCHOOL CHILDR   59
MORE WOMEN BORN THAN MEN." . . . .   485 STATISTICS   4
FOR CHILDREN BORN OF HER PAIN. . . . .   487 CRAZED MOON   6
WHAT, BE A SINGER BORN AND LACK A THEME? . . . . . .   502 VACILLATION   73
SELF-BORN, BORN ANEW? . . . .   507 STREAM AND SUN   15
THAT THE CRIME OF BEING BORN . . . .   534 CONSOLATION   9
WE IRISH, BORN INTO THAT ANCIENT SECT . . . .   611 STATUES   28
WERE WE NOT BORN IN THE PEASANT'S COT . . . .   615 MARCH SONGS 2   13
WE WERE NOT BORN IN THE PEASANT'S COT . . . .   615 MARCH SONGS 2   V   13
WHEN WERE YOU BORN? BEFORE YOUR GRANDAM EVE. . . . .   721 WITCH VIVIEN   32
BORN OUT OF IMMODERATE THOUGHT, ...   772 SONG DEIRDRE 1   12
BORNE   SEE SEA-BORNE CAR-BORNE
HAVE BORNE ME WHERE THE TEMPESTS BLIND . . . .   6 OISIN 1   V   58
CAME BALOR, AS OLD AS A FOREST, CAR BORNE, HIS MIGHTY HEAD   53 OISIN 3   V   91
   SUNK
WINGED LOVES BORNE ON IN GENTLE STRIFE, ...   135 TWO TREES   V   14
EVEN IN AN OLD STORY, IS A BURDEN NOT TO BE BORNE. . .   210 UNDER THE MOON   20
THAT IDLENESS HAD BORNE TO PRIDE, ...   296 THREE BEGGARS   40
HAVE BORNE YOU THROUGH THE SMOOTH AND ROUGH . . . . .   436 FOR MY SON   V   29
HOW ALL THAT DIE ARE BORNE ABOUT THE WORLD . . . . .   750 SHADOW WATER A   84
BORROW
FOR NOON AND MIDNIGHT FROM EACH OTHER BORROW, ...   735 QUATRAIN APHOR   26
BOSKY
BY BOSKY JUNE I SWEAR, AND BY THE BEE, HER MINISTER. . .   661 ISLE STAT II 1   74
BOSOM
AS HER SOFT BOSOM ROSE AND FELL. . . . .   4 OISIN 1   30
AND ON MY BOSOM LAID HER WEEPING HEAD. . . . .   46 OISIN 2   250
IN MIDST OF AN OLD MAN'S BOSOM; OWLS RUFFLING AND PACING   50 OISIN 3   47
   AROUND
IN THE MIDST OF AN OLD MAN'S BOSOM; OWLS RUFFLING   50 OISIN 3   V   47
   AND PACING AROUND
THRUSTING HIS NOSE TO MY SHOULDER; HE KNEW IN HIS BOSOM   54 OISIN 3   106
   DEEP
THAT ONCE MORE MOVED IN MY BOSOM THE ANCIENT SADNESS OF   54 OISIN 3   107
   MAN,
IN BOSOM AND HAIR. "AH, DO NOT MOURN," HE SAID, ...   80 EPHEMERA   20
IN BOSOM AND HAIR. THEN HE; "LET US NOT MOURN   80 EPHEMERA   V   20
OF THE MATCHING OF RIBBONS FOR BOSOM AND HEAD, . . .   151 OLD MOTHER   6
SHE LAID THEM UPON HER BOSOM, ...   160 CAP AND BELLS   25
SHE TOOK THEM INTO HER BOSOM, ...   160 CAP AND BELLS   V   25
TALL AND NOBLE BUT WITH FACE AND BOSOM . . . .   199 ARROW   5
AT THE MOTH HOUR AND HID IT IN HER BOSOM. . . . . .   199 ARROW   V   6
I, STARVED FOR THE BOSOM OF HIS FAERY BRIDE? . . . .   629 CIRCUS ANIMALS   16
IN THE BOSOM OF THE AIR-- . . . .   706 DAWN-SONG   30
DROPS ON HIS BOSOM, SOMBRE, MOIST AND SLOW. . . . . .   711 FERENCZ RENYI   40
UPON HIS BOSOM, SOMBRE, MOIST AND SLOW. . . . .   711 FERENCZ RENYI   V   40
IN THE BOSOM AFAR OF THE FRAGRANT WOOD. . . . .   717 LOVE SONG   9
BOTTLE
AND PASS THE BOTTLE ROUND. . . . .   586 PARNELLITES   8
SO PASS THE BOTTLE ROUND. . . . .   587 PARNELLITES   24
FOR PASSING ROUND THE BOTTLE WITH GIRLS IN RAGS OR SILK,   592 PILGRIM   2
FOR PASSING ROUND THE BOTTLE WITH GIRLS IN RAG OR SILK,   592 PILGRIM   V   2
BOTTLES
OLD KETTLES, OLD BOTTLES, AND A BROKEN CAN, ...   630 CIRCUS ANIMALS   36
BOTTLING
AND THOUGH AT BOTTLING OF YOUR WINE . . . .   271 GREY ROCK   9
THOUGH AT THE BOTTLING OF YOUR WINE . . . .   271 GREY ROCK   V   9
BOTTOM
ALL, ALL, THE VERY BOTTOM OF THE BOWL-- . . . . . .   227 SHADOW WATER B   118
MANACLE HIS SOUL UPON THE RED SEA BOTTOM. . . . . . .   372 ON GOING HOUSE   16
UPON THE BOTTOM OF A KING OF KINGS; . . . .   445 SCHOOL CHILDR   44
AT THE BOTTOM OF A PIT. . . . .   632 MAN AND ECHO   3
AT THE BOTTOM OF A LETTER, FIFTY MEN. . . . .   790 DEDICATION   10
BOUGH   SEE BEECH-BOUGH YEW-BOUGH
A BEECH BOUGH TO ME, AND MY HEART GREW SORE, ...   44 OISIN 2   V   226
FROM A BOUGH OVERHEAD, ...   215 HAPPY TOWNLAND   42
THE YEW BOUGH HAS BEEN BROKEN INTO TWO, ...   241 SHADOW WATER B V   394
THE YEW BOUGH HAS BEEN BROKEN INTO TWO, ...   251 SHADOW WATER B V   593
THE YEW BOUGH HAS BEEN BROKEN IN TWO, ...   251 SHADOW WATER B V   593
AND THREW HIM UP TO LAUGH ON THE BOUGH; . . . . . .   318 APPOINTMENT   11
A HUNGER FOR THE APPLE ON THE BOUGH . . . .   368 EGO DOMINUS   24
CREW FROM A BLOSSOMING APPLE BOUGH . . . .   387 SOLOMON WITCH   10
UPON A BLOSSOMING APPLE BOUGH . . . .   387 SOLOMON WITCH   V   10
CRIED FROM A BLOSSOMING APPLE BOUGH . . . .   387 SOLOMON WITCH   V   10
OR SET UPON A GOLDEN BOUGH TO SING . . . .   408 SAIL BYZANTIUM   30
WHEN EVENING STIRS THE JASMINE BOUGH, AND YET . . . .   463 HARUN RASHID   53
PLANTED ON THE STAR-LIT GOLDEN BOUGH, ...   497 BYZANTIUM   19
PLANTED ON THE STARLIT GOLDEN BOUGH, ...   497 BYZANTIUM   V   19
A TREE THERE IS THAT FROM ITS TOPMOST BOUGH . . . . .   500 VACILLATION   11

BOUGH   (CONTINUED)
  UNDER OAK AND BEECHEN BOUGH, ...   522 LULLABY   11
  UNDER OAK AND BEECHES BOUGH, ...   522 LULLABY   V   11
  OFTEN HE HAD BENT DOWN SOME BOUGH ALL BRIGHT . . . . .   710 FERENCZ RENYI   28
  OFTEN HE HAD BENT DOWN SOME BOUGH ALL BRIGHT WITH BERRIES: 710 FERENCZ RENYI   V   28
BOUGHS   SEE APPLE-BOUGHS
  AND GREAT BOUGHS DROP TRANQUILLITY: . . . .   77 INDIAN TO LOVE   2
  HID UNDER QUIET BOUGHS APART, ...   78 INDIAN TO LOVE   12
  THE HEAVY BOUGHS, THE BURNISHED DOVE   . . . . . .   78 INDIAN TO LOVE   16
  THE GREAT BOUGHS, AND THE BURNISHED DOVE   . . . .   78 INDIAN TO LOVE   V   16
  AND GREAT BOUGHS, AND THE BURNISHED DOVE   . . . .   78 INDIAN TO LOVE   V   16
  I FIND UNDER THE BOUGHS OF LOVE AND HATE, ...   101 ROSE UPON ROOD   10
  UNDER THAT WOVEN CHANGELESS ROOF OF BOUGHS: . . .   126 DREAM OF FAERY   11
  UNDER THE WOVEN ROOFS OF QUICKEN BOUGHS:--   . . .   126 DREAM OF FAERY   V   11
  I TORE IT FROM GREEN BOUGHS WINDS TORE AND TOSSED   . .   130 BOOK STORIES   13
  I TORE IT FROM THE BARREN BOUGHS OF EIRE, ...   130 BOOK STORIES   15
  I TORE IT FROM GREEN BOUGHS WINDS TOSSED AND HURLED,   . .   130 BOOK STORIES   V   13
  GREEN BOUGHS OF TOSSING ALWAYS, WEARY, WEARY, ...   130 BOOK STORIES   V   14
  I TORE IT FROM THE GREEN BOUGHS OF OLD ERI,   . . .   130 BOOK STORIES   V   15
  BROKEN BOUGHS AND BLACKENED LEAVES.   . . . .   135 TWO TREES   28
  WITH BROKEN BOUGHS AND BLACKENED LEAVES   . . . . .   135 TWO TREES   V   26
  IN SHAKEN BOUGHS, IN TIDE ON THE SHORE?   . . . . .   141 EVERLAST VOICE   7
  AND HE, BEING LAID UPON GREEN BOUGHS   . . . . . .   192 BAILE AILLINN   71
  OR TWO SWEET BLOSSOMING APPLE BOUGHS   . . . . . .   195 BAILE AILLINN   V 153
  THE WITHERING OF THE BOUGHS . . . . .   203 WITHER BOUGHS   T
  NO BOUGHS HAVE WITHERED BECAUSE OF THE WINTRY WIND: . .   203 WITHER BOUGHS   7
  THE BOUGHS HAVE WITHERED BECAUSE I HAVE TOLD THEM   203 WITHER BOUGHS   8
    MY DREAMS.
  NO BOUGHS HAVE WITHERED BECAUSE OF THE WINTRY WIND: . .   203 WITHER BOUGHS   15
  THE BOUGHS HAVE WITHERED BECAUSE I HAVE TOLD THEM   203 WITHER BOUGHS   16
    MY DREAMS.
  NO BOUGHS HAVE WITHERED BECAUSE OF THE WINTRY WIND: . .   204 WITHER BOUGHS   23
  THE BOUGHS HAVE WITHERED BECAUSE I HAVE TOLD THEM   204 WITHER BOUGHS   24
    MY DREAMS.
  BOUGHS HAVE THEIR FRUIT AND BLOSSOM . . . .   214 HAPPY TOWNLAND   5
  WHERE BOUGHS HAVE FRUIT AND BLOSSOM . . . .   214 HAPPY TOWNLAND   V   5
  FROM GOLDEN AND SILVER BOUGHS: . . . .   215 HAPPY TOWNLAND   24
  FROM THE GOLDEN AND SILVER BOUGHS. . . . .   215 HAPPY TOWNLAND   V   24
  AS THOUGH THEY HAD BEEN HIDDEN BY GREEN BOUGHS . . . .   217 WOODS OF COOLE   6
  AND DRUID MOONS, AND MURMURING OF BOUGHS, ...   219 HARP OF AENGUS   4
  AND SLEEPY BOUGHS, AND BOUGHS WHERE APPLES MADE . . .   219 HARP OF AENGUS   5
  AND SLEEPY BOUGHS, AND BOUGHS WHERE APPLES MADE . . .   219 HARP OF AENGUS   5
  I GROPED MY WAY THROUGH BOUGHS, AND OVER ROOTS, . . .   283 TWO KINGS   V 139
  TILL ALL THE BOUGHS ARE GAY, ...   366 HER CHRIS TREE   5
  AMONG THE BOUGHS, BLUE AS THE HALCYON'S WING, ...   683 SEEKER   38
  OF AENGUS' BIRDS GLEAM IN THEIR APPLE BOUGHS. . . . .   751 SHADOW WATER A   103
  THE TOPMOST BLOSSOM ON THE BOUGHS OF TIME . . . . .   756 SHADOW WATER A   178
  AND DRUID MOONS, AND MURMURING OF BOUGHS. . . . . .   762 SHADOW WATER A   299
  AND SLEEPY BOUGHS, AND BOUGHS WHERE APPLES MADE . . .   762 SHADOW WATER A   300
  AND SLEEPY BOUGHS, AND BOUGHS WHERE APPLES MADE . . .   762 SHADOW WATER A   300
  IMPERISHABLE FIRE UNDER THE BOUGHS . . . .   765 SHADOW WATER A   356
  WHERE ARE THESE BOUGHS? WHERE ARE THE HOLY WOODS . . .   765 SHADOW WATER A   359
  AND MINGLING HAIR FALL FROM THE FIERY BOUGHS, ...   765 SHADOW WATER A   368
  AND ONE LIVES UNDER THE BOUGHS . . . .   771 SPINNING SONG   8
BOUGHT
  TO SEE MEN'S SOULS BARTERED AND BOUGHT. . . . . . .   136 TWO TREES   V   36
  I BOUGHT AT THE SLIGO FAIR. . . . .   178 FIDDLER DOONEY   8
  AND HERE AND THERE HAVE BOUGHT . . . .   366 HER CHRIS TREE   4
  (FOR SINCE THE HORIZON'S BOUGHT STRANGE DOGS ARE STILL)   579 DOR WELLESLEY   7
  AND BOUGHT THE GRANDEST JEWELRY . . . .   595 COLONEL MARTIN   21
  THOSE CHEERS THAT CAN BE BOUGHT OR SOLD, ...   598 MODEL LAUREATE   19
  CRAMM'D ALL HER YOUTH: AND HATES HAVE BOUGHT AND SOLD . .   687 TWO TITANS   13
BOUND   SEE SPELL-BOUND OATH-BOUND SLUMBER-BOUND
  AND IT WAS BOUND WITH A PEARL-PALE SHELL . . . . .   4 OISIN 1   28
  FOR BROOCH 'TWAS BOUND WITH A BRIGHT SEA-SHELL, . . .   4 OISIN 1   V   28
  AND IT WAS BOUND WITH A PEARL PALE SHELL . . . . .   4 OISIN 1   V   28
  AND CAPTIVES BOUND WITH LEATHERN THONGS . . . . . .   7 OISIN 1   77
  MY CAPTIVES, BOUND IN LEATHERN THONGS, ...   8 OISIN 1   V   78
  AND THEN I MOUNTED AND SHE BOUND ME . . . .   9 OISIN 1   106
  LIES FAR." I MOUNTED, AND SHE BOUND ME . . . . . .   9 OISIN 1   V 106
  SOME FEASTING MAN THAT THE SAME OATH HAS BOUND." . . .   108 CUCHULAIN SEA   38
  SOME FEATING MAN THAT THE SAME OATH HAS BOUND." . . .   108 CUCHULAIN SEA   V   38
  SOME FEASTING MAN THAT THE SAME OATH HAS BOUND." . . .   109 CUCHULAIN SEA   54
  OF ALL THIS HOST SO BOUND FROM CHILDHOOD ON." . . . .   109 CUCHULAIN SEA   56
  "SOME FEATING MAN THAT THE SAME OATH HAS BOUND." . . .   109 CUCHULAIN SEA   V   54
  BUT KNOW YOUR HAIR WAS BOUND AND WOUND . . . . . .   176 BELOVED DEAD   9
  BUT KNOW YOUR HAIR WAS BOUND AND BOUND . . . . . .   176 BELOVED DEAD   V   9
  BUT KNOW YOUR HAIR WAS BOUND AND BOUND . . . . . .   176 BELOVED DEAD   V   9
  AND SO TO THE OTHER TREE AT A BOUND. . . . . . .   318 APPOINTMENT   7
  BOUND NEITHER TO CAUSE NOR TO STATE, ...   414 TOWER   129
  SUCH THOUGHT, THAT IN IT BOUND . . . .   474 ALL SOUL NIGHT   97
  THE WOODEN SCABBARD BOUND AND WOUND, ...   477 SELF AND SOUL   15
  BELOVED BOOKS THAT FAMOUS HANDS HAVE BOUND, ...   491 COOLE BALLYLEE   27
  FOR HADES' BOBBIN BOUND IN MUMMY-CLOTH . . . . . .   497 BYZANTIUM   11
  FOR HADES' BOBBIN BOUND IN MUMMY CLOTH . . . . . .   497 BYZANTIUM   V   11
  THE SKEIN SO BOUND US GHOST TO GHOST . . . . . .   511 JANE AND JACK   15
  BOUND A THONG ABOUT HIS HAND. . . . .   595 COLONEL MARTIN   25
  OUR VOICES CARRY: AND THOUGH SLUMBER BOUND, ...   622 HOUND VOICE   V   5
  OH, BOY, I'M BOUND ON A MOST FEARFUL QUEST! . . . .   653 ISLE STAT I 2   31
  TWO FIGURES CROUCHING ON THE BLACK ROCK, BOUND . . .   687 TWO TITANS   5
  WITH PITILESS MAGIC HAS BOUND YOU-- . . . .   708 FAIRY PEDANT   31

```
BOUND    (CONTINUED)                                              PAGE    TITLE        LINE
    BEFORE HIM ONE WELL GUARDED, WITH BOUND HANDS:  . . . .       709 FERENCZ RENYI      10
    I HAVE CUT THE ROPE THAT BOUND THIS GALLEY TO OURS,  . . .    768 SHADOW WATER A     421
    THIS SOD HAS BOUND US  . . . . . . . . . . . . . . .          769 BLOOD BOND          1
    THIS BOND HAS BOUND US  . . . . . . . . . . . . . .           769 BLOOD BOND     V    1
BOUNDS
    THAT SPRING FIVE PACES IN THEIR BOUNDS,  . . . . . . .          8 OISIN 1        V  86A
    FROM THESE EARTHLY BOUNDS."  . . . . . . . . . . . .           97 FOXHUNTER          12
    HER CHARITY HAD NO BOUNDS:  . . . . . . . . . . . .           392 EASTER 1916    V   21
BOUNTIFUL
    BE PASSIONATE, NOT BOUNTIFUL  . . . . . . . . . . . .         335 YOUNG BEAUTY        8
BOUNTY
    OR THOSE WHO NEED HIS BOUNTY OR HIS LAW,  . . . . . .         462 HARUN RASHID   V  25A
    AND THEREUPON HIS BOUNTY GAVE WHAT NOW  . . . . . . .         465 HARUN RASHID      103
BOW       SEE SADDLE-BOW FIDDLE-BOW
    AH, FENIANS, WITH THE SHIELD AND BOW?  . . . . . . .           10 OISIN 1           116
    TELL ON, NOR BOW THY HEATHEN CREST  . . . . . . . .           11 OISIN 1        V 131A
    I RODE AWAY ON THE SURGES, WHERE HIGH AS THE SADDLE BOW       57 OISIN 3        V  147
    THE SORROWS OF THE WORLD BOW DOWN MY HEAD,  . . . . .        104 FERGUS DRUID   V  38A
    I HAVE OFTEN HEARD THE SWEET SOUND OF HIS BOW.  . . .        109 CUCHULAIN SEA      50
    I OFTEN HEAR THE SWEET SOUND OF HIS BOW.  . . . . .          109 CUCHULAIN SEA  V   50
    BOW DOWN, ARCHANGELS, IN YOUR DIM ABODE:  . . . . . .        112 ROSE OF WORLD      11
    AND ALL FOLK SEEING HIM BOW DOWN,  . . . . . . . .           113 ROSE OF PEACE       9
    ALL THE HEAVENS BOW DOWN TO HEAVEN,  . . . . . . .           125 CATHLEEN PARA      15
    THE SAD BELLS BOW THE FOREHEAD ON THE HANDS.  . . . .        130 BOOK STORIES   V   20
    BEING WEARY OF THE WORLD'S EMPIRES, BOW DOWN TO YOU,         161 BLACK PIG           7
    AND THEREFORE MY HEART WILL BOW, WHEN DEW  . . . . .         164 PERFECT BEAUTY      6
    WITH BEAUTY LIKE A TIGHTENED BOW, A KIND  . . . . . .        256 NO SECOND TROY      8
    UNDER A BOW, HE CRIED, "WHAT HAPPINESS  . . . . . . .        284 TWO KINGS         177
    THE BURNING BOW THAT ONCE COULD SHOOT AN ARROW  . . .        377 PHASES OF MOON    119
    A BEAUTIFUL SEATED BOY: A SACRED BOW:  . . . . . . .         541 PARN FUNERAL 1     10
    A HOARY HUNTER LEANING ON HIS BOW,  . . . . . . . .          672 ISLE STAT II 3    157
    BEHOLD I BOW BEFORE THEE TO THE GROUND:  . . . . . .         684 SEEKER         V   67
    BEHOLD I BOW:  AROUND MY BEARD IN DRIFTS  . . . . . .        684 SEEKER         V   68
    THAT ALL MEN EVERMORE MAY HUMBLY BOW  . . . . . . . .        688 TWO TITANS         49
    HIS MOODS BOW LOW HIS SOMBRE CREST,  . . . . . . . .        723 GIRLS SONG A        2
    WHERE LONG GREY GRASSES BOW AND BEND,  . . . . . . .        736 SUMMER EVENING      6
    AND MADE THE TYRANT BOW. . . . . . . . . . . . .            738 MOURN THEN ON      12
BOWED
    AND SIGHING BOWED HER GENTLE HEAD,  . . . . . . . .           12 OISIN 1           149
    WITH BOWED HEAD, TREMBLING WHEN THE WHITE BLADE SHONE, .      38 OISIN 2           137
    ARE BOWED IN SORROW UNDER PENDULOUS LIDS,  . . . . .          79 EPHEMERA            2
    ARE BOWED IN SORROW UNDER THEIR TREMBLING LIDS,  . .          79 EPHEMERA       V    2
    WITH HEAD BOWED ON HIS KNEES CUCHULAIN STAYED:  . . .        110 CUCHULAIN SEA      71
    WITH HEAD BOWED ON HIS KNEES, CUCHULLIN STAID,  . . .        110 CUCHULAIN SEA  V   71
    AND THOUGH THE SEVEN LIGHTS BOWED IN THEIR DANCE AND WEPT,   174 ELEMENT POWERS      3
    HIS FACE BOWED LOW TO WEEP THE END  . . . . . . . .          192 BAILE AILLINN      75
    AND HARPERS PONDERING WITH BOWED HEAD  . . . . . . .         193 BAILE AILLINN  V  107
    CROW UPON TARA." KING EOCHAID BOWED HIS HEAD  . . . .        286 TWO KINGS         211
    WHAT'S BOWED YOUR SHOULDER AND MADE PALE YOUR CHEEK":        467 HARUN RASHID      133
    AND THE WAVES BOWED BEFORE IT LIKE MOWN CORN,  . . .         657 ISLE STAT I 3      56
    LOW BOWED AND DUMB UPON THE SAND.  . . . . . . . .           671 ISLE STAT II 3    130
BOWELS
    TILL HER BOWELS ARE IN HEAT,  . . . . . . . . . . .          638 BEN BULBEN         49
BOWERS
    COME FORTH, FOR IN A THOUSAND BOWERS  . . . . . . .          647 ISLE STAT I 1      64
    AND HANGING O'ER THE HUSH OF WILLOW BOWERS,  . . . .         705 REMEMBRANCE         8
BOWING
    FULL MANY BOWING KINGS BESOUGHT ME,  . . . . . . .            7 OISIN 1        V   67
    CUMHAL CALLED OUT, BOWING HIS HEAD,  . . . . . . .           167 BLESSED        V   4A
    BOWING NATIONS, PLUMED WARS--  . . . . . . . . .            737 IN FIRELIGHT       10
BOWL
    ALL, ALL, THE VERY BOTTOM OF THE BOWL--  . . . . .           227 SHADOW WATER B    118
    IT SEEMED A GOLD-FISH SWIMMING IN A BOWL.  . . . . .         472 ALL SOUL NIGHT     40
BOW-LEGGED
    THE BOW-LEGGED GOBAN HAD NO SAY:  . . . . . . . .            271 GREY ROCK      V   10
BOWLS     SEE DRINKING-BOWLS
    AND BOWLS OF BARLEY, HONEY, AND WINE,  . . . . . . .           3 OISIN 1             8
    I PROMISE YOU A HUNDRED DRINKING BOWLS,  . . . . . .         756 SHADOW WATER A V  187
BOWS
    AND A HUNDRED SPEARS AND A HUNDRED BOWS,  . . . . .            8 OISIN 1            91
    AND A HUNDRED SWORDS AND A HUNDRED BOWS:  . . . . .            8 OISIN 1        V   91
    WITH BENDING STERNS AND BENDING BOWS,  . . . . . .           14 OISIN 1           189
    WITH BENDING STERNS AND BENDING BOWS,  . . . . . .           23 OISIN 1           353
    HID UNDER QUIET BOWS APART,  . . . . . . . . . .             78 INDIAN TO LOVE V   12
    AND THEREFORE MY HEART BOWS DOWN ANEW.  . . . . . .         164 PERFECT BEAUTY V    6
    A SLAVE BOWS DOWN TO A SLAVE.  . . . . . . . . .            547 TO SAME TUNE 3      6
    A SLAVE BOWS DOWN TO A SLAVE.  . . . . . . . . .            614 MARCH SONGS 2       6
    ALONG THE WOOD WITH SUBTLE TREAD AND BENDED BOWS.           649 ISLE STAT I 1     111
    BOWS THE BEDOUIN'S WHITENING HAIR--  . . . . . . .          733 STREET DANCERS     45
    YOU HAVE DONE WELL, BECAUSE MY BOWS ARE TURNED  . . .       755 SHADOW WATER A    164
BOW-STRING'S
    AND FEARED ALWAYS THE BOW-STRING'S TWANGING.  . . . .         3 OISIN 1        V 7GG
BOWSTRINGS
    . . . AND THE QUIVER OF STRETCHED BOWSTRINGS,  . . .         62 OISIN 3           207
BOX-BORDERED
    ENCLOSE A QUIET PLACE OF BEDS BOX-BORDERED, BEES,  . .      710 FERENCZ RENYI      24
BOXES
    TREASURE ON TREASURE.  BOXES OF PRECIOUS SPICE.  . . .      247 SHADOW WATER B    533
    TREASURE AND TREASURE.  BOXES OF PRECIOUS SPICE.  . .       247 SHADOW WATER B V  533
    FOR PAINTED FORMS OR BOXES OF MAKE-UP  . . . . . .          564 GYRES              13
```

BOY   SEE PLAY-BOY SHEPHERD-BOY GARDEN-BOY
UNTIL ONE CAME, A TEARFUL BOY: . . . . 17 OISIN 1   237
AND ONE CAME CLOSE, A TEARFUL BOY. . . . . 17 OISIN 1   V 237
WITH ONE LONG GLANCE FOR GIRL AND BOY . . . . . . 19 OISIN 1   287
WITH ONE LONG GLANCE ON MAID AND BOY . . . . . . 19 OISIN 1   V 287
AROSE FROM EVERY MAID AND BOY, ... 20 OISIN 1   V 289
FROM GIRL AND BOY AND MAN AND BEAST: . . . . . . 82 MAD KING GOLL   6
A GRACIOUS, GENTLE, KINGLY BOY. . . . . 82 MAD KING GOLL V 8
PEACE-MAKING, MILD, A KINGLY BOY. . . . . 82 MAD KING GOLL V 8
WHEN I WAS A BOY WITH NEVER A CRACK IN MY HEART. . 91 OLD FISHERMAN   4
WHEN I WAS A BOY WITH NEVER A CRACK IN MY HEART. . 91 OLD FISHERMAN   8
WHEN I WAS A BOY WITH NEVER A CRACK IN MY HEART. . 91 OLD FISHERMAN   12
A BOY OF TWENTY YEARS:--A MOUND AND STONE . . . . 276 TWO KINGS   V F
WHERE HELEN WALKED WITH HER BOY, ... 293 HELEN LIVED   9
THE ATTACK ON THE "PLAY BOY" . . . . 294 HATED PLAYBOY V T
AND EVERY MAN AND MAID AND BOY . . . . 337 TOM OROUGHLEY   2
IS DEAD. THE BOY THAT BRINGS MY GRIDDLE-CAKE . . 339 SHEP GOATHERD   20
IS DEAD. THE BOY THAT BRINGS MY GRIDDLE CAKE . . 339 SHEP GOATHERD V 20
I SEE A SCHOOL BOY WHEN I THINK OF HIM . . . . 370 EGO DOMINUS   V 55
SUFFICE THE AGEING MAN AS ONCE THE GROWING BOY. . 427 PHANTOM HATRED   40
OFTEN AT EVENING WHEN A BOY . . . . 494 AT ALGECIRAS   7
A BEAUTIFUL SEATED BOY: A SACRED BOW: . . . . . 541 PARN FUNERAL 1   10
A PIERCED BOY, IMAGE OF A STAR LAID LOW. . . . . 541 PARN FUNERAL 1   12
STAMPED BOY AND TREE UPON SICILIAN COIN. . . . . 541 PARN FUNERAL 1   15
ETERNITY IS PASSION, GIRL OR BOY . . . . 560 WHENCE COME   1
SEVENTY YEARS MAN AND BOY, ... 567 FROM JAPANESE   8
AY, BOY. LET'S SEE IF THAT SAME HERON'S DEAD. . 651 ISLE STAT I 1   169
OH, BOY, I'M BOUND ON A MOST FEARFUL QUEST: . . 653 ISLE STAT I 2   31
AND, BOY, SAW YOU, WHEN THROUGH THE FOREST WE . . 662 ISLE STAT II 2   9
BUT, FOR A BOY, HOW LONG THINE HAIR HAS GROWN! . 670 ISLE STAT II 3 104
TOUCH NOT THIS BOY, FOR HE IS INNOCENT. . . . . 694 MOSADA 1   106
REITERANT. A BOY GOES BY THE TENT. . . . . . 711 FERENCZ RENYI V 46
A LITTLE BOY OUTSIDE THE SYCAMORE WOOD . . . . 715 DWELT SYCAMORE   1
A LITTLE BOY INSIDE THE SYCAMORE WOOD . . . . 715 DWELT SYCAMORE   5
A BOY AND GIRL HOLD ONE ANOTHER'S HANDS: . . . . 752 SHADOW WATER A 122
BOYHOOD
NO, NOT IN BOYHOOD WHEN WITH ROD AND FLY, . . . 409 TOWER   8
THE IGNOMINY OF BOYHOOD: THE DISTRESS . . . . . 478 SELF AND SOUL   45
OF BOYHOOD CHANGING INTO MAN: . . . . 479 SELF AND SOUL   46
EVEN FROM BOYHOOD, IN MY FATHER'S HOUSE, . . . 683 SEEKER   48
BOYISH
MY FANCY, AND SET MY BOYISH LIPS TO SAY, . . . 270 PARDON FATHERS 17
OR BOYISH INTELLECT APPROVED, ... 328 ROBERT GREGORY 92
"ACCORDING TO MY BOYISH PLAN: . . . . 577 WHAT THEN   17
BOYNE
BESIDE THE BRACKISH WATERS OF THE BOYNE . . . . . 270 PARDON FATHERS 11
BOY'S
OR, IT MAY BE, LIKE A BOY'S. . . . . 363 DOLLS DRAWINGS   9
FOR SHOULD YOU LEAVE MY LETTER THERE, A BOY'S . . 461 HARUN RASHID   13
A BOY'S LOVELORN INDIFFERENT HANDS MIGHT FIND . . 461 HARUN RASHID V 14
A BOY'S TURBULENT DAYS . . . . 496 MOHINI CHATTER 13
AS THE FOX IN THE OLD FABLE DESTROYED THE SPARTAN BOY'S, 580 CURSE CROMWELL 18
BOYS   SEE HORSE-BOYS
TIME FOR US ALL BOYS, TO HIT ON A TUNE BOYS, . . . 548 TO SAME TUNE 3   13
TIME FOR US ALL BOYS, TO HIT ON A TUNE BOYS, . . . 548 TO SAME TUNE 3 V 13
BUT BOYS AND GIRLS, PALE FROM THE IMAGINED LOVE . . 610 STATUES   4
WITH BOYS AND GIRLS ABOUT HIM. . . . . 627 STATES HOLIDAY 27
THOSE STILTED BOYS, THAT BURNISHED CHARIOT, . . . 629 CIRCUS ANIMALS   7
AND LITTLE BOYS PLAYED PITCH AND TOSS. . . . . . 725 LEGEND   4
THE BOYS, THE WOMEN, AND OLD MEN. . . . . . . 725 LEGEND   7
AND DROVE THE BOYS AND WOMEN OFF. . . . . . . 725 LEGEND   24
BRACE
COULD LIKE A BRACE OF BLACKBIRDS SING. . . . . 332 ROUND TOWER   24
BRACE ME AND MAKE ME STRONG: . . . . 607 SONGS BURDEN 2 24
BRACKISH
BESIDE THE BRACKISH WATERS OF THE BOYNE . . . . 270 PARDON FATHERS 11
BRAHMA
TO MIGHTY BRAHMA, HE WHO MADE YOU MANY AS THE SANDS, . . 72 ANASHU VIJAYA   21
TO MIGHTY BRAHMA--HE WHO MADE YE MANY AS THE SANDS, . . 72 ANASHU VIJAYA V 21
TO MIGHTY BRAHMA, WHO HAS MADE YOU MANY AS THE SANDS, . . 72 ANASHU VIJAYA V 21
WHOM BRAHMA, TOUCHING WITH HIS FINGER, PRAISES, FOR YOU 73 ANASHU VIJAYA   42
HOLD
WHOM BRAHMA, TOUCHING WITH HIS FINGER, PRAISES, FOR YE HOLD 73 ANASHU VIJAYA V 42
PRAYERS FOR THE LAND. O BRAHMA, GUARD IN SLEEP . . . 75 ANASHU VIJAYA   85
BRAHMA'S
BY MIGHTY BRAHMA'S EVER-RUSTLING ROBE, ... 71 ANASHU VIJAYA   14
STAND YOU. BY BRAHMA'S EVER-RUSTLING ROBE, . . . 71 ANASHU VIJAYA V 14
BY MIGHTY BRAHMA'S EVER RUSTLING ROBE, ... 71 ANASHU VIJAYA V 14
ON BRAHMA'S GATEWAY, "THEY WITHIN HAVE FED . . . 735 QUATRAIN APHOR 15
BRAHMIN
BUT THE BRAHMIN SAID, ... 495 MOHINI CHATTER   2
BRAID
HOW THEREFORE COULD SHE HELP BUT BRAID . . . . . 309 PLAYER QUEEN   17
I HAVE WET THIS BRAID OF HAIR WITH TEARS WHILE ASLEEP. . 762 SHADOW WATER A 294
BRAIN
IN EVERY BRAIN A WIZARD GLOW. . . . . 20 OISIN 1   V 291A
SHADOWS AND SHOWS THAT CAN BUT TURN THE BRAIN." . . 281 TWO KINGS   108
NOR THE TAME WILL, NOR TIMID BRAIN, ... 318 APPOINTMENT   8
ON THAT WOMAN'S REELING BRAIN? . . . . 632 MAN AND ECHO   14
ON MY POOR BRAIN YOUR BUSY TUMULTS CROWD. . . . 648 ISLE STAT I 1   100
MY SINKING BRAIN!--CEASE!--CEASE! HEARD YE YON SOUND? . . 665 ISLE STAT II 2   73

	PAGE	TITLE		LINE
BRAIN (CONTINUED)				
LAUGHTER-LIPPED, BUT FOR HER BRAIN	668	ISLE STAT II 3		58
THAT DREAMS. SHE MOVETH, FEELING IN HER BRAIN	687	TWO TITANS		10
CIRCLING THE BRAIN? MY BROTHERS WILL PASS DOWN	699	MOSADA 3		6
THE BRAIN. MY BROTHERS WILL BE PASSING DOWN	699	MOSADA 3	V	6
CIRCLING THE BRAIN? MY BROTHERS NOW PASS DOWN	699	MOSADA 3	V	6
SO ENDS A BRAIN--A WORLD! THE SMOKE GOES UP, ...	714	FERENCZ RENYI		111
OF FIRE. SO ENDS A BRAIN--A WORLD! THE SMOKE FLOATS UP,	714	FERENCZ RENYI	V	111
SORROWS SAPPING BRAIN AND HEART.	733	STREET DANCERS		60
BRAINS				
SMOTE ON THEIR BRAINS THAT DWELT REMEMBERING AYE. . . .	34	OISIN 2	V	77A
BRAKE				
AND SEDGY STREAM, AND IN EACH BABBLING BRAKE	675	ISLE STAT II 3		225
BRAN				
BRAN, SGEOLAN, AND LOMAIR, ...	2	OISIN 1	V	7D
AND BRAN, SGEOLAN, AND LOMAIR	2	OISIN 1	V	7R
WITH BRAN, SCEOLAN, AND LOMAIR, ...	3	OISIN 1		15
AND BRAN, SCEOLAN, AND LOMAIR, ...	11	OISIN 1		125
I MUSED ON THE CHASE WITH THE FENIANS, AND BRAN, SCEOLAN, LOMAIR,	47	OISIN 3		5
WHEN THE FENIANS MADE FORAY AT MORNING WITH BRAN, SCEOLAN, LOMAIR.	54	OISIN 3		104
WHAT PLACE HAVE CAOILTE AND CONAN, AND BRAN, SCEOLAN, LOMAIR?	61	OISIN 3		195
WHAT PLACE HAVE CAOLTE AND FIN, AND BRAN, SGEOLAN, LOMAIR?	61	OISIN 3	V	195
I WILL GO TO CAOILTE, AND CONAN, AND BRAN, SCEOLAN, LOMAIR,	63	OISIN 3		223
TO FIN, CAOLTE, AND CONAN, AND BRAN, SGEOLAN, LOMAIR. . .	63	OISIN 3	V	224
BRANCH SEE BELL-BRANCH CHERRY-BRANCH				
ROUND EVERY BRANCH THE SONG-BIRDS FLEW, ...	14	OISIN 1		180
FOR ROUND EACH BRANCH THE SONG-BIRDS FLEW, ...	14	OISIN 1		180
IN ONE WAS A BRANCH SOFT-SHINING WITH BELLS MORE MANY THAN SIGHS	50	OISIN 3		46
CAME BY ME THE KINGS OF THE RED BRANCH, ...	53	OISIN 3		87
CAME BY ME THE CANNS OF THE RED BRANCH	53	OISIN 3	V	87
WHAT WOULD YOU, KING OF THE PROUD RED BRANCH KINGS? . .	102	FERGUS DRUID		8
WHAT WOULD YOU, KING OF THE PROUD RED BRANCH KINGS? . .	102	FERGUS DRUID		15
WHAT WOULD YOU, KING OF THE PROUD RED BRANCH KINGS? . .	103	FERGUS DRUID	V	21
"THE RED BRANCH CAMP IN A GREAT COMPANY	108	CUCHULAIN SEA		33
"THE RED BRANCH KINGS A TIRELESS BANQUET KEEP, ...	108	CUCHULAIN SEA	V	33
"THE RED BRANCH GATHER A GREAT COMPANY	108	CUCHULAIN SEA	V	33
AND THE GREY TIDE, THE RED BRANCH MULTITUDE	108	CUCHULAIN SEA	V	38B
AND CONCHUBAR, THE RED BRANCH KING OF KINGS, ...	109	CUCHULAIN SEA		45
"I ONLY OF THE RED BRANCH HOSTED NOW,"	109	CUCHULAIN SEA	V	55
THERE WAS A GREEN BRANCH HUNG WITH MANY A BELL	129	BOOK STORIES		1
I ALSO BEAR A BELL BRANCH FULL OF EASE.	130	BOOK STORIES	V	12
MY BELL BRANCH MURMURS. THE GAY BELLS BRING LAUGHTER, .	130	BOOK STORIES	V	18
O FLOWER OF THE BRANCH, O BIRD AMONG THE LEAVES, . . .	251	SHADOW WATER B		608
O FLOWER OF THE BRANCH, O BIRD AMONG THE LEAVES, . . .	769	SHADOW WATER A		424
BRANCHES				
FROM JOY THE HOLY BRANCHES START, ...	134	TWO TREES		3
THERE, THROUGH THE BROKEN BRANCHES, GO	135	TWO TREES		33
THERE, THROUGH BEWILDERED BRANCHES, GO	135	TWO TREES	V	13
I TURNED ABOUT AND LOOKED WHERE BRANCHES BREAK	490	COOLE BALLYLEE		15
I TURNED ABOUT AND LOOKED WHERE BRANCHES BROKE	490	COOLE BALLYLEE	V	15
THOSE BRANCHES OF THE NIGHT AND DAY	502	VACILLATION		68
A FRENZIED CROWD, AND WHERE THE BRANCHES SPRANG	541	PARN FUNERAL 1		9
EYES STARED OUT OF THE BRANCHES AND WERE GONE.	634	CUCHULAIN COMF		3
AND THE BIRD IN THE BRANCHES WILL CRY FOR US CLEAR, . .	717	LOVE SONG		6
BRANCHING				
BUT THE STAG STOOPED ITS HEAVY BRANCHING HORNS, ...	277	TWO KINGS	V	12
BRAND				
A BRAND, OR FLAMING BREATH, ...	500	VACILLATION		3
BRAND-NEW				
UPON SOME BRAND-NEW HAPPY DAY!	432	NINETEEN 19	V	106
BRANWEN				
THEREIN ARE MANY QUEENS LIKE BRANWEN AND GUINEVERE! . .	209	UNDER THE MOON		11
BRASS				
BETWEEN THEM A GATEWAY OF BRASS, AND THE HOWL OF THE ANGELS WHO FELL.	61	OISIN 3		200
WE WILL TEAR OUT THE FLAMING STONES, AND BATTER THE GATEWAY OF BRASS	62	OISIN 3		209
. . . AND WILL BATTER THE GATEWAY OF BRASS	62	OISIN 3	V	209
SHE SNICKED THE BRASS BOLTS DOWN.	159	CAP AND BELLS	V	12
AND PUSHED THE BRASS BOLT DOWN.	159	CAP AND BELLS	V	12
A HUNDRED SHIELDS OF BRASS, A HUNDRED SWORDS, ...	756	SHADOW WATER A	V	188
BRATTA				
AND WHEN THEY SAW THAT THE BRATTA I WORE	15	OISIN 1	V	207
BRATTAS				
THEIR BRATTAS MADE OUT OF YELLOW SILK, ...	15	OISIN 1	V	205
BRAVE				
ALL THAT DELIRIUM OF THE BRAVE?	290	SEPTEMBER 1913		22
COULD TRUMPETER MICHAEL BE SO BRAVE?"	338	TOM OROUGHLEY		13
FLY! FLY! SO THESE BRAVE SHEPHERDS BOTH ARE GONE! . . .	649	ISLE STAT I 1		112
BRAVED				
BRAVED LIONS FOR MY SAKE, ...	789	SINGING HEAD		2
BRAVELY				
SHE WOULD AS BRAVELY SHOW	516	MANS SONG		9
BRAVEST				
WE, TOO, HAVE SEEN OUR BRAVEST AND OUR BEST	709	FERENCZ RENYI		1
THE BRAVEST FROM THE GODS BUT ASK!	788	BRAVEST ASK		1

		PAGE	TITLE	LINE
BRAWLING				
	THE BRAWLING OF A SPARROW IN THE EAVES,	119	SORROW OF LOVE	1
	WITH SKELPING HIS BIG BRAWLING LOUT,	301	RUN PARADISE	9
	WHAT ONE OF MAEVE'S NINE BRAWLING SONS	303	HOUR DAWN	36
	HAS ONE OF MAEVE'S NINE BRAWLING SONS	303	HOUR DAWN V	36
	"I TOOK YOU FOR A BRAWLING GHOST,	304	HOUR DAWN V	41
BRAY				
	TO HEAR A JACKASS BRAY!	455	HIS MEMORIES	10
BRAYED				
	HOWLED, MIAU-D, BARKED, BRAYED, BELLED, YELLED, CRIED, CROWED,	387	SOLOMON WITCH	8
BRAZEN				
	O PATRICK, BY YOUR BRAZEN BELL,	7	OISIN 1	71
	OF SWORD AND BRAZEN BATTLE-AXE, WHILE DAY	40	OISIN 2	171
	AND MY LOUD BRAZEN BATTLE-CARS	83	MAD KING GOLL	18
	WITH HIS OWN BRAZEN FINGERS TOUCHED THE BRAZEN STRINGS.	109	CUCHULAIN SEA	46
	WITH HIS OWN FINGER TOUCHED THE BRAZEN STRINGS.	109	CUCHULAIN SEA V	46
	FOR FERGUS RULES THE BRAZEN CARS,	126	GOES FERGUS	9
	THE BRAZEN PILLARS OF HIS DOOR,	192	BAILE AILLINN	74
	FROM ANY BRAZEN THROAT,	291	TO A FRIEND	3
	TO BRAZEN HAWKS, NOR SELF-DELIGHTING REVERIE,	427	PHANTOM HATRED	29
	THE BRAZEN SKY, SO BLAZE THE DAFFODILLS!	645	ISLE STAT I 1	11
BRAZEN-GATED				
	BEHOLD THE BRAZEN-GATED GLADE!	667	ISLE STAT II 3	43
	OF HIM ON YONDER BRAZEN-GATED SPOT,	675	ISLE STAT II 3	240
BREAD				
	THOSE TWO CAME CARRYING WINE AND MEAT AND BREAD,	41	OISIN 2	184
	HOPING AND FEARING, BROUGHT ME WINE AND BREAD.	41	OISIN 2 V	184A
	AND A YOUNG GIRL WHITE BREAD.	144	HOST OF AIR	20
	THE BREAD AND THE WINE HAD A DOOM,	144	HOST OF AIR	25
	TO CLIMB THAT STAIR AND EAT THAT BITTER BREAD,	369	EGO DOMINUS	35
	OF ALL THOSE TRUTHS THAT ARE YOUR DAILY BREAD!	373	PHASES OF MOON	24
	DID GOD IN PORTIONING WINE AND BREAD	386	ROBARTES DANCE	39
	A BIT OF BREAD THROWN UP INTO THE AIR!	400	DEMON BEAST	25
	MIND'S BREAD GROW SWEET.	554	CHURCH STATE	6
	BREAD TASTE SOUR.	554	CHURCH STATE	12
	I FASTED FOR SOME FORTY DAYS ON BREAD AND BUTTERMILK,	592	PILGRIM	1
	THAT PLUCKS THE TREES FOR BREAD?	621	JOHN KINSELLA	34
	AND WHEN THE FOOL AND BLIND MAN STOLE THE BREAD	630	CIRCUS ANIMALS	25
BREAK SEE DAY-BREAK HEART-BREAK				
	. . . WHO COULD BREAK UP THE WORLD IN THEIR RAGE!	62	OISIN 3	214
	A RAPTUROUS MUSIC, TILL THE MORNING BREAK	137	TO SOME I TALK	14
	CONTINUAL MUSIC TILL THE MORNING BREAK,	137	TO SOME I TALK V	14
	THE EAST HER HIDDEN JOY BEFORE THE MORNING BREAK,	154	BELOVED PEACE	4
	UNTIL THE AXLE BREAK	165	CRY OF SEDGE	4
	AND SCRUB A KITCHEN PAVEMENT, OR BREAK STONES	204	ADAMS CURSE	8
	THE OLD BROWN THORN-TREES BREAK IN TWO HIGH OVER CUMMEN STRAND,	206	HANRAHANS SONG	1
	THE OLD BROWN THORN TREES BREAK IN TWO HIGH OVER CUMANN'S STRAND,	206	HANRAHANS SONG V	1
	WHOSE HEART WOULD BREAK IN TWO,	213	HAPPY TOWNLAND	2
	FOR NEITHER I NOR YOU CAN BREAK A MESH	238	SHADOW WATER B	351
	NOR KNAVE NOR DOLT CAN BREAK	259	UNWORTH PRAISE	2
	WHAT DOES HE CARE IF MY HEART BREAK?	275	GREY ROCK	104
	I HAVE STOOD HERE FROM BREAK OF DAY,	294	THREE BEGGARS	2
	WHEN DAY BEGINS TO BREAK	316	FRIENDS	21
	TO HIS SPEECH AT THE BREAK OF DAY,	341	SHEP GOATHERD	68
	OR SICKNESS BREAK HER WILL	365	HER RACE	10
	IMAGES CAN BREAK THE SOLITUDE	375	PHASES OF MOON	82
	TOWARDS BREAK OF DAY	398	BREAK OF DAY	T
	I DREAMED TOWARDS BREAK OF DAY,	399	BREAK OF DAY	19
	TO BREAK UPON A SLEEPER'S REST .	412	TOWER	87
	WHERE THE SYMBOLIC ROSE CAN BREAK IN FLOWER,	419	MY HOUSE	4
	BUT BREAK UPON HIS GHOSTLY SOLITUDE.	429	NINETEEN 19	40
	OR BREAK IN BITS THE FAMOUS IVORIES	430	NINETEEN 19	47
	ALL BREAK AND VANISH, AND EVIL GATHERS HEAD!	433	NINETEEN 19	117
	WHERE WE WROUGHT THAT SHALL BREAK THE TEETH OF TIME.	435	NEW FACES	4
	AND YET THEY TOO BREAK HEARTS--O PRESENCES	445	SCHOOL CHILDR	53
	O BUT HER HEART WOULD BREAK TO LEARN MY THOUGHTS ARE FAR AWAY."	450	OWEN AHERNE	20
	I TURNED ABOUT AND LOOKED WHERE BRANCHES BREAK	490	COOLE BALLYLEE	15
	TILL THE DAWN BREAK UPON THOSE MINGLED SEAS.	494	AT ALGECIRAS	6
	UNTIL THE MORNING BREAK AS ON A DARK BREAST.	494	AT ALGECIRAS V	6
	SPIRIT AFTER SPIRIT! THE SMITHIES BREAK THE FLOOD,	498	BYZANTIUM	34
	BREAK BITTER FURIES OF COMPLEXITY,	498	BYZANTIUM	37
	I MADE, AND MAY NOT BREAK IT	520	HIS BARGAIN	9
	TO-MORROW NIGHT I WILL BREAK DOWN THE DOOR.	551	SONGS REWRIT 1	6
	TO-MORROW NIGHT I WILL BREAK DOWN THE DOOR.	551	SONGS REWRIT 1	12
	TO-MORROW NIGHT I WILL BREAK DOWN THE DOOR.	551	SONGS REWRIT 1	18
	TOMORROW NIGHT I WILL BREAK DOWN THE DOOR.	551	SONGS REWRIT 1 V	REF
	TO-MORROW NIGHT I WILL BREAK IN THE DOOR.	551	SONGS REWRIT 1 V	REF
	DO NOT BREAK UP THEIR LINES TO WEEP.	565	LAPIS LAZULI	15
	"IRELAND SHALL GET HER FREEDOM AND YOU STILL BREAK STONE."	590	PARNELL	2
	THROUGH THIS NIGHT-VESTED PLACE THE RED BEAMS BREAK.	662	ISLE STAT II 2	4
	"SHIELD BREAKER, BREAK A SHIELD TO-DAY,	739	EARL PAUL	1
	SHIELD-BREAKER, BREAK A SHIELD TO-DAY,	739	EARL PAUL V	1
	O! I WOULD BREAK THIS NET THE GODS HAVE WOVEN	765	SHADOW WATER A	361
BREAKER SEE PROMISE-BREAKER SHIELD-BREAKER				
	"SHIELD BREAKER, BREAK A SHIELD TO-DAY,	739	EARL PAUL	1
	MEN CRY "BRING PAUL, SHIELD BREAKER,	740	EARL PAUL	11
	"SHIELD BREAKER, GREAT SHIELD BREAKER,"	740	EARL PAUL	25

	PAGE	TITLE		LINE
BREAKER (CONTINUED)				
"SHIELD BREAKER, GREAT SHIELD BREAKER,"	740	EARL PAUL		25
BREAKERS				
BE BUT THE BREAKERS OF MEN'S HEARTS OR ENGINES OF DELIGHT!	354	HIS PHOENIX		23
BREAKING SEE BATTLE-BREAKING				
IN A WHITE BREAKING WAVE! THEY HAD THE LOOK	223	SHADOW WATER B		34
AND BARREN AS A BREAKING WAVE	456	FRIENDS YOUTH		11
BREAKS				
"AND BREAKS THE RIDGE OF BATTLE WITH HIS HANDS."	107	CUCHULAIN SEA	V	26
OUR COURAGE BREAKS LIKE AN OLD TREE IN A BLACK WIND AND	207	HANRAHANS SONG		3
DIES,				
. . . NIGHT SPLITS AND THE DAWN BREAKS LOOSE!	623	HIGH TALK		12
THE DIM SPEAR BREAKS THE BRIGHT SHIELD	741	EARL PAUL		49
LET HIM WHO BREAKS IT	770	BLOOD BOND		4
BREAST				
OF A DROWNED DRIPPING BODY TO MY BREAST!	40	OISIN 2		179
AND SUNKEN SHAPE, AGAINST MY FACE AND BREAST, ...	40	OISIN 2	V	179
AND DRIPPING AND SUNKEN SHAPE, TO FACE AND BREAST, . . .	40	OISIN 2	V	179
. . . HER BROW ON THE MIDST OF MY BREAST!	52	OISIN 3		74
SAD NIAM CAME NEAR ME, AND LAID HER BROWS ON THE MIDST	52	OISIN 3	V	74
OF MY BREAST				
AND PEARL-PALE NEAVE LAY BY ME, HER BROW ON THE MIDST OF	52	OISIN 3	V	74
MY BREAST!				
. . . FOR BREAST UNTO BREAST	56	OISIN 3		131
. . . FOR BREAST UNTO BREAST	56	OISIN 3		131
SING PEACE INTO HIS BREAST, ...	88	STOLEN CHILD		47
IN VAIN HER ARMS, IN VAIN HER SOFT WHITE BREAST. . . .	110	CUCHULAIN SEA		74
AND THE WHITE BREAST OF THE DIM SEA	126	GOES FERGUS		11
AND HIS NECK AND HIS BREAST AND HIS ARMS	145	HOST OF AIR		35
I KISS MY WAILING CHILD AND PRESS IT TO MY BREAST, . . .	147	UNAPPEAS HOST		5
AND MY BREAST LIES UPON HIS BREAST.	151	HEART OF WOMAN		4
AND MY BREAST LIES UPON HIS BREAST.	151	HEART OF WOMAN		4
AND MY WHITE BREAST ON HIS HE LAID.	151	HEART OF WOMAN	V	4
OVER MY HEART, AND YOUR HAIR FALL OVER MY BREAST, . . .	154	BELOVED PEACE		10
OVER MY HEART, AND YOUR HAIR FALL ABOUT MY BREAST . . .	154	BELOVED PEACE	V	10
THAT WAS SHAKEN OUT OVER MY BREAST!	155	REPROVE CURLEW		5
FOR THAT PALE BREAST AND LINGERING HAND	156	FORGOT BEAUTY		15
AND COVER THE PALE BLOSSOMS OF YOUR BREAST	163	ASKS FORGIVE		21
THEN COVER THE PALE BLOSSOM OF YOUR BREAST	163	ASKS FORGIVE	V	21
YOUR BREAST WILL NOT LIE BY THE BREAST	165	CRY OF SEDGE		9
YOUR BREAST WILL NOT LIE BY THE BREAST	165	CRY OF SEDGE		9
YOUR BREAST WILL NOT LIE ON THE BREAST	165	CRY OF SEDGE		9
YOUR BREAST WILL NOT LIE ON THE BREAST!	165	CRY OF SEDGE	V	9
AND I WOULD LAY MY HEAD ON YOUR BREAST!	175	BELOVED DEAD		4
MAY NOT LIE ON THE BREAST NOR HIS LIPS ON THE HAIR . .	177	PAST GREATNESS		9
WOULD NOT LIE ON THE BREAST, OR HIS LIPS ON THE HAIR, .	177	PAST GREATNESS	V	9
LIKE A GREY GULL UPON THE BREAST OF EACH.	223	SHADOW WATER B		24
A SPHINX WITH WOMAN BREAST AND LION PAW, ...	383	VISION ROBART		18
APPROPRIATE TO THAT BEATING BREAST	386	ROBARTES DANCE		22
WHILE UNDER ITS STORM-BEATEN BREAST	397	POLIT PRISONER		23
COME WITH LOUD CRY AND PANTING BREAST	412	TOWER		86
THE BREAST THRUST OUT IN PRIDE	430	NINETEEN 19		66
DROVE HORROR FROM HIS MOTHER'S BREAST.	440	WISDOM		20
HE HOLDS HER HELPLESS BREAST UPON HIS BREAST.	441	LEDA AND SWAN		4
HE HOLDS HER HELPLESS BREAST UPON HIS BREAST.	441	LEDA AND SWAN		4
HAS LAID HER HELPLESS FACE UPON HIS BREAST.	441	LEDA AND SWAN	V	4
A STONE UPON HER BREAST, ...	456	FRIENDS YOUTH		6
SO GREAT A SWEETNESS FLOWS INTO THE BREAST	479	SELF AND SOUL		69
SWIFT BEATING ON HIS BREAST IN SIBYLLINE FRENZY BLIND .	481	BLOOD AND MOON		19
BECAUSE THE HEART IN HIS BLOOD-SODDEN BREAST	481	BLOOD AND MOON		20
CANNOT LACERATE HIS BREAST.	493	SWIFTS EPITAPH		3
UNTIL THE MORNING BREAK AS ON A DARK BREAST.	494	AT ALGECIRAS	V	6
AND YET UPON MY BREAST	496	MOHINI CHATTER		10
UPON THE ABUNDANCE OF MY BREAST"!	521	THREE THINGS		5
ON THE MATERNAL MIDNIGHT OF MY BREAST	535	CHOSEN		7
I STARED UPON HIS BLOOD-BEDABBLED BREAST	537	HER VISION		23
I STARED UPON MY BLOOD-BEDABBLED BREAST	537	HER VISION	V	23
AND LAUGHED UPON HIS BREAST TO THINK	538	LAST CONFESS		11
DRINKING JOY AS IT WERE MILK UPON HIS BREAST.	559	MAGIC DRUM		3
DOWN LIMB AND BREAST OR DOWN THAT GLIMMERING BELLY . . .	560	MAGIC DRUM		5
ON BREAST OF MARS THE GODDESS SIGHED.	562	CONJUNCTIONS		4
PROPER TO MY BREAST, ...	573	LADYS 2ND SONG		16
WITH EVERY NOBLE BREAST, ...	573	LADYS 2ND SONG	V	18
ON MY COLD BREAST?	574	MAIDS 1ST SONG		4
UPON A WOMAN'S BREAST."	590	OLD WICKED MAN		62
THE SALT-FLAKES ON HIS BREAST, ...	612	NEWS ORACLE		10
THE SALT FLAKES ON HIS BREAST, ...	612	NEWS ORACLE	V	10
JOY'S BROTHER, FEAR, DWELLS EVER IN EACH BREAST-- . .	651	ISLE STAT I 1		155
FOR SO SHE WILLED--THOU HEARD'ST? UPON THE BREAST .	653	ISLE STAT I 2		32
ABODE, AS BANDED ADDERS IN MY BREAST.	683	SEEKER		50
ON HER BROAD BREAST! BENEATH HER WITHERED BROWS . . .	685	SEEKER		73
MADONNA FROM MY BREAST?	686	LIFE		12
I WAVE THEM HITHER, MY BREAST HEAVES WITH JOY.	694	MOSADA 1		98
A FEARFUL PALENESS CREEPS ACROSS HER BREAST	701	MOSADA 3		69
HANGS ON MY BREAST! LISTEN, WE SHALL BE SAFE.	701	MOSADA 3		73
SAFE ON THE BREAST OF GOMEZ LIES THY HEAD, ...	703	MOSADA 3		101
SAFE ON THE BREAST OF VALLENCE IS THY HEAD	703	MOSADA 3	V	101
SAFE ON THE BREAST OF GOMEZ IS THY HEAD, ...	703	MOSADA 3	V	101
THEREFORE, O NATION OF THE BLEEDING BREAST, ...	709	FERENCZ RENYI		4
AND HE SHALL SLUMBER ON MY BREAST.	723	GIRLS SONG A		4
AND PIERCED THE MIRTHFUL BREAST, ...	741	EARL PAUL		50

106

BREAST   (CONTINUED)
IN DAY OUT—LIVING BATTLE, ON THE BREAST . . . .   750 SHADOW WATER A   73
HIS TOO HUMAN BREAST. . . . .   786 YOUR HEART   21
BREASTPLATE
SAID THE MAN IN THE GOLDEN BREASTPLATE . . . .   598 STONE CROSS   7
SAID THE MAN IN THE GOLDEN BREASTPLATE . . . .   599 STONE CROSS   15
SAID THE MAN IN THE GOLDEN BREASTPLATE . . . .   599 STONE CROSS   23
SAID THE OLD MAN IN THE GOLDEN BREASTPLATE . . . . .   599 STONE CROSS   V 23
BREASTS
OUR BREASTS ARE HEAVING, OUR EYES ARE AGLEAM, ...   140 HOSTING SIDHE   8
FOR BREASTS ARE HEAVING AND EYES A-GLEAM; . . . . .   140 HOSTING SIDHE   V   7
OUR BREASTS ARE HEAVING, OUR EYES ARE A-GLEAM, . . .   140 HOSTING SIDHE   V   8
"THOSE BREASTS ARE FLAT AND FALLEN NOW, ...   513 JANE TALK BISH   3
(SWALLOWS WERE FLASHING THEIR WHITE BREASTS ABOVE . .   690 MOSADA 1   7
BREATH   SEE ROSE-BREATH AIR-BREATH WINE-BREATH
BUT ONLY KIND AND MERRY BREATH, ...   19 OISIN 1   285
WERE THE WINDS LESS SOFT THAN THE BREATH OF A PIGEON . . .   56 OISIN 3   134
. . . THEY WILL RISE, MAKING CLOUDS WITH THEIR BREATH, . .   61 OISIN 3   202
HE CAUGHT HIS BREATH AND CAST HIM WEEPING DOWN . . . .   106 CUCHULAIN SEA   V 14
AND PIERCED HIM. "SPEAK BEFORE YOUR BREATH IS DONE." . .   110 CUCHULAIN SEA   67
MY BREATH IS MIXED INTO HIS BREATH. . . . .   152 HEART OF WOMAN   12
MY BREATH IS MIXED INTO HIS BREATH. . . . .   152 HEART OF WOMAN   12
AND WITH A GROAN, AS IF THE MORTAL BREATH . . . .   185 QUEEN MAEVE   103
THAT HAPPIER BREATH HAD MOVED, HER HUSBAND TURNED . .   185 QUEEN MAEVE   105
I AM A WOMAN, I DIE AT EVERY BREATH. . . . . . .   250 SHADOW WATER B   583
NAMING IT WITH ECSTATIC BREATH, ...   254 HIS DREAM   18
BREATHED ON THE WORLD WITH TIMID BREATH. . . . . .   266 GALWAY RACES   9
THOUGH YOU MAY THINK I WASTE MY BREATH . . . . .   271 GREY ROCK   6
TOWARD PEOPLED TARA, NOR STOOD TO DRAW HIS BREATH . .   279 TWO KINGS   46
ON PEOPLED TARA, NOR STOOD TO DRAW HIS BREATH . . .   279 TWO KINGS   V 46
TOWARDS PEOPLED TARA, NOR STOOD TO DRAW HIS BREATH . .   279 TWO KINGS   V 46
FORBID, BESEECH AND WASTE MY BREATH." THEN I: . .   281 TWO KINGS   102
TO DRINK OF THAT SALT BREATH OUT OF THE SEA . . .   292 TO A SHADE   5
THE TIME FOR YOU TO TASTE OF THAT SALT BREATH . . .   293 TO A SHADE   21
I AM ACCUSTOMED TO THEIR LACK OF BREATH, ...   325 ROBERT GREGORY   45
THE YEARS TO COME SEEMED WASTE OF BREATH, ...   328 IRISH AIRMAN   14
A WASTE OF BREATH THE YEARS BEHIND . . . .   328 IRISH AIRMAN   15
YOUNG MEN NO LONGER SUDDENLY CATCH THEIR BREATH . .   355 BROKEN DREAMS   2
WHO HAD ENDED WHERE HIS BREATH BEGAN. . . . . . .   360 ALF POLLEXFEN   12
WHO HAD MURMURED OF GIORGIONE AT HIS LATEST BREATH-- . .   366 HER COURAGE   8
OBEDIENT TO SOME HIDDEN MAGICAL BREATH. . . . . .   382 VISION ROBART   13
"MAYBE A BREATH OF POLITIC WORDS . . . .   396 ROSE TREE   3
AND MURMUR IT WITH BATED BREATH, AS THOUGH . . . .   398 LEADERS CROWD   5
THAT MADE A CATCH IN THE BREATH-- . . . .   416 TOWER   191
CHAUCER HAD NOT DRAWN BREATH . . . .   421 MY TABLE   8
BUT VANISH WITH OUR BREATH . . . .   431 NINETEEN 19   76
NEVER TO HAVE DRAWN THE BREATH OF LIFE, ...   459 FROM OEDIPUS   11
NEVER TO HAVE DRUNK THE BREATH OF LIFE, ...   459 FROM OEDIPUS   V 11
WORDS WERE BUT WASTED BREATH; . . . .   471 ALL SOUL NIGHT   27
SUPERSESSION OF BREATH; . . . .   476 DEATH   10
A MOUTH THAT HAS NO MOISTURE AND NO BREATH . . .   497 BYZANTIUM   13
A BRAND, OR FLAMING BREATH, ...   500 VACILLATION   3
AND CALL THOSE WORKS EXTRAVAGANCE OF BREATH . . .   501 VACILLATION   32
SUCH EXACTING BREATH, ...   517 HER ANXIETY   8
LAY IN THE COFFIN, STOPPED HIS BREATH AND DIED. . .   609 IN TARAS HALLS   20
PROFOUND MCTAGGART THOUGHT SO, AND IN A BREATH . .   619 BRONZE HEAD   13
SHE WILL SAY WITH BATED BREATH, ...   680 LOVE AND DEATH   30
ALL THAT MINGLING OF OUR BREATH, ...   777 SONG DEIRDRE 2   10
BREATHE
BREATHE ON THE BURNISHED MIRROR OF THE WORLD . . .   228 SHADOW WATER B   132
BREATHE ON THE BURNISHED MIRROR OF THE WORLD . . . .   750 SHADOW WATER A   69
BREATHED
OR HAVE THEY BREATHED THE MORTAL AIR?" . . . . .   12 OISIN 1   147
BREATHED ON THE WORLD WITH TIMID BREATH. . . . .   266 GALWAY RACES   9
BREATHED OUT A DRUID VAPOUR, AND CRUMBLED AWAY . .   761 SHADOW WATER A   279
BREATHES
WHEN AN IMMORTAL PASSION BREATHES IN MORTAL CLAY; . . .   172 TRAV PASSION   2
BREATHING
THE BREATHING CAME FROM THOSE BODIES, . . .   49 OISIN 3   36
HE HOLDS HIM FROM DESIRE, ALL BUT STOPS HIS BREATHING LEST   559 MAGIC DRUM   1
ONE WHOSE BREATHING SHAKES THE AIR, ...   727 LOVERS QUARREL   31
THE BREATHING OF THE SMALLEST BIRD, ...   730 PRIEST FAIRY   68
BREATHLESS
AND NOW THEIR BREATHLESS FACES SEEM TO LOOK . . .   325 ROBERT GREGORY   43
AND THEIR BREATHLESS FACES SEEM TO LOOK . . . .   325 ROBERT GREGORY V   43
UPON THE BREATHLESS STARLIT AIR, ...   477 SELF AND SOUL   4
BREATHLESS MOUTHS MAY SUMMON; . . . .   497 BYZANTIUM   14
BRED   SEE COARSE-BRED PURE-BRED MIRACLE-BRED ILL-BRED ROCK-BRED THOROUGH-BRED
BRED TO BE A HERO'S WAGE. . . . .   258 PEACE   3
BEING HONOUR BRED, WITH ONE . . . .   291 TO A FRIEND   5
BRED TO A HARDER THING . . . .   291 TO A FRIEND   9
BRED THAT FIERCE TOOTH AND CLEANLY LIMB . . . .   318 APPOINTMENT   10
BRED ON THE ATLANTIC, CAN BE STAYED: . . . . . .   403 FOR DAUGHTER   6
HOW COULD SHE MATE WITH FIFTY YEARS THAT WAS SO WILDLY   450 OWEN AHERNE   15
  BRED?
BRED OUT OF THE CONTAGION OF THE THRONG, ...   542 PARN FUNERAL 1   27
BREECHED
THAT HE MIGHT BE NOBLY BREECHED . . . .   440 WISDOM   13
BREED
TO BREED THE LIDLESS EYE THAT LOVES THE SUN? . . .   264 HOUSE SHAKEN   4
THAT SOME NEW DAY MAY BREED THE BEST . . . . . .   288 TO WEALTHY MAN   34

107

                                                           PAGE   TITLE   LINE

BREED (CONTINUED)
    THAT NONE OF ANOTHER BREED . . . .   583 GHOST ROG CASE   24
BREEDING   SEE WOLF-BREEDING
BREEDS
    LEST ALL THY TOILING ONLY BREEDS . . . .   66 HAPPY SHEPHERD   25
    THE COMMON BREEDS THE COMMON, ...   605 SONGS BURDEN 1   5
BREEZE
    BUT NOW A WANDERING LAND BREEZE CAME . . . . . .   13 OISIN 1   165
    AND HEARD THE MOURNFUL BREEZE. . . . .   123 DREAM OF DEATH V   12
    THE SOUTH BREEZE NOW IN DYING FEARS . . . . . .   655 ISLE STAT I 3   13
    HAD FELT THE ISLAND BREEZE, MY LORE . . . . . .   668 ISLE STAT II 3   55
    HAD LEFT THE ISLAND BREEZE, MY LORE . . . . . .   668 ISLE STAT II 3 V   55
BREEZES
    'TIS HERE THE ARROW FELL: THE BREEZES LAUGHED . . . .   657 ISLE STAT I 3   70
BRESSEL
    BRESSEL THE FISHERMAN . . . .   146 FISH   V T
BRETHREN
    AND CAME TO WHERE HIS BRETHREN STOOD, ...   730 PRIEST FAIRY   63
BREW   SEE HOME-BREW
BREWED
    BREWED' BY THE SEA-GODS, FROM HUGE CUPS THAT LAY . . .   41 OISIN 2   189
    BREWED OF THE SEA-GODS, FROM HUGE CUPS THAT LAY . . .   41 OISIN 2   V 189
    BREWED BY THE SEA GODS, FROM HUGE CUPS THAT LAY . . .   41 OISIN 2   V 189
    THAT SACRED GOBAN BREWED," HE CRIED . . . .   304 HOUR DAWN   V 50
BREWS
    TO HOLD THE SACRED STUFF HE BREWS . . . .   272 GREY ROCK   24
BRIAR
    I ADMIT THE BRIAR . . . .   532 FIRST CONFESS   1
BRIBE
    TO BRIBE OR THREAT: HABITS THAT MADE OLD WRONG . . .   428 NINETEEN 19   11
    THOSE BANNERS COME TO BRIBE OR THREATEN, ...   635 BLACK TOWER   11
BRIDE
    LIKE A BRIDE BENDING OVER HER MIRROR ADORNING, . . .   28 OISIN 1   V 423E
    THE STOLEN BRIDE . . . .   143 HOST OF AIR   V T
    OF BRIDGET HIS BRIDE. . . . .   144 HOST OF AIR   8
    AND BRIDGET HIS BRIDE AMONG THEM, ...   144 HOST OF AIR   15
    UNTIL ONE BORE BRIDGET HIS BRIDE . . . .   145 HOST OF AIR   31
    AND FLINGS HERSELF OUT OF THE ROOM WHEN JULIET WOULD BE 354 HIS PHOENIX   13
        BRIDE
    AND FLINGS HERSELF OUT OF THE ROOM WHEN JULIET WOULD BE 354 HIS PHOENIX   V 13
        A BRIDE
    THE BRIDE IS CARRIED TO THE BRIDEGROOM'S CHAMBER . . . . 459 FROM OEDIPUS   8
    "I HAVE BROUGHT A SLENDER BRIDE INTO THE HOUSE: . . .   463 HARUN RASHID   49
    YOU KNOW THE SAYING, "CHANGE THE BRIDE WITH SPRING," .   463 HARUN RASHID   50
    THINK WHEN I CHOOSE A BRIDE I CHOOSE FOR EVER: . . .   464 HARUN RASHID   80
    BY SOME NEW-MARRIED BRIDE, I TAKE . . . .   535 CHOSEN   13
    BY SOME NEW MARRIED BRIDE I TAKE . . . .   535 CHOSEN   V 13
    THOUGHT IS A GARMENT AND THE SOUL'S A BRIDE . . .   558 RIBH CHRISTIAN   16
    I, STARVED FOR THE BOSOM OF HIS FAERY BRIDE? . . .   629 CIRCUS ANIMALS   16
BRIDE-BED
    IN OWING THEM THE BRIDE-BED THAT GIVES PEACE." . . . .   187 QUEEN MAEVE   148
    MAYBE THE BRIDE-BED BRINGS DESPAIR, ...   388 SOLOMON WITCH   25
BRIDEGROOM
    AND MAY HER BRIDEGROOM BRING HER TO A HOUSE . . . . .   405 FOR DAUGHTER   73
BRIDE-GROOM
    AND MAY HER BRIDE-GROOM BRING HER TO A HOUSE . . . . .   405 FOR DAUGHTER   V 73
BRIDEGROOM'S
    THE BRIDE IS CARRIED TO THE BRIDEGROOM'S CHAMBER . . . . 459 FROM OEDIPUS   8
BRIDELESS
    ARE BRIDELESS." "I AM FALLING INTO YEARS." . . . . .   463 HARUN RASHID   54
BRIDE'S
    AND EVERY BRIDE'S AMBITION SATISFIED. . . . .   491 COOLE BALLYLEE   37
BRIDGE
    THAT CAST THEIR SHADOWS UPON ROAD AND BRIDGE: . . . .   326 ROBERT GREGORY   51
    AN OLD MAN COCKED HIS EAR UPON A BRIDGE: . . . . .   372 PHASES OF MOON   1
    WE ARE ON THE BRIDGE: THAT SHADOW IS THE TOWER, . . .   372 PHASES OF MOON   10
    AND UNDER THE ARCHES OF THE BRIDGE, AND SCREAM . . .   403 FOR DAUGHTER   11
    AN ANCIENT BRIDGE, AND A MORE ANCIENT TOWER, ...   419 MY HOUSE   1
    THE WOMEN-SLINGERS ON THE NARROW BRIDGE, ...   749 SHADOW WATER A   41
    A CAPTIVE WOMAN FROM THE NARROW BRIDGE, ...   749 SHADOW WATER A   49
    THE WOMEN SLINGERS ON THE NARROW BRIDGE, ...   749 SHADOW WATER A V   41
BRIDGET
    OF BRIDGET HIS BRIDE. . . . .   144 HOST OF AIR   8
    AND BRIDGET HIS BRIDE AMONG THEM, ...   144 HOST OF AIR   15
    BUT BRIDGET DREW HIM BY THE SLEEVE . . . .   144 HOST OF AIR   21
    UNTIL ONE BORE BRIDGET HIS BRIDE . . . .   145 HOST OF AIR   31
BRIDLE
    ON A HORSE WITH BRIDLE OF FINDRINNY: . . . . . .   3 OISIN 1   21
    IS THERE A BRIDLE FOR THIS PROTEUS . . . .   265 ABBEY THEATRE   11
BRIDLED
    AND FOUND THE HORSE AND BRIDLED HIM, ...   25 OISIN 1   378
BRIDLE-PATH
    MAKING WAY FROM THE KINDLING SURGES, I RODE ON A   58 OISIN 3   161
        BRIDLE-PATH
BRIEF
    BUT A BRIEF, DREAMY, KIND DELIGHT. . . . .   202 NEVER GIVE ALL   7
    FOR THAT BRIEF SIGHING. IF YOU HAD LOVED SOME WOMAN-- . 228 SHADOW WATER B   135
    LOVES IN BRIEF LONGING AND DECEIVING HOPE . . . .   228 SHADOW WATER B   146
    IS THAT WE GIVE, ALTHOUGH IT BE BRIEF GIVING, . . .   282 TWO KINGS   120
    FOR WHAT IS DOUBLY BRIEF." AND NOW THE SHAPE . . .   285 TWO KINGS   207
    FOR WHAT IS DOUBLY BRIEF." "BUT NOW THE SHAPE, . . .   285 TWO KINGS   V 207

BRIEF   (CONTINUED)
    BEFORE THAT BRIEF GLEAM OF ITS LIFE BE GONE, ... 430 NINETEEN 19   63
    A BRIEF PARTING FROM THOSE DEAR . . . . 637 BEN BULBEN   19
    AND TURN BRIEF LONGING AND DECEIVING HOPE . . . . . 750 SHADOW WATER A   59
    THAN IN BRIEF LONGING AND DECEIVING HOPE . . . . . 750 SHADOW WATER A   65
    IS BUT BRIEF LONGING, AND DECEIVING HOPE, ... 765 SHADOW WATER A   354
    THEIR BRIEF LIVES I NEVER KNEW. . . . . 787 HUDDON DUDDON   5
BRIGAND
    ALL THAT THE BRIGAND APPLE BROUGHT . . . . 388 SOLOMON WITCH   15
BRIGHT
    FOR BROOCH 'TWAS BOUND WITH A BRIGHT SEA-SHELL, . . . 4 OISIN 1   V   28
    KEPT TIME WITH THEIR BRIGHT WINGS AND FEET; . . . . 26 OISIN 1   397
    BEAT TIME WITH THEIR BRIGHT WINGS AND FEET. . . . . 26 OISIN 1   V   397
    AND KISSED MY EYES; AND, SWAYING HER BRIGHT HEAD . . 29 OISIN 2   6
    AND HER BRIGHT BODY, SANG OF FAERY AND MAN . . . . . 29 OISIN 2   7
    AND NOW SANG NIAM, SWAYING HER BRIGHT HEAD . . . . . 29 OISIN 2   V   6
    AND HER BRIGHT BODY--NOW OF FAY AND MAN; . . . . . 29 OISIN 2   V   7
    SO SANG YOUNG NIAM, SWAYING HER BRIGHT HEAD, ... 30 OISIN 2   V   15
    LIKE DRIFTS OF LEAVES, IMMOVABLE AND BRIGHT, ... 40 OISIN 2   166
    LIKE DRIFTS OF LAUREL LEAVES, IMMOVABLE AND BRIGHT . 40 OISIN 2   V   166
    AND BECAUSE I WENT BY THEM SO HUGH AND SO SPEEDY WITH EYES
       SO BRIGHT, ... 59 OISIN 3   169
    AND BEFORE I WENT BY THEM SO HUGE AND SO SPEEDY WITH EYES
       SO BRIGHT, ... 59 OISIN 3   V   169
    "WHAT DO YOU MAKE SO FAIR AND BRIGHT?" . . . . . . 69 CLOAK BOAT   1
    "WHAT DO YOU WEAVE SO SOFT AND BRIGHT?" . . . . . . 69 CLOAK BOAT   V   1
    "WHAT DO YOU WEAVE SO FAIR AND BRIGHT?" . . . . . . 69 CLOAK BOAT   V   1
    BY GOD TO THE BRIGHT HEARTS OF THOSE LONG DEAD, . . . 101 ROSE UPON ROOD   20
    SHINING BRIGHT AS A NEW LANCE; . . . . 125 CATHLEEN PARA   V   14
    "AND BROOD NO MORE WHERE THE FIRE IS BRIGHT . . . . 140 HOSTING SIDHE   V   5
    TILL PRIDE HAD MADE HER EYES GROW BRIGHT, ... 314 MEMORY YOUTH   10
    SHOWS THROUGH OUR LINEAMENTS. MY CANDLE'S BRIGHT, . . 464 HARUN RASHID   70
    AND IF HER EYE SHOULD NOT GROW BRIGHT FOR MINE . . . 464 HARUN RASHID   81
    THAT NEVER KNEW THAT STRAIN WOULD SCARCE SEEM BRIGHT, . 465 HARUN RASHID   88
    AND THE EYES MORE BRIGHT . . . . 531 BEFORE WORLD   2
    SLEEPILY CLOSE HER ROUND BRIGHT EYNE; . . . . . . 646 ISLE STAT I 1   35
    AND THINE EYES MORE BRIGHT THAN FAERY'S, ... 647 ISLE STAT I 1   53
    NASCHINA, WHEREFORE ARE YOUR EYES SO BRIGHT . . . . 650 ISLE STAT I 1   141
    WHAT DO YOU WEAVE SO FAIR AND BRIGHT? . . . . . . 666 ISLE STAT II 3   1
    THY SOUL SHALL BE, THOUGH PITILESS AND BRIGHT . . . 674 ISLE STAT II 3   210
    AND WHEREFORE SHOULD THY BRIGHT BROW ROAM . . . . . 686 LIFE   11
    BRIGHT ON A GRASS BLADE'S UNDER SIDE, MIGHT HEAR, . . 689 NETTLESHIP   10
    A LITTLE NEARER THOSE BRIGHT STARS. TELL ME, . . . 701 MOSADA 3   59
    WHILE O'ER THE BUDS, AND O'ER THE GRASS-BLADES, BRIGHT . 704 REMEMBRANCE   3
    OFTEN HE HAD BENT DOWN SOME BOUGH ALL BRIGHT . . . . 710 FERENCZ RENYI   28
    OFTEN HE HAD BENT DOWN SOME BOUGH ALL BRIGHT WITH BERRIES; 710 FERENCZ RENYI   V   28
    IT SEEMS TO FONDLE, WITH A FINGER BRIGHT . . . . . 714 FERENCZ RENYI   114
    CHECK. AH! HOW BRIGHT YOUR EYES. HOW SWIFT YOUR MOVES. 722 WITCH VIVIEN   61
    AND FOR HIM MAKE ME WISE AND BRIGHT. . . . . . . 723 GIRLS SONG A   12
    ARE TWO RAGGED CHILDREN BRIGHT-- . . . . 731 STREET DANCERS   4
    STORM DARKENED OR STARRY BRIGHT. . . . . 739 WHERE BOOKS GO   8
    THE DIM SPEAR MET THE BRIGHT SPEAR, ... 741 EARL PAUL   45
    AND MADE THE BRIGHT SPEAR BEND, ... 741 EARL PAUL   46
    THE DIM SPEAR BREAKS THE BRIGHT SHIELD . . . . . . 741 EARL PAUL   49
    THE DIM SPEAR MET THE BRIGHT SPEAR . . . . 741 EARL PAUL   V   49
BRIGHTEN
    OR BRIGHTEN ONLY FOR SOME YOUNGER EYE, ... 464 HARUN RASHID   82
BRIGHTENED
    OR EYES THAT RAGE HAS BRIGHTENED, ARMS IT HAS MADE LEAN, 427 PHANTOM HATRED   27
    OF EYES THAT RAGE HAS BRIGHTENED, ARMS IT HAS MADE LEAN, 427 PHANTOM HATRED V   27
BRIGHTENING
    AND FADED THROUGH THE BRIGHTENING AIR. . . . . . . 150 WANDER AENGUS   16
    SHE DREW IN THE BRIGHTENING CASEMENT. . . . . . . 159 CAP AND BELLS   V   11
    THE CLOUDS WERE BRIGHTENING WITH THE DAWN. . . . . . 307 HOUR DAWN   122
    O BODY SWAYED TO MUSIC, O BRIGHTENING GLANCE, ... 446 SCHOOL CHILDR   63
    O BODY SWAYED TO MUSIC BRIGHTENING GLANCE . . . . . 446 SCHOOL CHILDR   V   63
    MY THOUGHTS, AND YONDER BRIGHTENING PATCH OF SKY . . . 700 MOSADA 3   31
BRIGHTER
    BRIGHTNESS REMAINS; A BRIGHTER STAR SHOOTS DOWN; . . . 541 PARN FUNERAL 1   4
BRIGHT-EYED
    YONDER HE COMES; BRIGHT-EYED, AND HOLLOW-CHEEKED . . . 697 MOSADA 2   35
BRIGHTNESS
    OF MILKY BRIGHTNESS TO AND FRO . . . . 22 OISIN 1   328
    AND GAZES AROUND HER WITH EYES OF BRIGHTNESS; . . . . 27 OISIN 1   413
    AND GAZES AROUND HER WITH EYES OF BRIGHTNESS; . . . . 28 OISIN 1   V   421
    BUT THEY MISTOOK THE BRIGHTNESS OF THE MOON . . . . 411 TOWER   45
    BACK TURNED UPON THE BRIGHTNESS OF THE SUN . . . . . 489 COOLE PARK 29   30
    BRIGHTNESS THAT I PULL BACK . . . . 533 FIRST CONFESS   13
    BRIGHTNESS REMAINS; A BRIGHTER STAR SHOOTS DOWN; . . . 541 PARN FUNERAL 1   4
    AH! WOE FOR YOUR EYES AND THEIR BRIGHTNESS-- . . . . 708 FAIRY PEDANT   35
BRILLIANT
    THE BRILLIANT MOON AND ALL THE MILKY SKY, ... 119 SORROW OF LOVE   2
    I HAVE LOOKED UPON THOSE BRILLIANT CREATURES, ... 322 SWANS AT COOLE   13
    I HAVE LOOKED UPON THESE BRILLIANT CREATURES . . . . 322 SWANS AT COOLE V   13
    OF EVERY BRILLIANT EYE . . . . 416 TOWER   190
    BUT BRILLIANT AS THE NIGHT'S EMBROIDERY, ... 461 HARUN RASHID   7
    ONE DEAR BRILLIANT WOMAN; . . . . 504 RESULT THOUGHT   2
    A FAMOUS, A BRILLIANT FIGURE . . . . 608 SONGS BURDEN 3   16
BRIM
    MY HEART WOULD BRIM WITH DREAMS ABOUT THE TIMES . . . 136 TO SOME I TALK   2
    O HEAVY SWOLLEN WATERS, BRIM THE FALL OF THE OAK TREES, 207 HANRAHANS SONG V   11

		PAGE	TITLE		LINE
BRIM	(CONTINUED)				
	AND AFTER RUNNING AT THE BRIM • • • • • • • • •	254	HIS DREAM		9
	AND FISHES, BUBBLING TO THE BRIM, • • • • • • •	254	HIS DREAM	V	9
	A HORSE-HOOF SLIDES ON THE BRIM, • • • • • • • •	393	EASTER 1916		51
BRIMFUL					
	BRIMFUL OF STARLIGHT, AND HE SAID: THE STAMPER OF THE SKIES,	76	INDIAN ON GOD		14
BRIMMED					
	THAT WAS BRIMMED UP WITH PRAYER AND REST: • • • • •	151	HEART OF WOMAN		2
	THAT IS BRIMMED FROM THE PALE FIRE OF TIME: • • • •	157	POET BELOVED		6
	BEING ALL BRIMMED WITH LIFE?" "WERE IT BUT TRUE • • •	465	HARUN RASHID		90
	BEING SO BRIMMED WITH LIFE. "IF THAT COULD BE • • •	465	HARUN RASHID	V	90
	AND TWO LONG GLASSES BRIMMED WITH MUSCATEL • • • •	470	ALL SOUL NIGHT		4
BRIMMING					
	UPON THE BRIMMING WATER AMONG THE STONES • • • • •	322	SWANS AT COOLE		5
	IN THAT MYSTERIOUS, ALWAYS BRIMMING LAKE • • • • •	356	BROKEN DREAMS		32
BRING					
	OF THE YOUNG. "YOUNG MAIDEN, WHAT MAY BRING • • • •	5	OISIN 1	V	50
	O WORN DEED-DOER." "WHAT MAY BRING • • • • • • • •	5	OISIN 1	V	50
	SHE BADE THEM BRING US TO THE HALL • • • • • • •	16	OISIN 1		217
	"I BRING DELIVERANCE," PEARL-PALE NIAMH SAID. • • • •	34	OISIN 2		78
	"I BRING THEE A DELIVERER FROM FAR AWAY, • • • • •	34	OISIN 2	V	78A
	BRING WHAT IS THERE TO BRING: • • • • • • • • • •	97	FOXHUNTER		6
	BRING WHAT IS THERE TO BRING: • • • • • • • • • •	97	FOXHUNTER		6
	BRING RODY AND HIS HOUNDS, • • • • • • • • • • •	97	FOXHUNTER		10
	AND SOME ONE FROM THE STABLE BRING • • • • • • • •	97	FOXHUNTER		5
	AND SOME ONE FROM THE STABLES BRING • • • • • • •	97	FOXHUNTER	V	5
	BRING MY BROWN HUNTER NEAR, • • • • • • • • • •	97	FOXHUNTER	V	6
	BRING HOUND AND HUNTSMAN HERE," • • • • • • • • •	97	FOXHUNTER	V	10
	HAS WON THE GOLD HIS CARS OF BATTLE BRING." • • • •	106	CUCHULAIN SEA		11
	AT THE SWORD POINT, AND BADE ME BRING HIM ONE • • •	109	CUCHULAIN SEA	V	53
	THAT HE'S A LOVELESS MAN: GAY BELLS BRING LAUGHTER • •	130	BOOK STORIES		18
	GAY BELLS OR SAD, THEY BRING YOU MEMORIES • • • • •	130	BOOK STORIES		21
	MY BELL BRANCH MURMURS: THE GAY BELLS BRING LAUGHTER, • •	130	BOOK STORIES	V	18
	THEY BRING YOU MEMORIES OF OLD VILLAGE FACES, • • • •	130	BOOK STORIES	V	22
	I BRING YOU WITH REVERENT HANDS • • • • • • • • •	157	POET BELOVED		1
	I BRING YOU MY PASSIONATE RHYME. • • • • • • • • •	157	POET BELOVED		8
	"I CAN BRING YOU SALMON OUT OF THE STREAMS • • • • •	167	BLESSED		9
	AND BRING US INTO POPULOUS SEAS AGAIN? • • • • • •	225	SHADOW WATER B		74
	BRING MADNESS? QUEEN, I AM NOT MAD. YET SAY • • •	236	SHADOW WATER B		316
	AND MEASURE OUT A COURSE AND BRING US HOME, • • • •	238	SHADOW WATER B		362
	AND THAT YOU'LL BRING ME THERE? I HAVE DECEIVED YOU: • •	245	SHADOW WATER B		471
	TO FANCY THAT SHE'D BRING YOU HOME AGAIN. • • • • •	248	SHADOW WATER B		549
	FOR HE WILL SHELTER YOU AND BRING YOU HOME. • • • •	250	SHADOW WATER B		590
	PLEASURE ITSELF CAN BRING NO WEARINESS. • • • • • •	284	TWO KINGS		181
	AND DO NOT KNOW THAT YOU WOULD BRING, • • • • • •	306	HOUR DAWN		93
	BRING ROSES IF THE ROSE BE YET IN BLOOM: • • • • •	311	MOUNTAIN TOMB		2
	PULL DOWN THE BLINDS: BRING FIDDLE AND CLARIONET • • •	311	MOUNTAIN TOMB		5
	I HAD THE WISDOM LOVE CAN BRING, • • • • • • • • •	313	MEMORY YOUTH	V	2
	FOR WHAT PROUD DEATH MAY BRING • • • • • • • • •	317	NIGHT COME		3
	THE MAN AND THE WOMAN BRING • • • • • • • • • •	319	DOLLS		10
	BUT NOT A FRIEND THAT I WOULD BRING • • • • • • •	324	ROBERT GREGORY		14
	NO LIKELY END COULD BRING THEM LOSS • • • • • • •	328	IRISH AIRMAN		7
	BRING THE BALLOON OF THE MIND • • • • • • • • • •	358	BALLOON MIND		2
	CERTAIN ARTISTS BRING HER DOLLS AND DRAWINGS • • • •	362	DOLLS DRAWINGS		T
	BRING WHERE OUR BEAUTY LIES • • • • • • • • • •	362	DOLLS DRAWINGS		T
	HER FRIENDS BRING HER A CHRISTMAS TREE • • • • • •	366	HER CHRIS TREE		T
	HER FRIENDS BRING HER A CHRISTMAS-TREE • • • • • •	366	HER CHRIS TREE	V	T
	THAT ANY NIGHT COULD BRING • • • • • • • • • •	390	IMAGE PAST		32
	AND MAY HER BRIDEGROOM BRING HER TO A HOUSE • • • •	405	FOR DAUGHTER		73
	AND MAY HER BRIDE-GROOM BRING HER TO A HOUSE • • • •	405	FOR DAUGHTER	V	73
	AND BRING BEAUTY'S BLIND RAMBLING CELEBRANT: • • • •	412	TOWER		91
	BRING UP OUT OF THAT DEEP CONSIDERING MIND • • • • •	413	TOWER		106
	THE MOTHER BIRDS BRING GRUBS AND FLIES. • • • • • •	424	STARES NEST		3
	AND PLANNED TO BRING THE WORLD UNDER A RULE, • • • •	429	NINETEEN 19		31
	THAT IMAGE CAN BRING WILDNESS, BRING A RAGE • • • •	431	NINETEEN 19		80
	THAT IMAGE CAN BRING WILDNESS, BRING A RAGE • • • •	431	NINETEEN 19		80
	BRING THAT TO NOUGHT. • • • • • • • • • • • • •	436	FOR MY SON		16
	I BRING FULL-FLAVOURED WINE OUT OF A BARREL FOUND • •	442	BLACK CENTAUR		10
	I BRING FULL FLAVOURED WINE OUT OF A BARREL FOUND • •	442	BLACK CENTAUR	V	10
	AND PRIDE BRING IN IMPURITY: • • • • • • • • • •	460	THREE MONUMENT		11
	NOTHING COULD BRING HIM, WHEN HIS LADY DIED, • • • •	471	ALL SOUL NIGHT		25
	BRING ME TO THE BLASTED OAK. • • • • • • • • • •	507	JANE BISHOP		1
	HATRED OF GOD MAY BRING THE SOUL TO GOD. • • • • •	558	RIBH CHRISTIAN		18
	AND I AM IN DESPAIR THAT TIME MAY BRING • • • • • •	602	GALLERY REVIS		30
	THAT PASSION COULD BRING CHARACTER ENOUGH, • • • • •	610	STATUES		6
	BRING THE SOUL OF MAN TO GOD, • • • • • • • • • •	638	BEN BULBEN		40
	I'LL BRING THAT FLOWER TO HER, AND SO MAY EARN • • •	653	ISLE STAT I 2		45
	AND SHOREWARD WAVES, WE NIGH HAVE FOUGHT: WAVES BRING •	660	ISLE STAT II 1		44
	THE ARCADIANS BRING, AND BID THE STONE BE RAISED • •	663	ISLE STAT II 2		25
	THAT SHEPHERDESS: ARISE, AND BRING TO ME: • • • • •	673	ISLE STAT II 3		191
	FOR THIS DID THE ETERNAL DARKNESS BRING • • • • • •	688	TWO TITANS		51
	I SAW HIS JOVIAL MOOD BRING ONCE A SMILE • • • • •	696	MOSADA 2		14
	OH, CAN MY KISSES BRING A FLUSH NO MORE • • • • • •	701	MOSADA 3		71
	AFRAID TO BE TOO FAR." "AY, BRING HER HERE!" • • • •	712	FERENCZ RENYI		69
	THAT MAIDEN BRING THEY. WHEN THE TALL RED DEER • • •	713	FERENCZ RENYI		79
	"BRING THE ROPES NOW! STAND YE BY NOW! • • • • • •	718	PHANTOM SHIP		13
	I DO NOT NEED YOUR SCYTHE. MAY THAT BRING PEACE • • •	721	WITCH VIVIEN		26
	WE WILL BRING A CROWN OF GOLD, • • • • • • • • •	726	LOVERS QUARREL		13
	MEN CRY "BRING PAUL, SHIELD BREAKER, • • • • • • •	740	EARL PAUL		11
	"GO BRING ME MY OLD ARMOUR • • • • • • • • • • •	740	EARL PAUL		19

110

		PAGE	TITLE		LINE
BRING	**(CONTINUED)**				
	MEN CRY: "BRING PAUL, SHIELD-BREAKER, ...	740	EARL PAUL	V	11
	GO BRING ME MY OWN ARMOUR	740	EARL PAUL	V	19
	AND TURN HIS GALLEY ABOUT AND BRING ME HOME.	751	SHADOW WATER A		108
	AND BRING HER TO HER KINGDOM AND HER PEOPLE.	755	SHADOW WATER A		170
	WE BRING YOU THIS GREAT QUEEN.	755	SHADOW WATER A	V	166
	AND BRING ME TO MY PEOPLE. I PROMISED THESE	756	SHADOW WATER A	V	185
	AND BRING ME WHERE THE CHILDREN OF AENGUS WIND . . .	763	SHADOW WATER A		317
	THAT THE VAST TROUBLED WATERS BRING	784	WOMANS BEAUTY		17
BRINGING					
	BRINGING ME HONEYED, WANDERING THOUGHT	7	OISIN 1	V	65
	SHEEP-GUIDING, OR THE BRINGING SOME STRANGE BIRD, . . .	650	ISLE STAT I 1		147
BRINGS					
	IT BRINGS NO SHAME UPON A HUMAN HEAD	35	OISIN 2	V	90A
	"HE BRINGS THE PEACEFUL AGE OF GOLD"--	82	MAD KING GOLL	V	11
	"THIS YOUNG MAN BRINGS THE AGE OF GOLD."	82	MAD KING GOLL	V	11
	NOR WON THE GOLD THAT NOW CUCHULAIN BRINGS."	106	CUCHULAIN SEA	V	11
	BECAUSE YOUR CRYING BRINGS TO MY MIND	155	REPROVE CURLEW		3
	KNOWING THAT SILENCE BRINGS NO GOOD TO KINGS, ...	279	TWO KINGS		57
	I HAD THE WISDOM LOVE BRINGS FORTH:	313	MEMORY YOUTH		2
	IS DEAD. THE BOY THAT BRINGS MY GRIDDLE-CAKE	339	SHEP GOATHERD		20
	IS DEAD. THE BOY THAT BRINGS MY GRIDDLE CAKE	339	SHEP GOATHERD	V	20
	BRINGS ME TO BIRTH AGAIN--	346	ON WOMAN		32
	MAYBE THE BRIDE-BED BRINGS DESPAIR, ...	388	SOLOMON WITCH		25
	FOR EACH AN IMAGINED IMAGE BRINGS	388	SOLOMON WITCH		26
	AND THAT MERE GROWING OLD, THAT BRINGS	401	DEMON BEAST		38
	THAT BRINGS MORE BLOSSOM TO AUTUMNAL CHILL	465	HARUN RASHID	V	104
	BRINGS SUCH SATISFACTION	533	FIRST CONFESS		11
	THAT DAY BRINGS ROUND THE NIGHT, THAT BEFORE DAWN . .	563	MERU		13
	THE BROWN WEED BURDEN, SO THE SWORD BRINGS FEAR . . .	660	ISLE STAT II 1		45
	HE DIGS HIS CABBAGES. HE BRINGS TO MIND	696	MOSADA 2		18
	HALF HID. HE BRINGS THE PEASANT'S ONLY KIN, ...	711	FERENCZ RENYI		50
	ACCURSED WHO BRINGS TO LIGHT OF DAY	779	ACCURSED WHO		1
BRINK					
	UPON THE STARRY BRINK.	216	HAPPY TOWNLAND		52
	TO EASE THEIR WORLD-OLD THIRST ALONG THE BRINK . . .	663	ISLE STAT II 2		41
BRISTLES					
	I WOULD THAT THE BOAR WITHOUT BRISTLES HAD COME FROM THE WEST	153	CHANGE BELOVED		10
BRITAIN					
	WHAT NAME HAD THAT DEAD KING? ARTHUR OF BRITAIN? . .	242	SHADOW WATER B		404
BRITISH					
	UPON THE BRITISH EMPIRE, ...	583	GHOST ROG CASE		17
BRITTLE					
	AS DANCE UPON THE SPEAR-GRASS BRITTLE, ...	731	PRIEST FAIRY		78
BROACHED					
	"IF YOU HAD BROACHED A MATTER	333	SOLOMON SHEBA		11
BROAD					
	ON CREVROE OR BROAD KNOCKFEFIN, WITH MANY OF OLD THEY FEAST	59	OISIN 3		179
	ON CREVROE OR ON BROAD KNOCKFEFIN, WITH MANY OF OLD THEY FAST	59	OISIN 3	V	179
	BY A BROAD WATER-LILY LEAF:	195	BAILE AILLINN		146
	THAT BROAD NOON HAS NEVER LIT, ...	632	MAN AND ECHO		4
	ON HER BROAD BREAST: BENEATH HER WITHERED BROWS . . .	685	SEEKER		73
	DANCING ON THE MOON'S BROAD STAIN.	731	STREET DANCERS		15
	YE ON THE BROAD HIGH MOUNTAINS OF OLD ERI, ...	737	MOURN THEN ON		1
BROKE					
	AND BROKE THE HEAVING RANKS OF BATTLE:	10	OISIN 1		124
	. . . FROM THE FOAM-PALE DISTANCE BROKE:	47	OISIN 3		3
	. . . FROM THE DISTANCE BROKE:	47	OISIN 3	V	3
	AND BROKE BETWEEN MY HANDS THE STAFF	84	MAD KING GOLL	V	33
	AND THROUGH THAT NEW BLADE'S GUARD THE OLD BLADE BROKE,	110	CUCHULAIN SEA		66
	AND THROUGH THE OTHER'S SHIELD HIS LONG BLADE BROKE, . .	110	CUCHULAIN SEA	V	66
	BROKE FROM HIS PARTED LIPS AND BROKE AGAIN, ...	182	QUEEN MAEVE		48
	BROKE FROM HIS PARTED LIPS AND BROKE AGAIN, ...	182	QUEEN MAEVE		48
	BEFORE HER LOVE-WORN HEART HAD BROKE, ...	194	BAILE AILLINN		127
	ABOUT THE STARS AND BROKE IN DAYS AND YEARS.	206	ADAMS CURSE		33
	ABOUT THE STARN AND BROKE IN DAYS AND YEARS.	206	ADAMS CURSE	V	33
	A SHELTER TILL THE DAYLIGHT BROKE.	302	HOUR DAWN		15
	WHO BROKE MY HEART FOR HER	336	YOUNG GIRL		6
	I TURNED ABOUT AND LOOKED WHERE BRANCHES BROKE . . .	490	COOLE BALLYLEE	V	15
	I BROKE MY HEART IN TWO	518	HIS CONFIDENCE		7
	AND BROKE THE CHAIN AND SET MY ANKLES FREE, ...	533	HER TRIUMPH		9
BROKEN	**SEE WIND-BROKEN STORM-BROKEN**				
	OF BATTLES BROKEN BY HIS HANDS, ...	7	OISIN 1		67
	WHERE BROKEN FAITH HAS NEVER BEEN KNOWN, ...	8	OISIN 1		84
	FROM SOME DEAD WARRIOR'S BROKEN LANCE:	24	OISIN 1		367
	AND DEMONS BE BROKEN IN PIECES, AND TRAMPLED BENEATH THEM IN DEATH.	61	OISIN 3		204
	AND DEMONS, ALL BROKEN IN PIECES, BE TRAMPLED BENEATH THEM IN DEATH.	61	OISIN 3	V	204
	AH ME! TO BE SHAKEN WITH COUGHING AND BROKEN WITH OLD AGE AND PAIN,	63	OISIN 3		217
	UNDER A BROKEN TREE	131	OLD PENSIONER		2
	UPON A BROKEN TREE, ...	131	OLD PENSIONER		14
	BROKEN BOUGHS AND BLACKENED LEAVES.	135	TWO TREES		28
	THERE, THROUGH THE BROKEN BRANCHES, GO	135	TWO TREES		33
	WITH BROKEN BOUGHS AND BLACKENED LEAVES	135	TWO TREES	V	26
	ALL THINGS UNCOMELY AND BROKEN, ALL THINGS WORN OUT AND OLD,	142	ROSE IN HEART		1
	ALL THINGS UNCOMELY AND BROKEN, ALL THINGS WORN AND OLD,	142	ROSE IN HEART	V	1

	PAGE	TITLE	LINE
BROKEN (CONTINUED)			
BECAUSE EARTH, CRAZY FOR ITS BROKEN POWER,	186	QUEEN MAEVE	124
ARE TRODDEN AND BROKEN BY THE HERDS,	190	BAILE AILLINN	43
BAILE'S HEART WAS BROKEN IN TWO:	192	BAILE AILLINN	70
WANDERING FROM BROKEN STREET TO STREET	196	BAILE AILLINN	167
WAKE ALL BELOW! WHY HAVE YOU BROKEN OUR SLEEP?	233	SHADOW WATER B	242
THE YEW-BOUGH HAS BEEN BROKEN INTO TWO,	241	SHADOW WATER B	394
THE YEW BOUGH HAS BEEN BROKEN INTO TWO,	241	SHADOW WATER B V	394
LET THE BIRDS SCATTER, FOR THE TREE IS BROKEN,	250	SHADOW WATER B	584
THE YEW-BOUGH HAS BEEN BROKEN INTO TWO,	251	SHADOW WATER B	593
YOU ARE BROKEN, YOU ARE BROKEN. THE WORLD DRIFTS AWAY,	251	SHADOW WATER B	599
YOU ARE BROKEN, YOU ARE BROKEN. THE WORLD DRIFTS AWAY,	251	SHADOW WATER B	599
THE YEW BOUGH HAS BEEN BROKEN INTO TWO,	251	SHADOW WATER B V	593
THE YEW BOUGH HAS BEEN BROKEN IN TWO,	251	SHADOW WATER B V	593
BE AS BROKEN IN THE END.	313	TWO YEAR LATER	10
I TOOK A BROKEN ROOT TO FLING	317	APPOINTMENT	2
AND SCATTER WHEELING IN GREAT BROKEN RINGS	322	SWANS AT COOLE	11
"IT'S CERTAIN THAT MY LUCK IS BROKEN,"	332	ROUND TOWER	25
IN THE BROKEN MIST	349	HAWK	11
BROKEN DREAMS	355	BROKEN DREAMS	T
WILL SCARCELY FIND FOR HIM A BROKEN CRUST	373	PHASES OF MOON	23
AND HAD BUT BROKEN KNEES FOR HIRE	411	TOWER	62
TILL IT WAS BROKEN BY	416	TOWER	179
A PEAR-TREE BROKEN BY THE STORM.	424	ROAD AT DOOR	10
A PEAR TREE BROKEN BY THE STORM.	424	ROAD AT DOOR V	10
I CLIMB TO THE TOWER-TOP AND LEAN UPON BROKEN STONE,	425	PHANTOM HATRED	1
I CLIMB TO THE TOWER TOP AND LEAN UPON BROKEN STONE,	425	PHANTOM HATRED V	1
THE BROKEN WALL, THE BURNING ROOF AND TOWER	441	LEDA AND SWAN	10
UNDER A BROKEN TREE.	452	HUMAN DIGNITY	8
AND BODIES BROKEN LIKE A THORN	454	HIS MEMORIES	3
FORGET ITS BROKEN TOYS	473	ALL SOUL NIGHT	59
UPON THE BROKEN, CRUMBLING BATTLEMENT,	477	SELF AND SOUL	3
AND SAPLINGS ROOT AMONG THE BROKEN STONE,	489	COOLE PARK 29	28
THOUGH SOMEWHAT BROKEN BY THE LEAVES, THAT LIGHT	555	RIBH AT TOMB	25
IN BROKEN SENTENCES. MY SOUL HAD FOUND	557	RIBH ECSTASY	3
FROM MARBLE OF A BROKEN SEPULCHRE,	565	GYRES	20
HER KNEE-CAP BROKEN, THAT GIRL I DECLARE	578	CRAZED GIRL	6
HER KNEE CAP BROKEN! THAT GIRL I DECLARE	578	CRAZED GIRL V	6
MAYBE AT LAST, BEING BUT A BROKEN MAN,	629	CIRCUS ANIMALS	3
OLD KETTLES, OLD BOTTLES, AND A BROKEN CAN,	630	CIRCUS ANIMALS	36
UNDER BROKEN STONE I HALT	632	MAN AND ECHO	2
WAS BROKEN IN HIS QUIVERING HAND.	671	ISLE STAT II 3	126
AS MOTHS WITH BROKEN WINGS, AND AS WE SIT	671	ISLE STAT II 3	142
MINE HEART-STRINGS ARE ALL BROKEN SAVING ONE,	684	SEEKER V	69B
WAKE ALL BELOW. WHY HAVE YOU BROKEN OUR SLEEP?	753	SHADOW WATER A	132
O SCENT OF THE BROKEN APPLES!	774	COME RIDE	14
TO THE LOUD SANDS BEFORE DAY HAS BROKEN.	784	WOMANS BEAUTY	18
AMID THE DARK BEFORE DAY HAD BROKEN.	784	WOMANS BEAUTY	20
BROKENHEARTED			
BROKENHEARTED, HAVING LOST HIS QUEEN	242	SHADOW WATER B V	407
BROKEN-HEARTED			
BROKEN-HEARTED, HAVING LOST HIS QUEEN	242	SHADOW WATER B	407
MATCHING OUR BROKEN-HEARTED WIT AGAINST HER WIT,	362	HER COURTESY	7
BRONZE			
. . . WITH BRONZE AND SILVER AND GOLD,	49	OISIN 3	32
BETWEEN THE WALLS COVERED WITH BEATEN BRONZE,	180	QUEEN MAEVE	10
THE POSTS OF POLISHED YEW, CIRCLED WITH BRONZE,	279	TWO KINGS	48
IN BRONZE, OR THAT IN DAZZLING MARBLE APPEARS,	334	LIVING BEAUTY	5
FOR ALL ITS BRONZE AND MARBLE, 'S BUT A MOUSE.	418	ANCEST HOUSES	24
AMID THE ORNAMENTAL BRONZE AND STONE	428	NINETEEN 19	5
BUT KEEP A MARBLE OR A BRONZE REPOSE.	445	SCHOOL CHILDR	52
WHO HANDLED MARBLE AS IF IT WERE BRONZE,	566	LAPIS LAZULI	30
IN MARBLE OR IN BRONZE, LACKED CHARACTER.	610	STATUES	3
A BRONZE HEAD	618	BRONZE HEAD	T
HERE AT RIGHT OF THE ENTRANCE THIS BRONZE HEAD,	618	BRONZE HEAD	1
BRONZED			
BRONZED PEACOCK FEATHERS, RED COMBS OF HER COCKS.	433	NINETEEN 19	130
BRONZE-RINGED			
ROSE ROUND THE WALLS, AND THROUGH THE BRONZE-RINGED DOOR	286	TWO KINGS	215
BROOCH			
FOR BROOCH 'TWAS BOUND WITH A BRIGHT SEA-SHELL,	4	OISIN 1 V	28
WITH THE PIN OF A BROOCH,	344	DAWN	4
BROOD			
SPAKE THUS: "CUCHULAIN WILL DWELL THERE AND BROOD	110	CUCHULAIN SEA	77
AND CRIED, "CUCHULLIN WILL DWELL THERE AND BROOD,	110	CUCHULAIN SEA V	77
AND BROOD ON HOPES AND FEAR NO MORE.	125	GOES FERGUS	6
AND NO MORE TURN ASIDE AND BROOD	125	GOES FERGUS	7
AND BROOD ON HOPES AND FEARS NO MORE.	125	GOES FERGUS V	6
AND MAY THE THOUGHTS OF IRELAND BROOD	138	TO IRELAND	15
AND STILL THE THOUGHTS OF IRELAND BROOD,	138	TO IRELAND V	15
"AND BROOD NO MORE WHERE THE FIRE IS BRIGHT	140	HOSTING SIDHE V	5
BROOD HER HIGH LONELY MYSTERIES,	156	FORGOT BEAUTY	24
AND BY THE UNLABOURING BROOD OF THE SKIES!	164	PERFECT BEAUTY	5
HAVE WRONG TO BROOD UPON--ENOUGH OF THAT,	444	SCHOOL CHILDR V	30
IN BEAUTY'S MURDEROUS BROOD.	451	FIRST LOVE	2
AND ROVE UNCEASING ROUND THEIR DREADFUL BROOD.	681	SEEKER	5
AND TRAILING CRIMSON VANS, A MUMBLING BROOD,	687	TWO TITANS	20
WHY THEY WHO WILL THE HIGHEST SOMETIMES BROOD,	711	FERENCZ RENYI	34
MAYBE NOW A BEDOUIN'S BROOD;	732	STREET DANCERS	40
MINE WHERE WATERS BROOD AND TOSS!	744	ROSY CROSS	7

112

BROODED
    BROODED UPON SANCTITY . . . . 324 ROBERT GREGORY   20
BROODING
    IN BROODING MEMORY, NOR WEEP. . . . . 11 OISIN 1   V 131B
    BROODING NO MORE UPON GOD'S WARS . . . . 113 ROSE OF PEACE   5
    OF SERAPHS, BROODING, EACH ALONE, ... 156 FORGOT BEAUTY   V 22
    WHERE GODS ARE BROODING IN A MOUNTAINOUS PLACE . . . . 757 SHADOW WATER A   198
BROODS
    AND SANG UNTO THE STARRY BROODS. . . . . 22 OISIN 1   326
    AND BY THE HEAVEN'S ALL-LABOURING BROODS! . . . . . 164 PERFECT BEAUTY V   5
    AND BY THE HEAVEN'S UN-LABOURING BROODS! . . . . . 164 PERFECT BEAUTY V   5
    THE FAERY BLOSSOM BROODS UPON THY LIPS. . . . . 678 ISLE STAT II 3   306
BROOK
    AND YOUNG HARES BROOK MY HARMLESS HOLD-- . . . 84 MAD KING GOLL   V 47
    THE FALLING HAWTHORN BLOOM. BY MERE AND BROOK . . . 677 ISLE STAT II 3   279
BROOM
    MAKE CLEAN AS A BROOM CLEANS, ... 62 OISIN 3   211
BROOM-STICKS
    FOR ALL THEIR BROOM-STICKS AND THEIR TEARS, ... 343 DEJECTION   5
BROTHER
    EACH ONE WOVEN TO HIS BROTHER . . . . 22 OISIN 1   335
    IN THE HOUSE OF A CHILD, OF A FRIEND, OF A BROTHER. . . . 26 OISIN 1   401
    IN THE HOUSE OF HIS FRIEND, OF HIS KIN, OF HIS BROTHER, 26 OISIN 1   V 405
    TRUE BROTHER OF A COMPANY . . . . 137 TO IRELAND   2
    TRUE BROTHER OF THAT COMPANY . . . . 137 TO IRELAND   V 2
    MY BROTHER IN MOCHARABUIEE. . . . . 178 FIDDLER DOONEY   4
    I PASSED MY BROTHER AND COUSIN! . . . . 178 FIDDLER DOONEY   5
    MY BROTHER IS PRIEST OF KILBARNET, ... 178 FIDDLER DOONEY V   3
    MY BROTHER IS PRIEST IN KILVARNET, ... 178 FIDDLER DOONEY V   3
    "YOU BROUGHT ME WHERE YOUR BROTHER ARDAN SAT . . . 280 TWO KINGS   79
    AND THANKED HER FOR HER KINDNESS TO HIS BROTHER, . . . 286 TWO KINGS   212
    AND IN THE MIDST KING EOCHAID'S BROTHER STOOD, . . . 286 TWO KINGS   217
    "I THANK YOU FOR YOUR KINDNESS TO MY BROTHER, . . . 286 TWO KINGS   V 212
    MY BROTHER MOURTEEN IS WORN OUT . . . . . . 301 RUN PARADISE   8
    BROTHER AND BROTHER, FRIEND AND FRIEND, ... 540 FROM ANTIGONE   10
    BROTHER AND BROTHER, FRIEND AND FRIEND, ... 540 FROM ANTIGONE   10
    JOY'S BROTHER, FEAR, DWELLS EVER IN EACH BREAST-- . . . 651 ISLE STAT I 1   155
    JOY'S BROTHER, FEAR, LURKS IN EACH LEAFY WAY. . . . 651 ISLE STAT I 1   156
    HARK! HE'S DEAD--MY DROWSY BROTHER, ... 656 ISLE STAT I 3   18
    O BROTHER, LAY THY FLUTE UPON THY LIPS! . . . . 681 SEEKER   6
    STAR-ENVIOUS. HE WAS A SPIRIT, BROTHER. . . . . 683 SEEKER   39
    WHERE IS OUR BROTHER PETER? WHEN YOU'RE NIGH, . . . 696 MOSADA 2   12
    HE LOVES OUR BROTHER PETER IN HIS HEART. . . . . 696 MOSADA 2   16
    SEE YOU, BROTHER, CRANBERRY FRUIT-- . . . . . 727 LOVERS QUARREL   25
    LIKE BROTHER TO BROTHER, ... 769 BLOOD BOND   2
    LIKE BROTHER TO BROTHER, ... 769 BLOOD BOND   2
BROTHERHOOD
    AND DIE A PEARLY BROTHERHOOD! . . . . 66 HAPPY SHEPHERD   42
    FOR RUTH AND JOY HAVE BROTHERHOOD, ... 66 HAPPY SHEPHERD V   42
    FOR THERE THE MYSTICAL BROTHERHOOD . . . . . . 148 INTO TWILIGHT   10
    FOR THERE LIVE THE MYSTIC BROTHERHOOD . . . . . 148 INTO TWILIGHT   V 10
BROTHER'S
    WITH HER DEAD BROTHER'S VALOUR . . . . 365 HER RACE   11
BROTHERS
    TO JOIN HIS BROTHERS IN THE HOME OF YEARS . . . 30 OISIN 2   V 17
    "MY BROTHERS SPRING OUT OF THEIR BEDS AT MORN, . . . 32 OISIN 2   51
    "MY BROTHERS AND MY SISTERS LIVE AND THRIVE, . . . 32 OISIN 2   V 50C
    CIRCLING THE BRAIN? MY BROTHERS WILL PASS DOWN . . . 699 MOSADA 3   6
    THE BRAIN. MY BROTHERS WILL BE PASSING DOWN . . . 699 MOSADA 3   V 6
    CIRCLING THE BRAIN? MY BROTHERS NOW PASS DOWN . . . 699 MOSADA 3   V 6
BROUGHT
    UNTIL THE DANAAN POETS BROUGHT . . . . 7 OISIN 1   63
    LOVE, TILL THE DANAAN POETS BROUGHT . . . . . . 7 OISIN 1   V 63
    I NE'ER LOVED ANY TILL SONG BROUGHT ME . . . . . 7 OISIN 1   V 69
    WHO BROUGHT US FOUND A TORCH, AND, WITH ITS FLARE . . . 37 OISIN 2   V 122
    HOPING AND FEARING, BROUGHT ME WINE AND BREAD. . . . 41 OISIN 2   V 184A
    VIJAYA, I HAVE BROUGHT MY EVENING RICE! . . . . . 72 ANASHU VIJAYA   23
    AND A YOUNG MAN BROUGHT HIM RED WINE . . . . . 144 HOST OF AIR   19
    IF HE HAD BROUGHT US AMONG PEOPLED SEAS, ... 225 SHADOW WATER B V 68C
    WHERE DO YOU COME FROM? WHO BROUGHT YOU TO THIS PLACE? 235 SHADOW WATER B   284
    YOU DID NOT KNOW WHAT BROUGHT HIM TO HIS END, . . . 240 SHADOW WATER B   382
    I DREAM THAT I HAVE BROUGHT . . . . 255 WOMAN HOMER   10
    SICKNESS BROUGHT ME THIS . . . . 267 FRIEND ILLNESS   1
    BY THE ANCIENT HOLY HANDS THAT BROUGHT THEM . . . 271 GREY ROCK   V 21
    "YOU BROUGHT ME WHERE YOUR BROTHER ARDAN SAT . . . 280 TWO KINGS   79
    OF YOUR OWN PASSIONATE SERVING KIND WHO HAD BROUGHT . 292 TO A SHADE   10
    OF YOUR OWN PASSIONATE SERVING KIND WHO HAS BROUGHT . 292 TO A SHADE   V 10
    AND WHEN THE SECOND TWILIGHT BROUGHT . . . . . 296 THREE BEGGARS   42
    I HAD BEEN HURT!; AND TOPPLING BROUGHT . . . . . 302 HOUR DAWN   19
    "WHEN I WAS BROUGHT TO BED," . . . . 308 PLAYER QUEEN   6
    TO BE BROUGHT . . . . 310 WITCH   5
    A LONG BLAST UPON THE HORN THAT BROUGHT . . . . 324 ROBERT GREGORY   22
    THAT SHAKES THE SHUTTER, TO HAVE BROUGHT TO MIND . . . 327 ROBERT GREGORY   90
    UNTIL IMAGINATION BROUGHT . . . . 328 ROBERT GREGORY   94
    I BALANCED ALL, BROUGHT ALL TO MIND, ... 328 IRISH AIRMAN   13
    LET THE YOUNG WISH. BUT WHAT HAS BROUGHT YOU HERE? . . 339 SHEP GOATHERD   6
    BROUGHT THE BARE NEWS. HE HAD THROWN THE CROOK AWAY . 339 SHEP GOATHERD   21
    LESS BITTER. THEY HAVE BROUGHT ME FROM THAT RIDGE . . 342 SHEP GOATHERD   87
    THAT COVERS ALL HE HAS BROUGHT . . . . 345 ON WOMAN   5
    AND NO KNAVE BROUGHT TO BOOK . . . . 347 FISHERMAN   17
    SINBAD THE SAILOR'S BROUGHT A PAINTED CHEST, ... 371 ON GOING HOUSE   10

	PAGE	TITLE		LINE

BROUGHT   (CONTINUED)

BODY PERFECTION BROUGHT, ... 383 VISION ROBART   40
TO SUCH A PITCH OF FOLLY I AM BROUGHT, ... 384 VISION ROBART   58
ALL THAT THE BRIGAND APPLE BROUGHT . . . . 388 SOLOMON WITCH   15
OF THE HOVERING THING NIGHT BROUGHT ME. . . . . . . 390 IMAGE PAST   42
FOR HOW SHOULD I FORGET THE WISDOM THAT YOU BROUGHT, . . 391 UNDER SATURN   4
YOUR COMING BROUGHT; THOUGH I ACKNOWLEDGE I HAVE GONE . . 391 UNDER SATURN   V   5
CHILLED BLOOD, THIS SWEETNESS BROUGHT; . . . . 401 DEMON BEAST   39
AND BROUGHT THEM IN A LITTLE COVERED DISH. . . . . . 410 TOWER   32
TO WHOM THE LOVE-LORN LADY KYTELER BROUGHT . . . . . 433 NINETEEN 19   129
THE BABYLONIAN STARLIGHT BROUGHT . . . . 438 SONGS PLAY 2   4
THE BABYLONIAN STAR-LIGHT BROUGHT . . . . 438 SONGS PLAY 2   V   4
THE SOUTH WIND BROUGHT IT LONGING, AND THE EAST WIND   449 OWEN AHERNE   5
    DESPAIR,
THE SOUTH WIND BROUGHT IT LONGING, AND THE EAST BROUGHT   449 OWEN AHERNE   V   5
    IN DESPAIR,
THE SOUTH WIND BROUGHT IT LONGING, AND THE EAST BROUGHT   449 OWEN AHERNE   V   5
    IN DESPAIR,
THE SOUTH WIND BROUGHT IT LONGING, AND THE EAST BROUGHT   449 OWEN AHERNE   V   5
    IT DESPAIR,
THE SOUTH WIND BROUGHT IT LONGING, AND THE EAST BROUGHT   449 OWEN AHERNE   V   5
    IT DESPAIR,
SHE WHO HAD BROUGHT GREAT HECTOR DOWN . . . . 455 HIS MEMORIES   15
"I HAVE BROUGHT A SLENDER BRIDE INTO THE HOUSE; . . . 463 HARUN RASHID   49
BROUGHT FACE TO FACE WITH HIS OWN CLUMSINESS; . . . . 479 SELF AND SOUL   48
THEY BROUGHT TO PASS; . . . . 505 GRAT INSTRUCT   2
THAT THEY HAD BROUGHT NO FABULOUS SYMBOL THERE . . . 537 HER VISION   31
STRONG DRINK I HAD, AND IT BROUGHT ME TO SORROW, . . 544 TO SAME TUNE 1   13
WHAT BROUGHT THEM THERE SO FAR FROM THEIR HOME, . . . 549 SEVERED HEAD   8
CIVILIZATION IS HOOPED TOGETHER, BROUGHT . . . . . . 563 MERU   1
SOMETHING TO PERFECTION BROUGHT"; . . . . 577 WHAT THEN   19
HE BROUGHT IT ALL TO PASS; . . . . 586 PARNELLITES   14
WE THREE ALONE IN MODERN TIMES HAD BROUGHT . . . . . 603 GALLERY REVIS   45
STRONG DRINK I HAD, AND IT BROUGHT ME TO SORROW, . . 616 MARCH SONGS 3   13
HAD SHATTERED HER SOUL. PROPINQUITY HAD BROUGHT . . 619 BRONZE HEAD   18
AND THIS BROUGHT FORTH A DREAM AND SOON ENOUGH . . . 630 CIRCUS ANIMALS   23
I HAVE BROUGHT HIS CROWN. AND I HAVE BROUGHT HIS QUEEN. 755 SHADOW WATER A   166
I HAVE BROUGHT HIS CROWN. AND I HAVE BROUGHT HIS QUEEN. 755 SHADOW WATER A   166
ANY THAT LIVED, AND I HAVE BROUGHT MY GALLEY . . . . 756 SHADOW WATER A   V 191A
YOU HAD BROUGHT DOWN BEFORE YOU DIED. . . . . 791 REPRISALS   2

BROW

. . . HER BROW ON THE MIDST OF MY BREAST; . . . . . 52 OISIN 3   74
AND PEARL-PALE NEAVE LAY BY ME, HER BROW ON THE MIDST OF   52 OISIN 3   V   74
    MY BREAST;
FOR FAIR ARE POPPIES ON THE BROW; . . . . 67 HAPPY SHEPHERD   56
WITH A KISS AND A TEAR ON THY DROOPING BROW. . . . . 79 FALLING LEAVES   8
YOUNG MAN, LIFT UP YOUR RUSSET BROW, ... 125 GOES FERGUS   4
PALE BROW, STILL HANDS, AND DIM HAIR, ... 152 LOSS OF LOVE   V   1
FOR THAT DIM BROW AND LINGERING HAND . . . . 156 FORGOT BEAUTY   V   15
NOR HEAVY KNITTING OF THE BROW . . . . 318 APPOINTMENT   9
WHOSE BEARD A MOONLIGHT RIVER IS, WHOSE BROW . . . . 657 ISLE STAT I 3   73
CAN ENTER THERE. SEE; SEE! ABOVE YON BROW . . . . . 659 ISLE STAT II 1   27
AND WHEREFORE SHOULD THY BRIGHT BROW ROAM . . . . . 686 LIFE   11
TO PLACE A KISS OF FIRE ON THE DIM BROW . . . . . . 688 TWO TITANS   47
FROM THE GREAT PAINTED WINDOW WRAPS HIS BROW, . . . 697 MOSADA 2   37
UPON THE MOUNTAIN'S BROW. YONDER HE TREADS . . . . 703 MOSADA 3   114
FLED FROM HIS BROW WHERE THE HAIR WAS GREY; . . . . 728 PRIEST FAIRY   10

BROWED   SEE CLEAR-BROWED PLACID-BROWED

SORROW-WORN, YET PLACID BROWED. . . . . 733 STREET DANCERS V   56

BROWN   SEE SQUIRREL-BROWN

AND NOW A MAID, ON A SWIFT BROWN STEED . . . . . . 12 OISIN 1   V 142
YET SANG NO MORE AS WHEN, LIKE A BROWN BEE . . . . 30 OISIN 2   15
BUT SANG NO MORE, AS WHEN, LIKE A BROWN BEE . . . . 30 OISIN 2   V   15
. . . AND LATER THE SHORE-WEEDS BROWN. . . . . . . 57 OISIN 3   156
OR SEE THE BROWN MICE BOB . . . . 88 STOLEN CHILD   48
THE LINES ARE NOT HEAVY, NOR HEAVY THE LONG NETS BROWN-- 91 OLD FISHERMAN V   5
BRING MY BROWN HUNTER NEAR, ... 97 FOXHUNTER   V   6
MY DERMOT DEAR AND BROWN, ... 97 FOXHUNTER   V   6
BROWN LOLLARD TREADS UPON THE LAWN, ... 98 FOXHUNTER   17
HE SMOOTHS THE LONG BROWN NOSE. . . . . 98 FOXHUNTER   20
BROWN DERMOT TREADS UPON THE LAWN, ... 98 FOXHUNTER   V   17
OVER THE WHITE-HORNED BULL AND THE BROWN BULL. . . 182 QUEEN MAEVE   58
AND THE BROWN BULL HAD NOT YET COME, ... 189 BAILE AILLINN   15
THE OLD BROWN THORN-TREES BREAK IN TWO HIGH OVER CUMMEN   206 HANRAHANS SONG   1
    STRAND,
THE OLD BROWN THORN TREES BREAK IN TWO HIGH OVER CUMANN'S   206 HANRAHANS SONG V   1
    STRAND,
WITH RED BEER AND BROWN BEER. . . . . 214 HAPPY TOWNLAND   8
WHEN WE HAVE NEITHER BROWN NOR YELLOW ALE? . . . . 240 SHADOW WATER B   387
I SAW A FLAGON OF BROWN ALE ABOARD HER. . . . . . 240 SHADOW WATER B   388
BROWN PENNY . . . . 268 BROWN PENNY   T
AH, PENNY, BROWN PENNY, BROWN PENNY, ... 268 BROWN PENNY   7
AH, PENNY, BROWN PENNY, BROWN PENNY, ... 268 BROWN PENNY   7
AH, PENNY, BROWN PENNY, BROWN PENNY, ... 268 BROWN PENNY   15
AH, PENNY, BROWN PENNY, BROWN PENNY, ... 268 BROWN PENNY   15
WHERE THE BROWN HARE MIGHT BE, ... 381 SONGS FOOL 2   4
A BROWN LIEUTENANT AND HIS MEN, ... 424 ROAD AT DOOR   6
BROWN, OR BLACK, OR CARROT, ... 492 ANNE GREGORY   9
OVER THE CROWN OF THE WILLOWS BROWN. . . . . 653 ISLE STAT I 2   30
OVER THE CROWN OF THE WILLOWS BROWN. . . . . 653 ISLE STAT I 2   51
THE BROWN WEED BURDEN, SO THE SWORD BRINGS FEAR . . 660 ISLE STAT II 1   45

	PAGE	TITLE		LINE

BROWN   (CONTINUED)
A LONG, BROWN GRASSHOPPER OF MAIDS! PEACE, SIR! . . . . . 661 ISLE STAT II 1 69
HE NUMBERS. HE A BROWN FARM-HOUSE SEES. . . . . . . 710 FERENCZ RENYI 22
RINGED ROUND AND FONDLED, A BROWN FARM HOUSE SEES. . . . 710 FERENCZ RENYI V 23
LIKE SMALL BROWN MOTHS, A-TREMBLE. "RENYI SAY . . . . 713 FERENCZ RENYI 82
LIKE SMALL BROWN MOTHS, A-TREMBLE CEASELESSLY. . . . . 713 FERENCZ RENYI V 82
NESTED 'MONG THE VAPOURS BROWN. . . . . 731 STREET DANCERS 6
I SAID THE ALE WAS BROWN. I HAVE FOUND THE ALE, . . . 759 SHADOW WATER A 244
IT IS THE BROWN ALE DOES IT. GIVE ME YOUR SWORDS. . . . 766 SHADOW WATER A V 372
AND TELL ITS STORY OVER THEIR BROWN ALE. . . . . . . 767 SHADOW WATER A 393
(O THE BROWN AND THE YELLOW BEER!) . . . . 779 GOING THE ROAD 2
(O THE BROWN AND THE YELLOW BEER!) . . . . 779 GOING THE ROAD 6
(O THE BROWN AND THE YELLOW BEER!) . . . . 779 GOING THE ROAD 10
BROWNING
WHAT ROBERT BROWNING MEANT . . . . 605 YOU CONTENT 22
BROWS
THEIR BROWS WERE WHITE AS FRAGRANT MILK, ... 15 OISIN 1 204
THEIR BROWS WERE WHITE AS THE FRAGRANT MILK . . . . . 15 OISIN 1 V 204
AND, GATHERING ON OUR BROWS A FROWN, ... 20 OISIN 1 296
AND, GATHERING ON OUR BROWS A FROWN, ... 20 OISIN 1 V 297
SAD NIAM CAME NEAR ME, AND LAID HER BROWS ON THE MIDST 52 OISIN 3 V 74
OF MY BREAST
AND CHAPLET THEIR CALM BROWS WITH LEAFAGE DIM, ... 127 DREAM OF FAERY 32
AND CHAPLET THEIR CALM BROWS WITH LEAFAGE COOL! . . . . 127 DREAM OF FAERY V 32
PALE BROWS, STILL HANDS AND DIM HAIR, ... 152 LOSS OF LOVE 1
ON HER BROAD BREAST! BENEATH HER WITHERED BROWS . . . . 685 SEEKER 73
BROWSE
WHERE MY GOATS BROWSE ON THE SCARCE GRASS OR LEAP . . . 339 SHEP GOATHERD 8
BROW-SHADING
ONE HAND BROW-SHADING, FAR ACROSS THE NIGHT, ... 663 ISLE STAT II 2 27
BROWSING
AND HIS OWN FLOCK WAS BROWSING AT THE DOOR. . . . . . 340 SHEP GOATHERD 27
NOW HER SHEEP ALL BROWSING MEET . . . . 646 ISLE STAT I 1 22
BRUISE
AND FILL ME WITH THY RAGE, THAT I MAY BRUISE . . . . . 698 MOSADA 2 54
BRUISED
THE BODY IS NOT BRUISED TO PLEASURE SOUL, ... 445 SCHOOL CHILDR 58
BRUISING
BRUISING THE DARKNESS WITH THEIR CRACKLING LIGHT! . . . 687 TWO TITANS 2
BRUSH
BRUSH LIGHTLY AS HAYMOUSE EARTH'S PEBBLES, ... 56 OISIN 3 128
BRUSH LIGHTLY AS HAY MOUSE EARTH'S PEBBLES, ... 56 OISIN 3 V 128
WHETHER WE HAVE CHOSEN CHISEL, PEN OR BRUSH, ... 368 EGO DOMINUS 14
THE PAINTER'S BRUSH CONSUMES HIS DREAMS! . . . . . 438 SONGS PLAY 2 12
BUT WHERE IS THE BRUSH THAT COULD SHOW ANYTHING . . . . 602 GALLERY REVIS 28
BRUSHED
WHEN BRUSHED WITH THE WINGS OF THE OWLS, ... 53 OISIN 3 98
BRUSHES
WHAT BRUSHES FLY AND MOTH ASIDE? . . . . 625 NATIVITY 7
BRUSHING
BRUSHING BACK HIS YELLOW HAIR! . . . . 729 PRIEST FAIRY 38
BRUTAL
THE HEART'S GROWN BRUTAL FROM THE FARE! . . . . . . 425 STARES NEST 17
THE HEART GROWS BRUTAL FROM THE FARE, ... 425 STARES NEST V 17
FOUL GOAT-HEAD, BRUTAL ARM APPEAR, ... 612 NEWS ORACLE 33
BRUTE
SO MASTERED BY THE BRUTE BLOOD OF THE AIR, ... 441 LEDA AND SWAN 12
AND THE BRUTE DOLPHINS PLUNGE . . . . 612 NEWS ORACLE 20
BRYCELINDE
I HAVE NO HAPPINESS IN DREAMING OF BRYCELINDE, ... 209 UNDER THE MOON 1
I FIND NO HAPPINESS IN SHADY BRYCELINDE . . . . . . 209 UNDER THE MOON V 1
BUAL'S
AND SET THEM DIGGING UNDER BUAL'S HILL. . . . . . . 184 QUEEN MAEVE 93
BUAN'S
ON THE HEIR OF ULADH, BUAN'S SON, ... 189 BAILE AILLINN 4
BUBBLE
BUBBLE UPON THE TABLE. A GHOST MAY COME! . . . . . 470 ALL SOUL NIGHT 5
AND NOW AND THEN A BUBBLE RISE. I HEAR . . . . . . 722 WITCH VIVIEN 63
BUBBLED
LONG SIGHS AROSE IN OUR SPIRITS, BENEATH US BUBBLED THE 48 OISIN 3 20
GROUND.
BUBBLES
LIKE BUBBLES IN A FROZEN POND! . . . . 22 OISIN 1 336
AND CHASE THE FROTHY BUBBLES. . . . . 87 STOLEN CHILD 21
"OR SEEK WHERE SWEETEST WATER BUBBLES, ... 731 PRIEST FAIRY 79
BUBBLING
A LITTLE RUNNEL MADE A BUBBLING STRAIN, ... 39 OISIN 2 156
DUSKY AND HERBLESS, WHERE A BUBBLING STRAIN . . . . 39 OISIN 2 V 156
IN A REVERIE FORGETFUL OF ALL THINGS, OVER THE BUBBLING 56 OISIN 3 140
GROUND.
IN REVERIE FORGETFUL OF ALL THINGS, OVER THE BUBBLING 56 OISIN 3 V 140
GROUND.
AND TRAMPLED IN THE BUBBLING MIRE, ... 83 MAD KING GOLL 26
AND TRAMPLED ON THE BUBBLING MIRE, ... 83 MAD KING GOLL V 26
AND FISHES, BUBBLING TO THE BRIM, ... 254 HIS DREAM V 9
AND LAUGH'D, SO, SO ALONG THE BUBBLING RILLS . . . . 645 ISLE STAT I 1 18
TO WANDER BY THE BUBBLING SHORE. . . . . 668 ISLE STAT II 3 57
MID BUBBLING LEAVES A WANDERING SONG-RAPT BIRD . . . . 672 ISLE STAT II 3 154
BUCKET
WHO DRAWS A BUCKET WITH THE REST . . . . 335 YOUNG BEAUTY 5

115

	PAGE	TITLE	LINE

BUCKLED
THAT NOBLE BLADE THE MUSES BUCKLED ON, ... 489 COOLE PARK 29 10

BUCKLERS
AND HEARD THE FOEMEN'S BUCKLERS RATTLE, ... 10 OISIN 1 123
AND HEARD THE FOEMAN'S BUCKLERS RATTLE, ... 10 OISIN 1 V 123

BUCKSKIN
FOR NATURE'S PULLED HER TRAGIC BUCKSKIN ON . . . . . . 490 COOLE BALLYLEE V 12

BUD
AND SHAKE THE BLOSSOM FROM THE BUD . . . . 396 ROSE TREE 11

BUDDHA
A BUDDHA, HAND AT REST, ... 383 VISION ROBART 19

BUDDHA'S
GRIMALKIN CRAWLS TO BUDDHA'S EMPTINESS. . . . . 611 STATUES 24

BUDDING
AND STIRS THE YOUNG KID'S BUDDING HORN, ... 18 OISIN 1 264

BUDS
WHILE O'ER THE BUDS, AND O'ER THE GRASS-BLADES, BRIGHT . . 704 REMEMBRANCE 3

BUFFETED
BUFFETED BY SUCH SEAS! . . . . 530 DELPHIC ORACLE 2

BUGLE
THUS FOR ANOTHER'S BUGLE CALL! . . . . 671 ISLE STAT II 3 136

BUILD
"WHAT DO YOU BUILD WITH SAILS FOR FLIGHT?" . . . . . . 69 CLOAK BOAT 6
"I BUILD A BOAT FOR SORROW! . . . . 70 CLOAK BOAT 7
A BOAT I BUILD FOR SORROW! . . . . 70 CLOAK BOAT V 7
AND A SMALL CABIN BUILD THERE, OF CLAY AND WATTLES MADE! 117 ISLE INNISFREE 2
I HUNGER TO BUILD THEM ANEW AND SIT ON A GREEN KNOLL APART, 143 ROSE IN HEART 6
I BADE MY HEART BUILD THESE POOR RHYMES! . . . . . . 158 BELOVED RHYMES 3
TO BUILD A PERFECT BEAUTY IN RHYME . . . . 164 PERFECT BEAUTY 3
TO BUILD THE PERFECT BEAUTY IN RHYME, ... 164 PERFECT BEAUTY V 3
MUST END AT THE DUMB STONE? BUT WHERE WE BUILD . . . 284 TWO KINGS 179
AMONG WHAT RUSHES WILL THEY BUILD, ... 323 SWANS AT COOLE 27
MAY BUILD IN THE CRACKED MASONRY AND CRY . . . . . 423 MY DESCENDANTS 15
THE BEES BUILD IN THE CREVICES . . . . 424 STARES NEST 1
COME BUILD IN THE EMPTY HOUSE OF THE STARE. . . . . . 424 STARES NEST 5
COME BUILD IN THE EMPTY HOUSE OF THE STARE. . . . . . 425 STARES NEST 10
COME BUILD IN THE EMPTY HOUSE OF THE STARE. . . . . . 425 STARES NEST 15
COME BUILD IN THE EMPTY HOUSE OF THE STARE. . . . . . 425 STARES NEST 20
AND THOSE THAT BUILD THEM AGAIN ARE GAY. . . . . 566 LAPIS LAZULI 36
HERE WHERE THE ROUND WAVES COME, HERE LET THEM BUILD, . . 663 ISLE STAT II 2 19
WHAT DO YOU BUILD WITH SAILS FOR FLIGHT? . . . . . 666 ISLE STAT II 3 6
A BOAT I BUILD FOR SORROW. . . . . 666 ISLE STAT II 3 7
TO BUILD THE CIRCLING SEATS, WHERE HIGH IN AIR . . . . 699 MOSADA 3 18

BUILDED
OF STORIES BUILDED BY HIS WORDS . . . . 7 OISIN 1 68
. . . THE OWLS HAD BUILDED THEIR NESTS IN THEIR LOCKS, . . 49 OISIN 3 39

BUILDER
(I WONDER IF THE BUILDER HAS BEEN PAID) . . . . 292 TO A SHADE 3

BUILDING
BUILDING A SORROWFUL LOVELINESS . . . . 158 BELOVED RHYMES 5
BUILDING YARD AND STORMY SHORE, ... 530 OLD TOM AGAIN V 5

BUILDINGS
AND BUILDINGS THAT A HAUGHTIER AGE DESIGNED, ... 418 ANCEST HOUSES 34

BUILDING-YARD
BUILDING-YARD AND STORMY SHORE, ... 530 OLD TOM AGAIN 5

BUILDS
SHE BUILDS HER NEST UPON A NARROW LEDGE . . . . 285 TWO KINGS 194

BUILT SEE HEAVILY-BUILT
OUT OF THE SEVENFOLD SEAS, BUILT THE DARK HALL . . . . 38 OISIN 2 131
OUT OF THE SEVEN-FOLD SEAS, BUILT THE DARK HALL . . . . 38 OISIN 2 V 131
AND A SMALL CABIN BUILT THERE, OF CLAY AND WATTLES MADE! 117 ISLE INNISFREE V 2
I HELPED YOUR FATHERS WHEN THEY BUILT THESE WALLS, . . . 184 QUEEN MAEVE 97
HE RAN TOWARDS THE HOUSE HIS FATHERS BUILT . . . . . 279 TWO KINGS V 45E
A HEAVILY BUILT FALSTAFFAN MAN, ... 423 ROAD AT DOOR V 2
THAT PURITY BUILT UP THE STATE . . . . 460 THREE MONUMENT 6
WE THE GREAT GAZEBO BUILT, ... 476 EVA GORE-BOOTH 30
ALL THINGS FALL AND ARE BUILT AGAIN, ... 566 LAPIS LAZULI 35
THAT HAVE BUILT ALL ARE DUST ON A MOTH'S WING. . . . . 757 SHADOW WATER A 205

BULBEN
UNDER BEN BULBEN TO THE MEET, ... 397 POLIT PRISONER 14
UPON BEN BULBEN SIDE . . . . 398 BREAK OF DAY 6
OUT OF BEN BULBEN AND KNOCKNAREA, ... 549 SEVERED HEAD 2
UNDER BEN BULBEN . . . . 636 BEN BULBEN T
WHERE BEN BULBEN SETS THE SCENE. . . . . 637 BEN BULBEN 11

BULBEN'S
OR THE HUMBLER WORM, I CLIMBED BEN BULBEN'S BACK . . . . 409 TOWER 9
UNDER BARE BEN BULBEN'S HEAD . . . . 640 BEN BULBEN 84

BULK
AND HIS LOOSE BULK BE THROWN IN THE LOUD TIDE." . . . . 35 OISIN 2 91
CAST THE LOOSE BULK, LEST NIAM FEAR HIM DEAD; . . . . 41 OISIN 2 V 183

BULL
OVER THE WHITE-HORNED BULL AND THE BROWN BULL. . . . . 182 QUEEN MAEVE 58
OVER THE WHITE-HORNED BULL AND THE BROWN BULL. . . . . 182 QUEEN MAEVE 58
AND THE BROWN BULL HAD NOT YET COME, ... 189 BAILE AILLINN 15
THAT CHANGED A LOVER FOR A BULL. . . . . 509 JANE REPROVED 6
JOHN BULL AND THE SEA ARE FRIENDS, ... 583 GHOST ROG CASE 4
JOHN BULL HAS STOOD FOR PARLIAMENT, ... 583 GHOST ROG CASE 11
JOHN BULL HAS GONE TO INDIA . . . . 583 GHOST ROG CASE 21

BULLETS
WHERE WORM THE REBELS, OR MY BULLETS LAY . . . . . . 713 FERENCZ RENYI 83

116

		PAGE	TITLE	LINE

BULLO
   LULLABULLOO, BULOO, BULOO, LULLABULLOO, BULLO. • • • • 594 COLONEL MARTIN V REF
BULOO
   LULLABULLOO, BULOO, BULOO, LULLABULLOO, BULLO. • • • • 594 COLONEL MARTIN V REF
   LULLABULLOO, BULOO, BULOO, LULLABULLOO, BULLO. • • • • 594 COLONEL MARTIN V REF
BULWARK
   AND BEAT THE BULWARK OF YOUR SHIP ON MINE. • • • • • • 236 SHADOW WATER B 312
   OR CROWD BEHIND THE BULWARK, THAT WE SEEM • • • • • • 751 SHADOW WATER A 94
   BULWARK TO BULWARK, AND SQUARE HER SAIL BY OURS. • • • • 752 SHADOW WATER A 129
   BULWARK TO BULWARK, AND SQUARE HER SAIL BY OURS. • • • • 752 SHADOW WATER A 129
BUM
   BELLY, SHOULDER, BUM, • • • • • • • • • • • • • 612 NEWS ORACLE 34
BUNCH
   OUT OF A NEIGHBOURING BUNCH OF HEATHER! • • • • • • • 728 PRIEST FAIRY 20
BUNCHES
   SEE! OH, SEE! THE DEW-DROWNED BUNCHES • • • • • • • 655 ISLE STAT I 3 1
BUNCHING
   MIGHT BE ACCOMPLISHED. BUNCHING THE CURTAIN UP • • • • 183 QUEEN MAEVE 68
BUNDLE
   A BUNDLE OF RAGS UPON A CRUTCH, • • • • • • • • • 302 HOUR DAWN 2
   TO BUNDLE TIME AWAY • • • • • • • • • • • • • 317 NIGHT COME 11
   A BUNDLE OF TEMPESTUOUS CLOUD IS BLOWN • • • • • • • 541 PARN FUNERAL 1 2
   A BUNDLE OF LINEN. SHROUDS BY TWO AND THREE • • • • • 634 CUCHULAIN COMF 9
BUNDLED
   THE WIND HAS BUNDLED UP THE CLOUDS HIGH OVER KNOCKNAREA 207 HANRAHANS SONG 6
   THE WINDS HAVE BUNDLED UP THE CLOUDS HIGH OVER KNOCKNAREA 207 HANRAHANS SONG V 6
   ANGERS THAT ARE LIKE BUNDLED CLOUDS HAVE SET OUR HEARTS 207 HANRAHANS SONG V 8
     ABEAT!
BUOYED
   AND GOD'S BELL BUOYED TO BE THE WATER'S CARE! • • • • • 114 ROSE OF BATTLE 4
   • • BUOYED OUT ON THE FOAM OF THE SEA! • • • • • • 122 WHITE BIRDS 12
BURDEN
   • • • BUT FELL WITH THEIR BURDEN AT LENGTH. • • • • • 60 OISIN 3 186
   AND LO! MY ANCIENT BURDEN MAY DEPART. • • • • • • • 69 SAD SHEPHERD 24
   AND WHAT TO ME WAS BURDEN WITHOUT END, • • • • • • • 102 FERGUS DRUID 12
   WHILE DAY ITS BURDEN ON TO EVENING BORE, • • • • • 110 CUCHULAIN SEA 70
   AND ALL THE BURDEN OF HER MYRIAD YEARS. • • • • • • 120 SORROW OF LOVE V 8
   EVEN IN AN OLD STORY, IS A BURDEN NOT TO BE BORNE. • • 210 UNDER THE MOON 20
   I BEAR A BURDEN THAT MIGHT WELL TRY • • • • • • • 380 SONGS FOOL 1 13
   SHOULD FIND NO BURDEN BUT ITSELF AND YET SHOULD BE WORN 449 OWEN AHERNE 3
     OUT.
   IT COULD NOT BEAR THAT BURDEN AND THEREFORE IT WENT MAD. 449 OWEN AHERNE 4
   THREE SONGS TO THE ONE BURDEN • • • • • • • • • 605 SONGS BURDEN 1 T
   THE BROWN WEED BURDEN, SO THE SWORD BRINGS FEAR • • • 660 ISLE STAT II 1 45
   BENEATH THE BURDEN OF THE INFINITE, • • • • • • • 674 ISLE STAT II 3 V 212
   LAY DOWN THE BURDEN OF THY RACE, • • • • • • • • 736 SUMMER EVENING 14
BURDENED
   BEYOND THE LAKE, WHOSE SMALLEST WAVE WAS BURDENED • • • 656 ISLE STAT I 3 31
BURDENS
   NOR LANDS THAT SEEM TOO DIM TO BE BURDENS ON THE HEART! 209 UNDER THE MOON 5
   OR LANDS THAT SEEMED TOO OLD TO BE BURDENS ON THE HEART, 209 UNDER THE MOON V 5
   THAT HAD SUCH BURDENS ON THE MIND • • • • • • • • 432 NINETEEN 19 94
   THEY PITCH THEIR BURDENS OFF. • • • • • • • • • 612 NEWS ORACLE 24
BURDENSOME
   BURDENSOME BEAUTY--FOR YOUR SOLE SAKE • • • • • • 356 BROKEN DREAMS 10
   BURDENSOME BEAUTY--BUT FOR YOUR SAKE • • • • • • 356 BROKEN DREAMS V 10
BURGHERS
   THE BURGHERS OF THE NIGHT FADE ONE BY ONE. • • • • • 700 MOSADA 3 40
BURIAL
   AND PASSING THE FIRBOLGS' BURIAL MOUNDS, • • • • • • 3 OISIN 1 V 16
   WHERE MEN HAVE HEAPED NO BURIAL MOUNDS, • • • • • • 8 OISIN 1 V 82
   AND SHOULD HE DIE TO HEAP HIS BURIAL MOUND • • • • • 280 TWO KINGS V 82
BURIAL-MOUND
   AND SHOULD HE DIE TO HEAP HIS BURIAL-MOUND • • • • • 280 TWO KINGS 82
BURIAL-MOUNDS
   AND PASSING THE FIRBOLGS' BURIAL-MOUNDS, • • • • • 3 OISIN 1 16
   WHERE MEN HAVE HEAPED NO BURIAL-MOUNDS, • • • • • • 8 OISIN 1 82
BURIED
   BURIED AND MIGHTY. WHEN THROUGH THE GREAT DOOR • • • • 39 OISIN 2 151
   BURIED AND MIGHTY. THENCE I JOURNEYED NOT • • • • • • 39 OISIN 2 V 151
   BURIED UNDER THE SLEEPY GROUND, • • • • • • • • 67 HAPPY SHEPHERD 48
   (WHO'S BURIED IN THE SLEEPY GROUND), • • • • • • • 67 HAPPY SHEPHERD V 48
   WHO HAS BEEN BURIED SOME TWO THOUSAND YEARS? • • • • 181 QUEEN MAEVE 35
   HAVE BURIED NOTHING BUT MY GOLDEN ARMS. • • • • • • 243 SHADOW WATER B 431
   WHERE THE O'BYRNES AND BYRNES ARE BURIED, • • • • • 331 ROUND TOWER 9
   WAS BURIED NEAR THE ASTROLOGER, • • • • • • • • 361 ALF POLLEXFEN 26
   AND YET, TWICE BORN, TWICE BURIED, GROW HE MUST, • • • 374 PHASES OF MOON 48
   BUT WHEN THE MASTER'S BURIED MICE CAN PLAY, • • • • 418 ANCEST HOUSES 22
   TO THINK OF BURIED HECTOR • • • • • • • • • • 455 HIS MEMORIES 5
   TIME I WERE BURIED," SAID THE OLD, OLD MAN. • • • • • 548 TO SAME TUNE 3 10
   TIME I WERE BURIED," SAID THE OLD, OLD MAN. • • • • • 548 TO SAME TUNE 3 20
   TIME I WERE BURIED," SAID THE OLD, OLD MAN. • • • • • 549 TO SAME TUNE 3 30
   THEY BUT THRUST THEIR BURIED MEN • • • • • • • • 637 BEN BULBEN 23
   "WE BURIED LATE IN A HAZEL DELL • • • • • • • • 729 PRIEST FAIRY 43
BURKE
   THE PEOPLE OF BURKE AND OF GRATTAN • • • • • • • 414 TOWER 132
   • • • BERKELEY AND BURKE HAVE TRAVELLED THERE. • • • 481 BLOOD AND MOON 18
   AND HAUGHTIER-HEADED BURKE THAT PROVED THE STATE A TREE, 481 BLOOD AND MOON 22
   AND HAUGHTIER HEADED BURKE THAT PROVED THE STATE A TREE 481 BLOOD AND MOON V 22
   MY GREAT-GRANDFATHER SPOKE TO EDMUND BURKE • • • • • 486 SEVEN SAGES 1
   BURKE WAS A WHIG. WHETHER THEY KNEW OR NOT, • • • • 486 SEVEN SAGES 8

117

```
                                                              PAGE    TITLE          LINE
BURKE  (CONTINUED)
     GOLDSMITH AND BURKE, SWIFT AND THE BISHOP OF CLOYNE . . .   486 SEVEN SAGES        9
BURKE'S
     HARRIED, AND BURKE'S GREAT MELODY AGAINST IT. . . . . .     487 SEVEN SAGES       16
BURN     SEE OUT-BURN
     YOUNG WARRIOR." "NAY," I ANSWERED: "MY HANDS BURN           35 OISIN 2        V  89B
     DREAM, UNTIL GOD BURN NATURE WITH A KISS? . . . . . .      128 DREAM OF FAERY     47
     UNTIL HE BURN UP NATURE WITH A KISS:—                      128 DREAM OF FAERY     47
     AND ALL MEN'S HEARTS MUST BURN AND BEAT:                   158 BELOVED RHYMES      9
     IS DROPPING SLEEP, UNTIL GOD BURN TIME . . . . . .         164 PERFECT BEAUTY      7
     AT HUSH OF EVENING TILL GOD BURN TIME . . . . . .          164 PERFECT BEAUTY V    7
     TO BURN US TO THE MARROW IF WE STRIKE. . . . . . .         239 SHADOW WATER B    372
     WAS THERE ANOTHER TROY FOR HER TO BURN? . . . . . .        257 NO SECOND TROY     12
     SOME BURN DAMP FAGGOTS, OTHERS MAY CONSUME . . . . .       327 ROBERT GREGORY     81
     I THOUGHT 'TWOULD BURN MY BODY . . . . . . . . .           335 SONG               15
     TO BURN THAT STUMP ON THE ACROPOLIS, . . . . . . .         430 NINETEEN 19        46
     CAN BURN OUT THAT SUFFERING . . . . . . . . . . .          589 OLD WICKED MAN     57
     THUS DO I BURN THESE PRECIOUS HERBS, WHOSE SMOKE . .       691 MOSADA 1           39
     THEY SAID I'D BURN IN HELL UNLESS I TOLD. . . . . .        694 MOSADA 1          108
     SO SHE MUST BURN, YOU SAY?  SHE MUST IN TRUTH. . . .       696 MOSADA 2            2
     I WILL BURN HERESY FROM THIS MAD EARTH, . . . . . .        697 MOSADA 2           40
     THAT SHALL BURN TIME WHEN TIMES HAVE EBBED AWAY. . .       750 SHADOW WATER A     61
     BURN THEIR BODIES UP FOR NOUGHT, . . . . . . . . .         787 HUDDON DUDDON      14
BURNED
     A DEMON'S LEISURE: EYES: FIRST WHITE, NOW BURNED . . .      40 OISIN 2           168
     WHEN WINDS HAVE GATHERED AND SUN AND MOON BURNED DIM . .   175 ELEMENT POWERS     15
     THOUGH FLAME HAD BURNED THE WHOLE . . . . . . . .          267 FRIEND ILLNESS      4
     THE MOTHS ARE WHEN THEY ARE BURNED? . . . . . . .          313 TWO YEAR LATER      4
     THAT SEEMED AS THOUGH ICE BURNED AND WAS BUT THE MORE ICE, 316 COLD HEAVEN         2
     THE WICK OF YOUTH BEING BURNED AND THE OIL SPENT, . . .    334 LIVING BEAUTY  V    3
     WHEN OIL AND WICK ARE BURNED IN ONE: . . . . . .           388 SOLOMON WITCH      30
     A MAN IS KILLED, OR A HOUSE BURNED, . . . . . . .          425 STARES NEST         8
     THOUGHT THAT UNLESS A LITTLE POWDER BURNED . . . . .       429 NINETEEN 19        21
     OR BURNED GREAT CITIES DOWN, . . . . . . . . . .           789 SINGING HEAD       16
BURNING
     BURNING BETWEEN HER FINGERS, AND IN MINE . . . . . .        37 OISIN 2           125
     TILL THE FAR DOORWAY GREW A BURNING BLOT . . . . . .        39 OISIN 2        V  152
     HOW THE HAMMERS SPRING ON THE ANVIL, ON THE SPEARHEAD'S     52 OISIN 3            83
        BURNING SPOT:
     . . . ON THE SPEAR-HEAD'S BURNING SPOT: . . . . . .         52 OISIN 3        V   83
     . . . ON THE BURNING STONES IS THEIR PLACE: . . . .         61 OISIN 3           197
     . . . ON THE BURNING STONES OF WIDE HELL, . . . . .         61 OISIN 3           198
     A METEOR OF THE BURNING HEART, . . . . . . . . .            78 INDIAN TO LOVE     14
     CAOILTE TOSSING HIS BURNING HAIR, . . . . . . . .          140 HOSTING SIDHE       3
     CAOILTE TOSSING HIS BURNING HAIR, . . . . . . . .          141 HOSTING SIDHE      15
     BURNING IN FIRES OF A SLANDEROUS TONGUE. . . . . .         148 INTO TWILIGHT       8
     BUT WITH THE BURNING, LIVE, UNSHAKEN VOICE . . . .         183 QUEEN MAEVE        75
     AND YOU HAVE GROWN TO BE A BURNING SOD . . . . . .         245 SHADOW WATER B    487
     "PUT OFF THAT MASK OF BURNING GOLD . . . . . . . .         263 MASK                1
     THE MAJESTY THAT SHUTS HIS BURNING EYE: . . . . . .        265 THESE CLOUDS        2
     THE MAJESTY THAT SHUTS HIS BURNING EYE. . . . . . .        265 THESE CLOUDS       12
     WOMEN CAN FIND." WITH A MOST BURNING VOICE . . . . .       284 TWO KINGS      V  175
     WHEREON A THING ONCE WALKED THAT SEEMED A BURNING CLOUD.   315 FALLEN MAJESTY      8
     ONCE WALKED A THING THAT SEEMED, AS IT WERE, A BURNING     315 FALLEN MAJESTY V    8
        CLOUD.
     WHEN I HAD MY BURNING YOUTH! . . . . . . . . . .           329 MEN IMPROVE        15
     AND THAT PROUD LOOK AS THOUGH SHE HAD GAZED INTO           354 HIS PHOENIX        29
        THE BURNING SUN,
     BURNING ALONE BESIDE AN OPEN BOOK, . . . . . . .           370 EGO DOMINUS        63
     THE BURNING BOW THAT ONCE COULD SHOOT AN ARROW . . .       377 PHASES OF MOON    119
     WHO NEVER GAVE THE BURNING TOWN A THOUGHT: . . . .         384 VISION ROBART      57
     THE BROKEN WALL, THE BURNING ROOF AND TOWER . . . .        441 LEDA AND SWAN      10
     THE BURNING TREE . . . . . . . . . . . . . .               499 VACILLATION    V    T
     BERENICE'S BURNING HAIR. . . . . . . . . . . . .           519 HER DREAM           8
     THE SKIES MORE DIM, THOUGH BURNING LIKE A SHIELD, . .      656 ISLE STAT I 3      26
     OR HER EVER BURNING EYES, . . . . . . . . . . .            658 ISLE STAT I 3      85
     THIS VISION OF PETER AND THE BURNING GATE. . . . . .       696 MOSADA 2           21
     OF HOLY PETER OF THE BURNING GATE: . . . . . . .           696 MOSADA 2       V   20
     HIS MEMORY NOW IS A TALL PILLAR, BURNING . . . . . .       738 MOURN THEN ON      15
     AT THE BURNING WHEEL OF LOVE . . . . . . . . . .           776 AGAINST WITCH      34
     I MOCK AT ALL SO BURNING OUT. . . . . . . . . .            787 HUDDON DUDDON      15
     BUT HOW THEY MOCK US BURNING OUT. . . . . . . . .          787 HUDDON DUDDON  V   15
BURNISHED
     THE HEAVY BOUGHS, THE BURNISHED DOVE . . . . . . .          78 INDIAN TO LOVE     16
     THE GREAT BOUGHS, AND THE BURNISHED DOVE . . . . .          78 INDIAN TO LOVE V   16
     AND GREAT BOUGHS, AND THE BURNISHED DOVE . . . . .          78 INDIAN TO LOVE V   16
     BREATHE ON THE BURNISHED MIRROR OF THE WORLD . . . .       228 SHADOW WATER B    132
     THOSE STILTED BOYS, THAT BURNISHED CHARIOT, . . . .        629 CIRCUS ANIMALS      7
     BREATHE ON THE BURNISHED MIRROR OF THE WORLD . . . .       750 SHADOW WATER A     69
BURNS
     AT HUSH OF EVENING TILL GOD BURNS TIME . . . . . .         164 PERFECT BEAUTY V    7
     BURNS BUT MORE CLEARLY.  O SHE HAD NOT THESE WAYS . . .    200 FOLLY COMFORT      11
     A LAMP BURNS ON BESIDE THE OPEN BOOK . . . . . . .         367 EGO DOMINUS         3
     A LAMP BURNS ON ABOVE THE OPEN BOOK . . . . . . .          367 EGO DOMINUS    V    3
BURNT
     LIKE A CANDLE BURNT OUT, . . . . . . . . . . . .           142 MOODS               2
     THAT THE TOPLESS TOWERS BE BURNT . . . . . . . .           617 LONG-LEG FLY       11
BURROW
     I CHOSE THIS BURROW UNDER GROUND. . . . . . . . .          305 HOUR DAWN          73
BURROWING
     WHO'S BURROWING SOMEWHERE IN THE GROUND, . . . . .         272 GREY ROCK          33
```

	PAGE	TITLE	LINE

BURST
BURST FROM A GREAT DOOR MARRED BY MANY A BLOW • • • • • • 31 OISIN 2   29
I BURST THE CHAIN: STILL EARLESS, NERVELESS, BLIND, • • • 36 OISIN 2   97
THERE IS NO MEASURE THAT IT WOULD NOT BURST• • • • • • • 245 SHADOW WATER B   484
AND HAVING SAID IT, BURST IN TEARS• • • • • • • • • • 273 GREY ROCK   48
OR EVERY BELLOWS BURST, BE HAPPY STILL• • • • • • • • 405 FOR DAUGHTER   72
THE TRUMPETERS MIGHT BURST WITH TRUMPETING • • • • • • • 429 NINETEEN 19   22
AND HIS BEATING HEART WOULD BURST• • • • • • • • • • • 454 EMPTY CUP   6
AND THE TRUMPETS ALL ARE BURST, • • • • • • • • • • • 527 AM OF IRELAND   22
HER SPIRIT• AS SHE MOVES, THE FOAM-GLOBES BURST • • • • 687 TWO TITANS   14

BURSTING
THAT UNDER BURSTING DAWN • • • • • • • • • • • • • • 416 TOWER   176
O WHAT A BURSTING OUT THERE WAS, • • • • • • • • • • 457 SUMMER SPRING   13
THAN ALL MY BURSTING SPRINGTIME KNEW• A GIRL • • • • 466 HARUN RASHID   105

BURSTS
YOUNG FERENCZ RENYI BURSTS HIS BONDS--AT LAST, • • • 714 FERENCZ RENYI V   116

BURTHEN
AND LO--MY HEAVY BURTHEN MAY DEPART:" • • • • • • • • 69 SAD SHEPHERD V   24
IS THE BURTHEN AND PERSISTENCE• • • • • • • • • • • • 647 ISLE STAT I 1   75
BENEATH THE BURTHEN OF THE INFINITE, • • • • • • • • 674 ISLE STAT II 3   212
FOR LONG THE BURTHEN OF THEIR TALKING GRIEFS• • • • • 693 MOSADA 1   71
THE BURTHEN OF THY TRUTH• REACH DOWN THY HANDS • • • 698 MOSADA 2   53

BURY
HE BADE THEM TAKE AND BURY HER • • • • • • • • • • • 571 THREE BUSHES   71

BUSH
THROUGH BUSH THEY PLUNGED AND OVER IVIED ROOT, • • • • 278 TWO KINGS   32

BUSHES   SEE CURRANT-BUSHES
BETWEEN TWO BUSHES UNDER THE RAIN: • • • • • • • • • 551 SONGS REWRIT 1   14
THE THREE BUSHES • • • • • • • • • • • • • • • • • 569 THREE BUSHES   T
AND THERE TWO BUSHES PLANTED • • • • • • • • • • • • 571 THREE BUSHES   59
HIVES, CURRANT BUSHES• THERE HIS KIN ARE• HIGH • • • 710 FERENCZ RENYI   25

BUSINESS
THEATRE BUSINESS, MANAGEMENT OF MEN• • • • • • • • • 260 FASC DIFFICULT   11
AND HAVE NO BUSINESS BUT DISPENSING ROUND • • • • • • 404 FOR DAUGHTER   43
MEN AND THEIR BUSINESS TOOK • • • • • • • • • • • • 421 MY TABLE   23
THROUGH TOO MUCH BUSINESS WITH THE PASSING HOUR, • • • 423 MY DESCENDANTS   11
WELL THEN, TO BUSINESS: WHAT IS IN YOUR BAG? • • • • 720 WITCH VIVIEN   19

BUSKIN
FOR NATURE'S PULLED HER TRAGIC BUSKIN ON • • • • • • 490 COOLE BALLYLEE   12
FOR NATURE'D PULLED HER TRAGIC BUSKIN ON • • • • • • 490 COOLE BALLYLEE V   12

BUST
WITH PATIENT BEAUTY YONDER ATTIC BUST • • • • • • • 685 DRAWING-ROOM   3
WITH PATIENT BEAUTY YONDER ATTIC BUST • • • • • • • 735 QUATRAIN APHOR   23

BUSTLE
THAT SCARES WITH HIS BUSTLE THE DELICATE NIGHT, • • • 28 OISIN 1   V 423B

BUSY
AND NEW FRIENDS BUSY WITH YOUR PRAISE, • • • • • • • 173 PLEADS FRIEND   3
THEY ARE TOO BUSY WITH EACH OTHER• LOOK: • • • • • 232 SHADOW WATER B   229
BEING TOO BUSY IN THE AIR AND THE HIGH AIR, • • • • 234 SHADOW WATER B   274
HANDS THAT ARE BUSY WITH HIS BEADS • • • • • • • • 588 OLD WICKED MAN   25
ON MY POOR BRAIN YOUR BUSY TUMULTS CROWD• • • • • • 648 ISLE STAT I 1   100
IN BUSY FLAKES: RE-SHINING FROM THE LAKE, • • • • • 662 ISLE STAT II 2   3
THE MEN ARE BUSY IN THE GLIMMERING SQUARE• • • • • • 699 MOSADA 3   16
OH, WOULD THE BUSY MINUTES MIGHT FOLD UP • • • • • • 702 MOSADA 3   97
NOW MAKING BUSY WITH THE OAR, • • • • • • • • • • • 742 DANAAN QUICK   2

BUTLER
A BUTLER OR AN ARMSTRONG THAT WITHSTOOD • • • • • • 270 PARDON FATHERS   10

BUTLERS
OLD BUTLERS WHEN YOU TOOK TO HORSE AND STOOD • • • • • 270 PARDON FATHERS V   10
THE SMUGGLER MIDDLETON, BUTLERS FAR BACK, • • • • • • 605 YOU CONTENT   15

BUTT   SEE WATER-BUTT
THE BUTT END OF A STEERING OAR, • • • • • • • • • • 253 HIS DREAM V   2
DROWN, DROWN IN THE WATER BUTT, • • • • • • • • • • 546 TO SAME TUNE 2 V   REF

BUTTED
BUTTED BELOW THE SINGLE AND SO PIERCED • • • • • • • 278 TWO KINGS   22

BUTT-END
THE BUTT-END OF A STEERING-OAR, • • • • • • • • • • 253 HIS DREAM   2

BUTTERFLIES
TORTOISESHELL BUTTERFLIES, PEACOCK BUTTERFLIES, • • • 482 BLOOD AND MOON   45
TORTOISESHELL BUTTERFLIES, PEACOCK BUTTERFLIES, • • • 482 BLOOD AND MOON   45
NOT GOOD: BUT YOU ARE LIKE THE BUTTERFLIES• • • • • 693 MOSADA 1   65

BUTTERFLY
"AND WISDOM IS A BUTTERFLY • • • • • • • • • • • • 338 TOM OROUGHLEY   7
THIS GREAT PURPLE BUTTERFLY• • • • • • • • • • • • 381 SONG OF FOOL   1
BUT EVERY BUTTERFLY TO A FRIEND• • • • • • • • • • 787 GARRET CELLAR   2

BUTTERMILK
I FASTED FOR SOME FORTY DAYS ON BREAD AND BUTTERMILK, • • 592 PILGRIM   1

BUTTING
HIS ROD AND ITS BUTTING HEAD • • • • • • • • • • • 575 MAIDS 2ND SONG   3

BUY
THAT ONLY GODS MAY BUY OF HIM• • • • • • • • • • • 272 GREY ROCK   25
TO HOLD THE WINE THEY BUY OF HIM• • • • • • • • • • 272 GREY ROCK V   25
THAT NOBODY CAN BUY OR BIND: • • • • • • • • • • • 301 RUN PARADISE   27
IT SEEMS I MUST BUY KNOWLEDGE WITH MY PEACE• • • • • 468 HARUN RASHID   169
UNDYING LOVE TO BUY • • • • • • • • • • • • • • • 517 HIS CONFIDENCE   1
COME HERE• BE SEATED NOW: I'D BUY OF YOU• • • • • • 720 WITCH VIVIEN   17
SOME DAY YOU'LL BUY THEM, MAYBE• NEVER: NEVER? • • • 721 WITCH VIVIEN   24
I'D BUY YOUR GLASS• MY GLASS I WILL NOT SELL• • • • 721 WITCH VIVIEN   28

BUYING
THE FOLK WHO ARE BUYING AND SELLING, • • • • • • • 119 PITY OF LOVE   3

BYE   SEE HUSH-A-BYE GOOD-BYE
BYRE
    BEYOND OLD MARTIN'S BYRE . . . .   95 MOLL MAGEE   34
BYRNE
    CRIED THE BEGGAR, BILLY BYRNE: . . . .   331 ROUND TOWER   4
BYRNES
    WHERE THE O'BYRNES AND BYRNES ARE BURIED, ... 331 ROUND TOWER   9
BYZANTINE
    GATHERED A CROWD IN SOME BYZANTINE LANE, ...   180 QUEEN MAEVE   2
    WHO HAVE ACCEPTED THE BYZANTINE FAITH, ...   464 HARUN RASHID   78
    SHARED THE BYZANTINE CROWN? . . . .   789 SINGING HEAD   14
BYZANTIUM
    SAILING TO BYZANTIUM . . . .   407 SAIL BYZANTIUM   T
    TO THE HOLY CITY OF BYZANTIUM. . . . . 408 SAIL BYZANTIUM   16
    TO LORDS AND LADIES OF BYZANTIUM . . . . 408 SAIL BYZANTIUM   31
    PASS BOOKS OF LEARNING FROM BYZANTIUM . . . . . .   461 HARUN RASHID   9
    BYZANTIUM . . . .   497 BYZANTIUM   T
CABBAGE
    GROUNDS WHERE PLUM AND CABBAGE GREW, ... 577 WHAT THEN   13
CABBAGES
    HE DIGS HIS CABBAGES. HE BRINGS TO MIND . . . . .   696 MOSADA 2   18
CABIN
    AND A SMALL CABIN BUILD THERE, OF CLAY AND WATTLES MADE: 117 ISLE INNISFREE   2
    AND A SMALL CABIN BUILT THERE, OF CLAY AND WATTLES MADE: 117 ISLE INNISFREE V 2
CABINS
    CABINS GONE NOW, OLD WELL-SIDES, OLD DEAR PLACES, . . 130 BOOK STORIES   V   23
CAER
    CAER, HIS BLUE-EYED DAUGHTER THAT I LOVE. . . . . . 184 QUEEN MAEVE   96
    CAER, HIS BLUE EYED DAUGHTER THAT I LOVE. . . . . . 184 QUEEN MAEVE   V   96
CAESAR
    A ROMAN CAESAR IS HELD DOWN . . . .   379 SAINT HUNCH   4
    AUGUSTUS CAESAR, AND AFTER THESE . . . . 379 SAINT HUNCH   11
    OUR MASTER CAESAR IS IN THE TENT . . . . 617 LONG-LEG FLY   5
CAESARS
    WHAT HAD THE CAESARS BUT THEIR THRONES? . . . . . . 401 DEMON BEAST   50
CAGE
    NOR A CAGE, NOR ALIGHT UPON WRIST, ... 349 HAWK   8
    LET THE CAGE BIRD AND THE CAGE BIRD MATE . . . . . 450 OWEN AHERNE   16
    LET THE CAGE BIRD AND THE CAGE BIRD MATE . . . . . 450 OWEN AHERNE   16
    I DID NOT FIND IN ANY CAGE THE WOMAN AT MY SIDE. . . 450 OWEN AHERNE   19
CAGED
    LET HIM BE HOODED OR CAGED . . . . 349 HAWK   2
    BECAUSE PIEBALD PONIES, LED BEARS, CAGED LIONS, MAKE BUT 623 HIGH TALK   5
       POOR SHOWS,
CAGES
    THE BIRDS, FOR HE OPENED THEIR CAGES . . . .   92 FATHER OHART   17
CAIRN
    . . . AND GUARDLESS THE SACRED CAIRN AND THE RATH, 58 OISIN 3   163
    THE GREY CAIRN ON THE HILL, WHEN DAY SINKS DROWNED IN DEW, 161 BLACK PIG   6
    UNDER A CAIRN OF SLEEPY STONE . . . .   192 BAILE AILLINN   81
    O TATTERED CLOUDS OF THE WORLD, CALL FROM THE HIGH CAIRN 207 HANRAHANS SONG V 6
       OF MAIVE,
    A HIGH, GREY CAIRN. WHAT MORE IS TO BE SAID? . . . 778 SONG DEIRDRE 3   5
CAIRN-HEAPED
    CAME TO THE CAIRN-HEAPED GRASSY HILL . . . .   3 OISIN 1   17
CAIRN'S
    FOR WHOM THE CAIRN'S BUT HEAPED ANEW. . . . . 192 BAILE AILLINN   84
CAKE   SEE GRIDDLE-CAKE
    IS DEAD. THE BOY THAT BRINGS MY GRIDDLE CAKE . . . 339 SHEP GOATHERD   V   20
CALAMITY
    HEAVEN KNOWS WHAT CALAMITY: . . . .   193 BAILE AILLINN   112
    THAT IN THE SAME CALAMITY . . . .   540 FROM ANTIGONE   9
    CALAMITY CAN HAVE ITS FLING. . . . . 782 HEART FRIGHT   18
CALCULATION
    WHAT CALCULATION, NUMBER, MEASUREMENT, REPLIED? . . 611 STATUES   27
CALCULATIONS
    CALCULATIONS THAT LOOK BUT CASUAL FLESH, PUT DOWN . . 610 STATUES   11
CALENDARS
    WITH ALL THOSE CALENDARS WHEREON . . . . 432 NINETEEN 19   99
CALF
    WHERE LIES THE COW AT PEACE BESIDE HER CALF, ... 715 FERENCZ RENYI   121
    CURES FOR CALF WITH 'PLAINING THROAT, ...   717 FAIRY DOCTOR   V   15
CALIF'S
    FOR THE GREAT CALIF'S TREASURER AND MY FRIEND, . . 460 HARUN RASHID   V   2
    WHERE GOLD-EMBROIDERED BANNERS OF THE CALIF'S . . . 461 HARUN RASHID   V   6
CALIPH
    BOOK I WHAT THE CALIPH PARTLY LEARNED . . . . . . 372 PHASES OF MOON   V   T
    BOOK II WHAT THE CALIPH REFUSED TO LEARN . . . . . 460 HARUN RASHID   V   T
    WHEN OUR BELOVED CALIPH PUT TO DEATH . . . . 462 HARUN RASHID   31
CALIPH'S
    NOW THE GOOD CALIPH'S LEARNED TREASURER, ... 461 HARUN RASHID   3
CALIPHS
    WHERE BANNERS OF THE CALIPHS HANG, NIGHT-COLOURED . 461 HARUN RASHID   6
    AND HIDE IT THERE, FOR CALIPHS TO WORLD'S END . . . 461 HARUN RASHID   17
CALL   SEE HUNTING-CALL
    I CALL, AS THEY GO BY ME ONE BY ONE, ... 114 ROSE OF BATTLE   8
    "TURN IF YE MAY," I CALL OUT TO EACH ONE, ... 114 ROSE OF BATTLE V   7
    THAT YOU CALL IN BIRDS, IN WIND ON THE HILL, . . . 141 EVERLAST VOICE   6
    WHEN OWLS BEGAN TO CALL: . . . .   159 CAP AND BELLS   6
    AND CALL TO MY BELOVED AND ME: "NO LONGER FLY . . . 173 SPEAKS HEARERS   7
    BUT CALL ME FIRST THROUGH THE GATE: . . . .   178 FIDDLER DOONEY   12

		PAGE	TITLE		LINE

CALL   (CONTINUED)
```
"I AM FROM THOSE RIVERS AND I BID YOU CALL . . . .        184 QUEEN MAEVE            91
"I COME FROM THE UNDIMMED RIVERS TO BID YOU CALL . . . .  184 QUEEN MAEVE       V    91
"I AM FROM THE UNDIMMED RIVERS.  I BID YOU CALL . . . .   184 QUEEN MAEVE       V    91
"I AM FROM THOSE RIVERS AND WOULD HAVE YOU CALL . . . .   184 QUEEN MAEVE       V    91
WHAT SHALL I CALL THEM? FISH THAT SWIM, . . . .           195 BAILE AILLINN         144
IT MIGHT CALL UP A NEW AGE, CALLING TO MIND  . . . .      201 OLD MEMORY              4
"LET PEEWIT CALL AND CURLEW CRY WHERE THEY WILL, . . . .  203 WITHER BOUGHS           2
THE MARTYRS CALL THE WORLD."  AND THEREUPON  . . . .      205 ADAMS CURSE            14
THE MARTYRS CALL THE WORLD."  THAT WOMAN THEN . . . .     205 ADAMS CURSE            14
O TATTERED CLOUDS OF THE WORLD, CALL FROM THE HIGH CAIRN  207 HANRAHANS SONG   V     6
   OF MAIVE,
LIKE TATTERED CLOUDS OF THE WORLD, PASSIONS CALL AND OUR  207 HANRAHANS SONG   V     8
   HEARTS BEAT,
LIKE PLOVERS THAT HAVE HEARD THE CALL. . . . . . .        213 BLESS PSALTER          13
WHAT DO YOU CALL IT?--THAT OLD PROMISE-BREAKER, . . .     228 SHADOW WATER B        122
A MAGIC THAT CAN CALL A DEMON UP, . . . . . .             238 SHADOW WATER B        344
WHAT NAME TO CALL HIM BY?  COME TO HIS SHIP. . . .        240 SHADOW WATER B        390
BY ANY OTHER MEANS.  YOU CALL IT PASSION, . . . .         244 SHADOW WATER B        455
AND WORDS OBEY MY CALL", . . . . . . . .                  256 WORDS                  12
I CALL FOR SPADE AND HORSE AND HOUND . . . .              275 GREY ROCK             105
AND CALL THOSE EXILES AS THEY WERE . . . . .              290 SEPTEMBER 1913         26
BUT I'LL HAVE NO MAN CALL ME GHOST." . . . .              304 HOUR DAWN              41
THERE IS NOT A FOOL CAN CALL ME FRIEND, . . .             336 YOUNG BEAUTY           16
THAT NOT A FOOL CAN CALL ME FRIEND, . . . .               336 YOUNG BEAUTY     V     16
TO CALL UP TO THE EYES . . . . . . .                      347 FISHERMAN               7
"CALL DOWN THE HAWK FROM THE AIR, . . . .                 349 HAWK                    1
I CALL TO MY OWN OPPOSITE, SUMMON ALL . . .               367 EGO DOMINUS             8
I CALL TO THE MYSTERIOUS ONE WHO YET . . .                371 EGO DOMINUS            70
WHAT BETTER THAN CALL A DANCE? . . . . .                  378 CAT AND MOON           13
AND HENS TO MOOR-COCKS CALL, . . . . .                    393 EASTER 1916            54
UNDER THE DAY'S DECLINING BEAM, AND CALL . .              410 TOWER                  21
OR SERVILE SHAPE, AT OTHERS' BECK AND CALL. .             417 ANCEST HOUSES           8
THROUGH WINTER-TIME WE CALL ON SPRING, . . .              434 WHEEL                   1
AND THROUGH THE SPRING ON SUMMER CALL, . . .              434 WHEEL                   2
EVEN WHERE HORRIBLE GREEN PARROTS CALL AND SWING. . .     442 BLACK CENTAUR           2
EVEN WHERE THE HORRIBLE GREEN PARROTS CALL AND SWING.     442 BLACK CENTAUR    V      2
IF KINDNESS I MAY CALL . . . . . . .                      452 HUMAN DIGNITY           2
AND SPEAK BUT LIES.  CALL UP TO MEMORY . . .              462 HARUN RASHID     V     30
HORTON'S THE FIRST I CALL.  HE LOVED STRANGE THOUGHT      471 ALL SOUL NIGHT         21
ON FLORENCE EMERY I CALL THE NEXT. . . . .                472 ALL SOUL NIGHT         41
AND I CALL UP MACGREGOR FROM THE GRAVE, . .               473 ALL SOUL NIGHT         61
I CALL MACGREGOR MATHERS FROM HIS GRAVE, . .              473 ALL SOUL NIGHT   V     61
I CALL IT DEATH-IN-LIFE AND LIFE-IN-DEATH. .              497 BYZANTIUM              16
AND CALL THOSE WORKS EXTRAVAGANCE OF BREATH .             501 VACILLATION            32
MAY CALL DOWN CURSES ON HIS HEAD . . . .                  508 JANE BISHOP             4
MAY CALL A CURSE OUT OF THE SKY . . . .                   508 JANE BISHOP            4
TILL TRUTH OBEYED HIS CALL, . . . . .                     576 ACRE OF GRASS          18
CALL THE MUSES HOME. . . . . .                            600 THOSE IMAGES            8
I CALL ON THOSE THAT CALL ME SON . . .                    604 YOU CONTENT             1
I CALL ON THOSE THAT CALL ME SON, . . .                   604 YOU CONTENT             1
AND IN THAT TERROR'S NAME OBEYED THE CALL, .              622 HOUND VOICE            12
ACH, CALL ME WHAT YOU PLEASE! . . . .                     627 STATES HOLIDAY         21
THE FAIRY'S CALL . . . . . . .                            654 ISLE STAT I 2    V      T
NO, NO, WHEN THAT SHALL BE, THEN MEN MAY CALL . .         662 ISLE STAT II 1         79
FOR SUCH A CALL.  LET THE WILD WORD BE CRIED .            669 ISLE STAT II 3         76
THUS FOR ANOTHER'S BUGLE CALL! . . . .                    671 ISLE STAT II 3        136
I SOUGHT THEE NOT.  MEN CALL ME INFAMY. . .               685 SEEKER                 75
DARK JOAN CALL THE BERRIES SWEET, . . .                   743 DANAAN QUICK           28
AND I HAVE HEARD THEM CALL FROM WIND TO WIND .            750 SHADOW WATER A         83
GIVE ME THE HELM! CALL HITHER THOSE WHO LIE . .           751 SHADOW WATER A         91
WE WILL GO CALL THESE SAILORS, AND ESCAPE . .             766 SHADOW WATER A        382
CAN CALL THE MILCH COWS . . . . .                         780 WELL AND TREE           5
CAN CALL THE MILCH-COWS . . . . .                         780 WELL AND TREE    V      5
```
CALLED
```
NOW, MAN OF CROZIERS, SHADOWS CALLED OUR NAMES . . .       29 OISIN 2                1
HALF LOST IN VAPOUR, SHADOWS CALLED OUR NAMES, . .         29 OISIN 2          V     3
AND CALLED HIM SWEETEST NAMES AND SOOTHED HIS FEARS. . .   30 OISIN 2          V    27
HOLDING THAT HORSE, AND SADLY CALLED MY NAME, . .          44 OISIN 2              230
AND HE CALLED LOUDLY TO THE STARS TO BEND . .              68 SAD SHEPHERD           5
HE CALLED ALOUD TO ALL THE STARS TO LEND . .               68 SAD SHEPHERD     V     5
I CALLED MY BATTLE-BREAKING MEN . . . .                    83 MAD KING GOLL         17
AND CALLED OUT TO HIM, "SON IT IS NOT MEET . .            107 CUCHULAIN SEA    V    20
AND SOME ONE CALLED ME BY MY NAME, . . .                  149 WANDER AENGUS          12
AND SOMEONE CALLED ME BY MY NAME. . . .                   149 WANDER AENGUS    V    12
WHO CALLED ME BY MY NAME AND RAN . . .                    150 WANDER AENGUS         15
THAT CALLED ME BY MY NAME AND RAN . . .                   150 WANDER AENGUS    V    15
WHEN THE OWLS CALLED OUT NO MORE! . . .                   159 CAP AND BELLS         14
CUMHAL CALLED OUT, BENDING HIS HEAD, . . .                166 BLESSED                1
CUMHAL CALLED OUT, BOWING HIS HEAD, . . .                 167 BLESSED          V    4A
NOW WORDS THAT CALLED UP THE LIGHTNING . . .              171 MAID QUIET             7
FOR THE WORDS THAT CALLED UP THE LIGHTNING . .            171 MAID QUIET       V     7
SHE COULD HAVE CALLED OVER THE RIM OF THE WORLD . .       181 QUEEN MAEVE           23
TILL MAEVE CALLED OUT, "THESE ARE BUT COMMON MEN.         186 QUEEN MAEVE          122
CALLED RATHER BAILE LITTLE-LAND, . . . .                  189 BAILE AILLINN         17
CALLED RATHER BAILE LITTLE LAND, . . . .                  189 BAILE AILLINN         17
WISE BIDDY EARLY CALLED THE WICKED WOOD, . .              218 WOODS OF COOLE        15
BEING AS DOUBTFUL?  I HAVE CALLED YOU MASTER .            227 SHADOW WATER B        110
HAVE CALLED ME THEIR BELOVED, I'LL NOT KISS THEM. .       237 SHADOW WATER B        336
OR CALLED BEFORE HIS EYES.  O CARRY ME . . .              249 SHADOW WATER B        568
ARDAN, AND THOUGH I CALLED TO HIM AND TRIED . . .         283 TWO KINGS            142
```

121

	PAGE	TITLE	LINE
CALLED (CONTINUED)			
CALLED CRUACHAN, AND IT WAS AS MUCH	302	HOUR DAWN	4
AND CALLED THE PLEASURES EVIL	365	HER RACE	3
AND CALLED HER NAME, SHE HAD HEARD, ...	381	SONGS FOOL 2	11
HAS CALLED UP THE COLD SPIRITS THAT ARE BORN	382	VISION ROBART	2
NEVER TO LEAVE THAT VALLEY HIS FATHERS CALLED THEIR HOME.	391	UNDER SATURN	16
OR ANYTHING CALLED CONSCIENCE ONCE:	413	TOWER	118
CALLED ARCHITECT AND ARTIST IN, THAT THEY, ...	418	ANCEST HOUSES	18
OUT OF THE FABULOUS DARKNESS CALLED.	437	SONGS PLAY 1	16
. . . "YOU HAVE CALLED ME MAD," IT SAID, ...	450	OWEN AHERNE	13
THAT'S CALLED PLATONIC LOVE, ...	471	ALL SOUL NIGHT	23
. . . THOUGHT'S CROWNED POWERS HE CALLED THEM ONCE. . . .	480	BLOOD AND MOON	15
I HAD THOUGHT TO HAVE CALLED HER OUT TO THE DOOR, . .	551	SONGS REWRIT 1 V	15
BUT THAT I CALLED ON HIM?	658	ISLE STAT I 3	80
MY LORD, YOU CALLED? NOT I. THIS MAID IS DEAD. . . .	704	MOSADA 3	125
"WATCHER, WHEREFORE HAVE YE CALLED US?" EYES GO AFTER HIS LEAN HAND,	718	PHANTOM SHIP	10
FOR HE WHO GAVE IT CALLED IT AENGUS' HARP	762	SHADOW WATER A	288
HAVE CALLED HIM MIGHTY. I WILL FOLLOW YOU	768	SHADOW WATER A	412
WE CALLED IT A GOOD DEATH. TODAY	791	REPRISALS	3
CALLED'ST			
THOU CALLED'ST ME FORTH. AND HOW THOU MADEST ME . . .	683	SEEKER	52
CALLEN			
YOUNG NIAM, AND THOU SHALT BE CALLEN	7	OISIN 1 V	75
CALLIMACHUS			
NO HANDIWORK OF CALLIMACHUS, ...	566	LAPIS LAZULI	29
CALLING			
FROM THE GREAT GRASS-BARNACLE CALLING, ...	57	OISIN 3	156
AND NIAMH CALLING AWAY, COME AWAY!	140	HOSTING SIDHE	4
AND NIAMH CALLING AWAY, COME AWAY.	141	HOSTING SIDHE	16
AND HEAR THE NARROW GRAVES CALLING MY CHILD AND ME. . .	147	UNAPPEAS HOST	6
DO YOU NOT HEAR ME CALLING, WHITE DEER WITH NO HORNS? . .	153	CHANGE BELOVED	1
AND NOW MY CALLING IS BUT THE CALLING OF A HOUND! . .	153	CHANGE BELOVED	8
AND NOW MY CALLING IS BUT THE CALLING OF A HOUND! . .	153	CHANGE BELOVED	8
AND SORROW AWAY, AND CALLING BARD AND CLOWN	170	SECRET ROSE	20
ARE CALLING THROUGH MY HEART.	171	MAID QUIET V	8
IT MIGHT CALL UP A NEW AGE, CALLING TO MIND	201	OLD MEMORY	4
WHAT ARE YOU CALLING OUT ABOVE THE MAST?	243	SHADOW WATER B	437
YOU'LL HEAR THEM CALLING OUT TO ONE ANOTHER	247	SHADOW WATER B	521
A VOICE CAME CALLING ME TO THIS YOUR LAND, ...	682	SEEKER	22
THE CALLING AFAR OF THE DOE AND THE DEER.	717	LOVE SONG	5
AH, WELL! THEY ARE CALLING ME--THEY ARE CALLING ME. . .	760	SHADOW WATER A	251
AH, WELL! THEY ARE CALLING ME--THEY ARE CALLING ME. . .	760	SHADOW WATER A	251
WHEN THE WINDS ARE CALLING THERE.	772	SONG DEIRDRE 1	4
OR THE GANNETS CALLING OUT	772	SONG DEIRDRE 1	5
CALLS			
THE BELL THAT CALLS US ON: THE SWEET FAR THING. . . .	115	ROSE OF BATTLE	28
WHAT THE EXULTANT HEART CALLS GOOD	288	TO WEALTHY MAN	33
THE BODY CALLS IT DEATH, ...	500	VACILLATION	7
THAT CALLS. O EVIL STARRED! IT COMES ALONG	653	ISLE STAT I 2	49
HUSH'D THE FISHERS, TILL A MOTHER CALLS BY NAME HER DROWNED SON!	719	PHANTOM SHIP	23
THEN EACH WIFE AND MAID AND MOTHER CALLS BY NAME SOME DROWNED ONE.	719	PHANTOM SHIP	24
CALM			
THE VAN OF WANDERING QUIET! ERE YOU BE TOO CALM AND OLD,	73	ANASHU VIJAYA	43
THE VAN OF WANDERING QUIET! ERE YE BE TOO CALM AND OLD,	73	ANASHU VIJAYA V	43
AND CHAPLET THEIR CALM BROWS WITH LEAFAGE DIM, . . .	127	DREAM OF FAERY V	32
AND CHAPLET THEIR CALM BROWS WITH LEAFAGE COOL: . . .	127	DREAM OF FAERY V	32
AND FROM ITS MURMURING GREENNESS, CALM OF FAERY, . . .	129	BOOK STORIES	3
O HOW COULD I BE SO CALM	171	MAID QUIET	5
SHE GOES ABOUT HER HOUSE ERECT AND CALM	340	SHEP GOATHERD	35
OF SWORD-BLUE WAVES OF CALM: WHILE O'ER HEAD BLINK . .	663	ISLE STAT II 2	42
IN THEIR COILING CALM AND SLOW.	680	LOVE AND DEATH	8
AND CALM, ROBED ALL IN RAIMENT MOONY WHITE.	693	MOSADA 1	77
CALUMNY			
OR CALUMNY A SONG. HOW CAN THEY KNOW	398	LEADERS CROWD	7
CALVARY'S			
BEING BY CALVARY'S TURBULENCE UNSATISFIED, ...	318	MAGI	7
CALVERT			
CALVERT AND WILSON, BLAKE AND CLAUDE, ...	639	BEN BULBEN	64
AND WILSON, BLAKE AND CALVERT, CLAUDE, ...	639	BEN BULBEN V	64
CALVES			
AND A HUNDRED CALVES AND A HUNDRED SHEEP	8	OISIN 1	89
OF THE CALVES ON THE WARM HILLSIDE	88	STOLEN CHILD	45
OF THE CALVES ON THE WARM HILL SIDE, ...	88	STOLEN CHILD V	45
OF THE CALVES ON THE WARM HILL-SIDE, ...	88	STOLEN CHILD V	45
CURES FOR CALVES WITH 'PLAINING THROAT, ...	717	FAIRY DOCTOR	15
CAME			
CAME TO THE CAIRN-HEAPED GRASSY HILL	3	OISIN 1	17
"WHAT DREAM CAME WITH YOU THAT YOU CAME	5	OISIN 1	50
"WHAT DREAM CAME WITH YOU THAT YOU CAME	5	OISIN 1	50
UNTIL THE DANAAN POETS CAME	7	OISIN 1 V	64
CAOILTE, CONAN, AND FINN CAME NEAR, ...	10	OISIN 1	111
BUT NOW A WANDERING LAND BREEZE CAME	13	OISIN 1	165
WHEN ROUND US SUDDENLY THERE CAME	13	OISIN 1 V	165
UNTIL ONE CAME, A TEARFUL BOY	17	OISIN 1	237
AND NOW, STILL SAD, WE CAME TO WHERE	17	OISIN 1	247
AND ONE CAME CLOSE, A TEARFUL BOY, ...	17	OISIN 1 V	237
THAT FROM THE SAFFRON MORNING CAME, ...	19	OISIN 1	277
AND CAME TO WHERE THE DEWDROPS FALL	20	OISIN 1	293

```
                                                    PAGE      TITLE            LINE
CAME   (CONTINUED)
     A SEA-WORN WAIF CAME FLOATING BY. . . . . . .    24  OISIN 1        V    365
     THEREON YOUNG NIAMH SOFTLY CAME   . . . . . .    25  OISIN 1             373
     THEN SOFTLY TO ME NIAM CAME,   . . . . . . .     25  OISIN 1        V    373
     LIKE DROPS OF HONEY CAME THEIR WORDS,  . . . .   26  OISIN 1             398
     NEARER THE CASTLE CAME WE.  A VAST TIDE,  . . .  31  OISIN 2        V    27A
     CAME SWIMMING SADLY DOWN THE MIGHTY STAIR. . . . 32  OISIN 2        V    50B
     AND TELL ME HOW YOU CAME TO ONE UNBID,  . . . .  33  OISIN 2        V    67
     LIKE A SMALL RIVER, AND WHERE FEET TOUCHED CAME  37  OISIN 2             117
     AND CAME AGAIN, HOLDING A SECOND LIGHT  . . . .  37  OISIN 2             124
     AND WHERE OUR FOOTFALL 'LIGHTED LAST THERE CAME  37  OISIN 2        V    119
     AWHILE, AND CAME AGAIN, A SECOND LIGHT  . . . .  37  OISIN 2        V    124
     AND AT HIS CRY THERE CAME NO MILK-PALE FACE   .  38  OISIN 2             134
     THE DAWN CAME IN, AND GLIMMERED ON THE FLOOR  .  39  OISIN 2             152
     THOSE TWO CAME CARRYING WINE AND MEAT AND BREAD, 41  OISIN 2             184
     OUTCRY OF BATS.  AND THEN YOUNG NIAMH CAME  . .  44  OISIN 2             229
     THE HARE LEAPED IN THE GRASS.  YOUNG NIAMH CAME  44  OISIN 2        V    229
     AND DRIFTING GREYNESS.  CAME THIS MONOTONE  . .  45  OISIN 2        V    232
     CAME TO MY TOWER AS AGE DRAGGED AFTER AGE  . . . 45  OISIN 2        V    242
     CAME NOW THE SLIDING OF TEARS AND SWEEPING OF MIST-COLD
                                                      47  OISIN 3             7
       HAIR,
     CAME NOW THE SLIDING OF TEARS AND SWEEPING OF MIST-COLD
                                                      47  OISIN 3        V    7
       AIR,
     CAME NOW THE SLIDING OF TEARS AND SWEEPING OF MIST COLD
                                                      47  OISIN 3        V    7
       HAIR,
     THE BREATHING CAME FROM THOSE BODIES, . . . . .  49  OISIN 3             36
     AND OVER THE LIMBS AND THE VALLEY THE SLOW OWLS WANDERED
                                                      49  OISIN 3             41
       AND CAME,
     CAME SOUND FROM THOSE MONSTROUS SLEEPERS, . . . . 51 OISIN 3             58
     HIS LIPS MOVED SLOWLY IN SILENCE, NO ANSWER OUT OF THEM
                                                      51  OISIN 3             66
       CAME:
     AND A SOFTNESS CAME FROM THE STARLIGHT . . . . . 52  OISIN 3             72
     SAD NIAM CAME NEAR ME, AND LAID HER BROWS ON THE MIDST
                                                      52  OISIN 3        V    74
       OF MY BREAST
     CAME BY ME THE KINGS OF THE RED BRANCH, . . . . . 53 OISIN 3             87
     CAME BLANAID, MAC NESSA, TALL FERGUS WHO FEASTWARD OF OLD
                                                      53  OISIN 3             89
       TIME SLUNK,
     CAME BY ME THE CANNS OF THE RED BRANCH . . . . . 53  OISIN 3        V    87
     CAME BLANID, MAC NESSA, CUCHULIN: . . . . . . .  53  OISIN 3        V    89
     . . . CAME FERGUS WHO FEASTWARD SAD SLUNK, . . . 53  OISIN 3        V    89
     CAME BLANID, MAC NESSA, AND FERGUS WHO FEASTWARD OF OLD
                                                      53  OISIN 3        V    89
       TIME SLUNK,
     CAME CAR-BORNE BALOR, AS OLD AS A FOREST, HIS VAST FACE
                                                      53  OISIN 3        V    91
       SUNK
     CAME BALOR, AS OLD AS A FOREST, CAR BORNE, HIS MIGHTY HEAD
                                                      53  OISIN 3        V    91
       SUNK
     CAME, AND MY FOREHEAD FELL LOW, AND MY TEARS LIKE BERRIES
                                                      57  OISIN 3             154
       FELL DOWN:
     LATER A SOUND CAME, HALF LOST IN THE SOUND OF A SHORE FAR
                                                      57  OISIN 3             155
       AWAY,
     CAME AFTER THE HARD GAZE OF YOUTH, OR AN OLD MAN LIFTED
                                                      59  OISIN 3             170
       HIS HEAD:
     A HERDSMAN CAME FROM INLAND VALLEYS, . . . . . . 82  MAD KING GOLL       14
     I CAME UPON A LITTLE TOWN  . . . . . . . . . .   85  MAD KING GOLL       49
     WITH EYES OF SADNESS CAME TO HEAR . . . . . . .  85  MAD KING GOLL  V    62
     CAME KEENERS HOARSER THAN ROOKS . . . . . . . .  92  FATHER OHART        22
     PEOPLE CAME INTO COLOONEY: . . . . . . . . . .   93  FATHER OHART        27
     CAME KEENING IN THAT DAY. . . . . . . . . . . .  93  FATHER OHART        32
     CAME FLYING, HEAVY AND SAD: . . . . . . . . . .  93  FATHER OHART        34
     A MAN CAME SLOWLY FROM THE SETTING SUN, . . . . 105  CUCHULAIN SEA       1
     HERDED THE CATTLE CAME WITH STUMBLING FEET,  . . 106  CUCHULAIN SEA      19
     WAS DRIVING CATTLE CAME SHE WITH SWIFT FEET, . . 106  CUCHULAIN SEA  V   19
     SEEK OUT WHAT MAN HE IS."  ONE WENT AND CAME. . . 109  CUCHULAIN SEA     51
     STOOD UP, AND CAME TO THE LONG SANDS ALONE: . . 111  CUCHULAIN SEA      84
     A WOVEN SILENCE, OR BUT CAME TO CAST . . . . . . 114  ROSE OF BATTLE     13
     AND THEN YOU CAME WITH THOSE RED MOURNFUL LIPS, . 120  SORROW OF LOVE V  5
     AND WITH YOU CAME THE WHOLE OF THE WORLD'S TEARS, 120  SORROW OF LOVE V  6
     I CAME AND WROTE UPON A CROSS OF WOOD-- . . . . 123  DREAM OF DEATH V    7
     WHEN THE MOTHS CAME ONCE MORE, . . . . . . . . . 133  FR GILLIGAN        22
     WHEN MOTHS CAME ONCE MORE, . . . . . . . . . .  133  FR GILLIGAN    V    22
     A MAN WITH A HAZEL WAND CAME WITHOUT SOUND: . . 153  CHANGE BELOVED      6
     A MAN WITH A WAND OF HAZEL CAME WITHOUT SOUND:  153  CHANGE BELOVED V    6
     AND THE HEART AND THE SOUL CAME THROUGH, . . . . 160  CAP AND BELLS      30
     TO HER RIGHT HAND CAME THE RED ONE, . . . . . . 160  CAP AND BELLS      31
     TO HER LEFT HAND CAME THE BLUE, . . . . . . . . 160  CAP AND BELLS      32
     THE HEART AND THE SOUL CAME THROUGH: . . . . . . 160  CAP AND BELLS      30
     THAT MURMURING AND LONGING CAME . . . . . . . . 162  ASKS FORGIVE        8
     THAT LONGING AND MURMURING CAME . . . . . . . . 162  ASKS FORGIVE   V    8
     AND I DREAMED MY LOST LOVE CAME STEALTHILY OUT OF THE WOOD
                                                     163  VALLEY LOVERS       3
     TILL DATHI CAME AND STOOD, . . . . . . . . . .  166  BLESSED             2
     CAME BY THE WOODY WAY . . . . . . . . . . . . . 166  BLESSED        V    2
     TILL DATHI CAME AND STOOD, . . . . . . . . . .  167  BLESSED        V    4B
     THE POWERS, NOT KIND LIKE YOU, CAME WHERE GOD'S GARDEN
                                                     174  ELEMENT POWERS V    1
       BLOWS,
     CAME TO THE THRESHOLD OF THE PAINTED HOUSE . . . 185  QUEEN MAEVE       108
     CAME UP OUT OF THE HOLE, AND RED-EARED HOUNDS . 185  QUEEN MAEVE        117
     WITH LONG WHITE BODIES CAME OUT OF THE AIR . . . 185  QUEEN MAEVE       118
     UNTIL TWO LOVERS CAME OUT OF THE AIR . . . . .  187  QUEEN MAEVE        143
     BUT OUT OF THE DARK AIR OVER HER HEAD THERE CAME 187  QUEEN MAEVE        153
     HE RAN AND LAUGHED UNTIL HE CAME . . . . . . .  194  BAILE AILLINN      128
     TWO SWANS CAME FLYING UP TO HIM, . . . . . . .  194  BAILE AILLINN      135
```

123

CAME   (CONTINUED)

	PAGE	TITLE		LINE
AND HURRYING TO THE SOUTH HE CAME	194	BAILE AILLINN	V	128
EDAIN CAME OUT OF MIDHIR'S HILL, AND LAY	219	HARP OF AENGUS		1
MY COURAGE CAME AGAIN. BUT THAT'S NOT ALL.	223	SHADOW WATER B		31
A BEAUTIFUL YOUNG MAN AND GIRL CAME UP	223	SHADOW WATER B		33
AND IF YOU SAY THAT SHE CAME WILLINGLY--	244	SHADOW WATER B		460
AND YOU SAY THAT SHE CAME WILLINGLY--	244	SHADOW WATER B	V	460
CAME WHEN TIME HAD TOUCHED HER FORM.	259	PEACE		11
AND THESE THINGS CAME, SO MUCH THE MORE THEREBY	265	THESE CLOUDS		8
'TWAS ROUNDLY SPOKE, BUT WHEN NIGHT CAME	275	GREY ROCK		95
KING EOCHAID CAME AT SUNDOWN TO A WOOD	276	TWO KINGS		1
AND CAME INTO A WOOD AS THE SUN SET	277	TWO KINGS	V	3
UNTIL HE CAME BEFORE THE PAINTED WALL,	279	TWO KINGS		47
AND WHEN OLD GUAIRE CAME AND STOOD	297	THREE BEGGARS		54
AS I CAME OVER WINDY GAP	300	RUN PARADISE		1
HE CAME, BUT MAN IS A FOOL."	341	SHEP GOATHERD		74
"HUNCHBACK AND SAINT AND FOOL," AND THAT THEY CAME	377	PHASES OF MOON		132
BEFORE THAT RUIN CAME, FOR CENTURIES,	412	TOWER		81
OUT OF NOTHING IT CAME,	439	FRAGMENTS		7
CAME TO THE LEAST CONSIDERED OF HIS COURTIERS;	462	HARUN RASHID		42
TRUTHS WITHOUT FATHER CAME, TRUTHS THAT NO BOOK	467	HARUN RASHID		138
BUT MINE SAW STELLA ONCE. WHENCE CAME OUR THOUGHT?	486	SEVEN SAGES		6
MINE SAW STELLA ONCE. WHENCE CAME OUR THOUGHT?	486	SEVEN SAGES	V	6
MINE SAW STELLA ONCE. WHEN CAME OUR THOUGHT?	486	SEVEN SAGES	V	6
THEY CAME LIKE SWALLOWS AND LIKE SWALLOWS WENT,	489	COOLE PARK 29		17
OR OUT OF FOLLY INTO FOLLY CAME.	491	COOLE BALLYLEE		32
CAME TO SO DEEP A THOUGHT	505	RESULT THOUGHT		10
CAME WHEN HE WOULD.	512	JANE ON GOD		2
ANOTHER CAME IN SIGHT	515	GIRLS SONG B		5
CAME WHERE YOU STOOD,	518	LOVES LONENESS		4
I DID THE DRAGON'S WILL UNTIL YOU CAME	533	HER TRIUMPH		1
WHAT FROM THE FOREST CAME? WHAT BEAST HAS LICKED ITS YOUNG?	560	MAGIC DRUM		6
CAME OUT OF A NEEDLE'S EYE;	562	NEEDLES EYE		2
ON THEIR OWN FEET THEY CAME, OR ON SHIPBOARD,	566	LAPIS LAZULI		25
"BECAUSE MY LADY CAME	570	THREE BUSHES		37
THE PRIEST CAME WHERE SHE WAS;	571	THREE BUSHES		65
HOW CAME THIS RANGER	574	MAIDS 1ST SONG		1
ALL HIS HAPPIER DREAMS CAME TRUE--	577	WHAT THEN		11
I CAME ON A GREAT HOUSE IN THE MIDDLE OF THE NIGHT,	581	CURSE CROMWELL		25
PARNELL CAME DOWN THE ROAD, HE SAID TO A CHEERING MAN;	590	PARNELL		1
AND HE CAME SAILING HOME.	594	COLONEL MARTIN		6
AND WHEN THEY CAME TO THE TOP STAIR	595	COLONEL MARTIN		41
PRAISE EVERY MAN THAT CAME AGAIN.	608	SONGS BURDEN 3		7
PLOTINUS CAME AND LOOKED ABOUT,	611	NEWS ORACLE		9
CAME AND WERE GONE. HE LEANT UPON A TREE	634	CUCHULAIN COMF		5
AMONG THOSE BIRD-LIKE THINGS CAME, AND LET FALL	634	CUCHULAIN COMF		8
CAME CREEPING UP BECAUSE THE MAN WAS STILL.	634	CUCHULAIN COMF		10
LOVE FROM HEAVEN CAME OF YORE	648	ISLE STAT I 1		77
AND TROUBLED EYES CAME MORNING'S FIRST-BORN GLOW;	648	ISLE STAT I 1		103
YON SHEPHERD--CAME YOUR SPIRIT TO BEGUILE	648	ISLE STAT I 1		105
AND, OH! THE WONDER OF THE THING! EACH CAME	656	ISLE STAT I 3		29
WITH CLINGING MIST, EACH STAR-FOUGHT WANDERER CAME	656	ISLE STAT I 3		33
AND THEN NEW MURMURS CAME NEW UTTERING	657	ISLE STAT I 3		50
HE PASSED ACROSS THE LAKE. WHEN WE TWO CAME	658	ISLE STAT II 1		5
AYE, VERY LATELY, SORROW CAME TO WEEP	659	ISLE STAT II 1		25
EACH CAME ONE MORN, WITH WELCOMING OF SONG,	660	ISLE STAT II 1		42
TWO CAME, HIS NAME AND MINE ON MANY A TREE	662	ISLE STAT II 2		10
YONDER'S THE ISLE IN SEARCH WHEREOF WE CAME;	662	ISLE STAT II 2		13
FOR THERE CAME AN AIR-BREATH COOL	667	ISLE STAT II 3		27
AND DOWN I CAME AS A FALCON SWOOPS	673	ISLE STAT II 3		178
AS HERE I CAME I SAW GOD PAN. HE PLAYED	678	ISLE STAT II 3		300
SHEPHERDS, I CAME THIS MORNING TO YOUR LAND	682	SEEKER		15
A VOICE CAME CALLING ME TO THIS YOUR LAND,	682	SEEKER		22
WHEN FLASH ON FLASH ONCE MORE THE LIGHTNING CAME,	688	TWO TITANS		39
I CAME THE FIRST TIME TO THY VILLAGE SCHOOL?	713	FERENCZ RENYI		90
CAME OLIVE FIRES OF MORNING AND ON THE DARKNESS FED,	719	PHANTOM SHIP		33
CAME THE OLIVE FIRE OF MORNING, AND ON THE DARKNESS FED,	719	PHANTOM SHIP	V	33
THE MAYOR CAME, LEANING HIS DEAF EAR--	725	LEGEND		13
THE BISHOP CAME WITH OPEN BOOK,	725	LEGEND		17
A COCK CAME BY UPON HIS TOES;	725	LEGEND		26
HE CAME TO THE HOME OF THE FOREST PEOPLE	728	PRIEST FAIRY		5
AND CAME TO WHERE HIS BRETHREN STOOD,	730	PRIEST FAIRY		63
EARL PAUL CAME WHERE THE KING SAT,	740	EARL PAUL		29
AND CAME AND DWELT IN HIS OWN HOUSE,	742	EARL PAUL		67
HIS FACE HAS NEVER GLADDENED SINCE HE CAME	747	SHADOW WATER A		1
AND WHEN YOU CAME, THE NORTH UNDER YOUR SAILS,	749	SHADOW WATER A		34
AND WHEN YOU CAME TO SCORN OUR LITTLE WARS	749	SHADOW WATER A	V	34
THE FOOL THAT CAME OUT OF THE WINTRY WOOD	750	SHADOW WATER A		75
WHERE I HAD HEARD NO FEET BUT THE GODS' CAME.	756	SHADOW WATER A	V	191B
EDAINE CAME OUT OF MIDHIR'S HILL, AND LAY	762	SHADOW WATER A		296

CAMEL
| AMONG THE COARSE GRASS AND THE CAMEL DUNG. | 369 | EGO DOMINUS | V | 31 |

CAMEL-BACK
| CAMEL-BACK, HORSE-BACK, ASS-BACK, MULE-BACK, | 566 | LAPIS LAZULI | | 26 |

CAMEL-DUNG
| AMONG THE COARSE GRASS AND THE CAMEL-DUNG. | 369 | EGO DOMINUS | | 31 |

CAMEL'S
| PAST THE CAMEL'S DREAMING EYE. | 733 | STREET DANCERS | | 43 |

CAMP
| "THE RED BRANCH CAMP IN A GREAT COMPANY | 108 | CUCHULAIN SEA | | 33 |

CAMP (CONTINUED)
GO THERE, AND CAMP UPON THE FOREST'S RIM: 108 CUCHULAIN SEA V 35
GO THERE, AND LIGHT A CAMP FIRE AT WOOD'S RIM: 108 CUCHULAIN SEA V 35
CAMP-FIRE
GO THERE, AND LIGHT A CAMP-FIRE AT WOOD'S RIM: 108 CUCHULAIN SEA 35
CAMPING
. . . THERE CAMPING IN GRASSES DEEP, 50 OISIN 3 54
LIKE SOME LAST COURTIER AT A GYPSY CAMPING PLACE 314 FALLEN MAJESTY V 3
CAMPING-PLACE
LIKE SOME LAST COURTIER AT A GYPSY CAMPING-PLACE 314 FALLEN MAJESTY 3
CAMP'S
A SOLDIER ANSWERS: "BY THE CAMP'S FAR END 712 FERENCZ RENYI 67
CANDLE
LIKE A CANDLE BURNT OUT, 142 MOODS 2
BUT PURER THAN A TALL CANDLE BEFORE THE HOLY ROOD 208 HANRAHANS SONG 14
BUT PURE AS A TALL CANDLE BEFORE THE TRINITY 208 HANRAHANS SONG V 14
BUT PURER THAN A TALL CANDLE BEFORE THE BLESSED ROOD 208 HANRAHANS SONG V 14
BECAUSE, IT MAY BE, OF THE CANDLE LIGHT 373 PHASES OF MOON V 14
HIS SLEEPLESS CANDLE AND LABORIOUS PEN, 375 PHASES OF MOON 86
A CANDLE AND WRITTEN PAGE, 419 MY HOUSE 13
HAVE SEEN HIS MIDNIGHT CANDLE GLIMMERING, 420 MY HOUSE 20
HAD SEEN HIS MIDNIGHT CANDLE GLIMMERING 420 MY HOUSE V 20
TOWER WHERE A CANDLE GLEAMS, 420 MY HOUSE V 20I
AND WROTE BY CANDLE LIGHT: BUT HER FORM MOVED 467 HARUN RASHID V 129
DAYBREAK AND A CANDLE END. 588 OLD WICKED MAN V REF
DAY-BREAK AND A CANDLE END. 588 OLD WICKED MAN V REF
CANDLE-END
DAYBREAK AND A CANDLE-END. 588 OLD WICKED MAN 9
DAYBREAK AND A CANDLE-END. 588 OLD WICKED MAN 18
DAYBREAK AND A CANDLE-END. 588 OLD WICKED MAN 27
DAYBREAK AND A CANDLE-END. 589 OLD WICKED MAN 36
DAYBREAK AND A CANDLE-END. 589 OLD WICKED MAN 45
DAYBREAK AND A CANDLE-END. 589 OLD WICKED MAN 54
DAYBREAK AND A CANDLE-END. 590 OLD WICKED MAN 63
CANDLE-LIGHT
BECAUSE, IT MAY BE, OF THE CANDLE-LIGHT 373 PHASES OF MOON 14
AND WROTE BY CANDLE-LIGHT: BUT HER FORM MOVED, 467 HARUN RASHID 129
CANDLE-LIKE
AND CANDLE-LIKE FOAM ON THE DIM SAND, 158 BELOVED RHYMES 10
CANDLE'S
SHOWS THROUGH OUR LINEAMENTS. MY CANDLE'S BRIGHT, 464 HARUN RASHID 70
CANDLES
SHE CARRIES IN THE CANDLES, 89 ISLE IN WATER 9
GOD LIGHTS THE STARS, HIS CANDLES, 96 MOLL MAGEE 51
AND TIME BADE ALL HIS CANDLES FLARE 138 TO IRELAND 13
AND STILL THE STARRY CANDLES FLARE 138 TO IRELAND V 13
IS COMELIER THAN CANDLES AT MOTHER MARY'S FEET. 147 UNAPPEAS HOST 12
IS COMELIER THAN CANDLES BEFORE MAURYA'S FEET. 147 UNAPPEAS HOST V 12
BUT THOSE THE CANDLES LIGHT ARE NOT AS THOSE 445 SCHOOL CHILDR 50
"HAVE NO LIT CANDLES IN YOUR ROOM," 569 THREE BUSHES 8
WHERE NO CANDLES ARE, 570 THREE BUSHES 25
WHERE NO LIT CANDLES ARE, 570 THREE BUSHES V 25
CANDLESTICK
WHEN EVERY SILVER CANDLESTICK OR SCONCE 410 TOWER 26
CANKER-WORM
AS THE CANKER-WORM ON A MILK-WHITE ROSE: 673 ISLE STAT II 3 177
CANN
. . . NO, NEITHER IN HOUSE OF A CANN 50 OISIN 3 V 49
I CRIED, "COME OUT OF THE SHADOW, CANN OF THE NAILS OF
GOLD! 51 OISIN 3 V 61
CANNON
THOUGH HE'D BUT CANNON--WHEREAS WE THAT HAD THOUGHT 258 KING NO KING 7
AND THE OUTRAGEOUS CANNON, 317 NIGHT COME 10
WHAT MATTER THAT NO CANNON HAD BEEN TURNED 429 NINETEEN 19 19
I NEED SOME MIND THAT, IF THE CANNON SOUND 471 ALL SOUL NIGHT 11
HURRAH FOR REVOLUTION AND CANNON COME AGAIN! 590 GREAT DAY 3
HURRAH FOR REVOLUTION AND MORE CANNON SHOT! 590 GREAT DAY V 1
CANNONADE
THAT SUCH CANNONADE 496 MOHINI CHATTER 24
CANNON-SHOT
HURRAH FOR REVOLUTION AND MORE CANNON-SHOT! 590 GREAT DAY 1
CANNS
"I LOVED NO MAN, THOUGH CANNS BESOUGHT, 7 OISIN 1 V 62
CAME BY ME THE CANNS OF THE RED BRANCH 53 OISIN 3 V 87
CANOPY
UPON THE CLOUDY CANOPY, 397 POLIT PRISONER 22
THAT SLEEPS UNDER THE CANOPY: 528 TOM LUNATIC 2
AND RULE TOGETHER UNDER A CANOPY. 767 SHADOW WATER A 385
CANTERED
WE CANTERED TO THE SHORE, AND KNEW 14 OISIN 1 178
CANVAS
AND ALL THEIR SWELLING CANVAS WEAR, 530 OLD TOM AGAIN 2
AND ALL THEIR YELLOW CANVAS WEAR, 530 OLD TOM AGAIN V 2
GOD! THEY'RE MAD TO FLY SUCH CANVAS!" 718 PHANTOM SHIP 14
CAOILTE
CAOILTE, AND CONAN, AND FINN WERE THERE, 3 OISIN 1 13
CAOILTE, CONAN, AND FINN CAME NEAR, 10 OISIN 1 111
WHAT PLACE HAVE CAOILTE AND CONAN, AND BRAN, SCEOLAN,
LOMAIR? 61 OISIN 3 195
I WILL GO TO CAOILTE, AND CONAN, AND BRAN, SCEOLAN, LOMAIR, 63 OISIN 3 223
CAOILTE TOSSING HIS BURNING HAIR, 140 HOSTING SIDHE 3

```
                                                     PAGE     TITLE        LINE
CAOILTE  (CONTINUED)
    CAOILTE TOSSING HIS BURNING HAIR, . . . . . . . .   141 HOSTING SIDHE       15
CAOLTE
    WHAT PLACE HAVE CAOLTE AND FIN, AND BRAN, SGEOLAN, LOMAIR?   61 OISIN 3    V 195
    TO FIN, CAOLTE, AND CONAN, AND BRAN, SGEOLAN, LOMAIR. . .   63 OISIN 3     V 224
    . . . FINVARRA, FEACRA, AND CAOLTE                  174 ELEMENT POWERS  V   T
CAP      SEE KNEE-CAP
    AND FOR THE PEEWIT PAINTS HIS CAP, . . . . . . . .    18 OISIN 1            266
    THE CAP AND BELLS . . . . . . . . . . . . . .       159 CAP AND BELLS       T
    CAP AND BELL . . . . . . . . . . . . . . . .        159 CAP AND BELLS  V    T
    "I HAVE CAP AND BELLS," HE PONDERED, . . . . . .     160 CAP AND BELLS      21
    "I'VE CAP AND BELL," HE PONDERED, . . . . . . .      160 CAP AND BELLS  V   21
    THEY THREW A HALFPENNY INTO MY CAP, . . . . . .      300 RUN PARADISE        2
    HER KNEE CAP BROKEN! THAT GIRL I DECLARE . . . . .   578 CRAZED GIRL    V    6
    BLEW MY CRIMSON CAP AWAY . . . . . . . . . . .       656 ISLE STAT I 3      16
    BENEATH A POINTED CAP OF GREEN! . . . . . . . .      728 PRIEST FAIRY       22
    HE DREW FROM HIS CAP A FEATHER GREY, . . . . . .     729 PRIEST FAIRY       29
CAPS
    IN THEIR DOWNY CAPS, AND STARTLE THE NAPS . . . .    644 SONG FAERIES       11
    IN THEIR DOWNY CAPS, AND STARTLE THE NAPS . . . . .  676 ISLE STAT II 3    258
CAPTAIN
    IF HE WERE DEAD! BUT WHO WILL BE OUR CAPTAIN, . . .  224 SHADOW WATER B     60
    BECOME OUR CAPTAIN, AIBRIC. I AM RESOLVED . . . .    225 SHADOW WATER B     64
    THE SOLDIER TAKES PRIDE IN SALUTING HIS CAPTAIN, .   547 TO SAME TUNE 3      1
    SOLDIERS TAKE PRIDE IN SALUTING THEIR CAPTAIN, . .   547 TO SAME TUNE 3 V    1
    SOLDIERS TAKE PRIDE IN SALUTING THEIR CAPTAIN, . .   548 TO SAME TUNE 3     21
    THE SOLDIER TAKES PRIDE IN SALUTING HIS CAPTAIN, .   614 MARCH SONGS 2       1
CAPTAIN'S
    AND TAKE THE CAPTAIN'S SHARE OF EVERYTHING . . . .   225 SHADOW WATER B     73
    YOU'LL HAVE THE CAPTAIN'S SHARE OF EVERYTHING. . .   225 SHADOW WATER B V  67A
CAPTAINS
    WHERE ARE THE CAPTAINS THAT GOVERN MANKIND? . . . .  548 TO SAME TUNE 3     22
    WHERE ARE THE CAPTAINS THAT GOVERN MANKIND? . . . .  615 MARCH SONGS 2      22
CAPTIVE
    SPRANG DRIPPING, AND, WITH CAPTIVE DEMONS SENT . .    38 OISIN 2           130
    AND DID THOSE WATCHERS BID YOU TAKE ME CAPTIVE? . .  236 SHADOW WATER B    322
    THE CAPTIVE FROM KINSALE. . . . . . . . . . .        740 EARL PAUL          28
    A CAPTIVE WOMAN FROM THE NARROW BRIDGE, . . . . .    749 SHADOW WATER A     49
CAPTIVE'S
    THE CAPTIVE'S JOURNEYS TO AND FRO WERE WRIT . . .     37 OISIN 2           116
CAPTIVES
    AND CAPTIVES BOUND WITH LEATHERN THONGS . . . . .      7 OISIN 1            77
    MY CAPTIVES, BOUND IN LEATHERN THONGS, . . . . .       8 OISIN 1         V  78
CAPTIVES'
    THE CAPTIVES' JOURNEYS TO AND FRO WERE WRIT . . .     37 OISIN 2         V 116
    THE CAPTIVES' FOOTSTEPS WRITTEN TO AND FRO! . . .     37 OISIN 2         V 118
CAR      SEE GLEN-CAR
    CAME BALOR, AS OLD AS A FOREST, CAR BORNE, HIS MIGHTY HEAD   53 OISIN 3  V  91
      SUNK
    . . . AND O'ER YOUR CAR HEADS PEER . . . . . . .     73 ANASHU VIJAYA   V  45
CAR-BORNE
    DARK BALOR, AS OLD AS A FOREST, CAR-BORNE, HIS MIGHTY HEAD   53 OISIN 3    91
      SUNK
    CAME CAR-BORNE BALOR, AS OLD AS A FOREST, HIS VAST FACE   53 OISIN 3     V  91
      SUNK
CARD
    THAT ALL BUT THE ONE CARD BECAME . . . . . . . .    411 TOWER              68
CARDINAL
    THAT MADE HER DIARMUID DEAR, AND SOME OLD CARDINAL  . .   366 HER COURAGE    6
    AND THAT MADE HER DERMUID DEAR, AND SOME OLD CARDINAL  . .   366 HER COURAGE  V  6
CARDS
    TO OLD MEN PLAYING AT CARDS . . . . . . . . .       144 HOST OF AIR        23
    O'DRISCOLL SCATTERED THE CARDS . . . . . . . .      145 HOST OF AIR        37
    AND SCATTERED THE CARDS WITH A CRY, . . . . . .     145 HOST OF AIR    V   38
    GOOD FELLOWS SHUFFLED CARDS IN AN OLD BAWN! . . .   411 TOWER              65
    HE SO BEWITCHED THE CARDS UNDER HIS THUMB . . . .   411 TOWER              67
    A PACK OF HOUNDS AND NOT A PACK OF CARDS, . . . .   411 TOWER              69
CARE
    WHERE CARE CANNOT TROUBLE THE LEAST OF OUR DAYS, . .  27 OISIN 1           409
    UPON HIS HEAD TO CAST AWAY MY CARE. . . . . . .     102 FERGUS DRUID   V   14
    AND FOUND HER DYEING CLOTH WITH SUBTLE CARE . . .   105 CUCHULAIN SEA  V   2A
    AND GOD'S BELL BUOYED TO BE THE WATER'S CARE! . .   114 ROSE OF BATTLE      4
    BEFORE EARTH TOOK HIM TO HER STONY CARE! . . . .    126 DREAM OF FAERY      4
    BEFORE EARTH MADE OF HIM HER SLEEPY CARE! . . . .   126 DREAM OF FAERY V    4
    AND RODE WITH LITTLE CARE. . . . . . . . . .        133 FR GILLIGAN        28
    WITH PLANETS IN HIS CARE, . . . . . . . . . .       134 FR GILLIGAN        46
    THINE EYES GROW FULL OF TENDER CARE! . . . . . .    135 TWO TREES          19
    O WHAT TO ME MY MOTHER'S CARE, . . . . . . . .      151 HEART OF WOMAN      5
    THAT MY OLD CARE MAY CEASE! . . . . . . . . .       174 ELEMENT POWERS     10
    THEIR LOVE WAS NEVER DROWNED IN CARE . . . . . .    189 BAILE AILLINN       8
    CARE MORE ABOUT THE KEGS OF SILVER AND GOLD . . .   232 SHADOW WATER B    234
    I WILL CONFESS IT ALL.  WHAT DO I CARE, . . . . .   245 SHADOW WATER B    485
    WHAT DOES HE CARE IF MY HEART BREAK? . . . . . .    275 GREY ROCK         104
    MY MARRIED SISTER PUT INTO MY CARE  . . . . . .     276 TWO KINGS      V    E
    HAVE BEEN THE MEASURE OF THAT CARE."  BUT EOCHAID,  .   276 TWO KINGS   V    H
    ALWAYS IN HIS ONE SEAT, AND BID ME CARE HIM . . .   280 TWO KINGS          80
    IF BUT I DO NOT SEEM TO CARE." . . . . . . . .      297 THREE BEGGARS      68
    "WHAT CARE I IF YOU SLEEP OR WAKE? . . . . . . .    304 HOUR DAWN          40
    THE GOLDEN TOP OF CARE? . . . . . . . . . . .       309 PLAYER QUEEN       20
    WHAT NEED HAVE YOU TO CARE . . . . . . . . . .      312 CHILD DANCING       2
    BY TENDERNESS AND CARE, . . . . . . . . . . .       346 ON WOMAN           37
```

CARE   (CONTINUED)
 O LITTLE DID THEY CARE WHO DANCED BETWEEN, ... 383 VISION ROBART   37
 SO THE CROWD COME THEY CARE NOT WHAT MAY COME. . . . . . 398 LEADERS CROWD   10
 BUT WHAT CARE I THAT LONG FOR A MAN'S LOVE? . . . . . . 448 HERO GIRL FOOL   17
 GAVE BUT MORE REASON FOR A WOMAN'S CARE. . . . . 466 HARUN RASHID   111
 PERPLEXED HER FANTASY AND PLANNED HER CARE? . . . . . . 466 HARUN RASHID   114
 PERPLEXED HER PHANTASY AND PLANNED HER CARE? . . . . . . 466 HARUN RASHID   V 114
 THAT STIRRED HER FANTASY AND PLANNED HER CARE, ... 466 HARUN RASHID   V 114
 BUT NAMES ARE NOTHING. I CARE NOT WHO IT BE. . . . . . 473 ALL SOUL NIGHT   V 81
 I CARE NOT WHAT THE SAILORS SAY! . . . . 509 JANE REPROVED   1
 CARE NOT A THRANEEN FOR WHAT CHANCED . . . . 514 JANE GROWN OLD   V 18
 BUT NOT FROM HER PROTECTING CARE. . . . . 522 LULLABY   18
 "WHO'D CARE TO DIG 'EM," SAID THE OLD, OLD MAN, ... 548 TO SAME TUNE 3   7
 "WHO'D CARE TO DIG 'EM," SAID THE OLD, OLD MAN, ... 548 TO SAME TUNE 3   17
 "WHO'D CARE TO DIG 'EM," SAID THE OLD, OLD MAN, ... 549 TO SAME TUNE 3   27
 BANISH AGE AND CARE. . . . . 620 JOHN KINSELLA   20
 IS SORROW IN HIS SONG, OR ANY CARE? . . . . 652 ISLE STAT I 2   20
 GROWETH THE GOBLIN FLOWER OF JOY, HER CARE, ... 653 ISLE STAT I 2   39
 AND NEVER HEARD OF GRIEF OR CARE . . . . 667 ISLE STAT II 3   21
 LEAD THEY ONE WITH FOOLISH CARE, ... 727 LOVERS QUARREL   29
 THE LIVING WOODS FOREGO THEIR CARE, ... 736 SUMMER EVENING   1
 CARE NOT IF BEYOND THE SHADOWS . . . . 737 IN FIRELIGHT   7
CARED
 THE VERSES THAT THEY CARED FOR ON THE DAY . . . . . . 257 RECONCILIATION   V   2
 WHAT CARED DUKE ERCOLE, THAT BID . . . . 287 TO WEALTHY MAN   9
 FOR ALL THE SLEEPER KNEW OR CARED! . . . . 307 HOUR DAWN   115
 CARED NOT A THRANEEN FOR WHAT CHANCED . . . . 514 JANE GROWN OLD   18
 BUT WHAT CARED I THAT SET HIM ON TO RIDE, ... 629 CIRCUS ANIMALS   15
CAREFUL
 WHOSE CAREFUL PASTERN PRESSED THE SOD . . . . 2 OISIN 1   V 7W
 A CAREFUL FIELD-MOUSE FINDS A FALLEN CRUMB! . . . . . 713 FERENCZ RENYI   77
 I MUST BE CAREFUL NOW. I HAVE SUCH PLOTS-- . . . . . 722 WITCH VIVIEN   65
CARELESS
 THE PROUD AND CARELESS NOTES LIVE ON, ... 213 BLESS PSALTER   19
 THE CARELESS PLANETS IN THEIR COURSES, ... 344 DAWN   7
 WHAT A STAR SANG AND CARELESS MUSES HEARD! . . . . . 445 SCHOOL CHILDR   47
CARES
 IMMEDIATE, MOURNFUL, WHITE WITH SUDDEN CARES, ... 44 OISIN 2   V 229A
 HIS MIND RAN ALL ON MONEY CARES AND FEARS, ... 127 DREAM OF FAERY   14
 NOR THOSE UNPASSING CARES, ... 315 FRIENDS   5
 . . . "SPEAK ALL YOUR MIND! WHO CARES, ... 450 OWEN AHERNE   21
 CARES WHAT KING SETS UP HIS RULE. . . . . 635 BLACK TOWER   14
 SHE CARES NO WHIT FOR EITHER, BUT HAS BLEST . . . . 660 ISLE STAT II 1   49
CARESSED
 BUT NIAM WITH HER HANDS CARESSED HIS EARS, ... 30 OISIN 2   V 26
 AND SHE, TO WIN HIM, HIS GREY HAIR CARESSED! . . . . 110 CUCHULAIN SEA   73
 ABOVE THE STAGGERING GIRL, HER THIGHS CARESSED . . . 441 LEDA AND SWAN   2
CARGO
 HIDING AMID THE CARGO OF A STEAMSHIP, ... 578 CRAZED GIRL   5
CARHEADS
 . . . AND FROM YOUR CARHEADS PEER, ... 73 ANASHU VIJAYA   45
CARICATURE
 O HEART, O TROUBLED HEART--THIS CARICATURE, ... 409 TOWER   2
CAROL
 SING, O YOU LITTLE STARS! O SING AND RAISE YOUR RAPTUROUS 72 ANASHU VIJAYA   20
  CAROL
 SING, OH YE LITTLE STARS! OH, SING, AND RAISE YOUR   72 ANASHU VIJAYA   V 20
  RAPTUROUS CAROL
CARP
 SAVE, WITH THE LITTLE GOLDEN GREEDY CARP, ... 720 WITCH VIVIEN   2
 HOW STILL IT IS! I HEAR THE CARP GO SPLASH, ... 722 WITCH VIVIEN   62
CARPENTER   SEE WORKING-CARPENTER
CARPENTERS
 SET CARPENTERS TO WORK ON NO WIDE TABLE, ... 340 SHEP GOATHERD   50
 AND DIRTY NAILS OF CARPENTERS. . . . . 440 WISDOM   V   7
 DIGGERS AND CARPENTERS MAKE GRAVE AND COFFIN! . . . . 609 IN TARAS HALLS   17
CARPET
 ALL WEAR THE CARPET WITH THEIR SHOES! . . . . 337 SCHOLARS   8
 WEAR OUT THE CARPET WITH THEIR SHOES . . . . 337 SCHOLARS   V   8
CARRAIG   SEE PAIRC-NA-CARRAIG
CARRIAGE
 CARRIAGE AND VOICE HAD HE! . . . . 608 SONGS BURDEN 3   13
 THERE IN A TWO-HORSED CARRIAGE . . . . 628 JANE MOUNTAIN   13
 THERE IN A TWO HORSED CARRIAGE . . . . 628 JANE MOUNTAIN   V 13
CARRIED
 . . . TWO CARRIED A SACK FULL OF SAND, ... 60 OISIN 3   185
 THAT CARRIED THE TAKE TO SLIGO TOWN TO BE SOLD, . . . 91 OLD FISHERMAN   7
 THAT CARRIED THE FISH FOR THE SALE IN THE FAR-AWAY TOWN, 91 OLD FISHERMAN   V   7
 WAS CARRIED TO THE GOODLY HOUSE . . . . 192 BAILE AILLINN   72
 HE CARRIED EDAIN OFF FROM A KING'S HOUSE, ... 224 SHADOW WATER B   48
 AND CARRIED HIM HIS FOOD WITH MY OWN HANDS, ... 280 TWO KINGS   88
 I SHALL BE CARRIED IN THE GUST, COMMAND, ... 281 TWO KINGS   101
 WHO CARRIED IN THEIR MEMORY . . . . 361 ALF POLLEXFEN   34
 WE'VE CARRIED IN OUR TREE. . . . . 366 HER CHRIS TREE   3
 THE BRIDE IS CARRIED TO THE BRIDEGROOM'S CHAMBER . . . 459 FROM OEDIPUS   8
 CARRIED BY THE WANDERING FOOL. . . . . 484 SYMBOLS   4
CARRIER   SEE LINEN-CARRIER
CARRIES
 SHE CARRIES IN THE DISHES, ... 89 ISLE IN WATER   5
 SHE CARRIES IN THE CANDLES, ... 89 ISLE IN WATER   9
 AND CARRIES IT BETWEEN US. HOLY FIRE . . . . 239 SHADOW WATER B   371

	PAGE	TITLE		LINE

CARRIES (CONTINUED)
AND SO A HUNTER CARRIES IN THE EYE . . . . 463 HARUN RASHID 61
CARRIES A MUSICAL INSTRUMENT. . . . . 566 LAPIS LAZULI 42
CARROT
BROWN, OR BLACK, OR CARROT, ... 492 ANNE GREGORY 9
CARRY
CARRY ME, YE FOUR, ... 97 FOXHUNTER 2
AND CARRY ME YE FOUR, ... 97 FOXHUNTER V 2
AND CARRY ME, YOU FOUR, ... 97 FOXHUNTER V 2
CARRY ALL THAT MOURNFUL BEAUTY . . . . 124 CATHLEEN PARA 7
WILL OVERTHROW HIS SHADOWS AND CARRY OFF . . . . 184 QUEEN MAEVE 95
TO TAKE HIM WHILE HE SLEEPS AND CARRY HIM . . . . 222 SHADOW WATER B 14
A SHADOW DOES NOT CARRY SWORD OR SPEAR. . . . . . 224 SHADOW WATER B 44
THAT EVERY MAN SHOULD CARRY HIS OWN SOUL . . . . 235 SHADOW WATER B 299
OR CALLED BEFORE HIS EYES. O CARRY ME . . . . . . 249 SHADOW WATER B 568
DID NOT THE POET CARRY HIM WITH AN AIR . . . . . 267 ALL TEMPT ME V 7
AND DREAM THAT I SHOULD CARRY . . . . 309 PLAYER QUEEN 19
WOULD CARRY IT AWAY TO BLASPHEMOUS MEN. . . . . . 371 EGO DOMINUS 79
AND FOR NO EAR BUT HIS. CARRY THIS LETTER . . . . 461 HARUN RASHID 4
OR CARRY THE RINGED MAIL UPON MY BACK, ... 463 HARUN RASHID 58
WOULD I CARRY TO A FRIEND-- . . . . 494 AT ALGECIRAS 8
I WOULD CARRY TO A FRIEND-- . . . . 494 AT ALGECIRAS V 8
I CARRY FROM MY MOTHER'S WOMB . . . . 506 REMORSE SPEECH 14
I CARRY THE SUN IN A GOLDEN CUP, ... 525 DANCING DAYS 7
I CARRY THE SUN IN A GOLDEN CUP, ... 525 DANCING DAYS 15
I CARRY THE SUN IN A GOLDEN CUP, ... 525 DANCING DAYS 23
MARK AND DIGEST MY TALE, CARRY IT AFAR . . . . . 554 RIBH AT TOMB 3
CARRY THE GOLD ABOUT THE TOWN, ... 596 COLONEL MARTIN 52
OUR VOICES CARRY: AND THOUGH SLUMBER-BOUND, . . . 622 HOUND VOICE 5
OUR VOICES CARRY: AND THOUGH SLUMBER BOUND, . . . 622 HOUND VOICE V 5
CARRY IT: SUDDENLY IT IS STILL. . . . . 783 GREY ROUND 5
CARRYING
THOSE TWO CAME CARRYING WINE AND MEAT AND BREAD, ... 41 OISIN 2 184
ALTHOUGH HE IS CARRYING STONE, BUT TWO . . . . . . 192 BAILE AILLINN 83
CARS   SEE BATTLE-CARS
ACROSS YOUR WANDERING RUBY CARS . . . . 22 OISIN 1 330
SING, TURNING IN YOUR CARS, ... 73 ANASHU VIJAYA 44
HAS WON THE GOLD HIS CARS OF BATTLE BRING." . . . 106 CUCHULAIN SEA 11
MY FATHER STANDS AMID HIS BATTLE CARS . . . . . . 107 CUCHULAIN SEA V 26
AND WEARY OF THE CRASH OF BATTLE CARS." . . . . . 107 CUCHULAIN SEA V 30
THE CARS OF BATTLE AND HIS OWN NAME CRIED: . . . 111 CUCHULAIN SEA 85
FOR FERGUS RULES THE BRAZEN CARS, ... 126 GOES FERGUS 9
OUT OF THEIR WHIRLING CARS, ... 175 ELEMENT POWERS V 16
CART
MY SORROW! FOR MANY A CREAK GAVE THE CREEL IN THE CART . . 91 OLD FISHERMAN 6
AH WOE! FULL MANY A CREAK GAVE THE CREEL IN THE CART . . 91 OLD FISHERMAN V 6
AH ME! FULL MANY A CREAK GAVE THE CREEL IN THE CART . . 91 OLD FISHERMAN V 6
THE CRY OF A CHILD BY THE ROADWAY, THE CREAK OF A LUMBERING 142 ROSE IN HEART 2
   CART.
THERE, STANDING ON THE CART, ... 544 TO SAME TUNE 1 5
"HARNESS AN ASS AND CART." . . . . 596 COLONEL MARTIN 51
THERE, STANDING ON THE CART, ... 616 MARCH SONGS 3 5
CART-HORSE
SHE KNOWS THAT IT WAS BUT THE CART-HORSE COUGHING . . . 230 SHADOW WATER B 176
CARVE
OR CARVE A DREADFUL SPEAR. . . . . 32 OISIN 2 V 56
AND CARVE HIS NAME IN OGHAM." EOCHAID SAID, ... 280 TWO KINGS 83
CARVED
UNTIL I CARVED THESE WORDS: . . . . 123 DREAM OF DEATH 10
TO BE CARVED ON A STONE AT THOOR BALLYLEE . . . . 406 CARVED STONE T
TO BE CARVED ON A STONE AT BALLYLEE . . . . 406 CARVED STONE V T
ARE CARVED IN LAPIS LAZULI, ... 566 LAPIS LAZULI 38
HE CARVED ON TREES, AND WITH A SUN-DRY WEED . . . 659 ISLE STAT II 1 8
CARVED: HERE, BEYOND THE LAKE'S SLOW-MUFFLED TREAD, . . 662 ISLE STAT II 2 11
CARVEN
AND CARVEN FIGURES ON THEIR PROWS . . . . 14 OISIN 1 190
AND CARVEN FIGURES ON THEIR PROWS . . . . 23 OISIN 1 354
A DOME MADE OUT OF ENDLESS CARVEN JAGS, ... 38 OISIN 2 144
WAITED. ABOVE, IN ENDLESS CARVEN JAGS, ... 38 OISIN 2 V 144
LIFTED THE DOME, WHERE FACE IN CARVEN FACE . . . 39 OISIN 2 V 145
IN MOULDED PLASTER OR IN CARVEN STONE? . . . . . 327 ROBERT GREGORY 77
AND GONE ARE PHIDIAS' CARVEN IVORIES . . . . . . 428 NINETEEN 19 V 7
CASE
DEAR CRAOIBHIN AOIBHIN, LOOK INTO OUR CASE. . . . 264 ABBEY THEATRE 1
"THAT'S CERTAINLY THE CASE," SAID HE. . . . . . . 510 JANE JUDGMENT 10
"THAT'S CERTAINLY THE CASE," SAID HE. . . . . . . 510 JANE JUDGMENT 20
"THAT'S CERTAINLY THE CASE," SAID SHE. . . . . . . 510 JANE JUDGMENT V 10
AND UNDERSTOOD HER CASE. . . . . 571 THREE BUSHES 69
CASEMENT
SHE DREW IN THE HEAVY CASEMENT . . . . 159 CAP AND BELLS 11
SHE DREW IN THE BRIGHTENING CASEMENT, ... 159 CAP AND BELLS V 11
ROGER CASEMENT . . . . 581 ROGER CASEMENT T
I SAY THAT ROGER CASEMENT . . . . 581 ROGER CASEMENT 1
THE GHOST OF ROGER CASEMENT . . . . 583 GHOST ROG CASE T
THE GHOST OF ROGER CASEMENT . . . . 583 GHOST ROG CASE 9
THE GHOST OF ROGER CASEMENT . . . . 583 GHOST ROG CASE 19
THE GHOST OF ROGER CASEMENT . . . . 584 GHOST ROG CASE 29
THE GHOST OF ROGER CASEMENT . . . . 584 GHOST ROG CASE 39
CASEMENT UPON TRIAL, HALF HIDDEN BY THE BARS, ... 601 GALLERY REVIS 3
CASHEL
ON THE GREY ROCK OF CASHEL THE MIND'S EYE . . . . . . 382 VISION ROBART 1

		PAGE	TITLE	LINE

CASHEL (CONTINUED)
ON THE GREY ROCK OF CASHEL I SUDDENLY SAW . . . . . . 383 VISION ROBART 17

CASKET
. . . REMADE, LIKE A CASKET OF GOLD . . . . 143 ROSE IN HEART 7
. . . RE-MADE LIKE A CASKET OF GOLD . . . . 143 ROSE IN HEART V 7

CAST
THROUGH HEART AND SPINE; AND CAST HIM IN THE WAVE . . . 41 OISIN 2 182
CAST THE LOOSE BULK, LEST NIAM FEAR HIM DEAD; . . . 41 OISIN 2 V 183
GO CAST YOUR BODY ON THE STONES AND PRAY, ... 42 OISIN 2 207
WHO CAST ROUND FERGUS DREAMS, AND RUIN UNTOLD; . . . 101 ROSE UPON ROOD 5
UPON HIS HEAD TO CAST AWAY MY SORROW. . . . . . . 102 FERGUS DRUID 14
UPON HIS HEAD TO CAST AWAY MY CARE. . . . . 102 FERGUS DRUID V 14
THEN EMER CAST THE WEB UPON THE FLOOR, ... 105 CUCHULAIN SEA 6
THEREON HE SHOOK THE MORE AND CAST HIM DOWN . . . . 106 CUCHULAIN SEA 14
ALEEL, THE SWINEHERD, WEPT AND CAST HIM DOWN . . . . 106 CUCHULAIN SEA V 14
HE CAUGHT HIS BREATH AND CAST HIM WEEPING DOWN . . . 106 CUCHULAIN SEA V 14
GO, CAST ON HIM DELUSIONS MAGICAL, ... 111 CUCHULAIN SEA V 80
A WOVEN SILENCE, OR BUT CAME TO CAST . . . . . . 114 ROSE OF BATTLE 13
I CAST MY HEART INTO MY RHYMES, ... 139 TO IRELAND 45
LET GO MY HANDS! WHY DO YOU CAST A SHADOW? . . . 235 SHADOW WATER B 283
TO CAST HIS DREAMS AWAY. NO OTHER'LL DO IT. . . . 239 SHADOW WATER B 366
THE IMMORTAL MOCKERS HAVE CAST INTO HIS MIND, . . . 249 SHADOW WATER B 567
SOLDIERS THAT GAVE, WHATEVER DIE WAS CAST! . . . . 269 PARDON FATHERS 9
SHE CAST HERSELF UPON THE GROUND . . . . . . 275 GREY ROCK 107
THEREON SHE CAST HERSELF UPON THE GROUND, ... 275 GREY ROCK V 107
THAT CAST THEIR SHADOWS UPON ROAD AND BRIDGE; . . . 326 ROBERT GREGORY 51
WOULD I COULD CAST A SAIL ON THE WATER . . . . . 330 BONE OF A HARE 1
FROM BEAUTY THAT IS CAST OUT OF A MOULD . . . . . 334 LIVING BEAUTY 4
AT DAWN TO CAST HIS FLIES. . . . . 347 FISHERMAN 5
BODY AND SOUL CAST OUT AND CAST AWAY . . . . . . 374 PHASES OF MOON 62
BODY AND SOUL CAST OUT AND CAST AWAY . . . . . . 374 PHASES OF MOON 62
THEY ARE CAST BEYOND THE VERGE, AND IN A CLOUD, . . . 376 PHASES OF MOON 105
I HAD THOUGHT THAT ALL MY DAYS WERE CAST . . . . . 389 IMAGE PAST 12
DROP THEIR CAST AT THE SIDE . . . . 414 TOWER 125
LIFE SCARCE CAN CAST A FRAGRANCE ON THE WIND, . . . 422 MY DESCENDANTS 5
WHERE WE SHOULD CAST OFF BODY AND TRADE . . . . . 431 NINETEEN 19 73
WHEN SUCH AS I CAST OUT REMORSE . . . . . . 479 SELF AND SOUL 68
CAST BUT DEAD LEAVES TO MATHEMATICAL EQUALITY; . . . 481 BLOOD AND MOON 24
BUT COULD NOT CAST A SINGLE JET THEREON. . . . . 482 BLOOD AND MOON 39
CAST YOUR MIND ON OTHER DAYS . . . . 640 BEN BULBEN 81
CAST A COLD EYE . . . . 640 BEN BULBEN 92
SOME CAST OF DIE, OR LET SOME ARROW GLANCE . . . . 656 ISLE STAT I 3 40
CAST ON THE SOUND, ON, ON. THIS NIGHT OF GRAVES, . . . 665 ISLE STAT II 2 71
HAVE LIT LONE TAPERS. NOW THE NIGHT WAS CAST; . . . 687 TWO TITANS 27
CAST OFF THY HERESIES, AND SAVE THY SOUL . . . . 701 MOSADA 3 64
HER HEAD CAST BACKWARD IN HER UNLOOSED HAIR. . . . 701 MOSADA 3 67
AND SOFT, ONE GLIMMERING STAR. RENYI HAS CAST . . . 714 FERENCZ RENYI 115
CAST OUT ALL HOPE, CAST OUT ALL FEAR, ... 743 DANAAN QUICK 25
CAST OUT ALL HOPE, CAST OUT ALL FEAR, ... 743 DANAAN QUICK 25
THE WRITINGS I HAVE CAST AWAY! . . . . 779 ACCURSED WHO 2

CASTAWAYS
HIS DWINDLING SCORE AND HE SEEMED CASTAWAYS . . . . . 420 MY HOUSE 25

CAST-A-WAYS
HIS DWINDLING SCORE AND HE SEEMED CAST-A-WAYS . . . . . 420 MY HOUSE V 25

CASTING
AND SAID, CASTING ASIDE HIS DRAGGLED HAIR, ... 105 CUCHULAIN SEA V 3
ABOUT THE CASTING OUT OF MY NET, ... 146 FISH 4
CRIED, CASTING OFF THE MOUNTAIN SNOW, ... 502 VACILLATION 60
OR THAN THE SHIVERING CASTING NET OF THE STARS. . . . 762 SHADOW WATER A V 290

CASTING-NET
OR THAN THE SHIVERING CASTING-NET OF THE STARS, ... 237 SHADOW WATER B 329
OR THAN THE SHIVERING CASTING-NET OF THE STARS. . . . . 762 SHADOW WATER A 290

CASTLE
NEARER THE CASTLE CAME WE. A VAST TIDE, ... 31 OISIN 2 V 27A
FROM CASTLE TAYLOR TO THE ROXBOROUGH SIDE . . . . 326 ROBERT GREGORY 58
BESIDE THE CASTLE DOOR, WHERE ALL IS STARK . . . . 377 PHASES OF MOON 126
CASTLE DARGAN'S RUIN ALL LIT. . . . . 788 HAWTHORN TREE 3

CASTLE'S
AND EVEN THE SUN, THE DAY CASTLE'S WARDER, ... 28 OISIN 1 V 423A

CASTS
CASTS UP A SHOW AND THE WINDS ANSWER IT . . . . . 186 QUEEN MAEVE 125
THEY WOULD NOT SEND ME ONE THAT CASTS A SHADOW. . . . 235 SHADOW WATER B 285
CASTS DERISION UPON . . . . 476 DEATH 9
CASTS UPON HIS EYES UNTIL AT LAST . . . . . . 479 SELF AND SOUL 53
CASTS BUT DEAD LEAVES TO MATHEMATICAL EQUALITY! . . . 481 BLOOD AND MOON V 24
IMAGINATION TO THAT PITCH WHERE IT CASTS OUT . . . 619 BRONZE HEAD 19

CASUAL
SO WILD THAT EVERY CASUAL THOUGHT OF THAT AND THIS . . . 316 COLD HEAVEN 4
IN THE CASUAL COMEDY; . . . . 393 EASTER 1916 37
BECAUSE I HAD FANCIED LOVE A CASUAL . . . . . 533 HER TRIUMPH 2
THAT ALL ATTENDANTS AND THE CASUAL CROWD MIGHT HEAR. . . 609 IN TARAS HALLS 13
CALCULATIONS THAT LOOK BUT CASUAL FLESH, PUT DOWN . . . 610 STATUES 11

CAT   SEE MARTEN-CAT
AND MARTIN CAT, AND BORDERS THAT OLD WOOD . . . . 218 WOODS OF COOLE V 14
SHE WILL BE LIKE A WILD CAT; FOR THESE QUEENS . . . 232 SHADOW WATER B 233
THE CAT AND THE MOON . . . . 378 CAT AND MOON T
THE CAT WENT HERE AND THERE . . . . 378 CAT AND MOON 1
THE CREEPING CAT, LOOKED UP. . . . . 378 CAT AND MOON 4
A SPECKLED CAT AND A TAME HARE . . . . . . 380 SONGS FOOL 1 1
THE SPECKLED CAT SLEPT ON MY KNEE; . . . . . 381 SONGS FOOL 2 2
"THEY KILLED MY GOOSE AND A CAT. . . . . . . 546 TO SAME TUNE 2 8

129

CAT   (CONTINUED)
    "THEY KILLED MY GOOSE AND A CAT.   . . . .   546 TO SAME TUNE 2   18
    "THEY KILLED MY GOOSE AND A CAT.   . . . .   547 TO SAME TUNE 2   28
    THAT CAN MAKE A CAT LAUGH, OR   . . . .   589 OLD WICKED MAN   39
CATALPA
    NEITHER CATALPA TREE NOR SCENTED LIME   . . . .   435 NEW FACES   V   2
CATALPA-TREE
    NEITHER CATALPA-TREE NOR SCENTED LIME   . . . .   435 NEW FACES   2
CATARACT
    THE CATARACT SMOKES UPON THE MOUNTAIN SIDE, ...   311 MOUNTAIN TOMB   3
    IN VAIN, IN VAIN; THE CATARACT STILL CRIES: . . . .   311 MOUNTAIN TOMB   9
    THE CATARACT SMOKES ON THE MOUNTAIN SIDE.   . . . . .   311 MOUNTAIN TOMB   V   3
CATCH
    YES, VOICES! BUT I DO NOT CATCH THE WORDS.   . . . .   233 SHADOW WATER B   251
    THE CATCH CRIES OF THE CLOWN, ...   347 FISHERMAN   V 22
    YOUNG MEN NO LONGER SUDDENLY CATCH THEIR BREATH   . .   355 BROKEN DREAMS   2
    THAT MADE A CATCH IN THE BREATH--   . . . .   416 TOWER   191
    AND STRIKE ANOTHER TILL TIME CATCH;   . . . .   476 EVA GORE-BOOTH   27
CATCH-CRIES
    THE CATCH-CRIES OF THE CLOWN, ...   347 FISHERMAN   22
CATCHERS   SEE FLY-CATCHERS
CATCHES
    PROCESSIONS THAT LACK HIGH STILTS HAVE NOTHING THAT CATCHES   622 HIGH TALK   1
       THE EYE.
CATCHING
    CATCHING SMALL BIRDS IN THE DEW OF THE MORN   . . . .   636 BLACK TOWER   22
CAT-HEADED
    AND THE EDDYING CAT-HEADED BIRD;   . . . .   783 GREY ROUND   23
CATHEDRAL
    AFTER GREAT CATHEDRAL GONG;   . . . .   497 BYZANTIUM   4
CATHLEEN
    THE COUNTESS CATHLEEN IN PARADISE   . . . .   124 CATHLEEN PARA   T
    OF CATHLEEN, THE DAUGHTER OF HOULIHAN.   . . . . . .   207 HANRAHANS SONG   5
    OF CATHLEEN, THE DAUGHTER OF HOULIHAN.   . . . . . .   207 HANRAHANS SONG   10
    IS CATHLEEN, THE DAUGHTER OF HOULIHAN.   . . . . . .   208 HANRAHANS SONG   15
    THE COUNTESS CATHLEEN WAS THE NAME I GAVE IT;   . . .   629 CIRCUS ANIMALS   18
CAT-O'-NINE-TAILS
    AS WITH THE CAT-O'-NINE-TAILS OF THE MIND, ...   374 PHASES OF MOON   42
CATS
    FROM THE WIVES, AND THE CATS, AND THE CHILDREN,   . .   92 FATHER OHART   15
    FROM THEIR WIVES, AND THEIR CATS, AND THEIR CHILDREN,   .   92 FATHER OHART   V   15
    AS MIDDLE NIGHT GREAT CATS WITH SILVER CLAWS,   . . .   185 QUEEN MAEVE   115
CATTLE
    HERDED THE CATTLE CAME WITH STUMBLING FEET, ...   106 CUCHULAIN SEA   19
    WAS DRIVING CATTLE CAME SHE WITH SWIFT FEET, ...   106 CUCHULAIN SEA V   19
    AND TURNED THE FARMER'S MEMORY FROM HIS CATTLE,   . .   129 BOOK STORIES   6
    TOILED WITH EMPOUNDED CATTLE THROUGH THE MIRE,   . . .   276 TWO KINGS   V   2
    THAT WITH EMPOUNDED CATTLE TROD THE MIRE, ...   277 TWO KINGS   4
    THE FORD WHERE DRINKING CATTLE MAKE A STIR   . . . .   326 ROBERT GREGORY   53
    ROADS FULL OF BEGGARS, CATTLE IN THE FIELDS, ...   487 SEVEN SAGES   18
    THE HERON-BILLED PALE CATTLE BIRD, ...   493 AT ALGECIRAS   V   1
    THE HERON-BILLED PALE CATTLE BIRDS, ...   493 AT ALGECIRAS   V   1
CATTLE-BIRDS
    THE HERON-BILLED PALE CATTLE-BIRDS   . . . .   493 AT ALGECIRAS   1
CATULLUS
    DID THEIR CATULLUS WALK THAT WAY?   . . . .   337 SCHOLARS   12
    SHOULD THEIR CATULLUS WALK THAT WAY!   . . . .   337 SCHOLARS   V   12
CAUGHT
    AND CAUGHT THE SILVER HARP AWAY, ...   17 OISIN 1   240
    THAN THIS STRANGE BARD," HE CRIED, AND CAUGHT   . . .   17 OISIN 1   V 239
    AND CAUGHT MY HANDS, BUT SPAKE NO WORD   . . . . . .   25 OISIN 1   374
    AND CAUGHT MY HANDS AND SPAKE NO WORD   . . . . . .   25 OISIN 1   V 374
    . . . CROZIERED ONE, CAUGHT IN YOUR NET!   . . . . .   58 OISIN 3   167
    . . . CROZIERED ONE, CAUGHT IN THY NET--   . . . . .   58 OISIN 3   V 167
    . . . CROZIERED ONE, CAUGHT IN THEIR NET!   . . . . .   58 OISIN 3   V 167
    HE CAUGHT HIS BREATH AND CAST HIM WEEPING DOWN   . . .   106 CUCHULAIN SEA V   14
    AND CAUGHT A LITTLE SILVER TROUT.   . . . .   149 WANDER AENGUS   8
    AND WISDOM THAT CAUGHT FIRE LIKE THE DRIED FLAX,   . .   181 QUEEN MAEVE   28
    AN OLD MAN CAUGHT THE HORSE'S HEAD   . . . .   191 BAILE AILLINN   57
    HE HAS CAUGHT THE CRESCENT MOON OUT OF THE SKY,   . .   239 SHADOW WATER B   370
    CAUGHT AND CRACKED HIS FLEA, THE THIRD, ...   299 THREE HERMITS   30
    BUT THE FOOLS CAUGHT IT, ...   320 COAT   5
    CAUGHT UP IN CONTEMPLATION, THE MIND'S EYE   . . . .   375 PHASES OF MOON   79
    I'D STAND AND MUTTER THERE UNTIL HE CAUGHT   . . . .   377 PHASES OF MOON   131
    BEING CAUGHT BETWEEN THE PULL   . . . .   384 VISION ROBART   59
    CAUGHT IN THAT SENSUAL MUSIC ALL NEGLECT   . . . . .   407 SAIL BYZANTIUM   7
    CAUGHT BY AN OLD MAN'S JUGGLERIES   . . . .   411 TOWER   60
    MIND FROM MIND HAS CAUGHT: . . . .   420 MY HOUSE   V 20G
    AND TURN TOWARDS MY CHAMBER, CAUGHT   . . . .   424 ROAD AT DOOR   14
    BY THE DARK WEBS, HER NAPE CAUGHT IN HIS BILL,   . . .   441 LEDA AND SWAN   3
    AND AGAMEMNON DEAD. BEING SO CAUGHT UP, ...   441 LEDA AND SWAN   11
    BUT O! MY HEART COULD BEAR NO MORE WHEN THE UPLAND CAUGHT   450 OWEN AHERNE   11
       THE WIND:
    NO LONGER IN LETHEAN FOLIAGE CAUGHT   . . . .   500 VACILLATION   27
    TILL SUDDENLY IN GRIEF'S CONTAGION CAUGHT, ...   537 HER VISION   22
    ALL THERE CAUGHT UP THE TUNE!   . . . .   545 TO SAME TUNE 1   15
    ALL THERE CAUGHT UP THE TUNE!   . . . .   616 MARCH SONGS 3   15
    I WOULD HAVE SPARED HER HANDMAID, BUT SHE CAUGHT   . .   755 SHADOW WATER A   167
    SHE CAUGHT THIS BLADE OUT OF MY BELT AND DIED.   . . .   755 SHADOW WATER A   168
    I AM CAUGHT IN WOVEN NETS OF ENCHANTMENT. LOOK!   . .   762 SHADOW WATER A   293

CAULDRON
CAULDRON AND SPEAR AND STONE AND SWORD, • • • • • • • • 196 BAILE AILLINN 165
CAUSE
AND MEN WHO LOVED THE CAUSE THAT NEVER DIES. • • • • • 130 BOOK STORIES V 24
NOR GAVE LOUD SERVICE TO A CAUSE • • • • • • • 273 GREY ROCK 57
BOUND NEITHER TO CAUSE NOR TO STATE, • • • • • • • 414 TOWER 129
BUT A GOOD STRONG CAUSE AND BLOWS ARE DELIGHT." • • • 545 TO SAME TUNE 1 14
BUT A GOOD STRONG CAUSE--THE ROPE GAVE A JERK THERE, • 545 TO SAME TUNE 1 23
BUT A GOOD STRONG CAUSE AND THE BLOWS ARE DELIGHT." • • 545 TO SAME TUNE 1 V 14
ALL HAPPINESS IN ITS OWN CAUSE OR GROUND. • • • • • 557 RIBH ECSTASY 4
BUT A GOOD STRONG CAUSE AND BLOWS ARE DELIGHT." • • • 616 MARCH SONGS 3 14
BUT A GOOD STRONG CAUSE--THE ROPE GAVE A JERK THERE, • 616 MARCH SONGS 3 23
TWO MEN WHO LOVE ONE MAID HAVE AMPLE CAUSE • • • • • 659 ISLE STAT II 1 30
UPON THE CAUSE YOU SERVED, THAT WE • • • • • 791 REPRISALS 13
CAVE
THE WEAK WORM HIDING DOWN IN ITS SMALL CAVE, • • • • • 101 ROSE UPON ROOD 16
TO THE CAVE, WHERE DATHI THE BLESSED HAD GONE, • • • • 166 BLESSED V 3
WITH A BLINK IN HIS EYES AT THE CAVE MOUTH, • • • • • 166 BLESSED V 3
CAVE-MOUTH
WITH A BLINK IN HIS EYES, AT THE CAVE-MOUTH, • • • • • 166 BLESSED 3
CAVERN
I WILL FIND OUT SOME CAVERN IN THE HILLS • • • • • • 448 HERO GIRL FOOL V 11
IN CAVERN, CREVICE, HOLE, • • • • • • • • • 546 TO SAME TUNE 2 V 5
IN CAVERN, CREVICE OR HOLE, • • • • • • • 546 TO SAME TUNE 2 V 5
WHAT MATTER? OUT OF CAVERN COMES A VOICE, • • • • • 564 GYRES 15
WHAT MATTER? OUT OF CAVERN COME A VOICE • • • • • 564 GYRES V 15
THE CAVERN OF THE MIND? • • • • • • • • • • 600 THOSE IMAGES 2
FROM WHERE PAN'S CAVERN IS • • • • • • • • 612 NEWS ORACLE 31
IN CAVERN, CREVICE, OR HOLE, • • • • • • • 613 MARCH SONGS 1 5
WHEN SHE IN A CAVERN LIES, • • • • • • • • 658 ISLE STAT I 3 86
CAVERNED
CAVERNED IN NIGHT UNDER THE DRIFTED SNOW, • • • • • 563 MERU 10
CAVERN-GLOOMS
WHERE TREES MADE SUDDEN CAVERN-GLOOMS • • • • • • 16 OISIN 1 V 224B
CAVERNS
EYED PANTHERS IN THEIR DESERT CAVERNS ROVE • • • • • 681 SEEKER V 4
CAVE'S
WITH BLINKING EYES, AT THE CAVE'S EDGE, • • • • • • 167 BLESSED V 4C
CAVES   SEE DESERT-CAVES
AND TOSS AND TURN IN NARROW CAVES! • • • • • • 19 OISIN 1 281
I PASSED BY MANY CAVES OF DRIPPING STONE, • • • • • 657 ISLE STAT I 3 47
CEASE
AND KISSED, AS THEY WOULD NEVER CEASE, • • • • • • 16 OISIN 1 215
AND THEY CEASE WITH A SIGH OF "UNJUST! UNJUST!" • • • • 27 OISIN 1 V 416
DARKEN: HEAVEN IS ANGRY. CEASE! UNTO MY MIND, • • • 42 OISIN 2 V 205
AND LIGHTNING FLASH FOR EVER? CEASE AND HEAR. • • • 42 OISIN 2 V 207
CEASE, CEASE, O MOURNFUL, LAUGHING FENIAN HORN! • • • 43 OISIN 2 213
CEASE, CEASE, O MOURNFUL, LAUGHING FENIAN HORN! • • • 43 OISIN 2 213
AH, CEASE, THOU MOURNFUL, LAUGHING FENIAN HORN! • • • 43 OISIN 2 V 213
AH, CEASE, YOU MOURNFUL, LAUGHING FENIAN HORN! • • • • 43 OISIN 2 V 213
ALL DRIPPING ON A GRASSY SLOPE, AND SAW THEM CEASE TO CHASE 76 INDIAN ON GOD 4
AND AH, THEY KNOW NOT, AS THEY PINE AND CEASE, • • • • 81 EPHEMERA 5
HE MADE FOR HER AN ARMY CEASE TO BE." • • • • • • 106 CUCHULAIN SEA V 16B
AND GOD WOULD BID HIS WARFARE CEASE, • • • • • • • 113 ROSE OF PEACE 13
AND GOD WOULD BID MAN'S WARFARE CEASE. • • • • • • 113 ROSE OF PEACE V 13
FOR HIM WHO HEARS LOVE SING AND NEVER CEASE, • • • • 114 ROSE OF BATTLE 10
OR HOPES THAT IN MERE HOPING FLICKER AND CEASE! • • • 162 ASKS FORGIVE 3
AND HOPES THAT IN MERE HOPING FLICKER AND CEASE! • • • 162 ASKS FORGIVE V 3
THAT MY OLD CARE MAY CEASE! • • • • • • • • • 174 ELEMENT POWERS 10
I SHALL NOT CEASE TO BLESS BECAUSE • • • • • • • 379 SAINT HUNCH 7
CEASE TO REMEMBER THE DELIGHTS OF YOUTH, TRAVEL-WEARIED 459 FROM OEDIPUS 2
   AGED MAN!
AND HE, DESPITE HIS TERROR, CANNOT CEASE • • • • • • 563 MERU 4
OH, CEASE YOUR SINGING! WILD AND SHRILL AND LOUD, • • • 648 ISLE STAT I 1 99
WITH THEIR UNHUMAN SORROWS. CEASE! NO MORE! • • • • 661 ISLE STAT II 1 58
CEASE! THERNOT'S WOUNDED, CEASE! THEY WILL NOT HEED.• • 665 ISLE STAT II 2 64
CEASE! THERNOT'S WOUNDED, CEASE! THEY WILL NOT HEED. • 665 ISLE STAT II 2 64
MY SINKING BRAIN!--CEASE!--CEASE! HEARD YE YON SOUND? • • 665 ISLE STAT II 2 73
MY SINKING BRAIN!--CEASE!--CEASE! HEARD YE YON SOUND? • • 665 ISLE STAT II 2 73
THE DIRGE OF HER YE LOVE. CEASE!--CEASE! • • • • • 665 ISLE STAT II 2 74
THE DIRGE OF HER YE LOVE. CEASE!--CEASE! • • • • • 665 ISLE STAT II 2 74
AH! YOU ARE WEEPING! HERE SHOULD ALL GRIEF CEASE. • • • 672 ISLE STAT II 3 149
SAD LADY, CEASE! • • • • • • • • • • • 672 ISLE STAT II 3 160
• • • CEASE THE WINDS, AND ON THEIR POLES • • • • • 719 PHANTOM SHIP 17
CEASE THE SAILS THEIR FLAPPING UPROAR, AND THE HULL NO 719 PHANTOM SHIP 18
   LONGER ROLLS.
CEASE THE SAILS, THEIR FLAPPING UPROAR TO THE HULL 719 PHANTOM SHIP V 18
   NO LONGER ROLLS.
CEASED
AND LOVE, IN THE HOURS WHEN YOUTH HAS CEASED! • • • • 2 OISIN 1 V 7A
NOR CEASED UNTIL WHITE NIAMH STROKED HIS EARS • • • • 30 OISIN 2 26
AN ENDLESS WAR. THE HUNDRED YEARS HAD CEASED! • • • • 44 OISIN 2 224
AN ENDLESS WAR. THE HUNDREDTH YEAR HAD CEASED. • • • • 44 OISIN 2 V 224
CEASED ON OUR HANDS AND OUR FACES, ON HAZEL AND OAK LEAF, 48 OISIN 3 23
   THE LIGHT.
• • • I MURMURED, "IN OLD AGE THEY CEASED"! • • • • • 59 OISIN 3 177
• • • WHEN LIFE IN MY BODY HAS CEASED, • • • • • • 63 OISIN 3 222
TILL OAK AND HAZEL CEASED AND BEECH BEGAN, • • • • • 283 TWO KINGS V 139A
I WISHED BEFORE IT CEASED. NOR BIRD NOR BEAST • • • • 338 SHEP GOATHERD 2
YEAR. I WISHED BEFORE IT CEASED. NOR BIRD NOR BEAST • • 338 SHEP GOATHERD V 2
AS THE SUMMER VOICE OF THE DAYTIME CEASED, • • • • • 728 PRIEST FAIRY 4

	PAGE	TITLE		LINE

CEASED   (CONTINUED)
    I CEASED TO BE A WOMAN, BEING A QUEEN. . . . .   758 SHADOW WATER A   228
CEASELESS
    AS AN HURT LEOPARD FILLS WITH CEASELESS MOAN, ...   674 ISLE STAT II 3   208
    AS A HURT LEOPARD FILLS WITH CEASELESS MOAN . . . .   674 ISLE STAT II 3 V   208
    OF CEASELESS LONELINESS AND HIGH REGRET . . . .   705 REMEMBRANCE   9
CEASELESSLY
    AND THEY WERE TREMBLING CEASELESSLY, ...   13 OISIN 1   173
    LIKE SMALL BROWN MOTHS, A-TREMBLE CEASELESSLY. . . . .   713 FERENCZ RENYI V   82
CEDAR
    CHRYSELEPHANTINE, CEDAR BOARDED, ...   440 WISDOM   V   10
CEDAR-BOARDED
    CHRYSELEPHANTINE, CEDAR-BOARDED, ...   440 WISDOM   10
CEILING
    WHAT MADE THE CEILING WATERPROOF? . . . .   625 NATIVITY   5
CELEBRANT
    AND BRING BEAUTY'S BLIND RAMBLING CELEBRANT; . . . . .   412 TOWER   91
CELEBRATE
    I CELEBRATE THE SILENT KISS THAT ENDS SHORT LIFE OR LONG.   459 FROM OEDIPUS   9
CELL
    DOWN TO HER CELL AND THERE ALIT, ...   397 POLIT PRISONER   4
CELLAR
    THEN DARKENING THROUGH "DARK" RAFTERY'S "CELLAR" DROP, . .   490 COOLE BALLYLEE   4
    BATTERED TO DEATH IN A CELLAR, ...   628 JANE MOUNTAIN   9
    AS WITHIN A CELLAR CHILLY . . . .   647 ISLE STAT I 1   57
    TO GARRET OR CELLAR A WHEEL I SEND, ...   787 GARRET CELLAR   1
CELTIC
    THE CELTIC TWILIGHT . . . .   147 INTO TWILIGHT V   T
CENTAUR
    OR BEEN FIT SPOIL FOR A CENTAUR . . . .   355 PROPERTIUS   7
    ON A PICTURE OF A BLACK CENTAUR BY EDMUND DULAC . . . .   442 BLACK CENTAUR   T
    SUGGESTED BY A PICTURE OF A BLACK CENTAUR . . . . . .   442 BLACK CENTAUR V   T
CENTAURS
    THE HOLY CENTAURS OF THE HILLS ARE VANISHED; . . . . .   344 DEJECTION   7
    THE HOLY CENTAURS OF THE HILLS ARE BANISHED; . . . . .   344 DEJECTION   V   7
CENTO   SEE QUINTO-CENTO QUATTRO-CENTO
CENTRAL
    OF THE GREAT ROUND SUN, FROM HIS CENTRAL FIRES. . . . .   13 OISIN 1   V 168
    UPON THE WOODY CENTRAL HILL; . . . .   22 OISIN 1   323
    TILL ON THE CENTRAL HILL WE HUSHED . . . .   22 OISIN 1   V 323
    THE SAGE, WHO DEEP IN CENTRAL NATURE DELVES, ...   686 LIFE   2
    THE SAGE WHO DEEP IN CENTRAL NATURE DELVES, ...   734 QUATRAIN APHOR   2
CENTRE
    UPON THE CENTRE OF THE SUN, ...   14 OISIN 1   175
    THINGS FALL APART; THE CENTRE CANNOT HOLD; . . . . . .   402 SECOND COMING   3
    THINGS FALL APART; THE CENTRE CAN NOT HOLD, ...   402 SECOND COMING V   3
CENTRES
    IN THE DEEP CENTRES OF THE SECRET WOODS. . . . . . .   661 ISLE STAT II 1   54
CENTURIES
    HAVE KNOWN THREE CENTURIES, POETS SING, ...   2 OISIN 1   3
    AND HOUNDS FOR CENTURIES DUST AND AIR. . . . .   11 OISIN 1   131
    FOR CENTURIES, AND STARS HAD DAWNED AND SET. . . . . .   31 OISIN 2   V   40
    NO CENTURIES COULD DIM, AND A WORD RAN . . . .   38 OISIN 2   127
    NOT LOADED CENTURIES MIGHT VAPOUR, RAN . . . .   38 OISIN 2   V 127
    THE MOIL OF MY CENTURIES FILLED ME; AND GONE LIKE . . .   51 OISIN 3   70
        A SEA-COVERED STONE
    MY SLEEP WERE NOW NINE CENTURIES . . . .   306 HOUR DAWN   75
    . . . THROUGH ALL THE CENTURIES, ...   354 HIS PHOENIX   25
    THERE'LL BE THAT CROWD TO MAKE MEN WILD THROUGH ALL THE   354 HIS PHOENIX   V   25
        CENTURIES,
    THROUGHOUT SO MANY VARYING CENTURIES . . . .   371 ON GOING HOUSE   8
    THAT TWENTY CENTURIES OF STONY SLEEP . . . .   402 SECOND COMING   19
    THAT THIRTY CENTURIES OF STONY SLEEP . . . .   402 SECOND COMING V   19
    BEFORE THAT RUIN CAME, FOR CENTURIES, ...   412 TOWER   81
    AND THROUGH THE CENTURIES RAN . . . .   421 MY TABLE   20
    UNSPOTTED BY THE CENTURIES; . . . .   477 SELF AND SOUL   12
    SEVEN CENTURIES HAVE PASSED AND IT IS PURE, ...   482 BLOOD AND MOON   33
    THROUGH SEVEN HEROIC CENTURIES; . . . .   640 BEN BULBEN   80
    HOW MANY CENTURIES SPENT . . . .   784 WOMANS BEAUTY   7
CENTURY   SEE EIGHTEENTH-CENTURY
    AND, MAN OF THE MANY WHITE CROZIERS, A CENTURY THERE I   52 OISIN 3   77
        FORGOT
    AND, MAN OF THE MANY WHITE CROZIERS, A CENTURY THERE I   52 OISIN 3   81
        FORGOT
    . . . AT THE HEEL OF A CENTURY FELL, ...   54 OISIN 3   102
    I'LL SLEEP ANOTHER CENTURY." . . . .   304 HOUR DAWN   43
    . . . CENTURY AFTER CENTURY, ...   481 BLOOD AND MOON   23
    . . . CENTURY AFTER CENTURY, ...   481 BLOOD AND MOON   23
    THE NINETEENTH CENTURY AND AFTER . . . .   485 NINETEENTH CEN   T
    RAVENING THROUGH CENTURY AFTER CENTURY, ...   563 MERU   5
    RAVENING THROUGH CENTURY AFTER CENTURY, ...   563 MERU   5
CEPHISUS
    WHO FINDS ABOUNDING CEPHISUS . . . .   447 COLONUS PRAISE   23
CEREMONIAL
    AS, CLOTHED IN CEREMONIAL GLOOM, ...   655 ISLE STAT I 3   10
CEREMONIOUS
    FOR PROUD, SOFT, CEREMONIOUS PROOF . . . .   386 ROBARTES DANCE   30
    WHERE ALL'S ACCUSTOMED, CEREMONIOUS; . . . .   405 FOR DAUGHTER   74
CEREMONY
    BEING BUT A PART OF ANCIENT CEREMONY-- . . . .   321 REED WHISPERER   12
    THE CEREMONY OF INNOCENCE IS DROWNED; . . . .   402 SECOND COMING   6

132

CEREMONY (CONTINUED)
        HOW BUT IN CUSTOM AND IN CEREMONY . . . .   406 FOR DAUGHTER   77
        WITH THE GREAT TOIL AND CEREMONY OF STATE, ... 462 HARUN RASHID   V   25
CEREMONY'S
        CEREMONY'S A NAME FOR THE RICH HORN, ...   406 FOR DAUGHTER   79
CERTAIN
        WORDS ALONE ARE CERTAIN GOOD. . . . .   65 HAPPY SHEPHERD   10
        FOR WORDS ALONE ARE CERTAIN GOOD! . . . .   66 HAPPY SHEPHERD   43
        AND WORDS ALONE ARE CERTAIN GOOD, ...   66 HAPPY SHEPHERD V   43
        HE GIVES HIS BELOVED CERTAIN RHYMES . . . . . .   157 BELOVED RHYMES   T
        AEDH GIVES HIS BELOVED CERTAIN RHYMES . . . . . .   157 BELOVED RHYMES V   T
        A CERTAIN POET IN OUTLANDISH CLOTHES . . . . . .   180 QUEEN MAEVE   1
        CERTAIN, AND THEY NEVER DREAM . . . .   202 NEVER GIVE ALL   4
        I SAID: "IT'S CERTAIN THERE IS NO FINE THING . .   205 ADAMS CURSE   21
        IT'S CERTAIN I'D SLEEP EASIER O' NIGHTS . . . .   224 SHADOW WATER B   59
        YOU'RE CERTAIN OF IT? I NEVER WAKE FROM SLEEP .   226 SHADOW WATER B   83
        IT'S CERTAIN THEY ARE LEADING YOU TO DEATH. . .   231 SHADOW WATER B   201
        THAT MUCH IS CERTAIN. I SHALL FIND A WOMAN, . .   231 SHADOW WATER B   209
        I DO NOT KNOW FOR CERTAIN, BUT I KNOW . . . .   249 SHADOW WATER B   564
        . . . CERTAIN BAD POETS, IMITATORS OF HIS AND MINE . 262 TO A POET   T
        . . . CERTAIN BAD POETS, IMITATORS OF HIS AND OF MINE 262 TO A POET   V   T
        TO A CERTAIN COUNTRY HOUSE IN TIME OF CHANGE . .   264 HOUSE SHAKEN   V   T
        WHERE CERTAIN BEECHES MIXED A PALE GREEN LIGHT . .   277 TWO KINGS   V   5
        IT'S CERTAIN THERE ARE TROUT SOMEWHERE . . . .   297 THREE BEGGARS   66
        BEING CERTAIN IT WAS NO RIGHT ROCK . . . . . .   303 HOUR DAWN   23
        BEING CERTAIN IT WAS NO RIGHT PLACE . . . . . .   303 HOUR DAWN   V   23
        TOWARDS NIGHTFALL UPON CERTAIN SET APART . . . .   325 ROBERT GREGORY   29
        "IT'S CERTAIN THAT MY LUCK IS BROKEN," . . . .   332 ROUND TOWER   25
        AND CERTAIN LOST COMPANIONS OF MY OWN. . . . .   342 SHEP GOATHERD   78
        CERTAIN ARTISTS BRING HER DOLLS AND DRAWINGS . .   362 DOLLS DRAWINGS   T
        BEING CERTAIN THAT THEY AND I . . . .   392 EASTER 1916   13
        FOR CERTAIN MINUTES AT THE LEAST . . . .   399 DEMON BEAST   1
        YET I AM CERTAIN AS CAN BE . . . .   401 DEMON BEAST   33
        IT'S CERTAIN THAT FINE WOMEN EAT . . . .   404 FOR DAUGHTER   30
        AND CERTAIN MEN, BEING MADDENED BY THOSE RHYMES,   410 TOWER   41
        AND CERTAIN MEN-AT-ARMS THERE WERE . . . . . .   412 TOWER   84
        AND CERTAIN MEN AT ARMS THERE WERE . . . . . .   412 TOWER   84
        FOR IT IS CERTAIN THAT YOU HAVE . . . .   413 TOWER   108
        HAD HE NOT FOUND IT CERTAIN BEYOND DREAMS . . .   417 ANCEST HOUSES   10
        THE EXTRAVAGANCE OF SPRING; OR CERTAIN TIMES . .   466 HARUN RASHID   V   125
        A CERTAIN MARVELLOUS THING . . . .   471 ALL SOUL NIGHT   16
        SO MUCH IS CERTAIN; . . . .   504 QUARREL IN AGE   10
        LIVES; THAT MUCH IS CERTAIN; . . . .   504 QUARREL IN AGE V   10
        AFTER CERTAIN YEARS HE WON . . . .   577 WHAT THEN   7
        CERTAIN MEN THE ENGLISH SHOT? . . . .   632 MAN AND ECHO   12
        THEN CERTAIN SHROUDS THAT MUTTERED HEAD TO HEAD .   634 CUCHULAIN COMF   4
        FOR I AM CERTAIN SOMEBODY IS DEAD. . . . . . .   760 SHADOW WATER A   254
        TILL CERTAIN SECOND THOUGHTS HAVE COME . . . .   791 REPRISALS   12
CERTAINLY
        FOR CERTAINLY HE SANK INTO HIS GRAVE . . . . .   370 EGO DOMINUS   57
        "THAT'S CERTAINLY THE CASE," SAID HE. . . . . .   510 JANE JUDGMENT   10
        "THAT'S CERTAINLY THE CASE," SAID HE. . . . . .   510 JANE JUDGMENT   20
        "THAT'S CERTAINLY THE CASE," SAID SHE. . . . .   510 JANE JUDGMENT   V   10
        A GREAT EBULLIENT PORTRAIT CERTAINLY; . . . . .   602 GALLERY REVIS   27
        AN EBULLIENT GREAT PORTRAIT CERTAINLY; . . . .   602 GALLERY REVIS   V   27
CERTAINTY
        THE CERTAINTY THAT I SHALL SEE THAT LADY . . .   356 BROKEN DREAMS   22
        THEY MUST TO KEEP THEIR CERTAINTY ACCUSE . . .   398 LEADERS CROWD   1
        FOUND CERTAINTY UPON THE DREAMING AIR, ...   489 COOLE PARK 29   22
CHAFF
        TILL ALL ELSE IS EMPTY CHAFF, ...   647 ISLE STAT I 1   60
CHAIN
        AND SHE WITH A WAVE-RUSTED CHAIN WAS TIED . . .   34 OISIN 2   73
        WITH CHAIN SEA-ROTTED, ROUND HER MIDDLE TIED, .   34 OISIN 2   V   75
        I BURST THE CHAIN: STILL EARLESS, NERVELESS, BLIND,   36 OISIN 2   97
        I THROW DOWN THE CHAIN OF SMALL STONES! . . . .   63 OISIN 3   222
        LINKED BY A GOLD CHAIN EACH TO EACH, ...   194 BAILE AILLINN   136
        AND BROKE THE CHAIN AND SET MY ANKLES FREE, . .   533 HER TRIUMPH   9
        WITH A MONKEY ON A CHAIN, ...   627 STATES HOLIDAY   36
        TO ONE ANOTHER WITH A COILING CHAIN; . . . . .   687 TWO TITANS   6
        I SAW HIM STAGGER WITH THE CLANKING CHAIN, . .   687 TWO TITANS   31
CHAINED
        CHAINED WAS SHE. ON THEIR WINGS THE HUNDREDTH YEAR .   34 OISIN 2   V   76
CHAINS
        COUPLED WITH GOLDEN CHAINS, AND SING AS THEY FLY. . . 204 WITHER BOUGHS   18
CHAIR
        MINE WAS A CHAIR OF SKINS AND GOLD, ...   81 MAD KING GOLL   V   1
        "LAY ME IN A CUSHIONED CHAIR! . . . .   97 FOXHUNTER   1
        "PUT THE CHAIR UPON THE GRASS! . . . .   97 FOXHUNTER   9
        "NOW LAY ME IN A CUSHIONED CHAIR, ...   97 FOXHUNTER   V   1
        "NOW LEAVE THE CHAIR DOWN ON THE GRASS, ...   97 FOXHUNTER   V   9
        "NOW LEAVE THE CHAIR UPON THE GRASS, ...   97 FOXHUNTER   V   9
        AND BY THE CHAIR HE GOES, ...   98 FOXHUNTER   V   18
        A KING SITTING UPON A CHAIR OF GOLD-- . . . .   104 FERGUS DRUID   36
        MY CHAIR WAS NEAREST TO THE FIRE . . . . . .   131 OLD PENSIONER   3
        I HAD A CHAIR AT EVERY HEARTH, ...   131 OLD PENSIONER   V   1
        ONCE, WHILE HE NODDED ON A CHAIR, ...   132 FR GILLIGAN   5
        HE KNELT, AND LEANING ON THE CHAIR . . . . .   132 FR GILLIGAN   13
        AND THEN, HALF-LYING ON THE CHAIR, ...   132 FR GILLIGAN   V   13
        WHILE I SLEPT ON THE CHAIR"; . . . .   133 FR GILLIGAN   26
        ASLEEP UPON A CHAIR." . . . .   134 FR GILLIGAN   48

	PAGE	TITLE		LINE
CHAIR (CONTINUED)				
BEFORE HIS CHAIR AND BENDING DOWN MY HEAD	282	TWO KINGS		132
AND CROUCHED BY THE ARM OF HIS CHAIR,	319	DOLLS		16
ALL DAY IN THE ONE CHAIR	357	BROKEN DREAMS		38
NO TABLE OR CHAIR OR STOOL NOT SIMPLE ENOUGH	371	ON GOING HOUSE		3
FROM SOMEBODY THAT TOILS FROM CHAIR TO CHAIR;	491	COOLE BALLYLEE		26
FROM SOMEBODY THAT TOILS FROM CHAIR TO CHAIR;	491	COOLE BALLYLEE		26
THE AUSTERE ARTHUR, RULE FROM UTHER'S CHAIR?	678	ISLE STAT II 3		296
CHAIRED				
CHAIRED IN THE CUSHIONED OTTER SKIN,	82	MAD KING GOLL	V	5
CHAIRED IN A CUSHIONED OTTER-SKIN	82	MAD KING GOLL	V	5
CHALK				
"THOSE SIX FEET MARKED IN CHALK?	548	TO SAME TUNE 3		8
"THOSE SIX FEET MARKED IN CHALK?	548	TO SAME TUNE 3		18
"THOSE SIX FEET MARKED IN CHALK?	549	TO SAME TUNE 3		28
CHAMBER				
TO THAT SMALL CHAMBER BY THE OUTER GATE.	181	QUEEN MAEVE		44
TO THE CHAMBER WHERE	310	WITCH		6
A WINDING STAIR, A CHAMBER ARCHED WITH STONE,	419	MY HOUSE		11
IN SOME LIKE CHAMBER, SHADOWING FORTH	419	MY HOUSE		15
AND TURN TOWARDS MY CHAMBER, CAUGHT	424	ROAD AT DOOR		14
THE BRIDE IS CARRIED TO THE BRIDEGROOM'S CHAMBER	459	FROM OEDIPUS		8
TAKE THIS LIGHT PARCHMENT, PASS THROUGH THE GREAT CHAMBER	461	HARUN RASHID	V	5
CLIMB TO YOUR CHAMBER FULL OF BOOKS AND WAIT,	579	DOR WELLESLEY		8
CHAMBERMAID				
DEAR CHAMBERMAID," SAID SHE.	569	THREE BUSHES		16
BUT HEAVED A SIGH IF THE CHAMBERMAID	570	THREE BUSHES		33
THE CHAMBERMAID LIVED LONG, AND TOOK	571	THREE BUSHES		57
CHAMBERMAID'S				
THE CHAMBERMAID'S FIRST SONG	574	MAIDS 1ST SONG		T
THE CHAMBERMAID'S SECOND SONG	575	MAIDS 2ND SONG		T
CHAMBERS				
AMID GREAT CHAMBERS AND LONG GALLERIES, LINED	418	ANCEST HOUSES		36
CHANCE				
WE MOCKED AT TIME AND FATE AND CHANCE	20	OISIN 1		291
EQUAL TO GOOD OR GRIEVOUS CHANCE;	24	OISIN 1		372
EQUAL TO GOOD OR EVIL CHANCE	24	OISIN 1	V	371
AND THOUGHT NOT OF EVIL CHANCE,	145	HOST OF AIR		30
SAVE BY AN EVIL CHANCE,	178	FIDDLER DOONEY		14
I'D DROWN HIM WHILE WE HAVE THE CHANCE TO DO IT.	224	SHADOW WATER B		58
I'D KILL HIM WHILE WE HAVE THE CHANCE TO DO IT.	224	SHADOW WATER B	V	58
WE'D BETTER GO, FOR WE HAVE LOST THIS CHANCE.	226	SHADOW WATER B		80
PERVERSE CREATURE OF CHANCE,	346	ON WOMAN		41
CHANCE BEING AT ONE WITH CHOICE AT LAST,	388	SOLOMON WITCH		14
WITH CRUELTIES OF CHOICE AND CHANCE;	388	SOLOMON WITCH		23
BEING BOTH CHANCE AND CHOICE;	472	ALL SOUL NIGHT		58
SOME THINK IT A MATTER OF COURSE THAT CHANCE	626	OLD MEN BE MAD		9
SOME THINK IT MATTER OF COURSE THAT CHANCE	626	OLD MEN BE MAD	V	9
ALL CHOICE, AND GIVE TO CHANCE FOR GUIDING CHANCE	656	ISLE STAT I 3		39
ALL CHOICE, AND GIVE TO CHANCE FOR GUIDING CHANCE	656	ISLE STAT I 3		39
WITH LOADED DICE. ANOTHER CHANCE! COME, FATHER;	721	WITCH VIVIEN		45
CHANCE, AND NOT SKILL, HAS FAVOURED YOU, OLD FATHER!	722	WITCH VIVIEN		60
CHANCE HATH A SKILL!	722	WITCH VIVIEN		69
CHANCED				
CARED NOT A THRANEEN FOR WHAT CHANCED	514	JANE GROWN OLD		18
CARE NOT A THRANEEN FOR WHAT CHANCED	514	JANE GROWN OLD	V	18
CHANCELLOR				
AM I A GREAT LORD CHANCELLOR	627	STATES HOLIDAY		14
CHANCES				
MAY WELL BE OF ALL EVIL CHANCES CHIEF.	405	FOR DAUGHTER		53
AT CHANCES AND AT MOMENTS WITH MANKIND.	721	WITCH VIVIEN		35
CHANGE				
WHERE THE VOICE OF CHANGE IS THE VOICE OF A TUNE,	8	OISIN 1	V	82
THERE WERE AN END OF CHANGE AND BIRTH,	18	OISIN 1		270
AND HERE THERE IS NOR CHANGE NOR DEATH,	19	OISIN 1		284
FOR NEITHER DEATH NOR CHANGE COMES NEAR US,	21	OISIN 1		316
FOR CHANGE AND DEATH THEY COME NOT NEAR US,	21	OISIN 1	V	316
NOR EVER CHANGE OR FEEL THE CLUTCHES	23	OISIN 1	V	341A
FROM CHANGE TO CHANGE! I HAVE BEEN MANY THINGS--	104	FERGUS DRUID		32
FROM CHANGE TO CHANGE! I HAVE BEEN MANY THINGS--	104	FERGUS DRUID		32
HE MOURNS FOR THE CHANGE THAT HAS COME UPON HIM	153	CHANGE BELOVED		T
MONGAN LAMENTS THE CHANGE THAT HAS COME UPON HIM AND HIS BELOVED	153	CHANGE BELOVED	V	T
AND TIME AND BIRTH AND CHANGE ARE HURRYING BY.	153	CHANGE BELOVED		9
O PITEOUS HEARTS, CHANGING TILL CHANGE BE DEAD	163	ASKS FORGIVE		19
AND NIAMH AND LABAN AND FAND, WHO COULD CHANGE TO AN OTTER OR FAWN,	209	UNDER THE MOON		12
AND FAND, AND NIAM, AND LABAN, WHO COULD CHANGE TO AN OTTER OR FAWN,	209	UNDER THE MOON	V	12
TO A CERTAIN COUNTRY HOUSE IN TIME OF CHANGE	264	HOUSE SHAKEN	V	T
HEARING THE WHOLE EARTH CHANGE ITS TUNE,	266	GALWAY RACES		12
"NEVER WILL I BELIEVE THERE IS ANY CHANGE	285	TWO KINGS		203
THE WATER-HEN MUST CHANGE HER GROUND;	326	ROBERT GREGORY		55
THE WATERHEN MUST CHANGE HER GROUND;	326	ROBERT GREGORY	V	55
TO CHANGE MY LOVES WHILE DANCING	330	BONE OF A HARE		7
BUT FOR HER GRANDSON NOW; THERE IS NO CHANGE	340	SHEP GOATHERD		39
THEY CHANGE THEIR BODIES AT A WORD. AND THEN?	376	PHASES OF MOON		113
WILL PASS FROM CHANGE TO CHANGE,	379	CAT AND MOON		22
WILL PASS FROM CHANGE TO CHANGE,	379	CAT AND MOON		22
MINUTE BY MINUTE THEY CHANGE;	393	EASTER 1916		48
MINUTE BY MINUTE CHANGE.	393	EASTER 1916	V	48

134

CHANGE   (CONTINUED)
    YET IF NO CHANGE APPEARS . . . .   421 MY TABLE   12
    YOU KNOW THE SAYING, "CHANGE THE BRIDE WITH SPRING," . . 463 HARUN RASHID   50
    AND WHAT IF MIND SEEMED CHANGE . . . .   473 ALL SOUL NIGHT V   66
    MUST VANISH ON THE INSTANT IF THE MIND BUT CHANGE   481 BLOOD AND MOON   27
        ITS THEME:
    "SHE WILL CHANGE," I CRIED, ...   516 MANS SONG   1
    CHANGE THEIR LOVES ABOUT. . . . .   520 HIS BARGAIN   6
    "WHAT CHANGE HAS PUT MY THOUGHTS ASTRAY . . . . .   529 TOM LUNATIC   3
    I COOK AND CHANGE MY PLATE, ...   607 SONGS BURDEN 2   6
    OF HIS DEATH AND CHANGE MALIGN. . . . .   648 ISLE STAT I 1   80
    A DEAL OF EVIL AND OF CHANGE HATH CROSSED . . .   676 ISLE STAT II 3   273
    MAKE GALLEYS OUT OF WIND THAT CHANGE TO WIND . .   751 SHADOW WATER A   105
    ENDS TIME AND CHANGE. . . . .   754 SHADOW WATER A V   163
    THAT CAN CHANGE LOVE TO IMPERISHABLE FIRE? . . .   765 SHADOW WATER A   360
    THEY WOULD CHANGE THEM INTO HOUNDS . . . . . .   775 AGAINST WITCH   15
    THOUGH THE CHANGE WERE BUT A WHIM: . . . . . .   775 AGAINST WITCH   17
    THOUGH THEIR CHANGE WERE BUT A WHIM: . . . . .   775 AGAINST WITCH V   17
CHANGED
    AMID THE SHADES OF NIGHT, HE CHANGED AND RAN . . . . 40 OISIN 2   174
    OF A GREAT EEL: IT CHANGED, AND I BUT SMOTE . . . .   40 OISIN 2   176
    CHANGED ALL HE SANG TO INARTICULATE MOAN . . . . .   69 SAD SHEPHERD   27
    CHANGED ALL HIS WORDS TO INARTICULATE MOAN . . . .   69 SAD SHEPHERD V   27
    AND YOU HAVE CHANGED AND FLOWED FROM SHAPE TO SHAPE, . . 102 FERGUS DRUID   2
    FOR I WOULD WE WERE CHANGED TO WHITE BIRDS . . . . . 122 WHITE BIRDS   8
    I HAVE BEEN CHANGED TO A HOUND WITH ONE RED EAR: . . . 153 CHANGE BELOVED   2
    HE CHANGED ME SUDDENLY: I WAS LOOKING ANOTHER WAY: . . 153 CHANGE BELOVED   7
    THEY KNEW HIM: HIS CHANGED BODY WAS . . . .   195 BAILE AILLINN   139
    AND THE WOOD-WOMAN, WHOSE LOVER WAS CHANGED TO A BLUE-EYED 209 UNDER THE MOON   13
        HAWK:
    AND THE WOOD WOMAN, WHOSE LOVER WAS CHANGED TO A BLUE-EYED 209 UNDER THE MOON V 13
        HAWK:
    BUT O, IN A MINUTE SHE CHANGED-- . . . .   212 O DO NOT LOVE   9
    WHEN MIDHIR'S WIFE HAD CHANGED HER TO A FLY, ... 220 HARP OF AENGUS   10
    AND WHEN ONE CHANGED HER TO A SILVER FLY, ... 220 HARP OF AENGUS V   10
    "HOW LIGHT WE ARE, NOW WE ARE CHANGED TO BIRDS!" . . . 233 SHADOW WATER B   253
    TILL THEY HAD CHANGED US TO LIKE STRENGTH?" . . . . 259 PEACE   V   9
    "THEY ARE NOT CHANGED TO ANYTHING, ...   299 THREE HERMITS   25
    SO CHANGED ME THAT I LIVE . . . .   315 FRIENDS   15
    ALL'S CHANGED SINCE I, HEARING AT TWILIGHT, ... 322 SWANS AT COOLE   15
    WHEN MY LUCK CHANGED AND THEY DARED MEET MY FACE, . . 352 PEOPLE   25
    WHEN MY LUCK CHANGED AND THEY DARED TO MEET MY FACE, . 352 PEOPLE   V   25
    SHUDDERS IN MANY CRADLES: ALL IS CHANGED, ... 375 PHASES OF MOON   89
    ALL CHANGED, CHANGED UTTERLY! . . . .   392 EASTER 1916   15
    ALL CHANGED, CHANGED UTTERLY! . . . .   392 EASTER 1916   15
    HE, TOO, HAS BEEN CHANGED IN HIS TURN, ...   393 EASTER 1916   38
    ARE CHANGED, CHANGED UTTERLY! . . . .   394 EASTER 1916   79
    ARE CHANGED, CHANGED UTTERLY! . . . .   394 EASTER 1916   79
    AND THAT HE CHANGED INTO A HARE. . . . .   412 TOWER   70
    THAT CHANGED SOME CHILDISH DAY TO TRAGEDY-- . . .   443 SCHOOL CHILDR   12
    HAVE CHANGED THEIR SILK FOR SACK. . . . .   458 HIS WILDNESS   6
    AND WHAT IF MIND SEEM CHANGED, ...   473 ALL SOUL NIGHT   66
    AND IT SEEM CHANGED WITH THE MIND, ...   473 ALL SOUL NIGHT   67
    AND IT SEEMED CHANGED WITH THE MIND, ...   473 ALL SOUL NIGHT V   67
    BUT ALL IS CHANGED, THAT HIGH HORSE RIDERLESS, . . . 492 COOLE BALLYLEE   46
    BUT FASHION'S CHANGED, THAT HIGH-HORSE RIDERLESS . . 492 COOLE BALLYLEE V   46
    THAT CHANGED A LOVER FOR A BULL. . . . .   509 JANE REPROVED   6
    THE ZODIAC IS CHANGED INTO A SPHERE. . . . . .   535 CHOSEN   18
    BUT THE DARK CHANGED TO RED, AND TORCHES SHONE, . . . 537 HER VISION   12
    THE BEGGARS HAVE CHANGED PLACES; BUT THE LASH GOES ON. . 590 GREAT DAY   4
    THEY HAD CHANGED THEIR THROATS AND HAD THE THROATS   635 CUCHULAIN COMF   25
        OF BIRDS.
    ARE CHANGED FOR EVER INTO MOON-WHITE STONE. . . . . 653 ISLE STAT I 2   43
    YOUR HOOD IS THREADBARE--SEE THAT IT BE CHANGED . . . 704 MOSADA 3   133
    BUT THAT THE WIND CHANGED: FOR I FOLLOWED HIM . . . 747 SHADOW WATER A   4
    THEY ARE CHANGED AND AS GREY BIRDS FLY OUT TO SEA, . 750 SHADOW WATER A   82
    "HOW LIGHT WE ARE NOW WE ARE CHANGED TO BIRDS!" . . . 753 SHADOW WATER A   143
    WHEN MIDHER'S WIFE HAD CHANGED HER TO A FLY . . . . 763 SHADOW WATER A   305
    AND WHEN ONE CHANGED HER TO A SILVER FLY, ... 763 SHADOW WATER A V   305
CHANGELESS
    UNDER THAT WOVEN CHANGELESS ROOF OF BOUGHS: . . . . 126 DREAM OF FAERY   11
    IN CHANGELESS OGHAM LETTERS WRIT-- . . . .   194 BAILE AILLINN   117
    WHERE PASSION GROWS TO BE A CHANGELESS THING, . . . 231 SHADOW WATER B   213
    WHEN WE HAVE PUT THEIR CHANGELESS IMAGE ON. . . . . 250 SHADOW WATER B   582
    WHERE SATO'S GIFT, A CHANGELESS SWORD, ...   421 MY TABLE   2
    CONCEIVES A CHANGELESS WORK OF ART. . . . . . .   421 MY TABLE   14
    IS A MAN'S MOCKERY OF THE CHANGELESS SOUL." . . .   465 HARUN RASHID   102
    IN GLORY OF CHANGELESS METAL . . . .   498 BYZANTIUM   22
CHANGERS   SEE SHAPE-CHANGERS
    THE SHAPE CHANGERS THAT CAN PUT . . . .   775 AGAINST WITCH V   2
CHANGES
    THAT TURNS AND CHANGES LIKE HIS DRAUGHTY SEAS? . . . 265 ABBEY THEATRE   12
    SING ME THE CHANGES OF THE MOON ONCE MORE: . . . . 373 PHASES OF MOON   29
    CHANGES MINUTE BY MINUTE: . . . .   393 EASTER 1916   50
CHANGING   SEE MANY-CHANGING
    OF ALL THE MANY CHANGING THINGS . . . .   65 HAPPY SHEPHERD   7
    AND LOVED THE SORROWS OF YOUR CHANGING FACE: . . . . 121 YOU ARE OLD   8
    THE CHANGING COLOURS OF ITS FRUIT . . . .   134 TWO TREES   5
    AND THE CHANGING MOON WORK OUT THEIR WILL. . . . . 148 INTO TWILIGHT V   12
    O WINDS, OLDER THAN CHANGING OF NIGHT AND DAY, . . . 162 ASKS FORGIVE   7
    O WINDS, ELDER THAN CHANGING OF NIGHT AND DAY, . . . 162 ASKS FORGIVE V   7

		PAGE	TITLE	LINE

CHANGING (CONTINUED)
O PITEOUS HEARTS, CHANGING TILL CHANGE BE DEAD • • •   163 ASKS FORGIVE   19
OR AS THE CHANGING SPEARS FLUNG BY THE GOLDEN STARS • • •   175 ELEMENT POWERS V   15
AND WONDERING WHO OF THE MANY CHANGING SIDHE • • • • •   181 QUEEN MAEVE   V   41
THAT LIFT US TO THE FLOWING, CHANGING WORLD • • • •   230 SHADOW WATER B   182
AND LIFTS TO THE CHANGING MOON • • • • • • • • •   379 CAT AND MOON   27
HIS CHANGING EYES. • • • • • • • • • • • • • •   379 CAT AND MOON   28
OF BOYHOOD CHANGING INTO MAN! • • • • • • • • •   479 SELF AND SOUL   46

CHANNELS
AND FROZEN ARE THE CHANNELS OF THE BLOOD, • • • • • •   333 LIVING BEAUTY   2

CHANT
• • • I WILL GO TO THE FENIANS, THOU CLERIC, AND CHANT • •   61 OISIN 3   V   201
AND LEARN TO CHANT A TONGUE MEN DO NOT KNOW. • • • •   101 ROSE UPON ROOD V   21

CHANTED
THE DRUIDS CHANTED, SWAYING IN THEIR HANDS • • • • •   111 CUCHULAIN SEA V   82
AND CHANTED FOR THREE DAYS. CUCHULAIN STIRRED, • • • •   111 CUCHULAIN SEA V   83

CHANTING
AND THE LOUD CHANTING OF THE UNQUIET LEAVES, • • • • •   120 SORROW OF LOVE V   11

CHANTS
AND CHANTS OF VICTORY AMID THE ENCIRCLING HOUNDS. • •   622 HOUND VOICE   21

CHAPEL
SHUT THE DOOR OF THE POPE'S CHAPEL, • • • • • • • •   618 LONG-LEG FLY   23
ON THE SISTINE CHAPEL ROOF, • • • • • • • • • • •   638 BEN BULBEN   46
SLOW THE CHAPEL BELL IS TOLLING AS THOUGH THE DEAD PASSED   718 PHANTOM SHIP   16
        BY•

CHAPLET
A CHAPLET FOR YOUR HEAD• • • • • • • • • • • • •   113 ROSE OF PEACE   8
AND CHAPLET THEIR CALM BROWS WITH LEAFAGE DIM, • • • •   127 DREAM OF FAERY V   32
AND CHAPLET THEIR CALM BROWS WITH LEAFAGE COOL! • • •   127 DREAM OF FAERY V   32

CHARACTER
AND YET A WOMAN'S POWERFUL CHARACTER • • • • • • •   489 COOLE PARK 29   18
HE HAD SUCH CHARACTER. • • • • • • • • • • • •   606 SONGS BURDEN 1   13
IN MARBLE OR IN BRONZE, LACKED CHARACTER. • • • • •   610 STATUES   3
THAT PASSION COULD BRING CHARACTER ENOUGH, • • • • •   610 STATUES   6
CHARACTER ISOLATED BY A DEED • • • • • • • • •   630 CIRCUS ANIMALS   29
BUT FIRST YOU MUST BE TOLD OUR CHARACTER! • • • • •   634 CUCHULAIN COMF   20

CHARACTERS
AND TRACE THESE CHARACTERS UPON THE SANDS? • • • •   370 EGO DOMINUS   64
AND TRACE THESE CHARACTERS UPON THE SAND? • • • •   370 EGO DOMINUS   V   64
AND, STANDING BY THESE CHARACTERS, DISCLOSE • • • •   371 EGO DOMINUS   75
AND MAY THESE CHARACTERS REMAIN • • • • • • • •   406 CARVED STONE   5
ALL THOSE TRAGIC CHARACTERS RIDE • • • • • • • •   549 SEVERED HEAD   4

CHARGE
WHAT TURNED SO GOOD A SHEPHERD FROM HIS CHARGE. • • • •   339 SHEP GOATHERD   16
"FOR ALL THAT I HAVE DONE AT MY OWN CHARGE? • • • •   351 PEOPLE   2
THEIR GRAVES INTO HER CHARGE, • • • • • • • • • •   571 THREE BUSHES   58

CHARGERS
THE GUARDSMEN'S DROWSY CHARGERS WOULD NOT PRANCE. • • •   429 NINETEEN 19   24

CHARIOT
AND PACE THE WOODS, AND DRIVE MY CHARIOT WHEELS • • •   103 FERGUS DRUID   V   18
THOSE STILTED BOYS, THAT BURNISHED CHARIOT. • • • •   629 CIRCUS ANIMALS   7

CHARIOT-WHEELS
AND PACE THE WOODS, AND DRIVE MY CHARIOT-WHEELS • • •   103 FERGUS DRUID   18

CHARITY
HER CHARITY HAD NO BOUNDS! • • • • • • • • • • •   392 EASTER 1916   V   21
"COME OUT OF CHARITY, • • • • • • • • • • • • •   526 AM OF IRELAND   4
"COME OUT OF CHARITY, • • • • • • • • • • • • •   527 AM OF IRELAND   17
"COME OUT OF CHARITY, • • • • • • • • • • • • •   527 AM OF IRELAND   30

CHARLEMAGNE
WHEN WORLD-TRANSFORMING CHARLEMAGNE WAS CONCEIVED? • • •   560 WHENCE COME   12

CHARM
ALL THAT STERNNESS AMID CHARM, • • • • • • • • •   259 PEACE   8
SO MUCH STERNNESS AND SUCH CHARM." • • • • • • •   259 PEACE   V   8
AND TWO OR THREE HAD CHARM, • • • • • • • • • •   350 MEMORY   2
BUT CHARM AND FACE WERE IN VAIN • • • • • • • • •   350 MEMORY   3
AND RUTH ST. DENIS HAD MORE CHARM ALTHOUGH SHE HAD POOR   353 HIS PHOENIX   10
        LUCK!
FOR BEAUTY'S VERY SELF, HAS CHARM MADE WISE, • • • •   404 FOR DAUGHTER   37

CHARMED
IT CHARMED AWAY THE MERCHANT FROM HIS GUILE, • • • •   129 BOOK STORIES   5
LIKE CHARMED APPLES MADE OF CHRYSOPRASE, • • • • •   231 SHADOW WATER B   214
ALL THAT TO THIS MOMENT CHARMED YOU? • • • • • •   390 IMAGE PAST   21
WELL NIGH IMMORTAL IN THIS CHARMED CLIME, • • • • •   674 ISLE STAT II 3   202
WELL-NIGH IMMORTAL IN THIS CHARMED CLIME! • • • •   674 ISLE STAT II 3 V   202
UNTIL WE DIE WITHIN THE CHARMED RING • • • • • • •   679 ISLE STAT II 3   322

CHARTER
A CHARTER TO COMMIT THE CRIME ONCE MORE. • • • • •   478 SELF AND SOUL   32

CHASE
THE STAG YE CHASE IS NOT MORE SAD, • • • • • •   4 OISIN 1   V   35
OF WAR, AND THE CHASE, AND HUNTING, AND PLEASURE! • • •   26 OISIN 1   V   403
THEY CHASE THE NOONTIDE DEER! • • • • • • • • • •   32 OISIN 2   53
AND CHASE THE WILD BEE HOMEWARD TO HIS HIVE • • • •   32 OISIN 2   V   50D
THEY CHASE AT NOON THE DEER. • • • • • • • • • •   32 OISIN 2   V   53
THEY CHASE THE NOON-TIDE DEER! • • • • • • • • •   32 OISIN 2   V   53
I MUSED ON THE CHASE WITH THE FENIANS, AND BRAN, SCEOLAN,   47 OISIN 3   5
        LOMAIR,
YON TALL ONE EYES MY SUPPER! CHASE HIM AWAY, • • • •   72 ANASHU VIJAYA   34
YON TALL ONE EYES MY SUPPER! SWIFTLY CHASE HIM • • •   72 ANASHU VIJAYA V   34
ALL DRIPPING ON A GRASSY SLOPE, AND SAW THEM CEASE TO CHASE   76 INDIAN ON GOD   4
AND CHASE THE FROTHY BUBBLES, • • • • • • • • • •   87 STOLEN CHILD   21
NOR BUT IN MERRIMENT BEGIN A CHASE, • • • • • • •   405 FOR DAUGHTER   45

	PAGE	TITLE		LINE
CHASED				
THE STAG WE CHASED WAS NOT MORE SAD, ...	2	OISIN 1	V	7J
THAN THE HORNLESS DEER WE CHASED THAT MORN, ...	2	OISIN 1	V	7P
I CHASED AT MORN THE FLYING DEER, ...	10	OISIN 1		121
I CHASED WITH HOUNDS THE FLYING DEER, ...	10	OISIN 1	V	121
PASSED BY US, CHASED BY A PHANTOM HOUND	11	OISIN 1		140
PASSED BY US, CHASED OF A PHANTOM HOUND	11	OISIN 1	V	140
I CHASED UPON THAT WOODY SHORE	23	OISIN 1		344
A HUNDRED YEARS I CHASED THE BOAR, ...	23	OISIN 1	V	344
SHAKING AND WAVING, VAPOUR VAPOUR CHASED, ...	39	OISIN 2		164
SHAKING AND WAVING, VAPOURS VAPOURS CHASED:	39	OISIN 2	V	164
CHASES				
"BUT NEVER WITH US WHERE THE WILD FOWL CHASES	27	OISIN 1	V	408
THE CHILD WHO CHASES LIZARDS IN THE GRASS, ...	734	QUATRAIN APHOR		1
IT CHASES OTHER THOUGHT AWAY, ...	791	REPRISALS		9
CHASTITY				
IF I LOST MY CHASTITY?	570	THREE BUSHES		20
CHAT				
YOU WILL WITH THE BANSHEE CHAT, ...	726	LOVERS QUARREL		9
CHATTER				
OF BEAUTY'S CRUELTY AND WISDOM'S CHATTER--	377	PHASES OF MOON		121
THE DAWS CHATTER AND SCREAM, ...	415	TOWER		167
CHATTERING				
A CHATTERING WISE AND SWEET, ...	161	CAP AND BELLS		34
THE WATERS OF SLEEP CAN MAKE A CHATTERING TONGUE	218	WOODS OF COOLE		25
PIERCED THROUGH, CHATTERING FROM HABIT IN THE SUN, . . .	664	ISLE STAT II 2		53
CHATTERJEE				
MOHINI CHATTERJEE	495	MOHINI CHATTER		T
MOHINI CHATTERJEE	496	MOHINI CHATTER		14
CHAUCER				
CHAUCER HAD NOT DRAWN BREATH	421	MY TABLE		8
CHAUNT				
COMING OUT OF THE SEA AS THE DAWN COMES, A CHAUNT OF LOVE	58	OISIN 3		158
ON MY LIPS,				
. . . FOR I GO TO THE FENIANS, O CLERIC, TO CHAUNT . . .	61	OISIN 3		201
AND LEARN TO CHAUNT A TONGUE MEN DO NOT KNOW.	101	ROSE UPON ROOD		21
CHAUNT IN HIS EAR DELUSIONS MAGICAL, ...	111	CUCHULAIN SEA		80
CHAUNTED				
AND CHAUNTED FOR THREE DAYS. CUCHULAIN STIRRED, ...	111	CUCHULAIN SEA		83
THE DRUIDS CHAUNTED, SWAYING IN THEIR HANDS	111	CUCHULAIN SEA	V	82
CHAUNTING				
AND THE LOUD CHAUNTING OF THE UNQUIET LEAVES, ...	120	SORROW OF LOVE	V	11
CHEATED				
AMONG THE OTHER CHEATED DEAD.	791	REPRISALS		24
CHECK				
I TRAP YOU. CHECK. I DO MISCALCULATE.	722	WITCH VIVIEN		58
CHECK. AH! HOW BRIGHT YOUR EYES. HOW SWIFT YOUR MOVES.	722	WITCH VIVIEN		61
A BIRD WALK ON THE DOORSTEP. CHECK ONCE MORE.	722	WITCH VIVIEN		64
CHECKED				
COULD MY SPOKEN WORDS HAVE CHECKED	632	MAN AND ECHO		15
CHEEK				
NOR CAN TIME WASTE THE CHEEK, NOR IS THERE FOOT	284	TWO KINGS		182
AND HAD THAT COLOUR UPON CHEEK OR HAIR, ...	444	SCHOOL CHILDR		22
HOLLOW OF CHEEK AS THOUGH IT DRANK THE WIND	444	SCHOOL CHILDR		27
WERE SOME DEAR CHEEK. UPON A MOONLESS NIGHT	466	HARUN RASHID		127
WHAT'S BOWED YOUR SHOULDER AND MADE PALE YOUR CHEEK"! . .	467	HARUN RASHID		133
INHABITANT OF THE SOFT CHEEK OF A GIRL--	540	FROM ANTIGONE		2
SAD HISTORIES ARE LETTERED ON THY CHEEK.	660	ISLE STAT II 1		52
I FEEL A FINGER DRAWN ACROSS MY CHEEK!	694	MOSADA 1		96
CHEEKED	SEE HOLLOW-CHEEKED			
CHEEKS				
LOOK ON MY THIN GREY HAIR AND HOLLOW CHEEKS	103	FERGUS DRUID		23
OUR CHEEKS ARE PALE, OUR HAIR IS UNBOUND, ...	140	HOSTING SIDHE		7
AND PLEASURE MADE HER CHEEKS GROW RED, ...	314	MEMORY YOUTH		11
A GREY-HAIRED YOUTH, WHOSE CHEEKS HAD NEVER FOUND, . . .	687	TWO TITANS		7
CHEER				
FILLED FULL OF ANCIENT CHEER."	97	FOXHUNTER	V	12
WHO HAS WON A DRUNKEN CHEER, ...	347	FISHERMAN		18
COULD, HE WAS SO HARRIED, CHEER!	412	TOWER		76
COULD, SO HE WAS HARRIED, CHEER!	412	TOWER	V	76
AND FULL HIS EYES OF FAIRY CHEER.	716	FAIRY DOCTOR		12
CHEERING				
NOR PUBLIC MEN, NOR CHEERING CROWDS, ...	328	IRISH AIRMAN		10
NOR PUBLIC MAN, NOR CHEERING CROWDS, ...	328	IRISH AIRMAN	V	10
PARNELL CAME DOWN THE ROAD, HE SAID TO A CHEERING MAN: . .	590	PARNELL		1
CHEERS				
THOSE CHEERS THAT CAN BE BOUGHT OR SOLD, ...	598	MODEL LAUREATE		19
CHEESE				
COMPANIONS OF THE CHESHIRE CHEESE, ...	270	GREY ROCK		2
CHERRIES				
AND OF REDDEST STOLEN CHERRIES.	87	STOLEN CHILD		8
CHERRY				
WHERE SHADOW OF CHERRY, AND SHADOW OF APPLE TREES, . . .	710	FERENCZ RENYI		23
CHERRY-BRANCH				
THOUGH DOUBTLESS PLUM OR CHERRY-BRANCH	567	LAPIS LAZULI		47
CHERUBIM				
WITH OLD EZEKIEL'S CHERUBIM	336	YOUNG BEAUTY		11
CHESHIRE				
COMPANIONS OF THE CHESHIRE CHEESE, ...	270	GREY ROCK		2
CHESS				
THAT SAT SO STILL AND PLAYED AT THE CHESS?	550	SEVERED HEAD		12

	PAGE	TITLE	LINE
CHESS (CONTINUED)			
COME TO THE CHESS, FOR YOUNG GIRLS' WITS ARE BETTER . . .	721 WITCH VIVIEN		46
CHESSBOARDS			
IN THE FENIANS' DWELLINGS OF WATTLE LEAN ON THE CHESSBOARDS AND PLAY,	55 OISIN 3		115
CHEST SEE LINEN-CHEST OATMEAL-CHEST			
ROUND AND ROUND THE OATMEAL CHEST.	88 STOLEN CHILD	V	49
BETWEEN THE PANTRY AND THE LINEN CHEST, ...	340 SHEP GOATHERD	V	36
SINBAD THE SAILOR'S BROUGHT A PAINTED CHEST, ...	371 ON GOING HOUSE		10
CHESTNUT			
O CHESTNUT TREE, GREAT ROOTED BLOSSOMER, ...	446 SCHOOL CHILDR	V	61
CHESTNUTS			
COOKING CHESTNUTS ON THE BARS--	737 IN FIRELIGHT		2
COOKING CHESTNUTS ON THE BARS.	737 IN FIRELIGHT		12
CHESTNUT-TREE			
O CHESTNUT-TREE, GREAT-ROOTED BLOSSOMER, ...	446 SCHOOL CHILDR		61
CHIDE			
OUR HEARTS CAN HEAR THE VOICES CHIDE.	192 BAILE AILLINN		94
OUR HEART CAN HEAR THE VOICES CHIDE.	192 BAILE AILLINN	V	94
CHIEF			
AND THE CHIEF OF THE HUGE WHITE CREATURES, ...	50 OISIN 3		43
THE CHIEF IMAGINATION OF CHRISTENDOM, ...	368 EGO DOMINUS		18
MAY WELL BE OF ALL EVIL CHANCES CHIEF.	405 FOR DAUGHTER		53
WHAT IS IT, FRIEND? HE LOST I' THE WOODS THE CHIEF . . .	661 ISLE STAT II 1		60
CHIEFLY			
IN COURTESY I'D HAVE HER CHIEFLY LEARNED:	404 FOR DAUGHTER		33
CHIEFS			
ARE STILL THE ACHAIANS' TENTED CHIEFS AT BAY?	679 ISLE STAT II 3		310
CHIEFTAINS			
. . . WITH BODIES UNGLORIOUS, THEIR CHIEFTAINS STOOD, . .	58 OISIN 3		166
CHILD			
"I AM NEAVE, A CHILD OF THE MIGHTY SHEE.	5 OISIN 1	V	48
IN THE HOUSE OF A CHILD, OF A FRIEND, OF A BROTHER. . . .	26 OISIN 1		401
AND DEW-BLANCHED HORNS, IN WHOSE HOLLOW A CHILD OF THREE YEARS OLD	49 OISIN 3		30
AND DEW-BLANCHED HORNS, IN WHOSE HOLLOWS A CHILD OF THREE YEARS OLD	49 OISIN 3	V	31
. . . HE SAD AS A CHILD WITHOUT MILK:	59 OISIN 3		174
WHEN THE POOR TIRED CHILD, PASSION, FALLS ASLEEP.	80 EPHEMERA		7
A GENTLE YET A KINGLY CHILD:	82 MAD KING GOLL	V	8
THE STOLEN CHILD	86 STOLEN CHILD		T
COME AWAY, O HUMAN CHILD!	87 STOLEN CHILD		9
COME AWAY, O HUMAN CHILD!	87 STOLEN CHILD		24
COME AWAY, O HUMAN CHILD!	88 STOLEN CHILD		38
FOR HE COMES, THE HUMAN CHILD, ...	88 STOLEN CHILD		50
COME, O HUMAN CHILD!	88 STOLEN CHILD	V	38
THE CRY OF A CHILD BY THE ROADWAY, THE CREAK OF A LUMBERING CART,	142 ROSE IN HEART		2
I KISS MY WAILING CHILD AND PRESS IT TO MY BREAST, . . .	147 UNAPPEAS HOST		5
AND HEAR THE NARROW GRAVES CALLING MY CHILD AND ME. . . .	147 UNAPPEAS HOST		6
HALF LION, HALF CHILD, IS AT PEACE.	260 UNWORTH PRAISE		20
I HAVE NO CHILD, I HAVE NOTHING BUT A BOOK, ...	270 PARDON FATHERS		21
BECAUSE SHE DREAMED WHEN BUT A CHILD	272 GREY ROCK		42
AND THEN, AS TERROR-STRICKEN AS A CHILD	279 TWO KINGS	V	45A
BEING WEARIED OUT, I LOVE IN MAN THE CHILD?	285 TWO KINGS		192
TO A CHILD DANCING IN THE WIND	312 CHILD DANCING		T
TO A CHILD DANCING UPON THE SHORE	312 CHILD DANCING	V	T
BUT NOT THE EXACT LIKENESS, THE SIMPLICITY OF A CHILD, . .	354 HIS PHOENIX		28
ONE IS A HARLOT, AND ONE A CHILD	358 PRESENCES		12
SHE IS PLAYING LIKE A CHILD	364 END OF DAY		1
AS A MOTHER NAMES HER CHILD	394 EASTER 1916		62
I WOULD HAVE TOUCHED IT LIKE A CHILD	399 BREAK OF DAY		12
MY CHILD SLEEPS ON. THERE IS NO OBSTACLE	403 FOR DAUGHTER		3
I HAVE WALKED AND PRAYED FOR THIS YOUNG CHILD AN HOUR . .	403 FOR DAUGHTER		9
I LOOK UPON ONE CHILD OR T'OTHER THERE	443 SCHOOL CHILDR		18
SHE STANDS BEFORE ME AS A LIVING CHILD.	444 SCHOOL CHILDR		24
"BECAUSE I MADE YOU TURN AWAY AND RUN FROM THAT YOUNG CHILD:	450 OWEN AHERNE		14
NOW THAT YOUR TONGUE CANNOT PERSUADE THE CHILD TILL SHE MISTAKE	450 OWEN AHERNE		22
THINKS THAT THE STONE'S A CHILD.	456 FRIENDS YOUTH		12
SHE SEEMED THE LEARNED MAN AND I THE CHILD:	467 HARUN RASHID		137
THAT IS TO AGE WHAT MILK IS TO A CHILD?	469 HARUN RASHID		174
SO ARROGANTLY PURE, A CHILD MIGHT THINK	491 COOLE BALLYLEE		23
"A CHILD FOUND ALL A CHILD CAN LACK, ...	521 THREE THINGS		3
"A CHILD FOUND ALL A CHILD CAN LACK, ...	521 THREE THINGS		3
FATHER AND CHILD	531 FATHER CHILD		T
A WOMAN YOUNG AND OLD I FATHER AND CHILD	531 FATHER CHILD	V	T
AND YET I WEEP--OEDIPUS' CHILD	540 FROM ANTIGONE		15
. . . MAN, WOMAN, CHILD (A DAUGHTER OR A SON), ...	556 RIBH PATRICK		2
RECALL HIS TRINITY. A FATHER, MOTHER, CHILD (A DAUGHTER OR A SON),	556 RIBH PATRICK	V	2
PRIMORDIAL MOTHERHOOD FORSAKE HIS LIMBS, THE CHILD NO LONGER REST,	559 MAGIC DRUM		2
OR CHILD HID IN THE WOMB.	589 OLD WICKED MAN		53
THE HARLOT AND THE CHILD.	601 THOSE IMAGES		12
SHE THINKS, PART WOMAN, THREE PARTS A CHILD, ...	617 LONG-LEG FLY		15
AND WANDERED MURMURING EVERYWHERE, "MY CHILD, MY CHILD!"	619 BRONZE HEAD		21
AND WANDERED MURMURING EVERYWHERE, "MY CHILD, MY CHILD!"	619 BRONZE HEAD		21
FROM COLLAR TO COLLAR, FROM STILT TO STILT, FROM FATHER TO CHILD.	623 HIGH TALK		10

138

	PAGE	TITLE	LINE

CHILD   (CONTINUED)
    MY PRETTY CHILD, SINCE HE HAS GONE, OH SAY . . . . 658 ISLE STAT II 1   3
    THE CHILD PURSUING LIZARDS IN THE GRASS, ... 686 LIFE   1
    HUNG ON HIS DOUBLET--DEAR AND MOURNFUL CHILD, ... 691 MOSADA 1   35
    THE VISION. YOU ARE PALE AND WEEPING. CHILD, ... 693 MOSADA 1   73
    AND KNOW YOU NOT SHE KISSED THAT PIOUS CHILD. . . . . 696 MOSADA 2   6
    A WEAK, THIN CHILD, WHEN LAST I SAW HIM THERE. . . . . 699 MOSADA 3   14
    AND EVIL STILL IS ACTION'S CHILD. . . . . 728 PRIEST FAIRY   14
    THE CHILD WHO CHASES LIZARDS IN THE GRASS, ... 734 QUATRAIN APHOR   1
    THE CHILD PURSUING LIZARDS IN THE GRASS, ... 734 QUATRAIN APHOR V   1
    THE LITTLE OLD GLOVE OF A CHILD: . . . . 744 GLOVE CLOAK   9
    DELIGHTED ME AS A CHILD. . . . . 787 HUDDON DUDDON   2
    DELIGHTED ME AS A CHILD. . . . . 787 HUDDON DUDDON   7
    DELIGHTED ME AS A CHILD. . . . . 787 HUDDON DUDDON   12
CHILD-BEARING
    CRAZED THROUGH MUCH CHILD-BEARING . . . . 487 CRAZED MOON   1
CHILDER
    COME ROUND ME, LITTLE CHILDER: . . . . 94 MOLL MAGEE   1
    YE LITTLE CHILDER DEAR, ... 95 MOLL MAGEE   18
    SO NOW, YE LITTLE CHILDER, ... 96 MOLL MAGEE   53
CHILDHOOD
    OF ALL THIS HOST SO BOUND FROM CHILDHOOD ON." . . . . 109 CUCHULAIN SEA   56
    AND HE MY MASTER FROM MY CHILDHOOD UP! . . . . . . 225 SHADOW WATER B   77
    FROM EARLIEST CHILDHOOD, BUT THAT BEING SO, ... 225 SHADOW WATER B V   77
    ALL THOSE THAT MANHOOD TRIED, OR CHILDHOOD LOVED . . . 327 ROBERT GREGORY   91
    HIS CHILDHOOD AND HIS FAMILY. . . . . 361 ALF POLLEXFEN   35
    FROM CHILDHOOD ON, HAD NOW SO MUCH . . . . 397 POLIT PRISONER   2
    THAT ALL MY CHILDHOOD COUNTED DEAR: . . . . . . 398 BREAK OF DAY   7
    AND CHILDHOOD A DELIGHT FOR EVERY SENSE, ... 418 ANCEST HOUSES   31
    THAT FROM CHILDHOOD STOOD . . . . 512 JANE ON GOD   14
CHILDISH
    THE NAMES THAT STILLED YOUR CHILDISH PLAY, ... 289 SEPTEMBER 1913   10
    BY CHILDISH MEMORIES OF AN OLD CROSS POLLEXFEN, . . . 391 UNDER SATURN   7
    SO MANY TIMES CHILDISH DELIGHT. . . . . 399 BREAK OF DAY   11
    THAT CHANGED SOME CHILDISH DAY TO TRAGEDY-- . . . . 443 SCHOOL CHILDR   12
    HER CHILDISH GRATITUDE FOR LOVE AND MATCH YOUR FIFTY YEARS? 450 OWEN AHERNE   23
    HAD SPOKEN OF THEIR CHILDISH DAYS . . . . 457 SUMMER SPRING   11
    IN CHILDISH IGNORANCE OF ALL THAT PASSED. . . . . . 468 HARUN RASHID   149
    IN CHILDISH IGNORANCE OF ALL THAT PASSED. . . . . . 468 HARUN RASHID   160
CHILDLESS
    CHILDLESS I THOUGHT, "MY CHILDREN MAY FIND HERE . . . 603 GALLERY REVIS   36
    CHILDLESS, I THOUGHT, "MY CHILDREN MAY LEARN HERE . . 603 GALLERY REVIS V   36
CHILDREN   SEE GRAND-CHILDREN
    HAPPY AS CHILDREN WITH UNWITHERING LIPS, ... 30 OISIN 2   V 14B
    WITHOUT LAUGHTER, A SHOW UNTO CHILDREN, ... 63 OISIN 3   218
    AH ME! TO BE OLD WITHOUT SUCCOUR, A SHOW UNTO CHILDREN, 63 OISIN 3   V 217
      A STAIN,
    BUT O, SICK CHILDREN OF THE WORLD, ... 65 HAPPY SHEPHERD   6
    YOU WAVES, THOUGH YOU DANCE BY MY FEET LIKE CHILDREN AT 90 OLD FISHERMAN   1
      PLAY,
    YE WAVES, THOUGH YE DANCE 'FORE MY FEET LIKE CHILDREN AT 90 OLD FISHERMAN V   1
      PLAY,
    FROM THE WIVES, AND THE CATS, AND THE CHILDREN, . . . 92 FATHER OHART   15
    FROM THEIR WIVES, AND THEIR CATS, AND THEIR CHILDREN, . 92 FATHER OHART V   15
    AND USNA'S CHILDREN DIED. . . . . 111 ROSE OF WORLD   5
    GIVE TO THESE CHILDREN, NEW FROM THE WORLD, ... 116 FAERY SONG   5
    GIVE TO THESE CHILDREN, NEW FROM THE WORLD, ... 116 FAERY SONG   9
    THE DANAAN CHILDREN LAUGH, IN CRADLES OF WROUGHT GOLD, . 146 UNAPPEAS HOST   1
    THE FAERY CHILDREN LAUGH IN CRADLES OF WROUGHT GOLD, . 146 UNAPPEAS HOST V   1
    THEIR CHILDREN'S CHILDREN SHALL SAY THEY HAVE LIED. . . 166 EVIL OF BELOV   6
    WOMEN AND CHILDREN, YOUNG MEN WITH BOOKS, ... 167 BLESSED   15
    CHILDREN AND WOMEN AND TONSURED YOUNG MEN, ... 167 BLESSED V   15
    FASHIONED TO BE THE MOTHER OF STRONG CHILDREN: . . . 181 QUEEN MAEVE   26
    THE CHILDREN OF THE MAINES OUT OF SLEEP, ... 184 QUEEN MAEVE   92
    THE MAINES' CHILDREN DROPPED THEIR SPADES, AND STOOD . 185 QUEEN MAEVE   120
    THE MAINES' CHILDREN HAVE NOT DROPPED THEIR SPADES . . 186 QUEEN MAEVE   123
    THAT WOULD BE HARSH FOR CHILDREN THAT HAVE STRAYED. . . 201 OLD MEMORY   12
    THAT HAD BEEN HARSH FOR CHILDREN THAT HAVE STRAYED. . . 201 OLD MEMORY V   12
    LAND FOR YOUR CHILDREN OR MONEY IN A POT." . . . . 228 SHADOW WATER B   125
    IN ISLANDS WHERE THE CHILDREN OF AENGUS WIND . . . . 245 SHADOW WATER B   469
    ALTHOUGH IT BE FOR CHILDREN THAT YOU SIGH: . . . . . 265 THESE CLOUDS   10
    HAPPINESS TO CHILDREN AND TO MEN." . . . . 282 TWO KINGS   121
    HAD GIVEN THEIR CHILDREN'S CHILDREN LOFTIER THOUGHT, . 292 TO A SHADE   12
    EVEN BEFORE HIS CHILDREN AND HIS WIFE? . . . . . . 340 SHEP GOATHERD   34
    AND CHILDREN WHEN THEY SPRING UP SHOULDER-HIGH. . . . 343 SHEP GOATHERD   119
    AND CHILDREN WHEN THEY SPRING UP SHOULDER HIGH. . . . 343 SHEP GOATHERD V   119
    AMONG SCHOOL CHILDREN . . . . 443 SCHOOL CHILDR   T
    THE CHILDREN LEARN TO CIPHER AND TO SING, ... 443 SCHOOL CHILDR   3
    AS THAT OLD WANDERING BEGGAR AND THESE GOD-HATED CHILDREN 459 FROM OEDIPUS   6
      KNOW,
    MIMICKING WHAT THEY HEARD, AS CHILDREN MIMIC: . . . . 487 SEVEN SAGES   25
    FOR CHILDREN BORN OF HER PAIN. . . . . 487 CRAZED MOON   6
    CHILDREN DAZED OR DEAD! . . . . 488 CRAZED MOON   7
    GREAT ROOMS WHERE TRAVELLED MEN AND CHILDREN FOUND . . 491 COOLE BALLYLEE   29
    ALTHOUGH THEIR CHILDREN NEED A RICH ESTATE: . . . . 500 VACILLATION   24
    THE CHILDREN THAT HE GAVE, ... 525 DANCING DAYS   12
    CHILDLESS I THOUGHT, "MY CHILDREN MAY FIND HERE . . . 603 GALLERY REVIS   36
    CHILDLESS, I THOUGHT, "MY CHILDREN MAY LEARN HERE . . 603 GALLERY REVIS V   36
    KEEP THOSE CHILDREN OUT. . . . . 618 LONG-LEG FLY   24
    BECAUSE CHILDREN DEMAND DADDY-LONG-LEGS UPON HIS TIMBER 623 HIGH TALK   6
      TOES,

		PAGE	TITLE	LINE

CHILDREN   (CONTINUED)
LIVE TO BEAR CHILDREN TO A DUNCE; . . . .   626 OLD MEN BE MAD   6
AND FLOWERS AND LITTLE CHILDREN. SUDDENLY . . . . . .   688 TWO TITANS   36
ONE SHOULDER TWISTED, AND THE CHILDREN CRY . . . . . .   695 MOSADA 1   116
MURMURS OF HER CHILDREN TALKING-- . . . .   705 DAWN-SONG   6
IN EVERY DANCE, BY CHILDREN SOUGHT. "ACCURST, . . .   709 FERENCZ RENYI   12
OF MY DEAD CHILDREN SOON, WHATE'ER BETIDE, ...   712 FERENCZ RENYI   58
NEVER STORM AROSE SO SWIFTLY; SCARCE THE CHILDREN WERE   718 PHANTOM SHIP   4
    IN BED,
DOWN THE VAPOURS FALL AND HIDE THEM FROM THE CHILDREN OF 719 PHANTOM SHIP   27
    A DAY,
ARE TWO RAGGED CHILDREN BRIGHT-- . . . .   731 STREET DANCERS   4
CHILDREN SING IN TWOS AND THREES. . . . .   732 STREET DANCERS   17
DANCE THE SAVAGE CHILDREN SMALL, ...   732 STREET DANCERS   29
AND BRING ME WHERE THE CHILDREN OF AENGUS WIND . . . .   763 SHADOW WATER A   317
BUT CHILDREN AND DOGS ON THE FLOOR. . . . .   780 WELL AND TREE   14
AMONG HIS CHILDREN, GRANDCHILDREN AND GREAT-GRANDCHILDREN; 790 DEDICATION   6
AND SUCKLE CHILDREN NOW? ARMED MEN . . . .   791 REPRISALS   20
CHILDREN'S
THEIR CHILDREN'S CHILDREN SHALL SAY THEY HAVE LIED. . . 166 EVIL OF BELOV   6
HAD GIVEN THEIR CHILDREN'S CHILDREN LOFTIER THOUGHT, . 292 TO A SHADE   12
IN THE BEST MODERN WAY--THE CHILDREN'S EYES . . . . .   443 SCHOOL CHILDR   6
OF CHILDREN'S GRATITUDE OR WOMAN'S LOVE. . . . .   500 VACILLATION   26
OF SOME MILD WOMAN, OR IN CHILDREN'S WAYS. . . . . . .   750 SHADOW WATER A   74
CHILD'S
A CHILD'S LAUGHTER, A WOMAN'S KISS. . . . .   190 BAILE AILLINN   40
WHERE NO CHILD'S BORN BUT TO OUTLIVE THE MOON." . . .   247 SHADOW WATER B   531
WITH ALL A WOMAN'S PASSION, A CHILD'S IMPERIOUS WAY, . 354 HIS PHOENIX   14
I AM THINKING OF A CHILD'S VOW SWORN IN VAIN . . . . .   391 UNDER SATURN   15
CHILL
CAN SHAKE MORE BLOSSOM FROM AUTUMNAL CHILL . . . . .   465 HARUN RASHID   104
THAT BRINGS MORE BLOSSOM TO AUTUMNAL CHILL . . . . .   465 HARUN RASHID   V 104
AN EVENING CHILL UPON THE AIR, ...   494 AT ALGECIRAS   14
OR STRIKES A SUDDEN CHILL INTO MY BONES . . . .   499 MOTHER OF GOD   14
TO DEATH. HIS DARKNESS AND HIS CHILL I FEEL. . . . .   684 SEEKER   63
MY SOUL. HIS DARKNESS AND HIS CHILL I FEEL. . . . . .   684 SEEKER   V 63B
CHILLED
MY BARREN THOUGHTS HAVE CHILLED ME TO THE BONE. . . .   257 RECONCILIATION   12
THIS BLAST HAS CHILLED ME TO THE BONE." . . . .   305 HOUR DAWN   62
WHEN AGE MIGHT WELL HAVE CHILLED HIS BLOOD." . . . . .   356 BROKEN DREAMS   19
CHILLED BLOOD, THIS SWEETNESS BROUGHT; . . . .   401 DEMON BEAST   39
CHILLING
THE WARMTH OF LIFE IS CHILLING, AND THE SHADOWS GROW . 675 ISLE STAT II 3   232
CHILLS
THIS SULLEN PEASANT CHILLS THE GOOD SUNSHINE. . . . .   711 FERENCZ RENYI   V   42
CHILLY
AS WITHIN A CELLAR CHILLY . . . .   647 ISLE STAT I 1   57
LIES A CHILLY FINGER TIP, ...   732 STREET DANCERS   19
CHIMAERAS
CHRONICLING CHIMAERAS FLED. . . . .   65 HAPPY SHEPHERD V   17
CHIME
AND THROUGH THE CHIME SHE'D SAY, ...   570 THREE BUSHES   30
WHEN THE CLOCK BEGINS TO CHIME." . . . .   570 THREE BUSHES   41
CHIMED
BUT NO DOGS BARKED, AND MIDNIGHTS CHIMED, ...   570 THREE BUSHES   29
AND NO DOGS BARKED THROUGH MIDNIGHTS CHIMED . . . . .   570 THREE BUSHES   V   29
CHIMES
AND YET THE SADDEST CHIMES ARE BEST ENJOYED. . . . . .   130 BOOK STORIES   20
CHIMNEY   SEE LAMP-CHIMNEY
HE HEARS THE STORM IN THE CHIMNEY ABOVE, ...   26 OISIN 1   404
THE BARE CHIMNEY IS GONE BLACK OUT . . . .   327 ROBERT GREGORY   84
CHIMNEY CORNER, GARDEN WALK. . . . .   499 MOTHER OF GOD   8
HIS LONG LAMP CHIMNEY SHAPED LIKE THE STEM . . . . . .   566 LAPIS LAZULI   V   33
CHIN
ONE HAND UPHELD HIS BEARDLESS CHIN, ...   17 OISIN 1   250
ONE HAND BENEATH HIS BEARDLESS CHIN, ...   17 OISIN 1   V 251
THE SUN HAS LAID HIS CHIN ON THE GREY WOOD, ...   72 ANASHU VIJAYA   24
THE SUN HATH LAID HIS CHIN ON THE GREY WOOD, ...   72 ANASHU VIJAYA   V   24
CHINA
THERE IS A QUEEN IN CHINA . . . .   353 HIS PHOENIX   V   T
THERE IS A QUEEN IN CHINA, OR MAYBE IT'S IN SPAIN, . .   353 HIS PHOENIX   1
THERE IS A QUEEN IN CHINA, OR MAY BE IT'S IN SPAIN, .   353 HIS PHOENIX   V   1
ON THRONES FROM CHINA TO PERU. . . . .   597 MODEL LAUREATE   1
CHINAMEN
TWO CHINAMEN, BEHIND THEM A THIRD, ...   566 LAPIS LAZULI   37
THOSE CHINAMEN CLIMB TOWARDS, AND I . . . .   567 LAPIS LAZULI   49
CHINESE
WHEN LOIE FULLER'S CHINESE DANCERS ENWOUND . . . . . .   430 NINETEEN 19   49
CHINS
LIFT THEIR CHINS AND TOSS THEIR CURLS, ...   726 LOVERS QUARREL   23
LIFT THEIR CHINS AND TURN AWAY. . . . .   726 LOVERS QUARREL   24
CHIRP   SEE SPARROW-CHIRP
UPON THE TIME OF SPARROW CHIRP, ...   133 FR GILLIGAN   V   21
CHISEL
WHETHER WE HAVE CHOSEN CHISEL, PEN OR BRUSH, ...   368 EGO DOMINUS   14
HE SET HIS CHISEL TO THE HARDEST STONE. . . . .   369 EGO DOMINUS   32
THAT WITH A MALLET OR A CHISEL MODELLED THESE . . . .   610 STATUES   10
THAT PATCHING OLD HEELS THEY MAY SHRIEK, I TAKE TO CHISEL 623 HIGH TALK   8
    AND PLANE.
CHIVALRY
AND MEASURE OUT THE WAYS OF CHIVALRY. . . . .   660 ISLE STAT II 1   37

140

<pre>
                                                PAGE   TITLE   LINE
CHIVALRY   (CONTINUED)
    AND ALL THE SAD FAY CHIVALRY . . . .   730 PRIEST FAIRY   71
CHOICE
    CHANCE BEING AT ONE WITH CHOICE AT LAST, ...   388 SOLOMON WITCH   14
    WITH CRUELTIES OF CHOICE AND CHANCE; . . . .   388 SOLOMON WITCH   23
    BEING BOTH CHANCE AND CHOICE, ...   472 ALL SOUL NIGHT   58
    THE CHOICE . . . .   495 CHOICE   T
    THE CHOICE . . . .   534 CHOSEN   V   T
    SOME FEW HALF WAKE AND HALF RENEW THEIR CHOICE, . .   622 HOUND VOICE   6
    IN THIS MY CHOICE, SOME GOD MIGHT HELP; IF SO . . .   656 ISLE STAT I 3   37
    ALL CHOICE, AND GIVE TO CHANCE FOR GUIDING CHANCE .   656 ISLE STAT I 3   39
    IF WRONG MY CHOICE, AS SILENT AS THOU ART. . . . .   657 ISLE STAT I 3   76
CHOIR
    WITH YOUR HARMONIOUS CHOIR . . . .   174 ELEMENT POWERS   8
    AND ALL THE CHOIR OF LOVE. . . . .   531 DELPHIC ORACLE   10
    THERE SIGHED AMID HIS CHOIR OF LOVE . . . .   611 NEWS ORACLE   7
    WHERE WADES THE CHOIR OF LOVE . . . .   612 NEWS ORACLE   22
    WHERE WADE THE CHOIR OF LOVE . . . .   612 NEWS ORACLE V   22
CHOIRS
    A FAR VAGUE SOUND OF FEATHERY CHOIRS. . . . . . .   13 OISIN 1   V   166
CHOKE
    BANNERS CHOKE THE SKY; . . . .   512 JANE ON GOD   7
CHOKED
    ARE CHOKED WITH THUNDER, LIGHTNING, AND FIERCE WIND, .   42 OISIN 2   205
    YET KNOWS THAT TO BE CHOKED WITH HATE . . . . . .   405 FOR DAUGHTER   52
CHOOSE
    YET NOW I CHOOSE, FOR THESE FOUR FEET . . . . . .   6 OISIN 1   57
    CHOOSE YOUR COMPANIONS FROM THE BEST; . . . . . .   335 YOUNG BEAUTY   4
    ANOTHER BOASTS, "I PICK AND CHOOSE AND HAVE BUT TWO OR   354 HIS PHOENIX   20
      THREE."
    SAID I WAS DEAD; AND DEAD I CHOOSE TO BE. . . . .   373 PHASES OF MOON   28
    CHOOSE PLATO AND PLOTINUS FOR A FRIEND . . . . . .   409 TOWER   12
    I CHOOSE UPSTANDING MEN . . . .   414 TOWER   122
    AS THOUGH TO CHOOSE WHATEVER SHAPE IT WILLS . . .   417 ANCEST HOUSES   6
    O LET HER CHOOSE A YOUNG MAN NOW AND ALL FOR HIS .   450 OWEN AHERNE   24
      WILD SAKE."
    THINK WHEN I CHOOSE A BRIDE I CHOOSE FOR EVER; . .   464 HARUN RASHID   80
    THINK WHEN I CHOOSE A BRIDE I CHOOSE FOR EVER; . .   464 HARUN RASHID   80
    THE INTELLECT OF MAN IS FORCED TO CHOOSE . . . . .   491 COOLE BALLYLEE V   40A
    THE INTELLECT OF MAN IS FORCED TO CHOOSE . . . . .   495 CHOICE   1
    DID I BECOME A CHRISTIAN MAN AND CHOOSE FOR MY BELIEF 503 VACILLATION   85
    I CHOOSE ANOTHER MARK, ...   588 OLD WICKED MAN   29
    I CHOOSE THE SECOND-BEST, ...   590 OLD WICKED MAN   60
    AND WERE THE LAST TO CHOOSE THE SETTLED GROUND, . .   621 HOUND VOICE   2
    KNOW HIS WORK OR CHOOSE HIS MATE. . . . .   638 BEN BULBEN   36
    AS I, TO CHOOSE BENEATH DAY'S DYING FLAMES; . . .   656 ISLE STAT I 3   34
    "CHOOSE!" RESTLESS HAYNAU'S FINGERS TAPPING GO. . .   711 FERENCZ RENYI   41
    THREE MOONS. IT WERE BEST TO KILL HIM, AND CHOOSE OUT .   748 SHADOW WATER A 15
CHOOSES
    THAT CHOOSES RIGHT, AND NEVER FIND A FRIEND. . . .   404 FOR DAUGHTER   24
CHOOSING
    CHOOSING WHATEVER TASK'S MOST DIFFICULT . . . . .   376 PHASES OF MOON   91
CHOP
    AND THEREUPON I DREW THE LIVID CHOP . . . .   40 OISIN 2   178
    ONCE HELD BETWEEN MY ARMS, WITH LIVID CHOP . . . .   40 OISIN 2   V   178
    I HELD A DRIPPING CORPSE, WITH LIVID CHOP . . . .   40 OISIN 2   V   178
    AND I BUT HELD A CORPSE, WITH LIVID CHOP . . . . .   40 OISIN 2   V   178
CHOPPERS   SEE LOGIC-CHOPPERS
    "THOUGH LOGIC CHOPPERS RULE THE TOWN, ...   337 TOM OROUGHLEY V   1
CHORUS
    CHORUS FOR A PLAY . . . .   771 SONG DEIRDRE 1 V   T
CHOSE
    SOUGHT ONCE AGAIN THE SHORE, AND CHOSE A SHELL . .   68 SAD SHEPHERD V   18
    I CHOSE THIS BURROW UNDER GROUND. . . . .   305 HOUR DAWN   73
    THAT DYING CHOSE THE LIVING WORLD FOR TEXT . . . .   324 ROBERT GREGORY   26
    SAID I WAS DEAD; AND DEAD I CHOSE TO BE. . . . . .   373 PHASES OF MOON V   28
    YET CHOSE A BANDY-LEGGED SMITH FOR MAN. . . . . .   404 FOR DAUGHTER   29
    WHEN MOCKING MUSES CHOSE THE COUNTRY WENCH. . . .   413 TOWER   96
    FOR AN OLD NEIGHBOUR'S FRIENDSHIP CHOSE THE HOUSE .   423 MY DESCENDANTS   21
    TWO CONTEMPLATING PASSIONS CHOSE ONE THEME . . . .   466 HARUN RASHID   117
    WE WERE THE LAST ROMANTICS--CHOSE FOR THEME . . .   491 COOLE BALLYLEE   41
    I CHOSE IT FOR MY LOT! IF QUESTIONED ON . . . . .   535 CHOSEN   11
    AMONG THE QUEENS, AND CHOSE THE MIGHTIEST . . . .   757 SHADOW WATER A   213
CHOSEN
    OLD SILENCE BIDS ITS CHOSEN RACE REJOICE, ...   127 DREAM OF FAERY   31
    HAD CHOSEN A HUSBAND ANYWHERE . . . .   191 BAILE AILLINN   54
    MY TRADE ALLOWS; CHOSEN MY COMPANY, ...   352 PEOPLE   20
    AND CHOSEN WHAT SCENERY HAD PLEASED ME BEST." . .   352 PEOPLE   21
    WHETHER WE HAVE CHOSEN CHISEL, PEN OR BRUSH, . . .   368 EGO DOMINUS   14
    MERE IMAGES; CHOSEN THIS PLACE TO LIVE IN . . . .   373 PHASES OF MOON   13
    HELEN BEING CHOSEN FOUND LIFE FLAT AND DULL . . .   404 FOR DAUGHTER   25
    DANCING WITH HER CHOSEN YOUTH, ...   514 JANE GROWN OLD   2
    CHOSEN . . . .   534 CHOSEN   T
    THE LOT OF LOVE IS CHOSEN. I LEARNT THAT MUCH . .   534 CHOSEN   1
    HIS CHOSEN COMRADES THOUGHT AT SCHOOL . . . . . .   576 WHAT THEN   1
    AND PRAISE OUR CHOSEN MAN; . . . .   586 PARNELLITES   2
CHOU
    IN HIS NOSTRILS, THE GREAT LORD OF CHOU . . . . .   502 VACILLATION   59
CHRIST
    ABOUT THE TIME WHEN CHRIST WAS BORN, ...   189 BAILE AILLINN   13
    BUT THAT OF CHRIST. AND DID HE FIND HIMSELF . . .   368 EGO DOMINUS   22
</pre>

	PAGE	TITLE	LINE

CHRIST   (CONTINUED)
    ODOUR OF BLOOD WHEN CHRIST WAS SLAIN . . . .   438 SONGS PLAY 2   6
    MIDNIGHT HAS COME, AND THE GREAT CHRIST CHURCH BELL . . .   470 ALL SOUL NIGHT   1
    IT IS ALL SOULS' NIGHT AND THE GREAT CHRIST CHURCH BELL   470 ALL SOUL NIGHT   V   1
    HIS FATHERS SERVED THEIR FATHERS BEFORE CHRIST WAS   580 CURSE CROMWELL   6
        CRUCIFIED.
    UPON THE CHURCH OF CHRIST. . . . .   583 GHOST ROG CASE   18
CHRISTENDOM
    THE CHIEF IMAGINATION OF CHRISTENDOM, ...   368 EGO DOMINUS   18
CHRISTENED
    HE CHRISTENED HIMSELF WITH BLOOD. . . . .   585 ORAHILLY   8
    IN A CLEFT THAT'S CHRISTENED ALT . . . .   632 MAN AND ECHO   1
CHRISTIAN
    DID I BECOME A CHRISTIAN MAN AND CHOOSE FOR MY BELIEF . .   503 VACILLATION   85
    RIBH CONSIDERS CHRISTIAN LOVE INSUFFICIENT . . . . . .   558 RIBH CHRISTIAN   T
    WITH CHRISTIAN AND WITH INFIDEL . . . .   594 COLONEL MARTIN   3
CHRISTMAS
    HER FRIENDS BRING HER A CHRISTMAS TREE . . . .   366 HER CHRIS TREE   T
CHRISTMAS-TREE
    HER FRIENDS BRING HER A CHRISTMAS-TREE . . . .   366 HER CHRIS TREE   V   T
CHRONICLER
    A MYSTERY THAT ELSE HAD FOUND NO CHRONICLER . . . . .   461 HARUN RASHID   21
CHRONICLERS
    THAT I COMMEND TO ALL THE CHRONICLERS . . . .   463 HARUN RASHID   46
CHRONICLING
    CHRONICLING CHIMAERAS FLED. . . . .   65 HAPPY SHEPHERD   V   17
CHRONOS
    TO THE CRACKED TUNE THAT CHRONOS SINGS, ...   65 HAPPY SHEPHERD   9
    TO THE OLD CRACKED TUNE THAT CHRONOS SINGS, ...   65 HAPPY SHEPHERD   V   9
CHRYSELEPHANTINE
    CHRYSELEPHANTINE, CEDAR-BOARDED, ...   440 WISDOM   10
    CHRYSELEPHANTINE, CEDAR BOARDED, ...   440 WISDOM   V   10
CHRYSOBERYL
    OR CHRYSOBERYL, OR BERYL, OR CHRYSOLITE: . . . . . .   231 SHADOW WATER B   215
    OF CHRYSOBERYL, OR BERYL, OR CHRYSOLITE: . . . . . .   231 SHADOW WATER B   V 215
    OF CHRYSOBERYL AND BERYL AND CHRYSOLITE, ...   765 SHADOW WATER A   357
CHRYSOLITE
    OF OPAL AND RUBY AND PALE CHRYSOLITE . . . .   219 HARP OF AENGUS   6
    OR CHRYSOBERYL, OR BERYL, OR CHRYSOLITE: . . . . . .   231 SHADOW WATER B   215
    OF CHRYSOBERYL, OR BERYL, OR CHRYSOLITE: . . . . . .   231 SHADOW WATER B   V 215
    OF OPAL AND RUBY AND PALE CHRYSOLITE . . . .   762 SHADOW WATER A   301
    OF CHRYSOBERYL AND BERYL AND CHRYSOLITE, ...   765 SHADOW WATER A   357
CHRYSOPRASE
    LIKE CHARMED APPLES MADE OF CHRYSOPRASE, ...   231 SHADOW WATER B   214
    AND CHRYSOPRASE AND RUBY AND SARDONYX. . . . . . .   765 SHADOW WATER A   358
CHUBBY
    LIES A CHUBBY FINGER-TIP, ...   732 STREET DANCERS   V   19
CHURCH
    HOW THE MEN OF THE SAND-SACK SHOWED ME A CHURCH . . . .   61 OISIN 3   193
    MIDNIGHT HAS COME, AND THE GREAT CHRIST CHURCH BELL . .   470 ALL SOUL NIGHT   1
    IT IS ALL SOULS' NIGHT AND THE GREAT CHRIST CHURCH BELL   470 ALL SOUL NIGHT   V   1
    CHURCH AND STATE . . . .   553 CHURCH STATE   T
    MIGHT OF THE CHURCH AND THE STATE, ...   554 CHURCH STATE   3
    WHAT IF THE CHURCH AND THE STATE . . . .   554 CHURCH STATE   9
    UPON THE CHURCH OF CHRIST. . . . .   583 GHOST ROG CASE   18
    I POKED ABOUT A VILLAGE CHURCH . . . .   584 GHOST ROG CASE   31
    LONG YEARS AGO, A CHURCH STANDS NEAR. . . . .   640 BEN BULBEN   87
    BENEATH THE SHELTERING SHADOW OF THY CHURCH: . . . . .   698 MOSADA 2   58
    IN CHURCH . . . .   735 IN CHURCH   T
    IN THE HOLY CHURCH OF GOD. . . . .   735 IN CHURCH   4
    IN THE HOLY CHURCH OF GOD. . . . .   736 IN CHURCH   16
CHURCHES
    YOUR BELL-MOUNTED CHURCHES, ...   58 OISIN 3   163
    THY BELL-MOUNTED CHURCHES, ...   58 OISIN 3   V 163
    AT THE OLD BITTER WORLD WHERE THEY MARRY IN CHURCHES, . .   330 BONE OF A HARE   13
    AT ALL WHO MARRY IN CHURCHES, ...   330 BONE OF A HARE   15
CHURCHMEN
    SOON WILL THE CHURCHMEN NOD ABOVE THE CROWD. . . . . .   699 MOSADA 3   19
CHURCH'S
    TAKEN IN MAGIC, IN THE CHURCH'S NAME . . . .   694 MOSADA 1   104
CHURCHYARD
    IN DRUMCLIFF CHURCHYARD YEATS IS LAID. . . . .   640 BEN BULBEN   85
CHURNED
    THE STREAM CHURNED, CHURNED, AND CHURNED--HIS LIPS APART,   31 OISIN 2   43
    THE STREAM CHURNED, CHURNED, AND CHURNED--HIS LIPS APART,   31 OISIN 2   43
    THE STREAM CHURNED, CHURNED, AND CHURNED--HIS LIPS APART,   31 OISIN 2   43
    THE STREAM CHURNED, CHURNED, ...   31 OISIN 2   V   43
    THE STREAM CHURNED, CHURNED, ...   31 OISIN 2   V   43
    . . . AND CHURNED. HIS LIPS WERE ROLLED APART, ...   31 OISIN 2   V   43
CICERO
    THAT EVEN CICERO . . . .   524 MAD AS MIST   16
CIDER
    WORK AT THE CIDER PRESS. . . . .   774 COME RIDE   12
CINCTURE
    AND GATHERED IN A SILVER CINCTURE: . . . .   3 OISIN 1   V 24A
CINNAMON
    NO: BUT OPOPONAX AND CINNAMON. . . . .   232 SHADOW WATER B   222
CIPHER
    THE CHILDREN LEARN TO CIPHER AND TO SING, ...   443 SCHOOL CHILDR   3
CIRCLE
    THERE THE LOVES A CIRCLE GO, ...   135 TWO TREES   13

CIRCLE   (CONTINUED)
```
    THE FLAMING CIRCLE OF OUR DAYS,  . . . . . . . .    135 TWO TREES             14
    THE FLAMING CIRCLE OF OUR LIFE.  . . . . . . . .    135 TWO TREES          V  16
    PROTECTED FROM THE CIRCLE OF THE MOON  . . . . .    428 NINETEEN 19           3
    LIES IN A CIRCLE ON THE GRASS: THEREIN . . . . .    555 RIBH AT TOMB         26
    WILL CIRCLE ROUND THE WORLD UPON A QUEST,  . . .    651 ISLE STAT I 1       159
    THE FLAMING CIRCLE OF THE OUTER LAW,  . . . . . .   689 NETTLESHIP           13
CIRCLED     SEE ORCHARD-CIRCLED
    THE POSTS OF POLISHED YEW, CIRCLED WITH BRONZE,  .  279 TWO KINGS            48
    AND CIRCLED ROUND HIM WITH ITS SQUEAKY CRY,  . . .  377 PHASES OF MOON      138
CIRCLES
    EACH OTHER ROUND IN CIRCLES, AND HEARD THE ELDEST SPEAK:
                                                         76 INDIAN ON GOD         5
    EACH OTHER ROUND IN CIRCLES: AND I HEARD THE ELDEST
        SPEAK:--                                         76 INDIAN ON GOD     V   5
    HAS MADE THE VERY OWLS IN CIRCLES MOVE:  . . . . .  423 MY DESCENDANTS       18
    OF APPLE BLOSSOM CIRCLES IN THE GLOOM.  . . . . .   700 MOSADA 3             42
    OF APPLE BLOSSOM CIRCLES IN THE GLOOM,  . . . . .   700 MOSADA 3         V   42
    AN APPLE BLOSSOM CIRCLES IN THE GLOOM,  . . . . .   700 MOSADA 3         V   42
    AND THROB WITHIN THE CIRCLES OF GREEN DAWN.  . . .  701 MOSADA 3             54
CIRCLING
    OF MISTY DAWN: WHEN, CIRCLING ROUND THE HALL,  . .   39 OISIN 2         V  153
    AND AFTER CIRCLING WITH STRANGE CRIES AWHILE  . .   223 SHADOW WATER B       26
    CIRCLING AND CIRCLING OVER THE MASTHEAD?  . . . .   234 SHADOW WATER B      266
    CIRCLING AND CIRCLING OVER THE MASTHEAD?  . . . .   234 SHADOW WATER B      266
    A MEANING IN THAT CIRCLING OVERHEAD?  . . . . . .   234 SHADOW WATER B      270
    THEY HAVE BEEN CIRCLING OVER OUR HEADS IN THE AIR,  247 SHADOW WATER B      525
    I SLEPT, 'TWAS SULTRY, AND SCARCE CIRCLING SHOOK .  677 ISLE STAT II 3      278
    SLID CIRCLING DOWN AND SOFTLY TOUCHED MY LIPS  . .  690 MOSADA 1             21
    CIRCLING THE BRAIN?  MY BROTHERS WILL PASS DOWN  .  699 MOSADA 3              6
    TO BUILD THE CIRCLING SEATS, WHERE HIGH IN AIR  .   699 MOSADA 3             18
    CIRCLING THE BRAIN? MY BROTHERS NOW PASS DOWN  . .  699 MOSADA 3         V    6
CIRCUIT
    THAN THE HEAVENLY CIRCUIT OF ITS STARS  . . . . .   451 FIRST LOVE           17
    THAN HEAVENLY CIRCUIT OF ITS STARS  . . . . . . .   451 FIRST LOVE       V   17
    THE HEAVENLY CIRCUIT: BERENICE'S HAIR:  . . . . .   483 VERONIC NAPKIN        1
    STOOD IN THE CIRCUIT OF A NEEDLE'S EYE.  . . . . .  483 VERONIC NAPKIN        6
CIRCUS
    THE CIRCUS ANIMALS' DESERTION  . . . . . . . . .    629 CIRCUS ANIMALS        T
    THE CIRCUS ANIMAL'S DESERTION  . . . . . . . . .    629 CIRCUS ANIMALS  V     T
    MY CIRCUS ANIMALS WERE ALL ON SHOW,  . . . . . .    629 CIRCUS ANIMALS        6
CISTERN
    OR ROCKY CISTERN WHERE WE TREAD THE CLOTHES  . . .  499 MOTHER OF GOD         9
CITIES
    FROM MARBLE CITIES LOUD WITH TABORS OF OLD . . . .  162 ASKS FORGIVE          9
    GIRLS THAT HAVE GOVERNED CITIES,  . . . . . . . .   789 SINGING HEAD         15
    OR BURNED GREAT CITIES DOWN,  . . . . . . . . . .   789 SINGING HEAD         16
CITRON
    A CITRON COLOUR GLOOMED IN HER HAIR,  . . . . . .     3 OISIN 1              24
    HER HAIR WAS OF A CITRON TINCTURE,  . . . . . . .     3 OISIN 1          V   24
    LONG CITRON COILS THAT HANG AROUND THEE, BLOWN  .   670 ISLE STAT II 3      105
CITY
    TO THE HOLY CITY OF BYZANTIUM.  . . . . . . . . .   408 SAIL BYZANTIUM       16
    CITY AND CITY MAY CONTEND,  . . . . . . . . . . .   540 FROM ANTIGONE        12
    CITY AND CITY MAY CONTEND,  . . . . . . . . . . .   540 FROM ANTIGONE        12
    OR ROUND THE CITY HALL,  . . . . . . . . . . . .    608 SONGS BURDEN 3        6
    CLOSE TO THE CITY HALL HE DIED:  . . . . . . . .    608 SONGS BURDEN 3       12
    AND ON THAT CITY DROPPED A TEAR,  . . . . . . . .   725 LEGEND               31
    AND NOW THAT CITY IS A LAKE.  . . . . . . . . . .   725 LEGEND               32
CIVIL
    MEDITATIONS IN TIME OF CIVIL WAR   ANCESTRAL HOUSES  417 ANCEST HOUSES  V     T
    COMES CRACKING JOKES OF CIVIL WAR  . . . . . . .    423 ROAD AT DOOR          3
    SOME FOURTEEN DAYS OF CIVIL WAR:  . . . . . . . .   425 STARES NEST          12
    NO CIVIL RANCOUR TORN THE LAND APART.  . . . . .    542 PARN FUNERAL 2        4
CIVILISATION
    THAT CIVILISATION MAY NOT SINK,  . . . . . . . .    617 LONG-LEG FLY          1
CIVILISATIONS
    OLD CIVILISATIONS PUT TO THE SWORD.  . . . . . .    566 LAPIS LAZULI         27
CIVILIZATION
    CIVILIZATION IS HOOPED TOGETHER, BROUGHT  . . . .   563 MERU                  1
CLAIM
    SOME OTHER WOMAN HAS A CLAIM ON YOU,  . . . . . .   245 SHADOW WATER B      474
    THAT I MAY CLAIM YOU AS MY WIFE AGAIN."  . . . . .  284 TWO KINGS           170
    AND CLAIM AS BY A SOLDIER'S RIGHT  . . . . . . .    478 SELF AND SOUL        31
CLAIMED
    GOD'S BELL HAS CLAIMED THEM BY THE LITTLE CRY  . .  114 ROSE OF BATTLE       23
    HE CLAIMED HIS COUNTRY'S NEED WAS MOST,  . . . . .  275 GREY ROCK           101
CLAMBER
    WHEN I CLAMBER TO THE HEIGHTS OF SLEEP,  . . . . .  357 DEEP-SWORN VOW        4
    THE TOWER'S OLD COOK THAT MUST CLIMB AND CLAMBER .  636 BLACK TOWER          21
CLAMBERING
    TILL, CLAMBERING AT THE CRADLE-SIDE,  . . . . . .   343 SHEP GOATHERD       109
    TILL, CLAMBERING AT THE CRADLE SIDE,  . . . . . .   343 SHEP GOATHERD  V    109
CLAMOROUS
    AROSE, AND ON THE INSTANT CLAMOROUS EAVES,  . . .   120 SORROW OF LOVE        9
    UPON THEIR CLAMOROUS WINGS.  . . . . . . . . . .    322 SWANS AT COOLE       12
CLAMOUR
    CRIED FROM THE PORTER'S LODGE, AND WITH LONG CLAMOUR 181 QUEEN MAEVE         37
    AND YET YOU MAKE A CLAMOUR OF REPROACH.  . . . .    243 SHADOW WATER B      444
    "THE WIND-BLOWN CLAMOUR OF THE BARNACLE-GEESE."  .  300 BEGGAR CRIED         20
    THOSE WINDS THAT CLAMOUR OF APPROACHING NIGHT.  .   431 NINETEEN 19          68
    AND CLAMOUR IN DRUNKEN FRENZY FOR THE MOON.  . . .  482 BLOOD AND MOON       42
```

143

	PAGE	TITLE		LINE
CLAMOUR (CONTINUED)				
ALL CLAMOUR-CLOTHED--WAS'T CLAMOUR WHEN I SUNG,	649	ISLE STAT I 1		108
CLAMOUR OF THE LONE NIGHTJAR.	732	STREET DANCERS		21
CLAMOUR-CLOTHED				
ALL CLAMOUR-CLOTHED--WAS'T CLAMOUR WHEN I SUNG,	649	ISLE STAT I 1		108
CLAN				
MINE WERE CLAN MORNA'S TRIBES UNTOLD,	81	MAD KING GOLL	V	3
BEFORE GOD MADE THE ANGELIC CLAN,	138	TO IRELAND		8
CLANG				
WITH SHOUTING AND THE CLANG OF UNHOOKED ARMS.	185	QUEEN MAEVE		111
WITH A CLANG OF HIS DIM MAIL,	742	EARL PAUL		66
CLANGING				
IN CLANGING SPACE A MOMENT HEARD,	65	HAPPY SHEPHERD		20
'MID CLANGING SPACE A MOMENT HEARD	65	HAPPY SHEPHERD	V	20
AND WITH THE CLANGING OF THEIR SWORD-BLADES MAKE	137	TO SOME I TALK	V	13
THE INNUMERABLE CLANGING WINGS THAT HAVE PUT OUT THE MOON.	427	PHANTOM HATRED		32
CLANGOUR				
INTO THE CLANGOUR OF THE WIND AND SEA.	45	OISIN 2		234
LIKE THE CLANGOUR OF A BELL,	382	SONG OF FOOL		9
GOES TO THE BARBAROUS CLANGOUR OF A GONG.	430	NINETEEN 19		58
GOES TO THE BARBAROUS CLANGOUR OF GONG.	430	NINETEEN 19	V	58
CLANKING				
I SAW HIM STAGGER WITH THE CLANKING CHAIN,	687	TWO TITANS		31
CLANN				
. . . FOR NOWHERE IN ANY CLANN	50	OISIN 3	V	49
CLAP SEE THUNDER-CLAP				
AND CLAP THEIR HANDS TOGETHER, AND HALF CLOSE THEIR EYES,	146	UNAPPEAS HOST		2
SOUL CLAP ITS HANDS AND SING, AND LOUDER SING	407	SAIL BYZANTIUM		11
THAT GATHERS VOLUME: NOW A THUNDER CLAP.	487	SEVEN SAGES	V	23
UP WITH THE NECK AND CLAP THE WING,	782	HEART FRIGHT		6
UP WITH THE NECK AND CLAP THE WING,	782	HEART FRIGHT		13
UP WITH THE NECK AND CLAP THE WING,	782	HEART FRIGHT		20
STRETCH NECK AND CLAP THE WING,	783	GREY ROUND		27
CLAPPED				
"I WILL NOT BE CLAPPED IN A HOOD,	349	HAWK		7
CLARE				
TO COLD CLARE ROCK AND GALWAY ROCK AND THORN,	326	ROBERT GREGORY		66
CLARE-GALWAY				
THE WINDS OUT OF CLARE-GALWAY	783	GREY ROUND		4
CLARIONET				
PULL DOWN THE BLINDS, BRING FIDDLE AND CLARIONET	311	MOUNTAIN TOMB		5
CLASH				
LAUGHTER AND CRIES. THE ARMIES CLASH AND SHOCK,	43	OISIN 2		211
AND THEN THE CLASH OF FALLEN HORSEMEN AND THE CRIES	161	BLACK PIG		3
CLASHING				
AND WITH THE CLASHING OF THEIR SWORD-BLADES MAKE	137	TO SOME I TALK		13
AND WITH THE CLASHING OF THEIR SWORD BLADES MAKE	137	TO SOME I TALK	V	13
AND FLUNG DOWN CLASHING ON THE FLOOR	740	EARL PAUL		15
CLASPING				
HELP THEM THAT WANDER WITH HAND CLASPING HAND,	184	QUEEN MAEVE		86
CLATTER				
TO MAKE A CLATTER IN THE HOLE	304	HOUR DAWN	V	54
CLAUDE				
CALVERT AND WILSON, BLAKE AND CLAUDE,	639	BEN BULBEN		64
AND WILSON, BLAKE AND CALVERT, CLAUDE,	639	BEN BULBEN	V	64
CLAW				
NOR SORROW WITH HER OSPREY CLAW.	19	OISIN 1	V	285
CRUEL CLAW AND HUNGRY THROAT,	136	TWO TREES		36
NOTHING BUT GRIP OF CLAW, AND THE EYE'S COMPLACENCY,	427	PHANTOM HATRED		31
CLAWS SEE BIRD-CLAWS				
. . . THEIR HANDS WERE THE CLAWS OF BIRDS,	49	OISIN 3		34
AS MIDDLE NIGHT GREAT CATS WITH SILVER CLAWS,	185	QUEEN MAEVE		115
THEY HAD HANDS LIKE CLAWS, AND THEIR KNEES	208	OLD MEN ADMIRE		4
AND DUG ITS CLAWS AND SHRIEKED AND FOUGHT.	385	ROBARTES DANCE		8
A WHITE BIRD HAS TORN ME WITH HIS SILVER CLAWS.	759	SHADOW WATER A		234
CLAY				
A HOUSE OF WATTLES, CLAY, AND SKIN:	17	OISIN 1		249
INNUMERABLE, SINGING, EXULTANT: THE CLAY UNDERNEATH THEM SHALL PANT,	61	OISIN 3		203
SPLASHED ALL WITH CLAY AND JOURNEY DULL,	82	MAD KING GOLL	V	13
AND A SMALL CABIN BUILD THERE, OF CLAY AND WATTLES MADE:	117	ISLE INNISFREE		2
AND A SMALL CABIN BUILT THERE, OF CLAY AND WATTLES MADE:	117	ISLE INNISFREE	V	2
IN FLOOD AND FIRE AND CLAY AND WIND,	138	TO IRELAND	V	25
THE HORSES OF DISASTER PLUNGE IN THE HEAVY CLAY:	154	BELOVED PEACE		8
THE HORSES OF DISASTER PLUNGE IN THE DESOLATE CLAY.	154	BELOVED PEACE	V	8
WHEN AN IMMORTAL PASSION BREATHES IN MORTAL CLAY:	172	TRAV PASSION		2
BUT UNDER HEAVY LOADS OF TRAMPLED CLAY	483	OIL AND BLOOD		4
THE LOVERS AND THE DANCERS ARE BEATEN INTO THE CLAY,	580	CURSE CROMWELL		3
OF ROOT, SHOOT, BLOSSOM OR CLAY	600	SPIRIT MEDIUM		21
THAT WERE BEATEN INTO THE CLAY	640	BEN BULBEN		79
MADE THEM OF FIRE AND CLAY.	680	LOVE AND DEATH		12
CLOGGED IN A MARSH WHERE THE SLOW MARSH CLAY CLINGS,	711	FERENCZ RENYI		35
WITH LIGHT IMAGES OF CLAY	775	AGAINST WITCH		12
CLAY-COLD				
AS QUIET AS THE CLAY-COLD DEAD.	670	ISLE STAT II 3		113
CLAY-PILED				
TO EMER OF BORDA, IN HER CLAY-PILED DUN,	105	CUCHULAIN SEA	V	2
CLEAN				
MAKE CLEAN AS A BROOM CLEANS,	62	OISIN 3		211
BESIDES HER CLEAN SWEPT HEARTH, HER QUIET SHADE:	114	ROSE OF BATTLE	V	11
TO HAVE LIT UPON AS CLEAN AND SWEET A TALE	258	KING NO KING		8

144

CLEAN   (CONTINUED)
    SHE SEEMED TO HAVE GROWN CLEAN AND SWEET . . . . . .   397 POLIT PRISONER   17
CLEANING
    THEN CLEANING OUT AND BANDAGING OF WOUNDS, ...   622 HOUND VOICE   20
CLEANLY
    BRED THAT FIERCE TOOTH AND CLEANLY LIMB . . . .   318 APPOINTMENT   10
CLEANS
    MAKE CLEAN AS A BROOM CLEANS, ...   62 OISIN 3   211
    AS THAT WHICH CLEANS MAN'S DIRTY SLATE. . . . . . .   633 MAN AND ECHO   24
CLEAN-SWEPT
    BESIDE HER CLEAN-SWEPT HEARTH, HER QUIET SHADE: . . .   114 ROSE OF BATTLE   11
CLEAR
    CLEAR FLUTED THEN THAT GOBLIN RARE-- . . . . . .   6 OISIN 1   V   54
    WITH A CLEAR VOICE THE YOUNG MAN CRIED, ...   18 OISIN 1   V 260
    WHEN THE MORN GREW FROSTY AND CLEAR. . . . . . .   95 MOLL MAGEE   20
    IN THE FROSTY MORNIN' CLEAR. . . . .   95 MOLL MAGEE   V   20
    COME CLEAR OF THE NETS OF WRONG AND RIGHT: . . . .   147 INTO TWILIGHT   2
    COME CLEAR OF THE NETS OF WRONG AND RIGHT: . . . .   147 INTO TWILIGHT   V   2
    OR BIRDS LOST IN THE ONE CLEAR SPACE . . . . . .   195 BAILE AILLINN   149
    OR BIRDS LOST IN ONE CLEAR SPACE . . . . . .   195 BAILE AILLINN   V 149
    THAT WERE CLEAR MESSAGES FROM THE EVER-LIVING, . . .   243 SHADOW WATER B   442
    A CLEAR ARTICULATION IN THE AIR, ...   320 REED WHISPERER   3
    AND NEVER WROTE A BOOK, YOUR THOUGHT IS CLEAR. . . .   376 PHASES OF MOON   97
    FOR ALL MEN'S THOUGHTS GREW CLEAR . . . .   400 DEMON BEAST   19
    FOR ALL MEN'S THOUGHT GREW CLEAR . . . .   400 DEMON BEAST   V   19
    YET NO CLEAR FACT TO BE DISCERNED: . . . .   425 STARES NEST   9
    ABOUT THE SKY: WHERE THAT IS CLEAR OF CLOUD . . . .   541 PARN FUNERAL 1   3
    A SORT OF BESOM THAT CAN CLEAR THE SOUL . . . . .   558 RIBH CHRISTIAN   5
    THAT ALL'S ARRANGED IN ONE CLEAR VIEW, ...   633 MAN AND ECHO   31
    EACH SHINING CLEAR AS SOME UNBAFFLED STAR: . . . .   656 ISLE STAT I 3   25
    AND NOT TOO CLEAR, HOW WILL THE NEW GOD KNOW . . .   658 ISLE STAT I 3   79
    'TIS CLEAR THAT YOU HAVE SEEN HER NOT. THE CROWN . .   661 ISLE STAT II 1   70
    I COULD GAZE, GAZE UPON THINE EYES' CLEAR GREY: . .   671 ISLE STAT II 3   147
    AGAIN THE WOODLAND LAUGHTER, AND THE CLEAR . . . .   674 ISLE STAT II 3   221
    AND THE BIRD IN THE BRANCHES WILL CRY FOR US CLEAR, . .   717 LOVE SONG   6
    . . . SEE, SHE ROUNDS THE HARBOUR CLEAR. . . . . .   718 PHANTOM SHIP   13
    UPON CLEAR NIGHTS THEY LEAVE THE UPPER AIR . . . .   750 SHADOW WATER A   87
CLEAR-BROWED
    CLEAR-BROWED ARCADIAN, THOU SHALT BE OUR KING! . . .   679 ISLE STAT II 3   318
    CLEAR-BROWED ARCADIAN, THOU SHALT BE OUR KING! . . .   679 ISLE STAT II 3   321
CLEARED
    UNTIL MY THOUGHTS CLEARED UP AGAIN, ...   256 WORDS   6
CLEARLY
    BURNS BUT MORE CLEARLY. O SHE HAD NOT THESE WAYS . . .   200 FOLLY COMFORT   11
CLEAR-SHINING
    AFAR, CLEAR-SHINING ON THE HERALD HILLS, ...   645 ISLE STAT I 1   14
CLEAVE
    AND MORE I MAY NOT WRITE OF, FOR THEY THAT CLEAVE . .   218 WOODS OF COOLE   24
    AND MORE I MAY NOT WRITE OF, FOR THEM THAT CLEAVE . .   218 WOODS OF COOLE V   24
    "WHAT TUMBLING CLOUD DID YOU CLEAVE, ...   349 HAWK   13
CLEFT
    LIKE SOME OLD RABBIT TO MY CLEFT . . . .   307 HOUR DAWN   105
    IN A CLEFT THAT'S CHRISTENED ALT . . . .   632 MAN AND ECHO   1
CLENCHED
    WITHIN HIS CLENCHED TEETH A SWORD. . . . .   673 ISLE STAT II 3   182
CLERGYMEN
    OF BANKERS, SCHOOLMASTERS, AND CLERGYMEN . . . . .   205 ADAMS CURSE   13
CLERIC
    . . . FOR I GO TO THE FENIANS, O CLERIC, TO CHAUNT . . .   61 OISIN 3   201
    . . . I WILL GO TO THE FENIANS, THOU CLERIC, AND CHANT . .   61 OISIN 3   V 201
CLERICS
    BUT NOW THE LYING CLERICS MURDER SONG . . . . . .   42 OISIN 2   196
CLERK
    BEFORE THE MERCHANT AND THE CLERK . . . .   266 GALWAY RACES   8
CLEVER
    THE CLEVER MAN WHO CRIES . . . .   347 FISHERMAN   21
    AND O HE WAS A CLEVER MAN. . . . .   595 COLONEL MARTIN   39
CLIFF
    FROM DOORED AND WINDOWED CLIFF, OR HALF UPTURNED . . .   368 EGO DOMINUS   30
    ON THE CLIFF BY THE SEA, ...   739 EARL PAUL   4
    ON THE CLIFF OF KINSALE. . . . .   742 EARL PAUL   68
CLIFF-ENCIRCLED
    HERE IS THE PLACE, THE CLIFF-ENCIRCLED WOOD: . . . .   651 ISLE STAT I 2   3
CLIFFS
    GO DWELL UPON THE SEA CLIFFS, VAPOUR HID, ...   105 CUCHULAIN SEA V   4
    GO DWELL UPON THE SEA CLIFFS, VAPOUR-HID . . . .   105 CUCHULAIN SEA V   4
    GO DWELL UPON THE CLIFFS AND WATCH THE TIDE: . . .   105 CUCHULAIN SEA V   4
CLIFF-SHELTERED
    UNTIL, IN SOME CLIFF-SHELTERED BAY . . . .   612 NEWS ORACLE   21
CLIMB
    COMPANIONABLE STREAMS OR CLIMB THE AIR: . . . . .   323 SWANS AT COOLE   21
    CLIMB UP THE NARROW WINDING STAIR TO BED: . . . .   324 ROBERT GREGORY   5
    TO CLIMB THAT STAIR AND EAT THAT BITTER BREAD, . . .   369 EGO DOMINUS   35
    THAT CLIMB THE STREAMS UNTIL . . . .   414 TOWER   123
    THAT CLIMB THE MOUNTAIN SIDE, ...   416 TOWER   V 175
    I CLIMB TO THE TOWER-TOP AND LEAN UPON BROKEN STONE, . .   425 PHANTOM HATRED   1
    I CLIMB TO THE TOWER TOP AND LEAN UPON BROKEN STONE, . .   425 PHANTOM HATRED V   1
    SHOULD THE CONFLAGRATION CLIMB, ...   476 EVA GORE-BOOTH   28
    THOSE CHINAMEN CLIMB TOWARDS, AND I . . . . . .   567 LAPIS LAZULI   49
    CLIMB TO YOUR CHAMBER FULL OF BOOKS AND WAIT, . . .   579 DOR WELLESLEY   8
    CLIMB TO OUR PROPER DARK, THAT WE MAY TRACE . . .   611 STATUES   31

145

CLIMB (CONTINUED)
    CLIMB ON A WAGONETTE TO SCREAM. . . . .   626 OLD MEN BE MAD   8
    THE TOWER'S OLD COOK THAT MUST CLIMB AND CLAMBER . . . .   636 BLACK TOWER   21
    "IF I DO BUT CLIMB THE STAIR . . . .   771 SONG DEIRDRE 1   2
CLIMBED
    HALF IN THE UNVESSELLED SEA, WE CLIMBED THE STAIR . . .   32 OISIN 2   47
    AND CLIMBED SO LONG, I THOUGHT THE LAST STEPS WERE . . .   32 OISIN 2   48
    HALF IN THE UNVESSELLED SEA, WE CLIMBED THE STAIRS . . .   32 OISIN 2   V 47
    AND THEN WE CLIMBED THE STAIR TO A HIGH DOOR! . . . . .   36 OISIN 2   101
    THAT OLD MAN CLIMBED; THE DAY GREW DIM; . . . . . .   194 BAILE AILLINN   134
    AND CLIMBED INTO THE AIR, CRUMBLING AWAY, ...   278 TWO KINGS   42
    OR CLIMBED AMONG THE IMAGES OF THE PAST—— . . . . .   352 PEOPLE   10
    CLIMBED UP MY CREAKING STAIR. THEY HAD READ . . . . .   358 PRESENCES   6
    OR THE HUMBLER WORM, I CLIMBED BEN BULBEN'S BACK . . .   409 TOWER   9
    OR SHOD IN IRON, CLIMBED THE NARROW STAIRS, ...   412 TOWER   83
    AND BOTH CLIMBED UP THE STAIR, ...   595 COLONEL MARTIN   38
    AS SLOWLY AUTUMN CLIMBED THE GOLDEN THRONE . . . . .   690 MOSADA 1   V 1A
CLIMBING
    A CLIMBING MOON UPON AN EMPTY SKY, ...   120 SORROW OF LOVE   10
    AND STARS CLIMBING THE DEW-DROPPING SKY, ...   158 BELOVED RHYMES   11
    CLIMBING UP TO A PLACE . . . .   348 FISHERMAN   31
    CLIMBING THE MOUNTAIN-SIDE, ...   416 TOWER   175
    CLIMBING, FALLING SHE KNEW NOT WHERE, ...   578 CRAZED GIRL   4
CLIMBS
    WHERE I WOULD BE WHEN THE WHITE MOON CLIMBS, ...   9 OISIN 1   104
    AND NOW LIES SUNK IN SLEEP. WHAT CLIMBS THE STAIR? . . .   579 DOR WELLESLEY   11
    BUT NOW LIES SUNK IN SLEEP. WHAT CLIMBS THE STAIR? . . .   579 DOR WELLESLEY V 11
CLIME
    LIAR AND FLATTERER OF THE WEAK, IN WHAT STRANGE CLIME . .   42 OISIN 2   V 198
    WELL NIGH IMMORTAL IN THIS CHARMED CLIME, ...   674 ISLE STAT II 3   202
    WELL-NIGH IMMORTAL IN THIS CHARMED CLIME! . . . . .   674 ISLE STAT II 3 V 202
    THE SUNFLOWERS WEAVE A GOLDEN CLIME, ...   736 SUMMER EVENING   9
CLING
    BUT, DEAR, CLING CLOSE TO ME! SINCE YOU WERE GONE, . . .   257 RECONCILIATION   11
    ADMONISH US TO CLING TO THAT . . . .   460 THREE MONUMENT   8
    UPON THE DUSTY, GLITTERING WINDOWS CLING, ...   482 BLOOD AND MOON   43
    AND SEEM TO CLING UPON THE MOONLIT SKIES, ...   482 BLOOD AND MOON   44
    CLOSE AND CLING SO TIGHT, ...   538 LAST CONFESS   22
    ABOUT A SUN-FLUSHED DOVE-COT, COOING, CLING . . . . .   710 FERENCZ RENYI   20
CLINGETH
    WHERE THE FLESH OF THE FOOTSOLE CLINGETH . . . . .   61 OISIN 3   197
    WHEN THE FLESH OF THE FOOTSOLE CLINGETH . . . . . .   61 OISIN 3   V 197
CLINGING
    AND WANDER IN THE STORMS AND CLINGING SNOWS, ...   42 OISIN 2   201
    THE NORTH UNFOLDS ABOVE THEM CLINGING, CREEPING NIGHT, . . 154 BELOVED PEACE   3
    THE NORTH UNROLLS ABOVE THEM CLINGING, CREEPING NIGHT, . . 154 BELOVED PEACE V   3
    FOR THE WET WINDS ARE BLOWING OUT OF THE CLINGING AIR! . . 207 HANRAHANS SONG   12
    FOR THE GREY WINDS ARE BLOWING UP, OUT OF THE CLINGING   207 HANRAHANS SONG V 12
      SEAS!
    AND CLINGING TO IT I COULD HEAR THE COCKS . . . . .   286 TWO KINGS   210
    WITH CLINGING MIST, EACH STAR-FOUGHT WANDERER CAME . . .   656 ISLE STAT I 3   33
    AND CLINGING WITH THE DEW OF ODOROUS SHOWERS, ...   704 REMEMBRANCE   4
    AWAY HER CLINGING HANDS, AND TURNS. SHE THROWS . . . .   714 FERENCZ RENYI   102
CLINGS
    CLOGGED IN A MARSH WHERE THE SLOW MARSH CLAY CLINGS, . .   711 FERENCZ RENYI   35
    AND BE SO HAPPY." TO HIS HANDS SHE CLINGS, ...   714 FERENCZ RENYI   100
    AND BE SO HAPPY." TO HIS HAND SHE CLINGS, ...   714 FERENCZ RENYI V 100
CLIP
    FOR THEY SHOULD CLIP AND CLIP AGAIN . . . .   194 BAILE AILLINN   122
    FOR THEY SHOULD CLIP AND CLIP AGAIN . . . .   194 BAILE AILLINN   122
CLIPPED
    CLIPPED AN INSOLENT FARMER'S EARS . . . .   410 TOWER   31
    NOR MUSIC NOR AN ENEMY'S CLIPPED EAR . . . . . .   412 TOWER   75
CLOAK
    AND WHEN THEY SAW THE CLOAK I WORE . . . .   15 OISIN 1   207
    ALL EMPTIED OF PURPLE HOURS AS A BEGGAR'S CLOAK IN THE   63 OISIN 3   219
      RAIN,
    THE CLOAK, THE BOAT, AND THE SHOES . . . .   69 CLOAK BOAT   T
    "I MAKE THE CLOAK OF SORROW! . . . .   69 CLOAK BOAT   2
    SHALL BE THE CLOAK OF SORROW! . . . .   69 CLOAK BOAT   4
    THE CLOAK I WEAVE OF SORROW! . . . .   69 CLOAK BOAT   V   2
    HE HAD HALF A CLOAK TO KEEP HIM DRY, ...   190 BAILE AILLINN   29
    GATHERING HIS CLOAK ABOUT HIM, RUN . . . .   193 BAILE AILLINN   101
    AND THERE'S A PLAYER IN THE STATES WHO GATHERS UP HER CLOAK 354 HIS PHOENIX   12
    AND THERE'S THE PLAYER IN THE STATES WHO GATHERS UP HER   354 HIS PHOENIX   V 12
      CLOAK
    AND A CLOAK WRAPPED ABOUT THE STONE, ...   456 FRIENDS YOUTH   7
    I WRAPPED HER IN A HOODED CLOAK, AND SHE, ...   468 HARUN RASHID   154
    I WRAPPED HER IN A HEAVY HOODED CLOAK, ...   468 HARUN RASHID   V 154
    I WRAPPED HER IN A HEAVY HOODED CLOAK, AND SHE . . . .   468 HARUN RASHID   V 154
    IN MASKER'S CLOAK AND HOOD, ...   539 MEETING   2
    IN COUNTRY SHAWL OR PARIS CLOAK, HAD PUT MY WITS ASTRAY,   592 PILGRIM   3
    SO COME IN RAGS OR COME IN SILK, IN CLOAK OR COUNTRY SHAWL, 593 PILGRIM   22
    SO COME IN RAG OR COME IN SILK, IN CLOAK OR COUNTRY SHAWL, 593 PILGRIM   V 22
    WITH A RAGGED BANDIT CLOAK, ...   627 STATES HOLIDAY   31
    THE CLOAK I WEAVE OF SORROW. . . . .   666 ISLE STAT II 3   2
    SHALL BE THE CLOAK OF SORROW, ...   666 ISLE STAT II 3   4
    I'LL DRAW MY CLOAK AROUND ME! IT IS COLD. . . . . .   704 MOSADA 3   123
    THE GLOVE AND THE CLOAK . . . .   744 GLOVE CLOAK   T
    I STOOD WITH HER CLOAK ON MY ARM . . . .   744 GLOVE CLOAK   5
    AND MURMURED: "O LONG GREY CLOAK, ...   744 GLOVE CLOAK   11

146

	PAGE	TITLE		LINE
CLOAKS				
THEIR CLOAKS MADE OUT OF YELLOW SILK, ...	15	OISIN 1		205
CLOCK				
SHOULD LAUGH AND WEEP AN HOUR UPON THE CLOCK.	471	ALL SOUL NIGHT		20
SHOULD LAUGH AND WEEP AN HOUR UPON THE CLOCK.	474	ALL SOUL NIGHT		90
SHOULD WEEP AND LAUGH AN HOUR UPON THE CLOCK.	474	ALL SOUL NIGHT	V	90
NOON UPON THE CLOCK, ...	525	DANCING DAYS		18
. . . "THE KING OF THE GREAT CLOCK TOWER"	549	SEVERED HEAD		T
WHAT SAYS THE CLOCK IN THE GREAT CLOCK TOWER?	549	SEVERED HEAD		3
WHAT SAYS THE CLOCK IN THE GREAT CLOCK TOWER?	549	SEVERED HEAD		3
WHAT SAYS THE CLOCK IN THE GREAT CLOCK TOWER?	550	SEVERED HEAD		10
WHAT SAYS THE CLOCK IN THE GREAT CLOCK TOWER?	550	SEVERED HEAD		10
WHAT SAYS THE CLOCK IN THE GREAT CLOCK TOWER?	550	SEVERED HEAD		17
WHAT SAYS THE CLOCK IN THE GREAT CLOCK TOWER?	550	SEVERED HEAD		17
"THAT I AT MIDNIGHT BY THE CLOCK	569	THREE BUSHES		10
WHEN THE CLOCK BEGINS TO CHIME."	570	THREE BUSHES		41
"BECAUSE I HELPED TO WIND THE CLOCK	585	ORAHILLY		25
"TILL THE SUN GOES DOWN AND AN HOUR OF THE CLOCK" . . .	779	GOING THE ROAD		7
"FOR A YEAR AND A DAY BY THE CLOCK OF THE SUN"	779	GOING THE ROAD		11
CLOGGED				
CLOGGED IN A MARSH WHERE THE SLOW MARSH CLAY CLINGS, . .	711	FERENCZ RENYI		35
CLOONE				
AND ONE WAS DROWNED IN THE GREAT BOG OF CLOONE.	411	TOWER		48
CLOOTH-NA-BARE				
AND OVER THE GRAVE OF CLOOTH-NA-BARE;	140	HOSTING SIDHE		2
THE YELLOW POOL HAS OVERFLOWED HIGH UP ON CLOOTH-NA-BARE,	207	HANRAHANS SONG		11
THE YELLOW POOL HAS OVERFLOWED HIGH UPON CLOOTH-NA-BARE,	207	HANRAHANS SONG	V	11
CLOSE				
OR CLUNG AS CLOSE AS SWARMS OF BEES, ...	14	OISIN 1	V	181
AND ONE CAME CLOSE, A TEARFUL BOY.	17	OISIN 1	V	237
AND GO YOU CLOSE TO THEM.	33	OISIN 1	V	59
HIS EYELIDS CLOSE, HIS HEAD DROOPS LOW, ...	98	FOXHUNTER	V	13
YOUNG SUBTLE CONCHUBAR SAT CLOSE BY ME	102	FERGUS DRUID		10
AND HIS YOUNG SWEETHEART CLOSE BESIDE HIM KNELT, ...	108	CUCHULAIN SEA		40
AND HIS YOUNG DEAR ONE CLOSE BESIDE HIM KNELT, ...	108	CUCHULAIN SEA	V	40
AND CLAP THEIR HANDS TOGETHER, AND HALF CLOSE THEIR EYES,	146	UNAPPEAS HOST		2
BELOVED, LET YOUR EYES HALF CLOSE, AND YOUR HEART BEAT . .	154	BELOVED PEACE		9
THAT ONLY GOD'S EYES DID NOT CLOSE;	156	FORGOT BEAUTY		14
THAT ONLY THE GODS' EYES DID NOT CLOSE;	156	FORGOT BEAUTY	V	14
HALF CLOSE YOUR EYELIDS, LOOSEN YOUR HAIR, ...	166	EVIL OF BELOV		1
WHEN WE COME AT THE CLOSE OF TIME	178	FIDDLER DOONEY	V	9
THAT BEAUTIFUL MILD WOMAN, YOUR CLOSE FRIEND, ...	204	ADAMS CURSE		11
BUT, DEAR, CLING CLOSE TO ME; SINCE YOU WERE GONE, . . .	257	RECONCILIATION		11
ALTHOUGH I HAVE COME CLOSE ON FORTY-NINE, ...	270	PARDON FATHERS		20
WHEN CUPS WENT ROUND AT CLOSE OF DAY--	271	GREY ROCK		12
CLOSE TO A CLUMP OF BEECH TREES IN THE WOOD	283	TWO KINGS	V	135
WHEN CLOSE TO HIS RIGHT HAND A HEAP	302	HOUR DAWN		11
THEY WERE MY CLOSE COMPANIONS MANY A YEAR, ...	325	ROBERT GREGORY		41
HANDS GRIPPED IN HANDS, TOES CLOSE TOGETHER, ...	332	ROUND TOWER		21
OF THE ANALYTIC MIND, CAN NEITHER CLOSE	353	PEOPLE		33
WHEN TWO CLOSE KINDRED MEET, ...	378	CAT AND MOON		12
I HAVE MET THEM AT CLOSE OF DAY	391	EASTER 1916		1
THE LADIES CLOSE THEIR MUSING EYES. NO PROPHECIES, . . .	426	PHANTOM HATRED		19
CLOSE AND CLING SO TIGHT, ...	538	LAST CONFESS		22
IN HATING GOD SHE MAY CREEP CLOSE TO GOD.	558	RIBH CHRISTIAN	V	18
THOSE HANDS TO CLOSE THESE EYES, ...	587	OLD WICKED MAN		6
CAN NEVER CLOSE THOSE EYES."	588	OLD WICKED MAN		26
CLOSE TO THE CITY HALL HE DIED;	608	SONGS BURDEN 3		12
SLEEPILY CLOSE HER ROUND BRIGHT EYNE;	646	ISLE STAT I 1		35
WHEN HIS SINEWY WINGS TOGETHER CLOSE.	673	ISLE STAT II 3		179
THOU'RT WELCOME. LIE THERE CLOSE AGAINST MY FINGERS, . .	700	MOSADA 3		44
NOW STEPS DRAW CLOSE, HE HIDES BENEATH A DRUM;	713	FERENCZ RENYI		78
CLOSE AND MORE CLOSE--I FEEL HIM IN MY HEART--	720	WITCH VIVIEN		11
CLOSE AND MORE CLOSE--I FEEL HIM IN MY HEART--	720	WITCH VIVIEN		11
YE BY THE WAVES THAT CLOSE IN OUR SAD NATION, ...	738	MOURN THEN ON		5
YET ONE JOY HAVE I, HID CLOSE, ...	744	ROSY CROSS		8
THEN CLOSE YOUR EARS WITH DUST AND LIE	791	REPRISALS		23
CLOSE-CROPPED				
OR ON THE CLOSE-CROPPED GRASS	343	SHEP GOATHERD		103
CLOSED SEE HALF-CLOSED				
CLOSED IN THE MISTY AIR PROFOUND.	10	OISIN 1	V	114D
THE MIST CLOSED ROUND US; PEARLY LIGHT	28	OISIN 1	V	427C
NONE CLOSED HIS BLOOD-SHOT EYES BUT SOUGHT	296	THREE BEGGARS		44
THEY CLOSED THEIR BLOOD-SHOT EYES FOR NAUGHT.	296	THREE BEGGARS	V	44
WE ARE CLOSED IN, AND THE KEY IS TURNED	425	STARES NEST		6
WE ARE CLOSED IN, AND THE KEY TURNED	425	STARES NEST	V	6
HAVE CLOSED THE LADIES' EYES, THEIR MINDS ARE BUT A POOL	426	PHANTOM HATRED		21
FOR CLOSED IN DARKNESS NOW	738	MOURN THEN ON		10
CLOSELY				
LULLED WEARINESS; AND CLOSELY ROUND	11	OISIN 1	V	137
IF YOU'LL BUT LISTEN CLOSELY TO THAT CRYING	247	SHADOW WATER B		520
CLOSELY ROUND US, BODY AND MIND--	717	FAIRY DOCTOR		23
CLOSER				
BUT THE TREES GREW TALLER AND CLOSER, ...	48	OISIN 3		17
BUT TALLER THE TREES GREW AND CLOSER, ...	48	OISIN 3	V	17
AS THOUGH TO DRAW THEM CLOSER YET. RAMMED FULL	579	DOR WELLESLEY		5
SHIVERING CLOSER TO THEIR DAMS	726	LOVERS QUARREL		7
CLOSES				
THE CROWD THAT CLOSES IN BEHIND;	266	GALWAY RACES		4
THE FIELD THAT CLOSES IN BEHIND.	266	GALWAY RACES	V	4

147

CLOSING
    CLOSING RHYMES . . . .   320 REED WHISPERER V   T
    CLOSING RHYME . . . .   320 REED WHISPERER V   T
CLOTH   SEE MUMMY-CLOTH
    WHEN THEY FROZE THE CLOTH ON MY BODY LIKE ARMOUR RIVETED   57 OISIN 3   151
      FAST,
    AND FOUND HER DYEING CLOTH WITH SUBTLE CARE . . . . .   105 CUCHULAIN SEA V   2A
    BY DREAMING LADIES UPON CLOTH . . . .   156 FORGOT BEAUTY   7
    AND GREY CONNEMARA CLOTH, ...   348 FISHERMAN   30
    THEIR CONNEMARA CLOTH WORN OUT OF SHAPE! . . . . .   372 PHASES OF MOON   4
    A SHINING WEB, A FLOATING RIBBON OF CLOTH, ...   430 NINETEEN 19   50
    I ROSE THAT I MIGHT SCREEN IT WITH A CLOTH. . . . .   467 HARUN RASHID   131
    AS MUMMIES IN THE MUMMY CLOTH ARE WOUND! . . . . .   471 ALL SOUL NIGHT V   14
    AS MUMMIES IN THE MUMMY CLOTH ARE WOUND. . . . . .   474 ALL SOUL NIGHT V   100
    FOR HADES' BOBBIN BOUND IN MUMMY CLOTH . . . . . .   497 BYZANTIUM   V   11
CLOTHED   SEE CLAMOUR-CLOTHED
    AND STOOD WITHIN! CLOTHED IN A MISTY RAY . . . . .   36 OISIN 2   104
    IN DAMASK CLOTHED AND ON A SEAT . . . .   440 WISDOM   9
    AS, CLOTHED IN CEREMONIAL GLOOM, ...   655 ISLE STAT I 3   10
    HAVE CLOTHED THEIR TONGUES WITH SONG OF SONGLESS DAYS? . .   666 ISLE STAT II 3   17
CLOTHES   SEE SWADDLING-CLOTHES
    A CERTAIN POET IN OUTLANDISH CLOTHES . . . . . .   180 QUEEN MAEVE   1
    AND RENT HER CLOTHES AND MADE HER MOAN! . . . . .   275 GREY ROCK   108
    SHE MAY HAVE WORN SILK CLOTHES, OR WORN A CROWN, . . .   282 TWO KINGS   117
    IN THEIR STIFF, PAINTED CLOTHES, THE PALE UNSATISFIED ONES   318 MAGI   2
    IN GREY CONNEMARA CLOTHES . . . .   347 FISHERMAN   4
    FOR SILKEN CLOTHES AND STATELY WALK, ...   422 MY TABLE   30
    OLD CLOTHES UPON OLD STICKS TO SCARE A BIRD. . . .   445 SCHOOL CHILDR   48
    OR ROCKY CISTERN WHERE WE TREAD THE CLOTHES . . .   499 MOTHER OF GOD   9
    WINDING-SHEET AND SWADDLING CLOTHES. . . . . . .   530 OLD TOM AGAIN V   6
    THAT STEPPED OUT OF THEIR CLOTHES, ...   538 LAST CONFESS   14
    AGREED THEIR CLOTHES TO SWOP, ...   595 COLONEL MARTIN   20
    A ROOF, GOOD CLOTHES, PASSION, LOVE PERHAPS, . . .   609 IN TARAS HALLS   8
    WITH ANY SORT OF CLOTHES, ...   627 STATES HOLIDAY   28
CLOTHING
    CLOTHING HIM ROUND, I SAW A SEAGULL FLOAT . . . . .   36 OISIN 2   V 105
CLOTHS
    HE WISHES FOR THE CLOTHS OF HEAVEN . . . .   176 CLOTHS HEAVEN   T
    AEDH WISHES FOR THE CLOTHS OF HEAVEN . . . . . .   176 CLOTHS HEAVEN V   T
    HAD I THE HEAVENS' EMBROIDERED CLOTHS, ...   176 CLOTHS HEAVEN   1
    THE BLUE AND THE DIM AND THE DARK CLOTHS! . . . .   176 CLOTHS HEAVEN   3
    I WOULD SPREAD THE CLOTHS UNDER YOUR FEET! . . . .   176 CLOTHS HEAVEN   5
    HAD I THE HEAVEN'S EMBROIDERED CLOTHS, ...   176 CLOTHS HEAVEN V   1
CLOTTED
    WHEN LOW THE SUN SANK DOWN IN CLOTTED FLAME . . . .   656 ISLE STAT I 3   30
    LIE STREWN THE YELLOW LEAVES--THE CLOTTED LEAVES. . .   684 SEEKER   69
    LIE STREWN THE CLOTTED LEAVES--THE DEAD OLD LEAVES. . .   684 SEEKER   V   69
CLOUD
    THE DARKNESS COMES. A CLOUD HANGS OVERHEAD-- . . .   43 OISIN 2   V 208A
    HIS OLD EYES CLOUD WITH DREAMS! . . . .   98 FOXHUNTER   14
    AS A CLOUD FADED INTO THE SKY. . . . .   145 HOST OF AIR   V   40
    UNDER A CLOUD OF HER HAIR. . . . .   160 CAP AND BELLS   26
    AS 'TWERE UPON A CLOUD, ...   255 WOMAN HOMER   18
    NOR ON OLYMPUS LEAPED FROM CLOUD TO CLOUD, ...   260 FASC DIFFICULT   6
    NOR ON OLYMPUS LEAPED FROM CLOUD TO CLOUD, ...   260 FASC DIFFICULT   6
    NOR ON AN OLYMPUS LEAPED FROM CLOUD TO CLOUD, . . .   260 FASC DIFFICULT V   6
    NOR ON AN OLYMPUS LEAPED FROM CLOUD TO CLOUD, . . .   260 FASC DIFFICULT V   6
    A CLOUD BLOWN FROM THE CUT-THROAT NORTH . . . . .   313 MEMORY YOUTH   6
    WHEREON A THING ONCE WALKED THAT SEEMED A BURNING CLOUD.   315 FALLEN MAJESTY   8
    ONCE WALKED A THING THAT SEEMED, AS IT WERE, A BURNING   315 FALLEN MAJESTY V   8
      CLOUD.
    OR TUMBLING CLOUD." . . . .   349 HAWK   12
    "WHAT TUMBLING CLOUD DID YOU CLEAVE, ...   349 HAWK   13
    THEY ARE CAST BEYOND THE VERGE, AND IN A CLOUD, . . .   376 PHASES OF MOON   105
    FROM CLOUD TO TUMBLING CLOUD, ...   393 EASTER 1916   47
    FROM CLOUD TO TUMBLING CLOUD, ...   393 EASTER 1916   47
    A SHADOW OF CLOUD ON THE STREAM . . . .   393 EASTER 1916   49
    "VENGENCE FOR JACQUES MOLAY." IN CLOUD PALE RAGS, OR IN   426 PHANTOM HATRED V   10
      LACE,
    THE QUIVERING HALF-CLOSED EYELIDS, THE RAGS OF CLOUD OR   427 PHANTOM HATRED   26
      OF LACE,
    THE CLOUD PALE UNICORNS, THE EYES OF AQUAMARINE, . . .   427 PHANTOM HATRED V   25
    WHEN IT HAS LOOKED IN GLORY FROM A CLOUD. . . . .   482 BLOOD AND MOON   54
    ALTHOUGH THAT WESTERN CLOUD IS LUMINOUS, ...   488 COOLE PARK 29   4
    WHETHER IN WOOD, WATER OR CLOUD, ...   528 DANCER CRUACH   7
    A BUNDLE OF TEMPESTUOUS CLOUD IS BLOWN . . . . .   541 PARN FUNERAL 1   2
    ABOUT THE SKY! WHERE THAT IS CLEAR OF CLOUD . . .   541 PARN FUNERAL 1   3
    OR OUT OF HER BLACK CLOUD. . . . .   568 SWEET DANCER   6
    WOULD HE TEACH ANY SIN? GAZE IN THE CLOUD . . . .   692 MOSADA 1   58
    THAT YOU SHALL SEE ON YONDER GLOWING CLOUD . . . .   692 MOSADA 1   V   43
    "ON THIS EMBROIDERED CLOUD," THE SUN HATH SAID, . . .   712 FERENCZ RENYI   74
    AMID A CLOUD OF BANNERS, ...   741 EARL PAUL   39
    MY HEAD IS IN A CLOUD! . . . .   782 HEART FRIGHT   8
CLOUDLESS
    FLOWERS AND GRASS AND CLOUDLESS SKY, ...   639 BEN BULBEN   57
CLOUDLETS
    WHILE HIGH FRAIL CLOUDLETS, FED WITH A GREEN LIGHT, . .   40 OISIN 2   165
    HUNG THE FRAIL LOFTIER CLOUDLETS. TURNED HE SLOW-- . .   40 OISIN 2   V 167
CLOUD-O'ER-MUFFLED
    AS WHEN UPON HER CLOUD-O'ER-MUFFLED STEEP . . . . .   645 ISLE STAT I 1   16

		PAGE	TITLE		LINE

CLOUD-PALE
  WITH HER CLOUD-PALE EYELIDS FALLING ON DREAM-DIMMED EYES: — 163 VALLEY LOVERS — 4
  WITH HER CLOUD-PALE EYELIDS HALF COVERING HER DIM EYES: — 163 VALLEY LOVERS V 4
  O CLOUD-PALE EYELIDS, DREAM-DIMMED EYES, — 164 PERFECT BEAUTY — 1
  "VENGEANCE FOR JACQUES MOLAY." IN CLOUD-PALE RAGS, OR IN LACE, — 426 PHANTOM HATRED — 10
  THE CLOUD-PALE UNICORNS, THE EYES OF AQUAMARINE, — 427 PHANTOM HATRED — 25
CLOUDS
  AND CLOUDS ARRAYED THEIR RANK ON RANK — 12 OISIN 1 — 154
  THE CLOUDS ARRAYED THEM RANK ON RANK — 12 OISIN 1 V 154
  OR OF THE FLAKED CLOUDS?" "NOT SO, FOR WE — 34 OISIN 2 V 78C
  ROOTED IN FOAM AND CLOUDS, AND CRIED TO ALL — 38 OISIN 2 — 132
  ROOTED IN FOAM AND CLOUDS. THERE MIGHTIER MASTERS MET — 38 OISIN 2 V 132
  . . . "WHERE WHITE CLOUDS LIE SPREAD — 59 OISIN 3 — 178
  . . . THEY WILL RISE, MAKING CLOUDS WITH THEIR BREATH, — 61 OISIN 3 — 202
  AND STARLIGHT GLEAMED, AND CLOUDS FLEW HIGH, — 84 MAD KING GOLL — 34
  THE CLOUDS ON THEIR JOURNEY ABOVE, — 119 PITY OF LOVE — 4
  WHERE SUCH GREY CLOUDS OF INCENSE ROSE — 156 FORGOT BEAUTY — 13
  IN OLD TIMES AMONG THE CLOUDS OF THE AIR. — 194 BAILE AILLINN — 133
  THE WIND HAS BUNDLED UP THE CLOUDS HIGH OVER KNOCKNAREA, — 207 HANRAHANS SONG — 6
  ANGERS THAT ARE LIKE NOISY CLOUDS HAVE SET OUR HEARTS ABEAT: — 207 HANRAHANS SONG — 8
  O TATTERED CLOUDS OF THE WORLD, CALL FROM THE HIGH CAIRN OF MAIVE, — 207 HANRAHANS SONG V 6
  THE WINDS HAVE BUNDLED UP THE CLOUDS HIGH OVER KNOCKNAREA, — 207 HANRAHANS SONG V 6
  LIKE TATTERED CLOUDS OF THE WORLD, PASSIONS CALL AND OUR HEARTS BEAT: — 207 HANRAHANS SONG V 8
  ANGERS THAT ARE LIKE BUNDLED CLOUDS HAVE SET OUR HEARTS ABEAT: — 207 HANRAHANS SONG V 8
  THESE ARE THE CLOUDS — 265 THESE CLOUDS — T
  THESE ARE THE CLOUDS ABOUT THE FALLEN SUN, — 265 THESE CLOUDS — 1
  THESE ARE THE CLOUDS ABOUT THE FALLEN SUN, — 265 THESE CLOUDS — 11
  THE CLOUDS WERE BRIGHTENING WITH THE DAWN. — 307 HOUR DAWN — 122
  TORE FROM THE CLOUDS HIS MARVELLOUS MOON. — 314 MEMORY YOUTH — 21
  SOMEWHERE AMONG THE CLOUDS ABOVE: — 328 IRISH AIRMAN — 2
  DROVE TO THIS TUMULT IN THE CLOUDS: — 328 IRISH AIRMAN — 12
  SEEM BUT THE CLOUDS OF THE SKY. — 416 TOWER — 192
  THAT CAN PIERCE THE CLOUDS, — 576 ACRE OF GRASS — 20
CLOUDY
  ABOVE ITS CLOUDY RIM: — 175 ELEMENT POWERS — 16
  A CLOUDY QUIVER OVER PAIRC-NA-LEE. — 198 SEVEN WOODS — 14
  ABOVE THE CLOUDY SHOULDERS OF THE HORSES: — 344 DAWN — 12
  UPON THE CLOUDY CANOPY, — 397 POLIT PRISONER — 22
  AMID THE CLOUDY WRACK, — 458 HIS WILDNESS — 2
  CLOUDY LEAFAGE OF THE SKY, — 501 VACILLATION — 46
  AMONG THOSE STREAMS, OR ON THEIR CLOUDY EDGE. — 750 SHADOW WATER A — 63
  THE CLOUDY WATERS AND THE GLIMMERING WINDS — 764 SHADOW WATER A — 327
  WHERE THE MOON MAKES A CLOUDY LIGHT IN THE MIST. — 764 SHADOW WATER A — 329
  EAGLES HAVE GONE INTO THEIR CLOUDY BED. — 778 SONG DEIRDRE 3 — 6
  AND HEAVEN'S A CLOUDY BLOT. — 782 HEART FRIGHT — 17
CLOVEN
  HAS CLOVEN AND RENT THEIR HEARTS IN TWAIN, — 66 HAPPY SHEPHERD — 33
  MY DREAMS WERE CLOVEN BY VOICES AND BY FIRES: — 218 WOODS OF COOLE — 20
  TREAD AND TREAD THEIR CLOVEN FEET — 646 ISLE STAT I 1 — 24
  I SEE WITHIN A CLOVEN ROCK DISPART — 673 ISLE STAT II 3 — 195
  A CLOVEN, DANCING JET, — 680 LOVE AND DEATH — 2
  WHY HAVE YOU CLOVEN ME WITH A MORTAL LOVE? — 768 SHADOW WATER A — 419
CLOVER
  WE PASSED BY WOODS, AND LAWNS OF CLOVER, — 25 OISIN 1 — 377
  BY WOODS OF MOSS, BY LAWNS OF CLOVER, — 25 OISIN 1 V 377
  UNDERNEATH THE GRASS AND CLOVER, — 124 CATHLEEN PARA — 3
CLOWN
  AND SORROW AWAY, AND CALLING BARD AND CLOWN — 170 SECRET ROSE — 20
  THE CATCH-CRIES OF THE CLOWN, — 347 FISHERMAN — 22
  THE CATCH CRIES OF THE CLOWN, — 347 FISHERMAN V 22
  DOWN THE FANATIC, DOWN THE CLOWN: — 544 TO SAME TUNE 1 — 8
  DOWN THE FANATIC, DOWN THE CLOWN: — 545 TO SAME TUNE 1 — 18
  DOWN THE FANATIC, DOWN THE CLOWN: — 545 TO SAME TUNE 1 — 28
  DOWN THE FANATIC, DOWN THE CLOWN: — 546 TO SAME TUNE 2 V REF
  DOWN THE FANATIC, DOWN THE CLOWN: — 548 TO SAME TUNE 3 V REF
  HEROIC REVERIE MOCKED BY CLOWN AND KNAVE, — 619 BRONZE HEAD — 27
  WITHOUT MY GLASS I'D BE A SORRY CLOWN. — 721 WITCH VIVIEN — 29
  WHETHER A KING OR CLOWN, — 789 SINGING HEAD — 18
  FOR PRAISE OF CLOWN OR KING, — 789 SINGING HEAD — 20
CLOYNE
  DRANK TAR-WATER WITH THE BISHOP OF CLOYNE. — 486 SEVEN SAGES — 5
  GOLDSMITH AND BURKE, SWIFT AND THE BISHOP OF CLOYNE — 486 SEVEN SAGES — 9
  SOFT AS THE RUSTLE OF A REED FROM CLOYNE — 487 SEVEN SAGES — 22
CLUB
  AROUND THE FIRE AT THE CLUB, — 392 EASTER 1916 — 12
CLUMP
  WE TIED THE HORSE IN A LEAFY CLUMP, — 14 OISIN 1 — 194
  AND RIVER, FERN AND FLOWERY CLUMP, — 15 OISIN 1 V 196
  A CLUMP OF BEECH TREES MADE AN EMPTY SPACE — 277 TWO KINGS V 4A
  CLOSE TO A CLUMP OF BEECH TREES IN THE WOOD — 283 TWO KINGS V 135
CLUMSINESS
  BROUGHT FACE TO FACE WITH HIS OWN CLUMSINESS: — 479 SELF AND SOUL — 48
CLUNG
  OR CLUNG THEREON LIKE SWARMING BEES: — 14 OISIN 1 — 181
  OR CLUNG AS CLOSE AS SWARMS OF BEES, — 14 OISIN 1 V 181

CLUSTER   SEE GRAPE-CLUSTER
CLUSTERING
   AND FLOWERS AROUND IN CLUSTERING THOUSANDS ARE, ...   656 ISLE STAT I 3   24
CLUSTERS
   THE HEAVY CLUSTERS OF THE GRAPES WERE FULL, ...   690 MOSADA 1   13
CLUTCHES
   NOR EVER CHANGE OR FEEL THE CLUTCHES . . . .   23 OISIN 1   V 341A
   THE OSPREY OF SORROW GOES AFTER AND CLUTCHES, ...   27 OISIN 1   V 415D
CLYTEMNESTRA
   AS ARGIVE CLYTEMNESTRA SAW OUT-BURN . . . .   645 ISLE STAT I 1   12
COACH
   THAT MERELY STOOD, ROCKING THE GLITTERING COACH . . .   344 DAWN   11
   YET DID BUT LOOK, ROCKING THE GLITTERING COACH . . .   344 DAWN   V 11
COAGULATE
   COAGULATE OF STUFF . . . .   449 HERO GIRL FOOL   26
COAL
   WORLD, AS IT WERE A COAL, ...   267 FRIEND ILLNESS   5
   ISAIAH'S COAL, WHAT MORE CAN MAN DESIRE? . . . . . .   502 VACILLATION   74
   EZEKIEL'S COAL, WHAT MORE CAN MAN DESIRE? . . . . . .   502 VACILLATION   V 74
COAL-BLACK
   BUT WHEN HE WOUND HER COAL-BLACK HAIR . . . . . .   514 JANE GROWN OLD   3
COALS
   WHEN WE BENT DOWN ABOVE THE FADING COALS . . . . .   136 TO SOME I TALK   3
   WHILE THE NIGHT GREW, ABOVE THE FADING COALS, ...   136 TO SOME I TALK V   3
COARSE
   AMONG THE COARSE GRASS AND THE CAMEL-DUNG. . . . .   369 EGO DOMINUS   31
   AMONG THE COARSE GRASS AND THE CAMEL DUNG. . . . .   369 EGO DOMINUS   V 31
   CONDUCT AND WORK GROW COARSE, AND COARSE THE SOUL, .   564 GYRES   17
   CONDUCT AND WORK GROW COARSE, AND COARSE THE SOUL, .   564 GYRES   17
   BUT A COARSE OLD MAN AM I. . . . .   590 OLD WICKED MAN   59
COARSE-BRED
   THE COARSE-BRED SON OF A LIVERY-STABLE KEEPER-- . . .   370 EGO DOMINUS   61
COARSENESS
   THE COARSENESS OF THE DRUDGE. BEFORE THE FULL . . .   376 PHASES OF MOON   94
COAST
   HELP! HELP! AND HURL HIM FROM OUR COAST . . . . .   83 MAD KING GOLL V   17
COAT
   IN SOME OUTLANDISH COAT BESIDE . . . .   303 HOUR DAWN   V 28
   A COAT . . . .   320 COAT   T
   I MADE MY SONG A COAT . . . .   320 COAT   1
   A TATTERED COAT UPON A STICK, UNLESS . . . . .   407 SAIL BYZANTIUM   10
   AND WEAR A COAT IN FASHION, ...   607 SONGS BURDEN 2   21
   THE WORST A COAT UPON A COAT-HANGER. . . . . .   624 APPARITIONS   8
   THE WORST A COAT UPON A COAT-HANGER. . . . . .   624 APPARITIONS   16
   THE WORST A COAT UPON A COAT-HANGER. . . . . .   624 APPARITIONS   24
   A COAT OF GILDED MAIL. . . . .   740 EARL PAUL   16
COATED   SEE LEATHER-COATED
COAT-HANGER
   THE WORST A COAT UPON A COAT-HANGER. . . . . .   624 APPARITIONS   8
   THE WORST A COAT UPON A COAT-HANGER. . . . . .   624 APPARITIONS   16
   THE WORST A COAT UPON A COAT-HANGER. . . . . .   624 APPARITIONS   24
COBWEB
   THAT SHAKES A MOULDERING COBWEB FROM THE RAFTER, . .   130 BOOK STORIES   19
   LEAPING TO SHAKE A COBWEB FROM THE RAFTER, ...   130 BOOK STORIES   19
   AND SHAKE A MOULDERING COBWEB FROM THE RAFTER, . . .   130 BOOK STORIES   V 19
   AT MORN, AND WITH HER FEET EACH COBWEB RENDS, . . .   670 ISLE STAT II 3   99
COBWEBS
   HANG THE MIST-THREADS FOR A LITTLE WHILE LIKE COBWEBS IN
     THE AIR, ...   719 PHANTOM SHIP   29
   HANG THE MIST THREADS FOR A LITTLE WHILE LIKE COBWEBS IN
     THE AIR, ...   719 PHANTOM SHIP   V 29
COCK   SEE HAY-COCK
   MARE OR STALLION, COCK OR HEN, ...   529 TOM LUNATIC   15
   A COCK CAME BY UPON HIS TOES, ...   725 LEGEND   26
   RED COCK, AND CROW! . . . .   782 HEART FRIGHT   7
   RED COCK, AND CROW! . . . .   782 HEART FRIGHT   14
   RED COCK, AND CROW! . . . .   782 HEART FRIGHT   21
COCK-A-DOODLE-DOODLE-DO
   "COCK-A-DOODLE-DOODLE-DO!" . . . .   697 MOSADA 2   29
COCKED
   AN OLD MAN COCKED HIS EAR UPON A BRIDGE, ...   372 PHASES OF MOON   1
   WERE DISTANT STILL. AN OLD MAN COCKED HIS EAR. . . .   372 PHASES OF MOON   7
   WERE DISTANT. AN OLD MAN COCKED HIS EAR. . . . .   372 PHASES OF MOON V   7
   AND COCKED A MALICIOUS EYE, ...   527 AM OF IRELAND   25
COCKEREL
   THEREON REPLIED: "A COCKEREL . . . .   387 SOLOMON WITCH   9
   ANSWERED: "A CRESTED COCKEREL CREW . . . . . .   387 SOLOMON WITCH   V 9
   THEREON EXPLAINED: "A COCKEREL . . . .   387 SOLOMON WITCH   V 9
   YOUR COCKEREL FOUND US IN THE WRONG . . . . . .   388 SOLOMON WITCH   34
COCK'S
   WITH A GREAT COCK'S FEATHER, ...   627 STATES HOLIDAY   37
COCKS   SEE MOOR-COCKS
   AND CLINGING TO IT I COULD HEAR THE COCKS . . . . .   286 TWO KINGS   210
   AND THERE'S NO MAN BUT COCKS HIS EAR . . . . . .   306 HOUR DAWN   99
   BRONZED PEACOCK FEATHERS, RED COMBS OF HER COCKS. . .   433 NINETEEN 19   130
   CAN LIKE THE COCKS OF HADES CROW, ...   498 BYZANTIUM   20
   SPOKE AND SET THE COCKS A-CROW. . . . .   637 BEN BULBEN   4
   RED COCKS, AND CROW! . . . .   783 GREY ROUND   28
CODGERS
   THERE ALL THE GOLDEN CODGERS LAY, ...   611 NEWS ORACLE   1

                                                              PAGE   TITLE   LINE

COFFIN
    DIGGERS AND CARPENTERS MAKE GRAVE AND COFFIN; . . . . .   609 IN TARAS HALLS   17
    SAW THAT THE GRAVE WAS DEEP, THE COFFIN SOUND, ... 609 IN TARAS HALLS   18
    LAY IN THE COFFIN, STOPPED HIS BREATH AND DIED. . . . .   609 IN TARAS HALLS   20
COGENT
    AND HERE'S A COGENT REASON, ...   586 PARNELLITES   9
COGNOMEN
    THAT COGNOMEN SOUNDED BEST . . . .   440 WISDOM   18
COIL
    THAT JUGGLING NATURE MOUNTS, HER COIL IN THEIR EMBRACES   556 RIBH PATRICK   9
        TWINED.
    IN COIL ON COIL OF AZURE. ALL IS READY. . . . . . .   691 MOSADA 1   41
    IN COIL ON COIL OF AZURE. ALL IS READY. . . . . . .   691 MOSADA 1   41
    NO SIN TO SEE IN COIL ON COIL OF AZURE . . . .   692 MOSADA 1   43
    NO SIN TO SEE IN COIL ON COIL OF AZURE . . . .   692 MOSADA 1   43
    I HAD THROWN IT DOWN BEHIND THIS COIL OF ROPE. . . . .   759 SHADOW WATER A   245
COILING
    IN THEIR COILING CALM AND SLOW. . . . .   680 LOVE AND DEATH   8
    TO ONE ANOTHER WITH A COILING CHAIN; . . . .   687 TWO TITANS   6
COILS
    LONG CITRON COILS THAT HANG AROUND THEE, BLOWN . . . .   670 ISLE STAT II 3   105
COIN
    THOSE BODIES FROM A PICTURE OR A COIN . . . .   537 HER VISION   28
    STAMPED BOY AND TREE UPON SICILIAN COIN. . . . . . .   541 PARN FUNERAL 1   15
COLA
    AMONG THE FRUIT! BUT THERE, LAME COLA CROUCHES . . . .   691 MOSADA 1   32
    AND COLA, SEEING, KNOWS THE SIGN AND COMES. . . . . .   691 MOSADA 1   38
    AMONG THE FRUIT. BUT YON, LAME COLA CROUCHES . . . .   691 MOSADA 1   V   32
    AND COLA, SEEING, KNOWS THE SIGN AND RISES. . . . . .   691 MOSADA 1   V   38
COLA'S
    OF SILVER HANGING ROUND LAME COLA'S NECK-- . . . . .   691 MOSADA 1   V   35
COLD   SEE MIST-COLD DEW-COLD CLAY-COLD
    AND BENDS TO THE FIRE AND SHAKES WITH THE COLD . . . .   26 OISIN 1   405
    NONE MAY BEGUILE HIM, AND HIS PASSIONS COLD . . . . .   35 OISIN 2   V 83A
    CAME NOW THE SLIDING OF TEARS AND SWEEPING OF MIST COLD   47 OISIN 3   V   7
        HAIR,
    NO WORD OF THEIRS--THE COLD STAR-BANE . . . .   66 HAPPY SHEPHERD   32
    "HE DRIVES AWAY THE NORTHERN COLD." . . . .   82 MAD KING GOLL   11
    THROUGH SUMMER'S HEAT AND WINTER'S COLD. . . . . . .   86 MAD KING GOLL   71
    I LOOKED ON MY COLD BABY . . . .   95 MOLL MAGEE   19
    THE COLD WET WINDS EVER BLOWING, ...   119 PITY OF LOVE   5
    AND THE COLD WET WINDS EVER BLOWING, ...   119 PITY OF LOVE   V   7
    UNDER THAT COLD AND VAPOUR-TURBANED STEEP, ...   128 DREAM OF FAERY   39
    WITH HEAVY WHITENING WINGS, AND A HEART FALLEN COLD;   147 UNAPPEAS HOST   4
    AND THE SEED OF THE FIRE GETS FEEBLE AND COLD. . . . .   151 OLD MOTHER   10
    BUT THE SEED OF THE FIRE GETS FEEBLE AND COLD, ...   151 OLD MOTHER   V   9
    WERE YOU BUT LYING COLD AND DEAD, ...   175 BELOVED DEAD   1
    NOR THE COLD NORTH HAS TROUBLED?" HE REPLIED, ...   184 QUEEN MAEVE   90
    OF THIS OR THAT THING, NOR GREW COLD . . . .   189 BAILE AILLINN   9
    OF THIS OR THAT THING, OR GREW COLD . . . .   189 BAILE AILLINN   V   9
    "FROM HEAT AND COLD AND WIND AND WAVE; . . . . . .   193 BAILE AILLINN   114
    WRUNG FROM THE COLD WOMEN OF THE SEA-- . . . . . .   237 SHADOW WATER B   343
    AND YET NOT COLD." . . . .   263 MASK   5
    HER EYES WERE COLD AND STEADY, HER LIPS TIGHT. . . . .   279 TWO KINGS   64
    BY A COLD AND DESOLATE SEA, ...   298 THREE HERMITS   2
    THE COLD HEAVEN . . . .   316 COLD HEAVEN   T
    SUDDENLY I SAW THE COLD AND ROOK-DELIGHTING HEAVEN . . .   316 COLD HEAVEN   1
    SUDDENLY I SAW THE COLD AND ROOK DELIGHTING HEAVEN . . .   316 COLD HEAVEN   V   1
    THEY PADDLE IN THE COLD . . . .   323 SWANS AT COOLE   20
    AND WE ARE HURT IF EITHER FRIEND SEEM COLD, ...   324 ROBERT GREGORY   10
    TO COLD CLARE ROCK AND GALWAY ROCK AND THORN, ...   326 ROBERT GREGORY   66
    POEM MAYBE AS COLD . . . .   348 FISHERMAN   39
    POEM MAY BE AS COLD . . . .   348 FISHERMAN   V   39
    THE PURE COLD LIGHT IN THE SKY . . . .   378 CAT AND MOON   7
    HAS CALLED UP THE COLD SPIRITS THAT ARE BORN . . . .   382 VISION ROBART   2
    UNDER THE FIRST COLD GLEAM OF DAY? . . . .   398 BREAK OF DAY   4
    COLD STONE AND WATER. I GREW WILD. . . . .   399 BREAK OF DAY   14
    THE COLD BLOWN SPRAY IN MY NOSTRIL. . . . .   399 BREAK OF DAY   20
    IN THE COLD SNOWS OF A DREAM. . . . .   424 ROAD AT DOOR   15
    COLD AS THE MARCH WIND HIS EYES. . . . .   531 FATHER CHILD   8
    AND MY BLOOD BE COLD THE WHILE . . . .   532 BEFORE WORLD   11
    ON MY COLD BREAST? . . . .   574 MAIDS 1ST SONG   4
    WHEN AN OLD MAN'S BLOOD GROWS COLD? . . . .   588 OLD WICKED MAN   13
    NO MAN GROWS OLD, NO GIRL GROWS COLD, ...   621 JOHN KINSELLA   31
    CAST A COLD EYE . . . .   640 BEN BULBEN   92
    AS A LEAF THAT IS OLD, AND WITHERED, AND COLD, ...   643 SONG FAERIES   3
    AS A LEAF THAT IS OLD, AND WITHERED, AND COLD, ...   644 SONG FAERIES   15
    AS A LEAF THAT IS OLD, AND WITHERED, AND COLD, ...   676 ISLE STAT II 3   250
    AS A LEAF THAT IS OLD, AND WITHERED, AND COLD, ...   676 ISLE STAT II 3   262
    I'M WEARY--WEARY, AND 'TIS VERY COLD. . . . .   703 MOSADA 3   122
    I'LL DRAW MY CLOAK AROUND ME; IT IS COLD. . . . . . .   704 MOSADA 3   123
    I NEVER KNEW A NIGHT SO BITTER COLD. . . . .   704 MOSADA 3   124
    IN THE COLD STREAMS, AND WAKE TO THEIR DESIRE, ...   750 SHADOW WATER A   85
    AND UNFORGOTTEN NAMES, AND THE COLD STARS . . . . .   757 SHADOW WATER A   204
    AND A COLD WIND IS BLOWING IN MY HAIR. . . . . . .   761 SHADOW WATER A   277
    WHETHER AMONG THE COLD WINDS OF THE DEAD. . . . . .   768 SHADOW WATER A V 413
    ARE BLOWN COLD DUST OR A BIT OF BONE. . . . . . .   788 HAWTHORN TREE   8
COLDER
    COLDER AND DUMBER AND DEAFER THAN A FISH. . . . . . .   267 ALL TEMPT ME   10
COLIN
    IF HER YE LOVE. AYE, COLIN, WE MUST FIGHT. . . . . .   662 ISLE STAT II 1   76

151

	PAGE	TITLE		LINE
COLLAR				
FROM COLLAR TO COLLAR, FROM STILT TO STILT, FROM FATHER TO CHILD.	623	HIGH TALK		10
FROM COLLAR TO COLLAR, FROM STILT TO STILT, FROM FATHER TO CHILD.	623	HIGH TALK		10
COLLAR-BONE				
THE COLLAR-BONE OF A HARE	330	BONE OF A HARE		T
THE COLLAR-BONE OF A HARE	330	BONE OF A HARE		10
COLLEENS				
O COLLEENS, KNEELING BY YOUR ALTAR RAILS LONG HENCE, . .	173	SPEAKS HEARERS	V	1
COLLEGE				
MAY I NOT PUT MYSELF TO COLLEGE?	385	ROBARTES DANCE		18
COLLOQUY				
AND THEREUPON A COLLOQUY TOOK PLACE	463	HARUN RASHID		45
THAT THEREUPON A COLLOQUY TOOK PLACE	463	HARUN RASHID	V	45
COLONEL				
COLONEL MARTIN	594	COLONEL MARTIN		T
THE COLONEL WENT OUT SAILING.	594	COLONEL MARTIN		1
THE COLONEL WENT OUT SAILING.	594	COLONEL MARTIN		9
THE COLONEL WENT OUT SAILING.	594	COLONEL MARTIN		18
THE COLONEL MET A PEDLAR,	595	COLONEL MARTIN		19
THE COLONEL WENT OUT SAILING.	595	COLONEL MARTIN		27
THE COLONEL KNOCKED ON THE RICH MAN'S DOOR,	595	COLONEL MARTIN		28
THE COLONEL WENT OUT SAILING.	595	COLONEL MARTIN		36
THE COLONEL KNOCKED ON A RICH MAN'S DOOR.	595	COLONEL MARTIN	V	28
THE COLONEL WENT OUT SAILING.	596	COLONEL MARTIN		45
THE COLONEL SAID TO TOM HIS MAN,	596	COLONEL MARTIN		50
THE COLONEL WENT OUT SAILING.	596	COLONEL MARTIN		54
TO SHOOT THE COLONEL DEAD,	596	COLONEL MARTIN		58
THE COLONEL WENT OUT SAILING.	596	COLONEL MARTIN		63
THE COLONEL WENT OUT SAILING.	597	COLONEL MARTIN		72
COLONIES				
AMERICAN COLONIES, IRELAND, FRANCE AND INDIA	487	SEVEN SAGES		15
COLONUS				
EVERY COLONUS LAD OR LASS DISCOURSES	447	COLONUS PRAISE		29
FROM "OEDIPUS AT COLONUS"	459	FROM OEDIPUS		T
COLONUS'				
COLONUS' PRAISE	446	COLONUS PRAISE		T
COME PRAISE COLONUS' HORSES, AND COME PRAISE	446	COLONUS PRAISE		1
COLOONEY				
PEOPLE CAME INTO COLOONEY, ...	93	FATHER OHART		27
COLOONY				
THE PRIEST OF COLOONY	91	FATHER OHART	V	T
COLOUR				
A CITRON COLOUR GLOOMED IN HER HAIR, ...	3	OISIN 1		24
KINGFISHER COLOUR GREW WITH RAGE. HE ROSE	40	OISIN 2	V	169
DELICATE IN COLOUR AS APPLE BLOSSOM.	199	ARROW		6
AND THOUGH THEY'RE BUT THE COLOUR OF GREY ASH, . . .	247	SHADOW WATER B		528
TO THAT STERN COLOUR AND THAT DELICATE LINE	326	ROBERT GREGORY		67
AND PRAISED THE COLOUR OF HER FACE, ...	410	TOWER		36
AND HAD THAT COLOUR UPON CHEEK OR HAIR, ...	444	SCHOOL CHILDR		22
AND SET SUCH COLOUR THERE, ...	492	ANNE GREGORY		8
COLOURED SEE LEOPARD-COLOURED SLATE-COLOURED MANY-COLOURED GRASS-COLOURED HONEY-COLOURED				
THAT ARE LIKE COLOURED ASIAN BIRDS	7	OISIN 1		69
LEAVE THE BODY'S COLOURED PRIDE	124	CATHLEEN PARA		2
COLOURS				
WITH ALL HIS COLOURS JOURNEY-DULL, ...	82	MAD KING GOLL	V	13
THE CHANGING COLOURS OF ITS FRUIT	134	TWO TREES		5
COLT				
OUT OF MY HEART. THERE'S SOMETHING AILS OUR COLT . . .	260	FASC DIFFICULT		4
COLTSFOOT				
COME YOU, COLTSFOOT, MOUSETAIL, COME!	727	LOVERS QUARREL		33
COMB SEE HONEY-COMB				
WHAT MADE US DREAM THAT HE COULD COMB GREY HAIR? . . .	327	ROBERT GREGORY		88
COMBS				
BRONZED PEACOCK FEATHERS, RED COMBS OF HER COCKS. . . .	433	NINETEEN 19		130
COMBUSTIBLE				
THE ENTIRE COMBUSTIBLE WORLD IN ONE SMALL ROOM	327	ROBERT GREGORY		82
ALL THE COMBUSTIBLE WORLD IN ONE SMALL ROOM	327	ROBERT GREGORY	V	82
COME				
FOR CHANGE AND DEATH THEY COME NOT NEAR US, ...	21	OISIN 1	V	316
WHEN GOD SHALL COME FROM THE SEA WITH A SIGH	28	OISIN 1		425
COME FROM THE ISLE OF THE LIVING." "THEN GET YE . . .	34	OISIN 2	V	79
AS THOUGH HIS HOUR WERE COME. WE SOUGHT THE PART . .	37	OISIN 2		112
I CRIED, "COME OUT OF THE SHADOW, KING OF THE NAILS OF GOLD!	51	OISIN 3		61
I CRIED, "COME OUT OF THE SHADOW, CANN OF THE NAILS OF GOLD!	51	OISIN 3	V	61
AND SOFTLY COME TO YOUR NIAMH OVER THE TOPS OF THE TIDE,	55	OISIN 3		126
AND SOFTLY COME TO THY NIAM OVER THE TOPS OF THE TIDE, . .	52	OISIN 3	V	126
. . . YOU WILL COME NO MORE TO MY SIDE.	56	OISIN 3		128
"IN THE ISLES OF THE FARTHEST SEAS WHERE ONLY THE SPIRITS COME.	56	OISIN 3		133
SEE HOW THE SACRED OLD FLAMINGOES COME, ...	72	ANASHU VIJAYA		29
MAYBE YOU HAVE NOT HEARD OF US, YOU HAVE COME FORTH SO NEWLY,	75	ANASHU VIJAYA		78
HATH COME A SEA-KING MASTERFUL, ...	82	MAD KING GOLL	V	15
COME AWAY, O HUMAN CHILD!	87	STOLEN CHILD		9
COME AWAY, O HUMAN CHILD!	87	STOLEN CHILD		24
COME AWAY, O HUMAN CHILD!	88	STOLEN CHILD		38
COME, O HUMAN CHILD!	88	STOLEN CHILD	V	38

COME   (CONTINUED)

COME ROUND ME, LITTLE CHILDER:	94	MOLL MAGEE		1
SHE SAYS MY MAN WILL SURELY COME,	96	MOLL MAGEE		41
SHE SAYS MY HUSBAND SURE WILL COME	96	MOLL MAGEE	V	41
COME NEAR ME, WHILE I SING THE ANCIENT WAYS:	100	ROSE UPON ROOD		2
COME NEAR, THAT NO MORE BLINDED BY MAN'S FATE,	101	ROSE UPON ROOD		9
COME NEAR, COME NEAR, COME NEAR--AH, LEAVE ME STILL	101	ROSE UPON ROOD		13
COME NEAR, COME NEAR, COME NEAR--AH, LEAVE ME STILL	101	ROSE UPON ROOD		13
COME NEAR, COME NEAR, COME NEAR--AH, LEAVE ME STILL	101	ROSE UPON ROOD		13
COME NEAR: I WOULD, BEFORE MY TIME TO GO,	101	ROSE UPON ROOD		22
THAT YOU HAVE COME AND DARED ME TO MY FACE?"	109	CUCHULAIN SEA		61
THAT YOU COME HERE TO MEET THIS ANCIENT SWORD?"	109	CUCHULAIN SEA	V	61
WOULD COME AT LAST TO GOD'S GREAT TOWN,	113	ROSE OF PEACE		11
YOU, TOO, HAVE COME WHERE THE DIM TIDES ARE HURLED	115	ROSE OF BATTLE		26
WHERE TIME WOULD SURELY FORGET US, AND SORROW COME NEAR US NO MORE:	122	WHITE BIRDS		10
WHERE SURELY TIME WOULD FORGET US AND SORROW COME NEAR US NO MORE:	122	WHITE BIRDS	V	10
"FATHER: YOU COME AGAIN!"	133	FR GILLIGAN		32
AND NIAMH CALLING AWAY, COME AWAY:	140	HOSTING SIDHE		4
AWAY, COME AWAY, TO THE DIM TWILIGHT.	140	HOSTING SIDHE	V	8
WE COME BETWEEN HIM AND THE DEED OF HIS HAND,	141	HOSTING SIDHE		11
WE COME BETWEEN HIM AND THE HOPE OF HIS HEART.	141	HOSTING SIDHE		12
AND NIAMH CALLING AWAY, COME AWAY.	141	HOSTING SIDHE		16
COME CLEAR OF THE NETS OF WRONG AND RIGHT:	147	INTO TWILIGHT		2
COME CLEAR OFF THE NETS OF WRONG AND RIGHT:	147	INTO TWILIGHT	V	2
COME, HEART, WHERE HILL IS HEAPED UPON HILL	148	INTO TWILIGHT		9
HE MOURNS FOR THE CHANGE THAT HAS COME UPON HIM	153	CHANGE BELOVED		T
MONGAN LAMENTS THE CHANGE THAT HAS COME UPON HIM AND HIS BELOVED	153	CHANGE BELOVED	V	T
I WOULD THAT THE BOAR WITHOUT BRISTLES HAD COME FROM THE WEST	153	CHANGE BELOVED		10
COME FROM A MORE DREAM-HEAVY LAND,	156	FORGOT BEAUTY		16
"I HAVE COME BY THE WINDY WAY	167	BLESSED		6
"I COME BY THE WINDY WAY	167	BLESSED	V	6
SURELY THINE HOUR HAS COME, THY GREAT WIND BLOWS,	170	SECRET ROSE		31
I WOULD THE PALE DEER HAD COME	171	MAID QUIET	V	4A
HAD COME THROUGH THE MOUNTAIN SIDE,	171	MAID QUIET	V	4B
YOU WOULD COME HITHER, AND BEND YOUR HEAD,	175	BELOVED DEAD		3
WHEN WE COME AT THE END OF TIME	178	FIDDLER DOONEY		9
WHEN WE COME AT THE CLOSE OF TIME	178	FIDDLER DOONEY	V	9
THEY WILL ALL COME UP TO ME,	179	FIDDLER DOONEY		18
WILL ALL COME UP TO ME,	179	FIDDLER DOONEY	V	18
HAD COME AS IN THE OLD TIMES TO COUNSEL HER,	181	QUEEN MAEVE		42
HAD COME, AS IN OLD TIMES, TO COUNSEL HER,	181	QUEEN MAEVE	V	42
OF THE FAR-WANDERING SHADOWS HAS COME TO ME	183	QUEEN MAEVE		80
AS IN THE OLD DAYS WHEN THEY WOULD COME AND GO	183	QUEEN MAEVE		81
OF THE FAR WANDERING SHADOWS HAS COME TO ME,	183	QUEEN MAEVE	V	80
KINGS OF THE GREAT PLAIN HAVE COME AND GONE	183	QUEEN MAEVE	V	81
"I COME FROM THE UNDIMMED RIVERS TO BID YOU CALL	184	QUEEN MAEVE		91
AND THE BROWN BULL HAD NOT YET COME,	189	BAILE AILLINN		15
WHEN THEY HAD COME TO THE MARRIAGE-BED:	193	BAILE AILLINN		106
WHEN THEY HAD COME TO THE MARRIAGE BED:	193	BAILE AILLINN	V	106
THEY COME WHERE SOME HUGE WATCHER IS,	196	BAILE AILLINN		168
A BETTER TIME HAD COME AGAIN	197	BAILE AILLINN		192
AND LITTLE SHADOWS COME ABOUT HER EYES:	199	FOLLY COMFORT		3
IT ALL, AND MORE THAN IT ALL, WOULD COME TO NAUGHT,	201	OLD MEMORY		8
IT ALL, MORE THAN IT ALL, WOULD COME TO NAUGHT:	201	OLD MEMORY	V	8
WHO COME WITH THEIR CROWNS OF PEARL AND THEIR SPINDLES OF WOOL,	203	WITHER BOUGHS		10
THAT THEY WOULD COME TO BLOWS,	214	HAPPY TOWNLAND		22
THAT THEY MUST COME TO BLOWS,	214	HAPPY TOWNLAND	V	22
GABRIEL WILL COME FROM THE WATER	215	HAPPY TOWNLAND		45
AND THAT YOU COME FROM EDEN ON FLYING FEET.	218	WOODS OF COOLE		29
WE HAVE NOT COME UPON A SHORE OR SHIP	222	SHADOW WATER B		3
I'D NEVER COME UPON THE HAPPINESS	226	SHADOW WATER B		87
HAS EVER COME BUT THOSE MAN-HEADED BIRDS,	226	SHADOW WATER B		99
AND THE HIGH FAME THAT COME TO THEM IN MARRIAGE,	232	SHADOW WATER B		235
ARMED MEN HAVE COME UPON US! O I AM SLAIN!	233	SHADOW WATER B		241
ARMED MEN HAVE COME UPON US! O I AM SLAIN!	233	SHADOW WATER B		243
THERE! THERE THEY COME! GULL, GANNET, OR DIVER!	233	SHADOW WATER B		244
TO WAIT THEIR FRIENDS! BUT WHEN THEIR FRIENDS HAVE COME	233	SHADOW WATER B		247
WHERE DO YOU COME FROM? WHO BROUGHT YOU TO THIS PLACE?	235	SHADOW WATER B		284
HAS COME INTO THE JEWELS OF THE HARP	239	SHADOW WATER B	V	371A
WHAT NAME TO CALL HIM BY? COME TO HIS SHIP.	240	SHADOW WATER B		390
HIS NAME WILL COME INTO OUR THOUGHTS IN A MINUTE.	241	SHADOW WATER B		391
FOR EVERYTHING IS GONE. COME HITHER, AIBRIC,	241	SHADOW WATER B		402
BUT HARRY US WITH HOPES THAT COME TO NOTHING,	250	SHADOW WATER B		579
BECAUSE I HAVE COME INTO MY STRENGTH,	256	WORDS		11
ALTHOUGH I HAVE COME CLOSE ON FORTY-NINE,	270	PARDON FATHERS		20
"COME OUT AND DIG FOR A DEAD MAN,	272	GREY ROCK		32
THAT EMPTIED ALL OUR DAYS TO COME.	272	GREY ROCK		40
BEING BETRAYED INTO A CRADLE, AND I COME	284	TWO KINGS		169
"SEEING THAT WHEN YOU COME TO THE DEATHBED	285	TWO KINGS		196
"SEEING THAT WHEN YOU COME TO THE DEATH-BED	285	TWO KINGS	V	196
WHAT NEED YOU, BEING COME TO SENSE,	289	SEPTEMBER 1913		1
TO A FRIEND WHOSE WORK HAS COME TO NOTHING	290	TO A FRIEND		T
AND LISTEN AT THE CORNERS HAS NOT COME:	293	TO A SHADE		22
COULD EVER COME BETWEEN	315	FRIENDS		8
THAT THE NIGHT COME	317	NIGHT COME		T
THAT THE NIGHT COME.	317	NIGHT COME		12

COME (CONTINUED)

		PAGE	TITLE		LINE
--BEN JONSON'S PHRASE--AND FIND WHEN JUNE IS COME		321	REED WHISPERER		6
THE NINETEENTH AUTUMN HAS COME UPON ME		322	SWANS AT COOLE		7
FOR ALL THAT COME INTO MY MIND ARE DEAD.		324	ROBERT GREGORY		16
BUT THAT, LONG TRAVELLING, HE HAD COME		325	ROBERT GREGORY		28
THE YEARS TO COME SEEMED WASTE OF BREATH,		328	IRISH AIRMAN		14
"STRETCH BONES TILL THE DAYLIGHT COME		331	ROUND TOWER		5
AND NOW THAT I HAVE COME TO FIFTY YEARS		344	DEJECTION		10
MANAGE THE TALK UNTIL HER NAME COME ROUND.		351	HER PRAISE		14
MANAGE TO TALK UNTIL HER NAME COME ROUND.		351	HER PRAISE	V	14
I WAS ABASHED, AND NOW THEY COME TO MIND		353	PEOPLE		36
COME PLAY WITH ME:		359	TO A SQUIRREL		1
NOW THAT HIS FIFTIETH YEAR HAD COME,		361	ALF POLLEXFEN		31
WILL COME FROM THE HOUSE, AND SAY--		364	END OF DAY		6
"COME IN AND LEAVE THE PLAY."		364	END OF DAY		8
AMID THE DREAMS OF YOUTH) LET HER COME FACE TO FACE,		366	HER COURAGE		3
COULD THE IMPOSSIBLE COME TO PASS		385	ROBARTES DANCE		9
THAT ALL MUST COME TO SIGHT AND TOUCH:		386	ROBARTES DANCE		31
NO, NO, NOT SAID, BUT CRIED IT OUT--"YOU HAVE COME AGAIN,		391	UNDER SATURN		13
AND SURELY AFTER TWENTY YEARS IT WAS TIME TO COME."		391	UNDER SATURN		14
WHEN SLEEP AT LAST HAS COME		394	EASTER 1916		63
"TO MAKE THE GREEN COME OUT AGAIN		396	ROSE TREE		9
SO THE CROWD COME THEY CARE NOT WHAT MAY COME.		398	LEADERS CROWD		10
SO THE CROWD COME THEY CARE NOT WHAT MAY COME.		398	LEADERS CROWD		10
AND WHAT ROUGH BEAST, ITS HOUR COME ROUND AT LAST,		402	SECOND COMING		21
THAT THE FUTURE YEARS HAD COME,		403	FOR DAUGHTER		14
AND THEREFORE I HAVE SAILED THE SEAS AND COME		408	SAIL BYZANTIUM		15
COME FROM THE HOLY FIRE, PERNE IN A GYRE,		408	SAIL BYZANTIUM		19
OF WHAT IS PAST, OR PASSING, OR TO COME.		408	SAIL BYZANTIUM		32
AND THEREFORE HAVE I SAILED THE SEAS AND COME		408	SAIL BYZANTIUM	V	15
COME WITH LOUD CRY AND PANTING BREAST		412	TOWER		86
AS I WOULD QUESTION ALL, COME ALL WHO CAN:		412	TOWER		89
COME OLD, NECESSITOUS, HALF-MOUNTED MAN:		412	TOWER		90
OR WHAT WORSE EVIL COME--		416	TOWER		188
COME BUILD IN THE EMPTY HOUSE OF THE STARE.		424	STARES NEST		5
COME BUILD IN THE EMPTY HOUSE OF THE STARE.		425	STARES NEST		10
COME BUILD IN THE EMPTY HOUSE OF THE STARE.		425	STARES NEST		15
COME BUILD IN THE EMPTY HOUSE OF THE STARE.		425	STARES NEST		20
NOR HATE OF WHAT'S TO COME, NOR PITY FOR WHAT'S GONE,		427	PHANTOM HATRED		30
COME LET US MOCK AT THE GREAT		432	NINETEEN 19		93
COME LET US MOCK AT THE WISE:		432	NINETEEN 19		98
COME LET US MOCK AT THE GOOD		432	NINETEEN 19		103
BECAUSE THE SPRING-TIME HAS NOT COME--		434	WHEEL		6
TILL HIS MORNING MEAL COME ROUND:		435	FOR MY SON		4
COME PRAISE COLONUS' HORSES, AND COME PRAISE		446	COLONUS PRAISE		1
COME PRAISE COLONUS' HORSES, AND COME PRAISE		446	COLONUS PRAISE		1
WHO COMES INTO THIS COUNTRY, AND HAS COME		447	COLONUS PRAISE		17
A STRANGE THING SURELY THAT MY HEART, WHEN LOVE HAD COME UNSOUGHT		449	OWEN AHERNE		1
LOVE-LORN, INDIFFERENT HANDS MIGHT COME UPON IT		461	HARUN RASHID		14
MIDNIGHT HAS COME, AND THE GREAT CHRIST CHURCH BELL		470	ALL SOUL NIGHT		1
BUBBLE UPON THE TABLE. A GHOST MAY COME:		470	ALL SOUL NIGHT		5
CAN COME UPON THE VISAGE OF THE MOON		482	BLOOD AND MOON		53
WHERE BLOOD-BEGOTTEN SPIRITS COME		498	BYZANTIUM		28
WHERE BLOOD BEGOTTEN SPIRITS COME		498	BYZANTIUM	V	28
THAT ARE NOT SUITED FOR SUCH MEN AS COME		501	VACILLATION		33
MY FIFTIETH YEAR HAD COME AND GONE,		501	VACILLATION		35
BATHED IN MIRACULOUS OIL, SWEET ODOURS FROM IT COME,		503	VACILLATION		81
OUT OF IRELAND HAVE WE COME.		506	REMORSE SPEECH		11
BUT SHOULD THAT OTHER COME, I SPIT:		509	JANE BISHOP		27
THAT TO GOD SHALL COME:		511	JANE AND JACK		8
MEN COME, MEN GO,		512	JANE ON GOD		5
ALL NIGHT'S FATHOMLESS WISDOM COME,		519	HER DREAM		2
COME, LET ME SING INTO YOUR EAR:		524	DANCING DAYS		1
"COME OUT OF CHARITY,		526	AM OF IRELAND		4
COME DANCE WITH ME IN IRELAND."		526	AM OF IRELAND		5
"COME OUT OF CHARITY,		527	AM OF IRELAND		17
"COME OUT OF CHARITY,		527	AM OF IRELAND		30
AND, THOUGH LOVE'S BITTER-SWEET HAD ALL COME BACK,		537	HER VISION		27
COME, FIX UPON ME THAT ACCUSING EYE.		542	PARN FUNERAL 1		24
COME MARCH, SINGING THIS SONG,		544	TO SAME TUNE 1	V	REF
THOSE THAT COME AFTER SHALL MOCK AT O'DONNELL,		546	TO SAME TUNE 2		23
THOSE THAT COME AFTER SHALL MOCK O'DONNELL,		546	TO SAME TUNE 2	V	23
WHAT MADE THEM MOUNT AND WHAT MADE THEM COME,		549	SEVERED HEAD	V	8
THOSE AMOROUS CRIES THAT OUT OF QUIET COME		557	RIBH ECSTASY		7
WHENCE HAD THEY COME?		560	WHENCE COME		T
WHAT MASTER MADE THE LASH. WHENCE HAD THEY COME,		560	WHENCE COME		9
RAVENING, RAGING, AND UPROOTING THAT HE MAY COME		563	MERU		6
WHAT MATTER? OUT OF CAVERN COME A VOICE		564	GYRES	V	15
AEROPLANE AND ZEPPELIN WILL COME OUT,		565	LAPIS LAZULI		6
IF STRANGE MEN COME FROM THE HOUSE		568	SWEET DANCER		8
STRANGE NIGHT HAS COME:		574	MAIDS 1ST SONG		6
COME TOM AND DICK, COME ALL THE TROOP		582	ROGER CASEMENT		17
COME TOM AND DICK, COME ALL THE TROOP		582	ROGER CASEMENT		17
COME FROM THE FORGER AND HIS DESK,		582	ROGER CASEMENT		19
COME SPEAK YOUR BIT IN PUBLIC		582	ROGER CASEMENT		21
COME ALFRED NOYES AND ALL THE TROUP		582	ROGER CASEMENT	V	17
I COME TO HEAR IT STRIKE."		585	ORAHILLY		26
COME GATHER ROUND ME, PARNELLITES		586	PARNELLITES		T
COME GATHER ROUND ME, PARNELLITES,		586	PARNELLITES		1
COME FILL UP ALL THOSE GLASSES		586	PARNELLITES		7

154

COME (CONTINUED)

	PAGE	TITLE		LINE
HURRAH FOR REVOLUTION AND CANNON COME AGAIN!	590	GREAT DAY		3
COME SWISH AROUND, MY PRETTY PUNK,	591	DRUNK SOBRIETY		1
SO COME IN RAGS OR COME IN SILK, IN CLOAK OR COUNTRY SHAWL,	593	PILGRIM		22
SO COME IN RAGS OR COME IN SILK, IN CLOAK OR COUNTRY SHAWL,	593	PILGRIM		22
AND COME WITH LEARNED LOVERS OR WITH WHAT MEN YOU MAY,	593	PILGRIM		23
SO COME IN RAG OR COME IN SILK, IN CLOAK OR COUNTRY SHAWL,	593	PILGRIM	V	22
SO COME IN RAG OR COME IN SILK, IN CLOAK OR COUNTRY SHAWL,	593	PILGRIM	V	22
AND COME WITH LEARNED LOVERS OR WITH WHAT MAN YOU MAY,	593	PILGRIM	V	23
THOSE WORDS COME TRUE IN THE END	597	COLONEL MARTIN	V	69
THAT COME INTO MY SOUL AND ESCAPE	599	SPIRIT MEDIUM		3
AND NOW THAT END HAS COME I HAVE NOT WEPT:	603	GALLERY REVIS		38
MUST COME FROM CONTACT WITH THE SOIL, FROM THAT	603	GALLERY REVIS		43
BUT NOW THAT END HAS COME I HAVE NOT WEPT:	603	GALLERY REVIS	V	38
THIS BOOK OR THAT, COME TO THIS HALLOWED PLACE	604	GALLERY REVIS		51
ALL MANNIONS COME FROM MANANNAN,	606	SONGS BURDEN 1		10
COME GATHER ROUND ME, PLAYERS ALL!	608	SONGS BURDEN 3		1
COME PRAISE NINETEEN-SIXTEEN,	608	SONGS BURDEN 3		2
AND YET WHO KNOWS WHAT'S YET TO COME?	608	SONGS BURDEN 3		23
COME PRAISE NINETEEN SIXTEEN,	608	SONGS BURDEN 3	V	2
OF GOD OR WOMAN, THE TIME WERE COME TO DIE."	609	IN TARAS HALLS		15
THOSE THAT COME AFTER SHALL MOCK AT O'DONNELL,	614	MARCH SONGS 1		23
WHENCE DID ALL THAT FURY COME?	619	STICK INCENSE		1
THOSE BANNERS COME NOT IN.	635	BLACK TOWER		6
BUT WINDS COME UP FROM THE SHORE!	635	BLACK TOWER		8
THOSE BANNERS COME TO BRIBE OR THREATEN,	635	BLACK TOWER		11
BUT WINDS COME UP FROM THE SHORE!	636	BLACK TOWER	V	REF
MAIDEN, COME FORTH! THE WOODS KEEP WATCH FOR THEE!	645	ISLE STAT I 1		1
COME FORTH! THE MORN IS FAIR! AS FROM THE PYRE	645	ISLE STAT I 1		8
COME FORTH, COME FORTH, MY MUSIC FLOWS FOR THEE,	645	ISLE STAT I 1		20
COME FORTH, COME FORTH, MY MUSIC FLOWS FOR THEE,	645	ISLE STAT I 1		20
SHEPHERD, TO MAR THE MORNING HAST THOU COME?	646	ISLE STAT I 1		30
COME THOU, COME, AND TO THIS STRING—	646	ISLE STAT I 1		37
COME THOU, COME, AND TO THIS STRING—	646	ISLE STAT I 1		37
COME FORTH, FOR IN A THOUSAND BOWERS	647	ISLE STAT I 1		64
AND WHEREFORE HAVE WE COME? A SONG TO HEAR.	652	ISLE STAT I 2		27
COME FOLLOW! COME FOLLOW!	654	ISLE STAT I 2		79
COME FOLLOW! COME FOLLOW!	654	ISLE STAT I 2		79
OF HILL TWO SHEPHERDS COME. FAREWELL! I'LL DON	659	ISLE STAT II 1		28
HERE WHERE THE ROUND WAVES COME, HERE LET THEM BUILD,	663	ISLE STAT II 2		19
AND ONCE A-YEAR LET THE ARCADIANS COME,	663	ISLE STAT II 2		29
ONCE MORE THOSE SHEPHERDS COME. MAYHAP SOME MIRTH	664	ISLE STAT II 2		49
THENCE HAVE I COME WINGING!	672	ISLE STAT II 3		170
NOW HERE I COME WINGING!	672	ISLE STAT II 3	V	170
A ROVER I, WHO COME FROM WHERE MEN'S EARS	678	ISLE STAT II 3		293
ALONG THE VELVET VALE I SAW HIM COME—	690	MOSADA 1		10
THE DARK STILL MAN, HAS COME AND SAYS 'TIS SIN.	692	MOSADA 1		47
THE PHANTOMS COME; HA! HA! THEY COME, THEY COME!	694	MOSADA 1		97
THE PHANTOMS COME; HA! HA! THEY COME, THEY COME!	694	MOSADA 1		97
THE PHANTOMS COME; HA! HA! THEY COME, THEY COME!	694	MOSADA 1		97
THE PHANTOMS COME; THEY COME, THEY COME, THEY COME!	694	MOSADA 1	V	97
THE PHANTOMS COME; THEY COME, THEY COME, THEY COME!	694	MOSADA 1	V	97
THE PHANTOMS COME; THEY COME, THEY COME, THEY COME!	694	MOSADA 1	V	97
THE PHANTOMS COME; THEY COME, THEY COME, THEY COME!	694	MOSADA 1	V	97
NAMES AFTER ME. LADY—I COME. FORGIVE,	695	MOSADA 1		117
YOU'RE FULL OF WORDINESS. COME, HEAR MY SONG.	696	MOSADA 2		8
AND NOT COME THENCE! FOR HERE IN THIS SMALL RING—	699	MOSADA 3		22
HE FADES AMONG THE MISTS! HOW FAST THEY COME,	703	MOSADA 3		117
COME AWAY WHILE THE MOON'S IN THE WOODLAND,	707	FAIRY PEDANT		9
COME AWAY WHILE THE MOON'S IN THE WOODLAND,	708	FAIRY PEDANT		37
HAYNAU, THINE HOUR HAS COME, THY FOLLOWERS FAR	715	FERENCZ RENYI		117
AND DEATH, OH MY FAIR ONE, WILL NEVER COME NEAR	717	LOVE SONG		8
AND THE WINDS COME DOWN AND BLOW THEM WITH THE VAPOURS FAR AWAY.	719	PHANTOM SHIP		28
COME HERE. BE SEATED NOW! I'D BUY OF YOU.	720	WITCH VIVIEN		17
COME, FATHER. LADY, I NOR REST NOR SIT.	720	WITCH VIVIEN		18
WITH LOADED DICE. ANOTHER CHANCE! COME, FATHER!	721	WITCH VIVIEN		45
COME TO THE CHESS, FOR YOUNG GIRLS' WITS ARE BETTER	721	WITCH VIVIEN		46
AND THEN THE GREAT ONES COME, AND LAST THE KING.	722	WITCH VIVIEN		54
COME YOU, COLTSFOOT, MOUSETAIL, COME!	727	LOVERS QUARREL		33
COME YOU, COLTSFOOT, MOUSETAIL, COME!	727	LOVERS QUARREL		33
COME I KNOW WHERE, FAR AWAY,	727	LOVERS QUARREL		34
COME AND TEASE THEM TILL THE DAY.	727	LOVERS QUARREL		36
COME, BESIDE A SANDY LAKE,	727	LOVERS QUARREL		41
AND COME KNEELING ON ONE KNEE,	727	LOVERS QUARREL		53
COME AND DREAM OF KINGS AND KINGDOMS,	737	IN FIRELIGHT		1
TILL THEY COME WHERE YOUR SAD, SAD HEART IS,	739	WHERE BOOKS GO		5
FOR A KNIGHT, COME FROM NORMANDY	740	EARL PAUL		7
BEST PLEASES YOU. ARMED MEN HAVE COME UPON US.	752	SHADOW WATER A		131
ARMED MEN HAVE COME UPON US. O! I AM SLAIN!	753	SHADOW WATER A		133
BECAUSE I HAD HOPED TO COME, AS DREAMS FORETOLD,	757	SHADOW WATER A		197
I HAVE COME HITHER BECAUSE I HOPED TO COME	757	SHADOW WATER A	V	197
I HAVE COME HITHER BECAUSE I HOPED TO COME	757	SHADOW WATER A	V	197
FORGAEL CAN DIE TO-MORROW. COME TO THE ALE.	759	SHADOW WATER A		246
COME TO THE ALE! FOR HE CAN DIE TO-MORROW.	760	SHADOW WATER A		247
AND I SHALL LAUGH WITH JOY. COME HITHER, AIBRIC,	760	SHADOW WATER A		249
THAT MY TRUE-LOVE WOULD COME IN A SHIP OF PEARL	763	SHADOW WATER A		315
BUT FAITHFUL LOVERS. WHITHER HAVE YOU COME,	763	SHADOW WATER A	V	309
THAT MY TRUE LOVE WOULD COME IN A SHIP OF PEARL	763	SHADOW WATER A	V	315
AND WE GO HOME. COME, AIBRIC! END YOUR TALE	766	SHADOW WATER A		374
WHEN THE DARK HOUNDS WERE LOOSED. COME TO THE ALE.	766	SHADOW WATER A		379

155

	PAGE	TITLE		LINE
COME (CONTINUED)				
FOR LOVE IS KIND AND HAPPY. O COME WITH ME! • • • • • •	767	SHADOW WATER A		396
COME RIDE AND RIDE TO THE GARDEN, • • • • • • • •	773	COME RIDE		1
COME RIDE AND RIDE WITH A WILL! • • • • • • • • •	773	COME RIDE		2
COME RIDE AND RIDE TO THE GARDEN, • • • • • • • •	774	COME RIDE		5
COME RIDE LIKE THE MARCH WIND! • • • • • • • • •	774	COME RIDE		6
COME RIDE AND RIDE TO THE GARDEN, • • • • • • • •	774	COME RIDE		13
COME RIDE AND RIDE TO THE GARDEN, • • • • • • • •	774	COME RIDE		18
FOR THE THINGS COME AFTER DEATH? • • • • • • • • •	777	SONG DEIRDRE 2		12
TILL CERTAIN SECOND THOUGHTS HAVE COME • • • • • • •	791	REPRISALS		12
COMEDIAN'S				
UNDER THE GREAT COMEDIAN'S TOMB THE CROWD. • • • • • •	541	PARN FUNERAL 1		1
COMEDIES				
FOR THE ITALIAN COMEDIES? • • • • • • • • • • • •	287	TO WEALTHY MAN		13
COMEDY				
IN THE CASUAL COMEDY! • • • • • • • • • • • • •	393	EASTER 1916		37
COMELIER				
IS COMELIER THAN CANDLES AT MOTHER MARY'S FEET. • • • •	147	UNAPPEAS HOST		12
IS COMELIER THAN CANDLES BEFORE MAURYA'S FEET. • • • • •	147	UNAPPEAS HOST	V	12
GROWS COMELIER. ELEVEN PASS, AND THEN • • • • • • •	374	PHASES OF MOON		44
COMELY				
AND MORE COMELY THAN MAN CAN MAKE THEM • • • • • • •	49	OISIN 3		32
MORE COMELY THAN MAN MAY MAKE THEM, INLAID WITH SILVER AND GOLD,	49	OISIN 3	V	29
"WHERE ALL ARE COMELY AND GOOD? • • • • • • • • •	167	BLESSED		22
"AND THOUGH I'D MARRY WITH A COMELY LASS, • • • • • •	300	BEGGAR CRIED		9
SHE NEED NOT BE TOO COMELY--LET IT PASS," • • • • • •	300	BEGGAR CRIED		10
AND ALIGHT AT THE COMELY TREES AND THE LAWN, • • • • •	330	BONE OF A HARE		4
COMER SEE NEW-COMER				
FLOATING FROM YON BARRED WINDOW. NEW COMER, • • • • •	700	MOSADA 3	V	43
COMES				
"HOW COMES IT, PRINCESS, THAT YOUR MIND • • • • • • •	6	OISIN 1	V	59A
FOR NEITHER DEATH NOR CHANGE COMES NEAR US, • • • • • •	21	OISIN 1		316
THE DARKNESS COMES. A CLOUD HANGS OVERHEAD-- • • • • •	43	OISIN 2	V	208A
YOUR QUESTIONER, OISIN, IS WORTHY, HE COMES FROM THE FENIAN LANDS."	51	OISIN 3		64
COMING OUT OF THE SEA AS THE DAWN COMES, A CHAUNT OF LOVE ON MY LIPS,	58	OISIN 3		158
COMES A SEA-KING MASTERFUL • • • • • • • • • • •	82	MAD KING GOLL	V	15
FOR HE COMES, THE HUMAN CHILD, • • • • • • • • •	88	STOLEN CHILD		50
"BUT IF YOUR MASTER COMES HOME TRIUMPHING • • • • • •	106	CUCHULAIN SEA		12
OR COMES IN LAUGHTER FROM THE SEA'S SAD LIPS, • • • • •	114	ROSE OF BATTLE		19
AND I SHALL HAVE SOME PEACE THERE, FOR PEACE COMES DROPPING SLOW.	117	ISLE INNISFREE		5
A WEARINESS COMES FROM THOSE DREAMERS, • • • • • • •	122	WHITE BIRDS		5
AND A WEARINESS COMES FROM THOSE DREAMERS • • • • • •	122	WHITE BIRDS	V	5
"O BLESSEDNESS COMES IN THE NIGHT AND THE DAY • • • • •	168	BLESSED		33
WHEN THE WIND COMES BLOWING ACROSS THE HILLY LAND! • • •	207	HANRAHANS SONG	V	7
I ONLY KNOW THAT ALL WE KNOW COMES FROM YOU, • • • • •	218	WOODS OF COOLE		28
THE COZENING FORTUNE-TELLER THAT COMES WHISPERING, • • •	228	SHADOW WATER B		123
COMES CRYING, "I HAVE RUN UPON THE SWORD. • • • • • •	234	SHADOW WATER B		261
AH, BUT PEACE THAT COMES AT LENGTH, • • • • • • • •	259	PEACE		10
I SWEAR BEFORE THE DAWN COMES ROUND AGAIN • • • • • •	260	FASC DIFFICULT		12
WINE COMES IN AT THE MOUTH • • • • • • • • • • •	261	DRINKING SONG		1
AND LOVE COMES IN AT THE EYE! • • • • • • • • • •	261	DRINKING SONG		2
THAT COMES OF THE BEST KNIT TO THE BEST? ALTHOUGH • • •	264	HOUSE SHAKEN		7
NOW NOTHING BUT COMES READIER TO THE HAND • • • • • •	267	ALL TEMPT ME		4
FOR ONLY RUBBISH COMES MY WAY. • • • • • • • • •	295	THREE BEGGARS		4
WHO COMES AT NEED, ALTHOUGH NOT NOW AS ONCE • • • • •	320	REED WHISPERER		2
LIONEL JOHNSON COMES THE FIRST TO MIND, • • • • • • •	324	ROBERT GREGORY		17
AND THAT ENQUIRING MAN JOHN SYNGE COMES NEXT, • • • • •	324	ROBERT GREGORY		25
THE STARS FADE OUT WHERE THE MOON COMES, • • • • • •	344	DAWN		8
PLEASURE THAT COMES WITH SLEEP, • • • • • • • • •	345	ON WOMAN		22
AND THEREUPON THERE COMES THAT SCREAM • • • • • • •	389	IMAGE PAST		5
THE HORSE THAT COMES FROM THE ROAD, • • • • • • • •	393	EASTER 1916		45
COMES CRACKING JOKES OF CIVIL WAR • • • • • • • •	423	ROAD AT DOOR		3
WHO COMES INTO THIS COUNTRY, AND HAS COME • • • • • •	447	COLONUS PRAISE		17
FOR THAT OLD MADGE COMES DOWN THE LANE, • • • • • •	456	FRIENDS YOUTH		5
THEY UNDERSTOOD THAT WISDOM COMES OF BEGGARY. • • • • •	487	SEVEN SAGES		26
MAY REND WHAT COMES IN REACH. • • • • • • • • • •	488	CRAZED MOON		18
COMES TO DESTROY • • • • • • • • • • • • • •	500	VACILLATION		4
AND ALL ALONE COMES RIDING THERE • • • • • • • • •	550	SEVERED HEAD		18
AND PRAYER COMES ROUND AGAIN-- • • • • • • • • •	553	PRAYER OLD AGE		10
WHAT MATTER? OUT OF CAVERN COMES A VOICE, • • • • • •	564	GYRES		15
WHAT HOUR OF TERROR COMES TO TEST THE SOUL, • • • • •	622	HOUND VOICE		11
BUT WIND COMES UP FROM THE SHORE! • • • • • • • •	636	BLACK TOWER		18
BUT WIND COMES UP FROM THE SHORE! • • • • • • • •	636	BLACK TOWER		28
HER LOVE! TO HER WHO WEARS THAT BLOOM COMES TRUTH. • • •	653	ISLE STAT I 2		46
THAT CALLS. O EVIL STARRED! IT COMES ALONG • • • • •	653	ISLE STAT I 2		49
THE HOUR OF INCANTATION COMES A-TIPTOE, • • • • • •	691	MOSADA 1		37
AND COLA, SEEING, KNOWS THE SIGN AND COMES. • • • • •	691	MOSADA 1		38
YONDER HE COMES! BRIGHT-EYED, AND HOLLOW-CHEEKED • • • •	697	MOSADA 2		35
IS IT YOUR MESSAGE, STARS, THAT WHEN DEATH COMES • • • •	701	MOSADA 3		60
FOR NIGHT COMES FAST. LOOK DOWN ON ME, MY LOVE, • • •	703	MOSADA 3		103
THE FAIRY DOCTOR COMES OUR WAY • • • • • • • • •	716	FAIRY DOCTOR		1
ROUND SHE COMES IN STAYS BEFORE THEM! • • • • • • •	719	PHANTOM SHIP		17
THEY ARE STILL WAITING! AND NOW THE LAGGARD COMES, • • •	754	SHADOW WATER A		150
WHOSE SHADOW IS THE SLEEP THAT COMES WITH LOVE, • • • •	754	SHADOW WATER A		162
THEY ARE STILL WAITING! AND A LAGGARD COMES, • • • • •	754	SHADOW WATER A	V	150
BUT NOW I WILL KILL HER. ALL COMES TO AN END. • • • •	755	SHADOW WATER A		176
THAT COMES WITH LOVE, COMES MURMURING OF AN HOUR • • • •	765	SHADOW WATER A		365

156

COMES   (CONTINUED)
    THAT COMES WITH LOVE, COMES MURMURING OF AN HOUR . . . .   765 SHADOW WATER A   365
    FOR THE FLOWER COMES WITH THE FRUIT THERE . . . .   774 COME RIDE   3
    TILL THE SIDE OF HATE COMES UP. . . . .   776 AGAINST WITCH   35
COMEST
    YES, ALL IS VERY WELL. WHENCE COMEST THOU? . . . . .   682 SEEKER   14
COMETH
    OR DEATH THAT COMETH WITH THE NEXT LIFE-KEY? . . . .   724 KANVA ON SELF   18
COMFORT
    FROM THEIR PALE THRONES AND COMFORT HIM, BUT THEY . . .   68 SAD SHEPHERD   6
    THEIR HEARING, AND SOME COMFORT GIVE, BUT THEY . . . .   68 SAD SHEPHERD   V   6
    THE MAN HAS FOUND NO COMFORT IN THE GRAVE. . . . . .   128 DREAM OF FAERY   48
    I HAVE NOT A CRUMB OF COMFORT, NOT A GRAIN. . . . . .   200 FOLLY COMFORT   7
    BUT HEART THERE IS NO COMFORT, NOT A GRAIN. . . . . .   200 FOLLY COMFORT V   7
    THE COMFORT THAT YOU MADE? ALTHOUGH MY WITS HAVE GONE . .   391 UNDER SATURN   5
    AND SO FORGET THE COMFORT THAT NO WORDS CAN TELL . . .   391 UNDER SATURN   V   4
    AND FIND A COMFORT IN IT? MAY THIS TOWER . . . . . .   423 MY DESCENDANTS V   13
    HAS BUT ONE COMFORT LEFT. ALL TRIUMPH WOULD . . . . .   429 NINETEEN 19   39
    BUT IS THERE ANY COMFORT TO BE FOUND? . . . .   429 NINETEEN 19   41
    AND OTHER COMFORT WERE A BITTER WOUND. . . . .   429 NINETEEN 19   V   41
    IN THE COMFORT OF A BED. . . . .   596 COLONEL MARTIN   44
COMFORTABLE
    IN COMFORTABLE SLEEP. ALL LIVING SLEPT . . . .   180 QUEEN MAEVE   15
    "AND GET A COMFORTABLE WIFE AND HOUSE . . . .   299 BEGGAR CRIED   5
    AND EVERY COMFORTABLE THING, ...   307 HOUR DAWN   111
    THERE IS A COMFORTABLE KIND OF OLD SCARECROW. . . . .   444 SCHOOL CHILDR   32
    TO THE COMFORTABLE DOOR OF HIS HOUSE. . . . .   780 WELL AND TREE   6
COMFORTED
    THE FOLLY OF BEING COMFORTED . . . .   199 FOLLY COMFORT   T
    YOU'D KNOW THE FOLLY OF BEING COMFORTED. . . . . . .   200 FOLLY COMFORT   14
    WHERE MAN IS COMFORTED. . . . .   534 CONSOLATION   6
    CUCHULAIN COMFORTED . . . .   634 CUCHULAIN COMF   T
COMFORTERS
    AND THEY THY COMFORTERS WILL BE, ...   66 HAPPY SHEPHERD   38
COMFORTING
    AND MY OWN WHISPERING WORDS BE COMFORTING, ...   68 SAD SHEPHERD   23
    AND MINE OWN WHISPERING WORDS BE COMFORTING, ...   68 SAD SHEPHERD   V   23
COMING
    COMING OUT OF THE SEA AS THE DAWN COMES, A CHAUNT OF LOVE   58 OISIN 3   158
        ON MY LIPS,
    COMING FORTH FROM THE SEA LIKE THE MORNING . . . . .   58 OISIN 3   V   158
    TO IRELAND IN THE COMING TIMES . . . .   137 TO IRELAND   T
    APOLOGIA ADDRESSED TO IRELAND IN THE COMING DAYS . . .   137 TO IRELAND   V   T
    THAT YOU, IN THE DIM COMING TIMES, ...   139 TO IRELAND   46
    AT THE COMING OF NIGHT-TIDE, ...   144 HOST OF AIR   6
    AT THE COMING OF NIGHT TIDE, ...   144 HOST OF AIR   V   6
    THE PEOPLE OF COMING DAYS WILL KNOW . . . .   146 FISH   3
    THE LOVER SPEAKS TO THE HEARERS OF HIS SONGS IN COMING DAYS 173 SPEAKS HEARERS   T
    HANRAHAN SPEAKS TO THE LOVERS OF HIS SONGS IN COMING DAYS 173 SPEAKS HEARERS V   T
    A LOVER SPEAKS TO THE HEARERS OF HIS SONGS IN COMING DAYS 173 SPEAKS HEARERS V   T
    AS FOR THIS WOMAN, I THINK SHE IS COMING WITH ME. . . .   248 SHADOW WATER B   545
    THAT COMING TIME CAN SAY, ...   255 WOMAN HOMER   12
    THE COMING OF WISDOM WITH TIME . . . .   261 COMING WISDOM   T
    YOUR COMING BROUGHT. THOUGH I ACKNOWLEDGE I HAVE GONE . . 391 UNDER SATURN   V   5
    COMING WITH VIVID FACES . . . .   391 EASTER 1916   2
    WAS COMING INTO HIS FORCE. . . . .   392 EASTER 1916   27
    THE SECOND COMING . . . .   401 SECOND COMING   T
    SURELY THE SECOND COMING IS AT HAND. . . . .   402 SECOND COMING   10
    THE SECOND COMING. HARDLY ARE THOSE WORDS OUT . . . .   402 SECOND COMING   11
    . . . FULLNESS AND OF THE COMING EMPTINESS . . . . .   425 PHANTOM HATRED   T
    ROMANTIC FISH SWAM IN NETS COMING TO THE HAND. . . . .   485 THREE MOVEMENT   2
    WHAT SORT OF MAN IS COMING . . . .   572 LADYS 2ND SONG   1
    THAT WE IN COMING DAYS MAY BE . . . .   640 BEN BULBEN   82
COMMAND
    I SHALL BE CARRIED IN THE GUST, COMMAND, ...   281 TWO KINGS   101
    IS NOT AT MY COMMAND. . . . .   588 OLD WICKED MAN   22
    BY HIS COMMAND THESE WORDS ARE CUT. . . . .   640 BEN BULBEN   91
COMMANDED
    I HAVE COMMANDED MEN IN DREAMS. BELOVED, ...   766 SHADOW WATER A   381
COMMANDING
    COMMANDING OFFICER THAT TORE . . . .   627 STATES HOLIDAY   16
COMMENCED
    ERE YONDER PALM COMMENCED HIS THOUSAND YEARS? . . . .   724 KANVA ON SELF   14
COMMEND
    FISH, FLESH, OR FOWL, COMMEND ALL SUMMER LONG . . . .   407 SAIL BYZANTIUM   5
    BUT WANDERING ARABS. I COMMEND THE ARABS . . . . .   462 HARUN RASHID   V   22
    THAT I COMMEND TO ALL THE CHRONICLERS . . . . . .   463 HARUN RASHID   46
    DID AN OLDER MIND COMMEND-- . . . .   494 AT ALGECIRAS   10
COMMENDED
    A PEASANT GIRL COMMENDED BY A SONG, ...   410 TOWER   34
COMMENTARY
    WITH SOME APPROPRIATE COMMENTARY ON EACH. . . . . .   328 ROBERT GREGORY   93
    I ADD IN COMMENTARY, ...   496 MOHINI CHATTER   16
COMMINGLING
    THEY WERE COMMINGLING LICE AND BLOOD. . . . . . .   297 THREE BEGGARS   56
COMMIT
    A CHARTER TO COMMIT THE CRIME ONCE MORE. . . . . .   478 SELF AND SOUL   32
COMMITTED
    BUT WHERE THE CRIME'S COMMITTED . . . .   534 CONSOLATION   11
COMMON
    LEST I NO MORE HEAR COMMON THINGS THAT CRAVE. . . . .   101 ROSE UPON ROOD   15

157

		PAGE	TITLE	LINE

COMMON   (CONTINUED)

TO IDLE LIFE AWAY, A COMMON HERD." . . . . 107 CUCHULAIN SEA 21'
TILL MAEVE CALLED OUT, "THESE ARE BUT COMMON MEN. . . . . 186 QUEEN MAEVE 122
NO COMMON LOVE IS TO OUR MIND, ... 190 BAILE AILLINN 34
THE HOURLY KINDNESS, THE DAY'S COMMON SPEECH, ... 258 KING NO KING 14
BECAUSE WE HAVE MADE OUR ART OF COMMON THINGS, ... 265 ABBEY THEATRE 5
AND ALL THINGS AT ONE COMMON LEVEL LIE. . . . . . . 265 THESE CLOUDS 6
THE COMMON GOOD OF LIFE, ... 317 NIGHT COME 5
AS COMMON BEAUTIES MAY, ... 336 YOUNG BEAUTY 9
UPON THE LIPS OF COMMON MEN . . . . 361 ALF POLLEXFEN 33
OR RANK, RAISED FROM A COMMON . . . . 365 HER RACE 7
WHO HAS AWAKENED FROM THE COMMON DREAM . . . . . . 369 EGO DOMINUS 50
AND THERE'S BUT COMMON GREENNESS AFTER THAT. . . . . . 422 MY DESCENDANTS 8
THAT PITCHES COMMON THINGS ABOUT.   THERE STOOD . . . . 428 NINETEEN 19 4
WITH A COMMON WRONG OR RIGHT. . . . . 476 EVA GORE-BOOTH 23
COMMON BIRD OR PETAL . . . . 498 BYZANTIUM 23
EVERY COMMON WOMAN KNOWS, ... 499 MOTHER OF GOD 7
SENSE THAN A COMMON MAN? . . . . 507 STREAM AND SUN 10
AND MUST THE COMMON ROUND OF DAY RESUME. . . . . . 557 RIBH ECSTASY 8
LIMBS A LOVE IN COMMON . . . . 573 LADYS 2ND SONG 17
NO COMMON INTELLIGIBLE SOUND . . . . 578 CRAZED GIRL 13
NOTHING THAT COMMON WOMEN PONDER ON . . . . 579 DOR WELLESLEY 12
(AN IMAGE OUT OF SPENSER AND THE COMMON TONGUE). . . . . 603 GALLERY REVIS 40
ALL THINGS DOWN TO THAT COMMON TEST AGAIN, ... 603 GALLERY REVIS V 46
AND I BEAT UP THE COMMON SORT . . . . 605 SONGS BURDEN 1 3
THE COMMON BREEDS THE COMMON, ... 605 SONGS BURDEN 1 5
THE COMMON BREEDS THE COMMON, ... 605 SONGS BURDEN 1 5
THOUGH ALL WAS DONE IN COMMON AS BEFORE: . . . . . . 635 CUCHULAIN COMF 24
AND COMMON MEN THAT SLEEP. . . . . 736 IN CHURCH 8

COMMONEST

AIMED AT THE COMMONEST EAR, ... 347 FISHERMAN 20

COMMONNESS

TARA UPROOTED, AND NEW COMMONNESS . . . . 198 SEVEN WOODS 6
THE COMMONNESS OF THOUGHT AND IMAGES . . . . . . 384 VISION ROBART 61

COMMONPLACE

WITH 'MINISHED BEAUTY, MULTIPLIED COMMONPLACE, ... 472 ALL SOUL NIGHT 45
DIMINISHED BEAUTY, MULTIPLIED COMMONPLACE: . . . . . . 472 ALL SOUL NIGHT V 45

COMMUNE

HE HOLDS DEEP COMMUNE WITH HIS HEART: . . . . . . 99 FOXHUNTER 43

COMMUNIST

AND TO HIMSELF CRIED, "COMMUNIST!" . . . . 725 LEGEND 15

COMPANIES

AND OF THE WAYWARD TWILIGHT COMPANIES . . . . . . 136 TO SOME I TALK 6
AND OF THE WANDERING TWILIGHT COMPANIES . . . . . . 136 TO SOME I TALK V 6

COMPANION

DID YOUR COMPANION WANDER AWAY . . . . 6 OISIN 1 52
IS THY COMPANION GONE FROM THEE?" . . . . 6 OISIN 1 V 52
HAVE YOU MADE GREATNESS YOUR COMPANION, ... 265 THESE CLOUDS 9
TO PLEASE A COMPANION . . . . 392 EASTER 1916 11
SEMELE'S LAD A GAY COMPANION. . . . . 446 COLONUS PRAISE 8
ACQUAINTANCE: COMPANION: . . . . 504 RESULT THOUGHT 1

COMPANIONABLE

COMPANIONABLE STREAMS OR CLIMB THE AIR: . . . . . . 323 SWANS AT COOLE 21
AND THAT A SLIGHT COMPANIONABLE GHOST, ... 472 ALL SOUL NIGHT 35

COMPANIONED

SO MANY YEARS COMPANIONED BY A HOUND, ... 621 HOUND VOICE 4

COMPANIONING

COMPANIONING THE RIVER'S PILGRIM TORCH. . . . . . . 703 MOSADA 3 112

COMPANIONS

COMPANIONS LONG ACCURST AND DEAD, ... 11 OISIN 1 130
NOR THY COMPANIONS. LET THEM REST. . . . . . . 11 OISIN 1 V 130
REMEMBERING ITS LONG-OARED COMPANIONS, ... 55 OISIN 3 118
AYE, HORSEMEN FOR COMPANIONS, ... 266 GALWAY RACES 7
COMPANIONS OF THE CHESHIRE CHEESE, ... 270 GREY ROCK 2
BUT INWARDLY, SURMISE COMPANIONS . . . . 320 REED WHISPERER 4
OR MERE COMPANIONS OF MY YOUTH, ... 324 ROBERT GREGORY 7
THEY WERE MY CLOSE COMPANIONS MANY A YEAR, ... 325 ROBERT GREGORY 41
CHOOSE YOUR COMPANIONS FROM THE BEST: . . . . . . 335 YOUNG BEAUTY 4
AND CERTAIN LOST COMPANIONS OF MY OWN. . . . . . . 342 SHEP GOATHERD 78
MY COMPANIONS, TWO AND TWO, ... 705 DAWN-SONG 7

COMPANIONSHIP

COMPANIONSHIP IN THOSE MYSTERIOUS THINGS . . . . . . 465 HARUN RASHID 92

COMPANIONSHIPS

UNLANGUID AS THE BIRDS, IN PROUD COMPANIONSHIPS: . . . . 30 OISIN 2 V 14C

COMPANY

"THE RED BRANCH CAMP IN A GREAT COMPANY . . . . . 108 CUCHULAIN SEA 33
"THE RED BRANCH GATHER A GREAT COMPANY . . . . . . 108 CUCHULAIN SEA V 33
IN EVERY COMPANY . . . . 131 OLD PENSIONER 4
TRUE BROTHER OF A COMPANY . . . . 137 TO IRELAND 2
TRUE BROTHER OF THAT COMPANY . . . . 137 TO IRELAND V 2
HAS TIRED OF HIS OWN COMPANY? . . . . 303 HOUR DAWN 35
GROWN TIRED OF HIS OWN COMPANY? . . . . 303 HOUR DAWN V 37
WITH EVERY SORT OF COMPANY, ... 335 YOUNG BEAUTY 2
MY TRADE ALLOWS: CHOSEN MY COMPANY, ... 352 PEOPLE 20
AND ALL HIS SACRED COMPANY . . . . 386 ROBARTES DANCE 27
BUT BECKONED TO SWEET COMPANY, ... 400 DEMON BEAST 18
A COMPANY OF FRIENDS, A CONSCIENCE SET AT EASE, ... 427 PHANTOM HATRED 37
A SCENE WELL SET AND EXCELLENT COMPANY. . . . . . 489 COOLE PARK 29 16
THAT THE SWORDSMEN AND THE LADIES CAN STILL KEEP COMPANY, . 581 CURSE CROMWELL 20
IN SOME GOOD COMPANY, ... 605 YOU CONTENT 18
THAT PALE, LONG-VISAGED COMPANY . . . . 637 BEN BULBEN 7

```
                                             PAGE    TITLE        LINE
COMPANY   (CONTINUED)
     THAT PALE, LONG VISAGED COMPANY  . . . . . . .  637 BEN BULBEN    V    7
     BY THOSE WAN STARS THAT SIT IN COMPANY . . . . . . .  691 MOSADA 1        26
     I'M NOT OF THAT PALE COMPANY WHOSE FEET . . . . . .  699 MOSADA 3        20
COMPARES
     COMPARES THE SOLITARY SOUL TO A SWAN; . . . . . . .  430 NINETEEN 19      60
COMPASS
     THAT SEEMED TO WHIRL UPON A COMPASS POINT, . . . . .  489 COOLE PARK 29  V  21
COMPASS-POINT
     THAT SEEMED TO WHIRL UPON A COMPASS-POINT, . . . . .  489 COOLE PARK 29     21
COMPEL
     BUT ALL THAT'S RAVING.  WHO IS THERE CAN COMPEL . . . .  237 SHADOW WATER B  333
COMPELLING
     COMPELLING IT TO STUDY  . . . . . . . . . . .  416 TOWER           182
COMPELS
     WHOSE BLADE COMPELS, AND WAIT TILL THEY HAVE FOUND . . .  108 CUCHULAIN SEA    37
     WHOSE BLADE COMPELS, AND BID THEM SEND YOU ONE . . . .  108 CUCHULAIN SEA  V  37
COMPENSATION
     A COMPENSATION FOR THE PANG OF HIS BIRTH, . . . . . .  444 SCHOOL CHILDR    39
COMPETE
     FOR HOW CAN YOU COMPETE, . . . . . . . . . . .  291 TO A FRIEND       4
COMPLACENCY
     NOTHING BUT GRIP OF CLAW, AND THE EYE'S COMPLACENCY, . .  427 PHANTOM HATRED   31
COMPLACENT
     THE MERRY LAMBS AND THE COMPLACENT KINE, . . . . . .  75 ANASHU VIJAYA    86
     THE MERRY LAMBS AND ALL THE KINE COMPLACENT, . . . .  75 ANASHU VIJAYA  V  86
     THE GIDDY BEE'S COMPLACENT CROON, . . . . . . . .  736 SUMMER EVENING    5
COMPLAIN
     I'VE NOTHING TO COMPLAIN OF BUT HEARTBURN, . . . . .  227 SHADOW WATER B V 116A
     STAND AT MY DOOR, AND I COMPLAIN . . . . . . . .  424 ROAD AT DOOR      8
COMPLAINED
     COMPLAINED OF THE PEOPLE." ALL I COULD REPLY . . . . .  352 PEOPLE           29
COMPLAINING
     BUT THERE'S NO GOOD COMPLAINING, FOR MONEY'S RANT IS ON.  580 CURSE CROMWELL   10
COMPLETE
     THOSE MASTERFUL IMAGES BECAUSE COMPLETE . . . . . .  630 CIRCUS ANIMALS   33
     WHEN BEAUTY IS COMPLETE  . . . . . . . . . . .  786 YOUR HEART       29
COMPLETED
     FOR PERFECTED, COMPLETED, AND IMMOVABLE . . . . . .  375 PHASES OF MOON V  81
COMPLETENESS
     COMPLETENESS OF THEIR PASSIONS WON; . . . . . . .  637 BEN BULBEN        9
COMPLETES
     HE COMPLETES HIS PARTIAL MIND, . . . . . . . . .  638 BEN BULBEN       30
COMPLEXION
     COMPLEXION AND FORM PROVE SUPERHUMAN, . . . . . .  637 BEN BULBEN        6
COMPLEXITIES
     ALL MERE COMPLEXITIES, . . . . . . . . . . .  497 BYZANTIUM         7
     AND ALL COMPLEXITIES OF MIRE OR BLOOD. . . . . . .  498 BYZANTIUM        24
     AND ALL COMPLEXITIES OF FURY LEAVE, . . . . . . .  498 BYZANTIUM        29
COMPLEXITY
     BREAK BITTER FURIES OF COMPLEXITY, . . . . . . .  498 BYZANTIUM        37
COMPLIMENT
     AND WHEN I PASS A COMPLIMENT . . . . . . . . .  453 DEATH OF HARE     3
COMPOSE
     COULD BUT COMPOSE MAN'S IMAGE AND HIS CRY. . . . . .  120 SORROW OF LOVE   12
COMPOSITE
     THAT BLEST SOULS ARE NOT COMPOSITE, . . . . . . .  387 ROBARTES DANCE   44
     OR MAYBE SUBSTANCE CAN BE COMPOSITE, . . . . . . .  619 BRONZE HEAD      12
     OR MAY BE SUBSTANCE CAN BE COMPOSITE, . . . . . .  619 BRONZE HEAD    V  12
COMPOUNDED
     SO MUCH COMPOUNDED OF HIGH COURTESY . . . . . . .  205 ADAMS CURSE      24
COMPREHENSION
     WHAT HAS NO COMPREHENSION IN'T, . . . . . . . .  452 HUMAN DIGNITY     3
     WHAT HAS NOT COMPREHENSION IN'T: . . . . . . . .  452 HUMAN DIGNITY  V  3
COMRADE
     AND HE, OF HIS HIGH COMRADE SORROW DREAMING, . . . . .  67 SAD SHEPHERD      2
COMRADES
     SINCE, TAVERN COMRADES, YOU HAVE DIED, . . . . . .  273 GREY ROCK        49
     FOR THOSE NEW COMRADES THEY HAVE FOUND, . . . . . .  395 SIXTEEN DEAD     15
     HIS CHOSEN COMRADES THOUGHT AT SCHOOL . . . . . .  576 WHAT THEN         1
     SLEW THEE, POOR SIBYL! COMRADES THOU AND I: . . . .  675 ISLE STAT II 3  235
CON
     IN MEMORY OF EVA GORE-BOOTH AND CON MARKIEWICZ . . . .  475 EVA GORE-BOOTH    T
CONAN
     CAOILTE, AND CONAN, AND FINN WERE THERE, . . . . . .  3 OISIN 1         13
     CAOILTE, CONAN, AND FINN CAME NEAR, . . . . . . .  10 OISIN 1        111
     FIN, CONAN, OSCAR, MANY MORE, THE TIDE . . . . . .  44 OISIN 2      V 228A
     WHAT PLACE HAVE CAOILTE AND CONAN, AND BRAN, SCEOLAN,    61 OISIN 3        195
          LOMAIR?
     I WILL GO TO CAOILTE, AND CONAN, AND BRAN, SCEOLAN, LOMAIR,  63 OISIN 3        223
     TO FIN, CAOLTE, AND CONAN, AND BRAN, SGEOLAN, LOMAIR. . .  63 OISIN 3      V  224
CONAN'S
     AH, SWEET TO ME NOW WERE EVEN BALD CONAN'S SLANDEROUS   55 OISIN 3        116
          TONGUE!
CONCEIVE
     CONCEIVE A THING SO SAD AND SOFT, A GENTLE THING LIKE ME?  77 INDIAN ON GOD    16
CONCEIVED
     WHEN WORLD-TRANSFORMING CHARLEMAGNE WAS CONCEIVED? . . .  560 WHENCE COME      12
CONCEIVES
     CONCEIVES A CHANGELESS WORK OF ART. . . . . . . .  421 MY TABLE         14
```

159

		PAGE	TITLE	LINE

CONCENTRATION
    BUT SEEMS A CONCENTRATION OF THE SKY; • • • • • • •   490 COOLE BALLYLEE   18
CONCERNING
    TWO POEMS CONCERNING PEASANT VISIONARIES A CRADLE SONG   146 UNAPPEAS HOST V   T
    TWO POEMS BY O'SULLIVAN THE RED CONCERNING MARY LAVELL.   157 POET BELOVED V   T
CONCH
    WHEN GONG AND CONCH DECLARE THE HOUR TO BLESS • • • • • 611 STATUES   23
CONCHUBAR
    YOUNG SUBTLE CONCHUBAR SAT CLOSE BY ME • • • • • 102 FERGUS DRUID   10
    AND CONCHUBAR, THE RED BRANCH KING OF KINGS, • • • • 109 CUCHULAIN SEA   45
    THEN CONCHUBAR SENT THAT SWEET-THROATED MAID, • • • • 110 CUCHULAIN SEA   72
    THEN CONCHUBAR, THE SUBTLEST OF ALL MEN, • • • • • 110 CUCHULAIN SEA   75
CONCHUBAR'S
    • • MADE CONCHUBAR'S SWORD-BLADE OF OLD. • • • • •   52 OISIN 3   80
CONCOBAR
    THEN CONCOBAR SENT THAT SWEET THROATED MAID • • • • 110 CUCHULAIN SEA V 72
CONDEMNED
    THE OLDER IS CONDEMNED TO DEATH, • • • • • • • • 475 EVA GORE-BOOTH   7
CONDUCT
    BETTER CONDUCT MYSELF OR HAVE MORE • • • • • • • 507 STREAM AND SUN   9
    CONDUCT AND WORK GROW COARSE, AND COARSE THE SOUL, • • • 564 GYRES   17
CONES
    THOSE CONES AND CUBES AND GYRES, THOSE MIDNIGHT THINGS, 469 HARUN RASHID V 184
CONEYS
    FROM HUMAN THOUGHT, AS HARES AND MICE AND CONEYS • • • 218 WOODS OF COOLE   31
CONFER
    SO GREAT A GLORY DID THE SONG CONFER. • • • • • • 410 TOWER   40
CONFESS
    I WILL CONFESS IT ALL. WHAT DO I CARE, • • • • • 245 SHADOW WATER B   485
CONFESSION
    A FIRST CONFESSION • • • • • • • • • • • • • 532 FIRST CONFESS   T
    A LAST CONFESSION • • • • • • • • • • • • • 538 LAST CONFESS   T
    SHE MADE A FULL CONFESSION. • • • • • • • • • 571 THREE BUSHES   66
CONFIDENCE
    HER CONFIDENCE IN MINE, OR EVEN LOSE • • • • • • 469 HARUN RASHID   176
    CAN WITH A FITTING CONFIDENCE REPLY. • • • • • • 494 AT ALGECIRAS   18
    HIS CONFIDENCE • • • • • • • • • • • • 517 HIS CONFIDENCE   T
CONFLAGRATION
    SHOULD THE CONFLAGRATION CLIMB, • • • • • • • 476 EVA GORE-BOOTH   28
    WHEN THE CONFLAGRATION OF THEIR PASSION SINKS, • • • 556 RIBH PATRICK   8
CONFRONTING
    CONFRONTING MURDEROUS MEN • • • • • • • • 476 DEATH   8
CONFUSEDLY
    A MAN CONFUSEDLY IN A HALF DREAM • • • • • • 351 HER PRAISE   8
    SHE MOVED HER LIMBS CONFUSEDLY AS THOUGH • • • 466 HARUN RASHID V 125A
CONFUSION
    THERE CANNOT BE, CONFUSION OF OUR SOUND FORGOT, • • • 291 PAUDEEN   7
    CONFUSION OF THE DEATH-BED OVER, IS IT SENT • • • 316 COLD HEAVEN   10
    IN THE CONFUSION OF ITS NIGHT-DARK FOLDS, • • • • 470 HARUN RASHID   192
    CONFUSION OF THE BED, • • • • • • • • • • 599 SPIRIT MEDIUM   4
    CONFUSION FELL UPON OUR THOUGHT. • • • • • • 639 BEN BULBEN   67
CONGEALED
    LONG YEARS AGO, AND UNTO STONE CONGEALED. • • • • • 656 ISLE STAT I 3   28
CONHOR
    • • MADE ARMOUR FOR CONHOR OF OLD. • • • • • •   52 OISIN 3   V 80
CONJUNCTIONS
    CONJUNCTIONS • • • • • • • • • • • • • • 562 CONJUNCTIONS   T
CONNACHT
    WELL KNOWN FOR HORSEMANSHIP TO CONNACHT MEN • • • • 325 ROBERT GREGORY V 34
CONNEMARA
    ON MUNSTER GRASS AND CONNEMARA SKIES. • • • • • 130 BOOK STORIES   24
    ON MUNSTER GRASS, OR CONNEMARA SKIES. • • • • • 130 BOOK STORIES V 24
    IN GREY CONNEMARA CLOTHES • • • • • • • • 347 FISHERMAN   4
    AND GREY CONNEMARA CLOTH, • • • • • • • • 348 FISHERMAN   30
    THEIR CONNEMARA CLOTH WORN OUT OF SHAPE; • • • • 372 PHASES OF MOON   4
CONNOLLY
    AND CONNOLLY AND PEARSE • • • • • • • • 394 EASTER 1916   76
    SAID PEARSE TO CONNOLLY, • • • • • • • • 396 ROSE TREE   2
    JAMES CONNOLLY REPLIED, • • • • • • • • 396 ROSE TREE   8
    SAID PEARSE TO CONNOLLY, • • • • • • • • 396 ROSE TREE   14
    HE TOLD PEARSE AND CONNOLLY • • • • • • • 585 ORAHILLY   12
    THEN ON PEARSE AND CONNOLLY • • • • • • • 585 ORAHILLY   23
    THE PLAYER CONNOLLY, • • • • • • • • • 608 SONGS BURDEN 3   11
CONOR
    • • MADE ARMOUR FOR CONOR THE OLD. • • • • • •   52 OISIN 3   V 80
CONQUER
    TO CONQUER AMONG THE COUNTRIES OF THE NORTH. • • • • 757 SHADOW WATER A   200
CONQUERED
    AND DROWNED THE TREASURES OF NINE CONQUERED NATIONS, • • 235 SHADOW WATER B   287
CONQUEROR
    ROSE; SOME CONQUEROR DREW REIN. • • • • • • • 502 VACILLATION   64
CONQUERORS
    CONQUERORS • • • • • • • • • • • • • 499 VACILLATION V T
CONQUEST
    PASSION OR CONQUEST, WANDER WHERE THEY WILL, • • • • 323 SWANS AT COOLE   23
CONSCIENCE
    A STERNER CONSCIENCE AND A FRIENDLIER HOME, • • • • 321 REED WHISPERER   8
    OR ANYTHING CALLED CONSCIENCE ONCE; • • • • • • 413 TOWER   118
    A COMPANY OF FRIENDS, A CONSCIENCE SET AT EASE, • • • 427 PHANTOM HATRED   37
    THAT NONE MIGHT KNOW THAT HE WAS CONSCIENCE STRUCK, • • 462 HARUN RASHID V 38
    CONSCIENCE • • • • • • • • • • • • • • 499 VACILLATION V T

	PAGE	TITLE	LINE

CONSCIENCE   (CONTINUED)
    MY CONSCIENCE OR MY VANITY APPALLED. . . . . 501 VACILLATION 56
    NOR SATISFIED CONSCIENCE, BUT THAT GREAT FAMILY . . . . 579 DOR WELLESLEY 14
CONSCIENCE-STRUCK
    THAT NONE MIGHT KNOW THAT HE WAS CONSCIENCE-STRUCK-- . . 462 HARUN RASHID 38
CONSECRATED
    THE CONSECRATED BLADE UPON MY KNEES . . . . 477 SELF AND SOUL 9
    THE CONSECRATED SWORD UPON MY KNEES . . . . 477 SELF AND SOUL V 9
CONSIDER
    CONSIDER BEAUTY A SUFFICIENT END, ... 403 FOR DAUGHTER 21
    CONSIDER MOST TO MAGNIFY, OR TO BLESS, ... 418 ANCEST HOUSES 39
CONSIDERATION
    CONSIDERATION, GENEROSITY, ... 244 SHADOW WATER B 456
CONSIDERED
    YET, NOW I HAVE CONSIDERED IT, I FIND . . . . 411 TOWER 50
    CAME TO THE LEAST CONSIDERED OF HIS COURTIERS; . . . . 462 HARUN RASHID 42
CONSIDERING
    CONSIDERING THAT, ALL HATRED DRIVEN HENCE, ... 405 FOR DAUGHTER 65
    BRING UP OUT OF THAT DEEP CONSIDERING MIND . . . . . . 413 TOWER 106
    CONSIDERING WHAT WILD INFANCY . . . . 440 WISDOM 19
CONSIDERS
    RIBH CONSIDERS CHRISTIAN LOVE INSUFFICIENT . . . . . . 558 RIBH CHRISTIAN T
CONSOLATION
    THE CONSOLATION . . . . 255 WORDS V T
    CONSOLATION . . . . 534 CONSOLATION T
CONSPIRACY
    FOR SOME CONSPIRACY, ... 131 OLD PENSIONER 8
CONSPIRING
    CONSPIRING AMONG THE IGNORANT. . . . . 475 EVA GORE-BOOTH 9
CONSTELLATIONS
    . . . WHEN A PART OF THE CONSTELLATIONS OF HEAVEN . . . 177 PAST GREATNESS T
    HER BEAUTY AS THE CONSTELLATIONS POUR . . . . 279 TWO KINGS V 62B
CONSTITUTE
    THAT CONSTITUTE THE WILD, ... 601 THOSE IMAGES 10
CONSTRAINED
    CONSTRAINED, ARRAIGNED, BAFFLED, BENT AND UNBENT . . . . 382 VISION ROBART 9
CONSTRUCTED
    GREAT WORKS CONSTRUCTED THERE IN NATURE'S SPITE . . . . 488 COOLE PARK 29 5
CONSUME
    SOME BURN DAMP FAGGOTS, OTHERS MAY CONSUME . . . . . . 327 ROBERT GREGORY 81
    CONSUME MY HEART AWAY; SICK WITH DESIRE . . . . 408 SAIL BYZANTIUM 21
    AND HALF AND HALF CONSUME WHAT THEY RENEW, ... 500 VACILLATION 15
CONSUMED
    EVERYTHING THAT IS NOT GOD CONSUMED WITH INTELLECTUAL FIRE. 481 BLOOD, AND MOON 30
    WHERE FOR ITS MOMENT BOTH SEEM LOST, CONSUMED. . . . . 555 RIBH AT TOMB 16
CONSUMES
    THE PAINTER'S BRUSH CONSUMES HIS DREAMS; . . . . . . 438 SONGS PLAY 2 12
CONSUMING
    IN TRUTH'S CONSUMING ECSTASY, ... 139 TO IRELAND 42
    CONSUMING ITS RAG AND BONE, ... 575 ACRE OF GRASS 11
CONSUMMATION
    A MEASURELESS CONSUMMATION THAT HE DREAMED. . . . . . 324 ROBERT GREGORY 24
CONTACT
    MUST COME FROM CONTACT WITH THE SOIL, FROM THAT . . . . 603 GALLERY REVIS 43
    CONTACT EVERYTHING ANTAEUS-LIKE GREW STRONG. . . . . . 603 GALLERY REVIS 44
    CONTACT ALL THINGS ANTAEUS-LIKE GREW STRONG; . . . . . 603 GALLERY REVIS V 44
CONTAGION
    TILL SUDDENLY IN GRIEF'S CONTAGION CAUGHT, ... 537 HER VISION 22
    BRED OUT OF THE CONTAGION OF THE THRONG, ... 542 PARN FUNERAL 1 27
CONTEMPLATING
    TWO CONTEMPLATING PASSIONS CHOSE ONE THEME . . . . . . 466 HARUN RASHID 117
CONTEMPLATION
    CAUGHT UP IN CONTEMPLATION, THE MIND'S EYE . . . . . . 375 PHASES OF MOON 79
    IN CONTEMPLATION HAD THOSE THREE SO WROUGHT . . . . . 384 VISION ROBART 45
    WHERE SLIPPERED CONTEMPLATION FINDS HIS EASE . . . . . 418 ANCEST HOUSES 30
CONTEMPLATIONS
    MY CONTEMPLATIONS ARE OF TIME . . . . 131 OLD PENSIONER 11
CONTEMPLATIVE
    HAVING GROWN SLUGGISH AND CONTEMPLATIVE. . . . . . . 325 ROBERT GREGORY 40
CONTEND
    CITY AND CITY MAY CONTEND, ... 540 FROM ANTIGONE 12
CONTENT
    BENEATH HAD PACED CONTENT; WE HELD OUR WAY . . . . . . 36 OISIN 2 103
    SHOUTED AND HAILED HIM. STILL HE HUNG CONTENT. . . . . 36 OISIN 2 V 107
    THAT SEA-GOD'S NAME, WHO IN A DEEP CONTENT . . . . . . 38 OISIN 2 129
    SEA-GOD, THAT ONCE, TO GIVE HIS SLAVES CONTENT, ... 38 OISIN 2 V 129
    THAT SEA GOD'S NAME, WHO IN A DEEP CONTENT . . . . . . 38 OISIN 2 V 129
    IS THE ISLAND OF CONTENT?" "NONE KNOW," SHE SAID; . . . 46 OISIN 2 249
    WHO SIGH WITH MINGLED SORROW AND CONTENT, ... 136 TO SOME I TALK 7
    TO FILL YOUR HEART WITH CONTENT." . . . . 167 BLESSED 20
    HOW COULD WE BE SO SOON CONTENT; . . . . 193 BAILE AILLINN 95
    AND BEEN CONTENT TO LIVE. . . . . 256 WORDS 16
    THE HABITUAL CONTENT OF EACH WITH EACH . . . . 258 KING NO KING 15
    SPONTANEOUS JOY AND NATURAL CONTENT . . . . 260 FASC DIFFICULT 3
    SO THAT THE WANDERING FOOT'S CONTENT. . . . . 276 GREY ROCK 131
    LET THESE CONTENT YOU AND BE GONE AGAIN; . . . . . . 292 TO A SHADE 8
    I'LL SAY AND MAYBE DREAM I HAVE DRAWN CONTENT, ... 333 LIVING BEAUTY V 1
    MY DISCONTENTED HEART TO DRAW CONTENT . . . . 334 LIVING BEAUTY 3
    CAN BE CONTENT WITH ARGUMENT AND DEAL . . . . 409 TOWER 14
    I AM CONTENT WITH THAT, ... 430 NINETEEN 19 V 61
    AND THAT SHE DREAMED AWAKE CONTENT TO TOUCH . . . . . 466 HARUN RASHID V 125C

161

		PAGE	TITLE		LINE

CONTENT   (CONTINUED)
```
    I AM CONTENT TO LIVE IT ALL AGAIN . . . . . . . .      479 SELF AND SOUL          57
    I AM CONTENT TO FOLLOW TO ITS SOURCE . . . . . . .      479 SELF AND SOUL          65
    CONTENT TO TRACE THAT MISERY TO ITS SOURCE, . . . .     479 SELF AND SOUL    V     65
    CONTENT OR JOY; A LAST INHERITOR . . . . . . . . .      491 COOLE BALLYLEE         30
    HAD I NOT FOUND CONTENT AMONG THE SHOWS . . . . . .     499 MOTHER OF GOD           6
    IF YOU ARE WORTH MY HOPE! NEITHER CONTENT . . . . .     579 DOR WELLESLEY          13
    ALL NEIGHBOURLY CONTENT AND EASY TALK ARE GONE, . .     580 CURSE CROMWELL          9
    I AM CONTENT TO STAND AND SING . . . . . . . . .       582 ROGER CASEMENT   V     21
    OR STAY CONTENT ON THE LOW, . . . . . . . . . .        589 OLD WICKED MAN         49
    ARE YOU CONTENT? . . . . . . . . . . . . . .           604 YOU CONTENT             T
    I CANNOT, BUT I AM NOT CONTENT. . . . . . . . . .      604 YOU CONTENT             8
    BUT I AM NOT CONTENT. . . . . . . . . . . . .          605 YOU CONTENT            24
    FORGAEL, SEEK OUT CONTENT, WHERE OTHER MEN . . . .      750 SHADOW WATER A         71
    AND CAN NEVER BE CONTENT . . . . . . . . . . .         777 SONG DEIRDRE 2          2
```
CONTENTED
```
    THAT I MAY CONTENTED PASS . . . . . . . . . .          97 FOXHUNTER              11
    I AM CONTENTED, FOR I KNOW THAT QUIET . . . . . .      198 SEVEN WOODS            10
    SINCE HE WHO HAD BEEN CONTENTED LONG, . . . . . .      361 ALF POLLEXFEN          28
    CONTENTED THAT A TROUBLED MIRROR SHOW IT, . . . . .     430 NINETEEN 19      V     62
    AND I GROW HALF CONTENTED TO BE BLIND! . . . . . .     473 ALL SOUL NIGHT         70
```
CONTEST
```
    THE SHEPHERDS' CONTEST OF SONG . . . . . . . . .       646 ISLE STAT I 1    V      T
```
CONTINUAL
```
    ARE LOVE, AND A CONTINUAL FAREWELL." . . . . . . .      81 EPHEMERA               24
    CONTINUAL MUSIC TILL THE MORNING BREAK, . . . . . .     137 TO SOME I TALK   V     14
```
CONTINUALLY
```
    AND NIAMH SANG CONTINUALLY . . . . . . . . . .         11 OISIN 1               134
    FOR FAIRY SONGS CONTINUALLY . . . . . . . . . .        11 OISIN 1          V    134
    FOR NEAVE SANG CONTINUALLY . . . . . . . . . .         11 OISIN 1          V    134
```
CONTRADICT
```
    HE CANNOT CONTRADICT ME.  IS THAT TRUE? . . . . . .     249 SHADOW WATER B V     563
```
CONTRAPUNTAL
```
    A CONTRAPUNTAL SERPENT HISS, . . . . . . . . .         573 LADYS 3RD SONG         10
```
CONTROL
```
    FOR THAT'S A PASSION IN MY OWN CONTROL, . . . . . .     558 RIBH CHRISTIAN          4
```
CONVENT
```
    I HAD BETTER FIND A CONVENT AND TURN NUN! . . . . .     448 HERO GIRL FOOL         11
```
CONVENTIONAL
```
    NO MARBLE, NO CONVENTIONAL PHRASE! . . . . . . .       640 BEN BULBEN             89
```
CONVERGE
```
    THERE ALL THE GYRES CONVERGE IN ONE, . . . . . . .     557 THERE                   3
```
CONVERSE
```
    THEN FEAST, MAKING CONVERSE OF WARS, . . . . . .       62 OISIN 3               212
    THEN FEAST, MAKING CONVERSE OF EIRE, OF WARS, . . . .   62 OISIN 3          V    212
    THAT CONVERSE BONE TO BONE? . . . . . . . . . .        395 SIXTEEN DEAD           18
```
CONVICTED
```
    THEY CONVICTED US OF GUILT! . . . . . . . . . .        476 EVA GORE-BOOTH         31
    CONVICTED COWARDS ALL, BY KINDRED SLAIN . . . . . .     634 CUCHULAIN COMF         21
```
CONVICTION
```
    THE BEST LACK ALL CONVICTION, WHILE THE WORST . . . .   402 SECOND COMING           7
    THE BEST LACK CONVICTION, WHILE THE WORST . . . . .     402 SECOND COMING    V      7
```
CONVINCE
```
    I TOOK NO TROUBLE TO CONVINCE, . . . . . . . . .       624 APPARITIONS             3
```
COOING
```
    ABOUT A SUN-FLUSHED DOVE-COT, COOING, CLING . . . .     710 FERENCZ RENYI          20
```
COOK
```
    COOK BARACH, THE TRAITOR! AND WARWARD, . . . . . .      53 OISIN 3                90
    THE OLD COOK ENRAGED, . . . . . . . . . . . .         349 HAWK                    5
    THAT IT CAN TAKE WHAT FORM COOK NATURE FANCIES . . .    377 PHASES OF MOON        115
    THAT IT CAN TAKE WHAT FORM COOK NATURE FANCY . . . .    377 PHASES OF MOON V      115
    I COOK AND CHANGE MY PLATE, . . . . . . . . . .        607 SONGS BURDEN 2          6
    THE TOWER'S OLD COOK THAT MUST CLIMB AND CLAMBER . .    636 BLACK TOWER            21
```
COOKING
```
    COOKING CHESTNUTS ON THE BARS-- . . . . . . . .       737 IN FIRELIGHT            2
    COOKING CHESTNUTS ON THE BARS. . . . . . . . .         737 IN FIRELIGHT           12
```
COOL
```
    LAY 'NEATH US; OF ITS HOLLOW COOL . . . . . . . .       17 OISIN 1          V    241
    AND CHAPLET THEIR CALM BROWS WITH LEAFAGE COOL! . . .   127 DREAM OF FAERY   V     32
    WIND AND UNWIND THEIR DANCES WHEN THE LIGHT GROWS COOL  203 WITHER BOUGHS          13
    WIND AND UNWIND DANCING WHEN THE LIGHT GROWS COOL . .   203 WITHER BOUGHS    V     13
    FOR THERE CAME AN AIR-BREATH COOL . . . . . . . .      667 ISLE STAT II 3         27
```
COOLE
```
    I WALKED AMONG THE SEVEN WOODS OF COOLE! . . . . .      217 WOODS OF COOLE          1
    THE WILD SWANS AT COOLE . . . . . . . . . . .         322 SWANS AT COOLE          T
    COOLE PARK, [NINETEEN-TWENTY-NINE] . . . . . . .       488 COOLE PARK 29           T
    COOLE PARK . . . . . . . . . . . . . . . .            488 COOLE PARK 29    V      T
    COOLE PARK AND BALLYLEE, [NINETEEN-THIRTY-ONE] . . .    490 COOLE BALLYLEE          T
    COOLE PARK AND BALLYLEE [NINETEEN-THIRTY-TWO] . . .     490 COOLE BALLYLEE   V      T
    COOLE AND BALLYLEE, [NINETEEN-THIRTY-ONE] . . . .      490 COOLE BALLYLEE   V      T
    IN COOLE DEMESNE, AND THERE TO FINISH UP . . . . .     490 COOLE BALLYLEE          6
```
COPIED
```
    HER DOMINO, HER PANNIERED SKIRT COPIED FROM LONGHI!    363 DOLLS FACES            7
    AND COPIED OUT WHAT I COULD READ . . . . . . . .      584 GHOST ROG CASE         33
```
COPIES
```
    FOR THINGS BELOW ARE COPIES, THE GREAT SMARAGDINE TABLET  556 RIBH PATRICK         6
        SAID.
    YET ALL MUST COPY COPIES, ALL INCREASE THEIR KIND! . .  556 RIBH PATRICK          7
```
COPSE
```
    AND IN A COPSE OF BEECHES THERE I STOOD, . . . . .     490 COOLE BALLYLEE         11
```

	PAGE	TITLE	LINE

COPULATE
    COPULATE IN THE FOAM. . . . . 612 NEWS ORACLE   36
COPY
    AND COPY THEIR PROUD STEADY GAZE. . . . . 273 GREY ROCK   64
    YET ALL MUST COPY COPIES, ALL INCREASE THEIR KIND! . . . 556 RIBH PATRICK   7
    BUT COPY SOME ONE ACTION. . . . . 600 SPIRIT MEDIUM   13
COQUETRY
    NOTHING BUT COQUETRY. . . . . 532 FIRST CONFESS   6
CORAL
    DROPPING AT EVE IN CORAL BAYS . . . . 78 INDIAN TO LOVE V   19
CORBETS
    SANDYMOUNT CORBETS, THAT NOTABLE MAN . . . . 604 YOU CONTENT   13
CORD
    UNLOOSE THE CORD, AND THEY WILL WRAP YOU ROUND. . . . 104 FERGUS DRUID   30
CORDELIA
    THAT'S OPHELIA, THAT CORDELIA! . . . . 565 LAPIS LAZULI   11
CORDS
    OVER THE LITTLE SILVER CORDS, ... 146 FISH   6
    FORGIVE ME! IT WAS ALLAH'S WILL. THE CORDS. . . . . 695 MOSADA 1   109
    FORGIVE ME! IT WAS ALLAH'S WILL. NOW CORDS. . . . . 695 MOSADA 1 V 109
    I HAVE CUT THE CORDS THAT HELD THIS GALLEY TO OURS. . . 768 SHADOW WATER A V 421
CORE
    I HEAR IT IN THE DEEP HEART'S CORE. . . . . 117 ISLE INNISFREE   12
    SHALL LIGHT UPON A PLACE IN THE WORLD'S CORE, ... 231 SHADOW WATER B   212
    YOU ARE NOT THE WORLD'S CORE. O NO, NO, NO! . . . . 234 SHADOW WATER B   277
    YOU ARE NOT ITS CORE. MY TEETH ARE IN THE WORLD, . . 235 SHADOW WATER B   279
CORMAC'S
    IN CORMAC'S RUINED HOUSE. . . . . 384 VISION ROBART   68
CORMORANTS
    THE CORMORANTS SHIVER ON THEIR ROCKS! . . . . 84 MAD KING GOLL   42
CORN
    AND WAKES THE SLUGGARD SEEDS OF CORN, ... 18 OISIN 1   263
    CRIES TO THE SLUGGARD SEEDS OF CORN, ... 18 OISIN 1 V 263
    SEND PEACE ON ALL THE LANDS AND FLICKERING CORN.-- . . 71 ANASHU VIJAYA   1
    THAT MEN THRESHED CORN AT MIDNIGHT BY A TRESS, . . . 170 SECRET ROSE   26
    AND THE WAVES BOWED BEFORE IT LIKE MOWN CORN, ... 657 ISLE STAT I 3   56
    AND THRICE THE CORN AROUND THE SICKLES FLAMED, . . . 690 MOSADA 1   3
CORNER
    CHIMNEY CORNER, GARDEN WALK, ... 499 MOTHER OF GOD   8
    WHEN SEA-WIND SWEPT THE CORNER, STANDS! . . . . . . 566 LAPIS LAZULI   32
CORNERS   SEE STREET-CORNERS
    AND LISTEN AT THE CORNERS HAS NOT COME! . . . . . . 293 TO A SHADE   22
    THE CORNERS OF THIS EYE . . . . 518 HIS CONFIDENCE   3
    AND THERE AT ALL STREET CORNERS . . . . 596 COLONEL MARTIN V 55
CORNFIELD
    QUITE SOON THE CORNFIELD, WHERE THE POPPIES GROW, . . 699 MOSADA 3   7
    ALONG THE CORNFIELD, WHERE THE POPPIES GROW, ... 699 MOSADA 3 V 7
CORPSE
    I HELD A DRIPPING CORPSE, WITH LIVID CHOP . . . . . 40 OISIN 2 V 178
    AND I BUT HELD A CORPSE, WITH LIVID CHOP . . . . . 40 OISIN 2 V 178
    AND SUNKEN SHAPE, A NINE DAYS' CORPSE SEA-DASHED-- . . 40 OISIN 2 V 179
CORRIDOR
    THROUGH MANY A SACRED CORRIDOR . . . . 156 FORGOT BEAUTY   12
COSGRAVE
    HAD COSGRAVE EATEN PARNELL'S HEART, THE LAND'S . . . 543 PARN FUNERAL 2   5
COSIMO
    AND WHEN THEY DROVE OUT COSIMO, ... 288 TO WEALTHY MAN   20
COSSETING
    THEY'D SOONER LEAVE THEIR COSSETING . . . . 455 HIS MEMORIES   9
COST
    HE THAT MADE THIS KNOWS ALL THE COST, ... 202 NEVER GIVE ALL   13
    PARDON, AND YOU THAT DID NOT WEIGH THE COST, ... 269 PARDON FATHERS V 9
COT   SEE DOVE-COT
    WERE WE NOT BORN IN THE PEASANT'S COT . . . . 615 MARCH SONGS 2   13
    WE WERE NOT BORN IN THE PEASANT'S COT . . . . 615 MARCH SONGS 2 V 13
COTTAGE
    GOD GRANT A BLESSING ON THIS TOWER AND COTTAGE . . . 371 ON GOING HOUSE   1
    THAT SHADES THE ROAD, OR SETTING UP A COTTAGE . . . 372 ON GOING HOUSE   14
COTTAGES
    FROM SOMEWHERE IN THE NEIGHBOURING COTTAGES. . . . . 411 TOWER   59
    STORM-BEATEN COTTAGES-- . . . . 480 BLOOD AND MOON   7
    STORMBEATEN COTTAGES. . . . . 480 BLOOD AND MOON V 7
COUCH
    COULD SLEEP ON A COUCH OF RUSHES, AND ALL INWROUGHT AND 49 OISIN 3   31
        INLAID,
    COULD SLEEP ON A COUCH OF RUSHES--ROUND AND ABOUT THEM 49 OISIN 3 V 32
        LAID.
COUGH
    ALL SHUFFLE THERE; ALL COUGH IN INK! . . . . 337 SCHOLARS   7
    THEY'LL COUGH IN THE INK TO THE WORLD'S END! . . . . 337 SCHOLARS V 7
COUGHING
    NOT COUGHING, MY HEAD ON MY KNEES, ... 58 OISIN 3   159
    AH ME! TO BE SHAKEN WITH COUGHING AND BROKEN WITH OLD AGE 63 OISIN 3   217
        AND PAIN!
    WITHOUT LAUGHTER, A COUGHING, ALONE WITH REMEMBRANCE AND 63 OISIN 3 V 218
        FEAR!
    SHE KNOWS THAT IT WAS BUT THE CART-HORSE COUGHING . . 230 SHADOW WATER B   176
COUNCIL
    AND SPOKEN IN THE COUNCIL, AND HEARD TALES . . . . . 748 SHADOW WATER A   28
COUNCILS
    YOU KNOW THE COUNCILS OF THE EVER-LIVING, ... 244 SHADOW WATER B V 450

	PAGE	TITLE		LINE

COUNSEL
    HAD COME AS IN THE OLD TIMES TO COUNSEL HER, • • • • •   181 QUEEN MAEVE   42
    HAD COME, AS IN OLD TIMES, TO COUNSEL HER, • • • • •   181 QUEEN MAEVE V   42
    ABOUT MY THRESHOLD TO COUNSEL AND TO HELP?" • • • • •   183 QUEEN MAEVE   82
    ABOUT MY DOOR TO COUNSEL AND TO HELP." • • • • •   183 QUEEN MAEVE V -82
    OUR GIVER OF GOOD COUNSEL AND GOOD LUCK." • • • • •   185 QUEEN MAEVE   102
COUNSELLED
    WHAT OTHER COULD SO WELL HAVE COUNSELLED US • • • • •   327 ROBERT GREGORY   73
COUNSELS
    YOU KNOW THE COUNSELS OF THE EVER-LIVING, • • • • •   244 SHADOW WATER B   450
COUNT
    I COUNT MY GOOD AND BAD, • • • • • • • • •   316 FRIENDS   22
    SINCE I FIRST MADE MY COUNT! • • • • • • •   322 SWANS AT COOLE   8
    COUNT ALL THE PRAISES DUE • • • • • • • •   345 ON WOMAN   15
    AND I, THAT COUNT MYSELF MOST PROSPEROUS, • • • •   423 MY DESCENDANTS   19
    I COUNT THOSE FEATHERED BALLS OF SOOT • • • • •   424 ROAD AT DOOR   11
    COUNT EVERY SIN OF ACTION OR OF THOUGHT! • • • • •   479 SELF AND SOUL V 66
COUNTED
    NOR MAY I LESS BE COUNTED ONE • • • • • • •   138 TO IRELAND   17
    HE HAD COUNTED, WHERE LONG YEARS AGO • • • • • •   302 HOUR DAWN   7
    HE COUNTED, WHERE LONG YEARS AGO • • • • • • •   302 HOUR DAWN V   7
    THEY SAY HE COUNTED GRASS, • • • • • • • •   345 ON WOMAN   14
    THAT ALL MY CHILDHOOD COUNTED DEAR! • • • • •   398 BREAK OF DAY   7
    THE GARDEN PATHS, NOR COUNTED UP THE ROOMS, • • • •   466 HARUN RASHID   119
COUNTENANCE
    LACKING THE COUNTENANCE OF OUR FRIENDS. AND YET • • •   368 EGO DOMINUS   17
    KEVIN O'HIGGINS' COUNTENANCE THAT WEARS • • • •   601 GALLERY REVIS   5
COUNTENANCES
    THEN THE STARS GROW OUT OF HEAVEN WITH THEIR COUNTENANCES   719 PHANTOM SHIP   30
        FAIR.
COUNTER
    FROM COUNTER OR DESK AMONG GREY • • • • • •   392 EASTER 1916   3
COUNTER-TRUTH
    AND THEN A COUNTER-TRUTH FILLED OUT ITS PLAY, • • • •   629 CIRCUS ANIMALS   17
COUNTESS
    THE COUNTESS CATHLEEN IN PARADISE • • • • • •   124 CATHLEEN PARA   T
    ALEEL, HIS COUNTESS! HANRAHAN • • • • • • •   550 SEVERED HEAD   15
    THE COUNTESS CATHLEEN WAS THE NAME I GAVE IT! • • •   629 CIRCUS ANIMALS   18
COUNTING-HOUSE
    AND THE FOOL HEART OF THE COUNTING-HOUSE FEARS ALL • •   181 QUEEN MAEVE   21
COUNTLESS
    ON OUR DARK PATHWAY, TILL A COUNTLESS FLIGHT • • • •   31 OISIN 2   34
COUNTRIES
    FLED TO FAR COUNTRIES, OR SHELTERED THEMSELVES • • •   546 TO SAME TUNE 2   4
    FLED TO FAR COUNTRIES, OR SHELTERED THEMSELVES • • •   613 MARCH SONGS 1   4
    TO CONQUER AMONG THE COUNTRIES OF THE NORTH. • • • •   757 SHADOW WATER A   200
COUNTRY
    AND FROM WHAT COUNTRY DO YOU RIDE?" • • • • • •   5 OISIN 1   45
    NIAMH, AND MY COUNTRY FAR • , • • • • • •   5 OISIN 1   48
    THY NAME, THY KIN, AND THY COUNTRY," • • • • •   5 OISIN 1 V 44
    AND INTO WHAT COUNTRY DO YOU RIDE?" • • • • • •   5 OISIN 1 V 45
    HIS SUDDEN VENGEANCE WERE A COUNTRY TALE, • • • •   127 DREAM OF FAERY   27
    THAT COUNTRY WHERE A MAN CAN BE SO CROSSED! • • •   130 BOOK STORIES   16
    I HAVE DRUNK ALE FROM THE COUNTRY OF THE YOUNG • •   177 PAST GREATNESS   1
    TALKED OF HIS COUNTRY AND ITS PEOPLE, SANG • • •   180 QUEEN MAEVE   3
    RODE FROM THE COUNTRY OF HER KIN, • • • • • •   191 BAILE AILLINN   50
    FOR ALL THAT COUNTRY HAD BEEN ASTIR, • • • • •   191 BAILE AILLINN   52
    I KNOW OF THE SLEEPY COUNTRY, WHERE SWANS FLY ROUND • •   204 WITHER BOUGHS   17
    TOWARDS THE COUNTRY OF THE DEAD. WHAT MATTER • •   231 SHADOW WATER B   206
    WHAT ARE THEY? UNTO WHAT COUNTRY DO THEY FLY? • •   247 SHADOW WATER B   523
    "THERE IS A COUNTRY AT THE END OF THE WORLD • • •   247 SHADOW WATER B   530
    WE WOULD RETURN TO OUR OWN COUNTRY, FORGAEL, • • •   248 SHADOW WATER B   539
    IT SHALL BE IN THE COUNTRY OF THE DEAD, • • • • •   249 SHADOW WATER B   557
    IF THERE BE SUCH A COUNTRY. NO, NOT THERE, • • •   249 SHADOW WATER B   558
    TO SOME SURE COUNTRY, SOME FAMILIAR PLACE. • • •   249 SHADOW WATER B   569
    TO A CERTAIN COUNTRY HOUSE IN TIME OF CHANGE • • •   264 HOUSE SHAKEN V T
    OLD COUNTRY SCHOLAR, ROBERT EMMET'S FRIEND, • • •   269 PARDON FATHERS   5
    AND COUNTRY SCHOLAR, ROBERT EMMET'S FRIEND, • • •   269 PARDON FATHERS V 5
    MY COUNTRY IS KILTARTAN CROSS, • • • • • • •   328 IRISH AIRMAN   5
    HE THAT WAS BEST IN EVERY COUNTRY SPORT • • • •   339 SHEP GOATHERD   17
    AND EVERY COUNTRY CRAFT, AND OF US ALL • • • •   339 SHEP GOATHERD   18
    ARE MET ON THE WASTE HILLS BY COUNTRY MEN • • • •   375 PHASES OF MOON V 76
    BUT TAKE ME FOR SOME DRUNKEN COUNTRY MAN! • • • •   377 PHASES OF MOON V 130
    THAT IS NO COUNTRY FOR OLD MEN. THE YOUNG • • •   407 SAIL BYZANTIUM   1
    WHEN MOCKING MUSES CHOSE THE COUNTRY WENCH. • • •   413 TOWER   96
    WHAT MORE IS THERE TO SAY? THAT COUNTRY ROUND • •   430 NINETEEN 19   43
    GREEKS WERE BUT LOVERS! ALL THAT COUNTRY ROUND • •   430 NINETEEN 19 V 43
    WHO COMES INTO THIS COUNTRY, AND HAS COME • • •   447 COLONUS PRAISE   17
    BECAUSE THIS COUNTRY HAS A PIOUS MIND • • • •   447 COLONUS PRAISE   25
    THE COUNTRY THINKS NO END OF HIM, • • • • •   583 GHOST ROG CASE   13
    AND PARNELL LOVED HIS COUNTRY, • • • • • •   587 PARNELLITES   31
    IN COUNTRY SHAWL OR PARIS CLOAK, HAD PUT MY WITS ASTRAY,   592 PILGRIM   3
    SO COME IN RAGS OR COME IN SILK, IN CLOAK OR COUNTRY SHAWL,   593 PILGRIM   22
    SO COME IN RAG OR COME IN SILK, IN CLOAK OR COUNTRY SHAWL,   593 PILGRIM V 22
    "I KEPT HER MUCH IN THE COUNTRY • • • • • •   594 COLONEL MARTIN   10
    ON COUNTRY AND ON TOWN, • • • • • • • •   606 SONGS BURDEN 1   24
    HARD-RIDING COUNTRY GENTLEMEN, • • • • • •   639 BEN BULBEN   75
    THE SISTER! "SELL THY COUNTRY, AND THE SHAME • • •   712 FERENCZ RENYI   60
    TOWARDS A COUNTRY WHERE THERE ARE NO KINGS. • • • •   755 SHADOW WATER A   165
    THERE—THERE—BY THE OAR. THE CROWN OF A FAR COUNTRY. • •   763 SHADOW WATER A   310
    AND BID HIM TO YOUR COUNTRY. I SHOULD WANDER • • • •   767 SHADOW WATER A   403

COUNTRY   (CONTINUED)
    LIVING OR DYING. BID AIBRIC TO YOUR COUNTRY, ...   768 SHADOW WATER A   413
COUNTRYMAN
    BUT TAKE ME FOR SOME DRUNKEN COUNTRYMAN!   377 PHASES OF MOON   130
    FOUR SONGS FROM THE YOUNG COUNTRYMAN . . . .   451 FIRST LOVE   V   T
    THE YOUNG COUNTRYMAN . . . .   451 FIRST LOVE   V   T
    TWO SONGS FROM THE OLD COUNTRYMAN . . . .   454 EMPTY CUP   V   T
    THE OLD COUNTRYMAN . . . .   454 EMPTY CUP   V   T
    MORE SONGS OF AN OLD COUNTRYMAN . . . .   454 HIS MEMORIES   V   T
COUNTRYMEN
    MY COUNTRYMEN KILTARTAN'S POOR,   328 IRISH AIRMAN   6
    ARE MET ON THE WASTE HILLS BY COUNTRYMEN . . . . .   375 PHASES OF MOON   76
COUNTRY'S
    HE CLAIMED HIS COUNTRY'S NEED WAS MOST, ...   275 GREY ROCK   101
    THAT HE, ALTHOUGH A COUNTRY'S TALK . . . .   422 MY TABLE   29
COUNTRYSIDE
    WHAT STIR RAN THROUGH THE COUNTRYSIDE . . . .   488 CRAZED MOON   10
COUNTRY-SIDE
    THE BEAUTY OF HER COUNTRY-SIDE . . . .   397 POLIT PRISONER   15
COUNTY
    THAT RED-HEADED RECTOR IN COUNTY DOWN, ...   604 YOU CONTENT   11
COUPLE
    ONE--AND ONE--A COUPLE--FIVE TOGETHER! . . . . . .   233 SHADOW WATER B   249
    A COUPLE OF NIGHT-MOTHS ARE ON THE WING. . . . . .   482 BLOOD AND MOON   46
    A COUPLE OF NIGHT MOTHS ARE ON THE WING, ...   482 BLOOD AND MOON V   46
COUPLED
    COUPLED WITH GOLDEN CHAINS, AND SING AS THEY FLY. . . .   204 WITHER BOUGHS   18
COUPLES
    THOSE MERRY COUPLES DANCING IN TUNE, ...   3 OISIN 1   9
    BUT ALL THAT RUN IN COUPLES, ON EARTH, IN FLOOD OR AIR,   556 RIBH PATRICK   11
    . . .
    THROW LIKELY COUPLES INTO BED . . . .   606 SONGS BURDEN 1   25
COURAGE
    WITH EQUAL COURAGE IN THAT WHIRLING ROUT! . . . . .   186 QUEEN MAEVE   131
    OUR COURAGE BREAKS LIKE AN OLD TREE IN A BLACK WIND AND   207 HANRAHANS SONG   3
      DIES.
    LIKE TUFTED REEDS OUR COURAGE DROOPS IN A BLACK WIND AND 207 HANRAHANS SONG V   3
      DIES!
    WEAK AND WORN AND WEARY OUR COURAGE DROOPS AND DIES . .   207 HANRAHANS SONG V   8
    MY COURAGE CAME AGAIN. BUT THAT'S NOT ALL. . . . .   223 SHADOW WATER B   31
    HAD THEY BUT COURAGE EQUAL TO DESIRE? . . . .   256 NO SECOND TROY   5
    HER COURAGE . . . .   365 HER COURAGE   T
    MUCH BOISTEROUS COURAGE, BEFORE LONELINESS . . . .   473 ALL SOUL NIGHT   72
    SUSTAINS HIS SOUL IN COURAGE OR IN MIGHT. . . . . .   650 ISLE STAT I 1   144
    WAS FORGAEL'S COURAGE THAT THE MUSIC KILLED. . . . .   747 SHADOW WATER A   9
COURAGEOUS
    COURAGEOUS MIRACLES! THE SUNLIGHT SHONE . . . . . .   649 ISLE STAT I 1   113
COURSE   SEE RACE-COURSE WATER-COURSE
    JUDGE OF THE STARS, AND FIND A COURSE FOR US? . . . .   224 SHADOW WATER B   61
    AND MEASURE OUT A COURSE AND BRING US HOME, ...   238 SHADOW WATER B   362
    THERE WHERE THE COURSE IS, ...   266 GALWAY RACES   1
    OUT YONDER, WHERE THE RACE COURSE IS, ...   266 GALWAY RACES   V   1
    CRYING ALOUD AS THE RACE COURSE IS, ...   266 GALWAY RACES   V   14
    THE THIRD! "I'LL HURRY TO THE COURSE . . . . . .   296 THREE BEGGARS   33
    BUT THE THIRD CRIED! "I'LL TO THE COURSE . . . . .   296 THREE BEGGARS   V   33
    MAN RUNS HIS COURSE! . . . .   499 VACILLATION   2
    LOVE LEAPS UPON ITS COURSE. . . . .   518 HIS CONFIDENCE   12
    SOME THINK IT A MATTER OF COURSE THAT CHANCE . . . .   626 OLD MEN BE MAD   9
    SOME THINK IT MATTER OF COURSE THAT CHANCE . . . . .   626 OLD MEN BE MAD V   9
    UPON THE WIND, AND GUIDE MINE ARROW'S COURSE. . . .   657 ISLE STAT I 3   62
    GO PILOT THE COURSE OF HIS ARROW'S DECEIT! . . . . .   657 ISLE STAT I 3   69
COURSES   SEE RACE-COURSES
    THE CARELESS PLANETS IN THEIR COURSES, ...   344 DAWN   7
    BUT WEARIED RUNNING ROUND AND ROUND IN THEIR COURSES .   433 NINETEEN 19   116
    BUT, WEARY RUNNING ROUND AND ROUND IN THEIR COURSES, . . 433 NINETEEN 19   V   116
COURT
    KING GUAIRE WALKED AMID HIS COURT . . . .   295 THREE BEGGARS   8
    COURT HIS SHEPHERD LASS, ...   343 SHEP GOATHERD   104
    THAT SPEECH WAS ALL THAT THE COURT KNOW, BUT HE . . . .   462 HARUN RASHID   V   35
    OR COURT A WOMAN! NEITHER ENEMY, ...   463 HARUN RASHID   59
    THE JUDGE AT THE ASSIZE COURT, ...   596 COLONEL MARTIN   46
    THEN TURNED HE FROM THE KING'S COURT, ...   742 EARL PAUL   65
COURTEOUS
    THOUGH COURTEOUS TO THE WORST! MUCH FALLING HE . . .   324 ROBERT GREGORY   19
    MOST COURTEOUS TO SLOW AGE AND HASTY YOUTH, ...   339 SHEP GOATHERD   19
    NOW BE COURTEOUS, NOW BE KIND, ...   717 FAIRY DOCTOR   21
    GREET HIM COURTEOUS, GREET HIM KIND, ...   717 FAIRY DOCTOR   V   21
COURTESIES
    THAT GRAMMAR SCHOOL OF COURTESIES . . . .   288 TO WEALTHY MAN   15
    --PEDANT IN PASSION, LEARNED IN OLD COURTESIES, . . .   363 DOLLS FACES   4
COURTESY
    SO MUCH COMPOUNDED OF HIGH COURTESY . . . .   205 ADAMS CURSE   24
    COURTESY AND PASSION INTO ONE LIKE THOSE . . . . . .   352 PEOPLE   17
    HER COURTESY . . . .   362 HER COURTESY   T
    IN COURTESY I'D HAVE HER CHIEFLY LEARNED! . . . . .   404 FOR DAUGHTER   33
COURTIER
    LIKE SOME LAST COURTIER AT A GYPSY CAMPING-PLACE . . . . 314 FALLEN MAJESTY   3
    LIKE SOME LAST COURTIER AT A GYPSY CAMPING PLACE . . . . 314 FALLEN MAJESTY V   3
COURTIERS
    AND "WAKEN, COURTIERS OF THE MORN!" . . . . . .   18 OISIN 1   V 262
    CAME TO THE LEAST CONSIDERED OF HIS COURTIERS! . . . .   462 HARUN RASHID   42

	PAGE	TITLE		LINE
COURT-LADIES'				
FROM SOME COURT-LADIES' DRESS AND ROUND	477	SELF AND SOUL	V	14
COURT-LADY'S				
FROM SOME COURT-LADY'S DRESS AND ROUND	477	SELF AND SOUL		14
COURTLY				
THE UNPERTURBED AND COURTLY IMAGES--	352	PEOPLE		11
TIRED OF THAT COURTLY FASHION,	378	CAT AND MOON		15
TIRED OF HER COURTLY FASHION,	378	CAT AND MOON	V	15
THAT MIGHT ADORN OLD SONGS OR COURTLY SHOWS;	629	CIRCUS ANIMALS		14
COUSIN				
MY COUSIN IS PRIEST IN KILVARNET,	178	FIDDLER DOONEY		3
I PASSED MY BROTHER AND COUSIN;	178	FIDDLER DOONEY		5
MY COUSIN OF ROSNAREE.	178	FIDDLER DOONEY	V	4
MY COUSIN IN ROSNAREE.	178	FIDDLER DOONEY	V	4
COUSINS				
MY COUSINS BY THE SCORE,	620	JOHN KINSELLA		6
A KING HAD SOME BEAUTIFUL COUSINS,	628	JANE MOUNTAIN		7
COVER				
THE SOUTH WOULD COVER THEM WITH ROSES OF CRIMSON FIRE!	154	BELOVED PEACE	V	6
COVER OVER AND HIDE, FOR HE HAS NO PART	158	TO HIS HEART		6
AND COVER YOUR LIPS WITH ODOROUS TWILIGHT AND SAY,	162	ASKS FORGIVE		5
COVER YOUR LIPS WITH ROSE-HEAVY TWILIGHT, AND SAY!	162	ASKS FORGIVE	V	5
AND COVER THE PALE BLOSSOMS OF YOUR BREAST	163	ASKS FORGIVE		21
THEN COVER THE PALE BLOSSOM OF YOUR BREAST	163	ASKS FORGIVE	V	21
UNFOLD YOUR FLAMING WINGS AND COVER OUT OF SIGHT	175	ELEMENT POWERS		11
AND WINDS AND PONDS COVER MORE QUIET WOODS,	218	WOODS OF COOLE		34
I LOVED HIM; I WOULD COVER UP MY EARS,	246	SHADOW WATER B		494
BUT I WILL COVER UP YOUR EYES AND EARS,	250	SHADOW WATER B		574
BEND LOWER, THAT I MAY COVER YOU WITH MY HAIR,	251	SHADOW WATER B		613
I TORE MY BODY THAT ITS WINE MIGHT COVER	537	HER VISION		7
COVER YOUR EARS; FOR ONCE WE HAD MOORED OUR GALLEY	756	SHADOW WATER A		187
COVER THEIR FACES WITH THEIR HAIR AND WEEP.	764	SHADOW WATER A		333
BEND LOWER, THAT I MAY COVER YOU WITH MY HAIR,	769	SHADOW WATER A		429
COVERED SEE RAVEN-COVERED SEAWEED-COVERED MIST-COVERED SEA-COVERED IVY-COVERED				
SORREL-COVERED				
A FIRWOOD HOUSE, ALL COVERED OVER	17	OISIN 1	V	248
AND GOD COVERED THE WORLD WITH SHADE,	133	FR GILLIGAN		19
BETWEEN THE WALLS COVERED WITH BEATEN BRONZE,	180	QUEEN MAEVE		10
THE MIST HAS COVERED THE HEAVENS, AND YOU AND I	251	SHADOW WATER B		604
COVERED WITH EMBROIDERIES	320	COAT		2
AND BROUGHT THEM IN A LITTLE COVERED DISH.	410	TOWER		32
MY HEART RECOVERING WITH COVERED EYES!	602	GALLERY REVIS		18
AND KEEP A COVERED HEAD."	742	EARL PAUL		64
KEEP HIDDEN AND COVERED HER HEART!"	744	GLOVE CLOAK		12
HAVE COVERED THEM. WHERE DID THEY VANISH AWAY?	764	SHADOW WATER A		328
COVERING				
HIGH AS THE SADDLE-GIRTH, COVERING AWAY FROM OUR GLANCES	47	OISIN 3		2
THE TIDE;				
HIGH AS THE SADDLE GIRTH, COVERING AWAY FROM OUR GLANCES	47	OISIN 3	V	2
THE TIDE;				
WITH HER CLOUD-PALE EYELIDS HALF COVERING HER DIM EYES!	163	VALLEY LOVERS	V	4
COVERLET				
AND SHAKE THEIR COVERLET.	33	OISIN 2		62
TO STIR THEIR COVERLET AND THEIR HAIR.	197	BAILE AILLINN		186
AND GATHER THE GLASNEVIN COVERLET	293	TO A SHADE		19
DRAW THE GLASNEVIN COVERLET ANEW	293	TO A SHADE	V	19
COVERLET'S				
AND SHAKE THEIR COVERLET'S HEM,	33	OISIN 2	V	62
COVERLID				
UNDER THIS CRADLE-HOOD AND COVERLID	403	FOR DAUGHTER		2
COVERS				
AND COVERS AWAY THE SMOKE OF MYRRH AND FRANKINCENSE!	173	SPEAKS HEARERS		4
THAT COVERS ALL HE HAS BROUGHT	345	ON WOMAN		5
COVERS ITS WOODEN SHEATH.	421	MY TABLE		7
COW				
HALF ASLEEP THE OLD COW CROPS,	706	DAWN-SONG		20
WHERE LIES THE COW AT PEACE BESIDE HER CALF,	715	FERENCZ RENYI		121
CURES HE HATH FOR COW OR GOAT	716	FAIRY DOCTOR		13
HE HAD DREAMED THE COW HAD GOT WITHIN	729	PRIEST FAIRY		33
COWARD				
A COWARD IN THE FIELD; AND ALL MEN CRIED!	684	SEEKER		53
COWARDICE				
COWARDICE, SOME SILLY OVER-SUBTLE THOUGHT	413	TOWER		117
COWARDICE, OVER SOME SILLY SUBTLE THOUGHT	413	TOWER	V	117
COWARDLY				
THAT WERE A COWARDLY SONG,	554	CHURCH STATE		7
COWARDS				
CONVICTED COWARDS ALL, BY KINDRED SLAIN	634	CUCHULAIN COMF		21
COWER				
AND IN THE FLAMING FORESTS COWER THE LION	73	ANASHU VIJAYA		52
THEY SEE IN FLAMING FORESTS COWER THE LION	73	ANASHU VIJAYA	V	52
COWERED				
I COWERED BACK UPON THE WALL IN TERROR,	284	TWO KINGS		164
COWS SEE MILCH-COWS				
WHIPS TO THE SEA THE COWS AND SWINE."	82	MAD KING GOLL	V	16
TO FILL WITH COWS HIS HOLLOW GALLEYS."	82	MAD KING GOLL	V	16
SCARED BY THE SPLASHING OF A DOZEN COWS;	419	MY HOUSE		10
SCARED BY THE SPLASHING OF A HUNDRED COWS.	419	MY HOUSE	V	10
TO MIND HIS COWS AND SWINE BY THE RED LAKE.	752	SHADOW WATER A		112
CAN CALL THE MILCH COWS	780	WELL AND TREE		5

166

COXCOMB
COXCOMB WAS THE LEAST HE SAID! . . . . 508 JANE BISHOP 6
THE SOLID MAN AND THE COXCOMB. . . . . 508 JANE BISHOP 7
THE SOLID MAN AND THE COXCOMB. . . . . 508 JANE BISHOP 14
THE SOLID MAN AND THE COXCOMB. . . . . 508 JANE BISHOP 21
THE SOLID MAN AND THE COXCOMB. . . . . 509 JANE BISHOP 28
COY
THE PROUDEST OR MOST COY OF SPIRIT THINGS, ... 720 WITCH VIVIEN 7
COZENING
THE COZENING FORTUNE-TELLER THAT COMES WHISPERING, . . . 228 SHADOW WATER B 123
CRABBED
YOUR THIRST FOR THOSE OLD CRABBED MYSTERIES, ... 465 HARUN RASHID 86
CRACK
WHEN I WAS A BOY WITH NEVER A CRACK IN MY HEART. . . . . 91 OLD FISHERMAN 4
WHEN I WAS A BOY WITH NEVER A CRACK IN MY HEART. . . . . 91 OLD FISHERMAN 8
WHEN I WAS A BOY WITH NEVER A CRACK IN MY HEART. . . . . 91 OLD FISHERMAN 12
AND THEN I'D STAGGER OUT. HE'D CRACK HIS WITS . . . . 377 PHASES OF MOON 134
AND PUT THAT CRACK IN IT, ... 455 FRIENDS YOUTH 2
MADE THE JOINTS OF HEAVEN CRACK! . . . . 509 JANE REPROVED 11
EVERY ACCIDENTAL CRACK OR DENT, ... 567 LAPIS LAZULI 44
CRACKED
TO THE CRACKED TUNE THAT CHRONOS SINGS, ... 65 HAPPY SHEPHERD 9
TO THE OLD CRACKED TUNE THAT CHRONOS SINGS, ... 65 HAPPY SHEPHERD V 9
CAUGHT AND CRACKED HIS FLEA, THE THIRD, ... 299 THREE HERMITS 30
MAY BUILD IN THE CRACKED MASONRY AND CRY . . . . . 423 MY DESCENDANTS 15
FOUR POEMS CRACKED MARY AND THE BISHOP . . . . . 507 JANE BISHOP V T
CRACKED MARY REPROVED . . . . 509 JANE REPROVED V T
CRACKED MARY AND THE DANCERS . . . . 514 JANE GROWN OLD V T
NOR HEARD THIS VOICE THAT NINETY YEARS HAVE CRACKED. . . 555 RIBH AT TOMB 5
CRACKING
COMES CRACKING JOKES OF CIVIL WAR . . . . 423 ROAD AT DOOR 3
CRACKLE
HEARING THE HARPERS PLAY, THE PINE-WOOD CRACKLE, . . . 759 SHADOW WATER A 241
HEARING THE HARPERS PLAY, THE PINE WOOD CRACKLE, . . . 759 SHADOW WATER A V 241
CRACKLING
BRUISING THE DARKNESS WITH THEIR CRACKLING LIGHT! . . . 687 TWO TITANS 2
CRACK-PATED
LEARN THAT WE WERE CRACK-PATED WHEN WE DREAMED. . . . 431 NINETEEN 19 88
CRADLE
A CRADLE SONG . . . . 118 CRADLE SONG T
TWO POEMS CONCERNING PEASANT VISIONARIES A CRADLE SONG 146 UNAPPEAS HOST V T
BEING BETRAYED INTO A CRADLE, AND I COME . . . . . 284 TWO KINGS 169
AND MADE A GOLDEN CRADLE . . . . 308 PLAYER QUEEN 3
LOOKS AT THE CRADLE AND BAWLS! . . . . 319 DOLLS 2
TILL, CLAMBERING AT THE CRADLE SIDE, ... 343 SHEP GOATHERD V 109
TOO PERFECT AT THE FULL TO LIE IN A CRADLE, ... 374 PHASES OF MOON 60
THEY RAN FROM CRADLE TO CRADLE TILL AT LAST . . . . 375 PHASES OF MOON 69
THEY RAN FROM CRADLE TO CRADLE TILL AT LAST . . . . 375 PHASES OF MOON 69
CRADLE UPON CRADLE, AND ALL IN FLIGHT AND ALL . . . . 376 PHASES OF MOON 100
CRADLE UPON CRADLE, AND ALL IN FLIGHT AND ALL . . . . 376 PHASES OF MOON 100
WERE VEXED TO NIGHTMARE BY A ROCKING CRADLE, ... 402 SECOND COMING 20
FROM CRADLE RUN TO GRAVE . . . . 449 HERO GIRL FOOL 19
FROM GRAVE TO CRADLE RUN INSTEAD! . . . . 449 HERO GIRL FOOL 20
WHEN CRADLE AND SPOOL ARE PAST . . . . 449 HERO GIRL FOOL 24
CRADLED
AND CRADLED ME HERE WHERE ARE SUNG, ... 708 FAIRY PEDANT 25
CRADLE-HOOD
UNDER THIS CRADLE-HOOD AND COVERLID . . . . 403 FOR DAUGHTER 2
CRADLES
THE DANAAN CHILDREN LAUGH, IN CRADLES OF WROUGHT GOLD, . . 146 UNAPPEAS HOST 1
THE FAERY CHILDREN LAUGH IN CRADLES OF WROUGHT GOLD, . . 146 UNAPPEAS HOST V 1
THE CRADLES THAT A MAN MUST NEEDS BE ROCKED IN! . . . 373 PHASES OF MOON 34
SHUDDERS IN MANY CRADLES! ALL IS CHANGED, ... 375 PHASES OF MOON 89
MAKE HIM FILL THE CRADLES RIGHT. . . . . 638 BEN BULBEN 41
CRADLE-SIDE
TILL, CLAMBERING AT THE CRADLE-SIDE, ... 343 SHEP GOATHERD 109
CRAFT
PATRICK, BEFORE THY CRAFT DIES EACH OLD SONG. . . . . 42 OISIN 2 V 196
YOU HAVE A DRUID CRAFT OF WICKED SOUND . . . . . . 237 SHADOW WATER B 342
YOU HAVE A DRUID CRAFT, WICKED SOUND . . . . . . 237 SHADOW WATER B V 342
ALL THINGS CAN TEMPT ME FROM THIS CRAFT OF VERSE! . . . 267 ALL TEMPT ME 1
UNDER THE EYELIDS OF ANOTHER, FOR IT WAS MY CRAFT . . . 284 TWO KINGS 156
WHERE I MAY SPEAK TO YOU ALONE, MY CRAFT . . . . . 284 TWO KINGS 159
UNDER AN ALIEN EYELID, FOR IT WAS MY CRAFT . . . . 284 TWO KINGS V 156
AND EVERY COUNTRY CRAFT, AND OF US ALL . . . . . . 339 SHEP GOATHERD 18
CRAFTY
FOR HE IS STRONG AND CRAFTY AS THE SEAS . . . . . . 35 OISIN 2 83
NOW HAD THAT OLD GAUNT CRAFTY ONE, ... 193 BAILE AILLINN 100
THAT CRAFTY DEMON AND THAT LOUD BEAST . . . . . . 399 DEMON BEAST 2
CRAM
LOVE CRAM LOVE'S TWO DIVISIONS . . . . 573 LADYS 2ND SONG 12
CRAMM'D
CRAMM'D ALL HER YOUTH! AND HATES HAVE BOUGHT AND SOLD . . 687 TWO TITANS 13
CRAMMED
ALL HIS TWENTIES CRAMMED WITH TOIL! . . . . 576 WHAT THEN 4
CRANBERRY
SEE YOU, BROTHER, CRANBERRY FRUIT-- . . . . 727 LOVERS QUARREL 25
CRANE
MUTTERED THE OLD CRANE OF GORT. . . . . 295 THREE BEGGARS 6
NOW THEY ARE SILENT," SAID THE CRANE. . . . . . . 297 THREE BEGGARS 62
ALONG THE LAKE. THE CRANE HAS HOMEWARD FLED. . . . . 656 ISLE STAT I 3 23

		PAGE	TITLE	LINE

CRAOIBHIN
   DEAR CRAOIBHIN AOIBHIN, LOOK INTO OUR CASE. • • • • • 264 ABBEY THEATRE 1
CRASH
   AND WEARY OF THE CRASH OF BATTLE CARS." • • • • • • • 107 CUCHULAIN SEA V 30
   OF THOSE STEEL TONGUES! CRASH, SWORDS! WELL THRUST! 665 ISLE STAT II 2 67
      WELL BENT
CRASHED
   CRASHED ON THE STONES, UPON THE GLIMMERING STONES, • • • 33 OISIN 2 V 68A
CRASHING   SEE LOUD-CRASHING
   OF THE LOUD CRASHING AND EARTH SHAKING FIGHT • • • • • • 38 OISIN 2 V 141
CRAVE
   LEST I NO MORE HEAR COMMON THINGS THAT CRAVE; • • • • 101 ROSE UPON ROOD 15
CRAVEN
   THE CRAVEN MAN IN HIS SEAT, • • • • • • • • • • • • • 347 FISHERMAN 15
   "AM I SUCH A CRAVEN THAT • • • • • • • • • • • • • 585 ORAHILLY 19
CRAVING
   TO THE CRAVING IN MY BONES. • • • • • • • • • • • • • 533 FIRST CONFESS 12
CRAWL
   NO MORE TO CRAWL ON THE SEAS WITH LONG OARS MILE AFTER 55 OISIN 3 119
      MILE,
   TO CRAWL IN HER OWN BLOOD, AND GO SCOT-FREE; • • • • • 429 NINETEEN 19 28
   I CANNOT EVEN CRAWL ALONG THE FLAGS • • • • • • • • 701 MOSADA 3 58
CRAWLED
   HE CRAWLED INTO THAT PLEASANT NOOK. • • • • • • • • • 303 HOUR DAWN 32
   CRAWLED FROM OBSCURITY, AND SET UPON ME • • • • • • • 352 PEOPLE 26
CRAWLING
   THE NETTED MARKS OF CRAWLING SCALES SEA-SPRUNG • • • 37 OISIN 2 V 115
   BUT TURN FROM ROSSES' CRAWLING TIDE, • • • • • • • • 549 SEVERED HEAD 5
CRAWLS
   GRIMALKIN CRAWLS TO BUDDHA'S EMPTINESS. • • • • • • • 611 STATUES 24
   A LIZARD CRAWLS--THE TWO MEN GAZE INTENT, • • • • • • 711 FERENCZ RENYI 47
   TIME GOES. THE FLAKED FIRE OF EVENING CRAWLS • • • • 712 FERENCZ RENYI 70
   TIME GOES. THE FLICKED FIRE OF EVENING CRAWLS • • • • 712 FERENCZ RENYI V 70
   FROM WHERE THE OLD IVY CRAWLS ROUND THE OLD STEEPLE, • • 728 PRIEST FAIRY 6
CRAZED   SEE PITY-CRAZED
   CRAZED WITH ITS OWN INTERMINABLE SOUND, • • • • • • • 30 OISIN 2 V 23A
   IN THE HID PLACE, BEING CRAZED BY LOVE. • • • • • • • 195 BAILE AILLINN 143
   WHERE ONE FOUND LANCELOT CRAZED AND HID HIM FOR A WHILE; 209 UNDER THE MOON 3
   WHERE ONE FOUND LANCELOT CRAZED, AND HID HIM FOR AWHILE, 209 UNDER THE MOON V 3
   AND FOR THAT REASON AM I CRAZED • • • • • • • • • • 454 EMPTY CUP 9
   HAD DRIVEN HIM CRAZED; • • • • • • • • • • • • • • 473 ALL SOUL NIGHT 73
   THE CRAZED MOON • • • • • • • • • • • • • • • • • 487 CRAZED MOON T
   CRAZED THROUGH MUCH CHILD-BEARING • • • • • • • • • 487 CRAZED MOON 1
   AN ABSTRACT GREEK ABSURDITY HAS CRAZED THE MAN-- • • • 556 RIBH PATRICK 1
   ABSTRACTIONS OF THE GREEK PHILOSOPHY HAVE CRAZED THE MAN, 556 RIBH PATRICK V 1
   A CRAZED GIRL • • • • • • • • • • • • • • • • • 578 CRAZED GIRL T
   THAT CRAZED GIRL IMPROVISING HER MUSIC, • • • • • • • 578 CRAZED GIRL 1
CRAZY
   AND CRAZY RASCALS RAGE THEIR FILL • • • • • • • • • 131 OLD PENSIONER 9
   BECAUSE EARTH, CRAZY FOR ITS BROKEN POWER, • • • • • • 186 QUEEN MAEVE 124
   HALF CRAZY WITH THE THOUGHT, SHE TOO HAS WEPT! • • • • 186 QUEEN MAEVE 140
   THE CRAZY HERDSMAN THAT WILL TELL HIS FELLOWS • • • • 229 SHADOW WATER B 167
   THE CRAZY NOTHING THAT I THINK IT IS, • • • • • • • • 248 SHADOW WATER B 556
   A CRAZY JUICE THAT MAKES THE PULSES BEAT • • • • • • 384 VISION ROBART 54
   A CRAZY SALAD WITH THEIR MEAT • • • • • • • • • • • 404 FOR DAUGHTER 31
   AND SHOULD SOME CRAZY HAND DARE TOUCH A DAUGHTER • • • 433 NINETEEN 19 122
   A CRAZY MAN THAT FOUND A CUP, • • • • • • • • • • • 454 EMPTY CUP 1
   CRAZY JANE AND THE BISHOP • • • • • • • • • • • • • 507 JANE BISHOP T
   EIGHT POEMS CRAZY JANE AND THE BISHOP • • • • • • • • 507 JANE BISHOP V T
   CRAZY JANE REPROVED • • • • • • • • • • • • • • • 509 JANE REPROVED T
   CRAZY JANE ON THE DAY OF JUDGMENT • • • • • • • • • 510 JANE JUDGMENT T
   CRAZY JANE AND JACK THE JOURNEYMAN • • • • • • • • • 511 JANE AND JACK T
   CRAZY JANE ON GOD • • • • • • • • • • • • • • • • 512 JANE ON GOD T
   CRAZY JANE TALKS WITH THE BISHOP • • • • • • • • • • 513 JANE TALK BISH T
   CRAZY JANE GROWN OLD LOOKS AT THE DANCERS • • • • • • 514 JANE GROWN OLD T
   CRAZY JANE AND THE DANCERS • • • • • • • • • • • • 514 JANE GROWN OLD V T
   I MOCKED, BEING CRAZY, BUT YOU MASTERED IT • • • • • 533 HER TRIUMPH 8
   ALONE WITH A CRAZY HEAD. • • • • • • • • • • • • • 552 SONGS REWRIT 2 V 12
   THAT SHE IS HAPPY BEING CRAZY; • • • • • • • • • • • 568 SWEET DANCER 10
   OUT OF THAT CRAZY FIGHT; • • • • • • • • • • • • • 585 ORAHILLY 15
   COULD CRAZY JANE PUT OFF OLD AGE • • • • • • • • • • 606 SONGS BURDEN 1 19
   CRAZY JANE ON THE MOUNTAIN • • • • • • • • • • • • 628 JANE MOUNTAIN T
   (SAID CRAZY JANE) • • • • • • • • • • • • • • • • 628 JANE MOUNTAIN 2
   (SAID CRAZY JANE) • • • • • • • • • • • • • • • • 628 JANE MOUNTAIN 12
   O! WHY IS LOVE SO CRAZY THAT IT LONGS • • • • • • • 765 SHADOW WATER A 363
   THOSE CRAZY FINGERS PLAY • • • • • • • • • • • • • 783 GREY ROUND 16
CREAK
   MY SORROW! FOR MANY A CREAK GAVE THE CREEL IN THE CART • 91 OLD FISHERMAN 6
   AH WOE! FULL MANY A CREAK GAVE THE CREEL IN THE CART • 91 OLD FISHERMAN V 6
   AH ME! FULL MANY A CREAK GAVE THE CREEL IN THE CART • • • 91 OLD FISHERMAN V 6
   THE CRY OF A CHILD BY THE ROADWAY, THE CREAK OF A LUMBERING 142 ROSE IN HEART 2
      CART,
CREAKING
   CLIMBED UP MY CREAKING STAIR. THEY HAD READ • • • • • 358 PRESENCES 6
   WITHIN THE FOLD TO HEAR THE CREAKING GATE-- • • • • • 646 ISLE STAT I 1 41
CREAKY
   OR CREAKY SHOES. AND AT THE END OF ALL • • • • • • • 228 SHADOW WATER B 128
CREAMY
   WILD FLAMES OF RED AND CREAMY WHITES, • • • • • • • 18 OISIN 1 V 255
CREASES
   AND THERE ARE LITTLE CREASES ABOUT HER EYES; • • • • • 199 FOLLY COMFORT V 3

		PAGE	TITLE	LINE

CREATE
WE ARE BUT CRITICS, OR BUT HALF CREATE, ... 368 EGO DOMINUS 15
DREAM AND SO CREATE . . . . 415 TOWER 155

CREATED
AND I MYSELF CREATED HANRAHAN . . . . 411 TOWER 57
MAN HAS CREATED DEATH. . . . . 476 DEATH 12

CREATION
ALL CREATION SHIVERS . . . . 559 HE AND SHE 11

CREATURE
A SWIFTER CREATURE NEVER WAS BORN, ... 2 OISIN 1 V 7Q
OF MANY A FIGURED CREATURE STRANGE, ... 4 OISIN 1 V 27
"A SADDER CREATURE NEVER STEPT . . . . 17 OISIN 1 238
NO CREATURE HAD FAMILIAR THOUGHT . . . . 17 OISIN 1 V 242
THE POWERS WHOSE NAME AND SHAPE NO LIVING CREATURE KNOWS 174 ELEMENT POWERS 1
PERVERSE CREATURE OF CHANCE, ... 346 ON WOMAN 41
A STUPID HAPPY CREATURE . . . . 400 DEMON BEAST 31

CREATURES
NO MIGHTIER CREATURES BAY AT THE MOON! . . . . . . 8 OISIN 1 87
FOR NO LIVE CREATURES LIVED THERE, NO WEASELS MOVED IN 48 OISIN 3 19
    THE DARK!
AND EACH OF THE HUGE WHITE CREATURES WAS HUGER THAN 49 OISIN 3 33
    FOURSCORE MEN!
AND EACH OF THE HUGE WHITE CREATURES WAS HUGER THAN 49 OISIN 3 V 33
    FOUR-SCORE MEN!
AND THE CHIEF OF THE HUGE WHITE CREATURES, ... 50 OISIN 3 43
. . . WITH CREATURES OF DREAMS, ... 53 OISIN 3 95
FOR NO LIVE CREATURES LIVE THERE, NO WEASELS MOVE IN THE 56 OISIN 3 139
    DARK!
FOR THE ELEMENTAL CREATURES GO . . . . 138 TO IRELAND 23
STRANGE CREATURES FLUTTER UP BEFORE ONE'S EYES, ... 222 SHADOW WATER B 18
I HAVE LOOKED UPON THOSE BRILLIANT CREATURES, ... 322 SWANS AT COOLE 13
I HAVE LOOKED UPON THESE BRILLIANT CREATURES . . . . 322 SWANS AT COOLE V 13
WHEN THE MOON'S FULL THOSE CREATURES OF THE FULL . . . 375 PHASES OF MOON 75
AND FOLLOWED UP THOSE BAYING CREATURES TOWARDS-- . . . 412 TOWER 72
WITH CREATURES OF OUR HEAVY NIGHT, ... 743 DANAAN QUICK 10
SIX HOLY CREATURES, ... 770 BLOOD BOND 14

CREEL
MY SORROW! FOR MANY A CREAK GAVE THE CREEL IN THE CART . . 91 OLD FISHERMAN 6
AH WOE! FULL MANY A CREAK GAVE THE CREEL IN THE CART . . 91 OLD FISHERMAN V 6
AH ME! FULL MANY A CREAK GAVE THE CREEL IN THE CART . . 91 OLD FISHERMAN V 6

CREEP
IN HATING GOD SHE MAY CREEP CLOSE TO GOD. . . . . . 558 RIBH CHRISTIAN V 18
MAY CREEP INTO YOUR BED, ... 569 THREE BUSHES 11
FOR IF I SAW MYSELF CREEP IN . . . . 569 THREE BUSHES 12
BACK THE SHADOWS CREEP AGHAST-- . . . . 648 ISLE STAT I 1 98

CREEPERS
AND TANGLED CREEPERS EVERY HOUR . . . . 16 OISIN 1 223
WHERE TANGLING CREEPERS EVERY HOUR . . . . 16 OISIN 1 V 223

CREEPING
A CREEPING OLD MAN, FULL OF SLEEP, ... 60 OISIN 3 192
THE NORTH UNFOLDS ABOVE THEM CLINGING, CREEPING NIGHT, . . 154 BELOVED PEACE 3
THE NORTH UNROLLS ABOVE THEM CLINGING, CREEPING NIGHT, . . 154 BELOVED PEACE V 3
THE CREEPING CAT, LOOKED UP. . . . . 378 CAT AND MOON 4
CAME CREEPING UP BECAUSE THE MAN WAS STILL. . . . . 634 CUCHULAIN COMF 10
A CREEPING HORROR IS ALL OVER ME. . . . . 681 SEEKER 12
CREEPING ALONG THE HEAVENS' PURPLE CUP, ... 714 FERENCZ RENYI 112

CREEPS
MINNALOUSHE CREEPS THROUGH THE GRASS . . . . . . 378 CAT AND MOON 17
MINNALOUSHE CREEPS THROUGH THE GRASS . . . . . . 379 CAT AND MOON 25
A FEARFUL PALENESS CREEPS ACROSS HER BREAST . . . . 701 MOSADA 3 69

CRESCENT
A GOLDEN CRESCENT LIT THE PLAIN, ... 2 OISIN 1 V 7BB
AND THE THIN CRESCENT OF THE MOON, ... 20 OISIN 1 V 288
HE HAS CAUGHT THE CRESCENT MOON OUT OF THE SKY, . . . 239 SHADOW WATER B 370
FROM THE FIRST CRESCENT TO THE HALF, THE DREAM . . . 373 PHASES OF MOON 36
BECAUSE THE HERO'S CRESCENT IS THE TWELFTH. . . . . 374 PHASES OF MOON 47
BECAUSE THE HEROES' CRESCENT IS THE TWELFTH. . . . 374 PHASES OF MOON V 47
THAT THE LAST SERVILE CRESCENT HAS SET FREE? . . . . 376 PHASES OF MOON 103
THE FIRST THIN CRESCENT IS WHEELED ROUND ONCE MORE. . . 377 PHASES OF MOON 116
AND THAT FROM ROUND TO CRESCENT, ... 379 CAT AND MOON 23
FROM CRESCENT TO ROUND THEY RANGE? . . . . . . 379 CAT AND MOON 24
OF RHYME! REMEMBERING THEE, THIS CRESCENT NIGHT, . . . 704 REMEMBRANCE 2

CRESCENTS
THE FULL AND THE MOON'S DARK AND ALL THE CRESCENTS, . . 373 PHASES OF MOON 32
HUNCHBACK AND SAINT AND FOOL ARE THE LAST CRESCENTS. . . 377 PHASES OF MOON 118
UNDER THE THREE LAST CRESCENTS OF THE MOON, ... 377 PHASES OF MOON 133

CREST
TELL ON, NOR BOW THY HEATHEN CREST . . . . . . 11 OISIN 1 V 131A
FROM MOUNTAIN CREST TO CREST. . . . . 536 PARTING 10
FROM MOUNTAIN CREST TO CREST. . . . . 536 PARTING 10
AS FLAMING MINSTREL-WORD UPON HIS CREST. . . . . . 679 ISLE STAT II 3 317
WHERE HOMES ONCE WHITENED VALE AND MOUNTAIN CREST! . . 709 FERENCZ RENYI 3
HIS MOODS BOW LOW HIS SOMBRE CREST, ... 723 GIRLS SONG A 2

CRESTED   SEE GOLDEN-CRESTED
ANSWERED! "A CRESTED COCKEREL CREW . . . . . . 387 SOLOMON WITCH V 9

CRETAN
RECALL THE CRETAN BARB THAT PIERCED A STAR? . . . . 541 PARN FUNERAL 1 7

CREVICE
IN CAVERN, CREVICE, HOLE, ... 546 TO SAME TUNE 2 5
IN CAVERN, CREVICE OR HOLE, ... 546 TO SAME TUNE 2 V 5
IN CAVERN, CREVICE, OR HOLE, ... 613 MARCH SONGS 1 5

169

	PAGE	TITLE		LINE

CREVICED
    IN CREVICED ROCKS, AND LAUGHED TO THE OLD SEA, ... 688 TWO TITANS   34
CREVICES
    THE BEES BUILD IN THE CREVICES . . . .   424 STARES NEST   1
CREVROE
    ON CREVROE OR BROAD KNOCKFEFIN, WITH MANY OF OLD THEY FEAST 59 OISIN 3   179
    ON CREVROE OR ON BROAD KNOCKFEFIN, WITH MANY OF OLD THEY   59 OISIN 3   V 179
        FAST
CREW
    AND OVERPOWER THE CREW WHILE YET ASLEEP! . . . . . . 233 SHADOW WATER B   240
    CREW FROM A BLOSSOMING APPLE BOUGH . . . . 387 SOLOMON WITCH   10
    ANSWERED! "A CRESTED COCKEREL CREW . . . .   387 SOLOMON WITCH   V   9
    AND NEVER CREW AGAIN TILL NOW, ... 388 SOLOMON WITCH   12
    NOTHING BUT CROMWELL'S HOUSE AND CROMWELL'S MURDEROUS CREW, 580 CURSE CROMWELL 2
    THEN THE STRANGER SOFTLY CREW-- . . . .   697 MOSADA 2   28
    BUT WHERE THAT ROARING, RANTING CREW . . . . 787 HUDDON DUDDON   3
CRICKET
    DROPPING FROM THE VEILS OF THE MORNING TO WHERE THE CRICKET 117 ISLE INNISFREE 6
        SINGS!
    'TWAS EVENING, AND THE CRICKET NATION SANG . . . . . 690 MOSADA 1   18
    A NEIGHBOURING CRICKET LIFTS HIS SHRILLY SHOUT . . . 711 FERENCZ RENYI   45
CRICKETS
    THEY SET UP A NOISE LIKE CRICKETS, ... 161 CAP AND BELLS   33
CRIED
    CRIED FIN! AND CRIED SHE, "MEN OF FAME, ...   5 OISIN 1   V 45
    CRIED FIN! AND CRIED SHE, "MEN OF FAME, ...   5 OISIN 1   V 45
    "YOU ONLY WILL I WED," I CRIED, ...   7 OISIN 1   74
    IN LOVE. I CRIED, "THEE WILL I WED, ...   7 OISIN 1   V 74
    AWAY, AWAY WITH ME," SHE CRIED, ...   8 OISIN 1   V 80B
    THAN THIS STRANGE HUMAN BARD," HE CRIED! . . . . . .   17 OISIN 1   239
    THAN THIS STRANGE BARD," HE CRIED, AND CAUGHT . . . . 17 OISIN 1   V 239
    WITH A CLEAR VOICE THE YOUNG MAN CRIED, ...   18 OISIN 1   V 260
    TO ALL THINGS CRIED! "I AM A SLAVE! . . . .   19 OISIN 1   V 280
    "FLEE FROM HIM," PEARL-PALE NIAMH WEEPING CRIED, . . . 35 OISIN 2   92
    ROOTED IN FOAM AND CLOUDS, AND CRIED TO ALL . . . .   38 OISIN 2   132
    I CRIED, "COME OUT OF THE SHADOW, KING OF THE NAILS OF 51 OISIN 3   61
        GOLD!
    I CRIED, "THOU ART SURELY A WARRIOR, FORGETTING HIS FAMOUS 51 OISIN 3   V   61
        LINE,
    I CRIED, "COME OUT OF THE SHADOW, CANN OF THE NAILS OF 51 OISIN 3   V   61
        GOLD!
    I CRIED, "O NIAMH! O WHITE ONE! IF ONLY A TWELVE-HOURED 55 OISIN 3   113
        DAY,
    AND I RODE AND I RODE, AND I CRIED OUT, ...   59 OISIN 3   171
    SO SLEEP THEE BY DAYTIME." A VOICE CRIED, ...   59 OISIN 3   172
    . . . HE CRIED, "NO, THE GODS A LONG TIME ARE DEAD."   59 OISIN 3   180
    SO SLEEP THEY BY DAYTIME." A VOICE CRIED, ...   59 OISIN 3   V 172
    . . . HE CRIED, "NAY, THE GODS A LONG TIME ARE DEAD." 59 OISIN 3   V 180
    CRIED OUT, DIM SEA! HEAR MY MOST PITEOUS STORY! . . . 68 SAD SHEPHERD   9
    THE SEA SWEPT ON AND CRIED HER OLD CRY STILL, ... 68 SAD SHEPHERD   10
    CRIED ALL HIS STORY TO THE DEWDROPS GLISTENING. . . . 68 SAD SHEPHERD   14
    THEN CRIED THE MAN WHOM SORROW NAMED HIS FRIEND! . .   68 SAD SHEPHERD   V 8
    THERE CRIED A HERALD, "TO OUR VALLEYS . . . .   82 MAD KING GOLL   V 14
    CRIED A HERALD, "PEACE WITH THINE! . . . .   82 MAD KING GOLL   14
    CRIED A HERALD, "TO OUR VALLEYS . . . .   82 MAD KING GOLL   14
    UPON THE WEB-HEAPED FLOOR, AND CRIED HIS WORD! . . . 106 CUCHULAIN SEA   15
    "WHO BADE YOU TELL THESE THINGS?" AND THEN SHE CRIED 106 CUCHULAIN SEA   V 17
    AND CRIED WITH ANGRY VOICE, "IT IS NOT MEET . . . . 107 CUCHULAIN SEA   20
    AND CRIED OUT TO HIM, "SON IT IS NOT MEET . . . . . 107 CUCHULAIN SEA   V 20
    CUCHULAIN CRIED, "I AM THE ONLY MAN . . . . 109 CUCHULAIN SEA   55
    CUCHULAIN CRIED, "HAVE MADE AND KEEP THAT VOW." . . . 109 CUCHULAIN SEA   V 56
    AND CRIED, "CUCHULLIN WILL DWELL THERE AND BROOD, . . 110 CUCHULAIN SEA   V 77
    THE CARS OF BATTLE AND HIS OWN NAME CRIED! . . . . . 111 CUCHULAIN SEA   85
    AND AFTER CRIED HE, "GOD FORGIVE! . . . . 132 FR GILLIGAN   11
    "AND IS THE POOR MAN DEAD?" HE CRIED. . . . . 133 FR GILLIGAN   33
    WHEN THE BATS CRIED OUT NO MORE! . . . . 159 CAP AND BELLS   V 14
    I CRIED IN MY DREAM, O WOMEN, BID THE YOUNG MEN LAY . 163 VALLEY LOVERS   5
    AND I CRIED IN MY DREAM "O WOMEN, BID THE YOUNG MEN LAY 163 VALLEY LOVERS   V 5
    CRIED FROM THE PORTER'S LODGE, AND WITH LONG CLAMOUR 181 QUEEN MAEVE   37
    WHERE HER GRANDCHILDREN SLEPT, AND CRIED ALOUD . . . 185 QUEEN MAEVE   109
    WHERE HER GRAND-CHILDREN SLEPT, AND CRIED ALOUD . . . 185 QUEEN MAEVE   V 109
    A YOUNG MAN CRIED AND KISSED HER HAND, ... 191 BAILE AILLINN   60
    "ANOTHER'S HURRIED OFF," CRIED HE, ... 193 BAILE AILLINN   113
    AND AMID LEAFY LIGHT HE CRIED, ... 193 BAILE AILLINN   V 113
    I CRIED WHEN THE MOON WAS MURMURING TO THE BIRDS! . . 203 WITHER BOUGHS   1
    CRIED OUT UPON THAT THING BENEATH . . . . 254 HIS DREAM   10
    CRIED OUT THE WHOLE NIGHT LONG, ... 254 HIS DREAM   16
    THAT EVERY YEAR I HAVE CRIED, "AT LENGTH . . . . . . 256 WORDS   9
    THE NO KING CRIED WHO AFTER THAT WAS KING, ... 258 KING NO KING   2
    TILL THE WILDERNESS CRIED ALOUD . . . . 259 UNWORTH PRAISE   8
    AND I BUT ASKED THE MORE, TILL HE CRIED OUT, ... 281 TWO KINGS   92
    FOR MEDICINE." THEREON HE CRIED ALOUD . . . . 281 TWO KINGS   98
    UNDER A BOW, HE CRIED, "WHAT HAPPINESS . . . . 284 TWO KINGS   177
    THRUST HIM AWAY WITH BOTH MY HANDS AND CRIED, ... 285 TWO KINGS   202
    UNTIL A CURLEW CRIED AND IN THE LUMINOUS WIND . . . . 291 PAUDEEN   4
    AN OLD FOUL MOUTH THAT ONCE CRIED OUT ON YOU . . . . 292 TO A SHADE   V 17
    WE HAVE CRIED IN OUR DESPAIR . . . . 293 HELEN-LIVED   1
    ONE TO ANOTHER SIGHED AND CRIED! . . . . 296 THREE BEGGARS   38
    BUT THE THIRD CRIED! "I'LL TO THE COURSE . . . . . 296 THREE BEGGARS   V 33
    ABOUT A FARM," THE SECOND CRIED. . . . . 296 THREE BEGGARS   V 38
    "TIME'S UP," HE CRIED, AND ALL THE THREE . . . . . . 297 THREE BEGGARS   57

170

CRIED   (CONTINUED)
```
"TIME'S UP," HE CRIED, AND ALL THE THREE  . . . . . .   297 THREE BEGGARS      59
ONE BEGGAR CRIED: "YOU'RE SHAMMING SLEEP,"  . . . . .   297 THREE BEGGARS   V  45
BEGGAR TO BEGGAR CRIED . . . . . . . . . . . . . . .    299 BEGGAR CRIED        1
BEGGAR TO BEGGAR CRIED, BEING FRENZY-STRUCK,  . . . .   299 BEGGAR CRIED        3
BEGGAR TO BEGGAR CRIED, BEING FRENZY-STRUCK,  . . . .   300 BEGGAR CRIED        7
BEGGAR TO BEGGAR CRIED, BEING FRENZY-STRUCK,  . . . .   300 BEGGAR CRIED       11
BEGGAR TO BEGGAR CRIED, BEING FRENZY-STRUCK,  . . . .   300 BEGGAR CRIED       15
BEGGAR TO BEGGAR CRIED, BEING FRENZY-STRUCK,  . . . .   300 BEGGAR CRIED       19
THAT SACRED GOBAN BREWED," HE CRIED . . . . . . . .     304 HOUR DAWN       V  50
BUT THE OTHER CRIED, "YOU LONG FOR SPRING . . . . .     306 HOUR DAWN       V  91
UNTIL I CRIED AND TREMBLED AND ROCKED TO AND FRO,  .    316 COLD HEAVEN         8
CRIED THE BEGGAR, BILLY BYRNE: . . . . . . . . . .      331 ROUND TOWER         4
THE EXULTATION OF THEIR STONE, THAT CRIED . . . . .     339 SHEP GOATHERD      25
AND CRIED, "BEFORE I AM OLD . . . . . . . . . . .       348 FISHERMAN          37
I SUDDENLY CRIED OUT IN A STRANGE TONGUE  . . . . .     387 SOLOMON WITCH       5
HOWLED, MIAU-D, BARKED, BRAYED, BELLED, YELLED, CRIED,  387 SOLOMON WITCH       8
   CROWED,
CRIED FROM A BLOSSOMING APPLE BOUGH . . . . . . . .     387 SOLOMON WITCH   V  10
NO, NO, NOT SAID, BUT CRIED IT OUT--"YOU HAVE COME AGAIN, 391 UNDER SATURN     13
CRIED OUT THE HOLLOWS OF THE SEA. . . . . . . . . .     397 POLIT PRISONER     24
BECAUSE OF ALL THAT SENSELESS TUMULT, ALL BUT CRIED .   426 PHANTOM HATRED     15
THAT SHE CRIED INTO THIS EAR, . . . . . . . . . .       455 HIS MEMORIES       17
CRIED, CASTING OFF THE MOUNTAIN SNOW, . . . . . . .     502 VACILLATION        60
AND CRIED TO BATTLE-WEARY MEN, . . . . . . . . . .      502 VACILLATION        65
CRIED THAT WE LIVED LIKE BEAST AND BEAST: . . . . .     508 JANE BISHOP        13
AND FAIR NEEDS FOUL," I CRIED. . . . . . . . . . .      513 JANE TALK BISH      8
I SAT AND CRIED. . . . . . . . . . . . . . . . . .      515 GIRLS SONG B        8
"SHE WILL CHANGE," I CRIED, . . . . . . . . . . .       516 MANS SONG           1
AND TIME RUNS ON," CRIED SHE. . . . . . . . . . .       526 AM OF IRELAND       3
AND TIME RUNS ON," CRIED SHE. . . . . . . . . . .       527 AM OF IRELAND      16
AND THE TROMBONE," CRIED HE, . . . . . . . . . . .      527 AM OF IRELAND      23
AND TIME RUNS ON," CRIED SHE. . . . . . . . . . .       527 AM OF IRELAND      29
I CRIED AND WHISTLED BUT VAIN, ALL VAIN. . . . . .      551 SONGS REWRIT 1  V  16
THAT CRIED IT FAR AND WIDE, . . . . . . . . . . .       582 ROGER CASEMENT     18
AND I CRIED TEARS DOWN. . . . . . . . . . . . . .       628 JANE MOUNTAIN      22
AND, LEAPING TO THEIR FEET, FAR ECHOES CRIED, . . .     659 ISLE STAT II 1     13
FOR SUCH A CALL. LET THE WILD WORD BE CRIED . . . .     669 ISLE STAT II 3     76
I CRIED THE THING YOU BADE ME CRY. . . . . . . . .      670 ISLE STAT II 3    114
I CRIED THE WORDS YOU BID ME CRY. . . . . . . . .       673 ISLE STAT II 3    186
A COWARD IN THE FIELD: AND ALL MEN CRIED! . . . . .     684 SEEKER             53
HIDING MY FACE, I CRIED LONG, BITTERLY. . . . . . .     690 MOSADA 1           17
THY SACRED DOOR!" BUT PETER CRIED, . . . . . . . .      697 MOSADA 2           25
A GREY PROFESSOR PASSING CRIED, . . . . . . . . .       725 LEGEND              9
AND TO HIMSELF CRIED, "COMMUNIST!" . . . . . . . .      725 LEGEND             15
"THEY ARE LOST, THEY ARE LOST, EACH ONE," CRIED HE. .   730 PRIEST FAIRY       58
WAS CRIED IN STREET AND LANE . . . . . . . . . . .      740 EARL PAUL          26
THE PEOPLE CRIED "SHIELD-BREAKER!" . . . . . . . .      741 EARL PAUL          53
```
CRIES   SEE CATCH-CRIES
```
CRIES TO THE SLUGGARD SEEDS OF CORN. . . . . . . .       18 OISIN 1         V 263
LAUGHTER AND CRIES. THE ARMIES CLASH AND SHOCK, . .      43 OISIN 2          211
OF ARMOUR--LAUGHTER AND CRIES--THE ARMIES' SHOCK. . .    43 OISIN 2         V 211
AND THEN THE CLASH OF FALLEN HORSEMEN AND THE CRIES .   161 BLACK PIG           3
WHERE WIND CRIES IN THE SEDGE! . . . . . . . . . .      165 CRY OF SEDGE        3
MUST I ENDURE YOUR AMOROUS CRIES? . . . . . . . .       177 PAST GREATNESS     12
CRY OF HIS LOVE WITH THEIR PITIFUL CRIES. . . . . .     177 PAST GREATNESS  V  12
ALL THAT YOU NEED IS PATIENCE." HEART CRIES, "NO, .     200 FOLLY COMFORT       6
AND AFTER CIRCLING WITH STRANGE CRIES AWHILE  . . .     223 SHADOW WATER B     26
THE LAPWING AT THEIR FOOLISH CRIES  . . . . . . .       306 HOUR DAWN          77
TO KNOW WHEN MICHAEL'S TRUMPET CRIES . . . . . . .      307 HOUR DAWN         100
IN VAIN, IN VAIN! THE CATARACT STILL CRIES: . . . .     311 MOUNTAIN TOMB       9
THE CLEVER MAN WHO CRIES . . . . . . . . . . . .        347 FISHERMAN          21
THE CATCH CRIES OF THE CLOWN, . . . . . . . . . .       347 FISHERMAN       V  22
THEIR MOMENTARY CRIES BEFORE IT IS DAWN, . . . . .      371 EGO DOMINUS        78
ALL TURN WITH AMOROUS CRIES, OR ANGRY CRIES, . . .      433 NINETEEN 19       123
ALL TURN WITH AMOROUS CRIES, OR ANGRY CRIES, . . .      433 NINETEEN 19       123
FOR THE HEART CRIES THAT WHAT DECEPTION WINS  . . .     448 HERO GIRL FOOL      6
THOSE AMOROUS CRIES THAT OUT OF QUIET COME  . . . .     557 RIBH ECSTASY        7
THEIR CRIES ARE SWEET AND STRANGE, . . . . . . . .      612 NEWS ORACLE        18
WILD CRIES, GROWN SWEET WITH LULLS AND LINGERINGS LONG. 674 ISLE STAT II 3    222
WITH LITTLE CRIES OF JOY HE KISSED THE RAIN . . . .     688 TWO TITANS         33
THAT ANCIENT MOTHER CRIES, "SPEAK NOT, MY SON. . .      711 FERENCZ RENYI      56
WITH CRIES AND MURMURS. SUDDENLY HE FLINGS  . . . .     714 FERENCZ RENYI     101
CRIES A VOICE AT ROARING MIDNIGHT BESIDE THE MOONLESS DEEP. 718 PHANTOM SHIP     8
"PRAY FOR THE SOULS IN PURGATORY," THE PALE PRIEST      719 PHANTOM SHIP       31
   TREMBLING CRIES.
AND SAID, "YON BITTERN CRIES, IN TRUTH, . . . . . .     731 PRIEST FAIRY       75
AND SHE CRIES OUT, "I HAVE FLED TO MY BELOVED  . . .    754 SHADOW WATER A    151
UPON THIS WORLD NO LONGER. THE HARP CRIES OUT. . . .    769 SHADOW WATER A  V 430
CRIES OUT THE EMPTY WELL, . . . . . . . . . . . .       780 WELL AND TREE       2
CRIES OUT THE LEAFLESS TREE, . . . . . . . . . . .       780 WELL AND TREE      10
```
CRIETH
```
LOUD FOR THEE THE MORNING CRIETH, . . . . . . . .       648 ISLE STAT I 1      86
```
CRIME
```
DELIVER FROM THE CRIME OF DEATH AND BIRTH. . . . .      478 SELF AND SOUL      24
A CHARTER TO COMMIT THE CRIME ONCE MORE. . . . . .      478 SELF AND SOUL      32
THAT THE CRIME OF BEING BORN . . . . . . . . . . .      534 CONSOLATION         9
THE CRIME CAN BE FORGOT. . . . . . . . . . . . .        534 CONSOLATION        12
```
CRIME'S
```
BUT WHERE THE CRIME'S COMMITTED . . . . . . . . .       534 CONSOLATION        11
```

		PAGE	TITLE		LINE

CRIMSON
AND WITH THE GLIMMERING CRIMSON GLOWED — 3 OISIN 1 — 26
AND WITH THE WOVEN CRIMSON GLOWED — 3 OISIN 1 V 26
ABOUT HIS FADING CRIMSON BALL: — 12 OISIN 1 — 155
IN SILENCE ROUND HIS CRIMSON BALL. — 12 OISIN 1 V 155
AND TRIMMED WITH MANY A CRIMSON FEATHER: — 15 OISIN 1 — 206
TRIMMED ROUND WITH MANY A CRIMSON FEATHER: — 15 OISIN 1 V 206
BLOSSOM IN SOME NEW CRIMSON FLOWER, — 16 OISIN 1 — 224
LIKE CRIMSON METEORS HANG IN THE GLOOM, — 21 OISIN 1 — 306
THE PEA-HENS DANCE, IN CRIMSON FEATHER — 77 INDIAN TO LOVE V 3
THE SOUTH IS POURING DOWN ROSES OF CRIMSON FIRE: — 154 BELOVED PEACE — 6
THE SOUTH WOULD COVER THEM WITH ROSES OF CRIMSON FIRE: — 154 BELOVED PEACE V 6
AND STOLE THE CRIMSON ROSE, — 174 ELEMENT POWERS V 2
AND SHE FORGET THE WANDERING AND ALL THE CRIMSON GLOOM — 175 ELEMENT POWERS V 11
AND SHE FORGET THE WANDERING AND THE CRIMSON GLOOM — 175 ELEMENT POWERS V 11
OVER THEM CRIMSON VAPOURS WINGING, — 648 ISLE STAT I 1 — 92
BLEW MY CRIMSON CAP AWAY — 656 ISLE STAT I 3 — 16
AND TRAILING CRIMSON VANS, A MUMBLING BROOD, — 687 TWO TITANS — 20

CRITIC
THE MEDITATIVE CRITIC: ALL ARE ON THEIR TOES, — 363 DOLLS FACES — 8

CRITICS
WE ARE BUT CRITICS, OR BUT HALF CREATE, — 368 EGO DOMINUS — 15

CROAGH
UPON CROAGH PATRICK SANG IT LOUD: — 528 DANCER CRUACH V 5

CROCUS
WHERE GOLDEN CROCUS AND NARCISSUS BLOOM, — 447 COLONUS PRAISE — 18

CROMLECH
WE WHO STILL LABOUR BY THE CROMLECH ON THE SHORE, — 161 BLACK PIG — 5
WE, WHO ARE LABOURING BY THE CROMLECH ON THE SHORE, — 161 BLACK PIG V 5

CROMWELL
THE CURSE OF CROMWELL — 580 CURSE CROMWELL — T

CROMWELL'S
NOTHING BUT CROMWELL'S HOUSE AND CROMWELL'S MURDEROUS CREW, — 580 CURSE CROMWELL — 2
NOTHING BUT CROMWELL'S HOUSE AND CROMWELL'S MURDEROUS CREW, — 580 CURSE CROMWELL — 2

CRONE
"INTO A WITHERED CRONE." — 516 MANS SONG — 2
NO WITHERED CRONE I SAW — 516 MANS SONG — 11

CROOK
BROUGHT THE BARE NEWS. HE HAD THROWN THE CROOK AWAY — 339 SHEP GOATHERD — 21
AND THOUGH I HAVE TURNED THE TALK BY HOOK OR CROOK — 350 HER PRAISE — 5

CROOKED
THE PILOT STAR AND THE CROOKED PLOUGH — 177 PAST GREATNESS — 4
AND THE GREY BIRD WITH CROOKED BILL — 192 BAILE AILLINN — 89
O LOVE IS THE CROOKED THING, — 268 BROWN PENNY — 9
SAID THE WICKED, CROOKED, HAWTHORN TREE: — 788 HAWTHORN TREE — 6
SAID THE WICKED, CROOKED, HAWTHORN TREE. — 788 HAWTHORN TREE — 14

CROON
THE GIDDY BEE'S COMPLACENT CROON, — 736 SUMMER EVENING — 5

CROONING
SWAYED, CROONING TO HIMSELF AN UNKNOWN TONGUE: — 39 OISIN 2 — 159

CROP
WHAT A CROP OF MUMMY WHEAT: — 562 CONJUNCTIONS — 2

CRO-PATRICK
THE DANCER AT CRUACHAN AND CRO-PATRICK — 528 DANCER CRUACH — T
UPON CRO-PATRICK SANG ALOUD: — 528 DANCER CRUACH — 5

CROPPED   SEE CLOSE-CROPPED

CROPS
HALF ASLEEP THE OLD COW CROPS, — 706 DAWN-SONG — 20

CROSIERED
. . . CROSIERED ONE, CAUGHT IN THY NET-- — 58 OISIN 3 V 167
THE REST THOU HAST HEARD OF, THOU CROSIERED ONE-- — 60 OISIN 3 V 189

CROSIERS
NOW, MAN OF CROSIERS, PHANTOMS DREW AROUND — 29 OISIN 2 V 1
LORD OF THE CROSIERS, THOU EVEN HADST LIFTED THY HANDS AND WEPT: — 54 OISIN 3 V 110

CROSS
A CROSS THEY HAD MADE OUT OF TWO BITS OF WOOD, — 123 DREAM OF DEATH — 7
I CAME AND WROTE UPON A CROSS OF WOOD-- — 123 DREAM OF DEATH V 7
AND THOUGH THEY HAVE TO CROSS THE LOUGHLAN WATERS — 282 TWO KINGS — 113
AND THOUGH THEY HAVE TO CROSS THE LOUGHLAN SEAS — 282 TWO KINGS V 113
MY COUNTRY IS KILTARTAN CROSS, — 328 IRISH AIRMAN — 5
BY CHILDISH MEMORIES OF AN OLD CROSS POLLEXFEN, — 391 UNDER SATURN — 7
THAT CUT THROUGH TIME OR CROSS IT WITHERSHINS. — 489 COOLE PARK 29 — 24
THAT CAN CROSS TIME AND CUT IT WITHERSHINS. — 489 COOLE PARK 29 V 24
CROSS THE NARROW STRAITS TO LIGHT — 494 AT ALGECIRAS — 4
CROSS THOSE NARROW STRAITS TO LIGHT — 494 AT ALGECIRAS V 4
THE SWORD'S A CROSS: THEREON HE DIED: — 562 CONJUNCTIONS — 3
THE OLD STONE CROSS — 598 STONE CROSS — T
UNDER THE OLD STONE CROSS. — 598 STONE CROSS — 8
UNDER THE OLD STONE CROSS. — 599 STONE CROSS — 16
UNDER THE OLD STONE CROSS. — 599 STONE CROSS — 24
SET UP THE OLD STONE CROSS, — 604 YOU CONTENT — 10
BY THE ROAD AN ANCIENT CROSS. — 640 BEN BULBEN — 88
I SPEAK ALONE WITH SERVANTS OF THE CROSS — 698 MOSADA 2 — 48
SAT UNDERNEATH THE MARKET CROSS, — 724 LEGEND — 2
A SONG OF THE ROSY CROSS — 744 ROSY CROSS — T
GAVE TO ME ALONE THE CROSS: — 744 ROSY CROSS — 3
GAVE TO ME ALONE THE CROSS. — 744 ROSY CROSS — 11
FLIT TO KILTARTAN CROSS AND STAY — 791 REPRISALS — 11

CROSS'D
FROM WASTE SEAS CROSS'D, YET EVER GARRULOUS) — 690 MOSADA 1 — 9

172

                                                                    PAGE   TITLE   LINE
CROSSED
      THAT HAS DRUNK FULL, SHE CROSSED THE MISTY SEA   . . . . .   30 OISIN 2   16
      THAT COUNTRY WHERE A MAN CAN BE SO CROSSED!   . . . . .   130 BOOK STORIES   16
      FOR I AM AENGUS, AND I AM CROSSED IN LOVE."   . . . . .   183 QUEEN MAEVE   84
      WHEN NEITHER SOUL NOR BODY HAS BEEN CROSSED.   . . . . .   258 KING NO KING   16
      JAMES AND HIS IRISH WHEN THE DUTCHMAN CROSSED!   . . . .   270 PARDON FATHERS   12
      WITH THE HOT BLOOD OF YOUTH, OF LOVE CROSSED LONG AGO! . .   316 COLD HEAVEN   6
      IT NEVER CROSSED THE SEA BECAUSE . . . .   583 GHOST ROG CASE   3
      ONE IMAGE CROSSED THE MANY-HEADED, SAT . . . .   610 STATUES   17
      TO SEEK NOT HOPELESS HAVE I CROSSED THE GLOOM, ...   656 ISLE STAT I 3   42
      AS THOUGH SHE WHOM YOU FEAR HAD CROSSED THE WIDE . . . .   669 ISLE STAT II 3   77
      A DEAL OF EVIL AND OF CHANGE HATH CROSSED . . . . . .   676 ISLE STAT II 3   273
      WITH THREE BARS CROSSED, AND THESE FOUR WALLS MY WORLD,   700 MOSADA 3   32
CROSSES
      CROSSES THE NARROW STRAITS TO LIGHT . . . .   494 AT ALGECIRAS   V   4
CROSS-GARTERED
      ROUGH MEN-AT-ARMS, CROSS-GARTERED TO THE KNEES   . . .   412 TOWER   82
      ROUGH MEN AT ARMS, CROSS-GARTERED TO THE KNEES   . . .   412 TOWER   V   82
CROSSING
      CROSSING STREAM AGAIN . . . .   419 MY HOUSE   9
CROUCH
      CROUCH UPON A STONE, ...   525 DANCING DAYS   4
      AND CROUCH IN SOME FAR STILLNESS OF THE ISLE, AND DIE. . .   675 ISLE STAT II 3   246
CROUCHED
      AND CROUCHED BY THE ARM OF HIS CHAIR, ...   319 DOLLS   16
      FIERCE MORTAL, AND CROUCHED LOW BESIDE THE LAKE   . . .   675 ISLE STAT II 3 V 245A
CROUCHES
      AMONG THE FRUIT! BUT THERE, LAME COLA CROUCHES   . . . .   691 MOSADA 1   32
      AMONG THE FRUIT. BUT YON, LAME COLA CROUCHES   . . . .   691 MOSADA 1   V   32
CROUCHING
      TWO FIGURES CROUCHING ON THE BLACK ROCK, BOUND   . . . .   687 TWO TITANS   5
      WHY NOT? HE IS HER OWN! AND CROUCHING NIGH   . . . . .   688 TWO TITANS   44
CROW   SEE A-CROW
      CROW UPON TARA." KING EOCHAID BOWED HIS HEAD   . . . .   286 TWO KINGS   211
      CROW UPON TARA." SHE HAD FIXED HER EYES   . . . . . .   286 TWO KINGS   V   211
      ALTHOUGH HE THOUGHT IT WORTH A CROW. . . . .   388 SOLOMON WITCH   35
      ANOTHER LINEAGE FEED THE CROW, ...   437 SONGS PLAY 1   10
      CAN LIKE THE COCKS OF HADES CROW, ...   498 BYZANTIUM   20
      BUT YONDER THING, YON IDLE NOISE, YON CROW, ...   648 ISLE STAT I 1   104
      RED BIRD OF MARCH, BEGIN TO CROW! . . . .   782 HEART FRIGHT   5
      RED COCK, AND CROW! . . . .   782 HEART FRIGHT   7
      RED BIRD OF MARCH, BEGIN TO CROW! . . . .   782 HEART FRIGHT   12
      RED COCK, AND CROW! . . . .   782 HEART FRIGHT   14
      RED BIRD OF MARCH, BEGIN TO CROW! . . . .   782 HEART FRIGHT   19
      RED COCK, AND CROW! . . . .   782 HEART FRIGHT   21
      RED COCKS, AND CROW! . . . .   783 GREY ROUND   28
CROWD
      AND HID HIS FACE AMID A CROWD OF STARS. . . . . . .   121 YOU ARE OLD   12
      HE STOOD AMONG A CROWD AT DROMAHAIR! . . . .   126 DREAM OF FAERY   1
      VOICES AMONG THE CROWD . . . .   172 PLEADS FRIEND   2
      AND THE TONGUES OF THE CROWD   . . . .   172 PLEADS FRIEND   V   2
      GATHERED A CROWD IN SOME BYZANTINE LANE, ...   180 QUEEN MAEVE   2
      ARE DANCING IN A CROWD. . . . .   214 HAPPY TOWNLAND   12
      ARE DANCING IN THE CROWD. . . . .   214 HAPPY TOWNLAND   V   12
      A CROWD UPON A SHORE. . . . .   253 HIS DREAM   4
      AND THOUGH I WOULD HAVE HUSHED THE CROWD, ...   253 HIS DREAM   5
      AND RUNNING CROWD AND GAUDY SHIP   . . . .   254 HIS DREAM   15
      AND FISH AND CROWD AND PAINTED SHIP, ...   254 HIS DREAM   V   15
      AND FISH AND CROWD AND GAUDY SHIP . . . .   254 HIS DREAM   V   15
      THE CROWD THAT CLOSES IN BEHIND! . . . .   266 GALWAY RACES   4
      THESE, THESE REMAIN, BUT I RECORD WHAT'S GONE. A CROWD   315 FALLEN MAJESTY   6
      ALL THE DISHONEST CROWD I HAD DRIVEN AWAY, ...   352 PEOPLE   24
      THERE'LL BE THAT CROWD, THAT BARBAROUS CROWD, ...   354 HIS PHOENIX   25
      THERE'LL BE THAT CROWD, THAT BARBAROUS CROWD, ...   354 HIS PHOENIX   25
      THERE'LL BE THAT CROWD TO MAKE MEN WILD THROUGH ALL THE   354 HIS PHOENIX   V   25
          CENTURIES,
      THE LEADERS OF THE CROWD . . . .   398 LEADERS CROWD   T
      SO THE CROWD COME THEY CARE NOT WHAT MAY COME.   . . . .   398 LEADERS CROWD   10
      UNDER THE GREAT COMEDIAN'S TOMB THE CROWD. . . . . .   541 PARN FUNERAL 1   1
      A FRENZIED CROWD, AND WHERE THE BRANCHES SPRANG   . . . .   541 PARN FUNERAL 1   9
      THEIR SCHOOL A CROWD, HIS MASTER SOLITUDE!   . . . . .   543 PARN FUNERAL 2   10
      THEIR SCHOOL THE CROWD, HIS MASTER SOLITUDE, ...   543 PARN FUNERAL 2   V   10
      THEIR SCHOOL A CROWD, HIS MASTER'S SOLITUDE!   . . . .   543 PARN FUNERAL 2   V   10
      ESCAPED OUT OF HER CROWD, ...   568 SWEET DANCER   5
      MY FATHER UPON THE ABBEY STAGE, BEFORE HIM A RAGING CROWD!   577 LOFTY THINGS   2
      THAT ALL ATTENDANTS AND THE CASUAL CROWD MIGHT HEAR. . .   609 IN TARAS HALLS   13
      ON MY POOR BRAIN YOUR BUSY TUMULTS CROWD. . . . . .   648 ISLE STAT I 1   100
      SOON WILL THE CHURCHMEN NOD ABOVE THE CROWD.   . . . . .   699 MOSADA 3   19
      BEFORE WE TAKE OUR SEATS ABOVE THE CROWD. . . . . .   704 MOSADA 3   134
      OR CROWD BEHIND THE BULWARK, THAT WE SEEM . . . . .   751 SHADOW WATER A   94
CROWDED   SEE MACKEREL-CROWDED
      THE DANCERS CROWDED ABOUT HIM . . . .   144 HOST OF AIR   17
      CROWDED WITH BITTER FACES, THE WOUNDS IN PALM AND SIDE,   172 TRAV PASSION   4
      OUR HEARTS ENDURE THE PLAITED THORN, THE CROWDED WAY, . .   172 TRAV PASSION   V   3
      ON EVERY CROWDED STREET TO STARE   . . . .   294 HATED PLAYBOY   3
      IN A CROWDED LONDON SHOP, ...   501 VACILLATION   37
CROWDS
      AND ARE PLAGUED BY CROWDS, UNTIL   . . . .   298 THREE HERMITS   20
      ALTHOUGH CROWDS GATHERED ONCE IF SHE BUT SHOWED HER FACE,   314 FALLEN MAJESTY   1
      NOR PUBLIC MEN, NOR CHEERING CROWDS, ...   328 IRISH AIRMAN   10
      NOR PUBLIC MAN, NOR ANGRY CROWDS, ...   328 IRISH AIRMAN   V   10

173

	PAGE	TITLE		LINE
CROWDS (CONTINUED)				
NOR PUBLIC MAN, NOR CHEERING CROWDS,	328	IRISH AIRMAN	V	10
CROWDS JOSTLED AT THE FAIR	410	TOWER	V	39
CROWED				
HOWLED, MIAU-D, BARKED, BRAYED, BELLED, YELLED, CRIED, CROWED,	387	SOLOMON WITCH		8
HE THAT CROWED OUT ETERNITY	388	SOLOMON WITCH		17
THOUGHT TO HAVE CROWED IT IN AGAIN.	388	SOLOMON WITCH		18
CROWN				
UNDER A CROWN OF THORNS AND DARK WITH BLOOD,	38	OISIN 2		135
TO HIM SEEMED EASY, SO I LAID THE CROWN	102	FERGUS DRUID		13
AND STILL I FEEL THE CROWN UPON MY HEAD.	103	FERGUS DRUID		20
BUT STILL I FEEL THE CROWN UPON MY HEAD.	103	FERGUS DRUID	V	20
WHY MUST YOU BLENCH AND SHAKE FROM FOOT TO CROWN?"	106	CUCHULAIN SEA		13
"WHY DO YOU TREMBLE THUS FROM FEET TO CROWN?".	106	CUCHULAIN SEA	V	13
WHY ARE YOU PALE AND SHAKE FROM FOOT TO CROWN?"	106	CUCHULAIN SEA	V	13
AND THE PROUD DREAMING KING WHO FLUNG THE CROWN	170	SECRET ROSE		19
THAT I MIGHT LAY IT ON YOUR HEAD AS A CROWN.	246	SHADOW WATER B		511
SHALL BE ALONE FOR EVER. WE TWO--THIS CROWN--	251	SHADOW WATER B		605
BEND LOWER, O KING, THAT I MAY CROWN YOU WITH IT.	251	SHADOW WATER B		607
SHE MAY HAVE WORN SILK CLOTHES, OR WORN A CROWN,	282	TWO KINGS		117
WAS BORN TO WEAR A CROWN.	308	PLAYER QUEEN		12
OVER THE CROWN OF THE WILLOWS BROWN.	653	ISLE STAT I 2		30
OVER THE CROWN OF THE WILLOWS BROWN.	653	ISLE STAT I 2		51
'TIS CLEAR THAT YOU HAVE SEEN HER NOT. THE CROWN	661	ISLE STAT II 1		70
OF FAILURE, AND TO CROWN HER CROWNLESS HEAD,	688	TWO TITANS		48
WE WILL BRING A CROWN OF GOLD,	726	LOVERS QUARREL		13
BEYOND THE SAIL A MAN WITH A RED CROWN	752	SHADOW WATER A		126
I HAVE BROUGHT HIS CROWN. AND I HAVE BROUGHT HIS QUEEN.	755	SHADOW WATER A		166
THERE--THERE--BY THE OAR. THE CROWN OF A FAR COUNTRY.	763	SHADOW WATER A		310
THAT CROWN WAS IN MY DREAMS--NO, NO--IN A RHYME.	763	SHADOW WATER A		311
I CROWN YOU WITH THIS CROWN. BEND LOWER, O KING,	768	SHADOW WATER A		423
I CROWN YOU WITH THIS CROWN. BEND LOWER, O KING,	768	SHADOW WATER A		423
SHARED THE BYZANTINE CROWN?	789	SINGING HEAD		14
CROWNED SEE LEAF-CROWNED				
HIS SHOUTING DAYS WITH MIRTH WERE CROWNED;	67	HAPPY SHEPHERD		50
OF THE CROWNED MAGI; AND THE KING WHOSE EYES	169	SECRET ROSE		9
OF THE CROWNED MAGI; AND THE HOUND OF CU	169	SECRET ROSE	V	9
OF THE CROWNED MAGI; AND THE KINGS WHOSE EYES	169	SECRET ROSE	V	9
. . . THOUGHT'S CROWNED POWERS HE CALLED THEM ONCE.	480	BLOOD AND MOON		15
CROWNLESS				
OF FAILURE, AND TO CROWN HER CROWNLESS HEAD,	688	TWO TITANS		48
CROWNS				
THE JEWELLED CROWNS THAT KINGS HAVE HURLED	155	FORGOT BEAUTY		4
WHO COME WITH THEIR CROWNS OF PEARL AND THEIR SPINDLES OF WOOL,	203	WITHER BOUGHS		10
HURL HELMETS, CROWNS, AND SWORDS INTO THE PIT.	257	RECONCILIATION		10
THE CROWNS OF NINEVEH.	439	FRAGMENTS		10
PROFFERING ITS SACRED LAUREL CROWNS,	612	NEWS ORACLE		23
THE STARS WOULD HURL THEIR CROWNS AMONG THE FOAM	761	SHADOW WATER A		265
CROZIER				
. . . THE CROZIER GLEAMS;	61	OISIN 3		194
. . . THAT CROZIER GLEAMS;	61	OISIN 3	V	194
CROZIERED				
. . . CROZIERED ONE, CAUGHT IN YOUR NET;	58	OISIN 3		167
. . . CROZIERED ONE, CAUGHT IN THEIR NET;	58	OISIN 3	V	167
THE REST YOU HAVE HEARD OF, O CROZIERED MAN;	60	OISIN 3		189
CROZIERS				
NOW, MAN OF CROZIERS, SHADOWS CALLED OUR NAMES	29	OISIN 2		1
FOR ALL YOUR CROZIERS, THEY HAVE LEFT THE PATH	42	OISIN 2		200
AND, MAN OF THE MANY WHITE CROZIERS, A CENTURY THERE I FORGOT	52	OISIN 3		77
AND, MAN OF THE MANY WHITE CROZIERS, A CENTURY THERE I FORGOT	52	OISIN 3		81
BUT IN DREAMS, MILD MAN OF THE CROZIERS,	53	OISIN 3		85
SO WATCHED I WHEN, MAN OF THE CROZIERS,	54	OISIN 3		101
LORD OF THE CROZIERS, YOU EVEN HAD LIFTED YOUR HANDS AND WEPT;	54	OISIN 3		110
AND OLD MEN WITH CROZIERS AND STOLES.	167	BLESSED		16
CRUACHAN				
IN HER HIGH HOUSE AT CRUACHAN; THE LONG HEARTH,	180	QUEEN MAEVE		11
HE SAID, "HIGH QUEEN OF CRUACHAN AND MAGH AI,	183	QUEEN MAEVE		77
HE SAID "QUEEN OF UNSHELTERED CRUACHAN,	183	QUEEN MAEVE	V	77
QUEEN OF HIGH CRUACHAN." "I OBEY YOUR WILL	184	QUEEN MAEVE		99
WITH THE FIRST KINGS OF MANY-PILLARED CRUACHAN.	187	QUEEN MAEVE		151
WITH THE FIRST KINGS OF MANY PILLARED CRUACHAN	187	QUEEN MAEVE	V	151
CALLED CRUACHAN, AND IT WAS AS MUCH	302	HOUR DAWN		4
STUMBLED ON WINDY CRUACHAN	302	HOUR DAWN	V	3
BUT THE HELL MOUTH AT CRUACHAN	303	HOUR DAWN	V	24
FROM THE HELL MOUTH AT CRUACHAN	307	HOUR DAWN	V	120
THE DANCER AT CRUACHAN AND CRO-PATRICK	528	DANCER CRUACH		T
TOM AT CRUACHAN	529	TOM CRUACHAN		T
OLD TOM AT CRUACHAN	529	TOM CRUACHAN	V	T
CRUACHAN'S				
DANCED ON CRUACHAN'S WINDY PLAIN,	528	DANCER CRUACH		4
DANCED IT ON CRUACHAN'S WINDY PLAIN,	528	DANCER CRUACH	V	4
ON CRUACHAN'S PLAIN SLEPT HE	529	TOM CRUACHAN		1
CRUCIFIED				
HIS FATHERS SERVED THEIR FATHERS BEFORE CHRIST WAS CRUCIFIED.	580	CURSE CROMWELL		6

174

		PAGE	TITLE		LINE
CRUCIFIX					
SINKS, SHINING ON THE LITTLE CRUCIFIX · · · · · · · ·		691	MOSADA 1		34
A-SHINING ON THE LITTLE CRUCIFIX · · · · · · · · · ·		691	MOSADA 1	V	34
CRUEL					
SANG WHERE--UNNECESSARY CRUEL VOICE-- · · · · · · ·		127	DREAM OF FAERY		30
CRUEL CLAW AND HUNGRY THROAT, · · · · · · · · ·		136	TWO TREES		36
FORGOT IN CRUEL HAPPINESS · · · · · · · · · · ·		453	MERMAID		5
"O CRUEL DEATH, GIVE THREE THINGS BACK," · · · · ·		521	THREE THINGS		1
WHY SHOULD HE THINK ME CRUEL · · · · · · · · ·		532	BEFORE WORLD		13
THOU WILT NOT SPEAK, OH CRUEL ART THOU YET! · · · · ·		684	SEEKER	V	69A
AH! CRUEL ONES, LEAVE ME ALONE NOW · · · · · · ·		707	FAIRY PEDANT		13
AH! CRUEL ONES, LEAVE ME ALONE · · · · · · · · ·		707	FAIRY PEDANT	V	13
AND LOVE WENCH WISDOM'S CRUEL FACE. · · · · · · ·		787	HUDDON DUDDON		10
AND LOVE WENCH-WISDOM'S CRUEL FACE. · · · · · · ·		787	HUDDON DUDDON	V	10
CRUELTIES					
WITH CRUELTIES OF CHOICE AND CHANCE! · · · · · · ·		388	SOLOMON WITCH		23
CRUELTY					
OF BEAUTY'S CRUELTY AND WISDOM'S CHATTER-- · · · · ·		377	PHASES OF MOON		121
CRUELTY MUST KEEP; THEREFORE BE WARNED AND GO · · · ·		448	HERO GIRL FOOL		7
AND NEEDS NO CRUELTY. I HAVE HEARD ONE SAY · · · · ·		448	HERO GIRL FOOL		13
MY CRUELTY MUST KEEP! AND SO BEGONE · · · · · · ·		448	HERO GIRL FOOL	V	7
AND HAVE NO NEED OF CRUELTY TO KEEP · · · · · · ·		448	HERO GIRL FOOL	V	12A
OR IN MERE WOMAN'S CRUELTY · · · · · · · · · ·		789	SINGING HEAD		11
CRUISE					
A GOOD ROUND SUM UPON THIS CRUISE, AND TURN-- · · · · ·		222	SHADOW WATER B		5
CRUMB					
I HAVE NOT A CRUMB OF COMFORT, NOT A GRAIN. · · · · ·		200	FOLLY COMFORT		7
A CAREFUL FIELD-MOUSE FINDS A FALLEN CRUMB; · · · · ·		713	FERENCZ RENYI		77
CRUMBLED					
BREATHED OUT A DRUID VAPOUR, AND CRUMBLED AWAY · · · ·		761	SHADOW WATER A		279
CRUMBLING					
THE CRUMBLING MOON, THE WHITE STARS IN THE SKY, · · · ·		120	SORROW OF LOVE	V	10
AND CLIMBED INTO THE AIR, CRUMBLING AWAY, · · · · · ·		278	TWO KINGS		42
AND AFTER THAT THE CRUMBLING OF THE MOON. · · · · ·		375	PHASES OF MOON		87
UPON THE BROKEN, CRUMBLING BATTLEMENT, · · · · · ·		477	SELF AND SOUL		3
CRUMPLE					
CRUMPLE THE ROSE IN YOUR HAIR! · · · · · · · · ·		162	ASKS FORGIVE		4
CRUMPLED					
AND CRUMPLED IN MY HANDS THE STAFF · · · · · · ·		84	MAD KING GOLL	V	33
CRUNCHES					
THERE WHERE YONDER SQUIRREL CRUNCHES · · · · · · ·		655	ISLE STAT I 3		4
CRUSH					
CRUSH THE ROSE IN YOUR HAIR, · · · · · · · · ·		162	ASKS FORGIVE	V	4
CRUSHED					
AS A GRASS SEED CRUSHED BY A PEBBLE, AS A WOLF SUCKED UNDER		63	OISIN 3	V	220
A WEIR.					
BUT THE CRUSHED GRASS WHERE WE HAVE LAIN! · · · · ·		389	SOLOMON WITCH		42
CRUSHING					
· · · THE STRONG HOOFS CRUSHING THE SAND AND THE SHELLS,		58	OISIN 3		157
· · · THE GOLD HOOVES CRUSHING THE SANDS AND THE SHELLS		58	OISIN 3	V	157
· · · THE STRONG HOOFS CRUSHING THE SANDS AND THE SHELLS		58	OISIN 3	V	157
ARE 'NEATH ITS PROW, AND CRUSHING SHELLS. · · · · · ·		663	ISLE STAT II 2		35
CRUST					
WILL SCARCELY FIND FOR HIM A BROKEN CRUST · · · · · ·		373	PHASES OF MOON		23
CRUTCH					
A BUNDLE OF RAGS UPON A CRUTCH, · · · · · · · ·		302	HOUR DAWN		2
WERE HERE, HE WOULD TURN DEATH INTO A CRUTCH! · · · ·		711	FERENCZ RENYI		38
CRUTCHES					
OF GRIEVOUS TIME ON HIS OLD CRUTCHES, · · · · · · ·		23	OISIN 1	V	341B
GREY HAIRS AND CRUTCHES, CRUTCHES AND GREY HAIRS, · · ·		721	WITCH VIVIEN		20
GREY HAIRS AND CRUTCHES, CRUTCHES AND GREY HAIRS, · · ·		721	WITCH VIVIEN		20
CRY					
BUT NOW HEARTS CRY THAT HEARTS ARE SLAVES, · · · · · ·		19	OISIN 1		280
AND THE CRY OF THE HOUNDS ON THE HILLS OF OLD. · · · ·		27	OISIN 1		407
FOR NO MAN'S CRY SHALL EVER MOUNT SO FAR! · · · · · ·		36	OISIN 2		108
FOR NEVER MORTAL CRY SO FAR HATH SENT. · · · · · ·		36	OISIN 2	V	108
NOR NO MAN'S CRY SHALL EVER MOUNT SO FAR! · · · · · ·		36	OISIN 2	V	108
AND AT HIS CRY THERE CAME NO MILK-PALE FACE · · · · ·		38	OISIN 2		134
THE SEA SWEPT ON AND CRIED HER OLD CRY STILL, · · · ·		68	SAD SHEPHERD		10
I KNOW THE WORD THEY CRY, "ETERNITY!" · · · · · ·		81	EPHEMERA	V	24F
NOT THEY ARE THE ETERNAL--'TIS THE CRY." · · · · ·		81	EPHEMERA	V	24J
A GAY WANDERING CRY. · · · · · · · · · · ·		98	FOXHUNTER		28
A GAY AND WANDERING CRY. · · · · · · · · · ·		98	FOXHUNTER	V	28
PARTED HER LIPS WITH A LOUD SUDDEN CRY. · · · · · ·		105	CUCHULAIN SEA		8
GOD'S BELL HAS CLAIMED THEM BY THE LITTLE CRY · · · ·		114	ROSE OF BATTLE		23
WE SHALL NO LONGER HEAR THE LITTLE CRY · · · · · ·		115	ROSE OF BATTLE		35
HAD BLOTTED OUT MAN'S IMAGE AND HIS CRY. · · · · · ·		120	SORROW OF LOVE		4
COULD BUT COMPOSE MAN'S IMAGE AND HIS CRY. · · · · ·		120	SORROW OF LOVE		12
HAD HID AWAY EARTH'S OLD AND WEARY CRY. · · · · · ·		120	SORROW OF LOVE	V	4
ARE SHAKEN WITH EARTH'S OLD AND WEARY CRY. · · · · ·		120	SORROW OF LOVE	V	12
PROCLAIM WITH THAT UNWEARIED, REEDY CRY · · · · · ·		128	DREAM OF FAERY		42
A-TELLING WITH THEIR LOW AND REEDY CRY · · · · · ·		128	DREAM OF FAERY	V	42
PROCLAIMING WITH A LOW AND REEDY CRY, · · · · · ·		128	DREAM OF FAERY	V	42
AND, LIKE A STORM, CRY THE INEFFABLE NAME, · · · · ·		137	TO SOME I TALK		12
THE CRY OF A CHILD BY THE ROADWAY, THE CREAK OF A LUMBERING		142	ROSE IN HEART		2
CART,					
AND SCATTERED THE CARDS WITH A CRY, · · · · · · ·		145	HOST OF AIR	V	38
DESOLATE WINDS THAT CRY OVER THE WANDERING SEA! · · · ·		147	UNAPPEAS HOST		7
O CURLEW, CRY NO MORE IN THE AIR, · · · · · · · ·		155	REPROVE CURLEW		1
HE HEARS THE CRY OF THE SEDGE · · · · · · · · ·		165	CRY OF SEDGE		T
AEDH HEARS THE CRY OF THE SEDGE · · · · · · · ·		165	CRY OF SEDGE	V	T

175

		PAGE	TITLE		LINE
CRY	(CONTINUED)				
TILL THE ATTORNEY FOR LOST SOULS CRY HER SWEET CRY,	• • •	173	SPEAKS HEARERS		6
TILL THE ATTORNEY FOR LOST SOULS CRY HER SWEET CRY,	• • •	173	SPEAKS HEARERS		6
TILL MAURYA OF THE WOUNDED HEART CRY A SWEET CRY,	• • •	173	SPEAKS HEARERS		6
TILL MAURYA OF THE WOUNDED HEART CRY A SWEET CRY,	• • •	173	SPEAKS HEARERS	V	6
CRY OF HIS LOVE WITH THEIR PITIFUL CRIES.	• • •	177	PAST GREATNESS	V	12
I HARDLY HEAR THE CURLEW CRY,	• • • • • • • •	189	BAILE AILLINN		1
LET RUSH AND BIRD CRY OUT THEIR FILL	• • • • • •	197	BAILE AILLINN		198
"LET PEEWIT CALL AND CURLEW CRY WHERE THEY WILL,	• •	203	WITHER BOUGHS		2
A QUEEN-WOMAN DRESSED OUT IN SILVER, CRY	• • •	210	RAGGED WOOD		2
I WILL DRIVE ALL THOSE LOVERS OUT AND CRY—	• •	211	RAGGED WOOD		10
FOR THERE THE TALL DEER AND HIS LEMAN CRY	• • •	211	RAGGED WOOD	V	6
I WILL DRIVE OUT THE DEER AND MOON AND CRY—	•	211	RAGGED WOOD	V	10
I'LL HOLLO ALL THOSE LOVERS OUT AND CRY—	• • •	211	RAGGED WOOD	V	10
OR CRY ABOUT ONE'S EARS. NOTHING TO FEAR.	• •	222	SHADOW WATER B		19
AND LISTENING TO THE CRY OF WIND AND WAVE	• • •	236	SHADOW WATER B		315
AND LISTENING TO THE CRY OF THE WIND AND WAVE	•	236	SHADOW WATER B	V	315
BUT NO, NO, NO! YOUR CRY IS NOT AGAINST ME.	• •	244	SHADOW WATER B		449
THAT YOU MAY NEVER HEAR THE CRY OF THE BIRDS.	• •	250	SHADOW WATER B		575
TO CRY ALOUD TO THE GREY BIRDS, AND DREAMS,	• •	252	SHADOW WATER B		618
IT VANISHED LIKE A SHADOW, AND A CRY	• • •	278	TWO KINGS		38
SO MOURNFUL THAT IT SEEMED THE CRY OF ONE	• • •	278	TWO KINGS		39
YOU'D CRY, "SOME WOMAN'S YELLOW HAIR	• • •	290	SEPTEMBER 1913		28
A SINGLE SOUL THAT LACKS A SWEET CRYSTALLINE CRY.	•	291	PAUDEEN		8
"YOU CRY ALOUD, O WOULD 'TWERE SPRING	• • •	306	HOUR DAWN		91
"I HEARD A SEA-MEW CRY,	• • • • • • • • •	308	PLAYER QUEEN		14
"I HEARD A SEAMEW CRY,	• • • • • • • • •	308	PLAYER QUEEN	V	14
WERE IT NOT THAT LOVE LIVE UPON THE CRY	• • •	314	MEMORY YOUTH		19
FROM NINETEEN HUNDRED NINE OR TEN, PAVLOVA'S HAD THE CRY,		354	HIS PHOENIX		11
AND WITH THAT CRY I HAVE RAISED MY CRY.	• • •	361	ALF POLLEXFEN		39
AND WITH THAT CRY I HAVE RAISED MY CRY.	• • •	361	ALF POLLEXFEN		39
HE WERE AFRAID THE BIRDS, WHO CRY ALOUD	• • •	371	EGO DOMINUS		77
AND CIRCLED ROUND HIM WITH ITS SQUEAKY CRY.	• •	377	PHASES OF MOON		138
COME WITH LOUD CRY AND PANTING BREAST	• • •	412	TOWER		86
AND CRY IN PLATO'S TEETH.	• • • • • • • •	415	TOWER		147
OR A BIRD'S SLEEPY CRY	• • • • • • • • •	416	TOWER		194
MAY BUILD IN THE CRACKED MASONRY AND CRY	• •	423	MY DESCENDANTS		15
"VENGEANCE UPON THE MURDERERS," THE CRY GOES UP,	• •	426	PHANTOM HATRED		9
NOR CRY, NOR TURN IN THE BED	• • • • • •	435	FOR MY SON		3
THE HERALD'S CRY, THE SOLDIER'S TREAD	• • •	438	SONGS PLAY 2		13
I'D HAVE A PEACOCK CRY,	• • • • • • • • •	458	HIS WILDNESS		8
WITH THAT SWEET CRY.	• • • • • • • • • •	559	HE AND SHE		12
CRY AT THE ONSET OF THEIR SEXUAL JOY	• • •	560	WHENCE COME		2
CRY AT THE ONSET OF THE SEXUAL JOY	• • •	560	WHENCE COME	V	2
AND ITS CRY DISTRACTS MY THOUGHT.	• • • •	633	MAN AND ECHO		46
AND ITS CRY DISTRACTS MY THOUGHTS.	• • • •	633	MAN AND ECHO		46
OF THINE CRY OVER WOLD AND WATER WHITE,	• • •	669	ISLE STAT II 3		73
I CRIED THE THING YOU BADE ME CRY.	• • • •	670	ISLE STAT II 3		114
I CRIED THE WORDS YOU BID ME CRY.	• • • •	673	ISLE STAT II 3		186
MAKE MOAN AND CRY. WITHIN YON SUNLESS VALLEY,	• •	682	SEEKER		26
THITHER THY DUST, AND KNEAD IT WITH A CRY,	• •	688	TWO TITANS		52
NOT AS HE SHAKES THE FOREST! BUT A CRY	• • •	689	NETTLESHIP		8
NOR HEEDS THE OLD, DIM PROTEST AND THE CRY	• •	689	NETTLESHIP		14
ONE SHOULDER TWISTED, AND THE CHILDREN CRY	• •	695	MOSADA 1		116
AND SEIZE HER, AND THUS FLOATS HER QUIVERING CRY!	•	714	FERENCZ RENYI		105
AND THE BIRD IN THE BRANCHES WILL CRY FOR US CLEAR,	•	717	LOVE SONG		6
MEN CRY "BRING PAUL, SHIELD BREAKER.	• • •	740	EARL PAUL		11
MEN CRY: "BRING PAUL, SHIELD-BREAKER,	• • •	740	EARL PAUL	V	11
THOUGH THE GLAD CRY "SHIELD-BREAKER,"	• • •	741	EARL PAUL		35
TO CRY HIS FOLDING CRY! NO, NO, BE SILENT,	• •	760	SHADOW WATER A		253
TO CRY HIS FOLDING CRY! NO, NO, BE SILENT,	• •	760	SHADOW WATER A		253
TO CRY HIS FOLDING CRY. THERE IS SOME MAN	• •	760	SHADOW WATER A		253
TO CRY HIS FOLDING CRY. THERE IS SOME MAN	• •	760	SHADOW WATER A	V	253
THE HARP-STRINGS HAVE BEGUN TO CRY OUT TO THE EAGLES.	•	769	SHADOW WATER A		431
IT HAS BEGUN TO CRY OUT TO THE EAGLES.	• • •	769	SHADOW WATER A	V	431
THAT I CRY, THAT I CRY?"	• • • • • • • •	772	SONG DEIRDRE 1		8
THAT I CRY, THAT I CRY?"	• • • • • • • •	772	SONG DEIRDRE 1		8
HAVE TO CRY, HAVE TO CRY."	• • • • • • •	772	SONG DEIRDRE 1		16
HAVE TO CRY, HAVE TO CRY."	• • • • • • •	772	SONG DEIRDRE 1		16
THOUGH WE WERE BIDDEN TO SING, CRY NOTHING LOUD.	• •	778	SONG DEIRDRE 3		2
THE DREAMING BONES CRY OUT	• • • • • • •	782	HEART FRIGHT		15
THE CURLEW CRY BEFORE DAWN	• • • • • • •	783	GREY ROUND		22
CRYING					
CRYING, THE PIRATES DROVE HIS SWINE	• • • •	82	MAD KING GOLL		15
FLYING, CRYING, TO AND FRO.	• • • • • •	136	TWO TREES		35
BECAUSE YOUR CRYING BRINGS TO MY MIND	• • •	155	REPROVE CURLEW		3
THERE IS ENOUGH EVIL IN THE CRYING OF WIND.	• •	155	REPROVE CURLEW		6
WITH ALL THIS CRYING IN THE WIND,	• • • •	190	BAILE AILLINN		33
UPON THE THRONE AND CRYING ABOUT THE STREETS	• •	198	SEVEN WOODS		7
COMES CRYING, "I HAVE RUN UPON THE SWORD.	• •	234	SHADOW WATER B		261
WHAT IS THERE BUT THE CRYING OF THE BIRDS?	• •	247	SHADOW WATER B		519
IF YOU'LL BUT LISTEN CLOSELY TO THAT CRYING	• •	247	SHADOW WATER B		520
THEY'RE CRYING OUT, COULD YOU BUT HEAR THEIR WORDS,	•	247	SHADOW WATER B		529
WITH ALL THOSE SIGHTS AND ALL THAT CRYING OUT?	• •	249	SHADOW WATER B		573
CRYING AMID THE GLITTERING SEA,	• • • •	254	HIS DREAM		17
CRYING ALOUD AS THE RACECOURSE IS,	• • • •	266	GALWAY RACES		14
CRYING ALOUD AS THE RACE COURSE IS,	• • • •	266	GALWAY RACES	V	14
CRYING ALOUD AS THE RACE-COURSE IS,	• • • •	266	GALWAY RACES	V	14
THE MONSTROUS CRYING OF WIND?	• • • • •	312	CHILD DANCING		12
CRYING TO ONE ANOTHER LIKE THE BATS!	• • •	376	PHASES OF MOON		106
"A LAUGHING, CRYING, SACRED SONG,	• • • •	570	THREE BUSHES		43

176

CRYING   (CONTINUED)
    A STRICKEN RABBIT IS CRYING OUT, ... 633 MAN AND ECHO   45
    AND CRYING, "I HAVE FLED TO MY BELOVED . . . . . . 754 SHADOW WATER A V   151
    AND NOW THE WAVES ARE CRYING IN MY EARS, ... 761 SHADOW WATER A   276
CRY'S
    THAT CRY'S FROM THE FIRST CUCKOO OF THE YEAR. . . . . 338 SHEP GOATHERD   1
    THAT CRY'S FROM THE FIRST CUCKOO OF THE . . . . . . 338 SHEP GOATHERD   V   1
CRYSTALLINE
    A SINGLE SOUL THAT LACKS A SWEET CRYSTALLINE CRY. . . . 291 PAUDEEN   8
CU
    OF THE CROWNED MAGI; AND THE HOUND OF CU . . . . . . 169 SECRET ROSE   V   9
CUB
    BUT HERE THE LIONESS LICKS HER SOFT CUB . . . . 688 NETTLESHIP   2
CUBES
    ALL, ALL THOSE GYRES AND CUBES AND MIDNIGHT THINGS . . . 469 HARUN RASHID   184
    THOSE CONES AND CUBES AND GYRES, THOSE MIDNIGHT THINGS, 469 HARUN RASHID   V   184
CUBS
    AND LIONESS, WITH ALL THEIR WHIMPERING CUBS; . . . . . 73 ANASHU VIJAYA   53
CUCHULAIN
    CUCHULAIN BATTLING WITH THE BITTER TIDE; . . . . . . 100 ROSE UPON ROOD   3
    THE DEATH OF CUCHULAIN . . . . 105 CUCHULAIN SEA   V   T
    NOR WON THE GOLD THAT NOW CUCHULAIN BRINGS." . . . . 106 CUCHULAIN SEA   V   11
    "NAY, YOU ARE TALLER THAN CUCHULAIN, SON." . . . . . 107 CUCHULAIN SEA   V   27
    AMONG THOSE FEASTING MEN CUCHULAIN DWELT, ... 108 CUCHULAIN SEA   39
    FEASTED, AND WITH THEM OLD CUCHULAIN DWELT, ... 108 CUCHULAIN SEA   V   39
    AMONG THOSE FEASTING KINGS CUCHULAIN DWELT, ... 108 CUCHULAIN SEA   V   39
    AT LAST CUCHULAIN SPAKE, "SOME MAN HAS MADE . . . . . 109 CUCHULAIN SEA   47
    CUCHULAIN CRIED, "I AM THE ONLY MAN . . . . 109 CUCHULAIN SEA   55
    AT LAST CUCHULAIN SPAKE, "A YOUNG MAN STRAYS . . . . . 109 CUCHULAIN SEA   V   47
    CUCHULAIN CRIED, "HAVE MADE AND KEEP THAT VOW." . . . . 109 CUCHULAIN SEA   V   56
    BUT NOW THE WAR-RAGE IN CUCHULAIN WOKE, ... 110 CUCHULAIN SEA   65
    "CUCHULAIN I, MIGHTY CUCHULAIN'S SON." . . . . . . 110 CUCHULAIN SEA   68
    WITH HEAD BOWED ON HIS KNEES CUCHULAIN STAYED; . . . . 110 CUCHULAIN SEA   71
    SPAKE THUS: "CUCHULAIN WILL DWELL THERE AND BROOD . . . 110 CUCHULAIN SEA   77
    BUT NOW THE WAR RAGE IN CUCHULAIN WOKE, ... 110 CUCHULAIN SEA   V   65
    AND CHAUNTED FOR THREE DAYS. CUCHULAIN STIRRED, ... 111 CUCHULAIN SEA   83
    IN THREE DAYS' TIME, CUCHULAIN WITH A MOAN . . . . . 111 CUCHULAIN SEA   V   83
    AND CHANTED FOR THREE DAYS. CUCHULAIN STIRRED, ... 111 CUCHULAIN SEA   V   83
    CUCHULAIN THE GIRL AND THE FOOL . . . . 447 HERO GIRL FOOL V   T
    CUCHULAIN THAT FOUGHT NIGHT LONG WITH THE FOAM, ... 549 SEVERED HEAD   9
    WHEN PEARSE SUMMONED CUCHULAIN TO HIS SIDE, ... 611 STATUES   25
    CUCHULAIN SAT AT HER SIDE; . . . . 628 JANE MOUNTAIN   17
    CUCHULAIN FOUGHT THE UNGOVERNABLE SEA; . . . . . . 630 CIRCUS ANIMALS   26
    CUCHULAIN COMFORTED . . . . 634 CUCHULAIN COMF   T
CUCHULAIN'S
    CUCHULAIN'S FIGHT WITH THE SEA . . . . 105 CUCHULAIN SEA   T
    "CUCHULAIN I, MIGHTY CUCHULAIN'S SON." . . . . . . 110 CUCHULAIN SEA   68
    "I AM FINMOLE, MIGHTY CUCHULAIN'S SON." . . . . . . 110 CUCHULAIN SEA   V   68
CUCHULIN
    CAME BLANID, MAC NESSA, CUCHULIN; . . . . 53 OISIN 3   V   89
CUCHULLIN
    WITH HEAD BOWED ON HIS KNEES, CUCHULLIN STAID, ... 110 CUCHULAIN SEA   V   71
    AND CRIED, "CUCHULLIN WILL DWELL THERE AND BROOD, . . . 110 CUCHULAIN SEA   V   77
    NEAR TO CUCHULLIN, ROUND A QUICKEN TREE, ... 111 CUCHULAIN SEA   V   81A
CUCKOO
    THAT CRY'S FROM THE FIRST CUCKOO OF THE YEAR. . . . . 338 SHEP GOATHERD   1
    THAT CRY'S FROM THE FIRST CUCKOO OF THE . . . . . . 338 SHEP GOATHERD   V   1
    AS THOUGH HE KNEW HIMSELF, AS IT WERE, A CUCKOO, . . . 341 SHEP GOATHERD   54
    AS ALIEN AS A CUCKOO IN A ROBIN'S NEST, ... 671 ISLE STAT II 3   138
    ALIEN AS CUCKOO IN A ROBIN'S NEST, ... 671 ISLE STAT II 3 V   138
    AND THE CUCKOO UNSEEN IN HIS FESTIVAL MOOD; . . . . . 717 LOVE SONG   7
CUFF
    NOW CUFF HIM OFF. HE'S OFF! A KISS FOR YOU, ... 73 ANASHU VIJAYA   39
CUMANN'S
    THE OLD BROWN THORN TREES BREAK IN TWO HIGH OVER CUMANN'S 206 HANRAHANS SONG V   1
        STRAND,
CUMBERED   SEE DEW-CUMBERED
    HE HAD SAT DOWN AND SIGHED WITH CUMBERED HEART, ... 37 OISIN 2   111
    HE HAD GONE WHISPERING FORTH WITH CUMBERED HEART, . . . 37 OISIN 2   V   111
CUMBROUS
    . . . FOR, CUMBROUS WITH STEMS OF THE HAZEL AND OAK, . . 48 OISIN 3   25
CUMHAL
    CUMHAL CALLED OUT, BENDING HIS HEAD, ... 166 BLESSED   1
    CUMHAL THE KING, BEING ANGRY AND SAD, ... 166 BLESSED   V   1
    AND CUMHAL SAID, BENDING HIS KNEES, ... 167 BLESSED   5
    AND CUMHAL SAW LIKE A DRIFTING SMOKE . . . . 167 BLESSED   13
    "AND WHICH IS THE BLESSEDEST," CUMHAL SAID, ... 167 BLESSED   21
    CUMHAL CALLED OUT, BOWING HIS HEAD, ... 167 BLESSED   V   4A
    "AND WHO IS THE BLESSEDEST," CUMHAL SAID, ... 167 BLESSED   V   21
CUMMEN
    THE OLD BROWN THORN-TREES BREAK IN TWO HIGH OVER CUMMEN 206 HANRAHANS SONG   1
        STRAND,
    WEAK AND WORN AND WEARY THE WAVES OF CUMMEN STRAND, . . . 207 HANRAHANS SONG V   6
CUP   SEE WINE-CUP
    AND FILLS WITH STARS NIGHT'S PURPLE CUP, ... 18 OISIN 1   262
    LIKE THE PALE CUP OF THE SEA, ... 175 ELEMENT POWERS   14
    THEIR HEARTS WOULD BE LIKE A CUP . . . . 215 HAPPY TOWNLAND   31
    FOR THEIR HEARTS WOULD BE LIKE A CUP . . . . 215 HAPPY TOWNLAND V   31
    THE ALE CUP IS MY FATHER AND MY MOTHER. . . . . . . 222 SHADOW WATER B V   11B
    A MELANCHOLY THAT A CUP OF WINE, ... 227 SHADOW WATER B   114
    IS NO MORE THAN A WINE CUP IN THE TASTING, ... 229 SHADOW WATER B V   150

	PAGE	TITLE		LINE

CUP   (CONTINUED)

OR ON SOME STILL UNEMPTIED CUP	271	GREY ROCK		21
AND STRETCHING FORTH HIS ARM AND CUP	275	GREY ROCK		118
THE EMPTY CUP	454	EMPTY CUP		T
A CRAZY MAN THAT FOUND A CUP,	454	EMPTY CUP		1
AN OPEN BOOK AND EMPTY CUP	501	VACILLATION		38
I CARRY THE SUN IN A GOLDEN CUP,	525	DANCING DAYS		7
I CARRY THE SUN IN A GOLDEN CUP,	525	DANCING DAYS		15
I CARRY THE SUN IN A GOLDEN CUP,	525	DANCING DAYS		23
MORN-BEWILDERED, AND THE CUP	646	ISLE STAT I 1		47
CREEPING ALONG THE HEAVENS' PURPLE CUP,	714	FERENCZ RENYI		112
THEREFORE IN THIS ANCIENT CUP	776	AGAINST WITCH		36
THEREFORE FROM THIS ANCIENT CUP	776	AGAINST WITCH	V	36
A GREY-GREEN CUP OF JADE,	781	MY HEART BEAT		15
OR MAYBE AN AGATE CUP.	781	MY HEART BEAT		16

CUPBOARDS

I HAVE CUPBOARDS OF DRIED FRAGRANCE,	572	LADYS 2ND SONG		5

CUPS

BREWED BY THE SEA-GODS, FROM HUGE CUPS THAT LAY	41	OISIN 2		189
BREWED OF THE SEA-GODS, FROM HUGE CUPS THAT LAY	41	OISIN 2	V	189
BREWED BY THE SEA GODS, FROM HUGE CUPS THAT LAY	41	OISIN 2	V	189
WHEN CUPS WENT ROUND AT CLOSE OF DAY--	271	GREY ROCK		12
FROM MURMURING MURIAS: ON CUPS--	271	GREY ROCK	V	22

CUR

BUT A THIEVING RASCALLY CUR--	552	SONGS REWRIT 2		7

CURD-PALE

THE CURD-PALE MOON, THE WHITE STARS IN THE SKY,	120	SORROW OF LOVE	V	10

CURDS

. . . LONG WARLESS, GROWN WHITER THAN CURDS.	49	OISIN 3		36
. . . LONG-WARLESS, GROWN WHITER THAN CURDS.	49	OISIN 3	V	36
WHITER THAN CURDS, ITS EYES THE TINT OF THE SEA.	277	TWO KINGS		7

CURE

SIGHED, "YOU, EVEN YOU YOURSELF, COULD WORK THE CURE!"	282	TWO KINGS		124
A FRIEND THAT COULD, HE HAD TOLD HER, WORK HIS CURE	283	TWO KINGS		137
THAT COULD, AS HE HAD TOLD HER, WORK HIS CURE,	283	TWO KINGS	V	137

CURED

AND THAT IS CURED BY A BOILED LIQUORICE ROOT.	227	SHADOW WATER B	V	116B

CURES

CURES HE HATH FOR COW OR GOAT	716	FAIRY DOCTOR		13
CURES FOR CALVES WITH 'PLAINING THROAT,	717	FAIRY DOCTOR		15
CURES FOR CALF WITH 'PLAINING THROAT,	717	FAIRY DOCTOR	V	15

CURLEW

HE REPROVES THE CURLEW	155	REPROVE CURLEW		T
WINDLE-STRAWS I. O'SULLIVAN RUA TO THE CURLEW	155	REPROVE CURLEW	V	T
HANRAHAN REPROVES THE CURLEW	155	REPROVE CURLEW	V	T
O CURLEW, CRY NO MORE IN THE AIR,	155	REPROVE CURLEW		1
I HARDLY HEAR THE CURLEW CRY,	189	BAILE AILLINN		1
"LET PEEWIT CALL AND CURLEW CRY WHERE THEY WILL,	203	WITHER BOUGHS		2
I KNOW, AND THE CURLEW AND PEEWIT ON ECHTGE OF STREAMS.	204	WITHER BOUGHS		22
AND THE CURLEW AND PEEWIT KNOW ON ECHTGE OF STREAMS.	204	WITHER BOUGHS	V	22
UNTIL A CURLEW CRIED AND IN THE LUMINOUS WIND	291	PAUDEEN		4
A CURLEW ANSWERED; AND SUDDENLY THEREUPON I THOUGHT	291	PAUDEEN		5
A CURLEW ANSWERED, AND I WAS STARTLED BY THE THOUGHT	291	PAUDEEN	V	5
THE CURLEW CRY BEFORE DAWN	783	GREY ROUND		22

CURLS

THE ODOROUS WEIGHT OF HIS CURLS OF LIGHT,	28	OISIN 1	V	423D
LIFT THEIR CHINS AND TOSS THEIR CURLS,	726	LOVERS QUARREL		23

CURRANT

HIVES, CURRANT BUSHES. THERE HIS KIN ARE. HIGH	710	FERENCZ RENYI		25
HE NUMBERS. HE, WITH FLOWERING CURRANT TREES,	710	FERENCZ RENYI		22

CURRANT-BUSHES

HIVES, CURRANT-BUSHES. THERE HIS KIN ARE. HIGH	710	FERENCZ RENYI	V	25

CURSE

AND GAVE HIS CURSE TO ME:	95	MOLL MAGEE		26
ADAM'S CURSE	204	ADAMS CURSE		T
AS THOUGH IT DRAGGED ROAD-METAL. MY CURSE ON PLAYS	260	FASC DIFFICULT		8
AS THOUGH IT DRAGGED ROAD METAL. MY CURSE ON PLAYS	260	FASC DIFFICULT	V	8
THOSE WINE-DRENCHED EYES, AND CURSE OUR LUCK	272	GREY ROCK		39
AND THOSE FIERCE EYES, AND CURSE OUR LUCK	272	GREY ROCK	V	39
'TWAS WINE OR WOMEN, OR SOME CURSE--	273	GREY ROCK		54
AND MURMURED "MAY GOD CURSE THE NIGHT	303	HOUR DAWN	V	32B
"THOSE PLATONISTS ARE A CURSE," HE SAID,	485	STATISTICS		1
MAY CALL A CURSE OUT OF THE SKY	508	JANE BISHOP	V	4
CURSE AS YOU MAY I SING IT THROUGH;	525	DANCING DAYS		9
THE CURSE OF CROMWELL	580	CURSE CROMWELL		T
I CURSE THEE--CURSE THEE!" RENYI SILENT STANDS,	714	FERENCZ RENYI		107
I CURSE THEE--CURSE THEE!" RENYI SILENT STANDS,	714	FERENCZ RENYI		107

CURSED   SEE A-CURSED

TO KEEP HIM UPRIGHT WHILE HE CURSED.	302	HOUR DAWN		6
AND THEN, GROWN WEARY, PRAYED AND CURSED	307	HOUR DAWN		117
AND PRAYED AND CURSED AND CURSED AND FLED	307	HOUR DAWN		119
AND PRAYED AND CURSED AND CURSED AND FLED	307	HOUR DAWN		119
AND CURSED AND PRAYED, AND PRAYED AND CURSED	307	HOUR DAWN	V	117
AND CURSED AND PRAYED, AND PRAYED AND CURSED	307	HOUR DAWN	V	117

CURSES

MAY CALL DOWN CURSES ON HIS HEAD	508	JANE BISHOP		4

CURSING

A CURSING ROGUE WITH A MERRY FACE,	302	HOUR DAWN		1
CURSING THE WIND. IT WAS AS MUCH	302	HOUR DAWN	V	4
I AM TIRED OF CURSING THE BISHOP,	628	JANE MOUNTAIN		1

178

CURTAIN
    LIFTED THE CURTAIN OF HER SLEEPING-ROOM, ...   182 QUEEN MAEVE   63
    LIFTED THE CURTAIN OF HER SLEEPING ROOM, ...   182 QUEEN MAEVE   V   63
    MIGHT BE ACCOMPLISHED. BUNCHING THE CURTAIN UP . . . .   183 QUEEN MAEVE   68
    SOMEWHERE BEYOND THE CURTAIN   . . . .   504 QUARREL IN AGE   12
    THE GREAT STAGE CURTAIN ABOUT TO DROP, ...   565 LAPIS LAZULI   13
CURTAINED
    AND LIGHTS THE CURTAINED ROOM, ...   89 ISLE IN WATER   10
CURTAINS
    THE CURTAINS DRAWN UPON UNFRIENDLY NIGHT, ...   523 LONG SILENCE   4
CURVED
    TO ONE VAST FOOT, FROTH-SPLASHED, WITH CURVED TOES LYING   32 OISIN 2   V 46A
    CURVED LIKE NEW MOON, MOON-LUMINOUS, ...   421 MY TABLE   10
    CURVED LIKE NEW MOON, MOON LUMINOUS, ...   421 MY TABLE   V   10
CURVING
    CURVING BENEATH THE PROW, AS SOME WILD DRAKE   . . . . .   659 ISLE STAT II 1   16
CUSHIONED
    I SAT ON CUSHIONED OTTER-SKIN, ...   81 MAD KING GOLL   1
    I SAT ON CUSHIONED OTTER SKIN, ...   81 MAD KING GOLL   V   1
    CHAIRED IN THE CUSHIONED OTTER SKIN, ...   82 MAD KING GOLL   V   5
    CHAIRED IN A CUSHIONED OTTER-SKIN   . . . .   82 MAD KING GOLL   V   5
    "LAY ME IN A CUSHIONED CHAIR, ...   97 FOXHUNTER   1
    "NOW LAY ME IN A CUSHIONED CHAIR, ...   97 FOXHUNTER   V   1
    SERVANTS ROUND HIS CUSHIONED PLACE   . . . .   99 FOXHUNTER   37
    THE SERVANTS ROUND HIS CUSHIONED PLACE   . . . .   99 FOXHUNTER   V   37
CUSHIONS
    WITH CUSHIONS HERE AND CUSHIONS THERE, ...   97 FOXHUNTER   3
    WITH CUSHIONS HERE AND CUSHIONS THERE, ...   97 FOXHUNTER   3
CUSHLA
    WAKE, MA CUSHLA, SLEEPY-HEADED, ...   705 DAWN-SONG   9
CUSTOM
    HOW BUT IN CUSTOM AND IN CEREMONY   . . . .   406 FOR DAUGHTER   77
    AND CUSTOM FOR THE SPREADING LAUREL TREE.   . . . . . .   406 FOR DAUGHTER   80
CUSTOMARY
    FAR FROM THE CUSTOMARY SKIES, ...   360 ALF POLLEXFEN   14
CUSTOMS
    WHO DIG OLD CUSTOMS UP.   . . . .   93 FATHER OHART   40
CUT
    AND CUT AND PEELED A HAZEL WAND, ...   149 WANDER AENGUS   3
    AND CUT AND PEELED A HAZEL ROD .   . . .   149 WANDER AENGUS   V   3
    AND I WILL FOLLOW YOU AND CUT THE ROPE   . . . .   250 SHADOW WATER B   586
    AND CUT THE ROPE, FOR I GO ON WITH FORGAEL.   . . . . .   250 SHADOW WATER B   592
    CUT OUT OUR RHYMES ON STRIPS OF NEW-TORN BARK   . . . .   343 SHEP GOATHERD   115
    CUT IN THE TURKISH FASHION, ...   363 DOLLS DRAWINGS   8
    TO CUT AND SEW, BE NEAT IN EVERYTHING   . . . .   443 SCHOOL CHILDR   5
    THAT CUT THROUGH TIME OR CROSS IT WITHERSHINS.   . . . .   489 COOLE PARK 29   24
    THAT CAN CROSS TIME AND CUT IT WITHERSHINS.   . . . . .   489 COOLE PARK 29   24
    THAT CUT THROUGH TIME AND CUT IT WITHERSHINS   . . . . .   489 COOLE PARK 29   V   24
    THAT CUT THROUGH TIME AND CUT IT WITHERSHINS   . . . . .   489 COOLE PARK 29   V   24
    CUT OUT HIS HEART. SOME MASTER OF DESIGN   . . . . . .   541 PARN FUNERAL 1   14
    BY HIS COMMAND THESE WORDS ARE CUT, ...   640 BEN BULBEN   91
    "AND CUT NO WOOD THE WHOLE DAY LONG, ...   731 PRIEST FAIRY   81
    I HAVE CUT THE ROPE THAT BOUND THIS GALLEY TO OURS. . .   768 SHADOW WATER A   421
    I HAVE CUT THE CORDS THAT HELD THIS GALLEY TO OURS. . .   768 SHADOW WATER A   V   421
CUTTER   SEE WOOD-CUTTER
CUT-THROAT
    A CLOUD BLOWN FROM THE CUT-THROAT NORTH   . . . .   313 MEMORY YOUTH   6
CUTTING
    DESTROY THE VIEW BY CUTTING DOWN AN ASH   . . . .   372 ON GOING HOUSE   13
CYPRESS
    AND PLANTED CYPRESS ROUND, ...   123 DREAM OF DEATH   8
    A CYPRESS AND A YEW.   . . . .   123 DREAM OF DEATH   V   6
    WHERE CYPRESS IS AND OOZY PINE, ...   670 ISLE STAT II 3   110
DA
    DA VINCI' FINGER SO HAD FASHIONED IT   . . . .   444 SCHOOL CHILDR   V   26
DABBLE
    THE FEET OF SUMMER DABBLE   . . . .   680 LOVE AND DEATH   7
DABBLED   SEE DEW-DABBLED SPRAY-DABBLED
    . . . DEW DABBLED, THE LILY AND ROSE, ...   122 WHITE BIRDS   V   5
DAD   SEE GRAND-DAD
DADDY-LONG-LEGS
    BECAUSE CHILDREN DEMAND DADDY-LONG-LEGS UPON HIS TIMBER   623 HIGH TALK   6
        TOES,
DAEMONIC
    HOW THE DAEMONIC RAGE   . . . .   419 MY HOUSE   16
    THE HALF-READ WISDOM OF DAEMONIC IMAGES, ...   427 PHANTOM HATRED   39
    THE HALF READ WISDOM OF DAEMONIC IMAGES, ...   427 PHANTOM HATRED   V   39
DAEMONS
    AND IN MY HEART THE DAEMONS AND THE GODS   . . . .   104 FERGUS DRUID   V 38B
DAFFODIL
    WHERE DAFFODIL AND LILY WAVE, ...   67 HAPPY SHEPHERD   46
DAFFODILLS
    THE BRAZEN SKY, SO BLAZE THE DAFFODILLS, ...   645 ISLE STAT I 1   11
    IN VALE AND DELL SO BLAZE THE DAFFODILLS, ...   645 ISLE STAT I 1   15
    IN LEMON-TINTED LINES, SO BLAZE THE DAFFODILLS.   . . .   645 ISLE STAT I 1   19
    LAPPED IN THE LEMON DAFFODILLS, A BEE   . . . .   716 DWELT SYCAMORE   10
DAILY
    QUIET'S WILD HEART, LIKE DAILY MEAT, ...   196 BAILE AILLINN   178
    BECAUSE THE DAILY SPECTACLE THAT STIRRED   . . . . . .   270 PARDON FATHERS   16
    MY DAILY THOUGHTS SINCE THE FIRST STUPOR OF YOUTH . . .   342 SHEP GOATHERD   83
    THE DAILY SPITE OF THIS UNMANNERLY TOWN, ...   351 PEOPLE   3

	PAGE	TITLE		LINE

DAILY   (CONTINUED)
    OF ALL THOSE TRUTHS THAT ARE YOUR DAILY BREAD: . . . .   373 PHASES OF MOON   24
    MY HEART COULD NEVER TURN FROM DAILY RUIN, ...   464 HARUN RASHID   83
    MY HEART MUST LOOK UPON A DAILY RUIN . . . .   464 HARUN RASHID   V   83
    HAD WATCHED MY DAILY PASSAGE TO AND FRO: . . . .   466 HARUN RASHID   107
    WHETHER FOR DAILY PITTANCE OR IN BLIND FEAR . . . . . .   482 BLOOD AND MOON   37
    I SOUGHT IT DAILY FOR SIX WEEKS OR SO. . . . .   629 CIRCUS ANIMALS   2
DAIRY
    WE'LL DANCE AND THEN FEAST IN A DAIRY. . . . .   707 FAIRY PEDANT   10
    WE'LL DANCE AND THEN FEAST IN A DAIRY. . . . .   708 FAIRY PEDANT   38
DAISY
    DEWY-TONGUED, THE DAISY TOPS-- . . . .   706 DAWN-SONG   22
DALLIANCE
    OF DALLIANCE WITH A DEMON THING. . . . .   2 OISIN 1   4
DAMAGES
    AWARDED HIM FOR DAMAGES . . . .   596 COLONEL MARTIN   48
DAMASK
    THE DAMASK ROSES, BLOOM ON BLOOM, ...   21 OISIN 1   305
    SHALL FALL THE LEAVES OF DAMASK ROSES. . . . .   21 OISIN 1   315
    DAMASK ROSES IN THE NIGHT, ...   21 OISIN 1   V 306A
    IN DAMASK CLOTHED AND ON A SEAT . . . .   440 WISDOM   9
DAMES
    TALL DAMES GO WALKING IN GRASS-GREEN AVALON. . . . . .   627 STATES HOLIDAY   13
    TALL DAMES GO WALKING IN GRASS-GREEN AVALON. . . . . .   627 STATES HOLIDAY   26
    TALL DAMES GO WALKING IN GRASS-GREEN AVALON. . . . . .   627 STATES HOLIDAY   39
    TALL DAMES GO WALKING IN GRASS GREEN AVALON. . . . . .   627 STATES HOLIDAY   V REF
DAMNED
    TO WHERE THE DAMNED HAVE HOWLED AWAY THEIR HEARTS, . . .   474 ALL SOUL NIGHT   95
DAMP
    SOME BURN DAMP FAGGOTS, OTHERS MAY CONSUME . . . . . .   327 ROBERT GREGORY   81
DAMPED
    . . . DAMPED BY THE BODY OR THE MIND, ...   556 RIBH PATRICK   8
DAMS
    SHIVERING CLOSER TO THEIR DAMS . . . .   726 LOVERS QUARREL   7
DAN
    DAN AND JERRY LOUT . . . .   520 HIS BARGAIN   5
    DAN AND JERRY TOUT, ...   520 HIS BARGAIN   V   5
DANAAN
    UNTIL THE DANAAN POETS BROUGHT . . . .   7 OISIN 1   63
    LOVE, TILL THE DANAAN POETS BROUGHT . . . .   7 OISIN 1   V   63
    UNTIL THE DANAAN POETS CAME. . . . .   7 OISIN 1   V   64
    AND YOU SHALL KNOW THE DANAAN LEISURE: . . . .   9 OISIN 1   100
    DANAAN SONGS, AND THEIR DEWY SHOWERS . . . .   11 OISIN 1   135
    "WERE THESE TWO BORN IN THE DANAAN LAND, ...   12 OISIN 1   146
    THAT SLOPING GREEN DE DANAAN SOD . . . .   20 OISIN 1   299
    OF DANAAN HOOVES WE URGED OUR WAY BETWEEN . . . . .   31 OISIN 2   V   31
    THAT FEED WHITE MOTHS BY SOME DE DANAAN SHRINE: . . .   41 OISIN 2   186
    I AM HAUNTED BY NUMBERLESS ISLANDS, AND MANY A DANAAN   122 WHITE BIRDS   9
        SHORE,
    A DANAAN FRUITAGE MAKES A SHOWER OF MOONS, ...   127 DREAM OF FAERY V   22
    WHILE I WROUGHT OUT THESE FITFUL DANAAN RHYMES, . . .   136 TO SOME I TALK V   1
    I DEDICATE THESE FITFUL DANAAN RHYMES . . . . . .   136 TO SOME I TALK V   1
    THE DANAAN CHILDREN LAUGH, IN CRADLES OF WROUGHT GOLD,   146 UNAPPEAS HOST   1
    I KNOW WHERE A DIM MOON DRIFTS, WHERE THE DANAAN KIND   203 WITHER BOUGHS   12
    AND I KNOW OF THE ISLES WHERE THE DANAAN KIND . . . .   203 WITHER BOUGHS V   12
    AND OF APPLE ISLANDS WHERE THE DANAAN KIND . . . . .   203 WITHER BOUGHS V   12
    THE DANAAN QUICKEN TREE . . . .   742 DANAAN QUICK   T
    (AH, MOURNFUL DANAAN QUICKEN TREE!) . . . .   742 DANAAN QUICK   6
    (AH, MOURNFUL DANAAN QUICKEN TREE!) . . . .   743 DANAAN QUICK   12
    (AH, MOURNFUL DANAAN QUICKEN TREE!) . . . .   743 DANAAN QUICK   18
    BELOVED, BLAME THE DANAAN WHIM, ...   743 DANAAN QUICK   22
    (AH, MOURNFUL DANAAN QUICKEN TREE!) . . . .   743 DANAAN QUICK   24
    (AH, MOURNFUL DANAAN QUICKEN TREE!) . . . .   743 DANAAN QUICK   30
DANCE
    WHO WHEN THEY DANCE TO A FITFUL MEASURE . . . . . .   9 OISIN 1   97
    AND IN A WILD AND SUDDEN DANCE . . . .   20 OISIN 1   290
    BENDING OVER THEM IN THE DANCE, ...   21 OISIN 1   308
    THE DANCE WOUND THROUGH THE WINDLESS WOODS: . . . . .   21 OISIN 1   320
    SANG WE SOFTLY IN THE DANCE, ...   21 OISIN 1   V 308
    THE PEAHENS DANCE ON A SMOOTH LAWN, ...   77 INDIAN TO LOVE   3
    THE PEA-HENS DANCE, IN CRIMSON FEATHER . . . . . .   77 INDIAN TO LOVE V   3
    YOU WAVES, THOUGH YOU DANCE BY MY FEET LIKE CHILDREN AT   90 OLD FISHERMAN   1
        PLAY,
    YE WAVES, THOUGH YE DANCE 'FORE MY FEET LIKE CHILDREN AT   90 OLD FISHERMAN V   1
        PLAY,
    WHILE YOUNG STARS ABOUT HER DANCE. . . . .   125 CATHLEEN PARA V   16
    AND DANCE UPON THE LEVEL SHORE? . . . .   125 GOES FERGUS   3
    AND DREAMING HOW THEY DANCE AND DART, ...   135 TWO TREES   V   18
    AWAY FROM THE MERRY DANCE. . . . .   145 HOST OF AIR   32
    AND THOUGH THE SEVEN LIGHTS BOWED IN THEIR DANCE AND WEPT,   174 ELEMENT POWERS   3
    FOLK DANCE LIKE A WAVE OF THE SEA: . . . .   178 FIDDLER DOONEY   2
    AND THE MERRY LOVE TO DANCE! . . . .   179 FIDDLER DOONEY   16
    AND DANCE LIKE A WAVE OF THE SEA. . . . .   179 FIDDLER DOONEY   20
    THAT HAS GROWN WEARY OF THE WANDERING DANCE, ...   285 TWO KINGS   183
    THAT HAS GROWN WEARY OF THE WHIRLING DANCE, ...   285 TWO KINGS   V 183
    POUR WINE AND DANCE IF MANHOOD STILL HAVE PRIDE, . . .   311 MOUNTAIN TOMB   1
    POUR WINE AND DANCE, IF MANKIND STILL HAVE PRIDE, . . .   311 MOUNTAIN TOMB V   1
    DANCE THERE UPON THE SHORE! . . . .   312 CHILD DANCING   1
    I'D DANCE A MEASURE ON HIS GRAVE." . . . .   338 TOM OROUGHLEY   16
    THAT SHEBA LED A DANCE. . . . .   346 ON WOMAN   43
    DO YOU DANCE, MINNALOUSHE, DO YOU DANCE? . . . . .   378 CAT AND MOON   11

	PAGE	TITLE	LINE

DANCE (CONTINUED)

	PAGE	TITLE	LINE
DO YOU DANCE, MINNALOUSHE, DO YOU DANCE?	378	CAT AND MOON	11
WHAT BETTER THAN CALL A DANCE?	378	CAT AND MOON	13
A NEW DANCE TURN.	378	CAT AND MOON	16
A NEW DANCE TUNE.	378	CAT AND MOON V	16
AND NEW DANCE TURN.	378	CAT AND MOON V	16
AND LITTLE SHE BY WHOM HER DANCE WAS SEEN	383	VISION ROBART	38
HOW CAN WE KNOW THE DANCER FROM THE DANCE?	446	SCHOOL CHILDR	64
AND WHERE THE BLESSED DANCE!	474	ALL SOUL NIGHT	96
WHAT MANHOOD LED THE DANCE!	488	CRAZED MOON	12
MEN DANCE ON DEATHLESS FEET."	496	MOHINI CHATTER	28
DYING INTO A DANCE,	498	BYZANTIUM	30
SUCH A DANCE AS THERE WAS DANCED--	515	JANE GROWN OLD	20
COME DANCE WITH ME IN IRELAND."	526	AM OF IRELAND	5
AND DANCE WITH ME IN IRELAND."	527	AM OF IRELAND	18
AND DANCE WITH ME IN IRELAND."	527	AM OF IRELAND	31
LET HER FINISH HER DANCE,	568	SWEET DANCER	12
LET HER FINISH HER DANCE.	568	SWEET DANCER	13
A DANCE FOR THE FISHER-LADS!	589	OLD WICKED MAN	33
A DANCE FOR THE FISHER LADS!	589	OLD WICKED MAN V	33
SHOULD DANCE ATTENTION UPON MY OLD AGE!	591	SPUR	2
SHOULD DANCE ATTENDANCE UPON MY OLD AGE!	591	SPUR V	2
THROUGH THEIR ANCESTRAL PATTERNS DANCE,	612	NEWS ORACLE	19
SO LET US DANCE WHERE THE YELLOW LANCE	643	SONG FAERIES	7
SO LET US DANCE ON FRINGED WAVES,	644	SONG FAERIES	9
SO LET US DANCE WHERE THE YELLOW LANCE	676	ISLE STAT II 3	254
SO LET US DANCE ON THE FRINGED WAVES,	676	ISLE STAT II 3	256
AND UNTO IT WE'LL DANCE UPON THE SWARD.	681	SEEKER	10
THOU KNOWEST THIS, AND HOW FROM 'MID THE DANCE	683	SEEKER	51
WE'LL DANCE AND THEN FEAST IN A DAIRY.	707	FAIRY PEDANT	10
WE'LL DANCE AND THEN FEAST IN A DAIRY.	708	FAIRY PEDANT	38
IN EVERY DANCE, BY CHILDREN SOUGHT. "ACCURST,	709	FERENCZ RENYI	12
SO WE DANCE A FAIRY JIG	726	LOVERS QUARREL	19
"THE SWIFTEST HE TO DANCE OR FLY,	729	PRIEST FAIRY	45
AS DANCE UPON THE SPEAR-GRASS BRITTLE,	731	PRIEST FAIRY	78
DANCE THE SAVAGE CHILDREN SMALL,	732	STREET DANCERS	29
THE FLIES THAT DANCE IN THREES, IN TWOS,	736	IN CHURCH	11

DANCED

	PAGE	TITLE	LINE
WE DANCED TO WHERE IN THE WINDING THICKET	20	OISIN 1	304
WE DANCED TO WHERE WITHIN THE GLOOM	21	OISIN 1 V	305
SOME DANCED LIKE SHADOWS ON THE MOUNTAINS,	25	OISIN 1	388
WHO DANCED ON A LEVEL PLACE,	144	HOST OF AIR	14
DANCED IN THE WHIRLING FOAM AND IN THE DUST,	284	TWO KINGS	167
THAT, IT MAY BE, HAD DANCED HER LIFE AWAY,	383	VISION ROBART	22
O LITTLE DID THEY CARE WHO DANCED BETWEEN,	383	VISION ROBART	37
THAT IT MAYBE HAD DANCED HER LIFE AWAY,	383	VISION ROBART V	22
SO THAT SHE DANCED. NO THOUGHT,	383	VISION ROBART V	39
I SAID THAT SHE HAD DANCED HEART'S TRUTH,	514	JANE GROWN OLD	9
SUCH A DANCE AS THERE WAS DANCED--	515	JANE GROWN OLD	20
DANCED ON CRUACHAN'S WINDY PLAIN.	528	DANCER CRUACH	4
DANCED IT ON CRUACHAN'S WINDY PLAIN,	528	DANCER CRUACH V	4
AND NEVER HAVE I DANCED FOR JOY,	567	FROM JAPANESE	9
AROUND MY HEAD AND DANCED AMONG THE GRASS!	690	MOSADA 1	19
DANCED, LAUGHED, LOVED, FOUGHT THROUGH	787	HUDDON DUDDON	4
WHAT THOUGH THEY DANCED! THOSE DAYS ARE GONE,	788	HAWTHORN TREE	5

DANCE-LIKE

	PAGE	TITLE	LINE
A DANCE-LIKE GLORY THAT THOSE WALLS BEGOT.	488	COOLE PARK 29	8

DANCER

	PAGE	TITLE	LINE
WHAT A DANCER GLIMMERING!	125	CATHLEEN PARA	14
THAT IF A DANCER STAYED HIS HUNGRY FOOT	127	DREAM OF FAERY	22
UPON THE DANCER BY THE DREAMLESS WAVE.	128	DREAM OF FAERY	45
AND NO ONE ANY LEAF-CROWNED DANCER MISS	128	DREAM OF FAERY V	46
MICHAEL ROBARTES AND THE DANCER	385	ROBARTES DANCE	T
HOW CAN WE KNOW THE DANCER FROM THE DANCE?	446	SCHOOL CHILDR	64
THE DANCER AT CRUACHAN AND CRO-PATRICK	528	DANCER CRUACH	T
SWEET DANCER	568	SWEET DANCER	T
AH, DANCER, AH, SWEET DANCER!	568	SWEET DANCER	7
AH, DANCER, AH, SWEET DANCER!	568	SWEET DANCER	7
AH, DANCER, AH, SWEET DANCER!	568	SWEET DANCER	14
AH, DANCER, AH, SWEET DANCER!	568	SWEET DANCER	14
AND UNDER EVERY DANCER	592	DRUNK SOBRIETY	11

DANCERS

	PAGE	TITLE	LINE
OF DANCERS LEAPING IN THE AIR!	18	OISIN 1	254
THE MANY-COLOURED DANCERS RUSHED,	21	OISIN 1 V	322
THE DANCERS CROWDED ABOUT HIM	144	HOST OF AIR	17
BUT THE OLD MEN AND DANCERS WERE GONE,	145	HOST OF AIR V	39
WHEN LOIE FULLER'S CHINESE DANCERS ENWOUND	430	NINETEEN 19	49
HAD FALLEN AMONG DANCERS, HAD WHIRLED THEM ROUND	430	NINETEEN 19	52
ALL MEN ARE DANCERS AND THEIR TREAD	430	NINETEEN 19	57
OWEN AHERNE AND HIS DANCERS	449	OWEN AHERNE	T
IN THE LONG ECHOING STREET THE LAUGHING DANCERS THRONG,	459	FROM OEDIPUS	7
IN THE LONG ECHOING STREETS THE LAUGHING DANCERS THRONG,	459	FROM OEDIPUS V	7
CRAZY JANE GROWN OLD LOOKS AT THE DANCERS	514	JANE GROWN OLD	T
CRACKED MARY AND THE DANCERS	514	JANE GROWN OLD V	T
CRAZY JANE AND THE DANCERS	514	JANE GROWN OLD V	T
THE LOVERS AND THE DANCERS ARE BEATEN INTO THE CLAY,	580	CURSE CROMWELL	3
STREET DANCERS	731	STREET DANCERS	T

DANCE'S

	PAGE	TITLE	LINE
SWEPT ON THE DANCE'S LINKED FLOW,	20	OISIN 1	V 291
ONCE MORE THE DANCE'S LINKED FLOW,	22	OISIN 1	V 323A

181

		PAGE	TITLE		LINE
DANCES					
AND WAVERING ARMS AND WANDERING DANCES.		19	OISIN 1		275
AND WAVING ARMS AND WANDERING DANCES.		19	OISIN 1	V	275
WEAVING OLDEN DANCES,		87	STOLEN CHILD		17
WIND AND UNWIND THEIR DANCES WHEN THE LIGHT GROWS COOL		203	WITHER BOUGHS		13
IN HAPPY DANCES UNDER A WINDY MOON,		245	SHADOW WATER B		470
IN HAPPY DANCES, UNDER A WINDY MOON:		763	SHADOW WATER A		318
DANCING					
THOSE MERRY COUPLES DANCING IN TUNE,		3	OISIN 1		9
AND FEET OF MAIDENS DANCING IN TUNE,		3	OISIN 1	V	9
THE FLOOR OF EMAN'S DANCING HALL		13	OISIN 1	V	156
THE ISLANDS OF DANCING AND OF VICTORIES		46	OISIN 2		247
IN DREARY DANCING PAST US WHIRLED,		65	HAPPY SHEPHERD		8
IN DANCING SILVER-SANDALLED ON THE SEA,		101	ROSE UPON ROOD		7
IN DANCING SILVER SANDALLED ON THE SEA,		101	ROSE UPON ROOD	V	7
AH, FAERIES, DANCING UNDER THE MOON,		139	TO IRELAND		31
WIND AND UNWIND DANCING WHEN THE LIGHT GROWS COOL		203	WITHER BOUGHS	V	13
ARE DANCING IN A CROWD.		214	HAPPY TOWNLAND		12
ARE DANCING IN THE CROWD.		214	HAPPY TOWNLAND	V	12
TO A CHILD DANCING IN THE WIND		312	CHILD DANCING		T
TO A CHILD DANCING UPON THE SHORE		312	CHILD DANCING	V	T
THE PLAYING UPON PIPES AND THE DANCING,		330	BONE OF A HARE		5
TO CHANGE MY LOVES WHILE DANCING		330	BONE OF A HARE		7
THAT SHE OF DANCING DREAMED.		383	VISION ROBART		24
DANCING TO A FRENZIED DRUM,		403	FOR DAUGHTER		15
LABOUR IS BLOSSOMING OR DANCING WHERE		445	SCHOOL CHILDR		57
MARBLES OF THE DANCING FLOOR		498	BYZANTIUM		36
DANCING WITH HER CHOSEN YOUTH,		514	JANE GROWN OLD		2
THOSE DANCING DAYS ARE GONE		524	DANCING DAYS		T
THOSE DANCING DAYS ARE GONE,		524	DANCING DAYS		2
THE GIRL GOES DANCING THERE		568	SWEET DANCER		1
HER POETRY, DANCING UPON THE SHORE,		578	CRAZED GIRL		2
AND KEEP ME DANCING STILL		591	DRUNK SOBRIETY		2
AND THEREFORE KEEP ME DANCING		592	DRUNK SOBRIETY		7
KEEP DANCING LIKE A WAVE,		592	DRUNK SOBRIETY		10
DANCING IN SOME MOONY PLACE,		647	ISLE STAT I 1		54
THE LIGHT IS DANCING O'ER THE KNOTTED TREES,		662	ISLE STAT II 2		2
A CLOVEN, DANCING JET,		680	LOVE AND DEATH		2
DANCING ON THE MOON'S BROAD STAIN,		731	STREET DANCERS		15
DANCING IN THE FEEBLE GLOW,		733	STREET DANCERS		49
LOVELY LADIES DANCING IN IT.		788	HAWTHORN TREE		4
LIVE, FOR I SAW THEM DANCING THERE.		788	HAWTHORN TREE		12
DANCING-PLACE					
WHEN HER SOUL FLIES TO THE PREDESTINED DANCING-PLACE		365	HER COURAGE		1
DANDLED					
YOU'VE DANDLED THEM AND FED THEM FROM THE BOOK		265	ABBEY THEATRE		8
MY MOTHER DANDLED ME AND SANG,		308	PLAYER QUEEN		1
DANE					
BUT A GREAT DANE THAT CANNOT BAY THE MOON		579	DOR WELLESLEY		10
DANES					
HAD PERISHED THERE, BUT THE DANES RAN,		274	GREY ROCK		74
AND MORE, IF YOU WILL WAR AGAINST THE DANES		756	SHADOW WATER A	V	190
DANGER					
DANGER NO REFUGE HOLDS, AND WAR NO PEACE,		114	ROSE OF BATTLE		9
THERE IS GREAT DANGER IN THE BODY.		386	ROBARTES DANCE		38
PROTECTING, TILL THE DANGER PAST,		436	FOR MY SON		31
AND DANGER NOT BE DIMINISHED:		786	YOUR HEART		31
DANGEROUS					
OF THE EVER-LIVING HALF SO DANGEROUS		224	SHADOW WATER B		46
AND HAS BEEN DANGEROUS TO HIM. I HAVE HEARD		224	SHADOW WATER B		52
DANGLING					
BUT NEVER, NEVER DANGLING LEAVE THE LIVER AND THE LIGHTS.		790	HEART SLEEVE		2
DANIEL					
"HUDDON AND DUDDON AND DANIEL O'LEARY,		529	TOM LUNATIC		7
HUDDON, DUDDON AND DANIEL O'LEARY		787	HUDDON DUDDON		1
HUDDON, DUDDON AND DANIEL O'LEARY		787	HUDDON DUDDON		6
HUDDON, DUDDON AND DANIEL O'LEARY		787	HUDDON DUDDON		11
DANISH					
"THE DANISH TROOP WAS DRIVEN OUT		273	GREY ROCK		65
DANTE					
DANTE ALIGHIERI, SO UTTERLY FOUND HIMSELF		368	EGO DOMINUS		19
A GIRL THAT KNEW ALL DANTE ONCE		626	OLD MEN BE MAD		5
DAPHNE					
A DAPHNE AND A MARY WHO LIVE IN PRIVACY:		354	HIS PHOENIX		18
DAPPLED					
AND WALK AMONG LONG DAPPLED GRASS,		150	WANDER AENGUS		21
ON DAPPLED SKINS IN A GLASS BOAT,		196	BAILE AILLINN		180
DARE					
"YOU DARE ME TO MY FACE," AND THEREUPON		106	CUCHULAIN SEA		17
AND DROP HIM FROM THE GUNNEL. I DARE NOT DO IT.		222	SHADOW WATER B		15
DARE MATCH IN LEARNING WITH US TWO,		333	SOLOMON SHEBA		21
AND SHOULD SOME CRAZY HAND DARE TOUCH A DAUGHTER		433	NINETEEN 19		122
IMITATE HIM IF YOU DARE,		493	SWIFTS EPITAPH		4
BUT WHAT AM I THAT DARE		507	STREAM AND SUN		7
OR BODILY MOVEMENT DID I DARE,		514	JANE GROWN OLD		5
THERE'S NOT A BIRD OF DAY THAT DARE		538	LAST CONFESS		23
"BUT NEVER DARE TO BOAST		539	MEETING		8
DARED					
THAT YOU HAVE COME AND DARED ME TO MY FACE?"		109	CUCHULAIN SEA		61
TO GRASP THE WOMAN. YOU HAVE DARED TO TOUCH HER?		223	SHADOW WATER B		39
WHEN MY LUCK CHANGED AND THEY DARED MEET MY FACE,		352	PEOPLE		25

182

		PAGE	TITLE		LINE
DARED (CONTINUED)					
WHEN MY LUCK CHANGED AND THEY DARED TO MEET MY FACE,		352	PEOPLE	V	25
NONE DARED ADMIT, IF SUCH A THOUGHT WERE HIS,		430	NINETEEN 19		44
HARDLY DARED TO WET HIS MOUTH		454	EMPTY CUP		3
MADGE TELLS ME WHAT I DARED NOT THINK		457	SECRETS OF OLD		3
DARED I STOP".		559	HE AND SHE		6
NO SHEPHERD FOOT HAS EVER DARED ITS DEPTHS.		682	SEEKER		32
DARGAN'S					
CASTLE DARGAN'S RUIN ALL LIT,		788	HAWTHORN TREE		3
DARING					
HAS NO ONE SAID THOSE DARING		312	TWO YEAR LATER		1
SO DARING AND SWEET HIS THOUGHT,		393	EASTER 1916		30
DARK SEE WINE-DARK BLOOD-DARK PITCH-DARK NIGHT-DARK					
OF OUR STRONG STEEDS WAS DARK WITH SWEAT,		2	OISIN 1	V	7T
TOGETHER, WHILE THE DARK WOODS RANG,		16	OISIN 1		227
WOVEN INTO HER HAIR, BEFORE DARK TOWERS		30	OISIN 2		22
WOVE IN HER FLOWER-LIKE HAIR, BEFORE DARK TOWERS		30	OISIN 2	V	22
AND BLACKNESS IN THE DARK. THE SEA ROLLED ROUND,		30	OISIN 2	V	23
ON OUR DARK PATHWAY, TILL A COUNTLESS FLIGHT		31	OISIN 2		34
DARK STATUES GLIMMERED OVER THE PALE TIDE		31	OISIN 2		36
UPON DARK THRONES. BETWEEN THE LIDS OF ONE		31	OISIN 2		37
OUT OF THE SEVENFOLD SEAS, BUILT THE DARK HALL		38	OISIN 2		131
UNDER A CROWN OF THORNS, AND DARK WITH BLOOD,		38	OISIN 2		135
OUT OF THE SEVEN-FOLD SEAS, BUILT THE DARK HALL		38	OISIN 2	V	131
AND MANANNAN'S DARK TOWER, STONE AFTER STONE,		45	OISIN 2		236
AND MANANAN'S DARK TOWER, STONE BY STONE,		45	OISIN 2	V	236
AND TRAMPLE MY DARK ISLE.		45	OISIN 2	V	239E
FOR NO LIVE CREATURES LIVED THERE, NO WEASELS MOVED IN THE DARK!		48	OISIN 3		19
DARK BALOR, AS OLD AS A FOREST, CAR-BORNE, HIS MIGHTY HEAD SUNK		53	OISIN 3		91
FOR NO LIVE CREATURES LIVE THERE, NO WEASELS MOVE IN THE DARK!		56	OISIN 3		139
ORCHIL SHAKES OUT HER LONG DARK HAIR		85	MAD KING GOLL		62
AND TALKED OF THE DARK FOLK WHO LIVE IN SOULS		136	TO SOME I TALK		4
OF THAT DARK FOLK WHO GATHER IN THE SOULS		136	TO SOME I TALK	V	4
AND HE SAW HOW THE REEDS GREW DARK		144	HOST OF AIR		5
THE BLUE AND THE DIM AND THE DARK CLOTHS		176	CLOTHS HEAVEN		3
UNTIL THE PILLARED DARK BEGAN TO STIR		185	QUEEN MAEVE		110
BUT OUT OF THE DARK AIR OVER HER HEAD THERE CAME		187	QUEEN MAEVE		153
DARK AND DULL AND EARTHY THE STREAM OF DRUMAHAIR		207	HANRAHANS SONG	V	11
DARK AND DULL AND EARTHY OUR SOULS AND BODIES BE!		208	HANRAHANS SONG	V	13
A DARK DEEP HOLLOW IN THE ROCK.		303	HOUR DAWN		21
A DARK DEEP HOLE IN THE ROCK'S FACE,		303	HOUR DAWN	V	21
OF THE DARK LEOPARDS OF THE MOON?		343	DEJECTION		3
WHERE STONE IS DARK UNDER FROTH,		348	FISHERMAN		32
WHERE STONE IS DARK WITH FROTH,		348	FISHERMAN	V	32
THE FULL AND THE MOON'S DARK AND ALL THE CRESCENTS,		373	PHASES OF MOON		32
FOR THERE'S NO HUMAN LIFE AT THE FULL OR THE DARK.		373	PHASES OF MOON		35
BECAUSE ALL DARK, LIKE THOSE THAT ARE ALL LIGHT,		376	PHASES OF MOON		104
OF THE DARK MOON AND THE FULL,		384	VISION ROBART		60
ON THE DARK STREAM,		389	IMAGE PAST		3
LIT UP THE DARK MAHOGANY AND THE WINE,		410	TOWER		27
OUT OF THE OBSCURE DARK OF THE RICH STREAMS,		417	ANCEST HOUSES		14
OUT OF DARK NIGHT WHERE LAY		439	FRAGMENTS		9
BY THE DARK WEBS, HER NAPE CAUGHT IN HIS BILL,		441	LEDA AND SWAN		3
IN THE MAD ABSTRACT DARK AND GROUND IT GRAIN BY GRAIN		442	BLACK CENTAUR		8
THE WINE DARK OF THE WOOD'S INTRICACIES,		446	COLONUS PRAISE	V	2
AMONG DARK SKINS, AND THERE		472	ALL SOUL NIGHT		48
THEN DARKENING THROUGH "DARK" RAFTERY'S "CELLAR" DROP,		490	COOLE BALLYLEE		4
A HEAVENLY MANSION, RAGING IN THE DARK,		491	COOLE BALLYLEE	V	40D
UNTIL THE MORNING BREAK AS ON A DARK BREAST.		494	AT ALGECIRAS	V	6
A HEAVENLY MANSION, RAGING IN THE DARK.		495	CHOICE		4
BETWEEN THE DARK AND DAWN.		511	JANE AND JACK		6
IF I MAKE THE LASHES DARK		531	BEFORE WORLD		1
MY DARK DECLIVITIES.		536	PARTING		14
STARED AT THE WINE-DARK NAIL, OR DARK THAT RAN		537	HER VISION		10
BUT THE DARK CHANGED TO RED, AND TORCHES SHONE,		537	HER VISION		12
THROUGH JONATHAN SWIFT'S DARK GROVE HE PASSED, AND THERE		543	PARN FUNERAL 2		11
BECAUSE YOU HAVE IT IN THE PITCH DARK NIGHT		554	RIBH AT TOMB	V	1
BECAUSE YOU HAVE FOUND ME IN THE PITCH DARK NIGHT		554	RIBH AT TOMB	V	1
HERE IN THE PITCH DARK ATMOSPHERE ABOVE		555	RIBH AT TOMB	V	17
OR DARK BETWIXT THE POLECAT AND THE OWL,		565	GYRES		21
OR ANY RICH, DARK NOTHING DISINTER		565	GYRES		22
WHO UNDERSTAND THE DARK!		588	OLD WICKED MAN		31
WHEN DARK HANGS UPON THE WATER		589	OLD WICKED MAN		34
"A YOUNG MAN IN THE DARK AM I,		589	OLD WICKED MAN		37
CLIMB TO OUR PROPER DARK, THAT WE MAY TRACE		611	STATUES		31
NO DARK TOMB-HAUNTER ONCE! HER FORM ALL FULL		618	BRONZE HEAD		8
THERE IN THE TOMB THE DARK GROWS BLACKER,		636	BLACK TOWER		27
OH, MORE DARK THY GLEAMING HAIR IS		647	ISLE STAT I 1		51
AS LIES DARK WATER IN A MURMUROUS GLADE,		650	ISLE STAT I 1		138
IN THE NEVER-LIFTING DARK.		658	ISLE STAT I 3		89
MORE DARK BENEATH THE POPLARS, WHERE YON OWL		675	ISLE STAT II 3		233
IN ENDLESS DARK, AND BY THE WEEDY MARGE		682	SEEKER		19
FEET OF DARK GOMEZ, WHERE NOW WANDER YE?		690	MOSADA 1		11
THE DARK STILL MAN, HAS COME AND SAYS 'TIS SIN.		692	MOSADA 1		47
THE FOOT-WORN WAY IS LONG, AND IT GROWS DARK.		702	MOSADA 3		92
THE FOOTWORN WAY IS LONG, AND IT GROWS DARK.		702	MOSADA 3	V	92
AND HIS HAIR WAS AS DARK AS A PLOVER'S EYE.		729	PRIEST FAIRY		46
DARK JOAN CALL THE BERRIES SWEET,		743	DANAAN QUICK		28

183

	PAGE	TITLE		LINE
DARK (CONTINUED)				
THAT LIVES AMONG THE WOODS OF THE DARK HOUNDS.	766	SHADOW WATER A		376
WHEN THE DARK HOUNDS WERE LOOSED. COME TO THE ALE.	766	SHADOW WATER A		379
BETWEEN DARK FURROWS UPON THE PLOUGHED LAND.	784	WOMANS BEAUTY		6
AMID THE DARK BEFORE DAY HAD BROKEN.	784	WOMANS BEAUTY		20
DARK-BEAKED				
TO FILL THEIR DARK-BEAKED HOLLOW GALLEYS.	82	MAD KING GOLL		16
DARKEN				
DARKEN: HEAVEN IS ANGRY. CEASE! UNTO MY MIND,	42	OISIN 2	V	205
THEY DREAM AND DARKEN OUR SUN.	783	GREY ROUND		15
DARKENED				
STORM DARKENED OR STARRY BRIGHT.	739	WHERE BOOKS GO		8
DARKENING SEE DAYLIGHT-DARKENING				
IN PITY FOR MAN'S DARKENING THOUGHT	438	SONGS PLAY 2		1
THEN DARKENING THROUGH "DARK" RAFTERY'S "CELLAR" DROP,	490	COOLE BALLYLEE		4
WHERE THE SWAN DRIFTS UPON A DARKENING FLOOD.	492	COOLE BALLYLEE		48
DARKER				
A DARKER KNOWLEDGE AND IN HATRED TURN	558	RIBH CHRISTIAN		14
DARKEST				
IT IS THE DARKEST EVE I EVER KNEW.	702	MOSADA 3		93
DARKNESS				
ROSE IN THE DARKNESS, AND THE WHITE SURF GLEAMED	30	OISIN 2		23
THE DARKNESS COMES. A CLOUD HANGS OVERHEAD--	43	OISIN 2	V	208A
AND DEMONS AFRAID IN THEIR DARKNESS:	62	OISIN 3		205
AND LAY IN THE DARKNESS, GRUNTING, AND TURNING TO HIS REST.	153	CHANGE BELOVED		12
HE HAS PUT A SUDDEN DARKNESS OVER THE MOON.	239	SHADOW WATER B		367
NOTHING BUT DARKNESS OVERHEAD.	314	MEMORY YOUTH		14
THE DARKNESS DROPS AGAIN: BUT NOW I KNOW	402	SECOND COMING		18
OUT OF THE FABULOUS DARKNESS CALLED.	437	SONGS PLAY 1		16
A FABULOUS, FORMLESS DARKNESS IN:	438	SONGS PLAY 2		5
WHO CAN DISTINGUISH DARKNESS FROM THE SOUL?	477	SELF AND SOUL		8
TO DEATH. HIS DARKNESS AND HIS CHILL I FEEL.	684	SEEKER		63
MY SOUL. HIS DARKNESS AND HIS CHILL I FEEL.	684	SEEKER	V	63B
BRUISING THE DARKNESS WITH THEIR CRACKLING LIGHT:	687	TWO TITANS		2
DROPT DOWN THE VELVET DARKNESS FROM ABOVE,	688	TWO TITANS		37
FOR THIS DID THE ETERNAL DARKNESS BRING	688	TWO TITANS		51
THE DARKNESS OF THE WHIRLWIND SHATTERED DEEP.	688	TWO TITANS		58
SEE THE DARKNESS SLOW DISGORGING A VESSEL BLIND WITH SQUALL.	718	PHANTOM SHIP		12
CAME OLIVE FIRES OF MORNING AND ON THE DARKNESS FED,	719	PHANTOM SHIP		33
CAME THE OLIVE FIRE OF MORNING, AND ON THE DARKNESS FED,	719	PHANTOM SHIP	V	33
AND AS THE TIME TO DARKNESS PLODDED	728	PRIEST FAIRY		11
FOR CLOSED IN DARKNESS NOW	738	MOURN THEN ON		10
LOVE WAS NOT MADE FOR DARKNESS AND THE WINDS	767	SHADOW WATER A		394
AMID THE DARKNESS, NOW THAT ALL MY STARS	767	SHADOW WATER A	V	404
DARLING				
"MY DARLING CANNOT UNDERSTAND	255	WORDS		2
MY DARLING UNDERSTANDS IT ALL,	256	WORDS		10
AND MANY A DARLING WIT'S GROWN DULL	301	RUN PARADISE		18
HER LABOURING MEN, AS THOUGH HER DARLING LIVED,	340	SHEP GOATHERD		38
"ON, ON, MY DARLING MAN."	545	TO SAME TUNE 1		16
"ON, ON, MY DARLING MAN."	616	MARCH SONGS 3		16
"OH, ON, MY DARLING MAN."	616	MARCH SONGS 3	V	16
DART				
ONE WITH THE TIDE THAT GLEAMS, THE WINGS THAT GLEAM AND DART,	78	INDIAN TO LOVE		15
ONE WITH THE WAVES THAT SOFTLY ROUND US LAUGH AND DART.	78	INDIAN TO LOVE	V	15
. . . THE WINGS THAT GLIMMER AND GLEAM AND DART:	78	INDIAN TO LOVE	V	15
. . . AND WINGS, THAT GLIMMER AND GLEAM AND DART,	78	INDIAN TO LOVE	V	15
THOUGH YOU GLOW AND YOU GLANCE, THOUGH YOU PURR AND YOU DART:	90	OLD FISHERMAN		2
THOUGH YE GLOW AND YE GLANCE, THOUGH YE PURR AND YE DART,	90	OLD FISHERMAN	V	2
AND HOW THE WINGED SANDALS DART,	135	TWO TREES		18
AND DREAMING HOW THEY DANCE AND DART,	135	TWO TREES	V	18
DARTING				
DARTING YOU WAVE THEM, DARTING IN THE VAPOUR.	694	MOSADA 1		94
DARTING YOU WAVE THEM, DARTING IN THE VAPOUR.	694	MOSADA 1		94
DASHED SEE SEA-DASHED				
I PAUSED--AND FAR AWAY I DASHED	83	MAD KING GOLL	V	31
DATE				
WILD INDOLENCE AND MUSIC HAVE NO DATE.	686	LIFE		20
WILD INDOLENCE AND MUSIC HAVE NO DATE,	735	QUATRAIN APHOR		18
AS THOUGH THEIR SEASON HAD NO DATE,	736	SUMMER EVENING		10
DATELESS				
FROM DATELESS PAIN. SHE SLEEPS--MOSADA--THOU--	701	MOSADA 3	V	65
DATHI				
TILL DATHI CAME AND STOOD,	166	BLESSED		2
TO THE CAVE, WHERE DATHI THE BLESSED HAD GONE,	166	BLESSED	V	3
BUT DATHI FOLDED HIS HANDS AND SMILED	167	BLESSED		11
"PRAISE GOD AND GOD'S MOTHER," DATHI SAID,	167	BLESSED		17
TILL DATHI CAME AND STOOD,	167	BLESSED	V	4B
"MY EYES ARE BLINKING," DATHI SAID,	168	BLESSED		25
DAUGHTER				
IS NIAM, DAUGHTER OF THE KING	5	OISIN 1	V	49
THE DAUGHTER OF THE GREY OLD WOOD-CUTTER,	74	ANASHU VIJAYA	V	63
TO FORGAIL'S DAUGHTER, EMER, IN HER DUN,	105	CUCHULAIN SEA		2
O DAUGHTER OF THE ISLAND OF WOODS:	164	PERFECT BEAUTY	V	1
CAER, HIS BLUE-EYED DAUGHTER THAT I LOVE.	184	QUEEN MAEVE		96
CAER, HIS BLUE EYED DAUGHTER THAT I LOVE.	184	QUEEN MAEVE	V	96
OF THE HARPER'S DAUGHTER AND HER FRIEND.	192	BAILE AILLINN		76
OF THE HARPER'S DAUGHTER IF THEY WILL,	197	BAILE AILLINN		199

184

DAUGHTER   (CONTINUED)

	PAGE	TITLE	LINE
OF CATHLEEN, THE DAUGHTER OF HOULIHAN.	207	HANRAHANS SONG	5
OF CATHLEEN, THE DAUGHTER OF HOULIHAN.	207	HANRAHANS SONG	10
IS CATHLEEN, THE DAUGHTER OF HOULIHAN.	208	HANRAHANS SONG	15
THE DAUGHTER AND THE GRANDDAUGHTER OF KINGS	237	SHADOW WATER B	334
THE DAUGHTER AND GRANDDAUGHTER OF KINGS	237	SHADOW WATER B V	334
AND MANY A KING'S DAUGHTER,	330	BONE OF A HARE	3
MANY A SON AND DAUGHTER LIES	360	ALF POLLEXFEN	13
A PRAYER FOR MY DAUGHTER	403	FOR DAUGHTER	T
AND SHOULD SOME CRAZY HAND DARE TOUCH A DAUGHTER	433	NINETEEN 19	122
WHERE THE GREAT MOTHER, MOURNING FOR HER DAUGHTER	447	COLONUS PRAISE	19
. . . MAN, WOMAN, CHILD (A DAUGHTER OR A SON),	556	RIBH PATRICK	2
RECALL HIS TRINITY. A FATHER, MOTHER, CHILD (A DAUGHTER OR A SON)	556	RIBH PATRICK V	2
A SMALL OLD HOUSE, WIFE, DAUGHTER, SON,	577	WHAT THEN	12
IN THY WAN FACE? HEAR THOU, O DAUGHTER OF THE DAYS,	674	ISLE STAT II 3	200
IN THOSE FAR YEARS, O DAUGHTER OF THE DAYS.	674	ISLE STAT II 3	213
IN THY WAN FACE? HEAR, DAUGHTER OF THE DAYS.	674	ISLE STAT II 3 V	200
IN THOSE FAIR YEARS, O DAUGHTER OF THE DAYS.	674	ISLE STAT II 3 V	213
O WHAT INNKEEPER'S DAUGHTER	789	SINGING HEAD	13

DAUGHTERS

	PAGE	TITLE	LINE
AND HE GAVE THEM AS DOWERS TO HIS DAUGHTERS,	92	FATHER OHART	7
HERODIAS' DAUGHTERS HAVE RETURNED AGAIN,	433	NINETEEN 19	118
FOR EVEN DAUGHTERS OF THE SWAN CAN SHARE	444	SCHOOL CHILDR	20

DAVIS

	PAGE	TITLE	LINE
WITH DAVIS, MANGAN, FERGUSON,	138	TO IRELAND	18

DAWN

	PAGE	TITLE	LINE
AND THINGS THAT FEAR THE DAWN OF THE MORROW	20	OISIN 1	302
THE DAWN CAME IN, AND GLIMMERED ON THE FLOOR	39	OISIN 2	152
OF MISTY DAWN; WHEN, CIRCLING ROUND THE HALL,	39	OISIN 2 V	153
HUNG IN THE PASSIONATE DAWN. HE SLOWLY TURNED;	40	OISIN 2	167
DAWN PASSIONED; FED WITH A FAINT GREEN LIGHT,	40	OISIN 2 V	165
FOR HE HAS WROUGHT MIDNIGHT AND DAWN AND DAY,	43	OISIN 2	208
AND MANY PATER NOSTERS SAID SINCE DAWN.	43	OISIN 2	V 208D
COMING OUT OF THE SEA AS THE DAWN COMES, A CHAUNT OF LOVE ON MY LIPS,	58	OISIN 3	158
WITH MIRTHFUL SONGS BEFORE THE DAWN.	67	HAPPY SHEPHERD	49
WITH MIRTHFUL SONGS TILL RISE THE DAWN.	67	HAPPY SHEPHERD V	49
THE ISLAND DREAMS UNDER THE DAWN	77	INDIAN TO LOVE	1
TO SMILE ON THE PALE DAWN; AND GATHER YOU	114	ROSE OF BATTLE	15
I RISE IN THE DAWN, AND I KNEEL AND BLOW	150	OLD MOTHER	1
I RISE AT THE DAWN, AND I KNEEL AND BLOW	150	OLD MOTHER V	1
AND WOOD-OF-WONDERS, WHERE ONE KILLS AN OX AT DAWN,	209	UNDER THE MOON	9
GATHERS THE WILD DUCK FROM THE WINTER DAWN;	217	WOODS OF COOLE	3
AMONG THE WINDY MEADOWS OF THE DAWN."	234	SHADOW WATER B	264
I SWEAR BEFORE THE DAWN COMES ROUND AGAIN	260	FASC DIFFICULT	12
BETWEEN THE DAWN AND DUSK," SHE SAID;	273	GREY ROCK	66
"WERE IT NOT THAT WHEN THE DAWN HAS LIT MY BED	285	TWO KINGS	187
THE HOUR BEFORE DAWN	302	HOUR DAWN	T
"NIGHT GROWS UNEASY NEAR THE DAWN	303	HOUR DAWN	33
THAT'S GROWN UNEASY NEAR THE DAWN	303	HOUR DAWN V	33
IN THE BAD HOUR BEFORE THE DAWN."	304	HOUR DAWN	55
THE CLOUDS WERE BRIGHTENING WITH THE DAWN.	307	HOUR DAWN	122
THE DAWN	344	DAWN	T
I WOULD BE IGNORANT AS THE DAWN	344	DAWN	1
I WOULD BE IGNORANT AS THE DAWN	344	DAWN	10
IGNORANT AND WANTON AS THE DAWN.	344	DAWN	14
I WOULD BE AS IGNORANT AS THE DAWN,	344	DAWN V	1
AT DAWN TO CAST HIS FLIES,	347	FISHERMAN	5
AND PASSIONATE AS THE DAWN."	348	FISHERMAN	40
IN THEIR GREAT WINDOW LOOKING AT THE DAWN;	352	PEOPLE	15
THAT SAW THE WICKS GROW YELLOW IN THE DAWN;	352	PEOPLE	18
THEIR MOMENTARY CRIES BEFORE IT IS DAWN,	371	EGO DOMINUS	78
AND DROVE HIM DRUNK OR SOBER THROUGH THE DAWN	411	TOWER	58
THE FOUNTAIN LEAP, AND AT DAWN	414	TOWER	124
THAT UNDER BURSTING DAWN	416	TOWER	176
TILL THE DAWN BREAK UPON THOSE MINGLED SEAS.	494	AT ALGECIRAS	6
BETWEEN THE DARK AND DAWN.	511	JANE AND JACK	6
THAT FIRST DAWN IN HELEN'S ARMS?	522	LULLABY	6
THAT SONG ANNOUNCES DAWN.	536	PARTING	4
THAT DAY BRINGS ROUND THE NIGHT, THAT BEFORE DAWN	563	MERU	13
SOME DAY WE SHALL GET UP BEFORE THE DAWN	622	HOUND VOICE	15
. . . NIGHT SPLITS AND THE DAWN BREAKS LOOSE;	623	HIGH TALK	12
THOSE GREAT SEA-HORSES BARE THEIR TEETH AND LAUGH AT THE DAWN.	623	HIGH TALK	14
NOW THEY RIDE THE WINTRY DAWN	637	BEN BULBEN	10
FOR THE DAWN THE FOLIAGE FINGERETH,	646	ISLE STAT I 1	26
FOR THE DAWN OF FOLIAGE FINGERETH,	646	ISLE STAT I 1 V	26
IN THE HEART OF THE DAWN THE RIVERS ARE SINGING,	648	ISLE STAT I 1	91
AND RULE THE SHADOWS OF THE EVE AND DAWN?	678	ISLE STAT II 3	304
AND THROB WITHIN THE CIRCLES OF GREEN DAWN.	701	MOSADA 3	54
ALONE AMONG THE MURMURS OF THE DAWN.	702	MOSADA 3	81
AMONG THE WINDY MEADOWS OF THE DAWN."	754	SHADOW WATER A	153
WHERE THE DEW IS MADE BEFORE DAWN;	771	SPINNING SONG	5
THE CURLEW CRY BEFORE DAWN	783	GREY ROUND	22

DAWNED

	PAGE	TITLE	LINE
AND THE FIXED STARS HAD DAWNED AND SHONE AND SET,	31	OISIN 2	40
FOR CENTURIES, AND STARS HAD DAWNED AND SET.	31	OISIN 2 V	40
FOR YEARS HIS DAYS HAD DAWNED AND FADED THUS	692	MOSADA 1	54

DAWNING

	PAGE	TITLE	LINE
AND WE FEAR NO DAWNING MORROW,	21	OISIN 1	318

| | | | PAGE | TITLE | | LINE |

DAWNING   (CONTINUED)
    OR TIRED ON ANY DAWNING MORROW, ... 23 OISIN 1 V 341
    WENT IN THE DAWNING LIGHT . . . . 512 JANE ON GOD 3
    THAT WILL BE LATER, DAY IS SCARCELY DAWNING. . . . . . 699 MOSADA 3 12
    THAT WILL BE LATER, DAY IS DAWNING. . . . . 699 MOSADA 3 V 12
DAWNS
    THE HUMAN SADNESS DAWNS ONCE MORE!" . . . . 25 OISIN 1 V 381
DAWN-SONG
    A DAWN-SONG. . . . . 705 DAWN-SONG T
DAWS
    THE DAWS CHATTER AND SCREAM, ... 415 TOWER 167
DAY   SEE TO-DAY MARRIAGE-DAY MID-DAY WELL-A-DAY
    WHEN ONE DAY BY THE TIDE I STOOD, ... 24 OISIN 1 364
    WHEN ONE DAY BY THE SHORE I STOOD, ... 24 OISIN 1 V 364
    BUT THE LOVE-DEW DIMS OUR EYES TILL THE DAY . . . . . . 28 OISIN 1 424
    AND EVEN THE SUN, THE DAY CASTLE'S WARDER. . . . . . . 28 OISIN 1 V 423A
    BEFORE THIS DAY; FOR NOW THE FALL OF TEARS . . . . . . 30 OISIN 2 18
    THOSE WARRIORS OF A LONG-FORGOTTEN DAY, ... 30 OISIN 2 V 14A
    AND THROUGH THEIR EYES NO LIGHT OF MOON OR DAY . . . . . 34 OISIN 2 V 77
    OF SWORD AND BRAZEN BATTLE-AXE, WHILE DAY . . . . . . 40 OISIN 2 171
    MINGLING OF SWORD AND WAR-AXE, WHILE THE DAY . . . . . 40 OISIN 2 V 171
    UPON THE LIPS OF SEA-GODS IN THEIR DAY; . . . . . . 41 OISIN 2 190
    FOR HE HAS WROUGHT MIDNIGHT AND DAWN AND DAY. . . . . . 43 OISIN 2 208
    TO LIE THERE 'TILL THE FOURTH DAY SAW EMERGE . . . . . 44 OISIN 2 V 220
    AND THE MOON GOAD THE WATERS NIGHT AND DAY, ... 45 OISIN 2 238
    I CRIED, "O NIAMH! O WHITE ONE! IF ONLY A TWELVE-HOURED
        DAY, 55 OISIN 3 113
    O SWIFT ON THE SEAS ALL DAY AND NIGHT . . . . 70 CLOAK BOAT 8
    ALL DAY AND NIGHT." . . . . 70 CLOAK BOAT 10
    THE FIELDS GREW FATTER DAY BY DAY, ... 82 MAD KING GOLL 7
    THE FIELDS GREW FATTER DAY BY DAY, ... 82 MAD KING GOLL 7
    HOW I HAVE FOLLOWED, NIGHT AND DAY, ... 85 MAD KING GOLL 53
    CAME KEENING IN THAT DAY. . . . . 93 FATHER OHART 32
    THE WHOLE OF THE LONG DAY. . . . . 94 MOLL MAGEE 8
    A NEIGHBOUR MINDED HER BY DAY, ... 94 MOLL MAGEE 15
    IN ALL POOR FOOLISH THINGS THAT LIVE A DAY, ... 101 ROSE UPON ROOD 11
    THIS WHOLE DAY HAVE I FOLLOWED IN THE ROCKS, ... 102 FERGUS DRUID 1
    THE WHOLE DAY HAVE I FOLLOWED IN THE ROCKS, ... 102 FERGUS DRUID V 1
    WHILE DAY ITS BURDEN ON TO EVENING BORE, ... 110 CUCHULAIN SEA 70
    AMID MEN'S SOULS THAT DAY BY DAY GIVE PLACE, ... 112 ROSE OF WORLD V 7
    AMID MEN'S SOULS THAT DAY BY DAY GIVE PLACE, ... 112 ROSE OF WORLD V 7
    I WILL ARISE AND GO NOW, FOR ALWAYS NIGHT AND DAY . . . 117 ISLE INNISFREE 9
    AND SANG HOW DAY A DRUID TWILIGHT SHEDS . . . . . . 126 DREAM OF FAERY V 7
    OR STORMY SILVER FRET THE GOLD OF DAY, ... 128 DREAM OF FAERY V 33
    AND HOW, WHEN FADES THE SEA-STREWN ROSE OF DAY, ... 128 DREAM OF FAERY V 33
    WAS WEARY NIGHT AND DAY; . . . . 132 FR GILLIGAN 2
    THE HOST IS RUSHING 'TWIXT NIGHT AND DAY, ... 141 HOSTING SIDHE 13
    HAVE THEIR DAY, HAVE THEIR DAY; . . . . 142 MOODS 4
    HAVE THEIR DAY, HAVE THEIR DAY; . . . . 142 MOODS 4
    AND THEIR DAY GOES OVER IN IDLENESS, ... 151 OLD MOTHER 7
    SHE LOOKED IN MY HEART ONE DAY . . . . 152 LOSS OF LOVE 5
    UNDER MY FEET THAT THEY FOLLOW YOU NIGHT AND DAY. . . . 153 CHANGE BELOVED 5
    UNDER MY FEET, THAT I FOLLOW YOU, NIGHT AND DAY. . . . . 153 CHANGE BELOVED V 5
    IT WORKED AT THEM, DAY OUT, DAY IN, ... 158 BELOVED RHYMES 4
    IT WORKED AT THEM, DAY OUT, DAY IN, ... 158 BELOVED RHYMES 4
    THE GREY CAIRN ON THE HILL, WHEN DAY SINKS DROWNED IN DEW, 161 BLACK PIG 6
    O WINDS, OLDER THAN CHANGING OF NIGHT AND DAY, ... 162 ASKS FORGIVE 7
    O WINDS, ELDER THAN CHANGING OF NIGHT AND DAY, ... 162 ASKS FORGIVE V 7
    TO HIDE FROM THE TROUBLED DAY. . . . . 166 BLESSED V 4
    "O BLESSEDNESS COMES IN THE NIGHT AND THE DAY . . . . . 168 BLESSED 33
    THE NETS OF DAY AND NIGHT. . . . . 175 ELEMENT POWERS 12
    AND ALL THAT NIGHT, AND ALL THROUGH THE NEXT DAY . . . 185 QUEEN MAEVE 113
    BUT WHERE IT COULD SEE HER EVERY DAY. . . . . 191 BAILE AILLINN 55
    HE ALWAYS WEPT THEM ON THAT DAY; . . . . 192 BAILE AILLINN 78
    FOR ON THAT DAY THEY HAD BEEN BETRAYED! . . . . . . 192 BAILE AILLINN 79
    THAT OLD MAN CLIMBED! THE DAY GREW DIM; . . . . . . 194 BAILE AILLINN 134
    O THOUGHT, FLY TO HER WHEN THE END OF DAY . . . . . 201 OLD MEMORY 1
    I THOUGHT TO FLY TO HER WHEN THE END OF DAY . . . . . 201 OLD MEMORY V 1
    THOUGHT FLY TO HER WHEN THE END OF DAY . . . . . . 201 OLD MEMORY V 1
    WHEN IN RAGGED VAPOUR THEY MUTTER NIGHT AND DAY, ... 206 HANRAHANS SONG V 2
    OF THE HUNTER'S MOON, THAT HUNG BETWEEN THE NIGHT AND THE 210 UNDER THE MOON 18
        DAY,
    OF THE THIRD MOON, THAT HUNG BETWEEN THE NIGHT AND THE DAY, 210 UNDER THE MOON V 18
    AS THAT WILD AENGUS. LONG BEFORE HER DAY . . . . . . 224 SHADOW WATER B 47
    AND IN A TOWER OF GLASS, AND FROM THAT DAY . . . . . 224 SHADOW WATER B 50
    BUT MY BELOVED--THAT NIGHT AND DAY HAD PERISHED, ... 246 SHADOW WATER B 504
    THE VERSES THAT COULD MOVE THEM ON THE DAY . . . . . 257 RECONCILIATION 2
    THE VERSES THAT THEY CARED FOR ON THE DAY . . . . . . 257 RECONCILIATION V 2
    WHILE THOSE SAME HUNDREDS MOCK ANOTHER DAY . . . . . 265 ABBEY THEATRE 4
    BUT SOME DAY AND AT SOME NEW MOON . . . . 266 GALWAY RACES V 10
    WHEN CUPS WENT ROUND AT CLOSE OF DAY-- . . . . . . 271 GREY ROCK 12
    ALL WAS ACCOMPLISHED. "WHEN THIS DAY . . . . 273 GREY ROCK 70
    THE MEANING OF THAT MONSTROUS DAY. THEN SHE! . . . . 280 TWO KINGS 78
    "DAY AFTER DAY YOU QUESTION ME, AND I, ... 281 TWO KINGS 99
    "DAY AFTER DAY YOU QUESTION ME, AND I, ... 281 TWO KINGS 99
    THAT SOME NEW DAY MAY BREED THE BEST . . . . 288 TO WEALTHY MAN 34
    OR HAPPIER-THOUGHTED WHEN THE DAY IS SPENT . . . . . 292 TO A SHADE 4
    OR HAPPIER THOUGHTED WHEN THE DAY IS SPENT . . . . . 292 TO A SHADE V 4
    I HAVE STOOD HERE FROM BREAK OF DAY, ... 294 THREE BEGGARS 2
    THEY MAULED AND BIT TILL THE DAY SHONE! . . . . . . 297 THREE BEGGARS 49
    THEY MAULED AND BIT THROUGH ALL THAT DAY . . . . . . 297 THREE BEGGARS 50

DAY   (CONTINUED)

		PAGE	TITLE		LINE
THREE TIMES IN A SINGLE DAY		298	THREE HERMITS		10
OR MAYBE TO MIDSUMMER DAY,"		305	HOUR DAWN		58
FOR ALL LIFE LONGS FOR THE LAST DAY		306	HOUR DAWN		98
WHEN DAY BEGINS TO BREAK		316	FRIENDS		21
THAT PACKED HIS MARRIAGE DAY		317	NIGHT COME		7
DELIGHT MEN'S EYES WHEN I AWAKE SOME DAY		323	SWANS AT COOLE		29
AND ALL DAY LONG I LOOK		329	MEN IMPROVE		4
"ALL DAY LONG FROM MID-DAY		332	SOLOMON SHEBA		3
ALL DAY LONG FROM SHADOWLESS NOON		332	SOLOMON SHEBA		5
"ALL DAY LONG FROM MIDDAY		332	SOLOMON SHEBA	V	3
AND ALL DAY LONG WE HAVE FOUND		333	SOLOMON SHEBA		22
COULD MAKE ME WISH FOR ANYTHING THIS DAY,		338	SHEP GOATHERD		3
YOU HAVE PUT THE THOUGHT IN RHYME. I WORKED ALL DAY,		341	SHEP GOATHERD		58
TO HIS SPEECH AT THE BREAK OF DAY,		341	SHEP GOATHERD		68
I MIGHT HAVE WISHED ON THE DAY		341	SHEP GOATHERD		73
I HAD WISHED A DEAR THING ON THAT DAY		341	SHEP GOATHERD	V	73
ALL DAY I'D LOOKED IN THE FACE		347	FISHERMAN		9
WHERE EVERY DAY MY FOOTFALL SHOULD HAVE LIT		352	PEOPLE		8
I KNEW A PHOENIX IN MY YOUTH, SO LET THEM HAVE THEIR DAY.		353	HIS PHOENIX		8
I KNEW A PHOENIX IN MY YOUTH, SO LET THEM HAVE THEIR DAY.		354	HIS PHOENIX		16
I KNEW A PHOENIX IN MY YOUTH, SO LET THEM HAVE THEIR DAY.		354	HIS PHOENIX		24
I KNEW A PHOENIX IN MY YOUTH, SO LET THEM HAVE THEIR DAY.		354	HIS PHOENIX		32
ALL DAY IN THE ONE CHAIR		357	BROKEN DREAMS		38
BECAUSE THE PRIEST MUST HAVE LIKE EVERY DOG HIS DAY		364	DOLLS FACES		10
THE END OF DAY		364	END OF DAY		T
BECAUSE THE END OF DAY		364	END OF DAY		4
DAY AFTER DAY, YET NEVER FIND THE MEANING.		377	PHASES OF MOON		135
DAY AFTER DAY, YET NEVER FIND THE MEANING.		377	PHASES OF MOON		135
SOME DAY I MAY FORGET		380	SONGS FOOL 1		8
DO NOT BECAUSE THIS DAY I HAVE GROWN SATURNINE		390	UNDER SATURN		1
I HAVE MET THEM AT CLOSE OF DAY		391	EASTER 1916		1
THEY HAVE LOUD MUSIC, HOPE EVERY DAY RENEWED		398	LEADERS CROWD		11
TOWARDS BREAK OF DAY		398	BREAK OF DAY		T
UNDER THE FIRST COLD GLEAM OF DAY?		398	BREAK OF DAY		4
I DREAMED TOWARDS BREAK OF DAY,		399	BREAK OF DAY		19
THAT PLAGUE ME DAY AND NIGHT		399	DEMON BEAST		3
TO MAKE IT LINGER HALF A DAY.		401	DEMON BEAST		42
AND HAD THE LIVELONG SUMMER DAY TO SPEND.		409	TOWER		10
FOR THE PROSAIC LIGHT OF DAY--		411	TOWER		46
WHEN HE FINISHED HIS DOG'S DAY!		412	TOWER		79
UNDER ECLIPSE AND THE DAY BLOTTED OUT.		414	TOWER		120
THE SWEETNESS THAT ALL LONGED FOR NIGHT AND DAY,		418	ANCEST HOUSES		20
UPON SOME BRAND-NEW HAPPY DAY!		432	NINETEEN 19	V	106
IN THE OLD ROOMS! NIGHT CAN OUTBALANCE DAY,		435	NEW FACES		6
FROM NOTHING EVERY DAY, AND TEACH		436	FOR MY SON		18
ENDURES A MOMENT OR A DAY.		438	SONGS PLAY 2		10
THAT CHANGED SOME CHILDISH DAY TO TRAGEDY--		443	SCHOOL CHILDR		12
SUMMER AND WINTER, DAY AND NIGHT,		447	COLONUS PRAISE		31
"YOU BUT IMAGINE LIES ALL DAY, O MURDERER," I REPLIED.		450	OWEN AHERNE		17
. . . NEVER TO HAVE LOOKED INTO THE EYE OF DAY!		459	FROM OEDIPUS		11
. . . AT ALL NOR LOOKED INTO THE EYE OF DAY.		459	FROM OEDIPUS	V	11
LIKE MEN WHO LIVE BY HABIT. EVERY DAY		463	HARUN RASHID		56
BUT WOKE AT THE FIRST GLEAM OF DAY, ROSE UP		467	HARUN RASHID		147
THAT DAY BY DAY I STUDY AND MARVEL AT,		468	HARUN RASHID		157
THAT DAY BY DAY I STUDY AND MARVEL AT,		468	HARUN RASHID		157
FOR EMBLEMS OF THE DAY AGAINST THE TOWER		478	SELF AND SOUL		29
THE UNPURGED IMAGES OF DAY RECEDE;		497	BYZANTIUM		1
OF DAY AND NIGHT!		500	VACILLATION		6
WEIGH ME DOWN, AND NOT A DAY		501	VACILLATION		54
THOSE BRANCHES OF THE NIGHT AND DAY		502	VACILLATION		68
ALL THAT STORM THAT BLOTS THE DAY		509	JANE REPROVED		3
ALL THOSE STORMS THAT BLOT THE DAY		509	JANE REPROVED	V	3
CRAZY JANE ON THE DAY OF JUDGMENT		510	JANE JUDGMENT		T
THAT BLACK DAY";		510	JANE JUDGMENT		14
I THOUGHT IT OUT THIS VERY DAY,		525	DANCING DAYS		17
THE MURDEROUS STEALTH OF DAY.		536	PARTING		8
THERE'S NOT A BIRD OF DAY THAT DARE		538	LAST CONFESS		23
NO LOOSE-LIPPED DEMAGOGUE HAD WON THE DAY,		542	PARN FUNERAL 2		3
NO LOOSE LIPPED DEMAGOGUE HAD WON THE DAY,		542	PARN FUNERAL 2	V	3
AND MUST THE COMMON ROUND OF DAY RESUME.		557	RIBH ECSTASY		8
THAT DAY BRINGS ROUND THE NIGHT; THAT BEFORE DAWN		563	MERU		13
OF A SLENDER PALM, STOOD BUT A DAY!		566	LAPIS LAZULI		34
LOOKED HALF ASLEEP ALL DAY.		570	THREE BUSHES		34
NO, BUT THAT DAY THEY DID.		570	THREE BUSHES		46
A DOG MUST HAVE HIS DAY,		582	ROGER CASEMENT	V	18
A DOG MUST HAVE HIS DAY,		583	GHOST ROG CASE		12
THE GREAT DAY		590	GREAT DAY		T
FRAGMENTS THE GREAT DAY		590	GREAT DAY	V	T
AND THERE I FOUND AN OLD MAN, AND THOUGH I PRAYED ALL DAY		593	PILGRIM		8
THEIR DRINK, THEIR PITCH-AND-TOSS BY DAY,		607	SONGS BURDEN 2		14
THEIR DRINK, THEIR PITCH AND TOSS BY DAY,		607	SONGS BURDEN 2	V	14
WHO WAS THE FIRST MAN SHOT THAT DAY?		608	SONGS BURDEN 3		10
SOME DAY WE SHALL GET UP BEFORE THE DAWN		622	HOUND VOICE		15
GROWS MORE DEEP DAY AFTER DAY,		624	APPARITIONS		18
GROWS MORE DEEP DAY AFTER DAY,		624	APPARITIONS		18
UNTO THE WANDERER'S SHIPS, OR AS DAY FILLS		645	ISLE STAT I 1		10
BY DAY AND NIGHT A LONELY FOUNTAIN SINGS,		650	ISLE STAT I 1		130
THE PALE ANEMONES. WE'VE SOUGHT ALL DAY,		651	ISLE STAT I 2		5
O'ER THE LAKE THIS VERY DAY.		656	ISLE STAT I 3		17
ONCE MORE HOW ON THAT MISERABLE DAY		658	ISLE STAT II 1		4

187

```
                                                  PAGE    TITLE           LINE

DAY  (CONTINUED)
     O SWIFT ON THE SEAS ALL DAY AND NIGHT  . . . . . .   666  ISLE STAT II 3      8
     ALL DAY AND NIGHT. . . . . . . . . . . . . . . . .   666  ISLE STAT II 3     10
     AND THE HAPPY WINGED DAY, . . . . . . . . . . . .    668  ISLE STAT II 3     64
     IT IS, YET SHALL IT FAIL THEE DAY AND NIGHT  . . .   674  ISLE STAT II 3    211
     O ARCADY, O ARCADY, THIS DAY  . . . . . . . . . .    676  ISLE STAT II 3    272
     AND WOE-BEGONE.  FOR THEM NO EVIL DAY!  . . . . .    677  ISLE STAT II 3    275
     BEAT ON IT WITH THEIR HAMMERS DAY AND NIGHT. . . .   687  TWO TITANS          4
     THAT WILL BE LATER, DAY IS SCARCELY DAWNING. . . .   699  MOSADA 3           12
     THAT WILL BE LATER, DAY IS DAWNING. . . . . . . .    699  MOSADA 3        V  12
     'TIS LATE, WAIT ONE MORE DAY! BELOW THE HILLS . . .  702  MOSADA 3           91
     AND POUR UPON THE WORLD! AH! WELL A DAY!  . . . .    703  MOSADA 3        V 118
     DOWN THE VAPOURS FALL AND HIDE THEM FROM THE CHILDREN OF 719 PHANTOM SHIP    27
        A DAY,
     SOME DAY YOU'LL BUY THEM, MAYBE.  NEVER!  NEVER? . . 721  WITCH VIVIEN       24
     THAN OLD MEN'S ANY DAY, AS MERLIN FOUND. . . . . .   721  WITCH VIVIEN       47
     COME AND TEASE THEM TILL THE DAY. . . . . . . . .    727  LOVERS QUARREL     36
     THE TANGLED THOUGHTS OF THE FINISHED DAY  . . . .    728  PRIEST FAIRY        9
     "AND CUT NO WOOD THE WHOLE DAY LONG, . . . . . . .   731  PRIEST FAIRY       81
     LONG THOU FOR NOTHING, NEITHER NIGHT NOR DAY! . . .  734  QUATRAIN APHOR     10
     MOURN ALL THE NIGHT AND DAY, . . . . . . . . . .     737  MOURN THEN ON       2
     TILL DAY AND NIGHT TIME END. . . . . . . . . . .     741  EARL PAUL          48
     IN DAY OUT-LIVING BATTLE, ON THE BREAST . . . . .    750  SHADOW WATER A     73
     THAT DIES OUT BEFORE 'TIS DAY. . . . . . . . . .     777  SONG DEIRDRE 2      8
     I WAS GOING THE ROAD ONE DAY  . . . . . . . . . .    779  GOING THE ROAD      1
     "FOR A YEAR AND A DAY BY THE CLOCK OF THE SUN" . .   779  GOING THE ROAD     11
     ACCURSED WHO BRINGS TO LIGHT OF DAY  . . . . . .     779  ACCURSED WHO        1
     TO THE LOUD SANDS BEFORE DAY HAS BROKEN. . . . .     784  WOMANS BEAUTY      18
     AMID THE DARK BEFORE DAY HAD BROKEN. . . . . . .     784  WOMANS BEAUTY      20
DAYBREAK
     THE EAST TELLS ALL HER SECRET JOY BEFORE DAYBREAK, . 154  BELOVED PEACE  V   4
     "SAY WHAT YOU PLEASE, BUT FROM DAYBREAK, . . . . .   304  HOUR DAWN          42
     I STRUGGLED WITH THE HORROR OF DAYBREAK, . . . . .   535  CHOSEN             10
     DAYBREAK AND A CANDLE-END. . . . . . . . . . . .     588  OLD WICKED MAN      9
     DAYBREAK AND A CANDLE-END. . . . . . . . . . . .     588  OLD WICKED MAN     18
     DAYBREAK AND A CANDLE-END. . . . . . . . . . . .     588  OLD WICKED MAN     27
     DAYBREAK AND A CANDLE END. . . . . . . . . . . .     588  OLD WICKED MAN V  REF
     DAYBREAK AND A CANDLE-END. . . . . . . . . . . .     589  OLD WICKED MAN     36
     DAYBREAK AND A CANDLE-END. . . . . . . . . . . .     589  OLD WICKED MAN     45
     DAYBREAK AND A CANDLE-END. . . . . . . . . . . .     589  OLD WICKED MAN     54
     DAYBREAK AND A CANDLE-END. . . . . . . . . . . .     590  OLD WICKED MAN     63
     HOW MANY HOURS TO DAYBREAK, BECAUSE LOVE . . . .     767  SHADOW WATER A    405
     AT DAYBREAK AFTER STORMY NIGHT . . . . . . . . .     784  WOMANS BEAUTY       3
DAY-BREAK
     "SAY WHAT YOU PLEASE, BUT FROM DAY-BREAK . . . . .   304  HOUR DAWN      V   42
     DAY-BREAK AND A CANDLE END. . . . . . . . . . .      588  OLD WICKED MAN V  REF
DAYLIGHT
     "WHETHER UNDER ITS DAYLIGHT OR ITS STARS . . . . .   107  CUCHULAIN SEA      25
     "NO, SOMEWHERE UNDER DAYLIGHT OR THE STARS . . . .   107  CUCHULAIN SEA  V   25
     "WHETHER UNDER ITS DAYLIGHT OR THE STARS . . . . .   107  CUCHULAIN SEA  V   25
     WE SAW THE LAST EMBERS OF DAYLIGHT DIE, . . . . .    205  ADAMS CURSE        29
     A SHELTER TILL THE DAYLIGHT BROKE. . . . . . . .     302  HOUR DAWN          15
     "STRETCH BONES TILL THE DAYLIGHT COME  . . . . .     331  ROUND TOWER         5
     AND MAKE THE DAYLIGHT SWEET ONCE MORE! BUT WHEN . .  339  SHEP GOATHERD      13
     THE NIGHTINGALE THAT DEAFENS DAYLIGHT THERE, . . .   446  COLONUS PRAISE      3
     IF DAYLIGHT EVER VISIT WHERE, . . . . . . . . .      446  COLONUS PRAISE      4
     DAYLIGHT ALREADY FLIES  . . . . . . . . . . . .      536  PARTING             9
     FOR I THAT AM HIS DAYLIGHT LADY  . . . . . . . .     573  LADYS 3RD SONG      5
DAYLIGHT-DARKENING
     AND NOW THE DAYLIGHT-DARKENING RAVENS FLOCK. . . .    43  OISIN 2           212
DAY-LONG
     AND ONCE MORE TO A DAY-LONG BATTLE FELL, . . . . .    43  OISIN 2           218
DAY'S
     I SANG HOW, WHEN DAY'S TOIL IS DONE, . . . . . .      85  MAD KING GOLL      61
     THE HOURLY KINDNESS, THE DAY'S COMMON SPEECH, . . .  258  KING NO KING       14
     ON THE DAY'S WAR WITH EVERY KNAVE AND DOLT, . . .    260  FASC DIFFICULT     10
     UNDER THE DAY'S DECLINING BEAM, AND CALL . . . .     410  TOWER              21
     OR THE DAY'S VANITY, THE NIGHT'S REMORSE. . . . .    491  COOLE BALLYLEE V  40H
     OR THE DAY'S VANITY, THE NIGHT'S REMORSE. . . . .    495  CHOICE              8
     A NEW DAY'S TROOP OF WASP AND BEE . . . . . . .      646  ISLE STAT I 1      44
     AS I, TO CHOOSE BENEATH DAY'S DYING FLAMES! . . .    656  ISLE STAT I 3      34
     DAY'S DEAD, ALL FLAME-BEWILDERED, AND THE HILLS . .  702  MOSADA 3           86
DAYS
     THE BAD OLD DAYS.  THOU WERT, MEN SING, . . . . .      2  OISIN 1        V    3
     AND THE DAYS PASS BY LIKE A WAYWARD TUNE, . . . .      8  OISIN 1            83
     I KNOW NOT IF DAYS PASSED OR HOURS, . . . . . .       11  OISIN 1           133
     I KNEW NOT IF DAYS PASSED OR HOURS, . . . . . .       11  OISIN 1        V  133
     A DRUID DREAM OF THE END OF DAYS  . . . . . . .       16  OISIN 1           219
     FOR HIS LAST DAYS TO LIE IN WAIT. . . . . . . .       24  OISIN 1           363
     HE HAS OVER-LINGERED HIS WELCOME! THE DAYS, . . .     26  OISIN 1           402
     WHERE CARE CANNOT TROUBLE THE LEAST OF OUR DAYS, . .  27  OISIN 1           409
     HE HATH OVER LINGERED HIS WELCOME! THE DAYS, . . .    27  OISIN 1        V  406
     WILL SCATTER IN RUIN THE LEAST OF OUR DAYS, . . .     27  OISIN 1        V 419B
     SHALL BLOW INTO RUIN OUR MUSICAL DAYS, . . . . .      28  OISIN 1        V  425
     ON THE OLD SORROWS OF HIS HUMAN DAYS. . . . . .       29  OISIN 2        V   12
     TROUBLED HER SONG.  I DO NOT KNOW IF DAYS . . . .     30  OISIN 2            19
     FLASHING--I KNOW NOT WERE IT HOURS OR DAYS, . . .     30  OISIN 2        V  19B
     WAS LOADED WITH THE MEMORY OF DAYS  . . . . . .       39  OISIN 2           150
     WE FEASTED FOR THREE DAYS.  ON THE FOURTH MORN . .    43  OISIN 2           214
     THREE DAYS WE FEASTED, WHEN ON THE FOURTH MORN . .    43  OISIN 2        V  214
     REMEMBERING HOW I PACED IN DAYS GONE O'ER, . . . .    44  OISIN 2        V  227

                                   188
```

		PAGE	TITLE		LINE

DAYS (CONTINUED)

	PAGE	TITLE		LINE
WERE WE DAYS LONG OR HOURS LONG IN RIDING,	47	OISIN 3		9
HIS SHOUTING DAYS WITH MIRTH WERE CROWNED;	67	HAPPY SHEPHERD		50
THAT MOANS AND SIGHS A HUNDRED DAYS!	78	INDIAN TO LOVE		17
IN PENAL DAYS RODE OUT	91	FATHER OHART		2
RED ROSE, PROUD ROSE, SAD ROSE OF ALL MY DAYS!	100	ROSE UPON ROOD		1
RED ROSE, PROUD ROSE, SAD ROSE OF ALL MY DAYS.	101	ROSE UPON ROOD		24
AND PONDERED ON THE GLORY OF HIS DAYS;	108	CUCHULAIN SEA		43
AND PONDERED ON THE WONDER OF HIS DAYS,	108	CUCHULAIN SEA	V	43
FOR THREE DAYS MORE IN DREADFUL QUIETUDE,	110	CUCHULAIN SEA		78
AND CHAUNTED FOR THREE DAYS. CUCHULAIN STIRRED,	111	CUCHULAIN SEA		83
AND CHANTED FOR THREE DAYS. CUCHULAIN STIRRED,	111	CUCHULAIN SEA	V	83
FOR FOUR DAYS WARRED HE WITH THE BITTER TIDE,	111	CUCHULAIN SEA	V	85
ALL THE HEAVY DAYS ARE OVER!	124	CATHLEEN PARA		1
AS IN THE OLD DAYS LONG GONE BY,	131	OLD PENSIONER	V	15
THE FLAMING CIRCLE OF OUR DAYS,	135	TWO TREES		14
APOLOGIA ADDRESSED TO IRELAND IN THE COMING DAYS	137	TO IRELAND	V	T
THE PEOPLE OF COMING DAYS WILL KNOW	146	FISH		3
OUT OF THE OLD DAYS	158	TO HIS HEART	V	T
REMEMBER THE WISDOM OUT OF THE OLD DAYS!	158	TO HIS HEART		2
THE POETS LABOURING ALL THEIR DAYS	164	PERFECT BEAUTY		2
WE POETS LABOUR ALL OUR DAYS,	164	PERFECT BEAUTY	V	2
THOUGH YOU ARE IN YOUR SHINING DAYS,	172	PLEADS FRIEND		1
ALTHOUGH YOU ARE IN YOUR SHINING DAYS,	172	PLEADS FRIEND	V	1
THE LOVER SPEAKS TO THE HEARERS OF HIS SONGS IN COMING DAYS	173	SPEAKS HEARERS		T
HANRAHAN SPEAKS TO THE LOVERS OF HIS SONGS IN COMING DAYS	173	SPEAKS HEARERS	V	T
A LOVER SPEAKS TO THE HEARERS OF HIS SONGS IN COMING DAYS	173	SPEAKS HEARERS	V	T
AND THOUGHT OF DAYS WHEN HE'D HAD A STRAIGHT BODY,	183	QUEEN MAEVE		70
AS IN THE OLD DAYS WHEN THEY WOULD COME AND GO	183	QUEEN MAEVE		81
THROUGH THE LONG DAYS OF YOUTH, AND WHO WOULD HAVE THOUGHT	201	OLD MEMORY	V	7
ABOUT THE STARS AND BROKE IN DAYS AND YEARS.	206	ADAMS CURSE		33
ABOUT THE STARN AND BROKE IN DAYS AND YEARS.	206	ADAMS CURSE	V	33
THESE MANY DAYS! AND YET THERE MUST BE MANY	226	SHADOW WATER B		89
WHY SHOULD I BLAME HER THAT SHE FILLED MY DAYS	256	NO SECOND TROY		1
THE LABYRINTH OF HER DAYS	260	UNWORTH PRAISE		13
THROUGH ALL THE LYING DAYS OF MY YOUTH	261	COMING WISDOM		2
THAT EMPTIED ALL OUR DAYS TO COME.	272	GREY ROCK		40
AND FOR NINE DAYS HE HAD FOOD FROM OTHER HANDS,	282	TWO KINGS		126
AND FOR NINE DAYS MY MIND WENT WHIRLING ROUND	282	TWO KINGS		127
BUT WHEN NINE DAYS HAD GONE I STOOD AGAIN	282	TWO KINGS		131
IN DAYS YOU HAVE NOT KEPT IN MEMORY,	284	TWO KINGS		168
WHAT JOY IS IN MY DAYS!	315	FRIENDS		3
AND BE WELL PLEASED REMEMBERING IT, FOR IN THE OLD DAYS,	351	HER PRAISE		16
HAPPIER DAYS THOUGHT GOOD!	365	HER RACE		4
IMAGINED BODIES ALL THEIR DAYS	386	ROBARTES DANCE		28
I HAD THOUGHT THAT ALL MY DAYS WERE CAST	389	IMAGE PAST		12
THAT WOMAN'S DAYS WERE SPENT	392	EASTER 1916		17
GATHERED A SCORE OF HORSE AND SPENT HIS DAYS	420	MY HOUSE		22
MY DAYS OUT OF THEIR AIMLESSNESS.	421	MY TABLE		5
SOME FOURTEEN DAYS OF CIVIL WAR!	425	STARES NEST		12
WE THOUGHT IT WOULD OUTLIVE ALL FUTURE DAYS.	428	NINETEEN 19		14
NOW DAYS ARE DRAGON-RIDDEN, THE NIGHTMARE	429	NINETEEN 19		25
NOW DAYS ARE DRAGON RIDDEN, THE NIGHTMARE	429	NINETEEN 19	V	25
THAT WAITS UPON HIS FUTURE DAYS,	436	FOR MY SON		14
WHEN MY DAYS THAT HAVE	449	HERO GIRL FOOL	V	18
HAD SPOKEN OF THEIR CHILDISH DAYS	457	SUMMER SPRING		11
AND OFTEN THOSE FIRST DAYS I SAW HER STARE	466	HARUN RASHID		122
A BOY'S TURBULENT DAYS	496	MOHINI CHATTER		13
THE TRIVIAL DAYS AND RAM THEM WITH THE SUN,	500	VACILLATION		21
OF DISTORTING DAYS	504	QUARREL IN AGE		13
THOSE DANCING DAYS ARE GONE	524	DANCING DAYS		T
THOSE DANCING DAYS ARE GONE,	524	DANCING DAYS		2
I FASTED FOR SOME FORTY DAYS ON BREAD AND BUTTERMILK,	592	PILGRIM		1
CAST YOUR MIND ON OTHER DAYS	640	BEN BULBEN		81
THAT WE IN COMING DAYS MAY BE	640	BEN BULBEN		82
NAY, NAY, I MISS'D HIM NOT! HIS DAYS	649	ISLE STAT I 1		117
HAVE CLOTHED THEIR TONGUES WITH SONG OF SONGLESS DAYS?	666	ISLE STAT II 3		17
IN THY WAN FACE? HEAR THOU, O DAUGHTER OF THE DAYS,	674	ISLE STAT II 3		200
YET EVER MORE, THROUGH ALL THY DAYS OF RUTH.	674	ISLE STAT II 3		206
IN THOSE FAR YEARS, O DAUGHTER OF THE DAYS.	674	ISLE STAT II 3		213
IN THY WAN FACE? HEAR, DAUGHTER OF THE DAYS.	674	ISLE STAT II 3	V	200
YET EVERMORE, THROUGH ALL THY DAYS OF RUTH,	674	ISLE STAT II 3	V	206
IN THOSE FAIR YEARS, O DAUGHTER OF THE DAYS.	674	ISLE STAT II 3	V	213
AND PEACE BE WITH YOU, PEACE AND WEALTH OF DAYS.	682	SEEKER		28
WERE ALL MY WANDERING DAYS OF NO AVAIL,	684	SEEKER		64
FOR YEARS HIS DAYS HAD DAWNED AND FADED THUS	692	MOSADA 1		54
LIKE HAPPY THOUGHTS GROWN SAD IN EVIL DAYS.	703	MOSADA 3		116
AND DREAM OF THE END OF THEIR DAYS,	707	FAIRY PEDANT		4
AND NUMBER THEIR DAYS AND THEIR HOURS--	707	FAIRY PEDANT		19
IN THEIR DAYS OF YOUTHFUL MIRTH!	727	LOVERS QUARREL		40
AS THOUGH HIS DAYS WERE FULL OF RUTH.	731	PRIEST FAIRY		76
HE HAS HEARD ME AND NOT YOU. NINE DAYS AGO	752	SHADOW WATER A		113
"LIVES ALL HIS DAYS	780	WELL AND TREE		3
WHAT THOUGH THEY DANCED! THOSE DAYS ARE GONE,	788	HAWTHORN TREE		5

DAYS'

	PAGE	TITLE		LINE
AND SUNKEN SHAPE, A NINE DAYS' CORPSE SEA-DASHED--	40	OISIN 2	V	179
IN THREE DAYS' TIME HE STOOD UP WITH A MOAN,	111	CUCHULAIN SEA	V	83
IN THREE DAYS' TIME, CUCHULAIN WITH A MOAN	111	CUCHULAIN SEA	V	83

DAYSPRING

	PAGE	TITLE		LINE
TO HIS OWN DAYSPRING,	342	SHEP GOATHERD		96

	PAGE	TITLE		LINE
DAYTIME				
SO SLEEP THEE BY DAYTIME." A VOICE CRIED, ...	59	OISIN 3		172
SO SLEEP THEY BY DAYTIME." A VOICE CRIED, ...	59	OISIN 3	V	172
TILL DAYTIME, PLAYTIME SEEM THE SAME;	343	SHEP GOATHERD		106
OR RUN WHERE LADS REFORM OUR DAYTIME	343	SHEP GOATHERD	V	105
AS THE SUMMER VOICE OF THE DAYTIME CEASED, ...	728	PRIEST FAIRY		4
DAZED				
WE SHOULD BE DAZED AND TERROR-STRUCK, ...	272	GREY ROCK		37
WE SHOULD BE DAZED AND TERROR STRUCK	272	GREY ROCK	V	37
OF THE STARK MYSTERY THAT HAS DAZED MY SIGHT, ...	466	HARUN RASHID		113
CHILDREN DAZED OR DEAD!	488	CRAZED MOON		7
DAZZLED				
NOR DAZZLED BY THE EMBROIDERY, NOR LOST	470	HARUN RASHID		191
NOT BLIND WITH GOLD, NOR DAZZLED BY THE GOLD	470	HARUN RASHID	V	191
DAZZLING				
IN BRONZE, OR THAT IN DAZZLING MARBLE APPEARS, ...	334	LIVING BEAUTY		5
DEAD SEE HALF-DEAD MUMMY-DEAD				
FOR OUR BEST WERE DEAD ON GAVRA'S GREEN.	2	OISIN 1	V	71
COMPANIONS LONG ACCURST AND DEAD, ...	11	OISIN 1		130
FROM DEWY EYES: "UPON THE DEAD	21	OISIN 1		310
ON THE DEAD DIM EARTH ENCLOSES:	21	OISIN 1		312
SANG WE SOFTLY, "ON THE DEAD, ...	21	OISIN 1	V	310
ON THE DEAD THE EARTH ENCLOSES.	21	OISIN 1	V	312
FROM SOME DEAD WARRIOR'S BROKEN LANCE!	24	OISIN 1		367
IT WAS OF SOME DEAD WARRIOR'S LANCE.	24	OISIN 1	V	367
"NEITHER THE LIVING, NOR THE UNLABOURING DEAD, ...	34	OISIN 2		79
THE DEAD GOD'S SWORD, TO MANY FORMS HE GREW, ...	40	OISIN 2	V	175
CAST THE LOOSE BULK, LEST NIAM FEAR HIM DEAD:	41	OISIN 2	V	183
A HUSH! AH, ME! IT HANGS TO STRIKE US DEAD.	43	OISIN 2	V	208B
. . . "THE FENIANS A LONG TIME ARE DEAD."	59	OISIN 3		172
. . . HE CRIED, "NO, THE GODS A LONG TIME ARE DEAD." . .	59	OISIN 3		180
. . . HE CRIED, "NAY, THE GODS A LONG TIME ARE DEAD." . .	59	OISIN 3	V	180
THE WOODS OF ARCADY ARE DEAD, ...	64	HAPPY SHEPHERD		1
THE KINGS OF THE OLD TIME ARE DEAD!	65	HAPPY SHEPHERD		17
AND DEAD IS ALL THEIR HUMAN TRUTH.	66	HAPPY SHEPHERD		34
WHEN WE ARE DEAD, BEYOND THE SETTING SUNS, ...	71	ANASHU VIJAYA		8
TURNING, HE SAW THAT SHE HAD THRUST DEAD LEAVES . . .	80	EPHEMERA		18
THE HOUNDS WAIL FOR THE DEAD.	99	FOXHUNTER		48
THE HOUNDS KEEN FOR THE DEAD.	99	FOXHUNTER	V	48
BY GOD TO THE BRIGHT HEARTS OF THOSE LONG DEAD, . . .	101	ROSE UPON ROOD		20
"NO MAN ALIVE, NO MAN AMONG THE DEAD, ...	106	CUCHULAIN SEA		10
"NOT ANY GOD ALIVE NOR MORTAL DEAD, ...	106	CUCHULAIN SEA	V	10
WITH THE WHIMPERING DEAD.	118	CRADLE SONG		4
THE SOULS OF THE DEAD.	118	CRADLE SONG	V	4
"AND IS THE POOR MAN DEAD?" HE CRIED.	133	FR GILLIGAN		33
OF PASSIONATE MEN, LIKE BATS IN THE DEAD TREES!	136	TO SOME I TALK		5
OLD WOMEN WERE KEENING THE DEAD!	145	HOST OF AIR	V	40D
O PITEOUS HEARTS, CHANGING TILL CHANGE BE DEAD	163	ASKS FORGIVE		19
AND WHEN IT IS GONE WE ARE DEAD!	168	BLESSED		30
FEASTED, AND WEPT THE BARROWS OF HIS DEAD!	170	SECRET ROSE		18
AND SMOKE FROM THIS DEAD HEART DRIFTS THROUGH THE VIOLET AIR	173	SPEAKS HEARERS		3
HE WISHES HIS BELOVED WERE DEAD	175	BELOVED DEAD		T
AEDH WISHES HIS BELOVED WERE DEAD	175	BELOVED DEAD	V	T
WERE YOU BUT LYING COLD AND DEAD, ...	175	BELOVED DEAD		1
FORGIVING ME, BECAUSE YOU WERE DEAD!	175	BELOVED DEAD		6
WHERE THE DEAD DRIFTED, I COULD SEE A BIRD	223	SHADOW WATER B		23
IF HE WERE DEAD: BUT WHO WILL BE OUR CAPTAIN.	224	SHADOW WATER B		60
NONE BUT THE DEAD, OR THOSE THAT NEVER LIVED, ...	231	SHADOW WATER B		202
TOWARDS THE COUNTRY OF THE DEAD. WHAT MATTER . . .	231	SHADOW WATER B		206
UNTIL THE OVERBURTHENED MOON IS DEAD.	231	SHADOW WATER B		218
NOW THAT HE'S DEAD I HAVE NO NEED OF IT, ...	241	SHADOW WATER B		401
WHAT NAME HAD THAT DEAD KING? ARTHUR OF BRITAIN? . . .	242	SHADOW WATER B		404
THAT YOU ARE WEEPING FOR. NO, FOR HE IS DEAD.	243	SHADOW WATER B		427
IT SHALL BE IN THE COUNTRY OF THE DEAD, ...	249	SHADOW WATER B		557
"COME OUT AND DIG FOR A DEAD MAN."	272	GREY ROCK		32
FOR HE IS THE WORST OF ALL DEAD MEN."	272	GREY ROCK		36
ALTHOUGH THE KING OF IRELAND'S DEAD	273	GREY ROCK		68
FOR HE AND THE KING'S SON WERE DEAD.	275	GREY ROCK		97
TOWARDS THE HOUR FOR SPEAKING OF THE DEAD?	276	TWO KINGS	V	D
ROMANTIC IRELAND'S DEAD AND GONE, ...	289	SEPTEMBER 1913		7
ROMANTIC IRELAND'S DEAD AND GONE, ...	289	SEPTEMBER 1913		15
ROMANTIC IRELAND'S DEAD AND GONE, ...	290	SEPTEMBER 1913		23
BUT LET THEM BE, THEY'RE DEAD AND GONE, ...	290	SEPTEMBER 1913		31
NOR THE BEST LABOURER DEAD	312	CHILD DANCING		9
AND HE, THE BEST WARRIOR, DEAD	312	CHILD DANCING	V	9
ALL, ALL ARE IN MY THOUGHTS TO-NIGHT BEING DEAD. . . .	324	ROBERT GREGORY		8
FOR ALL THAT COME INTO MY MIND ARE DEAD.	324	ROBERT GREGORY		16
"AND IF MY DEAREST FRIEND WERE DEAD	338	TOM OROUGHLEY		15
IS DEAD. THE BOY THAT BRINGS MY GRIDDLE-CAKE	339	SHEP GOATHERD		20
IS DEAD. THE BOY THAT BRINGS MY GRIDDLE CAKE	339	SHEP GOATHERD	V	20
THE DEAD MAN THAT I LOVED, ...	347	FISHERMAN		14
TO STRIKE YOU DEAD?	359	TO A SQUIRREL		5
WITH HER DEAD BROTHER'S VALOUR	365	HER RACE		11
SAID I WAS DEAD: AND DEAD I CHOOSE TO BE.	373	PHASES OF MOON		28
SAID I WAS DEAD: AND DEAD I CHOOSE TO BE.	373	PHASES OF MOON		28
SAID I WAS DEAD: AND DEAD I CHOSE TO BE.	373	PHASES OF MOON	V	28
SAID I WAS DEAD: AND DEAD I CHOSE TO BE.	373	PHASES OF MOON	V	28
SO DEAD BEYOND OUR DEATH, ...	382	VISION ROBART		15
FOR NOW BEING DEAD IT SEEMED	383	VISION ROBART		23
WERE DEAD YET FLESH AND BONE.	384	VISION ROBART		48

190

DEAD   (CONTINUED)
    AND THIS FOUL WORLD WERE DEAD AT LAST. . . . . . .   388 SOLOMON WITCH   16
    TO KNOW THEY DREAMED AND ARE DEAD! . . . .   394 EASTER 1916   71
    SIXTEEN DEAD MEN . . . .   395 SIXTEEN DEAD   T
    WHILE THOSE DEAD MEN ARE LOITERING THERE . . . . . 395 SIXTEEN DEAD   5
    THAT, BEING DEAD, WE RISE. . . . .   415 TOWER   154
    THAT DEAD YOUNG SOLDIER IN HIS BLOOD! . . . . 425 STARES NEST   14
    IF YOU, THAT HAVE GROWN OLD, WERE THE FIRST DEAD, . 435 NEW FACES   1
    AND AGAMEMNON DEAD. BEING SO CAUGHT UP, ...   441 LEDA AND SWAN   11
    WHEN ALL BUT DEAD OF THIRST. . . . .   454 EMPTY CUP   2
    WHEN ALL BUT DEAD WITH THIRST, ...   454 EMPTY CUP   V   2
    ONLY THE DEAD CAN BE FORGIVEN! . . . .   478 SELF AND SOUL   39
    HALF DEAD AT THE TOP. . . . .   480 BLOOD AND MOON   12
    CAST BUT DEAD LEAVES TO MATHEMATICAL EQUALITY! . .   481 BLOOD AND MOON   24
    CASTS BUT DEAD LEAVES TO MATHEMATICAL EQUALITY! . . 481 BLOOD AND MOON V   24
    HALF DEAD AT THE TOP? NO MATTER WHAT I SAID, . . . 482 BLOOD AND MOON   48
    FOR WISDOM IS THE PROPERTY OF THE DEAD, ... 482 BLOOD AND MOON   49
    CHILDREN DAZED OR DEAD! . . . .   488 CRAZED MOON   7
    BECAUSE OF MY DEAR JACK THAT'S DEAD. . . . .   508 JANE BISHOP   5
    MINE MUST WALK WHEN DEAD. . . . .   511 JANE AND JACK   18
    MINE WOULD WALK, BEING DEAD. . . . .   511 JANE AND JACK   18
    DREW A KNIFE TO STRIKE HIM DEAD, ...   514 JANE GROWN OLD   10
    ALL OTHER LOVERS BEING ESTRANGED OR DEAD, ... 523 LONG SILENCE   2
    HECTOR IS DEAD AND THERE'S A LIGHT IN TROY! . . . . 564 GYRES   7
    I THINK I SHOULD DROP DEAD." . . . .   569 THREE BUSHES   13
    "I KNOW THAT I MUST DROP DOWN DEAD . . . . 569 THREE BUSHES   17
    YET WHAT COULD I BUT DROP DOWN DEAD . . . . 569 THREE BUSHES   19
    SHAKE THE DEAD IN THEIR SHROUDS! . . . .   576 ACRE OF GRASS   22
    A DEAD MAN IN HIS GRAVE. . . . .   592 DRUNK SOBRIETY   12
    A DRUNKARD IS A DEAD MAN. . . . .   592 DRUNK SOBRIETY   15
    AND ALL DEAD MEN ARE DRUNK. . . . .   592 DRUNK SOBRIETY   16
    ALL KNOW THAT ALL THE DEAD IN THE WORLD ABOUT THAT PLACE 593 PILGRIM   11
      ARE STUCK,
    TO SHOOT THE COLONEL DEAD! . . . .   596 COLONEL MARTIN   58
    BECAUSE OF THOSE NEW DEAD . . . .   599 SPIRIT MEDIUM   2
    "THE DEAD IRELAND OF MY YOUTH, BUT AN IRELAND . . . 602 GALLERY REVIS   11
    NOW MY OLD BAWD IS DEAD? . . . .   620 JOHN KINSELLA   12
    NOW MY OLD BAWD IS DEAD? . . . .   621 JOHN KINSELLA   24
    NOW MY OLD BAWD IS DEAD? . . . .   621 JOHN KINSELLA   36
    VIOLENT AND FAMOUS, STRODE AMONG THE DEAD! . . . .   634 CUCHULAIN COMF   2
    THERE IN THE TOMB STAND THE DEAD UPRIGHT, ... 635 BLACK TOWER   7
    OR THE RIFLE KNOCKS HIM DEAD, ...   637 BEN BULBEN   18
    OR THE RIFLE KNOCK HIM DEAD, ...   637 BEN BULBEN   V   18
    AY, BOY. LET'S SEE IF THAT SAME HERON'S DEAD. . .   651 ISLE STAT I 1   169
    AS SOME DEAD MAIDEN'S SINGING IN A DREAM. . . . . . 654 ISLE STAT I 2   59
    HARK! HE'S DEAD--MY DROWSY BROTHER, ... 656 ISLE STAT I 3   18
    AS QUIET AS THE CLAY-COLD DEAD. . . . .   670 ISLE STAT II 3   113
    A MAN WHO BY A DEAD MAN STOOD. . . . .   671 ISLE STAT II 3   124
    I MUST BESTIR MYSELF. BOTH DEAD FOR ME! . . . . .   673 ISLE STAT II 3   189
    BOTH DEAD!--NO TIME TO THINK. I AM SHE, ...   673 ISLE STAT II 3   190
    BOTH DEAD!--NO TIME FOR THINKING. I AM SHE, . . .   673 ISLE STAT II 3 V 190
    AND DEAD AS ARE THE LOVERS OF OLD RIME . . . . . .   674 ISLE STAT II 3   204
    AND DEAD AS ARE THE LOVERS OF OLD RHYME. . . . . .   674 ISLE STAT II 3 V 204
    SAVING A GREEN FROG DEAD UPON THE GRASS, ...   676 ISLE STAT II 3   269
    HE IS LONG DEAD. WAKE! SOFT AS A BEE SIPS . . . .   678 ISLE STAT II 3   297
    LIE STREWN THE CLOTTED LEAVES--THE DEAD OLD LEAVES. . 684 SEEKER   V   69
    DOWN TO THE MOTHER OF THE FOILED AND DEAD. . . . .   688 TWO TITANS   50
    SOFT AS A LONG DEAD FOOTSTEP WHISPERING THROUGH . . 699 MOSADA 3   V   5
    DAY'S DEAD, ALL FLAME-BEWILDERED, AND THE HILLS . . 702 MOSADA 3   86
    THE PATH O'ER-MUFFLED WITH THE LEAVES--DEAD LEAVES, . 703 MOSADA 3   115
    THE PATH O'ER MUFFLED WITH THE LEAVES--DEAD LEAVES, . 703 MOSADA 3   V   115
    MY LORD, YOU CALLED? NOT I. THIS MAID IS DEAD. . . 704 MOSADA 3   125
    SILENCE! THOU SHALT BE DEAD!" NOW SUDDENLY . . . . 710 FERENCZ RENYI   16
    OF MY DEAD CHILDREN SOON, WHATE'ER BETIDE, ...   712 FERENCZ RENYI   58
    . . . GONE AND PUFFED AWAY AND DEAD. . . . .   718 PHANTOM SHIP   3
    SLOW THE CHAPEL BELL IS TOLLING AS THOUGH THE DEAD PASSED 718 PHANTOM SHIP 16
      BY,
    BY THE SLOW HEAVING OCEAN--MUMBLING MOTHER OF THE DEAD. 719 PHANTOM SHIP   34
    PRAYED BESIDE THE OCEAN, THE OLD MUMBLING MOTHER OF THE 719 PHANTOM SHIP V 34
      DEAD.
    AND THEN HIS HEART GREW WELL-NIGH DEAD . . . . . .   730 PRIEST FAIRY   59
    AND A STRING MURMURS AS THOUGH TIME WERE DEAD . . . 752 SHADOW WATER A   124
    THE FALLING BLOSSOMS, AND THE DEAD THE LIVING. . .   756 SHADOW WATER A   182
    I WAIT YOUR WORDS AS THE DEAD WAIT THE LIVING. . .   756 SHADOW WATER A V 182
    FOR THOSE AMONG YOUR PEOPLE THAT ARE DEAD? . . . .   758 SHADOW WATER A   224
    FOR I AM CERTAIN SOMEBODY IS DEAD. . . . .   760 SHADOW WATER A   254
    WHETHER AMONG THE COLD WINDS OF THE DEAD. . . . .   768 SHADOW WATER A V 413
    FROM THE DRY BONES OF THE DEAD? . . . .   781 MY HEART BEAT   8
    AND HEARD THE DEAD LIPS SING. . . . .   790 SINGING HEAD   24
    A MEMORY, EVEN TO THE DEAD, ...   791 REPRISALS   8
    AMONG THE OTHER CHEATED DEAD. . . . .   791 REPRISALS   24
DEADLY
    FRIEND! BUT 'TWERE A DEADLY SIN . . . .   697 MOSADA 2   31
DEAF
    BLIND AND NIGH DEAF, WITH WITHERED ARMS HE LIES . .   42 OISIN 2   V 203
    IF DEAF AND DUMB AND BLIND WITH LOVE? . . . . 202 NEVER GIVE ALL   12
    HAS MADE THEM SO HAPPY AND HOPELESS, SO DEAF AND SO BLIND 204 WITHER BOUGHS 20
    THE BEGGAR DEAF TO ALL BUT HOPE . . . .   304 HOUR DAWN   V   44
    NOW PEARSE IS DEAF AND DUMB? . . . .   395 SIXTEEN DEAD   10
    THAT MAN IS STRICKEN DEAF AND DUMB AND BLIND, . . . 478 SELF AND SOUL   35
    THAT MAN IS DEAF AND DRUNK AND BLIND . . . .   478 SELF AND SOUL V   35

	PAGE	TITLE		LINE
DEAF (CONTINUED)				
THE MAYOR CAME, LEANING HIS DEAF EAR--	725	LEGEND		13
I AM BLIND AND DEAF BECAUSE OF THE WHITE WINGS.	759	SHADOW WATER A		235
DEAFENED				
WHEN, THE EARS BEING DEAFENED, THE SIGHT OF THE EYES BLIND	257	RECONCILIATION		3
DEAFENING				
AND DEAFENING MUSIC SHOOK THE LEAVES; A TROOP	537	HER VISION		13
DEAFENING US WITH IDLE SOUND--	727	LOVERS QUARREL		30
DEAFENS				
THE NIGHTINGALE THAT DEAFENS DAYLIGHT THERE, ...	446	COLONUS PRAISE		3
DEAFER				
COLDER AND DUMBER AND DEAFER THAN A FISH.	267	ALL TEMPT ME		10
DEAL				
ON PAINTED PILLARS, ON A DEAL	271	GREY ROCK	V	19
A DEAL I'D SWEAT AND LITTLE EARN	331	ROUND TOWER		2
CAN BE CONTENT WITH ARGUMENT AND DEAL	409	TOWER		14
A DEAL OF EVIL AND OF CHANGE HATH CROSSED	676	ISLE STAT II 3		273
DEAN				
THAT GOLDSMITH AND THE DEAN, ...	481	BLOOD AND MOON		18
DEAR				
YE LITTLE CHILDER DEAR, ...	95	MOLL MAGEE		18
MY DERMOT DEAR AND BROWN, ...	97	FOXHUNTER	V	6
MY LOLLARD OLD AND DEAR.	97	FOXHUNTER	V	8
AND HIS YOUNG DEAR ONE CLOSE BESIDE HIM KNELT, ...	108	CUCHULAIN SEA	V	40
MY DEAR, WHEN YOU'RE GROWN!	118	CRADLE SONG	V	12
WHEN, DEAR, YOU HAVE GROWN.	118	CRADLE SONG	V	12
CABINS GONE NOW, OLD WELL-SIDES, OLD DEAR PLACES, ...	130	BOOK STORIES	V	23
AND HOPE IS LESS DEAR THAN THE DEW OF THE MORN.	148	INTO TWILIGHT		16
AND THAT DEAR WORDS MEANT NOTHING?" BUT ENOUGH, ...	201	OLD MEMORY		9
I THOUGHT, "HE HOLDS HER DEAR,"	254	WOMAN HOMER		3
BUT, DEAR, CLING CLOSE TO ME; SINCE YOU WERE GONE, ...	257	RECONCILIATION		11
"O NO, MY DEAR, YOU MAKE SO BOLD	263	MASK		3
"O NO, MY DEAR, LET ALL THAT BE;	263	MASK		13
DEAR CRAOIBHIN AOIBHIN, LOOK INTO OUR CASE.	264	ABBEY THEATRE		1
HOPELESS AND DEAR, OR TERRIBLE TO THINK ON, ...	281	TWO KINGS		96
"MY DEAR, MY DEAR, O DEAR, ...	319	DOLLS		19
"MY DEAR, MY DEAR, O DEAR, ...	319	DOLLS		19
"MY DEAR, MY DEAR, O DEAR, ...	319	DOLLS		19
BUT NOT THAT MY DEAR FRIEND'S DEAR SON, ...	325	ROBERT GREGORY		46
BUT NOT THAT MY DEAR FRIEND'S DEAR SON, ...	325	ROBERT GREGORY		46
DEAR FELLOW-ARTIST, WHY SO FREE	335	YOUNG BEAUTY		1
DEAR FELLOW ARTIST WHY SO FREE	335	YOUNG BEAUTY	V	1
MY DEAR, MY DEAR, I KNOW	336	YOUNG GIRL		1
MY DEAR, MY DEAR, I KNOW	336	YOUNG GIRL		1
I HAD WISHED A DEAR THING ON THAT DAY	341	SHEP GOATHERD	V	73
TO HOPE A THING SO DEAR	346	ON WOMAN		27
THAT MADE HER DIARMUID DEAR, AND SOME OLD CARDINAL	366	HER COURAGE		6
AND THAT MADE HER DERMUID DEAR, AND SOME OLD CARDINAL	366	HER COURAGE	V	6
THAT ALL MY CHILDHOOD COUNTED DEAR;	398	BREAK OF DAY		7
I COULD NOT FIND A THING SO DEAR."	398	BREAK OF DAY		9
BEING DEAR AS MINE ARE DEAR.	400	DEMON BEAST		20
BEING DEAR AS MINE ARE DEAR.	400	DEMON BEAST		20
ROOTED IN ONE DEAR PERPETUAL PLACE.	405	FOR DAUGHTER		48
WERE SOME DEAR CHEEK. UPON A MOONLESS NIGHT	466	HARUN RASHID		127
WERE SOME DEAR FACE. UPON A MOONLESS NIGHT	466	HARUN RASHID	V	127
ONE DEAR HOPE HAD HE!	471	ALL SOUL NIGHT		28
DEAR SHADOWS, NOW YOU KNOW IT ALL, ...	476	EVA GORE-BOOTH		21
SEEMED ONCE MORE DEAR THAN LIFE; ANCESTRAL TREES, ...	491	COOLE BALLYLEE		34
THAT ONLY GOD, MY DEAR, ...	492	ANNE GREGORY		16
ONE DEAR BRILLIANT WOMAN;	504	RESULT THOUGHT		2
BECAUSE OF MY DEAR JACK THAT'S DEAD.	508	JANE BISHOP		5
"THREE DEAR THINGS THAT WOMEN KNOW,"	521	THREE THINGS		7
DEAR, I MUST BE GONE	535	PARTING		1
WHAT MATTER? THOSE THAT ROCKY FACE HOLDS DEAR, ...	564	GYRES		18
O MY DEAR, O MY DEAR.	569	THREE BUSHES		7
O MY DEAR, O MY DEAR.	569	THREE BUSHES		7
O MY DEAR, O MY DEAR.	569	THREE BUSHES		14
O MY DEAR, O MY DEAR.	569	THREE BUSHES		14
DEAR CHAMBERMAID," SAID SHE.	569	THREE BUSHES		16
O MY DEAR, O MY DEAR.	570	THREE BUSHES		21
O MY DEAR, O MY DEAR.	570	THREE BUSHES		21
O MY DEAR, O MY DEAR.	570	THREE BUSHES		28
O MY DEAR, O MY DEAR.	570	THREE BUSHES		28
O MY DEAR, O MY DEAR.	570	THREE BUSHES		35
O MY DEAR, O MY DEAR.	570	THREE BUSHES		35
O MY DEAR, O MY DEAR.	570	THREE BUSHES		42
O MY DEAR, O MY DEAR.	570	THREE BUSHES		42
O MY DEAR, O MY DEAR.	571	THREE BUSHES		49
O MY DEAR, O MY DEAR.	571	THREE BUSHES		49
O MY DEAR, O MY DEAR.	571	THREE BUSHES		56
O MY DEAR, O MY DEAR.	571	THREE BUSHES		56
O MY DEAR, O MY DEAR.	571	THREE BUSHES		63
O MY DEAR, O MY DEAR.	571	THREE BUSHES		63
O MY DEAR, O MY DEAR.	571	THREE BUSHES		70
O MY DEAR, O MY DEAR.	571	THREE BUSHES		70
O MY DEAR, O MY DEAR.	571	THREE BUSHES		77
O MY DEAR, O MY DEAR.	571	THREE BUSHES		77
THAT IS ALL I ASK, MY DEAR, ...	587	OLD WICKED MAN		7
"KIND ARE ALL YOUR WORDS, MY DEAR, ...	588	OLD WICKED MAN		10
WHO CAN KNOW THE YEAR, MY DEAR, ...	588	OLD WICKED MAN		12
OF ALL THAT SCHOLARLY GENERATIONS HAD HELD DEAR;	603	GALLERY REVIS	V	37A

```
                                              PAGE    TITLE            LINE
DEAR   (CONTINUED)
     BUT MY DEAR MARY MOORE,  . . . . . . . . . . .   620 JOHN KINSELLA       8
     I THOUGHT MY DEAR MUST HER OWN SOUL DESTROY, . . . . .  630 CIRCUS ANIMALS   21
     A BRIEF PARTING FROM THOSE DEAR  . . . . . . .   637 BEN BULBEN          19
     I LAUGHED?  AND WHY IS THAT A THING SO DEAR? . . . .  670 ISLE STAT II 3   97
     SO BE THOU STILL, DEAR HEART, A LITTLE WHILE! . . . .  677 ISLE STAT II 3  283
     HUNG ON HIS DOUBLET--DEAR AND MOURNFUL CHILD, . . . .  691 MOSADA 1         35
     AND OUT-SPREAD ARMS.  BE NOT SO PALE, DEAR LOVE. . . .  701 MOSADA 3        70
     DEAR HEART, THERE IS A SECRET WAY THAT LEADS . . . .  702 MOSADA 3         75
     "NOW ANSWER, IF THIS LIFE BE DEAR TO THEE, . . . .  713 FERENCZ RENYI  V  83
     SHE PRAYS FOR FATHER, MOTHER DEAR, . . . . . . .  735 IN CHURCH            1
     HER PRAYER FOR FATHER, MOTHER DEAR, . . . . . .  736 IN CHURCH           13
     (O MY DEAR, MY DEAR). . . . . . . . . . . . .   779 GOING THE ROAD       4
     (O MY DEAR, MY DEAR). . . . . . . . . . . . .   779 GOING THE ROAD       4
     (O MY DEAR, MY DEAR). . . . . . . . . . . . .   779 GOING THE ROAD       8
     (O MY DEAR, MY DEAR). . . . . . . . . . . . .   779 GOING THE ROAD       8
     (O MY DEAR, MY DEAR). . . . . . . . . . . . .   779 GOING THE ROAD      12
     (O MY DEAR, MY DEAR). . . . . . . . . . . . .   779 GOING THE ROAD      12
     O MY DEAR, O MY DEAR! . . . . . . . . . . . .   779 GOING THE ROAD  V    4
     O MY DEAR, O MY DEAR! . . . . . . . . . . . .   779 GOING THE ROAD  V    4
     THOUGH BATTLE JOY MAY BE SO DEAR . . . . . . .   791 REPRISALS            7
DEARER
     DEARER THAN ANY THAT THE DUMB STONE HIDES, . . . .  281 TWO KINGS      V  96
     YET HAVE NO DEARER THOUGHT . . . . . . . . . .   401 DEMON BEAST         40
     I HOLD HIM DEARER THAN THE GLAD, . . . . . . .   723 GIRLS SONG A         3
     I HOLD HIM DEARER THAN THE GOOD, . . . . . . .   723 GIRLS SONG A         7
     I HOLD HIM DEARER THAN THE WISE, . . . . . . .   723 GIRLS SONG A        11
DEAREST
     "AND IF MY DEAREST FRIEND WERE DEAD . . . . . .   338 TOM OROUGHLEY       15
     THERE'S LITTLE I'D REFUSE THEE, DEAREST YOUTH. . . .  669 ISLE STAT II 3   71
DEARTH
     I'LL HAVE.  OH, ABSENT ONE 'TIS NOT FOR DEARTH . . .  664 ISLE STAT II 2   50
DEATH   SEE STRAW-DEATH LIFE-IN-DEATH
     THEN MOCK AT DEATH AND TIME WITH GLANCES . . . .   19 OISIN 1           274
     AND HERE THERE IS NOR CHANGE NOR DEATH, . . . . .   19 OISIN 1           284
     FOR NEITHER DEATH NOR CHANGE COMES NEAR US, . . . .   21 OISIN 1           316
     FOR CHANGE AND DEATH THEY COME NOT NEAR US, . . . .   21 OISIN 1       V  316
     SINCE GOD MADE TIME AND DEATH AND SLEEP! THE OTHER . .   31 OISIN 2        41
     AND DEMONS BE BROKEN IN PIECES, AND TRAMPLED BENEATH THEM  61 OISIN 3     204
       IN DEATH.
     AND DEMONS, ALL BROKEN IN PIECES, BE TRAMPLED BENEATH THEM  61 OISIN 3 V 204
       IN DEATH.
     THE DEATH OF CUCHULAIN . . . . . . . . . . . .   105 CUCHULAIN SEA  V   T
     A DREAM OF DEATH . . . . . . . . . . . . . .   123 DREAM OF DEATH      T
     I AM NO MORE WITH LIFE AND DEATH, . . . . . . .   152 HEART OF WOMAN     10
     ARE PLOTTING FOR YOUR DEATH.  HAVE I NOT GIVEN . . .  226 SHADOW WATER B  93
     TO DEATH! FOR THEY THAT PROMISED TO ME LOVE . . . .  230 SHADOW WATER B 192
     IT'S CERTAIN THEY ARE LEADING YOU TO DEATH. . . . .  231 SHADOW WATER B 201
     IF I AM GOING TO MY DEATH?--FOR THERE, . . . . .  231 SHADOW WATER B 207
     WE'LL PUT THIS MAN TO DEATH.  I PROMISE IT. . . . .  238 SHADOW WATER B 363
     TO HIM THAT WOUNDS HIM TO THE DEATH.  I'LL DO IT. . .  240 SHADOW WATER B 375
     THAT HE IS BEING DRIVEN TO HIS DEATH. . . . . . .  248 SHADOW WATER B 551
     HE KNOWS THAT HE IS TAKING YOU TO DEATH! . . . . .  249 SHADOW WATER B 562
     BY THE SWEET NAME OF DEATH. . . . . . . . . . .  254 HIS DREAM          12
     BY THE SWEET NAME OF DEATH. . . . . . . . . . .  254 HIS DREAM          20
     WE'LL LEARN THAT SLEEPING IS NOT DEATH, . . . . .  266 GALWAY RACES       11
     THAT HAS MORE LIFE IN IT THAN DEATH, . . . . . .  271 GREY ROCK           8
     SWEETENED BY DEATH, BUT IF I COULD BELIEVE, . . . .  285 TWO KINGS         205
     YOU HAD ENOUGH OF SORROW BEFORE DEATH-- . . . . .  293 TO A SHADE         23
     "THOUGH THE DOOR OF DEATH IS NEAR . . . . . . .   298 THREE HERMITS       8
     FOR WHAT PROUD DEATH MAY BRING . . . . . . . .   317 NIGHT COME          3
     COULD SHARE IN THAT DISCOURTESY OF DEATH. . . . .  325 ROBERT GREGORY     48
     OF THAT LATE DEATH TOOK ALL MY HEART FOR SPEECH. . .  328 ROBERT GREGORY   96
     AN IRISH AIRMAN FORESEES HIS DEATH . . . . . . .   328 IRISH AIRMAN        T
     IN BALANCE WITH THIS LIFE, THIS DEATH. . . . . .  328 IRISH AIRMAN       16
     LAID ON THE DEATH BED. . . . . . . . . . . . .   335 SONG           V   16
     RECOVERED HIM UPON THE BED OF DEATH. . . . . . .  355 BROKEN DREAMS       6
     YET ALWAYS WHEN I LOOK DEATH IN THE FACE, . . . .  357 DEEP-SWORN VOW      3
     LAID HIS STRONG BONES DOWN IN DEATH . . . . . . .  360 ALF POLLEXFEN       3
     LAID HIS STRONG BONES IN DEATH . . . . . . . .   360 ALF POLLEXFEN  V    3
     WE HAVE NAUGHT FOR DEATH BUT TOYS. . . . . . . .  363 DOLLS DRAWINGS     11
     WHO HAVE LIVED IN JOY AND LAUGHED INTO THE FACE OF DEATH.  366 HER COURAGE  10
     WHO LIVED IN SHAMELESS JOY AND LAUGHED INTO THE FACE OF  366 HER COURAGE V 10
       DEATH.
     THAT LIVED IN JOY AND LAUGHED INTO THE FACE OF DEATH. .  366 HER COURAGE V 10
     WHO HAVE LIVED IN JOY AND LAUGHED IN THE FACE OF DEATH. .  366 HER COURAGE V 10
     FROM DEATH, AND WOUNDS, OR ON SINAI'S TOP, . . . .  375 PHASES OF MOON   67
     SO DEAD BEYOND OUR DEATH, . . . . . . . . . . .  382 VISION ROBART      15
     NO, NO, NOT NIGHT BUT DEATH! . . . . . . . . .   394 EASTER 1916        66
     WAS IT NEEDLESS DEATH AFTER ALL? . . . . . . . .   394 EASTER 1916        67
     DEATH AND LIFE WERE NOT . . . . . . . . . . .   415 TOWER             148
     THE DEATH OF FRIENDS, OR DEATH . . . . . . . .   416 TOWER             189
     THE DEATH OF FRIENDS, OR DEATH . . . . . . . .   416 TOWER             189
     THAT WERE A LUCKY DEATH. . . . . . . . . . . .   431 NINETEEN 19        77
     AS THOUGH GOD'S DEATH WERE BUT A PLAY. . . . . .  437 SONGS PLAY 1        8
     THE DEATH OF THE HARE . . . . . . . . . . . .   453 DEATH OF HARE       T
     AT THE DEATH OF THE HARE. . . . . . . . . . . .  453 DEATH OF HARE      12
     DEATH, DESPAIR, DIVISION OF FAMILIES, . . . . . .  459 FROM OEDIPUS        5
     WHEN OUR BELOVED CALIPH PUT TO DEATH . . . . . .  462 HARUN RASHID       31
     BEING SHARPENED BY HIS DEATH. . . . . . . . . .  471 ALL SOUL NIGHT      8
     OF THAT OR THE NEXT WINTER WOULD BE DEATH. . . . .  471 ALL SOUL NIGHT    30
```

193

	PAGE	TITLE		LINE
DEATH (CONTINUED)				
THE OLDER IS CONDEMNED TO DEATH,	475	EVA GORE-BOOTH		7
DEATH	476	DEATH		T
HE KNOWS DEATH TO THE BONE--	476	DEATH		11
MAN HAS CREATED DEATH.	476	DEATH		12
DELIVER FROM THE CRIME OF DEATH AND BIRTH.	478	SELF AND SOUL		24
AT ALGECIRAS--A MEDITATION UPON DEATH	493	AT ALGECIRAS		T
MEDITATIONS UPON DEATH	493	AT ALGECIRAS	V	T
THE BODY CALLS IT DEATH,	500	VACILLATION		7
BEGIN THE PREPARATION FOR YOUR DEATH	500	VACILLATION		28
LOVE IS NEARER DEATH.	517	HER ANXIETY		11
"O CRUEL DEATH, GIVE THREE THINGS BACK,"	521	THREE THINGS		1
THE MIRACLE THAT GAVE THEM SUCH A DEATH,	555	RIBH AT TOMB		10
HERE ON THE ANNIVERSARY OF THEIR DEATH,	555	RIBH AT TOMB		19
BUT OF THE DEATH HE MET	585	ORAHILLY		29
EYES SPIRITUALISED BY DEATH CAN JUDGE,	604	YOU CONTENT		7
THOSE INNOCENTS RE-LIVE THEIR DEATH,	612	NEWS ORACLE		15
THESE INNOCENTS RELIVE THEIR DEATH,	612	NEWS ORACLE	V	15
STOOD, TOOK DEATH LIKE A TUNE	613	MARCH SONGS 1		15
A MOUTHFUL HELD THE EXTREME OF LIFE AND DEATH.	619	BRONZE HEAD		14
A MOUTHFUL HOLD THE EXTREME OF LIFE AND DEATH.	619	BRONZE HEAD	V	14
FOR DEATH WHO TAKES WHAT MAN WOULD KEEP,	620	JOHN KINSELLA		3
BATTERED TO DEATH IN A CELLAR,	628	JANE MOUNTAIN		9
ON LIFE, ON DEATH,	640	BEN BULBEN		93
OF HIS DEATH AND CHANGE MALIGN.	648	ISLE STAT I 1		80
BEFORE A DEATH, O'ER WAVE AND BANK	673	ISLE STAT II 3		185
OH DEATH IS HORRIBLE! AND FOUL, FOUL, FOUL!	675	ISLE STAT II 3		238
LOVE AND DEATH.	680	LOVE AND DEATH		T
AND THEY'LL ANSWER DEATH AND LOVE.	680	LOVE AND DEATH		16
ARE THE SPIRITS LOVE AND DEATH.	680	LOVE AND DEATH		32
TO DEATH. HIS DARKNESS AND HIS CHILL I FEEL.	684	SEEKER		63
TO DEATH. HIS LIPS ARE GLUED, WITH QUIVERING TOUCH,	684	SEEKER	V	63
WITH DEW, AS THOUGH 'TWERE SEALING THEM FOR DEATH.	691	MOSADA 1		22
THE WAGES OF SIN IS DEATH. NO USE. NO GOOD.	697	MOSADA 2		42
THE WAGE OF SIN IS DEATH. NO USE. NO USE.	697	MOSADA 2	V	42
TOO LATE, TOO LATE, FOR I AM NEAR TO DEATH.	701	MOSADA 3		55
THIS DEATH IS HEAVY IN MY VEINS LIKE SLEEP.	701	MOSADA 3		57
IS IT YOUR MESSAGE, STARS, THAT WHEN DEATH COMES	701	MOSADA 3		60
WERE HERE, HE WOULD TURN DEATH INTO A CRUTCH!	711	FERENCZ RENYI		38
THE MAN WHOSE HOUR OF DEATH DRAWS NIGH,	716	FAIRY DOCTOR		6
AND DEATH, OH MY FAIR ONE, WILL NEVER COME NEAR	717	LOVE SONG		8
DEFEAT IS DEATH. SHOULD MY PLOTS FAIL I'D DIE.	722	WITCH VIVIEN		52
OR DEATH THAT COMETH WITH THE NEXT LIFE-KEY?	724	KANVA ON SELF		18
THAT I WOULD BID MY PEOPLE PUT TO DEATH.	760	SHADOW WATER A	V	254
FOR THE THINGS COME AFTER DEATH?	777	SONG DEIRDRE 2		12
WHAT DEATH? WHAT DISCIPLINE?	784	WOMANS BEAUTY		21
THOUGH DEATH ITSELF FORBADE.	789	SINGING HEAD		8
WE CALLED IT A GOOD DEATH. TODAY	791	REPRISALS		3
DEATHBED				
"SEEING THAT WHEN YOU COME TO THE DEATHBED	285	TWO KINGS		196
DEATH-BED				
"SEEING THAT WHEN YOU COME TO THE DEATH-BED	285	TWO KINGS	V	196
CONFUSION OF THE DEATH-BED OVER, IS IT SENT	316	COLD HEAVEN		10
LAID ON THE DEATH-BED,	335	SONG		16
DEATHBEDS				
AT ALL THESE DEATHBEDS WOMEN HEARD	361	ALF POLLEXFEN	V	36
DEATH-BEDS				
AT ALL THESE DEATH-BEDS WOMEN HEARD	361	ALF POLLEXFEN		36
DEATHFUL				
I HEARD THE DEATHFUL MONOTONE,	673	ISLE STAT II 3		183
DEATH-HOUR				
BIRTH-HOUR AND DEATH-HOUR MEET,	496	MOHINI CHATTER		26
DEATH-IN-LIFE				
I CALL IT DEATH-IN-LIFE AND LIFE-IN-DEATH.	497	BYZANTIUM		16
DEATHLESS				
MEN DANCE ON DEATHLESS FEET."	496	MOHINI CHATTER		28
SIX THAT ARE DEATHLESS,	770	BLOOD BOND		13
DEATH-LONGING				
DELIGHT BECOMES DEATH-LONGING IF ALL LONGING ELSE BE VAIN.	459	FROM OEDIPUS		3
DEATH-MAKING				
HELPLESS, MEN LIFTING THE LIDS OF HIS WEARY AND DEATH-MAKING EYE.	53	OISIN 3		92
DEATH-PALE				
I WOULD THAT THE DEATH-PALE DEER	171	MAID QUIET	V	4A
LILIES OF DEATH-PALE HOPE, ROSES OF PASSIONATE DREAM.	172	TRAV PASSION		8
DEATH-POURING				
HELPLESS, MEN LIFTING THE LIDS OF HIS WEARY AND DEATH-POURING EYE.	53	OISIN 3	V	92
DEATH'S				
O DEATH'S OLD BONY FINGER	213	HAPPY TOWNLAND	V	1
THE GLITTERING EYES IN A DEATH'S HEAD	400	DEMON BEAST		9
FROM DEATH'S LATE LANGUOR AS THESE LINES I READ	734	QUATRAIN APHOR		14
DEATHS				
AFTER THE DEATHS OF MANY MEN,	197	BAILE AILLINN		193
DECAY				
"I HEAR MY SOUL DROP DOWN INTO DECAY,	45	OISIN 2		235
"AGE AFTER AGE I FEEL MY SOUL DECAY	45	OISIN 2	V	235
TIME DROPS IN DECAY,	142	MOODS		1
THOUGH HOPE FALL FROM YOU AND LOVE DECAY,	148	INTO TWILIGHT		7
THOUGH HOPE FALL FROM THEE OR LOVE DECAY	148	INTO TWILIGHT	V	7
SLOW DECAY OF BLOOD,	416	TOWER		185

194

	PAGE	TITLE	LINE
DECAY (CONTINUED)			
AND AFTER KEPT IT FROM DECAY:	460	THREE MONUMENT	7
GAZE ON TILL RAGGED TIME HIMSELF DECAY.	672	ISLE STAT II 3	148
THEY WOULD MAKE A PRINCE DECAY	775	AGAINST WITCH	11
DECAYETH			
WHILE THE MORNING STAR DECAYETH	706	DAWN-SONG	29
DECEIT SEE HALF-DECEIT			
BUT IT WAS ALL DECEIT, AND FLATTERY	244	SHADOW WATER B	457
LOVE OR DECEIT."	263	MASK	7
GO PILOT THE COURSE OF HIS ARROW'S DECEIT:	657	ISLE STAT I 3	69
DECEITLESS			
AND LOVE IS KINDLY AND DECEITLESS,	77	INDIAN TO LOVE V	5D
DECEIVE			
THE RHETORICIAN WOULD DECEIVE HIS NEIGHBOURS,	369	EGO DOMINUS	46
DECEIVED			
BETTER THAN MY OWN HANDS. I HAVE DECEIVED YOU	244	SHADOW WATER B	466
AND THAT YOU'LL BRING ME THERE? I HAVE DECEIVED YOU:	245	SHADOW WATER B	471
I HAVE DECEIVED YOU UTTERLY. HOW CAN THAT BE?	245	SHADOW WATER B	472
OLD SAGES WERE NOT DECEIVED:	504	QUARREL IN AGE	11
DECEIVING			
LOVES IN BRIEF LONGING AND DECEIVING HOPE	228	SHADOW WATER B	146
AND TURN BRIEF LONGING AND DECEIVING HOPE	750	SHADOW WATER A	59
THAN IN BRIEF LONGING AND DECEIVING HOPE	750	SHADOW WATER A	65
IS BUT BRIEF LONGING, AND DECEIVING HOPE,	765	SHADOW WATER A	354
DECENT			
FOR THINGS LIKE THESE WHAT DECENT MAN	598	MODEL LAUREATE	22
DECEPTION			
FOR THE HEART CRIES THAT WHAT DECEPTION WINS	448	HERO GIRL FOOL	6
WHAT NO DECEPTION WON. I HAVE HEARD THEM SAY	448	HERO GIRL FOOL V	13
FROM TERROR AND DECEPTION FREED IT CAN	558	RIBH CHRISTIAN	9
DECIDE			
AS RECOLLECTION OR THE DRUG DECIDE,	444	SCHOOL CHILDR	36
DECIDED			
DECIDED HE WOULD JOURNEY HOME,	361	ALF POLLEXFEN	30
DECIDED HE MUST JOURNEY HOME,	361	ALF POLLEXFEN V	30
DECK			
THERE IS A KING AND QUEEN UPON HER DECK,	232	SHADOW WATER B	226
UNTIL YOU STOOD BEFORE ME ON THE DECK--	236	SHADOW WATER B	313
NOW A SCREAM FROM ALL THOSE FISHERS, FOR THERE ON DECK THERE BE	719	PHANTOM SHIP	19
DECKED			
AND DECKED AND ALTERED IT FOR A GIRL'S LOVE,	423	MY DESCENDANTS	22
DECLAIMING			
ACCLAIMING, PROCLAIMING, DECLAIMING HIM.	528	DANCER CRUACH	8
DECLARE			
OF DRIPPING STONE: I DECLARE	414	TOWER	126
AND I DECLARE MY FAITH:	414	TOWER	145
DECLARE THAT WINTER'S BEST OF ALL:	434	WHEEL	4
I DECLARE THIS TOWER IS MY SYMBOL: I DECLARE	480	BLOOD AND MOON	16
I DECLARE THIS TOWER IS MY SYMBOL: I DECLARE	480	BLOOD AND MOON	16
BUT YESTERNIGHT DECLARE	492	ANNE GREGORY	14
HER KNEE-CAP BROKEN, THAT GIRL I DECLARE	578	CRAZED GIRL	6
HER KNEE CAP BROKEN: THAT GIRL I DECLARE	578	CRAZED GIRL V	6
WHEN GONG AND CONCH DECLARE THE HOUR TO BLESS	611	STATUES	23
AND WHEN IT'S VANISHED STILL DECLARE,	639	BEN BULBEN	60
DECLARED			
AND THUS DECLARED THAT ARAB LADY:	387	SOLOMON WITCH	1
ROSE FROM THE TABLE AND DECLARED IT RIGHT	410	TOWER	43
HE IN HIS RAGE DECLARED:	539	MEETING	14
DECLENSION			
THROUGH NATURAL DECLENSION OF THE SOUL,	423	MY DESCENDANTS	10
DECLINE			
AND KNOW WHATEVER FLOURISH AND DECLINE	423	MY DESCENDANTS	23
ON THIS FOUL WORLD IN ITS DECLINE AND FALL:	619	BRONZE HEAD	24
DECLINING			
FLOWED ON ANEW, AND OFT, ANEW DECLINING,	33	OISIN 2 V	68D
UNDER THE DAY'S DECLINING BEAM, AND CALL	410	TOWER	21
DECLIVITIES			
MY DARK DECLIVITIES.	536	PARTING	14
DECREED			
BUT THE GODS LONG AGO DECREED	194	BAILE AILLINN	119
THE STAR-TAUGHT MOOR, SAID THUS IT WAS DECREED	691	MOSADA 1	25
DECREES			
WHERE FASHION OR MERE FANTASY DECREES	491	COOLE BALLYLEE	38
DECREPIT			
DECREPIT AGE THAT HAS BEEN TIED TO ME	409	TOWER	3
DECREPIT AGE THAT HAS BEEN TIED UPON ME	409	TOWER V	3
DECREPITUDE			
OR DULL DECREPITUDE,	416	TOWER	187
BODILY DECREPITUDE IS WISDOM: YOUNG	523	LONG SILENCE	7
DECTORA			
AODH TO DECTORA THREE SONGS	152	LOSS OF LOVE V	T
AODH TO DECTORA	175	BELOVED DEAD V	T
OF FORGAEL AND DECTORA AND THE EMPTY WATERS	218	WOODS OF COOLE	22
BEFORE THEY READ OF FORGAEL AND DECTORA,	219	WOODS OF COOLE	42
DEDICATE			
I DEDICATE THESE FITFUL DANAAN RHYMES	136	TO SOME I TALK V	1
AND DEDICATE--EYES BENT UPON THE GROUND,	489	COOLE PARK 29	29
DEDICATION			
THE DEDICATION TO A BOOK OF STORIES SELECTED FROM THE IRISH NOVELISTS	129	BOOK STORIES	T

	PAGE	TITLE		LINE

DEDICATION (CONTINUED)
DEDICATION	129	BOOK STORIES	V	T
DEDICATION OF "IRISH TALES"	129	BOOK STORIES	V	T
DEDICATION TO THE "SHADOWY WATERS"	217	WOODS OF COOLE	V	T
DEDICATION	790	DEDICATION		T

DEED
WE COME BETWEEN HIM AND THE DEED OF HIS HAND, ...	141	HOSTING SIDHE		11
AND WHERE IS THERE HOPE OR DEED AS FAIR?	141	HOSTING SIDHE		14
WAS: "YOU, THAT HAVE NOT LIVED IN THOUGHT BUT DEED, . .	353	PEOPLE		30
OF SOME MOST HAUGHTY DEED OR THOUGHT	436	FOR MY SON		13
CHARACTER ISOLATED BY A DEED	630	CIRCUS ANIMALS		29
THE NOISY WORLD DIVIDES. HOW SOON A DEED	700	MOSADA 3		34

DEED-DOER
| O WORN DEED-DOER." "WHAT MAY BRING . . . . | 5 | OISIN 1 | V | 50 |

DEED-DOERS
| YE WORN DEED-DOERS, AND MY NAME . . . . | 5 | OISIN 1 | V | 48 |

DEEDS
BARD OISIN, BOAST NOT OF THY DEEDS	11	OISIN 1	V	129
THEN NOWISE WORSHIP DUSTY DEEDS, ...	65	HAPPY SHEPHERD		22
THEN NO WISE WORSHIP DUSTY DEEDS, ...	65	HAPPY SHEPHERD	V	22
HE WOULD HIS DEEDS FORGET.	112	ROSE OF PEACE		4
WHEN ALL THOUGHTS AND DEEDS ARE RECKONED, ...	298	THREE HERMITS		15
THOSE DEEDS WERE BEST THAT GAVE THE MINUTE WINGS . .	533	HER TRIUMPH		5

DEEM
| YET DIMLY DEEM I THAT THE MORNING RAYS . . . . . . | 30 | OISIN 2 | V | 20 |

DEEP
THEN, MOUNTED ON A HERON, O'ER THE DEEP	33	OISIN 2	V	64
THAT SEA-GOD'S NAME, WHO IN A DEEP CONTENT	38	OISIN 2		129
DEEP SUNKEN ON THE BLADE'S LENGTH, "MANANAN!" . . .	38	OISIN 2	V	128
THAT SEA GOD'S NAME, WHO IN A DEEP CONTENT	38	OISIN 2	V	129
AND FOUND A DOOR DEEP SUNKEN IN THE WALL, ...	39	OISIN 2		154
ROLLING HIS FLAGRANT WHEEL OUT OF THE DEEP, ...	42	OISIN 2		193
ROLLING HIS WHEEL, WE SANG BESIDE THE DEEP	42	OISIN 2	V	193
. . . THERE CAMPING IN GRASSES DEEP, ...	50	OISIN 3		54
THRUSTING HIS NOSE TO MY SHOULDER: HE KNEW IN HIS BOSOM DEEP	54	OISIN 3		106
. . . DEEP HORROR OF EYES AND OF WINGS, ...	62	OISIN 3		205
FELL ON THE PIRATES BY THE DEEP, ...	83	MAD KING GOLL		21
FELL ON THE ROBBERS BY THE DEEP, ...	83	MAD KING GOLL	V	21
FELL ON THE PIRATES OF THE DEEP, ...	83	MAD KING GOLL	V	21
HE HOLDS DEEP COMMUNE WITH HIS HEART:	99	FOXHUNTER		43
WHERE THE SUN FALLS INTO THE WESTERN DEEP.	108	CUCHULAIN SEA	V	34
I HEAR IT IN THE DEEP HEART'S CORE.	117	ISLE INNISFREE		12
YOUR EYES HAD ONCE, AND OF THEIR SHADOWS DEEP: . . .	121	YOU ARE OLD		4
AND ABOVE THE DEEP OF HEAVEN, ...	125	CATHLEEN PARA	V	15
AND PIERCE THE DEEP WOOD'S WOVEN SHADE, ...	125	GOES FERGUS		2
NOW THAT DEEP EARTH HAS DRUNK HIS BODY IN:	127	DREAM OF FAERY	V	28
OF THINGS DISCOVERED IN THE DEEP, ...	138	TO IRELAND		21
OF THE DIM WISDOMS OLD AND DEEP, ...	138	TO IRELAND	V	21
DROWNING LOVE'S LONELY HOUR IN DEEP TWILIGHT OF REST, .	154	BELOVED PEACE		11
BUT FLAME ON FLAME, AND DEEP ON DEEP, ...	156	FORGOT BEAUTY		21
BUT FLAME ON FLAME, AND DEEP ON DEEP, ...	156	FORGOT BEAUTY		21
BUT FLAME ON FLAME, DEEP UNDER DEEP, ...	156	FORGOT BEAUTY		21
BUT FLAME ON FLAME, DEEP UNDER DEEP, ...	156	FORGOT BEAUTY	V	21
ALL BUT THE FLAMES, AND DEEP ON DEEP, ...	156	FORGOT BEAUTY	V	21
ALL BUT THE FLAMES, AND DEEP ON DEEP, ...	156	FORGOT BEAUTY	V	21
AND HANDS HURL IN THE DEEP	165	CRY OF SEDGE		6
AND TUMULT OF DEFEATED DREAMS: AND DEEP	169	SECRET ROSE		5
DWELT AMONG WINE-STAINED WANDERERS IN DEEP WOODS: . .	170	SECRET ROSE		21
HIS HEAVY RINGS UNCOILED FROM GLIMMERING DEEP TO DEEP:	174	ELEMENT POWERS		5
HIS HEAVY RINGS UNCOILED FROM GLIMMERING DEEP TO DEEP:	174	ELEMENT POWERS		5
ON OLD DEEP SILVER ROLLING THERE	271	GREY ROCK		20
A DARK DEEP HOLLOW IN THE ROCK.	303	HOUR DAWN		21
A DARK DEEP HOLE IN THE ROCK'S FACE.	303	HOUR DAWN	V	21
HAD DIPPED THE WOODEN LADLE DEEP	304	HOUR DAWN		46
A DEEP SWORN VOW	357	DEEP-SWORN VOW	V	T
THAT DEEP SWORN VOW, HAVE BEEN FRIENDS OF MINE, . .	357	DEEP-SWORN VOW	V	2
BRING UP OUT OF THAT DEEP CONSIDERING MIND	413	TOWER		106
CAME TO SO DEEP A THOUGHT	505	RESULT THOUGHT		10
HOW COULD PASSION RUN SO DEEP	534	CONSOLATION		7
"FORGETTING HUMAN WORDS," A GRAVE DEEP FACE. . . .	603	GALLERY REVIS		49
WHAT DEEP ROOTS ARE," AND NEVER FORESAW THE END . .	603	GALLERY REVIS	V	37
SAW THAT THE GRAVE WAS DEEP, THE COFFIN SOUND, . .	609	IN TARAS HALLS		18
GROWS MORE DEEP DAY AFTER DAY, ...	624	APPARITIONS		18
SADNESS, SOUL OF JOY MOST DEEP, ...	647	ISLE STAT I 1		74
SAD LADY OF THE DEEP, POURS DOWN HER LIGHT: . . .	650	ISLE STAT I 1		127
LONE REGENT OF THE WOODS, DEEP MUTTERING.	657	ISLE STAT I 3		49
THE BARRED WOODPECKER'S MANSION IS AND DEEP, . . .	659	ISLE STAT II 1		23
OF THE WIDE WOODS. AND THE DEEP EARTH GATHERED THEM.	660	ISLE STAT II 1		33
IN THE DEEP CENTRES OF THE SECRET WOODS.	661	ISLE STAT II 1		54
FROM THE DEEP EARTH UNTO THE LURID SKY	662	ISLE STAT II 2		5
AND WHEN THE SUMMER'S DEEP, THEN TO THIS SPOT . . .	663	ISLE STAT II 2		24
WAS MY SLEEP LONG, OH, YOUTH? LONG, LONG AND DEEP. .	678	ISLE STAT II 3		299
IN THE DEEP ALCOVES DIMNESS SMILES AND HIDES. . . .	685	DRAWING-ROOM		4
THE SAGE, WHO DEEP IN CENTRAL NATURE DELVES, . . .	686	LIFE		2
THE DARKNESS OF THE WHIRLWIND SHATTERED DEEP. . . .	688	TWO TITANS		58
DEEP IN HIS SOUL, LIKE RAIN UPON A SOIL	692	MOSADA 1		56
DEEP IN THE WOODLAND PAUSED THEY, THE SIX FEET . . .	716	DWELT SYCAMORE		9
DEEP IN THE WOODLAND PASSED THEY. THE SIX FEET . . .	716	DWELT SYCAMORE	V	9
CRIES A VOICE AT ROARING MIDNIGHT BESIDE THE MOONLESS DEEP.	718	PHANTOM SHIP		8
WHAT SHALLOW THOUGHTS ABOUT DEEP THINGS!	725	LEGEND		11

	PAGE	TITLE	LINE

DEEP (CONTINUED)

THE SAGE WHO DEEP IN CENTRAL NATURE DELVES, ...	734 QUATRAIN APHOR	2
IN THE DEEP ALCOVE'S DIMNESS SMILES AND HIDES."	735 QUATRAIN APHOR	24
AND JOY, IN GROWING DEEPER AND MORE DEEP, ...	735 QUATRAIN APHOR	27
IN THE DEEP ALCOVES DIMNESS SMILES AND HIDES.	735 QUATRAIN APHOR V	24

DEEPENED

AND WOULD BE NO HARSH FRIEND. WHEN NIGHT HAD DEEPENED,   283 TWO KINGS   138

DEEPENING

AMONG THE DEEPENING SHADES. . . . .   416 TOWER   195

DEEPER

TO WATCH THEE PASS? YET DEEPER THAN MEN KNOW	672 ISLE STAT II 3	158
DEEPER THAN THE DEEPEST WELL."	697 MOSADA 2	27
AND JOY, IN GROWING DEEPER AND MORE DEEP, ...	735 QUATRAIN APHOR	27

DEEPEST

UNDER THE DEEPEST SHADOWS OF THE HALL	37 OISIN 2	119
WHEN NIGHT WAS AT ITS DEEPEST, A WILD GOOSE	181 QUEEN MAEVE	36
"NO, THY HOME IS DEEPEST HELL, ...	697 MOSADA 2	26
DEEPER THAN THE DEEPEST WELL."	697 MOSADA 2	27

DEEP-EYED

DEEP-EYED, SLOW-FOOTING DOWN THE EMPTY GLADE. . . . .   653 ISLE STAT I 2   55

DEEP-ROOTED

DEEP-ROOTED THINGS," BUT NEVER FORESAW ITS END, ...	603 GALLERY REVIS	37
A GUERDON OF DEEP-ROOTED PAIN, ...	668 ISLE STAT II 3	59

DEEPS

PIERCED WITH SOFT LIGHT THE SHALLOWING DEEPS.	13 OISIN 1	164
AND TOLD THE PURPLE DEEPS THEIR PRIDE, ...	14 OISIN 1	186
. . . IN THE DEEPS OF MY HEART.	143 ROSE IN HEART	4
. . . IN THE DEEPS OF MY HEART.	143 ROSE IN HEART	8
AND THEIR SECRET SMILE, OUT OF THE DEEPS OF THE LAKE: . .	203 WITHER BOUGHS V	11

DEEP-SUNKEN

I FOUND A DOOR DEEP-SUNKEN IN THE WALL, ...   39 OISIN 2   V   154

DEEP-SWORN

A DEEP-SWORN VOW	357 DEEP-SWORN VOW	T
THAT DEEP-SWORN VOW HAVE BEEN FRIENDS OF MINE:	357 DEEP-SWORN VOW	2

DEER

THAN THE HORNLESS DEER WE CHASED THAT MORN, ...	2 OISIN 1	V	7P
WHEN WE FOLLOWED A DEER WITH OUR BAYING HOUNDS, ...	3 OISIN 1		14
THE HORNLESS DEER IS NOT MORE SAD	4 OISIN 1		34
I CHASED AT MORN THE FLYING DEER, ...	10 OISIN 1		121
I CHASED WITH HOUNDS THE FLYING DEER, ...	10 OISIN 1	V	121
YOU GO NOT WHERE THE RED DEER FEEDS, ...	11 OISIN 1		127
WE GALLOPED: NOW A HORNLESS DEER	11 OISIN 1		139
YE GO NOT WHERE THE RED DEER FEEDS, ...	11 OISIN 1	V	127
ON, ON: AND NOW A HORNLESS DEER	11 OISIN 1	V	139
SAVE DEER TOWARDS NOON THAT WATER SOUGHT.	17 OISIN 1	V	243
THE DEER, THE BADGER, AND THE BOAR.	23 OISIN 1		345
AND SLEW THE BADGER AND THE DEER:	23 OISIN 1	V	345
THE YOUTH AND LADY AND THE DEER AND HOUND:	29 OISIN 2		4
ONCE MORE--THE YOUTH AND LADY, DEER AND HOUND:	29 OISIN 2	V	2
THEY CHASE THE NOONTIDE DEER:	32 OISIN 2		53
THEY CHASE AT NOON THE DEER.	32 OISIN 2	V	53
THEY CHASE THE NOON-TIDE DEER:	32 OISIN 2	V	53
THE DEER AND THE HOUND, AND THE LADY AND YOUTH, ...	47 OISIN 3		3
THE JOYOUS FLOCKS OF DEER AND ANTELOPE, ...	75 ANASHU VIJAYA		74
THE JOYOUS FLOCKS OF DEER AND ANTELOPES, ...	75 ANASHU VIJAYA	V	74
I LEAD ALONG THE WOODLAND DEER:	84 MAD KING GOLL		46
DRIVING THE DEER ALONG THE WOODY WAYS.	109 CUCHULAIN SEA	V	48
DO YOU NOT HEAR ME CALLING, WHITE DEER WITH NO HORNS? . .	153 CHANGE BELOVED		1
I WOULD THE PALE DEER HAD COME	171 MAID QUIET	V	4A
I WOULD THAT THE DEATH-PALE DEER	171 MAID QUIET	V	4A
FOR THERE THE TALL DEER AND HIS LEMAN SIGH	210 RAGGED WOOD	V	2
FOR THERE THE TALL DEER AND HIS LEMAN CRY	211 RAGGED WOOD	V	6
I WILL DRIVE OUT THE DEER AND MOON AND CRY--	211 RAGGED WOOD	V	10
THAT MAIDEN BRING THEY. WHEN THE TALL RED DEER	713 FERENCZ RENYI		79
THE CALLING AFAR OF THE DOE AND THE DEER.	717 LOVE SONG		5
A RED-EARED HOUND FOLLOWS A HORNLESS DEER.	764 SHADOW WATER A		325
THE PALE HOUND AND THE DEER WANDER FOR EVER	764 SHADOW WATER A		330
THE PALE HOUND AND THE DEER WANDER FOREVER	764 SHADOW WATER A V		330

DEER-HOUNDS

THE FENIANS. LET THEIR DEER-HOUNDS SLEEP. . . . . .   11 OISIN 1   V   131

DEFAMED

WHERE WHO HAS SERVED THE MOST IS MOST DEFAMED, ...   351 PEOPLE   4

DEFEAT

BE SECRET AND TAKE DEFEAT	290 TO A FRIEND	2
THE HEART NEED SUFFER NO DEFEAT: BUT I	464 HARUN RASHID	77
DEFEAT IS DEATH. SHOULD MY PLOTS FAIL I'D DIE. . . .	722 WITCH VIVIEN	52

DEFEATED

AND WHEN AT LAST, DEFEATED IN HIS WARS, ...	115 ROSE OF BATTLE	33
AND TUMULT OF DEFEATED DREAMS: AND DEEP	169 SECRET ROSE	5
HAVE BEEN DEFEATED BY THAT PLEDGE YOU GAVE	258 KING NO KING	9

DEFENCE

FOR LEARNING AND DEFENCE . . . .   380 SONGS FOOL 1   5

DEFENDING

DEFENDING IRELAND'S SOUL.	546 TO SAME TUNE 2	6
DEFENDING IRELAND'S SOUL.	613 MARCH SONGS 1	6

DEFILE

ARE BUT A POST THE PASSING DOGS DEFILE. . . . . . .   321 REED WHISPERER   14

DEFILED

WE KNOW WHAT RASCAL MIGHT HAS DEFILED, ...   614 MARCH SONGS 2   11

DEFILING

THAT DEFILING AND DISFIGURED SHAPE . . . .   479 SELF AND SOUL   51

		PAGE	TITLE	LINE

DEFINITIONS
    BUT I, WHOSE VIRTUES ARE THE DEFINITIONS • • • • • • •   353 PEOPLE   32
DEFORMED
    DEFORMED BECAUSE THERE IS NO DEFORMITY • • • • • • •   376 PHASES OF MOON   101
    DEFORMED BEYOND DEFORMITY, UNFORMED, •   376 PHASES OF MOON   111
DEFORMITY
    DEFORMED BECAUSE THERE IS NO DEFORMITY • • • • • • •   376 PHASES OF MOON   101
    DEFORMED BEYOND DEFORMITY, UNFORMED, • • • • • •   376 PHASES OF MOON   111
    DEFORMITY OF BODY AND OF MIND. • • • • • • • • • •   377 PHASES OF MOON   123
DEGREES
    HONOURED BY ALL IN THEIR DEGREES, • • • • • • • • •   380 SAINT HUNCH   15
DEIGN
    AND SHALL BE DONE, IF YOU WILL DEIGN TO KISS • • • • •   669 ISLE STAT II 3   79
DEIRDRE
    REMEMBER DEIRDRE AND HER MAN; • • • • • • • • • • •   192 BAILE AILLINN   91
    THE PRAISE OF DEIRDRE • • • • • • • • • • • • • •   771 SONG DEIRDRE 1 V   T
    THE ENTRANCE OF DEIRDRE • • • • • • • • • • • • •   771 SONG DEIRDRE 1 V   T
    SONGS FROM DEIRDRE • • • • • • • • • • • • • • •   771 SONG DEIRDRE 1 V   T
DEIRDRE'S
    AND THEY HAVE NEWS OF DEIRDRE'S EYES, • • • • • • •   193 BAILE AILLINN   97
DEITIES
    BEFORE THE INDIFFERENT GARDEN DEITIES; • • • • • • •   418 ANCEST HOUSES   28
DEJECTION
    LINES WRITTEN IN DEJECTION • • • • • • • • • • • •   343 DEJECTION   T
DELACROIX
    NOT A MAN BUT DELACROIX• • • • • • • • • • • • • •   625 NATIVITY   4
DELIBERATE
    REMEMBER HIS DELIBERATE HAPPINESS. • • • • • • • • •   370 EGO DOMINUS   53
DELIBERATELY
    GOLDSMITH DELIBERATELY SIPPING AT THE HONEY-POT OF HIS   481 BLOOD AND MOON   21
    MIND,
    GOLDSMITH DELIBERATELY SIPPING AT THE HONEY POT OF HIS   481 BLOOD AND MOON V   21
    MIND;
DELICATE
    THAT SCARES WITH HIS BUSTLE THE DELICATE NIGHT, • • • •   28 OISIN 1   V 423B
    DELICATE IN COLOUR AS APPLE BLOSSOM. • • • • • • •   199 ARROW   6
    THE DELICATE STEPPING STAG AND HIS LADY SIGH • • • •   210 RAGGED WOOD   V   2
    "SUCH A DELICATE HIGH HEAD, • • • • • • • • • •   259 PEACE   7
    TO THAT STERN COLOUR AND THAT DELICATE LINE • • • •   326 ROBERT GREGORY   67
    LIFTING HIS DELICATE FEET. • • • • • • • • • • •   378 CAT AND MOON   10
    AND LIFTS HIS DELICATE FEET. • • • • • • • • • •   378 CAT AND MOON   V   10
    WITH DELICATE FEET UPON OLD TERRACES, • • • • • •   418 ANCEST HOUSES   26
    THEIR LEGS LONG, DELICATE AND SLENDER, AQUAMARINE THEIR   426 PHANTOM HATRED   17
    EYES,
    ON DELICATE SENSITIVE EAR OR TOSSING MANE, • • • • •   433 NINETEEN 19   115
    WITH THE DELICATE MOTHER-OF-PEARL, • • • • • • • •   509 JANE REPROVED   10
    HER LIMBS ARE DELICATE AS AN EYELID, • • • • • • •   612 NEWS ORACLE   27
DELICATE-STEPPING
    THE DELICATE-STEPPING STAG AND HIS LADY SIGH, • • • •   210 RAGGED WOOD   2
DELIGHT   SEE SELF-DELIGHT
    AND MURMURED SNATCHES OF DELIGHT; • • • • • • • •   14 OISIN 1   187
    • • • REMEMBERING ALONE THAT DELIGHT • • • • • • •   54 OISIN 3   111
    BUT A BRIEF, DREAMY, KIND DELIGHT. • • • • • • • •   202 NEVER GIVE ALL   7
    BECOME ONE MOVEMENT, ENERGY, DELIGHT, • • • • • • •   231 SHADOW WATER B   217
    DELIGHT MAKES ALL OF THE ONE MIND, • • • • • • • •   266 GALWAY RACES   2
    DELIGHT IN ART WHOSE END IS PEACE, • • • • • • • •   288 TO WEALTHY MAN   26
    TAKING DELIGHT THAT HE COULD SPRING; • • • • • • •   317 APPOINTMENT   4
    DELIGHT MEN'S EYES WHEN I AWAKE SOME DAY • • • • •   323 SWANS AT COOLE   29
    TO HAVE PUBLISHED ALL TO BE A WORLD'S DELIGHT. • • • •   327 ROBERT GREGORY   72
    A LONELY IMPULSE OF DELIGHT • • • • • • • • • • •   328 IRISH AIRMAN   11
    BE BUT THE BREAKERS OF MEN'S HEARTS OR ENGINES OF DELIGHT;   354 HIS PHOENIX   23
    SO MANY TIMES CHILDISH DELIGHT. • • • • • • • • •   399 BREAK OF DAY   11
    THAT OUT OF LIFE'S OWN SELF DELIGHT HAD SPRUNG • • • •   417 ANCEST HOUSES   V   11
    AND CHILDHOOD A DELIGHT FOR EVERY SENSE, • • • • • •   418 ANCEST HOUSES   31
    DELIGHT BECOMES DEATH-LONGING IF ALL LONGING ELSE BE VAIN.   459 FROM OEDIPUS   3
    EVEN FROM THAT DELIGHT MEMORY TREASURES SO, • • • • •   459 FROM OEDIPUS   4
    AND SINK INTO ITS OWN DELIGHT AT LAST. • • • • • •   473 ALL SOUL NIGHT   60
    THERE'S KEEN DELIGHT IN WHAT WE HAVE; • • • • • • •   485 NINETEENTH CEN   2
    EXTINGUISH THAT DELIGHT. • • • • • • • • • • • •   538 LAST CONFESS   24
    BUT A GOOD STRONG CAUSE AND BLOWS ARE DELIGHT." • • •   545 TO SAME TUNE 1   14
    BUT A GOOD STRONG CAUSE AND THE BLOWS ARE DELIGHT." • •   545 TO SAME TUNE 1 V   14
    SOME TAKE DELIGHT IN ADORNING A WOMAN. • • • • • •   547 TO SAME TUNE 3 V   3
    DELIGHT TO IMAGINE THEM SEATED THERE; • • • • • • •   567 LAPIS LAZULI   50
    BUT A GOOD STRONG CAUSE AND BLOWS ARE DELIGHT." • • •   616 MARCH SONGS 3   14
    AND I DELIGHT TO SING; • • • • • • • • • • • •   627 STATES HOLIDAY   25
    HAST THOU NOT KNOWN ALL SORROW AND DELIGHT • • • • •   723 KANVA ON SELF   2
    HAVE FOUND DELIGHT, IN THE RESOUNDING OARS, • • • • •   750 SHADOW WATER A   72
DELIGHTED
    A RUMOUR OF DELIGHTED HEARTS. • • • • • • • • • •   16 OISIN 1   230
    FANNED THE DELIGHTED AIR LIKE WINGS OF BIRDS; • • • •   32 OISIN 2   50
    THAT FAN THE PULSES OF DELIGHTED AIR, • • • • • • •   32 OISIN 2   V 50A
    MIND AND DELIGHTED MIND; • • • • • • • • • • • •   315 FRIENDS   9
    HEART AND DELIGHTED HEART; • • • • • • • • • • •   315 FRIENDS   V   9
    FOR ALL THINGS THE DELIGHTED EYE NOW SEES • • • • •   326 ROBERT GREGORY   49
    DELIGHTED TO BE BUT WISE, • • • • • • • • • • • •   329 MEN IMPROVE   10
    DELIGHTED ME AS A CHILD; • • • • • • • • • • • •   787 HUDDON DUDDON   2
    DELIGHTED ME AS A CHILD. • • • • • • • • • • • •   787 HUDDON DUDDON   7
    DELIGHTED ME AS A CHILD. • • • • • • • • • • • •   787 HUDDON DUDDON   12
DELIGHTFUL
    DELIGHTFUL TO THE TOUCH; TIGHTEN THAT HAND • • • • • •   579 DOR WELLESLEY   4

```
                                                          PAGE      TITLE          LINE
DELIGHTING      SEE ROOK-DELIGHTING SELF-DELIGHTING
     SUDDENLY I SAW THE COLD AND ROOK DELIGHTING HEAVEN  . . .   316 COLD HEAVEN     V    1
DELIGHTS
     CEASE TO REMEMBER THE DELIGHTS OF YOUTH, TRAVEL-WEARIED     459 FROM OEDIPUS         2
          AGED MAN;
     BUT GOOD STRONG BLOWS ARE DELIGHTS TO THE MIND."  . . . .  544 TO SAME TUNE 1       4
     BUT GOOD STRONG BLOWS ARE DELIGHTS TO THE MIND."  . . . .  616 MARCH SONGS 3        4
DELIRIUM
     ALL THAT DELIRIUM OF THE BRAVE?  . . . . . . . . . .       290 SEPTEMBER 1913      22
     TESTY DELIRIUM  . . . . . . . . . . . . . . . . .          416 TOWER              186
DELIVER
     DELIVER FROM THE CRIME OF DEATH AND BIRTH. . . . . . .      478 SELF AND SOUL       24
DELIVERANCE
     "I BRING DELIVERANCE," PEARL-PALE NIAMH SAID. . . . . .      34 OISIN 2            78
DELIVERED
     THEN MY DELIVERED SOUL HERSELF SHALL LEARN . . . . . .      558 RIBH CHRISTIAN      13
DELIVERER
     "I BRING THEE A DELIVERER FROM FAR AWAY,  . . . . . . .      34 OISIN 2       V   78A
DELL
     IN VALE AND DELL SO BLAZE THE DAFFODILS;  . . . . . .       645 ISLE STAT I 1       15
     WERE FURLED THE WINGS OF SHIPS.  THERE IN A DELL,  . . .    693 MOSADA 1            82
     "WE BURIED LATE IN A HAZEL DELL  . . . . . . . . . .        729 PRIEST FAIRY        43
DELLS
     AND HATH HER HOME BY MANY-FOLDED DELLS. . . . . . . .       657 ISLE STAT I 3       46
DELPHIC
     THE DELPHIC ORACLE UPON PLOTINUS  . . . . . . . . . .       530 DELPHIC ORACLE       T
     NEWS FOR THE DELPHIC ORACLE . . . . . . . . . . . .         611 NEWS ORACLE          T
DELUSION
     ENTHRALLED BY THE UNCONQUERABLE DELUSION,  . . . . . .      367 EGO DOMINUS          6
DELUSIONS
     CHAUNT IN HIS EAR DELUSIONS MAGICAL,  . . . . . . . .       111 CUCHULAIN SEA       80
     GO, CAST ON HIM DELUSIONS MAGICAL,  . . . . . . . .         111 CUCHULAIN SEA  V    80
DELVES
     THE SAGE, WHO DEEP IN CENTRAL NATURE DELVES,  . . . .       686 LIFE                 2
     THE SAGE WHO DEEP IN CENTRAL NATURE DELVES,  . . . . .      734 QUATRAIN APHOR       2
DEMAGOGUE
     NO LOOSE-LIPPED DEMAGOGUE HAD WON THE DAY,  . . . . .       542 PARN FUNERAL 2       3
     NO LOOSE LIPPED DEMAGOGUE HAD WON THE DAY, . . . . . .      542 PARN FUNERAL 2 V     3
DEMAND
     MAKES NO DEMAND. . . . . . . . . . . . . . . . .           600 SPIRIT MEDIUM       22
     BECAUSE CHILDREN DEMAND DADDY-LONG-LEGS UPON HIS TIMBER     623 HIGH TALK            6
          TOES,
     BECAUSE WOMEN IN THE UPPER STOREYS DEMAND A FACE AT THE     623 HIGH TALK            7
          PANE,
DEMESNE
     IN COOLE DEMESNE, AND THERE TO FINISH UP  . . . . . .       490 COOLE BALLYLEE       6
     I HAVE A SMALL DEMESNE,  . . . . . . . . . . . . .          606 SONGS BURDEN 2       2
DEMON
     THE WANDERINGS OF OISIN AND HOW A DEMON TRAPPED HIM  . .      1 OISIN 1        V     T
     OF DALLIANCE WITH A DEMON THING. . . . . . . . . .           2 OISIN 1              4
     TRAPPED OF AN AMOROUS DEMON THING. . . . . . . . .           2 OISIN 1        V     4
     "THIS DEMON SHALL BE BATTERED TILL HE DIE, . . . . .        35 OISIN 2             90
     "THIS DEMON SHALL BE PIERCED AND DROP AND DIE,  . . .       35 OISIN 2        V    90
     A DUSKY DEMON DRY AS A WITHERED SEDGE  . . . . . . .        39 OISIN 2            158
     A DUSK DEMON, DRY AS A WITHERED SEDGE,  . . . . . .         39 OISIN 2        V   158
     A HUSKY DEMON, DRY AS A WITHERED SEDGE  . . . . . .         39 OISIN 2        V   158
     THROUGH HEART AND DEMON SPINE, AND IN THE WAVE  . . .       41 OISIN 2        V   182
     THAT DEMON DULL AND UNSUBDUABLE. . . . . . . . . .          43 OISIN 2            217
     AND THE NAME OF THE DEMON WHOSE HAMMER . . . . . . .        52 OISIN 3             80
     THROUGH THE DEMON LOVE OF ITS YOUTH . . . . . . . .         63 OISIN 3            216
     A MAGIC THAT CAN CALL A DEMON UP, . . . . . . . . .        238 SHADOW WATER B     344
     DEMON AND BEAST . . . . . . . . . . . . . . . .            399 DEMON BEAST          T
     THAT CRAFTY DEMON AND THAT LOUD BEAST  . . . . . . .       399 DEMON BEAST          2
     BELONGS TO BEAST OR DEMON,  . . . . . . . . . . .          401 DEMON BEAST         35
     AND OVERTURNED THE DEMON WITH A SOUND  . . . . . . .       762 SHADOW WATER A     283
DEMONIAC
     BEING NO MORE DEMONIAC  . . . . . . . . . . . . .          400 DEMON BEAST         30
DEMONIC
     HOW THE DEMONIC RAGE  . . . . . . . . . . . . .            419 MY HOUSE       V    16
     THE HALF-READ WISDOM OF DEMONIC IMAGES  . . . . . .        427 PHANTOM HATRED V    39
DEMON'S
     A DEMON'S LEISURE; EYES, FIRST WHITE, NOW BURNED . . . .    40 OISIN 2            168
     A DEMON'S LEISURE.  EYES FIRST WHITE AS SNOW, . . . .       40 OISIN 2        V   168
DEMONS
     MY ENEMY AND HOPE; DEMONS FOR FRIGHT . . . . . . . .        34 OISIN 2             81
     THE DEMONS OF THE WILDS AND WINDS FOR FRIGHT  . . . .       34 OISIN 2        V   81B
     UNTIL THE GODS AND DEMONS DROP ASLEEP,  . . . . . . .       35 OISIN 2             86
     "FOR ALL MEN FLEE THE DEMONS"; BUT MOVED NOT  . . . .       36 OISIN 2             93
     SPRANG DRIPPING, AND, WITH CAPTIVE DEMONS SENT  . . .       38 OISIN 2            130
     . . . NOR IN GLAMOURS BY DEMONS FLUNG,  . . . . . .         50 OISIN 3             50
     . . . OR IN GLAMOURS BY DEMONS FLUNG,  . . . . . .          50 OISIN 3        V    50
     OF THE HIGH PEOPLE OF SORACA NOR IN GLAMOUR BY DEMONS       50 OISIN 3        V    50
          FLUNG,
     AND THE NAMES OF THE DEMONS WHOSE HAMMERS . . . . . .       52 OISIN 3        V    80
     WHERE THE DEMONS WHIP THEM WITH WIRES . . . . . . .         61 OISIN 3            198
     AND DEMONS BE BROKEN IN PIECES, AND TRAMPLED BENEATH THEM   61 OISIN 3            204
          IN DEATH.
     AND DEMONS, ALL BROKEN IN PIECES, BE TRAMPLED BENEATH THEM  61 OISIN 3        V   204
          IN DEATH.
     AND DEMONS AFRAID IN THEIR DARKNESS; . . . . . . . .        62 OISIN 3            205
```

	PAGE	TITLE		LINE
DEMONS (CONTINUED)				
FOR THY YOUTH WITHOUT PEACE, AND THY YEARS WITH THE DEMONS,	63	OISIN 3	V	216
• • •				
THE DEMONS, WITH THEIR SUBTLE GUILE, • • • • • • • •	135	TWO TREES		22
IN THE DIM GLASS THE DEMONS HOLD, • • • • • • • • •	135	TWO TREES		30
DEMONSTRATE				
OR DEMONSTRATE IN MY OWN LIFE • • • • • • • • • •	605	YOU CONTENT		21
DENIED				
ALL THAT TIME DENIED-- • • • • • • • • • • •	496	MOHINI CHATTER		18
NOR GRAVE NOR BED DENIED, • • • • • • • • • • •	513	JANE TALK BISH		10
DENIES				
THAT SHE DENIES • • • • • • • • • • • • •	336	YOUNG GIRL		8
THOUGH PEDANTRY DENIES, • • • • • • • • • • • •	345	ON WOMAN		9
WHO IS MY BEAUTY'S EQUAL, THOUGH THAT MY HEART DENIES, • •	354	HIS PHOENIX		27
NO ONE DENIES TO KEATS LOVE OF THE WORLD! •- • • •	370	EGO DOMINUS		52
NO RIGHT-TAUGHT MAN DENIES. • • • • • • • • • • •	590	OLD WICKED MAN		58
NO RIGHT TAUGHT MAN DENIES. • • • • • • • • • • •	590	OLD WICKED MAN	V	58
DENIS				
AND RUTH ST. DENIS HAD MORE CHARM ALTHOUGH SHE HAD POOR	353	HIS PHOENIX		10
LUCK!				
DENOUNCES				
RIBH DENOUNCES PATRICK • • • • • • • • • • • •	556	RIBH PATRICK		T
DENT				
EVERY ACCIDENTAL CRACK OR DENT, • • • • • • • • •	567	LAPIS LAZULI		44
DENY				
SPEAK--HE WILL NOT DENY IT. IS THAT TRUE? • • • • •	249	SHADOW WATER B		563
DO NOT DENY HIS RIGHT! • • • • • • • • • • • •	584	ORAHILLY		2
DENYING				
WITH A STARK, DENYING LOOK! • • • • • • • • • •	381	SONG OF FOOL		6
DEPART				
AND LO! MY ANCIENT BURDEN MAY DEPART. • • • • • • •	69	SAD SHEPHERD		24
AND LO--MY HEAVY BURTHEN MAY DEPART!" • • • • • • •	69	SAD SHEPHERD	V	24
WHEN SHE ROSE UP TO DEPART? • • • • • • • • • •	171	MAID QUIET		6
INNOCENCE AND PEACE DEPART, • • • • • • • • • •	561	FOUR AGES MAN		4
OF MY SAD HUNTER-FRIEND WILL ALL DEPART • • • • • •	668	ISLE STAT II 3		45
I SAW HIM FROM SAD DIDO'S SHORES DEPART, • • • • • •	677	ISLE STAT II 3		288
DEPARTING				
AND MAY DEPARTING TWILIGHT KEEP • • • • • • • • •	435	FOR MY SON		5
DEPTH				
MORE MOURNFUL THAN THE DEPTH OF STARRY SKIES, • • • • •	108	CUCHULAIN SEA	V	42
APPEAR AND DISAPPEAR IN THE BLUE DEPTH OF THE SKY • • •	318	MAGI		3
DEPTHS				
AND THEIR SECRET SMILE, OUT OF THE DEPTHS OF THE LAKE! • •	203	WITHER BOUGHS		11
APPEAR AND DISAPPEAR IN THE BLUE DEPTHS OF THE SKY • • •	318	MAGI	V	3
NO SHEPHERD FOOT HAS EVER DARED ITS DEPTHS. • • • • •	682	SEEKER		32
DERG'S				
ROUND LOUGH DERG'S HOLY ISLAND I WENT UPON THE STONES, • •	593	PILGRIM		6
DERIDED				
DERIDED AND DERIDING, DRIVEN OUT • • • • • • • • •	369	EGO DOMINUS		34
IN ABSTRACT THINGS! OR BE DERIDED BY • • • • • • •	409	TOWER		15
IS HE WHO LABOURED ON, DERIDED, HATED, • • • • • • •	738	MOURN THEN ON		11
DERIDING				
DERIDED AND DERIDING, DRIVEN OUT • • • • • • • • •	369	EGO DOMINUS		34
DERISION				
CASTS DERISION UPON • • • • • • • • • • • •	476	DEATH		9
BECAUSE THERE IS SAFETY IN DERISION • • • • • • • •	624	APPARITIONS		1
DERMOT				
MY DERMOT DEAR AND BROWN, • • • • • • • • • •	97	FOXHUNTER	V	6
BROWN DERMOT TREADS UPON THE LAWN, • • • • • • • •	98	FOXHUNTER	V	17
DERMUID				
AND THAT MADE HER DERMUID DEAR, AND SOME OLD CARDINAL • •	366	HER COURAGE	V	6
DESCANT				
THAT WE DESCANT AND YET AGAIN DESCANT • • • • • • •	523	LONG SILENCE		5
THAT WE DESCANT AND YET AGAIN DESCANT • • • • • • •	523	LONG SILENCE		5
DESCEND				
MY LORD, IF IT MUST BE, I PRAY DESCEND • • • • • • •	697	MOSADA 2		43
DESCENDANTS				
MY DESCENDANTS • • • • • • • • • • • • • •	422	MY DESCENDANTS		T
AND WHAT IF MY DESCENDANTS LOSE THE FLOWER • • • • • •	423	MY DESCENDANTS		9
DESCENDS				
THE BIRD DESCENDS, AND HER FRAIL THIGHS ARE PRESSED • • •	441	LEDA AND SWAN	V	2
DESCENDS INTO THE LOVELESS DUST. • • • • • • • • •	540	FROM ANTIGONE		16
DESERT				
THAT MEN DESERT, • • • • • • • • • • • • •	293	HELEN LIVED		2
TROUBLES MY SIGHT! SOMEWHERE IN SANDS OF THE DESERT • • •	402	SECOND COMING		13
REEL SHADOWS OF THE INDIGNANT DESERT BIRDS. • • • • •	402	SECOND COMING		17
TROUBLES MY SIGHT! A WASTE OF DESERT SAND! • • • • • •	402	SECOND COMING	V	13
WIND SHADOWS OF THE INDIGNANT DESERT BIRDS. • • • • •	402	SECOND COMING	V	17
DESERT GEOMETRY OR THE GIFT OF HARUN AL-RASCHID • • • •	460	HARUN RASHID	V	T
THAT WANDERING IN A DESERT, FEATURELESS • • • • • •	462	HARUN RASHID		27
WANDERING IN A DESERT FEATURELESS • • • • • • • •	462	HARUN RASHID	V	27
HALF RUNNING, DROPPED AT THE FIRST RIDGE OF THE DESERT • •	468	HARUN RASHID		155
MURMURED THE WISDOM OF THE DESERT DJINNS, • • • • • •	468	HARUN RASHID		163
HAS SPOKEN THE WISDOM OF THE DESERT DJINS, • • • • • •	468	HARUN RASHID	V	163
HAS MURMURED WISDOM OF THE DESERT DJINNS, • • • • • •	468	HARUN RASHID	V	163
DESERT THE PERJURER'S SIDE! • • • • • • • • • •	582	ROGER CASEMENT		20
EYED PANTHERS IN THEIR DESERT CAVERNS ROVE • • • • • •	681	SEEKER	V	4
DESERT-CAVES				
OF DESERT-CAVES THE RED-EYED PANTHERS ROVE • • • • • •	681	SEEKER		4
DESERTED				
DESERTED ON A DOORWAY SEAT, • • • • • • • • • •	85	MAD KING GOLL		56

DESERTED   (CONTINUED)
       DESERTED IN A DOORWAY SEAT, ...   85 MAD KING GOLL V   56
DESERTION
       THE CIRCUS ANIMALS' DESERTION . . . . 629 CIRCUS ANIMALS   T
       THE CIRCUS ANIMAL'S DESERTION . . . . 629 CIRCUS ANIMALS V   T
DESIGN
       CUT OUT HIS HEART. SOME MASTER OF DESIGN . . . . . . 541 PARN FUNERAL 1   14
DESIGNED
       AND BUILDINGS THAT A HAUGHTIER AGE DESIGNED, ... 418 ANCEST HOUSES   34
DESIRE
       THE IMMORTAL DESIRE OF IMMORTALS WE SAW IN THEIR FACES, 47 OISIN 3   4
           AND SIGHED.
       THE DESIRE OF MAN AND OF WOMAN . . . . 153 CHANGE BELOVED V T
       FOR SOMEBODY HID HATRED AND HOPE AND DESIRE AND FEAR . 153 CHANGE BELOVED   4
       AND I HAVE HATRED AND HOPE AND DESIRE AND FEAR . . . . 153 CHANGE BELOVED V 4
       O VANITY OF SLEEP, HOPE, DREAM, ENDLESS DESIRE, ... 154 BELOVED PEACE   7
       AND THE SWEETNESS OF DESIRE, ... 168 BLESSED   38
       THE HEAVINESS OF DESIRE. . . . . 168 BLESSED   V 38
       BUT SOFT BEAUTY AND INDOLENT DESIRE. . . . . 181 QUEEN MAEVE   22
       OUR HEART'S DESIRE NOW THAT WE ARE SO LIGHT." . . . . 233 SHADOW WATER B 255
       WHAT POWER THAT IS MORE MIGHTY THAN DESIRE . . . . . . 234 SHADOW WATER B 267
       WHY LINGER? RUN TO YOUR DESIRE, ... 234 SHADOW WATER B 272
       WHY DO YOU NOT RUN TO YOUR DESIRE, ... 234 SHADOW WATER B V 272
       HAD THEY BUT COURAGE EQUAL TO DESIRE? . . . . 256 NO SECOND TROY   5
       DO MEN WHO LEAST DESIRE GET MOST, ... 295 THREE BEGGARS   13
       OR GET THE MOST WHO MOST DESIRE?" . . . . 295 THREE BEGGARS   14
       UNLESS DESIRE HAD MADE THEM SO?" . . . . 295 THREE BEGGARS   18
       HER SOUL HAD SUCH DESIRE . . . . 317 NIGHT COME   2
       I HAVE NOT LOST DESIRE . . . . 335 SONG   13
       HARSHNESS OF THEIR DESIRE . . . . 345 ON WOMAN   20
       THAT NEVER LOOKED UPON MAN WITH DESIRE, ... 358 PRESENCES   13
       AND HAVING NO DESIRE THEY CANNOT TELL . . . . 376 PHASES OF MOON 107
       BUT HAVING NO DESIRE THEY CANNOT TELL . . . . 376 PHASES OF MOON V 107
       BETWEEN MY HATRED AND DESIRE, ... 400 DEMON BEAST   6
       CONSUME MY HEART AWAY; SICK WITH DESIRE . . . . 408 SAIL BYZANTIUM   21
       AND HORRIBLE SPLENDOUR OF DESIRE; . . . . 411 TOWER   63
       . . . OF ITS OWN DESIRE; . . . . 481 BLOOD AND MOON   29
       ISAIAH'S COAL, WHAT MORE CAN MAN DESIRE? . . . . 502 VACILLATION   74
       EZEKIEL'S COAL, WHAT MORE CAN MAN DESIRE? . . . . . . 502 VACILLATION   V 74
       MY PAISTIN FINN IS MY SOLE DESIRE, ... 550 SONGS REWRIT 1   1
       MY PRETTY PAISTIN IS MY HEART'S DESIRE, ... 550 SONGS REWRIT 1 V 1
       THAT BLONDE GIRL THERE IS MY HEART'S DESIRE, ... 550 SONGS REWRIT 1 V 1
       HE HOLDS HIM FROM DESIRE, ALL BUT STOPS HIS BREATHING LEST 559 MAGIC DRUM   1
       HIS HEART'S DESIRE WHERE THE WORLD DWINDLES OUT? . . . 747 SHADOW WATER A   13
       IN THE COLD STREAMS, AND WAKE TO THEIR DESIRE, ... 750 SHADOW WATER A   85
       FORGAEL MAY FIND HIS HEART'S DESIRE ON BOARD . . . . . 751 SHADOW WATER A 107
       OUR HEARTS' DESIRE NOW THAT WE ARE SO LIGHT." . . . . 753 SHADOW WATER A 145
       YOUR HEART'S DESIRE AND THE END OF ALL OUR TROUBLE; . . 755 SHADOW WATER A 175
       AND NONE KNOWS WHEREFORE; BUT THE HEART'S DESIRE . . . 764 SHADOW WATER A 340
       FOLDING THEIR HEARTS' DESIRE TO THEIR GLAD HEARTS. . . 765 SHADOW WATER A 349
       THAT HE FOLLOW WITH DESIRE . . . . 776 AGAINST WITCH   19
DESISTED
       THOUGH FROM BESEECHING THEY DESISTED NOT, ...   36 OISIN 2   V 93
DESK
       FROM COUNTER OR DESK AMONG GREY . . . . 392 EASTER 1916   3
       COME FROM THE FORGER AND HIS DESK, ... 582 ROGER CASEMENT   19
       ITS BOREDOM OF THE DESK OR OF THE SPADE, BECAUSE . . . 621 HOUND VOICE   3
DESOLATE
       GROWN DESOLATE, WHISPER AND SIGH TO EACH OTHER; . . .   26 OISIN 1   403
       GROWN DESOLATE, WHISPER AND SIGH TO EACH OTHER. . . .   27 OISIN 1   V 407
       DESOLATE WINDS THAT CRY OVER THE WANDERING SEA; . . . 147 UNAPPEAS HOST   7
       DESOLATE WINDS THAT HOVER IN THE FLAMING WEST; . . . . 147 UNAPPEAS HOST   8
       DESOLATE WINDS THAT BEAT THE DOORS OF HEAVEN, AND BEAT 147 UNAPPEAS HOST   9
       THE HORSES OF DISASTER PLUNGE IN THE DESOLATE CLAY. . . 154 BELOVED PEACE V 8
       AND LINGERED IN THE HIDDEN DESOLATE PLACE . . . . . . 162 ASKS FORGIVE   15
       OF THIS DESOLATE LAKE . . . . 165 CRY OF SEDGE   2
       AS NOW. DOES WANDERING IN THESE DESOLATE SEAS . . . . 236 SHADOW WATER B 314
       BUT DESOLATE WATERS AND A BATTERED SHIP. . . . . 246 SHADOW WATER B 497
       BY A COLD AND DESOLATE SEA, ... 298 THREE HERMITS   2
       AND DESOLATE THREE ROCK . . . . 310 PEACOCK   5
       AND DESOLATE THREE-ROCK . . . . 310 PEACOCK   V 5
       IN A MOST DESOLATE STONY PLACE, ... 325 ROBERT GREGORY   30
       HER DESOLATION TO THE DESOLATE SKY. . . . . 423 MY DESCENDANTS   16
       THE SWAN HAS LEAPED INTO THE DESOLATE HEAVEN; . . . . 431 NINETEEN 19   79
       OUT OF A DESOLATE SOURCE, ... 518 HIS CONFIDENCE   11
       AND THE DESOLATE SHUDDERING SEA. . . . . 648 ISLE STAT I 1   85
DESOLATION
       HER DESOLATION TO THE DESOLATE SKY. . . . . 423 MY DESCENDANTS   16
       INTO THE DESOLATION OF REALITY; . . . . 563 MERU   7
DESPAIR
       A KING AND PROUD! AND THAT IS MY DESPAIR. . . . . . . 103 FERGUS DRUID   16
       AND DREAMED THAT THE OLD DESPAIR . . . . 152 LOSS OF LOVE   3
       WE HAVE CRIED IN OUR DESPAIR . . . . 293 HELEN LIVED   1
       WITH DESPAIR? . . . . 310 WITCH   8
       RHYMED OUT IN LOVE'S DESPAIR . . . . 337 SCHOLARS   5
       GNASHING OF TEETH, DESPAIR; . . . . 346 ON WOMAN   39
       BUT DISSIPATION AND DESPAIR? AND YET . . . . 369 EGO DOMINUS   51
       MAYBE THE BRIDE-BED BRINGS DESPAIR, ... 388 SOLOMON WITCH   25
       NOR BEAUTY BORN OUT OF ITS OWN DESPAIR, ... 445 SCHOOL CHILDR   59
       THE SOUTH WIND BROUGHT IT LONGING, AND THE EAST WIND   449 OWEN AHERNE   5
           DESPAIR,

		PAGE	TITLE		LINE

DESPAIR   (CONTINUED)
        THE SOUTH WIND BROUGHT IT LONGING, AND THE EAST BROUGHT   449 OWEN AHERNE   V   5
            IN DESPAIR,
        THE SOUTH WIND BROUGHT IT LONGING, AND THE EAST BROUGHT   449 OWEN AHERNE   V   5
            IT DESPAIR,
        DEATH, DESPAIR, DIVISION OF FAMILIES, ...   459 FROM OEDIPUS   5
        THROWN INTO DESPAIR . . . .   492 ANNE GREGORY   2
        THAT YOUNG MEN IN DESPAIR . . . .   492 ANNE GREGORY   10
        AND I AM IN DESPAIR THAT TIME MAY BRING . . . . . .   602 GALLERY REVIS   30
        THAT DESPAIR AND KEEP THE PACE . . . .   787 HUDDON DUDDON   9
DESPAIRING
        OR WARNED YOU HOW DESPAIRING . . . .   313 TWO YEAR LATER   3
        I HAVE FOUND OUT HOW DESPAIRING . . . .   313 TWO YEAR LATER V   3
        MOON-STRUCK BY THE DESPAIRING . . . .   487 CRAZED MOON   3
DESPERATE
        INTO A DESPERATE GULPH OF LOVE! . . . .   7 OISIN 1   73
        SHE STOOD IN DESPERATE MUSIC WOUND, ...   578 CRAZED GIRL   10
DESPITE
        TO WIN A WOMAN IN HER OWN DESPITE, ...   244 SHADOW WATER B   458
        TO WIN A WOMAN IS IN HER OWN DESPITE, ...   244 SHADOW WATER B V   458
        DESPITE A DWINDLING AND LATE-RISEN MOON, ...   372 PHASES OF MOON   6
        DESPITE A DWINDLING AND LATE RISEN MOON, ...   372 PHASES OF MOON V   6
        UNTIL THAT GLANCE RUN IN THE WORLD'S DESPITE . . . .   474 ALL SOUL NIGHT   94
        AND HE, DESPITE HIS TERROR, CANNOT CEASE . . . . . .   563 MERU   4
        ALLOW THAT HE, DESPITE . . . .   584 ORAHILLY   4
DESTINY
        AND ON THIS LOOM I WEAVE THY DESTINY." . . . .   716 DWELT SYCAMORE   14
DESTROY
        DESTROY THE VIEW BY CUTTING DOWN AN ASH . . . .   372 ON GOING HOUSE   13
        COMES TO DESTROY . . . .   500 VACILLATION   4
        I THOUGHT MY DEAR MUST HER OWN SOUL DESTROY, ...   630 CIRCUS ANIMALS   21
DESTROYED
        CAN BE SO BATTERED, BADGERED AND DESTROYED . . . . .   130 BOOK STORIES   17
        LAUGHTER NOT TIME DESTROYED MY VOICE . . . .   455 FRIENDS YOUTH   1
        AS THE FOX IN THE OLD FABLE DESTROYED THE SPARTAN BOY'S,   580 CURSE CROMWELL   18
DESTROYING   SEE ALL-DESTROYING
DESTROYS
        BUT THERE'S ANOTHER KNOWLEDGE THAT MY HEART DESTROYS, . .   580 CURSE CROMWELL   17
DEVIL
        WHOM MAN OR DEVIL CANNOT TIRE, ...   295 THREE BEGGARS   16
        TO RID ME OF THE DEVIL IN MY SHOES," . . . .   299 BEGGAR CRIED   6
        "AND THE WORSE DEVIL THAT IS BETWEEN MY THIGHS." . . .   300 BEGGAR CRIED   8
        "BUT THERE'S A DEVIL IN A LOOKING-GLASS." . . . . . .   300 BEGGAR CRIED   12
        THAT DREAM IS A NORM! AND SHOULD SOME LIMB OF THE DEVIL   372 ON GOING HOUSE   12
        AND MAY THE DEVIL TAKE THE REST. . . . .   386 ROBARTES DANCE   24
DEVILISH
        SUCH DEVILISH THINGS EXIST, ...   436 FOR MY SON   11
DEVIL'S
        HE TAKES THE DEVIL'S PAY. . . . .   582 ROGER CASEMENT V   20
        I KNOW WHAT DEVIL'S TRADE THEY LEARN . . . .   607 SONGS BURDEN 2   12
DEVILS
        WHOM THE DEVILS HAVE BY THE HAIR, ...   92 FATHER OHART   14
DEVIOUS
        WITHIN THE TEMPLE, DEVIOUS WALKING, MADE . . . . . .   72 ANASHU VIJAYA   32
DEVOTEE
        THE DEVOTEE PROFFERS A KNEE TO HIS LORD, ...   547 TO SAME TUNE 3   2
        THE DEVOTEE PROFFERS A KNEE TO HIS LORD, ...   614 MARCH SONGS 2   2
DEVOUR
        BUT NOW TWO THINGS DEVOUR MY LIFE! . . . .   24 OISIN 1   358
DEVOURED
        UPON A PAINTED STAGE WHEN WE DEVOURED HIS HEART. . . .   542 PARN FUNERAL 1   23
DEVOUTLY
        AND LEAN YOUR LIPS DEVOUTLY TO THIS HARP, ...   762 SHADOW WATER A   287
DEW   SEE LOVE-DEW
        WHERE DROPS OF DEW IN MYRIADS FALL, ...   16 OISIN 1   222
        "JOY DROWNS THE TWILIGHT IN THE DEW, ...   18 OISIN 1   261
        WALKING GHOSTLY IN THE DEW, ...   67 HAPPY SHEPHERD   52
        WALKING GHOSTLY 'MONG THE DEW, ...   67 HAPPY SHEPHERD V   52
        THE DEW DROPS, FOR THE SOUND OF THEIR OWN DROPPING-- . .   68 SAD SHEPHERD V   16
        IT QUENCHED, WITH SOUND LIKE FALLING DEW, ...   86 MAD KING GOLL   66
        OF DEW ON THE YOUNG STREAMS. . . . .   88 STOLEN CHILD V   37
        WHO HAVE SOUGHT MORE THAN IS IN RAIN OR DEW . . . . .   114 ROSE OF BATTLE   16
        . . . HUNG LOW IN THE FALL OF THE DEW! . . . .   122 WHITE BIRDS   7
        . . . DEW DABBLED, THE LILY AND ROSE! . . . .   122 WHITE BIRDS V   5
        SIGH, HEART, AGAIN IN THE DEW OF THE MORN. . . . . . .   147 INTO TWILIGHT   4
        DEW EVER SHINING AND TWILIGHT GREY! . . . .   148 INTO TWILIGHT   6
        AND HOPE IS LESS DEAR THAN THE DEW OF THE MORN. . . . .   148 INTO TWILIGHT   16
        THE WEST WEEPS IN PALE DEW AND SIGHS PASSING AWAY, . .   154 BELOVED PEACE   5
        FOR HOURS WHEN ALL MUST FADE LIKE DEW, ...   156 FORGOT BEAUTY   20
        THE GREY CAIRN ON THE HILL, WHEN DAY SINKS DROWNED IN DEW,   161 BLACK PIG   6
        THE DEW DROPS SLOWLY! THE DREAMS GATHER! UNKNOWN SPEARS   161 BLACK PIG V   1
        AND THEREFORE MY HEART WILL BOW, WHEN DEW . . . . . .   164 PERFECT BEAUTY   6
        IN TWILIGHTS OF DEW AND OF FIRE." . . . .   168 BLESSED   40
        IN TWILIGHTS OF DEW AND FIRE!" . . . .   168 BLESSED V   40
        WHO MET FAND WALKING AMONG FLAMING DEW . . . .   169 SECRET ROSE   13
        THAT IT MAY DROP FAINT PERFUME, AND BE HEAVY WITH DEW, .   172 TRAV PASSION   7
        ABOUNDING FOLIAGE MOISTENED WITH THE DEW! . . . . . .   500 VACILLATION   13
        ALL THINGS HANG LIKE A DROP OF DEW . . . .   505 GRAT INSTRUCT   3
        THERE THE SILVER DEW, ...   611 NEWS ORACLE   2
        CATCHING SMALL BIRDS IN THE DEW OF THE MORN . . . . .   636 BLACK TOWER   22
        WITH DEW, AS THOUGH 'TWERE SEALING THEM FOR DEATH. . .   691 MOSADA 1   22

202

	PAGE	TITLE	LINE
DEW (CONTINUED)			
AND SEE HOW THICK THE DEW LIES ON MY FACE.	703	MOSADA 3	104
AND CLINGING WITH THE DEW OF ODOROUS SHOWERS, ...	704	REMEMBRANCE	4
GATHERING MUSHROOMS IN THE DEW.	705	DAWN-SONG	8
GATHERING MUSHROOMS IN THE DEW.	705	DAWN-SONG	16
SHOWERED AWAY THE KEEN DEW DROPS!	705	DAWN-SONG	18
GATHERING MUSHROOMS IN THE DEW.	706	DAWN-SONG	24
GATHERING MUSHROOMS IN THE DEW.	706	DAWN-SONG	32
AND AWAY IN THE WOODS WE WILL SCATTER THE DEW!	717	LOVE SONG	2
FOR GOD IS WALKING IN THE DEW, ...	736	SUMMER EVENING	15
AND TEARS OF FIRE FALL GENTLY IN THE DEW.	738	YOU ARE SAD	4
IN A WOOD OF DEW AND MOSS, ...	744	ROSY CROSS	5
LET THE DEW BEAR WITNESS, ...	770	BLOOD BOND	11
WHERE THE DEW IS MADE BEFORE DAWN!	771	SPINNING SONG	5
DEW-BEDROWNED			
I NEVER KNEW A NIGHT SO DEW-BEDROWNED.	703	MOSADA 3	105
DEW-BLANCHED			
AND DEW-BLANCHED HORNS, IN WHOSE HOLLOW A CHILD OF THREE YEARS OLD	49	OISIN 3	30
AND DEW-BLANCHED HORNS, IN WHOSE HOLLOWS A CHILD OF THREE YEARS OLD	49	OISIN 3 V	31
DEW-COLD			
THE DEW-COLD LILIES LADIES BORE	156	FORGOT BEAUTY	11
DEW-CUMBERED			
. . . NOR GO FROM HIS DEW-CUMBERED SKIES!	49	OISIN 3	38
DEW-DABBLED			
. . . DEW-DABBLED, THE LILY AND ROSE!	122	WHITE BIRDS	5
DEW-DRENCH'D			
'TIS MORN, AND FROM THE DEW-DRENCH'D WOOD I'VE SPED . .	645	ISLE STAT I 1	6
DEW-DROP			
LOW, LONG AND MUSICAL. A DEW-DROP HUNG	689	NETTLESHIP	9
DEW-DROPPING			
AND THE LONG DEW-DROPPING HOURS OF THE NIGHT, ...	116	FAERY SONG	7
AND STARS CLIMBING THE DEW-DROPPING SKY, ...	158	BELOVED RHYMES	11
DEWDROPS			
HER EYES WERE SOFT AS DEWDROPS HANGING	3	OISIN 1 V	7HH
WHERE WHITE DEWDROPS IN MILLIONS FALL!	16	OISIN 1 V	222
AND CAME TO WHERE THE DEWDROPS FALL	20	OISIN 1	293
CRIED ALL HIS STORY TO THE DEWDROPS GLISTENING.	68	SAD SHEPHERD	14
THE DEWDROPS, FOR THE SOUND OF THEIR OWN DROPPING. . . .	68	SAD SHEPHERD	16
DEW-DROWNED			
AND WHEN THE DEW-DROWNED STARS HANG IN THE AIR	32	OISIN 2	54
SEE! OH, SEE! THE DEW-DROWNED BUNCHES	655	ISLE STAT I 3	1
DEWS			
. . . THEIR DIMNESS, THEIR DEWS DROPPING SLEEP.	54	OISIN 3	108
THE DEWS DROP SLOWLY AND DREAMS GATHER! UNKNOWN SPEARS . .	161	BLACK PIG	1
DEW-WASHED			
WHEN THE EARLIEST DEW-WASHED STAR FROM EVE HATH LEANT, . .	32	OISIN 2 V	54
DEWY			
OR DOWN THE DEWY FOREST ALLEYS, ...	10	OISIN 1	120
AND DOWN THE DEWY FOREST ALLEYS, ...	10	OISIN 1 V	120
DANAAN SONGS, AND THEIR DEWY SHOWERS	11	OISIN 1	135
SANG NIAM, AND THEIR DEWY SHOWERS	11	OISIN 1 V	135
FROM DEWY EYES: "UPON THE DEAD	21	OISIN 1	310
OR WRESTLE WITH THEIR PEERS IN DEWY VALLEYS.	30	OISIN 2 V	14E
GATHERED IN SILENCE, DEWY AS HER EYES, ...	80	EPHEMERA	19
O HIDING HAIR AND DEWY EYES, ...	152	HEART OF WOMAN	9
BLOSSOMS OPEN DEWY LIPS!	647	ISLE STAT I 1	65
IF SO I MIGHT, ALONG A DEWY VALE, ...	649	ISLE STAT I 1	123
WITH QUIET SHADE ITS EVER DEWY SPOT, ...	714	FERENCZ RENYI V	109
WITH QUIET SHADE ITS EVER DEWY PLOT.	714	FERENCZ RENYI V	109
DEWY-PLOT			
WITH QUIET SHADE ITS EVER DEWY-PLOT, ...	714	FERENCZ RENYI	109
DEWY-TONGUED			
DEWY-TONGUED, THE DAISY TOPS--	706	DAWN-SONG	22
DIAGRAM			
A DIAGRAM HUNG THERE INSTEAD, ...	485	STATISTICS	3
DIALOGUE			
A DIALOGUE OF SELF AND SOUL	477	SELF AND SOUL	T
A DIALOGUE	499	VACILLATION V	T
DIARMUID			
THAT MADE HER DIARMUID DEAR, AND SOME OLD CARDINAL . . .	366	HER COURAGE	6
DICE			
WHILE THEIR GREAT WOODEN DICE BEAT ON THE BOARD.	412	TOWER	88
I LOSE! THEY'RE LOADED DICE. TIME ALWAYS PLAYS	721	WITCH VIVIEN	44
WITH LOADED DICE. ANOTHER CHANCE! COME, FATHER! . . .	721	WITCH VIVIEN	45
DICK			
COME TOM AND DICK, COME ALL THE TROOP	582	ROGER CASEMENT	17
DIDO			
OF SAD QUEEN DIDO SHONE THE LAPPING FIRE	645	ISLE STAT I 1	9
DIDO'S			
I SAW HIM FROM SAD DIDO'S SHORES DEPART, ...	677	ISLE STAT II 3	288
DIE			
SLEEP THERE TILL THE MOON AND THE STARS DIE!"	17	OISIN 1	246
AND EARTH AND HEAVEN AND HELL WOULD DIE, ...	19	OISIN 1	271
THE UNIVERSE HERSELF WOULD DIE, ...	19	OISIN 1 V	271
O'ER MEN WHO SLEEP, AND WAKE, AND DIE, ...	22	OISIN 1 V	340B
OR LOVE'S FIRST TENDERNESS DIE IN OUR GAZE.	27	OISIN 1	411
OR LOVE'S FIRST TENDERNESS DIE IN OUR GAZE.	27	OISIN 1 V	419D
OR LOVE'S FIRST TENDERNESS DIE IN OUR GAZE."	28	OISIN 1 V	427
"THIS DEMON SHALL BE BATTERED TILL HE DIE, ...	35	OISIN 2	90

		PAGE	TITLE		LINE

DIE   (CONTINUED)

"THIS DEMON SHALL BE PIERCED AND DROP AND DIE, ...   35 OISIN 2   V   90
"I WOULD DIE LIKE A SMALL WITHERED LEAF IN THE AUTUMN,   56 OISIN 3   131
    . . .

AND DIE A PEARLY BROTHERHOOD: . . . .   66 HAPPY SHEPHERD   42
HOW WHEN WE DIE OUR SHADES WILL ROVE, ...   78 INDIAN TO LOVE   18
HOW WHEN WE DIE OUR SHADES MAY ROVE, ...   78 INDIAN TO LOVE   V   18
DIE OFF THE FEEBLE SOUNDS: . . . .   99 FOXHUNTER   V   42
BUT WHEREFORE NOW?" "THERE IS A MAN TO DIE: . . . .   107 CUCHULAIN SEA   23
OF THEIR SAD HEARTS, THAT MAY NOT LIVE NOR DIE. . . .   114 ROSE OF BATTLE   24
OF OUR SAD HEARTS, THAT MAY NOT LIVE NOR DIE. . . . .   115 ROSE OF BATTLE   36
HAS AWAKED IN OUR HEARTS, MY BELOVED, A SADNESS THAT MAY   122 WHITE BIRDS   4
    NOT DIE.
HAS AWAKED IN OUR HEARTS, MY BELOVED, A SADNESS THAT NEVER   122 WHITE BIRDS   V   4
    MAY DIE.
FOR PEOPLE DIE AND DIE", ...   132 FR GILLIGAN   10
FOR PEOPLE DIE AND DIE", ...   132 FR GILLIGAN   10
FROM OUR BIRTHDAY, UNTIL WE DIE, ...   139 TO IRELAND   35
"I WILL SEND THEM TO HER AND DIE": . . . .   160 CAP AND BELLS   22
AND WHEN IT IS GONE WE DIE: . . . .   168 BLESSED   V   30
LIKE THE SPARKS BLOWN OUT OF A SMITHY, AND DIE? . .   170 SECRET ROSE   30
"SHE WILL GROW OLD AND DIE, AND SHE HAS WEPT!" . . .   186 QUEEN MAEVE   138
WE SAW THE LAST EMBERS OF DAYLIGHT DIE, ...   205 ADAMS CURSE   29
I AM A WOMAN, I DIE AT EVERY BREATH. . . . . . .   250 SHADOW WATER B   583
BEFORE WE GROW OLD AND DIE. . . . .   261 DRINKING SONG   4
SOLDIERS THAT GAVE, WHATEVER DIE WAS CAST: . . . . .   269 PARDON FATHERS   9
HER LOVE, AND WOULD NOT HAVE ME DIE, ...   274 GREY ROCK   87
AND SHOULD HE DIE TO HEAP HIS BURIAL-MOUND . . . . .   280 TWO KINGS   82
AND SHOULD HE DIE TO HEAP HIS BURIAL MOUND . . . . .   280 TWO KINGS   V   82
LIVE HE OR DIE . . . .   310 PEACOCK   7
THAT EVEN THE BEST OF LOVE MUST DIE, ...   314 MEMORY YOUTH   17
BEING OLD, BUT THAT THE OLD ALONE MIGHT DIE, ...   339 SHEP GOATHERD   4
LAMENTING THAT A MAN SHOULD DIE: . . . .   361 ALF POLLEXFEN   38
IT IS ABOUT TO DIE. . . . .   367 HER CHRIS TREE   12
TO DIE INTO THE LABYRINTH OF ITSELF: . . . .   374 PHASES OF MOON   55
THERE CAN BE NOTHING SOLIDER TILL I DIE: . . . . .   383 VISION ROBART   26
AS THOUGH TO DIE BY GUNSHOT WERE . . . .   424 ROAD AT DOOR   4
ERE THE ONE OR T'OTHER DIE, ...   508 JANE BISHOP   V   5
DID HE DIE OR DID SHE DIE? . . . .   514 JANE GROWN OLD   15
DID HE DIE OR DID SHE DIE? . . . .   514 JANE GROWN OLD   15
SEEMED TO DIE OR DIED THEY BOTH? . . . .   514 JANE GROWN OLD   16
SEEM TO DIE OR DIED THEY BOTH? . . . .   514 JANE GROWN OLD   V   16
ALL TRUE LOVE MUST DIE, ...   517 HER ANXIETY   3
IN THAT FAITH I LIVE OR DIE." . . . .   529 TOM LUNATIC   18
SAVING THE RHYME RATS HEAR BEFORE THEY DIE. . . . .   542 PARN FUNERAL 1   28
THAT I MAY SEEM, THOUGH I DIE OLD, ...   553 PRAYER OLD AGE   11
WHAT CAN THEY KNOW THAT WE KNOW THAT KNOW THE TIME TO DIE?   580 CURSE CROMWELL   14
"NOT TO DIE ON THE STRAW AT HOME," . . . .   587 OLD WICKED MAN   5
"THEN WANT BEFORE YOU DIE." . . . .   596 COLONEL MARTIN   67
TO FOLLOW IS TO DIE: . . . .   600 SPIRIT MEDIUM   18
BUT HAD GONE OUT TO DIE . . . .   608 SONGS BURDEN 3   20
OF GOD OR WOMAN, THE TIME WERE COME TO DIE." . . . .   609 IN TARAS HALLS   15
(SOMETHING MAY LINGER THERE THOUGH ALL ELSE DIE:) . .   618 BRONZE HEAD   5
SLEEPLESS WOULD LIE DOWN AND DIE. . . . .   632 MAN AND ECHO   18
LIE DOWN AND DIE. THAT WERE TO SHIRK . . . . . .   632 MAN AND ECHO   19
"OR DRIVEN FROM HOME AND LEFT TO DIE IN FEAR." . . .   635 CUCHULAIN COMF   22
WHETHER MAN DIE IN HIS BED . . . .   637 BEN BULBEN   17
SOME CAST OF DIE, OR LET SOME ARROW GLANCE . . . . .   656 ISLE STAT I 3   40
TO DIE FOR HER IN AIR OR GROUND. . . . .   668 ISLE STAT II 3   52
THAT ONE SHALL DIE, UNLESS ONE DIE FOR HER. . . . .   669 ISLE STAT II 3   74
THAT ONE SHALL DIE, UNLESS ONE DIE FOR HER. . . . .   669 ISLE STAT II 3   74
I DREAM:--I CANNOT DIE:--NO: NO: . . . .   675 ISLE STAT II 3   227
AND CROUCH IN SOME FAR STILLNESS OF THE ISLE, AND DIE. .   675 ISLE STAT II 3   246
I DREAM:--I CANNOT DIE:--NOT DIE: NO: NO: . . . .   675 ISLE STAT II 3   V   227
I DREAM:--I CANNOT DIE:--NO: NO: . . . .   675 ISLE STAT II 3   V   227
IN A FAR STILLNESS OF THE ISLAND DIE. . . . . . .   675 ISLE STAT II 3   V   246
UNTIL WE DIE WITHIN THE CHARMED RING . . . .   679 ISLE STAT II 3   322
THEN LET ME SEE THY FACE BEFORE I DIE. . . . . . .   684 SEEKER   66
WHAT, LOVER, DIE BEFORE OUR LIPS HAVE MET? . . . .   685 SEEKER   80
WE TWO, BEFORE WE DIE: FOR AZOLAR, ...   691 MOSADA 1   24
FORGIVE, OR I WILL DIE. 'TWAS ALLAH'S WILL. . . . .   695 MOSADA 1   118
I WILL NOT HEAR: THE MOORISH GIRL MUST DIE. . . . .   697 MOSADA 2   39
OH, GOD:--AWAKE: THOU SHALT NOT DIE. SHE SLEEPS, .   701 MOSADA 3   66
LOVE, WILL YOU DIE WHEN WE HAVE MET? ONE LOOK . . .   703 MOSADA 3   109
WE GATHERED. FERENCZ, NAY, I MUST NOT DIE: . . . .   713 FERENCZ RENYI   96
WE GATHERED. FERENCZ, DO NOT LET ME DIE. . . . .   713 FERENCZ RENYI   V   96
"ASSASSIN, MY ASSASSIN: THOU WHO LET'ST ME DIE, . .   714 FERENCZ RENYI   106
DEFEAT IS DEATH. SHOULD MY PLOTS FAIL I'D DIE. . . .   722 WITCH VIVIEN   52
I HAVE GOOD PILOTS: AIBRIC. WHEN MEN DIE . . . . .   750 SHADOW WATER A   81
HOW ALL THAT DIE ARE BORNE ABOUT THE WORLD . . . .   750 SHADOW WATER A   84
BE PULLERS OF THE OAR UNTIL YOU DIE? . . . . . .   757 SHADOW WATER A   217
WITH ONE YOU HAVE KILLED AND DIE: FOR WHEN I LEFT .   758 SHADOW WATER A   226
WITH SOME YOU HAVE KILLED AND DIE: FOR WHEN I LEFT .   758 SHADOW WATER A   V   226
FORGAEL CAN DIE TO-MORROW. COME TO THE ALE. . . . .   759 SHADOW WATER A   246
COME TO THE ALE: FOR HE CAN DIE TO-MORROW. . . . .   760 SHADOW WATER A   247
MAYBE I SHALL NOT DIE AT ALL. . . . .   788 HAWTHORN TREE   16
MAY BE I SHALL NOT DIE AT ALL. . . . .   788 HAWTHORN TREE   V   16

DIED

UNDER THE SHADOWS TILL THE TUMULTS DIED . . . . .   38 OISIN 2   140
IT DIED AFAR. GREY SLEET THOSE TOWERS HID . . . .   46 OISIN 2   V   245
BUT IF WHEN ANYONE DIED . . . .   92 FATHER OHART   21

				PAGE	TITLE		LINE

DIED (CONTINUED)
```
    BUT IF WHEN ANY ONE DIED,  . . . . . . . . . . . . .      92  FATHER OHART    V   21
    FOR HE'D DIED AT NINETY-FOUR.  . . . . . . . . . . .      93  FATHER OHART        28
    AND THE WAVES FLOWED ABOVE HIM AND HE DIED.  . . . .     111  CUCHULAIN SEA   V   86
    AND USNA'S CHILDREN DIED.  . . . . . . . . . . . . .     111  ROSE OF WORLD        5
    I DREAMED THAT ONE HAD DIED IN A STRANGE PLACE  . . .    123  DREAM OF DEATH       1
    "MAVRONE, MAVRONE! THE MAN HAS DIED  . . . . . . . .     133  FR GILLIGAN         25
    "HE DIED AN HOUR AGO."  . . . . . . . . . . . . . .      133  FR GILLIGAN         34
    "WHEN YOU WERE GONE, HE TURNED AND DIED  . . . . . .     133  FR GILLIGAN         37
    "OCHONE, OCHONE! THE MAN HAS DIED,  . . . . . . . .      133  FR GILLIGAN     V   25
    WHERE THE LAST PHOENIX DIED,  . . . . . . . . . . .      162  ASKS FORGIVE        16
    TILL VAIN FRENZY AWOKE AND HE DIED! AND HIM  . . . .     169  SECRET ROSE         12
    TILL IT DIED OUT WHERE AN OLD THORN-TREE STOOD.  . .     186  QUEEN MAEVE        129
    AND WHEN I'VE HEARD HOW THEY GREW OLD AND DIED,  . .     186  QUEEN MAEVE        136
    TILL IT DIED OUT WHERE AN OLD THORN TREE STOOD.  . .     186  QUEEN MAEVE     V  129
    SHE FELL AND DIED OF THE HEART-BREAK."  . . . . . .      191  BAILE AILLINN       64
    AND THEN ONE ASKS ANOTHER HOW HE DIED,  . . . . . .      234  SHADOW WATER B     256
    MY HUSBAND AND MY KING DIED AT MY FEET,  . . . . . .     237  SHADOW WATER B     337
    I KNOW THAT HE DIED A THOUSAND YEARS AGO,  . . . . .     241  SHADOW WATER B     392
    IT WAS GOLDEN-ARMED IOLLAN, AND HE DIED  . . . . . .     242  SHADOW WATER B     406
    AND THAT HE DIED A THOUSAND YEARS AGO.  . . . . . .      242  SHADOW WATER B     417
    SINCE, TAVERN COMRADES, YOU HAVE DIED,  . . . . . .      273  GREY ROCK           49
    AND THE WORLD'S ALTERED SINCE YOU DIED,  . . . . . .     276  GREY ROCK          126
    FOR THIS EDWARD FITZGERALD DIED,  . . . . . . . . .      290  SEPTEMBER 1913      20
    AND DIED IN THE GREAT WAR BEYOND THE SEA. . . . . .      339  SHEP GOATHERD       22
    AND OF A RED-HAIRED YEATS WHOSE LOOKS, ALTHOUGH HE DIED  391  UNDER SATURN         9
    BEWILDERED THEM TILL THEY DIED?  . . . . . . . . . .     394  EASTER 1916         73
    THAT THE WORST ROGUES AND RASCALS HAD DIED OUT.  . .     428  NINETEEN 19         16
    WHERE HOLY DIONYSUS DIED,  . . . . . . . . . . . .       437  SONGS PLAY 1         2
    THE GARDEN DIED!  . . . . . . . . . . . . . . . .        439  FRAGMENTS            2
    NOTHING COULD BRING HIM, WHEN HIS LADY DIED,  . . .      471  ALL SOUL NIGHT      25
    MANY TIMES HE DIED,  . . . . . . . . . . . . . . .       476  DEATH                5
    A SPOT WHEREON THE FOUNDERS LIVED AND DIED  . . . .      491  COOLE BALLYLEE      33
    SEEMED TO DIE OR DIED THEY BOTH?  . . . . . . . . .      514  JANE GROWN OLD      16
    SEEM TO DIE OR DIED THEY BOTH?  . . . . . . . . . .      514  JANE GROWN OLD  V   16
    O'HIGGINS ITS SOLE STATESMAN HAD NOT DIED. . . . . .     543  PARN FUNERAL 2       8
    BUT HE KICKED BEFORE HE DIED,  . . . . . . . . . .       545  TO SAME TUNE 1      25
    JUSTIFY ALL THAT HAVE DIED ON THE SCAFFOLD,  . . . .     546  TO SAME TUNE 2      13
    TROY BACKED ITS HELEN! TROY DIED AND ADORED!  . . .      547  TO SAME TUNE 3       4
    TROY LOOKED ON HELEN, IT DIED AND ADORED!  . . . . .     547  TO SAME TUNE 3  V    4
    THE SWORD'S A CROSS! THEREON HE DIED!  . . . . . . .     562  CONJUNCTIONS         3
    HE DROPPED UPON HIS HEAD AND DIED.  . . . . . . . .      571  THREE BUSHES        52
    AND DROPPED AND DIED THEREON, FOR SHE  . . . . . . .     571  THREE BUSHES        54
    "THIS LAND OF SAINTS." AND THEN AS THE APPLAUSE DIED OUT,  577  LOFTY THINGS       3
    HE DIED UPON THE GALLOWS.  . . . . . . . . . . . .       581  ROGER CASEMENT       3
    "HERE DIED THE O'RAHILLY.  . . . . . . . . . . . .       585  ORAHILLY            34
    CLOSE TO THE CITY HALL HE DIED!  . . . . . . . . . .     608  SONGS BURDEN 3      12
    LAY IN THE COFFIN, STOPPED HIS BREATH AND DIED.  . .     609  IN TARAS HALLS      20
    REMEMBER ALL THAT HAVE DIED ON THE SCAFFOLD,  . . .      613  MARCH SONGS 1       13
    TROY BACKED ITS HELEN! TROY DIED AND ADORED!  . . .      614  MARCH SONGS 2        4
    BUT HE KICKED BEFORE HE DIED,  . . . . . . . . . .       616  MARCH SONGS 3       25
    IF HE DIED LONG AGO  . . . . . . . . . . . . . . .       635  BLACK TOWER         15
    AND MANNED AN ARGOSY AND SAILING DIED.  . . . . . .      693  MOSADA 1            89
    HOW MANY MOONS HAVE DIED FROM THE FULL MOON  . . . .     747  SHADOW WATER A      10
    AND THEN ONE ASKS ANOTHER HOW HE DIED,  . . . . . .      753  SHADOW WATER A     146
    THIS BLADE OUT OF MY HAND AND DIED OF A SUDDEN.  . .     755  SHADOW WATER A     168
    SHE CAUGHT THIS BLADE OUT OF MY BELT AND DIED.  . .      755  SHADOW WATER A  V  168
    UNTIL HE HAD DIED OF HIS WOUNDS.  . . . . . . . . .      775  AGAINST WITCH       16
    YOUR OWN THOUGHT WILL HAVE DIED  . . . . . . . . .       786  YOUR HEART          30
    HER OWN THOUGHT WILL HAVE DIED . . . . . . . . . .       786  YOUR HEART      V   30
    YOU HAD BROUGHT DOWN BEFORE YOU DIED.  . . . . . .       791  REPRISALS            2
DIES
    UPON THE LIFE THAT FADES AND FLICKERS AND DIES,  . .      29  OISIN 2             12
    PATRICK, BEFORE THY CRAFT DIES EACH OLD SONG. . . .       42  OISIN 2         V  196
    HIS PURPOSE DRIFTS AND DIES."  . . . . . . . . . .        45  OISIN 2            244
    AND WHEN THE WANDERING MUSIC DIES  . . . . . . . .        99  FOXHUNTER           31
    AND ALL THEIR TROUBLE DIES INTO ITS PEACE!--  . . .      128  DREAM OF FAERY  V   35
    AND MEN WHO LOVED THE CAUSE THAT NEVER DIES.  . . .      130  BOOK STORIES    V   24
    OF THE WOMAN THAT HE LOVES, UNTIL HE DIES. . . . . .     177  PAST GREATNESS      10
    OUR COURAGE BREAKS LIKE AN OLD TREE IN A BLACK WIND AND  207  HANRAHANS SONG       3
      DIES,
    LIKE TUFTED REEDS OUR COURAGE DROOPS IN A BLACK WIND AND  207  HANRAHANS SONG V    3
      DIES!
    WEAK AND WORN AND WEARY OUR COURAGE DROOPS AND DIES  . .  207  HANRAHANS SONG V    8
    FOR ALL HIS SPELLS WILL VANISH WHEN HE DIES.  . . .      240  SHADOW WATER B     376
    THE LAST STROKE OF MIDNIGHT DIES. . . . . . . . . .      357  BROKEN DREAMS       37
    WHATEVER IS BEGOTTEN, BORN, AND DIES.  . . . . . .       407  SAIL BYZANTIUM       6
    WHATEVER IS BEGOTTEN BORN OR DIES,  . . . . . . . .      407  SAIL BYZANTIUM V     6
    FOR BEAUTY DIES OF BEAUTY, WORTH OF WORTH,  . . . . .    564  GYRES                3
    MANY TIMES MAN LIVES AND DIES  . . . . . . . . . .       637  BEN BULBEN          13
    BUT SOULLESS A FAIRY DIES,  . . . . . . . . . . . .      643  SONG FAERIES         2
    FOR SOULLESS A FAIRY DIES,  . . . . . . . . . . . .      644  SONG FAERIES        14
    BUT SOULLESS A FAERY DIES,  . . . . . . . . . . . .      676  ISLE STAT II 3     249
    FOR SOULLESS A FAERY DIES,  . . . . . . . . . . . .      676  ISLE STAT II 3     261
    THE VERY SQUIRREL DIES THAT ENTERS THERE.  . . . . .     682  SEEKER              33
    THE VERY SQUIRREL DIES THAT ENTERS IT.  . . . . . .      682  SEEKER          V   33
    A LITTLE WHILE AND--RED EVE DIES--  . . . . . . . .      686  LIFE                13
    ALL DIES AMONG THOSE STREAMS.  THE FOOL HAS MADE  . .    764  SHADOW WATER A     335
    THAT DIES OUT BEFORE 'TIS DAY,  . . . . . . . . . .      777  SONG DEIRDRE 2       8
DIETH
    AND MY SOUL IN WAITING DIETH,  . . . . . . . . . .       648  ISLE STAT I 1       87
```

		PAGE	TITLE		LINE

DIETH (CONTINUED)
EVER DIETH, DIETH, DIETH. . . . .   648 ISLE STAT I 1   88
EVER DIETH, DIETH, DIETH. . . . .   648 ISLE STAT I 1   88
EVER DIETH, DIETH, DIETH. . . . .   648 ISLE STAT I 1   88
THAT DIETH SLOW WITH SUNSICK DOOM. . . . .   655 ISLE STAT I 3   12
DIFFERENT
YET THEY WERE OF A DIFFERENT KIND, ...   289 SEPTEMBER 1913   9
SO WE SPEAK A DIFFERENT TONGUE. . . . .   313 TWO YEAR LATER   6
ACCORDING TO A DIFFERENT PLAN. . . . .   379 SAINT HUNCH   6
THEY SAY SUCH DIFFERENT THINGS AT SCHOOL. . . . .   387 ROBARTES DANCE   52
ALL THAT ARE DIFFERENT OF A BASE INTENT; . . . .   398 LEADERS CROWD   2
SOME FOUND A DIFFERENT POLE, AND WHERE IT STOOD . .   483 VERONIC NAPKIN   7
DIFFERENTLY
I'LL SHOW YOU THAT I AM MADE DIFFERENTLY, ...   227 SHADOW WATER B   119
DIFFICULT
THAT WORK TOO DIFFICULT FOR MORTAL HANDS . . . .   182 QUEEN MAEVE   67
THE FASCINATION OF WHAT'S DIFFICULT . . . .   260 FASC DIFFICULT   T
THE FASCINATION OF WHAT'S DIFFICULT . . . .   260 FASC DIFFICULT   1
THAT IS MOST DIFFICULT. . . . .   291 TO A FRIEND   16
HE FOLLOWS WHATEVER WHIM'S MOST DIFFICULT . . . .   374 PHASES OF MOON   40
CHOOSING WHATEVER TASK'S MOST DIFFICULT . . . . .   376 PHASES OF MOON   91
DIG
WHO DIG OLD CUSTOMS UP. . . . .   93 FATHER OHART   40
"COME OUT AND DIG FOR A DEAD MAN, ...   272 GREY ROCK   32
"WHO'D CARE TO DIG 'EM," SAID THE OLD, OLD MAN, .   548 TO SAME TUNE 3   7
"WHO'D CARE TO DIG 'EM," SAID THE OLD, OLD MAN, .   548 TO SAME TUNE 3   17
"WHO'D CARE TO DIG 'EM," SAID THE OLD, OLD MAN, .   549 TO SAME TUNE 3   27
DIGEST
MARK AND DIGEST MY TALE, CARRY IT AFAR . . . . .   554 RIBH AT TOMB   3
DIGGERS   SEE GRAVE-DIGGERS GRAVE-DIGGERS;
DIGGERS AND CARPENTERS MAKE GRAVE AND COFFIN; . .   609 IN TARAS HALLS   17
DIGGES
THEN THAT OLD ABBEY ACTOR, DUDLEY DIGGES, ...   790 DEDICATION   7
DIGGING
AND SET THEM DIGGING UNDER BUAL'S HILL. . . . . .   184 QUEEN MAEVE   93
AND SET THEM DIGGING INTO ANBUAL'S HILL. . . . .   184 QUEEN MAEVE   V 93
AND SET THEM DIGGING IN THE WEST OF THE HILL. . .   184 QUEEN MAEVE   V 93
DIGNITY
--IT HAD SUCH DIGNITY OF LIMB-- . . . .   254 HIS DREAM   11
BECAUSE IT HAD SUCH DIGNITY. . . . .   254 HIS DREAM   19
A FARMER HAS MORE DIGNITY." . . . .   296 THREE BEGGARS   37
THERE IS A SOLID DIGNITY . . . .   296 THREE BEGGARS   V 37
HUMAN DIGNITY . . . .   452 HUMAN DIGNITY   T
FROM HUMAN DIGNITY. . . . .   452 HUMAN DIGNITY   12
DIGS
HE DIGS HIS CABBAGES. HE BRINGS TO MIND . . . .   696 MOSADA 2   18
DILIGENCE
I STUDY HATRED WITH GREAT DILIGENCE, ...   558 RIBH CHRISTIAN   3
DIM
TO THIS DIM SHORE THOSE GENTLE FEET? . . . . . .   5 OISIN 1   V 51
TO THIS DIM SHORE ON FOAM WET FEET? . . . .   5 OISIN 1   V 51
TO THIS DIM SHORE ON FOAM-WET FEET? . . . .   5 OISIN 1   V 51
THE RED SUN FALLS AND THE WORLD GROWS DIM." . . .   9 OISIN 1   105
WAS DIM WITH MIRE OF A MORTAL SHORE, ...   15 OISIN 1   208
WAS DIM WITH THE MIRE OF A MORTAL SHORE, ...   15 OISIN 1   V 208
THAT KEPT DIM WATERS FROM THE SKY; . . . .   17 OISIN 1   243
AND SHOWED THEIR EYES WITH TEARDROPS DIM, ...   18 OISIN 1   256
ON THE DEAD DIM EARTH ENCLOSES; . . . .   21 OISIN 1   312
UNCHAINABLE AS THE DIM TIDE, ...   22 OISIN 1   338
I HEARD ONE SAY, "HIS EYES GROW DIM . . . .   25 OISIN 1   380
YET LOVE AND KISS ON DIM SHORES FAR AWAY . . . .   29 OISIN 2   13
BUT LOVE AND KISS ON DIM SHORES FAR AWAY . . . .   29 OISIN 2   V 13
THAT WITH DIM EYEBALLS STOOD ON EITHER SIDE. . .   34 OISIN 2   75
FOR THEIR DIM MINDS WERE WITH THE ANCIENT THINGS.   34 OISIN 2   77
STOOD LONELY, WITH DIM EYEBALLS ON EACH SIDE, . .   34 OISIN 2   V 74
IN SOME DIM MEMORY OR ANCIENT MOOD, ...   36 OISIN 2   99
WRAPT ROUND IN SOME DIM MEMORY, IT SEEMED-- . . .   36 OISIN 2   V 99
PASSED UNDER THE DIM DOORWAY, OUT OF SIGHT, . . .   37 OISIN 2   123
PASSED UNDER A DIM DOORWAY, OUT OF SIGHT, ...   37 OISIN 2   V 123
NO CENTURIES COULD DIM, AND A WORD RAN . . . . .   38 OISIN 2   127
THE LEAST OF DOORS; BEYOND ON A DIM PLAIN . . . .   39 OISIN 2   155
THEN IN THAT HALL, LIT BY THE DIM SEA-SHINE, . .   41 OISIN 2   187
THEN IN THAT HALL, LIT BY THE DIM SEA SHINE, . .   41 OISIN 2   V 187
. . . FLUNG LOOSELY ALONG THE DIM GROUND; . . . .   50 OISIN 3   45
SORRY PLACE, WHERE FOR SWING OF THE WAR-AXE IN MY DIM EYES   61 OISIN 3   194

CRIED OUT, DIM SEA, HEAR MY MOST PITEOUS STORY! . . .   68 SAD SHEPHERD   9
RAGING AT HIS OWN IMAGE IN THE DIM ENAMELLED SEA . .   77 INDIAN TO LOVE   V 5
THE DIM GREY SANDS WITH LIGHT, ...   87 STOLEN CHILD   14
OR DO YOU LONG FOR THE DIM SLEEPY GROUND, ...   109 CUCHULAIN SEA   60
BOW DOWN, ARCHANGELS, IN YOUR DIM ABODE; . . . .   112 ROSE OF WORLD   11
YOU, TOO, HAVE COME WHERE THE DIM TIDES ARE HURLED   115 ROSE OF BATTLE   26
MADE YOU OF US, AND OF THE DIM GREY SEA. . . . .   115 ROSE OF BATTLE   30
AND THE WHITE BREAST OF THE DIM SEA . . . .   126 GOES FERGUS   11
UPON A DIM, GREEN, WELL-BELOVED ISLE, ...   126 DREAM OF FAERY   V 8
AND CHAPLET THEIR CALM BROWS WITH LEAFAGE DIM, .   127 DREAM OF FAERY   V 32
IN THE DIM GLASS THE DEMONS HOLD, ...   135 TWO TREES   30
OF THE DIM WISDOMS OLD AND DEEP, ...   138 TO IRELAND   V 21
THAT YOU, IN THE DIM COMING TIMES, ...   139 TO IRELAND   46
AND DREAMED OF THE LONG DIM HAIR . . . .   144 HOST OF AIR   7
OF HER LONG DIM HAIR. . . . .   145 HOST OF AIR   28

206

DIM   (CONTINUED)
    WERE DROWNED IN HER LONG DIM HAIR. . . . .   145 HOST OF AIR   36
    PALE BROWS, STILL HANDS AND DIM HAIR, ...   152 LOSS OF LOVE   1
    PALE BROW, STILL HANDS, AND DIM HAIR, ...   152 LOSS OF LOVE   V   1
    FOR THAT DIM BROW AND LINGERING HAND . . . . . .   156 FORGOT BEAUTY   V   15
    AND CANDLE—LIKE FOAM ON THE DIM SAND, ...   158 BELOVED RHYMES   10
    WITH YOUR DIM HEAVY HAIR, ...   163 ASKS FORGIVE   22
    WITH YOUR DIM SHADOWY HAIR, ...   163 ASKS FORGIVE   V   22
    WITH HER CLOUD—PALE EYELIDS HALF COVERING HER DIM EYES! 163 VALLEY LOVERS   V   4
    IN DRUID VAPOUR AND MAKE THE TORCHES DIM! . . . .   169 SECRET ROSE   11
    DIM POWERS OF DROWSY THOUGHT, LET HER NO LONGER BE .   175 ELEMENT POWERS   13
    WHEN WINDS HAVE GATHERED AND SUN AND MOON BURNED DIM   175 ELEMENT POWERS   15
    THE BLUE AND THE DIM AND THE DARK CLOTHS . . . . .   176 CLOTHS HEAVEN   3
    THEIR BODICES IN SOME DIM PLACE . . . .   193 BAILE AILLINN   105
    THAT OLD MAN CLIMBED! THE DAY GREW DIM! . . . . .   194 BAILE AILLINN   134
    SCALE RUBBING SCALE WHERE LIGHT IS DIM . . . . .   195 BAILE AILLINN   145
    OF MORNING LIGHT IN A DIM SKY! . . . .   195 BAILE AILLINN   150
    I KNOW WHERE A DIM MOON DRIFTS, WHERE THE DANAAN KIND   203 WITHER BOUGHS   12
    NOR LANDS THAT SEEM TOO DIM TO BE BURDENS ON THE HEART! 209 UNDER THE MOON   5
    DIM PAIRC—NA—CARRAIG, WHERE THE WILD BEES FLING . .   217 WOODS OF COOLE   9
    DIM PAIRC—NA—TARAV, WHERE ENCHANTED EYES . . . .   217 WOODS OF COOLE   11
    DIM INCHY WOOD, THAT HIDES BADGER AND FOX . . . .   218 WOODS OF COOLE   13
    MADE OF DIM GOLD RAVE OUT IN SECRET TOMBS! . . . .   235 SHADOW WATER B   295
    ALL THOSE HAD LIFTED UP THE DIM . . . .   272 GREY ROCK   27
    AND EVEN OLD MEN'S EYES GREW DIM, THIS HAND ALONE, . . 314 FALLEN MAJESTY   2
    BUT THE GOLDEN RACE LOOKS DIM, ...   530 DELPHIC ORACLE   4
    THE SKIES MORE DIM, THOUGH BURNING LIKE A SHIELD, .   656 ISLE STAT I 3   26
    NOURISH THE PANTHERS IN DIM SOLITUDES! . . . . .   657 ISLE STAT I 3   44
    FROM THE DIM WOOD'S FOUNDATION—— . . . .   672 ISLE STAT II 3   162
    TO PLACE A KISS OF FIRE ON THE DIM BROW . . . . .   688 TWO TITANS   47
    NOR HEEDS THE OLD, DIM PROTEST AND THE CRY . . . .   689 NETTLESHIP   14
    AND YON FEW STARS GROWN DIM, LIKE EYES OF LOVERS .   700 MOSADA 3   33
    AND HER DIM WAVE BIDS MAN BE NO MORE GLAD, ...   738 YOU ARE SAD   11
    THAT THE RED RUST MAKES DIM." . . . .   740 EARL PAUL   20
    AND STOOD IN HIS DIM ARMOUR, ...   741 EARL PAUL   33
    THE DIM SPEAR MET THE BRIGHT SPEAR, ...   741 EARL PAUL   45
    THE DIM SPEAR BREAKS THE BRIGHT SHIELD . . . . .   741 EARL PAUL   49
    THE DIM SPEAR MET THE BRIGHT SPEAR . . . .   741 EARL PAUL   V   49
    WITH A CLANG OF HIS DIM MAIL, ...   742 EARL PAUL   66
    I FLING AWAY MY SWORD, BLOOD DIM, ...   743 DANAAN QUICK   20
    MADE OF DIM GOLD, RAVE OUT IN SECRET TOMBS, ...   765 SHADOW WATER A   345
DIMINISHED
    DIMINISHED BEAUTY, MULTIPLIED COMMONPLACE! . . . .   472 ALL SOUL NIGHT V   45
    AND DANGER NOT BE DIMINISHED! . . . .   786 YOUR HEART   31
DIMLY
    YET DIMLY DEEM I THAT THE MORNING RAYS . . . . .   30 OISIN 2   V   20
DIMMED   SEE BLOOD—DIMMED PASSION—DIMMED DREAM—DIMMED
    BY RIVERS WHERE THE RAIN HAS NEVER DIMMED . . . .   184 QUEEN MAEVE   V   87
    BY RIVERS WHERE NOR RAIN NOR HAIL HAS DIMMED . . .   184 QUEEN MAEVE   V   87
    DIMMED AT THREE-QUARTER LIGHT, ...   786 YOUR HEART   32
    DIMMED AT THREE QUARTER LIGHT . . . .   786 YOUR HEART   V   32
DIMNESS
    FILLING THE FIBROUS DIMNESS WITH LONG GENERATIONS OF EYES.   49 OISIN 3   40
    . . . IN THE DIMNESS THEY LOVE GOING BY! . . . . .   53 OISIN 3   98
    . . . THEIR DIMNESS, THEIR DEWS DROPPING SLEEP. . . .   54 OISIN 3   108
    IN SHADOWY DIMNESS. TO BE FAIR AS THEE . . . . .   670 ISLE STAT II 3   106
    IN THE DEEP ALCOVES DIMNESS SMILES AND HIDES. . .   685 DRAWING-ROOM   4
    AND ALL WAS DIMNESS, TILL A DYING LEAF . . . . .   690 MOSADA 1   20
    IN THE DEEP ALCOVE'S DIMNESS SMILES AND HIDES." . .   735 QUATRAIN APHOR   24
    IN THE DEEP ALCOVES DIMNESS SMILES AND HIDES. . .   735 QUATRAIN APHOR V   24
DIMS
    BUT THE LOVE-DEW DIMS OUR EYES TILL THE DAY . . .   28 OISIN 1   424
    LEAPS AND TIME'S OLD LANTHORN DIMS. . . . . . .   777 SONG DEIRDRE 2   5
DIN
    WHILE THE WOOD—PECKER MADE A MERRY DIN, ...   44 OISIN 2   V   228
    THE BLIND HOUND WITH A MOURNFUL DIN . . . .   99 FOXHUNTER   45
    THE OLDEST HOUND WITH MOURNFUL DIN. . . . . . .   99 FOXHUNTER   V   45
    HE'D HEARD THAT DIN ON THE HORIZON'S EDGE . . . .   286 TWO KINGS   V 217A
DINE
    AND I MAY DINE AT JOURNEY'S END . . . .   336 YOUNG BEAUTY   17
    THAT I MAY DINE AT JOURNEY'S END . . . .   336 YOUNG BEAUTY   V   17
DIONYSUS
    WHERE HOLY DIONYSUS DIED, ...   437 SONGS PLAY 1   2
DIP
    SHALL DIP HIS NOSE INTO MY LADLE . . . .   304 HOUR DAWN   53
    TILL IT DIP AN AGEING WING . . . .   777 SONG DEIRDRE 2   3
DIPPED
    LED BY A FOOTSOLE DIPPED IN BLOOD . . . .   274 GREY ROCK   78
    LED BY A FOOT—SOLE DIPPED IN BLOOD . . . .   274 GREY ROCK   V   78
    HAD DIPPED THE WOODEN LADLE DEEP . . . .   304 HOUR DAWN   46
    "BEFORE YOU HAVE DIPPED IT IN THE BEER . . . . .   304 HOUR DAWN   49
    AND WOULD HAVE DIPPED IT IN THE BEER . . . . . .   304 HOUR DAWN   V   47
    HE DIPPED HIS LADLE IN THE TUB . . . .   307 HOUR DAWN   107
    A PATTERN ON A NAPKIN DIPPED IN BLOOD. . . . . .   483 VERONIC NAPKIN   8
DIPPING
    DIPPING HIS NOSE INTO MY LADLE . . . .   304 HOUR DAWN   V   53
DIPS
    WHERE DIPS THE ROCKY HIGHLAND . . . .   86 STOLEN CHILD   1
DIRGE
    OH, HEART! HER DIRGE! WITH RUSHING ARMS THE WAVES . . 665 ISLE STAT II 2   70
    THE DIRGE OF HER YE LOVE. CEASE!——CEASE! . . . .   665 ISLE STAT II 2   74

		PAGE	TITLE	LINE

DIRT
I KNELT IN THE DIRT. . . . . 516 MANS SONG 15
I LAY STRETCHED OUT IN THE DIRT . . . . 628 JANE MOUNTAIN 21

DIRTY
AND DIRTY NAILS OF CARPENTERS. . . . . 440 WISDOM V 7
OR GROPE WITH A DIRTY HAND. . . . . 599 SPIRIT MEDIUM 8
OR GROPE WITH A DIRTY HAND. . . . . 600 SPIRIT MEDIUM 16
OR GROPE WITH A DIRTY HAND. . . . . 600 SPIRIT MEDIUM 24
AS THAT WHICH CLEANS MAN'S DIRTY SLATE. . . . 633 MAN AND ECHO 24

DISAPPEAR
THAT FLESH AND BONE MAY DISAPPEAR, ... 307 HOUR DAWN 101
APPEAR AND DISAPPEAR IN THE BLUE DEPTH OF THE SKY . . . 318 MAGI 3
APPEAR AND DISAPPEAR IN THE BLUE DEPTHS OF THE SKY . . . 318 MAGI V 3

DISASTER
THE HORSES OF DISASTER PLUNGE IN THE HEAVY CLAY. . . . 154 BELOVED PEACE 8
THE HORSES OF DISASTER PLUNGE IN THE DESOLATE CLAY. . . 154 BELOVED PEACE V 8
NO MATTER WHAT DISASTER OCCURRED . . . . . . 578 CRAZED GIRL 9

DISASTROUS
THE ONE DISASTROUS ZODIAC, MUTTERING . . . . 282 TWO KINGS 128

DISCARD
COULD WE BOTH DISCARD . . . . 539 MEETING 16

DISCERNED
SO IT'S PLAIN TO BE DISCERNED . . . . 298 THREE HERMITS 16
YET NO CLEAR FACT TO BE DISCERNED! . . . . . 425 STARES NEST 9

DISCERNING
OR THE DISCERNING EARS, ... 329 MEN IMPROVE 9

DISCIPLINE
THAT ARE OUR SECRET DISCIPLINE . . . . 326 ROBERT GREGORY 68
THE STRANGE REWARD OF ALL THAT DISCIPLINE. . 374 PHASES OF MOON 57
AND VAIN ALL DORIC DISCIPLINE. . . . . 438 SONGS PLAY 2 8
AND VAIN THE DORIC DISCIPLINE. . . . . 438 SONGS PLAY 2 V 8
IN VAIN THE DORIC DISCIPLINE. . . . . 438 SONGS PLAY 2 V 8
WHAT DEATH? WHAT DISCIPLINE? . . . . 784 WOMANS BEAUTY 21

DISCLOSE
AND, STANDING BY THESE CHARACTERS, DISCLOSE . . . 371 EGO DOMINUS 75
HIS "MORNING" AND HIS "NIGHT" DISCLOSE . . . 386 ROBARTES DANCE 33
THE PARCHMENT WILL DISCLOSE TO SOME LEARNED MAN . . . 461 HARUN RASHID 20

DISCOLORATION
EVERY DISCOLORATION OF THE STONE, ... 567 LAPIS LAZULI 43

DISCONTENTED
MY DISCONTENTED HEART TO DRAW CONTENT . . . 334 LIVING BEAUTY 3

DISCORD
AND DISCORD FOLLOW UPON UNISON, ... 265 THESE CLOUDS 5

DISCOURSE
FROM A DISCOURSE IN FIGURATIVE SPEECH . . . 472 ALL SOUL NIGHT 52

DISCOURSES
EVERY COLONUS LAD OR LASS DISCOURSES . . . . 447 COLONUS PRAISE 29

DISCOURTESY
COULD SHARE IN THAT DISCOURTESY OF DEATH. . 325 ROBERT GREGORY 48

DISCOVER
DISCOVER IMPURITIES, CAN SHOW AT LAST . . . 558 RIBH CHRISTIAN 10

DISCOVERED
OF THINGS DISCOVERED IN THE DEEP, ... 138 TO IRELAND 21
DISCOVERED THAT MY THOUGHTS, NOT IT, ... 333 SOLOMON SHEBA 15
ALL THAT YOU HAVE DISCOVERED IN THE GRAVE, . 413 TOWER 107
THE TRUE FAITH DISCOVERED WAS . . . . 440 WISDOM 1

DISCOVERERS
DISCOVERERS OF FORGOTTEN TRUTH . . . . 324 ROBERT GREGORY 6

DISDAINS
A STARLIT OR A MOONLIT DOME DISDAINS . . . . 497 BYZANTIUM 5

DISEASE
IN A BODKIN OR DISEASE, ... 632 MAN AND ECHO 22

DISEMBOWELLED
THE DISEMBOWELLED HORSE. KING EOCHAID RAN . 278 TWO KINGS 45
THE DISEMBOWELLED HORSE. KING EOCHAID GAZED, . . . 278 TWO KINGS V 45

DISFIGURED
THAT DEFILING AND DISFIGURED SHAPE . . . . . 479 SELF AND SOUL 51

DISFIGURING
LIVED AT MY SIDE: THOUGHT TIME'S DISFIGURING TOUCH . . . 466 HARUN RASHID 110
LIVED AT MY SIDE: THAT TIME'S DISFIGURING TOUCH . . . 466 HARUN RASHID V 110

DISGORGING
SEE THE DARKNESS SLOW DISGORGING A VESSEL BLIND WITH
SQUALL. . . . 718 PHANTOM SHIP 12

DISGRACE
AND FOR HIS OPEN-HANDEDNESS, DISGRACE: . . . 292 TO A SHADE 16
HITHER, TO OUR DISGRACE, ... 319 DOLLS 11

DISGUISED
HE, DISGUISED AS A SAILOR BEFORE THE MAST, . 790 DEDICATION 2

DISH
AND SOMEBODY PUTS HIS HAND IN THE DISH . . . 301 RUN PARADISE 5
AND BROUGHT THEM IN A LITTLE COVERED DISH. . 410 TOWER 32

DISHES
SHE CARRIES IN THE DISHES, ... 89 ISLE IN WATER 5

DISHEVELLED
FEW FEATHERS WERE ON THEIR DISHEVELLED WINGS, . . . 34 OISIN 2 76
AND ALL DISHEVELLED WANDERING STARS. . . . . 126 GOES FERGUS 12

DISHONEST
ALL THE DISHONEST CROWD I HAD DRIVEN AWAY, . 352 PEOPLE 24

DISINTER
OR ANY RICH, DARK NOTHING DISINTER . . . . . 565 GYRES 22

		PAGE	TITLE		LINE

DISK
    OF THE ALHAMBRA BLACK ATHWART HIS DISK: • • • • • • • 691 MOSADA 1   V   37
DISLIKE
    ON THOSE WHO DISLIKE THE PLAYBOY • • • • • • • • • • 294 HATED PLAYBOY V   T
DISMAY
    TO DREAM OF WOMEN WHOSE BEAUTY WAS FOLDED IN DISMAY, • • 210 UNDER THE MOON   19
    HEARD THE VOICE OF THEIR DISMAY, • • • • • • • • • • 730 PRIEST FAIRY   74
DISMAYED
    WHY SHOULD I BE DISMAYED • • • • • • • • • • • • • 267 FRIEND ILLNESS   3
DISMISSES
    AND, ALL WORK DONE, DISMISSES ALL • • • • • • • • • 633 MAN AND ECHO   34
DISOWNS
    MY BETTER SELF DISOWNS, • • • • • • • • • • • • • 533 FIRST CONFESS   9
DISPART
    I SEE WITHIN A CLOVEN ROCK DISPART • • • • • • • • 673 ISLE STAT II 3   195
DISPENSING
    AND HAVE NO BUSINESS BUT DISPENSING ROUND • • • • • 404 FOR DAUGHTER   43
DISPLAY
    WITH FLOPPING AND WITH FLAPPING IT MADE A GREAT DISPLAY, 593 PILGRIM   18
    WITH THEIR FLOPPING AND THEIR FLAPPING IT MADE A GREAT   593 PILGRIM   V   18
        DISPLAY
    ALL THEIR JEALOUSY DISPLAY, • • • • • • • • • • • 726 LOVERS QUARREL   22
DISPLAYED
    NO VANITY'S DISPLAYED: • • • • • • • • • • • • • 532 BEFORE WORLD   6
DISPLAYS
    OR ELSE ALL JUNO FROM AN URN DISPLAYS • • • • • • 418 ANCEST HOUSES   27
DISPLEASE
    MY MEN, WHETHER IT PLEASE HER OR DISPLEASE, • • • • 281 TWO KINGS   112
DISPORTED
    AND HAD DISPORTED IN THE STILLY JET, • • • • • • • 31 OISIN 2   39
    AND HAD DISPORTED IN THE EYES STILL JET • • • • • • 31 OISIN 2   V   39
DISSEMBLING
    NOTHING BUT DISSEMBLING, • • • • • • • • • • • • 532 FIRST CONFESS   5
DISSIPATION
    BUT DISSIPATION AND DESPAIR? AND YET • • • • • • • 369 EGO DOMINUS   51
DISSOLVE
    I WILL DISSOLVE AWAY THE FAERIES' GUILE: • • • • • 677 ISLE STAT II 3   282
DISTAFF
    FROM THE DISTAFF OF THE MOON. • • • • • • • • • • 743 WISDOM DREAMS   4
DISTAINS
    A STARLIGHT OR A MOONLIT DOME DISTAINS • • • • • • 497 BYZANTIUM   V   5
DISTANCE
    • • • FROM THE FOAM-PALE DISTANCE BROKE: • • • • • • 47 OISIN 3   3
    • • • FROM THE DISTANCE BROKE: • • • • • • • • • • 47 OISIN 3   V   3
    AND THE HORSE WAS GONE IN THE DISTANCE, • • • • • • 52 OISIN 3   75
    I AWOKE: THE STRANGE HORSE WITHOUT SUMMONS OUT OF   54 OISIN 3   105
        THE DISTANCE RAN,
    FORTH, PIERCING THE DISTANCE— • • • • • • • • • • 54 OISIN 3   V 112
DISTANT
    AND MADE IN ALL THEIR DISTANT PARTS, • • • • • • • 16 OISIN 1   228
    AND ROSE FROM ALL THEIR DISTANT PARTS, • • • • • • 16 OISIN 1   V 228
    THAT WAS MOST DISTANT FROM THE DOOR: GREEN SLIME • 37 OISIN 2   113
    MOST DISTANT STRODE WE. ON THE FLOOR LAY SLIME, • • 37 OISIN 2   V 113
    SURLY AND DISTANT, MIXED INSEPARABLY • • • • • • • 45 OISIN 2   233
    SURLY AND DISTANT, WITH THE WINDS AND SEA:— • • • • 45 OISIN 2   V 234
    I SAW FROM A DISTANT SADDLE: FROM THE EARTH SHE MADE HER 56 OISIN 3   130
        MOAN:
    THE WAILING GREW DISTANT: I RODE BY THE WOODS OF   56 OISIN 3   137
        THE WRINKLING BARK,
    HAS MARKED A DISTANT OBJECT DOWN, • • • • • • • • 337 TOM OROUGHLEY   3
    WERE DISTANT STILL. AN OLD MAN COCKED HIS EAR. • • 372 PHASES OF MOON   7
    WERE DISTANT. AN OLD MAN COCKED HIS EAR. • • • • • 372 PHASES OF MOON V   7
    TO A DISTANT POST: • • • • • • • • • • • • • • • 617 LONG-LEG FLY   4
    WHAT GREAT TOMB-HAUNTER SWEEPS THE DISTANT SKY • • 618 BRONZE HEAD   4
DISTINGUISH
    WHO CAN DISTINGUISH DARKNESS FROM THE SOUL? • • • • 477 SELF AND SOUL   8
DISTINGUISHED
    WITH THE OLD KINDNESS, THE OLD DISTINGUISHED GRACE, • • 362 HER COURTESY   1
DISTORTING
    OF DISTORTING DAYS • • • • • • • • • • • • • • • 504 QUARREL IN AGE   13
DISTRACTED
    BY HER DISTRACTED AIR • • • • • • • • • • • • • 453 DEATH OF HARE   8
    DISTRACTED GENTLENESS THAT CANNOT HIDE • • • • • • 601 GALLERY REVIS V   6
DISTRACTION
    DISTRACTION • • • • • • • • • • • • • • • • • 267 ALL TEMPT ME   V   T
DISTRACTS
    AND ITS CRY DISTRACTS MY THOUGHT. • • • • • • • • 633 MAN AND ECHO   46
    AND ITS CRY DISTRACTS MY THOUGHTS. • • • • • • • 633 MAN AND ECHO   V 46
DISTRAUGHT   SEE GRIEF-DISTRAUGHT
    BEAUTY TO MAKE A STRANGER'S EYE DISTRAUGHT, • • • • 403 FOR DAUGHTER   18
    WITH LOOSENED HAIR OR FOREHEADS GRIEF DISTRAUGHT, • • 537 HER VISION   V   18
DISTRESS
    BUT NIAMH WITH A SWIFT DISTRESS • • • • • • • • 15 OISIN 1   211
    BUT NIAM, WITH A SAD DISTRESS, • • • • • • • • • 15 OISIN 1   V 211
    BUT LITTLE NEED THE GRAVE DISTRESS. • • • • • • • 338 TOM OROUGHLEY   10
    AND LITTLE NEED THE GRAVE DISTRESS. • • • • • • • 338 TOM OROUGHLEY V 10
    FROM VAGUE DISTRESS • • • • • • • • • • • • • 390 IMAGE PAST   24
    THE IGNOMINY OF BOYHOOD: THE DISTRESS • • • • • • 478 SELF AND SOUL   45
DISTRUSTFUL
    DISTRUSTFUL OF THAT POPULAR EYE • • • • • • • • • 624 APPARITIONS   5

		PAGE	TITLE	LINE
DISTURB				
CAN DISTURB GLOBE-TROTTING MADAM • • • • • • •		638	BEN BULBEN	48
DISTURBED				
AND FEARING THAT MY LIGHT DISTURBED HER SLEEP • • • • •		467	HARUN RASHID	130
DISTURBS				
NOR KNOW THAT WHAT DISTURBS OUR BLOOD • • • • • •		434	WHEEL	7
NOR STORM DISTURBS, FLAMES BEGOTTEN OF FLAME, • • • • •		498	BYZANTIUM	27
DITCH				
DRINKING THE FOUL DITCH WHERE THEY LIE? • • • • • • •		397	POLIT PRISONER	12
INTO THE FROG-SPAWN OF A BLIND MAN'S DITCH, • • • • •		479	SELF AND SOUL	59
OR INTO THAT MOST FECUND DITCH OF ALL, • • • • • •		479	SELF AND SOUL	61
ENGENDER IN THE DITCH, • • • • • • • • • • •		598	STONE CROSS	10
DITCHES				
WHAT MATTER IF THE DITCHES ARE IMPURE? • • • • • •		478	SELF AND SOUL	42
DIVE				
THE LONG-LEGGED MOOR-HENS DIVE, • • • • • • • • •		393	EASTER 1916	53
WHERE LONG-LEGGED MOOR-HENS DIVE. • • • • • • • •		393	EASTER 1916 V	53
DIVER				
THERE! THERE THEY COME! GULL, GANNET, OR DIVER, • • • •		233	SHADOW WATER B	244
DIVIDED				
• • • HOW, WHEN DIVIDED THE GIRTH, • • • • • • • •		60	OISIN 3	189
DIVIDES				
THE NOISY WORLD DIVIDES. HOW SOON A DEED • • • • •		700	MOSADA 3	34
DIVINE				
IN HIS DIVINE HOMESTEAD, • • • • • • • • • • •		113	ROSE OF PEACE	6
REMEMBERING THAT SHE TOO HAD SEEMED DIVINE • • • • • •		182	QUEEN MAEVE	64
A SERVING-MAN, THAT COULD DIVINE • • • • • • • •		410	TOWER	28
A SERVING MAN THAT COULD DIVINE • • • • • • • • •		410	TOWER V	28
DIVINITY				
WILD WITH DIVINITY, • • • • • • • • • • • • •		472	ALL SOUL NIGHT	36
DIVISION				
DEATH, DESPAIR, DIVISION OF FAMILIES, • • •		459	FROM OEDIPUS	5
HER SOUL IN DIVISION FROM ITSELF • • • • • • • • •		578	CRAZED GIRL	3
DIVISIONS				
LOVE CRAM LOVE'S TWO DIVISIONS • • • • • • • • • •		573	LADYS 2ND SONG	12
DIZZY				
AND NOW I AM DIZZY WITH THE THOUGHT • • • • • • •		7	OISIN 1	65
AND MOUNTS MORE DIZZY HIGH THE MORE IT RAINS • • • • •		417	ANCEST HOUSES	5
DIZZY WITH HARMONIOUS SOUND, • • • • • • • • •		446	COLONUS PRAISE	7
HALF DIZZY WITH THE LIGHTNING THERE RUNS A GATHERING BAND--		718	PHANTOM SHIP	9
NOW HALF DIZZY WITH THE LIGHTNING THERE RUNS A GATHERING BAND!		718	PHANTOM SHIP V	9
THAT DIZZY DREAMS CAN SPRING • • • • • • • • • •		781	MY HEART BEAT	7
DJIN				
I SAY THAT A DJIN SPOKE. A LIVE LONG HOUR • • • •		467	HARUN RASHID V	136
DJINN				
OR WAS IT SHE THAT SPOKE OR SOME GREAT DJINN? • • • •		467	HARUN RASHID	135
I SAY THAT A DJINN SPOKE. A LIVELONG HOUR • • • • •		467	HARUN RASHID	136
DJINNS				
MURMURED THE WISDOM OF THE DESERT DJINNS, • • • • • •		468	HARUN RASHID	163
HAS MURMURED WISDOM OF THE DESERT DJINNS, • • • • • •		468	HARUN RASHID V	163
DJINS				
HAS SPOKEN THE WISDOM OF THE DESERT DJINS, • • • • •		468	HARUN RASHID V	163
DOCK-LFAVES				
UNDER THE DOCK-LEAVES IN THE GROUND, • • • • • • •		176	BELOVED DEAD	12
DOCTOR				
THE FAIRY DOCTOR. • • • • • • • • • • • • •		716	FAIRY DOCTOR	T
THE FAIRY DOCTOR COMES OUR WAY • • • • • • • • •		716	FAIRY DOCTOR	1
DOE				
THE WILD STAG AND THE DOE: THAT MOUTH TO MOUTH • • • •		465	HARUN RASHID	101
ROE COULD RUN OR DOE COULD LEAP • • • • • • • • •		522	LULLABY	10
ROE COULD LEAP OR DOE COULD RUN! • • • • • • • •		522	LULLABY	12
IN TROUBLE IS, THE DOE WILL LINGER NEAR. • • • • • •		713	FERENCZ RENYI	80
THE CALLING AFAR OF THE DOE AND THE DEER. • • • • •		717	LOVE SONG	5
DOER SEE DEED-DOER				
DOERS SEE DEED-DOERS				
DOG				
BUT WAS THERE EVER DOG THAT PRAISED HIS FLEAS? • • • •		262	TO A POET	4
BUT WHERE'S THE WILD DOG THAT HAS PRAISED HIS FLEAS? • •		262	TO A POET V	4
BUT HAVE YOU KNOWN A DOG TO PRAISE HIS FLEAS? • • • •		262	TO A POET V	4
AND THOUGH HE KEEP A DOG AND A GUN, • • • • • • •		301	RUN PARADISE	12
BECAUSE THE PRIEST MUST HAVE LIKE EVERY DOG HIS DAY • • •		364	DOLLS FACES	10
A DOG MUST HAVE HIS DAY, • • • • • • • • • • •		582	ROGER CASEMENT V	18
A DOG MUST HAVE HIS DAY, • • • • • • • • • • •		583	GHOST ROG CASE	12
QUIET THE DOG, TETHER THE PONY • • • • • • • • •		617	LONG-LEG FLY	3
DOG'S				
AS TO A DOG'S TAIL? NEVER HAD I MORE • • • • • • •		409	TOWER	4
AS UPON A DOG'S TAIL. NEVER HAD I MORE • • • • • •		409	TOWER V	4
WHEN HE FINISHED HIS DOG'S DAY! • • • • • • • • •		412	TOWER	79
DOGS				
WAS THAT, THE AIR BEING HEAVY AND THE DOGS • • • • •		182	QUEEN MAEVE	53
ARE BUT A POST THE PASSING DOGS DEFILE. • • • • • •		321	REED WHISPERER	14
"DROWN ALL THE DOGS," SAID THE FIERCE YOUNG WOMAN, • • •		546	TO SAME TUNE 2	7
DROWN ALL THE DOGS," SAID THE FIERCE YOUNG WOMAN. • • •		546	TO SAME TUNE 2	10
"DROWN ALL THE DOGS," SAID THE FIERCE YOUNG WOMAN, • • •		546	TO SAME TUNE 2	17
DROWN ALL THE DOGS," SAID THE FIERCE YOUNG WOMAN. • • •		546	TO SAME TUNE 2	20
"DROWN ALL THE DOGS," SAID THE FIERCE YOUNG WOMAN. • • •		547	TO SAME TUNE 2	27
DROWN ALL THE DOGS," SAID THE FIERCE YOUNG WOMAN. • • •		547	TO SAME TUNE 2	30
BUT NO DOGS BARKED, AND MIDNIGHTS CHIMED, • • • • • •		570	THREE BUSHES	29
AND NO DOGS BARKED THROUGH MIDNIGHTS CHIMED • • • • •		570	THREE BUSHES V	29
(FOR SINCE THE HORIZON'S BOUGHT STRANGE DOGS ARE STILL)		579	DOR WELLESLEY	7

PAGE   TITLE   LINE

DOGS (CONTINUED)
    AMONG THE DOGS AND HORSES THAT UNDERSTAND MY TALK. • • •   581 CURSE CROMWELL   30
    BUT CHILDREN AND DOGS ON THE FLOOR. • • • • • • • •   780 WELL AND TREE   14
DOING
    AS I AM DOING NOW. WHY DO YOU WEEP? • • • • • • •   246 SHADOW WATER B   495
    AS IF IT WERE NOT WORTH THE DOING. • • • • • • •   306 HOUR DAWN   84
DOLL
    A DOLL IN THE DOLL-MAKER'S HOUSE • • • • • • • • •   319 DOLLS   1
    A NEW MODELLED DOLL, OR DRAWING, • • • • • • • • •   362 DOLLS DRAWINGS   2
    NOW THY GREAT WHITE DOLL TO HOLD-- • • • • • • • •   726 LOVERS QUARREL   15
DOLL-MAKER'S
    A DOLL IN THE DOLL-MAKER'S HOUSE • • • • • • • • •   319 DOLLS   1
    THE DOLL-MAKER'S WIFE IS AWARE • • • • • • • • •   319 DOLLS   14
DOLLS
    THE DOLLS • • • • • • • • • • • • • • • •   319 DOLLS   T
    BUT THE OLDEST OF ALL THE DOLLS, • • • • • • •   319 DOLLS   4
    CERTAIN ARTISTS BRING HER DOLLS AND DRAWINGS • • • •   362 DOLLS DRAWINGS   T
    WE AND OUR DOLLS BEING BUT THE WORLD WERE BEST AWAY. • •   364 DOLLS FACES   12
DOLLS'
    SHE TURNS THE DOLLS' FACES TO THE WALL • • • • • • •   363 DOLLS FACES   T
DOLOROUS
    THE HARP AWAY. A DOLOROUS POOL • • • • • • • •   17 OISIN 1   V   240
    UNTO THE DOLOROUS BORDER OF THE FAIRY LAKE. • • • •   655 ISLE STAT I 2   85
    WE SAW THE DOLOROUS LAKE; AND THEN THY NAME • • • •   659 ISLE STAT II 1   7
DOLPHIN
    PAINTINGS OF THE DOLPHIN DRAWN; • • • • • • • •   309 REALISTS   V   4
DOLPHIN-DRAWN
    PAINTINGS OF THE DOLPHIN-DRAWN • • • • • • • •   309 REALISTS   4
DOLPHIN'S
    ASTRADDLE ON THE DOLPHIN'S MIRE AND BLOOD, • • • •   498 BYZANTIUM   33
    A STRADDLE ON THE DOLPHIN'S MIRE AND BLOOD • • • •   498 BYZANTIUM   V   33
    STRADDLING EACH A DOLPHIN'S BACK • • • • • • • •   612 NEWS ORACLE   13
DOLPHINS
    AND THE BRUTE DOLPHINS PLUNGE • • • • • • • •   612 NEWS ORACLE   20
DOLPHIN-TORN
    THAT DOLPHIN-TORN, THAT GONG-TORMENTED SEA. • • • •   498 BYZANTIUM   40
DOLT
    NOR KNAVE NOR DOLT CAN BREAK • • • • • • • •   259 UNWORTH PRAISE   2
    FROM SELF-SAME DOLT AND KNAVE; • • • • • • • •   260 UNWORTH PRAISE   17
    ON THE DAY'S WAR WITH EVERY KNAVE AND DOLT, • • • •   260 FASC DIFFICULT   10
    WHAT HURRIES OUT THE KNAVE AND DOLT? • • • • • •   625 NATIVITY   9
DOME
    A DOME MADE OUT OF ENDLESS CARVEN JAGS, • • • •   38 OISIN 2   144
    I WAITED HOUR BY HOUR, AND THE HIGH DOME, • • • •   39 OISIN 2   147
    LIFTED THE DOME, WHERE FACE IN CARVEN FACE • • • •   39 OISIN 2   V   145
    HOUR AFTER HOUR I WAITED, AND THE DOME • • • • •   39 OISIN 2   V   147
    A STARLIT OR A MOONLIT DOME DISDAINS • • • • •   497 BYZANTIUM   5
    A STARLIGHT OR A MOONLIT DOME DISTAINS • • • • •   497 BYZANTIUM   V   5
DOMINATE
    TO ENGROSS THE PRESENT AND DOMINATE MEMORY. • • • •   630 CIRCUS ANIMALS   30
DOMINION
    YOU MOVE IN ANOTHER DOMINION • • • • • • • • •   707 FAIRY PEDANT   5
DOMINIONS
    I RULED O'ER ALL MY FAIR DOMINIONS, • • • • • •   82 MAD KING GOLL V   7
DOMINO
    HER DOMINO, HER PANNIERED SKIRT COPIED FROM LONGHI; • •   363 DOLLS FACES   7
DOMINUS
    EGO DOMINUS TUUS • • • • • • • • • • • •   367 EGO DOMINUS   T
DON
    OF HILL TWO SHEPHERDS COME. FAREWELL! I'LL DON • • • •   659 ISLE STAT II 1   28
DONE   SEE HALF-DONE
    YOUR MORTAL SHORES TILL TIME IS DONE!" • • • • • •   6 OISIN 1   V   59
    AND, NOW OUR WANDERING HOURS WERE DONE, • • • • • •   14 OISIN 1   177
    SUNG OF THE BIRDS. OUR TOIL WAS DONE! • • • • •   14 OISIN 1   V   177
    WHEN THE STARS ARE TO WANE AND THE WORLD BE DONE. • • •   16 OISIN 1   220
    BEFORE THE SWIFT THINGS THAT SHE DREAMED OF WERE DONE • •   27 OISIN 1   414
    ERE HALF THE SWIFT THINGS THAT SHE DREAMT ON WERE DONE, •   28 OISIN 1   V   422
    MAY SLEEP IN THE END WITH THE WHOLE OF HIS FATE DONE, • •   28 OISIN 1   V 423F
    THINGS DONE ERE GOD FIRST WAS OR MY OLD LINE BEGAN; • • •   29 OISIN 2   V   8
    ALL IS DONE NOW--I SEE THE RAVENS FLOCK-- • • • •   43 OISIN 2   V   212
    I SANG HOW, WHEN DAY'S TOIL IS DONE, • • • • • •   85 MAD KING GOLL   61
    FOR MY REMEMBERING HOUR IS DONE! • • • • • • •   86 MAD KING GOLL V   69
    AND PIERCED HIM. "SPEAK BEFORE YOUR BREATH IS DONE." • •   110 CUCHULAIN SEA   67
    TURN IF YOU MAY FROM BATTLES NEVER DONE. • • • •   114 ROSE OF BATTLE   7
    AND PLUCK TILL TIME AND TIMES ARE DONE • • • • •   150 WANDER AENGUS   22
    WHEN ALL THIS HEAVY HISTORY'S DONE; • • • • • •   213 BLESS PSALTER   17
    OR WAVE TO DROWN. BUT I HAVE DONE WITH WORDS, • • •   238 SHADOW WATER B   348
    I HAVE DONE RIGHT. WHAT COULD I BUT OBEY? • • • •   243 SHADOW WATER B   443
    BUT I HAVE DONE SO GREAT A WRONG AGAINST YOU, • • •   245 SHADOW WATER B   483
    WHAT I HAVE DONE, OR WHAT WOULD DO • • • • • •   256 WORDS   3
    REMEMBERING THAT THE BEST I HAVE DONE • • • • •   256 WORDS   7
    WAS DONE TO MAKE IT PLAIN! • • • • • • • •   256 WORDS   8
    THAT HAD SHE DONE SO WHO CAN SAY • • • • • •   256 WORDS   13
    WHY, WHAT COULD SHE HAVE DONE, BEING WHAT SHE IS? • • •   257 NO SECOND TROY   11
    THE WEAK LAY HAND ON WHAT THE STRONG HAS DONE, • • •   265 THESE CLOUDS   3
    AND WHEN FOR ALL I'D DONE OR SAID-- • • • • •   275 GREY ROCK   99
    AND EVIL MUST IT BE, IF DONE 'TWERE WORSE • • • •   281 TWO KINGS   105
    AND ALL HE DID DONE PERFECTLY • • • • • • • •   327 ROBERT GREGORY   79
    REMEMBERING KINDNESS DONE, AND HOW CAN I, • • • •   340 SHEP GOATHERD   30
    AND TILL THAT'S DONE CAN NEITHER WORK NOR WAIT. • • • •   340 SHEP GOATHERD   45
    AND WHEN 'TWAS DONE SO LITTLE HAD I DONE • • • •   341 SHEP GOATHERD   59

211

DONE   (CONTINUED)
  AND WHEN 'TWAS DONE SO LITTLE HAD I DONE . . . . . .   341 SHEP GOATHERD   59
  "FOR ALL THAT I HAVE DONE AT MY OWN CHARGE? . . . . .   351 PEOPLE   2
  I MOURN FOR THAT MOST LONELY THING: AND YET GOD'S WILL 354 HIS PHOENIX   31
    BE DONE:
  A YOUNG MAN WHEN THE OLD MEN ARE DONE TALKING . . . .   356 BROKEN DREAMS   16
  THOUGH PLAY IS BUT HALF DONE-- . . . .   364 END OF DAY   7
  AND THOUGHT BEFORE I HAD DONE . . . .   392 EASTER 1916   9
  HE HAD DONE MOST BITTER WRONG . . . .   393 EASTER 1916   33
  FOR ALL THAT IS DONE AND SAID. . . . .   394 EASTER 1916   69
  FOR ALL SHE HAD DONE AND SAID. . . . .   394 EASTER 1916   V   69
  AND NOT A THING IS DONE, ...   451 FIRST LOVE   10
  TOLD ALL THAT HAD BEEN SAID OR DONE . . . .   456 SUMMER SPRING   3
  THAT QUARTER WHERE ALL THOUGHT IS DONE: . . . . .   477 SELF AND SOUL   7
  WE THAT HAVE DONE AND THOUGHT, ...   484 SPILT MILK   1
  THAT HAVE THOUGHT AND DONE, ...   484 SPILT MILK   2
  THINGS SAID OR DONE LONG YEARS AGO, ...   501 VACILLATION   51
  NOTHING SAID OR DONE CAN REACH . . . .   506 REMORSE SPEECH   9
  SOME STUPID THING THAT I HAD DONE . . . .   507 STREAM AND SUN   4
  ALL WRONGS DONE. . . . .   518 HIS CONFIDENCE   4
  WHEN, THE POTION'S WORK BEING DONE, ...   522 LULLABY   9
  THAT IF NOTHING DRASTIC IS DONE . . . .   565 LAPIS LAZULI   5
  THAT IF NOTHING DRASTIC CAN BE DONE . . . .   565 LAPIS LAZULI   V   5
  "THE WORK IS DONE," GROWN OLD HE THOUGHT, ...   577 WHAT THEN   16
  TO JUDGE WHAT I HAVE DONE. . . . .   604 YOU CONTENT   4
  ALL THAT I HAVE SAID AND DONE, ...   632 MAN AND ECHO   6
  AND, ALL WORK DONE, DISMISSES ALL . . . .   633 MAN AND ECHO   34
  ALL MUST TOGETHER DO." THAT DONE, THE MAN . . . . .   634 CUCHULAIN COMF   17
  THOUGH ALL WAS DONE IN COMMON AS BEFORE: . . . . .   635 CUCHULAIN COMF   24
  AND OUR LAUGHTER OVER AND DONE: . . . .   643 SONG FAERIES   6
  OF FLIGHT ARE DONE. MOST FAIR OF ALL WHO GRAZE . . .   649 ISLE STAT I 1   118
  HAVE DONE THIS PHRASING, AND SAY WHY, IN SOOTH, . .   652 ISLE STAT I 2   25
  TILL HIS LAST WRETCHEDNESS WAS O'ER AND DONE." . .   664 ISLE STAT II 2   54
  AND SHALL BE DONE, IF YOU WILL DEIGN TO KISS . . .   669 ISLE STAT II 3   79
  AND OUR LAUGHTER OVER AND DONE: . . . .   676 ISLE STAT II 3   253
  BUT NOW MY WANDERING SHALL BE DONE, I KNOW. . . .   682 SEEKER   21
  BUT SOON MY WANDERING SHALL BE DONE I KNOW. . . .   682 SEEKER   V   21
  MY BIDDING. NOW 'TIS DONE, AND I AM GLAD . . . .   700 MOSADA 3   29
  YOU HAVE DONE WELL, BECAUSE MY BOWS ARE TURNED . . .   755 SHADOW WATER A   164
DONNE
  WITH LANDOR AND WITH DONNE. . . . .   336 YOUNG BEAUTY   18
DOODLE   SEE COCK-A-DOODLE-DOODLE-DO
DOOM
  "GOD ONLY SEES WHAT DOOM FOR ME LIES STORED." . . .   110 CUCHULAIN SEA V   62
  THE BREAD AND THE WINE HAD A DOOM, ...   144 HOST OF AIR   25
  OF THE ROSE IN ITS DOOM. . . . .   175 ELEMENT POWERS V   12
  HEAVEN HAS PUT AWAY THE STROKE OF HER DOOM, ...   356 BROKEN DREAMS   11
  THAT DIETH SLOW WITH SUNSICK DOOM. . . . .   655 ISLE STAT I 3   12
DOOMED
  A STORMY SUNSET ON DOOMED SHIPS: . . . .   3 OISIN 1   23
  A STORMY SUNSET O'ER DOOMED SHIPS. . . . .   3 OISIN 1   V   23
  DOOMED LIKE ODYSSEUS AND THE LABOURING SHIPS . . .   120 SORROW OF LOVE   7
  HOW THEY WHO SEEK ARE EVER DOOMED TO FAIL. . . . .   653 ISLE STAT I 2   41
DOOMS
  "THE DOOMS OF MEN ARE IN GOD'S HIDDEN PLACE." . . .   110 CUCHULAIN SEA   62
  "THE DOOMS OF MEN ARE IN GOD'S HIDDEN HOARD." . . .   110 CUCHULAIN SEA V   62
DOONEY
  THE FIDDLER OF DOONEY . . . .   178 FIDDLER DOONEY   T
  WHEN I PLAY ON MY FIDDLE IN DOONEY, ...   178 FIDDLER DOONEY   1
  WITH "HERE IS THE FIDDLER OF DOONEY!" . . . . . .   179 FIDDLER DOONEY   19
DOOR
  BURST FROM A GREAT DOOR MARRED BY MANY A BLOW . . .   31 OISIN 2   29
  AND THEN WE CLIMBED THE STAIR TO A HIGH DOOR: . . .   36 OISIN 2   101
  AND UP THE STAIR WE TOILED TO A HIGH DOOR, ...   36 OISIN 2   V 101
  THAT WAS MOST DISTANT FROM THE DOOR: GREEN SLIME . .   37 OISIN 2   113
  BURIED AND MIGHTY, WHEN THROUGH THE GREAT DOOR . . .   39 OISIN 2   151
  AND FOUND A DOOR DEEP SUNKEN IN THE WALL, ...   39 OISIN 2   154
  I FOUND A DOOR DEEP-SUNKEN IN THE WALL, ...   39 OISIN 2   V 154
  THE LEAST OF DOORS: BEYOND THE DOOR A PLAIN, . . .   39 OISIN 2   155
  I SAW HER STANDING IN HER DOOR BUT NOW. . . . .   74 ANASHU VIJAYA   64
  HE DROVE ME OUT AND SHUT THE DOOR, ...   95 MOLL MAGEE   25
  HE DROVE ME FORTH AND SHUT THE DOOR, ...   95 MOLL MAGEE   V   25
  WHEN, OPENIN' WIDE HIS DOOR, ...   96 MOLL MAGEE   50
  THEN TO HER SERVANTS: "BEAT HIM FROM THE DOOR . . .   106 CUCHULAIN SEA V 17A
  AND DRIVE HIM FROM THE DOOR." AND THUS IT WAS: . .   106 CUCHULAIN SEA V 17B
  THE SICK MAN'S WIFE OPENED THE DOOR: . . . . . .   133 FR GILLIGAN   31
  AND HE RAN TO THE DOOR OF HIS HOUSE: . . . . . .   145 HOST OF AIR   V 40C
  IT SANG TO HER THROUGH THE DOOR. . . . .   160 CAP AND BELLS   16
  SHE OPENED HER DOOR AND HER WINDOW, ...   160 CAP AND BELLS   29
  MASTER OF THE STILL STARS AND OF THE FLAMING DOOR. .   161 BLACK PIG   8
  WHEN THE FLAMING LUTE-THRONGED ANGELIC DOOR IS WIDE: 172 TRAV PASSION   1
  HAD PACED FROM DOOR TO FIRE AND FIRE TO DOOR. . . .   180 QUEEN MAEVE   17
  HAD PACED FROM DOOR TO FIRE AND FIRE TO DOOR. . . .   180 QUEEN MAEVE   17
  ABOUT MY DOOR TO COUNSEL AND TO HELP." . . . . .   183 QUEEN MAEVE   V   82
  THE BRAZEN PILLARS OF HIS DOOR, ...   192 BAILE AILLINN   74
  OR THE DOOR PILLARS OF ONE HOUSE, ...   195 BAILE AILLINN V 152
  BECAUSE OF THAT OLD DRAUGHT UNDER THE DOOR. . . .   228 SHADOW WATER B   127
  OF THE GREAT DOOR: BUT THOUGH THE HANGING LAMPS . .   279 TWO KINGS   49
  NOR DOOR, NOR MOUTH, NOR SLIPPER MADE A NOISE, . .   279 TWO KINGS   51
  IN THE HALF LIGHT, AND RUNS TO ITS OWN DOOR . . .   279 TWO KINGS   V 45C
  ROSE ROUND THE WALLS, AND THROUGH THE BRONZE-RINGED DOOR 286 TWO KINGS   215

212

DOOR   (CONTINUED)
"THOUGH THE DOOR OF DEATH IS NEAR • • • • • • • • • •   298 THREE HERMITS   8
AND WHAT WAITS BEHIND THE DOOR, • • • • • • • • •   298 THREE HERMITS   9
PASS THE DOOR OF BIRTH AGAIN, • • • • • • • • • • •   298 THREE HERMITS   19
AND HIS OWN FLOCK WAS BROWSING AT THE DOOR. • • • • •   340 SHEP GOATHERD   27
BUT PUT NO NAME AND LEAVE THEM AT HER DOOR. • • • •   343 SHEP GOATHERD   116
THEY STOOD IN THE DOOR AND STOOD BETWEEN • • • • • •   358 PRESENCES   9
WHO KNOW IT ALL RING AT HIS DOOR, AND SPEAK • • • • •   373 PHASES OF MOON   21
BESIDE THE CASTLE DOOR, WHERE ALL IS STARK • • • • •   377 PHASES OF MOON   126
OR, THE HOUSE DOOR LEFT UNSHUT, • • • • • • • • •   380 SONGS FOOL 1   10
AND WHETHER THE DOOR WERE SHUT. • • • • • • •   381 SONGS FOOL 2   5
WHO TROD UPON THESE ROCKS OR PASSED THIS DOOR, • • • •   413 TOWER   98
KNOWING THAT NONE COULD PASS HEAVEN'S DOOR • • • • •   422 MY TABLE   26
KNOWING THAT NONE WHO PASS HEAVEN'S DOOR • • • • •   422 MY TABLE   V 26
KNOWING THAT NONE CAN PASS HEAVEN'S DOOR • • • • •   422 MY TABLE   V 26
THE ROAD AT MY DOOR • • • • • • • • •   423 ROAD AT DOOR   T
STAND AT MY DOOR, AND I COMPLAIN • • • • • • • •   424 ROAD AT DOOR   8
I TURN AWAY AND SHUT THE DOOR, AND ON THE STAIR • •   427 PHANTOM HATRED   33
CAN LEAVE THE MOTHER, MURDERED AT HER DOOR, • • • •   429 NINETEEN 19   27
THE MORE I LEAVE THE DOOR UNLATCHED • • • • • •   511 JANE AND JACK   3
FROM DOOR TO TOP! • • • • • • • • • • • •   512 JANE ON GOD   17
TO-MORROW NIGHT I WILL BREAK DOWN THE DOOR. • • •   551 SONGS REWRIT 1   6
TO-MORROW NIGHT I WILL BREAK DOWN THE DOOR. • • •   551 SONGS REWRIT 1   12
TO-MORROW NIGHT I WILL BREAK DOWN THE DOOR. • • •   551 SONGS REWRIT 1   18
TO-MORROW NIGHT I WILL BREAK IN THE DOOR. • • • •   551 SONGS REWRIT 1 V REF
TOMORROW NIGHT I WILL BREAK DOWN THE DOOR. • • •   551 SONGS REWRIT 1 V REF
I HAD THOUGHT TO HAVE CALLED HER OUT TO THE DOOR, • •   551 SONGS REWRIT 1 V 15
ARE THE MOB THAT HOWLS AT THE DOOR! • • • • • •   554 CHURCH STATE   10
IS BEATING ON THE DOOR. • • • • • • • • • • •   583 GHOST ROG CASE   10
IS BEATING ON THE DOOR. • • • • • • • • • • •   583 GHOST ROG CASE   20
IS BEATING ON THE DOOR. • • • • • • • • • • •   584 GHOST ROG CASE   30
IS BEATING ON THE DOOR. • • • • • • • • • • •   584 GHOST ROG CASE   40
THE DOOR ABOVE HIS HEAD • • • • • • • • • • •   585 ORAHILLY   33
THE COLONEL KNOCKED ON THE RICH MAN'S DOOR, • • • •   595 COLONEL MARTIN   28
THE COLONEL KNOCKED ON A RICH MAN'S DOOR. • • • • •   595 COLONEL MARTIN V 28
SHUT THE DOOR OF THE POPE'S CHAPEL, • • • • • •   618 LONG-LEG FLY   23
AND FIND OUR ANCIENT HOUNDS BEFORE THE DOOR, • • •   622 HOUND VOICE   16
UNTO HER DOOR! FOR THIS, WHERE NOD THE LONG • • •   660 ISLE STAT II 1   43
BY THE DOOR OF MARY'S GARDEN • • • • • • • • •   680 LOVE AND DEATH   31
TENDING THE ROSES ROUND HIS LATTICE DOOR. • • • •   692 MOSADA 1   53
UNDER A LEMON TREE BESIDE YOUR DOOR: • • • • • •   693 MOSADA 1   68
BY THE DOOR OF PETER'S GATE, • • • • • • • • •   696 MOSADA 2   23
BESIDE THE DOOR OF PETER'S GATE. • • • • • • •   696 MOSADA 2   V 23
THY SACRED DOOR!" BUT PETER CRIED, • • • • • •   697 MOSADA 2   25
OF DREAMING AND OF WATCHING BY THE DOOR • • • • •   700 MOSADA 3   26
AND HURRIED TO THE GUARD-HOUSE DOOR. • • • • • •   725 LEGEND   16
"SAY AND THRICE ANIGH THY DOOR • • • • • • • •   730 PRIEST FAIRY   54
THE HANDMAIDS LAUGH AND WHISPER IN THE DOOR. • • •   759 SHADOW WATER A   242
TO THE COMFORTABLE DOOR OF HIS HOUSE. • • • • • •   780 WELL AND TREE   6
ALTHOUGH THE DOOR BE SHUT • • • • • • • • •   786 YOUR HEART   14
DOORED
FROM DOORED AND WINDOWED CLIFF, OR HALF UPTURNED • • • • 368 EGO DOMINUS   30
DOORMAT
WHERE THE MOSS WAS SPREAD LIKE HIS OWN DOORMAT. • • • •   728 PRIEST FAIRY   8
DOOR-PILLARS
OR THE DOOR-PILLARS OF ONE HOUSE, • • • • • • • • •   195 BAILE AILLINN   152
DOOR-PIN
RAISE THE DOOR-PIN WITH ALARM, • • • • • • • • • •   727 LOVERS QUARREL   52
DOOR-POST
LOOKED DOWN ON YOU FROM HEAVEN'S DOOR-POST • • • • • •   112 ROSE OF PEACE   3
DOOR-POSTS
LOOKED DOWN ON YOU FROM HEAVEN'S DOOR-POSTS, • • • • •   112 ROSE OF PEACE V   3
DOORS
AND THROUGH THE DOORS, A RUSTLING ROUT, • • • • • •   20 OISIN 1   V 290
THE LEAST OF DOORS; BEYOND ON A DIM PLAIN • • • • •   39 OISIN 2   155
THE LEAST OF DOORS; BEYOND THE DOOR A PLAIN, • • • • •   39 OISIN 2   V 155
THE WINDOWS AND THE DOORS WERE SHUT, • • • • • • •   95 MOLL MAGEE   29
WITHOUT DOORS OR WITHIN, • • • • • • • • •   96 MOLL MAGEE   44
DESOLATE WINDS THAT BEAT THE DOORS OF HEAVEN, AND BEAT • • 147 UNAPPEAS HOST   9
THE DOORS OF HELL AND BLOW THERE MANY A WHIMPERING GHOST; 147 UNAPPEAS HOST   10
WHAT IF THE GLORY OF ESCUTCHEONED DOORS, • • • • • • •   418 ANCEST HOUSES   33
SCARCE THE OLD AND WIZEN HOUSES HAD THEIR DOORS AND WINDOWS 718 PHANTOM SHIP   5
    SHUT.
SCARCE THE OLD AND WIZENED HOUSES HAD THEIR DOORS   718 PHANTOM SHIP   V   5
    AND WINDOWS SHUT.
THE HARVEST'S IN! THE GRANARY DOORS ARE SHUT! • • • • •   755 SHADOW WATER A   177
DOORSTEP
A BIRD WALK ON THE DOORSTEP. CHECK ONCE MORE. • • • •   722 WITCH VIVIEN   64
DOOR-STEP
OVER THE DOOR-STEP INTO THE AIR, • • • • • • • •   97 FOXHUNTER   V   3
DOORWAY
PASSED UNDER THE DIM DOORWAY, OUT OF SIGHT, • • • • •   37 OISIN 2   123
PASSED UNDER A DIM DOORWAY, OUT OF SIGHT, • • • • • •   37 OISIN 2   V 123
TILL THE FAR DOORWAY GREW A BURNING BLOT • • • • •   39 OISIN 2   152
DESERTED ON A DOORWAY SEAT, • • • • • • • • •   85 MAD KING GOLL   56
DESERTED IN A DOORWAY SEAT, • • • • • • • • •   85 MAD KING GOLL V 56
SHY IN THE DOORWAY • • • • • • • • •   89 ISLE IN WATER   11
ITS OPEN LIGHTED DOORWAY AND ITS WINDOWS ALL ALIGHT, • • 581 CURSE CROMWELL   26
STRETCHED UNDER A DOORWAY • • • • • • • • •   585 ORAHILLY   30
DORIC
AND VAIN ALL DORIC DISCIPLINE. • • • • • • • • • •   438 SONGS PLAY 2   8

213

		PAGE	TITLE		LINE

DORIC (CONTINUED)
    AND VAIN THE DORIC DISCIPLINE. . . . . 438 SONGS PLAY 2 V '8
    IN VAIN THE DORIC DISCIPLINE. . . . . 438 SONGS PLAY 2 V   8
DOROTHY
    THERE'S MARGARET AND MARJORIE AND DOROTHY AND NAN, . . . 354 HIS PHOENIX 17
    TO DOROTHY WELLESLEY . . . . 579 DOR WELLESLEY T
DORTHA   SEE KYLE-DORTHA
DOTE
    ALL WOMEN DOTE UPON AN IDLE MAN . . . . 500 VACILLATION 23
DOUBLE
    UNTIL AT LAST THE DOUBLE HORNS, DRAWN BACKWARD, ... 278 TWO KINGS 21
    THAT WERE A DOUBLE HUNGER IN MY LIPS . . . . 285 TWO KINGS 206
    THAT WERE A DOUBLE HUNGER ON MY LIPS . . . . 285 TWO KINGS V 206
    AND LOOK MOST LIKE ME, BEING INDEED MY DOUBLE, ... 371 EGO DOMINUS 72
    THE DOUBLE VISION OF MICHAEL ROBARTES . . . . 382 VISION ROBART T
    WAS IT THE DOUBLE OF MY DREAM . . . . 398 BREAK OF DAY 1
    DOUBLE SIXES! . . . . 721 WITCH VIVIEN 43
DOUBLES
    WHEREIN THE GAZING HEART DOUBLES HER MIGHT. . . . . . 326 ROBERT GREGORY 69
DOUBLET
    HUNG ON HIS DOUBLET--DEAR AND MOURNFUL CHILD, ... 691 MOSADA 1 35
DOUBLING
    DRIPPING AND DOUBLING LANDWARD, AS THOUGH THEY WOULD HASTEN 48 OISIN 3 15
      AWAY.
    DRIPPING AND DOUBLING LANDWARD, AS THOUGH THEY WOULD HASTEN 57 OISIN 3 143
      AWAY.
DOUBLY
    FOR WHAT IS DOUBLY BRIEF." AND NOW THE SHAPE . . . 285 TWO KINGS 207
    FOR WHAT IS DOUBLY BRIEF." "BUT NOW THE SHAPE, . . . 285 TWO KINGS V 207
DOUBT
    DO YOU, TOO, DOUBT ME? HAVE YOU JOINED THEIR PLOT? . . 227 SHADOW WATER B 106
    MAYBE IT IS BUT NATURAL TO DOUBT ME. . . . . 227 SHADOW WATER B 112
    YOU'D NEVER DOUBT THAT IT WAS LIFE THEY PROMISED . . 231 SHADOW WATER B 197
    "ALTHOUGH THE EVENT WAS LONG IN DOUBT, ... 273 GREY ROCK 67
    BEING AS THE MOON OF BIRTH, MAY END OUR DOUBT. . . . 748 SHADOW WATER A 24
    I DOUBT YOUR WISDOM, BUT DO NOT DOUBT MY LOVE. . . . 748 SHADOW WATER A 31
    I DOUBT YOUR WISDOM, BUT DO NOT DOUBT MY LOVE. . . . 748 SHADOW WATER A 31
    ALTHOUGH I DOUBT YOUR WISDOM, DO NOT DOUBT . . . . 748 SHADOW WATER A 31
    ALTHOUGH I DOUBT YOUR WISDOM, DO NOT DOUBT . . . . 748 SHADOW WATER A V 31
DOUBTFUL
    BEING AS DOUBTFUL? I HAVE CALLED YOU MASTER . . . . 227 SHADOW WATER B 110
    ARE DOUBTFUL LIKE THESE PULLERS OF THE OAR! . . . . 748 SHADOW WATER A 30
DOUBTING
    NOT DOUBTING TO HAVE SHOULDERED IT AWAY. . . . . . 277 TWO KINGS V 11A
DOUBTLESS
    DOUBTLESS I SPOKE OR SANG WHAT I HAD HEARD . . . . . 557 RIBH ECSTASY 2
    THE THIRD, DOUBTLESS A SERVING-MAN, ... 566 LAPIS LAZULI 41
    THOUGH DOUBTLESS PLUM OR CHERRY-BRANCH . . . . . . 567 LAPIS LAZULI 47
DOUBTS
    BUT WOULD TURN HOME AGAIN. NO MAN HAD DOUBTS . . . . 749 SHADOW WATER A 38
DOUGH
    IS BUT HALF YOURS! HE KNEADED IN THE DOUGH . . . . . 201 OLD MEMORY 6
    INSIPID AS THE DOUGH BEFORE IT IS BAKED, ... 376 PHASES OF MOON 112
    WHEN ALL THE DOUGH HAS BEEN SO KNEADED UP . . . . . 377 PHASES OF MOON 114
DOVE
    THE HEAVY BOUGHS, THE BURNISHED DOVE . . . . 78 INDIAN TO LOVE 16
    LIKE SWARMING BEES, ONE WITH THE DOVE . . . . 78 INDIAN TO LOVE V 16
    ONE WITH THE LEAVES, ONE WITH THE DOVE . . . . . . 78 INDIAN TO LOVE V 16
    THE GREAT BOUGHS, AND THE BURNISHED DOVE . . . . . 78 INDIAN TO LOVE V 16
    AND GREAT BOUGHS, AND THE BURNISHED DOVE . . . . . 78 INDIAN TO LOVE V 16
    BOOK III DOVE OR SWAN I LEDA . . . . 441 LEDA AND SWAN V T
    BOOK V: DOVE OR SWAN I LEDA . . . . 441 LEDA AND SWAN V T
DOVE-COT
    ABOUT A SUN-FLUSHED DOVE-COT, COOING, CLING . . . . 710 FERENCZ RENYI 20
DOVE-GREY
    AND FOUND ON THE DOVE-GREY EDGE OF THE SEA . . . . . 3 OISIN 1 19
    AS THE TIDE WEARS THE DOVE-GREY SANDS, ... 157 POET BELOVED 4
    AS THE TIDE HAS THE DOVE-GREY SANDS, ... 157 POET BELOVED V 4
    IN DOVE-GREY FAERY LANDS! . . . . 162 ASKS FORGIVE 10
DOVE'S   SEE RING-DOVE'S
DOVES
    THAN DOVES THAT MOANED ROUND EMAN'S HALL . . . . . 3 OISIN 1 V 7EE
    THE DOVES WHOSE GROWING FORMS HE'D WATCHED. NOT THESE . . 710 FERENCZ RENYI V 21
    THE DOVES WHOSE GROWING FORM HE'D WATCHED. NOT THESE . . 710 FERENCZ RENYI V 21
DOWERED
    HAVE DOWERED THE STARS WITH MERRY LIGHT! . . . . . 134 TWO TREES 6
DOWERS
    AND HE GAVE THEM AS DOWERS TO HIS DAUGHTERS, ... 92 FATHER OHART 7
DOWN   SEE GOING-DOWN
    WHEN AMBLING DOWN THE VALE WE MET . . . . 2 OISIN 1 V 7U
    BUT DOWN TO HER FEET WHITE VESTURE FLOWED, ... 3 OISIN 1 25
    DOWN TO HER FEET WHITE VESTURE FLOWED, ... 3 OISIN 1 V 25
    AND WAS BORN WHERE THE SUN DROPS DOWN IN THE TIDE, . . 5 OISIN 1 V 49
    BEFORE THY FEET SHALL KNEEL DOWN ALL . . . . 7 OISIN 1 V 77
    OR DOWN THE DEWY FOREST ALLEYS, ... 10 OISIN 1 120
    AND DOWN THE DEWY FOREST ALLEYS, ... 10 OISIN 1 V 120
    IT DOWN IN A LEAF-HID, HOLLOW PLACE . . . . 17 OISIN 1 242
    BENT ALL OUR SWAYING BODIES DOWN, ... 20 OISIN 1 297
    PASSED A-TIPTOE UP AND DOWN . . . . 20 OISIN 1 V 294
    BENT DOWN ABOVE EACH HOOKED KNEE, ... 26 OISIN 1 392
    AND BID THE STARS DROP DOWN FROM THE SKY, ... 28 OISIN 1 426

DOWN (CONTINUED)

CAME SWIMMING SADLY DOWN THE MIGHTY STAIR.	32 OISIN 2	V	50B
DOWN ON US WITH HER EYES LIKE FUNERAL TAPERS.	33 OISIN 2	V	69
AS ANY RUDDY MOTH, LOOKED DOWN ON US.	34 OISIN 2		72
NOT EVEN YOUR GOD COULD HAVE THROWN DOWN THAT HALL. . . .	36 OISIN 2		109
NOT E'EN THY GOD COULD HAVE THROWN DOWN THAT HALL. . . .	36 OISIN 2	V	109
HE HAD SAT DOWN AND SIGHED WITH CUMBERED HEART, ...	37 OISIN 2		111
SHOWED PRINTS OF SEA-BORN SCALES, WHILE DOWN THROUGH IT	37 OISIN 2		115
ANOINTING, TORCH JAMMED DOWN BETWEEN THE FLAGS, ...	38 OISIN 2	V	143
LOOKED DOWN ON ME. AND IN THE SELF-SAME PLACE	39 OISIN 2		146
BARKING. WE TRAMPLED UP AND DOWN WITH BLOWS	40 OISIN 2		170
WHEN I HAD TORN IT DOWN. BUT WHEN THE WEST	41 OISIN 2	V	180
WHEN I TORE DOWN THE TREE. BUT WHEN THE WEST	41 OISIN 2		180
WHEN I'D TORE DOWN THAT TREE. BUT WHEN THE WEST	41 OISIN 2	V	180
WHEN I TORE DOWN THAT TREE. BUT WHEN THE WEST	41 OISIN 2	V	180
"I HEAR MY SOUL DROP DOWN INTO DECAY, ...	45 OISIN 2		235
A VALLEY FLOWED DOWN FROM HIS HOOFS, AND THERE IN THE LONG GRASS LAY,	48 OISIN 3		26
SQUARE LEAVES OF THE IVY MOVED OVER US, BINDING US DOWN TO OUR REST.	52 OISIN 3		76
CAME, AND MY FOREHEAD FELL LOW, AND MY TEARS LIKE BERRIES FELL DOWN.	57 OISIN 3		154
LEANING DOWN FROM THE GEM-STUDDED SADDLE, ...	60 OISIN 3		187
I THROW DOWN THE CHAIN OF SMALL STONES.	63 OISIN 3		222
A RABBIT OLD AND LAME LIMPED DOWN THE PATH.	80 EPHEMERA		15
WHILE HE BENT DOWN HIS FADING HEAD, ...	82 MAD KING GOLL		10
AND SONG THAT DOWN THE VALLEYS ROLLED--	84 MAD KING GOLL	V	35
AND SONG THAT DOWN THE VALLEY ROLLED--	84 MAD KING GOLL	V	35
THAT DOWN THE ECHOING VALLEYS ROLLED.	84 MAD KING GOLL	V	35
AND PASSED A-TIPTOE UP AND DOWN, ...	85 MAD KING GOLL		51
I PASSED A-TIP-TOE UP AND DOWN, ...	85 MAD KING GOLL	V	51
I PASSED A-TIPTOE UP AND DOWN, ...	85 MAD KING GOLL	V	51
DOWN BY THE SALLEY GARDENS	90 SALLEY GARDENS		T
DOWN BY THE SALLEY GARDENS MY LOVE AND I DID MEET. . .	90 SALLEY GARDENS		1
AND FATHER JOHN WENT DOWN.	92 FATHER OHART		10
AS HE WENT UP AND DOWN.	92 FATHER OHART		18
AND SLOWLY UP AND DOWN.	97 FOXHUNTER	V	8
AND GENTLY UP AND DOWN.	97 FOXHUNTER	V	8
"NOW LEAVE THE CHAIR DOWN ON THE GRASS, ...	97 FOXHUNTER	V	9
THE WEAK WORM HIDING DOWN IN ITS SMALL CAVE, ...	101 ROSE UPON ROOD		16
THE SORROWS OF THE WORLD BOW DOWN MY HEAD, ...	104 FERGUS DRUID	V	38A
AND THE WHOLE WORLD WEIGHS DOWN UPON MY HEART-- . . .	104 FERGUS DRUID	V	38A
THEREON HE SHOOK THE MORE AND CAST HIM DOWN	106 CUCHULAIN SEA		14
ALEEL, THE SWINEHERD, WEPT AND CAST HIM DOWN	106 CUCHULAIN SEA	V	14
HE CAUGHT HIS BREATH AND CAST HIM WEEPING DOWN	106 CUCHULAIN SEA	V	14
AND WENT DOWN TO THE LONG SANDS ALONE, ...	111 CUCHULAIN SEA	V	84
AND HE WENT DOWN TO THE LONG SANDS ALONE, ...	111 CUCHULAIN SEA	V	84
BOW DOWN, ARCHANGELS, IN YOUR DIM ABODE.	112 ROSE OF WORLD		11
LOOKED DOWN ON YOU FROM HEAVEN'S DOOR-POST	112 ROSE OF PEACE		3
LOOKED DOWN ON YOU FROM HEAVEN'S DOOR-POSTS, ...	112 ROSE OF PEACE	V	3
AND ALL FOLK SEEING HIM BOW DOWN, ...	113 ROSE OF PEACE		9
THEY HAVE GONE DOWN UNDER THE SAME WHITE STARS, . . .	115 ROSE OF BATTLE		34
AND NODDING BY THE FIRE, TAKE DOWN THIS BOOK, ...	120 YOU ARE OLD		2
AND BENDING DOWN BESIDE THE GLOWING BARS, ...	121 YOU ARE OLD		9
ALL THE HEAVENS BOW DOWN TO HEAVEN, ...	125 CATHLEEN PARA		15
SHE GOES DOWN THE FLOOR OF HEAVEN, ...	125 CATHLEEN PARA	V	13
SENT ONE OF HIS GREAT ANGELS DOWN	134 FR GILLIGAN		43
WHEN WE BENT DOWN ABOVE THE FADING COALS	136 TO SOME I TALK		3
HE SAT DOWN AND PLAYED IN A DREAM	145 HOST OF AIR	V	27
THE SOUTH IS POURING DOWN ROSES OF CRIMSON FIRE. . .	154 BELOVED PEACE		6
AND PUSHED THE LATCHES DOWN.	159 CAP AND BELLS		12
SHE SNICKED THE BRASS BOLTS DOWN.	159 CAP AND BELLS	V	12
AND PUSHED THE BRASS BOLT DOWN.	159 CAP AND BELLS	V	12
BEING WEARY OF THE WORLD'S EMPIRES, BOW DOWN TO YOU, .	161 BLACK PIG		7
AND THEREFORE MY HEART BOWS DOWN ANEW, ...	164 PERFECT BEAUTY	V	6
WE WILL BEND DOWN AND LOOSEN OUR HAIR OVER YOU, . . .	172 TRAV PASSION		6
BEND DOWN AND PRAY FOR ALL THAT SIN I WOVE IN SONG, .	173 SPEAKS HEARERS		5
BEND DOWN AND PRAY FOR THE GREAT SIN I WOVE IN SONG, .	173 SPEAKS HEARERS	V	5
BLOSSOM PALE, SHE PULLED DOWN THE PALE BLOSSOM . . .	199 ARROW	V	5
BETTER GO DOWN UPON YOUR MARROW-BONES	204 ADAMS CURSE		7
BETTER GO DOWN UPON YOUR MARROW BONES	204 ADAMS CURSE	V	7
AND SHAKE DOWN THUNDER ON THE STONES BECAUSE THE RED WINDS RAVE.	207 HANRAHANS SONG	V	7
O. LAY THE SHRILLY TRUMPET DOWN, ...	212 BLESS PSALTER		4
O NO, O NO. THEY HURRY DOWN	213 BLESS PSALTER		12
HE HAS STOOPED DOWN AND KISSED HER ON THE LIPS. . . .	232 SHADOW WATER B		230
AGAINST A BEECH-BOLE, HE THREW DOWN THE BEAST	278 TWO KINGS		36
AGAINST A BEECH BOLE, HE THREW DOWN THE BEAST	278 TWO KINGS	V	36
BUT FINDING HIM STILL SILENT I STOOPED DOWN	281 TWO KINGS		109
BEFORE HIS CHAIR AND BENDING DOWN MY HEAD	282 TWO KINGS		132
BEFORE YOU'LL PUT YOUR GUINEAS DOWN, ...	287 TO WEALTHY MAN		5
BEFORE YOU'VE PUT YOUR GUINEAS DOWN, ...	287 TO WEALTHY MAN	V	5
FELL DOWN UPON THE DUST AND SNORED.	297 THREE BEGGARS		60
WENT DOWN UPON A HAND AND KNEE	304 HOUR DAWN	V	45
I SHOULD NOT BE TOO DOWN IN THE MOUTH	306 HOUR DAWN		88
PULL DOWN THE BLINDS, BRING FIDDLE AND CLARIONET . .	311 MOUNTAIN TOMB		5
SOON TOPPLES DOWN THE HILL.	335 YOUNG BEAUTY		6
HAS MARKED A DISTANT OBJECT DOWN, ...	337 TOM OROUGHLEY		3
THAT HAS LOOKED DOWN	344 DAWN		2
THE BEATING DOWN OF THE WISE	348 FISHERMAN		23
AND GREAT ART BEATEN DOWN.	348 FISHERMAN		24

DOWN   (CONTINUED)

```
                                                              PAGE   TITLE            LINE
AND THE DOWN TURN OF HIS WRIST . . . . . . . . .               348  FISHERMAN     V    33
"CALL DOWN THE HAWK FROM THE AIR: . . . . . . .               349  HAWK               1
I HAVE GONE ABOUT THE HOUSE, GONE UP AND DOWN . . . .         350  HER PRAISE         2
FROM GOING DOWN OF THE SUN I HAVE DREAMED . . . .            358  PRESENCES     V    3
LAID HIS STRONG BONES DOWN IN DEATH . . . . . .               360  ALF POLLEXFEN      3
DESTROY THE VIEW BY CUTTING DOWN AN ASH . . . .              372  ON GOING HOUSE     13
OUT OF THE UP AND DOWN, THE WAGON-WHEEL . . . .              377  PHASES OF MOON    120
OUT OF THE UP AND DOWN, THE WAGON WHEEL . . . .              377  PHASES OF MOON V  120
A ROMAN CAESAR IS HELD DOWN . . . . . . . . . .              379  SAINT HUNCH        4
DOWN TO HER CELL AND THERE ALIT, . . . . . . .               397  POLIT PRISONER     4
PULL DOWN ESTABLISHED HONOUR: HAWK FOR NEWS . .              398  LEADERS CROWD      3
IT HAD SET DOWN AMONG ITS LAWS: . . . . . . . .              399  BREAK OF DAY      16
NOW GYRING DOWN AND PERNING THERE . . . . . . .              400  DEMON BEAST       26
AND RAINS DOWN LIFE UNTIL THE BASIN SPILLS, . .             417  ANCEST HOUSES      4
LAST NIGHT THEY TRUNDLED DOWN THE ROAD . . . .              425  STARES NEST       13
MELT DOWN, AS IT WERE WAX IN THE SUN'S RAYS: . .            428  NINETEEN 19       12
MY WORKS ARE ALL STAMPED DOWN INTO THE SULTRY MUD,         442  BLACK CENTAUR      3
LAUGHED: AND PLUNGING DOWN . . . . . . . . . . .            453  MERMAID            4
AM SET DOWN STANDING IN THE WOOD . . . . . . .              453  DEATH OF HARE     11
SHE WHO HAD BROUGHT GREAT HECTOR DOWN . . . .               455  HIS MEMORIES      15
FOR THAT OLD MADGE COMES DOWN THE LANE, . . . .            456  FRIENDS YOUTH      5
AND THEN I LAUGH TILL TEARS RUN DOWN . . . . .             456  FRIENDS YOUTH     17
OR THE BED OF DOWN . . . . . . . . . . . . . .             458  SECRETS OF OLD    18
SAT DOWN UPON THE FOUNTAIN'S MARBLE EDGE, . . .            463  HARUN RASHID      43
AND SHE LAY DOWN UPON HER BED AND SLEPT, . . .            467  HARUN RASHID     146
. . . HAD DRAGGED HIM DOWN INTO MANKIND, . . .            481  BLOOD AND MOON    20
RESPONSIBILITY SO WEIGHS ME DOWN. . . . . . . .            501  VACILLATION       50
WEIGH ME DOWN, AND NOT A DAY . . . . . . . . .            501  VACILLATION       54
MAY CALL DOWN CURSES ON HIS HEAD . . . . . . .            508  JANE BISHOP        4
AND LAY DOWN THAT HEAD . . . . . . . . . . . .            534  CONSOLATION        4
DOWN EVERY WITHERED FINGER FROM THE TOP: . . .            537  HER VISION        11
BRIGHTNESS REMAINS: A BRIGHTER STAR SHOOTS DOWN:          541  PARN FUNERAL 1     4
HYSTERICA PASSIO DRAGGED THIS QUARRY DOWN. . .            542  PARN FUNERAL 1    21
DOWN THE FANATIC, DOWN THE CLOWN: . . . . . . .            544  TO SAME TUNE 1     8
DOWN THE FANATIC, DOWN THE CLOWN: . . . . . . .            544  TO SAME TUNE 1     8
DOWN, DOWN, HAMMER THEM DOWN, . . . . . . . . .            544  TO SAME TUNE 1     9
DOWN, DOWN, HAMMER THEM DOWN, . . . . . . . . .            544  TO SAME TUNE 1     9
DOWN, DOWN, HAMMER THEM DOWN, . . . . . . . . .            544  TO SAME TUNE 1     9
DOWN TO THE TUNE OF O'DONNELL ABU. . . . . . .            544  TO SAME TUNE 1    10
DOWN THE FANATIC, DOWN THE CLOWN: . . . . . . .            545  TO SAME TUNE 1    18
DOWN THE FANATIC, DOWN THE CLOWN: . . . . . . .            545  TO SAME TUNE 1    18
DOWN, DOWN, HAMMER THEM DOWN, . . . . . . . . .            545  TO SAME TUNE 1    19
DOWN, DOWN, HAMMER THEM DOWN, . . . . . . . . .            545  TO SAME TUNE 1    19
DOWN, DOWN, HAMMER THEM DOWN, . . . . . . . . .            545  TO SAME TUNE 1    19
DOWN TO THE TUNE OF O'DONNELL ABU. . . . . . .            545  TO SAME TUNE 1    20
DOWN THE FANATIC, DOWN THE CLOWN: . . . . . . .            545  TO SAME TUNE 1    28
DOWN THE FANATIC, DOWN THE CLOWN: . . . . . . .            545  TO SAME TUNE 1    28
DOWN, DOWN, HAMMER THEM DOWN, . . . . . . . . .            545  TO SAME TUNE 1    29
DOWN, DOWN, HAMMER THEM DOWN, . . . . . . . . .            545  TO SAME TUNE 1    29
DOWN, DOWN, HAMMER THEM DOWN, . . . . . . . . .            545  TO SAME TUNE 1    29
DOWN TO THE TUNE OF O'DONNELL ABU. . . . . . .            545  TO SAME TUNE 1    30
DOWN THE FANATIC, DOWN THE CLOWN: . . . . . . .            546  TO SAME TUNE 2 V  REF
DOWN THE FANATIC, DOWN THE CLOWN: . . . . . . .            546  TO SAME TUNE 2 V  REF
DOWN, DOWN, HAMMER THEM DOWN, . . . . . . . . .            546  TO SAME TUNE 2 V  REF
DOWN, DOWN, HAMMER THEM DOWN, . . . . . . . . .            546  TO SAME TUNE 2 V  REF
DOWN, DOWN, HAMMER THEM DOWN, . . . . . . . . .            546  TO SAME TUNE 2 V  REF
DOWN TO THE TUNE OF O'DONNELL ABU. . . . . . .            546  TO SAME TUNE 2 V  REF
A SLAVE BOWS DOWN TO A SLAVE. . . . . . . . . .            547  TO SAME TUNE 3     6
DOWN THE FANATIC, DOWN THE CLOWN: . . . . . . .            548  TO SAME TUNE 3 V  REF
DOWN THE FANATIC, DOWN THE CLOWN: . . . . . . .            548  TO SAME TUNE 3 V  REF
DOWN, DOWN, HAMMER THEM DOWN, . . . . . . . . .            548  TO SAME TUNE 3 V  REF
DOWN, DOWN, HAMMER THEM DOWN, . . . . . . . . .            548  TO SAME TUNE 3 V  REF
DOWN, DOWN, HAMMER THEM DOWN, . . . . . . . . .            548  TO SAME TUNE 3 V  REF
DOWN TO THE TUNE OF O'DONNELL ABU. . . . . . .            548  TO SAME TUNE 3 V  REF
TO-MORROW NIGHT I WILL BREAK DOWN THE DOOR. . .            551  SONGS REWRIT 1     6
TO-MORROW NIGHT I WILL BREAK DOWN THE DOOR. . .            551  SONGS REWRIT 1    12
I THOUGHT TO HAVE WHISTLED HER DOWN THAT WAY, .            551  SONGS REWRIT 1    15
TO-MORROW NIGHT I WILL BREAK DOWN THE DOOR. . .            551  SONGS REWRIT 1    18
TOMORROW NIGHT I WILL BREAK DOWN THE DOOR. . .            551  SONGS REWRIT 1 V  REF
DOWN LIMB AND BREAST OR DOWN THAT GLIMMERING BELLY         560  MAGIC DRUM         5
DOWN LIMB AND BREAST OR DOWN THAT GLIMMERING BELLY         560  MAGIC DRUM         5
THE HAND AND LASH THAT BEAT DOWN FRIGID ROME?            560  WHENCE COME       10
BEAT DOWN UPON THEIR NAKED BODIES, KNOW . . . .            563  MERU              12
"I KNOW THAT I MUST DROP DOWN DEAD . . . . . .            569  THREE BUSHES      17
YET WHAT COULD I BUT DROP DOWN DEAD . . . . . .            569  THREE BUSHES      19
GIRLS DOWN ON THE SEASHORE . . . . . . . . . .            588  OLD WICKED MAN    30
THEY TURN DOWN THEIR BEDS. . . . . . . . . . .            589  OLD WICKED MAN    35
PARNELL CAME DOWN THE ROAD, HE SAID TO A CHEERING MAN:    590  PARNELL            1
FOR I CAN PUT THE WHOLE LOT DOWN. AND ALL I HAVE TO SAY   593  PILGRIM           24
BUT THEY THREW DOWN THEIR PISTOLS . . . . . . .            596  COLONEL MARTIN    59
HEART-SMITTEN WITH EMOTION I SINK DOWN, . . . .            602  GALLERY REVIS     17
HEART SMITTEN WITH EMOTION, I SINK DOWN, . . .            602  GALLERY REVIS  V  17
EVERYTHING DOWN TO THAT SOLE TEST AGAIN, . . .            603  GALLERY REVIS     46
ALL THINGS DOWN TO THAT COMMON TEST AGAIN, . .            603  GALLERY REVIS  V  46
THAT RED-HEADED RECTOR IN COUNTY DOWN, . . . .            604  YOU CONTENT       11
AND KNOCK THE OTHERS DOWN. . . . . . . . . . .            606  SONGS BURDEN 1    26
CALCULATIONS THAT LOOK BUT CASUAL FLESH, PUT DOWN         610  STATUES           11
DOWN THE MOUNTAIN WALLS . . . . . . . . . . . .            612  NEWS ORACLE       30
A SLAVE BOWS DOWN TO A SLAVE. . . . . . . . . .            614  MARCH SONGS 2      6
WHAT MARCHES DOWN THE MOUNTAIN PASS? . . . . .            615  MARCH SONGS 2     17
```

216

		PAGE	TITLE		LINE

DOWN   (CONTINUED)

	PAGE	TITLE		LINE
WHAT TEARS DOWN A TREE THAT HAS NOTHING WITHIN IT?	615	MARCH SONGS 2		23
WHAT MARCHES DOWN THE MOUNTAIN PASS?	615	MARCH SONGS 2		27
WHAT TEARS DOWN A TREE HAS NOTHING WITHIN IT?	615	MARCH SONGS 2	V	23
BUT HE TOOK DOWN THE MOON	616	MARCH SONGS 3		8
BUT HE TOOK DOWN THE MOON	616	MARCH SONGS 3		18
BUT HE TOOK DOWN THE MOON	616	MARCH SONGS 3		28
AND I CRIED TEARS DOWN.	628	JANE MOUNTAIN		22
I MUST LIE DOWN WHERE ALL THE LADDERS START,	630	CIRCUS ANIMALS		39
SLEEPLESS WOULD LIE DOWN AND DIE.	632	MAN AND ECHO		18
LIE DOWN AND DIE. THAT WERE TO SHIRK	632	MAN AND ECHO		19
'TIS MORN: THY SHEEP ARE WANDERING DOWN THE VALE--	645	ISLE STAT I 1		3
SAD LADY OF THE DEEP, POURS DOWN HER LIGHT:	650	ISLE STAT I 1		127
OUT OF THE AIR. AND WHEN? WHEN THE SUN GOES DOWN	652	ISLE STAT I 2		29
THE WIND AT EVENING WHEN THE SUN GOES DOWN	653	ISLE STAT I 2		50
DEEP-EYED, SLOW-FOOTING DOWN THE EMPTY GLADE.	653	ISLE STAT I 2		55
WHEN LOW THE SUN SANK DOWN IN CLOTTED FLAME	656	ISLE STAT I 3		30
DOWN TO THEIR FEET THE STARS THAT SHINE ALONE,	662	ISLE STAT II 1		80
AND WHO WILL THROW HIS MANSION DOWN	671	ISLE STAT II 3		135
AND DOWN I CAME AS A FALCON SWOOPS	673	ISLE STAT II 3		178
GO UP AND DOWN, AND RAISE THEIR HEADS AND SING	682	SEEKER		30
DROPT DOWN THE VELVET DARKNESS FROM ABOVE,	688	TWO TITANS		37
DOWN TO THE MOTHER OF THE FOILED AND DEAD.	688	TWO TITANS		50
FAILURE FOR GLORY DOWN ON THEE, AND MOULD	688	TWO TITANS		54
DOWN LOW THE HEAD OF HIS MAGNIFICENCE	689	NETTLESHIP	V	6
IN AUTUMN, WHEN FAR DOWN THE MOUNTAIN SLOPES	690	MOSADA 1		12
OF HIS SAD GOD: AND DOWN AMONG THE GRASS	690	MOSADA 1		16
SLID CIRCLING DOWN AND SOFTLY TOUCHED MY LIPS	690	MOSADA 1		21
DOWN THE LONG VALLEYS FROM MY PEOPLE'S TENTS,	691	MOSADA 1		30
SINKS DOWN AT LAST WITH YONDER MINARET,	691	MOSADA 1	V	36
STAY, STAY, OR I WILL HOLD YOUR WHITE ARMS DOWN.	694	MOSADA 1		92
FROM FASTING--SEE, THE RED LIGHT SLANTING DOWN	697	MOSADA 2		36
THE BURTHEN OF THY TRUTH. REACH DOWN THY HANDS	698	MOSADA 2		53
CIRCLING THE BRAIN? MY BROTHERS WILL PASS DOWN	699	MOSADA 3		6
THE BRAIN. MY BROTHERS WILL BE PASSING DOWN	699	MOSADA 3	V	6
CIRCLING THE BRAIN? MY BROTHERS NOW PASS DOWN	699	MOSADA 3	V	6
WHERE SHALL I LAY ME DOWN? THAT QUESTION IS	700	MOSADA 3		36
NAY HERE, I'LL LAY ME DOWN WHERE I CAN WATCH	700	MOSADA 3		39
FOR NIGHT COMES FAST. LOOK DOWN ON ME, MY LOVE,	703	MOSADA 3		103
OFTEN HE HAD BENT DOWN SOME BOUGH ALL BRIGHT	710	FERENCZ RENYI		28
OFTEN HE HAD BENT DOWN SOME BOUGH ALL BRIGHT WITH BERRIES:	710	FERENCZ RENYI	V	28
I SAT ME DOWN BESIDE THEE, AND I KNEW	713	FERENCZ RENYI		92
DOWN THE VAPOURS FALL AND HIDE THEM FROM THE CHILDREN OF A DAY,	719	PHANTOM SHIP		27
AND THE WINDS COME DOWN AND BLOW THEM WITH THE VAPOURS FAR AWAY.	719	PHANTOM SHIP		28
LAY DOWN THE BURDEN OF THY RACE,	736	SUMMER EVENING		14
"AND ALL DOWN FROM NORTHUMBERLAND	740	EARL PAUL		9
AND FLUNG DOWN CLASHING ON THE FLOOR	740	EARL PAUL		15
AND FLY AMONG THE FOAM. THRUST DOWN THE HELM,	750	SHADOW WATER A		88
I SWEAR IT, THOUGH I GLADLY WOULD LIE DOWN	758	SHADOW WATER A		225
I HAD THROWN IT DOWN BEHIND THIS COIL OF ROPE.	759	SHADOW WATER A		245
"TILL THE SUN GOES DOWN AND AN HOUR OF THE CLOCK"	779	GOING THE ROAD		7
OR BURNED GREAT CITIES DOWN,	789	SINGING HEAD		16
YOU HAD BROUGHT DOWN BEFORE YOU DIED.	791	REPRISALS		2

DOWNS

	PAGE	TITLE		LINE
THAT HAS LESS UPS AND DOWNS THAN ROBBERY.	222	SHADOW WATER B		7
NO UPS AND DOWNS, MY PRETTY,	592	DRUNK SOBRIETY		13

DOWN-TURN

	PAGE	TITLE		LINE
AND THE DOWN-TURN OF HIS WRIST	348	FISHERMAN		33

DOWNWARD

	PAGE	TITLE		LINE
FACE DOWNWARD, TOSSING IN A TROUBLED SLEEP:	185	QUEEN MAEVE		106

DOWNY

	PAGE	TITLE		LINE
AND DOWNY BEES HAVE AMBUSCADE,	67	HAPPY SHEPHERD	V	46A
IN THEIR DOWNY CAPS, AND STARTLE THE NAPS	644	SONG FAERIES		11
IN THEIR DOWNY CAPS, AND STARTLE THE NAPS	676	ISLE STAT II 3		258

DOWSON

	PAGE	TITLE		LINE
DOWSON AND JOHNSON MOST I PRAISE--	273	GREY ROCK		62

DOZEN

	PAGE	TITLE		LINE
THESE DOZEN WEEKS. AND I HAD THOUGHT TO MAKE	222	SHADOW WATER B		4
AND FOR A DOZEN HOURS HAVE BEEN A PART	230	SHADOW WATER B		171
SCARED BY THE SPLASHING OF A DOZEN COWS:	419	MY HOUSE		10
A DOZEN NIGHTS OF NATURAL SLEEP, AND THEN	468	HARUN RASHID		150
AND HALF A DOZEN IN FORMATION THERE,	489	COOLE PARK 29		20

DRAG

	PAGE	TITLE		LINE
I SCARCE COULD DRAG MY FEET,	94	MOLL MAGEE		10

DRAGGED

	PAGE	TITLE		LINE
CAME TO MY TOWER AS AGE DRAGGED AFTER AGE	45	OISIN 2	V	242
BELOVED, HAVING DRAGGED THE NET ABOUT US,	252	SHADOW WATER B		615
AS THOUGH IT DRAGGED ROAD-METAL. MY CURSE ON PLAYS	260	FASC DIFFICULT		8
AS THOUGH IT DRAGGED ROAD METAL. MY CURSE ON PLAYS	260	FASC DIFFICULT	V	8
I DRAGGED FROM GOBAN'S MOUNTAIN-TOP	304	HOUR DAWN		50
. . . HAD DRAGGED HIM DOWN INTO MANKIND,	481	BLOOD AND MOON		20
HYSTERICA PASSIO DRAGGED THIS QUARRY DOWN.	542	PARN FUNERAL 1		21
AND HE IS DRAGGED AGAIN BEFORE HER FEET.	688	TWO TITANS		43
AND SHE IS DRAGGED TO WHERE THE WILLOW BANDS	714	FERENCZ RENYI		108
DRAGGED INTO BEING	785	WOMANS BEAUTY		27

DRAGGLED

	PAGE	TITLE		LINE
AND SAID, CASTING ASIDE HIS DRAGGLED HAIR,	105	CUCHULAIN SEA	V	3

DRAGON

	PAGE	TITLE		LINE
THE POLAR DRAGON SLEPT,	174	ELEMENT POWERS		4

217

```
                                                        PAGE    TITLE              LINE

DRAGON  (CONTINUED)
    DRAGON THAT LOVED THE WORLD AND HELD US TO IT,  .  .  .  .  .    251 SHADOW WATER B      598
    THAT DRAGON THROUGH THE FADING LIGHT,  .  .  .  .  .  .  .  .    385 ROBARTES DANCE        4
    THE HALF-DEAD DRAGON WAS HER THOUGHT,  .  .  .  .  .  .  .  .    385 ROBARTES DANCE        6
    MY WRETCHED DRAGON IS PERPLEXED.  .  .  .  .  .  .  .  .  .  .    386 ROBARTES DANCE       41
    NOW DAYS ARE DRAGON RIDDEN, THE NIGHTMARE  .  .  .  .  .  .  .    429 NINETEEN 19      V   25
    IT SEEMED THAT A DRAGON OF AIR  .  .  .  .  .  .  .  .  .  .  .    430 NINETEEN 19          51
    AND THEN YOU STOOD AMONG THE DRAGON RINGS.  .  .  .  .  .  .  .    533 HER TRIUMPH      V    7
DRAGON-GUARDED
    IN A DRAGON-GUARDED LAND,  .  .  .  .  .  .  .  .  .  .  .  .  .    309 REALISTS              3
DRAGON-RIDDEN
    NOW DAYS ARE DRAGON-RIDDEN, THE NIGHTMARE  .  .  .  .  .  .  .    429 NINETEEN 19          25
DRAGON-RINGS
    AND THEN YOU STOOD AMONG THE DRAGON-RINGS.  .  .  .  .  .  .  .    533 HER TRIUMPH           7
DRAGON'S
    I DID THE DRAGON'S WILL UNTIL YOU CAME  .  .  .  .  .  .  .  .    533 HER TRIUMPH           1
DRAGONS
    DRAGONS WITH EYES OF RUBY.  THE WHOLE SHIP  .  .  .  .  .  .  .    248 SHADOW WATER B      535
    WITH THE DRAGONS?  .  .  .  .  .  .  .  .  .  .  .  .  .  .  .  .    309 REALISTS              8
DRAGON-SCALES
    UNTIL AFAR APPEAR THE GLEAMING DRAGON-SCALES!  .  .  .  .  .  .    651 ISLE STAT I 1       160
DRAGS
    AND DRAGS HIM THROUGH THE SEA.  WELL, NET OR NONE,  .  .  .  .    224 SHADOW WATER B       57
    THAT BELLIES AND DRAGS IN THE WIND  .  .  .  .  .  .  .  .  .    358 BALLOON MIND          3
    PARDONED, DRAGS OUT LONELY YEARS  .  .  .  .  .  .  .  .  .  .    475 EVA GORE-BOOTH        8
DRAIN
    UNLESS WE DRAIN MORE FLAGONS IN A YEAR  .  .  .  .  .  .  .  .    225 SHADOW WATER B       70
DRAINED
    AND AFTER, DRAINED DRY,  .  .  .  .  .  .  .  .  .  .  .  .  .    310 WITCH                 4
DRAKE
    THE WILD DUCK AND THE DRAKE  .  .  .  .  .  .  .  .  .  .  .  .    143 HOST OF AIR           2
    CURVING BENEATH THE PROW; AS SOME WILD DRAKE  .  .  .  .  .  .    659 ISLE STAT II 1       16
DRAMA
    WHAT SACRED DRAMA THROUGH HER BODY HEAVED  .  .  .  .  .  .  .    560 WHENCE COME          11
DRAMATIC
    INTRODUCTION TO A DRAMATIC POEM  .  .  .  .  .  .  .  .  .  .    217 WOODS OF COOLE V      T
DRAMATIS
    IGNORANT WHAT DRAMATIS PERSONAE SPAKE!  .  .  .  .  .  .  .  .    560 WHENCE COME           4
DRAMATIST
    IGNORANT WHAT THAT DRAMATIST ENJOINS,  .  .  .  .  .  .  .  .    560 WHENCE COME           8
DRANK
    WE LAY ON SKINS OF OTTERS, AND DRANK WINE,  .  .  .  .  .  .  .     41 OISIN 2             188
    I SAT AND MUSED AND DRANK SWEET WINE!  .  .  .  .  .  .  .  .     82 MAD KING GOLL        13
    AND DRANK AND YAWNED AND STRETCHED HIM OUT,  .  .  .  .  .  .  .    307 HOUR DAWN           108
    WHO KNOWS HOW SHE DRANK THE WIND  .  .  .  .  .  .  .  .  .  .    381 SONGS FOOL 2          6
    HOLLOW OF CHEEK AS THOUGH IT DRANK THE WIND  .  .  .  .  .  .  .    444 SCHOOL CHILDR.       27
    DRANK TAR-WATER WITH THE BISHOP OF CLOYNE,  .  .  .  .  .  .  .    486 SEVEN SAGES           5
    I WOULD THAT I DRANK WITH MY LOVE ON MY KNEE,  .  .  .  .  .  .    551 SONGS REWRIT 1        9
DRAPERIES
    MADE DRAPERIES THAT SEEMED TO RISE  .  .  .  .  .  .  .  .  .    566 LAPIS LAZULI         31
    STRANGE DRAPERIES DID ALL THE SIDES ADORN,  .  .  .  .  .  .  .    657 ISLE STAT I 3        55
DRAPERY
    TENT-POLE OF EDEN; THE TENT'S DRAPERY;  .  .  .  .  .  .  .  .    483 VERONIC NAPKIN        2
    TENT POLE OF EDEN; THE TENT'S DRAPERY;  .  .  .  .  .  .  .  .    483 VERONIC NAPKIN V      2
    WHAT MADE THE DRAPERY GLISTEN SO?  .  .  .  .  .  .  .  .  .    625 NATIVITY              3
DRASTIC
    THAT IF NOTHING DRASTIC IS DONE  .  .  .  .  .  .  .  .  .  .    565 LAPIS LAZULI          5
    THAT IF NOTHING DRASTIC CAN BE DONE  .  .  .  .  .  .  .  .  .    565 LAPIS LAZULI   V      5
DRAUGHT
    BECAUSE OF THAT OLD DRAUGHT UNDER THE DOOR,  .  .  .  .  .  .    228 SHADOW WATER B      127
DRAUGHTY
    THAT TURNS AND CHANGES LIKE HIS DRAUGHTY SEAS?  .  .  .  .  .    265 ABBEY THEATRE        12
DRAVE
    HAD SURGED UP IN A PLUMY FIRE, I DRAVE  .  .  .  .  .  .  .  .     41 OISIN 2             181
    WITH SURGE OF PLUMY FIRE, LUNGING I DRAVE  .  .  .  .  .  .  .     41 OISIN 2             181
    SURGED UP IN PLUMY FIRE, I LUNGED AND DRAVE  .  .  .  .  .  .     41 OISIN 2         V   181
DRAW
    AMRITA.  DRAW YOU NEAR, AND 'NEATH YON PILLAR  .  .  .  .  .     71 ANASHU VIJAYA  V    13A
    IF YOU WILL DRAW THAT SWORD OUT OF ITS SCABBARD  .  .  .  .    225 SHADOW WATER B       78
    TOWARD PEOPLED TARA, NOR STOOD TO DRAW HIS BREATH  .  .  .    279 TWO KINGS            46
    ON PEOPLED TARA, NOR STOOD TO DRAW HIS BREATH  .  .  .  .    279 TWO KINGS      V     46
    TOWARDS PEOPLED TARA, NOR STOOD TO DRAW HIS BREATH  .  .  .    279 TWO KINGS      V     46
    WHENCE TURBULENT ITALY SHOULD DRAW  .  .  .  .  .  .  .  .    288 TO WEALTHY MAN       25
    DRAW THE GLASNEVIN COVERLET ANEW  .  .  .  .  .  .  .  .  .    293 TO A SHADE     V     19
    MY DISCONTENTED HEART TO DRAW CONTENT  .  .  .  .  .  .  .    334 LIVING BEAUTY         3
    "BUT WHERE CAN WE DRAW WATER."  .  .  .  .  .  .  .  .  .    396 ROSE TREE            13
    AS THOUGH TO DRAW THEM CLOSER YET.  RAMMED FULL  .  .  .    579 DOR WELLESLEY         5
    DRAW ROUND, BELOVED AND BITTER MEN,  .  .  .  .  .  .  .    584 GHOST ROG CASE       37
    DRAW ROUND AND RAISE A SHOUT!  .  .  .  .  .  .  .  .  .    584 GHOST ROG CASE       38
    SOME BARBAROUS, UN-FAERY THING DRAW NEAR.  .  .  .  .  .    656 ISLE STAT I 3        21
    OF WONDERS! EVE OF PRODIGIES! DRAW! DRAW!  .  .  .  .  .    664 ISLE STAT II 2       62
    OF WONDERS! EVE OF PRODIGIES! DRAW! DRAW!  .  .  .  .  .    664 ISLE STAT II 2       62
    DRAW STAR TO STAR, AS ON THAT EVE HE PASSED  .  .  .  .  .    691 MOSADA 1             29
    I'LL DRAW MY CLOAK AROUND ME! IT IS COLD.  .  .  .  .  .    704 MOSADA 3            123
    NOW STEPS DRAW CLOSE, HE HIDES BENEATH A DRUM.  .  .  .  .    713 FERENCZ RENYI        78
    FROM HAYNAU'S LIFTED FINGERS--TWO DRAW NIGH  .  .  .  .  .    714 FERENCZ RENYI       104
    I SWEAR IT.  LET EVERY MAN DRAW OUT HIS SWORD.  .  .  .  .    758 SHADOW WATER A      230
DRAWETH
    AND YONDER HUDDLING BLACKNESS DRAWETH NIGH--  .  .  .  .  .    663 ISLE STAT II 2       15
DRAWING
    A NEW MODELLED DOLL, OR DRAWING,  .  .  .  .  .  .  .  .  .    362 DOLLS DRAWINGS        2
```

DRAWING-ROOM
   IN A DRAWING-ROOM. . . . .   685 DRAWING-ROOM   T
   IN A DRAWING-ROOM . . . .   734 QUATRAIN APHOR V   T
DRAWINGS
   CERTAIN ARTISTS BRING HER DOLLS AND DRAWINGS . . . . .   362 DOLLS DRAWINGS   T
DRAWN   SEE DOLPHIN-DRAWN
   UNTIL AT LAST THE DOUBLE HORNS, DRAWN BACKWARD, . . .   278 TWO KINGS   21
   AND KNELT ABOVE IT WITH DRAWN KNIFE. ON THE INSTANT . .   278 TWO KINGS   37
   AND WHEN I HAD GOT MY WILL AND DRAWN YOU HERE, ...   284 TWO KINGS   158
   PAINTINGS OF THE DOLPHIN DRAWN: . . . .   309 REALISTS   V   4
   I'LL SAY AND MAYBE DREAM I HAVE DRAWN CONTENT, . . .   333 LIVING BEAUTY   V   1
   OUT OF THAT RAVING TIDE--IS DRAWN BETWIXT . . . . .   377 PHASES OF MOON   122
   CHAUCER HAD NOT DRAWN BREATH . . . .   421 MY TABLE   8
   BUT O! AMBITIOUS HEART, HAD SUCH A PROOF DRAWN FORTH . .   427 PHANTOM HATRED   36
   ALL TEETH WERE DRAWN, ALL ANCIENT TRICKS UNLEARNED, . .   429 NINETEEN 19   17
   NEVER TO HAVE DRAWN THE BREATH OF LIFE, ...   459 FROM OEDIPUS   11
   DRAWN THROUGH THE WANDERING VEGETATIVE DREAM, ...   467 HARUN RASHID   143
   AND I LEFT SHIVERING. THE VOICE HAS DRAWN . . . . .   469 HARUN RASHID   179
   WHEELS BY MILK-WHITE ASSES DRAWN . . . .   502 VACILLATION   62
   THE CURTAINS DRAWN UPON UNFRIENDLY NIGHT, ...   523 LONG SILENCE   4
   THE BLINDS DRAWN UP"! MAUD GONNE AT HOWTH STATION WAITING   578 LOFTY THINGS   10
    A TRAIN,
   NASCHINA'S GONE, DRAWN BY A THIRST OF LOVE, ...   664 ISLE STAT II 2   59
   I FEEL A FINGER DRAWN ACROSS MY CHEEK! . . . . . .   694 MOSADA 1   96
   OF SOLDIERS DRAWN IS ON A GRASSY SPOT, ...   712 FERENCZ RENYI   V   64
DRAWS
   WHO DRAWS A BUCKET WITH THE REST . . . .   335 YOUNG BEAUTY   5
   THE BOAT DRAWS NEAR AND NEAR. YOU HEED ME NOT! . . .   663 ISLE STAT II 2   23
   THE MAN WHOSE HOUR OF DEATH DRAWS NIGH, ...   716 FAIRY DOCTOR   6
DREAD
   "FRET NOT WITH SPEECH THE PHANTOMS DREAD," . . . . .   12 OISIN 1   V   148
   "THESE FORMS?" "VEX NOT WITH SPEECH THE PHANTOMS DREAD."   29 OISIN 2   V   5
   LONG WHILE, ARE WHIPS OF STEEL." "IS HE SO DREAD?" . .   35 OISIN 2   V   88
   FOR BATTLE." "FLY YE FROM A THING SO DREAD. . . . .   35 OISIN 2   V   90
   LEST NIAMH SHUDDER. FULL OF HOPE AND DREAD . . . . .   41 OISIN 2   183
   DREAD OATH, WHO DWELL ON SACRED HIMALAY, ...   74 ANASHU VIJAYA   67
   AND HIS HEART WAS BLACKENED BY DREAD, ...   145 HOST OF AIR   V 40B
   WHAT NEED HAVE YOU TO DREAD . . . .   312 CHILD DANCING   11
   WHAT NEED THAT YOU SHOULD DREAD . . . .   312 CHILD DANCING   V   11
   ALL DREAD AFAR TILL MORNING'S BACK, ...   435 FOR MY SON   6
   AND WHEN I WAKE TOWARDS MORN I DREAD MYSELF, ...   448 HERO GIRL FOOL   5
   NOR DREAD NOR HOPE ATTEND . . . .   476 DEATH   1
   DREAD HAS FOLLOWED LONGING, ...   519 LOVES LONENESS   11
   GAIETY TRANSFIGURING ALL THAT DREAD. . . . . . .   565 LAPIS LAZULI   17
   I SING WHAT WAS LOST AND DREAD WHAT WAS WON, ...   591 WHAT WAS LOST   1
   MORE DREAD THE LIFE THAT WE LIVE, ...   615 MARCH SONGS 2   15
   WHY DO YOU DREAD US SO? . . . .   635 BLACK TOWER   16
   OF THE DREAD WOODS! ALONG THEIR RUSSET FLOOR . . . .   675 ISLE STAT II 3   243
   ALL THESE ARE SOULS THAT FLY FROM THEIR DREAD SELVES. .   686 LIFE   4
   ALL THESE ARE SOULS WHO FLY FROM THEIR DREAD SELVES. .   734 QUATRAIN APHOR   4
   ALL THESE ARE SOULS THAT FLY FROM THEIR DREAD SELVES. .   734 QUATRAIN APHOR V   4
   THEIR DREAD OF AUTUMN'S MORTAL WING, ...   736 SUMMER EVENING   2
   AND DREAD NO MORE FOUL AUTUMN'S WING, ...   737 SUMMER EVENING   18
DREADFUL
   OR CARVE A DREADFUL SPEAR. . . . .   32 OISIN 2   V   56
   "IS HE SO DREADFUL?" "BE NOT OVER-BOLD, ...   35 OISIN 2   88
   "IS HE SO DREADFUL?" "BE NOT OVER BOLD, ...   35 OISIN 2   V   88
   LEST THEY SHOULD LOOK UPON SOME DREADFUL SIGHT! . . .   38 OISIN 2   142
   AND MAY SOME SUDDEN DREADFUL ILL BEFALL HER! . . . .   74 ANASHU VIJAYA   59
   AND MAY SOME DREADFUL ILL BEFALL HER QUICK! . . . .   74 ANASHU VIJAYA   V   59
   FOR THREE DAYS MORE IN DREADFUL QUIETUDE. . . . .   110 CUCHULAIN SEA   78
   ALL THOSE DREADFUL THUNDER-STONES, ...   509 JANE REPROVED   2
   ALL THOSE DREADFUL THUNDERSTONES, ...   509 JANE REPROVED   V   2
   OR WHERE THAT SNOW AND WINTER'S DREADFUL BLAST . . .   563 MERU   11
   AND ROVE UNCEASING ROUND THEIR DREADFUL BROOD. . . .   681 SEEKER   5
DREADING
   DREADING AND HOPING ALL! . . . .   476 DEATH   4
DREADS
   HE DREADS THE WEIGHT OF MORTAL HOURS. . . . . . .   212 BLESS PSALTER   11
DREAM
   "WHAT DREAM CAME WITH YOU THAT YOU CAME . . . . .   5 OISIN 1   50
   A DRUID DREAM OF THE END OF DAYS . . . .   16 OISIN 1   219
   AND STILL I DREAM HE TREADS THE LAWN. . . . . .   67 HAPPY SHEPHERD   51
   BUT AH! SHE DREAMS NOT NOW! DREAM THOU! . . . . .   67 HAPPY SHEPHERD   55
   DREAM, DREAM, FOR THIS IS ALSO SOOTH. . . . . .   67 HAPPY SHEPHERD   57
   DREAM, DREAM, FOR THIS IS ALSO SOOTH. . . . . .   67 HAPPY SHEPHERD   57
   WHO WASTES HIS BLOOD TO BE ANOTHER'S DREAM. . . . .   103 FERGUS DRUID   28
   BECAUSE I BE NOT OF THE THINGS I DREAM. . . . . .   103 FERGUS DRUID   V 26A
   TO DO AND DO AND DO AND NEVER DREAM. . . . . .   103 FERGUS DRUID   V   28
   WHO DREAMED THAT BEAUTY PASSES LIKE A DREAM? . . . .   111 ROSE OF WORLD   1
   AND SLOWLY READ, AND DREAM OF THE SOFT LOOK . . . .   121 YOU ARE OLD   3
   AH, DREAM NOT OF THEM, MY BELOVED, THE FLAME OF THE METEOR 122 WHITE BIRDS   6
    THAT GOES,
   A DREAM OF DEATH . . . .   123 DREAM OF DEATH   T
   A DREAM OF A BLESSED SPIRIT . . . .   124 CATHLEEN PARA   V   T
   DREAM, UNTIL GOD BURN NATURE WITH A KISS? . . . . .   128 DREAM OF FAERY   47
   THE LOVE I LIVED, THE DREAM I KNEW. . . . . . .   139 TO IRELAND   34
   NO PLACE FOR LOVE AND DREAM AT ALL! . . . . . .   139 TO IRELAND   43
   EMPTY YOUR HEART OF ITS MORTAL DREAM. . . . . .   140 HOSTING SIDHE   5
   FILLING THY HEART WITH A MORTAL DREAM, ...   140 HOSTING SIDHE   V   6
   HE SAT AND PLAYED IN A DREAM . . . .   145 HOST OF AIR   27

219

	PAGE	TITLE		LINE

DREAM   (CONTINUED)

AND OUT OF HIS DREAM AWOKE: . . . . 145 HOST OF AIR   38
HE SAT DOWN AND PLAYED IN A DREAM . . . . 145 HOST OF AIR   V   27
AND THE YOUNG LIE LONG AND DREAM IN THEIR BED . . . . 150 OLD MOTHER   5
WHILE THE YOUNG LIE LONG AND DREAM IN THEIR BED . . . 150 OLD MOTHER   V   5
BUT THE YOUNG LIE LONG AND DREAM IN THEIR BED . . . . 150 OLD MOTHER   V   5
O VANITY OF SLEEP, HOPE, DREAM, ENDLESS DESIRE, . . . 154 BELOVED PEACE   7
I CRIED IN MY DREAM, O WOMEN, BID THE YOUNG MEN LAY . 163 VALLEY LOVERS   5
AND I CRIED IN MY DREAM "O WOMEN, BID THE YOUNG MEN LAY 163 VALLEY LOVERS V   5
AND DREAM ABOUT THE GREAT AND THEIR PRIDE: . . . . . 166 EVIL OF BELOV   2
LILIES OF DEATH-PALE HOPE, ROSES OF PASSIONATE DREAM. 172 TRAV PASSION   8
FOR ALL THEIR BEAUTY'S LIKE A HOLLOW DREAM . . . . . 184 QUEEN MAEVE   88
FOR ALL THEIR BEAUTY, LIKE A HOLLOW DREAM?" . . . . . 184 QUEEN MAEVE   V   89
ALTHOUGH THEIR BEAUTY'S LIKE A HOLLOW DREAM" . . . . 184 QUEEN MAEVE   V   89
CERTAIN, AND THEY NEVER DREAM . . . . 202 NEVER GIVE ALL   4
TO DREAM OF WOMEN WHOSE BEAUTY WAS FOLDED IN DISMAY, . 210 UNDER THE MOON   19
AND LET THE DREAM GO BY. IT'S NOT A DREAM, ... 229 SHADOW WATER B   158
AND LET THE DREAM GO BY. IT'S NOT A DREAM, ... 229 SHADOW WATER B   158
OR FUMBLING IN A DREAM ABOUT THE HOUSE? . . . . 230 SHADOW WATER B   174
COULD WE BUT MIX OURSELVES INTO A DREAM, ... 230 SHADOW WATER B   188
NOW THAT MY BODY HAS BEGUN TO DREAM, ... 245 SHADOW WATER B   486
HIS DREAM . . . . 253 HIS DREAM   T
A DREAM . . . . 253 HIS DREAM   V   T
I DREAM THAT I HAVE BROUGHT . . . . 255 WOMAN HOMER   10
BUT AN HEROIC DREAM. . . . . 255 WOMAN HOMER   21
A DREAM THAT A LION HAD DREAMED . . . . 259 UNWORTH PRAISE   7
SO BITTERLY, YOU'D DREAM THEY LONGED TO LOOK . . . . 265 ABBEY THEATRE   6
AND DREAM THAT I SHOULD CARRY . . . . 309 PLAYER QUEEN   19
AND DREAM THAT ALL THE WORLD'S A FRIEND, ... 313 TWO YEAR LATER   8
WHAT MADE US DREAM THAT HE COULD COMB GREY HAIR? . . 327 ROBERT GREGORY   88
IS THIS MY DREAM, OR THE TRUTH? . . . . 329 MEN IMPROVE   13
HE STRETCHED HIS BONES AND FELL IN A DREAM . . . . . 331 ROUND TOWER   10
I'LL SAY AND MAYBE DREAM I HAVE DRAWN CONTENT, . . . 333 LIVING BEAUTY V   1
A MAN WHO IS BUT A DREAM: . . . . 348 FISHERMAN   36
A MAN CONFUSEDLY IN A HALF DREAM . . . . 351 HER PRAISE   8
A MAN—SO VAGUELY THAT HE SEEMED TO DREAM—— . . . . . 351 HER PRAISE   V   8
FROM DREAM TO DREAM AND RHYME TO RHYME I HAVE RANGED . 357 BROKEN DREAMS   39
FROM DREAM TO DREAM AND RHYME TO RHYME I HAVE RANGED . 357 BROKEN DREAMS   39
WHO HAS AWAKENED FROM THE COMMON DREAM . . . . 369 EGO DOMINUS   50
WE TAKE IT FOR THE NORM! YET SHOULD I DREAM . . . . 371 ON GOING HOUSE   9
THAT DREAM IS A NORM! AND SHOULD SOME LIMB OF THE DEVIL 372 ON GOING HOUSE   12
FROM THE FIRST CRESCENT TO THE HALF, THE DREAM . . . 373 PHASES OF MOON   36
BUT SAVES US FROM A DREAM. AND WHAT OF THOSE . . . . 376 PHASES OF MOON   102
WE KNOW THEIR DREAM: ENOUGH . . . . 394 EASTER 1916   70
HOW COULD YOU DREAM THEY'D LISTEN . . . . 395 SIXTEEN DEAD   13
WAS IT THE DOUBLE OF MY DREAM . . . . 398 BREAK OF DAY   1
DREAMED, OR DID WE HALVE A DREAM . . . . 398 BREAK OF DAY   3
DREAM AND SO CREATE . . . . 415 TOWER   155
MIRROR-RESEMBLING DREAM. . . . . 415 TOWER   165
IN THE COLD SNOWS OF A DREAM. . . . . 424 ROAD AT DOOR   15
FEW DREAM THAT THEY EXIST, ... 436 FOR MY SON   V   11
DREAM OF SHAVINGS ON A FLOOR . . . . 440 WISDOM   V   6
I DREAM OF A LEDAEAN BODY, BENT . . . . 443 SCHOOL CHILDR   9
THAT THEY HAVE WELCOMED IN THEIR TENTS THE DREAM . . 462 HARUN RASHID V   23
DRAWN THROUGH THE WANDERING VEGETATIVE DREAM, ... 467 HARUN RASHID   143
DREAM THAT I LOVE HER ONLY FOR THE VOICE, ... 469 HARUN RASHID   171
DREAM THAT I LOVE HER ONLY FOR THAT VOICE, ... 469 HARUN RASHID V 171
AND GOD-APPOINTED BERKELEY THAT PROVED ALL THINGS A DREAM, 481 BLOOD AND MOON 25
BLENCHED BY THAT MALICIOUS DREAM . . . . 488 CRAZED MOON   16
HER DREAM . . . . 519 HER DREAM   T
DREAM OF THE NOBLE AND THE BEGGAR-MAN. . . . . 603 GALLERY REVIS   47
DREAM OF THE NOBLE AND THE BEGGARMAN. . . . . 603 GALLERY REVIS V   47
A HELEN OF SOCIAL WELFARE DREAM, ... 626 OLD MEN BE MAD   7
AND THIS BROUGHT FORTH A DREAM AND SOON ENOUGH . . . 630 CIRCUS ANIMALS   23
THIS DREAM ITSELF HAD ALL MY THOUGHT AND LOVE. . . . 630 CIRCUS ANIMALS   24
IT WAS THE DREAM ITSELF ENCHANTED ME: . . . . 630 CIRCUS ANIMALS   28
ITS JOY OR NIGHT SEEM BUT A DREAM: . . . . 633 MAN AND ECHO   42
ITS JOY OR NIGHT SEEMS BUT A DREAM. . . . . 633 MAN AND ECHO V   42
WHEN SLEEPERS WAKE AND YET STILL DREAM, ... 639 BEN BULBEN   59
WHEN THAT GREATER DREAM HAD GONE . . . . 639 BEN BULBEN   63
AS SOME DEAD MAIDEN'S SINGING IN A DREAM. . . . . . 654 ISLE STAT I 2   59
I DREAM!—I CANNOT DIE!—NO! NO! . . . . 675 ISLE STAT II 3   227
I DREAM!—I CANNOT DIE!—NOT DIE! NO! NO! . . . . . . 675 ISLE STAT II 3 V 227
AND DREAM OF THE END OF THEIR DAYS, ... 707 FAIRY PEDANT   4
COME AND DREAM OF KINGS AND KINGDOMS, ... 737 IN FIRELIGHT   1
OF FOLLOWING FORGAEL'S DREAM FROM WIND TO WIND. . . . 758 SHADOW WATER A   219
HE HAS THROWN A DRUID DREAM UPON THE AIR. . . . . . 759 SHADOW WATER A   237
AND THAT DREAM ONLY SHINE BEFORE HER FEET. . . . . . 761 SHADOW WATER A   258
THEY DREAM THAT LAUGHED IN THE SUN. . . . . 783 GREY ROUND   13
DRY BONES THAT DREAM ARE BITTER, ... 783 GREY ROUND   14
THEY DREAM AND DARKEN OUR SUN. . . . . 783 GREY ROUND   15

DREAM-AWAKENED

SUDDENLY HURTLE BEFORE MY DREAM-AWAKENED EYES, . . . 161 BLACK PIG   2

DREAM-DIMMED

WITH HER CLOUD-PALE EYELIDS FALLING ON DREAM-DIMMED EYES: 163 VALLEY LOVERS   4
O CLOUD-PALE EYELIDS, DREAM-DIMMED EYES, ... 164 PERFECT BEAUTY   1

DREAMED

A BEAUTIFUL YOUNG MAN DREAMED WITHIN . . . . 17 OISIN 1   248
BEFORE THE SWIFT THINGS THAT SHE DREAMED OF WERE DONE 27 OISIN 1   414
STILL EARLESS, NERVELESS, BLIND, THE EAGLES DREAMED. 36 OISIN 2   V 100
WHO DREAMED THAT BEAUTY PASSES LIKE A DREAM? . . . . 111 ROSE OF WORLD   1

	PAGE	TITLE		LINE
DREAMED (CONTINUED)				
I DREAMED THAT ONE HAD DIED IN A STRANGE PLACE	123	DREAM OF DEATH		1
THE MAN WHO DREAMED OF FAERYLAND	126	DREAM OF FAERY		T
A MAN WHO DREAMED OF FAIRYLAND	126	DREAM OF FAERY	V	T
FOR ALL WHO HEARD IT DREAMED A LITTLE WHILE.	129	BOOK STORIES	V	8
AND DREAMED OF THE LONG DIM HAIR	144	HOST OF AIR		7
HE HEARD WHILE HE SANG AND DREAMED	144	HOST OF AIR		9
AND DREAMED THAT THE OLD DESPAIR	152	LOSS OF LOVE		3
I DREAMED THAT I STOOD IN A VALLEY, AND AMID SIGHS,	163	VALLEY LOVERS		1
AND I DREAMED MY LOST LOVE CAME STEALTHILY OUT OF THE WOOD	163	VALLEY LOVERS		3
HE HAD FALLEN ASLEEP, AND, THOUGH HE HAD DREAMED NOTHING,	182	QUEEN MAEVE		55
DREAMED OF THE HANDS THAT WOULD UNLACE	193	BAILE AILLINN		104
YET DREAMED THAT BEINGS HAPPIER THAN MEN	218	WOODS OF COOLE		18
A DREAM THAT A LION HAD DREAMED	259	UNWORTH PRAISE		7
BECAUSE SHE DREAMED WHEN BUT A CHILD	272	GREY ROCK		42
A MEASURELESS CONSUMMATION THAT HE DREAMED.	324	ROBERT GREGORY		24
WE DREAMED THAT A GREAT PAINTER HAD BEEN BORN	326	ROBERT GREGORY		65
BECAUSE OF WHAT HE HAD DREAMED,	342	SHEP GOATHERD		92
FROM GOING-DOWN OF THE SUN I HAVE DREAMED	358	PRESENCES		3
FROM GOING DOWN OF THE SUN I HAVE DREAMED	358	PRESENCES	V	3
THAT SHE OF DANCING DREAMED.	383	VISION ROBART		24
THIS OTHER MAN I HAD DREAMED	393	EASTER 1916		31
TO KNOW THEY DREAMED AND ARE DEAD;	394	EASTER 1916		71
DREAMED, OR DID WE HALVE A DREAM	398	BREAK OF DAY		3
I DREAMED TOWARDS BREAK OF DAY,	399	BREAK OF DAY		19
O BUT WE DREAMED TO MEND	431	NINETEEN 19		84
LEARN THAT WE WERE CRACK-PATED WHEN WE DREAMED.	431	NINETEEN 19		88
AND THAT SHE DREAMED AWAKE CONTENT TO TOUCH	466	HARUN RASHID	V	125C
I DREAMED AS IN MY BED I LAY,	519	HER DREAM		1
HE HAD DREAMED THE COW HAD GOT WITHIN	729	PRIEST FAIRY		33
WHEN SHE DREAMED FIRST OF LOVE, SHALL FLICKER OUT	760	SHADOW WATER A	V	257
THEY DREAMED THAT LAUGHED IN THE SUN.	783	GREY ROUND	V	13
DREAMER				
DREAMER OF THE MIDDLE-AGES. EMPTY EYEBALLS KNEW	610	STATUES		20
DREAMER OF THE MIDDLE-AGES. EMPTY EYE-BALLS KNEW	610	STATUES	V	20
SCHOOLMASTER HE, A DREAMER, FIDDLER, FIRST	709	FERENCZ RENYI		11
DREAMERS				
A WEARINESS COMES FROM THOSE DREAMERS,	122	WHITE BIRDS		5
AND A WEARINESS COMES FROM THOSE DREAMERS	122	WHITE BIRDS	V	5
DREAM-FED				
WHERE DREAM-FED PASSION IS AND PEACE ENCLOSES,	669	ISLE STAT II 3		85
DREAM-HEAVY				
COME FROM A MORE DREAM-HEAVY LAND,	156	FORGOT BEAUTY		16
A MORE DREAM-HEAVY HOUR THAN THIS!	156	FORGOT BEAUTY		17
DREAMING				
DREAMING OF HER OWN MELTING HUES,	13	OISIN 1		162
OF OLD THE WORLD ON DREAMING FED!	64	HAPPY SHEPHERD		3
AND HE, OF HIS HIGH COMRADE SORROW DREAMING,	67	SAD SHEPHERD		2
AND HE, OF HIS HIGH KINSMAN SORROW DREAMING,	67	SAD SHEPHERD	V	2
BUT LEARN THE DREAMING WISDOM THAT IS YOURS.	103	FERGUS DRUID		22
AND DREAMING HOW THEY DANCE AND DART,	135	TWO TREES	V	18
BY DREAMING LADIES UPON CLOTH	156	FORGOT BEAUTY		7
IT HAD GROWN SWEET-TONGUED BY DREAMING	160	CAP AND BELLS		17
THE TONGUE OF IT SWEET WITH DREAMING	160	CAP AND BELLS	V	17
AND THE PROUD DREAMING KING WHO FLUNG THE CROWN	170	SECRET ROSE		19
I HAVE NO HAPPINESS IN DREAMING OF BRYCELINDE,	209	UNDER THE MOON		1
AND SET YOU DREAMING. HOW CAN WE HAVE A WAKE	240	SHADOW WATER B		386
AND HOW WHAT HER DREAMING GAVE	260	UNWORTH PRAISE		15
THAT VIGOROUS THIGH, THAT DREAMING EYE?	386	ROBARTES DANCE		23
FOUND CERTAINTY UPON THE DREAMING AIR,	489	COOLE PARK 29		22
OF THE DREAMING WATER-FOWLS,	644	SONG FAERIES		12
DREAMING IN THEIR SOFT ODOUR-LADEN SLEEP!	650	ISLE STAT I 1		125
DREAMING THE LIVE-LONG SUMMER IN THE SHADE,	650	ISLE STAT I 1		139
DREAMING OF FLASHING FLIGHT AND OF THE PLUMED WAVE.	650	ISLE STAT I 1		140
OF THE DREAMING WATER-FOWLS,	676	ISLE STAT II 3		259
THE OTTERS DREAMING LAY. AYE!	677	ISLE STAT II 3		280
THE OTTERS DREAMING LAY. NASCHINA! AY!	677	ISLE STAT II 3	V	280
WHO, DREAMING TO A WONDROUS AGE, LIVED ON,	692	MOSADA 1		52
THE WORLD WERE DREAMING IN ITS SUMMER SLEEP!	699	MOSADA 3		11
OF DREAMING AND OF WATCHING BY THE DOOR	700	MOSADA 3		26
PAST THE CAMEL'S DREAMING EYE.	733	STREET DANCERS		43
WEIGH THEM IN AN HOUR OF DREAMING,	737	IN FIRELIGHT		11
AND LEAVE HER DREAMING. WHEN I LOOKED ON HER,	761	SHADOW WATER A	V	258
THE DREAMING BONES CRY OUT	782	HEART FRIGHT		15
DREAM-LED				
FROM THREESCORE YEARS OF DREAM-LED WANDERING	682	SEEKER		16
DREAMLESS				
UPON THE DANCER BY THE DREAMLESS WAVE.	128	DREAM OF FAERY		45
SHALL GROW THY BEAUTY AND THY DREAMLESS TRUTH,	674	ISLE STAT II 3		207
OF LOVE FROM OUT A DREAMLESS RACE FOR STRIFE,	684	SEEKER		58
HAST THOU NOT KNOWN A RAJA'S DREAMLESS SLUMBER?	724	KANVA ON SELF		8
DREAMS SEE LOVE-DREAMS				
YOU ARE STILL WRECKED AMONG HEATHEN DREAMS.	4	OISIN 1		31
AND DREAMS OF HER OWN MELTING HUES,	13	OISIN 1	V	162
WHERE AENGUS DREAMS, FROM SUN TO SUN,	16	OISIN 1		218
AND WRAPPED IN DREAMS RODE OUT AGAIN	25	OISIN 1		382
OR SAT IN DREAMS ON THE PALE STRAND,	25	OISIN 1		390
MY DREAMS WERE LIVING. NOW THE HOOF	25	OISIN 1	V	382
THE WARRIOR DREAMS IN AN AGED LEISURE	26	OISIN 1	V	401
WHILE HIS HEART STILL DREAMS OF BATTLE AND LOVE	27	OISIN 1		406
SO WARRED, SO FEASTED, WITH NOR DREAMS NOR FEARS,	44	OISIN 2		222

221

		PAGE	TITLE		LINE
DREAMS (CONTINUED)					
SO WARRED, SO FEASTED WE. NO DREAMS, NO FEARS,	• • •	44	OISIN 2	V	222
• • • DULL WITH THE SMOKE OF THEIR DREAMS!	• • • • •	51	OISIN 3		65
BUT IN DREAMS, MILD MAN OF THE CROZIERS,	• • •	53	OISIN 3		85
• • • WITH CREATURES OF DREAMS,	• • • • •	53	OISIN 3		95
AND THE DREAMS OF THE ISLANDS WERE GONE,	• • • • •	59	OISIN 3		175
AND THE DREAMS OF THE ISLANDS WENT OUT OF ME,	• • •	59	OISIN 3	V	175
• • • AN OLD MAN SURROUNDED WITH DREAMS.	• • • •	61	OISIN 3		196
NEW DREAMS, NEW DREAMS! THERE IS NO TRUTH	• • •	66	HAPPY SHEPHERD		26
NEW DREAMS, NEW DREAMS! THERE IS NO TRUTH	• • •	66	HAPPY SHEPHERD		26
BUT AH! SHE DREAMS NOT NOW! DREAM THOU!	• • • • •	67	HAPPY SHEPHERD		55
ROLLING ALONG IN DREAMS FROM HILL TO HILL.	• • • • •	68	SAD SHEPHERD		11
ON THEIR VAST FACES MYSTERY AND DREAMS!	• • • •	74	ANASHU VIJAYA		70
TROUBLE HIS SLEEPING! GIVE HIM DREAMS OF ME.	• • •	75	ANASHU VIJAYA		91
THE ISLAND DREAMS UNDER THE DAWN	• • • • •	77	INDIAN TO LOVE		1
GIVE THEM UNQUIET DREAMS!	• • • • • • •	88	STOLEN CHILD		34
WE GIVE THEM EVIL DREAMS,	• • • • • • •	88	STOLEN CHILD	V	34
HIS OLD EYES CLOUD WITH DREAMS!	• • • • •	98	FOXHUNTER		14
AND NOW THE OLD MAN'S DREAMS ARE GONE,	• • • • •	98	FOXHUNTER		19
WHO CAST ROUND FERGUS DREAMS, AND RUIN UNTOLD!	• •	101	ROSE UPON ROOD		5
TAKE, IF YOU MUST, THIS LITTLE BAG OF DREAMS!	• •	104	FERGUS DRUID		29
TAKE THEN THIS SMALL SLATE-COLOURED BAG OF DREAMS!	•	104	FERGUS DRUID	V	29
MY HEART WOULD BRIM WITH DREAMS ABOUT THE TIMES	• •	136	TO SOME I TALK		2
BECAUSE THEIR BLOSSOMING DREAMS HAVE NEVER BENT	• • •	136	TO SOME I TALK		8
FOR MY DREAMS OF YOUR IMAGE THAT BLOSSOMS A ROSE	• • •	143	ROSE IN HEART		8
THE BOOKS OF MY NUMBERLESS DREAMS,	• • • • •	157	POET BELOVED		2
WHITE WOMAN WITH NUMBERLESS DREAMS,	• • • •	157	POET BELOVED		7
THE DEWS DROP SLOWLY AND DREAMS GATHER! UNKNOWN SPEARS	• •	161	BLACK PIG		1
THE DEW DROPS SLOWLY! THE DREAMS GATHER! UNKNOWN SPEARS		161	BLACK PIG	V	1
AND TUMULT OF DEFEATED DREAMS! AND DEEP	• • • • •	169	SECRET ROSE		5
BUT I, BEING POOR, HAVE ONLY MY DREAMS!	• • •	176	CLOTHS HEAVEN		6
I HAVE SPREAD MY DREAMS UNDER YOUR FEET!	• • •	176	CLOTHS HEAVEN		7
TREAD SOFTLY BECAUSE YOU TREAD ON MY DREAMS.	• • • •	176	CLOTHS HEAVEN		8
HE COULD REMEMBER WHEN HE HAD HAD FINE DREAMS.	• • •	182	QUEEN MAEVE		56
THE BOUGHS HAVE WITHERED BECAUSE I HAVE TOLD THEM MY DREAMS.		203	WITHER BOUGHS		8
THE BOUGHS HAVE WITHERED BECAUSE I HAVE TOLD THEM MY DREAMS.		203	WITHER BOUGHS		16
THE BOUGHS HAVE WITHERED BECAUSE I HAVE TOLD THEM MY DREAMS.		204	WITHER BOUGHS		24
AND WHETHER I GO IN MY DREAMS BY WOODLAND, OR DUN, OR SHORE,		210	UNDER THE MOON		14
MY DREAMS WERE CLOVEN BY VOICES AND BY FIRES!	• • • • •	218	WOODS OF COOLE		20
WE HAVE FALLEN IN THE DREAMS THE EVER-LIVING	• • • • •	228	SHADOW WATER B		131
COULD WE BUT GIVE US WHOLLY TO THE DREAMS.	• • • •	230	SHADOW WATER B		178
AMONG SUBSTANTIAL THINGS! FOR IT IS DREAMS	• • • • •	230	SHADOW WATER B		181
BUT DREAMS THAT HURRY FROM BEYOND THE WORLD	• • • •	230	SHADOW WATER B		185
TO CAST HIS DREAMS AWAY. NO OTHER'LL DO IT.	• • • • •	239	SHADOW WATER B		366
BEING DRIVEN ON BY VOICES AND BY DREAMS	• • • • •	243	SHADOW WATER B		441
AND IF THAT HAPPINESS BE MORE THAN DREAMS,	• • • •	248	SHADOW WATER B		554
I HALF REMEMBER. IT HAS BEEN IN MY DREAMS.	• • • •	251	SHADOW WATER B		606
TO CRY ALOUD TO THE GREY BIRDS, AND DREAMS,	• • • •	252	SHADOW WATER B		618
THAT HAVE HAD DREAMS FOR FATHER, LIVE IN US.	• • • •	252	SHADOW WATER B		619
IF WE BUT SAW IN DREAMS THAT ROOM,	• • • •	272	GREY ROCK		38
AND LOOSEN ON US DREAMS THAT WASTE OUR LIFE,	• • • •	281	TWO KINGS		107
THE EXORBITANT DREAMS OF BEGGARY,	• • • • •	296	THREE BEGGARS		39
I AM WORN OUT WITH DREAMS!	• • • • • • •	329	MEN IMPROVE		1
BUT I GROW OLD AMONG DREAMS.	• • • • • • •	329	MEN IMPROVE		16
HE DREAMS HIMSELF HIS MOTHER'S PRIDE,	• • • • •	343	SHEP GOATHERD		110
BROKEN DREAMS	• • • • • • • • •	355	BROKEN DREAMS		T
AMID THE DREAMS OF YOUTH! LET HER COME FACE TO FACE,	• •	366	HER COURAGE		3
BEYOND THE VISIBLE WORLD. ALL DREAMS OF THE SOUL	• •	374	PHASES OF MOON		63
OR ELSE MY DREAMS THAT FLY	• • • • •	384	VISION ROBART		51
MIRROR RESEMBLING DREAMS.	• • • • • •	415	TOWER	V	165
MERE DREAMS, MERE DREAMS! YET HOMER HAD NOT SUNG	• •	417	ANCEST HOUSES		9
MERE DREAMS, MERE DREAMS! YET HOMER HAD NOT SUNG	• •	417	ANCEST HOUSES		9
HAD HE NOT FOUND IT CERTAIN BEYOND DREAMS	• • • •	417	ANCEST HOUSES		10
BUT THAT HE FOUND MORE SUBSTANCE THERE THAN DREAMS,	• •	417	ANCEST HOUSES	V	10
FROM MY OLD FATHERS, I MUST NOURISH DREAMS.	• • • •	422	MY DESCENDANTS		2
THE PAINTER'S BRUSH CONSUMES HIS DREAMS!	• • • • •	438	SONGS PLAY 2		12
I KNOW NOT WHAT THE YOUNGER DREAMS--	• • • • •	475	EVA GORE-BOOTH		10
WANDER IN DREAMS NO MORE!	• • • • • • •	554	CHURCH STATE		8
ALL HIS HAPPIER DREAMS CAME TRUE--	• • • •	577	WHAT THEN		11
GAVE WOMEN DREAMS AND DREAMS THEIR LOOKING-GLASS.	• •	610	STATUES		16
GAVE WOMEN DREAMS AND DREAMS THEIR LOOKING-GLASS.	• •	610	STATUES		16
GAVE WOMEN DREAMS AND DREAMS THEIR LOOKING GLASS.	• •	610	STATUES	V	16
GAVE WOMEN DREAMS AND DREAMS THEIR LOOKING GLASS.	• •	610	STATUES	V	16
THROUGH THREE ENCHANTED ISLANDS, ALLEGORICAL DREAMS,	• •	629	CIRCUS ANIMALS		11
MY DREAMS ROUND THOUGHTS OF PLENTY, AS IN GLOOM	• • •	681	SEEKER		3
MY DREAMS O'ER THOUGHTS OF PLENTY, AS THE RED-	• • •	681	SEEKER	V	3
THAT DREAMS. SHE MOVETH, FEELING IN HER BRAIN	• •	687	TWO TITANS		10
HER DREAMS ARE TALKING WITH OLD YEARS. AWAKE,	• •	702	MOSADA 3		89
FIRST DREAMS, AND GOBLINS, AND THE LESSER SPRITES,	• •	722	WITCH VIVIEN		56
WISDOM AND DREAMS	• • • • • • •	743	WISDOM DREAMS		T
WISDOM AND DREAMS ARE ONE,	• • • • •	743	WISDOM DREAMS		5
FOR DREAMS ARE THE FLOWERS ABLOW,	• • • • •	743	WISDOM DREAMS		6
BECAUSE A GOD HAS MADE HIM WISE WITH DREAMS!	• • •	748	SHADOW WATER A		26
WOULD OVERCOME YOUR SORROW AND YOUR DREAMS.	• • •	749	SHADOW WATER A		52
AND FALLS AMONG THE DREAMS THE DROWSY GODS	• • •	750	SHADOW WATER A		68
AND WERE ALL DREAMS, IT WOULD NOT WEIGH IN THE HAND.	• •	750	SHADOW WATER A		77
BECAUSE I HAD HOPED TO COME, AS DREAMS FORETOLD,	• • •	757	SHADOW WATER A		197

222

		PAGE	TITLE		LINE

DREAMS (CONTINUED)
I HAVE FORGOT IT ALL. HOW SOON DREAMS FADE!	• • • • •	761	SHADOW WATER A		272
THAT CROWN WAS IN MY DREAMS--NO, NO--IN A RHYME.	• • • •	763	SHADOW WATER A		311
OF VOICES AND OF DREAMS. O HEART, BE STILL!	• • • • •	765	SHADOW WATER A		362
I HAVE BEGUN REMEMBERING MY DREAMS.	• • • • • •	766	SHADOW WATER A		380
I HAVE COMMANDED MEN IN DREAMS. BELOVED,	• • • • • •	766	SHADOW WATER A		381
AND EDDY TO EDDY. MASTERS OF OUR DREAMS,	• • • • •	768	SHADOW WATER A		418
THAT DIZZY DREAMS CAN SPRING	• • • • • • •	781	MY HEART BEAT		7
WITH THOSE FANTASTIC DREAMS.	• • • • • • •	781	MY HEART BEAT		11

DREAMT
ERE HALF THE SWIFT THINGS THAT SHE DREAMT ON WERE DONE,		28	OISIN 1	V	422
AND WEPT BECAUSE SHE HAD DREAMT THAT I	• • • • •	308	PLAYER QUEEN		11
I DREAMT SOME GREAT ONE. AH, MY BEAUTIFUL,	• • • •	720	WITCH VIVIEN		14
WHEN SHE DREAMT FIRST OF LOVE, SHALL FLICKER OUT	• • • •	760	SHADOW WATER A		257

DREAMY
OF DREAMY FOAM A STAFF OF WOOD.	• • • • • • • •	24	OISIN 1		366
AND SANG, AND WITH A DREAMY GAZE	• • • • • •	26	OISIN 1		393
MY SONGS OF OLD EARTH'S DREAMY YOUTH.	• • • • • •	67	HAPPY SHEPHERD		54
THERE DREAMY TIME LETS FALL HIS SICKLE	• • • • •	77	INDIAN TO LOVE	V	5A
VEILED IN A DREAMY SORROW FOR THEIR LOVE	• • • •	79	EPHEMERA	V	2A
BUT A BRIEF, DREAMY, KIND DELIGHT.	• • • • •	202	NEVER GIVE ALL		7
THAT THE GRAVE-DIGGERS IN A DREAMY FRENZY	• • • • •	243	SHADOW WATER B		430
YOUTH'S DREAMY LOAD, TILL SHE	• • • • • • •	315	FRIENDS		14

DREAR
| OF THE DREAR HART LAKE. | • • • • • • • • • • | 143 | HOST OF AIR | | 4 |

DREARY
| IN DREARY DANCING PAST US WHIRLED, | • • • • • • | 65 | HAPPY SHEPHERD | | 8 |
| A DREARY, DREEPY BEGGAR | • • • • • • • • | 552 | SONGS REWRIT 2 | | 5 |

DREEPY
| A DREARY, DREEPY BEGGAR | • • • • • • • • • | 552 | SONGS REWRIT 2 | | 5 |

DRENCH'D   SEE DEW-DRENCH'D
DRENCHED   SEE WINE-DRENCHED
| SUDDENLY DRENCHED HER TO THE SKIN! | • • • • • • • | 275 | GREY ROCK | | 120 |

DRESS
AND WHEN THEY SAW MY EARTHLY DRESS,	• • • • •	15	OISIN 1	V	207
HER PEARL-PALE HAND AND THE HEM OF HER DRESS.	• • •	16	OISIN 1		216
SHE'LL NOT ASK A HAUGHTY DRESS!	• • • • • •	124	CATHLEEN PARA		6
BEAR THE GOLD-EMBROIDERED DRESS--	• • • • •	124	CATHLEEN PARA	V	6
BEAR THE GOLD EMBROIDERED DRESS--	• • • • •	124	CATHLEEN PARA	V	6
HIS HEART HUNG ALL UPON A SILKEN DRESS,	• • • • •	126	DREAM OF FAERY		2
OVER SOME SILKEN DRESS	• • • • • • • • •	363	DOLLS DRAWINGS		7
FOR EVERY TATTER IN ITS MORTAL DRESS,	• • • • •	407	SAIL BYZANTIUM		12
A BIT OF AN EMBROIDERED DRESS	• • • • • • •	421	MY TABLE		6
FROM SOME COURT-LADY'S DRESS AND ROUND	• • • •	477	SELF AND SOUL		14
FROM SOME COURT-LADIES' DRESS AND ROUND	• • • •	477	SELF AND SOUL	V	14
I PLUCKED HER BACKWARDS BY HER DRESS OF GREEN.	• • •	676	ISLE STAT II 3		264

DRESSED
A QUEEN-WOMAN DRESSED OUT IN SILVER, CRY	• • • •	210	RAGGED WOOD	V	2
OR A YOUNG GIRL DRESSED OUT IN HER NEW GOWN,	• • •	350	HER PRAISE		4
HALF DRESSED IN NATIONAL UNIFORM,	• • • • • •	424	ROAD AT DOOR		7
EARTH IN BEAUTY DRESSED	• • • • • • • • •	517	HER ANXIETY		1
I, AS A SHEPHERD DRESSED, WILL SEEK AND SEEK	• • •	658	ISLE STAT II 1		1
I FOUGHT TWELVE BATTLES DRESSED IN GOLDEN ARMOUR.	• •	761	SHADOW WATER A		271

DREW
AND NOW STILL SAD OUR TROOP DREW NIGH	• • • • •	17	OISIN 1	V	247
AND NIGH UNTO HIM EACH ONE DREW,	• • • • • •	18	OISIN 1	V	257
I DREW OUT OF THE NUMBERLESS	• • • • • • • •	24	OISIN 1	V	365
I DREW IT FORTH! THE STAFF OF WOOD,	• • • • •	24	OISIN 1	V	366
NOW, MAN OF CROSIERS, PHANTOMS DREW AROUND	• • • •	29	OISIN 2	V	1
AND THEREUPON I DREW THE LIVID CHOP	• • • • •	40	OISIN 2		178
LAY LOOSE IN A PLACE OF SHADOW! WE DREW THE REINS BY HIS		50	OISIN 3		44
SIDE.					
I DREW AT EVENING MY MAILED MEN,	• • • • •	83	MAD KING GOLL	V	19
SHE DREW FROM ME MY STORY--	• • • • • •	96	MOLL MAGEE		37
BUT BRIDGET DREW HIM BY THE SLEEVE	• • • • •	144	HOST OF AIR		21
SHE DREW IN THE HEAVY CASEMENT	• • • • •	159	CAP AND BELLS		11
SHE DREW IN THE BRIGHTENING CASEMENT,	• • • • •	159	CAP AND BELLS	V	11
IF ANY MAN DREW NEAR	• • • • • • • •	254	WOMAN HOMER		1
THEN DREW HIS SWORD TO HOLD ITS LEVELLED POINT	• • •	277	TWO KINGS		14
BUT DREW HIS SWORD, AND THOUGHT WITH LEVELLED POINT	• •	277	TWO KINGS	V	14
ROSE! SOME CONQUEROR DREW REIN	• • • • •	502	VACILLATION		64
DREW A KNIFE TO STRIKE HIM DEAD,	• • • • •	514	JANE GROWN OLD		10
POETS AND WITS ABOUT HIM DREW!	• • • • •	577	WHAT THEN		14
MY MOTHER DREW FORTH FROM THE LONG GRASS	• • • •	708	FAIRY PEDANT		23
HE DREW FROM HIS CAP A FEATHER GREY, •--	• • •	729	PRIEST FAIRY		29
I DREW MY SWORD TO FLING IT IN A POOL, •--	• • •	747	SHADOW WATER A		7

DRIED
• • • THE FLESH OF HIS FACE AS DRIED GRASS,	• • •	59	OISIN 3		173
AND WISDOM THAT CAUGHT FIRE LIKE THE DRIED FLAX,	• •	181	QUEEN MAEVE		28
HAS DRIED THE SAP OUT OF MY VEINS, AND RENT	• • •	260	FASC DIFFICULT		2
YOU HAVE DRIED THE MARROW FROM THE BONE?	• • • •	289	SEPTEMBER 1913		5
AS THOUGH DRIED STRAW, AND IF WE TURN ABOUT	• • •	327	ROBERT GREGORY		83
PROSPER BUT LITTLE, HAS DRIED UP OF LATE,	• • • •	405	FOR DAUGHTER		51
A BONE WAVE-WHITENED AND DRIED IN THE WIND.	• • •	521	THREE THINGS		6
A BONE WAVE-WHITENED AND DRIED IN THE WIND.	• • •	521	THREE THINGS		12
A BONE WAVE-WHITENED AND DRIED IN THE WIND.	• • •	521	THREE THINGS		18
I HAVE CUPBOARDS OF DRIED FRAGRANCE,	• • • • •	572	LADYS 2ND SONG		5
HAS ROLLED AWAY THE STARS AND DRIED THE SEA	• • •	671	ISLE STAT II 3		146

DRIFT
| I SAW A FOAM-WHITE SEAGULL DRIFT AND FLOAT | • • • • | 36 | OISIN 2 | | 105 |
| FOR, AS DRIFT FROM A SAILOR SLOW DROWNING | • • • • | 48 | OISIN 3 | | 22 |

```
                                                          PAGE      TITLE            LINE

DRIFT   (CONTINUED)
    ALL THEIR LIVES THROUGH INTO SOME DRIFT OF WINGS.   .   .   .   265 ABBEY THEATRE          7
    BUT NOW THEY DRIFT ON THE STILL WATER,  .  .  .  .  .  .  .  .   323 SWANS AT COOLE        25
    DRIFT AND FLOAT LIKE SILVER SHIPS;  .  .  .  .  .  .  .  .  .    647 ISLE STAT I 1         67
DRIFTED
    WHERE THE DEAD DRIFTED, I COULD SEE A BIRD  .  .  .  .  .  .  .  223 SHADOW WATER B        23
    CAVERNED IN NIGHT UNDER THE DRIFTED SNOW.  .  .  .  .  .  .  .   563 MERU                  10
DRIFTING
    DRIFTING ON HIGH, AND WITH A STRAINING THROAT  .  .  .  .  .     36 OISIN 2          V   106
    AND DRIFTING GREYNESS, WHILE THIS MONOTONE,  .  .  .  .  .  .    45 OISIN 2              232
    AND DRIFTING GREYNESS.  CAME THIS MONOTONE .  .  .  .  .  .  .   45 OISIN 2          V   232
    I SEE MY LIFE GO DRIFTING LIKE A RIVER  .  .  .  .  .  .  .     104 FERGUS DRUID          31
    WERE GONE LIKE A DRIFTING SMOKE;  .  .  .  .  .  .  .  .  .  .   145 HOST OF AIR           40
    AND CUMHAL SAW LIKE A DRIFTING SMOKE .  .  .  .  .  .  .  .  .   167 BLESSED               13
DRIFTS
    LIKE DRIFTS OF LEAVES, IMMOVABLE AND BRIGHT,  .  .  .  .  .  .   40 OISIN 2              166
    LIKE DRIFTS OF LAUREL LEAVES, IMMOVABLE AND BRIGHT  .  .  .     40 OISIN 2          V   166
    HIS PURPOSE DRIFTS AND DIES."  .  .  .  .  .  .  .  .  .  .  .   45 OISIN 2              244
    HIS PURPOSE DRIFTS AWAY."  .  .  .  .  .  .  .  .  .  .  .  .    45 OISIN 2          V   244
    AND SMOKE FROM THIS DEAD HEART DRIFTS THROUGH THE VIOLET       173 SPEAKS HEARERS         3
        AIR
    I KNOW WHERE A DIM MOON DRIFTS, WHERE THE DANAAN KIND  .  .     203 WITHER BOUGHS         12
    "ALL THAT'S BEAUTIFUL DRIFTS AWAY  .  .  .  .  .  .  .  .  .     208 OLD MEN ADMIRE         8
    YOU ARE BROKEN, YOU ARE BROKEN. THE WORLD DRIFTS AWAY,         251 SHADOW WATER B       599
    WHERE THE SWAN DRIFTS UPON A DARKENING FLOOD.  .  .  .  .  .    492 COOLE BALLYLEE        48
    BEHOLD, I BEND!  AROUND MY BEARD IN DRIFTS  .  .  .  .  .  .    684 SEEKER                68
    BEHOLD I BOW!  AROUND MY BEARD IN DRIFTS  .  .  .  .  .  .      684 SEEKER           V    68
DRINK
    OF HAMMERED SILVER, AND DRINK  .  .  .  .  .  .  .  .  .  .  .   215 HAPPY TOWNLAND        50
    TO MAKE LOW LAUGHTER MORE THAN MEAT AND DRINK,  .  .  .  .  .   230 SHADOW WATER B       186
    TO DRINK OF THAT SALT BREATH OUT OF THE SEA  .  .  .  .  .      292 TO A SHADE             5
    AND DRINK BEFORE I TALK."  AND HE .  .  .  .  .  .  .  .  .  .   304 HOUR DAWN             45
    AND DRINK, AND YOU WILL SLEEP THAT LENGTH."  .  .  .  .  .  .   305 HOUR DAWN             59
    YOU'VE BUT TO DRINK THE BEER AND SAY .  .  .  .  .  .  .  .     305 HOUR DAWN        V    56
    IF YOU BUT DRINK THAT BEER AND SAY  .  .  .  .  .  .  .  .  .   305 HOUR DAWN        V    56
    THEIR FOOD AND DRINK:  .  .  .  .  .  .  .  .  .  .  .  .  .  .  380 SONGS FOOL 1           9
    TO DRINK FROM THE WINE-BREATH  .  .  .  .  .  .  .  .  .  .      471 ALL SOUL NIGHT         9
    WHILE OUR GROSS PALATES DRINK FROM THE WHOLE WINE,  .  .  .     471 ALL SOUL NIGHT        10
    NO LIVING MAN CAN DRINK FROM THE WHOLE WINE.  .  .  .  .  .     474 ALL SOUL NIGHT        85
    WHAT MATTER IF A BLIND MAN DRINK HIS DROP?  .  .  .  .  .  .    478 SELF AND SOUL    V    41
    STRONG DRINK I HAD, AND IT BROUGHT ME TO SORROW,  .  .  .  .    544 TO SAME TUNE 1        13
    COULD I BUT DRINK, MY LOVE ON MY KNEE  .  .  .  .  .  .  .  .    551 SONGS REWRIT 1 V       9
    O COULD I DRINK, MY LOVE ON MY KNEE,  .  .  .  .  .  .  .  .    551 SONGS REWRIT 1 V       9
    ALTHOUGH I DRINK MY FILL.  .  .  .  .  .  .  .  .  .  .  .  .    592 DRUNK SOBRIETY         4
    SO STAY AT HOME AND DRINK YOUR BEER  .  .  .  .  .  .  .  .  .   598 STONE CROSS            5
    WE'D DRINK A CAN OR TWO,  .  .  .  .  .  .  .  .  .  .  .  .  .  606 SONGS BURDEN 1        22
    THEIR DRINK, THEIR PITCH-AND-TOSS BY DAY,  .  .  .  .  .  .     607 SONGS BURDEN 2        14
    THEIR DRINK, THEIR PITCH AND TOSS BY DAY,  .  .  .  .  .  .     607 SONGS BURDEN 2 V      14
    STRONG DRINK I HAD, AND IT BROUGHT ME TO SORROW,  .  .  .  .    616 MARCH SONGS 3         13
    AWAY FROM ME WHERE MISTS OF EVENING DRINK  .  .  .  .  .  .     663 ISLE STAT II 2        40
    AND TELL ME A LOVE-STORY WHILE I DRINK.  .  .  .  .  .  .  .    760 SHADOW WATER A       250
    AND TELL ME A LOVE STORY WHILE I DRINK.  .  .  .  .  .  .  .    760 SHADOW WATER A V     250
    I WILL DRINK OUT OF THE STREAM.  THE STREAM IS GONE!  .  .      761 SHADOW WATER A       273
    MAY THE SWORD-BLADES DRINK THEIR FILL  .  .  .  .  .  .  .  .    776 AGAINST WITCH         37
    MAY THE SWORD BLADES DRINK THEIR FILL  .  .  .  .  .  .  .  .    776 AGAINST WITCH    V    37
DRINKERS'      SEE PORTER-DRINKERS'
DRINKING
    A DRINKING SONG  .  .  .  .  .  .  .  .  .  .  .  .  .  .  .  .  261 DRINKING SONG          T
    THE FORD WHERE DRINKING CATTLE MAKE A STIR  .  .  .  .  .  .    326 ROBERT GREGORY        53
    DRINKING THE FOUL DITCH WHERE THEY LIE?  .  .  .  .  .  .  .    397 POLIT PRISONER        12
    WENCHING, DRINKING, STILL REMAIN  .  .  .  .  .  .  .  .  .     529 TOM LUNATIC            9
    IS DRINKING HER HEALTH WHEN LONE, ALONE--  .  .  .  .  .  .     551 SONGS REWRIT 1 V       4
    DRINKING ALONE WITH A SPECKLED SHIN?  .  .  .  .  .  .  .  .    551 SONGS REWRIT 1 V       8
    DRINKING JOY AS IT WERE MILK UPON HIS BREAST.  .  .  .  .  .    559 MAGIC DRUM             3
    I PROMISE YOU A HUNDRED DRINKING BOWLS,  .  .  .  .  .  .  .    756 SHADOW WATER A V     187
DRINKING-BOWLS
    A HUNDRED SWORDS, A HUNDRED DRINKING-BOWLS.  .  .  .  .  .  .    756 SHADOW WATER A       186
DRINKS
    A LIVING MAN IS BLIND AND DRINKS HIS DROP.  .  .  .  .  .  .    478 SELF AND SOUL         41
    O'ER GRIEF.  THE WORLD DRINKS SORROW FROM THE BEAMS  .  .  .    664 ISLE STAT II 2        46
DRIP
    HOW THE FETLOCKS DRIP BLOOD IN THE BATTLE,  .  .  .  .  .  .     52 OISIN 3               78
DRIPPED
    DRIPPED ON THE EARTH; BUT SOON, AH! SOON,  .  .  .  .  .  .      19 OISIN 1          V   279
DRIPPING     SEE FOG-DRIPPING
    SPRANG DRIPPING, AND, WITH CAPTIVE DEMONS SENT  .  .  .  .       38 OISIN 2              130
    OF A DROWNED DRIPPING BODY TO MY BREAST;  .  .  .  .  .  .       40 OISIN 2              179
    I HELD A DRIPPING CORPSE, WITH LIVID CHOP  .  .  .  .  .  .      40 OISIN 2          V   178
    AND DRIPPING AND SUNKEN SHAPE, TO FACE AND BREAST,  .  .  .      40 OISIN 2          V   179
    AN ISLE LAY LEVEL BEFORE US, WITH DRIPPING HAZEL AND OAK?       47 OISIN 3               10
    AN ISLE LAY LEVEL BEFORE US, DRIPPING WITH HAZEL AND OAK?       47 OISIN 3          V    10
    GREY SAND ON THE GREEN OF THE GRASSES AND OVER THE DRIPPING     48 OISIN 3               14
        TREES,
    DRIPPING AND DOUBLING LANDWARD, AS THOUGH THEY WOULD HASTEN     48 OISIN 3               15
        AWAY,
    GREY SANDS ON THE GREEN OF THE GRASSES AND OVER THE            48 OISIN 3          V    14
        DRIPPING TREES,
    GREY SAND ON THE GREEN OF THE GRASSES AND OVER THE DRIPPING     57 OISIN 3              142
        TREES,
    DRIPPING AND DOUBLING LANDWARD, AS THOUGH THEY WOULD HASTEN     57 OISIN 3              143
        AWAY,
```

224

		PAGE	TITLE		LINE

DRIPPING   (CONTINUED)
    GREY SANDS ON THE GREEN OF THE GRASSES AND OVER THE   57 OISIN 3   V 142
        DRIPPING TREES,
    ALL DRIPPING ON A GRASSY SLOPE, AND SAW THEM CEASE TO CHASE   76 INDIAN ON GOD   4
    THE RAINS ARE FROM HIS DRIPPING WING, THE MOONBEAMS FROM   76 INDIAN ON GOD   8
        HIS EYE.
    I SEE MY LIFE GO DRIPPING LIKE A STREAM . . . .   104 FERGUS DRUID   V   31
    OF DRIPPING STONE; I DECLARE . . . .   414 TOWER   126
    I PASSED BY MANY CAVES OF DRIPPING STONE, ...   657 ISLE STAT I 3   47
    ABOVE, SALIVA DRIPPING FROM HIS JAWS, ...   689 NETTLESHIP   4
    HE TURNS WHERE, HUNG LIKE DROPS OF DRIPPING GOLD, ...   710 FERENCZ RENYI   18
    AND THE FISHER MEN AND WOMEN FROM THE DRIPPING HARBOUR WALL   718 PHANTOM SHIP   11
DRIVE
    AND PACE THE WOODS, AND DRIVE MY CHARIOT-WHEELS . . . .   103 FERGUS DRUID   18
    AND PACE THE WOODS, AND DRIVE MY CHARIOT-WHEELS . . . .   103 FERGUS DRUID   V   18
    AND DRIVE HIM FROM THE DOOR." AND THUS IT WAS: . . . .   106 CUCHULAIN SEA   V 17B
    WHO WILL GO DRIVE WITH FERGUS NOW, ...   125 GOES FERGUS   1
    I WILL DRIVE ALL THOSE LOVERS OUT AND CRY-- . . . . .   211 RAGGED WOOD   10
    I WILL DRIVE OUT THE DEER AND MOON AND CRY-- . . . . .   211 RAGGED WOOD   V   10
    DRIVE TO A FLASHIER BAUBLE YET. . . . .   437 SONGS PLAY 1   12
    MUST DRIVE THE ARABIAN HOST. THE VOICE GREW STILL,   467 HARUN RASHID   145
    MADE DRIVE THE ARABIAN HOST. THE VOICE GREW STILL,   467 HARUN RASHID   V 145
    NASCHINA, HAIL! I'D DRIVE THY WOOLLY SHEEP, ...   649 ISLE STAT I 1   122
    GATHER ON THE WIND AND DRIVE . . . .   775 AGAINST WITCH   7
DRIVEN   SEE RAGE-DRIVEN FOOL-DRIVEN PASSION-DRIVEN
    DRIVEN BY A STORM THAT EVER GRIEVES. . . . .   135 TWO TREES   V   28
    HAVE DRIVEN TRAVELLERS MAD FOR THEIR OWN SPORT. . . .   227 SHADOW WATER B   105
    MAY NOT HAVE DRIVEN YOU MAD FOR THEIR OWN SPORT? . . .   227 SHADOW WATER B   V 105
    BEING DRIVEN ON BY VOICES AND BY DREAMS . . . . . .   243 SHADOW WATER B   441
    THAT HE IS BEING DRIVEN TO HIS DEATH. . . . . . .   248 SHADOW WATER B   551
    "THE DANISH TROOP WAS DRIVEN OUT . . . .   273 GREY ROCK   65
    THEN HE, DRIVEN BY HIS THOUGHT BEYOND HIS THOUGHT,   282 TWO KINGS   122
    THEN HE, DRIVEN BY THIS THOUGHT BEYOND HIS THOUGHT,   282 TWO KINGS   V 122
    LIKE GENTLE BLOOD, HAS BEEN DRIVEN FROM THE PLACE, . .   292 TO A SHADE   14
    ARE DRIVEN BY WEALTH AS BEGGARS BY THE ITCH," . . . .   300 BEGGAR CRIED   14
    AND THEREUPON IMAGINATION AND HEART WERE DRIVEN . . .   316 COLD HEAVEN   3
    I HAD DRIVEN EVERY RHYME INTO ITS PLACE . . . . .   339 SHEP GOATHERD   14
    UNTIL I AM DRIVEN MAD, ...   346 ON WOMAN   35
    SLEEP DRIVEN FROM MY BED, ...   346 ON WOMAN   36
    ALL THE DISHONEST CROWD I HAD DRIVEN AWAY, ...   352 PEOPLE   24
    DERIDED AND DERIDING, DRIVEN OUT . . . .   369 EGO DOMINUS   34
    EVEN TO EYES THAT BEAUTY HAD DRIVEN MAD, ...   390 IMAGE PAST   34
    CONSIDERING THAT, ALL HATRED DRIVEN HENCE, ...   405 FOR DAUGHTER   65
    MUSIC HAD DRIVEN THEIR WITS ASTRAY-- . . . .   411 TOWER   47
    THE RAGE DRIVEN, RAGE TORMENTED, AND RAGE HUNGRY TROOP,   426 PHANTOM HATRED V   11
    AND THAT ALONE; YET I, BEING DRIVEN HALF INSANE . . .   442 BLACK CENTAUR   6
    AND THEREUPON MY HEART IS DRIVEN WILD! . . . . .   444 SCHOOL CHILDR   23
    HAD DRIVEN HIM CRAZED! . . . .   473 ALL SOUL NIGHT   73
    BY THAT GREAT GLORY DRIVEN WILD. . . . . . .   540 FROM ANTIGONE   13
    "OR DRIVEN FROM HOME AND LEFT TO DIE IN FEAR." . . .   635 CUCHULAIN COMF   22
    HAD DRIVEN HER FORTH, FOR EVER MORE . . . . .   668 ISLE STAT II 3   56
    HAD DRIVEN HER FORTH, FOR EVERMORE . . . . . .   668 ISLE STAT II 3 V   56
    BE DRIVEN FROM THE THRESHOLD . . . .   770 BLOOD BOND   5
    BE DRIVEN FROM THE THRESHOLDS . . . .   770 BLOOD BOND   V   4
    MAY THIS FIRE HAVE DRIVEN OUT . . . . . .   775 AGAINST WITCH   1
    MAY THIS FLAME HAVE DRIVEN OUT . . . . . .   775 AGAINST WITCH   V   1
DRIVES
    "HE DRIVES AWAY THE NORTHERN COLD." . . . .   82 MAD KING GOLL   11
    LOVE'S PLEASURE DRIVES HIS LOVE AWAY, ...   438 SONGS PLAY 2   11
DRIVING
    . . . DRIVING THE DUST WITH THEIR THRONGS, ...   53 OISIN 3   85
    WAS DRIVING CATTLE CAME SHE WITH SWIFT FEET, ...   106 CUCHULAIN SEA   V   19
    DRIVING THE DEER ALONG THE WOODY WAYS. . . . . .   109 CUCHULAIN SEA   V   48
    FLAMES THE SHUTTLE OF THE LIGHTNING ACROSS THE DRIVING 718 PHANTOM SHIP   1
        SLEET,
DROMAHAIR
    HE STOOD AMONG A CROWD AT DROMAHAIR: . . . . . .   126 DREAM OF FAERY   1
DROOP
    "AND EVERY HERO DROOP HIS HEAD? . . . .   4 OISIN 1   33
    HIS EYELIDS DROOP, HIS HEAD FALLS LOW, ...   98 FOXHUNTER   13
    IN THE LONG GRASS--FOUR EYES DROOP LOW--A SEAT . . .   716 DWELT SYCAMORE   11
DROOPED
    GLIMMERING IN HER DROOPED EYES, SAW HER LIPS MOVE . .   81 EPHEMERA   V 24D
DROOPETH
    DROOPETH NOW HIS FOREHEAD LOW . . . .   711 FERENCZ RENYI   V   39
DROOPING
    BOAST NOT, NOR MOURN WITH DROOPING HEAD . . . .   11 OISIN 1   129
    WITH A KISS AND A TEAR ON THY DROOPING BROW. . . .   79 FALLING LEAVES   8
    AT THE DROOPING OF AN EYE, ...   453 DEATH OF HARE   5
    AND 'MONG THE STUNTED ASH-TREES' DROOPING RINGS, . .   650 ISLE STAT I 1   128
    AS THEY GO WITH DROOPING FEATHER. . . . . . .   667 ISLE STAT II 3   33
DROOPS
    "WHY, AS YE RIDE, DROOPS LOW EACH HEAD? . . . . .   4 OISIN 1   V   32
    HIS EYELIDS CLOSE, HIS HEAD DROOPS LOW, ...   98 FOXHUNTER   V   13
    LIKE TUFTED REEDS OUR COURAGE DROOPS IN A BLACK WIND AND 207 HANRAHANS SONG V   3
        DIES!
    WEAK AND WORN AND WEARY OUR COURAGE DROOPS AND DIES . . 207 HANRAHANS SONG V   8
DROP   SEE TEAR-DROP FROTH-DROP DEW-DROP
    "THE SOUL IS A DROP OF JOY AFAR. . . . .   19 OISIN 1   V 276
    AND BID THE STARS DROP DOWN FROM THE SKY, ...   28 OISIN 1   426
    UNTIL THE GODS AND DEMONS DROP ASLEEP, ...   35 OISIN 2   86

225

	PAGE	TITLE		LINE

DROP   (CONTINUED)

"THIS DEMON SHALL BE PIERCED AND DROP AND DIE, ...   35 OISIN 2   V   90
"I HEAR MY SOUL DROP DOWN INTO DECAY, ...   45 OISIN 2   235
WITH ALL YOUR WHIRLING HAIR, AND DROP MANY AN AZURE TEAR.   73 ANASHU VIJAYA   46
WITH ALL YOUR WHIRLING HAIR, AND DROP THROUGH SPACE AN   73 ANASHU VIJAYA V 46
   AZURE TEAR.
WITH ALL YOUR WHIRLING HAIR, AND DROP TEAR UPON AZURE TEAR. 73 ANASHU VIJAYA V 46
WITH ALL OUR WHIRLING HAIR, AND DROP MANY AN AZURE TEAR.   73 ANASHU VIJAYA   46
IS BUT A SLIDING DROP OF RAIN BETWEEN HIS PETALS WIDE. . . 76 INDIAN ON GOD   12
IS BUT A SLIDING DROP OF RAIN WITHIN HIS PETALS WIDE." . . 76 INDIAN ON GOD V 12
AND GREAT BOUGHS DROP TRANQUILLITY: . . . .   77 INDIAN TO LOVE   2
AND DROP A VAPOURY FOOTFALL IN THE WATER'S DROWSY BLAZE. .   78 INDIAN TO LOVE V 20
FROM FERNS THAT DROP THEIR TEARS . . . .   88 STOLEN CHILD   36
FROM FERNS THAT DROP THEIR TEAR . . . .   88 STOLEN CHILD   V 36
A GREEN DROP IN THE SURGE, A GLEAM OF LIGHT . . . . .   104 FERGUS DRUID   33
THE DEWS DROP SLOWLY AND DREAMS GATHER: UNKNOWN SPEARS . . 161 BLACK PIG   1
"THE ROSE THAT MUST DROP, OUT OF SWEET LEAVES, ... 168 BLESSED   V 37
THAT IT MAY DROP FAINT PERFUME, AND BE HEAVY WITH DEW, . . 172 TRAV PASSION   7
AND ONE BY ONE WE DROP AWAY." . . . . 208 OLD MEN ADMIRE   3
AND DROP HIM FROM THE GUNNEL. I DARE NOT DO IT. . . . . 222 SHADOW WATER B   15
WHEN THE FLIES DROP IN THE STREAM: . . . . 348 FISHERMAN   34
DROP THEIR CAST AT THE SIDE . . . . 414 TOWER   125
AND DROP TWIGS LAYER UPON LAYER. . . . . 415 TOWER   168
THEY MAY DROP A FLY: . . . . 416 TOWER   177
BEFORE THE INDIFFERENT BEAK COULD LET HER DROP? . . . . 441 LEDA AND SWAN   14
A LIVING MAN IS BLIND AND DRINKS HIS DROP. . . . . . . 478 SELF AND SOUL   41
WHAT MATTER IF A BLIND MAN DRINK HIS DROP? . . . . . . 478 SELF AND SOUL V 41
THEN DARKENING THROUGH "DARK" RAFTERY'S "CELLAR" DROP, . . 490 COOLE BALLYLEE   4
SPREAD TO A LAKE AND DROP INTO A HOLE. . . . . 490 COOLE BALLYLEE   7
ALL THINGS HANG LIKE A DROP OF DEW . . . .   505 GRAT INSTRUCT   3
MAY SING, AND SING UNTIL HE DROP, ... 525 DANCING DAYS   21
THERE ALL THE PLANETS DROP IN THE SUN. . . . . 557 THERE   4
WHAT MATTER? HEAVE NO SIGH, LET NO TEAR DROP, ... 564 GYRES   11
THE GREAT STAGE CURTAIN ABOUT TO DROP, ... 565 LAPIS LAZULI   13
AND ALL THE DROP-SCENES DROP AT ONCE . . . . 566 LAPIS LAZULI   22
AND ALL THE DROP SCENES DROP AT ONCE . . . . 566 LAPIS LAZULI   V 22
AND ALL THE DROP SCENES DROP AT ONCE . . . . 566 LAPIS LAZULI   V 22
I THINK I SHOULD DROP DEAD." . . . . 569 THREE BUSHES   13
"I KNOW THAT I MUST DROP DOWN DEAD . . . . 569 THREE BUSHES   17
YET WHAT COULD I BUT DROP DOWN DEAD . . . . 569 THREE BUSHES   19
A POISON DROP. A TOY, A FANCY ONCE, ... 700 MOSADA 3   24
A POISON DROP. THE TOY OF FANCY ONCE, ... 700 MOSADA 3   V 24

DROPPED

I DROPPED THE BERRY IN A STREAM . . . . 149 WANDER AENGUS   7
THE MAINES' CHILDREN DROPPED THEIR SPADES, AND STOOD . . 185 QUEEN MAEVE   120
THE MAINES' CHILDREN HAVE NOT DROPPED THEIR SPADES . . . 186 QUEEN MAEVE   123
THAT DROPPED UPON THY THIGH," . . . . 309 PLAYER QUEEN   16
THEIR BEAUTY DROPPED OUT OF THE LONELINESS . . . . . . 375 PHASES OF MOON   70
IT DROPPED THE REINS OF PEACE AND WAR . . . . 437 SONGS PLAY 1   14
HALF RUNNING, DROPPED AT THE FIRST RIDGE OF THE DESERT . . 468 HARUN RASHID   155
HE DROPPED UPON HIS HEAD AND DIED. . . . . 571 THREE BUSHES   52
AND DROPPED AND DIED THEREON, FOR SHE . . . . 571 THREE BUSHES   54
AND ON THAT CITY DROPPED A TEAR, ... 725 LEGEND   31
BEFORE I DROPPED ASLEEP, A KINGFISHER . . . . 761 SHADOW WATER A   274

DROPPING   SEE DEW-DROPPING

GOES DROPPING FROM HIS EYES A LANGUID LIGHT, ...   34 OISIN 2   V 81A
I FOUND, DROPPING SEA-FOAM ON THE WIDE STAIR, ...   43 OISIN 2   V 215
I FOUND, DROPPING SEA FOAM ON THE WIDE STAIR, ...   43 OISIN 2   V 215
DROPPING: A MURMUROUS DROPPING: OLD SILENCE AND THAT ONE   48 OISIN 3   18
   SOUND:
DROPPING: A MURMUROUS DROPPING: OLD SILENCE AND THAT ONE   48 OISIN 3   18
   SOUND:
. . . SLOW DROPPING A SOUND IN FAINT STREAMS . . . .   51 OISIN 3   67
. . . THEIR DIMNESS, THEIR DEWS DROPPING SLEEP. . . .   54 OISIN 3   108
WHERE EVER IS MURMUROUS DROPPING, OLD SILENCE AND THAT   56 OISIN 3   138
   ONE SOUND:
THE DEWDROPS, FOR THE SOUND OF THEIR OWN DROPPING. . . .   68 SAD SHEPHERD   16
THE DEW DROPS, FOR THE SOUND OF THEIR OWN DROPPING-- . .   68 SAD SHEPHERD   V 16
DROPPING AT EVE IN CORAL BAYS . . . .   78 INDIAN TO LOVE V 19
DROPPING A VAPOURY FOOTSOLE ON THE TIDE'S DROWSY BLAZE. .   78 INDIAN TO LOVE V 20
AND I SHALL HAVE SOME PEACE THERE, FOR PEACE COMES DROPPING 117 ISLE INNISFREE   5
   SLOW,
DROPPING FROM THE VEILS OF THE MORNING TO WHERE THE CRICKET 117 ISLE INNISFREE   6
   SINGS:
IS DROPPING SLEEP, UNTIL GOD BURN TIME, ... 164 PERFECT BEAUTY   7
THE ENTRAILS OF THE HORSE. DROPPING HIS SWORD . . . . 278 TWO KINGS   23
THROUGH THE ENTRAILS OF THE HORSE. DROPPING HIS SWORD . . 278 TWO KINGS   V 23
DROPPING OUT OF SKY OR ROCK, ... 633 MAN AND ECHO   44
DROPPING LIQUID RAINBOW LIGHT, ... 732 STREET DANCERS   33

DROPS   SEE MIST-DROPS

AND WAS BORN WHERE THE SUN DROPS DOWN IN THE TIDE, . . .   5 OISIN 1   V 49
AND DROPS OF HONEY ARE HIS WORDS, ...   7 OISIN 1   V 64
LIKE DROPS OF FROZEN RAINBOW LIGHT, ...   14 OISIN 1   183
WHERE DROPS OF DEW IN MYRIADS FALL. . . . .   16 OISIN 1   222
"MEN'S HEARTS OF OLD WERE DROPS OF FLAME . . . . . .   19 OISIN 1   276
OR DROPS OF SILVER JOY THAT FELL . . . .   19 OISIN 1   278
LIKE DROPS OF HONEY CAME THEIR WORDS, ...   26 OISIN 1   398
THE DEW DROPS, FOR THE SOUND OF THEIR OWN DROPPING-- . .   68 SAD SHEPHERD   V 16
TIME DROPS IN DECAY. . . . . 142 MOODS   1
THE DEW DROPS SLOWLY: THE DREAMS GATHER: UNKNOWN SPEARS   161 BLACK PIG   V   1
"THAT DROWSILY DROPS FAINT LEAVES ON HIM . . . . . . 168 BLESSED   37

226

DROPS   (CONTINUED)

	PAGE	TITLE	LINE
THAT THE SALT DROPS HAVE WET:	312	CHILD DANCING	5
THE DARKNESS DROPS AGAIN: BUT NOW I KNOW	402	SECOND COMING	18
BUT NOW WIND DROPS, DUST SETTLES: THEREUPON	433	NINETEEN 19	125
THERE IN THE TOMB DROPS THE FAINT MOONLIGHT,	636	BLACK TOWER	17
SOMETHING DROPS FROM EYES LONG BLIND,	638	BEN BULBEN	29
SHOWERED AWAY THE KEEN DEW DROPS:	705	DAWN-SONG	18
HE TURNS WHERE, HUNG LIKE DROPS OF DRIPPING GOLD,	710	FERENCZ RENYI	18
HE TURNS WHERE, HUNG LIKE DROPS OF LIQUID GOLD,	710	FERENCZ RENYI V	18
BUT THIS ONE--THIS ONE. NOW HIS HEAD DROPS LOW,	711	FERENCZ RENYI	39
DROPS ON HIS BOSOM, SOMBRE, MOIST AND SLOW.	711	FERENCZ RENYI	40

DROP-SCENES

	PAGE	TITLE	LINE
AND ALL THE DROP-SCENES DROP AT ONCE	566	LAPIS LAZULI	22

DROPT

	PAGE	TITLE	LINE
DROPT DOWN THE VELVET DARKNESS FROM ABOVE,	688	TWO TITANS	37
THE FATHER DROPT HIS ROSARY--	730	PRIEST FAIRY	57

DROUGHT

	PAGE	TITLE	LINE
WHEN LOVE LONGING IS BUT DROUGHT	777	SONG DEIRDRE 2 V	11

DROUTH

	PAGE	TITLE	LINE
WHEN LOVE-LONGING IS BUT DROUTH	777	SONG DEIRDRE 2	11

DROVE

	PAGE	TITLE	LINE
AND DROVE TUMULT AND WAR AWAY	82	MAD KING GOLL	5
CRYING, THE PIRATES DROVE HIS SWINE	82	MAD KING GOLL	15
HE DROVE ME OUT AND SHUT THE DOOR,	95	MOLL MAGEE	25
HE DROVE ME FORTH AND SHUT THE DOOR,	95	MOLL MAGEE V	25
THE TALE DROVE HIS FINE ANGRY MOOD AWAY.	128	DREAM OF FAERY	36
O'DRISCOLL DROVE WITH A SONG	143	HOST OF AIR	1
AND HIM WHO DROVE THE GODS OUT OF THEIR LISS,	170	SECRET ROSE	16
THAT DROVE YOU TO IT, AND I FOOL ENOUGH	248	SHADOW WATER B	548
UPON HIS TREMBLING HORSE, THEN DROVE THE SPUR:	277	TWO KINGS	11
TREMBLING BENEATH HIM, AND THEN DROVE THE SPUR	277	TWO KINGS V	11
AND WHEN THEY DROVE OUT COSIMO,	288	TO WEALTHY MAN	20
DROVE TO THIS TUMULT IN THE CLOUDS:	328	IRISH AIRMAN	12
AND MASONS DROVE FROM MILES AWAY	360	ALF POLLEXFEN	9
AND DROVE HIM DRUNK OR SOBER THROUGH THE DAWN	411	TOWER	58
DROVE HORROR FROM HIS MOTHER'S BREAST.	440	WISDOM	20
RICHES DROVE OUT RANK,	626	STATES HOLIDAY	2
BASE DROVE OUT THE BETTER BLOOD,	626	STATES HOLIDAY	3
AND DROVE THE BOYS AND WOMEN OFF.	725	LEGEND	24

DROWN

	PAGE	TITLE	LINE
AND SLEEP DROWN SUN AND MOON AND STAR."	5	OISIN 1 V	49
THEIR HEADS ON YOUR KNEES, AND DROWN THEIR EYES WITH YOUR HAIR,	163	VALLEY LOVERS	6
THAT I MAY DROWN MYSELF? BETTER STEER HOME,	222	SHADOW WATER B	12
I'D DROWN HIM WHILE WE HAVE THE CHANCE TO DO IT.	224	SHADOW WATER B	58
OR WAVE TO DROWN. BUT I HAVE DONE WITH WORDS,	238	SHADOW WATER B	348
NO NEED TO DROWN, FOR, IF YOU WILL PARDON US	238	SHADOW WATER B	361
THAT EVEN LOVERS DROWN.	453	MERMAID	6
"DROWN ALL THE DOGS," SAID THE FIERCE YOUNG WOMAN,	546	TO SAME TUNE 2	7
DROWN, DROWN IN THE WATER-BUTT,	546	TO SAME TUNE 2	9
DROWN, DROWN IN THE WATER-BUTT,	546	TO SAME TUNE 2	9
DROWN ALL THE DOGS," SAID THE FIERCE YOUNG WOMAN.	546	TO SAME TUNE 2	10
"DROWN ALL THE DOGS," SAID THE FIERCE YOUNG WOMAN,	546	TO SAME TUNE 2	17
DROWN, DROWN IN THE WATER-BUTT,	546	TO SAME TUNE 2	19
DROWN, DROWN IN THE WATER-BUTT,	546	TO SAME TUNE 2	19
DROWN ALL THE DOGS," SAID THE FIERCE YOUNG WOMAN.	546	TO SAME TUNE 2	20
DROWN, DROWN IN THE WATER BUTT,	546	TO SAME TUNE 2 V	REF
DROWN, DROWN IN THE WATER BUTT,	546	TO SAME TUNE 2 V	REF
"DROWN ALL THE DOGS," SAID THE FIERCE YOUNG WOMAN,	547	TO SAME TUNE 2	27
DROWN, DROWN IN THE WATER-BUTT,	547	TO SAME TUNE 2	29
DROWN, DROWN IN THE WATER-BUTT,	547	TO SAME TUNE 2	29
DROWN ALL THE DOGS," SAID THE FIERCE YOUNG WOMAN.	547	TO SAME TUNE 2	30
WITH FIERY SONG I'LL DROWN YON PUNY VOICE.	648	ISLE STAT I 1	81
TO DROWN IN ITS OWN IMAGE? EVEN THAT SLEEP	765	SHADOW WATER A	364

DROWNED   SEE DEW-DROWNED

	PAGE	TITLE	LINE
OF A DROWNED DRIPPING BODY TO MY BREAST:	40	OISIN 2	179
WERE DROWNED IN HER LONG DIM HAIR.	145	HOST OF AIR	36
BEFORE THEY DROWNED THEIR LOVERS' EYES	156	FORGOT BEAUTY V	10A
THE GREY CAIRN ON THE HILL, WHEN DAY SINKS DROWNED IN DEW,	161	BLACK PIG	6
THEIR LOVE WAS NEVER DROWNED IN CARE	189	BAILE AILLINN	8
WHERE TIME IS DROWNED IN ODOUR-LADEN WINDS	219	HARP OF AENGUS	3
AND DROWNED THE TREASURES OF NINE CONQUERED NATIONS,	235	SHADOW WATER B	287
HAD DROWNED ME ALSO. BUT, BEING YET ALIVE,	235	SHADOW WATER B	289
THE CEREMONY OF INNOCENCE IS DROWNED:	402	SECOND COMING	6
AND ONE WAS DROWNED IN THE GREAT BOG OF CLOONE.	411	TOWER	48
THE MAN DROWNED IN A BOG'S MIRE,	413	TOWER	95
AND WHAT HAD DROWNED A LOVER ONCE	457	SECRETS OF OLD	5
TO SEE THEM DROWNED BY THOSE VAST SOLITUDES,	661	ISLE STAT II 1	57
ALL THE DROWNED THAT EVER WERE DROWNED FROM THAT VILLAGE BY THE SEA:	719	PHANTOM SHIP	20
ALL THE DROWNED THAT EVER WERE DROWNED FROM THAT VILLAGE BY THE SEA:	719	PHANTOM SHIP	20
ON THE DROWNED MEN'S HANDS AND FACES, ON THE SPARS AND ON THE SAILS.	719	PHANTOM SHIP	22
HUSH'D THE FISHERS, TILL A MOTHER CALLS BY NAME HER DROWNED SON:	719	PHANTOM SHIP	23
THEN EACH WIFE AND MAID AND MOTHER CALLS BY NAME SOME DROWNED ONE.	719	PHANTOM SHIP	24
WHERE TIME IS DROWNED IN ODOUR-LADEN WINDS	762	SHADOW WATER A	298

DROWNING

	PAGE	TITLE	LINE
FOR, AS DRIFT FROM A SAILOR SLOW DROWNING	48	OISIN 3	22

227

	PAGE	TITLE	LINE
DROWNING (CONTINUED)			
DROWNING LOVE'S LONELY HOUR IN DEEP TWILIGHT OF REST, . .	154	BELOVED PEACE	11
DROWNS			
"JOY DROWNS THE TWILIGHT IN THE DEW, ...	18	OISIN 1	261
WHERE EVEN LONGING DROWNS UNDER ITS OWN EXCESS:	426	PHANTOM HATRED	22
DROWSILY			
"THAT DROWSILY DROPS FAINT LEAVES ON HIM	168	BLESSED	37
DROWSY			
WITH VAPOURY FOOTSOLE BY THE WATER'S DROWSY BLAZE.	78	INDIAN TO LOVE	20
AND DROP A VAPOURY FOOTFALL IN THE WATER'S DROWSY BLAZE. .	78	INDIAN TO LOVE	20
WITH VAPOURY FOOTSOLE AMONG THE WATER'S DROWSY BLAZE. . .	78	INDIAN TO LOVE V	20
DROPPING A VAPOURY FOOTSOLE ON THE TIDE'S DROWSY BLAZE. .	78	INDIAN TO LOVE V	20
THE DROWSY WATER-RATS!	87	STOLEN CHILD	5
THE DROWSY WATER RATS!	87	STOLEN CHILD V	5
DIM POWERS OF DROWSY THOUGHT, LET HER NO LONGER BE . .	175	ELEMENT POWERS	13
THEY SANG A DROWSY SONG, OR SNORED, ...	271	GREY ROCK	16
AND SANG A DROWSY SONG, OR SNORED, ...	271	GREY ROCK V	16
TO KEEP A DROWSY EMPEROR AWAKE!	408	SAIL BYZANTIUM	29
THE GUARDSMEN'S DROWSY CHARGERS WOULD NOT PRANCE. . .	429	NINETEEN 19	24
WITHIN THE DROWSY BLOSSOM HANGS THE BEE!	645	ISLE STAT I 1	2
HARK! HE'S DEAD--MY DROWSY BROTHER, ...	656	ISLE STAT I 3	18
FAR OFF IN DROWSY VALLEYS	680	LOVE AND DEATH	5
AND FALLS AMONG THE DREAMS THE DROWSY GODS	750	SHADOW WATER A	68
DRUDGE			
THE COARSENESS OF THE DRUDGE. BEFORE THE FULL	376	PHASES OF MOON	94
DRUDGERY			
RENOUNCE THAT DRUDGERY, ...	600	THOSE IMAGES	7
DRUG			
AS RECOLLECTION OR THE DRUG DECIDE, ...	444	SCHOOL CHILDR	36
WINE OR LOVE DRUG HIM TO SLEEP, ...	633	MAN AND ECHO	26
DRUGS			
WINE OR LOVE DRUGS HIM TO SLEEP, ...	633	MAN AND ECHO V	26
DRUID			
A DRUID DREAM OF THE END OF DAYS	16	OISIN 1	219
HE FELL INTO A DRUID SWOON.	20	OISIN 1	289
WHO WEDDED MEN WITH RINGS OF DRUID GOLD!	29	OISIN 2	10
THE DRUID SWORD OF MANANAN, HE GREW	40	OISIN 2 V	174
AND EVERY WHISPERING DRUID SAID, ...	82	MAD KING GOLL V	9
THE DRUID, GREY, WOOD-NURTURED, QUIET-EYED, ...	101	ROSE UPON ROOD	4
THE DRUID, GREY, WOOD NURTURED, QUIET EYED, ...	101	ROSE UPON ROOD V	4
FERGUS AND THE DRUID	102	FERGUS DRUID	T
AH! DRUID, DRUID, HOW GREAT WEBS OF SORROW	104	FERGUS DRUID	39
AH! DRUID, DRUID, HOW GREAT WEBS OF SORROW	104	FERGUS DRUID	39
AND SANG HOW DAY A DRUID TWILIGHT SHEDS	126	DREAM OF FAERY V	7
A DRUID KINDNESS, ON ALL HEARERS FELL.	129	BOOK STORIES	4
A DRUID LAND, A DRUID TUNE!	139	TO IRELAND	32
A DRUID LAND, A DRUID TUNE!	139	TO IRELAND	32
IN DRUID VAPOUR AND MAKE THE TORCHES DIM!	169	SECRET ROSE	11
HAD FILLED THE HOUSE WITH DRUID HEAVINESS!	181	QUEEN MAEVE	40
AND DRUID MOONS, AND MURMURING OF BOUGHS, ...	219	HARP OF AENGUS	4
HE MADE A HARP WITH DRUID APPLE-WOOD	220	HARP OF AENGUS	11
HE MADE A HARP WITH DRUID APPLE WOOD	220	HARP OF AENGUS V	11
YOU HAVE A DRUID CRAFT OF WICKED SOUND	237	SHADOW WATER B	342
YOU HAVE A DRUID CRAFT, WICKED SOUND	237	SHADOW WATER B V	342
HE HAS FLUNG A DRUID SPELL UPON THE AIR, ...	240	SHADOW WATER B	385
HE HAS THROWN A DRUID DREAM UPON THE AIR.	759	SHADOW WATER A	237
BREATHED OUT A DRUID VAPOUR, AND CRUMBLED AWAY . . .	761	SHADOW WATER A	279
AND DRUID MOONS, AND MURMURING OF BOUGHS, ...	762	SHADOW WATER A	299
HE MADE A HARP WITH DRUID APPLE WOOD	763	SHADOW WATER A	306
HE MADE A HARP WITH DRUID APPLE-WOOD	763	SHADOW WATER A V	306
DRUIDS			
RANKING HIS DRUIDS ROUND HIM TEN BY TEN, ...	110	CUCHULAIN SEA	76
SENT FOR HIS DRUIDS TWENTY SCORE AND TEN, ...	110	CUCHULAIN SEA V	76
THE DRUIDS TOOK THEM TO THEIR MYSTERY, ...	111	CUCHULAIN SEA	82
THE DRUIDS CHANTED, SWAYING IN THEIR HANDS	111	CUCHULAIN SEA	82
THE DRUIDS CHAUNTED, SWAYING IN THEIR HANDS	111	CUCHULAIN SEA V	82
MUST BE SUBSTANTIAL SOMEWHERE. I HAVE HEARD THE DRUIDS	229	SHADOW WATER B	162
THAT DRUIDS WRITE ON YEW AND APPLE WOOD, ...	748	SHADOW WATER A	29
AND HEARS THE ROAR OF THE STREAMS WHERE, DRUIDS SAY, . .	749	SHADOW WATER A	46
DRUM			
. . , THE SOUND OF THE SEA'S VAGUE DRUM?	56	OISIN 3	135
TO DRUM WITH HER HEEL AND TO LEAP?	381	SONGS FOOL 2	9
DANCING TO A FRENZIED DRUM, ...	403	FOR DAUGHTER	15
WHAT MAGIC DRUM?	559	MAGIC DRUM	T
THROUGH LIGHT-OBLITERATING GARDEN FOLIAGE WHAT MAGIC DRUM?	560	MAGIC DRUM	4
NOW STEPS DRAW CLOSE, HE HIDES BENEATH A DRUM.	713	FERENCZ RENYI	78
DRUMAHAIR			
DARK AND DULL AND EARTHY THE STREAM OF DRUMAHAIR . . .	207	HANRAHANS SONG V	11
DRUMCLIFF			
HE THAT IN SLIGO AT DRUMCLIFF	604	YOU CONTENT	9
IN DRUMCLIFF CHURCHYARD YEATS IS LAID.	640	BEN BULBEN	85
DRUMS			
THE DRUMS AND THE KETTLEDRUMS	527	AM OF IRELAND	21
THE DRUMS AND THE KETTLE DRUMS	527	AM OF IRELAND	21
THE DRUMS AND THE KETTLE DRUMS	527	AM OF IRELAND V	21
DRUNK SEE HALF-DRUNK			
THAT HAS DRUNK FULL, SHE CROSSED THE MISTY SEA	30	OISIN 2	16
WHEN EARTHY NIGHT HAD DRUNK HIS BODY IN!	127	DREAM OF FAERY	28
NOW THAT DEEP EARTH HAS DRUNK HIS BODY IN!	127	DREAM OF FAERY	28
AND DRUNK UP THE MURMURING TIDE!	171	MAID QUIET V	4D
I HAVE DRUNK ALE FROM THE COUNTRY OF THE YOUNG	177	PAST GREATNESS	1

228

```
                                                        PAGE    TITLE              LINE

DRUNK   (CONTINUED)
        THAT SOMEBODY HAD DRUNK DRY.  . . . . . . . .   215 HAPPY TOWNLAND         32
        BUT WHEN I HAD EATEN AND DRUNK MYSELF ASLEEP  . . . .  223 SHADOW WATER B   30
        BUT WHEN I HAD EATEN AND DRUNK A BELLYFUL  . . . . .   223 SHADOW WATER B V 30
        DRUNK WITH THE UNMIXED WINE.  . . . . . . . .   355 PROPERTIUS              8
        DRUNK WITH THE UN-MIXED WINE.  . . . . . . . .  355 PROPERTIUS         V    8
        AND DROVE HIM DRUNK OR SOBER THROUGH THE DAWN  . . .   411 TOWER            58
        NEVER TO HAVE DRUNK THE BREATH OF LIFE,  . . . . .    459 FROM OEDIPUS  V   11
        DRUNK WITH THE BITTER SWEETNESS OF HER YOUTH.  . . .   469 HARUN RASHID    186
        DRUNK WITH THE BITTER-SWEETNESS OF HER YOUTH.  . . .   469 HARUN RASHID  V 186
        THAT MAN IS DEAF AND DRUNK AND BLIND  . . . . . .     478 SELF AND SOUL V   35
        AND ALL DEAD MEN ARE DRUNK.  . . . . . . . . .  592 DRUNK SOBRIETY         16
        AND DRUNK OR SOBER LIVE AT EASE  . . . . . . . .      597 MODEL LAUREATE    13
DRUNKARD
        A DRUNKARD IS A DEAD MAN,  . . . . . . . . .    592 DRUNK SOBRIETY         15
DRUNKARD'S
        OR OUT OF DRUNKARD'S EYE.  ALL'S WHIGGERY NOW,  . . .  486 SEVEN SAGES      13
        OR DRUNKARD'S EYE.  ALL'S WHIGGERY NOW,  . . . .     486 SEVEN SAGES   V   13
        OR OUT OF A DRUNKARD'S EYE.  ALL'S WHIGGERY NOW,  . .  486 SEVEN SAGES   V  13
DRUNKARDS
        "THE DRUNKARDS, PILFERERS OF PUBLIC FUNDS,  . . . .   352 PEOPLE           23
        THOUGH DRUNKARDS LIE AND SNORE.  . . . . . . .  592 DRUNK SOBRIETY          8
DRUNKEN      SEE BEAUTY-DRUNKEN
        AND HE NODS A DRUNKEN HEAD.  . . . . . . . . .  168 BLESSED                32
        THOUGH DRUNKEN WITH THE FLAGS THAT SWAY  . . . . .    212 BLESS PSALTER     5
        AND WAIT HIM IN A DRUNKEN SLEEP."  . . . . . .  307 HOUR DAWN             106
        WHO HAS WON A DRUNKEN CHEER,  . . . . . . . . . 347 FISHERMAN              18
        BUT TAKE ME FOR SOME DRUNKEN COUNTRYMAN:  . . . . .   377 PHASES OF MOON   130
        BUT TAKE ME FOR SOME DRUNKEN COUNTRY MAN:  . . . . .  377 PHASES OF MOON V 130
        A DRUNKEN, VAINGLORIOUS LOUT.  . . . . . . . .  393 EASTER 1916            32
        A DRUNKEN, VAIN-GLORIOUS LOUT.  . . . . . . . .  393 EASTER 1916   V       32
        RIDES UPON SLEEP; A DRUNKEN SOLDIERY  . . . . . .     429 NINETEEN 19      26
        AND CLAMOUR IN DRUNKEN FRENZY FOR THE MOON.  . . . .  482 BLOOD AND MOON   42
        THE EMPEROR'S DRUNKEN SOLDIERY ARE ABED;  . . . . .   497 BYZANTIUM         2
        THE EMPEROR'S DRUNKEN SOLDIERY ARE A-BED;  . . . . .  497 BYZANTIUM     V   2
        NOR KNEW, DRUNKEN WITH SINGING AS WITH WINE,  . . . . 537 HER VISION       30
        SPEAKING TO A DRUNKEN AUDIENCE HIGH NONSENSICAL WORDS: 577 LOFTY THINGS     6
        A DRUNKEN MAN'S PRAISE OF SOBRIETY  . . . . . . .     591 DRUNK SOBRIETY    T
        TURN TO A DRUNKEN JOURNALIST:  . . . . . . . .  626 OLD MEN BE MAD          4
DRY      SEE SUN-DRY
        A DUSKY DEMON DRY AS A WITHERED SEDGE  . . . . . .    39 OISIN 2          158
        A DUSK DEMON, DRY AS A WITHERED SEDGE,  . . . . . .   39 OISIN 2       V  158
        A HUSKY DEMON, DRY AS A WITHERED SEDGE  . . . . . .   39 OISIN 2       V  158
        . . . THE SPITTLE ON HIS BEARD NEVER DRY,  . . . .    53 OISIN 3           90
        . . . WITH THE SPITTLE ON HIS BEARD NEVER DRY.  . . . 60 OISIN 3          192
        HE HAD HALF A CLOAK TO KEEP HIM DRY,  . . . . . .     190 BAILE AILLINN    29
        THAT SOMEBODY HAD DRUNK DRY.  . . . . . . . . . 215 HAPPY TOWNLAND         32
        AND AFTER, DRAINED DRY,  . . . . . . . . . .    310 WITCH                   4
        THE WOODLAND PATHS ARE DRY,  . . . . . . . . .  322 SWANS AT COOLE          2
        BUT WALK BY THE DRY THORN UNTIL I HAVE FOUND  . . . . 351 HER PRAISE       12
        WHEN ALL STREAMS ARE DRY,  . . . . . . . . . .  414 TOWER                 138
        BUT FOUND IT DRY AS BONE,  . . . . . . . . . .  454 EMPTY CUP               8
        ON OLD DRY WRITING IN A LEARNED TONGUE,  . . . . .    466 HARUN RASHID    123
        ON OLD DRY FAGGOTS THAT COULD NEVER PLEASE  . . . . . 466 HARUN RASHID    124
        NOW ALL DRY STICKS UNDER A WINTRY SUN,  . . . . . .   490 COOLE BALLYLEE   10
        THOSE VEINS MUST SOON BE DRY:  . . . . . . . .  513 JANE TALK BISH          4
        DRY TIMBER UNDER THAT RICH FOLIAGE,  . . . . . .     536 HER VISION        1
        ON GANGLING STOCKS GROWN GREAT, GREAT STOCKS RUN DRY, 619 BRONZE HEAD      25
        AND ALL HIS VEINS HAD NEAR RUN DRY,  . . . . . .     670 ISLE STAT II 3  119
        WITH FAIRY-SMITTEN UDDERS DRY--  . . . . . . . .     716 FAIRY DOCTOR     14
        PAST THE SPEARS AND PALM-STEMS DRY,  . . . . . .     733 STREET DANCERS   42
        WERE HIS MEASURE RUNNING DRY.  . . . . . . . .  772 SONG DEIRDRE 1         14
        WERE HIS MEASURES RUNNING DRY.  . . . . . . . . 772 SONG DEIRDRE 1 V       14
        DRY STONES IN A WELL?"  . . . . . . . . . . .   780 WELL AND TREE           8
        FROM THE DRY BONES OF THE DEAD?  . . . . . . . .     781 MY HEART BEAT     8
        DRY BONES THAT DREAM ARE BITTER,  . . . . . . .  783 GREY ROUND           14
DUACH'S
        NOT I, NOR MAINE THERE, NOR DUACH'S SON.  . . . . .   748 SHADOW WATER A   22
DUBLIN
        OLD DUBLIN MERCHANT "FREE OF TEN AND FOUR"  . . . . . 269 PARDON FATHERS    3
        OLD DUBLIN MERCHANT "FREE OF THE TEN AND FOUR"  . . . 269 PARDON FATHERS V  3
        . . . TO THE DUBLIN MUNICIPAL GALLERY IF IT WERE PROVED 287 TO WEALTHY MAN  T
        . . .
DUCHESS
        TO WHERE THE DUCHESS AND HER PEOPLE TALKED  . . . . . 352 PEOPLE           13
DUCHESSES
        AND THERE'S A SCORE OF DUCHESSES, SURPASSING WOMANKIND,  353 HIS PHOENIX    5
        AND THERE'S A SCORE OF DUCHESSES, SURPASSING WOMAN-KIND,  353 HIS PHOENIX V 5
DUCK
        THE WILD DUCK AND THE DRAKE  . . . . . . . . .  143 HOST OF AIR             2
        GATHERS THE WILD DUCK FROM THE WINTER DAWN:  . . . .  217 WOODS OF COOLE    3
DUDDON
        "HUDDON AND DUDDON AND DANIEL O'LEARY,  . . . . . .   529 TOM LUNATIC       7
        HUDDON, DUDDON AND DANIEL O'LEARY  . . . . . . .  787 HUDDON DUDDON        1
        HUDDON, DUDDON AND DANIEL O'LEARY  . . . . . . .  787 HUDDON DUDDON        6
        HUDDON, DUDDON AND DANIEL O'LEARY  . . . . . . .  787 HUDDON DUDDON       11
DUDLEY
        THEN THAT OLD ABBEY ACTOR, DUDLEY DIGGES,  . . . . .  790 DEDICATION        7
DUE
        COUNT ALL THE PRAISES DUE  . . . . . . . . . .  345 ON WOMAN               15
```

229

	PAGE	TITLE		LINE
DUG				
TO MIDDLE NIGHT, THEY DUG INTO THE HILL.	185	QUEEN MAEVE		114
AND DUG ITS CLAWS AND SHRIEKED AND FOUGHT.	385	ROBARTES DANCE		8
DUGS				
BY SUCKING AT THE DUGS OF GREECE.	288	TO WEALTHY MAN		28
DUKE				
WHAT CARED DUKE ERCOLE, THAT BID	287	TO WEALTHY MAN		9
DULAC				
ON A PICTURE OF A BLACK CENTAUR BY EDMUND DULAC	442	BLACK CENTAUR		T
DULL SEE JOURNEY-DULL				
THAT DEMON DULL AND UNSUBDUABLE!	43	OISIN 2		217
. . . DULL WITH THE SMOKE OF THEIR DREAMS!	51	OISIN 3		65
SPLASHED ALL WITH CLAY AND JOURNEY DULL,	82	MAD KING GOLL	V	13
DARK AND DULL AND EARTHY THE STREAM OF DRUMAHAIR.	207	HANRAHANS SONG	V	11
DARK AND DULL AND EARTHY OUR SOULS AND BODIES BE!	208	HANRAHANS SONG	V	13
AND MANY A DARLING WIT'S GROWN DULL	301	RUN PARADISE		18
BEYOND THE FLING OF THE DULL ASS'S HOOF	321	REED WHISPERER		5
SHE LIES, HER LOVELY PITEOUS HEAD AMID DULL RED HAIR	362	HER COURTESY		2
OF DULL RED HAIR WAS FLOWING	363	DOLLS DRAWINGS		6
HELEN BEING CHOSEN FOUND LIFE FLAT AND DULL	404	FOR DAUGHTER		25
OR DULL DECREPITUDE,	416	TOWER		187
DULL AS A WORM,	575	MAIDS 2ND SONG		2
BLENCHING ON HIGH THE DULL STARS SICKEN	646	ISLE STAT I 1		46
I'LL SILENCE THIS DULL SINGER--	647	ISLE STAT I 1		50
THAT DULL AND FADED ARE.	680	LOVE AND DEATH		26
SHINE DULL UNMOVING EYES. WHAT THING ART THOU?	685	SEEKER		74
UNQUENCHABLE STILL GLOWS IN HER DULL STARE,	687	TWO TITANS		17
I AM DULL TO-DAY, OR YOU WERE NOW ALL LOST.	722	WITCH VIVIEN		59
DULL-EYED				
THAT TURN DULL-EYED AWAY,	505	RESULT THOUGHT		14
DULL-WITTED				
DULL-WITTED THING, WITH FACE RED SQUIRREL-BROWN.	661	ISLE STAT II 1		68
DUMB				
IN A LONG IRON SLEEP, AS A FISH IN THE WATER GOES DUMB AS A STONE.	53	OISIN 3		96
IF DEAF AND DUMB AND BLIND WITH LOVE?	202	NEVER GIVE ALL		12
THAT MAKE THE HEART AKIN TO THE DUMB STONE."	281	TWO KINGS		94
DEARER THAN ANY THAT THE DUMB STONE HIDES,	281	TWO KINGS	V	96
MUST END AT THE DUMB STONE? BUT WHERE WE BUILD	284	TWO KINGS		179
THAN DUMB BELL AND FOIL	334	SONG	V	3
NOW PEARSE IS DEAF AND DUMB?	395	SIXTEEN DEAD		10
TO PASSING BIRD, BUT I AM DUMB	452	HUMAN DIGNITY		11
THOUGH MARGERY IS STRICKEN DUMB	457	SECRETS OF OLD		7
THAT MAN IS STRICKEN DEAF AND DUMB AND BLIND,	478	SELF AND SOUL		35
STRUCK DUMB IN THE SIMPLICITY OF FIRE!	502	VACILLATION		75
LIKE A DUMB BEAST IN A SHOW,	572	LADYS 1ST SONG		2
HEAR ME, AND, SHEPHERD, HEARING ME, GROW DUMB.	646	ISLE STAT I 1		31
I AM NOT DUMB! I'D SOONER SILENT WAIT	646	ISLE STAT I 1		40
A WHITE, DUMB THING OF TEARS, HERE LET IT STAND,	663	ISLE STAT II 2		21
LOW BOWED AND DUMB UPON THE SAND.	671	ISLE STAT II 3		130
AT ARM'S LENGTH, THUS TILL DUMB ETERNITY	671	ISLE STAT II 3		145
AND WE THOUGH ASTONISHED ARE DUMB	785	YOUR HEART		11
AND WE THOUGH ASTONISHED ARE DUMB	786	YOUR HEART		24
AND WE THOUGH ASTONISHED ARE DUMB	786	YOUR HEART		37
DUMB-BELL				
THAN DUMB-BELL AND FOIL	334	SONG		3
DUMBER				
COLDER AND DUMBER AND DEAFER THAN A FISH.	267	ALL TEMPT ME		10
DUMBFOUNDED				
DUMBFOUNDED BEFORE A KNAVE,	349	HAWK		16
DUN				
AT EVENING IN MY WESTERN DUN."	8	OISIN 1		79
TO EMER, RADDLING RAIMENT IN HER DUN,	105	CUCHULAIN SEA		2
TO EMER OF BORDA, IN HER CLAY-PILED DUN,	105	CUCHULAIN SEA	V	2
TO FORGAIL'S DAUGHTER, EMER, IN HER DUN,	105	CUCHULAIN SEA	V	2
"HE IS THE MIGHTIEST MAN IN SHIP OR DUN."	107	CUCHULAIN SEA	V	28
WHO HAS A LIKE VOW FROM THEIR TRIPLE DUN."	108	CUCHULAIN SEA	V	38
WHO HAD A LIKE VOW FROM OUR TRIPLE DUN."	109	CUCHULAIN SEA	V	54
AND WHETHER I GO IN MY DREAMS BY WOODLAND, OR DUN, OR SHORE,	210	UNDER THE MOON		14
DUNCE				
LIVE TO BEAR CHILDREN TO A DUNCE!	626	OLD MEN BE MAD		6
DUNG SEE CAMEL-DUNG				
AMONG THE COARSE GRASS AND THE CAMEL DUNG.	369	EGO DOMINUS	V	31
DUNGEON				
YOURSELF INTO THE DUNGEON 'NEATH OUR FEET	697	MOSADA 2		44
DURAS				
BETWEEN THE WOOD OF DURAS AND MAGAI	276	TWO KINGS	V	G
DURING				
A MEDITATION WRITTEN DURING SICKNESS AT ALGECIRAS	493	AT ALGECIRAS	V	T
DUSK				
A DUSK DEMON, DRY AS A WITHERED SEDGE,	39	OISIN 2	V	158
BETWEEN THE DAWN AND DUSK," SHE SAID!	273	GREY ROCK		66
DUSKY				
A DUSKY DEMON DRY AS A WITHERED SEDGE	39	OISIN 2		158
DUSKY AND HERBLESS, WHERE A BUBBLING STRAIN	39	OISIN 2	V	156
AND KISSED HER DUSKY FACE,	332	SOLOMON SHEBA		2
I'LL SING THE SONGS THE DUSKY LOVERS SING,	694	MOSADA 1		101
DUST				
AND HOUNDS FOR CENTURIES DUST AND AIR.	11	OISIN 1		131
AND THE KINGFISHER TURNS TO A BALL OF DUST,	27	OISIN 1	V	418

		PAGE	TITLE	LINE
DUST	(CONTINUED)			
AND THE KINGFISHER TURNS TO A BALL OF DUST,		28	OISIN 1	422
. . . DRIVING THE DUST WITH THEIR THRONGS,		53	OISIN 3	85
ARE DUST ON THE MOTH'S WING! THAT NOTHING MATTERS		235	SHADOW WATER B	297
DANCED IN THE WHIRLING FOAM AND IN THE DUST,		284	TWO KINGS	167
ABOUT YOUR HEAD TILL THE DUST STOPS YOUR EAR,		293	TO A SHADE	20
FELL DOWN UPON THE DUST AND SNORED.		297	THREE BEGGARS	60
HECTOR IS IN THE DUST, NIETZSCHE IS BORN,		374	PHASES OF MOON	46
BUT NOW WIND DROPS, DUST SETTLES; THEREUPON		433	NINETEEN 19	125
EVEN THOSE TRUTHS THAT WHEN MY BONES ARE DUST		467	HARUN RASHID	144
TRUTHS THAT WHEN MY VERY BONES ARE DUST		467	HARUN RASHID V	144
DESCENDS INTO THE LOVELESS DUST.		540	FROM ANTIGONE	16
MOULDING IT OF DUST OR SAND,		600	SPIRIT MEDIUM	14
THOSE TWAIN ARE DUST. WAKE! LIGHT AS A BEE SIPS		678	ISLE STAT II 3	290
SHE IS LONG AGES DUST. AH, WOE IS ME!		679	ISLE STAT II 3	313
AROUND THE TWITTER OF THE LIPS OF DUST		685	DRAWING-ROOM	1
THITHER THY DUST, AND KNEAD IT WITH A CRY,		688	TWO TITANS	52
BY TABLES THAT WERE FALLEN INTO DUST		724	KANVA ON SELF	13
"AROUND, THE TWITTER OF THE LIPS OF DUST		735	QUATRAIN APHOR	21
THAT HAVE BUILT ALL ARE DUST ON A MOTH'S WING.		757	SHADOW WATER A	205
ARE BLOWN COLD DUST OR A BIT OF BONE.		788	HAWTHORN TREE	8
THEN CLOSE YOUR EARS WITH DUST AND LIE		791	REPRISALS	23
DUSTWHIRL				
MORE THAN THE FROTH, THE FEATHER, THE DUSTWHIRL,		248	SHADOW WATER B V	555
DUST-WHIRL				
MORE THAN THE FROTH, THE FEATHER, THE DUST-WHIRL,		248	SHADOW WATER B	555
DUSTY				
THEN NOWISE WORSHIP DUSTY DEEDS,		65	HAPPY SHEPHERD	22
THEN NO WISE WORSHIP DUSTY DEEDS,		65	HAPPY SHEPHERD V	22
A SUDDEN BLAST OF DUSTY WIND AND AFTER		433	NINETEEN 19	119
UPON THE DUSTY, GLITTERING WINDOWS CLING,		482	BLOOD AND MOON	43
DUTCHMAN				
JAMES AND HIS IRISH WHEN THE DUTCHMAN CROSSED;		270	PARDON FATHERS	12
DUTIFUL				
DUTIFUL HUSBAND, HONEST WIFE BY TURN,		376	PHASES OF MOON	99
DUTY				
BATHED IN FLAMING FOUNTS OF DUTY		124	CATHLEEN PARA	5
ONE WITH HER ARE MIRTH AND DUTY;		124	CATHLEEN PARA V	5
NOR LAW, NOR DUTY BADE ME FIGHT,		328	IRISH AIRMAN	9
DWELL				
AND DWELL IN THE HOUSE OF THE FENIANS, BE THEY IN FLAMES OR AT FEAST.		63	OISIN 3	224
DREAD OATH, WHO DWELL ON SACRED HIMALAY,		74	ANASHU VIJAYA	67
GO DWELL UPON THE SEA CLIFFS, VAPOUR HID,		105	CUCHULAIN SEA V	4
GO DWELL UPON THE SEA CLIFFS, VAPOUR-HID,		105	CUCHULAIN SEA V	4
GO DWELL UPON THE CLIFFS AND WATCH THE TIDE;		105	CUCHULAIN SEA V	4
GO THERE AND DWELL ON THE GREEN FOREST RIM.		108	CUCHULAIN SEA V	35
SPAKE THUS: "CUCHULAIN WILL DWELL THERE AND BROOD		110	CUCHULAIN SEA	77
AND CRIED, "CUCHULLIN WILL DWELL THERE AND BROOD,		110	CUCHULAIN SEA V	77
OR IN THE WINE-VAT, DWELL BEYOND THE STIR		169	SECRET ROSE	4
OR IN THE WINE VAT, DWELL BEYOND THE STIR		169	SECRET ROSE V	4
DOES THE IMAGINATION DWELL THE MOST		413	TOWER	113
DOTH HE STILL DWELL WITHIN THE WOODY SHADE,		678	ISLE STAT II 3	303
WHERE DWELL THE MINDS OF OLD MEN HAVING PEACE,		721	WITCH VIVIEN	22
AND THOU CANST DWELL IN THINE OWN HOME,		739	EARL PAUL	3
DWELLER				
BUT THE SAD DWELLER BY THE SEA-WAYS LONE		69	SAD SHEPHERD	26
BUT THE SAD DWELLER BY THE SEAWAYS LONE		69	SAD SHEPHERD V	26
DWELLETH				
OF EVENING AND GLAD SILENCE DWELLETH AYE,		653	ISLE STAT I 2	37
DWELLING				
WHOSE DWELLING WAS A TREE-WRAPT ISLAND, LULLED		693	MOSADA 1	79
DWELLINGS				
IN THE FENIANS' DWELLINGS OF WATTLE LEAN ON THE CHESSBOARDS AND PLAY,		55	OISIN 3	115
DWELLS				
"MY FATHER DWELLS AMONG THE SEA-WORN BANDS,		107	CUCHULAIN SEA V	25
JOY'S BROTHER, FEAR, DWELLS EVER IN EACH BREAST--		651	ISLE STAT I 1	155
VAST GREENNESS, WHERE ETERNAL RUMOUR DWELLS,		657	ISLE STAT I 3	45
LAUGHS NOT. IT DWELLS ALONE ON MORTAL LIPS!		670	ISLE STAT II 3	100
THERE DWELLS A LITTLE FAIR-HAIRED MAID I LOVE.		679	ISLE STAT II 3 V	312
DWELT				
SMOTE ON THEIR BRAINS THAT DWELT REMEMBERING AYE.		34	OISIN 2 V	77A
AMONG THOSE FEASTING MEN CUCHULAIN DWELT,		108	CUCHULAIN SEA	39
FEASTED, AND WITH THEM OLD CUCHULAIN DWELT,		108	CUCHULAIN SEA V	39
AMONG THOSE FEASTING KINGS CUCHULAIN DWELT,		108	CUCHULAIN SEA V	39
THERE DWELT A GAY, EXULTING, GENTLE RACE.		127	DREAM OF FAERY	20
DWELT AMONG WINE-STAINED WANDERERS IN DEEP WOODS;		170	SECRET ROSE	21
THE RED SQUIRREL SHALL REAR HER YOUNG WHERE THOU HAST DWELT--		674	ISLE STAT II 3	215
SHE WHO DWELT AMONG THE SYCAMORES.		715	DWELT SYCAMORE	T
SHE DWELT AMONG THE SYCAMORES.		715	DWELT SYCAMORE V	T
AH! IT DWELT WITHIN THE TWILIGHT AS THE WORM WITHIN THE NUT.		718	PHANTOM SHIP	6
AND CAME AND DWELT IN HIS OWN HOUSE,		742	EARL PAUL	67
DWINDLE				
ETERNITY MAY DWINDLE,		520	HIS BARGAIN	3
TIME AND THE WORLD AND ALL THINGS DWINDLE OUT.		749	SHADOW WATER A	47
DWINDLES				
HIS HEART'S DESIRE WHERE THE WORLD DWINDLES OUT?		747	SHADOW WATER A	13

		PAGE	TITLE		LINE
DWINDLING					
DESPITE A DWINDLING AND LATE-RISEN MOON,		372	PHASES OF MOON		6
DESPITE A DWINDLING AND LATE RISEN MOON,		372	PHASES OF MOON	V	6
HIS DWINDLING SCORE AND HE SEEMED CASTAWAYS		420	MY HOUSE		25
HIS DWINDLING SCORE AND HE SEEMED CAST-A-WAYS		420	MY HOUSE	V	25
DYE SEE HAIR-DYE					
AND RAISING ARMS ALL RADDLED WITH THE DYE,		105	CUCHULAIN SEA		7
AND STRETCHING OUT HER ARMS, RED WITH THE DYE,		105	CUCHULAIN SEA	V	7
DYEING					
AND FOUND HER DYEING CLOTH WITH SUBTLE CARE		105	CUCHULAIN SEA	V	2A
DYING					
TO SHORES WHERE DYING HAS NEVER BEEN KNOWN,		8	OISIN 1	V	84
IT SEEMED TO BLOW FROM THE DYING FLAME,		13	OISIN 1		167
THAT HIDES AWAY THE DYING SUN		85	MAD KING GOLL		63
DYING AT EVERY MOMENT IN THE WORLD,		226	SHADOW WATER B		90
THAT DYING CHOSE THE LIVING WORLD FOR TEXT		324	ROBERT GREGORY		26
WHAT'S DYING BUT A SECOND WIND?		338	TOM OROUGHLEY		11
SEVEN POEMS I UPON A DYING LADY		362	HER COURTESY	V	T
--THOSE DYING GENERATIONS--AT THEIR SONG,		407	SAIL BYZANTIUM		3
AND FASTENED TO A DYING ANIMAL		408	SAIL BYZANTIUM		22
AND FASTENED TO THIS DYING ANIMAL		408	SAIL BYZANTIUM	V	22
A DYING ANIMAL;		476	DEATH		2
DYING INTO A DANCE		498	BYZANTIUM		30
WHEN SHE WAS OLD AND DYING,		571	THREE BUSHES		64
HAZEL LAVERY LIVING AND DYING, THAT TALE		602	GALLERY REVIS		23
THE SOUTH BREEZE NOW IN DYING FEARS		655	ISLE STAT I 3		13
AS I, TO CHOOSE BENEATH DAY'S DYING FLAMES;		656	ISLE STAT I 3		34
OH FAMOUS DYING MINION OF THE SUN,		673	ISLE STAT II 3		197
I'M DYING! OH, FORGIVE ME IF I TOUCH		684	SEEKER		70
AND ALL WAS DIMNESS, TILL A DYING LEAF		690	MOSADA 1		20
AND DYING MEN--AND YET--BUT NO, FAREWELL.		698	MOSADA 2		49
MY BLOSSOM, I AM DYING, AND THE STARS		700	MOSADA 3		47
ARE DYING TOO. THEY WERE FULL SEVEN STARS;		700	MOSADA 3		48
LIVING OR DYING. BID AIBRIC TO YOUR COUNTRY,		768	SHADOW WATER A		413
EADES'S					
THE MALL AND EADES'S GRAMMAR SCHOOL,		360	ALF POLLEXFEN		15
EAGER					
YON EAGER LARK, THAT FILLS WITH SONG THE WHOLE		652	ISLE STAT I 2		18
AND PART HIS FOAMING MOUTH WITH EAGER EYE--		688	TWO TITANS		46
EAGERLY					
O'ER HER YOUNG SO EAGERLY		658	ISLE STAT I 3		93
EAGLE SEE GER-EAGLE GIER-EAGLE					
FOR WINDS WILL BEAR THEM GENTLY WHEN THE EAGLE FLIES,		146	UNAPPEAS HOST	V	3
AND THE SWEET LAUGHING EAGLE THOUGHTS THAT GROW		264	HOUSE SHAKEN		5
WHAT EAGLE LOOK STILL SHOWS,		316	FRIENDS		25
AN OLD MAN'S EAGLE MIND.		576	ACRE OF GRASS		24
AN EAGLE ON THE WING,		601	THOSE IMAGES		14
BEYOND EAGLE OR MOLE,		784	WOMANS BEAUTY		10
EAGLE'S					
BUT THE RIGHT TWIGS FOR AN EAGLE'S NEST!		288	TO WEALTHY MAN		36
EAGLES					
TO TWO OLD EAGLES, FULL OF ANCIENT PRIDE,		34	OISIN 2		74
TO EAGLES TWAIN THAT, FULL OF ANCIENT PRIDE,		34	OISIN 2	V	73
STILL EARLESS, NERVELESS, BLIND, THE EAGLES STOOD.		36	OISIN 2		100
STILL EARLESS, NERVELESS, BLIND, THE EAGLES DREAMED.		36	OISIN 2	V	100
HAS TOLD ME THAT THE UNDYING SEND THEIR EAGLES		765	SHADOW WATER A		346
THE HARP-STRINGS HAVE BEGUN TO CRY OUT TO THE EAGLES.		769	SHADOW WATER A		431
IT HAS BEGUN TO CRY OUT TO THE EAGLES.		769	SHADOW WATER A	V	431
EAGLES HAVE GONE INTO THEIR CLOUDY BED.		778	SONG DEIRDRE 3		6
EAR SEE WHEAT-EAR					
ALL PEARLY WHITE, SAVE ONE RED EAR;		12	OISIN 1		141
THE GREY WOLF KNOWS ME; BY ONE EAR		84	MAD KING GOLL		45
THE WILD BOAR KNOWS ME, BY ONE EAR		84	MAD KING GOLL	V	45
CHAUNT IN HIS EAR DELUSIONS MAGICAL,		111	CUCHULAIN SEA		80
I HAVE BEEN CHANGED TO A HOUND WITH ONE RED EAR!		153	CHANGE BELOVED		2
ABOUT YOUR HEAD TILL THE DUST STOPS YOUR EAR,		293	TO A SHADE		20
AND THERE'S NO MAN BUT COCKS HIS EAR		306	HOUR DAWN		99
SHE MURMURS INTO HIS EAR,		319	DOLLS		17
TO FLATTER BEAUTY'S IGNORANT EAR.		337	SCHOLARS		6
AIMED AT THE COMMONEST EAR,		347	FISHERMAN		20
AN OLD MAN COCKED HIS EAR UPON A BRIDGE;		372	PHASES OF MOON		1
WERE DISTANT STILL. AN OLD MAN COCKED HIS EAR.		372	PHASES OF MOON		7
WERE DISTANT. AN OLD MAN COCKED HIS EAR.		372	PHASES OF MOON	V	7
FOR WHAT BUT EYE AND EAR SILENCE THE MIND		384	VISION ROBART		41
THAT HAVE AN EAR ALONE		395	SIXTEEN DEAD		14
IMAGINATION, NOR AN EAR AND EYE		409	TOWER		6
UNTIL IMAGINATION, EAR AND EYE,		409	TOWER		13
NOR MUSIC NOR AN ENEMY'S CLIPPED EAR		412	TOWER		75
GIFTED WITH SO FINE AN EAR!		412	TOWER		94
ON DELICATE SENSITIVE EAR OR TOSSING MANE,		433	NINETEEN 19		115
THAT SHE CRIED INTO THIS EAR,		455	HIS MEMORIES		17
AND FOR NO EAR BUT HIS. CARRY THIS LETTER		461	HARUN RASHID		4
FARISTAH, AND NO LIVING EAR BUT HIS.		461	HARUN RASHID	V	4
OLD FELLOW-STUDENT, WHOSE MOST PATIENT EAR		468	HARUN RASHID		167
OLD FELLOW STUDENT, WHOSE MOST PATIENT EAR		468	HARUN RASHID	V	167
THOUGH NOT FOR SOBER EAR;		471	ALL SOUL NIGHT		18
THOUGH NOT FOR SOBER EAR,		474	ALL SOUL NIGHT		88
RAMPARTS AT YOUR EAR,		492	ANNE GREGORY		4
THROUGH THE HOLLOW OF AN EAR;		499	MOTHER OF GOD		2
COME, LET ME SING INTO YOUR EAR;		524	DANCING DAYS		1
THOUGH NOT FOR THE PRIEST'S EAR,		620	JOHN KINSELLA		18

232

EAR   (CONTINUED)
```
    ANOTHER STAR HAS SHOT AN EAR.  . . . . . . . .         625 NATIVITY            2
    A KID, HELD BY ONE SOFT WHITE EAR FOR TETHER, . . . . .  715 DWELT SYCAMORE      3
    THE MAYOR CAME, LEANING HIS DEAF EAR--  . . . . . . .    725 LEGEND             13
EARED      SEE RED-EARED
EARL
    THE BALLAD OF EARL PAUL  . . . . . . . . . . . .        739 EARL PAUL           T
    TO THE EARL OF KINSALE,  . . . . . . . . . . . .        740 EARL PAUL          14
    EARL PAUL STOOD ON THE BED OF STRAW,  . . . . . . .     740 EARL PAUL          17
    EARL PAUL CAME WHERE THE KING SAT,  . . . . . . . .     740 EARL PAUL          29
    SAYING "EARL PAUL IS PARDONED  . . . . . . . . . .      741 EARL PAUL          55
    THE EARL OF KINSALE SAID,  . . . . . . . . . . .        742 EARL PAUL          62
EARLESS
    I BURST THE CHAIN: STILL EARLESS, NERVELESS, BLIND, . .  36 OISIN 2           97
    STILL EARLESS, NERVELESS, BLIND, THE EAGLES STOOD. . .   36 OISIN 2          100
    STILL EARLESS, NERVELESS, BLIND, THE EAGLES DREAMED. . . 36 OISIN 2        V 100
EARLIEST
    WHEN THE EARLIEST DEW-WASHED STAR FROM EVE HATH LEANT, .  32 OISIN 2       V  54
    FROM EARLIEST CHILDHOOD, BUT THAT BEING SO,  . . . . .  225 SHADOW WATER B V  77
EARLY
    WISE BIDDY EARLY CALLED THE WICKED WOOD:  . . . . . .   218 WOODS OF COOLE    15
    THAT IN THE EARLY SUMMER OF THE YEAR  . . . . . . .     462 HARUN RASHID      40
    THAT IN THE EARLY SUMMER OF THAT YEAR  . . . . . .      462 HARUN RASHID   V  40
EARN
    "ONLY THE WASTEFUL VIRTUES EARN THE SUN":  . . . . .    270 PARDON FATHERS    18
    A DEAL I'D SWEAT AND LITTLE EARN  . . . . . . . . .     331 ROUND TOWER        2
    I'LL BRING THAT FLOWER TO HER, AND SO MAY EARN  . . .   653 ISLE STAT I 2     45
EARNED
    "YOU WILL HAVE ALL YOU HAVE WISHED FOR WHEN YOU HAVE EARNED  228 SHADOW WATER B 124
    EARNED SLANDER, INGRATITUDE,  . . . . . . . . . .       260 UNWORTH PRAISE    16
    AND THEREFORE EARNED THE RIGHT--AND YET  . . . . . .    273 GREY ROCK         61
    "WE'RE BUT GIVEN WHAT WE HAVE EARNED  . . . . . . .     298 THREE HERMITS     14
    "WHAT HAVE I EARNED FOR ALL THAT WORK," I SAID,  . . .  351 PEOPLE             1
    HEARTS ARE NOT HAD AS A GIFT BUT HEARTS ARE EARNED  . . 404 FOR DAUGHTER      34
EARNING
    EARNING RESPECT: HAVE NO STRANGE FRIEND:  . . . . . .   337 SCHOLARS       V   9
EAR-PIERCING
    MAEVE WAITED, AND WHEN THAT EAR-PIERCING NOISE  . . . . 182 QUEEN MAEVE       47
EARS
    AND 'TWEEN HIS EARS, ABOVE HIS MANE,  . . . . . . .       2 OISIN 1        V 7AA
    NOR CEASED UNTIL WHITE NIAMH STROKED HIS EARS . . . . .  30 OISIN 2           26
    BUT NIAM WITH HER HANDS CARESSED HIS EARS,  . . . . .    30 OISIN 2        V  26
    AND THE EARS OF THE HORSE WENT SINKING AWAY IN THE HOLLOW 48 OISIN 3          21
       NIGHT,
    THE TOPS OF THEIR EARS WERE FEATHERED,  . . . . . .      49 OISIN 3           34
    AFRAID, THEIR EARS ON THE EARTH LAID, . . . . . . .      62 OISIN 3          206
    IN ALL MEN'S EARS OF SORROW,  . . . . . . . . . .        70 CLOAK BOAT        14
    IN EACH MAN'S EARS OF SORROW--  . . . . . . . . .        70 CLOAK BOAT     V  14
    AND WHISPERING IN THEIR EARS  . . . . . . . . . .        88 STOLEN CHILD      33
    OF UNKNOWN PERISHING ARMIES BEAT ABOUT MY EARS. . . . . 161 BLACK PIG          4
    I HAD A THOUGHT FOR NO ONE'S BUT YOUR EARS:  . . . . .  206 ADAMS CURSE       34
    I HAD A THOUGHT FOR NO ONE BUT YOUR EARS!  . . . . .    206 ADAMS CURSE    V  34
    OR CRY ABOUT ONE'S EARS.  NOTHING TO FEAR.  . . . .     222 SHADOW WATER B    19
    I LOVED HIM: I WOULD COVER UP MY EARS,  . . . . . .     246 SHADOW WATER B   494
    BUT I WILL COVER UP YOUR EYES AND EARS,  . . . . . .    250 SHADOW WATER B   574
    WHEN, THE EARS BEING DEAFENED, THE SIGHT OF THE EYES BLIND 257 RECONCILIATION   3
    YOUR EARS THAN STORIES NOW IN FASHION,  . . . . . .     271 GREY ROCK          5
    OR THE DISCERNING EARS,  . . . . . . . . . . . .        329 MEN IMPROVE        9
    HAD SCARCELY ACCUSTOMED OUR EARS  . . . . . . . .       341 SHEP GOATHERD     67
    WHEN HE VANISHED FROM EARS AND EYES.  . . . . . . .     341 SHEP GOATHERD     72
    CLIPPED AN INSOLENT FARMER'S EARS  . . . . . . . .      410 TOWER             31
    TELLS ALL HIS SINNING IN THEIR EARS.  . . . . . . .     655 ISLE STAT I 3     14
    TELLS ALL HER SINNING IN THEIR EARS.  . . . . . . .     655 ISLE STAT I 3  V  14
    IN ALL SUCH THINGS, PRAY LET THINE EARS BE TURNED,  . . 660 ISLE STAT II 1    39
    IN EACH MAN'S EARS OF SORROW,  . . . . . . . . .        666 ISLE STAT II 3    14
    A ROVER I, WHO COME FROM WHERE MEN'S EARS  . . . . .    678 ISLE STAT II 3   293
    FOR THERE ARE SUDDEN VOICES IN MY EARS. . . . . . .     753 SHADOW WATER A   141
    COVER YOUR EARS! FOR ONCE WE HAD MOORED OUR GALLEY  . . 756 SHADOW WATER A   187
    AND NOW THE WAVES ARE CRYING IN MY EARS,  . . . . .     761 SHADOW WATER A   276
    THEN CLOSE YOUR EARS WITH DUST AND LIE  . . . . . .     791 REPRISALS         23
EAR-SHOT
    SOMEWHERE IN EAR-SHOT FOR THE STORY'S END,  . . . . .   269 PARDON FATHERS     2
EARTH
    AND IF JOY WERE NOT ON THE EARTH,  . . . . . . . .       18 OISIN 1          269
    IF JOY WERE NOWHERE ON THE EARTH  . . . . . . . .        18 OISIN 1        V 269
    AND EARTH AND HEAVEN AND HELL WOULD DIE,  . . . . .      19 OISIN 1          271
    DRIPPED ON THE EARTH: BUT SOON, AH! SOON,  . . . . .     19 OISIN 1        V 279
    TRICKLING ALONG THE EARTH, I RAVE:  . . . . . . .        19 OISIN 1        V 281
    ON THE DEAD DIM EARTH ENCLOSES:  . . . . . . . .         21 OISIN 1          312
    ON THE DEAD THE EARTH ENCLOSES,  . . . . . . . .         21 OISIN 1        V 312
    OF THE LOUD CRASHING AND EARTH SHAKING FIGHT  . . . . .  38 OISIN 2        V 141
    WRAPT IN THE WAVE OF THAT MUSIC, WITH WEARINESS MORE THAN 51 OISIN 3          69
       OF EARTH,
    . . . THE FLUTTERING SADNESS OF EARTH.  . . . . . .      55 OISIN 3          124
    FOR MOVETH ALIVE IN THY FINGERS THE FLUTTERING SADNESS   55 OISIN 3        V 124
       OF EARTH.
    I SAW FROM A DISTANT SADDLE: FROM THE EARTH SHE MADE HER 56 OISIN 3          130
       MOAN:
    . . . AND I ROSE, AND WALKED ON THE EARTH,  . . . . .    60 OISIN 3          191
    AFRAID, THEIR EARS ON THE EARTH LAID,  . . . . . .       62 OISIN 3          206
    THE WANDERING EARTH HERSELF MAY BE  . . . . . . .        65 HAPPY SHEPHERD    18
```

		PAGE	TITLE	LINE

EARTH   (CONTINUED)

```
    OR IN THE SUN AND MOON, OR ON THE EARTH,          114 ROSE OF BATTLE        17
    BEFORE EARTH TOOK HIM TO HER STONY CARE:          126 DREAM OF FAERY         4
    BEFORE EARTH MADE OF HIM HER SLEEPY CARE:         126 DREAM OF FAERY V       4
    NOW THAT DEEP EARTH HAS DRUNK HIS BODY IN:        127 DREAM OF FAERY V      28
    NOW THAT THE EARTH HAD TAKEN MAN AND ALL:         128 DREAM OF FAERY        40
    NOW THAT OLD EARTH HAD TAKEN MAN AND ALL:         128 DREAM OF FAERY V      40
    WITH THE EARTH AND THE SKY AND THE WATER,         143 ROSE IN HEART          7
    BECAUSE EARTH, CRAZY FOR ITS BROKEN POWER,        186 QUEEN MAEVE          124
    BEING FORBID TO MARRY ON EARTH,                   189 BAILE AILLINN         11
    WAS ROBBED BEFORE EARTH GAVE THE WHEAT:           196 BAILE AILLINN        166
    WANDER WHERE EARTH WITHERS AWAY,                  196 BAILE AILLINN        171
    HEARING THE WHOLE EARTH CHANGE ITS TUNE,          266 GALWAY RACES          12
    TREE, LIKE A SOOTY FINGER, STARTS FROM THE EARTH: 410 TOWER                 19
    IF BUT IMAGINATION SCORN THE EARTH                478 SELF AND SOUL         21
    SYMBOLICAL GLORY OF THE EARTH AND AIR:            483 VERONIC NAPKIN         3
    OVER THE BLACKENED EARTH                          496 MOHINI CHATTER        21
    EARTH IN BEAUTY DRESSED                           517 HER ANXIETY            1
    HEAVEN AND EARTH OUT OF THEIR PLACES,             540 FROM ANTIGONE          8
    WITHOUT A FRIEND ON THE EARTH                     552 SONGS REWRIT 2         6
    WITHOUT A FRIEND ON THIS EARTH                    552 SONGS REWRIT 2 V       6
    BUT ALL THAT RUN IN COUPLES, ON EARTH, IN FLOOD OR AIR,
                                                      556 RIBH PATRICK          11
    IRRATIONAL STREAMS OF BLOOD ARE STAINING EARTH:   564 GYRES                  5
    OF THE WIDE WOODS.  AND THE DEEP EARTH GATHERED THEM.
                                                      660 ISLE STAT II 1        33
    FROM THE DEEP EARTH UNTO THE LURID SKY            662 ISLE STAT II 2         5
    SHOUTED A MOMENT 'TWEEN THE EARTH AND SKY.        675 ISLE STAT II 3       237
    I WILL BURN HERESY FROM THIS MAD EARTH,           697 MOSADA 2              40
    FROM THE HILLS OF EARTH HAVE PEALED               705 DAWN-SONG              5
    JOYS AND FEARS IN THEIR GREY FACES THAT THE LIVE EARTH
                                                      719 PHANTOM SHIP          26
      KNOWETH NOT:
    SCOFF THEY AT THE MODERN EARTH--                  727 LOVERS QUARREL        38
    REMOTE FROM ALL THE HARD EARTH TROUBLES,          731 PRIEST FAIRY          80
    HANGS O'ER ALL THE WOODED EARTH.                  731 STREET DANCERS         8
    OTHERS KNOW THE HEALING EARTH.                    733 STREET DANCERS        53
    ALL THE HEALING EARTH MAY-TREASURE,               733 STREET DANCERS        63
    ALL THE HEALING EARTH MAY TREASURE,               733 STREET DANCERS V      63
    AND HAVE BEEN WOOED BY THE TWELVE KINGS OF THE EARTH,
                                                      757 SHADOW WATER A V     214
    WHEN EARTH AND HEAVEN HAVE BEEN FOLDED UP:        765 SHADOW WATER A       366
    THAT BLOW WHEN HEAVEN AND EARTH ARE WITHERING,    767 SHADOW WATER A       395
    LET THE EARTH BEAR WITNESS,                       770 BLOOD BOND             9
EARTH-ENKINDLED
    POOR EARTH-ENKINDLED PAIR,                        680 LOVE AND DEATH        22
EARTHLY
    AS THOUGH HE HELD AN EARTHLY MEAD                   2 OISIN 1        V     7X
    AND WHEN THEY SAW MY EARTHLY DRESS,                15 OISIN 1        V    207
    AND BADE ME SING OF EARTHLY LANDS:                 17 OISIN 1        V    233
    WEDDING THE QUEENS OF EARTHLY LANDS WITH RINGS     29 OISIN 2        V     10
    FROM THESE EARTHLY BOUNDS."                        97 FOXHUNTER            12
    OF ANY UNBLESSED EARTHLY BIRD."                   697 MOSADA 2             33
    DO NOT FEAR US, EARTHLY MAID:                     726 LOVERS QUARREL        1
EARTH'S
    BRUSH LIGHTLY AS HAYMOUSE EARTH'S PEBBLES,         56 OISIN 3             128
    BRUSH LIGHTLY AS HAY MOUSE EARTH'S PEBBLES,        56 OISIN 3        V    128
    MY SONGS OF OLD EARTH'S DREAMY YOUTH:              67 HAPPY SHEPHERD       54
    MURMURING HOW FAR AWAY ARE ALL EARTH'S FEVERISH LANDS.
                                                       78 INDIAN TO LOVE V     10
    HID IN THE EARTH'S MOST HIDDEN PART,               78 INDIAN TO LOVE V     12
    EARTH'S ALIENS.  WHY SO SORROWFUL?  OUR SOULS      80 EPHEMERA       V    12A
    HAD HID AWAY EARTH'S OLD AND WEARY CRY.           120 SORROW OF LOVE V      4
    ARE SHAKEN WITH EARTH'S OLD AND WEARY CRY.        120 SORROW OF LOVE V     12
    FULL OF EARTH'S OLD TIMID GRACE.                  124 CATHLEEN PARA        12
    PEACE, PEACE, THE EARTH'S A-QUAKE.  I HEAR        656 ISLE STAT I 3        20
EARTH-SHAKING
    OF THE LOUD-CRASHING AND EARTH-SHAKING FIGHT,      38 OISIN 2             141
EARTHY
    WHEN EARTHY NIGHT HAD DRUNK HIS BODY IN:          127 DREAM OF FAERY       28
    WE SHADOWS, WHILE THEY UPROOT HIS EARTHY HOUSE,   184 QUEEN MAEVE          94
    WE SHADOWS, WHILE THEY UPROOT THE EARTHY HOUSE    184 QUEEN MAEVE    V     94
    DARK AND DULL AND EARTHY THE STREAM OF DRUMAHAIR  207 HANRAHANS SONG V     11
    DARK AND DULL AND EARTHY OUR SOULS AND BODIES BE: 208 HANRAHANS SONG V     13
EASE
    THE SINGING SHOOK HIM OUT OF HIS NEW EASE.        126 DREAM OF FAERY       12
    I ALSO BEAR A BELL-BRANCH FULL OF EASE.           130 BOOK STORIES         12
    I ALSO BEAR A BELL BRANCH FULL OF EASE.           130 BOOK STORIES   V     12
    WROUGHT OF HIGH LAUGHTER, LOVELINESS AND EASE?    264 HOUSE SHAKEN         12
    "AND THERE I'LL GROW RESPECTED AT MY EASE,        300 BEGGAR CRIED         17
    BUT PRAY TO GOD THAT HE EASE                      380 SONGS FOOL 1         17
    WHERE SLIPPERED CONTEMPLATION FINDS HIS EASE      418 ANCEST HOUSES        30
    A COMPANY OF FRIENDS, A CONSCIENCE SET AT EASE,   427 PHANTOM HATRED       37
    AND DRUNK OR SOBER LIVE AT EASE                   597 MODEL LAUREATE       13
    FOR AN INSTANT STANDS AT EASE,                    638 BEN BULBEN           31
    GARDENS WHERE A SOUL'S AT EASE:                   639 BEN BULBEN           55
    TO EASE THEIR WORLD-OLD THIRST ALONG THE BRINK    663 ISLE STAT II 2       41
    WILL WONDERING LISTEN, AND THIS TALE SHALL EASE   693 MOSADA 1             70
    HE NOW GETS NOVELS AT HIS EASE.                   792 GEORGE MOORE          4
EASIER
    TIME CAN BUT MAKE IT EASIER TO BE WISE            200 FOLLY COMFORT         4
    IT'S CERTAIN I'D SLEEP EASIER O' NIGHTS           224 SHADOW WATER B       59
EAST
    SANG HOW SOMEWHERE TO NORTH OR EAST OR SOUTH      127 DREAM OF FAERY V     19
    THE EAST HER HIDDEN JOY BEFORE THE MORNING BREAK, 154 BELOVED PEACE         4
```

EAST   (CONTINUED)
   THE EAST TELLS ALL HER SECRET JOY BEFORE DAYBREAK, . . . 154 BELOVED PEACE V   4
   THE BANNERS OF EAST AND WEST, ... 165 CRY OF SEDGE   7
   A GLITTERING SWORD OUT OF THE EAST. A PUFF OF WIND . . . 426 PHANTOM HATRED   5
   THE SOUTH WIND BROUGHT IT LONGING, AND THE EAST WIND
     DESPAIR,   449 OWEN AHERNE   5
   THE SOUTH WIND BROUGHT IT LONGING, AND THE EAST BROUGHT
     IN DESPAIR,   449 OWEN AHERNE V   5
   THE SOUTH WIND BROUGHT IT LONGING, AND THE EAST BROUGHT
     IT DESPAIR,   449 OWEN AHERNE V   5
   ENFOLDEN IN THE SHADOWS OF THE EAST, ... 705 REMEMBRANCE   11
   SHE OFFERS GREAT REWARDS IF WE TURN EAST . . . . . 755 SHADOW WATER A   169
EASTER
   IF A GOOD EASTER WIND WERE BLOWING, ... 306 HOUR DAWN   86
   EASTER [NINETEEN-SIXTEEN] . . . . 391 EASTER 1916   T
EASTERN
   FEEDING WHITE MOTHS AROUND SOME EASTERN SHRINE, ...   41 OISIN 2   V   186
   PRAYED THOSE FORGOTTEN FISHERS, TILL IN THE EASTERN SKIES 719 PHANTOM SHIP   32
   ALL THOSE LONG FORGOTTEN FISHERS, TILL IN THE EASTERN SKIES 719 PHANTOM SHIP V   32
EASTERN-HEARTED
   AH! NOW I'M EASTERN-HEARTED ONCE AGAIN, ... 694 MOSADA 1   99
EASY
   SHE BID ME TAKE LOVE EASY, AS THE LEAVES GROW ON THE TREE!   90 SALLEY GARDENS   3
   SHE BID ME TAKE LIFE EASY, AS THE GRASS GROWS ON THE WEIRS!   90 SALLEY GARDENS   7
   SHE BID ME TAKE LOVE EASY, AS THE LEAVES GROW ON THE TREE!   90 SALLEY GARDENS V   3
   TO HIM SEEMED EASY, SO I LAID THE CROWN . . . . . . 102 FERGUS DRUID   13
   ALL NEIGHBOURLY CONTENT AND EASY TALK ARE GONE, ... 580 CURSE CROMWELL   9
   A STATESMAN IS AN EASY MAN, ... 598 STONE CROSS   1
EAT
   EAT AWAY THE SLOPING SOD, ...   20 OISIN 1   V   299
   WHAT WERE OUR PRAISE TO THEM? THEY EAT . . . . . . 196 BAILE AILLINN   177
   I HAVE NOT FOUND A THING TO EAT, ... 294 THREE BEGGARS   3
   TO CLIMB THAT STAIR AND EAT THAT BITTER BREAD, ... 369 EGO DOMINUS   35
   EAT AT MY HEARTHSTONE . . . . 380 SONGS FOOL 1   2
   IT'S CERTAIN THAT FINE WOMEN EAT . . . . 404 FOR DAUGHTER   30
   WHAT WHOLESOME SUN HAS RIPENED IS WHOLESOME FOOD TO EAT, 442 BLACK CENTAUR   5
EATEN
   BUT WHEN I HAD EATEN AND DRUNK MYSELF ASLEEP . . . . . 223 SHADOW WATER B   30
   BUT WHEN I HAD EATEN AND DRUNK A BELLYFUL . . . . . 223 SHADOW WATER B V   30
   AND THE SHADOWS EATEN THE MOON, ... 268 BROWN PENNY   14
   HAD DE VALERA EATEN PARNELL'S HEART . . . . 542 PARN FUNERAL 2   2
   HAD COSGRAVE EATEN PARNELL'S HEART, THE LAND'S . . . . 543 PARN FUNERAL 2   5
   AND MANY A PURPLE GILLYFLOWER EATEN, ... 729 PRIEST FAIRY   35
EATING   SEE FISH-EATING
   WANDERS LAUGHING AND EATING HER WILD HEART . . . . . 198 SEVEN WOODS   11
   NO HAMLET THIN FROM EATING FLIES, A FAT . . . . . . 610 STATUES   19
EAVES
   THE BRAWLING OF A SPARROW IN THE EAVES, ... 119 SORROW OF LOVE   1
   THE QUARREL OF THE SPARROWS IN THE EAVES, ... 119 SORROW OF LOVE V   1
   AROSE, AND ON THE INSTANT CLAMOROUS EAVES, ... 120 SORROW OF LOVE   9
   AND NOW THE SPARROWS WARRING IN THE EAVES, ... 120 SORROW OF LOVE V   9
EBB
   ALTHOUGH YOU HIDE IN THE EBB AND FLOW . . . . 146 FISH   1
   OF THE EBB OF ALL THINGS TO MAKE LOVE . . . . . . 193 BAILE AILLINN V   109
   OUR HANDS, OUR HANDS MUST EBB AWAY. . . . . 213 BLESS PSALTER   18
   BUT BLESS OUR HANDS THAT EBB AWAY. . . . . 213 BLESS PSALTER   20
   OR ALL THAT WAYWARD EBB AND FLOW. THERE STOOD . . . . 428 NINETEEN 19 V   4
   ON ALL THAT WAYWARD EBB AND FLOW. THERE STOOD . . . . 428 NINETEEN 19 V   4
   HAVE I NOT SEEN A THOUSAND SEASONS EBB AND FLOW . . . 675 ISLE STAT II 3   229
EBBED
   UNTIL TIME AND THE WORLD HAVE EBBED AWAY . . . . . . 168 BLESSED   V   39
   THAT SHALL BURN TIME WHEN TIMES HAVE EBBED AWAY. . . . . 750 SHADOW WATER A   61
EBBING
   WHILE TIME AND THE WORLD ARE EBBING AWAY . . . . . . 168 BLESSED   39
EBREMAR
   WHY THESE NEW FEARS? THE GREAT MONK EBREMAR, ... 692 MOSADA 1   46
   WHEN THERE ARE MANY? EBREMAR WILL STAMP . . . . . 696 MOSADA 2   17
   BE STILL! I HEAR THE STEP OF EBREMAR. . . . . . . 697 MOSADA 2   34
   WAS EBREMAR, WHOSE THOUGHTS WERE FIXED ON GOD, ... 702 MOSADA 3   83
EBREMAR'S
   TO SAINTED EBREMAR'S SAD EYES. I THINK . . . . . . 696 MOSADA 2   15
EBULLIENT
   A GREAT EBULLIENT PORTRAIT CERTAINLY! . . . . 602 GALLERY REVIS   27
   AN EBULLIENT GREAT PORTRAIT CERTAINLY! . . . . 602 GALLERY REVIS V   27
ECHO
   THE MAN AND THE ECHO . . . . 632 MAN AND ECHO   T
   MAN AND THE ECHO . . . . 632 MAN AND ECHO V   T
   AND HEARD EACH UNSEEN ECHO ON HER THRONE, ... 657 ISLE STAT I 3   48
ECHOES
   OR SAD SEA-SHELLS WHERE LITTLE ECHOES SIT? . . . . . 650 ISLE STAT I 1   149
   AND, LEAPING TO THEIR FEET, FAR ECHOES CRIED, ... 659 ISLE STAT II 1   13
ECHO-HARBOURING
   SOME TWISTED, ECHO-HARBOURING SHELL, ...   66 HAPPY SHEPHERD   36
ECHOING   SEE RE-ECHOING
   THAT DOWN THE ECHOING VALLEYS ROLLED. . . . .   84 MAD KING GOLL V   35
   IN THE LONG ECHOING STREET THE LAUGHING DANCERS THRONG, 459 FROM OEDIPUS   7
   IN THE LONG ECHOING STREETS THE LAUGHING DANCERS THRONG, 459 FROM OEDIPUS V   7
   MY ECHOING HEART. NOW RAISE THY VOICE AND SPEAK! . . . 683 SEEKER   47
ECHTGE
   ECHTGE OF STREAMS . . . . 203 WITHER BOUGHS V   T
   AND I FELL ASLEEP UPON LONELY ECHTGE OF STREAMS. . . . . 203 WITHER BOUGHS   6

	PAGE	TITLE	LINE

ECHTGE (CONTINUED)
    I KNOW, AND THE CURLEW AND PEEWIT ON ECHTGE OF STREAMS.   204 WITHER BOUGHS   22
    AND THE CURLEW AND PEEWIT KNOW ON ECHTGE OF STREAMS. • • 204 WITHER BOUGHS V 22
ECLIPSE
    UNDER ECLIPSE AND THE DAY BLOTTED OUT. • • • • • • • 414 TOWER   120
ECSTACY
    GIVE TO HIS SHARPENED PALATE ECSTACY • • • • • • • 474 ALL SOUL NIGHT V 84
ECSTASY
    IN TRUTH'S CONSUMING ECSTASY, • • • • • • • • 139 TO IRELAND   42
    MIRACLE, ECSTASY, THE IMPOSSIBLE HOPE, • • • • • 227 SHADOW WATER B 102
    CAN KNOW THAT ECSTASY. FORGAEL! FORGAEL! • • • 231 SHADOW WATER B 203
    LABOURING IN ECSTASY. • • • • • • • • • 315 FRIENDS   16
    CAN GIVE HIS SHARPENED PALATE ECSTASY • • • • 474 ALL SOUL NIGHT   84
    RIBH IN ECSTASY • • • • • • • • • • 557 RIBH ECSTASY   T
ECSTATIC
    NAMING IT WITH ECSTATIC BREATH, • • • • • • 254 HIS DREAM   18
    THE ECSTATIC WATERS LAUGH BECAUSE • • • • • 612 NEWS ORACLE   17
EDAIN
    AENGUS AND EDAIN, MY OWN NAME • • • • • • • 5 OISIN 1   47
    AENGUS AND EDAIN, AND MY NAME • • • • • • 5 OISIN 1 V 47
    THAT EDAIN, MIDHIR'S WIFE, HAD WOVE • • • • 195 BAILE AILLINN 142
    EDAIN CAME OUT OF MIDHIR'S HILL, AND LAY • • • 219 HARP OF AENGUS   1
    'TWAS AENGUS AND EDAIN, THE WANDERING LOVERS, • • 224 SHADOW WATER B 42
    HE CARRIED EDAIN OFF FROM A KING'S HOUSE, • • • 224 SHADOW WATER B 48
    AENGUS AND EDAIN, THOSE PASSIONATE WANDERERS, • • 228 SHADOW WATER B 138
    AENGUS AND EDAIN RAN UP OUT OF THE WAVE— • • 231 SHADOW WATER B 196
    HAVING NO THOUGHT BUT FOR HIS QUEEN EDAIN, • • 276 TWO KINGS V I
    PALE-FACED, ALONE UPON A BENCH, EDAIN • • • 279 TWO KINGS   61
    "WHY IS IT," QUEEN EDAIN SAID, • • • • • 771 SONG DEIRDRE 1   1
    BUT IS EDAIN WORTH A SONG • • • • • • • 773 SONG DEIRDRE 1   17
EDAINE
    WHEN AENGUS AND HIS EDAINE WAKE FROM SLEEP • • • 749 SHADOW WATER A 57
    TILL HIS EDAINE, NO LONGER A GOLDEN FLY • • • 757 SHADOW WATER A 210
    TILL HIS EDAINE, NO MORE A SILVER FLY • • • 757 SHADOW WATER A V 210
    EDAINE CAME OUT OF MIDHIR'S HILL, AND LAY • • 762 SHADOW WATER A 296
    QUEEN EDAINE • • • • • • • • • • 771 SONG DEIRDRE 1 V T
EDDIES
    TILL ALL THE EDDIES GLEAM! • • • • • • • 389 IMAGE PAST   4
    AMONG THE STARRY EDDIES OF HER HAIR • • • • • 390 IMAGE PAST   27
EDDY
    AND EDDY TO EDDY. MASTERS OF OUR DREAMS, • • • 768 SHADOW WATER A 418
    AND EDDY TO EDDY. MASTERS OF OUR DREAMS, • • • 768 SHADOW WATER A 418
EDDYING
    AND THE EDDYING CAT-HEADED BIRD! • • • • • 783 GREY ROUND   23
EDEN
    AND THAT YOU COME FROM EDEN ON FLYING FEET. • • • 218 WOODS OF COOLE 29
    IS EDEN FAR AWAY, OR DO YOU HIDE • • • • 218 WOODS OF COOLE 30
    IS EDEN OUT OF TIME AND OUT OF SPACE? • • • 218 WOODS OF COOLE 36
    TENT-POLE OF EDEN! THE TENT'S DRAPERY! • • • 483 VERONIC NAPKIN 2
    TENT POLE OF EDEN! THE TENT'S DRAPERY! • • • 483 VERONIC NAPKIN V 2
EDEN'S
    EDEN'S GARDEN WOULD BE THERE • • • • • • 621 JOHN KINSELLA   27
EDEN-SOD
    O'ER THE GREEN EDEN-SOD! • • • • • • • 654 ISLE STAT I 2 65
    O'ER THE GREEN EDEN-SOD, • • • • • • • 654 ISLE STAT I 2 75
EDGE
    AND FOUND ON THE DOVE-GREY EDGE OF THE SEA • • • 3 OISIN 1   19
    AND ON THE RUNNEL'S STONY AND BARE EDGE • • • 39 OISIN 2   157
    ROSE FROM A LITTLE RUNNEL ON WHOSE EDGE • • • 39 OISIN 2 V 157
    AND WE STOOD ON A SEA'S EDGE WE SAW NOT! • • • 47 OISIN 3   11
    AND WE RODE ON THE PLAINS OF THE SEA'S EDGE! • • • 48 OISIN 3   13
    • • THE SEA'S EDGE BARREN AND GREY, • • • 48 OISIN 3   13
    AND I RODE BY THE PLAINS OF THE SEA'S EDGE, • • • 56 OISIN 3   141
    AND THE WINDS MADE THE SANDS ON THE SEA'S EDGE • • 57 OISIN 3   145
    I PASSED ALONG THE WATER'S EDGE BELOW THE HUMID TREES, • 76 INDIAN ON GOD   1
    I WANDER BY THE EDGE • • • • • • • • 165 CRY OF SEDGE   1
    WITH BLINKING EYES, AT THE CAVE'S EDGE, • • • 167 BLESSED V 4C
    ON THE HORIZON EDGE BELLOWED THE HERDS. • • • 279 TWO KINGS   56
    HE'D HEARD THAT DIN ON THE HORIZON'S EDGE • • • 286 TWO KINGS V 217A
    AND NOT A HOUSE TO THE PLAIN'S EDGE, • • • • 302 HOUR DAWN   10
    BY THE WOOD'S EDGE WHERE ONLY EQUALS MEET, • • • 321 REED WHISPERER V 8
    BY WHAT LAKE'S EDGE OR POOL • • • • • • 323 SWANS AT COOLE 28
    THE TOWER SET ON THE STREAM'S EDGE! • • • • 326 ROBERT GREGORY 52
    THE TOWER SET BY THE STREAM'S EDGE! • • • • 326 ROBERT GREGORY V 52
    I WOULD FIND BY THE EDGE OF THAT WATER • • • 330 BONE OF A HARE   9
    SHALL WALK THE WET SANDS BY THE EDGE OF THE STREAM • 371 EGO DOMINUS   71
    SHALL WALK THE WET SAND BY THE WATER'S EDGE, • • 371 EGO DOMINUS V 71
    SAT DOWN UPON THE FOUNTAIN'S MARBLE EDGE, • • • 463 HARUN RASHID 43
    I RIDE WITH FALCON TO THE RIVER'S EDGE • • • 463 HARUN RASHID 57
    I RIDE WITH FALCON TO THE WATER'S EDGE • • • 463 HARUN RASHID V 57
    BY THE SINGING WATERS' EDGE! • • • • • • 646 ISLE STAT I 1 23
    SAW ON THE WOOD'S EDGE GLEAM AN ASH-GREY FEATHER! • 715 DWELT SYCAMORE 2
    AMONG THOSE STREAMS, OR ON THEIR CLOUDY EDGE. • • 750 SHADOW WATER A 63
EDIT
    EDIT AND ANNOTATE THE LINES • • • • • • • 337 SCHOLARS   3
EDMUND
    ON A PICTURE OF A BLACK CENTAUR BY EDMUND DULAC • • 442 BLACK CENTAUR   T
    MY GREAT-GRANDFATHER SPOKE TO EDMUND BURKE • • 486 SEVEN SAGES   1
EDWARD
    FOR THIS EDWARD FITZGERALD DIED, • • • • • 290 SEPTEMBER 1913 20
    LORD EDWARD AND WOLFE TONE, • • • • • • 395 SIXTEEN DEAD 16

	PAGE	TITLE		LINE

EEL
    OF A GREAT EEL; IT CHANGED, AND I BUT SMOTE • • • • •   40 OISIN 2   176
E'EN
    NOT E'EN THY GOD COULD HAVE THROWN DOWN THAT HALL; • •   36 OISIN 2   V 109
    E'EN THEN, BEFORE HER SHEPHERD HAIR • • • • • • • •   668 ISLE STAT II 3   54
    FROM THEE I SNATCHED IT; E'EN THE FAY THAT TRIPS • • •   670 ISLE STAT II 3   98
    E'EN THOUGH HIS WINGS WERE PLUMELESS STUMPS, • • • • •   670 ISLE STAT II 3   118
E'ER
    WITH SINGING SWEET AS E'ER ROUND LAKE-LULLED ISLE • • •   649 ISLE STAT I 1   106
EGG
    A PIECE OF A NIGHTINGALE'S EGG, • • • • • • • • • •   708 FAIRY PEDANT   24
EGGED
    'TWAS YOU THAT EGGED HIM TO IT, FOR YOU KNOW • • • • •   248 SHADOW WATER B   550
EGO
    EGO DOMINUS TUUS • • • • • • • • • • • • • • •   367 EGO DOMINUS   T
EGYPT
    EGYPT AND GREECE, GOOD-BYE, AND GOOD-BYE, ROME! • • • •   563 MERU   8
EGYPTIAN
    FORMS A STARK EGYPTIAN THOUGHT, • • • • • • • • • •   638 BEN BULBEN   43
EIGHT   SEE TWENTY-AND-EIGHT
    EIGHT POEMS CRAZY JANE AND THE BISHOP • • • • • • •   507 JANE BISHOP   V T
EIGHTEENTH-CENTURY
    EIGHTEENTH-CENTURY HOUSES. • • • • • • • • • • • •   392 EASTER 1916   4
EIGHTIETH
    HER EIGHTIETH WINTER APPROACHING! "YESTERDAY HE THREATENED   578 LOFTY THINGS   8
        MY LIFE.
EIRE
    THEN FEAST, MAKING CONVERSE OF EIRE, OF WARS, • • • • •   62 OISIN 3   V 212
    SING OF OLD EIRE AND THE ANCIENT WAYS! • • • • • •   101 ROSE UPON ROOD   23
    WHEN HER OWN PEOPLE RULED THIS TRAGIC EIRE! • • • • •   129 BOOK STORIES   2
    I TORE IT FROM THE BARREN BOUGHS OF EIRE, • • • • • •   130 BOOK STORIES   15
    YOUR MOTHER EIRE IS ALWAYS YOUNG, • • • • • • • • •   148 INTO TWILIGHT   5
EL
    BELOVED HAROUN EL RASHID, OCCUPIED • • • • • • •   462 HARUN RASHID   V 24
    THAT YEAR WHEN GREAT HAROUN EL RASHID KILLED • • • •   462 HARUN RASHID   V 31
ELABORATE
    AMID THE ELABORATE WILDERNESS OF THE AIR. • • • • • •   278 TWO KINGS   31
    THE ELABORATE STARLIGHT THROWS A REFLECTION • • • • •   389 IMAGE PAST   2
    THE ELABORATE STAR-LIGHT HAS THROWN REFLECTIONS • • • •   389 IMAGE PAST   V 2
    TO ROUND THAT SHELL'S ELABORATE WHORL, • • • • • • •   509 JANE REPROVED   8
ELBOW
    O MAY TRANQUILLITY WALK BY HIS ELBOW • • • • • • • •   71 ANASHU VIJAYA   2
ELBOWS
    LEANS ON HIS ELBOWS, GAZING AT THE SEA. • • • • • • •   752 SHADOW WATER A   127
ELDER
    O WINDS, ELDER THAN CHANGING OF NIGHT AND DAY, • • •   162 ASKS FORGIVE   V 7
    SAW THE PIERCED HANDS AND ROOD OF ELDER RISE • • • •   169 SECRET ROSE   10
ELDERS
    AND ALL THE ELDERS SITTING IN THE SUN • • • • • • •   693 MOSADA 1   69
ELDEST
    EACH OTHER ROUND IN CIRCLES, AND HEARD THE ELDEST SPEAK!   76 INDIAN ON GOD   5
    EACH OTHER ROUND IN CIRCLES! AND I HEARD THE ELDEST   76 INDIAN ON GOD   V 5
        SPEAK!——
ELECT
    THE BEST-ENDOWED, THE ELECT, • • • • • • • • • •   504 RESULT THOUGHT   3
    THE ENDOWED, THE ELECT! • • • • • • • • • • • •   504 RESULT THOUGHT V   3
ELEGANCE
    AND SMOOTH OUT STAIN AND BLEMISH WITH THE ELEGANCE OF HIS   353 HIS PHOENIX   7
        MIND!
    IF FOLLY LINK WITH ELEGANCE • • • • • • • • • • •   598 STONE CROSS   13
    IF FOLLY LINKS WITH ELEGANCE • • • • • • • • • • •   598 STONE CROSS   V 13
ELEMENT
    HIS ELEMENT IS SO FINE • • • • • • • • • • • •   470 ALL SOUL NIGHT   7
    WHERE SOME LAUGHING ELEMENT • • • • • • • • • • •   777 SONG DEIRDRE 2   4
ELEMENTAL
    FOR THE ELEMENTAL CREATURES GO • • • • • • • • • •   138 TO IRELAND   23
    FOR THE ELEMENTAL BEINGS GO • • • • • • • • • • •   138 TO IRELAND   V 23
    THE POET PLEADS WITH THE ELEMENTAL POWERS • • • • • •   174 ELEMENT POWERS   T
    AODH PLEADS WITH THE ELEMENTAL POWERS • • • • • • •   174 ELEMENT POWERS V   T
    GREAT ELEMENTAL POWERS OF WIND, AND WAVE, AND FIRE, • • •   174 ELEMENT POWERS V   7
ELEMENTS
    A MYSTICAL PRAYER TO THE MASTERS OF THE ELEMENTS, • • •   174 ELEMENT POWERS V   T
    SO THAT HIS ELEMENTS HAVE GROWN SO FINE • • • • • • •   473 ALL SOUL NIGHT   82
ELEVATE
    THE MIND OF MAN OR ELEVATE A RHYME! • • • • • • • •   492 COOLE BALLYLEE   45
ELEVEN
    GROWS COMELIER, ELEVEN PASS, AND THEN • • • • • • •   374 PHASES OF MOON   44
ELF
    REPLY LIKE MOANING OF IMPRISONED ELF! • • • • • • •   652 ISLE STAT I 2   11
ELFIN-SIGHTS
    AND THEY WILL WAR, 'MID WONDROUS ELFIN-SIGHTS! • • • •   651 ISLE STAT I 1   164
ELIZABETH
    BY HIS WIFE ELIZABETH • • • • • • • • • • • • •   360 ALF POLLEXFEN   4
ELMS
    IN THE ELMS ABOVE THE FLOODED STREAM! • • • • • • •   403 FOR DAUGHTER   12
    OLD RAGGED ELMS, OLD THORNS INNUMERABLE, • • • • • •   419 MY HOUSE   5
    VALLEY, RIVER, AND ELMS, UNDER THE LIGHT OF A MOON • • •   426 PHANTOM HATRED   3
    VALLEY, RIVER, ELMS, UNDER THE LIGHT OF A MOON • • • •   426 PHANTOM HATRED V   3
ELSE
    TWO THINGS THAT 'FORE ALL ELSE I HATE, • • • • • • •   24 OISIN 1   V 359
    HE IS A GENTLE ROEBUCK! FOR HOW ELSE, I PRAY, COULD HE • •   76 INDIAN ON GOD   15

		PAGE	TITLE		LINE
ELSE	(CONTINUED)				
	OR ELSE THEY STAND AND SNIFF THE WIND,	136	TWO TREES		37
	OR ELSE AT MEADOW OR AT GRAZING OVERLOOKS	340	SHEP GOATHERD		37
	OLD GOATHERDS AND OLD GOATS, IF IN ALL ELSE	340	SHEP GOATHERD		46
	WHAT ELSE HE GIVE OR KEEP	346	ON WOMAN		24
	OR ELSE MY DREAMS THAT FLY	384	VISION ROBART		51
	OR ELSE BY TOASTING HER A SCORE OF TIMES,	410	TOWER		42
	OR ELSE ALL JUNO FROM AN URN DISPLAYS	418	ANCEST HOUSES		27
	OR ELSE, TO ALTER PLATO'S PARABLE,	443	SCHOOL CHILDR		15
	DELIGHT BECOMES DEATH-LONGING IF ALL LONGING ELSE BE VAIN.	459	FROM OEDIPUS		3
	A MYSTERY THAT ELSE HAD FOUND NO CHRONICLER	461	HARUN RASHID		21
	SAINT GEORGE OR ELSE A PAGAN PERSEUS!	533	HER TRIUMPH		10
	OR ANYTHING ELSE BUT A RHYMER	552	SONGS REWRIT 2		9
	OR ANYTHING ELSE BUT A MAN	552	SONGS REWRIT 2	V	9
	FOR EVERYBODY KNOWS OR ELSE SHOULD KNOW	565	LAPIS LAZULI		4
	FORGOTTEN ELSE BY MANKIND,	576	ACRE OF GRASS		23
	WHAT ELSE HAVE I TO SPUR ME INTO SONG?	591	SPUR		4
	EVERYTHING ELSE WITHERED AND MUMMY-DEAD,	618	BRONZE HEAD		3
	(SOMETHING MAY LINGER THERE THOUGH ALL ELSE DIE!)	618	BRONZE HEAD		5
	OR ELSE I THOUGHT HER SUPERNATURAL!	619	BRONZE HEAD		22
	TILL ALL ELSE IS EMPTY CHAFF,	647	ISLE STAT I 1		60
ELSEWHERE					
	AS THOUGH TO SAY "IT IS THE SWORD ELSEWHERE,"	267	ALL TEMPT ME	V	8
ELVISH					
	AND ELVISH WISDOM, AND LONG YEARS OF YOUTH	653	ISLE STAT I 2		47
EMAIN					
	MY WORD WAS LAW FROM ITH TO EMAIN,	81	MAD KING GOLL		2
	RODE OUT OF EMAIN WITH A BAND	189	BAILE AILLINN		18
EMAN					
	AT EMAN, 'NEATH THE BEECH TREES, ON EACH SIDE,	44	OISIN 2	V	228
	WOLF-BREEDING MOUNTAINS, GALLERIED EMAN,	81	MAD KING GOLL	V	2
EMAN'S					
	THAN DOVES THAT MOANED ROUND EMAN'S HALL	3	OISIN 1	V	7EE
	THE FLOOR OF EMAN'S DANCING HALL	13	OISIN 1	V	156
	MINE WAS THE THRONE IN EMAN'S HALL,	81	MAD KING GOLL	V	2
EMBASSY					
	WITH PERSIAN EMBASSY OR GRECIAN WAR,	462	HARUN RASHID		25
EMBATTLED					
	AND OF THE EMBATTLED FLAMING MULTITUDE	137	TO SOME I TALK		10
	AND OF THE PROUD EMBATTLED MULTITUDE	137	TO SOME I TALK	V	10
EMBERS					
	WE SAW THE LAST EMBERS OF DAYLIGHT DIE,	205	ADAMS CURSE		29
EMBITTERED					
	I HAVE NOTHING BUT THE EMBITTERED SUN!	344	DEJECTION		8
	OR, BY THE MOON EMBITTERED, SCORN ALOUD	498	BYZANTIUM		21
	THEMES OF THE EMBITTERED HEART, OR SO IT SEEMS,	629	CIRCUS ANIMALS		13
EMBLEM					
	A POWERFUL EMBLEM UP,	480	BLOOD AND MOON		9
	ANOTHER EMBLEM THERE! THAT STORMY WHITE	490	COOLE BALLYLEE		17
EMBLEMATICAL					
	EMBLEMATICAL OF LOVE AND WAR?	477	SELF AND SOUL		19
	EMBLEMATICAL OF THE NIGHT,	478	SELF AND SOUL		30
EMBLEMS					
	BEFITTING EMBLEMS OF ADVERSITY.	420	MY HOUSE		30
	AND THERE MARKED OUT THOSE EMBLEMS ON THE SAND	468	HARUN RASHID		156
	AND THERE MARKED OUT EMBLEMS ON THE SAND	468	HARUN RASHID	V	156
	FOR EMBLEMS OF THE DAY AGAINST THE TOWER	478	SELF AND SOUL		29
	AND NOT THOSE THINGS THAT THEY WERE EMBLEMS OF.	630	CIRCUS ANIMALS		32
EMBOSOMED	SEE LAKE-EMBOSOMED				
	SNATCHING THE BIRD IN SECRET! NOR KNEW I, EMBOSOMED APART,	57	OISIN 3		150
	OF THIS WIDE VALE, EMBOSOMED IN THE AIR,	652	ISLE STAT I 2		19
EMBRACE					
	FOR THE EMBRACE OF NOTHING! AND I, MY WITS ASTRAY	426	PHANTOM HATRED		14
	THE ANNIVERSARY OF THEIR FIRST EMBRACE,	555	RIBH AT TOMB		20
EMBRACED					
	THOSE WILD HANDS THAT HAVE EMBRACED	776	AGAINST WITCH		32
EMBRACES					
	THAT JUGGLING NATURE MOUNTS, HER COIL IN THEIR EMBRACES TWINED.	556	RIBH PATRICK		9
EMBROIDERED	SEE GOLD-EMBROIDERED				
	BEAR THE GOLD EMBROIDERED DRESS--	124	CATHLEEN PARA	V	6
	HAD I THE HEAVENS' EMBROIDERED CLOTHS,	176	CLOTHS HEAVEN		1
	HAD I THE HEAVEN'S EMBROIDERED CLOTHS,	176	CLOTHS HEAVEN	V	1
	A BIT OF AN EMBROIDERED DRESS	421	MY TABLE		6
	IS BUT A HEAVY, GOLD EMBROIDERED BANNER,	469	HARUN RASHID	V	188
	"ON THIS EMBROIDERED CLOUD," THE SUN HATH SAID,	712	FERENCZ RENYI		74
EMBROIDERIES					
	COVERED WITH EMBROIDERIES	320	COAT		2
	A WOMAN LIES AMONG EMBROIDERIES.	752	SHADOW WATER A		120
EMBROIDERY					
	OF MANY A FIGURED EMBROIDERY!	4	OISIN 1		27
	BUT BRILLIANT AS THE NIGHT'S EMBROIDERY,	461	HARUN RASHID		7
	NOR DAZZLED BY THE EMBROIDERY, NOR LOST	470	HARUN RASHID		191
	THAT FLOWERING, SILKEN, OLD EMBROIDERY, TORN	477	SELF AND SOUL		13
	FLOWERS FROM I KNOW NOT WHAT EMBROIDERY--	478	SELF AND SOUL		27
EMEN'S					
	THE FLOOR OF EMEN'S HOISTING HALL	13	OISIN 1	V	156
EMER					
	TO EMER, RADDLING RAIMENT IN HER DUN,	105	CUCHULAIN SEA		2
	THEN EMER CAST THE WEB UPON THE FLOOR,	105	CUCHULAIN SEA		6
	TO EMER OF BORDA, IN HER CLAY-PILED DUN,	105	CUCHULAIN SEA	V	2

EMER   (CONTINUED)
   TO FORGAIL'S DAUGHTER, EMER, IN HER DUN, ...   105 CUCHULAIN SEA V   2
   AND LOST THE WORLD AND EMER FOR A KISS! . . . . . .   170 SECRET ROSE   15
   GREAT-BLADDERED EMER SAT, ...   628 JANE MOUNTAIN   15
   GREAT BLADDERED EMER SAT, ...   628 JANE MOUNTAIN V   15
EMERALD
   WITH EMERALD EYES." . . . .   263 MASK   2
EMERGE
   TO LIE UNTIL THE FOURTH MORN SAW EMERGE . . . . . .   44 OISIN 2   220
   TO LIE THERE 'TILL THE FOURTH DAY SAW EMERGE . . . .   44 OISIN 2   V 220
   TO LIE UNTIL THE FOURTH MORN SUN EMERGE . . . . .   44 OISIN 2   V 220
EMERY
   ON FLORENCE EMERY I CALL THE NEXT, ...   472 ALL SOUL NIGHT   41
EMMET
   AND ROBERT EMMET AND WOLFE TONE, ...   290 SEPTEMBER 1913   21
   WHEN STRANGERS MURDERED EMMET, FITZGERALD, TONE, . . .   541 PARN FUNERAL 1   17
   MOCK EMMET, MOCK PARNELL! . . . .   547 TO SAME TUNE 2   25
   MOCK EMMET, MOCK PARNELL, ...   614 MARCH SONGS 1   25
EMMET'S
   OLD COUNTRY SCHOLAR, ROBERT EMMET'S FRIEND, ...   269 PARDON FATHERS   5
   AND COUNTRY SCHOLAR, ROBERT EMMET'S FRIEND, ...   269 PARDON FATHERS V   5
EMOTION
   SWEETER EMOTION, WORKING IN THEIR VEINS . . . . . .   292 TO A SHADE   13
   HEART-SMITTEN WITH EMOTION I SINK DOWN, ...   602 GALLERY REVIS   17
   HEART SMITTEN WITH EMOTION, I SINK DOWN, ...   602 GALLERY REVIS V   17
EMPEDOCLES
   EMPEDOCLES HAS THROWN ALL THINGS ABOUT! . . . . . .   564 GYRES   6
EMPEROR
   TO KEEP A DROWSY EMPEROR AWAKE! . . . .   408 SAIL BYZANTIUM   29
   THE GOLDEN SMITHIES OF THE EMPEROR! . . . .   498 BYZANTIUM   35
EMPEROR'S
   THE EMPEROR'S DRUNKEN SOLDIERY ARE ABED! . . . . .   497 BYZANTIUM   2
   THE EMPEROR'S DRUNKEN SOLDIERY ARE A-BED! . . . . .   497 BYZANTIUM   V   2
   AT MIDNIGHT ON THE EMPEROR'S PAVEMENT FLIT . . . .   498 BYZANTIUM   25
EMPIRE
   THE ROMAN EMPIRE STOOD APPALLED! . . . .   437 SONGS PLAY 1   13
   WHEN ALEXANDER'S EMPIRE PASSED, THEY SLEPT SO SOUND. . .   442 BLACK CENTAUR   12
   WHEN ALEXANDER'S EMPIRE PAST, THEY SLEPT SO SOUND. . .   442 BLACK CENTAUR V   12
   UPON THE BRITISH EMPIRE, ...   583 GHOST ROG CASE   17
EMPIRES
   BEING WEARY OF THE WORLD'S EMPIRES, BOW DOWN TO YOU, . .   161 BLACK PIG   7
EMPOUNDED
   TOILED WITH EMPOUNDED CATTLE THROUGH THE MIRE, ...   276 TWO KINGS   V   2
   THAT WITH EMPOUNDED CATTLE TROD THE MIRE, ...   277 TWO KINGS   4
   THEREON THE BELLOWING OF THE EMPOUNDED HERDS . . . .   286 TWO KINGS   214
EMPTIED
   ALL EMPTIED OF PURPLE HOURS AS A BEGGAR'S CLOAK IN THE   63 OISIN 3   219
     RAIN,
   THAT EMPTIED ALL OUR DAYS TO COME. . . . .   272 GREY ROCK   40
   AND EMPTIED MANY A CAN! . . . .   620 JOHN KINSELLA   16
   EMPTIED, RUINED, WRACKED, AND LOST, ...   776 AGAINST WITCH   27
   GAVE THEIR BODIES, EMPTIED PURSES . . . .   789 SINGING HEAD   19
EMPTIER
   EMPTIER OF THOUGHT . . . .   451 FIRST LOVE   16
EMPTINESS
   . . . FULLNESS AND OF THE COMING EMPTINESS . . . .   425 PHANTOM HATRED   T
   GRIMALKIN CRAWLS TO BUDDHA'S EMPTINESS. . . . . . .   611 STATUES   24
   HYSTERICA PASSIO OF ITS OWN EMPTINESS? . . . . . .   618 BRONZE HEAD   7
   HYSTERICO-PASSIO OF ITS OWN EMPTINESS? . . . . . .   618 BRONZE HEAD   V   7
EMPTY
   ARE EMPTY OF ALL POWER." "AND WHICH OF THESE . . . .   46 OISIN 2   248
   WE SHALL MINGLE NO MORE, NOR OUR GAZES EMPTY THEIR   56 OISIN 3   132
     SWEETNESS LONE
   A CLIMBING MOON UPON AN EMPTY SKY, ...   120 SORROW OF LOVE   10
   EMPTY YOUR HEART OF ITS MORTAL DREAM. . . . . . .   140 HOSTING SIDHE   5
   THAT EMPTY THE HEART. I HAVE FORGOT AWHILE . . . .   198 SEVEN WOODS   5
   OF FORGAEL AND DECTORA AND THE EMPTY WATERS . . . .   218 WOODS OF COOLE   22
   A CLUMP OF BEECH TREES MADE AN EMPTY SPACE . . . .   277 TWO KINGS   V   4A
   TO AN OLD EMPTY WOODMAN'S HOUSE THAT'S HIDDEN . . . .   282 TWO KINGS   134
   YOUR EMPTY BED." "HOW SHOULD I LOVE," I ANSWERED, . .   285 TWO KINGS   186
   TIMID, ENTANGLED, EMPTY AND ABASHED, ...   368 EGO DOMINUS   16
   AS IF SOME MARVELLOUS EMPTY SEA-SHELL FLUNG . . . .   417 ANCEST HOUSES   13
   COME BUILD IN THE EMPTY HOUSE OF THE STARE. . . . .   424 STARES NEST   5
   COME BUILD IN THE EMPTY HOUSE OF THE STARE. . . . .   425 STARES NEST   10
   COME BUILD IN THE EMPTY HOUSE OF THE STARE. . . . .   425 STARES NEST   15
   COME BUILD IN THE EMPTY HOUSE OF THE STARE. . . . .   425 STARES NEST   20
   THE EMPTY CUP . . . .   454 EMPTY CUP   T
   AND FOLLOWED THROUGH THE EMPTY STREET, AND SHE, . .   468 HARUN RASHID   V 154A
   THAT OLD PERPLEXITY AN EMPTY PURSE, ...   491 COOLE BALLYLEE V 40G
   THAT OLD PERPLEXITY AN EMPTY PURSE, ...   495 CHOICE   7
   AN OPEN BOOK AND EMPTY CUP . . . .   501 VACILLATION   38
   IN AN EMPTY BED, ...   511 JANE AND JACK   14
   IF EMPTY NIGHT REPLIES? . . . .   533 FIRST CONFESS   18
   WHEN NATIONS ARE EMPTY UP THERE AT THE TOP, ...   548 TO SAME TUNE 3   11
   AND FOUND AN EMPTY ROOM. . . . .   594 COLONEL MARTIN   8
   DREAMER OF THE MIDDLE AGES. EMPTY EYEBALLS KNEW . .   610 STATUES   20
   DREAMER OF THE MIDDLE-AGES. EMPTY EYE-BALLS KNEW . .   610 STATUES   V   20
   FROM EMPTY TOMB OR VIRGIN WOMB? . . . .   619 STICK INCENSE   2
   HIS EMPTY HEART IS FULL AT LENGTH, ...   624 APPARITIONS   19
   TILL ALL ELSE IS EMPTY CHAFF, ...   647 ISLE STAT I 1   60
   DEEP-EYED, SLOW-FOOTING DOWN THE EMPTY GLADE. . . .   653 ISLE STAT I 2   55

		PAGE	TITLE	LINE
EMPTY (CONTINUED)				
THE PLACE WAS EMPTY NOW OF PEOPLE.		725	LEGEND	25
HAVE THE WINDS BLOWN YOU AMONG THESE EMPTY WATERS?		756	SHADOW WATER A	192
I HAVE FOUND NOTHING BUT THESE EMPTY WATERS!		757	SHADOW WATER A	201
CRIES OUT THE EMPTY WELL,		780	WELL AND TREE	2
EMPTYING				
BUT WILL IT HOLD WHILE WE ARE EMPTYING HER?		754	SHADOW WATER A	156
EMPYREAN				
OVERCOME THE EMPYREAN! HURL		540	FROM ANTIGONE	7
ENAMELLED				
RAGING AT HIS OWN IMAGE IN THE ENAMELLED SEA.		77	INDIAN TO LOVE	5
RAGES AT HIS OWN IMAGE IN THE ENAMELLED SEA		77	INDIAN TO LOVE V	5
RAGING AT HIS OWN IMAGE IN THE DIM ENAMELLED SEA		77	INDIAN TO LOVE V	5
ENAMELLING				
OF HAMMERED GOLD AND GOLD ENAMELLING		408	SAIL BYZANTIUM	28
ENAMOURED				
ENAMOURED OF THE WAVES' IMPETUOUS LIPS.		677	ISLE STAT II 3	289
ENCHANTED				
DIM PAIRC-NA-TARAV, WHERE ENCHANTED EYES		217	WOODS OF COOLE	11
I HAD NOT EYES LIKE THOSE ENCHANTED EYES,		218	WOODS OF COOLE	17
ENCHANTED TO A STONE		393	EASTER 1916	43
THROUGH THREE ENCHANTED ISLANDS, ALLEGORICAL DREAMS,		629	CIRCUS ANIMALS	11
IT WAS THE DREAM ITSELF ENCHANTED ME!		630	CIRCUS ANIMALS	28
IF ON HIS LIPS THE ENCHANTED FLOWER BE LAID!		668	ISLE STAT II 3	46
THE ENCHANTED FLOWER WERE,		668	ISLE STAT II 3	62
ENCHANTER				
WILL STRUGGLE. OR HE'LL SEEK ENCHANTER OLD,		651	ISLE STAT I 1	162
ENCHANTMENT				
I AM CAUGHT IN WOVEN NETS OF ENCHANTMENT. LOOK!		762	SHADOW WATER A	293
ENCHANTRESS				
FOR THERE THE GREAT ENCHANTRESS LIVES. AND THERE		653	ISLE STAT I 2	38
SHE WAS A GREAT ENCHANTRESS ONCE OF YORE,		693	MOSADA 1	78
ENCIRCLE				
ENCIRCLE HER I LOVE AND SING HER INTO PEACE,		174	ELEMENT POWERS	9
ENCIRCLED SEE CLIFF-ENCIRCLED				
ENCIRCLING				
AND CHANTS OF VICTORY AMID THE ENCIRCLING HOUNDS.		622	HOUND VOICE	21
ENCLOSE				
ENCLOSE A QUIET PLACE OF BEDS BOX-BORDERED, BEES,		710	FERENCZ RENYI	24
ENCLOSES				
ON THE DEAD DIM EARTH ENCLOSES!		21	OISIN 1	312
ON THE DEAD THE EARTH ENCLOSES.		21	OISIN 1 V	312
WHERE DREAM-FED PASSION IS AND PEACE ENCLOSES,		669	ISLE STAT II 3	85
FROM FLOOD-TIME ENCLOSES		672	ISLE STAT II 3	167
END SEE BUTT-END CANDLE-END				
A DRUID DREAM OF THE END OF DAYS		16	OISIN 1	219
THERE WERE AN END OF CHANGE AND BIRTH,		18	OISIN 1	270
MAY SLEEP IN THE END WITH THE WHOLE OF HIS FATE DONE,		28	OISIN 1 V	423F
I THOUGHT THE END HAD RESTED, WHEN THESE WORDS		32	OISIN 2 V	49
MAY PANTHERS END HIM.——HEAR, AND LOAD OUR KING		71	ANASHU VIJAYA	6
AND WHAT TO ME WAS BURDEN WITHOUT END,		102	FERGUS DRUID	12
AND THE WHITE HUSH END ALL BUT THE LOUD BEAT		137	TO SOME I TALK	15
AND THE WHITE HUSH END ALL THINGS BUT THE BEAT		137	TO SOME I TALK V	15
WOULD END IN LOVE IN THE END!		152	LOSS OF LOVE	4
WOULD END IN LOVE IN THE END!		152	LOSS OF LOVE	4
MIGHT FADE IN LOVE IN THE END!		152	LOSS OF LOVE V	4
. . . AND HIS BELOVED, AND LONGS FOR THE END OF THE WORLD		153	CHANGE BELOVED	T
WHEN WE COME AT THE END OF TIME		178	FIDDLER DOONEY	9
HIS FACE BOWED LOW TO WEEP THE END		192	BAILE AILLINN	75
HAVE HAPPINESS WITHOUT AN END,		195	BAILE AILLINN	158
THOUGH NOW IT'S HARD, TILL TROUBLE IS AT AN END!		200	FOLLY COMFORT V	5
O THOUGHT, FLY TO HER WHEN THE END OF DAY		201	OLD MEMORY	1
I THOUGHT TO FLY TO HER WHEN THE END OF DAY		201	OLD MEMORY V	1
THOUGHT FLY TO HER WHEN THE END OF DAY		201	OLD MEMORY V	1
WE SAT TOGETHER AT ONE SUMMER'S END,		204	ADAMS CURSE	1
TO MAKE AN END WHILE HE IS SLEEPING THERE.		222	SHADOW WATER B V	14
TO MAKE AN END OF FORGAEL WHILE HE SLEEPS.		225	SHADOW WATER B	65
KNOWING IT FOR THE WORLD'S END? WHERE THE WORLD ENDS		226	SHADOW WATER B	100
OR CREAKY SHOES. AND AT THE END OF ALL		228	SHADOW WATER B	128
SHE MAY NOT BE TOO SORRY IN THE END.		232	SHADOW WATER B	232
AND FOR THIS END THEY GAVE ME MY OLD HARP		237	SHADOW WATER B	327
YOU DID NOT KNOW WHAT BROUGHT HIM TO HIS END,		240	SHADOW WATER B	382
I WILL END ALL YOUR MAGIC ON THE INSTANT.		242	SHADOW WATER B	411
"THERE IS A COUNTRY AT THE END OF THE WORLD		247	SHADOW WATER B	530
I CANNOT——I AM GOING ON TO THE END.		248	SHADOW WATER B	544
THE BUTT END OF A STEERING OAR,		253	HIS DREAM V	2
SOMEWHERE IN EAR-SHOT FOR THE STORY'S END,		269	PARDON FATHERS	2
MUST END AT THE DUMB STONE? BUT WHERE WE BUILD		284	TWO KINGS	179
DELIGHT IN ART WHOSE END IS PEACE,		288	TO WEALTHY MAN	26
BEFORE THE THREE TO END THIS TALE,		297	THREE BEGGARS	55
AND WHEN AT ONE YEAR'S END I FOUND		305	HOUR DAWN	71
BE AS BROKEN IN THE END.		313	TWO YEAR LATER	10
NO LIKELY END COULD BRING THEM LOSS		328	IRISH AIRMAN	7
AND I MAY DINE AT JOURNEY'S END		336	YOUNG BEAUTY	17
THAT I MAY DINE AT JOURNEY'S END		336	YOUNG BEAUTY V	17
THEY'LL COUGH IN THE INK TO THE WORLD'S END!		337	SCHOLARS V	7
THE END OF DAY .		364	END OF DAY	T
BECAUSE THE END OF DAY		364	END OF DAY	4
SING OUT THE SONG; SING TO THE END, AND SING		374	PHASES OF MOON	56
END IN A BEAUTIFUL MAN'S OR WOMAN'S BODY.		374	PHASES OF MOON	64
HE MIGHT HAVE WON FAME IN THE END,		392	EASTER 1916	28

240

END   (CONTINUED)
        CONSIDER BEAUTY A SUFFICIENT END, ...   403 FOR DAUGHTER   21
        TO END ALL THINGS, TO END . . . .   431 NINETEEN 19   81
        TO END ALL THINGS, TO END . . . .   431 NINETEEN 19   81
        "AND ALL THOSE LIES HAVE BUT ONE END, POOR WRETCHES TO 450 OWEN AHERNE   18
           BETRAY:
        AND HIDE IT THERE, FOR CALIPHS TO WORLD'S END . . . .   461 HARUN RASHID   17
        HIDDEN FROM EYESIGHT TO THE UNNOTICED END. . . . . .   472 ALL SOUL NIGHT   50
        BEFORE THAT END MUCH HAD SHE RAVELLED OUT . . . . .   472 ALL SOUL NIGHT   51
        A MAN AWAITS HIS END . . . .   476 DEATH   3
        WINE SHALL RUN THICK TO THE END, ...   554 CHURCH STATE   11
        HERE AT LIFE'S END . . . .   575 ACRE OF GRASS   8
        THE COUNTRY THINKS NO END OF HIM, ...   583 GHOST ROG CASE   13
        DAYBREAK AND A CANDLE END. . . . .   588 OLD WICKED MAN V   REF
        DAY-BREAK AND A CANDLE END. . . . .   588 OLD WICKED MAN V   REF
        SAW THE STORY'S END, ...   597 COLONEL MARTIN   69
        THOSE WORDS COME TRUE IN THE END . . . .   597 COLONEL MARTIN V   69
        DEEP-ROOTED THINGS," BUT NEVER FORESAW ITS END, . .   603 GALLERY REVIS   37
        AND NOW THAT END HAS COME I HAVE NOT WEPT: . . . . .   603 GALLERY REVIS   38
        WHAT DEEP ROOTS ARE," AND NEVER FORESAW THE END . .   603 GALLERY REVIS V   37
        BUT NOW I WILL KILL HER. ALL COMES TO AN END. . . .   603 GALLERY REVIS V   38
        MY HUNDREDTH YEAR IS AT AN END. I THINK . . . . .   609 IN TARAS HALLS   3
        HE BADE, HIS HUNDRED AND FIRST YEAR AT END, ...   609 IN TARAS HALLS   16
        A BLOODY AND A SUDDEN END, ...   620 JOHN KINSELLA   1
        ASIDE!--THE WILD HORNS TOLD ALMINTOR'S END, ...   665 ISLE STAT II 2   68
        AND DREAM OF THE END OF THEIR DAYS, ...   707 FAIRY PEDANT   4
        A SOLDIER ANSWERS: "BY THE CAMP'S FAR END . . . .   712 FERENCZ RENYI   67
        HAS NO WORD OF THE SULPHUROUS END. . . . .   736 SUMMER EVENING   8
        TILL DAY AND NIGHT TIME END. . . . .   741 EARL PAUL   48
        BEING THE MOON OF BIRTH, MAY END OUR DOUBT. . . . .   748 SHADOW WATER A   24
        WOULD END THIS PEACEFUL LIFE THAT ROTS THE BONES, .   752 SHADOW WATER A   110
        YOUR HEART'S DESIRE AND THE END OF ALL OUR TROUBLE: 755 SHADOW WATER A   175
        BUT NOW I WILL KILL HER. ALL COMES TO AN END. . . .   755 SHADOW WATER A   176
        AND WE GO HOME. COME, AIBRIC: END YOUR TALE . . . .   766 SHADOW WATER A   374
        SHOULD LOOK UPON HIS EYES WITH LOVE, IN THE END . .   768 SHADOW WATER A   409
        SHOULD LOOK UPON HIS EYES WITH LOVE UNTO THE END . .   768 SHADOW WATER A V 409
ENDAPPLED   SEE LIGHT-ENDAPPLED
ENDED
        WHO HAD ENDED WHERE HIS BREATH BEGAN. . . . .   360 ALF POLLEXFEN   12
ENDLESS
        A DOME MADE OUT OF ENDLESS CARVEN JAGS, ...   38 OISIN 2   144
        WAITED. ABOVE, IN ENDLESS CARVEN JAGS, ...   38 OISIN 2   V 144
        NOR LANGUOR NOR FATIGUE: AN ENDLESS FEAST, ...   44 OISIN 2   223
        AN ENDLESS WAR. THE HUNDRED YEARS HAD CEASED: . . .   44 OISIN 2   224
        NO LANGUOR, NO FATIGUE: AN ENDLESS FEAST, ...   44 OISIN 2   V 223
        NOR LANGUOR NOR FATIGUE: AND ENDLESS FEAST, ...   44 OISIN 2   V 223
        AN ENDLESS WAR. THE HUNDREDTH YEAR HAD CEASED. . .   44 OISIN 2   V 224
        TROUBLING THE ENDLESS REVERIE. . . . .   65 HAPPY SHEPHERD   21
        O VANITY OF SLEEP, HOPE, DREAM, ENDLESS DESIRE, . .   154 BELOVED PEACE   7
        IN ENDLESS DARK, AND BY THE WEEDY MARGE . . . . . .   682 SEEKER   19
        HER SOUL FROM SEAS OF ENDLESS FLAME IN HELL. . . .   698 MOSADA 2   47
        ROUND US THE WHITE ROADS ARE ENDLESS, ...   737 IN FIRELIGHT   3
        AND PRAISED YOUR WAR AMONG THE ENDLESS SEAS, . . .   749 SHADOW WATER A   35
        AND PRAISE A WAR AMONG THE ENDLESS SEAS. . . . . . .   749 SHADOW WATER A V   35
ENDLESSLY
        WHEN YOU HAVE TOLD HOW I WEEP ENDLESSLY, ...   33 OISIN 2   63
ENDOWED   SEE BEST-ENDOWED
        THE ENDOWED, THE ELECT: . . . .   504 RESULT THOUGHT V   3
ENDS
        KNOWING IT FOR THE WORLD'S END? WHERE THE WORLD ENDS 226 SHADOW WATER B   100
        YOU HAD TO FACE YOUR ENDS WHEN YOUNG-- . . . . . .   273 GREY ROCK   53
        AND UNREPENTING FACED YOUR ENDS, ...   273 GREY ROCK   60
        YET THE WORLD ENDS WHEN THESE TWO THINGS, ...   388 SOLOMON WITCH   28
        I CELEBRATE THE SILENT KISS THAT ENDS SHORT LIFE OR LONG. 459 FROM OEDIPUS   9
        AND TOLD HIM SO, BUT FRIENDSHIP NEVER ENDS: . . . .   473 ALL SOUL NIGHT   65
        THINK WHERE MAN'S GLORY MOST BEGINS AND ENDS, . . .   604 GALLERY REVIS   54
        NO PLEASING HABIT ENDS. . . . .   621 JOHN KINSELLA   30
        TALKED OF ODDS AND ENDS. . . . .   627 STATES HOLIDAY   8
        SO ENDS A BRAIN--A WORLD! THE SMOKE GOES UP, . . .   714 FERENCZ RENYI   111
        OF FIRE. SO ENDS A BRAIN--A WORLD! THE SMOKE FLOATS UP, 714 FERENCZ RENYI V 111
        ENDS ALL THINGS. I HAVE SLAIN THE LOCHLANN KING. .   754 SHADOW WATER A   163
        ENDS TIME AND CHANGE. . . . .   754 SHADOW WATER A V 163
        THEY LURE US TO THE STREAMS WHERE THE WORLD ENDS. .   764 SHADOW WATER A   334
        TO LEAD US TO THE STREAMS WHERE THE WORLD ENDS. . .   765 SHADOW WATER A   369
        WHERE THE WORLD ENDS, OR RUNS FROM WIND TO WIND . .   768 SHADOW WATER A   417
ENDURE
        AND I MUST NEEDS ENDURE AND HATE AND WEEP, ...   35 OISIN 2   85
        OUR HEARTS ENDURE THE SCOURGE, THE PLAITED THORNS, THE WAY 172 TRAV PASSION   3
        OUR HEARTS ENDURE THE PLAITED THORN, THE CROWDED WAY, . 172 TRAV PASSION V   3
        MUST I ENDURE YOUR AMOROUS CRIES? . . . .   177 PAST GREATNESS   12
        THAT IT COULD NOT ENDURE . . . .   317 NIGHT COME   4
        I MUST ENDURE THE TIMID SUN. . . . .   344 DEJECTION   11
        ENDURE WHAT LIFE GOD GIVES AND ASK NO LONGER SPAN: 459 FROM OEDIPUS   1
        CANNOT ENDURE TO THINK YOU TREAD THESE PATHS, . . .   463 HARUN RASHID   52
        ENDURE THAT TOIL OF GROWING UP: . . . .   478 SELF AND SOUL   44
        AT STROKE OF MIDNIGHT SOUL CANNOT ENDURE . . . . .   558 RIBH CHRISTIAN   19
ENDURED
        AND THERE ENDURED HER FINGERS' TOUCH . . . .   397 POLIT PRISONER   5
        AND THERE ENDURED HER FINGER'S TOUCH . . . .   397 POLIT PRISONER V   5
ENDURES
        ENDURES A MOMENT OR A DAY. . . . .   438 SONGS PLAY 2   10

		PAGE	TITLE		LINE

ENDURING
NO USE. AWAY! HEAR, THOU ENDURING GOD, ... 698 MOSADA 2 — 50
AND THOU SHALT BEND, ENDURING GOD, THE KNEES . . . . 698 MOSADA 2 — 59
NO USE. AWAY! HEAR OH! THOU ENDURING GOD, ... 698 MOSADA 2 V 50
AND THOU SHALL BEND, ENDURING GOD, THE KNEES . . . . 698 MOSADA 2 V 59

ENEMIES
THE FINISHED MAN AMONG HIS ENEMIES?-- . . . . 479 SELF AND SOUL — 49

ENEMY
MY ENEMY AND HOPE; DEMONS FOR FRIGHT . . . . . . 34 OISIN 2 — 81
WITH HOPE, MINE ENEMY. AS HE BY NIGHT . . . . . . 34 OISIN 2 V 81
MY ENEMY? I LOOKED UPON THE MOON, ... 246 SHADOW WATER B — 509
"BUT LEST YOU ARE MY ENEMY, ... 263 MASK — 11
YOUR ENEMY, AN OLD FOUL MOUTH, HAD SET . . . . 292 TO A SHADE — 17
PARDON, GREAT ENEMY, ... 366 HER CHRIS TREE — 1
THE SERVANTS OF YOUR ENEMY, ... 436 FOR MY SON — 26
OR COURT A WOMAN: NEITHER ENEMY, ... 463 HARUN RASHID — 59
HAVE NO ENEMY BUT TIME: . . . . 476 EVA GORE-BOOTH — 25

ENEMY'S
WITH A FRIEND'S OR AN ENEMY'S . . . . . . 362 DOLLS DRAWINGS — 3
NOR MUSIC NOR AN ENEMY'S CLIPPED EAR . . . . . . 412 TOWER — 75

ENERGY
BECOME ONE MOVEMENT, ENERGY, DELIGHT, ... 231 SHADOW WATER B — 217

ENFOLD
AND MIDNIGHT THERE ENFOLD THEM LIKE A FLEECE . . . 128 DREAM OF FAERY — 34
ENFOLD ME IN MY HOUR OF HOURS: WHERE THOSE . . . 169 SECRET ROSE — 2
MEN HAVE NAMED BEAUTY. THY GREAT LEAVES ENFOLD . . 169 SECRET ROSE — 7
MEN HAVE NAMED BEAUTY. YOUR HEAVY LEAVES ENFOLD . . 169 SECRET ROSE V 7
MEN HAVE NAMED BEAUTY. YOUR GREAT LEAVES ENFOLD . . 169 SECRET ROSE V 7

ENFOLDEN
ENFOLDEN IN THE SHADOWS OF THE EAST, ... 705 REMEMBRANCE — 11

ENGAGED
"IT WAS THE MASK ENGAGED YOUR MIND, ... 263 MASK — 8

ENGENDER
ENGENDER IN THE DITCH, ... 598 STONE CROSS — 10

ENGENDERS
A SHUDDER IN THE LOINS ENGENDERS THERE . . . . . . 441 LEDA AND SWAN — 9

ENGINES
BE BUT THE BREAKERS OF MEN'S HEARTS OR ENGINES OF DELIGHT: 354 HIS PHOENIX — 23

ENGLAND
FOR ENGLAND MAY KEEP FAITH . . . . . . 394 EASTER 1916 — 68
HE FOUGHT THE MIGHT OF ENGLAND . . . . . . 586 PARNELLITES — 11

ENGLISH
CERTAIN MEN THE ENGLISH SHOT? . . . . . . 632 MAN AND ECHO — 12

ENGRAVED
THE LONELY LIGHT THAT SAMUEL PALMER ENGRAVED, . . . 373 PHASES OF MOON — 17

ENGROSS
TO ENGROSS THE PRESENT AND DOMINATE MEMORY. . . . . 630 CIRCUS ANIMALS — 30

ENJOINS
IGNORANT WHAT THAT DRAMATIST ENJOINS, ... 560 WHENCE COME — 8

ENJOYED
AND YET THE SADDEST CHIMES ARE BEST ENJOYED. . . . . 130 BOOK STORIES — 20

ENKINDLED   SEE EARTH-ENKINDLED

ENMITIES
MORE SUBSTANCE IN OUR ENMITIES . . . . . . 425 STARES NEST — 18

ENMITY
HER THOUGHT SOME POPULAR ENMITY! . . . . . . 397 POLIT PRISONER — 10
FOR THOUGHT SOME POPULAR ENMITY, ... 397 POLIT PRISONER V 10

ENORMOUS
ON THE FAR GOLDEN PEAK: ENORMOUS SHAPES, ... 74 ANASHU VIJAYA — 68
THE WAVES, ENORMOUS WANDERERS OF THE WORLD, ... 687 TWO TITANS — 3

ENOUGH
THERE IS ENOUGH EVIL IN THE CRYING OF WIND. . . . . 155 REPROVE CURLEW — 6
THAT IS BAD ENOUGH TO BE TRUE, IS TRUE, ... 191 BAILE AILLINN — 69
AS THOUGH THEIR MUSIC WERE ENOUGH . . . . . . 193 BAILE AILLINN — 108
A MUSIC THAT HAD THOUGHT ENOUGH . . . . . . 193 BAILE AILLINN V 108
AND THAT DEAR WORDS MEANT NOTHING?" BUT ENOUGH, . . 201 OLD MEMORY — 9
AND WHO COULD PLAY IT WELL ENOUGH . . . . . . 202 NEVER GIVE ALL — 11
AND WHO CAN PLAY IT WELL ENOUGH . . . . . . 202 NEVER GIVE ALL V 11
YET NOW IT SEEMS AN IDLE TRADE ENOUGH." . . . . . 205 ADAMS CURSE — 27
FOR LONG ENOUGH? AYE, LONG AND LONG ENOUGH. . . . . 221 SHADOW WATER B — 2
FOR LONG ENOUGH? AYE, LONG AND LONG ENOUGH. . . . . 221 SHADOW WATER B — 2
COULD NOT AMEND. I HAVE GOOD SPIRITS ENOUGH. . . . 227 SHADOW WATER B — 116
THAT DROVE YOU TO IT, AND I FOOL ENOUGH . . . . . 248 SHADOW WATER B — 548
ENOUGH IF THE WORK HAS SEEMED, ... 259 UNWORTH PRAISE — 5
HOW SHOULD THEIR LUCK RUN HIGH ENOUGH TO REACH . . . 264 HOUSE SHAKEN — 9
AND THEN, "I AM OLD ENOUGH": . . . . . . 268 BROWN PENNY — 2
THERE IS NOBODY WISE ENOUGH . . . . . . 268 BROWN PENNY — 10
UNTIL ENOUGH OF PAUDEEN'S PENCE . . . . . . 287 TO WEALTHY MAN — 2
YOU HAD ENOUGH OF SORROW BEFORE DEATH-- . . . . . 293 TO A SHADE — 23
I'D HAVE A MERRY LIFE ENOUGH . . . . . . 306 HOUR DAWN — 85
IF THERE BE RAGS ENOUGH HE WILL KNOW HER NAME . . . 351 HER PRAISE — 15
HE HAS HAD ENOUGH OF MEDDLING WHO CAN PLEASE . . . 359 WAR POEM — 4
NO TABLE OR CHAIR OR STOOL NOT SIMPLE ENOUGH . . . 371 ON GOING HOUSE — 3
JUST TRUTH ENOUGH TO SHOW THAT HIS WHOLE LIFE . . . 373 PHASES OF MOON — 22
OR MAYBE IS NOT STRONG ENOUGH." . . . . . . 388 SOLOMON WITCH — 37
WE KNOW THEIR DREAM; ENOUGH . . . . . . 394 EASTER 1916 — 70
O TOWARDS I HAVE FORGOTTEN WHAT--ENOUGH! . . . . . 412 TOWER — 73
SEEING THAT LOVE AND FRIENDSHIP ARE ENOUGH, ... 423 MY DESCENDANTS — 20
HAD PRETTY PLUMAGE ONCE--ENOUGH OF THAT, ... 444 SCHOOL CHILDR — 30
HAVE WRONG TO BROOD UPON--ENOUGH OF THAT, ... 444 SCHOOL CHILDR V 30
BUT THAT'S A TRAITOR'S THOUGHT. ENOUGH FOR ME . . . 462 HARUN RASHID — 39

242

ENOUGH   (CONTINUED)
   IT SEEMS ENOUGH THAT I AM THERE: AND YET, ... 468 HARUN RASHID   166
   NO MAN HAS EVER LIVED THAT HAD ENOUGH . . . . . 500 VACILLATION   25
   I HAD FORGIVEN ENOUGH . . . . 504 QUARREL IN AGE   7
   WHAT PAYMENT WERE ENOUGH . . . . 518 HIS CONFIDENCE   5
   WHAT PAYMENTS WERE ENOUGH . . . . 518 HIS CONFIDENCE V   5
   TILL EITHER NEITHER HAVE ENOUGH, ... 573 LADYS 3RD SONG   8
   THAT PASSION COULD BRING CHARACTER ENOUGH, . . . 610 STATUES   6
   AND THIS BROUGHT FORTH A DREAM AND SOON ENOUGH . 630 CIRCUS ANIMALS   23
   AND SAID: "SHE HAS FOOLED ME ENOUGH," . . . . 744 GLOVE CLOAK   3
   HAD I NOT GOLD AND SILVER, AND ENOUGH . . . . . 748 SHADOW WATER A   32
   THEY ARE GONE, THEY ARE GONE. WHISPERING WERE ENOUGH. . 778 SONG DEIRDRE 3   3
   AND ALL SEEM WELL ENOUGH, ... 786 YOUR HEART   15
ENQUIRE
   I MUST ENQUIRE." . . . . 263 MASK   12
   WE NEVER THOUGHT TO ENQUIRE . . . . 381 SONGS FOOL 2   3
ENQUIRING
   AND THAT ENQUIRING MAN JOHN SYNGE COMES NEXT, . . . 324 ROBERT GREGORY   25
ENRAGED
   THE OLD COOK ENRAGED, ... 349 HAWK   5
ENRICHED
   PLUCKED BITTER WISDOM THAT ENRICHED HIS BLOOD. . . . 543 PARN FUNERAL 2   12
ENSLAVE
   SO DID FANATICISM AND HATE ENSLAVE IT, ... 630 CIRCUS ANIMALS   22
ENTANGLED
   READING SOME ENTANGLED STORY: . . . . 65 HAPPY SHEPHERD   16
   TIMID, ENTANGLED, EMPTY AND ABASHED, ... 368 EGO DOMINUS   16
   ENTANGLED IN MY HAIR . . . . 532 FIRST CONFESS   2
ENTANGLEMENTS
   . . . ALL ENTANGLEMENTS OF MANKIND GROW, ... 459 FROM OEDIPUS   5
ENTER
   AND ENTER, AND NONE SAYETH "NO" . . . . . . 62 OISIN 3   210
   AND ENTER, AND NONE SAYETH "NAY" . . . . . . 62 OISIN 3   V 210
   AWAIT THE HOUR OF WAR, ENTER THE SMALL, ... 461 HARUN RASHID V   8
   NO OTHER BIRD MAY ENTER IN. WELL? LATE-- . . . 659 ISLE STAT II 1   24
   CAN ENTER THERE. SEE: SEE: ABOVE YON BROW . . . 659 ISLE STAT II 1   27
   ANSWERED PETER: "ENTER IN, ... 697 MOSADA 2   30
ENTERPRISE
   FOR THERE'S MORE ENTERPRISE . . . . 320 COAT   9
   O SELF-BORN MOCKERS OF MAN'S ENTERPRISE: . . . . 445 SCHOOL CHILDR   56
ENTERS
   . . . WHEN THERE ENTERS THE STRONGLY ARMED GUEST: . . . 62 OISIN 3   210
   THE VERY SQUIRREL DIES THAT ENTERS THERE. . . . . 682 SEEKER   33
   THE VERY SQUIRREL DIES THAT ENTERS IT. . . . . . 682 SEEKER   V 33
ENTHRALLED
   ENTHRALLED BY THE UNCONQUERABLE DELUSION, ... 367 EGO DOMINUS   6
ENTIRE
   THE ENTIRE COMBUSTIBLE WORLD IN ONE SMALL ROOM . . . 327 ROBERT GREGORY   82
ENTIRELY
   BY THOSE THAT ARE NOT ENTIRELY BEAUTIFUL: . . . . 404 FOR DAUGHTER   35
ENTRAILS
   THE ENTRAILS OF THE HORSE. DROPPING HIS SWORD . . . 278 TWO KINGS   23
   THROUGH THE ENTRAILS OF THE HORSE. DROPPING HIS SWORD . . 278 TWO KINGS   V 23
ENTRANCE
   HERE AT RIGHT OF THE ENTRANCE THIS BRONZE HEAD, . . . 618 BRONZE HEAD   1
   THE ENTRANCE OF DEIRDRE . . . . 771 SONG DEIRDRE 1 V T
ENTRANCED
   FLOATED IN ALL HER SINGING. HALF ENTRANCED . . . . 30 OISIN 2   V 19
ENTWINED
   OF LANGUID EVENING THAT ENTWINED US. . . . . . . 25 OISIN 1   V 385A
ENUMERATE
   WHAT CAN I BUT ENUMERATE OLD THEMES? . . . . . . 629 CIRCUS ANIMALS   9
ENVIOUS   SEE STAR-ENVIOUS
ENVY
   TO SILENCE THE ENVY IN MY THOUGHT: . . . . 424 ROAD AT DOOR   13
ENWOUND
   AND WHISPERING TO HERSELF ENWOUND ME: . . . . . 9 OISIN 1   108
   AND WHEN TUMULTUOUS FEET ENWOUND ME . . . . . 83 MAD KING GOLL V 20
   WHEN LOIE FULLER'S CHINESE DANCERS ENWOUND . . . . 430 NINETEEN 19   49
ENWROUGHT
   BUT LET A GENTLE SILENCE ENWROUGHT WITH MUSIC FLOW . . 175 ELEMENT POWERS V 17
   ENWROUGHT WITH GOLDEN AND SILVER LIGHT, ... 176 CLOTHS HEAVEN   2
EOCHA
   EOCHA AND MAINE ARE ALWAYS QUARRELLING. . . . . . 766 SHADOW WATER A 371
EOCHAID
   KING EOCHAID CAME AT SUNDOWN TO A WOOD . . . . . 276 TWO KINGS   1
   KING EOCHAID SAID, AND HE THAT BORE HIS SHIELD . . . 276 TWO KINGS   V B
   HAVE BEEN THE MEASURE OF THAT CARE." BUT EOCHAID, . . . 276 TWO KINGS   V H
   RENDING THE HORSE'S FLANK. KING EOCHAID REELED, . . . 277 TWO KINGS   13
   RIPPED THROUGH THE HORSE'S FLANKS. KING EOCHAID REELED, 277 TWO KINGS   V 13
   KING EOCHAID SEIZED THE HORNS IN HIS STRONG HANDS . . 278 TWO KINGS   24
   THE DISEMBOWELLED HORSE. KING EOCHAID RAN . . . . 278 TWO KINGS   45
   EOCHAID SEIZED BOTH THE HORNS IN HIS STRONG HANDS . . 278 TWO KINGS   V 24
   THE DISEMBOWELLED HORSE. KING EOCHAID GAZED, . . . 278 TWO KINGS   V 45
   AND CARVE HIS NAME IN OGHAM." EOCHAID SAID, . . . 280 TWO KINGS   83
   AND RAISE HIS PILLAR STONE." KING EOCHAID SAID, . . 280 TWO KINGS   V 83
   CROW UPON TARA." KING EOCHAID BOWED HIS HEAD . . . . 286 TWO KINGS   211
EOCHAID'S
   YET ANSWERED HIM, "I AM KING EOCHAID'S WIFE . . . . 284 TWO KINGS   173
   AND IN THE MIDST KING EOCHAID'S BROTHER STOOD . . . 286 TWO KINGS   217
   UPON KING EOCHAID'S FACE, WHO LOWERED HIS FACE . . . 286 TWO KINGS   V 211A

243

	PAGE	TITLE	LINE

EPHEMERA
    EPHEMERA . . . .   79 EPHEMERA   T
EPHEMERAL
    AS MAN, AS BEAST, AS AN EPHEMERAL FLY BEGETS, GODHEAD   556 RIBH PATRICK   5
        BEGETS GODHEAD,
EPHESIAN
    WHERE SEVEN EPHESIAN TOPERS SLEPT AND NEVER KNEW . . . .   442 BLACK CENTAUR   11
EPILOGUE
    AN EPILOGUE TO "THE ISLAND OF STATUES" AND "THE SEEKER"   64 HAPPY SHEPHERD V   T
EPITAPH
    AN EPITAPH . . . .   123 DREAM OF DEATH V   T
    SWIFT'S EPITAPH . . . .   493 SWIFTS EPITAPH   T
EPITOME
    AS 'TWERE ALL LIFE'S EPITOME. . . . .   327 ROBERT GREGORY   87
EQUAL
    EQUAL TO GOOD OR GRIEVOUS CHANCE: . . . .   24 OISIN 1   372
    EQUAL TO GOOD OR EVIL CHANCE . . . .   24 OISIN 1   V 371
    FOR GOD HAS BID THEM SHARE AN EQUAL FATE: . . . . .   115 ROSE OF BATTLE   32
    WITH EQUAL COURAGE IN THAT WHIRLING ROUT: . . . . .   186 QUEEN MAEVE   131
    HAD THEY BUT COURAGE EQUAL TO DESIRE? . . . . . .   256 NO SECOND TROY   5
    WHO IS MY BEAUTY'S EQUAL, THOUGH THAT MY HEART DENIES, .   354 HIS PHOENIX   27
    IN SPACE, MADE EQUAL WITH A SIGH, WE MET. . . . . .   705 REMEMBRANCE   14
    OF EQUAL POWER IN SPELLS AND SECRET RITES. . . . .   720 WITCH VIVIEN   6
EQUALITY
    CAST BUT DEAD LEAVES TO MATHEMATICAL EQUALITY: . . .   481 BLOOD AND MOON   24
    CASTS BUT DEAD LEAVES TO MATHEMATICAL EQUALITY: . . .   481 BLOOD AND MOON V   24
    WHAT'S EQUALITY?--MUCK IN THE YARD: . . . .   547 TO SAME TUNE 3 V   4
EQUALS
    BY THE WOOD'S EDGE WHERE ONLY EQUALS MEET, ...   321 REED WHISPERER V   8
ERCOLE
    WHAT CARED DUKE ERCOLE, THAT BID . . . .   287 TO WEALTHY MAN   9
ERE
    ERE LONG AN ANSWERING WHISPER FLEW, ...   15 OISIN 1   V 197
    ERE HALF THE SWIFT THINGS THAT SHE DREAMT ON WERE DONE,   28 OISIN 1   V 422
    THINGS DONE ERE GOD FIRST WAS OR MY OLD LINE BEGAN: .   29 OISIN 2   V 8
    THE VAN OF WANDERING QUIET: ERE YOU BE TOO CALM AND OLD,   73 ANASHU VIJAYA   43
    THE VAN OF WANDERING QUIET: ERE YE BE TOO CALM AND OLD,   73 ANASHU VIJAYA   V 43
    LET US PART, ERE THE SEASON OF PASSION FORGET US, . .   79 FALLING LEAVES   7
    ERE FALL OF EVENING, MY MAILED HOST, ...   83 MAD KING GOLL V   19
    ERE TIME TRANSFIGURED ME. . . . .   131 OLD PENSIONER   6
    IT TALKED, ERE THE MORN GREW WHITE. . . . .   159 CAP AND BELLS V   6
    ERE THE ONE OR T'OTHER DIE, ...   508 JANE BISHOP   V 5
    LONG ERE AN ARROW WHIZZED OR SWORD LEFT SHEATH . . .   650 ISLE STAT I 1   135
    OR LONG ERE THIS HAD LOST THEIR RUDDY STAIN: . . . .   687 TWO TITANS   8
    ERE LONG SHALL FALTER THROUGH THE NOISY SQUARE, . . .   699 MOSADA 3   21
    ERE YONDER PALM COMMENCED HIS THOUSAND YEARS? . . . .   724 KANVA ON SELF   14
ERECT
    SHE GOES ABOUT HER HOUSE ERECT AND CALM . . . . . .   340 SHEP GOATHERD   35
    WITH MOTIONLESS HEAD ERECT. . . . .   383 VISION ROBART   32
    HORSEMAN ERECT UPON HORSEBACK . . . .   589 OLD WICKED MAN   52
ERI
    AFAR IN ANCIENT ERI, ...   32 OISIN 2   V 50E
    SAY HOW HE WEEPS IN ERI." . . . .   33 OISIN 2   V 68
    WHEN HER OWN PEOPLE RULED IN WAVE-WORN ERI, ...   129 BOOK STORIES V   2
    I TORE IT FROM THE GREEN BOUGHS OF OLD ERI, ...   130 BOOK STORIES V   15
    THY MOTHER ERI IS ALWAYS YOUNG, ...   148 INTO TWILIGHT V   5
    YE ON THE BROAD HIGH MOUNTAINS OF OLD ERI, ...   737 MOURN THEN ON   1
    MOURN YE ON GRASS-GREEN PLAINS OF ERI FATED, ...   738 MOURN THEN ON   9
ERI'S
    SPINNING AT ALL TIMES ERI'S GOOD TO-MORROW, ...   129 BOOK STORIES V   10
ERROR
    FOR GREAT OUR ERROR, GREAT OUR GUILT." . . . . . .   43 OISIN 2   V 208H
ESCAPE
    THEY'VE THE PASSION TO ESCAPE." . . . .   299 THREE HERMITS   21
    BUT THE ESCAPE: THE SONG'S NOT FINISHED YET. . . . .   377 PHASES OF MOON   117
    AND THAT MUST SLEEP, SHRIEK, STRUGGLE TO ESCAPE . . .   444 SCHOOL CHILDR   35
    HOW IN THE NAME OF HEAVEN CAN HE ESCAPE . . . . . .   479 SELF AND SOUL   50
    AND WHAT'S THE GOOD OF AN ESCAPE . . . .   479 SELF AND SOUL   55
    THAT COME INTO MY SOUL AND ESCAPE . . . .   599 SPIRIT MEDIUM   3
    SO THEY ESCAPE FROM HELL. BUT, PARDON ME, ...   704 MOSADA 3   132
    NONE SHOULD ESCAPE MY SWORD: I WOULD SEND ALL . . .   752 SHADOW WATER A   111
    I PROMISED HIM THAT NONE SHOULD ESCAPE MY SWORD . . .   752 SHADOW WATER A   114
    WE WILL GO CALL THESE SAILORS, AND ESCAPE . . . . .   766 SHADOW WATER A   382
ESCAPED
    ESCAPED FROM BITTER YOUTH, ...   568 SWEET DANCER   4
    ESCAPED OUT OF HER CROWD, ...   568 SWEET DANCER   5
ESCUTCHEONED
    WHAT IF THE GLORY OF ESCUTCHEONED DOORS, ...   418 ANCEST HOUSES   33
ESERKELLY
    AND ESERKELLY PLAINS, FEW KEPT HIS PACE: . . . . .   326 ROBERT GREGORY V   59
    OR ESERKELLY PLAINS, FEW KEPT HIS PACE: . . . . . .   326 ROBERT GREGORY V   59
ESSERKELLY
    OR ESSERKELLY PLAIN, FEW KEPT HIS PACE: . . . . .   326 ROBERT GREGORY   59
ESTABLISHED
    PULL DOWN ESTABLISHED HONOUR: HAWK FOR NEWS . . . .   398 LEADERS CROWD   3
    FOUND PRIDE ESTABLISHED IN HUMILITY, ...   489 COOLE PARK 29   15
    ESTABLISHED IT FOR GOOD: . . . .   584 ORAHILLY   6
ESTATE
    ALTHOUGH THEIR CHILDREN NEED A RICH ESTATE: . . . .   500 VACILLATION   24
ESTEEMS
    EVERYTHING THAT MAN ESTEEMS . . . .   438 SONGS PLAY 2   9

	PAGE	TITLE		LINE
ESTRANGED				
ESTRANGED AMID THE STRANGENESS OF THEMSELVES, • • • • •	375	PHASES OF MOON		78
ALTHOUGH OF LATE ESTRANGED• • • • • • • • • • •	473	ALL SOUL NIGHT		63
ALL OTHER LOVERS BEING ESTRANGED OR DEAD, • • • • •	523	LONG SILENCE		2
ETERNAL				
NOT THEY ARE THE ETERNAL——'TIS THE CRY." • • • • • •	81	EPHEMERA	V	24J
ETERNAL BEAUTY WANDERING ON HER WAY• • • • • • • •	101	ROSE UPON ROOD		12
WAGE AN ETERNAL BATTLE, AND I FEEL • • • • • • •	104	FERGUS DRUID	V	38C
VAST GREENNESS, WHERE ETERNAL RUMOUR DWELLS, • • • • •	657	ISLE STAT I 3		45
FOR THIS DID THE ETERNAL DARKNESS BRING • • • • • •	688	TWO TITANS		51
GIVES FORTH. HE, THE ETERNAL, WORKS HIS WILL• • • • •	689	NETTLESHIP		16
ETERNALISED				
ETERNALISED THE BODY OF A MODERN SAINT THAT ONCE • • • •	503	VACILLATION		83
ETERNITIES				
BETWEEN HIS TWO ETERNITIES, • • • • • • • • • • •	637	BEN BULBEN		14
ETERNITY				
BEFORE US LIES ETERNITY: OUR SOULS • • • • • • •	81	EPHEMERA		23
THAT WORD OF THE SOUL'S PEACE——"ETERNITY•" • • • • •	81	EPHEMERA	V	24B
I KNOW THE WORD THEY CRY, "ETERNITY!" • • • • • •	81	EPHEMERA	V	24F
BEAUTY GROWN SAD WITH ITS ETERNITY • • • • • • •	115	ROSE OF BATTLE		29
HE THAT CROWED OUT ETERNITY • • • • • • • • • •	388	SOLOMON WITCH		17
INTO THE ARTIFICE OF ETERNITY• • • • • • • • • •	408	SAIL BYZANTIUM		24
ETERNITY MAY DWINDLE, • • • • • • • • • • • •	520	HIS BARGAIN		3
■THE STALLION ETERNITY • • • • • • • • • • • •	529	TOM CRUACHAN		4
ETERNITY IS PASSION, GIRL OR BOY • • • • • • • •	560	WHENCE COME		1
HAS FENCED US ROUND FOR ALL ETERNITY• • • • • • •	670	ISLE STAT II 3		95
AT ARM'S LENGTH, THUS TILL DUMB ETERNITY • • • • •	671	ISLE STAT II 3		145
EUNUCHS				
EUNUCHS RAN THROUGH HELL AND MET • • • • • • • • •	294	HATED PLAYBOY		2
EUROPA				
GREAT EUROPA PLAYED THE FOOL • • • • • • • • • •	509	JANE REPROVED		5
EUROPE				
EUROPE PUT OFF THAT FOAM WHEN PHIDIAS • • • • • • •	610	STATUES		15
EUROTAS'				
UPON EUROTAS' GRASSY BANK • • • • • • • • • • •	522	LULLABY		14
EVA				
IN MEMORY OF EVA GORE-BOOTH AND CON MARKIEWICZ • • • •	475	EVA GORE-BOOTH		T
EVADING				
EVADING, TURNING: ONCE DID I HEW AND HEW • • • • • •	40	OISIN 2	V	176
EVE				
WHEN THE EARLIEST DEW-WASHED STAR FROM EVE HATH LEANT, • •	32	OISIN 2	V	54
GAVE TO THE NOON, AND NOON TO EVE GAVE WAY, • • • • •	40	OISIN 2	V	172
AND IN THE EVE I THREW HIM IN THE SURGE, • • • • •	44	OISIN 2	V	219
AMRITA. THIS SAME EVE SHE WATCHED ME PASS• • • • • •	74	ANASHU VIJAYA	V	64
WHEN EVE HAS HUSHED THE FEATHERED WAYS, • • • • • •	78	INDIAN TO LOVE		19
DROPPING AT EVE IN CORAL BAYS • • • • • • • • •	78	INDIAN TO LOVE	V	19
WHERE EVE HAS HUSHED THE FEATHERED WAYS, • • • • • •	78	INDIAN TO LOVE	V	19
WHO PACED IN THE EVE BY THE NETS ON THE PEBBLY SHORE, • •	91	OLD FISHERMAN		11
AT THE MOTH-HOUR OF EVE, • • • • • • • • • • •	132	FR GILLIGAN		6
OF WONDERS! EVE OF PRODIGIES! DRAW! DRAW! • • • • •	664	ISLE STAT II 2		62
AND RULE THE SHADOWS OF THE EVE AND DAWN? • • • • •	678	ISLE STAT II 3		304
A LITTLE WHILE AND——RED EVE DIES—— • • • • • • •	686	LIFE		13
DRAW STAR TO STAR, AS ON THAT EVE HE PASSED • • • • •	691	MOSADA 1		29
SEER OF VISIONS! NOW EVE FALLS ASLEEP, • • • • • •	691	MOSADA 1		36
THIS EVE, TO-MORROW, OR TO-MORROW NIGHT • • • • • •	699	MOSADA 3		2
I NEVER KNEW AN EVE SO MARVELLOUS STILL• • • • • •	702	MOSADA 3		88
IT IS THE DARKEST EVE I EVER KNEW• • • • • • • •	702	MOSADA 3		93
WHEN WERE YOU BORN? BEFORE YOUR GRANDAM EVE• • • • •	721	WITCH VIVIEN		32
EVEN				
AND EVEN THE SUN, THE DAY CASTLE'S WARDER, • • • • •	28	OISIN 1	V	423A
NOT EVEN YOUR GOD COULD HAVE THROWN DOWN THAT HALL: • •	36	OISIN 1		109
AND EVEN THE NAMES OF HIS FATHERS, AND EVEN THE WORKS OF HIS HANDS?	51	OISIN 3	V	62
AND EVEN THE NAMES OF HIS FATHERS, AND EVEN THE WORKS OF HIS HANDS?	51	OISIN 3	V	62
LORD OF THE CROZIERS, YOU EVEN HAD LIFTED YOUR HANDS AND WEPT:	54	OISIN 3		110
LORD OF THE CROSIERS, THOU EVEN HADST LIFTED THY HANDS AND WEPT:	54	OISIN 3	V	110
AH, SWEET TO ME NOW WERE EVEN BALD CONAN'S SLANDEROUS TONGUE!	55	OISIN 3		116
EVEN AS SPRING UPON THE ANCIENT SKIES, • • • • • •	108	CUCHULAIN SEA		42
EVEN IN AN OLD STORY, IS A BURDEN NOT TO BE BORNE• • • •	210	UNDER THE MOON		20
EVEN IF FORGAEL HAD NOT BEEN MY MASTER • • • • •	225	SHADOW WATER B	V	76
AND BODILY TENDERNESS, AND FINDS THAT EVEN • • • • •	228	SHADOW WATER B		147
EVEN THOUGH IT BE THE LIGHTEST OF LIGHT LOVE, • • • • ■	230	SHADOW WATER B		184
SIGHED, "YOU, EVEN YOU YOURSELF, COULD WORK THE CURE!"➤ •	282	TWO KINGS		124
OUR QUESTIONING, BEYOND OUR PITY EVEN• • • ╱ • • • •	282	TWO KINGS		130
QUESTION OF OURS, BEYOND OUR PITY EVEN• • • • • • •	282	TWO KINGS	V	130
EVEN LIKE THESE TO RAIL AND SWEAT • • • • • • •	294	HATED PLAYBOY		5
TILL EVEN I SLEEP LIGHT: BUT WHO • • • • • • •	303	HOUR DAWN		34
SO THAT IT SEEMS EVEN I SLEEP LIGHT: • • • • • • •	303	HOUR DAWN	V	34
EVEN A HALF-HOUR'S NOTHINGNESS• • • • • • • • • •	305	HOUR DAWN		70
EVEN A HALF HOUR'S NOTHINGNESS• • • • • • • • • •	305	HOUR DAWN	V	70
THAT EVEN THE BEST OF LOVE MUST DIE, • • • • • • •	314	MEMORY YOUTH		17
AND EVEN OLD MEN'S EYES GREW DIM, THIS HAND ALONE, • • •	314	FALLEN MAJESTY		2
I CAN FORGIVE EVEN THAT WRONG OF WRONGS, • • • • •	321	REED WHISPERER		9
NOT EVEN YOUR OWN MOTHER • • • • • • • • • •	336	YOUNG GIRL		4
EVEN BEFORE HIS CHILDREN AND HIS WIFE? • • • • • •	340	SHEP GOATHERD		34
THEY HAD A PRIEST SAY MASS, AND EVEN THE JAPANESE, • • •	363	DOLLS FACES		2
EVEN OUR BEAUTY WITH HER TURKISH TROUSERS ON• • • • •	364	DOLLS FACES		9

	PAGE	TITLE		LINE
EVEN (CONTINUED)				
THEY DO NOT EVEN FEEL, SO ABSTRACT ARE THEY,	382	VISION ROBART		14
EVEN FROM THE FOOT-SOLE THINK IT TOO.	387	ROBARTES DANCE		51
EVEN TO EYES THAT BEAUTY HAD DRIVEN MAD,	390	IMAGE PAST		34
EVEN ACCUSING HEAVEN BECAUSE	399	BREAK OF DAY		15
AND EVEN STRAFFORD SMILED AS THOUGH	400	DEMON BEAST		13
AND EVEN STAFFORD SMILED AS THOUGH	400	DEMON BEAST	V	13
WHERE EVEN LONGING DROWNS UNDER ITS OWN EXCESS;	426	PHANTOM HATRED		22
WHAT MY LABORIOUS LIFE IMAGINED, EVEN	431	NINETEEN 19		82
EVEN WHERE HORRIBLE GREEN PARROTS CALL AND SWING.	442	BLACK CENTAUR		2
EVEN WHERE THE HORRIBLE GREEN PARROTS CALL AND SWING.	442	BLACK CENTAUR	V	2
FOR EVEN DAUGHTERS OF THE SWAN CAN SHARE	444	SCHOOL CHILDR		20
EVEN THE GREY-LEAVED OLIVE-TREE	446	COLONUS PRAISE		12
EVEN THE GREY-LEAVED OLIVE TREE	446	COLONUS PRAISE	V	12
IT IS AS THOUGH YOU PRAISED ANOTHER, OR EVEN	448	HERO GIRL FOOL		3
IT IS AS THOUGH YOU PRAISE ANOTHER, OR EVEN	448	HERO GIRL FOOL	V	3
THAT EVEN LOVERS DROWN.	453	MERMAID		6
EVEN FROM THAT DELIGHT MEMORY TREASURES SO,	459	FROM OEDIPUS		4
EVEN THOSE TRUTHS THAT WHEN MY BONES ARE DUST	467	HARUN RASHID		144
EVEN TO-DAY, AFTER SOME SEVEN YEARS	468	HARUN RASHID		161
EVEN TODAY, AFTER SOME SEVEN YEARS	468	HARUN RASHID	V	161
HER CONFIDENCE IN MINE, OR EVEN LOSE	469	HARUN RASHID		176
THAT EVEN CICERO	524	MAD AS MIST		16
HAD EVEN O'DUFFY--BUT I NAME NO MORE--	543	PARN FUNERAL 2		9
BUT EVEN AT THE STARTING-POST, ALL SLEEK AND NEW,	619	BRONZE HEAD		15
EVEN THE WISEST MAN GROWS TENSE	638	BEN BULBEN		33
AND EVEN SHE SHALL NEVER HOLD	668	ISLE STAT II 3		50
EVEN FROM BOYHOOD, IN MY FATHER'S HOUSE,	683	SEEKER		48
I CANNOT EVEN CRAWL ALONG THE FLAGS	701	MOSADA 3		58
OF BIRDS EVEN, LONGINGS FOR AERY	708	FAIRY PEDANT		26
NOT EVEN "I LONG TO SEE THY LONGING OVER,"	734	QUATRAIN APHOR		11
EVEN THE WANDERING ISLANDS OF THE GODS,	749	SHADOW WATER A		45
TO DROWN IN ITS OWN IMAGE? EVEN THAT SLEEP	765	SHADOW WATER A		364
A MEMORY, EVEN TO THE DEAD,	791	REPRISALS		8
EVENING				
AT EVENING IN THEIR RAINLESS LANDS."	7	OISIN 1		70
AT EVENING IN THEIR RAINLESS LANDS."	7	OISIN 1	V	66
AT EVENING IN MY WESTERN DUN."	8	OISIN 1		79
AT EVENING ON THE GLIMMERING SANDS.	23	OISIN 1		347
UNDER THE GOLDEN EVENING LIGHT,	25	OISIN 1		385
OF LANGUID EVENING THAT ENTWINED US.	25	OISIN 1	V	385A
HIS SHADOW ALONG IN THE EVENING BLAZE,	27	OISIN 1	V	409
SO MUCH REMAINED THAT ON THE EVENING STAR	32	OISIN 2	V	48
HOW THE SLOW, BLUE-EYED OXEN OF FINN LOW SADLY AT EVENING TIDE.	52	OISIN 3		84
AND LAID YOU ON THE GATES OF EVENING WITH HIS QUIET HANDS.	72	ANASHU VIJAYA		22
VIJAYA, I HAVE BROUGHT MY EVENING RICE;	72	ANASHU VIJAYA		23
AND LAID YE ON THE GATES OF EVENING WITH HIS QUIET HANDS.	72	ANASHU VIJAYA	V	22
MY SPIRIT ROCKED IN EVENING LIGHT, THE RUSHES ROUND MY KNEES,	76	INDIAN ON GOD		2
THE LITTLE WAVES THAT WALKED IN EVENING WHITENESS,	81	EPHEMERA	V	24C
ERE FALL OF EVENING, MY MAILED HOST,	83	MAD KING GOLL	V	19
I DREW AT EVENING MY MAILED MEN,	83	MAD KING GOLL	V	19
IN ALL HIS EVENING VAPOURS ROLLED--	86	MAD KING GOLL	V	71
HIS EVENING FIRE AMID THE LEAFY SHADE.	109	CUCHULAIN SEA		48
WHILE DAY ITS BURDEN ON TO EVENING BORE,	110	CUCHULAIN SEA		70
AND EVENING FULL OF THE LINNET'S WINGS.	117	ISLE INNISFREE		8
AND EVENING FULL OF THE LINNETS' WINGS.	117	ISLE INNISFREE	V	8
AND SANG WHAT GOLD MORNING OR EVENING SHEDS	126	DREAM OF FAERY		7
AT HUSH OF EVENING TILL GOD BURNS TIME	164	PERFECT BEAUTY	V	7
AT HUSH OF EVENING TILL GOD BURN TIME	164	PERFECT BEAUTY	V	7
AMONG THE EVENING SHADOWS,	341	SHEP GOATHERD		71
LAST EVENING? THAT I, WHO HAD SAT	349	HAWK		15
EVENING AND MORNING, THE STEEP STREET OF URBINO	352	PEOPLE		12
EVENING AND MORN, THE STEEP STREET OF URBINO	352	PEOPLE	V	12
WHEN EVENING STIRS THE JASMINE BOUGH, AND YET	463	HARUN RASHID		53
WHEN EVENING STIRS THE JASMINE, AND YET	463	HARUN RASHID	V	53
THE LIGHT OF EVENING, LISSADELL,	475	EVA GORE-BOOTH		1
OFTEN AT EVENING WHEN A BOY	494	AT ALGECIRAS		7
AN EVENING CHILL UPON THE AIR,	494	AT ALGECIRAS		14
FROM MORN THE TWAIN UNTIL THE EVENING PALES	651	ISLE STAT I 1		161
OF EVENING AND GLAD SILENCE DWELLETH AYE,	653	ISLE STAT I 2		37
THE WIND AT EVENING WHEN THE SUN GOES DOWN	653	ISLE STAT I 2		50
THE EVENING GLEAMS ARE GREEN AND GOLD AND RED	656	ISLE STAT I 3		22
AWAY FROM ME WHERE MISTS OF EVENING DRINK	663	ISLE STAT II 2		40
'TWAS EVENING, AND THE CRICKET NATION SANG	690	MOSADA 1		18
RETURNS THAT SOLDIER IN THE EVENING RAYS	711	FERENCZ RENYI		49
TIME GOES. THE FLAKED FIRE OF EVENING CRAWLS	712	FERENCZ RENYI		70
TIME GOES. THE FLICKED FIRE OF EVENING CRAWLS	712	FERENCZ RENYI	V	70
HIGHER AND HIGHER GOLD WITH EVENING LIGHT;	714	FERENCZ RENYI		113
A SUMMER EVENING	736	SUMMER EVENING		T
AN EVENING PRESENCE FILLS THE PLACE.	736	SUMMER EVENING		16
EVENING'S				
MY SPIRIT ROCKED IN EVENING'S HUSH, THE RUSHES ROUND MY KNEES,	76	INDIAN ON GOD	V	2
EVENINGS				
SHALL FEED. I SHALL NOT IN THE EVENINGS HEAR	674	ISLE STAT II 3		220
EVENT				
"ALTHOUGH THE EVENT WAS LONG IN DOUBT,	273	GREY ROCK		67
TOLD OF A HARSH REPROOF, OR TRIVIAL EVENT	443	SCHOOL CHILDR		11
EVERY EVENT IN ACTION OR IN THOUGHT;	479	SELF AND SOUL		66

246

EVENT (CONTINUED)
```
    WHY DO I HATE MAN, WOMAN OR EVENT?  . . . . . . . . .    558 RIBH CHRISTIAN        7
EVENTS
    WHERE I AM RID OF LIFE--THE EVENTS OF THE WORLD--  . . .  227 SHADOW WATER B      121
EVER
    ROSE EVER OUT OF THE WARM SEA:  . . . . . . . . . . .     13 OISIN 1             172
    AND, AS THE SUN SANK EVER LOWER,  . . . . . . . . . .     13 OISIN 1           V 170A
    ROSE EVER FROM THE SEA'S WARM FLOOR,  . . . . . . . .     13 OISIN 1           V 172
    AND EVER NEARER, NEARER GREW:  . . . . . . . . . . .      15 OISIN 1             200
    THE EVER SUMMERED SOLITUDES,  . . . . . . . . . . .       21 OISIN 1           V 321
    NOR EVER CHANGE OR FEEL THE CLUTCHES  . . . . . . . .     23 OISIN 1           V 341A
    SOME WANDERED EVER HAND IN HAND:  . . . . . . . . . .     25 OISIN 1             389
    FOR NO MAN'S CRY SHALL EVER MOUNT SO FAR:  . . . . .      36 OISIN 2             108
    NOR NO MAN'S CRY SHALL EVER MOUNT SO FAR:  . . . . .      36 OISIN 2           V 108
    HOPELESS FOR EVER: ANCIENT OISIN KNOWS,  . . . . . .      42 OISIN 2             202
    HOPELESS FOR EVER, THEY ALONE SHALL SEEK  . . . . . .     42 OISIN 2             200
    AND LIGHTNING FLASH FOR EVER?  CEASE AND HEAR.  . . .     42 OISIN 2           V 207
    WHERE EVER IS MURMUROUS DROPPING, OLD SILENCE AND THAT    56 OISIN 3             138
        ONE SOUND:
    BUT NAUGHT THEY HEARD, FOR THEY ARE EVER LISTENING,  . .  68 SAD SHEPHERD      V  15
    BY MIGHTY BRAHMA'S EVER RUSTLING ROBE,  . . . . . . .     71 ANASHU VIJAYA     V  14
    AND, EVER PACING ON THE VERGE OF THINGS,  . . . . . .     73 ANASHU VIJAYA        54
    SHOOT ON HIM SHAFTS OF QUIETNESS, THAT HE MAY EVER KEEP   75 ANASHU VIJAYA        81
    AND WANDER EVER WITH WOVEN HANDS,  . . . . . . . . .      78 INDIAN TO LOVE        7
    THE COLD WET WINDS EVER BLOWING,  . . . . . . . . .      119 PITY OF LOVE          5
    AND THE COLD WET WINDS EVER BLOWING,  . . . . . . .      119 PITY OF LOVE        V  7
    DRIVEN BY A STORM THAT EVER GRIEVES.  . . . . . . .      135 TWO TREES         V  28
    MAN JOURNEYS ON WITH THEM  . . . . . . . . . . . .       139 TO IRELAND           29
    DEW EVER SHINING AND TWILIGHT GREY:  . . . . . . .       148 INTO TWILIGHT         6
    AND TIME AND THE WORLD ARE EVER IN FLIGHT:  . . . .      148 INTO TWILIGHT        14
    NO WAITING-MAID SHOULD EVER SPREAD  . . . . . . . .      194 BAILE AILLINN       120
    NO WAITING MAID SHOULD EVER SPREAD  . . . . . . . .      194 BAILE AILLINN     V 120
    ONE THAT IS EVER KIND SAID YESTERDAY,  . . . . . . .     199 FOLLY COMFORT         1
    WOULD NONE HAD EVER LOVED BUT YOU AND I:  . . . . .      210 RAGGED WOOD           4
    O THAT NONE EVER LOVED BUT YOU AND I:  . . . . . .       210 RAGGED WOOD       V   4
    O THAT NONE EVER LOVED BUT YOU AND I:  . . . . . .       211 RAGGED WOOD           8
    NO ONE HAS EVER LOVED BUT YOU AND I.  . . . . . . .      211 RAGGED WOOD          12
    OF THOSE THAT ARE ALIVE FOR EVER AND EVER.  . . . .      223 SHADOW WATER B       35
    OF THOSE THAT ARE ALIVE FOR EVER AND EVER.  . . . .      223 SHADOW WATER B       35
    MORE RICHES THAN THEY EVER HOPED TO FIND?  . . . . .     226 SHADOW WATER B       94
    HAS EVER COME BUT THOSE MAN-HEADED BIRDS?  . . . . .     226 SHADOW WATER B       99
    AND AS SOON FINISHED.  ALL THAT EVER LOVED  . . . .      229 SHADOW WATER B      151
    THAT I WOULD LOOK UPON FOR EVER?  MY GRIEF:  . . . .     244 SHADOW WATER B      462
    WHO CANNOT PUT ME FROM HIS SIGHT FOR EVER.  . . . .      251 SHADOW WATER B      601
    WE ARE ALONE FOR EVER, AND I LAUGH,  . . . . . . .      251 SHADOW WATER B      602
    SHALL BE ALONE FOR EVER.  WE TWO--THIS CROWN--  . .      251 SHADOW WATER B      605
    BUT WAS THERE EVER DOG THAT PRAISED HIS FLEAS?  . .      262 TO A POET             4
    COULD EVER COME BETWEEN  . . . . . . . . . . . . .       315 FRIENDS               8
    THE GENTLENESS NONE THERE HAD EVER KNOWN:  . . . . .     418 ANCEST HOUSES        21
    WHAT EVER MISCHIEF SEEMED  . . . . . . . . . . . .       431 NINETEEN 19       V  85
    IF DAYLIGHT EVER VISIT WHERE,  . . . . . . . . . .       446 COLONUS PRAISE        4
    THINK WHEN I CHOOSE A BRIDE I CHOOSE FOR EVER:  . .      464 HARUN RASHID         80
    NO MAN HAS EVER LIVED THAT HAD ENOUGH  . . . . . .       500 VACILLATION          25
    IF EVER LOVER'S LONELINESS  . . . . . . . . . . . .      518 LOVES LONENESS        3
    WHY SHOULD THEY THINK THAT ARE FOR EVER YOUNG?  . .      537 HER VISION           21
    "FOR EVER AND FOR EVER": THEN AWAKE  . . . . . . .       560 WHENCE COME           3
    "FOR EVER AND FOR EVER": THEN AWAKE  . . . . . . .       560 WHENCE COME           3
    DID EVER MEN HEAR SUCH A SONG?  . . . . . . . . .        570 THREE BUSHES         45
    DID EVER MAN RIDE SUCH A RACE?  . . . . . . . . .        570 THREE BUSHES         47
    NOR EVER MADE AN IRON RED  . . . . . . . . . . . .       606 SONGS BURDEN 1       14
    EVER RINGING, RINGING, RINGING,  . . . . . . . . .       647 ISLE STAT I 1        68
    EVER DIETH, DIETH, DIETH.  . . . . . . . . . . . .       648 ISLE STAT I 1        88
    AND THERE TO ITS OWN HEART FOR EVER MOANS.  . . . .      650 ISLE STAT I 1       131
    JOY'S BROTHER, FEAR, DWELLS EVER IN EACH BREAST--  . .   651 ISLE STAT I 1       155
    HOW THEY WHO SEEK ARE EVER DOOMED TO FAIL.  . . . .      653 ISLE STAT I 2        41
    ARE CHANGED FOR EVER INTO MOON-WHITE STONE.  . . .       653 ISLE STAT I 2        43
    SAD FAERY TONES.  'TIS THUS THEY EVER SEEM,  . . .       654 ISLE STAT I 2        58
    OR HER EVER BURNING EYES,  . . . . . . . . . . . .       658 ISLE STAT I 3        85
    THAT OF OLD WERT MOVING EVER,  . . . . . . . . . .       658 ISLE STAT I 3        91
    MORE GRIEF IS MINE.  NO MAN SHALL EVER STOOP  . . .      661 ISLE STAT II 1       62
    HAD DRIVEN HER FORTH, FOR EVER MORE  . . . . . . .       668 ISLE STAT II 3       56
    I' FAITH THOU EVER WAST A WORDY SPIRIT:  . . . . .       673 ISLE STAT II 3      175
    YET EVER MORE, THROUGH ALL THY DAYS OF RUTH,  . . .      674 ISLE STAT II 3      206
    FOR EVER FOAM AND FRET:  . . . . . . . . . . . . .       680 LOVE AND DEATH        4
    THE BANKS ARE WORN FOR EVER.  . . . . . . . . . .        680 LOVE AND DEATH        9
    NO SHEPHERD FOOT HAS EVER DARED ITS DEPTHS.  . . .       682 SEEKER               32
    THAT FROM THE FIRE IS EVER POURING UP  . . . . . .       683 SEEKER               37
    THROUGH MISERIES UNHUMAN EVER ON  . . . . . . . .        684 SEEKER               59
    THROUGH HIS SAD SOUL FOR EVER OLD AND YOUNG,  . . .      687 TWO TITANS           25
    FOR EVER ROUND THY WAKING AND THY SLEEP  . . . . .       688 TWO TITANS           57
    RE-SHINING IN HIS EYES.  SO EVER MOVES  . . . . . .      689 NETTLESHIP           12
    FROM WASTE SEAS CROSS'D, YET EVER GARRULOUS)  . . .      690 MOSADA 1              9
    EVER MORE TO SPEAK A WORD  . . . . . . . . . . . .       697 MOSADA 2             32
    IT IS THE DARKEST EVE I EVER KNEW.  . . . . . . .        702 MOSADA 3             93
    FLASHING AND FLICKERING, WITH EVER UNDULANT WING,  . .   710 FERENCZ RENYI     V  19
    OF TRAITOR EVER MORE IS ON OUR NAME."  . . . . . .       712 FERENCZ RENYI     V  61
    WITH QUIET SHADE ITS EVER DEWY-PLOT.  . . . . . .        714 FERENCZ RENYI       109
    WITH QUIET SHADE ITS EVER DEWY SPOT,  . . . . . .        714 FERENCZ RENYI       109
    WITH QUIET SHADE ITS EVER DEWY PLOT.  . . . . . .        714 FERENCZ RENYI     V 109
    ALL THE DROWNED THAT EVER WERE DROWNED FROM THAT VILLAGE 719 PHANTOM SHIP         20
        BY THE SEA:
```

		PAGE	TITLE	LINE

EVER   (CONTINUED)
FOR AS THINGS WERE SO SHALL THINGS EVER BE.   •   •   •   •   •   •   724 KANVA ON SELF   20.
"OF OUR GREAT QUEEN IS EVER HEARD   •   •   •   •   •   •   •   •   729 PRIEST FAIRY   41
AND HER OLD WIND THAT NO MIRTH EVER HAD,   •   •   •   •   •   738 YOU ARE SAD   7
I PRAY THAT I EVER BE WEAVING   •   •   •   •   •   •   •   •   743 WISDOM DREAMS   1
THE WINDS AND WATERS TO BE YOUR HOME FOR EVER!   •   •   •   762 SHADOW WATER A   282
THE PALE HOUND AND THE DEER WANDER FOR EVER   •   •   •   •   764 SHADOW WATER A   330
WHEN EVER I REMAKE A SONG,   •   •   •   •   •   •   •   •   •   778 FRIENDS WRONG   2
EVEREST
HERMITS UPON MOUNT MERU OR EVEREST,   •   •   •   •   •   •   563 MERU   9
EVERLASTING
THE EVERLASTING VOICES   •   •   •   •   •   •   •   •   •   •   141 EVERLAST VOICE   T
EVERLASTING VOICES   •   •   •   •   •   •   •   •   •   •   •   •   141 EVERLAST VOICE V   T
O SWEET EVERLASTING VOICES, BE STILL!   •   •   •   •   •   •   141 EVERLAST VOICE   1
O SWEET EVERLASTING VOICES, BE STILL.   •   •   •   •   •   •   141 EVERLAST VOICE   8
THE EVERLASTING TAPER LIGHTS THE GLOOM!   •   •   •   •   •   311 MOUNTAIN TOMB   10
EVER-LAUGHING
THAT THE SHAPE-CHANGERS, THE EVER-LAUGHING ONES,   •   •   •   249 SHADOW WATER B   566
EVER-LIVING
OF THE EVER-LIVING HALF SO DANGEROUS   •   •   •   •   •   •   224 SHADOW WATER B   46
WE HAVE FALLEN IN THE DREAMS THE EVER-LIVING   •   •   •   •   228 SHADOW WATER B   131
IT MAY BE THAT THE EVER-LIVING KNOW IT--   •   •   •   •   •   229 SHADOW WATER B   164
WITH THE EVER-LIVING.   WHAT IF HE SPEAK THE TRUTH,   •   •   229 SHADOW WATER B   170
ONE OF THE EVER-LIVING, AS I THINK--   •   •   •   •   •   •   231 SHADOW WATER B   210
THE EVER-LIVING HAVE KEPT MY BARGAIN FOR ME,   •   •   •   •   232 SHADOW WATER B   223
WITHHOLDS THEM NOW? HAVE THE EVER-LIVING ONES   •   •   •   234 SHADOW WATER B   269
THE EVER-LIVING HOLD US. DO WHAT YOU WILL,   •   •   •   238 SHADOW WATER B   359
THAT WERE CLEAR MESSAGES FROM THE EVER-LIVING,   •   •   •   243 SHADOW WATER B   442
YOU KNOW THE COUNSELS OF THE EVER-LIVING,   •   •   •   •   244 SHADOW WATER B   450
YOU KNOW THE COUNCILS OF THE EVER-LIVING,   •   •   •   •   244 SHADOW WATER B V   450
THE EVER-LIVING HAVE MADE YOU MAD! BUT NO,   •   •   •   248 SHADOW WATER B   546
EVER-LONGING
TO THE EVER-LONGING AND MOURNFUL SPIRIT SAY.   •   •   •   •   734 QUATRAIN APHOR   12
EVERMORE
HAD DRIVEN HER FORTH, FOR EVERMORE   •   •   •   •   •   •   668 ISLE STAT II 3 V   56
YET EVERMORE, THROUGH ALL THY DAYS OF RUTH,   •   •   •   674 ISLE STAT II 3 V   206
THAT ALL MEN EVERMORE MAY HUMBLY BOW   •   •   •   •   •   688 TWO TITANS   49
OF TRAITOR EVERMORE IS ON OUR NAME."   •   •   •   •   •   •   712 FERENCZ RENYI   61
EVER-MOVING
FROM THE EVER-MOVING PINIONS   •   •   •   •   •   •   •   •   •   667 ISLE STAT II 3   28
EVER-RUSTLING
BY MIGHTY BRAHMA'S EVER-RUSTLING ROBE,   •   •   •   •   •   71 ANASHU VIJAYA   14
STAND YOU.   BY BRAHMA'S EVER-RUSTLING ROBE,   •   •   •   71 ANASHU VIJAYA V   14
EVER-SINGING
AND THE LOUD SONG OF THE EVER-SINGING LEAVES   •   •   •   •   120 SORROW OF LOVE V   3
EVER-SUMMERED
THE EVER-SUMMERED SOLITUDES!   •   •   •   •   •   •   •   •   •   21 OISIN 1   321
EVER-TREMBLING
PRESSED ON THE EVER-TREMBLING ROOF   •   •   •   •   •   •   25 OISIN 1   V   383
EVER-UNDULANT
FLASHING AND FLICKERING WITH EVER-UNDULANT WING   •   •   •   710 FERENCZ RENYI   19
EVER-WINDING
THE EVER-WINDING WAKEFUL SEA,   •   •   •   •   •   •   •   •   22 OISIN 1   V   338
EVERY
"AND EVERY HERO DROOP HIS HEAD?   •   •   •   •   •   •   •   4 OISIN 1   33
ROUND EVERY BRANCH THE SONG-BIRDS FLEW,   •   •   •   •   •   14 OISIN 1   180
AND KNELT THERE, EVERY GIRL AND MAN,   •   •   •   •   •   •   15 OISIN 1   214
AND KNELT THEM, EVERY MAID AND MAN,   •   •   •   •   •   •   15 OISIN 1   V   214
AND TANGLED CREEPERS EVERY HOUR   •   •   •   •   •   •   •   16 OISIN 1   223
WHERE TANGLING CREEPERS EVERY HOUR   •   •   •   •   •   •   16 OISIN 1   V   223
THEY HUSHED THEM, EVERY MAN AND MAID.   •   •   •   •   •   17 OISIN 1   V   235
AROSE FROM EVERY MAID AND BOY,   •   •   •   •   •   •   •   20 OISIN 1   V   289
IN EVERY BRAIN A WIZARD GLOW,   •   •   •   •   •   •   •   •   20 OISIN 1   V 291A
OF EVERY FOAMDROP ON ITS MISTY WAY.   •   •   •   •   •   •   32 OISIN 2   45
HE TOLD OF EVERY FROTH-DROP HISSING, FLYING.   •   •   •   32 OISIN 2   V   45
AND SING FROM SHORE TO SHORE, AND EVERY YEAR   •   •   •   81 EPHEMERA   V   24G
AND EVERY ANCIENT OLLAVE SAID,   •   •   •   •   •   •   •   82 MAD KING GOLL   9
AND MINE WAS EVERY TROPHIED WALL,   •   •   •   •   •   •   82 MAD KING GOLL   V   4
AND EVERY WHISPERING DRUID SAID,   •   •   •   •   •   •   82 MAD KING GOLL   V   9
AND EVERY MUMBLING OLD MAN SAID,   •   •   •   •   •   •   82 MAD KING GOLL   V   9
AND EVERY WHISPERING OLD MAN SAID,   •   •   •   •   •   •   82 MAD KING GOLL   V   9
AND TOADS AND EVERY OUTLAWED THING   •   •   •   •   •   •   85 MAD KING GOLL   V   61
IN EVERY COMPANY   •   •   •   •   •   •   •   •   •   •   •   131 OLD PENSIONER   4
I HAD A CHAIR AT EVERY HEARTH,   •   •   •   •   •   •   •   131 OLD PENSIONER   V   1
AND BIND UP EVERY WANDERING TRESS!   •   •   •   •   •   •   157 BELOVED RHYMES   2
BUT WHERE IT COULD SEE HER EVERY DAY.   •   •   •   •   •   191 BAILE AILLINN   55
WHO PEERED ABOUT ON EVERY SIDE!   •   •   •   •   •   •   •   193 BAILE AILLINN   V 112
HAS HATED EVERY MAN THAT'S NOT IN LOVE,   •   •   •   •   •   224 SHADOW WATER B   51
DYING AT EVERY MOMENT IN THE WORLD,   •   •   •   •   •   •   226 SHADOW WATER B   90
HAS BEAUTIFUL WOMEN TO PLEASE EVERY MAN.   •   •   •   •   228 SHADOW WATER B   144
THAT EVERY MAN SHOULD CARRY HIS OWN SOUL   •   •   •   •   235 SHADOW WATER B   299
I AM A WOMAN; I DIE AT EVERY BREATH.   •   •   •   •   •   250 SHADOW WATER B   583
THAT EVERY YEAR I HAVE CRIED, "AT LENGTH   •   •   •   •   256 WORDS   9
ON THE DAY'S WAR WITH EVERY KNAVE AND DOLT,   •   •   •   260 FASC DIFFICULT   10
BUT THEREON EVERY GOD STOOD UP   •   •   •   •   •   •   •   275 GREY ROCK   116
ITS TERROR GROWING WILDER AT EVERY FOOT-FALL,   •   •   •   279 TWO KINGS   V 45D
ITS TERROR GROWING WILDER AT EVERY FOOTFALL   •   •   •   279 TWO KINGS   V 45D
AND WITH HIM HAVE FOUND EVERY HAPPINESS   •   •   •   •   284 TWO KINGS   174
THE GREY WING UPON EVERY TIDE!   •   •   •   •   •   •   •   290 SEPTEMBER 1913   18
HAS MADDENED EVERY MOTHER'S SON"!   •   •   •   •   •   •   290 SEPTEMBER 1913   29
ON EVERY CROWDED STREET TO STARE   •   •   •   •   •   •   294 HATED PLAYBOY   3

	PAGE	TITLE	LINE
EVERY (CONTINUED)			
MY LIFE OF EVERY PLEASANT THOUGHT	307	HOUR DAWN	110
AND EVERY COMFORTABLE THING,	307	HOUR DAWN	111
BELIEVING EVERY WORD I SAID,	314	MEMORY YOUTH	8
SO WILD THAT EVERY CASUAL THOUGHT OF THAT AND THIS	316	COLD HEAVEN	4
WITH EVERY SORT OF COMPANY,	335	YOUNG BEAUTY	2
WITH EVERY JACK AND JILL?	335	YOUNG BEAUTY	3
AND EVERY MAN AND MAID AND BOY	337	TOM OROUGHLEY	2
I HAD DRIVEN EVERY RHYME INTO ITS PLACE	339	SHEP GOATHERD	14
HE THAT WAS BEST IN EVERY COUNTRY SPORT	339	SHEP GOATHERD	17
AND EVERY COUNTRY CRAFT, AND OF US ALL	339	SHEP GOATHERD	18
"HE GROWS YOUNGER EVERY SECOND	342	SHEP GOATHERD	89
WHERE EVERY DAY MY FOOTFALL SHOULD HAVE LIT	352	PEOPLE	8
THE YOUNG MEN EVERY NIGHT APPLAUD THEIR GABY'S LAUGHING EYE,	353	HIS PHOENIX	9
BECAUSE THE PRIEST MUST HAVE LIKE EVERY DOG HIS DAY	364	DOLLS FACES	10
THAT EVERY MORNING ROSE AGAIN	385	ROBARTES DANCE	7
WILL BANISH EVERY THOUGHT, UNLESS	387	ROBARTES DANCE	48
FOR EVERY NERVE, AND TESTS A LOVER	388	SOLOMON WITCH	22
FOR EVERY NERVE: LOVER TESTS LOVER	388	SOLOMON WITCH V	22
AND THE MOON IS WILDER EVERY MINUTE,	389	SOLOMON WITCH	43
AND SPREAD ON EVERY SIDE,	396	ROSE TREE	10
THEY HAVE LOUD MUSIC, HOPE EVERY DAY RENEWED	398	LEADERS CROWD	11
THAT EVERY NATURAL VICTORY	401	DEMON BEAST	34
BARTER THAT HORN AND EVERY GOOD	405	FOR DAUGHTER	62
SHE CAN, THOUGH EVERY FACE SHOULD SCOWL	405	FOR DAUGHTER	70
AND EVERY WINDY QUARTER HOWL	405	FOR DAUGHTER	71
OR EVERY BELLOWS BURST, BE HAPPY STILL,	405	FOR DAUGHTER	72
FOR EVERY TATTER IN ITS MORTAL DRESS,	407	SAIL BYZANTIUM	12
WHEN EVERY SILVER CANDLESTICK OR SCONCE	410	TOWER	26
THAT MOST RESPECTED LADY'S EVERY WISH	410	TOWER	29
OLD LECHER WITH A LOVE ON EVERY WIND,	413	TOWER	105
RECKONED UP EVERY UNFOREKNOWN, UNSEEING	413	TOWER	109
OF EVERY BRILLIANT EYE	416	TOWER	190
AND CHILDHOOD A DELIGHT FOR EVERY SENSE,	418	ANCEST HOUSES	31
OF EVERY WIND THAT BLOWS:	419	MY HOUSE	7
FROM NOTHING EVERY DAY, AND TEACH	436	FOR MY SON	18
SOMETHING OF EVERY PADDLER'S HERITAGE--	444	SCHOOL CHILDR	21
EVERY COLONUS LAD OR LASS DISCOURSES	447	COLONUS PRAISE	29
FOR EVERY HAND IS LUNATIC	451	FIRST LOVE	11
LIKE MEN WHO LIVE BY HABIT. EVERY DAY	463	HARUN RASHID	56
EVERY PHILOSOPHER SHOULD PRAISE THAT LOVE,	465	HARUN RASHID	97
WHEN MAYBE THRICE IN EVERY MOON HER MOUTH	468	HARUN RASHID	162
THAT EVERY GIFT AND EVERY WORD OF PRAISE	469	HARUN RASHID	172
THAT EVERY GIFT AND EVERY WORD OF PRAISE	469	HARUN RASHID	172
FOR EVERY SEPARATE QUALITY OF LOVE:	469	HARUN RASHID V	189A
FROM EVERY QUARTER OF THE WORLD, CAN STAY	471	ALL SOUL NIGHT	12
FIX EVERY WANDERING THOUGHT UPON	477	SELF AND SOUL	6
EVERY EVENT IN ACTION OR IN THOUGHT:	479	SELF AND SOUL	66
COUNT EVERY SIN OF ACTION OR OF THOUGHT:	479	SELF AND SOUL V	66
IS EVERY MODERN NATION LIKE THE TOWER,	482	BLOOD AND MOON	47
IS EVERY NATION LIKE THE TOWER	482	BLOOD AND MOON V	47
WHERE EVERY FOOT OBEYED HER GLANCE:	488	CRAZED MOON	11
AND EVERY BRIDE'S AMBITION SATISFIED.	491	COOLE BALLYLEE	37
EVERY NIGHT IN BED,	495	MOHINI CHATTER	4
EVERY COMMON WOMAN KNOWS,	499	MOTHER OF GOD	7
TEST EVERY WORK OF INTELLECT OR FAITH,	501	VACILLATION	30
EVERY THING THAT HAS LIVED	504	QUARREL IN AGE V	9
ADORNING EVERY SECRET TRACK	509	JANE REPROVED	9
EVERY TOUCH THEY GIVE,	517	HER ANXIETY	10
DOWN EVERY WITHERED FINGER FROM THE TOP:	537	HER VISION	11
LIFT, EVERY MOTHER'S SON,	548	TO SAME TUNE 3 V	15
FROM EVERY THOUGHT OF GOD MANKIND HAS HAD,	558	RIBH CHRISTIAN	15
EVERY DISCOLORATION OF THE STONE,	567	LAPIS LAZULI	43
EVERY ACCIDENTAL CRACK OR DENT,	567	LAPIS LAZULI	44
WITH EVERY NOBLE BEAST,	573	LADYS 2ND SONG	18
WITH EVERY NOBLE BREAST,	573	LADYS 2ND SONG V	18
EVERY MAN THAT SINGS A SONG	586	PARNELLITES	19
AND UNDER EVERY DANCER	592	DRUNK SOBRIETY	11
THROW IT IN EVERY PART."	596	COLONEL MARTIN	53
THOUGH RICH ON EVERY SHORE	606	SONGS BURDEN 1	11
WHEN EVERY SUNDAY AFTERNOON	607	SONGS BURDEN 2	19
PRAISE EVERY MAN THAT CAME AGAIN,	608	SONGS BURDEN 3	7
PRAISE EVERY MAN THAT FELL.	608	SONGS BURDEN 3	8
THAT IN EVERY GENERATION	608	SONGS BURDEN 3	25
HIS SLEUTH-HOUNDS FOLLOW EVERY FAERY THING.	675	ISLE STAT II 3	244
IN EVERY DANCE, BY CHILDREN SOUGHT. "ACCURST,	709	FERENCZ RENYI	12
AND EVERY FLOWER ABOVE ITS SHADOW SITS,	712	FERENCZ RENYI	73
AND EVERY FLOWER ABOVE A SHADOW SITS.	712	FERENCZ RENYI V	73
SUCH WAR PLOTS, PEACE PLOTS, LOVE PLOTS--EVERY SIDE:	722	WITCH VIVIEN	66
BENDING HUMBLY EVERY KNEE,	726	LOVERS QUARREL	14
TEASING EVERY WILFUL MAID.	727	LOVERS QUARREL	28
"EVERY SUMMER WILT THOU SEE	730	PRIEST FAIRY	55
HUSH! HUSH! HUSH! ON EVERY LIP	732	STREET DANCERS	18
SHE PRAYS FOR EVERY FALLING TEAR	735	IN CHURCH	3
A PRAYER FOR EVERY FALLING TEAR	736	IN CHURCH	15
I SWEAR IT. LET EVERY MAN DRAW OUT HIS SWORD.	758	SHADOW WATER A	230
BUT EVERY BUTTERFLY TO A FRIEND.	787	GARRET CELLAR	2
EVERYBODY			
FOR EVERYBODY KNOWS OR ELSE SHOULD KNOW	565	LAPIS LAZULI	4

EVERYTHING
  EVERYTHING THAT'S SAD IS WICKED-- . . . .   20 OISIN 1   V 301
  EVERYTHING THAT FEARS TO-MORROW . . . .   20 OISIN 1   V 302
  FOR EVERYTHING THAT'S LOVELY IS . . . . 202 NEVER GIVE ALL   6
  "EVERYTHING ALTERS, ... 208 OLD MEN ADMIRE   2
  AND TAKE THE CAPTAIN'S SHARE OF EVERYTHING . . . . . . 225 SHADOW WATER B   73
  YOU'LL HAVE THE CAPTAIN'S SHARE OF EVERYTHING . . . . 225 SHADOW WATER B V 67A
  FOR EVERYTHING IS GONE. COME HITHER, AIBRIC, ... 241 SHADOW WATER B   402
  HAVE WE NOT EVERYTHING THAT LIFE CAN GIVE . . . . . . 249 SHADOW WATER B   570
  TO MOCK AT EVERYTHING I LOVE . . . . 306 HOUR DAWN   83
  IMAGINED EVERYTHING. . . . . 419 MY HOUSE   17
  THOUGH YOU CAN FASHION EVERYTHING . . . . 436 FOR MY SON   17
  EVERYTHING THAT MAN ESTEEMS . . . . 438 SONGS PLAY 2   9
  TO CUT AND SEW, BE NEAT IN EVERYTHING . . . . 443 SCHOOL CHILDR   5
  WE ARE BLEST BY EVERYTHING, ... 479 SELF AND SOUL   71
  EVERYTHING WE LOOK UPON IS BLEST. . . . . 479 SELF AND SOUL   72
  EVERYTHING THAT IS NOT GOD CONSUMED WITH INTELLECTUAL FIRE. 481 BLOOD AND MOON   30
  LIKE EVERYTHING THAT HAS THE STAIN OF BLOOD. . . . . . 482 BLOOD AND MOON   51
  AND EVERYTHING THAT YOUR OWN HANDS HAVE WROUGHT, . . . 501 VACILLATION   31
  WHEN EVERYTHING IS TOLD, ... 515 GIRLS SONG B   10
  THAT EVERYTHING OUTSIDE US IS . . . . 523 MAD AS MIST   5
  OF EVERYTHING THAT IS NOT MIND OR SENSE. . . . . 558 RIBH CHRISTIAN   6
  EVERYTHING HE WROTE WAS READ, ... 577 WHAT THEN   6
  CONTACT EVERYTHING ANTAEUS-LIKE GREW STRONG. . . . . . 603 GALLERY REVIS   44
  EVERYTHING DOWN TO THAT SOLE TEST AGAIN, ... 603 GALLERY REVIS   46
  AND GIVEN EVERYTHING A WOMAN NEEDS, ... 609 IN TARAS HALLS   7
  EVERYTHING ELSE WITHERED AND MUMMY-DEAD. . . . . 618 BRONZE HEAD   3
  ON EVERYTHING SHE SAID. . . . . 621 JOHN KINSELLA   22
  WHERE EVERYTHING THAT MEETS THE EYE, ... 639 BEN BULBEN   56
  FORGIVE! FOR I HAVE TOLD THEM EVERYTHING. . . . . . . 694 MOSADA 1   107
EVERYWHERE
  THEY HAVE SPOKEN AGAINST YOU EVERYWHERE, ... 166 EVIL OF BELOV   3
  AND EVERYWHERE THAT I COULD TURN . . . . 253 HIS DREAM   V   3
  THE BLOOD-DIMMED TIDE IS LOOSED, AND EVERYWHERE . . . . 402 SECOND COMING   5
  OLD MARBLE HEADS, OLD PICTURES EVERYWHERE! . . . . . . 491 COOLE BALLYLEE   28
  I EVERYWHERE PROCLAIMED THERE IS . . . . 528 DANCER CRUACH   V   1
  AND WANDERED MURMURING EVERYWHERE, "MY CHILD, MY CHILD!" 619 BRONZE HEAD   21
  THEY PASSED A-TIP-TOE EVERYWHERE, ... 667 ISLE STAT II 3   20
  THEY PASSED A-TIPTOE EVERYWHERE, ... 667 ISLE STAT II 3 V 20
EVE'S
  FOR MOTHER EVE'S WINNING . . . . 654 ISLE STAT I 2   61
  ALL THINGS ARE QUIET IN THE EVE'S WIDE EYE. . . . . . 662 ISLE STAT II 2   6
EVE-SOOTHED
  EVE-SOOTHED IN SOME FAR LEAFY REST, ... 686 LIFE   10
EVIDENCE
  TO BE "SOME SORT OF EVIDENCE", ... 287 TO WEALTHY MAN   4
EVIL
  EQUAL TO GOOD OR EVIL CHANCE . . . .   24 OISIN 1   V 371
  WE GIVE THEM EVIL DREAMS. . . . .   88 STOLEN CHILD   V   34
  UNDER THE FRUIT OF EVIL AND OF GOOD! . . . . 137 TO SOME I TALK   9
  AND THOUGHT NOT OF EVIL CHANCE, ... 145 HOST OF AIR   30
  THERE IS ENOUGH EVIL IN THE CRYING OF WIND. . . . . . 155 REPROVE CURLEW   6
  AND BLOWING US EVIL AND GOOD . . . . 158 TO HIS HEART   V   4A
  HE THINKS OF THOSE WHO HAVE SPOKEN EVIL OF HIS BELOVED . 166 EVIL OF BELOV   T
  AEDH THINKS OF THOSE WHO HAVE SPOKEN EVIL OF HIS BELOVED 166 EVIL OF BELOV   V   T
  SAVE BY AN EVIL CHANCE. . . . . 178 FIDDLER DOONEY   14
  WHAT MAN YOU HAVE LOST, WHAT EVIL YOU HAVE FOUND." . . 280 TWO KINGS   86
  "ALTHOUGH THE THING THAT YOU HAVE HID WERE EVIL, . . . 281 TWO KINGS   103
  AND EVIL MUST IT BE, IF DONE 'TWERE WORSE . . . . . . 281 TWO KINGS   105
  EVIL OF THIS PLACE, ... 319 DOLLS   9
  AND CALLED THE PLEASURES EVIL . . . . 365 HER RACE   3
  KNOWING NOT EVIL AND GOOD! . . . . 382 VISION ROBART   12
  MAY WELL BE OF ALL EVIL CHANCES CHIEF. . . . . 405 FOR DAUGHTER   53
  OR WHAT WORSE EVIL COME-- . . . . 416 TOWER   188
  ALL BREAK AND VANISH, AND EVIL GATHERS HEAD! . . . . . 433 NINETEEN 19   117
  SPEAK NO EVIL OF THE SOUL, ... 573 LADYS 3RD SONG   3
  KNOW WORSE EVIL OF THE BODY! . . . . 573 LADYS 3RD SONG   6
  AND ALL SEEMS EVIL UNTIL I . . . . 632 MAN AND ECHO   17
  THAT CALLS. O EVIL STARRED! IT COMES ALONG . . . . . 653 ISLE STAT I 2   49
  A DEAL OF EVIL AND OF CHANGE HATH CROSSED . . . . . . 676 ISLE STAT II 3   273
  AND WOE-BEGONE. FOR THEM NO EVIL DAY! . . . . 677 ISLE STAT II 3   275
  THE PREACHER WATCHING FOR THE EVIL HOUR TO PASS, . . . 686 LIFE   3
  IN TRUTH, AN EVIL RACE. WHY STRIVE FOR HER, ... 696 MOSADA 2   9
  LIKE HAPPY THOUGHTS GROWN SAD IN EVIL DAYS. . . . . . 703 MOSADA 3   116
  MY LOVE HATH MANY AN EVIL MOOD, ... 723 GIRLS SONG A   5
  AND EVIL STILL IS ACTION'S CHILD. . . . . 728 PRIEST FAIRY   14
  THE PREACHER WATCHING FOR THE EVIL HOUR TO PASS, . . . 734 QUATRAIN APHOR V   3
  AND EVIL FORTUNE HAVE OVERTHROWN SAILED HITHER . . . . 757 SHADOW WATER A   196
EVIL-STARRED
  I, TOO, WILL FOLLOW FOR THIS EVIL-STARRED ONE'S SAKE . . 655 ISLE STAT I 2   84
EWES
  WHEN I HAVE SHUT THESE EWES AND THIS OLD RAM . . . . . 343 SHEP GOATHERD   113
EXACT
  BUT NOT THE EXACT LIKENESS, THE SIMPLICITY OF A CHILD, . . 354 HIS PHOENIX   28
EXACTING
  SUCH EXACTING BREATH, ... 517 HER ANXIETY   8
EXALT
  TO EXALT A LONELY MIND, ... 420 MY HOUSE   29
EXALTED
  THE MOST EXALTED LADY LOVED BY A MAN. . . . . 369 EGO DOMINUS   37

		PAGE	TITLE	LINE

EXAMPLE
  FOR AN EXAMPLE STILL? • • • • • • • • • • • • • •   365 HER RACE   12
  HOMER IS MY EXAMPLE AND HIS UNCHRISTENED HEART• • • • •   503 VACILLATION   87
EXCEL
  YOUTH CAN EXCEL THEM IN ACCOMPLISHMENT, • • • • • • • •   340 SHEP GOATHERD   47
EXCELLENCE
  BUT NOT THAT SELFSAME EXCELLENCE AGAIN• • • • • • • •   602 GALLERY REVIS   32
  BUT NOT THAT SELF—SAME EXCELLENCE AGAIN• • • • • • •   602 GALLERY REVIS V 32
EXCELLENT
  A SCENE WELL SET AND EXCELLENT COMPANY• • • • • • • •   489 COOLE PARK 29   16
EXCESS
  AND WHAT IF EXCESS OF LOVE • • • • • • • • • • • • •   394 EASTER 1916   72
  WHERE EVEN LONGING DROWNS UNDER ITS OWN EXCESS! • • • •   426 PHANTOM HATRED   22
EXCHANGE
  I CAN EXCHANGE OPINION WITH ANY NEIGHBOURING MIND, • • •   450 OWEN AHERNE   9
EXCITE
  DO MOST EXCITE MY SPLEEN • • • • • • • • • • • • • •   599 STONE CROSS   18
EXCITED
  OR WHEN I GROW EXCITED WITH WINE, • • • • • • • • • •   357 DEEP-SWORN VOW   5
  IMAGINING IN EXCITED REVERIE • • • • • • • • • • •   403 FOR DAUGHTER   13
  EXCITED, PASSIONATE, FANTASTICAL • • • • • • • • •   409 TOWER   5
EXCITING
  ALTHOUGH YOUR LAST EXCITING YEAR • • • • • • • • • •   791 REPRISALS   5
EXCREMENT
  THE PLACE OF EXCREMENT! • • • • • • • • • • • • •   513 JANE TALK BISH   16
EXECUTIONER
  SOLDIER, ASSASSIN, EXECUTIONER, • • • • • • • • •   482 BLOOD AND MOON   36
EXERCISE
  FOR AIR AND EXERCISE, • • • • • • • • • • • • • •   575 ACRE OF GRASS   3
  THERE'S BETTER EXERCISE • • • • • • • • • • • •   600 THOSE IMAGES   3
EXHAUST
  EXHAUST HIS GLORY AND HIS MIGHT! • • • • • • • • •   438 SONGS PLAY 2   14
EXILES
  AH, EXILES WANDERING OVER LANDS AND SEAS, • • • • •   129 BOOK STORIES   9
  AH, EXILES, WANDERING OVER MANY SEAS, • • • • • •   129 BOOK STORIES   V 9
  AH, EXILES, WANDERING OVER MANY LANDS, • • • • • •   130 BOOK STORIES   V 17
  AND CALL THOSE EXILES AS THEY WERE • • • • • • •   290 SEPTEMBER 1913   26
EXIST
  A MAN WHO DOES NOT EXIST, • • • • • • • • • • •   348 FISHERMAN   35
  SUCH DEVILISH THINGS EXIST, • • • • • • • • • •   436 FOR MY SON   11
  FEW DREAM THAT THEY EXIST, • • • • • • • • • •   436 FOR MY SON   V 11
EXISTENCE
  JOY AND LOVE ARE ONE EXISTENCE• • • • • • • •   647 ISLE STAT I 1   71
  LOVE AND SORROW, ONE EXISTENCE, • • • • • • •   647 ISLE STAT I 1   73
EXORBITANT
  THE EXORBITANT DREAMS OF BEGGARY, • • • • • • •   296 THREE BEGGARS   39
EXPECTATION
  NO EXPECTATION FAILS THERE, • • • • • • • • •   621 JOHN KINSELLA   29
EXPECTED
  THAT MORE EXPECTED THE IMPOSSIBLE-- • • • • • •   409 TOWER   7
EXPENSE
  HE'D GONE TO GREAT EXPENSE • • • • • • • • •   585 ORAHILLY   13
EXPLAINED
  THEREON EXPLAINED! "A COCKEREL • • • • • • •   387 SOLOMON WITCH V 9
EXPLORE
  YOU, SHOULD HAND EXPLORE A THIGH, • • • • • •   573 LADYS 3RD SONG   11
EXPOUND
  I HEARD HER VOICE, "TURN THAT I MAY EXPOUND • • • •   467 HARUN RASHID   132
EXPRESSION
  ARE BUT A NEW EXPRESSION OF HER BODY • • • • • •   469 HARUN RASHID   185
EXQUISITE
  A FRAGILE, EXQUISITE, PALE SHELL, • • • • • • •   784 WOMANS BEAUTY   16
EXTINGUISH
  EXTINGUISH THAT DELIGHT• • • • • • • • • • •   538 LAST CONFESS   24
EXTRAVAGANCE
  THE EXTRAVAGANCE OF SPRING! OR MOVE A HAND • • • •   466 HARUN RASHID   125
  THE EXTRAVAGANCE OF SPRING! OR CERTAIN TIMES • • • •   466 HARUN RASHID V 125
  AND CALL THOSE WORKS EXTRAVAGANCE OF BREATH • • • •   501 VACILLATION   32
EXTRAVAGANT
  HE WROTE OF ME IN THAT EXTRAVAGANT STYLE • • • •   373 PHASES OF MOON   26
EXTREME
  A MOUTHFUL HELD THE EXTREME OF LIFE AND DEATH• • • •   619 BRONZE HEAD   14
  A MOUTHFUL HOLD THE EXTREME OF LIFE AND DEATH• • • •   619 BRONZE HEAD   V 14
EXTREMITIES
  BETWEEN EXTREMITIES • • • • • • • • • • • •   499 VACILLATION   1
EXTREMITY
  AND KNEW THAT SWEET EXTREMITY OF PRIDE • • • • • •   471 ALL SOUL NIGHT   22
EXUDE
  BODIES OF HOLY MEN AND WOMEN EXUDE • • • • • • •   483 OIL AND BLOOD   2
EXULT
  BE SECRET AND EXULT, • • • • • • • • • • • •   291 TO A FRIEND   14
EXULTANT
  AND SWANS WITH THEIR EXULTANT THROATS! • • • • •   14 OISIN 1   192
  WARS SHADOWY, VAST, EXULTANT! FAERIES OF OLD • • • •   29 OISIN 2   9
  WARS SHADOWY, VAST, EXULTANT! FAIRY KINGS • • • •   29 OISIN 2   V 9
  BUT ONLY EXULTANT FACES• NIAMH STOOD • • • • •   38 OISIN 2   136
  AND ALL THE EXULTANT LABOURS OF THE STRONG• • • • •   42 OISIN 2   195
  INNUMERABLE, SINGING, EXULTANT! THE CLAY UNDERNEATH THEM   61 OISIN 3   203
      SHALL PANT,
  WHAT THE EXULTANT HEART CALLS GOOD • • • • • • •   288 TO WEALTHY MAN   33
  WHEN THAT EXULTANT ANTHONY • • • • • • • • •   401 DEMON BEAST   46

		PAGE	TITLE		LINE
EXULTANT (CONTINUED)					
A PASSION-DRIVEN EXULTANT MAN SINGS OUT	• • • • • • •	560	WHENCE COME		'5
EXULTATION					
THE EXULTATION OF THEIR STONE, THAT CRIED	• • • • • •	339	SHEP GOATHERD		25
WHERE IN WHITE EXULTATION	• • • • • • • • • • •	672	ISLE STAT II 3		164
EXULTING					
THERE DWELT A GAY, EXULTING, GENTLE RACE	• • • • • •	127	DREAM OF FAERY		20
EYE					
HAVE FACES ALIVE WITH SUCH BEAUTY BEEN KNOWN TO THE SALT EYE OF MAN.		50	OISIN 3		51
ARE FACES ALIVE WITH SUCH BEAUTY MADE KNOWN TO THE SALT EYE OF MAN.		50	OISIN 3	V	51
ARE FACES ALIVE WITH SUCH BEAUTY MADE KNOWN TO THE SOFT EYE OF MAN.		50	OISIN 3	V	51
HELPLESS, MEN LIFTING THE LIDS OF HIS WEARY AND DEATH-MAKING EYE.		53	OISIN 3		92
HELPLESS, MEN LIFTING THE LIDS OF HIS WEARY AND DEATH-POURING EYE.		53	OISIN 3	V	92
THE RAINS ARE FROM HIS DRIPPING WING, THE MOONBEAMS FROM HIS EYE.		76	INDIAN ON GOD		8
AND STILL, WITH PITYIN', SCORNIN' EYE,	• • • • • • •	96	MOLL MAGEE		39
IS BUT THE WINKING OF AN EYE!	• • • • • • • •	139	TO IRELAND		36
ALTHOUGH HE HAD A SQUIRREL'S EYE.	• • • • • • • •	190	BAILE AILLINN		30
OR, IT MAY BE, THE EYELIDS OF ONE EYE,	• • • • • •	195	BAILE AILLINN		151
THAT HAD BUT THE ONE EYE. CAN NO BEWITCHMENT	• • • • •	222	SHADOW WATER B		10
FOR THAT RED MOLL THAT HAD BUT THE ONE EYE.	• • • •	222	SHADOW WATER B	V	10
WITH AN INDIFFERENT EYE.	• • • • • • • • • • •	255	WOMAN HOMER		7
AND LOVE COMES IN AT THE EYE!	• • • • • • • • •	261	DRINKING SONG		2
TO BREED THE LIDLESS EYE THAT LOVES THE SUN?	• • • •	264	HOUSE SHAKEN		4
THE MAJESTY THAT SHUTS HIS BURNING EYE!	• • • • • •	265	THESE CLOUDS		2
THE MAJESTY THAT SHUTS HIS BURNING EYE.	• • • • • •	265	THESE CLOUDS		12
THEREON A YOUNG MAN MET HIS EYE,	• • • • • • •	274	GREY ROCK		85
AND STARED INTO THE SEA-GREEN EYE, AND SO	• • • • •	278	TWO KINGS		25
LOOK UP IN THE SUN'S EYE AND GIVE	• • • • • • •	288	TO WEALTHY MAN		32
THAT ON THE LONELY HEIGHT WHERE ALL ARE IN GOD'S EYE,	• •	291	PAUDEEN		6
WITH THE PRIDE OF HIS EYE?	• • • • • • • • • •	310	PEACOCK		3
FOR THE PRIDE OF HIS EYE.	• • • • • • • • • •	311	PEACOCK		11
NOW AS AT ALL TIMES I CAN SEE IN THE MIND'S EYE,	• • •	318	MAGI		1
WORE IT IN THE WORLD'S EYE	• • • • • • • • •	320	COAT	V	6
FOR ALL THINGS THE DELIGHTED EYE NOW SEES	• • • • • •	326	ROBERT GREGORY		49
TILL THE YELLOW EYE HAS GROWN MILD,	• • • • • • •	349	HAWK		3
THE EYE OF THE MIND NOR KEEP MY TONGUE FROM SPEECH."	• •	353	PEOPLE		34
THE YOUNG MEN EVERY NIGHT APPLAUD THEIR GABY'S LAUGHING EYE,		353	HIS PHOENIX		9
WHAT IF A LAUGHING EYE	• • • • • • • • •	367	HER CHRIS TREE		10
MORE PLAIN TO THE MIND'S EYE THAN ANY FACE	• • • • •	368	EGO DOMINUS		21
CAUGHT UP IN CONTEMPLATION, THE MIND'S EYE	• • • • •	375	PHASES OF MOON		79
HAS A LEARNING IN HIS EYE	• • • • • • • •	381	SONG OF FOOL		3
ON THE GREY ROCK OF CASHEL THE MIND'S EYE	• • • • •	382	VISION ROBART		1
ALTHOUGH I SAW IT ALL IN THE MIND'S EYE.	• • • • •	383	VISION ROBART		25
FOR WHAT BUT EYE AND EAR SILENCE THE MIND	• • • • •	384	VISION ROBART		41
IF I SHOULD RUB AN EYE,	• • • • • • • • •	384	VISION ROBART		52
THAT VIGOROUS THIGH, THAT DREAMING EYE?	• • • • • •	386	ROBARTES DANCE		23
FOR THOUGH LOVE HAS A SPIDER'S EYE	• • • • • • •	388	SOLOMON WITCH		19
A LOVER WITH A SPIDER'S EYE	• • • • • • • •	388	SOLOMON WITCH	V	19
BEAUTY TO MAKE A STRANGER'S EYE DISTRAUGHT,	• • • • •	403	FOR DAUGHTER		18
IMAGINATION, NOR AN EAR AND EYE	• • • • • • •	409	TOWER		6
UNTIL IMAGINATION, EAR AND EYE,	• • • • • • • •	409	TOWER		13
PLUNGE, LURED BY A SOFTENING EYE,	• • • • • • •	413	TOWER		110
WHEN THE SWAN MUST FIX HIS EYE	• • • • • • •	414	TOWER		140
OF EVERY BRILLIANT EYE	• • • • • • • • •	416	TOWER		190
MONSTROUS FAMILIAR IMAGES SWIM TO THE MIND'S EYE.	• • •	426	PHANTOM HATRED		8
AT THE DROOPING OF AN EYE,	• • • • • • • •	453	DEATH OF HARE		5
• • • NEVER TO HAVE LOOKED INTO THE EYE OF DAY!	• • •	459	FROM OEDIPUS		11
• • • AT ALL NOR LOOKED INTO THE EYE OF DAY.	• • •	459	FROM OEDIPUS	V	11
AND SO A HUNTER CARRIES IN THE EYE	• • • • • • •	463	HARUN RASHID		61
AND IF HER EYE SHOULD NOT GROW BRIGHT FOR MINE	• • •	464	HARUN RASHID		81
OR BRIGHTEN ONLY FOR SOME YOUNGER EYE,	• • • • • •	464	HARUN RASHID		82
SO STRAINS TO LOOK BEYOND OUR LIFE, AN EYE	• • • • •	465	HARUN RASHID		87
SO LONGS TO LOOK BEYOND OUR LIFE, AN EYE	• • • • •	465	HARUN RASHID	V	87
BUT THINK THAT HIS MIND'S EYE,	• • • • • • • •	471	ALL SOUL NIGHT		33
STOOD IN THE CIRCUIT OF A NEEDLE'S EYE,	• • • • •	483	VERONIC NAPKIN		6
THAT NEVER LOOKED OUT OF THE EYE OF A SAINT	• • • •	486	SEVEN SAGES		12
OR OUT OF DRUNKARD'S EYE. ALL'S WHIGGERY NOW,	• • •	486	SEVEN SAGES		13
OR DRUNKARD'S EYE. ALL'S WHIGGERY NOW,	• • • •	486	SEVEN SAGES	V	13
OR OUT OF A DRUNKARD'S EYE. ALL'S WHIGGERY NOW,	• • •	486	SEVEN SAGES	V	13
GLANCES OF HER WANDERING EYE	• • • • • • • •	487	CRAZED MOON		4
THE CORNERS OF THIS EYE	• • • • • • • • •	518	HIS CONFIDENCE		3
AND COCKED A MALICIOUS EYE,	• • • • • • • •	527	AM OF IRELAND		25
STANDS IN GOD'S UNCHANGING EYE	• • • • • • •	529	TOM LUNATIC		16
HALF TURNED AND FIXED A GLAZING EYE ON MINE,	• • • •	537	HER VISION		26
COME, FIX UPON ME THAT ACCUSING EYE.	• • • • •	542	PARN FUNERAL 1		24
ROLLING A BLIND PEARL EYE,	• • • • • • • •	552	SONGS REWRIT 2		2
A NEEDLE'S EYE	• • • • • • • • • •	562	NEEDLES EYE		T
CAME OUT OF A NEEDLE'S EYE!	• • • • • • • •	562	NEEDLES EYE		2
FROM NEEDLE'S EYE STILL GOAD IT ON.	• • • • • •	562	NEEDLES EYE		4
HUMAN, SUPERHUMAN, A BIRD'S ROUND EYE,	• • • • • •	618	BRONZE HEAD		2
HUMAN, SUPER-HUMAN, A BIRD'S ROUND EYE,	• • • • •	618	BRONZE HEAD	V	2
AS THOUGH A STERNER EYE LOOKED THROUGH HER EYE	• • •	619	BRONZE HEAD		23
AS THOUGH A STERNER EYE LOOKED THROUGH HER EYE	• • • •	619	BRONZE HEAD		23

252

		PAGE	TITLE	LINE

EYE   (CONTINUED)

PROCESSIONS THAT LACK HIGH STILTS HAVE NOTHING THAT CATCHES THE EYE.		622	HIGH TALK		1
DISTRUSTFUL OF THAT POPULAR EYE		624	APPARITIONS		5
WITH AN EYE LIKE A HAWK,		627	STATES HOLIDAY		32
WHERE EVERYTHING THAT MEETS THE EYE,		639	BEN BULBEN		56
CAST A COLD EYE		640	BEN BULBEN		92
ALL THINGS ARE QUIET IN THE EYE'S WIDE EYE.		662	ISLE STAT II 2		6
AND PART HIS FOAMING MOUTH WITH EAGER EYE--		688	TWO TITANS		46
ABOVE, THE WOODS WHERE WITH THE SOFT MILD EYE		710	FERENCZ RENYI		26
STAGGERING WITH LANGUID EYE.		717	FAIRY DOCTOR	V	16
AND HIS HAIR WAS AS DARK AS A PLOVER'S EYE.		729	PRIEST FAIRY		46
PAST THE CAMEL'S DREAMING EYE.		733	STREET DANCERS		43

EYEBALLS

THAT WITH DIM EYEBALLS STOOD ON EITHER SIDE.		34	OISIN 2		75
STOOD LONELY, WITH DIM EYEBALLS ON EACH SIDE,		34	OISIN 2	V	74
THEIR MOTIONLESS EYEBALLS OF SPIRITS		55	OISIN 3		121
THAT OTHER'S MOONLIT EYEBALLS NEVER MOVED,		383	VISION ROBART		33
SOMETHING MADE THESE EYEBALLS WEARY		529	TOM LUNATIC		11
DREAMER OF THE MIDDLE AGES. EMPTY EYEBALLS KNEW		610	STATUES		20
BENEATH THE FLAMING EYEBALLS OF THE NIGHT,		723	KANVA ON SELF		4

EYE-BALLS

| DREAMER OF THE MIDDLE-AGES. EMPTY EYE-BALLS KNEW | | 610 | STATUES | V | 20 |

EYED   SEE YELLOW-EYED ONE-EYED BLEAR-EYED GREY-EYED SOLEMN-EYED BLUE-EYED
         QUIET-EYED DEEP-EYED BRIGHT-EYED GRAVE-EYED RED-EYED WIDE-EYED
         OPEN-EYED DULL-EYED

| THE DRUID, GREY, WOOD NURTURED, QUIET EYED, | | 101 | ROSE UPON ROOD | V | 4 |
| CAER, HIS BLUE EYED DAUGHTER THAT I LOVE. | | 184 | QUEEN MAEVE | V | 96 |

EYELID

UNDER AN ALIEN EYELID, FOR IT WAS MY CRAFT		284	TWO KINGS	V	156
OR EYELID SHOT THE GLEAM		507	STREAM AND SUN		12
HER LIMBS ARE DELICATE AS AN EYELID,		612	NEWS ORACLE		27

EYELIDS

AH, TOUCH THEIR BLUE-VEINED EYELIDS IF THEY SLEEP,		33	OISIN 2		61
IF THEY STILL SLUMBER, TOUCH THEIR EYELIDS BLUE,		33	OISIN 2	V	61
AH, TOUCH THEIR BLUE VEINED EYELIDS IF THEY SLEEP,		33	OISIN 2	V	61
HALF WAKENING, WE LIFTED OUR EYELIDS,		54	OISIN 3		100
HALF-WAKENING, WE LIFTED OUR EYELIDS,		54	OISIN 3	V	100
HIS EYELIDS DROOP, HIS HEAD FALLS LOW,		98	FOXHUNTER		13
HIS EYELIDS CLOSE, HIS HEAD DROOPS LOW,		98	FOXHUNTER	V	13
AND LIFT YOUR TENDER EYELIDS, MAID,		125	GOES FERGUS		5
WITH HER CLOUD-PALE EYELIDS FALLING ON DREAM-DIMMED EYES!		163	VALLEY LOVERS		4
WITH HER CLOUD-PALE EYELIDS HALF COVERING HER DIM EYES!		163	VALLEY LOVERS	V	4
O CLOUD-PALE EYELIDS, DREAM-DIMMED EYES,		164	PERFECT BEAUTY		1
HALF CLOSE YOUR EYELIDS, LOOSEN YOUR HAIR,		166	EVIL OF BELOV		1
AMONG PALE EYELIDS, HEAVY WITH THE SLEEP		169	SECRET ROSE		6
OR, IT MAY BE, THE EYELIDS OF ONE EYE,		195	BAILE AILLINN		151
BEFORE THEIR SLEEPY EYELIDS RAN		272	GREY ROCK		30
UNDER THE EYELIDS OF ANOTHER, FOR IT WAS MY CRAFT		284	TWO KINGS		156
PACING WITH HALF-CLOSED EYELIDS IN A SUNNY SPOT		366	HER COURAGE		7
THE QUIVERING HALF-CLOSED EYELIDS, THE RAGS OF CLOUD OR LACE,		427	PHANTOM HATRED		26
EYES UNDER EYELIDS DID SO GLEAM!		514	JANE GROWN OLD		6
LOOK ON ME ONCE. WHY SINK YOUR EYELIDS THUS?		703	MOSADA 3		107
LOOK ON ME ONCE. WHY SINK YOUR EYELIDS SO?		703	MOSADA 3	V	107
AMONG THE WINDS, LOOKS UNDER YOUR PALE EYELIDS.		757	SHADOW WATER A		211
HER EYELIDS TREMBLE AND THE WHITE FOAM FADES!		761	SHADOW WATER A		264
AND UNDER LOVERS' EYELIDS. BEND YOUR HEAD		762	SHADOW WATER A		286

EYE'S

| NOTHING BUT GRIP OF CLAW, AND THE EYE'S COMPLACENCY, | | 427 | PHANTOM HATRED | | 31 |

EYES

HER EYES WERE SOFT AS DEWDROPS HANGING		3	OISIN 1	V	7HH
AND WITH QUENCHLESS EYES AND FLUTTERING HAIR		12	OISIN 1	V	144
AND SHOWED THEIR EYES WITH TEARDROPS DIM,		18	OISIN 1		256
FROM DEWY EYES "UPON THE DEAD"		21	OISIN 1		310
IN OUR RAISED EYES THERE FLASHED A GLOW		22	OISIN 1		327
I HEARD ONE SAY, "HIS EYES GROW DIM		25	OISIN 1		380
I HEARD ONE SAY, "WITHIN HIS EYES		25	OISIN 1	V	380
AND GAZES AROUND HER WITH EYES OF BRIGHTNESS!		27	OISIN 1		413
BUT THE LOVE-DEW DIMS OUR EYES TILL THE DAY		28	OISIN 1		424
AND GAZES AROUND HER WITH EYES OF BRIGHTNESS!		28	OISIN 1	V	421
AND KISSED MY EYES, AND, SWAYING HER BRIGHT HEAD		29	OISIN 2		6
AND HOW THOSE LOVERS NEVER TURN THEIR EYES		29	OISIN 2		11
AND HAD DISPORTED IN THE EYES STILL JET		31	OISIN 2	V	39
A LADY WITH SOFT EYES LIKE FUNERAL TAPERS,		33	OISIN 2		69
DOWN ON US WITH HER EYES LIKE FUNERAL TAPERS.		33	OISIN 2	V	69
A MAIDEN WITH SOFT EYES LIKE FUNERAL TAPERS,		33	OISIN 2	V	69
AND THROUGH THEIR EYES NO LIGHT OF MOON OR DAY		34	OISIN 2	V	77
GOES DROPPING FROM HIS EYES A LANGUID LIGHT,		34	OISIN 2	V	81A
A DEMON'S LEISURE! EYES, FIRST WHITE, NOW BURNED		40	OISIN 2		168
A DEMON'S LEISURE. EYES FIRST WHITE AS SNOW,		40	OISIN 2	V	168
FILLING THE FIBROUS DIMNESS WITH LONG GENERATIONS OF EYES.		49	OISIN 3		40
SIDLED THEIR BODIES AGAINST HIM, FILLING THE SHADE WITH THEIR EYES.		50	OISIN 3		48
WATCHED ME WITH MOURNFUL WONDER OUT OF THE WELLS OF HIS EYES.		51	OISIN 3		60
HALF OPEN HIS EYES WERE, AND HELD ME,		51	OISIN 3		65
AND BECAUSE I WENT BY THEM SO HUGH AND SO SPEEDY WITH EYES SO BRIGHT,		59	OISIN 3		169
AND IN FOLDS ROUND HIS EYES AND HIS MOUTH,		59	OISIN 3		174
. . . AND THEIR EYES THAT GLIMMER LIKE SILK.		59	OISIN 3		176

PAGE   TITLE   LINE

EYES   (CONTINUED)
AND BEFORE I WENT BY THEM SO HUGE AND SO SPEEDY WITH EYES   59 OISIN 3   V 169
    SO BRIGHT,
. . . AND THEIR YOUTH, AND THEIR EYES SOFT AS SILK . . .   59 OISIN 3   V 176
SORRY PLACE, WHERE FOR SWING OF THE WAR-AXE IN MY DIM EYES   61 OISIN 3   194

. . . DEEP HORROR OF EYES AND OF WINGS, ...   62 OISIN 3   205
FOR LONELY TO MOVE 'MONG THE SOFT EYES . . . . . .   63 OISIN 3   V 222
YON TALL ONE EYES MY SUPPER! CHASE HIM AWAY, ...   72 ANASHU VIJAYA   34
YON TALL ONE EYES MY SUPPER! SWIFTLY CHASE HIM . . . .   72 ANASHU VIJAYA   V 34
THEIR FACES ARE ALL WORN, AND IN THEIR EYES . . . . .   73 ANASHU VIJAYA   48
A LITTLE WAY WITHIN THE GLOOM A ROEBUCK RAISED HIS EYES   76 INDIAN ON GOD   13
"YOUR EYES THAT ONCE WERE NEVER WEARY OF MINE . . . .   79 EPHEMERA   1
GATHERED IN SILENCE, DEWY AS HER EYES, ...   80 EPHEMERA   19
GLIMMERING IN HER DROOPED EYES, SAW HER LIPS MOVE . . .   81 EPHEMERA   V 24D
AROUND ME SHONE KEEN EYES OF MEN! . . . .   83 MAD KING GOLL   30
AND SHONE AROUND THE EYES OF MEN! . . . .   83 MAD KING GOLL   V 30
WITH EYES OF SADNESS CAME TO HEAR, ...   85 MAD KING GOLL   V 62
WITH EYES OF SADNESS ROSE TO HEAR, ...   85 MAD KING GOLL   V 62
HIS OLD EYES CLOUD WITH DREAMS! . . . .   98 FOXHUNTER   14
FIRE IS IN THE OLD MAN'S EYES, ...   98 FOXHUNTER   29
A FIRE IS IN THE OLD MAN'S EYES, ...   98 FOXHUNTER   V 29
STARED ON THE MOURNFUL WONDER OF HIS EYES, ...   108 CUCHULAIN SEA   41
AND GAZED UPON THE WISDOM OF HIS EYES, ...   108 CUCHULAIN SEA   V 41
UPON THE MOURNFUL WONDER OF HIS EYES, ...   108 CUCHULAIN SEA   V 42
YOUR EYES HAD ONCE, AND OF THEIR SHADOWS DEEP! . . . .   121 YOU ARE OLD   4
THINE EYES GROW FULL OF TENDER CARE! . . . .   135 TWO TREES   19
THY TENDER EYES GROW ALL UNKIND! . . . .   136 TWO TREES   39
OUR BREASTS ARE HEAVING, OUR EYES ARE AGLEAM, ...   140 HOSTING SIDHE   8
FOR BREASTS ARE HEAVING AND EYES A-GLEAM! . . . . . .   140 HOSTING SIDHE   V 7
OUR BREASTS ARE HEAVING, OUR EYES ARE A-GLEAM, ...   140 HOSTING SIDHE   V 8
AND CLAP THEIR HANDS TOGETHER, AND HALF CLOSE THEIR EYES,   146 UNAPPEAS HOST   2
O HIDING HAIR AND DEWY EYES, ...   152 HEART OF WOMAN   9
THEIR HOOFS HEAVY WITH TUMULT, THEIR EYES GLIMMERING WHITE!   154 BELOVED PEACE   2
BELOVED, LET YOUR EYES HALF CLOSE, AND YOUR HEART BEAT . .   154 BELOVED PEACE   9
PASSION-DIMMED EYES AND LONG HEAVY HAIR . . . .   155 REPROVE CURLEW   4
THAT ONLY GOD'S EYES DID NOT CLOSE! . . . .   156 FORGOT BEAUTY   14
BEFORE THEY DROWNED THEIR LOVERS' EYES . . . .   156 FORGOT BEAUTY   V 10A
THAT ONLY THE GODS' EYES DID NOT CLOSE! . . . .   156 FORGOT BEAUTY   V 14
SUDDENLY HURTLE BEFORE MY DREAM-AWAKENED EYES, ...   161 BLACK PIG   2
WITH HER CLOUD-PALE EYELIDS FALLING ON DREAM-DIMMED EYES!   163 VALLEY LOVERS   4
THEIR HEADS ON YOUR KNEES, AND DROWN THEIR EYES WITH YOUR   163 VALLEY LOVERS   6
    HAIR,
WITH HER CLOUD-PALE EYELIDS HALF COVERING HER DIM EYES!   163 VALLEY LOVERS   V 4
O CLOUD-PALE EYELIDS, DREAM-DIMMED EYES, ...   164 PERFECT BEAUTY   1
WITH A BLINK IN HIS EYES, AT THE CAVE-MOUTH, ...   166 BLESSED   3
WITH A BLINK IN HIS EYES AT THE CAVE MOUTH, ...   166 BLESSED   V 3
WITH THE SECRETS OF GOD IN HIS EYES, ...   167 BLESSED   12
WITH BLINKING EYES, AT THE CAVE'S EDGE, ...   167 BLESSED   V 4C
"MY EYES ARE BLINKING," DATHI SAID, ...   168 BLESSED   25
OF THE CROWNED MAGI! AND THE KING WHOSE EYES . . . . .   169 SECRET ROSE   9
OF THE CROWNED MAGI! AND THE KINGS WHOSE EYES . . . .   169 SECRET ROSE   V 9
FOR ALL EYES BUT THESE EYES . . . .   173 PLEADS FRIEND   8
FOR ALL EYES BUT THESE EYES. . . . .   173 PLEADS FRIEND   8
AND SHE'D HAD LUCKY EYES AND A HIGH HEART, ...   181 QUEEN MAEVE   27
WITH STILL AND STONY LIMBS AND OPEN EYES. . . . . .   182 QUEEN MAEVE   46
TO MANY THOUSAND EYES, AND TO HER OWN . . . . . .   182 QUEEN MAEVE   65
BODIES OF SHADOW AND BLIND EYES LIKE PEARLS, ...   185 QUEEN MAEVE   116
BEFORE HIS EYES, HE HAS TEARS FOR NONE, ...   192 BAILE AILLINN   82
AND THEY HAVE NEWS OF DEIRDRE'S EYES, ...   193 BAILE AILLINN   97
AND LITTLE SHADOWS COME ABOUT HER EYES! . . . . . .   199 FOLLY COMFORT   3
AND THERE ARE LITTLE CREASES ABOUT HER EYES! . . . .   199 FOLLY COMFORT   V 3
BUT WE HAVE HIDDEN IN OUR HEARTS THE FLAME OUT OF THE EYES   207 HANRAHANS SONG   4
BUT OUR HEARTS ARE LIGHTED FROM THE FLAME IN THE EYES . .   207 HANRAHANS SONG   V 9
QUEENS, THEIR EYES BLUE LIKE THE ICE, ...   214 HAPPY TOWNLAND   11
DIM PAIRC-NA-TARAV, WHERE ENCHANTED EYES . . . . . .   217 WOODS OF COOLE   11
I HAD NOT EYES LIKE THOSE ENCHANTED EYES, ...   218 WOODS OF COOLE   17
I HAD NOT EYES LIKE THOSE ENCHANTED EYES, ...   218 WOODS OF COOLE   17
STRANGE CREATURES FLUTTER UP BEFORE ONE'S EYES, ...   222 SHADOW WATER B   18
AND HAVING SUCH WIDE-OPEN, SHINING EYES. . . . . . .   231 SHADOW WATER B   200
WHY ARE YOU STANDING WITH YOUR EYES UPON ME? . . . . .   234 SHADOW WATER B   276
IS IT THAT THOUGH YOUR EYES ARE FULL OF LOVE . . . . .   245 SHADOW WATER B   473
I WEEP BECAUSE I'VE NOTHING FOR YOUR EYES . . . . . .   246 SHADOW WATER B   496
O WHY DO YOU NOT LIFT YOUR EYES TO MINE? . . . . . .   246 SHADOW WATER B   498
IVORY IMAGES WITH AMETHYST EYES. . . . .   248 SHADOW WATER B   534
DRAGONS WITH EYES OF RUBY. THE WHOLE SHIP . . . . .   248 SHADOW WATER B   535
THERE'S SOMEBODY I'D GIVE THE AMETHYST EYES TO. . . . .   248 SHADOW WATER B   538
OR CALLED BEFORE HIS EYES. O CARRY ME . . . .   249 SHADOW WATER B   568
BUT I WILL COVER UP YOUR EYES AND EARS, ...   250 SHADOW WATER B   574
WHEN, THE EARS BEING DEAFENED, THE SIGHT OF THE EYES BLIND   257 RECONCILIATION   3
WITH EMERALD EYES." . . . .   263 MASK   2
IMAGINATIONS OF THEIR EYES, ...   272 GREY ROCK   28
THOSE WINE-DRENCHED EYES, AND CURSE OUR LUCK . . . . .   272 GREY ROCK   39
AND THOSE FIERCE EYES, AND CURSE OUR LUCK . . . . .   272 GREY ROCK   V 39
AND THESE IMMORTAL EYES SHED TEARS-- . . . .   275 GREY ROCK   100
WHITER THAN CURDS, ITS EYES THE TINT OF THE SEA. . . .   277 TWO KINGS   7
AND STARED INTO THE SEA-GREEN EYES, AND SO . . . . .   278 TWO KINGS   V 25
HER EYES WERE COLD AND STEADY, HER LIPS TIGHT. . . . .   279 TWO KINGS   64
GAZING UPON HER WITH BEWILDERED EYES! . . . . . .   280 TWO KINGS   V 84
WHO HAD UNNATURAL MAJESTY, AND EYES . . . .   283 TWO KINGS   149
LIKE THE EYES OF SOME GREAT KITE SCOURING THE WOODS,   283 TWO KINGS   150

EYES   (CONTINUED)

	PAGE	TITLE		LINE
PUSH OUT HIS VIGOROUS LIMBS AND RUB HIS EYES,	284	TWO KINGS		162
CROW UPON TARA." SHE HAD FIXED HER EYES	286	TWO KINGS	V	211
NOR IN HIS NEIGHBOURS' EYES?	291	TO A FRIEND		8
NONE CLOSED HIS BLOOD-SHOT EYES BUT SOUGHT	296	THREE BEGGARS		44
THEY CLOSED THEIR BLOOD-SHOT EYES FOR NAUGHT.	296	THREE BEGGARS	V	44
WITH BLOOD-SHOT EYES UPON HIM STARED.	297	THREE BEGGARS		58
BEFORE HIS EYES, WHERE STONES HAD BEEN,	302	HOUR DAWN		20
ALL WISDOM SHUT INTO HIS ONYX EYES,	311	MOUNTAIN TOMB		11
ALL WISDOM SHUT INTO ITS ONYX EYES.	311	MOUNTAIN TOMB	V	11
KIND EYES SHOULD BE MORE LEARN'D?	312	TWO YEAR LATER		2
TILL PRIDE HAD MADE HER EYES GROW BRIGHT,	314	MEMORY YOUTH		10
AND EVEN OLD MEN'S EYES GREW DIM, THIS HAND ALONE,	314	FALLEN MAJESTY		2
AND ALL THEIR EYES STILL FIXED, HOPING TO FIND ONCE MORE,	318	MAGI		6
WORE IT IN THE WORLD'S EYES	320	COAT		6
DELIGHT MEN'S EYES WHEN I AWAKE SOME DAY	323	SWANS AT COOLE		29
HAD SHUT THEIR EYES; AND WHERE WAS IT	326	ROBERT GREGORY		62
PLEASED TO HAVE FILLED THE EYES	329	MEN IMPROVE		8
AND KISSED HER ARAB EYES,	333	SOLOMON SHEBA		18
AND GLITTERED IN HER EYES.	336	YOUNG GIRL		11
HAD SCARCELY ACCUSTOMED OUR EYES	341	SHEP GOATHERD		69
WHEN HE VANISHED FROM EARS AND EYES.	341	SHEP GOATHERD		72
WHEN IT HAS VANISHED FROM OUR NATURAL EYES;	342	SHEP GOATHERD		81
THE ROUND GREEN EYES AND THE LONG WAVERING BODIES	343	DEJECTION		2
TO CALL UP TO THE EYES	347	FISHERMAN		7
AND WITH THE FERVOUR OF MY YOUTHFUL EYES,	356	BROKEN DREAMS		25
AND WHEN SHE MEETS OUR GAZE HER EYES ARE LAUGHTER-LIT,	362	HER COURTESY		5
AND WHEN SHE MEETS OUR GAZE HER EYES ARE LAUGHTER LIT	362	HER COURTESY	V	5
MAY HANDLE NOTHING AND SET EYES ON NOTHING	371	ON GOING HOUSE		6
IT MUST BE THAT THE TERROR IN THEIR EYES	375	PHASES OF MOON		72
OF LOVELY, SATISFIED, INDIFFERENT EYES.	375	PHASES OF MOON		83
HIS CHANGING EYES.	379	CAT AND MOON		28
UNDER BLANK EYES AND FINGERS NEVER STILL	382	VISION ROBART		5
ONE LASHED HER TAIL; HER EYES LIT BY THE MOON	383	VISION ROBART		29
SHE WOULD HAVE TIME TO TURN HER EYES,	385	ROBARTES DANCE		10
WHY HAVE YOU LAID YOUR HANDS UPON MY EYES?	389	IMAGE PAST		15
MY EYES SHOULD NEVER REST?	389	IMAGE PAST		18
EVEN TO EYES THAT BEAUTY HAD DRIVEN MAD,	390	IMAGE PAST		34
THE GLITTERING EYES IN A DEATH'S HEAD	400	DEMON BEAST		9
FROM A GLAD KINDNESS CANNOT TAKE HIS EYES.	404	FOR DAUGHTER		40
BUT I HAVE FOUND AN ANSWER IN THOSE EYES	413	TOWER		101
THEIR LEGS LONG, DELICATE AND SLENDER, AQUAMARINE THEIR EYES,	426	PHANTOM HATRED		17
THE LADIES CLOSE THEIR MUSING EYES. NO PROPHECIES,	426	PHANTOM HATRED		19
HAVE CLOSED THE LADIES' EYES, THEIR MINDS ARE BUT A POOL	426	PHANTOM HATRED		21
THE CLOUD-PALE UNICORNS, THE EYES OF AQUAMARINE,	427	PHANTOM HATRED		25
OR EYES THAT RAGE HAS BRIGHTENED, ARMS IT HAS MADE LEAN,	427	PHANTOM HATRED		27
THE CLOUD PALE UNICORNS, THE EYES OF AQUAMARINE,	427	PHANTOM HATRED	V	25
OF EYES THAT RAGE HAS BRIGHTENED, ARMS IT HAS MADE LEAN,	427	PHANTOM HATRED	V	27
THEY FIXED OLD ACHING EYES,	432	NINETEEN 19		100
THERE LURCHES PAST, HIS GREAT EYES WITHOUT THOUGHT	433	NINETEEN 19		126
UNWEARIED EYES UPON THOSE HORRIBLE GREEN BIRDS.	442	BLACK CENTAUR		16
IN THE BEST MODERN WAY--THE CHILDREN'S EYES	443	SCHOOL CHILDR		6
WE SHOULD BE HIDDEN FROM THEIR EYES;	454	HIS MEMORIES		1
SHE ROSE, AND WITH HER EYES SHUT FAST IN SLEEP	468	HARUN RASHID		152
THE MIRROR OF MALICIOUS EYES	479	SELF AND SOUL		52
CASTS UPON HIS EYES UNTIL AT LAST	479	SELF AND SOUL		53
AND DEDICATE--EYES BENT UPON THE GROUND,	489	COOLE PARK 29		29
THAT SHONE BEFORE THESE EYES	504	QUARREL IN AGE		15
BEFORE THEIR EYES A HOUSE	512	JANE ON GOD		13
EYES UNDER EYELIDS DID SO GLEAM;	514	JANE GROWN OLD		6
"UPLIFT THOSE EYES AND THROW	516	MANS SONG		7
AND EYES THAT HAD SO KEEN A SIGHT?	529	TOM LUNATIC		4
SALT BLOOD BLOCKS HIS EYES.	530	DELPHIC ORACLE		5
COLD AS THE MARCH WIND HIS EYES.	531	FATHER CHILD		8
AND THE EYES MORE BRIGHT	531	BEFORE WORLD		2
WHY THOSE QUESTIONING EYES	533	FIRST CONFESS		15
WHILE NIGHT SHUTS THE EYES	535	PARTING		2
HURRY INTO EACH OTHER'S ARMS; THESE EYES,	555	RIBH AT TOMB		22
THEIR EYES MID MANY WRINKLES, THEIR EYES,	567	LAPIS LAZULI		55
THEIR EYES MID MANY WRINKLES, THEIR EYES,	567	LAPIS LAZULI		55
THEIR ANCIENT, GLITTERING EYES, ARE GAY.	567	LAPIS LAZULI		56
THOSE HANDS TO CLOSE THESE EYES,	587	OLD WICKED MAN		6
CAN NEVER CLOSE THOSE EYES."	588	OLD WICKED MAN		26
MY HEART RECOVERING WITH COVERED EYES;	602	GALLERY REVIS		18
EYES SPIRITUALISED BY DEATH CAN JUDGE,	604	YOU CONTENT		7
HIS EYES FIXED UPON NOTHING,	617	LONG-LEG FLY		7
EYES STARED OUT OF THE BRANCHES AND WERE GONE.	634	CUCHULAIN COMF		3
"WE THREAD THE NEEDLES' EYES, AND ALL WE DO	634	CUCHULAIN COMF		16
SOMETHING DROPS FROM EYES LONG BLIND,	638	BEN BULBEN		29
'TIS MORN; LIKE OLD MEN'S EYES THE STARS ARE PALE,	645	ISLE STAT I 1		4
AND THINE EYES MORE BRIGHT THAN FAERY'S,	647	ISLE STAT I 1		53
AND TROUBLED EYES CAME MORNING'S FIRST-BORN GLOW;	648	ISLE STAT I 1		103
NASCHINA, WHEREFORE ARE YOUR EYES SO BRIGHT	650	ISLE STAT I 1		141
ACORNS GREEN, WITH EYES AWAKE.	655	ISLE STAT I 3		5
BUT WIDE AWAKE HIS TWO EYES WERE.	655	ISLE STAT I 3		7
OR HER EVER BURNING EYES;	658	ISLE STAT I 3		85
AND LET THEM TELL SAD HISTORIES, TILL THEIR EYES	663	ISLE STAT II 2		32
AND PENETRATION OF THEIR EYES. WHERE YONDER BLOTCH	664	ISLE STAT II 2		47
AND IN HER EYES A LIGHTLESS STARE,	668	ISLE STAT II 3		60
YOUR EYES ARE ALL A-FLASH. SHE IS NOT HERE.	669	ISLE STAT II 3		68

255

EYES (CONTINUED)
   YOUR EYES ARE ALL AFLASH. SHE IS NOT HERE.   669 ISLE STAT II 3 V 68
   I COULD GAZE, GAZE UPON THINE EYES OF GREY;   671 ISLE STAT II 3 V 147
   BUT ART THOU HAPPY? THOSE GREY EYES OF THINE.   672 ISLE STAT II 3   151
   HAVE THEY NE'ER SEEN THE EYES OF LYNX OR KINE, 672 ISLE STAT II 3   152
   AS LIGHT OF TRIUMPH IN THY GOBLIN EYES——   674 ISLE STAT II 3   199
   WHOSE INSOLENT EYES UNUSED TO TEARS WOULD WEEP. 678 ISLE STAT II 3   302
   BEFORE THE WIND. SAW YOU HIS EYES A-GLITTER?   683 SEEKER   35
   SHINE DULL UNMOVING EYES. WHAT THING ART THOU? 685 SEEKER   74
   AND WHEREFORE, THEN, SHOULD THY GREY EYES   686 LIFE   7
   AH, LET US KISS EACH OTHER'S EYES,   686 LIFE   15
   TILL THEIR FIERCE MISERIES WITHIN HIS EYES   687 TWO TITANS   26
   AND IN THE SIBYL'S EYES A LANGUID FLAME   688 TWO TITANS   41
   RE-SHINING IN HIS EYES. SO EVER MOVES   689 NETTLESHIP   12
   TO SAINTED EBREMAR'S SAD EYES. I THINK   696 MOSADA 2   15
   AND YON FEW STARS GROWN DIM, LIKE EYES OF LOVERS 700 MOSADA 3   33
   THE FLAME THAT SHONE WITHIN HIS EYES BUT NOW 704 MOSADA 3   128
   AH! WOE FOR YOUR EYES AND THEIR BRIGHTNESS—— 708 FAIRY PEDANT   35
   A PEASANT PALE AND PRETTY, HER EYES FOR FEAR, 713 FERENCZ RENYI   81
   A PEASANT YOUNG AND FAIR, HER EYES FOR FEAR 713 FERENCZ RENYI V 81
   A PEASANT, PALE AND PRETTY, HER EYES FROM FEAR, 713 FERENCZ RENYI V 81
   IN THE LONG GRASS--FOUR EYES DROOP LOW--A SEAT 716 DWELT SYCAMORE 11
   AND FULL HIS EYES OF FAIRY CHEER.   716 FAIRY DOCTOR   12
   "WATCHER, WHEREFORE HAVE YE CALLED US?" EYES GO AFTER 718 PHANTOM SHIP   10
     HIS LEAN HAND,
   CHECK. AH! HOW BRIGHT YOUR EYES. HOW SWIFT YOUR MOVES. 722 WITCH VIVIEN   61
   NO TENDER WISDOM FLOODS THE EYES   723 GIRLS SONG A   9
   HE BLINKED AND BLINKED HIS EYES   740 EARL PAUL   22
   AND GAZE ON ONE ANOTHER THROUGH OUR EYES,   749 SHADOW WATER A 58
   A TRADING GALLEY IN HER HELMSMAN'S EYES.   751 SHADOW WATER A 95
   I HAVE TURNED HOMEWARDS. IN THE EYES OF THE GODS, 757 SHADOW WATER A 202
   AGAINST MY FACE AND EYES. MINE TOO ARE BEATEN. 759 SHADOW WATER A V 233
   MY EYES ARE TROUBLED BY THE SILVER ARROWS; 761 SHADOW WATER A 269
   I KNOW YOU NOW, BESEECHING HANDS AND EYES. 763 SHADOW WATER A 312
   HIS WELL-BELOVED THROUGH A MORTAL'S EYES; 763 SHADOW WATER A 322
   IS LAUGHING THROUGH A MORTAL'S EYES. O LOOK! 763 SHADOW WATER A 324
   BESEECHING HANDS AND MORE BESEECHING EYES? 763 SHADOW WATER A V 312
   I THINK THAT THERE IS LOVE IN AIBRIC'S EYES. 768 SHADOW WATER A 407
   I KNOW HE WILL OBEY YOU; AND IF YOUR EYES 768 SHADOW WATER A 408
   SHOULD LOOK UPON HIS EYES WITH LOVE, IN THE END 768 SHADOW WATER A 409
   PITY THESE WEEPING EYES! I WILL FOLLOW YOU. 768 SHADOW WATER A 420
   SHOULD LOOK UPON HIS EYES WITH LOVE UNTO THE END 768 SHADOW WATER A V 409
   THAT HAVE ONE ANOTHER'S EYES?   773 SONG DEIRDRE 1 24
EYES'
   I COULD GAZE, GAZE UPON THINE EYES' CLEAR GREY; 671 ISLE STAT II 3   147
EYESIGHT
   HIDDEN FROM EYESIGHT TO THE UNNOTICED END.   472 ALL SOUL NIGHT 50
EYNE
   SLEEPILY CLOSE HER ROUND BRIGHT EYNE;   646 ISLE STAT I 1   35
EZEKIEL'S
   WITH OLD EZEKIEL'S CHERUBIM   336 YOUNG BEAUTY   11
   EZEKIEL'S COAL, WHAT MORE CAN MAN DESIRE?   502 VACILLATION   V 74
FABLE
   AS THE FOX IN THE OLD FABLE DESTROYED THE SPARTAN BOY'S, 580 CURSE CROMWELL 18
FABRIC
   DID ALL THE FABRIC FADE;   516 MANS SONG   10
FABULOUS
   IF SOMETHING THAT'S MOST FABULOUS WERE TRUE—— 245 SHADOW WATER B 489
   A FIGURE THAT HAS GROWN SO FABULOUS   412 TOWER   77
   OR THAT OF THE FABULOUS HORN,   414 TOWER   136
   OUT OF THE FABULOUS DARKNESS CALLED.   437 SONGS PLAY 1   16
   A FABULOUS, FORMLESS DARKNESS IN;   438 SONGS PLAY 2   5
   THAT THEY HAD BROUGHT NO FABULOUS SYMBOL THERE 537 HER VISION   31
FACE
   A SORROW WRAPPED EACH MERRY FACE,   17 OISIN 1   235
   AND FACE THAT SEEMED WROUGHT OUT OF MOONLIT VAPOURS, 33 OISIN 2   70
   HER FACE SEEMED FASHIONED ALL OF MOONLIT VAPOURS, 33 OISIN 2   V   70
   AND AT HIS CRY THERE CAME NO MILK-PALE FACE   38 OISIN 2   134
   WHERE SHADOWY FACE FLOWED INTO SHADOWY FACE,   39 OISIN 2   145
   WHERE SHADOWY FACE FLOWED INTO SHADOWY FACE,   39 OISIN 2   145
   LIFTED THE DOME, WHERE FACE IN CARVEN FACE   39 OISIN 2   145
   LIFTED THE DOME, WHERE FACE IN CARVEN FACE   39 OISIN 2   V 145
   AND SUNKEN SHAPE, AGAINST MY FACE AND BREAST,   40 OISIN 2   179
   AND DRIPPING AND SUNKEN SHAPE, TO FACE AND BREAST, 40 OISIN 2   V 179
   CAME CAR-BORNE BALOR, AS OLD AS A FOREST, HIS VAST FACE 53 OISIN 3   V   91
     SUNK
   . . . THE FLESH OF HIS FACE AS DRIED GRASS,   59 OISIN 3   173
   AND WRAPPING MY FACE IN MY HAIR,   59 OISIN 3   177
   WATCHING THE BLESSED ONES MOVE FAR OFF, AND THE SMILE ON 61 OISIN 3   199
     GOD'S FACE,
   HOUNDS ARE GAZING ON HIS FACE,   99 FOXHUNTER   39
   THE HOUNDS ARE GAZING ON HIS FACE,   99 FOXHUNTER   V 39
   AND HOUNDS ARE GAZING ON HIS FACE,   99 FOXHUNTER   V 39
   THAT SWINEHERD STARED UPON HER FACE AND SAID, 106 CUCHULAIN SEA   9
   "YOU DARE ME TO MY FACE," AND THEREUPON   106 CUCHULAIN SEA 17
   THAT YOU HAVE COME AND DARED ME TO MY FACE?" 109 CUCHULAIN SEA 61
   LIVES ON THIS LONELY FACE.   112 ROSE OF WORLD   10
   MORE FLEETING THAN THE SEA'S FOAM-FICKLE FACE, 112 ROSE OF WORLD V 8
   MORE FLEETING THAN THE SEA'S FOAM FICKLE FACE, 112 ROSE OF WORLD V 8
   AND LOVED THE SORROWS OF YOUR CHANGING FACE; 121 YOU ARE OLD   8
   AND HID HIS FACE AMID A CROWD OF STARS.   121 YOU ARE OLD   12

FACE   (CONTINUED)
    AND THEY HAD NAILED THE BOARDS ABOVE HER FACE,   • • •   123 DREAM OF DEATH   3
    PUT THAT MUSIC IN HER FACE? • • • • • • • • •   124 CATHLEEN PARA   10
    THE LONG HAIR IS ON HER FACE! • • • • • • • •   124 CATHLEEN PARA   V 10
    THE LONG HAIR SHADOWS HER FACE! • • • • • • •   124 CATHLEEN PARA   V 10
    THERE'S NOT A WOMAN TURNS HER FACE • • • • • •   131 OLD PENSIONER   13
    I SPIT INTO THE FACE OF TIME • • • • • • • • •   132 OLD PENSIONER   17
    WITH A SAD AND A GAY FACE. • • • • • • • • •   144 HOST OF AIR   16
    THAT SAW YOUNG NIAMH HOVER WITH LOVE-LORN FACE • • •   162 ASKS FORGIVE   13
    OR REMEMBERING HERS THEY WILL FIND NO OTHER FACE FAIR • 163 VALLEY LOVERS   7
    OR, REMEMBERING HERS, THEY WILL HOLD NO OTHER FACE FAIR   163 VALLEY LOVERS   V   7
    FACE DOWNWARD, TOSSING IN A TROUBLED SLEEP! • • • •   185 QUEEN MAEVE   106
    ABOUT WHOSE FACE BIRDS WAGGED THEIR FIERY WINGS, • • • 187 QUEEN MAEVE   145
    AND WHEN NO FACE GREW PITEOUS • • • • • • • •   191 BAILE AILLINN   62
    HIS FACE BOWED LOW TO WEEP THE END • • • • • • •   192 BAILE AILLINN   75
    TALL AND NOBLE BUT WITH FACE AND BOSOM • • • • • •   199 ARROW   5
    HAD YOU LOOKED ON THEM FACE TO FACE AS I DID, • • • • 231 SHADOW WATER B   198
    HAD YOU LOOKED ON THEM FACE TO FACE AS I DID, • • • • 231 SHADOW WATER B   198
    AND I WOULD HAVE YOU LOOK INTO MY FACE • • • • • •   238 SHADOW WATER B   349
    FOOL, FOOL! ALTHOUGH YOU HAVE LOOKED INTO MY FACE • •   238 SHADOW WATER B   356
    AND YOU WILL RECOLLECT MY FACE AND VOICE, • • • • •   243 SHADOW WATER B   433
    WHY DO YOU TURN AWAY AND HIDE YOUR FACE, • • • • •   244 SHADOW WATER B   461
    I DO NOT UNDERSTAND. I KNOW YOUR FACE • • • • • •   244 SHADOW WATER B   465
    WILL LOOK UPON HIS FACE AGAIN. GO WITH HIM, • • • •   250 SHADOW WATER B   589
    ONE TIME IT WAS A WOMAN'S FACE, OR WORSE-- • • • •   267 ALL TEMPT ME   2
    AND MOCK HIM TO HIS FACE AND THEN • • • • • • •   272 GREY ROCK   34
    YOU HAD TO FACE YOUR ENDS WHEN YOUNG-- • • • • • •   273 GREY ROCK   53
    SHE WOULD NOT LOOK IN ANY KNOWN MAN'S FACE • • • • • 280 TWO KINGS   73
    WOULD NEVER LOOK AGAIN ON KNOWN MAN'S FACE." • • • •   280 TWO KINGS   75
    WILL NEVER LOOK AGAIN ON KNOWN MAN'S FACE." • • • •   280 TWO KINGS   V 75
    UPON KING EOCHAID'S FACE, WHO LOWERED HIS FACE • • •   286 TWO KINGS   V 211A
    UPON KING EOCHAID'S FACE, WHO LOWERED HIS FACE • • •   286 TWO KINGS   V 211A
    A CURSING ROGUE WITH A MERRY FACE, • • • • • • •   302 HOUR DAWN   1
    A GREAT LAD WITH A BEERY FACE • • • • • • • • •   303 HOUR DAWN   27
    A DARK DEEP HOLE IN THE ROCK'S FACE, • • • • • •   303 HOUR DAWN   V 21
    ALTHOUGH CROWDS GATHERED ONCE IF SHE BUT SHOWED HER FACE, 314 FALLEN MAJESTY   1
    AND KISSED HER DUSKY FACE, • • • • • • • • • •   332 SOLOMON SHEBA   2
    BUT SUCH AS I HAVE SEEN UPON HER FACE • • • • • •   340 SHEP GOATHERD   40
    ALL DAY I'D LOOKED IN THE FACE • • • • • • • •   347 FISHERMAN   9
    AND HIS SUN-FRECKLED FACE, • • • • • • • • • •   348 FISHERMAN   29
    ONE HAD A LOVELY FACE, • • • • • • • • • • •   350 MEMORY   1
    BUT CHARM AND FACE WERE IN VAIN • • • • • • • •   350 MEMORY   3
    WHEN MY LUCK CHANGED AND THEY DARED MEET MY FACE, • •   352 PEOPLE   25
    WHEN MY LUCK CHANGED AND THEY DARED TO MEET MY FACE, •   352 PEOPLE   V 25
    YET ALWAYS WHEN I LOOK DEATH IN THE FACE, • • • • •   357 DEEP-SWORN VOW   3
    SUDDENLY I MEET YOUR FACE. • • • • • • • • • •   357 DEEP-SWORN VOW   6
    PROPPED UPON PILLOWS, ROUGE ON THE PALLOR OF HER FACE. • 362 HER COURTESY   3
    HEEL UP AND WEIGHT ON TOE, MUST FACE THE WALL • • • • 363 DOLLS FACES   3
    NO RED AND WHITE OF A FACE, • • • • • • • • •   365 HER RACE   6
    AMID THE DREAMS OF YOUTH! LET HER COME FACE TO FACE, •   366 HER COURAGE   3
    AMID THE DREAMS OF YOUTH! LET HER COME FACE TO FACE, •   366 HER COURAGE   3
    WHO HAVE LIVED IN JOY AND LAUGHED INTO THE FACE OF DEATH. 366 HER COURAGE   10
    WHO LIVED IN SHAMELESS JOY AND LAUGHED INTO THE FACE OF   366 HER COURAGE   V 10
        DEATH.
    THAT LIVED IN JOY AND LAUGHED INTO THE FACE OF DEATH. • 366 HER COURAGE   V 10
    WHO HAVE LIVED IN JOY AND LAUGHED IN THE FACE OF DEATH.   366 HER COURAGE   V 10
    HAVE LOOKED INTO YOUR FACE? • • • • • • • • •   367 HER CHRIS TREE   11
    THAT HE HAS MADE THAT HOLLOW FACE OF HIS • • • • •   368 EGO DOMINUS   20
    MORE PLAIN TO THE MIND'S EYE THAN ANY FACE • • • •   368 EGO DOMINUS   21
    AN IMAGE THAT MIGHT HAVE BEEN A STONY FACE • • • •   368 EGO DOMINUS   28
    WITH FACE AND NOSE PRESSED TO A SWEET-SHOP WINDOW, • •   370 EGO DOMINUS   56
    WITH FACE AND NOSE PRESSED TO A SWEETSHOP WINDOW. • •   370 EGO DOMINUS   V 56
    SHE CAN, THOUGH EVERY FACE SHOULD SCOWL • • • • •   405 FOR DAUGHTER   70
    AND PRAISED THE COLOUR OF HER FACE, • • • • • • •   410 TOWER   36
    TROOPER BELABOURING TROOPER, BITING AT ARM OR AT FACE, • 426 PHANTOM HATRED   12
    HAS LAID HER HELPLESS FACE UPON HIS BREAST. • • • •   441 LEDA AND SWAN   V   4
    WERE SOME DEAR FACE. UPON A MOONLESS NIGHT • • • •   466 HARUN RASHID   V 127
    WHO FINDING THE FIRST WRINKLES ON A FACE • • • • •   472 ALL SOUL NIGHT   42
    BROUGHT FACE TO FACE WITH HIS OWN CLUMSINESS! • • • • 479 SELF AND SOUL   48
    BROUGHT FACE TO FACE WITH HIS OWN CLUMSINESS! • • • • 479 SELF AND SOUL   48
    RUN FOR A MILE UNDIMMED IN HEAVEN'S FACE • • • • •   490 COOLE BALLYLEE   3
    FACE TO FACE MY RIGHTFUL MAN • • • • • • • • •   521 THREE THINGS   16
    FACE TO FACE MY RIGHTFUL MAN • • • • • • • • •   521 THREE THINGS   16
    I'M LOOKING FOR THE FACE I HAD • • • • • • • • •   532 BEFORE WORLD   7
    FACE TO FACE WE STOOD! • • • • • • • • • • •   539 MEETING   4
    FACE TO FACE WE STOOD! • • • • • • • • • • •   539 MEETING   4
    THE GYRES! THE GYRES! OLD ROCKY FACE, LOOK FORTH! • •   564 GYRES   1
    WHAT MATTER? THOSE THAT ROCKY FACE HOLDS DEAR, • • •   564 GYRES   18
    LONG LOOKED HE IN HER FACE, • • • • • • • • • •   571 THREE BUSHES   67
    "FORGETTING HUMAN WORDS," A GRAVE DEEP FACE. • • • •   603 GALLERY REVIS   49
    LIVE LIPS UPON A PLUMMET-MEASURED FACE. • • • • • •   610 STATUES   8
    THE LINEAMENTS OF A PLUMMET-MEASURED FACE. • • • • •   611 STATUES   32
    AND MEN RECALL THAT FACE, • • • • • • • • • •   617 LONG-LEG FLY   12
    BECAUSE WOMEN IN THE UPPER STOREYS DEMAND A FACE AT THE   623 HIGH TALK   7
        PANE,
    WHAT DO WE KNOW BUT THAT WE FACE • • • • • • • •   633 MAN AND ECHO   39
    THAN THE PEEPING PANSY'S FACE, • • • • • • • • •   647 ISLE STAT I 1   52
    DULL-WITTED THING, WITH FACE RED SQUIRREL-BROWN. • • • 661 ISLE STAT II 1   68
    IS ROLLED AS VERDANT SMOKE! O THOU WHOSE FACE • • •   667 ISLE STAT II 3   35
    IS IN THY FACE, AND LIPS TOGETHER PRESSED! • • • • • 671 ISLE STAT II 3   139
    IN THY WAN FACE? HEAR THOU, O DAUGHTER OF THE DAYS, • • 674 ISLE STAT II 3   200

257

FACE   (CONTINUED)
      IN THY WAN FACE? HEAR, DAUGHTER OF THE DAYS. . . . .   674 ISLE STAT II 3 V   200
      THEN LET ME SEE THY FACE BEFORE I DIE. . . . .   684 SEEKER   66
      A SIBYL, WITH FIERCE FACE AS OF A HOUND . . . .   687 TWO TITANS   9
      BENDING HER FACE O'ER HIS, SHE WATCHES MEET . . . .   688 TWO TITANS   45
      HIDING MY FACE, I CRIED LONG, BITTERLY. . . . .   690 MOSADA 1   17
      UPON THY FACE? HOW HEAVILY THY HEAD . . . .   701 MOSADA 3   72
      AFAR ALONG THE FLEET WHITE RIVER'S FACE-- . . . .   702 MOSADA 3   79
      AND SEE HOW THICK THE DEW LIES ON MY FACE. . . . .   703 MOSADA 3   104
      AH! WOE FOR THE LOSS OF YOUR FACE. . . . .   708 FAIRY PEDANT   32
      AND NOW WITH FATHER TIME I'M FACE TO FACE. . . . .   722 WITCH VIVIEN   57
      AND NOW WITH FATHER TIME I'M FACE TO FACE. . . . .   722 WITCH VIVIEN   57
      AND THEN A POINTED FACE WAS SEEN . . . .   728 PRIEST FAIRY   21
      WITH MANY A LOVELY FACE . . . .   740 EARL PAUL   30
      HIS FACE HAS NEVER GLADDENED SINCE HE CAME . . . .   747 SHADOW WATER A   1
      A WHITE BIRD BEATS HIS WINGS UPON MY FACE. . . . .   759 SHADOW WATER A   233
      AGAINST MY FACE AND EYES, MINE TOO ARE BEATEN. . . . . . .   759 SHADOW WATER A V   233
      AND LOVE WENCH WISDOM'S CRUEL FACE. . . . .   787 HUDDON DUDDON   10
      AND LOVE WENCH-WISDOM.'S CRUEL FACE. . . . .   787 HUDDON DUDDON V   10
FACED   SEE PALE-FACED
      AND UNREPENTING FACED YOUR ENDS, ...   273 GREY ROCK   60
FACES
      OR THE SOFTNESS OF YOUTH BE GONE FROM OUR FACES, ...   27 OISIN 1   410
      WILL THE SOFTNESS OF YOUTH BE GONE FROM OUR FACES, . . .   27 OISIN 1   V 410
      OR THE SOFTNESS OF YOUTH BE GONE FROM OUR FACES, ...   27 OISIN 1   V 419C
      OR THE SOFTNESS OF YOUTH BE GONE FROM OUR FACES, ...   28 OISIN 1   V 426
      BUT ONLY EXULTANT FACES. NIAMH STOOD . . . .   38 OISIN 2   136
      OF FACES, WAITED: AND THE LEISURED GAZE . . . .   39 OISIN 2   149
      OF FACES, WATCHED ME, AND THE LEISURED GAZE . . . . . .   39 OISIN 2   V 149
      THE SEASHINE ON OUR FACES, WE OUR WAY . . . .   41 OISIN 2   V 184B
      THE IMMORTAL DESIRE OF IMMORTALS WE SAW IN THEIR FACES,   47 OISIN 3   4
         AND SIGHED,
      CEASED ON OUR HANDS AND OUR FACES, ON HAZEL AND OAK LEAF,   48 OISIN 3   23
         THE LIGHT,
      HAVE FACES ALIVE WITH SUCH BEAUTY BEEN KNOWN TO THE SALT   50 OISIN 3   51
         EYE OF MAN,
      ARE FACES ALIVE WITH SUCH BEAUTY MADE KNOWN TO THE SALT   50 OISIN 3   V 51
         EYE OF MAN,
      ARE FACES ALIVE WITH SUCH BEAUTY MADE KNOWN TO THE SOFT   50 OISIN 3   V 51
         EYE OF MAN,
      WATCHED HER THOSE SEAMLESS FACES FROM THE VALLEY'S   55 OISIN 3   122
         GLIMMERING GIRTH;
      WATCHED HER THOSE SEAMLESS FACES FROM THE VALLEY'S MURAL   55 OISIN 3   V 122
         GIRTH
      OR WEEDING OR PLOUGHING WITH FACES A-SHINING WITH MUCH-TOIL   58 OISIN 3   165
         WET:
      THEIR FACES ARE ALL WORN, AND IN THEIR EYES . . . . . .   73 ANASHU VIJAYA   48
      ON THEIR VAST MYSTERY AND DREAMS! . . . .   74 ANASHU VIJAYA   70
      THEY BRING YOU MEMORIES OF OLD VILLAGE FACES, ...   130 BOOK STORIES   V   22
      THE WELL-KNOWN FACES ARE ALL GONE, ...   132 OLD PENSIONER   V   17
      CROWDED WITH BITTER FACES, THE WOUNDS IN PALM AND SIDE,   172 TRAV PASSION   4
      WITH QUAKING JOINTS AND TERROR-STRICKEN FACES, ...   185 QUEEN MAEVE   121
      WITH QUAKING JOINTS AND TERROR STRUCKEN FACES, ...   185 QUEEN MAEVE   V 121
      WITH QUAKING JOINTS AND TERROR-STRUCKEN FACES, ...   185 QUEEN MAEVE   V 121
      THE BITTER SWEETNESS OF FALSE FACES? . . . .   275 GREY ROCK   113
      WITH ALL THEIR ANCIENT FACES LIKE RAIN-BEATEN STONES,   318 MAGI   4
      AND NOW THEIR BREATHLESS FACES SEEM TO LOOK . . . . . .   325 ROBERT GREGORY   43
      AND THEIR BREATHLESS FACES SEEM TO LOOK . . . .   325 ROBERT GREGORY V   43
      SHE TURNS THE DOLLS' FACES TO THE WALL . . . .   363 DOLLS FACES   T
      HE AND HIS FRIEND, THEIR FACES TO THE SOUTH, ...   372 PHASES OF MOON   2
      COMING WITH VIVID FACES . . . .   391 EASTER 1916   2
      THE NEW FACES . . . .   435 NEW FACES   T
      LET THE NEW FACES PLAY WHAT TRICKS THEY WILL . . . . .   435 NEW FACES   5
      ON THE DROWNED MEN'S HANDS AND FACES, ON THE SPARS AND   719 PHANTOM SHIP   22
         ON THE SAILS.
      JOYS AND FEARS IN THEIR GREY FACES THAT THE LIVE EARTH   719 PHANTOM SHIP   26
         KNOWETH NOT:
      COVER THEIR FACES WITH THEIR HAIR AND WEEP. . . . . .   764 SHADOW WATER A   333
FACING
      HERE, FACING TO THE LAKE, AND NO NAME GILD: . . . . . .   663 ISLE STAT II 2   20
FACT
      YET NO CLEAR FACT TO BE DISCERNED: . . . .   425 STARES NEST   9
FACTION
      WHEN ORDER HAS WEAKENED OR FACTION IS STRONG, ...   548 TO SAME TUNE 3   12
FADE
      TILL THEY SHALL SINGING FADE IN RUTH . . . .   66 HAPPY SHEPHERD   41
      WE TIRE OF THE FLAME OF THE METEOR, BEFORE IT CAN FADE   122 WHITE BIRDS   2
         AND FLEE!
      MIGHT FADE IN LOVE IN THE END! . . . .   152 LOSS OF LOVE   V   4
      FOR HOURS WHEN ALL MUST FADE LIKE DEW, ...   156 FORGOT BEAUTY   20
      OF THOSE THAT IT MAY BE SHALL NEVER FADE. . . . .   183 QUEEN MAEVE   V   76
      THEIR HAUGHTY IMAGES THAT CANNOT FADE. . . . .   184 QUEEN MAEVE   V   88
      SANG TILL STARS BEGAN TO FADE, ...   332 ROUND TOWER   20
      THE OUTRAGEOUS WAR SHALL FADE! . . . .   342 SHEP GOATHERD   100
      THE STARS FADE OUT WHERE THE MOON COMES, ...   344 DAWN   8
      DID ALL THE FABRIC FADE! . . . .   516 MANS SONG   10
      ALL THAT IS FINISHED, LET IT FADE. . . . .   613 MARCH SONGS 1   10
      AND ALL THAT'S FINISHED, LET IT FADE. . . . .   613 MARCH SONGS 1   20
      AND ALL THAT'S FINISHED, LET IT FADE. . . . .   614 MARCH SONGS 1   30
      I FADE, AND SHALL NOT SEE THE MORNINGS WAKE, ...   674 ISLE STAT II 3   223
      THE BURGHERS OF THE NIGHT FADE ONE BY ONE. . . . . . .   700 MOSADA 3   40

	PAGE	TITLE	LINE

FADE   (CONTINUED)
    STRIKE QUICKLY, IT WILL FADE OUT WHEN YOU STRIKE. • • •   759 SHADOW WATER A   238
    I HAVE FORGOT IT ALL. HOW SOON DREAMS FADE! • • • •   761 SHADOW WATER A   272
FADED
    YET WEARY WITH PASSIONS THAT FADED • • • •   50 OISIN 3   52
    PENSIVE THEY PACED ALONG THE FADED LEAVES, • • •   80 EPHEMERA   10
    AS A CLOUD FADED INTO THE SKY. • • • • • •   145 HOST OF AIR V 40
    AND FADED THROUGH THE BRIGHTENING AIR. • • •   150 WANDER AENGUS   16
    THAT HAS LONG FADED FROM THE WORLD! • • • •   155 FORGOT BEAUTY   3
    THAT HAS LONG FADED IN THE WORLD! • • • •   155 FORGOT BEAUTY V 3
    CAN, TATTERED, STILL PROTECT, FADED ADORN. • •   477 SELF AND SOUL   16
    AND FADED NOW IS ALL THY WONDROUS ART. • • • •   673 ISLE STAT II 3   194
    FADED AND VANISHED, NOTHING NOW IS SEEN, • •   676 ISLE STAT II 3   268
    THAT DULL AND FADED ARE. • • • • • •   680 LOVE AND DEATH   26
    THE PHANTOMS OF HER FADED PLEASURES WALK! • •   687 TWO TITANS   19
    FOR YEARS HIS DAYS HAD DAWNED AND FADED THUS • • •   692 MOSADA 1   54
FADES
    UPON THE LIFE THAT FADES AND FLICKERS AND DIES, • • •   29 OISIN 2   12
    MY SINGING FADES, THE STRINGS ARE TORN, • • •   86 MAD KING GOLL V 66
    AND HOW, WHEN FADES THE SEA-STREWN ROSE OF DAY, • •   128 DREAM OF FAERY V 33
    THAT IT FADES OUT FROM KISS TO KISS! • • • •   202 NEVER GIVE ALL   5
    WHEN THE HORIZON FADES. • • • • • •   416 TOWER   193
    HE FADES AMONG THE MISTS! HOW FAST THEY COME. • •   703 MOSADA 3   117
    REMEMBERING THEE, I MUSE, WHILE FADES IN FLIGHT • •   705 REMEMBRANCE   6
    ARE BETTER THAN THE WOODS WHERE NO LOVE FADES • • •   754 SHADOW WATER A   160
    HER EYELIDS TREMBLE AND THE WHITE FOAM FADES! • •   761 SHADOW WATER A   264
    AND WHILE SHE FADES AND LIFE WITHERS AWAY, • • •   768 SHADOW WATER A   422
FADETH
    SLOWLY, SLOWLY FADETH SHE, • • • • • •   648 ISLE STAT I 1   83
FADING
    ABOUT HIS FADING CRIMSON BALL! • • • •   12 OISIN 1   155
    "THOUGH OUR SAD LOVE IS FADING, LET US YET • •   79 EPHEMERA V 4
    WHILE HE BENT DOWN HIS FADING HEAD, • • • •   82 MAD KING GOLL V 10
    BENDING LOW HIS FADING HEAD, • • • • •   82 MAD KING GOLL V 10
    WHEN WE BENT DOWN ABOVE THE FADING COALS • •   136 TO SOME I TALK   3
    WHILE THE NIGHT GREW, ABOVE THE FADING COALS, • •   136 TO SOME I TALK V 3
    THAT DRAGON THROUGH THE FADING LIGHT, • • •   385 ROBARTES DANCE   4
    WHAT IS THERE BUT THE SLOWLY FADING WEST, • •   390 IMAGE PAST   19
    UPON A FADING GLEAM, • • • • • •   414 TOWER   141
    WHERE SAT OLD SUMMER FADING INTO SONG, • •   690 MOSADA 1 V 18
    SHE IS ALREADY FADING, AS THOUGH THE GODS • •   768 SHADOW WATER A V 422
FAERIES
    WARS SHADOWY, VAST, EXULTANT! FAERIES OF OLD • • •   29 OISIN 2   9
    AH, FAERIES, DANCING UNDER THE MOON, • • • •   139 TO IRELAND   31
    SONG OF THE FAERIES • • • • • • •   643 SONG FAERIES V T
    NOR FAERIES IN THE HONEY-HEART OF JUNE ASTIR. • •   661 ISLE STAT II 1   73
FAERIES!
    I WILL DISSOLVE AWAY THE FAERIES' GUILE! • • •   677 ISLE STAT II 3   282
    AND TASTE WITH ME THE FAERIES' MEAT, • • • •   743 DANAAN QUICK   26
FAERY   SEE UN-FAERY
    AND MANY A MILE IS THE FAERY STATE. • • • •   9 OISIN 1 V 103
    AND HER BRIGHT BODY, SANG OF FAERY AND MAN • • •   29 OISIN 2   7
    ABOUT THEM! AND THE HORSE OF FAERY SCREAMED • •   30 OISIN 2   24
    THERE WE'VE HID OUR FAERY VATS, • • • •   87 STOLEN CHILD   6
    WITH A FAERY, HAND IN HAND, • • • • •   87 STOLEN CHILD   11
    WITH A FAERY, HAND IN HAND, • • • • •   87 STOLEN CHILD   26
    WITH A FAERY, HAND IN HAND, • • • • •   88 STOLEN CHILD   40
    WITH A FAERY, HAND IN HAND, • • • • •   89 STOLEN CHILD   52
    WITH A FAERY, HAND AND HAND, • • • • •   89 STOLEN CHILD V 52
    A FAERY SONG • • • • • • • •   115 FAERY SONG   T
    HOW TIME MAY NEVER MAR THEIR FAERY VOWS • •   126 DREAM OF FAERY V 10
    AND FROM ITS MURMURING GREENNESS, CALM OF FAERY, • •   129 BOOK STORIES   3
    THE FAERY HOST • • • • • • • •   140 HOSTING SIDHE V T
    THE FAERY CHILDREN LAUGH IN CRADLES OF WROUGHT GOLD, •   146 UNAPPEAS HOST V 1
    IN DOVE-GREY FAERY LANDS! • • • • • •   162 ASKS FORGIVE   10
    I, STARVED FOR THE BOSOM OF HIS FAERY BRIDE? • •   629 CIRCUS ANIMALS   16
    SAD FAERY TONES. 'TIS THUS THEY EVER SEEM, • •   654 ISLE STAT I 2   58
    THE WINGED WONDER OF ALL FAERY LAND. • • •   657 ISLE STAT I 3   57
    THE FAERY SHIP THAT SWIMS ATHWART THE SKY. • •   663 ISLE STAT II 2   16
    ALL SWIM WITH TEARS. THE FAERY BOAT'S AT HAND! •   663 ISLE STAT II 2   33
    THE FAERY THING FLEW WITH HER O'ER THE GRAY • •   663 ISLE STAT II 2   38
    I'D GIVE MY FAERY FLEETNESS, THOUGH I BE • •   670 ISLE STAT II 3   107
    HIS SLEUTH-HOUNDS FOLLOW EVERY FAERY THING. • •   675 ISLE STAT II 3   244
    BUT SOULLESS A FAERY DIES, • • • • •   676 ISLE STAT II 3   249
    FOR SOULLESS A FAERY DIES, • • • • •   676 ISLE STAT II 3   261
    THE FAERY FLOWER LIES UPON THY LIPS. • • •   677 ISLE STAT II 3   277
    THE FAERY BLOSSOM LIES UPON THY LIPS. • • •   677 ISLE STAT II 3   285
    THE FAERY BLOSSOM LIES UPON THY LIPS! • • •   678 ISLE STAT II 3   291
    THE FAERY BLOSSOM BROODS UPON THY LIPS. • • •   678 ISLE STAT II 3   306
    A MURMURING FAERY MULTITUDE, • • • • •   742 DANAAN QUICK   7
FAERYLAND
    THE MAN WHO DREAMED OF FAERYLAND • • • •   126 DREAM OF FAERY   T
FAERY'S
    AND THINE EYES MORE BRIGHT THAN FAERY'S, • • •   647 ISLE STAT I 1   53
FAGGOT
    FLAMES THAT NO FAGGOT FEEDS, NOR STEEL HAS LIT, • •   498 BYZANTIUM   26
FAGGOTS
    SOME BURN DAMP FAGGOTS, OTHERS MAY CONSUME • •   327 ROBERT GREGORY   81
    ON OLD DRY FAGGOTS THAT COULD NEVER PLEASE • •   466 HARUN RASHID   124
FAIL
    HE MUSED UPON HIS MOCKERS! WITHOUT FAIL • • • •   127 DREAM OF FAERY   26

	PAGE	TITLE	LINE

FAIL   (CONTINUED)
AND HOW SHOULD HER HEART FAIL HER . . . .   365 HER RACE   9
NOR SHALL THE SELF-BEGOTTEN FAIL . . . .   530 OLD TOM AGAIN   3
FAIL, AND THAT HISTORY TURNS INTO RUBBISH, ...   546 TO SAME TUNE 2   21
FAIL, AND THAT HISTORY TURNS INTO RUBBISH, ...   614 MARCH SONGS 1   21
HOW THEY WHO SEEK ARE EVER DOOMED TO FAIL. . . . . .   653 ISLE STAT I 2   41
IT IS, YET SHALL IT FAIL THEE DAY AND NIGHT . . . . .   674 ISLE STAT II 3   211
DEFEAT IS DEATH. SHOULD MY PLOTS FAIL I'D DIE. . . .   722 WITCH VIVIEN   52
FAILED
WHO HAVE FAILED, BEING WEAK OF WILL, ...   298 THREE HERMITS   18
FAILS
NO EXPECTATION FAILS THERE, ...   621 JOHN KINSELLA   29
FAILURE
OF FAILURE, AND TO CROWN HER CROWNLESS HEAD, ...   688 TWO TITANS   48
FAILURE FOR GLORY DOWN ON THEE, AND MOULD . . . . . .   688 TWO TITANS   54
FAIN
I FAIN HAD BEEN THE FIRST OF SINGING THINGS . . . . .   648 ISLE STAT I 1   101
FAINT
DAWN PASSIONED, FED WITH A FAINT GREEN LIGHT, ...   40 OISIN 2   V 165
. . . SLOW DROPPING A SOUND IN FAINT STREAMS . . . . .   51 OISIN 3   67
FELL LIKE FAINT METEORS IN THE GLOOM, AND ONCE . . .   80 EPHEMERA   14
AND SHEDS FAINT ODOURS THROUGH THE AIR! . . . .   85 MAD KING GOLL   64
AND SHEDS FAINT ODOUR THROUGH THE AIR! . . . .   85 MAD KING GOLL V 64
ONE STAR SHONE FAINT AND GREEN, ...   95 MOLL MAGEE   30
"THAT DROWSILY DROPS FAINT LEAVES ON HIM . . . . . .   168 BLESSED   37
THAT IT MAY DROP FAINT PERFUME, AND BE HEAVY WITH DEW,   172 TRAV PASSION   7
MAKE THEIR FAINT THUNDER, AND THE GARDEN BEES . . . .   198 SEVEN WOODS   2
SHOWED THEIR FAINT LIGHT THROUGH THE UNSHUTTERED WINDOWS,   279 TWO KINGS   50
I AM NO LONGER FAINT . . . .   335 SONG   9
THERE IN THE TOMB DROPS THE FAINT MOONLIGHT, ...   636 BLACK TOWER   17
WILL BE THE FAINT FAR THUNDER-SOUND, AS THOUGH . . .   699 MOSADA 3   10
WILL MOVE THE FAINT FAR THUNDER-SOUND, AS THOUGH . .   699 MOSADA 3   V 10
REMEMBERING THEE, I SEARCH OUT THESE FAINT FLOWERS . .   704 REMEMBRANCE   1
FAINTER
BUT FAINTER THAN A YOUNG LAMB'S BLEAT. . . . .   26 OISIN 1   399
AND FAINTER THAN A YOUNG LAMB'S BLEAT. . . . .   26 OISIN 1   V 399
FAIR
ON A MORNING MISTY AND MILD AND FAIR. . . . .   2 OISIN 1   V   7E
HIS MISTRESS WAS MORE MILD AND FAIR . . . .   3 OISIN 1   V 7DD
SHE SAID: "FOR HE IS FAIR ABOVE . . . .   7 OISIN 1   V 62A
FOR FAIR ARE POPPIES ON THE BROW! . . . .   67 HAPPY SHEPHERD   56
"WHAT DO YOU MAKE SO FAIR AND BRIGHT?" . . . .   69 CLOAK BOAT   1
"WHAT DO YOU WEAVE SO FAIR AND BRIGHT?" . . . .   69 CLOAK BOAT   V   1
I RULED O'ER ALL MY FAIR DOMINIONS, ...   82 MAD KING GOLL V   7
AND AH, YOU PROUD MAIDEN, YOU ARE NOT SO FAIR WHEN HIS OAR   91 OLD FISHERMAN   9
PROUD MAIDEN, YE ARE NOT SO FAIR, WHEN HIS OAR . . .   91 OLD FISHERMAN V   9
AND, AH, YE PROUD MAIDENS, YOU ARE NOT SO FAIR, WHEN HIS OAR   91 OLD FISHERMAN V 9
AND WHERE IS THERE HOPE OR DEED AS FAIR? . . . . . .   141 HOSTING SIDHE   14
OR REMEMBERING HERS THEY WILL FIND NO OTHER FACE FAIR .   163 VALLEY LOVERS   7
OR, REMEMBERING HERS, THEY WILL HOLD NO OTHER FACE FAIR   163 VALLEY LOVERS V   7
I BOUGHT AT THE SLIGO FAIR. . . . .   178 FIDDLER DOONEY   8
IF ANYBODY HALF AS FAIR . . . .   191 BAILE AILLINN   53
BUT WITH A MAN'S HEAD, OR A FAIR WOMAN'S, ...   233 SHADOW WATER B   245
IF THE LADY BE YOUNG AND FAIR." . . . .   268 BROWN PENNY   6
FARMERS JOSTLED AT THE FAIR . . . .   410 TOWER   39
CROWDS JOSTLED AT THE FAIR . . . .   410 TOWER   V 39
"FAIR AND FOUL ARE NEAR OF KIN, ...   513 JANE TALK BISH   7
AND FAIR NEEDS FOUL," I CRIED. . . . .   513 JANE TALK BISH   8
COME FORTH! THE MORN IS FAIR! AS FROM THE PYRE . . .   645 ISLE STAT I 1   8
OF FLIGHT ARE DONE. MOST FAIR OF ALL WHO GRAZE . . .   649 ISLE STAT I 1   118
NASCHINA, HAIL! MOST FAIR OF ALL WHO GRAZE . . . . .   649 ISLE STAT I 1   120
AS FAIR AS ANY THAT ON IDA'S MOUNT . . . .   650 ISLE STAT I 1   134
IS NOT MORE FAIR AND JOYOUS THAN SHE IS . . . . . .   661 ISLE STAT II 1   71
WHAT DO YOU WEAVE SO FAIR AND BRIGHT? . . . .   666 ISLE STAT II 3   1
FAIR YOUTH, ALONG A WANDERING WAY . . . .   667 ISLE STAT II 3   38
MY LIPS, FAIR YOUTH. IT SHALL BE AS YOU ASK. . . .   669 ISLE STAT II 3   80
FAIR SHEPHERD, AS WE WANDERED HITHER, ...   669 ISLE STAT II 3   83
IN SHADOWY DIMNESS. TO BE FAIR AS THEE . . . . . .   670 ISLE STAT II 3   106
IN THOSE FAIR YEARS, O DAUGHTER OF THE DAYS, ...   674 ISLE STAT II 3 V 213
THUS BECKON TO OUR AID A PHANTOM FAIR . . . .   693 MOSADA 1   76
A PEASANT YOUNG AND FAIR, HER EYES FOR FEAR . . . . .   713 FERENCZ RENYI V 81
AND DEATH, OH MY FAIR ONE, WILL NEVER COME NEAR . . .   717 LOVE SONG   8
THEN THE STARS GROW OUT OF HEAVEN WITH THEIR COUNTENANCES   719 PHANTOM SHIP   30
      FAIR.
ILL WORDS FOR ALL THINGS SOFT AND FAIR, ...   723 GIRLS SONG A   6
FAIR-HAIRED
THE PLAIN, A LITTLE FAIR-HAIRED MAID I LOVE. . . . .   679 ISLE STAT II 3   312
THERE DWELLS A LITTLE FAIR-HAIRED MAID I LOVE. . . .   679 ISLE STAT II 3 V 312
FAIRIES
THE FAIRIES MOVED AMONG THE FOUNTAINS, ...   25 OISIN 1   V 386
GLAMOURED BY FAIRIES FOR THEIR OWN. . . . .   717 FAIRY DOCTOR   20
A LOVER'S QUARREL AMONG THE FAIRIES. . . . .   726 LOVERS QUARREL   T
WHERE THE SOULS OF FAIRIES GO?" . . . .   729 PRIEST FAIRY   48
FAIRIES'
THE FAIRIES' HERALD SPAKE ONCE MORE! . . . .   730 PRIEST FAIRY   53
FAIRS
FROM MARKETS AND FROM FAIRS . . . .   420 MY HOUSE   19
FAIRY
MOUNT MY WHITE STEED, FOR THE FAIRY STATE . . . . . .   9 OISIN 1   V 103
FOR FAIRY SONGS CONTINUALLY . . . .   11 OISIN 1   V 134
WARS SHADOWY, VAST, EXULTANT! FAIRY KINGS . . . . . .   29 OISIN 2   V   9

260

		PAGE	TITLE		LINE
FAIRY (CONTINUED)					
OF SEA-SPRUNG PEARL, AND QUEENS OF FAIRY LANDS		29	OISIN 2	V	10A
BUT SOULLESS A FAIRY DIES,		643	SONG FAERIES		2
FOR SOULLESS A FAIRY DIES,		644	SONG FAERIES		14
UNTO THE DOLOROUS BORDER OF THE FAIRY LAKE.		655	ISLE STAT I 2		85
THE FAIRY VOICES		655	ISLE STAT I 3	V	T
THE FAIRY PEDANT.		706	FAIRY PEDANT		T
THE SOLITARY FAIRY		706	FAIRY PEDANT	V	T
YOU ARE WASTING AWAY, LITTLE FAIRY.		707	FAIRY PEDANT		12
YOU ARE WASTING AWAY, LITTLE FAIRY.		707	FAIRY PEDANT		20
YOU ARE WASTING AWAY, LITTLE FAIRY.		708	FAIRY PEDANT		28
SHE IS WASTING AWAY, LITTLE FAIRY.		708	FAIRY PEDANT		40
THE FAIRY DOCTOR.		716	FAIRY DOCTOR		T
THE FAIRY DOCTOR COMES OUR WAY		716	FAIRY DOCTOR		1
HE SEES THE FAIRY HOSTING MOVE		716	FAIRY DOCTOR		9
AND FULL HIS EYES OF FAIRY CHEER.		716	FAIRY DOCTOR		12
SO WE DANCE A FAIRY JIG		726	LOVERS QUARREL		19
YONDER SEE THE FAIRY GIRLS		726	LOVERS QUARREL		21
THE PRIEST AND THE FAIRY.		728	PRIEST FAIRY		T
NOW, WHAT HAS A FAIRY TO DO WITH A PRIEST		729	PRIEST FAIRY		27
A FAIRY WHOM WE LOVED FULL WELL!		729	PRIEST FAIRY		44
THE FAIRY VANISHED FROM HIS SIGHT,		730	PRIEST FAIRY		62
WERE YOU A FAIRY YOU'D HAVE HEARD		730	PRIEST FAIRY		67
FAIRY-HAUNTED					
IN THE FAIRY-HAUNTED RATH,		706	DAWN-SONG		21
FAIRYLAND					
A MAN WHO DREAMED OF FAIRYLAND		126	DREAM OF FAERY	V	
FAIRY'S					
THE FAIRY'S CALL		126	DREAM OF FAERY	V	T
FAIRY-SMITTEN					
WITH FAIRY-SMITTEN UDDERS DRY--		654	ISLE STAT I 2	V	T
FAITH		716	FAIRY DOCTOR		14
WHERE BROKEN FAITH HAS NEVER BEEN KNOWN,		8	OISIN 1		84
AND I THAT HAVE NOT YOUR FAITH, HOW SHALL I KNOW		258	KING NO KING		11
I HAVE KEPT MY FAITH, THOUGH FAITH WAS TRIED,		276	GREY ROCK		124
I HAVE KEPT MY FAITH, THOUGH FAITH WAS TRIED,		276	GREY ROCK		124
FOR ENGLAND MAY KEEP FAITH		394	EASTER 1916		68
AND I DECLARE MY FAITH!		414	TOWER		145
I LEAVE BOTH FAITH AND PRIDE		416	TOWER		173
THE TRUE FAITH DISCOVERED WAS		440	WISDOM		1
WHO HAVE ACCEPTED THE BYZANTINE FAITH,		464	HARUN RASHID		78
TEST EVERY WORK OF INTELLECT OR FAITH,		501	VACILLATION		30
IN THAT FAITH I LIVE OR DIE."		529	TOM LUNATIC		18
I' FAITH THOU EVER WAST A WORDY SPIRIT!		673	ISLE STAT II 3		175
SHE WOULD WEAVE A NET TO TAKE US. SHE MIGHT KEEP FAITH!		756	SHADOW WATER A		190
FAITHFUL					
BUT FAITHFUL LOVERS.		220	HARP OF AENGUS		14
WHY SHOULD YOU BE MORE FAITHFUL THAN THE REST,		227	SHADOW WATER B		109
A FAITHFUL LOVE, A FAITHFUL LOVE.		449	HERO GIRL FOOL		29
A FAITHFUL LOVE, A FAITHFUL LOVE.		449	HERO GIRL FOOL		29
HE WATCHES OVER NONE BUT FAITHFUL LOVERS.		762	SHADOW WATER A		295
BUT FAITHFUL LOVERS. SOMETHING GLITTERS THERE--		763	SHADOW WATER A		309
BUT FAITHFUL LOVERS. WHITHER HAVE YOU COME,		763	SHADOW WATER A	V	309
FAITHFULLEST					
WHY SHOULD THE FAITHFULLEST HEART MOST LOVE		275	GREY ROCK		112
FAITHLESS					
"WHY ARE THEY FAITHLESS WHEN THEIR MIGHT		275	GREY ROCK		109
FALCON					
HOW THE FALCONER FOLLOWS THE FALCON IN THE WEEDS OF THE HERON'S PLOT,		52	OISIN 3		79
THE FALCON CANNOT HEAR THE FALCONER!		401	SECOND COMING		2
THE FALCON CAN NOT HEAR THE FALCONER!		401	SECOND COMING	V	2
I RIDE WITH FALCON TO THE RIVER'S EDGE		463	HARUN RASHID		57
I RIDE WITH FALCON TO THE WATER'S EDGE		463	HARUN RASHID	V	57
AND DOWN I CAME AS A FALCON SWOOPS		673	ISLE STAT II 3		178
FALCONER					
HOW THE FALCONER FOLLOWS THE FALCON IN THE WEEDS OF THE HERON'S PLOT,		52	OISIN 3		79
THE FALCON CANNOT HEAR THE FALCONER!		401	SECOND COMING		2
THE FALCON CAN NOT HEAR THE FALCONER!		401	SECOND COMING	V	2
FALIAS					
AND FINDRIAS AND FALIAS,		196	BAILE AILLINN		162
FALL SEE FOOT-FALL					
IT SEEMED TO FALL FROM THE VERY FLAME		13	OISIN 1	V	167
WHERE DROPS OF DEW IN MYRIADS FALL,		16	OISIN 1		222
WHERE WHITE DEWDROPS IN MILLIONS FALL!		16	OISIN 1	V	222
AND CAME TO WHERE THE DEWDROPS FALL		20	OISIN 1		293
FALL THE LEAVES OF OTHER ROSES.		21	OISIN 1		311
SHALL FALL THE LEAVES OF DAMASK ROSES.		21	OISIN 1		315
BEFORE THIS DAY! FOR NOW THE FALL OF TEARS		30	OISIN 2		18
TREMBLING, ON THE FLAGS WE FALL,		43	OISIN 2	V	208E
GATHER SEA-SLIME AND FALL THE SEAWARD WAY,		45	OISIN 2		237
GATHER SEA SLIME AND FALL THE SEAWARD WAY,		45	OISIN 2	V	237
MY PILLARS TOWARDS THEIR FALL.		44	OISIN 2	V	239
THERE DREAMY TIME LETS FALL HIS SICKLE		77	INDIAN TO LOVE	V	5A
ERE FALL OF EVENING, MY MAILED HOST,		83	MAD KING GOLL	V	19
. . . HUNG LOW IN THE FALL OF THE DEW!		122	WHITE BIRDS		7
WHATEVER RAVELLED WATERS RISE AND FALL		127	DREAM OF FAERY		32
THE LIGHT FALL OF HER FLYING FEET		138	TO IRELAND	V	11
THOUGH HOPE FALL FROM YOU AND LOVE DECAY,		148	INTO TWILIGHT		7
THOUGH HOPE FALL FROM THEE OR LOVE DECAY		148	INTO TWILIGHT	V	7

FALL   (CONTINUED)
    OVER MY HEART, AND YOUR HAIR FALL OVER MY BREAST,   154 BELOVED PEACE   10
    OVER MY HEART, AND YOUR HAIR FALL ABOUT MY BREAST   154 BELOVED PEACE   V   10
    AND YOUR HIGH BEAUTY FALL AND BE LOST   173 PLEADS FRIEND   V   7
    SINCE ADAM'S FALL BUT NEEDS MUCH LABOURING.   205 ADAMS CURSE   22
    O HEAVY SWOLLEN WATERS, BRIM THE FALL OF THE OAK TREES,   207 HANRAHANS SONG   V   11
    MEAN ROOF-TREES WERE THE STURDIER FOR ITS FALL.   264 HOUSE SHAKEN   8
    I STAGGERED, BUT A BEECH-TREE STAYED MY FALL,   286 TWO KINGS   209
    I STAGGERED, BUT A BEECH TREE STAYED MY FALL,   286 TWO KINGS   V   209
    FALL ASLEEP WHEN I SHOULD PRAY."   298 THREE HERMITS   12
    THREE HUNDRED YEARS BEFORE THE FALL,   388 SOLOMON WITCH   11
    THINGS FALL APART; THE CENTRE CANNOT HOLD;   402 SECOND COMING   3
    THINGS FALL APART; THE CENTRE CAN NOT HOLD,   402 SECOND COMING   V   3
    AND LET IT FALL UNNOTICED TO THE FLOOR.   461 HARUN RASHID   15
    AND IT WOULD FALL UNNOTICED ON THE FLOOR.   461 HARUN RASHID   V   15
    THAT FOLLOWED IF I LET THE KERCHIEF FALL!   533 HER TRIUMPH   4
    NOR SAW MY BODY FALL NOR HEARD IT SHRIEK,   537 HER VISION   29
    NO MATTER WHAT HAPPENS AND WHO TAKES THE FALL,   545 TO SAME TUNE 1   22
    NO MATTER WHAT HAPPENS OR WHO TAKES THE FALL,   545 TO SAME TUNE 1 V   22
    ALL THINGS FALL AND ARE BUILT AGAIN,   566 LAPIS LAZULI   35
    NO MATTER WHAT HAPPENS AND WHO TAKES THE FALL,   616 MARCH SONGS 3   22
    ON THIS FOUL WORLD IN ITS DECLINE AND FALL   619 BRONZE HEAD   24
    AMONG THOSE BIRD-LIKE THINGS CAME, AND LET FALL   634 CUCHULAIN COMF   8
    THEY GET THEM SWORDS, AND BOTH OR EITHER FALL?   662 ISLE STAT II 1   78
    NOR TREMBLE TO ITS FALL. THE FIRE SWEEPS ROUND   689 NETTLESHIP   11
    I TRY TO LIFT MINE ARMS--THEY FALL AGAIN.   701 MOSADA 3   56
    DOWN THE VAPOURS FALL AND HIDE THEM FROM THE CHILDREN OF 719 PHANTOM SHIP   27
        A DAY,
    TO THE FIDDLE'S RISE AND FALL.   726 LOVERS QUARREL   20
    AND TEARS OF FIRE FALL GENTLY IN THE DEW.   738 YOU ARE SAD   4
    AND MINGLING HAIR FALL FROM THE FIERY BOUGHS,   765 SHADOW WATER A   368
    AND, HURRYING HOMEWARD, FALL UPON SOME LAND   767 SHADOW WATER A   384
FALLEN
    NO LIMB OF ME THAT WAS NOT FALLEN   7 OISIN 1   V   72
    AND NOW HAVE FALLEN ON MY LIFE   24 OISIN 1   V   358
    AND THEY HAVE FALLEN OR FLED, AGE AFTER AGE,   45 OISIN 2   242
    . . . WHEN THE FALLEN ON FALLEN LIE ROLLED!   52 OISIN 3   78
    . . . WHEN THE FALLEN ON FALLEN LIE ROLLED!   52 OISIN 3   78
    FROM POND AND FALLEN TREE--ME SING   85 MAD KING GOLL   V   63
    HAS FALLEN AWAY?   142 MOODS   7
    WITH HEAVY WHITENING WINGS, AND A HEART FALLEN COLD! 147 UNAPPEAS HOST   4
    THE GARDEN HAD FALLEN STILL!   159 CAP AND BELLS   2
    AND THEN THE CLASH OF FALLEN HORSEMEN AND THE CRIES   161 BLACK PIG   3
    HE HAD FALLEN ASLEEP, AND, THOUGH HE HAD DREAMED NOTHING, 182 QUEEN MAEVE   55
    TILL HE HAS FALLEN ASLEEP   216 HAPPY TOWNLAND   51
    SHINING ON WATER AND FALLEN AMONG LEAVES,   218 WOODS OF COOLE   38
    WE HAVE FALLEN IN THE DREAMS THE EVER-LIVING   228 SHADOW WATER B   131
    THESE ARE THE CLOUDS ABOUT THE FALLEN SUN,   265 THESE CLOUDS   1
    THESE ARE THE CLOUDS ABOUT THE FALLEN SUN,   265 THESE CLOUDS   11
    THAT WHEN HE HAS FALLEN ASLEEP WITHIN MY ARMS,   285 TWO KINGS   191
    FALLEN MAJESTY   314 FALLEN MAJESTY   T
    BABBLING OF FALLEN MAJESTY, RECORDS WHAT'S GONE.   314 FALLEN MAJESTY   4
    "THE NIGHT HAS FALLEN! NOT A SOUND   389 SOLOMON WITCH   38
    HAD FALLEN AMONG DANCERS, HAD WHIRLED THEM ROUND   430 NINETEEN 19   52
    THE THREEFOLD TERROR OF LOVE; A FALLEN FLARE   499 MOTHER OF GOD   1
    THIS FALLEN STAR MY MILK SUSTAINS,   499 MOTHER OF GOD   12
    THE THREE-FOLD TERROR OF LOVE; A FALLEN FLARE   499 MOTHER OF GOD   V   1
    "THOSE BREASTS ARE FLAT AND FALLEN NOW,   513 JANE TALK BISH   3
    A CAREFUL FIELD-MOUSE FINDS A FALLEN CRUMB!   713 FERENCZ RENYI   77
    BY TABLES THAT WERE FALLEN INTO DUST   724 KANVA ON SELF   13
    FOR ALL GOOD MEN NOW FALLEN ILL,   736 IN CHURCH   5
    HAVE FALLEN AND MY SUN AND MOON GONE OUT.   767 SHADOW WATER A V   405
FALLING
    RISING AND FALLING, MIXED INSEPARABLY,   45 OISIN 2   V   233
    THE FALLING OF THE LEAVES   79 FALLING LEAVES   T
    FALLING OF THE LEAVES   79 FALLING LEAVES   V   T
    IT QUENCHED, WITH SOUND LIKE FALLING DEW,   86 MAD KING GOLL   66
    WITH HER CLOUD-PALE EYELIDS FALLING ON DREAM-DIMMED EYES! 163 VALLEY LOVERS   4
    GREAT POWERS OF FALLING WAVE AND WIND AND WINDY FIRE, 174 ELEMENT POWERS   7
    THOUGH COURTEOUS TO THE WORST; MUCH FALLING HE   324 ROBERT GREGORY   19
    ARE BRIDELESS." "I AM FALLING INTO YEARS."   463 HARUN RASHID   54
    CLIMBING, FALLING SHE KNEW NOT WHERE,   578 CRAZED GIRL   4
    THE FALLING HAWTHORN BLOOM. BY MERE AND BROOK   677 ISLE STAT II 3   279
    SHE PRAYS FOR EVERY FALLING TEAR   735 IN CHURCH   3
    A PRAYER FOR EVERY FALLING TEAR   736 IN CHURCH   15
    KINGDOMS RISING! KINGDOMS FALLING!   737 IN FIRELIGHT   9
    THE FALLING BLOSSOMS, AND THE DEAD THE LIVING. 756 SHADOW WATER A   182
FALLS   SEE SALMON-FALLS
    THE RED SUN FALLS AND THE WORLD GROWS DIM."   9 OISIN 1   105
    AND THE ROOF FALLS IN OF HIS TUNNELLED HOUSE.   27 OISIN 1   V   419
    AND THE ROOF FALLS IN OF HIS TUNNELLED HOUSE.   28 OISIN 1   423
    WHEN THE POOR TIRED CHILD, PASSION, FALLS ASLEEP. 80 EPHEMERA   7
    HIS EYELIDS DROOP, HIS HEAD FALLS LOW,   98 FOXHUNTER   13
    FALLS IN SLEEPY STREAMS.   98 FOXHUNTER   16
    WHERE THE SUN FALLS INTO THE WESTERN DEEP.   108 CUCHULAIN SEA   V   34
    AND AS IT FALLS AWAKENS LEAFY TUNES!--   127 DREAM OF FAERY   V   5
    TO FIND IT WHEN NIGHT FALLS LAID ON A GOLDEN BIER. 209 UNDER THE MOON   10
    THE ROPE'S IN TWO--IT FALLS INTO THE SEA.   251 SHADOW WATER B   596
    THE SALMON FALLS, THE MACKEREL-CROWDED SEAS, 407 SAIL BYZANTIUM   V   4
    THAT SPRINGS FROM BODY AND IN BODY FALLS   463 HARUN RASHID   63
    AND FALLS INTO THE BASIN OF THE MIND   478 SELF AND SOUL   34

PAGE   TITLE   LINE

FALLS   (CONTINUED)
    INTOLERABLE MUSIC FALLS. . . . .   612 NEWS ORACLE   32
    THE NIGHEST BLOSSOM WHERE IT FALLS I'LL TAKE. . . . . .   657 ISLE STAT I 3   65
    SEER OF VISIONS! NOW EVE FALLS ASLEEP, ...   691 MOSADA 1   36
    AND FALLS AMONG THE DREAMS THE DROWSY GODS . . . . . .   750 SHADOW WATER A   68
FALSE
    AND LOVED YOUR BEAUTY WITH LOVE FALSE OR TRUE, . . .   121 YOU ARE OLD   6
    AND LOVED YOUR BEAUTY WILL LOVE FALSE OR TRUE! . . . .   121 YOU ARE OLD   V   6
    THE BITTER SWEETNESS OF FALSE FACES? . . . .   275 GREY ROCK   113
FALSTAFFAN
    A HEAVILY BUILT FALSTAFFAN MAN, ...   423 ROAD AT DOOR   V   2
FALSTAFFIAN
    A HEAVILY-BUILT FALSTAFFIAN MAN, ...   423 ROAD AT DOOR   2
FALTER
    ERE LONG SHALL FALTER THROUGH THE NOISY SQUARE, ...   699 MOSADA 3   21
FALTERS
    AND "MY SPEED IS A WEARINESS," FALTERS THE MOUSE, . . .   28 OISIN 1   421
FAME
    CRIED FIN! AND CRIED SHE, "MEN OF FAME, ...   5 OISIN 1   V   45
    OF ALL THAT WISDOM AND THE FAME . . . .   7 OISIN 1   66
    OF NOBLE OISIN AND HIS FAME, ...   7 OISIN 1   V   66
    TO PEAK AND PINE O'ER OISIN'S FAME." . . . .   7 OISIN 1   V   70
    AND THE HIGH FAME THAT COME TO THEM IN MARRIAGE, . . .   232 SHADOW WATER B   235
    --SEEING THAT FAME HAS PERISHED THIS LONG WHILE, . . .   321 REED WHISPERER   11
    HE MIGHT HAVE WON FAME IN THE END, ...   392 EASTER 1916   28
    SO GREAT ITS FAME. WHEN FITTING TIME HAS PASSED . . .   461 HARUN RASHID   19
    WHERE NONE HAS REIGNED THAT LACKED A NAME AND FAME . . .   491 COOLE BALLYLEE   31
    BUT FAME AND VIRTUE ROT. . . . .   584 GHOST ROG CASE   36
FAMED
    IN SILENCE, THAT FAMED FLOWER OF WIZARDRY, ...   673 ISLE STAT II 3   192
FAMILIAR
    NO CREATURE HAD FAMILIAR THOUGHT . . . .   17 OISIN 1   V   242
    TO SOME SURE COUNTRY, SOME FAMILIAR PLACE. . . . . .   249 SHADOW WATER B   569
    MONSTROUS FAMILIAR IMAGES SWIM TO THE MIND'S EYE. . . .   426 PHANTOM HATRED   8
FAMILIES
    DEATH, DESPAIR, DIVISION OF FAMILIES, ...   459 FROM OEDIPUS   5
    MARRIAGES, ALLIANCES AND FAMILIES, ...   491 COOLE BALLYLEE   36
FAMILY
    HIS CHILDHOOD AND HIS FAMILY, ...   361 ALF POLLEXFEN   35
    MONTASHIGI, THIRD OF HIS FAMILY, FASHIONED IT . . . .   478 SELF AND SOUL   25
    FAMILY AND FAMILY, ...   540 FROM ANTIGONE   11
    FAMILY AND FAMILY, ...   540 FROM ANTIGONE   11
    NOR SATISFIED CONSCIENCE, BUT THAT GREAT FAMILY . . .   579 DOR WELLESLEY   14
    AND FOUND HIS FAMILY TOMB . . . .   584 GHOST ROG CASE   32
FAMISH
    THE ICICLES THAT FAMISH ALL THE NORTH, ...   73 ANASHU VIJAYA   50
FAMISHED
    BECAUSE OF SOMETHING TOLD UNDER THE FAMISHED HORN . . .   210 UNDER THE MOON   17
    HE HAD FAMISHED IN A WILDERNESS, ...   789 SINGING HEAD   1
FAMOUS   SEE WORLD-FAMOUS
    OISIN, TELL ME THE FAMOUS STORY . . . .   2 OISIN 1   V   1
    I CRIED, "THOU ART SURELY A WARRIOR, FORGETTING HIS FAMOUS   51 OISIN 3   V   61
        LINE,
    HE IS A FAMOUS FISHER! HOUR BY HOUR . . . .   73 ANASHU VIJAYA   36
    AND ALL THAT FAMOUS HARMONY OF LEAVES, ...   120 SORROW OF LOVE   3
    AND OF THAT FAMOUS FERGUS, NESSA'S HUSBAND, ...   183 QUEEN MAEVE   71
    WITH FAMOUS PORTRAITS OF OUR ANCESTORS! . . . . .   418 ANCEST HOUSES   37
    AND GONE ARE PHIDIAS' FAMOUS IVORIES . . . .   428 NINETEEN 19   7
    OR BREAK IN BITS THE FAMOUS IVORIES . . . .   430 NINETEEN 19   47
    BELOVED BOOKS THAT FAMOUS HANDS HAVE BOUND, ...   491 COOLE BALLYLEE   27
    HE MUST GROW A FAMOUS MAN! . . . .   576 WHAT THEN   2
    AND THEY BUT FAMOUS OLD UPHOLSTERIES . . . .   579 DOR WELLESLEY   3
    SOME ANCIENT FAMOUS AUTHORS MISREPRESENT, ...   579 DOR WELLESLEY   15
    FOUND MANY A FAMOUS MAN THERE! . . . .   584 GHOST ROG CASE   35
    A FAMOUS, A BRILLIANT FIGURE . . . .   608 SONGS BURDEN 3   16
    VIOLENT AND FAMOUS, STRODE AMONG THE DEAD! . . . .   634 CUCHULAIN COMF   2
    OH FAMOUS DYING MINION OF THE SUN, ...   673 ISLE STAT II 3   197
    FAMOUS, A MAN OF RULES, A VICTOR.   STANDS . . . .   709 FERENCZ RENYI   9
FAN
    THAT FAN THE PULSES OF DELIGHTED AIR, ...   32 OISIN 2   V   50A
    BUT SHE TOOK UP HER FAN FROM THE TABLE . . . . . .   160 CAP AND BELLS   19
    BUT SHE TOOK HER FAN FROM THE TABLE, ...   160 CAP AND BELLS   V   19
    OF OCEAN FAN THEE INTO LIFE, AND FOLD . . . . . .   688 TWO TITANS   56
FANATIC
    MY FANATIC HEART. . . . .   506 REMORSE SPEECH   5
    MY FANATIC HEART. . . . .   506 REMORSE SPEECH   10
    A FANATIC HEART. . . . .   506 REMORSE SPEECH   15
    DOWN THE FANATIC, DOWN THE CLOWN! . . . .   544 TO SAME TUNE 1   8
    DOWN THE FANATIC, DOWN THE CLOWN! . . . .   545 TO SAME TUNE 1   18
    DOWN THE FANATIC, DOWN THE CLOWN! . . . .   545 TO SAME TUNE 1   28
    DOWN THE FANATIC, DOWN THE CLOWN! . . . .   546 TO SAME TUNE 2   V   REF
    DOWN THE FANATIC, DOWN THE CLOWN! . . . .   548 TO SAME TUNE 3   V   REF
FANATICISM
    SO DID FANATICISM AND HATE ENSLAVE IT, ...   630 CIRCUS ANIMALS   22
FANATICS
    WHAT FANATICS INVENT . . . .   503 QUARREL IN AGE   2
    THOSE FANATICS ALL THAT WE DO WOULD UNDO! . . . .   544 TO SAME TUNE 1   7
    THOSE FANATICS ALL THAT WE DO WOULD UNDO! . . . .   545 TO SAME TUNE 1   17
    THOSE FANATICS ALL THAT WE DO WOULD UNDO! . . . .   545 TO SAME TUNE 1   27
    THOSE FANATICS ALL THAT WE DO WOULD UNDO! . . . .   546 TO SAME TUNE 2   V   REF
    THOSE FANATICS ALL THAT WE DO WOULD UNDO! . . . .   548 TO SAME TUNE 3   V   REF

263

	PAGE	TITLE		LINE
FANCIED				
THAT FANCIED GOODNESS MIGHT BE GAY,	432	NINETEEN 19		104
ALL THOSE ABSTRACTIONS THAT YOU FANCIED WERE	469	HARUN RASHID		182
AND THOSE ABSTRACTIONS THAT YOU FANCIED WERE	469	HARUN RASHID	V	182
BECAUSE I HAD FANCIED LOVE A CASUAL	533	HER TRIUMPH		2
HE FANCIED THAT I GAVE A SOUL	538	LAST CONFESS		9
FANCIES				
THAT IT CAN TAKE WHAT FORM COOK NATURE FANCIES	377	PHASES OF MOON		115
FANCY				
WHATEVER WOMAN'S LOVER HAD HIT HER FANCY,	181	QUEEN MAEVE		24
THE ONLY RICHES THAT HAVE HIT MY FANCY.	226	SHADOW WATER B		96
THAT SET HIM TO THE FANCY. ALL WOULD BE WELL	230	SHADOW WATER B		177
TO FANCY THAT SHE'D BRING YOU HOME AGAIN.	248	SHADOW WATER B		549
MY FANCY, AND SET MY BOYISH LIPS TO SAY,	270	PARDON FATHERS		17
TO TAKE MY FANCY LIKE THE WIND	301	RUN PARADISE		26
HAD SOUNDED BETTER TO YOUR MOUNTAIN FANCY.	341	SHEP GOATHERD		61
THAT IT CAN TAKE WHAT FORM COOK NATURE FANCY	377	PHASES OF MOON	V	115
TO TEST THEIR FANCY BY THEIR SIGHT:	410	TOWER		44
FANCY THAT I CAN	507	STREAM AND SUN		8
MY FANCY ON A MAN,	515	GIRLS SONG B		3
A POISON DROP. A TOY, A FANCY ONCE,	700	MOSADA 3		24
A POISON DROP. THE TOY OF FANCY ONCE,	700	MOSADA 3	V	24
FANCY-MAN				
HAVE BEDDED WITH THEIR FANCY-MAN	789	SINGING HEAD		17
FAND				
WHO MET FAND WALKING AMONG FLAMING DEW	169	SECRET ROSE		13
AND NIAMH AND LABAN AND FAND, WHO COULD CHANGE TO AN OTTER OR FAWN,	209	UNDER THE MOON		12
AND FAND, AND NIAM, AND LABAN, WHO COULD CHANGE TO AN OTTER OR FAWN,	209	UNDER THE MOON	V	12
FAN-FORMED				
WHITENED AFAR WITH SURGE, FAN-FORMED AND WIDE,	31	OISIN 2		28
WHITENING THE SURGE AFAR, FAN-FORMED AND WIDE,	31	OISIN 2	V	28
FANGLED SEE NEW-FANGLED				
FANNED				
FANNED THE DELIGHTED AIR LIKE WINGS OF BIRDS!	32	OISIN 2		50
FANTASIES				
WE HAD FED THE HEART ON FANTASIES,	425	STARES NEST		16
WE HAVE FED THE HEART ON FANTASIES,	425	STARES NEST	V	16
FANTASTIC				
PLEASE A FANTASTIC HEAD.	366	HER CHRIS TREE		8
ON A FANTASTIC RIDE, MY HORSE'S FLANKS ARE SPURRED	391	UNDER SATURN		6
ON A FANTASTIC RIDE I SWEAR MY HORSE'S FLANKS WERE SPURRED	391	UNDER SATURN	V	6
THOUGH FANTASTIC MEN SUPPOSE	530	OLD TOM AGAIN		4
WITH THOSE FANTASTIC DREAMS.	781	MY HEART BEAT		11
FANTASTICAL				
FANTASTICAL AND WILD	364	END OF DAY		3
EXCITED, PASSIONATE, FANTASTICAL	409	TOWER		5
FANTASY				
AS, FULL OF LOVING FANTASY.	13	OISIN 1		158
WHATEVER THEIR LOOSE FANTASY INVENT	398	LEADERS CROWD		4
MANKIND INANIMATE FANTASY.	406	IN TIME OF WAR	V	5
AND SPEAK BUT FANTASY. RECALL THE YEAR	462	HARUN RASHID		30
PERPLEXED HER FANTASY AND PLANNED HER CARE?	466	HARUN RASHID		114
THAT STIRRED HER FANTASY AND PLANNED HER CARE,	466	HARUN RASHID	V	114
WHERE FASHION OR MERE FANTASY DECREES	491	COOLE BALLYLEE		38
FANTASY OR INCIDENT	504	QUARREL IN AGE		4
FAR				
NIAMH, AND MY COUNTRY FAR	5	OISIN 1		48
MY HOME IS FAR FROM WHERE THE TIDE	5	OISIN 1	V	46
LIES FAR." I MOUNTED, AND SHE BOUND ME	9	OISIN 1	V	106
IN WHAT FAR KINGDOM DO YOU GO,	10	OISIN 1		115
AND FAR BEHIND US, SLOWLY ROUND	10	OISIN 1	V	114B
IN WHAT FAR KINGDOM DO YE GO,	10	OISIN 1	V	115
AND A FAR SOUND OF FEATHERY QUIRES:	13	OISIN 1		166
A FAR VAGUE SOUND OF FEATHERY CHOIRS,	13	OISIN 1	V	166
THUS ON THE WATERS, FAR AND SWEET,	26	OISIN 1	V	398A
YET LOVE AND KISS ON DIM SHORES FAR AWAY	29	OISIN 2		13
THEY LOVE AND KISS IN ISLANDS FAR AWAY,	29	OISIN 2	V	13
BUT LOVE AND KISS ON DIM SHORES FAR AWAY	29	OISIN 2	V	13
HALF IN THE UNVESSELLED SEA. WE'D MOUNTED FAR:	32	OISIN 2	V	47
"I BRING THEE A DELIVERER FROM FAR AWAY,	34	OISIN 2	V	78A
FOR NO MAN'S CRY SHALL EVER MOUNT SO FAR:	36	OISIN 2		108
FOR NEVER MORTAL CRY SO FAR HATH SENT.	36	OISIN 2	V	108
NOR NO MAN'S CRY SHALL EVER MOUNT SO FAR:	36	OISIN 2	V	108
THE STRANGER WATCHED THE SWORD: BUT NIAM FAR,	38	OISIN 2	V	136
THE FLOWERS STILL GREW THERE: FAR ON THE SEA'S WASTE	39	OISIN 2		163
TILL THE FAR DOORWAY GREW A BURNING BLOT	39	OISIN 2	V	152
'TIS OVER: FAR WITH MEMORY I SWAY AND ROCK.	43	OISIN 2	V	212
. . . FAR SUNG BY THE SENNACHIES.	50	OISIN 3		53
. . . FAR SUNG OF THE SENNACHIES.	50	OISIN 3	V	53
"LIKE ME WERE SOME GALLEY FORSAKEN FAR OFF IN MERIDIAN ISLE,	55	OISIN 3		117
. . . FAR FROM THE HAZEL AND OAK,	57	OISIN 3		146
LATER A SOUND CAME, HALF LOST IN THE SOUND OF A SHORE FAR AWAY,	57	OISIN 3		155
WATCHING THE BLESSED ONES MOVE FAR OFF, AND THE SMILE ON GOD'S FACE,	61	OISIN 3		199
FAR, FAR AWAY. I NAMED HIM AFTER YOU.	72	ANASHU VIJAYA		35
FAR, FAR AWAY. I NAMED HIM AFTER YOU.	72	ANASHU VIJAYA		35
FAR, FAR AWAY. I'VE NAMED HIM AFTER YOU.	72	ANASHU VIJAYA	V	35

FAR   (CONTINUED)
    FAR, FAR AWAY. I'VE NAMED HIM AFTER YOU. . . . .   72 ANASHU VIJAYA V   35
    ON THE FAR GOLDEN PEAK! ENORMOUS SHAPES, ...   74 ANASHU VIJAYA   68
    MURMURING HOW FAR AWAY ARE THE UNQUIET LANDS! . . . . .   78 INDIAN TO LOVE   10
    MURMURING HOW FAR AWAY ARE ALL EARTH'S FEVERISH LANDS. .   78 INDIAN TO LOVE V   10
    MURMURING GENTLY HOW FAR OFF ARE THE UNQUIET LANDS! . .   78 INDIAN TO LOVE V   10
    HOW FAR AWAY THE STARS SEEM, AND HOW FAR . . . .   80 EPHEMERA   8
    HOW FAR AWAY THE STARS SEEM, AND HOW FAR . . . .   80 EPHEMERA   8
    WITH HORSEMEN HURRYING NEAR AND FAR, ...   83 MAD KING GOLL V   18
    I PAUSED--AND FAR AWAY I DASHED . . . .   83 MAD KING GOLL V   31
    I PAUSED--AND FAR AWAY RUSHED ON, ...   83 MAD KING GOLL V   31
    FAR OFF BY FURTHEST ROSSES . . . .   87 STOLEN CHILD   15
    THE BELL THAT CALLS US ON! THE SWEET FAR THING. . . . .   115 ROSE OF BATTLE   28
    REST FAR FROM MEN. . . . .   116 FAERY SONG   10
    HE PACED UPON THE MOUNTAINS FAR ABOVE, ...   121 YOU ARE OLD V   11
    SOON FAR FROM THE ROSE AND THE LILY . . . .   122 WHITE BIRDS   11
    FAR OFF, MOST SECRET, AND INVIOLATE ROSE, ...   169 SECRET ROSE V   1
    FAR OFF, MOST SECRET, AND INVIOLATE ROSE? . . . . . .   170 SECRET ROSE V   32
    OF THE FAR WANDERING SHADOWS HAS COME TO ME, ...   183 QUEEN MAEVE V   80
    FAR OUT UNDER A WINDLESS SKY! . . . .   197 BAILE AILLINN   181
    IS EDEN FAR AWAY, OR DO YOU HIDE . . . .   218 WOODS OF COOLE   30
    STRAYING TOO FAR INTO THE NORTH OR SOUTH, ...   226 SHADOW WATER B   86
    BEFORE HIM OR BEHIND, BUT THAT FAR OFF . . . .   279 TWO KINGS   55
    "YOU THAT HAVE WANDERED FAR AND WIDE . . . .   295 THREE BEGGARS   11
    "YOU HAVE WANDERED FAR AND WIDE, ...   295 THREE BEGGARS V   11
    FAR FROM THE CUSTOMARY SKIES, ...   360 ALF POLLEXFEN   14
    FROM THE FAR TOWER WHERE MILTON'S PLATONIST . . . . .   373 PHASES OF MOON   15
    WERE NOT OUR BEDS FAR OFF I'D RING THE BELL, ...   377 PHASES OF MOON   124
    WERE I TO TRAVEL FAR AND WIDE . . . .   398 BREAK OF DAY   8
    ONE HEARS THE RUMBLE OF IT FAR BELOW . . . .   420 MY HOUSE V   20B
    O BUT HER HEART WOULD BREAK TO LEARN MY THOUGHTS ARE FAR   450 OWEN AHERNE   20
      AWAY."
    SHAKESPEAREAN FISH SWAM THE SEA, FAR AWAY FROM LAND! . .   485 THREE MOVEMENT   1
    FLED TO FAR COUNTRIES, OR SHELTERED THEMSELVES . . . .   546 TO SAME TUNE 2   4
    WHAT BROUGHT THEM THERE SO FAR FROM THEIR HOME, ...   549 SEVERED HEAD   8
    YOU ASK WHAT I HAVE FOUND, AND FAR AND WIDE I GO! . . .   580 CURSE CROMWELL   1
    THAT CRIED IT FAR AND WIDE, ...   582 ROGER CASEMENT   18
    THE SMUGGLER MIDDLETON, BUTLERS FAR BACK, ...   605 YOU CONTENT   15
    FLED TO FAR COUNTRIES, OR SHELTERED THEMSELVES . . . .   613 MARCH SONGS 1   4
    FAR UP IN THE STRETCHES OF NIGHT! . . . .   623 HIGH TALK   12
    FAR THE MORNING VAPOURS SHATTER, ...   648 ISLE STAT I 1   89
    AND FAR AWAY THE HERON SAILS, I WIS. . . . .   649 ISLE STAT I 1   116
    AND, LEAPING TO THEIR FEET, FAR ECHOES CRIED, ...   659 ISLE STAT II 1   13
    ONE HAND BROW-SHADING, FAR ACROSS THE NIGHT, ...   663 ISLE STAT II 2   27
    I WOULD HAVE GONE ALSO! BUT FAR AWAY . . . .   663 ISLE STAT II 2   37
    IN THE FAR WORLD WILL VANISH FROM THY MIND, ...   670 ISLE STAT II 3   93
    FAR FLEETER THAN THE MILLION-FOOTED SEA. . . . . . .   670 ISLE STAT II 3   108
    FOR I AM MIGHTIER NOW BY FAR THAN THEE, ...   673 ISLE STAT II 3   193
    IN THOSE FAR YEARS, O DAUGHTER OF THE DAYS. . . . . .   674 ISLE STAT II 3   213
    AND CROUCH IN SOME FAR STILLNESS OF THE ISLE, AND DIE. .   675 ISLE STAT II 3   246
    IN A FAR STILLNESS OF THE ISLAND DIE. . . . .   675 ISLE STAT II 3 V   246
    FAR OFF IN DROWSY VALLEYS . . . .   680 LOVE AND DEATH   5
    THE OTHER IS NOT FAR. . . . .   680 LOVE AND DEATH   28
    EVE-SOOTHED IN SOME FAR LEAFY REST, ...   686 LIFE   10
    IN AUTUMN, WHEN FAR DOWN THE MOUNTAIN SLOPES . . . . .   690 MOSADA 1   12
    FAR OUT UPON THE WATER WORLD AND RINGED . . . . . .   693 MOSADA 1   80
    HEARING THE FAR OFF SINGING GUILE AND GROANED, ...   693 MOSADA 1 V   88
    IN THE FAR ISLE SHE SANG HERSELF ASLEEP, ...   694 MOSADA 1   90
    HE IS NOT FAR. I'D HAVE HIM SPEAK FOR HER. . . . . .   696 MOSADA 2   13
    WILL BE THE FAINT FAR THUNDER-SOUND, AS THOUGH . . . .   699 MOSADA 3   10
    WILL MOVE THE FAINT FAR THUNDER-SOUND, AS THOUGH . . .   699 MOSADA 3 V   10
    JUST NOW MY SOUL ROSE UP AND TOUCHED IT, FAR . . . . .   705 REMEMBRANCE   13
    SLEEP IN SOME FAR OTHER FIELD . . . .   705 DAWN-SONG   3
    A SOLDIER ANSWERS! "BY THE CAMP'S FAR END . . . . .   712 FERENCZ RENYI   67
    AFRAID TO BE TOO FAR." "AY, BRING HER HERE!" . . . .   712 FERENCZ RENYI   69
    AND LOST AND FAR IN YONDER HILLS I KNOW! . . . . . .   713 FERENCZ RENYI   98
    THERE FAR AWAY FROM ALL WE TWO WILL GO, ...   714 FERENCZ RENYI   99
    HAYNAU, THINE HOUR HAS COME, THY FOLLOWERS FAR . . .   715 FERENCZ RENYI   .17
    AND THE WINDS COME DOWN AND BLOW THEM WITH THE VAPOURS   719 PHANTOM SHIP   28
      FAR AWAY.
    COME I KNOW WHERE, FAR AWAY, ...   727 LOVERS QUARREL   34
    FAR AWAY THE STARRY MIRTH . . . .   731 STREET DANCERS   7
    MAYBE NOW IN SOME FAR LANE, ...   731 STREET DANCERS   14
    THERE--THERE--BY THE OAR. THE CROWN OF A FAR COUNTRY. .   763 SHADOW WATER A   310
    I HAVE HEARD FROM FAR BELOW . . . .   783 GREY ROUND   25
FAR-AWAY
    THAT CARRIED THE FISH FOR THE SALE IN THE FAR-AWAY TOWN,   91 OLD FISHERMAN V   7
FARE
    THE HEART'S GROWN BRUTAL FROM THE FARE! . . . . . .   425 STARES NEST   17
    THE HEART GROWS BRUTAL FROM THE FARE, ...   425 STARES NEST V   17
FAREWELL
    FAREWELL! I MUST BE GONE I-WIS, ...   67 HAPPY SHEPHERD V   46D
    FAREWELL, VIJAYA. NAY, NO WORD, NO WORD! . . . . .   75 ANASHU VIJAYA   83
    ARE LOVE, AND A CONTINUAL FAREWELL." . . . .   81 EPHEMERA   24
    WHEN I HAVE SAID FAREWELL TO THIS MAN HERE, ...   250 SHADOW WATER B   587
    FAREWELL! FAREWELL! THE SWORD IS IN THE ROPE-- . . .   251 SHADOW WATER B   595
    FAREWELL! FAREWELL! THE SWORD IS IN THE ROPE-- . . .   251 SHADOW WATER B   595
    OF HILL TWO SHEPHERDS COME. FAREWELL! I'LL DON . . .   659 ISLE STAT II 1   28
    BETWEEN THE HORNED HILLS--SHEPHERDS, FAREWELL! . . .   682 SEEKER   27
    SHEPHERDS, FAREWELL! HE SOON WILL BE--ASHES . . . .   682 SEEKER   34
    AND DYING MEN--AND YET--BUT NO, FAREWELL. . . . . .   698 MOSADA 2   49

265

	PAGE	TITLE	LINE

FAREWELL (CONTINUED)
OUT OF THEIR HATRED. MY BELOVED, FAREWELL. • • • • •   767 SHADOW WATER A   400
FARISTAH
FARISTAH, AND NO LIVING EAR BUT HIS. • • • • • • • •   461 HARUN RASHID   V   4
FARM
THE MILKING-PLACE, THE SHELTERED FARM? • • • • • •   151 HEART OF WOMAN V   6
ABOUT A FARM," THE SECOND CRIED. • • • • •   296 THREE BEGGARS   V   38
TO THEIR FARM WORK! HOW SILENT ALL WILL BE!   699 MOSADA 3   8
RINGED ROUND AND FONDLED, A BROWN FARM HOUSE SEES. • •   710 FERENCZ RENYI V   23
TO THE ORCHARD-CIRCLED FARM! • • • • • • • •   727 LOVERS QUARREL   50
FARMER
THERE'S MANY A STRONG FARMER • • • • • • • •   213 HAPPY TOWNLAND   1
A FARMER HAS MORE DIGNITY.'" • • • • • • • •   296 THREE BEGGARS   37
FARMER'S
AND TURNED THE FARMER'S MEMORY FROM HIS CATTLE,   129 BOOK STORIES   6
CLIPPED AN INSOLENT FARMER'S EARS • • • • • •   410 TOWER   31
WHATEVER GOOD A FARMER'S GOT • • • • • • •   586 PARNELLITES   13
FARMERS
FOR O, THE STRONG FARMERS • • • • • • • •   215 HAPPY TOWNLAND   29
FARMERS JOSTLED AT THE FAIR • • • • • • • •   410 TOWER   39
FARMHOUSE
A FARMHOUSE THAT IS SHELTERED BY ITS WALL, • • • • •   419 MY HOUSE   2
FARM-HOUSE
A FARM-HOUSE THAT IS SHELTERED BY ITS WALL,   419 MY HOUSE   V   2
ABOVE THE FARM-HOUSE BY THE LITTLE LAKE • • • • •   699 MOSADA 3   3
HE NUMBERS. HE A BROWN FARM-HOUSE SEES, • • • • •   710 FERENCZ RENYI   22
FARM-WORK
TO THEIR FARM-WORK! HOW SILENT ALL WILL BE.   699 MOSADA 3   V   8
FAR-OFF
AND THEY WHO TO A FAR-OFF PLACE HAD FLED, • • • •   41 OISIN 2   V 184
AND, IN A FAR-OFF, GENTLE VALLEY STOPPING, • • • •   68 SAD SHEPHERD   13
HE FLED, AND IN A FAR-OFF VALLEY STOPPING, • • • •   68 SAD SHEPHERD   V   13
FAR-OFF, MOST SECRET, AND INVIOLATE ROSE, • • • •   169 SECRET ROSE   1
FAR-OFF, MOST SECRET, AND INVIOLATE ROSE? • • • •   170 SECRET ROSE   32
BEFORE HIM OR BEHIND, BUT THAT FAR-OFF • • • • •   279 TWO KINGS   V   55
HEARING THE FAR-OFF SINGING GUILE, AND GROANED, • • • •   693 MOSADA 1   88
FARRELL
THEN FARRELL, STEEL KING, MASTER OF MEN, • • • • •   790 DEDICATION   5
FARROW
• • • ITS FARROW THAT SO SOLID SEEM, • • • • • • •   481 BLOOD AND MOON   26
FARTHEST
"IN THE ISLES OF THE FARTHEST SEAS WHERE ONLY THE SPIRITS   56 OISIN 3   133
COME.
FAR-WANDERING
OF THE FAR-WANDERING SHADOWS HAS COME TO ME • • • • •   183 QUEEN MAEVE   80
FASCINATION
THE FASCINATION OF WHAT'S DIFFICULT • • • • • • •   260 FASC DIFFICULT   T
THE FASCINATION OF WHAT'S DIFFICULT • • • • • • •   260 FASC DIFFICULT   1
FASHION
AND GREW TO BE OUT OF FASHION • • • • • •   211 O DO NOT LOVE   3
OR YOU WILL GROW OUT OF FASHION • • • • •   212 O DO NOT LOVE   11
BUT HE THAT GETS THEIR LOVE AFTER THE FASHION • • • •   228 SHADOW WATER B 145
I SHALL HAVE LOVE IN THEIR IMMORTAL FASHION! • • • •   237 SHADOW WATER B 326
YOUR EARS THAN STORIES NOW IN FASHION, • • • • •   271 GREY ROCK   5
CUT IN THE TURKISH FASHION, • • • • • •   363 DOLLS DRAWINGS   8
TIRED OF THAT COURTLY FASHION, • • • • • •   378 CAT AND MOON   15
TIRED OF HER COURTLY FASHION, • • • • • •   378 CAT AND MOON   V   15
THOUGH YOU CAN FASHION EVERYTHING • • • • •   436 FOR MY SON   17
DID QUATTROCENTO FINGER FASHION IT • • • • •   444 SCHOOL CHILDR   26
WHERE FASHION OR MERE FANTASY DECREES • • • •   491 COOLE BALLYLEE   38
AND WEAR A COAT IN FASHION, • • • • • • •   607 SONGS BURDEN 2   21
WITH A HAT OUT OF FASHION, • • • • • • •   627 STATES HOLIDAY   29
A FASHION WITH US MOORISH MAIDS, BEGOT • • • •   700 MOSADA 3   25
FASHIONED
HER FACE SEEMED FASHIONED ALL OF MOONLIT VAPOURS, • •   33 OISIN 2   V   70
FASHIONED TO BE THE MOTHER OF STRONG CHILDREN! • • •   181 QUEEN MAEVE   26
I THINK HE FASHIONED FROM HIS OPPOSITE • • • •   368 EGO DOMINUS   27
THE PRIMUM MOBILE THAT FASHIONED US • • • •   423 MY DESCENDANTS   17
WHAT QUINTO-CENTO FINGER FASHIONED IT, • • • •   444 SCHOOL CHILDR   V   26
DA VINCI' FINGER SO HAD FASHIONED IT • • • • •   444 SCHOOL CHILDR   V   26
MONTASHIGI, THIRD OF HIS FAMILY, FASHIONED IT • •   478 SELF AND SOUL   25
MONTASHIGI OF OSAFUME FASHIONED IT • • • • •   478 SELF AND SOUL   V   25
FASHION'S
BUT FASHION'S CHANGED, THAT HIGH-HORSE RIDERLESS • • •   492 COOLE BALLYLEE V   46
I PRAY—FOR FASHION'S WORD IS OUT • • • • • • •   553 PRAYER OLD AGE   9
FAST
WHEN THEY FROZE THE CLOTH ON MY BODY LIKE ARMOUR RIVETED   57 OISIN 3   151
FAST,
ON CREVROE OR ON BROAD KNOCKFEFIN, WITH MANY OF OLD THEY   59 OISIN 3   V 179
FAST
TO MAKE HER FAST WHILE WE ARE PLUNDERING HER. • • • •   232 SHADOW WATER B 225
THAT GIRL MY UNREMEMBERING NIGHTS HOLD FAST • • •   384 VISION ROBART   50
SHE ROSE, AND WITH HER EYES SHUT FAST IN SLEEP • •   468 HARUN RASHID   152
AND THERE, FREE AND YET FAST, • • • • • • •   472 ALL SOUL NIGHT   57
AND WHITHER, UNCOUTH HUNTER? WHY SO FAST? • • • •   651 ISLE STAT I 2   1
FOR NIGHT COMES FAST. LOOK DOWN ON ME, MY LOVE, • • •   703 MOSADA 3   103
HE FADES AMONG THE MISTS! HOW FAST THEY COME, • • • •   703 MOSADA 3   117
ITS STRANGE HEART BEATING FAST • • • • • • • •   785 YOUR HEART   6
FASTED
I FASTED FOR SOME FORTY DAYS ON BREAD AND BUTTERMILK, • •   592 PILGRIM   1

FASTEN
    FASTEN YOUR HAIR WITH A GOLDEN PIN, ... 157 BELOVED RHYMES 1
FASTENED
    AND FASTENED TO A DYING ANIMAL . . . . 408 SAIL BYZANTIUM 22
    AND FASTENED TO THIS DYING ANIMAL . . . . 408 SAIL BYZANTIUM V 22
FASTING
    FASTING AND PRAYERS. TELL ON. YES, YES, ... 24 OISIN 1 360
    FASTING AND PRAYERS. TELL ON. AY, AY! . . . . 24 OISIN 1 V 360
    A SAINT OF MUNSTER, WHEN MUCH FASTING, SAW . . . . . 696 MOSADA 2 20
    FROM FASTING—SEE, THE RED LIGHT SLANTING DOWN . . . . 697 MOSADA 2 36
FAT
    THAT HAS MADE FAT THE MURDEROUS MOTH; . . . . 156 FORGOT BEAUTY 8
    THE FAT FLOCKS AND THE FIELDS' FATNESS, ... 540 FROM ANTIGONE 4
    NO HAMLET THIN FROM EATING FLIES, A FAT . . . . . . 610 STATUES 19
FATAL
    FOR THERE A FATAL IMAGE GROWS . . . . 135 TWO TREES 25
    SANG OF THE BEAST THAT GAVE THE FATAL WOUND. . . . . 537 HER VISION 16
FATE
    WE MOCKED AT TIME AND FATE AND CHANCE . . . . 20 OISIN 1 291
    FOR THESE WERE ANCIENT OISIN'S FATE . . . . 24 OISIN 1 361
    MAY SLEEP IN THE END WITH THE WHOLE OF HIS FATE DONE, . . 28 OISIN 1 V 423F
    COME NEAR, THAT NO MORE BLINDED BY MAN'S FATE, . . . 101 ROSE UPON ROOD 9
    FOR GOD HAS BID THEM SHARE AN EQUAL FATE! . . . . . 115 ROSE OF BATTLE 32
    I KNOW THAT I SHALL MEET MY FATE . . . . 328 IRISH AIRMAN 1
    I COULD BUT LEAVE HIM TO HIS FATE! . . . . 514 JANE GROWN OLD 11
    BEFORE HE CAN ACCOMPLISH FATE, ... 638 BEN BULBEN 35
    I GO AS SOFT AS FOLLY! I AM FATE." . . . . 686 LIFE 18
    I GO AS SOFT AS FOLLY! I AM FATE." . . . . 735 QUATRAIN APHOR 20
FATED
    MOURN YE ON GRASS-GREEN PLAINS OF ERI FATED, ... 738 MOURN THEN ON 9
FATHER
    "MY FATHER AND MY MOTHER ARE . . . . 5 OISIN 1 46
    HAD KISSED MY FATHER, LONG-ARMED FIN, ... 10 OISIN 1 V 112B
    WITH HER OLD FATHER THE BLIND WOOD-CUTTER; . . . . 74 ANASHU VIJAYA 63
    THE BALLAD OF FATHER O'HART . . . . 91 FATHER OHART T
    FATHER O'HART . . . . 91 FATHER OHART V T
    GOOD FATHER JOHN O'HART . . . . 91 FATHER OHART 1
    BUT FATHER JOHN WENT UP, ... 92 FATHER OHART 9
    AND FATHER JOHN WENT DOWN! . . . . 92 FATHER OHART 10
    MY FATHER STANDS AMID HIS BATTLE-CARS." . . . . . 107 CUCHULAIN SEA 26
    MY FATHER STANDS." "AGED, WORN OUT WITH WARS . . . 107 CUCHULAIN SEA 29
    "MY FATHER," MADE HE, SMILING, ANSWER THEN, . . . 107 CUCHULAIN SEA V 25
    "MY FATHER DWELLS AMONG THE SEA-WORN BANDS, . . . 107 CUCHULAIN SEA V 25
    MY FATHER STANDS AMID HIS BATTLE CARS." . . . . . 107 CUCHULAIN SEA V 26
    THE BALLAD OF FATHER GILLIGAN . . . . 132 FR GILLIGAN T
    FATHER GILLIGAN . . . . 132 FR GILLIGAN V T
    "FATHER! YOU COME AGAIN!" . . . . 133 FR GILLIGAN 32
    THE ALE CUP IS MY FATHER AND MY MOTHER. . . . . . 222 SHADOW WATER B V 11B
    THAT HAVE HAD DREAMS FOR FATHER, LIVE IN US. . . . 252 SHADOW WATER B 619
    OUR FATHER ROSICROSS IS IN HIS TOMB. . . . . . . 311 MOUNTAIN TOMB 4
    OUR FATHER ROSICROSS IS IN HIS TOMB. . . . . . . 311 MOUNTAIN TOMB 8
    OUR FATHER ROSICROSS SLEEPS IN HIS TOMB. . . . . . 311 MOUNTAIN TOMB 12
    FROM FATHER UNTO SON . . . . 421 MY TABLE 19
    TRUTHS WITHOUT FATHER CAME, TRUTHS THAT NO BOOK . . 467 HARUN RASHID 138
    THE FATHER AND HIS ANGELIC HIERARCHY . . . . . . 483 VERONIC NAPKIN 4
    MY GREAT-GRANDFATHER'S FATHER TALKED OF MUSIC, . . 486 SEVEN SAGES 4
    MY GREAT-GRANDFATHER'S FATHER TALKED OF MUSIC AND PAINTING, . 486 SEVEN SAGES V 4
    FATHER AND CHILD . . . . 531 FATHER CHILD T
    A WOMAN YOUNG AND OLD I FATHER AND CHILD . . . . . 531 FATHER CHILD V T
    RECALL HIS TRINITY. A FATHER, MOTHER, CHILD (A DAUGHTER 556 RIBH PATRICK V 2
     OR A SON)
    MY FATHER UPON THE ABBEY STAGE, BEFORE HIM A RAGING CROWD! 577 LOFTY THINGS 2
    MY FATHER SANG THAT SONG, ... 613 MARCH SONGS 1 8
    MY FATHER SANG THAT SONG, ... 613 MARCH SONGS 1 18
    MY FATHER SANG THAT SONG, ... 614 MARCH SONGS 1 28
    FROM COLLAR TO COLLAR, FROM STILT TO STILT, FROM FATHER 623 HIGH TALK 10
     TO CHILD.
    YET 'TIS NO SIN! MY FATHER TAUGHT IT ME. . . . . . 692 MOSADA 1 50
    COME, FATHER. LADY, I NOR REST NOR SIT. . . . . . 720 WITCH VIVIEN 18
    AND—NO! I'LL NONE OF THESE, OLD FATHER WRINKLES. . . 721 WITCH VIVIEN 23
    WITH LOADED DICE. ANOTHER CHANCE! COME, FATHER! . . 721 WITCH VIVIEN 45
    AND NOW WITH FATHER TIME I'M FACE TO FACE. . . . . 722 WITCH VIVIEN 57
    CHANCE, AND NOT SKILL, HAS FAVOURED YOU, OLD FATHER! . 722 WITCH VIVIEN 60
    THE FATHER DROPT HIS ROSARY— . . . . 730 PRIEST FAIRY 57
    SHE PRAYS FOR FATHER, MOTHER DEAR, ... 735 IN CHURCH 1
    HER PRAYER FOR FATHER, MOTHER DEAR, ... 736 IN CHURCH 13
    LIKE SON TO FATHER . . . . 769 BLOOD BOND V 2
    LIKE SON TO FATHER. . . . . 770 BLOOD BOND 3
    MEN THAT REVERE YOUR FATHER YET . . . . 791 REPRISALS 17
FATHERLESS
    BEING FATHERLESS COULD HAVE HER WAY . . . . 404 FOR DAUGHTER 28
FATHER'S
    BUT LEFT THE HOUSE AS IN HIS FATHER'S TIME . . . . . 341 SHEP GOATHERD 53
    THAT IT WAS MADE IN YOUR GREAT FATHER'S REIGN." . . . 464 HARUN RASHID 72
    EVEN FROM BOYHOOD, IN MY FATHER'S HOUSE, ... 683 SEEKER 48
FATHERS
    AND EVEN THE NAMES OF HIS FATHERS, AND EVEN THE WORKS OF 51 OISIN 3 V 62
     HIS HANDS?
    I HELPED YOUR FATHERS WHEN THEY BUILT THESE WALLS, . . . 184 QUEEN MAEVE 97
    PARDON, OLD FATHERS, IF YOU STILL REMAIN . . . . . . 269 PARDON FATHERS 1
    HE RAN TOWARDS THE HOUSE HIS FATHERS BUILT . . . . . 279 TWO KINGS V 45E

	PAGE	TITLE		LINE

FATHERS   (CONTINUED)

NEVER TO LEAVE THAT VALLEY HIS FATHERS CALLED THEIR HOME.	391	UNDER SATURN		16
FROM MY OLD FATHERS, I MUST NOURISH DREAMS	422	MY DESCENDANTS		2
OLD FATHERS, GREAT-GRANDFATHERS,	518	LOVES LONENESS		1
OLD FATHERS, GREAT GRANDFATHERS,	518	LOVES LONENESS	V	1
HIS FATHERS SERVED THEIR FATHERS BEFORE CHRIST WAS CRUCIFIED.	580	CURSE CROMWELL		6
HIS FATHERS SERVED THEIR FATHERS BEFORE CHRIST WAS CRUCIFIED.	580	CURSE CROMWELL		6

FATHOMLESS

ALL NIGHT'S FATHOMLESS WISDOM COME,	519	HER DREAM		2

FATIGUE

NOR LANGUOR NOR FATIGUE! AN ENDLESS FEAST,	44	OISIN 2		223
NO LANGUOR, NO FATIGUE! AN ENDLESS FEAST,	44	OISIN 2	V	223
NOR LANGUOR NOR FATIGUE! AND ENDLESS FEAST,	44	OISIN 2	V	223

FATNESS

THE FAT FLOCKS AND THE FIELDS' FATNESS,	540	FROM ANTIGONE		4

FATTEN

THEY LEFT THEIR BODIES TO FATTEN THE WOLVES,	545	TO SAME TUNE 2		2
THEY LEFT THEIR HOMESTEADS TO FATTEN THE FOXES,	546	TO SAME TUNE 2		3
THEY LEFT THEIR BODIES TO FATTEN THE WOLVES,	613	MARCH SONGS 1		2
THEY LEFT THEIR HOMESTEADS TO FATTEN THE FOXES,	613	MARCH SONGS 1		3

FATTENING

TILL, FATTENING THE WINDS OF THE MORNING, AN ODOUR OF NEW-MOWN HAY	57	OISIN 3		153
FIELDS FATTENING SLOW, MEN WISE IN JOY,	82	MAD KING GOLL	V	6

FATTER

THE FIELDS GREW FATTER DAY BY DAY,	82	MAD KING GOLL		7

FAUN

AND I WOULD PLEASE THE HAPLESS FAUN,	67	HAPPY SHEPHERD		47
THAT I MAY SOOTHE THAT HAPLESS FAUN,	67	HAPPY SHEPHERD	V	47
AN OATEN PIPE UNTO A LISTENING FAUN,	678	ISLE STAT II 3	V	301

FAVOURED

CHANCE, AND NOT SKILL, HAS FAVOURED YOU, OLD FATHER!	722	WITCH VIVIEN		60

FAVOURITE

WE WILL FIND HER FAVOURITE LAIR,	706	DAWN-SONG		26

FAWN

AND NIAMH AND LABAN AND FAND, WHO COULD CHANGE TO AN OTTER OR FAWN,	209	UNDER THE MOON		12
AND FAND, AND NIAM, AND LABAN, WHO COULD CHANGE TO AN OTTER OR FAWN,	209	UNDER THE MOON	V	12
TREMBLING IN THE BLUE HEAVENS LIKE A WHITE FAWN	251	SHADOW WATER B		611
AN OATEN PIPE UNTO A LISTENING FAWN,	678	ISLE STAT II 3		301
TREMBLING IN THE BLUE HEAVENS LIKE A WHITE FAWN	769	SHADOW WATER A		427

FAY

MY HUMAN SADNESS FAY ARMS WOUND.	11	OISIN 1	V	138
AND HER BRIGHT BODY--NOW OF FAY AND MAN!	29	OISIN 2	V	7
AND MAY NO RESTLESS FAY WITH FIDGET FINGER	75	ANASHU VIJAYA		90
MAY NEVER RESTLESS FAY WITH FIDGET FINGER	75	ANASHU VIJAYA	V	90
FROM THEE I SNATCHED IT! E'EN THE FAY THAT TRIPS	670	ISLE STAT II 3		98
AND THEN THE FAY QUEEN SOBBED APART,	730	PRIEST FAIRY		70
AND ALL THE SAD FAY CHIVALRY	730	PRIEST FAIRY		71

FEACRA

. . FINVARRA, FEACRA, AND CAOLTE	174	ELEMENT POWERS	V	T

FEAR

AND THINGS THAT FEAR THE DAWN OF THE MORROW	20	OISIN 1		302
AND ALL LISTLESS HOURS FEAR US,	21	OISIN 1		317
AND WE FEAR NO DAWNING MORROW,	21	OISIN 1		318
AND WE NEVER FEAR THE MORROW	21	OISIN 1	V	318
OR FEAR THE WILD GREY OSPREY SORROW."	23	OISIN 1	V	342
AND A SAD MOUTH, THAT FEAR MADE TREMULOUS	34	OISIN 2		71
HAD NEITHER HOPE NOR FEAR. I BADE THEM HIDE	38	OISIN 2		139
OF FEAR, I BADE THEM GO! AND FOR THE FIGHT	38	OISIN 2	V	142
CAST THE LOOSE BULK, LEST NIAM FEAR HIM DEAD!	41	OISIN 2	V	183
. . . ALONE WITH REMEMBRANCE AND FEAR!	63	OISIN 3		218
WITHOUT LAUGHTER, A COUGHING, ALONE WITH REMEMBRANCE AND FEAR!	63	OISIN 3	V	218
THE SONG OF OUTLAWS AND THEIR FEAR!	85	MAD KING GOLL	V	64
WHILE HUSHED FROM FEAR, OR LOUD WITH HOPE, A BAND	114	ROSE OF BATTLE		5
AND PRESSING ON, OR LINGERING SLOW WITH FEAR,	114	ROSE OF BATTLE	V	5
AND BROOD ON HOPES AND FEAR NO MORE.	125	GOES FERGUS		6
FOR SOMEBODY HID HATRED AND HOPE AND DESIRE AND FEAR	153	CHANGE BELOVED		4
AND I HAVE HATRED AND HOPE AND DESIRE AND FEAR	153	CHANGE BELOVED	V	4
TO HIS HEART, BIDDING IT HAVE NO FEAR	158	TO HIS HEART		T
TO MY HEART, BIDDING IT HAVE NO FEAR	158	TO HIS HEART	V	T
OR CRY ABOUT ONE'S EARS. NOTHING TO FEAR.	222	SHADOW WATER B		19
THAT MAKES ME FEAR TO RAISE A HAND AGAINST HIM,	222	SHADOW WATER B	V	16A
BUT WERE YOU NOT AFRAID? WHY SHOULD I FEAR?	224	SHADOW WATER B		41
THERE'S NOTHING IN THE WORLD THAT'S WORTH A FEAR.	238	SHADOW WATER B		353
I CAN PUT FEAR AWAY AS A QUEEN SHOULD.	238	SHADOW WATER B		355
AM I TO FEAR THE WAVES, OR IS THE MOON	246	SHADOW WATER B		508
AND SHOOK WITH HATE AND FEAR.	254	WOMAN HOMER		4
SO WITH A LAUGH AT HIS OWN FEAR	303	HOUR DAWN		31
A STRING OF SCHOLARS WENT IN FEAR	381	SONG OF FOOL		7
A GREY GULL LOST ITS FEAR AND FLEW	397	POLIT PRISONER		3
WHETHER FOR DAILY PITTANCE OR IN BLIND FEAR	482	BLOOD AND MOON		37
"OR DRIVEN FROM HOME AND LEFT TO DIE IN FEAR."	635	CUCHULAIN COMF		22
IS THE WORST MAN HAS TO FEAR.	637	BEN BULBEN		20
JOY'S BROTHER, FEAR, DWELLS EVER IN EACH BREAST--	651	ISLE STAT I 1		155
JOY'S BROTHER, FEAR, LURKS IN EACH LEAFY WAY.	651	ISLE STAT I 1		156
THE BROWN WEED BURDEN, SO THE SWORD BRINGS FEAR	660	ISLE STAT II 1		45

268

FEAR (CONTINUED)

I'D KILL HER IF SHE WERE. NAY, DO NOT FEAR! . . . . . 669 ISLE STAT II 3   69
AS THOUGH SHE WHOM YOU FEAR HAD CROSSED THE WIDE . . . . 669 ISLE STAT II 3   77
TO QUESTION HER--OH NO, I DID NOT FEAR, ... 676 ISLE STAT II 3   265
A PEASANT PALE AND PRETTY, HER EYES FOR FEAR, ... 713 FERENCZ RENYI   81
A PEASANT YOUNG AND FAIR, HER EYES FOR FEAR . . . . 713 FERENCZ RENYI V   81
A PEASANT, PALE AND PRETTY, HER EYES FROM FEAR, . . . 713 FERENCZ RENYI V   81
THEN WHEREFORE FEAR THE USURY OF TIME, ... 724 KANVA ON SELF   17
DO NOT FEAR US, EARTHLY MAID! . . . . 726 LOVERS QUARREL   1
NIGH OF HIS WITS BY FEAR BEREFT. . . . . 730 PRIEST FAIRY   50
CAST OUT ALL HOPE, CAST OUT ALL FEAR, ... 743 DANAAN QUICK   25

FEARED

AND FEARED ALWAYS THE BOW-STRING'S TWANGING. . . . . . 3 OISIN 1 V 7GG
IT FEARED TO GIVE ITS LOVE A HURT WITH ALL THE TEMPEST   450 OWEN AHERNE   7
   THERE!
IT FEARED THE HURT THAT SHE COULD GIVE AND THEREFORE IT   450 OWEN AHERNE   8
   WENT MAD.

FEARFUL

FEARFUL OF THE THUNDER-BALL, ... 43 OISIN 2 V 208F
INTO SOME MOST FEARFUL SHAPE." . . . . 299 THREE HERMITS   23
OH, BOY, I'M BOUND ON A MOST FEARFUL QUEST! . . . . . 653 ISLE STAT I 2   31
WITH LITTLE VOICES SONGS OF FEARFUL THINGS. . . . . . 682 SEEKER   31
BE NOT AFRAID, YOU'LL SEE NO FEARFUL THING. . . . . . 693 MOSADA 1   74
A FEARFUL PALENESS CREEPS ACROSS HER BREAST . . . . . 701 MOSADA 3   69

FEARING

HOPING AND FEARING, BROUGHT ME WINE AND BREAD. . . . . 41 OISIN 2 V 184A
THEN FEARING THAT SOME LABOURER, ON HIS WAY . . . . . 283 TWO KINGS   145
AND FEARING THAT MY LIGHT DISTURBED HER SLEEP . . . . 467 HARUN RASHID   130
BUT FEARING THAT SHE WOULD REFUSE . . . . 792 GEORGE MOORE   2

FEARLESS

AND KNOW THAT IT IS FEARLESS. DO WHAT YOU WILL, . . . 238 SHADOW WATER B   350
TENDER AND FEARLESS ON HER FUNERAL PYRE! . . . . . . 688 NETTLESHIP   3

FEARS

EVERYTHING THAT FEARS TO-MORROW . . . . 20 OISIN 1 V 302
FOLDED IN LOVE THAT FEARS NO MORROW, ... 23 OISIN 1 V 341
AND SHIVERED, KNOWING THE ISLE OF MANY FEARS, ... 30 OISIN 2   25
AND CALLED HIM SWEETEST NAMES AND SOOTHED HIS FEARS. . . 30 OISIN 2 V 27
SO WARRED, SO FEASTED, WITH NOR DREAMS NOR FEARS, . . . 44 OISIN 2   222
SO WARRED, SO FEASTED WE. NO DREAMS, NO FEARS, ... 44 OISIN 2 V 222
AND BROOD ON HOPES AND FEARS NO MORE. . . . . 125 GOES FERGUS V 6
HIS MIND RAN ALL ON MONEY CARES AND FEARS, ... 127 DREAM OF FAERY   14
AND THE FOOL HEART OF THE COUNTING-HOUSE FEARS ALL . . . 181 QUEEN MAEVE   21
THE SOUTH BREEZE NOW IN DYING FEARS, ... 655 ISLE STAT I 3   13
I HURL AWAY THESE ALL UNFAERY FEARS, ... 675 ISLE STAT II 3   228
DOTH STILL THE MAN WHOM EACH STERN ROVER FEARS, ... 678 ISLE STAT II 3   295
WHY THESE NEW FEARS? THE GREAT MONK EBREMAR, ... 692 MOSADA 1   46
WHY THESE NEW FEARS? THE SERVANT OF THE CHURCH, . . . 692 MOSADA 1 V 46
JOYS AND FEARS IN THEIR GREY FACES THAT THE LIVE EARTH   719 PHANTOM SHIP   26
   KNOWETH NOT!
OF ANCIENT PASSIONS AND OF ANCIENT FEARS? . . . . . 724 KANVA ON SELF   16
BE FULL OF SUDDEN FEARS, ... 738 MOURN THEN ON   6

FEAST

THE LONG-HAIRED WARRIORS, THE SPREAD FEAST! . . . . . 2 OISIN 1 V 7
NOR LANGUOR NOR FATIGUE! AN ENDLESS FEAST, ... 44 OISIN 2   223
NO LANGUOR, NO FATIGUE! AN ENDLESS FEAST, ... 44 OISIN 2 V 223
NOR LANGUOR NOR FATIGUE! AND ENDLESS FEAST, ... 44 OISIN 2 V 223
ON CREVROE OR BROAD KNOCKFEFIN, WITH MANY OF OLD THEY FEAST 59 OISIN 3   179
THEN FEAST, MAKING CONVERSE OF WARS, ... 62 OISIN 3   212
THEN FEAST, MAKING CONVERSE OF EIRE, OF WARS, ... 62 OISIN 3 V 212
AND DWELL IN THE HOUSE OF THE FENIANS, BE THEY IN FLAMES   63 OISIN 3   224
   OR AT FEAST,
I WILL GO TO THE HOUSE OF THE FENIANS, BE THEY IN FLAMES   63 OISIN 3 V 223
   OR AT FEAST,
I FEAST AMID MY PEOPLE ON THE HILL, ... 103 FERGUS DRUID   17
AND SILENCE HOLDING REVELRY AND FEAST! . . . . . . 705 REMEMBRANCE   12
WE'LL DANCE AND THEN FEAST IN A DAIRY. . . . . . . 707 FAIRY PEDANT   10
WE'LL DANCE AND THEN FEAST IN A DAIRY. . . . . . . 708 FAIRY PEDANT   38

FEASTED

WE FEASTED FOR THREE DAYS. ON THE FOURTH MORN . . . . 43 OISIN 2   214
THREE DAYS WE FEASTED, WHEN ON THE FOURTH MORN . . . . 43 OISIN 2 V 214
SO WARRED, SO FEASTED, WITH NOR DREAMS NOR FEARS, . . . 44 OISIN 2   222
SO WARRED, SO FEASTED WE. NO DREAMS, NO FEARS, ... 44 OISIN 2 V 222
FEASTED, AND WITH THEM OLD CUCHULAIN DWELT, ... 108 CUCHULAIN SEA V 39
FEASTED, AND WEPT THE BARROWS OF HIS DEAD! . . . . . 170 SECRET ROSE   18

FEASTING

SOME FEASTING MAN THAT THE SAME OATH HAS BOUND." . . . 108 CUCHULAIN SEA   38
AMONG THOSE FEASTING MEN CUCHULAIN DWELT, ... 108 CUCHULAIN SEA   39
AMONG THOSE FEASTING KINGS CUCHULAIN DWELT, ... 108 CUCHULAIN SEA V 39
SOME FEASTING MAN THAT THE SAME OATH HAS BOUND." . . . 109 CUCHULAIN SEA   54

FEASTWARD

CAME BLANAID, MAC NESSA, TALL FERGUS WHO FEASTWARD OF OLD   53 OISIN 3   89
   TIME SLUNK,
. . . CAME FERGUS WHO FEASTWARD SAD SLUNK, ... 53 OISIN 3 V 89
CAME BLANID, MAC NESSA, AND FERGUS WHO FEASTWARD OF OLD   53 OISIN 3 V 89
   TIME SLUNK,

FEATHER

AND TRIMMED WITH MANY A CRIMSON FEATHER! . . . . . . 15 OISIN 1   206
TRIMMED ROUND WITH MANY A CRIMSON FEATHER! . . . . . 15 OISIN 1 V 206
SCARCE LEFT A WHITENING FEATHER, GREY AND SERE! . . . . 34 OISIN 2 V 76A
THE PEA-HENS DANCE, IN CRIMSON FEATHER . . . . 77 INDIAN TO LOVE V 3
SCARCELY A FEATHER LINGERED, THEN YOU SEEMED . . . . . 102 FERGUS DRUID   4

269

                                                          PAGE   TITLE   LINE

FEATHER   (CONTINUED)
    MORE THAN THE FROTH, THE FEATHER, THE DUST-WHIRL, . . .   248 SHADOW WATER B   555
    MORE THAN THE FROTH, THE FEATHER, THE DUSTWHIRL, ... 248 SHADOW WATER B V 555
    ADDING FEATHER TO FEATHER . . . .   311 PEACOCK   10
    ADDING FEATHER TO FEATHER . . . .   311 PEACOCK   10
    AND SNUG IT IN A FEATHER BED. . . . .   332 ROUND TOWER   28
    WITH A GREAT COCK'S FEATHER, ...   627 STATES HOLIDAY   37
    AS THEY GO WITH DROOPING FEATHER. . . . .   667 ISLE STAT II 3   33
    SAW ON THE WOOD'S EDGE GLEAM AN ASH-GREY FEATHER;   715 DWELT SYCAMORE   2
    FOLLOWED A RINGDOVE'S ASH-GREY GLEAM OF FEATHER. . .   715 DWELT SYCAMORE   6
    FOLLOWED THE RING-DOVE'S ASH-GREY GLEAM OF FEATHER. . .   715 DWELT SYCAMORE V   6
    A FULL HOUR LONG, WHEN ROSE A FEATHER . . . . . .   728 PRIEST FAIRY   19
    HE DREW FROM HIS CAP A FEATHER GREY, ...   729 PRIEST FAIRY   29
FEATHER-BED
    AND SNUG IT IN A FEATHER-BED, ...   332 ROUND TOWER   V   28
FEATHERED
    THE TOPS OF THEIR EARS WERE FEATHERED, ...   49 OISIN 3   34
    WHEN EVE HAS HUSHED THE FEATHERED WAYS, ...   78 INDIAN TO LOVE   19
    WHERE EVE HAS HUSHED THE FEATHERED WAYS. . . . . .   78 INDIAN TO LOVE V 19
    I COUNT THOSE FEATHERED BALLS OF SOOT . . . . . .   424 ROAD AT DOOR   11
    THE FEATHERED GLORY FROM HER LOOSENING THIGHS? . . .   441 LEDA AND SWAN   6
FEATHERS
    FROM HIGH ABOVE, LIKE FEATHERS OF YOUNG BIRDS . . . .   32 OISIN 2   V 50
    FEW FEATHERS WERE ON THEIR DISHEVELLED WINGS, ...   34 OISIN 2   76
    WHO MADE THE GRASS AND MADE THE WORMS AND MADE MY FEATHERS 77 INDIAN ON GOD   18
        GAY,
    AND WINDS BLOWING FROM FLOWERS, AND WHIRR OF FEATHERS . . 219 WOODS OF COOLE   39
    "THOUGH TO MY FEATHERS IN THE WET, ...   294 THREE BEGGARS   1
    "THOUGH TO MY FEATHERS IN THE WET, ...   297 THREE BEGGARS   63
    BRONZED PEACOCK FEATHERS, RED COMBS OF HER COCKS. . . .   433 NINETEEN 19   130
    ALL MY FINE FEATHERS WOULD BE PLUCKED AWAY . . . .   469 HARUN RASHID   178
    BECAUSE HE HAD FEATHERS INSTEAD OF HAIR. . . . . .   550 SEVERED HEAD   20
FEATHERY
    AND A FAR SOUND OF FEATHERY QUIRES; . . . .   13 OISIN 1   166
    A FAR VAGUE SOUND OF FEATHERY CHOIRS. . . . . . .   13 OISIN 1   V 166
    AROUND THE FEATHERY TIP. UNTO THE SHAFT . . . . .   657 ISLE STAT I 3   71
FEATING
    SOME FEATING MAN THAT THE SAME OATH HAS BOUND." . . .   108 CUCHULAIN SEA V   38
    "SOME FEATING MAN THAT THE SAME OATH HAS BOUND." . . .   109 CUCHULAIN SEA V   54
FEATURELESS
    THAT WANDERING IN A DESERT, FEATURELESS . . . . . .   462 HARUN RASHID   27
    WANDERING IN A DESERT FEATURELESS . . . .   462 HARUN RASHID   V   27
FEATURES
    FEATURES, OR MAYBE SHOWING . . . .   363 DOLLS DRAWINGS   4
    HER FEATURES WHEN A TRESS . . . .   363 DOLLS DRAWINGS   5
    FEATURES, OR MAY BE SHOWING . . . .   363 DOLLS DRAWINGS V   4
    PICK OUT MY FEATURES IN SUCH LIGHT AND SHADE . . .   466 HARUN RASHID   116
FECUND
    OR INTO THAT MOST FECUND DITCH OF ALL, ...   479 SELF AND SOUL   61
FED   SEE DREAM-FED
    WHILE HIGH FRAIL CLOUDLETS, FED WITH A GREEN LIGHT, . .   40 OISIN 2   165
    DAWN PASSIONED, FED WITH A FAINT GREEN LIGHT, . . .   40 OISIN 2   V 165
    . . . AND FED OF UNHUMAN SLEEP. . . . .   51 OISIN 3   56
    OF OLD THE WORLD ON DREAMING FED; . . . .   64 HAPPY SHEPHERD   3
    YOU'VE DANDLED THEM AND FED THEM FROM THE BOOK . . .   265 ABBEY THEATRE   8
    THOSE I HAD SERVED AND SOME THAT I HAD FED; . . . .   352 PEOPLE   27
    WHEN ALL IS FED WITH LIGHT AND HEAVEN IS BARE. . . .   375 PHASES OF MOON   74
    WE HAD FED THE HEART ON FANTASIES, ...   425 STARES NEST   16
    WE HAVE FED THE HEART ON FANTASIES. . . . .   425 STARES NEST   V 16
    MAN'S OWN RESINOUS HEART HAS FED. . . . .   438 SONGS PLAY 2   16
    THAT HAVE FOUND IT WHERE YOU FED. . . . .   522 LULLABY   2
    CAME OLIVE FIRES OF MORNING AND ON THE DARKNESS FED, . . 719 PHANTOM SHIP   33
    CAME THE OLIVE FIRE OF MORNING, AND ON THE DARKNESS FED, 719 PHANTOM SHIP   V 33
    ON BRAHMA'S GATEWAY, "THEY WITHIN HAVE FED . . . . .   735 QUATRAIN APHOR   15
FEE
    OH I WOULD THINK THAT I HAD MY FEE, ...   551 SONGS REWRIT 1 V   7
FEEBLE
    AND A SMALL AND A FEEBLE POPULACE STOOPING WITH MATTOCK   58 OISIN 3   164
        AND SPADE,
    AND A SMALL AND A FEEBLE RACE STOOPING WITH MATTOCK AND   58 OISIN 3   V 164
        SPADE.
    AND A SMALL AND FEEBLE RACE STOOPING WITH MATTOCK   58 OISIN 3   V 164
        AND SPADE.
    DIE OFF THE FEEBLE SOUNDS; . . . .   99 FOXHUNTER   V 42
    AND THE SEED OF THE FIRE GETS FEEBLE AND COLD. . . .   151 OLD MOTHER   10
    BUT THE SEED OF THE FIRE GETS FEEBLE AND COLD, . . .   151 OLD MOTHER   V   9
    BUT MAEVE, AND NOT WITH A SLOW FEEBLE FOOT. . . . .   185 QUEEN MAEVE   107
    BY A WINDOW'S FEEBLE LIGHT . . . .   731 STREET DANCERS   3
    FOOTING IN THE FEEBLE GLOW, ...   731 STREET DANCERS   10
    FOOTING IN THE FEEBLE GLOW, ...   732 STREET DANCERS   23
    FOOTING IN THE FEEBLE GLOW, ...   732 STREET DANCERS   36
    DANCING IN THE FEEBLE GLOW, ...   733 STREET DANCERS   49
    FOOTING IN THE FEEBLE GLOW, ...   733 STREET DANCERS   62
    FOOTING IN THE FEEBLE GLOW, ...   733 STREET DANCERS V 49
FEEBLER
    FEEBLER AND FEEBLER SHONE THE MISTY GLARE. . . . .   37 OISIN 2   V 121
    FEEBLER AND FEEBLER SHONE THE MISTY GLARE. . . . .   37 OISIN 2   V 121
FEEBLY
    THEY HEAR HIM FEEBLY SAY, ...   99 FOXHUNTER   32
FEED
    THAT FEED WHITE MOTHS BY SOME DE DANAAN SHRINE; . . .   41 OISIN 2   186

270

FEED   (CONTINUED)
  ANOTHER LINEAGE FEED THE CROW, ... 437 SONGS PLAY 1   10
  THAT FEED ON SOME FOUL PARASITE . . . . 493 AT ALGECIRAS   2
  THOUGH THEY BUT FEED AS THE GOATHERD FEEDS, ... 635 BLACK TOWER   2
  SHALL FEED. I SHALL NOT IN THE EVENINGS HEAR . . . 674 ISLE STAT II 3 220
  WHERE THEY ALL SUMMER FEED THEIR WANDERING FLOCKS, . . 690 MOSADA 1   5
  FEED A FIRE WITH STEMS OF GRASS! . . . . 727 LOVERS QUARREL   42
FEEDING
  FEEDING WHITE MOTHS AROUND SOME EASTERN SHRINE, . . . 41 OISIN 2   V 186
  NAY, GRIEF IN FEEDING ON OLD GRIEF GROWS LESS. . . . . 659 ISLE STAT II 1   19
  GRIEF NEEDS MUCH FEEDING THEN. OF HIM I SWEAR . . . . 659 ISLE STAT II 1   20
FEEDS
  YOU GO NOT WHERE THE RED DEER FEEDS, ... 11 OISIN 1   127
  YE GO NOT WHERE THE RED DEER FEEDS, ... 11 OISIN 1   V 127
  THAT FEEDS ON SOME FOUL PARASITE . . . . 493 AT ALGECIRAS   V 2
  FLAMES THAT NO FAGGOT FEEDS, NOR STEEL HAS LIT, . . . 498 BYZANTIUM   26
  THOUGH THEY BUT FEED AS THE GOATHERD FEEDS, ... 635 BLACK TOWER   2
FEEL
  NOR EVER CHANGE OR FEEL THE CLUTCHES . . . . 23 OISIN 1   V 341A
  "AGE AFTER AGE I FEEL MY SOUL DECAY . . . . 45 OISIN 2   V 235
  AND FEEL THE SOFTNESS OF EACH OTHER'S HAND, ... 74 ANASHU VIJAYA   57
  AND FEEL THE SOFTNESS OF EACH OTHER'S HANDS, ... 74 ANASHU VIJAYA   V 57
  AND STILL I FEEL THE CROWN UPON MY HEAD. . . . . . . 103 FERGUS DRUID   20
  BUT STILL I FEEL THE CROWN UPON MY HEAD. . . . . . . 103 FERGUS DRUID   V 20
  WAGE AN ETERNAL BATTLE, AND I FEEL . . . . 104 FERGUS DRUID   V 38C
  THAT NONE MAY FEEL THE POWER OF SQUALL AND WAVE, . . . 128 DREAM OF FAERY V   45
  THEY DO NOT EVEN FEEL, SO ABSTRACT ARE THEY, ... 382 VISION ROBART   14
  BUT FEEL THE STRANGE HEART BEATING WHERE IT LIES? . . . 441 LEDA AND SWAN   8
  TO DEATH. HIS DARKNESS AND HIS CHILL I FEEL. . . . . 684 SEEKER   63
  MY SOUL. HIS DARKNESS AND HIS CHILL I FEEL. . . . . 684 SEEKER   V 63B
  I FEEL A FINGER DRAWN ACROSS MY CHEEK! . . . . 694 MOSADA 1   96
  CLOSE AND MORE CLOSE--I FEEL HIM IN MY HEART-- . . . . 720 WITCH VIVIEN   11
  MY FINGERS FEEL HIS AMBER HAIR. . . . . 723 GIRLS SONG A   8
  THE HOLLOW WOODLANDS FEEL HIM THERE, ... 737 SUMMER EVENING   17
FEELING
  A GENTLE FEELING WRAPS THEM LIKE A FLEECE, ... 128 DREAM OF FAERY V   34
  THAT DREAMS. SHE MOVETH, FEELING IN HER BRAIN . . . . 687 TWO TITANS   10
FEELS
  AND FEELS THE STRANGE HEART BEATING WHERE IT LIES! . . . 441 LEDA AND SWAN V   8
FEET
  BUT DOWN TO HER FEET WHITE VESTURE FLOWED, ... 3 OISIN 1   25
  AND FEET OF MAIDENS DANCING IN TUNE, ... 3 OISIN 1 V   9
  DOWN TO HER FEET WHITE VESTURE FLOWED, ... 3 OISIN 1 V   25
  THROUGH BITTER TIDE ON FOAM-WET FEET? . . . . 5 OISIN 1   51
  TO THIS DIM SHORE THOSE GENTLE FEET? . . . . 5 OISIN 1 V   51
  TO THIS DIM SHORE ON FOAM WET FEET? . . . . 5 OISIN 1 V   51
  TO THIS DIM SHORE ON FOAM-WET FEET? . . . . 5 OISIN 1 V   51
  YET NOW I CHOOSE, FOR THESE FOUR FEET . . . . 6 OISIN 1   57
  FOR LOVE OF USHEEN MY FEET RAN . . . . 6 OISIN 1 V   57
  FOR LOVE OF OISIN FOAM WET FEET . . . . 6 OISIN 1 V   57
  FOR LOVE OF OISIN FOAM-WET FEET . . . . 6 OISIN 1 V   57
  BEFORE THY FEET SHALL KNEEL DOWN ALL . . . . 7 OISIN 1 V   77
  A WHISPER OF IMPETUOUS FEET, ... 15 OISIN 1   199
  KEPT TIME WITH THEIR BRIGHT WINGS AND FEET! . . . . . 26 OISIN 1   397
  BEAT TIME WITH THEIR BRIGHT WINGS AND FEET, ... 26 OISIN 1 V   397
  HIS TOOTHLESS HOUND AT HIS NERVELESS FEET, ... 26 OISIN 1 V   400
  THAT OLD, SEA-WEEDY, SQUARED, THREE HUNDRED FEET . . . 31 OISIN 2 V   30C
  SOBBED INTO SILENCE. WE HAD MOUNTED FEET . . . . . . 33 OISIN 2 V   68E
  LIKE A SMALL RIVER, AND WHERE FEET TOUCHED CAME . . . 37 OISIN 2   117
  OF AWELESS BIRDS, AND ROUND THEIR STIRLESS FEET . . . 74 ANASHU VIJAYA   73
  AND WHEN TUMULTUOUS FEET ENWOUND ME . . . . 83 MAD KING GOLL V   20
  A TRAMPING OF TREMENDOUS FEET, ... 85 MAD KING GOLL V   54
  THE TRAMPING OF TREMENDOUS FEET, ... 85 MAD KING GOLL V   54
  SHE PASSED THE SALLEY GARDENS WITH LITTLE SNOW-WHITE FEET. 90 SALLEY GARDENS   2
  YOU WAVES, THOUGH YOU DANCE BY MY FEET LIKE CHILDREN AT 90 OLD FISHERMAN   1
    PLAY,
  YE WAVES, THOUGH YE DANCE 'FORE MY FEET LIKE CHILDREN AT 90 OLD FISHERMAN V   1
    PLAY,
  I SCARCE COULD DRAG MY FEET, ... 94 MOLL MAGEE   10
  HERDED THE CATTLE CAME WITH STUMBLING FEET, ... 106 CUCHULAIN SEA   19
  "WHY DO YOU TREMBLE THUS FROM FEET TO CROWN?" . . . . 106 CUCHULAIN SEA V   13
  WAS DRIVING CATTLE CAME SHE WITH SWIFT FEET, ... 106 CUCHULAIN SEA V   19
  BEFORE HER WANDERING FEET. . . . . 112 ROSE OF WORLD   15
  WITH THE FEET LAID SIDE BY SIDE. . . . . 124 CATHLEEN PARA   4
  'MONG THE FEET OF ANGELS SEVEN . . . . 125 CATHLEEN PARA   13
  WITH WHITE FEET OF ANGELS SEVEN . . . . 125 CATHLEEN PARA V   13
  HER WHITE FEET GO GLIMMERING! . . . . 125 CATHLEEN PARA V   14
  OF THEIR LONG WINGS, THE FLASH OF THEIR WHITE FEET. . . 137 TO SOME I TALK   16
  OF THEIR LONG WINGS, THE FLASH OF THEIR SWIFT FEET. . . 137 TO SOME I TALK V   16
  THE MEASURE OF HER FLYING FEET . . . . 138 TO IRELAND   11
  THE LIGHT FALL OF HER FLYING FEET . . . . 138 TO IRELAND V   11
  IS COMELIER THAN CANDLES AT MOTHER MARY'S FEET. . . . 147 UNAPPEAS HOST   12
  IS COMELIER THAN CANDLES BEFORE MAURYA'S FEET. . . . . 147 UNAPPEAS HOST V   12
  UNDER MY FEET THAT THEY FOLLOW YOU NIGHT AND DAY. . . . 153 CHANGE BELOVED   5
  UNDER MY FEET, THAT I FOLLOW YOU, NIGHT AND DAY. . . . 153 CHANGE BELOVED V   5
  AND HIDING THEIR TOSSING MANES AND THEIR TUMULTUOUS FEET. 154 BELOVED PEACE   12
  AND HIDE THEIR TOSSING MANES AND THEIR TUMULTUOUS FEET. 154 BELOVED PEACE V   12
  LIVE BUT TO LIGHT YOUR PASSING FEET, ... 158 BELOVED RHYMES   12
  AND THE QUIET OF LOVE IN HER FEET. . . . . 161 CAP AND BELLS   36
  I WOULD SPREAD THE CLOTHS UNDER YOUR FEET! . . . . . . 176 CLOTHS HEAVEN   5
  I HAVE SPREAD MY DREAMS UNDER YOUR FEET! . . . . . . 176 CLOTHS HEAVEN   7

271

FEET   (CONTINUED)

Line	Page	Title	Line
WITH SPEEDY FEET AND A MOST THANKFUL HEART'	185	QUEEN MAEVE	100
ON THE ISLAND LAWNS, THEIR FEET WHERE THE PALE FOAM GLEAMS.	203	WITHER BOUGHS	14
BUT WE HAVE ALL BENT LOW AND LOW AND KISSED THE QUIET FEET	207	HANRAHANS SONG	9
BUT WE BEND TOGETHER AND KISS THE QUIET FEET	207	HANRAHANS SONG V	4
AND THAT YOU COME FROM EDEN ON FLYING FEET.	218	WOODS OF COOLE	29
WITH SO RED LIPS, AND RUNNING ON SUCH FEET,	231	SHADOW WATER B	199
MY HUSBAND AND MY KING DIED AT MY FEET,	237	SHADOW WATER B	337
BLUE-EYED, AND A QUICK RUNNER ON BARE FEET,	242	SHADOW WATER B	416
THEY KILLED HIM AT MY FEET. O! O! O! O!	242	SHADOW WATER B	420
AND KILLED A LOVER OR HUSBAND AT MY FEET--	246	SHADOW WATER B	491
SAT UPRIGHT WITH A SWORD BEFORE HER FEET.	279	TWO KINGS	62
BEN JONSON'S PHRASE--AND STILL MAY TURN MY FEET	321	REED WHISPERER V	6
AND YET HIS MIND OUTRAN THE HORSES' FEET.	326	ROBERT GREGORY	64
HAVE FOUND THE PATH MY GOATS' FEET CANNOT FIND.	342	SHEP GOATHERD	84
HAVE FOUND THE PATH MY GOAT'S FEET CANNOT FIND.	342	SHEP GOATHERD V	84
LIFTING HIS DELICATE FEET.	378	CAT AND MOON	10
AND LIFTS HIS DELICATE FEET.	378	CAT AND MOON V	10
WITH DELICATE FEET UPON OLD TERRACES,	418	ANCEST HOUSES	26
THUNDER OF FEET, TUMULT OF IMAGES,	433	NINETEEN 19	120
SHOULD HEAR MY LIVING FEET, NOR WOULD I TREAD	435	NEW FACES	3
MEN DANCE ON DEATHLESS FEET."	496	MOHINI CHATTER	28
"THOSE SIX FEET MARKED IN CHALK?	548	TO SAME TUNE 3	8
"THOSE SIX FEET MARKED IN CHALK?	548	TO SAME TUNE 3	18
"THOSE SIX FEET MARKED IN CHALK?	549	TO SAME TUNE 3	28
THEIR MOBS PUT UNDER THEIR FEET.	554	CHURCH STATE	4
ON THEIR OWN FEET THEY CAME, OR ON SHIPBOARD,	566	LAPIS LAZULI	25
TO LIE BETWEEN YOUR FEET?	572	LADYS 2ND SONG	2
AND HE PLAYS TUNES BETWEEN YOUR FEET,	573	LADYS 3RD SONG	2
FEET TO THE RISING AND SETTING MAY RUN,	591	WHAT WAS LOST	4
O MIND YOUR FEET, O MIND YOUR FEET,	592	DRUNK SOBRIETY	9
O MIND YOUR FEET, O MIND YOUR FEET,	592	DRUNK SOBRIETY	9
SOME TWENTY FEET FROM TIP TO TIP HAD IT STRETCHED RIGHTLY OUT,	593	PILGRIM	17
SOME TWENTY FEET FROM TIP TO TIP HAD ITS WINGS STRETCHED RIGHTLY OUT,	593	PILGRIM V	17
THAT NOBODY LOOKS, HER FEET	617	LONG-LEG FLY	16
TREAD AND TREAD THEIR CLOVEN FEET	646	ISLE STAT I 1	24
AND, LEAPING TO THEIR FEET, FAR ECHOES CRIED,	659	ISLE STAT II 1	13
DOWN TO THEIR FEET THE STARS THAT SHINE ALONE,	662	ISLE STAT II 1	80
AT THEIR FEET THE WAVES IN RINGS	667	ISLE STAT II 3	25
AT MORN, AND WITH HER FEET EACH COBWEB RENDS,	670	ISLE STAT II 3	99
THE FEET OF SUMMER DABBLE	680	LOVE AND DEATH	7
AS ROUND HER, SLOW ON FEET THAT HAVE NO BLOOD,	687	TWO TITANS	18
AND HE IS DRAGGED AGAIN BEFORE HER FEET.	688	TWO TITANS	43
FEET OF DARK GOMEZ, WHERE NOW WANDER YE?	690	MOSADA 1	11
PICTURED, WHERE WANDER THE BELOVED FEET	692	MOSADA 1	44
YOURSELF INTO THE DUNGEON 'NEATH OUR FEET	697	MOSADA 2	44
I'M NOT OF THAT PALE COMPANY WHOSE FEET	699	MOSADA 3	20
FOR YOUR FEET THE MORNING PRAYETH!	706	DAWN-SONG	25
IN TERROR FLINGS HER AT HER LOVER'S FEET.	713	FERENCZ RENYI V	85
HER ARMS AROUND HIS FEET. THE SIGNAL GOES	714	FERENCZ RENYI	103
DEEP IN THE WOODLAND PAUSED THEY, THE SIX FEET	716	DWELT SYCAMORE	9
DEEP IN THE WOODLAND PASSED THEY. THE SIX FEET	716	DWELT SYCAMORE V	9
FROM THE RUSTLING OF OUR FEET.	726	LOVERS QUARREL	8
THREE SPANS HIGH AS HE ROSE TO HIS FEET,	729	PRIEST FAIRY	25
WHO IS SIX FEET HIGH IN HIS SOCKS AT LEAST?	729	PRIEST FAIRY	28
TO THE RHYTHM OF THEIR FEET,	731	STREET DANCERS	2
FELL AT MY FEET ON THE FLOOR,--	744	GLOVE CLOAK	8
WHERE I HAD HEARD NO FEET BUT THE GODS' CAME.	756	SHADOW WATER A V	191B
AND THAT DREAM ONLY SHINE BEFORE HER FEET.	761	SHADOW WATER A	258
HAS MADE MY FEET UNSTEADY, AND BLINDED ME.	767	SHADOW WATER A	406

FELL

Line	Page	Title	Line
AS HER SOFT BOSOM ROSE AND FELL.	4	OISIN 1	30
THERE WAS NO LIMB OF MINE BUT FELL	7	OISIN 1	72
OR DROPS OF SILVER JOY THAT FELL	19	OISIN 1	278
IT FELL, OR FROM THE TWISTED MOON	19	OISIN 1 V	278
HE FELL INTO A DRUID SWOON.	20	OISIN 1	289
OUR TREAD, AS ROSE AND FELL THE LIQUID TONES	33	OISIN 2 V	68B
AND ONCE MORE TO A DAY-LONG BATTLE FELL.	43	OISIN 2	218
AND WE ONCE MORE UNTO OUR FIGHTING FELL.	43	OISIN 2 V	218
. . . AT THE HEEL OF A CENTURY FELL,	54	OISIN 3	102
CAME, AND MY FOREHEAD FELL LOW, AND MY TEARS LIKE BERRIES FELL DOWN!	57	OISIN 3	154
CAME, AND MY FOREHEAD FELL LOW, AND MY TEARS LIKE BERRIES FELL DOWN!	57	OISIN 3	154
. . . BUT FELL WITH THEIR BURDEN AT LENGTH.	60	OISIN 3	186
I FELL ON THE PATH, AND THE HORSE WENT AWAY LIKE A SUMMER FLY!	60	OISIN 3	190
AND MY YEARS THREE HUNDRED FELL ON ME,	60	OISIN 3	191
BETWEEN THEM A GATEWAY OF BRASS, AND THE HOWL OF THE ANGELS WHO FELL.	61	OISIN 3	200
FELL LIKE FAINT METEORS IN THE GLOOM, AND ONCE	80	EPHEMERA	14
FELL ON THE PIRATES BY THE DEEP,	83	MAD KING GOLL	21
FELL ON THE ROBBERS BY THE DEEP,	83	MAD KING GOLL V	21
FELL ON THE PIRATES OF THE DEEP,	83	MAD KING GOLL V	21
THEY WENT FORTH TO THE BATTLE, BUT THEY ALWAYS FELL	113	ROSE OF BATTLE V	T
A DRUID KINDNESS, ON ALL HEARERS FELL.	129	BOOK STORIES	4
HE PRAYED AND FELL ASLEEP!	132	FR GILLIGAN	14
HE KNELT, PRAYED, FELL ASLEEP!	132	FR GILLIGAN V	14
OR FELL INTO UNHAPPINESS, I'VE SAID,	186	QUEEN MAEVE	137

	PAGE	TITLE	LINE

FELL (CONTINUED)

THAT ALL THINGS FELL OUT HAPPILY, ... 189 BAILE AILLINN 22
SHE FELL AND DIED OF THE HEART-BREAK." . . . . 191 BAILE AILLINN 64
AND I FELL ASLEEP UPON LONELY ECHTGE OF STREAMS. . . . 203 WITHER BOUGHS 6
WASHED BY TIME'S WATERS AS THEY ROSE AND FELL . . . . . 206 ADAMS CURSE 32
WHERE IS MY SWORD THAT FELL OUT OF MY HAND . . . . . . 241 SHADOW WATER B 397
FELL DOWN UPON THE DUST AND SNORED. . . . . 297 THREE BEGGARS 60
HE STRETCHED HIS BONES AND FELL IN A DREAM . . . . . . 331 ROUND TOWER 10
AND FELL THE ONE IN T'OTHER'S ARMS . . . . 457 SUMMER SPRING 7
WHEN UPWARD TURNED, ON ONE SOLE IMAGE FELL: . . . . . . 471 ALL SOUL NIGHT 34
WHEN UPWARD TURNED ON ONE SOUL IMAGE FELL, ... 471 ALL SOUL NIGHT V 34
SUCH A SLEEP AND SOUND AS FELL . . . . 522 LULLABY 13
BELOVED SUCH A SLEEP AS FELL . . . . 522 LULLABY V 13
ALL THE RENOWN THAT FELL. . . . . 547 TO SAME TUNE 2 26
GODHEAD. SOME SHADOW FELL. MY SOUL FORGOT . . . . . . 557 RIBH ECSTASY 6
PRAISE EVERY MAN THAT FELL. . . . . 608 SONGS BURDEN 3 8
ALL THE RENOWN THAT FELL. . . . . 614 MARCH SONGS 1 26
CONFUSION FELL UPON OUR THOUGHT. . . . . 639 BEN BULBEN 67
'TIS HERE THE ARROW FELL! THE BREEZES LAUGHED . . . . 657 ISLE STAT I 3 70
AMONG THE PLANTS! THE FLOWERY SILENCE FELL . . . . . . 692 MOSADA 1 55
FOR ALL SAVE HIM WHO PINING FELL, ... 717 FAIRY DOCTOR 19
FOR ALL SAVE HE WHO PINING FELL, ... 717 FAIRY DOCTOR V 19
FELL AT MY FEET ON THE FLOOR,-- . . . . 744 GLOVE CLOAK 8
THE STORM AROSE AND SUDDENLY FELL . . . . 784 WOMANS BEAUTY 19

FELLOW

WITH "LOOK AT THAT OLD FELLOW THERE! . . . . 131 OLD PENSIONER V 3
THOUGH IT BUT SET US SIGHING. FELLOW WANDERER . . . . 230 SHADOW WATER B V 187
DEAR FELLOW ARTIST WHY SO FREE . . . . 335 YOUNG BEAUTY V 1
TO ABD-AL-RABBAN! FELLOW ROYSTERER ONCE . . . . 460 HARUN RASHID V 2
OLD FELLOW STUDENT, WHOSE MOST PATIENT EAR . . . . . . 468 HARUN RASHID V 167

FELLOW-ARTIST

DEAR FELLOW-ARTIST, WHY SO FREE . . . . 335 YOUNG BEAUTY 1

FELLOW-ROYSTERER

TO ABD AL-RABBAN! FELLOW-ROYSTERER ONCE, ... 460 HARUN RASHID 2

FELLOWS

THE CRAZY HERDSMAN THAT WILL TELL HIS FELLOWS . . . . 229 SHADOW WATER B 167
TO KEEP HIS FELLOWS FROM THEIR SLEEP: . . . . 297 THREE BEGGARS 45
GOOD FELLOWS SHUFFLED CARDS IN AN OLD BAWN! . . . . . 411 TOWER 65

FELLOW-STUDENT

OLD FELLOW-STUDENT, WHOSE MOST PATIENT EAR . . . . . . 468 HARUN RASHID 167

FELLOW-WANDERER

THOUGH IT BUT SET US SIGHING? FELLOW-WANDERER, ... 230 SHADOW WATER B 187

FELT

BUT WHEN THE HORSE HAD FELT MY WEIGHT, ... 9 OISIN 1 109
AND WHEN THE WHITE STEED FELT MY WEIGHT, ... 9 OISIN 1 V 109
HAD FELT THE ISLAND BREEZE, MY LORE . . . . 668 ISLE STAT II 3 55
AND WHEN THOU HAST THESE THINGS FOR MANY AGES FELT, . 674 ISLE STAT II 3 214
AND WHEN THOU HAST THESE THINGS FOR AGES FELT, ... 674 ISLE STAT II 3 V 214
I FELT A SUDDEN TEAR START, ... 744 GLOVE CLOAK 10

FEN

BY ROCKY SHORE AND RUSHY FEN! . . . . 83 MAD KING GOLL 32
O'ER HILL AND HEATH AND SPONGY FEN, ... 83 MAD KING GOLL V 32
OVER THE HEATH AND SPONGY FEN, ... 83 MAD KING GOLL V 32
BY ROCKY LANE AND FEN! . . . . 133 FR GILLIGAN 30

FENCE

SOME ROGUE OF THE WORLD STOLE THEM TO PATCH UP A FENCE 623 HIGH TALK 4
    OR A FIRE.
AN OLD HORSE LOOKED ACROSS A FENCE, ... 725 LEGEND 27

FENCED

HAS FENCED US ROUND FOR ALL ETERNITY. . . . . 670 ISLE STAT II 3 95

FENIAN

THE FENIAN HORSES! ARMOUR TORN ASUNDER! . . . . 43 OISIN 2 210
CEASE, CEASE, O MOURNFUL, LAUGHING FENIAN HORN! . . . 43 OISIN 2 213
AH, CEASE, THOU MOURNFUL, LAUGHING FENIAN HORN! . . . 43 OISIN 2 V 213
AH, CEASE, YOU MOURNFUL, LAUGHING FENIAN HORN! . . . . 43 OISIN 2 V 213
YOUR QUESTIONER, OISIN, IS WORTHY, HE COMES FROM THE FENIAN 51 OISIN 3 64
    LANDS."
WORTHY'S THY QUESTIONER, OISIN, HE FROM THE FENIAN LANDS." 51 OISIN 3 V 64

FENIANS

AH, FENIANS, WITH THE SHIELD AND BOW? . . . . 10 OISIN 1 116
NEAR BY, THE FENIANS SAW, AND KNEW . . . . 10 OISIN 1 V 111
AND THE FENIANS ALL HAD WEPT WITH ME, ... 10 OISIN 1 V 113
THE FENIANS ON THE HUMAN GROUND . . . . 10 OISIN 1 V 114C
THE FENIANS. LET THEIR DEER-HOUNDS SLEEP. . . . . . . 11 OISIN 1 V 131
REMEMBERING HOW THE FENIANS STEPT . . . . 24 OISIN 1 370
IN WAR, THE NOBLE FENIANS STEPT. . . . . 24 OISIN 1 V 372
THE HORSES OF THE FENIANS--TEARING ASUNDER . . . . . . 43 OISIN 2 V 210
I MUSED ON THE CHASE WITH THE FENIANS, AND BRAN, SCEOLAN, 47 OISIN 3 5
    LOMAIR,
AND BY ME, IN SOFT RED RAIMENT, THE FENIANS MOVED IN LOUD 53 OISIN 3 93
    STREAMS,
WHEN THE FENIANS MADE FORAY AT MORNING WITH BRAN, SCEOLAN, 54 OISIN 3 104
    LOMAIR.
AS MY MIND MADE THE NAMES OF THE FENIANS. . . . . . . 57 OISIN 3 146
. . . "THE FENIANS HUNT WOLVES IN THE NIGHT, ... 59 OISIN 3 171
. . . "THE FENIANS A LONG TIME ARE DEAD." . . . . . . 59 OISIN 3 172
. . . FOR I GO TO THE FENIANS, O CLERIC, TO CHAUNT . . 61 OISIN 3 201
. . . I WILL GO TO THE FENIANS, THOU CLERIC, AND CHANT . 61 OISIN 3 V 201
. . . THE LIMBS OF THE FENIANS ARE TOST! . . . . 62 OISIN 3 213
AND DWELL IN THE HOUSE OF THE FENIANS, BE THEY IN FLAMES 63 OISIN 3 224
    OR AT FEAST.

273

	PAGE	TITLE		LINE

FENIANS (CONTINUED)
I WILL GO TO THE HOUSE OF THE FENIANS, BE THEY IN FLAMES   63 OISIN 3   V 223
    OR AT FEAST,

FENIANS'
IN THE FENIANS' DWELLINGS OF WATTLE LEAN ON THE CHESSBOARDS   55 OISIN 3   115
    AND PLAY,
. . . A SOB FOR THE FENIANS' OLD STRENGTH. . . . . . .   60 OISIN 3   188

FERENCZ
HOW FERENCZ RENYI KEPT SILENT. . . . .   709 FERENCZ RENYI   T
THY NAME IS?" "FERENCZ RENYI." "OF?" "THIS VILLAGE."   709 FERENCZ RENYI   V 13
    "GOOD!
SPEAK, FERENCZ, SPEAK. WE LOVE EACH OTHER. SEE, .   713 FERENCZ RENYI   87
WE GATHERED. FERENCZ, NAY, I MUST NOT DIE! . . . .   713 FERENCZ RENYI   96
"AH, FERENCZ, SPEAK AND SAVE THYSELF AND ME! . . . .   713 FERENCZ RENYI   V 86
WE GATHERED. FERENCZ, DO NOT LET ME DIE. . . . .   713 FERENCZ RENYI   V 96
YOUNG FERENCZ RENYI BURSTS HIS BONDS--AT LAST, . . .   714 FERENCZ RENYI   V 116

FERGUS
CAME BLANAID, MAC NESSA, TALL FERGUS WHO FEASTWARD OF OLD   53 OISIN 3   89
    TIME SLUNK,
. . . CAME FERGUS WHO FEASTWARD SAD SLUNK, ...   53 OISIN 3   V 89
CAME BLANID, MAC NESSA, AND FERGUS WHO FEASTWARD OF OLD   53 OISIN 3   V 89
    TIME SLUNK,
WHO CAST ROUND FERGUS DREAMS, AND RUIN UNTOLD! . . .   101 ROSE UPON ROOD   5
FERGUS AND THE DRUID . . . .   102 FERGUS DRUID   T
WHAT WOULD YOU, FERGUS? BE NO MORE A KING, ...   103 FERGUS DRUID   21
WHO GOES WITH FERGUS? . . . .   125 GOES FERGUS   T
WHO WILL GO DRIVE WITH FERGUS NOW, ...   125 GOES FERGUS   1
FOR FERGUS RULES THE BRAZEN CARS, ...   126 GOES FERGUS   9
AND OF THAT FAMOUS FERGUS, NESSA'S HUSBAND, ...   183 QUEEN MAEVE   71

FERGUSON
WITH DAVIS, MANGAN, FERGUSON, ...   138 TO IRELAND   18

FERN
AMONG THE FIELDS OF WAVING FERN. . . . .   2 OISIN 1   V 7N
AMONG THE WAVING FIELDS OF FERN! . . . .   4 OISIN 1   38
AND RIVER, FERN AND FLOWERY CLUMP, ...   15 OISIN 1   V 196

FERNS
AND MAKES THE INFANT FERNS UNWRAP, ...   18 OISIN 1   265
FROM FERNS THAT DROP THEIR TEARS . . . .   88 STOLEN CHILD   36
FROM FERNS THAT DROP THEIR TEAR . . . .   88 STOLEN CHILD   V 36

FERRARA
IN THE GREEN SHADOW OF FERRARA WALL! . . . . . .   352 PEOPLE   9
IN THE GREEN SHADOW ON FERRARA WALL! . . . . . .   352 PEOPLE   V 9

FERTILE
AND THROUGH THE FERTILE AND WASTE, ...   436 FOR MY SON   30

FERVOUR
AND WITH THE FERVOUR OF MY YOUTHFUL EYES, ...   356 BROKEN DREAMS   25

FESTIVAL
BECAUSE TO-DAY IS SOME RELIGIOUS FESTIVAL . . . . .   363 DOLLS FACES   1
HOLD FESTIVAL ACROSS THE LAND, ...   671 ISLE STAT II 3   128
AND THE CUCKOO UNSEEN IN HIS FESTIVAL MOOD! . . . .   717 LOVE SONG   7

FETCH
AND FETCH ME HOME AGIN! . . . .   96 MOLL MAGEE   42
I BADE THEM FETCH HIS HEAD. . . . .   789 SINGING HEAD   12

FETLOCKS
HOW THE FETLOCKS DRIP BLOOD IN THE BATTLE, ...   52 OISIN 3   78

FEVER
A FEVER AND A WHIRLING FIRE! . . . .   83 MAD KING GOLL   V 28
MY SINGING SANG ME FEVER FREE, ...   86 MAD KING GOLL   V 65
OF FEVER. NOW THE STRINGS ARE TORN . . . . . .   86 MAD KING GOLL   V 66

FEVER-FREE
MY SINGING SANG ME FEVER-FREE! . . . .   86 MAD KING GOLL   V 65

FEVERISH
MURMURING HOW FAR AWAY ARE ALL EARTH'S FEVERISH LANDS. . .   78 INDIAN TO LOVE   V 10

FEW
FEW FEATHERS WERE ON THEIR DISHEVELLED WINGS, ...   34 OISIN 2   76
SING YOU OF HER, O FIRST FEW STARS, ...   73 ANASHU VIJAYA   41
SING YE OF HER, OH FIRST FEW STARS, ...   73 ANASHU VIJAYA   V 41
IF HE BUT SHIFTED A FEW STONES, ...   302 HOUR DAWN   14
OR ESSERKELLY PLAIN, FEW KEPT HIS PACE! . . . . .   326 ROBERT GREGORY   V 59
AND ESERKELLY PLAINS, FEW KEPT HIS PACE! . . . . .   326 ROBERT GREGORY   V 59
OR ESERKELLY PLAINS, FEW KEPT HIS PACE! . . . . .   326 ROBERT GREGORY   V 59
SOME FEW REMEMBERED STILL WHEN I WAS YOUNG . . . .   410 TOWER   33
SOME FEW HAVE HANDSOME RIDERS, ARE GARLANDED . . . .   432 NINETEEN 19   114
FEW DREAM THAT THEY EXIST, ...   436 FOR MY SON   V 11
THOUGH BUT A FEW LEARNED MEN SHALL LOOK WITHIN, . . .   461 HARUN RASHID   V 18A
I KNOW AS FEW CAN KNOW, ...   589 OLD WICKED MAN   47
SOME FEW HALF WAKE AND HALF RENEW THEIR CHOICE, . . .   622 HOUND VOICE   6
AND YON FEW STARS GROWN DIM, LIKE EYES OF LOVERS . . .   700 MOSADA 3   33
"HOW FEW THE MIND'S INTEMPERANCE RULE! . . . . . .   725 LEGEND   10

FIBROUS
FILLING THE FIBROUS DIMNESS WITH LONG GENERATIONS OF EYES.   49 OISIN 3   40

FICKLE   SEE FOAM-FICKLE
AND SLEEK YOUNG JOY IS NO MORE FICKLE, ...   77 INDIAN TO LOVE   V 5C
MORE FLEETING THAN THE SEA'S FOAM FICKLE FACE, ...   112 ROSE OF WORLD   V 8
VEERING, FLEETING, FICKLE, THE WINDS OF KNOCKNAREA, . .   206 HANRAHANS SONG   V 1
VEERING, FLEETING, FICKLE, OUR LOVES AND ANGERS MEET! . .   207 HANRAHANS SONG   V 3
FICKLE THE GUIDING HIS ARROW SHALL FIND! . . . . .   657 ISLE STAT I 3   66

FIDDLE
WHEN I PLAY ON MY FIDDLE IN DOONEY, ...   178 FIDDLER DOONEY   1
AND THE MERRY LOVE THE FIDDLE, ...   179 FIDDLER DOONEY   15
PULL DOWN THE BLINDS, BRING FIDDLE AND CLARIONET . . .   311 MOUNTAIN TOMB   5

	PAGE	TITLE		LINE

FIDDLE (CONTINUED)
FINGERED UPON A FIDDLE STICK OR STRING . . . . 445 SCHOOL CHILDR V 46
OR THE FIDDLE STRING ACCURSED, ... 527 AM OF IRELAND V 20
CAN PAY THE POET FOR A VERSE AND HEAR THE FIDDLE SOUND, 581 CURSE CROMWELL 21

FIDDLE-BOW
THEY ARE SICK OF THE PALETTE AND FIDDLE-BOW, ... 565 LAPIS LAZULI 2

FIDDLER
THE FIDDLER OF DOONEY . . . . 178 FIDDLER DOONEY T
WITH "HERE IS THE FIDDLER OF DOONEY!" . . . . 179 FIDDLER DOONEY 19
SCHOOLMASTER HE, A DREAMER, FIDDLER, FIRST . . . . . . 709 FERENCZ RENYI 11

FIDDLERS
"THE FIDDLERS ARE ALL THUMBS, ... 527 AM OF IRELAND 19

FIDDLE'S
TO THE FIDDLE'S RISE AND FALL. . . . . 726 LOVERS QUARREL 20

FIDDLES
OF FIDDLES AND OF FLUTES HUNG THERE . . . . 271 GREY ROCK V 20

FIDDLE-STICK
FINGERED UPON A FIDDLE-STICK OR STRINGS . . . . 445 SCHOOL CHILDR 46

FIDDLE-STRING
OR THE FIDDLE-STRING ACCURSED, ... 527 AM OF IRELAND 20

FIDGET
AND MAY NO RESTLESS FAY WITH FIDGET FINGER . . . . . . 75 ANASHU VIJAYA 90
MAY NEVER RESTLESS FAY WITH FIDGET FINGER . . . . . . 75 ANASHU VIJAYA V 90
AND MAY NO RESTLESS PITRI'S FIDGET FINGER . . . . . . 75 ANASHU VIJAYA V 90

FIELD
IN A FIELD BY THE RIVER MY LOVE AND I DID STAND, ... 90 SALLEY GARDENS 5
THE FIELD MOUSE RUNNING BY ME IN THE GRASS, ... 101 ROSE UPON ROOD V 17
THE FIELD THAT CLOSES IN BEHIND. . . . . 266 GALWAY RACES V 4
OR WINTRY MOONLIGHT SINK THE FIELD . . . . 501 VACILLATION 47
A RIVERY FIELD SPREAD OUT BELOW, ... 502 VACILLATION 57
"WHATEVER STANDS IN FIELD OR FLOOD, ... 529 TOM LUNATIC 13
A COWARD IN THE FIELD! AND ALL MEN CRIED! . . . . . . 684 SEEKER 53
SLEEP IN SOME FAR OTHER FIELD . . . . 705 DAWN-SONG 3
ALONG THE TENTS, FIELD, THE VILLAGE WALLS. . . . . . . 712 FERENCZ RENYI V 71

FIELD-MOUSE
THE FIELD-MOUSE RUNNING BY ME IN THE GRASS, ... 101 ROSE UPON ROOD 17
A CAREFUL FIELD-MOUSE FINDS A FALLEN CRUMB! . . . . . 713 FERENCZ RENYI 77

FIELDS
AMONG THE FIELDS OF WAVING FERN. . . . . 2 OISIN 1 V 7N
AMONG THE WAVING FIELDS OF FERN, ... 4 OISIN 1 38
YOU HUNTER OF THE FIELDS AFAR! . . . . 75 ANASHU VIJAYA 79
THE FIELDS GREW FATTER DAY BY DAY, ... 82 MAD KING GOLL 7
FIELDS FATTENING SLOW, MEN WISE IN JOY, ... 82 MAD KING GOLL V 6
AND THE MOTH-HOUR WENT FROM THE FIELDS, ... 133 FR GILLIGAN 15
"I HAVE SENT AMONG THE FIELDS OR TO THE WOODS . . . . 280 TWO KINGS 69
"I HAVE SENT OUT INTO THE FIELDS AND WOODS . . . . . 280 TWO KINGS V 69
ROADS FULL OF BEGGARS, CATTLE IN THE FIELDS, ... 487 SEVEN SAGES 18
THE AVENGING LEAF THOSE FIELDS RAISED UP AGAINST IT. . 487 SEVEN SAGES 20
A MAN HAS THE FIELDS OF HEAVEN, ... 643 SONG FAERIES 1
THUS, THUS I BECKON FROM HER VIEWLESS FIELDS-- . . . 693 MOSADA 1 75
ALONG THE TENTS, THE FIELDS, THE VILLAGE WALLS. . . . 712 FERENCZ RENYI 71
AND OVER TILLAGE FIELDS AND PASTURE LANDS . . . . . 715 FERENCZ RENYI 120
AND FOLLOWING O'ER THE FIELDS AND PASTURE LANDS, . . 715 FERENCZ RENYI V 120
AS THERE FLOATS FROM FIELDS AFAR . . . . 732 STREET DANCERS 20
WELL SHELTERED FROM THE WINDS, AND FRUITFUL FIELDS, . 758 SHADOW WATER A 221

FIELDS'
THE FAT FLOCKS AND THE FIELDS' FATNESS, ... 540 FROM ANTIGONE 4

FIEND
OF SOME FORGOTTEN FIEND. NOW NONE ASSAILS . . . . . 31 OISIN 2 V 30B
THAT INSOLENT FIEND ROBERT ARTISSON . . . . 433 NINETEEN 19 128

FIERCE
ARE CHOKED WITH THUNDER, LIGHTNING, AND FIERCE WIND, . 42 OISIN 2 205
AT NEED, AND MADE HER BEAUTIFUL AND FIERCE, ... 181 QUEEN MAEVE 29
"YOUR STRENGTH, THAT IS SO LOFTY AND FIERCE AND KIND, 201 OLD MEMORY 3
YOU MOST OF ALL, SILENT AND FIERCE OLD MAN, ... 270 PARDON FATHERS 15
AND THOSE FIERCE EYES, AND CURSE OUR LUCK . . . . . 272 GREY ROCK V 39
BRED THAT FIERCE TOOTH AND CLEANLY LIMB . . . . . . 318 APPOINTMENT 10
WHEN THAT FIERCE VIRGIN AND HER STAR . . . . 437 SONGS PLAY 1 15
WHEN THE FIERCE VIRGIN AND HER STAR . . . . 437 SONGS PLAY 1 V 15
"DROWN ALL THE DOGS," SAID THE FIERCE YOUNG WOMAN, . 546 TO SAME TUNE 2 7
DROWN ALL THE DOGS," SAID THE FIERCE YOUNG WOMAN. . 546 TO SAME TUNE 2 10
"DROWN ALL THE DOGS," SAID THE FIERCE YOUNG WOMAN, . 546 TO SAME TUNE 2 17
DROWN ALL THE DOGS," SAID THE FIERCE YOUNG WOMAN, . 546 TO SAME TUNE 2 20
"DROWN ALL THE DOGS," SAID THE FIERCE YOUNG WOMAN, . 547 TO SAME TUNE 2 27
DROWN ALL THE DOGS," SAID THE FIERCE YOUNG WOMAN. . 547 TO SAME TUNE 2 30
FROM MOUNTAIN TO MOUNTAIN RIDE THE FIERCE HORSEMEN. . 605 SONGS BURDEN 1 9
FROM MOUNTAIN TO MOUNTAIN RIDE THE FIERCE HORSEMEN. . 606 SONGS BURDEN 1 18
FROM MOUNTAIN TO MOUNTAIN RIDE THE FIERCE HORSEMEN. . 606 SONGS BURDEN 1 27
FROM MOUNTAIN TO MOUNTAIN RIDE THE FIERCE HORSEMEN. . 607 SONGS BURDEN 2 9
FROM MOUNTAIN TO MOUNTAIN RIDE THE FIERCE HORSEMEN. . 607 SONGS BURDEN 2 18
FROM MOUNTAIN TO MOUNTAIN RIDE THE FIERCE HORSEMEN. . 607 SONGS BURDEN 2 27
FROM MOUNTAIN TO MOUNTAIN RIDE THE FIERCE HORSEMEN. . 608 SONGS BURDEN 3 9
FROM MOUNTAIN TO MOUNTAIN RIDE THE FIERCE HORSEMEN. . 608 SONGS BURDEN 3 18
FROM MOUNTAIN TO MOUNTAIN RIDE THE FIERCE HORSEMEN. . 608 SONGS BURDEN 3 27
FIERCE THRUST! A TARDY BLOSSOM HAD THE SEED, ... 665 ISLE STAT II 2 65
LIES TORN AND ROTTING. THE FIERCE KESTREL BIRDS . . 675 ISLE STAT II 3 234
BEFORE I AM TOO WEAK, FIERCE MORTAL, LET ME FLY, . . 675 ISLE STAT II 3 245
FIERCE MORTAL, AND CROUCHED LOW BESIDE THE LAKE . . 675 ISLE STAT II 3 V 245A
A SIBYL, WITH FIERCE FACE AS OF A HOUND . . . . . . 687 TWO TITANS 9
TILL THEIR FIERCE MISERIES WITHIN HIS EYES . . . . . 687 TWO TITANS 26
WORN BY THE SOLSTICE FIERCE, AND MADE IT PURE. . . . 692 MOSADA 1 57

		PAGE	TITLE	LINE

FIERCE (CONTINUED)
THE WORLD TO ITS FIERCE INFANCY AGAIN. . . . .   698 MOSADA 2   61
OBEYS. SOME FIERCE MAGICIAN FLIES OR WALKS . . . . .   720 WITCH VIVIEN   9
FIERCELY
TO HUNGER FIERCELY AFTER TRUTH, ...   66 HAPPY SHEPHERD   24
FIERY
ABOUT WHOSE FACE BIRDS WAGGED THEIR FIERY WINGS, . . .   187 QUEEN MAEVE   145
FOR SHE HAD FIERY BLOOD . . . .   255 WOMAN HOMER   15
WITH FIERY SONG I'LL DROWN YON PUNY VOICE. . . . . .   648 ISLE STAT I 1   81
BEHOLD, HOW LIKE A SWARM OF FIERY BEES . . . .   662 ISLE STAT II 2   1
THAT WITH THEIR FIERY RUIN FILL THE HALL, ...   683 SEEKER   45
AND MINGLING HAIR FALL FROM THE FIERY BOUGHS, ...   765 SHADOW WATER A   368
FIFTEEN
NO, NOT IN THESE FIFTEEN . . . .   315 FRIENDS   6
AND MINE WERE BUT FIFTEEN FOOT, NO MODERN STALKS   623 HIGH TALK   3
    UPON HIGHER,
FIFTEEN APPARITIONS HAVE I SEEN: . . . .   624 APPARITIONS   7
FIFTEEN APPARITIONS HAVE I SEEN: . . . .   624 APPARITIONS   15
FIFTEEN APPARITIONS HAVE I SEEN: . . . .   624 APPARITIONS   23
FIFTEENTH
NOW AT ITS FIFTEENTH NIGHT. . . . .   383 VISION ROBART   28
FIFTIETH
NOW THAT HIS FIFTIETH YEAR HAD COME, ...   361 ALF POLLEXFEN   31
MY FIFTIETH YEAR HAD COME AND GONE, ...   501 VACILLATION   35
FIFTY   SEE NINE-AND-FIFTY
THAT HAVE TO BE SET UP IN FIFTY WAYS, ...   260 FASC DIFFICULT   9
ARE NINE AND FIFTY SWANS. . . . .   322 SWANS AT COOLE V   6
AND NOW THAT I HAVE COME TO FIFTY YEARS . . . . . .   344 DEJECTION   10
HOW COULD SHE MATE WITH FIFTY YEARS THAT WAS SO WILDLY   450 OWEN AHERNE   15
    BRED?
HER CHILDISH GRATITUDE FOR LOVE AND MATCH YOUR FIFTY YEARS?   450 OWEN AHERNE   23
I MET HER ALL BUT FIFTY YEARS AGO . . . .   602 GALLERY REVIS   15
AT THE BOTTOM OF A LETTER, FIFTY MEN. . . . .   790 DEDICATION   10
FIGHT
NOR THE HIGH GODS WHO NEVER LIVED, MAY FIGHT . . . .   34 OISIN 2   80
ONCE MORE UNTO YOUR FLOWERS, FOR NONE MAY FIGHT, . . .   34 OISIN 2   V   80
OF THE LOUD-CRASHING AND EARTH-SHAKING FIGHT, ...   38 OISIN 2   141
OF THE LOUD CRASHING AND EARTH SHAKING FIGHT . . . .   38 OISIN 2   V   141
OF FEAR, I BADE THEM GO; AND FOR THE FIGHT . . . . .   38 OISIN 2   V   142
CUCHULAIN'S FIGHT WITH THE SEA . . . .   105 CUCHULAIN SEA   T
THAT HE MAY FIGHT THE HORSES OF THE SEA." . . . . .   111 CUCHULAIN SEA   81
THAT HE MAY FIGHT THE WAVES OF THE LOUD SEA." . . . .   111 CUCHULAIN SEA   V   81
THAT HE MIGHT FIGHT THE WAVES OF THE LOUD SEA." . . .   111 CUCHULAIN SEA   V   81
THOSE THAT I FIGHT I DO NOT HATE, ...   328 IRISH AIRMAN   3
NOR LAW, NOR DUTY BADE ME FIGHT, ...   328 IRISH AIRMAN   9
ALL THE FOLLY OF A FIGHT . . . .   476 EVA GORE-BOOTH   22
HE WITH BODY WAGED A FIGHT, ...   561 FOUR AGES MAN   1
OUT OF THAT CRAZY FIGHT: . . . .   585 ORAHILLY   15
AND FIGHT FOR THE BLACK SLOE-BERRIES. . . . .   644 SONG FAERIES   13
THIS THING WE ASK: MUST WE TWO FIGHT?--JUDGE THOU. . .   660 ISLE STAT II 1   41
FOR THIS THING FIGHT--WE LOVE ONE MAID? HER NAME? . .   661 ISLE STAT II 1   66
THERE IS NO WAY BUT THAT YE FIGHT I WIS. . . . . . .   662 ISLE STAT II 1   75
IF HER YE LOVE. AYE, COLIN, WE MUST FIGHT. . . . .   662 ISLE STAT II 1   76
AYE, FIGHT WE MUST. TELL ME, ANTONIO, MIGHT . . . .   662 ISLE STAT II 1   77
ANTONIO! WE HAVE RESOLVED TO FIGHT. . . . .   664 ISLE STAT II 2   55
AND FIGHT FOR THE BLACK SLOE-BERRIES, ...   676 ISLE STAT II 3   260
FIGHTING
AND WE ONCE MORE UNTO OUR FIGHTING FELL. . . . . . .   43 OISIN 2   V   218
AFTER SHORT FIGHTING IN THE LEAFY SHADE, ...   109 CUCHULAIN SEA   57
THAT I LOVED ONCE." AGAIN THE FIGHTING SPED, ...   110 CUCHULAIN SEA   64
AND THAT LONG FIGHTING AT THE FORD, ...   197 BAILE AILLINN   194
THE FIGHTING MEN AND SERVANTS OF THIS HOUSE, ...   280 TWO KINGS   V   70
WHO ARE BUT WEASELS FIGHTING IN A HOLE . . . .   429 NINETEEN 19   32
AND A MAN IS FIGHTING MAD, ...   638 BEN BULBEN   28
FIGHTING-MEN
THE FIGHTING-MEN AND SERVANTS OF THIS HOUSE, ...   280 TWO KINGS   70
FIGURATIVE
FROM A DISCOURSE IN FIGURATIVE SPEECH . . . .   472 ALL SOUL NIGHT   52
FIGURE
"WHAT IS THE FIGURE IN A SHROUD . . . .   253 HIS DREAM   7
A FIGURE THAT HAS GROWN SO FABULOUS . . . .   412 TOWER   77
A FAMOUS, A BRILLIANT FIGURE . . . .   608 SONGS BURDEN 3   16
FIGURED
OF MANY A FIGURED EMBROIDERY: . . . .   4 OISIN 1   27
OF MANY A FIGURED CREATURE STRANGE, ...   4 OISIN 1   V   27
AS IF THAT WRITING OR THE FIGURED PAGE . . . .   466 HARUN RASHID   126
THAT IF THEIR NEIGHBOURS FIGURED PLAIN, ...   626 OLD MEN BE MAD   11
FIGURES
AND CARVEN FIGURES ON THEIR PROWS . . . .   14 OISIN 1   190
AND CARVEN FIGURES ON THEIR PROWS . . . .   23 OISIN 1   354
AS FIGURES MOVING MIRRORED IN A GLASS, ...   676 ISLE STAT II 3   270
TWO FIGURES CROUCHING ON THE BLACK ROCK, BOUND . . .   687 TWO TITANS   5
FILL
TO FILL THEIR DARK-BEAKED HOLLOW GALLEYS. . . . . .   82 MAD KING GOLL   16
THAT HE MAY FILL HIS HOLLOW GALLEYS. . . . .   82 MAD KING GOLL   V   16
TO FILL WITH COWS HIS HOLLOW GALLEYS." . . . . . .   82 MAD KING GOLL   V   16
A LITTLE SPACE FOR THE ROSE-BREATH TO FILL! . . . .   101 ROSE UPON ROOD   14
AND CRAZY RASCALS RAGE THEIR FILL . . . .   131 OLD PENSIONER   9
TO FILL YOUR HEART WITH CONTENT." . . . .   167 BLESSED   20
LET RUSH AND BIRD CRY OUT THEIR FILL . . . .   197 BAILE AILLINN   198
WOULD HAVE HIS FILL OUT OF MY LADLE . . . .   304 HOUR DAWN   V   53

276

		PAGE	TITLE	LINE
FILL	(CONTINUED)			
ONE'S HAD HER FILL OF LOVERS, ANOTHER'S HAD BUT ONE,		354	HIS PHOENIX	19
HER FILL OF SLEEP.		435	FOR MY SON	8
"LET OTHERS BOAST THEIR FILL," SAID I,		539	MEETING	7
COME FILL UP ALL THOSE GLASSES		586	PARNELLITES	7
ALTHOUGH I DRINK MY FILL.		592	DRUNK SOBRIETY	4
MAKE HIM FILL THE CRADLES RIGHT.		638	BEN BULBEN	41
THAT WITH THEIR FIERY RUIN FILL THE HALL,		683	SEEKER	45
THAT FILL THE BLAZING HOLLOWS OF MY HEART.		684	SEEKER V	69D
AND FILL ME WITH THY RAGE, THAT I MAY BRUISE		698	MOSADA 2	54
MAY THE SWORD-BLADES DRINK THEIR FILL		776	AGAINST WITCH	37
MAY THE SWORD BLADES DRINK THEIR FILL		776	AGAINST WITCH V	37
FILLED				
THE MOIL OF MY CENTURIES FILLED ME; AND GONE LIKE A SEA-COVERED STONE		51	OISIN 3	70
. . . AND FILLED ME FULL TO THE BONE.		52	OISIN 3	72
THEIR HAIR ALONG THE MOUNTAINS ROLLED AND FILLED		74	ANASHU VIJAYA	71
FILLED FULL OF ANCIENT CHEER."		97	FOXHUNTER V	12
HAD FILLED THE HOUSE WITH DRUID HEAVINESS;		181	QUEEN MAEVE	40
WHY SHOULD I BLAME HER THAT SHE FILLED MY DAYS		256	NO SECOND TROY	1
NOW IT HAS FILLED AN OLD SOCK FULL:		301	RUN PARADISE	20
PLEASED TO HAVE FILLED THE EYES		329	MEN IMPROVE	8
AND THEN A COUNTER-TRUTH FILLED OUT ITS PLAY,		629	CIRCUS ANIMALS	17
FILLED THEM AS THEY SAT TOGETHER:		667	ISLE STAT II 3	31
AS WORDS OF THINE THROUGH FOURSCORE YEARS HAVE FILLED		683	SEEKER	46
FILLING				
FILLING THE FIBROUS DIMNESS WITH LONG GENERATIONS OF EYES.		49	OISIN 3	40
SIDLED THEIR BODIES AGAINST HIM, FILLING THE SHADE WITH THEIR EYES.		50	OISIN 3	48
FILLING THY HEART WITH A MORTAL DREAM,		140	HOSTING SIDHE V	6
FILLS				
AND FILLS WITH STARS NIGHT'S PURPLE CUP,		18	OISIN 1	262
ANOTHER FILLS YOUR MIND. MY MOTHER'S NAME.		71	ANASHU VIJAYA	16
SOME OTHER FILLS YOUR MIND. MY MOTHER'S NAME.		71	ANASHU VIJAYA V	16
UNTO THE WANDERER'S SHIPS, OR AS DAY FILLS		645	ISLE STAT I 1	10
YON EAGER LARK, THAT FILLS WITH SONG THE WHOLE		652	ISLE STAT I 2	18
AS AN HURT LEOPARD FILLS WITH CEASELESS MOAN,		674	ISLE STAT II 3	208
AS A HURT LEOPARD FILLS WITH CEASELESS MOAN		674	ISLE STAT II 3 V	208
AND THEN HIS HEART FILLS FULL OF LOVE,		716	FAIRY DOCTOR	11
AN EVENING PRESENCE FILLS THE PLACE.		736	SUMMER EVENING	16
THAT ALL THE VALLEY FILLS		781	MY HEART BEAT	10
LIKE WINE THAT FILLS TO THE TOP		781	MY HEART BEAT	14
FILTHY				
A NOISY AND FILTHY THING."		319	DOLLS	12
OR SHIFT TIME'S FILTHY LOAD,		505	RESULT THOUGHT	15
BUT THROWN UPON THIS FILTHY MODERN TIDE		611	STATUES	29
FIN				
CRIED FIN, AND CRIED SHE, "MEN OF FAME,		5	OISIN 1 V	45
HAD KISSED MY FATHER, LONG-ARMED FIN,		10	OISIN 1 V	112B
FIN, CONAN, OSCAR, MANY MORE, THE TIDE		44	OISIN 2 V	228A
WHAT PLACE HAVE CAOLTE AND FIN, AND BRAN, SGEOLAN, LOMAIR?		61	OISIN 3 V	195
TO FIN, CAOLTE, AND CONAN, AND BRAN, SGEOLAN, LOMAIR.		63	OISIN 3 V	224
AND STEADIED BY A FIN,		612	NEWS ORACLE	14
FINAL				
THE FINAL PARADISE.		415	TOWER V	156
AND HERE'S A FINAL REASON,		586	PARNELLITES	17
YOUNG MOORISH GIRL, THY FINAL HOUR IS HERE;		701	MOSADA 3	63
FIND				
WENT WE TO FIND THEIR PRINCE'S HALL--		16	OISIN 1 V	217
AND NEVER FIND, THOUGH YE IN MUSIC SPEAK.		42	OISIN 2 V	201
I FIND UNDER THE BOUGHS OF LOVE AND HATE,		101	ROSE UPON ROOD	10
I WILL FIND OUT WHERE SHE HAS GONE,		150	WANDER AENGUS	19
I WILL FIND OUT WHERE SHE IS GONE		150	WANDER AENGUS V	19
OR REMEMBERING HERS THEY WILL FIND NO OTHER FACE FAIR		163	VALLEY LOVERS	7
THERE'S MANY A ONE SHALL FIND OUT ALL HEARTACHE		205	ADAMS CURSE	16
TO FIND IT WHEN NIGHT FALLS LAID ON A GOLDEN BIER.		209	UNDER THE MOON	10
I FIND NO HAPPINESS IN SHADY BRYCELINDE		209	UNDER THE MOON V	1
WILL NEVER FIND US THERE		213	HAPPY TOWNLAND V	2
WHERE OLD AGE CANNOT FIND THEM: PAIRC-NA-LEE,		217	WOODS OF COOLE	7
JUDGE OF THE STARS, AND FIND A COURSE FOR US?		224	SHADOW WATER B	61
MORE RICHES THAN THEY EVER HOPED TO FIND?		226	SHADOW WATER B	94
WHAT RICHES CAN YOU FIND IN THIS WASTE SEA		226	SHADOW WATER B	97
AND FIND THEIR LAUGHTER SWEETER TO THE TASTE		228	SHADOW WATER B	134
AND ALMOST WEPT BECAUSE THEY COULD NOT FIND IT.		229	SHADOW WATER B	155
OR SOMEWHERE, I SHALL FIND THE LOVE THEY HAVE PROMISED.		231	SHADOW WATER B	208
THAT MUCH IS CERTAIN. I SHALL FIND A WOMAN,		231	SHADOW WATER B	209
ANOTHER ANSWERS, "MAYBE WE SHALL FIND		233	SHADOW WATER B	254
WITH LIGHTNING, YOU WENT FROM ME, AND I COULD FIND		257	RECONCILIATION	4
WE'LL FIND SO GOOD A THING AS THAT WE HAVE LOST?		258	KING NO KING	13
I'LL FIND THE STABLE AND PULL OUT THE BOLT.		260	FASC DIFFICULT	13
TO FIND IF HEARTS BE WILD AND WISE,		263	MASK	4
"I WOULD BUT FIND WHAT'S THERE TO FIND,		263	MASK	6
"I WOULD BUT FIND WHAT'S THERE TO FIND,		263	MASK	6
AND WE FIND HEARTENERS AMONG MEN		266	GALWAY RACES	15
AND FIND HEARTENERS AMONG MEN		266	GALWAY RACES V	15
TO FIND OUT IF I MIGHT LOVE.		268	BROWN PENNY	4
TO FIND OUT ALL THAT IS IN IT,		268	BROWN PENNY	11
KNOWING THAT HE SHOULD FIND UPON HER LIPS		280	TWO KINGS	77
AND I, THAT I MIGHT FIND AND STUB IT OUT,		281	TWO KINGS V	92
WOMEN CAN FIND." WITH A MOST MASTERFUL VOICE,		284	TWO KINGS	175
WOMEN CAN FIND." WITH A MOST BURNING VOICE		284	TWO KINGS V	175

	PAGE	TITLE		LINE
FIND (CONTINUED)				
AND FIND MY HEALTH AGAIN IN THE SEA AIR,"	299	BEGGAR CRIED		2
THAT I MAY FIND THE SLEEP I HAVE LOST."	303	HOUR DAWN		39
I HAVE TO FIND THE SLEEP I HAVE LOST."	303	HOUR DAWN	V	39
BUT FOR THOSE MORNINGS WHEN I FIND	306	HOUR DAWN		76
YET WE, FOR ALL THAT PRAISE, COULD FIND	314	MEMORY YOUTH		13
AND ALL THEIR EYES STILL FIXED, HOPING TO FIND ONCE MORE,	318	MAGI		6
--BEN JONSON'S PHRASE--AND FIND WHEN JUNE IS COME	321	REED WHISPERER		6
TO FIND THEY HAVE FLOWN AWAY?	323	SWANS AT COOLE		30
I WOULD FIND BY THE EDGE OF THAT WATER	330	BONE OF A HARE		9
I CANNOT FIND THE PEACE OF HOME	332	ROUND TOWER		29
HAVE FOUND THE PATH MY GOATS' FEET CANNOT FIND.	342	SHEP GOATHERD		84
HAVE FOUND THE PATH MY GOAT'S FEET CANNOT FIND.	342	SHEP GOATHERD	V	84
A MAN MAY FIND IN NO MAN	345	ON WOMAN		3
TO FIND WHAT ONCE I HAD	346	ON WOMAN		33
AND I WOULD FIND MYSELF AND NOT AN IMAGE.	367	EGO DOMINUS		10
BUT THAT OF CHRIST. AND DID HE FIND HIMSELF	368	EGO DOMINUS		22
WHAT HE SHALL NEVER FIND. WHY SHOULD NOT YOU	373	PHASES OF MOON		20
WILL SCARCELY FIND FOR HIM A BROKEN CRUST	373	PHASES OF MOON		23
THAT HE WILL NEVER FIND! I'D PLAY A PART!	377	PHASES OF MOON		128
DAY AFTER DAY, YET NEVER FIND THE MEANING.	377	PHASES OF MOON		135
TO FIND OUT SOME APPROPRIATE PAIN--	388	SOLOMON WITCH		20
WILL FIND OUT SOME APPROPRIATE PAIN,	388	SOLOMON WITCH	V	20
OR BUT TO FIND,	390	IMAGE PAST		38
I COULD NOT FIND A THING SO DEAR."	398	BREAK OF DAY		9
THAN THAT I MAY FIND OUT A WAY	401	DEMON BEAST		41
THAT CHOOSES RIGHT, AND NEVER FIND A FRIEND.	404	FOR DAUGHTER		24
YET, NOW I HAVE CONSIDERED IT, I FIND	411	TOWER		50
MY BODILY HEIRS MAY FIND,	420	MY HOUSE		28
AND FIND A COMFORT IN IT? MAY THIS TOWER	423	MY DESCENDANTS	V	13
I HAD BETTER FIND A CONVENT AND TURN NUN!	448	HERO GIRL FOOL		11
I WILL FIND OUT SOME CAVERN IN THE HILLS	448	HERO GIRL FOOL	V	11
I THINK THAT I MAY FIND	449	HERO GIRL FOOL		28
SHOULD FIND NO BURDEN BUT ITSELF AND YET SHOULD BE WORN OUT.	449	OWEN AHERNE		3
I DID NOT FIND IN ANY CAGE THE WOMAN AT MY SIDE.	450	OWEN AHERNE		19
A BOY'S LOVELORN INDIFFERENT HANDS MIGHT FIND	461	HARUN RASHID	V	14
THEIR BITTERNESS AND FIND THE HONEYCOMB.	463	HARUN RASHID		48
NOR FIND A REMEDY." "BUT WHAT IF I	464	HARUN RASHID		84
AND FIND NO REMEDY. "BUT WHAT IF I	464	HARUN RASHID	V	84
IF HONOUR FIND HIM IN THE WINTRY BLAST?	479	SELF AND SOUL		56
HAD SCOOPED OUT PHARAOH'S MUMMY. I--THOUGH HEART MIGHT FIND RELIEF	503	VACILLATION		84
(ALL FIND SAFETY IN THE TOMB.)	508	JANE BISHOP		3
(ALL FIND SAFETY IN THE TOMB.)	508	JANE BISHOP		10
(ALL FIND SAFETY IN THE TOMB.)	508	JANE BISHOP		17
(ALL FIND SAFETY IN THE TOMB.)	508	JANE BISHOP		24
OR BUT TO FIND IF WITHERED VEIN RAN BLOOD,	537	HER VISION		6
HE IT HAS FOUND SHALL FIND THEREIN	538	LAST CONFESS		17
"I THINK THAT I SHALL FIND HER	594	COLONEL MARTIN		16
FIND IN MIDDLE AIR	601	THOSE IMAGES		13
CHILDLESS I THOUGHT, "MY CHILDREN MAY FIND HERE	603	GALLERY REVIS		36
THAT GIRLS AT PUBERTY MAY FIND	617	LONG-LEG FLY		21
AND FIND OUR ANCIENT HOUNDS BEFORE THE DOOR,	622	HOUND VOICE		16
NO SINGLE STORY WOULD THEY FIND	626	OLD MEN BE MAD		13
FICKLE THE GUIDING HIS ARROW SHALL FIND!	657	ISLE STAT I 3		66
UNTIL I FIND HIM. WHAT A WEARY WEEK,	658	ISLE STAT II 1		2
WHO SEEK MAY FIND, SAVE ONLY ONE,	668	ISLE STAT II 3		48
AND THOU WILT STAY. ALL THOUGHT OF WHAT THEY FIND	670	ISLE STAT II 3		92
THEM ALL, AND LET THEM FIND YOU IN THE VAPOUR.	694	MOSADA 1	V	108A
WE WILL FIND HER FAVOURITE LAIR,	706	DAWN-SONG		26
AND WILL FIND HER GOOD AT HEART,	726	LOVERS QUARREL		10
HE'D FIND FOR THIS SOME HOLY TEXT.	728	PRIEST FAIRY		16
THE FOOL FORETOLD ME I WOULD FIND THIS LOVE	750	SHADOW WATER A		62
FORGAEL MAY FIND HIS HEART'S DESIRE ON BOARD	751	SHADOW WATER A		107
NOW RUSH UPON HER AND FIND OUT WHAT PREY	752	SHADOW WATER A		130
I SHALL FIND OUT IF I HAVE LOST MY WAY	753	SHADOW WATER A		137
AND THE OTHER ANSWERS, "MAYBE WE SHALL FIND	753	SHADOW WATER A		144
I SHALL FIND OUT IF I HAVE LOST THE WAY	753	SHADOW WATER A	V	137
WE WILL FIND OUT VALLEYS AND WOODS AND MEADOWS	767	SHADOW WATER A		388
FINDING				
ON FINDING THAT HER VOICE IS SWEET AND LOW	205	ADAMS CURSE		17
IN FINDING THAT IT'S YOUNG AND MILD AND LOW.	205	ADAMS CURSE	V	17
BUT FINDING HIM STILL SILENT I STOOPED DOWN	281	TWO KINGS		109
WHO FINDING THE FIRST WRINKLES ON A FACE	472	ALL SOUL NIGHT		42
FINDRIAS				
AND FINDRIAS AND FALIAS,	196	BAILE AILLINN		162
FINDRINNY				
ON A HORSE WITH BRIDLE OF FINDRINNY!	3	OISIN 1		21
WITH HOOFS OF THE PALE FINDRINNY	25	OISIN 1		383
WITH HOOFS OF THE RUDDY FINDRINNY	25	OISIN 1	V	383
FINDS				
THE SOUL IS FREE, AND FINDS NO FLAW,	19	OISIN 1	V	284
THE MIND IS MADE UNCHANGING, FOR IT FINDS	227	SHADOW WATER B		101
AND BODILY TENDERNESS, AND FINDS THAT EVEN	228	SHADOW WATER B		147
WHEN SHE FINDS OUT WE HAVE BETTER MEN ABOARD	232	SHADOW WATER B		231
WHEN SHE FINDS OUT I WILL NOT LET HER GO--	236	SHADOW WATER B		302
A MAN THAT FINDS GREAT BITTERNESS	379	SAINT HUNCH		2
AND FINDS A REAL IMAGE THERE!	388	SOLOMON WITCH		27
WHERE SLIPPERED CONTEMPLATION FINDS HIS EASE	418	ANCEST HOUSES		30
WHO FINDS ABOUNDING CEPHISUS	447	COLONUS PRAISE		23

278

	PAGE	TITLE	LINE
FINDS (CONTINUED)			
AND FINDS THERE NOTHING TO MAKE ITS TERROR LESS	618	BRONZE HEAD	6
A CAREFUL FIELD-MOUSE FINDS A FALLEN CRUMB:	713	FERENCZ RENYI	77
FOR HAPPIER LOVE BUT FINDS UNHAPPINESS.	750	SHADOW WATER A	67
FINE			
THE TALE DROVE HIS FINE ANGRY MOOD AWAY.	128	DREAM OF FAERY	36
HE COULD REMEMBER WHEN HE HAD HAD FINE DREAMS.	182	QUEEN MAEVE	56
I SAID: "IT'S CERTAIN THERE IS NO FINE THING	205	ADAMS CURSE	21
AND YET COULD GIVE SO FINE A STROKE?"	274	GREY ROCK	84
IT'S CERTAIN THAT FINE WOMEN EAT	404	FOR DAUGHTER	30
GIFTED WITH SO FINE AN EAR:	412	TOWER	94
O WHAT FINE THOUGHT WE HAD BECAUSE WE THOUGHT	428	NINETEEN 19	15
O WHAT FINE THOUGHTS WE HAD BECAUSE WE THOUGHT	428	NINETEEN 19 V	15
ALL MY FINE FEATHERS WOULD BE PLUCKED AWAY	469	HARUN RASHID	178
HIS ELEMENT IS SO FINE	470	ALL SOUL NIGHT	7
SO THAT HIS ELEMENTS HAVE GROWN SO FINE	473	ALL SOUL NIGHT	82
FINE MANNERS, LIBERAL SPEECH,	506	REMORSE SPEECH	7
IMAGINED SUCH A FINE AFFAIR:	791	REPRISALS	14
FINEST			
THE FINEST PLAY UNDER THE SUN.	424	ROAD AT DOOR	5
FINGER			
OF ONE LONG FINGER ON MY LIP.	12	OISIN 1	151
WHOM BRAHMA, TOUCHING WITH HIS FINGER, PRAISES, FOR YOU HOLD	73	ANASHU VIJAYA	42
WHOM BRAHMA, TOUCHING WITH HIS FINGER, PRAISES, FOR YE HOLD	73	ANASHU VIJAYA V	42
AND MAY NO RESTLESS FAY WITH FIDGET FINGER	75	ANASHU VIJAYA	90
MAY NEVER RESTLESS FAY WITH FIDGET FINGER	75	ANASHU VIJAYA V	90
AND MAY NO RESTLESS PITRI'S FIDGET FINGER	75	ANASHU VIJAYA V	90
WITH HIS OWN FINGER TOUCHED THE BRAZEN STRINGS.	109	CUCHULAIN SEA V	46
WHERE THAT WISE HARPER'S FINGER RAN.	195	BAILE AILLINN	156
O DEATH'S OLD BONY FINGER	213	HAPPY TOWNLAND V	1
THOUGH I'D MY FINGER ON MY LIP,	254	HIS DREAM	13
UPON THE PALENESS OF A FINGER.	390	IMAGE PAST	28
BUT KNEW MY FINGER COULD BUT HAVE TOUCHED	399	BREAK OF DAY	13
BUT KNEW MY FINGER WOULD HAVE TOUCHED	399	BREAK OF DAY V	13
TREE, LIKE A SOOTY FINGER, STARTS FROM THE EARTH:	410	TOWER	19
DID QUATTROCENTO FINGER FASHION IT	444	SCHOOL CHILDR	26
WHAT QUINTO-CENTO FINGER FASHIONED IT:	444	SCHOOL CHILDR V	26
DA VINCI' FINGER SO HAD FASHIONED IT	444	SCHOOL CHILDR V	26
WITH HER WHITE FINGER. I LED HER HOME ASLEEP	468	HARUN RASHID	158
DOWN EVERY WITHERED FINGER FROM THE TOP:	537	HER VISION	11
BUT LIKED THE WAY HIS FINGER SMELT.	619	STICK INCENSE	4
AND JOY, THE TOUCHING OF WHOSE FINGER LENDS	686	DRAWING-ROOM	7
I FEEL A FINGER DRAWN ACROSS MY CHEEK:	694	MOSADA 1	96
IT SEEMS TO FONDLE, WITH A FINGER BRIGHT	714	FERENCZ RENYI	114
LIES A CHILLY FINGER TIP,	732	STREET DANCERS	19
AND JOY, THE TOUCHING OF WHOSE FINGER LENDS	734	QUATRAIN APHOR	7
WHAT FINGER FIRST BEGAN	783	GREY ROUND	11
FINGERED			
THEY FINGERED IT AND GAZED ON ME	15	OISIN 1	209
THEY FINGERED IT AND GAZED AT ME,	15	OISIN 1 V	209
FINGERED UPON A FIDDLE-STICK OR STRINGS	445	SCHOOL CHILDR	46
FINGERED UPON A FIDDLE STICK OR STRING	445	SCHOOL CHILDR V	46
FINGERETH			
FOR THE DAWN THE FOLIAGE FINGERETH,	646	ISLE STAT I 1	26
FOR THE DAWN OF FOLIAGE FINGERETH,	646	ISLE STAT I 1 V	26
FINGER'S			
AND THERE ENDURED HER FINGER'S TOUCH	397	POLIT PRISONER V	5
FINGERS			
LIKE SOOTY FINGERS, MANY A TREE	13	OISIN 1	171
HER FINGERS AND HER GARMENTS' HEM.	16	OISIN 1 V	216
BURNING BETWEEN HER FINGERS, AND IN MINE	37	OISIN 2	125
COULD FONDLE THE LEAVES WITH HIS FINGERS,	49	OISIN 3	38
THEN HE SWAYED IN HIS FINGERS THE BELL-BRANCH,	51	OISIN 3	67
BUT, THE BIRD IN MY FINGERS, I MOUNTED,	54	OISIN 3	111
BUT, THE BIRD IN MY FINGERS, I MOUNTED, MINDFUL ONLY TO LAUNCH	54	OISIN 3 V	111
FOR THERE MOVES ALIVE IN YOUR FINGERS	55	OISIN 3	124
FOR MOVETH ALIVE IN THY FINGERS THE FLUTTERING SADNESS OF EARTH.	55	OISIN 3 V	124
HIS FINGERS MOVE AND SWAY,	98	FOXHUNTER	30
WITH HIS OWN FINGERS TOUCHED THE BRAZEN STRINGS.	109	CUCHULAIN SEA	46
THAT GOD HAS LAID HIS FINGERS ON THE SKY:	128	DREAM OF FAERY	43
THAT FROM THOSE FINGERS GLITTERING SUMMER RUNS	128	DREAM OF FAERY	44
WHERE THAT WISE HARPER'S FINGERS RAN.	195	BAILE AILLINN V	156
WHEREON MAD FINGERS PLAY	291	TO A FRIEND	12
UNDER HIS FINGERS. I HAD IT FROM HIS MOTHER,	339	SHEP GOATHERD	26
THAT THOSE THAT WE HAVE LOVED GOT THEIR LONG FINGERS	375	PHASES OF MOON	66
UNDER BLANK EYES AND FINGERS NEVER STILL	382	VISION ROBART	5
NOW THAT NO FINGERS BIND,	390	IMAGE PAST	39
AND FROM HER FINGERS ATE ITS BIT.	397	POLIT PRISONER	6
PLUNGES TOWARDS NOTHING, ARMS AND FINGERS SPREADING WIDE	426	PHANTOM HATRED	13
HOW CAN THOSE TERRIFIED VAGUE FINGERS PUSH	441	LEDA AND SWAN	5
OUR HANDS ARE BLENCHED, OUR FINGERS SEEM	488	CRAZED MOON	14
AND AFTER THAT I HELD MY FINGERS UP,	537	HER VISION	9
ACCOMPLISHED FINGERS BEGIN TO PLAY.	567	LAPIS LAZULI	54
WITH INFANTINE FINGERS	672	ISLE STAT II 3	168
THOU'RT WELCOME. LIE THERE CLOSE AGAINST MY FINGERS.	700	MOSADA 3	44
"CHOOSE!" RESTLESS HAYNAU'S FINGERS TAPPING GO.	711	FERENCZ RENYI	41
FROM HAYNAU'S LIFTED FINGERS—TWO DRAW NIGH	714	FERENCZ RENYI	104
WHAT ROSEATE FINGERS! NO: NOR IS THERE ONE	720	WITCH VIVIEN	5

279

FINGERS   (CONTINUED)
   WHAT ROSEATE FINGERS! HA, HA! HA, HA, HA! . . . . . .   720 WITCH VIVIEN   15
   MY FINGERS FEEL HIS AMBER HAIR. . . . .   723 GIRLS SONG A   8
   THOSE CRAZY FINGERS PLAY . . . .   783 GREY ROUND   16
FINGERS'
   AND THERE ENDURED HER FINGERS' TOUCH . . . .   397 POLIT PRISONER   5
FINGER-TIP
   LIES A CHUBBY FINGER-TIP. . . . .   732 STREET DANCERS V   19
FINGER-TIPS
   AND TOUCHED IT WITH THEIR FINGER-TIPS. . . . .   18 OISIN 1   259
   AND TOUCHED IT WITH HIS FINGER-TIPS. . . . .   18 OISIN 1   V 259
   AND NEVER A SONG SANG NIAMH, AND OVER MY FINGER-TIPS . .   47 OISIN 3   6
FINISH
   IN COOLE DEMESNE, AND THERE TO FINISH UP . . . .   490 COOLE BALLYLEE   6
   LET HER FINISH HER DANCE. . . . .   568 SWEET DANCER   12
   LET HER FINISH HER DANCE. . . . .   568 SWEET DANCER   13
   A FINISH WORTHY OF THE START. . . . .   626 OLD MEN BE MAD   15
FINISHED
   AND AS SOON FINISHED. ALL THAT EVER LOVED . . . . .   229 SHADOW WATER B   151
   I SAW, BEFORE I HAD WELL FINISHED. . . . .   322 SWANS AT COOLE   9
   BECAUSE THE WORK HAD FINISHED IN THAT FLARE. . . . .   327 ROBERT GREGORY   85
   BUT THE ESCAPE; THE SONG'S NOT FINISHED YET. . . . .   377 PHASES OF MOON   117
   WHEN HE FINISHED HIS DOG'S DAY! . . . .   412 TOWER   79
   THE FINISHED MAN AMONG HIS ENEMIES?-- . . . . . .   479 SELF AND SOUL   49
   AND WHEN THE STORY'S FINISHED, WHAT'S THE NEWS? . . .   491 COOLE BALLYLEE V   40E
   WHEN ALL THAT STORY'S FINISHED, WHAT'S THE NEWS? . .   495 CHOICE   5
   ALL THAT IS FINISHED, LET IT FADE. . . . .   613 MARCH SONGS 1   10
   AND ALL THAT'S FINISHED, LET IT FADE. . . . . . .   613 MARCH SONGS 1   20
   AND ALL THAT'S FINISHED, LET IT FADE. . . . . . .   614 MARCH SONGS 1   30
   BE ONE? I THINK ALL'S FINISHED NOW AND SEALED. . . .   701 MOSADA 3   62
   THE TANGLED THOUGHTS OF THE FINISHED DAY . . . . .   728 PRIEST FAIRY   9
   WHEN MOON'S ROUND IS FINISHED . . . .   786 YOUR HEART   33
FINMOLE
   AND WHERE HER SON, FINMOLE, ON THE SMOOTH GRASS . . .   106 CUCHULAIN SEA V   18
   "I AM FINMOLE, MIGHTY CUCHULAIN'S SON." . . . . . .   110 CUCHULAIN SEA V   68
FINN
   CAOILTE, AND CONAN, AND FINN WERE THERE, ...   3 OISIN 1   13
   "O PLEASANT WOMAN," ANSWERED FINN, ...   5 OISIN 1   40
   "O PLEASANT MAIDEN," ANSWERED FINN, ...   5 OISIN 1   V   40
   CAOILTE, CONAN, AND FINN CAME NEAR, ...   10 OISIN 1   111
   REMEMBERING HOW I HAD STOOD BY WHITE-HAIRED FINN . .   44 OISIN 2   227
   REMEMBERING HOW I STOOD BY WHITE-HAIRED FINN . . . .   44 OISIN 2   V 227
   HOW THE SLOW, BLUE-EYED OXEN OF FINN LOW SADLY AT EVENING
     TIDE. . . . .   52 OISIN 3   84
   I MUST GAZE ON THE BEARD OF FINN, ...   55 OISIN 3   114
   MY PAISTIN FINN IS MY SOLE DESIRE, ...   550 SONGS REWRIT 1   1
FINVARRA
   . . . FINVARRA, FEACRA, AND CAOLTE . . . . . .   174 ELEMENT POWERS V   T
FIR
   A FIR TREE ROARING IN ITS LEAFLESS TOP, ...   40 OISIN 2   V 177
   UPON A SWORD, A FIR TREE ON A HILL, ...   104 FERGUS DRUID   V   34
   OF BEAMS A-FLICKER ON YON LONELY FIR, ...   661 ISLE STAT II 1   72
FIRBOLGS'
   AND PASSING THE FIRBOLGS' BURIAL-MOUNDS, ...   3 OISIN 1   16
   AND PASSING THE FIRBOLGS' BURIAL MOUNDS, ...   3 OISIN 1   V   16
FIRE   SEE STAR-FIRE CAMP-FIRE
   "AN OLD MAN STIRS THE FIRE TO A BLAZE, ...   26 OISIN 1   400
   AND BENDS TO THE FIRE AND SHAKES WITH THE COLD . . .   26 OISIN 1   405
   SHOUTED. WITH FIRE OF HAIR ABOUT HER SWIRLED, . . .   38 OISIN 2   V 134
   HAD SURGED UP IN A PLUMY FIRE, I DRAVE . . . .   41 OISIN 2   181
   WITH SURGE OF PLUMY FIRE, LUNGING I DRAVE . . . .   41 OISIN 2   181
   SURGED UP IN PLUMY FIRE, I LUNGED AND DRAVE . . .   41 OISIN 2   181
   FLASHES THE FIRE OF SADNESS, FOR THEY SEE . . . .   73 ANASHU VIJAYA   49
   A WHIRLING AND A WANDERING FIRE, ...   83 MAD KING GOLL   28
   A FEVER AND A WHIRLING FIRE! . . . . . .   83 MAD KING GOLL V   28
   THE WHIRLING AND THE WANDERING FIRE! . . . . .   86 MAD KING GOLL   67
   BLOWIN' HER MORNIN' FIRE. . . . .   95 MOLL MAGEE   36
   A-BLOWIN' OF HER MORNIN' FIRE, ...   95 MOLL MAGEE   V   35
   FIRE IS IN THE OLD MAN'S EYES, ...   98 FOXHUNTER   29
   A FIRE IS IN THE OLD MAN'S EYES. . . . . .   98 FOXHUNTER   V   29
   GO THERE, AND LIGHT A CAMP FIRE AT WOOD'S RIM! . . .   108 CUCHULAIN SEA V   35
   HIS EVENING FIRE AMID THE LEAFY SHADE. . . . . .   109 CUCHULAIN SEA   48
   AND NODDING BY THE FIRE, TAKE DOWN THIS BOOK, . . .   120 YOU ARE OLD   2
   MY CHAIR WAS NEAREST TO THE FIRE . . . . .   131 OLD PENSIONER   3
   TO SOME I HAVE TALKED WITH BY THE FIRE . . . . .   136 TO SOME I TALK   T
   IN FLOOD AND FIRE AND CLAY AND WIND, ...   138 TO IRELAND   V   25
   "AND BROOD NO MORE WHERE THE FIRE IS BRIGHT . . .   140 HOSTING SIDHE V   5
   BECAUSE A FIRE WAS IN MY HEAD, ...   149 WANDER AENGUS   2
   I WENT TO BLOW THE FIRE AFLAME, ...   149 WANDER AENGUS   10
   I BENT TO BLOW THE FIRE AFLAME! . . . . . .   149 WANDER AENGUS V   10
   I WENT TO BLOW THE FIRE A-FLAME, ...   149 WANDER AENGUS V   10
   I STOOPED TO BLOW THE FIRE AFLAME, ...   149 WANDER AENGUS V   10
   TILL THE SEED OF THE FIRE FLICKER AND GLOW! . . .   150 OLD MOTHER   2
   AND THE SEED OF THE FIRE GETS FEEBLE AND COLD. . . .   151 OLD MOTHER   10
   BUT THE SEED OF THE FIRE GETS FEEBLE AND COLD, . . .   151 OLD MOTHER   V   9
   THE SOUTH IS POURING DOWN ROSES OF CRIMSON FIRE! . .   154 BELOVED PEACE   6
   THE SOUTH WOULD COVER THEM WITH ROSES OF CRIMSON FIRE! .   154 BELOVED PEACE V   6
   THAT IS BRIMMED FROM THE PALE FIRE OF TIME! . . .   157 POET BELOVED   6
   IN TWILIGHTS OF DEW AND OF FIRE." . . . . . .   168 BLESSED   40
   IN TWILIGHTS OF DEW AND FIRE!" . . . . . .   168 BLESSED   V   40
   GREAT POWERS OF FALLING WAVE AND WIND AND WINDY FIRE, . .   174 ELEMENT POWERS   7

FIRE   (CONTINUED)
     YOU GREAT ANGELIC POWERS OF WIND, AND WAVE, AND FIRE, . . .   174 ELEMENT POWERS V   7
     GREAT ELEMENTAL POWERS OF WIND, AND WAVE, AND FIRE, ...   174 ELEMENT POWERS V   7
     HAD PACED FROM DOOR TO FIRE AND FIRE TO DOOR. . . . . . .   180 QUEEN MAEVE   17
     HAD PACED FROM DOOR TO FIRE AND FIRE TO DOOR. . . . . . .   180 QUEEN MAEVE   17
     AND WISDOM THAT CAUGHT FIRE LIKE THE DRIED FLAX, ...   181 QUEEN MAEVE   28
     WITH BODIES MADE OUT OF SOFT FIRE. THE ONE, ...   187 QUEEN MAEVE   144
     THE FIRE THAT STIRS ABOUT HER, WHEN SHE STIRS, ...   200 FOLLY COMFORT   10
     THE FLAGSTONE UNDER ALL, THE FIRE OF FIRES, ...   227 SHADOW WATER B   103
     AND CARRIES IT BETWEEN US. HOLY FIRE . . . .   239 SHADOW WATER B   371
     THAT NOBLENESS MADE SIMPLE AS A FIRE, ...   256 NO SECOND TROY   7
     WHAT MATTER, SO THERE IS BUT FIRE . . . .   263 MASK   14
     AND WHERE THE STONE STRUCK FIRE, WHILE IN THE LEAVES . .   278 TWO KINGS   33
     BESIDE A FIRE OF TURF IN TH' ANCIENT TOWER, ...   324 ROBERT GREGORY   3
     NEW WELCOME AND OLD WISDOM AT HER FIRE . . . .   340 SHEP GOATHERD   32
     WHEN FROM THE SMITHY FIRE . . . .   345 ON WOMAN   18
     MY GREAT WOOD LECTERN AND THE FIRE . . . .   358 PRESENCES   10
     I SLEPT ON MY THREE-LEGGED STOOL BY THE FIRE, ...   381 SONGS FOOL 2   1
     AROUND THE FIRE AT THE CLUB, ...   392 EASTER 1916   12
     O SAGES STANDING IN GOD'S HOLY FIRE . . . .   408 SAIL BYZANTIUM   17
     COME FROM THE HOLY FIRE, PERNE IN A GYRE. . . . .   408 SAIL BYZANTIUM   19
     ABOVE A SINKING FIRE, A TALE THAT SHE . . . .   443 SCHOOL CHILDR   10
     ABOVE A SINKING FIRE, SOME TALE THAT SHE . . . .   443 SCHOOL CHILDR V   10
     I'D TEAR IT OFF AND THROW IT IN THE FIRE." . . . .   462 HARUN RASHID   34
     EVERYTHING THAT IS NOT GOD CONSUMED WITH INTELLECTUAL FIRE.   481 BLOOD AND MOON   30
     "GOD'S FIRE UPON THE WANE, ...   485 STATISTICS   2
     STRUCK DUMB IN THE SIMPLICITY OF FIRE! . . . .   502 VACILLATION   75
     LOOK ON THAT FIRE, SALVATION WALKS WITHIN. . . . . . .   502 VACILLATION   76
     SOME ROGUE OF THE WORLD STOLE THEM TO PATCH UP A FENCE   623 HIGH TALK   4
        OR A FIRE.
     OF SAD QUEEN DIDO SHONE THE LAPPING FIRE . . . . . .   645 ISLE STAT I 1   9
     WITH ROLLING FIRE, BEYOND THE HIGH TREES TURBANED . . .   656 ISLE STAT I 3   32
     IS WORN AS THOUGH WITH FIRE. OH, GOBLIN QUEEN, ...   667 ISLE STAT II 3   36
     MADE THEM OF FIRE AND CLAY. . . . .   680 LOVE AND DEATH   12
     THAT FROM THE FIRE IS EVER POURING UP . . . .   683 SEEKER   37
     WEARY OF WATCHING ROUND THE FIRE AT NIGHT. . . . . .   683 SEEKER   42
     TO PLACE A KISS OF FIRE ON THE DIM BROW . . . .   688 TWO TITANS   47
     NOR TREMBLE TO ITS FALL. THE FIRE SWEEPS ROUND . . . .   689 NETTLESHIP   11
     TIME GOES. THE FLAKED FIRE OF EVENING CRAWLS . . . . .   712 FERENCZ RENYI   73
     TIME GOES. THE FLICKED FIRE OF EVENING CRAWLS . . . .   712 FERENCZ RENYI V   70
     OF FIRE. SO ENDS A BRAIN--A WORLD! THE SMOKE FLOATS UP,   714 FERENCZ RENYI V   111
     CAME THE OLIVE FIRE OF MORNING, AND ON THE DARKNESS FED,   719 PHANTOM SHIP V   33
     FEED A FIRE WITH STEMS OF GRASS! . . . .   727 LOVERS QUARREL   42
     LONG BEFORE THE MORNING FIRE . . . .   727 LOVERS QUARREL   45
     AND TEARS OF FIRE FALL GENTLY IN THE DEW. . . . . . .   738 YOU ARE SAD   4
     AND BODILY TENDERNESS TO THE SOFT FIRE . . . .   750 SHADOW WATER A   60
     IMPERISHABLE FIRE UNDER THE BOUGHS . . . .   765 SHADOW WATER A   356
     THAT CAN CHANGE LOVE TO IMPERISHABLE FIRE? . . . . . .   765 SHADOW WATER A   360
     LET THE FIRE BEAR WITNESS. . . . .   770 BLOOD BOND   10
     MAY THIS FIRE HAVE DRIVEN OUT . . . .   775 AGAINST WITCH   1
FIRE-BORN
     OF THE FIRE-BORN MOODS . . . .   142 MOODS   6
FIRED
     THAT SHE MAY QUENCH THE RICK SHE HAS FIRED! AND THOUGH . .   282 TWO KINGS   116
FIRELIGHT
     SHE MOVES IN THE FIRELIGHT . . . .   89 ISLE IN WATER   3
     IN THE FIRELIGHT . . . .   737 IN FIRELIGHT   T
FIRELIT
     "O, WHAT TO ME THE FIRELIT ROOM, ...   151 HEART OF WOMAN V   1
FIREPLACE
     A GREY STONE FIREPLACE WITH AN OPEN HEARTH, ...   419 MY HOUSE   V   12
FIRE-PLACE
     A GREY STONE FIRE-PLACE WITH AN OPEN HEARTH, ...   419 MY HOUSE   12
FIRE'S
     AND BLOWS ON HIS HANDS IN THE FIRE'S WARM BLAZE! . . . .   26 OISIN 1   V 404
FIRES   SEE STAR-FIRES
     THEY SEEMED TO SING IN THE SMOULDERING FIRES. . . . . .   13 OISIN 1   168
     OF THE GREAT ROUND SUN, FROM HIS CENTRAL FIRES. . . . .   13 OISIN 1   V 168
     . . . AND THE GODLESS FIRES OF THINE AGE. . . . . . .   63 OISIN 3   V 216
     BURNING IN FIRES OF A SLANDEROUS TONGUE. . . . . . .   148 INTO TWILIGHT   8
     MY DREAMS WERE CLOVEN BY VOICES AND BY FIRES! . . . .   218 WOODS OF COOLE   20
     MOVED ROUND ME IN THE VOICES AND THE FIRES, ...   218 WOODS OF COOLE   23
     AWAKE UNSLEEPING FIRES! AND WOVE SEVEN STRINGS, ...   219 HARP OF AENGUS   7
     THE FLAGSTONE UNDER ALL, THE FIRE OF FIRES, ...   227 SHADOW WATER B   103
     BECAUSE THE FIRES OF PURGATORY HAVE ATE THEIR SHAPES AWAY!   593 PILGRIM   13
     OENONE SAW THE FIRES OF TROIA LEAP, ...   645 ISLE STAT I 1   17
     CAME OLIVE FIRES OF MORNING AND ON THE DARKNESS FED, . .   719 PHANTOM SHIP   33
     AWAKE UNSLEEPING FIRES! AND WOVE SEVEN STRINGS, ...   762 SHADOW WATER A   302
FIRM
     NOR SHOOK MY FIRM AND SPACIOUS SOUL ONE JOT! . . . . .   36 OISIN 2   V   94
FIRST
     AND THE BLUSHES OF FIRST LOVE NEVER HAVE FLOWN! . . . .   8 OISIN 1   85
     AND THE FLUSHES OF FIRST LOVE NEVER HAVE FLOWN! . . . .   8 OISIN 1   V   85
     OR LOVE'S FIRST TENDERNESS DIE IN OUR GAZE. . . . . .   27 OISIN 1   411
     OR LOVE'S FIRST TENDERNESS DIE IN OUR GAZE. . . . . .   27 OISIN 1   V 419D
     OR LOVE'S FIRST TENDERNESS DIE IN OUR GAZE." . . . . .   28 OISIN 1   V 427
     THINGS DONE ERE GOD FIRST WAS OR MY OLD LINE BEGAN! . .   29 OISIN 2   V   8
     A DEMON'S LEISURE! EYES, FIRST WHITE, NOW BURNED . . .   40 OISIN 2   168
     A DEMON'S LEISURE. EYES FIRST WHITE AS SNOW, ...   40 OISIN 2   V 168
     SING YOU OF HER, O FIRST FEW STARS, ...   73 ANASHU VIJAYA   41
     SING YE OF HER, OH FIRST FEW STARS, ...   73 ANASHU VIJAYA V   41

FIRST   (CONTINUED)
```
    IS OUR FIRST KISS, AND AH, HOW OLD MY HEART!"  . . . . .    80 EPHEMERA            9
    FIRST AS A RAVEN ON WHOSE ANCIENT WINGS . . . . . .        102 FERGUS DRUID        3
    SHE WAS MORE BEAUTIFUL THAN THY FIRST LOVE, . . . . .      123 DREAM OF DEATH     11
    FOR IN THE WORLD'S FIRST BLOSSOMING AGE . . . . . .        138 TO IRELAND     V   10
    BUT CALL ME FIRST THROUGH THE GATE! . . . . . . .         178 FIDDLER DOONEY     12
    WITH THE FIRST KINGS OF MANY-PILLARED CRUACHAN. . . . .    187 QUEEN MAEVE       151
    WITH THE FIRST KINGS OF MANY PILLARED CRUACHAN . . . .     187 QUEEN MAEVE    V  151
    TO HIM THAT STRIKES HIM FIRST!  I WILL STRIKE HIM FIRST.   239 SHADOW WATER B    369
    TO HIM THAT STRIKES HIM FIRST!  I WILL STRIKE HIM FIRST.   239 SHADOW WATER B    369
    WHEN I FIRST HEARD THE NEWS? AH, THERE IT IS! . . . .     241 SHADOW WATER B    398
    WHO IS FIRST ASLEEP, IF BUT HE CAN  . . . . . . .         295 THREE BEGGARS      23
    FIRST WAS MUTTERING A PRAYER, . . . . . . . . .           298 THREE HERMITS       3
    SO THE FIRST, BUT NOW THE SECOND! . . . . . . . .         298 THREE HERMITS      13
    "I HAD NO BETTER PLAN AT FIRST. . . . . . . . .           305 HOUR DAWN          63
    AND SO IT WILL BE.  AT THE FIRST . . . . . .              305 HOUR DAWN      V   59
    YOU WILL SLEEP THAT LENGTH; AND AT THE FIRST . . . .      305 HOUR DAWN      V   59
    SINCE I FIRST MADE MY COUNT! . . . . . . . . .            322 SWANS AT COOLE      8
    THE FIRST TIME ON THIS SHORE, . . . . . . . .             323 SWANS AT COOLE     16
    LIONEL JOHNSON COMES THE FIRST TO MIND, . . . . .         324 ROBERT GREGORY     17
    THAT CRY'S FROM THE FIRST CUCKOO OF THE YEAR. . . . .     338 SHEP GOATHERD       1
    THAT CRY'S FROM THE FIRST CUCKOO OF THE . . . . .         338 SHEP GOATHERD  V    1
    AS OTHERS WILL, WHEN FIRST THEY TAKE POSSESSION, . . .    341 SHEP GOATHERD      52
    I HEARD HIM FIRST, BUT MAN IS A FOOL." . . . . .          341 SHEP GOATHERD  V   74
    MY DAILY THOUGHTS SINCE THE FIRST STUPOR OF YOUTH         342 SHEP GOATHERD      83
    IN THE FIRST LOVELINESS OF WOMANHOOD, . . . . .           356 BROKEN DREAMS      24
    AMID THAT FIRST ASTONISHMENT, WITH GRANIA'S SHADE, . .    366 HER COURAGE         4
    FROM THE FIRST CRESCENT TO THE HALF, THE DREAM . . .      373 PHASES OF MOON     36
    THE FIRST THIN CRESCENT IS WHEELED ROUND ONCE MORE. . .   377 PHASES OF MOON    116
    WHEN FIRST IT SPRANG OUT OF THE NEST . . . . .            397 POLIT PRISONER     20
    UNDER THE FIRST COLD GLEAM OF DAY? . . . . . .            398 BREAK OF DAY        4
    IF YOU, THAT HAVE GROWN OLD, WERE THE FIRST DEAD, . .     435 NEW FACES           1
    FIRST LOVE . . . . . . . . . . . . . . .                 451 FIRST LOVE          T
    A MAN YOUNG AND OLD  FIRST LOVE . . . . . . .             451 FIRST LOVE     V    T
    THE FIRST OF ALL THE TRIBE LAY THERE . . . . .            455 HIS MEMORIES       13
    SINCE FIRST WE SAW THE LIGHT, . . . . . . . .             456 SUMMER SPRING       4
    AND OFTEN THOSE FIRST DAYS I SAW HER STARE . . . .        466 HARUN RASHID      122
    BUT WOKE AT THE FIRST GLEAM OF DAY, ROSE UP  . . . .      467 HARUN RASHID      147
    HALF RUNNING, DROPPED AT THE FIRST RIDGE OF THE DESERT .  468 HARUN RASHID      155
    THAT FIRST UNNATURAL INTEREST IN MY BOOKS. . . . .        468 HARUN RASHID      165
    THAT FIRST STRANGE INTEREST IN MY BOOKS AND STUDIES. . .  468 HARUN RASHID   V  165
    ITS FIRST SIMPLICITY, LOVE, VOICE AND ALL, . . . .        469 HARUN RASHID      177
    ITS FIRST SIMPLICITY, LOVE AND ALL, . . . . . .           469 HARUN RASHID   V  177
    HORTON'S THE FIRST I CALL.  HE LOVED STRANGE THOUGHT      471 ALL SOUL NIGHT     21
    WHO FINDING THE FIRST WRINKLES ON A FACE . . . .          472 ALL SOUL NIGHT     42
    FOR IN MY FIRST HARD SPRINGTIME WE WERE FRIENDS, . .      473 ALL SOUL NIGHT     62
    FOR IN MY FIRST HARD SPRING-TIME WE WERE FRIENDS, . .     473 ALL SOUL NIGHT V   62
    FIRST TROD ON THE MOUNTAIN'S HEAD . . . . . .             488 CRAZED MOON         9
    COULD KEEP A SWALLOW TO ITS FIRST INTENT! . . . .         489 COOLE PARK 29      19
    THAT FIRST DAWN IN HELEN'S ARMS? . . . . . .              522 LULLABY             6
    THAT FIRST NIGHT IN HELEN'S ARMS. . . . . . .             522 LULLABY        V    6
    A FIRST CONFESSION . . . . . . . . . . .                 532 FIRST CONFESS       T
    FIRST SONG . . . . . . . . . . . . . .                   545 TO SAME TUNE 2 V    T
    THE ANNIVERSARY OF THEIR FIRST EMBRACE, . . . .           555 RIBH AT TOMB       20
    A YEAR AGO FOR THE FIRST TIME . . . . . . .              570 THREE BUSHES       38
    THE LADY'S FIRST SONG . . . . . . . . . .                572 LADYS 1ST SONG      T
    THE CHAMBERMAID'S FIRST SONG . . . . . . .               574 MAIDS 1ST SONG      T
    WHO WAS THE FIRST MAN SHOT THAT DAY? . . . .             608 SONGS BURDEN 3     10
    HE BADE, HIS HUNDRED AND FIRST YEAR AT END, . . .        609 IN TARAS HALLS     16
    THE FIRST ADAM IN THEIR THOUGHT, . . . . . .             617 LONG-LEG FLY       22
    FIRST THAT SEA-RIDER OISIN LED BY THE NOSE . . . .       629 CIRCUS ANIMALS     10
    BUT FIRST YOU MUST BE TOLD OUR CHARACTER! . . . .        634 CUCHULAIN COMF     20
    I FAIN HAD BEEN THE FIRST OF SINGING THINGS . . .        648 ISLE STAT I 1     101
    SCHOOLMASTER HE, A DREAMER, FIDDLER, FIRST . . . .       709 FERENCZ RENYI      11
    I CAME THE FIRST TIME TO THY VILLAGE SCHOOL? . . .       713 FERENCZ RENYI      90
    THUS PLAY WE FIRST WITH PAWNS, POOR THINGS AND WEAK! .   722 WITCH VIVIEN       53
    FIRST DREAMS, AND GOBLINS, AND THE LESSER SPRITES, . .   722 WITCH VIVIEN       56
    FROM ITS FIRST SIGHS AND LAUGHTER, BEFORE THE SLEEP, .   754 SHADOW WATER A    161
    WHEN SHE DREAMT FIRST OF LOVE, SHALL FLICKER OUT . . .   760 SHADOW WATER A    257
    WHEN SHE DREAMED FIRST OF LOVE, SHALL FLICKER OUT . .    760 SHADOW WATER A V  257
    WHAT FINGER FIRST BEGAN . . . . . . . . . .              783 GREY ROUND         11
    FIRST I GREET MACCARTAN, REVOLUTIONARY LEADER. . . .     790 DEDICATION          1
FIRST-BORN
    AND TROUBLED EYES CAME MORNING'S FIRST-BORN GLOW! . . .  648 ISLE STAT I 1     103
FIR-TREE
    A FIR-TREE ROARING IN ITS LEAFLESS TOP! . . . . .         40 OISIN 2           177
    UPON A SWORD, A FIR-TREE ON A HILL, . . . . . .          104 FERGUS DRUID       34
FIRWOOD
    A FIRWOOD HOUSE, ALL COVERED OVER . . . . . . .           17 OISIN 1        V  248
FISH      SEE GOLD-FISH
    IN A LONG IRON SLEEP, AS A FISH IN THE WATER GOES DUMB    53 OISIN 3            96
      AS A STONE.
    THAT CARRIED THE FISH FOR THE SALE IN THE FAR-AWAY TOWN,  91 OLD FISHERMAN V     7
    BUT WHEN A MAN POURED FISH INTO A PILE, . . . . .        126 DREAM OF FAERY      5
    THE FISH . . . . . . . . . . . . . . .                   146 FISH                T
    WHAT SHALL I CALL THEM? FISH THAT SWIM, . . . .          195 BAILE AILLINN     144
    WITH A FISH TAIL, AND TALK . . . . . . . .               215 HAPPY TOWNLAND V   46
    O SILVER FISH THAT MY TWO HANDS HAVE TAKEN . . . .       251 SHADOW WATER B    609
    AND FISH AND CROWD AND PAINTED SHIP, . . . . .           254 HIS DREAM      V   15
    AND FISH AND CROWD AND GAUDY SHIP . . . . .              254 HIS DREAM      V   15
    COLDER AND DUMBER AND DEAFER THAN A FISH. . . . .        267 ALL TEMPT ME       10
```

		PAGE	TITLE	LINE

FISH   (CONTINUED)
TO THROW ME A BIT OF SALTED FISH! . . . .   301 RUN PARADISE   6
FISH, FLESH, OR FOWL, COMMEND ALL SUMMER LONG . . . . . .   407 SAIL BYZANTIUM   V
THOUGH MARGERY IS LIKE A FISH . . . .   457 SECRETS OF OLD V   7
SHAKESPEAREAN FISH SWAM THE SEA, FAR AWAY FROM LAND! . . .   485 THREE MOVEMENT   1
ROMANTIC FISH SWAM IN NETS COMING TO THE HAND! . . . .   485 THREE MOVEMENT   2
WHAT ARE ALL THOSE FISH THAT LIE GASPING ON THE STRAND?   485 THREE MOVEMENT   3
BIRD, BEAST, FISH OR MAN, ...   529 TOM LUNATIC   14
O SILVER FISH THAT MY TWO HANDS HAVE TAKEN . . . . . .   769 SHADOW WATER A   425
FISH-EATING
OF BITTERNS, AND FISH-EATING STOATS, ...   14 OISIN 1   191
OF BITTERNS AND FISH-EATING STOATS. . . . .   23 OISIN 1   355
FISHER
HE IS A FAMOUS FISHER! HOUR BY HOUR . . . .   73 ANASHU VIJAYA   36
MY MAN WAS A POOR FISHER . . . .   94 MOLL MAGEE   5
MY HUSBAND WAS A FISHER POOR . . . .   94 MOLL MAGEE   V 5
A DANCE FOR THE FISHER LADS! . . . .   589 OLD WICKED MAN V 33
AND THE FISHER MEN AND WOMEN FROM THE DRIPPING HARBOUR WALL   718 PHANTOM SHIP   11
FISHER-LADS
A DANCE FOR THE FISHER-LADS! . . . .   589 OLD WICKED MAN   33
FISHERMAN
THE MEDITATION OF THE OLD FISHERMAN . . . .   90 OLD FISHERMAN   T
BRESSEL THE FISHERMAN . . . .   146 FISH   V   T
THE FISHERMAN . . . .   146 FISH   V   T
THE FISHERMAN . . . .   347 FISHERMAN   T
FISHERMEN
BAWDY TALK FOR THE FISHERMEN! . . . .   588 OLD WICKED MAN   32
FISHER'S   SEE FLY-FISHER'S
THAT HAD A SOUND FLY FISHER'S WRIST . . . .   625 OLD MEN BE MAD V   3
FISHERS
"WAKEN, WAKEN, SLEEPY FISHERS! NO HOUR IS THIS FOR SLEEP,"   718 PHANTOM SHIP   7
NOW A SCREAM FROM ALL THOSE FISHERS, FOR THERE ON DECK   719 PHANTOM SHIP   19
    THERE BE
HUSH'D THE FISHERS, TILL A MOTHER CALLS BY NAME HER DROWNED   719 PHANTOM SHIP   23
    SON!
PRAYED THOSE FORGOTTEN FISHERS, TILL IN THE EASTERN SKIES   719 PHANTOM SHIP   32
ALL THOSE LONG FORGOTTEN FISHERS, TILL IN THE EASTERN SKIES   719 PHANTOM SHIP   V 32
FISHERS'
AY, AND SHAKES IN SEA-GREEN WAVERINGS ALONG THE FISHERS'   718 PHANTOM SHIP   2
    STREET!
AYE AND SHAKES IN SEA GREEN WAVERINGS, ALONG THE FISHERS'   718 PHANTOM SHIP   V 2
    STREET.
FISHES
AND FISHES, BUBBLING TO THE BRIM, ...   254 HIS DREAM   V   9
FISHES'
NOW BATHING LILY LEAF AND FISHES' SCALE, ...   464 HARUN RASHID   V 65
FISHING   SEE A-FISHING
FISHING-LINES
LOOK TO LONG FISHING-LINES, OR POINT AND PARE . . . .   32 OISIN 2   55
FISHLIKE
FLASH FISHLIKE! NYMPHS AND SATYRS . . . .   612 NEWS ORACLE   35
FISH'S
NOW BATHING LILY LEAF AND FISH'S SCALE, ...   464 HARUN RASHID   65
FISH-TAIL
WITH A FISH-TAIL, AND TALK . . . .   215 HAPPY TOWNLAND   46
FIST
SHE SMOTE WITH RADDLED FIST, AND WHERE HER SON . . . .   106 CUCHULAIN SEA   18
BID THE GHOST HAVE SWORD IN FIST! . . . .   435 FOR MY SON   9
YET HE, AN OLD BOOK IN HIS FIST, ...   508 JANE BISHOP   12
FIT
AND WHILE WE'RE IN OUR LAUGHING, WEEPING FIT, ...   257 RECONCILIATION   9
OR BEEN FIT SPOIL FOR A CENTAUR . . . .   355 PROPERTIUS   7
AND THERE IS NONE SO FIT TO KEEP A WATCH AND KEEP . . .   442 BLACK CENTAUR   15
AND THINKING OF THAT FIT OF GRIEF OR RAGE . . . . . .   443 SCHOOL CHILDR   17
I GET A LAUGHING FIT, ...   455 FRIENDS YOUTH   4
FIT AUDIENCE FOUND, BUT CANNOT RULE . . . .   506 REMORSE SPEECH   4
FITFUL
WHO WHEN THEY DANCE TO A FITFUL MEASURE . . . .   9 OISIN 1   97
MURMURING, TO A FITFUL TUNE, ...   85 MAD KING GOLL   52
WHILE I WROUGHT OUT THESE FITFUL DANAAN RHYMES, ...   136 TO SOME I TALK   1
I DEDICATE THESE FITFUL DANAAN RHYMES . . . .   136 TO SOME I TALK V   1
FITS
YOUR WEEPING FITS! LOOK YOU, SO VERY STRAIT . . . . .   659 ISLE STAT II 1   22
FITTER
A FITTER WELCOME! BUT A THOUGHT . . . .   328 ROBERT GREGORY   95
FITTING
I ASK A FITTING PUNISHMENT FOR ALL . . . .   235 SHADOW WATER B   290
SO GREAT ITS FAME. WHEN FITTING TIME HAS PASSED . . . .   461 HARUN RASHID   19
CAN WITH A FITTING CONFIDENCE REPLY. . . . .   494 AT ALGECIRAS   18
FITZGERALD
FOR THIS EDWARD FITZGERALD DIED, ...   290 SEPTEMBER 1913   20
WHEN STRANGERS MURDERED EMMET, FITZGERALD, TONE, ...   541 PARN FUNERAL 1   17
FIVE
THAT SPRING FIVE PACES IN THEIR BOUNDS, ...   8 OISIN 1   V 86A
. . . I FLUNG IT FIVE YARDS WITH MY HAND, ...   60 OISIN 3   187
ONE--AND ONE--A COUPLE--FIVE TOGETHER! . . . .   233 SHADOW WATER B   249
FIVE AND TWENTY YEARS HAVE GONE . . . .   360 ALF POLLEXFEN V   1
IT LAY FIVE HUNDRED YEARS. . . . .   421 MY TABLE   11
FIVE HUNDRED YEARS AGO, ABOUT IT LIE . . . .   478 SELF AND SOUL   26
RECOGNIZE THE FIVE . . . .   601 THOSE IMAGES   15

283

		PAGE	TITLE	LINE

FIVE-AND-TWENTY
FIVE-AND-TWENTY YEARS HAVE GONE . . . . 360 ALF POLLEXFEN 1
FIVE-SIX
FIVE-SIX. HA, TIME! . . . . 721 WITCH VIVIEN 42
FIX
WHEN THE SWAN MUST FIX HIS EYE . . . . 414 TOWER 140
FIX EVERY WANDERING THOUGHT UPON . . . . 477 SELF AND SOUL 6
COME, FIX UPON ME THAT ACCUSING EYE. . . . . 542 PARN FUNERAL 1 24
MY ATTENTION FIX . . . . 631 POLITICS 2
FIXED
AND THE FIXED STARS HAD DAWNED AND SHONE AND SET, . . . 31 OISIN 2 40
THROUGH THAT STRANGE ILLNESS THAT HAD FIXED HIM THERE, . . 280 TWO KINGS 81
CROW UPON TARA." SHE HAD FIXED HER EYES . . . . . . 286 TWO KINGS V 211
AND ALL THEIR EYES STILL FIXED, HOPING TO FIND ONCE MORE, 318 MAGI 6
FIXED UPON IMAGES THAT ONCE WERE THOUGHT: . . . . . 375 PHASES OF MOON 80
BEING FIXED ON ALL THINGS LOVED, ALL THINGS UNLOVED, . . 383 VISION ROBART 34
THEY FIXED OLD ACHING EYES, ... 432 NINETEEN 19 100
THAT ARE FIXED UPON ME? . . . . 533 FIRST CONFESS 16
HALF TURNED AND FIXED A GLAZING EYE ON MINE, ... 537 HER VISION 26
HE FIXED A BITTER LOOK: . . . . 585 ORAHILLY 24
HIS EYES FIXED UPON NOTHING, ... 617 LONG-LEG FLY 7
WAS EBREMAR, WHOSE THOUGHTS WERE FIXED ON GOD, . . . 702 MOSADA 3 83
OF HER HE LOVED FIXED ON HIM FULL OF LIGHT, ... 710 FERENCZ RENYI 27
FLAG
UNDER A MARBLE FLAG? . . . . 525 DANCING DAYS 14
AND THIS HARD FLAG OF STONE, ... 739 EARL PAUL 6
A GALLEY FROM THE LOCHLANN SEAS: HER FLAG . . . . . 751 SHADOW WATER A 98
FLAGELLANT
THE FLAGELLANT LASHES THOSE SUBMISSIVE LOINS . . . . . 560 WHENCE COME 7
FLAGON
I SAW A FLAGON OF BROWN ALE ABOARD HER. . . . . . . 240 SHADOW WATER B 388
FLAGONS
UNLESS WE DRAIN MORE FLAGONS IN A YEAR . . . . . . 225 SHADOW WATER B 70
FLAGRANT
AND WHEN THE SUN IN ALL HIS FLAGRANT SAFFRON STEPT, . . 41 OISIN 2 V 192
ROLLING HIS FLAGRANT WHEEL OUT OF THE DEEP, ... 42 OISIN 2 193
THE FLAGRANT SIGNAL OF HER LORD'S RETURN, ... 645 ISLE STAT I 1 13
FLAGS
AND THRUST THE TORCH BETWEEN THE SLIMY FLAGS. . . . . 38 OISIN 2 143
ANOINTING, TORCH JAMMED DOWN BETWEEN THE FLAGS, . . . 38 OISIN 2 V 143
TREMBLING, ON THE FLAGS WE FALL, ... 43 OISIN 2 V 208E
BUT TO BE AMID SHOOTING OF FLIES AND FLOWERING OF RUSHES 55 OISIN 3 120
AND FLAGS."
. . . AND THE FLOWERING OF RUSHES AND FLAGS." . . . . 55 OISIN 3 V 120
BUT KNEEL AND WEAR OUT THE FLAGS AND PRAY FOR YOUR SOUL 63 OISIN 3 215
THAT IS LOST
BUT WEEP THOU, AND WEAR THOU THE FLAGS WITH THY KNEES, 63 OISIN 3 V 215
. . .
BUT WEEP YOU, AND WEAR YOU THE FLAGS WITH YOUR KNEES, . . 63 OISIN 3 V 215
BUT WEEP YOU AND KNEEL: WEAR OUT THE FLAGS! . . . . 63 OISIN 3 V 215
KNEEL, USHEEN, WEAR OUT THE FLAGS AND PRAY FOR YOUR SOUL 63 OISIN 3 V 215
THAT IS LOST
THOUGH DRUNKEN WITH THE FLAGS THAT SWAY . . . . . . 212 BLESS PSALTER 5
I CANNOT EVEN CRAWL ALONG THE FLAGS . . . . 701 MOSADA 3 58
FLAGSTONE
THE FLAGSTONE UNDER ALL, THE FIRE OF FIRES, ... 227 SHADOW WATER B 103
FLAKE
AND SAW A FLAKE OF THE YELLOW FOAM . . . . 309 PLAYER QUEEN 15
I SAW A FLAKE OF YELLOW FOAM . . . . 309 PLAYER QUEEN V 15
FLAKED
OR OF THE FLAKED CLOUDS?" "NOT SO, FOR WE . . . . . 34 OISIN 2 V 78C
TIME GOES. THE FLAKED FIRE OF EVENING CRAWLS . . . . 712 FERENCZ RENYI 70
FLAKES   SEE FOAM-FLAKES SNOW-FLAKES SALT-FLAKES
THE SALT FLAKES ON HIS BREAST, ... 612 NEWS ORACLE V 10
IN BUSY FLAKES: RE-SHINING FROM THE LAKE, ... 662 ISLE STAT II 2 3
FLAME   SEE STAR-FLAME A-FLAME
IT SEEMED TO BLOW FROM THE DYING FLAME, ... 13 OISIN 1 167
IT SEEMED TO FALL FROM THE VERY FLAME . . . . . . 13 OISIN 1 V 167
"MEN'S HEARTS OF OLD WERE DROPS OF FLAME . . . . . . 19 OISIN 1 276
A MOMENTARY GLEAM OF PHOSPHORUS FLAME. . . . . . . 37 OISIN 2 118
A MOMENTARY GLIMMER OF VAGUE PHOSPHORUS FLAME. . . . 37 OISIN 2 V 120
SOFTER THAN SNOW-FLAKES IN APRIL AND PIERCING THE MARROW 51 OISIN 3 68
LIKE FLAME.
SOFTER THAN SNOWFLAKES IN APRIL, AND PIERCING THE MARROW 51 OISIN 3 V 68
LIKE FLAME.
SHALL WARM THEIR LIVES AT MANY A RUSTLING FLAME." . . . 80 EPHEMERA V 12B
WE TIRE OF THE FLAME OF THE METEOR, BEFORE IT CAN FADE 122 WHITE BIRDS 2
AND FLEE:
AND THE FLAME OF THE BLUE STAR OF TWILIGHT, ... 122 WHITE BIRDS 3
AH, DREAM NOT OF THEM, MY BELOVED, THE FLAME OF THE METEOR 122 WHITE BIRDS 6
THAT GOES,
OR THE FLAME OF THE BLUE STAR THAT LINGERS . . . . . 122 WHITE BIRDS 7
FOR WE TIRE OF THE FLAME OF THE METEOR BEFORE IT CAN PASS 122 WHITE BIRDS V 2
BY AND FLEE
WE TIRE OF THE FLAME OF THE METEOR, BEFORE IT CAN PASS 122 WHITE BIRDS V 2
BY AND FLEE:
FLAME TO FLAME AND WING TO WING. . . . . 125 CATHLEEN PARA 16
FLAME TO FLAME AND WING TO WING. . . . . 125 CATHLEEN PARA 16
FLAME ON FLAME AND WING ON WING. . . . . 125 CATHLEEN PARA V 16
FLAME ON FLAME AND WING ON WING. . . . . 125 CATHLEEN PARA V 16
WHO RISE, WING ABOVE WING, FLAME ABOVE FLAME, ... 137 TO SOME I TALK 11

		PAGE	TITLE	LINE

FLAME   (CONTINUED)
```
    WHO RISE, WING ABOVE WING, FLAME ABOVE FLAME, . . . . .     137 TO SOME I TALK      11
    FLAME UNDER FLAME, TILL TIME BE NO MORE!   . . . . .        141 EVERLAST VOICE       4
    FLAME UNDER FLAME, TILL TIME BE NO MORE!   . . . . .        141 EVERLAST VOICE       4
    OF THE FLOOD AND FLAME, OF THE HEIGHT AND WOOD, . . . .     148 INTO TWILIGHT  V    11
    BUT FLAME ON FLAME, AND DEEP ON DEEP, . . . . . . .         156 FORGOT BEAUTY       21
    BUT FLAME ON FLAME, AND DEEP ON DEEP, . . . . . . .         156 FORGOT BEAUTY       21
    BUT FLAME ON FLAME, DEEP UNDER DEEP, . . . . . . .          156 FORGOT BEAUTY  V    21
    BUT FLAME ON FLAME, DEEP UNDER DEEP, . . . . . . .          156 FORGOT BEAUTY  V    21
    HIM WHO TREMBLES BEFORE THE FLAME AND THE FLOOD, . . . .    158 TO HIS HEART         3
    LET THE STARRY WINDS AND THE FLAME AND THE FLOOD . . . .    158 TO HIS HEART         5
    WHO TREMBLES BEFORE THE FLAME AND THE FLOOD, . . . .       158 TO HIS HEART   V     3
    "O HEARTS OF WIND-BLOWN FLAME! . . . . . . . . .           162 ASKS FORGIVE         6
    BUT WE HAVE HIDDEN IN OUR HEARTS THE FLAME OUT OF THE EYES  207 HANRAHANS SONG       4
    BUT OUR HEARTS ARE LIGHTED FROM THE FLAME IN THE EYES . .   207 HANRAHANS SONG V     9
    THOUGH FLAME HAD BURNED THE WHOLE . . . . . . . .          267 FRIEND ILLNESS       4
    NOR STORM DISTURBS, FLAMES BEGOTTEN OF FLAME, . . . . .     498 BYZANTIUM           27
    AN AGONY OF FLAME THAT CANNOT SINGE A SLEEVE. . . . . .     498 BYZANTIUM           32
    IS HALF ALL GLITTERING FLAME AND HALF ALL GREEN . . . .     500 VACILLATION         12
    IS HALF ALL GLITTERING FLAME AND HALF A GREEN . . . .       500 VACILLATION    V    12
    WHEN LOW THE SUN SANK DOWN IN CLOTTED FLAME . . . . .       656 ISLE STAT I 3       30
    FROM THE WOOD'S WAYS, THEN, LIKE A SILVER FLAME, . . . .    658 ISLE STAT II 1       6
    THE WHITE WAVES WRAP IT IN A SHEET OF FLAME, . . . .        662 ISLE STAT II 2      14
    AND IN THE SIBYL'S EYES A LANGUID FLAME . . . . . . .       688 TWO TITANS          41
    HER SOUL FROM SEAS OF ENDLESS FLAME IN HELL. . . . . .      698 MOSADA 2            47
    THE FLAME THAT SHONE WITHIN HIS EYES BUT NOW . . . . .      704 MOSADA 2           128
    MAY THIS FLAME HAVE DRIVEN OUT . . . . . . . . .           775 AGAINST WITCH  V     1
FLAME-BEWILDERED
    DAY'S DEAD, ALL FLAME-BEWILDERED, AND THE HILLS . . . .     702 MOSADA 3            86
FLAMED
    AND THRICE THE CORN AROUND THE SICKLES FLAMED, . . . .      690 MOSADA 1             3
FLAME-LIKE
    ALL FLAME-LIKE GUSHING FROM THE HOLLOW STONES, . . . .      650 ISLE STAT I 1      129
FLAMES   SEE GHOST-FLAMES
    WILD FLAMES OF RED AND GOLD AND BLUE, . . . . . . .          18 OISIN 1            252
    WILD FLAMES OF RED AND CREAMY WHITES, . . . . . . .          18 OISIN 1       V    255
    AND THEN AWAY, AWAY, LIKE WHIRLING FLAMES! . . . . . .       29 OISIN 2              2
    AND THEN AWAY, AWAY, LIKE SPIRAL FLAMES! . . . . . .         29 OISIN 2       V      2
    AND DWELL IN THE HOUSE OF THE FENIANS, BE THEY IN FLAMES     63 OISIN 3            224
        OR AT FEAST,
    I WILL GO TO THE HOUSE OF THE FENIANS, BE THEY IN FLAMES     63 OISIN 3       V    223
        OR AT FEAST,
    . . . AND FRET OF THE FLAMES WOULD WE BE, . . . . .         122 WHITE BIRDS         11
    . . . AND FREE OF THE FLAMES WOULD WE BE, . . . . .         122 WHITE BIRDS   V     11
    ALL BUT THE FLAMES, AND DEEP ON DEEP, . . . . . . .         156 FORGOT BEAUTY  V    21
    AND WRAPPED THE FLAMES ABOVE HIS HOLY HEAD! . . . . .       162 ASKS FORGIVE        17
    AND GATHERED THE FLAMES ABOVE HIS HOLY HEAD, . . . .        162 ASKS FORGIVE  V     17
    WHATEVER FLAMES UPON THE NIGHT . . . . . . . . .           438 SONGS PLAY 2        15
    FLAMES THAT NO FAGGOT FEEDS, NOR STEEL HAS LIT, . . . .     498 BYZANTIUM           26
    NOR STORM DISTURBS, FLAMES BEGOTTEN OF FLAME, . . . .       498 BYZANTIUM           27
    AS I, TO CHOOSE BENEATH DAY'S DYING FLAMES! . . . . .       656 ISLE STAT I 3       34
    MY SOUL SHALL TOUCH WITH HIS, AND THE TWO FLAMES . . .      701 MOSADA 3            61
    FLAMES THE SHUTTLE OF THE LIGHTNING ACROSS THE DRIVING      718 PHANTOM SHIP         1
        SLEET,
    AND THE GHASTLY GHOST FLAMES GLIMMER ALONG THE TAFFREL      719 PHANTOM SHIP  V     21
        RAILS,
FLAMING
    "O FLAMING LION OF THE WORLD, O WHEN WILL YOU TURN TO YOUR   56 OISIN 3            129
        REST?"
    O FLAMING LION OF THE WORLD, O WHEN WILL YOU TURN TO YOUR    56 OISIN 3            136
        REST?"
    "OH, FLAMING LION OF THE WORLD, OH, WHEN WILT THOU TURN      56 OISIN 3       V    129
        TO THY REST?"
    WE WILL TEAR OUT THE FLAMING STONES, AND BATTER THE GATEWAY  62 OISIN 3            209
        OF BRASS
    ON THE FLAMING STONES, WITHOUT REFUGE, . . . . . . .        62 OISIN 3            213
    WE WILL TEAR OUT THE RED FLAMING STONES, . . . . . .        62 OISIN 3       V    209
    WE WILL TEAR THE RED FLAMING STONES OUT, . . . . . .        62 OISIN 3       V    209
    ON THE RED FLAMING STONES WITHOUT REFUGE . . . . . .        62 OISIN 3       V    213
    ONLY A SUDDEN FLAMING WORD, . . . . . . . . . .             65 HAPPY SHEPHERD      19
    AND IN THE FLAMING FORESTS COWER THE LION . . . . . .       73 ANASHU VIJAYA       52
    THEY SEE IN FLAMING FORESTS COWER THE LION . . . . . .      73 ANASHU VIJAYA  V    52
    BATHED IN FLAMING FOUNTS OF DUTY . . . . . . . . .         124 CATHLEEN PARA        5
    THE FLAMING CIRCLE OF OUR DAYS, . . . . . . . . .          135 TWO TREES           14
    THE FLAMING CIRCLE OF OUR LIFE. . . . . . . . . .          135 TWO TREES     V     16
    AND OF THE EMBATTLED FLAMING MULTITUDE . . . . . . .       137 TO SOME I TALK      10
    DESOLATE WINDS THAT HOVER IN THE FLAMING WEST! . . . .     147 UNAPPEAS HOST        8
    MASTER OF THE STILL STARS AND OF THE FLAMING DOOR. . . .   161 BLACK PIG            8
    WHO MET FAND WALKING AMONG FLAMING DEW . . . . . .         169 SECRET ROSE         13
    WHEN THE FLAMING LUTE-THRONGED ANGELIC DOOR IS WIDE! . .   172 TRAV PASSION         1
    UNFOLD YOUR FLAMING WINGS AND COVER OUT OF SIGHT . . . .   175 ELEMENT POWERS      11
    A BRAND, OR FLAMING BREATH. . . . . . . . . . .           500 VACILLATION          3
    AS FLAMING MINSTREL-WORD UPON HIS CREST. . . . . . .      679 ISLE STAT II 3     317
    THE FLAMING CIRCLE OF THE OUTER LAW, . . . . . . .         689 NETTLESHIP          13
    BENEATH THE FLAMING EYEBALLS OF THE NIGHT, . . . . .       723 KANVA ON SELF        4
FLAMINGO
    OF RED FLAMINGO! AND MY LOVE, VIJAYA, . . . . . .          75 ANASHU VIJAYA  V    89
FLAMINGOES
    SEE HOW THE SACRED OLD FLAMINGOES COME, . . . . . .        72 ANASHU VIJAYA       29
    OF RED FLAMINGOES! AND MY LOVE, VIJAYA! . . . . . .        75 ANASHU VIJAYA       89
```

		PAGE	TITLE		LINE
FLANK					
RENDING THE HORSE'S FLANK. KING EOCHAID REELED,	• • • •	277	TWO KINGS		13
FLANKS					
RIPPED THROUGH THE HORSE'S FLANKS. KING EOCHAID REELED,		277	TWO KINGS	V	13
BUT WHEN AT LAST HE FORCED THOSE SINEWY FLANKS	• • • •	278	TWO KINGS		35
ON A FANTASTIC RIDE, MY HORSE'S FLANKS ARE SPURRED	• • •	391	UNDER SATURN		6
ON A FANTASTIC RIDE I SWEAR MY HORSE'S FLANKS WERE SPURRED		391	UNDER SATURN	V	6
FLAP					
THE TALL THOUGHT-WOVEN SAILS, THAT FLAP UNFURLED	• • • •	113	ROSE OF BATTLE		2
FLAPPING					
WHERE FLAPPING HERONS WAKE	• • • • • • • • •	86	STOLEN CHILD		4
WITH FLOPPING AND WITH FLAPPING IT MADE A GREAT DISPLAY,		593	PILGRIM		18
WITH THEIR FLOPPING AND THEIR FLAPPING IT MADE A GREAT DISPLAY		593	PILGRIM	V	18
CEASE THE SAILS THEIR FLAPPING UPROAR, AND THE HULL NO LONGER ROLLS.		719	PHANTOM SHIP		18
CEASE THE SAILS, THEIR FLAPPING UPROAR TO THE HULL NO LONGER ROLLS.		719	PHANTOM SHIP	V	18
LOOK! THERE SHE LIES UNDER A FLAPPING SAIL.	• • • •	751	SHADOW WATER A		90
FLAPT					
AND LOUDLY TWICE THE LIVING WINGS FLAPT WIDE,	• • • • •	659	ISLE STAT II 1		12
HALF LIT, SO FLAPT THE WINGS ACROSS THE LAKE--	• • • •	659	ISLE STAT II 1		17
FLARE					
AND IN THE RING A TORCH, AND WITH ITS FLARE	• • • •	37	OISIN 2		121
WHO BROUGHT US FOUND A TORCH, AND, WITH ITS FLARE	• •	37	OISIN 2	V	122
AND TIME BADE ALL HIS CANDLES FLARE	• • • • •	138	TO IRELAND		13
AND STILL THE STARRY CANDLES FLARE	• • • • •	138	TO IRELAND	V	13
BECAUSE THE WORK HAD FINISHED IN THAT FLARE.	• • • •	327	ROBERT GREGORY		85
THE THREEFOLD TERROR OF LOVE: A FALLEN FLARE	• • • •	499	MOTHER OF GOD		1
THE THREE-FOLD TERROR OF LOVE: A FALLEN FLARE	• • • •	499	MOTHER OF GOD	V	1
LOVE STORM: AND STAINED WITH MIST THE NEW MOONS FLARE.	• •	678	ISLE STAT II 3		294
LOVE STORM AND STAINED WITH MIST THE NEW MOON'S FLARE	• •	678	ISLE STAT II 3	V	294
FLASH SEE A-FLASH					
AND LIGHTNING FLASH FOR EVER? CEASE AND HEAR.	• • • •	42	OISIN 2	V	207
OF THEIR LONG WINGS, THE FLASH OF THEIR WHITE FEET.	• • •	137	TO SOME I TALK		16
OF THEIR LONG WINGS, THE FLASH OF THEIR SWIFT FEET.	• • •	137	TO SOME I TALK	V	16
FLASH FISHLIKE: NYMPHS AND SATYRS	• • • • • • •	612	NEWS ORACLE		35
WHEN FLASH ON FLASH ONCE MORE THE LIGHTNING CAME,	• •	688	TWO TITANS		39
WHEN FLASH ON FLASH ONCE MORE THE LIGHTNING CAME,	• •	688	TWO TITANS		39
NOISE! AND A FLASH, A MOMENTARY BLOT.	• • • • • •	714	FERENCZ RENYI		110
FLASHED					
IN OUR RAISED EYES THERE FLASHED A GLOW	• • • • • • •	22	OISIN 1		327
THE IMAGED METEORS HAD FLASHED AND RUN	• • • • • •	31	OISIN 2		38
FORMS WITHOUT NUMBER! WHEN THE LIVE WEST FLASHED	• • •	41	OISIN 2	V	180
I PAUSED--THE STARS ABOVE ME FLASHED,	• • • • • • •	83	MAD KING GOLL	V	29
FLASHES					
FLASHES THE FIRE OF SADNESS, FOR THEY SEE	• • • • •	73	ANASHU VIJAYA		49
FLASHES AS IF IT WERE A NET OF HERRINGS.	• • • • • •	248	SHADOW WATER B		536
FLASHIER					
DRIVE TO A FLASHIER BAUBLE YET.	• • • • • • • • •	437	SONGS PLAY 1		12
FLASHING					
AND ONE A SCEPTRE FLASHING OUT	• • • • • • • • •	17	OISIN 1		251
HE HELD THAT FLASHING SCEPTRE UP.	• • • • • • • •	18	OISIN 1		260
FLASHING--I KNOW NOT WERE IT HOURS OR DAYS,	• • • •	30	OISIN 2	V	198
UPLIFTED GATEWAY. WITH THE FLASHING BEAT	• • • • •	31	OISIN 2	V	30D
THE RIVER IMAGING THE FLASHING SKIES,	• • • • • • •	390	IMAGE PAST		20
DREAMING OF FLASHING FLIGHT AND OF THE PLUMED WAVE.	• • •	650	ISLE STAT I 1		140
BEHOLD THE FLASHING WATERS.	• • • • • • • • • •	680	LOVE AND DEATH		1
(SWALLOWS WERE FLASHING THEIR WHITE BREASTS ABOVE	• •	690	MOSADA 1		7
FLASHING AND FLICKERING WITH EVER-UNDULANT WING	• • •	710	FERENCZ RENYI		19
FLASHING AND FLICKERING, WITH EVER UNDULANT WING,	• • •	710	FERENCZ RENYI	V	19
FLAT					
HELEN BEING CHOSEN FOUND LIFE FLAT AND DULL	• • • • •	404	FOR DAUGHTER		25
"THOSE BREASTS ARE FLAT AND FALLEN NOW,	• • • • • • •	513	JANE TALK BISH		3
UNTIL THE TOWN LIE BEATEN FLAT.	• • • • • • • • •	565	LAPIS LAZULI		8
FLATTER					
TO FLATTER BEAUTY'S IGNORANT EAR.	• • • • • • • • •	337	SCHOLARS		6
NAY, RISE AND FLATTER HER WITH GOLDEN RHYME,	• • • • •	724	KANVA ON SELF		19
FLATTERER					
LIAR AND FLATTERER OF THE WEAK, IN WHAT STRANGE CLIME	• •	42	OISIN 2	V	198
FLATTERIES					
WITH BARREN WORDS AND FLATTERIES OF THE WEAK.	• • • • •	42	OISIN 2		197
FLATTERING					
BUT NOW WITH FLATTERING TONGUE	• • • • • • • • •	434	YOUTH AND AGE		3
FLATTERY					
BUT IT WAS ALL DECEIT, AND FLATTERY	• • • • • • • •	244	SHADOW WATER B		457
THEIR HEADS BEING TURNED WITH PRAISE AND FLATTERY!	• • •	245	SHADOW WATER B		480
FLAVOUR					
THAT HAS THE HEADY FLAVOUR OF NEW WINE,	• • • • • • •	240	SHADOW WATER B		374
FLAVOURED SEE FULL-FLAVOURED					
I BRING FULL FLAVOURED WINE OUT OF A BARREL FOUND	• • •	442	BLACK CENTAUR	V	10
FLAW					
THE SOUL IS FREE, AND FINDS NO FLAW.	• • • • • • • •	19	OISIN 1	V	284
AND YET YOUR BODY HAD A FLAW!	• • • • • • • • • •	356	BROKEN DREAMS		28
AND YET YOUR BEAUTY HAD A FLAW!	• • • • • • • • •	356	BROKEN DREAMS	V	28
FLAX					
AND WISDOM THAT CAUGHT FIRE LIKE THE DRIED FLAX,	• • • •	181	QUEEN MAEVE		28
FLEA					
SECOND RUMMAGED FOR A FLEA:	• • • • • • • • • • •	298	THREE HERMITS		4
CAUGHT AND CRACKED HIS FLEA, THE THIRD,	• • • • • • •	299	THREE HERMITS		30

286

	PAGE	TITLE		LINE
FLEAS				
BUT WAS THERE EVER DOG THAT PRAISED HIS FLEAS?	262	TO A POET		4
BUT WHERE'S THE WILD DOG THAT HAS PRAISED HIS FLEAS?	262	TO A POET	V	4
BUT HAVE YOU KNOWN A DOG TO PRAISE HIS FLEAS?	262	TO A POET	V	4
FLED				
AND NOW FLED BY, MIST-COVERED, WITHOUT SOUND,	29	OISIN 2		3
AND THEY WHO TO A FAR-OFF PLACE HAD FLED,	41	OISIN 2	V	184
AND THEY HAVE FALLEN OR FLED, AGE AFTER AGE.	45	OISIN 2		242
FLED FOAM UNDERNEATH US, AND ROUND US, A WANDERING AND MILKY SMOKE,	47	OISIN 3		1
AND THOSE THAT FLED, AND THAT FOLLOWED,	47	OISIN 3		3
FLED FOAM UNDERNEATH US, AND ROUND US, A WANDERING AND MILKY SMOKE,	47	OISIN 3		12
FLED FOAM UNDERNEATH US, AND AROUND US, A WANDERING AND MILKY SMOKE,	47	OISIN 3	V	1
FLED FOAM UNDERNEATH ME, AND ROUND ME, A WANDERING AND MILKY SMOKE.	57	OISIN 3		148
LONG FLED THE FOAM-FLAKES AROUND ME, THE WINDS FLED OUT OF THE VAST,	57	OISIN 3		149
LONG FLED THE FOAM-FLAKES AROUND ME, THE WINDS FLED OUT OF THE VAST,	57	OISIN 3		149
CHRONICLING CHIMAERAS FLED.	65	HAPPY SHEPHERD	V	17
THE KINGS OF THE OLD TIME ARE FLED.	65	HAPPY SHEPHERD	V	17
HE FLED THE PERSECUTION OF HER GLORY	68	SAD SHEPHERD		12
HE FLED, AND IN A FAR-OFF VALLEY STOPPING,	68	SAD SHEPHERD	V	13
MURMUR, A LITTLE SADLY, HOW LOVE FLED	121	YOU ARE OLD		10
MURMUR, A LITTLE SAD, "FROM US FLED LOVE.	121	YOU ARE OLD	V	10
IN SHADOWY POOLS, WHEN ARMIES FLED;	155	FORGOT BEAUTY		5
I HAVE FLED TO MY BELOVED IN THE AIR,	234	SHADOW WATER B		262
HE GAVE A GASP AND THOUGHT TO HAVE FLED,	303	HOUR DAWN		22
AND PRAYED AND CURSED AND CURSED AND FLED	307	HOUR DAWN		119
IN FURY AND IN PANIC FLED	307	HOUR DAWN	V	119
FLED TO FAR COUNTRIES, OR SHELTERED THEMSELVES	546	TO SAME TUNE 2		4
JUSTIFY ALL THAT HAVE FLED, THAT HAVE STOOD,	546	TO SAME TUNE 2		14
JUSTIFY ALL THAT HAVE FLED OR HAVE STOOD,	546	TO SAME TUNE 2	V	14
HIS SPIRIT THAT HAS FLED	575	MAIDS 2ND SONG		5
FLED TO FAR COUNTRIES, OR SHELTERED THEMSELVES	613	MARCH SONGS 1		4
REMEMBER ALL THAT HAVE FLED, THAT HAVE STOOD,	613	MARCH SONGS 1		14
ALONG THE LAKE. THE CRANE HAS HOMEWARD FLED.	656	ISLE STAT I 3		23
FLED FROM HIS BROW WHERE THE HAIR WAS GREY;	728	PRIEST FAIRY		10
AND SHE CRIES OUT, "I HAVE FLED TO MY BELOVED	754	SHADOW WATER A		151
AND CRYING, "I HAVE FLED TO MY BELOVED	754	SHADOW WATER A	V	151
WERE THEY BUT LIFTED UP. THE RED HOUND IS FLED.	761	SHADOW WATER A		266
FLEE				
"FLEE.FROM HIM," PEARL-PALE NIAMH WEEPING CRIED,	35	OISIN 2		92
BUT FLEE WHILE YOU STILL MAY." THEN I:	35	OISIN 2		89
BUT FLEE WHILE YOU MAY FLEE FROM HIM." THEN I:	35	OISIN 2	V	89
BUT FLEE WHILE YOU MAY FLEE FROM HIM." THEN I:	35	OISIN 2	V	89
"FOR ALL MEN FLEE THE DEMONS"; BUT MOVED NOT	36	OISIN 2		93
WE TIRE OF THE FLAME OF THE METEOR, BEFORE IT CAN FADE AND FLEE;	122	WHITE BIRDS		2
FOR WE TIRE OF THE FLAME OF THE METEOR BEFORE IT CAN PASS BY AND FLEE	122	WHITE BIRDS	V	2
WE TIRE OF THE FLAME OF THE METEOR, BEFORE IT CAN PASS BY AND FLEE;	122	WHITE BIRDS	V	2
FLEECE				
. . . FOR WHITER THAN NEW-WASHED FLEECE	47	OISIN 3		11
AND MIDNIGHT THERE ENFOLD THEM LIKE A FLEECE	128	DREAM OF FAERY		34
A GENTLE FEELING WRAPS THEM LIKE A FLEECE,	128	DREAM OF FAERY	V	34
HERE WHERE LABURNUM HANGS HER GOLDEN FLEECE;	670	ISLE STAT II 3		102
FLEEING				
WHAT PURSUING OR FLEEING,	785	WOMANS BEAUTY		25
FLEET				
SOME GOBLIN, MY SERVANT, ON WINGS THAT ARE FLEET,	657	ISLE STAT I 3		67
AFAR ALONG THE FLEET WHITE RIVER'S FACE--	702	MOSADA 3		79
WOULD THEY FOOT SO FLEET A MEASURE?	731	STREET DANCERS		12
WOULD THEY FOOT SO FLEET A MEASURE?	732	STREET DANCERS		25
WOULD THEY FOOT SO FLEET A MEASURE?	732	STREET DANCERS		38
WOULD THEY FOOT SO FLEET A MEASURE?	733	STREET DANCERS		51
WOULD THEY FOOT SO FLEET A MEASURE?	733	STREET DANCERS		64
FLEETER				
FAR FLEETER THAN THE MILLION-FOOTED SEA.	670	ISLE STAT II 3		108
FLEETING				
MORE FLEETING THAN THE SEA'S FOAM-FICKLE FACE,	112	ROSE OF WORLD	V	8
MORE FLEETING THAN THE SEA'S FOAM FICKLE FACE,	112	ROSE OF WORLD	V	8
VEERING, FLEETING, FICKLE, THE WINDS OF KNOCKNAREA,	206	HANRAHANS SONG	V	1
VEERING, FLEETING, FICKLE, OUR LOVES AND ANGERS MEET!	207	HANRAHANS SONG	V	3
FLEETNESS				
AND LIFE THE SANDALS OF HER FLEETNESS,	77	INDIAN TO LOVE	V	5B
I'D GIVE MY FAERY FLEETNESS, THOUGH I BE	670	ISLE STAT II 3		107
FLESH				
LIKE ROTTED FLESH, AND STONE BY STONE MY HALL	45	OISIN 2	V	236
. . . THE FLESH OF HIS FACE AS DRIED GRASS,	59	OISIN 3		173
WHERE THE FLESH OF THE FOOTSOLE CLINGETH	61	OISIN 3		197
WHEN THE FLESH OF THE FOOTSOLE CLINGETH	61	OISIN 3	V	197
ITS FLESH BEING WILD, AND IT AGAIN	266	GALWAY RACES		13
FLESH WILD AGAIN, AND IT AGAIN	266	GALWAY RACES	V	13
THAT FLESH AND BONE MAY DISAPPEAR,	307	HOUR DAWN		101
AS WITH HER FLESH AND BONE,	345	ON WOMAN		6
GREEK ALEXANDER FROM MY FLESH,	379	SAINT HUNCH		10
TO ALL THAT IN YOUR FLESH HAVE STOOD	380	SAINT HUNCH		13

FLESH   (CONTINUED)
    WERE DEAD YET FLESH AND BONE. . . . .   384 VISION ROBART   48
    FISH, FLESH, OR FOWL, COMMEND, ALL SUMMER LONG . . . . . 407 SAIL BYZANTIUM   9
    OF FLESH AND BONE; . . . .   436 FOR MY SON   24
    I HAVE AS HEALTHY FLESH AND BLOOD AS ANY RHYMER'S HAD, . . 450 OWEN AHERNE   10
    A HEART OF FLESH AND BLOOD. . . . .   451 FIRST LOVE   6
    WHAT IS THIS FLESH I PURCHASED WITH MY PAINS, . . . 499 MOTHER OF GOD   11
    CALCULATIONS THAT LOOK BUT CASUAL FLESH, PUT DOWN . . . 610 STATUES   11
    OVER HER SPOTTED FLESH AND FLYING HAIR . . . . . . 687 TWO TITANS   15
FLEW
    ROUND EVERY BRANCH THE SONG-BIRDS FLEW, ... 14 OISIN 1   180
    FOR ROUND EACH BRANCH THE SONG-BIRDS FLEW, ... 14 OISIN 1   V   180
    AND THEN AN ANSWERING WHISPERING FLEW . . . . . . 15 OISIN 1   197
    ERE LONG AN ANSWERING WHISPER FLEW, ... 15 OISIN 1   V   197
    AND THEN AN ANSWERING WHISPER FLEW . . . . . . 15 OISIN 1   V   197
    AND STARLIGHT GLEAMED, AND CLOUDS FLEW HIGH, ... 84 MAD KING GOLL   34
    FLEW WESTWARD! AND MANY A TIME SINCE THEN . . . . 223 SHADOW WATER B   27
    A GREY GULL LOST ITS FEAR AND FLEW . . . . . . 397 POLIT PRISONER   3
    WHERE IS THE OWL THAT LATELY FLEW . . . . . . 646 ISLE STAT I 1   32
    THE FAERY THING FLEW WITH HER O'ER THE GRAY . . . . 663 ISLE STAT II 2   38
    WHITE LILIES, AND HER SONG FLEW FORTH AFAR . . . . 693 MOSADA 1   85
FLICKED
    TIME GOES. THE FLICKED FIRE OF EVENING CRAWLS . . . 712 FERENCZ RENYI   V   70
FLICKER   SEE A-FLICKER
    TILL THE SEED OF THE FIRE FLICKER AND GLOW; . . . . 150 OLD MOTHER   2
    OR HOPES THAT IN MERE HOPING FLICKER AND CEASE! . . . 162 ASKS FORGIVE   3
    AND HOPES THAT IN MERE HOPING FLICKER AND CEASE! . . . 162 ASKS FORGIVE   V   3
    WHEN SHE DREAMT FIRST OF LOVE, SHALL FLICKER OUT . . . 760 SHADOW WATER A   257
    WHEN SHE DREAMED FIRST OF LOVE, SHALL FLICKER OUT . . 760 SHADOW WATER A V   257
FLICKERED
    HAS FLICKERED AND GONE OUT. I AM NOT WELL. . . . . 704 MOSADA 3   129
FLICKERING
    SEND PEACE ON ALL THE LANDS AND FLICKERING CORN.— . . 71 ANASHU VIJAYA   1
    AND MOTH-LIKE STARS WERE FLICKERING OUT, ... 149 WANDER AENGUS   6
    FLICKERING WITH ASH AND HAZEL, BUT HALF SHOWED . . . 180 QUEEN MAEVE   12
    FLICKERING UNDER THE WHITE MOONSHINE? . . . . . . 646 ISLE STAT I 1   33
    GOES FLICKERING IN REVERBERATED LIGHT. . . . . . 653 ISLE STAT I 2   53
    NODDING BY THE FLICKERING LAKE. . . . . 655 ISLE STAT I 3   3
    THY FLICKERING HAND? WHAT MEAN THE LIGHTS THAT RISE . . 674 ISLE STAT II 3   198
    TRAILING AND SHINING 'NEATH THE FLICKERING GLARE. . . 688 TWO TITANS   32
    FLASHING AND FLICKERING WITH EVER-UNDULANT WING . . . 710 FERENCZ RENYI   19
    FLASHING AND FLICKERING, WITH EVER UNDULANT WING, . . 710 FERENCZ RENYI V   19
    THE SUNLIGHT FLICKERING ON THE PEWS, ... 736 IN CHURCH   9
FLICKERS
    UPON THE LIFE THAT FADES AND FLICKERS AND DIES, ... 29 OISIN 2   12
FLIES   SEE HALF-FLIES
    . . . A SOUND LIKE THE STIRRING OF FLIES. . . . . . 51 OISIN 3   58
    BUT TO BE AMID SHOOTING OF FLIES AND FLOWERING OF RUSHES
      AND FLAGS." . . . . 55 OISIN 3   120
    BUT TO BE 'MID THE SHOOTING OF FLIES . . . . 55 OISIN 3   V 120
    THE FLIES BELOW THE LEAVES, AND THE YOUNG MICE . . . 75 ANASHU VIJAYA   87
    FOR THEY WILL RIDE THE NORTH WHEN THE GER-EAGLE FLIES, . 146 UNAPPEAS HOST   3
    FOR WINDS WILL BEAR THEM GENTLY WHEN THE EAGLE FLIES, . 146 UNAPPEAS HOST V   3
    FOR THEY WILL RIDE THE WINDS WHEN THE GIER-EAGLE FLIES . 146 UNAPPEAS HOST V   3
    AT DAWN TO CAST HIS FLIES, ... 347 FISHERMAN   5
    WHEN THE FLIES DROP IN THE STREAM! . . . . . . 348 FISHERMAN   34
    WHEN HER SOUL FLIES TO THE PREDESTINED DANCING-PLACE . 365 HER COURAGE   1
    THE MOTHER BIRDS BRING GRUBS AND FLIES. . . . . . 424 STARES NEST   3
    DAYLIGHT ALREADY FLIES . . . . 536 PARTING   9
    OVER THEM FLIES A LONG-LEGGED BIRD, ... 566 LAPIS LAZULI   39
    NO HAMLET THIN FROM EATING FLIES, A FAT . . . . . 610 STATUES   19
    WAVES OFF THE FLIES, AND WARMS HIM IN THE SHINE. . . 709 FERENCZ RENYI   7
    OBEYS. SOME FIERCE MAGICIAN FLIES OR WALKS . . . . 720 WITCH VIVIEN   9
    THE FLIES THAT DANCE IN THREES, IN TWOS, ... 736 IN CHURCH   11
FLIETH
    FLIETH FORTUNE'S FURIOUS WHEEL. . . . . 737 IN FIRELIGHT   8
FLIGHT
    ON OUR DARK PATHWAY, TILL A COUNTLESS FLIGHT . . . . 31 OISIN 2   34
    AT LAST THE MOON AND STARS SHONE, AND A FLIGHT . . . . 31 OISIN 2   V   34
    "WHAT DO YOU BUILD WITH SAILS FOR FLIGHT?" . . . . . 69 CLOAK BOAT   6
    TILL THE MOON HAS TAKEN FLIGHT! . . . . 87 STOLEN CHILD   19
    AND TIME AND THE WORLD ARE EVER IN FLIGHT! . . . . 148 INTO TWILIGHT   14
    THAT IF WE HOLD THAT FLIGHT THEY'LL LEAVE THE PLACE, . 265 ABBEY THEATRE   3
    ALL BUT THE TERRORS OF THE WOODLAND FLIGHT FORGOT . . 366 HER COURAGE   5
    ALL BUT THE PERILS OF THE WOODLAND FLIGHT FORGOT, . . 366 HER COURAGE V   5
    CRADLE UPON CRADLE, AND ALL IN FLIGHT AND ALL . . . 376 PHASES OF MOON   100
    THE WINGS HALF SPREAD FOR FLIGHT, ... 430 NINETEEN 19   65
    I MEDITATE UPON A SWALLOW'S FLIGHT, ... 488 COOLE PARK 29   1
    OF FLIGHT ARE DONE. MOST FAIR OF ALL WHO GRAZE . . 649 ISLE STAT I 1   118
    DREAMING OF FLASHING FLIGHT AND OF THE PLUMED WAVE. . 650 ISLE STAT I 1   140
    WHAT DO YOU BUILD WITH SAILS FOR FLIGHT? . . . . . 666 ISLE STAT II 3   6
    REMEMBERING THEE, I MUSE, WHILE FADES IN FLIGHT . . . 705 REMEMBRANCE   6
    AS A WREATH OF SMOKE IN WIND-BLOWN FLIGHT . . . . 730 PRIEST FAIRY   61
    AND NEVER REST IN THEIR FLIGHT, ... 739 WHERE BOOKS GO   4
FLING
    OR FLING MY LAUGHTER TO THE SUN . . . . 86 MAD KING GOLL V   69
    AND FLING MY LAUGHTER TO THE SUN . . . . 86 MAD KING GOLL V   69
    THERE, DON'T FLING STONES AT ME . . . . 94 MOLL MAGEE   2
    YE WON'T FLING STONES AT ME! . . . . 96 MOLL MAGEE   54
    DIM PAIRC-NA-CARRAIG, WHERE THE WILD BEES FLING . . . 217 WOODS OF COOLE   9
    I TOOK A BROKEN ROOT TO FLING . . . . 317 APPOINTMENT   2

	PAGE	TITLE		LINE

FLING (CONTINUED)
BEYOND THE FLING OF THE DULL ASS'S HOOF . . . . 321 REED WHISPERER   5
AND YET IN FLYING FLING INTO MY MEAT . . . . 384 VISION ROBART   53
THE SUMMERS FLING THEIR SCENTS? AH, SUBTILE AND SLOW, . . 675 ISLE STAT II 3   231
GATHERED ON HER OWN LIPS, OH YOUTH, AND FLING . . . . . 688 TWO TITANS   53
I FLING AWAY MY SWORD, BLOOD DIM, ... 743 DANAAN QUICK   20
I DREW MY SWORD TO FLING IT IN A POOL,—— . . . . . . 747 SHADOW WATER A   7
CALAMITY CAN HAVE ITS FLING. . . . . 782 HEART FRIGHT   18
O THEY HAD THEIR FLING, ... 790 SINGING HEAD   22
FLINGING
FLINGING FROM HIS ARMS I LAUGHED . . . . 538 LAST CONFESS   7
NOW FLINGING LOOSE THE SLANTING SAIL, ... 742 DANAAN QUICK   3
FLINGS
AND FLINGS HERSELF OUT OF THE ROOM WHEN JULIET WOULD BE   354 HIS PHOENIX   13
  BRIDE
AND FLINGS HERSELF OUT OF THE ROOM WHEN JULIET WOULD BE   354 HIS PHOENIX   V   13
  A BRIDE
FLINGS HER BEFORE HIM. "SAVE THYSELF AND ME. . . . . . 713 FERENCZ RENYI   86
IN TERROR FLINGS HER AT HER LOVER'S FEET. . . . . . 713 FERENCZ RENYI   V   85
WITH CRIES AND MURMURS. SUDDENLY HE FLINGS . . . . 714 FERENCZ RENYI   101
FLIT
WHEN GREY GULLS FLIT ABOUT INSTEAD OF MEN, ... 292 TO A SHADE   6
AT MIDNIGHT ON THE EMPEROR'S PAVEMENT FLIT . . . . . 498 BYZANTIUM   25
FLIT TO KILTARTAN CROSS AND STAY . . . . 791 REPRISALS   11
FLITTING
WITHIN HIS OTHER HAND WERE FLITTING . . . . 18 OISIN 1   V 253
FLOAT
I SAW A FOAM-WHITE SEAGULL DRIFT AND FLOAT . . . . . 36 OISIN 2   105
CLOTHING HIM ROUND, I SAW A SEAGULL FLOAT . . . . . 36 OISIN 2   V 105
FLOAT OUT UPON A LONG . . . . 414 TOWER   142
DRIFT AND FLOAT LIKE SILVER SHIPS! . . . . . . 647 ISLE STAT I 1   67
LIVING, WIDE WINGED, ON THE WATERS FLOAT. . . . . 657 ISLE STAT I 3   54
FLOATED
FLOATED IN ALL HER SINGING. HALF ENTRANCED . . . . 30 OISIN 2   V   19
AND RODE ON TILL OVER THE WORLD'S RIM FLOATED THE SEA'S   60 OISIN 3   V 183
  OLD SHOUT,
FLOATING
THE HORSEMEN WITH THEIR FLOATING HAIR, ...   2 OISIN 1   7
A SEA-WORN WAIF CAME FLOATING BY. . . . . 24 OISIN 1   V 365
A SHINING WEB, A FLOATING RIBBON OF CLOTH, ... 430 NINETEEN 19   50
FLOATING FROM YON BARRED WINDOW. SMALL NEW-COMER, . . 700 MOSADA 3   43
FLOATING FROM YON BARRED WINDOW. NEW COMER, . . 700 MOSADA 3   V   43
FLOATING-HAIRED
AND FLOATING-HAIRED AND PROUD IN STRIFE: . . . . . .   9 OISIN 1   V   99
FLOATS
A SWEETHEART FROM ANOTHER LIFE FLOATS THERE . . . . 390 IMAGE PAST   22
HER PRESENT IMAGE FLOATS INTO THE MIND—— . . . . 444 SCHOOL CHILDR   25
BEFORE ME FLOATS AN IMAGE, MAN OR SHADE, ... 497 BYZANTIUM   9
POURS UP AND FLOATS IN FRAGRANCE ROUND MY HEAD . . . 691 MOSADA 1   40
POURS UP AND FLOATS IN FRAGRANCE O'ER MY HEAD . . . 691 MOSADA 1   V   40
AND SEIZE HER, AND THUS FLOATS HER QUIVERING CRY! . . 714 FERENCZ RENYI   105
OF FIRE. SO ENDS A BRAIN——A WORLD! THE SMOKE FLOATS UP, 714 FERENCZ RENYI   V 111
AS THERE FLOATS FROM FIELDS AFAR . . . . 732 STREET DANCERS   20
FLOCK
AND NOW THE DAYLIGHT-DARKENING RAVENS FLOCK. . . . . 43 OISIN 2   212
ALL IS DONE NOW——I SEE THE RAVENS FLOCK—— . . . . 43 OISIN 2   V 212
THAT YOU STAY IDLING HERE WITH FLOCK AND HERDS." . . 107 CUCHULAIN SEA   21
FOR HALF HIS FLOCK WERE IN THEIR BEDS, ... 132 FR GILLIGAN   3
FOR HALF HIS FLOCK LAY IN THEIR BEDS . . . . . 132 FR GILLIGAN   V   3
AND HIS OWN FLOCK WAS BROWSING AT THE DOOR. . . . 340 SHEP GOATHERD   27
OF A MOROCCAN FLOCK OR HERD, ... 493 AT ALGECIRAS   V   3
FLOCKS
. . . THAT HE WHO HAS STARS FOR HIS FLOCKS . . . . . 49 OISIN 3   37
. . . THAT HE WHO HAD STARS FOR HIS FLOCKS . . . . . 49 OISIN 3   V   37
NO OTHER.——HEAR, AND MAY THE INDOLENT FLOCKS . . . 71 ANASHU VIJAYA   4
THE JOYOUS FLOCKS OF DEER AND ANTELOPE, ... 75 ANASHU VIJAYA   74
IN THE TREE ROOTS, AND ALL THE SACRED FLOCKS . . . 75 ANASHU VIJAYA   88
THE JOYOUS FLOCKS OF DEER AND ANTELOPES, ... 75 ANASHU VIJAYA   V   74
IN THE TREE ROOTS, AND ALL THY SACRED FLOCKS . . . 75 ANASHU VIJAYA   V   88
THAT YOU STAY IDLING HERE WITH FLOCKS AND HERDS." . . 107 CUCHULAIN SEA   21
TO IDLE LIFE AWAY WITH FLOCKS AND HERDS." . . . . 107 CUCHULAIN SEA   V   21
OF THE MOROCCAN FLOCKS AND HERDS . . . . . . 493 AT ALGECIRAS   3
THE FAT FLOCKS AND THE FIELDS' FATNESS, ... 540 FROM ANTIGONE   4
HIDING AWAY THE OCEAN'S YELPING FLOCKS. . . . . . 688 TWO TITANS   38
WHERE THEY ALL SUMMER FEED THEIR WANDERING FLOCKS, . 690 MOSADA 1   5
WHO MIGHT HAVE FLOCKS AND HERDS AND MANY THRALLS, . . 757 SHADOW WATER A   216
FLOOD
TWO WALLS, A ROOF, A FLOOD! THERE TREMBLING GREEN . . 31 OISIN 2   V   32
AS A HAY-COCK OUT ON THE FLOOD, OR A WOLF SUCKED UNDER 63 OISIN 3   220
  A WEIR.
TO RANT AND RAGE IN FLOOD AND WIND! . . . . . 138 TO IRELAND   26
IN FLOOD AND FIRE AND CLAY AND WIND, ... 138 TO IRELAND   V   25
OF THE FLOOD AND FLAME, OF THE HEIGHT AND WOOD, . . 148 INTO TWILIGHT   V   11
HIM WHO TREMBLES BEFORE THE FLAME AND THE FLOOD, . . 158 TO HIS HEART   3
LET THE STARRY WINDS AND THE FLAME AND THE FLOOD . . 158 TO HIS HEART   5
WHO TREMBLES BEFORE THE FLAME AND THE FLOOD, . . . 158 TO HIS HEART   V   3
TIME'S BITTER FLOOD WILL RISE, ... 173 PLEADS FRIEND   6
WHERE THE SWAN DRIFTS UPON A DARKENING FLOOD. . . . 492 COOLE BALLYLEE   48
SPIRIT AFTER SPIRIT! THE SMITHIES BREAK THE FLOOD, . 498 BYZANTIUM   34
"WHATEVER STANDS IN FIELD OR FLOOD, ... 529 TOM LUNATIC   13

289

```
                                    PAGE    TITLE          LINE

FLOOD   (CONTINUED)
     BUT ALL THAT RUN IN COUPLES, ON EARTH, IN FLOOD OR AIR,    556 RIBH PATRICK      11
          . . .
FLOODED
     LIKE HEAVY FLOODED WATERS OUR BODIES AND OUR BLOOD, . . .  208 HANRAHANS SONG    13
     IN THE ELMS ABOVE THE FLOODED STREAM, . . . . . . . .      403 FOR DAUGHTER      12
     THE GLITTERING REACHES OF THE FLOODED LAKE. . . . . .      490 COOLE BALLYLEE    16
FLOODS
     NO TENDER WISDOM FLOODS THE EYES . . . . . . . . . .       723 GIRLS SONG A       9
FLOOD-TIME
     FROM FLOOD-TIME ENCLOSES . . . . . . . . . . . . .         672 ISLE STAT II 3   167
FLOOR
     THE FLOOR OF ALMHUIN'S HOSTING HALL . . . . . . . .         13 OISIN 1          156
     THE FLOOR OF EMAN'S DANCING HALL . . . . . . . . .          13 OISIN 1        V 156
     THE FLOOR OF EMEN'S HOISTING HALL . . . . . . . . .         13 OISIN 1        V 156
     THE FLOOR OF ALLEN'S HOSTING HALL . . . . . . . . .         13 OISIN 1        V 172
     ROSE EVER FROM THE SEA'S WARM FLOOR, . . . . . . .          36 OISIN 2          102
     A HUNDRED HORSEMEN ON THE BASALT FLOOR . . . . . .          36 OISIN 2        V 102
     WHERETHROUGH A HUNDRED HORSEMEN ON THE FLOOR . . . .        37 OISIN 2        V 113
     MOST DISTANT STRODE WE.  ON THE FLOOR LAY SLIME, . .        39 OISIN 2          152
     THE DAWN CAME IN, AND GLIMMERED ON THE FLOOR . . . .       105 CUCHULAIN SEA      6
     THEN EMER CAST THE WEB UPON THE FLOOR, . . . . . .         106 CUCHULAIN SEA     15
     UPON THE WEB-HEAPED FLOOR, AND CRIED HIS WORD, . . .       106 CUCHULAIN SEA   V 15
     UPON THE WEB-HEAPED FLOOR, AND THUS HIS WORD, . . .        106 CUCHULAIN SEA   V 17
     "WHO BADE YOU TELL THESE THINGS UPON MY FLOOR?" . .        125 CATHLEEN PARA   V 13
     SHE GOES DOWN THE FLOOR OF HEAVEN, . . . . . . . .         133 FR GILLIGAN       24
     STOOD UPRIGHT ON THE FLOOR. . . . . . . . . . . .          149 WANDER AENGUS      9
     WHEN I HAD LAID IT ON THE FLOOR . . . . . . . . .          149 WANDER AENGUS     11
     BUT SOMETHING RUSTLED ON THE FLOOR, . . . . . . . .        318 MAGI               8
     THE UNCONTROLLABLE MYSTERY ON THE BESTIAL FLOOR, . .       440 WISDOM             6
     SWEPT THE SAWDUST FROM THE FLOOR . . . . . . . . .         440 WISDOM          V  6
     DREAM OF SHAVINGS ON A FLOOR . . . . . . . . . . .         440 WISDOM          V  6
     IMAGINED HIM UPON THE FLOOR . . . . . . . . . . .          461 HARUN RASHID      15
     AND LET IT FALL UNNOTICED TO THE FLOOR. . . . . . .        461 HARUN RASHID    V 15
     AND IT WOULD FALL UNNOTICED ON THE FLOOR. . . . . .        482 BLOOD AND MOON    32
     HAS FLUNG ITS ARROWY SHAFT UPON THE FLOOR. . . . .         482 BLOOD AND MOON  V 32
     HAD FLUNG ITS ARROWY SHAFT UPON THE FLOOR, . . . .         491 COOLE BALLYLEE    25
     SOUND OF A STICK UPON THE FLOOR, A SOUND . . . . .         498 BYZANTIUM         36
     MARBLES OF THE DANCING FLOOR . . . . . . . . . . .         675 ISLE STAT II 3   243
     OF THE DREAD WOODS, ALONG THEIR RUSSET FLOOR . . . .       705 DAWN-SONG         11
     ALL HEAVEN'S FLOOR, WITH VAPOURS BEDDED—— . . . . .        740 EARL PAUL         15
     AND FLUNG DOWN CLASHING ON THE FLOOR . . . . . . .         744 GLOVE CLOAK        8
     FELL AT MY FEET ON THE FLOOR,—— . . . . . . . . .          780 WELL AND TREE     14
     BUT CHILDREN AND DOGS ON THE FLOOR. . . . . . . .
FLOORS
     ON THE FLOORS OF THE GODS." . . . . . . . . . .             59 OISIN 3          180
     THE PACING TO AND FRO ON POLISHED FLOORS . . . . .         418 ANCEST HOUSES     35
     I SCRUB ITS FLOORS AND MAKE MY BED, . . . . . . .          607 SONGS BURDEN 2     5
FLOPPING
     WITH FLOPPING AND WITH FLAPPING IT MADE A GREAT DISPLAY,   593 PILGRIM           18
     WITH THEIR FLOPPING AND THEIR FLAPPING IT MADE A GREAT     593 PILGRIM         V 18
          DISPLAY
FLORENCE
     ON FLORENCE EMERY I CALL THE NEXT, . . . . . . . .         472 ALL SOUL NIGHT    41
FLOURISH
     AND KNOW WHATEVER FLOURISH AND DECLINE . . . . . .         423 MY DESCENDANTS    23
FLOURISHES
     TRUTH FLOURISHES WHERE THE STUDENT'S LAMP HAS SHONE,       398 LEADERS CROWD      8
FLOURISHING
     MAY SHE BECOME A FLOURISHING HIDDEN TREE . . . . .         404 FOR DAUGHTER      41
FLOUT
     WHETHER SHE THREW THEM UP TO FLOUT ME, . . . . . .         390 IMAGE PAST        37
FLOW
     SWEPT ON THE DANCE'S LINKED FLOW, . . . . . . . .           20 OISIN 1        V 291
     WHISPERED TO THE SEA WHOSE FLOW . . . . . . . . .           20 OISIN 1        V 298
     ONCE MORE THE DANCE'S LINKED FLOW, . . . . . . . .          22 OISIN 1        V 323A
     GREY IN THE MIDST LIKE A SMALL RIVULET'S FLOW, . . .        37 OISIN 2        V 117
     . . . AND YEARS AFTER YEARS 'GAN FLOW, . . . . . .          52 OISIN 3           75
     . . . AND YEARS AFTER YEARS 'GAN THEIR FLOW, . . .          52 OISIN 3        V 75
     ALTHOUGH YOU HIDE IN THE EBB AND FLOW . . . . . .          146 FISH               1
     BUT LET A GENTLE SILENCE WROUGHT WITH MUSIC FLOW . .       175 ELEMENT POWERS    17
     BUT LET A GENTLE SILENCE ENWROUGHT WITH MUSIC FLOW .       175 ELEMENT POWERS V 17
     OR ALL THAT WAYWARD EBB AND FLOW.  THERE STOOD            428 NINETEEN 19        4
     ON ALL THAT WAYWARD EBB AND FLOW.  THERE STOOD            428 NINETEEN 19      V  4
     HAVE I NOT SEEN A THOUSAND SEASONS EBB AND FLOW . .       675 ISLE STAT II 3   229
     UPON THEIR THRONES.  THE LIVES OF MEN SHALL FLOW . .      698 MOSADA 2          56
FLOWED
     BUT DOWN TO HER FEET WHITE VESTURE FLOWED, . . . .          3 OISIN 1           25
     DOWN TO HER FEET WHITE VESTURE FLOWED . . . . . .           3 OISIN 1        V 25
     FLOWED ON ANEW, AND OFT, ANEW DECLINING, . . . . .         33 OISIN 2        V 68D
     WHERE SHADOWY FACE FLOWED INTO SHADOWY FACE, . . .         39 OISIN 2          145
     MELTED AND FLOWED, AND IN THE SELF-SAME PLACE . . .        39 OISIN 2        V 146
     A VALLEY FLOWED DOWN FROM HIS HOOFS, AND THERE IN THE LONG 48 OISIN 3           26
          GRASS LAY,
     AND YOU HAVE CHANGED AND FLOWED FROM SHAPE TO SHAPE, . .  102 FERGUS DRUID       2
     AND THE WAVES FLOWED ABOVE HIM AND HE DIED, . . . .       111 CUCHULAIN SEA  V 86
     AS THOUGH THE WATERS HAD FLOWED UP BETWEEN, . . .         749 SHADOW WATER A    55
FLOWER
     BLOSSOM IN SOME NEW CRIMSON FLOWER, . . . . . . . .        16 OISIN 1          224
     AND HER HAIR WAS A FOLDED FLOWER . . . . . . . .          161 CAP AND BELLS     35
     O FLOWER OF THE BRANCH, O BIRD AMONG THE LEAVES, . .      251 SHADOW WATER B   608
```

		PAGE	TITLE	LINE

FLOWER   (CONTINUED)
```
    WHERE THE SYMBOLIC ROSE CAN BREAK IN FLOWER,  . . . . .   419 MY HOUSE              4
    AND WHAT IF MY DESCENDANTS LOSE THE FLOWER . . . . . .    423 MY DESCENDANTS        9
    HAS PLUCKED A FLOWER AND SUNG HER LOSS!  . . . . . . .    447 COLONUS PRAISE       22
    GROWETH THE GOBLIN FLOWER OF JOY, HER CARE,  . . . . .    653 ISLE STAT I 2        39
    THAT FLOWER I SEEK.   THOU NEVER WILT RETURN.  . . . .    653 ISLE STAT I 2        44
    I'LL BRING THAT FLOWER TO HER, AND SO MAY EARN  . . . .   653 ISLE STAT I 2        45
    OF THE HAPPY FLOWER MINIONS.  . . . . . . . . . . .      667 ISLE STAT II 3       29
    IF ON HIS LIPS THE ENCHANTED FLOWER BE LAID!  . . . .    668 ISLE STAT II 3       46
    O LET ME PASS!   THAT FLOWER NONE  . . . . . . . . .     668 ISLE STAT II 3       47
    THE FLOWER, SAVE SOME THING BE FOUND . . . . . . . .     668 ISLE STAT II 3       51
    THE ENCHANTED FLOWER WERE,  . . . . . . . . . . .       668 ISLE STAT II 3       62
    IN SILENCE, THAT FAMED FLOWER OF WIZARDRY,  . . . . .    673 ISLE STAT II 3      192
    BEHOLD THE LOVING LOVELESS FLOWER OF LONE WAYS,  . . .   674 ISLE STAT II 3      201
    THE FAERY FLOWER LIES UPON THY LIPS.  . . . . . . .     677 ISLE STAT II 3      277
    THE GOBLIN FLOWER LIETH ON THY LIPS.  . . . . . . .     678 ISLE STAT II 3      298
    AND EVERY FLOWER ABOVE ITS SHADOW SITS.  . . . . . .    712 FERENCZ RENYI        73
    AND EVERY FLOWER ABOVE A SHADOW SITS.  . . . . . . .    712 FERENCZ RENYI    V   73
    O FLOWER OF THE BRANCH, O BIRD AMONG THE LEAVES,  . . .  769 SHADOW WATER A      424
    FOR THE FLOWER COMES WITH THE FRUIT THERE  . . . . .    774 COME RIDE             3
FLOWERED
    AND TILL A HUNDRED MORNS HAD FLOWERED RED  . . . . . .   170 SECRET ROSE          17
FLOWERING
    BUT TO BE AMID SHOOTING OF FLIES AND FLOWERING OF RUSHES   55 OISIN 3            120
        AND FLAGS."
    . . . AND THE FLOWERING OF RUSHES AND FLAGS."  . . . .    55 OISIN 3         V  120
    SURELY AMONG A RICH MAN'S FLOWERING LAWNS,  . . . . .    417 ANCEST HOUSES         1
    THAT FLOWERING, SILKEN, OLD EMBROIDERY, TORN  . . . .    477 SELF AND SOUL        13
    HE NUMBERS.  HE, WITH FLOWERING CURRANT TREES,  . . .    710 FERENCZ RENYI    V   22
FLOWER-LIKE
    WOVE IN HER FLOWER-LIKE HAIR, BEFORE DARK TOWERS  . . .   30 OISIN 2         V   22
    OF A FLUTTER OF FLOWER-LIKE HAIR!  . . . . . . . . .    160 CAP AND BELLS        18
    ON A FLUTTER OF FLOWER-LIKE HAIR!  . . . . . . . . .    160 CAP AND BELLS    V   18
FLOWERS       SEE WATER-FLOWERS
    WHITE FLOWERS OF THE FOAM A STAFF OF WOOD  . . . . .      24 OISIN 1         V  366
    SHONE MANY TIMES AMONG THE GLIMMERING FLOWERS  . . . .    30 OISIN 2             21
    ONCE MORE UNTO YOUR FLOWERS; FOR NONE MAY FIGHT,  . . .   34 OISIN 2         V   80
    THE FLOWERS STILL GREW THERE! FAR ON THE SEA'S WASTE  . .  39 OISIN 2            163
    THE FLOWERS STILL GREW THERE.  MOVED BEYOND HIM THE SEA'S   39 OISIN 2        V  163
        WASTE!
    AND HEALED MY WOUNDS WITH UNGUENTS OUT OF FLOWERS  . . .   41 OISIN 2            185
    WITH WITCHERY AND UNGUENTS FROM THE FLOWERS  . . . . .    41 OISIN 2         V  185
    AND ALL THE TREMBLING FLOWERS THEY BEAR.  . . . . . .    134 TWO TREES             4
    THE VINEGAR-HEAVY SPONGE, THE FLOWERS BY KEDRON STREAM!   172 TRAV PASSION          5
    THE HISSOP-HEAVY SPONGE, THE FLOWERS BY KIDRON STREAM!    172 TRAV PASSION     V    5
    HUM IN THE LIME-TREE FLOWERS! AND PUT AWAY  . . . . .    198 SEVEN WOODS           8
    AND HANGING ITS PAPER FLOWERS FROM POST TO POST,  . . .   198 SEVEN WOODS           8
    HUM IN THE LIME TREE FLOWERS! AND PUT AWAY  . . . . .    198 SEVEN WOODS      V    3
    AND WINDS BLOWING FROM FLOWERS, AND WHIRR OF FEATHERS     219 WOODS OF COOLE       39
    I SWAYED MY LEAVES AND FLOWERS IN THE SUN!  . . . . .    261 COMING WISDOM         3
    SEED-PODS AND FLOWERS THAT ARE NOT ALL WILD POPPY.  . .   342 SHEP GOATHERD        88
    SEED PODS AND FLOWERS THAT ARE NOT ALL WILD POPPY.  . .   342 SHEP GOATHERD    V   88
    FLOWERS FROM I KNOW NOT WHAT EMBROIDERY—  . . . . .      478 SELF AND SOUL        27
    (HURRAH FOR THE FLOWERS OF SPRING,  . . . . . . . .     567 FROM JAPANESE         3
    FLOWERS AND GRASS AND CLOUDLESS SKY,  . . . . . . .     639 BEN BULBEN           57
    AND FLOWERS AROUND IN CLUSTERING THOUSANDS ARE,  . . .   656 ISLE STAT I 3        24
    GO ASK THE SPRINGING FLOWERS,  . . . . . . . . . .      680 LOVE AND DEATH       13
    WITH WREATHS OF WITHERED FLOWERS,  . . . . . . . .      680 LOVE AND DEATH       17
    WITH WREATHS OF WITHERED FLOWERS,  . . . . . . . .      680 LOVE AND DEATH       19
    STILL STARING AT THEIR FLOWERS,  . . . . . . . . .      680 LOVE AND DEATH       25
    AND FLOWERS AND LITTLE CHILDREN.  SUDDENLY  . . . . .    688 TWO TITANS           36
    REMEMBERING THEE, I SEARCH OUT THESE FAINT FLOWERS  . .   704 REMEMBRANCE           1
    AND MEASURE THE MINDS OF THE FLOWERS.  . . . . . . .    707 FAIRY PEDANT         17
    FOR DREAMS ARE THE FLOWERS ABLOW,  . . . . . . . . .    743 WISDOM DREAMS         6
FLOWERS'
    THEY ARE THE FLOWERS' GUARDIAN SPRIGHTS!  . . . . .     666 ISLE STAT II 3       18
FLOWERY
    AND RIVER, FERN AND FLOWERY CLUMP,  . . . . . . . .      15 OISIN 1         V  196
    WHAT ARE THE VOICES THAT IN FLOWERY WAYS  . . . . . .    666 ISLE STAT II 3       16
    AMONG THE PLANTS! THE FLOWERY SILENCE FELL  . . . . .    692 MOSADA 1             55
FLOWING
    AND FLOWING STRENGTH, WITH AGE IS SUBTLE-SOULED.  . .     35 OISIN 2         V   83
    WHERE MOUSE-GREY WATERS ARE FLOWING,  . . . . . . .     119 PITY OF LOVE          7
    THE MOUSE-GREY WATERS ON FLOWING,  . . . . . . . .      119 PITY OF LOVE     V    5
    THAT LIFT US TO THE FLOWING, CHANGING WORLD  . . . .     230 SHADOW WATER B      182
    THE LONG FLOWING LINE,  . . . . . . . . . . . . .       355 PROPERTIUS            3
    OF DULL RED HAIR WAS FLOWING  . . . . . . . . . .       363 DOLLS DRAWINGS        6
    AND THE FLOWING AIR ABOVE,  . . . . . . . . . . .       680 LOVE AND DEATH       14
FLOWN
    AND THE BLUSHES OF FIRST LOVE NEVER HAVE FLOWN!  . . .     8 OISIN 1             85
    AND THE FLUSHES OF FIRST LOVE NEVER HAVE FLOWN!  . . .     8 OISIN 1         V   85
    TO FIND THEY HAVE FLOWN AWAY?  . . . . . . . . . .      323 SWANS AT COOLE       30
    HOW HAVE THE YEARS IN TROIA FLOWN AWAY?  . . . . . .    679 ISLE STAT II 3      309
    A GREY BIRD HAS FLOWN BY.  HE HAS FLOWN UPWARD.  . . .   753 SHADOW WATER A      134
    A GREY BIRD HAS FLOWN BY.  HE HAS FLOWN UPWARD.  . . .   753 SHADOW WATER A      134
    THEY HAVE FLOWN AWAY TOGETHER.  WE ARE NEARLY  . . . .   754 SHADOW WATER A      154
FLOWS
    WHOSE LONG WOOL WHITER THAN SEA-FROTH FLOWS,  . . . .      8 OISIN 1             90
    WHOSE LONG WOOL WHITER THAN SEA FROTH FLOWS,  . . . .      8 OISIN 1         V   90
    SO GREAT A SWEETNESS FLOWS  . . . . . . . . . . .       316 FRIENDS              27
    SO GREAT A SWEETNESS FLOWS INTO THE BREAST . . . . .     479 SELF AND SOUL        69
```

FLOWS   (CONTINUED)
   COME FORTH, COME FORTH, MY MUSIC FLOWS FOR THEE, • • • •   645 ISLE STAT I 1   20
FLUNG
   WE FLUNG ON HIGH EACH WAVING HAND, • • • • • • • •   22 OISIN 1   325
   FLUNG ON HIGH EACH WAVING HAND, • • • • • • • • •   22 OISIN 1 V 325
   AND FLUNG THE JOYOUS HUNTING-SPEAR! • • • • • • •   23 OISIN 1 V 345A
   • • • FLUNG LOOSELY ALONG THE DIM GROUND! • • • • • •   50 OISIN 3   45
   • • • NOR IN GLAMOURS BY DEMONS FLUNG, • • • • • •   50 OISIN 3   50
   • • • OR IN GLAMOURS BY DEMONS FLUNG, • • • • • •   50 OISIN 3 V 50
   OF THE HIGH PEOPLE OF SORACA NOR IN GLAMOUR BY DEMONS
      FLUNG,   50 OISIN 3 V 50
   • • • I FLUNG IT FIVE YARDS WITH MY HAND, • • • • •   60 OISIN 3   187
   AND THE PROUD DREAMING KING WHO FLUNG THE CROWN • • •   170 SECRET ROSE   19
   OR AS THE CHANGING SPEARS FLUNG BY THE GOLDEN STARS • •   175 ELEMENT POWERS V 15
   HE HAS FLUNG A DRUID SPELL UPON THE AIR, • • • •   240 SHADOW WATER B 385
   AS IF SOME MARVELLOUS EMPTY SEA-SHELL FLUNG • • • •   417 ANCEST HOUSES   13
   HAS FLUNG ITS ARROWY SHAFT UPON THE FLOOR, • • • •   482 BLOOD AND MOON   32
   HAD FLUNG ITS ARROWY SHAFT UPON THE FLOOR, • • • •   482 BLOOD AND MOON V 32
   THE YOUTH HAD FLUNG HIS ARMS AROUND THE ROCKS, • • •   688 TWO TITANS   40
   AND FLUNG DOWN CLASHING ON THE FLOOR • • • • • •   740 EARL PAUL   15
FLUSH
   OH, CAN MY KISSES BRING A FLUSH NO MORE • • • • • •   701 MOSADA 3   71
FLUSHED   SEE SUN-FLUSHED
   AND THRICE THE PEACHES FLUSHED UPON THE WALLS, • • • •   690 MOSADA 1   2
FLUSHES
   AND THE FLUSHES OF FIRST LOVE NEVER HAVE FLOWN! • • •   8 OISIN 1 V 85
FLUTE
   HE'LL PRACTISE ON THE SHEPHERD'S FLUTE, • • • • •   343 SHEP GOATHERD   102
   O BROTHER, LAY THY FLUTE UPON THY LIPS! • • • • •   681 SEEKER   6
FLUTED
   CLEAR FLUTED THEN THAT GOBLIN RARE-- • • • • • •   6 OISIN 1 V 54
   IN THE POPPY-HUNG HOUSE OF THE TWILIGHT FLUTED! • • •   8 OISIN 1 V 83
FLUTES
   OF FIDDLES AND OF FLUTES HUNG THERE • • • • • •   271 GREY ROCK V 20
FLUTINGS
   GOING THE FOREST THROUGH, WITH FLUTINGS WEAK! • • • •   672 ISLE STAT II 3 155
FLUTTER   SEE A-FLUTTER
   FLUTTER ALONG THE FROTH LIPS OF THE SEA, • • • • •   33 OISIN 2   58
   FLUTTER ALONG THE FROTH LIPS OF THE SEA • • • • •   33 OISIN 2   64
   FLUTTER ALONG THE FROTH-LIPS OF THE SEA, • • • • •   33 OISIN 2 V 58
   (THEY WILL NOT HUSH, THE LEAVES THAT ROUND ME FLUTTER--   82 MAD KING GOLL V REF
   OF A FLUTTER OF FLOWER-LIKE HAIR! • • • • • • •   160 CAP AND BELLS   18
   ON A FLUTTER OF FLOWER-LIKE HAIR! • • • • • • •   160 CAP AND BELLS V 18
   STRANGE CREATURES FLUTTER UP BEFORE ONE'S EYES, • • •   222 SHADOW WATER B 18
FLUTTERED
   AS LIKE A RUDDY MOTH THEY WAVED AND FLUTTERED. • • • •   34 OISIN 2 V 72
   I LAUGHED BECAUSE BIRDS FLUTTERED BY, • • • • • •   84 MAD KING GOLL   33
   HIS RUEFUL SPIRIT FLUTTERED BY. • • • • • • • •   673 ISLE STAT II 3 188
FLUTTERING   SEE A-FLUTTERING
   WITH QUENCHLESS GAZE AND FLUTTERING HAIR. • • • • •   12 OISIN 1   145
   AND WITH QUENCHLESS EYES AND FLUTTERING HAIR • • • •   12 OISIN 1 V 144
   O SIGH, O FLUTTERING SIGH, BE KIND TO ME! • • • • •   33 OISIN 2   57
   • • • THE FLUTTERING SADNESS OF EARTH. • • • • •   55 OISIN 3   124
   FOR MOVETH ALIVE IN THY FINGERS THE FLUTTERING SADNESS
      OF EARTH.   55 OISIN 3 V 124
FLUTTERS
   HER RAVEN FLUTTERS. ROB HIM OF HIS FOOD • • • • • •   751 SHADOW WATER A 100
FLY
   FOLDED LIKE A FROZEN FLY! • • • • • • • • •   19 OISIN 1   273
   BUT FLY WHILE STILL YOU MAY." AND THEREON I! • • • •   35 OISIN 2   89
   FOR BATTLE." "FLY YE FROM A THING SO DREAD. • • • •   35 OISIN 2 V 90
   TO FLY A SPIRIT," NIAM WEEPING SAID. • • • • • •   35 OISIN 2 V 92
   I FELL ON THE PATH, AND THE HORSE WENT AWAY LIKE A SUMMER
      FLY!   60 OISIN 3   190
   WITH HER WOULD I FLY. • • • • • • • • • •   89 ISLE IN WATER   16
   AND CALL TO MY BELOVED AND ME! "NO LONGER FLY • • • •   173 SPEAKS HEARERS   7
   WHILE OVER THEM BIRDS OF AENGUS FLY. • • • • • •   197 BAILE AILLINN 182
   O THOUGHT, FLY TO HER WHEN THE END OF DAY • • • •   201 OLD MEMORY   1
   I THOUGHT TO FLY TO HER WHEN THE END OF DAY • • • •   201 OLD MEMORY V 1
   THOUGHT FLY TO HER WHEN THE END OF DAY • • • • •   201 OLD MEMORY V 1
   I KNOW OF THE SLEEPY COUNTRY, WHERE SWANS FLY ROUND • •   204 WITHER BOUGHS   17
   COUPLED WITH GOLDEN CHAINS, AND SING AS THEY FLY. • •   204 WITHER BOUGHS   18
   WHEN MIDHIR'S WIFE HAD CHANGED HER TO A FLY, • • • •   220 HARP OF AENGUS   10
   AND WHEN ONE CHANGED HER TO A SILVER FLY, • • • •   220 HARP OF AENGUS V 10
   THEY'LL FLY UPON THAT SECRET WAY OF THEIRS. • • • •   233 SHADOW WATER B 248
   AND NOW THEY ALL WHEEL SUDDENLY AND FLY • • • • •   234 SHADOW WATER B 258
   THAT FLY INTO THE WEST? BUT LISTEN, LISTEN! • • • •   247 SHADOW WATER B 518
   WHAT ARE THEY? UNTO WHAT COUNTRY DO THEY FLY? • • •   247 SHADOW WATER B 523
   WHEN GREY GULLS FLY ABOUT INSTEAD OF MEN, • • • •   292 TO A SHADE V 6
   THE STRUGGLE OF THE FLY IN MARMALADE. • • • • •   369 EGO DOMINUS   45
   OR ELSE MY DREAMS THAT FLY • • • • • • • •   384 VISION ROBART   51
   NO, NOT IN BOYHOOD WHEN WITH ROD AND FLY, • • • •   409 TOWER   8
   THEY MAY DROP A FLY! • • • • • • • • •   416 TOWER   177
   AS MAN, AS BEAST, AS AN EPHEMERAL FLY BEGETS, GODHEAD
      BEGETS GODHEAD,   556 RIBH PATRICK   5
   THE FURTHER THAT I FLY". • • • • • • • •   559 HE AND SHE   10
   LONG-LEGGED FLY • • • • • • • • • •   617 LONG-LEG FLY   T
   LIKE A LONG-LEGGED FLY UPON THE STREAM • • • • •   617 LONG-LEG FLY   9
   LIKE A LONG-LEGGED FLY UPON THE STREAM • • • • •   617 LONG-LEG FLY   19
   LIKE A LONG-LEGGED FLY UPON THE STREAM • • • • •   618 LONG-LEG FLY   29

FLY   (CONTINUED)
   WHAT BRUSHES FLY AND MOTH ASIDE? . . . .   625 NATIVITY   7
   THAT HAD A SOUND FLY FISHER'S WRIST . . . .   625 OLD MEN BE MAD V   3
   FLY! FLY! SO THESE BRAVE SHEPHERDS BOTH ARE GONE!   649 ISLE STAT I 1   112
   FLY! FLY! SO THESE BRAVE SHEPHERDS BOTH ARE GONE!   649 ISLE STAT I 1   112
   BEFORE I AM TOO WEAK, FIERCE MORTAL, LET ME FLY, .   675 ISLE STAT II 3   245
   BEFORE I AM TOO WEAK, OH LET ME FLY, ...   675 ISLE STAT II 3 V 245
   ALL THESE ARE SOULS THAT FLY FROM THEIR DREAD SELVES. .   686 LIFE   4
   OH, SWALLOWS, SWALLOWS, SWALLOWS, WILL YE FLY . .   699 MOSADA 3   1
   WE'LL FLY FROM THIS BEFORE THE MORNING STAR. . . .   702 MOSADA 3   74
   GOD! THEY'RE MAD TO FLY SUCH CANVAS!" . . . . . .   718 PHANTOM SHIP   14
   "THE SWIFTEST HE TO DANCE OR FLY, ...   729 PRIEST FAIRY   45
   ALL THESE ARE SOULS WHO FLY FROM THEIR DREAD SELVES. .   734 QUATRAIN APHOR   4
   ALL THESE ARE SOULS THAT FLY FROM THEIR DREAD SELVES. .   734 QUATRAIN APHOR V 4
   THEY ARE CHANGED AND AS GREY BIRDS FLY OUT TO SEA, .   750 SHADOW WATER A   82
   AND FLY AMONG THE FOAM. THRUST DOWN THE HELM. . .   750 SHADOW WATER A   88
   WHEN ALL GATHER THEY WILL FLY UPON THEIR WAY. . . .   753 SHADOW WATER A   136
   AND NOW THEY ALL WHEEL SUDDENLY AND FLY . . . . .   753 SHADOW WATER A   148
   TILL HIS EDAINE, NO LONGER A GOLDEN FLY . . . . .   757 SHADOW WATER A   210
   TILL HIS EDAINE, NO MORE A SILVER FLY . . . . . .   757 SHADOW WATER A V 210
   WHEN MIDHER'S WIFE HAD CHANGED HER TO A FLY . . .   763 SHADOW WATER A   305
   AND WHEN ONE CHANGED HER TO A SILVER FLY, ...   763 SHADOW WATER A V 305
FLY-CATCHERS
   FLY-CATCHERS OF THE MOON, ...   488 CRAZED MOON   13
FLY-FISHER'S
   THAT HAD A SOUND FLY-FISHER'S WRIST . . . .   625 OLD MEN BE MAD   3
FLYING
   I CHASED AT MORN THE FLYING DEER, ...   10 OISIN 1   121
   I CHASED WITH HOUNDS THE FLYING DEER, ...   10 OISIN 1   V 121
   AFAR FROM WHERE THE YEARS ARE FLYING . . . . . .   22 OISIN 1   V 340A
   HE TOLD OF EVERY FROTH-DROP HISSING, FLYING. . . .   32 OISIN 2   V 45
   CAME FLYING, HEAVY AND SAD! . . . .   93 FATHER OHART   34
   FLYING, CRYING, TO AND FRO, ...   136 TWO TREES   35
   PEERING AND FLYING TO AND FRO, ...   136 TWO TREES   V 35
   THE MEASURE OF HER FLYING FEET . . . .   138 TO IRELAND   11
   THE LIGHT FALL OF HER FLYING FEET . . . .   138 TO IRELAND   V 11
   TWO SWANS CAME FLYING UP TO HIM, ...   194 BAILE AILLINN   135
   AND THAT YOU COME FROM EDEN ON FLYING FEET. . . .   218 WOODS OF COOLE   29
   AND FLYING TOWARDS THEIR PEACE. PUT BY THESE THOUGHTS,   226 SHADOW WATER B 91
   AND YET IN FLYING FLING INTO MY MEAT . . . . . .   384 VISION ROBART   53
   OVER HER SPOTTED FLESH AND FLYING HAIR . . . . .   687 TWO TITANS   15
   WHEN FLYING TO THE HEART OF LIGHT . . . .   742 DANAAN QUICK   8
FOAL
   'GAT THE FOAL OF THE WORLD." . . . .   529 TOM CRUACHAN   6
FOAM   SEE SEA-FOAM
   TO THIS DIM SHORE ON FOAM WET FEET? . . . .   5 OISIN 1   V 51
   RAN THROUGH THE FOAM AND RAN TO THIS . . . . . .   6 OISIN 1   58
   THAT YOU THROUGH ALL THAT FOAM SHOULD RUN?" . . .   6 OISIN 1   61
   FOR LOVE OF OISIN FOAM WET FEET . . . .   6 OISIN 1   V 57
   OF DREAMY FOAM A STAFF OF WOOD . . . .   24 OISIN 1   366
   WHITE FLOWERS OF THE FOAM A STAFF OF WOOD . . . .   24 OISIN 1   V 366
   ROOTED IN FOAM AND CLOUDS, AND CRIED TO ALL . . .   38 OISIN 2   132
   ROOTED IN FOAM AND CLOUDS. THERE MIGHTIER MASTERS MET .   38 OISIN 2   V 132
   I FOUND, DROPPING SEA FOAM ON THE WIDE STAIR, . .   43 OISIN 2   V 215
   FLED FOAM UNDERNEATH US, AND ROUND US, A WANDERING AND
     MILKY SMOKE,   47 OISIN 3   1
   FLED FOAM UNDERNEATH US, AND ROUND US, A WANDERING AND
     MILKY SMOKE.   47 OISIN 3   12
   FLED FOAM UNDERNEATH US, AND AROUND US, A WANDERING AND
     MILKY SMOKE,   47 OISIN 3   V 1
   FLED FOAM UNDERNEATH ME, AND ROUND ME, A WANDERING AND
     MILKY SMOKE.   57 OISIN 3   148
   LIKE AN ARMY OF OLD MEN LOUNGING FOR REST FROM THE FOAM
     OF THE SEAS.   57 OISIN 3   V 144
   UNDER THE PASSING STARS, FOAM OF THE SKY, ...   112 ROSE OF WORLD   9
   MORE FLEETING THAN THE SEA'S FOAM FICKLE FACE, . .   112 ROSE OF WORLD V 8
   I WOULD THAT WE WERE, MY BELOVED, WHITE BIRDS ON THE FOAM
     OF THE SEA!   121 WHITE BIRDS   1
   O WOULD THAT WE WERE, MY BELOVED, WHITE BIRDS ON THE FOAM
     OF THE SEA,   121 WHITE BIRDS   V 1
   . . . ON THE WANDERING FOAM! I AND YOU! . . . . .   122 WHITE BIRDS   8
   . . . BUOYED OUT ON THE FOAM OF THE SEA! . . . .   122 WHITE BIRDS   12
   AND CANDLE-LIKE FOAM ON THE DIM SAND, ...   158 BELOVED RHYMES   10
   ON THE ISLAND LAWNS, THEIR FEET WHERE THE PALE FOAM GLEAMS.   203 WITHER BOUGHS 14
   IT WHIRLS INTO THE FOAM. O ANCIENT WORM, ...   251 SHADOW WATER B   597
   DANCED IN THE WHIRLING FOAM AND IN THE DUST, . . .   284 TWO KINGS   167
   AND SAW A FLAKE OF THE YELLOW FOAM . . . .   309 PLAYER QUEEN   15
   I SAW A FLAKE OF YELLOW FOAM . . . .   309 PLAYER QUEEN   V 15
   CUCHULAIN THAT FOUGHT NIGHT LONG WITH THE FOAM, .   549 SEVERED HEAD   9
   THE MANY-HEADED FOAM AT SALAMIS, ...   610 STATUES   14
   EUROPE PUT OFF THAT FOAM WHEN PHIDIAS . . . . . .   610 STATUES   15
   COPULATE IN THE FOAM. . . . .   612 NEWS ORACLE   36
   FOR EVER FOAM AND FRET! . . . .   680 LOVE AND DEATH   4
   AND FLY AMONG THE FOAM. THRUST DOWN THE HELM, . .   750 SHADOW WATER A   88
   THE WHITE FOOL MAKES AT MORNING OUT OF FOAM! . . .   761 SHADOW WATER A 261
   HER EYELIDS TREMBLE AND THE WHITE FOAM FADES! . .   761 SHADOW WATER A   264
   THE STARS WOULD HURL THEIR CROWNS AMONG THE FOAM .   761 SHADOW WATER A   265
FOAMDROP
   OF EVERY FOAMDROP ON ITS MISTY WAY. . . . .   32 OISIN 2   45
FOAMDROPS
   AMONG THE FOAMDROPS OF THE SEA, ...   20 OISIN 1   294

	PAGE	TITLE		LINE

FOAM-FICKLE
MORE FLEETING THAN THE SEA'S FOAM-FICKLE FACE, ... 112 ROSE OF WORLD V 8
FOAM-FLAKES
LONG FLED THE FOAM-FLAKES AROUND ME, THE WINDS FLED OUT 57 OISIN 3 149
OF THE VAST,
FOAM-GLOBES
HER SPIRIT. AS SHE MOVES, THE FOAM-GLOBES BURST . . . . 687 TWO TITANS 14
FOAMING
AND NAMED HIM BY SWEET NAMES. A FOAMING TIDE . . . . 30 OISIN 2 27
AND PART HIS FOAMING MOUTH WITH EAGER EYE— . . . . . 688 TWO TITANS 46
FOAM-OOZY
I FOUND, FOAM-OOZY ON THE VASTY STAIR, ... 43 OISIN 2 V 215
FOAM-PALE
. . . FROM THE FOAM-PALE DISTANCE BROKE: . . . . . . 47 OISIN 3 3
FOAM-WET
THROUGH BITTER TIDE ON FOAM-WET FEET? . . . . 5 OISIN 1 51
TO THIS DIM SHORE ON FOAM-WET FEET? . . . . 5 OISIN 1 V 51
FOR LOVE OF OISIN FOAM-WET FEET . . . . 6 OISIN 1 V 57
FOAM-WHITE
I SAW A FOAM-WHITE SEAGULL DRIFT AND FLOAT . . . . . . 36 OISIN 2 105
FOE
THY WITHERED FOE, AND WITH THE PURPLE WING . . . . . 688 TWO TITANS 55
FOEMAN'S
AND HEARD THE FOEMAN'S BUCKLERS RATTLE, ... 10 OISIN 1 V 123
FOEMEN
NOR TEAR THE FOEMEN FROM THEIR STEEDS. . . . . 11 OISIN 1 128
FOEMEN'S
AND HEARD THE FOEMEN'S BUCKLERS RATTLE, ... 10 OISIN 1 123
FOG
FOR I HAVE SEEN A SHIP HID IN THE FOG. . . . . 751 SHADOW WATER A 89
FOG-DRIPPING
FOG-DRIPPING, PEDESTALLED ABOVE THE TIDE, ... 31 OISIN 2 V 36
FOIL
THAN DUMB-BELL AND FOIL . . . . 334 SONG 3
THAN DUMB BELL AND FOIL . . . . 334 SONG V 3
FOILED
DOWN TO THE MOTHER OF THE FOILED AND DEAD. . . . . . 688 TWO TITANS 50
FOLD   SEE SEVEN-FOLD THREE-FOLD
HE, SHAKING THE FOLD OF HIS LIPS, ... 51 OISIN 3 59
GO TO THE GUARDS OF THE HEAVENLY FOLD . . . . . . 141 EVERLAST VOICE 2
FROM BATTLE-BANNERS, FOLD UPON PURPLE FOLD, ... 162 ASKS FORGIVE 11
FROM BATTLE-BANNERS, FOLD UPON PURPLE FOLD, ... 162 ASKS FORGIVE 11
FROM BATTLE BANNERS FOLD UPON PURPLE FOLD, ... 162 ASKS FORGIVE V 11
FROM BATTLE BANNERS FOLD UPON PURPLE FOLD, ... 162 ASKS FORGIVE V 11
INTO THE FOLD, WE'LL TO THE WOODS AND THERE . . . . 343 SHEP GOATHERD 114
WITHIN THE FOLD TO HEAR THE CREAKING GATE— . . . . 646 ISLE STAT I 1 41
OF OCEAN FAN THEE INTO LIFE, AND FOLD . . . . . . 688 TWO TITANS 56
OH, WOULD THE BUSY MINUTES MIGHT FOLD UP . . . . . 702 MOSADA 3 97
LEST HE MAY SOME GLAMOUR FOLD . . . . . . 717 FAIRY DOCTOR 22
LEST SOME GLAMOUR HE MAY FOLD . . . . . . 717 FAIRY DOCTOR V 22
FOLDED   SEE MANY-FOLDED
FOLDED LIKE A FROZEN FLY: . . . . . . 19 OISIN 1 273
FOLDED IN LOVE THAT FEARS NO MORROW, ... 23 OISIN 1 341
AND HER HAIR WAS A FOLDED FLOWER . . . . 161 CAP AND BELLS 35
BUT DATHI FOLDED HIS HANDS AND SMILED . . . . . 167 BLESSED 11
TO DREAM OF WOMEN WHOSE BEAUTY WAS FOLDED IN DISMAY, . 210 UNDER THE MOON 19
THE WORLD, WITHIN HIS FOLDED HEART. . . . . . 671 ISLE STAT II 3 133
WHEN SOMETHING FOLDED AND SMALL . . . . 744 GLOVE CLOAK 7
WHEN EARTH AND HEAVEN HAVE BEEN FOLDED UP: . . . . 765 SHADOW WATER A 366
FOL DE ROL
FOL DE ROL, FOL DE ROL. . . . . . . 509 JANE REPROVED 7
FOL DE ROL, FOL DE ROL. . . . . . . 509 JANE REPROVED 7
FOL DE ROL, FOL DE ROL. . . . . . . 509 JANE REPROVED 14
FOL DE ROL, FOL DE ROL. . . . . . . 509 JANE REPROVED 14
IS FOL DE ROL DE ROLLY O. . . . . . 592 PILGRIM 5
BUT FOL DE ROL DE ROLLY O. . . . . . 593 PILGRIM 10
WAS FOL DE ROL DE ROLLY O. . . . . . 593 PILGRIM 15
BUT FOL DE ROL DE ROLLY O. . . . . . 593 PILGRIM 20
IS FOL DE ROL DE ROLLY O. . . . . . 593 PILGRIM 25
FOLDING
IS FOLDING AND UNFOLDING, AND IN ITS FOLDS . . . . 751 SHADOW WATER A 99
TO CRY HIS FOLDING CRY! NO, NO, BE SILENT, ... 760 SHADOW WATER A 253
TO CRY HIS FOLDING CRY. THERE IS SOME MAN . . . . 760 SHADOW WATER A V 253
FOLDING THEIR HEARTS' DESIRE TO THEIR GLAD HEARTS. . . 765 SHADOW WATER A 349
FOLDS
HE, SHAKING THE FOLDS OF HIS LIPS, ... 51 OISIN 3 V 59
AND IN FOLDS ROUND HIS EYES AND HIS MOUTH, ... 59 OISIN 3 174
IN THE CONFUSION OF ITS NIGHT-DARK FOLDS, ... 470 HARUN RASHID 192
THE HEART OF NOON FOLDS SILENCE AND FOLDS SLEEP, . . 735 QUATRAIN APHOR 25
THE HEART OF NOON FOLDS SILENCE AND FOLDS SLEEP, . . 735 QUATRAIN APHOR 25
IS FOLDING AND UNFOLDING, AND IN ITS FOLDS . . . . 751 SHADOW WATER A 99
FOLIAGE
ABOUNDING FOLIAGE MOISTENED WITH THE DEW: . . . . 500 VACILLATION 13
NO LONGER IN LETHEAN FOLIAGE CAUGHT . . . . . 500 VACILLATION 27
DRY TIMBER UNDER THAT RICH FOLIAGE, ... 536 HER VISION 1
RICH FOLIAGE THAT THE STARLIGHT GLITTERED THROUGH, . . 541 PARN FUNERAL 1 8
THROUGH LIGHT-OBLITERATING GARDEN FOLIAGE WHAT MAGIC DRUM? 560 MAGIC DRUM 4
FOR THE DAWN THE FOLIAGE FINGERETH. . . . . . 646 ISLE STAT I 1 26
FOR THE DAWN OF FOLIAGE FINGERETH, ... 646 ISLE STAT I 1 V 26
FOLK
UNDER THE STARLIGHT AND SHADOW, A MONSTROUS SLUMBERING 48 OISIN 3 27
FOLK,

```
                                                    PAGE    TITLE              LINE
FOLK   (CONTINUED)
     FROM HIS HOOVES IN THE HEAVY GRASSES, WITH MONSTROUS    48 OISIN 3          V   27
        SLUMBERING FOLK,
     AND ALL FOLK SEEING HIM BOW DOWN,  . . . . . .   .    113 ROSE OF PEACE         9
     THE FOLK WHO ARE BUYING AND SELLING,  . . . .   .    119 PITY OF LOVE          3
     OLD SILENCE BIDS A LONELY FOLK REJOICE,  . . .   .    127 DREAM OF FAERY  V   31
     AND TALKED OF THE DARK FOLK WHO LIVE IN SOULS  .   .  136 TO SOME I TALK       4
     OF THAT DARK FOLK WHO GATHER IN THE SOULS  . .   .    136 TO SOME I TALK       4
     THE FOLK OF THE AIR  . . . . . .   .               143 HOST OF AIR     V     T
     FOR THESE WERE THE FOLK OF THE AIR;  . . . .   .    144 HOST OF AIR     V   26
     HE KNEW NOW THE FOLK OF THE AIR,  . . . . .   .    145 HOST OF AIR     V  40A
     FOLK DANCE LIKE A WAVE OF THE SEA;  . . . .   .    178 FIDDLER DOONEY       2
     AND WHEN THE FOLK THERE SPY ME,  . . . . .   .    179 FIDDLER DOONEY      17
     AND THE FOLK THERE WHEN THEY SPY ME  . . .   .    179 FIDDLER DOONEY  V   17
FOLKS
     AND WHEN THE FOLKS THERE SPY ME,  . . . . .   .    179 FIDDLER DOONEY  V   17
FOLKS'
     I'D GLAD FOLKS' HEARTS WITH BLITHER SONG."  . . .  731 PRIEST FAIRY        82
FOLLOW
     SHALL FOLLOW YOUR HORN AND OBEY YOUR WHIM,  . . .     9 OISIN 1            99
     WHO FOLLOW WITH THE OPTIC GLASS  . . . . .   .      66 HAPPY SHEPHERD      29
     UNDER MY FEET THAT THEY FOLLOW YOU NIGHT AND DAY.  .  153 CHANGE BELOVED      5
     UNDER MY FEET, THAT I FOLLOW YOU, NIGHT AND DAY.  .   153 CHANGE BELOVED  V   5
     AND FOLLOW THE WAY OF THE WIND;  . . . .   .      168 BLESSED            28
     AND NOW THEY WILL NOT FOLLOW, WHILE I SEEK  .  .   .  226 SHADOW WATER B      95
     THEY HAVE MADE YOU FOLLOW THE MAN-HEADED BIRDS,  .   231 SHADOW WATER B     204
     THEY HAVE BADE YOU FOLLOW THE MAN-HEADED BIRDS,  .   231 SHADOW WATER B     204
     WE HAVE TO FOLLOW, FOR THEY ARE OUR PILOTS;  .   .   231 SHADOW WATER B  V  204
     AND I WILL FOLLOW YOU AND CUT THE ROPE  . . .   .   247 SHADOW WATER B     527
     AND DISCORD FOLLOW UPON UNISON,   . . . .   .      250 SHADOW WATER B     586
     I AM CONTENT TO FOLLOW TO ITS SOURCE  . . .   .    265 THESE CLOUDS         5
     TO FOLLOW IS TO DIE;  . . . . . .   .             479 SELF AND SOUL       65
     ARISE THOU AND FOLLOW!  . . . . . . .   .         600 SPIRIT MEDIUM       18
     AND FOLLOW, AND FOLLOW!  . . . . . . .   .        654 ISLE STAT I 2       57
     AND FOLLOW, AND FOLLOW!  . . . . . . .   .        654 ISLE STAT I 2       69
     COME FOLLOW! COME FOLLOW!  . . . . . .   .        654 ISLE STAT I 2       69
     COME FOLLOW! COME FOLLOW!  . . . . . .   .        654 ISLE STAT I 2       79
     ARISE, WORM, AND FOLLOW!  . . . . . . .   .       654 ISLE STAT I 2       79
     I, TOO, WILL FOLLOW FOR THIS EVIL-STARRED ONE'S SAKE  .  655 ISLE STAT I 2       83
     HIS SLEUTH-HOUNDS FOLLOW EVERY FAERY THING.  .   .   655 ISLE STAT I 2       84
     DID I NOT FOLLOW WITH A SCORE OF SHIPS?  . .   .    675 ISLE STAT II 3     244
     AND NOW THEY ARE ALL GONE, I FOLLOW STILL.  .   .   749 SHADOW WATER A      36
     OR BE HIS FOOD, I FOLLOW THE GREY WINGS,  . .   .   749 SHADOW WATER A      37
     SHE BIDS US FOLLOW HER. I HAVE GROWN WEARY  .   .   751 SHADOW WATER A     101
     HAVE CALLED HIM MIGHTY. I WILL FOLLOW YOU.  .   .   758 SHADOW WATER A     218
     I WILL FOLLOW YOU. I WILL HAVE NONE OF YOU.  .   .  768 SHADOW WATER A     412
     PITY THESE WEEPING EYES! I WILL FOLLOW YOU.  .   .  768 SHADOW WATER A     415
     SO WORTHY AMONG MEN. I FOLLOW YOU,  . . .   .     768 SHADOW WATER A     420
     THAT HE FOLLOW WITH DESIRE  . . . . .   .         768 SHADOW WATER A  V  412
     THAT THEY FOLLOW, FOR AT MOST  . . . . .   .      776 AGAINST WITCH       19
                                                        776 AGAINST WITCH       28
FOLLOWED
     WHEN WE FOLLOWED A DEER WITH OUR BAYING HOUNDS,  .     3 OISIN 1            14
     AND A BEAUTIFUL YOUNG MAN FOLLOWED BEHIND  . .   .    12 OISIN 1           144
     A BEAUTIFUL YOUNG MAN FOLLOWED BEHIND.  . . .   .    12 OISIN 1         V 145
     THAT FOLLOWED MY KEEN HUNTING-CALL--  . . .   .     23 OISIN 1         V 345F
     FOR LOVE THEY FOLLOWED ONE AND ALL!  . . .   .      23 OISIN 1         V 345G
     AND THOSE THAT FLED, AND THAT FOLLOWED,  . . .   .   47 OISIN 3             3
     I TURNED AND RODE TO THE WESTWARD, AND FOLLOWED THE SEA'S  60 OISIN 3          183
        OLD SHOUT
     HOW I HAVE FOLLOWED, NIGHT AND DAY,  . . .   .      85 MAD KING GOLL       53
     THIS WHOLE DAY HAVE I FOLLOWED IN THE ROCKS,  .   .  102 FERGUS DRUID         1
     THE WHOLE DAY HAVE I FOLLOWED IN THE ROCKS,  .   .   102 FERGUS DRUID    V    1
     SHE FOLLOWED WITH LIGHT FOOTFALL IN THE MIDST,  .   186 QUEEN MAEVE        128
     AND FOLLOWED UP THOSE BAYING CREATURES TOWARDS--  .  412 TOWER               72
     AND FOLLOWED THROUGH THE EMPTY STREET, AND SHE,  .   468 HARUN RASHID    V 154A
     DREAD HAS FOLLOWED LONGING,  . . . . .   .        519 LOVES LONENESS      11
     THAT FOLLOWED IF I LET THE KERCHIEF FALL!  .   .    533 HER TRIUMPH          4
     "A GIRL I HAD, BUT SHE FOLLOWED ANOTHER,  . .   .   544 TO SAME TUNE 1      11
     "A GIRL I HAD, BUT SHE FOLLOWED ANOTHER,  . .   .   616 MARCH SONGS 3       11
     I FOLLOWED HIM FROM MY GREEN LAIR,  . . .   .      655 ISLE STAT I 3        6
     FOLLOWED A RINGDOVE'S ASH-GREY GLEAM OF FEATHER.  .  715 DWELT SYCAMORE       6
     FOLLOWED THE RING-DOVE'S ASH-GREY GLEAM OF FEATHER.  715 DWELT SYCAMORE  V    6
     BUT THAT THE WIND CHANGED: FOR I FOLLOWED HIM  .   .  747 SHADOW WATER A       4
     WHY DID YOU SAY THAT I HAVE FOLLOWED HIM  . .   .   761 SHADOW WATER A     267
     THAT FORGAEL HAS FOLLOWED THE GREY BIRDS ALONE,  .   767 SHADOW WATER A     402
FOLLOWERS
     HAYNAU, THINE HOUR HAS COME, THY FOLLOWERS FAR  .   .  715 FERENCZ RENYI      117
FOLLOWING
     AND FOLLOWING HER AT A HEADLONG SPEED  . . .   .    12 OISIN 1         V 144
     AND FOLLOWING O'ER THE FIELDS AND PASTURE LANDS,  .  715 FERENCZ RENYI   V 120
     OF FOLLOWING FORGAEL'S DREAM FROM WIND TO WIND.  .   758 SHADOW WATER A     219
FOLLOWS
     HOW THE FALCONER FOLLOWS THE FALCON IN THE WEEDS OF THE  52 OISIN 3          79
        HERON'S PLOT,
     THAT FOLLOWS AFTER. I UNDERSTAND YOU NOW.  . .   .   237 SHADOW WATER B     341
     HE FOLLOWS WHATEVER WHIM'S MOST DIFFICULT  . .   .   374 PHASES OF MOON      40
     IT FOLLOWS FROM THIS LATIN TEXT  . . . .   .      386 ROBARTES DANCE      43
     MUST NEEDS BE IN THIS LIFE AND IN WHAT FOLLOWS  .   465 HARUN RASHID        95
     A RED-EARED HOUND FOLLOWS A HORNLESS DEER.  . .   .  764 SHADOW WATER A     325
FOLLY
     YOU PUT SUCH FOLLY IN OUR HEADS  . . . . .   .    190 BAILE AILLINN       32
```

	PAGE	TITLE	LINE

FOLLY   (CONTINUED)
THE FOLLY OF BEING COMFORTED . . . . 199 FOLLY COMFORT   T
YOU'D KNOW THE FOLLY OF BEING COMFORTED. . . . . . 200 FOLLY COMFORT   14
TO SUCH A PITCH OF FOLLY I AM BROUGHT, ... 384 VISION ROBART   58
ALL THE FOLLY OF A FIGHT . . . . 476 EVA GORE-BOOTH   22
THE FOLLY THAT MAN DOES . . . . 479 SELF AND SOUL   62
OR OUT OF FOLLY INTO FOLLY CAME. . . . . 491 COOLE BALLYLEE   32
OR OUT OF FOLLY INTO FOLLY CAME. . . . . 491 COOLE BALLYLEE   32
IF FOLLY LINK WITH ELEGANCE . . . . 598 STONE CROSS   13
IF FOLLY LINKS WITH ELEGANCE . . . . 598 STONE CROSS   V   13
I GO AS SOFT AS FOLLY! I AM FATE." . . . . 686 LIFE   18
I GO AS SOFT AS FOLLY! I AM FATE." . . . . 735 QUATRAIN APHOR   20

FOND
OF KNITTED MUSIC. OFT THE FOND REPINING . . . . . 33 OISIN 2   V   68C

FONDER
BUT IMAGES TO MAKE ME FONDER? . . . . 390 IMAGE PAST   35

FONDLE
COULD FONDLE THE LEAVES WITH HIS FINGERS, ... 49 OISIN 3   38
IT SEEMS TO FONDLE, WITH A FINGER BRIGHT . . . . . 714 FERENCZ RENYI   114

FONDLED
HE SPAKE ONCE MORE AND FONDLED WITH HIS LIPS . . . 81 EPHEMERA   V   24A
RINGED ROUND AND FONDLED, A BROWN FARM HOUSE SEES. . 710 FERENCZ RENYI V   23

FOOD
AND CARRIED HIM HIS FOOD WITH MY OWN HANDS, ... 280 TWO KINGS   88
AND FOR NINE DAYS HE HAD FOOD FROM OTHER HANDS. . . 282 TWO KINGS   126
THEIR FOOD AND DRINK! . . . . 380 SONGS FOOL 1   9
WHAT WHOLESOME SUN HAS RIPENED IS WHOLESOME FOOD TO EAT, . 442 BLACK CENTAUR   5
A LOVE THAT LACKS ITS PROPER FOOD! . . . . 569 THREE BUSHES   3
I KEEP SUCH THINGS ABOUT ME! THEY ARE FOOD . . . . 721 WITCH VIVIEN   37
HER RAVEN FLUTTERS. ROB HIM OF HIS FOOD . . . . . 751 SHADOW WATER A   100
OR BE HIS FOOD, I FOLLOW THE GREY WINGS, ... 751 SHADOW WATER A   101

FOOL
AND THE FOOL HEART OF THE COUNTING-HOUSE FEARS ALL . . 181 QUEEN MAEVE   21
HOW ARE WE BETTER OFF THAN SEAGHAN THE FOOL, . . . 228 SHADOW WATER B   129
WE HAVE BEEN NO BETTER OFF THAN SEAGHAN THE FOOL, . 228 SHADOW WATER B V 129
FOOL, FOOL! ALTHOUGH YOU HAVE LOOKED INTO MY FACE . 238 SHADOW WATER B   356
FOOL, FOOL! ALTHOUGH YOU HAVE LOOKED INTO MY FACE . 238 SHADOW WATER B   356
THAT DROVE YOU TO IT, AND I FOOL ENOUGH . . . . . 248 SHADOW WATER B   548
TO VALUE BEER! NO HALF-LEGGED FOOL . . . . 304 HOUR DAWN   52
TO JUDGE IF A LIGHT SLEEPING FOOL . . . . 304 HOUR DAWN   V   52
TO VALUE BEER--I WILL HAVE NO FOOL . . . . 304 HOUR DAWN   V   52
AS WHEN I ALSO PLAYED THE FOOL." . . . . 306 HOUR DAWN   79
THERE IS NOT A FOOL CAN CALL ME FRIEND, ... 336 YOUNG BEAUTY   16
THAT NOT A FOOL CAN CALL ME FRIEND, ... 336 YOUNG BEAUTY   V   16
HE CAME, BUT MAN IS A FOOL." . . . . 341 SHEP GOATHERD   74
I HEARD HIM FIRST, BUT MAN IS A FOOL." . . . . . 341 SHEP GOATHERD V   74
HAS SET ME MUTTERING LIKE A FOOL. . . . . 356 BROKEN DREAMS   26
HUNCHBACK AND SAINT AND FOOL ARE THE LAST CRESCENTS. . 377 PHASES OF MOON 118
"HUNCHBACK AND SAINT AND FOOL," AND THAT THEY CAME . 377 PHASES OF MOON   132
TWO SONGS OF A FOOL . . . . 380 SONGS FOOL 1   T
THAT AM A WANDERING-WITTED FOOL . . . . 380 SONGS FOOL 1   16
THAT AM A WANDERING WITTED FOOL . . . . 380 SONGS FOOL 1   V   16
ANOTHER SONG OF A FOOL . . . . 381 SONG OF FOOL   T
NOT A POOR FOOL UNDERSTANDS. . . . . 381 SONG OF FOOL   4
AND LATER HAD MUCH TROUBLE FROM A FOOL, ... 404 FOR DAUGHTER   26
YET MANY, THAT HAVE PLAYED THE FOOL . . . . 404 FOR DAUGHTER   36
THROUGH TOO MUCH PLAY, OR MARRIAGE WITH A FOOL? . . 423 MY DESCENDANTS   12
THE HERO, THE GIRL, AND THE FOOL . . . . 447 HERO GIRL FOOL   T
CUCHULAIN THE GIRL AND THE FOOL . . . . 447 HERO GIRL FOOL V   T
BOOK IV THE GATES OF PLUTO I. THE FOOL BY THE ROADSIDE . 447 HERO GIRL FOOL V   T
WHEN THOUGHTS THAT A FOOL . . . . 449 HERO GIRL FOOL   21
CARRIED BY THE WANDERING FOOL. . . . . 484 SYMBOLS   4
BEAUTY AND FOOL TOGETHER LAID. . . . . 484 SYMBOLS   6
FOOL, RASCAL, KNAVE, ... 496 MOHINI CHATTER   8
I RANTED TO THE KNAVE AND FOOL, ... 506 REMORSE SPEECH   1
GREAT EUROPA PLAYED THE FOOL . . . . 509 JANE REPROVED   5
FOR THE SONG'S SAKE A FOOL? . . . . 553 PRAYER OLD AGE   8
BUT NOTHING SATISFIED THE FOOL . . . . 620 JOHN KINSELLA   7
AND WHEN THE FOOL AND BLIND MAN STOLE THE BREAD . . 630 CIRCUS ANIMALS   25
OR WHISPER THAT A MAN'S A FOOL . . . . 635 BLACK TOWER   12
THE WORLD GROWS OLD AND PLAYS THE FOOL." . . . . . 725 LEGEND   12
OUT OF THAT ISLAND WHERE THE FOOL OF THE WOOD . . . 747 SHADOW WATER A   2
NINE MOONS. AND FROM THE HARPING OF THE FOOL? . . 747 SHADOW WATER A   14
I HAD KILLED HIM LONG AGO, BUT THAT THE FOOL . . . 748 SHADOW WATER A   17
THE FOOL FORETOLD ME I WOULD FIND THIS LOVE . . . 750 SHADOW WATER A   62
THE FOOL THAT CAME OUT OF THE WINTRY WOOD . . . . 750 SHADOW WATER A   75
IT WAS A FOOL THAT GAVE IT, AND MAY BE . . . . . 750 SHADOW WATER A   78
THE WHITE FOOL MAKES AT MORNING OUT OF FOAM! . . . 761 SHADOW WATER A   261
ALL DIES AMONG THOSE STREAMS. THE FOOL HAS MADE . 764 SHADOW WATER A   335
THE FOOL, WHO HAS MADE THE WISDOM THAT MEN WRITE . . 764 SHADOW WATER A   342

FOOL-DRIVEN
THE SEEMING NEEDS OF MY FOOL-DRIVEN LAND! . . . . . 267 ALL TEMPT ME   3

FOOLED
AND SAID! "SHE HAS FOOLED ME ENOUGH," . . . . . . 744 GLOVE CLOAK   3

FOOLISH
BUT I, BEING YOUNG AND FOOLISH, WITH HER WOULD NOT AGREE. 90 SALLEY GARDENS   4
BUT I WAS YOUNG AND FOOLISH, AND NOW AM FULL OF TEARS. . 90 SALLEY GARDENS   8
IN ALL POOR FOOLISH THINGS THAT LIVE A DAY, . . . 101 ROSE UPON ROOD   11
A KING IS BUT A FOOLISH LABOURER . . . . 103 FERGUS DRUID   27
I'D PUT AWAY THE FOOLISH MIGHT OF A KING, ... 103 FERGUS DRUID   V 21A
A WILD AND FOOLISH LABOURER IS A KING . . . . . . 103 FERGUS DRUID   V   27

296

	PAGE	TITLE	LINE

FOOLISH (CONTINUED)
THE LAPWING AT THEIR FOOLISH CRIES . . . . 306 HOUR DAWN 77
A FOOLISH, PASSIONATE MAN. . . . . 553 PRAYER OLD AGE 12
A FOOLISH WORD THOU GAVEST ME! . . . . 671 ISLE STAT II 3 131
OH, I AM WEARY OF THAT FOOLISH TALE. . . . . 721 WITCH VIVIEN 33
LEAD THEY ONE WITH FOOLISH CARE, ... 727 LOVERS QUARREL 29
YONDER FOOLISH ONES WILL TIRE . . . . 727 LOVERS QUARREL 47
FOOL'S
THE FOOL'S TRIUMPH, NOR YET . . . . 312 CHILD DANCING 7
FOOLS
AND THERE, FOR ALL THAT FOOLS HAD SAID, ... 190 BAILE AILLINN 23
ALL THAT GREAT PAST TO A TROUBLE OF FOOLS; . . . . . 546 TO SAME TUNE 2 22
LET THE FOOLS RAGE, I SWERVED IN NAUGHT, ... 577 WHAT THEN 18
THAT OFFICE FOOLS HAVE RUN, ... 598 MODEL LAUREATE 20
ALL THAT GREAT PAST TO A TROUBLE OF FOOLS; . . . . . 614 MARCH SONGS 1 22
AND I MUST LOSE MORE TIME BECAUSE THESE FOOLS . . . . 754 SHADOW WATER A 158
FOOT
TYING THE HORSE TO HIS VAST FOOT THAT LAY . . . . . 32 OISIN 2 46
TO ONE VAST FOOT, FROTH-SPLASHED, WITH CURVED TOES LYING 32 OISIN 2 V 46A
AND THERE AT THE FOOT OF THE MOUNTAIN, ... 60 OISIN 3 185
WE FOOT IT ALL THE NIGHT, ... 87 STOLEN CHILD 16
WHY MUST YOU BLENCH AND SHAKE FROM FOOT TO CROWN?" . . 106 CUCHULAIN SEA 13
WHY ARE YOU PALE AND SHAKE FROM FOOT TO CROWN?" . . . 106 CUCHULAIN SEA V 13
ON FOOT, ON HORSEBACK OR IN BATTLE-CARS." . . . . . 107 CUCHULAIN SEA 30
THAT IF A DANCER STAYED HIS HUNGRY FOOT . . . . . . 127 DREAM OF FAERY 22
TO HELP HER LIGHT FOOT HERE AND THERE, ... 138 TO IRELAND V 14
BUT MAEVE, AND NOT WITH A SLOW FEEBLE FOOT, ... 185 QUEEN MAEVE 107
FOOT AFTER FOOT WAS GIVING WAY, ... 274 GREY ROCK 72
FOOT AFTER FOOT WAS GIVING WAY, ... 274 GREY ROCK 72
TO THAT ROCK-BORN, ROCK-WANDERING FOOT, ... 276 GREY ROCK 125
SOME PASSION HAD MADE HER STONE. HEARING A FOOT . . . 279 TWO KINGS 65
SHE STARTED AND THEN KNEW WHOSE FOOT IT WAS; . . . . 280 TWO KINGS 66
STOOD ON MY PATH. TREMBLING FROM HEAD TO FOOT . . . . 283 TWO KINGS 151
STOOD ON MY PATH. TREMBLING FROM HAND TO FOOT . . . . 283 TWO KINGS V 151
NOR CAN TIME WASTE THE CHEEK, NOR IS THERE FOOT . . . 284 TWO KINGS 182
THAT THERE BE NO FOOT SILENT IN THE ROOM . . . . . 311 MOUNTAIN TOMB 6
LET THERE BE NO FOOT SILENT IN THE ROOM, ... 311 MOUNTAIN TOMB V 6
I SHAKE FROM HEAD TO FOOT. . . . . 316 FRIENDS 28
WHERE EVERY FOOT OBEYED HER GLANCE! . . . . 488 CRAZED MOON 11
WHERE VERY FOOT OBEYED HER GLANCE! . . . . 488 CRAZED MOON V 11
WRINKLED LIKE THE FOOT OF A GOOSE, ... 508 JANE BISHOP 16
A BEGGAR UPON HORSEBACK LASHES A BEGGAR ON FOOT. . . . 590 GREAT DAY 2
A BEGGAR UPON HORSEBACK LASHES A BEGGAR UPON FOOT; . . 590 GREAT DAY V 2
WHAT IF MY GREAT-GRANDDAD HAD A PAIR THAT WERE TWENTY FOOT 622 HIGH TALK 2
    HIGH,
AND MINE WERE BUT FIFTEEN FOOT, NO MODERN STALKS 623 HIGH TALK 3
    UPON HIGHER,
NO SHEPHERD FOOT HAS EVER DARED ITS DEPTHS. . . . . 682 SEEKER 32
WOULD THEY FOOT SO FLEET A MEASURE? . . . . 731 STREET DANCERS 12
WOULD THEY FOOT SO FLEET A MEASURE? . . . . 732 STREET DANCERS 25
WOULD THEY FOOT SO FLEET A MEASURE? . . . . 732 STREET DANCERS 38
WOULD THEY FOOT SO FLEET A MEASURE? . . . . 733 STREET DANCERS 51
WOULD THEY FOOT SO FLEET A MEASURE? . . . . 733 STREET DANCERS 64
FOOTED   SEE RESTLESS-FOOTED TUMULTUOUS-FOOTED MILLION-FOOTED LAME-FOOTED
FOOTFALL
AND WHERE OUR FOOTFALL 'LIGHTED LAST THERE CAME . . . 37 OISIN 2 V 119
SOUNDLESS SHALL BE THE FOOTFALL LIGHT . . . . 70 CLOAK BOAT 13
A VAPOURY FOOTFALL ON THE OCEAN'S SLEEPY BLAZE. . . . 78 INDIAN TO LOVE V 20
AND DROP A VAPOURY FOOTFALL IN THE WATER'S DROWSY BLAZE. 78 INDIAN TO LOVE V 20
FOR GOD GOES BY WITH WHITE FOOTFALL. . . . . 139 TO IRELAND 44
OF A QUIET AND LIGHT FOOTFALL; . . . . 159 CAP AND BELLS 8
OF A FOOTFALL HUSHED AND LIGHT . . . . 159 CAP AND BELLS V 8
MAEVE WALKED, YET WITH SLOW FOOTFALL, BEING OLD, . . . 181 QUEEN MAEVE 43
SHE FOLLOWED WITH LIGHT FOOTFALL IN THE MIDST, . . . 186 QUEEN MAEVE 128
ITS TERROR GROWING WILDER AT EVERY FOOTFALL . . . . 279 TWO KINGS V 45D
AND VANITY HER FOOTFALL LIGHT, ... 314 MEMORY YOUTH 12
WHERE EVERY DAY MY FOOTFALL SHOULD HAVE LIT . . . . 352 PEOPLE 8
SOUNDLESS SHALL BE THE FOOTFALL LIGHT . . . . 666 ISLE STAT II 3 13
WHOSE FOOTFALL I HAVE LONGED FOR, THREE SAD SUMMERS. . 692 MOSADA 1 45
ONE WHOSE FOOTFALL SHAKES THE GROUND. . . . . . . 727 LOVERS QUARREL 32
SINGING TO THEIR LIGHT FOOTFALL. . . . . 732 STREET DANCERS 30
FOOT-FALL
FOR GOD GOES BY WITH WHITE FOOT-FALL. . . . . . . 139 TO IRELAND V 44
ON A FOOT-FALL HUSHED AND LIGHT, ... 159 CAP AND BELLS V 8
OF A QUIET AND LIGHT FOOT-FALL; . . . . 159 CAP AND BELLS V 8
ITS TERROR GROWING WILDER AT EVERY FOOT-FALL, ... 279 TWO KINGS V 45D
FOOTING   SEE SLOW-FOOTING
FOOTING IN THE FEEBLE GLOW, ... 731 STREET DANCERS 10
FOOTING IN THE FEEBLE GLOW, ... 732 STREET DANCERS 23
FOOTING IN THE FEEBLE GLOW, ... 732 STREET DANCERS 36
FOOTING IN THE FEEBLE GLOW, ... 733 STREET DANCERS 62
FOOTING IN THE FEEBLE GLOW, ... 733 STREET DANCERS V 49
FOOT'S
SO THAT THE WANDERING FOOT'S CONTENT. . . . . . . 276 GREY ROCK 131
FOOTSOLE
WHERE THE FLESH OF THE FOOTSOLE CLINGETH . . . . . 61 OISIN 3 197
WHEN THE FLESH OF THE FOOTSOLE CLINGETH . . . . . . 61 OISIN 3 V 197
WITH VAPOURY FOOTSOLE BY THE WATER'S DROWSY BLAZE. . . 78 INDIAN TO LOVE 20
WITH VAPOURY FOOTSOLE AMONG THE WATER'S DROWSY BLAZE. . 78 INDIAN TO LOVE V 20
DROPPING A VAPOURY FOOTSOLE ON THE TIDE'S DROWSY BLAZE. 78 INDIAN TO LOVE V 20
LED BY A FOOTSOLE DIPPED IN BLOOD . . . . 274 GREY ROCK 78

		PAGE	TITLE		LINE

FOOT-SOLE
LED BY A FOOT-SOLE DIPPED IN BLOOD . . . . 274 GREY ROCK V 78
EVEN FROM THE FOOT-SOLE THINK IT TOO. . . . . 387 ROBARTES DANCE 51

FOOTSORE
YET SOMEWHERE IN THE FOOTSORE WORLD WE MEET, ... 691 MOSADA 1 23

FOOTSTEP
YET SHE GOES WITH FOOTSTEP WARY, ... 124 CATHLEEN PARA 11
SOFT AS THE WHISPERING OF A LONG-LOST FOOTSTEP . . . . 699 MOSADA 3 5
SOFT AS A LONG DEAD FOOTSTEP WHISPERING THROUGH . . . . 699 MOSADA 3 V 5
SOFT AS THE WHISPERING OF A LOST FOOTSTEP . . . . . . 699 MOSADA 3 V 5

FOOTSTEPS
THE CAPTIVES' FOOTSTEPS WRITTEN TO AND FRO; . . . . . 37 OISIN 2 V 118
STILL SHE GOES WITH FOOTSTEPS WARY, ... 124 CATHLEEN PARA 11
WHITHER HER FOOTSTEPS GO. . . . . 175 ELEMENT POWERS 18
WHERE HER SOFT FOOTSTEPS GO. . . . . 175 ELEMENT POWERS V 18

FOOTSTOOL
UPON HIS KNEES BY MY FOOTSTOOL . . . . 82 MAD KING GOLL V 13
AND HURLED IT FROM ITS PLACE BEFORE HIS FOOTSTOOL WHITE, 174 ELEMENT POWERS V 3

FOOTWORN
THE FOOTWORN WAY IS LONG, AND IT GROWS DARK. . . . . . 702 MOSADA 3 V 92

FOOT-WORN
THE FOOT-WORN WAY IS LONG, AND IT GROWS DARK. . . . . . 702 MOSADA 3 92

FORAY
WHEN THE FENIANS MADE FORAY AT MORNING WITH BRAN, SCEOLAN, 54 OISIN 3 104
LOMAIR.

FORBADE
THOUGH DEATH ITSELF FORBADE. . . . . 789 SINGING HEAD 8

FORBID
BEING FORBID TO MARRY ON EARTH, ... 189 BAILE AILLINN 11
FORBID, BESEECH AND WASTE MY BREATH." THEN I; . . . . 281 TWO KINGS 102

FORBIDDEN
IN THE FORBIDDEN SACRED GROVE . . . . 389 SOLOMON WITCH 39

FORCE
CAN HAVE THE PURITY OF A NATURAL FORCE, ... 353 PEOPLE 31
WAS COMING INTO HIS FORCE; . . . . 392 EASTER 1916 27

FORCED
BUT WHEN AT LAST HE FORCED THOSE SINEWY FLANKS . . . . 278 TWO KINGS 35
AS THOUGH SHE HAD BEEN FORCED TO LINGER . . . . . . 390 IMAGE PAST 23
THE INTELLECT OF MAN IS FORCED TO CHOOSE . . . . . . 491 COOLE BALLYLEE V 40A
THE INTELLECT OF MAN IS FORCED TO CHOOSE . . . . . . 495 CHOICE 1

FORD
AND THAT LONG FIGHTING AT THE FORD, ... 197 BAILE AILLINN 194
THE FORD WHERE DRINKING CATTLE MAKE A STIR . . . . . 326 ROBERT GREGORY 53

'FORE
TWO THINGS THAT 'FORE ALL ELSE I HATE, ... 24 OISIN 1 V 359
YE WAVES, THOUGH YE DANCE 'FORE MY FEET LIKE CHILDREN AT 90 OLD FISHERMAN V 1
PLAY,
'FORE PARADISE'S GATE. . . . . 680 LOVE AND DEATH 20

FOREBEAR
AND I GAZED ON THE BELL-BRANCH, SLEEP'S FOREBEAR, . . . 50 OISIN 3 53

FOREFATHERS
WHAT HIS GREAT FOREFATHERS DID, ... 638 BEN BULBEN 39

FOREGATHER
AND WHO FOREGATHER IN THE SKY. . . . . 716 FAIRY DOCTOR 8

FOREGO
THE LIVING WOODS FOREGO THEIR CARE, ... 736 SUMMER EVENING 1

FOREHEAD
EACH FOREHEAD LIKE AN OBSCURE STAR . . . . 26 OISIN 1 391
CAME, AND MY FOREHEAD FELL LOW, AND MY TEARS LIKE BERRIES 57 OISIN 3 154
FELL DOWN;
THE SAD BELLS BOW THE FOREHEAD ON THE HANDS. . . . . . 130 BOOK STORIES V 20
AND TOUCHED HER FOREHEAD WITH HIS LIPS AND SAID: . . . 286 TWO KINGS V 211B
DROOPETH NOW HIS FOREHEAD LOW . . . . 711 FERENCZ RENYI V 39

FOREHEADS
WITH LOOSENED HAIR OR FOREHEADS GRIEF-DISTRAUGHT, . . . 537 HER VISION 18
WITH LOOSENED HAIR OR FOREHEADS GRIEF DISTRAUGHT, . . . 537 HER VISION V 18

FOREKNOWLEDGE
IS MEMORY OR FOREKNOWLEDGE OF THE HOUR . . . . 375 PHASES OF MOON 73
AND BY FOREKNOWLEDGE OF THE FUTURE VEXED; . . . . . . 472 ALL SOUL NIGHT V 44

FOREMOST
SHE IS FOREMOST OF THOSE THAT I WOULD HEAR PRAISED. . . 350 HER PRAISE 1
SHE IS FOREMOST OF THOSE THAT I WOULD HEAR PRAISED. . . 351 HER PRAISE 10

FORESAW
DEEP-ROOTED THINGS," BUT NEVER FORESAW ITS END, ... 603 GALLERY REVIS 37
WHAT DEEP ROOTS ARE," AND NEVER FORESAW THE END . . . . 603 GALLERY REVIS V 37

FORESEES
AN IRISH AIRMAN FORESEES HIS DEATH . . . . 328 IRISH AIRMAN T

FOREST
IN HIS OWN LEAFY FOREST HOUSE, ... 2 OISIN 1 V 7L
IN HIS OWN LEAFY FOREST HOUSE . . . . 4 OISIN 1 37
OR DOWN THE DEWY FOREST ALLEYS, ... 10 OISIN 1 120
AND DOWN THE DEWY FOREST ALLEYS, ... 10 OISIN 1 V 120
OF MANY A SLAUGHTERED FOREST ROVER. . . . . 17 OISIN 1 V 249A
DARK BALOR, AS OLD AS A FOREST, CAR-BORNE, HIS MIGHTY HEAD 53 OISIN 3 91
SUNK
CAME CAR-BORNE BALOR, AS OLD AS A FOREST, HIS VAST FACE 53 OISIN 3 V 91
SUNK
CAME BALOR, AS OLD AS A FOREST, CAR BORNE, HIS MIGHTY HEAD 53 OISIN 3 V 91
SUNK
WHEN WANDERING IN THE FOREST, IF HE LOVE . . . . . . 71 ANASHU VIJAYA 3
GO THERE AND DWELL ON THE GREEN FOREST RIM. . . . . . 108 CUCHULAIN SEA V 35

298

FOREST (CONTINUED)	PAGE	TITLE	LINE
OUT OF THE FOREST LOAM, ...	439	FRAGMENTS	8
WHAT FROM THE FOREST CAME? WHAT BEAST HAS LICKED ITS YOUNG?	560	MAGIC DRUM	6
SUCH MAY I LOVE. THE SHUDDERING FOREST LIGHTS	651	ISLE STAT I 1	165
BY MANY SOUGHT, AND 'TIS A FOREST TALE, . . .	653	ISLE STAT I 2	40
AND, BOY, SAW YOU, WHEN THROUGH THE FOREST WE .	662	ISLE STAT II 2	9
BETWEEN THE LONELY FOREST AND THE SAND.	663	ISLE STAT II 2	22
GOING THE FOREST THROUGH, WITH FLUTINGS WEAK; .	672	ISLE STAT II 3	155
WHERE LIES THE LONG-LOST FOREST OF THE SPRITE, .	682	SEEKER	23
THERE LIES THE LONG-LOST FOREST OF THE SPRITE, .	682	SEEKER	V 23
NOT AS HE SHAKES THE FOREST; BUT A CRY	689	NETTLESHIP	8
HE CAME TO THE HOME OF THE FOREST PEOPLE . . .	728	PRIEST FAIRY	5
FOREST'S			
GO THERE, AND CAMP UPON THE FOREST'S RIM; . . .	108	CUCHULAIN SEA	V 35
FORESTS			
AND IN THE FLAMING FORESTS COWER THE LION . . .	73	ANASHU VIJAYA	52
THEY SEE IN FLAMING FORESTS COWER THE LION . .	73	ANASHU VIJAYA	V 52
OF THE FORESTS ALL THE PRIDE, ...	658	ISLE STAT I 3	84
WANDERING OF YORE IN FORESTS RUMOROUS.	723	KANVA ON SELF	3
FORETOLD			
O WHO COULD HAVE FORETOLD	334	SONG	5
O WHO COULD HAVE FORETOLD	335	SONG	11
FOR WHO COULD HAVE FORETOLD	335	SONG	17
BUT WHO COULD HAVE FORETOLD	335	SONG	V 17
A SHEPHERDESS LONG YEARS FORETOLD;	668	ISLE STAT II 3	49
THE FOOL FORETOLD ME I WOULD FIND THIS LOVE . .	750	SHADOW WATER A	62
BECAUSE I HAD HOPED TO COME, AS DREAMS FORETOLD,	757	SHADOW WATER A	197
FOREVER			
THE WINDS AND WATERS TO BE YOUR HOME FOREVER; .	762	SHADOW WATER A	V 282
THE PALE HOUND AND THE DEER WANDER FOREVER . .	764	SHADOW WATER A	V 330
FORGAEL			
OF FORGAEL AND DECTORA AND THE EMPTY WATERS . .	218	WOODS OF COOLE	22
BEFORE THEY READ OF FORGAEL AND DECTORA, . . .	219	WOODS OF COOLE	42
I SAW THEM, TOO, ONE NIGHT. FORGAEL WAS PLAYING,	223	SHADOW WATER B	36
I THINK THAT HE HAS FORGAEL IN HIS NET.	224	SHADOW WATER B	56
FOR HE CAN JUDGE THE STARS AS WELL AS FORGAEL. .	225	SHADOW WATER B	63
TO MAKE AN END OF FORGAEL WHILE HE SLEEPS. . .	225	SHADOW WATER B	65
AND FORGAEL IN THE OTHER SCALE; KILL FORGAEL, .	225	SHADOW WATER B	76
AND FORGAEL IN THE OTHER SCALE; KILL FORGAEL, .	225	SHADOW WATER B	76
EVEN IF FORGAEL HAD NOT BEEN MY MASTER	225	SHADOW WATER B	V 76
CAN KNOW THAT ECSTASY. FORGAEL; FORGAEL; . .	231	SHADOW WATER B	203
CAN KNOW THAT ECSTASY. FORGAEL; FORGAEL; . .	231	SHADOW WATER B	203
WE WOULD RETURN TO OUR OWN COUNTRY, FORGAEL, .	248	SHADOW WATER B	539
AND CUT THE ROPE, FOR I GO ON WITH FORGAEL. . .	250	SHADOW WATER B	592
FORGAEL, BECAUSE YOU CANNOT PUT ME FROM YOU. .	251	SHADOW WATER B	603
WALKED ON THE WATERS AND BID FORGAEL SEEK . .	747	SHADOW WATER A	12
FORGAEL, SEEK OUT CONTENT; WHERE OTHER MEN . .	748	SHADOW WATER A	25
FORGAEL MAY FIND HIS HEART'S DESIRE ON BOARD .	750	SHADOW WATER A	71
FORGAEL CAN DIE TO-MORROW. COME TO THE ALE. .	751	SHADOW WATER A	107
THAT FORGAEL HAS FOLLOWED THE GREY BIRDS ALONE,	759	SHADOW WATER A	246
FORGAEL'S	767	SHADOW WATER A	402
SILENCE! FOR YOU HAVE TAKEN FORGAEL'S PAY. . .	225	SHADOW WATER B	V 68
WHEN FORGAEL'S IN THE OTHER SCALE. I'D SAY IT	225	SHADOW WATER B	V 75
WAS FORGAEL'S COURAGE THAT THE MUSIC KILLED. .	747	SHADOW WATER A	9
OF FOLLOWING FORGAEL'S DREAM FROM WIND TO WIND.	758	SHADOW WATER A	219
FORGAIL'S			
TO FORGAIL'S DAUGHTER, EMER, IN HER DUN, . . .	105	CUCHULAIN SEA	V 2
FORGATHERED			
A STARLING LIKE THEM THAT FORGATHERED 'NEATH A MOON . . .	54	OISIN 3	103
FORGE			
AND SMITHY WORK FROM THE GORT FORGE, ...	406	CARVED STONE	3
FORGED			
WHEN IT WAS FORGED. IN SATO'S HOUSE, ...	421	MY TABLE	9
THAT WHEN AND WHERE 'TWAS FORGED	421	MY TABLE	16
FORGER			
COME FROM THE FORGER AND HIS DESK, ...	582	ROGER CASEMENT	19
FORGERY			
THEY TURNED A TRICK BY FORGERY	582	ROGER CASEMENT	7
TO PROVE THEIR FORGERY TRUE;	582	ROGER CASEMENT	10
THEY TURNED A TRICK OF FORGERY	582	ROGER CASEMENT	V 7
FORGET			
LET US PART, ERE THE SEASON OF PASSION FORGET US,	79	FALLING LEAVES	7
HE WOULD HIS DEEDS FORGET!	112	ROSE OF PEACE	4
WHERE TIME WOULD SURELY FORGET US, AND SORROW COME NEAR US NO MORE;	122	WHITE BIRDS	10
WHERE SURELY TIME WOULD FORGET US AND SORROW COME NEAR US NO MORE!	122	WHITE BIRDS	V 10
AND SHE FORGET THE WANDERING AND ALL THE CRIMSON GLOOM . .	175	ELEMENT POWERS	V 11
AND SHE FORGET THE WANDERING AND THE CRIMSON GLOOM . .	175	ELEMENT POWERS	V 11
BUT I'D HAVE BIRD AND RUSH FORGET	197	BAILE AILLINN	204
BUT I'D HAVE BIRDS AND RUSH FORGET	197	BAILE AILLINN	V 204
SOME DAY I MAY FORGET	380	SONGS FOOL 1	8
FOR HOW SHOULD I FORGET THE WISDOM THAT YOU BROUGHT,	391	UNDER SATURN	4
AND SO FORGET THE COMFORT THAT NO WORDS CAN TELL . .	391	UNDER SATURN	V 4
FORGET ITS BROKEN TOYS	473	ALL SOUL NIGHT	59
I FORGET IT ALL AWHILE	590	OLD WICKED MAN	61
"AND HALF FORGET THIS BED OF STRAW	739	EARL PAUL	5
FORGETFUL			
IN A REVERIE FORGETFUL OF ALL THINGS, OVER THE BUBBLING GROUND.	56	OISIN 3	140

299

	PAGE	TITLE		LINE

FORGETFUL (CONTINUED)
IN REVERIE FORGETFUL OF ALL THINGS, OVER THE BUBBLING   56 OISIN 3   V 140
   GROUND.
BALD HEADS FORGETFUL OF THEIR SINS,   337 SCHOLARS   1
FORGETFULNESS
I FOUND IN THAT FORGETFULNESS   24 OISIN 1   365
TO THE ISLAND OF FORGETFULNESS, FOR LO!   46 OISIN 2   246
THE ISLAND OF FORGETFULNESS   47 OISIN 3   V   T
FORGETTING
I CRIED, "THOU ART SURELY A WARRIOR, FORGETTING HIS FAMOUS   51 OISIN 3   V 61
   LINE,
AMONG HER WILDERING WHIRLS, FORGETTING HIM.   69 SAD SHEPHERD   28
WITHIN HER WILDERING WHIRLS--FORGETTING HIM.   69 SAD SHEPHERD V 28
FORGETTING AND FORGOT!   420 MY HOUSE   26
"FORGETTING HUMAN WORDS," A GRAVE DEEP FACE.   603 GALLERY REVIS   49
SHE HAS BEGUN FORGETTING. WHEN SHE WAKES,   760 SHADOW WATER A 255
FORGIVE
AND AFTER CRIED HE, "GOD FORGIVE!   132 FR GILLIGAN   11
I CAN FORGIVE EVEN THAT WRONG OF WRONGS,   321 REED WHISPERER   9
"GREAT PRINCE, FORGIVE THE FREEDOM OF MY SPEECH!   464 HARUN RASHID   74
MEASURE THE LOT! FORGIVE MYSELF THE LOT!   479 SELF AND SOUL   67
WHERE MEN FORGIVE IF THE BELLY GAIN?   615 MARCH SONGS 2   14
HOW CAN THE MIND FORGIVE?   615 MARCH SONGS 2   16
I'M DYING! OH, FORGIVE ME IF I TOUCH   684 SEEKER   70
FORGIVE! FOR I HAVE TOLD THEM EVERYTHING.   694 MOSADA 1   107
FORGIVE ME! IT WAS ALLAH'S WILL. THE CORDS.   695 MOSADA 1   109
NAMES AFTER ME, LADY--I COME. FORGIVE,   695 MOSADA 1   117
FORGIVE, OR I WILL DIE. 'TWAS ALLAH'S WILL.   695 MOSADA 1   118
FORGIVE ME! IT WAS ALLAH'S WILL. NOW CORDS.   695 MOSADA 1   V 109
FORGIVEN
I HAVE FORGIVEN, O NEW STAR!   75 ANASHU VIJAYA 77
ONLY THE DEAD CAN BE FORGIVEN!   478 SELF AND SOUL   39
I HAD FORGIVEN ENOUGH   504 QUARREL IN AGE   7
THAT HAD FORGIVEN OLD AGE.   504 QUARREL IN AGE   8
FORGIVENESS
THE LOVER ASKS FORGIVENESS BECAUSE OF HIS MANY MOODS   162 ASKS FORGIVE   T
THE TWILIGHT OF FORGIVENESS   162 ASKS FORGIVE V T
MICHAEL ROBARTES ASKS FORGIVENESS BECAUSE OF HIS MANY MOODS 162 ASKS FORGIVE V T
FORGIVING
FORGIVING ME, BECAUSE YOU WERE DEAD!   175 BELOVED DEAD   6
FORGO
GAVE ME SUCH PLEASURE I'D FORGO   305 HOUR DAWN   69
FORGOT
AND, MAN OF THE MANY WHITE CROZIERS, A CENTURY THERE I   52 OISIN 3   77
   FORGOT
AND, MAN OF THE MANY WHITE CROZIERS, A CENTURY THERE I   52 OISIN 3   81
   FORGOT
AND OUR MOTHER OF PEACE HAS FORGOT ME   171 MAID QUIET   V   7
THAT EMPTY THE HEART. I HAVE FORGOT AWHILE   198 SEVEN WOODS   5
SOMEWHERE OR SOMEHOW THAT I HAVE FORGOT,   258 KING NO KING   6
TO TROOP WITH THOSE THE WORLD'S FORGOT,   273 GREY ROCK   63
THERE CANNOT BE, CONFUSION OF OUR SOUND FORGOT,   291 PAUDEEN   7
AND HAS FORGOT,   336 YOUNG GIRL   9
ALL BUT THE TERRORS OF THE WOODLAND FLIGHT FORGOT   366 HER COURAGE   5
ALL BUT THE PERILS OF THE WOODLAND FLIGHT FORGOT,   366 HER COURAGE   V 5
FORGETTING AND FORGOT!   420 MY HOUSE   26
FORGOT IN CRUEL HAPPINESS   453 MERMAID   5
NOR HAD FORGOT THE STRANGENESS OF MY PRESENCE   466 HARUN RASHID V 119A
THE CRIME CAN BE FORGOT.   534 CONSOLATION   12
GODHEAD. SOME SHADOW FELL. MY SOUL FORGOT   557 RIBH ECSTASY   6
I HAVE FORGOT IT ALL. HOW SOON DREAMS FADE!   761 SHADOW WATER A 272
FORGOTTEN   SEE HALF-FORGOTTEN LONG-FORGOTTEN WORLD-FORGOTTEN
OF SOME FORGOTTEN FIEND. NOW NONE ASSAILS   31 OISIN 2   V 30B
HE REMEMBERS FORGOTTEN BEAUTY   155 FORGOT BEAUTY   T
MICHAEL ROBARTES REMEMBERS FORGOTTEN BEAUTY   155 FORGOT BEAUTY V T
FORGOTTEN AT THE THRESHING-PLACE!   195 BAILE AILLINN 148
FORGOTTEN AT THE THRESHING PLACE!   195 BAILE AILLINN V 148
I HAD FORGOTTEN THAT WE MUST GO WAKE HIM.   240 SHADOW WATER B 384
DISCOVERERS OF FORGOTTEN TRUTH   324 ROBERT GREGORY   6
BECAUSE YOU ARE FORGOTTEN, HALF OUT OF LIFE,   376 PHASES OF MOON 96
O TOWARDS I HAVE FORGOTTEN WHAT--ENOUGH!   412 TOWER   73
FORGOTTEN ELSE BY MANKIND,   576 ACRE OF GRASS   23
A SMALL FORGOTTEN HOUSE THAT'S SET   606 SONGS BURDEN 2   3
WHO, WHEN HIS OWN RIGHT KING'S FORGOTTEN,   635 BLACK TOWER   13
ON A GIRL'S FORGOTTEN LUTE,   668 ISLE STAT I? 3 66
THOU HAST FORGOTTEN. ON THE OAKEN STOOL   713 FERENCZ RENYI   91
PRAYED THOSE FORGOTTEN FISHERS, TILL IN THE EASTERN SKIES 719 PHANTOM SHIP   32
ALL THOSE LONG FORGOTTEN FISHERS, TILL IN THE EASTERN SKIES 719 PHANTOM SHIP V 32
I HAVE FORGOTTEN WHEREFORE. THE RED HOUND   747 SHADOW WATER A   8
FORLORN
OR PACE AND WEEP IN WOODS FORLORN,   86 MAD KING GOLL V 68
AND LIFT AN ULULU FORLORN,   86 MAD KING GOLL V 68
BUT THE MAN IS THRICE FORLORN,   776 AGAINST WITCH   26
BUT THE MAN IS TWICE FORLORN,   776 AGAINST WITCH V 26
FORM
AH, THAT TIME COULD TOUCH A FORM   258 PEACE   1
AH, BUT TIME HAS TOUCHED A FORM   258 PEACE   V   1
WOULD NOT PAINTERS PAINT A FORM   259 PEACE   5
CAME WHEN TIME HAD TOUCHED HER FORM.   259 PEACE   11
CANNOT BUT KEEP THE FORM   350 MEMORY   5
THAT IT CAN TAKE WHAT FORM COOK NATURE FANCIES   377 PHASES OF MOON 115

300

FORM - (CONTINUED)

	PAGE	TITLE		LINE
THAT IT CAN TAKE WHAT FORM COOK NATURE FANCY	377	PHASES OF MOON	V	115
MY BODILY FORM FROM ANY NATURAL THING,	408	SAIL BYZANTIUM		26
BUT SUCH A FORM AS GRECIAN GOLDSMITHS MAKE	408	SAIL BYZANTIUM		27
I SAT WHERE I COULD WATCH HER SLEEPING FORM,	467	HARUN RASHID		128
AND WROTE BY CANDLE-LIGHT: BUT HER FORM MOVED,	467	HARUN RASHID		129
AND WROTE BY CANDLE LIGHT: BUT HER FORM MOVED	467	HARUN RASHID	V	129
NO DARK TOMB-HAUNTER ONCE: HER FORM ALL FULL	618	BRONZE HEAD		8
COMPLEXION AND FORM PROVE SUPERHUMAN,	637	BEN BULBEN		6
THE DOVES WHOSE GROWING FORM HE'D WATCHED. NOT THESE	710	FERENCZ RENYI	V	21

FORMATION

AND HALF A DOZEN IN FORMATION THERE,	489	COOLE PARK 29		20

FORMED   SEE FAN-FORMED

FORMLESS

A FABULOUS, FORMLESS DARKNESS IN:	438	SONGS PLAY 2		5
AND BY ITS FORMLESS SPAWNING FURY WRECKED,	611	STATUES		30

FORMS

"THESE FORMS?" "VEX NOT WITH SPEECH THE PHANTOMS DREAD."	29	OISIN 2	V	5
HUGE FORMS OF STONE: BETWEEN THE LIDS OF ONE	31	OISIN 2	V	37
THE DEAD GOD'S SWORD, TO MANY FORMS HE GREW,	40	OISIN 2	V	175
FORMS WITHOUT NUMBER! WHEN THE LIVE WEST FLASHED	41	OISIN 2	V	180
FOR PAINTED FORMS OR BOXES OF MAKE-UP	564	GYRES		13
WHICH OF HER FORMS HAS SHOWN HER SUBSTANCE RIGHT?	618	BRONZE HEAD		11
FORMS A STARK EGYPTIAN THOUGHT,	638	BEN BULBEN		43
FORMS THAT GENTLER PHIDIAS WROUGHT.	638	BEN BULBEN		44
RESEMBLE FORMS THAT ARE OR SEEM	639	BEN BULBEN		58
THE DOVES WHOSE GROWING FORMS HE'D WATCHED. NOT THESE	710	FERENCZ RENYI		21

FORSAKE

PRIMORDIAL MOTHERHOOD FORSAKE HIS LIMBS, THE CHILD			
NO LONGER REST,	559	MAGIC DRUM	2

FORSAKEN   SEE GOD-FORSAKEN

"LIKE ME WERE SOME GALLEY FORSAKEN FAR OFF IN MERIDIAN			
ISLE,	55	OISIN 3	117

FORSWEAR

THAT SHE FORSWEAR HER HERESIES AND SAVE	698	MOSADA 2	46

FORSWEARS

FORSWEARS HIS WANDERING 'MONG THE PINE,	686	LIFE	6

FORTH

I DREW IT FORTH: THE STAFF OF WOOD,	24	OISIN 1	V	366
"OH, SIGH, AWAKE AND GO YOU FORTH FOR ME:	33	OISIN 2	V	57
HE HAD GONE WHISPERING FORTH WITH CUMBERED HEART,	37	OISIN 2	V	111
SNATCHING THE HORN OF NIAM, I BLEW FORTH A LINGERING NOTE:	51	OISIN 3	V	57
FORTH, PIERCING THE DISTANCE--	54	OISIN 3	V	112
COMING FORTH FROM THE SEA LIKE THE MORNING	58	OISIN 3	V	158
LEANING FORTH FROM THE GEM-STUDDED SADDLE,	60	OISIN 3	V	187
MAYBE YOU HAVE NOT HEARD OF US, YOU HAVE COME FORTH SO	75	ANASHU VIJAYA		78
NEWLY,				
HE DROVE ME FORTH AND SHUT THE DOOR,	95	MOLL MAGEE	V	25
THEY WENT FORTH TO THE BATTLE, BUT THEY ALWAYS FELL	113	ROSE OF BATTLE	V	T
AND STRETCHING FORTH HIS ARM AND CUP	275	GREY ROCK		118
I HAD THE WISDOM LOVE BRINGS FORTH:	313	MEMORY YOUTH		2
AND SEND IMAGINATION FORTH	410	TOWER		20
IN SOME LIKE CHAMBER, SHADOWING FORTH	419	MY HOUSE		15
BUT O! AMBITIOUS HEART, HAD SUCH A PROOF DRAWN FORTH	427	PHANTOM HATRED		36
OR THE UNCERTAINTY OF HIS SETTING FORTH?	444	SCHOOL CHILDR		40
THE GYRES! THE GYRES! OLD ROCKY FACE, LOOK FORTH:	564	GYRES		1
AND THIS BROUGHT FORTH A DREAM AND SOON ENOUGH	630	CIRCUS ANIMALS		23
MAIDEN, COME FORTH! THE WOODS KEEP WATCH FOR THEE:	645	ISLE STAT I 1		1
COME FORTH! THE MORN IS FAIR! AS FROM THE PYRE	645	ISLE STAT I 1		8
COME FORTH, COME FORTH, MY MUSIC FLOWS FOR THEE:	645	ISLE STAT I 1		20
COME FORTH, COME FORTH, MY MUSIC FLOWS FOR THEE,	645	ISLE STAT I 1		20
COME FORTH, FOR IN A THOUSAND BOWERS	647	ISLE STAT I 1		64
HAD DRIVEN HER FORTH, FOR EVER MORE	668	ISLE STAT II 3		56
HAD DRIVEN HER FORTH, FOR EVERMORE	668	ISLE STAT II 3	V	56
FORTH! FORTH! O SPIRITS, YE HAVE HEARD YOUR TASK!	669	ISLE STAT II 3		81
FORTH! FORTH! O SPIRITS, YE HAVE HEARD YOUR TASK!	669	ISLE STAT II 3	V	81
FORTH FROM THE HOLLOW ALDER TRUNK	670	ISLE STAT II 3		120
THOU CALLED'ST ME FORTH. AND HOW THOU MADEST ME	683	SEEKER		52
TO MINE, AND HE IS SLOWLY SUCKING FORTH	684	SEEKER	V	63A
GIVES FORTH. HE, THE ETERNAL, WORKS HIS WILL.	689	NETTLESHIP		16
WHITE LILIES, AND HER SONG FLEW FORTH AFAR	693	MOSADA 1		85
MY MOTHER DREW FORTH FROM THE LONG GRASS	708	FAIRY PEDANT		23
NOR, GAZING FORTH WHERE LIFE'S SAD SICKLES REAP,	710	FERENCZ RENYI		31

FORTIETH

AND FROM THE FORTIETH WINTER BY THAT THOUGHT	501	VACILLATION	29

FORTUNE

THE FORTUNE THAT HAD BEEN MY SHAME	274	GREY ROCK	93
AND EVIL FORTUNE HAVE OVERTHROWN SAILED HITHER	757	SHADOW WATER A	196

FORTUNE'S

FLIETH FORTUNE'S FURIOUS WHEEL.	737	IN FIRELIGHT	8

FORTUNE-TELLER

THE COZENING FORTUNE-TELLER THAT COMES WHISPERING,	228	SHADOW WATER B	123

FORTY

WHY MUST I LIVE SOME THIRTY, FORTY YEARS,	285	TWO KINGS	199
FORTY YEARS LATER	542	PARN FUNERAL 2	V T
I FASTED FOR SOME FORTY DAYS ON BREAD AND BUTTERMILK,	592	PILGRIM	1

FORTY-NINE

ALTHOUGH I HAVE COME CLOSE ON FORTY-NINE,	270	PARDON FATHERS	20

FOSTER

MY FOSTER MOTHER'S GARDEN IN THE SOUTH	758	SHADOW WATER A	V	227
I SAT BESIDE MY FOSTER MOTHER, AND NOW	762	SHADOW WATER A	V	292

	PAGE	TITLE		LINE
FOSTER (CONTINUED)				
MY FOSTER MOTHER SANG IN AN OLD RHYME	763	SHADOW WATER A	V	314
FOSTER-MOTHER				
I SAT BESIDE MY FOSTER-MOTHER, AND NOW	762	SHADOW WATER A		292
MY FOSTER-MOTHER SANG IN AN OLD RHYME	763	SHADOW WATER A		314
FOSTER-MOTHER'S				
MY FOSTER-MOTHER'S GARDEN IN THE SOUTH	758	SHADOW WATER A		227
FOUGHT SEE STAR-FOUGHT				
AND FOUGHT WITH THE INVULNERABLE TIDE.	111	CUCHULAIN SEA		86
AND DUG ITS CLAWS AND SHRIEKED AND FOUGHT.	385	ROBARTES DANCE		8
CUCHULAIN THAT FOUGHT NIGHT LONG WITH THE FOAM,	549	SEVERED HEAD		9
HE FOUGHT THE MIGHT OF ENGLAND.	586	PARNELLITES		11
I WALK IN A BATTLE FOUGHT OVER AGAIN,	591	WHAT WAS LOST		2
THAT FOUGHT IN THE POST OFFICE	608	SONGS BURDEN 3		5
CUCHULAIN FOUGHT THE UNGOVERNABLE SEA;	630	CIRCUS ANIMALS		26
FOUGHT ONCE FOR SELF-SAME REASON ON THE HEM	660	ISLE STAT II 1		32
AND SHOREWARD WAVES, WE NIGH HAVE FOUGHT; WAVES BRING	660	ISLE STAT II 1		44
I FOUGHT TWELVE BATTLES DRESSED IN GOLDEN ARMOUR.	761	SHADOW WATER A		271
DANCED, LAUGHED, LOVED, FOUGHT THROUGH	787	HUDDON DUDDON		4
FOUL				
YOUR ENEMY, AN OLD FOUL MOUTH, HAD SET	292	TO A SHADE		17
AN OLD FOUL MOUTH THAT ONCE CRIED OUT ON YOU	292	TO A SHADE	V	17
AN OLD FOUL MOUTH THAT SLANDERED YOU HAD SET	292	TO A SHADE	V	17
WITH A FOUL WITCH	310	WITCH		3
AND THIS FOUL WORLD WERE DEAD AT LAST.	388	SOLOMON WITCH		16
DRINKING THE FOUL DITCH WHERE THEY LIE?	397	POLIT PRISONER		12
OF THE FOUL WEATHER, HAIL AND RAIN,	424	ROAD AT DOOR		9
TO BAR THAT FOUL STORM OUT, FOR WE	432	NINETEEN 19		111
PERMIT FOUL YEARS TO WEAR	472	ALL SOUL NIGHT		49
THAT FEED ON SOME FOUL PARASITE	493	AT ALGECIRAS		2
THAT FEEDS ON SOME FOUL PARASITE	493	AT ALGECIRAS	V	2
NOT IN SOME FOUL STY."	513	JANE TALK BISH		6
"FAIR AND FOUL ARE NEAR OF KIN,	513	JANE TALK BISH		7
AND FAIR NEEDS FOUL," I CRIED.	513	JANE TALK BISH		8
FOR THE FOUL WINDS BLOW:	523	MAD AS MIST		2
WRAPPING THAT FOUL BODY UP	525	DANCING DAYS		5
IN AS FOUL A RAG:	525	DANCING DAYS		6
NO FOX CAN FOUL THE LAIR THE BADGER SWEPT--	603	GALLERY REVIS		39
FOUL GOAT-HEAD, BRUTAL ARM APPEAR,	612	NEWS ORACLE		33
ON THIS FOUL WORLD IN ITS DECLINE AND FALL:	619	BRONZE HEAD		24
WITH AN OLD FOUL TUNE.	627	STATES HOLIDAY		38
IN THE FOUL RAG-AND-BONE SHOP OF THE HEART.	630	CIRCUS ANIMALS		40
IN THE FOUL RAG AND BONE SHOP OF THE HEART.	630	CIRCUS ANIMALS	V	40
OH DEATH IS HORRIBLE: AND FOUL, FOUL, FOUL:	675	ISLE STAT II 3		238
OH DEATH IS HORRIBLE: AND FOUL, FOUL, FOUL:	675	ISLE STAT II 3		238
OH DEATH IS HORRIBLE: AND FOUL, FOUL, FOUL:	675	ISLE STAT II 3		238
AND DREAD NO MORE FOUL AUTUMN'S WING,	737	SUMMER EVENING		18
FOUND				
AND FOUND ON THE DOVE-GREY EDGE OF THE SEA	3	OISIN 1		19
I FOUND IN THAT FORGETFULNESS	24	OISIN 1		365
AND FOUND THE HORSE AND BRIDLED HIM,	25	OISIN 1		378
AND TELL ME THAT YOU FOUND A MAN UNBID,	33	OISIN 2		67
THAT WOMAN FOUND A RING HUNG ON THE WALL,	37	OISIN 2		120
THAT MAIDEN FOUND A RING HUNG ON THE WALL,	37	OISIN 2	V	120
WHO BROUGHT US FOUND A TORCH, AND, WITH ITS FLARE	37	OISIN 2	V	122
AND FOUND A DOOR DEEP SUNKEN IN THE WALL,	39	OISIN 2		154
I FOUND A DOOR DEEP-SUNKEN IN THE WALL,	39	OISIN 2	V	154
I FOUND, DROPPING SEA-FOAM ON THE WIDE STAIR,	43	OISIN 2		215
I FOUND, FOAM-OOZY ON THE VASTY STAIR,	43	OISIN 2	V	215
I FOUND, DROPPING SEA FOAM ON THE WIDE STAIR,	43	OISIN 2	V	215
SOUGHT ONCE AGAIN THE SHORE, AND FOUND A SHELL,	68	SAD SHEPHERD		18
AND FOUND HER DYEING CLOTH WITH SUBTLE CARE	105	CUCHULAIN SEA	V	2A
WHOSE BLADE COMPELS, AND WAIT, TILL THE HAVE FOUND	108	CUCHULAIN SEA		37
AT THE SWORD-POINT, AND WAITS TILL WE HAVE FOUND	109	CUCHULAIN SEA		53
AT THE SWORD POINT, AND WAITS TILL WE HAVE FOUND	109	CUCHULAIN SEA	V	53
THE MAN HAS FOUND NO COMFORT IN THE GRAVE.	128	DREAM OF FAERY		48
IN HER HEART SHE FOUND A TUNE,	160	CAP AND BELLS	V	26
BUT I HAVE FOUND WHERE THE WIND GOES	168	BLESSED	V	27
UNTIL HE FOUND, WITH LAUGHTER AND WITH TEARS,	170	SECRET ROSE		24
THEY FOUND AN OLD MAN RUNNING THERE:	190	BAILE AILLINN		25
AND POETS FOUND, OLD WRITERS SAY,	197	BAILE AILLINN		187
WHERE ONE FOUND LANCELOT CRAZED AND HID HIM FOR A WHILE:	209	UNDER THE MOON		3
WHERE ONE FOUND LANCELOT CRAZED, AND HID HIM FOR AWHILE,	209	UNDER THE MOON	V	3
FOR WE HAVE FOUND A TREASURE THAT'S SO GREAT	248	SHADOW WATER B		540
AND BEING THANKFUL MURROUGH FOUND,	274	GREY ROCK		77
WHAT MAN YOU HAVE LOST, WHAT EVIL YOU HAVE FOUND."	280	TWO KINGS		86
FOUND THAT OLD HOUSE, A SPUTTERING TORCH WITHIN,	283	TWO KINGS		140
AND FOUND THE HOUSE, A SPUTTERING TORCH WITHIN,	283	TWO KINGS	V	140
AND WITH HIM HAVE FOUND EVERY HAPPINESS	284	TWO KINGS		174
I HAVE NOT FOUND A THING TO EAT,	294	THREE BEGGARS		3
BUT YEAR BY YEAR I FOUND THAT LESS	305	HOUR DAWN		68
AND WHEN AT ONE YEAR'S END I FOUND	305	HOUR DAWN		71
I HAVE FOUND OUT HOW DESPAIRING	313	TWO YEAR LATER	V	3
AS THOUGH I HAD FOUND IN A BOOK	329	MEN IMPROVE		6
AS THOUGH I HAD FOUND IN BOOK	329	MEN IMPROVE	V	6
AND ALL DAY LONG WE HAVE FOUND	333	SOLOMON SHEBA		22
THAT FOUND WHEN I HAD NEITHER GOAT NOR GRAZING	340	SHEP GOATHERD		31
IS HOT TO SHOW WHATEVER IT HAS FOUND.	340	SHEP GOATHERD		44
HAVE FOUND THE PATH MY GOATS' FEET CANNOT FIND.	342	SHEP GOATHERD		84
HAVE FOUND THE PATH MY GOAT'S FEET CANNOT FIND.	342	SHEP GOATHERD	V	84
BUT WALK BY THE DRY THORN UNTIL I HAVE FOUND	351	HER PRAISE		12

302

		PAGE	TITLE	LINE

FOUND (CONTINUED)
OR WHO HAVE FOUND A PAINTER TO MAKE THEM SO FOR PAY . . .   353 HIS PHOENIX   6
HE NEVER FOUND HIS REST ASHORE. . . . .   361 ALF POLLEXFEN   21
DANTE ALIGHIERI, SO UTTERLY FOUND HIMSELF . . . . .   368 EGO DOMINUS   19
HE FOUND THE UNPERSUADABLE JUSTICE, HE FOUND . . . .   369 EGO DOMINUS   36
HE FOUND THE UNPERSUADABLE JUSTICE, HE FOUND . . . .   369 EGO DOMINUS   36
AND SING WHEN THEY HAVE FOUND IT. NO, NOT SING, . .   369 EGO DOMINUS   41
A STYLE IS FOUND BY SEDENTARY TOIL . . . .   370 EGO DOMINUS   65
HE HAS FOUND, AFTER THE MANNER OF HIS KIND, ...   373 PHASES OF MOON   12
THE HARE MAY RUN TILL IT'S FOUND . . . .   380 SONGS FOOL 1   11
THAT NOW, IT MAY BE, HAS FOUND . . . .   381 SONGS FOOL 2   13
YOUR COCKEREL FOUND US IN THE WRONG . . . .   388 SOLOMON WITCH   34
FOR THOSE NEW COMRADES THEY HAVE FOUND, ...   395 SIXTEEN DEAD   15
HELEN BEING CHOSEN FOUND LIFE FLAT AND DULL . . . .   404 FOR DAUGHTER   25
BUT I HAVE FOUND AN ANSWER IN THOSE EYES . . . . .   413 TOWER   101
HAD HE NOT FOUND IT CERTAIN BEYOND DREAMS . . . . .   417 ANCEST HOUSES   10
BUT THAT HE FOUND MORE SUBSTANCE THERE THAN DREAMS, .   417 ANCEST HOUSES   V   10
TWO MEN HAVE FOUND IT HERE. A MAN-AT-ARMS . . . .   420 MY HOUSE   V   21
BUT IS THERE ANY COMFORT TO BE FOUND? . . . . . .   429 NINETEEN 19   41
INCENDIARY OR BIGOT COULD BE FOUND . . . .   430 NINETEEN 19   45
I BRING FULL-FLAVOURED WINE OUT OF A BARREL FOUND .   442 BLACK CENTAUR   10
I BRING FULL FLAVOURED WINE OUT OF A BARREL FOUND .   442 BLACK CENTAUR   V   10
HAS FOUND THE LOVELIEST SPECTACLE THERE IS. . . . .   447 COLONUS PRAISE   24
AND FOUND A HEART OF STONE . . . .   451 FIRST LOVE   8
A MERMAID FOUND A SWIMMING LAD, ...   452 MERMAID   1
A CRAZY MAN THAT FOUND A CUP, ...   454 EMPTY CUP   1
OCTOBER LAST I FOUND IT TOO . . . .   454 EMPTY CUP   7
BUT FOUND IT DRY AS BONE. . . . .   454 EMPTY CUP   8
A MYSTERY THAT ELSE HAD FOUND NO CHRONICLER . . . .   461 HARUN RASHID   21
I WOULD HAVE FOUND THE BEST THAT LIFE CAN GIVE, . .   465 HARUN RASHID   91
SOME FOUND A DIFFERENT POLE, AND WHERE IT STOOD . .   483 VERONIC NAPKIN   7
FOUND PRIDE ESTABLISHED IN HUMILITY. . . . . . .   489 COOLE PARK 29   15
FOUND CERTAINTY UPON THE DREAMING AIR, ...   489 COOLE PARK 29   22
GREAT ROOMS WHERE TRAVELLED MEN AND CHILDREN FOUND .   491 COOLE BALLYLEE   29
THAT HE HAD FOUND A TEXT TO PROVE . . . .   492 ANNE GREGORY   15
HAD I NOT FOUND CONTENT AMONG THE SHOWS . . . . .   499 MOTHER OF GOD   6
FIT AUDIENCE FOUND, BUT CANNOT RULE . . . .   506 REMORSE SPEECH   4
I FOUND THAT IVORY IMAGE THERE . . . .   514 JANE GROWN OLD   1
"A CHILD FOUND ALL A CHILD CAN LACK," . . . . . .   521 THREE THINGS   3
FOUND ALL THE PLEASURE THAT LIFE GAVE"! . . . . .   521 THREE THINGS   11
THAT HAVE FOUND IT WHERE YOU FED. . . . .   522 LULLABY   2
TO MIGHTY PARIS WHEN HE FOUND . . . .   522 LULLABY   4
WHAT WERE THEY WHEN PARIS FOUND . . . .   522 LULLABY   V   4
OR FOUND A SUBTERRANEAN REST . . . .   535 CHOSEN   6
HE IT HAS FOUND SHALL FIND THEREIN . . . .   538 LAST CONFESS   17
HAD FOUND A SWEETER WORD. . . . .   539 MEETING   18
BECAUSE YOU HAVE FOUND ME IN THE PITCH-DARK NIGHT .   554 RIBH AT TOMB   1
BECAUSE YOU HAVE FOUND ME IN THE PITCH DARK NIGHT .   554 RIBH AT TOMB   V   1
IN BROKEN SENTENCES. MY SOUL HAD FOUND . . . . .   557 RIBH ECSTASY   3
ALL MEN HAVE AIMED AT, FOUND AND LOST! . . . . .   566 LAPIS LAZULI   18
HEROICALLY LOST, HEROICALLY FOUND. . . . .   578 CRAZED GIRL   8
YOU ASK WHAT I HAVE FOUND, AND FAR AND WIDE I GO! .   580 CURSE CROMWELL   1
AND FOUND HIS FAMILY TOMB . . . .   584 GHOST ROG CASE   32
FOUND MANY A FAMOUS MAN THERE! . . . .   584 GHOST ROG CASE   35
THEY THAT FOUND HIM FOUND UPON . . . .   585 ORAHILLY   32
THEY THAT FOUND HIM FOUND UPON . . . .   585 ORAHILLY   32
AND THERE I FOUND AN OLD MAN, AND THOUGH I PRAYED ALL DAY   593 PILGRIM   8
AND FOUND AN EMPTY ROOM. . . . .   594 COLONEL MARTIN   8
HIS WIFE HE FOUND AND THE RICH MAN . . . .   595 COLONEL MARTIN   43
HONOUR HAD LIVED SO LONG, ALL LACKING FOUND. . . .   603 GALLERY REVIS   35
HONOUR HAD LIVED SO LONG, THEIR HEALTH I FOUND. . .   603 GALLERY REVIS   V   35
I HAVE FOUND NOTHING HALF SO GOOD . . . .   624 APPARITIONS   9
I HAVE FOUND SOMETHING WORSE . . . .   628 JANE MOUNTAIN   5
AND FOUND. 'TIS WELL!—ANOTHER MILE OF WAY . . .   651 ISLE STAT I 2   6
THE FLOWER, SAVE SOME THING BE FOUND . . . . . .   668 ISLE STAT II 3   51
THE TALKING WINDS HAVE FOUND THEIR HOME, ...   686 LIFE   9
A GREY-HAIRED YOUTH, WHOSE CHEEKS HAD NEVER FOUND, .   687 TWO TITANS   7
THAN OLD MEN'S ANY DAY, AS MERLIN FOUND. . . . .   721 WITCH VIVIEN   47
HAVE FOUND DELIGHT, IN THE RESOUNDING OARS, ...   750 SHADOW WATER A   72
I LEFT HER LIVING, THINKING THAT I HAD FOUND . . .   755 SHADOW WATER A   174
I HAVE FOUND NOTHING BUT THESE EMPTY WATERS! . . .   757 SHADOW WATER A   201
I SAID THE ALE WAS BROWN. I HAVE FOUND THE ALE, .   759 SHADOW WATER A   244
HAVE FOUND IT LIKE THE FROTH UPON THE ALE. . . . .   767 SHADOW WATER A   387
FOUNDATION
FROM THE DIM WOOD'S FOUNDATION— . . . .   672 ISLE STAT II 3   162
FOUNDATIONS
ON THE FOUNDATIONS OF A HOUSE, OR WHERE . . . . .   409 TOWER   18
FOUNDED
TWO MEN HAVE FOUNDED HERE. A MAN-AT-ARMS . . . .   420 MY HOUSE   21
FOUNDERS
A SPOT WHEREON THE FOUNDERS LIVED AND DIED . . . .   491 COOLE BALLYLEE   33
FOUNT
I'D BE ALONE. WE TWO, BY THAT PALE FOUNT, ...   650 ISLE STAT I 1   132
FOUNTAIN
HAD RUN INTO ONE FOUNTAIN. SPEAK TO HIM. . . . .   249 SHADOW WATER B   561
THE FOUNTAIN LEAP, AND AT DAWN . . . .   414 TOWER   124
AND NOT A FOUNTAIN, WERE THE SYMBOL WHICH . . . .   418 ANCEST HOUSES   15
AND YET HERSELF CAN SEEM YOUTH'S VERY FOUNTAIN, . .   465 HARUN RASHID   89
BY DAY AND NIGHT A LONELY FOUNTAIN SINGS, ...   650 ISLE STAT I 1   130
FOUNTAIN'S
SAT DOWN UPON THE FOUNTAIN'S MARBLE EDGE, ...   463 HARUN RASHID   43

303

FOUNTAINS
    THE IMMORTALS MOVED AMONG THE FOUNTAINS • • • • •   25 OISIN 1   386
    THE FAIRIES MOVED AMONG THE FOUNTAINS, • • • • • •   25 OISIN 1   V 386
FOUNTS
    BATHED IN FLAMING FOUNTS OF DUTY • • • • • • • • • 124 CATHLEEN PARA   5
FOUR   SEE NINETY-FOUR
    YET NOW I CHOOSE, FOR THESE FOUR FEET • • • • • •   6 OISIN 1   57
    CARRY ME, YE FOUR, • • • • • • • • • • • • •   97 FOXHUNTER   2
    AND CARRY ME YE FOUR, • • • • • • • • • • • •   97 FOXHUNTER   V   2
    AND CARRY ME, YOU FOUR, • • • • • • • • • • •   97 FOXHUNTER   V   2
    FOR FOUR DAYS WARRED HE WITH THE BITTER TIDE, • • 111 CUCHULAIN SEA V 85
    OLD DUBLIN MERCHANT "FREE OF TEN AND FOUR" • • • • 269 PARDON FATHERS   3
    OLD DUBLIN MERCHANT "FREE OF THE TEN AND FOUR" • • 269 PARDON FATHERS V 3
    FOUR SONGS FROM THE YOUNG COUNTRYMAN • • • • • • 451 FIRST LOVE   T
    FROM FOUR GREAT MINDS THAT HATED WHIGGERY, • • • 486 SEVEN SAGES   7
    WHAT SCHOOLING HAD THESE FOUR? THEY WALKED THE ROADS • • 487 SEVEN SAGES   24
    FOUR POEMS CRACKED MARY AND THE BISHOP • • • • 507 JANE BISHOP   V T
    THE FOUR AGES OF MAN • • • • • • • • • • • • • 561 FOUR AGES MAN   T
    HE NEVER LAY BEHIND FOUR WALLS • • • • • • • • • 606 SONGS BURDEN 1   12
    WITH THREE BARS CROSSED, AND THESE FOUR WALLS MY WORLD, 700 MOSADA 3   32
    IN THE LONG GRASS--FOUR EYES DROOP LOW--A SEAT • 716 DWELT SYCAMORE 11
    AMONG THESE MISTY WATERS. TWO! NOW FOUR! • • • • 753 SHADOW WATER A 138
    NOW FOUR TOGETHER! I SHALL HEAR THEIR WORDS • • • 753 SHADOW WATER A 139
FOURS
    UPON ALL FOURS• • • • • • • • • • • • • • • • 572 LADYS 1ST SONG   12
FOURSCORE
    AND EACH OF THE HUGE WHITE CREATURES WAS HUGER THAN
        FOURSCORE MEN!   49 OISIN 3   33
    AS WORDS OF THINE THROUGH FOURSCORE YEARS HAVE FILLED • • 683 SEEKER   46
FOUR-SCORE
    AND EACH OF THE HUGE WHITE CREATURES WAS HUGER THAN
        FOUR-SCORE MEN!   49 OISIN 3   V 33
FOUR-SIX
    FOUR-SIX• • • • • • • • • • • • • • • • • 721 WITCH VIVIEN   41
FOURTEEN
    SOME FOURTEEN DAYS OF CIVIL WAR! • • • • • • • • 425 STARES NEST   12
FOURTEENTH
    UNDER THE FRENZY OF THE FOURTEENTH MOON, • • • • • 374 PHASES OF MOON   53
FOURTH
    WE FEASTED FOR THREE DAYS. ON THE FOURTH MORN • •   43 OISIN 2   214
    THREE DAYS WE FEASTED, WHEN ON THE FOURTH MORN • •   43 OISIN 2   V 214
    TO LIE UNTIL THE FOURTH MORN SAW EMERGE • • • •   44 OISIN 2   220
    TO LIE THERE 'TILL THE FOURTH DAY SAW EMERGE • •   44 OISIN 2   V 220
    TO LIE UNTIL THE FOURTH MORN SUN EMERGE • • • • •   44 OISIN 2   V 220
FOWL
    "BUT NEVER WITH US WHERE THE WILD FOWL CHASES • •   27 OISIN 1   V 408
    THE WILD FOWL OF THE AIR INCREASED! • • • • • • •   82 MAD KING GOLL   8
    ALTHOUGH THE RUSHES AND THE FOWL OF THE AIR • • • 177 PAST GREATNESS V 11
    FISH, FLESH, OR FOWL, COMMEND ALL SUMMER LONG • • 407 SAIL BYZANTIUM   5
FOWLS   SEE WATER-FOWLS
FOX
                             214 HAPPY TOWNLAND   13
    THE LITTLE FOX HE MURMURED, • • • • • • • • • 214 HAPPY TOWNLAND   17
    BUT THE LITTLE RED FOX MURMURED, • • • • • • • • 215 HAPPY TOWNLAND   33
    THE LITTLE FOX HE MURMURED, • • • • • • • • • 215 HAPPY TOWNLAND   37
    BUT THE LITTLE RED FOX MURMURED, • • • • • • • • 216 HAPPY TOWNLAND   53
    THE LITTLE FOX HE MURMURED, • • • • • • • • • 216 HAPPY TOWNLAND   57
    BUT THE LITTLE RED FOX MURMURED, • • • • • • • • 218 WOODS OF COOLE   13
    DIM INCHY WOOD, THAT HIDES BADGER AND FOX • • • • 580 CURSE CROMWELL   18
    AS THE FOX IN THE OLD FABLE DESTROYED THE SPARTAN BOY'S, 603 GALLERY REVIS   39
    NO FOX CAN FOUL THE LAIR THE BADGER SWEPT-- • • • • •
FOXES
    THEY LEFT THEIR HOMESTEADS TO FATTEN THE FOXES, • • • 546 TO SAME TUNE 2   3
    THEY LEFT THEIR HOMESTEADS TO SHELTER THE FOXES, • • • 546 TO SAME TUNE 2 V 3
    THEY LEFT THEIR HOMESTEADS TO FATTEN THE FOXES, • • • 613 MARCH SONGS 1   3
FOXGLOVE
    WHERE REVEL OF FOXGLOVE IS AND REVEL OF ROSES." • • • • 669 ISLE STAT II 3 V 86
FOX-GLOVE
    WHERE REVEL OF FOX-GLOVE IS AND REVEL OF ROSES." • • • • 669 ISLE STAT II 3   86
FOXHOUNDS
    WHEN WITH THE GALWAY FOXHOUNDS HE WOULD RIDE • • • • 326 ROBERT GREGORY   57
FOXHUNTER
    THE BALLAD OF THE FOXHUNTER • • • • • • • • • •   97 FOXHUNTER   T
    THE BALLAD OF THE OLD FOXHUNTER • • • • • • • • •   97 FOXHUNTER   V T
FOX-HUNTER
    THE BALLAD OF THE OLD FOX-HUNTER • • • • • • • • •   97 FOXHUNTER   V T
FRAGILE
    A FRAGILE, EXQUISITE, PALE SHELL, • • • • • • • • 784 WOMANS BEAUTY   16
FRAGMENT
    ISLAND OF STATUES A FRAGMENT • • • • • • • • • 666 ISLE STAT II 3 V T
FRAGMENTS
    AND THOSE WHITE GLIMMERING FRAGMENTS OF THE MIST SWEEP BY, 426 PHANTOM HATRED   6
    FRAGMENTS • • • • • • • • • • • • • • • • • • 439 FRAGMENTS   T
    FRAGMENTS THE GREAT DAY • • • • • • • • • • • 590 GREAT DAY   V T
FRAGRANCE
    LIFE SCARCE CAN CAST A FRAGRANCE ON THE WIND, • • • 422 MY DESCENDANTS   5
    I HAVE CUPBOARDS OF DRIED FRAGRANCE, • • • • • • • 572 LADYS 2ND SONG   5
    POURS UP AND FLOATS IN FRAGRANCE ROUND MY HEAD • • 691 MOSADA 1   40
    POURS UP AND FLOATS IN FRAGRANCE O'ER MY HEAD • • • 691 MOSADA 1   V 40
FRAGRANCES
    THEIR SUDDEN FRAGRANCES ON THE GREEN AIR! • • • • • 217 WOODS OF COOLE   10

```
                                                         PAGE     TITLE             LINE
FRAGRANT
    THE MIST-DROPS HUNG ON THE FRAGRANT TREES,  . . . . . .   2 OISIN 1         V    7F
    THEIR BROWS WERE WHITE AS FRAGRANT MILK,  . . . . . . .  15 OISIN 1              204
    THEIR BROWS WERE WHITE AS THE FRAGRANT MILK  . . . . .   15 OISIN 1         V    204
    RISES, AND SHOWERS ABROAD HIS FRAGRANT ARROWS,  . . . .  72 ANASHU VIJAYA        27
    IN THE BOSOM AFAR OF THE FRAGRANT WOOD.  . . . . . . .  717 LOVE SONG             9
FRAIL
    WHILE HIGH FRAIL CLOUDLETS, FED WITH A GREEN LIGHT,  . .  40 OISIN 2             165
    HUNG THE FRAIL LOFTIER CLOUDLETS.  TURNED HE SLOW--  . .  40 OISIN 2         V   167
    THE BIRD DESCENDS, AND HER FRAIL THIGHS ARE PRESSED  . . 441 LEDA AND SWAN   V    2
    FRAIL BIRD, LIKE A WHITE SEA-BIRD ALONE  . . . . . . .  784 WOMANS BEAUTY         2
FRANCE
    AMONG THE KINGS OF GREECE AND FRANCE."  . . . . . . .   296 THREE BEGGARS   V  32A
    AMERICAN COLONIES, IRELAND, FRANCE AND INDIA  . . . . . 487 SEVEN SAGES          15
FRANKINCENSE
    AND COVERS AWAY THE SMOKE OF MYRRH AND FRANKINCENSE;  . 173 SPEAKS HEARERS        4
FRAY         SEE SUN-FRECKLED
    THUNDERING, AND THE WIDE USELESS WATERS FRAY  . . . . .  45 OISIN 2         V  238
FRECKLED
    THE FRECKLED MAN WHO GOES  . . . . . . . . . . . . .   347 FISHERMAN             2
FREE         SEE SCOT-FREE FEVER-FREE
    THE SOUL IS FREE, AND FINDS NO FLAW,  . . . . . . . .    19 OISIN 1         V  284
    BUT WE, OH ROLLING STARS, ARE FREE.  . . . . . . . . .   22 OISIN 1         V  337
    IS NOT SO FREE, SO FREE, SO FREE.  . . . . . . . . . .   22 OISIN 1         V 338B
    IS NOT SO FREE, SO FREE, SO FREE.  . . . . . . . . . .   22 OISIN 1         V 338B
    IS NOT SO FREE, SO FREE, SO FREE.  . . . . . . . . . .   22 OISIN 1         V 338B
    AND AS I SANG MY SOUL WAS FREE,  . . . . . . . . . . .   86 MAD KING GOLL   V   65
    MY SINGING SANG ME FEVER FREE,  . . . . . . . . . . .    86 MAD KING GOLL   V   65
    TO A SHONEEN WHO HAD FREE LANDS  . . . . . . . . . . .   92 FATHER OHART          3
    . . . AND FREE OF THE FLAMES WOULD WE BE,  . . . . . .  122 WHITE BIRDS     V   11
    OLD DUBLIN MERCHANT "FREE OF TEN AND FOUR"  . . . . . . 269 PARDON FATHERS        3
    OLD DUBLIN MERCHANT "FREE OF THE TEN AND FOUR"  . . . . 269 PARDON FATHERS   V    3
    HE GAVE THE HOURS THEY HAD SET FREE  . . . . . . . . .  288 TO WEALTHY MAN       22
    DEAR FELLOW-ARTIST, WHY SO FREE  . . . . . . . . . . .  335 YOUNG BEAUTY          1
    DEAR FELLOW ARTIST WHY SO FREE  . . . . . . . . . . .   335 YOUNG BEAUTY    V    1
    THAT THE LAST SERVILE CRESCENT HAS SET FREE?  . . . . . 376 PHASES OF MOON      103
    THAT GAVE, THOUGH FREE TO REFUSE--  . . . . . . . . .   414 TOWER               133
    AND THERE, FREE AND YET FAST,  . . . . . . . . . . . .  472 ALL SOUL NIGHT       57
    AND BROKE THE CHAIN AND SET MY ANKLES FREE,  . . . . .  533 HER TRIUMPH           9
    AND FREE--'TWILL THIEVE AWAY WITH SLEEPY MOOD  . . . .  700 MOSADA 3             30
    OR YONDER MOUNTAINS.  WHERE?  THOU SHALT BE FREE--  . . 710 FERENCZ RENYI        15
    OR YONDER MOUNTAIN.  WHERE?  THOU SHALT BE FREE--  . .  710 FERENCZ RENYI   V   15
    "IF I WERE FREE TO DO AS LITTLE  . . . . . . . . . . .  731 PRIEST FAIRY         77
FREED
    FROM TERROR AND DECEPTION FREED IT CAN  . . . . . . .   558 RIBH CHRISTIAN        9
FREEDOM
    I SAW MY FREEDOM WON  . . . . . . . . . . . . . . . .   400 DEMON BEAST           7
    "GREAT PRINCE, FORGIVE THE FREEDOM OF MY SPEECH;  . . . 464 HARUN RASHID         74
    "IRELAND SHALL GET HER FREEDOM AND YOU STILL BREAK STONE."  590 PARNELL           2
FREELANDS
    TO A SHONEEN IN HIS FREELANDS,  . . . . . . . . . . .    92 FATHER OHART    V    3
FREEMAN
    THAT NEVER YET HAD FREEMAN  . . . . . . . . . . . . .   401 DEMON BEAST          36
FRENCH
    BEYOND THAT RIDGE LIVED MRS. FRENCH, AND ONCE  . . . .  410 TOWER                25
    THROUGH GOD-FORSAKEN MEADOWS; MRS. FRENCH,  . . . . .   412 TOWER                93
FRENZIED
    DANCING TO A FRENZIED DRUM,  . . . . . . . . . . . .   403 FOR DAUGHTER         15
    A FRENZIED CROWD, AND WHERE THE BRANCHES SPRANG  . . .  541 PARN FUNERAL 1        9
FRENZIES
    FRENZIES BEWILDER, REVERIES PERTURB THE MIND;  . . . .  426 PHANTOM HATRED        7
FRENZY
    TILL VAIN FRENZY AWOKE AND HE DIED; AND HIM  . . . . .  169 SECRET ROSE          12
    THAT THE GRAVE-DIGGERS IN A DREAMY FRENZY,  . . . . .   243 SHADOW WATER B      430
    THAT HE, WHEN FRENZY STIRRED HIS THEWS,  . . . . . . .  271 GREY ROCK            22
    THE FRENZY OF THE BEGGARS' MOON  . . . . . . . . . . .  296 THREE BEGGARS        43
    THE FRENZY OF THE BEGGAR'S MOON  . . . . . . . . . . .  296 THREE BEGGARS   V   43
    UNDER THE FRENZY OF THE FOURTEENTH MOON,  . . . . . .   374 PHASES OF MOON       53
    THAT HAVE THE FRENZY OF OUR WESTERN SEAS.  . . . . . .  384 VISION ROBART        62
    HANRAHAN ROSE IN FRENZY THERE  . . . . . . . . . . .   412 TOWER                71
    SWIFT BEATING ON HIS BREAST IN SIBYLLINE FRENZY BLIND  . 481 BLOOD AND MOON      19
    AND CLAMOUR IN DRUNKEN FRENZY FOR THE MOON.  . . . . .  482 BLOOD AND MOON       42
    GRANT ME AN OLD MAN'S FRENZY,  . . . . . . . . . . . .  576 ACRE OF GRASS        13
    OR INSPIRED BY FRENZY  . . . . . . . . . . . . . . .   576 ACRE OF GRASS        21
FRENZY-STRUCK
    BEGGAR TO BEGGAR CRIED, BEING FRENZY-STRUCK,  . . . . . 299 BEGGAR CRIED          3
    BEGGAR TO BEGGAR CRIED, BEING FRENZY-STRUCK,  . . . . . 300 BEGGAR CRIED          7
    BEGGAR TO BEGGAR CRIED, BEING FRENZY-STRUCK,  . . . . . 300 BEGGAR CRIED         11
    BEGGAR TO BEGGAR CRIED, BEING FRENZY-STRUCK,  . . . . . 300 BEGGAR CRIED         15
    BEGGAR TO BEGGAR CRIED, BEING FRENZY-STRUCK,  . . . . . 300 BEGGAR CRIED         19
FRESH
    FRESH IMAGES BEGET,  . . . . . . . . . . . . . . . .   498 BYZANTIUM            39
    HERE IS FRESH MATTER, POET,  . . . . . . . . . . . . .  553 CHURCH STATE          1
FRESHET
    NOAH'S FRESHET NEVER REACHED.  . . . . . . . . . . .   553 WISDOM               15
FRET
    "FRET NOT WITH SPEECH THE PHANTOMS DREAD,"  . . . . .    12 OISIN 1         V  148
    . . . AND FRET OF THE FLAMES WOULD WE BE,  . . . . . .  122 WHITE BIRDS          11
    OR STORMY SILVER FRET THE GOLD OF DAY,  . . . . . . .   128 DREAM OF FAERY       33
    AND THE FRET IS ON ME.  . . . . . . . . . . . . . . .  131 OLD PENSIONER   V    6
    AND THE FRET LIES ON ME.  . . . . . . . . . . . . . .  131 OLD PENSIONER   V    6
```

FRET   (CONTINUED)
        AND THE FRET IS ON ME.   132 OLD PENSIONER V   18
        AND THE FRET LIES ON ME.   132 OLD PENSIONER V   18
        FOR EVER FOAM AND FRET!   680 LOVE AND DEATH   4
FRETFUL
        THY FRETFUL WORDS A LITTLE WHILE,   66 HAPPY SHEPHERD   40
FRIEND   SEE HUNTER-FRIEND
        IN THE HOUSE OF A CHILD, OF A FRIEND, OF A BROTHER.   26 OISIN 1   401
        IN THE HOUSE OF HIS FRIEND, OF HIS KIN, OF HIS BROTHER,   26 OISIN 1   V 405
        THERE WAS A MAN WHOM SORROW NAMED HIS FRIEND,   67 SAD SHEPHERD   1
        AND THEN THE MAN WHOM SORROW NAMED HIS FRIEND   68 SAD SHEPHERD   8
        AND THEN THE MAN WHOM SORROW NAMED HIS FRIEND   68 SAD SHEPHERD   17
        THEN CRIED THE MAN WHOM SORROW NAMED HIS FRIEND!   68 SAD SHEPHERD   V   8
        I HAD A BEAUTIFUL FRIEND   152 LOSS OF LOVE   2
        THE LOVER PLEADS WITH HIS FRIEND FOR OLD FRIENDS   172 PLEADS FRIEND   T
        THE POET PLEADS WITH HIS FRIEND FOR OLD FRIENDS   172 PLEADS FRIEND   V T
        OF ONE WHO IS NO FRIEND TO ME OR TO MINE,   184 QUEEN MAEVE   V 94A
        FRIEND OF THESE MANY YEARS, YOU TOO HAD STOOD   186 QUEEN MAEVE   130
        FRIEND OF THESE MANY YEARS, YOU TO HAVE STOOD   186 QUEEN MAEVE   V 130
        OF THE HARPER'S DAUGHTER AND HER FRIEND.   192 BAILE AILLINN   76
        BECAUSE THEY HAVE MADE SO GOOD A FRIEND.   195 BAILE AILLINN   159
        AND SO BE PATIENT! BE WISE AND PATIENT FRIEND."   200 FOLLY COMFORT   V 6
        THAT BEAUTIFUL MILD WOMAN, YOUR CLOSE FRIEND.   204 ADAMS CURSE   2
        AND THEREFORE, FRIEND, IF YOUR GREAT RACE WERE RUN   265 THESE CLOUDS   7
        OLD COUNTRY SCHOLAR, ROBERT EMMET'S FRIEND,   269 PARDON FATHERS   5
        AND COUNTRY SCHOLAR, ROBERT EMMET'S FRIEND,   269 PARDON FATHERS   V 5
        "WHO IS THE FRIEND THAT SEEMS BUT AIR   274 GREY ROCK   83
        OF A NEW FRIEND HE HAS TURNED A GHOST.   275 GREY ROCK   103
        A FRIEND THAT COULD, HE HAD TOLD HER, WORK HIS CURE.   283 TWO KINGS   137
        AND WOULD BE NO HARSH FRIEND. WHEN NIGHT HAD DEEPENED,   283 TWO KINGS   138
        WESTWARD OF TARA, THERE TO AWAIT A FRIEND   283 TWO KINGS   V 136
        TO A FRIEND WHOSE WORK HAS COME TO NOTHING   290 TO A FRIEND   T
        YET NEVER HAVE I LIT ON A FRIEND   301 RUN PARADISE   25
        AND DREAM THAT ALL THE WORLD'S A FRIEND,   313 TWO YEAR LATER   8
        ALWAYS WE'D HAVE THE NEW FRIEND MEET THE OLD   324 ROBERT GREGORY   9
        AND WE ARE HURT IF EITHER FRIEND SEEM COLD,   324 ROBERT GREGORY   10
        BUT NOT A FRIEND THAT I WOULD BRING   324 ROBERT GREGORY   14
        THERE IS NOT A FOOL CAN CALL ME FRIEND,   336 YOUNG BEAUTY   16
        THAT NOT A FOOL CAN CALL ME FRIEND,   336 YOUNG BEAUTY   V 16
        EARNING RESPECT! HAVE NO STRANGE FRIEND!   337 SCHOLARS   V 9
        "AND IF MY DEAREST FRIEND WERE DEAD   338 TOM OROUGHLEY   15
                                                                  349 HAWK   17
        SHOULD GIVE TO MY FRIEND   352 PEOPLE   16
        I MIGHT HAVE HAD NO FRIEND THAT COULD NOT MIX   372 PHASES OF MOON   2
        HE AND HIS FRIEND, THEIR FACES TO THE SOUTH,   392 EASTER 1916   26
        THIS OTHER HIS HELPER AND FRIEND   404 FOR DAUGHTER   24
        THAT CHOOSES RIGHT, AND NEVER FIND A FRIEND.   409 TOWER   12
        CHOOSE PLATO AND PLOTINUS FOR A FRIEND   460 HARUN RASHID   V 2
        FOR THE GREAT CALIF'S TREASURER AND MY FRIEND,   472 ALL SOUL NIGHT   47
        AWAY FROM NEIGHBOUR OR FRIEND,   494 AT ALGECIRAS   8
        WOULD I CARRY TO A FRIEND--   494 AT ALGECIRAS   V 8
        I WOULD CARRY TO A FRIEND--   524 MAD AS MIST   13
        YOU ASK WHAT MAKES ME SIGH, OLD FRIEND,   540 FROM ANTIGONE   10
        BROTHER AND BROTHER, FRIEND AND FRIEND,   540 FROM ANTIGONE   10
        BROTHER AND BROTHER, FRIEND AND FRIEND,   552 SONGS REWRIT 2   6
        WITHOUT A FRIEND ON THE EARTH   552 SONGS REWRIT 2 V   6
        WITHOUT A FRIEND ON THIS EARTH   579 DOR WELLESLEY   V T
        TO A FRIEND   624 APPARITIONS   12
        WITH SOME FRIEND THAT HAS THE WIT   624 APPARITIONS   V 12
        WITH SOME FRIEND WHO HAS THE WIT   660 ISLE STAT II 1   38
        SIR PAGE, ALMINTOR'S FRIEND, AND THEREFORE LEARNED   661 ISLE STAT II 1   60
        WHAT IS IT, FRIEND? HE LOST I' THE WOODS THE CHIEF   695 MOSADA 1   115
        SHE WAS MY ONLY FRIEND! I'M LAME, YOU KNOW--   696 MOSADA 2   11
        I HAD A SISTER LIKE HER ONCE, MY FRIEND.   697 MOSADA 2   31
        FRIEND! BUT 'TWERE A DEADLY SIN   712 FERENCZ RENYI   66
        "NOW HATH HE KITH OR KIN, OR ANY FRIEND?"   787 GARRET CELLAR   2
        BUT EVERY BUTTERFLY TO A FRIEND.
FRIENDLIER
        A STERNER CONSCIENCE AND A FRIENDLIER HOME,   321 REED WHISPERER   8
FRIENDLY
        WITH A SWIFT AND FRIENDLY GLANCE   21 OISIN 1   309
        AND ALL GREW FRIENDLY FOR A LITTLE WHILE.   129 BOOK STORIES   8
        AND ALL WHO HEARD GREW FRIENDLY FOR A WHILE.   129 BOOK STORIES   V 8
FRIEND'S
        A FRIEND'S ILLNESS   267 FRIEND ILLNESS   T
        BUT NOT THAT MY DEAR FRIEND'S DEAR SON,   325 ROBERT GREGORY   46
        WITH A FRIEND'S OR AN ENEMY'S   362 DOLLS DRAWINGS   3
FRIENDS
        THE LOVER PLEADS WITH HIS FRIEND FOR OLD FRIENDS   172 PLEADS FRIEND   T
        THE POET PLEADS WITH HIS FRIEND FOR OLD FRIENDS   172 PLEADS FRIEND   V T
        AND NEW FRIENDS BUSY WITH YOUR PRAISE,   173 PLEADS FRIEND   3
        BUT THINK ABOUT OLD FRIENDS THE MOST!   173 PLEADS FRIEND   5
        AND OF NEW FRIENDS ARE GLAD WITH YOUR PRAISE,   173 PLEADS FRIEND   V 3
        BUT THINK OF YOUR OLD FRIENDS THE MOST!   173 PLEADS FRIEND   V 5
        TO WAIT THEIR FRIENDS! BUT WHEN THEIR FRIENDS HAVE COME   233 SHADOW WATER B   247
        TO WAIT THEIR FRIENDS! BUT WHEN THEIR FRIENDS HAVE COME   233 SHADOW WATER B   247
        THAT YOU MIGHT HAVE A TROOP OF FRIENDS.   273 GREY ROCK   58
        FRIENDS   315 FRIENDS   T
        I'LL NAME THE FRIENDS THAT CANNOT SUP WITH US   323 ROBERT GREGORY   2
        THAT DEEP-SWORN VOW HAVE BEEN FRIENDS OF MINE!   357 DEEP-SWORN VOW   2
        THAT DEEP SWORN VOW, HAVE BEEN FRIENDS OF MINE,   357 DEEP-SWORN VOW V   2
        HER FRIENDS BRING HER A CHRISTMAS TREE   366 HER CHRIS TREE   T

FRIENDS   (CONTINUED)
      HER FRIENDS BRING HER A CHRISTMAS-TREE . . . . . .   366 HER CHRIS TREE V   T
      LACKING THE COUNTENANCE OF OUR FRIENDS. AND YET . . . . .   368 EGO DOMINUS   17
      THE DEATH OF FRIENDS, OR DEATH . . . .   416 TOWER   189
      A COMPANY OF FRIENDS, A CONSCIENCE SET AT EASE, ...   427 PHANTOM HATRED   37
      THE FRIENDS OF HIS YOUTH . . . .   455 FRIENDS YOUTH   T
      OF FRIENDS THAT ARE GONE, ...   458 SECRETS OF OLD V   14
      SEEMED SO ON PURPOSE, MUTTERED JAFFER'S FRIENDS, ...   462 HARUN RASHID   37
      FOR IN MY FIRST HARD SPRINGTIME WE WERE FRIENDS, ...   473 ALL SOUL NIGHT   62
      FOR IN MY FIRST HARD SPRING-TIME WE WERE FRIENDS, ...   473 ALL SOUL NIGHT V   62
      "MY FRIENDS ARE GONE, BUT THAT'S A TRUTH . . . . . .   513 JANE TALK BISH   9
      FRIENDS THAT HAVE BEEN FRIENDS INDEED: . . . . . .   577 WHAT THEN   9
      FRIENDS THAT HAVE BEEN FRIENDS INDEED: . . . . . .   577 WHAT THEN   9
      AND ALL MY FRIENDS WERE THERE AND MADE ME WELCOME TOO: . .   581 CURSE CROMWELL   27
      JOHN BULL AND THE SEA ARE FRIENDS: . . . .   583 GHOST ROG CASE   4
      AND SAY MY GLORY WAS I HAD SUCH FRIENDS. . . . . . .   604 GALLERY REVIS   55
      BUT FRIENDS WALK BY FRIENDS. . . . .   621 JOHN KINSELLA   32
      BUT FRIENDS WALK BY FRIENDS. . . . .   621 JOHN KINSELLA   32
      BUT I'D A TROOP OF FRIENDS . . . .   626 STATES HOLIDAY   6
      FOR PEACE AND LAUGHTER HAVE BEEN SELDOM FRIENDS. . . .   670 ISLE STAT II 3   103
      TWO SPIRIT THINGS A MAN HATH FOR HIS FRIENDS! . . . .   686 DRAWING-ROOM   5
      AND SPIDERS ARE MY FRIENDS: I'M THEIRS, AND THEY ARE . .   693 MOSADA 1   64
      TWO SPIRIT-THINGS A MAN HATH FOR HIS FRIENDS-- . . . .   734 QUATRAIN APHOR   5
      TWO SPIRIT THINGS A MAN HATH FOR HIS FRIENDS! . . . .   734 QUATRAIN APHOR V   5
      THE HAND THAT WOUNDS HIM, BECAUSE THE GODS ARE HIS FRIENDS.   758 SHADOW WATER A   232
      THE FRIENDS THAT HAVE IT I DO WRONG . . . .   778 FRIENDS WRONG   1
FRIENDS'
      WHERE MY FRIENDS' PORTRAITS HANG AND LOOK THEREON: . . .   604 GALLERY REVIS   52
FRIENDSHIP
      A FRIENDSHIP OF HER KIND . . . .   345 ON WOMAN   4
      SEEING THAT LOVE AND FRIENDSHIP ARE ENOUGH, ...   423 MY DESCENDANTS   20
      FOR AN OLD NEIGHBOUR'S FRIENDSHIP CHOSE THE HOUSE . . .   423 MY DESCENDANTS   21
      AND TOLD HIM SO, BUT FRIENDSHIP NEVER ENDS: . . . .   473 ALL SOUL NIGHT   65
FRIGHT
      MY ENEMY AND HOPE: DEMONS FOR FRIGHT . . . . . .   34 OISIN 2   81
      THE DEMONS OF THE WILDS AND WINDS FOR FRIGHT . . . .   34 OISIN 2   V   81B
      PUTS ALL MEN IN A FRIGHT, ...   597 MODEL LAUREATE   12
      THAT OPENS HER MYSTERY AND FRIGHT. . . . .   624 APPARITIONS   22
      YE SAID THAT YE WOULD FRIGHT HER FROM HER SIN-- . . . .   695 MOSADA 1   113
      WHY SHOULD THE HEART TAKE FRIGHT? . . . .   781 HEART FRIGHT   1
FRIGHTED
      IN MURMURS, LIKE A FRIGHTED BIRD. . . . .   25 OISIN 1   376
FRIGID
      THE HAND AND LASH THAT BEAT DOWN FRIGID ROME? . . . .   560 WHENCE COME   10
FRINGED
      SO LET US DANCE ON FRINGED WAVES, ...   644 SONG FAERIES   9
      SO LET US DANCE ON THE FRINGED WAVES, ...   676 ISLE STAT II 3   256
FRO
      OF MILKY BRIGHTNESS TO AND FRO . . . .   22 OISIN 1   328
      THE CAPTIVE'S JOURNEYS TO AND FRO WERE WRIT . . . .   37 OISIN 2   116
      THE CAPTIVES' JOURNEYS TO AND FRO WERE WRIT . . . .   37 OISIN 2   V   116
      THE CAPTIVES' FOOTSTEPS WRITTEN TO AND FRO: . . . .   37 OISIN 2   V   118
      BACCHANT AND MOURNFUL, PASSING TO AND FRO . . . . .   39 OISIN 2   161
      WE TRAMPLED TO AND FRO. WHEN HIS MIND KNEW . . . .   40 OISIN 2   V   173
      TO AND FRO WE LEAP . . . .   87 STOLEN CHILD   20
      LEAD MY LOLLARD TO AND FRO, ...   97 FOXHUNTER   7
      AND LEAD HIM SLOWLY TO AND FRO, ...   97 FOXHUNTER   V   7
      I HAVE OFTEN HEARD HIM SINGING TO AND FRO, ...   109 CUCHULAIN SEA   49
      I OFTEN HEAR HIM SINGING TO AND FRO, ...   109 CUCHULAIN SEA   49
      IN GRIEF SWAYED TO AND FRO. . . . .   133 FR GILLIGAN   36
      GYRING, SPIRING TO AND FRO . . . .   135 TWO TREES   15
      TOSSING AND TOSSING TO AND FRO . . . .   135 TWO TREES   V   15
      FLYING, CRYING, TO AND FRO, ...   136 TWO TREES   35
      PEERING AND FLYING TO AND FRO, ...   136 TWO TREES   V   35
      ABOUT MY TABLE TO AND FRO, ...   138 TO IRELAND   24
      THE MAGICAL POWERS TO AND FRO. . . . .   138 TO IRELAND   V   24
      ABOUT MY TABLE TO AND FRO, ...   139 TO IRELAND   40
      MAEVE THE GREAT QUEEN WAS PACING TO AND FRO, ...   180 QUEEN MAEVE   9
      THE NORTH WIND TUMBLES TO AND FRO . . . .   191 BAILE AILLINN   45
      THAT NORTH WIND TUMBLES TO AND FRO . . . .   191 BAILE AILLINN V   45
      AND WAVING WHITE WINGS TO AND FRO . . . .   197 BAILE AILLINN   184
      HITHER AND THITHER TO AND FRO THEY TROD . . . . .   278 TWO KINGS   26
      HAD SENT NO RUNNERS TO AND FRO . . . .   288 TO WEALTHY MAN   18
      UNTIL I CRIED AND TREMBLED AND ROCKED TO AND FRO, . . .   316 COLD HEAVEN   8
      HE STUMBLED, TUMBLED, FUMBLED TO AND FRO . . . . .   411 TOWER   61
      THE PACING TO AND FRO ON POLISHED FLOORS . . . . .   418 ANCEST HOUSES   35
      HAD WATCHED MY DAILY PASSAGE TO AND FRO: . . . . .   466 HARUN RASHID   107
      HIS HAND MOVES TO AND FRO. . . . .   618 LONG-LEG FLY   28
      AND, NODDING TO AND FRO, SANG SONGS OF LOVE, ...   688 TWO TITANS   35
      TRAVELLED TO AND FRO ACROSS THE ATLANTIC, ...   790 DEDICATION   3
FROG
      SAVING A GREEN FROG DEAD UPON THE GRASS. . . . . .   676 ISLE STAT II 3   269
FROG-SPAWN
      INTO THE FROG-SPAWN OF A BLIND MAN'S DITCH, ...   479 SELF AND SOUL   59
FROLIC
      THE HARE HATH LAID ASLEEP HER FROLIC WITS, ...   712 FERENCZ RENYI   72
FROSTY
      WHEN THE MORN GREW FROSTY AND CLEAR. . . . . . .   95 MOLL MAGEE   20
      IN THE FROSTY MORNIN' CLEAR. . . . .   95 MOLL MAGEE   V   20
FROTH   SEE SEA-FROTH
      WHOSE LONG WOOL WHITER THAN SEA FROTH FLOWS, ...   8 OISIN 1   V   90

FROTH   (CONTINUED)

	PAGE	TITLE		LINE
FLUTTER ALONG THE FROTH LIPS OF THE SEA,	33	OISIN 2		58
AND SHORES THE FROTH LIPS WET!	33	OISIN 2		59
FLUTTER ALONG THE FROTH LIPS OF THE SEA	33	OISIN 2		64
MORE THAN THE FROTH, THE FEATHER, THE DUST-WHIRL,	248	SHADOW WATER B		555
MORE THAN THE FROTH, THE FEATHER, THE DUSTWHIRL,	248	SHADOW WATER B	V	555
WHERE STONE IS DARK UNDER FROTH,	348	FISHERMAN		32
WHERE STONE IS DARK WITH FROTH,	348	FISHERMAN	V	32
HAVE FOUND IT LIKE THE FROTH UPON THE ALE.	767	SHADOW WATER A		387

FROTH-DROP

	PAGE	TITLE		LINE
HE TOLD OF EVERY FROTH-DROP HISSING, FLYING.	32	OISIN 2	V	45

FROTH-LIPS

	PAGE	TITLE		LINE
FLUTTER ALONG THE FROTH-LIPS OF THE SEA,	33	OISIN 2	V	58

FROTH-SPLASHED

	PAGE	TITLE		LINE
TO ONE VAST FOOT, FROTH-SPLASHED, WITH CURVED TOES LYING	32	OISIN 2	V	46A

FROTHY

	PAGE	TITLE		LINE
AND CHASE THE FROTHY BUBBLES,	87	STOLEN CHILD		21

FROWN

	PAGE	TITLE		LINE
AND, GATHERING ON OUR BROWS A FROWN,	20	OISIN 1		296
AND, GATHERING ON OUR BROWS A FROWN,	20	OISIN 1	V	297
AND HE WENT HIS WAY WITH A FROWN.	92	FATHER OHART		20
AND WENT ON HIS WAY WITH A FROWN.	92	FATHER OHART	V	20
AND WENT HIS WAY WITH A FROWN.	92	FATHER OHART	V	20

FROZE

	PAGE	TITLE		LINE
WHEN THEY FROZE THE CLOTH ON MY BODY LIKE ARMOUR RIVETED FAST,	57	OISIN 3		151

FROZEN

	PAGE	TITLE		LINE
LIKE DROPS OF FROZEN RAINBOW LIGHT,	14	OISIN 1		183
FOLDED LIKE A FROZEN FLY!	19	OISIN 1		273
LIKE BUBBLES IN A FROZEN POND!	22	OISIN 1		336
WHERE MEN LIE FROZEN IN THE GLIMMERING SNOW!	73	ANASHU VIJAYA		51
AND FROZEN ARE THE CHANNELS OF THE BLOOD,	333	LIVING BEAUTY		2
SEEING THAT TIME HAS FROZEN UP THE BLOOD	333	LIVING BEAUTY	V	2

FRUIT

	PAGE	TITLE		LINE
IT SEEMED THE SUN AND MOON WERE IN THE FRUIT!	127	DREAM OF FAERY		23
THE CHANGING COLOURS OF ITS FRUIT	134	TWO TREES		5
UNDER THE FRUIT OF EVIL AND OF GOOD!	137	TO SOME I TALK		9
BUT FRUIT THAT IS OF PRECIOUS STONE,	196	BAILE AILLINN		175
BOUGHS HAVE THEIR FRUIT AND BLOSSOM	214	HAPPY TOWNLAND		5
WHERE BOUGHS HAVE FRUIT AND BLOSSOM	214	HAPPY TOWNLAND	V	5
I'LL GIVE A GOLDEN GALLEY FULL OF FRUIT,	240	SHADOW WATER B		373
BUT HEAVY FRUIT. HOW SWIFT THE ARGUMENT	665	ISLE STAT II 2		66
AMONG THE FRUIT! BUT THERE, LAME COLA CROUCHES	691	MOSADA 1		32
AMONG THE FRUIT. BUT YON, LAME COLA CROUCHES	691	MOSADA 1	V	32
SEE YOU, BROTHER, CRANBERRY FRUIT--	727	LOVERS QUARREL		25
AND THEREON GREW THE RUDDY FRUIT	743	DANAAN QUICK		15
AND WISDOM THE FRUIT OF THE GARDEN!	743	WISDOM DREAMS		7
FOR THE FLOWER COMES WITH THE FRUIT THERE	774	COME RIDE		3

FRUITAGE

	PAGE	TITLE		LINE
A DANAAN FRUITAGE MAKES A SHOWER OF MOONS,	127	DREAM OF FAERY	V	22

FRUITFUL

	PAGE	TITLE		LINE
A FRUITFUL LAND UNDER THE AIBHLIN HILLS?	748	SHADOW WATER A	V	33
WELL SHELTERED FROM THE WINDS, AND FRUITFUL FIELDS,	758	SHADOW WATER A		221

FRUITS

	PAGE	TITLE		LINE
AND HID HER AMONG FRUITS OF JEWEL-STONE.	224	SHADOW WATER B		49
AND PLUCKED SMALL FRUITS ON INNISFREE.	742	DANAAN QUICK		5

FULL

	PAGE	TITLE		LINE
FULL MANY BOWING KINGS BESOUGHT ME,	7	OISIN 1	V	67
AS, FULL OF LOVING FANTASY,	13	OISIN 1		158
THAT HAS DRUNK FULL, SHE CROSSED THE MISTY SEA	30	OISIN 2		16
FULL MANY MORE, WHEN PEERED A MAIDEN SWEET	33	OISIN 2	V	68F
TO TWO OLD EAGLES, FULL OF ANCIENT PRIDE,	34	OISIN 2		74
TO EAGLES TWAIN THAT, FULL OF ANCIENT PRIDE,	34	OISIN 2	V	73
LEST NIAMH SHUDDER. FULL OF HOPE AND DREAD	41	OISIN 2		183
. . . AND FILLED ME FULL TO THE BONE.	52	OISIN 3		72
. . . TWO CARRIED A SACK FULL OF SAND,	60	OISIN 3		185
A CREEPING OLD MAN, FULL OF SLEEP,	60	OISIN 3		192
. . . THEY LIFTED AND SHOULDERED A SACK FULL OF SAND,	60	OISIN 3	V	185
THE HOUR WHEN KAMA, FULL OF SLEEPY LAUGHTER,	72	ANASHU VIJAYA		26
FULL OF BERRIES	87	STOLEN CHILD		7
FOR THE WORLD'S MORE FULL OF WEEPING THAN YOU CAN UNDERSTAND.	87	STOLEN CHILD		12
WHILE THE WORLD IS FULL OF TROUBLES	87	STOLEN CHILD		22
FOR THE WORLD'S MORE FULL OF WEEPING THAN YOU CAN UNDERSTAND.	87	STOLEN CHILD		27
FOR THE WORLD'S MORE FULL OF WEEPING THAN YOU CAN UNDERSTAND.	88	STOLEN CHILD		41
FROM A WORLD MORE FULL OF WEEPING THAN HE CAN UNDERSTAND.	89	STOLEN CHILD		53
FOR THE WORLD'S MORE FULL OF WEEPING THAN HE CAN UNDERSTAND	89	STOLEN CHILD	V	53
BUT I WAS YOUNG AND FOOLISH, AND NOW AM FULL OF TEARS.	90	SALLEY GARDENS		8
AH WOE! FULL MANY A CREAK GAVE THE CREEL IN THE CART	91	OLD FISHERMAN	V	6
AH ME! FULL MANY A CREAK GAVE THE CREEL IN THE CART	91	OLD FISHERMAN	V	6
FILLED FULL OF ANCIENT CHEER."	97	FOXHUNTER	V	12
AND EVENING FULL OF THE LINNET'S WINGS.	117	ISLE INNISFREE		8
AND EVENING FULL OF THE LINNETS' WINGS.	117	ISLE INNISFREE	V	8
THE FULL ROUND MOON AND THE STAR-LADEN SKY,	119	SORROW OF LOVE		2
WHEN YOU ARE OLD AND GREY AND FULL OF SLEEP,	120	YOU ARE OLD		1
FULL OF EARTH'S OLD TIMID GRACE.	124	CATHLEEN PARA		12
I ALSO BEAR A BELL-BRANCH FULL OF EASE.	130	BOOK STORIES		12
I ALSO BEAR A BELL BRANCH FULL OF EASE.	130	BOOK STORIES	V	12
THINE EYES GROW FULL OF TENDER CARE!	135	TWO TREES		19

FULL (CONTINUED)

	PAGE	TITLE		LINE
HE TELLS OF A VALLEY FULL OF LOVERS	163	VALLEY LOVERS		T
AEDH TELLS OF A VALLEY FULL OF LOVERS	163	VALLEY LOVERS	V	T
SO FULL OF THAT THING AND OF THIS,	192	BAILE AILLINN		86
AT THE FULL MOON? HE PLAYED ALL THROUGH THE NIGHT.	223	SHADOW WATER B		21
I'LL GIVE A GOLDEN GALLEY FULL OF FRUIT,	240	SHADOW WATER B		373
THAT I SHOULD KEEN HIM FROM THE FULL OF THE MOON	243	SHADOW WATER B		446
IS IT THAT THOUGH YOUR EYES ARE FULL OF LOVE	245	SHADOW WATER B		473
THE HOLD IS FULL OF TREASURE. FULL TO THE HATCHES.	247	SHADOW WATER B		532
THE HOLD IS FULL OF TREASURE. FULL TO THE HATCHES.	247	SHADOW WATER B		532
FOR ALL WERE FULL OF WINE AND MEAT.	271	GREY ROCK		17
IN HIS FULL HANDS WHAT, HAD THEY ONLY KNOWN,	292	TO A SHADE		11
NOW IT HAS FILLED AN OLD SOCK FULL,	301	RUN PARADISE		20
GROW RICH, POPULAR AND FULL OF INFLUENCE,	369	EGO DOMINUS		43
THE FULL AND THE MOON'S DARK AND ALL THE CRESCENTS,	373	PHASES OF MOON		32
FOR THERE'S NO HUMAN LIFE AT THE FULL OR THE DARK.	373	PHASES OF MOON		35
BUT WHILE THE MOON IS ROUNDING TOWARDS THE FULL	373	PHASES OF MOON		39
BEFORE THE FULL MOON, HELPLESS AS A WORM,	374	PHASES OF MOON		49
TOO PERFECT AT THE FULL TO LIE IN A CRADLE,	374	PHASES OF MOON		60
WHEN THE MOON'S FULL THOSE CREATURES OF THE FULL	375	PHASES OF MOON		75
WHEN THE MOON'S FULL THOSE CREATURES OF THE FULL	375	PHASES OF MOON		75
THE COARSENESS OF THE DRUDGE. BEFORE THE FULL	376	PHASES OF MOON		94
OF THE DARK MOON AND THE FULL,	384	VISION ROBART		60
WHEN THE LONG LOOKING-GLASS IS FULL,	387	ROBARTES DANCE		50
ARE FULL OF PASSIONATE INTENSITY.	402	SECOND COMING		8
FOR AN OLD BELLOWS FULL OF ANGRY WIND?	405	FOR DAUGHTER		64
NOTHING BUT STILLNESS CAN REMAIN WHEN HEARTS ARE FULL	426	PHANTOM HATRED		23
I BRING FULL FLAVOURED WINE OUT OF A BARREL FOUND	442	BLACK CENTAUR	V	10
WHEN THE FULL MOON SWAM TO ITS GREATEST HEIGHT	468	HARUN RASHID		151
LIE BODIES OF THE VAMPIRES FULL OF BLOOD!	483	OIL AND BLOOD		5
ROADS FULL OF BEGGARS, CATTLE IN THE FIELDS,	487	SEVEN SAGES		18
SHE MADE A FULL CONFESSION.	571	THREE BUSHES		66
AS THOUGH TO DRAW THEM CLOSER YET. RAMMED FULL	579	DOR WELLESLEY		5
CLIMB TO YOUR CHAMBER FULL OF BOOKS AND WAIT,	579	DOR WELLESLEY		8
NO DARK TOMB-HAUNTER ONCE; HER FORM ALL FULL	618	BRONZE HEAD		8
HIS EMPTY HEART IS FULL AT LENGTH,	624	APPARITIONS		19
WITH A BAG FULL OF PENNIES,	627	STATES HOLIDAY		35
ALMINTOR, THOU HAST GROWN SO FULL OF RUTH,	652	ISLE STAT I 2		26
SMALL ISLAND, WHERE THE FULL SOFT SHEEN	653	ISLE STAT I 2		36
AND FULL OF WISDOM IS EACH BLOOM,	655	ISLE STAT I 3		9
THE HEAVY CLUSTERS OF THE GRAPES WERE FULL,	690	MOSADA 1		13
THEN HAS THIS ONE BEEN SINNED FULL MANY TIMES.	692	MOSADA 1		49
YOU'RE FULL OF WORDINESS. COME, HEAR MY SONG.	696	MOSADA 2		8
ARE DYING TOO. THEY WERE FULL SEVEN STARS;	700	MOSADA 3		48
OF HER HE LOVED FIXED ON HIM FULL OF LIGHT,	710	FERENCZ RENYI		27
AND THEN HIS HEART FILLS FULL OF LOVE,	716	FAIRY DOCTOR		11
AND FULL HIS EYES OF FAIRY CHEER.	716	FAIRY DOCTOR		12
AND THEN HIS HEART IS FULL OF LOVE,	716	FAIRY DOCTOR	V	11
FULL MOODY IS MY LOVE AND SAD,	723	GIRLS SONG A		1
A FULL HOUR LONG, WHEN ROSE A FEATHER	728	PRIEST FAIRY		19
A FAIRY WHOM WE LOVED FULL WELL;	729	PRIEST FAIRY		44
AS THOUGH HIS DAYS WERE FULL OF RUTH.	731	PRIEST FAIRY		76
BE FULL OF SUDDEN FEARS,	738	MOURN THEN ON		6
HOW MANY MOONS HAVE DIED FROM THE FULL MOON	747	SHADOW WATER A		10

FULLER'S

WHEN LOIE FULLER'S CHINESE DANCERS ENWOUND	430	NINETEEN 19		49

FULL-FLAVOURED

I BRING FULL-FLAVOURED WINE OUT OF A BARREL FOUND	442	BLACK CENTAUR		10

FULLNESS

. . . FULLNESS AND OF THE COMING EMPTINESS	425	PHANTOM HATRED		T
SUCH FULLNESS IN THAT QUARTER OVERFLOWS	478	SELF AND SOUL		33

FUMBLE

BUT FUMBLE IN A GREASY TILL	289	SEPTEMBER 1913		2

FUMBLED

BUT WHILE HE FUMBLED WITH THE STONES	302	HOUR DAWN		16
HE STUMBLED, TUMBLED, FUMBLED TO AND FRO	411	TOWER		61

FUMBLING

OR FUMBLING IN A DREAM ABOUT THE HOUSE?	230	SHADOW WATER B		174
INDIGNANT AT THE FUMBLING WITS, THE OBSCURE SPITE	291	PAUDEEN		1

FUME

THE FUME OF MUSCATEL	473	ALL SOUL NIGHT		83

FUNDS

"THE DRUNKARDS, PILFERERS OF PUBLIC FUNDS,	352	PEOPLE		23

FUNERAL

A LADY WITH SOFT EYES LIKE FUNERAL TAPERS,	33	OISIN 2		69
DOWN ON US WITH HER EYES LIKE FUNERAL TAPERS.	33	OISIN 2	V	69
A MAIDEN WITH SOFT EYES LIKE FUNERAL TAPERS,	33	OISIN 2	V	69
TROY PASSED AWAY IN ONE HIGH FUNERAL GLEAM,	111	ROSE OF WORLD		4
PARNELL'S FUNERAL	541	PARN FUNERAL 1		T
A PARNELLITE AT PARNELL'S FUNERAL	541	PARN FUNERAL 1	V	T
TENDER AND FEARLESS ON HER FUNERAL PYRE;	688	NETTLESHIP		3

FUNEREAL

AND IN SOME URN FUNEREAL LIE	19	OISIN 1	V	272

FURIES

BREAK BITTER FURIES OF COMPLEXITY,	498	BYZANTIUM		37
THE PROUD FURIES EACH WITH HER TORCH ON HIGH.	579	DOR WELLESLEY		16

FURIOUS

OR HURRIED THEM OFF ON ITS OWN FURIOUS PATH;	430	NINETEEN 19		53
FLIETH FORTUNE'S FURIOUS WHEEL.	737	IN FIRELIGHT		8

FURLED

TO YONDER ISLE, WHERE NEVER SAIL WAS FURLED,	664	ISLE STAT II 2		56

	PAGE	TITLE	LINE

FURLED (CONTINUED)
WERE FURLED THE WINGS OF SHIPS. THERE IN A DELL, • • • 693 MOSADA 1 82
FURNITURE
A BODILY OR MENTAL FURNITURE. • • • • • • • • • 558 RIBH CHRISTIAN 20
FURR'D
OR SOME SMALL BEAST MOST WONDERFULLY FURR'D, • • • • • 650 ISLE STAT I 1 148
FURROWS
AS THE SEA'S FURROWS ON A SEA-TOST SHELL, • • • • • • 660 ISLE STAT II 1 51
BETWEEN TWO FURROWS UPON THE PLOUGHED LAND! • • • • • 784 WOMANS BEAUTY 4
BETWEEN DARK FURROWS UPON THE PLOUGHED LAND. • • • • • 784 WOMANS BEAUTY 6
FURTHER
I PASSED A LITTLE FURTHER ON AND HEARD A LOTUS TALK! • • 76 INDIAN ON GOD 9
I PACED A LITTLE FURTHER ON AND HEARD A LOTUS TALK!— • 76 INDIAN ON GOD V 9
I PASSED A LITTLE FURTHER ON AND HEARD A PEACOCK SAY! • • 77 INDIAN ON GOD 17
I PACED A LITTLE FURTHER AND I HEARD A PEACOCK SAY! • • 77 INDIAN ON GOD V 17
I PASSED A LITTLE FURTHER AND I HEARD A PEACOCK SAY!— • 77 INDIAN ON GOD V 17
AND FURTHER ADD TO THAT" • • • • • • • • • • • 415 TOWER 153
THE FURTHER THAT I FLY". • • • • • • • • • • • • 559 HE AND SHE 10
FURTHEST
FAR OFF BY FURTHEST ROSSES • • • • • • • • • • • 87 STOLEN CHILD 15
FURY
IN FURY AND IN PANIC FLED • • • • • • • • • • • 307 HOUR DAWN V 119
THE FURY AND THE MIRE OF HUMAN VEINS. • • • • • • • 497 BYZANTIUM 8
AND ALL COMPLEXITIES OF FURY LEAVE, • • • • • • • • 498 BYZANTIUM 29
THAT STARING FURY AND THE BLIND LUSH LEAF • • • • • • 500 VACILLATION 17
AND BY ITS FORMLESS SPAWNING FURY WRECKED, • • • • • • 611 STATUES 30
WHENCE DID ALL THAT FURY COME? • • • • • • • • • • 619 STICK INCENSE 1
FURZE
WE RODE BEYOND THE FURZE AND HEATHER, • • • • • • • 9 OISIN 1 V 101A
FUTURE
THAT THE FUTURE YEARS HAD COME, • • • • • • • • • 403 FOR DAUGHTER 14
WE THOUGHT IT WOULD OUTLIVE ALL FUTURE DAYS. • • • • • 428 NINETEEN 19 14
THAT WAITS UPON HIS FUTURE DAYS, • • • • • • • • • 436 FOR MY SON 14
AND KNOWING THAT THE FUTURE WOULD BE VEXED • • • • • • 472 ALL SOUL NIGHT 44
AND BY FOREKNOWLEDGE OF THE FUTURE VEXED! • • • • • • 472 ALL SOUL NIGHT V 44
GABHRA'S
ON GABHRA'S RAVEN-COVERED PLAIN! • • • • • • • • • 5 OISIN 1 43
GABRIEL
• • • MICHAEL, GABRIEL, AND RAPHAEL • • • • • • • • 174 ELEMENT POWERS V T
GABRIEL WILL COME FROM THE WATER • • • • • • • • • 215 HAPPY TOWNLAND 45
GABY'S
THE YOUNG MEN EVERY NIGHT APPLAUD THEIR GABY'S LAUGHING 353 HIS PHOENIX 9
EYE,
GAFFER
BUT MAYBE SOME OLD GAFFER MUTTERS A BLESSING • • • • • 355 BROKEN DREAMS 4
GAIETY
GAIETY TRANSFIGURING ALL THAT DREAD. • • • • • • • • 565 LAPIS LAZULI 17
VAIN GAIETY, VAIN BATTLE, VAIN REPOSE, • • • • • • • 629 CIRCUS ANIMALS 12
GAIN
WHERE MEN FORGIVE IF THE BELLY GAIN? • • • • • • • • 615 MARCH SONGS 2 14
HE WHO MEASURES GAIN AND LOSS, • • • • • • • • • • 744 ROSY CROSS 1
HE WHO MEASURES GAIN AND LOSS, • • • • • • • • • • 744 ROSY CROSS 9
GAINSAY
WHERE NONE GAINSAY THEIR RIGHT, • • • • • • • • • 597 MODEL LAUREATE 14
GALILEAN
IN GALILEAN TURBULENCE! • • • • • • • • • • • • 438 SONGS PLAY 2 3
GALILEE
FOR SHEPHERD LADS IN GALILEE! AND GRANT • • • • • • • 371 ON GOING HOUSE 4
GALLANT
TO THIS MOST GALLANT GENTLEMAN • • • • • • • • • • 582 ROGER CASEMENT 23
LOVELY LADY OR GALLANT MAN • • • • • • • • • • • 788 HAWTHORN TREE 7
LOVELY LADY AND GALLANT MAN • • • • • • • • • • • 788 HAWTHORN TREE V 7
GALLERIED
WOLF-BREEDING MOUNTAINS, GALLERIED EMAN, • • • • • • 81 MAD KING GOLL V 2
GALLERIES
AMID GREAT CHAMBERS AND LONG GALLERIES, LINED • • • • • 418 ANCEST HOUSES 36
GALLERY
• • • TO THE DUBLIN MUNICIPAL GALLERY IF IT WERE PROVED 287 TO WEALTHY MAN T
• • •
THERE WAS NO PORTRAIT IN THE GALLERY • • • • • • • 400 DEMON BEAST 17
THROUGH THE GREAT GALLERY OF THE TREASURE HOUSE • • • 461 HARUN RASHID 5
AND WAIT WAR'S MUSIC! PASS THE LITTLE GALLERY! • • • 461 HARUN RASHID 8
THE MUNICIPAL GALLERY REVISITED • • • • • • • • • 601 GALLERY REVIS T
THE MUNICIPAL GALLERY RE-VISITED • • • • • • • • • 601 GALLERY REVIS V T
THOSE FROM THE PIT AND GALLERY • • • • • • • • • • 608 SONGS BURDEN 3 3
GALLEY
"LIKE ME WERE SOME GALLEY FORSAKEN FAR OFF IN MERIDIAN 55 OISIN 3 117
ISLE,
DO YOU REMEMBER WHEN WE SANK THAT GALLEY • • • • • 223 SHADOW WATER B 20
I'LL GIVE A GOLDEN GALLEY FULL OF FRUIT, • • • • • • 240 SHADOW WATER B 373
A TRADING GALLEY IN HER HELMSMAN'S EYES. • • • • • • 751 SHADOW WATER A 95
A GALLEY FROM THE LOCHLANN SEAS! HER FLAG • • • • • • 751 SHADOW WATER A 98
AND TURN HIS GALLEY ABOUT AND BRING ME HOME. • • • • 751 SHADOW WATER A 108
WHEN YOU ARE ABOARD THE LOCHLANN GALLEY, LASH • • • • 752 SHADOW WATER A 128
COVER YOUR EARS! FOR ONCE WE HAD MOORED OUR GALLEY • • 756 SHADOW WATER A 187
ANY THAT LIVED, AND I HAVE BROUGHT MY GALLEY • • • • 756 SHADOW WATER A V 191A
AND A STRONG GALLEY. I GIVE YOU ALL AS MUCH. • • • • 758 SHADOW WATER A 222
SEEK AIBRIC ON THE LOCHLANN GALLEY, AND TELL HIM • • • 767 SHADOW WATER A 401
I HAVE CUT THE ROPE THAT BOUND THIS GALLEY TO OURS, • • 768 SHADOW WATER A 421
I HAVE CUT THE CORDS THAT HELD THIS GALLEY TO OURS. • • 768 SHADOW WATER A V 421

310

```
                                                     PAGE    TITLE           LINE
GALLEYS
    THEY WALK ON SHORES UNSEEN OF OARING GALLEYS,  . . . . .  30 OISIN 2       V 14D
    TO FILL THEIR DARK-BEAKED HOLLOW GALLEYS. . . . . . . .   82 MAD KING GOLL    16
    THAT HE MAY FILL HIS HOLLOW GALLEYS. . . . . . . . .      82 MAD KING GOLL V  16
    TO FILL WITH COWS HIS HOLLOW GALLEYS." . . . . . . .      82 MAD KING GOLL V  16
    MAKE GALLEYS OUT OF WIND THAT CHANGE TO WIND . . . . .   751 SHADOW WATER A   105
    WAR-LADEN GALLEYS, AND ARMIES ON WHITE ROADS, . . . .    757 SHADOW WATER A   203
    WAR LADEN GALLEYS, AND ARMIES ON WHITE ROADS, . . . .    757 SHADOW WATER A V 203
GALLIVANTING
    GO GALLIVANTING BY! . . . . . . . . . . . . . .         552 SONGS REWRIT 2     4
GALLOPED
    WE GALLOPED OVER THE GLOSSY SEA! . . . . . . . . .       11 OISIN 1          132
    WE GALLOPED! NOW A HORNLESS DEER . . . . . . . . .       11 OISIN 1          139
    ON, ON, WE GALLOPED O'ER THE SEA. . . . . . . . .       11 OISIN 1        V 132
    WHILE THAT GREAT JUAN GALLOPED BY! . . . . . . . .      294 HATED PLAYBOY  V   4
GALLOPING
    THE RIDERS UPON THE GALLOPING HORSES, . . . . . . .     266 GALWAY RACES       3
    THE RIDERS AND THE GALLOPING HORSES, . . . . . . .      266 GALWAY RACES   V   3
GALLOWS
    GRANDFATHER SANG IT UNDER THE GALLOWS! . . . . . . .    544 TO SAME TUNE 1     1
    HE DIED UPON THE GALLOWS. . . . . . . . . . . .         581 ROGER CASEMENT     3
    GRANDFATHER SANG IT UNDER THE GALLOWS! . . . . . . .    615 MARCH SONGS 3      1
GALWAY      SEE CLARE-GALWAY
    AT GALWAY RACES . . . . . . . . . . . . . . .          266 GALWAY RACES       T
    GALWAY RACES . . . . . . . . . . . . . . . .           266 GALWAY RACES   V   T
    OR TRADING OUT OF GALWAY INTO SPAIN! . . . . . . .      269 PARDON FATHERS     4
    WHEN WITH THE GALWAY FOXHOUNDS HE WOULD RIDE . . . .    326 ROBERT GREGORY    57
    TO COLD CLARE ROCK AND GALWAY ROCK AND THORN, . . . .   326 ROBERT GREGORY    66
    IN A GALWAY SHOP! . . . . . . . . . . . . . .          595 COLONEL MARTIN    22
GAMBLER
    THEY SAY YOU ARE A GAMBLER AND A PLAYER . . . . . .     721 WITCH VIVIEN      34
GAME
    BETWEEN THE GAME AND THE HORSES OF THE SEA. . . . .     108 CUCHULAIN SEA  V  34
    OR PUT HIS HEART INTO SOME GAME . . . . . . . . .       343 SHEP GOATHERD    105
    GAME BIRD, OR WOMAN DOES THE SAME THING TWICE! . . .    463 HARUN RASHID   V  60
    THAN SOULS THAT START NO GAME AND TURN NO RHYME! . . .  464 HARUN RASHID      68
    IMPROVISATION, OR A SETTLED GAME . . . . . . . .        533 HER TRIUMPH        3
GAMEBIRD
    GAMEBIRD, NOR WOMAN DOES THE SAME THING TWICE! . . .    463 HARUN RASHID   V  60
GAME-BIRD
    GAME-BIRD, NOR WOMAN DOES THE SAME THING TWICE! . . .   463 HARUN RASHID      60
'GAN
    . . . AND YEARS AFTER YEARS 'GAN FLOW! . . . . . .      52 OISIN 3           75
    . . . AND YEARS AFTER YEARS 'GAN THEIR FLOW! . . . .    52 OISIN 3        V  75
    THEN 'GAN TO SPEAK THAT GOBLIN RARE, . . . . . . .     729 PRIEST FAIRY      37
GANGLING
    ON GANGLING STOCKS GROWN GREAT, GREAT STOCKS RUN DRY, . 619 BRONZE HEAD       25
GANNET
    THERE! THERE THEY COME! GULL, GANNET, OR DIVER, . . .   233 SHADOW WATER B   244
GANNETS
    OR THE GANNETS CALLING OUT . . . . . . . . . .         772 SONG DEIRDRE 1     5
GAP
    AS I CAME OVER WINDY GAP . . . . . . . . . . .         300 RUN PARADISE       1
    I HAVE STOOD SO LONG BY A GAP IN THE WALL . . . . .     788 HAWTHORN TREE     15
    I HAVE STOPPED SO LONG A GAP IN THE WALL . . . . .      788 HAWTHORN TREE  V  15
GAPE
    AND NOW BUT GAPE AT THE SUN. . . . . . . . . .         432 NINETEEN 19      102
GARDEN
    THE JESTER WALKED IN THE GARDEN! . . . . . . . .       159 CAP AND BELLS      1
    THE GARDEN HAD FALLEN STILL! . . . . . . . . .         159 CAP AND BELLS      2
    THE POWERS, NOT KIND LIKE YOU, CAME WHERE GOD'S GARDEN  174 ELEMENT POWERS V   1
        BLOWS,
    MAKE THEIR FAINT THUNDER, AND THE GARDEN BEES . . . .   198 SEVEN WOODS        2
    WHO HAS SEEN A GARDEN IMAGE OR TWISTED TREE . . . .     279 TWO KINGS      V 45B
    RAN AND WITH THE GARDEN SHEARS . . . . . . . . .       410 TOWER             30
    BEFORE THE INDIFFERENT GARDEN DEITIES! . . . . . .      418 ANCEST HOUSES     28
    BUT THE TORN PETALS STREW THE GARDEN PLOT! . . . . .    422 MY DESCENDANTS     7
    WHEN THE TORN PETALS STREW THE GARDEN PLOT! . . . .     422 MY DESCENDANTS V   7
    OUR SHADOWS ROVE THE GARDEN GRAVEL STILL, . . . . .     435 NEW FACES          7
    THE GARDEN DIED! . . . . . . . . . . . . . .           439 FRAGMENTS          2
    AND YONDER IN THE GYMNASTS' GARDEN THRIVES . . . . .    446 COLONUS PRAISE     9
    THE GARDEN PATHS, NOR COUNTED UP THE ROOMS, . . . .     466 HARUN RASHID     119
    IN THE RICH MIDNIGHT OF THE GARDEN TREES . . . . .      494 AT ALGECIRAS       5
    IN THE RICH MIDNIGHT OF THE GARDEN TREE . . . . . .     494 AT ALGECIRAS   V   5
    CHIMNEY CORNER, GARDEN WALK, . . . . . . . . .         499 MOTHER OF GOD      8
    THROUGH LIGHT-OBLITERATING GARDEN FOLIAGE WHAT MAGIC DRUM? 560 MAGIC DRUM       4
    GRASS PLOT OF THE GARDEN! . . . . . . . . . . .        568 SWEET DANCER       3
    EDEN'S GARDEN WOULD BE THERE . . . . . . . . .         621 JOHN KINSELLA     27
    BY THE DOOR OF MARY'S GARDEN . . . . . . . . .         680 LOVE AND DEATH    31
    HIS GARDEN RINGED WITH JESSAMINE, . . . . . . . .       729 PRIEST FAIRY      34
    AND WISDOM THE FRUIT OF THE GARDEN! . . . . . . .       743 WISDOM DREAMS      7
    FOR I HAVE ALL HIS GARDEN WISDOM. O SPEAK! . . . .      756 SHADOW WATER A   180
    MY FOSTER-MOTHER'S GARDEN IN THE SOUTH . . . . . .      758 SHADOW WATER A   227
    MY FOSTER MOTHER'S GARDEN IN THE SOUTH . . . . . .      758 SHADOW WATER A V 227
    COME RIDE AND RIDE TO THE GARDEN, . . . . . . . .       773 COME RIDE          1
    COME RIDE AND RIDE TO THE GARDEN, . . . . . . . .       774 COME RIDE          5
    AND ALL THE GARDEN BLESS, . . . . . . . . . .          774 COME RIDE         10
    COME RIDE AND RIDE TO THE GARDEN, . . . . . . . .       774 COME RIDE         13
    COME RIDE AND RIDE TO THE GARDEN, . . . . . . . .       774 COME RIDE         18
GARDEN-BOY
    THE POST AND GARDEN-BOY ALONE . . . . . . . . .        607 SONGS BURDEN 2     7
```

311

```
                                                      PAGE      TITLE              LINE
GARDEN'S
    AND HEAR AMID THE GARDEN'S NIGHTLY PEACE," . . . . . . .   300 BEGGAR CRIED         18
    TO BE THE GARDEN'S PRIDE." . . . . . . . . . . . .         396 ROSE TREE            12
GARDENS
    DOWN BY THE SALLEY GARDENS . . . . . . . . . . . .          90 SALLEY GARDENS        T
    DOWN BY THE SALLEY GARDENS MY LOVE AND I DID MEET! . . .    90 SALLEY GARDENS        1
    SHE PASSED THE SALLEY GARDENS WITH LITTLE SNOW-WHITE FEET.  90 SALLEY GARDENS        2
    O WHAT IF GARDENS WHERE THE PEACOCK STRAYS . . . . . .     418 ANCEST HOUSES        25
    OR GARDENS RICH IN MEMORY GLORIFIED . . . . . . . .        491 COOLE BALLYLEE       35
    IN ALGECIRAS GARDENS, AND THERE REST . . . . . . . .       494 AT ALGECIRAS     V    5
    GARDENS WHERE A SOUL'S AT EASE! . . . . . . . . . .        639 BEN BULBEN           55
GARLANDED
    SOME FEW HAVE HANDSOME RIDERS, ARE GARLANDED . . . . .     432 NINETEEN 19         114
GARMENT
    IT ROSE IN A STRAIGHT BLUE GARMENT, . . . . . . . .        159 CAP AND BELLS         5
    IN A LONG AND STRAIGHT BLUE GARMENT . . . . . . . .        159 CAP AND BELLS    V    5
    IN A RED AND QUIVERING GARMENT . . . . . . . . . .         160 CAP AND BELLS        15
    IN A GARMENT RED AND QUIVERING, . . . . . . . . .          160 CAP AND BELLS    V   15
    THOUGHT IS A GARMENT AND THE SOUL'S A BRIDE . . . . .      558 RIBH CHRISTIAN       16
GARMENT'S
    THY GARMENT'S HEM, THOU VISIONARY ONE! . . . . . .         684 SEEKER           V   71
GARMENTS
    MY SHEPHERD GARMENTS, AND RETURN ANON. . . . . . . .       659 ISLE STAT II 1       29
GARMENTS'
    HER FINGERS AND HER GARMENTS' HEM. . . . . . . . .          16 OISIN 1          V  216
    THY GARMENTS' HEM, THOU VISIONARY ONE! . . . . . .         684 SEEKER               71
GARNERED
    IS NOT THY BODY BUT THE GARNERED RUST . . . . . . .        724 KANVA ON SELF        15
GARRET
    TO GARRET OR CELLAR A WHEEL I SEND, . . . . . . . .        787 GARRET CELLAR         1
GARRULOUS
    FROM WASTE SEAS CROSS'D, YET EVER GARRULOUS) . . . . .     690 MOSADA 1              9
GARTERED        SEE CROSS-GARTERED
GASP
    HE GAVE A GASP AND THOUGHT TO HAVE FLED, . . . . . .       303 HOUR DAWN            22
    HE GAVE A GASP AND THOUGHT TO RUN, . . . . . . . .         303 HOUR DAWN        V   22
GASPED
    TREMBLED AND GASPED AND SHOULD HAVE RUN . . . . . .        303 HOUR DAWN        V   22
GASPING
    WHAT ARE ALL THOSE FISH THAT LIE GASPING ON THE STRAND?    485 THREE MOVEMENT        3
'GAT
    'GAT THE FOAL OF THE WORLD.'" . . . . . . . . . .          529 TOM CRUACHAN          6
GATE
    LOOSED LONG AGO FROM HEAVEN'S GATE. . . . . . . . .         24 OISIN 1             362
    BUT CALL ME FIRST THROUGH THE GATE! . . . . . . . .        178 FIDDLER DOONEY       12
    TO THAT SMALL CHAMBER BY THE OUTER GATE. . . . . . .       181 QUEEN MAEVE          44
    ROUND ABOUT HELL'S GATE TO STARE . . . . . . . . .         294 HATED PLAYBOY    V    3
    HAVE KEYS TO MY OLD GATE. . . . . . . . . . . .            607 SONGS BURDEN 2        8
    THOUGH I HAVE LOCKED MY GATE ON THEM, . . . . . . .        607 SONGS BURDEN 2       10
    WITHIN THE FOLD TO HEAR THE CREAKING GATE-- . . . . .      646 ISLE STAT I 1        41
    'FORE PARADISE'S GATE. . . . . . . . . . . . .             680 LOVE AND DEATH       20
    THIS VISION OF PETER AND THE BURNING GATE. . . . . .       696 MOSADA 2             21
    BY THE DOOR OF PETER'S GATE, . . . . . . . . . .           696 MOSADA 2             23
    OF HOLY PETER OF THE BURNING GATE! . . . . . . . .         696 MOSADA 2         V   20
    BESIDE THE DOOR OF PETER'S GATE. . . . . . . . .           696 MOSADA 2         V   23
GATED           SEE BRAZEN-GATED
GATES
    . . . KEENED IN THE GATES OF MY HEART. . . . . . . .        57 OISIN 3             152
    AND LAID YOU ON THE GATES OF EVENING WITH HIS QUIET HANDS.  72 ANASHU VIJAYA        22
    AND LAID YE ON THE GATES OF EVENING WITH HIS QUIET HANDS.   72 ANASHU VIJAYA    V   22
    THE TOWERY GATES OF GORIAS, . . . . . . . . . .            196 BAILE AILLINN       161
    LAND-OF-THE-TOWER, WHERE AENGUS HAS THROWN THE GATES APART, 209 UNDER THE MOON   V    8
    LAND OF THE TOWER, WHEN AENGUS HAS THROWN THE GATES APART,  209 UNDER THE MOON   V    8
    BOOK IV  THE GATES OF PLUTO  I.  THE FOOL BY THE ROADSIDE   447 HERO GIRL FOOL   V    T
GATEWAY
    SPRANG FROM A GATEWAY WALLED AROUND WITH BLACK . . . .      31 OISIN 2          V   29
    UPLIFTED GATEWAY.  WITH THE FLASHING BEAT . . . . .         31 OISIN 2          V   30D
    BETWEEN THEM A GATEWAY OF BRASS, AND THE HOWL OF THE ANGELS 61 OISIN 3             200
        WHO FELL.
    WE WILL TEAR OUT THE FLAMING STONES, AND BATTER THE GATEWAY 62 OISIN 3             209
        OF BRASS
    . . . AND WILL BATTER THE GATEWAY OF BRASS . . . . .        62 OISIN 3          V  209
    BEYOND THE GATEWAY--BY THE SENTRIES NOW-- . . . . .        720 WITCH VIVIEN         10
    ON BRAHMA'S GATEWAY, "THEY WITHIN HAVE FED . . . . .       735 QUATRAIN APHOR       15
GATHER
    GATHER SEA-SLIME AND FALL THE SEAWARD WAY, . . . . .        45 OISIN 2             237
    GATHER SEA SLIME AND FALL THE SEAWARD WAY, . . . . .        45 OISIN 2          V  237
    GO GATHER BY THE HUMMING SEA . . . . . . . . . .            66 HAPPY SHEPHERD       35
    GO GATHER BY THE HUMMING-SEA . . . . . . . . . .            66 HAPPY SHEPHERD   V   35
    BUT GATHER WITH YOUR SHININ' LOOKS . . . . . . . .          96 MOLL MAGEE           55
    "THE RED BRANCH GATHER A GREAT COMPANY . . . . . .         108 CUCHULAIN SEA    V   33
    WITH BLOWN, SPRAY-DABBLED HAIR GATHER AT HAND. . . . .     114 ROSE OF BATTLE        6
    BUT GATHER ALL FOR WHOM NO LOVE HATH MADE . . . . .        114 ROSE OF BATTLE       12
    TO SMILE ON THE PALE DAWN: AND GATHER YOU . . . . .        114 ROSE OF BATTLE       15
    TO SMILE UPON THEIR STARS! AND GATHER YOU, . . . . .       114 ROSE OF BATTLE   V   15
    OF THAT DARK FOLK WHO GATHER IN THE SOULS . . . . .        136 TO SOME I TALK   V    4
    THE DEWS DROP SLOWLY AND DREAMS GATHER! UNKNOWN SPEARS .   161 BLACK PIG             1
    THE DEW DROPS SLOWLY! THE DREAMS GATHER! UNKNOWN SPEARS    161 BLACK PIG        V    1
    TO GATHER THE HALF OF YOUR BLESSEDNESS . . . . . .         167 BLESSED               7
    AND DO YOU GATHER ABOUT US WHEN PALE LIGHT . . . . .       218 WOODS OF COOLE       37
    AND GATHER THE GLASNEVIN COVERLET . . . . . . . .          293 TO A SHADE           19
```

312

GATHER   (CONTINUED)
    WILL GATHER, AND NOT KNOW IT WALKS THE VERY STREET . . .   315 FALLEN MAJESTY   7
    WILL GATHER AND NOT KNOW THAT THROUGH ITS VERY STREET . .   315 FALLEN MAJESTY V   7
    IT KNOWS NOT WHAT IT IS, AND GATHER ME . . . .   408 SAIL BYZANTIUM   23
    IT KNOWS NOT WHAT IT IS, GATHER ME . . . .   408 SAIL BYZANTIUM V   23
    AND WE THAT HAVE SHED NONE MUST GATHER THERE . . . . .   482 BLOOD AND MOON   41
    AND GATHER ALL THE TALK? . . . .   499 MOTHER OF GOD   10
    COME GATHER ROUND ME, PARNELLITES . . . .   586 PARNELLITES   7
    COME GATHER ROUND ME, PARNELLITES, ...   586 PARNELLITES   1
    COME GATHER ROUND ME, PLAYERS ALL! . . . .   608 SONGS BURDEN 3   1
    AND, WHILE THEY GATHER ROUND MY BECKONING ARMS, ...   694 MOSADA 1   100
    ALL THE WORDS THAT I GATHER, ...   739 WHERE BOOKS GO   1
    WHEN ALL GATHER THEY WILL FLY UPON THEIR WAY. . . . . .   753 SHADOW WATER A   136
    GATHER ABOUT HIM, THAT THE GODS MAY NOT KNOW . . . . .   758 SHADOW WATER A   231
    AND GATHER ROUND HIM, THAT NO GOD MAY KNOW . . . . . .   758 SHADOW WATER A V   231
    GATHER ON THE WIND AND DRIVE . . . .   775 AGAINST WITCH   7
GATHERED
    AND GATHERED IN A SILVER CINCTURE! . . . .   3 OISIN 1   V 24A
    MOURNFUL, AND GATHERED ON THE SANDS, ...   10 OISIN 1   V 111B
    AND, GATHERED IN A PANTING BAND, ...   22 OISIN 1   324
    WEARY, WITH ALL HIS POPPIES GATHERED ROUND HIM. . . . .   72 ANASHU VIJAYA   25
    GATHERED IN SILENCE, DEWY AS HER EYES, ...   80 EPHEMERA   19
    TO HIS OWN ICE!" I GATHERED ROUND ME, ...   83 MAD KING GOLL V   18
    AND GATHERED THE FLAMES ABOVE HIS HOLY HEAD, ...   162 ASKS FORGIVE V   17
    WHEN WINDS HAVE GATHERED AND SUN AND MOON BURNED DIM . .   175 ELEMENT POWERS   15
    GATHERED A CROWD IN SOME BYZANTINE LANE, ...   180 QUEEN MAEVE   2
    HAD THE WORLD'S TOTAL LIFE GATHERED UP, IT SEEMED, . . .   231 SHADOW WATER B   194
    THE HANDS THAT GATHERED UP THE MIGHT OF THE WORLD, . . .   278 TWO KINGS   29
    ALTHOUGH CROWDS GATHERED ONCE IF SHE BUT SHOWED HER FACE,   314 FALLEN MAJESTY   1
    THAT HE ALONE HAD GATHERED UP NO GEAR, ...   340 SHEP GOATHERD   49
    GATHERED A SCORE OF HORSE AND SPENT HIS DAYS . . . . .   420 MY HOUSE   22
    BECAUSE OF SOME GREEN WING, GATHERED OLD MUMMY WHEAT . .   442 BLACK CENTAUR   7
    OF THE WIDE WOODS. AND THE DEEP EARTH GATHERED THEM. . .   660 ISLE STAT II 1   33
    HEAVY WITH WOOL THE SHEEP ARE GATHERED IN, ...   681 SEEKER   1
    GATHERED ON HER OWN LIPS, OH YOUTH, AND FLING . . . . .   688 TWO TITANS   53
    WE GATHERED. FERENCZ, NAY, I MUST NOT DIE! . . . . . .   713 FERENCZ RENYI   96
    WE GATHERED. FERENCZ, DO NOT LET ME DIE. . . . . . .   713 FERENCZ RENYI V   96
GATHERING
    AND, GATHERING ON OUR BROWS A FROWN, ...   20 OISIN 1   296
    AND, GATHERING ON OUR BROWS A FROWN, ...   20 OISIN 1   V 297
    A THIN GREY MAN HALF LOST IN GATHERING NIGHT. . . . . .   102 FERGUS DRUID   7
    A THIN, GREY MAN, HALF-LOST IN GATHERING NIGHT. . . . .   102 FERGUS DRUID V   7
    THE THRONGS WITH BLOWN WET HAIR ARE GATHERING NEAR. . . .   114 ROSE OF BATTLE V   6
    GATHERING HIS CLOAK ABOUT HIM, RUN . . . .   193 BAILE AILLINN   101
    GATHERING MUSHROOMS IN THE DEW. . . . .   705 DAWN-SONG   8
    GATHERING MUSHROOMS IN THE DEW. . . . .   705 DAWN-SONG   16
    GATHERING MUSHROOMS IN THE DEW. . . . .   706 DAWN-SONG   24
    GATHERING MUSHROOMS IN THE DEW. . . . .   706 DAWN-SONG   32
    HALF DIZZY WITH THE LIGHTNING THERE RUNS A GATHERING BAND--   718 PHANTOM SHIP   9
    NOW HALF DIZZY WITH THE LIGHTNING THERE RUNS A GATHERING   718 PHANTOM SHIP V   9
        BAND!
GATHERS
    GATHERS SEA-SLIME AND GOES THE SEAWARD WAY, ...   45 OISIN 2   V 237
    ONE GATHERS UP HIS PURPLE GOWN! . . . .   212 BLESS PSALTER   9
    GATHERS THE WILD DUCK FROM THE WINTER DAWN! . . . . . .   217 WOODS OF COOLE   3
    AND THERE'S A PLAYER IN THE STATES WHO GATHERS UP HER CLOAK   354 HIS PHOENIX   12
    AND THERE'S THE PLAYER IN THE STATES WHO GATHERS UP HER   354 HIS PHOENIX V   12
        CLOAK
    ALL BREAK AND VANISH, AND EVIL GATHERS HEAD! . . . . . .   433 NINETEEN 19   117
    THAT GATHERS VOLUME! NOW A THUNDER-CLAP. . . . .   487 SEVEN SAGES   23
    THAT GATHERS VOLUME! NOW A THUNDER CLAP. . . . .   487 SEVEN SAGES V   23
GAUDY
    I SWAYED UPON THE GAUDY STERN . . . .   253 HIS DREAM   1
    UPON A GAUDY BED?" . . . .   253 HIS DREAM   8
    AND RUNNING CROWD AND GAUDY SHIP . . . .   254 HIS DREAM   15
    AND FISH AND CROWD AND GAUDY SHIP . . . .   254 HIS DREAM V   15
    WHERE THE GAUDY MOON IS HUNG. . . . .   502 VACILLATION   69
GAUGE
    LET HIM BETWEEN US JUDGE, FOR HE CAN GAUGE . . . . . .   660 ISLE STAT II 1   36
GAUNT   SEE SKELETON-GAUNT.
    NOW HAD THAT OLD GAUNT CRAFTY ONE, ...   193 BAILE AILLINN   100
    AND THE GAUNT HOUSES PUT ON MAJESTY! . . . .   292 TO A SHADE   7
GAVE
    GAVE ME A HARP, AND BID ME SING, ...   16 OISIN 1   232
    GAVE ME A HARP, AND BADE ME SING, ...   16 OISIN 1   V 232
    AND SURGING PHOSPHORUS ALONE GAVE LIGHT . . . .   31 OISIN 2   33
    OF SURGING PHOSPHORUS ALONE GAVE LIGHT. . . . .   31 OISIN 2   V 33
    GAVE TO HIGH NOON AND NOON TO NIGHT GAVE WAY! . . . . .   40 OISIN 2   172
    GAVE TO HIGH NOON AND NOON TO NIGHT GAVE WAY! . . . . .   40 OISIN 2   172
    GAVE TO THE NOON, AND NOON TO EVE GAVE WAY, ...   40 OISIN 2   V 172
    GAVE TO THE NOON, AND NOON TO EVE GAVE WAY, ...   40 OISIN 2   V 172
    TILL THE HORSE GAVE A WHINNY! . . . .   48 OISIN 3   25
    MY SORROW! FOR MANY A CREAK GAVE THE CREEL IN THE CART . .   91 OLD FISHERMAN   6
    AH WOE! FULL MANY A CREAK GAVE THE CREEL IN THE CART . .   91 OLD FISHERMAN V   6
    AH ME! FULL MANY A CREAK GAVE THE CREEL IN THE CART . . .   91 OLD FISHERMAN V   6
    AND HE GAVE THEM AS DOWERS TO HIS DAUGHTERS, ...   92 FATHER OHART   7
    AND GAVE ME MONEY, AND BADE ME GO . . . .   95 MOLL MAGEE   23
    AND GAVE HIS CURSE TO ME! . . . .   95 MOLL MAGEE   26
    WHEN I GAVE JUDGMENT, AND HIS WORDS WERE WISE, ...   102 FERGUS DRUID   11
    WAS ROBBED BEFORE EARTH GAVE THE WHEAT! . . . .   196 BAILE AILLINN   166
    FOR HE GAVE ALL HIS HEART AND LOST. . . . .   202 NEVER GIVE ALL   14

313

		PAGE	TITLE	LINE
GAVE	(CONTINUED)			
	AND FOR THIS END THEY GAVE ME MY OLD HARP	237	SHADOW WATER B	327
	THEY GAVE ME THAT OLD HARP OF THE NINE SPELLS	237	SHADOW WATER B V	327
	HAVE BEEN DEFEATED BY THAT PLEDGE YOU GAVE	258	KING NO KING	9
	AND HOW WHAT HER DREAMING GAVE	260	UNWORTH PRAISE	15
	SOLDIERS THAT GAVE, WHATEVER DIE WAS CAST!	269	PARDON FATHERS	9
	NOR GAVE LOUD SERVICE TO A CAUSE	273	GREY ROCK	57
	PRAISED THEIR GREAT VICTORIES AND GAVE THEM JOY	286	TWO KINGS V	218B
	YOU GAVE, BUT WILL NOT GIVE AGAIN	287	TO WEALTHY MAN	1
	HE GAVE THE HOURS THEY HAD SET FREE	288	TO WEALTHY MAN	22
	BECAUSE YOU GAVE, NOT WHAT THEY WOULD,	288	TO WEALTHY MAN	35
	THEY WEIGHED SO LIGHTLY WHAT THEY GAVE.	290	SEPTEMBER 1913	30
	HE GAVE A GASP AND THOUGHT TO HAVE FLED,	303	HOUR DAWN	22
	HE GAVE A GASP AND THOUGHT TO RUN.	303	HOUR DAWN V	22
	GAVE ME SUCH PLEASURE I'D FORGO	305	HOUR DAWN	69
	HE GAVE HIM A GREAT PUMMELLING.	307	HOUR DAWN	113
	NOR GAVE GOD THANKS TILL OVERHEAD	307	HOUR DAWN	121
	AND GAVE GOD THANKS THAT OVERHEAD	307	HOUR DAWN V	121
	AMONG THE POOR BOTH OLD AND YOUNG GAVE HER PRAISE.	351	HER PRAISE	18
	WHO NEVER GAVE THE BURNING TOWN A THOUGHT:	384	VISION ROBART	57
	GAVE SHEBA TO HER SOLOMON."	388	SOLOMON WITCH	32
	THAT GAVE, THOUGH FREE TO REFUSE--	414	TOWER	133
	POSEIDON GAVE IT BIT AND OAR,	447	COLONUS PRAISE	28
	THAT IF THE SPRING BEAR OFF WHAT THE SPRING GAVE	464	HARUN RASHID	76
	AND THEREUPON HIS BOUNTY GAVE WHAT NOW	465	HARUN RASHID	103
	GAVE BUT MORE REASON FOR A WOMAN'S CARE.	466	HARUN RASHID	111
	FOUND ALL THE PLEASURE THAT LIFE GAVE"!	521	THREE THINGS	11
	THE CHILDREN THAT HE GAVE,	525	DANCING DAYS	12
	THOSE DEEDS WERE BEST THAT GAVE THE MINUTE WINGS	533	HER TRIUMPH	5
	AND HEAVENLY MUSIC IF THEY GAVE IT WIT!	533	HER TRIUMPH	6
	SANG OF THE BEAST THAT GAVE THE FATAL WOUND.	537	HER VISION	16
	I ANSWER THAT I GAVE MY SOUL	538	LAST CONFESS	3
	HE FANCIED THAT I GAVE A SOUL	538	LAST CONFESS	9
	BEAST GAVE BEAST AS MUCH.	538	LAST CONFESS	12
	I GAVE WHAT OTHER WOMEN GAVE	538	LAST CONFESS	13
	I GAVE WHAT OTHER WOMEN GAVE	538	LAST CONFESS	13
	BUT A GOOD STRONG CAUSE--THE ROPE GAVE A JERK THERE,	545	TO SAME TUNE 1	23
	THE MIRACLE THAT GAVE THEM SUCH A DEATH	555	RIBH AT TOMB	10
	THEY GAVE IT OUT TO ALL THE WORLD,	582	ROGER CASEMENT	11
	WHAT GAVE THAT ROAR OF MOCKERY.	583	GHOST ROG CASE	7
	I GAVE IT ALL TO AN OLDER MAN.	588	OLD WICKED MAN	23
	GAVE WOMEN DREAMS AND DREAMS THEIR LOOKING-GLASS.	610	STATUES	16
	GAVE WOMEN DREAMS AND DREAMS THEIR LOOKING-GLASS.	610	STATUES V	16
	BUT A GOOD STRONG CAUSE--THE ROPE GAVE A JERK THERE,	616	MARCH SONGS 3	23
	AND YET GAVE TONGUE. "HOUND VOICES" WERE THEY ALL.	622	HOUND VOICE	9
	THE COUNTESS CATHLEEN WAS THE NAME I GAVE IT!	629	CIRCUS ANIMALS	18
	THE SPIRITS STOLE, AND GAVE HIM IN ITS STEAD	684	SEEKER	55
	FOR ALL I GAVE THE VOICE, FOR ALL MY YOUTH,	685	SEEKER	78
	WHEN HE GAVE TO THEE THE ROSE,	744	ROSY CROSS	2
	GAVE TO ME ALONE THE CROSS!	744	ROSY CROSS	3
	WHEN HE GAVE TO THEE THE ROSE,	744	ROSY CROSS	10
	GAVE TO ME ALONE THE CROSS.	744	ROSY CROSS	11
	GAVE HIM HIS HARP. NOW THAT HE IS ASLEEP,	748	SHADOW WATER A	18
	AND, THOUGH YOU LOVED HER, GAVE HER UP TO ME?	749	SHADOW WATER A	50
	TAUGHT ME WISE MUSIC, AND GAVE ME THIS OLD HARP!	750	SHADOW WATER A	76
	IT WAS A FOOL THAT GAVE IT, AND MAY BE	750	SHADOW WATER A	78
	FOR HE WHO GAVE IT CALLED IT AENGUS' HARP	762	SHADOW WATER A	288
	GAVE THEIR BODIES, EMPTIED PURSES.	789	SINGING HEAD	19
	GAVE ALL THE LOVE THAT WOMEN KNOW!	789	SINGING HEAD	21
GAVEST				
	A FOOLISH WORD THOU GAVEST ME!	671	ISLE STAT II 3	131
GAVRA				
	AND THOSE ON GAVRA LYING LOW,	5	OISIN 1 V	41
GAVRA'S				
	FOR OUR BEST WERE DEAD ON GAVRA'S GREEN.	2	OISIN 1 V	71
GAY				
	HELD TO THE TOWERS WITH BOASTING SONGS AND GAY.	41	OISIN 2 V	184C
	WHO MADE THE GRASS AND MADE THE WORMS AND MADE MY FEATHERS GAY,	77	INDIAN ON GOD	18
	. . . THE WAVES WERE MORE GAY,	91	OLD FISHERMAN	3
	A GAY WANDERING CRY.	98	FOXHUNTER	28
	A GAY AND WANDERING CRY.	98	FOXHUNTER V	28
	WE WHO ARE OLD, OLD AND GAY,	116	FAERY SONG	1
	US WHO ARE OLD, OLD AND GAY,	116	FAERY SONG	13
	ARE GAY WITH HIS MOOD.	118	CRADLE SONG	8
	GROW GAY WITH HIS MOOD.	118	CRADLE SONG V	8
	THERE DWELT A GAY, EXULTING, GENTLE RACE	127	DREAM OF FAERY	20
	THAT HE'S A LOVELESS MAN! GAY BELLS BRING LAUGHTER	130	BOOK STORIES	18
	GAY BELLS OR SAD, THEY BRING YOU MEMORIES	130	BOOK STORIES	21
	MY BELL BRANCH MURMURS! THE GAY BELLS BRING LAUGHTER,	130	BOOK STORIES V	18
	AND NEVER WAS PIPING SO GAY.	144	HOST OF AIR	12
	WITH A SAD AND A GAY FACE.	144	HOST OF AIR	16
	AND NEVER WAS PIPING SO GAY.	145	HOST OF AIR	44
	HIS GHOST WILL BE GAY.	311	PEACOCK	9
	TILL ALL THE BOUGHS ARE GAY.	366	HER CHRIS TREE	5
	THAT FANCIED GOODNESS MIGHT BE GAY.	432	NINETEEN 19	104
	SEMELE'S LAD A GAY COMPANION.	446	COLONUS PRAISE	8
	THE SECOND BEST'S A GAY GOODNIGHT AND QUICKLY TURN AWAY.	459	FROM OEDIPUS	12
	AND ALL MY HEART SEEMED GAY!	507	STREAM AND SUN	3
	OF POETS THAT ARE ALWAYS GAY,	565	LAPIS LAZULI	3
	THEY KNOW THAT HAMLET AND LEAR ARE GAY;	565	LAPIS LAZULI	16

314

	PAGE	TITLE	LINE

GAY (CONTINUED)

AND THOSE THAT BUILD THEM AGAIN ARE GAY. 566 LAPIS LAZULI 36
THEIR ANCIENT, GLITTERING EYES, ARE GAY. 567 LAPIS LAZULI 56
MY LOVER LOOKED SO GAY"; 570 THREE BUSHES 32
MY LOVER LOOKS SO GAY." 570 THREE BUSHES V 32
THE POETS HAVE IMAGINED, TERRIBLE AND GAY." 602 GALLERY REVIS 12
SING THE LORDS AND LADIES GAY 640 BEN BULBEN 78
BY A PEOPLE SADLY GAY! 680 LOVE AND DEATH 10
NOW SADLY, NOW UNEARTHLY GAY, 716 FAIRY DOCTOR 3
LONG THOU FOR NOTHING, NEITHER SAD NOR GAY; 734 QUATRAIN APHOR 9

GAYEST

GAYEST WANDERERS, I AND YOU, 706 DAWN-SONG 31

GAZE

WITH QUENCHLESS GAZE AND FLUTTERING HAIR. 12 OISIN 1 145
AND SANG, AND WITH A DREAMY GAZE 26 OISIN 1 393
OR LOVE'S FIRST TENDERNESS DIE IN OUR GAZE. 27 OISIN 1 411
OR LOVE'S FIRST TENDERNESS DIE IN OUR GAZE. 27 OISIN 1 V 419D
AS THEY GAZE AT EACH OTHER, "OH, WHERE IS THAT GREAT ONE?" 28 OISIN 1 V 423H
OR LOVE'S FIRST TENDERNESS DIE IN OUR GAZE." 28 OISIN 1 V 427
"GAZE NO MORE ON THE PHANTOMS," NIAMH SAID, 29 OISIN 2 5
HOW SUCH A WARRIOR NEVER TURNED HIS GAZE 29 OISIN 2 V 11
WHERE GOES TO GAZE THE RESTLESS-FOOTED STAR 32 OISIN 2 V 50G
OF FACES, WAITED! AND THE LEISURED GAZE 39 OISIN 2 149
OF FACES, WATCHED ME, AND THE LEISURED GAZE 39 OISIN 2 V 149
AND MY GAZE WAS THRONGED WITH THE SLEEPERS; 50 OISIN 3 49
I MUST GAZE ON THE BEARD OF FINN, 55 OISIN 3 114
CAME AFTER THE HARD GAZE OF YOUTH, OR AN OLD MAN LIFTED HIS HEAD! 59 OISIN 3 170
IT WERE SAD TO GAZE ON THE BLESSED AND NO MAN I LOVED OF OLD THERE; 63 OISIN 3 221
IT WAS SAD TO GAZE ON THE BLESSED AND NO MAN I LOVED OF OLD THERE; 63 OISIN 3 V 221
BELOVED, GAZE IN THINE OWN HEART, 134 TWO TREES 1
BELOVED, GAZE IN THINE OWN HEART. 135 TWO TREES 20
GAZE NO MORE IN THE BITTER GLASS 135 TWO TREES 21
OR ONLY GAZE A LITTLE WHILE; 135 TWO TREES 24
GAZE NO MORE IN THE BITTER GLASS. 136 TWO TREES 40
MAY SURELY BARTER GAZE FOR GAZE. 139 TO IRELAND 28
MAY SURELY BARTER GAZE FOR GAZE. 139 TO IRELAND 28
MAY SURELY MEET THEIR ANCIENT GAZE. 139 TO IRELAND V 28
AND IF ANY GAZE ON OUR RUSHING BAND, 141 HOSTING SIDHE 10
ARE OVERTHROWN BY A WOMAN'S GAZE 164 PERFECT BEAUTY 4
STILL OVERTHROWN BY A WOMAN'S GAZE, 164 PERFECT BEAUTY V 4
WHEN ALL THE WILD SUMMER WAS IN HER GAZE." 200 FOLLY COMFORT 12
FOR WE WILL GAZE UPON THIS WORLD NO LONGER. 251 SHADOW WATER B 614
FOR HE WILL GAZE UPON THIS WORLD NO LONGER. 251 SHADOW WATER B 614
FOR HE WILL GAZE UPON THE WORLD NO LONGER. 251 SHADOW WATER B V 614
AND COPY THEIR PROUD STEADY GAZE. 273 GREY ROCK 64
AND WHEN SHE MEETS OUR GAZE HER EYES ARE LAUGHTER-LIT, 362 HER COURTESY 5
AND WHEN SHE MEETS OUR GAZE HER EYES ARE LAUGHTER LIT 362 HER COURTESY V 5
A GAZE BLANK AND PITILESS AS THE SUN, 402 SECOND COMING 15
THE POPLARS GAZE ACROSS THE WATERS GREY 653 ISLE STAT I 2 34
EACH ONE AT GAZE FOR AYE UPON HIS WHIRLING THRONE. 662 ISLE STAT II 1 81
BUT ART THOU HAPPY? LET ME GAZE ON THEE 671 ISLE STAT II 3 144
I COULD GAZE, GAZE UPON THINE EYES' CLEAR GREY; 671 ISLE STAT II 3 147
I COULD GAZE, GAZE UPON THINE EYES' CLEAR GREY; 671 ISLE STAT II 3 147
I COULD GAZE, GAZE UPON THINE EYES OF GREY; 671 ISLE STAT II 3 147
I COULD GAZE, GAZE UPON THINE EYES OF GREY; 671 ISLE STAT II 3 V 147
GAZE ON TILL RAGGED TIME HIMSELF DECAY. 672 ISLE STAT II 3 148
WOULD HE TEACH ANY SIN? GAZE IN THE CLOUD 692 MOSADA 1 58
O SISTER OF SORROWFUL GAZE! 706 FAIRY PEDANT 2
AND GAZE ON THE MEADOW-MICE WARY, 707 FAIRY PEDANT 18
A LIZARD CRAWLS--THE TWO MEN GAZE INTENT, 711 FERENCZ RENYI 47
AND GAZE ON ONE ANOTHER THROUGH OUR EYES, 749 SHADOW WATER A 58
FOR WE WILL GAZE UPON THIS WORLD NO LONGER. 769 SHADOW WATER A 430
I HIDE YOU WITH MY HAIR, THAT WE MAY GAZE 769 SHADOW WATER A V 429

GAZEBO

WE THE GREAT GAZEBO BUILT, 476 EVA GORE-BOOTH 30

GAZED

THEY FINGERED IT AND GAZED ON ME 15 OISIN 1 209
THEY FINGERED IT AND GAZED AT ME, 15 OISIN 1 V 209
AND I GAZED ON THE BELL-BRANCH, SLEEP'S FOREBEAR, 50 OISIN 3 53
. . . AND GAZED ON THE GRASS WITH A SIGH. 54 OISIN 3 100
AND GAZED UPON THE WISDOM OF HIS EYES, 108 CUCHULAIN SEA V 41
AND GAZED UPON THE MOURNFUL STARS ABOVE, 123 DREAM OF DEATH V 11
AND THOUGH WHEN HE GAZED HERE AND THERE, 274 GREY ROCK 81
HE HAD BUT GAZED ON THORN-TREES, SPOKE, 274 GREY ROCK 82
HE HAD BUT GAZED ON THORN TREES, SPOKE! 274 GREY ROCK V 82
THE DISEMBOWELLED HORSE. KING EOCHAID GAZED, 278 TWO KINGS V 45
I GAZED AT HIM LIKE GROUSE UPON A KITE! 283 TWO KINGS 152
AND THAT PROUD LOOK AS THOUGH SHE HAD GAZED INTO THE BURNING SUN, 354 HIS PHOENIX 29
GAZED UPON ALL THINGS KNOWN, ALL THINGS UNKNOWN, 383 VISION ROBART 30
WHILE ON THE SHOP AND STREET I GAZED 501 VACILLATION 40
AS I AM STANDING NOW--AS THOUGH I GAZED, 663 ISLE STAT II 2 26

GAZELLE

BEAUTIFUL, ONE A GAZELLE. 475 EVA GORE-BOOTH 4
BEAUTIFUL, ONE A GAZELLE. 475 EVA GORE-BOOTH 20

GAZES

AND GAZES AROUND HER WITH EYES OF BRIGHTNESS; 27 OISIN 1 413
AND GAZES AROUND HER WITH EYES OF BRIGHTNESS; 28 OISIN 1 V 421

315

		PAGE	TITLE		LINE

GAZES   (CONTINUED)
WE SHALL MINGLE NO MORE, NOR OUR GAZES EMPTY THEIR   56 OISIN 3   132
  SWEETNESS LONE
GAZING
HOUNDS ARE GAZING ON HIS FACE,   99 FOXHUNTER   39
THE HOUNDS ARE GAZING ON HIS FACE,   99 FOXHUNTER   V   39
AND HOUNDS ARE GAZING ON HIS FACE,   99 FOXHUNTER   V   39
AND GAZING ON HIS VISAGE WORN,   99 FOXHUNTER   V   43
GAZING UPON HER WITH BEWILDERED EYES: 280 TWO KINGS   V   84
WHEREIN THE GAZING HEART DOUBLES HER MIGHT.   326 ROBERT GREGORY   69
IN LIST'NING SILENCE GAZING ON OUR GRIEF.   702 MOSADA 3   87
NOR, GAZING FORTH WHERE LIFE'S SAD SICKLES REAP,   710 FERENCZ RENYI   31
LEANS ON HIS ELBOWS, GAZING AT THE SEA.   752 SHADOW WATER A   127
GEAR
THAT HE ALONE HAD GATHERED UP NO GEAR,   340 SHEP GOATHERD   49
ALL THAT SILK AND SATIN GEAR: 525 DANCING DAYS   3
IN THAT OUTLANDISH GEAR,   526 AM OF IRELAND   7
GEESE   SEE BARNACLE-GEESE
WAS IT FOR THIS THE WILD GEESE SPREAD   290 SEPTEMBER 1913   17
AN ANCIENT LECHER TOOK TO GEESE   792 GEORGE MOORE   3
GEM-STUDDED
LEANING DOWN FROM THE GEM-STUDDED SADDLE,   60 OISIN 3   187
LEANING FORTH FROM THE GEM-STUDDED SADDLE,   60 OISIN 3   V   187
GENERAL
BEFORE HIS TENT THE GENERAL SIPS HIS WINE,   709 FERENCZ RENYI   6
GENERATED
WHAT'S WATER BUT THE GENERATED SOUL?   490 COOLE BALLYLEE   8
GENERATION
HONEY OF GENERATION HAD BETRAYED,   444 SCHOOL CHILDR   34
THAT IN EVERY GENERATION   608 SONGS BURDEN 3   25
GENERATIONS
FILLING THE FIBROUS DIMNESS WITH LONG GENERATIONS OF EYES.   49 OISIN 3   40
ONE THAT THE GENERATIONS HAD LONG WAITED   182 QUEEN MAEVE   66
GENERATIONS OF HIS SORT,   319 DOLLS   6
—THOSE DYING GENERATIONS—AT THEIR SONG,   407 SAIL BYZANTIUM   3
JUSTIFY ALL THOSE RENOWNED GENERATIONS,   545 TO SAME TUNE 2   1
JUSTIFY ALL THOSE RENOWNED GENERATIONS,   546 TO SAME TUNE 2   11
OF ALL THAT SCHOLARLY GENERATIONS HAD HELD DEAR: 603 GALLERY REVIS   V   37A
SUMMONED THE GENERATIONS OF HIS HOUSE,   609 IN TARAS HALLS   19
REMEMBER ALL THOSE RENOWNED GENERATIONS,   613 MARCH SONGS 1   1
REMEMBER ALL THOSE RENOWNED GENERATIONS,   613 MARCH SONGS 1   11
REMEMBER ALL THESE RENOWNED GENERATIONS,   613 MARCH SONGS 1   V   11
GENEROSITY
CONSIDERATION, GENEROSITY,   244 SHADOW WATER B   456
GENEROUS
ON GENEROUS THINGS THAT HE DID   473 ALL SOUL NIGHT   69
GENII
AND WHEN ONCE MORE THE LIGHTNING GENII PASSED,   687 TWO TITANS   29
GENTLE
TO THIS DIM SHORE THOSE GENTLE FEET?   5 OISIN 1   V   51
AND SIGHING BOWED HER GENTLE HEAD,   12 OISIN 1   149
THE GENTLE NIAMH WAS MY WIFE,   24 OISIN 1   357
AND THE GENTLE WAVES OF THE SUMMER SEAS,   27 OISIN 1   418
AND, IN A FAR-OFF, GENTLE VALLEY STOPPING,   68 SAD SHEPHERD   13
HE IS A GENTLE ROEBUCK: FOR HOW ELSE, I PRAY, COULD HE   76 INDIAN ON GOD   15
CONCEIVE A THING SO SAD AND SOFT, A GENTLE THING LIKE ME?   77 INDIAN ON GOD   16
A GENTLE YET A KINGLY CHILD: 82 MAD KING GOLL   V   8
A GRACIOUS, GENTLE, KINGLY BOY.   82 MAD KING GOLL   V   8
LED ON BY GENTLE WAYS: 113 ROSE OF PEACE   12
THERE DWELT A GAY, EXULTING, GENTLE RACE,   127 DREAM OF FAERY   20
A GENTLE FEELING WRAPS THEM LIKE A FLEECE,   128 DREAM OF FAERY   V   34
WINGED LOVES BORNE ON IN GENTLE STRIFE,   135 TWO TREES   14
BUT LET A GENTLE SILENCE WROUGHT WITH MUSIC FLOW   175 ELEMENT POWERS   17
BUT LET A GENTLE SILENCE ENWROUGHT WITH MUSIC FLOW   175 ELEMENT POWERS   V   17
FOR ANY GENTLE THING SHE SPAKE,   191 BAILE AILLINN   63
GROW GENTLE WITHOUT SORROWING,   193 BAILE AILLINN   110
GROW GENTLE WITHOUT SORROWINGS: 193 BAILE AILLINN   V   110
LIKE GENTLE BLOOD, HAS BEEN DRIVEN FROM THE PLACE,   292 TO A SHADE   14
BUT GROWS MORE GENTLE WHEN HE SPEAKS HER NAME,   340 SHEP GOATHERD   29
WE HAVE LIT UPON THE GENTLE, SENSITIVE MIND   368 EGO DOMINUS   12
A GENTLE QUESTIONING LOOK THAT CANNOT HIDE   601 GALLERY REVIS   6
BEAUTIFUL AND GENTLE IN HER VENETIAN WAY.   602 GALLERY REVIS   14
YET A MOST GENTLE WOMAN: WHO CAN TELL   618 BRONZE HEAD   10
GENTLEMAN
TO THIS MOST GALLANT GENTLEMAN   582 ROGER CASEMENT   23
GENTLEMEN
AMONG THE OTHER GENTLEMEN,   296 THREE BEGGARS   34
"HEAR, GENTLEMEN, LADIES, AND ALL MANKIND: 544 TO SAME TUNE 1   2
"HEAR, GENTLEMEN, LADIES, AND ALL MANKIND: 615 MARCH SONGS 3   2
HARD-RIDING COUNTRY GENTLEMEN,   639 BEN BULBEN   75
GENTLENESS
TOGETHER IN THAT HOUR OF GENTLENESS   80 EPHEMERA   6
THE GENTLENESS NONE THERE HAD EVER KNOWN: 418 ANCEST HOUSES   21
DISTRACTED GENTLENESS THAT CANNOT HIDE   601 GALLERY REVIS   V   6
WITH YOU I AM ALL GENTLENESS: IN TRUTH,   669 ISLE STAT II 3   70
GENTLER
FORMS THAT GENTLER PHIDIAS WROUGHT.   638 BEN BULBEN   44
GENTLY
THEN SHE SIGHED GENTLY, "IT GROWS LATE.   9 OISIN 1   102
MURMURING GENTLY HOW FAR OFF ARE THE UNQUIET LANDS: 78 INDIAN TO LOVE   V   10
OR GENTLY IN A RING.   97 FOXHUNTER   8

316

		PAGE	TITLE		LINE

GENTLY   (CONTINUED)
    AND LEAD HIM GENTLY IN A RING, ...   97 FOXHUNTER   V   7
    AND GENTLY UP AND DOWN. . . . .   97 FOXHUNTER   V   8
    FOR WINDS WILL BEAR THEM GENTLY WHEN THE EAGLE FLIES, . .   146 UNAPPEAS HOST   V   3
    LEAD THEM GENTLY ASTRAY! . . . .   568 SWEET DANCER   11
    MOVE MOST GENTLY IF MOVE YOU MUST . . . .   617 LONG-LEG FLY   13
    GENTLY SHOOK THEIR MOTH-LIKE WINGS; . . . .   667 ISLE STAT II 3   26
    AND TEARS OF FIRE FALL GENTLY IN THE DEW. . . . . .   738 YOU ARE SAD   4
GEOMETRY
    DESERT GEOMETRY OR THE GIFT OF HARUN AL-RASCHID . . . .   460 HARUN RASHID   V   T
GEORGE
    AND THEN I THINK OF OLD GEORGE POLLEXFEN, ...   325 ROBERT GREGORY   33
    HIS SON GEORGE, THE ASTROLOGER; . . . .   360 ALF POLLEXFEN   8
    RESTORED THIS TOWER FOR MY WIFE GEORGE; . . . . . .   406 CARVED STONE   4
    SAINT GEORGE OR ELSE A PAGAN PERSEUS! . . . . . .   533 HER TRIUMPH   10
    ON GEORGE MOORE! . . . .   792 GEORGE MOORE   T
GEORGIAN
    OF THAT OLD GEORGIAN MANSION, MIX . . . .   475 EVA GORE-BOOTH   16
GER-EAGLE
    FOR THEY WILL RIDE THE NORTH WHEN THE GER-EAGLE FLIES, . .   146 UNAPPEAS HOST   3
GERMAN
    SOME NINETEEN GERMAN PLANES, THEY SAY, ...   791 REPRISALS   1
GERMANY'S
    TILL GERMANY'S OVERCOME! . . . .   395 SIXTEEN DEAD   8
GET
    COME FROM THE ISLE OF THE LIVING." "THEN GET YE . . . .   34 OISIN 2   V   79
    AND GET INTO THEIR WORLD THAT TO THE SENSE . . . . .   230 SHADOW WATER B   179
    DO MEN WHO LEAST DESIRE GET MOST, ...   295 THREE BEGGARS   13
    OR GET THE MOST WHO MOST DESIRE?" . . . .   295 THREE BEGGARS   14
    A BEGGAR SAID, "THEY GET THE MOST . . . .   295 THREE BEGGARS   15
    "AND GET A COMFORTABLE WIFE AND HOUSE . . . . . .   299 BEGGAR CRIED   5
    I GET A LAUGHING FIT, ...   455 FRIENDS YOUTH   4
    AND SHE CAN GET NO REST . . . .   456 FRIENDS YOUTH   8
    "BUT I CAN GET A HAIR-DYE . . . .   492 ANNE GREGORY   7
    GET ALL THE GOLD AND SILVER THAT YOU CAN, ...   500 VACILLATION   19
    SO GET YOU GONE, VON HUEGEL, THOUGH WITH BLESSINGS ON YOUR   503 VACILLATION   89
        HEAD.
    I SHOULD NOT GET THE WORD . . . .   585 ORAHILLY   20
    "IRELAND SHALL GET HER FREEDOM AND YOU STILL BREAK STONE."   590 PARNELL   2
    SOME DAY WE SHALL GET UP BEFORE THE DAWN . . . . .   622 HOUND VOICE   15
    AND NEVER GET THE ANSWERS RIGHT. . . . .   632 MAN AND ECHO   10
    WE MUST GET SWORDS. IS'T THE ONLY WAY? OH, SEE, . . .   660 ISLE STAT II 1   34
    THEY GET THEM SWORDS, AND BOTH OR EITHER FALL? . . .   662 ISLE STAT II 1   78
GETS
    AND THE SEED OF THE FIRE GETS FEEBLE AND COLD. . . . .   151 OLD MOTHER   10
    BUT THE SEED OF THE FIRE GETS FEEBLE AND COLD, ...   151 OLD MOTHER   V   9
    BUT HE THAT GETS THEIR LOVE AFTER THE FASHION . . . .   228 SHADOW WATER B   145
    HE NOW GETS NOVELS AT HIS EASE. . . . .   792 GEORGE MOORE   4
GETTING
    FOR I AM GETTING ON IN LIFE--TO SOMETHING . . . . .   222 SHADOW WATER B   6
GHASTLY
    AND THE GHASTLY GHOST-FLAMES GLIMMER ALL ALONG THE TAFFRAIL   719 PHANTOM SHIP   21
        RAILS
    AND THE GHASTLY GHOST FLAMES GLIMMER ALONG THE TAFFREL   719 PHANTOM SHIP   V   21
        RAILS,
GHOST
    THE DOORS OF HELL AND BLOW THERE MANY A WHIMPERING GHOST;   147 UNAPPEAS HOST   10
    OF A NEW FRIEND HE HAS TURNED A GHOST. . . . . . .   275 GREY ROCK   103
    BUT I'LL HAVE NO MAN CALL ME GHOST." . . . .   304 HOUR DAWN   41
    "I TOOK YOU FOR A BRAWLING GHOST, ...   304 HOUR DAWN   V   41
    HIS GHOST WILL BE GAY . . . .   311 PEACOCK   9
    RIDDLED WITH LIGHT. AH! WHEN THE GHOST BEGINS TO QUICKEN,   316 COLD HEAVEN   9
    BID A STRONG GHOST STAND AT THE HEAD . . . .   435 FOR MY SON   1
    BID THE GHOST HAVE SWORD IN FIST! . . . .   435 FOR MY SON   9
    BID THE GHOST HAVE SWORD IN HAND! . . . .   435 FOR MY SON   V   9
    BUBBLE UPON THE TABLE. A GHOST MAY COME! . . . . .   470 ALL SOUL NIGHT   5
    AND THAT A SLIGHT COMPANIONABLE GHOST, ...   472 ALL SOUL NIGHT   35
    AND MAY HAVE GROWN MORE ARROGANT BEING A GHOST. . . .   473 ALL SOUL NIGHT   80
    A LONELY GHOST THE GHOST IS . . . .   511 JANE AND JACK   7
    A LONELY GHOST THE GHOST IS . . . .   511 JANE AND JACK   7
    THE SKEIN SO BOUND US GHOST TO GHOST . . . .   511 JANE AND JACK   15
    THE SKEIN SO BOUND US GHOST TO GHOST . . . .   511 JANE AND JACK   15
    "WHAT THEN?"   SANG PLATO'S GHOST.   "WHAT THEN?" . . .   576 WHAT THEN   5
    "WHAT THEN?"   SANG PLATO'S GHOST.   "WHAT THEN?" . . .   577 WHAT THEN   10
    "WHAT THEN?"   SANG PLATO'S GHOST.   "WHAT THEN?" . . .   577 WHAT THEN   15
    BUT LOUDER SANG THAT GHOST, "WHAT THEN?" . . . . .   577 WHAT THEN   20
    THE GHOST OF ROGER CASEMENT . . . .   583 GHOST ROG CASE   T
    THE GHOST OF ROGER CASEMENT . . . .   583 GHOST ROG CASE   9
    THE GHOST OF ROGER CASEMENT . . . .   583 GHOST ROG CASE   19
    THE GHOST OF ROGER CASEMENT . . . .   584 GHOST ROG CASE   29
    THE GHOST OF ROGER CASEMENT . . . .   584 GHOST ROG CASE   39
    AND THE GHASTLY GHOST FLAMES GLIMMER ALONG THE TAFFREL   719 PHANTOM SHIP   V   21
        RAILS,
    CAN GHOST OR MAN BE SATISFIED? . . . .   791 REPRISALS   4
GHOST-FLAMES
    AND THE GHASTLY GHOST-FLAMES GLIMMER ALL ALONG THE TAFFRAIL   719 PHANTOM SHIP   21
        RAILS
GHOST-LOVER
    A GHOST-LOVER HE WAS . . . .   473 ALL SOUL NIGHT   79
GHOSTLY
    WALKING GHOSTLY IN THE DEW, ...   67 HAPPY SHEPHERD   52

317

GHOSTLY   (CONTINUED)
    WALKING GHOSTLY 'MONG THE DEW, ...   67 HAPPY SHEPHERD V   52
    BUT BREAK UPON HIS GHOSTLY SOLITUDE. . . . . 429 NINETEEN 19   40
    UPON A GHOSTLY PARADIGM OF THINGS: . . . . 445 SCHOOL CHILDR   42
    UPON THE GHOSTLY IMAGES OF THINGS . . . . 445 SCHOOL CHILDR V 42
GHOST'S
    FOR IT IS A GHOST'S RIGHT, ... 470 ALL SOUL NIGHT   6
    AN OLD GHOST'S THOUGHTS ARE LIGHTNING, ... 600 SPIRIT MEDIUM   17
GHOSTS
    GHOSTS OF HER VANISHED GLORIES, MUSE AND STALK . . . . 687 TWO TITANS   21
    AMONG THE WHIMPERING GHOSTS. MATE THUS. ALREADY? . . . 722 WITCH VIVIEN   68
    THE GHOSTS WENT BY ME WITH THEIR LIPS APART . . . . . 734 QUATRAIN APHOR   13
GIANT
    AMONG THE GIANT KINGS WHOSE HOARD, ... 196 BAILE AILLINN   164
GIANTS
    WHEN GODS AND GIANTS WARRED. WE RODE BETWEEN . . . .   31 OISIN 2   31
GIBE
    OF A MOCKING TALE OR A GIBE . . . . 392 EASTER 1916   10
GIDDY
    GIDDY WITH HIS HUNDREDTH YEAR, ... 298 THREE HERMITS   6
    GIDDY WITH HIS HUNDREDTH YEAR, ... 299 THREE HERMITS   31
    THE GIDDY BEE'S COMPLACENT CROON, ... 736 SUMMER EVENING   5
GIER-EAGLE
    FOR THEY WILL RIDE THE WINDS WHEN THE GIER-EAGLE FLIES . . 146 UNAPPEAS HOST V   3
GIFT
    TO GRADUAL TIME'S LAST GIFT, A WRITTEN SPEECH . . . . 264 HOUSE SHAKEN   11
    THE GIFT . . . . 287 TO WEALTHY MAN V   T
    WE HAVE NO GIFT TO SET A STATESMAN RIGHT: . . . . . 359 WAR POEM   3
    HEARTS ARE NOT HAD AS A GIFT BUT HEARTS ARE EARNED . . 404 FOR DAUGHTER   34
    WHERE SATO'S GIFT, A CHANGELESS SWORD, ... 421 MY TABLE   2
    THE GIFT OF HARUN AL-RASHID . . . . 460 HARUN RASHID   T
    DESERT GEOMETRY OR THE GIFT OF HARUN AL-RASCHID . . . 460 HARUN RASHID V   T
    THAT EVERY GIFT AND EVERY WORD OF PRAISE . . . . . . 469 HARUN RASHID   172
    "I BID HIM ASK WHAT GIFT HE WILL, ... 741 EARL PAUL   57
GIFTED
    GIFTED WITH SO FINE AN EAR: . . . . 412 TOWER   94
GIFTS
    THE GIFTS THAT GOVERN MEN, AND AFTER THESE . . . . . 264 HOUSE SHAKEN   10
GIGANTIC
    AND HER GIGANTIC LIMBS. THE WEARY THIRST . . . . . . 687 TWO TITANS   16
GILD
    ALTHOUGH THE SUMMER SUNLIGHT GILD . . . . 501 VACILLATION   45
    HERE, FACING TO THE LAKE, AND NO NAME GILD: . . . . 663 ISLE STAT II 2   20
GILDED
    HAST THOU NOT RULED AMONG THE GILDED WALLS? . . . . 724 KANVA ON SELF   7
    A COAT OF GILDED MAIL. . . . . 740 EARL PAUL   16
GILLIGAN
    THE BALLAD OF FATHER GILLIGAN . . . . 132 FR GILLIGAN   T
    FATHER GILLIGAN . . . . 132 FR GILLIGAN V   T
    THE OLD PRIEST PETER GILLIGAN . . . . 132 FR GILLIGAN   1
    THE OLD PRIEST PETER GILLIGAN . . . . 133 FR GILLIGAN   23
    THE OLD PRIEST PETER GILLIGAN . . . . 133 FR GILLIGAN   35
    THE OLD PRIEST PETER GILLIGAN . . . . 133 FR GILLIGAN   39
GILLYFLOWER
    AND MANY A PURPLE GILLYFLOWER EATEN, ... 729 PRIEST FAIRY   35
GIMLET
    AND PIERCE IT THROUGH WITH A GIMLET, AND STARE . . . 330 BONE OF A HARE   12
GIORGIONE
    WHO HAD MURMURED OF GIORGIONE AT HIS LATEST BREATH-- . . 366 HER COURAGE   8
GIRDLE
    AND THE GIRDLE OF LIGHT IS UNBOUND, ... 165 CRY OF SEDGE   8
    BINDS, AS WITHIN A GIRDLE OR A RING, ... 657 ISLE STAT I 3   59
GIRL
    AND KNELT THERE, EVERY GIRL AND MAN, ...   15 OISIN 1   214
    WITH ONE LONG GLANCE FOR GIRL AND BOY . . . .   19 OISIN 1   287
    FROM GIRL AND BOY AND MAN AND BEAST: . . . .   82 MAD KING GOLL   6
    A GIRL AROSE THAT HAD RED MOURNFUL LIPS . . . . . . 120 SORROW OF LOVE   5
    AND A YOUNG GIRL WHITE BREAD. . . . . 144 HOST OF AIR   20
    IT HAD BECOME A GLIMMERING GIRL . . . . 149 WANDER AENGUS   13
    IT HAD BECOME A LAUGHING GIRL. . . . . 149 ANDER AENGUS V   13
    TO TELL HIM HOW THE GIRL AILLINN . . . . 191 BAILE AILLINN   49
    FOR THIS YOUNG GIRL AND THIS YOUNG MAN . . . . 195 BAILE AILLINN   157
    A BEAUTIFUL YOUNG MAN AND GIRL CAME UP . . . . 223 SHADOW WATER B   33
    A PRETTY GIRL TO SHARE MY BED". . . . . 296 THREE BEGGARS   31
    TO A YOUNG GIRL . . . . 336 YOUNG GIRL   T
    OR A YOUNG GIRL DRESSED OUT IN HER NEW GOWN, ... 350 HER PRAISE   4
    THAT SHE MIGHT BE THAT SPRIGHTLY GIRL TRODDEN BY A BIRD: . 353 HIS PHOENIX   4
    THAT SHE MIGHT BE THAT SPRIGHTLY GIRL WHO HAD MARRIED WITH 353 HIS PHOENIX V   4
      A BIRD:
    THAT SHE MIGHT BE THAT SPRIGHTLY GIRL WHO WAS TRODDEN BY 353 HIS PHOENIX V   4
      A BIRD:
    A YOUNG GIRL IN THE INDOLENCE OF HER YOUTH, ... 359 WAR POEM   5
    AND RIGHT BETWEEN THESE TWO A GIRL AT PLAY . . . . . 383 VISION ROBART   21
    THAT GIRL MY UNREMEMBERING NIGHTS HOLD FAST . . . . 384 VISION ROBART   50
    A PEASANT GIRL COMMENDED BY A SONG, ... 410 TOWER   34
    ABOVE THE STAGGERING GIRL, HER THIGHS CARESSED . . . 441 LEDA AND SWAN   2
    THE HERO, THE GIRL, AND THE FOOL . . . . 447 HERO GIRL FOOL   T
    CUCHULAIN THE GIRL AND THE FOOL . . . . 447 HERO GIRL FOOL V   T
    THAN ALL MY BURSTING SPRINGTIME KNEW. A GIRL . . . . 466 HARUN RASHID   105
    INHABITANT OF THE SOFT CHEEK OF A GIRL-- . . . . . . 540 FROM ANTIGONE   2
    MONEY IS GOOD AND A GIRL MIGHT BE BETTER, ... 544 TO SAME TUNE 1   3

GIRL   (CONTINUED)   PAGE   TITLE   LINE

"A GIRL I HAD, BUT SHE FOLLOWED ANOTHER, ...   544 TO SAME TUNE 1   11
"MONEY IS GOOD AND A GIRL MIGHT BE BETTER, ...   545 TO SAME TUNE 1   21
THAT BLONDE GIRL THERE IS MY HEART'S DESIRE, ...   550 SONGS REWRIT 1 V   1
ETERNITY IS PASSION, GIRL OR BOY . . . .   560 WHENCE COME   1
THE GIRL GOES DANCING THERE . . . .   568 SWEET DANCER   1
A CRAZED GIRL . . . .   578 CRAZED GIRL   T
THAT CRAZED GIRL IMPROVISING HER MUSIC, ...   578 CRAZED GIRL   1
HER KNEE-CAP BROKEN, THAT GIRL I DECLARE . . . .   578 CRAZED GIRL   6
HER KNEE CAP BROKEN, THAT GIRL I DECLARE . . . .   578 CRAZED GIRL   V   6
MONEY IS GOOD AND A GIRL MIGHT BE BETTER, ...   616 MARCH SONGS 3   3
"A GIRL I HAD, BUT SHE FOLLOWED ANOTHER, ...   616 MARCH SONGS 3   11
"MONEY IS GOOD AND A GIRL MIGHT BE BETTER, ...   616 MARCH SONGS 3   21
NO MAN GROWS OLD, NO GIRL GROWS COLD, ...   621 JOHN KINSELLA   31
A GIRL THAT KNEW ALL DANTE ONCE . . . .   626 OLD MEN BE MAD   5
HOW CAN I, THAT GIRL STANDING THERE, ...   631 POLITICS   1
A LOTUS IN THEIR HANDS—YOUNG MOORISH GIRL . . . . . .   694 MOSADA 1   103
A LITTLE MOORISH GIRL? SMALL WORTH. MY SONG— . . . .   696 MOSADA 2   10
I WILL NOT HEAR! THE MOORISH GIRL MUST DIE. . . . . .   697 MOSADA 2   39
YOUNG MOORISH GIRL, THY FINAL HOUR IS HERE! . . . . .   701 MOSADA 3   63
I SAW A GIRL AFRAID TO BE TOO NEAR, ...   712 FERENCZ RENYI   68
A BOY AND GIRL HOLD ONE ANOTHER'S HANDS! . . . . . .   752 SHADOW WATER A   122
GIRLHOOD'S
FROM MEAGRE GIRLHOOD'S PUTTING ON . . . .   356 BROKEN DREAMS   9
GIRL'S
AND DECKED AND ALTERED IT FOR A GIRL'S LOVE, ...   423 MY DESCENDANTS   22
GIRL'S SONG . . . .   515 GIRLS SONG B   T
SEVEN POEMS GIRL'S SONG . . . .   515 GIRLS SONG B   V   T
ON A GIRL'S FORGOTTEN LUTE, ...   668 ISLE STAT II 3   66
GIRL'S SONG . . . .   723 GIRLS SONG A   V   T
GIRLS
AND HE SAW YOUNG MEN AND YOUNG GIRLS . . . .   144 HOST OF AIR   13
OLD MEN AND YOUNG MEN AND YOUNG GIRLS . . . .   145 HOST OF AIR   39
TWO GIRLS IN SILK KIMONOS, BOTH . . . .   475 EVA GORE-BOOTH   3
TWO GIRLS IN SILK KIMONOS, BOTH . . . .   475 EVA GORE-BOOTH   19
GIRLS DOWN ON THE SEASHORE . . . .   588 OLD WICKED MAN   30
FOR PASSING ROUND THE BOTTLE WITH GIRLS IN RAGS OR SILK,   592 PILGRIM   2
FOR PASSING ROUND THE BOTTLE WITH GIRLS IN RAG OR SILK,   592 PILGRIM   V   2
BUT BOYS AND GIRLS, PALE FROM THE IMAGINED LOVE . . .   610 STATUES   4
THAT GIRLS AT PUBERTY MAY FIND . . . .   617 LONG-LEG FLY   21
WHAT SHALL I DO FOR PRETTY GIRLS . . . .   620 JOHN KINSELLA   11
WHAT SHALL I DO FOR PRETTY GIRLS . . . .   621 JOHN KINSELLA   23
WHAT SHALL I DO FOR PRETTY GIRLS . . . .   621 JOHN KINSELLA   35
WITH BOYS AND GIRLS ABOUT HIM, ...   627 STATES HOLIDAY   27
YONDER SEE THE FAIRY GIRLS . . . .   726 LOVERS QUARREL   21
GIRLS THAT HAVE GOVERNED CITIES, ...   789 SINGING HEAD   15
GIRLS'
    SEE SADDLE-GIRTH
COME TO THE CHESS, FOR YOUNG GIRLS' WITS ARE BETTER . .   721 WITCH VIVIEN   46
GIRTH
HIGH AS THE SADDLE GIRTH, COVERING AWAY FROM OUR GLANCES
    THE TIDE! . . . .   47 OISIN 3   V   2
WATCHED HER THOSE SEAMLESS FACES FROM THE VALLEY'S
    GLIMMERING GIRTH! . . . .   55 OISIN 3   122
WATCHED HER THOSE SEAMLESS FACES FROM THE VALLEY'S MURAL
    GIRTH . . . .   55 OISIN 3   V   122
. . . HOW, WHEN DIVIDED THE GIRTH, ...   60 OISIN 3   189
GIST
HERE'S THE GIST OF WHAT THEY MEAN. . . . .   637 BEN BULBEN   12
GIVE
AND THERE I WILL GIVE YOU A HUNDRED HOUNDS! . . . . .   8 OISIN 1   86
SEA-GOD, THAT ONCE, TO GIVE HIS SLAVES CONTENT, . . .   38 OISIN 2   V   129
THEIR HEARING, AND SOME COMFORT GIVE, BUT THEY . . .   68 SAD SHEPHERD   V   6
TROUBLE HIS SLEEPING! GIVE HIM DREAMS OF ME. . . . .   75 ANASHU VIJAYA   91
GIVE THEM UNQUIET DREAMS! . . . .   88 STOLEN CHILD   34
WE GIVE THEM EVIL DREAMS, ...   88 STOLEN CHILD   V   34
HE BADE THEM GIVE OVER THEIR KEENING! . . . .   93 FATHER OHART   23
AMID MEN'S SOULS, THAT WAVER AND GIVE PLACE . . . . .   112 ROSE OF WORLD   7
AMID MEN'S SOULS THAT DAY BY DAY GIVE PLACE, ...   112 ROSE OF WORLD V   7
GIVE TO THESE CHILDREN, NEW FROM THE WORLD, ...   116 FAERY SONG   5
GIVE TO THESE CHILDREN, NEW FROM THE WORLD, ...   116 FAERY SONG   9
SAID, "AENGUS AND HIS SWEETHEART GIVE THEIR THANKS . .   187 QUEEN MAEVE   146
THAT ALL THIS LIFE CAN GIVE US IS . . . .   190 BAILE AILLINN   39
THAT ALL LIFE HAS TO GIVE US IS . . . .   190 BAILE AILLINN V   39
THAT ALL LIFE HAD TO GIVE US IS . . . .   190 BAILE AILLINN V   39
NEVER GIVE ALL THE HEART . . . .   202 NEVER GIVE ALL   T
NEVER GIVE ALL THE HEART, FOR LOVE . . . .   202 NEVER GIVE ALL   1
O NEVER GIVE THE HEART OUTRIGHT, ...   202 NEVER GIVE ALL   8
WHERE LOVE'S TO GIVE AND TO SPARE! . . . .   214 HAPPY TOWNLAND   4
I COULD GIVE ALL MY HEART TO THAT RED MOLL . . . . .   222 SHADOW WATER B   9
I'D GIVE THE PROFIT OF NINE VOYAGES . . . .   222 SHADOW WATER B   9
I'LL GIVE MY ANSWER. YOU HAVE AWAKENED HIM. . . . .   225 SHADOW WATER B   79
I'LL GIVE MY ANSWER. YOU HAVE AWAKED HIM. . . . . .   225 SHADOW WATER B V   79
IF YOU WILL GIVE ME ALL YOUR MIND AWHILE— . . . . .   227 SHADOW WATER B   117
NO MORTAL CAN. YES! IF THEY GIVE US HELP. . . . . .   229 SHADOW WATER B   165
COULD WE BUT GIVE US WHOLLY TO THE DREAMS, ...   230 SHADOW WATER B   178
AND I WOULD KNOW IF YOU WILL GIVE ME VENGEANCE. . . .   235 SHADOW WATER B   301
UNTIL MY BODY GIVE YOU KISS FOR KISS. . . . .   238 SHADOW WATER B   345
YOUR SOUL SHALL GIVE THE KISS. I AM NOT AFRAID, . .   238 SHADOW WATER B   346
I'LL STRIKE A BLOW FOR HIM TO GIVE HIM TIME . . . . .   239 SHADOW WATER B   365
I'LL GIVE A GOLDEN GALLEY FULL OF FRUIT. . . . . . .   240 SHADOW WATER B   373
QUEEN, GIVE IT ME. NO, I HAVE NEED OF IT. . . . . .   241 SHADOW WATER B   399

319

GIVE   (CONTINUED)
    I'LL NEVER GIVE ANOTHER THOUGHT TO IT.   .   .   .   .   .   .   245 SHADOW WATER B   477
    LET'S HOME: I'D GIVE SOME RUBIES TO A WOMAN.   .   .   .   .   .   248 SHADOW WATER B   537
    THERE'S SOMEBODY I'D GIVE THE AMETHYST EYES TO.   .   .   .   .   248 SHADOW WATER B   538
    HAVE WE NOT EVERYTHING THAT LIFE CAN GIVE   .   .   .   .   .   .   249 SHADOW WATER B   570
    THAT LONG TO GIVE THEMSELVES FOR WAGE, ...   262 STUDENTS AGIT   2
    AND YET COULD GIVE SO FINE A STROKE?"   .   .   .   .   274 GREY ROCK   84
    IS THAT WE GIVE, ALTHOUGH IT BE BRIEF GIVING, ...   282 TWO KINGS   120
    TO GO—FOR HOPE WOULD GIVE HIS LIMBS THE POWER—   .   .   .   .   282 TWO KINGS   V 133A
    FOR HOPE WOULD GIVE HIS LIMBS THE POWER—AND AWAIT   .   .   .   283 TWO KINGS   136
    YOU GAVE, BUT WILL NOT GIVE AGAIN   .   .   .   .   287 TO WEALTHY MAN   1
    THAT THINGS IT WERE A PRIDE TO GIVE   .   .   .   .   287 TO WEALTHY MAN   6
    LOOK UP IN THE SUN'S EYE AND GIVE   .   .   .   .   288 TO WEALTHY MAN   32
    WHAT ELSE HE GIVE OR KEEP   .   .   .   .   346 ON WOMAN   24
    SHOULD GIVE TO MY FRIEND   .   .   .   .   349 HAWK   17
    GIVE HER A LITTLE GRACE, ...   367 HER CHRIS TREE   9
    AND BLESSED, I GIVE MY GRATITUDE, ...   380 SAINT HUNCH   14
    GIVE MAN HIS THOUGHT OR HIS MERE BODY?   .   .   .   .   .   .   386 ROBARTES DANCE   40
    BUT WHO CAN TALK OF GIVE AND TAKE   .   .   .   .   395 SIXTEEN DEAD   3
    OR MEDDLE WITH OUR GIVE AND TAKE   .   .   .   .   395 SIXTEEN DEAD   17
    GIVE PLACE TO AN INDIFFERENT MULTITUDE, GIVE PLACE   .   .   .   427 PHANTOM HATRED   28
    GIVE PLACE TO AN INDIFFERENT MULTITUDE, GIVE PLACE   .   .   .   427 PHANTOM HATRED   28
    IT FEARED TO GIVE ITS LOVE A HURT WITH ALL THE TEMPEST   450 OWEN AHERNE   7
        THERE:
    IT FEARED THE HURT THAT SHE COULD GIVE AND THEREFORE IT   450 OWEN AHERNE   8
        WENT MAD.
    AS AIR UNDER A WING, CAN GIVE BIRDS' WIT.   .   .   .   .   .   .   462 HARUN RASHID   28
    AS AIR UNDER A WING, CAN GIVE BIRD'S WIT.   .   .   .   .   .   .   462 HARUN RASHID   V 28
    I WOULD HAVE FOUND THE BEST THAT LIFE CAN GIVE, ...   465 HARUN RASHID   91
    CAN GIVE HIS SHARPENED PALATE ECSTASY   .   .   .   .   474 ALL SOUL NIGHT   84
    GIVE TO HIS SHARPENED PALATE ECSTACY   .   .   .   .   474 ALL SOUL NIGHT V   84
    EVERY TOUCH THEY GIVE, ...   517 HER ANXIETY   10
    "O CRUEL DEATH, GIVE THREE THINGS BACK,"   .   .   .   .   .   .   521 THREE THINGS   1
    AND GIVE HIS OWN AND TAKE HIS OWN   .   .   .   .   538 LAST CONFESS   19
    WHAT CAN SHE TAKE UNTIL HER MASTER GIVE: .   .   .   .   .   .   558 RIBH CHRISTIAN   21
    "LOVE TO GIVE OR TO WITHHOLD   .   .   .   .   588 OLD WICKED MAN   21
    GIVE TONGUE, PROCLAIM THEIR HIDDEN NAME—"HOUND VOICE."   622 HOUND VOICE   7
    ALL CHOICE, AND GIVE TO CHANCE FOR GUIDING CHANCE   .   .   .   656 ISLE STAT I 3   39
    I'D GIVE MY FAERY FLEETNESS, THOUGH I BE   .   .   .   .   .   .   670 ISLE STAT II 3   107
    NAY, GIVE IT ME, AND I WILL SOUND A MEASURE: .   .   .   .   .   681 SEEKER   9
    HER HANGING MANSION. GIVE TO ME, I PRAY, ...   698 MOSADA 2   52
    GIVE TO THY GOMEZ. GOMEZ—HE HAS GONE   .   .   .   .   .   .   703 MOSADA 3   110
    GIVE TO THY VALLENCE. VALLENCE—HE HAS GONE   .   .   .   .   703 MOSADA 3   V 110
    THEN GIVE ME TRIUMPH IN MY MANY PLOTS.   .   .   .   .   .   .   722 WITCH VIVIEN   51
    AND YET, THERE IS A LOVE THAT THE GODS GIVE, ...   749 SHADOW WATER A   56
    GIVE ME THE HELM: CALL HITHER THOSE WHO LIE   .   .   .   .   .   751 SHADOW WATER A   91
    GIVE HER TO AIBRIC, IF HE WILL. I WAIT   .   .   .   .   .   .   755 SHADOW WATER A   172
    AND TO GIVE WEALTH OF OXEN AND SHEEP TO ALL: .   .   .   .   756 SHADOW WATER A   184
    AND TO GIVE YOU BESIDES A HUNDRED SHIELDS, ...   756 SHADOW WATER A   185
    GIVE ME A HUNDRED SHEEP. GIVE ME A HOUSE   .   .   .   .   .   758 SHADOW WATER A   220
    GIVE ME A HUNDRED SHEEP. GIVE ME A HOUSE   .   .   .   .   .   758 SHADOW WATER A   220
    AND A STRONG GALLEY. I GIVE YOU ALL AS MUCH.   .   .   .   .   758 SHADOW WATER A   222
    THEY ARE ALWAYS QUARRELLING. GIVE ME YOUR SWORDS.   .   .   766 SHADOW WATER A   370
    ALE SETS THEM QUARRELLING. GIVE ME YOUR SWORDS.   .   .   .   766 SHADOW WATER A   372
    GIVE ME YOUR SWORDS. THEY ARE ALWAYS QUARRELLING.   .   .   766 SHADOW WATER A V   370
    IT IS THE BROWN ALE DOES IT. GIVE ME YOUR SWORDS.   .   .   .   766 SHADOW WATER A V   372
    THEY WILL GIVE HIM KISS FOR KISS   .   .   .   .   776 AGAINST WITCH   29
    "GIVE ME YOUR WIFE," SAID HE.   .   .   .   .   779 GOING THE ROAD   5
    OR GIVE BUT A SIGH AND A WORD, ...   786 YOUR HEART   12
    A MAN BUT WILL GIVE YOU HIS LOVE   .   .   .   .   786 YOUR HEART   17
    OR GIVE BUT A SIGH AND A WORD, ...   786 YOUR HEART   25
    OR GIVE BUT A SIGH AND A WORD, ...   786 YOUR HEART   38
GIVEN
    HAS GIVEN THE WAVES THEIR MELODY, ...   134 TWO TREES   10
    HAVE GIVEN THEIR HEARTS UP TO THE PLAY.   .   .   .   .   .   .   202 NEVER GIVE ALL   10
    ARE PLOTTING FOR YOUR DEATH. HAVE I NOT GIVEN   .   .   .   .   226 SHADOW WATER B   93
    IT WAS SO GIVEN OUT, BUT I WILL PROVE   .   .   .   .   243 SHADOW WATER B   429
    YOU SAY, AS I HAVE OFTEN GIVEN TONGUE   .   .   .   .   262 TO A POET   1
    I HAD NOT GIVEN A PENNY FOR A SONG   .   .   .   .   267 ALL TEMPT ME   6
    HE THOUGHT TO HAVE GIVEN HIS HORSE THE SPUR, BUT SAW   .   .   277 TWO KINGS   V 48
    TILL JUDGMENT HAS BEEN GIVEN, AND IF GUILTY, ...   280 TWO KINGS   74
    HAD GIVEN THEIR CHILDREN'S CHILDREN LOFTIER THOUGHT,   .   .   292 TO A SHADE   12
    HAD GIVEN BUT AS THE REST   .   .   .   .   293 HELEN LIVED   10
    "WE'RE BUT GIVEN WHAT WE HAVE EARNED   .   .   .   .   298 THREE HERMITS   14
    AND GIVEN TO OTHERS ALL HEART'S ACHE, ...   355 BROKEN DREAMS   8
    WE HAVE GIVEN THE WORLD OUR PASSION, ...   363 DOLLS DRAWINGS   10
    AND GIVEN EVERYTHING A WOMAN NEEDS, ...   609 IN TARAS HALLS   7
    SHE, PITY-CRAZED, HAD GIVEN HER SOUL AWAY, ...   629 CIRCUS ANIMALS   19
GIVER
    OUR GIVER OF GOOD COUNSEL AND GOOD LUCK."   .   .   .   .   .   185 QUEEN MAEVE   102
    HAD SEEMED TO BE THE GIVER OF ALL PEACE, ...   228 SHADOW WATER B   149
GIVES
    BE PLENTY.—IF HE GIVES ANOTHER LOVE, ...   71 ANASHU VIJAYA V   5
    SHE GIVES ME BITE AND SUP.   .   .   .   .   96 MOLL MAGEE   40
    "HE BADE ME LET ALL KNOW HE GIVES HIS NAME   .   .   .   .   .   109 CUCHULAIN SEA   52
    THAT GOD GIVES UNTO MAN IN SLEEP.   .   .   .   .   138 TO IRELAND   V 22
    HE GIVES HIS BELOVED CERTAIN RHYMES   .   .   .   .   157 BELOVED RHYMES   T
    AEDH GIVES HIS BELOVED CERTAIN RHYMES   .   .   .   .   .   .   157 BELOVED RHYMES V   T
    IN OWING THEM THE BRIDE-BED THAT GIVES PEACE."   .   .   .   .   187 QUEEN MAEVE   148
    I KNOW WHAT WAGES BEAUTY GIVES, ...   336 YOUNG BEAUTY   13
    THAT GIVES UP ALL HER MIND, ...   345 ON WOMAN   2

		PAGE	TITLE		LINE
GIVES (CONTINUED)					
THE SELF-SOWN, SELF-BEGOTTEN SHAPE THAT GIVES		446	COLONUS PRAISE		10
ENDURE WHAT LIFE GOD GIVES AND ASK NO LONGER SPAN; . . .		459	FROM OEDIPUS		1
THE STRENGTH THAT GIVES OUR BLOOD AND STATE MAGNANIMITY . . .		481	BLOOD AND MOON		29
SORROW THAT GIVES FOR GUERDON LIBERTY, ...		686	DRAWING-ROOM		6
GIVES FORTH, HE, THE ETERNAL, WORKS HIS WILL.		689	NETTLESHIP		16
SORROW, THAT GIVES FOR GUERDON LIBERTY, ...		734	QUATRAIN APHOR		6
FOR GOD GIVES POWER TO THE SAD		741	EARL PAUL		47
FOR GOD GIVES POWER TO THE SAD		741	EARL PAUL		51
GIVETH					
WHO GIVETH TO THE GOLDEN-CRESTED WREN		698	MOSADA 2		51
GIVING					
FOOT AFTER FOOT WAS GIVING WAY, ...		274	GREY ROCK		72
IS THAT WE GIVE, ALTHOUGH IT BE BRIEF GIVING, ...		282	TWO KINGS		120
GIVING HIS HAND TO THAT MAN AND TO THIS, ...		286	TWO KINGS	V	218A
GLAD					
THE HUNTING OF HEROES SHOULD BE GLAD."		4	OISIN 1		39
"THE HUNTING OF HEROES SHOULD BE GLAD!		4	OISIN 1	V	32
"FOR HUNTING HEROES SHOULD BE GLAD.		4	OISIN 1	V	34
WE ONLY KNOW THAT WE WERE GLAD		22	OISIN 1	V	340D
NO LONGER GLAD AS ON THAT MORNING, SPED		30	OISIN 2	V	16
PIERCED BY MY GLAD SINGING THROUGH, ...		67	HAPPY SHEPHERD		53
HOW MANY LOVED YOUR MOMENTS OF GLAD GRACE, ...		121	YOU ARE OLD		5
AND OF NEW FRIENDS ARE GLAD WITH YOUR PRAISE, ...		173	PLEADS FRIEND	V	3
AND WITH GLAD VOICE MAEVE ANSWERED HIM, "WHAT KING		183	QUEEN MAEVE		79
AND WITH GLAD VOICE MAEVE ANSWERED "MANY A TIME		183	QUEEN MAEVE	V	79
WITH HOLY SHADOWS," HER HIGH HEART WAS GLAD, ...		186	QUEEN MAEVE		126
THERE'S NOT A MAN BUT WILL BE GLAD OF IT		225	SHADOW WATER B		66
FROM A GLAD KINDNESS CANNOT TAKE HIS EYES.		404	FOR DAUGHTER		40
HERE IN THE SHADE, WHY? WHY? FOR WHAT IS GLAD?		652	ISLE STAT I 2		8
POOR SAD WOOD-RHAPSODISTS, NOT SO! THEY'RE GLAD. . . .		652	ISLE STAT I 2		16
NAY, NAY, ALMINTOR, YONDER SONG IS GLAD.		652	ISLE STAT I 2		23
OF EVENING AND GLAD SILENCE DWELLETH AYE.		653	ISLE STAT I 2		37
(HOW GLAD WAS HER MIEN!), ...		654	ISLE STAT I 2		72
TO MAKE US GLAD WITH WONDER AS WE SAT		683	SEEKER		41
MY BIDDING. NOW 'TIS DONE, AND I AM GLAD		700	MOSADA 3		29
GLAD, SIMPLE—NAY, HE SOUGHT NOT MYSTERY, ...		710	FERENCZ RENYI		30
I HOLD HIM DEARER THAN THE GLAD, ...		723	GIRLS SONG A		3
I'D GLAD FOLKS' HEARTS WITH BLITHER SONG."		731	PRIEST FAIRY		82
AND HER DIM WAVE BIDS MAN BE NO MORE GLAD, ...		738	YOU ARE SAD		11
THOUGH THE GLAD CRY "SHIELD-BREAKER,"		741	EARL PAUL		35
FOLDING THEIR HEARTS' DESIRE TO THEIR GLAD HEARTS. . . .		765	SHADOW WATER A		349
GLADDENED					
HIS FACE HAS NEVER GLADDENED SINCE HE CAME		747	SHADOW WATER A		1
GLADE SEE WILLOW-GLADE					
THROUGH ALL THE WELL-BELOVED GLADE.		67	HAPPY SHEPHERD	V	46C
AND LIVE ALONE IN THE BEE-LOUD GLADE.		117	ISLE INNISFREE		4
AS LIES DARK WATER IN A MURMUROUS GLADE, ...		650	ISLE STAT I 1		138
DEEP-EYED, SLOW-FOOTING DOWN THE EMPTY GLADE. . . .		653	ISLE STAT I 2		55
BEHOLD THE BRAZEN-GATED GLADE!		667	ISLE STAT II 3		43
BY THE WILLOWS IN THE GLADE, ...		726	LOVERS QUARREL		3
GLADLY					
I SWEAR IT, THOUGH I GLADLY WOULD LIE DOWN		758	SHADOW WATER A		225
GLAMOUR					
OF THE HIGH PEOPLE OF SORACA NOR IN GLAMOUR BY DEMONS FLUNG,		50	OISIN 3	V	50
LEST HE MAY SOME GLAMOUR FOLD		717	FAIRY DOCTOR		22
LEST SOME GLAMOUR HE MAY FOLD		717	FAIRY DOCTOR	V	22
GLAMOURED					
GLAMOURED BY FAIRIES FOR THEIR OWN.		717	FAIRY DOCTOR		20
GLAMOURS					
. . . NOR IN GLAMOURS BY DEMONS FLUNG, ...		50	OISIN 3		50
. . . OR IN GLAMOURS BY DEMONS FLUNG, ...		50	OISIN 3	V	50
GLANCE					
WITH ONE LONG GLANCE FOR GIRL AND BOY		19	OISIN 1		287
WITH ONE LONG GLANCE ON MAID AND BOY		19	OISIN 1	V	287
WITH A SWIFT AND FRIENDLY GLANCE		21	OISIN 1		309
WITH NO RETURNING GLANCE, IN WORDLESS MOOD		44	OISIN 2	V	230A
THOUGH YOU GLOW AND YOU GLANCE, THOUGH YOU PURR AND YOU DART!		90	OLD FISHERMAN		2
THOUGH YE GLOW AND YE GLANCE, THOUGH YE PURR AND YE DART,		90	OLD FISHERMAN	V	2
A LATTICED WINDOW. HIS GLANCE WENT UP AT TIMES		180	QUEEN MAEVE		6
AYE, THOUGH ALL PASSION'S IN THE GLANCE—		388	SOLOMON WITCH		21
O BODY SWAYED TO MUSIC, O BRIGHTENING GLANCE, ...		446	SCHOOL CHILDR		63
O BODY SWAYED TO MUSIC BRIGHTENING GLANCE		446	SCHOOL CHILDR	V	63
NOTHING CAN STAY MY GLANCE		474	ALL SOUL NIGHT		93
UNTIL THAT GLANCE RUN IN THE WORLD'S DESPITE		474	ALL SOUL NIGHT		94
WHERE EVERY FOOT OBEYED HER GLANCE!		488	CRAZED MOON		11
WHERE VERY FOOT OBEYED HER GLANCE!		488	CRAZED MOON	V	11
SOME CAST OF DIE, OR LET SOME ARROW GLANCE		656	ISLE STAT I 3		40
GLANCED					
I LAY, AS OVER SEA THE LIGHT HOOVES GLANCED		30	OISIN 2	V	19A
GLANCES					
THEN MOCK AT DEATH AND TIME WITH GLANCES		19	OISIN 1		274
HIGH AS THE SADDLE-GIRTH, COVERING AWAY FROM OUR GLANCES THE TIDE;		47	OISIN 3		2
HIGH AS THE SADDLE GIRTH, COVERING AWAY FROM OUR GLANCES THE TIDE;		47	OISIN 3	V	2
MINGLING HANDS AND MINGLING GLANCES		87	STOLEN CHILD		18
GLANCES OF HER WANDERING EYE		487	CRAZED MOON		4

	PAGE	TITLE	LINE

GLANCES   (CONTINUED)
    THOSE GLANCES UNAFRAID: . . . . • . 516 MANS SONG   8
GLARE
    FEEBLER AND FEEBLER SHONE THE MISTY GLARE. . . . . . 37 OISIN 2   V 121
    THE SMOKY TORCHES MADE A GLARE • . . . . 271 GREY ROCK   18
    AND SMOKY TORCHES MADE A GLARE . . . . 271 GREY ROCK   V   18
    TRAILING AND SHINING 'NEATH THE FLICKERING GLARE. . . 688 TWO TITANS   32
GLASNEVIN
    AND GATHER THE GLASNEVIN COVERLET . . . . 293 TO A SHADE   19
    DRAW THE GLASNEVIN COVERLET ANEW . . . . 293 TO A SHADE   V   19
GLASS   SEE WINDOW-GLASS LOOKING-GLASS HOUR-GLASS
    WHO FOLLOW WITH THE OPTIC GLASS . . . . 66 HAPPY SHEPHERD   29
    GAZE NO MORE IN THE BITTER GLASS . . . . 135 TWO TREES   21
    IN THE DIM GLASS THE DEMONS HOLD• . . . . 135 TWO TREES   30
    THE GLASS OF OUTER WEARINESS, ... 135 TWO TREES   31
    GAZE NO MORE IN THE BITTER GLASS. . . . . 136 TWO TREES   40
    ON DAPPLED SKINS IN A GLASS BOAT• . . . . 196 BAILE AILLINN   180
    BESIDE YOUNG AENGUS IN HIS TOWER OF GLASS, ... 219 HARP OF AENGUS   2
    AND IN A TOWER OF GLASS, AND FROM THAT DAY . . . . . 224 SHADOW WATER B   50
    "HE SHADOWED IN A GLASS . . . . 255 WOMAN HOMER   13
    I LIFT THE GLASS TO MY MOUTH, ... 261 DRINKING SONG   5
    HER LOVER THOUGHT, UPON THE GLASS . . . . 385 ROBARTES DANCE   11
    I RAGE AT MY OWN IMAGE IN THE GLASS . . . . 447 HERO GIRL FOOL   1
    THE GLASS BECAUSE MY GLASS: . . . . 473 ALL SOUL NIGHT   78
    THE GLASS BECAUSE MY GLASS: . . . . 473 ALL SOUL NIGHT   78
    STILL RAZOR-KEEN, STILL LIKE A LOOKING GLASS . . . . 477 SELF AND SOUL   V 11
    ARE SUNG ABOVE THE GLASS, ... 587 PARNELLITES   30
    ARE SUNG ABOVE A GLASS: . . . . 587 PARNELLITES   V 30
    GAVE WOMEN DREAMS AND DREAMS THEIR LOOKING GLASS. . . 610 STATUES   16
    AS FIGURES MOVING MIRRORED IN A GLASS, ... 676 ISLE STAT II 3   270
    TREMBLES AS A BELL OF GLASS • . . . . 705 DAWN-SONG   10
    I'D BUY YOUR GLASS. MY GLASS I WILL NOT SELL• . . . 721 WITCH VIVIEN   28
    I'D BUY YOUR GLASS. MY GLASS I WILL NOT SELL• . . . 721 WITCH VIVIEN   28
    WITHOUT MY GLASS I'D BE A SORRY CLOWN• . . . . . . 721 WITCH VIVIEN   29
    FOR OTHER STAKES WE PLAY. YOU LOST THE GLASS. . . . 722 WITCH VIVIEN   50
    BESIDE YOUNG AENGUS IN HIS TOWER OF GLASS, ... 762 SHADOW WATER A   297
GLASSES
    AND TWO LONG GLASSES BRIMMED WITH MUSCATEL . . . . . 470 ALL SOUL NIGHT   4
    COME FILL UP ALL THOSE GLASSES . . . . 586 PARNELLITES   7
GLASS-MOSAIC
    GLASS-MOSAIC, WINDOW-GLASS, ... 440 WISDOM   3
GLAZING
    HALF TURNED AND FIXED A GLAZING EYE ON MINE, ... 537 HER VISION   26
GLEAM   SEE A-GLEAM
    A MOMENTARY GLEAM OF PHOSPHORUS FLAME• . . . . . . 37 OISIN 2   118
    ONE WITH THE TIDE THAT GLEAMS, THE WINGS THAT GLEAM AND
        DART, ... 78 INDIAN TO LOVE   15
    . . . THE WINGS THAT GLIMMER AND GLEAM AND DART: . . 78 INDIAN TO LOVE V   15
    . . . AND WINGS, THAT GLIMMER AND GLEAM AND DART, . . 78 INDIAN TO LOVE V   15
    A GREEN DROP IN THE SURGE, A GLEAM OF LIGHT . . . . 104 FERGUS DRUID   33
    TROY PASSED AWAY IN ONE HIGH FUNERAL GLEAM, ... 111 ROSE OF WORLD   4
    TILL ALL THE EDDIES GLEAM: . . . . 389 IMAGE PAST   4
    UNDER THE FIRST COLD GLEAM OF DAY? . . . . 398 BREAK OF DAY   4
    BEFORE THAT BRIEF GLEAM OF ITS LIFE BE GONE, ... 414 TOWER   141
    UPON A FADING GLEAM, ... 430 NINETEEN 19   63
    BUT WOKE AT THE FIRST GLEAM OF DAY, ROSE UP . . . . 467 HARUN RASHID   147
    OR EYELID SHOT THE GLEAM • . . . . 507 STREAM AND SUN   12
    EYES UNDER EYELIDS DID SO GLEAM: . . . . 514 JANE GROWN OLD   6
    SAW ON THE WOOD'S EDGE GLEAM AN ASH-GREY FEATHER: . . 715 DWELT SYCAMORE   2
    FOLLOWED A RINGDOVE'S ASH-GREY GLEAM OF FEATHER. . . 715 DWELT SYCAMORE   6
    FOLLOWED THE RING-DOVE'S ASH-GREY GLEAM OF FEATHER• . 715 DWELT SYCAMORE V   6
    GOLD UNTO GOLD, A GLEAM IN ITS LONG HAIR, ... 720 WITCH VIVIEN   3
    A HURTING GLEAM OF LIGHT, ... 741 EARL PAUL   V 38
    I SAW HER GLITTER AND GLEAM, ... 744 GLOVE CLOAK   1
    OF AENGUS' BIRDS GLEAM IN THEIR APPLE BOUGHS. . . . 751 SHADOW WATER A   103
GLEAMED
    ROSE IN THE DARKNESS, AND THE WHITE SURF GLEAMED . . 30 OISIN 2   23
    AND WHEN THE WHITE STEED SAW WHAT BLACKNESS GLEAMED, . 30 OISIN 2   V   24
    AND STARLIGHT GLEAMED, AND CLOUDS FLEW HIGH. . . . . 84 MAD KING GOLL   34
GLEAMING
    THEIR NAKED AND GLEAMING BODIES POURED OUT AND HEAPED IN
        THE WAY. . . . . 48 OISIN 3   28
    THEIR MIGHTY AND NAKED AND GLEAMING BODIES . . . . . 48 OISIN 3   V   28
    WENT WALKING WITH SLOW STEPS ALONG THE GLEAMING . . . 68 SAD SHEPHERD   3
    OH, MORE DARK THY GLEAMING HAIR IS . . . . 647 ISLE STAT I 1   51
    UNTIL AFAR APPEAR THE GLEAMING DRAGON-SCALES: . . . 651 ISLE STAT I 1   160
GLEAMS
    . . . THE GLEAMS OF THE WORLD AND THE SUN, ... 48 OISIN 3   22
    . . . THE CROZIER GLEAMS: . . . . 61 OISIN 3   194
    . . . THAT CROZIER GLEAMS: . . . . 61 OISIN 3   V 194
    ONE WITH THE TIDE THAT GLEAMS, THE WINGS THAT GLEAM AND
        DART, ... 78 INDIAN TO LOVE   15
    BUT LIGHT FROM THE PALE STARS, AND GLEAMS . . . . . 196 BAILE AILLINN   173
    ON THE ISLAND LAWNS, THEIR FEET WHERE THE PALE FOAM GLEAMS. 203 WITHER BOUGHS   14
    TOWER WHERE A CANDLE GLEAMS, ... 420 MY HOUSE   V 201
    THE EVENING GLEAMS ARE GREEN AND GOLD AND RED . . . 656 ISLE STAT I 3   22
    OF LILAC O'ER THE PULSING WATER GLEAMS, ... 664 ISLE STAT II 2   48
GLEN
    . . . AND THE LEAVES OF THE MURAL GLEN, ... 49 OISIN 3   35
    FROM ROLLING VALE AND RIVERY GLEN: . . . . 83 MAD KING GOLL   19
    FROM ROLLING VALLEY AND RIVERY GLEN, ... 83 MAD KING GOLL   V   17

322

	PAGE	TITLE	LINE
GLEN-CAR			
FROM THE HILLS ABOVE GLEN-CAR, • • • • • • • • • •	88	STOLEN CHILD	29
GLENDALOUGH			
IN GLENDALOUGH BESIDE THE STREAM, • • • • • • • •	331	ROUND TOWER	8
STREAM AND SUN AT GLENDALOUGH • • • • • • • • • •	506	STREAM AND SUN	T
GLIDE			
WHO HAD SEEMED TO GLIDE TO SOME INTRIGUE IN HER RED SHOES,	363	DOLLS FACES	6
GLIDING			
STREAM AND GLIDING SUN • • • • • • • • •	506	STREAM AND SUN	2
GLIMMER			
AND TO THE WAVES THAT GLIMMER BY • • • • • • •	20	OISIN 1	298
A MOMENTARY GLIMMER OF VAGUE PHOSPHORUS FLAME• • • • •	37	OISIN 2 V	120
• • • AND THEIR EYES THAT GLIMMER LIKE SILK. • • • •	59	OISIN 3	176
• • • THE WINGS THAT GLIMMER AND GLEAM AND DART; • • •	78	INDIAN TO LOVE V	15
• • • AND WINGS, THAT GLIMMER AND GLEAM AND DART, • • •	78	INDIAN TO LOVE V	15
THERE MIDNIGHT'S ALL A GLIMMER, AND NOON A PURPLE GLOW,	117	ISLE INNISFREE	7
AND THE GHASTLY GHOST-FLAMES GLIMMER ALL ALONG THE TAFFRAIL RAILS	719	PHANTOM SHIP	21
AND THE GHASTLY GHOST FLAMES GLIMMER ALONG THE TAFFREL RAILS,	719	PHANTOM SHIP V	21
BEND LOWER LEST YOUR BATTLE-AXES GLIMMER. • • • • • •	752	SHADOW WATER A	117
BEND LOWER LEST YOUR BATTLE AXES GLIMMER. • • • • • •	752	SHADOW WATER A V	117
GLIMMERED			
OF MOONLIT STEPS GLIMMERED; AND LEFT AND RIGHT • • • •	31	OISIN 2	35
DARK STATUES GLIMMERED OVER THE PALE TIDE • • • • •	31	OISIN 2	36
THE DAWN CAME IN, AND GLIMMERED ON THE FLOOR • • • • •	39	OISIN 2	152
GLIMMERING SEE STAR-GLIMMERING			
AND WITH THE GLIMMERING CRIMSON GLOWED • • • • • • •	3	OISIN 1	26
HEAPED BESIDE THE GLIMMERING WAVES, • • • • • • • •	21	OISIN 1	314
HEAVED BESIDE THE GLIMMERING WAVES, • • • • • • • •	21	OISIN 1 V	314
AT EVENING ON THE GLIMMERING SANDS, • • • • • • • •	23	OISIN 1	347
OVER THE GLIMMERING PURPLE SEA. • • • • • • • •	25	OISIN 1	384
SHONE MANY TIMES AMONG THE GLIMMERING FLOWERS • • • • •	30	OISIN 2	21
CRASHED ON THE STONES, UPON THE GLIMMERING STONES, • • •	33	OISIN 2 V	68A
WATCHED HER THOSE SEAMLESS FACES FROM THE VALLEY'S GLIMMERING GIRTH;	55	OISIN 3	122
WHERE MEN LIE FROZEN IN THE GLIMMERING SNOW; • • • • •	73	ANASHU VIJAYA	51
ONE WITH THE GLIMMERING TIDE, • • • • • • • •	78	INDIAN TO LOVE V	15
GLIMMERING IN HER DROOPED EYES, SAW HER LIPS MOVE • • •	81	EPHEMERA V	24D
WHAT A DANCER GLIMMERING! • • • • • • • • • • •	125	CATHLEEN PARA	14
HER WHITE FEET GO GLIMMERING; • • • • • • • • •	125	CATHLEEN PARA V	14
IT HAD BECOME A GLIMMERING GIRL • • • • • • • •	149	WANDER AENGUS	13
THEIR HOOFS HEAVY WITH TUMULT, THEIR EYES GLIMMERING WHITE;	154	BELOVED PEACE	2
QUEENS WROUGHT WITH GLIMMERING HANDS; • • • • • • •	162	ASKS FORGIVE	12
HIS HEAVY RINGS UNCOILED FROM GLIMMERING DEEP TO DEEP; • •	174	ELEMENT POWERS	5
HAVE SEEN HIS MIDNIGHT CANDLE GLIMMERING. • • • • • •	420	MY HOUSE	20
HAD SEEN HIS MIDNIGHT CANDLE GLIMMERING • • • • • •	420	MY HOUSE V	20
AND THOSE WHITE GLIMMERING FRAGMENTS OF THE MIST SWEEP BY.	426	PHANTOM HATRED	6
DOWN LIMB AND BREAST OR DOWN THAT GLIMMERING BELLY • • •	560	MAGIC DRUM	5
THE MEN ARE BUSY IN THE GLIMMERING SQUARE. • • • • •	699	MOSADA 3	16
AND SOFT, ONE GLIMMERING STAR. RENYI HAS CAST • • • •	714	FERENCZ RENYI	115
AND SOFT, ONE GLIMMERING STAR—WITH POWER VAST; • • • •	714	FERENCZ RENYI V	115
THE CLOUDY WATERS AND THE GLIMMERING WINDS • • • • • •	764	SHADOW WATER A	327
GLISTEN			
WHAT MADE THE DRAPERY GLISTEN SO? • • • • • • • • •	625	NATIVITY	3
GLISTENING			
CRIED ALL HIS STORY TO THE DEWDROPS GLISTENING. • • • •	68	SAD SHEPHERD	14
GLITTER SEE A-GLITTER			
I SAW HER GLITTER AND GLEAM, • • • • • • • • • •	744	GLOVE CLOAK	1
GLITTERED			
AND GLITTERED IN HER EYES. • • • • • • • • • • •	336	YOUNG GIRL	11
RICH FOLIAGE THAT THE STARLIGHT GLITTERED THROUGH, • • •	541	PARN FUNERAL 1	8
GLITTERING			
SCARED OF ITS GLITTERING LIKE A METEOR STAR, • • • • •	38	OISIN 2 V	137
THAT FROM THOSE FINGERS GLITTERING SUMMER RUNS • • • •	128	DREAM OF FAERY	44
O MASTERS OF THE GLITTERING TOWN! • • • • • • • •	212	BLESS PSALTER	3
CRYING AMID THE GLITTERING SEA. • • • • • • • •	254	HIS DREAM	17
THAT MERELY STOOD, ROCKING THE GLITTERING COACH • • • •	344	DAWN	11
YET DID BUT LOOK, ROCKING THE GLITTERING COACH • • • •	344	DAWN V	11
THE GLITTERING EYES IN A DEATH'S HEAD • • • • • • •	400	DEMON BEAST	9
LAST REACH OF GLITTERING STREAM • • • • • • • •	414	TOWER	143
THE ABOUNDING GLITTERING JET; THOUGH NOW IT SEEMS • • •	417	ANCEST HOUSES	12
A GLITTERING SWORD OUT OF THE EAST. A PUFF OF WIND • •	426	PHANTOM HATRED	5
GLITTERING AMONG GREY-LEAVED OLIVE-TREES, • • • • • •	447	COLONUS PRAISE	21
GLITTERING AMONG GREY-LEAVED OLIVE TREES, • • • • • •	447	COLONUS PRAISE V	21
UPON THE DUSTY, GLITTERING WINDOWS CLING, • • • • • •	482	BLOOD AND MOON	43
THE GLITTERING REACHES OF THE FLOODED LAKE. • • • • •	490	COOLE BALLYLEE	16
IS HALF ALL GLITTERING FLAME AND HALF ALL GREEN • • • •	500	VACILLATION	12
IS HALF ALL GLITTERING FLAME AND HALF A GREEN • • • •	500	VACILLATION V	12
THEIR ANCIENT, GLITTERING EYES, ARE GAY. • • • • • •	567	LAPIS LAZULI	56
GLITTERS			
BUT FAITHFUL LOVERS. SOMETHING GLITTERS THERE— • • • •	763	SHADOW WATER A	309
GLOBES SEE FOAM-GLOBES			
GLOBE-TROTTING			
CAN DISTURB GLOBE-TROTTING MADAM • • • • • • • • •	638	BEN BULBEN	48
GLOOM			
LIKE CRIMSON METEORS HANG IN THE GLOOM, • • • • • • •	21	OISIN 1	306
WE DANCED TO WHERE WITHIN THE GLOOM • • • • • • • •	21	OISIN 1 V	305
A LITTLE WAY WITHIN THE GLOOM A ROEBUCK RAISED HIS EYES	76	INDIAN ON GOD	13
FELL LIKE FAINT METEORS IN THE GLOOM, AND ONCE • • • •	80	EPHEMERA	14
AND SHY IN THE GLOOM; • • • • • • • • • • • • •	89	ISLE IN WATER	12

		PAGE	TITLE		LINE

GLOOM   (CONTINUED)
HE BADE ME OUT INTO THE GLOOM, ... 151 HEART OF WOMAN   3
AND SHE FORGET THE WANDERING AND ALL THE CRIMSON GLOOM . 175 ELEMENT POWERS V   11
AND SHE FORGET THE WANDERING AND THE CRIMSON GLOOM . . . 175 ELEMENT POWERS V   11
THE EVERLASTING TAPER LIGHTS THE GLOOM! . . . . . 311 MOUNTAIN TOMB   10
BECAUSE OF THE GREAT GLOOM THAT IS IN MY MIND. . . . 403 FOR DAUGHTER   8
IN THAT RELIGIOUS GLOOM! . . . . 584 GHOST ROG CASE   34
AS, CLOTHED IN CEREMONIAL GLOOM, ... 655 ISLE STAT I 3   10
TO SEEK NOT HOPELESS HAVE I CROSSED THE GLOOM, . . . 656 ISLE STAT I 3   42
MY DREAMS ROUND THOUGHTS OF PLENTY, AS IN GLOOM . . . 681 SEEKER   3
OF APPLE-BLOSSOM CIRCLES IN THE GLOOM, ... 700 MOSADA 3   42
OF APPLE BLOSSOM CIRCLES IN THE GLOOM, ... 700 MOSADA 3   V   42
AN APPLE BLOSSOM CIRCLES IN THE GLOOM, ... 700 MOSADA 3   V   42
BEFORE US IN THE GLOOM! . . . . 738 MOURN THEN ON   16

GLOOMED
A CITRON COLOUR GLOOMED IN HER HAIR, ... 3 OISIN 1   24

GLOOMS   SEE CAVERN-GLOOMS

GLOOMY
AND IN SOME GLOOMY BARROW LIE . . . . 19 OISIN 1   272
AND NOT A GLOOMY BIRD OF PREY. . . . . 338 TOM OROUGHLEY   8

GLORIES
GHOSTS OF HER VANISHED GLORIES, MUSE AND STALK . . . . 687 TWO TITANS   21

GLORIFIED
OR GARDENS RICH IN MEMORY GLORIFIED . . . . 491 COOLE BALLYLEE   35

GLORIOUS   SEE VAIN-GLORIOUS
AND GLORIOUS AS ASIAN BIRDS . . . . 7 OISIN 1   V   65

GLORY
MY SOUL, ONCE GLORY OF ITS ANCIENT LINE, ... 36 OISIN 2   V   95
AN IDLE WORD IS NOW THEIR GLORY, ... 65 HAPPY SHEPHERD   14
HE FLED THE PERSECUTION OF HER GLORY . . . . . . 68 SAD SHEPHERD   12
AND FROM THE PERSECUTION OF HER GLORY . . . . . . 68 SAD SHEPHERD   V   12
AND PONDERED ON THE GLORY OF HIS DAYS! . . . . . 108 CUCHULAIN SEA   43
SO GREAT A GLORY DID THE SONG CONFER. . . . . . 410 TOWER   40
SHADOWS THE INHERITED GLORY OF THE RICH. . . . . 418 ANCEST HOUSES   16
WHAT IF THE GLORY OF ESCUTCHEONED DOORS, ... 418 ANCEST HOUSES   33
SCARCE SPREAD A GLORY TO THE MORNING BEAMS, ... 422 MY DESCENDANTS   6
AND YET IT LACK ALL GLORY! AND PERCHANCE . . . . 429 NINETEEN 19   23
EXHAUST HIS GLORY AND HIS MIGHT! . . . . 438 SONGS PLAY 2   14
THE FEATHERED GLORY FROM HER LOOSENING THIGHS? . . . 441 LEDA AND SWAN   6
AND THAT ALL HEAVENLY GLORY SYMBOLISE-- . . . . . 445 SCHOOL CHILDR   55
WHEN IT HAS LOOKED IN GLORY FROM A CLOUD. . . . . 482 BLOOD AND MOON   54
SYMBOLICAL GLORY OF THE EARTH AND AIR! . . . . . 483 VERONIC NAPKIN   3
THAT MADE THE MAGNITUDE AND GLORY THERE . . . . . 483 VERONIC NAPKIN   5
A DANCE-LIKE GLORY THAT THOSE WALLS BEGOT. . . . . 488 COOLE PARK 29   8
WE SHIFT ABOUT--ALL THAT GREAT GLORY SPENT-- . . . 491 COOLE BALLYLEE   39
MAN SHIFTS ABOUT--ALL THAT GREAT GLORY SPENT-- . . . 491 COOLE BALLYLEE V   39
GREATER GLORY IN THE SUN, ... 494 AT ALGECIRAS   13
IN GLORY OF CHANGELESS METAL . . . . 498 BYZANTIUM   22
BITTER GLORY WRECKED. . . . . 504 RESULT THOUGHT   6
BY THAT GREAT GLORY DRIVEN WILD, ... 540 FROM ANTIGONE   13
HIS GLORY AND HIS MONUMENTS ARE GONE. . . . . . 563 MERU   14
THINK WHERE MAN'S GLORY MOST BEGINS AND ENDS, . . . 604 GALLERY REVIS   54
AND SAY MY GLORY WAS I HAD SUCH FRIENDS. . . . . 604 GALLERY REVIS   55
FAILURE FOR GLORY DOWN ON THEE, AND MOULD . . . . 688 TWO TITANS   54
AND MADE THEIR GLORY NAUGHT. . . . . 741 EARL PAUL   44

GLOSSES
WHERE THE WAVE OF MOONLIGHT GLOSSES . . . . 87 STOLEN CHILD   13

GLOSSY
ACROSS THE GLOSSY SEA." "OH, WILD . . . . . 6 OISIN 1   V   58
OVER THE GLOSSY SEA." "O, WILD . . . . . . 6 OISIN 1   V   58
WE GALLOPED OVER THE GLOSSY SEA! . . . . . 11 OISIN 1   132

GLOVE   SEE FOX-GLOVE
THE GLOVE AND THE CLOAK . . . . 744 GLOVE CLOAK   T
THE LITTLE OLD GLOVE OF A CHILD! . . . . . . 744 GLOVE CLOAK   9

GLOW
WHOSE LIPS HAD LIFE'S MOST PROSPEROUS GLOW? . . . . 10 OISIN 1   118
IN EVERY BRAIN A WIZARD GLOW. . . . . 20 OISIN 1   V 291A
IN OUR RAISED EYES THERE FLASHED A GLOW . . . . . 22 OISIN 1   327
THOUGH YOU GLOW AND YOU GLANCE, THOUGH YOU PURR AND YOU 90 OLD FISHERMAN   2
   DART!
THOUGH YE GLOW AND YE GLANCE, THOUGH YE PURR AND YE DART, 90 OLD FISHERMAN V   2
THERE MIDNIGHT'S ALL A GLIMMER, AND NOON A PURPLE GLOW, 117 ISLE INNISFREE   7
TILL THE SEED OF THE FIRE FLICKER AND GLOW! . . . . 150 OLD MOTHER   2
AND TROUBLED EYES CAME MORNING'S FIRST-BORN GLOW! . . 648 ISLE STAT I 1   103
FOOTING IN THE FEEBLE GLOW. . . . . 731 STREET DANCERS   10
FOOTING IN THE FEEBLE GLOW, ... 732 STREET DANCERS   23
FOOTING IN THE FEEBLE GLOW, ... 732 STREET DANCERS   36
FOOTING IN THE FEEBLE GLOW, ... 733 STREET DANCERS   49
DANCING IN THE FEEBLE GLOW, ... 733 STREET DANCERS   62
FOOTING IN THE FEEBLE GLOW, ... 733 STREET DANCERS V   49
FOOTING IN THE FEEBLE GLOW, ...

GLOWED
AND WITH THE GLIMMERING CRIMSON GLOWED . . . . . 3 OISIN 1   26
AND WITH THE WOVEN CRIMSON GLOWED . . . . . . 3 OISIN 1   V   26

GLOWING
AND BENDING DOWN BESIDE THE GLOWING BARS, ... 121 YOU ARE OLD   9
THAT YOU SHALL SEE ON YONDER GLOWING CLOUD . . . . 692 MOSADA 1   V   43

GLOWS
UNQUENCHABLE STILL GLOWS IN HER DULL STARE, ... 687 TWO TITANS   17

GLOW-WORM
WHEN A GLOW-WORM WAS GREEN ON A GRASS-LEAF, ... 53 OISIN 3   99
WHEN A GLOW-WORM WAS GREEN ON A GRASS LEAF, ... 53 OISIN 3   V   99

GLUED

	PAGE	TITLE		LINE

GLUED
  TO DEATH. HIS LIPS ARE GLUED, WITH QUIVERING TOUCH, . . . 684 SEEKER V 63
GLUTS
  WHEN SUMMER GLUTS THE GOLDEN BEES, ... 84 MAD KING GOLL 38
  WHERE SUMMER GLUTS THE GOLDEN BEES, ... 84 MAD KING GOLL V 38
GNASHING
  GNASHING OF TEETH, DESPAIR; . . . . 346 ON WOMAN 39
GO
  WHERE ROUND AND ROUND THE RAVENS GO. . . . . 5 OISIN 1 V 42
  IN WHAT FAR KINGDOM DO YOU GO, ... 10 OISIN 1 115
  THAT I WOULD GO WITH HER, THEY GREW . . . . 10 OISIN 1 V 111A
  IN WHAT FAR KINGDOM DO YE GO; . . . . 10 OISIN 1 V 115
  YOU GO NOT WHERE THE RED DEER FEEDS, ... 11 OISIN 1 127
  YE GO NOT WHERE THE RED DEER FEEDS, ... 11 OISIN 1 V 127
  "OH, SIGH, AWAKE AND GO YOU FORTH FOR ME; . . . . . . 33 OISIN 2 V 57
  AND GO YOU CLOSE TO THEM. . . . . 33 OISIN 2 V 59
  AND ONE WHOM YOU WILL GO TO WITHOUT TELLING, ... 33 OISIN 2 V 67
  OF FEAR, I BADE THEM GO; AND FOR THE FIGHT . . . . . 38 OISIN 2 V 142
  GO CAST YOUR BODY ON THE STONES AND PRAY, ... 42 OISIN 2 207
  AND THEN LOST NIAMH MURMURED, "LOVE, WE GO . . . . . 46 OISIN 2 245
  LOST NIAM MOURN AND SAY, "AH, LOVE, WE GO . . . . . . 46 OISIN 2 V 245B
  . . . NOR GO FROM HIS DEW-CUMBERED SKIES! . . . . . . 49 OISIN 3 38
  "THEN GO THROUGH THE LANDS IN THE SADDLE AND SEE WHAT THE
    MORTALS DO, 55 OISIN 3 125
  . . . TURNING AND TURNING GO, ... 57 OISIN 3 145
  . . . FOR I GO TO THE FENIANS, O CLERIC, TO CHAUNT . . . 61 OISIN 3 201
  . . . I WILL GO TO THE FENIANS, THOU CLERIC, AND CHANT . . 61 OISIN 3 V 201
  I WILL GO TO CAOILTE, AND CONAN, AND BRAN, SCEOLAN, LOMAIR, . 63 OISIN 3 223
  I WILL GO TO THE HOUSE OF THE FENIANS, BE THEY IN FLAMES 63 OISIN 3 V 223
    OR AT FEAST,
  GO GATHER BY THE HUMMING SEA . . . . 66 HAPPY SHEPHERD 35
  GO GATHER BY THE HUMMING-SEA . . . . 66 HAPPY SHEPHERD V 35
  OH, MAY TRANQUILLITY BESIDE HIM GO, ... 71 ANASHU VIJAYA V 2
  WITH HER WOULD I GO. . . . . 89 ISLE IN WATER 8
  BECAUSE I MUTTER AS I GO; . . . . 94 MOLL MAGEE 3
  AND GAVE ME MONEY, AND BADE ME GO . . . . 95 MOLL MAGEE 23
  "TO STABLE AND TO KENNEL GO; . . . . 97 FOXHUNTER 5
  "AND OF MY SERVANTS SOME ONE GO; . . . . 97 FOXHUNTER V 5
  COME NEAR; I WOULD, BEFORE MY TIME TO GO, ... 101 ROSE UPON ROOD 22
  I SEE MY LIFE GO DRIFTING LIKE A RIVER . . . . 104 FERGUS DRUID 31
  I SEE MY LIFE GO DRIPPING LIKE A STREAM . . . . 104 FERGUS DRUID V 31
  GO WATCH THE ROAD BETWEEN THE WOOD AND TIDE, ... 105 CUCHULAIN SEA 4
  GO DWELL UPON THE SEA CLIFFS, VAPOUR HID, ... 105 CUCHULAIN SEA V 4
  GO DWELL UPON THE SEA CLIFFS, VAPOUR-HID . . . . . . 105 CUCHULAIN SEA V 4
  GO DWELL UPON THE CLIFFS AND WATCH THE TIDE, ... 105 CUCHULAIN SEA V 4
  GO THERE, AND LIGHT A CAMP-FIRE AT WOOD'S RIM; . . . 108 CUCHULAIN SEA 35
  GO THERE AND DWELL ON THE GREEN FOREST RIM. . . . . . 108 CUCHULAIN SEA V 35
  GO THERE, AND CAMP UPON THE FOREST'S RIM; . . . . . . 108 CUCHULAIN SEA V 35
  GO THERE, AND LIGHT A CAMP FIRE AT WOOD'S RIM; . . . 108 CUCHULAIN SEA V 35
  GO, CAST ON HIM DELUSIONS MAGICAL, ... 111 CUCHULAIN SEA V 80
  HE WOULD GO WEAVE OUT OF THE STARS . . . . 113 ROSE OF PEACE 7
  I CALL, AS THEY GO BY ME ONE BY ONE, ... 114 ROSE OF BATTLE 8
  I WILL ARISE AND GO NOW, AND GO TO INNISFREE, ... 117 ISLE INNISFREE 1
  I WILL ARISE AND GO NOW, AND GO TO INNISFREE, ... 117 ISLE INNISFREE 1
  I WILL ARISE AND GO NOW, FOR ALWAYS NIGHT AND DAY . . 117 ISLE INNISFREE 9
  HER WHITE FEET GO GLIMMERING. . . . . 125 CATHLEEN PARA V 14
  WHO WILL GO DRIVE WITH FERGUS NOW, ... 125 GOES FERGUS 1
  THERE HE LOVES A CIRCLE GO, ... 135 TWO TREES 13
  THERE, THROUGH THE BROKEN BRANCHES, GO . . . . 135 TWO TREES 33
  THERE, THROUGH BEWILDERED BRANCHES, GO . . . . 135 TWO TREES V 13
  FOR THE ELEMENTAL CREATURES GO . . . . 138 TO IRELAND 23
  FOR ROUND ABOUT MY TABLE GO . . . . 138 TO IRELAND V 23
  FOR THE ELEMENTAL BEINGS GO . . . . 138 TO IRELAND V 23
  AND ALL BENIGHTED THINGS THAT GO . . . . 139 TO IRELAND 39
  AND ALL THE WIZARD THINGS THAT GO . . . . 139 TO IRELAND V 39
  GO TO THE GUARDS OF THE HEAVENLY FOLD . . . . 141 EVERLAST VOICE 2
  HE BADE HIS HEART GO TO HER, ... 159 CAP AND BELLS 13
  HE MADE HIS SOUL GO UPWARD . . . . 159 CAP AND BELLS V 3
  WHITHER HER FOOTSTEPS GO. . . . . 175 ELEMENT POWERS V 18
  WHERE HER SOFT FOOTSTEPS GO. . . . . 175 ELEMENT POWERS V 18
  AS IN THE OLD DAYS WHEN THEY WOULD COME AND GO . . . 183 QUEEN MAEVE 81
  BETTER GO DOWN UPON YOUR MARROW-BONES . . . . 204 ADAMS CURSE 7
  BETTER GO DOWN UPON YOUR MARROW BONES . . . . 204 ADAMS CURSE V 7
  AND WHETHER I GO IN MY DREAMS BY WOODLAND, OR DUN, . 210 UNDER THE MOON 14
    OR SHORE,
  WE'D BETTER GO, FOR WE HAVE LOST THIS CHANCE. . . . . 226 SHADOW WATER B 80
  AND LET THE DREAM GO BY. IT'S NOT A DREAM. . . . . . 229 SHADOW WATER B 158
  LET GO MY HANDS! WHY DO YOU CAST A SHADOW? . . . . . 235 SHADOW WATER B 283
  WHEN SHE FINDS OUT I WILL NOT LET HER GO-- . . . . . 236 SHADOW WATER B 302
  THAT YOU'LL NOT LET ME GO? I AM A QUEEN. . . . . . . 236 SHADOW WATER B 304
  I HAD FORGOTTEN THAT WE MUST GO WAKE HIM. . . . . . . 236 SHADOW WATER B 384
  WILL LOOK UPON HIS FACE AGAIN. GO WITH HIM, ... 240 SHADOW WATER B 589
  AND CUT THE ROPE, FOR I GO ON WITH FORGAEL. . . . . . 250 SHADOW WATER B 589
  "GO AND LOVE, GO AND LOVE, YOUNG MAN, ... 250 SHADOW WATER B 592
  "GO AND LOVE, GO AND LOVE, YOUNG MAN, ... 268 BROWN PENNY 5
  I BADE HIM GO WHEN ALL HIS HOUSEHOLD SLEPT . . . . . 268 BROWN PENNY 5
  TO GO--FOR HOPE WOULD GIVE HIS LIMBS THE POWER-- . . 282 TWO KINGS 133
  THE PACK UPON HIM. GO, UNQUIET WANDERER, ... 282 TWO KINGS V 133A
  "TIME TO PUT OFF THE WORLD AND GO SOMEWHERE . . . . . 292 TO A SHADE 18
  AND LET YOU GO, ... 299 BEGGAR CRIED 1
  GO PLUCK ATHENE BY THE HAIR! . . . . 359 TO A SQUIRREL 8
    386 ROBARTES DANCE 19

325

		PAGE	TITLE		LINE
GO	(CONTINUED)				
IT SEEMS THAT I MUST BID THE MUSE GO PACK,		409	TOWER		11
GO THEREFORE; BUT LEAVE HANRAHAN,		413	TOWER		103
TO CRAWL IN HER OWN BLOOD, AND GO SCOT-FREE;		429	NINETEEN 19		28
CRUELTY MUST KEEP; THEREFORE BE WARNED AND GO		448	HERO GIRL FOOL		7
MEN COME, MEN GO,		512	JANE ON GOD		5
TAKE TO THE ROADS AND GO MARCHING ALONG.		548	TO SAME TUNE 3		14
GO GALLIVANTING BY;		552	SONGS REWRIT 2		4
NOR WHERE I GO,		572	LADYS 1ST SONG		4
YOU ASK WHAT I HAVE FOUND, AND FAR AND WIDE I GO;		580	CURSE CROMWELL		1
"GO YOUR WAYS, O GO YOUR WAYS,		588	OLD WICKED MAN		28
"GO YOUR WAYS, O GO YOUR WAYS,		588	OLD WICKED MAN		28
I NEVER BADE YOU GO		600	THOSE IMAGES		5
HOW CAN THE YOUNG GO STRAIGHT?		607	SONGS BURDEN 2		17
HE LACKED THOSE YEARS THAT GO WITH SKILL,		608	SONGS BURDEN 3		14
TALL DAMES GO WALKING IN GRASS-GREEN AVALON.		627	STATES HOLIDAY		13
TALL DAMES GO WALKING IN GRASS-GREEN AVALON.		627	STATES HOLIDAY		26
TALL DAMES GO WALKING IN GRASS-GREEN AVALON.		627	STATES HOLIDAY		39
TALL DAMES GO WALKING IN GRASS GREEN AVALON.		627	STATES HOLIDAY	V	REF
I COULD NOT GO. LET'S TALK, AND LET'S BE SAD,		651	ISLE STAT I 2		7
GO PILOT THE COURSE OF HIS ARROW'S DECEIT!		657	ISLE STAT I 3		69
AS THEY GO WITH DROOPING FEATHER.		667	ISLE STAT II 3		33
AH, WOE IS ME! I GO FROM SUN AND SHADE,		674	ISLE STAT II 3		216
GO ASK THE SPRINGING FLOWERS,		680	LOVE AND DEATH		13
GO ASK THE YOUNGEST ANGEL,		680	LOVE AND DEATH		29
GO UP AND DOWN, AND RAISE THEIR HEADS AND SING		682	SEEKER		30
I GO AS SOFT AS FOLLY! I AM FATE."		686	LIFE		18
SO YOU MUST GO; KISS ME BEFORE YOU GO?		702	MOSADA 3		96
SO YOU MUST GO; KISS ME BEFORE YOU GO.		702	MOSADA 3		96
THERE IS NO LEAVE-TAKING. I GO NO MORE.		702	MOSADA 3		100
THERE IS NO LEAVE TAKING. I GO NO MORE.		702	MOSADA 3	V	100
UNHAPPY ONE. GO NOT, GO NOT, GO NOT;		703	MOSADA 3		102
UNHAPPY ONE. GO NOT, GO NOT, GO NOT;		703	MOSADA 3		102
UNHAPPY ONE. GO NOT, GO NOT, GO NOT!		703	MOSADA 3		102
EACH OTHER'S NECKS, AND WHISPERING AS THEY GO,		703	MOSADA 3		120
TO PRISONS GO, AND MOSSY RUIN REST		709	FERENCZ RENYI		2
TO PRISON GO, AND MOSSY RUIN REST		709	FERENCZ RENYI	V	2
"CHOOSE!" RESTLESS HAYNAU'S FINGERS TAPPING GO.		711	FERENCZ RENYI		41
THERE FAR AWAY FROM ALL WE TWO WILL GO,		714	FERENCZ RENYI		99
MY LOVE, WE WILL GO, WE WILL GO, I AND YOU,		717	LOVE SONG		1
MY LOVE, WE WILL GO, WE WILL GO, I AND YOU,		717	LOVE SONG		1
"WATCHER, WHEREFORE HAVE YE CALLED US?" EYES GO AFTER		718	PHANTOM SHIP		10
HIS LEAN HAND,					
HOW STILL IT IS! I HEAR THE CARP GO SPLASH,		722	WITCH VIVIEN		62
I CANNOT GO INTO THE BLOODLESS LAND		722	WITCH VIVIEN		67
WHERE THE SOULS OF FAIRIES GO?"		729	PRIEST FAIRY		48
I GO AS SOFT AS FOLLY! I AM FATE."		735	QUATRAIN APHOR		20
WHERE MY BOOKS GO.		739	WHERE BOOKS GO		T
"GO BRING ME MY OLD ARMOUR		740	EARL PAUL		19
GO BRING ME MY OWN ARMOUR		740	EARL PAUL	V	19
THEN GO TO HIS OWN LAND,		741	EARL PAUL		58
IT MAY BE NOW THAT I CAN GO MY WAY		751	SHADOW WATER A		96
IF I GO NEARER TO THE WINDWARD SIDE,		753	SHADOW WATER A		140
AND WE GO HOME. COME, AIBRIC; END YOUR TALE		766	SHADOW WATER A		374
WE WILL GO CALL THESE SAILORS, AND ESCAPE		766	SHADOW WATER A		382
BUT I AM NEW TO LOVE. GO AMONG THESE		767	SHADOW WATER A		391
OR GO BESIDE HIM TO HIS MOUNTAIN WARS.		768	SHADOW WATER A		414
I'D LET THE WHOLE WORLD GO!		782	HEART FRIGHT		9
GOAD					
AND THE MOON GOAD THE WATERS NIGHT AND DAY,		45	OISIN 2		238
FROM NEEDLE'S EYE STILL GOAD IT ON.		562	NEEDLES EYE		4
GOAT					
THAT FOUND WHEN I HAD NEITHER GOAT NOR GRAZING		340	SHEP GOATHERD		31
CURES HE HATH FOR COW OR GOAT		716	FAIRY DOCTOR		13
WHEN SOMETHING THAT WAS BEARDED LIKE A GOAT		747	SHADOW WATER A		11
WHEN SOMETHING, HALF A LAMB AND HALF A GOAT,		747	SHADOW WATER A	V	11
GOAT-HEAD					
FOUL GOAT-HEAD, BRUTAL ARM APPEAR,		612	NEWS ORACLE		33
GOATHERD					
SHEPHERD AND GOATHERD		338	SHEP GOATHERD		T
THOUGH THEY BUT FEED AS THE GOATHERD FEEDS,		635	BLACK TOWER		2
GOATHERDS					
OLD GOATHERDS AND OLD GOATS, IF IN ALL ELSE		340	SHEP GOATHERD		46
GOAT'S					
HAVE FOUND THE PATH MY GOAT'S FEET CANNOT FIND.		342	SHEP GOATHERD	V	84
GOATS					
WHERE MY GOATS BROWSE ON THE SCARCE GRASS OR LEAP		339	SHEP GOATHERD		8
OLD GOATHERDS AND OLD GOATS, IF IN ALL ELSE		340	SHEP GOATHERD		46
GOATS'					
HAVE FOUND THE PATH MY GOATS' FEET CANNOT FIND.		342	SHEP GOATHERD		84
GOBAN					
OLD WHOLESOME GOBAN HAD NO SAY;		271	GREY ROCK		10
THE BOW-LEGGED GOBAN HAD NO SAY;		271	GREY ROCK	V	10
OLD GOBAN HAMMERED THEM AND WROUGHT THEM,		271	GREY ROCK	V	23
THAT SACRED GOBAN BREWED," HE CRIED		304	HOUR DAWN		50
GOBAN'D					
ON METAL GOBAN'D HAMMERED AT,		271	GREY ROCK		19
GOBAN'S					
AND SHE WITH GOBAN'S WINE ADRIP,		276	GREY ROCK		121
I DRAGGED FROM GOBAN'S MOUNTAIN-TOP		304	HOUR DAWN		50

	PAGE	TITLE		LINE

GOBLIN
    CLEAR FLUTED THEN THAT GOBLIN RARE--   6 OISIN 1   V   54
    GROWETH THE GOBLIN FLOWER OF JOY, HER CARE,   653 ISLE STAT I 2   39
    IN SONG, FROM GOBLIN WATERS SWAYING WHITE,   657 ISLE STAT I 3   51
    SOME GOBLIN, MY SERVANT, ON WINGS THAT ARE FLEET,   657 ISLE STAT I 3   67
    IS WORN AS THOUGH WITH FIRE. OH, GOBLIN QUEEN,   667 ISLE STAT II 3   36
    AS LIGHT OF TRIUMPH IN THY GOBLIN EYES--   674 ISLE STAT II 3   199
    UPON MY NECKLACE. BUT THE GOBLIN QUEEN   676 ISLE STAT II 3   267
    THE GOBLIN FLOWER LIETH ON THY LIPS.   678 ISLE STAT II 3   298
    THE YEARS OF GOBLIN SLEEP. AH! WHILE I SLUMBERED,   679 ISLE STAT II 3   308
    SEEK NOT THAT WOOD, FOR THERE THE GOBLIN SNAKES   682 SEEKER   29
    THEN 'GAN TO SPEAK THAT GOBLIN RARE,   729 PRIEST FAIRY   37
GOBLINS
    FIRST DREAMS, AND GOBLINS, AND THE LESSER SPRITES,   722 WITCH VIVIEN   56
GOD   SEE SEA-GOD
    FOR JOY IS GOD AND GOD IS JOY."   19 OISIN 1   286
    FOR JOY IS GOD AND GOD IS JOY."   19 OISIN 1   286
    SANG, "GOD IS JOY AND JOY IS GOD,   20 OISIN 1   300
    SANG, "GOD IS JOY AND JOY IS GOD,   20 OISIN 1   300
    SHAKE THE LOOSE REINS! YOU SLAVES OF GOD,   22 OISIN 1   331
    SHAKE THE LOOSE REINS! YE SLAVES OF GOD,   22 OISIN 1   331
    WHEN GOD SHALL COME FROM THE SEA WITH A SIGH   28 OISIN 1   V   425
    BEFORE GOD WAS OR MY OLD LINE BEGAN;   29 OISIN 2   8
    THINGS DONE ERE GOD FIRST WAS OR MY OLD LINE BEGAN;   29 OISIN 2   V   8
    SINCE GOD MADE TIME AND DEATH AND SLEEP: THE OTHER   31 OISIN 2   41
    NOT EVEN YOUR GOD COULD HAVE THROWN DOWN THAT HALL: 36 OISIN 2   109
    NOT E'EN THY GOD COULD HAVE THROWN DOWN THAT HALL: 36 OISIN 2   V   109
    FOR GOD HAS HEARD, AND SPEAKS HIS ANGRY MIND;   42 OISIN 2   V   206
    GOD SHAKES THE WORLD WITH RESTLESS HANDS. MORE NEAR   43 OISIN 2   V   208
    THE INDIAN UPON GOD   76 INDIAN ON GOD   T
    FROM THE BOOK OF KAURI THE INDIAN-- SECTION V. ON THE   76 INDIAN ON GOD   V   T
    NATURE OF GOD
    KANVA, THE INDIAN, ON GOD   76 INDIAN ON GOD   V   T
    GOD LIGHTS THE STARS, HIS CANDLES,   96 MOLL MAGEE   51
    BY GOD TO THE BRIGHT HEARTS OF THOSE LONG DEAD,   101 ROSE UPON ROOD   20
    "NOT ANY GOD ALIVE NOR MORTAL DEAD,   106 CUCHULAIN SEA   V   10
    FOR GOD WHO MADE YOU BITTER MADE YOU WISE."   108 CUCHULAIN SEA   V   32
    "GOD ONLY SEES WHAT DOOM FOR ME LIES STORED."   110 CUCHULAIN SEA   V   62
    AND GOD WOULD BID HIS WARFARE CEASE,   113 ROSE OF PEACE   13
    AND GOD WOULD BID MAN'S WARFARE CEASE,   113 ROSE OF PEACE   V   13
    FOR GOD HAS BID THEM SHARE AN EQUAL FATE: 115 ROSE OF BATTLE   32
    GOD SMILES IN HIGH HEAVEN   118 CRADLE SONG   V   5
    THE STARS OF GOD WHERE THEY MOVE,   119 PITY OF LOVE   V   4
    THAT GOD HAS LAID HIS FINGERS ON THE SKY,   128 DREAM OF FAERY   43
    DREAM, UNTIL GOD BURN NATURE WITH A KISS?   128 DREAM OF FAERY   47
    OF HOW GOD LEANS HIS HANDS OUT OF THE SKY,   128 DREAM OF FAERY V   43
    THAT GOD HAD LEANED HIS HANDS OUT OF THE SKY,   128 DREAM OF FAERY V   43
    THAT GOD HAD LEANT HIS HANDS OUT OF THE SKY,   128 DREAM OF FAERY V   43
    AND AFTER CRIED HE, "GOD FORGIVE!   132 FR GILLIGAN   11
    AND GOD COVERED THE WORLD WITH SHADE,   133 FR GILLIGAN   19
    MADE WHEN GOD SLEPT IN TIMES OF OLD.   135 TWO TREES   32
    BEFORE GOD MADE THE ANGELIC CLAN,   138 TO IRELAND   8
    THAT GOD GIVES UNTO MAN IN SLEEP.   138 TO IRELAND   V   22
    FOR GOD GOES BY WITH WHITE FOOTFALL.   139 TO IRELAND   44
    FOR GOD GOES BY WITH WHITE FOOT-FALL.   139 TO IRELAND   V   44
    AND GOD STANDS WINDING HIS LONELY HORN,   148 INTO TWILIGHT   13
    IS DROPPING SLEEP, UNTIL GOD BURN TIME,   164 PERFECT BEAUTY   7
    AT HUSH OF EVENING TILL GOD BURNS TIME   164 PERFECT BEAUTY V   7
    AT HUSH OF EVENING TILL GOD BURN TIME   164 PERFECT BEAUTY V   7
    WITH THE SECRETS OF GOD IN HIS EYES.   167 BLESSED   12
    "PRAISE GOD AND GOD'S MOTHER," DATHI SAID,   167 BLESSED   17
    "FOR GOD AND GOD'S MOTHER HAVE SENT   167 BLESSED   18
    "WITH THE SECRETS OF GOD HALF BLIND,   168 BLESSED   26
    THAT NO GOD TROUBLED NOW, AND, WONDERING   182 QUEEN MAEVE   60
    SOME GOD OR KING HAD MADE THE LAWS   194 BAILE AILLINN   131
    BUT THEREON EVERY GOD STOOD UP   275 GREY ROCK   116
    AND WHAT, GOD HELP US, COULD THEY SAVE?   289 SEPTEMBER 1913   14
    HAVING LOVED GOD ONCE, BUT MAYBE   299 THREE HERMITS   26
    AND MURMURED "MAY GOD CURSE THE NIGHT   303 HOUR DAWN   V   32B
    AND THERE BE NOTHING BUT GOD LEFT;   307 HOUR DAWN   103
    NOR GAVE GOD THANKS TILL OVERHEAD   307 HOUR DAWN   121
    "OH GOD IF HE GOT LOOSE!" AND THEN   307 HOUR DAWN   V   118
    AND GAVE GOD THANKS THAT OVERHEAD   307 HOUR DAWN   V   121
    MAY GOD BE PRAISED FOR WOMAN   345 ON WOMAN   1
    GOD GRANT ME--NO, NOT HERE,   346 ON WOMAN   25
    GOD GRANT A BLESSING ON THIS TOWER AND COTTAGE   371 ON GOING HOUSE   1
    UNDER THIS HUMP. GOD TRIES EACH MAN   379 SAINT HUNCH   5
    BUT PRAY TO GOD THAT HE EASE   380 SONGS FOOL 1   17
    DID GOD IN PORTIONING WINE AND BREAD   386 ROBARTES DANCE   39
    GOD TOOK THE SPINNING-JENNY   439 FRAGMENTS   3
    THAT ONLY GOD HAS LOVED US FOR OURSELVES,   448 HERO GIRL FOOL   16
    AND NOT THEIR WORTH. GOD LOVES US FOR OUR WORTH;   448 HERO GIRL FOOL V   15
    ENDURE WHAT LIFE GOD GIVES AND ASK NO LONGER SPAN;   459 FROM OEDIPUS   1
    WHETHER OF HER OR GOD HE THOUGHT THE MOST,   471 ALL SOUL NIGHT   32
    EVERYTHING THAT IS NOT GOD CONSUMED WITH INTELLECTUAL FIRE.   481 BLOOD AND MOON   30
    THAT ONLY GOD, MY DEAR,   492 ANNE GREGORY   16
    THE MOTHER OF GOD   499 MOTHER OF GOD   T
    THE BISHOP HAS A SKIN, GOD KNOWS,   508 JANE BISHOP   15
    THAT TO GOD SHALL COME;   511 JANE AND JACK   8
    CRAZY JANE ON GOD   512 JANE ON GOD   T
    ALL THINGS REMAIN IN GOD.   512 JANE ON GOD   6

327

PAGE   TITLE   LINE

GOD   (CONTINUED)
ALL THINGS REMAIN IN GOD. . . . . 512 JANE ON GOD 12
ALL THINGS REMAIN IN GOD. . . . . 512 JANE ON GOD 18
ALL THINGS REMAIN IN GOD. . . . . 512 JANE ON GOD 24
GOD BE WITH THE TIMES WHEN I . . . . 514 JANE GROWN OLD 17
GOD GUARD ME FROM THOSE THOUGHTS MEN THINK . . . . . 553 PRAYER OLD AGE 1
. . . SHARE GOD THAT IS BUT THREE, ... 556 RIBH PATRICK 11
IT IS OF GOD AND PASSES HUMAN WIT. . . . . 558 RIBH CHRISTIAN 2
FROM EVERY THOUGHT OF GOD MANKIND HAS HAD. . . . . . 558 RIBH CHRISTIAN 15
HATRED OF GOD MAY BRING THE SOUL TO GOD. . . . . . . 558 RIBH CHRISTIAN 18
HATRED OF GOD MAY BRING THE SOUL TO GOD. . . . . . . 558 RIBH CHRISTIAN 18
IN HATING GOD SHE MAY CREEP CLOSE TO GOD. . . . . . 558 RIBH CHRISTIAN V 18
IN HATING GOD SHE MAY CREEP CLOSE TO GOD. . . . . . 558 RIBH CHRISTIAN V 18
NOW HIS WARS ON GOD BEGIN; . . . . 561 FOUR AGES MAN 7
AT STROKE OF MIDNIGHT GOD SHALL WIN. . . . . 561 FOUR AGES MAN 8
WHO TRAVELS WHERE GOD WILLS. . . . . 587 OLD WICKED MAN 4
I SWEAR TO GOD I QUESTIONED THEM, AND ALL THEY HAD TO SAY 593 PILGRIM 14
I SWEAR TO GOD I QUESTIONED THEM ALL AND ALL THEY HAD TO 593 PILGRIM V 14
SAY
COULD THAT OLD GOD RISE UP AGAIN . . . . 606 SONGS BURDEN 1 21
"GOD I HAVE LOVED, BUT SHOULD I ASK RETURN . . . . 609 IN TARAS HALLS 14
OF GOD OR WOMAN, THE TIME WERE COME TO DIE." . . . 609 IN TARAS HALLS 15
BRING THE SOUL OF MAN TO GOD. . . . . 638 BEN BULBEN 40
ON BACKGROUNDS FOR A GOD OR SAINT . . . . 639 BEN BULBEN 54
PREPARED A REST FOR THE PEOPLE OF GOD, ... 639 BEN BULBEN 65
UNLESS SOME PITYING GOD SHALL SUCCOUR ME . . . . . 656 ISLE STAT I 3 36
IN THIS MY CHOICE. SOME GOD MIGHT HELP; IF SO . . 656 ISLE STAT I 3 37
SHALL NOT SO HOPELESS PROVE; SOME GOD MAY REST . . 657 ISLE STAT I 3 61
HE WAS OUR ANCIENT GOD. IF I SPEAK LOW, ... 658 ISLE STAT I 3 78
AND NOT TOO CLEAR, HOW WILL THE NEW GOD KNOW . . . 658 ISLE STAT I 3 79
AS HERE I CAME I SAW GOD PAN. HE PLAYED . . . . . 678 ISLE STAT II 3 300
THE BLESSED GOD WAS GOOD TO SEND US SUCH, ... 683 SEEKER 40
OF HIS SAD GOD; AND DOWN AMONG THE GRASS . . . . . 690 MOSADA 1 16
THE VAPOUR IS MUCH THICKER. GOD! THE STAKE! . . . 695 MOSADA 1 112
NO USE. AWAY! HEAR, THOU ENDURING GOD, ... 698 MOSADA 2 50
AND THOU SHALT BEND, ENDURING GOD, THE KNEES . . . 698 MOSADA 2 59
NO USE. AWAY! HEAR OH! THOU ENDURING GOD, . . . 698 MOSADA 2 V 50
AND THOU SHALL BEND, ENDURING GOD, THE KNEES . . . 698 MOSADA 2 V 59
OH, GOD!--AWAKE! THOU SHALT NOT DIE. SHE SLEEPS, 701 MOSADA 3 66
WAS EBREMAR, WHOSE THOUGHTS WERE FIXED ON GOD, . . 702 MOSADA 3 83
GOD! THEY'RE MAD TO FLY SUCH CANVAS!" . . . . . . 718 PHANTOM SHIP 14
THERE WAS SOME TALKING OF MAN'S GOD, ... 725 LEGEND 19
HIS GOD OF STUPOR AND OF WRATH. . . . . 725 LEGEND 20
IN THE HOLY CHURCH OF GOD. . . . . 735 IN CHURCH 4
IN THE HOLY CHURCH OF GOD. . . . . 736 IN CHURCH 16
FOR GOD IS WALKING IN THE DEW, ... 736 SUMMER EVENING 15
FOR GOD GIVES POWER TO THE SAD . . . . 741 EARL PAUL 47
FOR GOD GIVES POWER TO THE SAD . . . . 741 EARL PAUL 51
GOD PLANTED HIM LONG AGO. . . . . 743 WISDOM DREAMS 8
HE CANNOT WAKE THE GOD THAT HIDES IN IT. . . . . . 748 SHADOW WATER A 19
BECAUSE A GOD HAS MADE HIM WISE WITH DREAMS; . . . 748 SHADOW WATER A 26
I SWORE BUT YESTERDAY IF THE RED GOD . . . . 751 SHADOW WATER A 109
OR A GOD HID THEM UNDER THE SHADOW OF WINGS. . . . 752 SHADOW WATER A 125
AND GATHER ROUND HIM, THAT NO GOD MAY KNOW . . . . 758 SHADOW WATER A V 231
HOW LITTLE AND REEDY A SOUND AWAKES A GOD . . . . 760 SHADOW WATER A 252
GOD-APPOINTED
AND GOD-APPOINTED BERKELEY THAT PROVED ALL THINGS A DREAM, 481 BLOOD AND MOON 25
GODDESS
ON BREAST OF MARS THE GODDESS SIGHED. . . . . . . 562 CONJUNCTIONS 4
GOD-FORSAKEN
THROUGH GOD-FORSAKEN MEADOWS; MRS. FRENCH, ... 412 TOWER 93
GOD-HATED
AS THAT OLD WANDERING BEGGAR AND THESE GOD-HATED CHILDREN 459 FROM OEDIPUS 6
KNOW.
GODHEAD
AS MAN, AS BEAST, AS AN EPHEMERAL FLY BEGETS, GODHEAD 556 RIBH PATRICK 5
BEGETS GODHEAD,
AS MAN, AS BEAST, AS AN EPHEMERAL FLY BEGETS, GODHEAD 556 RIBH PATRICK 5
BEGETS GODHEAD,
GODHEAD ON GODHEAD IN SEXUAL SPASM BEGOT . . . . . 557 RIBH ECSTASY 5
GODHEAD ON GODHEAD IN SEXUAL SPASM BEGOT . . . . . 557 RIBH ECSTASY 5
GODHEAD. SOME SHADOW FELL. MY SOUL FORGOT . . . . 557 RIBH ECSTASY 6
GOD-KIND
OF GOD-KIND AND MAN-KIND. . . . . 770 BLOOD BOND 6
GODLESS
. . . AND ITS GODLESS AND PASSIONATE AGE. . . . . 63 OISIN 3 216
. . . AND THE GODLESS FIRES OF THINE AGE. . . . . 63 OISIN 3 V 216
GOD'S   SEE SEA-GOD'S
THAT SEA GOD'S NAME, WHO IN A DEEP CONTENT . . . . 38 OISIN 2 V 129
THE DEAD GOD'S SWORD, TO MANY FORMS HE GREW, . . . 40 OISIN 2 V 175
WATCHING THE BLESSED ONES MOVE FAR OFF, AND THE SMILE ON 61 OISIN 3 199
GOD'S FACE,
"THE DOOMS OF MEN ARE IN GOD'S HIDDEN PLACE." . . 110 CUCHULAIN SEA 62
"THE DOOMS OF MEN ARE IN GOD'S HIDDEN HOARD." . . 110 CUCHULAIN SEA V 62
IF MICHAEL, LEADER OF GOD'S HOST . . . . 112 ROSE OF PEACE 1
IF MICHAEL, LEADER OF GOD'S HOSTS . . . . 112 ROSE OF PEACE V 1
BROODING NO MORE UPON GOD'S WARS . . . . 113 ROSE OF PEACE 5
WOULD COME AT LAST TO GOD'S GREAT TOWN, ... 113 ROSE OF PEACE 11
AND GOD'S BELL BUOYED TO BE THE WATER'S CARE; . . 114 ROSE OF BATTLE 4
AND WAGE GOD'S BATTLES IN THE LONG GREY SHIPS. . . 114 ROSE OF BATTLE 20
GOD'S BELL HAS CLAIMED THEM BY THE LITTLE CRY . . 114 ROSE OF BATTLE 23

328

GOD'S   (CONTINUED)   PAGE   TITLE   LINE

GOD'S LAUGHING IN HEAVEN . . . .   118 CRADLE SONG   5
THAT ONLY GOD'S EYES DID NOT CLOSE; . . . .   156 FORGOT BEAUTY   14
"PRAISE GOD AND GOD'S MOTHER," DATHI SAID, ...   167 BLESSED   17
"FOR GOD AND GOD'S MOTHER HAVE SENT . . . .   167 BLESSED   18
THE POWERS, NOT KIND LIKE YOU, CAME WHERE GOD'S GARDEN   174 ELEMENT POWERS V   1
  BLOWS.
THAT ON THE LONELY HEIGHT WHERE ALL ARE IN GOD'S EYE,   291 PAUDEEN   6
AND THAT WOULD BE AGAINST GOD'S PROVIDENCE. . . . .   339 SHEP GOATHERD   5
I MOURN FOR THAT MOST LONELY THING; AND YET GOD'S WILL   354 HIS PHOENIX   31
  BE DONE!
O SAGES STANDING IN GOD'S HOLY FIRE . . . .   408 SAIL BYZANTIUM   17
AS THOUGH GOD'S DEATH WERE BUT A PLAY. . . . .   437 SONGS PLAY 1   8
"GOD'S FIRE UPON THE WANE, ...   485 STATISTICS   2
STANDS IN GOD'S UNCHANGING EYE . . . .   529 TOM LUNATIC   16
GOD'S LOVE HAS HIDDEN HIM . . . .   574 MAIDS 1ST SONG   7
GODS   SEE SEA-GODS
WHEN GODS AND GIANTS WARRED. WE RODE BETWEEN . . . .   31 OISIN 2   31
NOR THE HIGH GODS WHO NEVER LIVED, MAY FIGHT . . . .   34 OISIN 2   80
UNTIL THE GODS AND DEMONS DROP ASLEEP. . . . .   35 OISIN 2   86
BREWED BY THE SEA GODS, FROM HUGE CUPS THAT LAY . . .   41 OISIN 2   V   189
ON THE FLOORS OF THE GODS." . . . .   59 OISIN 3   180
. . . HE CRIED, "NO, THE GODS A LONG TIME ARE DEAD."   59 OISIN 3   180
. . . HE CRIED, "NAY, THE GODS A LONG TIME ARE DEAD."   59 OISIN 3   V   180
AY, AY. SWEAR BY THE PARENTS OF THE GODS, ...   74 ANASHU VIJAYA   66
SWEAR! BY THE PARENTS OF THE GODS, I SWEAR. . . . .   75 ANASHU VIJAYA   76
AND IN MY HEART THE DAEMONS AND THE GODS . . . . . .   104 FERGUS DRUID   V   38B
AND HIM WHO DROVE THE GODS OUT OF THEIR LISS, ...   170 SECRET ROSE   16
BUT THE GODS LONG AGO DECREED . . . .   194 BAILE AILLINN   119
PROTECT ME NOW, GODS THAT MY PEOPLE SWEAR BY. . . . .   241 SHADOW WATER B   396
THE GODS WERE SITTING AT THE BOARD . . . .   271 GREY ROCK   14
BUT LET THAT BE--THE GODS WERE STILL . . . .   271 GREY ROCK   V   16
THAT ONLY GODS MAY BUY OF HIM. . . . .   272 GREY ROCK   25
WHY ARE THE GODS BY MEN BETRAYED?" . . . .   275 GREY ROCK   115
STARED AT THE GODS WITH LAUGHING LIP. . . . .   276 GREY ROCK   123
OVERCOME GODS UPON PARNASSUS! . . . .   540 FROM ANTIGONE   6
BY AN OLD HUNTER TALKING WITH GODS; . . . .   605 YOU CONTENT   23
FOR GUIDING OF THE GODS. THE SACRED BLOOM . . . . .   656 ISLE STAT I 3   41
EVEN THE WANDERING ISLANDS OF THE GODS, ...   749 SHADOW WATER A   45
AND YET, THERE IS A LOVE THAT THE GODS GIVE, ...   749 SHADOW WATER A   56
AND FALLS AMONG THE DREAMS THE DROWSY GODS . . . . .   750 SHADOW WATER A   68
IT WERE BETTER TO PASS BY, BECAUSE THE GODS . . . . .   751 SHADOW WATER A   104
BECAUSE THE UNAMBITIOUS THAT HATE THE GODS . . . . .   754 SHADOW WATER A V   158
BY SUN AND MOON AND A HUNDRED GODS AS WELL, ...   756 SHADOW WATER A   189
THE GODS HOLD WATCH ABOUT THE WORDS OF A QUEEN. . . .   756 SHADOW WATER A   191
WHERE GODS ARE BROODING IN A MOUNTAINOUS PLACE . . .   757 SHADOW WATER A   198
I HAVE TURNED HOMEWARDS. IN THE EYES OF THE GODS, .   757 SHADOW WATER A   202
GATHER ABOUT HIM, THAT THE GODS MAY NOT KNOW . . . .   758 SHADOW WATER A   231
THE HAND THAT WOUNDS HIM, BECAUSE THE GODS ARE HIS FRIENDS. 758 SHADOW WATER A   232
THE MOUNTAIN OF THE GODS, THE UNAPPEASABLE GODS . . .   764 SHADOW WATER A   332
THE MOUNTAIN OF THE GODS, THE UNAPPEASABLE GODS . . .   764 SHADOW WATER A   332
THE GODS WEAVE NETS, AND TAKE US IN THEIR NETS, . . .   764 SHADOW WATER A   339
O! I WOULD BREAK THIS NET THE GODS HAVE WOVEN . . .   765 SHADOW WATER A   361
THE NETS THE GODS HAVE WOVEN AND OUR OWN HEARTS, . .   766 SHADOW WATER A   383
THE GODS HATE HAPPINESS, AND WEAVE THEIR NETS, . . .   767 SHADOW WATER A   399
SHE IS ALREADY FADING, AS THOUGH THE GODS . . . . .   768 SHADOW WATER A V   422
THE BRAVEST FROM THE GODS BUT ASK! . . . .   788 BRAVEST ASK   1
GODS'
THAT ONLY THE GODS' EYES DID NOT CLOSE! . . . . . .   156 FORGOT BEAUTY   V   14
WHERE I HAD HEARD NO FEET BUT THE GODS' CAME. . . .   756 SHADOW WATER A V 191B
GOES
THE OSPREY OF SORROW GOES AFTER AND CLUTCHES, . . .   27 OISIN 1   V 415D
WHERE YOU GO TO GAZE THE RESTLESS-FOOTED STAR . . .   32 OISIN 2   V 50G
GOES DROPPING FROM HIS EYES A LANGUID LIGHT, ...   34 OISIN 2   V 81A
GATHERS SEA-SLIME AND GOES THE SEAWARD WAY, ...   45 OISIN 2   V 237
IN A LONG IRON SLEEP, AS A FISH IN THE WATER GOES DUMB   53 OISIN 3   96
  AS A STONE.
NO LIVE MAN GOES THITHER, ...   62 OISIN 3   V 214
AND TO THE ARMCHAIR GOES, ...   98 FOXHUNTER   18
AND BY THE CHAIR HE GOES, ...   98 FOXHUNTER   V 18
AH, DREAM NOT OF THEM, MY BELOVED, THE FLAME OF THE METEOR 122 WHITE BIRDS   6
  THAT GOES,
YET SHE GOES WITH FOOTSTEP WARY, ...   124 CATHLEEN PARA   11
STILL SHE GOES WITH FOOTSTEPS WARY, ...   124 CATHLEEN PARA   V 11
SHE GOES DOWN THE FLOOR OF HEAVEN, ...   125 CATHLEEN PARA   V 13
WHO GOES WITH FERGUS? . . . .   125 GOES FERGUS   T
FOR GOD GOES BY WITH WHITE FOOTFALL, ...   139 TO IRELAND   44
FOR GOD GOES BY WITH WHITE FOOT-FALL. . . . .   139 TO IRELAND   V 44
AND THEIR DAY GOES OVER IN IDLENESS, ...   151 OLD MOTHER   7
BUT I CAN SEE WHERE THE WIND GOES . . . .   168 BLESSED   27
"AND BLESSEDNESS GOES WHERE THE WIND GOES, ...   168 BLESSED   29
"AND BLESSEDNESS GOES WHERE THE WIND GOES, ...   168 BLESSED   29
BUT I HAVE FOUND WHERE THE WIND GOES . . . .   168 BLESSED   V 27
SHE GOES ABOUT HER HOUSE ERECT AND CALM . . . . . .   340 SHEP GOATHERD   35
THE FRECKLED MAN WHO GOES . . . .   347 FISHERMAN   2
"VENGEANCE UPON THE MURDERERS," THE CRY GOES UP, . .   426 PHANTOM HATRED   9
GOES TO THE BARBAROUS CLANGOUR OF A GONG, ...   430 NINETEEN 19   58
GOES TO THE BARBAROUS CLANGOUR OF GONG. . . . . . .   430 NINETEEN 19   V 58
NAKED TO NAKED GOES, ...   538 LAST CONFESS   16
THE GIRL GOES DANCING THERE . . . .   568 SWEET DANCER   1
NOW STRENGTH OF BODY GOES! . . . .   575 ACRE OF GRASS   4

329

	PAGE	TITLE		LINE

GOES (CONTINUED)

HOW GOES THE WEATHER?	585	ORAHILLY		9
HOW GOES THE WEATHER?	585	ORAHILLY		18
HOW GOES THE WEATHER?	585	ORAHILLY		27
HOW GOES THE WEATHER?	585	ORAHILLY		36
THE BEGGARS HAVE CHANGED PLACES, BUT THE LASH GOES ON.	590	GREAT DAY		4
A HORN! SOME TROOP OF ROBBERS WINDING GOES	649	ISLE STAT I 1		110
YON WIND GOES SADLY, AND THE GRASS AND TREES	652	ISLE STAT I 2		10
OUT OF THE AIR. AND WHEN? WHEN THE SUN GOES DOWN	652	ISLE STAT I 2		29
THE WIND AT EVENING WHEN THE SUN GOES DOWN	653	ISLE STAT I 2		50
GOES FLICKERING IN REVERBERATED LIGHT.	653	ISLE STAT I 2		53
GOES HIS POPPIES NOW A-HAWKING;	705	DAWN-SONG		4
HE WHISPERS TO A SOLDIER, WHO GOES OUT—	711	FERENCZ RENYI		44
REITERANT. A BIRD GOES BY THE TENT	711	FERENCZ RENYI		46
REITERANT. A BOY GOES BY THE TENT,	711	FERENCZ RENYI	V	46
TIME GOES. THE FLAKED FIRE OF EVENING CRAWLS	712	FERENCZ RENYI		70
TIME GOES. THE FLICKED FIRE OF EVENING CRAWLS	712	FERENCZ RENYI	V	70
HER ARMS AROUND HIS FEET. THE SIGNAL GOES	714	FERENCZ RENYI		103
SO ENDS A BRAIN—A WORLD! THE SMOKE GOES UP,	714	FERENCZ RENYI		111
LAUGHING GOES IN WILDEST MOOD;	732	STREET DANCERS		41
THERE THY WANDERING PATHWAY GOES,	744	ROSY CROSS		6
"TILL THE SUN GOES DOWN AND AN HOUR OF THE CLOCK"	779	GOING THE ROAD		7

GOIN'

| OR GOIN' TO THE WELL, | 96 | MOLL MAGEE | | 46 |

GOING

. . . IN THE DIMNESS THEY LOVE GOING BY;	53	OISIN 3		98
AWAY WITH US HE'S GOING,	88	STOLEN CHILD		42
IF I AM GOING TO MY DEATH?—FOR THERE,	231	SHADOW WATER B		207
I CANNOT—I AM GOING ON TO THE END.	248	SHADOW WATER B		544
FROM GOING DOWN OF THE SUN I HAVE DREAMED	358	PRESENCES	V	3
A PRAYER ON GOING INTO MY HOUSE	371	ON GOING HOUSE		T
GOING THE FOREST THROUGH, WITH FLUTINGS WEAK;	672	ISLE STAT II 3		155
I WAS GOING THE ROAD ONE DAY	779	GOING THE ROAD		1

GOING-DOWN

| FROM GOING-DOWN OF THE SUN I HAVE DREAMED | 358 | PRESENCES | | 3 |

GOLD

FOR GOLD HIS HOOVES AND SILK HIS REIN,	2	OISIN 1	V	72
WITH AN APPLE OF GOLD IN HER TOSSING HAND;	12	OISIN 1		143
AN APPLE OF GOLD IN HER TOSSING HAND;	12	OISIN 1	V	143
WILD FLAMES OF RED AND GOLD AND BLUE,	18	OISIN 1		252
WHO WEDDED MEN WITH RINGS OF DRUID GOLD;	29	OISIN 2		10
HEARING AEDH TOUCH THE MOURNFUL STRINGS OF GOLD."	35	OISIN 2		87
. . . WITH BRONZE AND SILVER AND GOLD.	49	OISIN 3		32
MORE COMELY THAN MAN MAY MAKE THEM; INLAID WITH SILVER AND GOLD,	49	OISIN 3	V	29
I CRIED, "COME OUT OF THE SHADOW, KING OF THE NAILS OF GOLD!	51	OISIN 3		61
I CRIED, "COME OUT OF THE SHADOW, CANN OF THE NAILS OF GOLD!	51	OISIN 3	V	61
. . . WHEN THE SUN WAS ON SILVER OR GOLD;	53	OISIN 3		97
. . . THE GOLD HOOVES CRUSHING THE SANDS AND THE SHELLS	58	OISIN 3	V	157
MINE WAS A CHAIR OF SKINS AND GOLD,	81	MAD KING GOLL	V	1
OF PURPLE AND OF HEAVY GOLD;	81	MAD KING GOLL	V	3
"HE BRINGS THE PEACEFUL AGE OF GOLD"—	82	MAD KING GOLL	V	11
"THIS YOUNG MAN BRINGS THE AGE OF GOLD."	82	MAD KING GOLL	V	11
THESE HANDS WON MANY A TORQUE OF GOLD.	83	MAD KING GOLL		23
A KING SITTING UPON A CHAIR OF GOLD—	104	FERGUS DRUID		36
HAS WON THE GOLD HIS CARS OF BATTLE BRING."	106	CUCHULAIN SEA		11
NOR WON THE GOLD THAT NOW CUCHULAIN BRINGS."	106	CUCHULAIN SEA		11
BEAR THE GOLD EMBROIDERED DRESS—	124	CATHLEEN PARA	V	6
AND SANG WHAT GOLD MORNING OR EVENING SHEDS	126	DREAM OF FAERY		7
OR STORMY SILVER FRET THE GOLD OF DAY,	128	DREAM OF FAERY		33
. . . REMADE, LIKE A CASKET OF GOLD	143	ROSE IN HEART		7
. . . RE-MADE LIKE A CASKET OF GOLD	143	ROSE IN HEART	V	7
THE DANAAN CHILDREN LAUGH, IN CRADLES OF WROUGHT GOLD,	146	UNAPPEAS HOST		1
THE FAERY CHILDREN LAUGH IN CRADLES OF WROUGHT GOLD,	146	UNAPPEAS HOST	V	1
THE ANCIENT BEARDS, THE HELMS OF RUBY AND GOLD	169	SECRET ROSE		8
LINKED BY A GOLD CHAIN EACH TO EACH,	194	BAILE AILLINN		136
IN A GOLD AND SILVER WOOD;	214	HAPPY TOWNLAND	V	10
CARE MORE ABOUT THE KEGS OF SILVER AND GOLD	232	SHADOW WATER B		234
MADE OF DIM GOLD RAVE OUT IN SECRET TOMBS;	235	SHADOW WATER B		295
AND NOT A ROOF OF IVORY AND GOLD.	246	SHADOW WATER B		500
"PUT OFF THAT MASK OF BURNING GOLD	263	MASK		1
THE GOLD AND SILVER THREAD,	308	PLAYER QUEEN		8
THE GOLD INTO MY HAIR,	309	PLAYER QUEEN		18
THE GOLD UPON MY HAIR,	309	PLAYER QUEEN	V	18
AS IN THE GOLD MOSAIC OF A WALL,	408	SAIL BYZANTIUM		18
OF HAMMERED GOLD AND GOLD ENAMELLING	408	SAIL BYZANTIUM		28
OF HAMMERED GOLD AND GOLD ENAMELLING	408	SAIL BYZANTIUM		28
WRITTEN IN GOLD UPON A PURPLE STAIN,	461	HARUN RASHID		10
IS BUT A HEAVY, GOLD EMBROIDERED BANNER,	469	HARUN RASHID	V	188
NOT BLIND WITH GOLD, NOR DAZZLED BY THE GOLD	470	HARUN RASHID	V	191
NOT BLIND WITH GOLD, NOR DAZZLED BY THE GOLD	470	HARUN RASHID	V	191
IN TOMBS OF GOLD AND LAPIS LAZULI	483	OIL AND BLOOD		1
IN TOMBS OF GOLD AND LAPIS-LAZULI	483	OIL AND BLOOD	V	1
GET ALL THE GOLD AND SILVER THAT YOU CAN,	500	VACILLATION		19
THREE KEGS OF GOLD.	596	COLONEL MARTIN		49
CARRY THE GOLD ABOUT THE TOWN,	596	COLONEL MARTIN		52
"AND DID YOU KEEP NO GOLD, TOM?	596	COLONEL MARTIN		64
WHO SITS IN LONELY SPLENDOUR, MAIL'D IN GOLD,	651	ISLE STAT I 1		163
THE EVENING GLEAMS ARE GREEN AND GOLD AND RED	656	ISLE STAT I 3		22

GOLD   (CONTINUED)   PAGE   TITLE   LINE

THE MOBS OF STARS IN GOLD AND GREEN AND BLUE,   663 ISLE STAT II 2   43
HE TURNS WHERE, HUNG LIKE DROPS OF DRIPPING GOLD,   710 FERENCZ RENYI   18
HE TURNS WHERE, HUNG LIKE DROPS OF LIQUID GOLD,   710 FERENCZ RENYI   V   18
AMONG THE GOLD, THE AMBER, AND THE RED,"   712 FERENCZ RENYI   76
HIGHER AND HIGHER GOLD WITH EVENING LIGHT: 714 FERENCZ RENYI   113
GOLD UNTO GOLD, A GLEAM IN ITS LONG HAIR,   720 WITCH VIVIEN   3
GOLD UNTO GOLD, A GLEAM IN ITS LONG HAIR,   720 WITCH VIVIEN   3
WE WILL BRING A CROWN OF GOLD,   726 LOVERS QUARREL   13
WITH SHIELD AND ARMOUR WROUGHT WITH GOLD,   741 EARL PAUL   37
HAD I NOT GOLD AND SILVER, AND ENOUGH   748 SHADOW WATER A   32
ARMLETS OF GOLD OR SHIELDS WITH GOLDEN NAILS   749 SHADOW WATER A   43
BELIEVE THAT GOLD AND WOMEN TAKEN IN WAR   754 SHADOW WATER A   159
MADE OF DIM GOLD, RAVE OUT IN SECRET TOMBS,   765 SHADOW WATER A   345
GOLD-EMBROIDERED
BEAR THE GOLD-EMBROIDERED DRESS--   124 CATHLEEN PARA   V   6
WHERE GOLD-EMBROIDERED BANNERS OF THE CALIF'S   461 HARUN RASHID   V   6
GOLDEN
A GOLDEN CRESCENT LIT THE PLAIN,   2 OISIN 1   V   788
TO THE MUSIC OF THE GOLDEN RHYME   14 OISIN 1   V   176
UNDER THE GOLDEN EVENING LIGHT,   25 OISIN 1   385
GOLDEN THE NAILS OF HIS BIRD-CLAWS,   50 OISIN 3   45
ON THE FAR GOLDEN PEAK: ENORMOUS SHAPES,   74 ANASHU VIJAYA   68
WHEN SUMMER GLUTS THE GOLDEN BEES,   84 MAD KING GOLL   38
WHERE SUMMER GLUTS THE GOLDEN BEES,   84 MAD KING GOLL   V   38
UNDER THE GOLDEN OR THE SILVER SKIES: 127 DREAM OF FAERY   21
THE GOLDEN APPLES OF THE SUN.   150 WANDER AENGUS   24
FASTEN YOUR HAIR WITH A GOLDEN PIN,   157 BELOVED RHYMES   1
IS IT THESE THAT WITH GOLDEN THURIBLES   167 BLESSED   23
IS IT THOSE THAT WITH GOLDEN THURIBLES   167 BLESSED   V   23
OR AS THE CHANGING SPEARS FLUNG BY THE GOLDEN STARS   175 ELEMENT POWERS   V   15
ENWROUGHT WITH GOLDEN AND SILVER LIGHT,   176 CLOTHS HEAVEN   2
COUPLED WITH GOLDEN CHAINS, AND SING AS THEY FLY.   204 WITHER BOUGHS   18
TO FIND IT WHEN NIGHT FALLS LAID ON A GOLDEN BIER.   209 UNDER THE MOON   10
WHEN THE SUN LOOKED OUT OF HIS GOLDEN HOOD,   210 RAGGED WOOD   V   3
WHEN THE SUN LOOKED OUT OF HIS GOLDEN HOOD?--   211 RAGGED WOOD   7
IN A GOLDEN AND SILVER WOOD: 214 HAPPY TOWNLAND   10
FROM GOLDEN AND SILVER BOUGHS: 215 HAPPY TOWNLAND   24
FROM THE GOLDEN AND SILVER BOUGHS.   215 HAPPY TOWNLAND   V   24
OF THE GREAT GOLDEN NET THAT IS ABOUT US.   238 SHADOW WATER B   352
YOU CANNOT LEAP OUT OF THE GOLDEN NET.   238 SHADOW WATER B   360
I'LL GIVE A GOLDEN GALLEY FULL OF FRUIT.   240 SHADOW WATER B   373
AND BEAT THE GOLDEN HELMET WITH THEIR SWORDS?   243 SHADOW WATER B   425
HAVE BURIED NOTHING BUT MY GOLDEN ARMS.   243 SHADOW WATER B   431
AND STRIKE THE GOLDEN PILLARS WITH MY HANDS.   246 SHADOW WATER B   502
AND MADE A GOLDEN CRADLE   308 PLAYER QUEEN   3
AND MADE A GOLDEN GOWN,   308 PLAYER QUEEN   10
THE GOLDEN TOP OF CARE?   309 PLAYER QUEEN   20
OF GOLDEN KING AND SILVER LADY,   331 ROUND TOWER   13
THAT GOLDEN KING AND THAT WILD LADY   332 ROUND TOWER   19
THAT LADY AND THAT GOLDEN KING   332 ROUND TOWER   23
OR SET UPON A GOLDEN BOUGH TO SING   408 SAIL BYZANTIUM   30
AND ALL THE GOLDEN GRASSHOPPERS AND BEES.   428 NINETEEN 19   8
AND ALL HIS GOLDEN GRASSHOPPERS AND BEES.   428 NINETEEN 19   V   8
WORLD-FAMOUS GOLDEN THIGHED PYTHAGORAS   445 SCHOOL CHILDR   V   45
WHERE GOLDEN CROCUS AND NARCISSUS BLOOM,   447 COLONUS PRAISE   18
MIRACLE, BIRD OR GOLDEN HANDIWORK,   497 BYZANTIUM   17
PLANTED ON THE STAR-LIT GOLDEN BOUGH,   497 BYZANTIUM   19
MIRACLE, BIRD OR GOLDEN HANDY-WORK,   497 BYZANTIUM   V   17
PLANTED ON THE STARLIT GOLDEN BOUGH,   497 BYZANTIUM   V   19
THE GOLDEN SMITHIES OF THE EMPEROR!   498 BYZANTIUM   35
SLEEP UPON A GOLDEN BED   522 LULLABY   5
I CARRY THE SUN IN A GOLDEN CUP,   525 DANCING DAYS   7
I CARRY THE SUN IN A GOLDEN CUP,   525 DANCING DAYS   15
I CARRY THE SUN IN A GOLDEN CUP,   525 DANCING DAYS   23
BUT THE GOLDEN RACE LOOKS DIM,   530 DELPHIC ORACLE   4
SAID THE MAN IN THE GOLDEN BREASTPLATE   598 STONE CROSS   7
SAID THE MAN IN THE GOLDEN BREASTPLATE   599 STONE CROSS   15
SAID THE MAN IN THE GOLDEN BREASTPLATE   599 STONE CROSS   23
SAID THE OLD MAN IN THE GOLDEN BREASTPLATE   599 STONE CROSS   V   23
THE GOLDEN PLOUGH AND HARROW AND SPOKE ALOUD   609 IN TARAS HALLS   12
THERE ALL THE GOLDEN CODGERS LAY,   611 NEWS ORACLE   1
HERE WHERE LABURNUM HANGS HER GOLDEN FLEECE: 670 ISLE STAT II 3   102
AS SLOWLY AUTUMN CLIMBED THE GOLDEN THRONE.   690 MOSADA 1   V   1A
SAVE, WITH THE LITTLE GOLDEN GREEDY CARP,   720 WITCH VIVIEN   2
NAY, RISE AND FLATTER HER WITH GOLDEN RHYME,   724 KANVA ON SELF   19
THE SUNFLOWERS WEAVE A GOLDEN CLIME,   736 SUMMER EVENING   9
ARMLETS OF GOLD OR SHIELDS WITH GOLDEN NAILS   749 SHADOW WATER A   43
TILL HIS EDAINE, NO LONGER A GOLDEN FLY.   757 SHADOW WATER A   210
I FOUGHT TWELVE BATTLES DRESSED IN GOLDEN ARMOUR.   761 SHADOW WATER A   271
OF GOLDEN ARMED AOLAN AND THE QUEEN   766 SHADOW WATER A   V   375
OF THE GOLDEN APPLE TREE: 771 SPINNING SONG   9
GOLDEN-ARMED
IT WAS GOLDEN-ARMED IOLLAN, AND HE DIED   242 SHADOW WATER B   406
FOR GOLDEN-ARMED IOLLAN HAS BEEN KILLED.   242 SHADOW WATER B   410
FOR GOLDEN-ARMED IOLLAN THAT I LOVED.   242 SHADOW WATER B   421
O! O! O! O! FOR GOLDEN-ARMED IOLLAN,   243 SHADOW WATER B   428
I NEVER HAVE BEEN GOLDEN-ARMED IOLLAN.   244 SHADOW WATER B   464
OF GOLDEN-ARMED IOLAN AND THE QUEEN   766 SHADOW WATER A   375
GOLDEN-CRESTED
WHO GIVETH TO THE GOLDEN-CRESTED WREN   698 MOSADA 2   51

	PAGE	TITLE	LINE

GOLDEN-THIGHED
WORLD-FAMOUS GOLDEN-THIGHED PYTHAGORAS • • • • • • • • 445 SCHOOL CHILDR 45

GOLDFISH
ONE HAND AMID THE GOLDFISH IN THE POOL! • • • • • • • • 463 HARUN RASHID 44

GOLD-FISH
IT SEEMED A GOLD-FISH SWIMMING IN A BOWL• • • • • • 472 ALL SOUL NIGHT 40

GOLDS
HER GOLDS, HER AMBERS, AND HER BLUES, • • • • • • • 13 OISIN 1 163
HER GOLDS, HER AZURES, AND HER BLUES, • • • • • • • 13 OISIN 1 V 163

GOLD-SEWN
GOLD-SEWN SILK ON THE SWORD-BLADE, • • • • • • • • • 484 SYMBOLS 5

GOLD-SHOD
SCARCE WORTHY OF A HOOF GOLD-SHOD. • • • • • • • • • 2 OISIN 1 V 7Y

GOLDSMITH
THAT GOLDSMITH AND THE DEAN, • • • • • • • • • • 481 BLOOD AND MOON 18
GOLDSMITH DELIBERATELY SIPPING AT THE HONEY-POT OF HIS 481 BLOOD AND MOON 21
MIND,
GOLDSMITH DELIBERATELY SIPPING AT THE HONEY POT OF HIS 481 BLOOD AND MOON V 21
MIND!
A POT-HOUSE BENCH WITH OLIVER GOLDSMITH ONCE• • • • • 486 SEVEN SAGES 3
GOLDSMITH AND BURKE, SWIFT AND THE BISHOP OF CLOYNE • • • 486 SEVEN SAGES 9
OLIVER GOLDSMITH SANG WHAT HE HAD SEEN, • • • • • • • 487 SEVEN SAGES 17

GOLDSMITHS
BUT SUCH A FORM AS GRECIAN GOLDSMITHS MAKE • • • • • • 408 SAIL BYZANTIUM 27

GOLD-SOWN
GOLD-SOWN SILK ON THE SWORD BLADE! • • • • • • • 484 SYMBOLS V 5

GOLL
THE MADNESS OF KING GOLL • • • • • • • • • 81 MAD KING GOLL T

GOMEZ
FEET OF DARK GOMEZ, WHERE NOW WANDER YE? • • • • • 690 MOSADA 1 11
WHEN MY LOST LOVER LEFT THESE ARMS. MY GOMEZ • • • • 701 MOSADA 3 51
LOOK UP, LOOK UP, THY GOMEZ IS BY THEE• • • • • • 701 MOSADA 3 68
GRIEVE NOT, FOR GOMEZ KNEELS BESIDE THEE—GOMEZ, • • • 702 MOSADA 3 90
GRIEVE NOT, FOR GOMEZ KNEELS BESIDE THEE—GOMEZ, • • • 702 MOSADA 3 90
SAFE ON THE BREAST OF GOMEZ LIES THY HEAD, • • • • 703 MOSADA 3 101
GIVE TO THY GOMEZ. GOMEZ—HE HAS GONE • • • • 703 MOSADA 3 110
GIVE TO THY GOMEZ. GOMEZ—HE HAS GONE • • • • 703 MOSADA 3 110
SAFE ON THE BREAST OF GOMEZ IS THY HEAD, • • • • 703 MOSADA 3 V 101

GONE
IS THY COMPANION GONE FROM THEE!" • • • • • • 6 OISIN 1 V 52
OR THE SOFTNESS OF YOUTH BE GONE FROM OUR FACES, • • • 27 OISIN 1 410
WILL THE SOFTNESS OF YOUTH BE GONE FROM OUR FACES, • • • 27 OISIN 1 V 410
OR THE SOFTNESS OF YOUTH BE GONE FROM OUR FACES, • • • 27 OISIN 1 V 419C
OR THE SOFTNESS OF YOUTH BE GONE FROM OUR FACES, • • • 28 OISIN 1 V 426
THE ISLE WAS OVER NOW AND GONE! • • • • • • 28 OISIN 1 V 427B
HE HAD GONE WHISPERING FORTH WITH CUMBERED HEART, • • • 37 OISIN 2 111
BUT SHE WHOSE HOURS OF TENDERNESS WERE GONE • • • • 38 OISIN 2 138
REMEMBERING HOW I PACED IN DAYS GONE O'ER, • • • • 44 OISIN 2 V 227
THE MOIL OF MY CENTURIES FILLED ME! AND GONE LIKE 51 OISIN 3 70
A SEA-COVERED STONE
AND THE HORSE WAS GONE IN THE DISTANCE, • • • • • 52 OISIN 3 75
OF TWILIGHT AND SLUMBER WERE GONE, AND THAT HOOFS 54 OISIN 3 112
IMPATIENTLY STEPT.
AND THE DREAMS OF THE ISLANDS WERE GONE, • • • • • 59 OISIN 3 175
I MUST BE GONE! THERE IS A GRAVE • • • • • • 67 HAPPY SHEPHERD 45
FAREWELL! I MUST BE GONE I-WIS, • • • • • • 67 HAPPY SHEPHERD V 46D
THE SAD, SAD THOUGHT HAS GONE FROM ME NOW WHOLLY! • • • 72 ANASHU VIJAYA 19
AND NOW THE OLD MAN'S DREAMS ARE GONE, • • • • • 98 FOXHUNTER 19
THEY HAVE GONE DOWN UNDER THE SAME WHITE STARS, • • • 115 ROSE OF BATTLE 34
CABINS GONE NOW, OLD WELL-SIDES, OLD DEAR PLACES, • • • 130 BOOK STORIES V 23
AS IN THE OLD DAYS LONG GONE BY, • • • • • 131 OLD PENSIONER V 15
THE WELL-KNOWN FACES ARE ALL GONE, • • • • • 132 OLD PENSIONER V 17
"WHEN YOU WERE GONE, HE TURNED AND DIED • • • • 133 FR GILLIGAN 37
WERE GONE LIKE A DRIFTING SMOKE! • • • • • 145 HOST OF AIR 40
BUT THE OLD MEN AND DANCERS WERE GONE, • • • • 145 HOST OF AIR V 39
I WILL FIND OUT WHERE SHE HAS GONE, • • • • • 150 WANDER AENGUS 19
I WILL FIND OUT WHERE SHE IS GONE • • • • • 150 WANDER AENGUS V 19
SHE HAS GONE WEEPING AWAY, • • • • • • 152 LOSS OF LOVE 7
TO THE CAVE, WHERE DATHI THE BLESSED HAD GONE, • • • 166 BLESSED V 3
AND WHEN IT IS GONE WE ARE DEAD! • • • • • 168 BLESSED 30
AND WHEN IT IS GONE WE DIE! • • • • • • 168 BLESSED V 30
WHERE HAS MAID QUIET GONE TO, • • • • • 171 MAID QUIET 1
THAT'S ALL BUT GONE! FOR THE PROUD HEART IS GONE, • • • 181 QUEEN MAEVE 20
THAT'S ALL BUT GONE! FOR THE PROUD HEART IS GONE, • • • 181 QUEEN MAEVE 20
KINGS OF THE GREAT PLAIN HAVE COME AND GONE • • • 183 QUEEN MAEVE V 81
WITH WISDOM, THEY WANDER TILL ALL THE YEARS HAVE GONE BY! 204 WITHER BOUGHS 21
YOU DO NOT SEE MY PURPOSE. I SHALL HAVE GONE • • • 238 SHADOW WATER B 357
YOU DID NOT SEE MY PURPOSE. I SHALL HAVE GONE • • • 238 SHADOW WATER B V 357
FOR EVERYTHING IS GONE. COME HITHER, AIBRIC, • • • 241 SHADOW WATER B 402
BUT, DEAR, CLING CLOSE TO ME! SINCE YOU WERE GONE, • • • 257 RECONCILIATION 11
BUT THERE IT'S GONE! I WILL NOT TAKE • • • • 274 GREY ROCK 92
BUT WHEN NINE DAYS HAD GONE I STOOD AGAIN • • • 282 TWO KINGS 131
ROMANTIC IRELAND'S DEAD AND GONE, • • • • 289 SEPTEMBER 1913 7
THEY HAVE GONE ABOUT THE WORLD LIKE WIND, • • • 289 SEPTEMBER 1913 11
ROMANTIC IRELAND'S DEAD AND GONE, • • • • 289 SEPTEMBER 1913 15
ROMANTIC IRELAND'S DEAD AND GONE, • • • • 290 SEPTEMBER 1913 23
BUT LET THEM BE, THEY'RE DEAD AND GONE, • • • 290 SEPTEMBER 1913 31
LET THESE CONTENT YOU AND BE GONE AGAIN! • • • 292 TO A SHADE 8
AND TILL ANOTHER NIGHT HAD GONE, • • • • 297 THREE BEGGARS 51
"I'LL SLEEP UNTIL THE WINTER'S GONE • • • • 305 HOUR DAWN 57
"I'D LIKE TO SLEEP TILL WINTER'S GONE • • • • 305 HOUR DAWN 60

		PAGE	TITLE	LINE

GONE (CONTINUED)

	PAGE	TITLE	LINE
THAT HAD GONE	309	REALISTS	7
BABBLING OF FALLEN MAJESTY, RECORDS WHAT'S GONE.	314	FALLEN MAJESTY	4
THESE, THESE REMAIN, BUT I RECORD WHAT'S GONE. A CROWD	315	FALLEN MAJESTY	6
ALL TILL MY YOUTH WAS GONE	315	FRIENDS	18
THE BARE CHIMNEY IS GONE BLACK OUT	327	ROBERT GREGORY	84
WHERE MANY A KING HAS GONE	330	BONE OF A HARE	2
WE HAVE GONE ROUND AND ROUND	332	SOLOMON SHEBA	6
APPEARS, BUT WHEN WE HAVE GONE IS GONE AGAIN,	334	LIVING BEAUTY	6
APPEARS, BUT WHEN WE HAVE GONE IS GONE AGAIN,	334	LIVING BEAUTY	6
APPEARS, AND WHEN WE HAVE GONE IS GONE AGAIN,	334	LIVING BEAUTY V	6
APPEARS, AND WHEN WE HAVE GONE IS GONE AGAIN,	334	LIVING BEAUTY V	6
YET PRAISE THE WINTERS GONE!	336	YOUNG BEAUTY	15
THE SHEEP HAD GONE FROM THEIRS. I KNOW RIGHT WELL	339	SHEP GOATHERD	15
TILL WINTER BLASTS WERE GONE, BUT SPEAK OF HER	340	SHEP GOATHERD	33
NO SETTLED MAN. AND NOW THAT HE IS GONE	341	SHEP GOATHERD	55
THEIR ANGRY TEARS, ARE GONE.	344	DEJECTION	6
THE SCULLION GONE WILD."	349	HAWK	6
I HAVE GONE ABOUT THE HOUSE, GONE UP AND DOWN	350	HER PRAISE	2
I HAVE GONE ABOUT THE HOUSE, GONE UP AND DOWN	350	HER PRAISE	2
AND ALL THE SHAPELY BODY NO TITTLE GONE ASTRAY.	354	HIS PHOENIX	30
FIVE-AND-TWENTY YEARS HAVE GONE	360	ALF POLLEXFEN	1
FIVE AND TWENTY YEARS HAVE GONE	360	ALF POLLEXFEN V	1
THE COMFORT THAT YOU MADE? ALTHOUGH MY WITS HAVE GONE	391	UNDER SATURN	5
YOUR COMING BROUGHT; THOUGH I ACKNOWLEDGE I HAVE GONE	391	UNDER SATURN V	5
THAT ARE IMPATIENT TO BE GONE;	413	TOWER	102
NOR HATE OF WHAT'S TO COME, NOR PITY FOR WHAT'S GONE,	427	PHANTOM HATRED	30
MANY INGENIOUS LOVELY THINGS ARE GONE	428	NINETEEN 19	1
AND GONE ARE PHIDIAS' FAMOUS IVORIES	428	NINETEEN 19	7
MANY INGENUOUS LOVELY THINGS ARE GONE	428	NINETEEN 19 V	1
AND GONE ARE PHIDIAS' CARVEN IVORIES	428	NINETEEN 19 V	7
BEFORE THAT BRIEF GLEAM OF ITS LIFE BE GONE,	430	NINETEEN 19	63
AND MY SLEEP IS GONE.	454	EMPTY CUP	10
OF ALL THAT ARE GONE;	458	SECRETS OF OLD	14
OF FRIENDS THAT ARE GONE,	458	SECRETS OF OLD V	14
ARE GONE AWAY, AND SOME THAT STAY	458	HIS WILDNESS	5
WHEN ALL THOSE ROOMS AND PASSAGES ARE GONE,	489	COOLE PARK 29	26
AND IN THE MORNING'S GONE, NO MAN KNOWS WHY;	490	COOLE BALLYLEE	20
MY FIFTIETH YEAR HAD COME AND GONE,	501	VACILLATION	35
SO GET YOU GONE, VON HUEGEL, THOUGH WITH BLESSINGS ON YOUR HEAD.	503	VACILLATION	89
WHERE HAD HER SWEETNESS GONE?	503	QUARREL IN AGE	1
IF TIME WERE BUT GONE."	510	JANE JUDGMENT	19
THE SOONER LOVE IS GONE,	511	JANE AND JACK	4
"MY FRIENDS ARE GONE, BUT THAT'S A TRUTH	513	JANE TALK BISH	9
THOSE DANCING DAYS ARE GONE	524	DANCING DAYS	T
THOSE DANCING DAYS ARE GONE;	524	DANCING DAYS	2
DEAR, I MUST BE GONE	535	PARTING	1
WHAT MATTER FOR THE SCENE, THE SCENE ONCE GONE!	542	PARN FUNERAL 1	19
THINGS UNBORN, THINGS THAT ARE GONE,	562	NEEDLES EYE	3
HIS GLORY AND HIS MONUMENTS ARE GONE.	563	MERU	14
A GREATER, A MORE GRACIOUS TIME HAS GONE;	564	GYRES	12
AND IF YOUR LOVE WERE GONE	569	THREE BUSHES	4
ALL NEIGHBOURLY CONTENT AND EASY TALK ARE GONE,	580	CURSE CROMWELL	9
JOHN BULL HAS GONE TO INDIA	583	GHOST ROG CASE	21
HE'D GONE TO GREAT EXPENSE	585	ORAHILLY	13
THE WISDOM OF THE PEOPLE'S GONE,	607	SONGS BURDEN 2	16
BUT HAD GONE OUT TO DIE	608	SONGS BURDEN 3	20
THAT KNOWING BETTER TALK HAD GONE	627	STATES HOLIDAY	7
BUT WHERE ARE THEY GONE?	628	JANE MOUNTAIN	3
WHO KEEPS THE TILL. NOW THAT MY LADDER'S GONE,	630	CIRCUS ANIMALS	38
BUT BODY GONE HE SLEEPS NO MORE.	633	MAN AND ECHO	29
EYES STARED OUT OF THE BRANCHES AND WERE GONE.	634	CUCHULAIN COMF	3
CAME AND WERE GONE. HE LEANT UPON A TREE	634	CUCHULAIN COMF	5
THEIR MONEY SPENT, THEIR WINE GONE SOUR,	635	BLACK TOWER	3
WHEN THAT GREATER DREAM HAD GONE	639	BEN BULBEN	63
FLY! FLY! SO THESE BRAVE SHEPHERDS BOTH ARE GONE!	649	ISLE STAT I 1	112
MY PRETTY CHILD, SINCE HE HAS GONE, OH SAY	658	ISLE STAT II 1	3
YOU MUST BE GONE! THE ROLLING GRAINS OF SAND	663	ISLE STAT II 2	34
I WOULD HAVE GONE ALSO! BUT FAR AWAY	663	ISLE STAT II 2	37
NASCHINA'S GONE, DRAWN BY A THIRST OF LOVE,	664	ISLE STAT II 2	59
WE ARE GONE!	669	ISLE STAT II 3	82
NAY, HE IS GONE. WAKE! WAKE! AS A BEE SIPS	678	ISLE STAT II 3	305
GIVE TO THY GOMEZ. GOMEZ--HE HAS GONE	703	MOSADA 3	110
GIVE TO THY VALLENCE. VALLENCE--HE HAS GONE	703	MOSADA 3 V	110
STILL WANDER THROUGH THE WORLD. HE'S GONE, HE'S GONE.	703	MOSADA 3	121
STILL WANDER THROUGH THE WORLD. HE'S GONE, HE'S GONE.	703	MOSADA 3	121
HAS FLICKERED AND GONE OUT. I AM NOT WELL.	704	MOSADA 3	129
GONE THE STARS AND GONE THE WHITE MOON,	718	PHANTOM SHIP	3
GONE THE STARS AND GONE THE WHITE MOON,	718	PHANTOM SHIP	3
. . . GONE AND PUFFED AWAY AND DEAD.	718	PHANTOM SHIP	3
THE MAN IS GONE WHO GUIDED YE, UNWEARY,	738	MOURN THEN ON	3
THE MAN IS GONE WHO FROM HIS LONELY STATION	738	MOURN THEN ON	7
AND NOW THEY ARE ALL GONE, I FOLLOW STILL.	749	SHADOW WATER A	37
THE YEARS THAT HAVE GONE OVER HER FROM THE HOUR	760	SHADOW WATER A	256
I WILL DRINK OUT OF THE STREAM. THE STREAM IS GONE!	761	SHADOW WATER A	273
THERE! THERE! THEY HAVE GONE QUICKLY, FOR ALREADY	764	SHADOW WATER A	326
THAT HAVE GONE THITHER TO LOOK FOR THE LOUD STREAMS,	765	SHADOW WATER A	348
HAVE FALLEN AND MY SUN AND MOON GONE OUT.	767	SHADOW WATER A V	405
THEY ARE GONE, THEY ARE GONE. THE PROUD MAY LIE BY THE PROUD.	777	SONG DEIRDRE 3	1

	PAGE	TITLE		LINE

GONE (CONTINUED)

THEY ARE GONE, THEY ARE GONE. THE PROUD MAY LIE BY THE PROUD.	777	SONG DEIRDRE 3		1
THEY ARE GONE, THEY ARE GONE. WHISPERING WERE ENOUGH.	778	SONG DEIRDRE 3		3
THEY ARE GONE, THEY ARE GONE. WHISPERING WERE ENOUGH.	778	SONG DEIRDRE 3		3
	778	SONG DEIRDRE 3		6
EAGLES HAVE GONE INTO THEIR CLOUDY BED.	783	GREY ROUND		24
BUT NOW THE NIGHT IS GONE.	788	HAWTHORN TREE		5
WHAT THOUGH THEY DANCED! THOSE DAYS ARE GONE.				

GONG

GOES TO THE BARBAROUS CLANGOUR OF A GONG.	430	NINETEEN 19		58
GOES TO THE BARBAROUS CLANGOUR OF GONG.	430	NINETEEN 19	V	58
AFTER GREAT CATHEDRAL GONG!	497	BYZANTIUM		4
WHEN GONG AND CONCH DECLARE THE HOUR TO BLESS	611	STATUES		23

GONG-TORMENTED

| THAT DOLPHIN-TORN, THAT GONG-TORMENTED SEA. | 498 | BYZANTIUM | | 40 |

GONNE

| THE BLINDS DRAWN UP"! MAUD GONNE AT HOWTH STATION WAITING A TRAIN, | 578 | LOFTY THINGS | | 10 |

GOOD

"GOOD REASON HAVE I FOR MY LOVE,"	7	OISIN 1	V	62
EQUAL TO GOOD OR GRIEVOUS CHANCE!	24	OISIN 1		372
EQUAL TO GOOD OR EVIL CHANCE	24	OISIN 1	V	371
A GOOD NAME IS GOODLY TO HEAR OF, AND A GOOD NAME SURELY IS THINE.	51	OISIN 3	V	63
A GOOD NAME IS GOODLY TO HEAR OF, AND A GOOD NAME SURELY IS THINE.	51	OISIN 3	V	63
WORDS ALONE ARE CERTAIN GOOD.	65	HAPPY SHEPHERD		10
FOR WORDS ALONE ARE CERTAIN GOOD!	66	HAPPY SHEPHERD		43
AND WORDS ALONE ARE CERTAIN GOOD,	66	HAPPY SHEPHERD	V	43
GOOD FATHER JOHN O'HART	91	FATHER OHART		1
I SAW A NEIGHBOUR GOOD.	95	MOLL MAGEE	V	36
TO SEE YOU SO GOOD!	118	CRADLE SONG		6
SPINNING AT ALL TIMES ERI'S GOOD TO-MORROW,	129	BOOK STORIES	V	10
UNDER THE FRUIT OF EVIL AND OF GOOD!	137	TO SOME I TALK		9
AND BLOWING US EVIL AND GOOD!	158	TO HIS HEART	V	4A
"WHERE ALL ARE COMELY AND GOOD"	167	BLESSED		22
FOR THE GOOD ARE ALWAYS THE MERRY,	178	FIDDLER DOONEY		13
MORE STILL THAN THEY HAD BEEN FOR A GOOD MONTH,	182	QUEEN MAEVE		54
OUR GIVER OF GOOD COUNSEL AND GOOD LUCK."	185	QUEEN MAEVE		102
OUR GIVER OF GOOD COUNSEL AND GOOD LUCK."	185	QUEEN MAEVE		102
BECAUSE THEY HAVE MADE SO GOOD A FRIEND.	195	BAILE AILLINN		159
AND BEING IN GOOD HEART, BECAUSE	197	BAILE AILLINN		191
A GOOD ROUND SUM UPON THIS CRUISE, AND TURN--	222	SHADOW WATER B		5
WHAT GOOD IS THERE IN THIS HARD WAY OF LIVING,	225	SHADOW WATER B		69
YOU'LL BE AS GOOD A LEADER. BE OF YOUR TROOP!	225	SHADOW WATER B	V	73
COULD NOT AMEND. I HAVE GOOD SPIRITS ENOUGH.	227	SHADOW WATER B		116
I HAVE GOOD REASON FOR THAT THOUGHT. AND NOW	238	SHADOW WATER B		354
WE'LL FIND SO GOOD A THING AS THAT WE HAVE LOST?	258	KING NO KING		13
WE, TOO, HAD GOOD ATTENDANCE ONCE,	266	GALWAY RACES		5
IS NOT THAT HOW GOOD STORIES RUN?--	271	GREY ROCK		13
BEFORE THAT ROOMFUL OR AS GOOD.	273	GREY ROCK		52
AND I AM IN NO GOOD REPUTE	276	GREY ROCK		127
KNOWING THAT SILENCE BRINGS NO GOOD TO KINGS,	279	TWO KINGS		57
WHAT THE EXULTANT HEART CALLS GOOD	288	TO WEALTHY MAN		33
IF A GOOD EASTER WIND WERE BLOWING,	306	HOUR DAWN		86
I COUNT MY GOOD AND BAD,	316	FRIENDS		22
THE COMMON GOOD OF LIFE,	317	NIGHT COME		5
OF SUN AND MOON THAT A GOOD HOUR	331	ROUND TOWER		11
WHAT TURNED SO GOOD A SHEPHERD FROM HIS CHARGE.	339	SHEP GOATHERD		16
HAPPIER DAYS THOUGHT GOOD!	365	HER RACE		4
WHAT'S GOOD OR BAD, OR WHAT IT IS TO TRIUMPH	376	PHASES OF MOON		108
KNOWING NOT EVIL AND GOOD!	382	VISION ROBART		12
IN IGNORANT GOOD WILL,	392	EASTER 1916	V	18
HAD IGNORANT GOOD WILL!	392	EASTER 1916	V	19
BARTER THAT HORN AND EVERY GOOD	405	FOR DAUGHTER		62
GOOD FELLOWS SHUFFLED CARDS IN AN OLD BAWN!	411	TOWER		65
COME LET US MOCK AT THE GOOD	432	NINETEEN 19		103
TO HELP GOOD, WISE OR GREAT	432	NINETEEN 19		110
AND AFTER THAT THERE'S NOTHING GOOD	434	WHEEL		5
NOW THE GOOD CALIPH'S LEARNED TREASURER,	461	HARUN RASHID		3
AND WHAT'S THE GOOD OF AN ESCAPE	479	SELF AND SOUL		55
OF ALL GOOD MEN AND WOMEN,	531	FATHER CHILD		3
"BODES ME LITTLE GOOD."	539	MEETING		6
MONEY IS GOOD AND A GIRL MIGHT BE BETTER,	544	TO SAME TUNE 1		3
BUT GOOD STRONG BLOWS ARE DELIGHTS TO THE MIND."	544	TO SAME TUNE 1		4
BUT A GOOD STRONG CAUSE AND BLOWS ARE DELIGHT."	545	TO SAME TUNE 1		14
"MONEY IS GOOD AND A GIRL MIGHT BE BETTER,	545	TO SAME TUNE 1		21
BUT A GOOD STRONG CAUSE"--THE ROPE GAVE A JERK THERE,	545	TO SAME TUNE 1		23
BUT A GOOD STRONG CAUSE AND THE BLOWS ARE DELIGHT."	545	TO SAME TUNE 1	V	14
TIME FOR US ALL TO PICK OUT A GOOD TUNE,	548	TO SAME TUNE 3		13
WHAT IS THE GOOD OF A MAN AND HE	551	SONGS REWRIT 1		7
WHAT IS THE GOOD OF A MAN IF HE	551	SONGS REWRIT 1	V	7
AND O HE WAS A GOOD MAN	571	THREE BUSHES		68
BUT THERE'S NO GOOD COMPLAINING, FOR MONEY'S RANT IS ON.	580	CURSE CROMWELL		10
AND BLACKENED HIS GOOD NAME.	582	ROGER CASEMENT		8
ESTABLISHED IT FOR GOOD!	584	ORAHILLY		6
WHATEVER GOOD A FARMER'S GOT	586	PARNELLITES		13
AND WHAT'S THE GOOD OF WOMEN, FOR ALL THAT THEY CAN SAY	592	PILGRIM		4
PROCLAIMED BOTH GOOD AND GREAT!	597	MODEL LAUREATE		4
A GOOD MAN ON A HORSE,	604	YOU CONTENT		12
IN SOME GOOD COMPANY,	605	YOU CONTENT		18

	PAGE	TITLE		LINE

GOOD   (CONTINUED)
A ROOF, GOOD CLOTHES, PASSION, LOVE PERHAPS, ...   609 IN TARAS HALLS   8
MONEY IS GOOD AND A GIRL MIGHT BE BETTER, ...   616 MARCH SONGS 3   3
BUT GOOD STRONG BLOWS ARE DELIGHTS TO THE MIND." . . .   616 MARCH SONGS 3   4
BUT A GOOD STRONG CAUSE AND BLOWS ARE DELIGHT." . . . .   616 MARCH SONGS 3   14
"MONEY IS GOOD AND A GIRL MIGHT BE BETTER, ...   616 MARCH SONGS 3   21
BUT A GOOD STRONG CAUSE"--THE ROPE GAVE A JERK THERE, . .   616 MARCH SONGS 3   23
I HAVE FOUND NOTHING HALF SO GOOD . . . .   624 APPARITIONS   9
SHOULD STARVE GOOD MEN AND BAD ADVANCE, ...   626 OLD MEN BE MAD   10
THE BLESSED GOD WAS GOOD TO SEND US SUCH, ...   683 SEEKER   40
SHOULD I BE GOOD? BUT YOU ARE BEAUTIFUL. . . . . .   692 MOSADA 1   62
NOT GOOD; BUT YOU ARE LIKE THE BUTTERFLIES. . . . . .   693 MOSADA 1   65
THE WAGES OF SIN IS DEATH. NO USE. NO GOOD. . . . . .   697 MOSADA 2   42
THOUGH YOUNGEST OF ALL IN OUR GOOD BAND, ...   707 FAIRY PEDANT   11
THOUGH YOUNGEST OF ALL IN OUR GOOD BAND, ...   708 FAIRY PEDANT   39
THY NAME IS?" "RENYI." "OF?" "THIS VILLAGE." "GOOD!   709 FERENCZ RENYI   13
THY NAME IS?" "FERENCZ RENYI." "OF?" "THIS VILLAGE."   709 FERENCZ RENYI   V   13
     "GOOD!
SEARCHED THE UNSEARCHABLE--WHY GOOD MEN WEEP; . . . .   710 FERENCZ RENYI   32
WHY THOSE WHO DO GOOD OFTEN BE NOT GOOD, ...   710 FERENCZ RENYI   33
WHY THOSE WHO DO GOOD OFTEN BE NOT GOOD, ...   710 FERENCZ RENYI   33
THIS SULLEN PEASANT SPOILS THE GOOD SUNSHINE, ...   711 FERENCZ RENYI   42
THIS SULLEN PEASANT SPOILS THE GOOD RED WINE. . . . . .   711 FERENCZ RENYI   43
THIS SULLEN PEASANT CHILLS THE GOOD SUNSHINE. . . . . .   711 FERENCZ RENYI   V   42
THIS SULLEN PEASANT SOURS THE GOOD RED WINE. . . . . .   711 FERENCZ RENYI   V   43
I HOLD HIM DEARER THAN THE GOOD. . . . .   723 GIRLS SONG A   7
ARE PRAYERS OF PATIENT MEN AND GOOD." . . . . . .   725 LEGEND   6
AND WILL FIND HER GOOD AT HEART, ...   726 LOVERS QUARREL   10
HOW "THE ONLY GOOD IS MUSING MILD, ...   728 PRIEST FAIRY   13
FOR ALL GOOD MEN NOW FALLEN ILL, ...   736 IN CHURCH   5
I HAVE GOOD PILOTS, AIBRIC. WHEN MEN DIE . . . . . .   750 SHADOW WATER A   81
BUT HER GOOD MAN ANSWERED HER . . . .   772 SONG DEIRDRE 1 V   9
WE CALLED IT A GOOD DEATH. TODAY . . . .   791 REPRISALS   3
GOOD-BYE
EGYPT AND GREECE, GOOD-BYE, AND GOOD-BYE, ROME! . . . .   563 MERU   8
EGYPT AND GREECE, GOOD-BYE, AND GOOD-BYE, ROME! . . . .   563 MERU   8
"GOOD-BYE, GOOD-BYE, MY HUSBAND," . . . .   779 GOING THE ROAD   9
"GOOD-BYE, GOOD-BYE, MY HUSBAND," . . . .   779 GOING THE ROAD   9
GOODLY
AND TELL OF YOUR GOODLY HOUSEHOLD AND THE GOODLY WORKS   51 OISIN 3   62
     OF YOUR HANDS,
AND TELL OF YOUR GOODLY HOUSEHOLD AND THE GOODLY WORKS   51 OISIN 3   62
     OF YOUR HANDS,
A GOOD NAME IS GOODLY TO HEAR OF, AND A GOOD NAME SURELY   51 OISIN 3   V   63
     IS THINE.
WAS CARRIED TO THE GOODLY HOUSE . . . .   192 BAILE AILLINN   72
GOODMAN
BUT HER GOODMAN ANSWERED HER; . . . .   772 SONG DEIRDRE 1   9
GOODNESS
THAT FANCIED GOODNESS MIGHT BE GAY, ...   432 NINETEEN 19   104
GOODNIGHT
THE SECOND BEST'S A GAY GOODNIGHT AND QUICKLY TURN AWAY.   459 FROM OEDIPUS   12
GOODS
AND HIM WHO SOLD TILLAGE, AND HOUSE, AND GOODS, ...   170 SECRET ROSE   22
GOOD-WILL
IN IGNORANT GOOD-WILL, ...   392 EASTER 1916   18
GOOSE
WHEN NIGHT WAS AT ITS DEEPEST, A WILD GOOSE . . . . .   181 QUEEN MAEVE   36
WRINKLED LIKE THE FOOT OF A GOOSE, ...   508 JANE BISHOP   16
"THEY KILLED MY GOOSE AND A CAT." . . . .   546 TO SAME TUNE 2   8
"THEY KILLED MY GOOSE AND A CAT. . . . .   546 TO SAME TUNE 2   18
"THEY KILLED MY GOOSE AND A CAT. . . . .   547 TO SAME TUNE 2   28
ALL METAPHOR, MALACHI, STILTS AND ALL. A BARNACLE GOOSE   623 HIGH TALK   11
GORE-BOOTH
IN MEMORY OF EVA GORE-BOOTH AND CON MARKIEWICZ . . . .   475 EVA GORE-BOOTH   T
GORIAS
THE TOWERY GATES OF GORIAS, ...   196 BAILE AILLINN   161
GORSE
BY THE GORSE ON THE HIGH LAND, ...   726 LOVERS QUARREL   4
GORT
MUTTERED THE OLD CRANE OF GORT. . . . .   295 THREE BEGGARS   6
AND SMITHY WORK FROM THE GORT FORGE, ...   406 CARVED STONE   3
GOSPELLER
BY SOME PEASANT GOSPELLER; . . . .   440 WISDOM   5
WHEN SOME PEASANT GOSPELLER . . . .   440 WISDOM   V   5
GOSPELLERS'
THROUGH THE PEASANT GOSPELLERS' . . . .   440 WISDOM   V   5
GOT
O'DRISCOLL GOT UP FROM THE GRASS, ...   145 HOST OF AIR   V   37
AND WHEN I HAD GOT MY WILL AND DRAWN YOU HERE, ...   284 TWO KINGS   158
"OH GOD IF HE GOT LOOSE!" AND THEN . . . . . .   307 HOUR DAWN   V   118
"WHEN SHE WAS GOT," MY MOTHER SANG, ...   308 PLAYER QUEEN   13
THAT THOSE THAT WE HAVE LOVED GOT THEIR LONG FINGERS . .   375 PHASES OF MOON   66
ALL THAT SHE GOT SHE SPENT, ...   392 EASTER 1916   V   20
WHERE GOT I THAT TRUTH? . . . .   439 FRAGMENTS   5
KING ABUNDANCE GOT HIM ON . . . .   440 WISDOM   16
AND THEN THE SPEAKERS GOT IT . . . .   582 ROGER CASEMENT   15
WHATEVER GOOD A FARMER'S GOT . . . .   586 PARNELLITES   13
THE PRIESTS HAVE GOT A BOOK THAT SAYS . . . . .   621 JOHN KINSELLA   25
HE HAD DREAMED THE COW HAD GOT WITHIN . . . . . .   729 PRIEST FAIRY   33

335

	PAGE	TITLE		LINE
GOVERN				
THE GIFTS THAT GOVERN MEN, AND AFTER THESE	264	HOUSE SHAKEN		10
WHERE ARE THE CAPTAINS THAT GOVERN MANKIND?	548	TO SAME TUNE 3		22
WHERE ARE THE CAPTAINS THAT GOVERN MANKIND?	615	MARCH SONGS 2		22
GOVERNED				
GIRLS THAT HAVE GOVERNED CITIES,	789	SINGING HEAD		15
GOVERNMENT				
ON A RECENT GOVERNMENT APPOINTMENT IN IRELAND	317	APPOINTMENT	V	T
BEING OUT OF HEART WITH GOVERNMENT	317	APPOINTMENT		1
BEING OUT OF HEART AT GOVERNMENT	317	APPOINTMENT	V	1
NO GOVERNMENT APPOINTED HIM.	318	APPOINTMENT		12
PLANNED IN A GOVERNMENT OFFICE, SHORTEN HIS LIFE,	372	ON GOING HOUSE		15
OR LACKING THAT, GOVERNMENT IN SUCH HANDS,	543	PARN FUNERAL 2		7
GOWN SEE NIGHT-GOWN				
AND HE WORE LARGE HOLES IN HIS GOWN.	92	FATHER OHART		12
SHE ROSE IN HER PALE NIGHT GOWN,	159	CAP AND BELLS	V	10
ONE GATHERS UP HIS PURPLE GOWN;	212	BLESS PSALTER		9
AND MADE A GOLDEN GOWN,	308	PLAYER QUEEN		10
OR A YOUNG GIRL DRESSED OUT IN HER NEW GOWN,	350	HER PRAISE		4
GRACE				
HOW MANY LOVED YOUR MOMENTS OF GLAD GRACE,	121	YOU ARE OLD		5
FULL OF EARTH'S OLD TIMID GRACE.	124	CATHLEEN PARA		12
WITH THE OLD KINDNESS, THE OLD DISTINGUISHED GRACE,	362	HER COURTESY		1
GIVE HER A LITTLE GRACE,	367	HER CHRIS TREE		9
GRACIOUS				
A GRACIOUS, GENTLE, KINGLY BOY.	82	MAD KING GOLL	V	8
A GREATER, A MORE GRACIOUS TIME HAS GONE;	564	GYRES		12
BEAUTIFUL, GRACIOUS, IN HER VENETIAN WAY,	602	GALLERY REVIS	V	14
HERE, WHERE MEN KNOW THE GRACIOUS WOODLAND JOYS,	651	ISLE STAT I 1		154
OH! GRACIOUS PAN, TAKE NOW THY SERVANT'S PART.	657	ISLE STAT I 3		77
GRADUAL				
TO GRADUAL TIME'S LAST GIFT, A WRITTEN SPEECH	264	HOUSE SHAKEN		11
GRAIN				
I HAVE NOT A CRUMB OF COMFORT, NOT A GRAIN.	200	FOLLY COMFORT		7
BUT HEART THERE IS NO COMFORT, NOT A GRAIN;	200	FOLLY COMFORT	V	7
IN THE MAD ABSTRACT DARK AND GROUND IT GRAIN BY GRAIN	442	BLACK CENTAUR		8
IN THE MAD ABSTRACT DARK AND GROUND IT GRAIN BY GRAIN	442	BLACK CENTAUR		8
GRAINS				
YOU MUST BE GONE: THE ROLLING GRAINS OF SAND	663	ISLE STAT II 2		34
THE PASSING OF THOSE LITTLE GRAINS IS SNOW	722	WITCH VIVIEN		48
GRAMMAR				
THAT GRAMMAR SCHOOL OF COURTESIES	288	TO WEALTHY MAN		15
THE MALL AND EADES'S GRAMMAR SCHOOL,	360	ALF POLLEXFEN		15
GRANARY				
SLEEK AS ANY GRANARY MOUSE	2	OISIN 1	V	7M
MORE SLEEK THAN ANY GRANARY MOUSE,	4	OISIN 1		36
SLEEK AS ANY GRANARY MOUSE,	4	OISIN 1	V	37
THE HARVEST'S IN; THE GRANARY DOORS ARE SHUT;	755	SHADOW WATER A		177
GRAND				
JEWELRY SO GRAND."	595	COLONEL MARTIN		33
GRANDAM				
WHEN WERE YOU BORN? BEFORE YOUR GRANDAM EVE.	721	WITCH VIVIEN		32
GRANDCHILDREN SEE GREAT-GRANDCHILDREN				
WHERE HER GRANDCHILDREN SLEPT, AND CRIED ALOUD,	185	QUEEN MAEVE		109
AMONG HIS CHILDREN, GRANDCHILDREN AND GREAT-GRANDCHILDREN;	790	DEDICATION		6
GRAND-CHILDREN				
WHERE HER GRAND-CHILDREN SLEPT, AND CRIED ALOUD	185	QUEEN MAEVE	V	109
GRAND-DAD				
AND WANT HE DID: FOR MY OWN GRAND-DAD	596	COLONEL MARTIN		68
AND WANT HE DID FOR MY GRAND-DAD SAW	596	COLONEL MARTIN	V	68
GRANDDAD SEE GREAT-GRANDDAD				
GRANDDAUGHTER				
THE DAUGHTER AND THE GRANDDAUGHTER OF KINGS	237	SHADOW WATER B		334
THE DAUGHTER AND GRANDDAUGHTER OF KINGS	237	SHADOW WATER B	V	334
GRANDEST				
AND BOUGHT THE GRANDEST JEWELRY	595	COLONEL MARTIN		21
GRANDFATHER SEE GREAT-GRANDFATHER				
GRANDFATHER SANG IT UNDER THE GALLOWS:	544	TO SAME TUNE 1		1
GRANDFATHER SAID IN THE GREAT REBELLION:	544	TO SAME TUNE 1	V	1
GRANDFATHER SANG IT UNDER THE GALLOWS:	615	MARCH SONGS 3		1
GRANDFATHER'S SEE GREAT-GRANDFATHER'S				
ON GREAT GRANDFATHER'S BATTERED TOMB."	332	ROUND TOWER	V	30
GRANDFATHERS SEE GREAT-GRANDFATHERS				
OLD FATHERS, GREAT GRANDFATHERS,	518	LOVES LONENESS	V	1
GRANDSON SEE GREAT-GRANDSON				
BUT FOR HER GRANDSON NOW: THERE IS NO CHANGE	340	SHEP GOATHERD		39
GRANDSON, OR GREAT-GRANDSON,	604	YOU CONTENT		2
GRANIA				
AND GRANIA, WALKING AND SMILING, SEWED WITH HER NEEDLE OF BONE.	53	OISIN 3		94
GRANIA'S				
AMID THAT FIRST ASTONISHMENT, WITH GRANIA'S SHADE,	366	HER COURAGE		4
WHILE WONDERING STILL TO BE A SHADE, WITH GRANIA'S SHADE,	366	HER COURAGE	V	4
GRANT				
GOD GRANT ME--NO, NOT HERE,	346	ON WOMAN		25
GOD GRANT A BLESSING ON THIS TOWER AND COTTAGE	371	ON GOING HOUSE		1
FOR SHEPHERD LADS IN GALILEE: AND GRANT	371	ON GOING HOUSE		4
FOR WHAT MERE BOOK CAN GRANT A KNOWLEDGE	386	ROBARTES DANCE		20
GRANT ME AN OLD MAN'S FRENZY,	576	ACRE OF GRASS		13
GRANTED				
MAY SHE BE GRANTED BEAUTY AND YET NOT	403	FOR DAUGHTER		17

336

	PAGE	TITLE		LINE
GRAPE-CLUSTER				
HANG ON THE SIDE OF THE ROUND GRAPE-CLUSTER; • • • • •	646	ISLE STAT I 1		45
GRAPES				
THE HEAVY CLUSTERS OF THE GRAPES WERE FULL, • • • • •	690	MOSADA 1		13
GRASP				
TO GRASP THE WOMAN. YOU HAVE DARED TO TOUCH HER? • • •	223	SHADOW WATER B		39
WAS MOVING. BLEEDING NOW, HIS GRASP UNLOCKS, • • • • •	688	TWO TITANS		42
GRASS SEE KNOT-GRASS SPEAR-GRASS				
THE HARE LEAPED IN THE GRASS. YOUNG NIAMH CAME • • • •	44	OISIN 2	V	229
A VALLEY FLOWED DOWN FROM HIS HOOFS, AND THERE IN THE LONG GRASS LAY,	48	OISIN 3		26
WHEN A GLOW-WORM WAS GREEN ON A GRASS LEAF, • • •	53	OISIN 3	V	99
• • • AND GAZED ON THE GRASS WITH A SIGH. • • • • • •	54	OISIN 3		100
• • • THE FLESH OF HIS FACE AS DRIED GRASS, • • • • • •	59	OISIN 3		173
• • • AND MARCH ON AS OXEN MOVE OVER YOUNG GRASS; • • •	62	OISIN 3		211
AS A GRASS SEED CRUSHED BY A PEBBLE, AS A WOLF SUCKED UNDER A WEIR.	63	OISIN 3	V	220
WHO MADE THE GRASS AND MADE THE WORMS AND MADE MY FEATHERS GAY,	77	INDIAN ON GOD		18
ALONG THE GRASS, ALONG THE SANDS, • • • • • • •	78	INDIAN TO LOVE		9
SHE BID ME TAKE LIFE EASY, AS THE GRASS GROWS ON THE WEIRS;	90	SALLEY GARDENS		7
"PUT THE CHAIR UPON THE GRASS; • • • • • • • • • •	97	FOXHUNTER		9
"NOW LEAVE THE CHAIR DOWN ON THE GRASS, • • • • • • •	97	FOXHUNTER	V	9
"NOW LEAVE THE CHAIR UPON THE GRASS, • • • • • • • •	97	FOXHUNTER	V	9
ON THE SUN-SMITTEN GRASS; • • • • • • • • • •	99	FOXHUNTER		42
THE FIELD-MOUSE RUNNING BY ME IN THE GRASS, • • • • •	101	ROSE UPON ROOD		17
THE FIELD-MOUSE RUNNING BY ME IN THE GRASS, • • • •	101	ROSE UPON ROOD	V	17
AND WHERE HER SON, FINMOLE, ON THE SMOOTH GRASS • • •	106	CUCHULAIN SEA	V	18
UNDERNEATH THE GRASS AND CLOVER, • • • • • • • •	124	CATHLEEN PARA		3
ON MUNSTER GRASS AND CONNEMARA SKIES. • • • • • •	130	BOOK STORIES		24
ON MUNSTER GRASS, OR CONNEMARA SKIES. • • • • • •	130	BOOK STORIES	V	24
O'DRISCOLL GOT UP FROM THE GRASS, • • • • • • • •	145	HOST OF AIR	V	37
AND WALK AMONG LONG DAPPLED GRASS, • • • • • • •	150	WANDER AENGUS		21
AND WALK AND WALK THROUGH SUMMER GRASS, • • • • • •	150	WANDER AENGUS	V	21
AND WHEN THE UPROAR RAN ALONG THE GRASS • • • • • •	186	QUEEN MAEVE		127
ALIGHTED ON THE WINDY GRASS. • • • • • • • • •	195	BAILE AILLINN		138
BUT A WILD APPLE HID THE GRASS • • • • • • • • •	197	BAILE AILLINN		189
OR AVALLON THE GRASS GREEN HOLLOW, OR JOYOUS ISLE • •	209	UNDER THE MOON	V	2
WHERE MY GOATS BROWSE ON THE SCARCE GRASS OR LEAP • •	339	SHEP GOATHERD		8
OR ON THE CLOSE-CROPPED GRASS • • • • • • • • •	343	SHEP GOATHERD		103
THEY SAY HE COUNTED GRASS, • • • • • • • • • •	345	ON WOMAN		14
BECAUSE THE MOUNTAIN GRASS • • • • • • • • •	350	MEMORY		4
AMONG THE COARSE GRASS AND THE CAMEL-DUNG. • • • • •	369	EGO DOMINUS		31
AMONG THE COARSE GRASS AND THE CAMEL DUNG. • • • • •	369	EGO DOMINUS	V	31
MINNALOUSHE RUNS IN THE GRASS • • • • • • • •	378	CAT AND MOON		9
MINNALOUSHE CREEPS THROUGH THE GRASS • • • • • • •	378	CAT AND MOON		17
MINNALOUSHE CREEPS THROUGH THE GRASS • • • • • • •	379	CAT AND MOON		25
BUT THE CRUSHED GRASS WHERE WE HAVE LAIN; • • • • •	389	SOLOMON WITCH		42
UPON A BLADE OF GRASS. • • • • • • • • • • •	505	GRAT INSTRUCT		4
THE GRASS MY BED; • • • • • • • • • • • •	510	JANE JUDGMENT		12
SCATTERED ON THE LEVEL GRASS • • • • • • • •	530	DELPHIC ORACLE		6
LIES IN A CIRCLE ON THE GRASS; THEREIN • • • • • •	555	RIBH AT TOMB		26
GRASS PLOT OF THE GARDEN; • • • • • • • • • •	568	SWEET DANCER		3
AN ACRE OF GRASS • • • • • • • • • • •	575	ACRE OF GRASS		T
AN ACRE OF GREEN GRASS • • • • • • • • • •	575	ACRE OF GRASS		2
BY OISIN ON THE GRASS; • • • • • • • • • •	611	NEWS ORACLE		6
AND NO MAN KNOWS WHAT TREADS THE GRASS. • • • • •	614	MARCH SONGS 2		10
AND NO MAN KNOWS WHAT TREADS THE GRASS. • • • • •	615	MARCH SONGS 2		20
AND NO MAN KNOWS WHAT TREADS THE GRASS. • • • • •	615	MARCH SONGS 2		30
TALL DAMES GO WALKING IN GRASS GREEN AVALON. • • • •	627	STATES HOLIDAY	V	REF
FLOWERS AND GRASS AND CLOUDLESS SKY. • • • • • •	639	BEN BULBEN		57
YON WIND GOES SADLY, AND THE GRASS AND TREES • • •	652	ISLE STAT I 2		10
O'ER THE GRASS LIGHT-ENDAPPLED • • • • • • • •	654	ISLE STAT I 2		63
SAVING A GREEN FROG DEAD UPON THE GRASS. • • • • •	676	ISLE STAT II 3		269
THE CHILD PURSUING LIZARDS IN THE GRASS, • • • • •	686	LIFE		1
BRIGHT ON A GRASS BLADE'S UNDER SIDE, MIGHT HEAR, • • •	689	NETTLESHIP		10
OF HIS SAD GOD; AND DOWN AMONG THE GRASS • • • • •	690	MOSADA 1		16
AROUND MY HEAD AND DANCED AMONG THE GRASS; • • • • •	690	MOSADA 1		19
ON THEIR SWAYING BLADES OF GRASS, • • • • • • •	705	DAWN-SONG		14
MY MOTHER DREW FORTH FROM THE LONG GRASS • • • • •	708	FAIRY PEDANT		23
IN THE LONG GRASS—FOUR EYES DROOP LOW—A SEAT • • •	716	DWELT SYCAMORE		11
FEED A FIRE WITH STEMS OF GRASS; • • • • • • •	727	LOVERS QUARREL		42
THE CHILD WHO CHASES LIZARDS IN THE GRASS, • • • • •	734	QUATRAIN APHOR		1
THE CHILD PURSUING LIZARDS IN THE GRASS, • • • • •	734	QUATRAIN APHOR	V	1
I AWAIT YOUR WORDS AS THE BLIND GRASS AWAITS • • • •	756	SHADOW WATER A		181
THE GRASS AND THE BLUE SHADOW ON THE STREAM • • • •	761	SHADOW WATER A		280
WHO CAN HAVE TROD IN THE GRASS? • • • • • • •	781	MY HEART BEAT		4
GRASS-BARNACLE				
FROM THE GREAT GRASS-BARNACLE CALLING, • • • • • • •	57	OISIN 3		156
GRASS-BLADES				
WHILE O'ER THE BUDS, AND O'ER THE GRASS-BLADES, BRIGHT • •	704	REMEMBRANCE		3
GRASS-BLADES'				
UPON THE GRASS-BLADES' BENDING TIPS, • • • • • • • •	3	OISIN 1	V	711
GRASS-COLOURED				
HE HAD RAGGED LONG GRASS-COLOURED HAIR; • • • • • •	190	BAILE AILLINN		26
GRASSES				
AMONG THE WOODLAND GRASSES SWEET, • • • • • • •	15	OISIN 1	V	199
AND THE LONG GREY GRASSES, WHOSE TENDEREST TOUCHES • • •	27	OISIN 1	V	415B
GREY SAND ON THE GREEN OF THE GRASSES AND OVER THE DRIPPING TREES,	48	OISIN 3		14

337

	PAGE	TITLE		LINE

GRASSES   (CONTINUED)
    GREY SANDS ON THE GREEN OF THE GRASSES AND OVER THE   48 OISIN 3   V   14
        DRIPPING TREES,
    FROM HIS HOOVES IN THE HEAVY GRASSES, WITH MONSTROUS   48 OISIN 3   V   27
        SLUMBERING FOLK,
    AND, SHAKING THE PLUMES OF THE GRASSES . . . .   49 OISIN 3   35
    . . . THERE CAMPING IN GRASSES DEEP . . . .   50 OISIN 3   54
    IN THE ROOTS OF THE GRASSES, THE SORRELS, I LAID MY BODY   52 OISIN 3   73
        AS LOW:
    GREY SAND ON THE GREEN OF THE GRASSES AND OVER THE DRIPPING 57 OISIN 3   142
        TREES,
    GREY SANDS ON THE GREEN OF THE GRASSES AND OVER THE   57 OISIN 3   V 142
        DRIPPING TREES,
    WHERE LONG GREY GRASSES BOW AND BEND, ...   736 SUMMER EVENING   6
GRASS-GREEN
    NOR AVALON THE GRASS-GREEN HOLLOW, NOR JOYOUS ISLE, . . .   209 UNDER THE MOON   2
    TALL DAMES GO WALKING IN GRASS-GREEN AVALON. . . . . .   627 STATES HOLIDAY   13
    TALL DAMES GO WALKING IN GRASS-GREEN AVALON. . . . . .   627 STATES HOLIDAY   26
    TALL DAMES GO WALKING IN GRASS-GREEN AVALON. . . . . .   627 STATES HOLIDAY   39
    MOURN YE ON GRASS-GREEN PLAINS OF ERI FATED, ...   738 MOURN THEN ON   9
GRASSHOPPER
    THE HEART IN ME LONGING TO LEAP LIKE A GRASSHOPPER INTO   60 OISIN 3   182
        HER HEART:
    A LONG, BROWN GRASSHOPPER OF MAIDS! PEACE, SIR! . . .   661 ISLE STAT II 1   69
    BUT LOUD THE GRASSHOPPER THAT SITS BENEATH. . . . . .   662 ISLE STAT II 2   8
GRASSHOPPERS
    AND ALL THE GOLDEN GRASSHOPPERS AND BEES. . . . . . .   428 NINETEEN 19   8
    AND ALL HIS GOLDEN GRASSHOPPERS AND BEES. . . . . . .   428 NINETEEN 19   V   8
    OR TRAFFIC IN THE GRASSHOPPERS OR BEES. . . . .   430 NINETEEN 19   48
    OR TRAFFIC IN THE GRASSHOPPERS AND BEES? . . . . . .   430 NINETEEN 19   V 48
GRASS-LEAF
    WHEN A GLOW-WORM WAS GREEN ON A GRASS-LEAF, ...   53 OISIN 3   99
GRASSY
    CAME TO THE CAIRN-HEAPED GRASSY HILL . . . .   3 OISIN 1   17
    "BUT WE ARE APART IN THE GRASSY PLACES, ...   27 OISIN 1   408
    ALL DRIPPING ON A GRASSY SLOPE, AND SAW THEM CEASE TO CHASE 76 INDIAN ON GOD   4
    HE MADE THE WORLD TO BE A GRASSY ROAD . . . .   112 ROSE OF WORLD   14
    ON GRASSY MATTRESS I HAD LAID ME, ...   387 SOLOMON WITCH   3
    UPON EUROTAS' GRASSY BANK . . . .   522 LULLABY   14
    OF SOLDIERS RANKED IS ON A GRASSY SPOT, ...   712 FERENCZ RENYI   64
    OF SOLDIERS DRAWN IS ON A GRASSY SPOT, ...   712 FERENCZ RENYI V 64
GRASS-YELLOW
    HE HAD RAGGED, LONG GRASS-YELLOW HAIR! . . . .   190 BAILE AILLINN V 26
GRATED
    THE BOAT'S PROW GRATED ON THE SHALLOW SAND, ...   659 ISLE STAT II 1   11
GRATITUDE
    AND BLESSED, I GIVE MY GRATITUDE. . . . .   380 SAINT HUNCH   14
    HER CHILDISH GRATITUDE FOR LOVE AND MATCH YOUR FIFTY YEARS? 450 OWEN AHERNE   23
    OF CHILDREN'S GRATITUDE OR WOMAN'S LOVE. . . . . . .   500 VACILLATION   26
    GRATITUDE TO THE UNKNOWN INSTRUCTORS . . . .   505 GRAT INSTRUCT   T
    GRATITUDE TO THE UNKNOWN POWERS . . . .   505 GRAT INSTRUCT V   T
GRATTAN
    THE PEOPLE OF BURKE AND OF GRATTAN . . . .   414 TOWER   132
GRATTAN'S
    IN GRATTAN'S HOUSE. MY GREAT-GRANDFATHER SHARED . . . .   486 SEVEN SAGES   2
GRAVE
    I MUST BE GONE: THERE IS A GRAVE . . . .   67 HAPPY SHEPHERD   45
    BEFORE THEY HEAPED HIS GRAVE UNDER THE HILL: . . . . .   127 DREAM OF FAERY   16
    THE MAN HAS FOUND NO COMFORT IN THE GRAVE. . . . . . .   128 DREAM OF FAERY   48
    AND OVER THE GRAVE OF CLOOTH-NA-BARE: . . . .   140 HOSTING SIDHE   2
    THEY HAVE HEAPED THE STONES ABOVE HIS GRAVE . . . . .   193 BAILE AILLINN   115
    THIS SWORD IS TO LIE BESIDE HIM IN THE GRAVE. . . . . .   242 SHADOW WATER B   412
    THAT IN THE BLINDING LIGHT BEYOND THE GRAVE . . . . .   258 KING NO KING   12
    HE HAD BETRAYED ME TO HIS GRAVE, ...   275 GREY ROCK   96
    IT'S WITH O'LEARY IN THE GRAVE. . . . .   289 SEPTEMBER 1913   8
    IT'S WITH O'LEARY IN THE GRAVE. . . . .   289 SEPTEMBER 1913   16
    IT'S WITH O'LEARY IN THE GRAVE. . . . .   290 SEPTEMBER 1913   24
    THEY'RE WITH O'LEARY IN THE GRAVE. . . . .   290 SEPTEMBER 1913   32
    SICK OF HIS GRAVE HAS WAKENED ME? . . . .   303 HOUR DAWN   37
    BUT LET HIM KEEP HIS GRAVE FOR ONCE . . . .   303 HOUR DAWN   38
    BUT LITTLE NEED THE GRAVE DISTRESS. . . . .   338 TOM OROUGHLEY   10
    I'D DANCE A MEASURE ON HIS GRAVE." . . . .   338 TOM OROUGHLEY   16
    AND LITTLE NEED THE GRAVE DISTRESS. . . . .   338 TOM OROUGHLEY V 10
    BUT IN THE GRAVE ALL, ALL, SHALL BE RENEWED. . . . .   356 BROKEN DREAMS   21
    FOR CERTAINLY HE SANK INTO HIS GRAVE . . . .   370 EGO DOMINUS   57
    ALL THAT YOU HAVE DISCOVERED IN THE GRAVE, ...   413 TOWER   107
    FROM CRADLE RUN TO GRAVE . . . .   449 HERO GIRL FOOL   19
    FROM GRAVE TO CRADLE RUN INSTEAD: . . . .   449 HERO GIRL FOOL   20
    AND I CALL UP MACGREGOR FROM THE GRAVE, ...   473 ALL SOUL NIGHT   61
    I CALL MACGREGOR MATHERS FROM HIS GRAVE, ...   473 ALL SOUL NIGHT V 61
    GRAVE IS HEAPED ON GRAVE . . . .   496 MOHINI CHATTER   19
    GRAVE IS HEAPED ON GRAVE . . . .   496 MOHINI CHATTER   19
    NOR GRAVE NOR BED DENIED, ...   513 JANE TALK BISH   10
    OUT OF THE GRAVE. SADDLE AND RIDE . . . .   549 SEVERED HEAD   V   4
    AND SET A ROSE-TREE ON HER GRAVE, ...   571 THREE BUSHES   73
    A DEAD MAN IN HIS GRAVE. . . . .   592 DRUNK SOBRIETY   12
    "FORGETTING HUMAN WORDS," A GRAVE DEEP FACE. . . . . .   603 GALLERY REVIS   49
    DIGGERS AND CARPENTERS MAKE GRAVE AND COFFIN! . . . .   609 IN TARAS HALLS   17
    SAW THAT THE GRAVE WAS DEEP, THE COFFIN SOUND, ...   609 IN TARAS HALLS   18
GRAVE-DIGGERS
    THAT THE GRAVE-DIGGERS IN A DREAMY FRENZY . . . . . .   243 SHADOW WATER B   430

		PAGE	TITLE	LINE

GRAVE-DIGGERS'
    THOUGH GRAVE-DIGGERS' TOIL IS LONG, ...   637 BEN BULBEN   21

GRAVE-EYED
    WITH PURPLE SANDALS SWEEP THE GRAVE-EYED HOURS-- . . . .   705 REMEMBRANCE   5

GRAVEL
    OUR SHADOWS ROVE THE GARDEN GRAVEL STILL, ...   435 NEW FACES   7

GRAVELLED
    O WHAT IF LEVELLED LAWNS AND GRAVELLED WAYS . . . . .   418 ANCEST HOUSES   29

GRAVES
    BUT NEVER, NEVER ON OUR GRAVES, ...   21 OISIN 1   313
    NEVER, NEVER ON OUR GRAVES, ...   21 OISIN 1   V 313
    AND HEAR THE NARROW GRAVES CALLING MY CHILD AND ME. . .   147 UNAPPEAS HOST   6
    THEIR GRAVES INTO HER CHARGE, ...   571 THREE BUSHES   58
    CAST ON THE SOUND, ON, ON. THIS NIGHT OF GRAVES, . . .   665 ISLE STAT II 2   71

GRAVITY
    WITH AN IMPASSIONED GRAVITY. . . . .   386 ROBARTES DANCE   21

GRAY
    THE FAERY THING FLEW WITH HER O'ER THE GRAY . . . . .   663 ISLE STAT II 2   38
    AND ONE IN THE OLD GRAY HOUSE . . . .   771 SPINNING SONG   4

GRAZE
    OF FLIGHT ARE DONE. MOST FAIR OF ALL WHO GRAZE . . . .   649 ISLE STAT I 1   118
    NASCHINA, HAIL! MOST FAIR OF ALL WHO GRAZE . . . . . .   649 ISLE STAT I 1   120

GRAZED
    WHOSE HOOVES THE TOPS OF THE SURGES GRAZED, ...   12 OISIN 1   V 142A

GRAZING
    THAT FOUND WHEN I HAD NEITHER GOAT NOR GRAZING . . . .   340 SHEP GOATHERD   31
    OR ELSE AT MEADOW OR AT GRAZING OVERLOOKS . . . . . .   340 SHEP GOATHERD   37

GREASE
    THAT IS MADE OUT OF THE GREASE . . . .   776 AGAINST WITCH   24

GREASY
    BUT FUMBLE IN A GREASY TILL . . . .   289 SEPTEMBER 1913   2

GREAT
    "NOT SO, GREAT KING; FOR I HAVE NE'ER . . . .   6 OISIN 1   V   55
    OF THE GREAT ROUND SUN, FROM HIS CENTRAL FIRES. . . . .   13 OISIN 1   V 168
    AS THEY GAZE AT EACH OTHER, "OH, WHERE IS THAT GREAT ONE?"   28 OISIN 1   V 423H
    BURST FROM A GREAT DOOR MARRED BY MANY A BLOW . . . . .   31 OISIN 2   29
    BURIED AND MIGHTY. WHEN THROUGH THE GREAT DOOR . . . .   39 OISIN 2   151
    OF A GREAT EEL; IT CHANGED, AND I BUT SMOTE . . . . .   40 OISIN 2   176
    FOR GREAT OUR ERROR, GREAT OUR GUILT." . . . .   43 OISIN 2   V 208H
    FOR GREAT OUR ERROR, GREAT OUR GUILT." . . . .   43 OISIN 3   V 208H
    FROM THE GREAT GRASS-BARNACLE CALLING . . . .   57 OISIN 3   156
    WHO STILL WERE OLD WHEN THE GREAT SEA WAS YOUNG; . . .   74 ANASHU VIJAYA   69
    AND GREAT BOUGHS DROP TRANQUILLITY; . . . .   77 INDIAN TO LOVE   2
    THE GREAT BOUGHS, AND THE BURNISHED DOVE . . . . . .   78 INDIAN TO LOVE V   16
    AND GREAT BOUGHS, AND THE BURNISHED DOVE . . . . . .   78 INDIAN TO LOVE V   16
    AND THEY INHERIT THE GREAT SLEEP. . . . .   83 MAD KING GOLL   V   22
    AND ALL THESE THINGS WERE WONDERFUL AND GREAT; . . . .   104 FERGUS DRUID   37
    AH! DRUID, DRUID, HOW GREAT WEBS OF SORROW . . . . .   104 FERGUS DRUID   39
    HAS SLAIN SO MIGHTY ARMIES, SO GREAT KINGS, ...   106 CUCHULAIN SEA   V 10A
    "THE RED BRANCH CAMP IN A GREAT COMPANY . . . .   108 CUCHULAIN SEA   33
    "THE RED BRANCH GATHER A GREAT COMPANY . . . .   108 CUCHULAIN SEA   V 33
    WOULD COME AT LAST TO GOD'S GREAT TOWN, ...   113 ROSE OF PEACE   11
    SENT ONE OF HIS GREAT ANGELS DOWN . . . .   134 FR GILLIGAN   43
    IN THOSE GREAT IGNORANT LEAFY WAYS; . . . .   135 TWO TREES   16
    THE WRONG OF UNSHAPELY THINGS IS A WRONG TOO GREAT TO BE
      TOLD; . . . .   143 ROSE IN HEART   5
    THE WRONG OF THE THINGS MISSHAPEN IS WRONG TOO GREAT TO
      BE TOLD;   143 ROSE IN HEART   V   5
    AND DREAM ABOUT THE GREAT AND THEIR PRIDE; . . . . .   166 EVIL OF BELOV   2
    BUT WEIGH THIS SONG WITH THE GREAT AND THEIR PRIDE; . .   166 EVIL OF BELOV   4
    MEN HAVE NAMED BEAUTY. THY GREAT LEAVES ENFOLD . . . .   169 SECRET ROSE   7
    MEN HAVE NAMED BEAUTY. YOUR GREAT LEAVES ENFOLD . . . .   169 SECRET ROSE   V   7
    THE HOUR OF THY GREAT WIND OF LOVE AND HATE. . . . . .   170 SECRET ROSE   28
    SURELY THINE HOUR HAS COME, THY GREAT WIND BLOWS, . . .   170 SECRET ROSE   31
    BEND DOWN AND PRAY FOR THE GREAT SIN I WOVE IN SONG, . .   173 SPEAKS HEARERS V   5
    GREAT POWERS OF FALLING WAVE AND WIND AND WINDY FIRE, .   174 ELEMENT POWERS V   7
    YOU GREAT ANGELIC POWERS OF WIND, AND WAVE, AND FIRE, .   174 ELEMENT POWERS V   7
    GREAT ELEMENTAL POWERS OF WIND, AND WAVE, AND FIRE, . .   174 ELEMENT POWERS V   7
    GREAT RULERS OF THE STILLNESS, LET HER NO LONGER BE . .   175 ELEMENT POWERS V   13
    GREAT RULERS OF STILLNESS, LET HER NO LONGER BE . . . .   175 ELEMENT POWERS V   13
    MAEVE THE GREAT QUEEN WAS PACING TO AND FRO, ...   180 QUEEN MAEVE   9
    BUT THAT GREAT QUEEN, WHO MORE THAN HALF THE NIGHT . .   180 QUEEN MAEVE   16
    HAVE I NOT BID YOU TELL OF THAT GREAT QUEEN . . . . .   181 QUEEN MAEVE   34
    AND YET HAD BEEN GREAT BODIED AND GREAT LIMBED, ...   181 QUEEN MAEVE   V   25
    AND YET HAD BEEN GREAT BODIED AND GREAT LIMBED, ...   181 QUEEN MAEVE   V   25
    IT WAS BEFORE THE TIME OF THE GREAT WAR . . . .   182 QUEEN MAEVE   57
    MAEVE WALKED THROUGH THAT GREAT HALL, AND WITH A SIGH .   182 QUEEN MAEVE   62
    A KING OF THE GREAT PLAIN WOULD SPEAK WITH YOU." . . .   183 QUEEN MAEVE   78
    KINGS OF THE GREAT PLAIN HAVE COME AND GONE . . . . .   183 QUEEN MAEVE   V   81
    AND I WOULD HAVE YOUR HELP IN MY GREAT NEED, ...   184 QUEEN MAEVE   98
    AS MIDDLE NIGHT GREAT CATS WITH SILVER CLAWS, ...   185 QUEEN MAEVE   115
    OUTRUN THE MEASURE. I'D TELL OF THAT GREAT QUEEN . . .   187 QUEEN MAEVE   141
    WHO WAS IT PUT SO GREAT A SCORN . . . .   190 BAILE AILLINN   41
    WHERE WILD BEES HIVE ON THE GREAT PLAIN. . . . . . .   194 BAILE AILLINN   123
    THOUGH NOTHING TROUBLES THE GREAT STREAMS . . . . . .   196 BAILE AILLINN   172
    AMONG PIGEONS AND BEES, WHILE THAT GREAT ARCHER, . . .   198 SEVEN WOODS   12
    BECAUSE OF THAT GREAT NOBLENESS OF HERS . . . .   200 FOLLY COMFORT   9
    INTO THEIR SHINING LIMBS--I'VE HAD GREAT TEACHERS. . .   231 SHADOW WATER B   195
    OF THE GREAT GOLDEN NET THAT IS ABOUT US. . . . . . .   238 SHADOW WATER B   352
    BUT I HAVE DONE SO GREAT A WRONG AGAINST YOU, ...   245 SHADOW WATER B   483
    HOW GREAT A WRONG IT IS TO LET ONE'S THOUGHT . . . . .   246 SHADOW WATER B   514

339

		PAGE	TITLE	LINE

GREAT   (CONTINUED)

Text	PAGE	TITLE	LINE
FOR WE HAVE FOUND A TREASURE THAT'S SO GREAT	248	SHADOW WATER B	540
OR HURLED THE LITTLE STREETS UPON THE GREAT,	256	NO SECOND TROY	4
AND THEREFORE, FRIEND, IF YOUR GREAT RACE WERE RUN	265	THESE CLOUDS	7
IN THEIR GREAT HOUSE AT SLIEVENAMON,	271	GREY ROCK	15
OF THE GREAT DOOR; BUT THOUGH THE HANGING LAMPS	279	TWO KINGS	49
AND SAW WHERE IN THE MIDST OF THE GREAT HALL	279	TWO KINGS	60
THE SPEAKING OF IT COULD BE NO GREAT WRONG,	281	TWO KINGS	104
LIKE THE EYES OF SOME GREAT KITE SCOURING THE WOODS,	283	TWO KINGS	150
PRAISED THEIR GREAT VICTORIES AND GAVE THEM JOY	286	TWO KINGS	V 218B
UPON GREAT JUAN RIDING BY!	294	HATED PLAYBOY	4
AT GREAT JUAN RIDING BY!	294	HATED PLAYBOY	V 4
WHILE THAT GREAT JUAN GALLOPED BY!	294	HATED PLAYBOY	V 4
A GREAT LAD WITH A BEERY FACE	303	HOUR DAWN	27
HE GAVE HIM A GREAT PUMMELLING,	307	HOUR DAWN	113
THAT HAS MADE A GREAT PEACOCK	310	PEACOCK	2
SO GREAT A SWEETNESS FLOWS	316	FRIENDS	27
AND SCATTER WHEELING IN GREAT BROKEN RINGS	322	SWANS AT COOLE	11
WE DREAMED THAT A GREAT PAINTER HAD BEEN BORN	326	ROBERT GREGORY	65
ON GREAT GRANDFATHER'S BATTERED TOMB."	332	ROUND TOWER	V 30
AND DIED IN THE GREAT WAR BEYOND THE SEA.	339	SHEP GOATHERD	22
AND GREAT ART BEATEN DOWN.	348	FISHERMAN	24
AND YOU KNOW WELL HOW GREAT THE LONGING HAS BEEN,	352	PEOPLE	7
IN THEIR GREAT WINDOW LOOKING AT THE DAWN!	352	PEOPLE	15
TO GREAT SHAPELY KNEES	355	PROPERTIUS	2
SO GREAT HER PORTION IN THAT PEACE YOU MAKE	356	BROKEN DREAMS	12
MY GREAT WOOD LECTERN AND THE FIRE	358	PRESENCES	10
A NOBODY IN A GREAT THRONG,	361	ALF POLLEXFEN	29
PARDON, GREAT ENEMY,	366	HER CHRIS TREE	1
AND BY THE IMITATION OF GREAT MASTERS.	370	EGO DOMINUS	66
BUT WHAT THE GREAT AND PASSIONATE HAVE USED	371	ON GOING HOUSE	7
A MAN THAT FINDS GREAT BITTERNESS	379	SAINT HUNCH	2
THAT GREAT ROGUE ALCIBIADES.	379	SAINT HUNCH	12
MY GREAT RESPONSIBILITIES?	380	SONGS FOOL 1	18
THIS GREAT PURPLE BUTTERFLY,	381	SONG OF FOOL	1
OF HIS GREAT BIRCH AND HIS GREAT BOOK.	381	SONG OF FOOL	8
OF HIS GREAT BIRCH AND HIS GREAT BOOK.	381	SONG OF FOOL	8
THERE IS GREAT DANGER IN THE BODY.	386	ROBARTES DANCE	38
WITHIN MY ARMS GREAT SOLOMON,	387	SOLOMON WITCH	4
BECAUSE OF THE GREAT GLOOM THAT IS IN MY MIND.	403	FOR DAUGHTER	8
WHILE THAT GREAT QUEEN, THAT ROSE OUT OF THE SPRAY,	404	FOR DAUGHTER	27
SO GREAT A GLORY DID THE SONG CONFER.	410	TOWER	40
AND ONE WAS DROWNED IN THE GREAT BOG OF CLOONE.	411	TOWER	48
WHOSE IMAGES, IN THE GREAT MEMORY STORED,	412	TOWER	85
WHILE THEIR GREAT WOODEN DICE BEAT ON THE BOARD.	412	TOWER	88
FROM A GREAT LABYRINTH OUT OF PRIDE,	413	TOWER	116
FROM SOME GREAT LABYRINTH OUT OF PRIDE,	413	TOWER	V 116
AMID GREAT CHAMBERS AND LONG GALLERIES, LINED	418	ANCEST HOUSES	36
AND A GREAT ARMY BUT A SHOWY THING!	429	NINETEEN 19	18
COME LET US MOCK AT THE GREAT	432	NINETEEN 19	93
TO HELP GOOD, WISE OR GREAT	432	NINETEEN 19	110
THERE LURCHES PAST, HIS GREAT EYES WITHOUT THOUGHT	433	NINETEEN 19	126
A SUDDEN BLOW! THE GREAT WINGS BEATING STILL	441	LEDA AND SWAN	1
O CHESTNUT TREE, GREAT ROOTED BLOSSOMER,	446	SCHOOL CHILDR	V 61
THE GREAT GREY-EYED ATHENE STARES THEREON.	447	COLONUS PRAISE	16
WHERE THE GREAT MOTHER, MOURNING FOR HER DAUGHTER	447	COLONUS PRAISE	19
SHE WHO HAD BROUGHT GREAT HECTOR DOWN	455	HIS MEMORIES	15
AND PETER THAT HAD GREAT AFFAIRS	456	FRIENDS YOUTH	13
FOR THE GREAT CALIF'S TREASURER AND MY FRIEND,	460	HARUN RASHID	V 2
THROUGH THE GREAT GALLERY OF THE TREASURE HOUSE	461	HARUN RASHID	5
AT THE GREAT BOOK OF SAPPHO'S SONG! BUT NO,	461	HARUN RASHID	12
SO GREAT ITS FAME. WHEN FITTING TIME HAS PASSED	461	HARUN RASHID	19
TAKE THIS LIGHT PARCHMENT, PASS THROUGH THE GREAT CHAMBER	461	HARUN RASHID	V 5
WHAT GREAT HARUN AL-RASHID, OCCUPIED	462	HARUN RASHID	24
WITH THE GREAT TOIL AND CEREMONY OF STATE,	462	HARUN RASHID	V 25
THAT YEAR WHEN GREAT HAROUN EL RASHID KILLED	462	HARUN RASHID	V 31
TO SHOW HOW VIOLENT GREAT HEARTS CAN LOSE	463	HARUN RASHID	47
THAT IT WAS MADE IN YOUR GREAT FATHER'S REIGN."	464	HARUN RASHID	72
"GREAT PRINCE, FORGIVE THE FREEDOM OF MY SPEECH!	464	HARUN RASHID	74
OR WAS IT SHE THAT SPOKE OR SOME GREAT DJINN?	467	HARUN RASHID	135
FROM THE GREAT TREATISE OF PARMENIDES!	469	HARUN RASHID	183
MIDNIGHT HAS COME, AND THE GREAT CHRIST CHURCH BELL	470	ALL SOUL NIGHT	1
IT IS ALL SOULS' NIGHT AND THE GREAT CHRIST CHURCH BELL	470	ALL SOUL NIGHT	V 1
GREAT WINDOWS OPEN TO THE SOUTH,	475	EVA GORE-BOOTH	2
WE THE GREAT GAZEBO BUILT,	476	EVA GORE-BOOTH	30
A GREAT MAN IN HIS PRIDE	476	DEATH	7
SO GREAT A SWEETNESS FLOWS INTO THE BREAST	479	SELF AND SOUL	69
THOUGH THE GREAT SONG RETURN NO MORE	485	NINETEENTH CEN	1
FROM FOUR GREAT MINDS THAT HATED WHIGGERY.	486	SEVEN SAGES	7
HARRIED, AND BURKE'S GREAT MELODY AGAINST IT.	487	SEVEN SAGES	16
GREAT WORKS CONSTRUCTED THERE IN NATURE'S SPITE	488	COOLE PARK 29	5
GREAT ROOMS WHERE TRAVELLED MEN AND CHILDREN FOUND	491	COOLE BALLYLEE	29
WE SHIFT ABOUT—ALL THAT GREAT GLORY SPENT—	491	COOLE BALLYLEE	39
MAN SHIFTS ABOUT—ALL THAT GREAT GLORY SPENT—	491	COOLE BALLYLEE	V 39
BY THOSE GREAT HONEY-COLOURED	492	ANNE GREGORY	3
MUCH ON THE GREAT QUESTIONER!	494	AT ALGECIRAS	16
OR, AS GREAT SAGES SAY,	496	MOHINI CHATTER	27
AFTER GREAT CATHEDRAL GONG!	497	BYZANTIUM	4
IT SEEMED, SO GREAT MY HAPPINESS,	501	VACILLATION	43
IN HIS NOSTRILS, THE GREAT LORD OF CHOU	502	VACILLATION	59
GREAT HATRED, LITTLE ROOM,	506	REMORSE SPEECH	12

	PAGE	TITLE	LINE
GREAT (CONTINUED)			
GREAT EUROPA PLAYED THE FOOL	509	JANE REPROVED	5
WHERE THE GREAT BATTLE WAS	512	JANE ON GOD	10
OLD FATHERS, GREAT GRANDFATHERS,	518	LOVES LONENESS V	1
IN A GREAT TUMULT OF THE AIR,	519	HER DREAM	6
BEHOLD THAT GREAT PLOTINUS SWIM,	530	DELPHIC ORACLE	1
BUT HAD GREAT PLEASURE WITH A LAD	538	LAST CONFESS	5
BY THAT GREAT GLORY DRIVEN WILD.	540	FROM ANTIGONE	13
UNDER THE GREAT COMEDIAN'S TOMB THE CROWD.	541	PARN FUNERAL 1	1
THAT WOMAN, THE GREAT MOTHER IMAGING,	541	PARN FUNERAL 1	13
GRANDFATHER SAID IN THE GREAT REBELLION!	544	TO SAME TUNE 1 V	1
ALL THAT GREAT PAST TO A TROUBLE OF FOOLS!	546	TO SAME TUNE 2	22
GREAT NATIONS BLOSSOM ABOVE!	547	TO SAME TUNE 3	5
. . . "THE KING OF THE GREAT CLOCK TOWER"	549	SEVERED HEAD	T
WHAT SAYS THE CLOCK IN THE GREAT CLOCK TOWER?	549	SEVERED HEAD	3
WHAT SAYS THE CLOCK IN THE GREAT CLOCK TOWER?	550	SEVERED HEAD	10
WHAT SAYS THE CLOCK IN THE GREAT CLOCK TOWER?	550	SEVERED HEAD	17
FOR THINGS BELOW ARE COPIES, THE GREAT SMARAGDINE TABLET SAID.	556	RIBH PATRICK	6
I STUDY HATRED WITH GREAT DILIGENCE,	558	RIBH CHRISTIAN	3
THE GREAT STAGE CURTAIN ABOUT TO DROP,	565	LAPIS LAZULI	13
AUGUSTA GREGORY SEATED AT HER GREAT ORMOLU TABLE,	577	LOFTY THINGS	7
BUT A GREAT DANE THAT CANNOT BAY THE MOON	579	DOR WELLESLEY	10
NOR SATISFIED CONSCIENCE, BUT THAT GREAT FAMILY	579	DOR WELLESLEY	14
I CAME ON A GREAT HOUSE IN THE MIDDLE OF THE NIGHT,	581	CURSE CROMWELL	25
HE'D GONE TO GREAT EXPENSE	585	ORAHILLY	13
THE GREAT DAY	590	GREAT DAY	T
FRAGMENTS THE GREAT DAY	590	GREAT DAY V	T
A GREAT BLACK RAGGED BIRD APPEARED WHEN I WAS IN THE BOAT!	593	PILGRIM	16
WITH FLOPPING AND WITH FLAPPING IT MADE A GREAT DISPLAY,	593	PILGRIM	18
A GREAT BLACK BIRD APPEARED WHEN I WAS IN THE BOAT,	593	PILGRIM V	16
WITH THEIR FLOPPING AND THEIR FLAPPING IT MADE A GREAT DISPLAY	593	PILGRIM V	18
PROCLAIMED BOTH GOOD AND GREAT!	597	MODEL LAUREATE	4
A GREAT EBULLIENT PORTRAIT CERTAINLY!	602	GALLERY REVIS	27
AN EBULLIENT GREAT PORTRAIT CERTAINLY!	602	GALLERY REVIS V	27
AND THE GREAT WATER SIGHED FOR LOVE,	611	NEWS ORACLE	3
ALL THAT GREAT PAST TO A TROUBLE OF FOOLS!	614	MARCH SONGS 1	22
GREAT NATIONS BLOSSOM ABOVE!	614	MARCH SONGS 2	5
ITS GREAT BATTLE LOST,	617	LONG-LEG FLY	2
WHAT GREAT TOMB-HAUNTER SWEEPS THE DISTANT SKY	618	BRONZE HEAD	4
ON GANGLING STOCKS GROWN GREAT, GREAT STOCKS RUN DRY,	619	BRONZE HEAD	25
ON GANGLING STOCKS GROWN GREAT, GREAT STOCKS RUN DRY,	619	BRONZE HEAD	25
THOSE GREAT SEA-HORSES BARE THEIR TEETH AND LAUGH AT THE DAWN.	623	HIGH TALK	14
I LIVED AMONG GREAT HOUSES,	626	STATES HOLIDAY	1
AM I A GREAT LORD CHANCELLOR	627	STATES HOLIDAY	14
WITH A GREAT COCK'S FEATHER,	627	STATES HOLIDAY	37
GREAT BLADDERED EMER SAT,	628	JANE MOUNTAIN V	15
DID WORDS OF MINE PUT TOO GREAT STRAIN	632	MAN AND ECHO	13
THE SPIRITUAL INTELLECT'S GREAT WORK,	632	MAN AND ECHO	20
NOR CAN THERE BE WORK SO GREAT	632	MAN AND ECHO	23
NOR CAN THERE BE A WORK SO GREAT	632	MAN AND ECHO V	23
SHALL WE IN THAT GREAT NIGHT REJOICE?	633	MAN AND ECHO	38
SWEARS THAT HE HEARS THE KING'S GREAT HORN.	636	BLACK TOWER	24
WHAT HIS GREAT FOREFATHERS DID,	638	BEN BULBEN	39
AND THE GREAT GREY LYNX'S SKIN! IN SOOTH, METHINKS	650	ISLE STAT I 1	151
THAT I MYSELF COULD SHOOT A GREAT GREY LYNX.	650	ISLE STAT I 1	152
FOR THERE THE GREAT ENCHANTRESS LIVES. AND THERE	653	ISLE STAT I 2	38
WILL HE HAVE HAPPINESS? GREAT SOBS HER BEING SHAKE.	676	ISLE STAT II 3	247
THE LION, THE WORLD'S GREAT SOLITARY, BENDS	689	NETTLESHIP	5
WHY THESE NEW FEARS? THE GREAT MONK EBREMAR,	692	MOSADA 1	46
SHE WAS A GREAT ENCHANTRESS ONCE OF YORE,	693	MOSADA 1	78
NO MORE! TAKE ME INSTEAD OF HER, GREAT SIRS.	695	MOSADA 1	114
FROM THE GREAT PAINTED WINDOW WRAPS HIS BROW,	697	MOSADA 2	37
OF THE GREAT WARRIORS WHOSE NAMES HAVE SUNG	698	MOSADA 2	60
SOME GREAT ONE. NO! I HEAR THE WAVERING STEPS	720	WITCH VIVIEN	12
I DREAMT SOME GREAT ONE. AH, MY BEAUTIFUL,	720	WITCH VIVIEN	14
AND THEN THE GREAT ONES COME, AND LAST THE KING.	722	WITCH VIVIEN	54
NOW THY GREAT WHITE DOLL TO HOLD--	726	LOVERS QUARREL	15
"OF OUR GREAT QUEEN IS EVER HEARD	729	PRIEST FAIRY	41
"SHIELD BREAKER, GREAT SHIELD BREAKER,"	740	EARL PAUL	25
FOR HIS GREAT HARDIHOOD.	741	EARL PAUL	56
SHE OFFERS GREAT REWARDS IF WE TURN EAST	755	SHADOW WATER A	169
WE BRING YOU THIS GREAT QUEEN.	755	SHADOW WATER A V	166
AMONG GREAT TREES, AND IN THE WINGS OF OWLS,	762	SHADOW WATER A	285
RUIN ON A GREAT KING'S HOUSE	775	AGAINST WITCH	3
OR BURNED GREAT CITIES DOWN,	789	SINGING HEAD	16
GREAT-AUNTS			
ON UNCLES, AUNTS, GREAT-UNCLES OR GREAT-AUNTS,	604	YOU CONTENT	3
GREAT-BLADDERED			
GREAT-BLADDERED EMER SAT,	628	JANE MOUNTAIN	15
GREAT-BODIED			
AND YET HAD BEEN GREAT-BODIED AND GREAT-LIMBED,	181	QUEEN MAEVE	25
GREATER			
AND HAD THE GREATER JOY IN PRAISING HER,	410	TOWER	37
GREATER GLORY IN THE SUN,	494	AT ALGECIRAS	13
A GREATER WITH A LESSER PANG ASSUAGE	537	HER VISION	5
THE GREATER GROWS MY LIGHT	559	HE AND SHE	9
A GREATER, A MORE GRACIOUS TIME HAS GONE!	564	GYRES	12
THAT IRELAND'S MIND BE GREATER,	608	SONGS BURDEN 3	21

341

	PAGE	TITLE	LINE

GREATER   (CONTINUED)
NO! GREATER THAN PYTHAGORAS, FOR THE MEN . . . . . . 610 STATUES 9
WHEN THAT GREATER DREAM HAD GONE . . . . 639 BEN BULBEN 63
BENEATH THE WEIGHT OF GREATER GRIEF THAN I! . . . . . 661 ISLE STAT II 1 63

GREATEST
WHAT IF THOSE THINGS THE GREATEST OF MANKIND . . . . 418 ANCEST HOUSES 38
WHEN THE FULL MOON SWAM TO ITS GREATEST HEIGHT . . . 468 HARUN RASHID 151
"GREATEST SINCE REMBRANDT," ACCORDING TO JOHN SYNGE! . 602 GALLERY REVIS 26

GREAT-GRANDCHILDREN
AMONG HIS CHILDREN, GRANDCHILDREN AND GREAT-GRANDCHILDREN! 790 DEDICATION 6

GREAT-GRANDDAD
WHAT IF MY GREAT-GRANDDAD HAD A PAIR THAT WERE TWENTY FOOT 622 HIGH TALK 2
HIGH,

GREAT-GRANDFATHER
MY GREAT-GRANDFATHER SPOKE TO EDMUND BURKE . . . . . 486 SEVEN SAGES 1
IN GRATTAN'S HOUSE. MY GREAT-GRANDFATHER SHARED . . . . 486 SEVEN SAGES 2

GREAT-GRANDFATHER'S
ON GREAT-GRANDFATHER'S BATTERED TOMB." . . . . 331 ROUND TOWER 6
ON GREAT-GRANDFATHER'S BATTERED TOMB." . . . . 332 ROUND TOWER 30
MY GREAT-GRANDFATHER'S FATHER TALKED OF MUSIC, ... 486 SEVEN SAGES 4
MY GREAT-GRANDFATHER'S FATHER TALKED OF MUSIC AND PAINTING, 486 SEVEN SAGES V 4

GREAT-GRANDFATHERS
OLD FATHERS, GREAT-GRANDFATHERS, ... 518 LOVES LONENESS 1

GREAT-GRANDSON
AND MAYBE THE GREAT-GRANDSON OF THAT HOUSE, ... 418 ANCEST HOUSES 23
GRANDSON, OR GREAT-GRANDSON, ... 604 YOU CONTENT 2

GREAT-LIMBED
AND YET HAD BEEN GREAT-BODIED AND GREAT-LIMBED, . . . 181 QUEEN MAEVE 25

GREATNESS
AND SEEMED THE GREATNESS OF THE WORLD IN TEARS, ... 120 SORROW OF LOVE 6
HE THINKS OF HIS PAST GREATNESS . . . . 177 PAST GREATNESS T
MONGAN THINKS OF HIS PAST GREATNESS . . . . 177 PAST GREATNESS V T
HAVE ALL THAT GREATNESS, AND NOT HERS ALONE, ... 186 QUEEN MAEVE 133
HAVE YOU MADE GREATNESS YOUR COMPANION, ... 265 THESE CLOUDS 9
BUT TAKE OUR GREATNESS WITH OUR VIOLENCE? . . . . . . 418 ANCEST HOUSES 32
BUT TAKE OUR GREATNESS WITH OUR BITTERNESS? . . . . . 418 ANCEST HOUSES 40
THE GREATNESS OF MY LOVE. DID I NOT RULE . . . . . . 748 SHADOW WATER A V 32

GREAT-ROOTED
O CHESTNUT-TREE, GREAT-ROOTED BLOSSOMER, ... 446 SCHOOL CHILDR 61

GREAT-UNCLES
ON UNCLES, AUNTS, GREAT-UNCLES OR GREAT-AUNTS, ... 604 YOU CONTENT 3

GRECIAN
BUT SUCH A FORM AS GRECIAN GOLDSMITHS MAKE . . . . . 408 SAIL BYZANTIUM 27
WITH PERSIAN EMBASSY OR GRECIAN WAR, ... 462 HARUN RASHID 25

GREECE
BY SUCKING AT THE DUGS OF GREECE. . . . . 288 TO WEALTHY MAN 28
AMONG THE KINGS OF GREECE AND FRANCE." . . . . . . 296 THREE BEGGARS V 32A
AND THE PROUD STONES OF GREECE, ... 415 TOWER 159
EGYPT AND GREECE, GOOD-BYE, AND GOOD-BYE, ROME! . . . . 563 MERU 8
OR THE KING OF GREECE, ... 627 STATES HOLIDAY 19

GREEDY
SAVE, WITH THE LITTLE GOLDEN GREEDY CARP, ... 720 WITCH VIVIEN 2

GREEK
TILL ALL HIS GREEK AND LATIN LEARNING SEEMED . . . . . 324 ROBERT GREGORY 21
GREEK ALEXANDER FROM MY FLESH, ... 379 SAINT HUNCH 10
WITH PERSIAN WARS OR GREEK AMBASSADORS . . . . . . 462 HARUN RASHID V 25
AN ABSTRACT GREEK ABSURDITY HAS CRAZED THE MAN— . . . 556 RIBH PATRICK 1
ABSTRACTIONS OF THE GREEK PHILOSOPHY HAVE CRAZED THE MAN, 556 RIBH PATRICK V 1

GREEKS
GREEKS WERE BUT LOVERS! ALL THAT COUNTRY ROUND . . . . 430 NINETEEN 19 V 43

GREEN   SEE SEA-GREEN BLUE-GREEN GRASS-GREEN GREY-GREEN
FOR OUR BEST WERE DEAD ON GAVRA'S GREEN. . . . . . . 2 OISIN 1 V 71
THAT SLOPING GREEN DE DANAAN SOD . . . . 20 OISIN 1 299
THE SEAWEED-COVERED PILLARS! AND THE GREEN . . . . . 31 OISIN 2 32
TWO WALLS, A ROOF, A FLOOD! THERE TREMBLING GREEN . . 31 OISIN 2 V 32
THAT WAS MOST DISTANT FROM THE DOOR! GREEN SLIME . . . 37 OISIN 2 113
WHILE HIGH FRAIL CLOUDLETS, FED WITH A GREEN LIGHT, . . . 40 OISIN 2 165
DAWN PASSIONED! FED WITH A FAINT GREEN LIGHT, ... 40 OISIN 2 V 165
GREY SAND ON THE GREEN OF THE GRASSES AND OVER THE DRIPPING 48 OISIN 3 14
TREES,
GREY SANDS ON THE GREEN OF THE GRASSES AND OVER THE 48 OISIN 3 V 14
DRIPPING TREES,
WHEN A GLOW-WORM WAS GREEN ON A GRASS-LEAF, ... 53 OISIN 3 99
WHEN A GLOW-WORM WAS GREEN ON A GRASS LEAF, ... 53 OISIN 3 V 99
GREY SAND ON THE GREEN OF THE GRASSES AND OVER THE DRIPPING 57 OISIN 3 142
TREES,
GREY SANDS ON THE GREEN OF THE GRASSES AND OVER THE 57 OISIN 3 V 142
DRIPPING TREES,
ONE STAR SHONE FAINT AND GREEN, ... 95 MOLL MAGEE 30
A GREEN DROP IN THE SURGE, A GLEAM OF LIGHT . . . . 104 FERGUS DRUID 33
GO THERE AND DWELL ON THE GREEN FOREST RIM. . . . . 108 CUCHULAIN SEA V 35
UPON A DIM, GREEN, WELL-BELOVED ISLE, ... 126 DREAM OF FAERY V 8
THERE WAS A GREEN BRANCH HUNG WITH MANY A BELL . . . 129 BOOK STORIES 1
I TORE IT FROM GREEN BOUGHS WINDS TORE AND TOSSED . . 130 BOOK STORIES 13
I TORE IT FROM GREEN BOUGHS WINDS TOSSED AND HURLED, . 130 BOOK STORIES V 13
GREEN BOUGHS OF TOSSING ALWAYS, WEARY, WEARY, . . . 130 BOOK STORIES 14
I TORE IT FROM THE GREEN BOUGHS OF OLD ERI, ... 130 BOOK STORIES V 15
GREEN OAK AND POPLAR TREE! . . . . 132 OLD PENSIONER V 16
OR UNDER GREEN SODS LAY. . . . . 132 FR GILLIGAN 4
I HUNGER TO BUILD THEM ANEW AND SIT ON A GREEN KNOLL APART, 143 ROSE IN HEART 6
AND HE, BEING LAID UPON GREEN BOUGHS, ... 192 BAILE AILLINN 71

GREEN   (CONTINUED)   PAGE   TITLE   LINE
   O TUFTED REEDS, BEND LOW AND LOW IN POOLS ON THE GREEN
      LAND,   206 HANRAHANS SONG V   1
   OR AVALLON THE GRASS GREEN HOLLOW, OR JOYOUS ISLE   209 UNDER THE MOON V   2
   AS THOUGH THEY HAD BEEN HIDDEN BY GREEN BOUGHS   217 WOODS OF COOLE   6
   THEIR SUDDEN FRAGRANCES ON THE GREEN AIR: 217 WOODS OF COOLE   10
   AND THE GREEN QUIET, HAVE UPLIFTED THE HEART?   219 WOODS OF COOLE   40
   AND WHERE BEECH-TREES HAD MIXED A PALE GREEN LIGHT   277 TWO KINGS   5
   BETWEEN THE PALE GREEN LIGHT OF THE BEECH LEAVES   277 TWO KINGS   5
   WHERE CERTAIN BEECHES MIXED A PALE GREEN LIGHT   277 TWO KINGS   V   5
   AND WHERE BEECH TREES HAD MIXED A PALE GREEN LIGHT   277 TWO KINGS   V   5
   WANDERED BETWEEN THE BLUE AND THE GREEN LEAF   278 TWO KINGS   41
   THE ROUND GREEN EYES AND THE LONG WAVERING BODIES   343 DEJECTION   2
   IN THE GREEN SHADOW OF FERRARA WALL: 352 PEOPLE   9
   IN THE GREEN SHADOW ON FERRARA WALL: 352 PEOPLE   V   9
   AND THAT HE WILL TURN GREEN WITH RAGE   385 ROBARTES DANCE   16
   WHEREVER GREEN IS WORN,   394 EASTER 1916   78
   "TO MAKE THE GREEN COME OUT AGAIN   396 ROSE TREE   9
   O MAY SHE LIVE LIKE SOME GREEN LAUREL   405 FOR DAUGHTER   47
   EVEN WHERE HORRIBLE GREEN PARROTS CALL AND SWING.   442 BLACK CENTAUR   2
   BECAUSE OF SOME GREEN WING, GATHERED OLD MUMMY WHEAT   442 BLACK CENTAUR   7
   UNWEARIED EYES UPON THOSE HORRIBLE GREEN BIRDS.   442 BLACK CENTAUR   16
   EVEN WHERE THE HORRIBLE GREEN PARROTS CALL AND SWING.   442 BLACK CENTAUR V   2
   IS HALF ALL GLITTERING FLAME AND HALF ALL GREEN   500 VACILLATION   12
   IS HALF ALL GLITTERING FLAME AND HALF A GREEN   500 VACILLATION   V   12
   AN ACRE OF GREEN GRASS   575 ACRE OF GRASS   2
   ON A STORM-BITTEN GREEN.   606 SONGS BURDEN 2   4
   ON THE GREEN LANDS I WALK   607 SONGS BURDEN 2   20
   TALL DAMES GO WALKING IN GRASS GREEN AVALON.   627 STATES HOLIDAY V REF
   UPON HIS WINGS. THRO' YONDER GREEN ABYSS   649 ISLE STAT I 1   114
   OF GREEN ARCADIA DO NOT HIDE, I TROW,   651 ISLE STAT I 1   166
   OF YONDER LAKE, FROM WHOSE GREEN BANKS ALWAY   653 ISLE STAT I 2   33
   AND NOD TO ONE ANOTHER, LIES A GREEN,   653 ISLE STAT I 2   35
   O'ER THE GREEN EDEN-SOD: 654 ISLE STAT I 2   65
   AWAY IN THE GREEN PARADISE,   654 ISLE STAT I 2   70
   O'ER THE GREEN EDEN-SOD,   654 ISLE STAT I 2   75
   FROM THE GREEN SHADED HOLLOW   655 ISLE STAT I 2   82
   ACORNS GREEN, WITH EYES AWAKE.   655 ISLE STAT I 3   5
   I FOLLOWED HIM FROM MY GREEN LAIR,   655 ISLE STAT I 3   6
   THE EVENING GLEAMS ARE GREEN AND GOLD AND RED   656 ISLE STAT I 3   22
   THE MOBS OF STARS IN GOLD AND GREEN AND BLUE,   663 ISLE STAT II 2   43
   FROM WHOSE GREEN BANKS NO LIVING THING MAY ROVE,   664 ISLE STAT II 2   57
   O, LADY, THOU WHOSE VESTITURE OF GREEN   667 ISLE STAT II 3   34
   I PLUCKED HER BACKWARDS BY HER DRESS OF GREEN.   676 ISLE STAT II 3   264
   SAVING A GREEN FROG DEAD UPON THE GRASS.   676 ISLE STAT II 3   269
   AND THROB WITHIN THE CIRCLES OF GREEN DAWN.   701 MOSADA 3   54
   AYE AND SHAKES IN SEA GREEN WAVERINGS, ALONG THE FISHERS'
      STREET.   718 PHANTOM SHIP   V   2
   IN THE GREEN HILL'S INMOST PART.   726 LOVERS QUARREL   12
   WAKE THE LARKS UPON THE GREEN.   727 LOVERS QUARREL   46
   BENEATH A POINTED CAP OF GREEN: 728 PRIEST FAIRY   22
   TO THE GREEN ISLE OF WIGHT   740 EARL PAUL   10
GREENISH
   GREENISH AND SLIPPERY. TIME AFTER TIME   37 OISIN 2   V 114
GREENNESS
   AND FROM ITS MURMURING GREENNESS, CALM OF FAERY,   129 BOOK STORIES   3
   AND THERE'S BUT COMMON GREENNESS AFTER THAT.   422 MY DESCENDANTS   8
   VAST GREENNESS, WHERE ETERNAL RUMOUR DWELLS,   657 ISLE STAT I 3   45
GREEN-PATED
   PORTLY GREEN-PATED BIRD   400 DEMON BEAST   28
GREET
   GREET HIM COURTEOUS, GREET HIM KIND,   717 FAIRY DOCTOR   V   21
   GREET HIM COURTEOUS, GREET HIM KIND,   717 FAIRY DOCTOR   V   21
   FIRST I GREET MACCARTAN, REVOLUTIONARY LEADER.   790 DEDICATION   1
GREGORY
   IN MEMORY OF MAJOR ROBERT GREGORY   323 ROBERT GREGORY   T
   IN MEMORY OF ROBERT GREGORY   323 ROBERT GREGORY V   T
   FOR ANNE GREGORY   492 ANNE GREGORY   T
   ANNE GREGORY   492 ANNE GREGORY   V   T
   AUGUSTA GREGORY SEATED AT HER GREAT ORMOLU TABLE,   577 LOFTY THINGS   7
   MANCINI'S PORTRAIT OF AUGUSTA GREGORY,   602 GALLERY REVIS   25
   JOHN SYNGE, I AND AUGUSTA GREGORY, THOUGHT   603 GALLERY REVIS   41
GREGORY'S
   BUT GREGORY'S WOOD AND ONE BARE HILL   403 FOR DAUGHTER   4
   BUT GREGORY'S WOODS AND ONE BARE HILL   403 FOR DAUGHTER   V   4
   AUGUSTA GREGORY'S SON: HER SISTER'S SON,   602 GALLERY REVIS   21
GREW
   THAT I WOULD GO WITH HER, THEY GREW   10 OISIN 1   V 111A
   AND EVER NEARER, NEARER GREW: 15 OISIN 1   200
   UNTIL THE TOSSING ARMS GREW STILL   21 OISIN 1   322
   THE FLOWERS STILL GREW THERE: FAR ON THE SEA'S WASTE   39 OISIN 2   163
   TILL THE FAR DOORWAY GREW A BURNING BLOT   39 OISIN 2   V   152
   THE FLOWERS STILL GREW THERE. MOVED BEYOND HIM THE SEA'S
      WASTE: 39 OISIN 2   V   163
   KINGFISHER COLOUR GREW WITH RAGE. HE ROSE   40 OISIN 2   169
   THE DRUID SWORD OF MANANAN, HE GREW   40 OISIN 2   V   174
   THE DEAD GOD'S SWORD, TO MANY FORMS HE GREW,   40 OISIN 2   V   175
   HORROR FROM HORROR GREW: BUT WHEN THE WEST   41 OISIN 2   180
   A BEECH-BOUGH TO ME, AND MY HEART GREW SORE,   44 OISIN 2   226
   A BEECH BOUGH TO ME, AND MY HEART GREW SORE,   44 OISIN 2   V   226
   BUT THE TREES GREW TALLER AND CLOSER,   48 OISIN 3   17

GREW   (CONTINUED)
        BUT TALLER THE TREES GREW AND CLOSER, ...   48 OISIN 3   V   17
        THE WAILING GREW DISTANT: I RODE BY THE WOODS OF   56 OISIN 3   137
           THE WRINKLING BARK,
        THE FIELDS GREW FATTER DAY BY DAY, ...   82 MAD KING GOLL   7
        IN MY MOST SECRET SPIRIT GREW . . . .   83 MAD KING GOLL   27
        WHEN THE MORN GREW FROSTY AND CLEAR. . . . .   95 MOLL MAGEE   20
        MY MAN GREW RED AND PALE, ...   95 MOLL MAGEE   22
        AND ALL GREW FRIENDLY FOR A LITTLE WHILE. . . . . . .   129 BOOK STORIES   8
        AND ALL WHO HEARD GREW FRIENDLY FOR A WHILE. . . . . .   129 BOOK STORIES   V   8
        THEY SLOWLY INTO MILLIONS GREW. . . . .   133 FR GILLIGAN   17
        WHILE THE NIGHT GREW, ABOVE THE FADING COALS, ...   136 TO SOME I TALK V   3
        AND HE SAW HOW THE REEDS GREW DARK . . . .   144 HOST OF AIR   5
        AND ONCE, WHEN THE OWLS GREW STILL, ...   159 CAP AND BELLS V   2
        IT TALKED, ERE THE MORN GREW WHITE. . . . .   159 CAP AND BELLS V   6
        TILL STARS GREW OUT OF THE AIR. . . . .   160 CAP AND BELLS   28
        THE STARS GREW OUT OF THE AIR. . . . .   160 CAP AND BELLS V 28
        WHILE BIRDS GREW SILENT ONE BY ONE. . . . .   176 BELOVED DEAD   V 13
        AND WHEN I'VE HEARD HOW THEY GREW OLD AND DIED, . . .   186 QUEEN MAEVE   136
        OF THIS OR THAT THING, NOR GREW COLD . . . .   189 BAILE AILLINN   9
        OF THIS OR THAT THING, OR GREW COLD . . . .   189 BAILE AILLINN V   9
        AND WHEN NO FACE GREW PITEOUS . . . .   191 BAILE AILLINN   62
        THAT OLD MAN CLIMBED: THE DAY GREW DIM: . . . . . .   194 BAILE AILLINN   134
        AND GREW TO BE OUT OF FASHION . . . .   211 O DO NOT LOVE   3
        AND I GREW WEARY OF THE SUN . . . .   256 WORDS   5
        THOUGH ALWAYS AT MY WORDS HIS TROUBLE GREW: . . . .   281 TWO KINGS   91
        ALL SHOUTED TILL THEIR ANGER GREW . . . .   297 THREE BEGGARS   46
        AND THEREUPON THEIR ANGER GREW, ...   297 THREE BEGGARS V 46
        AND EVEN OLD MEN'S EYES GREW DIM, THIS HAND ALONE, . .   314 FALLEN MAJESTY   2
        THAT SOLOMON GREW WISE . . . .   345 ON WOMAN   11
        UNTIL HER VOICE GREW SHRILL. . . . .   392 EASTER 1916   20
        COLD STONE AND WATER. I GREW WILD, ...   399 BREAK OF DAY   14
        FOR ALL MEN'S THOUGHTS GREW CLEAR . . . .   400 DEMON BEAST   19
        FOR ALL MEN'S THOUGHT GREW CLEAR . . . .   400 DEMON BEAST   V 19
        MUST DRIVE THE ARABIAN HOST. THE VOICE GREW STILL, . .   467 HARUN RASHID   145
        MADE DRIVE THE ARABIAN HOST. THE VOICE GREW STILL, . .   467 HARUN RASHID   V 145
        GROUNDS WHERE PLUM AND CABBAGE GREW, ...   577 WHAT THEN   13
        CONTACT EVERYTHING ANTAEUS-LIKE GREW STRONG. . . . .   603 GALLERY REVIS   44
        CONTACT ALL THINGS ANTAEUS-LIKE GREW STRONG: . . .   603 GALLERY REVIS V 44
        UNDER THE TROPIC SHADE, GREW ROUND AND SLOW, . . .   610 STATUES   18
        GREW IN PURE MIND, BUT OUT OF WHAT BEGAN? . . . .   630 CIRCUS ANIMALS   34
        ALONG THE SEA: AND MANY A MAN GREW HUSHED . . . .   693 MOSADA 1   86
        SO LITTLE. AS THE MONTHS PASSED BY WE GREW . . . .   713 FERENCZ RENYI   93
        AND THEN HIS HEART GREW WELL-NIGH DEAD . . . . .   730 PRIEST FAIRY   59
        THEY GREW SO VERY STILL, I WIS . . . .   730 PRIEST FAIRY   66
        AND THEREON GREW A TENDER ROOT, ...   743 DANAAN QUICK   13
        AND THEREON GREW A TENDER STEM, ...   743 DANAAN QUICK   14
        AND THEREON GREW THE RUDDY FRUIT . . . .   743 DANAAN QUICK   15
        BUT YOU GREW WEARY OF HER. WHEN I HOLD . . . . .   749 SHADOW WATER A   53
        I GREW AS OLD AS TIME, AND SHE GROWS YOUNG . . . .   761 SHADOW WATER A   259

GREY   SEE STONE-GREY DOVE-GREY MOUSE-GREY ASH-GREY
        OR THE GREY WANDERING OSPREY SORROW." . . . . .   20 OISIN 1   303
        OR THE WILD GREY OSPREY SORROW," . . . .   20 OISIN 1   V 303
        NOR THE GREY WANDERING OSPREY SORROW." . . . . .   21 OISIN 1   319
        OR THE WILD GREY OSPREY SORROW." . . . .   21 OISIN 1   V 319
        NOR THE GREY WANDERING OSPREY SORROW." . . . . .   23 OISIN 1   342
        OR FEAR THE WILD GREY OSPREY SORROW." . . . . . .   23 OISIN 1   V 342
        AND THE LONG GREY GRASSES, WHOSE TENDEREST TOUCHES . .   27 OISIN 1   V 415B
        SCARCE LEFT A WHITENING FEATHER, GREY AND SERE: . . .   34 OISIN 2   V 76A
        GREY IN THE MIDST LIKE A SMALL RIVULET'S FLOW, . . .   37 OISIN 2   V 117
        IT DIED AFAR. GREY SLEET THOSE TOWERS HID . . . . .   46 OISIN 2   V 245
        . . . THE SEA'S EDGE BARREN AND GREY, ...   48 OISIN 3   13
        GREY SAND ON THE GREEN OF THE GRASSES AND OVER THE DRIPPING   48 OISIN 3   14
           TREES,
        GREY SANDS ON THE GREEN OF THE GRASSES AND OVER THE   48 OISIN 3   V   14
           DRIPPING TREES,
        . . . WHERE ALL IS BARREN AND GREY, ...   56 OISIN 3   141
        GREY SAND ON THE GREEN OF THE GRASSES AND OVER THE DRIPPING   57 OISIN 3   142
           TREES,
        GREY SANDS ON THE GREEN OF THE GRASSES AND OVER THE   57 OISIN 3   V 142
           DRIPPING TREES,
        GREY TRUTH IS NOW HER PAINTED TOY: . . . .   65 HAPPY SHEPHERD   4
        THE SUN HAS LAID HIS CHIN ON THE GREY WOOD, ...   72 ANASHU VIJAYA   24
        THE SUN HATH LAID HIS CHIN ON THE GREY WOOD, ...   72 ANASHU VIJAYA V 24
        THE DAUGHTER OF THE GREY OLD WOOD-CUTTER, ...   74 ANASHU VIJAYA V 63
        THE GREY WOLF KNOWS ME: BY ONE EAR . . . . . .   84 MAD KING GOLL   45
        THE DIM GREY SANDS WITH LIGHT, ...   87 STOLEN CHILD   14
        THE DRUID, GREY, WOOD-NURTURED, QUIET-EYED, ...   101 ROSE UPON ROOD   4
        THE DRUID, GREY, WOOD NURTURED, QUIET EYED, ...   101 ROSE UPON ROOD V   4
        A THIN GREY MAN HALF LOST IN GATHERING NIGHT. . . .   102 FERGUS DRUID   7
        A THIN, GREY MAN, HALF-LOST IN GATHERING NIGHT. . . .   102 FERGUS DRUID   V   7
        LOOK ON MY THIN GREY HAIR AND HOLLOW CHEEKS . . . .   103 FERGUS DRUID   23
        AND THE GREY TIDE, THE RED BRANCH MULTITUDE . . . .   108 CUCHULAIN SEA V 38B
        AND SHE, TO WIN HIM, HIS GREY HAIR CARESSED: . . . .   110 CUCHULAIN SEA   73
        AND WAGE GOD'S BATTLES IN THE LONG GREY SHIP'S. . . .   114 ROSE OF BATTLE   20
        "FROM THE GREY SHIPS AND BATTLES NEVER WON. . . . . .   114 ROSE OF BATTLE V   8
        MADE YOU OF US, AND OF THE DIM GREY SEA. . . . . .   115 ROSE OF BATTLE   30
        WHILE I STAND ON THE ROADWAY, OR ON THE PAVEMENTS GREY,   117 ISLE INNISFREE   11
        WHILE I STAND ON THE ROADWAY, OR ON THE PAVEMENT GREY, . .   117 ISLE INNISFREE V 11
        WHEN YOU ARE OLD AND GREY AND FULL OF SLEEP, ...   120 YOU ARE OLD   1
        A LUG-WORM WITH ITS GREY AND MUDDY MOUTH . . . . .   127 DREAM OF FAERY   18

	PAGE	TITLE		LINE

GREY   (CONTINUED)
LAUGH, HEART, AGAIN IN THE GREY TWILIGHT, ... 147 INTO TWILIGHT   3
DEW EVER SHINING AND TWILIGHT GREY; . . . . 148 INTO TWILIGHT   6
AND LOVE IS LESS KIND THAN THE GREY TWILIGHT, ... 148 INTO TWILIGHT   15
WHERE SUCH GREY CLOUDS OF INCENSE ROSE . . . . 156 FORGOT BEAUTY   13
THE GREY CAIRN ON THE HILL, WHEN DAY SINKS DROWNED IN DEW, 161 BLACK PIG   6
BY A GREY SHORE WHERE THE WIND NEVER BLEW, ... 170 SECRET ROSE   14
NOR THE GREY RUSH WHEN THE WIND IS HIGH . . . . 189 BAILE AILLINN   2
NOR THE GREY RUSH WHEN WIND IS HIGH . . . . 189 BAILE AILLINN   V   2
IN THE GREY REEDS THAT NIGHT AND MORN . . . . 190 BAILE AILLINN   42
BUT THE GREY RUSH UNDER THE WIND . . . . 192 BAILE AILLINN   88
AND THE GREY BIRD WITH CROOKED BILL . . . . 192 BAILE AILLINN   89
"YOUR WELL-BELOVED'S HAIR HAS THREADS OF GREY, ... 199 FOLLY COMFORT   V   2
"YOUR WELL BELOVED'S HAIR HAS A THREAD OF GREY, . . . 199 FOLLY COMFORT   V   2
"YOUR WELL BELOVED'S HAIR HAS THREADS OF GREY, ... 199 FOLLY COMFORT   V   2
FOR THE GREY WINDS ARE BLOWING UP, OUT OF THE CLINGING   207 HANRAHANS SONG V   12
    SEAS!
LIKE A GREY GULL UPON THE BREAST OF EACH. . . . . . . 223 SHADOW WATER B   24
AND THOUGH THEY'RE BUT THE COLOUR OF GREY ASH, ... 247 SHADOW WATER B   528
TO CRY ALOUD TO THE GREY BIRDS, AND DREAMS, ... 252 SHADOW WATER B   618
AND NOW, BEING GREY, ... 255 WOMAN HOMER   9
THE GREY ROCK . . . . 270 GREY ROCK   T
THE GREY ROCK AND THE WINDY LIGHT? . . . . 275 GREY ROCK   111
THE GREY WING UPON EVERY TIDE! . . . . 290 SEPTEMBER 1913   18
WHEN GREY GULLS FLIT ABOUT INSTEAD OF MEN, ... 292 TO A SHADE   6
WHEN GREY GULLS FLY ABOUT INSTEAD OF MEN, ... 292 TO A SHADE   V   6
OF GREY STONES AND A ROCKY LEDGE . . . . 302 HOUR DAWN   12
WHAT MADE US DREAM THAT HE COULD COMB GREY HAIR? . . . 327 ROBERT GREGORY   88
UPON A GREY OLD BATTERED TOMBSTONE . . . . 331 ROUND TOWER   7
UPON THE GREY OLD BATTERED TOMBSTONE . . . . 331 ROUND TOWER   V   7
TO A GREY PLACE ON A HILL . . . . 347 FISHERMAN   3
IN GREY CONNEMARA CLOTHES . . . . 347 FISHERMAN   4
AND GREY CONNEMARA CLOTH, ... 348 FISHERMAN   30
THERE IS GREY IN YOUR HAIR. . . . . 355 BROKEN DREAMS   1
IN THE GREY STONE TOMB HE MADE. . . . . 360 ALF POLLEXFEN   5
ON THE GREY SAND BESIDE THE SHALLOW STREAM . . . . . 367 EGO DOMINUS   1
ON THE GREY ROCK OF CASHEL THE MIND'S EYE . . . . . . 382 VISION ROBART   1
ON THE GREY ROCK OF CASHEL I SUDDENLY SAW . . . . . . 383 VISION ROBART   17
FROM COUNTER OR DESK AMONG GREY . . . . 392 EASTER 1916   3
A GREY GULL LOST ITS FEAR AND FLEW . . . . 397 POLIT PRISONER   3
WHILE ON THAT OLD GREY STONE I SAT . . . . 406 IN TIME OF WAR   2
A GREY STONE FIREPLACE WITH AN OPEN HEARTH, ... 419 MY HOUSE   12
A GREY STONE FIRE-PLACE WITH AN OPEN HEARTH, ... 419 MY HOUSE   V   12
AND THE GREAT GREY LYNX'S SKIN! IN SOOTH, METHINKS . . 650 ISLE STAT I 1   151
THAT I MYSELF COULD SHOOT A GREAT GREY LYNX . . . . . 650 ISLE STAT I 1   152
THE POPLARS GAZE ACROSS THE WATERS GREY, ... 653 ISLE STAT I 2   34
I COULD GAZE, GAZE UPON THINE EYES' CLEAR GREY; . . . 671 ISLE STAT II 3   147
I COULD GAZE, GAZE UPON THINE EYES OF GREY; . . . . . 671 ISLE STAT II 3 V   147
BUT ART THOU HAPPY? THOSE GREY EYES OF THINE . . . . 672 ISLE STAT II 3   151
AND WHEREFORE, THEN, SHOULD THY GREY EYES . . . . . . 686 LIFE   7
IN HIS OWN HOUSE OR 'MONG THE MERCHANTS GREY, ... 693 MOSADA 1   87
STANDS EACH GREY AND SILENT PHANTOM ON THE SAME REGARDLESS 719 PHANTOM SHIP   25
    SPOT--
JOYS AND FEARS IN THEIR GREY FACES THAT THE LIVE EARTH   719 PHANTOM SHIP   26
  - KNOWETH NOT!
GREY HAIRS AND CRUTCHES, CRUTCHES AND GREY HAIRS, . . . 721 WITCH VIVIEN   20
GREY HAIRS AND CRUTCHES, CRUTCHES AND GREY HAIRS, . . . 721 WITCH VIVIEN   20
A GREY PROFESSOR PASSING CRIED, ... 725 LEGEND   9
FLED FROM HIS BROW WHERE THE HAIR WAS GREY; . . . . . 728 PRIEST FAIRY   10
HE THOUGHT WISE THINGS AS HIS GREY HEAD NODDED. . . . 728 PRIEST FAIRY   12
HE DREW FROM HIS CAP A FEATHER GREY, ... 729 PRIEST FAIRY   29
WHERE LONG GREY GRASSES BOW AND BEND, ... 736 SUMMER EVENING   6
LIKE A GREY OWL MEN HARRY OUT . . . . 740 EARL PAUL   23
AND MURMURED! "O LONG GREY CLOAK, ... 744 GLOVE CLOAK   11
THEY ARE CHANGED AND AS GREY BIRDS FLY OUT TO SEA, . . 750 SHADOW WATER A   82
OR BE HIS FOOD, I FOLLOW THE GREY WINGS. . . . . . . 751 SHADOW WATER A   101
A GREY BIRD HAS FLOWN BY. HE HAS FLOWN UPWARD. . . . 753 SHADOW WATER A   134
THAT FORGAEL HAS FOLLOWED THE GREY BIRDS ALONE, . . . 767 SHADOW WATER A   402
A HIGH, GREY CAIRN. WHAT MORE IS TO BE SAID? . . . . 778 SONG DEIRDRE 3   5
AT THE GREY ROUND OF THE HILL . . . . 782 GREY ROUND   1
GREY-EYED
THE GREAT GREY-EYED ATHENE STARES THEREON. . . . . . 447 COLONUS PRAISE   16
GREY-GREEN
A GREY-GREEN CUP OF JADE, ... 781 MY HEART BEAT   15
GREY-HAIRED
A GREY-HAIRED YOUTH, WHOSE CHEEKS HAD NEVER FOUND, . . 687 TWO TITANS   7
GREY-LEAVED
EVEN THE GREY-LEAVED OLIVE-TREE . . . . 446 COLONUS PRAISE   12
EVEN THE GREY-LEAVED OLIVE TREE . . . . 446 COLONUS PRAISE V   12
GLITTERING AMONG GREY-LEAVED OLIVE-TREES, ... 447 COLONUS PRAISE   21
GLITTERING AMONG GREY-LEAVED OLIVE TREES, ... 447 COLONUS PRAISE V   21
GREYNESS
AND DRIFTING GREYNESS, WHILE THIS MONOTONE, ... 45 OISIN 2   232
AND DRIFTING GREYNESS. CAME THIS MONOTONE . . . . . 45 OISIN 2   V 232
GRIDDLE
IS DEAD. THE BOY THAT BRINGS MY GRIDDLE CAKE . . . . 339 SHEP GOATHERD V   20
GRIDDLE-CAKE
IS DEAD. THE BOY THAT BRINGS MY GRIDDLE-CAKE . . . . 339 SHEP GOATHERD   20
GRIEF
IN GRIEF SWAYED TO AND FRO. . . . . 133 FR GILLIGAN   36
THAT I WOULD LOOK UPON FOR EVER? MY GRIEF! . . . . . 244 SHADOW WATER B   462

345

		PAGE	TITLE		LINE
GRIEF (CONTINUED)					
HOW DOES SHE BEAR HER GRIEF? THERE IS NOT A SHEPHERD	• •	340	SHEP GOATHERD		28
SOME MEDICABLE HERB TO MAKE OUR GRIEF	• • • • • •	342	SHEP GOATHERD		86
AND THINKING OF THAT FIT OF GRIEF OR RAGE	• • • • •	443	SCHOOL CHILDR		17
MAY KNOW NOT WHAT HE KNOWS, BUT KNOWS NOT GRIEF.	• •	500	VACILLATION		18
WITH LOOSENED HAIR OR FOREHEADS GRIEF DISTRAUGHT,	• •	537	HER VISION	V	18
NAY, GRIEF IN FEEDING ON OLD GRIEF GROWS LESS.	• • •	659	ISLE STAT II 1		19
NAY, GRIEF IN FEEDING ON OLD GRIEF GROWS LESS.	• • •	659	ISLE STAT II 1		19
GRIEF NEEDS MUCH FEEDING THEN. OF HIM I SWEAR	• • •	659	ISLE STAT II 1		20
OLD MISER HOARDS OF GRIEF TO TELL AND TELL!	• • • •	661	ISLE STAT II 1		55
THOU HAST AN OVER-NIMBLE TONGUE. THY GRIEF,	• • •	661	ISLE STAT II 1		59
MORE GRIEF IS MINE. NO MAN SHALL EVER STOOP	• • •	661	ISLE STAT II 1		62
BENEATH THE WEIGHT OF GREATER GRIEF THAN I:	• • • •	661	ISLE STAT II 1		63
O'ER GRIEF. THE WORLD DRINKS SORROW FROM THE BEAMS	• •	664	ISLE STAT II 2		46
OF GRIEF. AND IF THEY SAY, "ANTONIO LAUGHED,"	• •	664	ISLE STAT II 2		51
AND NEVER HEARD OF GRIEF OR CARE	• • • • • • •	667	ISLE STAT II 3		21
AH! YOU ARE WEEPING! HERE SHOULD ALL GRIEF CEASE.	• •	672	ISLE STAT II 3		149
IN LIST'NING SILENCE GAZING ON OUR GRIEF	• • • •	702	MOSADA 3		87
GRIEF-DISTRAUGHT					
WITH LOOSENED HAIR OR FOREHEADS GRIEF-DISTRAUGHT,	• •	537	HER VISION		18
GRIEF'S					
TILL SUDDENLY IN GRIEF'S CONTAGION CAUGHT,	• • • •	537	HER VISION		22
SAY THEN,--"A POPINJAY BEFORE GRIEF'S SHAFT	• • •	664	ISLE STAT II 2		52
GRIEFS					
FOR LONG THE BURTHEN OF THEIR TALKING GRIEFS.	• • •	693	MOSADA 1		71
SHE SMILES--IS HAPPY WITH HER WANDERING GRIEFS.	• •	702	MOSADA 3		95
GRIEVE					
AND HE BEGAN TO GRIEVE.	• • • • • • • •	132	FR GILLIGAN		8
TO KNOW THE MOUNTAIN AND THE VALLEY GRIEVE	• • •	343	SHEP GOATHERD	V	117
AND HEAVEN, AND HOLINESS. LET'S TALK AND GRIEVE.	• •	702	MOSADA 3		84
GRIEVE NOT, FOR GOMEZ KNEELS BESIDE THEE--GOMEZ,	• •	702	MOSADA 3		90
GRIEVE NOT, FOR VALLENCE KNEELS BESIDE THEE--VALLENCE,	• •	702	MOSADA 3	V	90
GRIEVED					
TO KNOW THE MOUNTAIN AND THE VALLEY HAVE GRIEVED	• • •	343	SHEP GOATHERD		117
GRIEVES					
DRIVEN BY A STORM THAT EVER GRIEVES.	• • • • • •	135	TWO TREES	V	28
GRIEVING					
A QUENCHLESS GRIEVING OF LOVE MELODY.	• • • • • •	645	ISLE STAT I 1		21
GRIEVOUS					
OF GRIEVOUS TIME ON HIS OLD CRUTCHES,	• • • • •	23	OISIN 1	V	341B
EQUAL TO GOOD OR GRIEVOUS CHANCE!	• • • • • • •	24	OISIN 1		372
GRIFFITH					
GUARDED: GRIFFITH STARING IN HYSTERICAL PRIDE:	• • •	601	GALLERY REVIS		4
GRIMALKIN					
GRIMALKIN CRAWLS TO BUDDHA'S EMPTINESS.	• • • • •	611	STATUES		24
GRINDING					
AN OLD SLAVE GRINDING AT A HEAVY QUERN,	• • • •	104	FERGUS DRUID		35
GRIP					
NOTHING BUT GRIP OF CLAW, AND THE EYE'S COMPLACENCY,	• •	427	PHANTOM HATRED		31
GRIPPED					
HER HANDS ON EITHER SIDE HAD GRIPPED THE BENCH,	• • •	279	TWO KINGS		63
HANDS GRIPPED IN HANDS, TOES CLOSE TOGETHER,	• • • •	332	ROUND TOWER		21
GRIPS					
WHO GRIPS HIS LONG SPEAR SO TO PUSH	• • • • • •	385	ROBARTES DANCE		3
GRISLY					
• • WHEN, ROLLED IN A GRISLY PEACE,	• • • • • •	47	OISIN 3		9
GROAN					
AND WITH A GROAN, AS IF THE MORTAL BREATH	• • • •	185	QUEEN MAEVE		103
HEARING HIM GROAN AND STRETCH	• • • • • • •	319	DOLLS		13
TO SHUFFLE, GRUNT AND GROAN,	• • • • • • • •	599	STONE CROSS		20
GROANED					
HEARING THE FAR-OFF SINGING GUILE, AND GROANED,	• • • •	693	MOSADA 1		88
HEARING THE FAR OFF SINGING GUILE AND GROANED,	• • •	693	MOSADA 1	V	88
GROOM SEE BRIDE-GROOM					
GROOMED SEE WELL-GROOMED					
GROPE					
WE GROPE, AND GROPE IN VAIN,	• • • • • • • •	487	CRAZED MOON		5
WE GROPE, AND GROPE IN VAIN,	• • • • • • • • •	487	CRAZED MOON		5
OR GROPE WITH A DIRTY HAND.	• • • • • • • •	599	SPIRIT MEDIUM		8
OR GROPE WITH A DIRTY HAND.	• • • • • • • •	600	SPIRIT MEDIUM		16
OR GROPE WITH A DIRTY HAND.	• • • • • • • •	600	SPIRIT MEDIUM		24
GROPED					
I GROPED MY WAY FROM BEECH TO HAZEL WOOD,	• • • •	283	TWO KINGS		139
I GROPED MY WAY THROUGH BOUGHS, AND OVER ROOTS,	• • •	283	TWO KINGS	V	139
GROSS					
WHILE OUR GROSS PALATES DRINK FROM THE WHOLE WINE,	• •	471	ALL SOUL NIGHT		10
GROUND					
THE FENIANS ON THE HUMAN GROUND	• • • • • • •	10	OISIN 1	V	114C
LONG SIGHS AROSE IN OUR SPIRITS, BENEATH US BUBBLED THE GROUND.		48	OISIN 3		20
• • FLUNG LOOSELY ALONG THE DIM GROUND:	• • • •	50	OISIN 3		45
IN A REVERIE FORGETFUL OF ALL THINGS, OVER THE BUBBLING GROUND.		56	OISIN 3		140
IN REVERIE FORGETFUL OF ALL THINGS, OVER THE BUBBLING GROUND.		56	OISIN 3	V	140
BURIED UNDER THE SLEEPY GROUND,	• • • • • • •	67	HAPPY SHEPHERD		48
(WHO'S BURIED IN THE SLEEPY GROUND),	• • • • •	67	HAPPY SHEPHERD	V	48
OR DO YOU LONG FOR THE DIM SLEEPY GROUND,	• • • •	109	CUCHULAIN SEA		60
UNDER THE DOCK-LEAVES IN THE GROUND,	• • • • •	176	BELOVED DEAD		12
THAT HAVE ONE SHADOW ON THE GROUND:	• • • • •	195	BAILE AILLINN		154
WHO'S BURROWING SOMEWHERE IN THE GROUND,	• • • •	272	GREY ROCK		33

346

GROUND   (CONTINUED)

		PAGE	TITLE	LINE
THAT HAD MADE PRINTS UPON THE GROUND,		274	GREY ROCK	79
SHE CAST HERSELF UPON THE GROUND		275	GREY ROCK	107
TO WHERE SHE MOANED UPON THE GROUND,		275	GREY ROCK	119
THEREON SHE CAST HERSELF UPON THE GROUND,		275	GREY ROCK V	107
AND THE GROUND IVY'S BLUER LIGHT, A STAG		277	TWO KINGS V	6
I CHOSE THIS BURROW UNDER GROUND.		305	HOUR DAWN	73
THE WATER-HEN MUST CHANGE HER GROUND;		326	ROBERT GREGORY	55
THE WATERHEN MUST CHANGE HER GROUND;		326	ROBERT GREGORY V	55
OUR SHADOWS ON THE GROUND		333	SOLOMON SHEBA	14
UNLESS A PETAL HIT THE GROUND,		389	SOLOMON WITCH	40
AN ACRE OF STONY GROUND,		419	MY HOUSE	3
IN THE MAD ABSTRACT DARK AND GROUND IT GRAIN BY GRAIN		442	BLACK CENTAUR	8
IMMORTAL LADIES TREAD THE GROUND		446	COLONUS PRAISE	6
THERE, ON BLOOD-SATURATED GROUND, HAVE STOOD		482	BLOOD AND MOON	35
THERE, ON BLOOD SATURATED GROUND, HAVE STOOD		482	BLOOD AND MOON V	35
AND DEDICATE--EYES BENT UPON THE GROUND,		489	COOLE PARK 29	29
I--LOVE'S SKEIN UPON THE GROUND,		511	JANE AND JACK	9
ALL HAPPINESS IN ITS OWN CAUSE OR GROUND.		557	RIBH ECSTASY	4
NO PROUDER TROD THE GROUND,		587	PARNELLITES	22
AND WERE THE LAST TO CHOOSE THE SETTLED GROUND,		621	HOUND VOICE	2
TO DIE FOR HER IN AIR OR GROUND.		668	ISLE STAT II 3	52
BEHOLD, I BEND BEFORE THEE TO THE GROUND		683	SEEKER	43
BEHOLD, I BEND BEFORE THEE TO THE GROUND;		684	SEEKER	61
BEHOLD, I BEND BEFORE THEE TO THE GROUND!		684	SEEKER	67
BEHOLD I BOW BEFORE THEE TO THE GROUND!		684	SEEKER V	67
ONE WHOSE FOOTFALL SHAKES THE GROUND.		727	LOVERS QUARREL	32

GROUND-IVY'S
| WITH THE GROUND-IVY'S BLUE, HE SAW A STAG | | 277 | TWO KINGS | 6 |

GROUNDS
| GROUNDS WHERE PLUM AND CABBAGE GREW, | | 577 | WHAT THEN | 13 |

GROUSE
| I GAZED AT HIM LIKE GROUSE UPON A KITE; | | 283 | TWO KINGS | 152 |

GROVE
AND THE SHADOWY HAZEL GROVE		119	PITY OF LOVE	6
IN THE FORBIDDEN SACRED GROVE		389	SOLOMON WITCH	39
OR WINDING THROUGH THE GROVE		530	DELPHIC ORACLE	7
THROUGH JONATHAN SWIFT'S DARK GROVE HE PASSED, AND THERE		543	PARN FUNERAL 2	11

GROW
AFORETIME, AND SHALL NOT GROW SAD		22	OISIN 1 V	340E
I HEARD ONE SAY, "HIS EYES GROW DIM		25	OISIN 1	380
O HAD YOU SEEN BEAUTIFUL NIAMH GROW WHITE AS THE WATERS ARE WHITE,		54	OISIN 3	109
SHE BID ME TAKE LOVE EASY, AS THE LEAVES GROW ON THE TREE;		90	SALLEY GARDENS	3
SHE BID ME TAKE LOVE EASY, AS THE LEAVES GROW ON THE TREES;		90	SALLEY GARDENS V	3
THE SUN UPON ALL THINGS THAT GROW		98	FOXHUNTER	15
GROW SWEET WITH HIS MOOD.		118	CRADLE SONG V	8
GROW GAY WITH HIS MOOD.		118	CRADLE SONG V	8
THINE EYES GROW FULL OF TENDER CARE!		135	TWO TREES	19
THY TENDER EYES GROW ALL UNKIND!		136	TWO TREES	39
"SHE WILL GROW OLD AND DIE, AND SHE HAS WEPT!"		186	QUEEN MAEVE	138
O WHEN WILL YOU GROW WEARY?" THEY HAD VANISHED;		187	QUEEN MAEVE	152
GROW GENTLE WITHOUT SORROWING,		193	BAILE AILLINN	110
GROW GENTLE WITHOUT SORROWINGS;		193	BAILE AILLINN V	110
OR YOU WILL GROW OUT OF FASHION		212	O DO NOT LOVE	11
I WOULD GROW JEALOUS OF THE IVORY ROOF,		246	SHADOW WATER B	501
AND KNITTED MESH TO MESH, WE GROW IMMORTAL;		252	SHADOW WATER B	616
AND KNITTING MESH TO MESH, WE GROW IMMORTAL;		252	SHADOW WATER B V	616
BEFORE WE GROW OLD AND DIE.		261	DRINKING SONG	4
AND THE SWEET LAUGHING EAGLE THOUGHTS THAT GROW		264	HOUSE SHAKEN	5
"AND THERE I'LL GROW RESPECTED AT MY EASE,		300	BEGGAR CRIED	17
TOIL AND GROW RICH,		310	WITCH	1
TILL PRIDE HAD MADE HER EYES GROW BRIGHT,		314	MEMORY YOUTH	10
AND PLEASURE MADE HER CHEEKS GROW RED,		314	MEMORY YOUTH	11
BUT I GROW OLD AMONG DREAMS,		329	MEN IMPROVE	16
THAT SAW THE WICKS GROW YELLOW IN THE DAWN;		352	PEOPLE	18
OR WHEN I GROW EXCITED WITH WINE,		357	DEEP-SWORN VOW	5
GROW RICH, POPULAR AND FULL OF INFLUENCE,		369	EGO DOMINUS	43
AND YET, TWICE BORN, TWICE BURIED, GROW HE MUST,		374	PHASES OF MOON	48
AND ON THE INSTANT WOULD GROW WISE.		385	ROBARTES DANCE	12
BUT WHY SHOULD YOU GROW SUDDENLY AFRAID		390	IMAGE PAST	29
. . . ALL ENTANGLEMENTS OF MANKIND GROW,		459	FROM OEDIPUS	5
AND IF HER EYE SHOULD NOT GROW BRIGHT FOR MINE		464	HARUN RASHID	81
AND I GROW HALF CONTENTED TO BE BLIND!		473	ALL SOUL NIGHT	70
MAKE HUMAN INTERCOURSE GROW LESS AND LESS;		473	ALL SOUL NIGHT	75
HISTORIC NATIONS GROW		547	TO SAME TUNE 3 V	5
MIND'S BREAD GROW SWEET.		554	CHURCH STATE	6
CONDUCT AND WORK GROW COARSE, AND COARSE THE SOUL,		564	GYRES	17
IT CANNOT GROW BY AN INCH OR AN OUNCE.		566	LAPIS LAZULI	24
HE MUST GROW A FAMOUS MAN;		576	WHAT THEN	2
"YOUR LIFE CAN GROW MUCH SWEETER IF YOU WILL		634	CUCHULAIN COMF	12
HEAR ME, AND, SHEPHERD, HEARING ME, GROW DUMB.		646	ISLE STAT I 1	31
HERE GROW THAT SHY, RETIRING SISTERHOOD,		651	ISLE STAT I 2	4
SHALL GROW THY BEAUTY AND THY DREAMLESS TRUTH,		674	ISLE STAT II 3	207
THE WARMTH OF LIFE IS CHILLING, AND THE SHADOWS GROW		675	ISLE STAT II 3	232
QUITE SOON THE CORNFIELD, WHERE THE POPPIES GROW,		699	MOSADA 3	7
ALONG THE CORNFIELD, WHERE THE POPPIES GROW,		699	MOSADA 3 V	7
SO SMALL MAKES ONE GROW WEAK AND TOTTERING!		700	MOSADA 3	35
THEN THE STARS GROW OUT OF HEAVEN WITH THEIR COUNTENANCES FAIR.		719	PHANTOM SHIP	30
HAS BLOSSOMED, AND I GROW AS OLD AS TIME.		756	SHADOW WATER A	179

347

```
                                                           PAGE    TITLE           LINE
GROW   (CONTINUED)
     OR GROW KIND, FOR THEY ANOINT  . . . . . . . . .       776 AGAINST WITCH        21
GROWETH
     GROWETH THE GOBLIN FLOWER OF JOY, HER CARE,  . . . .    653 ISLE STAT I 2       39
GROWING
     THE HARES RUN BY ME GROWING BOLD. . . . . . . .          84 MAD KING GOLL       47
     THE HARE RUNS BY ME GROWING BOLD-- . . . . . . . .       84 MAD KING GOLL   V   47
     AND HARES RUN NEAR ME GROWING BOLD. . . . . . . .        84 MAD KING GOLL   V   47
     BUT ONE SMALL KNOT-GRASS GROWING BY THE POOL . . . .    127 DREAM OF FAERY      29
     BUT ONE SMALL KNOT-GRASS GROWING BY THE RIM . . . .     127 DREAM OF FAERY  V   29
     AH, WORLD-WIDE NATION, ALWAYS GROWING SORROW, . . .     130 BOOK STORIES    V   11
     AH, WORLDWIDE NATION, ALWAYS GROWING SORROW! . . .      130 BOOK STORIES    V   11
     THE HOLY TREE IS GROWING THERE! . . . . . . . . .       134 TWO TREES            2
     ITS TERROR GROWING WILDER AT EVERY FOOT-FALL, . . .     279 TWO KINGS       V  45D
     ITS TERROR GROWING WILDER AT EVERY FOOTFALL . . .       279 TWO KINGS       V  45D
     NOW I AM GROWING OLD, . . . . . . . . . . . .           346 ON WOMAN            28
     AND THAT MERE GROWING OLD, THAT BRINGS . . . .          401 DEMON BEAST         38
     SUFFICE THE AGEING MAN AS ONCE THE GROWING BOY. . .     427 PHANTOM HATRED      40
     AND WHEN WE TALKED OF GROWING UP . . . . . . . .        456 SUMMER SPRING        5
     ENDURE THAT TOIL OF GROWING UP; . . . . . . . .         478 SELF AND SOUL       44
     SCORN THE SORT NOW GROWING UP . . . . . . . .           639 BEN BULBEN          70
     THE DOVES WHOSE GROWING FORMS HE'D WATCHED.  NOT THESE . 710 FERENCZ RENYI      21
     THE DOVES WHOSE GROWING FORM HE'D WATCHED.  NOT THESE .  710 FERENCZ RENYI  V   21
     AND JOY, IN GROWING DEEPER AND MORE DEEP, . . . .       735 QUATRAIN APHOR      27
GROWN
     AND THINGS THAT HAVE GROWN SAD ARE WICKED, . . . .       20 OISIN 1            301
     GROWN DESOLATE, WHISPER AND SIGH TO EACH OTHER; . . .    26 OISIN 1            403
     GROWN DESOLATE, WHISPER AND SIGH TO EACH OTHER. . . .    27 OISIN 1        V   407
     . . . LONG WARLESS, GROWN WHITER THAN CURDS. . . .       49 OISIN 3             36
     . . . LONG-WARLESS, GROWN WHITER THAN CURDS. . . .       49 OISIN 3        V    36
     I SAW HOW THOSE SLUMBERERS, GROWN WEARY, . . . .         50 OISIN 3             54
     . . . GROWN MILD WITH MYSTERIOUS THOUGHT, . . . .        55 OISIN 3            121
     AND THINE OWN SADNESS, WHEREOF STARS, GROWN OLD . . .   101 ROSE UPON ROOD       6
     BUT NOW I HAVE GROWN NOTHING, KNOWING ALL. . . . .      104 FERGUS DRUID        38
     BUT NOW I HAVE GROWN NOTHING, BEING ALL! . . . .        104 FERGUS DRUID   V    38
     "BUT YOU HAVE GROWN TO BE THE TALLER MAN." . . . .      107 CUCHULAIN SEA       27
     BEAUTY GROWN SAD WITH ITS ETERNITY . . . . . .          115 ROSE OF BATTLE      29
     WHEN YOU HAVE GROWN. . . . . . . . . . . . .            118 CRADLE SONG         12
     MY DEAR, WHEN YOU'RE GROWN! . . . . . . . . .           118 CRADLE SONG    V    12
     WHEN, DEAR, YOU HAVE GROWN. . . . . . . . .             118 CRADLE SONG    V    12
     UNTIL THE SAP OF SUMMER HAD GROWN WEARY! . . . .        130 BOOK STORIES        14
     IT HAD GROWN WISE-TONGUED BY THINKING . . . . . .       159 CAP AND BELLS        7
     IT HAD GROWN MOST WISE WITH THINKING . . . . . .        159 CAP AND BELLS  V     7
     AND IT HAD GROWN WISE BY THINKING . . . . . .           159 CAP AND BELLS  V     7
     IT HAD GROWN SWEET-TONGUED BY DREAMING . . . .          160 CAP AND BELLS       17
     BECAUSE THEIR BODIES HAD GROWN OLD. . . . . . .         189 BAILE AILLINN       10
     AS WHEN NEWLY GROWN TO BE A WOMAN. . . . . . .          199 ARROW                4
     WE SAT GROWN QUIET AT THE NAME OF LOVE; . . . .         205 ADAMS CURSE         28
     THAT IT HAD ALL SEEMED HAPPY, AND YET WE'D GROWN . . .  206 ADAMS CURSE         37
     AND YOU HAVE GROWN TO BE A BURNING SOD . . . .          245 SHADOW WATER B     487
     THAT HAS GROWN WEARY OF THE WANDERING DANCE, . . . .    285 TWO KINGS          183
     THAT HAS GROWN WEARY OF THE WHIRLING DANCE, . . .       285 TWO KINGS      V   183
     POOR MEN HAVE GROWN TO BE RICH MEN, . . . . . .         301 RUN PARADISE        15
     AND RICH MEN GROWN TO BE POOR AGAIN, . . . . .          301 RUN PARADISE        16
     AND MANY A DARLING WIT'S GROWN DULL . . . . . .         301 RUN PARADISE        18
     THAT'S GROWN UNEASY NEAR THE DAWN . . . . . . .         303 HOUR DAWN      V    33
     GROWN TIRED OF HIS OWN COMPANY? . . . . . . .           303 HOUR DAWN      V    37
     AND THEN, GROWN WEARY, PRAYED AND CURSED . . . .        307 HOUR DAWN          117
     THEIR HEARTS HAVE NOT GROWN OLD; . . . . . . .          323 SWANS AT COOLE      22
     HAVING GROWN SLUGGISH AND CONTEMPLATIVE. . . . .        325 ROBERT GREGORY      40
     TILL THE YELLOW EYE HAS GROWN MILD, . . . . . .         349 HAWK                 3
     SHE HAS NOT GROWN UNCIVIL . . . . . . . . . .           365 HER RACE             1
     DO NOT BECAUSE THIS DAY I HAVE GROWN SATURNINE . . .    390 UNDER SATURN         1
     SHE SEEMED TO HAVE GROWN CLEAN AND SWEET . . . .        397 POLIT PRISONER      17
     A FIGURE THAT HAS GROWN SO FABULOUS . . . . . .         412 TOWER               77
     THE HEART'S GROWN BRUTAL FROM THE FARE; . . . .         425 STARES NEST         17
     GROWN TIRED OF THEIR SOLITUDE. . . . . . . . .          432 NINETEEN 19    V   105
     IF YOU, THAT HAVE GROWN OLD, WERE THE FIRST DEAD, . .   435 NEW FACES            1
     SEEMED FOR A WHILE TO HAVE GROWN YOUNG AGAIN; . . .     462 HARUN RASHID        36
     AND MAY HAVE GROWN MORE ARROGANT BEING A GHOST. . . .   473 ALL SOUL NIGHT      80
     SO THAT HIS ELEMENTS HAVE GROWN SO FINE . . . .         473 ALL SOUL NIGHT      82
     CRAZY JANE GROWN OLD LOOKS AT THE DANCERS . . . .       514 JANE GROWN OLD       T
     THAT WHEN THEY HAD GROWN LARGE . . . . . . . .          571 THREE BUSHES        60
     "THE WORK IS DONE," GROWN OLD HE THOUGHT. . . . .       577 WHAT THEN           16
     ALL THAT IS NOT ITSELF!  I HAD GROWN WILD . . . .       619 BRONZE HEAD         20
     ON GANGLING STOCKS GROWN GREAT, GREAT STOCKS RUN DRY, . 619 BRONZE HEAD         25
     ALMINTOR, THOU HAST GROWN SO FULL OF RUTH, . . .        652 ISLE STAT I 2       26
     AND STONY-HEARTED; NOW THOU HAST GROWN KIND, . . .      670 ISLE STAT II 3      91
     BUT, FOR A BOY, HOW LONG THINE HAIR HAS GROWN! . . .    670 ISLE STAT II 3     104
     WILD CRIES, GROWN SWEET WITH LULLS AND LINGERINGS LONG. 674 ISLE STAT II 3     222
     THREE TIMES THE ROSES HAVE GROWN LESS AND LESS, . . .   690 MOSADA 1             1
     AND YON FEW STARS GROWN DIM, LIKE EYES OF LOVERS . . .  700 MOSADA 3            33
     'TIS THOU, FOR THEY'VE GROWN BLUE AROUND THE NAILS. . . 700 MOSADA 3            46
     LIKE HAPPY THOUGHTS GROWN SAD IN EVIL DAYS. . . .       703 MOSADA 3           116
     THE SPIRIT OF YOUNG RENYI HAS GROWN OLD. . . . .        710 FERENCZ RENYI       17
     SHE BIDS US FOLLOW HER.  I HAVE GROWN WEARY . . .       758 SHADOW WATER A     218
     IT MAY BE, AND HAVE GROWN WEARY OF LOVE. . . . .        767 SHADOW WATER A     390
GROWS
     THEN SHE SIGHED GENTLY, "IT GROWS LATE. . . . . .         9 OISIN 1            102
     THE RED SUN FALLS AND THE WORLD GROWS DIM." . . . .       9 OISIN 1            105
     THE HARE GROWS OLD AS SHE PLAYS IN THE SUN . . . .       27 OISIN 1            412
```

GROWS   (CONTINUED)
"OLD GROWS THE HARE AS SHE PLAYS IN THE SUN,   28 OISIN 1   V 420
WHILE OUR LOVE GROWS AN INDIAN STAR,   78 INDIAN TO LOVE   13
WHILE GROWS OUR LOVE AN INDIAN STAR,   78 INDIAN TO LOVE V   13
SHE BID ME TAKE LIFE EASY, AS THE GRASS GROWS ON THE WEIRS, 90 SALLEY GARDENS 7
FOR THERE A FATAL IMAGE GROWS   135 TWO TREES   25
WIND AND UNWIND THEIR DANCES WHEN THE LIGHT GROWS COOL 203 WITHER BOUGHS   13
WIND AND UNWIND DANCING WHEN THE LIGHT GROWS COOL 203 WITHER BOUGHS V 13
WHERE PASSION GROWS TO BE A CHANGELESS THING,   231 SHADOW WATER B   213
"NIGHT GROWS UNEASY NEAR THE DAWN   303 HOUR DAWN   33
THAT THE HEART GROWS OLD?   334 SONG   6
THAT THE HEART GROWS OLD?   335 SONG   12
THAT THE HEART GROWS OLD?   335 SONG   18
BUT GROWS MORE GENTLE WHEN HE SPEAKS HER NAME,   340 SHEP GOATHERD   29
"HE GROWS YOUNGER EVERY SECOND   342 SHEP GOATHERD   89
GROWS COMELIER. ELEVEN PASS, AND THEN   374 PHASES OF MOON   44
THE HEART GROWS BRUTAL FROM THE FARE,   425 STARES NEST   V   17
"AND THE NIGHT GROWS ROUGH."   526 AM OF IRELAND   13
THE GREATER GROWS MY LIGHT   559 HE AND SHE   9
WHEN AN OLD MAN'S BLOOD GROWS COLD?   588 OLD WICKED MAN   13
NO MAN GROWS OLD, NO GIRL GROWS COLD,   621 JOHN KINSELLA   31
NO MAN GROWS OLD, NO GIRL GROWS COLD,   621 JOHN KINSELLA   31
WHEN A MAN GROWS OLD HIS JOY   624 APPARITIONS   17
GROWS MORE DEEP DAY AFTER DAY,   624 APPARITIONS   18
AND TILL HIS INTELLECT GROWS SURE,   633 MAN AND ECHO   30
THERE IN THE TOMB THE DARK GROWS BLACKER,   636 BLACK TOWER   27
EVEN THE WISEST MAN GROWS TENSE   638 BEN BULBEN   33
NAY, GRIEF IN FEEDING ON OLD GRIEF GROWS LESS.   659 ISLE STAT II 1   19
I, AS MUSIC THAT GROWS MUTE,   668 ISLE STAT II 3   65
THE FOOT-WORN WAY IS LONG, AND IT GROWS DARK.   702 MOSADA 3   92
THE FOOTWORN WAY IS LONG, AND IT GROWS DARK.   702 MOSADA 3   V   92
THE WORLD GROWS OLD AND PLAYS THE FOOL."   725 LEGEND   12
I GREW AS OLD AS TIME, AND SHE GROWS YOUNG   761 SHADOW WATER A   259
GROWS YOUNG AND A MAN'S HEART GROWS OLD IN A TWINKLING. 761 SHADOW WATER A 263
GROWS YOUNG AND A MAN'S HEART GROWS OLD IN A TWINKLING. 761 SHADOW WATER A 263
IS THIS POOR BODY THAT REDDENS AND GROWS PALE.   764 SHADOW WATER A   341
GRUBS
THE MOTHER BIRDS BRING GRUBS AND FLIES.   424 STARES NEST   3
GRUMBLE
WHEN IT IS OVER, NOR ONE TO GRUMBLE AT US.   225 SHADOW WATER B   67
GRUNT
TO SHUFFLE, GRUNT AND GROAN,   599 STONE CROSS   20
GRUNTING
AND LAY IN THE DARKNESS, GRUNTING, AND TURNING TO HIS REST. 153 CHANGE BELOVED 12
GUAIRE
KING GUAIRE WALKED AMID HIS COURT   295 THREE BEGGARS   8
BUT GUAIRE LAUGHED WITH SECRET THOUGHT,   295 THREE BEGGARS   19
WITH HIS OLD THOUGHTS, KING GUAIRE WENT   296 THREE BEGGARS   26
AND WHEN OLD GUAIRE CAME AND STOOD   297 THREE BEGGARS   54
GUARD
PRAYERS FOR THE LAND. O BRAHMA, GUARD IN SLEEP   75 ANASHU VIJAYA   85
AND THROUGH THAT NEW BLADE'S GUARD THE OLD BLADE BROKE, 110 CUCHULAIN SEA 66
THOSE THAT I GUARD I DO NOT LOVE,   328 IRISH AIRMAN   4
GOD GUARD ME FROM THOSE THOUGHTS MEN THINK   553 PRAYER OLD AGE   1
STAND WE ON GUARD OATH-BOUND!   636 BLACK TOWER   26
GUARDED   SEE DRAGON-GUARDED
GUARDED, GRIFFITH STARING IN HYSTERICAL PRIDE,   601 GALLERY REVIS   4
BEFORE HIM ONE WELL GUARDED, WITH BOUND HANDS,   709 FERENCZ RENYI   10
GUARD-HOUSE
AND HURRIED TO THE GUARD-HOUSE DOOR.   725 LEGEND   16
GUARDIAN
THEY ARE THE FLOWERS' GUARDIAN SPRIGHTS,   666 ISLE STAT II 3   18
GUARDLESS
. . . AND GUARDLESS THE SACRED CAIRN AND THE RATH,   58 OISIN 3   163
GUARDS
GO TO THE GUARDS OF THE HEAVENLY FOLD   141 EVERLAST VOICE   2
GUARDSMEN'S
THE GUARDSMEN'S DROWSY CHARGERS WOULD NOT PRANCE. 429 NINETEEN 19   24
GUARIMOND
IT IS THE SHEPHERD GUARIMOND, WHO LOVETH WELL   661 ISLE STAT II 1   53
YOUNG GUARIMOND HE TELLS THEM O'ER AND O'ER,   661 ISLE STAT II 1   56
GUERDON
A GUERDON OF DEEP-ROOTED PAIN,   668 ISLE STAT II 3   59
SORROW THAT GIVES FOR GUERDON LIBERTY,   686 DRAWING-ROOM   6
SORROW, THAT GIVES FOR GUERDON LIBERTY,   734 QUATRAIN APHOR   6
GUESS
OR ARCHIMEDES' GUESS,   784 WOMANS BEAUTY   12
GUEST
. . . WHEN THERE ENTERS THE STRONGLY ARMED GUEST,   62 OISIN 3   210
IT SPEEDS THE PARTING GUEST.   434 YOUTH AND AGE   4
GUIDE
UPON THE WIND, AND GUIDE MINE ARROW'S COURSE.   657 ISLE STAT I 3   62
GUIDED
THE MAN IS GONE WHO GUIDED YE, UNWEARY,   738 MOURN THEN ON   3
GUIDES
AND HER GUIDES ARE ANGELS SEVEN,   125 CATHLEEN PARA   V   15
THE MOOR-HEN GUIDES UPON THE STREAM,   424 ROAD AT DOOR   12
HE GUIDES YE FROM THE TOMB,   738 MOURN THEN ON   14
GUIDING   SEE SHEEP-GUIDING
ALL CHOICE, AND GIVE TO CHANCE FOR GUIDING CHANCE   656 ISLE STAT I 3   39
FOR GUIDING OF THE GODS. THE SACRED BLOOM   656 ISLE STAT I 3   41

		PAGE	TITLE	LINE

GUIDING   (CONTINUED)
    FICKLE THE GUIDING HIS ARROW SHALL FIND! . . . . . .   657 ISLE STAT I 3   66
GUIDO
    THE MAN THAT LAPO AND THAT GUIDO KNEW? . . . .   368 EGO DOMINUS   26
    BEING MOCKED BY GUIDO FOR HIS LECHEROUS LIFE, ...   369 EGO DOMINUS   33
GUIDOBALDO
    AND GUIDOBALDO, WHEN HE MADE . . . .   287 TO WEALTHY MAN   14
GUILE
    REWORDING IN MELODIOUS GUILE . . . .   66 HAPPY SHEPHERD   39
    REWARDING IN MELODIOUS GUILE . . . .   66 HAPPY SHEPHERD V   39
    IT CHARMED AWAY THE MERCHANT FROM HIS GUILE, ...   129 BOOK STORIES   5
    THE DEMONS, WITH THEIR SUBTLE GUILE, ...   135 TWO TREES   22
    I WILL DISSOLVE AWAY THE FAERIES' GUILE; . . . . . .   677 ISLE STAT II 3.   282
    HEARING THE FAR-OFF SINGING GUILE, AND GROANED, . . .   693 MOSADA 1   88
    HEARING THE FAR OFF SINGING GUILE AND GROANED, . . .   693 MOSADA 1   V   88
GUILT
    FOR GREAT OUR ERROR, GREAT OUR GUILT." . . . . . .   43 OISIN 2   V 208H
    BECAUSE THAT WERE A GUILT AGAINST HER KING, ...   280 TWO KINGS   V 74A
    THEY CONVICTED US OF GUILT; . . . .   476 EVA GORE-BOOTH   31
    NONE SHARED OUR GUILT; NOR DID WE PLAY A PART . . . .   542 PARN FUNERAL 1   22
GUILTY
    TILL JUDGMENT HAS BEEN GIVEN, AND IF GUILTY, ...   280 TWO KINGS   74
GUINEAS
    BEFORE YOU'LL PUT YOUR GUINEAS DOWN, ...   287 TO WEALTHY MAN   5
    BEFORE YOU'VE PUT YOUR GUINEAS DOWN, ...   287 TO WEALTHY MAN V   5
GUINEVERE
    THEREIN ARE MANY QUEENS LIKE BRANWEN AND GUINEVERE; . .   209 UNDER THE MOON   11
GULL
    LIKE A GREY GULL UPON THE BREAST OF EACH. . . . . .   223 SHADOW WATER B   24
    THERE! THERE THEY COME! GULL, GANNET, OR DIVER, . . .   233 SHADOW WATER B   244
    A GREY GULL LOST ITS FEAR AND FLEW . . . .   397 POLIT PRISONER   3
    TO WATCH A WHITE GULL TAKE . . . .   400 DEMON BEAST   24
GULLEON'S
    FROM GULLEON'S PLACE OF PRIDE, ...   171 MAID QUIET   V   4B
GULLS
    WHEN GREY GULLS FLIT ABOUT INSTEAD OF MEN, ...   292 TO A SHADE   6
    WHEN GREY GULLS FLY ABOUT INSTEAD OF MEN, ...   292 TO A SHADE   V   6
GULPH
    INTO A DESPERATE GULPH OF LOVE! . . . .   7 OISIN 1   73
    AND HURLED THEM IN THE GULPH OF SLEEP! . . . . . .   83 MAD KING GOLL   22
GUN
    AND THOUGH HE KEEP A DOG AND A GUN, ...   301 RUN PARADISE   12
    AS THOUGH I'D A GUN . . . .   359 TO A SQUIRREL   4
GUNNEL
    AND DROP HIM FROM THE GUNNEL. I DARE NOT DO IT. . . .   222 SHADOW WATER B   15
GUNSHOT
    AS THOUGH TO DIE BY GUNSHOT WERE . . . .   424 ROAD AT DOOR   4
    GUNSHOT OR A NOOSE, ...   620 JOHN KINSELLA   2
GUSHES
    WHERE THE WANDERING WATER GUSHES . . . .   88 STOLEN CHILD   28
GUSHING
    ALL FLAME-LIKE GUSHING FROM THE HOLLOW STONES, ...   650 ISLE STAT I 1   129
GUST
    I SHALL BE CARRIED IN THE GUST, COMMAND, ...   281 TWO KINGS   101
GUTTER
    THE ABOUNDING GUTTER HAD BEEN HELICON . . . . . .   398 LEADERS CROWD   6
GUTTERS
    "HOW MAY A MORTAL WHOSE LIFE GUTTERS OUT . . . . . .   184 QUEEN MAEVE   85
GYMNASTS'
    AND YONDER IN THE GYMNASTS' GARDEN THRIVES . . . . .   446 COLONUS PRAISE   9
GYPSY
    LIKE SOME LAST COURTIER AT A GYPSY CAMPING-PLACE . . .   314 FALLEN MAJESTY   3
    LIKE SOME LAST COURTIER AT A GYPSY CAMPING PLACE . . .   314 FALLEN MAJESTY V   3
GYRE
    THOUGH I HAD LONG PERNED IN THE GYRE, ...   400 DEMON BEAST   5
    TURNING AND TURNING IN THE WIDENING GYRE . . . . .   401 SECOND COMING   1
    COME FROM THE HOLY FIRE, PERNE IN A GYRE, ...   408 SAIL BYZANTIUM   19
    ON THAT UNFASHIONABLE GYRE AGAIN. . . . .   565 GYRES   24
GYRES
    ALL, ALL THOSE GYRES AND CUBES AND MIDNIGHT THINGS . . .   469 HARUN RASHID   184
    THOSE CONES AND CUBES AND GYRES, THOSE MIDNIGHT THINGS,   469 HARUN RASHID   V 184
    THERE ALL THE GYRES CONVERGE IN ONE, ...   557 THERE   3
    THE GYRES . . . .   564 GYRES   T
    THE GYRES! THE GYRES! OLD ROCKY FACE, LOOK FORTH! . .   564 GYRES   1
    THE GYRES! THE GYRES! OLD ROCKY FACE, LOOK FORTH! . .   564 GYRES   1
    THAT HEAVENS HAD OPENED. GYRES RUN ON! . . . . .   639 BEN BULBEN   62
GYRING
    GYRING, SPIRING TO AND FRO . . . .   135 TWO TREES   15
    NOW GYRING DOWN AND PERNING THERE . . . .   400 DEMON BEAST   26
    THIS WINDING, GYRING, SPIRING TREADMILL OF A STAIR . . .   480 BLOOD AND MOON   17
HA
    THE PHANTOMS COME; HA! HA! THEY COME, THEY COME! . . .   694 MOSADA 1   97
    THE PHANTOMS COME; HA! HA! THEY COME, THEY COME! . . .   694 MOSADA 1   97
    WHAT ROSEATE FINGERS! HA, HA! HA, HA, HA! . . . .   720 WITCH VIVIEN   15
    WHAT ROSEATE FINGERS! HA, HA! HA, HA, HA! . . . .   720 WITCH VIVIEN   15
    WHAT ROSEATE FINGERS! HA, HA! HA, HA, HA! . . . .   720 WITCH VIVIEN   15
    WHAT ROSEATE FINGERS! HA, HA! HA, HA, HA! . . . .   720 WITCH VIVIEN   15
    WHAT ROSEATE FINGERS! HA, HA! HA, HA, HA! . . . .   720 WITCH VIVIEN   15
    WHAT ROSEATE FINGERS! HA, HA! HA, HA, HA! . . . .   720 WITCH VIVIEN   15
    FIVE-SIX. HA, TIME! . . . .   721 WITCH VIVIEN   42
HABILIMENT
    THIS BEGGARLY HABILIMENT-- . . . .   539 MEETING   17

HABIT
    THE ANCIENT HABIT STICKS, ...   431 NINETEEN 19   74
    LIKE MEN WHO LIVE BY HABIT. EVERY DAY . . . .   463 HARUN RASHID   56
    NO PLEASING HABIT ENDS, ...   621 JOHN KINSELLA   30
    PIERCED THROUGH, CHATTERING FROM HABIT IN THE SUN, . .   664 ISLE STAT II 2   53
HABITS
    TO BRIBE OR THREAT: HABITS THAT MADE OLD WRONG . . . .   428 NINETEEN 19   11
HABITUAL
    THE HABITUAL CONTENT OF EACH WITH EACH . . . .   258 KING NO KING   15
HACK
    BASALTIC PILLARS MARRED WITH HEW AND HACK . . . . . .   31 OISIN 2   V   30
HADES
    CAN LIKE THE COCKS OF HADES CROW, ...   498 BYZANTIUM   20
HADES'
    FOR HADES' BOBBIN BOUND IN MUMMY-CLOTH . . . .   497 BYZANTIUM   11
    FOR HADES' BOBBIN BOUND IN MUMMY CLOTH . . . .   497 BYZANTIUM   V   11
HAG
    WHETHER TO MAID OR HAG: . . . .   525 DANCING DAYS   22
HAIL
    HAIL! HAIL, MY ANASHUYA. NO! BE STILL. . . . . . .   71 ANASHU VIJAYA   11
    HAIL! HAIL, MY ANASHUYA. NO! BE STILL. . . . . .   71 ANASHU VIJAYA   11
    HAIL! HAIL, MY ANASHUYA. NAY! BE STILL. . . . . .   71 ANASHU VIJAYA   V   11
    HAIL! HAIL, MY ANASHUYA, NAY! BE STILL. . . . . .   71 ANASHU VIJAYA   V   11
    MIRRORED IN STREAMS THAT NEITHER HAIL NOR RAIN . . . .   184 QUEEN MAEVE   89
    BY RIVERS WHERE NOR RAIN NOR HAIL HAS DIMMED . . . .   184 QUEEN MAEVE   V   87
    MIRRORED IN WATERS THAT NOR HAIL NOR RAIN . . . . .   184 QUEEN MAEVE   V   89
    AND PINCHES AMONG HAIL AND SNOW? . . . .   191 BAILE AILLINN   46
    OF THE FOUL WEATHER, HAIL AND RAIN, ...   424 ROAD AT DOOR   9
    I HAIL THE SUPERHUMAN: . . . .   497 BYZANTIUM   15
    THEIR SHEEP IN ARCADY, NASCHINA, HAIL! . . . . .   649 ISLE STAT I 1   119
    NASCHINA, HAIL! MOST FAIR OF ALL WHO GRAZE . . . . .   649 ISLE STAT I 1   120
    THEIR SHEEP IN ARCADY, NASCHINA, HAIL! . . . . .   649 ISLE STAT I 1   121
    NASCHINA, HAIL! I'D DRIVE THY WOOLLY SHEEP, ...   649 ISLE STAT I 1   122
HAILED
    SHOUTED, AND HAILED HIM! HE HUNG THERE A STAR, ...   36 OISIN 2   107
    SHOUTED AND HAILED HIM. STILL HE HUNG CONTENT, ...   36 OISIN 2   V 107
HAIR   SEE HORSE-HAIR
    THE HORSEMEN WITH THEIR FLOATING HAIR, ...   2 OISIN 1   7
    WERE LOLLING THEIR TONGUES, AND THE SILKEN HAIR . . . .   2 OISIN 1   V   7S
    A CITRON COLOUR GLOOMED IN HER HAIR, ...   3 OISIN 1   24
    AND PEARLY WHITE HIS WELL-GROOMED HAIR. . . . . . .   3 OISIN 1   V 7CC
    HER HAIR WAS OF A CITRON TINCTURE, ...   3 OISIN 1   24
    WHERE ARE YOU WITH YOUR LONG ROUGH HAIR? . . . . .   11 OISIN 1   126
    WHERE ARE YE WITH YOUR LONG ROUGH HAIR? . . . . .   11 OISIN 1   V 126
    WITH QUENCHLESS GAZE AND FLUTTERING HAIR. . . . . .   12 OISIN 1   145
    AND WITH QUENCHLESS EYES AND FLUTTERING HAIR . . . .   12 OISIN 1   V 144
    WOVEN INTO HER HAIR, BEFORE DARK TOWERS . . . . . .   30 OISIN 2   22
    IN NIAM'S HAIR--WHEN ROSE A WORLD OF TOWERS . . . .   30 OISIN 2   V   22
    WOVE IN HER FLOWER-LIKE HAIR, BEFORE DARK TOWERS . . .   30 OISIN 2   V   22
    AND IN THE SHADOW OF MY HAIR LIE HID, ...   33 OISIN 2   66
    SHOUTED. WITH FIRE OF HAIR ABOUT HER SWIRLED, ...   38 OISIN 2   V 134
    AND HUNG WITH SLIME, AND WHISPERING IN HIS HAIR, . . .   43 OISIN 2   216
    HUNG ROUND WITH SLIME, AND WHISPERING IN HIS HAIR, . .   43 OISIN 2   V 216
    CAME NOW THE SLIDING OF TEARS AND SWEEPING OF MIST-COLD   47 OISIN 3   7
        HAIR,
    CAME NOW THE SLIDING OF TEARS AND SWEEPING OF MIST COLD   47 OISIN 3   V   7
        HAIR,
    AND WRAPPING MY FACE IN MY HAIR, ...   59 OISIN 3   177
    WITH MINGLING HAIR, AND PLAY UPON ONE LUTE. . . . .   71 ANASHU VIJAYA   10
    WITH ALL YOUR WHIRLING HAIR, AND DROP MANY AN AZURE TEAR.   73 ANASHU VIJAYA   46
    WITH ALL YOUR WHIRLING HAIR, AND DROP THROUGH SPACE AN   73 ANASHU VIJAYA   V   46
        AZURE TEAR.
    WITH ALL YOUR WHIRLING HAIR, AND DROP TEAR UPON AZURE TEAR.   73 ANASHU VIJAYA   V   46
    WITH ALL OUR WHIRLING HAIR, AND DROP MANY AN AZURE TEAR.   73 ANASHU VIJAYA   V   46
    THEIR HAIR ALONG THE MOUNTAINS ROLLED AND FILLED . .   74 ANASHU VIJAYA   71
    IN BOSOM AND HAIR. "AH, DO NOT MOURN," HE SAID, . . .   80 EPHEMERA   20
    IN BOSOM AND HAIR. THEN HE: "LET US NOT MOURN . . .   80 EPHEMERA   V   20
    ORCHIL SHAKES OUT HER LONG DARK HAIR . . . .   85 MAD KING GOLL   62
    WHOM THE DEVILS HAVE BY THE HAIR, ...   92 FATHER OHART   14
    LOOK ON MY THIN GREY HAIR AND HOLLOW CHEEKS . . . .   103 FERGUS DRUID   23
    AND SAID, CASTING ASIDE HIS DRAGGLED HAIR, ...   105 CUCHULAIN SEA   V   3
    AND SHE, TO WIN HIM, HIS GREY HAIR CARESSED: . . . .   110 CUCHULAIN SEA   73
    WITH BLOWN, SPRAY-DABBLED HAIR GATHER AT HAND. . . . .   114 ROSE OF BATTLE   6
    THE THRONGS WITH BLOWN WET HAIR ARE GATHERING NEAR. . . .   114 ROSE OF BATTLE V   6
    THE LONG HAIR IS ON HER FACE! . . . .   124 CATHLEEN PARA   V   10
    THE LONG HAIR SHADOWS HER FACE: . . . .   124 CATHLEEN PARA   V   10
    REMEMBERING ALL THAT SHAKEN HAIR . . . .   135 TWO TREES   17
    WHEN LOOKING ON THEIR SHAKEN HAIR . . . .   135 TWO TREES   V   17
    CAOILTE TOSSING HIS BURNING HAIR, ...   140 HOSTING SIDHE   3
    OUR CHEEKS ARE PALE, OUR HAIR IS UNBOUND, ...   140 HOSTING SIDHE   7
    CAOILTE TOSSING HIS BURNING HAIR, ...   141 HOSTING SIDHE   15
    AND DREAMED OF THE LONG DIM HAIR . . . .   144 HOST OF AIR   7
    OF HER LONG DIM HAIR. . . . .   145 HOST OF AIR   28
    WERE DROWNED IN HER LONG DIM HAIR. . . . .   145 HOST OF AIR   36
    WITH APPLE BLOSSOM IN HER HAIR . . . .   150 WANDER AENGUS   14
    WITH APPLE-BLOSSOM IN HER HAIR, ...   150 WANDER AENGUS   V   14
    WITH APPLE BLOSSOMS IN HER HAIR, ...   150 WANDER AENGUS   V   14
    THE SHADOWY BLOSSOM OF MY HAIR . . . .   152 HEART OF WOMAN   7
    O HIDING HAIR AND DEWY EYES, ...   152 HEART OF WOMAN   9
    PALE BROWS, STILL HANDS AND DIM HAIR, ...   152 LOSS OF LOVE   1
    PALE BROW, STILL HANDS, AND DIM HAIR, ...   152 LOSS OF LOVE   V   1

```
                                                        PAGE    TITLE            LINE
HAIR   (CONTINUED)
    OVER MY HEART, AND YOUR HAIR FALL OVER MY BREAST,  .  .  .   154  BELOVED PEACE        10
    OVER MY HEART, AND YOUR HAIR FALL ABOUT MY BREAST  .  .  .   154  BELOVED PEACE     V  10
    PASSION-DIMMED EYES AND LONG HEAVY HAIR  .  .  .  .  .  .    155  REPROVE CURLEW        4
    WOVEN BY LADIES IN THEIR HAIR  .  .  .  .  .  .  .  .  .     156  FORGOT BEAUTY        10
    FASTEN YOUR HAIR WITH A GOLDEN PIN,  .  .  .  .  .  .  .     157  BELOVED RHYMES        1
    AND BIND UP YOUR LONG HAIR AND SIGH,  .  .  .  .  .  .  .    158  BELOVED RHYMES        8
    OF A FLUTTER OF FLOWER-LIKE HAIR,  .  .  .  .  .  .  .  .    160  CAP AND BELLS        18
    UNDER A CLOUD OF HER HAIR,  .  .  .  .  .  .  .  .  .  .     160  CAP AND BELLS        26
    ON A FLUTTER OF FLOWER-LIKE HAIR,  .  .  .  .  .  .  .  .    160  CAP AND BELLS     V  18
    AND HER HAIR WAS A FOLDED FLOWER  .  .  .  .  .  .  .  .     161  CAP AND BELLS        35
    CRUMPLE THE ROSE IN YOUR HAIR,  .  .  .  .  .  .  .  .  .    162  ASKS FORGIVE          4
    CRUSH THE ROSE IN YOUR HAIR,  .  .  .  .  .  .  .  .  .  .   162  ASKS FORGIVE      V   4
    WITH YOUR DIM HEAVY HAIR,  .  .  .  .  .  .  .  .  .  .  .   163  ASKS FORGIVE         22
    WITH YOUR DIM SHADOWY HAIR,  .  .  .  .  .  .  .  .  .  .    163  ASKS FORGIVE      V  22
    THEIR HEADS ON YOUR KNEES, AND DROWN THEIR EYES WITH YOUR   163  VALLEY LOVERS         6
       HAIR,
    HALF CLOSE YOUR EYELIDS, LOOSEN YOUR HAIR,  .  .  .  .  .   166  EVIL OF BELOV         1
    WE WILL BEND DOWN AND LOOSEN OUR HAIR OVER YOU,  .  .  .    172  TRAV PASSION          6
    BUT KNOW YOUR HAIR WAS BOUND AND WOUND  .  .  .  .  .  .     176  BELOVED DEAD          9
    BUT KNOW YOUR HAIR WAS BOUND AND BOUND  .  .  .  .  .  .     176  BELOVED DEAD      V   9
    MAY NOT LIE ON THE BREAST NOR HIS LIPS ON THE HAIR  .  .    177  PAST GREATNESS        9
    WOULD NOT LIE ON THE BREAST, OR HIS LIPS ON THE HAIR,  .    177  PAST GREATNESS    V   9
    HE HAD RAGGED LONG GRASS-COLOURED HAIR,  .  .  .  .  .  .    190  BAILE AILLINN        26
    HE HAD RAGGED, LONG GRASS-YELLOW HAIR,  .  .  .  .  .  .     190  BAILE AILLINN     V  26
    TO STIR THEIR COVERLET AND THEIR HAIR,  .  .  .  .  .  .     197  BAILE AILLINN       186
    "YOUR WELL-BELOVED'S HAIR HAS THREADS OF GREY,  .  .  .     199  FOLLY COMFORT         2
    "YOUR WELL-BELOVED'S HAIR HAS A THREAD OF GREY,  .  .  .    199  FOLLY COMFORT     V   2
    "YOUR WELL BELOVED'S HAIR HAS THREADS OF GREY,  .  .  .     199  FOLLY COMFORT     V   2
    O MY SHARE OF THE WORLD, O YELLOW HAIR!  .  .  .  .  .  .    211  RAGGED WOOD          11
    SWEET WITH ALL MUSIC, OUT OF HIS LONG HAIR,  .  .  .  .     219  HARP OF AENGUS        8
    IT WAS IN ALL HIS BATTLES.  I WILL SPREAD MY HAIR,  .  .    242  SHADOW WATER B      413
    BEND LOWER, THAT I MAY COVER YOU WITH MY HAIR,  .  .  .     251  SHADOW WATER B      613
    I AM LOOPED IN THE LOOPS OF HER HAIR.  .  .  .  .  .  .     268  BROWN PENNY           8
    YOU'D CRY, "SOME WOMAN'S YELLOW HAIR,  .  .  .  .  .  .  .   290  SEPTEMBER 1913       28
    WHILE HE'D RUMMAGED RAGS AND HAIR,  .  .  .  .  .  .  .  .   299  THREE HERMITS        29
    THE GOLD INTO MY HAIR,  .  .  .  .  .  .  .  .  .  .  .  .   309  PLAYER QUEEN         18
    THE GOLD UPON MY HAIR,  .  .  .  .  .  .  .  .  .  .  .  .   309  PLAYER QUEEN      V  18
    AND TUMBLE OUT YOUR HAIR.  .  .  .  .  .  .  .  .  .  .  .   312  CHILD DANCING         4
    WHAT MADE US DREAM THAT HE COULD COMB GREY HAIR?  .  .  .   327  ROBERT GREGORY       88
    HAIR SPREAD ON THE WIND THEY MADE;  .  .  .  .  .  .  .  .   332  ROUND TOWER          22
    THERE IS GREY IN YOUR HAIR.  .  .  .  .  .  .  .  .  .  .    355  BROKEN DREAMS         1
    AS IF THE HAIR STOOD UP ON MY HEAD.  .  .  .  .  .  .  .     358  PRESENCES             2
    SHE LIES, HER LOVELY PITEOUS HEAD AMID DULL RED HAIR  .     362  HER COURTESY          2
    OF DULL RED HAIR WAS FLOWING  .  .  .  .  .  .  .  .  .  .   363  DOLLS DRAWINGS        6
    ATHENE TAKES ACHILLES BY THE HAIR,  .  .  .  .  .  .  .  .   374  PHASES OF MOON       45
    GO PLUCK ATHENE BY THE HAIR!  .  .  .  .  .  .  .  .  .  .   386  ROBARTES DANCE       19
    AMONG THE STARRY EDDIES OF HER HAIR  .  .  .  .  .  .  .     390  IMAGE PAST           27
    THAT HER HAIR STREAMS UPON THE WIND,  .  .  .  .  .  .  .    390  IMAGE PAST           40
    AND HAD THAT COLOUR UPON CHEEK OR HAIR,  .  .  .  .  .  .    444  SCHOOL CHILDR        22
    THE HEAVENLY CIRCUIT; BERENICE'S HAIR;  .  .  .  .  .  .     483  VERONIC NAPKIN        1
    AND NOT YOUR YELLOW HAIR."  .  .  .  .  .  .  .  .  .  .     492  ANNE GREGORY          6
    AND NOT MY YELLOW HAIR."  .  .  .  .  .  .  .  .  .  .  .    492  ANNE GREGORY         12
    AND NOT YOUR YELLOW HAIR."  .  .  .  .  .  .  .  .  .  .     492  ANNE GREGORY         18
    AND BIDS MY HAIR STAND UP?  .  .  .  .  .  .  .  .  .  .     499  MOTHER OF GOD        15
    AND MAKES MY HAIR STAND UP?  .  .  .  .  .  .  .  .  .  .    499  MOTHER OF GOD     V  15
    BUT WHEN HE WOUND HER COAL-BLACK HAIR  .  .  .  .  .  .  .   514  JANE GROWN OLD        3
    BERENICE'S BURNING HAIR.  .  .  .  .  .  .  .  .  .  .  .    519  HER DREAM             8
    A BARGAIN WITH THAT HAIR  .  .  .  .  .  .  .  .  .  .  .    520  HIS BARGAIN          11
    THAT HIS HAIR IS BEAUTIFUL,  .  .  .  .  .  .  .  .  .  .    531  FATHER CHILD          7
    ENTANGLED IN MY HAIR  .  .  .  .  .  .  .  .  .  .  .  .     532  FIRST CONFESS         2
    WITH LOOSENED HAIR OR FOREHEADS GRIEF-DISTRAUGHT,  .  .     537  HER VISION           18
    WITH LOOSENED HAIR OR FOREHEADS GRIEF DISTRAUGHT,  .  .     537  HER VISION        V  18
    BECAUSE HE HAD FEATHERS INSTEAD OF HAIR.  .  .  .  .  .     550  SEVERED HEAD         20
    OH, MORE DARK THY GLEAMING HAIR IS  .  .  .  .  .  .  .     647  ISLE STAT I 1        51
    WITH STREAMING HAIR AS WANDERING LIGHTS  .  .  .  .  .  .   667  ISLE STAT II 3       19
    E'EN THEN, BEFORE HER SHEPHERD HAIR  .  .  .  .  .  .  .     668  ISLE STAT II 3       54
    BUT, FOR A BOY, HOW LONG THINE HAIR HAS GROWN!  .  .  .     670  ISLE STAT II 3      104
    OVER HER SPOTTED FLESH AND FLYING HAIR  .  .  .  .  .  .     687  TWO TITANS           15
    STREWING UPON THE ROCKS THEIR STEEL-BLUE HAIR,  .  .  .     687  TWO TITANS           30
    HER HEAD CAST BACKWARD IN HER UNLOOSED HAIR,  .  .  .  .    701  MOSADA 3             67
    GOLD UNTO GOLD, A GLEAM IN ITS LONG HAIR,  .  .  .  .  .    720  WITCH VIVIEN          3
    MY FINGERS FEEL HIS AMBER HAIR.  .  .  .  .  .  .  .  .      723  GIRLS SONG A          8
    FLED FROM HIS BROW WHERE THE HAIR WAS GREY,  .  .  .  .     728  PRIEST FAIRY         10
    AND HIS HAIR WAS AS YELLOW AS WAVING WHEAT.  .  .  .  .     729  PRIEST FAIRY         26
    BRUSHING BACK HIS YELLOW HAIR!  .  .  .  .  .  .  .  .  .    729  PRIEST FAIRY         38
    AND HIS HAIR WAS AS DARK AS A PLOVER'S EYE.  .  .  .  .     729  PRIEST FAIRY         46
    BOWS THE BEDOUIN'S WHITENING HAIR--  .  .  .  .  .  .  .     733  STREET DANCERS       45
    THEIR HAIR MINGLES ON SOME STRINGED INSTRUMENT,  .  .  .    752  SHADOW WATER A      123
    AND A COLD WIND IS BLOWING IN MY HAIR.  .  .  .  .  .  .     761  SHADOW WATER A      277
    I HAVE WET THIS BRAID OF HAIR WITH TEARS WHILE ASLEEP.  .   762  SHADOW WATER A      294
    SWEET WITH ALL MUSIC, OUT OF HIS LONG HAIR,  .  .  .  .     762  SHADOW WATER A      303
    COVER THEIR FACES WITH THEIR HAIR AND WEEP.  .  .  .  .     764  SHADOW WATER A      333
    THAT I WOULD MIX WITH YOURS, AND IN THIS HAIR  .  .  .      765  SHADOW WATER A      351
    AND MINGLING HAIR FALL FROM THE FIERY BOUGHS,  .  .  .      765  SHADOW WATER A      368
    LOOK ON THIS BODY AND THIS HEAVY HAIR!  .  .  .  .  .  .     767  SHADOW WATER A      397
    MY LOVE SHAKES OUT HER HAIR UPON THE STREAMS  .  .  .  .    768  SHADOW WATER A      416
    BEND LOWER, THAT I MAY COVER YOU WITH MY HAIR,  .  .  .     769  SHADOW WATER A      429
    I HIDE YOU WITH MY HAIR, THAT WE MAY GAZE  .  .  .  .  .    769  SHADOW WATER A V    429
HAIR-DYE
    "BUT I CAN GET A HAIR-DYE  .  .  .  .  .  .  .  .  .  .  .   492  ANNE GREGORY          7
```

HAIRED   SEE RED-HAIRED FLOATING-HAIRED WHITE-HAIRED LONG-HAIRED FAIR-HAIRED GREY-HAIRED
HAIRS
      HAIRS SPREAD ON THE WIND THEY MADE: . . . .   332 ROUND TOWER   V   22
      GREY HAIRS AND CRUTCHES, CRUTCHES AND GREY HAIRS, . . . 721 WITCH VIVIEN   20
      GREY HAIRS AND CRUTCHES, CRUTCHES AND GREY HAIRS, . . . 721 WITCH VIVIEN   20
HALCYON'S
      YON ARCHER, HE WHO HATH THE HALCYON'S WING . . . . . . 679 ISLE STAT II 3   316
      AMONG THE BOUGHS, BLUE AS THE HALCYON'S WING, ... 683 SEEKER   38
      WITHIN THE WOODWAYS, BLUE AS THE HALCYON'S WING, . . . 683 SEEKER   V   38
HALE
      TO THE HORN, AND HE BE HALE AND HEARTY. . . . . 243 SHADOW WATER B   447
      WHEN WE HALE MEN LIE STRETCHED IN SLUMBER . . . . . . 636 BLACK TOWER   23
HALF
      OISIN, THOU ART HALF HEATHEN STILL! . . . .   4 OISIN 1   V   31
      WAS SLUMBERING HALF IN THE SEA-WAYS: . . . .   26 OISIN 1   395
      HALF SLUMBERED WITH HIS SAFFRON BLAZE: . . . .   26 OISIN 1   V 395
      WAS SLUMBERING HALF IN THE SEA-WAYS: . . . .   26 OISIN 1   V 395
      ERE HALF THE SWIFT THINGS THAT SHE DREAMT ON WERE DONE, 28 OISIN 1   V 422
      HALF LOST IN VAPOUR, SHADOWS CALLED OUR NAMES, ... 29 OISIN 2   V   3
      FLOATED IN ALL HER SINGING. HALF ENTRANCED . . . . . 30 OISIN 2   V   19
      HALF IN THE UNVESSELLED SEA. WE CLIMBED THE STAIR . . 32 OISIN 2   47
      HALF IN THE UNVESSELLED SEA. WE'D MOUNTED FAR: . . . 32 OISIN 2   V   47
      HALF IN THE UNVESSELLED SEA, WE CLIMBED THE STAIRS . . 32 OISIN 2   V   47
      HALF OPEN HIS EYES WERE, AND HELD ME, ... 51 OISIN 3   65
      HALF WAKENING, WE LIFTED OUR EYELIDS, ... 54 OISIN 3   100
      LATER A SOUND CAME, HALF LOST IN THE SOUND OF A SHORE FAR 57 OISIN 3   155
         AWAY,
      LIE NOW HALF HIDDEN UNDER PENDULOUS LIDS, ... 79 EPHEMERA   V   2
      A THIN GREY MAN HALF LOST IN GATHERING NIGHT. . . . . . 102 FERGUS DRUID   7
      FOR HALF HIS FLOCK WERE IN THEIR BEDS, ... 132 FR GILLIGAN   3
      FOR HALF HIS FLOCK LAY IN THEIR BEDS . . . . 132 FR GILLIGAN   V   3
      ROOTS HALF HIDDEN UNDER SNOWS, ... 135 TWO TREES   27
      AND ROOTS HALF HIDDEN UNDER SNOWS . . . . 135 TWO TREES   V   27
      AND CLAP THEIR HANDS TOGETHER, AND HALF CLOSE THEIR EYES, 146 UNAPPEAS HOST   2
      BELOVED, LET YOUR EYES HALF CLOSE, AND YOUR HEART BEAT . 154 BELOVED PEACE   9
      THRONE OVER THRONE WHERE IN HALF SLEEP, ... 156 FORGOT BEAUTY   22
      WITH HER CLOUD-PALE EYELIDS HALF COVERING HER DIM EYES: 163 VALLEY LOVERS   V   4
      HALF CLOSE YOUR EYELIDS, LOOSEN YOUR HAIR, ... 166 EVIL OF BELOV   1
      TO GATHER THE HALF OF YOUR BLESSEDNESS . . . . 167 BLESSED   7
      "WITH THE SECRETS OF GOD HALF BLIND, ... 168 BLESSED   26
      OF NIGHT AND LIGHT AND THE HALF LIGHT, ... 176 CLOTHS HEAVEN   V   4
      FLICKERING WITH ASH AND HAZEL, BUT HALF SHOWED . . . 180 QUEEN MAEVE   12
      BUT THAT GREAT QUEEN, WHO MORE THAN HALF THE NIGHT . . 180 QUEEN MAEVE   16
      HALF CRAZY WITH THE THOUGHT, SHE TOO HAS WEPT! . . . 186 QUEEN MAEVE   140
      HE HAD HALF A CLOAK TO KEEP HIM DRY, ... 190 BAILE AILLINN   29
      IF ANYBODY HALF AS FAIR . . . . 191 BAILE AILLINN   53
      IS BUT HALF YOURS; HE KNEADED IN THE DOUGH . . . . . . 201 OLD MEMORY   6
      HEAVY LIKE STONE, THEIR WISDOM BEING HALF SILENCE, . . 218 WOODS OF COOLE   26
      OF THE EVER-LIVING HALF SO DANGEROUS . . . . 224 SHADOW WATER B   46
      MORE MIGHTY THAN THE STARS HALF TROUBLED ME, ... 237 SHADOW WATER B   332
      AND I'VE BUT HALF? O NO! AND IF THERE IS, ... 245 SHADOW WATER B   475
      IF THERE BE HALF A HUNDRED MORE, WHAT MATTER? . . . . . 245 SHADOW WATER B   476
      NO, NO, NOR HALF A THOUGHT: BUT DO NOT SPEAK. . . . . 245 SHADOW WATER B   478
      I HALF REMEMBER. IT HAS BEEN IN MY DREAMS. . . . . . 251 SHADOW WATER B   606
      HALF LION, HALF CHILD, IS AT PEACE. . . . . 260 UNWORTH PRAISE   20
      HALF LION, HALF CHILD, IS AT PEACE. . . . . 260 UNWORTH PRAISE   20
      AND HALF THE KINGS, BEFORE SUNDOWN . . . . 273 GREY ROCK   69
      AND HALF HIS KINGS, BEFORE SUNDOWN . . . . 273 GREY ROCK   V   69
      IN THE HALF LIGHT, AND RUNS TO ITS OWN DOOR . . . . . 279 TWO KINGS   V 45C
      BUT IF NOT LIVING, HALF THE WORLD IS LOST." . . . . . 280 TWO KINGS   V   86
      HAD HALF AWAKENED SOME OLD MEMORY-- . . . . 284 TWO KINGS   172
      HAD HALF WAKENED SOME OLD MEMORY, ... 284 TWO KINGS   V 172
      SO SLEPT FOR HALF A YEAR OR SO: . . . . 305 HOUR DAWN   67
      AND SLEPT FOR HALF A YEAR OR SO: . . . . 305 HOUR DAWN   V   67
      EVEN A HALF HOUR'S NOTHINGNESS, ... 305 HOUR DAWN   V   70
      SO PERILOUS THAT HALF THE ASTONISHED MEET . . . . . . 326 ROBERT GREGORY   61
      THERE'S NOTHING OF HIM LEFT BUT HALF A SCORE . . . . 341 SHEP GOATHERD   56
      A MAN CONFUSEDLY IN A HALF DREAM . . . . 351 HER PRAISE   8
      THOUGH PLAY IS BUT HALF DONE-- . . . . 364 END OF DAY   7
      WE ARE BUT CRITICS, OR BUT HALF CREATE, ... 368 EGO DOMINUS   15
      FROM DOORED AND WINDOWED CLIFF, OR HALF UPTURNED . . . 368 EGO DOMINUS   30
      FROM THE FIRST CRESCENT TO THE HALF, THE DREAM . . . 373 PHASES OF MOON   36
      BECAUSE YOU ARE FORGOTTEN: HALF OUT OF LIFE, ... 376 PHASES OF MOON   96
      TO MAKE IT LINGER HALF A DAY. . . . . 401 DEMON BEAST   42
      ONCE MORE THE STORM IS HOWLING, AND HALF HID . . . . 403 FOR DAUGHTER   1
      HALF DRESSED IN NATIONAL UNIFORM, ... 424 ROAD AT DOOR   7
      THE HALF READ WISDOM OF DAEMONIC IMAGES, ... 427 PHANTOM HATRED   V   39
      THE WINGS HALF SPREAD FOR FLIGHT, ... 430 NINETEEN 19   65
      THE HALF IMAGINED, THE HALF WRITTEN PAGE. . . . . . . 431 NINETEEN 19   V   83
      THE HALF IMAGINED, THE HALF WRITTEN PAGE. . . . . . . 431 NINETEEN 19   V   83
      AND THAT ALONE: YET I, BEING DRIVEN HALF INSANE . . . 442 BLACK CENTAUR   6
      HALF RUNNING, DROPPED AT THE FIRST RIDGE OF THE DESERT   468 HARUN RASHID   155
      I THOUGHT HIM HALF A LUNATIC, HALF KNAVE, ... 473 ALL SOUL NIGHT   64
      I THOUGHT HIM HALF A LUNATIC, HALF KNAVE, ... 473 ALL SOUL NIGHT   64
      AND I GROW HALF CONTENTED TO BE BLIND: . . . . 473 ALL SOUL NIGHT   70
      HALF DEAD AT THE TOP. . . . . 480 BLOOD AND MOON   12
      HALF DEAD AT THE TOP? NO MATTER WHAT I SAID, ... 482 BLOOD AND MOON   48
      AND HALF A DOZEN IN FORMATION THERE, ... 489 COOLE PARK 29   20
      IS HALF ALL GLITTERING FLAME AND HALF ALL GREEN . . . 500 VACILLATION   12
      IS HALF ALL GLITTERING FLAME AND HALF ALL GREEN . . . 500 VACILLATION   12

		PAGE	TITLE		LINE
HALF (CONTINUED)					
	AND HALF IS HALF AND YET IS ALL THE SCENE;	500	VACILLATION		14
	AND HALF IS HALF AND YET IS ALL THE SCENE;	500	VACILLATION		14
	AND HALF AND HALF CONSUME WHAT THEY RENEW,	500	VACILLATION		15
	AND HALF AND HALF CONSUME WHAT THEY RENEW,	500	VACILLATION		15
	IS HALF ALL GLITTERING FLAME AND HALF A GREEN	500	VACILLATION	V	12
	IS HALF ALL GLITTERING FLAME AND HALF A GREEN	500	VACILLATION	V	12
	HALF TURNED AND FIXED A GLAZING EYE ON MINE,	537	HER VISION		26
	LOOKED HALF ASLEEP ALL DAY.	570	THREE BUSHES		34
	HAD TRAVELLED HALF THE NIGHT.	585	ORAHILLY		17
	CASEMENT UPON TRIAL, HALF HIDDEN BY THE BARS,	601	GALLERY REVIS		3
	HALF LEGENDARY MEN.	605	YOU CONTENT		16
	SO WHEN I TAKE ON HALF A SCORE.	605	SONGS BURDEN 1		7
	SOME FEW HALF WAKE AND HALF RENEW THEIR CHOICE,	622	HOUND VOICE		6
	SOME FEW HALF WAKE AND HALF RENEW THEIR CHOICE,	622	HOUND VOICE		6
	I HAVE FOUND NOTHING HALF SO GOOD.	624	APPARITIONS		9
	AS MY LONG-PLANNED HALF SOLITUDE,	624	APPARITIONS		10
	WHERE I CAN SIT UP HALF THE NIGHT.	624	APPARITIONS		11
	AS MY LONG PLANNED HALF SOLITUDE,	624	APPARITIONS	V	10
	HALF LIT, SO FLAPT THE WINGS ACROSS THE LAKE--	659	ISLE STAT II 1		17
	A STAR-LIT RAPIER, HALF BLOOD-DARK,	671	ISLE STAT II 3		125
	THEY SAY THE WISH ITSELF IS HALF THE SIN;	692	MOSADA 1		48
	HALF ASLEEP THE OLD COW CROPS,	706	DAWN-SONG		20
	HALF HID. HE BRINGS THE PEASANT'S ONLY KIN,	711	FERENCZ RENYI		50
	HALF DIZZY WITH THE LIGHTNING THERE RUNS A GATHERING BAND--	718	PHANTOM SHIP		9
	NOW HALF DIZZY WITH THE LIGHTNING THERE RUNS A GATHERING BAND;	718	PHANTOM SHIP	V	9
	"AND HALF FORGET THIS BED OF STRAW	739	EARL PAUL		5
	IF WHEN THE BATTLE IS HALF WON,	743	DANAAN QUICK		19
	WHEN SOMETHING, HALF A LAMB AND HALF A GOAT,	747	SHADOW WATER A V		11
	WHEN SOMETHING, HALF A LAMB AND HALF A GOAT,	747	SHADOW WATER A V		11
	I SPARED HER HANDMAID, TOO; BUT HALF WAY HITHER	755	SHADOW WATER A V		167
	I AM HALF BLINDED, TOO.	759	SHADOW WATER A V		235
	I AM HALF BLINDED. I AM HALF BLINDED, TOO.	759	SHADOW WATER A V		235
	WERE HE ANYTHING BY HALF,	772	SONG DEIRDRE 1		13
HALF-AWAKENED					
	WHERE BUT HALF-AWAKENED ADAM	638	BEN BULBEN		47
HALF-CLOSED					
	PACING WITH HALF-CLOSED EYELIDS IN A SUNNY SPOT	366	HER COURAGE		7
	THE QUIVERING HALF-CLOSED EYELIDS, THE RAGS OF CLOUD OR OF LACE,	427	PHANTOM HATRED		26
HALF-DEAD					
	THE HALF-DEAD DRAGON WAS HER THOUGHT,	385	ROBARTES DANCE		6
HALF-DECEIT					
	INTO THE HALF-DECEIT OF SOME INTOXICANT	429	NINETEEN 19		34
HALF-DONE					
	THOUGH PLAY IS BUT HALF-DONE--	364	END OF DAY	V	7
HALF-DRUNK					
	HALF-DRUNK OR WHOLE-MAD SOLDIERY	791	REPRISALS		15
HALF-FLIES					
	AND RUNS OR A WHILE HALF-FLIES	341	SHEP GOATHERD		64
	AND RUNS FOR A WHILE OR A WHILE HALF-FLIES	341	SHEP GOATHERD	V	64
HALF-FORGOTTEN					
	OF HALF-FORGOTTEN INNOCENT OLD PLACES;	130	BOOK STORIES		22
	HELMETS, AND SWORDS, AND HALF-FORGOTTEN THINGS	257	RECONCILIATION		6
HALF-HOUR'S					
	EVEN A HALF-HOUR'S NOTHINGNESS,	305	HOUR DAWN		70
HALF-IMAGINED					
	THE HALF-IMAGINED, THE HALF-WRITTEN PAGE;	431	NINETEEN 19		83
HALF-LEGENDARY					
	HALF-LEGENDARY MEN.	605	YOU CONTENT	V	16
HALF-LEGGED					
	TO VALUE BEER; NO HALF-LEGGED FOOL	304	HOUR DAWN		52
HALF-LIGHT					
	OF NIGHT AND LIGHT AND THE HALF-LIGHT,	176	CLOTHS HEAVEN		4
HALF-LOST					
	A THIN, GREY MAN, HALF-LOST IN GATHERING NIGHT.	102	FERGUS DRUID	V	7
HALF-LYING					
	AND THEN, HALF-LYING ON THE CHAIR,	132	FR GILLIGAN	V	13
HALF-MOUNTED					
	COME OLD, NECESSITOUS, HALF-MOUNTED MAN;	412	TOWER		90
HALFPENCE					
	AND ADD THE HALFPENCE TO THE PENCE	289	SEPTEMBER 1913		3
HALFPENNIES					
	BY BIDDY'S HALFPENNIES HAVE LAIN	287	TO WEALTHY MAN		3
	WHO QUARRELS OVER HALFPENNIES	621	JOHN KINSELLA		33
HALF-PENNIES					
	BY BIDDY'S HALF-PENNIES HAVE LAIN	287	TO WEALTHY MAN	V	3
	WHO QUARRELS OVER HALF-PENNIES	621	JOHN KINSELLA	V	33
HALFPENNY					
	THEY THREW A HALFPENNY INTO MY CAP,	300	RUN PARADISE		2
HALF-READ					
	THE HALF-READ WISDOM OF DAEMONIC IMAGES,	427	PHANTOM HATRED		39
	THE HALF-READ WISDOM OF DEMONIC IMAGES,	427	PHANTOM HATRED	V	39
HALF-WAKENING					
	HALF-WAKENING, WE LIFTED OUR EYELIDS,	54	OISIN 3	V	100
HALFWAY					
	SWEETEN THE LITTLE HALFWAY HOUSE	567	LAPIS LAZULI	V	48
HALF-WAY					
	SWEETENS THE LITTLE HALF-WAY HOUSE	567	LAPIS LAZULI		48

354

HALF-WRITTEN
    THE HALF-IMAGINED, THE HALF-WRITTEN PAGE: • • • • • •   431 NINETEEN 19   83
HALL
    THAN DOVES THAT MOANED ROUND EMAN'S HALL • • • • • • •   3 OISIN 1   V   7EE
    AND PRAISE THEE IN MY WESTERN HALL." • • • • • • • •   8 OISIN 1   V   79
    THE FLOOR OF ALMHUIN'S HOSTING HALL • • • • • • • •   13 OISIN 1   156
    THE FLOOR OF EMAN'S DANCING HALL • • • • • • • • •   13 OISIN 1   V   156
    THE FLOOR OF EMEN'S HOISTING HALL • • • • • • • •   13 OISIN 1   V   156
    THE FLOOR OF ALLEN'S HOSTING HALL • • • • • • • •   13 OISIN 1   V   156
    SHE BADE THEM BRING US TO THE HALL • • • • • • • •   16 OISIN 1   217
    WENT WE TO FIND THEIR PRINCE'S HALL-- • • • • • •   16 OISIN 1   V   217
    AND SWEPT OUT OF THE WATTLED HALL • • • • • • • •   20 OISIN 1   292
    NOT EVEN YOUR GOD COULD HAVE THROWN DOWN THAT HALL: 36 OISIN 2   109
    AND STOOD WITHIN THE HALL.   A MISTY RAY • • • • •   36 OISIN 2   V   104
    NOT E'EN THY GOD COULD HAVE THROWN DOWN THAT HALL: • •   36 OISIN 2   V   109
    UNDER THE DEEPEST SHADOWS OF THE HALL • • • • • •   37 OISIN 2   119
    OUT OF THE SEVENFOLD SEAS, BUILT THE DARK HALL • • •   38 OISIN 2   131
    OUT OF THE SEVEN-FOLD SEAS, BUILT THE DARK HALL • • •   38 OISIN 2   V   131
    WITH A PALE LIGHT, I JOURNEYED ROUND THE HALL • • •   39 OISIN 2   153
    OF MISTY DAWN: WHEN, CIRCLING ROUND THE HALL, • •   39 OISIN 2   V   153
    THEN IN THAT HALL, LIT BY THE DIM SEA-SHINE, • • •   41 OISIN 2   187
    THEN IN THAT HALL, LIT BY THE DIM SEA SHINE, • • •   41 OISIN 2   V   187
    LIKE ROTTED FLESH, AND STONE BY STONE MY HALL • •   45 OISIN 2   V   236
    MINE WAS THE THRONE IN EMAN'S HALL, • • • • • • •   81 MAD KING GOLL   V   2
    MAEVE WALKED THROUGH THAT GREAT HALL, AND WITH A SIGH   182 QUEEN MAEVE   62
    AND SAW WHERE IN THE MIDST OF THE GREAT HALL • •   279 TWO KINGS   60
    STAND UNDER THE ROUGH ROOF-TIMBERS OF THE HALL • •   377 PHASES OF MOON   125
    OR ROUND THE CITY HALL, • • • • • • • • • • •   608 SONGS BURDEN 3   6
    CLOSE TO THE CITY HALL HE DIED: • • • • • • •   608 SONGS BURDEN 3   12
    HIS TEMPLE AND HIS BANQUET HALL, • • • • • • •   671 ISLE STAT II 3   134
    THAT WITH THEIR FIERY RUIN FILL THE HALL, • • • •   683 SEEKER   45
HALLOWED
    THIS BOOK OR THAT, COME TO THIS HALLOWED PLACE • • • •   604 GALLERY REVIS   51
HALLS
    AMONG THE RINGING HALLS A SHOUT • • • • • • • • • •   20 OISIN 1   V   288
    IN TARA'S HALLS • • • • • • • • • • • • • •   609 IN TARAS HALLS   T
    A MAN I PRAISE THAT ONCE IN TARA'S HALLS • • • •   609 IN TARAS HALLS   1
    AND AS A SLAVE BEEN WAKEFUL IN THE HALLS • • • •   724 KANVA ON SELF   5
HALT
    UNDER BROKEN STONE I HALT • • • • • • • • • •   632 MAN AND ECHO   2
HALVE
    DREAMED, OR DID WE HALVE A DREAM • • • • • • • • •   398 BREAK OF DAY   3
HALVED
    KNEW THAT WE'D HALVED A SOUL • • • • • • • • • •   457 SUMMER SPRING   6
HAMLET
    THERE STRUTS HAMLET, THERE IS LEAR, • • • • • •   565 LAPIS LAZULI   10
    THEY KNOW THAT HAMLET AND LEAR ARE GAY: • • • • •   565 LAPIS LAZULI   16
    THOUGH HAMLET RAMBLES AND LEAR RAGES, • • • • •   566 LAPIS LAZULI   21
    NO HAMLET THIN FROM EATING FLIES, A FAT • • • • •   610 STATUES   19
HAMMER
    AND THE NAME OF THE DEMON WHOSE HAMMER • • • • • •   52 OISIN 3   80
    DOWN, DOWN, HAMMER THEM DOWN, • • • • • • • • •   544 TO SAME TUNE 1   9
    DOWN, DOWN, HAMMER THEM DOWN, • • • • • • • • •   545 TO SAME TUNE 1   19
    DOWN, DOWN, HAMMER THEM DOWN, • • • • • • • • •   545 TO SAME TUNE 1   29
    DOWN, DOWN, HAMMER THEM DOWN, • • • • • • • • •   546 TO SAME TUNE 2 V REF
    DOWN, DOWN, HAMMER THEM DOWN, • • • • • • • • •   548 TO SAME TUNE 3 V REF
HAMMERED
    OF HAMMERED SILVER, AND DRINK • • • • • • • • •   215 HAPPY TOWNLAND   50
    ON METAL GOBAN'D HAMMERED AT, • • • • • • • •   271 GREY ROCK   19
    HAD HAMMERED OUT ON MOUNTAIN TOP • • • • • • • •   271 GREY ROCK   23
    OLD GOBAN HAMMERED THEM AND WROUGHT THEM, • • • •   271 GREY ROCK   V   23
    OF HAMMERED GOLD AND GOLD ENAMELLING • • • • • •   408 SAIL BYZANTIUM   28
HAMMERS
    HOW THE HAMMERS SPRING ON THE ANVIL, ON THE SPEARHEAD'S   52 OISIN 3   83
        BURNING SPOT:
    AND THE NAMES OF THE DEMONS WHOSE HAMMERS • • • • •   52 OISIN 3   V   80
    BEAT ON IT WITH THEIR HAMMERS DAY AND NIGHT. • • • •   687 TWO TITANS   4
HAND
    WITH AN APPLE OF GOLD IN HER TOSSING HAND: • • • •   12 OISIN 1   143
    AN APPLE OF GOLD IN HER TOSSING HAND: • • • • • •   12 OISIN 1   V   143
    OF MEN AND LADIES, HAND IN HAND, • • • • • • • •   15 OISIN 1   202
    OF MEN AND LADIES, HAND IN HAND, • • • • • • • •   15 OISIN 1   202
    OF YOUTHS AND MAIDENS HAND IN HAND, • • • • • •   15 OISIN 1   V   202
    OF YOUTHS AND MAIDENS HAND IN HAND, • • • • • •   15 OISIN 1   V   202
    OF MEN AND MAIDENS, HAND IN HAND, • • • • • • •   15 OISIN 1   V   202
    OF MEN AND MAIDENS, HAND IN HAND, • • • • • • •   15 OISIN 1   V   202
    HER PEARL-PALE HAND AND THE HEM OF HER DRESS. • • •   16 OISIN 1   216
    ONE HAND UPHELD HIS BEARDLESS CHIN, • • • • • •   17 OISIN 1   250
    ONE HAND BENEATH HIS BEARDLESS CHIN, • • • • • •   17 OISIN 1   V   251
    WITHIN HIS OTHER HAND WERE FLITTING • • • • • •   18 OISIN 1   V   253
    WE FLUNG ON HIGH EACH WAVING HAND, • • • • • • •   22 OISIN 1   325
    FLUNG ON HIGH EACH WAVING HAND, • • • • • • • •   22 OISIN 1   V   325
    SOME WANDERED EVER HAND IN HAND: • • • • • • • •   25 OISIN 1   389
    SOME WANDERED EVER HAND IN HAND: • • • • • • • •   25 OISIN 1   389
    HIS HAND ALONG THE RUNNEL'S SIDE, AS THOUGH • •   39 OISIN 2   162
    OF RAVENING SORROW, OR THE HAND OF WRATH? • • •   42 OISIN 2   199
    . . . I FLUNG IT FIVE YARDS WITH MY HAND, • • •   60 OISIN 3   187
    AND FEEL THE SOFTNESS OF EACH OTHER'S HAND, • • •   74 ANASHU VIJAYA   57
    WHILE SLOWLY HE WHOSE HAND HELD HERS REPLIED: • •   80 EPHEMERA   11
    WHILE SLOWLY ANSWERED HE WHOSE HAND HELD HERS-- • •   80 EPHEMERA   V   11
    WHEN MY HAND PASSED FROM WIRE TO WIRE • • • • • •   86 MAD KING GOLL   65

HAND (CONTINUED)

		PAGE	TITLE	LINE
WITH A FAERY, HAND IN HAND,	. . . .	87	STOLEN CHILD	11
WITH A FAERY, HAND IN HAND,	. . . .	87	STOLEN CHILD	11
WITH A FAERY, HAND IN HAND,	. . . .	87	STOLEN CHILD	26
WITH A FAERY, HAND IN HAND,	. . . .	87	STOLEN CHILD	26
WITH A FAERY, HAND IN HAND,	. . . .	88	STOLEN CHILD	40
WITH A FAERY, HAND IN HAND,	. . . .	88	STOLEN CHILD	40
WITH A FAERY, HAND IN HAND,	. . . .	89	STOLEN CHILD	52
WITH A FAERY, HAND IN HAND,	. . . .	89	STOLEN CHILD	52
WITH A FAERY, HAND AND HAND,	. . . .	89	STOLEN CHILD	V 52
WITH A FAERY, HAND AND HAND,	. . . .	89	STOLEN CHILD	V 52
AND ON MY LEANING SHOULDER SHE LAID HER SNOW-WHITE HAND.		90	SALLEY GARDENS	6
WITH BLOWN, SPRAY-DABBLED HAIR GATHER AT HAND.	. . . .	114	ROSE OF BATTLE	6
NEAR NO ACCUSTOMED HAND;	. . . .	123	DREAM OF DEATH	2
WE COME BETWEEN HIM AND THE DEED OF HIS HAND,	. . . .	141	HOSTING SIDHE	11
AND KISS HER LIPS AND TAKE HER HAND,	. . . .	150	WANDER AENGUS	V 20
FOR THAT PALE BREAST AND LINGERING HAND	. . . . . .	156	FORGOT BEAUTY	15
FOR THAT DIM BROW AND LINGERING HAND	. . . .	156	FORGOT BEAUTY	V 15
YOU NEED BUT LIFT A PEARL-PALE HAND,	. . . .	158	BELOVED RHYMES	7
TO HER RIGHT HAND CAME THE RED ONE,	. . . .	160	CAP AND BELLS	31
TO HER LEFT HAND CAME THE BLUE.	. . . .	160	CAP AND BELLS	32
WITH BEAUTY HAND IN HAND?	. . . .	174	ELEMENT POWERS	V 6
WITH BEAUTY HAND IN HAND?	. . . .	174	ELEMENT POWERS	V 6
SHE LAID A HAND ON EITHER OF HIS SHOULDERS,	. . . .	182	QUEEN MAEVE	49
HELP THEM THAT WANDER WITH HAND CLASPING HAND,	. . .	184	QUEEN MAEVE	86
HELP THEM THAT WANDER WITH HAND CLASPING HAND,	. . .	184	QUEEN MAEVE	86
HELP THEM THAT PACE, HAND IN UNWITHERING HAND,	. . .	184	QUEEN MAEVE	V 86
HELP THEM THAT PACE, HAND IN UNWITHERING HAND,	. . .	184	QUEEN MAEVE	V 86
A YOUNG MAN CRIED AND KISSED HER HAND,	. . . . . .	191	BAILE AILLINN	60
UNDER A BITTER BLACK WIND THAT BLOWS FROM THE LEFT HAND;		206	HANRAHANS SONG	2
UNDER THE BITTER BLACK WINDS BLOWING OUT OF THE LEFT HAND;		206	HANRAHANS SONG	V 2
THAT MAKES ME FEAR TO RAISE A HAND AGAINST HIM,	. . .	222	SHADOW WATER B	V 16A
THAT I WILL NEVER LIFT A HAND AGAINST YOU.	. . . .	227	SHADOW WATER B	108
TOO MANY YEARS TO LIFT A HAND AGAINST YOU.	. . . .	227	SHADOW WATER B	111
BELIEVED THERE WAS SOME OTHER NEAR AT HAND,	. . . .	229	SHADOW WATER B	154
THAN A STRONG BODY AND A READY HAND.	. . . .	232	SHADOW WATER B	236
BEFORE A HAND CAN TOUCH ME. MY HANDS ARE STILL;	. .	238	SHADOW WATER B	358
WHERE IS MY SWORD THAT FELL OUT OF MY HAND.	. . . .	241	SHADOW WATER B	397
THE WEAK LAY HAND ON WHAT THE STRONG HAS DONE,	. . .	265	THESE CLOUDS	3
NOW NOTHING BUT COMES READIER TO THE HAND	. . . . .	267	ALL TEMPT ME	4
STOOD ON MY PATH. TREMBLING FROM HAND TO FOOT	. . .	283	TWO KINGS	V 151
GIVING HIS HAND TO THAT MAN AND TO THIS,	. . . . .	286	TWO KINGS	V 218A
YOUR OPEN HAND BUT SHOWS OUR LOSS,	. . . .	288	TO WEALTHY MAN	29
AND SOMEBODY PUTS HIS HAND IN THE DISH	. . . . . .	301	RUN PARADISE	5
WHEN CLOSE TO HIS RIGHT HAND A HEAP	. . . .	302	HOUR DAWN	11
WENT DOWN UPON A HAND AND KNEE	. . . .	304	HOUR DAWN	V 45
BUT THE OTHER PUSHED HIS HAND ASIDE,	. . . .	304	HOUR DAWN	V 48
AND EVEN OLD MEN'S EYES GREW DIM, THIS HAND ALONE,	. .	314	FALLEN MAJESTY	2
AND ONE BECAUSE HER HAND	. . . .	315	FRIENDS	10
AND LOST THE OLD NONCHALANCE OF THE HAND;	. . . . .	368	EGO DOMINUS	13
STAND UP AND LIFT YOUR HAND AND BLESS	. . . . . .	379	SAINT HUNCH	1
A BUDDHA, HAND AT REST,	. . . .	383	VISION ROBART	19
HAND LIFTED UP THAT BLEST!	. . . .	383	VISION ROBART	20
SURELY SOME REVELATION IS AT HAND;	. . . .	402	SECOND COMING	9
SURELY THE SECOND COMING IS AT HAND.	. . . .	402	SECOND COMING	10
ON MASTER-WORK OF INTELLECT OR HAND,	. . . .	429	NINETEEN 19	37
ON MASTER WORK OF INTELLECT OR HAND,	. . . .	429	NINETEEN 19	V 37
THAT WOULD NOT LIFT A HAND MAYBE	. . . .	432	NINETEEN 19	109
THAT WOULD NOT LIFT A HAND MAY BE	. . . .	432	NINETEEN 19	V 109
AND SHOULD SOME CRAZY HAND DARE TOUCH A DAUGHTER	. . .	433	NINETEEN 19	122
BID THE GHOST HAVE SWORD IN HAND;	. . . .	435	FOR MY SON	V 9
AND LAY THE HEART UPON HER HAND	. . . .	437	SONGS PLAY 1	4
BUT SINCE I LAID A HAND THEREON	. . . .	451	FIRST LOVE	7
FOR EVERY HAND IS LUNATIC	. . . .	451	FIRST LOVE	11
A STUMPIER ON EITHER HAND	. . . .	460	THREE MONUMENT	4
ONE HAND AMID THE GOLDFISH IN THE POOL;	. . . . . .	463	HARUN RASHID	44
THE EXTRAVAGANCE OF SPRING; OR MOVE A HAND	. . . . .	466	HARUN RASHID	125
ROMANTIC FISH SWAM IN NETS COMING TO THE HAND;	. . .	485	THREE MOVEMENT	2
THE HAND AND LASH THAT BEAT DOWN FRIGID ROME?	. . . .	560	WHENCE COME	10
YOU, SHOULD HAND EXPLORE A THIGH,	. . . .	573	LADYS 3RD SONG	11
AS THOUGH THAT HAND COULD REACH TO WHERE THEY STAND,	. .	579	DOR WELLESLEY	2
DELIGHTFUL TO THE TOUCH; TIGHTEN THAT HAND	. . . . .	579	DOR WELLESLEY	4
HIS STOUT STICK UNDER HIS HAND,	. . . .	588	OLD WICKED MAN	20
BOUND A THONG ABOUT HIS HAND,	. . . .	595	COLONEL MARTIN	25
AND HE LAID THEM ON HER HAND.	. . . .	595	COLONEL MARTIN	35
OR GROPE WITH A DIRTY HAND.	. . . .	599	SPIRIT MEDIUM	8
OR GROPE WITH A DIRTY HAND.	. . . .	600	SPIRIT MEDIUM	16
OR GROPE WITH A DIRTY HAND.	. . . .	600	SPIRIT MEDIUM	24
AN ABBOT OR ARCHBISHOP WITH AN UPRAISED HAND	. . . .	601	GALLERY REVIS	9
A HAND UNDER HIS HEAD.	. . . .	617	LONG-LEG FLY	8
HIS HAND MOVES TO AND FRO.	. . . .	618	LONG-LEG FLY	28
THE WAVES IN YONDER LAKE WHERE POINTS MY HAND	. . . .	652	ISLE STAT I 2	13
AND PONDER IT IF THEY WILL); THEN NEAR AT HAND	. . .	659	ISLE STAT II 2	10
ONE HAND BROW-SHADING, FAR ACROSS THE NIGHT,	. . . .	663	ISLE STAT II 2	27
ALL SWIM WITH TEARS. THE FAERY BOAT'S AT HAND;	. . .	663	ISLE STAT II 2	33
WAS BROKEN IN HIS QUIVERING HAND.	. . . .	671	ISLE STAT II 3	126
THY FLICKERING HAND? WHAT MEAN THE LIGHTS THAT RISE	. .	674	ISLE STAT II 3	198
HAYNAU, THE MAN OF SYSTEM, LIFTS HIS HAND	. . . . .	712	FERENCZ RENYI	62
I'M WEAK, AND BY THE HAND SHALL HOLD EACH ONE	. . .	712	FERENCZ RENYI	V 57
AND BE SO HAPPY." TO HIS HAND SHE CLINGS,	. . . . .	714	FERENCZ RENYI	V 100

356

	PAGE	TITLE		LINE
HAND (CONTINUED)				
"WATCHER, WHEREFORE HAVE YE CALLED US?" EYES GO AFTER HIS LEAN HAND,	718	PHANTOM SHIP		10
WE WILL LEAD YOU HAND IN HAND	726	LOVERS QUARREL		2
WE WILL LEAD YOU HAND IN HAND	726	LOVERS QUARREL		2
SITTING ON MY RIGHT HAND."	741	EARL PAUL		60
AND WERE ALL DREAMS, IT WOULD NOT WEIGH IN THE HAND. . .	750	SHADOW WATER A		77
THIS BLADE OUT OF MY HAND AND DIED OF A SUDDEN.	755	SHADOW WATER A		168
THE HAND THAT WOUNDS HIM, BECAUSE THE GODS ARE HIS FRIENDS.	758	SHADOW WATER A		232
THE HAND THAT WOUNDS. A WHITE BIRD BEATS HIS WINGS . . .	758	SHADOW WATER A	V	232
WHERE A HAND ON THE BELL	780	WELL AND TREE		4
HANDIWORK				
SHALL MAKE HER LOOK UPON HER HANDIWORK, ...	282	TWO KINGS		115
MIRACLE, BIRD OR GOLDEN HANDIWORK, ...	497	BYZANTIUM		17
MORE MIRACLE THAN BIRD OR HANDIWORK, ...	497	BYZANTIUM		18
NO HANDIWORK OF CALLIMACHUS, ...	566	LAPIS LAZULI		29
HANDLE				
MAY HANDLE NOTHING AND SET EYES ON NOTHING	371	ON GOING HOUSE		6
HANDLED				
THAT I HAVE HANDLED LEAST, LEAST LOOKED UPON.	367	EGO DOMINUS		9
WHO HANDLED MARBLE AS IF IT WERE BRONZE, ...	566	LAPIS LAZULI		30
HANDLES				
NINE SWORDS WITH HANDLES OF RHINOCEROS HORN	239	SHADOW WATER B		368
HANDMAID				
I WOULD HAVE SPARED HER HANDMAID, BUT SHE CAUGHT . . .	755	SHADOW WATER A		167
I SPARED HER HANDMAID, TOO; BUT HALF WAY HITHER . . .	755	SHADOW WATER A	V	167
HANDMAIDS				
THE HANDMAIDS LAUGH AND WHISPER IN THE DOOR.	759	SHADOW WATER A		242
HAND'S				
THAT NEVER DID A HAND'S TURN? AIBRIC! AIBRIC! . . .	228	SHADOW WATER B		130
HANDS				
OF BATTLES BROKEN BY HIS HANDS, ...	7	OISIN 1		67
ALL MEN, AND STRONGER OF HIS HANDS, ...	7	OISIN 1	V	63
AND WEPT, AND RAISED THEIR LAMENTING HANDS, ...	10	OISIN 1		112
THEY WEPT, AND RAISED LAMENTING HANDS.	10	OISIN 1	V	112
A HARP OF SILVER IN MY HANDS, ...	16	OISIN 1	V	232
NOR HAVE HANDS HELD A WEARY TOOL;	19	OISIN 1		283
AND HANDS THAT HOLD NO WEARISOME TOOL, ...	22	OISIN 1		340
OUR HANDS HAVE KNOWN NO WEARYING TOOL, ...	22	OISIN 1	V	339
THESE NOW OUTWORN AND WITHERED HANDS, ...	23	OISIN 1		349
THESE NOW O'ERWORN AND WITHERED HANDS, ...	23	OISIN 1	V	348
I TURNED IT IN MY HANDS; THE STAINS	24	OISIN 1		368
AND CAUGHT MY HANDS, BUT SPAKE NO WORD	25	OISIN 1		374
AND CAUGHT MY HANDS AND SPAKE NO WORD	25	OISIN 1	V	374
AND BLOWS ON HIS HANDS IN THE FIRE'S WARM BLAZE; . . .	26	OISIN 1	V	404
TAKING THE MORTAL WARRIORS BY THE HANDS:	29	OISIN 2	V	108
BUT NIAM WITH HER HANDS CARESSED HIS EARS, ...	30	OISIN 2	V	26
YOUNG WARRIOR." "NAY," I ANSWERED; "MY HANDS BURN . .	35	OISIN 2	V	89B
GOD SHAKES THE WORLD WITH RESTLESS HANDS. MORE NEAR . .	43	OISIN 2	V	208
CEASED ON OUR HANDS AND OUR FACES, ON HAZEL AND OAK LEAF, THE LIGHT,	48	OISIN 3		23
. . . THEIR HANDS WERE THE CLAWS OF BIRDS, ...	49	OISIN 3		34
LAID HANDS ON THE BELL-BRANCH AND SWAYED IT, ...	51	OISIN 3		56
AND TELL OF YOUR GOODLY HOUSEHOLD AND THE GOODLY WORKS OF YOUR HANDS,	51	OISIN 3		62
AND EVEN THE NAMES OF HIS FATHERS, AND EVEN THE WORKS OF HIS HANDS?	51	OISIN 3	V	62
LORD OF THE CROZIERS, YOU EVEN HAD LIFTED YOUR HANDS AND WEPT!	54	OISIN 3		110
LORD OF THE CROSIERS, THOU EVEN HADST LIFTED THY HANDS AND WEPT;	54	OISIN 3	V	110
MUCH WONDERING TO SEE UPON ALL HANDS, OF WATTLES AND WOODWORK MADE,	58	OISIN 3		162
MUCH WONDERING TO SEE UPON ALL HANDS, OF WATTLES AND WOOD-WORK MADE,	58	OISIN 3	V	162
PUT THE STAFF IN MY HANDS!	61	OISIN 3		201
AND LAID YOU ON THE GATES OF EVENING WITH HIS QUIET HANDS.	72	ANASHU VIJAYA		22
AND LAID YE ON THE GATES OF EVENING WITH HIS QUIET HANDS.	72	ANASHU VIJAYA	V	22
SING, TILL YOU RAISE YOUR HANDS AND SIGH, ...	73	ANASHU VIJAYA		45
SING, TILL YE RAISE YOUR HANDS AND SIGH, ...	73	ANASHU VIJAYA	V	45
AND FEEL THE SOFTNESS OF EACH OTHER'S HANDS, ...	74	ANASHU VIJAYA	V	57
A LONELY LAUGHTER, AND MAY KISS HIS HANDS TO ME IN SLEEP.	75	ANASHU VIJAYA		82
AN INNER LAUGHTER, AND MAY KISS HIS HANDS TO ME IN SLEEP.	75	ANASHU VIJAYA	V	82
A LONELY LAUGHTER, THAT HE MAY KISS HANDS TO ME IN SLEEP.	75	ANASHU VIJAYA	V	82
AND WANDER EVER WITH WOVEN HANDS.	78	INDIAN TO LOVE		7
THESE HANDS WON MANY A TORQUE OF GOLD.	83	MAD KING GOLL		23
THESE HANDS SLEW MANY WARRIORS BOLD—	83	MAD KING GOLL	V	23
THESE HANDS SLEW MANY ROBBERS BOLD—	83	MAD KING GOLL	V	23
THESE HANDS SLEW MANY A SEAMAN BOLD—	83	MAD KING GOLL	V	23
I WANDER ON, AND WAVE MY HANDS, ...	84	MAD KING GOLL		43
AND CRUMPLED IN MY HANDS THE STAFF	84	MAD KING GOLL		33
AND BROKE BETWEEN MY HANDS THE STAFF	84	MAD KING GOLL	V	33
MINGLING HANDS AND MINGLING GLANCES	87	STOLEN CHILD		18
UPON HIS WASTED HANDS.	98	FOXHUNTER		22
UPON HIS WASTED HANDS.	98	FOXHUNTER	V	24
AND ON THESE HANDS THAT MAY NOT LIFT THE SWORD, . . .	103	FERGUS DRUID		24
"AND BREAKS THE RIDGE OF BATTLE WITH HIS HANDS." . . .	107	CUCHULAIN SEA	V	26
THE DRUIDS CHANTED, SWAYING IN THEIR HANDS	111	CUCHULAIN SEA	V	82
THE DRUIDS CHAUNTED, SWAYING IN THEIR HANDS	111	CUCHULAIN SEA	V	82
OF HOW GOD LEANS HIS HANDS OUT OF THE SKY, ...	128	DREAM OF FAERY	V	43
THAT GOD HAD LEANED HIS HANDS OUT OF THE SKY, ...	128	DREAM OF FAERY	V	43

357

                                                              PAGE   TITLE   LINE
HANDS   (CONTINUED)
THAT GOD HAD LEANT HIS HANDS OUT OF THE SKY, ...   128 DREAM OF FAERY V   43
THE SAD BELLS BOW THE FOREHEAD ON THE HANDS. . . . . .   130 BOOK STORIES   V   20
WITH A TWINKLING OF ANCIENT HANDS. . . . .   144 HOST OF AIR   24
AND CLAP THEIR HANDS TOGETHER, AND HALF CLOSE THEIR EYES, 146 UNAPPEAS HOST   2
AND KISS HER LIPS AND TAKE HER HANDS; . . . .   150 WANDER AENGUS   20
PALE BROWS, STILL HANDS AND DIM HAIR, ...   152 LOSS OF LOVE   1
PALE BROW, STILL HANDS, AND DIM HAIR, ...   152 LOSS OF LOVE   V   1
I BRING YOU WITH REVERENT HANDS . . . .   157 POET BELOVED   1
QUEENS WROUGHT WITH GLIMMERING HANDS; . . . .   162 ASKS FORGIVE   12
AND HANDS HURL IN THE DEEP . . . .   165 CRY OF SEDGE   6
BUT DATHI FOLDED HIS HANDS AND SMILED . . . .   167 BLESSED   11
SAW THE PIERCED HANDS AND ROOD OF ELDER RISE . . . .   169 SECRET ROSE   10
THE KNOTTED SCOURGE, THE NAIL-PIERCED HANDS, THE WOUNDED 172 TRAV PASSION   V   4
   SIDE,
THAT WORK TOO DIFFICULT FOR MORTAL HANDS . . . . . .   182 QUEEN MAEVE   67
DREAMED OF THE HANDS THAT WOULD UNLACE . . . . . .   193 BAILE AILLINN   104
THEY HAD HANDS LIKE CLAWS, AND THEIR KNEES . . . .   208 OLD MEN ADMIRE   4
HURRY TO BLESS THE HANDS THAT PLAY. . . . .   212 BLESS PSALTER   1
O KINSMEN, BLESS THE HANDS THAT PLAY. . . . .   213 BLESS PSALTER   15
OUR HANDS, OUR HANDS MUST EBB AWAY. . . . .   213 BLESS PSALTER   18
OUR HANDS, OUR HANDS MUST EBB AWAY. . . . .   213 BLESS PSALTER   18
BUT BLESS OUR HANDS THAT EBB AWAY. . . . .   213 BLESS PSALTER   20
BECAUSE HER HANDS HAD BEEN MADE WILD BY LOVE. . . . .   219 HARP OF AENGUS   9
HE COULD NOT SEE THEM, BUT I HELD OUT MY HANDS . . .   223 SHADOW WATER B   38
AND THEN SMOOTH OUT WITH IVORY HANDS AND SIGH, . . .   228 SHADOW WATER B   133
WHO HAVE SLAIN MY HUSBAND AND LAID HANDS UPON ME. . .   235 SHADOW WATER B   282
LET GO MY HANDS! WHY DO YOU CAST A SHADOW? . . . .   235 SHADOW WATER B   283
THAT RAISED THEIR HANDS AGAINST HIM. THERE ARE SOME .   235 SHADOW WATER B   291
IT WAS THEIR HANDS THAT PLUCKED THE WINDS AWAKE . . .   237 SHADOW WATER B   324
BEFORE A HAND CAN TOUCH ME. MY HANDS ARE STILL; . .   238 SHADOW WATER B   358
AND WRING MY HANDS, AND WAIL HIM BITTERLY, ...   242 SHADOW WATER B   414
BETTER THAN MY OWN HANDS. I HAVE DECEIVED YOU . . .   244 SHADOW WATER B   466
AND STRIKE THE GOLDEN PILLARS WITH MY HANDS. . . . .   246 SHADOW WATER B   502
O SILVER FISH THAT MY TWO HANDS HAVE TAKEN . . . . .   251 SHADOW WATER B   609
BY THE ANCIENT HOLY HANDS THAT BROUGHT THEM . . . .   271 GREY ROCK   V   21
MORE HANDS IN HEIGHT THAN ANY STAG IN THE WORLD . . .   277 TWO KINGS   9
KING EOCHAID SEIZED THE HORNS IN HIS STRONG HANDS . .   278 TWO KINGS   24
THE HANDS THAT GATHERED UP THE MIGHT OF THE WORLD, . .   278 TWO KINGS   29
EOCHAID SEIZED BOTH THE HORNS IN HIS STRONG HANDS . .   278 TWO KINGS   V   24
HER HANDS ON EITHER SIDE HAD GRIPPED THE BENCH, . . .   279 TWO KINGS   63
AND CARRIED HIM HIS FOOD WITH MY OWN HANDS, ...   280 TWO KINGS   88
AND FOR NINE DAYS HE HAD FOOD FROM OTHER HANDS, . . .   282 TWO KINGS   126
THRUST HIM AWAY WITH BOTH MY HANDS AND CRIED, ...   285 TWO KINGS   202
MY HANDS WERE PRESSED TO VANISHED SUDDENLY. . . . . .   286 TWO KINGS   208
IN HIS FULL HANDS WHAT, HAD THEY ONLY KNOWN, ...   292 TO A SHADE   11
HANDS GRIPPED IN HANDS, TOES CLOSE TOGETHER, ...   332 ROUND TOWER   21
HANDS GRIPPED IN HANDS, TOES CLOSE TOGETHER, ...   332 ROUND TOWER   21
YOUR SMALL HANDS WERE NOT BEAUTIFUL, ...   356 BROKEN DREAMS   29
THE HANDS THAT I HAVE KISSED, ...   357 BROKEN DREAMS   35
HANDS, DO WHAT YOU'RE BID; . . . .   358 BALLOON MIND   1
OR FROM SOME BLOODY WHIP IN THEIR OWN HANDS. . . . .   375 PHASES OF MOON   68
IN THE PRISON OF MY HANDS. . . . .   381 SONG OF FOOL   2
WHY HAVE YOU LAID YOUR HANDS UPON MY EYES? . . . .   389 IMAGE PAST   15
SOUL CLAP ITS HANDS AND SING, AND LOUDER SING . . .   407 SAIL BYZANTIUM   11
LOVE-LORN, INDIFFERENT HANDS MIGHT COME UPON IT . .   461 HARUN RASHID   14
A BOY'S LOVELORN INDIFFERENT HANDS MIGHT FIND . . .   461 HARUN RASHID   V   14
HANDS UPON EITHER SHOULDER MADE HER MOVE, ...   466 HARUN RASHID   V 125B
OUR HANDS ARE BLENCHED, OUR FINGERS SEEM . . . . .   488 CRAZED MOON   14
BELOVED BOOKS THAT FAMOUS HANDS HAVE BOUND, ...   491 COOLE BALLYLEE   27
AND EVERYTHING THAT YOUR OWN HANDS HAVE WROUGHT, . . .   501 VACILLATION   31
HEALING FROM ITS LETTERED SLAB. THOSE SELF-SAME HANDS   503 VACILLATION   82
   PERCHANCE
OR LACKING THAT, GOVERNMENT IN SUCH HANDS, ...   543 PARN FUNERAL 2   7
THOSE HANDS TO CLOSE THESE EYES, ...   587 OLD WICKED MAN   6
HANDS THAT ARE BUSY WITH HIS BEADS . . . .   588 OLD WICKED MAN   25
OF THE PIED PANTHER-KITTENS FROM MY HANDS . . . . .   674 ISLE STAT II 3   219
A LOTUS IN THEIR HANDS--YOUNG MOORISH GIRL . . . . .   694 MOSADA 1   103
NO NEED TO BIND MY HANDS. WHERE ARE YE, SIRS? . . .   695 MOSADA 1   110
THE BURTHEN OF THY TRUTH. REACH DOWN THY HANDS . .   698 MOSADA 2   53
BEFORE HIM ONE WELL GUARDED, WITH BOUND HANDS; . . .   709 FERENCZ RENYI   10
I'M WEAK, AND BY THE HANDS SHALL HOLD EACH ONE . . .   712 FERENCZ RENYI   57
AND BE SO HAPPY." TO HIS HANDS SHE CLINGS, ...   714 FERENCZ RENYI   100
AWAY HER CLINGING HANDS, AND TURNS. SHE THROWS . . .   714 FERENCZ RENYI   102
YON BAUBLE OF THE HEAVENS, HE LIFTS HIS HANDS, . . .   715 FERENCZ RENYI   119
ON THE DROWNED MEN'S HANDS AND FACES, ON THE SPARS AND   719 PHANTOM SHIP   22
   ON THE SAILS.
AND THEN SMOOTH OUT WITH IVORY HANDS AND SIGH. . . .   750 SHADOW WATER A   70
A BOY AND GIRL HOLD ONE ANOTHER'S HANDS; . . . . .   752 SHADOW WATER A   122
BECAUSE HER HANDS HAD BEEN MADE WILD BY LOVE; . . .   762 SHADOW WATER A   304
I KNOW YOU NOW, BESEECHING HANDS AND EYES. . . . .   763 SHADOW WATER A   312
BESEECHING HANDS AND MORE BESEECHING EYES? . . . .   763 SHADOW WATER A V   312
THE LOVE I KNOW IS HIDDEN IN THESE HANDS . . . . .   765 SHADOW WATER A   350
AND LANGUORS THAT AWAKE IN MINGLING HANDS . . . .   765 SHADOW WATER A   367
O SILVER FISH THAT MY TWO HANDS HAVE TAKEN . . . .   769 SHADOW WATER A   425
THOSE WILD HANDS THAT HAVE EMBRACED . . . .   776 AGAINST WITCH   32
HANDSOME
IN REALMS WHERE THE HANDSOME WERE MANY, ...   50 OISIN 3   50
IN A REALM WHERE THE HANDSOME ARE MANY, ...   50 OISIN 3   V   50
IN REALMS WHERE THE HANDSOME ARE MANY, ...   50 OISIN 3   V   50
SOME FEW HAVE HANDSOME RIDERS, ARE GARLANDED . . .   432 NINETEEN 19   114

	PAGE	TITLE		LINE

HANDSOMEST
    THE HANDSOMEST YOUNG MAN THERE, ... 145 HOST OF AIR 34
HANDY-WORK
    MIRACLE, BIRD OR GOLDEN HANDY-WORK . . . . . . 497 BYZANTIUM V 17
    MORE MIRACLE THAN BIRD OR HANDY-WORK . . . . . . 497 BYZANTIUM V 18
HANG
    LIKE CRIMSON METEORS HANG IN THE GLOOM, ... 21 OISIN 1 306
    AND WHEN THE DEW-DROWNED STARS HANG IN THE AIR . . . 32 OISIN 2 54
    WHERE BANNERS OF THE CALIPHS HANG, NIGHT-COLOURED . . 461 HARUN RASHID 6
    ALL THINGS HANG LIKE A DROP OF DEW . . . . . . 505 GRAT INSTRUCT 3
    SO NEVER HANG YOUR HEART UPON . . . . 509 JANE REPROVED 12
    THAT ALL MUST HANG THEIR TRUST . . . . 583 GHOST ROG CASE 16
    WHERE MY FRIENDS' PORTRAITS HANG AND LOOK THEREON; . . 604 GALLERY REVIS 52
    HANG ON THE SIDE OF THE ROUND GRAPE-CLUSTER; . . . . 646 ISLE STAT I 1 45
    LONG CITRON COILS THAT HANG AROUND THEE, BLOWN . . . 670 ISLE STAT II 3 105
    OF OUR NATIVITY HANG SIDE BY SIDE, ... 701 MOSADA 3 53
    WHY DO YOU HANG SO HEAVY IN MY ARMS? . . . . . . 703 MOSADA 3 108
    AND HANG O'ER THE HISTORIED STONE? . . . . . . 707 FAIRY PEDANT 6
    HANG THE MIST-THREADS FOR A LITTLE WHILE LIKE COBWEBS IN 719 PHANTOM SHIP 29
        THE AIR;
    HANG THE MIST THREADS FOR A LITTLE WHILE LIKE COBWEBS IN 719 PHANTOM SHIP V 29
        THE AIR,
HANGER   SEE COAT-HANGER
HANGETH
    WHO MADE THE WORLD AND RULETH IT, HE HANGETH ON A STALK, 76 INDIAN ON GOD 10
    BECAUSE ST. JOSEPH'S IMAGE HANGETH HERE . . . . . . 676 ISLE STAT II 3 266
HANGING
    HER EYES WERE SOFT AS DEWDROPS HANGING . . . . . . 3 OISIN 1 V 7HH
    AND HANGING ITS PAPER FLOWERS FROM POST TO POST, . . . 198 SEVEN WOODS 8
    OF THE GREAT DOOR; BUT THOUGH THE HANGING LAMPS . . . 279 TWO KINGS 49
    OF SILVER HANGING ROUND LAME COLA'S NECK-- . . . . . 691 MOSADA 1 V 35
    HER HANGING MANSION. GIVE TO ME, I PRAY, ... 698 MOSADA 2 52
    AND HANGING O'ER THE HUSH OF WILLOW BOWERS, ... 705 REMEMBRANCE 8
HANGMAN'S
    FOR WHOM THE HANGMAN'S ROPE WAS SPUN, ... 289 SEPTEMBER 1913 13
HANGS
    THE DARKNESS COMES. A CLOUD HANGS OVERHEAD-- . . . . 43 OISIN 2 V 208A
    A HUSH! AH, ME! IT HANGS TO STRIKE US DEAD. . . . . 43 OISIN 2 V 208B
    WHO BUT AWAITS HIS HOUR TO SHOOT, STILL HANGS . . . . 198 SEVEN WOODS 13
    AND HE THAT ATTIS' IMAGE HANGS BETWEEN . . . . . . 500 VACILLATION 16
    WHEN DARK HANGS UPON THE WATER . . . . 589 OLD WICKED MAN 34
    WITHIN THE DROWSY BLOSSOM HANGS THE BEE; . . . . . 645 ISLE STAT I 1 2
    HERE WHERE LABURNUM HANGS HER GOLDEN FLEECE; . . . . 670 ISLE STAT II 3 102
    HANGS ON MY BREAST! LISTEN, WE SHALL BE SAFE. . . . 701 MOSADA 3 73
    HANGS O'ER ALL THE WOODED EARTH. . . . . 731 STREET DANCERS 8
HANRAHAN
    HANRAHAN REPROVES THE CURLEW . . . . 155 REPROVE CURLEW V T
    HANRAHAN LAMENTS BECAUSE OF HIS WANDERINGS . . . . . 171 MAID QUIET V T
    HANRAHAN SPEAKS TO THE LOVERS OF HIS SONGS IN COMING DAYS 173 SPEAKS HEARERS V T
    THE SONG OF RED HANRAHAN . . . . 206 HANRAHANS SONG V T
    AND I MYSELF CREATED HANRAHAN . . . . 411 TOWER 57
    HANRAHAN ROSE IN FRENZY THERE . . . . 412 TOWER 71
    GO THEREFORE; BUT LEAVE HANRAHAN, ... 413 TOWER 103
    ALEEL, HIS COUNTESS; HANRAHAN . . . . 550 SEVERED HEAD 15
HANRAHAN'S
    RED HANRAHAN'S SONG ABOUT IRELAND . . . . 206 HANRAHANS SONG T
HAPLESS
    AND I WOULD PLEASE THE HAPLESS FAUN, ... 67 HAPPY SHEPHERD 47
    THAT I MAY SOOTHE THAT HAPLESS FAUN . . . . . . 67 HAPPY SHEPHERD V 47
    BEHOLD THE HAPLESS SLEEPERS STANDING BY. . . . . . 677 ISLE STAT II 3 281
HAPPEN
    THAT SOMETHING IS ABOUT TO HAPPEN, I THINK . . . . . 609 IN TARAS HALLS 4
HAPPENED
    OF WONDERS THAT HAVE HAPPENED . . . . 215 HAPPY TOWNLAND 47
HAPPENS
    NO MATTER WHAT HAPPENS AND WHO TAKES THE FALL, . . . 545 TO SAME TUNE 1 22
    NO MATTER WHAT HAPPENS OR WHO TAKES THE FALL, . . . 545 TO SAME TUNE 1 V 22
    WHAT HAPPENS A TREE THAT HAS NOTHING WITHIN IT? . . . 548 TO SAME TUNE 3 23
    WHAT HAPPENS TO A TREE THAT HAS NOTHING WITHIN IT? . . 548 TO SAME TUNE 3 V 23
    NO MATTER WHAT HAPPENS AND WHO TAKES THE FALL, . . . 616 MARCH SONGS 3 22
HAPPIER
    THAT HAPPIER BREATH HAD MOVED, HER HUSBAND TURNED . . 185 QUEEN MAEVE 105
    YET DREAMED THAT BEINGS HAPPIER THAN MEN . . . . . 218 WOODS OF COOLE 18
    AND WHEN WE HAVE IT WE ARE NO HAPPIER, ... 228 SHADOW WATER B 126
    OR HAPPIER THOUGHTED WHEN THE DAY IS SPENT . . . . . 292 TO A SHADE V 4
    OR LEAVE THEM HAPPIER THAN BEFORE. . . . . . . 328 IRISH AIRMAN 8
    HAPPIER DAYS THOUGHT GOOD; . . . . 365 HER RACE 4
    IT MADE HIM HAPPIER TO KNOW . . . . 400 DEMON BEAST 14
    ALL HIS HAPPIER DREAMS CAME TRUE-- . . . . 577 WHAT THEN 11
    FOR HAPPIER LOVE BUT FINDS UNHAPPINESS, ... 750 SHADOW WATER A 67
HAPPIER-THOUGHTED
    OR HAPPIER-THOUGHTED WHEN THE DAY IS SPENT . . . . . 292 TO A SHADE 4
HAPPIEST
    THAT WOULD BE HAPPIEST. HE IS A KING . . . . . . 768 SHADOW WATER A 410
    THAT WOULD BE HAPPIEST, FOR THERE IS NONE . . . . . 768 SHADOW WATER A V 410
HAPPILY
    THAT ALL THINGS FELL OUT HAPPILY, ... 189 BAILE AILLINN 22
HAPPINESS
    HAVE HAPPINESS WITHOUT AN END, ... 195 BAILE AILLINN 158
    I HAVE NO HAPPINESS IN DREAMING OF BRYCELINDE, . . . 209 UNDER THE MOON 1
    I FIND NO HAPPINESS IN SHADY BRYCELINDE . . . . . 209 UNDER THE MOON V 1

359

	PAGE	TITLE		LINE

HAPPINESS (CONTINUED)
        I'D NEVER COME UPON THE HAPPINESS . . . . 226 SHADOW WATER B   87
        TO HURRY TO THEIR HIDDEN HAPPINESS . . . . 234 SHADOW WATER B   268
        TO UNIMAGINABLE HAPPINESS. . . . . 247 SHADOW WATER B   524
        AN UNIMAGINABLE HAPPINESS. . . . . 248 SHADOW WATER B   553
        AND IF THAT HAPPINESS BE MORE THAN DREAMS, ... 248 SHADOW WATER B   554
        HAPPINESS TO CHILDREN AND TO MEN." . . . . 282 TWO KINGS   121
        AND WITH HIM HAVE FOUND EVERY HAPPINESS . . . . . 284 TWO KINGS   174
        UNDER A BOW, HE CRIED, "WHAT HAPPINESS . . . . . 284 TWO KINGS   177
        CAN LOVERS HAVE THAT KNOW THEIR HAPPINESS . . . . 284 TWO KINGS   178
        ALONE WITH ALL THIS USELESS HAPPINESS?" . . . . . 285 TWO KINGS   200
        IMPULSIVE MEN THAT LOOK FOR HAPPINESS . . . . . . 369 EGO DOMINUS   40
        REMEMBER HIS DELIBERATE HAPPINESS. . . . . 370 EGO DOMINUS   53
        FORGOT IN CRUEL HAPPINESS . . . . 453 MERMAID   5
        AND SHE AND I, BEING SUNK IN HAPPINESS, ... 463 HARUN RASHID   51
        HAPPINESS . . . . 499 VACILLATION   V   T
        IT SEEMED, SO GREAT MY HAPPINESS, ... 501 VACILLATION   43
        ALL HAPPINESS IN ITS OWN CAUSE OR GROUND. . . . . 557 RIBH ECSTASY   4
        WILL HE HAVE HAPPINESS? GREAT SOBS HER BEING SHAKE. 676 ISLE STAT II 3   247
        THE GODS HATE HAPPINESS, AND WEAVE THEIR NETS . . . 767 SHADOW WATER A   399
HAPPY
        HAPPY AS CHILDREN WITH UNWITHERING LIPS, ... 30 OISIN 2   V 14B
        THE SONG OF THE HAPPY SHEPHERD . . . . 64 HAPPY SHEPHERD   T
        FOR HAPPY LOVERS PASSED TWO BY TWO WHERE I STOOD; . . 163 VALLEY LOVERS   2
        BECAUSE IT IS ALONE OF ALL THINGS HAPPY. . . . . 198 SEVEN WOODS   9
        HAS MADE THEM SO HAPPY AND HOPELESS, SO DEAF AND SO BLIND 204 WITHER BOUGHS   20
        THAT IT HAD ALL SEEMED HAPPY, AND YET WE'D GROWN . . 206 ADAMS CURSE   37
        THE HAPPY TOWNLAND . . . . 213 HAPPY TOWNLAND   T
        WHERE MANY HUNDRED SQUIRRELS ARE AS HAPPY . . . . 217 WOODS OF COOLE   5
        ARE YOU NOT HAPPY WINGED BODIES NOW? . . . . . . 234 SHADOW WATER B   273
        NOW THAT YOU HAVE HAPPY WINGED BODIES? . . . . . 234 SHADOW WATER B V 273
        IN HAPPY DANCES UNDER A WINDY MOON, ... 245 SHADOW WATER B   470
        "AND CANNOT HAVE A HUMOROUS HAPPY SPEECH." . . . . 300 BEGGAR CRIED   16
        AND SHE SEEMED HAPPY AS A KING, ... 313 MEMORY YOUTH   V   6
        HIS ART IS HAPPY, BUT WHO KNOWS HIS MIND? . . . . 370 EGO DOMINUS   54
        IS ALWAYS HAPPY LIKE A BIRD OR A BEAST; . . . . . 373 PHASES OF MOON   38
        A STUPID HAPPY CREATURE . . . . 400 DEMON BEAST   31
        OR EVERY BELLOWS BURST, BE HAPPY STILL. . . . . . 405 FOR DAUGHTER   72
        UPON SOME BRAND-NEW HAPPY DAY; . . . . 432 NINETEEN 19   V 106
        THAT SHE IS HAPPY BEING CRAZY; . . . . 568 SWEET DANCER   10
        NO MAN CAN KNOW A HAPPY MAN . . . . 598 STONE CROSS   11
        OF AN UNBROKEN HAPPY MIND. . . . . 626 OLD MEN BE MAD   14
        AND SEE AGAIN THE HAPPY WOODLAND LIGHT, ... 664 ISLE STAT II 2   58
        OF THE HAPPY FLOWER MINIONS. . . . . 667 ISLE STAT II 3   29
        AND THE HAPPY WINGED DAY. . . . . 668 ISLE STAT II 3   64
        BUT ART THOU HAPPY? LET ME GAZE ON THEE . . . . . 671 ISLE STAT II 3   144
        BUT ART THOU HAPPY? YOUTH, I AM AT PEACE. . . . . 672 ISLE STAT II 3   150
        BUT ART THOU HAPPY? THOSE GREY EYES OF THINE . . . 672 ISLE STAT II 3   151
        THOU SHALT OUTLIVE THINE AMOROUS HAPPY TIME, . . . 674 ISLE STAT II 3   203
        SHE SMILES--IS HAPPY WITH HER WANDERING GRIEFS. . . 702 MOSADA 3   95
        LIKE HAPPY THOUGHTS GROWN SAD IN EVIL DAYS. . . . 703 MOSADA 3   116
        AND BE SO HAPPY." TO HIS HANDS SHE CLINGS, ... 714 FERENCZ RENYI   100
        AND BE SO HAPPY." TO HIS HAND SHE CLINGS, ... 714 FERENCZ RENYI V 100
        OH, SO HAPPY WOULD WE BE! . . . . 726 LOVERS QUARREL   16
        IN HAPPY DANCES, UNDER A WINDY MOON; . . . . . . 763 SHADOW WATER A   318
        FOR LOVE IS KIND AND HAPPY. O COME WITH ME! . . . 767 SHADOW WATER A   396
HARBOUR
        AND THE FISHER MEN AND WOMEN FROM THE DRIPPING HARBOUR WALL 718 PHANTOM SHIP   11
        . . . SEE, SHE ROUNDS THE HARBOUR CLEAR. . . . . 718 PHANTOM SHIP   13
HARBOURING   SEE ECHO-HARBOURING
HARD
        CAME AFTER THE HARD GAZE OF YOUTH, OR AN OLD MAN LIFTED   59 OISIN 3   170
            HIS HEAD;
        A WEARY WOMAN SLEEPS SO HARD! . . . . 95 MOLL MAGEE   21
        AND THINK THAT YOU WERE HARD AND UNKIND, ... 146 FISH   7
        THOUGH NOW IT'S HARD, TILL TROUBLE IS AT AN END; . . 200 FOLLY COMFORT V   5
        WHAT GOOD IS THERE IN THIS HARD WAY OF LIVING, . . 225 SHADOW WATER B   69
        WOMEN ARE HARD AND PROUD AND STUBBORN-HEARTED, . . 245 SHADOW WATER B   479
        HOW HARD A LIFE HER SERVANT LIVES. . . . . . . 336 YOUNG BEAUTY   14
        AND THEN HE LAUGHED TO THINK THAT WHAT SEEMED HARD . 377 PHASES OF MOON   136
        AND TOILED SO HARD AND LATE . . . . 432 NINETEEN 19   95
        FOR IN MY FIRST HARD SPRINGTIME WE WERE FRIENDS, . 473 ALL SOUL NIGHT   62
        FOR IN MY FIRST HARD SPRING-TIME WE WERE FRIENDS, . 473 ALL SOUL NIGHT V 62
        SO HARD I STRUCK. . . . . 518 HIS CONFIDENCE   8
        REMOTE FROM ALL THE HARD EARTH TROUBLES, ... 731 PRIEST FAIRY   80
        HAS MOULDED THE HARD YEARS. . . . . 738 MOURN THEN ON   8
        AND THIS HARD FLAG OF STONE, ... 739 EARL PAUL   6
HARDER
        IS TO WORK HARDER THAN ALL THESE, AND YET . . . . 205 ADAMS CURSE   11
        BRED TO A HARDER THING . . . . 291 TO A FRIEND   9
        BLINDER SORROWS, HARDER WAGE-- . . . . 733 STREET DANCERS   58
HARDEST
        HE SET HIS CHISEL TO THE HARDEST STONE. . . . . . 369 EGO DOMINUS   32
HARDIHOOD
        FOR HIS GREAT HARDIHOOD. . . . . 741 EARL PAUL   56
HARD-LIVING
        HARD-LIVING MEN AND MEN OF THOUGHT . . . . . . 787 HUDDON DUDDON   13
HARDLY
        I HARDLY HEAR THE CURLEW CRY, ... 189 BAILE AILLINN   1
        WILL HARDLY SEEM WORTH THINKING OF . . . . . . 202 NEVER GIVE ALL   2
        THE SECOND COMING! HARDLY ARE THOSE WORDS OUT . . . 402 SECOND COMING   11

HARDLY (CONTINUED)
```
    HARDLY DARED TO WET HIS MOUTH  . . . . . . .              454 EMPTY CUP              3
    WHILE THE WIND IS LIGHT.  THE OAR CAN HARDLY MOVE HER, . .  754 SHADOW WATER A      157
HARD-RIDING
    HARD-RIDING COUNTRY GENTLEMEN, . . . . . . . .            639 BEN BULBEN            75
HARE
    THE HARE GROWS OLD AS SHE PLAYS IN THE SUN . . . . .       27 OISIN 1             412
    "OLD GROWS THE HARE AS SHE PLAYS IN THE SUN, . . . . .     28 OISIN 1          V 420
    THE HARE LEAPED IN THE GRASS.  YOUNG NIAMH CAME . . .      44 OISIN 2          V 229
    THE HARE RUNS BY ME GROWING BOLD-- . . . . . . .          84 MAD KING GOLL    V  47
    THE COLLAR-BONE OF A HARE  . . . . . . . . . . .         330 BONE OF A HARE        T
    THE COLLAR-BONE OF A HARE  . . . . . . . . . . .         330 BONE OF A HARE       10
    THROUGH THE WHITE THIN BONE OF A HARE. . . . . . .       330 BONE OF A HARE       16
    WHERE THE MOUNTAIN HARE HAS LAIN. . . . . . . .          350 MEMORY                6
    A SPECKLED CAT AND A TAME HARE . . . . . . . . .         380 SONGS FOOL 1          1
    THE HARE MAY RUN TILL IT'S FOUND . . . . . . . .         380 SONGS FOOL 1         11
    WHERE THE BROWN HARE MIGHT BE, . . . . . . . . .         381 SONGS FOOL 2          4
    AND THAT HE CHANGED INTO A HARE. . . . . . . . .         412 TOWER                70
    THE DEATH OF THE HARE . . . . . . . . . . . .           453 DEATH OF HARE         T
    THE HARE LEAP TO THE WOOD, . . . . . . . . . .          453 DEATH OF HARE         2
    AT THE DEATH OF THE HARE. . . . . . . . . . .           453 DEATH OF HARE        12
    AS THE MOORFOWL AND THE HARE, . . . . . . . . .         706 DAWN-SONG            28
    THE HARE HATH LAID ASLEEP HER FROLIC WITS, . . . . .    712 FERENCZ RENYI        72
HARE'S
    A PEERING HARE'S;" AND YET I MURMURED NOT, . . . . . .  684 SEEKER               56
HARES
    OF PLANETS WATCHING, WATCHING THE RACE OF HARES . . .    44 OISIN 2          V 228B
    THE HARES RUN BY ME GROWING BOLD. . . . . . . .          84 MAD KING GOLL        47
    AND YOUNG HARES BROOK MY HARMLESS HOLD-- . . . . . .     84 MAD KING GOLL    V  47
    AND HARES RUN NEAR ME GROWING BOLD. . . . . . . .        84 MAD KING GOLL    V  47
    FROM HUMAN THOUGHT, AS HARES AND MICE AND CONEYS . . .  218 WOODS OF COOLE       31
HARK
    HARK! HE'S DEAD--MY DROWSY BROTHER, . . . . . . .       656 ISLE STAT I 3        18
    AND ONE ALONE OF ALL WOULD HARK, . . . . . . . .       671 ISLE STAT II 3      123
HARLOT
    ONE IS A HARLOT, AND ONE A CHILD . . . . . . . .       358 PRESENCES            12
    THE HARLOT AND THE CHILD. . . . . . . . . . .         601 THOSE IMAGES         12
HARM
    OUT OF ALL HARM, . . . . . . . . . . . . .            574 MAIDS 1ST SONG        8
HARMLESS
    AND YOUNG HARES BROOK MY HARMLESS HOLD-- . . . . . .     84 MAD KING GOLL    V  47
HARMONIC
    WITH THAT SONG LEADING WHERE HARMONIC WOODS . . . .    657 ISLE STAT I 3        43
HARMONIOUS
    WITH YOUR HARMONIOUS CHOIR . . . . . . . . . .        174 ELEMENT POWERS        8
    WITH YOUR HARMONIOUS QUIRE, . . . . . . . . . .       174 ELEMENT POWERS V      8
    DIZZY WITH HARMONIOUS SOUND, . . . . . . . . .        446 COLONUS PRAISE        7
HARMONY
    AND ALL THAT FAMOUS HARMONY OF LEAVES, . . . . . .    120 SORROW OF LOVE        3
HARNESS
    "HARNESS AN ASS AND CART, . . . . . . . . . .        596 COLONEL MARTIN       51
HAROUN
    BELOVED HAROUN EL RASHID, OCCUPIED  . . . . . . .     462 HARUN RASHID     V   24
    THAT YEAR WHEN GREAT HAROUN EL RASHID KILLED . . . .  462 HARUN RASHID     V   31
HARP
    GAVE ME A HARP, AND BID ME SING, . . . . . . . .      16 OISIN 1             232
    A HARP OF SILVER IN MY HANDS, . . . . . . . . .       16 OISIN 1             232
    GAVE ME A HARP, AND BADE ME SING, . . . . . . . .     16 OISIN 1          V 232
    AND CAUGHT THE SILVER HARP AWAY, . . . . . . . .      17 OISIN 1             240
    "O SADDEST HARP IN ALL THE WORLD, . . . . . . . .     17 OISIN 1             245
    THE HARP AWAY.  A DOLOROUS POOL . . . . . . . .       17 OISIN 1          V 240
    THEREIN THE SILVER HARP HE HURLED . . . . . . . .     17 OISIN 1          V 244
    "THE SADDEST HARP IN ALL THE WORLD!" . . . . . .      17 OISIN 1             246
    I SAW THIS HARP ALL SONGLESS LIE, . . . . . . . .     85 MAD KING GOLL    V  55
    AND ALL AROUND THE HARP STRING TOLD HIS PRAISE, . .  109 CUCHULAIN SEA    V  44
    AWOKE THE HARP STRINGS LONG AGO. . . . . . . . .     190 BAILE AILLINN    V  37
    WERE HOVERING OVER THE HARP STRINGS . . . . . . .    195 BAILE AILLINN    V 141
    I HEAR THE HARP STRINGS PRAISE THEM, OR HEAR THEIR MOURNFUL  210 UNDER THE MOON V  16
        TALK.
    I HEAR THE HARP STRING PRAISE THEM OR HEAR THEIR MOURNFUL    210 UNDER THE MOON V  16
        TALK.
    AS MEN IN THE OLD TIMES, BEFORE THE HARP BEGAN, . . . .   219 WOODS OF COOLE V  43
    THE HARP OF AENGUS . . . . . . . . . . . .           219 HARP OF AENGUS        T
    HE MADE A HARP WITH DRUID APPLE-WOOD . . . . . .      220 HARP OF AENGUS       11
    HE MADE A HARP WITH DRUID APPLE WOOD . . . . . .      220 HARP OF AENGUS V     11
    WERE'T NOT THAT THERE IS MAGIC IN HIS HARP, . . . .   222 SHADOW WATER B       16
    THAT THERE IS MAGIC IN THAT HARP OF HIS, . . . . .    222 SHADOW WATER B V     16
    AND FOR THIS END THEY GAVE ME MY OLD HARP . . . .     237 SHADOW WATER B      327
    YOUR RAVING OF A MESSAGE AND A HARP . . . . . .       237 SHADOW WATER B      331
    THEY GAVE ME THAT OLD HARP OF THE NINE SPELLS . . .   237 SHADOW WATER B V    327
    HAS COME INTO THE JEWELS OF THE HARP . . . . . .      239 SHADOW WATER B V 371A
    AND THAT OLD HARP AWAKENS OF ITSELF . . . . . .       252 SHADOW WATER B      617
    PLAYED ON HIS HARP.  AND I WOULD BE AS SAD . . . .    747 SHADOW WATER A        3
    GAVE HIM HIS HARP.  NOW THAT HE IS ASLEEP, . . . .    748 SHADOW WATER A       18
    TAUGHT ME WISE MUSIC, AND GAVE ME THIS OLD HARP; . .  750 SHADOW WATER A       76
    BUT WOMEN AND JUGGLERS AND PLAYERS ON THE HARP, . .   752 SHADOW WATER A      115
    I AM AFRAID OF THE HARP.  O! WINGS ON WINGS! . . .    759 SHADOW WATER A      236
    I AM AFRAID OF HIS LOW-LAUGHING HARP. . . . . .       759 SHADOW WATER A      239
    I AM AFRAID OF HIS LOW LAUGHING HARP. . . . . .       759 SHADOW WATER A V    239
    AND LEAN YOUR LIPS DEVOUTLY TO THIS HARP, . . . .     762 SHADOW WATER A      287
    FOR HE WHO GAVE IT CALLED IT AENGUS' HARP . . . .     762 SHADOW WATER A      288
```

		PAGE	TITLE	LINE

HARP   (CONTINUED)
    HE MADE A HARP WITH DRUID APPLE WOOD . . . . 763 SHADOW WATER A   306
    HE MADE A HARP WITH DRUID APPLE-WOOD . . . . 763 SHADOW WATER A V 306
    UPON THIS WORLD NO LONGER. THE HARP CRIES OUT. . . . . 769 SHADOW WATER A V 430
HARPER
    IT WAS THAT HARPER PUT IT IN MY THOUGHTS, ... 243 SHADOW WATER B   423
HARPER'S
    OF THE HARPER'S DAUGHTER AND HER FRIEND. . . . . . . 192 BAILE AILLINN   76
    WHERE THAT WISE HARPER'S FINGER RAN. . . . . . . 195 BAILE AILLINN   156
    WHERE THAT WISE HARPER'S FINGERS RAN. . . . . . . 195 BAILE AILLINN V 156
    OF THE HARPER'S DAUGHTER IF THEY WILL, ... 197 BAILE AILLINN   199
HARPERS
    OF HARPERS AND YOUNG MEN; AND THEY . . . . . . 189 BAILE AILLINN   19
    AND HARPERS, PACING WITH HIGH HEAD . . . . . . 193 BAILE AILLINN   107
    AND HARPERS PONDERING WITH BOWED HEAD . . . . . 193 BAILE AILLINN V 107
    HEARING THE HARPERS PLAY, THE PINE-WOOD CRACKLE, . . . 759 SHADOW WATER A   241
    HEARING THE HARPERS PLAY, THE PINE WOOD CRACKLE, . . . 759 SHADOW WATER A V 241
HARPING
    NINE MOONS. AND FROM THE HARPING OF THE FOOL? . . . . 747 SHADOW WATER A   14
HARPS
    AS MEN IN THE OLD TIMES, BEFORE THE HARPS BEGAN, . . . 219 WOODS OF COOLE   43
HARPSTRING
    AND ALL AROUND THE HARPSTRING TOLD HIS PRAISE, ... 109 CUCHULAIN SEA V   44
    I HEAR THE HARPSTRING PRAISE THEM OR HEAR THEIR MOURNFUL 210 UNDER THE MOON V   16
        TALK.
HARP-STRING
    AND ALL AROUND THE HARP-STRING TOLD HIS PRAISE, . . . 109 CUCHULAIN SEA   44
    I HEAR THE HARP-STRING PRAISE THEM, OR HEAR THEIR MOURNFUL 210 UNDER THE MOON   16
        TALK.
HARP-STRINGS
    AWOKE THE HARP-STRINGS LONG AGO. . . . . . . 190 BAILE AILLINN   37
    WERE HOVERING OVER THE HARP-STRINGS . . . . . . 195 BAILE AILLINN   141
    THE HARP-STRINGS HAVE BEGUN TO CRY OUT TO THE EAGLES. . . 769 SHADOW WATER A   431
HARRIED
    SUDDENLY, AND RAN AT THEM AND HARRIED THEM. . . . . 185 QUEEN MAEVE   119
    COULD; HE WAS SO HARRIED, CHEER; . . . . . . 412 TOWER   76
    COULD, SO HE WAS HARRIED, CHEER; . . . . . . 412 TOWER   V 76
    HARRIED, AND BURKE'S GREAT MELODY AGAINST IT. . . . . 487 SEVEN SAGES   16
    AND HARRIED ALBAN TOWNS, AND OVERTHREW . . . . . 749 SHADOW WATER A   40
HARRIERS
    SHE RODE TO HARRIERS? . . . . 392 EASTER 1916   23
HARROW
    THE GOLDEN PLOUGH AND HARROW AND SPOKE ALOUD . . . . 609 IN TARAS HALLS   12
HARRY
    BUT HARRY US WITH HOPES THAT COME TO NOTHING, . . . 250 SHADOW WATER B   579
    THAT WE MAY HARRY HIM." THEREON . . . . . . 275 GREY ROCK   106
    LIKE A GREY OWL MEN HARRY OUT . . . . . . 740 EARL PAUL   23
HARSH
    THAT WOULD BE HARSH FOR CHILDREN THAT HAVE STRAYED. . . 201 OLD MEMORY   12
    THAT HAD BEEN HARSH FOR CHILDREN THAT HAVE STRAYED. . . 201 OLD MEMORY   V 12
    AND WOULD BE NO HARSH FRIEND. WHEN NIGHT HAD DEEPENED, 283 TWO KINGS   138
    AND I HAVE NOTHING BUT HARSH SUN; . . . . . . 344 DEJECTION   V   8
    SWEET AND HARSH, HARSH AND SWEET, ... 382 SONG OF FOOL   10
    SWEET AND HARSH, HARSH AND SWEET, ... 382 SONG OF FOOL   10
    TOLD OF A HARSH REPROOF, OR TRIVIAL EVENT . . . . 443 SCHOOL CHILDR   11
HARSHNESS
    HARSHNESS OF THEIR DESIRE . . . . 345 ON WOMAN   20
HART
    OF THE DREAR HART LAKE. . . . . 143 HOST OF AIR   4
HARUN
    THE GIFT OF HARUN AL-RASHID . . . . 460 HARUN RASHID   T
    DESERT GEOMETRY OR THE GIFT OF HARUN AL-RASCHID . . . 460 HARUN RASHID   V   T
    WHAT GREAT HARUN AL-RASHID, OCCUPIED . . . . . 462 HARUN RASHID   24
HARVEST
    THAT SLUMBERED IN THE HARVEST MOON, ...   85 MAD KING GOLL   50
    THAT SLUMBERED 'NEATH THE HARVEST MOON, ...   85 MAD KING GOLL V 50
HARVESTERS
    MARINERS, ROUGH HARVESTERS! . . . . 540 FROM ANTIGONE   5
    MARINERS, WILD HARVESTERS! . . . . 540 FROM ANTIGONE V   5
HARVEST'S
    THE HARVEST'S IN; THE GRANARY DOORS ARE SHUT; . . . 755 SHADOW WATER A   177
HARVEST-TIME
    WATCHING OUR SHEPHERD SPORTS AT HARVEST-TIME . . . . 340 SHEP GOATHERD   41
HASSAN
    AND HASSAN WILL BE WITH THEM--HE WAS SO SMALL, . . . 699 MOSADA 3   13
    HASSAN IS WITH THEM TOO--HE WAS SO SMALL, ... 699 MOSADA 3   V 13
HASTE
    SIGHING REPLIED: "WHAT NEED HAVE WE FOR HASTE . . . 276 TWO KINGS   V   C
    DID I ON QUIVERING PINIONS HASTE, ... 670 ISLE STAT II 3   111
HASTEN
    DRIPPING AND DOUBLING LANDWARD, AS THOUGH THEY WOULD HASTEN   48 OISIN 3   15
        AWAY,
    DRIPPING AND DOUBLING LANDWARD, AS THOUGH THEY WOULD HASTEN   57 OISIN 3   143
        AWAY,
    NOR WOULD YOU RISE AND HASTEN AWAY, ... 176 BELOVED DEAD   7
HASTY
    MOST COURTEOUS TO SLOW AGE AND HASTY YOUTH, ... 339 SHEP GOATHERD   19
HAT
    AFTER A RAGGED HAT IN BISCAY BAY; . . . . . . 270 PARDON FATHERS   14
    WITH A HAT OUT OF FASHION, ... 627 STATES HOLIDAY   29

		PAGE	TITLE	LINE

HATCHES
THE HOLD IS FULL OF TREASURE. FULL TO THE HATCHES. • • •   247 SHADOW WATER B   532
HATE
BY KNOWING NOR TUMULT NOR HATE NOR STRIFE, • • • • • •   9 OISIN 1   95
THE THINGS THAT MOST OF ALL I HATE: • • • • • • • •   24 OISIN 1   359
TWO THINGS THAT 'FORE ALL ELSE I HATE, • • • • • • •   24 OISIN 1   V   359
AND I MUST NEEDS ENDURE AND HATE AND WEEP, • • • • •   35 OISIN 2   85
HATE ON AND LOVE THROUGH UNREPINING HOURS. • • • • • •   80 EPHEMERA   22
I FIND UNDER THE BOUGHS OF LOVE AND HATE, • • • • • •   101 ROSE UPON ROOD   10
THE HOUR OF THY GREAT WIND OF LOVE AND HATE. • • • • •   170 SECRET ROSE   28
HE DOES NOT HATE SEAFARERS AS HE HATES • • • • • • •   224 SHADOW WATER B   53
AND SHOOK WITH HATE AND FEAR. • • • • • • • • • •   254 WOMAN HOMER   4
THOSE THAT I FIGHT I DO NOT HATE, • • • • • • • •   328 IRISH AIRMAN   3
THE LIVING MEN THAT I HATE, • • • • • • • • • •   347 FISHERMAN   13
YET KNOWS THAT TO BE CHOKED WITH HATE • • • • • • •   405 FOR DAUGHTER   52
NOR HATE OF WHAT'S TO COME, NOR PITY FOR WHAT'S GONE, • •   427 PHANTOM HATRED   30
THEY HAD ALL THAT HAD THEIR HATE: • • • • • • • •   514 JANE GROWN OLD   13
SAY THAT OF LIVING MEN I HATE • • • • • • • • • •   539 MEETING   11
WHY DO I HATE MAN, WOMAN OR EVENT? • • • • • • • •   558 RIBH CHRISTIAN   7
SO DID FANATICISM AND HATE ENSLAVE IT, • • • • • •   630 CIRCUS ANIMALS   22
AND PLAY WITH HIS IMMORTAL HATE. • • • • • • • •   736 SUMMER EVENING   12
BECAUSE THE UNAMBITIOUS THAT HATE THE GODS • • • • •   754 SHADOW WATER A   V   158
THE GODS HATE HAPPINESS, AND WEAVE THEIR NETS • • • •   767 SHADOW WATER A   399
TILL THE SIDE OF HATE COMES UP. • • • • • • • •   776 AGAINST WITCH   35
HATED   SEE GOD-HATED
HAS HATED EVERY MAN THAT'S NOT IN LOVE, • • • • • •   224 SHADOW WATER B   51
ON THOSE THAT HATED "THE PLAYBOY • • • • • • • •   294 HATED PLAYBOY   T
ON THOSE THAT HATED "THE PLAY-BOY • • • • • • • •   294 HATED PLAYBOY   V   T
FROM FOUR GREAT MINDS THAT HATED WHIGGERY. • • • • •   486 SEVEN SAGES   7
ALL HATED WHIGGERY: BUT WHAT IS WHIGGERY? • • • • •   486 SEVEN SAGES   10
I WHO HAVE ALWAYS HATED WORK, • • • • • • • • •   605 YOU CONTENT   19
IS HE WHO LABOURED ON, DERIDED, HATED, • • • • • •   738 MOURN THEN ON   11
HATER
I BECAME A MAN, A HATER OF THE WIND, • • • • • • •   177 PAST GREATNESS   7
HATES
HE DOES NOT HATE SEAFARERS AS HE HATES • • • • • •   224 SHADOW WATER B   53
CRAMM'D ALL HER YOUTH: AND HATES HAVE BOUGHT AND SOLD • •   687 TWO TITANS   13
HATING
EACH HATING WHAT THE OTHER LOVED, • • • • • • • •   539 MEETING   3
IN HATING GOD SHE MAY CREEP CLOSE TO GOD. • • • • •   558 RIBH CHRISTIAN   V   18
HATRED
FOR SOMEBODY HID HATRED AND HOPE AND DESIRE AND FEAR • •   153 CHANGE BELOVED   4
AND I HAVE HATRED AND HOPE AND DESIRE AND FEAR • • •   153 CHANGE BELOVED   V   4
FOR LOVE IS WAR, AND THERE IS HATRED IN IT: • • • •   244 SHADOW WATER B   459
BETWEEN MY HATRED AND DESIRE, • • • • • • • • •   400 DEMON BEAST   6
IF THERE'S NO HATRED IN A MIND • • • • • • • • •   405 FOR DAUGHTER   54
AN INTELLECTUAL HATRED IS THE WORST, • • • • • • •   405 FOR DAUGHTER   57
CONSIDERING THAT, ALL HATRED DRIVEN HENCE, • • • • •   405 FOR DAUGHTER   65
FOR ARROGANCE AND HATRED ARE THE WARES • • • • • •   406 FOR DAUGHTER   75
I SEE PHANTOMS OF HATRED AND OF THE HEART'S • • •   425 PHANTOM HATRED   T
AND WOULD THROUGH HATRED OF THE BAYS • • • • • • •   436 FOR MY SON   15
OR OUT OF ABSTRACT HATRED, AND SHED BLOOD, • • • •   482 BLOOD AND MOON   38
TURN HATRED INTO SPORT, • • • • • • • • • • •   506 REMORSE SPEECH   8
GREAT HATRED, LITTLE ROOM, • • • • • • • • • •   506 REMORSE SPEECH   12
I STUDY HATRED WITH GREAT DILIGENCE, • • • • • • •   558 RIBH CHRISTIAN   3
A DARKER KNOWLEDGE AND IN HATRED TURN • • • • • •   558 RIBH CHRISTIAN   14
HATRED OF GOD MAY BRING THE SOUL TO GOD. • • • • •   558 RIBH CHRISTIAN   18
OUT OF THEIR HATRED. MY BELOVED, FAREWELL. • • • •   767 SHADOW WATER A   400
HATRED MAY BE SWEET TO THE TASTE." • • • • • • •   776 AGAINST WITCH   31
HATRED MAY BE SWEET IN THE TASTE." • • • • • • •   776 AGAINST WITCH   V   31
HATS
NINE BOOKS OR NINE HATS • • • • • • • • • • •   628 JANE MOUNTAIN   3
HAUGHTIER
BUT HERE'S A HAUGHTIER TEXT, • • • • • • • • •   259 UNWORTH PRAISE   12
AND BUILDINGS THAT A HAUGHTIER AGE DESIGNED, • • • •   418 ANCEST HOUSES   34
AND HAUGHTIER HEADED BURKE THAT PROVED THE STATE A TREE   481 BLOOD AND MOON   V   22
HAUGHTIER-HEADED
AND HAUGHTIER-HEADED BURKE THAT PROVED THE STATE A TREE,   481 BLOOD AND MOON   22
HAUGHTY
THEREON DID SHE LOOK HAUGHTY AND SWEET: • • • • •   6 OISIN 1   54
SHE'LL NOT ASK A HAUGHTY DRESS: • • • • • • • •   124 CATHLEEN PARA   6
THEIR HAUGHTY IMAGES THAT CANNOT WITHER, • • • • •   184 QUEEN MAEVE   87
THEIR HAUGHTY IMAGES THAT CANNOT FADE, • • • • • •   184 QUEEN MAEVE   V   88
THE HAUGHTY IMAGES, THAT CANNOT PERISH • • • • •   184 QUEEN MAEVE   V   88
OF SOME MOST HAUGHTY DEED OR THOUGHT • • • • • •   436 FOR MY SON   13
HAUNTED   SEE FAIRY-HAUNTED
I AM HAUNTED BY NUMBERLESS ISLANDS, AND MANY A DANAAN   122 WHITE BIRDS   9
SHORE,
HAUNTER   SEE TOMB-HAUNTER
HAUNTS
AMONG THE HAUNTS OF BEE AND BIRD. • • • • • • •   729 PRIEST FAIRY   42
HAVING
AND HAVING SUCH WIDE-OPEN, SHINING EYES. • • • • •   231 SHADOW WATER B   200
HAVING THEIR LIFE IN HIM. THOUGH IT BE THE MOON • • •   240 SHADOW WATER B   377
BROKEN-HEARTED, HAVING LOST HIS QUEEN • • • • • •   242 SHADOW WATER B   407
BROKENHEARTED, HAVING LOST HIS QUEEN • • • • • •   242 SHADOW WATER B   V   407
AND HAVING LIT UPON THIS WOMAN THERE, • • • • • •   248 SHADOW WATER B   542
AND HAVING LIT UPON THIS WOMAN HERE, • • • • •   248 SHADOW WATER B   V   542
IN HAVING ONE ANOTHER? HOW COULD I REST • • • •   249 SHADOW WATER B   571
BELOVED, HAVING DRAGGED THE NET ABOUT US, • • • •   252 SHADOW WATER B   615
AND SLEEPY HAVING HAD THEIR MEAL: • • • • • • •   271 GREY ROCK   V   17

	PAGE	TITLE		LINE
HAVING (CONTINUED)				
AND HAVING SAID IT, BURST IN TEARS.	273	GREY ROCK		48
HAVING NO THOUGHT BUT FOR HIS QUEEN EDAIN,	276	TWO KINGS	V	1
HAVING LOVED GOD ONCE, BUT MAYBE	299	THREE HERMITS		26
AND HAVING TALKED TO SOME LATE HOUR	324	ROBERT GREGORY		4
HAVING GROWN SLUGGISH AND CONTEMPLATIVE.	325	ROBERT GREGORY		40
AND HAVING NO DESIRE THEY CANNOT TELL	376	PHASES OF MOON		107
BUT HAVING NO DESIRE THEY CANNOT TELL	376	PHASES OF MOON	V	107
HAVING INHERITED A VIGOROUS MIND	422	MY DESCENDANTS		1
AND HAVING STRETCHED AND YAWNED AWHILE	612	NEWS ORACLE		11
WHERE DWELL THE MINDS OF OLD MEN HAVING PEACE,	721	WITCH VIVIEN		22
HAWK				
AND THE WOOD-WOMAN, WHOSE LOVER WAS CHANGED TO A BLUE-EYED HAWK;	209	UNDER THE MOON		13
AND THE WOOD WOMAN, WHOSE LOVER WAS CHANGED TO A BLUE-EYED HAWK;	209	UNDER THE MOON	V	13
THE HAWK	349	HAWK		T
"CALL DOWN THE HAWK FROM THE AIR;	349	HAWK		1
YELLOW-EYED HAWK OF THE MIND,	349	HAWK		14
PULL DOWN ESTABLISHED HONOUR; HAWK FOR NEWS	398	LEADERS CROWD		3
WITH AN EYE LIKE A HAWK.	627	STATES HOLIDAY		32
UP THERE SOME HAWK OR OWL HAS STRUCK,	633	MAN AND ECHO		43
HAWKING SEE A-HAWKING				
HAWKS				
TO BRAZEN HAWKS. NOR SELF-DELIGHTING REVERIE,	427	PHANTOM HATRED		29
HAWTHORN				
THE FALLING HAWTHORN BLOOM. BY MERE AND BROOK	677	ISLE STAT II 3		279
THE WICKED HAWTHORN TREE.	788	HAWTHORN TREE	V	T
SAID THE WICKED, CROOKED, HAWTHORN TREE;	788	HAWTHORN TREE		6
SAID THE WICKED, CROOKED, HAWTHORN TREE.	788	HAWTHORN TREE		14
HAY				
BRUSH LIGHTLY AS HAY MOUSE EARTH'S PEBBLES,	56	OISIN 3	V	128
TILL, FATTENING THE WINDS OF THE MORNING, AN ODOUR OF NEW-MOWN HAY	57	OISIN 3		153
AN ODOUR OF THE NEW-MOWN HAY	502	VACILLATION		58
HAY-COCK				
AS A HAY-COCK OUT ON THE FLOOD, OR A WOLF SUCKED UNDER A WEIR.	63	OISIN 3		220
HAYMOUSE				
BRUSH LIGHTLY AS HAYMOUSE EARTH'S PEBBLES,	56	OISIN 3		128
HAYNAU				
THE AUSTRIAN HAYNAU HE, IN MANY LANDS	709	FERENCZ RENYI		8
THE SOLDIER THUS, AND HAYNAU--"PEASANT, SPEAK	711	FERENCZ RENYI		54
HAYNAU, THE MAN OF SYSTEM, LIFTS HIS HAND	712	FERENCZ RENYI		62
HAYNAU, THINE HOUR HAS COME, THY FOLLOWERS FAR	715	FERENCZ RENYI		117
HAYNAU'S				
"CHOOSE!" RESTLESS HAYNAU'S FINGERS TAPPING GO.	711	FERENCZ RENYI		41
FROM HAYNAU'S LIFTED FINGERS--TWO DRAW NIGH	714	FERENCZ RENYI		104
HAYSTACK				
WHEREBY THE HAYSTACK- AND ROOF-LEVELLING WIND,	403	FOR DAUGHTER		5
HAZEL				
THAT SPRANG UNDER THE SEVEN HAZEL TREES,	35	OISIN 2		84
AN ISLE LAY LEVEL BEFORE US, WITH DRIPPING HAZEL AND OAK?	47	OISIN 3		10
AN ISLE LAY LEVEL BEFORE US, DRIPPING WITH HAZEL AND OAK?	47	OISIN 3	V	10
CEASED ON OUR HANDS AND OUR FACES, ON HAZEL AND OAK LEAF, THE LIGHT,	48	OISIN 3		23
. . . FOR, CUMBROUS WITH STEMS OF THE HAZEL AND OAK,	48	OISIN 3		25
. . . FAR FROM THE HAZEL AND OAK,	57	OISIN 3		146
AND THE SHADOWY HAZEL GROVE	119	PITY OF LOVE		6
I WENT OUT TO THE HAZEL WOOD,	149	WANDER AENGUS		1
AND CUT AND PEELED A HAZEL WAND,	149	WANDER AENGUS		3
AND CUT AND PEELED A HAZEL ROD,	149	WANDER AENGUS	V	3
A MAN WITH A HAZEL WAND CAME WITHOUT SOUND;	153	CHANGE BELOVED		6
A MAN WITH A WAND OF HAZEL CAME WITHOUT SOUND;	153	CHANGE BELOVED	V	6
I HAVE BEEN A HAZEL TREE, AND THEY HUNG	177	PAST GREATNESS		3
WHERE HAZEL AND ASH AND PRIVET BLIND THE PATHS;	180	QUEEN MAEVE		12
FLICKERING WITH ASH AND HAZEL, BUT HALF SHOWED	217	WOODS OF COOLE		8
I GROPED MY WAY FROM BEECH TO HAZEL WOOD,	283	TWO KINGS		139
WESTWARD OF TARA, AMONG THE HAZEL TREES--	283	TWO KINGS	V	135
TILL OAK AND HAZEL CEASED AND BEECH BEGAN,	283	TWO KINGS	V	139A
HAZEL LAVERY LIVING AND DYING, THAT TALE	602	GALLERY REVIS		23
"WE BURIED LATE IN A HAZEL DELL	729	PRIEST FAIRY		43
HAZELS				
OF HOLLIES, AND HAZELS, AND OAK TREES, A VALLEY WAS SLOPING AWAY	48	OISIN 3	V	26
SHOULD BE SO SIMPLE--A BAT ROSE FROM THE HAZELS	377	PHASES OF MOON		137
HAZEL-TREE				
I HAVE BEEN A HAZEL-TREE, AND THEY HUNG	177	PAST GREATNESS		3
HAZEL-TREES				
WESTWARD OF TARA, AMONG THE HAZEL-TREES--	283	TWO KINGS		135
HEAD SEE RED-HEAD MAST-HEAD GOAT-HEAD				
"AND EVERY HERO DROOP HIS HEAD?	4	OISIN 1		33
"WHY, AS YE RIDE, DROOPS LOW EACH HEAD?	4	OISIN 1	V	32
THERE WAS, OH PATRICK, BY THY HEAD,	7	OISIN 1		71
BOAST NOT, NOR MOURN WITH DROOPING HEAD	11	OISIN 1		129
AND SIGHING BOWED HER GENTLE HEAD,	12	OISIN 1		149
AS WE KISSED EACH ROSE'S HEAD;	21	OISIN 1	V	307
AND KISSED MY EYES, AND, SWAYING HER BRIGHT HEAD	29	OISIN 2		6
AND NOW SANG NIAM, SWAYING HER BRIGHT HEAD	29	OISIN 2	V	6
SO SANG YOUNG NIAM, SWAYING HER BRIGHT HEAD,	30	OISIN 2		15
HE SHIVERING PAUSED, AND RAISED HIS HEAD AND SCREAMED.	30	OISIN 2	V	25

364

HEAD (CONTINUED)

	PAGE	TITLE		LINE
IT BRINGS NO SHAME UPON A HUMAN HEAD	35	OISIN 2	V	90A
WITH BOWED HEAD, TREMBLING WHEN THE WHITE BLADE SHONE, . .	38	OISIN 2		137
AND ON MY BOSOM LAID HER WEEPING HEAD.	46	OISIN 2		250
DARK BALOR, AS OLD AS A FOREST, CAR-BORNE, HIS MIGHTY HEAD SUNK	53	OISIN 3		91
CAME BALOR, AS OLD AS A FOREST, CAR BORNE, HIS MIGHTY HEAD SUNK	53	OISIN 3	V	91
NOT COUGHING, MY HEAD ON MY KNEES.	58	OISIN 3		159
I WOULD LEAVE NO SAINT'S HEAD ON HIS BODY	58	OISIN 3		160
CAME AFTER THE HARD GAZE OF YOUTH, OR AN OLD MAN LIFTED HIS HEAD!	59	OISIN 3		170
. . . OR WAS LIFTED AN OLD MAN'S MILD HEAD.	59	OISIN 3	V	170
YET STILL SHE TURNS HER RESTLESS HEAD!	65	HAPPY SHEPHERD		5
WHILE HE BENT DOWN HIS FADING HEAD	82	MAD KING GOLL		10
BENDING LOW HIS PIOUS HEAD, ...	82	MAD KING GOLL	V	10
BENDING LOW HIS FADING HEAD, ...	82	MAD KING GOLL	V	10
HIS EYELIDS DROOP, HIS HEAD FALLS LOW, ...	98	FOXHUNTER		13
HIS EYELIDS CLOSE, HIS HEAD DROOPS LOW, ...	98	FOXHUNTER	V	13
LIFTS SLOW HIS WINTRY HEAD!	99	FOXHUNTER		46
UPON HIS HEAD TO CAST AWAY MY SORROW.	102	FERGUS DRUID		14
UPON HIS HEAD TO CAST AWAY MY CARE.	102	FERGUS DRUID	V	14
AND STILL I FEEL THE CROWN UPON MY HEAD.	103	FERGUS DRUID		20
BUT STILL I FEEL THE CROWN UPON MY HEAD.	103	FERGUS DRUID	V	20
THE SORROWS OF THE WORLD BOW DOWN MY HEAD.	104	FERGUS DRUID	V	38A
"YOUR HEAD A WHILE SEEMED LIKE A WOMAN'S HEAD	110	CUCHULAIN SEA		63
"YOUR HEAD A WHILE SEEMED LIKE A WOMAN'S HEAD	110	CUCHULAIN SEA		63
WITH HEAD BOWED ON HIS KNEES CUCHULAIN STAYED!	110	CUCHULAIN SEA		71
WITH HEAD BOWED ON HIS KNEES, CUCHULLIN STAID, ...	110	CUCHULAIN SEA	V	71
A CHAPLET FOR YOUR HEAD.	113	ROSE OF PEACE		8
THREATEN THE HEAD THAT I LOVE.	119	PITY OF LOVE		8
ALL THREATEN THE HEAD THAT I LOVE.	119	PITY OF LOVE	V	8
THE SHAKING OF ITS LEAFY HEAD.	134	TWO TREES		9
BECAUSE A FIRE WAS IN MY HEAD, ...	149	WANDER AENGUS		2
OF THE MATCHING OF RIBBONS FOR BOSOM AND HEAD, ...	151	OLD MOTHER		6
AND WRAPPED THE FLAMES ABOVE HIS HOLY HEAD!	162	ASKS FORGIVE		17
AND GATHERED THE FLAMES ABOVE HIS HOLY HEAD	162	ASKS FORGIVE	V	17
CUMHAL CALLED OUT, BENDING HIS HEAD, ...	166	BLESSED		1
CUMHAL CALLED OUT, BOWING HIS HEAD, ...	167	BLESSED	V	4A
AND HE NODS A DRUNKEN HEAD.	168	BLESSED		32
YOU WOULD COME HITHER, AND BEND YOUR HEAD, ...	175	BELOVED DEAD		3
AND I WOULD LAY MY HEAD ON YOUR BREAST!	175	BELOVED DEAD		4
KNOWING ONE, OUT OF ALL THINGS, ALONE, THAT HIS HEAD . .	177	PAST GREATNESS		8
A WALL BEHIND HIS BACK, OVER HIS HEAD	180	QUEEN MAEVE		5
BUT OUT OF THE DARK AIR OVER HER HEAD THERE CAME	187	QUEEN MAEVE		153
AN OLD MAN CAUGHT THE HORSE'S HEAD	191	BAILE AILLINN		57
AND HARPERS, PACING WITH HIGH HEAD	193	BAILE AILLINN		107
AND HARPERS PONDERING WITH BOWED HEAD	193	BAILE AILLINN	V	107
O HEART! O HEART! IF SHE'D BUT TURN HER HEAD, ...	200	FOLLY COMFORT		13
BUT WITH A MAN'S HEAD, OR A FAIR WOMAN'S, ...	233	SHADOW WATER B		245
AND NOW A LAGGARD WITH A WOMAN'S HEAD	234	SHADOW WATER B		260
THAT I MIGHT LAY IT ON YOUR HEAD AS A CROWN.	246	SHADOW WATER B		511
"SUCH A DELICATE HIGH HEAD, ...	259	PEACE		7
BEFORE HIS CHAIR AND BENDING DOWN MY HEAD	282	TWO KINGS		132
STOOD ON MY PATH. TREMBLING FROM HEAD TO FOOT	283	TWO KINGS		151
CROW UPON TARA." KING EOCHAID BOWED HIS HEAD	286	TWO KINGS		211
ABOUT YOUR HEAD TILL THE DUST STOPS YOUR EAR, ...	293	TO A SHADE		20
CAN RAVEL OUT WHAT'S IN MY HEAD.	295	THREE BEGGARS		12
I SHAKE FROM HEAD TO FOOT.	316	FRIENDS		28
HEAD UPON SHOULDER LEANT!	319	DOLLS		18
THE BELL-BEAT OF THEIR WINGS ABOVE MY HEAD, ...	323	SWANS AT COOLE		17
AND QUARRELS ARE BLOWN UP UPON THAT HEAD!	324	ROBERT GREGORY		13
PITY, AN ACHING HEAD, ...	346	ON WOMAN		38
AS THOUGH SOME OTHER NAME RAN IN HIS HEAD.	351	HER PRAISE		9
OF SOME STRANGE WOMAN'S NAME THAT RAN IN HIS HEAD. . . .	351	HER PRAISE	V	9
AFTER NINE YEARS, I SINK MY HEAD ABASHED.	353	PEOPLE		37
IF HEAD AND LIMB HAVE BEAUTY AND THE INSTEP'S HIGH AND LIGHT	354	HIS PHOENIX		21
SHE MIGHT, SO NOBLE FROM HEAD	355	PROPERTIUS		1
AS IF THE HAIR STOOD UP ON MY HEAD.	358	PRESENCES		2
IS TO SCRATCH YOUR HEAD	359	TO A SQUIRREL		7
SHE LIES, HER LOVELY PITEOUS HEAD AMID DULL RED HAIR . .	362	HER COURTESY		2
PLEASE A FANTASTIC HEAD.	366	HER CHRIS TREE		8
WITH MOTIONLESS HEAD ERECT.	383	VISION ROBART		32
NOW SHE HAS THROWN HER ARMS ABOVE HER HEAD!	390	IMAGE PAST		36
I HAVE PASSED WITH A NOD OF THE HEAD	392	EASTER 1916		5
THE GLITTERING EYES IN A DEATH'S HEAD	400	DEMON BEAST		9
A SHAPE WITH LION BODY AND THE HEAD OF A MAN, ...	402	SECOND COMING		14
ALL BREAK AND VANISH, AND EVIL GATHERS HEAD!	433	NINETEEN 19		117
BID A STRONG GHOST STAND AT THE HEAD	435	FOR MY SON		1
WITH SIXTY OR MORE WINTERS ON ITS HEAD, ...	444	SCHOOL CHILDR		38
FIRST TROD ON THE MOUNTAIN'S HEAD	488	CRAZED MOON		9
A MOMENT'S MEMORY TO THAT LAURELLED HEAD.	489	COOLE ARK 29		32
SO GET YOU GONE, VON HUEGEL, THOUGH WITH BLESSINGS ON YOUR HEAD.	503	VACILLATION		89
MAY CALL DOWN CURSES ON HIS HEAD	508	JANE BISHOP		4
WHEN HE TURNED HIS HEAD	511	JANE AND JACK		16
WHEN YOU TURNED YOUR HEAD	511	JANE AND JACK	V	16
HAD TURNED HIS STATELY HEAD.	526	AM OF IRELAND		10
AND LAY DOWN THAT HEAD	534	CONSOLATION		4
ALTERNATIVE SONG FOR THE SEVERED HEAD IN	549	SEVERED HEAD		T

		PAGE	TITLE	LINE

HEAD   (CONTINUED)

WITHOUT A THING IN HIS HEAD . . . . 552 SONGS REWRIT 2   10
ALONE WITH A CRAZY HEAD. . . . . 552 SONGS REWRIT 2 V 12
TO THOSE THAT NEVER SAW THIS TONSURED HEAD . . . . 555 RIBH AT TOMB   4
BLACK OUT! HEAVEN BLAZING INTO THE HEAD! . . . . . 566 LAPIS LAZULI   19
HE DROPPED UPON HIS HEAD AND DIED. . . . . 571 THREE BUSHES   52
HIS ROD AND ITS BUTTING HEAD . . . . 575 MAIDS 2ND SONG   3
BEAUTIFUL LOFTY THINGS! O'LEARY'S NOBLE HEAD! . . . 577 LOFTY THINGS   1
"OF PLASTER SAINTS"! HIS BEAUTIFUL MISCHIEVOUS HEAD THROWN   577 LOFTY THINGS   4
BACK.
PALLAS ATHENE IN THAT STRAIGHT BACK AND ARROGANT HEAD! . . 578 LOFTY THINGS   11
THE DOOR ABOVE HIS HEAD . . . . 585 ORAHILLY   33
A HAND UNDER HIS HEAD. . . . . 617 LONG-LEG FLY   8
A BRONZE HEAD . . . . 618 BRONZE HEAD   T
HERE AT RIGHT OF THE ENTRANCE THIS BRONZE HEAD, . . 618 BRONZE HEAD   1
THEN CERTAIN SHROUDS THAT MUTTERED HEAD TO HEAD . . 634 CUCHULAIN COMF   4
THEN CERTAIN SHROUDS THAT MUTTERED HEAD TO HEAD . . 634 CUCHULAIN COMF   4
UNDER BARE BEN BULBEN'S HEAD . . . . 640 BEN BULBEN   84
OF SWORD-BLUE WAVES OF CALM; WHILE O'ER HEAD BLINK . . 663 ISLE STAT II 2   42
A BEARDED WITCH, HER SLUGGISH HEAD LOW BENT . . . 685 SEEKER   72
OF FAILURE, AND TO CROWN HER CROWNLESS HEAD, . . . 688 TWO TITANS   48
LOWLY THE HEAD OF HIS MAGNIFICENCE . . . . 689 NETTLESHIP   6
DOWN LOW THE HEAD OF HIS MAGNIFICENCE . . . . . . 689 NETTLESHIP   V   6
AROUND MY HEAD AND DANCED AMONG THE GRASS; . . . . 690 MOSADA 1   19
POURS UP AND FLOATS IN FRAGRANCE ROUND MY HEAD . . 691 MOSADA 1   40
POURS UP AND FLOATS IN FRAGRANCE O'ER MY HEAD . . . 691 MOSADA 1   V   40
AND IN HER SINGING WOVE AROUND HER HEAD . . . . . 693 MOSADA 1   84
HER HEAD CAST BACKWARD IN HER UNLOOSED HAIR. . . . 701 MOSADA 3   67
UPON THY FACE? HOW HEAVILY THY HEAD . . . . 701 MOSADA 3   72
SAFE ON THE BREAST OF GOMEZ LIES THY HEAD, ... 703 MOSADA 3   101
SAFE ON THE BREAST OF VALLENCE IS THY HEAD . . . . 703 MOSADA 3   V   101
SAFE ON THE BREAST OF GOMEZ IS THY HEAD, ... 703 MOSADA 3   V   101
AH! WOE FOR YOUR WINGS AND YOUR HEAD-- . . . . . 708 FAIRY PEDANT   34
BUT THIS ONE--THIS ONE. NOW HIS HEAD DROPS LOW, . . 711 FERENCZ RENYI   39
"A LITTLE WILL I LAY MY WEARY HEAD, ... 712 FERENCZ RENYI   75
HE THOUGHT WISE THINGS AS HIS GREY HEAD NODDED, . . 728 PRIEST FAIRY   12
AND KEEP A COVERED HEAD." . . . . 742 EARL PAUL   64
AND UNDER LOVERS' EYELIDS. BEND YOUR HEAD . . . . 762 SHADOW WATER A   286
IN THE TOWER OVER HEAD, ... 772 SONG DEIRDRE 1 V   3
TO THE TOWER OVER HEAD, ... 772 SONG DEIRDRE 1 V   3
MY HEAD IS IN A CLOUD! . . . . 782 HEART FRIGHT   8
THE SINGING HEAD AND THE LADY . . . . 789 SINGING HEAD   V   T
HIS HEAD FROM OFF HIS BODY . . . . 789 SINGING HEAD   5
I BADE THEM FETCH HIS HEAD. . . . . 789 SINGING HEAD   12
HEADED   SEE MAN-HEADED SLEEPY-HEADED CAT-HEADED MANY-HEADED HAUGHTIER-HEADED
AND HAUGHTIER HEADED BURKE THAT PROVED THE STATE A TREE   481 BLOOD AND MOON V   22
HEADLONG
AND FOLLOWING HER AT A HEADLONG SPEED . . . . . . 12 OISIN 1   V   144
WHEN THE HEADLONG LIGHT IS LOOSE, ... 414 TOWER   135
HEAD'S   SEE SPEAR-HEAD'S
HEADS   SEE HILL-HEADS
THAT RAISE THEIR HEADS AND WANDER SINGING, ... 27 OISIN 1   419
. . . AND O'ER YOUR CAR HEADS PEER . . . . 73 ANASHU VIJAYA V   45
OF HOW I HEAR ON HILL HEADS HIGH . . . . 85 MAD KING GOLL V   53
IT SEEMED THEY RAISED THEIR LITTLE SILVER HEADS, . . . 126 DREAM OF FAERY   6
THEIR HEADS ON YOUR KNEES, AND DROWN THEIR EYES WITH YOUR   163 VALLEY LOVERS   6
HAIR,
YOU PUT SUCH FOLLY IN OUR HEADS . . . . 190 BAILE AILLINN   32
THEIR HEADS BEING TURNED WITH PRAISE AND FLATTERY; . . 245 SHADOW WATER B   480
THEY HAVE BEEN CIRCLING OVER OUR HEADS IN THE AIR, . . 247 SHADOW WATER B   525
BALD HEADS FORGETFUL OF THEIR SINS, ... 337 SCHOLARS   1
OLD, LEARNED, RESPECTABLE BALD HEADS . . . . . . 337 SCHOLARS   2
OLD MARBLE HEADS, OLD PICTURES EVERYWHERE; . . . . 491 COOLE BALLYLEE   28
A MYRIAD HEADS HAVE LAIN." " . . . . 496 MOHINI CHATTER   11
WHAT HEADS SHAKE OR NOD? . . . . 505 RESULT THOUGHT   18
I KNOCK THEIR HEADS ABOUT. . . . . 605 SONGS BURDEN 1   8
THEIR UNREMEMBERING HEARTS AND HEADS . . . . . . 639 BEN BULBEN   72
GO UP AND DOWN, AND RAISE THEIR HEADS AND SING . . 682 SEEKER   30
WHILE WE SHAKE OUR HEADS AND SCOLD . . . . 727 LOVERS QUARREL   54
AND PLUMED HEADS ABOUT HIM, ... 740 EARL PAUL   31
WHERE NIAM HEADS THE REVELRY. . . . . 743 DANAAN QUICK   29
HEADY
THAT HAS THE HEADY FLAVOUR OF NEW WINE, ... 240 SHADOW WATER B   374
BEING TOO HIGH, THEIR HEADY PROPHECIES . . . . . . 250 SHADOW WATER B   578
HEALED   SEE NEW-HEALED
AND HEALED MY WOUNDS WITH UNGUENTS OUT OF FLOWERS . . 41 OISIN 2   185
THEY HEALED MY WOUNDS! AND ON THE SKIN SUPINE . . . 41 OISIN 2   V   187
HIS HEALED SHAPE! AND FOR A HUNDRED YEARS . . . . 44 OISIN 2   V   221
HIS NEW HEALED SHAPE! AND FOR A HUNDRED YEARS . . . 44 OISIN 2   V   221
HEALING
HEALING FROM ITS LETTERED SLAB. THOSE SELF-SAME HANDS   503 VACILLATION   82
PERCHANCE
OTHERS KNOW THE HEALING EARTH, ... 733 STREET DANCERS   53
ALL THE HEALING EARTH MAY-TREASURE, ... 733 STREET DANCERS   63
ALL THE HEALING EARTH MAY TREASURE, ... 733 STREET DANCERS V   63
HEALTH
AND FIND MY HEALTH AGAIN IN THE SEA AIR," . . . . 299 BEGGAR CRIED   2
WHETHER HEALTH, WEALTH OR PEACE OF MIND WERE SPENT . . 429 NINETEEN 19   36
IS DRINKING HER HEALTH WHEN LONE, ALONE-- . . . . 551 SONGS REWRIT 1 V   4
MY MEDIAEVAL KNEES LACK HEALTH UNTIL THEY BEND, . . 603 GALLERY REVIS   33
HONOUR HAD LIVED SO LONG, THEIR HEALTH I FOUND. . . 603 GALLERY REVIS V   35

366

		PAGE	TITLE	LINE

HEALTHY
    "HE LIVES?" "HE LIVES AND IS A HEALTHY MAN." . . . . . 280 TWO KINGS   84
    I HAVE AS HEALTHY FLESH AND BLOOD AS ANY RHYMER'S HAD, . . 450 OWEN AHERNE   10
HEAP
    AND SHOULD HE DIE TO HEAP HIS BURIAL-MOUND . . . . . . 280 TWO KINGS   82
    AND SHOULD HE DIE TO HEAP HIS BURIAL MOUND . . . . . . 280 TWO KINGS V 82
    AND THEY WERE WHIRLING IN A HEAP. . . . . 297 THREE BEGGARS 47
    TILL THEY WERE WHIRLING IN A HEAP. . . . . 297 THREE BEGGARS V 47
    WHEN CLOSE TO HIS RIGHT HAND A HEAP . . . . 302 HOUR DAWN   11
HEAPED   SEE WEB-HEAPED CAIRN-HEAPED
    WHERE MEN HAVE HEAPED NO BURIAL-MOUNDS, ...   8 OISIN 1   82
    WHERE MEN HAVE HEAPED NO BURIAL-MOUNDS, ...   8 OISIN 1 V 82
    HEAPED BESIDE THE GLIMMERING WAVES, ... 21 OISIN 1   314
    MY SOUL, MY PREY, AND THIS MY HEAPED PILE. . . . . . . 45 OISIN 2 V 239B
    THEIR NAKED AND GLEAMING BODIES POURED OUT AND HEAPED IN 48 OISIN 3   28
      THE WAY.
    . . . HEAPED LOOSE WHERE THEY LAY. . . . . 48 OISIN 3 V 28
    BEFORE THEY HEAPED HIS GRAVE UNDER THE HILL; . . . . . 127 DREAM OF FAERY 16
    COME, HEART, WHERE HILL IS HEAPED UPON HILL; . . . . . 148 INTO TWILIGHT   9
    FOR WHOM THE CAIRN'S BUT HEAPED ANEW. . . . . 192 BAILE AILLINN 84
    THEY HAVE HEAPED THE STONES ABOVE HIS GRAVE . . . . . 193 BAILE AILLINN 115
    AND INSULT HEAPED UPON HIM FOR HIS PAINS, ... 292 TO A SHADE   15
    AND AFTER HEAPED UP STONE ON STONE, ... 307 HOUR DAWN   116
    AND HEAPED UP STONE ON STONE AGAIN, ... 307 HOUR DAWN   118
    AND AFTER HEAPED THE STONES AGAIN . . . . 307 HOUR DAWN V 116
    GRAVE IS HEAPED ON GRAVE . . . . 496 MOHINI CHATTER 19
    BIRTH IS HEAPED ON BIRTH . . . . 496 MOHINI CHATTER 23
HEAPED-UP
    AND THEN ON HEAPED-UP SKINS OF OTTERS SLEPT. . . . . . 41 OISIN 2   191
HEAR
    AND LIGHTNING FLASH FOR EVER? CEASE AND HEAR. . . . . 42 OISIN 2 V 207
    SAINT, DO YOU WEEP? I HEAR AMID THE THUNDER . . . . . 43 OISIN 2   209
    SAINT, DOST THOU WEEP? I HEAR AMID THE THUNDER . . . . 43 OISIN 2 V 209
    "I HEAR MY SOUL DROP DOWN INTO DECAY, ... 45 OISIN 2   235
    A GOOD NAME IS GOODLY TO HEAR OF, AND A GOOD NAME SURELY 51 OISIN 3 V 63
      IS THINE.
    CRIED OUT, DIM SEA, HEAR MY MOST PITEOUS STORY! . . . 68 SAD SHEPHERD   9
    "OH SEA, OLD SEA, HEAR THOU MY PITEOUS STORY!" . . . . 68 SAD SHEPHERD V 9
    NO OTHER.—HEAR, AND MAY THE INDOLENT FLOCKS . . . . . 71 ANASHU VIJAYA   4
    MAY PANTHERS END HIM.—HEAR, AND LOAD OUR KING . . . . 71 ANASHU VIJAYA   6
    WHO NEVER HEAR THE UNFORGIVING HOUND. . . . . 75 ANASHU VIJAYA   75
    OF HOW I HEAR ON HILL-HEADS HIGH . . . . 85 MAD KING GOLL V 53
    OF HOW I HEAR ON HILL HEADS HIGH . . . . 85 MAD KING GOLL V 53
    WITH EYES OF SADNESS CAME TO HEAR . . . . 85 MAD KING GOLL V 62
    WITH EYES OF SADNESS ROSE TO HEAR, ... 85 MAD KING GOLL V 62
    IN SOLEMN REVERIE ROSE TO HEAR . . . . 85 MAD KING GOLL V 62
    HE'LL HEAR NO MORE THE LOWING . . . . 88 STOLEN CHILD   44
    THEY HEAR HIM FEEBLY SAY, ... 99 FOXHUNTER   32
    LEST I NO MORE HEAR COMMON THINGS THAT CRAVE! . . . . 101 ROSE UPON ROOD 15
    BUT SEEK ALONE TO HEAR THE STRANGE THINGS SAID . . . . 101 ROSE UPON ROOD 19
    I OFTEN HEAR HIM SINGING TO AND FRO, ... 109 CUCHULAIN SEA V 49
    I OFTEN HEAR THE SWEET SOUND OF HIS BOW. . . . . . . 109 CUCHULAIN SEA V 50
    WE SHALL NO LONGER HEAR THE LITTLE CRY . . . . 115 ROSE OF BATTLE 35
    I HEAR LAKE WATER LAPPING WITH LOW SOUNDS BY THE SHORE; 117 ISLE INNISFREE 10
    I HEAR IT IN THE DEEP HEART'S CORE. . . . . 117 ISLE INNISFREE 12
    I HEAR LAKE WATER LAPPING WITH LOW SOUNDS ON THE SHORE; 117 ISLE INNISFREE V 10
    AND HEAR THE NARROW GRAVES CALLING MY CHILD AND ME. . . 147 UNAPPEAS HOST   6
    AND HEAR THE WINDS HAVE SHAKEN, THE UNAPPEASABLE HOST . 147 UNAPPEAS HOST V 11
    DO YOU NOT HEAR ME CALLING, WHITE DEER WITH NO HORNS? . 153 CHANGE BELOVED 1
    I HEAR THE SHADOWY HORSES, THEIR LONG MANES A-SHAKE, . 154 BELOVED PEACE   1
    I HEAR WHITE BEAUTY SIGHING, TOO, ... 156 FORGOT BEAUTY 19
    I HEAR PALE BEAUTY SIGHING TOO, ... 156 FORGOT BEAUTY V 19
    I HARDLY HEAR THE CURLEW CRY, ... 189 BAILE AILLINN 1
    OUR HEARTS CAN HEAR THE VOICES CHIDE. . . . . 192 BAILE AILLINN 94
    OUR HEART CAN HEAR THE VOICES CHIDE. . . . . 192 BAILE AILLINN V 94
    I HEAR THE HARP-STRING PRAISE THEM, OR HEAR THEIR MOURNFUL 210 UNDER THE MOON 16
      TALK.
    I HEAR THE HARP-STRING PRAISE THEM, OR HEAR THEIR MOURNFUL 210 UNDER THE MOON 16
      TALK.
    I HEAR THE HARP STRINGS PRAISE THEM, OR HEAR THEIR MOURNFUL 210 UNDER THE MOON V 16
      TALK.
    I HEAR THE HARP STRINGS PRAISE THEM, OR HEAR THEIR MOURNFUL 210 UNDER THE MOON V 16
      TALK.
    I HEAR THE HARPSTRING PRAISE THEM OR HEAR THEIR MOURNFUL 210 UNDER THE MOON V 16
      TALK.
    I HEAR THE HARPSTRING PRAISE THEM OR HEAR THEIR MOURNFUL 210 UNDER THE MOON V 16
      TALK.
    I HEAR THE HARP STRING PRAISE THEM OR HEAR THEIR MOURNFUL 210 UNDER THE MOON V 16
      TALK.
    I HEAR THE HARP STRING PRAISE THEM OR HEAR THEIR MOURNFUL 210 UNDER THE MOON V 16
      TALK.
    HAVE THE BIRDS PASSED US? I COULD HEAR YOUR VOICE, . . 226 SHADOW WATER B 81
    AND IF SHE HEAR HIM MUTTER OF WILD RIDERS, ... 230 SHADOW WATER B 175
    SPEAK LOWER, OR THEY'LL HEAR. THEY CANNOT HEAR; . . . 232 SHADOW WATER B 228
    SPEAK LOWER, OR THEY'LL HEAR. THEY CANNOT HEAR; . . . 232 SHADOW WATER B 228
    AND I WILL HEAR THEM TALKING IN A MINUTE. . . . . . . 233 SHADOW WATER B 250
    NOW I CAN HEAR. THERE'S ONE OF THEM THAT SAYS, . . . 233 SHADOW WATER B 252
    THEY CANNOT HEAR MY VOICE; BUT WHAT'S THE MEANING? . . 234 SHADOW WATER B 275
    YOU'LL HEAR THEM CALLING OUT TO ONE ANOTHER . . . . . 247 SHADOW WATER B 521
    WITH HUMAN VOICES. O I CAN HEAR THEM NOW. . . . . . . 247 SHADOW WATER B 522
    THEY'RE CRYING OUT, COULD YOU BUT HEAR THEIR WORDS, . . 247 SHADOW WATER B 529

		PAGE	TITLE	LINE

HEAR (CONTINUED)

Text	PAGE	TITLE	LINE
THAT YOU MAY NEVER HEAR THE CRY OF THE BIRDS,	250	SHADOW WATER B	575
AND WHISPERING THAT NONE BUT HE SHOULD HEAR,	281	TWO KINGS	110
AND CLINGING TO IT I COULD HEAR THE COCKS	286	TWO KINGS	210
AND HEAR AMID THE GARDEN'S NIGHTLY PEACE,"	300	BEGGAR CRIED	18
SHE IS FOREMOST OF THOSE THAT I WOULD HEAR PRAISED.	350	HER PRAISE	1
SHE IS FOREMOST OF THOSE THAT I WOULD HEAR PRAISED.	351	HER PRAISE	10
TILL I COULD HEAR THEIR HEARTS BEATING.	358	PRESENCES	11
THE FALCON CANNOT HEAR THE FALCONER;	401	SECOND COMING	2
THE FALCON CAN NOT HEAR THE FALCONER;	401	SECOND COMING V	2
SHOULD HEAR MY LIVING FEET, NOR WOULD I TREAD	435	NEW FACES	3
TO HEAR A JACKASS BRAY;	455	HIS MEMORIES	10
WERE I BUT THERE AND NONE TO HEAR	458	HIS WILDNESS	7
CAN HEAR THE ARMED MAN SPEAK.	470	HARUN RASHID	193
THAT STORMS ARE SHAKING, HEAR THE ARMED MAN SPEAK.	470	HARUN RASHID V	193
IT MAY BE ALL THAT HEAR	471	ALL SOUL NIGHT	19
FOR MAYBE ALL THAT HEAR	474	ALL SOUL NIGHT	89
SAVING THE RHYME RATS HEAR BEFORE THEY DIE.	542	PARN FUNERAL 1	28
"HEAR, GENTLEMEN, LADIES, AND ALL MANKIND!	544	TO SAME TUNE 1	2
DID EVER MEN HEAR SUCH A SONG?	570	THREE BUSHES	45
THAT I MAY HEAR IF WE SHOULD KISS	573	LADYS 3RD SONG	9
CAN PAY THE POET FOR A VERSE AND HEAR THE FIDDLE SOUND.	581	CURSE CROMWELL	21
I COME TO HEAR IT STRIKE."	585	ORAHILLY	26
THAT ALL ATTENDANTS AND THE CASUAL CROWD MIGHT HEAR.	609	IN TARAS HALLS	13
"HEAR, GENTLEMEN, LADIES, AND ALL MANKIND!	615	MARCH SONGS 3	2
HEAR ME, AND, SHEPHERD, HEARING ME, GROW DUMB.	646	ISLE STAT I 1	31
WITHIN THE FOLD TO HEAR THE CREAKING GATE—	646	ISLE STAT I 1	41
I HEAR THE WHOLE SKY'S SORROW IN ONE VOICE.	652	ISLE STAT I 2	22
AND WHEREFORE HAVE WE COME? A SONG TO HEAR.	652	ISLE STAT I 2	27
THEY HEAR THE STORY OF THE WIND,	655	ISLE STAT I 3	11
PEACE, PEACE, THE EARTH'S A-QUAKE. I HEAR	656	ISLE STAT I 3	20
AND HEAR, AND JUDGE. MY POPINJAY, WHAT NOW?	660	ISLE STAT II 1	40
BUT WHY ART THOU SO SILENT? DID'ST THOU HEAR	670	ISLE STAT II 3	96
HOW SPED THY QUEST? THIS PRELUDE WE'LL NOT HEAR IT.	673	ISLE STAT II 3	174
IN THY WAN FACE? HEAR THOU, O DAUGHTER OF THE DAYS,	674	ISLE STAT II 3	200
SHALL FEED. I SHALL NOT IN THE EVENINGS HEAR	674	ISLE STAT II 3	220
IN THY WAN FACE? HEAR, DAUGHTER OF THE DAYS.	674	ISLE STAT II 3 V	200
BRIGHT ON A GRASS BLADE'S UNDER SIDE, MIGHT HEAR,	689	NETTLESHIP	10
WILL YOU NOT HEAR MY LAST NEW SONG? HUSH, HUSH!	695	MOSADA 2	1
YOU'RE FULL OF WORDINESS. COME, HEAR MY SONG.	696	MOSADA 2	8
BE STILL! I HEAR THE STEP OF EBREMAR.	697	MOSADA 2	34
I WILL NOT HEAR! THE MOORISH GIRL MUST DIE.	697	MOSADA 2	39
NO USE. AWAY! HEAR, THOU ENDURING GOD,	698	MOSADA 2	50
NO USE. AWAY! HEAR OH! THOU ENDURING GOD,	698	MOSADA 2 V	50
I HEAR THE MURMUR AS THEY RAISE THE BEAMS	699	MOSADA 3	17
MY LOVE, WE WILL HEAR, I AND YOU, WE WILL HEAR,	717	LOVE SONG	4
MY LOVE, WE WILL HEAR, I AND YOU, WE WILL HEAR,	717	LOVE SONG	4
. . . AH! WHAT BELL-NOTES DO THEY HEAR?	718	PHANTOM SHIP	14
SOME GREAT ONE. NO! I HEAR THE WAVERING STEPS	720	WITCH VIVIEN	12
HOW STILL IT IS! I HEAR THE CARP GO SPLASH.	722	WITCH VIVIEN	62
AND NOW AND THEN A BUBBLE RISE. I HEAR	722	WITCH VIVIEN	63
BELOVED, HEAR MY BITTER TALE!—	742	DANAAN QUICK	1
FOR WHILE I BLAMED THEM I COULD HEAR	743	DANAAN QUICK	27
NOW FOUR TOGETHER! I SHALL HEAR THEIR WORDS	753	SHADOW WATER A	139

HEARD

Text	PAGE	TITLE	LINE
AND HEARD THE FOEMEN'S BUCKLERS RATTLE,	10	OISIN 1	123
AND HEARD THE FOEMAN'S BUCKLERS RATTLE,	10	OISIN 1 V	123
AND WHEN THEY HEARD HER VOICE THEY RAN	15	OISIN 1	213
I HEARD ONE SAY, "HIS EYES GROW DIM	25	OISIN 1	380
I HEARD ONE SAY, "WITHIN HIS EYES	25	OISIN 1 V	380
IT PASSETH AWAY, AND IS HEARD OF NO LONGER.	26	OISIN 1 V	3998
FOR GOD HAS HEARD, AND SPEAKS HIS ANGRY MIND!	42	OISIN 2	206
UNDER A BEECH AT ALMHUIN AND HEARD THE THIN	44	OISIN 2	228
THE REST YOU HAVE HEARD OF, O CROZIERED MAN;	60	OISIN 3	189
THE REST THOU HAST HEARD OF, THOU CROSIERED ONE—	60	OISIN 3 V	189
IN CLANGING SPACE A MOMENT HEARD,	65	HAPPY SHEPHERD	20
'MID CLANGING SPACE A MOMENT HEARD	65	HAPPY SHEPHERD V	20
BUT NAUGHT THEY HEARD, FOR THEY ARE ALWAYS LISTENING,	68	SAD SHEPHERD	15
BUT NAUGHT THEY HEARD, FOR THEY ARE EVER LISTENING,	68	SAD SHEPHERD V	15
MAYBE YOU HAVE NOT HEARD OF US, YOU HAVE COME FORTH SO NEWLY,	75	ANASHU VIJAYA	78
WHO NEVER HEARD THE UNFORGIVING HOUND.	75	ANASHU VIJAYA V	75
EACH OTHER ROUND IN CIRCLES, AND HEARD THE ELDEST SPEAK!	76	INDIAN ON GOD	5
I PASSED A LITTLE FURTHER ON AND HEARD A LOTUS TALK!	76	INDIAN ON GOD	9
EACH OTHER ROUND IN CIRCLES! AND I HEARD THE ELDEST SPEAK!—	76	INDIAN ON GOD V	5
I PACED A LITTLE FURTHER ON AND HEARD A LOTUS TALK!—	76	INDIAN ON GOD V	9
I PASSED A LITTLE FURTHER ON AND I HEARD A PEACOCK SAY!	77	INDIAN ON GOD	17
I PACED A LITTLE FURTHER ON AND I HEARD A PEACOCK SAY!	77	INDIAN ON GOD V	17
I PASSED A LITTLE FURTHER AND I HEARD A PEACOCK SAY!—	77	INDIAN ON GOD V	17
IS HEARD ON THE WATER, AS THEY WERE, THE PROUD AND APART.	91	OLD FISHERMAN	10
I HAVE OFTEN HEARD HIM SINGING TO AND FRO,	109	CUCHULAIN SEA	49
I HAVE OFTEN HEARD THE SWEET SOUND OF HIS BOW.	109	CUCHULAIN SEA	50
STARED ON THE HORSES OF THE SEA, AND HEARD	111	CUCHULAIN SEA	84
UPON THE WHARVES OF SORROW, AND HEARD RING	115	ROSE OF BATTLE	27
AND HEARD THE MOURNFUL BREEZE.	123	DREAM OF DEATH V	12
FOR ALL WHO HEARD IT DREAMED A LITTLE WHILE.	129	BOOK STORIES	8
AND ALL WHO HEARD GREW FRIENDLY FOR A WHILE.	129	BOOK STORIES V	8
WHEN THEY ARE HEARD UPON THE WIND,	136	TWO TREES V	37
HAVE YOU NOT HEARD THAT OUR HEARTS ARE OLD,	141	EVERLAST VOICE	5
HE HEARD WHILE HE SANG AND DREAMED	144	HOST OF AIR	9

```
                                                        PAGE    TITLE            LINE
HEARD   (CONTINUED)
    BUT HE HEARD HIGH UP IN THE AIR  . . . . . . . . .   145 HOST OF AIR           41
    AND WHEN I'VE HEARD HOW THEY GREW OLD AND DIED, . . . .  186 QUEEN MAEVE       136
    I HAVE HEARD THE PIGEONS OF THE SEVEN WOODS . . . . .  198 SEVEN WOODS          1
    ALTHOUGH WE NEVER HEARD OF IT AT SCHOOL . . . . . .  205 ADAMS CURSE      V   19
    I HEARD THE OLD, OLD MEN SAY, . . . . . . . . .  208 OLD MEN ADMIRE           1
    I HEARD THE OLD, OLD MEN SAY, . . . . . . . . .  208 OLD MEN ADMIRE           7
    BECAUSE OF SOMETHING I HEARD OF UNDER THE THIN HORN . .  210 UNDER THE MOON V  17
    BECAUSE OF A STORY I HEARD UNDER THE THIN HORN . . .  210 UNDER THE MOON V     17
    BECAUSE OF A STORY I HEARD UNDER A THIN HORN . . .  210 UNDER THE MOON V       17
    I HEARD UNDER A RAGGED HOLLOW WOOD, . . . . . . .  210 RAGGED WOOD      V       1
    OR HAVE YOU HEARD THAT SLIDING SILVER-SHOED . . . .  211 RAGGED WOOD            5
    LIKE PLOVERS THAT HAVE HEARD THE CALL. . . . . . .  213 BLESS PSALTER         13
    I'VE HEARD A RUSTLING OVERHEAD IN THE WIND. . . . .  223 SHADOW WATER B        28
    AND HAS BEEN DANGEROUS TO HIM. I HAVE HEARD . . . .  224 SHADOW WATER B        52
    YOU SAY THAT ALSO? YOU HAVE HEARD THE VOICES, . . .  228 SHADOW WATER B       136
    MUST BE SUBSTANTIAL SOMEWHERE. I HAVE HEARD THE DRUIDS  229 SHADOW WATER B     162
    WHEN I FIRST HEARD THE NEWS? AH, THERE IT IS! . . .  241 SHADOW WATER B       398
    FOR I HAVE HEARD THAT HE WAS PROUD AND LAUGHING, . .  242 SHADOW WATER B      415
    I KNEW HIM WELL, AND WHILE I HEARD HIM LAUGHING . .  242 SHADOW WATER B       419
    BECAUSE HE HAD NOT HEARD OF ANYTHING . . . . . . .  258 KING NO KING          3
    HE'D HEARD THAT DIN ON THE HORIZON'S EDGE . . . . .  286 TWO KINGS      V 217A
    "I HEARD A SEA-MEW CRY, . . . . . . . . . . . .  308 PLAYER QUEEN            14
    "I HEARD A SEAMEW CRY, . . . . . . . . . . . .  308 PLAYER QUEEN     V      14
    HER HUSBAND HAS HEARD THE WRETCH, . . . . . . . .  319 DOLLS                 15
    I HEARD HIM FIRST, BUT MAN IS A FOOL." . . . . . .  341 SHEP GOATHERD    V    74
    AND BIRTHDAYS AND HOLIDAYS SUCH PRAISES CAN BE HEARD  353 HIS PHOENIX          2
    AT ALL THESE DEATH-BEDS WOMEN HEARD . . . . . . .  361 ALF POLLEXFEN         36
    AT ALL THESE DEATHBEDS WOMEN HEARD . . . . . . .  361 ALF POLLEXFEN    V     36
    AND CALLED HER NAME, SHE HAD HEARD, . . . . . . .  381 SONGS FOOL 2          11
    YET BE BUT SINEW. I HAVE HEARD SAID . . . . . . .  386 ROBARTES DANCE        37
    AND OF A MIDDLETON, WHOSE NAME YOU NEVER HEARD, . .  391 UNDER SATURN          8
    YOU HEARD THAT LABOURING MAN WHO HAD SERVED MY PEOPLE.  391 UNDER SATURN      11
        HE SAID
    AND HEARD THE SEA-WIND SCREAM UPON THE TOWER, . . .  403 FOR DAUGHTER         10
    WHAT A STAR SANG AND CARELESS MUSES HEARD! . . . .  445 SCHOOL CHILDR         47
    AND NEEDS NO CRUELTY. I HAVE HEARD ONE SAY . . . .  448 HERO GIRL FOOL        13
    WHAT NO DECEPTION WON. I HAVE HEARD THEM SAY . . .  448 HERO GIRL FOOL V      13
    HAD HEARD IMPOSSIBLE HISTORY OF MY PAST! . . . . .  466 HARUN RASHID        108
    I HEARD HER VOICE, "TURN THAT I MAY EXPOUND . . . .  467 HARUN RASHID        132
    HEARD ALL THE ANXIETY OF MY PASSIONATE YOUTH, . . .  468 HARUN RASHID        168
    MIMICKING WHAT THEY HEARD, AS CHILDREN MIMIC! . . .  487 SEVEN SAGES           25
    "I HEARD AN OLD RELIGIOUS MAN . . . . . . . . .  492 ANNE GREGORY           13
    NOR SAW MY BODY FALL NOR HEARD IT SHRIEK, . . . .  537 HER VISION            29
    SADDLE AND RIDE, I HEARD A MAN SAY, . . . . . . .  549 SEVERED HEAD           1
    IMAGES RIDE, I HEARD A MAN SAY, . . . . . . . .  549 SEVERED HEAD     V      1
    NOR HEARD THIS VOICE THAT NINETY YEARS HAVE CRACKED.  555 RIBH AT TOMB         5
    SURMOUNT THEIR BONES! BUT SPEAK WHAT NONE HAVE HEARD.  555 RIBH AT TOMB        9
    SURMOUNTS THEIR BONES! BUT SPEAK WHAT NONE HAVE HEARD.  555 RIBH AT TOMB  V    9
    DOUBTLESS I SPOKE OR SANG WHAT I HAD HEARD . . . .  557 RIBH ECSTASY           2
    I HAVE HEARD THAT HYSTERICAL WOMEN SAY . . . . . .  565 LAPIS LAZULI           1
    HAD HEARD I HAD NOT HEARD?" . . . . . . . . . .  585 ORAHILLY               22
    HAD HEARD I HAD NOT HEARD?" . . . . . . . . . .  585 ORAHILLY               22
    WHEN HE HEARD THAT STORY TOLD, . . . . . . . . .  596 COLONEL MARTIN        47
    AND ALL MEN HEARD THEM SWEAR . . . . . . . . . .  596 COLONEL MARTIN        60
    WHEN HE HAD HEARD THAT STORY TOLD . . . . . . . .  596 COLONEL MARTIN   V    47
    YOU THAT MITCHEL'S PRAYER HAVE HEARD, . . . . . .  638 BEN BULBEN            25
    AND HAS NOT HEARD ABSOLVO TE. . . . . . . . . .  656 ISLE STAT I 3         19
    AND HEARD EACH UNSEEN ECHO ON HER THRONE, . . . .  657 ISLE STAT I 3         48
    HE SAT, AND THEN I HEARD THE WHITE LAKE SING, . . .  659 ISLE STAT II 1       15
    MY SINKING BRAIN!--CEASE!--CEASE! HEARD YE YON SOUND?  665 ISLE STAT II 2      73
    AND NEVER HEARD OF GRIEF OR CARE . . . . . . . .  667 ISLE STAT II 3        21
    FORTH! FORTH! O SPIRITS, YE HAVE HEARD YOUR TASK! .  669 ISLE STAT II 3        81
    OR AUGHT REMOTE! OR HAST THOU NEVER HEARD . . . .  672 ISLE STAT II 3       153
    I HEARD THE DEATHFUL MONOTONE, . . . . . . . . .  673 ISLE STAT II 3       183
    THIS HEARD I WHERE AMONG THE APPLE TREES, . . . .  686 LIFE                  19
    HEARD YOU? YOUR LUTE HUNG IN THE WINDOW SOUNDED! .  694 MOSADA 1              95
    HEARD YOU? YOUR LUTE UPON THE WALL HAS SOUNDED! . .  694 MOSADA 1         V   95
    "OF OUR GREAT QUEEN IS EVER HEARD . . . . . . . .  729 PRIEST FAIRY          41
    AND WHEN THEY HEARD THAT TALE OF HIS . . . . . . .  730 PRIEST FAIRY          65
    WERE YOU A FAIRY YOU'D HAVE HEARD, . . . . . . . .  730 PRIEST FAIRY          67
    HEARD THE VOICE OF THEIR DISMAY, . . . . . . . .  730 PRIEST FAIRY          74
    THIS HEARD I WHERE, AMID THE APPLE TREES, . . . .  735 QUATRAIN APHOR        17
    THIS HEARD I WHERE AMONG THE APPLE TREES, . . . .  735 QUATRAIN APHOR V      19
    AND HEARD THE MUSIC IN THE WIND, AND SAW . . . . .  747 SHADOW WATER A         5
    AND SPOKEN IN THE COUNCIL, AND HEARD TALES . . . .  748 SHADOW WATER A        28
    AND I HAVE HEARD THEM CALL FROM WIND TO WIND . . .  750 SHADOW WATER A        83
    HE HAS HEARD ME AND NOT YOU. NINE DAYS AGO . . . .  752 SHADOW WATER A       113
    HE HAS HEARD ME BECAUSE I PROMISED ALL. . . . . .  752 SHADOW WATER A       116
    WHERE I HAD HEARD NO FEET BUT THE GODS' CAME. . . .  756 SHADOW WATER A V 191B
    I HAVE HEARD IN THE NIGHT AIR . . . . . . . . .  783 GREY ROUND             6
    MY HEART RAN WILD WHEN IT HEARD . . . . . . . . .  783 GREY ROUND            21
    I HAVE HEARD FROM FAR BELOW . . . . . . . . . .  783 GREY ROUND            25
    AND HEARD THE DEAD LIPS SING. . . . . . . . . .  790 SINGING HEAD          24
HEARD'ST
    FOR SO SHE WILLED--THOU HEARD'ST? UPON THE BREAST . .  653 ISLE STAT I 2       32
HEARERS
    A DRUID KINDNESS, ON ALL HEARERS FELL. . . . . . .  129 BOOK STORIES          4
    THE LOVER SPEAKS TO THE HEARERS OF HIS SONGS IN COMING DAYS  173 SPEAKS HEARERS  T
    A LOVER SPEAKS TO THE HEARERS OF HIS SONGS IN COMING DAYS  173 SPEAKS HEARERS V  T
    HEARERS AND HEARTENERS OF THE WORK! . . . . . . .  266 GALWAY RACES          6
```

		PAGE	TITLE		LINE
HEARERS	**(CONTINUED)**				
HEARERS, HEARTENERS OF THE WORK,	. . . .	266	GALWAY RACES	V	6
HEARING					
HEARING AEDH TOUCH THE MOURNFUL STRINGS OF GOLD."	. . .	35	OISIN		87
HEARING THE SHAKING OF SHIELDS		62	OISIN 3		207
HEARING HELL LOUD WITH A MURMUR, AS SHOUTING AND MOCKING		62	OISIN 3		208
WE SWEEP.					
THEIR HEARING, AND SOME COMFORT GIVE, BUT THEY	. . . .	68	SAD SHEPHERD	V	6
IF IT BE NOT THAT HEARING MESSAGES	. . . . . .	236	SHADOW WATER B		319
ON HEARING THAT THE STUDENTS OF OUR NEW UNIVERSITY	. . .	262	STUDENTS AGIT		T
HEARING THE WHOLE EARTH CHANGE ITS TUNE,	. . . . .	266	GALWAY RACES		12
SOME PASSION HAD MADE HER STONE. HEARING A FOOT	. . .	279	TWO KINGS		65
HEARING HIM GROAN AND STRETCH	. . . .	319	DOLLS		13
ALL'S CHANGED SINCE I, HEARING AT TWILIGHT,	. . . .	322	SWANS AT COOLE		15
HEARING IT NOW HAVE SIGHED FOR THAT YOUNG MAN	. . . .	342	SHEP GOATHERD		77
HEAR ME, AND, SHEPHERD, HEARING ME, GROW DUMB.	. . .	646	ISLE STAT I 1		31
HEARING THE FAR-OFF SINGING GUILE, AND GROANED,	. . .	693	MOSADA 1		88
HEARING THE FAR OFF SINGING GUILE AND GROANED,	. . . .	693	MOSADA 1	V	88
HEARING THE HARPERS PLAY, THE PINE-WOOD CRACKLE,	. . .	759	SHADOW WATER A		241
HEARING THE HARPERS PLAY, THE PINE WOOD CRACKLE,	. . .	759	SHADOW WATER A	V	241
BEYOND HEARING OR SEEING,	. . . .	784	WOMANS BEAUTY		11
HEARKEN					
HEARKEN, YE SWALLOWS!--I HAVE HOARDED UP	. . . . .	699	MOSADA 3		23
HEARS					
HE HEARS THE STORM IN THE CHIMNEY ABOVE,	. . . .	26	OISIN 1		404
FOR HIM WHO HEARS LOVE SING AND NEVER CEASE,	. . . .	114	ROSE OF BATTLE		10
HE HEARS THE CRY OF THE SEDGE	. . . .	165	CRY OF SEDGE		T
AEDH HEARS THE CRY OF THE SEDGE	. . . . .	165	CRY OF SEDGE	V	T
ONE HEARS THE RUMBLE OF IT FAR BELOW	. . . . . .	420	MY HOUSE	V	20B
SHE HEARS ME STRIKE THE BOARD AND SAY	. . . . .	531	FATHER CHILD		1
SWEARS THAT HE HEARS THE KING'S GREAT HORN.	. . . .	636	BLACK TOWER		24
AND HEARS THE ROAR OF THE STREAMS WHERE, DRUIDS SAY,	. .	749	SHADOW WATER A		46
HEART	**SEE HONEY-HEART**				
WITH A HEAVY HEART AND A WANDERING MIND,	. . . .	2	OISIN 1		2
OF THE THINGS THAT HIS HEART STILL KNOWS WERE SWEET--	. .	26	OISIN 1	V	402
WHILE HIS HEART STILL DREAMS OF BATTLE AND LOVE	. . .	27	OISIN 1		406
AS THOUGH HE TOLD HIS NEVER-SLUMBERING HEART	. . . .	32	OISIN 2		44
AS THOUGH UNTO HIS NEVER SLUMBERING HEART	. . . .	32	OISIN 2	V	44
AS THOUGH HE TOLD HIS NEVER SLUMBERING HEART	. . . .	32	OISIN 2	V	44
HE HAD SAT DOWN AND SIGHED WITH CUMBERED HEART,	. . .	37	OISIN 2		111
HE HAD GONE WHISPERING FORTH WITH CUMBERED HEART,	. . .	37	OISIN 2	V	111
THROUGH HEART AND SPINE: AND CAST HIM IN THE WAVE	. . .	41	OISIN 2		182
THROUGH HEART AND DEMON SPINE, AND IN THE WAVE	. . .	41	OISIN 2	V	182
A BEECH-BOUGH TO ME, AND MY HEART GREW SORE,	. . .	44	OISIN 2		226
A BEECH BOUGH TO ME, AND MY HEART GREW SORE,	. . .	44	OISIN 2	V	226
. . . KEENED IN THE GATES OF MY HEART.	. . . . .	57	OISIN 3		152
THE HEART IN ME LONGING TO LEAP LIKE A GRASSHOPPER INTO		60	OISIN 3		182
HER HEART!					
THE HEART IN ME LONGING TO LEAP LIKE A GRASSHOPPER INTO		60	OISIN 3		182
HER HEART!					
SAVING IN THINE OWN HEART. SEEK, THEN,	. . . . .	66	HAPPY SHEPHERD		27
THEIR SADNESS THROUGH A HOLLOW, PEARLY HEART:	. . .	68	SAD SHEPHERD		21
THEIR SADNESS THROUGH THE HOLLOWS OF ITS HEART,	. . .	68	SAD SHEPHERD	V	21
A METEOR OF THE BURNING HEART,	. . . . . .	78	INDIAN TO LOVE		14
IS OUR FIRST KISS, AND AH, HOW OLD MY HEART!"	. . .	80	EPHEMERA		9
SHY ONE OF MY HEART,	. . . .	89	ISLE IN WATER		2
WHEN I WAS A BOY WITH NEVER A CRACK IN MY HEART.	. . .	91	OLD FISHERMAN		4
WHEN I WAS A BOY WITH NEVER A CRACK IN MY HEART.	. . .	91	OLD FISHERMAN		8
WHEN I WAS A BOY WITH NEVER A CRACK IN MY HEART.	. . .	91	OLD FISHERMAN		12
HE HOLDS DEEP COMMUNE WITH HIS HEART!	. . . . .	99	FOXHUNTER		43
AND THE WHOLE WORLD WEIGHS DOWN UPON MY HEART--	. . .	104	FERGUS DRUID	V	38A
AND IN MY HEART THE DAEMONS AND THE GODS	. . . .	104	FERGUS DRUID	V	38B
IS HID IN THE HEART OF LOVE!	. . . . . .	119	PITY OF LOVE		2
HIS HEART HUNG ALL UPON A SILKEN DRESS,	. . . . .	126	DREAM OF FAERY		2
BELOVED, GAZE IN THINE OWN HEART,	. . . . .	134	TWO TREES		1
BELOVED, GAZE IN THINE OWN HEART.	. . . . .	135	TWO TREES		20
MY HEART WOULD BRIM WITH DREAMS ABOUT THE TIMES	. . .	136	TO SOME I TALK		2
MADE IRELAND'S HEART BEGIN TO BEAT:	. . . . .	138	TO IRELAND		12
I CAST MY HEART INTO MY RHYMES,	. . . . .	139	TO IRELAND		45
MAY KNOW HOW MY HEART WENT WITH THEM	. . . . .	139	TO IRELAND		47
EMPTY YOUR HEART OF ITS MORTAL DREAM,	. . . . .	140	HOSTING SIDHE		5
FILLING THY HEART WITH A MORTAL DREAM,	. . . . .	140	HOSTING SIDHE	V	6
WE COME BETWEEN HIM AND THE HOPE OF HIS HEART.	. . .	141	HOSTING SIDHE		12
THE LOVER TELLS OF THE ROSE IN HIS HEART	. . . .	142	ROSE IN HEART		T
THE ROSE IN MY HEART	. . . .	142	ROSE IN HEART	V	T
AEDH TELLS OF THE ROSE IN HIS HEART	. . . . .	142	ROSE IN HEART	V	T
. . . IN THE DEEPS OF MY HEART.	. . . . . .	143	ROSE IN HEART		4
. . . IN THE DEEPS OF MY HEART.	. . . . . .	143	ROSE IN HEART		8
AND HIS HEART WAS BLACKENED BY DREAD,	. . . .	145	HOST OF AIR	V	40B
WITH HEAVY WHITENING WINGS, AND A HEART FALLEN COLD!	. .	147	UNAPPEAS HOST		4
O HEART THE WINDS HAVE SHAKEN, THE UNAPPEASABLE HOST	. .	147	UNAPPEAS HOST		11
AND HEART THE WINDS HAVE SHAKEN: THE UNAPPEASABLE HOST	. .	147	UNAPPEAS HOST	V	11
OUT-WORN HEART, IN A TIME OUT-WORN,	. . . . .	147	INTO TWILIGHT		1
LAUGH, HEART, AGAIN IN THE GREY TWILIGHT,	. . . .	147	INTO TWILIGHT		3
SIGH, HEART, AGAIN IN THE DEW OF THE MORN.	. . . .	147	INTO TWILIGHT		4
OUTWORN HEART IN A TIME OUTWORN,	. . . . .	147	INTO TWILIGHT	V	1
COME, HEART, WHERE HILL IS HEAPED UPON HILL!	. . .	148	INTO TWILIGHT		9
THE HEART OF THE WOMAN	. . . .	151	HEART OF WOMAN		T
MY HEART UPON HIS WARM HEART LIES,	. . . . .	152	HEART OF WOMAN		11
MY HEART UPON HIS WARM HEART LIES,	. . . . .	152	HEART OF WOMAN		11
SHE LOOKED IN MY HEART ONE DAY	. . . . .	152	LOSS OF LOVE		5

HEART   (CONTINUED)

	PAGE	TITLE		LINE
BELOVED, LET YOUR EYES HALF CLOSE, AND YOUR HEART BEAT	154	BELOVED PEACE		9
OVER MY HEART, AND YOUR HAIR FALL OVER MY BREAST,	154	BELOVED PEACE		10
OVER MY HEART, AND YOUR HAIR FALL ABOUT MY BREAST	154	BELOVED PEACE	V	10
MY HEART UPON THE LOVELINESS	155	FORGOT BEAUTY		2
AND WITH HEART MORE OLD THAN THE HORN	157	POET BELOVED		5
AND WITH THE HEART MORE OLD THAN THE HORN	157	POET BELOVED	V	5
I BADE MY HEART BUILD THESE POOR RHYMES:	158	BELOVED RHYMES		3
TO HIS HEART, BIDDING IT HAVE NO FEAR	158	TO HIS HEART		T
TO MY HEART, BIDDING IT HAVE NO FEAR	158	TO HIS HEART	V	T
BE YOU STILL, BE YOU STILL, TREMBLING HEART:	158	TO HIS HEART		1
HE BADE HIS HEART GO TO HER,	159	CAP AND BELLS		13
AND THE HEART AND THE SOUL CAME THROUGH,	160	CAP AND BELLS		30
IN HER HEART SHE FOUND A TUNE.	160	CAP AND BELLS	V	26
THE HEART AND THE SOUL CAME THROUGH:	160	CAP AND BELLS	V	30
IF THIS IMPORTUNATE HEART TROUBLE YOUR PEACE	162	ASKS FORGIVE		1
AND THEREFORE MY HEART WILL BOW, WHEN DEW	164	PERFECT BEAUTY		6
AND THEREFORE MY HEART BOWS DOWN ANEW.	164	PERFECT BEAUTY	V	6
TO FILL YOUR HEART WITH CONTENT."	167	BLESSED		20
AND WHITHER THE WISE HEART KNOWS.	168	BLESSED		34
ARE HURTLING THROUGH MY HEART.	171	MAID QUIET		8
ARE CALLING THROUGH MY HEART.	171	MAID QUIET	V	8
AND SMOKE FROM THIS DEAD HEART DRIFTS THROUGH THE VIOLET AIR	173	SPEAKS HEARERS		3
TILL MAURYA OF THE WOUNDED HEART CRY A SWEET CRY,	173	SPEAKS HEARERS	V	6
THAT'S ALL BUT GONE: FOR THE PROUD HEART IS GONE,	181	QUEEN MAEVE		20
AND THE FOOL HEART OF THE COUNTING-HOUSE FEARS ALL	181	QUEEN MAEVE		21
AND SHE'D HAD LUCKY EYES AND A HIGH HEART,	181	QUEEN MAEVE		27
SUDDEN AND LAUGHING, O UNQUIET HEART,	181	QUEEN MAEVE		30
WITH SPEEDY FEET AND A MOST THANKFUL HEART:	185	QUEEN MAEVE		100
WITH HOLY SHADOWS." HER HIGH HEART WAS GLAD,	186	QUEEN MAEVE		126
FOR YOU, ALTHOUGH YOU'VE NOT HER WANDERING HEART,	186	QUEEN MAEVE		132
BAILE'S HEART WAS BROKEN IN TWO:	192	BAILE AILLINN		70
OUR HEART CAN HEAR THE VOICES CHIDE.	192	BAILE AILLINN	V	94
AH! WISE, MY HEART KNOWS WELL HOW WISE.	193	BAILE AILLINN		99
TO MAKE THE SAVAGE HEART OF LOVE	193	BAILE AILLINN		109
BEFORE HER LOVE-WORN HEART HAD BROKE,	194	BAILE AILLINN		127
QUIET'S WILD HEART, LIKE DAILY MEAT:	196	BAILE AILLINN		178
AND BEING IN GOOD HEART, BECAUSE	197	BAILE AILLINN		191
AND YOU ARE MORE HIGH OF HEART THAN SHE,	197	BAILE AILLINN		202
THAT EMPTY THE HEART. I HAVE FORGOT AWHILE	198	SEVEN WOODS		5
WANDERS LAUGHING AND EATING HER WILD HEART .	198	SEVEN WOODS		11
ALL THAT YOU NEED IS PATIENCE." HEART CRIES, "NO,	200	FOLLY COMFORT		6
O HEART! O HEART! IF SHE'D BUT TURN HER HEAD,	200	FOLLY COMFORT		13
O HEART! O HEART! IF SHE'D BUT TURN HER HEAD,	200	FOLLY COMFORT		13
BUT HEART THERE IS NO COMFORT, NOT A GRAIN:	200	FOLLY COMFORT	V	7
NEVER GIVE ALL THE HEART	202	NEVER GIVE ALL		T
NEVER GIVE ALL THE HEART, FOR LOVE	202	NEVER GIVE ALL		1
O NEVER GIVE THE HEART OUTRIGHT,	202	NEVER GIVE ALL		8
FOR HE GAVE ALL HIS HEART AND LOST.	202	NEVER GIVE ALL		14
NOR LANDS THAT SEEM TOO DIM TO BE BURDENS ON THE HEART:	209	UNDER THE MOON		5
OR LANDS THAT SEEMED TOO OLD TO BE BURDENS ON THE HEART,	209	UNDER THE MOON	V	5
WHOSE HEART WOULD BREAK IN TWO,	213	HAPPY TOWNLAND		2
AND THE GREEN QUIET, HAVE UPLIFTED THE HEART?	219	WOODS OF COOLE		40
I COULD GIVE ALL MY HEART TO THAT RED MOLL	222	SHADOW WATER B		9
THAT THE HEART LONGS FOR. WHAT IS LOVE ITSELF,	230	SHADOW WATER B		183
O HEART, BE AT PEACE, BECAUSE	259	UNWORTH PRAISE		1
OUT OF MY HEART. THERE'S SOMETHING AILS OUR COLT	260	FASC DIFFICULT		4
AND AFTER SET YOUR HEART TO BEAT,	263	MASK		5
WHAT DOES HE CARE IF MY HEART BREAK?	275	GREY ROCK		104
WHY SHOULD THE FAITHFULLEST HEART MOST LOVE	275	GREY ROCK		112
BETWEEN THE PILLARS WITH A BEATING HEART	279	TWO KINGS		59
THAT MAKE THE HEART AKIN TO THE DUMB STONE."	281	TWO KINGS		94
SHE'LL NOT BE PROUD, KNOWING WITHIN HER HEART	282	TWO KINGS		118
WHAT THE EXULTANT HEART CALLS GOOD	288	TO WEALTHY MAN		33
THE LINEAMENTS, A HEART THAT LAUGHTER HAS MADE SWEET,	315	FALLEN MAJESTY		5
THE LINEAMENTS, THE HEART THAT LAUGHTER HAS MADE SWEET,	315	FALLEN MAJESTY	V	5
HEART AND DELIGHTED HEART:	315	FRIENDS		9
HEART AND DELIGHTED HEART:	315	FRIENDS	V	9
AND THEREUPON IMAGINATION AND HEART WERE DRIVEN	316	COLD HEAVEN		3
BEING OUT OF HEART WITH GOVERNMENT	317	APPOINTMENT		1
BEING OUT OF HEART AT GOVERNMENT	317	APPOINTMENT	V	1
AND NOW MY HEART IS SORE.	322	SWANS AT COOLE		14
IN THE AFFECTIONS OF OUR HEART.	324	ROBERT GREGORY		12
PASSIONATE AND SIMPLE LIKE HIS HEART.	325	ROBERT GREGORY		32
WHEREIN THE GAZING HEART DOUBLES HER MIGHT.	326	ROBERT GREGORY		69
OF THAT LATE DEATH TOOK ALL MY HEART FOR SPEECH.	328	ROBERT GREGORY		96
MY DISCONTENTED HEART TO DRAW CONTENT	334	LIVING BEAUTY		3
THAN 'TWERE AN APPARITION. O HEART, WE ARE OLD:	334	LIVING BEAUTY		8
THAT THE HEART GROWS OLD?	334	SONG		6
THAT THE HEART GROWS OLD?	335	SONG		12
BUT THE HEART THAT I HAD:	335	SONG		14
THAT THE HEART GROWS OLD?	335	SONG		18
WHAT MAKES YOUR HEART BEAT SO!	336	YOUNG GIRL		3
WHO BROKE MY HEART FOR HER	336	YOUNG GIRL		6
OR PUT HIS HEART INTO SOME GAME	343	SHEP GOATHERD		105
AND YET, BECAUSE MY HEART LEAPED AT HER WORDS,	353	PEOPLE		35
WHO IS MY BEAUTY'S EQUAL, THOUGH THAT MY HEART DENIES,	354	HIS PHOENIX		27
AND HOW SHOULD HER HEART FAIL HER	365	HER RACE		9
HIS SENSES AND HIS HEART UNSATISFIED,	370	EGO DOMINUS		58
OF BODY AND SOUL. THE LOVER'S HEART KNOWS THAT.	375	PHASES OF MOON		71

	PAGE	TITLE	LINE
HEART (CONTINUED)			
AN IMAGE OF MY HEART THAT IS SMITTEN THROUGH	389	IMAGE PAST	8
TO SOME WHO ARE NEAR MY HEART.	393	EASTER 1916	34
CAN MAKE A STONE OF THE HEART.	394	EASTER 1916	58
CONSUME MY HEART AWAY; SICK WITH DESIRE	408	SAIL BYZANTIUM	21
O HEART, O TROUBLED HEART--THIS CARICATURE,	409	TOWER	2
O HEART, O TROUBLED HEART--THIS CARICATURE,	409	TOWER	2
NO MOON; ONLY AN ACHING HEART	421	MY TABLE	13
HAD SUCH AN ACHING HEART	422	MY TABLE	28
WE HAD FED THE HEART ON FANTASIES,	425	STARES NEST	16
WE HAVE FED THE HEART ON FANTASIES,	425	STARES NEST V	16
THE HEART GROWS BRUTAL FROM THE FARE.	425	STARES NEST V	17
BUT O! AMBITIOUS HEART, HAD SUCH A PROOF DRAWN FORTH	427	PHANTOM HATRED	36
AND TEAR THE HEART OUT OF HIS SIDE,	437	SONGS PLAY 1	3
AND LAY THE HEART UPON HER HAND	437	SONGS PLAY 1	4
AND BEAR THAT BEATING HEART AWAY!	437	SONGS PLAY 1	5
MAN'S OWN RESINOUS HEART HAS FED.	438	SONGS PLAY 2	16
BUT FEEL THE STRANGE HEART BEATING WHERE IT LIES?	441	LEDA AND SWAN	8
AND FEELS THE STRANGE HEART BEATING WHERE IT LIES!	441	LEDA AND SWAN V	8
AND THEREUPON MY HEART IS DRIVEN WILD:	444	SCHOOL CHILDR	23
FOR THE HEART CRIES THAT WHAT DECEPTION WINS	448	HERO GIRL FOOL	6
THE HEART REPLIES	449	OWEN AHERNE V	T
A STRANGE THING SURELY THAT MY HEART, WHEN LOVE HAD COME UNSOUGHT	449	OWEN AHERNE	1
BUT O! MY HEART COULD BEAR NO MORE WHEN THE UPLAND CAUGHT THE WIND:	450	OWEN AHERNE	11
I RAN, I RAN, FROM MY LOVE'S SIDE BECAUSE MY HEART WENT MAD.	450	OWEN AHERNE	12
THE HEART BEHIND ITS RIB LAUGHED OUT.	450	OWEN AHERNE	13
O BUT HER HEART WOULD BREAK TO LEARN MY THOUGHTS ARE FAR AWAY."	450	OWEN AHERNE	20
"SPEAK ALL YOUR MIND," MY HEART SANG OUT,	450	OWEN AHERNE	21
A HEART OF FLESH AND BLOOD.	451	FIRST LOVE	6
AND FOUND A HEART OF STONE	451	FIRST LOVE	8
THEN SUDDENLY MY HEART IS WRUNG	453	DEATH OF HARE	7
AND HIS BEATING HEART WOULD BURST.	454	EMPTY CUP	6
AND THE HEART THUMPS AT MY SIDE,	456	FRIENDS YOUTH	18
THE HEART NEED SUFFER NO DEFEAT! BUT I	464	HARUN RASHID	77
MY HEART COULD NEVER TURN FROM DAILY RUIN,	464	HARUN RASHID	83
MY HEART MUST LOOK UPON A DAILY RUIN	464	HARUN RASHID V	83
BECAUSE THE HEART IN HIS BLOOD-SODDEN BREAST	481	BLOOD AND MOON	20
FOR ALL HIS TIMID HEART, THERE THAT SLOW MAN,	489	COOLE PARK 29	12
THE HEART REMORSE.	500	VACILLATION	8
FROM MAN'S BLOOD-SODDEN HEART ARE SPRUNG	502	VACILLATION	67
HAD SCOOPED OUT PHARAOH'S MUMMY. I--THOUGH HEART MIGHT FIND RELIEF	503	VACILLATION	84
HOMER IS MY EXAMPLE AND HIS UNCHRISTENED HEART.	503	VACILLATION	87
MY FANATIC HEART.	506	REMORSE SPEECH	5
MY FANATIC HEART.	506	REMORSE SPEECH	10
A FANATIC HEART.	506	REMORSE SPEECH	15
AND ALL MY HEART SEEMED GAY:	507	STREAM AND SUN	3
REPENTANCE KEEPS MY HEART IMPURE:	507	STREAM AND SUN	6
SO NEVER HANG YOUR HEART UPON	509	JANE REPROVED	12
THE HEART IN MY SIDE,	516	MANS SONG	3
FOR THE HEART CANNOT LIE,	516	MANS SONG	14
TO MY OFFENDED HEART	516	MANS SONG	17
I BROKE MY HEART IN TWO	518	HIS CONFIDENCE	7
AND MY HEART UNMOVED?	532	BEFORE WORLD	12
WHERE HIS HEART MY HEART DID SEEM	535	CHOSEN	15
WHERE HIS HEART MY HEART DID SEEM	535	CHOSEN	15
CUT OUT HIS HEART. SOME MASTER OF DESIGN	541	PARN FUNERAL 1	14
UPON A PAINTED STAGE WHEN WE DEVOURED HIS HEART.	542	PARN FUNERAL 1	23
HAD DE VALERA EATEN PARNELL'S HEART	542	PARN FUNERAL 2	2
HAD COSGRAVE EATEN PARNELL'S HEART, THE LAND'S	543	PARN FUNERAL 2	5
HE SANG IT FROM HIS HEART.	544	TO SAME TUNE 1	6
FOR ALL MY HEART HAS HAD FOR ITS HIRE	551	SONGS REWRIT 1	3
FOR ALL THAT MY HEART HAS HAD FOR ITS HIRE	551	SONGS REWRIT 1 V	3
THEN HE STRUGGLED WITH THE HEART:	561	FOUR AGES MAN	3
HIS PROUD HEART HE LEFT BEHIND.	561	FOUR AGES MAN	6
BUT THERE'S ANOTHER KNOWLEDGE THAT MY HEART DESTROYS,	580	CURSE CROMWELL	17
WORDS I HAVE THAT CAN PIERCE THE HEART,	588	OLD WICKED MAN	16
MY HEART RECOVERING WITH COVERED EYES:	602	GALLERY REVIS	18
HEART SMITTEN WITH EMOTION, I SINK DOWN,	602	GALLERY REVIS V	17
HER HEART MOUNT UP ON HIGH:	608	SONGS BURDEN 3	22
HE SANG IT FROM HIS HEART.	616	MARCH SONGS 3	6
HIS EMPTY HEART IS FULL AT LENGTH,	624	APPARITIONS	19
I MUST BE SATISFIED WITH MY HEART, ALTHOUGH	629	CIRCUS ANIMALS	4
THEMES OF THE EMBITTERED HEART, OR SO IT SEEMS,	629	CIRCUS ANIMALS	13
IN THE FOUL RAG-AND-BONE SHOP OF THE HEART.	630	CIRCUS ANIMALS	40
HEART MYSTERIES THERE, AND YET WHEN ALL IS SAID	630	CIRCUS ANIMALS V	27
IN THE FOUL RAG AND BONE SHOP OF THE HEART.	630	CIRCUS ANIMALS V	40
LAUGHS ALOUD, HIS HEART AT PEACE.	638	BEN BULBEN	32
THOUGH MY LOVE-SICK HEART IS RENDING,	646	ISLE STAT I 1	38
IN THE HEART OF THE DAWN THE RIVERS ARE SINGING,	648	ISLE STAT I 1	91
AND THERE TO ITS OWN HEART FOR EVER MOANS.	650	ISLE STAT I 1	131
WITHIN MINE HEART, AND NAUGHT BUT SORROW NOW	659	ISLE STAT II 1	26
OH, HEART! HER DIRGE! WITH RUSHING ARMS THE WAVES	665	ISLE STAT II 2	70
LEST ON THINE HEART THE STONY SEAL	667	ISLE STAT II 3	41
O LET ME PASS! THE SPELLS FROM OFF THE HEART	668	ISLE STAT II 3	44
THE WORLD, WITHIN HIS FOLDED HEART,	671	ISLE STAT II 3	133
THE WATER-SERPENT SINGS HIS HEART	673	ISLE STAT II 3	184

HEART   (CONTINUED)   PAGE   TITLE   LINE

SO BE THOU STILL, DEAR HEART, A LITTLE WHILE! . . . . .   677 ISLE STAT II 3   283
HAVE I SLEPT LONG? LONG YEARS. WITH HUNGRY HEART . . . .   677 ISLE STAT II 3   286
MY ECHOING HEART. NOW RAISE THY VOICE AND SPEAK! . . . .   683 SEEKER   47
"BEHOLD THE KNIGHT OF THE WATERFALL, WHOSE HEART . . . .   684 SEEKER   54
THAT FILL THE BLAZING HOLLOWS OF MY HEART. . . . .   684 SEEKER   V 69D
THE ORB OF THE MOST INNER LIVING HEART . . . .   689 NETTLESHIP   15
HE LOVES OUR BROTHER PETER IN HIS HEART. . . . .   696 MOSADA 2   16
DEAR HEART, THERE IS A SECRET WAY THAT LEADS . . . . .   702 MOSADA 3   75
THE HEART OF THE PITILESS PLACE . . . .   708 FAIRY PEDANT   V 30
AND THEN HIS HEART FILLS FULL OF LOVE, ...   716 FAIRY DOCTOR   11
AND THEN HIS HEART IS FULL OF LOVE, ...   716 FAIRY DOCTOR   V 11
CLOSE AND MORE CLOSE--I FEEL HIM IN MY HEART-- . . . .   720 WITCH VIVIEN   11
AND WILL FIND HER GOOD AT HEART, ...   726 LOVERS QUARREL   10
UNTO THE HEART OF THE WOODLAND STRAYING, ...   728 PRIEST FAIRY   1
WITH OPEN MOUTH AND BEATING HEART. . . . .   729 PRIEST FAIRY   32
AND THEN HIS HEART GREW WELL-NIGH DEAD . . . .   730 PRIEST FAIRY   59
AWAY IN THE HEART OF THE ANTIQUE WOOD! . . . .   730 PRIEST FAIRY   64
THE BEATING OF A LEV'RET'S HEART! . . . .   730 PRIEST FAIRY   69
SORROWS SAPPING BRAIN AND HEART. . . . .   733 STREET DANCERS   60
THE SOUL UPON THE ASHES OF THE HEART." . . . .   735 QUATRAIN APHOR   16
THE HEART OF NOON FOLDS SILENCE AND FOLDS SLEEP, . . .   735 QUATRAIN APHOR   25
WANDERS AND WAILS BEFORE MY HEART MOST TRUE . . . . .   738 YOU ARE SAD   8
TILL THEY COME WHERE YOUR SAD, SAD HEART IS, ...   739 WHERE BOOKS GO   5
WHEN FLYING TO THE HEART OF LIGHT . . . .   742 DANAAN QUICK   8
AND THOUGHT THAT SHE HAD NO HEART. . . . .   744 GLOVE CLOAK   4
KEEP HIDDEN AND COVERED HER HEART!" . . . .   744 GLOVE CLOAK   12
FOR LOVE IS A-WEAVING WHEN A WOMAN'S HEART . . . . .   761 SHADOW WATER A   262
GROWS YOUNG AND A MAN'S HEART GROWS OLD IN A TWINKLING.   761 SHADOW WATER A   263
AH, THEY HAVE PIERCED HIS HEART! I HAVE SLEPT LONG!   761 SHADOW WATER A   270
OF VOICES AND OF DREAMS. O HEART, BE STILL! . . . .   765 SHADOW WATER A   362
HEART ON HEART, OR MOUTH ON MOUTH, ...   777 SONG DEIRDRE 2   9
HEART ON HEART, OR MOUTH ON MOUTH, ...   777 SONG DEIRDRE 2   9
WHY DOES MY HEART BEAT SO? . . . .   781 MY HEART BEAT   1
WHY SHOULD THE HEART TAKE FRIGHT? . . . .   781 HEART FRIGHT   1
MY RASCAL HEART IS PROUD . . . .   782 HEART FRIGHT   10
MY HEART RAN WILD WHEN IT HEARD . . . .   783 GREY ROUND   21
WHY DOES YOUR HEART BEAT THUS? . . . .   785 YOUR HEART   1
ITS STRANGE HEART BEATING FAST . . . .   785 YOUR HEART   6
O STILL THAT HEART AT LAST . . . .   785 YOUR HEART   8
WHAT MAKES HER HEART BEAT THUS, ...   785 YOUR HEART   8
WHAT MAKES YOUR HEART SO BEAT? . . . .   785 YOUR HEART   V   1
THE HEART WELL WORN UPON THE SLEEVE MAY BE THE BEST OF   786 YOUR HEART   27
    SIGHTS,   790 HEART SLEEVE   1
HEARTACHE
    THERE'S MANY A ONE SHALL FIND OUT ALL HEARTACHE . . .   205 ADAMS CURSE   16
HEART-BREAK
    SHE FELL AND DIED OF THE HEART-BREAK." . . . .   191 BAILE AILLINN   64
HEARTBURN
    I'VE NOTHING TO COMPLAIN OF BUT HEARTBURN, ...   227 SHADOW WATER B V 116A
HEARTED   SEE BROKEN-HEARTED WEARY-HEARTED STUBBORN-HEARTED STONY-HEARTED HONEY-HEARTED
             EASTERN-HEARTED
    AS WEARY HEARTED AS THAT HOLLOW MOON. . . . .   206 ADAMS CURSE   V 38
HEARTENERS
    HEARERS AND HEARTENERS OF THE WORK! . . . .   266 GALWAY RACES   6
    AND WE FIND HEARTENERS AMONG MEN . . . .   266 GALWAY RACES   15
    HEARERS, HEARTENERS OF THE WORK, ...   266 GALWAY RACES   V   6
    AND FIND HEARTENERS AMONG MEN . . . .   266 GALWAY RACES   V 15
HEARTH
    BESIDE HER CLEAN-SWEPT HEARTH, HER QUIET SHADE! . . .   114 ROSE OF BATTLE   11
    BESIDES HER CLEAN SWEPT HEARTH, HER QUIET SHADE! . .   114 ROSE OF BATTLE V 11
    I HAD A CHAIR AT EVERY HEARTH, ...   131 OLD PENSIONER   V   1
    IN HER HIGH HOUSE AT CRUACHAN! THE LONG HEARTH, . . .   180 QUEEN MAEVE   11
    A GREY STONE FIREPLACE WITH AN OPEN HEARTH, ...   419 MY HOUSE   12
    A GREY STONE FIRE-PLACE WITH AN OPEN HEARTH, ...   419 MY HOUSE   V 12
    BY AN OLD HEARTH, AND HE . . . .   780 WELL AND TREE   12
HEARTHSTONE
    EAT AT MY HEARTHSTONE! . . . .   380 SONGS FOOL 1   2
    THE THRESHOLD AND THE HEARTHSTONE, ...   775 AGAINST WITCH   6
    BUT THE THRESHOLD AND HEARTHSTONE. . . . .   776 AGAINST WITCH   40
HEARTIER
    AND HEARTIER LOVES! THAT LAMP IS FROM THE TOMB. . . .   398 LEADERS CROWD   12
HEARTIEST
    HE MIGHT HAVE BEEN YOUR HEARTIEST WELCOMER. . . . .   326 ROBERT GREGORY   56
HEART-MYSTERIES
    HEART-MYSTERIES THERE, AND YET WHEN ALL IS SAID . . .   630 CIRCUS ANIMALS   27
HEART-REVEALING
    THE HEART-REVEALING INTIMACY . . . .   404 FOR DAUGHTER   23
HEART'S
    I HEAR IT IN THE DEEP HEART'S CORE. . . . .   117 ISLE INNISFREE   12
    BECAUSE A LOVER'S HEART'S WORN OUT, ...   191 BAILE AILLINN   65
    OUR HEART'S DESIRE NOW THAT WE ARE SO LIGHT." . . .   233 SHADOW WATER B   255
    WHILE UP FROM MY HEART'S ROOT . . . .   316 FRIENDS   26
    FOR YOUR SOLE SAKE--THAT ALL HEART'S ACHE HAVE KNOWN,   355 BROKEN DREAMS   7
    AND GIVEN TO OTHERS ALL HEART'S ACHE, ...   355 BROKEN DREAMS   8
    BUT FOR YOUR SAKE--THAT ALL HEART'S ACHE HAVE KNOWN,   355 BROKEN DREAMS   V   7
    THE HEART'S GROWN BRUTAL FROM THE FARE! . . . . . .   425 STARES NEST   17
    I SEE PHANTOMS OF HATRED AND OF THE HEART'S . . . .   425 PHANTOM HATRED   T
    MY HEART'S AGONY . . . .   452 HUMAN DIGNITY   10
    HEART'S PURPLE--AND ALL THESE I SET . . . .   478 SELF AND SOUL   28
    THIS LOVE THAT MAKES MY HEART'S BLOOD STOP . . . . .   499 MOTHER OF GOD   13

	PAGE	TITLE	LINE
HEART'S (CONTINUED)			
AND IN THE HEART'S PRIDE.	513	JANE TALK BISH	12
I SAID THAT SHE HAD DANCED HEART'S TRUTH.	514	JANE GROWN OLD	9
BUT MY HEART'S VICTIM AND ITS TORTURER.	537	HER VISION	32
MY PRETTY PAISTIN IS MY HEART'S DESIRE.	550	SONGS REWRIT 1 V	1
THAT BLONDE GIRL THERE IS MY HEART'S DESIRE,	550	SONGS REWRIT 1 V	1
O BUT HEART'S WINE SHALL RUN PURE.	554	CHURCH STATE	5
HIS HEART'S DESIRE WHERE THE WORLD DWINDLES OUT?	747	SHADOW WATER A	13
FORGAEL MAY FIND HIS HEART'S DESIRE ON BOARD	751	SHADOW WATER A	107
YOUR HEART'S DESIRE AND THE END OF ALL OUR TROUBLE!	755	SHADOW WATER A	175
AND NONE KNOWS WHEREFORE; BUT THE HEART'S DESIRE	764	SHADOW WATER A	340
HEARTS			
A RUMOUR OF DELIGHTED HEARTS.	16	OISIN 1	230
"MEN'S HEARTS OF OLD WERE DROPS OF FLAME	19	OISIN 1	276
BUT NOW HEARTS CRY THAT HEARTS ARE SLAVES,	19	OISIN 1	280
BUT NOW HEARTS CRY THAT HEARTS ARE SLAVES,	19	OISIN 1	280
WITH HEARTS THAT KNOW NOR LAW NOR RULE,	22	OISIN 1	339
HAS CLOVEN AND RENT THEIR HEARTS IN TWAIN,	66	HAPPY SHEPHERD	33
HAS TORN AND RENT THEIR HEARTS IN TWAIN,	66	HAPPY SHEPHERD V	33
"PASSION HAS OFTEN WORN OUR WANDERING HEARTS."	80	EPHEMERA	12
"OFTEN HAS PASSION WORN OUR WANDERING HEARTS,	80	EPHEMERA V	12
THE HEARTS OF THE WORLD-TROUBLING SEAMEN,	82	MAD KING GOLL	4
BY GOD TO THE BRIGHT HEARTS OF THOSE LONG DEAD,	101	ROSE UPON ROOD	20
BEFORE YOU WERE, OR ANY HEARTS TO BEAT,	112	ROSE OF WORLD	12
BEFORE YE WERE, OR ANY HEARTS TO BEAT,	112	ROSE OF WORLD V	12
OF THEIR SAD HEARTS, THAT MAY NOT LIVE NOR DIE.	114	ROSE OF BATTLE	24
OF OUR SAD HEARTS, THAT MAY NOT LIVE NOR DIE.	115	ROSE OF BATTLE	36
HAS AWAKED IN OUR HEARTS, MY BELOVED, A SADNESS THAT MAY NOT DIE.	122	WHITE BIRDS	4
HAS AWAKED IN OUR HEARTS, MY BELOVED, A SADNESS THAT NEVER MAY DIE.	122	WHITE BIRDS V	4
HAVE YOU NOT HEARD THAT OUR HEARTS ARE OLD,	141	EVERLAST VOICE	5
AND ALL MEN'S HEARTS MUST BURN AND BEAT!	158	BELOVED RHYMES	9
"O HEARTS OF WIND-BLOWN FLAME!	162	ASKS FORGIVE	6
O PITEOUS HEARTS, CHANGING TILL CHANGE BE DEAD	163	ASKS FORGIVE	19
AND TROUBLE WITH SIGHS FOR ALL HEARTS WITHOUT REST	163	ASKS FORGIVE V	23
OUR HEARTS ENDURE THE SCOURGE, THE PLAITED THORNS, THE WAY	172	TRAV PASSION	3
OUR HEARTS ENDURE THE PLAITED THORN, THE CROWDED WAY,	172	TRAV PASSION V	3
OUR HEARTS CAN HEAR THE VOICES CHIDE.	192	BAILE AILLINN	94
HAVE GIVEN THEIR HEARTS UP TO THE PLAY.	202	NEVER GIVE ALL	10
BUT WE HAVE HIDDEN IN OUR HEARTS THE FLAME OUT OF THE EYES	207	HANRAHANS SONG	4
ANGERS THAT ARE LIKE NOISY CLOUDS HAVE SET OUR HEARTS ABEAT!	207	HANRAHANS SONG	8
LIKE TATTERED CLOUDS OF THE WORLD, PASSIONS CALL AND OUR HEARTS BEAT!	207	HANRAHANS SONG V	8
ANGERS THAT ARE LIKE BUNDLED CLOUDS HAVE SET OUR HEARTS ABEAT!	207	HANRAHANS SONG V	8
BUT OUR HEARTS ARE LIGHTED FROM THE FLAME IN THE EYES	207	HANRAHANS SONG V	9
WHEN THEIR HEARTS ARE SO HIGH	214	HAPPY TOWNLAND	21
THEIR HEARTS WOULD BE LIKE A CUP	215	HAPPY TOWNLAND	31
FOR THEIR HEARTS WOULD BE LIKE A CUP	215	HAPPY TOWNLAND V	31
TO FIND IF HEARTS BE WILD AND WISE,	263	MASK	4
THEIR HEARTS HAVE NOT GROWN OLD;	323	SWANS AT COOLE	22
BE BUT THE BREAKERS OF MEN'S HEARTS OR ENGINES OF DELIGHT!	354	HIS PHOENIX	23
TILL I COULD HEAR THEIR HEARTS BEATING!	358	PRESENCES	11
OWN NOTHING BUT THEIR BLIND, STUPEFIED HEARTS.	370	EGO DOMINUS	69
HEARTS WITH ONE PURPOSE ALONE	393	EASTER 1916	41
HEARTS ARE NOT HAD AS A GIFT BUT HEARTS ARE EARNED	404	FOR DAUGHTER	34
HEARTS ARE NOT HAD AS A GIFT BUT HEARTS ARE EARNED	404	FOR DAUGHTER	34
AND HELEN HAS ALL LIVING HEARTS BETRAYED.	411	TOWER	53
NOTHING BUT STILLNESS CAN REMAIN WHEN HEARTS ARE FULL	426	PHANTOM HATRED	23
AND YET THEY TOO BREAK HEARTS--O PRESENCES	445	SCHOOL CHILDR	53
TO SHOW HOW VIOLENT GREAT HEARTS CAN LOSE	463	HARUN RASHID	47
TO WHERE THE DAMNED HAVE HOWLED AWAY THEIR HEARTS,	474	ALL SOUL NIGHT	95
AND OUR HEARTS ARE TORN.	519	LOVES LONENESS	12
THEIR UNREMEMBERING HEARTS AND HEADS	639	BEN BULBEN	72
SUCH MEN, SUCH HEARTS. BUT, UNCOUTH HUNTER, THOU	651	ISLE STAT I 1	167
AS ON THOSE OTHER HEARTS WERE LAID.	667	ISLE STAT II 3	42
IT IS THE VOICE OF ALL OUR HEARTS THAT LAUGH.	681	SEEKER	7
I'D GLAD FOLKS' HEARTS WITH BLITHER SONG."	731	PRIEST FAIRY	82
THESE ARE THEIR LURES, BUT THEY HAVE SET THEIR HEARTS	757	SHADOW WATER A	206
FOLDING THEIR HEARTS' DESIRE TO THEIR GLAD HEARTS.	765	SHADOW WATER A	349
THE NETS THE GODS HAVE WOVEN AND OUR OWN HEARTS,	766	SHADOW WATER A	383
HEARTS'			
OUR HEARTS' DESIRE NOW THAT WE ARE SO LIGHT."	753	SHADOW WATER A	145
FOLDING THEIR HEARTS' DESIRE TO THEIR GLAD HEARTS.	765	SHADOW WATER A	349
HEART-SMITTEN			
HEART-SMITTEN WITH EMOTION I SINK DOWN,	602	GALLERY REVIS	17
HEART-STRINGS			
MINE HEART-STRINGS ARE ALL BROKEN SAVING ONE,	684	SEEKER V	69B
HEARTY			
TO THE HORN, AND HE BE HALE AND HEARTY.	243	SHADOW WATER B	447
HEAT			
THROUGH SUMMER'S HEAT AND WINTER'S COLD.	86	MAD KING GOLL	71
"FROM HEAT AND COLD AND WIND AND WAVE!	193	BAILE AILLINN	114
TILL HER BOWELS ARE IN HEAT,	638	BEN BULBEN	49
HEATH			
O'ER HILL AND HEATH AND SPONGY FEN,	83	MAD KING GOLL V	32
OVER THE HEATH AND SPONGY FEN,	83	MAD KING GOLL V	32
BY HEATH OR HOLLOW OR RUSHY MERE,	716	FAIRY DOCTOR	10

	PAGE	TITLE		LINE
HEATHEN				
YOU ARE STILL WRECKED AMONG HEATHEN DREAMS.	4	OISIN 1		31
OISIN, THOU ART HALF HEATHEN STILL!	4	OISIN 1	V	31
TELL ON, NOR BOW THY HEATHEN CREST	11	OISIN 1	V	131A
THIS HEATHEN HORDE AWAY. YOU NEED NOT HOPE:	696	MOSADA 2		5
THE HEATHEN. YEA, AND SHAKE THE SULLEN KINGS	698	MOSADA 2		55
HEATHER				
WE RODE BEYOND THE FURZE AND HEATHER,	9	OISIN 1	V	101A
AMID WET ROCKS AND HEATHER,	311	PEACOCK		8
BETWEEN ROCK AND WET HEATHER,	311	PEACOCK	V	8
OUT OF A NEIGHBOURING BUNCH OF HEATHER:	728	PRIEST FAIRY		20
HEAVE				
WHAT MATTER? HEAVE NO SIGH, LET NO TEAR DROP,	564	GYRES		11
HEAVED				
HEAVED BESIDE THE GLIMMERING WAVES,	21	OISIN 1	V	314
WHAT SACRED DRAMA THROUGH HER BODY HEAVED	560	WHENCE COME		11
BUT HEAVED A SIGH IF THE CHAMBERMAID	570	THREE BUSHES		33
HEAVEN				
AND EARTH AND HEAVEN AND HELL WOULD DIE,	19	OISIN 1		271
DARKEN: HEAVEN IS ANGRY. CEASE! UNTO MY MIND,	42	OISIN 2	V	205
WHEN HEAVEN AND HELL ARE MET,	112	ROSE OF PEACE		2
A PEACE OF HEAVEN WITH HELL.	113	ROSE OF PEACE		16
GOD'S LAUGHING IN HEAVEN.	118	CRADLE SONG		5
GOD SMILES IN HIGH HEAVEN	118	CRADLE SONG	V	5
ALL THE HEAVENS BOW DOWN TO HEAVEN,	125	CATHLEEN PARA		15
SHE GOES DOWN THE FLOOR OF HEAVEN,	125	CATHLEEN PARA	V	13
AND ABOVE THE DEEP OF HEAVEN,	125	CATHLEEN PARA	V	15
DESOLATE WINDS THAT BEAT THE DOORS OF HEAVEN, AND BEAT	147	UNAPPEAS HOST		9
HE WISHES FOR THE CLOTHS OF HEAVEN	176	CLOTHS HEAVEN		T
AEDH WISHES FOR THE CLOTHS OF HEAVEN	176	CLOTHS HEAVEN	V	T
. . . WHEN A PART OF THE CONSTELLATIONS OF HEAVEN	177	PAST GREATNESS		T
HEAVEN KNOWS WHAT CALAMITY:	193	BAILE AILLINN		112
THE COLD HEAVEN .	316	COLD HEAVEN		T
SUDDENLY I SAW THE COLD AND ROOK-DELIGHTING HEAVEN	316	COLD HEAVEN		1
SUDDENLY I SAW THE COLD AND ROOK DELIGHTING HEAVEN	316	COLD HEAVEN	V	1
HEAVEN HAS PUT AWAY THE STROKE OF HER DOOM,	356	BROKEN DREAMS		11
WHEN ALL IS FED WITH LIGHT AND HEAVEN IS BARE.	375	PHASES OF MOON		74
EVEN ACCUSING HEAVEN BECAUSE	399	BREAK OF DAY		15
THE SWAN HAS LEAPED INTO THE DESOLATE HEAVEN:	431	NINETEEN 19		79
THAT IS TO SAY, ASCENDS TO HEAVEN:	478	SELF AND SOUL		38
HOW IN THE NAME OF HEAVEN CAN HE ESCAPE	479	SELF AND SOUL		50
CAN BUT SHOW THAT HEAVEN YAWNS:	509	JANE REPROVED		4
MADE THE JOINTS OF HEAVEN CRACK!	509	JANE REPROVED		11
PRAY THAT HEAVEN PROTECT US .	518	LOVES LONENESS		5
HEAVEN AND EARTH OUT OF THEIR PLACES,	540	FROM ANTIGONE		8
BLACK OUT: HEAVEN BLAZING INTO THE HEAD:	566	LAPIS LAZULI		19
BUT MASTERFUL HEAVEN HAD INTERVENED TO SAVE IT.	630	CIRCUS ANIMALS		20
A MAN HAS THE FIELDS OF HEAVEN,	643	SONG FAERIES		1
A MAN HAS A HOPE FOR HEAVEN,	643	SONG FAERIES	V	1
LOVE FROM HEAVEN CAME OF YORE	648	ISLE STAT I 1		77
A MAN HAS A HOPE FOR HEAVEN,	676	ISLE STAT II 3		248
AND HEAVEN, AND HOLINESS. LET'S TALK AND GRIEVE,	702	MOSADA 3		84
THEN THE STARS GROW OUT OF HEAVEN WITH THEIR COUNTENANCES FAIR.	719	PHANTOM SHIP		30
WHEN EARTH AND HEAVEN HAVE BEEN FOLDED UP:	765	SHADOW WATER A		366
THAT BLOW WHEN HEAVEN AND EARTH ARE WITHERING,	767	SHADOW WATER A		395
HEAVENLY				
GO TO THE GUARDS OF THE HEAVENLY FOLD	141	EVERLAST VOICE		2
AND THAT ALL HEAVENLY GLORY SYMBOLISE--	445	SCHOOL CHILDR		55
THAN THE HEAVENLY CIRCUIT OF ITS STARS	451	FIRST LOVE		17
THAN HEAVENLY CIRCUIT OF ITS STARS	451	FIRST LOVE	V	17
THE HEAVENLY CIRCUIT: BERENICE'S HAIR:	483	VERONIC NAPKIN		1
A HEAVENLY MANSION, RAGING IN THE DARK,	491	COOLE BALLYLEE	V	40D
A HEAVENLY MANSION, RAGING IN THE DARK.	495	CHOICE		4
LIVE IN A HEAVENLY MANSION,	513	JANE TALK BISH		5
AND HEAVENLY MUSIC IF THEY GAVE IT WIT:	533	HER TRIUMPH		6
HEAVEN'S				
LOOSED LONG AGO FROM HEAVEN'S GATE!	24	OISIN 1		362
LOOKED DOWN ON YOU FROM HEAVEN'S DOOR-POST	112	ROSE OF PEACE		3
LOOKED DOWN ON YOU FROM HEAVEN'S DOOR-POSTS,	112	ROSE OF PEACE	V	3
AND BY THE HEAVEN'S ALL-LABOURING BROODS:	164	PERFECT BEAUTY	V	5
AND BY THE HEAVEN'S UN-LABOURING BROODS:	164	PERFECT BEAUTY	V	5
HAD I THE HEAVEN'S EMBROIDERED CLOTHS,	176	CLOTHS HEAVEN	V	1
THAT IS HEAVEN'S PART, OUR PART	394	EASTER 1916		60
AND THAT ITS OWN SWEET WILL IS HEAVEN'S WILL:	405	FOR DAUGHTER		69
KNOWING THAT NONE COULD PASS HEAVEN'S DOOR	422	MY TABLE		26
KNOWING THAT NONE WHO PASS HEAVEN'S DOOR	422	MY TABLE	V	26
KNOWING THAT NONE CAN PASS HEAVEN'S DOOR	422	MY TABLE	V	26
RUN FOR A MILE UNDIMMED IN HEAVEN'S FACE	490	COOLE BALLYLEE		3
ALL HEAVEN'S FLOOR, WITH VAPOURS BEDDED--	705	DAWN-SONG		11
AND HEAVEN'S A CLOUDY BLOT.	782	HEART FRIGHT		17
HEAVENS				
ALL THE HEAVENS BOW DOWN TO HEAVEN,	125	CATHLEEN PARA		15
THE MIST HAS COVERED THE HEAVENS, AND YOU AND I	251	SHADOW WATER B		604
TREMBLING IN THE BLUE HEAVENS LIKE A WHITE FAWN	251	SHADOW WATER B		611
AN IMAGE OF THE MOVING HEAVENS,	480	BLOOD AND MOON		14
THE HEAVENS IN MY WOMB.	499	MOTHER OF GOD		5
ALL THE LABOURING HEAVENS SIGH.	573	LADYS 3RD SONG		12
THAT HEAVENS HAD OPENED. GYRES RUN ON:	639	BEN BULBEN		62
WHERE ALL NIGHT LONG THE HEAVENS WEEP AND WEEP,	649	ISLE STAT I 1		124
THE HEAVENS ALL STAR-THROBBING ARE A-LIT.	671	ISLE STAT II 3		143

375

HEAVENS (CONTINUED)
  THE HEAVENS ALL STAR-THROBBING ARE ALIT. . . . . . . 671 ISLE STAT II 3 V 143
  YON BAUBLE OF THE HEAVENS, HE LIFTS HIS HANDS, ... 715 FERENCZ RENYI 119
  A QUARTER OF THE HEAVENS FROM OUR RIGHT WAY. . . . . 754 SHADOW WATER A 155
  TREMBLING IN THE BLUE HEAVENS LIKE A WHITE FAWN . . . 769 SHADOW WATER A 427
HEAVENS'
  HAD I THE HEAVENS' EMBROIDERED CLOTHS, ... 176 CLOTHS HEAVEN 1
  CREEPING ALONG THE HEAVENS' PURPLE CUP, ... 714 FERENCZ RENYI 112
HEAVES
  I WAVE THEM HITHER, MY BREAST HEAVES WITH JOY. . . . . 694 MOSADA 1 98
HEAVIER
  THAT YOU MIGHT HAVE A HEAVIER PURSE, ... 273 GREY ROCK 56
HEAVIEST
  YOU HAVE THE HEAVIEST ARM UNDER THE SKY." . . . . . 107 CUCHULAIN SEA 24
HEAVILY
  A HEAVILY BUILT FALSTAFFAN MAN, ... 423 ROAD AT DOOR V 2
  UPON THY FACE? HOW HEAVILY THY HEAD . . . . 701 MOSADA 3 72
HEAVILY-BUILT
  A HEAVILY-BUILT FALSTAFFIAN MAN, ... 423 ROAD AT DOOR 2
HEAVINESS
  THE HEAVINESS OF DESIRE, ... 168 BLESSED V 38
  HAD FILLED THE HOUSE WITH DRUID HEAVINESS; . . . . . 181 QUEEN MAEVE 40
HEAVING
  AND BROKE THE HEAVING RANKS OF BATTLE! . . . . . . 10 OISIN 1 124
  . . . AND HEAVING THE PILLAR OF HIS THROAT, ... 51 OISIN 3 59
  OUR BREASTS ARE HEAVING, OUR EYES ARE AGLEAM, ... 140 HOSTING SIDHE 8
  FOR BREASTS ARE HEAVING AND EYES A-GLEAM: . . . . . 140 HOSTING SIDHE V 7
  OUR BREASTS ARE HEAVING, OUR EYES ARE A-GLEAM, . . . 140 HOSTING SIDHE V 8
  BY THE SLOW HEAVING OCEAN--MUMBLING MOTHER OF THE DEAD. 719 PHANTOM SHIP 34
HEAVY   SEE VINEGAR-HEAVY DREAM-HEAVY HISSOP-HEAVY ROSE-HEAVY
  WITH A HEAVY HEART AND A WANDERING MIND, ... 2 OISIN 1 2
  FROM HIS HOOVES IN THE HEAVY GRASSES, WITH MONSTROUS   48 OISIN 3 V 27
      SLUMBERING FOLK,
  AND THOUGHT, I WILL MY HEAVY STORY TELL . . . . . 68 SAD SHEPHERD 19
  AND LO--MY HEAVY BURTHEN MAY DEPART!" . . . . . . 69 SAD SHEPHERD V 24
  THE HEAVY BOUGHS, THE BURNISHED DOVE . . . . . . 78 INDIAN TO LOVE 16
  OF PURPLE AND OF HEAVY GOLD; . . . . 81 MAD KING GOLL V 3
  AND SING, AND SHAKE MY HEAVY LOCKS. . . . . . . 84 MAD KING GOLL 44
  THE LINES ARE NOT HEAVY, NOR HEAVY THE LONG NETS BROWN-- 91 OLD FISHERMAN 5
  THE LINES ARE NOT HEAVY, NOR HEAVY THE LONG NETS BROWN-- 91 OLD FISHERMAN V 5
  CAME FLYING, HEAVY AND SAD; . . . . 93 FATHER OHART 34
  AND HEAVY MORTAL HOPES THAT TOIL AND PASS; . . . . . 101 ROSE UPON ROOD 18
  AN OLD SLAVE GRINDING AT A HEAVY QUERN, ... 104 FERGUS DRUID 35
  ALL THE HEAVY DAYS ARE OVER; . . . . 124 CATHLEEN PARA 1
  THE HEAVY STEPS OF THE PLOUGHMAN, SPLASHING THE WINTRY 143 ROSE IN HEART 3
      MOULD,
  THE HEAVY STEPS OF THE PLOUGHMAN SPLASHING THE WINTER   143 ROSE IN HEART V 3
      MOULD,
  WITH HEAVY WHITENING WINGS, AND A HEART FALLEN COLD! . 147 UNAPPEAS HOST 4
  THEIR HOOFS HEAVY WITH TUMULT, THEIR EYES GLIMMERING WHITE! 154 BELOVED PEACE 2
  THE HORSES OF DISASTER PLUNGE IN THE HEAVY CLAY! . . . 154 BELOVED PEACE 8
  PASSION-DIMMED EYES AND LONG HEAVY HAIR . . . . . 155 REPROVE CURLEW 4
  SHE DREW IN THE HEAVY CASEMENT . . . . 159 CAP AND BELLS 11
  WITH YOUR DIM HEAVY HAIR, ... 163 ASKS FORGIVE 22
  AMONG PALE EYELIDS, HEAVY WITH THE SLEEP . . . . . 169 SECRET ROSE 6
  MEN HAVE NAMED BEAUTY. YOUR HEAVY LEAVES ENFOLD . . 169 SECRET ROSE V 7
  THAT IT MAY DROP FAINT PERFUME, AND BE HEAVY WITH DEW, 172 TRAV PASSION 7
  HIS HEAVY RINGS UNCOILED FROM GLIMMERING DEEP TO DEEP; 174 ELEMENT POWERS 5
  WAS THAT, THE AIR BEING HEAVY AND THE DOGS . . . . 182 QUEEN MAEVE 53
  O HEAVY SWOLLEN WATERS, BRIM THE FALL OF THE OAK TREES, 207 HANRAHANS SONG V 11
  LIKE HEAVY FLOODED WATERS OUR BODIES AND OUR BLOOD; . 208 HANRAHANS SONG 13
  LIKE HEAVY SWOLLEN WATERS ARE OUR BODIES AND OUR BLOOD; 208 HANRAHANS SONG V 13
  WHEN ALL THIS HEAVY HISTORY'S DONE; . . . . . . 213 BLESS PSALTER 17
  THEY UNHOOK THEIR HEAVY SWORDS . . . . 215 HAPPY TOWNLAND 23
  HEAVY LIKE STONE, THEIR WISDOM BEING HALF SILENCE. . . 218 WOODS OF COOLE 26
  BUT THE STAG STOOPED ITS HEAVY BRANCHING HORNS, . . . 277 TWO KINGS V 12
  NOR HEAVY KNITTING OF THE BROW . . . . 318 APPOINTMENT 9
  TWO HEAVY TRESTLES, AND A BOARD . . . . 421 MY TABLE 1
  I WRAPPED HER IN A HEAVY HOODED CLOAK, ... 468 HARUN RASHID V 154
  I WRAPPED HER IN A HEAVY HOODED CLOAK, AND SHE . . . 468 HARUN RASHID V 154
  IS BUT A HEAVY, GOLD EMBROIDERED BANNER, ... 469 HARUN RASHID V 188
  BUT UNDER HEAVY LOADS OF TRAMPLED CLAY . . . . . 483 OIL AND BLOOD 4
  BUT HEAVY FRUIT. HOW SWIFT THE ARGUMENT . . . . . 665 ISLE STAT II 2 66
  HEAVY WITH WOOL THE SHEEP ARE GATHERED IN, ... 681 SEEKER 1
  THE HEAVY CLUSTERS OF THE GRAPES WERE FULL, ... 690 MOSADA 1 13
  THIS DEATH IS HEAVY IN MY VEINS LIKE SLEEP. . . . . 701 MOSADA 3 57
  WHY DO YOU HANG SO HEAVY IN MY ARMS? . . . . . . 703 MOSADA 3 108
  WHERE THE ROSES IN SCARLET ARE HEAVY . . . . . . 707 FAIRY PEDANT 3
  WITH CREATURES OF OUR HEAVY NIGHT, ... 743 DANAAN QUICK 10
  LOOK ON THIS BODY AND THIS HEAVY HAIR; . . . . . . 767 SHADOW WATER A 397
HEBER'S
  THERE WAS NO MIGHTIER SOUL OF HEBER'S LINE; . . . . 36 OISIN 2 95
HEBRIDES
  AND PASSED THE OUTER HEBRIDES, AND TOOK . . . . . 749 SHADOW WATER A 42
  AND PASSED THE NORTHERN HEBRIDES, AND TOOK . . . . 749 SHADOW WATER A V 42
  AMONG THE HEBRIDES. WHEN SHE AWAKENS, ... 760 SHADOW WATER A V 255
HECTOR
  HECTOR IS IN THE DUST, NIETZSCHE IS BORN, ... 374 PHASES OF MOON 46
  TO THINK OF BURIED HECTOR . . . . 455 HIS MEMORIES 5
  SHE WHO HAD BROUGHT GREAT HECTOR DOWN . . . . . 455 HIS MEMORIES 15
  HECTOR IS DEAD AND THERE'S A LIGHT IN TROY; . . . . 564 GYRES 7

	PAGE	TITLE	LINE
HEDGES			
AND WHEN ABOUNDING HEDGES RING	434	WHEEL	3
AND WHEN ABOUNDING HEDGES SING	434	WHEEL V	3
HEED			
AND ALL MUST PAY HIM HEED, ...	583	GHOST ROG CASE	22
THE BOAT DRAWS NEAR AND NEAR. YOU HEED ME NOT!	663	ISLE STAT II 2	23
CEASE! THERNOT'S WOUNDED, CEASE! THEY WILL NOT HEED. . .	665	ISLE STAT II 2	64
NOR LAW NOR PARLIAMENT TAKE HEED.	791	REPRISALS	22
HEEDS			
NOR HEEDS THE OLD, DIM PROTEST AND THE CRY	689	NETTLESHIP	14
HEEL			
. . . AT THE HEEL OF A CENTURY FELL, ...	54	OISIN 3	102
THAT TOSSED A BARE HEEL WHEN AT SCHOOL, ...	301	RUN PARADISE	19
FROM HEEL TO THROAT:	320	COAT	4
HEEL UP AND WEIGHT ON TOE, MUST FACE THE WALL	363	DOLLS FACES	3
TO DRUM WITH HER HEEL AND TO LEAP?	381	SONGS FOOL 2	9
A SORT OF BATTERED KETTLE AT THE HEEL.	409	TOWER	16
HEELS			
THEY SAT UPON THEIR HEELS TO RAIL, ...	297	THREE BEGGARS	53
OR SAT UPON THEIR HEELS TO RAIL	297	THREE BEGGARS V	53
THAT PATCHING OLD HEELS THEY MAY SHRIEK, I TAKE TO CHISEL	623	HIGH TALK	8
AND PLANE.			
HEIGHT			
OF THE FLOOD AND FLAME, OF THE HEIGHT AND WOOD, ...	148	INTO TWILIGHT V	11
MORE HANDS IN HEIGHT THAN ANY STAG IN THE WORLD	277	TWO KINGS	9
THAT ON THE LONELY HEIGHT WHERE ALL ARE IN GOD'S EYE, . .	291	PAUDEEN	6
WHEN THE FULL MOON SWAM TO ITS GREATEST HEIGHT	468	HARUN RASHID	151
HEIGHTS			
WHEN I CLAMBER TO THE HEIGHTS OF SLEEP, ...	357	DEEP-SWORN VOW	4
HEIR			
ON THE HEIR OF ULADH, BUAN'S SON, ...	189	BAILE AILLINN	4
AILLINN, WHO WAS KING LUGAIDH'S HEIR.	189	BAILE AILLINN	7
HEIRS			
AND ON MY HEIRS, IF ALL REMAIN UNSPOILED, ...	371	ON GOING HOUSE	2
MY BODILY HEIRS MAY FIND, ...	420	MY HOUSE	28
HELD			
AS THOUGH HE HELD AN EARTHLY MEAD	2	OISIN 1 V	7X
HE HELD THAT FLASHING SCEPTRE UP.	18	OISIN 1	260
NOR HAVE HANDS HELD A WEARY TOOL:	19	OISIN 1	283
BENEATH HAD PACED CONTENT! WE HELD OUR WAY	36	OISIN 2	103
BASALTIC, MIGHT HAVE PACED. WE HELD OUR WAY	36	OISIN 2 V	103
LAID IT AND SIGHED: I HELD A SWORD WHOSE SHINE	37	OISIN 2	126
ONCE HELD BETWEEN MY ARMS, WITH LIVID CHOP	40	OISIN 2 V	178
I HELD A DRIPPING CORPSE, WITH LIVID CHOP	40	OISIN 2 V	178
AND I BUT HELD A CORPSE, WITH LIVID CHOP	40	OISIN 2 V	178
HELD TO THE TOWERS WITH BOASTING SONGS AND GAY.	41	OISIN 2 V	184C
HALF OPEN HIS EYES WERE, AND HELD ME, ...	51	OISIN 3	65
WHILE SLOWLY HE WHOSE HAND HELD HERS REPLIED:	80	EPHEMERA	11
WHILE SLOWLY ANSWERED HE WHOSE HAND HELD HERS--	80	EPHEMERA V	11
A THOUSAND YEARS AGO YOU HELD HIGH TALK	187	QUEEN MAEVE	150
THAT HELD THE LAND TOGETHER THERE, ...	194	BAILE AILLINN	132
HE COULD NOT SEE THEM, BUT I HELD OUT MY HANDS	223	SHADOW WATER B	38
DRAGON THAT LOVED THE WORLD AND HELD US TO IT, ...	251	SHADOW WATER B	598
I HELD A PAINTED STEERING OAR, ...	253	HIS DREAM V	2
WHO SAID, "BECAUSE SHE HELD ME IN	274	GREY ROCK	86
A ROMAN CAESAR IS HELD DOWN	379	SAINT HUNCH	4
"A MAN IF I BUT HELD HIM SO	521	THREE THINGS	9
AND AFTER THAT I HELD MY FINGERS UP, ...	537	HER VISION	9
OF ALL THAT SCHOLARLY GENERATIONS HAD HELD DEAR:	603	GALLERY REVIS V	37A
A MOUTHFUL HELD THE EXTREME OF LIFE AND DEATH.	619	BRONZE HEAD	14
AND HELD HER IN MY ARMS!	631	POLITICS	12
A KID, HELD BY ONE SOFT WHITE EAR FOR TETHER, ...	715	DWELT SYCAMORE	3
I HAVE CUT THE CORDS THAT HELD THIS GALLEY TO OURS. . . .	768	SHADOW WATER A V	421
HELEN			
WHEN HELEN LIVED	293	HELEN LIVED	T
WHERE HELEN WALKED WITH HER BOY, ...	293	HELEN LIVED	9
HELEN BEING CHOSEN FOUND LIFE FLAT AND DULL	404	FOR DAUGHTER	25
AND HELEN HAS ALL LIVING HEARTS BETRAYED.	411	TOWER	53
FROM THE LIMBS OF HELEN SANK	522	LULLABY V	17
TROY BACKED ITS HELEN: TROY DIED AND ADORED:	547	TO SAME TUNE 3	4
TROY LOOKED ON HELEN, IT DIED AND ADORED:	547	TO SAME TUNE 3 V	4
TROY BACKED ITS HELEN: TROY DIED AND ADORED:	614	MARCH SONGS 2	4
A HELEN OF SOCIAL WELFARE DREAM, ...	626	OLD MEN BE MAD	7
HELEN'S			
THAT FIRST DAWN IN HELEN'S ARMS?	522	LULLABY	6
THAT FIRST NIGHT IN HELEN'S ARMS.	522	LULLABY V	6
HELICON			
THE ABOUNDING GUTTER HAD BEEN HELICON	398	LEADERS CROWD	6
HELL			
AND EARTH AND HEAVEN AND HELL WOULD DIE, ...	19	OISIN 1	271
. . . ON THE BURNING STONES OF WIDE HELL, ...	61	OISIN 3	198
HEARING HELL LOUD WITH A MURMUR, AS SHOUTING AND MOCKING	62	OISIN 3	208
WE SWEEP.			
NONE WAR ON THE MASTERS OF HELL, ...	62	OISIN 3	214
WHEN HEAVEN AND HELL ARE MET, ...	112	ROSE OF PEACE	2
A PEACE OF HEAVEN WITH HELL.	113	ROSE OF PEACE	16
THE DOORS OF HELL AND BLOW THERE MANY A WHIMPERING GHOST:	147	UNAPPEAS HOST	10
EUNUCHS RAN THROUGH HELL AND MET	294	HATED PLAYBOY	2
HELL MOUTH LAY OPEN NEAR THAT PLACE, ...	303	HOUR DAWN	25
BUT THE HELL MOUTH AT CRUACHAN	303	HOUR DAWN V	24
FROM THE HELL MOUTH AT CRUACHAN	307	HOUR DAWN V	120

	PAGE	TITLE		LINE

HELL (CONTINUED)
THEY SAID I'D BURN IN HELL UNLESS I TOLD. . . . . 694 MOSADA 1 — 108
"NO, THY HOME IS DEEPEST HELL, ... 697 MOSADA 2 — 26
HER SOUL FROM SEAS OF ENDLESS FLAME IN HELL. . . . . . 698 MOSADA 2 — 47
SO THEY ESCAPE FROM HELL. BUT, PARDON ME, ... 704 MOSADA 3 — 132

HELL'S
ROUND ABOUT HELL'S GATE TO STARE . . . . 294 HATED PLAYBOY V 3

HELM
AND FLY AMONG THE FOAM. THRUST DOWN THE HELM, ... 750 SHADOW WATER A 88
GIVE ME THE HELM! CALL HITHER THOSE WHO LIE . . . . 751 SHADOW WATER A 91
NODS BY THE HELM, AND NEARER TO THE SAIL . . . . . . 752 SHADOW WATER A 119

HELMET
AND BEAT THE GOLDEN HELMET WITH THEIR SWORDS? . . . . 243 SHADOW WATER B 425

HELMETS
HELMETS, AND SWORDS, AND HALF-FORGOTTEN THINGS . . . 257 RECONCILIATION 6
HURL HELMETS, CROWNS, AND SWORDS INTO THE PIT. . . 257 RECONCILIATION 10

HELMS
THE ANCIENT BEARDS, THE HELMS OF RUBY AND GOLD . . . 169 SECRET ROSE 8
AND ALL THEIR HELMS OF SILVER HOVERING SIDE BY SIDE, . . 318 MAGI 5

HELMSMAN'S
A TRADING GALLEY IN HER HELMSMAN'S EYES. . . . . . 751 SHADOW WATER A 95

HELP
HELP! HELP! AND HURL HIM FROM OUR COAST . . . . . 83 MAD KING GOLL V 17
HELP! HELP! AND HURL HIM FROM OUR COAST . . . . . 83 MAD KING GOLL V 17
NO WOMAN'S LOVED ME, NO MAN SOUGHT MY HELP. . . . 103 FERGUS DRUID 26
NO MAIDEN LOVES ME, NO MAN SEEKS MY HELP, ... 103 FERGUS DRUID V 26
NO WOMAN LOVES ME, NO MAN SEEKS MY HELP, ... 103 FERGUS DRUID V 26
TO HELP ME IN MY NEED. . . . . 134 FR GILLIGAN 44
TO HELP HER LIGHT FOOT HERE AND THERE, ... 138 TO IRELAND V 14
ABOUT MY THRESHOLD TO COUNSEL AND TO HELP?" . . . 183 QUEEN MAEVE 82
THE PARTED LIPS REPLIED, "I SEEK YOUR HELP, . . . 183 QUEEN MAEVE 83
ABOUT MY DOOR TO COUNSEL AND TO HELP." . . . . 183 QUEEN MAEVE V 82
HELP THEM THAT WANDER WITH HAND CLASPING HAND, . . 184 QUEEN MAEVE 86
AND I WOULD HAVE YOUR HELP IN MY GREAT NEED, . . . 184 QUEEN MAEVE 98
HELP THEM THAT PACE, HAND IN UNWITHERING HAND, . . 184 QUEEN MAEVE V 86
NO MORTAL CAN. YES! IF THEY GIVE US HELP. . . . 229 SHADOW WATER B 165
AND THERE'S NO HELP IN WORDS. TO THE OTHER SHIP, . 250 SHADOW WATER B 585
AND WHAT, GOD HELP US, COULD THEY SAVE? . . . . 289 SEPTEMBER 1913 14
HOW THEREFORE COULD SHE HELP BUT BRAID . . . . 309 PLAYER QUEEN 17
MAGICAL SHAPES. BY THE HELP OF AN IMAGE . . . 367 EGO DOMINUS 7
TO HELP GOOD, WISE OR GREAT . . . . 432 NINETEEN 19 110
IN THIS MY CHOICE. SOME GOD MIGHT HELP! IF SO . . 656 ISLE STAT I 3 37
THAT MURMURS WITH HOLY WOODS, AND WIN THEIR HELP . 757 SHADOW WATER A 199

HELPED
I HELPED YOUR FATHERS WHEN THEY BUILT THESE WALLS, . . 184 QUEEN MAEVE 97
"BECAUSE I HELPED TO WIND THE CLOCK . . . . . . 585 ORAHILLY 25

HELPER
THIS OTHER HIS HELPER AND FRIEND . . . . 392 EASTER 1916 26

HELPFUL
HELPFUL AND SHY. . . . . 89 ISLE IN WATER 14

HELPLESS
HELPLESS, MEN LIFTING THE LIDS OF HIS WEARY
AND DEATH-MAKING EYE. . . . . 53 OISIN 3 92
HELPLESS, MEN LIFTING THE LIDS OF HIS WEARY
AND DEATH-POURING EYE. . . . . 53 OISIN 3 V 92
BEFORE THE FULL MOON. HELPLESS AS A WORM. . . . 374 PHASES OF MOON 49
HE HOLDS HER HELPLESS BREAST UPON HIS BREAST. . . 441 LEDA AND SWAN 4
HAS LAID HER HELPLESS FACE UPON HIS BREAST. . . 441 LEDA AND SWAN V 4

HEM
HER PEARL-PALE HAND AND THE HEM OF HER DRESS. . . 16 OISIN 1 216
HER FINGERS AND HER GARMENTS' HEM. . . . . . 16 OISIN 1 V 216
AND SHAKE THEIR COVERLET'S HEM, ... 33 OISIN 2 V 62
BECAUSE THE RED-ROSE-BORDERED HEM . . . . . 137 TO IRELAND 6
BECAUSE THE RED ROSE BORDERED HEM . . . . . 137 TO IRELAND V 6
AFTER THE RED-ROSE-BORDERED HEM. . . . . 139 TO IRELAND 30
AFTER THE RED-ROSE-BORDERED HEM. . . . . 139 TO IRELAND 48
AFTER THE RED ROSE BORDERED HEM. . . . . 139 TO IRELAND V 30
AFTER THE RED ROSE BORDERED HEM. . . . . 139 TO IRELAND V 48
FOUGHT ONCE FOR SELF-SAME REASON ON THE HEM . . 660 ISLE STAT II 1 32
THY GARMENTS' HEM, THOU VISIONARY ONE! . . . 684 SEEKER 71
THY GARMENT'S HEM, THOU VISIONARY ONE! . . . 684 SEEKER V 71

HEN   SEE MOOR-HEN WATER-HEN
MARE OR STALLION, COCK OR HEN, ... 529 TOM LUNATIC 15
OF HEN WIVES AND OF QUEER OLD MEN . . . . . 607 SONGS BURDEN 2 V 23

HENCE
O WOMEN, KNEELING BY YOUR ALTAR-RAILS LONG HENCE, . . 173 SPEAKS HEARERS 1
O COLLEENS, KNEELING BY YOUR ALTAR RAILS LONG HENCE, . 173 SPEAKS HEARERS V 1
O, WOMEN, KNEELING BY YOUR ALTAR RAILS LONG HENCE, . 173 SPEAKS HEARERS V 1
CONSIDERING THAT, ALL HATRED DRIVEN HENCE, . . . 405 FOR DAUGHTER 65
MEETING LONG HENCE THE PHANTOM HERDSMAN, KING . . . 675 ISLE STAT II 3 242

HENRY
SOMEWHERE OFF HENRY STREET! . . . . 585 ORAHILLY 31
MY NAME IS HENRY MIDDLETON. . . . . 606 SONGS BURDEN 2 1

HENS   SEE MOOR-HENS PEA-HENS
AND HENS TO MOOR-COCKS CALL! . . . . 393 EASTER 1916 54
OTTERS BELOW AND MOOR HENS ON THE TOP, ... 490 COOLE BALLYLEE V 2

HENWIVES
OF HENWIVES AND OF QUEER OLD MEN . . . . . . 607 SONGS BURDEN 2 23

HERALD
THERE CRIED A HERALD, "TO OUR VALLEYS . . . . 82 MAD KING GOLL V 14
CRIED A HERALD, "PEACE WITH THINE! . . . . . 82 MAD KING GOLL V 14

378

		PAGE	TITLE		LINE
HERALD (CONTINUED)

CRIED A HERALD, "TO OUR VALLEYS . . . . 82 MAD KING GOLL V 14
AFAR, CLEAR-SHINING ON THE HERALD HILLS, ... 645 ISLE STAT I 1 14
THE FAIRIES' HERALD SPAKE ONCE MORE! . . . . 730 PRIEST FAIRY 53

HERALD'S

THE HERALD'S CRY, THE SOLDIER'S TREAD . . . . 438 SONGS PLAY 2 13

HERB

SOME MEDICABLE HERB TO MAKE OUR GRIEF . . . . 342 SHEP GOATHERD 86
BY WATER, HERB AND SOLITARY PRAYER . . . . 555 RIBH AT TOMB 23
AND MANY A HERB AND MANY A SPELL . . . . 717 FAIRY DOCTOR 17

HERBLESS

DUSKY AND HERBLESS, WHERE A BUBBLING STRAIN . . . . . 39 OISIN 2 V 156
BARKING, ALONG THE HERBLESS PLAIN, WITH BLOWS . . . . 40 OISIN 2 V 170

HERBS

THUS DO I BURN THESE PRECIOUS HERBS, WHOSE SMOKE . . . 691 MOSADA 1 39
AND MANY HERBS AND MANY A SPELL . . . . 717 FAIRY DOCTOR V 17

HERD

TO IDLE LIFE AWAY, A COMMON HERD." . . . . 107 CUCHULAIN SEA 21
OF A MOROCCAN FLOCK OR HERD, ... 493 AT ALGECIRAS V 3

HERDED

HERDED THE CATTLE CAME WITH STUMBLING FEET, ... 106 CUCHULAIN SEA 19

HERDING

HERDING THE PACK. UNQUIET WANDERER . . . . 292 TO A SHADE V 18

HERDS

HAVE A SPEED LIKE THE SPEED OF THE SALMON HERDS, . . . 9 OISIN 1 98
AND SWIFTER THAN THE SALMON HERDS: . . . . 9 OISIN 1 V 96
THAT YOU STAY IDLING HERE WITH FLOCKS AND HERDS." . . 107 CUCHULAIN SEA V 21
THAT YOU STAY IDLING HERE WITH FLOCK AND HERDS." . . 107 CUCHULAIN SEA V 21
TO IDLE LIFE AWAY WITH FLOCKS AND HERDS." . . . . . 107 CUCHULAIN SEA V 21
ARE TRODDEN AND BROKEN BY THE HERDS, ... 190 BAILE AILLINN 43
ON THE HORIZON EDGE BELLOWED THE HERDS. . . . . . . 279 TWO KINGS 56
THEREON THE BELLOWING OF THE EMPOUNDED HERDS . . . . 286 TWO KINGS 214
OF THE MOROCCAN FLOCKS AND HERDS . . . . 493 AT ALGECIRAS 3
ROUND US HERDS OF SHADOWS STEAL-- . . . . 737 IN FIRELIGHT 6
WHO MIGHT HAVE FLOCKS AND HERDS AND MANY THRALLS, . . 757 SHADOW WATER A 216
O, AENGUS OF THE HERDS, WATCH OVER ME! . . . . 762 SHADOW WATER A 291

HERDSMAN

A HERDSMAN CAME FROM INLAND VALLEYS, ... 82 MAD KING GOLL 14
THE CRAZY HERDSMAN THAT WILL TELL HIS FELLOWS . . . . 229 SHADOW WATER B 167
MEETING LONG HENCE THE PHANTOM HERDSMAN, KING . . . 675 ISLE STAT II 3 242

HERDSMEN

TO THAT HIGH HILL THE HERDSMEN NAME . . . . 194 BAILE AILLINN 129

HERESIES

THAT SHE FORSWEAR HER HERESIES AND SAVE . . . . . . 698 MOSADA 2 46
CAST OFF THY HERESIES, AND SAVE THY SOUL . . . . . . 701 MOSADA 3 64

HERESY

I WILL BURN HERESY FROM THIS MAD EARTH, ... 697 MOSADA 2 40

HERITAGE

SOMETHING OF EVERY PADDLER'S HERITAGE-- . . . . . . 444 SCHOOL CHILDR 21
LONDON STREETS HAVE HERITAGE, ... 733 STREET DANCERS 57

HERMIT

A BLIND HERMIT RINGS THE HOUR. . . . . 484 SYMBOLS 2

HERMITS

THE THREE HERMITS . . . . 298 THREE HERMITS T
THREE OLD HERMITS TOOK THE AIR . . . . 298 THREE HERMITS 1
HERMITS UPON MOUNT MERU OR EVEREST, ... 563 MERU 9

HERO

"AND EVERY HERO DROOP HIS HEAD? . . . . 4 OISIN 1 33
THE HERO, THE GIRL, AND THE FOOL . . . . 447 HERO GIRL FOOL T

HERODIAS'

HERODIAS' DAUGHTERS HAVE RETURNED AGAIN, ... 433 NINETEEN 19 118

HEROES

THE HUNTING OF HEROES SHOULD BE GLAD." . . . . . . 4 OISIN 1 39
"THE HUNTING OF HEROES SHOULD BE GLAD: . . . . . . 4 OISIN 1 V 32
"FOR HUNTING HEROES SHOULD BE GLAD. . . . . 4 OISIN 1 V 34
AND ON THE HEROES LYING SLAIN . . . . 5 OISIN 1 42

HEROES'

BECAUSE THE HEROES' CRESCENT IS THE TWELFTH. . . . . 374 PHASES OF MOON V 47

HEROIC

BUT AN HEROIC DREAM. . . . . 255 WOMAN HOMER 21
BANISHED HEROIC MOTHER MOON AND VANISHED, ... 344 DEJECTION 9
HEROIC MOTHER MOON HAS VANISHED, ... 344 DEJECTION V 9
WHAT BUT HEROIC WANTONNESS? . . . . 550 SEVERED HEAD 13
HEROIC REVERIE MOCKED BY CLOWN AND KNAVE, ... 619 BRONZE HEAD 27
THROUGH SEVEN HEROIC CENTURIES, ... 640 BEN BULBEN 80

HEROICALLY

HEROICALLY LOST, HEROICALLY FOUND. . . . . 578 CRAZED GIRL 8
HEROICALLY LOST, HEROICALLY FOUND. . . . . 578 CRAZED GIRL 8

HERON

THEN, MOUNTED ON A HERON, O'ER THE DEEP . . . . . . 33 OISIN 2 V 64
AND HERON OUT OF THE SKIES." . . . . 167 BLESSED 10
AND FAR AWAY THE HERON SAILS, I WIS. . . . . 649 ISLE STAT I 1 116
WAKE! THE HERON, RISING, HATH . . . . 705 DAWN-SONG 17
STRAYING AS THE HERON STRAYETH, ... 706 DAWN-SONG 27

HERON-BILLED

THE HERON-BILLED PALE CATTLE-BIRDS . . . . 493 AT ALGECIRAS 1
THE HERON-BILLED PALE CATTLE BIRD, ... 493 AT ALGECIRAS V 1
THE HERON-BILLED PALE CATTLE BIRDS, ... 493 AT ALGECIRAS V 1

HERON'S

HOW THE FALCONER FOLLOWS THE FALCON IN THE WEEDS OF THE 52 OISIN 3 79
HERON'S PLOT,

379

	PAGE	TITLE	LINE
HERON'S (CONTINUED)			
THE HERON'S HUNCH UPON HIS BACK, ...	508	JANE BISHOP	19
AY, BOY. LET'S SEE IF THAT SAME HERON'S DEAD.	651	ISLE STAT I 1	169
HERONS			
WHERE FLAPPING HERONS WAKE	86	STOLEN CHILD	4
AND THE JOY OF THE STREAMS WHERE LONG-LIMBED HERONS WADE:	674	ISLE STAT II 3	217
HERO'S			
BRED TO BE A HERO'S WAGE.	258	PEACE	3
BECAUSE THE HERO'S CRESCENT IS THE TWELFTH.	374	PHASES OF MOON	47
HERRING			
THE HERRING ARE NOT IN THE TIDES AS THEY WERE OF OLD: . .	91	OLD FISHERMAN	5
HERRINGS			
MY WORK WAS SALTIN' HERRINGS	94	MOLL MAGEE	7
FLASHES AS IF IT WERE A NET OF HERRINGS.	248	SHADOW WATER B	536
HESITATE			
HESITATE OR STAY?	505	RESULT THOUGHT	17
HEW			
BASALTIC PILLARS MARRED WITH HEW AND HACK	31	OISIN 2 V	30
EVADING, TURNING: ONCE DID I HEW AND HEW	40	OISIN 2	176
EVADING, TURNING: ONCE DID I HEW AND HEW	40	OISIN 2 V	176
HIBERNIAN			
ON MR. NETTLESHIP'S PICTURE AT THE ROYAL HIBERNIAN ACADEMY.	688	NETTLESHIP	T
HIBERNIANS			
. . . HAVE JOINED THE ANCIENT ORDER OF HIBERNIANS AND THE	262	STUDENTS AGIT V	T
. . .			
HID SEE LEAF-HID VAPOUR-HID			
AND IN THE SHADOW OF MY HAIR LIE HID, ...	33	OISIN 2	66
IT DIED AFAR. GREY SLEET THOSE TOWERS HID	46	OISIN 2 V	245
HID UNDER QUIET BOUGHS APART, ...	78	INDIAN TO LOVE	12
HID IN THE EARTH'S MOST HIDDEN PART, ...	78	INDIAN TO LOVE V	12
HID UNDER QUIET BOWS APART, ...	78	INDIAN TO LOVE V	12
THERE WE'VE HID OUR FAERY VATS, ...	87	STOLEN CHILD	6
GO DWELL UPON THE SEA CLIFFS, VAPOUR HID, ...	105	CUCHULAIN SEA V	4
IS HID IN THE HEART OF LOVE:	119	PITY OF LOVE	2
HAD HID AWAY EARTH'S OLD AND WEARY CRY.	120	SORROW OF LOVE V	4
AND HID HIS FACE AMID A CROWD OF STARS.	121	YOU ARE OLD	12
FOR SOMEBODY HID HATRED AND HOPE AND DESIRE AND FEAR . .	153	CHANGE BELOVED	4
IN THE HID PLACE, BEING CRAZED BY LOVE.	195	BAILE AILLINN	143
BUT A WILD APPLE HID THE GRASS	197	BAILE AILLINN	189
AT THE MOTH HOUR AND HID IT IN HER BOSOM.	199	ARROW V	6
WHERE ONE FOUND LANCELOT CRAZED AND HID HIM FOR A WHILE:	209	UNDER THE MOON	3
WHERE ONE FOUND LANCELOT CRAZED, AND HID HIM FOR AWHILE,	209	UNDER THE MOON V	3
AND HID HER AMONG FRUITS OF JEWEL-STONE	224	SHADOW WATER B	49
"ALTHOUGH THE THING THAT YOU HAVE HID WERE EVIL, . . .	281	TWO KINGS	103
SUDDENLY HID LOVE'S MOON AWAY.	313	MEMORY YOUTH	7
ONCE MORE THE STORM IS HOWLING, AND HALF HID	403	FOR DAUGHTER	1
UNFRIENDLY LAMPLIGHT HID UNDER ITS SHADE, ...	523	LONG SILENCE	3
THINGS HID IN THEIR MARROW-BONES	589	OLD WICKED MAN	41
HID FROM ALL THOSE WARTY LADS	589	OLD WICKED MAN	43
OR CHILD HID IN THE WOMB.	589	OLD WICKED MAN	53
THINGS HID IN THEIR MARROWBONES	589	OLD WICKED MAN V	41
THINGS HID IN THEIR MARROW BONES	589	OLD WICKED MAN V	41
FOR YE ARE HID WITH VAPOUR. ROUND THE STAKE	695	MOSADA 1	111
FOR YE ARE HID WITH VAPOURS? ROUND THE STAKE	695	MOSADA 1 V	111
HALF HID. HE BRINGS THE PEASANT'S ONLY KIN, ...	711	FERENCZ RENYI	50
YET ONE JOY HAVE I, HID CLOSE, ...	744	ROSY CROSS	8
FOR I HAVE SEEN A SHIP HID IN THE FOG.	751	SHADOW WATER A	89
OR A GOD HID THEM UNDER THE SHADOW OF WINGS.	752	SHADOW WATER A	125
HIDDEN			
HID IN THE EARTH'S MOST HIDDEN PART, ...	78	INDIAN TO LOVE V	12
LIE NOW HALF HIDDEN UNDER PENDULOUS LIDS, ...	79	EPHEMERA V	2
LAY HIDDEN IN THE SMALL SLATE-COLOURED THING:	104	FERGUS DRUID	40
LAY HIDDEN IN THE SMALL SLATE-COLOURED BAG:	104	FERGUS DRUID V	40
"THE DOOMS OF MEN ARE IN GOD'S HIDDEN PLACE."	110	CUCHULAIN SEA	62
"THE DOOMS OF MEN ARE IN GOD'S HIDDEN HOARD."	110	CUCHULAIN SEA V	62
THE SURETY OF ITS HIDDEN ROOT	134	TWO TREES	7
ROOTS HALF HIDDEN UNDER SNOWS, ...	135	TWO TREES	27
AND ROOTS HALF HIDDEN UNDER SNOWS	135	TWO TREES V	27
THE EAST HER HIDDEN JOY BEFORE THE MORNING BREAK, . . .	154	BELOVED PEACE	4
AND LINGERED IN THE HIDDEN DESOLATE PLACE	162	ASKS FORGIVE	15
BUT WE HAVE HIDDEN IN OUR HEARTS THE FLAME OUT OF THE EYES	207	HANRAHANS SONG	4
AS THOUGH THEY HAD BEEN HIDDEN BY GREEN BOUGHS	217	WOODS OF COOLE	6
TO HURRY TO THEIR HIDDEN HAPPINESS	234	SHADOW WATER B	268
TO AN OLD EMPTY WOODMAN'S HOUSE THAT'S HIDDEN	282	TWO KINGS	134
OBEDIENT TO SOME HIDDEN MAGICAL BREATH.	382	VISION ROBART	13
MAY SHE BECOME A FLOURISHING HIDDEN TREE	404	FOR DAUGHTER	41
WE SHOULD BE HIDDEN FROM THEIR EYES, ...	454	HIS MEMORIES	1
HIDDEN FROM EYESIGHT TO THE UNNOTICED END.	472	ALL SOUL NIGHT	50
UPON THE STAR THAT MARKS THE HIDDEN POLE:	477	SELF AND SOUL	5
NAKED AND HIDDEN AWAY, ...	510	JANE JUDGMENT	13
HIDDEN BY OLD AGE AWHILE	539	MEETING	1
GOD'S LOVE HAS HIDDEN HIM	574	MAIDS 1ST SONG	7
CASEMENT UPON TRIAL, HALF HIDDEN BY THE BARS, ...	601	GALLERY REVIS	3
GIVE TONGUE, PROCLAIM THEIR HIDDEN NAME——"HOUND VOICE."	622	HOUND VOICE	7
KEEP HIDDEN AND COVERED HER HEART!"	744	GLOVE CLOAK	12
THE LOVE I KNOW IS HIDDEN IN THESE HANDS	765	SHADOW WATER A	350
HIDE			
HAD NEITHER HOPE NOR FEAR. I BADE THEM HIDE	38	OISIN 2	139
. . . THE SHIELD OUT OF OSIER AND HIDE:	52	OISIN 3	82
TO THOSE ABOUT, "BEAT HIM WITH THONGS OF HIDE	106	CUCHULAIN SEA V	17A
ALTHOUGH YOU HIDE IN THE EBB AND FLOW	146	FISH	1

HIDE   (CONTINUED)
      WILL HIDE US FROM THE BITTER STORM. . . . .   152 HEART OF WOMAN   8
      SHALL HIDE US FROM THE BITTER STORM. . . . . 152 HEART OF WOMAN V   8
      AND HIDE THEIR TOSSING MANES AND THEIR TUMULTUOUS FEET. 154 BELOVED PEACE V   12
      COVER OVER AND HIDE, FOR HE HAS NO PART . . . . . .   158 TO HIS HEART   6
      TO HIDE FROM THE TROUBLED DAY. . . . .   166 BLESSED   V   4
      WHEN SONGS I WOVE FOR MY BELOVED HIDE THE PRAYER, . . . 173 SPEAKS HEARERS   2
      IS EDEN FAR AWAY, OR DO YOU HIDE . . . .   218 WOODS OF COOLE   30
      WHY DO YOU TURN AWAY AND HIDE YOUR FACE, ...   244 SHADOW WATER B   461
      THEN I.REPLIED, "ALTHOUGH YOU HIDE A SECRET, ... 281 TWO KINGS   95
      AND HIDE IT THERE, FOR CALIPHS TO WORLD'S END . . .   461 HARUN RASHID   17
      IF YOU SHOULD HIDE MY PARCHMENT IN THAT BOOK . . . . 461 HARUN RASHID V   13
      MUST NEEDS NEGLECT, I CANNOT HIDE THE TRUTH . . . .   462 HARUN RASHID   26
      MUST NEEDS NEGLECT, BUT CANNOT HIDE THE TRUTH, . . . 462 HARUN RASHID V   26
      NOR CAN HE HIDE IN HOLY BLACK . . . .   508 JANE BISHOP   18
      THAT CANNOT IN THAT TRASH AND TINSEL HIDE! . . . .   558 RIBH CHRISTIAN   17
      A GENTLE QUESTIONING LOOK THAT CANNOT HIDE . . . .   601 GALLERY REVIS   6
      DISTRACTED GENTLENESS THAT CANNOT HIDE . . . . . .   601 GALLERY REVIS V   6
      OF GREEN ARCADIA DO NOT HIDE, I TROW. . . . . . .   651 ISLE STAT I 1   166
      THE PANTHER WITH HER YELLOW HIDE, ...   658 ISLE STAT I 3   83
      DOWN THE VAPOURS FALL AND HIDE THEM FROM THE CHILDREN OF 719 PHANTOM SHIP   27
         A DAY,
      HIDE WHERE HE WILL, IN WAVE OR WRINKLED MOON, . . .   720 WITCH VIVIEN   8
      AND BID THEM HIDE IN SHADOW OF THE SAIL, ...   751 SHADOW WATER A   93
      I HIDE YOU WITH MY HAIR, THAT WE MAY GAZE . . . . . 769 SHADOW WATER A V   429
HIDES
      THAT HIDES US FROM ALL HUMAN SPYING, ...   22 OISIN 1   V 338A
      THAT HIDES AWAY THE DYING SUN . . . .   85 MAD KING GOLL   63
      WHEN SONG I WOVE FOR MY BELOVED HIDES THE PRAYER, . . 173 SPEAKS HEARERS V   2
      DIM INCHY WOOD, THAT HIDES BADGER AND FOX . . . .   218 WOODS OF COOLE   13
      DEARER THAN ANY THAT THE DUMB STONE HIDES, ...   281 TWO KINGS   V   96
      AND THE NEW STILL HIDES HER HORN. . . . .   382 VISION ROBART   4
      IN THE DEEP ALCOVES DIMNESS SMILES AND HIDES. . . .   685 DRAWING-ROOM   4
      NOW STEPS DRAW CLOSE, HE HIDES BENEATH A DRUM. . . . 713 FERENCZ RENYI   78
      IN THE DEEP ALCOVE'S DIMNESS SMILES AND HIDES." . .   735 QUATRAIN APHOR   24
      IN THE DEEP ALCOVES DIMNESS SMILES AND HIDES. . . .   735 QUATRAIN APHOR V   24
      HE CANNOT WAKE THE GOD THAT HIDES IN IT. . . . . .   748 SHADOW WATER A   19
HIDING
      THE WEAK WORM HIDING DOWN IN ITS SMALL CAVE, . . .   101 ROSE UPON ROOD   16
      O HIDING HAIR AND DEWY EYES, ...   152 HEART OF WOMAN   9
      AND HIDING THEIR TOSSING MANES AND THEIR TUMULTUOUS FEET. 154 BELOVED PEACE   12
      HIDING AMID THE CARGO OF A STEAMSHIP. . . . . . .   578 CRAZED GIRL   5
      HIDING AWAY THE OCEAN'S YELPING FLOCKS. . . . . . .   688 TWO TITANS   38
      HIDING MY FACE, I CRIED LONG, BITTERLY. . . . . .   690 MOSADA 1   17
      HIDING THE REBELS WORM IN YONDER WOOD . . . . . .   709 FERENCZ RENYI   14
      HIDING THE REBELS SWARM IN YONDER WOOD . . . . . .   709 FERENCZ RENYI V   14
      HIDING THE REBEL WORMS IN YONDER WOOD . . . . . .   709 FERENCZ RENYI V   14
HIERARCHY
      THE FATHER AND HIS ANGELIC HIERARCHY . . . .   483 VERONIC NAPKIN   4
HIGH   SEE SHOULDER-HIGH
      AND MANY PRINCES OF HIGH NAME. . . . .   7 OISIN 1   V   68
      WE FLUNG ON HIGH EACH WAVING HAND, ...   22 OISIN 1   325
      FLUNG ON HIGH EACH WAVING HAND, ...   22 OISIN 1   V   325
      FROM HIGH ABOVE, LIKE FEATHERS OF YOUNG BIRDS . . .   32 OISIN 2   V   50
      NOR THE HIGH GODS WHO NEVER LIVED, MAY FIGHT . . .   34 OISIN 2   80
      AND THEN WE CLIMBED THE STAIR TO A HIGH DOOR! . . .   36 OISIN 2   101
      AND UP THE STAIR WE TOILED TO A HIGH DOOR, ...   36 OISIN 2   V   101
      DRIFTING ON HIGH, AND WITH A STRAINING THROAT . . .   36 OISIN 2   106
      I WAITED HOUR BY HOUR, AND THE HIGH DOME . . . . .   39 OISIN 2   147
      WHILE HIGH FRAIL CLOUDLETS, FED WITH A GREEN LIGHT, .   40 OISIN 2   165
      GAVE TO HIGH NOON AND NOON TO NIGHT GAVE WAY! . . .   40 OISIN 2   172
      HIGH AS THE SADDLE-GIRTH, COVERING AWAY FROM OUR GLANCES   47 OISIN 3   2
         THE TIDE!
      HIGH AS THE SADDLE GIRTH, COVERING AWAY FROM OUR GLANCES   47 OISIN 3   V   2
         THE TIDE!
      OF THE HIGH PEOPLE OF SORACA NOR IN GLAMOUR BY DEMONS   50 OISIN 3   V   50
         FLUNG,
      I RODE AWAY ON THE SURGES, WHERE, HIGH AS THE SADDLE-BOW,   57 OISIN 3   147
      I RODE AWAY ON THE SURGES, WHERE HIGH AS THE SADDLE BOW   57 OISIN 3   V   147
      I RODE AWAY ON THE SURGES, WHERE, HIGH AS THE SADDLEBOW,   57 OISIN 3   V   147
      AND HE, OF HIS HIGH COMRADE SORROW DREAMING, ...   67 SAD SHEPHERD   2
      AND HE, OF HIS HIGH KINSMAN SORROW DREAMING, . . .   67 SAD SHEPHERD V   2
      AND STARLIGHT GLEAMED, AND CLOUDS FLEW HIGH, . . .   84 MAD KING GOLL   34
      OF HOW I HEAR ON HILL-HEADS HIGH . . . .   85 MAD KING GOLL   53
      OF HOW I HEAR ON HILL HEADS HIGH . . . .   85 MAD KING GOLL V   53
      SING IN THEIR HIGH AND LONELY MELODY. . . . . . .   101 ROSE UPON ROOD   8
      TROY PASSED AWAY IN ONE HIGH FUNERAL GLEAM, ...   111 ROSE OF WORLD   4
      GOD SMILES IN HIGH HEAVEN . . . .   118 CRADLE SONG   V   5
      BUT HE HEARD HIGH UP IN THE AIR . . . .   145 HOST OF AIR   41
      BROOD HER HIGH LONELY MYSTERIES. . . . .   156 FORGOT BEAUTY   24
      AND YOUR HIGH BEAUTY FALL AND BE LOST . . . . . .   173 PLEADS FRIEND V   7
      IN HER HIGH HOUSE AT CRUACHAN, THE LONG HEARTH, . .   180 QUEEN MAEVE   11
      AND SHE'D HAD LUCKY EYES AND A HIGH HEART, ...   181 QUEEN MAEVE   27
      HE SAID, "HIGH QUEEN OF CRUACHAN AND MAGH AI, . . .   183 QUEEN MAEVE   77
      QUEEN OF HIGH CRUACHAN." "I OBEY YOUR WILL . . . .   184 QUEEN MAEVE   99
      WITH HOLY SHADOWS." HER HIGH HEART WAS GLAD, . . .   186 QUEEN MAEVE   126
      FOR THERE IS NO HIGH STORY ABOUT QUEENS . . . . .   186 QUEEN MAEVE   134
      A THOUSAND YEARS AGO YOU HELD HIGH TALK . . . . .   187 QUEEN MAEVE   150
      NOR THE GREY RUSH WHEN THE WIND IS HIGH, ...   189 BAILE AILLINN   2
      NOR THE GREY RUSH WHEN WIND IS HIGH . . . .   189 BAILE AILLINN V   2
      AND HARPERS, PACING WITH HIGH HEAD . . . .   193 BAILE AILLINN   107

		PAGE	TITLE	LINE

HIGH (CONTINUED)
TO THAT HIGH HILL THE HERDSMEN NAME		194	BAILE AILLINN	129
AND YOU ARE MORE HIGH OF HEART THAN SHE,		197	BAILE AILLINN	202
SO MUCH COMPOUNDED OF HIGH COURTESY		205	ADAMS CURSE	24
TO LOVE YOU IN THE OLD HIGH WAY OF LOVE;		206	ADAMS CURSE	36
THE OLD BROWN THORN-TREES BREAK IN TWO HIGH OVER CUMMEN STRAND		206	HANRAHANS SONG	1
THE OLD BROWN THORN TREES BREAK IN TWO HIGH OVER CUMANN'S STRAND,		206	HANRAHANS SONG V	1
THE WIND HAS BUNDLED UP THE CLOUDS HIGH OVER KNOCKNAREA,		207	HANRAHANS SONG	6
THE YELLOW POOL HAS OVERFLOWED HIGH UP ON CLOOTH-NA-BARE,		207	HANRAHANS SONG	11
O TATTERED CLOUDS OF THE WORLD, CALL FROM THE HIGH CAIRN OF MAIVE,		207	HANRAHANS SONG V	6
THE WINDS HAVE BUNDLED UP THE CLOUDS HIGH OVER KNOCKNAREA		207	HANRAHANS SONG V	6
THE YELLOW POOL HAS OVERFLOWED HIGH UPON CLOOTH-NA-BARE,		207	HANRAHANS SONG V	11
WHEN THEIR HEARTS ARE SO HIGH		214	HAPPY TOWNLAND	21
IN THE HIGH HOLLOW TOWNLAND		214	HAPPY TOWNLAND	3
POURED OUT WINE FOR THE HIGH INVISIBLE ONES.		219	WOODS OF COOLE	44
AND THE HIGH FAME THAT COME TO THEM IN MARRIAGE,		232	SHADOW WATER B	235
IN THE WASTE OF THE HIGH AIR, THAT WE MAY WANDER		234	SHADOW WATER B	263
BEING TOO BUSY IN THE AIR AND THE HIGH AIR,		234	SHADOW WATER B	274
I'D DO YOUR WILL, BUT THEY ARE TOO HIGH--TOO HIGH.		250	SHADOW WATER B	577
I'D DO YOUR WILL, BUT THEY ARE TOO HIGH--TOO HIGH.		250	SHADOW WATER B	577
BEING TOO HIGH, THEIR HEADY PROPHECIES		250	SHADOW WATER B	578
THERE ON THE HIGH AND PAINTED STERN		253	HIS DREAM V	1
BEING HIGH AND SOLITARY AND MOST STERN?		257	NO SECOND TROY	10
"SUCH A DELICATE HIGH HEAD,		259	PEACE	7
HOW SHOULD THEIR LUCK RUN HIGH ENOUGH TO REACH		264	HOUSE SHAKEN	9
WROUGHT OF HIGH LAUGHTER, LOVELINESS AND EASE?		264	HOUSE SHAKEN	12
WHEN WE ARE HIGH AND AIRY HUNDREDS SAY		265	ABBEY THEATRE	2
TILL THAT BE TUMBLED THAT WAS LIFTED HIGH		265	THESE CLOUDS	4
AND CHILDREN WHEN THEY SPRING UP SHOULDER HIGH.		343	SHEP GOATHERD V	119
IF HEAD AND LIMB HAVE BEAUTY AND THE INSTEP'S HIGH AND LIGHT		354	HIS PHOENIX	21
AND MOUNTS MORE DIZZY HIGH THE MORE IT RAINS		417	ANCEST HOUSES	5
BUT ALL IS CHANGED, THAT HIGH HORSE RIDERLESS,		492	COOLE BALLYLEE	46
SPEAKING TO A DRUNKEN AUDIENCE HIGH NONSENSICAL WORDS;		577	LOFTY THINGS	6
THE PROUD FURIES EACH WITH HER TORCH ON HIGH.		579	DOR WELLESLEY	16
HER HEART MOUNT UP ON HIGH;		608	SONGS BURDEN 3	22
HIGH TALK		622	HIGH TALK	T
PROCESSIONS THAT LACK HIGH STILTS HAVE NOTHING THAT CATCHES THE EYE,		622	HIGH TALK	1
WHAT IF MY GREAT-GRANDDAD HAD A PAIR THAT WERE TWENTY FOOT HIGH,		622	HIGH TALK	2
BLENCHING ON HIGH THE DULL STARS SICKEN		646	ISLE STAT I 1	46
WITH ROLLING FIRE, BEYOND THE HIGH TREES TURBANED		656	ISLE STAT I 3	32
TO BUILD THE CIRCLING SEATS, WHERE HIGH IN AIR		699	MOSADA 3	18
OF CEASELESS LONELINESS AND HIGH REGRET		705	REMEMBRANCE	9
HIVES, CURRANT BUSHES. THERE HIS KIN ARE. HIGH		710	FERENCZ RENYI	25
THERE LIVE HIS SISTER AND HIS MOTHER. HIGH		710	FERENCZ RENYI	25
HIVES, CURRANT-BUSHES. THERE HIS KIN ARE. HIGH		710	FERENCZ RENYI V	25
I AM TO BE YOUR WIFE. A VILLAGE HIGH		713	FERENCZ RENYI	97
I WAS TO BE YOUR WIFE. A VILLAGE HIGH		713	FERENCZ RENYI V	97
SAY WHAT RINGER RINGS AT MIDNIGHT; FOR, IN THE BELFRY HIGH,		718	PHANTOM SHIP	15
BY THE GORSE ON THE HIGH LAND,		726	LOVERS QUARREL	4
THREE SPANS HIGH AS HE ROSE TO HIS FEET,		729	PRIEST FAIRY	25
WHO IS SIX FEET HIGH IN HIS SOCKS AT LEAST?		729	PRIEST FAIRY	28
YE ON THE BROAD HIGH MOUNTAINS OF OLD ERI,		737	MOURN THEN ON	1
HITHER AND THITHER AND SAY AT THE HIGH NOON		767	SHADOW WATER A	404
AMONG HIGH MOUNTAINS, AND THE MOUNTAIN ROBBERS		768	SHADOW WATER A	411
A HIGH, GREY CAIRN. WHAT MORE IS TO BE SAID?		778	SONG DEIRDRE 3	5

HIGH-BORN
A PEARL-PALE, HIGH-BORN LADY, WHO RODE		3	OISIN 1	20
SELF-BORN, HIGH-BORN, AND SOLITARY TRUTHS,		467	HARUN RASHID	141
BEGOT; SELF-BORN, HIGH-BORN, AND SOLITARY.		467	HARUN RASHID V	141

HIGHER
TO THE OTHER SIDE, AND HIGHER IN THE AIR.		234	SHADOW WATER B	259
AND MINE WERE BUT FIFTEEN FOOT, NO MODERN STALKS UPON HIGHER,		623	HIGH TALK	3
HIGHER AND HIGHER GOLD WITH EVENING LIGHT;		714	FERENCZ RENYI	113
HIGHER AND HIGHER GOLD WITH EVENING LIGHT;		714	FERENCZ RENYI V	113
TO THE OTHER SIDE AND HIGHER IN THE AIR.		753	SHADOW WATER A	149

HIGHEST
| WHY THEY WHO WILL THE HIGHEST SOMETIMES BROOD, | | 711 | FERENCZ RENYI | 34 |

HIGH-HORSE
| BUT FASHION'S CHANGED, THAT HIGH-HORSE RIDERLESS | | 492 | COOLE BALLYLEE V | 46 |

HIGHLAND
| WHERE DIPS THE ROCKY HIGHLAND | | 86 | STOLEN CHILD | 1 |

HIGH-PITCHED
| AND THEREUPON WITH AGED, HIGH-PITCHED VOICE | | 375 | PHASES OF MOON | 84 |

HIGHWAY
| TO LOVE YOU IN THE OLD HIGHWAY OF LOVE; | | 206 | ADAMS CURSE   V | 36 |

HILL
CAME TO THE CAIRN-HEAPED GRASSY HILL		3	OISIN 1	17
UPON THE WOODY CENTRAL HILL;		22	OISIN 1	323
TILL ON THE CENTRAL HILL WE HUSHED		22	OISIN 1	323
ROLLING ALONG IN DREAMS FROM HILL TO HILL.		68	SAD SHEPHERD	11
ROLLING ALONG IN DREAMS FROM HILL TO HILL.		68	SAD SHEPHERD	11
O'ER HILL AND HEATH AND SPONGY FEN,		83	MAD KING GOLL V	32
OF HOW I HEAR ON HILL HEADS HIGH		85	MAD KING GOLL	53
AND I MUST WANDER WOOD AND HILL		86	MAD KING GOLL	70

HILL   (CONTINUED)
      OF THE CALVES ON THE WARM HILL SIDE, ...   88 STOLEN CHILD   V   45
      I FEAST AMID MY PEOPLE ON THE HILL, ... 103 FERGUS DRUID   17
      UPON A SWORD, A FIR-TREE ON A HILL, ... 104 FERGUS DRUID   34
      UPON A SWORD, A FIR TREE ON A HILL, ... 104 FERGUS DRUID   V   34
      BEFORE THEY HEAPED HIS GRAVE UNDER THE HILL . . . . . . 127 DREAM OF FAERY   16
      HE SLEPT UNDER THE HILL OF LUGNAGALL; . . . . 128 DREAM OF FAERY   37
      THAT YOU CALL IN BIRDS, IN WIND ON THE HILL, ... 141 EVERLAST VOICE   6
      COME, HEART, WHERE HILL IS HEAPED UPON HILL! . . . . . 148 INTO TWILIGHT   9
      COME, HEART, WHERE HILL IS HEAPED UPON HILL! . . . . . 148 INTO TWILIGHT   9
      THE GREY CAIRN ON THE HILL, WHEN DAY SINKS DROWNED IN DEW, 161 BLACK PIG   6
      AND SET THEM DIGGING UNDER BUAL'S HILL. . . . . 184 QUEEN MAEVE   93
      AND SET THEM DIGGING INTO ANBUAL'S HILL. . . . . 184 QUEEN MAEVE   V   93
      AND SET THEM DIGGING IN THE WEST OF THE HILL. . . . . . 184 QUEEN MAEVE   V   93
      TO MIDDLE NIGHT, THEY DUG INTO THE HILL. . . . . 185 QUEEN MAEVE   114
      TO THAT HIGH HILL THE HERDSMEN NAME . . . . 194 BAILE AILLINN   129
      THE HILL SEAT OF LAIGHEN, BECAUSE . . . . 194 BAILE AILLINN   130
      THE HONEY-PALE MOON LAY LOW ON THE SLEEPY HILL, ... 203 WITHER BOUGHS   5
      THE HONEY PALE MOON HUNG LOW ON THE SLEEPY HILL, . . . 203 WITHER BOUGHS   V   5
      EDAIN CAME OUT OF MIDHIR'S HILL, AND LAY . . . . 219 HARP OF AENGUS   1
      SOMEWHERE WITHIN SOME HOLLOW HILL, ... 271 GREY ROCK   V   14
      UPON URBINO'S WINDY HILL, ... 288 TO WEALTHY MAN   17
      SOON TOPPLES DOWN THE HILL. . . . . 335 YOUNG BEAUTY   6
      TO A GREY PLACE ON A HILL . . . . 347 FISHERMAN   3
      BUT GREGORY'S WOOD AND ONE BARE HILL . . . . 403 FOR DAUGHTER   4
      BUT GREGORY'S WOODS AND ONE BARE HILL . . . . 403 FOR DAUGHTER   V   4
      OF HILL TWO SHEPHERDS COME.   FAREWELL! I'LL DON . . . 659 ISLE STAT II 1   28
      THE VIOLETS ARE THAT ON THE WOODED HILL . . . . 713 FERENCZ RENYI   95
      EDAINE CAME OUT OF MIDHIR'S HILL, AND LAY . . . . 762 SHADOW WATER A   296
      BEYOND A HILL AND A HILL. . . . . 774 COME RIDE   4
      BEYOND A HILL AND A HILL. . . . . 774 COME RIDE   4
      BEYOND A HILL AND A HILL THERE . . . . 774 COME RIDE   16
      BEYOND A HILL AND A HILL THERE . . . . 774 COME RIDE   16
      AT THE GREY ROUND OF THE HILL . . . . 782 GREY ROUND   1
HILL-HEADS
      OF HOW I HEAR ON HILL-HEADS HIGH . . . .   85 MAD KING GOLL   V   53
HILL'S
      IN THE GREEN HILL'S INMOST PART. . . . . 726 LOVERS QUARREL   12
HILLS
      AND THE CRY OF THE HOUNDS ON THE HILLS OF OLD. . . . .   27 OISIN 1   407
      FROM THE HILLS ABOVE GLEN-CAR, ...   88 STOLEN CHILD   29
      MAKE THE HILLS REPLY." . . . .   98 FOXHUNTER   26
      AND MAKE THE HILLS REPLY." . . . .   98 FOXHUNTER   V   26
      MAKE THE HILLS REPLY." . . . .   99 FOXHUNTER   34
      AND MAKE THE HILLS REPLY." . . . .   99 FOXHUNTER   V   34
      IN BARREN HILLS AND MARSHY LAND, ... 150 WANDER AENGUS   V   18
      THAT HE HAS BEEN ALL NIGHT UPON THE HILLS, ... 229 SHADOW WATER B   168
      HE HAD OFTEN PLAYED HIS PIPES AMONG MY HILLS, ... 339 SHEP GOATHERD   23
      THE HOLY CENTAURS OF THE HILLS ARE VANISHED; . . . . . 344 DEJECTION   7
      THE HOLY CENTAURS OF THE HILLS ARE BANISHED; . . . . . 344 DEJECTION   V   7
      ARE MET ON THE WASTE HILLS BY COUNTRYMEN . . . . 375 PHASES OF MOON   76
      ARE MET ON THE WASTE HILLS BY COUNTRY MEN . . . . 375 PHASES OF MOON   V   76
      AMID THE RUSTLE OF HIS PLANTED HILLS. . . . . 417 ANCEST HOUSES   2
      I WILL FIND OUT SOME CAVERN IN THE HILLS . . . . 448 HERO GIRL FOOL   V   11
      I AM MAD ABOUT THE HILLS," . . . . 587 OLD WICKED MAN   2
      BECAUSE WE LOVE BARE HILLS AND STUNTED TREES . . . . . 621 HOUND VOICE   1
      AFAR, CLEAR-SHINING ON THE HERALD HILLS, ... 645 ISLE STAT I 1   14
      BETWEEN THE HORNED HILLS--SHEPHERDS, FAREWELL! . . . . 682 SEEKER   27
      SINCE 'MONG MY PEOPLE, TENTED ON THE HILLS, ... 690 MOSADA 1   4
      BUT NO, IN THIS WARM WEATHER, 'MONG THE HILLS, ... 699 MOSADA 3   9
      DAY'S DEAD, ALL FLAME-BEWILDERED, AND THE HILLS . . . . 702 MOSADA 3   86
      'TIS LATE, WAIT ONE MORE DAY; BELOW THE HILLS . . . . 702 MOSADA 3   91
      FROM THE HILLS OF EARTH HAVE PEALED . . . . 705 DAWN-SONG   5
      AND LOST AND FAR IN YONDER HILLS I KNOW; . . . . 713 FERENCZ RENYI   98
      WHERE IN THE WOODS OR HILLS THE REBELS BE?" . . . . . . 713 FERENCZ RENYI   V 83A
      OF PASTURE-LAND AND PLOUGH-LAND AMONG THE HILLS? . . . 748 SHADOW WATER A   33
      A FRUITFUL LAND UNDER THE AIBHLIN HILLS? . . . . 748 SHADOW WATER A V   33
      THEY OVERFLOW THE HILLS, ... 781 MY HEART BEAT   12
HILLSIDE
      OF THE CALVES ON THE WARM HILLSIDE . . . .   88 STOLEN CHILD   45
HILL-SIDE
      OF THE CALVES ON THE WARM HILL-SIDE. . . . .   88 STOLEN CHILD   V   45
HILLY
      OF HOLLOW WOOD AND THE HILLY WOOD . . . . 148 INTO TWILIGHT   V   11
      THROUGH HOLLOW LANDS AND HILLY LANDS, ... 150 WANDER AENGUS   18
      THROUGH HILLY LANDS AND HOLLOW LANDS, ... 150 WANDER AENGUS   V   18
      WHEN THE WIND COMES BLOWING ACROSS THE HILLY LAND! . . 207 HANRAHANS SONG V   7
      FROM HILLY LOCHLANN; BUT OUR SAIL HAS PASSED . . . . . 749 SHADOW WATER A   44
HIMALAY
      DREAD OATH, WHO DWELL ON SACRED HIMALAY, ...   74 ANASHU VIJAYA   67
HIRE
      AND HAD BUT BROKEN KNEES FOR HIRE . . . . 411 TOWER   62
      SAEVA INDIGNATIO AND THE LABOURER'S HIRE, ... 481 BLOOD AND MOON   28
      FOR ALL MY HEART HAS HAD FOR ITS HIRE . . . . 551 SONGS REWRIT 1   3
      FOR ALL MY TOIL HAS HAD FOR ITS HIRE . . . . 551 SONGS REWRIT 1 V   3
      FOR ALL THAT MY HEART HAS HAD FOR ITS HIRE . . . . . . 551 SONGS REWRIT 1 V   3
HISS
      A CONTRAPUNTAL SERPENT HISS, ... 573 LADYS 3RD SONG   10
HISSING
      HE TOLD OF EVERY FROTH-DROP HISSING, FLYING. . . . . .   32 OISIN 2   V   45

383

	PAGE	TITLE	LINE

HISSOP-HEAVY
THE HISSOP-HEAVY SPONGE, THE FLOWERS BY KIDRON STREAM: . . . 172 TRAV PASSION V 5
HISTORIANS
ALL THOSE LEARNED HISTORIANS, ... 584 ORAHILLY 5
HISTORIC
HISTORIC NATIONS GROW . . . . 547 TO SAME TUNE 3 V 5
HISTORIED
AND HANG O'ER THE HISTORIED STONE: . . . . 707 FAIRY PEDANT 6
HISTORIES
TO STUDY READING BOOKS AND HISTORIES, ... 443 SCHOOL CHILDR V 4
FOR HISTORIES ARE THERE TO PROVE . . . . 583 GHOST ROG CASE 23
SAD HISTORIES ARE LETTERED ON THY CHEEK. . . . . . . 660 ISLE STAT II 1 52
AND LET THEM TELL SAD HISTORIES, TILL THEIR EYES . . . 663 ISLE STAT II 2 32
HISTORY
OF HER, WHOSE HISTORY BEGAN . . . . 137 TO IRELAND 7
BECAUSE AN ANCIENT HISTORY SAID . . . . 303 HOUR DAWN 24
TO STUDY READING-BOOKS AND HISTORY, ... 443 SCHOOL CHILDR 4
TO STUDY READING BOOKS AND HISTORY . . . . 443 SCHOOL CHILDR V 4
HAD HEARD IMPOSSIBLE HISTORY OF MY PAST: . . . . . . 466 HARUN RASHID 108
IMAGINED SOME IMPOSSIBLE HISTORY . . . . 466 HARUN RASHID 109
FAIL, AND THAT HISTORY TURNS INTO RUBBISH, ... 546 TO SAME TUNE 2 21
IRELAND'S HISTORY IN THEIR LINEAMENTS TRACE: . . . . 604 GALLERY REVIS 53
FAIL, AND THAT HISTORY TURNS INTO RUBBISH. . . . . . 614 MARCH SONGS 1 21
THE HISTORY HERE IN THE STONE NOW: . . . . 707 FAIRY PEDANT 15
THE HISTORY HERE IN THE STONE-- . . . . 707 FAIRY PEDANT V 15
HISTORY'S
WHEN ALL THIS HEAVY HISTORY'S DONE: . . . . 213 BLESS PSALTER 17
HIT
WHATEVER WOMAN'S LOVER HAD HIT HER FANCY. . . . . . 181 QUEEN MAEVE 24
THE ONLY RICHES THAT HAVE HIT MY FANCY. . . . . . . 226 SHADOW WATER B 96
UNLESS A PETAL HIT THE GROUND, ... 389 SOLOMON WITCH 40
TIME FOR US ALL BOYS, TO HIT ON A TUNE BOYS, ... 548 TO SAME TUNE 3 V 13
HITCHED
HITCHED IT ON HIS BACK. . . . . 595 COLONEL MARTIN 26
HITHER
YOU WOULD COME HITHER, AND BEND YOUR HEAD, ... 175 BELOVED DEAD 3
AND BLEW ME HITHER TO MY LASTING SORROW, ... 235 SHADOW WATER B 288
AND BLEW YOU HITHER: AND THEIR MOUTHS HAVE PROMISED . 237 SHADOW WATER B 325
FOR EVERYTHING IS GONE. COME HITHER, AIBRIC, ... 241 SHADOW WATER B 402
HITHER AND THITHER TO AND FRO THEY TROD . . . . . . 278 TWO KINGS 26
HITHER, TO OUR DISGRACE, ... 319 DOLLS 11
FAIR SHEPHERD, AS WE WANDERED HITHER, ... 669 ISLE STAT II 3 83
BUT NOW I WAVE HER HITHER TO MY SIDE. . . . . 694 MOSADA 1 91
I WAVE THEM HITHER, MY BREAST HEAVES WITH JOY. . . . 694 MOSADA 1 98
GIVE ME THE HELM: CALL HITHER THOSE WHO LIE . . . . 751 SHADOW WATER A 91
I SPARED HER HANDMAID, TOO: BUT HALF WAY HITHER . . . 755 SHADOW WATER A V 167
AND EVIL FORTUNE HAVE OVERTHROWN SAILED HITHER . . . 757 SHADOW WATER A 196
ON TEARS AND LAUGHTER: THEY HAVE LURED YOU HITHER . . 757 SHADOW WATER A 207
AND LURED ME HITHER, THAT YOU MIGHT BE MY LOVE. . . . 757 SHADOW WATER A 208
I HAVE COME HITHER BECAUSE I HOPED TO COME . . . . . 757 SHADOW WATER A V 197
AND I SHALL LAUGH WITH JOY. COME HITHER, AIBRIC, . . 760 SHADOW WATER A 249
HITHER AND THITHER AND SAY AT THE HIGH NOON . . . . . 767 SHADOW WATER A 404
HIVE
AND CHASE THE WILD BEE HOMEWARD TO HIS HIVE . . . . . 32 OISIN 2 V 50D
NINE BEAN-ROWS WILL I HAVE THERE, A HIVE FOR THE HONEY-BEE, 117 ISLE INNISFREE 3
NINE BEAN ROWS WILL I HAVE THERE, A HIVE FOR THE HONEY BEE, 117 ISLE INNISFREE V 3
WHERE WILD BEES HIVE ON THE GREAT PLAIN. . . . . . . 194 BAILE AILLINN 123
HIVES
HIVES, CURRANT BUSHES. THERE HIS KIN ARE. HIGH . . . 710 FERENCZ RENYI 25
HIVES, CURRANT-BUSHES. THERE HIS KIN ARE. HIGH . . . 710 FERENCZ RENYI V 25
HO
HO: HO: HO: THE MERRY BLADE:-- . . . . 727 LOVERS QUARREL 26
HO: HO: HO: THE MERRY BLADE:-- . . . . 727 LOVERS QUARREL 26
HO: HO: HO: THE MERRY BLADE:-- . . . . 727 LOVERS QUARREL 26
HOARD
"THE DOOMS OF MEN ARE IN GOD'S HIDDEN HOARD." . . . . 110 CUCHULAIN SEA V 62
AMONG THE GIANT KINGS WHOSE HOARD, ... 196 BAILE AILLINN 164
HOARDED
STITCHING AT A PURPLE HOARDED . . . . 440 WISDOM 12
HEARKEN, YE SWALLOWS:--I HAVE HOARDED UP . . . . . . 699 MOSADA 3 23
HOARDS
OLD MISER HOARDS OF GRIEF TO TELL AND TELL: . . . . 661 ISLE STAT II 1 55
HOARIEST
BENT LOW WITH TOIL AND HOARIEST YEARS. THE OTHER . . 711 FERENCZ RENYI 52
HOARSER
CAME KEENERS HOARSER THAN ROOKS, ... 92 FATHER OHART 22
HOARY
WHY THOU OUTLIVEST, BLIND AND HOARY, ... 2 OISIN 1 V 2
WHERE ARE NOW THE OLD KINGS HOARY? . . . . 65 HAPPY SHEPHERD V 13
A HOARY HUNTER LEANING ON HIS BOW, ... 672 ISLE STAT II 3 157
HOB
OR THE KETTLE ON THE HOB . . . . 88 STOLEN CHILD 46
HOISTING
THE FLOOR OF EMEN'S HOISTING HALL . . . . 13 OISIN 1 V 156
HOLD
BID THEM AWAY AND HOLD THEIR PEACE: . . . . 15 OISIN 1 212
AND HANDS THAT HOLD NO WEARISOME TOOL, ... 22 OISIN 1 340
OR HOURS PASSED BY, YET HOLD THE MORNING RAYS . . . 30 OISIN 2 20
WHOM BRAHMA, TOUCHING WITH HIS FINGER, PRAISES, FOR YOU 73 ANASHU VIJAYA 42
HOLD
WHOM BRAHMA, TOUCHING WITH HIS FINGER, PRAISES, FOR YE HOLD 73 ANASHU VIJAYA V 42

384

HOLD (CONTINUED)   PAGE TITLE   LINE

AND YOUNG HARES BROOK MY HARMLESS HOLD--   84 MAD KING GOLL   V   47
IN THE DIM GLASS THE DEMONS HOLD,   135 TWO TREES   30
OR, REMEMBERING HERS, THEY WILL HOLD NO OTHER FACE FAIR   163 VALLEY LOVERS   V   7
WE HOLD, BECAUSE OUR MEMORY IS   192 BAILE AILLINN   85
THE EVER-LIVING HOLD US. DO WHAT YOU WILL,   238 SHADOW WATER B   359
THE HOLD IS FULL OF TREASURE. FULL TO THE HATCHES.   247 SHADOW WATER B   532
THAT IF WE HOLD THAT FLIGHT THEY'LL LEAVE THE PLACE,   265 ABBEY THEATRE   3
TO HOLD THE SACRED STUFF HE BREWS   272 GREY ROCK   24
TO HOLD THE WINE THEY BUY OF HIM.   272 GREY ROCK   V   25
THEN DREW HIS SWORD TO HOLD ITS LEVELLED POINT   277 TWO KINGS   14
THAT GIRL MY UNREMEMBERING NIGHTS HOLD FAST   384 VISION ROBART   50
THINGS FALL APART; THE CENTRE CANNOT HOLD;   402 SECOND COMING   3
THINGS FALL APART; THE CENTRE CAN NOT HOLD,   402 SECOND COMING   V   3
THEY HOLD THEIR PUBLIC MEETINGS WHERE   460 THREE MONUMENT   1
SUCH THOUGHT--SUCH THOUGHT HAVE I THAT HOLD IT TIGHT   474 ALL SOUL NIGHT   91
TO HOLD HIMSELF UPRIGHT.   515 GIRLS SONG B   7
A MOUTHFUL HOLD THE EXTREME OF LIFE AND DEATH.   619 BRONZE HEAD   V   14
THE AGELESS SENTINELS WHO HOLD THEIR WATCH   664 ISLE STAT II 2   45
AND EVEN SHE SHALL NEVER HOLD   668 ISLE STAT II 3   50
HOLD FESTIVAL ACROSS THE LAND,   671 ISLE STAT II 3   128
STAY, STAY, OR I WILL HOLD YOUR WHITE ARMS DOWN.   694 MOSADA 1   92
I'M WEAK, AND BY THE HANDS SHALL HOLD EACH ONE   712 FERENCZ RENYI   57
I'M WEAK, AND BY THE HAND SHALL HOLD EACH ONE   712 FERENCZ RENYI   V   57
I HOLD HIM DEARER THAN THE GLAD,   723 GIRLS SONG A   3
I HOLD HIM DEARER THAN THE GOOD,   723 GIRLS SONG A   7
I HOLD HIM DEARER THAN THE WISE,   723 GIRLS SONG A   11
NOW THY GREAT WHITE DOLL TO HOLD--   726 LOVERS QUARREL   15
BUT YOU GREW WEARY OF HER. WHEN I HOLD   749 SHADOW WATER A   53
A BOY AND GIRL HOLD ONE ANOTHER'S HANDS;   752 SHADOW WATER A   122
BUT WILL IT HOLD WHILE WE ARE EMPTYING HER?   754 SHADOW WATER A   156
THE GODS HOLD WATCH ABOUT THE WORDS OF A QUEEN.   756 SHADOW WATER A   191
ALTHOUGH WIDE WORLD HOLD NOT   786 YOUR HEART   16
HOLDING
AND CAME AGAIN, HOLDING A SECOND LIGHT   37 OISIN 2   124
HOLDING THAT HORSE, AND SADLY CALLED MY NAME;   44 OISIN 2   230
HOLDING THAT HORSE LONG SEEN NOT, NIAM STOOD.   44 OISIN 2   V   230
THAT HE IS HOLDING UP BETWEEN US THERE,   240 SHADOW WATER B   378
AND SILENCE HOLDING REVELRY AND FEAST;   705 REMEMBRANCE   12
HOLDS
HE HOLDS YOU WITH AN IRON BOND,   22 OISIN 1   333
WHO HOLDS THE WORLD BETWEEN HIS BILL AND MADE US STRONG
OR WEAK   76 INDIAN ON GOD   6
WHO HOLDS THE WORLD BETWEEN HIS BILL AND MAKES US STRONG
OR WEAK   76 INDIAN ON GOD   V   6
HE HOLDS DEEP COMMUNE WITH HIS HEART;   99 FOXHUNTER   43
DANGER NO REFUGE HOLDS, AND WAR NO PEACE,   114 ROSE OF BATTLE   9
I THOUGHT, "HE HOLDS HER DEAR,"   254 WOMAN HOMER   3
HE HOLDS HER HELPLESS BREAST UPON HIS BREAST,   441 LEDA AND SWAN   4
HE HOLDS HIM FROM DESIRE, ALL BUT STOPS HIS BREATHING LEST   559 MAGIC DRUM   1
WHAT MATTER? THOSE THAT ROCKY FACE HOLDS DEAR,   564 GYRES   18
HOLE   SEE RABBIT-HOLE
CAME UP OUT OF THE HOLE, AND RED-EARED HOUNDS   185 QUEEN MAEVE   117
A DARK DEEP HOLE IN THE ROCK'S FACE,   303 HOUR DAWN   V   21
MERELY FOR STUMBLING ON THIS HOLE   304 HOUR DAWN   54
TO MAKE A CLATTER IN THE HOLE   304 HOUR DAWN   V   54
BECAUSE HE HAS STUMBLED ON THIS HOLE,   304 HOUR DAWN   V   54
UPON HIS HUNKERS IN THE HOLE,   306 HOUR DAWN   81
UNDER ITS ROCKY HOLE.   420 MY HOUSE   V   20C
WHO ARE BUT WEASELS FIGHTING IN A HOLE.   429 NINETEEN 19   32
SPREAD TO A LAKE AND DROP INTO A HOLE.   490 COOLE BALLYLEE   7
SPREAD TO A LAKE AND RUN INTO A HOLE.   490 COOLE BALLYLEE   V   7
IN CAVERN, CREVICE, HOLE,   546 TO SAME TUNE 2   5
IN CAVERN, CREVICE OR HOLE,   546 TO SAME TUNE 2   V   5
INTO A RABBIT HOLE   571 THREE BUSHES   V   51
IN CAVERN, CREVICE, OR HOLE,   613 MARCH SONGS 1   5
HOLES
AND HE WORE SMALL HOLES IN HIS SHOES,   92 FATHER OHART   11
AND HE WORE LARGE HOLES IN HIS GOWN.   92 FATHER OHART   12
HOLIDAY
MIGHT PROCLAIM A HOLIDAY;   432 NINETEEN 19   106
THE STATESMAN'S HOLIDAY   626 STATES HOLIDAY   T
HOLIDAYS
AND BIRTHDAYS AND HOLIDAYS SUCH PRAISES CAN BE HEARD   353 HIS PHOENIX   2
HOLIEST
FOR HOLIEST TEACHERS OF HIS WILL,   736 IN CHURCH   7
HOLIEST, HOLIEST SEVEN,   771 SPINNING SONG   11
HOLIEST, HOLIEST SEVEN,   771 SPINNING SONG   11
HOLINESS
THAT MEN HAVE REVERENCE FOR THEIR HOLINESS   448 HERO GIRL FOOL   14
THE HOLINESS OF MONKS, AND AFTER   640 BEN BULBEN   76
THE HOLINESS OF THE MONKS, AND AFTER   640 BEN BULBEN   V   76
AND HEAVEN, AND HOLINESS. LET'S TALK AND GRIEVE,   702 MOSADA 3   84
HOLLIES
OF HOLLIES, AND HAZELS, AND OAK TREES, A VALLEY WAS SLOPING
AWAY   48 OISIN 3   V   26
HOLLO
I'LL HOLLO ALL THOSE LOVERS OUT AND CRY--   211 RAGGED WOOD   V   10
HOLLO HIM ON WITH HORSE AND HOUND,   272 GREY ROCK   35
HOLLOW
IT DOWN IN A LEAF-HID, HOLLOW PLACE   17 OISIN 1   242

		PAGE	TITLE		LINE
HOLLOW	(CONTINUED)				
LAY 'NEATH US, OF ITS HOLLOW COOL		17	OISIN 1	V	241
AND THE EARS OF THE HORSE WENT SINKING AWAY IN THE HOLLOW		48	OISIN 3		21
NIGHT,					
AND DEW-BLANCHED HORNS, IN WHOSE HOLLOW A CHILD OF THREE		49	OISIN 3		30
YEARS OLD					
THEIR SADNESS THROUGH A HOLLOW, PEARLY HEART,		68	SAD SHEPHERD		21
TO FILL THEIR DARK-BEAKED HOLLOW GALLEYS,		82	MAD KING GOLL		16
THAT HE MAY FILL HIS HOLLOW GALLEYS. .		82	MAD KING GOLL	V	16
TO FILL WITH COWS HIS HOLLOW GALLEYS."		82	MAD KING GOLL	V	16
LOOK ON MY THIN GREY HAIR AND HOLLOW CHEEKS		103	FERGUS DRUID		23
OF SUN AND MOON AND HOLLOW AND WOOD		148	INTO TWILIGHT		11
OF HOLLOW WOOD AND THE HILLY WOOD		148	INTO TWILIGHT	V	11
THROUGH HOLLOW LANDS AND HILLY LANDS, . . .		150	WANDER AENGUS		18
THROUGH HILLY LANDS AND HOLLOW LANDS, . . .		150	WANDER AENGUS	V	18
FOR ALL THEIR BEAUTY'S LIKE A HOLLOW DREAM,		184	QUEEN MAEVE		88
FOR ALL THEIR BEAUTY, LIKE A HOLLOW DREAM?"		184	QUEEN MAEVE	V	89
ALTHOUGH THEIR BEAUTY'S LIKE A HOLLOW DREAM"		184	QUEEN MAEVE	V	89
AS WEARY-HEARTED AS THAT HOLLOW MOON . . .		206	ADAMS CURSE		38
AS WEARY HEARTED AS THAT HOLLOW MOON. . .		206	ADAMS CURSE	V	38
NOR AVALON THE GRASS-GREEN HOLLOW, NOR JOYOUS ISLE,		209	UNDER THE MOON		2
OR AVALLON THE GRASS GREEN HOLLOW, OR JOYOUS ISLE		209	UNDER THE MOON	V	2
THE HOLLOW WOOD		210	RAGGED WOOD	V	T
I HEARD UNDER A RAGGED HOLLOW WOOD,		210	RAGGED WOOD	V	1
O HURRY TO THE HOLLOW WOOD, FOR THERE		211	RAGGED WOOD	V	9
IN THE HIGH HOLLOW TOWNLAND		214	HAPPY TOWNLAND	V	3
SOMEWHERE WITHIN SOME HOLLOW HILL, ...		271	GREY ROCK		14
A DARK DEEP HOLLOW IN THE ROCK.		303	HOUR DAWN		21
THAT HE HAS MADE THAT HOLLOW FACE OF HIS		368	EGO DOMINUS		20
OR WAS THE HUNGER THAT HAD MADE IT HOLLOW		368	EGO DOMINUS		23
ON THEIR HOLLOW TOP, ...		415	TOWER		171
HOLLOW OF CHEEK AS THOUGH IT DRANK THE WIND		444	SCHOOL CHILDR		27
THROUGH THE HOLLOW OF AN EAR;		499	MOTHER OF GOD		2
ALL FLAME-LIKE GUSHING FROM THE HOLLOW STONES,		650	ISLE STAT I 1		129
FROM THE SHADOWY HOLLOW		654	ISLE STAT I 2		56
ARISE FROM THE HOLLOW, ...		654	ISLE STAT I 2		68
FROM THE SHADOWY HOLLOW		654	ISLE STAT I 2		78
FROM THE GREEN SHADED HOLLOW		655	ISLE STAT I 2		82
FORTH FROM THE HOLLOW ALDER TRUNK . . .		670	ISLE STAT II 3		120
AND HOLLOW LULLING THE YOUNG WINDS WITH SONG.		675	ISLE STAT II 3		226
BY HEATH OR HOLLOW OR RUSHY MERE, . . .		716	FAIRY DOCTOR		10
THE HOLLOW WOODLANDS FEEL HIM THERE, . . .		737	SUMMER EVENING		17
HOLLOW-CHEEKED					
YONDER HE COMES, BRIGHT-EYED, AND HOLLOW-CHEEKED		697	MOSADA 2		35
HOLLOWS					
AND DEW-BLANCHED HORNS, IN WHOSE HOLLOWS A CHILD OF THREE		49	OISIN 3	V	31
YEARS OLD					
THEIR SADNESS THROUGH THE HOLLOWS OF ITS HEART, . . .		68	SAD SHEPHERD	V	21
CRIED OUT THE HOLLOWS OF THE SEA. . .		397	POLIT PRISONER		24
THAT FILL THE BLAZING HOLLOWS OF MY HEART. .		684	SEEKER	V	69D
HOLY					
THE HOLY TREE IS GROWING THERE, ...		134	TWO TREES		2
FROM JOY THE HOLY BRANCHES START, . . .		134	TWO TREES		3
UPON HER HOLY QUIETUDE. . . .		138	TO IRELAND	V	16
AND WRAPPED THE FLAMES ABOVE HIS HOLY HEAD;		162	ASKS FORGIVE		17
AND GATHERED THE FLAMES ABOVE HIS HOLY HEAD,		162	ASKS FORGIVE	V	17
WHO SOUGHT THEE IN THE HOLY SEPULCHRE, . .		169	SECRET ROSE		3
WHO SOUGHT THEE AT THE HOLY SEPULCHRE, . .		169	SECRET ROSE	V	3
WITH HOLY SHADOWS." HER HIGH HEART WAS GLAD,		186	QUEEN MAEVE		126
FROM THE HOLY ORCHARDS, WHERE THERE IS NONE		196	BAILE AILLINN		174
BUT PURER THAN A TALL CANDLE BEFORE THE HOLY ROOD		208	HANRAHANS SONG		14
AND CARRIES IT BETWEEN US. HOLY FIRE		239	SHADOW WATER B		371
THAT MUST, AS IF IT HAD NOT HOLY BLOOD		260	FASC DIFFICULT		5
BY THE ANCIENT HOLY HANDS THAT BROUGHT THEM		271	GREY ROCK	V	21
IS FROM THE HOLY SHADES THAT ROVE . .		275	GREY ROCK		110
THAT THE SHADES OF HOLY MEN		298	THREE HERMITS		17
THE HOLY CENTAURS OF THE HILLS ARE VANISHED;		344	DEJECTION		7
THE HOLY CENTAURS OF THE HILLS ARE BANISHED;		344	DEJECTION	V	7
THROUGH THE HOLY IMAGES		355	PROPERTIUS		5
WHERE THOSE THAT HAVE OBEYED THE HOLY LAW		356	BROKEN DREAMS		33
TO THE HOLY CITY OF BYZANTIUM. . . .		408	SAIL BYZANTIUM		16
O SAGES STANDING IN GOD'S HOLY FIRE		408	SAIL BYZANTIUM		17
COME FROM THE HOLY FIRE, PERNE IN A GYRE, .		408	SAIL BYZANTIUM		19
UNLESS THE HOLY WRITINGS LIE, ...		436	FOR MY SON		28
WHERE HOLY DIONYSUS DIED, . . .		437	SONGS PLAY 1		2
AND LIVE AMONG THE ANCIENT HOLY MEN, . . .		448	HERO GIRL FOOL	V	11A
BEING BUT HOLY SHOWS		454	HIS MEMORIES		2
BODIES OF HOLY MEN AND WOMEN EXUDE . . .		483	OIL AND BLOOD		2
NOR CAN HE HIDE IN HOLY BLACK		508	JANE BISHOP		18
WHEN THE HOLY BIRD, THAT THERE . . .		522	LULLABY		15
AND THE HOLY LAND OF IRELAND, . . .		526	AM OF IRELAND		2
AND THE HOLY LAND OF IRELAND, . . .		526	AM OF IRELAND		15
AND THE HOLY LAND OF IRELAND, . . .		527	AM OF IRELAND		28
HOLY JOE, THE BEGGAR-MAN, ...		529	TOM LUNATIC		8
I TURN THE PAGES OF MY HOLY BOOK. . .		555	RIBH AT TOMB		27
ROUND LOUGH DERG'S HOLY ISLAND I WENT UPON THE STONES,		593	PILGRIM		6
OF HOLY PETER OF THE BURNING GATE; . . .		696	MOSADA 2	V	20
HE'D FIND FOR THIS SOME HOLY TEXT. . . .		728	PRIEST FAIRY		16
IN THE HOLY CHURCH OF GOD.		735	IN CHURCH		4
IN THE HOLY CHURCH OF GOD. . . .		736	IN CHURCH		16
THAT MURMURS WITH HOLY WOODS, AND WIN THEIR HELP . . .		757	SHADOW WATER A		199

HOLY   (CONTINUED)
WHERE TRUE-LOVE WANDERS AMONG THE HOLY WOODS. . . . . .   764 SHADOW WATER A   337
WHERE TRUE LOVE WANDERS AMONG THE HOLY WOODS. . . . . .   764 SHADOW WATER A V   337
WHERE ARE THESE BOUGHS? WHERE ARE THE HOLY WOODS . . . . .   765 SHADOW WATER A   359
SIX HOLY CREATURES, ...   770 BLOOD BOND   14
O SHUFFLING OF HOLY SHOES! . . . .   774 COME RIDE   15
HOME
MY HOME IS FAR FROM WHERE THE TIDE . . . .   5 OISIN 1   V   46
TO JOIN HIS BROTHERS IN THE HOME OF YEARS . . . .   30 OISIN 2   V   17
AND HOME TO ME AGAIN, ...   33 OISIN 2   65
WINDOWLESS, PILLARLESS, MULTITUDINOUS HOME . . . .   39 OISIN 2   148
HOME IN THE BLESSED MOONLIGHT . . . .   94 MOLL MAGEE   V   11
AND FETCH ME HOME AGIN! . . . .   96 MOLL MAGEE   42
"BUT IF YOUR MASTER COMES HOME TRIUMPHING . . . . .   106 CUCHULAIN SEA   12
THE HOME WHERE I WAS SAFE AND WARM? . . . . . .   151 HEART OF WOMAN V   6
WITH: "YOU MUST HOME AGAIN, AND WED . . . . . .   191 BAILE AILLINN   58
THAT I MAY DROWN MYSELF? BETTER STEER HOME, . . .   222 SHADOW WATER B   12
IT WOULD BE BETTER TO TURN HOME AGAIN, ...   222 SHADOW WATER B V   12
AND YOU HAD SPREAD A SAIL FOR HOME, A WIND . . .   236 SHADOW WATER B   309
AND MEASURE OUT A COURSE AND BRING US HOME, . . .   238 SHADOW WATER B   362
LET'S HOME! I'D GIVE SOME RUBIES TO A WOMAN. . . .   248 SHADOW WATER B   537
TO FANCY THAT SHE'D BRING YOU HOME AGAIN. . . . .   248 SHADOW WATER B   549
LET'S HOME AND SPEND IT IN OUR VILLAGES. . . . . .   248 SHADOW WATER B V 538A
FOR HE WILL SHELTER YOU AND BRING YOU HOME. . . .   250 SHADOW WATER B   590
"WE RIDE BUT SLOWLY THOUGH SO NEAR OUR HOME," . . .   276 TWO KINGS   V   A
A STERNER CONSCIENCE AND A FRIENDLIER HOME, . . .   321 REED WHISPERER   8
I CANNOT FIND THE PEACE OF HOME . . . .   332 ROUND TOWER   29
DECIDED HE WOULD JOURNEY HOME, ...   361 ALF POLLEXFEN   30
DECIDED HE MUST JOURNEY HOME, ...   361 ALF POLLEXFEN   V   30
NEVER TO LEAVE THAT VALLEY HIS FATHERS CALLED THEIR HOME. 391 UNDER SATURN   16
WITH HER WHITE FINGER. I LED HER HOME ASLEEP . . . .   468 HARUN RASHID   158
WHAT BROUGHT THEM THERE SO FAR FROM THEIR HOME, . .   549 SEVERED HEAD   8
"NOT TO DIE ON THE STRAW AT HOME, ...   587 OLD WICKED MAN   5
AND HE CAME SAILING HOME. . . . .   594 COLONEL MARTIN   6
SO STAY AT HOME AND DRINK YOUR BEER . . . . . .   598 STONE CROSS   5
CALL THE MUSES HOME. . . . .   600 THOSE IMAGES   8
"OR DRIVEN FROM HOME AND LEFT TO DIE IN FEAR." . . .   635 CUCHULAIN COMF   22
AND HATH HER HOME BY MANY-FOLDED DELLS. . . . .   657 ISLE STAT I 3   46
THE TALKING WINDS HAVE FOUND THEIR HOME, ...   686 LIFE   9
"NO, THY HOME IS DEEPEST HELL, ...   697 MOSADA 2   26
THEY WILL LEAD HER HOME AGAIN . . . .   727 LOVERS QUARREL   49
HE CAME TO THE HOME OF THE FOREST PEOPLE . . . .   728 PRIEST FAIRY   5
AND THOU CANST DWELL IN THINE OWN HOME, ...   739 EARL PAUL   3
ANOTHER LEADER, AND TURN HOME AGAIN. . . . . .   748 SHADOW WATER A   16
BUT WOULD TURN HOME AGAIN. NO MAN HAD DOUBTS . .   749 SHADOW WATER A   38
AND TURN HIS GALLEY ABOUT AND BRING ME HOME. . . .   751 SHADOW WATER A   108
I SHALL BE HOME NOW IN A LITTLE WHILE, ...   759 SHADOW WATER A   240
THE WINDS AND WATERS TO BE YOUR HOME FOR EVER! . .   762 SHADOW WATER A   282
THE WINDS AND WATERS TO BE YOUR HOME FOREVER! . .   762 SHADOW WATER A V   282
AND WE GO HOME. COME, AIBRIC, END YOUR TALE . . .   766 SHADOW WATER A   374
HOMEBREW
OF THE HOMEBREW THERE, UNTIL . . . .   776 AGAINST WITCH   V   38
HOME-BREW
OF THE HOME-BREW THERE, UNTIL . . . .   776 AGAINST WITCH   38
HOMER
A WOMAN HOMER SUNG . . . .   254 WOMAN HOMER   T
A WOMAN HOMER SUNG, ...   255 WOMAN HOMER   19
WITH HOMER THAT WAS A BLIND MAN, ...   411 TOWER   52
MERE DREAMS, MERE DREAMS! YET HOMER HAD NOT SUNG . .   417 ANCEST HOUSES   9
THOUGH MOUNTED IN THAT SADDLE HOMER RODE . . . .   492 COOLE BALLYLEE   47
WHAT THEME HAD HOMER BUT ORIGINAL SIN? . . . . .   502 VACILLATION   77
HOMER IS MY EXAMPLE AND HIS UNCHRISTENED HEART. . . .   503 VACILLATION   87
HORACE THERE BY HOMER STANDS, ...   524 MAD AS MIST   7
AND MANY-MINDED HOMER WERE . . . .   524 MAD AS MIST   17
HOMER'S
THAT COULD SHOW WHAT HOMER'S AGE . . . .   258 PEACE   2
BY HOMER'S PARAGON . . . .   384 VISION ROBART   56
HOMES
WHERE HOMES ONCE WHITENED VALE AND MOUNTAIN CREST! . . . 709 FERENCZ RENYI   3
HOMESTEAD
IN HIS DIVINE HOMESTEAD, ...   113 ROSE OF PEACE   6
HOMESTEADS
THEY LEFT THEIR HOMESTEADS TO FATTEN THE FOXES, . . .   546 TO SAME TUNE 2   3
THEY LEFT THEIR HOMESTEADS TO SHELTER THE FOXES, . . .   546 TO SAME TUNE 2 V   3
THEY LEFT THEIR HOMESTEADS TO FATTEN THE FOXES, . . .   613 MARCH SONGS 1   3
HOMEWARD
AND CHASE THE WILD BEE HOMEWARD TO HIS HIVE . . .   32 OISIN 2   V 50D
ALONG THE LAKE. THE CRANE HAS HOMEWARD FLED. . . .   656 ISLE STAT I 3   23
WITH BERRIES. PLACID AS A HOMEWARD BEE. . . . .   710 FERENCZ RENYI   29
A WOODMAN ON HIS HOMEWARD WAY . . . .   730 PRIEST FAIRY   73
AND, HURRYING HOMEWARD, FALL UPON SOME LAND . . .   767 SHADOW WATER A   384
HOMEWARDS
I HAVE TURNED HOMEWARDS. IN THE EYES OF THE GODS, . .   757 SHADOW WATER A   202
HONEST
DUTIFUL HUSBAND, HONEST WIFE BY TURN, ...   376 PHASES OF MOON   99
HONESTY
IF IT LACK HONESTY. . . . .   584 GHOST ROG CASE   28
HONEY
AND BOWLS OF BARLEY, HONEY, AND WINE, ...   3 OISIN 1   8
AND DROPS OF HONEY ARE HIS WORDS, ...   7 OISIN 1   V   64
AND OIL AND WINE AND HONEY AND MILK, ...   8 OISIN 1   92

```
                                                           PAGE      TITLE              LINE
HONEY    (CONTINUED)
        AND HONEY, AND OIL, AND WINE, AND MILK,  . . . . . . . .     8 OISIN 1        V    92
        FROM BEES AMONG THEIR HONEY MARTS,  . . . . . . . . .       16 OISIN 1        V   229
        WITH BOOM OF BEES IN HONEY MARTS,  . . . . . . . . .        16 OISIN 1        V   229
        LIKE DROPS OF HONEY CAME THEIR WORDS,  . . . . . . .        26 OISIN 1             398
        NINE BEAN ROWS WILL I HAVE THERE, A HIVE FOR THE HONEY BEE, 117 ISLE INNISFREE V     3
        TO BLESS THAT ISLE WITH HONEY IN HIS TONES,  . . . .       128 DREAM OF FAERY  V    44
        BAILE, WHO HAD THE HONEY MOUTH;  . . . . . . . . .         189 BAILE AILLINN   V     5
        YOUNG BAILE HONEY MOUTH, WHOM SOME  . . . . . . . .        189 BAILE AILLINN   V    16
        I RUN TO BAILE HONEY MOUTH  . . . . . . . . . . .          191 BAILE AILLINN   V    48
        AND NOW THAT HONEY MOUTH IS LAID  . . . . . . . . .        192 BAILE AILLINN   V    80
        THE HONEY PALE MOON HUNG LOW ON THE SLEEPY HILL,  . .      203 WITHER BOUGHS   V     5
        MY WALL IS LOOSENING, HONEY BEES  . . . . . . . . .        424 STARES NEST     V     4
        HONEY OF GENERATION HAD BETRAYED,  . . . . . . . .         444 SCHOOL CHILDR        34
        GOLDSMITH DELIBERATELY SIPPING AT THE HONEY POT OF HIS     481 BLOOD AND MOON  V    21
            MIND;
        I NEVER KNEW A NIGHT SO HONEY SWEET.  . . . . . . .        702 MOSADA 3        V    99
        WILD BEES' HONEY LAID FOR THEE."  . . . . . . . . .        730 PRIEST FAIRY         56
HONEY-BEE
        NINE BEAN-ROWS WILL I HAVE THERE, A HIVE FOR THE HONEY-BEE, 117 ISLE INNISFREE        3
HONEY-BEES
        MY WALL IS LOOSENING; HONEY-BEES,  . . . . . . . .        424 STARES NEST            4
        THAN IN OUR LOVE! O HONEY-BEES,  . . . . . . . . .        425 STARES NEST           19
        THAN IN OUR LOVES; OH, HONEY-BEES,  . . . . . . . .       425 STARES NEST     V    19
HONEY-COLOURED
        BY THOSE GREAT HONEY-COLOURED  . . . . . . . . .          492 ANNE GREGORY          3
HONEYCOMB
        THEIR BITTERNESS AND FIND THE HONEYCOMB.  . . . . .       463 HARUN RASHID         48
        THE LION AND THE HONEYCOMB, WHAT HAS SCRIPTURE SAID?  . .  503 VACILLATION          88
HONEY-COMB
        THE LION AND THE HONEY-COMB, WHAT HAS SCRIPTURE SAID?  . . 503 VACILLATION     V    88
HONEYED
        BRINGING ME HONEYED, WANDERING THOUGHT  . . . . . .        7 OISIN 1          V    65
HONEY-HEART
        NOR FAERIES IN THE HONEY-HEART OF JUNE ASTIR.  . . . .    661 ISLE STAT II 1       73
HONEY-HEARTED
        THE HONEY-HEARTED LEISURE OF THE LIGHT,  . . . . . .      705 REMEMBRANCE           7
HONEY-MARTS
        WITH BOOM OF BEES IN HONEY-MARTS,  . . . . . . . .         16 OISIN 1             229
HONEY-MOUTH
        YOUNG BAILE HONEY-MOUTH, WHOM SOME  . . . . . . . .       189 BAILE AILLINN        16
        I RUN TO BAILE HONEY-MOUTH  . . . . . . . . . . .         191 BAILE AILLINN        48
        AND NOW THAT HONEY-MOUTH IS LAID  . . . . . . . . .       192 BAILE AILLINN        80
HONEY-PALE
        THE HONEY-PALE MOON LAY LOW ON THE SLEEPY HILL,  . . .    203 WITHER BOUGHS         5
HONEY-POT
        GOLDSMITH DELIBERATELY SIPPING AT THE HONEY-POT OF HIS     481 BLOOD AND MOON       21
            MIND,
HONEY-SWEET
        I NEVER KNEW A NIGHT SO HONEY-SWEET.  . . . . . . .       702 MOSADA 3             99
HONEY-THICKENED
        IN ALL ITS HONEY-THICKENED TUNE  . . . . . . . .         736 SUMMER EVENING        7
HONIED
        A HONIED RINGING! UNDER THE NEW SKIES  . . . . . . .      130 BOOK STORIES    V    21
HONOUR
        IN HONOUR SOON BY HIS MASTER'S SIDE  . . . . . .           26 OISIN 1         V  399C
        BEING HONOUR BRED, WITH ONE . . . . . . . . . .           291 TO A FRIEND           5
        PULL DOWN ESTABLISHED HONOUR; HAWK FOR NEWS  . . . .      398 LEADERS CROWD         3
        NO HONOUR LEAVE ITS MIGHTY MONUMENT,  . . . . . . .       429 NINETEEN 19          38
        TALKED OF HONOUR AND OF TRUTH,  . . . . . . . . .         431 NINETEEN 19          90
        IF HONOUR FIND HIM IN THE WINTRY BLAST?  . . . . . .      479 SELF AND SOUL        56
        ACCEPT THE MIRACLES OF THE SAINTS AND HONOUR SANCTITY?  . .503 VACILLATION          79
        BUT IN HONOUR SPLIT HIS LOVE  . . . . . . . . . .         573 LADYS 3RD SONG        7
        HONOUR HAD LIVED SO LONG, ALL LACKING FOUND.  . . . .     603 GALLERY REVIS        35
        HONOUR HAD LIVED SO LONG, THEIR HEALTH I FOUND.  . . .    603 GALLERY REVIS   V    35
HONOURED
        HONOURED BY ALL IN THEIR DEGREES;  . . . . . . . .        380 SAINT HUNCH          15
HOOD     SEE CRADLE-HOOD MONK'S-HOOD
        NODDING HER RUSSET HOOD?  . . . . . . . . . . .           171 MAID QUIET            2
        NODDING HER PURPLE HOOD?  . . . . . . . . . . .           171 MAID QUIET      V     2
        UNDER HER PURPLE HOOD.  . . . . . . . . . . . .           171 MAID QUIET      V     8
        WHEN THE SUN LOOKED OUT OF HIS GOLDEN HOOD,  . . . .      210 RAGGED WOOD     V     3
        WHEN THE SUN LOOKED OUT OF HIS GOLDEN HOOD?--  . . .      211 RAGGED WOOD           7
        "I WILL NOT BE CLAPPED IN A HOOD,  . . . . . . . .        349 HAWK                  7
        A KIND OLD NUN IN A WHITE HOOD REPLIES;  . . . . . .      443 SCHOOL CHILDR         2
        IN MASKER'S CLOAK AND HOOD,  . . . . . . . . . .          539 MEETING               2
        YOUR HOOD IS THREADBARE--SEE THAT IT BE CHANGED  . . .    704 MOSADA 3            133
HOODED
        LET HIM BE HOODED OR CAGED . . . . . . . . . .            349 HAWK                  2
        I WRAPPED HER IN A HOODED CLOAK, AND SHE,  . . . . .      468 HARUN RASHID        154
        I WRAPPED HER IN A HEAVY HOODED CLOAK,  . . . . . .       468 HARUN RASHID    V   154
        I WRAPPED HER IN A HEAVY HOODED CLOAK, AND SHE  . . .     468 HARUN RASHID    V   154
HOOD'S    SEE MONK'S-HOOD'S
HOOF      SEE HORSE-HOOF
        SCARCE WORTHY OF A HOOF GOLD-SHOD.  . . . . . . . .         2 OISIN 1         V    7Y
        MY DREAMS WERE LIVING.  NOW THE HOOF . . . . . . .         25 OISIN 1         V   382
        AND HOOF AND HORN THAT HAD SUCKED IN THEIR SPEED  . .     278 TWO KINGS            30
        BEYOND THE FLING OF THE DULL ASS'S HOOF  . . . . .        321 REED WHISPERER        5
        BUT WHEN HIS HORSE HAD PUT ITS HOOF  . . . . . . .        571 THREE BUSHES         50
HOOFS
        WITH HOOFS OF THE PALE FINDRINNY  . . . . . . . . .        25 OISIN 1             383
```

HOOFS   (CONTINUED)
   WITH HOOFS OF THE RUDDY FINDRINNY . . . .   25 OISIN 1   V 383
   A VALLEY FLOWED DOWN FROM HIS HOOFS, AND THERE IN THE LONG   48 OISIN 3   26
      GRASS LAY,
   OF TWILIGHT AND SLUMBER WERE GONE, AND THAT HOOFS   54 OISIN 3   112
      IMPATIENTLY STEPT.
   . . . THE STRONG HOOFS CRUSHING THE SAND AND THE SHELLS,   58 OISIN 3   157
   . . . THE STRONG HOOFS CRUSHING THE SANDS AND THE SHELLS   58 OISIN 3   V 157
   THEIR HOOFS HEAVY WITH TUMULT, THEIR EYES GLIMMERING WHITE; 154 BELOVED PEACE   2
   AND UNDER HER HOOFS THE MARIGOLDS BEATEN. . . . . . . 729 PRIEST FAIRY   36
HOOK   SEE REAPING-HOOK
   THAT RUN BEFORE THE REAPING HOOK AND LIE . . . . 218 WOODS OF COOLE V 32
   AND THOUGH I HAVE TURNED THE TALK BY HOOK OR CROOK . . . 350 HER PRAISE   5
HOOKED
   BENT DOWN ABOVE EACH HOOKED KNEE, ...   26 OISIN 1   392
   BENT LOW ABOVE EACH HOOKED KNEE, ...   26 OISIN 1   V 392
   AND HOOKED A BERRY TO A THREAD; . . . . 149 WANDER AENGUS   4
   AND HOOKED A LITTLE SILVER TROUT. . . . . 149 WANDER AENGUS V 8
HOOKS
   SHOOK THE ALE-HORNS AND SHIELDS UPON THEIR HOOKS; . . . 181 QUEEN MAEVE   38
   SHOOK THE ALE HORNS AND SHIELDS UPON THEIR HOOKS; . . . 181 QUEEN MAEVE   V 38
HOOLIHAN   SEE KATHLEEN-NY-HOOLIHAN
HOOPED
   CIVILIZATION IS HOOPED TOGETHER, BROUGHT . . . . 563 MERU   1
NO MAIN ITEM   SEE BARREL-HOOPS
HOOTED
   HAD HOOTED FOR AN HUNDRED YEARS, ... 670 ISLE STAT II 3 116
   UP-RAISED HIS VOICE, AND HOOTED ME. . . . . 670 ISLE STAT II 3 117
   HE HOOTED AS I WANDERED BY. . . . . 670 ISLE STAT II 3 121
   UPRAISED HIS VOICE, AND HOOTED ME. . . . . 670 ISLE STAT II 3 V 117
HOOVES
   FOR GOLD HIS HOOVES AND SILK HIS REIN, ...   2 OISIN 1   V 7Z
   FOR THE SPARKLING HOOVES THEY SANK NOT IN; . . . . . .   10 OISIN 1   V 114A
   WHOSE HOOVES THE TOPS OF THE SURGES GRAZED, ...   12 OISIN 1   V 142A
   I LAY, AS OVER SEA THE LIGHT HOOVES GLANCED . . . . . .   30 OISIN 2   V 19A
   OF DANAAN HOOVES WE URGED OUR WAY BETWEEN . . . .   31 OISIN 2   V 31
   FROM HIS HOOVES IN THE HEAVY GRASSES, WITH MONSTROUS   48 OISIN 3   V 27
      SLUMBERING FOLK,
   . . . BENEATH ME THE HOOVES IMPATIENTLY STEPT. . . . .   54 OISIN 3   V 112
   . . . THE GOLD HOOVES CRUSHING THE SANDS AND THE SHELLS   58 OISIN 3   V 157
   YOUR HOOVES HAVE STAMPED AT THE BLACK MARGIN OF THE WOOD, 442 BLACK CENTAUR   1
HOPE
   MY ENEMY AND HOPE; DEMONS FOR FRIGHT . . . .   34 OISIN 2   81
   WITH HOPE, MINE ENEMY. AS HE BY NIGHT . . . .   34 OISIN 2   V 81
   HAD NEITHER HOPE NOR FEAR. I BADE THEM HIDE . . . . .   38 OISIN 2   139
   LEST NIAMH SHUDDER. FULL OF HOPE AND DREAD . . . . . .   41 OISIN 2   183
   WHILE HUSHED FROM FEAR, OR LOUD WITH HOPE, A BAND . . . 114 ROSE OF BATTLE   5
   WE COME BETWEEN HIM AND THE HOPE OF HIS HEART. . . . . 141 HOSTING SIDHE   12
   AND WHERE IS THERE HOPE OR DEED AS FAIR? . . . . 141 HOSTING SIDHE   14
   THOUGH HOPE FALL FROM YOU AND LOVE DECAY, ... 148 INTO TWILIGHT   7
   AND HOPE IS LESS DEAR THAN THE DEW OF THE MORN. . . . . 148 INTO TWILIGHT   16
   THOUGH HOPE FALL FROM THEE OR LOVE DECAY . . . . 148 INTO TWILIGHT V 7
   FOR SOMEBODY HID HATRED AND HOPE AND DESIRE AND FEAR . . 153 CHANGE BELOVED V 4
   AND I HAVE HATRED AND HOPE AND DESIRE AND FEAR . . . . 153 CHANGE BELOVED V 4
   O VANITY OF SLEEP, HOPE, DREAM, ENDLESS DESIRE, ... 154 BELOVED PEACE   7
   LILIES OF DEATH-PALE HOPE, ROSES OF PASSIONATE DREAM. . 172 TRAV PASSION   8
   MIRACLE, ECSTASY, THE IMPOSSIBLE HOPE, ... 227 SHADOW WATER B 102
   LOVES IN BRIEF LONGING AND DECEIVING HOPE . . . . 228 SHADOW WATER B 146
   TO GO--FOR HOPE WOULD GIVE HIS LIMBS THE POWER-- . . . . 282 TWO KINGS   V 133A
   FOR HOPE WOULD GIVE HIS LIMBS THE POWER--AND AWAIT . . . 283 TWO KINGS   136
   THE BEGGAR DEAF TO ALL BUT HOPE . . . . 304 HOUR DAWN   V 44
   HOPE THAT YOU MAY UNDERSTAND! . . . . 309 REALISTS   1
   DO, BUT AWAKE A HOPE TO LIVE . . . . 309 REALISTS   6
   DO BUT WAKE THE HOPE TO LIVE . . . . 309 REALISTS   V 6
   TO HOPE A THING SO DEAR . . . . 346 ON WOMAN   27
   THAT IS OUR MODERN HOPE, AND BY ITS LIGHT . . . . . . 368 EGO DOMINUS   11
   THEY HAVE LOUD MUSIC, HOPE EVERY DAY RENEWED . . . . . 398 LEADERS CROWD   11
   ONE DEAR HOPE HAD HE; . . . . 471 ALL SOUL NIGHT   28
   NOR DREAD NOR HOPE ATTEND . . . . 476 DEATH   1
   A VAIN HOPE . . . . 553 CHURCH STATE V T
   IF YOU ARE WORTH MY HOPE! NEITHER CONTENT . . . . . . 579 DOR WELLESLEY   13
   A MAN HAS A HOPE FOR HEAVEN, ... 643 SONG FAERIES V 1
   A MAN HAS A HOPE FOR HEAVEN, ... 676 ISLE STAT II 3 248
   THIS HEATHEN HORDE AWAY. YOU NEED NOT HOPE; . . . . . 696 MOSADA 2   5
   CAST OUT ALL HOPE, CAST OUT ALL FEAR, ... 743 DANAAN QUICK   25
   AND TURN BRIEF LONGING AND DECEIVING HOPE . . . . . . 750 SHADOW WATER A   59
   THAN IN BRIEF LONGING AND DECEIVING HOPE . . . . . . 750 SHADOW WATER A   65
   WHEN ONE HAS LEAPT ON BOARD. NO, FOR I HAVE HOPE . . 751 SHADOW WATER A 106
   HAVE BID ME HOPE, SAIL TO THE LOCHLANN SHORE . . . . 756 SHADOW WATER A 184
   IS BUT BRIEF LONGING, AND DECEIVING HOPE, ... 765 SHADOW WATER A 354
HOPED
   MORE RICHES THAN THEY EVER HOPED TO FIND? . . . . . . 226 SHADOW WATER B   94
   WHAT I HAD HOPED 'TWOULD BE . . . . 347 FISHERMAN   10
   BECAUSE I HAD HOPED TO COME, AS DREAMS FORETOLD, . . . 757 SHADOW WATER A 197
   I HAVE COME HITHER BECAUSE I HOPED TO COME . . . . . . 757 SHADOW WATER A V 197
HOPELESS
   HOPELESS FOR EVER; ANCIENT OISIN KNOWS, ...   42 OISIN 2   202
   HOPELESS FOR EVER, THEY ALONE SHALL SEEK . . . .   42 OISIN 2   V 200
   HAS MADE THEM SO HAPPY AND HOPELESS, SO DEAF AND SO BLIND 204 WITHER BOUGHS   20
   HOPELESS AND DEAR, OR TERRIBLE TO THINK ON, ... 281 TWO KINGS   96
   TO SEEK NOT HOPELESS HAVE I CROSSED THE GLOOM, ... 656 ISLE STAT I 3   42

		PAGE	TITLE		LINE
HOPELESS	(CONTINUED)				
	SHALL NOT SO HOPELESS PROVE! SOME GOD MAY REST	657	ISLE STAT I 3		61
HOPES					
	AND HEAVY MORTAL HOPES THAT TOIL AND PASS!	101	ROSE UPON ROOD		18
	AND BROOD ON HOPES AND FEAR NO MORE.	125	GOES FERGUS		6
	AND BROOD ON HOPES AND FEARS NO MORE.	125	GOES FERGUS	V	6
	OR HOPES THAT IN MERE HOPING FLICKER AND CEASE!	162	ASKS FORGIVE		3
	AND HOPES THAT IN MERE HOPING FLICKER AND CEASE!	162	ASKS FORGIVE	V	3
	BUT HARRY US WITH HOPES THAT COME TO NOTHING, ...	250	SHADOW WATER B		579
HOPING					
	HOPING AND FEARING, BROUGHT ME WINE AND BREAD.	41	OISIN 2	V	184A
	OR HOPES THAT IN MERE HOPING FLICKER AND CEASE!	162	ASKS FORGIVE		3
	AND HOPES THAT IN MERE HOPING FLICKER AND CEASE!	162	ASKS FORGIVE	V	3
	AND ALL THEIR EYES STILL FIXED, HOPING TO FIND ONCE MORE,	318	MAGI		6
	DREADING AND HOPING ALL!	476	DEATH		4
	HOPING MORE SUBSTANTIAL JOY	494	AT ALGECIRAS		9
	HOPING A MORE SUBSTANTIAL JOY	494	AT ALGECIRAS	V	9
HORACE					
	HORACE THERE BY HOMER STANDS, ...	524	MAD AS MIST		7
HORDE					
	THIS HEATHEN HORDE AWAY. YOU NEED NOT HOPE!	696	MOSADA 2		5
HORIZON					
	ON THE HORIZON EDGE BELLOWED THE HERDS.	279	TWO KINGS		56
	WHEN THE HORIZON FADES, ...	416	TOWER		193
HORIZON'S					
	HE'D HEARD THAT DIN ON THE HORIZON'S EDGE	286	TWO KINGS	V	217A
	(FOR SINCE THE HORIZON'S BOUGHT STRANGE DOGS ARE STILL)	579	DOR WELLESLEY		7
HORN					
	"WHY DO YOU WIND NO HORN?" SHE SAID, ...	4	OISIN 1		32
	WHY DO YE SOUND NO HORN?" SHE SAID, ...	4	OISIN 1	V	33
	WHY DO YOU WIND NO HORN?" SHE SAID, ...	4	OISIN 1	V	33
	SHALL FOLLOW YOUR HORN AND OBEY YOUR WHIM, ...	9	OISIN 1		99
	AND STIRS THE YOUNG KID'S BUDDING HORN, ...	18	OISIN 1		264
	A-MURMUR LIKE YOUNG PARTRIDGE! WITH LOUD HORN	32	OISIN 2		52
	WHEN THEY AWAKE UPSPRINGING! WITH LOUD HORN	32	OISIN 2	V	52
	CEASE, CEASE, O MOURNFUL, LAUGHING FENIAN HORN!	43	OISIN 2		213
	AH, CEASE, THOU MOURNFUL, LAUGHING FENIAN HORN!	43	OISIN 2	V	213
	AH, CEASE, YOU MOURNFUL, LAUGHING FENIAN HORN!	43	OISIN 2	V	213
	SNATCHING THE HORN OF NIAMH, I BLEW A LONG LINGERING NOTE.	51	OISIN 3		57
	SNATCHING THE HORN OF NIAM, I BLEW FORTH A LINGERING NOTE!	51	OISIN 3	V	57
	SNATCHING THE HORN OF NIAM, I BLEW A LINGERING NOTE! . .	51	OISIN 3	V	57
	"HUNTSMAN RODY, BLOW THE HORN, ...	98	FOXHUNTER		25
	"NOW HUNTSMAN RODY, BLOW THY HORN, ...	98	FOXHUNTER	V	REF
	"MY HUNTSMAN RODY, BLOW THE HORN, ...	98	FOXHUNTER	V	REF
	"HUNTSMAN RODY, BLOW THE HORN, ...	99	FOXHUNTER		33
	"I CANNOT BLOW UPON MY HORN, ...	99	FOXHUNTER		35
	AND GOD STANDS WINDING HIS LONELY HORN, ...	148	INTO TWILIGHT		13
	AND WITH HEART MORE OLD THAN THE HORN	157	POET BELOVED		5
	AND WITH THE HEART MORE OLD THAN THE HORN	157	POET BELOVED	V	5
	WHEN THE LONG WARS FOR THE WHITE HORN	189	BAILE AILLINN		14
	BECAUSE OF SOMETHING TOLD UNDER THE FAMISHED HORN . . .	210	UNDER THE MOON		17
	BECAUSE OF SOMETHING I HEARD OF UNDER THE THIN HORN . .	210	UNDER THE MOON V		17
	BECAUSE OF A STORY I HEARD UNDER THE THIN HORN	210	UNDER THE MOON V		17
	BECAUSE OF A STORY I HEARD UNDER A THIN HORN	210	UNDER THE MOON V		17
	AND LIFT UP AN OLD HORN	215	HAPPY TOWNLAND		49
	NINE SWORDS WITH HANDLES OF RHINOCEROS HORN	239	SHADOW WATER B		368
	TO THE HORN, AND HE BE HALE AND HEARTY.	243	SHADOW WATER B		447
	AGAINST THE STAG. WHEN HORN AND STEEL WERE MET	277	TWO KINGS		15
	THE HORN RESOUNDED AS THOUGH IT HAD BEEN SILVER, . . .	277	TWO KINGS		16
	HORN LOCKED IN SWORD, THEY TUGGED AND STRUGGLED THERE . .	277	TWO KINGS		18
	TO STAY THE STAG'S NEXT RUSH. WHEN SWORD MET HORN . . .	277	TWO KINGS	V	15
	AND HOOF AND HORN THAT HAD SUCKED IN THEIR SPEED . . .	278	TWO KINGS		30
	UNTIL AT LAST THE UNLOCKED HORN HAD TORN	278	TWO KINGS	V	21
	A LONG BLAST UPON THE HORN THAT BROUGHT	324	ROBERT GREGORY		22
	AND THE NEW STILL HIDES HER HORN.	382	VISION ROBART		4
	WHEREBY THE HORN OF PLENTY IS UNDONE.	404	FOR DAUGHTER		32
	OUT OF THE MOUTH OF PLENTY'S HORN.	405	FOR DAUGHTER		60
	BARTER THAT HORN AND EVERY GOOD	405	FOR DAUGHTER		62
	CEREMONY'S A NAME FOR THE RICH HORN, ...	406	FOR DAUGHTER		79
	OR THAT OF THE FABULOUS HORN.	414	TOWER		136
	THIN IS THE MOON'S HORN!	519	LOVES LONENESS		8
	SWEARS THAT HE HEARS THE KING'S GREAT HORN.	636	BLACK TOWER		24
	A HORN! SOME TROOP OF ROBBERS WINDING GOES	649	ISLE STAT I 1		110
HORNED	SEE WHITE-HORNED				
	BETWEEN THE HORNED HILLS--SHEPHERDS, FAREWELL!	682	SEEKER		27
HORNLESS					
	THAN THE HORNLESS DEER WE CHASED THAT MORN, ...	2	OISIN 1	V	7P
	THE HORNLESS DEER IS NOT MORE SAD	4	OISIN 1		34
	WE GALLOPED! NOW A HORNLESS DEER	11	OISIN 1		139
	ON, ON! AND NOW A HORNLESS DEER	11	OISIN 1	V	139
	A RED-EARED HOUND FOLLOWS A HORNLESS DEER.	764	SHADOW WATER A		325
HORN'S					
	THE HORN'S SWEET NOTE AND THE TOOTH OF THE HOUND. . . .	380	SONGS FOOL 1		12
	THE HORN'S SWEET NOTE AND THE TOOTH OF THE HOUND. . . .	381	SONGS FOOL 2		14
HORNS	SEE ALE-HORNS				
	AND DEW-BLANCHED HORNS, IN WHOSE HOLLOW A CHILD OF THREE	49	OISIN 3		30
	YEARS OLD				
	AND DEW-BLANCHED HORNS, IN WHOSE HOLLOWS A CHILD OF THREE	49	OISIN 3	V	31
	YEARS OLD				
	THE HORNS AND SHIELDS AND WILD SWAN'S PINIONS!	82	MAD KING GOLL V		5
	DO YOU NOT HEAR ME CALLING, WHITE DEER WITH NO HORNS? . .	153	CHANGE BELOVED		1

		PAGE	TITLE		LINE
HORNS (CONTINUED)					
SHOOK THE ALE HORNS AND SHIELDS UPON THEIR HOOKS;	• • •	181	QUEEN MAEVE	V	38
BUT THE STAG STOOPED ITS HEAVY BRANCHING HORNS,	• • • •	277	TWO KINGS	V	12
UNTIL AT LAST THE DOUBLE HORNS, DRAWN BACKWARD,	• • •	278	TWO KINGS		21
KING EOCHAID SEIZED THE HORNS IN HIS STRONG HANDS	• •	278	TWO KINGS		24
EOCHAID SEIZED BOTH THE HORNS IN HIS STRONG HANDS	• •	278	TWO KINGS	V	24
ASIDE!--THE WILD HORNS TOLD ALMINTOR'S END,	• • • •	665	ISLE STAT II 2		68
HORRIBLE					
AND HORRIBLE SPLENDOUR OF DESIRE;	• • • • •	411	TOWER		63
EVEN WHERE HORRIBLE GREEN PARROTS CALL AND SWING.	• • •	442	BLACK CENTAUR		2
UNWEARIED EYES UPON THOSE HORRIBLE GREEN BIRDS.	• • • •	442	BLACK CENTAUR		16
EVEN WHERE THE HORRIBLE GREEN PARROTS CALL AND SWING.	• • •	442	BLACK CENTAUR	V	2
YOU THINK IT HORRIBLE THAT LUST AND RAGE	• • • • • •	591	SPUR		1
OH DEATH IS HORRIBLE! AND FOUL, FOUL, FOUL!	• • • •	675	ISLE STAT II 3		238
HORROR					
HORROR FROM HORROR GREW; BUT WHEN THE WEST	• • • • •	41	OISIN 2		180
HORROR FROM HORROR GREW; BUT WHEN THE WEST	• • • • •	41	OISIN 2		180
• • • DEEP HORROR OF EYES AND OF WINGS,	• • • • • • •	62	OISIN 3		205
DROVE HORROR FROM HIS MOTHER'S BREAST,	• • • • • •	440	WISDOM		20
I STRUGGLED WITH THE HORROR OF DAYBREAK,	• • • • •	535	CHOSEN		10
A CREEPING HORROR IS ALL OVER ME.	• • • • • • •	681	SEEKER		12
HORSE SEE CART-HORSE HIGH-HORSE					
ON A HORSE WITH BRIDLE OF FINDRINNY;	• • • • • •	3	OISIN 1		21
BUT WHEN THE HORSE HAD FELT MY WEIGHT,	• • • • •	9	OISIN 1		109
THE HORSE TOWARDS THE MUSIC RACED,	• • • • • • •	13	OISIN 1		169
WE TIED THE HORSE IN A LEAFY CLUMP,	• • • • • •	14	OISIN 1		194
AND FOUND THE HORSE AND BRIDLED HIM,	• • • • •	25	OISIN 1		378
ON HORSE AND SEA AND SADDLE SHONE.	• • • • • •	28	OISIN 1	V	427D
ABOUT THEM; AND THE HORSE OF FAERY SCREAMED	• • • • •	30	OISIN 2		24
TYING THE HORSE TO HIS VAST FOOT THAT LAY	• • • • •	32	OISIN 2		46
HOLDING THAT HORSE, AND SADLY CALLED MY NAME;	• • • •	44	OISIN 2		230
HOLDING THAT HORSE LONG SEEN NOT, NIAM STOOD.	• • • •	44	OISIN 2	V	230
AND THE EARS OF THE HORSE WENT SINKING AWAY IN THE HOLLOW NIGHT,		48	OISIN 3		21
TILL THE HORSE GAVE A WHINNY;	• • • • • • • •	48	OISIN 3		25
AND THE HORSE WAS GONE IN THE DISTANCE,	• • • • •	52	OISIN 3		75
I AWOKE! THE STRANGE HORSE WITHOUT SUMMONS OUT OF THE DISTANCE RAN,		54	OISIN 3		105
AND THEIR HOUND, AND THEIR HORSE, AND THEIR LOVE,	• • •	59	OISIN 3		176
I FELL ON THE PATH, AND THE HORSE WENT AWAY LIKE A SUMMER FLY;		60	OISIN 3		190
HE ROUSED HIS HORSE OUT OF ITS SLEEP,	• • • • • •	133	FR GILLIGAN		27
OLD BUTLERS WHEN YOU TOOK TO HORSE AND STOOD	• • • •	270	PARDON FATHERS	V	10
HOLLO HIM ON WITH HORSE AND HOUND,	• • • • • •	272	GREY ROCK		35
I CALL FOR SPADE AND HORSE AND HOUND,	• • • • •	275	GREY ROCK		105
UPON HIS TREMBLING HORSE, THEN DROVE THE SPUR;	• • •	277	TWO KINGS		11
HE THOUGHT TO HAVE GIVEN HIS HORSE THE SPUR, BUT SAW	• •	277	TWO KINGS	V	4B
HE SAT WITH TIGHTENED REIN AMAZED, HIS HORSE	• • • •	277	TWO KINGS	V	10
THE ENTRAILS OF THE HORSE, DROPPING HIS SWORD	• • •	278	TWO KINGS		23
THE DISEMBOWELLED HORSE. KING EOCHAID RAN	• • • •	278	TWO KINGS		45
THROUGH THE ENTRAILS OF THE HORSE. DROPPING HIS SWORD	• •	278	TWO KINGS	V	23
THE DISEMBOWELLED HORSE. KING EOCHAID GAZED,	• • •	278	TWO KINGS	V	45
AND LAY IT ALL UPON A HORSE";	• • • • • • • •	296	THREE BEGGARS		35
LIKE AN OLD HORSE IN A POUND."	• • • • • • •	333	SOLOMON SHEBA		8
AND RODE OUR WINGED HORSE;	• • • • • • • •	392	EASTER 1916		25
AND OUR WINGED METTLESOME HORSE.	• • • • • •	392	EASTER 1916	V	25
THE HORSE THAT COMES FROM THE ROAD,	• • • • • •	393	EASTER 1916		45
AND A HORSE PLASHES WITHIN IT;	• • • • • • •	393	EASTER 1916		52
GATHERED A SCORE OF HORSE AND SPENT HIS DAYS	• • • •	420	MY HOUSE		22
I KNEW THAT HORSE PLAY, KNEW IT FOR A MURDEROUS THING.	• •	442	BLACK CENTAUR	V	4
BUT ALL IS CHANGED, THAT HIGH HORSE RIDERLESS,	• • • •	492	COOLE BALLYLEE		46
BUT WHEN HIS HORSE HAD PUT ITS HOOF	• • • • • •	571	THREE BUSHES		50
A GOOD MAN ON A HORSE,	• • • • • • • • •	604	YOU CONTENT		12
AN OLD HORSE LOOKED ACROSS A FENCE,	• • • • • •	725	LEGEND		27
HORSEBACK					
ON FOOT, ON HORSEBACK OR IN BATTLE-CARS."	• • • •	107	CUCHULAIN SEA		30
HORSEMAN ERECT UPON HORSEBACK	• • • • • • • •	589	OLD WICKED MAN		52
A BEGGAR UPON HORSEBACK LASHES A BEGGAR ON FOOT.	• • •	590	GREAT DAY		2
A BEGGAR UPON HORSEBACK LASHES A BEGGAR UPON FOOT;	• •	590	GREAT DAY	V	2
HORSE-BACK					
CAMEL-BACK, HORSE-BACK, ASS-BACK, MULE-BACK,	• • • •	566	LAPIS LAZULI		26
HORSE-BOYS					
WHERE THE TIRED HORSE-BOYS LAY UPON THE RUSHES,	• • •	180	QUEEN MAEVE		13
BUT THE HORSE-BOYS SLEPT ON, AS THOUGH SOME POWER	• •	181	QUEEN MAEVE		39
HORSED SEE TWO-HORSED					
THERE IN A TWO HORSED CARRIAGE	• • • • • • • •	628	JANE MOUNTAIN	V	13
HORSEHAIR					
"EACH ONE A HORSEHAIR SHIRT HATH ON,	• • • • • • •	43	OISIN 2	V	208C
HORSE-HAIR					
STARING UPON A BEDOUIN'S HORSE-HAIR ROOF	• • • • •	368	EGO DOMINUS		29
HORSE-HOOF					
A HORSE-HOOF SLIDES ON THE BRIM,	• • • • • • •	393	EASTER 1916		51
HORSEMAN					
SOLDIER, SCHOLAR, HORSEMAN, HE,	• • • • • •	327	ROBERT GREGORY		70
SOLDIER, SCHOLAR, HORSEMAN, HE,	• • • • • •	327	ROBERT GREGORY		78
SOLDIER, SCHOLAR, HORSEMAN, HE,	• • • • • •	327	ROBERT GREGORY		86
HORSEMAN ERECT UPON HORSEBACK	• • • • • • • •	589	OLD WICKED MAN		52
HORSEMAN, PASS BY!	• • • • • • • • •	640	BEN BULBEN		94
HORSEMANSHIP					
FOR HORSEMANSHIP AT MEETS OR AT RACECOURSES,	• • • •	325	ROBERT GREGORY		35
WELL KNOWN FOR HORSEMANSHIP TO CONNACHT MEN	• • • •	325	ROBERT GREGORY	V	34

391

HORSEMANSHIP   (CONTINUED)
FOR HORSEMANSHIP AT MEETS OR AT RACE-COURSES, ... 325 ROBERT GREGORY V   35
HORSEMEN
THE HORSEMEN WITH THEIR FLOATING HAIR, ...   2 OISIN 1   7
A HUNDRED HORSEMEN ON THE BASALT FLOOR . . . .   36 OISIN 2   102
WHERETHROUGH A HUNDRED HORSEMEN ON THE FLOOR . . . . . .   36 OISIN 2   V 102
WITH HORSEMEN HURRYING NEAR AND FAR, ...   83 MAD KING GOLL V 18
AND THEN THE CLASH OF FALLEN HORSEMEN AND THE CRIES . . . 161 BLACK PIG   3
AYE, HORSEMEN FOR COMPANIONS, ... 266 GALWAY RACES   7
AND THE TALL MEN AND THE SWORDSMEN AND THE HORSEMEN, WHERE   580 CURSE CROMWELL 4
   ARE THEY?
FROM MOUNTAIN TO MOUNTAIN RIDE THE FIERCE HORSEMEN. . . . 605 SONGS BURDEN 1 9
FROM MOUNTAIN TO MOUNTAIN RIDE THE FIERCE HORSEMEN. . . . 606 SONGS BURDEN 1 18
FROM MOUNTAIN TO MOUNTAIN RIDE THE FIERCE HORSEMEN. . . . 606 SONGS BURDEN 1 27
FROM MOUNTAIN TO MOUNTAIN RIDE THE FIERCE HORSEMEN. . . . 607 SONGS BURDEN 2 9
FROM MOUNTAIN TO MOUNTAIN RIDE THE FIERCE HORSEMEN. . . . 607 SONGS BURDEN 2 18
FROM MOUNTAIN TO MOUNTAIN RIDE THE FIERCE HORSEMEN. . . . 607 SONGS BURDEN 2 27
FROM MOUNTAIN TO MOUNTAIN RIDE THE FIERCE HORSEMEN. . . . 608 SONGS BURDEN 3 9
FROM MOUNTAIN TO MOUNTAIN RIDE THE FIERCE HORSEMEN. . . . 608 SONGS BURDEN 3 18
FROM MOUNTAIN TO MOUNTAIN RIDE THE FIERCE HORSEMEN. . . . 608 SONGS BURDEN 3 27
SWEAR BY THOSE HORSEMEN, BY THOSE WOMEN . . . . 637 BEN BULBEN   5
HORSE-PLAY
I KNEW THAT HORSE-PLAY, KNEW IT FOR A MURDEROUS THING. . . 442 BLACK CENTAUR 4
HORSE'S
AN OLD MAN CAUGHT THE HORSE'S HEAD . . . . 191 BAILE AILLINN 57
RENDING THE HORSE'S FLANK. KING EOCHAID REELED, ... 277 TWO KINGS   13
RIPPED THROUGH THE HORSE'S FLANKS. KING EOCHAID REELED, . 277 TWO KINGS   V 13
ON A FANTASTIC RIDE, MY HORSE'S FLANKS ARE SPURRED . . . 391 UNDER SATURN   6
ON A FANTASTIC RIDE I SWEAR MY HORSE'S FLANKS WERE SPURRED 391 UNDER SATURN V 6
HORSES   SEE SEA-HORSES
THE FENIAN HORSES! ARMOUR TORN ASUNDER! . . . .   43 OISIN 2   210
THE HORSES OF THE FENIANS--TEARING ASUNDER. . . . . . .   43 OISIN 2   V 210
BETWEEN WOOD'S RIM AND THE HORSES OF THE SEA. . . . . . . 108 CUCHULAIN SEA 34
BETWEEN THE GAME AND THE HORSES OF THE SEA. . . . . . . 108 CUCHULAIN SEA V 34
THAT HE MAY FIGHT THE HORSES OF THE SEA." . . . . 111 CUCHULAIN SEA 81
STARED ON THE HORSES OF THE SEA, AND HEARD . . . . 111 CUCHULAIN SEA 84
TWO LOVE POEMS   THE SHADOWY HORSES . . . . 154 BELOVED PEACE V T
I HEAR THE SHADOWY HORSES, THEIR LONG MANES A-SHAKE, . . 154 BELOVED PEACE 1
THE HORSES OF DISASTER PLUNGE IN THE HEAVY CLAY! . . . . 154 BELOVED PEACE 8
THE HORSES OF DISASTER PLUNGE IN THE DESOLATE CLAY. . . . 154 BELOVED PEACE V 8
I BECAME A RUSH THAT HORSES TREAD! . . . . 177 PAST GREATNESS 6
THE RIDERS UPON THE GALLOPING HORSES, ... 266 GALWAY RACES   3
THAT RIDE UPON HORSES. . . . . 266 GALWAY RACES 16
THE RIDERS UPON THE SWIFT HORSES . . . . 266 GALWAY RACES V 3
RIDERS UPON THE SWIFT HORSES, ... 266 GALWAY RACES V 3
THE RIDERS AND THE GALLOPING HORSES, ... 266 GALWAY RACES V 3
THAT COULD HAVE SHOWN HOW PURE-BRED HORSES . . . . 325 ROBERT GREGORY 36
THAT COULD HAVE SHOWN HOW PUREBRED HORSES . . . . 325 ROBERT GREGORY V 36
ABOVE THE CLOUDY SHOULDERS OF THE HORSES! . . . . 344 DAWN   12
VIOLENCE UPON THE ROADS! VIOLENCE OF HORSES! . . . . . . 432 NINETEEN 19 113
COME PRAISE COLONUS' HORSES, AND COME PRAISE . . . . . . 446 COLONUS PRAISE 1
OF HORSES AND HORSES OF THE SEA, WHITE HORSES. . . . . . 447 COLONUS PRAISE 32
OF HORSES AND HORSES OF THE SEA, WHITE HORSES. . . . . . 447 COLONUS PRAISE 32
OF HORSES AND HORSES OF THE SEA, WHITE HORSES. . . . . . 447 COLONUS PRAISE 32
ARMOURED HORSES NEIGH . . . . 512 JANE ON GOD   9
LOVERS OF HORSES AND OF WOMEN, SHALL, ... 564 GYRES   19
AMONG THE DOGS AND HORSES THAT UNDERSTAND MY TALK. . . . 581 CURSE CROMWELL 30
HORSES'
AND YET HIS MIND OUTRAN THE HORSES' FEET. . . . . 326 ROBERT GREGORY 64
HORTON'S
HORTON'S THE FIRST I CALL. HE LOVED STRANGE THOUGHT . . 471 ALL SOUL NIGHT 21
HOSE
HE HAD KNEES THAT STUCK OUT OF HIS HOSE! . . . . 190 BAILE AILLINN 27
HOST   SEE BATTLE-HOST
ERE FALL OF EVENING, MY MAILED HOST, ...   83 MAD KING GOLL V 19
OF ALL THIS HOST SO BOUND FROM CHILDHOOD ON." . . . . . 109 CUCHULAIN SEA 56
IF MICHAEL, LEADER OF GOD'S HOST . . . . 112 ROSE OF PEACE 1
THE FAERY HOST . . . . 140 HOSTING SIDHE V T
THE HOST . . . . 140 HOSTING SIDHE V T
THE HOST IS RIDING FROM KNOCKNAREA . . . . 140 HOSTING SIDHE 1
THE HOST IS RUSHING 'TWIXT NIGHT AND DAY, ... 141 HOSTING SIDHE 13
THE HOST OF THE AIR . . . . 143 HOST OF AIR   T
FOR THESE WERE THE HOST OF THE AIR! . . . . 144 HOST OF AIR   26
THE UNAPPEASABLE HOST . . . . 146 UNAPPEAS HOST T
O HEART THE WINDS HAVE SHAKEN, THE UNAPPEASABLE HOST . . 147 UNAPPEAS HOST 11
AND HEART THE WINDS HAVE SHAKEN, THE UNAPPEASABLE HOST . 147 UNAPPEAS HOST V 11
AND HEAR THE WINDS HAVE SHAKEN, THE UNAPPEASABLE HOST . 147 UNAPPEAS HOST V 11
WITH THE LOUD HOST BEFORE THE SEA, ... 276 GREY ROCK   128
MUST DRIVE THE ARABIAN HOST. THE VOICE GREW STILL, . . 467 HARUN RASHID 145
MADE DRIVE THE ARABIAN HOST. THE VOICE GREW STILL, . . 467 HARUN RASHID V 145
BUT HE'D OBJECT TO THE HOST, ... 473 ALL SOUL NIGHT 77
HOSTED
"I ONLY OF THE RED BRANCH HOSTED NOW," . . . . 109 CUCHULAIN SEA V 55
HOSTING
THE FLOOR OF ALMHUIN'S HOSTING HALL . . . . 13 OISIN 1   156
THE FLOOR OF ALLEN'S HOSTING HALL . . . . 13 OISIN 1   V 156
THE HOSTING OF THE SIDHE . . . . 140 HOSTING SIDHE T
HE SEES THE FAIRY HOSTING MOVE . . . . 716 FAIRY DOCTOR   9
HOSTS
IF MICHAEL, LEADER OF GOD'S HOSTS . . . . 112 ROSE OF PEACE V 1

	PAGE	TITLE		LINE
AND KISSED THE SCEPTRE WITH HOT LIPS,	18	OISIN 1	V	258
WITH THE HOT BLOOD OF YOUTH, OF LOVE CROSSED LONG AGO;	316	COLD HEAVEN		6
IS HOT TO SHOW WHATEVER IT HAS FOUND,	340	SHEP GOATHERD		44
HOULIHAN				
OF CATHLEEN, THE DAUGHTER OF HOULIHAN,	207	HANRAHANS SONG		5
OF CATHLEEN, THE DAUGHTER OF HOULIHAN,	207	HANRAHANS SONG		10
IS CATHLEEN, THE DAUGHTER OF HOULIHAN,	208	HANRAHANS SONG		15
HOUND				
PASSED BY US, CHASED BY A PHANTOM HOUND	11	OISIN 1		140
PASSED BY US, CHASED OF A PHANTOM HOUND	11	OISIN 1	V	140
HIS TOOTHLESS HOUND AT HIS NERVELESS FEET,	26	OISIN 1	V	400
THE YOUTH AND LADY AND THE DEER AND HOUND;	29	OISIN 2		4
ONCE MORE--THE YOUTH AND LADY, DEER AND HOUND;	29	OISIN 2	V	2
THE DEER AND THE HOUND, AND THE LADY AND YOUTH,	3	OISIN 3	V	3
AND THEIR HOUND, AND THEIR HORSE, AND THEIR LOVE,	47	OISIN 3		176
WHO NEVER HEAR THE UNFORGIVING HOUND.	59	OISIN 3		
WHO NEVER HEARD THE UNFORGIVING HOUND.	75	ANASHU VIJAYA		75
BRING HOUND AND HUNTSMAN HERE,	75	ANASHU VIJAYA	V	75
ONE BLIND HOUND ONLY LIES APART	97	FOXHUNTER	V	10
THE BLIND HOUND WITH A MOURNFUL DIN	99	FOXHUNTER		41
THE OLDEST HOUND WITH MOURNFUL DIN	99	FOXHUNTER		45
I HAVE BEEN CHANGED TO A HOUND WITH ONE RED EAR;	99	FOXHUNTER	V	45
AND NOW MY CALLING IS BUT THE CALLING OF A HOUND;	153	CHANGE BELOVED		2
OF THE CROWNED MAGI; AND THE HOUND OF CU	153	CHANGE BELOVED		8
WHERE THE HOUND OF ULADH SAT BEFORE	169	SECRET ROSE	V	9
HOLLO HIM ON WITH HORSE AND HOUND.	192	BAILE AILLINN		73
I CALL FOR SPADE AND HORSE AND HOUND	272	GREY ROCK		35
THE HORN'S SWEET NOTE AND THE TOOTH OF THE HOUND.	275	GREY ROCK		105
THE HORN'S SWEET NOTE AND THE TOOTH OF THE HOUND.	380	SONGS FOOL 1		12
HOUND VOICE	381	SONGS FOOL 2		14
SO MANY YEARS COMPANIONED BY A HOUND,	621	HOUND VOICE		T
GIVE TONGUE, PROCLAIM THEIR HIDDEN NAME--"HOUND VOICE."	621	HOUND VOICE		4
AND YET GAVE TONGUE. "HOUND VOICES" WERE THEY ALL.	621	HOUND VOICE		7
BUT HE'S A LYING HOUND!	622	HOUND VOICE		9
A SIBYL, WITH FIERCE FACE AS OF A HOUND	636	BLACK TOWER		25
A RED HOUND RUNNING FROM A SILVER ARROW.	687	TWO TITANS		9
I HAVE FORGOTTEN WHEREFORE. THE RED HOUND	747	SHADOW WATER A		6
WERE THEY BUT LIFTED UP. THE RED HOUND IS FLED.	747	SHADOW WATER A		8
A HOUND THAT HAD LAIN IN THE RED RUSHES	761	SHADOW WATER A		266
A RED-EARED HOUND FOLLOWS A HORNLESS DEER.	761	SHADOW WATER A		278
THE PALE HOUND AND THE DEER WANDER FOR EVER	764	SHADOW WATER A		325
THE PALE HOUND AND THE DEER WANDER FOREVER	764	SHADOW WATER A		330
HOUNDS SEE DEER-HOUNDS SLEUTH-HOUNDS	764	SHADOW WATER A	V	330
WE RODE IN SORROW, WITH STRONG HOUNDS THREE,	2	OISIN 1	V	7C
WHEN WE FOLLOWED A DEER WITH OUR BAYING HOUNDS,	3	OISIN 1		14
AND THERE I WILL GIVE YOU A HUNDRED HOUNDS;	8	OISIN 1		86
THERE SHALT THOU HAVE, AND A HUNDRED HOUNDS	8	OISIN 1	V	86
I CHASED WITH HOUNDS THE FLYING DEER,	10	OISIN 1	V	121
AND HOUNDS FOR CENTURIES DUST AND AIR.	11	OISIN 1		131
AND THE CRY OF THE HOUNDS ON THE HILLS OF OLD.	27	OISIN 1		407
AND THEIR HOUNDS, AND THEIR STEEDS, AND THEIR LOVES,	59	OISIN 3	V	176
BRING RODY AND HIS HOUNDS,	97	FOXHUNTER		10
FOR LEADING AGED HOUNDS AND YOUNG	98	FOXHUNTER		23
AND NOW WITH AGED HOUNDS AND YOUNG	98	FOXHUNTER	V	21
HOUNDS ARE GAZING ON HIS FACE,	99	FOXHUNTER		39
AGED HOUNDS AND YOUNG.	99	FOXHUNTER		40
THE HOUNDS WAIL FOR THE DEAD.	99	FOXHUNTER		48
THE HOUNDS ARE GAZING ON HIS FACE,	99	FOXHUNTER	V	39
AND HOUNDS ARE GAZING ON HIS FACE,	99	FOXHUNTER	V	39
THE OLD HOUNDS AND THE YOUNG.	99	FOXHUNTER	V	40
BOTH AGED HOUNDS AND YOUNG.	99	FOXHUNTER	V	40
ARE OLD AND PUPPY HOUNDS;	99	FOXHUNTER	V	44
THE HOUNDS KEEN FOR THE DEAD.	99	FOXHUNTER	V	48
CAME UP OUT OF THE HOLE, AND RED-EARED HOUNDS	185	QUEEN MAEVE		117
SHE HAD RIDDEN WELL TO HOUNDS.	392	EASTER 1916	V	23
A PACK OF HOUNDS AND NOT A PACK OF CARDS,	411	TOWER		69
AND FIND OUR ANCIENT HOUNDS BEFORE THE DOOR,	622	HOUND VOICE		16
AND CHANTS OF VICTORY AMID THE ENCIRCLING HOUNDS.	622	HOUND VOICE		21
THAT LIVES AMONG THE WOODS OF THE DARK HOUNDS.	766	SHADOW WATER A		376
WHEN THE DARK HOUNDS WERE LOOSED. COME TO THE ALE.	766	SHADOW WATER A		379
THEY WOULD CHANGE THEM INTO HOUNDS	775	AGAINST WITCH		15
HOUR SEE MOTH-HOUR DEATH-HOUR BIRTH-HOUR				
AND TANGLED CREEPERS EVERY HOUR	16	OISIN 1		223
WHERE TANGLING CREEPERS EVERY HOUR	16	OISIN 1	V	223
AS THOUGH HIS HOUR WERE COME. WE SOUGHT THE PART	37	OISIN 2		112
AS THOUGH HIS HOUR WERE ON HIM. TO THE PART	37	OISIN 2	V	112
I WAITED HOUR BY HOUR, AND THE HIGH DOME,	39	OISIN 2		147
I WAITED HOUR BY HOUR, AND THE HIGH DOME,	39	OISIN 2		147
HOUR AFTER HOUR I WAITED, AND THE DOME	39	OISIN 2		147
HOUR AFTER HOUR I WAITED, AND THE DOME	39	OISIN 2	V	147
WITH WISDOM HOUR BY HOUR.--MAY WE TWO STAND,	39	OISIN 2	V	147
WITH WISDOM HOUR BY HOUR.--MAY WE TWO STAND,	71	ANASHU VIJAYA		7
WITH WISDOM HOUR BY HOUR.--MAY WE TOO STAND,	71	ANASHU VIJAYA		7
WITH WISDOM HOUR BY HOUR.--MAY WE TOO STAND,	71	ANASHU VIJAYA	V	7
THE HOUR WHEN KAMA, FULL OF SLEEPY LAUGHTER,	71	ANASHU VIJAYA	V	7
THE HOUR WHEN KAMA, WITH A SUMPTUOUS SMILE,	72	ANASHU VIJAYA		26
HE IS A FAMOUS FISHER; HOUR BY HOUR	72	ANASHU VIJAYA	V	26
HE IS A FAMOUS FISHER; HOUR BY HOUR	73	ANASHU VIJAYA		36
THE HOUR OF THE WANING OF LOVE HAS BESET US,	73	ANASHU VIJAYA		36
TOGETHER IN THAT HOUR OF GENTLENESS	79	FALLING LEAVES		5
	80	EPHEMERA		6

HOUR (CONTINUED)
```
      FOR MY REMEMBERING HOUR IS DONE:  . . . . . . . . .          86 MAD KING GOLL    V    69
      "HE DIED AN HOUR AGO."  . . . . . . . . . . . . .           133 FR GILLIGAN           34
      DROWNING LOVE'S LONELY HOUR IN DEEP TWILIGHT OF REST,  . .   154 BELOVED PEACE         11
      A MORE DREAM-HEAVY HOUR THAN THIS:  . . . . . . . .         156 FORGOT BEAUTY         17
      ENFOLD ME IN MY HOUR OF HOURS: WHERE THOSE  . . . . .       169 SECRET ROSE            2
      THE HOUR OF THY GREAT WIND OF LOVE AND HATE.  . . . .       170 SECRET ROSE           28
      SURELY THINE HOUR HAS COME, THY GREAT WIND BLOWS,  . .      170 SECRET ROSE           31
      WHO BUT AWAITS HIS HOUR TO SHOOT, STILL HANGS  . . . .      198 SEVEN WOODS           13
      AT THE MOTH HOUR AND HID IT IN HER BOSOM.  . . . . .        199 ARROW            V     6
      AND FROM THAT HOUR HE HAS WATCHED OVER NONE  . . . . .      220 HARP OF AENGUS        13
      TOWARDS THE HOUR FOR SPEAKING OF THE DEAD?  . . . . .       276 TWO KINGS        V     0
      THE HOUR BEFORE DAWN . . . . . . . . . . . . . .           302 HOUR DAWN              T
      IN THE BAD HOUR BEFORE THE DAWN."  . . . . . . . .         304 HOUR DAWN             55
      BUT THE HOUR WHEN YOU SHALL PASS AWAY  . . . . . . .        306 HOUR DAWN             96
      AND HAVING TALKED TO SOME LATE HOUR  . . . . . . . .        324 ROBERT GREGORY         4
      OF SUN AND MOON THAT A GOOD HOUR  . . . . . . . . .         331 ROUND TOWER           11
      IS MEMORY OR FOREKNOWLEDGE OF THE HOUR  . . . . . . .       375 PHASES OF MOON        73
      AND WHAT ROUGH BEAST, ITS HOUR COME ROUND AT LAST,  . .     402 SECOND COMING         21
      AND FOR AN HOUR I HAVE WALKED AND PRAYED  . . . . . .       403 FOR DAUGHTER           7
      I HAVE WALKED AND PRAYED FOR THIS YOUNG CHILD AN HOUR  . .  403 FOR DAUGHTER           9
      OR THAT OF THE HOUR  . . . . . . . . . . . . . . .         414 TOWER                139
      THROUGH TOO MUCH BUSINESS WITH THE PASSING HOUR,  . .       423 MY DESCENDANTS        11
      AWAIT THE HOUR OF WAR, ENTER THE SMALL,  . . . . . .        461 HARUN RASHID     V     8
      I SAY THAT A DJINN SPOKE.  A LIVELONG HOUR  . . . . .       467 HARUN RASHID         136
      I SAY THAT A DJIN SPOKE.  A LIVE LONG HOUR  . . . . .       467 HARUN RASHID     V   136
      I SAY THAT A JINN SPOKE.  A LIVE-LONG HOUR  . . . . .       467 HARUN RASHID     V   136
      SHOULD LAUGH AND WEEP AN HOUR UPON THE CLOCK.  . . . .      471 ALL SOUL NIGHT        20
      SHOULD LAUGH AND WEEP AN HOUR UPON THE CLOCK.  . . . .      474 ALL SOUL NIGHT        90
      SHOULD WEEP AND LAUGH AN HOUR UPON THE CLOCK.  . . . .      474 ALL SOUL NIGHT   V    90
      A BLIND HERMIT RINGS THE HOUR.  . . . . . . . . .          484 SYMBOLS                2
      AND SCOLD FOR AN HOUR:  . . . . . . . . . . . . .          510 JANE JUDGMENT          9
      WHEN GONG AND CONCH DECLARE THE HOUR TO BLESS  . . . .      611 STATUES               23
      WHAT HOUR OF TERROR COMES TO TEST THE SOUL.  . . . .        622 HOUND VOICE           11
      THE PREACHER WATCHING FOR THE EVIL HOUR TO PASS,  . .       686 LIFE                   3
      THE HOUR OF INCANTATION COMES A-TIPTOE,  . . . . .          691 MOSADA 1              37
      YOUNG MOORISH GIRL, THY FINAL HOUR IS HERE:  . . . .        701 MOSADA 3              63
      HAYNAU, THINE HOUR HAS COME, THY FOLLOWERS FAR  . . .       715 FERENCZ RENYI        117
      THE MAN WHOSE HOUR OF DEATH DRAWS NIGH,  . . . . . .        716 FAIRY DOCTOR           6
      "WAKEN, WAKEN, SLEEPY FISHERS: NO HOUR IS THIS FOR SLEEP," . 718 PHANTOM SHIP          7
      A FULL HOUR LONG, WHEN ROSE A FEATHER  . . . . . .          728 PRIEST FAIRY          19
      THE PREACHER WATCHING FOR THE ILL HOUR TO PASS--  . .       734 QUATRAIN APHOR         3
      THE PREACHER WATCHING FOR THE EVIL HOUR TO PASS,  . .       734 QUATRAIN APHOR   V     3
      WEIGH THEM IN AN HOUR OF DREAMING.  . . . . . . . .         737 IN FIRELIGHT          11
      THE YEARS THAT HAVE GONE OVER HER FROM THE HOUR  . . .      760 SHADOW WATER A       256
      AND FROM THAT HOUR HE HAS WATCHED OVER NONE  . . . .        763 SHADOW WATER A       308
      THAT COMES WITH LOVE, COMES MURMURING OF AN HOUR  . .       765 SHADOW WATER A       365
      "TILL THE SUN GOES DOWN AND AN HOUR OF THE CLOCK"  . . .    779 GOING THE ROAD         7
HOURED      SEE TWELVE-HOURED
HOUR-GLASS
      I'LL PLAY YOU FOR YOUR OLD HOUR-GLASS.  YOU SEE  . . . .    721 WITCH VIVIEN          36
HOURLY
      THE HOURLY KINDNESS, THE DAY'S COMMON SPEECH,  . . . .      258 KING NO KING          14
HOUR'S      SEE HALF-HOUR'S
      EVEN A HALF HOUR'S NOTHINGNESS,  . . . . . . . . .          305 HOUR DAWN        V    70
HOURS
      AND LOVE, IN THE HOURS WHEN YOUTH HAS CEASED:  . . . .        2 OISIN 1          V    7A
      I KNOW NOT IF DAYS PASSED OR HOURS,  . . . . . . . .         11 OISIN 1              133
      I KNEW NOT IF DAYS PASSED OR HOURS,  . . . . . . . .         11 OISIN 1          V   133
      AND, NOW OUR WANDERING HOURS WERE DONE,  . . . . . .         14 OISIN 1              177
      AND ALL LISTLESS HOURS FEAR US,  . . . . . . . . .           21 OISIN 1              317
      OR HOURS PASSED BY, YET HOLD THE MORNING RAYS  . . . .       30 OISIN 2               20
      FLASHING--I KNOW NOT WERE IT HOURS OR DAYS,  . . . .         30 OISIN 2          V  19B
      BUT SHE WHOSE HOURS OF TENDERNESS WERE GONE  . . . .         38 OISIN 2              138
      THAT LACKEY THE WORN MOON IN MIDNIGHT HOURS,  . . . .        41 OISIN 2          V 185A
      WERE WE DAYS LONG OR HOURS LONG IN RIDING,  . . . . .        47 OISIN 3                9
      ALL EMPTIED OF PURPLE HOURS AS A BEGGAR'S CLOAK IN THE       63 OISIN 3              219
        RAIN,
      HATE ON AND LOVE THROUGH UNREPINING HOURS.  . . . .         80 EPHEMERA              22
      ABOVE THE TIDE OF HOURS, TROUBLE THE AIR,  . . . . .        114 ROSE OF BATTLE         3
      ABOVE THE TIDE OF HOURS, RISE ON THE AIR,  . . . . .        114 ROSE OF BATTLE   V     3
      AND THE LONG DEW-DROPPING HOURS OF THE NIGHT,  . . . .      116 FAERY SONG             7
      FOR HOURS WHEN ALL MUST FADE LIKE DEW.  . . . . . .         156 FORGOT BEAUTY         20
      ENFOLD ME IN MY HOUR OF HOURS: WHERE THOSE  . . . . .       169 SECRET ROSE            2
      I SAID: "A LINE WILL TAKE US HOURS MAYBE:  . . . . .        204 ADAMS CURSE            4
      HE DREADS THE WEIGHT OF MORTAL HOURS.  . . . . . . .        212 BLESS PSALTER         11
      AND FOR A DOZEN HOURS HAVE BEEN A PART  . . . . . .         230 SHADOW WATER B       171
      HE GAVE THE HOURS THEY HAD SET FREE  . . . . . . . .        288 TO WEALTHY MAN        22
      FROM BITTEREST HOURS:  . . . . . . . . . . . . .           293 HELEN LIVED            6
      WITH PURPLE SANDALS SWEEP THE GRAVE-EYED HOURS--  . .       705 REMEMBRANCE            5
      AND NUMBER THEIR DAYS AND THEIR HOURS--  . . . . . .        707 FAIRY PEDANT          19
      TALKING HOURS SWIFTLY PASS:  . . . . . . . . . .           727 LOVERS QUARREL        44
      HOW MANY HOURS TO DAYBREAK, BECAUSE LOVE  . . . . . .       767 SHADOW WATER A       405
HOUSE       SEE FARM-HOUSE COUNTING-HOUSE GUARD-HOUSE PUBLIC-HOUSE POT-HOUSE
      IN HIS OWN LEAFY FOREST HOUSE.  . . . . . . . . .            2 OISIN 1          V    7L
      IN HIS OWN LEAFY FOREST HOUSE  . . . . . . . . . .           4 OISIN 1               37
      IN THE POPPY-HUNG HOUSE OF THE TWILIGHT FLUTED:  . . .        8 OISIN 1          V    83
      A HOUSE OF WATTLES, CLAY, AND SKIN:  . . . . . . .          17 OISIN 1              249
      A FIRWOOD HOUSE, ALL COVERED OVER  . . . . . . . .          17 OISIN 1          V   248
      IN THE HOUSE OF A CHILD, OF A FRIEND, OF A BROTHER.  . .     26 OISIN 1              401
      IN THE HOUSE OF HIS FRIEND, OF HIS KIN, OF HIS BROTHER,      26 OISIN 1              405
```

HOUSE   (CONTINUED)

	PAGE	TITLE		LINE
AND THE ROOF FALLS IN OF HIS TUNNELLED HOUSE.	27	OISIN 1	V	419
AND THE ROOF FALLS IN OF HIS TUNNELLED HOUSE.	28	OISIN 1		423
. . . NO, NEITHER IN HOUSE OF A CANN .	50	OISIN 3	V	49
AND DWELL IN THE HOUSE OF THE FENIANS, BE THEY IN FLAMES OR AT FEAST.	63	OISIN 3		224
I WILL GO TO THE HOUSE OF THE FENIANS, BE THEY IN FLAMES OR AT FEAST,	63	OISIN 3	V	223
BUT TELL ALONE YOUR NAME AND HOUSE TO HIM	108	CUCHULAIN SEA	V	36
AND HE RAN TO THE DOOR OF HIS HOUSE!	145	HOST OF AIR	V	40C
THE HOUSE WHERE I WAS SAFE AND WARM!	151	HEART OF WOMAN		6
AND HIM WHO SOLD TILLAGE, AND HOUSE, AND GOODS,	170	SECRET ROSE		22
IN HER HIGH HOUSE AT CRUACHAN! THE LONG HEARTH,	180	QUEEN MAEVE		11
HAD FILLED THE HOUSE WITH DRUID HEAVINESS!	181	QUEEN MAEVE		40
WE SHADOWS, WHILE THEY UPROOT HIS EARTHY HOUSE,	184	QUEEN MAEVE		94
WE SHADOWS, WHILE THEY UPROOT THE EARTHY HOUSE	184	QUEEN MAEVE	V	94
CAME TO THE THRESHOLD OF THE PAINTED HOUSE	185	QUEEN MAEVE		108
WAS CARRIED TO THE GOODLY HOUSE	192	BAILE AILLINN		72
OR THE DOOR-PILLARS OF ONE HOUSE,	195	BAILE AILLINN		152
OR THE DOOR PILLARS OF ONE HOUSE,	195	BAILE AILLINN	V	152
HE CARRIED EDAIN OFF FROM A KING'S HOUSE,	224	SHADOW WATER B		48
OR FUMBLING IN A DREAM ABOUT THE HOUSE?	230	SHADOW WATER B		174
UPON A HOUSE SHAKEN BY THE LAND AGITATION	264	HOUSE SHAKEN		T
TO A CERTAIN COUNTRY HOUSE IN TIME OF CHANGE	264	HOUSE SHAKEN	V	T
UPON A THREATENED HOUSE	264	HOUSE SHAKEN	V	T
HOW SHOULD THE WORLD BE LUCKIER IF THIS HOUSE,	264	HOUSE SHAKEN		T
IN THEIR GREAT HOUSE AT SLIEVENAMON.	271	GREY ROCK		15
HE RAN TOWARDS THE HOUSE HIS FATHERS BUILT	279	TWO KINGS	V	45E
THE FIGHTING-MEN AND SERVANTS OF THIS HOUSE,	280	TWO KINGS		70
THE FIGHTING MEN AND SERVANTS OF THIS HOUSE,	280	TWO KINGS	V	70
TO AN OLD EMPTY WOODMAN'S HOUSE THAT'S HIDDEN	282	TWO KINGS		134
FOUND THAT OLD HOUSE, A SPUTTERING TORCH WITHIN,	283	TWO KINGS		140
AND FOUND THE HOUSE, A SPUTTERING TORCH WITHIN,	283	TWO KINGS	V	140
OF THEIR RETURN TO THAT ANCESTRAL HOUSE.	286	TWO KINGS	V	218C
"AND GET A COMFORTABLE WIFE AND HOUSE	299	BEGGAR CRIED		5
AND NOT A HOUSE TO THE PLAIN'S EDGE,	302	HOUR DAWN		10
A DOLL IN THE DOLL-MAKER'S HOUSE	319	DOLLS		1
NOW THAT WE'RE ALMOST SETTLED IN OUR HOUSE	323	ROBERT GREGORY		1
NOW THAT WE'VE ALMOST SETTLED IN OUR HOUSE	323	ROBERT GREGORY	V	1
IN ALL LOVELY INTRICACIES OF A HOUSE .	327	ROBERT GREGORY		74
SHE GOES ABOUT HER HOUSE ERECT AND CALM	340	SHEP GOATHERD		35
BUT LEFT THE HOUSE AS IN HIS FATHER'S TIME .	341	SHEP GOATHERD		53
I HAVE GONE ABOUT THE HOUSE, GONE UP AND DOWN	350	HER PRAISE		2
WILL COME FROM THE HOUSE, AND SAY—	364	END OF DAY		6
A PRAYER ON GOING INTO MY HOUSE	371	ON GOING HOUSE		T
OR, THE HOUSE DOOR LEFT UNSHUT,	380	SONGS FOOL 1		10
IN CORMAC'S RUINED HOUSE.	384	VISION ROBART		68
AND MAY HER BRIDEGROOM BRING HER TO A HOUSE	405	FOR DAUGHTER		73
AND MAY HER BRIDE-GROOM BRING HER TO A HOUSE	405	FOR DAUGHTER	V	73
ON THE FOUNDATIONS OF A HOUSE, OR WHERE	409	TOWER		18
AN ANCIENT BANKRUPT MASTER OF THIS HOUSE.	412	TOWER		80
AND MAYBE THE GREAT-GRANDSON OF THAT HOUSE,	418	ANCEST HOUSES		23
MY HOUSE .	419	MY HOUSE		T
WHEN IT WAS FORGED. IN SATO'S HOUSE,	421	MY TABLE		9
FOR AN OLD NEIGHBOUR'S FRIENDSHIP CHOSE THE HOUSE	423	MY DESCENDANTS		21
COME BUILD IN THE EMPTY HOUSE OF THE STARE.	424	STARES NEST		5
A MAN IS KILLED, OR A HOUSE BURNED,	425	STARES NEST		8
COME BUILD IN THE EMPTY HOUSE OF THE STARE.	425	STARES NEST		10
COME BUILD IN THE EMPTY HOUSE OF THE STARE.	425	STARES NEST		15
COME BUILD IN THE EMPTY HOUSE OF THE STARE.	425	STARES NEST		20
THROUGH THE GREAT GALLERY OF THE TREASURE HOUSE	461	HARUN RASHID		5
"I HAVE BROUGHT A SLENDER BRIDE INTO THE HOUSE!	463	HARUN RASHID		49
PERCHED IN SOME WINDOW OF HER MOTHER'S HOUSE	466	HARUN RASHID		106
AND SWEPT THE HOUSE AND SANG ABOUT HER WORK	468	HARUN RASHID		148
WALKED THROUGH THE HOUSE. UNNOTICED AND UNFELT	468	HARUN RASHID		153
AND ONCE AGAIN SHE ROSE AND SWEPT THE HOUSE	468	HARUN RASHID		159
IMMENSE MIRACULOUS HOUSE .	472	ALL SOUL NIGHT		38
IN GRATTAN'S HOUSE. MY GREAT-GRANDFATHER SHARED	486	SEVEN SAGES		2
UPON AN AGED WOMAN AND HER HOUSE,	488	COOLE PARK 29		2
BEFORE THEIR EYES A HOUSE	512	JANE ON GOD		13
SWEETENS THE LITTLE HALF-WAY HOUSE	567	LAPIS LAZULI		48
SWEETEN THE LITTLE HALFWAY HOUSE	567	LAPIS LAZULI	V	48
IF STRANGE MEN COME FROM THE HOUSE	568	SWEET DANCER		8
MIDNIGHT, AN OLD HOUSE	575	ACRE OF GRASS		5
A SMALL OLD HOUSE, WIFE, DAUGHTER, SON,	577	WHAT THEN		12
NOTHING BUT CROMWELL'S HOUSE AND CROMWELL'S MURDEROUS CREW,	580	CURSE CROMWELL		2
I CAME ON A GREAT HOUSE IN THE MIDDLE OF THE NIGHT,	581	CURSE CROMWELL		25
AND THERE'S NO LUCK ABOUT A HOUSE .	584	GHOST ROG CASE		27
NOW I AM IN THE PUBLIC HOUSE AND LEAN UPON THE WALL,	593	PILGRIM	V	21
A SMALL FORGOTTEN HOUSE THAT'S SET	606	SONGS BURDEN 2		3
WENT TO THE SACRED HOUSE AND STOOD BETWEEN	609	IN TARAS HALLS		11
SUMMONED THE GENERATIONS OF HIS HOUSE,	609	IN TARAS HALLS		19
THAT WHEREBY A HOUSE LAY WRECKED?	632	MAN AND ECHO		16
THAT WHEREBY A HOUSE WAS WRECKED?	632	MAN AND ECHO	V	16
EVEN FROM BOYHOOD, IN MY FATHER'S HOUSE,	683	SEEKER		48
IN HIS OWN HOUSE OR 'MONG THE MERCHANTS GREY,	693	MOSADA 1		87
RINGED ROUND AND FONDLED, A BROWN FARM HOUSE SEES.	710	FERENCZ RENYI	V	23
TO HIS OWN HOUSE DID HIM BETAKE.	725	LEGEND		30
AT THE HOUSE OF WEARY MEN	727	LOVERS QUARREL		51
AND CAME AND DWELT IN HIS OWN HOUSE,	742	EARL PAUL		67
GIVE ME A HUNDRED SHEEP. GIVE ME A HOUSE	758	SHADOW WATER A		220

	PAGE	TITLE	LINE

HOUSE (CONTINUED)
  AND ONE IN THE OLD GRAY HOUSE . . . . 771 SPINNING SONG 4
  ONE LIVES IN THE HOUSE OF THE SUN, ... 771 SPINNING SONG 6
  AND ONE IN THE HOUSE OF THE MOON, ... 771 SPINNING SONG 7
  I HAVE SPUN IN THE HOUSE THIS NIGHT! . . . . 771 SPINNING SONG 13
  RUIN ON A GREAT KING'S HOUSE . . . . 775 AGAINST WITCH 3
  TO THE COMFORTABLE DOOR OF HIS HOUSE. . . . . 780 WELL AND TREE 6
  I HAVE MET IN A MAN'S HOUSE . . . . 785 YOUR HEART 3
  A HOUSE, A SWORD, A SHIP, A MASK. . . . . . . 788 BRAVEST ASK 2

HOUSEHOLD
  THEN MUSE THEY ON THE HOUSEHOLD WOOL INTENT, . . 32 OISIN 2 V 55
  . . . NO, NEITHER IN HOUSEHOLD OF CAN, ... 50 OISIN 3 V 49
  AND TELL OF YOUR GOODLY HOUSEHOLD AND THE GOODLY WORKS 51 OISIN 3 62
    OF YOUR HANDS,
  TO MAEVE AND TO MAEVE'S HOUSEHOLD, OWING ALL . . 187 QUEEN MAEVE 147
  I BADE HIM GO WHEN ALL HIS HOUSEHOLD SLEPT . . 282 TWO KINGS 133
  THE WOMEN OF HIS HOUSEHOLD WERE ASLEEP . . . . 282 TWO KINGS V 133
  OF THE HOUSEHOLD SPIES! . . . . 536 PARTING 3
  BUT IN THAT WOMAN, IN THAT HOUSEHOLD WHERE . . . 603 GALLERY REVIS 34

HOUSES
  AND THE GAUNT HOUSES PUT ON MAJESTY! . . . . . 292 TO A SHADE 7
  EIGHTEENTH-CENTURY HOUSES. . . . . 392 EASTER 1916 4
  ANCESTRAL HOUSES . . . . 417 ANCEST HOUSES T
  ANCESTRAL HOUSES . . . . 417 ANCEST HOUSES V T
  MEDITATIONS IN TIME OF CIVIL WAR ANCESTRAL HOUSES . 626 STATES HOLIDAY 1
  I LIVED AMONG GREAT HOUSES, ... 718 PHANTOM SHIP 5
  SCARCE THE OLD AND WIZEN HOUSES HAD THEIR DOORS AND WINDOWS
    SHUT.
  SCARCE THE OLD AND WIZENED HOUSES HAD THEIR DOORS 718 PHANTOM SHIP V 5
    AND WINDOWS SHUT.

HOVER
  DESOLATE WINDS THAT HOVER IN THE FLAMING WEST! . . 147 UNAPPEAS HOST 8
  THAT SAW YOUNG NIAMH HOVER WITH LOVE-LORN FACE . 162 ASKS FORGIVE 13
  THEY HOVER OVER THE MASTHEAD AWHILE . . . . . 233 SHADOW WATER B 246
  TWO HOVER THERE TOGETHER, AND ONE SAYS, ... 753 SHADOW WATER A 142

HOVERING
  AMID THE HOVERING, PITEOUS, PENITENTIAL THRONG." . 173 SPEAKS HEARERS 8
  WERE HOVERING OVER THE HARP-STRINGS . . . . . 195 BAILE AILLINN 141
  WERE HOVERING OVER THE HARP STRINGS . . . . . 195 BAILE AILLINN V 141
  AND ALL THEIR HELMS OF SILVER HOVERING SIDE BY SIDE, . 318 MAGI 5
  HOVERING OVER THE WOOD . . . . 349 HAWK 10
  OF THE HOVERING THING NIGHT BROUGHT ME. . . . . 390 IMAGE PAST 42
  A RUSH, A SUDDEN WHEEL, AND HOVERING STILL . . . 441 LEDA AND SWAN V 1

HOVERS
  HE HOVERS ABOVE THE MAST AND WAITS HIS KIND! . . 753 SHADOW WATER A 135

HOWEVER
  HOWEVER THEY MAY TAKE IT, ... 520 HIS BARGAIN 7

HOWL
  BETWEEN THEM A GATEWAY OF BRASS, AND THE HOWL OF THE ANGELS 61 OISIN 3 200
    WHO FELL.
  AND EVERY WINDY QUARTER HOWL . . . . 405 FOR DAUGHTER 71

HOWLED
  HOWLED, MIAU-D, BARKED, BRAYED, BELLED, YELLED, CRIED, 387 SOLOMON WITCH 8
    CROWED,
  TO WHERE THE DAMNED HAVE HOWLED AWAY THEIR HEARTS, . . 474 ALL SOUL NIGHT 95
  BUT I WOKE IN AN OLD RUIN THAT THE WINDS HOWLED THROUGH! 581 CURSE CROMWELL 28

HOWLING
  ONCE MORE THE STORM IS HOWLING, AND HALF HID . . . 403 FOR DAUGHTER 1

HOWLS
  ARE THE MOB THAT HOWLS AT THE DOOR! . . . . . 554 CHURCH STATE 10

HOWTH
  THE BLINDS DRAWN UP"! MAUD GONNE AT HOWTH STATION WAITING 578 LOFTY THINGS 10
    A TRAIN,

HUCKSTER'S
  THAT HAS NOT PASSED THROUGH ANY HUCKSTER'S LOIN, ... 269 PARDON FATHERS 8

HUDDLE
  THEY HUDDLE FROM MAN'S PONDERING MIND, ... 138 TO IRELAND V 26

HUDDLING
  AND YONDER HUDDLING BLACKNESS DRAWETH NIGH— . . . . 663 ISLE STAT II 2 15

HUDDON
  "HUDDON AND DUDDON AND DANIEL O'LEARY, ... 529 TOM LUNATIC 7
  HUDDON, DUDDON AND DANIEL O'LEARY . . . . . . 787 HUDDON DUDDON 1
  HUDDON, DUDDON AND DANIEL O'LEARY . . . . . . 787 HUDDON DUDDON 6
  HUDDON, DUDDON AND DANIEL O'LEARY . . . . . . 787 HUDDON DUDDON 11

HUEGEL
  VON HUEGEL . . . . 499 VACILLATION V T
  MUST WE PART, VON HUEGEL, THOUGH MUCH ALIKE, FOR WE . . 503 VACILLATION 78
  SO GET YOU GONE, VON HUEGEL, THOUGH WITH BLESSINGS ON YOUR 503 VACILLATION 89
    HEAD.

HUES
  DREAMING OF HER OWN MELTING HUES, ... 13 OISIN 1 162
  AND DREAMS OF HER OWN MELTING HUES, ... 13 OISIN 1 V 162

HUGE
  HUGE FORMS OF STONE! BETWEEN THE LIDS OF ONE . . . 31 OISIN 2 V 37
  SAID NIAM. "AY, AND HUGE, WHEN YE HAVE LED . . . 35 OISIN 2 V 89
  BREWED BY THE SEA-GODS, FROM HUGE CUPS THAT LAY . . 41 OISIN 2 189
  BREWED OF THE SEA-GODS, FROM HUGE CUPS THAT LAY . . 41 OISIN 2 V 189
  BREWED BY THE SEA GODS, FROM HUGE CUPS THAT LAY . . 41 OISIN 2 V 189
  AND EACH OF THE HUGE WHITE CREATURES WAS HUGER THAN 49 OISIN 3 33
    FOURSCORE MEN!
  AND EACH OF THE HUGE WHITE CREATURES WAS HUGER THAN 49 OISIN 3 V 33
    FOUR-SCORE MEN!

		PAGE	TITLE		LINE
HUGE (CONTINUED)					
AND THE CHIEF OF THE HUGE WHITE CREATURES, ...		50	OISIN 3		43
AND BEFORE I WENT BY THEM SO HUGE AND SO SPEEDY WITH EYES SO BRIGHT,		59	OISIN 3	V	169
THEY COME WHERE SOME HUGE WATCHER IS, ...		196	BAILE AILLINN		168
WOULD RISE OF A SUDDEN, OR A WAVE SO HUGE		236	SHADOW WATER B		310
HUGER					
AND EACH OF THE HUGE WHITE CREATURES WAS HUGER THAN FOURSCORE MEN;		49	OISIN 3		33
AND EACH OF THE HUGE WHITE CREATURES WAS HUGER THAN FOUR-SCORE MEN;		49	OISIN 3	V	33
HUGH					
AND BECAUSE I WENT BY THEM SO HUGH AND SO SPEEDY WITH EYES SO BRIGHT,		59	OISIN 3		169
IMPETUOUS MEN, SHAWE-TAYLOR AND HUGH LANE, ...		489	COOLE PARK 29		14
HUGH LANE, "ONLIE BEGETTER" OF ALL THESE;		602	GALLERY REVIS		22
HUGS					
WHAT WOMAN HUGS HER INFANT THERE?		625	NATIVITY		1
HUGS AND PETS AND PATS YON NEWT, ...		727	LOVERS QUARREL		27
HULL					
CEASE THE SAILS THEIR FLAPPING UPROAR, AND THE HULL NO LONGER ROLLS.		719	PHANTOM SHIP		18
CEASE THE SAILS, THEIR FLAPPING UPROAR TO THE HULL NO LONGER ROLLS.		719	PHANTOM SHIP	V	18
HUM					
HUM IN THE LIME-TREE FLOWERS; AND PUT AWAY		198	SEVEN WOODS		3
HUM IN THE LIME TREE FLOWERS; AND PUT AWAY		198	SEVEN WOODS	V	3
HUMAN SEE SUPER-HUMAN					
BUT WE RODE OUT FROM THE HUMAN LANDS.		10	OISIN 1		114
THE FENIANS ON THE HUMAN GROUND		10	OISIN 1	V	114C
MY HUMAN SORROW HER WHITE ARMS WOUND.		11	OISIN 1		138
MY HUMAN SADNESS FAY ARMS WOUND.		11	OISIN 1	V	138
BUT WHEN I SANG OF HUMAN JOY , ...		17	OISIN 1		234
THAN THIS STRANGE HUMAN BARD," HE CRIED;		17	OISIN 1		239
AND WHEN I SANG OF HUMAN JOY		17	OISIN 1	V	234
THAT HIDES US FROM ALL HUMAN SPYING, ...		22	OISIN 1	V	338A
THE HUMAN SADNESS DAWNS ONCE MORE;"		25	OISIN 1	V	381
ON THE OLD SORROWS OF HIS HUMAN DAYS.		29	OISIN 2	V	12
IT BRINGS NO SHAME UPON A HUMAN HEAD		35	OISIN 2	V	90A
AND DEAD IS ALL THEIR HUMAN TRUTH.		66	HAPPY SHEPHERD		34
COME AWAY, O HUMAN CHILD!		87	STOLEN CHILD		9
COME AWAY, O HUMAN CHILD!		87	STOLEN CHILD		24
COME AWAY, O HUMAN CHILD!		88	STOLEN CHILD		38
FOR HE COMES, THE HUMAN CHILD, ...		88	STOLEN CHILD		50
COME, O HUMAN CHILD!		88	STOLEN CHILD	V	38
THERE WAS NO HUMAN KEENING;		93	FATHER OHART		29
AND NOW AT LAST YOU WEAR A HUMAN SHAPE.		102	FERGUS DRUID		6
AND NOW AT LAST YOU TAKE ON HUMAN SHAPE--		102	FERGUS DRUID	V	6
AT HUMAN TYRANNY.		131	OLD PENSIONER		10
FROM HUMAN THOUGHT, AS HARES AND MICE AND CONEYS . . .		218	WOODS OF COOLE		31
WITH HUMAN VOICES. O I CAN HEAR THEM NOW.		247	SHADOW WATER B		522
THIS HUMAN LIFE BLOTTED FROM MEMORY, ...		285	TWO KINGS		198
FOR THERE'S NO HUMAN LIFE AT THE FULL OR THE DARK. . . .		373	PHASES OF MOON		35
NOR ANY HUMAN SIGHT WITHIN IT		389	SOLOMON WITCH		41
WITH HUMAN LOVE.		436	FOR MY SON		32
HUMAN DIGNITY		452	HUMAN DIGNITY		T
FROM HUMAN DIGNITY.		452	HUMAN DIGNITY		12
MAKE HUMAN INTERCOURSE GROW LESS AND LESS;		473	ALL SOUL NIGHT		75
SERVED HUMAN LIBERTY.		493	SWIFTS EPITAPH		6
THE FURY AND THE MIRE OF HUMAN VEINS.		497	BYZANTIUM		8
IT IS OF GOD AND PASSES HUMAN WIT.		558	RIBH CHRISTIAN		2
THEY SAY IT IS MORE HUMAN		599	STONE CROSS		19
"FORGETTING HUMAN WORDS," A GRAVE DEEP FACE.		603	GALLERY REVIS		49
HUMAN, SUPERHUMAN, A BIRD'S ROUND EYE, ...		618	BRONZE HEAD		2
HUMAN, SUPER-HUMAN, A BIRD'S ROUND EYE, ...		618	BRONZE HEAD	V	2
THEY SANG, BUT HAD NOR HUMAN TUNES NOR WORDS, ...		635	CUCHULAIN COMF		23
BACK IN THE HUMAN MIND AGAIN.		637	BEN BULBEN		24
OF HUMAN SORROW LET THEM MORALIZE;		663	ISLE STAT II 2		31
UNTOUCHED OF HUMAN JOY OR HUMAN LOVE?		684	SEEKER		65
UNTOUCHED OF HUMAN JOY OR HUMAN LOVE?		684	SEEKER		65
THE WRINKLED SQUANDERER OF HUMAN WEALTH.		720	WITCH VIVIEN		16
HIS TOO HUMAN BREAST.		786	YOUR HEART		21
HUMBLER					
OR THE HUMBLER WORM, I CLIMBED BEN BULBEN'S BACK		409	TOWER		9
HUMBLY					
THAT ALL MEN EVERMORE MAY HUMBLY BOW		688	TWO TITANS		49
BENDING HUMBLY EVERY KNEE, ...		726	LOVERS QUARREL		14
HUMID					
I PASSED ALONG THE WATER'S EDGE BELOW THE HUMID TREES, . .		76	INDIAN ON GOD		1
HUMILITY					
FOUND PRIDE ESTABLISHED IN HUMILITY, ...		489	COOLE PARK 29		15
OF ALL THAT PRIDE AND THAT HUMILITY?		602	GALLERY REVIS		29
HUMMING					
GO GATHER BY THE HUMMING SEA		66	HAPPY SHEPHERD		35
AND HUMMING SANDS, WHERE WINDY SURGES WEND;		68	SAD SHEPHERD		4
HUMMING-SEA					
GO GATHER BY THE HUMMING-SEA		66	HAPPY SHEPHERD	V	35
HUMOROUS					
"AND CANNOT HAVE A HUMOROUS HAPPY SPEECH."		300	BEGGAR CRIED		16
A HUMOROUS, UNAMBITIOUS MAN, ...		361	ALF POLLEXFEN		25

	PAGE	TITLE		LINE

HUMP
UNDER THIS HUMP. GOD TRIES EACH MAN . . . . 379 SAINT HUNCH   5

HUNCH
THE HERON'S HUNCH UPON HIS BACK, ... 508 JANE BISHOP   19

HUNCHBACK
HUNCHBACK AND SAINT AND FOOL ARE THE LAST CRESCENTS. . . 377 PHASES OF MOON   118
"HUNCHBACK AND SAINT AND FOOL," AND THAT THEY CAME . . . 377 PHASES OF MOON   132
THE SAINT AND THE HUNCHBACK . . . . 379 SAINT HUNCH   T

HUNDRED
AND THERE I WILL GIVE YOU A HUNDRED HOUNDS! . . . . . .   8 OISIN 1   86
AND A HUNDRED ROBES OF MURMURING SILK, ...   8 OISIN 1   88
AND A HUNDRED CALVES AND A HUNDRED SHEEP . . . .   8 OISIN 1   89
AND A HUNDRED CALVES AND A HUNDRED SHEEP . . . .   8 OISIN 1   89
AND A HUNDRED SPEARS AND A HUNDRED BOWS, ...   8 OISIN 1   91
AND A HUNDRED SPEARS AND A HUNDRED BOWS, ...   8 OISIN 1   91
WHILE A HUNDRED YOUTHS, MIGHTY OF LIMB, ...   8 OISIN 1   94
AND A HUNDRED STEEDS, TUMULTUOUS-FOOTED, ...   8 OISIN 1   V 85A
THERE SHALT THOU HAVE, AND A HUNDRED HOUNDS . . . . .   8 OISIN 1   V 86
AND A HUNDRED ROBES OF THE SOFTEST SILK, ...   8 OISIN 1   V 88
AND A HUNDRED SWORDS AND A HUNDRED BOWS! . . . . . .   8 OISIN 1   V 91
AND A HUNDRED SWORDS AND A HUNDRED BOWS! . . . . . .   8 OISIN 1   V 91
AND A HUNDRED MAIDENS WISE AND YOUNG, ...   8 OISIN 1   V 94
AND A HUNDRED LADIES, MERRY AS BIRDS, ...   9 OISIN 1   96
AND A HUNDRED MAIDENS, MERRY AS BIRDS, ...   9 OISIN 1   V 96
AND A HUNDRED YOUTHS, WHOSE LIMBS ARE STRUNG . . . .   9 OISIN 1   97
O PATRICK! FOR A HUNDRED YEARS . . . .   23 OISIN 1   343
O PATRICK! FOR A HUNDRED YEARS . . . .   23 OISIN 1   346
O PATRICK! FOR A HUNDRED YEARS . . . .   23 OISIN 1   351
O PATRICK! FOR A HUNDRED YEARS . . . .   23 OISIN 1   356
A HUNDRED YEARS I CHASED THE BOAR, ...   23 OISIN 1   V 344
OH, PATRICK, THERE A HUNDRED SEASONS . . . .   23 OISIN 1   V 345B
AND TWICE A HUNDRED WERE THE VASSALS . . . .   23 OISIN 1   V 345E
OH, PATRICK, THERE A HUNDRED YEARS, ...   23 OISIN 1   V 346
WITH ME IN HER WHITE ARMS A HUNDRED YEARS . . . . .   30 OISIN 2   17
A HUNDRED SEASONS! FOR A SOUND OF TEARS . . . . . .   30 OISIN 2   V 18
THAT OLD, SEA-WEEDY, SQUARED, THREE HUNDRED FEET . . .   31 OISIN 2   V 30C
A HUNDRED HORSEMEN ON THE BASALT FLOOR . . . . . .   36 OISIN 2   102
WHERETHROUGH A HUNDRED HORSEMEN ON THE FLOOR . . . .   36 OISIN 2   V 102
HIS NEW-HEALED SHAPE! AND FOR A HUNDRED YEARS . . . .   44 OISIN 2   221
AN ENDLESS WAR. THE HUNDRED YEARS HAD CEASED! . . .   44 OISIN 2   224
HIS HEALED SHAPE! AND FOR A HUNDRED YEARS . . . . .   44 OISIN 2   221
HIS NEW HEALED SHAPE! AND FOR A HUNDRED YEARS . . .   44 OISIN 2   V 221
AND MY YEARS THREE HUNDRED FELL ON ME, ...   60 OISIN 3   191
THAT MOANS AND SIGHS A HUNDRED DAYS! . . . .   78 INDIAN TO LOVE   17
AND TILL A HUNDRED MORNS HAD FLOWERED RED . . . . . 170 SECRET ROSE   17
WHERE MANY HUNDRED SQUIRRELS ARE AS HAPPY . . . . . 217 WOODS OF COOLE   5
NO, NOR WITH A HUNDRED MEN LIKE YOU . . . . 225 SHADOW WATER B V 74
IF THERE BE HALF A HUNDRED MORE, WHAT MATTER? . . . . 245 SHADOW WATER B   476
I'D PROMISED HIM TWO HUNDRED YEARS, ... 275 GREY ROCK   98
FROM NINETEEN HUNDRED NINE OR TEN, PAVLOVA'S HAD THE CRY, 354 HIS PHOENIX   11
THREE HUNDRED YEARS BEFORE THE FALL, ... 388 SOLOMON WITCH   11
SCARED BY THE SPLASHING OF A HUNDRED COWS. . . . . . 419 MY HOUSE   V 10
IT LAY FIVE HUNDRED YEARS. . . . . 421 MY TABLE   11
NINETEEN HUNDRED AND NINETEEN . . . . 428 NINETEEN 19   T
FIVE HUNDRED YEARS AGO, ABOUT IT LIE . . . . 478 SELF AND SOUL   26
UPON A HUNDRED THOUSAND STAGES, ... 566 LAPIS LAZULI   23
HE BADE, HIS HUNDRED AND FIRST YEAR AT END, ... 609 IN TARAS HALLS   T
HAD HOOTED FOR AN HUNDRED YEARS, ... 670 ISLE STAT II 3   116
AND TO GIVE YOU BESIDES A HUNDRED SHIELDS, ... 756 SHADOW WATER A   185
A HUNDRED SWORDS, A HUNDRED DRINKING-BOWLS, ... 756 SHADOW WATER A   186
A HUNDRED SWORDS, A HUNDRED DRINKING-BOWLS, ... 756 SHADOW WATER A   186
BY SUN AND MOON AND A HUNDRED GODS AS WELL, ... 756 SHADOW WATER A   189
I PROMISE YOU A HUNDRED DRINKING BOWLS, ... 756 SHADOW WATER A V 187
A HUNDRED SHIELDS OF BRASS, A HUNDRED SWORDS, ... 756 SHADOW WATER A V 188
A HUNDRED SHIELDS OF BRASS, A HUNDRED SWORDS, ... 756 SHADOW WATER A V 188
A HUNDRED OXEN AND A HUNDRED SHEEP, ... 756 SHADOW WATER A V 189
A HUNDRED OXEN AND A HUNDRED SHEEP, ... 756 SHADOW WATER A V 189
GIVE ME A HUNDRED SHEEP. GIVE ME A HOUSE . . . . . 758 SHADOW WATER A   220

HUNDREDS
WHEN WE ARE HIGH AND AIRY HUNDREDS SAY . . . . . . 265 ABBEY THEATRE   2
WHILE THOSE SAME HUNDREDS MOCK ANOTHER DAY . . . . . 265 ABBEY THEATRE   4
WHEN HUNDREDS STOOD ABOUT TO SEE . . . . 740 EARL PAUL   27

HUNDREDTH
CHAINED WAS SHE. ON THEIR WINGS THE HUNDREDTH YEAR . .   34 OISIN 2   V 76
AN ENDLESS WAR. THE HUNDREDTH YEAR HAD CEASED. . . .   44 OISIN 2   V 224
GIDDY WITH HIS HUNDREDTH YEAR, ... 298 THREE HERMITS   6
GIDDY WITH HIS HUNDREDTH YEAR, ... 299 THREE HERMITS   31
MY HUNDREDTH YEAR IS AT AN END. I THINK . . . . . 609 IN TARAS HALLS   3

HUNDRED-THROATED
HUNDRED-THROATED MORN IS SINGING, ... 647 ISLE STAT I 1   70

HUNDRED-YEAR-OLD
A HUNDRED-YEAR-OLD MEMORY TO THE POOR! . . . . . . 269 PARDON FATHERS   6

HUNG   SEE POPPY-HUNG
THE MIST-DROPS HUNG ON THE FRAGRANT TREES, ...   2 OISIN 1   V 7F
AND IN THE BLOSSOMS HUNG THE BEES. . . . .   2 OISIN 1   V 7G
HUNG, LIKE METEORS OF RED LIGHT, ...   21 OISIN 1   V 306
HUNG FROM THE MORNING STAR! WHEN THESE MILD WORDS . .   32 OISIN 2   49
SHOUTED, AND HAILED HIM! HE HUNG THERE A STAR, . . .   36 OISIN 2   107
SHOUTED AND HAILED HIM. STILL HE HUNG CONTENT, . . .   36 OISIN 2   V 107
THAT WOMAN FOUND 'A RING HUNG ON THE WALL, ...   37 OISIN 2   120
THAT MAIDEN FOUND A RING HUNG ON THE WALL, ...   37 OISIN 2   V 120

398

		PAGE	TITLE		LINE

HUNG (CONTINUED)
HUNG IN THE PASSIONATE DAWN. HE SLOWLY TURNED! . . . .   40 OISIN 2   167
HUNG THE FRAIL LOFTIER CLOUDLETS. TURNED HE SLOW-- . . .   40 OISIN 2   V 167
AND HUNG WITH SLIME, AND WHISPERING IN HIS HAIR, ...   43 OISIN 2   216
HUNG ROUND WITH SLIME, AND WHISPERING IN HIS HAIR, . . .   43 OISIN 2   V 216
. . . HUNG LOW ON THE RIM OF THE SKY, ...   122 WHITE BIRDS   3
. . . HUNG LOW IN THE FALL OF THE DEW. . . . . . .   122 WHITE BIRDS   7
HIS HEART HUNG ALL UPON A SILKEN DRESS, ...   126 DREAM OF FAERY   2
THERE WAS A GREEN BRANCH HUNG WITH MANY A BELL . . . .   129 BOOK STORIES   1
I HAVE BEEN A HAZEL-TREE, AND THEY HUNG . . . . .   177 PAST GREATNESS   3
I HAVE BEEN A HAZEL TREE, AND THEY HUNG . . . .   177 PAST GREATNESS V 3
THE HONEY PALE MOON HUNG LOW ON THE SLEEPY HILL, . . .   203 WITHER BOUGHS   V 5
OR ULADH WHEN NAISI HAD HUNG A SAIL UPON THE WIND! . .   209 UNDER THE MOON V 4
OF THE HUNTER'S MOON, THAT HUNG BETWEEN THE NIGHT AND THE   210 UNDER THE MOON   18
  DAY,
OF THE THIRD MOON, THAT HUNG BETWEEN THE NIGHT AND THE DAY,   210 UNDER THE MOON V 18
OF OLD STRINGED INSTRUMENTS, HUNG THERE . . . . . .   271 GREY ROCK   V 20
OF FIDDLES AND OF FLUTES HUNG THERE . . . .   271 GREY ROCK   V 20
A DIAGRAM HUNG THERE INSTEAD, ...   485 STATISTICS   3
WHERE THE GAUDY MOON IS HUNG. . . . .   502 VACILLATION   69
LOW, LONG AND MUSICAL. A DEW-DROP HUNG . . . . . .   689 NETTLESHIP   9
HUNG ON HIS DOUBLET--DEAR AND MOURNFUL CHILD, ...   691 MOSADA 1   35
HEARD YOU? YOUR LUTE HUNG IN THE WINDOW SOUNDED! . . .   694 MOSADA 1   95
HE TURNS WHERE, HUNG LIKE DROPS OF DRIPPING GOLD, . . .   710 FERENCZ RENYI   18
HE TURNS WHERE, HUNG LIKE DROPS OF LIQUID GOLD, . . .   710 FERENCZ RENYI   V 18
HUNGARY
LIBATIONS, FROM THE HUNGARY OF THE WEST. . . . . . .   709 FERENCZ RENYI   5
HUNGER
TO HUNGER FIERCELY AFTER TRUTH, ...   66 HAPPY SHEPHERD   24
I HUNGER TO BUILD THEM ANEW AND SIT ON A GREEN KNOLL APART,   143 ROSE IN HEART   6
THAT WERE A DOUBLE HUNGER IN MY LIPS . . . .   285 TWO KINGS   206
THAT WERE A DOUBLE HUNGER ON MY LIPS . . . .   285 TWO KINGS   V 206
OR WAS THE HUNGER THAT HAD MADE IT HOLLOW . . . . .   368 EGO DOMINUS   23
A HUNGER FOR THE APPLE ON THE BOUGH . . . .   368 EGO DOMINUS   24
HUNGRY   SEE RAGE-HUNGRY
THAT IF A DANCER STAYED HIS HUNGRY FOOT . . . . . .   127 DREAM OF FAERY   22
CRUEL CLAW AND HUNGRY THROAT, ...   136 TWO TREES   36
THE RAGE DRIVEN, RAGE TORMENTED, AND RAGE HUNGRY TROOP,   426 PHANTOM HATRED V 11
BUT SANG, "O SEA-STARVED, HUNGRY SEA." . . . . . .   578 CRAZED GIRL   14
"O SEA--STARVED, HUNGRY SEA." . . . .   578 CRAZED GIRL   V 14
HAVE I SLEPT LONG? LONG YEARS. WITH HUNGRY HEART . .   677 ISLE STAT II 3   286
HUNKERS
UPON HIS HUNKERS IN THE HOLE, ...   306 HOUR DAWN   81
HUNT
. . . "THE FENIANS HUNT WOLVES IN THE NIGHT, ...   59 OISIN 3   171
AND WIDE AWAKE KNOW THAT THE HUNT IS ON! . . . . .   622 HOUND VOICE   17
NOW THE HUNT BEGINS ANEW? . . . .   773 SONG DEIRDRE 1   18
HUNTER   SEE FOX-HUNTER
YOU HUNTER OF THE FIELDS AFAR! . . . .   75 ANASHU VIJAYA   79
BRING MY BROWN HUNTER NEAR, ...   97 FOXHUNTER   V 6
AND SO A HUNTER CARRIES IN THE EYE . . . .   463 HARUN RASHID   61
BY AN OLD HUNTER TALKING WITH GODS! . . . .   605 YOU CONTENT   23
SUCH MEN, SUCH HEARTS. BUT, UNCOUTH HUNTER, THOU . .   651 ISLE STAT I 1   167
KNOW'ST NAUGHT OF THIS. AND, UNCOUTH HUNTER, NOW-- .   651 ISLE STAT I 1   168
AND WHITHER, UNCOUTH HUNTER? WHY SO FAST? . . . .   651 ISLE STAT I 2   1
A HOARY HUNTER LEANING ON HIS BOW, ...   672 ISLE STAT II 3   157
HUNTER-FRIEND
OF MY SAD HUNTER-FRIEND WILL ALL DEPART . . . . . .   668 ISLE STAT II 3   45
HUNTER-LOVER
SHALL BE THE HUNTER-LOVER OF THY YOUTH. . . . . .   674 ISLE STAT II 3   205
HUNTER'S
AH, YOU WILL KNOW MY LOVED ONE BY HIS HUNTER'S ARROWS   75 ANASHU VIJAYA   80
  TRULY,
OF THE HUNTER'S MOON, THAT HUNG BETWEEN THE NIGHT AND THE   210 UNDER THE MOON   18
  DAY,
I WEARY OF YOUR SONGS AND HUNTER'S TOYS. . . . . .   651 ISLE STAT I 1   157
YON IS THE HUNTER'S, SIR ALMINTOR'S, PAGE! . . . .   660 ISLE STAT II 1   35
HUNTING
THE HUNTING OF HEROES SHOULD BE GLAD." . . . . . .   4 OISIN 1   39
"THE HUNTING OF HEROES SHOULD BE GLAD! . . . . . .   4 OISIN 1   V 32
"FOR HUNTING HEROES SHOULD BE GLAD. . . . . . .   4 OISIN 1   V 34
BESIDE THE PILED-UP HUNTING SPEARS, ...   23 OISIN 1   348
OF WAR, AND THE CHASE, AND HUNTING, AND PLEASURE! . .   26 OISIN 1   V 403
AN ASHEN HUNTING SPEAR. . . . .   32 OISIN 2   56
A LARCH-WOOD HUNTING SPEAR. . . . .   32 OISIN 2   56
AN ASH-WOOD HUNTING SPEAR. . . . .   32 OISIN 2   V 56
HUNTING-CALL
THAT FOLLOWED MY KEEN HUNTING-CALL-- . . . .   23 OISIN 1   V 345F
HUNTING-SPEAR
AND FLUNG THE JOYOUS HUNTING-SPEAR! . . . .   23 OISIN 1   V 345A
HUNTING-SPEARS
BESIDE THE PILED-UP HUNTING-SPEARS, ...   23 OISIN 1   V 349
HUNTSMAN
BRING HOUND AND HUNTSMAN HERE, ...   97 FOXHUNTER   V 10
THE HUNTSMAN NEAR HIM STANDS. . . . .   98 FOXHUNTER   24
"HUNTSMAN RODY, BLOW THE HORN, ...   98 FOXHUNTER   25
THE HUNTSMAN LOOSENS ON THE MORN . . . .   98 FOXHUNTER   27
THE HUNTSMAN NEAR HIM STANDS. . . . .   98 FOXHUNTER   V 22
"NOW HUNTSMAN RODY, BLOW THY HORN, ...   98 FOXHUNTER   V REF
"MY HUNTSMAN RODY, BLOW THE HORN, ...   98 FOXHUNTER   V REF
"HUNTSMAN RODY, BLOW THE HORN, ...   99 FOXHUNTER   33

399

		PAGE	TITLE		LINE

HURL
HELP! HELP! AND HURL HIM FROM OUR COAST . . . . 83 MAD KING GOLL V 17
AND HANDS HURL IN THE DEEP . . . . 165 CRY OF SEDGE 6
HURL HELMETS, CROWNS, AND SWORDS INTO THE PIT. . . . . 257 RECONCILIATION 10
OVERCOME THE EMPYREAN! HURL . . . . 540 FROM ANTIGONE 7
I HURL AWAY THESE ALL UNFAERY FEARS. . . . . 675 ISLE STAT II 3 228
THE STARS WOULD HURL THEIR CROWNS AMONG THE FOAM . . . 761 SHADOW WATER A 265
OR THEY'D HURL A SPELL AT HIM, ... 775 AGAINST WITCH 18

HURLED
WITH WHOM I HURLED THE HURRYING SPEAR, ... 10 OISIN 1 122
AND, WEEPING OVER THE WHITE STRINGS, HURLED . . . . . 17 OISIN 1 241
THEREIN THE SILVER HARP HE HURLED, ... 17 OISIN 1 V 244
AND HURLED THEM IN THE GULPH OF SLEEP! . . . . 83 MAD KING GOLL 22
YOU, TOO, HAVE COME WHERE THE DIM TIDES ARE HURLED . . 115 ROSE OF BATTLE 26
I TORE IT FROM GREEN BOUGHS WINDS TOSSED AND HURLED, . 130 BOOK STORIES V 13
THE JEWELLED CROWNS THAT KINGS HAVE HURLED . . . . . 155 FORGOT BEAUTY 4
AND HURLED IT FROM ITS PLACE BEFORE HIS FOOTSTOOL WHITE, 174 ELEMENT POWERS V 3
AND HURLED IT FROM ITS PLACE AMID THE PEARLY LIGHT . . 174 ELEMENT POWERS V 3
OR HURLED THE LITTLE STREETS UPON THE GREAT, ... 256 NO SECOND TROY 4

HURLEY
RIDING TO HURLEY, OR IN THE BATTLE-HOST . . . . . . 229 SHADOW WATER B 169
FROM PLAYING HURLEY IN THE WOOD . . . . 743 DANAAN QUICK 9

HURLS
HURLS THEIR SWOONING LUSTRE UP. . . . . 647 ISLE STAT I 1 49

HURRAH
(HURRAH FOR THE FLOWERS OF SPRING, ... 567 FROM JAPANESE 3
HURRAH FOR REVOLUTION AND MORE CANNON-SHOT! . . . . 590 GREAT DAY 1
HURRAH FOR REVOLUTION AND CANNON COME AGAIN! . . . . 590 GREAT DAY 3
HURRAH FOR REVOLUTION AND MORE CANNON SHOT, ... 590 GREAT DAY V 1

HURRIED
HURRIED AWAY, AND OVER HER RAISED . . . . 12 OISIN 1 V 142B
I LAUGHED ALOUD AND HURRIED ON . . . . 83 MAD KING GOLL 31
"ANOTHER'S HURRIED OFF," CRIED HE, ... 193 BAILE AILLINN 113
OR HURRIED THEM OFF ON ITS OWN FURIOUS PATH! . . . 430 NINETEEN 19 53
HURRIED THROUGH THE SMOOTH AND ROUGH . . . . 436 FOR MY SON 29
AND HURRIED TO THE GUARD-HOUSE DOOR. . . . . 725 LEGEND 16
I HURRIED FROM THE WOODY SHORE, ... 742 DANAAN QUICK 4

HURRIEDLY
WHILE I WAS LOOKING THEY ROSE HURRIEDLY, ... 223 SHADOW WATER B 25

HURRIES
WHAT HURRIES OUT THE KNAVE AND DOLT? . . . . 625 NATIVITY 9

HURRY
THAT HURRY FROM UNMEASURED MIND . . . . 138 TO IRELAND 25
THAT PUT THIS HURRY IN MY SHOES." . . . . 194 BAILE AILLINN 125
O HURRY WHERE BY WATER AMONG THE TREES . . . . . . 210 RAGGED WOOD 1
O HURRY TO THE WATER AMID THE TREES, ... 210 RAGGED WOOD V 1
O HURRY WHERE BY WATER AMONG TREES, ... 210 RAGGED WOOD V 1
O HURRY TO THE RAGGED WOOD, FOR THERE . . . . 211 RAGGED WOOD 9
O HURRY TO THE WATER AMID THE TREES, ... 211 RAGGED WOOD V 5
O HURRY TO THE HOLLOW WOOD, FOR THERE . . . . 211 RAGGED WOOD V 9
HURRY TO BLESS THE HANDS THAT PLAY, ... 212 BLESS PSALTER 1
O NO, O NO! THEY HURRY DOWN . . . . 213 BLESS PSALTER 12
BUT DREAMS THAT HURRY FROM BEYOND THE WORLD . . . . 230 SHADOW WATER B 185
TO HURRY TO THEIR HIDDEN HAPPINESS . . . . 234 SHADOW WATER B 268
THE THIRD: "I'LL HURRY TO THE COURSE . . . . 296 THREE BEGGARS 33
WHILE I MUST HURRY UPON MY WAY, ... 301 RUN PARADISE 23
WHO SHUDDER AND HURRY BY! BODY AND SOUL . . . . . . 375 PHASES OF MOON 77
HURRY INTO EACH OTHER'S ARMS! THESE EYES, ... 555 RIBH AT TOMB 22
HURRY, HURRY, HURRY, ... 774 COME RIDE V REF
HURRY, HURRY, HURRY, ... 774 COME RIDE V REF
HURRY, HURRY, HURRY, ... 774 COME RIDE V REF

HURRYING
WITH WHOM I HURLED THE HURRYING SPEAR, ... 10 OISIN 1 122
WITH HORSEMEN HURRYING NEAR AND FAR, ... 83 MAD KING GOLL V 18
AND TIME AND BIRTH AND CHANGE ARE HURRYING BY. . . . 153 CHANGE BELOVED 9
AND HURRYING TO THE SOUTH HE CAME . . . . 194 BAILE AILLINN V 128
WESTWARD OF TARA. HURRYING TO HIS QUEEN . . . . . 276 TWO KINGS 2
AND, HURRYING HOMEWARD, FALL UPON SOME LAND . . . . 767 SHADOW WATER A 384

HURT
NO MAN SHOULD SEE TO DO ME HURT! . . . . 274 GREY ROCK 91
I HAD BEEN HURT"! AND TOPPLING BROUGHT . . . . . . 302 HOUR DAWN 19
I HAD BEEN HURT," THE OLD BEGGAR THOUGHT . . . . . 302 HOUR DAWN V 19
AND WE ARE HURT IF EITHER FRIEND SEEM COLD, ... 324 ROBERT GREGORY 10
IT FEARED TO GIVE ITS LOVE A HURT WITH ALL THE TEMPEST 450 OWEN AHERNE 7
  THERE!
IT FEARED THE HURT THAT SHE COULD GIVE AND THEREFORE IT 450 OWEN AHERNE 8
  WENT MAD.
AS AN HURT LEOPARD FILLS WITH CEASELESS MOAN, ... 674 ISLE STAT II 3 208
AS A HURT LEOPARD FILLS WITH CEASELESS MOAN . . . . 674 ISLE STAT II 3 V 208

HURTING
A HURTING BEAM OF LIGHT, ... 741 EARL PAUL 38
A HURTING GLEAM OF LIGHT, ... 741 EARL PAUL V 38

HURTLE
SUDDENLY HURTLE BEFORE MY DREAM-AWAKENED EYES, ... 161 BLACK PIG 2

HURTLING
ARE HURTLING THROUGH MY HEART. . . . . 171 MAID QUIET 8

HURTS
WHAT HURTS THE SOUL . . . . 572 LADYS 1ST SONG 9
FOR HURTS AND AILS AND LOVER'S MOAN-- . . . . 717 FAIRY DOCTOR 18

HUSBAND
MY HUSBAND WAS A FISHER POOR . . . . 94 MOLL MAGEE V 5

400

```
                                                          PAGE      TITLE          LINE
HUSBAND   (CONTINUED)
     MY HUSBAND STOOD UP PALE,  . . . . . . . . . . . .    95 MOLL MAGEE      V   22
     SHE SAYS MY HUSBAND SURE WILL COME  . . . . . . . .    96 MOLL MAGEE      V   41
     SHE SAW HER HUSBAND AILELL SLEEPING THERE, . . . .    183 QUEEN MAEVE         69
     AND OF THAT FAMOUS FERGUS, NESSA'S HUSBAND,  . . .    183 QUEEN MAEVE         71
     THAT HAPPIER BREATH HAD MOVED, HER HUSBAND TURNED  . .  185 QUEEN MAEVE       105
     HAD CHOSEN A HUSBAND ANYWHERE  . . . . . . . . . .    191 BAILE AILLINN       54
     WHO HAVE SLAIN MY HUSBAND AND LAID HANDS UPON ME.  .  235 SHADOW WATER B     282
     MY HUSBAND AND MY KING DIED AT MY FEET,  . . . . .    237 SHADOW WATER B     337
     AND KILLED A LOVER OR HUSBAND AT MY FEET--   . . .    246 SHADOW WATER B     491
     I WAS YOUR HUSBAND WHEN YOU RODE THE AIR,  . . . .    284 TWO KINGS          166
     AND SHOWN MY HUSBAND SLEEPING THERE, I HAVE SIGHED, . .  285 TWO KINGS        188
     HER HUSBAND HAS HEARD THE WRETCH,  . . . . . . . .    319 DOLLS               15
     DUTIFUL HUSBAND, HONEST WIFE BY TURN,  . . . . . .    376 PHASES OF MOON      99
     A HUSBAND THAT HAD SOLD HIS WIFE . . . . . . . . .    587 PARNELLITES         27
     A HUSBAND WHO HAD SOLD HIS WIFE  . . . . . . . . .    587 PARNELLITES     V   27
     "GOOD-BYE, GOOD-BYE, MY HUSBAND,"  . . . . . . . .    779 GOING THE ROAD       9
HUSH
     A HUSH! AH, ME! IT HANGS TO STRIKE US DEAD.  . . . .    43 OISIN 2         V 208B
     MY SPIRIT ROCKED IN EVENING'S HUSH, THE RUSHES ROUND MY    76 INDIAN ON GOD   V    2
       KNEES,
     THEY WILL NOT HUSH, THE LEAVES A-FLUTTER ROUND ME, . . .    82 MAD KING GOLL    12
     (THEY WILL NOT HUSH, THE LEAVES THAT ROUND ME FLUTTER--    82 MAD KING GOLL   V  REF
       . . .
     THEY WILL NOT HUSH, THE LEAVES A-FLUTTER ROUND ME, . . .    83 MAD KING GOLL    24
     THEY WILL NOT HUSH, THE LEAVES A-FLUTTER ROUND ME, . . .    84 MAD KING GOLL    36
     THEY WILL NOT HUSH, THE LEAVES A-FLUTTER ROUND ME, . . .    84 MAD KING GOLL    48
     THEY WILL NOT HUSH, THE LEAVES A-FLUTTER ROUND ME, . . .    85 MAD KING GOLL    60
     THEY WILL NOT HUSH, THE LEAVES A-FLUTTER ROUND ME, . . .    86 MAD KING GOLL    72
     AND THE WHITE HUSH END ALL BUT THE LOUD BEAT . . .    137 TO SOME I TALK      15
     AND THE WHITE HUSH END ALL THINGS BUT THE BEAT . .    137 TO SOME I TALK  V   15
     AT HUSH OF EVENING TILL GOD BURNS TIME . . . . . .    164 PERFECT BEAUTY  V    7
     AT HUSH OF EVENING TILL GOD BURN TIME  . . . . . .    164 PERFECT BEAUTY  V    7
     WITH SINGING HUSH AND HUSH-A-BYE;  . . . . . . . .    456 FRIENDS YOUTH        9
     BUT HUSH, FOR I HAVE LOST THE THEME, . . . . . . .    633 MAN AND ECHO        41
     WILL YOU NOT HEAR MY LAST NEW SONG?  HUSH, HUSH! . .    695 MOSADA 2           1
     WILL YOU NOT HEAR MY LAST NEW SONG?  HUSH, HUSH! . .    695 MOSADA 2           1
     OH, HUSH THE WANDERING MUSIC OF THY MIND.  . . . .    703 MOSADA 3          106
     AND HANGING O'ER THE HUSH OF WILLOW BOWERS,  . . .    705 REMEMBRANCE          8
     HUSH! HUSH! HUSH! ON EVERY LIP . . . . . . . . . .    732 STREET DANCERS      18
     HUSH! HUSH! HUSH! ON EVERY LIP . . . . . . . . . .    732 STREET DANCERS      18
     HUSH! HUSH! HUSH! ON EVERY LIP . . . . . . . . . .    732 STREET DANCERS      18
     HUSH! HUSH! HUSH! THEY PAUSE AND POINT . . . . . .    732 STREET DANCERS      31
     HUSH! HUSH! HUSH! THEY PAUSE AND POINT . . . . . .    732 STREET DANCERS      31
     HUSH! HUSH! HUSH! THEY PAUSE AND POINT . . . . . .    732 STREET DANCERS      31
     HUSH! HUSH! HUSH! THEY PAUSE THEM WHERE . . . . . .    733 STREET DANCERS      44
     HUSH! HUSH! HUSH! THEY PAUSE THEM WHERE . . . . . .    733 STREET DANCERS      44
     HUSH! HUSH! HUSH! THEY PAUSE THEM WHERE . . . . . .    733 STREET DANCERS      44
HUSH-A-BYE
     WITH SINGING HUSH AND HUSH-A-BYE;  . . . . . . . .    456 FRIENDS YOUTH        9
HUSH'D
     HUSH'D THE FISHERS, TILL A MOTHER CALLS BY NAME HER DROWNED    719 PHANTOM SHIP    23
       SON;
HUSHED
     THEY HUSHED THEM, EVERY MAN AND MAID.  . . . . . .     17 OISIN 1         V  235
     AND THERE WE HUSHED THE REVELRY; . . . . . . . . .     20 OISIN 1         V  295
     BESIDE THE SEA, WHERE, HUSHED AND SLOW,  . . . . .     20 OISIN 1         V  292
     WE HUSHED THE SINGING AND THE ROMP,  . . . . . . .     20 OISIN 1         V  296
     TILL ON THE CENTRAL HILL WE HUSHED . . . . . . . .     22 OISIN 1         V  323
     A WHITEBEARD STOOD HUSHED ON THE PATHWAY, . . . . .    59 OISIN 3          173
     WHEN EVE HAS HUSHED THE FEATHERED WAYS,  . . . . .     78 INDIAN TO LOVE      19
     WHERE EVE HAS HUSHED THE FEATHERED WAYS, . . . . .     78 INDIAN TO LOVE  V   19
     WHILE HUSHED FROM FEAR, OR LOUD WITH HOPE, A BAND  .  114 ROSE OF BATTLE       5
     AND HUSHED IN SLEEP THE ROARING RANKS OF BATTLE; .    129 BOOK STORIES         7
     ON A FOOT-FALL HUSHED AND LIGHT, . . . . . . . . .    159 CAP AND BELLS   V    8
     OF A FOOTFALL HUSHED AND LIGHT . . . . . . . . . .    159 CAP AND BELLS   V    8
     AND THOUGH I WOULD HAVE HUSHED THE CROWD, . . . . .   253 HIS DREAM            5
     THE SQUIRREL YONDER, HUSHED AND WISE,  . . . . . .    686 LIFE                 5
     ALONG THE SEA; AND MANY A MAN GREW HUSHED  . . . .    693 MOSADA 1            86
HUSKY
     A HUSKY DEMON, DRY AS A WITHERED SEDGE . . . . . .     39 OISIN 2         V  158
HYDE
     THERE HYDE BEFORE HE HAD BEATEN INTO PROSE . . . . .   489 COOLE PARK 29        9
HYMNS
     THAT TREMBLES AND RESOUNDS WITH HYMNS TO THEE, . . .   684 SEEKER          V  69C
HYSTERICA
     HYSTERICA PASSIO DRAGGED THIS QUARRY DOWN. . . . . .   542 PARN FUNERAL 1      21
     HYSTERICA PASSIO OF ITS OWN EMPTINESS? . . . . . .    618 BRONZE HEAD          7
HYSTERICAL
     I HAVE HEARD THAT HYSTERICAL WOMEN SAY . . . . . .    565 LAPIS LAZULI         1
     GUARDED; GRIFFITH STARING IN HYSTERICAL PRIDE; . . .   601 GALLERY REVIS       4
HYSTERICO-PASSIO
     HYSTERICO-PASSIO OF ITS OWN EMPTINESS? . . . . . .    618 BRONZE HEAD     V    7
ICE
     TO HIS OWN ICE!"  I GATHERED ROUND ME, . . . . . .     83 MAD KING GOLL   V   18
     QUEENS, THEIR EYES BLUE LIKE THE ICE,  . . . . . .    214 HAPPY TOWNLAND      11
     THAT SEEMED AS THOUGH ICE BURNED AND WAS BUT THE MORE ICE,    316 COLD HEAVEN    2
     THAT SEEMED AS THOUGH ICE BURNED AND WAS BUT THE MORE ICE,    316 COLD HEAVEN    2
ICICLES
     THE ICICLES THAT FAMISH ALL THE NORTH, . . . . . .     73 ANASHU VIJAYA       50
```

IDA'S
   AS FAIR AS ANY THAT ON IDA'S MOUNT . . . .   650 ISLE STAT I 1   134
IDIOT
   WHO BUT AN IDIOT WOULD PRAISE . . . .   780 WELL AND TREE   7
   WHO BUT AN IDIOT WOULD PRAISE . . . .   780 WELL AND TREE   15
IDLE
   AN IDLE WORD IS NOW THEIR GLORY, ...   65 HAPPY SHEPHERD   14
   TO IDLE LIFE AWAY, A COMMON HERD." . . . .   107 CUCHULAIN SEA   21
   TO IDLE LIFE AWAY WITH FLOCKS AND HERDS." . . . . . .   107 CUCHULAIN SEA   V   21
   YET NOW IT SEEMS AN IDLE TRADE ENOUGH." . . . .   205 ADAMS CURSE   27
   "SOME POLITICIANS IDLE WORDS . . . .   396 ROSE TREE   V   3
   ALL WOMEN DOTE UPON AN IDLE MAN . . . .   500 VACILLATION   23
   BUT YONDER THING, YON IDLE NOISE, YON CROW, ...   648 ISLE STAT I 1   104
   DEAFENING US WITH IDLE SOUND-- . . . .   727 LOVERS QUARREL   30
IDLENESS
   AND THEIR DAY GOES OVER IN IDLENESS, ...   151 OLD MOTHER   7
   THAT IDLENESS HAD BORNE TO PRIDE, ...   296 THREE BEGGARS   40
IDLER
   BE THOUGHT AN IDLER BY THE NOISY SET . . . .   205 ADAMS CURSE   12
IDLING
   THAT YOU STAY IDLING HERE WITH FLOCKS AND HERDS." . .   107 CUCHULAIN SEA   21
   THAT YOU STAY IDLING HERE WITH FLOCK AND HERDS." . . .   107 CUCHULAIN SEA   V   21
IGNOBLE
   IGNOBLE JOY, AND MORE IGNOBLE PAIN . . . .   687 TWO TITANS   12
   IGNOBLE JOY, AND MORE IGNOBLE PAIN . . . .   687 TWO TITANS   12
IGNOMINY
   ALL OF THAT WORST IGNOMINY . . . .   436 FOR MY SON   23
   THE IGNOMINY OF BOYHOOD; THE DISTRESS . . . .   478 SELF AND SOUL   45
IGNORANCE
   OF SWEETER IGNORANCE." . . . .   343 SHEP GOATHERD   112
   IN CHILDISH IGNORANCE OF ALL THAT PASSED. . . . . . .   468 HARUN RASHID   149
   IN CHILDISH IGNORANCE OF ALL THAT PASSED. . . . . . .   468 HARUN RASHID   160
   SHE KEEPS THAT IGNORANCE, NOR HAS SHE NOW . . . . . .   468 HARUN RASHID   164
   WHAT IF SHE LOSE HER IGNORANCE AND SO . . . .   468 HARUN RASHID   170
IGNORANT
   IN THOSE GREAT IGNORANT LEAFY WAYS; . . . .   135 TWO TREES   16
   HAVE TAUGHT TO IGNORANT MEN MOST VIOLENT WAYS, ...   256 NO SECOND TROY   3
   AND BADE ALL WELCOME, BEING IGNORANT. . . . .   286 TWO KINGS   218
   AND RIDDEN TOWARDS IT, BEING IGNORANT. . . . .   286 TWO KINGS   V   218
   ARE WHAT THE BLIND AND IGNORANT TOWN . . . .   287 TO WEALTHY MAN   7
   TO FLATTER BEAUTY'S IGNORANT EAR. . . . .   337 SCHOLARS   6
   I WOULD BE IGNORANT AS THE DAWN . . . .   344 DAWN   1
   I WOULD BE IGNORANT AS THE DAWN . . . .   344 DAWN   10
   IGNORANT AND WANTON AS THE DAWN. . . . .   344 DAWN   14
   I WOULD BE AS IGNORANT AS THE DAWN, ...   344 DAWN   V   1
   AND MADE--BEING POOR, AILING AND IGNORANT, ...   370 EGO DOMINUS   59
   SEEING THAT I, IGNORANT FOR SO LONG, ...   384 VISION ROBART   66
   IN IGNORANT GOOD-WILL, ...   392 EASTER 1916   18
   IN IGNORANT GOOD-WILL, ...   392 EASTER 1916   V   18
   HAD IGNORANT GOOD WILL; . . . .   392 EASTER 1916   V   19
   CONSPIRING AMONG THE IGNORANT. . . . .   475 EVA GORE-BOOTH   9
   WE LOVED EACH OTHER AND WERE IGNORANT. . . . .   523 LONG SILENCE   8
   IGNORANT WHAT DRAMATIS PERSONAE SPAKE; . . . .   560 WHENCE COME   4
   IGNORANT WHAT THAT DRAMATIST ENJOINS. . . . .   560 WHENCE COME   8
IL
   IL PENSEROSO'S PLATONIST TOILED ON . . . .   419 MY HOUSE   14
ILL
   AND MAY SOME SUDDEN DREADFUL ILL BEFALL HER! . . . . .   74 ANASHU VIJAYA   59
   AND MAY SOME DREADFUL ILL BEFALL HER QUICK! . . . . .   74 ANASHU VIJAYA   V   59
   NOW THAT I AM OLD AND ILL, ...   632 MAN AND ECHO   7
   ILL WORDS FOR ALL THINGS SOFT AND FAIR, ...   723 GIRLS SONG A   6
   THE PREACHER WATCHING FOR THE ILL HOUR TO PASS-- . . .   734 QUATRAIN APHOR   3
   FOR ALL GOOD MEN NOW FALLEN ILL, ...   736 IN CHURCH   5
ILL-BRED
   THE ILL-BRED SON OF A LIVERY STABLE KEEPER-- . . . . .   370 EGO DOMINUS   V   61
   THE ILL-BRED SON OF A LIVERY STABLE-KEEPER-- . . . . .   370 EGO DOMINUS   V   61
ILLNESS
   A FRIEND'S ILLNESS . . . .   267 FRIEND ILLNESS   T
   THROUGH THAT STRANGE ILLNESS THAT HAD FIXED HIM THERE, .   280 TWO KINGS   81
ILLUSION
   BY MANIFOLD ILLUSION; BUT MAN'S LIFE IS THOUGHT, ...   563 MERU   3
ILLUSIONS
   THAT I HAVE THE BEST OF PILOTS. SHADOWS, ILLUSIONS, . .   249 SHADOW WATER B   565
IMAGE
   FOR I AM IN HIS IMAGE MADE, AND ALL THIS TINKLING TIDE . .   76 INDIAN ON GOD   11
   RAGING AT HIS OWN IMAGE IN THE ENAMELLED SEA. . . . . .   77 INDIAN TO LOVE   5
   RAGES AT HIS OWN IMAGE IN THE ENAMELLED SEA . . . . .   77 INDIAN TO LOVE V   5
   RAGING AT HIS OWN IMAGE IN THE DIM ENAMELLED SEA . . .   77 INDIAN TO LOVE V   5
   HAD BLOTTED OUT MAN'S IMAGE AND HIS CRY. . . . . . .   120 SORROW OF LOVE   4
   COULD BUT COMPOSE MAN'S IMAGE AND HIS CRY. . . . . .   120 SORROW OF LOVE   12
   FOR THERE A FATAL IMAGE GROWS . . . .   135 TWO TREES   25
   ARE WRONGING YOUR IMAGE THAT BLOSSOMS A ROSE . . . . .   143 ROSE IN HEART   4
   FOR MY DREAMS OF YOUR IMAGE THAT BLOSSOMS A ROSE . . .   143 ROSE IN HEART   8
   AND SAW YOUR IMAGE WAS THERE; . . . .   152 LOSS OF LOVE   6
   NOT IN ITS IMAGE ON THE MIRROR! WHILE . . . .   230 SHADOW WATER B   189
   WHEN WE HAVE PUT THEIR CHANGELESS IMAGE ON. . . . . .   250 SHADOW WATER B   582
   WHO HAS SEEN A GARDEN IMAGE OR TWISTED TREE . . . . .   279 TWO KINGS   V   45B
   IN RAMBLING TALK WITH AN IMAGE OF AIR; . . . .   357 BROKEN DREAMS   40
   MAGICAL SHAPES. BY THE HELP OF AN IMAGE . . . . . .   367 EGO DOMINUS   7
   AND I WOULD FIND MYSELF AND NOT AN IMAGE. . . . . . .   367 EGO DOMINUS   10
   MOST OUT OF REACH? AND IS THAT SPECTRAL IMAGE . . . .   368 EGO DOMINUS   25

402

IMAGE   (CONTINUED)   PAGE   TITLE   LINE

AN IMAGE THAT MIGHT HAVE BEEN A STONY FACE . . . .   368 EGO DOMINUS   28
BECAUSE I SEEK AN IMAGE, NOT A BOOK. . . . .   370 EGO DOMINUS   67
OR IMAGE, FROM BEYOND THE LOADSTONE MOUNTAIN, ...   371 ON GOING HOUSE   11
AN IMAGE OF MYSTERIOUS WISDOM WON BY TOIL; . . . .   373 PHASES OF MOON   18
ALL THOUGHT BECOMES AN IMAGE AND THE SOUL . . . .   374 PHASES OF MOON   58
FOR EACH AN IMAGINED IMAGE BRINGS . . . .   388 SOLOMON WITCH   26
AND FINDS A REAL IMAGE THERE; . . . .   388 SOLOMON WITCH   27
MAYBE AN IMAGE IS TOO STRONG . . . .   388 SOLOMON WITCH   36
AN IMAGE FROM A PAST LIFE . . . .   389 IMAGE PAST   T
IMAGE OF POIGNANT RECOLLECTION. . . . .   389 IMAGE PAST   7
AN IMAGE OF MY HEART THAT IS SMITTEN THROUGH . . . .   389 IMAGE PAST   8
AN IMAGE UP, OR ANYTHING . . . .   390 IMAGE PAST   33
WHEN A VAST IMAGE OUT OF SPIRITUS MUNDI . . . .   402 SECOND COMING   12
AN ANCIENT IMAGE MADE OF OLIVE WOOD-- . . . .   428 NINETEEN 19   6
AN IMAGE OF ITS STATE; . . . .   430 NINETEEN 19   64
THAT IMAGE CAN BRING WILDNESS, BRING A RAGE . . . .   431 NINETEEN 19   80
HER PRESENT IMAGE FLOATS INTO THE MIND-- . . . .   444 SCHOOL CHILDR   25
I RAGE AT MY OWN IMAGE IN THE GLASS . . . .   447 HERO GIRL FOOL   1
AT MY OWN IMAGE IN THE LOOKING-GLASS . . . .   447 HERO GIRL FOOL V   1
IF YOU HAVE SEEN THAT IMAGE AND NOT THE WOMAN. . . . .   448 HERO GIRL FOOL   8
IF YOU HAVE SEEN THAT IMAGE AND NOT MY WORTH. . . . .   448 HERO GIRL FOOL V   8
WHEN UPWARD TURNED, ON ONE SOLE IMAGE FELL; . . . .   471 ALL SOUL NIGHT   34
WHEN UPWARD TURNED ON ONE SOUL IMAGE FELL, ...   471 ALL SOUL NIGHT V   34
AN IMAGE OF SUCH POLITICS. . . . .   475 EVA GORE-BOOTH   13
AN IMAGE OF THE MOVING HEAVENS, ...   480 BLOOD AND MOON   14
BEFORE ME FLOATS AN IMAGE, MAN OR SHADE, ...   497 BYZANTIUM   9
SHADE MORE THAN MAN, MORE IMAGE THAN A SHADE; . . . .   497 BYZANTIUM   10
AND HE THAT ATTIS' IMAGE HANGS BETWEEN . . . .   500 VACILLATION   16
I FOUND THAT IVORY IMAGE THERE . . . .   514 JANE GROWN OLD   1
STRUGGLING FOR AN IMAGE ON THE TRACK . . . .   534 CHOSEN   2
A THOUGHTLESS IMAGE OF MANTEGNA'S THOUGHT-- . . . .   537 HER VISION   20
A PIERCED BOY, IMAGE OF A STAR LAID LOW. . . . .   541 PARN FUNERAL 1   12
(AN IMAGE OUT OF SPENSER AND THE COMMON TONGUE). . . . . . .   603 GALLERY REVIS   40
ONE IMAGE CROSSED THE MANY-HEADED, SAT . . . .   610 STATUES   17
BECAUSE ST. JOSEPH'S IMAGE HANGETH HERE . . . .   676 ISLE STAT II 3   266
MY IMAGE YONDER? AH, MY BEAUTIFUL, ...   720 WITCH VIVIEN   4
TO DROWN IN ITS OWN IMAGE? EVEN THAT SLEEP . . . .   765 SHADOW WATER A   364
IMAGED

THE IMAGED METEORS HAD FLASHED AND RUN . . . .   31 OISIN 2   38
THE IMAGED METEORS HAD SHONE AND RUN, ...   31 OISIN 2   V   38
IMAGES

THEIR HAUGHTY IMAGES THAT CANNOT WITHER, ...   184 QUEEN MAEVE   87
THEIR HAUGHTY IMAGES THAT CANNOT FADE, ...   184 QUEEN MAEVE   V   88
THE HAUGHTY IMAGES, THAT CANNOT PERISH . . . .   184 QUEEN MAEVE   V   88
WHEN THEY HAVE BUT LOOKED UPON THEIR IMAGES-- . . . .   210 RAGGED WOOD   3
WHEN THEY HAVE BUT LOOKED UPON THEIR IMAGES, ...   211 RAGGED WOOD   V   7
AND THE IMAGES I HAVE WOVEN IN THIS STORY . . . .   218 WOODS OF COOLE   21
AND ALL THAT PROPHESYING IMAGES . . . .   235 SHADOW WATER B   294
IVORY IMAGES WITH AMETHYST EYES. . . . .   248 SHADOW WATER B   534
MAYBE YOUR IMAGES HAVE STOOD, ...   273 GREY ROCK   50
OR CLIMBED AMONG THE IMAGES OF THE PAST-- . . . .   352 PEOPLE   10
THE UNPERTURBED AND COURTLY IMAGES-- . . . .   352 PEOPLE   11
THROUGH THE HOLY IMAGES . . . .   355 PROPERTIUS   5
MERE IMAGES; CHOSEN THIS PLACE TO LIVE IN . . . .   373 PHASES OF MOON   13
FIXED UPON IMAGES THAT ONCE WERE THOUGHT; . . . .   375 PHASES OF MOON   80
IMAGES CAN BREAK THE SOLITUDE . . . .   375 PHASES OF MOON   82
THE COMMONNESS OF THOUGHT AND IMAGES . . . .   384 VISION ROBART   61
BUT IMAGES TO MAKE ME FONDER? . . . .   390 IMAGE PAST   35
IMAGES AND MEMORIES . . . .   410 TOWER   22
WHOSE IMAGES, IN THE GREAT MEMORY STORED, ...   412 TOWER   85
MONSTROUS FAMILIAR IMAGES SWIM TO THE MIND'S EYE. . . . . . .   426 PHANTOM HATRED   8
THE HALF-READ WISDOM OF DAEMONIC IMAGES, ...   427 PHANTOM HATRED   39
THE HALF-READ WISDOM OF DEMONIC IMAGES, ...   427 PHANTOM HATRED V   39
THE HALF READ WISDOM OF DAEMONIC IMAGES, ...   427 PHANTOM HATRED V   39
THUNDER OF FEET, TUMULT OF IMAGES, ...   433 NINETEEN 19   120
BOTH NUNS AND MOTHERS WORSHIP IMAGES . . . .   445 SCHOOL CHILDR   49
UPON THE GHOSTLY IMAGES OF THINGS . . . .   445 SCHOOL CHILDR   V   42
THE UNPURGED IMAGES OF DAY RECEDE; . . . .   497 BYZANTIUM   1
THOSE IMAGES THAT YET . . . .   498 BYZANTIUM   38
FRESH IMAGES BEGET, ...   498 BYZANTIUM   39
WHAT IMAGES ARE THESE, ...   505 RESULT THOUGHT   13
IMAGES RIDE, I HEARD A MAN SAY, ...   549 SEVERED HEAD   V   1
THOSE IMAGES . . . .   600 THOSE IMAGES   T
SEEK THOSE IMAGES . . . .   601 THOSE IMAGES   9
AROUND ME THE IMAGES OF THIRTY YEARS; . . . .   601 GALLERY REVIS   1
MY PERMANENT OR IMPERMANENT IMAGES; . . . .   602 GALLERY REVIS   20
THOSE IMAGES THAT WAKEN IN THE BLOOD. . . . .   622 HOUND VOICE   14
THOSE MASTERFUL IMAGES BECAUSE COMPLETE . . . .   630 CIRCUS ANIMALS   33
AND ALL THE WISDOM THAT OLD IMAGES, ...   764 SHADOW WATER A   344
AND ALL THAT PROPHESYING IMAGES . . . .   764 SHADOW WATER A V   344
WITH LIGHT IMAGES OF CLAY . . . .   775 AGAINST WITCH   12
IMAGINABLE

AND PROVE OF ALL IMAGINABLE THINGS . . . .   371 EGO DOMINUS   73
AND PROVE IF ALL IMAGINABLE THINGS . . . .   371 EGO DOMINUS   V   73
IMAGINATION

THE BED OF LOVE, THAT IN THE IMAGINATION . . . .   228 SHADOW WATER B   148
IN THE IMAGINATION AND INTELLECT? . . . .   245 SHADOW WATER B   488
IMAGINATION CANNOT RECKON IT. . . . .   248 SHADOW WATER B   541
AND THEREUPON IMAGINATION AND HEART WERE DRIVEN . . . . . .   316 COLD HEAVEN   3
UNTIL IMAGINATION BROUGHT . . . .   328 ROBERT GREGORY   94

		PAGE	TITLE	LINE
IMAGINATION (CONTINUED)				
	THE CHIEF IMAGINATION OF CHRISTENDOM,	368	EGO DOMINUS	18
	IMAGINATION, NOR AN EAR AND EYE	409	TOWER	6
	UNTIL IMAGINATION, EAR AND EYE,	409	TOWER	13
	AND SEND IMAGINATION FORTH	410	TOWER	20
	DOES THE IMAGINATION DWELL THE MOST	413	TOWER	113
	WHY SHOULD THE IMAGINATION OF A MAN	477	SELF AND SOUL	17
	IF BUT IMAGINATION SCORN THE EARTH	478	SELF AND SOUL	21
	BID IMAGINATION RUN	494	AT ALGECIRAS	15
	IMAGINATION HAD BEEN SATISFIED,	543	PARN FUNERAL 2	6
	NEITHER LOOSE IMAGINATION,	575	ACRE OF GRASS	9
	IMAGINATION TO THAT PITCH WHERE IT CASTS OUT	619	BRONZE HEAD	19
IMAGINATIONS				
	IMAGINATIONS OF THEIR EYES,	272	GREY ROCK	28
IMAGINE				
	IMAGINE THAT LOST LOVE, INSEPARABLE FROM MY THOUGHT	390	UNDER SATURN	2
	IMAGINE THAT SOME LOST LOVE, UNASSAILABLE	390	UNDER SATURN V	2
	"YOU BUT IMAGINE LIES ALL DAY, O MURDERER," I REPLIED.	450	OWEN AHERNE	17
	DELIGHT TO IMAGINE THEM SEATED THERE;	567	LAPIS LAZULI	50
IMAGINED SEE HALF-IMAGINED				
	IMAGINED, AS THEY STRUCK THE WAY	189	BAILE AILLINN	20
	THE QUEENS THAT WERE IMAGINED LONG AGO,	201	OLD MEMORY	5
	IMAGINED BODIES ALL THEIR DAYS	386	ROBARTES DANCE	28
	FOR EACH AN IMAGINED IMAGE BRINGS	388	SOLOMON WITCH	26
	IMAGINED EVERYTHING.	419	MY HOUSE	17
	WHAT MY LABORIOUS LIFE IMAGINED, EVEN	431	NINETEEN 19	82
	THE HALF IMAGINED, THE HALF WRITTEN PAGE.	431	NINETEEN 19 V	83
	IMAGINED HIM UPON THE FLOOR	440	WISDOM V	6
	IMAGINED SOME IMPOSSIBLE HISTORY	466	HARUN RASHID	109
	THE POETS HAVE IMAGINED, TERRIBLE AND GAY,"	602	GALLERY REVIS	12
	BUT BOYS AND GIRLS, PALE FROM THE IMAGINED LOVE	610	STATUES	4
	BEING IMAGINED WITHIN	785	WOMANS BEAUTY	23
	IMAGINED SUCH A FINE AFFAIR!	791	REPRISALS	14
IMAGINES				
	IMAGINES BEST TO MAKE IT THRIVE.	287	TO WEALTHY MAN	8
IMAGING				
	THE RIVER IMAGING THE FLASHING SKIES,	390	IMAGE PAST	20
	THAT WOMAN, THE GREAT MOTHER IMAGING,	541	PARN FUNERAL 1	13
IMAGINING				
	BY ITS OWN BLIND IMAGINING,	191	BAILE AILLINN	67
	IMAGINING AND PONDERING	193	BAILE AILLINN	111
	IMAGINING 'TWOULD BETTER PLEASE	271	GREY ROCK	4
	IMAGINING A MAN,	348	FISHERMAN	28
	IMAGINING.	390	IMAGE PAST	31
	IMAGINING IN EXCITED REVERIE	403	FOR DAUGHTER	13
	IMAGINING, MOON-ACCURSED,	454	EMPTY CUP	4
	IMAGINING MOON ACCURSED,	454	EMPTY CUP V	4
	IMAGINING MEN. IMAGINING THAT I COULD	537	HER VISION	4
	IMAGINING MEN. IMAGINING THAT I COULD	537	HER VISION	4
IMAGININGS				
	POET'S IMAGININGS	415	TOWER	160
IMITATE				
	IMITATE HIM IF YOU DARE,	493	SWIFTS EPITAPH	4
IMITATED				
	IMITATED FROM THE JAPANESE	567	FROM JAPANESE	T
IMITATION				
	AND BY THE IMITATION OF GREAT MASTERS.	370	EGO DOMINUS	66
IMITATORS				
	. . . CERTAIN BAD POETS, IMITATORS OF HIS AND MINE	262	TO A POET	T
	. . . CERTAIN BAD POETS, IMITATORS OF HIS AND OF MINE	262	TO A POET V	T
IMMEDIATE				
	IMMEDIATE, MOURNFUL, WHITE WITH SUDDEN CARES,	44	OISIN 2	V 229A
IMMEDICABLE				
	THAT THE IMMEDICABLE MOUND'S BEYOND	282	TWO KINGS	129
	THAT THE IMMEDICABLE WOUND'S BEYOND	282	TWO KINGS V	129
IMMENSE				
	. . . IMMENSE IN THEIR WRINKLING BARK;	48	OISIN 3	17
	IMMENSE MIRACULOUS HOUSE .	472	ALL SOUL NIGHT	38
IMMENSITIES				
	ALL ASIATIC VAGUE IMMENSITIES,	610	STATUES	12
IMMODERATE				
	BORN OUT OF IMMODERATE THOUGHT;	772	SONG DEIRDRE 1	12
	LOVE IS AN IMMODERATE THING	777	SONG DEIRDRE 2	1
IMMORAL				
	. . . HAVE JOINED THE AGITATION AGAINST IMMORAL LITERATURE	262	STUDENTS AGIT	T
	. . . AGITATION AGAINST IMMORAL LITERATURE	262	STUDENTS AGIT V	T
IMMORTAL				
	THAT IN IMMORTAL SILENCE SLEEPS	13	OISIN 1	161
	THE IMMORTAL DESIRE OF IMMORTALS WE SAW IN THEIR FACES, AND SIGHED.	47	OISIN 3	4
	WHEN AN IMMORTAL PASSION BREATHES IN MORTAL CLAY;	172	TRAV PASSION	2
	HAVE PULLED THE IMMORTAL ROSE;	174	ELEMENT POWERS	2
	THEY BLOSSOMED TO IMMORTAL MIRTH.	189	BAILE AILLINN	12
	HAVE SEEN IMMORTAL, MILD, PROUD SHADOWS WALK;	217	WOODS OF COOLE	12
	HOW SHALL I NAME YOU, IMMORTAL, MILD, PROUD SHADOWS?	218	WOODS OF COOLE	27
	I SHALL HAVE LOVE IN THEIR IMMORTAL FASHION;	237	SHADOW WATER B	326
	THE IMMORTAL MOCKERS HAVE CAST INTO HIS MIND,	249	SHADOW WATER B	567
	AND KNITTED MESH TO MESH, WE GROW IMMORTAL;	252	SHADOW WATER B	616
	AND KNITTING MESH TO MESH, WE GROW IMMORTAL;	252	SHADOW WATER B V	616
	AND THESE IMMORTAL EYES SHED TEARS--	275	GREY ROCK	100
	IMMORTAL LADIES TREAD THE GROUND	446	COLONUS PRAISE	6

		PAGE	TITLE	LINE

IMMORTAL (CONTINUED)
  WELL NIGH IMMORTAL IN THIS CHARMED CLIME, ... 674 ISLE STAT II 3   202
  WELL-NIGH IMMORTAL IN THIS CHARMED CLIME; . . . . . . 674 ISLE STAT II 3 V   202
  AND PLAY WITH HIS IMMORTAL HATE. . . . . 736 SUMMER EVENING   12
  FOR AN IMMORTAL WOMAN, AS I THINK. . . . . 755 SHADOW WATER A   173
IMMORTALITY
  THAT AIR IN IMMORTALITY . . . . 637 BEN BULBEN   8
  THAT AIRS IN IMMORTALITY . . . . 637 BEN BULBEN   V   8
  THAT AIRS AN IMMORTALITY . . . . 637 BEN BULBEN   V   8
IMMORTALS
  THE IMMORTALS MOVED AMONG THE FOUNTAINS . . . .   25 OISIN 1   386
  THE IMMORTAL DESIRE OF IMMORTALS WE SAW IN THEIR FACES, 47 OISIN 3   4
      AND SIGHED.
  AND THAT I WOULD LEAVE THE IMMORTALS, ...   54 OISIN 3   108
IMMORTALS'
  AND THOU SHALT KNOW THE IMMORTALS' LEISURE, ...   9 OISIN 1   V   100
IMMOVABLE
  LIKE DRIFTS OF LEAVES, IMMOVABLE AND BRIGHT, ...   40 OISIN 2   166
  LIKE DRIFTS OF LAUREL LEAVES, IMMOVABLE AND BRIGHT . . . 40 OISIN 2   V   166
  FOR SEPARATE, PERFECT, AND IMMOVABLE . . . .   375 PHASES OF MOON   81
  FOR PERFECTED, COMPLETED, AND IMMOVABLE . . . . . .   375 PHASES OF MOON V   81
IMPART
  AND KNOW THEM TO THE BONE; IMPART TO US-- . . . . . . 265 ABBEY THEATRE   9
IMPASSIONED
  WITH AN IMPASSIONED GRAVITY . . . .   386 ROBARTES DANCE   21
IMPATIENT
  THAT ARE IMPATIENT TO BE GONE; . . . .   413 TOWER   102
IMPATIENTLY
  OF TWILIGHT AND SLUMBER WERE GONE, AND THAT HOOFS   54 OISIN 3   112
      IMPATIENTLY STEPT.
  . . . BENEATH ME THE HOOVES IMPATIENTLY STEPT. . . . .   54 OISIN 3   V   112
IMPERIOUS
  WITH ALL A WOMAN'S PASSION, A CHILD'S IMPERIOUS WAY, . . 354 HIS PHOENIX   14
IMPERISHABLE
  BECAUSE WE ARE NOT PROUD, IMPERISHABLE, ... 250 SHADOW WATER B   580
  IMPERISHABLE FIRE UNDER THE BOUGHS . . . .   765 SHADOW WATER A   356
  THAT CAN CHANGE LOVE TO IMPERISHABLE FIRE? . . . . .   765 SHADOW WATER A   360
IMPERMANENT
  MY PERMANENT OR IMPERMANENT IMAGES; . . . .   602 GALLERY REVIS   20
IMPETUOUS
  A WHISPER OF IMPETUOUS FEET, ...   15 OISIN 1   199
  IMPETUOUS MEN, SHAWE-TAYLOR AND HUGH LANE, ... 489 COOLE PARK 29   14
  ENAMOURED OF THE WAVES' IMPETUOUS LIPS. . . . . 677 ISLE STAT II 3   289
IMPLACABLE
  THOSE TERRIBLE IMPLACABLE STRAIGHT LINES . . . . . .   467 HARUN RASHID   142
IMPORTANT
  ALONE, IMPORTANT AND WISE, ...   379 CAT AND MOON   26
IMPORTUNATE
  IF THIS IMPORTUNATE HEART TROUBLE YOUR PEACE . . . . . 162 ASKS FORGIVE   1
IMPORTUNE
  AND IMPORTUNE WITH WEIGHTY WORDS THIS MOOR, ... 698 MOSADA 2   45
  AND IMPORTUNE THEIR SOULS TO PENITENCE, ... 704 MOSADA 3   131
IMPOSSIBLE
  THOUGH NOW IT SEEM IMPOSSIBLE, AND SO . . . .   200 FOLLY COMFORT   5
  THOUGH NOW IT SEEMS IMPOSSIBLE, AND SO . . . .   200 FOLLY COMFORT   V   5
  MIRACLE, ECSTASY, THE IMPOSSIBLE HOPE, ...   227 SHADOW WATER B   102
  WE'RE IN THE BODY THAT'S IMPOSSIBLE. . . . .   230 SHADOW WATER B   190
  AMONG WHIMS NOT IMPOSSIBLE, AND THOUGH SCARRED, . . . 374 PHASES OF MOON   41
  AMONG TASKS NOT IMPOSSIBLE, IT TAKES . . . .   376 PHASES OF MOON   92
  COULD THE IMPOSSIBLE COME TO PASS . . . .   385 ROBARTES DANCE   9
  THAT MORE EXPECTED THE IMPOSSIBLE-- . . . .   409 TOWER   7
  HAD HEARD IMPOSSIBLE HISTORY OF MY PAST; . . . . . .   466 HARUN RASHID   108
  IMAGINED SOME IMPOSSIBLE HISTORY . . . .   466 HARUN RASHID   109
IMPRISONED
  REPLY LIKE MOANING OF IMPRISONED ELF; . . . . 652 ISLE STAT I 2   11
IMPROVE
  MEN IMPROVE WITH THE YEARS . . . .   329 MEN IMPROVE   T
  FOR MEN IMPROVE WITH THE YEARS; . . . .   329 MEN IMPROVE   11
IMPROVISATION
  IMPROVISATION, OR A SETTLED GAME . . . .   533 HER TRIUMPH   3
IMPROVISING
  THAT CRAZED GIRL IMPROVISING HER MUSIC, ... 578 CRAZED GIRL   1
IMPULSE
  A LONELY IMPULSE OF DELIGHT . . . .   328 IRISH AIRMAN   11
IMPULSIVE
  IMPULSIVE MEN THAT LOOK FOR HAPPINESS . . . .   369 EGO DOMINUS   40
IMPURE
  WHAT MATTER IF THE DITCHES ARE IMPURE? . . . .   478 SELF AND SOUL   42
  REPENTANCE KEEPS MY HEART IMPURE; . . . .   507 STREAM AND SUN   6
IMPURITIES
  DISCOVER IMPURITIES, CAN SHOW AT LAST . . . .   558 RIBH CHRISTIAN   10
IMPURITY
  AND PRIDE BRING IN IMPURITY; . . . .   460 THREE MONUMENT   11
INANIMATE
  MANKIND INANIMATE PHANTASY. . . . .   406 IN TIME OF WAR   5
  MANKIND INANIMATE FANTASY. . . . .   406 IN TIME OF WAR V   5
INARTICULATE
  CHANGED ALL HE SANG TO INARTICULATE MOAN . . . . . .   69 SAD SHEPHERD   27
  CHANGED ALL HIS WORDS TO INARTICULATE MOAN . . . . .   69 SAD SHEPHERD   V   27
INCANTATION
  THE HOUR OF INCANTATION COMES A-TIPTOE, ... 691 MOSADA 1   37

405

```
                                              PAGE      TITLE          LINE
INCAPABLE
    A SOUL INCAPABLE OF REMORSE OR REST;  . . . . . . . .    601  GALLERY REVIS        7
INCENDIARY
    INCENDIARY OR BIGOT COULD BE FOUND   . . . . . . . .     430  NINETEEN 19         45
INCENSE
    WHERE SUCH GREY CLOUDS OF INCENSE ROSE  . . . . . . .    156  FORGOT BEAUTY       13
    WHERE A SO SLEEPY INCENSE ROSE  . . . . . . . . . .      156  FORGOT BEAUTY  V    13
    A STICK OF INCENSE  . . . . . . . . . . . . . .          619  STICK INCENSE        T
INCH
    IT CANNOT GROW BY AN INCH OR AN OUNCE.  . . . . . .      566  LAPIS LAZULI        24
INCHY
    DIM INCHY WOOD, THAT HIDES BADGER AND FOX  . . . . .     218  WOODS OF COOLE      13
INCIDENT
    FANTASY OR INCIDENT  . . . . . . . . . . . . .          504  QUARREL IN AGE       4
INCLEMENCY
    THE INCLEMENCY  . . . . . . . . . . . . . .             471  ALL SOUL NIGHT      29
INCLINE
    BUT AS THE OUTRAGEOUS STARS INCLINE  . . . . . . .      325  ROBERT GREGORY      38
INCOMPATIBLE
    A SOMETHING INCOMPATIBLE WITH LIFE; AND POWER,  . . .    482  BLOOD AND MOON      50
INCORRUPTIBLE
    THE INCORRUPTIBLE ROSE,  . . . . . . . . . . .          168  BLESSED             36
INCREASE
    YET ALL MUST COPY COPIES, ALL INCREASE THEIR KIND;  . .  556  RIBH PATRICK         7
INCREASED
    THE WILD FOWL OF THE AIR INCREASED;  . . . . . . .       82  MAD KING GOLL        8
INCREASES
    THAT KNOWLEDGE INCREASES UNREALITY, THAT  . . . . .     610  STATUES             21
INCREASING
    BECAUSE OF THE INCREASING NIGHT  . . . . . . . .        624  APPARITIONS         21
IND
    WANDERING IN SULTRY PALACES OF IND,  . . . . . . .      694  MOSADA 1           102
INDEED
    THAT YOU HAVE TALKED WITH APPARITIONS.  INDEED  . . .    342  SHEP GOATHERD       82
    AND LOOK MOST LIKE ME, BEING INDEED MY DOUBLE,  . . .    371  EGO DOMINUS         72
    FRIENDS THAT HAVE BEEN FRIENDS INDEED;  . . . . .       577  WHAT THEN            9
    I SHALL BE OLD INDEED." THEREON THE MAN  . . . . .      609  IN TARAS HALLS      10
INDIA
    AMERICAN COLONIES, IRELAND, FRANCE AND INDIA  . . . .    487  SEVEN SAGES         15
    JOHN BULL HAS GONE TO INDIA . . . . . . . . . .         583  GHOST ROG CASE      21
INDIAN
    THE INDIAN UPON GOD  . . . . . . . .                     76  INDIAN ON GOD        T
    FROM THE BOOK OF KAURI THE INDIAN-- SECTION V.  ON THE   76  INDIAN ON GOD  V     T
        NATURE OF GOD
    KANVA, THE INDIAN, ON GOD  . . . . . . . . . .           76  INDIAN ON GOD  V     T
    THE INDIAN TO HIS LOVE  . . . . . . . . . .              77  INDIAN TO LOVE       T
    AN INDIAN SONG  . . . . . . . . . . . . . .              77  INDIAN TO LOVE  V    T
    WHILE OUR LOVE GROWS AN INDIAN STAR,  . . . . . .        78  INDIAN TO LOVE      13
    WHILE GROWS OUR LOVE AN INDIAN STAR,  . . . . . .        78  INDIAN TO LOVE  V   13
    BY SOME LEARNED INDIAN  . . . . . . . . . .             472  ALL SOUL NIGHT      53
INDIANS
    WHERE THE INDIANS TRADE OR JAPANESE?  . . . . . . .     361  ALF POLLEXFEN       20
INDIA'S
    OF INDIA'S RIVERS, ROLLING ON IN LIGHT. . . . . . .     682  SEEKER         V    20
INDIFFERENT
    AND LEFT HER TO THE INDIFFERENT STARS ABOVE  . . . .    123  DREAM OF DEATH       9
    WITH AN INDIFFERENT EYE. . . . . . . . . . . .          255  WOMAN HOMER          7
    INDIFFERENT HOW THE RANCOUR RAN,  . . . . . . . .       288  TO WEALTHY MAN      21
    BEING MORE INDIFFERENT TO OUR SOLITUDE  . . . . . .     334  LIVING BEAUTY        7
    OF LOVELY, SATISFIED, INDIFFERENT EYES. . . . . . .     375  PHASES OF MOON      83
    BEFORE THE INDIFFERENT GARDEN DEITIES;  . . . . . .     418  ANCEST HOUSES       28
    GIVE PLACE TO AN INDIFFERENT MULTITUDE, GIVE PLACE  . .  427  PHANTOM HATRED      28
    A LAW INDIFFERENT TO BLAME OR PRAISE,  . . . . . .      428  NINETEEN 19         10
    BEFORE THE INDIFFERENT BEAK COULD LET HER DROP?  . . .   441  LEDA AND SWAN       14
    LOVE-LORN, INDIFFERENT HANDS MIGHT COME UPON IT  . . .   461  HARUN RASHID        14
    A BOY'S LOVELORN INDIFFERENT HANDS MIGHT FIND  . . . .   461  HARUN RASHID  V     14
INDIGNANT
    INDIGNANT AT THE FUMBLING WITS, THE OBSCURE SPITE  . .   291  PAUDEEN              1
    REEL SHADOWS OF THE INDIGNANT DESERT BIRDS.  . . . .    402  SECOND COMING       17
    WIND SHADOWS OF THE INDIGNANT DESERT BIRDS.  . . . .    402  SECOND COMING  V    17
INDIGNATIO
    SAEVA INDIGNATIO AND THE LABOURER'S HIRE,  . . . . .    481  BLOOD AND MOON      28
INDIGNATION
    SAVAGE INDIGNATION THERE . . . . . . . . . .            493  SWIFTS EPITAPH       2
INDIVIDUAL
    ARE NOT INDIVIDUAL,  . . . . . . . . . . . .            600  SPIRIT MEDIUM       12
INDOLENCE
    A YOUNG GIRL IN THE INDOLENCE OF HER YOUTH,  . . . .    359  WAR POEM             5
    WILD INDOLENCE AND MUSIC HAVE NO DATE, . . . . . .      686  LIFE                20
    WILD INDOLENCE AND MUSIC HAVE NO DATE, . . . . . .      735  QUATRAIN APHOR      18
INDOLENT
    NO OTHER.--HEAR, AND MAY THE INDOLENT FLOCKS  . . .      71  ANASHU VIJAYA        4
    BUT SOFT BEAUTY AND INDOLENT DESIRE. . . . . . .        181  QUEEN MAEVE         22
INDOMITABLE
    STILL THE INDOMITABLE IRISHRY. . . . . . . . .          640  BEN BULBEN          83
INDUSTRY
    HE HAD MUCH INDUSTRY AT SETTING OUT,  . . . . . . .     473  ALL SOUL NIGHT      71
INEFFABLE
    AND, LIKE A STORM, CRY THE INEFFABLE NAME,  . . . . .   137  TO SOME I TALK      12
INEXTRICABLE
    ONE INEXTRICABLE BEAM,  . . . . . . . . . . . .         411  TOWER               55
```

406

	PAGE	TITLE		LINE

INFAMY
    I SOUGHT THEE NOT. MEN CALL ME INFAMY. • • • • • • • • 685 SEEKER 75
INFANCY
    CONSIDERING WHAT WILD INFANCY • • • • • 440 WISDOM 19
    THE WORLD TO ITS FIERCE INFANCY AGAIN. • • • • • • • 698 MOSADA 2 61
INFANT
    AND MAKES THE INFANT FERNS UNWRAP, • • • • • • • • 18 OISIN 1 265
    WHAT WOMAN HUGS HER INFANT THERE? • • • • • • • • 625 NATIVITY 1
INFANTINE
    WITH INFANTINE FINGERS • • • • • • • • • • • • 672 ISLE STAT II 3 168
INFERIOR
    THAT LOVED INFERIOR ART. • • • • • • • • • • • 422 MY TABLE 27
    HAVE LOVED INFERIOR ART, • • • • • • • • • • • 422 MY TABLE V 27
INFIDEL
    WITH CHRISTIAN AND WITH INFIDEL, • • • • • • • • • 594 COLONEL MARTIN 3
INFINITE
    BENEATH THE BURTHEN OF THE INFINITE, • • • • • • 674 ISLE STAT II 3 212
    BENEATH THE BURDEN OF THE INFINITE, • • • • • • 674 ISLE STAT II 3 V 212
INFIRM
    INFIRM AND AGED I MIGHT STAY • • • • • • • • 605 YOU CONTENT 17
INFLUENCE
    GROW RICH, POPULAR AND FULL OF INFLUENCE, • • • • • 369 EGO DOMINUS 43
INGENIOUS
    MANY INGENIOUS LOVELY THINGS ARE GONE • • • • • • 428 NINETEEN 19 1
INGENUOUS
    MANY INGENUOUS LOVELY THINGS ARE GONE • • • • • • 428 NINETEEN 19 V 1
INGRATITUDE
    EARNED SLANDER, INGRATITUDE, • • • • • • • • 260 UNWORTH PRAISE 16
INHABITANT
    INHABITANT OF THE SOFT CHEEK OF A GIRL-- • • • • • 540 FROM ANTIGONE 2
INHERIT
    AND THEY INHERIT THE GREAT SLEEP. • • • • • • • 83 MAD KING GOLL V 22
    THEY SHALL INHERIT MY PRIDE, • • • • • • • • • • 414 TOWER 127
INHERITANCE
    HAS HAD A LIKE INHERITANCE, • • • • • • • • • 584 GHOST ROG CASE 25
INHERITED
    SHADOWS THE INHERITED GLORY OF THE RICH. • • • • • 418 ANCEST HOUSES 16
    HAVING INHERITED A VIGOROUS MIND • • • • • • • • 422 MY DESCENDANTS 1
INHERITOR
    FOR THE MOST RICH INHERITOR. • • • • • • • • • 422 MY TABLE 25
    CONTENT OR JOY; A LAST INHERITOR • • • • • • • • 491 COOLE BALLYLEE 30
INHUMAN
    OF SOME INHUMAN MISERY • • • • • • • • • 85 MAD KING GOLL 58
    ALL, ALL, BY THAT INHUMAN • • • • • • • • • • 504 RESULT THOUGHT 5
INISHMURRAY
    KEENING FROM INISHMURRAY, • • • • • • • • • • 93 FATHER OHART 37
INJURE
    DID NOT INJURE ME; • • • • • • • • • • • • 532 FIRST CONFESS 3
INJUSTICE
    BY THE INJUSTICE OF THE SKIES FOR PUNISHMENT? • • • • • 316 COLD HEAVEN 12
INK
    ALL SHUFFLE THERE; ALL COUGH IN INK; • • • • • • 337 SCHOLARS 7
    THEY'LL COUGH IN THE INK TO THE WORLD'S END; • • • • 337 SCHOLARS V 7
    IT CAN BE MURDERED WITH A SPOT OF INK. • • • • • • 491 COOLE BALLYLEE 24
INLAID
    COULD SLEEP ON A COUCH OF RUSHES, AND ALL INWROUGHT AND   49 OISIN 3 31
        INLAID,
    MORE COMELY THAN MAN MAY MAKE THEM, INLAID WITH SILVER   49 OISIN 3 V 29
        AND GOLD,
    COULD SLEEP ON A BED OF RUSHES, AND ALL INWROUGHT   49 OISIN 3 V 31
        AND INLAID,
INLAND
    A HERDSMAN CAME FROM INLAND VALLEYS, • • • • • • • 82 MAD KING GOLL 14
INMOST
    IN THE GREEN HILL'S INMOST PART. • • • • • • • • • 726 LOVERS QUARREL 12
INN
    BETWEEN TWO BARRELS AT THE INN. • • • • • • • • 551 SONGS REWRIT 1 10
INNER
    AN INNER LAUGHTER, AND MAY KISS HIS HANDS TO ME IN SLEEP. 75 ANASHU VIJAYA V 82
    THE ORB OF THE MOST INNER LIVING HEART • • • • • • 689 NETTLESHIP 15
INNISFREE
    THE LAKE ISLE OF INNISFREE • • • • • • • • • 117 ISLE INNISFREE T
    I WILL ARISE AND GO NOW, AND GO TO INNISFREE, • • • • 117 ISLE INNISFREE 1
    AND PLUCKED SMALL FRUITS ON INNISFREE. • • • • • • 742 DANAAN QUICK 5
INNKEEPER'S
    O WHAT INNKEEPER'S DAUGHTER • • • • • • • • • 789 SINGING HEAD 13
INNOCENCE
    THE CEREMONY OF INNOCENCE IS DROWNED; • • • • • • 402 SECOND COMING 6
    OUT OF THE MURDEROUS INNOCENCE OF THE SEA. • • • • • 403 FOR DAUGHTER 16
    THE SOUL RECOVERS RADICAL INNOCENCE • • • • • • 405 FOR DAUGHTER 66
    ARE INNOCENCE AND BEAUTY BORN? • • • • • • • • 406 FOR DAUGHTER 78
    INNOCENCE; AND WISDOM HE. • • • • • • • • • • 440 WISDOM 17
    THE BLOOD OF INNOCENCE HAS LEFT NO STAIN. • • • • • 482 BLOOD AND MOON 34
    INNOCENCE AND PEACE DEPART. • • • • • • • • • 561 FOUR AGES MAN 4
    THE LOFTY INNOCENCE THAT IT HAS SLAIN, • • • • • • 614 MARCH SONGS 2 12
INNOCENT
    OF HALF-FORGOTTEN INNOCENT OLD PLACES; • • • • • • 130 BOOK STORIES 22
    WHO IS SELF-ACCUSED. IF SHE BE INNOCENT • • • • • 280 TWO KINGS 72
    THE INNOCENT AND THE BEAUTIFUL • • • • • • • • 476 EVA GORE-BOOTH 24
    YOURSELF. NONE BUT THE INNOCENT CAN SEE. • • • • • 692 MOSADA 1 59
    TOUCH NOT THIS BOY, FOR HE IS INNOCENT. • • • • • • 694 MOSADA 1 106

	PAGE	TITLE		LINE
INNOCENTS				
THOSE INNOCENTS RE-LIVE THEIR DEATH,	612	NEWS ORACLE		15
THESE INNOCENTS RELIVE THEIR DEATH,	612	NEWS ORACLE	V	15
INNUMERABLE				
THE SWIFT INNUMERABLE SPEARS,	2	OISIN 1		6
INNUMERABLE, SINGING, EXULTANT; THE CLAY UNDERNEATH THEM SHALL PANT,	61	OISIN 3		203
AND WHISPER, "THE INNUMERABLE REEDS	81	EPHEMERA	V	24E
OLD RAGGED ELMS, OLD THORNS INNUMERABLE,	419	MY HOUSE		5
THE INNUMERABLE CLANGING WINGS THAT HAVE PUT OUT THE MOON.	427	PHANTOM HATRED		32
WHERE TO THEMSELVES INNUMERABLE BIRDS	682	SEEKER		25
INNUMEROUS				
NOW WHEREFORE HAST THOU TEARS INNUMEROUS?	723	KANVA ON SELF		1
INO SEE KYLE-NA-INO				
INSANE				
AND THAT ALONE; YET I, BEING DRIVEN HALF INSANE	442	BLACK CENTAUR		6
INSATIABLE				
THE SAD, THE LONELY, THE INSATIABLE,	114	ROSE OF BATTLE		21
INSEPARABLE				
IMAGINE THAT LOST LOVE, INSEPARABLE FROM MY THOUGHT	390	UNDER SATURN		2
INSEPARABLY				
SURLY AND DISTANT, MIXED INSEPARABLY	45	OISIN 2		233
RISING AND FALLING, MIXED INSEPARABLY,	45	OISIN 2	V	233
INSIDE				
AND YET STOOD STILL, BECAUSE INSIDE	303	HOUR DAWN		26
A LITTLE BOY INSIDE THE SYCAMORE WOOD	715	DWELT SYCAMORE		5
INSIPID				
INSIPID AS THE DOUGH BEFORE IT IS BAKED,	376	PHASES OF MOON		112
INSOLENT				
OR NOISY, INSOLENT SPORT,	293	HELEN LIVED		4
THE INSOLENT UNREPROVED,	347	FISHERMAN		16
CLIPPED AN INSOLENT FARMER'S EARS	410	TOWER		31
THAT INSOLENT FIEND ROBERT ARTISSON	433	NINETEEN 19		128
WHOSE INSOLENT EYES UNUSED TO TEARS WOULD WEEP.	678	ISLE STAT II 3		302
INSPIRED				
OR INSPIRED BY FRENZY	576	ACRE OF GRASS		21
INSTANT				
AROSE, AND ON THE INSTANT CLAMOROUS EAVES,	120	SORROW OF LOVE		9
I WILL END ALL YOUR MAGIC ON THE INSTANT.	242	SHADOW WATER B		411
AND KNELT ABOVE IT WITH DRAWN KNIFE. ON THE INSTANT	278	TWO KINGS		37
AND ON THE INSTANT WOULD GROW WISE.	385	ROBARTES DANCE		12
MUST VANISH ON THE INSTANT IF THE MIND BUT CHANGE ITS THEME;	481	BLOOD AND MOON		27
FOR AN INSTANT STANDS AT EASE,	638	BEN BULBEN		31
INSTEAD				
WHEN GREY GULLS FLIT ABOUT INSTEAD OF MEN,	292	TO A SHADE		6
WHEN GREY GULLS FLY ABOUT INSTEAD OF MEN,	292	TO A SHADE	V	6
WHIRLS IN THE OLD INSTEAD;	430	NINETEEN 19		56
FROM GRAVE TO CRADLE RUN INSTEAD;	449	HERO GIRL FOOL		20
A DIAGRAM HUNG THERE INSTEAD,	485	STATISTICS		3
BECAUSE HE HAD FEATHERS INSTEAD OF HAIR.	550	SEVERED HEAD		20
INSTEAD OF THREAD AND NEEDLE	595	COLONEL MARTIN		23
NO MORE; TAKE ME INSTEAD OF HER, GREAT SIRS.	695	MOSADA 1		114
AND THE PALE BLOSSOM; BUT I WOKE INSTEAD	761	SHADOW WATER A		281
INSTEP'S				
IF HEAD AND LIMB HAVE BEAUTY AND THE INSTEP'S HIGH AND LIGHT	354	HIS PHOENIX		21
INSTRUCTORS				
GRATITUDE TO THE UNKNOWN INSTRUCTORS	505	GRAT INSTRUCT		T
INSTRUMENT				
TO SOME STRINGED INSTRUMENT NONE THERE HAD SEEN,	180	QUEEN MAEVE		4
CARRIES A MUSICAL INSTRUMENT.	566	LAPIS LAZULI		42
THEIR HAIR MINGLES ON SOME STRINGED INSTRUMENT,	752	SHADOW WATER A		123
INSTRUMENTS				
OF OLD STRINGED INSTRUMENTS, HUNG THERE	271	GREY ROCK	V	20
INSUFFICIENT				
RIBH CONSIDERS CHRISTIAN LOVE INSUFFICIENT	558	RIBH CHRISTIAN		T
INSULT				
AND INSULT HEAPED UPON HIM FOR HIS PAINS,	292	TO A SHADE		15
"THAT IS AN INSULT TO US."	319	DOLLS		7
INTELLECT				
IN THE IMAGINATION AND INTELLECT?	245	SHADOW WATER B		488
OR BOYISH INTELLECT APPROVED,	328	ROBERT GREGORY		92
IN TRIUMPH OF INTELLECT	383	VISION ROBART		31
MONUMENTS OF UNAGEING INTELLECT.	407	SAIL BYZANTIUM		8
ON MASTER-WORK OF INTELLECT OR HAND,	429	NINETEEN 19		37
ON MASTER WORK OF INTELLECT OR HAND,	429	NINETEEN 19	V	37
ATHENIAN INTELLECT ITS MASTERY,	446	COLONUS PRAISE		11
FOR INTELLECT WOULD MAKE US PROUD	460	THREE MONUMENT		10
AND INTELLECT ITS WANDERING	478	SELF AND SOUL		22
FOR INTELLECT NO LONGER KNOWS	478	SELF AND SOUL		36
THE INTELLECT OF MAN IS FORCED TO CHOOSE	491	COOLE BALLYLEE	V	40A
THE INTELLECT OF MAN IS FORCED TO CHOOSE	495	CHOICE		1
TEST EVERY WORK OF INTELLECT OR FAITH,	501	VACILLATION.		30
WHAT STALKED THROUGH THE POST OFFICE? WHAT INTELLECT,	611	STATUES		26
AND TILL HIS INTELLECT GROWS SURE	633	MAN AND ECHO		30
OUT OF INTELLECT AND SIGHT	633	MAN AND ECHO		35
INTELLECT'S				
THE SPIRITUAL INTELLECT'S GREAT WORK,	632	MAN AND ECHO		20
INTELLECTUAL				
AN INTELLECTUAL HATRED IS THE WORST,	405	FOR DAUGHTER		57

408

	PAGE	TITLE	LINE

INTELLECTUAL   (CONTINUED)
    EVERYTHING THAT IS NOT GOD CONSUMED WITH INTELLECTUAL FIRE.   481 BLOOD AND MOON   30
    THE INTELLECTUAL SWEETNESS OF THOSE LINES   489 COOLE PARK 29   23
    AN INTELLECTUAL TUNE,   743 WISDOM DREAMS   2
INTELLIGIBLE
    NO COMMON INTELLIGIBLE SOUND   578 CRAZED GIRL   13
INTEMPERANCE
    "HOW FEW THE MIND'S INTEMPERANCE RULE!   725 LEGEND   10
INTEMPERATE
    REMORSE FOR INTEMPERATE SPEECH   506 REMORSE SPEECH   T
INTENSITY
    AND YET HE HAD THE INTENSITY   327 ROBERT GREGORY   71
    ARE FULL OF PASSIONATE INTENSITY.   402 SECOND COMING   8
INTENT
    THEN MUSE THEY ON THE HOUSEHOLD WOOL INTENT,   32 OISIN 2   V   55
    ALL THAT ARE DIFFERENT OF A BASE INTENT!   398 LEADERS CROWD   2
    COULD KEEP A SWALLOW TO ITS FIRST INTENT!   489 COOLE PARK 29   19
    WHEN ON LOVE INTENT!   513 JANE TALK BISH   14
    A LIZARD CRAWLS--THE TWO MEN GAZE INTENT,   711 FERENCZ RENYI   47
INTERCOURSE
    MAKE HUMAN INTERCOURSE GROW LESS AND LESS!   473 ALL SOUL NIGHT   75
    FOR THE INTERCOURSE OF ANGELS IS A LIGHT   555 RIBH AT TOMB   15
INTEREST
    THAT FIRST UNNATURAL INTEREST IN MY BOOKS.   468 HARUN RASHID   165
    THAT FIRST STRANGE INTEREST IN MY BOOKS AND STUDIES.   468 HARUN RASHID   V   165
INTERMINABLE
    CRAZED WITH ITS OWN INTERMINABLE SOUND,   30 OISIN 2   V   23A
INTERVENED
    BUT MASTERFUL HEAVEN HAD INTERVENED TO SAVE IT.   630 CIRCUS ANIMALS   20
INTIMACY
    THE HEART-REVEALING INTIMACY   404 FOR DAUGHTER   23
INTOLERABLE
    INTOLERABLE MUSIC FALLS.   612 NEWS ORACLE   32
INTOXICANT
    INTO THE HALF-DECEIT OF SOME INTOXICANT   429 NINETEEN 19   34
INTRICACIES
    IN ALL LOVELY INTRICACIES OF A HOUSE   327 ROBERT GREGORY   74
    THE WINE-DARK OF THE WOOD'S INTRICACIES,   446 COLONUS PRAISE   2
    THE WINE DARK OF THE WOOD'S INTRICACIES,   446 COLONUS PRAISE   V   2
INTRICACY
    IN STORM-SCATTERED INTRICACY,   501 VACILLATION   48
INTRICATE
    THROUGH INTRICATE MOTIONS RAN   506 STREAM AND SUN   1
INTRIGUE
    WHO HAD SEEMED TO GLIDE TO SOME INTRIGUE IN HER RED SHOES,   363 DOLLS FACES   6
INTRODUCTION
    INTRODUCTION TO A DRAMATIC POEM   217 WOODS OF COOLE   V   T
INTRODUCTORY
    INTRODUCTORY RHYMES   217 WOODS OF COOLE   V   T
    INTRODUCTORY LINES   217 WOODS OF COOLE   V   T
    INTRODUCTORY RHYMES   269 PARDON FATHERS   V   T
    INTRODUCTORY RHYME   269 PARDON FATHERS   V   T
INVENT
    WHATEVER THEIR LOOSE FANTASY INVENT   398 LEADERS CROWD   4
    WHATEVER THEIR LOOSE PHANTASY INVENT   398 LEADERS CROWD   V   4
    WHAT FANATICS INVENT   503 QUARREL IN AGE   2
INVER
    AND SHOOK AT INVER AMERGIN   81 MAD KING GOLL   3
INVIOLATE
    FAR-OFF, MOST SECRET, AND INVIOLATE ROSE,   169 SECRET ROSE   1
    FAR-OFF, MOST SECRET, AND INVIOLATE ROSE,   169 SECRET ROSE   V   1
    FAR-OFF, MOST SECRET, AND INVIOLATE ROSE?   170 SECRET ROSE   32
    FAR-OFF, MOST SECRET, AND INVIOLATE ROSE?   170 SECRET ROSE   V   32
INVISIBLE
    POURED OUT WINE FOR THE HIGH INVISIBLE ONES.   219 WOODS OF COOLE   44
    FROM TERRIFIED, INVISIBLE BEAST OR BIRD!   389 IMAGE PAST   6
INVULNERABLE
    AND FOUGHT WITH THE INVULNERABLE TIDE.   111 CUCHULAIN SEA   86
INWARDLY
    BUT INWARDLY, SURMISE COMPANIONS   320 REED WHISPERER   4
INWROUGHT
    COULD SLEEP ON A COUCH OF RUSHES, AND ALL INWROUGHT AND
      INLAID,   49 OISIN 3   31
    COULD SLEEP ON A BED OF RUSHES, AND ALL INWROUGHT
      AND INLAID,   49 OISIN 3   V   31
IOLAN
    OF GOLDEN-ARMED IOLAN AND THE QUEEN   766 SHADOW WATER A   375
IOLLAN
    IT WAS GOLDEN-ARMED IOLLAN, AND HE DIED   242 SHADOW WATER B   406
    FOR GOLDEN-ARMED IOLLAN HAS BEEN KILLED.   242 SHADOW WATER B   410
    FOR GOLDEN-ARMED IOLLAN THAT I LOVED.   242 SHADOW WATER B   421
    O! O! O! O! FOR GOLDEN-ARMED IOLLAN.   243 SHADOW WATER B   428
    I NEVER HAVE BEEN GOLDEN-ARMED IOLLAN.   244 SHADOW WATER B   464
IRELAND
    TO IRELAND IN THE COMING TIMES   137 TO IRELAND   T
    APOLOGIA ADDRESSED TO IRELAND IN THE COMING DAYS   137 TO IRELAND   V   T
    AND MAY THE THOUGHTS OF IRELAND BROOD   138 TO IRELAND   15
    AND STILL THE THOUGHTS OF IRELAND BROOD,   138 TO IRELAND   V   15
    RED HANRAHAN'S SONG ABOUT IRELAND   206 HANRAHANS SONG   T
    ROMANCE IN IRELAND   289 SEPTEMBER 1913   V   T
    ROMANTIC IRELAND   289 SEPTEMBER 1913   V   T

		PAGE	TITLE		LINE

IRELAND   (CONTINUED)
ON A RECENT GOVERNMENT APPOINTMENT IN IRELAND . . . . . .   317 APPOINTMENT   V   T
AMERICAN COLONIES, IRELAND, FRANCE AND INDIA . . . .   487 SEVEN SAGES   15
OUT OF IRELAND HAVE WE COME. . . . .   506 REMORSE SPEECH   11
"I AM OF IRELAND" . . . .   526 AM OF IRELAND   T
"I AM OF IRELAND, ...   526 AM OF IRELAND   1
AND THE HOLY LAND OF IRELAND, ...   526 AM OF IRELAND   2
COME DANCE WITH ME IN IRELAND." . . . .   526 AM OF IRELAND   5
"I AM OF IRELAND, ...   526 AM OF IRELAND   14
AND THE HOLY LAND OF IRELAND, ...   526 AM OF IRELAND   15
AND DANCE WITH ME IN IRELAND." . . . .   527 AM OF IRELAND   18
"I AM OF IRELAND, ...   527 AM OF IRELAND   27
AND THE HOLY LAND OF IRELAND, ...   527 AM OF IRELAND   28
AND DANCE WITH ME IN IRELAND." . . . .   527 AM OF IRELAND   31
ALL THAT WAS SAID IN IRELAND IS A LIE . . . .   542 PARN FUNERAL 1   26
"IRELAND SHALL GET HER FREEDOM AND YOU STILL BREAK STONE."   590 PARNELL   2
"THE DEAD IRELAND OF MY YOUTH, BUT AN IRELAND . . . . . .   602 GALLERY REVIS   11
"THE DEAD IRELAND OF MY YOUTH, BUT AN IRELAND . . . . . .   602 GALLERY REVIS   11
IRELAND AFTER THE REVOLUTION   IV . . . .   628 JANE MOUNTAIN   V   T
AND ANCIENT IRELAND KNEW IT ALL. . . . .   637 BEN BULBEN   16
IRELAND'S
THAT SANG, TO SWEETEN IRELAND'S WRONG, ...   137 TO IRELAND   3
WHO SANG TO SWEETEN IRELAND'S WRONG, ...   137 TO IRELAND   V   3
MADE IRELAND'S HEART BEGIN TO BEAT; . . . .   138 TO IRELAND   12
ALTHOUGH THE KING OF IRELAND'S DEAD . . . .   273 GREY ROCK   68
MURROUGH, THE KING OF IRELAND'S SON, ...   274 GREY ROCK   71
ROMANTIC IRELAND'S DEAD AND GONE, ...   289 SEPTEMBER 1913   7
ROMANTIC IRELAND'S DEAD AND GONE, ...   289 SEPTEMBER 1913   15
ROMANTIC IRELAND'S DEAD AND GONE, ...   290 SEPTEMBER 1913   23
DEFENDING IRELAND'S SOUL. . . . .   546 TO SAME TUNE 2   6
IRELAND'S HISTORY IN THEIR LINEAMENTS TRACE; . . . .   604 GALLERY REVIS   53
THAT IRELAND'S MIND BE GREATER, ...   608 SONGS BURDEN 3   21
MUST IRELAND'S BLOOD BE SHED. . . . .   608 SONGS BURDEN 3   26
DEFENDING IRELAND'S SOUL. . . . .   613 MARCH SONGS 1   6
IRISH
THE DEDICATION TO A BOOK OF STORIES SELECTED FROM THE IRISH   129 BOOK STORIES   T
    NOVELISTS
DEDICATION OF "IRISH TALES" . . . .   129 BOOK STORIES   V   T
JAMES AND HIS IRISH WHEN THE DUTCHMAN CROSSED; . . . . . .   270 PARDON FATHERS   12
AN IRISH AIRMAN FORESEES HIS DEATH . . . .   328 IRISH AIRMAN   T
AND SAVED THE IRISH POOR, ...   586 PARNELLITES   12
WE IRISH, BORN INTO THAT ANCIENT SECT . . . .   611 STATUES   28
IRISH POETS, LEARN YOUR TRADE, ...   639 BEN BULBEN   68
THAT SONG I'VE MADE. 'TIS OF AN IRISH TALE. . . . .   696 MOSADA 2   19
IRISHRY
STILL THE INDOMITABLE IRISHRY. . . . .   640 BEN BULBEN   83
IRON
HE RULES YOU WITH AN IRON ROD, ...   22 OISIN 1   332
HE HOLDS YOU WITH AN IRON BOND, ...   22 OISIN 1   333
IN A LONG IRON SLEEP, AS A FISH IN THE WATER GOES DUMB   53 OISIN 3   96
    AS A STONE.
THEIR SWORDS UPON THEIR IRON KNEES, ...   156 FORGOT BEAUTY   23
A SWORD UPON HIS IRON KNEES, ...   156 FORGOT BEAUTY   V   23
WHEN SHE THE IRON WROUGHT, OR . . . .   345 ON WOMAN   17
OR SHOD IN IRON, CLIMBED THE NARROW STAIRS, ...   412 TOWER   83
A SLOW LOW NOTE AND AN IRON BELL. . . . .   549 SEVERED HEAD   7
A SLOW LOW NOTE AND AN IRON BELL. . . . .   550 SEVERED HEAD   14
A SLOW LOW NOTE AND AN IRON BELL. . . . .   550 SEVERED HEAD   21
NOR EVER MADE AN IRON RED . . . .   606 SONGS BURDEN 1   14
OLD IRON, OLD BONES, OLD RAGS, THAT RAVING SLUT . . . . .   630 CIRCUS ANIMALS   37
NOD TO THE IRON SHOES OF TIME, ...   736 SUMMER EVENING   11
IRRATIONAL
IRRATIONAL STREAMS OF BLOOD ARE STAINING EARTH; . . . . .   564 GYRES   5
IRREGULAR
AN AFFABLE IRREGULAR, ...   423 ROAD AT DOOR   1
IRVING
IRVING AND HIS PLUME OF PRIDE. . . . .   625 NATIVITY   8
ISAIAH'S
ISAIAH'S COAL, WHAT MORE CAN MAN DESIRE? . . . .   502 VACILLATION   74
ISLAND
THE ISLAND OF THE LIVING . . . .   1 OISIN 1   V   T
WRESTLED AMONG THE ISLAND BANDS. . . . .   23 OISIN 1   350
THE ISLAND OF VICTORIES . . . .   29 OISIN 2   V   T
TO THE ISLAND OF FORGETFULNESS, FOR LO; . . . .   46 OISIN 2   246
IS THE ISLAND OF CONTENT?" "NONE KNOW," SHE SAID; . . . .   46 OISIN 2   249
THE ISLAND OF FORGETFULNESS . . . .   47 OISIN 3   V   T
AN EPILOGUE TO "THE ISLAND OF STATUES" AND "THE SEEKER"   64 HAPPY SHEPHERD   V   T
THE ISLAND DREAMS UNDER THE DAWN . . . .   77 INDIAN TO LOVE   1
THERE LIES A LEAFY ISLAND . . . .   86 STOLEN CHILD   3
O DAUGHTER OF THE ISLAND OF WOODS; . . . .   164 PERFECT BEAUTY   V   1
ON THE ISLAND LAWNS, THEIR FEET WHERE THE PALE FOAM GLEAMS.   203 WITHER BOUGHS   14
BUT IN SOME ISLAND WHERE THE LIFE OF THE WORLD . . . . . .   249 SHADOW WATER B   559
ROUND LOUGH DERG'S HOLY ISLAND I WENT UPON THE STONES, . .   593 PILGRIM   6
THE ISLAND OF STATUES. . . . .   644 ISLE STAT I 1   T
LYRICS FROM "THE ISLAND OF STATUES" . . . .   646 ISLE STAT I 1   V   T
SMALL ISLAND, WHERE THE FULL SOFT SHEEN . . . .   653 ISLE STAT I 2   36
SOME SAY THAT ALL WHO TOUCH THE ISLAND LONE . . . .   653 ISLE STAT I 2   42
ISLAND OF STATUES   A FRAGMENT . . . .   666 ISLE STAT II 3   V   T
HAD FELT THE ISLAND BREEZE, MY LORE . . . .   668 ISLE STAT II 3   55
FROM MY WIZARD ISLAND LAIR, ...   668 ISLE STAT II 3   63
HAD LEFT THE ISLAND BREEZE, MY LORE . . . .   668 ISLE STAT II 3   V   55

410

		PAGE	TITLE	LINE

ISLAND   (CONTINUED)
    WILT ROAM AWAY FROM THIS RICH ISLAND REST? • • • • •   669 ISLE STAT II 3   88
    WHO, SWIMMING, SOUGHT THE ISLAND LONE: • • • • • • •   673 ISLE STAT II 3   181
    IN A FAR STILLNESS OF THE ISLAND DIE. • • • • • • •   675 ISLE STAT II 3 V 246
    WHOSE DWELLING WAS A TREE-WRAPT ISLAND, LULLED • •   693 MOSADA 1   79
    OUT OF THAT ISLAND WHERE THE FOOL OF THE WOOD • • • •   747 SHADOW WATER A   2
ISLANDS
    THEY LOVE AND KISS IN ISLANDS FAR AWAY, • • • • • •   29 OISIN 2   V   13
    THE ISLANDS OF DANCING AND OF VICTORIES • • • • • •   46 OISIN 2   247
    AND THE DREAMS OF THE ISLANDS WERE GONE, • • • • •   59 OISIN 3   175
    AND THE DREAMS OF THE ISLANDS WENT OUT OF ME, • • • •   59 OISIN 3   V 175
    I AM HAUNTED BY NUMBERLESS ISLANDS, AND MANY A DANAAN   122 WHITE BIRDS   9
        SHORE,
    AND SOUGHT THROUGH LANDS AND ISLANDS NUMBERLESS YEARS, • •   170 SECRET ROSE   23
    AND OF APPLE ISLANDS WHERE THE DANAAN KIND • • • •   203 WITHER BOUGHS V   12
    IN ISLANDS WHERE THE CHILDREN OF AENGUS WIND • • • •   245 SHADOW WATER B   469
    THROUGH THREE ENCHANTED ISLANDS, ALLEGORICAL DREAMS,   629 CIRCUS ANIMALS   11
    EVEN THE WANDERING ISLANDS OF THE GODS, • • • • •   749 SHADOW WATER A   45
ISLE
    THE ISLE LOOMED LARGELY IN THE LIGHT • • • • • • •   25 OISIN 1   V 385
    THE ISLE WAS OVER NOW AND GONE: • • • • • • • • •   28 OISIN 1   V 427B
    AND SHIVERED, KNOWING THE ISLE OF MANY FEARS, • • •   30 OISIN 2   25
    COME FROM THE ISLE OF THE LIVING." "THEN GET YE • •   34 OISIN 2   V 79
    AND TRAMPLE MY DARK ISLE. • • • • • • • • • • • •   45 OISIN 2   V 239E
    WHICH IS THE ISLE OF YOUTH?" "NONE KNOW," SHE SAID,   46 OISIN 2   V 249
    AN ISLE LAY LEVEL BEFORE US, WITH DRIPPING HAZEL AND OAK?   47 OISIN 3   10
    AN ISLE LAY LEVEL BEFORE US, DRIPPING WITH HAZEL AND OAK?   47 OISIN 3   V 10
    "LIKE ME WERE SOME GALLEY FORSAKEN FAR OFF IN MERIDIAN   55 OISIN 3   117
        ISLE,
    OUR ISLE AWAITS US, ON EACH LEA • • • • • • • •   77 INDIAN TO LOVE V   2
    TO AN ISLE IN THE WATER • • • • • • • • • • • •   89 ISLE IN WATER   T
    TO AN ISLE IN THE WATER • • • • • • • • • • • •   89 ISLE IN WATER   7
    TO AN ISLE IN THE WATER • • • • • • • • • • • •   89 ISLE IN WATER   15
    THE LAKE ISLE OF INNISFREE • • • • • • • • • • •   117 ISLE INNISFREE   T
    UPON A WOVEN WORLD-FORGOTTEN ISLE • • • • • • • •   126 DREAM OF FAERY   8
    UPON A DIM, GREEN, WELL-BELOVED ISLE, • • • • • •   126 DREAM OF FAERY V   8
    TO BLESS THAT ISLE WITH HONEY IN HIS TONES, • • •   128 DREAM OF FAERY V   44
    NOR AVALON THE GRASS-GREEN HOLLOW, NOR JOYOUS ISLE,   209 UNDER THE MOON   2
    OR AVALLON THE GRASS GREEN HOLLOW, OR JOYOUS ISLE •   209 UNDER THE MOON V   2
    WITH SINGING SWEET AS E'ER ROUND LAKE-LULLED ISLE   649 ISLE STAT I 1   106
    THE LAKE-EMBOSOMED ISLE. NAY, THIS MY QUEST • • •   657 ISLE STAT I 3   60
    YONDER'S THE ISLE IN SEARCH WHEREOF WE CAME: • • •   662 ISLE STAT II 2   13
    TO YONDER ISLE, WHERE NEVER SAIL WAS FURLED, • • •   664 ISLE STAT II 2   56
    AND CROUCH IN SOME FAR STILLNESS OF THE ISLE, AND DIE. • •   675 ISLE STAT II 3   246
    OF THIS LAKE-NURTURED ISLE: LET THY KING BE • • •   679 ISLE STAT II 3   315
    IN THE FAR ISLE SHE SANG HERSELF ASLEEP, • • • •   694 MOSADA 1   90
    MAYBE IN SOME ISLE OF ISLES, • • • • • • • • • •   732 STREET DANCERS   27
    TO THE GREEN ISLE OF WIGHT • • • • • • • • • • •   740 EARL PAUL   10
ISLE'S
    "BUT NEVER THE YEARS IN THE ISLE'S SOFT PLACES • • •   27 OISIN 1   V 419A
    "BUT NEVER THE YEARS IN OUR ISLE'S SOFT PLACES • •   28 OISIN 1   V 424
ISLES   SEE SPICE-ISLES
    ISLES OF THE LIVING AND OF VICTORIES • • • • • •   46 OISIN 2   V 247
    "IN THE ISLES OF THE FARTHEST SEAS WHERE ONLY THE SPIRITS   56 OISIN 3   133
        COME.
    AND I KNOW OF THE ISLES WHERE THE DANAAN KIND • • •   203 WITHER BOUGHS V   12
    MAYBE IN SOME ISLE OF ISLES, • • • • • • • • •   732 STREET DANCERS   27
ISOLATED
    CHARACTER ISOLATED BY A DEED • • • • • • • •   630 CIRCUS ANIMALS   29
ISSUE
    SHOULD KNOW WHAT ISSUE IS AT STAKE: • • • • • •   778 FRIENDS WRONG   3
ISSUED
    HE WALKED THAT ROOM AND ISSUED THENCE • • • • •   438 SONGS PLAY 2   2
ITALIAN
    FOR THE ITALIAN COMEDIES? • • • • • • • • • •   287 TO WEALTHY MAN   13
    WITH LEARNED ITALIAN THINGS • • • • • • • • • •   415 TOWER   158
    YET RISE FROM YOUR ITALIAN TOMB, • • • • • • •   791 REPRISALS   10
ITALY
    WHENCE TURBULENT ITALY SHOULD DRAW • • • • • •   288 TO WEALTHY MAN   25
ITCH
    ARE DRIVEN BY WEALTH AS BEGGARS BY THE ITCH," • • • •   300 BEGGAR CRIED   14
ITERATION
    AND BIRDLY ITERATION IS • • • • • • • • • •   67 HAPPY SHEPHERD V 46B
ITH
    MY WORD WAS LAW FROM ITH TO EMAIN, • • • • • •   81 MAD KING GOLL   2
IVIED
    THROUGH BUSH THEY PLUNGED AND OVER IVIED ROOT, • • •   278 TWO KINGS   32
IVORIES
    AND GONE ARE PHIDIAS' FAMOUS IVORIES • • • • • •   428 NINETEEN 19   7
    AND GONE ARE PHIDIAS' CARVEN IVORIES • • • • • •   428 NINETEEN 19   V   7
    OR BREAK IN BITS THE FAMOUS IVORIES • • • • • •   430 NINETEEN 19   47
IVORY
    AND THEN SMOOTH OUT WITH IVORY HANDS AND SIGH, • •   228 SHADOW WATER B   133
    AND NOT A ROOF OF IVORY AND GOLD. • • • • • •   246 SHADOW WATER B   500
    I WOULD GROW JEALOUS OF THE IVORY ROOF, • • • •   246 SHADOW WATER B   501
    IVORY IMAGES WITH AMETHYST EYES. • • • • • • •   248 SHADOW WATER B   534
    I FOUND THAT IVORY IMAGE THERE • • • • • • •   514 JANE GROWN OLD   1
    AND THEN SMOOTH OUT WITH IVORY HANDS AND SIGH. • • •   750 SHADOW WATER A   70
IVY
    SQUARE LEAVES OF THE IVY MOVED OVER US, BINDING US DOWN   52 OISIN 3   76
        TO OUR REST.

IVY   (CONTINUED)
    FROM WHERE THE OLD IVY CRAWLS ROUND THE OLD STEEPLE, . .   728 PRIEST FAIRY   6
IVY-COVERED
    WENT OUT. AMONG THE IVY-COVERED ROCKS, ...   283 TWO KINGS   147
IVY'S   SEE GROUND-IVY'S
    AND THE GROUND IVY'S BLUER LIGHT, A STAG . . . . . .   277 TWO KINGS   V   6
I-WIS
    FAREWELL: I MUST BE GONE I-WIS, ...   67 HAPPY SHEPHERD V   46D
JABBER
    JABBER AND SCREAM ABOUT HIM IN THE NIGHT: . . . . . .   34 OISIN 2   82
    JABBER AND SCREAM. YET HE, FOR ALL HIS BOLD . . . .   34 OISIN 2   V   82
JACK   SEE STILT-JACK
    WITH EVERY JACK AND JILL? . . . .   335 YOUNG BEAUTY   3
    BECAUSE OF MY DEAR JACK THAT'S DEAD. . . . .   508 JANE BISHOP   5
    BANISHED JACK THE JOURNEYMAN, ...   508 JANE BISHOP   9
    BUT A BIRCH-TREE STOOD MY JACK: . . . .   508 JANE BISHOP   20
    JACK HAD MY VIRGINITY. . . . .   508 JANE BISHOP   22
    BUT A BIRCH TREE STOOD MY JACK: . . . .   508 JANE BISHOP   V   20
    CRAZY JANE AND JACK THE JOURNEYMAN . . . .   511 JANE AND JACK   T
    I HAD WILD JACK FOR A LOVER: . . . .   512 JANE ON GOD   19
JACKASS
    TO HEAR A JACKASS BRAY: . . . .   455 HIS MEMORIES   10
JACQUES
    "VENGEANCE FOR JACQUES MOLAY." IN CLOUD-PALE RAGS, OR   426 PHANTOM HATRED   10
        IN LACE,
    FOR VENGEANCE ON THE MURDERERS OF JACQUES MOLAY. . . . .   426 PHANTOM HATRED   16
    "VENGENCE FOR JACQUES MOLAY." IN CLOUD PALE RAGS, OR IN   426 PHANTOM HATRED V   10
        LACE,
JADE
    A GREY-GREEN CUP OF JADE, ...   781 MY HEART BEAT   15
JAFFER
    HIS VIZIR JAFFER FOR AN UNKNOWN REASON: . . . .   462 HARUN RASHID   32
JAFFER'S
    SEEMED SO ON PURPOSE, MUTTERED JAFFER'S FRIENDS, ...   462 HARUN RASHID   37
JAGS
    A DOME MADE OUT OF ENDLESS CARVEN JAGS, ...   38 OISIN 2   144
    WAITED. ABOVE, IN ENDLESS CARVEN JAGS, ...   38 OISIN 2   V   144
JAILBIRD
    THAT RAMBLING JAILBIRD BILLY SAID: . . . .   332 ROUND TOWER   26
JAILOR
    THUS SPAKE THE TOWN JAILOR . . . .   740 EARL PAUL   13
JAMES
    JAMES AND HIS IRISH WHEN THE DUTCHMAN CROSSED: . . . .   270 PARDON FATHERS   12
    JAMES CONNOLLY REPLIED, ...   396 ROSE TREE   8
JAMMED
    ANOINTING, TORCH JAMMED DOWN BETWEEN THE FLAGS, ...   38 OISIN 2   V   143
JANE
    CRAZY JANE AND THE BISHOP . . . .   507 JANE BISHOP   T
    EIGHT POEMS CRAZY JANE AND THE BISHOP . . . .   507 JANE BISHOP   V   T
    CRAZY JANE REPROVED . . . .   509 JANE REPROVED   T
    CRAZY JANE ON THE DAY OF JUDGMENT . . . .   510 JANE JUDGMENT   T
    AND THAT IS WHAT JANE SAID. . . . .   510 JANE JUDGMENT   5
    AND THAT IS WHAT JANE SAID. . . . .   510 JANE JUDGMENT   15
    CRAZY JANE AND JACK THE JOURNEYMAN . . . .   511 JANE AND JACK   T
    CRAZY JANE ON GOD . . . .   512 JANE ON GOD   T
    CRAZY JANE TALKS WITH THE BISHOP . . . .   513 JANE TALK BISH   T
    CRAZY JANE GROWN OLD LOOKS AT THE DANCERS . . . . . .   514 JANE GROWN OLD   T
    CRAZY JANE AND THE DANCERS . . . .   514 JANE GROWN OLD V   T
    COULD CRAZY JANE PUT OFF OLD AGE . . . .   606 SONGS BURDEN 1   19
    CRAZY JANE ON THE MOUNTAIN . . . .   628 JANE MOUNTAIN   T
    (SAID CRAZY JANE) . . . .   628 JANE MOUNTAIN   2
    (SAID CRAZY JANE) . . . .   628 JANE MOUNTAIN   12
JAPANESE
    WHERE THE INDIANS TRADE OR JAPANESE? . . . .   361 ALF POLLEXFEN   20
    THEY HAD A PRIEST SAY MASS, AND EVEN THE JAPANESE, . . .   363 DOLLS FACES   2
    IMITATED FROM THE JAPANESE . . . .   567 FROM JAPANESE   T
JASMINE
    WHEN EVENING STIRS THE JASMINE BOUGH, AND YET . . . . .   463 HARUN RASHID   53
    WHEN EVENING STIRS THE JASMINE, AND YET . . . .   463 HARUN RASHID   V   53
    "AND YET THE JASMINE SEASON WARMS OUR BLOOD." . . . .   464 HARUN RASHID   73
JAUNTING
    JAUNTING, JOURNEYING . . . .   342 SHEP GOATHERD   95
JAWS
    BY THESE WIRE-JOINTED JAWS AND LIMBS OF WOOD, ...   382 VISION ROBART   10
    ABOVE, SALIVA DRIPPING FROM HIS JAWS, ...   689 NETTLESHIP   4
JAY'S
    THE JAY'S NEST BY MY WINDOW . . . .   424 STARES NEST   V   T
JEALOUS
    I WOULD GROW JEALOUS OF THE IVORY ROOF, ...   246 SHADOW WATER B   501
    I AM JEALOUS OF THE LOOK MEN TURN ON YOU . . . . .   447 HERO GIRL FOOL V   A
    THAT IS A LIGHT MY JEALOUS SOUL HAS SENT. . . . . .   558 RIBH CHRISTIAN   8
JEALOUSY
    JEALOUSY . . . .   70 ANASHU VIJAYA V   T
    ALL THEIR JEALOUSY DISPLAY, ...   726 LOVERS QUARREL   22
JENNY   SEE SPINNING-JENNY
JERK
    BUT A GOOD STRONG CAUSE"--THE ROPE GAVE A JERK THERE, . .   545 TO SAME TUNE 1   23
    BUT A GOOD STRONG CAUSE"--THE ROPE GAVE A JERK THERE, . .   616 MARCH SONGS 3   23
JERRY
    DAN AND JERRY LOUT . . . .   520 HIS BARGAIN   5
    DAN AND JERRY TOUT, ...   520 HIS BARGAIN   V   5

JESSAMINE
HIS GARDEN RINGED WITH JESSAMINE, ... 729 PRIEST FAIRY 34
JEST
A WORD AND A JEST. . . . . 293 HELEN LIVED 12
JESTER
THE JESTER WALKED IN THE GARDEN: . . . . 159 CAP AND BELLS 1
A QUEEN WAS LOVED BY A JESTER, ... 159 CAP AND BELLS V 1
A QUEEN WAS BELOVED BY A JESTER, ... 159 CAP AND BELLS V 1
JET
AND HAD DISPORTED IN THE STILLY JET, ... 31 OISIN 2 39
AND HAD DISPORTED IN THE EYES STILL JET . . . . . . 31 OISIN 2 V 39
THE ABOUNDING GLITTERING JET: THOUGH NOW IT SEEMS . . . 417 ANCEST HOUSES 12
LIKE THIS PURE JET, NOW LOST AMID BLUE SKY, ... 464 HARUN RASHID 64
BUT COULD NOT CAST A SINGLE JET THEREON. . . . . . 482 BLOOD AND MOON 39
A CLOVEN, DANCING JET, ... 680 LOVE AND DEATH 2
JEW
HE SPOKE WITH TURK AND JEW, ... 594 COLONEL MARTIN 2
LIKE AN OLD JEW MAN, ... 620 JOHN KINSELLA 14
JEWEL
SOBRIETY IS A JEWEL . . . . 592 DRUNK SOBRIETY 5
JEWELLED
THE JEWELLED CROWNS THAT KINGS HAVE HURLED . . . . . 155 FORGOT BEAUTY 4
JEWELRY
AND BOUGHT THE GRANDEST JEWELRY . . . . 595 COLONEL MARTIN 21
PUT JEWELRY IN THE PACK, ... 595 COLONEL MARTIN 24
JEWELRY SO GRAND." . . . . 595 COLONEL MARTIN 33
JEWELS
HAS COME INTO THE JEWELS OF THE HARP . . . . . . 239 SHADOW WATER B V 371A
JEWEL-STONE
AND HID HER AMONG FRUITS OF JEWEL-STONE . . . . . . 224 SHADOW WATER B 49
JIG
SO WE DANCE A FAIRY JIG . . . . 726 LOVERS QUARREL 19
JILL
WITH EVERY JACK AND JILL? . . . . 335 YOUNG BEAUTY 3
JINN
I SAY THAT A JINN SPOKE. A LIVE-LONG HOUR . . . . . 467 HARUN RASHID V 136
JOAN
DARK JOAN CALL THE BERRIES SWEET, ... 743 DANAAN QUICK 28
JOE
HOLY JOE, THE BEGGAR-MAN, ... 529 TOM LUNATIC 8
JOHN
GOOD FATHER JOHN O'HART . . . . 91 FATHER OHART 1
BUT FATHER JOHN WENT UP, ... 92 FATHER OHART 9
AND FATHER JOHN WENT DOWN: . . . . 92 FATHER OHART 10
AND THESE WERE THE WORKS OF JOHN, ... 93 FATHER OHART 25
AND THAT ENQUIRING MAN JOHN SYNGE COMES NEXT, ... 324 ROBERT GREGORY 25
BUT WHERE IS LAID THE SAILOR JOHN . . . . 360 ALF POLLEXFEN 17
WHERE HAVE THEY LAID THE SAILOR JOHN? . . . . . . 361 ALF POLLEXFEN 23
THAT MEDITATIVE MAN, JOHN SYNGE, AND THOSE . . . . . 489 COOLE PARK 29 13
JOHN BULL AND THE SEA ARE FRIENDS: . . . . 583 GHOST ROG CASE 4
JOHN BULL HAS STOOD FOR PARLIAMENT, ... 583 GHOST ROG CASE 11
JOHN BULL HAS GONE TO INDIA . . . . 583 GHOST ROG CASE 21
"GREATEST SINCE REMBRANDT," ACCORDING TO JOHN SYNGE: . . 602 GALLERY REVIS 26
JOHN SYNGE, I AND AUGUSTA GREGORY, THOUGHT . . . . . 603 GALLERY REVIS 41
AND HERE'S JOHN SYNGE HIMSELF, THAT ROOTED MAN, . . . 603 GALLERY REVIS 48
AND HERE'S JOHN SYNGE, A MEDITATIVE MAN, ... 603 GALLERY REVIS V 48
JOHN KINSELLA'S LAMENT FOR MRS. MARY MOORE . . . . . 620 JOHN KINSELLA T
AND JOHN WILL PARDON THEE, ... 739 EARL PAUL 2
AND JOHN ROSE UP AND STOOD, ... 741 EARL PAUL 54
JOHN'S
IN TRUST TOOK HE JOHN'S LANDS: . . . . 92 FATHER OHART 5
JOHNSON
DOWSON AND JOHNSON MOST I PRAISE-- . . . . 273 GREY ROCK 62
LIONEL JOHNSON COMES THE FIRST TO MIND, ... 324 ROBERT GREGORY 17
JOIN
TO JOIN HIS BROTHERS IN THE HOME OF YEARS . . . . . 30 OISIN 2 V 17
BEEN BONE AND SINEW: WHEN SUCH BODIES JOIN . . . . . 555 RIBH AT TOMB 12
THEY SEEM TO JOIN HER PRAYER-- . . . . 736 IN CHURCH 12
JOINED
BY ROOTS THAT JOINED ABOVE OUR PLUMES-- . . . . . 16 OISIN 1 V 224C
WE JOINED HIM FOR HIS PAY, BUT HAVE HAD NONE . . . . 225 SHADOW WATER B V 68A
DO YOU, TOO, DOUBT ME? HAVE YOU JOINED THEIR PLOT? . . 227 SHADOW WATER B 106
. . . HAVE JOINED THE AGITATION AGAINST IMMORAL LITERATURE 262 STUDENTS AGIT T
. . . HAVE JOINED THE ANCIENT ORDER OF HIBERNIANS AND THE 262 STUDENTS AGIT V T
. . .
NOR STRAINING JOY, BUT WHOLE IS JOINED TO WHOLE: . . . 555 RIBH AT TOMB 14
JOINT
IF TIME WERE SUPPLER IN THE JOINT, ... 306 HOUR DAWN 94
ALL THEIR BODIES, JOINT BY JOINT, ... 776 AGAINST WITCH 22
ALL THEIR BODIES, JOINT BY JOINT, ... 776 AGAINST WITCH 22
JOINTED SEE WIRE-JOINTED
JOINTS
WITH QUAKING JOINTS AND TERROR-STRICKEN FACES, . . . 185 QUEEN MAEVE 121
WITH QUAKING JOINTS AND TERROR STRUCKEN FACES, . . . 185 QUEEN MAEVE V 121
WITH QUAKING JOINTS AND TERROR-STRUCKEN FACES, . . . 185 QUEEN MAEVE V 121
MADE THE JOINTS OF HEAVEN CRACK: . . . . 509 JANE REPROVED 11
JOKE
THE WITTY MAN AND HIS JOKE . . . . 347 FISHERMAN 19
JOKES
COMES CRACKING JOKES OF CIVIL WAR . . . . 423 ROAD AT DOOR 3

413

JOLLY
    HE HAD SEEN A RED-HAIRED JOLLY LAD . . . .   303 HOUR DAWN   V   27
JOLT
    SHIVER UNDER THE LASH, STRAIN, SWEAT AND JOLT . . . . .   260 FASC DIFFICULT   7
JONATHAN
    "JONATHAN SWIFT'S AT REST! . . . .   493 SWIFTS EPITAPH V   1
    THROUGH JONATHAN SWIFT'S DARK GROVE HE PASSED, AND THERE   543 PARN FUNERAL 2   11
JONSON'S
    --BEN JONSON'S PHRASE--AND FIND WHEN JUNE IS COME . .   321 REED WHISPERER   6
    BEN JONSON'S PHRASE--AND STILL MAY TURN MY FEET . . . .   321 REED WHISPERER V   6
JOSEPH
    SAINT JOSEPH THOUGHT THE WORLD WOULD MELT . . . . . .   619 STICK INCENSE   3
JOSEPH'S
    BECAUSE ST. JOSEPH'S IMAGE HANGETH HERE . . . .   676 ISLE STAT II 3   266
JOSTLED
    JOSTLED AND SHOUTED THOSE WAR-WASTED MEN, ...   286 TWO KINGS   216
    FARMERS JOSTLED AT THE FAIR . . . .   410 TOWER   39
    CROWDS JOSTLED AT THE FAIR . . . .   410 TOWER   V   39
JOT
    MY ANGRY KING-REMEMBERING SOUL ONE JOT. . . . . . .   36 OISIN 2   94
    THEY STIRRED MY SPACIOUS SOUL IN ME NO JOT-- . . . . .   36 OISIN 2   V   94
    NOR SHOOK MY FIRM AND SPACIOUS SOUL ONE JOT! . . . . .   36 OISIN 2   V   94
    MY ANGRY, KING REMEMBERING SOUL ONE JOT! . . . . . .   36 OISIN 2   V   94
JOURNALIST
    A JOURNALIST MAKES UP HIS LIES . . . .   598 STONE CROSS   3
    TURN TO A DRUNKEN JOURNALIST! . . . .   626 OLD MEN BE MAD   4
JOURNEY
    SPLASHED ALL WITH CLAY AND JOURNEY DULL, ...   82 MAD KING GOLL V   13
    "I ONLY ASK WHAT WAY MY JOURNEY LIES, ...   108 CUCHULAIN SEA   31
    THE CLOUDS ON THEIR JOURNEY ABOVE, ...   119 PITY OF LOVE   4
    AND YOU HAVE TOLD ME THAT THEIR JOURNEY LIES . . . . .   231 SHADOW WATER B   205
    DECIDED HE WOULD JOURNEY HOME, ...   361 ALF POLLEXFEN   30
    DECIDED HE MUST JOURNEY HOME, ...   361 ALF POLLEXFEN V   30
    ON THE SOUL'S JOURNEY. HOW IT IS WHIRLED ABOUT, . . .   472 ALL SOUL NIGHT   54
    . . . A LOG-BOOK OF THE SUN'S JOURNEY AND THE MOON'S!   480 BLOOD AND MOON   14
    . . . A LOG BOOK OF THE SUN'S JOURNEY AND THE MOON'S,   480 BLOOD AND MOON V 14
JOURNEY-DULL
    WITH ALL HIS COLOURS JOURNEY-DULL, ...   82 MAD KING GOLL V   13
JOURNEYED
    WITH A PALE LIGHT, I JOURNEYED ROUND THE HALL . . . . .   39 OISIN 2   153
    BURIED AND MIGHTY. THENCE I JOURNEYED NOT . . . . . .   39 OISIN 2   V 151
JOURNEYING
    JAUNTING, JOURNEYING . . . .   342 SHEP GOATHERD   95
JOURNEYMAN
    BANISHED JACK THE JOURNEYMAN, ...   508 JANE BISHOP   9
    A ROARING, RANTING JOURNEYMAN. . . . .   509 JANE REPROVED   13
    CRAZY JANE AND JACK THE JOURNEYMAN . . . .   511 JANE AND JACK   T
JOURNEY-MAN
    A ROARING RANTING JOURNEY-MAN. . . . .   509 JANE REPROVED V 13
JOURNEY'S
    AND I MAY DINE AT JOURNEY'S END . . . .   336 YOUNG BEAUTY   17
    THAT I MAY DINE AT JOURNEY'S END . . . .   336 YOUNG BEAUTY V 17
JOURNEYS
    THE CAPTIVE'S JOURNEYS TO AND FRO WERE WRIT . . . . .   37 OISIN 2   116
    THE CAPTIVES' JOURNEYS TO AND FRO WERE WRIT . . . . .   37 OISIN 2   V 116
    MAN EVER JOURNEYS ON WITH THEM . . . .   139 TO IRELAND   29
JOVIAL
    I SAW HIS JOVIAL MOOD BRING ONCE A SMILE . . . . . .   696 MOSADA 2   14
JOY
    BUT WHEN I SANG OF HUMAN JOY . . . .   17 OISIN 1   234
    AND WHEN I SANG OF HUMAN JOY . . . .   17 OISIN 1   V 234
    "JOY DROWNS THE TWILIGHT IN THE DEW, ...   18 OISIN 1   261
    AND IF JOY WERE NOT ON THE EARTH, ...   18 OISIN 1   269
    "'TIS JOY MAKES SWIM THE SAPPY TIDE, ...   18 OISIN 1   V 261
    FOR JOY THE LITTLE PLANETS RUN . . . .   18 OISIN 1   V 267
    IF JOY WERE NOWHERE ON THE EARTH . . . .   18 OISIN 1   V 269
    OR DROPS OF SILVER JOY THAT FELL . . . .   19 OISIN 1   278
    FOR JOY IS GOD AND GOD IS JOY." . . . .   19 OISIN 1   286
    FOR JOY IS GOD AND GOD IS JOY." . . . .   19 OISIN 1   286
    "THE SOUL IS A DROP OF JOY AFAR. . . . .   19 OISIN 1   V 276
    SANG, "GOD IS JOY AND JOY IS GOD, ...   20 OISIN 1   300
    SANG, "GOD IS JOY AND JOY IS GOD, ...   20 OISIN 1   300
    AND OVER IS THEIR ANTIQUE JOY! . . . .   64 HAPPY SHEPHERD   2
    FOR RUTH AND JOY HAVE BROTHERHOOD, ...   66 HAPPY SHEPHERD V 42
    AND SLEEK YOUNG JOY IS NO MORE FICKLE, ...   77 INDIAN TO LOVE V 5C
    FIELDS FATTENING SLOW, MEN WISE IN JOY, ...   82 MAD KING GOLL V   6
    "I HAVE NO REST, NOR JOY, NOR PEACE, ...   132 FR GILLIGAN   9
    FROM JOY THE HOLY BRANCHES START, ...   134 TWO TREES   3
    THE EAST HER HIDDEN JOY BEFORE THE MORNING BREAK, . . .   154 BELOVED PEACE   4
    THE EAST TELLS ALL HER SECRET JOY BEFORE DAYBREAK, . .   154 BELOVED PEACE V   4
    AND ALL THAT TOSSING OF YOUR WINGS IS JOY, ...   244 SHADOW WATER B   451
    SPONTANEOUS JOY AND NATURAL CONTENT . . . .   260 FASC DIFFICULT   3
    PRAISED THEIR GREAT VICTORIES AND GAVE THEM JOY . . .   286 TWO KINGS   V 218B
    WHAT JOY IS IN MY DAYS! . . . .   315 FRIENDS   3
    AN AIMLESS JOY IS A PURE JOY," . . . .   338 TOM OROUGHLEY   4
    AN AIMLESS JOY IS A PURE JOY," . . . .   338 TOM OROUGHLEY   4
    OF ALL 'TWAS PAIN OR JOY TO LEARN, ...   342 SHEP GOATHERD   98
    WHO HAVE LIVED IN JOY AND LAUGHED INTO THE FACE OF DEATH.   366 HER COURAGE   10
    WHO LIVED IN SHAMELESS JOY AND LAUGHED INTO THE FACE OF   366 HER COURAGE   V 10
      DEATH.
    THAT LIVED IN JOY AND LAUGHED INTO THE FACE OF DEATH. . .   366 HER COURAGE   V 10

JOY (CONTINUED)
    WHO HAVE LIVED IN JOY AND LAUGHED IN THE FACE OF DEATH.   366 HER COURAGE V 10
    FOR AIMLESS JOY HAD MADE ME STOP . . . . 400 DEMON BEAST   22
    AND HAD THE GREATER JOY IN PRAISING HER, ... 410 TOWER   37
    IT HAD BUT MADE US PINE THE MORE. THE ABSTRACT JOY, . . 427 PHANTOM HATRED   38
    AND THAT WAS THE BEGINNING OF A JOY . . . . 465 HARUN RASHID V 103
    CONTENT OR JOY: A LAST INHERITOR . . . . 491 COOLE BALLYLEE   30
    HOPING MORE SUBSTANTIAL JOY . . . . 494 AT ALGECIRAS   9
    HOPING A MORE SUBSTANTIAL JOY . . . . 494 AT ALGECIRAS V 9
    WHAT IS JOY . . . . 499 VACILLATION V T
    WHAT IS JOY? . . . . 500 VACILLATION   10
    NOR STRAINING JOY, BUT WHOLE IS JOINED TO WHOLE: . . . 555 RIBH AT TOMB   14
    DRINKING JOY AS IT WERE MILK UPON HIS BREAST. . . . . 559 MAGIC DRUM   3
    CRY AT THE ONSET OF THEIR SEXUAL JOY . . . . 560 WHENCE COME   2
    CRY AT THE ONSET OF THE SEXUAL JOY . . . . 560 WHENCE COME V 2
    WE THAT LOOK ON BUT LAUGH IN TRAGIC JOY. . . . . . 564 GYRES   8
    AND NEVER HAVE I DANCED FOR JOY. . . . . 567 FROM JAPANESE   9
    WHEN A MAN GROWS OLD HIS JOY . . . . 624 APPARITIONS   17
    ITS JOY OR NIGHT SEEM BUT A DREAM: . . . . 633 MAN AND ECHO   42
    ITS JOY OR NIGHT SEEMS BUT A DREAM. . . . . 633 MAN AND ECHO V 42
    JOY AND LOVE ARE ONE EXISTENCE. . . . . 647 ISLE STAT I 1   71
    SADNESS, SOUL OF JOY MOST DEEP, ... 647 ISLE STAT I 1   74
    GROWETH THE GOBLIN FLOWER OF JOY, HER CARE, ... 653 ISLE STAT I 2   39
    AND THE JOY OF THE STREAMS WHERE LONG-LIMBED HERONS WADE: 674 ISLE STAT II 3   217
    UNTOUCHED OF HUMAN JOY OR HUMAN LOVE? . . . . . . 684 SEEKER   65
    FOR ALL MY JOY--AH, WOE: . . . . 685 SEEKER   79
    AND JOY, THE TOUCHING OF WHOSE FINGER LENDS . . . . 686 DRAWING-ROOM   7
    IGNOBLE JOY, AND MORE IGNOBLE PAIN . . . . 687 TWO TITANS   12
    WITH LITTLE CRIES OF JOY HE KISSED THE RAIN . . . . 688 TWO TITANS   33
    I WAVE THEM HITHER, MY BREAST HEAVES WITH JOY. . . . 694 MOSADA 1   98
    THOUGHTLESS JOY AND SORROW SAGE. . . . . 733 STREET DANCERS   47
    AND JOY, THE TOUCHING OF WHOSE FINGER LENDS . . . . 734 QUATRAIN APHOR   7
    AND JOY, IN GROWING DEEPER AND MORE DEEP, ... 735 QUATRAIN APHOR   27
    YET ONE JOY HAVE I, HID CLOSE, ... 744 ROSY CROSS   8
    AND I SHALL LAUGH WITH JOY. COME HITHER, AIBRIC, . . 760 SHADOW WATER A   249
    THOUGH BATTLE JOY MAY BE SO DEAR . . . . 791 REPRISALS   7
JOYOUS
    AND FLUNG THE JOYOUS HUNTING-SPEAR! . . . . 23 OISIN 1 V 345A
    THE JOYOUS FLOCKS OF DEER AND ANTELOPE, ... 75 ANASHU VIJAYA   74
    THE JOYOUS FLOCKS OF DEER AND ANTELOPES, ... 75 ANASHU VIJAYA V 74
    NOR AVALON THE GRASS-GREEN HOLLOW, NOR JOYOUS ISLE. . 209 UNDER THE MOON   2
    OR AVALLON THE GRASS GREEN HOLLOW, OR JOYOUS ISLE . . 209 UNDER THE MOON V 2
    IS NOT MORE FAIR AND JOYOUS THAN SHE IS . . . . . 661 ISLE STAT II 1   71
JOY'S
    JOY'S BROTHER, FEAR, DWELLS EVER IN EACH BREAST-- . . 651 ISLE STAT I 1   155
    JOY'S BROTHER, FEAR, LURKS IN EACH LEAFY WAY. . . . 651 ISLE STAT I 1   156
JOYS
    HERE, WHERE MEN KNOW THE GRACIOUS WOODLAND JOYS, . . 651 ISLE STAT I 1   154
    TO JOYS UNHUMAN, AND TO THEE--SPEAK! SPEAK! . . . . 684 SEEKER   60
    JOYS AND FEARS IN THEIR GREY FACES THAT THE LIVE EARTH 719 PHANTOM SHIP   26
        KNOWETH NOT:
    THOUGHTLESS JOYS AND SORROWS SAGE. . . . . 733 STREET DANCERS V 47
JUAN
    UPON GREAT JUAN RIDING BY: . . . . 294 HATED PLAYBOY   4
    AT GREAT JUAN RIDING BY: . . . . 294 HATED PLAYBOY V 4
    WHILE THAT GREAT JUAN GALLOPED BY: . . . . 294 HATED PLAYBOY V 4
JUBILANT
    A JUBILANT LIFE AMONG THE LEAVES, RETURN, ... 35 OISIN 2 V 89A
JUDGE
    JUDGE OF THE STARS, AND FIND A COURSE FOR US? . . . 224 SHADOW WATER B   61
    FOR HE CAN JUDGE THE STARS AS WELL AS FORGAEL. . . . 225 SHADOW WATER B   63
    TO JUDGE IF A LIGHT SLEEPING FOOL . . . . 304 HOUR DAWN V 52
    TO THIS BARE SOUL, LET ALL MEN JUDGE THAT CAN . . . 542 PARN FUNERAL 1   30
    THE JUDGE AT THE ASSIZE COURT, ... 596 COLONEL MARTIN   46
    YOU THAT WOULD JUDGE ME, DO NOT JUDGE ALONE . . . . 603 GALLERY REVIS   50
    YOU THAT WOULD JUDGE ME, DO NOT JUDGE ALONE . . . . 603 GALLERY REVIS   50
    TO JUDGE WHAT I HAVE DONE. . . . . 604 YOU CONTENT   4
    EYES SPIRITUALISED BY DEATH CAN JUDGE, ... 604 YOU CONTENT   7
    LET HIM BETWEEN US JUDGE, FOR HE CAN GAUGE . . . . 660 ISLE STAT II 1   36
    AND HEAR, AND JUDGE. MY POPINJAY, WHAT NOW? . . . 660 ISLE STAT II 1   40
    THIS THING WE ASK: MUST WE TWO FIGHT?--JUDGE THOU. . 660 ISLE STAT II 1   41
    BEING ALMINTOR'S PAGE. NOW JUDGE YOU HERE. . . . . 660 ISLE STAT II 1   47
    NOW, JUDGE, MUST SHEPHERD THERNOT THERE AND I . . . 661 ISLE STAT II 1   65
JUDGMENT
    WHEN I GAVE JUDGMENT, AND HIS WORDS WERE WISE, . . . 102 FERGUS DRUID   11
    FOR I WOULD HAVE YOUR JUDGMENT UPON ONE . . . . . 280 TWO KINGS   71
    TILL JUDGMENT HAS BEEN GIVEN, AND IF GUILTY, . . . 280 TWO KINGS   74
    CRAZY JANE ON THE DAY OF JUDGMENT . . . . 510 JANE JUDGMENT   T
    THEN STANDS IN JUDGMENT ON HIS SOUL, ... 633 MAN AND ECHO   33
JUGGLER
    THE RED MAN THE JUGGLER SENT . . . . 412 TOWER   92
JUGGLERIES
    AND THERE, IN JUGGLERIES OF SIGHT AND SENSE, . . . 231 SHADOW WATER B   216
    CAUGHT BY AN OLD MAN'S JUGGLERIES . . . . 411 TOWER   60
JUGGLERS
    BUT WOMEN AND JUGGLERS AND PLAYERS ON THE HARP. . . 752 SHADOW WATER A   115
JUGGLING
    FROM MAEVE AND ALL THAT JUGGLING PLAIN, ... 307 HOUR DAWN   120
    THAT JUGGLING NATURE MOUNTS, HER COIL IN THEIR EMBRACES 556 RIBH PATRICK   9
        TWINED.

                                                        PAGE   TITLE   LINE

JUICE
    NOW FROM THAT JUICE THAT MADE THEM WISE . . . .   272 GREY ROCK   26
    BUT FROM THE JUICE THAT MADE THEM WISE . . . .   272 GREY ROCK   V 26
    A CRAZY JUICE THAT MAKES THE PULSES BEAT . . . . . .   384 VISION ROBART   54
    WITH A MIRACLE-WORKING JUICE . . . .   776 AGAINST WITCH   23
JULIET
    AND FLINGS HERSELF OUT OF THE ROOM WHEN JULIET WOULD BE 354 HIS PHOENIX   13
        BRIDE
    AND FLINGS HERSELF OUT OF THE ROOM WHEN JULIET WOULD BE 354 HIS PHOENIX V 13
        A BRIDE
JUNCTURE
    WHAT JUNCTURE OF THE APPLE AND THE YEW, ...   555 RIBH AT TOMB   8
JUNE
    THE NIGHT SMELLED RICH WITH JUNE. . . . . . .   160 CAP AND BELLS V 28
    --BEN JONSON'S PHRASE--AND FIND WHEN JUNE IS COME . . .   321 REED WHISPERER   6
    NOR FAERIES IN THE HONEY-HEART OF JUNE ASTIR. . . .   661 ISLE STAT II 1   73
    BY BOSKY JUNE I SWEAR, AND BY THE BEE, HER MINISTER. . .   661 ISLE STAT II 1   74
JUNES
    IN THE JUNES THAT WERE WARMER THAN THESE ARE, ...   91 OLD FISHERMAN   3
JUNO
    OR ELSE ALL JUNO FROM AN URN DISPLAYS . . . . . .   418 ANCEST HOUSES   27
JUNO'S
    JUNO'S PEACOCK SCREAMED. . . . .   422 MY TABLE   32
JUPITER
    IF JUPITER AND SATURN MEET, ...   562 CONJUNCTIONS   1
JUST
    AND MY BABY WAS JUST BORN: . . . .   94 MOLL MAGEE   14
    JUST TRUTH ENOUGH TO SHOW THAT HIS WHOLE LIFE . . . . .   373 PHASES OF MOON   22
    JUST NOW MY SOUL ROSE UP AND TOUCHED IT, FAR . . . . .   705 REMEMBRANCE   13
JUSTICE
    HE FOUND THE UNPERSUADABLE JUSTICE, HE FOUND . . . . .   369 EGO DOMINUS   36
JUSTIFY
    JUSTIFY ALL THOSE RENOWNED GENERATIONS: . . . . .   545 TO SAME TUNE 2   1
    JUSTIFY ALL THOSE RENOWNED GENERATIONS, ...   546 TO SAME TUNE 2   11
    JUSTIFY ALL THAT HAVE SUNK IN THEIR BLOOD, ...   546 TO SAME TUNE 2   12
    JUSTIFY ALL THAT HAVE DIED ON THE SCAFFOLD, ...   546 TO SAME TUNE 2   13
    JUSTIFY ALL THAT HAVE FLED, THAT HAVE STOOD, ...   546 TO SAME TUNE 2   14
    JUSTIFY ALL THAT HAVE FLED OR HAVE STOOD, ...   546 TO SAME TUNE 2 V 14
KAMA
    THE HOUR WHEN KAMA, FULL OF SLEEPY LAUGHTER, ...   72 ANASHU VIJAYA   26
    THE HOUR WHEN KAMA, WITH A SUMPTUOUS SMILE, ...   72 ANASHU VIJAYA V 26
KANVA
    KANVA, THE INDIAN, ON GOD . . . .   76 INDIAN ON GOD V T
    KANVA ON HIMSELF. . . . .   723 KANVA ON SELF   T
KATE
    AND OUR POOR KATE OR NAN IS LESS . . . .   190 BAILE AILLINN   35
    AND WHEN WE WALK WITH KATE OR NAN . . . .   192 BAILE AILLINN   92
KATHLEEN
    KATHLEEN . . . .   124 CATHLEEN PARA V T
KATHLEEN-NY-HOOLIHAN
    OF KATHLEEN-NY-HOOLIHAN. . . . .   207 HANRAHANS SONG V REF
    OUR KATHLEEN-NY-HOOLIHAN. . . . .   208 HANRAHANS SONG V 15
KAURI
    FROM THE BOOK OF KAURI THE INDIAN-- SECTION V. ON THE 76 INDIAN ON GOD V T
        NATURE OF GOD
KEATS
    NO ONE DENIES TO KEATS LOVE OF THE WORLD: . . . . . .   370 EGO DOMINUS   52
KEDRON
    THE VINEGAR-HEAVY SPONGE, THE FLOWERS BY KEDRON STREAM: 172 TRAV PASSION   5
KEEN   SEE RAZOR-KEEN
    THAT FOLLOWED MY KEEN HUNTING-CALL-- . . . . . .   23 OISIN 1   V 345F
    I STOOD: KEEN STARS ABOVE ME SHONE, ...   83 MAD KING GOLL   29
    AROUND ME SHONE KEEN EYES OF MEN: . . . . . .   83 MAD KING GOLL   30
    THE HOUNDS KEEN FOR THE DEAD. . . . . . .   99 FOXHUNTER V 48
    HOW CAN WE RAISE THE KEEN THAT DO NOT KNOW . . . .   240 SHADOW WATER B   389
    THAT I SHOULD KEEN HIM FROM THE FULL OF THE MOON . . .   243 SHADOW WATER B   446
    THERE'S KEEN DELIGHT IN WHAT WE HAVE: . . . . .   485 NINETEENTH CEN   2
    AND EYES THAT HAD SO KEEN A SIGHT? . . . . . .   529 TOM LUNATIC   4
    SHOWERED AWAY THE KEEN DEW DROPS: . . . .   705 DAWN-SONG   18
KEENED
    . . . KEENED IN THE GATES OF MY HEART. . . . . . .   57 OISIN 3   152
KEENERS
    CAME KEENERS HOARSER THAN ROOKS, ...   92 FATHER OHART   22
KEENIN'
    AND KEENIN' TO MYSEL'. . . . .   96 MOLL MAGEE   48
KEENING
    HE BADE THEM GIVE OVER THEIR KEENING: . . . . . .   93 FATHER OHART   23
    THERE WAS NO HUMAN KEENING: . . . .   93 FATHER OHART   29
    CAME KEENING IN THAT DAY. . . . .   93 FATHER OHART   32
    KEENING IN FROM TIRARAGH, ...   93 FATHER OHART   35
    KEENING FROM BALLINAFAD: . . . .   93 FATHER OHART   36
    KEENING FROM INISHMURRAY, ...   93 FATHER OHART   37
    OLD WOMEN WERE KEENING THE DEAD: . . . .   145 HOST OF AIR V 40D
KEEP
    SHOOT ON HIM SHAFTS OF QUIETNESS, THAT HE MAY EVER KEEP   75 ANASHU VIJAYA   81
    SHOOT ON HIM SHAFTS OF QUIETNESS, AND ORDER HIM TO KEEP   75 ANASHU VIJAYA V 81
    "THE RED BRANCH KINGS A TIRELESS BANQUET KEEP, ...   108 CUCHULAIN SEA V 33
    CUCHULAIN CRIED, "HAVE MADE AND KEEP THAT VOW." . . .   109 CUCHULAIN SEA V 56
    THE ROAD-SIDE TREES KEEP MURMURING-- . . . . .   131 OLD PENSIONER V 13
    HE HAD HALF A CLOAK TO KEEP HIM DRY, ...   190 BAILE AILLINN   29
    AND KEEP TO THE ONE WEARY MARRIAGE-BED. . . . . . .   224 SHADOW WATER B   55

		PAGE	TITLE	LINE
KEEP (CONTINUED)				
AND KEEP TO THE ONE WEARY MARRIAGE BED.		224	SHADOW WATER B V	55
WHY DO YOU NEED A SWORD? BUT YOU MAY KEEP IT.		241	SHADOW WATER B	400
WE'LL KEEP THE SECRET—A NEW TRICK TO PLEASE.		265	ABBEY THEATRE	10
THAN MOUND AND STONE THAT KEEP ALL VIRTUE IN,		281	TWO KINGS	106
TO KEEP HIS FELLOWS FROM THEIR SLEEP;		297	THREE BEGGARS	45
AND THOUGH HE KEEP A DOG AND A GUN,		301	RUN PARADISE	12
TO KEEP HIM UPRIGHT WHILE HE CURSED;		302	HOUR DAWN	6
BUT LET HIM KEEP HIS GRAVE FOR ONCE		303	HOUR DAWN	38
BUT I ALONE BEING BLESSED KEEP		307	HOUR DAWN	104
TO KEEP THE BODY YOUNG.		334	SONG	4
WHO WERE NOT BORN TO KEEP IN TRIM		336	YOUNG BEAUTY	10
WHAT ELSE HE GIVE OR KEEP		346	ON WOMAN	24
CANNOT BUT KEEP THE FORM		350	MEMORY	5
THE EYE OF THE MIND NOR KEEP MY TONGUE FROM SPEECH."		353	PEOPLE	34
OTHERS BECAUSE YOU DID NOT KEEP		357	DEEP-SWORN VOW	1
WE POETS KEEP OUR MOUTHS SHUT, FOR IN TRUTH		359	WAR POEM V	2
A POET KEEP HIS MOUTH SHUT, FOR IN TRUTH		359	WAR POEM V	2
OR KEEP US ALL AWAKE WITH BAYING AT THE MOON,		364	DOLLS FACES	11
FOR ENGLAND MAY KEEP FAITH		394	EASTER 1916	68
THEY MUST TO KEEP THEIR CERTAINTY ACCUSE		398	LEADERS CROWD	1
TO KEEP A DROWSY EMPEROR AWAKE;		408	SAIL BYZANTIUM	29
AND MAY DEPARTING TWILIGHT KEEP		435	FOR MY SON	5
AND THERE IS NONE SO FIT TO KEEP A WATCH AND KEEP		442	BLACK CENTAUR	15
AND THERE IS NONE SO FIT TO KEEP A WATCH AND KEEP		442	BLACK CENTAUR	15
BUT KEEP A MARBLE OR A BRONZE REPOSE.		445	SCHOOL CHILDR	52
CRUELTY MUST KEEP; THEREFORE BE WARNED AND GO		448	HERO GIRL FOOL	7
MY CRUELTY MUST KEEP; AND SO BEGONE		448	HERO GIRL FOOL V	7
AND HAVE NO NEED OF CRUELTY TO KEEP		448	HERO GIRL FOOL V	12A
MUST KEEP THAT PERFECT, AS THEY KEEP HER SONG,		461	HARUN RASHID	18
MUST KEEP THAT PERFECT, AS THEY KEEP HER SONG,		461	HARUN RASHID	18
COULD KEEP A SWALLOW TO ITS FIRST INTENT;		489	COOLE PARK 29	19
YET KEEP HIS SUBSTANCE WHOLE.		573	LADYS 2ND SONG	13
THAT THE SWORDSMEN AND THE LADIES CAN STILL KEEP COMPANY,		581	CURSE CROMWELL	20
AND KEEP ME DANCING STILL		591	DRUNK SOBRIETY	2
AND THEREFORE KEEP ME DANCING		592	DRUNK SOBRIETY	7
KEEP DANCING LIKE A WAVE,		592	DRUNK SOBRIETY	10
"AND DID YOU KEEP NO GOLD, TOM?		596	COLONEL MARTIN	64
SHOULD KEEP THEIR LOVERS WAITING?		597	MODEL LAUREATE	7
KEEP THEIR LOVERS WAITING?		597	MODEL LAUREATE	8
AND KEEP THEIR LOVERS WAITING.		597	MODEL LAUREATE	15
KEEP THEIR LOVERS WAITING.		597	MODEL LAUREATE	16
WOULD KEEP HIS LOVER WAITING,		598	MODEL LAUREATE	23
KEEP HIS LOVER WAITING?		598	MODEL LAUREATE	24
KEEP THOSE CHILDREN OUT.		618	LONG-LEG FLY	24
FOR DEATH WHO TAKES WHAT MAN WOULD KEEP,		620	JOHN KINSELLA	3
TO KEEP THE SOUL OF MAN ALIVE,		620	JOHN KINSELLA	19
WHILE MAN CAN STILL HIS BODY KEEP		633	MAN AND ECHO	25
MAIDEN, COME FORTH! THE WOODS KEEP WATCH FOR THEE;		645	ISLE STAT I 1	1
AND THY MEMORY I KEEP,		647	ISLE STAT I 1	59
I KEEP SUCH THINGS ABOUT ME; THEY ARE FOOD		721	WITCH VIVIEN	37
AND KEEP A COVERED HEAD."		742	EARL PAUL	64
KEEP HIDDEN AND COVERED HER HEART!"		744	GLOVE CLOAK	12
SHE WOULD WEAVE A NET TO TAKE US. SHE MIGHT KEEP FAITH;		756	SHADOW WATER A	190
THAT DESPAIR AND KEEP THE PACE		787	HUDDON DUDDON	9
KEEPER SEE STABLE-KEEPER				
THE COARSE-BRED SON OF A LIVERY-STABLE KEEPER—		370	EGO DOMINUS	61
THE ILL-BRED SON OF A LIVERY STABLE KEEPER—		370	EGO DOMINUS V	61
KEEPING				
A REASON FOR KEEPING SILENT		359	WAR POEM V	T
KEEPING ALL THE KERRY MEN		585	ORAHILLY	14
I THERE HAD BEEN KEEPING		672	ISLE STAT II 3	171
KEEPS				
THAT KEEPS THE STARS IN THEIR ROUND,		165	CRY OF SEDGE	5
SHE KEEPS THAT IGNORANCE, NOR HAS SHE NOW		468	HARUN RASHID	164
REPENTANCE KEEPS MY HEART IMPURE;		507	STREAM AND SUN	6
KEEPS PARNELL IN HIS MIND.		586	PARNELLITES	20
WHO KEEPS THE TILL. NOW THAT MY LADDER'S GONE,		630	CIRCUS ANIMALS	38
KEGS				
CARE MORE ABOUT THE KEGS OF SILVER AND GOLD		232	SHADOW WATER B	234
THREE KEGS OF GOLD.		596	COLONEL MARTIN	49
YOU HAD THREE KEGS" SAID HE.		596	COLONEL MARTIN	65
KENNEL				
"TO STABLE AND TO KENNEL GO;		97	FOXHUNTER	5
KEPT				
THAT KEPT DIM WATERS FROM THE SKY;		17	OISIN 1	243
KEPT TIME WITH THEIR BRIGHT WINGS AND FEET;		26	OISIN 1	397
THE EVER-LIVING HAVE KEPT MY BARGAIN FOR ME,		232	SHADOW WATER B	223
YOU KEPT THE MUSES' STERNER LAWS,		273	GREY ROCK	59
I HAVE KEPT MY FAITH, THOUGH FAITH WAS TRIED,		276	GREY ROCK	124
IN DAYS YOU HAVE NOT KEPT IN MEMORY,		284	TWO KINGS	168
WHO HAD SEEN, BEING KEPT FOR SHOW		319	DOLLS	5
OR ESSERKELLY PLAIN, FEW KEPT HIS PACE;		326	ROBERT GREGORY	59
AND ESERKELLY PLAINS, FEW KEPT HIS PACE;		326	ROBERT GREGORY V	59
OR ESERKELLY PLAINS, FEW KEPT HIS PACE;		326	ROBERT GREGORY V	59
THEY HAD KEPT A STEADY PACE AS THOUGH THEIR BEDS,		372	PHASES OF MOON	5
THIS MAN HAD KEPT A SCHOOL		392	EASTER 1916	24
AND AFTER KEPT IT FROM DECAY;		460	THREE MONUMENT	7
"I KEPT HER MUCH IN THE COUNTRY		594	COLONEL MARTIN	10
HOW FERENCZ RENYI KEPT SILENT.		709	FERENCZ RENYI	T

417

		PAGE	TITLE	LINE

KERCHIEF
THAT FOLLOWED IF I LET THE KERCHIEF FALL' • • • • • •   533 HER TRIUMPH   4
KERRY
KEEPING ALL THE KERRY MEN • • • • • • • • • •   585 ORAHILLY   14
KESTREL
LIES TORN AND ROTTING. THE FIERCE KESTREL BIRDS • • •   675 ISLE STAT II 3   234
KETTLE
OR THE KETTLE ON THE HOB • • • • • • • • •   88 STOLEN CHILD   46
A SORT OF BATTERED KETTLE AT THE HEEL• • • • • • •   409 TOWER   16
THE DRUMS AND THE KETTLE DRUMS • • • • • • •   527 AM OF IRELAND V   21
KETTLEDRUM
TRUMPET AND KETTLEDRUM, • • • • • • • • • •   317 NIGHT COME   9
KETTLEDRUMS
THE DRUMS AND THE KETTLEDRUMS • • • • • • • •   527 AM OF IRELAND   21
KETTLES
OLD KETTLES, OLD BOTTLES, AND A BROKEN CAN, • • • •   630 CIRCUS ANIMALS   36
KEVIN
KEVIN O'HIGGINS' COUNTENANCE THAT WEARS • • • • •   601 GALLERY REVIS   5
KEVIN O'HIGGINS, AND THAT LOOK HE WEARS, • • • • •   601 GALLERY REVIS V   5
KEY   SEE LIFE-KEY
WE ARE CLOSED IN, AND THE KEY IS TURNED • • • • • •   425 STARES NEST   6
WE ARE CLOSED IN, AND THE KEY TURNED • • • • • •   425 STARES NEST V   6
KEYS
HAVE KEYS TO MY OLD GATE• • • • • • • • • •   607 SONGS BURDEN 2   8
KHAKI
THE KHAKI FROM HIS BACK? • • • • • • • • • •   627 STATES HOLIDAY   17
KICKED
BUT HE KICKED BEFORE HE DIED, • • • • • • • • •   545 TO SAME TUNE 1   25
BUT HE KICKED BEFORE HE DIED, • • • • • • • • •   616 MARCH SONGS 3   25
KID
A KID, HELD BY ONE SOFT WHITE EAR FOR TETHER, • • • •   715 DWELT SYCAMORE   3
KIDRON
THE HISSOP-HEAVY SPONGE, THE FLOWERS BY KIDRON STREAM: • •   172 TRAV PASSION V   5
KID'S
AND STIRS THE YOUNG KID'S BUDDING HORN, • • • • • •   18 OISIN 1   264
KILBARNET
MY BROTHER IS PRIEST OF KILBARNET, • • • • • • •   178 FIDDLER DOONEY V   3
KILL
I'D KILL HIM WHILE WE HAVE THE CHANCE TO DO IT• • • •   224 SHADOW WATER B V   58
AND FORGAEL IN THE OTHER SCALE: KILL FORGAEL, • • • •   225 SHADOW WATER B   76
THEN STUMBLING TO THE KILL BESIDE THE SHORE: • • • •   622 HOUND VOICE   19
THAT STUMBLING TO THE KILL BESIDE THE SHORE: • • • •   622 HOUND VOICE V   19
I'D KILL HER IF SHE WERE. NAY, DO NOT FEAR! • • • •   669 ISLE STAT II 3   69
THREE MOONS. IT WERE BEST TO KILL HIM, AND CHOOSE OUT • •   748 SHADOW WATER A   15
AND NO MAN KILL ME: FOR SOME WIND HAS BLOWN • • • •   751 SHADOW WATER A   97
BUT NOW I WILL KILL HER. ALL COMES TO AN END• • • •   755 SHADOW WATER A   176
KILLED
BUT ALL THAT ARE KILLED IN BATTLE • • • • • •   215 HAPPY TOWNLAND   25
FOR HE WAS KILLED. O! O! O! O! O! O! • • • • •   242 SHADOW WATER B   409
FOR GOLDEN-ARMED IOLLAN HAS BEEN KILLED. • • • • •   242 SHADOW WATER B   410
THEY KILLED HIM AT MY FEET. O! O! O! O! • • • •   242 SHADOW WATER B   420
AND KILLED A LOVER OR HUSBAND AT MY FEET-- • • • •   246 SHADOW WATER B   491
A MAN IS KILLED, OR A HOUSE BURNED, • • • • • •   425 STARES NEST   8
THAT YEAR WHEN GREAT HAROUN EL RASHID KILLED • • • •   462 HARUN RASHID V   31
"THEY KILLED MY GOOSE AND A CAT. • • • • • • •   546 TO SAME TUNE 2   8
"THEY KILLED MY GOOSE AND A CAT. • • • • • • •   546 TO SAME TUNE 2   18
"THEY KILLED MY GOOSE AND A CAT. • • • • • • •   547 TO SAME TUNE 2   28
WAS FORGAEL'S COURAGE THAT THE MUSIC KILLED. • • • •   747 SHADOW WATER A   9
I HAD KILLED HIM LONG AGO, BUT THAT THE FOOL • • • •   748 SHADOW WATER A   17
SO THESE WOULD HAVE KILLED FORGAEL WHILE ASLEEP • • • •   748 SHADOW WATER A   25
WITH ONE YOU HAVE KILLED AND DIE: FOR WHEN I LEFT • • •   758 SHADOW WATER A   226
WITH SOME YOU HAVE KILLED AND DIE: FOR WHEN I LEFT • • •   758 SHADOW WATER A V   226
KILLS
AND WOOD-OF-WONDERS, WHERE ONE KILLS AN OX AT DAWN, • • •   209 UNDER THE MOON   9
KILTARTAN
MY COUNTRY IS KILTARTAN CROSS, • • • • • • • •   328 IRISH AIRMAN   5
FLIT TO KILTARTAN CROSS AND STAY • • • • • • •   791 REPRISALS   11
KILTARTAN'S
MY COUNTRYMEN KILTARTAN'S POOR, • • • • • • • •   328 IRISH AIRMAN   6
KILVARNET
MY COUSIN IS PRIEST IN KILVARNET, • • • • • • •   178 FIDDLER DOONEY   3
MY BROTHER IS PRIEST IN KILVARNET, • • • • • • •   178 FIDDLER DOONEY V   3
KIMONOS
TWO GIRLS IN SILK KIMONOS, BOTH • • • • • • •   475 EVA GORE-BOOTH   3
TWO GIRLS IN SILK KIMONOS, BOTH • • • • • • •   475 EVA GORE-BOOTH   19
KIN
BUT WHERE ARE YOUR NOBLE KITH AND KIN, • • • • •   5 OISIN 1   44
THY NAME, THY KIN, AND THY COUNTRY," • • • • • •   5 OISIN 1 V   44
IN THE HOUSE OF HIS FRIEND, OF HIS KIN, OF HIS BROTHER,   26 OISIN 1 V   405
RODE FROM THE COUNTRY OF HER KIN, • • • • • •   191 BAILE AILLINN   50
AND THE NEAREST KIN OF THE MOON, • • • • • •   378 CAT AND MOON   3
"FAIR AND FOUL ARE NEAR OF KIN, • • • • • • •   513 JANE TALK BISH   7
HIVES, CURRANT BUSHES. THERE HIS KIN ARE. HIGH • •   710 FERENCZ RENYI   25
HIVES, CURRANT-BUSHES. THERE HIS KIN ARE. HIGH • •   710 FERENCZ RENYI V   25
HALF HID. HE BRINGS THE PEASANT'S ONLY KIN, • • •   711 FERENCZ RENYI   50
"NOW HATH HE KITH OR KIN, OR ANY FRIEND?" • • • •   712 FERENCZ RENYI   66
KIND   SEE WOMAN-KIND MAN-KIND GOD-KIND
BUT ONLY KIND AND MERRY BREATH, • • • • • • •   19 OISIN 1   285
O SIGH, O FLUTTERING SIGH, BE KIND TO ME: • • • •   33 OISIN 2   57
FOR THE KIND WIRES ARE TORN AND STILL, • • • • •   86 MAD KING GOLL   69
WEARY AND KIND ONE LINGERED BY HIS SEAT: • • • • •   112 ROSE OF WORLD   13

		PAGE	TITLE	LINE

KIND (CONTINUED)
    WEARY AND KIND ONE STOOD BESIDE HIS SEAT!   112 ROSE OF WORLD   V   13
    AND LOVE IS LESS KIND THAN THE GREY TWILIGHT,   148 INTO TWILIGHT   15
    THE POWERS, NOT KIND LIKE YOU, CAME WHERE GOD'S GARDEN   174 ELEMENT POWERS V   1
        BLOWS,
    ONE THAT IS EVER KIND SAID YESTERDAY!   199 FOLLY COMFORT   1
    "YOUR STRENGTH, THAT IS SO LOFTY AND FIERCE AND KIND,   201 OLD MEMORY   3
    BUT A BRIEF, DREAMY, KIND DELIGHT.   202 NEVER GIVE ALL   7
    I KNOW WHERE A DIM MOON DRIFTS, WHERE THE DANAAN KIND   203 WITHER BOUGHS   12
    AND I KNOW OF THE ISLES WHERE THE DANAAN KIND   203 WITHER BOUGHS   V   12
    AND OF APPLE ISLANDS WHERE THE DANAAN KIND   203 WITHER BOUGHS   12
    BUT OF A BEAUTIFUL, UNHEARD-OF KIND   228 SHADOW WATER B   142
    WITH BEAUTY LIKE A TIGHTENED BOW, A KIND   256 NO SECOND TROY   8
    YET OLD ROMANCE BEING KIND, LET HIM PREVAIL   258 KING NO KING   5
    A KIND MILD WOMAN HAD SHE BEEN, WHO POURED   279 TWO KINGS   V   62A
    BUT NOW SHE HAD NO MILD AND NO KIND LOOK!   279 TWO KINGS   V   62D
    YET THEY WERE OF A DIFFERENT KIND,   289 SEPTEMBER 1913   9
    OF YOUR OWN PASSIONATE SERVING KIND WHO HAD BROUGHT   292 TO A SHADE   10
    OF YOUR OWN PASSIONATE SERVING KIND WHO HAS BROUGHT   292 TO A SHADE   10
    KIND EYES SHOULD BE MORE LEARN'D?   312 TWO YEAR LATER   2
    A FRIENDSHIP OF HER KIND   345 ON WOMAN   4
    HE HAS FOUND, AFTER THE MANNER OF HIS KIND,   373 PHASES OF MOON   12
    A KIND OLD NUN IN A WHITE HOOD REPLIES!   443 SCHOOL CHILDR   2
    AND I THOUGH NEVER OF LEDAEAN KIND   444 SCHOOL CHILDR   29
    THERE IS A COMFORTABLE KIND OF OLD SCARECROW.   444 SCHOOL CHILDR   32
    YET ALL MUST COPY COPIES, ALL INCREASE THEIR KIND!   556 RIBH PATRICK   7
    HE WAS OF SUCH A KIND   586 PARNELLITES   18
    "KIND ARE ALL YOUR WORDS, MY DEAR,   588 OLD WICKED MAN   10
    AND STONY-HEARTED; NOW THOU HAST GROWN KIND,   670 ISLE STAT II 3   91
    NOW BE COURTEOUS, NOW BE KIND,   717 FAIRY DOCTOR   21
    GREET HIM COURTEOUS, GREET HIM KIND,   717 FAIRY DOCTOR   V   21
    HE HOVERS ABOVE THE MAST AND WAITS HIS KIND!   753 SHADOW WATER A   135
    FOR LOVE IS KIND AND HAPPY. O COME WITH ME!   767 SHADOW WATER A   396
    OR GROW KIND, FOR THEY ANOINT   776 AGAINST WITCH   21
    AND LETS THE KIND WORM TAKE THE LOT!   779 ACCURSED WHO   4
KINDER
    THIS BEAUTY'S KINDER, YET FOR A REASON   199 ARROW   7
KINDLING
    MAKING WAY FROM THE KINDLING SURGES, I RODE ON A   58 OISIN 3   161
        BRIDLE-PATH
KINDLY
    AND LOVE IS KINDLY AND DECEITLESS,   77 INDIAN TO LOVE V   5D
    I SAW A KINDLY NEIGHBOUR   95 MOLL MAGEE   35
    BUT, KINDLY OLD ROUT   142 MOODS   V   5
KINDNESS
    A DRUID KINDNESS, ON ALL HEARERS FELL.   129 BOOK STORIES   4
    THE HOURLY KINDNESS, THE DAY'S COMMON SPEECH,   258 KING NO KING   14
    AND THANKED HER FOR HER KINDNESS TO HIS BROTHER,   286 TWO KINGS   212
    "I THANK YOU FOR YOUR KINDNESS TO MY BROTHER,   286 TWO KINGS   V   212
    REMEMBERING KINDNESS DONE, AND HOW CAN I,   340 SHEP GOATHERD   30
    WITH THE OLD KINDNESS, THE OLD DISTINGUISHED GRACE,   362 HER COURTESY   1
    LOSE NATURAL KINDNESS AND MAYBE   404 FOR DAUGHTER   22
    FROM A GLAD KINDNESS CANNOT TAKE HIS EYES.   404 FOR DAUGHTER   40
    LIKE THE MOON HER KINDNESS IS,   452 HUMAN DIGNITY   1
    IF KINDNESS I MAY CALL   452 HUMAN DIGNITY   2
KINDRED
    WHEN TWO CLOSE KINDRED MEET,   378 CAT AND MOON   12
    A PROUD WOMAN NOT KINDRED OF HIS SOUL.   479 SELF AND SOUL   64
    RISE AS KINDRED SHOULD.   518 LOVES LONENESS   2
    CONVICTED COWARDS ALL, BY KINDRED SLAIN   634 CUCHULAIN COMF   21
KINDRED'S
    AND TELL ME HOW MY KINDRED'S TEARS ARE WELLING,   33 OISIN 2   V   66
KINDS
    LIKE AN OLD PAUPER, IN ALL KINDS OF WEATHER!   205 ADAMS CURSE   9
KINE
    THE MERRY LAMBS AND THE COMPLACENT KINE,   75 ANASHU VIJAYA   86
    THE MERRY LAMBS AND ALL THE KINE COMPLACENT,   75 ANASHU VIJAYA V   86
    HAVE THEY NE'ER SEEN THE EYES OF LYNX OR KINE,   672 ISLE STAT II 3   152
KING   SEE SEA-KING
    IS NIAM, DAUGHTER OF THE KING   5 OISIN 1   V   49
    "I HAVE NOT YET, WAR-WEARY KING,   6 OISIN 1   55
    "NOT SO, GREAT KING! FOR I HAVE NE'ER   6 OISIN 1   V   55
    MY ANGRY, KING REMEMBERING SOUL ONE JOT!   36 OISIN 2   V   94
    I CRIED, "COME OUT OF THE SHADOW, KING OF THE NAILS OF   51 OISIN 3   61
        GOLD!
    MAY PANTHERS END HIM.--HEAR, AND LOAD OUR KING   71 ANASHU VIJAYA   6
    THE MADNESS OF KING GOLL   81 MAD KING GOLL   T
    I WAS A WISE YOUNG KING OF OLD!   81 MAD KING GOLL V   1
    WHAT WOULD YOU, KING OF THE PROUD RED BRANCH KINGS?   102 FERGUS DRUID   8
    WHAT WOULD YOU, KING OF THE PROUD RED BRANCH KINGS?   102 FERGUS DRUID   15
    A KING AND PROUD! AND THAT IS MY DESPAIR.   103 FERGUS DRUID   16
    WHAT WOULD YOU, FERGUS? BE NO MORE A KING,   103 FERGUS DRUID   21
    A KING IS BUT A FOOLISH LABOURER   103 FERGUS DRUID   27
    WHAT WOULD YOU? I WOULD BE NO MORE A KING,   103 FERGUS DRUID   V   21
    WHAT WOULD YOU, KING OF THE PROUD RED BRANCH KINGS?   103 FERGUS DRUID V   21
    I'D PUT AWAY THE FOOLISH MIGHT OF A KING,   103 FERGUS DRUID   V   21A
    A WILD AND FOOLISH LABOURER IS A KING   103 FERGUS DRUID   V   27
    A KING SITTING UPON A CHAIR OF GOLD--   104 FERGUS DRUID   36
    AND CONCHUBAR, THE RED BRANCH KING OF KINGS,   109 CUCHULAIN SEA   .45
    CUMHAL THE KING, BEING ANGRY AND SAD,   166 BLESSED   V   1
    OF THE CROWNED MAGI; AND THE KING WHOSE EYES   169 SECRET ROSE   9

	PAGE	TITLE		LINE
KING (CONTINUED)				
AND THE PROUD DREAMING KING WHO FLUNG THE CROWN	170	SECRET ROSE		19
A KING OF THE GREAT PLAIN WOULD SPEAK WITH YOU."	183	QUEEN MAEVE		78
AND WITH GLAD VOICE MAEVE ANSWERED HIM, "WHAT KING	183	QUEEN MAEVE		79
AILLINN, WHO WAS KING LUGAIDH'S HEIR.	189	BAILE AILLINN		7
SOME GOD OR KING HAD MADE THE LAWS	194	BAILE AILLINN		131
A KING AND A QUEEN ARE WANDERING THERE, AND THE SOUND	204	WITHER BOUGHS		19
THERE IS A KING AND QUEEN UPON HER DECK,	232	SHADOW WATER B		226
MY HUSBAND AND MY KING DIED AT MY FEET,	237	SHADOW WATER B		337
WHAT NAME HAD THAT DEAD KING? ARTHUR OF BRITAIN?	242	SHADOW WATER B		404
BEND LOWER, O KING, THAT I MAY CROWN YOU WITH IT.	251	SHADOW WATER B		607
KING AND NO KING	258	KING NO KING		T
KING AND NO KING	258	KING NO KING		T
THE NO KING CRIED WHO AFTER THAT WAS KING,	258	KING NO KING		2
THE NO KING CRIED WHO AFTER THAT WAS KING,	258	KING NO KING		2
ALTHOUGH THE KING OF IRELAND'S DEAD	273	GREY ROCK		68
MURROUGH, THE KING OF IRELAND'S SON.	274	GREY ROCK		71
KING EOCHAID CAME AT SUNDOWN TO A WOOD	276	TWO KINGS		1
KING EOCHAID SAID, AND HE THAT BORE HIS SHIELD	276	TWO KINGS	V	8
RENDING THE HORSE'S FLANK. KING EOCHAID REELED,	277	TWO KINGS		13
RIPPED THROUGH THE HORSE'S FLANKS. KING EOCHAID REELED,	277	TWO KINGS	V	13
KING EOCHAID SEIZED THE HORNS IN HIS STRONG HANDS	278	TWO KINGS		24
THE DISEMBOWELLED HORSE. KING EOCHAID RAN	278	TWO KINGS		45
THE DISEMBOWELLED HORSE. KING EOCHAID GAZED,	278	TWO KINGS	V	45
BECAUSE THAT WERE A GUILT AGAINST HER KING,	280	TWO KINGS	V	74A
AND RAISE HIS PILLAR STONE." KING EOCHAID SAID,	280	TWO KINGS	V	83
YET ANSWERED HIM, "I AM KING EOCHAID'S WIFE	284	TWO KINGS		173
CROW UPON TARA." KING EOCHAID BOWED HIS HEAD	286	TWO KINGS		211
AND IN THE MIDST KING EOCHAID'S BROTHER STOOD,	286	TWO KINGS		217
UPON KING EOCHAID'S FACE, WHO LOWERED HIS FACE	286	TWO KINGS	V	211A
AND FOR THE LOVE THAT YOU HAVE SHOWN YOUR KING,	286	TWO KINGS	V	212A
KING GUAIRE WALKED AMID HIS COURT	295	THREE BEGGARS		8
WITH HIS OLD THOUGHTS; KING GUAIRE WENT	296	THREE BEGGARS		26
TO A POET OR A KING	299	THREE HERMITS		27
AND THERE THE KING IS BUT AS THE BEGGAR.	301	RUN PARADISE		7
AND THERE THE KING IS BUT AS THE BEGGAR.	301	RUN PARADISE		14
AND THERE THE KING IS BUT AS THE BEGGAR.	301	RUN PARADISE		21
AND THERE THE KING IS BUT AS THE BEGGAR.	301	RUN PARADISE		28
AND SHE SEEMED HAPPY AS A KING,	313	MEMORY YOUTH	V	6
BUT LIVED AS 'TWERE A KING	317	NIGHT COME		6
WHERE MANY A KING HAS GONE	330	BONE OF A HARE		2
OF GOLDEN KING AND SILVER LADY,	331	ROUND TOWER		13
THAT GOLDEN KING AND THAT WILD LADY	332	ROUND TOWER		19
THAT LADY AND THAT GOLDEN KING	332	ROUND TOWER		23
INTO A PLOUGHSHARE? PARLIAMENT AND KING	429	NINETEEN 19		20
KING ABUNDANCE GOT HIM ON	440	WISDOM		16
UPON THE BOTTOM OF A KING OF KINGS;	445	SCHOOL CHILDR		44
SHRIEKS, "I AM KING OF THE PEACOCKS,"	456	FRIENDS YOUTH		15
"I HAVE BEEN A KING,	495	MOHINI CHATTER		5
. . . "THE KING OF THE GREAT CLOCK TOWER"	549	SEVERED HEAD		T
THE KING THAT COULD MAKE HIS PEOPLE STARE,	550	SEVERED HEAD		19
PITCH LIKE KING BILLY BOMB-BALLS IN	565	LAPIS LAZULI		7
MY KING A LOST KING, AND LOST SOLDIERS MY MEN;	591	WHAT WAS LOST		3
MY KING A LOST KING, AND LOST SOLDIERS MY MEN;	591	WHAT WAS LOST		3
OR THE KING OF GREECE,	627	STATES HOLIDAY		19
A KING HAD SOME BEAUTIFUL COUSINS,	628	JANE MOUNTAIN		7
CARES WHAT KING SETS UP HIS RULE.	635	BLACK TOWER		14
MEETING LONG HENCE THE PHANTOM HERDSMAN, KING	675	ISLE STAT II 3		242
YOUTH, HERE WILL WE ABIDE, AND BE THOU KING	679	ISLE STAT II 3		314
OF THIS LAKE-NURTURED ISLE! LET THY KING BE	679	ISLE STAT II 3		315
CLEAR-BROWED ARCADIAN, THOU SHALT BE OUR KING!	679	ISLE STAT II 3		318
CLEAR-BROWED ARCADIAN, THOU SHALT BE OUR KING!	679	ISLE STAT II 3		321
AND THEN THE GREAT ONES COME, AND LAST THE KING.	722	WITCH VIVIEN		54
EARL PAUL CAME WHERE THE KING SAT,	740	EARL PAUL		29
AND YOU, MY AIBRIC, WHO HAVE BEEN A KING	748	SHADOW WATER A		27
ENDS ALL THINGS. I HAVE SLAIN THE LOCHLANN KING.	754	SHADOW WATER A		163
I AND THAT MIGHTY KING A SUDDEN BLOW	757	SHADOW WATER A		195
OF THE TWELVE KINGS OF THE WORLD TO BE MY KING,	757	SHADOW WATER A		214
THAT WOULD BE HAPPIEST. HE IS A KING	768	SHADOW WATER A		410
I CROWN YOU WITH THIS CROWN. BEND LOWER, O KING,	768	SHADOW WATER A		423
WHETHER A KING OR CLOWN!	789	SINGING HEAD		18
FOR PRAISE OF CLOWN OR KING,	789	SINGING HEAD		20
THEN FARRELL, STEEL KING, MASTER OF MEN,	790	DEDICATION		5
KINGDOM				
TO MY OWN KINGDOM IN THE SEA—	8	OISIN 1	V	80A
IN WHAT FAR KINGDOM DO YOU GO,	10	OISIN 1		115
IN WHAT FAR KINGDOM DO YE GO,	10	OISIN 1	V	115
AND BRING HER TO HER KINGDOM AND HER PEOPLE.	755	SHADOW WATER A		170
MUSIC OF A LOST KINGDOM	782	GREY ROUND		2
MUSIC OF A LOST KINGDOM?	783	GREY ROUND		12
KINGDOMS				
COME AND DREAM OF KINGS AND KINGDOMS,	737	IN FIRELIGHT		1
KINGDOMS RISING, KINGDOMS FALLING,	737	IN FIRELIGHT		9
KINGDOMS RISING, KINGDOMS FALLING.	737	IN FIRELIGHT		9
KINGFISHER				
AND THE KINGFISHER TURNS TO A BALL OF DUST,	27	OISIN 1	V	418
AND THE KINGFISHER TURNS TO A BALL OF DUST,	28	OISIN 1		422
KINGFISHER COLOUR GREW WITH RAGE. HE ROSE	40	OISIN 2	V	169
BEFORE I DROPPED ASLEEP, A KINGFISHER	761	SHADOW WATER A		274
KINGFISHERS				
LIKE WINGS OF KINGFISHERS; AND HE AROSE	40	OISIN 2		169

420

```
                                                PAGE    TITLE          LINE
KINGLY
  A GENTLE YET A KINGLY CHILD!  . . . . . . . . .  82 MAD KING GOLL  V    8
  A GRACIOUS, GENTLE, KINGLY BOY. . . . . . . . .  82 MAD KING GOLL  V    8
  PEACE-MAKING, MILD, A KINGLY BOY. . . . . . . .  82 MAD KING GOLL  V    8
KING-REMEMBERING
  MY ANGRY KING-REMEMBERING SOUL ONE JOT. . . . .  36 OISIN 2            94
KING'S
  HE CARRIED EDAIN OFF FROM A KING'S HOUSE, . . . 224 SHADOW WATER B    48
  SEEING, KING'S SON, WHAT WOUNDS YOU HAVE." . . . 275 GREY ROCK        94
  FOR HE AND THE KING'S SON WERE DEAD. . . . . . . 275 GREY ROCK        97
  AND MANY A KING'S DAUGHTER, . . . . . . . . . . 330 BONE OF A HARE     3
  WHO, WHEN HIS OWN RIGHT KING'S FORGOTTEN, . . . 635 BLACK TOWER       13
  SWEARS THAT HE HEARS THE KING'S GREAT HORN. . . 636 BLACK TOWER       24
  THEN TURNED HE FROM THE KING'S COURT, . . . . . 742 EARL PAUL         65
  RUIN ON A GREAT KING'S HOUSE  . . . . . . . . . 775 AGAINST WITCH      3
KINGS        SEE BEGGAR-KINGS
  "I LOVED NO MAN, THOUGH KINGS BESOUGHT, . . . .   7 OISIN 1           62
  FULL MANY BOWING KINGS BESOUGHT ME, . . . . . .   7 OISIN 1        V  67
  WARS SHADOWY, VAST, EXULTANT: FAIRY KINGS . . .  29 OISIN 2        V   9
  CAME BY ME THE KINGS OF THE RED BRANCH. . . . .  53 OISIN 3           87
  WHERE ARE NOW THE WARRING KINGS . . . . . . . .  65 HAPPY SHEPHERD    11
  WHERE ARE NOW THE WARRING KINGS? . . . . . . .   65 HAPPY SHEPHERD    13
  THE KINGS OF THE OLD TIME ARE DEAD! . . . . . .  65 HAPPY SHEPHERD    17
  WHERE ARE NOW THE OLD KINGS HOARY? . . . . . .   65 HAPPY SHEPHERD V  13
  THE KINGS OF THE OLD TIME ARE FLED. . . . . . .  65 HAPPY SHEPHERD V  17
  WHAT WOULD YOU, KING OF THE PROUD RED BRANCH KINGS? . . . 102 FERGUS DRUID   8
  WHAT WOULD YOU, KING OF THE PROUD RED BRANCH KINGS? . . . 102 FERGUS DRUID  15
  WHAT WOULD YOU, KING OF THE PROUD RED BRANCH KINGS? . . . 103 FERGUS DRUID V 21
  HAS SLAIN SO MIGHTY ARMIES, SO GREAT KINGS, . . 106 CUCHULAIN SEA  V 10A
  "THE RED BRANCH KINGS A TIRELESS BANQUET KEEP, . 108 CUCHULAIN SEA  V  33
  AMONG THOSE FEASTING KINGS CUCHULAIN DWELT, . . 108 CUCHULAIN SEA  V  39
  AND CONCHUBAR, THE RED BRANCH KING OF KINGS, . . 109 CUCHULAIN SEA     45
  THE JEWELLED CROWNS THAT KINGS HAVE HURLED . . . 155 FORGOT BEAUTY      4
  OF THE CROWNED MAGI! AND THE KINGS WHOSE EYES . 169 SECRET ROSE    V   9
  KINGS OF THE GREAT PLAIN HAVE COME AND GONE . . 183 QUEEN MAEVE       81
  WITH THE FIRST KINGS OF MANY-PILLARED CRUACHAN. 187 QUEEN MAEVE      151
  WITH THE FIRST KINGS OF MANY PILLARED CRUACHAN. 187 QUEEN MAEVE    V 151
  AMONG THE GIANT KINGS WHOSE HOARD, . . . . . . 196 BAILE AILLINN    164
  OR ON THE UNPEOPLED WAVES WITH KINGS TO PULL AT THE OAR, 210 UNDER THE MOON 15
  THEY HAVE IT THAT THE PLANS OF KINGS AND QUEENS . . 235 SHADOW WATER B 296
  THE DAUGHTER AND THE GRANDDAUGHTER OF KINGS . . 237 SHADOW WATER B   334
  THE DAUGHTER AND GRANDDAUGHTER OF KINGS . . . . 237 SHADOW WATER B V 334
  NOTHING TO MAKE A SONG ABOUT BUT KINGS, . . . . 257 RECONCILIATION     5
  AND HALF THE KINGS, BEFORE SUNDOWN . . . . . . 273 GREY ROCK         69
  AND HALF HIS KINGS, BEFORE SUNDOWN . . . . . . 273 GREY ROCK      V  69
  THE TWO KINGS . . . . . . . . . . . . . . . . . 276 TWO KINGS          T
  KNOWING THAT SILENCE BRINGS NO GOOD TO KINGS, . 279 TWO KINGS         57
  AMONG THE KINGS OF GREECE AND FRANCE." . . . . 296 THREE BEGGARS  V 32A
  UPON THE BOTTOM OF A KING OF KINGS! . . . . . . 445 SCHOOL CHILDR     44
  ALL SORTS OF KINGS HAVE SAT . . . . . . . . . . 597 MODEL LAUREATE     2
  SOME BOAST OF BEGGAR-KINGS AND KINGS . . . . . 597 MODEL LAUREATE     9
  THE HEATHEN.  YEA, AND SHAKE THE SULLEN KINGS . 698 MOSADA 2          55
  COME AND DREAM OF KINGS AND KINGDOMS, . . . . . 737 IN FIRELIGHT       1
  TOWARDS A COUNTRY WHERE THERE ARE NO KINGS. . . 755 SHADOW WATER A   165
  OF THE TWELVE KINGS OF THE WORLD TO BE MY KING, 757 SHADOW WATER A   214
  AND HAVE BEEN WOOED BY THE TWELVE KINGS OF THE EARTH, . . 757 SHADOW WATER A V 214
KINSALE
  TO MY OWN PLACE, KINSALE. . . . . . . . . . . .  95 MOLL MAGEE        24
  TO THE EARL OF KINSALE, . . . . . . . . . . . . 740 EARL PAUL         14
  THE CAPTIVE FROM KINSALE. . . . . . . . . . . . 740 EARL PAUL         28
  THE EARL OF KINSALE SAID, . . . . . . . . . . . 742 EARL PAUL         62
  ON THE CLIFF OF KINSALE. . . . . . . . . . . . 742 EARL PAUL         68
KINSELLA'S
  JOHN KINSELLA'S LAMENT FOR MRS. MARY MOORE . . . 620 JOHN KINSELLA      T
KINSMAN
  AND HE, OF HIS HIGH KINSMAN SORROW DREAMING, . .  67 SAD SHEPHERD   V   2
KINSMEN
  O KINSMEN OF THE THREE IN ONE, . . . . . . . . 213 BLESS PSALTER     14
  O KINSMEN, BLESS THE HANDS THAT PLAY. . . . . . 213 BLESS PSALTER     15
KISS
  THAT I MIGHT HAVE YOUR SON TO KISS." . . . . . .   6 OISIN 1           59
  YET LOVE AND KISS ON DIM SHORES FAR AWAY  . . .  29 OISIN 2           13
  THEY LOVE AND KISS IN ISLANDS FAR AWAY, . . . .  29 OISIN 2           13
  BUT LOVE AND KISS ON DIM SHORES FAR AWAY  . . .  29 OISIN 2        V  13
  NOW CUFF HIM OFF.  HE'S OFF!  A KISS FOR YOU, . .  73 ANASHU VIJAYA    39
  A LONELY LAUGHTER, AND MAY KISS HIS HANDS TO ME IN SLEEP. 75 ANASHU VIJAYA 82
  AN INNER LAUGHTER, AND MAY KISS HIS HANDS TO ME IN SLEEP. 75 ANASHU VIJAYA V 82
  A LONELY LAUGHTER, THAT HE MAY KISS HANDS TO ME IN SLEEP. 75 ANASHU VIJAYA V 82
  WITH A KISS AND A TEAR ON THY DROOPING BROW, . .  79 FALLING LEAVES     8
  IS OUR FIRST KISS, AND AH, HOW OLD MY HEART!" . .  80 EPHEMERA           9
  I SIGH THAT KISS YOU, . . . . . . . . . . . . . 118 CRADLE SONG        9
  I KISS YOU AND KISS YOU, . . . . . . . . . . . 118 CRADLE SONG        9
  I KISS YOU AND KISS YOU, . . . . . . . . . . . 118 CRADLE SONG    V   9
  DID THE KISS OF MOTHER MARY . . . . . . . . . . 124 CATHLEEN PARA      9
  HERS THE KISS OF MOTHER MARY, . . . . . . . . . 124 CATHLEEN PARA  V   9
  DREAM, UNTIL GOD BURN NATURE WITH A KISS? . . . 128 DREAM OF FAERY    47
  UNTIL HE BURN UP NATURE WITH A KISS:-- . . . . 128 DREAM OF FAERY V  47
  I KISS MY WAILING CHILD AND PRESS IT TO MY BREAST, . . 147 UNAPPEAS HOST 5
  AND KISS HER LIPS AND TAKE HER HANDS! . . . . . 150 WANDER AENGUS     20
  AND KISS HER LIPS AND TAKE HER HAND, . . . . . 150 WANDER AENGUS  V  20
  AND WHEN YOU SIGH FROM KISS TO KISS . . . . . . 156 FORGOT BEAUTY     18
```

421

KISS   (CONTINUED)
```
    AND WHEN YOU SIGH FROM KISS TO KISS  . . . . . . .     156 FORGOT BEAUTY        18
    AND LOST THE WORLD AND EMER FOR A KISS; . . . . . .     170 SECRET ROSE         15
    A CHILD'S LAUGHTER, A WOMAN'S KISS. . . . . . . . .     190 BAILE AILLINN       40
    AND TREMBLE WITH THEIR LOVE AND KISS. . . . . . . .     196 BAILE AILLINN      169
    THAT IT FADES OUT FROM KISS TO KISS; . . . . . . .      202 NEVER GIVE ALL       5
    THAT IT FADES OUT FROM KISS TO KISS; . . . . . . .      202 NEVER GIVE ALL       5
    BUT WE BEND TOGETHER AND KISS THE QUIET FEET  . . .     207 HANRAHANS SONG V     4
    AND KISS MORE LIPS THAN LASTING PEACEABLE MEN . . .     225 SHADOW WATER B      71
    A LUCKY BATTLE, OR A WOMAN'S KISS . . . . . . . . .     227 SHADOW WATER B     115
    THEY TAKE A KISS FOR WHAT A KISS IS WORTH, . . . .      229 SHADOW WATER B     157
    THEY TAKE A KISS FOR WHAT A KISS IS WORTH, . . . .      225 SHADOW WATER B     157
    HAVE CALLED ME THEIR BELOVED, I'LL NOT KISS THEM. .     237 SHADOW WATER B     336
    UNTIL MY BODY GIVE YOU KISS FOR KISS. . . . . . . .     238 SHADOW WATER B     345
    UNTIL MY BODY GIVE YOU KISS FOR KISS. . . . . . . .     238 SHADOW WATER B     345
    YOUR SOUL SHALL GIVE THE KISS.  I AM NOT AFRAID, .      238 SHADOW WATER B     346
    OR I HAD NO WOMAN THERE TO KISS; . . . . . . . . .      305 HOUR DAWN           66
    AND PAY BUT A KISS FOR A KISS. . . . . . . . . . .      330 BONE OF A HARE       8
    AND PAY BUT A KISS FOR A KISS. . . . . . . . . . .      330 BONE OF A HARE       8
    I CELEBRATE THE SILENT KISS THAT ENDS SHORT LIFE OR LONG.  459 FROM OEDIPUS     9
    THAT I MAY HEAR IF WE SHOULD KISS . . . . . . . .       573 LADYS 3RD SONG       9
    AND SHALL BE DONE, IF YOU WILL DEIGN TO KISS . . .      669 ISLE STAT II 3      79
    AH, LET US KISS EACH OTHER'S EYES, . . . . . . . .      686 LIFE                15
    TO PLACE A KISS OF FIRE ON THE DIM BROW . . . . . .     688 TWO TITANS          47
    SO YOU MUST GO; KISS ME BEFORE YOU GO. . . . . . .      702 MOSADA 3            96
    THE WOMEN NONE CAN KISS AND THRIVE . . . . . . . .      775 AGAINST WITCH        8
    WOMEN, THAT NONE CAN KISS AND THRIVE, . . . . . .       775 AGAINST WITCH  V     8
    THEY WILL GIVE HIM KISS FOR KISS . . . . . . . . .      776 AGAINST WITCH       29
    THEY WILL GIVE HIM KISS FOR KISS . . . . . . . . .      776 AGAINST WITCH       29
```
KISSED
```
    HAD KISSED MY FATHER, LONG-ARMED FIN, . . . . . . .      10 OISIN 1        V 112B
    AND KISSED, AS THEY WOULD NEVER CEASE. . . . . . .       16 OISIN 1          215
    AND KISSED THE SCEPTRE WITH RED LIPS, . . . . . . .      18 OISIN 1          258
    AND KISSED THE SCEPTRE WITH HOT LIPS, . . . . . . .      18 OISIN 1        V 258
    AS WE KISSED EACH ROSE'S HEAD; . . . . . . . . . .       21 OISIN 1        V 307
    AND KISSED MY EYES; AND, SWAYING HER BRIGHT HEAD . .     29 OISIN 2            6
    A YOUNG MAN CRIED AND KISSED HER HAND, . . . . . .      191 BAILE AILLINN      60
    BUT WE HAVE ALL BENT LOW AND LOW AND KISSED THE QUIET FEET 207 HANRAHANS SONG  9
    YET NEVER HAVE TWO LOVERS KISSED BUT THEY  . . . .      229 SHADOW WATER B     153
    HE HAS STOOPED DOWN AND KISSED HER ON THE LIPS. . .     232 SHADOW WATER B     230
    AND KISSED HER DUSKY FACE, . . . . . . . . . . . .      332 SOLOMON SHEBA        2
    AND KISSED HER ARAB EYES, . . . . . . . . . . . .      333 SOLOMON SHEBA       18
    THE HANDS THAT I HAVE KISSED, . . . . . . . . . .      357 BROKEN DREAMS       35
    AND AFTER KISSED A STONE, . . . . . . . . . . . .      384 VISION ROBART       64
    I KISSED A STONE; . . . . . . . . . . . . . . . .      628 JANE MOUNTAIN       20
    WITH LITTLE CRIES OF JOY HE KISSED THE RAIN . . . .     688 TWO TITANS          33
    AND KNOW YOU NOT SHE KISSED THAT PIOUS CHILD . . .      696 MOSADA 2             6
```
KISSES
```
    OH, CAN MY KISSES BRING A FLUSH NO MORE . . . . .      701 MOSADA 3            71
```
KISSING
```
    NOR MOUTH FROM KISSING, NOR FROM WINE UNWET; . . .      311 MOUNTAIN TOMB        7
    NOR MOUTH WITH KISSING NOR WITH WINE UNWET. . . . .     311 MOUNTAIN TOMB V      7
    NOR MOUTH WITH KISSING NOR WITH THE WINE UNWET. . .     311 MOUNTAIN TOMB V      7
```
KITCHEN
```
    AND SCRUB A KITCHEN PAVEMENT, OR BREAK STONES . . .     204 ADAMS CURSE          8
```
KITE
```
    LIKE THE EYES OF SOME GREAT KITE SCOURING THE WOODS, .  283 TWO KINGS          150
    I GAZED AT HIM LIKE GROUSE UPON A KITE; . . . . . .     283 TWO KINGS          152
```
KITH
```
    BUT WHERE ARE YOUR NOBLE KITH AND KIN . . . . . . .       5 OISIN 1            44
    "NOW HATH HE KITH OR KIN, OR ANY FRIEND?" . . . . .     712 FERENCZ RENYI       66
```
KITTENS   SEE PANTHER-KITTENS
KNAVE
```
    NOR KNAVE NOR DOLT CAN BREAK . . . . . . . . . . .      259 UNWORTH PRAISE       2
    FROM SELF-SAME DOLT AND KNAVE; . . . . . . . . . .      260 UNWORTH PRAISE      17
    ON THE DAY'S WAR WITH EVERY KNAVE AND DOLT, . . . .     260 FASC DIFFICULT      10
    AND NO KNAVE BROUGHT TO BOOK . . . . . . . . . . .      347 FISHERMAN           17
    DUMBFOUNDED BEFORE A KNAVE, . . . . . . . . . . . .     349 HAWK                16
    I THOUGHT HIM HALF A LUNATIC, HALF KNAVE, . . . . .     473 ALL SOUL NIGHT      64
    FOOL, RASCAL, KNAVE, . . . . . . . . . . . . . . .      496 MOHINI CHATTER       8
    I RANTED TO THE KNAVE AND FOOL, . . . . . . . . .      506 REMORSE SPEECH       1
    WHAT MATTER IF THE KNAVE . . . . . . . . . . . . .      525 DANCING DAYS        10
    HEROIC REVERIE MOCKED BY CLOWN AND KNAVE, . . . . .     619 BRONZE HEAD         27
    WHAT HURRIES OUT THE KNAVE AND DOLT? . . . . . . .      625 NATIVITY             9
```
KNEAD
```
    LONGING TO KNEAD AND PULL IT INTO SHAPE . . . . . .     246 SHADOW WATER B     510
    THITHER THY DUST, AND KNEAD IT WITH A CRY, . . . .      688 TWO TITANS          52
```
KNEADED
```
    IS BUT HALF YOURS; HE KNEADED IN THE DOUGH . . . .      201 OLD MEMORY           6
    WHEN ALL THE DOUGH HAS BEEN SO KNEADED UP . . . .      377 PHASES OF MOON     114
```
KNEE
```
    BENT DOWN ABOVE EACH HOOKED KNEE, . . . . . . . . .      26 OISIN 1          392
    BENT LOW ABOVE EACH HOOKED KNEE, . . . . . . . . .       26 OISIN 1          392
    WENT DOWN UPON A HAND AND KNEE . . . . . . . . . .      304 HOUR DAWN      V    45
    THE SPECKLED CAT SLEPT ON MY KNEE; . . . . . . . .      381 SONGS FOOL 2         2
    WAILING UPON A WOMAN'S KNEE . . . . . . . . . . . .     436 FOR MY SON          22
    AND ALL SHALL BEND THE KNEE . . . . . . . . . . . .     516 MANS SONG           16
    THE DEVOTEE PROFFERS A KNEE TO HIS LORD, . . . . .      547 TO SAME TUNE 3       2
    I WOULD THAT I DRANK WITH MY LOVE ON MY KNEE, . . .     551 SONGS REWRIT 1       9
    COULD I BUT DRINK, MY LOVE ON MY KNEE . . . . . . .     551 SONGS REWRIT 1 V     9
    O COULD I DRINK, MY LOVE ON MY KNEE, . . . . . . .      551 SONGS REWRIT 1 V     9
```

	PAGE	TITLE		LINE
KNEE (CONTINUED)				
HER KNEE CAP BROKEN; THAT GIRL I DECLARE	578	CRAZED GIRL	V	6
NO BOOKS UPON THE KNEE, AND NO ONE THERE	579	DOR WELLESLEY		9
THE DEVOTEE PROFFERS A KNEE TO HIS LORD,	614	MARCH SONGS 2		2
BENDING HUMBLY EVERY KNEE,	726	LOVERS QUARREL		14
AND COME KNEELING ON ONE KNEE,	727	LOVERS QUARREL		53
KNEE-CAP				
HER KNEE-CAP BROKEN, THAT GIRL I DECLARE	578	CRAZED GIRL		6
KNEEL				
BEFORE THY FEET SHALL KNEEL DOWN ALL	7	OISIN 1	V	77
SHALL KNEEL AND PRAISE YOU, ONE BY ONE,	8	OISIN 1		78
BUT KNEEL AND WEAR OUT THE FLAGS AND PRAY FOR YOUR SOUL THAT IS LOST	63	OISIN 3		215
BUT WEEP YOU AND KNEEL; WEAR OUT THE FLAGS;	63	OISIN 3	V	215
KNEEL, USHEEN, WEAR OUT THE FLAGS AND PRAY FOR YOUR SOUL THAT IS LOST	63	OISIN 3	V	215
I RISE IN THE DAWN, AND I KNEEL AND BLOW	150	OLD MOTHER		1
I RISE AT THE DAWN, AND I KNEEL AND BLOW	150	OLD MOTHER	V	1
I KNEEL BY THEE--NO PARTING NOW--LOOK UP.	702	MOSADA 3		94
KNEELING				
O WOMEN, KNEELING BY YOUR ALTAR-RAILS LONG HENCE,	173	SPEAKS HEARERS		1
O COLLEENS, KNEELING BY YOUR ALTAR RAILS LONG HENCE,	173	SPEAKS HEARERS	V	1
O, WOMEN, KNEELING BY YOUR ALTAR RAILS LONG HENCE,	173	SPEAKS HEARERS	V	1
A REVOLUTIONARY SOLDIER KNEELING TO BE BLESSED;	601	GALLERY REVIS		8
AND COME KNEELING ON ONE KNEE,	727	LOVERS QUARREL		53
KNEELS				
GRIEVE NOT, FOR GOMEZ KNEELS BESIDE THEE--GOMEZ,	702	MOSADA 3		90
GRIEVE NOT, FOR VALLENCE KNEELS BESIDE THEE--VALLENCE,	702	MOSADA 3	V	90
KNEES				
. . . HIS KNEES IN THE SOFT STAR-FLAME,	50	OISIN 3		43
NOT COUGHING, MY HEAD ON MY KNEES,	58	OISIN 3		159
BUT WEEP THOU, AND WEAR THOU THE FLAGS WITH THY KNEES, . . .	63	OISIN 3	V	215
BUT WEEP YOU, AND WEAR YOU THE FLAGS WITH YOUR KNEES,	63	OISIN 3	V	215
MY SPIRIT ROCKED IN EVENING LIGHT, THE RUSHES ROUND MY KNEES,	76	INDIAN ON GOD		2
MY SPIRIT ROCKED IN EVENING'S HUSH, THE RUSHES ROUND MY KNEES,	76	INDIAN ON GOD	V	2
UPON HIS KNEES BY MY FOOTSTOOL	82	MAD KING GOLL	V	13
WITH HEAD BOWED ON HIS KNEES CUCHULAIN STAYED;	110	CUCHULAIN SEA		71
WITH HEAD BOWED ON HIS KNEES, CUCHULLIN STAID,	110	CUCHULAIN SEA	V	71
THEIR SWORDS UPON THEIR IRON KNEES,	156	FORGOT BEAUTY		23
A SWORD UPON HIS IRON KNEES,	156	FORGOT BEAUTY	V	23
THEIR HEADS ON YOUR KNEES, AND DROWN THEIR EYES WITH YOUR HAIR,	163	VALLEY LOVERS		6
AND CUMHAL SAID, BENDING HIS KNEES,	167	BLESSED		5
HE HAD KNEES THAT STUCK OUT OF HIS HOSE;	190	BAILE AILLINN		27
THEY HAD HANDS LIKE CLAWS, AND THEIR KNEES	208	OLD MEN ADMIRE		4
PLANTED ON HIS KNEES,	333	SOLOMON SHEBA		10
TO GREAT SHAPELY KNEES	355	PROPERTIUS		2
AND HAD BUT BROKEN KNEES FOR HIRE	411	TOWER		62
ROUGH MEN-AT-ARMS, CROSS-GARTERED TO THE KNEES	412	TOWER		82
ROUGH MEN AT ARMS, CROSS-GARTERED TO THE KNEES	412	TOWER	V	82
BEFORE SHE HAD SPREAD A BOOK UPON HER KNEES	466	HARUN RASHID		120
THE CONSECRATED BLADE UPON MY KNEES	477	SELF AND SOUL		9
THE CONSECRATED SWORD UPON MY KNEES	477	SELF AND SOUL	V	9
STRAIGHTEN AGED KNEES,	505	RESULT THOUGHT		16
MY MEDIAEVAL KNEES LACK HEALTH UNTIL THEY BEND,	603	GALLERY REVIS		33
SAID TO THE WOMAN ON HIS KNEES, "LIE STILL.	609	IN TARAS HALLS		2
PROPPED UPON MY TWO KNEES,	628	JANE MOUNTAIN		19
UPON MY KNEES I PRAY YOU, LET IT SLEEP,	693	MOSADA 2		72
AND THOU SHALT BEND, ENDURING GOD, THE KNEES	698	MOSADA 2		59
AND THOU SHALL BEND, ENDURING GOD, THE KNEES	698	MOSADA 2	V	59
HAST THOU NOT SAT OF YORE UPON THE KNEES	724	KANVA ON SELF		9
KNELT				
AND KNELT THERE, EVERY GIRL AND MAN,	15	OISIN 1		214
AND KNELT THEM, EVERY MAID AND MAN,	15	OISIN 1	V	214
AND MEN AND LADIES KNELT THEM THERE	18	OISIN 1		255
AND MEN AND MAIDENS KNELT THEM THERE	18	OISIN 1	V	255
AND HIS YOUNG SWEETHEART CLOSE BESIDE HIM KNELT,	108	CUCHULAIN SEA		40
AND HIS YOUNG DEAR ONE CLOSE BESIDE HIM KNELT,	108	CUCHULAIN SEA	V	40
HE KNELT, AND LEANING ON THE CHAIR	132	FR GILLIGAN		13
HE KNELT, PRAYED, FELL ASLEEP;	132	FR GILLIGAN	V	14
HE KNELT HIM AT THAT WORD.	133	FR GILLIGAN		40
AND KNELT ABOVE IT WITH DRAWN KNIFE. ON THE INSTANT	278	TWO KINGS		37
I KNELT IN THE DIRT.	516	MANS SONG		15
KNEW				
NEAR BY, THE FENIANS SAW, AND KNEW	10	OISIN 1	V	111
I KNEW NOT IF DAYS PASSED OR HOURS,	11	OISIN 1	V	133
WE CANTERED TO THE SHORE, AND KNEW	14	OISIN 1		178
FOR WE KNEW WELL THE OLD WAS OVER.	25	OISIN 1		379
FOR WELL WE KNEW THE OLD WAS OVER.	25	OISIN 1	V	379
AND WHEN HE KNEW THE SWORD OF MANANNAN	40	OISIN 2		173
WE TRAMPLED TO AND FRO. WHEN HIS MIND KNEW	40	OISIN 2	V	173
BUT WHEN AT WITHERING OF THE SUN HE KNEW	40	OISIN 2		173
AND WHEN AT WITHERING OF THE SUN HE KNEW	40	OISIN 2	V	173
THRUSTING HIS NOSE TO MY SHOULDER; HE KNEW IN HIS BOSOM DEEP	54	OISIN 3		106
SNATCHING THE BIRD IN SECRET; NOR KNEW I, EMBOSOMED APART,	57	OISIN 3		150
. . . AND I KNEW HOW MEN SORROW AND PASS,	59	OISIN 3		175
. . . AND I KNEW HOW MEN PASS,	59	OISIN 3	V	175

		PAGE	TITLE		LINE
KNEW (CONTINUED)					
THE LOVE I LIVED, THE DREAM I KNEW.		139	TO IRELAND		34
HE KNEW NOW THE FOLK OF THE AIR,		145	HOST OF AIR	V	40A
THEY KNEW HIM, HIS CHANGED BODY WAS		195	BAILE AILLINN		139
ALL THE LOVE STORIES THAT THEY KNEW.		197	BAILE AILLINN		197
I KNEW HIM WELL, AND WHILE I HEARD HIM LAUGHING		242	SHADOW WATER B		419
I KNEW A WOMAN NONE COULD PLEASE,		272	GREY ROCK		41
SHE STARTED AND THEN KNEW WHOSE FOOT IT WAS,		280	TWO KINGS		66
FOR HE KNEW BETTER HOW TO LIVE.		288	TO WEALTHY MAN		30
FOR ALL THE SLEEPER KNEW OR CARED,		307	HOUR DAWN		115
WE KNEW, THOUGH SHE'D NOT SAID A WORD,		314	MEMORY YOUTH		16
AND KNEW, THOUGH SHE'D NOT SAID A WORD,		314	MEMORY YOUTH	V	16
AS THOUGH HE KNEW HIMSELF, AS IT WERE, A CUCKOO,		341	SHEP GOATHERD		54
I KNEW A PHOENIX IN MY YOUTH, SO LET THEM HAVE THEIR DAY.		353	HIS PHOENIX		8
I KNEW A PHOENIX IN MY YOUTH, SO LET THEM HAVE THEIR DAY.		354	HIS PHOENIX		16
I KNEW A PHOENIX IN MY YOUTH, SO LET THEM HAVE THEIR DAY.		354	HIS PHOENIX		24
I KNEW A PHOENIX IN MY YOUTH, SO LET THEM HAVE THEIR DAY.		354	HIS PHOENIX		32
THE MAN THAT LAPO AND THAT GUIDO KNEW?		368	EGO DOMINUS		26
I KNEW THAT I HAD SEEN, HAD SEEN AT LAST		384	VISION ROBART		49
NOT HIS, NOT MINE." AND HE THAT KNEW		387	SOLOMON WITCH	V	6
SHE THAT BUT LITTLE PATIENCE KNEW,		397	POLIT PRISONER		1
BUT KNEW MY FINGER COULD BUT HAVE TOUCHED		399	BREAK OF DAY		13
BUT KNEW MY FINGER WOULD HAVE TOUCHED		399	BREAK OF DAY	V	13
I KNEW THAT ONE IS ANIMATE,		406	IN TIME OF WAR		4
I KNEW THAT HORSE-PLAY, KNEW IT FOR A MURDEROUS THING.		442	BLACK CENTAUR		4
I KNEW THAT HORSE-PLAY, KNEW IT FOR A MURDEROUS THING.		442	BLACK CENTAUR		4
WHERE SEVEN EPHESIAN TOPERS SLEPT AND NEVER KNEW		442	BLACK CENTAUR		11
I KNEW THAT HORSE PLAY, KNEW IT FOR A MURDEROUS THING.		442	BLACK CENTAUR	V	4
I KNEW THAT HORSE PLAY, KNEW IT FOR A MURDEROUS THING.		442	BLACK CENTAUR	V	4
KNEW THAT WE'D HALVED A SOUL		457	SUMMER SPRING		6
"IF BUT THE SHIRT UPON MY BODY KNEW IT		462	HARUN RASHID		33
THAT SPEECH WAS ALL THAT THE TOWN KNEW, BUT HE		462	HARUN RASHID		35
THAT NEVER KNEW THAT STRAIN WOULD SCARCE SEEM BRIGHT,		465	HARUN RASHID		88
THAN ALL MY BURSTING SPRINGTIME KNEW. A GIRL		466	HARUN RASHID		105
AND KNEW THAT SWEET EXTREMITY OF PRIDE		471	ALL SOUL NIGHT		22
BURKE WAS A WHIG. WHETHER THEY KNEW OR NOT,		486	SEVEN SAGES		8
NOR KNEW, DRUNKEN WITH SINGING AS WITH WINE,		537	HER VISION		30
A MIND MICHAEL ANGELO KNEW		576	ACRE OF GRASS		19
CLIMBING, FALLING SHE KNEW NOT WHERE,		578	CRAZED GIRL		4
FOR ALL TONGUES HE KNEW.		594	COLONEL MARTIN		4
OF SOLITARY BEDS, KNEW WHAT THEY WERE,		610	STATUES		5
DREAMER OF THE MIDDLE AGES. EMPTY EYEBALLS KNEW		610	STATUES		20
DREAMER OF THE MIDDLE-AGES. EMPTY EYE-BALLS KNEW		610	STATUES	V	20
WE PICKED EACH OTHER FROM AFAR AND KNEW		622	HOUND VOICE		10
A GIRL THAT KNEW ALL DANTE ONCE		626	OLD MEN BE MAD		5
SOME KNEW WHAT AILED THE WORLD		627	STATES HOLIDAY		9
THAT THE WITCH OF ATLAS KNEW,		637	BEN BULBEN		3
AND ANCIENT IRELAND KNEW IT ALL.		637	BEN BULBEN		16
I NEVER KNEW AN EVE SO MARVELLOUS STILL.		702	MOSADA 3		88
IT IS THE DARKEST EVE I EVER KNEW.		702	MOSADA 3		93
I NEVER KNEW A NIGHT SO HONEY-SWEET.		702	MOSADA 3		99
I NEVER KNEW A NIGHT SO HONEY SWEET.		702	MOSADA 3	V	99
I NEVER KNEW A NIGHT SO DEW-BEDROWNED.		703	MOSADA 3		105
I NEVER KNEW A NIGHT SO BITTER COLD.		704	MOSADA 3		124
I SAT ME DOWN BESIDE THEE, AND I KNEW		713	FERENCZ RENYI		92
THEIR BRIEF LIVES I NEVER KNEW.		787	HUDDON DUDDON		5
KNIFE					
AND KNELT ABOVE IT WITH DRAWN KNIFE. ON THE INSTANT		278	TWO KINGS		37
DREW A KNIFE TO STRIKE HIM DEAD,		514	JANE GROWN OLD		10
KNIGHT					
IN THIS ALTAR-PIECE THE KNIGHT,		385	ROBARTES DANCE		2
TO PROVE HIS LOVE A KNIGHT WITH LANCE IN REST		651	ISLE STAT I 1		158
"BEHOLD THE KNIGHT OF THE WATERFALL, WHOSE HEART		684	SEEKER		54
FOR A KNIGHT, COME FROM NORMANDY		740	EARL PAUL		7
TO THROW THE NORMAN KNIGHT." "		740	EARL PAUL		12
STOOD THERE THE NORMAN KNIGHT.		741	EARL PAUL		40
KNIGHTLY					
YEA, NOBLE AND MOST KNIGHTLY HATH IT BEEN.		679	ISLE STAT II 3		320
KNIGHTS					
HAS TWELVE KNIGHTS OVERTHROWN,		740	EARL PAUL		8
FOR HE HAD OVERTHROWN TWELVE KNIGHTS		741	EARL PAUL		43
KNIT					
THAT COMES OF THE BEST KNIT TO THE BEST? ALTHOUGH		264	HOUSE SHAKEN		7
THERE ALL THE BARREL-HOOPS ARE KNIT,		557	THERE		1
KNITTED					
OF KNITTED MUSIC. OFT THE FOND REPINING		33	OISIN 2	V	68C
AND KNITTED MESH TO MESH, WE GROW IMMORTAL,		252	SHADOW WATER B		616
THOUGHTS LONG KNITTED INTO A SINGLE THOUGHT,		488	COOLE PARK 29		7
KNITTING					
WORTH KNITTING TO A MEASURE OF SWEET SOUND?		181	QUEEN MAEVE		33
AND KNITTING MESH TO MESH, WE GROW IMMORTAL,		252	SHADOW WATER B	V	616
NOR HEAVY KNITTING OF THE BROW		318	APPOINTMENT		9
KNOCK					
I KNOCK THEIR HEADS ABOUT.		605	SONGS BURDEN 1		8
AND KNOCK THE OTHERS DOWN.		606	SONGS BURDEN 1		26
OR THE RIFLE KNOCK HIM DEAD,		637	BEN BULBEN	V	18
KNOCKED					
THE COLONEL KNOCKED ON THE RICH MAN'S DOOR,		595	COLONEL MARTIN		28
THE COLONEL KNOCKED ON A RICH MAN'S DOOR.		595	COLONEL MARTIN	V	28
KNOCKFEFIN					
ON CREVROE OR BROAD KNOCKFEFIN, WITH MANY OF OLD THEY FEAST		59	OISIN 3		179

KNOCKFEFIN   (CONTINUED)
     ON CREVROE OR ON BROAD KNOCKFEFIN, WITH MANY OF OLD THEY   59 OISIN 3   V 179
          FAST
KNOCKNAREA
     THE BIRDS FROM KNOCKNAREA . . . .   93 FATHER OHART   30
     THE HOST IS RIDING FROM KNOCKNAREA . . . .   140 HOSTING SIDHE   1
     VEERING, FLEETING, FICKLE, THE WINDS OF KNOCKNAREA, . . .   206 HANRAHANS SONG V   1
     THE WIND HAS BUNDLED UP THE CLOUDS HIGH OVER KNOCKNAREA,   207 HANRAHANS SONG   6
     THE WINDS HAVE BUNDLED UP THE CLOUDS HIGH OVER KNOCKNAREA   207 HANRAHANS SONG V   6
     OUT OF BEN BULBEN AND KNOCKNAREA, ...   549 SEVERED HEAD   2
KNOCKNASHEE
     AND THE WORLD ROUND KNOCKNASHEE . . . .   93 FATHER OHART   31
KNOCKS
     OR THE RIFLE KNOCKS HIM DEAD, ...   637 BEN BULBEN   18
KNOLL
     I HUNGER TO BUILD THEM ANEW AND SIT ON A GREEN KNOLL APART,   143 ROSE IN HEART   6
KNOT-GRASS
     BUT ONE SMALL KNOT-GRASS GROWING BY THE POOL . . . . .   127 DREAM OF FAERY   29
     BUT ONE SMALL KNOT-GRASS GROWING BY THE RIM . . . . .   127 DREAM OF FAERY V   29
KNOTTED
     THE KNOTTED SCOURGE, THE NAIL-PIERCED HANDS, THE WOUNDED   172 TRAV PASSION   V   4
          SIDE,
     THE LIGHT IS DANCING O'ER THE KNOTTED TREES, ...   662 ISLE STAT II 2   2
KNOW
     AND YOU SHALL KNOW THE DANAAN LEISURE! . . . .   9 OISIN 1   100
     AND THOU SHALT KNOW THE IMMORTALS' LEISURE, ...   9 OISIN 1   V 100
     I KNOW NOT IF DAYS PASSED OR HOURS, ...   11 OISIN 1   133
     WITH HEARTS THAT KNOW NOR LAW NOR RULE, ...   22 OISIN 1   339
     AND PEAK AND PINE WE KNOW NOT WHY, ...   22 OISIN 1   V 340C
     WE ONLY KNOW THAT WE WERE GLAD . . . .   22 OISIN 1   V 340D
     TROUBLED HER SONG. I DO NOT KNOW IF DAYS . . . . .   30 OISIN 2   19
     FLASHING--I KNOW NOT WERE IT HOURS OR DAYS, ...   30 OISIN 2   V 19B
     IS THE ISLAND OF CONTENT?" "NONE KNOW," SHE SAID! . . .   46 OISIN 2   249
     WHICH IS THE ISLE OF YOUTH?" "NONE KNOW," SHE SAID, . .   46 OISIN 2   V 249
     WHAT KNOW THE PILOTS OF THE STARS OF TEARS? . . . .   73 ANASHU VIJAYA   47
     AH, YOU WILL KNOW MY LOVED ONE BY HIS HUNTER'S ARROWS   75 ANASHU VIJAYA   80
          TRULY,
     I KNOW THE WORD THEY CRY, "ETERNITY!" . . . .   81 EPHEMERA   V 24F
     AND AH, THEY KNOW NOT, AS THEY PINE AND CEASE, ...   81 EPHEMERA   V 24I
     AND LEARN TO CHAUNT A TONGUE MEN DO NOT KNOW, ...   101 ROSE UPON ROOD   21
     AND LEARN TO CHANT A TONGUE MEN DO NOT KNOW. . . . . .   101 ROSE UPON ROOD V   21
     "HE BADE ME LET ALL KNOW HE GIVES HIS NAME . . . . .   109 CUCHULAIN SEA   52
     KNOW, THAT I WOULD ACCOUNTED BE . . . .   137 TO IRELAND   1
     MAY KNOW HOW MY HEART WENT WITH THEM . . . .   139 TO IRELAND   47
     THE PEOPLE OF COMING DAYS WILL KNOW . . . .   146 FISH   3
     BUT KNOW YOUR HAIR WAS BOUND AND WOUND . . . .   176 BELOVED DEAD   9
     BUT KNOW YOUR HAIR WAS BOUND AND BOUND . . . .   176 BELOVED DEAD   V   9
     AND WEEP BECAUSE I KNOW ALL THINGS NOW! . . . .   177 PAST GREATNESS   2
     YET THEY THAT KNOW ALL THINGS BUT KNOW . . . .   190 BAILE AILLINN   38
     YET THEY THAT KNOW ALL THINGS BUT KNOW . . . .   190 BAILE AILLINN   38
     WHO KNOW THE WAY THAT NAOISE WENT? . . . .   193 BAILE AILLINN   96
     THEY KNOW ALL WONDERS, FOR THEY PASS . . . .   196 BAILE AILLINN   160
     THEY KNOW UNDYING THINGS, FOR THEY . . . .   196 BAILE AILLINN   170
     I AM CONTENTED, FOR I KNOW THAT QUIET . . . .   198 SEVEN WOODS   10
     YOU'D KNOW THE FOLLY OF BEING COMFORTED. . . . .   200 FOLLY COMFORT   14
     I KNOW OF THE LEAFY PATHS THAT THE WITCHES TAKE . . . .   203 WITHER BOUGHS   9
     I KNOW WHERE A DIM MOON DRIFTS, WHERE THE DANAAN KIND . .   203 WITHER BOUGHS   12
     I KNOW OF THE LEAFY PATH THAT THE WITCHES TAKE, ...   203 WITHER BOUGHS V   9
     AND I KNOW OF THE ISLES WHERE THE DANAAN KIND . . . .   203 WITHER BOUGHS V   12
     I KNOW OF THE SLEEPY COUNTRY, WHERE SWANS FLY ROUND . .   204 WITHER BOUGHS   17
     I KNOW, AND THE CURLEW AND PEEWIT ON ECHTGE OF STREAMS.   204 WITHER BOUGHS   22
     AND THE CURLEW AND PEEWIT NOW KNOW ON ECHTGE OF STREAMS.   204 WITHER BOUGHS V   22
     REPLIED! "TO BE BORN WOMAN IS TO KNOW-- . . . . . .   205 ADAMS CURSE   18
     "THERE IS ONE THING THAT ALL WE WOMEN KNOW . . . . . .   205 ADAMS CURSE   V   18
     I ONLY KNOW THAT ALL WE KNOW COMES FROM YOU, ...   218 WOODS OF COOLE   28
     I ONLY KNOW THAT ALL WE KNOW COMES FROM YOU, ...   218 WOODS OF COOLE   28
     THAT SHE AMONG HER WINDS MIGHT KNOW HE WEPT! . . . . .   220 HARP OF AENGUS   12
     THAT SHE AMONG HER WOODS MIGHT KNOW HE WEPT! . . . . .   220 HARP OF AENGUS V   12
     NO, NO, DO NOT SAY THAT. YOU KNOW RIGHT WELL . . . .   227 SHADOW WATER B   107
     IT MAY BE THAT THE EVER-LIVING KNOW IT-- . . . . . .   229 SHADOW WATER B   164
     CAN KNOW THAT ECSTASY. FORGAEL! FORGAEL! . . . . .   231 SHADOW WATER B   203
     AND I WOULD KNOW IF YOU WILL GIVE ME VENGEANCE. . . . .   235 SHADOW WATER B   301
     AND KNOW THAT IT IS FEARLESS. DO WHAT YOU WILL, ...   238 SHADOW WATER B   350
     YOU DID NOT KNOW WHAT BROUGHT HIM TO HIS END, ...   240 SHADOW WATER B   382
     HOW CAN WE RAISE THE KEEN THAT DO NOT KNOW . . . . .   240 SHADOW WATER B   389
     I KNOW THAT HE DIED A THOUSAND YEARS AGO, ...   241 SHADOW WATER B   392
     DO YOU NOT KNOW ME, LADY? I AM HE . . . .   243 SHADOW WATER B   426
     YOU KNOW THE COUNSELS OF THE EVER-LIVING, ...   244 SHADOW WATER B   450
     I DO NOT UNDERSTAND. I KNOW YOUR FACE . . . .   244 SHADOW WATER B   465
     YOU KNOW THE COUNCILS OF THE EVER-LIVING, ...   244 SHADOW WATER B V 450
     I WOULD NOT LET YOU SPEAK, FOR I WOULD KNOW . . . . .   246 SHADOW WATER B   492
     FOR YOU ARE LOOKING AT THE SEA. DO YOU NOT KNOW . . . .   246 SHADOW WATER B   513
     'TWAS YOU THAT EGGED HIM TO IT, FOR YOU KNOW . . . . .   248 SHADOW WATER B   550
     I DO NOT KNOW FOR CERTAIN, BUT I KNOW . . . .   249 SHADOW WATER B   564
     I DO NOT KNOW FOR CERTAIN, BUT I KNOW . . . .   249 SHADOW WATER B   564
     AND I THAT HAVE NOT YOUR FAITH, HOW SHALL I KNOW . . . .   258 KING NO KING   11
     THAT'S ALL WE SHALL KNOW FOR TRUTH . . . .   261 DRINKING SONG   3
     AND KNOW THEM TO THE BONE! IMPART TO US-- . . . . . .   265 ABBEY THEATRE   9
     I KNOW A WOMAN NONE COULD PLEASE, ...   272 GREY ROCK   V   41
     CAN LOVERS HAVE THAT KNOW THEIR HAPPINESS . . . . . .   284 TWO KINGS   178
     WHAT CAN THEY KNOW OF LOVE THAT DO NOT KNOW . . . . .   285 TWO KINGS   193

425

	PAGE	TITLE		LINE

KNOW   (CONTINUED)

	PAGE	TITLE		LINE
WHAT CAN THEY KNOW OF LOVE THAT DO NOT KNOW	285	TWO KINGS		193
AND DO NOT KNOW THAT YOU WOULD BRING,	306	HOUR DAWN		93
TO KNOW WHEN MICHAEL'S TRUMPET CRIES	307	HOUR DAWN		100
WILL GATHER, AND NOT KNOW IT WALKS THE VERY STREET	315	FALLEN MAJESTY		7
WILL GATHER AND NOT KNOW THAT THROUGH ITS VERY STREET	315	FALLEN MAJESTY	V	7
I KNOW THAT I SHALL MEET MY FATE	328	IRISH AIRMAN		1
I KNOW WHAT WAGES BEAUTY GIVES,	336	YOUNG BEAUTY		13
MY DEAR, MY DEAR, I KNOW	336	YOUNG GIRL		1
CAN KNOW IT AS I KNOW,	336	YOUNG GIRL		5
CAN KNOW IT AS I KNOW,	336	YOUNG GIRL		5
ALL KNOW THE MAN THEIR NEIGHBOUR KNOWS.	337	SCHOLARS		10
THE SHEEP HAD GONE FROM THEIRS. I KNOW RIGHT WELL	339	SHEP GOATHERD		15
TO KNOW THE MOUNTAIN AND THE VALLEY HAVE GRIEVED	343	SHEP GOATHERD		117
TO KNOW THE MOUNTAIN AND THE VALLEY GRIEVE	343	SHEP GOATHERD	V	117
AND KNOW WHAT ONCE I HAVE KNOWN,	346	ON WOMAN		34
IF THERE BE RAGS ENOUGH HE WILL KNOW HER NAME	351	HER PRAISE		15
AND YOU KNOW WELL HOW GREAT THE LONGING HAS BEEN,	352	PEOPLE		7
WHO KNOW IT ALL RING AT HIS DOOR, AND SPEAK	373	PHASES OF MOON		21
HE WOULD NEVER KNOW ME AFTER ALL THESE YEARS	377	PHASES OF MOON		129
DOES MINNALOUSHE KNOW THAT HIS PUPILS	379	CAT AND MOON		21
I DO NOT KNOW, THAT KNOW I AM AFRAID	390	IMAGE PAST		41
I DO NOT KNOW, THAT KNOW I AM AFRAID	390	IMAGE PAST		41
WE KNOW THEIR DREAM; ENOUGH	394	EASTER 1916		70
TO KNOW THEY DREAMED AND ARE DEAD;	394	EASTER 1916		71
OR CALUMNY A SONG. HOW CAN THEY KNOW	398	LEADERS CROWD		7
IT MADE HIM HAPPIER TO KNOW	400	DEMON BEAST		14
THE DARKNESS DROPS AGAIN; BUT NOW I KNOW	402	SECOND COMING		18
AND KNOW WHATEVER FLOURISH AND DECLINE	423	MY DESCENDANTS		23
NOR KNOW THAT WHAT DISTURBS OUR BLOOD	434	WHEEL		7
WHO HAVE PLANNED HIS MURDER, FOR THEY KNOW	436	FOR MY SON		12
TO TELL YOUR SIMPLEST WANT, AND KNOW,	436	FOR MY SON	V	21
HOW CAN WE KNOW THE DANCER FROM THE DANCE?	446	SCHOOL CHILDR		64
CAN KNOW THE STORIES THAT WE KNOW	458	SECRETS OF OLD		11
CAN KNOW THE STORIES THAT WE KNOW	458	SECRETS OF OLD		11
AS THAT OLD WANDERING BEGGAR AND THESE GOD-HATED CHILDREN	459	FROM OEDIPUS		6

KNOW,

	PAGE	TITLE		LINE
THAT NONE MIGHT KNOW THAT HE WAS CONSCIENCE-STRUCK--	462	HARUN RASHID		38
THAT SPEECH WAS ALL THAT THE COURT KNOW, BUT HE	462	HARUN RASHID	V	35
THAT NONE MIGHT KNOW THAT HE WAS CONSCIENCE STRUCK,	462	HARUN RASHID	V	38
YOU KNOW THE SAYING, "CHANGE THE BRIDE WITH SPRING,"	463	HARUN RASHID		50
I KNOW NOT WHAT THE YOUNGER DREAMS--	475	EVA GORE-BOOTH		10
DEAR SHADOWS, NOW YOU KNOW IT ALL,	476	EVA GORE-BOOTH		21
RUN TILL ALL THE SAGES KNOW.	476	EVA GORE-BOOTH		29
FLOWERS FROM I KNOW NOT WHAT EMBROIDERY--	478	SELF AND SOUL		27
MAY KNOW NOT WHAT HE KNOWS, BUT KNOWS NOT GRIEF.	500	VACILLATION		18
I KNOW, ALTHOUGH WHEN LOOKS MEET	511	JANE AND JACK		1
AND YOU KNOW WHO—	515	GIRLS SONG B		4
WHAT MATTER? FOR I KNOW	518	HIS CONFIDENCE		9
"THREE DEAR THINGS THAT WOMEN KNOW,"	521	THREE THINGS		7
AS DID THAT WILD TRISTRAM KNOW	522	LULLABY		8
AND I SEEM TO KNOW	523	MAD AS MIST		4
ALL KNOW THEIR TALE, ALL KNOW WHAT LEAF AND TWIG,	555	RIBH AT TOMB		7
ALL KNOW THEIR TALE, ALL KNOW WHAT LEAF AND TWIG,	555	RIBH AT TOMB		7
WHAT CAN SHE KNOW UNTIL HE BID HER KNOW!	558	RIBH CHRISTIAN		23
WHAT CAN SHE KNOW UNTIL HE BID HER KNOW!	558	RIBH CHRISTIAN		23
BEAT DOWN UPON THEIR NAKED BODIES, KNOW —	563	MERU		12
FOR EVERYBODY KNOWS OR ELSE SHOULD KNOW	565	LAPIS LAZULI		4
THEY KNOW THAT HAMLET AND LEAR ARE GAY;	565	LAPIS LAZULI		16
"I KNOW THAT I MUST DROP DOWN DEAD	569	THREE BUSHES		17
KNOW WHERE ITS ROOTS BEGAN.	571	THREE BUSHES		76
NEITHER KNOW WHAT I AM	572	LADYS 1ST SONG		3
KNOW WORSE EVIL OF THE BODY;	573	LADYS 3RD SONG		6
THOUGHT FOR I KNOW NOT WHERE,	574	LOVERS SONG		2
WHAT CAN THEY KNOW THAT WE KNOW THAT KNOW THE TIME TO DIE?	580	CURSE CROMWELL		14
WHAT CAN THEY KNOW THAT WE KNOW THAT KNOW THE TIME TO DIE?	580	CURSE CROMWELL		14
WHAT CAN THEY KNOW THAT WE KNOW THAT KNOW THE TIME TO DIE?	580	CURSE CROMWELL		14
WHO CAN KNOW THE YEAR, MY DEAR,	588	OLD WICKED MAN		12
I KNOW AS FEW CAN KNOW,	589	OLD WICKED MAN		47
I KNOW AS FEW CAN KNOW,	589	OLD WICKED MAN		47
ALL KNOW THAT ALL THE DEAD IN THE WORLD ABOUT THAT PLACE ARE STUCK,	593	PILGRIM		11
NO MAN CAN KNOW A HAPPY MAN	598	STONE CROSS		11
I KNOW WHAT DEVIL'S TRADE THEY LEARN	607	SONGS BURDEN 2		12
WE KNOW WHAT RASCAL MIGHT HAS DEFILED,	614	MARCH SONGS 2		11
AND WIDE AWAKE KNOW THAT THE HUNT IS ON;	622	HOUND VOICE		17
YOUNG MEN KNOW NOTHING OF THIS SORT,	626	OLD MEN BE MAD		16
OBSERVANT OLD MEN KNOW IT WELL!	626	OLD MEN BE MAD		17
AND WHEN THEY KNOW WHAT OLD BOOKS TELL,	626	OLD MEN BE MAD		18
KNOW WHY AN OLD MAN SHOULD BE MAD.	626	OLD MEN BE MAD		20
WHAT DO WE KNOW BUT THAT WE FACE	633	MAN AND ECHO		39
MAINLY BECAUSE OF WHAT WE ONLY KNOW	634	CUCHULAIN COMF		14
KNOW THAT WHEN ALL WORDS ARE SAID	638	BEN BULBEN		27
KNOW HIS WORK OR CHOOSE HIS MATE.	638	BEN BULBEN		36
HERE, WHERE MEN KNOW THE GRACIOUS WOODLAND JOYS,	651	ISLE STAT I 1		154
AND NOT TOO CLEAR, HOW WILL THE NEW GOD KNOW	658	ISLE STAT I 3		79
I LIKE YOU, AND, IN SOOTH I KNOW NOT WHY.	661	ISLE STAT II 1		64
NASCHINA. OH, I KNOW HER WELL—A LAME,	661	ISLE STAT II 1		67
TO WATCH THEE PASS? YET DEEPER THAN MEN KNOW	672	ISLE STAT II 3		158
I KNOW NOT OF THE THINGS YOU SPEAK. BUT WHAT	675	ISLE STAT II 3		239
BY THEE SPELL-BOUND? THOU SHALT KNOW MORE!	675	ISLE STAT II 3		241

KNOW   (CONTINUED)
BUT NOW MY WANDERING SHALL BE DONE, I KNOW.   682 SEEKER   21
BUT SOON MY WANDERING SHALL BE DONE I KNOW.   682 SEEKER   V 21
I KNOW NOT WHAT I AM. I SOUGHT THEE NOT.   685 SEEKER   76
SHE WAS MY ONLY FRIEND: I'M LAME, YOU KNOW--   695 MOSADA 1   115
AND KNOW YOU NOT SHE KISSED THAT PIOUS CHILD   696 MOSADA 2   6
ONCE IN THY NATION NONE SHALL KNOW THAT I   702 MOSADA 3   82
AMONG THY NATION NONE SHALL KNOW THAT I   702 MOSADA 3   V 82
I AM SO YOUNG. DOST THOU NO LONGER KNOW,   713 FERENCZ RENYI 88
AND LOST AND FAR IN YONDER HILLS I KNOW: 713 FERENCZ RENYI 98
COME I KNOW WHERE, FAR AWAY.   727 LOVERS QUARREL   34
"MAN OF WISDOM, DOST THOU KNOW   729 PRIEST FAIRY   47
IF THESE MERRY ONES SHOULD KNOW,   731 STREET DANCERS   9
IF THESE MERRY ONES SHOULD KNOW,   732 STREET DANCERS   22
IF THESE MERRY ONES SHOULD KNOW,   732 STREET DANCERS   35
IF THESE MERRY ONES SHOULD KNOW,   733 STREET DANCERS   48
OTHERS KNOW THE HEALING EARTH,   733 STREET DANCERS   53
OTHERS KNOW THE STARRY MIRTH: 733 STREET DANCERS   54
IF THESE MERRY ONES SHOULD KNOW,   733 STREET DANCERS   61
AND I AM OLD AS TIME, BECAUSE I KNOW   756 SHADOW WATER A V 179
GATHER ABOUT HIM, THAT THE GODS MAY NOT KNOW   758 SHADOW WATER A   231
AND GATHER ROUND HIM, THAT NO GOD MAY KNOW   758 SHADOW WATER A V 231
THAT SHE AMONG HER WINDS MIGHT KNOW HE WEPT: 763 SHADOW WATER A   307
I KNOW YOU NOW, BESEECHING HANDS AND EYES.   763 SHADOW WATER A   312
THE LOVE I KNOW IS HIDDEN IN THESE HANDS   765 SHADOW WATER A   350
ALL THAT KNOW LOVE AMONG THE WINDS OF THE WORLD   767 SHADOW WATER A   386
I KNOW HE WILL OBEY YOU; AND IF YOUR EYES   768 SHADOW WATER A   408
SHOULD KNOW WHAT ISSUE IS AT STAKE: 778 FRIENDS WRONG   3
GAVE ALL THE LOVE THAT WOMEN KNOW!   789 SINGING HEAD   21
KNOWER
IS FROM THE OUGHT, OR KNOWER FROM THE KNOWN--   478 SELF AND SOUL   37
KNOWEST
THOU KNOWEST THIS, AND HOW FROM 'MID THE DANCE   683 SEEKER   51
KNOWETH
JOYS AND FEARS IN THEIR GREY FACES THAT THE LIVE EARTH   719 PHANTOM SHIP   26
KNOWETH NOT:
KNOWING
BY KNOWING NOR TUMULT NOR HATE NOR STRIFE,   9 OISIN 1   95
AND SHIVERED, KNOWING THE ISLE OF MANY FEARS,   30 OISIN 2   25
BUT NOW I HAVE GROWN NOTHING, KNOWING ALL.   104 FERGUS DRUID   38
KNOWING ONE, OUT OF ALL THINGS, ALONE, THAT HIS HEAD   177 PAST GREATNESS   8
KNOWING IT FOR THE WORLD'S END? WHERE THE WORLD ENDS   226 SHADOW WATER B   100
KNOWING THAT SILENCE BRINGS NO GOOD TO KINGS,   279 TWO KINGS   57
KNOWING THAT HE SHOULD FIND UPON HER LIPS   280 TWO KINGS   77
SHE'LL NOT BE PROUD, KNOWING WITHIN HER HEART   282 TWO KINGS   118
KNOWING NOT EVIL AND GOOD: 382 VISION ROBART   12
KNOWING THAT NONE COULD PASS HEAVEN'S DOOR   422 MY TABLE   26
KNOWING THAT NONE WHO PASS HEAVEN'S DOOR   422 MY TABLE   V 26
KNOWING THAT NONE CAN PASS HEAVEN'S DOOR   422 MY TABLE   V 26
AND KNOWING THAT THE FUTURE WOULD BE VEXED   472 ALL SOUL NIGHT   44
NOT KNOWING WHAT UNEARTHLY STUFF   599 STONE CROSS   21
THAT KNOWING BETTER TALK HAD GONE   627 STATES HOLIDAY   7
KNOWING THAT THOU HADST SINGLED ME WITH WORD   684 SEEKER   57
KNOWLEDGE
KNOWLEDGE HE SHALL UNWIND   343 SHEP GOATHERD   107
ALL KNOWLEDGE LOST IN TRANCE   343 SHEP GOATHERD   111
I WOULD BE--FOR NO KNOWLEDGE IS WORTH A STRAW--   344 DAWN   13
FOR WHAT MERE BOOK CAN GRANT A KNOWLEDGE   386 ROBARTES DANCE   20
DID SHE PUT ON HIS KNOWLEDGE WITH HIS POWER   441 LEDA AND SWAN   13
IT SEEMS I MUST BUY KNOWLEDGE WITH MY PEACE.   468 HARUN RASHID   169
WHAT KNOWLEDGE OR ITS LACK HAD SET AWRY,   490 COOLE BALLYLEE   22
WHAT KNOWLEDGE OR ITS LACK HAS SET AWRY,   490 COOLE BALLYLEE V 22
A DARKER KNOWLEDGE AND IN HATRED TURN   558 RIBH CHRISTIAN   14
BUT THERE'S ANOTHER KNOWLEDGE THAT MY HEART DESTROYS,   580 CURSE CROMWELL   17
THAT KNOWLEDGE INCREASES UNREALITY, THAT   610 STATUES   21
KNOWN   SEE WELL-KNOWN
HAVE KNOWN THREE CENTURIES, POETS SING,   2 OISIN 1   3
WHERE BROKEN FAITH HAS NEVER BEEN KNOWN,   8 OISIN 1   84
TO SHORES WHERE DYING HAS NEVER BEEN KNOWN,   8 OISIN 1   V 84
OUR HANDS HAVE KNOWN NO WEARYING TOOL,   22 OISIN 1   V 339
OUR LIVES HAVE KNOWN NO LAW NOR RULE: 22 OISIN 1   V 340
HAVE FACES ALIVE WITH SUCH BEAUTY BEEN KNOWN TO THE SALT   50 OISIN 3   51
EYE OF MAN,
ARE FACES ALIVE WITH SUCH BEAUTY MADE KNOWN TO THE SALT   50 OISIN 3   V 51
EYE OF MAN,
ARE FACES ALIVE WITH SUCH BEAUTY MADE KNOWN TO THE SOFT   50 OISIN 3   V 51
EYE OF MAN,
AND HE HAD KNOWN AT LAST SOME TENDERNESS,   126 DREAM OF FAERY   3
AND HE HAD KNOWN AT LAST SOME PRUDENT YEARS   127 DREAM OF FAERY   15
AND MIGHT HAVE KNOWN AT LAST UNHAUNTED SLEEP   128 DREAM OF FAERY   38
NEITHER COULD HAVE KNOWN   211 O DO NOT LOVE   6
IS NOT KNOWN AMONG MEN,   215 HAPPY TOWNLAND   28
YOU'VE NEVER KNOWN, I'D LAY A WAGER ON IT,   227 SHADOW WATER B   113
AS THEY HAVE KNOWN IT. NOW THE SECRET'S OUT: 228 SHADOW WATER B   140
AS THOSE THAT CAN OUTLIVE THE MOON HAVE KNOWN IT,   230 SHADOW WATER B   193
AND WE ARE ALMOST ON HER! WE HAD NOT KNOWN   232 SHADOW WATER B   220
BUT HAVE YOU KNOWN A DOG TO PRAISE HIS FLEAS?   262 TO A POET   V 4
SHE WOULD NOT LOOK IN ANY KNOWN MAN'S FACE   280 TWO KINGS   73
WOULD NEVER LOOK AGAIN ON KNOWN MAN'S FACE."   280 TWO KINGS   75
WILL NEVER LOOK AGAIN ON KNOWN MAN'S FACE."   280 TWO KINGS   V 75
BECAUSE OF ALL THINGS KNOWN   291 TO A FRIEND   15

	PAGE	TITLE		LINE

KNOWN   (CONTINUED)
IN HIS FULL HANDS WHAT, HAD THEY ONLY KNOWN, ...   292 TO A SHADE   11
BEING YOUNG YOU HAVE NOT KNOWN   . . . . . .   312 CHILD DANCING   6
IN MUSCULAR YOUTH WELL KNOWN TO MAYO MEN   . . . .   325 ROBERT GREGORY   34
WELL KNOWN FOR HORSEMANSHIP TO CONNACHT MEN   . . . .   325 ROBERT GREGORY V   34
AND KNOW WHAT ONCE I HAVE KNOWN, ...   346 ON WOMAN   34
FOR YOUR SOLE SAKE--THAT ALL HEART'S ACHE HAVE KNOWN,   . .   355 BROKEN DREAMS   7
BUT FOR YOUR SAKE--THAT ALL HEART'S ACHE HAVE KNOWN,   . .   355 BROKEN DREAMS V   7
THAT SO MANY LANDS HAD KNOWN, ...   360 ALF POLLEXFEN   18
HAVE YOU NOT ALWAYS KNOWN IT? THE SONG WILL HAVE IT   .   374 PHASES OF MOON   65
GAZED UPON ALL THINGS KNOWN, ALL THINGS UNKNOWN,   . .   383 VISION ROBART   30
THE GENTLENESS NONE THERE HAD EVER KNOWN!   . . .   418 ANCEST HOUSES   21
TO TELL YOUR SIMPLEST WANT, AND KNOWN, ...   436 FOR MY SON   21
IS FROM THE OUGHT, OR KNOWER FROM THE KNOWN--   . .   478 SELF AND SOUL   37
ALL COULD BE KNOWN OR SHOWN   . . . .   510 JANE JUDGMENT   18
CAN MAKE THE TRUTH KNOWN.   . . . .   575 ACRE OF GRASS   12
ALL THE OLYMPIANS! A THING NEVER KNOWN AGAIN.   . . .   578 LOFTY THINGS   12
SOME HAVE KNOWN A LIKELY LAD   . . . .   625 OLD MEN BE MAD   2
HAST THOU NOT KNOWN ALL SORROW AND DELIGHT   . . .   723 KANVA ON SELF   2
HAST THOU NOT KNOWN A RAJA'S DREAMLESS SLUMBER?   . .   724 KANVA ON SELF   8
THAT HAVE KNOWN LOVE AMONG THE WINDS OF THE WORLD   . .   767 SHADOW WATER A   392
NAMES WHEREBY A MAN HAS KNOWN   . . . . . .   775 AGAINST WITCH   5

KNOWS
OF THE THINGS THAT HIS HEART STILL KNOWS WERE SWEET--   . .   26 OISIN 1   V   402
HOPELESS FOR EVER! ANCIENT OISIN KNOWS, ...   42 OISIN 2   202
AY! OISIN KNOWS, FOR HE IS OF THE WEAK, ...   42 OISIN 2   V   202
THE GREY WOLF KNOWS ME! BY ONE EAR   . . . . .   84 MAD KING GOLL   45
THE WILD BOAR KNOWS ME, BY ONE EAR   . . . . .   84 MAD KING GOLL   V   45
AND SOMETIMES I AM SURE SHE KNOWS   . . . . . .   96 MOLL MAGEE   49
AND WHITHER THE WISE HEART KNOWS!   . . . . . .   168 BLESSED   34
THE POWERS WHOSE NAME AND SHAPE NO LIVING CREATURE KNOWS   174 ELEMENT POWERS   1
AH! WISE, MY HEART KNOWS WELL HOW WISE, ...   193 BAILE AILLINN   99
HEAVEN KNOWS WHAT CALAMITY!   . . . .   193 BAILE AILLINN   112
HE THAT MADE THIS KNOWS ALL THE COST, ...   202 NEVER GIVE ALL   13
THE ROOTS OF THE WORLD. WHO KNOWS THAT SHADOWS   . .   227 SHADOW WATER B V   104
OF THAT MORE POWERFUL LIFE? HIS WIFE KNOWS BETTER.   . .   230 SHADOW WATER B   172
SHE KNOWS THAT IT WAS BUT THE CART-HORSE COUGHING   . .   230 SHADOW WATER B   176
WHEN SHE KNOWS THAT. WHAT IS IT THAT YOU ARE MUTTERING--   236 SHADOW WATER B   303
HE KNOWS THAT HE IS TAKING YOU TO DEATH!   . . . .   249 SHADOW WATER B   562
ALL KNOW THE MAN THEIR NEIGHBOUR KNOWS.   . . . . .   337 SCHOLARS   10
IF THEY HAVE SINNED NOBODY KNOWS!   . . . . . .   337 SCHOLARS   V   10
SHE KNOWS HERSELF A WOMAN, ...   365 HER RACE   5
HIS ART IS HAPPY, BUT WHO KNOWS HIS MIND?   . . . .   370 EGO DOMINUS   54
OF BODY AND SOUL. THE LOVER'S HEART KNOWS THAT.   . .   375 PHASES OF MOON   71
WHO KNOWS HOW SHE DRANK THE WIND   . . . . . .   381 SONGS FOOL 2   6
YET KNOWS THAT TO BE CHOKED WITH HATE   . . . . .   405 FOR DAUGHTER   52
IT KNOWS NOT WHAT IT IS! AND GATHER ME   . . . .   408 SAIL BYZANTIUM   23
IT KNOWS NOT WHAT IT IS! GATHER ME   . . . . .   408 SAIL BYZANTIUM V   23
FROM SHALLOW WITS! WHO KNOWS NO WORK CAN STAND,   . .   429 NINETEEN 19   35
THAT PASSION, PIETY OR AFFECTION KNOWS, ...   445 SCHOOL CHILDR   54
AND THAT NONE LIVING KNOWS.   . . . .   455 HIS MEMORIES   6
HE KNOWS DEATH TO THE BONE--   . . . .   476 DEATH   11
FOR INTELLECT NO LONGER KNOWS   . . . .   478 SELF AND SOUL   36
AND IN THE MORNING'S GONE, NO MAN KNOWS WHY!   . . .   490 COOLE BALLYLEE   20
EVERY COMMON WOMAN KNOWS, ...   499 MOTHER OF GOD   7
MAY KNOW NOT WHAT HE KNOWS, BUT KNOWS NOT GRIEF.   . .   500 VACILLATION   18
MAY KNOW NOT WHAT HE KNOWS, BUT KNOWS NOT GRIEF.   . .   500 VACILLATION   18
THE BISHOP HAS A SKIN, GOD KNOWS, ...   508 JANE BISHOP   15
WHAT NONE OTHER KNOWS, ...   538 LAST CONFESS   18
AND ALL IT KNOWS IS THAT ONE WORD "REJOICE!"   . . .   564 GYRES   16
FOR EVERYBODY KNOWS OR ELSE SHOULD KNOW   . . . .   565 LAPIS LAZULI   4
FOR HE KNOWS HOW TO SAY, ...   583 GHOST ROG CASE   14
NO MAN KNOWS WHICH IS WHICH, ...   599 STONE CROSS   14
KNOWS I HAVE LIVED SO LONG, ...   607 SONGS BURDEN 2   26
AND YET WHO KNOWS WHAT'S YET TO COME?   . . . . .   608 SONGS BURDEN 3   23
AND NO MAN KNOWS WHAT TREADS THE GRASS.   . . . .   614 MARCH SONGS 2   10
AND NO MAN KNOWS WHAT TREADS THE GRASS.   . . . .   615 MARCH SONGS 2   20
AND NO MAN KNOWS WHAT TREADS THE GRASS.   . . . .   615 MARCH SONGS 2   30
NONE OTHER KNOWS WHAT PLEASURES MAN   . . . . .   620 JOHN KINSELLA   9
LION AND WOMAN AND THE LORD KNOWS WHAT.   . . . .   629 CIRCUS ANIMALS   8
YET HERE'S A TRAVELLED MAN THAT KNOWS   . . . . .   631 POLITICS   5
AND COLA, SEEING, KNOWS THE SIGN AND COMES.   . . .   691 MOSADA 1   38
AND COLA, SEEING, KNOWS THE SIGN AND RISES.   . . .   691 MOSADA 1   V   38
IF PETER WOULD BUT ASK HER LIFE--WHO KNOWS?   . . .   696 MOSADA 2   17
HE KNOWS BY SIGNS OF SECRET WIT   . . . . . .   716 FAIRY DOCTOR   5
AMONG THE WATERS THAT NO PILOT KNOWS.   . . . . .   750 SHADOW WATER A   80
ALL THAT TIME KNOWS. SPEAK TO ME, QUEEN. O SPEAK!   . .   756 SHADOW WATER A V   180
AND NONE KNOWS WHEREFORE! BUT THE HEART'S DESIRE   . .   764 SHADOW WATER A   340
IN THE LAND THAT NO ONE KNOWS.   . . . . . .   774 COME RIDE   17
IN THE LAND THAT NO-ONE KNOWS.   . . . . . .   774 COME RIDE   V   17
NOBODY KNOWS WHAT MAY BEFALL, ...   788 HAWTHORN TREE   13

KNOW'ST
KNOW'ST NAUGHT OF THIS. AND, UNCOUTH HUNTER, NOW--   . .   651 ISLE STAT I 1   168

KUSTA
KUSTA BEN LUKA IS MY NAME, I WRITE   . . . . .   460 HARUN RASHID   1

KYLE-DORTHA
SHADY KYLE-DORTHA! SUNNIER KYLE-NA-NO, ...   217 WOODS OF COOLE   4

KYLE-NA-INO
TO KYLE-NA-INO AND TO THAT ANCIENT ROOF   . . . .   321 REED WHISPERER V   7

KYLE-NA-NO
SHADY KYLE-DORTHA! SUNNIER KYLE-NA-NO, ...   217 WOODS OF COOLE   4

428

	PAGE	TITLE	LINE

KYLE-NA-NO   (CONTINUED)
    AT KYLE-NA-NO UNDER THAT ANCIENT ROOF . . . . 321 REED WHISPERER 7
    TO A SQUIRREL AT KYLE-NA-NO . . . . 359 TO A SQUIRREL T
KYTELER
    TO WHOM THE LOVE-LORN LADY KYTELER BROUGHT . . . . . 433 NINETEEN 19 129
LABAN
    AND NIAMH AND LABAN AND FAND, WHO COULD CHANGE TO AN OTTER 209 UNDER THE MOON 12
      OR FAWN,
    AND FAND, AND NIAM, AND LABAN, WHO COULD CHANGE TO AN OTTER 209 UNDER THE MOON V 12
      OR FAWN,
LABORIOUS
    HIS SLEEPLESS CANDLE AND LABORIOUS PEN. . . . . 375 PHASES OF MOON 86
    MAY THIS LABORIOUS STAIR AND THIS STARK TOWER . . . . . 423 MY DESCENDANTS 13
    WHAT MY LABORIOUS LIFE IMAGINED, EVEN . . . . 431 NINETEEN 19 82
LABOUR
    THE PAIN OF WOUNDS, THE LABOUR OF THE SPEAR, ... 104 FERGUS DRUID V 38D
    WE WHO STILL LABOUR BY THE CROMLECH ON THE SHORE, . . . 161 BLACK PIG 5
    WE POETS LABOUR ALL OUR DAYS, ... 164 PERFECT BEAUTY V 2
    THAT WE MUST LABOUR TO BE BEAUTIFUL." . . . . 205 ADAMS CURSE 20
    LABOUR IS BLOSSOMING OR DANCING WHERE . . . . 445 SCHOOL CHILDR 57
LABOURED
    IS HE WHO LABOURED ON, DERIDED, HATED, ... 738 MOURN THEN ON 11
LABOURER
    A KING IS BUT A FOOLISH LABOURER . . . . 103 FERGUS DRUID 27
    A WILD AND FOOLISH LABOURER IS A KING . . . . . . 103 FERGUS DRUID V 27
    THEN FEARING THAT SOME LABOURER, ON HIS WAY . . . . 283 TWO KINGS 145
    NOR THE BEST LABOURER DEAD . . . . 312 CHILD DANCING 9
LABOURER'S
    SAEVA INDIGNATIO AND THE LABOURER'S HIRE, ... 481 BLOOD AND MOON 28
LABOURING   SEE UN-LABOURING ALL-LABOURING
    WE AND THE LABOURING WORLD ARE PASSING BY; . . . . . 112 ROSE OF WORLD 6
    DOOMED LIKE ODYSSEUS AND THE LABOURING SHIPS . . . . 120 SORROW OF LOVE 7
    AND ALL THE SORROWS OF HER LABOURING SHIPS, ... 120 SORROW OF LOVE V 7
    AND ALL THE TROUBLE OF HER LABOURING SHIPS, ... 120 SORROW OF LOVE V 7
    WE, WHO ARE LABOURING BY THE CROMLECH ON THE SHORE, . . 161 BLACK PIG V 5
    THE POETS LABOURING ALL THEIR DAYS . . . . 164 PERFECT BEAUTY 2
    SINCE ADAM'S FALL BUT NEEDS MUCH LABOURING. . . . . 205 ADAMS CURSE 22
    LABOURING IN ECSTASY. . . . . 315 FRIENDS 16
    HER LABOURING MEN, AS THOUGH HER DARLING LIVED, . . . 340 SHEP GOATHERD 38
    YOU HEARD THAT LABOURING MAN WHO HAD SERVED MY PEOPLE. 391 UNDER SATURN 11
      HE SAID
    A SUFFERING PASSION AND A LABOURING THOUGHT? . . . . 420 MY HOUSE V 20J
    ALL THE LABOURING HEAVENS SIGH. . . . . 573 LADYS 3RD SONG 12
LABOURS
    AND ALL THE EXULTANT LABOURS OF THE STRONG. . . . . 42 OISIN 2 195
    OF ANCIENT WARRIORS, THE LABOURS OF THE STRONG. . . . 42 OISIN 2 V 195
LABURNUM
    HERE WHERE LABURNUM HANGS HER GOLDEN FLEECE; . . . . 670 ISLE STAT II 3 102
LABYRINTH
    THE LABYRINTH OF HER DAYS . . . . 260 UNWORTH PRAISE 13
    TO DIE INTO THE LABYRINTH OF ITSELF! . . . . 374 PHASES OF MOON 55
    INTO THE LABYRINTH OF ANOTHER'S BEING! . . . . . . 413 TOWER 112
    FROM A GREAT LABYRINTH OUT OF PRIDE, ... 413 TOWER 116
    FROM SOME GREAT LABYRINTH OUT OF PRIDE, ... 413 TOWER V 116
    IS LOST AMID THE LABYRINTH THAT HE HAS MADE . . . . 431 NINETEEN 19 70
    THEIR PURPOSE IN THE LABYRINTH OF THE WIND; . . . . 433 NINETEEN 19 121
    THAT THIS UNCONQUERABLE LABYRINTH OF THE BIRDS, . . . 481 BLOOD AND MOON 23
    THE LABYRINTH OF THE MIND. . . . . 785 WOMANS BEAUTY 24
LACE
    IN RUSTLE OF LACE OR SILKEN STUFF, ... 358 PRESENCES 5
    "VENGEANCE FOR JACQUES MOLAY." IN CLOUD-PALE RAGS, OR 426 PHANTOM HATRED 10
      IN LACE,
    "VENGENCE FOR JACQUES MOLAY." IN CLOUD PALE RAGS, OR IN 426 PHANTOM HATRED V 10
      LACE,
    THE QUIVERING HALF-CLOSED EYELIDS, THE RAGS OF CLOUD OR 427 PHANTOM HATRED 26
      OF LACE,
LACERATE
    CANNOT LACERATE HIS BREAST. . . . . 493 SWIFTS EPITAPH 3
LACK
    I AM ACCUSTOMED TO THEIR LACK OF BREATH, ... 325 ROBERT GREGORY 45
    THE BEST LACK ALL CONVICTION, WHILE THE WORST . . . . 402 SECOND COMING 7
    THE BEST LACK CONVICTION, WHILE THE WORST . . . . . 402 SECOND COMING V 7
    AND YET IT LACK ALL GLORY; AND PERCHANCE . . . . . 429 NINETEEN 19 23
    THAT HIS MOTHER MAY NOT LACK . . . . 435 FOR MY SON 7
    WHAT KNOWLEDGE OR ITS LACK HAD SET AWRY, ... 490 COOLE BALLYLEE 22
    WHAT KNOWLEDGE OR ITS LACK HAS SET AWRY, ... 490 COOLE BALLYLEE V 22
    WHAT, BE A SINGER BORN AND LACK A THEME? . . . . . 502 VACILLATION 73
    "A CHILD FOUND ALL A CHILD CAN LACK, ... 521 THREE THINGS 3
    IF IT LACK HONESTY. . . . . 584 GHOST ROG CASE 28
    MY MEDIAEVAL KNEES LACK HEALTH UNTIL THEY BEND, . . . 603 GALLERY REVIS 33
    PROCESSIONS THAT LACK HIGH STILTS HAVE NOTHING THAT CATCHES 622 HIGH TALK 1
      THE EYE.
    LACK NOTHING THAT A SOLDIER NEEDS, ... 635 BLACK TOWER 4
LACKED
    YOU HAVE LACKED ARTICULATE SPEECH . . . . 436 FOR MY SON 20
    WHERE NONE HAS REIGNED THAT LACKED A NAME AND FAME . . 491 COOLE BALLYLEE 31
    HE LACKED THOSE YEARS THAT GO WITH SKILL, ... 608 SONGS BURDEN 3 14
    IN MARBLE OR IN BRONZE, LACKED CHARACTER. . . . . . 610 STATUES 3
LACKEY
    THAT LACKEY THE WORN MOON IN MIDNIGHT HOURS, ... 41 OISIN 2 V 185A

		PAGE	TITLE	LINE

LACKING
    LACKING THE COUNTENANCE OF OUR FRIENDS. AND YET . . . . .   368 EGO DOMINUS   17
    OR LACKING THAT, GOVERNMENT IN SUCH HANDS, ...   543 PARN FUNERAL 2   7
    BUT ACTORS LACKING MUSIC . . . .   599 STONE CROSS   17
    HONOUR HAD LIVED SO LONG, ALL LACKING FOUND. . . . . . .   603 GALLERY REVIS   35
LACKS
    A SINGLE SOUL THAT LACKS A SWEET CRYSTALLINE CRY. . . . .   291 PAUDEEN   8
    A LOVE THAT LACKS ITS PROPER FOOD; . . . .   569 THREE BUSHES   3
LAD
    A GREAT LAD WITH A BEERY FACE . . . .   303 HOUR DAWN   27
    HE HAD SEEN A RED-HAIRED JOLLY LAD . . . .   303 HOUR DAWN   V   27
    SEMELE'S LAD A GAY COMPANION. . . . .   446 COLONUS PRAISE   8
    EVERY COLONUS LAD OR LASS DISCOURSES . . . .   447 COLONUS PRAISE   29
    A MERMAID FOUND A SWIMMING LAD, ...   452 MERMAID   1
    WHAT LIVELY LAD MOST PLEASURED ME . . . .   538 LAST CONFESS   1
    BUT HAD GREAT PLEASURE WITH A LAD . . . .   538 LAST CONFESS   5
    NIAMH THAT RODE ON IT; LAD AND LASS . . . .   550 SEVERED HEAD   11
    SOME HAVE KNOWN A LIKELY LAD . . . .   625 OLD MEN BE MAD   2
LADDER'S
    WHO KEEPS THE TILL. NOW THAT MY LADDER'S GONE, ...   630 CIRCUS ANIMALS   38
LADDERS
    I MUST LIE DOWN WHERE ALL THE LADDERS START, ...   630 CIRCUS ANIMALS   39
LADEN   SEE STAR-LADEN ODOUR-LADEN WAR-LADEN
    WAR LADEN GALLEYS, AND ARMIES ON WHITE ROADS, ...   757 SHADOW WATER A V   203
LADIES   SEE COURT-LADIES'
    AND A HUNDRED LADIES, MERRY AS BIRDS, ...   9 OISIN 1   96
    OF MEN AND LADIES, HAND IN HAND, ...   15 OISIN 1   202
    AND MEN AND LADIES KNELT THEM THERE . . . .   18 OISIN 1   255
    BY DREAMING LADIES UPON CLOTH . . . .   156 FORGOT BEAUTY   7
    WOVEN BY LADIES IN THEIR HAIR, ...   156 FORGOT BEAUTY   10
    THE DEW-COLD LILIES LADIES BORE . . . .   156 FORGOT BEAUTY   11
    ALL THE WILD WITCHES, THOSE MOST NOBLE LADIES, ...   343 DEJECTION   4
    TO LORDS AND LADIES OF BYZANTIUM . . . .   408 SAIL BYZANTIUM   31
    MAGICAL UNICORNS BEAR LADIES ON THEIR BACKS. . . . .   426 PHANTOM HATRED   18
    THE LADIES CLOSE THEIR MUSING EYES. NO PROPHECIES, . .   426 PHANTOM HATRED   19
    IMMORTAL LADIES TREAD THE GROUND . . . .   446 COLONUS PRAISE   6
    "HEAR, GENTLEMEN, LADIES, AND ALL MANKIND! . . . . .   544 TO SAME TUNE 1   2
    THAT THE SWORDSMEN AND THE LADIES CAN STILL KEEP COMPANY,   581 CURSE CROMWELL   20
    "HEAR, GENTLEMEN, LADIES, AND ALL MANKIND! . . . . .   615 MARCH SONGS 3   2
    SING THE LORDS AND THE LADIES GAY . . . .   640 BEN BULBEN   78
    LOVELY LADIES DANCING IN IT. . . . .   788 HAWTHORN TREE   4
LADIES'
    HAVE CLOSED THE LADIES' EYES, THEIR MINDS ARE BUT A POOL   426 PHANTOM HATRED   21
LADLE
    A LADLE AND A TUB OF BEER, ...   303 HOUR DAWN   29
    HAD DIPPED THE WOODEN LADLE DEEP . . . .   304 HOUR DAWN   46
    SHALL DIP HIS NOSE INTO MY LADLE . . . .   304 HOUR DAWN   53
    AND TOOK THE WOODEN LADLE UP . . . .   304 HOUR DAWN   V   46
    WOULD HAVE HIS FILL OUT OF MY LADLE . . . .   304 HOUR DAWN   V   53
    DIPPING HIS NOSE INTO MY LADLE . . . .   304 HOUR DAWN   V   53
    HE DIPPED HIS LADLE IN THE TUB . . . .   307 HOUR DAWN   107
LADS   SEE FISHER-LADS
    THOUGH LADS ARE MAKING PIKES AGAIN . . . .   131 OLD PENSIONER   7
    OR RUN WHERE LADS REFORM OUR DAYTIME . . . .   343 SHEP GOATHERD V   105
    FOR SHEPHERD LADS IN GALILEE; AND GRANT . . . . . .   371 ON GOING HOUSE   4
    WERE YOU AND I UNLETTERED LADS . . . .   524 MAD AS MIST   11
    HID FROM ALL THOSE WARTY LADS . . . .   589 OLD WICKED MAN   43
    A DANCE FOR THE FISHER LADS; . . . .   589 OLD WICKED MAN V   33
    LADS AND LASSES, TWO AND TWO, ...   705 DAWN-SONG   15
LADY
    A PEARL-PALE, HIGH-BORN LADY, WHO RODE . . . .   3 OISIN 1   20
    AND NOW A LADY RODE LIKE THE WIND . . . .   12 OISIN 1   142
    AND ONCE A LADY BY MY SIDE . . . .   16 OISIN 1   231
    THE YOUTH AND LADY AND THE DEER AND HOUND! . . . . .   29 OISIN 2   4
    ONCE MORE—THE YOUTH AND LADY, DEER AND HOUND! . . . .   29 OISIN 2   V   2
    A LADY WITH SOFT EYES LIKE FUNERAL TAPERS, ...   33 OISIN 2   69
    THE DEER AND THE HOUND, AND THE LADY AND YOUTH, . . .   47 OISIN 3   V   3
    THIS LADY BY THE TREES"; . . . .   123 DREAM OF DEATH V   10
    "O LADY, WED WITH ONE OF US"; . . . .   191 BAILE AILLINN   61
    THE DELICATE-STEPPING STAG AND HIS LADY SIGH . . . .   210 RAGGED WOOD   2
    THE DELICATE STEPPING STAG AND HIS LADY SIGH . . . .   210 RAGGED WOOD   V   2
    DO YOU NOT KNOW ME, LADY? I AM HE . . . .   243 SHADOW WATER B   426
    IF THE LADY BE YOUNG AND FAIR." . . . .   268 BROWN PENNY   6
    OR A WITTY LOVELY LADY." . . . .   299 THREE HERMITS   28
    OF GOLDEN KING AND SILVER LADY, ...   331 ROUND TOWER   13
    THAT GOLDEN KING AND THAT WILD LADY . . . .   332 ROUND TOWER   19
    THAT LADY AND THAT GOLDEN KING . . . .   332 ROUND TOWER   23
    WILL SAY TO AN OLD MAN, "TELL ME OF THAT LADY . . . .   356 BROKEN DREAMS   17
    THE CERTAINTY THAT I SHALL SEE THAT LADY . . . . . .   356 BROKEN DREAMS   22
    SEVEN POEMS I UPON A DYING LADY . . . .   362 HER COURTESY   V   T
    VEHEMENT AND WITTY SHE HAD SEEMED—; THE VENETIAN LADY .   363 DOLLS FACES   5
    THE MOST EXALTED LADY LOVED BY A MAN. . . . .   369 EGO DOMINUS   37
    LOVED THE LADY; AND IT'S PLAIN . . . .   385 ROBARTES DANCE   5
    AND THUS DECLARED THAT ARAB LADY! . . . .   387 SOLOMON WITCH   1
    TO WHOM THE LOVE-LORN LADY KYTELER BROUGHT . . . . .   433 NINETEEN 19   129
    NOTHING COULD BRING HIM, WHEN HIS LADY DIED, ...   471 ALL SOUL NIGHT   25
    FOR HE CANNOT SEE MY LADY . . . .   552 SONGS REWRIT 2   3
    BUT RHYMES FOR A BEAUTIFUL LADY, ...   552 SONGS REWRIT 2   11
    SAID LADY ONCE TO LOVER. . . . .   569 THREE BUSHES   1
    THAT LOVELY LADY SAID, ...   569 THREE BUSHES   9
    "BECAUSE MY LADY CAME . . . .   570 THREE BUSHES   37

430

	PAGE	TITLE		LINE

LADY   (CONTINUED)
HIS LADY SAW IT ALL . . . . 571 THREE BUSHES 53
FOR I THAT AM HIS DAYLIGHT LADY . . . . 573 LADYS 3RD SONG 5
SHE ALONE, MY LADY, LINGERETH . . . . 646 ISLE STAT I 1 28
SAD LADY OF THE DEEP, POURS DOWN HER LIGHT; . . . . . . 650 ISLE STAT I 1 127
O, LADY, THOU WHOSE VESTITURE OF GREEN . . . . 667 ISLE STAT II 3 34
SAD LADY, CEASE! . . . . 672 ISLE STAT II 3 160
NAMES AFTER ME, LADY—I COME, FORGIVE, ... 695 MOSADA 1 117
"I AM LONE LADY QUIETNESS, MY SWEET, ... 716 DWELT SYCAMORE 13
COME, FATHER, LADY, I NOR REST NOR SIT. . . . . 720 WITCH VIVIEN 18
LOVELY LADY OR GALLANT MAN . . . . 788 HAWTHORN TREE 7
LOVELY LADY AND GALLANT MAN . . . . 788 HAWTHORN TREE V 7
THE SINGING HEAD AND THE LADY . . . . 789 SINGING HEAD T
LADY'S   SEE COURT-LADY'S
UPON THIS LADY'S BEAUTY . . . . 329 MEN IMPROVE 5
THAT MOST RESPECTED LADY'S EVERY WISH, ... 410 TOWER 29
BESIDE HER LADY'S MAN, ... 571 THREE BUSHES 72
THE LADY'S FIRST SONG . . . . 572 LADYS 1ST SONG T
THE LADY'S SECOND SONG . . . . 572 LADYS 2ND SONG T
THE LADY'S THIRD SONG . . . . 573 LADYS 3RD SONG T
LAEN
WE RODE IN SADNESS ABOVE LOUGH LAEN, ... 2 OISIN 1 V 7H
LAGGARD
AND NOW A LAGGARD WITH A WOMAN'S HEAD . . . . 234 SHADOW WATER B 260
THEY ARE STILL WAITING; AND NOW THE LAGGARD COMES, . . 754 SHADOW WATER A 150
THEY ARE STILL WAITING; AND A LAGGARD COMES, ... 754 SHADOW WATER A V 150
LAGOON
BY THE LAGOON YOU LOVE SO MUCH, ... 386 ROBARTES DANCE 29
LAID
AND SIGHING LAID THE PEARLY TIP . . . . 12 OISIN 1 150
SAID NIAM, AS SHE LAID THE TIP . . . . 12 OISIN 1 V 150
AND WHILE THEY SANG, A SINGER LAID . . . . 16 OISIN 1 V 231
LAID IT AND SIGHED; I HELD A SWORD WHOSE SHINE . . . . 37 OISIN 2 126
LAID IT AND SIGHED—A SWORD WHOSE WIZARD SHINE . . . . 37 OISIN 2 V 126
AND ON MY BOSOM LAID HER WEEPING HEAD. . . . . 46 OISIN 2 250
COULD SLEEP ON A COUCH OF RUSHES—ROUND AND ABOUT THEM 49 OISIN 3 V 32
     LAID.
LAID HANDS ON THE BELL-BRANCH AND SWAYED IT, ... 51 OISIN 3 56
IN THE ROOTS OF THE GRASSES, THE SORRELS, I LAID MY BODY 52 OISIN 3 73
     AS LOW;
SAD NIAM CAME NEAR ME, AND LAID HER BROWS ON THE MIDST 52 OISIN 3 V 74
     OF MY BREAST
AFRAID, THEIR EARS ON THE EARTH LAID, ... 62 OISIN 3 206
AND LAID YOU ON THE GATES OF EVENING WITH HIS QUIET HANDS. 72 ANASHU VIJAYA 22
THE SUN HAS LAID HIS CHIN ON THE GREY WOOD, ... 72 ANASHU VIJAYA 24
AND LAID YE ON THE GATES OF EVENING WITH HIS QUIET HANDS. 72 ANASHU VIJAYA 22
THE SUN HATH LAID HIS CHIN ON THE GREY WOOD, ... 72 ANASHU VIJAYA 24
AND ON MY LEANING SHOULDER SHE LAID HER SNOW-WHITE HAND, 90 SALLEY GARDENS 6
TO HIM SEEMED EASY, SO I LAID THE CROWN . . . . 102 FERGUS DRUID 13
WITH THE FEET LAID SIDE BY SIDE. . . . . 124 CATHLEEN PARA 4
THAT GOD HAS LAID HIS FINGERS ON THE SKY; . . . . . . 128 DREAM OF FAERY 43
WHERE ONLY BODY'S LAID ASLEEP. . . . . 138 TO IRELAND 22
WHEN I HAD LAID IT ON THE FLOOR . . . . 149 WANDER AENGUS 9
WHEN I HAD LAID IT ON A STOOL . . . . 149 WANDER AENGUS V 9
AND MY WHITE BREAST ON HIS HE LAID. . . . . 151 HEART OF WOMAN V 4
SHE LAID THEM UPON HER BOSOM, ... 160 CAP AND BELLS 25
SHE LAID A HAND ON EITHER OF HIS SHOULDERS, ... 182 QUEEN MAEVE 49
AND HE, BEING LAID UPON GREEN BOUGHS, ... 192 BAILE AILLINN 71
AND NOW THAT HONEY-MOUTH IS LAID . . . . 192 BAILE AILLINN 80
AND NOW THAT HONEY MOUTH IS LAID . . . . 192 BAILE AILLINN V 80
TO FIND IT WHEN NIGHT FALLS LAID ON A GOLDEN BIER. . . 209 UNDER THE MOON 10
WHO HAVE SLAIN MY HUSBAND AND LAID HANDS UPON ME. . . 235 SHADOW WATER B 282
LAID ON THE DEATH-BED, ... 335 SONG 16
LAID ON THE DEATH BED. . . . . 335 SONG V 16
LAID HIS STRONG BONES DOWN IN DEATH . . . . 360 ALF POLLEXFEN 3
AND AFTER TWENTY YEARS THEY LAID . . . . 360 ALF POLLEXFEN 6
BUT WHERE IS LAID THE SAILOR JOHN . . . . 360 ALF POLLEXFEN 17
LAID HIS STRONG BONES IN DEATH . . . . 360 ALF POLLEXFEN V 3
WHERE HAVE THEY LAID THE SAILOR JOHN? . . . . 361 ALF POLLEXFEN 23
ON GRASSY MATTRESS I HAD LAID ME, ... 387 SOLOMON WITCH 3
WHY HAVE YOU LAID YOUR HANDS UPON MY EYES? . . . . . 389 IMAGE PAST 15
AND HOW CAN BODY, LAID IN THAT WHITE RUSH, ... 441 LEDA AND SWAN 7
HAS LAID HER HELPLESS FACE UPON HIS BREAST. . . . . . 441 LEDA AND SWAN 4
ALL THE STRETCHED BODY'S LAID ON THE WHITE RUSH . . . 441 LEDA AND SWAN V 7
BUT SINCE I LAID A HAND THEREON . . . . 451 FIRST LOVE 7
BEAUTY AND FOOL TOGETHER LAID. . . . . 484 SYMBOLS 6
AND LAID THEM ON LOVE'S LETTERED TOMB; . . . . 519 HER DREAM 4
A PIERCED BOY, IMAGE OF A STAR LAID LOW. . . . . . . 541 PARN FUNERAL 1 12
THAT IS IN QUICKLIME LAID. . . . . 582 ROGER CASEMENT 24
THAT IS IN THE QUICK-LIME LAID. . . . . 582 ROGER CASEMENT V 24
FOR SOON WE LIE WHERE HE IS LAID, ... 586 PARNELLITES 5
AND HE LAID THEM ON HER HAND. . . . . 595 COLONEL MARTIN 35
IN DRUMCLIFF CHURCHYARD YEATS IS LAID. . . . . 640 BEN BULBEN 85
AS ON THOSE OTHER HEARTS WERE LAID. . . . . 667 ISLE STAT II 3 42
IF ON HIS LIPS THE ENCHANTED FLOWER BE LAID; . . . . 668 ISLE STAT II 3 46
THE HARE HATH LAID ASLEEP HER FROLIC WITS, ... 712 FERENCZ RENYI 72
WILD BEES' HONEY LAID FOR THEE." . . . . 730 PRIEST FAIRY 56
LAIGHEN
THE HILL SEAT OF LAIGHEN, BECAUSE . . . . 194 BAILE AILLINN 130
LAIN
WHEN I HAD LAIN IT ON A STOOL, ... 149 WANDER AENGUS V 9

	PAGE	TITLE		LINE
LAIN (CONTINUED)				
BY BIDDY'S HALFPENNIES HAVE LAIN	287	TO WEALTHY MAN		3
BY BIDDY'S HALF-PENNIES HAVE LAIN	287	TO WEALTHY MAN	V	3
WHERE THE MOUNTAIN HARE HAS LAIN.	350	MEMORY		6
BUT THE CRUSHED GRASS WHERE WE HAVE LAIN!	389	SOLOMON WITCH		42
A MYRIAD HEADS HAVE LAIN." "	496	MOHINI CHATTER		11
THAT SO STILL HAD LAIN,	516	MANS SONG		4
A HOUND THAT HAD LAIN IN THE RED RUSHES	761	SHADOW WATER A		278
LAIR				
. . LURED FROM HIS LAIR IN THE MOULD!	53	OISIN 3		99
NO FOX CAN FOUL THE LAIR THE BADGER SWEPT--	603	GALLERY REVIS		39
I FOLLOWED HIM FROM MY GREEN LAIR,	655	ISLE STAT I 3		6
FROM MY WIZARD ISLAND LAIR,	668	ISLE STAT II 3		63
WE WILL FIND HER FAVOURITE LAIR,	706	DAWN-SONG		26
LAKE				
BY THE LONE BORDER OF THE LAKE ONCE MORE,	79	EPHEMERA		5
STAND BY THE BORDER OF THE LAKE ONCE MORE,	79	EPHEMERA	V	5
ON THE LONE BORDER OF THE LAKE ONCE MORE!	80	EPHEMERA		17
ON THE LONE BORDER OF THE SULLEN LAKE.	80	EPHEMERA	V	17
OF SLEUTH WOOD IN THE LAKE.	86	STOLEN CHILD		2
THE LAKE ISLE OF INNISFREE	117	ISLE INNISFREE		T
I HEAR LAKE WATER LAPPING WITH LOW SOUNDS BY THE SHORE!	117	ISLE INNISFREE		10
I HEAR LAKE WATER LAPPING WITH LOW SOUNDS ON THE SHORE!	117	ISLE INNISFREE	V	10
OF THE DREAR HART LAKE.	143	HOST OF AIR		4
OF THIS DESOLATE LAKE	165	CRY OF SEDGE		2
AND THEIR SECRET SMILE, OUT OF THE DEPTHS OF THE LAKE!	203	WITHER BOUGHS		11
AND THEIR SECRET SMILE, OUT OF THE DEEPS OF THE LAKE!	203	WITHER BOUGHS	V	11
IN THAT MYSTERIOUS, ALWAYS BRIMMING LAKE	356	BROKEN DREAMS		32
BESIDE THE LITTLE LAKE	400	DEMON BEAST		23
SPREAD TO A LAKE AND DROP INTO A HOLE.	490	COOLE BALLYLEE		7
THE GLITTERING REACHES OF THE FLOODED LAKE.	490	COOLE BALLYLEE		16
SPREAD TO A LAKE AND RUN INTO A HOLE.	490	COOLE BALLYLEE	V	7
ROUND THE MAREOTIC LAKE	636	BEN BULBEN		2
OVER THE LAKE THE WATER-FLOWERS	647	ISLE STAT I 1		66
THE WAVES IN YONDER LAKE WHERE POINTS MY HAND	652	ISLE STAT I 2		13
OF YONDER LAKE, FROM WHOSE GREEN BANKS ALWAY	653	ISLE STAT I 2		33
UNTO THE DOLOROUS BORDER OF THE FAIRY LAKE.	655	ISLE STAT I 2		85
NODDING BY THE FLICKERING LAKE,	655	ISLE STAT I 3		3
O'ER THE LAKE THIS VERY DAY.	656	ISLE STAT I 3		17
ALONG THE LAKE. THE CRANE HAS HOMEWARD FLED.	656	ISLE STAT I 3		23
BEYOND THE LAKE, WHOSE SMALLEST WAVE WAS BURDENED	656	ISLE STAT I 3		31
FROM YONDER PINNACLE ABOVE THE LAKE	657	ISLE STAT I 3		63
HE PASSED ACROSS THE LAKE. WHEN WE TWO CAME	658	ISLE STAT II 1		5
WE SAW THE DOLOROUS LAKE! AND THEN THY NAME	659	ISLE STAT II 1		7
HE SAT, AND THEN I HEARD THE WHITE LAKE SING,	659	ISLE STAT II 1		15
HALF LIT, SO FLAPT THE WINGS ACROSS THE LAKE--	659	ISLE STAT II 1		17
IN BUSY FLAKES! RE-SHINING FROM THE LAKE,	662	ISLE STAT II 2		3
HERE, FACING TO THE LAKE, AND NO NAME GILD!	663	ISLE STAT II 2		20
SWIFT LAKE. A VERY LITTLE THING THAT IS,	669	ISLE STAT II 3		78
A WRIGGLING THING ON THE WHITE LAKE MOVED,	673	ISLE STAT II 3		176
A-FLUTTERING THE PAINTED POPULACE OF LAKE	675	ISLE STAT II 3		224
FIERCE MORTAL, AND CROUCHED LOW BESIDE THE LAKE	675	ISLE STAT II 3	V	245A
ABOVE THE FARM-HOUSE BY THE LITTLE LAKE.	699	MOSADA 3		3
AND NOW THAT CITY IS A LAKE.	725	LEGEND		32
COME, BESIDE A SANDY LAKE.	727	LOVERS QUARREL		41
TO MIND HIS COWS AND SWINE BY THE RED LAKE.	752	SHADOW WATER A		112
LAKE-EMBOSOMED				
THE LAKE-EMBOSOMED ISLE. NAY, THIS MY QUEST	657	ISLE STAT I 3		60
LAKE-LULLED				
WITH SINGING SWEET AS E'ER ROUND LAKE-LULLED ISLE	649	ISLE STAT I 1		106
LAKE-NURTURED				
OF THIS LAKE-NURTURED ISLE! LET THY KING BE	679	ISLE STAT II 3		315
LAKE'S				
BY WHAT LAKE'S EDGE OR POOL	323	SWANS AT COOLE		28
UPON THE BORDER OF THAT LAKE'S A WOOD	490	COOLE BALLYLEE		9
CARVED! HERE, BEYOND THE LAKE'S SLOW-MUFFLED TREAD,	662	ISLE STAT II 2		11
LAKES				
BY LAKES AND MEADOW LANDS AND LAWNS AFAR,	32	OISIN 2	V	50F
LAMB				
WHEN SOMETHING, HALF A LAMB AND HALF A GOAT,	747	SHADOW WATER A	V	11
LAMB'S				
BUT FAINTER THAN A YOUNG LAMB'S BLEAT.	26	OISIN 1		399
AND FAINTER THAN A YOUNG LAMB'S BLEAT.	26	OISIN 1	V	399
LAMBS				
THE MERRY LAMBS AND THE COMPLACENT KINE,	75	ANASHU VIJAYA		86
THE MERRY LAMBS AND ALL THE KINE COMPLACENT,	75	ANASHU VIJAYA	V	86
BY THE PASTURE WHERE THE LAMBS	726	LOVERS QUARREL		5
LAME				
A RABBIT OLD AND LAME LIMPED DOWN THE PATH!	80	EPHEMERA		15
NASCHINA. OH, I KNOW HER WELL--A LAME,	661	ISLE STAT II 1		67
AMONG THE FRUIT! BUT THERE, LAME COLA CROUCHES	691	MOSADA 1		32
AMONG THE FRUIT. BUT YON, LAME COLA CROUCHES	691	MOSADA 1	V	32
OF SILVER HANGING ROUND LAME COLA'S NECK--	691	MOSADA 1	V	35
SHE WAS MY ONLY FRIEND! I'M LAME, YOU KNOW--	695	MOSADA 1		115
LAME-FOOTED				
THEY SAY I AM ALL UGLINESS! LAME-FOOTED	692	MOSADA 1		60
LAMENT				
JOHN KINSELLA'S LAMENT FOR MRS. MARY MOORE	620	JOHN KINSELLA		T
LAMENTATION				
AND ALL THAT LAMENTATION OF THE LEAVES,	120	SORROW OF LOVE		11
THE LAMENTATION OF THE OLD PENSIONER	131	OLD PENSIONER		T

	PAGE	TITLE		LINE

LAMENTING
AND WEPT, AND RAISED THEIR LAMENTING HANDS, ... 10 OISIN 1 112
THEY WEPT, AND RAISED LAMENTING HANDS. . . . . 10 OISIN 1 V 112
LAMENTING THAT A MAN SHOULD DIE; . . . . 361 ALF POLLEXFEN 38
BEAT OUT THEIR LIVES LAMENTING O'ER THE SAND; . . . . . 652 ISLE STAT I 2 14
LAMENTS
AEDH LAMENTS THE LOSS OF LOVE . . . . 152 LOSS OF LOVE V T
MONGAN LAMENTS THE CHANGE THAT HAS COME UPON HIM AND HIS 153 CHANGE BELOVED V T
BELOVED
HANRAHAN LAMENTS BECAUSE OF HIS WANDERINGS . . . . . 171 MAID QUIET V T
LAMP
AS A LAMP SHADOW--NO--NO LAMP, THE SUN. . . . . . . 229 SHADOW WATER B 160
AS A LAMP SHADOW--NO--NO LAMP, THE SUN. . . . . . . 229 SHADOW WATER B 160
A LAMP BURNS ON BESIDE THE OPEN BOOK . . . . 367 EGO DOMINUS 3
A LAMP BURNS ON ABOVE THE OPEN BOOK . . . . 367 EGO DOMINUS V 3
LUXURIANT SONG. WHY SHOULD YOU LEAVE THE LAMP . . . . 370 EGO DOMINUS 62
TRUTH FLOURISHES WHERE THE STUDENT'S LAMP HAS SHONE, . . 398 LEADERS CROWD 8
AND HEARTIER LOVES; THAT LAMP IS FROM THE TOMB. . . . 398 LEADERS CROWD 12
HIS LONG LAMP CHIMNEY SHAPED LIKE THE STEM . . . . . 566 LAPIS LAZULI V 33
LAMP-CHIMNEY
HIS LONG LAMP-CHIMNEY SHAPED LIKE THE STEM . . . . . 566 LAPIS LAZULI 33
LAMPLIGHT
UNFRIENDLY LAMPLIGHT HID UNDER ITS SHADE, ... 523 LONG SILENCE 3
LAMPS
OF THE GREAT DOOR, BUT THOUGH THE HANGING LAMPS . . . 279 TWO KINGS 49
LANCE
FROM SOME DEAD WARRIOR'S BROKEN LANCE; . . . . 24 OISIN 1 367
IT WAS OF SOME DEAD WARRIOR'S LANCE. . . . . 24 OISIN 1 V 367
SHINING BRIGHT AS A NEW LANCE; . . . . 125 CATHLEEN PARA V 14
SO LET US DANCE WHERE THE YELLOW LANCE . . . . . . 643 SONG FAERIES 7
TO PROVE HIS LOVE A KNIGHT WITH LANCE IN REST . . . . 651 ISLE STAT I 1 158
SO LET US DANCE WHERE THE YELLOW LANCE . . . . . . 676 ISLE STAT II 3 254
LANCELOT
WHERE ONE FOUND LANCELOT CRAZED AND HID HIM FOR A WHILE; 209 UNDER THE MOON 3
WHERE ONE FOUND LANCELOT CRAZED, AND HID HIM FOR AWHILE, 209 UNDER THE MOON V 3
LAND   SEE PLOUGH-LAND PASTURE-LAND LITTLE-LAND
IS NIAMH, AND MY LAND WHERE TIDE . . . . 5 OISIN 1 V 48
"WERE THESE TWO BORN IN THE DANAAN LAND, ... 12 OISIN 1 146
WAS A BEAUTIFUL YOUTH FROM AN UNKNOWN LAND. . . . . . 12 OISIN 1 V 145
BUT NOW A WANDERING LAND BREEZE CAME . . . . 13 OISIN 1 165
OVER THE BARE AND WOODY LAND, ... 15 OISIN 1 198
BUT WE IN A LONELY LAND ABIDE . . . . 22 OISIN 1 337
IN WHAT LAND DO THE POWERLESS TURN THE BEAK . . . . . 42 OISIN 2 198
PRAYERS FOR THE LAND. I WILL WAIT HERE, AMRITA, . . . 71 ANASHU VIJAYA 13
PRAYERS FOR THE LAND. PRAY ON, AND I WILL WAIT YOU, . . 71 ANASHU VIJAYA 13
PRAYERS FOR THE LAND. O BRAHMA, GUARD IN SLEEP . . . 75 ANASHU VIJAYA 85
THE PEASANTS OF THAT LAND, ... 123 DREAM OF DEATH 4
A DRUID LAND, A DRUID TUNE; . . . . 139 TO IRELAND 32
IN BARREN HILLS AND MARSHY LAND, ... 150 WANDER AENGUS V 18
COME FROM A MORE DREAM-HEAVY LAND, ... 156 FORGOT BEAUTY 16
O, WHEN SHALL SORROW WANDER NO MORE IN THE LAND . . . 174 ELEMENT POWERS V 5
CALLED RATHER BAILE LITTLE LAND, ... 189 BAILE AILLINN V 17
WITH SOMEBODY IN YOUR OWN LAND." . . . . 191 BAILE AILLINN 59
THAT HELD THE LAND TOGETHER THERE, ... 194 BAILE AILLINN 132
O TUFTED REEDS, BEND LOW AND LOW IN POOLS ON THE GREEN 206 HANRAHANS SONG V 1
LAND,
WHEN THE WIND COMES BLOWING ACROSS THE HILLY LAND; . . 207 HANRAHANS SONG V 7
LAND OF THE TOWER, WHEN AENGUS HAS THROWN THE GATES APART, 209 UNDER THE MOON V 8
LAND FOR YOUR CHILDREN OR MONEY IN A POT." . . . . . 228 SHADOW WATER B 125
IN THIS BLIND BITTER LAND." . . . . 256 WORDS 4
UPON A HOUSE SHAKEN BY THE LAND AGITATION . . . . . 264 HOUSE SHAKEN T
THE SEEMING NEEDS OF MY FOOL-DRIVEN LAND; . . . . . 267 ALL TEMPT ME 3
FROM WELL SIDE OR FROM PLOUGH LAND, WAS THEIR NOISE; . . 279 TWO KINGS 53
TO PLOUGH OR PASTURE LAND, MIGHT SEE ME THERE . . . . 283 TWO KINGS V 146
IN A DRAGON-GUARDED LAND, ... 309 REALISTS 3
YOU SAY THAT WE SHOULD STILL THE LAND . . . . 395 SIXTEEN DEAD 7
SHAKESPEAREAN FISH SWAM THE SEA, FAR AWAY FROM LAND; . . 485 THREE MOVEMENT 1
AND THE HOLY LAND OF IRELAND, ... 526 AM OF IRELAND 2
AND THE HOLY LAND OF IRELAND, ... 526 AM OF IRELAND 15
AND THE HOLY LAND OF IRELAND, ... 527 AM OF IRELAND 28
NO CIVIL RANCOUR TORN THE LAND APART. . . . . 542 PARN FUNERAL 2 4
"THIS LAND OF SAINTS," AND THEN AS THE APPLAUSE DIED OUT, 577 LOFTY THINGS 3
THE WINGED WONDER OF ALL FAERY LAND. . . . . 657 ISLE STAT I 3 57
HOLD FESTIVAL ACROSS THE LAND, ... 671 ISLE STAT II 3 128
SHEPHERDS, I CAME THIS MORNING TO YOUR LAND . . . . . 682 SEEKER 15
A VOICE CAME CALLING ME TO THIS YOUR LAND, ... 682 SEEKER 22
A VOICE HAS TOLD ME HOW WITHIN THIS LAND . . . . . . 682 SEEKER V 22
I CANNOT GO INTO THE BLOODLESS LAND . . . . 722 WITCH VIVIEN 67
BY THE GORSE ON THE HIGH LAND, ... 726 LOVERS QUARREL 4
THEN GO TO HIS OWN LAND, ... 741 EARL PAUL 58
A FRUITFUL LAND UNDER THE AIBHLIN HILLS? . . . . . . 748 SHADOW WATER A V 33
AND, HURRYING HOMEWARD, FALL UPON SOME LAND . . . . . 767 SHADOW WATER A 384
IN THE LAND THAT NO ONE KNOWS. . . . . 774 COME RIDE 17
IN THE LAND THAT NO-ONE KNOWS. . . . . 774 COME RIDE V 17
BETWEEN TWO FURROWS UPON THE PLOUGHED LAND; . . . . . 784 WOMANS BEAUTY 4
BETWEEN DARK FURROWS UPON THE PLOUGHED LAND. . . . . 784 WOMANS BEAUTY 6
LAND-OF-THE-TOWER
LAND-OF-THE-TOWER, WHERE AENGUS HAS THROWN THE GATES APART, 209 UNDER THE MOON 8
LANDOR
WITH LANDOR AND WITH DONNE. . . . . 336 YOUNG BEAUTY 18

		PAGE	TITLE	LINE

LANDOR'S
LANDOR'S TARPAULIN ON THE ROOF. . . . . 625 NATIVITY   6
LAND'S
HAD COSGRAVE EATEN PARNELL'S HEART, THE LAND'S . . . . 543 PARN FUNERAL 2   5
LANDS
AT EVENING IN THEIR RAINLESS LANDS." . . . . 7 OISIN 1   70
AT EVENING IN THEIR RAINLESS LANDS. . . . . 7 OISIN 1   V   66
BUT WE RODE OUT FROM THE HUMAN LANDS. . . . . 10 OISIN 1   114
AND BADE ME SING OF EARTHLY LANDS! . . . . 17 OISIN 1   V   233
WEDDING THE QUEENS OF EARTHLY LANDS WITH RINGS . . . . 29 OISIN 2   10
OF SEA-SPRUNG PEARL, AND QUEENS OF FAIRY LANDS . . . . 29 OISIN 2   V   10A
BY LAKES AND MEADOW LANDS AND LAWNS AFAR, ... 32 OISIN 2   V   50F
YOUR QUESTIONER, OISIN, IS WORTHY, HE COMES FROM THE FENIAN 51 OISIN 3   64
    LANDS."
WORTHY'S THY QUESTIONER, OISIN, HE FROM THE FENIAN LANDS." 51 OISIN 3   V   64
"THEN GO THROUGH THE LANDS IN THE SADDLE AND SEE WHAT THE 55 OISIN 3   125
    MORTALS DO,
. . . THOUGH SPACIOUS HIS LANDS WERE AND STRONG. . . . . 58 OISIN 3   V   160
SEND PEACE ON ALL THE LANDS AND FLICKERING CORN.-- . . . 71 ANASHU VIJAYA   1
MURMURING HOW FAR AWAY ARE THE UNQUIET LANDS! . . . . 78 INDIAN TO LOVE   10
MURMURING HOW FAR AWAY ARE ALL EARTH'S FEVERISH LANDS. . 78 INDIAN TO LOVE   V   10
MURMURING GENTLY HOW FAR OFF ARE THE UNQUIET LANDS! . . 78 INDIAN TO LOVE   V   10
TO A SHONEEN WHO HAD FREE LANDS . . . . 92 FATHER OHART   3
IN TRUST TOOK HE JOHN'S LANDS! . . . . 92 FATHER OHART   5
AH, EXILES WANDERING OVER LANDS AND SEAS, ... 129 BOOK STORIES   9
AH, EXILES, WANDERING OVER MANY LANDS, ... 130 BOOK STORIES   V   17
THROUGH HOLLOW LANDS AND HILLY LANDS, ... 150 WANDER AENGUS   18
THROUGH HOLLOW LANDS AND HILLY LANDS, ... 150 WANDER AENGUS   18
THROUGH HILLY LANDS AND HOLLOW LANDS, ... 150 WANDER AENGUS   V   18
THROUGH HILLY LANDS AND HOLLOW LANDS, ... 150 WANDER AENGUS   V   18
IN DOVE-GREY FAERY LANDS! . . . . 162 ASKS FORGIVE   10
AND SOUGHT THROUGH LANDS AND ISLANDS NUMBERLESS YEARS, . 170 SECRET ROSE   23
NOR LANDS THAT SEEM TOO DIM TO BE BURDENS ON THE HEART! 209 UNDER THE MOON   5
OR LANDS THAT SEEMED TOO OLD TO BE BURDENS ON THE HEART, 209 UNDER THE MOON V   5
THAT SO MANY LANDS HAD KNOWN, ... 360 ALF POLLEXFEN   18
QUIET LANDS OR UNQUIET SEAS . . . . 360 ALF POLLEXFEN   19
ON THE GREEN LANDS I WALK . . . . 607 SONGS BURDEN 2   20
THE AUSTRIAN HAYNAU HE, IN MANY LANDS . . . . 709 FERENCZ RENYI   8
AND OVER TILLAGE FIELDS AND PASTURE LANDS, ... 715 FERENCZ RENYI   120
AND FOLLOWING O'ER THE FIELDS AND PASTURE LANDS, ... 715 FERENCZ RENYI   120
LANDSMAN
MANY A LANDSMAN, MANY A SEAMAN. . . . . 82 MAD KING GOLL   V   4
HE, THOUGH BUT A LANDSMAN, WENT TO THE MAST-HEAD! . . . 790 DEDICATION   4
LANDSMEN
MOVED ROUND ME, OF SEAMEN OR LANDSMEN, ALL WHO ARE WINTER 53 OISIN 3   86
    TALES!
LAND-UNDER-WAVE
LAND-UNDER-WAVE, WHERE OUT OF THE MOON'S LIGHT AND THE 209 UNDER THE MOON   6
    SUN'S
LANDWARD
DRIPPING AND DOUBLING LANDWARD, AS THOUGH THEY WOULD HASTEN 48 OISIN 3   15
    AWAY,
DRIPPING AND DOUBLING LANDWARD, AS THOUGH THEY WOULD HASTEN 57 OISIN 3   143
    AWAY,
LANE
BY ROCKY LANE AND FEN! . . . . 133 FR GILLIGAN   30
GATHERED A CROWD IN SOME BYZANTINE LANE, ... 180 QUEEN MAEVE   2
FOR THAT OLD MADGE COMES DOWN THE LANE, ... 456 FRIENDS YOUTH   5
IMPETUOUS MEN, SHAWE-TAYLOR AND HUGH LANE, ... 489 COOLE PARK 29   14
HUGH LANE, "ONLIE BEGETTER" OF ALL THESE! . . . . . 602 GALLERY REVIS   22
MAYBE NOW IN SOME FAR LANE, ... 731 STREET DANCERS   14
WAS CRIED IN STREET AND LANE . . . . 740 EARL PAUL   26
LANGUAGE
MY LANGUAGE BEATEN . . . . 572 LADYS 1ST SONG   5
LANGUID
OF LANGUID EVENING THAT ENTWINED US. . . . . 25 OISIN 1   V 385A
GOES DROPPING FROM HIS EYES A LANGUID LIGHT, ... 34 OISIN 1   V 81A
HIS LANGUID TAIL ABOVE US, LIT WITH MYRIAD SPOTS OF LIGHT. 77 INDIAN ON GOD   20
AND IN THE SIBYL'S EYES A LANGUID FLAME . . . . . . 688 TWO TITANS   41
STAGGERING WITH LANGUID EYE. . . . . 717 FAIRY DOCTOR   V   16
LANGUOR
NOR LANGUOR NOR FATIGUE! AN ENDLESS FEAST, ... 44 OISIN 2   223
NO LANGUOR, NO FATIGUE! AN ENDLESS FEAST, ... 44 OISIN 2   V   223
NOR LANGUOR NOR FATIGUE! AND ENDLESS FEAST, ... 44 OISIN 2   V   223
FROM DEATH'S LATE LANGUOR AS THESE LINES I READ . . . . 734 QUATRAIN APHOR   14
LANGUORS
AND LANGUORS THAT AWAKE IN MINGLING HANDS . . . . . . 765 SHADOW WATER A   367
LANTERN
MY LANTERN IS TOO LOYAL NOT TO SHOW . . . . 464 HARUN RASHID   71
LANTHORN
LEAPS AND TIME'S OLD LANTHORN DIMS. . . . . 777 SONG DEIRDRE 2   5
LAP
WHAT YOUTHFUL MOTHER, A SHAPE UPON HER LAP . . . . . 444 SCHOOL CHILDR   33
LAPIS
IN TOMBS OF GOLD AND LAPIS LAZULI . . . . 483 OIL AND BLOOD   1
LAPIS LAZULI . . . . 565 LAPIS LAZULI   T
ARE CARVED IN LAPIS LAZULI, ... 566 LAPIS LAZULI   38
LAPIS-LAZULI
IN TOMBS OF GOLD AND LAPIS-LAZULI . . . . 483 OIL AND BLOOD   V   1
LAPO
THE MAN THAT LAPO AND THAT GUIDO KNEW? . . . . . . 368 EGO DOMINUS   26

434

| | PAGE | TITLE | LINE |

LAPPED
"ALTHOUGH I'D LIE LAPPED UP IN LINEN . . . . 331 ROUND TOWER 1
LAPPED IN THE LEMON DAFFODILLS; A BEE . . . . 716 DWELT SYCAMORE 10
LAPPING
I HEAR LAKE WATER LAPPING WITH LOW SOUNDS BY THE SHORE; 117 ISLE INNISFREE 10
I HEAR LAKE WATER LAPPING WITH LOW SOUNDS ON THE SHORE; 117 ISLE INNISFREE V 10
WORN THIN BY THE LAPPING OF WATER, ... 330 BONE OF A HARE 11
OF SAD QUEEN DIDO SHONE THE LAPPING FIRE . . . . . 645 ISLE STAT I 1 9
LAPWING
THE LAPWING AT THEIR FOOLISH CRIES . . . . 306 HOUR DAWN 77
LAPWINGS
A PAIR OF LAPWINGS, ONE OLD SHEEP, ... 302 HOUR DAWN 9
LARCH-WOOD
A LARCH-WOOD HUNTING SPEAR. . . . . 32 OISIN 2 V 56
LARDER
FOR LARDER AND SPIT ARE BARE, ... 349 HAWK 4
LARGE
AND MY TEARS WERE LARGE LIKE TO BERRIES, AND I MURMURED, 59 OISIN 3 V 178
. . .
AND HE WORE LARGE HOLES IN HIS GOWN. . . . . 92 FATHER OHART 12
O BUT WE TALKED AT LARGE BEFORE . . . . 395 SIXTEEN DEAD 1
THAT WHEN THEY HAD GROWN LARGE . . . . 571 THREE BUSHES 60
AH! HOW LARGE MICE USED TO BE . . . . 727 LOVERS QUARREL 39
LARGELY
THE ISLE LOOMED LARGELY IN THE LIGHT . . . . 25 OISIN 1 V 385
LARGER
AND MY TEARS WERE LARGER THAN BERRIES, AND I MURMURED, 59 OISIN 3 178
. . .
LARGER SPARROWS OF THE TOWN, ... 731 STREET DANCERS 5
LARK
YON EAGER LARK, THAT FILLS WITH SONG THE WHOLE . . . 652 ISLE STAT I 2 18
LARKS
WAKE THE LARKS UPON THE GREEN. . . . . 727 LOVERS QUARREL 46
LASH
SHIVER UNDER THE LASH, STRAIN, SWEAT AND JOLT . . . 260 FASC DIFFICULT 7
WHAT MASTER MADE THE LASH. WHENCE HAD THEY COME, . . . 560 WHENCE COME 9
THE HAND AND LASH THAT BEAT DOWN FRIGID ROME? . . . 560 WHENCE COME 10
THE BEGGARS HAVE CHANGED PLACES; BUT THE LASH GOES ON. . 590 GREAT DAY 4
WHEN YOU ARE ABOARD THE LOCHLANN GALLEY, LASH . . . . 752 SHADOW WATER A 128
LASHED
ONE LASHED HER TAIL; HER EYES LIT BY THE MOON . . . . 383 VISION ROBART 29
LASHES
IF I MAKE THE LASHES DARK . . . . 531 BEFORE WORLD 1
THE FLAGELLANT LASHES THOSE SUBMISSIVE LOINS . . . . 560 WHENCE COME 7
A BEGGAR UPON HORSEBACK LASHES A BEGGAR ON FOOT. . . . 590 GREAT DAY 2
A BEGGAR UPON HORSEBACK LASHES A BEGGAR UPON FOOT; . . 590 GREAT DAY V 2
LASS
"AND THOUGH I'D MARRY WITH A COMELY LASS, ... 300 BEGGAR CRIED 9
COURT HIS SHEPHERD LASS, ... 343 SHEP GOATHERD 104
WHEN SHEBA WAS HIS LASS, ... 345 ON WOMAN 16
EVERY COLONUS LAD OR LASS DISCOURSES . . . . 447 COLONUS PRAISE 29
NIAMH THAT RODE ON IT; LAD AND LASS . . . . 550 SEVERED HEAD 11
THAT PARNELL LOVED A LASS. . . . . 586 PARNELLITES 16
AND PARNELL LOVED HIS LASS. . . . . 587 PARNELLITES 32
AND PARNELL LOVED A LASS. . . . . 587 PARNELLITES V 32
LASSES
LADS AND LASSES, TWO AND TWO, ... 705 DAWN-SONG 15
LAST
FOR HIS LAST DAYS TO LIE IN WAIT. . . . . 24 OISIN 1 363
MUST MURMUR AT LAST, "UNJUST, UNJUST"! . . . . . 28 OISIN 1 420
AT LAST THE MOON AND STARS SHONE, AND A FLIGHT . . . 31 OISIN 2 V 34
AND CLIMBED SO LONG, I THOUGHT THE LAST STEPS WERE . . 32 OISIN 2 48
AND WHERE OUR FOOTFALL 'LIGHTED LAST THERE CAME . . . 37 OISIN 2 V 119
"LAST OF MY RACE, THREE THINGS I RULE ALONE-- . . . 45 OISIN 2 V 239A
SONG OF THE LAST ARCADIAN . . . . 64 HAPPY SHEPHERD V T
AND NOW AT LAST YOU WEAR A HUMAN SHAPE, ... 102 FERGUS DRUID 6
AND NOW AT LAST YOU TAKE ON HUMAN SHAPE-- . . . . 102 FERGUS DRUID V 6
AT LAST CUCHULAIN SPAKE, "SOME MAN HAS MADE . . . . 109 CUCHULAIN SEA 47
AT LAST CUCHULAIN SPAKE, "A YOUNG MAN STRAYS . . . 109 CUCHULAIN SEA V 47
WOULD COME AT LAST TO GOD'S GREAT TOWN, ... 113 ROSE OF PEACE 11
AND WHEN AT LAST, DEFEATED IN HIS WARS, ... 115 ROSE OF BATTLE 33
AND HE HAD KNOWN AT LAST SOME TENDERNESS, ... 126 DREAM OF FAERY 3
AND HE HAD KNOWN AT LAST SOME PRUDENT YEARS . . . . 127 DREAM OF FAERY 15
AND MIGHT HAVE KNOWN AT LAST UNHAUNTED SLEEP . . . 128 DREAM OF FAERY 38
WHERE THE LAST PHOENIX DIED, ... 162 ASKS FORGIVE 16
WE SAW THE LAST EMBERS OF DAYLIGHT DIE . . . . . 205 ADAMS CURSE 29
IN THE LAST RIDGE OF THE BARLEY? DO OUR WOODS . . 218 WOODS OF COOLE 33
TO GRADUAL TIME'S LAST GIFT, A WRITTEN SPEECH . . . 264 HOUSE SHAKEN 11
UNTIL AT LAST THE DOUBLE HORNS, DRAWN BACKWARD, . . 278 TWO KINGS 21
BUT WHEN AT LAST HE FORCED THOSE SINEWY FLANKS . . 278 TWO KINGS 35
UNTIL AT LAST THE UNLOCKED HORN HAD TORN . . . . 278 TWO KINGS V 21
AND THEN AT LAST BEING WIDE AWAKE . . . . . . 304 HOUR DAWN V 40
FOR ALL LIFE LONGS FOR THE LAST DAY . . . . . 306 HOUR DAWN 98
LIKE SOME LAST COURTIER AT A GYPSY CAMPING-PLACE . . 314 FALLEN MAJESTY 3
LIKE SOME LAST COURTIER AT A GYPSY CAMPING PLACE . . 314 FALLEN MAJESTY V 3
WHEN HAVE I LAST LOOKED ON . . . . 343 DEJECTION 1
LAST EVENING? THAT I, WHO HAD SAT . . . . . . 349 HAWK 15
THE LAST STROKE OF MIDNIGHT DIES. . . . . . . 357 BROKEN DREAMS 37
THEY RAN FROM CRADLE TO CRADLE TILL AT LAST . . . 375 PHASES OF MOON 69
THAT THE LAST SERVILE CRESCENT HAS SET FREE? . . . 376 PHASES OF MOON 103
HUNCHBACK AND SAINT AND FOOL ARE THE LAST CRESCENTS. . 377 PHASES OF MOON 118

435

```
                                                            PAGE    TITLE            LINE
LAST   (CONTINUED)
    UNDER THE THREE LAST CRESCENTS OF THE MOON,   . . . . .   377  PHASES OF MOON    133
    I KNEW THAT I HAD SEEN, HAD SEEN AT LAST . . . . . . .    384  VISION ROBART      49
    "LAST NIGHT, WHERE UNDER THE WILD MOON . . . . . . . .    387  SOLOMON WITCH       2
    CHANCE BEING AT ONE WITH CHOICE AT LAST, . . . . . . .    388  SOLOMON WITCH      14
    AND THIS FOUL WORLD WERE DEAD AT LAST. . . . . . . . .    388  SOLOMON WITCH      16
    AND WHEN AT LAST THAT MURDER'S OVER . . . . . . . . .     388  SOLOMON WITCH      24
    THEREFORE A BLESSED MOON LAST NIGHT . . . . . . . . .     388  SOLOMON WITCH      31
    AND WHEN AT LAST, . . . . . . . . . . . . . . . . .      389  IMAGE PAST         10
    WHEN SLEEP AT LAST HAS COME . . . . . . . . . . . . .     394  EASTER 1916        63
    AND WHAT ROUGH BEAST, ITS HOUR COME ROUND AT LAST, . .    402  SECOND COMING      21
    AND LEARNS AT LAST THAT IT IS SELF-DELIGHTING, . . . .    405  FOR DAUGHTER       67
    LAST REACH OF GLITTERING STREAM . . . . . . . . . . .     414  TOWER             143
    AND THERE SING HIS LAST SONG. . . . . . . . . . . . .     414  TOWER             144
    LAST NIGHT THEY TRUNDLED DOWN THE ROAD . . . . . . . .    425  STARES NEST        13
    AND I MERE SHADE AT LAST . . . . . . . . . . . . . .     449  HERO GIRL FOOL     25
    OCTOBER LAST I FOUND IT TOO . . . . . . . . . . . . .     454  EMPTY CUP           7
    AND PAUSE AT LAST, I WAS ABOUT TO SAY, . . . . . . . .    461  HARUN RASHID       11
    AND SINK INTO ITS OWN DELIGHT AT LAST. . . . . . . . .    473  ALL SOUL NIGHT     60
    CASTS UPON HIS EYES UNTIL AT LAST . . . . . . . . . .     479  SELF AND SOUL      53
    CONTENT OR JOY, A LAST INHERITOR . . . . . . . . . .      491  COOLE BALLYLEE     30
    WE WERE THE LAST ROMANTICS--CHOSE FOR THEME . . . . .     491  COOLE BALLYLEE     41
    WHEN THE LAST THREAD HAS RUN, . . . . . . . . . . . .     520  HIS BARGAIN        10
    A LAST CONFESSION . . . . . . . . . . . . . . . . .      538  LAST CONFESS        T
    DISCOVER IMPURITIES, CAN SHOW AT LAST . . . . . . . .     558  RIBH CHRISTIAN     10
    YET THEY, SHOULD THE LAST SCENE BE THERE, . . . . . .     565  LAPIS LAZULI       12
    AND WERE THE LAST TO CHOOSE THE SETTLED GROUND, . . .     621  HOUND VOICE         2
    LAST NIGHT I LAY ON THE MOUNTAIN, . . . . . . . . . .     628  JANE MOUNTAIN      11
    MAYBE AT LAST, BEING BUT A BROKEN MAN, . . . . . . . .    629  CIRCUS ANIMALS      3
    AND SINKS AT LAST INTO THE NIGHT. . . . . . . . . . .     633  MAN AND ECHO       36
    SO! MID THE WILLOW-GLADE YOU PAUSE AT LAST. . . . . .     651  ISLE STAT I 2       2
    TILL HIS LAST WRETCHEDNESS WAS O'ER AND DONE." . . . .    664  ISLE STAT II 2     54
    SINKS DOWN AT LAST WITH YONDER MINARET, . . . . . . .     691  MOSADA 1        V  36
    AT LAST.  BUT NOW I WAVE HER TO MY SIDE. . . . . . . .    694  MOSADA 1        V  91
    WILL YOU NOT HEAR MY LAST NEW SONG?  HUSH, HUSH! . . .    695  MOSADA 2            1
    A WEAK, THIN CHILD, WHEN LAST I SAW HIM THERE. . . . .    699  MOSADA 3           14
    A WEIGHTY QUESTION, FOR IT IS THE LAST. . . . . . . .     700  MOSADA 3           37
    WE MEET AT LAST, THE MINISTERING STARS . . . . . . .     701  MOSADA 3           52
    HIS BONDS AWAY, SORE STRUGGLING.  NOW AT LAST . . . .     714  FERENCZ RENYI     116
    YOUNG FERENCZ RENYI BURSTS HIS BONDS--AT LAST, . . . .    714  FERENCZ RENYI   V 116
    WHY DO YOU LAUGH?  I LAUGH THE LAST ALWAYS. . . . . .     721  WITCH VIVIEN       25
    AND THEN THE GREAT ONES COME, AND LAST THE KING. . . .    722  WITCH VIVIEN       54
    O STILL THAT HEART AT LAST. . . . . . . . . . . . .      785  YOUR HEART          8
    ALTHOUGH YOUR LAST EXCITING YEAR . . . . . . . . . .      791  REPRISALS           5
LASTING
    AND KISS MORE LIPS THAN LASTING PEACEABLE MEN . . . .     225  SHADOW WATER B     71
    AND BLEW ME HITHER TO MY LASTING SORROW, . . . . . .      235  SHADOW WATER B    288
    FROM LASTING WATCHERS, THAT OUTLIVE THE MOON, . . . .     236  SHADOW WATER B    320
    WHY MUST THE LASTING LOVE WHAT PASSES, . . . . . . .      275  GREY ROCK         114
    HE THAT SINGS A LASTING SONG . . . . . . . . . . . .     553  PRAYER OLD AGE      3
LATCH
    HE ROSE THE LATCH AND WENT UPSTAIRS . . . . . . . . .     594  COLONEL MARTIN      7
LATCHES
    AND PUSHED THE LATCHES DOWN. . . . . . . . . . . . .     159  CAP AND BELLS      12
LATE
    THEN SHE SIGHED GENTLY, "IT GROWS LATE. . . . . . . .       9  OISIN 1           102
    THEN SIGHED SHE SOFTLY, "LATE! 'TIS LATE! . . . . . .       9  OISIN 1           102
    THEN SIGHED SHE SOFTLY, "LATE! 'TIS LATE! . . . . . .       9  OISIN 1         V 102
    WITH MISERY, OR THAT SHE WOULD OF LATE . . . . . . .     256  NO SECOND TROY      2
    AND HAVING TALKED TO SOME LATE HOUR . . . . . . . . .     324  ROBERT GREGORY      4
    OF THAT LATE DEATH TOOK ALL MY HEART FOR SPEECH. . . .    328  ROBERT GREGORY     96
    DESPITE A DWINDLING AND LATE RISEN MOON, . . . . . .     372  PHASES OF MOON  V   6
    SAT LATE, OR SHELLEY'S VISIONARY PRINCE, . . . . . .     373  PHASES OF MOON     16
    PROSPER BUT LITTLE, HAS DRIED UP OF LATE, . . . . . .     405  FOR DAUGHTER       51
    AND TOILED SO HARD AND LATE . . . . . . . . . . . .      432  NINETEEN 19        95
    ALTHOUGH OF LATE ESTRANGED. . . . . . . . . . . . .      473  ALL SOUL NIGHT     63
    NO OTHER BIRD MAY ENTER IN.  WELL?  LATE-- . . . . .     659  ISLE STAT II 1     24
    TOO LATE, TOO LATE, FOR I AM NEAR TO DEATH. . . . . .     701  MOSADA 3           55
    TOO LATE, TOO LATE, FOR I AM NEAR TO DEATH. . . . . .     701  MOSADA 3           55
    'TIS LATE, WAIT ONE MORE DAY! BELOW THE HILLS . . . .     702  MOSADA 3           91
    "WE BURIED LATE IN A HAZEL DELL . . . . . . . . . . .     729  PRIEST FAIRY       43
    FROM DEATH'S LATE LANGUOR AS THESE LINES I READ . . .     734  QUATRAIN APHOR     14
LATE-LOST
    AND THUS, MY LATE-LOST NIAM, DIDST THOU SAY! . . . . .     34  OISIN 2         V  78
LATELY
    WHERE IS THE OWL THAT LATELY FLEW . . . . . . . . . .     646  ISLE STAT I 1      32
    AYE, VERY LATELY, SORROW CAME TO WEEP . . . . . . . .     659  ISLE STAT II 1     25
LATER
    LATER A SOUND CAME, HALF LOST IN THE SOUND OF A SHORE FAR
        AWAY. . . . . . . . . . . . . . . . . . . . . .      57  OISIN 3           155
    . . . AND LATER THE SHORE-WEEDS BROWN. . . . . . . . .     57  OISIN 3           156
    TWO YEARS LATER . . . . . . . . . . . . . . . . . .      312  TWO YEAR LATER      T
    AND LATER HAD MUCH TROUBLE FROM A FOOL, . . . . . . .     404  FOR DAUGHTER       26
    FORTY YEARS LATER . . . . . . . . . . . . . . . . .      542  PARN FUNERAL 2  V   T
    BUT LATER MIGHT HAVE BEEN . . . . . . . . . . . . .      608  SONGS BURDEN 3     15
    THAT WILL BE LATER, DAY IS SCARCELY DAWNING. . . . . .    699  MOSADA 3           12
    THAT WILL BE LATER, DAY IS DAWNING. . . . . . . . . .     699  MOSADA 3        V  12
LATE-RISEN
    DESPITE A DWINDLING AND LATE-RISEN MOON, . . . . . .     372  PHASES OF MOON      6
LATEST
    TO MICHELOZZO'S LATEST PLAN . . . . . . . . . . . . .     288  TO WEALTHY MAN     23
```

	PAGE	TITLE	LINE
LATEST (CONTINUED)			
WHO HAD MURMURED OF GIORGIONE AT HIS LATEST BREATH--	366	HER COURAGE	8
LATIN			
TILL ALL HIS GREEK AND LATIN LEARNING SEEMED	324	ROBERT GREGORY	21
IT FOLLOWS FROM THIS LATIN TEXT	386	ROBARTES DANCE	43
LATTICE			
TENDING THE ROSES ROUND HIS LATTICE DOOR.	692	MOSADA 1	53
LATTICED			
A LATTICED WINDOW. HIS GLANCE WENT UP AT TIMES	180	QUEEN MAEVE	6
LAUGH			
AMONG THEMSELVES LAUGH ON AND SING ALWAY!	68	SAD SHEPHERD	7
ONE WITH THE WAVES THAT SOFTLY ROUND US LAUGH AND DART.	78	INDIAN TO LOVE V	15
OF MY LONG SPEAR, WITH SCREAM AND LAUGH,	84	MAD KING GOLL V	34
OF MY LONG SPEAR WITH SONG AND LAUGH	84	MAD KING GOLL V	34
THE DANAAN CHILDREN LAUGH, IN CRADLES OF WROUGHT GOLD,	146	UNAPPEAS HOST	1
THE FAERY CHILDREN LAUGH IN CRADLES OF WROUGHT GOLD,	146	UNAPPEAS HOST V	1
LAUGH, HEART, AGAIN IN THE GREY TWILIGHT,	147	INTO TWILIGHT	3
AND LAUGH OUT THEIR WHIMSEY AND WORK OUT THEIR WILL.	148	INTO TWILIGHT	12
LAUGH OUT THEIR WHIMSEY AND WORK OUT THEIR WILL.	148	INTO TWILIGHT V	12
WE ARE ALONE FOR EVER, AND I LAUGH,	251	SHADOW WATER B	602
SO WITH A LAUGH AT HIS OWN FEAR	303	HOUR DAWN	31
AND THREW HIM UP TO LAUGH ON THE BOUGH;	318	APPOINTMENT	11
AND LAUGH OVER THE UNTROUBLED WATER	330	BONE OF A HARE	14
AND ALL LAUGH IN THE SUN.	400	DEMON BEAST	8
AND THEN I LAUGH TILL TEARS RUN DOWN	456	FRIENDS YOUTH	17
THE THREE OLD RASCALS LAUGH ALOUD.	460	THREE MONUMENT	12
SHOULD LAUGH AND WEEP AN HOUR UPON THE CLOCK.	471	ALL SOUL NIGHT	20
SHOULD LAUGH AND WEEP AN HOUR UPON THE CLOCK.	474	ALL SOUL NIGHT	90
SHOULD WEEP AND LAUGH AN HOUR UPON THE CLOCK.	474	ALL SOUL NIGHT V	90
WE MUST LAUGH AND WE MUST SING,	479	SELF AND SOUL	70
WE THAT LOOK ON BUT LAUGH IN TRAGIC JOY.	564	GYRES	8
THAT CAN MAKE A CAT LAUGH, OR	589	OLD WICKED MAN	39
THE ECSTATIC WATERS LAUGH BECAUSE	612	NEWS ORACLE	17
THOSE GREAT SEA-HORSES BARE THEIR TEETH AND LAUGH AT THE DAWN.	623	HIGH TALK	14
TILL I LAUGH WHEN OTHERS WEEP,	647	ISLE STAT I 1	61
WEEPING WHEN ALL OTHERS LAUGH.	647	ISLE STAT I 1	62
IT IS THE VOICE OF ALL OUR HEARTS THAT LAUGH.	681	SEEKER	7
A TOSSING LAUGH BETWEEN THEIR REDNESS 'BIDES--	685	DRAWING-ROOM	2
AND LAUGH OUR LOVE AWAY.	686	LIFE	16
AND LOSS OF YOUR LAUGH AND ITS LIGHTNESS--	708	FAIRY PEDANT	33
HE RUSHES, ROLLING FROM HIS LIPS A MADMAN'S LAUGH.	715	FERENCZ RENYI	122
WHY DO YOU LAUGH? I LAUGH THE LAST ALWAYS.	721	WITCH VIVIEN	25
WHY DO YOU LAUGH? I LAUGH THE LAST ALWAYS.	721	WITCH VIVIEN	25
A TOSSING LAUGH BETWEEN THEIR RED ABIDES;	735	QUATRAIN APHOR	22
A TOSSING LAUGH BETWEEN THEIR REDNESS 'BIDES--	735	QUATRAIN APHOR V	22
THE HANDMAIDS LAUGH AND WHISPER IN THE DOOR.	759	SHADOW WATER A	242
AND I SHALL LAUGH WITH JOY. COME HITHER, AIBRIC,	760	SHADOW WATER A	249
LOVERS, IF THEY MAY NOT LAUGH,	772	SONG DEIRDRE 1	15
LAUGH'D			
AND LAUGH'D, SO, SO ALONG THE BUBBLING RILLS	645	ISLE STAT I 1	18
LAUGHED			
AND LAUGHED LIKE MURMURS OF THE SEA;	15	OISIN 1	210
I LAUGHED AT TIMES UNNUMBERED TREASONS,	23	OISIN 1 V	345D
I LAUGHED ALOUD AND HURRIED ON.	83	MAD KING GOLL	31
I LAUGHED BECAUSE BIRDS FLUTTERED BY,	84	MAD KING GOLL	33
WHERE I HAVE LAUGHED AND SPUN AND PLAYED?	151	HEART OF WOMAN V	2
HE RAN AND LAUGHED UNTIL HE CAME	194	BAILE AILLINN	128
BUT GUAIRE LAUGHED WITH SECRET THOUGHT,	295	THREE BEGGARS	19
WHO HAVE LIVED IN JOY AND LAUGHED INTO THE FACE OF DEATH.	366	HER COURAGE	10
WHO LIVED IN SHAMELESS JOY AND LAUGHED INTO THE FACE OF DEATH.	366	HER COURAGE V	10
THAT LIVED IN JOY AND LAUGHED INTO THE FACE OF DEATH.	366	HER COURAGE V	10
WHO HAVE LIVED IN JOY AND LAUGHED IN THE FACE OF DEATH.	366	HER COURAGE V	10
AHERNE LAUGHED, THINKING OF THE MAN WITHIN,	375	PHASES OF MOON	85
AND THEN HE LAUGHED TO THINK THAT WHAT SEEMED HARD	377	PHASES OF MOON	136
THE HEART BEHIND ITS RIB LAUGHED OUT.	450	OWEN AHERNE	13
LAUGHED; AND PLUNGING DOWN	453	MERMAID	4
FLINGING FROM HIS ARMS I LAUGHED	538	LAST CONFESS	7
AND LAUGHED UPON HIS BREAST TO THINK	538	LAST CONFESS	11
HER BARGAIN STRUCK WE LAUGHED AND TALKED	620	JOHN KINSELLA	15
'TIS HERE THE ARROW.FELL! THE BREEZES LAUGHED	657	ISLE STAT I 3	70
OF GRIEF. AND IF THEY SAY, "ANTONIO LAUGHED,"	664	ISLE STAT II 2	51
I LAUGHED? AND WHY IS THAT A THING SO DEAR?	670	ISLE STAT II 3	97
"I LAUGHED UPON THE LIPS OF SOPHOCLES,	686	LIFE	17
IN CREVICED ROCKS, AND LAUGHED TO THE OLD SEA,	688	TWO TITANS	34
"I LAUGHED UPON THE LIPS OF SOPHOCLES,	735	QUATRAIN APHOR	19
THEY DREAM THAT LAUGHED IN THE SUN.	783	GREY ROUND	13
THEY DREAMED THAT LAUGHED IN THE SUN.	783	GREY ROUND V	13
DANCED, LAUGHED, LOVED, FOUGHT THROUGH	787	HUDDON DUDDON	4
LAUGHING SEE LOW-LAUGHING EVER-LAUGHING			
TO THAT LOW LAUGHING WOODLAND RHYME.	14	OISIN 1	176
AND TOUCH THE LAUGHING SILVER STRING;	17	OISIN 1	233
CEASE, CEASE, O MOURNFUL, LAUGHING FENIAN HORN!	43	OISIN 2	213
AH, CEASE, THOU MOURNFUL, LAUGHING FENIAN HORN!	43	OISIN 2 V 213	
AH, CEASE, YOU MOURNFUL, LAUGHING FENIAN HORN!	43	OISIN 2 V 213	
GOD'S LAUGHING IN HEAVEN.	118	CRADLE SONG	5
IT HAD BECOME A LAUGHING GIRL.	149	WANDER AENGUS V	13
SUDDEN AND LAUGHING. O UNQUIET HEART,	181	QUEEN MAEVE	30
AND WITH LOW MURMURING LAUGHING SPEECH	195	BAILE AILLINN	137
WANDERS LAUGHING AND EATING HER WILD HEART	198	SEVEN WOODS	11

437

LAUGHING   (CONTINUED)
  THE SUN WAS LAUGHING SWEETLY, ... 214 HAPPY TOWNLAND   15
  THE SUN WAS LAUGHING SWEETLY, ... 215 HAPPY TOWNLAND   35
  THE SUN WAS LAUGHING SWEETLY, ... 216 HAPPY TOWNLAND   55
  ONE OF THE LAUGHING PEOPLE--AND SHE AND I . . . . 231 SHADOW WATER B   211
  FOR I HAVE HEARD THAT HE WAS PROUD AND LAUGHING, . . . 242 SHADOW WATER B   415
  I KNEW HIM WELL, AND WHILE I HEARD HIM LAUGHING . . . . 242 SHADOW WATER B   419
  AND WHILE WE'RE IN OUR LAUGHING, WEEPING FIT, ... 257 RECONCILIATION   9
  AND THE SWEET LAUGHING EAGLE THOUGHTS THAT GROW . . . 264 HOUSE SHAKEN   5
  STARED AT THE GODS WITH LAUGHING LIP. . . . . 276 GREY ROCK   123
  AND LIKE A LAUGHING STRING . . . . 291 TO A FRIEND   11
  THE YOUNG MEN EVERY NIGHT APPLAUD THEIR GABY'S LAUGHING 353 HIS PHOENIX   9
    EYE,
  THAT WOMEN LAUGHING, OR TIMID OR WILD, ... 358 PRESENCES   4
  WHAT IF A LAUGHING EYE . . . . 367 HER CHRIS TREE   10
  I GET A LAUGHING FIT. . . . . 455 FRIENDS YOUTH   4
  IN THE LONG ECHOING STREET THE LAUGHING DANCERS THRONG, 459 FROM OEDIPUS   7
  IN THE LONG ECHOING STREETS THE LAUGHING DANCERS THRONG, 459 FROM OEDIPUS V 7
  PROUD, OPEN-EYED AND LAUGHING TO THE TOMB. . . . . . . 501 VACILLATION   34
  "A LAUGHING, CRYING, SACRED SONG, ... 570 THREE BUSHES   43
  THOU'LT TEACH ME LAUGHING, AND I'LL TEACH THEE PEACE, . 670 ISLE STAT II 3 101
  LAUGHING GOES IN WILDEST MOOD, ... 732 STREET DANCERS   41
  I AM AFRAID OF HIS LOW LAUGHING HARP. . . . . 759 SHADOW WATER A V 239
  IS LAUGHING THROUGH A MORTAL'S EYES. O LOOK! . . . . 763 SHADOW WATER A   324
  WHERE SOME LAUGHING ELEMENT . . . . 777 SONG DEIRDRE 2   4
LAUGHS
  LAUGHS ALOUD, HIS HEART AT PEACE. . . . . 638 BEN BULBEN   32
  LAUGHS NOT. IT DWELLS ALONE ON MORTAL LIPS! . . . . . 670 ISLE STAT II 3 100
LAUGHTER
  WITH LAUGHTER LOW, AND TENDER, AND SWEET! . . . . . . 6 OISIN 1   V 54
  SHE SAID, WITH LAUGHTER TENDER AND SWEET! . . . . . . 6 OISIN 1   V 54
  OF PENSIVE LAUGHTER, UNHUMAN SOUND, ... 11 OISIN 1   136
  AND ONCE A SUDDEN LAUGHTER SPRANG . . . . 16 OISIN 1   225
  LAUGHTER AND CRIES. THE ARMIES CLASH AND SHOCK, . . . 43 OISIN 2   211
  OF ARMOUR--LAUGHTER AND CRIES--THE ARMIES' SHOCK. . . 43 OISIN 2   V 211
  . . . WITH ROARING OF LAUGHTER AND SONGS, ... 53 OISIN 3   87
  WENT THE LAUGHTER OF SCORN FROM MY MOUTH . . . . . . 58 OISIN 3   168
  WITHOUT LAUGHTER, A SHOW UNTO CHILDREN, ... 63 OISIN 3   218
  WITHOUT LAUGHTER, A COUGHING, ALONE WITH REMEMBRANCE AND 63 OISIN 3   V 218
    FEAR!
  THE HOUR WHEN KAMA, FULL OF SLEEPY LAUGHTER, ... 72 ANASHU VIJAYA   26
  A LONELY LAUGHTER, AND MAY KISS HIS HANDS TO ME IN SLEEP. 75 ANASHU VIJAYA   82
  AN INNER LAUGHTER, AND MAY KISS HIS HANDS TO ME IN SLEEP. 75 ANASHU VIJAYA V 82
  A LONELY LAUGHTER, THAT HE MAY KISS HANDS TO ME IN SLEEP. 75 ANASHU VIJAYA V 82
  OR FLING MY LAUGHTER TO THE SUN . . . . 86 MAD KING GOLL V 69
  AND FLING MY LAUGHTER TO THE SUN . . . . 86 MAD KING GOLL V 69
  OR COMES IN LAUGHTER FROM THE SEA'S SAD LIPS, ... 114 ROSE OF BATTLE   19
  THAT HE'S A LOVELESS MAN! GAY BELLS BRING LAUGHTER . . 130 BOOK STORIES   18
  MY BELL BRANCH MURMURS! THE GAY BELLS BRING LAUGHTER, 130 BOOK STORIES V 18
  UNTIL HE FOUND, WITH LAUGHTER AND WITH TEARS, ... 170 SECRET ROSE   24
  A CHILD'S LAUGHTER, A WOMAN'S KISS. . . . . 190 BAILE AILLINN   40
  AND FIND THEIR LAUGHTER SWEETER TO THE TASTE . . . . . 228 SHADOW WATER B   134
  TO MAKE LOW LAUGHTER MORE THAN MEAT AND DRINK, . . . 230 SHADOW WATER B   186
  BUT LAUGHTER AND TEARS--LAUGHTER, LAUGHTER, AND TEARS! 235 SHADOW WATER B   298
  BUT LAUGHTER AND TEARS--LAUGHTER, LAUGHTER, AND TEARS! 235 SHADOW WATER B   298
  BUT LAUGHTER AND TEARS--LAUGHTER, LAUGHTER, AND TEARS! 235 SHADOW WATER B   298
  WROUGHT OF HIGH LAUGHTER, LOVELINESS AND EASE? . . . 264 HOUSE SHAKEN   12
  THE LINEAMENTS, A HEART THAT LAUGHTER HAS MADE SWEET, 315 FALLEN MAJESTY   5
  THE LINEAMENTS, THE HEART THAT LAUGHTER HAS MADE SWEET, 315 FALLEN MAJESTY V 5
  THAT IS LIKE LAUGHTER, SPRANG AGAIN . . . . 318 APPOINTMENT   6
  AND WHEN SHE MEETS OUR GAZE HER EYES ARE LAUGHTER LIT 362 HER COURTESY V 5
  LAUGHTER NOT TIME DESTROYED MY VOICE . . . . 455 FRIENDS YOUTH   1
  PORTER-DRINKERS' RANDY LAUGHTER! . . . . 640 BEN BULBEN   77
  AND OUR LAUGHTER OVER AND DONE! . . . . 643 SONG FAERIES   6
  MOCKING WITH PATIENT LAUGHTER ALL THE NIGHT . . . . . 657 ISLE STAT I 3 52
  FOR PEACE AND LAUGHTER HAVE BEEN SELDOM FRIENDS. . . 670 ISLE STAT II 3 103
  AGAIN THE WOODLAND LAUGHTER, AND THE CLEAR . . . . . 674 ISLE STAT II 3 221
  AND OUR LAUGHTER OVER AND DONE! . . . . 676 ISLE STAT II 3 253
  A TITAN, WITH LOUD LAUGHTER, ... 680 LOVE AND DEATH   11
  FROM ITS FIRST SIGHS AND LAUGHTER, BEFORE THE SLEEP, . 754 SHADOW WATER A   161
  ON TEARS AND LAUGHTER. THEY HAVE LURED YOU HITHER . . 757 SHADOW WATER A   207
LAUGHTER-LIPPED
  LAUGHTER-LIPPED, BUT FOR HER BRAIN . . . . 668 ISLE STAT II 3 58
LAUGHTER-LIT
  AND WHEN SHE MEETS OUR GAZE HER EYES ARE LAUGHTER-LIT, 362 HER COURTESY   5
LAUNCH
  BUT, THE BIRD IN MY FINGERS, I MOUNTED, MINDFUL ONLY TO 54 OISIN 3   V 111
    LAUNCH
LAUREATE
  A MODEL FOR THE LAUREATE . . . . 597 MODEL LAUREATE   T
LAUREL
  AMONG THE LEAVES OF THE LAUREL WALL, ... 3 OISIN 1   V 7FF
  LIKE DRIFTS OF LAUREL LEAVES, IMMOVABLE AND BRIGHT . . 40 OISIN 2   V 166
  O MAY SHE LIVE LIKE SOME GREEN LAUREL . . . . 405 FOR DAUGHTER   47
  AND CUSTOM FOR THE SPREADING LAUREL TREE. . . . . . . 406 FOR DAUGHTER   80
  PROFFERING ITS SACRED LAUREL CROWNS, ... 612 NEWS ORACLE   23
LAURELLED
  A MOMENT'S MEMORY TO THAT LAURELLED HEAD. . . . . . . 489 COOLE PARK 29   32
LAVELL
  O'SULLIVAN RUA TO MARY LAVELL . . . . 155 FORGOT BEAUTY V T
  O'SULLIVAN THE RED TO MARY LAVELL. . . . . 157 POET BELOVED V T

		PAGE	TITLE	LINE

LAVELL   (CONTINUED)
    TWO POEMS BY O'SULLIVAN THE RED CONCERNING MARY LAVELL.   157 POET BELOVED   V   T
LAVERY
    HAZEL LAVERY LIVING AND DYING, THAT TALE . . . . . .   602 GALLERY REVIS   23
LAVISH
    BETWEEN THE LAVISH SHELTER OF A WOOD . . . .   108 CUCHULAIN SEA   V   38A
LAW
    BUT HERE THERE IS NOR LAW NOR RULE, ...   19 OISIN 1   282
    BUT, WARRIOR, HERE THERE IS NO LAW; . . . .   19 OISIN 1   V   283
    WITH HEARTS THAT KNOW NOR LAW NOR RULE, ...   22 OISIN 1   339
    OUR LIVES HAVE KNOWN NO LAW NOR RULE; . . . .   22 OISIN 1   V   340
    MY WORD WAS LAW FROM ITH TO EMAIN, ...   81 MAD KING GOLL   2
    IN LOGIC AND IN NATURAL LAW . . . .   288 TO WEALTHY MAN   27
    NOR LAW, NOR DUTY BADE ME FIGHT, ...   328 IRISH AIRMAN   9
    WHERE THOSE THAT HAVE OBEYED THE HOLY LAW . . . . . .   356 BROKEN DREAMS   33
    A LAW INDIFFERENT TO BLAME OR PRAISE, ...   428 NINETEEN 19   10
    OR THOSE WHO NEED HIS BOUNTY OR HIS LAW, ...   462 HARUN RASHID   V   25A
    THE FLAMING CIRCLE OF THE OUTER LAW, ...   689 NETTLESHIP   13
    NOR LAW NOR PARLIAMENT TAKE HEED. . . . .   791 REPRISALS   22
LAWN
    AND STILL I DREAM HE TREADS THE LAWN, ...   67 HAPPY SHEPHERD   51
    THE PEAHENS DANCE ON A SMOOTH LAWN, ...   77 INDIAN TO LOVE   3
    BROWN LOLLARD TREADS UPON THE LAWN, ...   98 FOXHUNTER   17
    HIS LOLLARD LEAD THEY ROUND THE LAWN, ...   98 FOXHUNTER   V   17
    BROWN DERMOT TREADS UPON THE LAWN, ...   98 FOXHUNTER   V   17
    AND ALIGHT AT THE COMELY TREES AND THE LAWN, ...   330 BONE OF A HARE   4
    AFAR FROM OUR LAWN AND OUR LEVEE, ...   706 FAIRY PEDANT   1
LAWNS
    WE PASSED BY WOODS, AND LAWNS OF CLOVER, ...   25 OISIN 1   377
    BY WOODS OF MOSS, BY LAWNS OF CLOVER, ...   25 OISIN 1   V   377F
    BY LAKES AND MEADOW LANDS AND LAWNS AFAR, ...   32 OISIN 2   V   50F
    ON THE ISLAND LAWNS, THEIR FEET WHERE THE PALE FOAM GLEAMS.   203 WITHER BOUGHS   14
    SURELY AMONG A RICH MAN'S FLOWERING LAWNS, ...   417 ANCEST HOUSES   1
    O WHAT IF LEVELLED LAWNS AND GRAVELLED WAYS . . . .   418 ANCEST HOUSES   29
LAWS
    SOME GOD OR KING HAD MADE THE LAWS . . . .   194 BAILE AILLINN   131
    YOU KEPT THE MUSES' STERNER LAWS, ...   273 GREY ROCK   59
    IT HAD SET DOWN AMONG ITS LAWS! . . . .   399 BREAK OF DAY   16
LAY
    AND THE WHITE BODY THAT LAY BY MINE: . . . .   3 OISIN 1   10
    LAY 'NEATH US: OF ITS HOLLOW COOL . . . .   17 OISIN 1   V   241
    I LAY, AS OVER SEA THE LIGHT HOOVES GLANCED . . . .   30 OISIN 2   V   19A
    TYING THE HORSE TO HIS VAST FOOT THAT LAY . . . . .   32 OISIN 2   46
    MOST DISTANT STRODE WE. ON THE FLOOR LAY SLIME, . .   37 OISIN 2   V   113
    WE LAY ON SKINS OF OTTERS, AND DRANK WINE, ...   41 OISIN 2   188
    BREWED BY THE SEA-GODS, FROM HUGE CUPS THAT LAY . .   41 OISIN 2   189
    BREWED BY THE SEA-GODS, FROM HUGE CUPS THAT LAY . .   41 OISIN 2   V   189
    BREWED BY THE SEA GODS, FROM HUGE CUPS THAT LAY . . .   41 OISIN 2   V   189
    AN ISLE LAY LEVEL BEFORE US, WITH DRIPPING HAZEL AND OAK?   47 OISIN 3   10
    AN ISLE LAY LEVEL BEFORE US, DRIPPING WITH HAZEL AND OAK?   47 OISIN 3   V   10
    A VALLEY FLOWED DOWN FROM HIS HOOFS, AND THERE IN THE LONG   48 OISIN 3   26
        GRASS LAY,
    . . . HEAPED LOOSE WHERE THEY LAY. . . . .   48 OISIN 3   V   28
    LAY LOOSE IN A PLACE OF SHADOW: WE DREW THE REINS BY HIS   50 OISIN 3   44
        SIDE.
    AND THE PEARL-PALE NIAMH LAY BY ME, ...   52 OISIN 3   74
    AND PEARL-PALE NEAVE LAY BY ME, HER BROW ON THE MIDST OF   52 OISIN 3   V   74
        MY BREAST:
    . . . THEY LAY 'NEATH THE SAND-SACK AT LENGTH . . .   60 OISIN 3   V   186
    AND SAW WHERE THIS OLD TYMPAN LAY . . . .   85 MAD KING GOLL   55
    I LAY UPON MY BABY: . . . .   95 MOLL MAGEE   17
    "LAY ME IN A CUSHIONED CHAIR: . . . .   97 FOXHUNTER   1
    "NOW LAY ME IN A CUSHIONED CHAIR, ...   97 FOXHUNTER   V   1
    LAY HIDDEN IN THE SMALL SLATE-COLOURED THING! . . .   104 FERGUS DRUID   40
    LAY HIDDEN IN THE SMALL SLATE-COLOURED BAG! . . . .   104 FERGUS DRUID   V   40
    WONDERING TO LAY HER IN THAT SOLITUDE, ...   123 DREAM OF DEATH   5
    OR UNDER GREEN SODS LAY. . . . .   132 FR GILLIGAN   4
    FOR HALF HIS FLOCK LAY IN THEIR BEDS . . . .   132 FR GILLIGAN   V   3
    I CRIED IN MY DREAM, O WOMEN, BID THE YOUNG MEN LAY .   163 VALLEY LOVERS   5
    AND I CRIED IN MY DREAM "O WOMEN, BID THE YOUNG MEN LAY   163 VALLEY LOVERS   V   5
    AND I WOULD. LAY MY HEAD ON YOUR BREAST! . . . . .   175 BELOVED DEAD   4
    O WOULD, BELOVED, THAT YOU LAY . . . .   176 BELOVED DEAD   11
    WHERE THE TIRED HORSE-BOYS LAY UPON THE RUSHES, . .   180 QUEEN MAEVE   13
    A YEW-TREE WHERE HIS BODY LAY: . . . .   197 BAILE AILLINN   188
    A YEW TREE WHERE HIS BODY LAY, ...   197 BAILE AILLINN   V   188
    THE HONEY-PALE MOON LAY LOW ON THE SLEEPY HILL, . .   203 WITHER BOUGHS   5
    O: LAY THE SHRILLY TRUMPET DOWN, ...   212 BLESS PSALTER   4
    EDAIN CAME OUT OF MIDHIR'S HILL, AND LAY . . . . .   219 HARP OF AENGUS   1
    YOU'VE NEVER KNOWN, I'D LAY A WAGER ON IT, ...   227 SHADOW WATER B   113
    THAT I MIGHT LAY IT ON YOUR HEAD AS A CROWN. . . . .   246 SHADOW WATER B   511
    THE WEAK LAY HAND ON WHAT THE STRONG HAS DONE, . . .   265 THESE CLOUDS   3
    AND LAY IT ALL UPON A HORSE"! . . . .   296 THREE BEGGARS   35
    HELL MOUTH LAY OPEN NEAR THAT PLACE, ...   303 HOUR DAWN   25
    I LAY ABOUT ME WITH THE TAWS . . . .   379 SAINT HUNCH   8
    THE WOMAN THAT BY ME LAY . . . .   398 BREAK OF DAY   2
    BUT SHE THAT BESIDE ME LAY . . . .   399 BREAK OF DAY   21
    IT LAY FIVE HUNDRED YEARS. . . . .   421 MY TABLE   11
    AND LAY THE HEART UPON HER HAND . . . .   437 SONGS PLAY 1   4
    OUT OF DARK NIGHT WHERE LAY . . . .   439 FRAGMENTS   9
    AND YET THERE BEAUTY LAY: . . . .   455 HIS MEMORIES   12

439

		PAGE	TITLE	LINE

LAY   (CONTINUED)
THE FIRST OF ALL THE TRIBE LAY THERE • • • • • • • •   455 HIS MEMORIES   13
AND SHE LAY DOWN UPON HER BED AND SLEPT, • • • • • •   467 HARUN RASHID   146
"NAKED I LAY. • • • • • • • • • • • • • • •   510 JANE JUDGMENT   11
I DREAMED AS IN MY BED I LAY, • • • • • • • • • •   519 HER DREAM   1
AND LAY DOWN THAT HEAD • • • • • • • • • • • •   534 CONSOLATION   4
AND SEEMED TO STAND ALTHOUGH IN BED I LAY• • • • • •   535 CHOSEN   9
OF ALL THAT WITH ME LAY? • • • • • • • • • • • •   538 LAST CONFESS   2
ALONE AND ALONE NINE NIGHTS I LAY • • • • • • • •   551 SONGS REWRIT 1   13
NINE NIGHTS I LAY IN LONGING SORE • • • • • • • •   551 SONGS REWRIT 1 V   13
NINE NIGHTS I LAY AND IN LONGING SORE • • • • • • •   551 SONGS REWRIT 1 V   13
BUT THERE I LAY AND I WHISTLED IN VAIN. • • • • • •   551 SONGS REWRIT 1 V   16
WHERE THE BALES AND THE BASKETS LAY • • • • • • •   578 CRAZED GIRL   12
THAT BY THEIR BODIES LAY. • • • • • • • • • • •   589 OLD WICKED MAN   44
HE NEVER LAY BEHIND FOUR WALLS • • • • • • • • •   606 SONGS BURDEN 1   12
AND OUT AND LAY OUR LEADERSHIP • • • • • • • • •   606 SONGS BURDEN 1   23
LAY IN THE COFFIN, STOPPED HIS BREATH AND DIED. • • •   609 IN TARAS HALLS   20
THERE ALL THE GOLDEN CODGERS LAY, • • • • • • • •   611 NEWS ORACLE   1
LAY SIGHING LIKE THE REST. • • • • • • • • • • •   612 NEWS ORACLE   12
LAST NIGHT I LAY ON THE MOUNTAIN, • • • • • • • •   628 JANE MOUNTAIN   11
I LAY STRETCHED OUT IN THE DIRT • • • • • • • • •   628 JANE MOUNTAIN   21
THAT WHEREBY A HOUSE LAY WRECKED? • • • • • • • •   632 MAN AND ECHO   16
THE OTTERS DREAMING LAY.   AYE! • • • • • • • • •   677 ISLE STAT II 3   280
THE OTTERS DREAMING LAY.   NASCHINA!   AY! • • • • •   677 ISLE STAT II 3 V   280
O BROTHER, LAY THY FLUTE UPON THY LIPS! • • • • • •   681 SEEKER   6
WHERE SHALL I LAY ME DOWN?   THAT QUESTION IS • • • •   700 MOSADA 3   36
NAY HERE, I'LL LAY ME DOWN WHERE I CAN WATCH • • • •   700 MOSADA 3   39
"A LITTLE WILL I LAY MY WEARY HEAD, • • • • • • •   712 FERENCZ RENYI   75
WHERE WORM THE REBELS, OR MY BULLETS LAY • • • • •   713 FERENCZ RENYI   83
LAY DOWN THE BURDEN OF THY RACE, • • • • • • • •   736 SUMMER EVENING   14
EDAINE CAME OUT OF MIDHER'S HILL, AND LAY • • • • •   762 SHADOW WATER A   296

LAYER
AND DROP TWIGS LAYER UPON LAYER. • • • • • • • •   415 TOWER   168
AND DROP TWIGS LAYER UPON LAYER. • • • • • • • •   415 TOWER   168

LAYS
AND LAYS THEM IN A ROW. • • • • • • • • • • • •   89 ISLE IN WATER   6

LAZULI   SEE LAPIS-LAZULI
IN TOMBS OF GOLD AND LAPIS LAZULI • • • • • • • •   483 OIL AND BLOOD   1
LAPIS LAZULI • • • • • • • • • • • • • • • •   565 LAPIS LAZULI   T
ARE CARVED IN LAPIS LAZULI, • • • • • • • • • • •   566 LAPIS LAZULI   38

LAZY
WHEN THE LAZY THREAD HAS RUN-- • • • • • • • • •   520 HIS BARGAIN   V   10

LEA
OUR ISLE AWAITS US, ON EACH LEA • • • • • • • • •   77 INDIAN TO LOVE V   2

LEAD
THEY LEAD US BY LONG AND SHADOWY WAYS • • • • • •   16 OISIN 1   V   221
I LEAD ALONG THE WOODLAND DEER! • • • • • • • • •   84 MAD KING GOLL   46
LEAD MY LOLLARD TO AND FRO, • • • • • • • • • •   97 FOXHUNTER   7
AND LEAD HIM SLOWLY TO AND FRO, • • • • • • • • •   97 FOXHUNTER   V   7
AND LEAD HIM GENTLY IN A RING, • • • • • • • • •   97 FOXHUNTER   V   7
HIS LOLLARD LEAD THEY ROUND THE LAWN, • • • • • •   98 FOXHUNTER   V   17
AND LEAD US TO THE LIKE--IF THEY • • • • • • • •   387 ROBARTES DANCE   47
TO LEAD HER AWAY, DO NOT SAY • • • • • • • • • •   568 SWEET DANCER   9
LEAD THEM GENTLY ASTRAY. • • • • • • • • • • •   568 SWEET DANCER   11
LEAD ME, I PRAY THEE, TO THE STATUED PLACE! • • • •   667 ISLE STAT II 3   37
WE WILL LEAD YOU IN HAND • • • • • • • • • • •   726 LOVERS QUARREL   2
LEAD THEY ONE WITH FOOLISH CARE, • • • • • • • •   727 LOVERS QUARREL   29
THEY WILL LEAD HER HOME AGAIN • • • • • • • • •   727 LOVERS QUARREL   49
TO LEAD US TO THE STREAMS WHERE THE WORLD ENDS. • • •   765 SHADOW WATER A   369

LEADER
IF MICHAEL, LEADER OF GOD'S HOST • • • • • • • •   112 ROSE OF PEACE   1
IF MICHAEL, LEADER OF GOD'S HOSTS • • • • • • • •   112 ROSE OF PEACE   V   1
YOU'LL BE AS GOOD A LEADER.   BE OF YOUR TROOP! • • •   225 SHADOW WATER B V   73
BLIND AND LEADER OF THE BLIND • • • • • • • • • •   397 POLIT PRISONER   11
ANOTHER LEADER, AND TURN HOME AGAIN. • • • • • • •   748 SHADOW WATER A   16
AND WHOM WILL YOU MAKE LEADER?   WHO WILL MAKE • • •   748 SHADOW WATER A   20
FIRST I GREET MACCARTAN, REVOLUTIONARY LEADER. • • • •   790 DEDICATION   1

LEADERS
THE LEADERS OF THE CROWD • • • • • • • • • • •   398 LEADERS CROWD   T

LEADERSHIP
AND OUT AND LAY OUR LEADERSHIP • • • • • • • • •   606 SONGS BURDEN 1   23

LEADING
FOR LEADING AGED HOUNDS AND YOUNG • • • • • • •   98 FOXHUNTER   23
AND YET I CANNOT THINK THEY'RE LEADING ME • • • • •   230 SHADOW WATER B   191
IT'S CERTAIN THEY ARE LEADING YOU TO DEATH. • • • • •   231 SHADOW WATER B   201
WITH THAT SONG LEADING WHERE HARMONIC WOODS • • • •   657 ISLE STAT I 3   43

LEADS
DEAR HEART, THERE IS A SECRET WAY THAT LEADS • • • •   702 MOSADA 3   75

LEAF   SEE GRASS-LEAF
CEASED ON OUR HANDS AND OUR FACES, ON HAZEL AND OAK LEAF,   48 OISIN 3   23
  THE LIGHT.
WHEN A GLOW-WORM WAS GREEN ON A GRASS LEAF, • • • •   53 OISIN 3   V   99
"I WOULD DIE LIKE A SMALL WITHERED LEAF IN THE AUTUMN,   56 OISIN 3   131
  • • •
BY A BROAD WATER-LILY LEAF! • • • • • • • • • •   195 BAILE AILLINN   146
WANDERED BETWEEN THE BLUE AND THE GREEN LEAF • • • •   278 TWO KINGS   41
CAN NEVER TEAR THE LINNET FROM THE LEAF. • • • • •   405 FOR DAUGHTER   56
ARE YOU THE LEAF, THE BLOSSOM OR THE BOLE? • • • •   446 SCHOOL CHILDR   62
NOW BATHING LILY LEAF AND FISH'S SCALE, • • • • • •   464 HARUN RASHID   65
NOW BATHING LILY LEAF AND FISHES' SCALE, • • • • •   464 HARUN RASHID   V   65
THE AVENGING LEAF THOSE FIELDS RAISED UP AGAINST IT. • •   487 SEVEN SAGES   20

	PAGE	TITLE	LINE

LEAF   (CONTINUED)

THAT STARING FURY AND THE BLIND LUSH LEAF . . . . 500 VACILLATION 17
ALL KNOW THEIR TALE, ALL KNOW WHAT LEAF AND TWIG, . . . 555 RIBH AT TOMB 7
AS A LEAF THAT IS OLD, AND WITHERED, AND COLD, ... 643 SONG FAERIES 3
AS A LEAF THAT IS OLD, AND WITHERED, AND COLD, ... 644 SONG FAERIES 15
THE AIR IS STILL ABOVE, AND STILL EACH LEAF, ... 662 ISLE STAT II 2 7
AS A LEAF THAT IS OLD, AND WITHERED, AND COLD, ... 676 ISLE STAT II 3 250
AS A LEAF THAT IS OLD, AND WITHERED, AND COLD, ... 676 ISLE STAT II 3 262
AND ALL WAS DIMNESS, TILL A DYING LEAF . . . . 690 MOSADA 1 20
YONDER A LEAF . . . . 700 MOSADA 3 41
WHERE THE SHAKING LEAF WITH THE BEAM WAS PLAYING, . . . 728 PRIEST FAIRY 2

LEAFAGE

AND CHAPLET THEIR CALM BROWS WITH LEAFAGE DIM, ... 127 DREAM OF FAERY V 32
AND CHAPLET THEIR CALM BROWS WITH LEAFAGE COOL: . . . . 127 DREAM OF FAERY V 32
CLOUDY LEAFAGE OF THE SKY, ... 501 VACILLATION 46

LEAF-CROWNED

AND NO ONE ANY LEAF-CROWNED DANCER MISS . . . . 128 DREAM OF FAERY V 46

LEAF-HID

IT DOWN IN A LEAF-HID, HOLLOW PLACE . . . . 17 OISIN 1 242

LEAFLESS

A FIR-TREE ROARING IN ITS LEAFLESS TOP: . . . . 40 OISIN 2 177
A FIR TREE ROARING IN ITS LEAFLESS TOP, ... 40 OISIN 2 V 177
CRIES OUT THE LEAFLESS TREE, ... 780 WELL AND TREE 10

LEAF-SOWN

ON THE LEAF-SOWN, NEW-MOWN, SMOOTH . . . . 568 SWEET DANCER 2
ON THE LEAF-SOWN, NEW MOWN, SMOOTH . . . . 568 SWEET DANCER V 2

LEAFY

IN HIS OWN LEAFY FOREST HOUSE, ... 2 OISIN 1 V 7L
IN HIS OWN LEAFY FOREST HOUSE . . . . 4 OISIN 1 37
WE TIED THE HORSE IN A LEAFY CLUMP, ... 14 OISIN 1 194
THERE LIES A LEAFY ISLAND . . . . 86 STOLEN CHILD 3
HIS EVENING FIRE AMID THE LEAFY SHADE. . . . . 109 CUCHULAIN SEA 48
AFTER SHORT FIGHTING IN THE LEAFY SHADE, ... 109 CUCHULAIN SEA 57
AND AS IT FALLS AWAKENS LEAFY TUNES:— . . . . 127 DREAM OF FAERY V 23
THE SHAKING OF ITS LEAFY HEAD . . . . 134 TWO TREES 9
IN THOSE GREAT IGNORANT LEAFY WAYS: . . . . 135 TWO TREES 16
WHO AMID LEAFY LIGHTS AND SHADES . . . . 193 BAILE AILLINN 103
AND AMID LEAFY LIGHT HE CRIED, ... 193 BAILE AILLINN V 113
I KNOW OF THE LEAFY PATHS THAT THE WITCHES TAKE . . . . 203 WITHER BOUGHS 9
I KNOW OF THE LEAFY PATH THAT THE WITCHES TAKE, ... 203 WITHER BOUGHS V 9
POOR RACE OF LEAFY ARCADY, YOUR LOVE . . . . 650 ISLE STAT I 1 145
JOY'S BROTHER, FEAR, LURKS IN EACH LEAFY WAY. . . . . . 651 ISLE STAT I 1 156
EVE-SOOTHED IN SOME FAR LEAFY REST, ... 686 LIFE 10
OF A WIDE WOOD'S LEAFY LEISURE, ... 731 STREET DANCERS 11

LEAGUES

THOUSANDS OF LEAGUES OVERSEA, ... 341 SHEP GOATHERD 63

LEAN

IN THE FENIANS' DWELLINGS OF WATTLE LEAN ON THE CHESSBOARDS 55 OISIN 3 115
    AND PLAY,
I CLIMB TO THE TOWER-TOP AND LEAN UPON BROKEN STONE, . . 425 PHANTOM HATRED 1
I CLIMB TO THE TOWER TOP AND LEAN UPON BROKEN STONE, . . 425 PHANTOM HATRED V 1
OR EYES THAT RAGE HAS BRIGHTENED, ARMS IT HAS MADE LEAN, 427 PHANTOM HATRED 27
OF EYES THAT RAGE HAS BRIGHTENED, ARMS IT HAS MADE LEAN, 427 PHANTOM HATRED V 27
NOW I AM IN THE PUBLIC-HOUSE AND LEAN UPON THE WALL, . . 593 PILGRIM 21
NOW I AM IN THE TAVERN AND LEAN AGAINST THE WALL, . . . 593 PILGRIM V 21
NOW I AM IN THE PUBLIC HOUSE AND LEAN UPON THE WALL, . . 593 PILGRIM V 21
"WATCHER, WHEREFORE HAVE YE CALLED US?" EYES GO AFTER 718 PHANTOM SHIP 10
    HIS LEAN HAND,
AND LEAN YOUR LIPS DEVOUTLY TO THIS HARP, ... 762 SHADOW WATER A 287

LEANED

THAT GOD HAD LEANED HIS HANDS OUT OF THE SKY, ... 128 DREAM OF FAERY V 43

LEANING

LEANING DOWN FROM THE GEM-STUDDED SADDLE, ... 60 OISIN 3 187
LEANING FORTH FROM THE GEM-STUDDED SADDLE, ... 60 OISIN 3 V 187
LEANING SOFTLY OUT . . . . 88 STOLEN CHILD 35
AND ON MY LEANING SHOULDER SHE LAID HER SNOW-WHITE HAND. 90 SALLEY GARDENS 6
HE KNELT, AND LEANING ON THE CHAIR . . . . 132 FR GILLIGAN 13
LEANING OR STANDING OR WALKING . . . . 356 BROKEN DREAMS 23
A HOARY HUNTER LEANING ON HIS BOW, ... 672 ISLE STAT II 3 157
THE MAYOR CAME, LEANING HIS DEAF EAR— . . . . 725 LEGEND 13

LEANNESS

FOR REMEMBRANCE, LIFTING HER LEANNESS, ... 57 OISIN 3 152

LEANS

OF HOW GOD LEANS HIS HANDS OUT OF THE SKY, ... 128 DREAM OF FAERY V 43
ONE LEANS AND MUTTERS BY THE WALL— . . . . 212 BLESS PSALTER 10
WHO LEANS UPON A STICK, ... 525 DANCING DAYS 20
LEANS ON HIS ELBOWS, GAZING AT THE SEA. . . . . 752 SHADOW WATER A 127

LEANT

WHEN THE EARLIEST DEW-WASHED STAR FROM EVE HATH LEANT, . . 32 OISIN 2 V 54
THAT GOD HAD LEANT HIS HANDS OUT OF THE SKY, ... 128 DREAM OF FAERY V 43
HEAD UPON SHOULDER LEANT: . . . . 319 DOLLS 18
MAN-PICKER NIAMH LEANT AND SIGHED . . . . 611 NEWS ORACLE 5
CAME AND WERE GONE. HE LEANT UPON A TREE . . . . . . 634 CUCHULAIN COMF 5

LEAP

LEAP IN THE MEADOW. ON THE MISTY STAIRS . . . . 44 OISIN 2 V 229
THE HEART IN ME LONGING TO LEAP LIKE A GRASSHOPPER INTO 60 OISIN 3 182
    HER HEART:
TO AND FRO WE LEAP . . . . 87 STOLEN CHILD 20
YOU CANNOT LEAP OUT OF THE GOLDEN NET. . . . . 238 SHADOW WATER B 360
WHERE MY GOATS BROWSE ON THE SCARCE GRASS OR LEAP . . . 339 SHEP GOATHERD 8
TO DRUM WITH HER HEEL AND TO LEAP? . . . . 381 SONGS FOOL 2 9

441

		PAGE	TITLE		LINE

LEAP (CONTINUED)
```
    THAT LOFTY WHITE STAG, LEAP . . . . . . . . . .      399 BREAK OF DAY        24
    THE FOUNTAIN LEAP, AND AT DAWN . . . . . . . . .      414 TOWER              124
    THE HARE LEAP TO THE WOOD, . . . . . . . . . . .      453 DEATH OF HARE        2
    SHALL LEAP INTO THE LIGHT LOST . . . . . . . . .      511 JANE AND JACK       11
    ROE COULD RUN OR DOE COULD LEAP . . . . . . . .       522 LULLABY             10
    ROE COULD LEAP OR DOE COULD RUN: . . . . . . . .      522 LULLABY             12
    STAG COULD RUN AND ROE LEAP . . . . . . . . . .       522 LULLABY        V    10
    STAG COULD LEAP AND ROE COULD RUN. . . . . . . .      522 LULLABY        V    12
    ALL THAT COULD RUN OR LEAP OR SWIM . . . . . . .      528 DANCER CRUACH        6
    ALL THAT RUN OR LEAP OR SWIM . . . . . . . . . .      528 DANCER CRUACH  V     6
    OENONE SAW THE FIRES OF TROIA LEAP, . . . . . .       645 ISLE STAT I 1       17
LEAPED
    THE HARE LEAPED IN THE GRASS.  YOUNG NIAMH CAME . . .  44 OISIN 2        V   229
    AND HOW YOU HAVE LEAPED TIMES OUT OF MIND. . . .      146 FISH                 5
    NOR ON OLYMPUS LEAPED FROM CLOUD TO CLOUD, . . .      260 FASC DIFFICULT       6
    NOR ON AN OLYMPUS LEAPED FROM CLOUD TO CLOUD, . .     260 FASC DIFFICULT V     6
    OLD MERCHANT SKIPPER THAT LEAPED OVERBOARD . . .      270 PARDON FATHERS      13
    YOU MERCHANT SKIPPER THAT LEAPED OVERBOARD . . .      270 PARDON FATHERS V    13
    AND MERCHANT SKIPPER THAT LEAPED OVERBOARD . . .      270 PARDON FATHERS V    13
    AT MOONEEN HE HAD LEAPED A PLACE . . . . . . . .      326 ROBERT GREGORY      60
    AND YET, BECAUSE MY HEART LEAPED AT HER WORDS, .      353 PEOPLE              35
    THE SWAN HAS LEAPED INTO THE DESOLATE HEAVEN! . .     431 NINETEEN 19         79
    LEAPED UP INTO THE AIR. . . . . . . . . . . . .       741 EARL PAUL           36
LEAPING
    OF DANCERS LEAPING IN THE AIR: . . . . . . . . .       18 OISIN 1            254
    LEAPING TO SHAKE A COBWEB FROM THE RAFTER: . . .      130 BOOK STORIES   V    19
    AND THE WAVES ARE LEAPING WHITE, . . . . . . . .      646 ISLE STAT I 1       27
    AND, LEAPING TO THEIR FEET, FAR ECHOES CRIED, . .     659 ISLE STAT II 1      13
LEAPS
    LEAPS UPWARD, AS IF ALL THE STREAMS O' THE WORLD . . . 249 SHADOW WATER B    560
    LOVE LEAPS UPON ITS COURSE. . . . . . . . . . .       518 HIS CONFIDENCE      12
    LEAPS AND TIME'S OLD LANTHORN DIMS. . . . . . .       777 SONG DEIRDRE 2       5
LEAPT
    WHEN ONE HAS LEAPT ON BOARD.  NO, FOR I HAVE HOPE . . 751 SHADOW WATER A     106
LEAR
    THERE STRUTS HAMLET, THERE IS LEAR, . . . . . .       565 LAPIS LAZULI        10
    THEY KNOW THAT HAMLET AND LEAR ARE GAY: . . . .       565 LAPIS LAZULI        16
    THOUGH HAMLET RAMBLES AND LEAR RAGES, . . . . .       566 LAPIS LAZULI        21
    TILL I AM TIMON AND LEAR . . . . . . . . . . . .      576 ACRE OF GRASS       15
LEARN
    AND LEARN TO CHAUNT A TONGUE MEN DO NOT KNOW. . .     101 ROSE UPON ROOD      21
    AND LEARN TO CHANT A TONGUE MEN DO NOT KNOW. . .      101 ROSE UPON ROOD V    21
    BUT LEARN THE DREAMING WISDOM THAT IS YOURS, . .      103 FERGUS DRUID        22
    AND LEARN TO PRAY WHEN YOU PRAY. . . . . . . . .      167 BLESSED              8
    AND LEARN THE PRAYERS THAT YOU SAY. . . . . . .       167 BLESSED        V     8
    WE'LL LEARN THAT SLEEPING IS NOT DEATH, . . . .       266 GALWAY RACES        11
    THAT HE MIGHT LEARN THE SHEPHERDS' WILL. . . . .      288 TO WEALTHY MAN      19
    THE SECOND: "I SHALL LEARN A TRADE": . . . . . .      296 THREE BEGGARS       32
    AND LEARN THAT THE BEST THING IS . . . . . . . .      330 BONE OF A HARE       6
    OF ALL 'TWAS PAIN OR JOY TO LEARN, . . . . . . .      342 SHEP GOATHERD       98
    MAYBE THE MOON MAY LEARN. . . . . . . . . . . .       378 CAT AND MOON        14
    LEARN THAT WE WERE CRACK-PATED WHEN WE DREAMED, .     431 NINETEEN 19         88
    THE CHILDREN LEARN TO CIPHER AND TO SING, . . .      443 SCHOOL CHILDR        3
    O BUT HER HEART WOULD BREAK TO LEARN MY THOUGHTS ARE FAR 450 OWEN AHERNE      20
        AWAY."
    BOOK II  WHAT THE CALIPH REFUSED TO LEARN . . . .    460 HARUN RASHID   V     T
    THEN MY DELIVERED SOUL HERSELF SHALL LEARN . . .     558 RIBH CHRISTIAN      13
    SOUL MUST LEARN A LOVE THAT IS . . . . . . . . .     573 LADYS 2ND SONG      15
    CHILDLESS, I THOUGHT, "MY CHILDREN MAY LEARN HERE    603 GALLERY REVIS  V    36
    I KNOW WHAT DEVIL'S TRADE THEY LEARN . . . . . .     607 SONGS BURDEN 2      12
    IRISH POETS, LEARN YOUR TRADE, . . . . . . . . .     639 BEN BULBEN          68
LEARN'D
    KIND EYES SHOULD BE MORE LEARN'D? . . . . . . .      312 TWO YEAR LATER       2
LEARNED
    THAT THEY WOULD SIGH AND QUOTE WITH LEARNED LOOKS . . 205 ADAMS CURSE        25
    POETS WITH WHOM I LEARNED MY TRADE. . . . . . .      270 GREY ROCK            1
    WHERE WIT AND BEAUTY LEARNED THEIR TRADE . . . .     288 TO WEALTHY MAN      16
    THAT MIGHT THE LEARNED PLEASE, . . . . . . . . .     333 SOLOMON SHEBA       12
    OLD, LEARNED, RESPECTABLE BALD HEADS . . . . . .     337 SCHOLARS             2
    ARE LEARNED IN WAITING.  YOU CANNOT BUT HAVE SEEN .  340 SHEP GOATHERD       48
    --PEDANT IN PASSION, LEARNED IN OLD COURTESIES, .    363 DOLLS FACES          4
    BOOK I  WHAT THE CALIPH PARTLY LEARNED . . . . .     372 PHASES OF MOON V     T
    REFORMER, MERCHANT, STATESMAN, LEARNED MAN, . .      376 PHASES OF MOON      98
    LEARNED LIKE A MAN?  PAUL VERONESE . . . . . . .     386 ROBARTES DANCE      26
    IT HAD NOT LEARNED ITS LESSON. . . . . . . . . .     389 IMAGE PAST          14
    IN COURTESY I'D HAVE HER CHIEFLY LEARNED: . . .      404 FOR DAUGHTER        33
    WITH LEARNED ITALIAN THINGS . . . . . . . . . .      415 TOWER              158
    IN A LEARNED SCHOOL . . . . . . . . . . . . . .      416 TOWER              183
    OUR LEARNED MEN HAVE URGED . . . . . . . . . . .     421 MY TABLE            15
    NOW THE GOOD CALIPH'S LEARNED TREASURER, . . . .     461 HARUN RASHID         3
    THE PARCHMENT WILL DISCLOSE TO SOME LEARNED MAN . .  461 HARUN RASHID        20
    THOUGH BUT A FEW LEARNED MEN SHALL LOOK WITHIN, .    461 HARUN RASHID   V   18A
    ON OLD DRY WRITING IN A LEARNED TONGUE, . . . .      466 HARUN RASHID       123
    SHE SEEMED THE LEARNED MAN AND I THE CHILD: . .      467 HARUN RASHID       137
    BY SOME LEARNED INDIAN . . . . . . . . . . . . .     472 ALL SOUL NIGHT      53
    LEARNED IN BODILY LOWLINESS . . . . . . . . . .      513 JANE TALK BISH      11
    WHERE--WROTE A LEARNED ASTROLOGER-- . . . . . .      535 CHOSEN              17
    ALL THOSE LEARNED HISTORIANS, . . . . . . . . .      584 ORAHILLY             5
    AND COME WITH LEARNED LOVERS OR WITH WHAT MEN YOU MAY, . 593 PILGRIM         23
    AND COME WITH LEARNED LOVERS OR WITH WHAT MAN YOU MAY, . 593 PILGRIM      V  23
```

	PAGE	TITLE	LINE
LEARNED (CONTINUED)			
MALACHI STILT-JACK AM I, WHATEVER I LEARNED HAS RUN WILD,	623	HIGH TALK	9
OH, LEARNED IS EACH MONK'S-HOOD'S MIND,	655	ISLE STAT I 3	8
SIR PAGE, ALMINTOR'S FRIEND, AND THEREFORE LEARNED	660	ISLE STAT II 1	38
HE WAS A MAN MOST LEARNED AND MOST MILD,	692	MOSADA 1	51
LEARNING			
NO LEARNING FROM THE STARRY MEN,	66	HAPPY SHEPHERD	28
THAT LOVED HIS LEARNING BETTER THAN MANKIND,	324	ROBERT GREGORY	18
TILL ALL HIS GREEK AND LATIN LEARNING SEEMED	324	ROBERT GREGORY	21
DARE MATCH IN LEARNING WITH US TWO,	333	SOLOMON SHEBA	21
FOR LEARNING AND DEFENCE	380	SONGS FOOL 1	5
HAS A LEARNING IN HIS EYE	381	SONG OF FOOL	3
PASS BOOKS OF LEARNING FROM BYZANTIUM	461	HARUN RASHID	9
LEARNS			
AND LEARNS AT LAST THAT IT IS SELF-DELIGHTING,	405	FOR DAUGHTER	67
LEARNT			
NOW I HAVE LEARNT TO BE PROUD	349	HAWK	9
HE HAD LEARNT FROM PATER, AND TO ROUND HIS TALE	373	PHASES OF MOON	27
THAT IS HOW HE LEARNT SO WELL	382	SONG OF FOOL	11
THE LOT OF LOVE IS CHOSEN. I LEARNT THAT MUCH	534	CHOSEN	1
LEAST			
WHERE CARE CANNOT TROUBLE THE LEAST OF OUR DAYS,	27	OISIN 1	409
WILL SCATTER IN RUIN THE LEAST OF OUR DAYS,	27	OISIN 1	V 419B
THE LEAST OF DOORS! BEYOND ON A DIM PLAIN	39	OISIN 2	155
THE LEAST OF DOORS! BEYOND THE DOOR A PLAIN,	39	OISIN 2	V 155
HAD PITY ON THE LEAST OF THINGS	134	FR GILLIGAN	47
DO MEN WHO LEAST DESIRE GET MOST,	295	THREE BEGGARS	13
THAT I HAVE HANDLED LEAST, LEAST LOOKED UPON.	367	EGO DOMINUS	9
THAT I HAVE HANDLED LEAST, LEAST LOOKED UPON.	367	EGO DOMINUS	9
FOR CERTAIN MINUTES AT THE LEAST	399	DEMON BEAST	1
A NUN AT LEAST HAS ALL MEN'S REVERENCE	448	HERO GIRL FOOL	12
FOR THEY AT LEAST HAVE ALL MEN'S REVERENCE	448	HERO GIRL FOOL V	12
CAME TO THE LEAST CONSIDERED OF HIS COURTIERS!	462	HARUN RASHID	42
COXCOMB WAS THE LEAST HE SAID!	508	JANE BISHOP	6
THERE STOOD A MAN, OF MEN THE LEAST--	729	PRIEST FAIRY	24
WHO IS SIX FEET HIGH IN HIS SOCKS AT LEAST?	729	PRIEST FAIRY	28
LEATHER			
WITH THONGS OF LEATHER." AS SHE SPAKE IT WAS!	106	CUCHULAIN SEA	V 17B
LEATHER-COATED			
AND LEATHER-COATED MEN WITH SLINGS	193	BAILE AILLINN	V 111
LEATHERN			
AND CAPTIVES BOUND WITH LEATHERN THONGS	7	OISIN 1	77
MY CAPTIVES, BOUND IN LEATHERN THONGS,	8	OISIN 1	V 78
LEAVE			
AND THAT I WOULD LEAVE THE IMMORTALS,	54	OISIN 3	108
I WOULD LEAVE NO SAINT'S HEAD ON HIS BODY	58	OISIN 3	160
"NOW LEAVE THE CHAIR DOWN ON THE GRASS,	97	FOXHUNTER V	9
"NOW LEAVE THE CHAIR UPON THE GRASS,	97	FOXHUNTER V	9
COME NEAR, COME NEAR, COME NEAR--AH, LEAVE ME STILL	101	ROSE UPON ROOD	13
LEAVE THE BODY'S COLOURED PRIDE	124	CATHLEEN PARA	2
THAT IF WE HOLD THAT FLIGHT THEY'LL LEAVE THE PLACE,	265	ABBEY THEATRE	3
LEAVE PAUDEENS TO THEIR PITCH AND TOSS!	288	TO WEALTHY MAN V	31
AND LEAVE NO SMOKING WICK BEHIND,	306	HOUR DAWN	97
OR LEAVE THEM HAPPIER THAN BEFORE.	328	IRISH AIRMAN	8
BUT PUT NO NAME AND LEAVE THEM AT HER DOOR.	343	SHEP GOATHERD	116
YOUR BEAUTY CAN BUT LEAVE AMONG US	356	BROKEN DREAMS	14
PADDLE AND ARE PERFECT. LEAVE UNCHANGED	357	BROKEN DREAMS	34
"COME IN AND LEAVE THE PLAY."	364	END OF DAY	8
LUXURIANT SONG. WHY SHOULD YOU LEAVE THE LAMP	370	EGO DOMINUS	62
NEVER TO LEAVE THAT VALLEY HIS FATHERS CALLED THEIR HOME.	391	UNDER SATURN	16
GO THEREFORE! BUT LEAVE HANRAHAN,	413	TOWER	103
I LEAVE BOTH FAITH AND PRIDE	416	TOWER	173
AND LEAVE A WOMAN AND A MAN BEHIND	422	MY DESCENDANTS	3
TO LEAVE A WOMAN AND A MAN BEHIND	422	MY DESCENDANTS V	3
CAN LEAVE THE MOTHER, MURDERED AT HER DOOR,	429	NINETEEN 19	27
NO HONOUR LEAVE ITS MIGHTY MONUMENT,	429	NINETEEN 19	38
TO LEAVE SOME MONUMENT BEHIND,	432	NINETEEN 19	96
THEY'D SOONER LEAVE THEIR COSSETING	455	HIS MEMORIES	9
FOR SHOULD YOU LEAVE MY LETTER THERE, A BOY'S	461	HARUN RASHID	13
AND ALL COMPLEXITIES OF FURY LEAVE,	498	BYZANTIUM	29
SEEK OUT REALITY, LEAVE THINGS THAT SEEM.	502	VACILLATION	72
THE MORE I LEAVE THE DOOR UNLATCHED	511	JANE AND JACK	3
I COULD BUT LEAVE HIM TO HIS FATE!	514	JANE GROWN OLD	11
LEAVE NOTHING BUT THE NOTHINGS THAT BELONG	542	PARN FUNERAL 1	29
WHAT IF I BADE YOU LEAVE	600	THOSE IMAGES	1
TO PASS AND LEAVE THEM THERE	680	LOVE AND DEATH	24
THERE IS NO LEAVE TAKING. I GO NO MORE.	702	MOSADA 3	V 100
AH! CRUEL ONES, LEAVE ME ALONE NOW	707	FAIRY PEDANT	13
AH! CRUEL ONES, LEAVE ME ALONE.	707	FAIRY PEDANT	V 13
AH! LEAVE ME, I PRAY YOU AND BEG.	708	FAIRY PEDANT	22
OR LEAVE SOME SERVICE ALL UNDONE,	743	DANAAN QUICK	21
UPON CLEAR NIGHTS THEY LEAVE THE UPPER AIR	750	SHADOW WATER A	87
AND LEAVE HER DREAMING. WHEN I LOOKED ON HER,	761	SHADOW WATER A V	258
BUT NEVER, NEVER DANGLING LEAVE THE LIVER AND THE LIGHTS.	790	HEART SLEEVE	2
LEAVED SEE GREY-LEAVED			
LEAVES SEE BEECH-LEAVES DOCK-LEAVES			
AMONG THE LEAVES OF THE LAUREL WALL,	3	OISIN 1	V 7FF
FALL THE LEAVES OF OTHER ROSES,	21	OISIN 1	311
SHALL FALL THE LEAVES OF DAMASK ROSES.	21	OISIN 1	315
A JUBILANT LIFE AMONG THE LEAVES, RETURN,	35	OISIN 2	V 89A
LIKE DRIFTS OF LEAVES, IMMOVABLE AND BRIGHT,	40	OISIN 2	166

443

LEAVES   (CONTINUED)
  LIKE DRIFTS OF LAUREL LEAVES, IMMOVABLE AND BRIGHT . . . . 40 OISIN 2 V 166
  . . . AND THE LEAVES OF THE MURAL GLEN, ... 49 OISIN 3 35
  COULD FONDLE THE LEAVES WITH HIS FINGERS, ... 49 OISIN 3 38
  SQUARE LEAVES OF THE IVY MOVED OVER US, BINDING US DOWN 52 OISIN 3 76
    TO OUR REST.
  THE FLIES BELOW THE LEAVES, AND THE YOUNG MICE . . . . 75 ANASHU VIJAYA 87
  ONE WITH THE LEAVES; ONE WITH THE DOVE . . . . 78 INDIAN TO LOVE V 16
  THE FALLING OF THE LEAVES . . . . 79 FALLING LEAVES T
  FALLING OF THE LEAVES . . . . 79 FALLING LEAVES V T
  AUTUMN IS OVER THE LONG LEAVES THAT LOVE US, ... 79 FALLING LEAVES 1
  YELLOW THE LEAVES OF THE ROWAN ABOVE US, ... 79 FALLING LEAVES 3
  AND YELLOW THE WET WILD-STRAWBERRY LEAVES. . . . . 79 FALLING LEAVES 4
  PENSIVE THEY PACED ALONG THE FADED LEAVES. . . . . 80 EPHEMERA 10
  THE WOODS WERE ROUND THEM, AND THE YELLOW LEAVES . . 80 EPHEMERA 13
  TURNING, HE SAW THAT SHE HAD THRUST DEAD LEAVES . . . . 80 EPHEMERA 18
  THEY WILL NOT HUSH, THE LEAVES A-FLUTTER ROUND ME, . . . 82 MAD KING GOLL 12
  . . . THE BEECH LEAVES OLD. . . . . 82 MAD KING GOLL 12
  (THEY WILL NOT HUSH, THE LEAVES THAT ROUND ME FLUTTER-- 82 MAD KING GOLL V REF
    . . .
  THEY WILL NOT HUSH, THE LEAVES A-FLUTTER ROUND ME, . . . 83 MAD KING GOLL 24
  . . . THE BEECH LEAVES OLD. . . . . 83 MAD KING GOLL 24
  THEY WILL NOT HUSH, THE LEAVES A-FLUTTER ROUND ME, . . . 84 MAD KING GOLL 36
  . . . THE BEECH LEAVES OLD. . . . . 84 MAD KING GOLL 36
  THEY WILL NOT HUSH, THE LEAVES A-FLUTTER ROUND ME, . . . 84 MAD KING GOLL 48
  . . . THE BEECH LEAVES OLD. . . . . 84 MAD KING GOLL 48
  THEY WILL NOT HUSH, THE LEAVES A-FLUTTER ROUND ME, . . . 85 MAD KING GOLL 60
  . . . THE BEECH LEAVES OLD. . . . . 85 MAD KING GOLL 60
  --FROM POOLS AND ROTTING LEAVES--ME SING . . . . 85 MAD KING GOLL V 63
  THEY WILL NOT HUSH, THE LEAVES A-FLUTTER ROUND ME, . . . 86 MAD KING GOLL 72
  . . . THE BEECH LEAVES OLD. . . . . 86 MAD KING GOLL 72
  SHE BID ME TAKE LOVE EASY, AS THE LEAVES GROW ON THE TREE; 90 SALLEY GARDENS 3
  SHE BID ME TAKE LOVE EASY, AS THE LEAVES GROW ON THE TREES; 90 SALLEY GARDENS V 3
  AND ALL THAT FAMOUS HARMONY OF LEAVES, ... 120 SORROW OF LOVE 3
  AND ALL THAT LAMENTATION OF THE LEAVES, ... 120 SORROW OF LOVE 11
  AND THE LOUD SONG OF THE EVER-SINGING LEAVES . . . . 120 SORROW OF LOVE V 3
  AND THE LOUD CHANTING OF THE UNQUIET LEAVES, ... 120 SORROW OF LOVE 11
  AND THE LOUD CHAUNTING OF THE UNQUIET LEAVES, ... 120 SORROW OF LOVE V 11
  AND LEAVES SHOOK IN THE WIND; . . . . 133 FR GILLIGAN 18
  BROKEN BOUGHS AND BLACKENED LEAVES. . . . . . . 135 TWO TREES 28
  WITH BROKEN BOUGHS AND BLACKENED LEAVES . . . . . 135 TWO TREES V 26
  THE WINDS AWAKEN, THE LEAVES WHIRL ROUND, ... 140 HOSTING SIDHE 6
  "THAT DROWSILY DROPS FAINT LEAVES ON HIM . . . . . 168 BLESSED 37
  "THE ROSE THAT MUST DROP, OUT OF SWEET LEAVES, . . . 168 BLESSED V 37
  MEN HAVE NAMED BEAUTY. THY GREAT LEAVES ENFOLD . . . . 169 SECRET ROSE 7
  MEN HAVE NAMED BEAUTY. YOUR HEAVY LEAVES ENFOLD . . . 169 SECRET ROSE V 7
  MEN HAVE NAMED BEAUTY. YOUR GREAT LEAVES ENFOLD . . . 169 SECRET ROSE V 7
  AMONG MY LEAVES IN TIMES OUT OF MIND; . . . . . 177 PAST GREATNESS 5
  SHINING ON WATER AND FALLEN AMONG LEAVES, ... 218 WOODS OF COOLE 38
  O FLOWER OF THE BRANCH, O BIRD AMONG THE LEAVES, ... 251 SHADOW WATER B 608
  THOUGH LEAVES ARE MANY, THE ROOT IS ONE; . . . . 261 COMING WISDOM 1
  I SWAYED MY LEAVES AND FLOWERS IN THE SUN; . . . . 261 COMING WISDOM 3
  BETWEEN THE PALE GREEN LIGHT OF THE BEECH LEAVES . . . 277 TWO KINGS V 5
  AND WHERE THE STONE STRUCK FIRE, WHILE IN THE LEAVES . . 278 TWO KINGS 33
  CAST BUT DEAD LEAVES TO MATHEMATICAL EQUALITY; . . . . 481 BLOOD AND MOON 24
  CASTS BUT DEAD LEAVES TO MATHEMATICAL EQUALITY; . . . . 481 BLOOD AND MOON V 24
  AND DEAFENING MUSIC SHOOK THE LEAVES; A TROOP . . . . 537 HER VISION 13
  THOUGH SOMEWHAT BROKEN BY THE LEAVES, THAT LIGHT . . . 555 RIBH AT TOMB 25
  LEAVES WHAT MAN WOULD LOSE. . . . . 620 JOHN KINSELLA 4
  AS THE LEAVES IN AUTUMN SCATTER. . . . . 648 ISLE STAT I 1 90
  THE BIRDS THAT NESTLE IN THE LEAVES ARE SAD, ... 652 ISLE STAT I 2 15
  MID BUBBLING LEAVES A WANDERING SONG-RAPT BIRD . . . 672 ISLE STAT II 3 154
  MID BABBLING LEAVES A WANDERING SONG-RAPT BIRD . . . 672 ISLE STAT II 3 V 154
  UNTIL MY BEARD IS IN THE TWISTED LEAVES . . . . . 683 SEEKER 44
  LIE STREWN THE YELLOW LEAVES--THE CLOTTED LEAVES. . . 684 SEEKER 69
  LIE STREWN THE YELLOW LEAVES--THE CLOTTED LEAVES. . . 684 SEEKER 69
  LIE STREWN THE CLOTTED LEAVES--THE DEAD OLD LEAVES. . . 684 SEEKER V 69
  LIE STREWN THE CLOTTED LEAVES--THE DEAD OLD LEAVES. . . 684 SEEKER V 69
  THE PATH O'ER-MUFFLED WITH THE LEAVES--DEAD LEAVES, . . 703 MOSADA 3 115
  THE PATH O'ER MUFFLED WITH THE LEAVES--DEAD LEAVES, . . 703 MOSADA 3 115
  THE PATH O'ER MUFFLED WITH THE LEAVES--DEAD LEAVES, . . 703 MOSADA 3 V 115
  THE PATH O'ER MUFFLED WITH THE LEAVES--DEAD LEAVES, . . 703 MOSADA 3 V 115
  O FLOWER OF THE BRANCH, O BIRD AMONG THE LEAVES, ... 769 SHADOW WATER A 424
LEAVE-TAKING
  THERE IS NO LEAVE-TAKING. I GO NO MORE. . . . . . . 702 MOSADA 3 100
LEBEEN-LONE
  AM I TO LIVE ON LEBEEN-LONE?" . . . . 295 THREE BEGGARS 5
  "FOR ALL MY PAINS ON LEBEEN-LONE?" . . . . 295 THREE BEGGARS 7
LECHER
  OLD LECHER WITH A LOVE ON EVERY WIND, ... 413 TOWER 105
  AN ANCIENT LECHER TOOK TO GEESE . . . . . . 792 GEORGE MOORE 3
LECHEROUS
  I AM SO LECHEROUS WITH ABSTINENCE . . . . . . 222 SHADOW WATER B V 8
  BEING MOCKED BY GUIDO FOR HIS LECHEROUS LIFE, ... 369 EGO DOMINUS 33
LECHING
  A LECHING SONG," THEY SAID. . . . . 570 THREE BUSHES 44
LECTERN
  MY GREAT WOOD LECTERN AND THE FIRE . . . . . . 358 PRESENCES 10
LED   SEE DREAM-LED
  THEY LED US BY LONG AND SHADOWY WAYS . . . . . . 16 OISIN 1 221
  SAID NIAM. "AY, AND HUGE. WHEN YE HAVE LED . . . . 35 OISIN 2 V 89

PAGE   TITLE   LINE

LED   (CONTINUED)
HOW THE MEN OF THE SAND-SACK LED ME TO SHAUL, • • • • •   61 OISIN 3   V   193
LED ON BY GENTLE WAYS: • • • • • • • • • • • •   113 ROSE OF PEACE   12
HAS HE NOT LED US INTO THESE WASTE SEAS • • • • • • •   221 SHADOW WATER B   1
LED BY A FOOTSOLE DIPPED IN BLOOD • • • • • • • • •   274 GREY ROCK   78
LED BY A FOOT-SOLE DIPPED IN BLOOD • • • • • • • •   274 GREY ROCK   V   78
THAT SHEBA LED A DANCE. • • • • • • • • • • •   346 ON WOMAN   43
WITH HER WHITE FINGER. I LED HER HOME ASLEEP • • • •   468 HARUN RASHID   158
WHAT MANHOOD LED THE DANCE! • • • • • • • • • •   488 CRAZED MOON   12
BECAUSE PIEBALD PONIES, LED BEARS, CAGED LIONS, MAKE BUT 623 HIGH TALK   5
    POOR SHOWS,
FIRST THAT SEA-RIDER OISIN LED BY THE NOSE • • • • • •   629 CIRCUS ANIMALS   10
I'VE LED THEE HERE, AND AS A WHEEL • • • • • • • •   667 ISLE STAT II 3   39
SERENE. THEY'RE LED AWAY, AND WHERE A BAND • • • • •   712 FERENCZ RENYI   63

LEDA
LEDA AND THE SWAN • • • • • • • • • • • • • •   441 LEDA AND SWAN   T
BOOK III DOVE OR SWAN I. LEDA • • • • • • •   441 LEDA AND SWAN   V   T
BOOK V: DOVE OR SWAN I LEDA • • • • • • • •   441 LEDA AND SWAN   V   T
FROM THE LIMBS OF LEDA SANK • • • • • • • • • •   522 LULLABY   17

LEDAEAN
I DREAM OF A LEDAEAN BODY, BENT • • • • • • • •   443 SCHOOL CHILDR   9
AND I THOUGH NEVER OF LEDAEAN KIND • • • • • • • •   444 SCHOOL CHILDR   29

LEDGE   SEE WINDOW-LEDGE
SHE BUILDS HER NEST UPON A NARROW LEDGE • • • • • •   285 TWO KINGS   194
OF GREY STONES AND A ROCKY LEDGE • • • • • • • •   302 HOUR DAWN   12

LEE   SEE PAIRC-NA-LEE

LEFT
OF MOONLIT STEPS GLIMMERED: AND LEFT AND RIGHT • • • •   31 OISIN 2   35
SCARCE LEFT A WHITENING FEATHER, GREY AND SERE: • • • •   34 OISIN 2   V   76A
FOR ALL YOUR CROZIERS, THEY HAVE LEFT THE PATH • • •   42 OISIN 2   200
AND LEFT HER TO THE INDIFFERENT STARS ABOVE • • • •   123 DREAM OF DEATH   9
WE AND OUR BITTERNESS HAVE LEFT NO TRACES • • • • •   130 BOOK STORIES   23
HE LEFT THEM WHERE SHE WENT BY. • • • • • • • •   160 CAP AND BELLS   24
TO HER LEFT HAND CAME THE BLUE. • • • • • • • •   160 CAP AND BELLS   32
UNDER A BITTER BLACK WIND THAT BLOWS FROM THE LEFT HAND: 206 HANRAHANS SONG   2
UNDER THE BITTER BLACK WINDS BLOWING OUT OF THE LEFT HAND! 206 HANRAHANS SONG V   2
AND I AM LEFT ALONE WITH MY BELOVED, • • • • • • •   251 SHADOW WATER B   600
MERCHANT AND SCHOLAR WHO HAVE LEFT ME BLOOD • • • • •   269 PARDON FATHERS   7
TRADERS OR SOLDIERS WHO HAVE LEFT ME BLOOD • • • • •   269 PARDON FATHERS   V   7
AND LEFT MERE SLEEP. HE'LL WAKE WHEN THE SUN WAKES,   284 TWO KINGS   161
AND LEFT THEM TO THEIR ARGUMENT. • • • • • • • •   296 THREE BEGGARS   28
AND THERE BE NOTHING BUT GOD LEFT: • • • • • • • •   307 HOUR DAWN   103
VANISHED, AND LEFT BUT MEMORIES, THAT SHOULD BE OUT OF   316 COLD HEAVEN   5
    SEASON
BUT LEFT THE HOUSE AS IN HIS FATHER'S TIME • • • • •   341 SHEP GOATHERD   53
THERE'S NOTHING OF HIM LEFT BUT HALF A SCORE • • • •   341 SHEP GOATHERD   56
THAT MICHAEL ROBARTES LEFT, YOU WALK IN THE MOON, • •   367 EGO DOMINUS   4
OR, THE HOUSE DOOR LEFT UNSHUT, • • • • • • • • •   380 SONGS FOOL 1   10
THERE'S NOT A NEIGHBOUR LEFT TO SAY • • • • • • • •   412 TOWER   78
HAS BUT ONE COMFORT LEFT: ALL TRIUMPH WOULD • • • •   429 NINETEEN 19   39
AND LEFT ME BUT A LOUT, • • • • • • • • • • •   451 FIRST LOVE   14
AND I LEFT SHIVERING. THE VOICE HAS DRAWN • • • •   469 HARUN RASHID   179
THE BLOOD OF INNOCENCE HAS LEFT NO STAIN. • • • • •   482 BLOOD AND MOON   34
IN LUCK OR OUT THE TOIL HAS LEFT ITS MARK: • • • •   491 COOLE BALLYLEE V   40F
IN LUCK OR OUT THE TOIL HAS LEFT ITS MARK: • • • •   495 CHOICE   6
BUT WERE I LEFT TO LIE ALONE • • • • • • • • • •   511 JANE AND JACK   13
THEY LEFT THEIR BODIES TO FATTEN THE WOLVES, • • • •   545 TO SAME TUNE 2   2
THEY LEFT THEIR HOMESTEADS TO FATTEN THE FOXES, • • •   546 TO SAME TUNE 2   3
THEY LEFT THEIR HOMESTEADS TO SHELTER THE FOXES, • • •   546 TO SAME TUNE 2 V   3
HIS PROUD HEART HE LEFT BEHIND. • • • • • • • • •   561 FOUR AGES MAN   6
WHAT'S LEFT TO SIGH FOR? • • • • • • • • • •   574 MAIDS 1ST SONG   5
WHAT IS THERE LEFT TO SAY? • • • • • • • • •   580 CURSE CROMWELL   8
WHAT IS THERE LEFT TO SAY? • • • • • • • • •   580 CURSE CROMWELL   16
WHAT IS THERE LEFT TO SAY? • • • • • • • • •   581 CURSE CROMWELL   24
WHAT IS THERE LEFT TO SAY? • • • • • • • • •   581 CURSE CROMWELL   32
THEY LEFT THEIR BODIES TO FATTEN THE WOLVES, • • • •   613 MARCH SONGS 1   2
THEY LEFT THEIR HOMESTEADS TO FATTEN THE FOXES, • • •   613 MARCH SONGS 1   3
AND WONDERED WHAT WAS LEFT FOR MASSACRE TO SAVE. • • •   619 BRONZE HEAD   28
"OR DRIVEN FROM HOME AND LEFT TO DIE IN FEAR." • •   635 CUCHULAIN COMF   22
MICHAEL ANGELO LEFT A PROOF • • • • • • • • • •   638 BEN BULBEN   45
MICHAELANGELO LEFT A PROOF • • • • • • • • • •   638 BEN BULBEN   V 45
LONG ERE AN ARROW WHIZZED OR SWORD LEFT SHEATH • • •   650 ISLE STAT I 1   135
HAD LEFT THE ISLAND BREEZE, MY LORE • • • • • •   668 ISLE STAT II 3 V   55
WHEN MY LOST LOVER LEFT THESE ARMS. MY GOMEZ • • •   701 MOSADA 3   51
WHEN MY LOST LOVER LEFT THESE ARMS. MY VALLENCE, • •   701 MOSADA 3   V 51
THE PRIEST LOOKED NEITHER TO RIGHT NOR LEFT, • • • •   730 PRIEST FAIRY   49
I LEFT HER LIVING, THINKING THAT I HAD FOUND • • • •   755 SHADOW WATER A   174
WITH ONE YOU HAVE KILLED AND DIE: FOR WHEN I LEFT • •   758 SHADOW WATER A   226
WITH SOME YOU HAVE KILLED AND DIE: FOR WHEN I LEFT • •   758 SHADOW WATER A V   226

LEG
AS THE ONE STURDY LEG COULD DO • • • • • • • • •   302 HOUR DAWN   5

LEGEND
A LEGEND OF THE PHANTOM SHIP. • • • • • • • • •   718 PHANTOM SHIP   V   T
A LEGEND. • • • • • • • • • • • • • • • •   724 LEGEND   T

LEGENDARY   SEE HALF-LEGENDARY
HALF LEGENDARY MEN. • • • • • • • • • • • • •   605 YOU CONTENT   16

LEGGED   SEE BANDY-LEGGED LONG-LEGGED THREE-LEGGED HALF-LEGGED ONE-LEGGED BOW-LEGGED

LEGS   SEE DADDY-LONG-LEGS
UPON ITS BANDY LEGS. RUN AT THEM NOW, • • • • • • •   233 SHADOW WATER B   239
ON HIS YELLOW LEGS THROUGH OUR MEADOWS, • • • • • •   341 SHEP GOATHERD   65

		PAGE	TITLE		LINE

LEGS (CONTINUED)
```
    UPON HIS YELLOW LEGS THROUGH OUR MEADOWS, . . . . .     341  SHEP GOATHERD  V   65
    STRETCHED UP ON TWO LEGS FROM THE MAT, . . . . . . .    381  SONGS FOOL 2        7
    THEIR LEGS LONG, DELICATE AND SLENDER, AQUAMARINE THEIR 426  PHANTOM HATRED     17
      EYES,
    STAND UPRIGHT ON YOUR LEGS AWHILE, . . . . . . . .     586  PARNELLITES         3
LEISURE
    AND YOU SHALL KNOW THE DANAAN LEISURE! . . . . . .       9  OISIN 1           100
    AND THOU SHALT KNOW THE IMMORTALS' LEISURE, . . . . .    9  OISIN 1        V  100
    THE WARRIOR DREAMS IN AN AGED LEISURE . . . . . . .     26  OISIN 1        V  401
    A DEMON'S LEISURE! EYES, FIRST WHITE, NOW BURNED . . .  40  OISIN 2           168
    A DEMON'S LEISURE, EYES FIRST WHITE AS SNOW, . . . .    40  OISIN 2        V  168
    THE HONEY-HEARTED LEISURE OF THE LIGHT, . . . . . .    705  REMEMBRANCE         7
    OF A WIDE WOOD'S LEAFY LEISURE, . . . . . . . . .      731  STREET DANCERS     11
LEISURED
    OF FACES, WAITED! AND THE LEISURED GAZE . . . . . .     39  OISIN 2           149
    OF FACES, WATCHED ME, AND THE LEISURED GAZE . . . .     39  OISIN 2        V  149
LEMAN
    FOR THERE THE TALL DEER AND HIS LEMAN SIGH . . . . .   210  RAGGED WOOD     V    2
    FOR THERE THE TALL DEER AND HIS LEMAN CRY . . . . .    211  RAGGED WOOD     V    6
    BECOME A STRANGER'S LEMAN! AND THAT YOU, . . . . .     757  SHADOW WATER A    215
LEMON
    UNDER A LEMON TREE BESIDE YOUR DOOR! . . . . . . .     693  MOSADA 1           68
    LAPPED IN THE LEMON DAFFODILLS; A BEE . . . . . .      716  DWELT SYCAMORE     10
LEMON-TINTED
    IN LEMON-TINTED LINES, SO BLAZE THE DAFFODILLS. . . .  645  ISLE STAT I 1      19
LEND
    HE CALLED ALOUD TO ALL THE STARS TO LEND . . . . .     68  SAD SHEPHERD    V    5
LENDS
    AND JOY, THE TOUCHING OF WHOSE FINGER LENDS . . . .    686  DRAWING-ROOM        7
    AND JOY, THE TOUCHING OF WHOSE FINGER LENDS . . . .    734  QUATRAIN APHOR      7
LENGTH
    DEEP SUNKEN ON THE BLADE'S LENGTH, "MANANAN!" . . . .   38  OISIN 2        V  128
    . . . BUT FELL WITH THEIR BURDEN AT LENGTH. . . . .     60  OISIN 3           186
    . . . THEY LAY 'NEATH THE SAND-SACK AT LENGTH . . .     60  OISIN 3        V  186
    THAT EVERY YEAR I HAVE CRIED, "AT LENGTH . . . . .     256  WORDS               9
    AH, BUT PEACE THAT COMES AT LENGTH, . . . . . . .      259  PEACE              10
    AND DRINK, AND YOU WILL SLEEP THAT LENGTH." . . . .    305  HOUR DAWN          59
    YOU WILL SLEEP THAT LENGTH; AND AT THE FIRST . . .     305  HOUR DAWN       V   59
    I TOILED LONG YEARS AND AT LENGTH . . . . . . . .      505  RESULT THOUGHT      9
    TOILED LONG YEARS AND AT LENGTH . . . . . . . .        505  RESULT THOUGHT  V   9
    HIS EMPTY HEART IS FULL AT LENGTH, . . . . . . .       624  APPARITIONS        19
    AT ARM'S LENGTH, THUS TILL DUMB ETERNITY . . . . .     671  ISLE STAT II 3    145
    ITS PAVEN LENGTH TOWARDS THE RIVER'S MARGE . . . .     702  MOSADA 3           76
LENGTHEN
    AND THERE IS SALT TO LENGTHEN OUT THE SMART . . . .    324  ROBERT GREGORY     11
LENGTHENING
    TO HIS SHAPE IN THE LENGTHENING SHADOWS, . . . . .     341  SHEP GOATHERD   V   70
LEOPARD
    AS AN HURT LEOPARD FILLS WITH CEASELESS MOAN, . . .    674  ISLE STAT II 3    208
    AS A HURT LEOPARD FILLS WITH CEASELESS MOAN . . . .    674  ISLE STAT II 3  V  208
LEOPARD-COLOURED
    ARISE THE LEOPARD-COLOURED TREES! . . . . . . . .      84  MAD KING GOLL      40
LEOPARDS
    OF THE DARK LEOPARDS OF THE MOON? . . . . . . . .     343  DEJECTION           3
LESS
    WERE THE WINDS LESS SOFT THAN THE BREATH OF A PIGEON . . 56  OISIN 3         134
    NOR BE I ANY LESS OF THEM, . . . . . . . . . .        137  TO IRELAND          5
    NOR MAY I LESS BE COUNTED ONE . . . . . . . . .       138  TO IRELAND         17
    AND LOVE IS LESS KIND THAN THE GREY TWILIGHT, . . .    148  INTO TWILIGHT      15
    AND HOPE IS LESS DEAR THAN THE DEW OF THE MORN. . .    148  INTO TWILIGHT      16
    AND OUR POOR KATE OR NAN IS LESS . . . . . . . .      190  BAILE AILLINN      35
    THAT HAS LESS UPS AND DOWNS FROM ROBBERY. . . . .      222  SHADOW WATER B      7
    BUT YEAR BY YEAR I FOUND THAT LESS . . . . . . .      305  HOUR DAWN          68
    LESS BITTER.  THEY HAVE BROUGHT ME FROM THAT RIDGE .   342  SHEP GOATHERD      87
    MAKE HUMAN INTERCOURSE GROW LESS AND LESS! . . . .     473  ALL SOUL NIGHT     75
    MAKE HUMAN INTERCOURSE GROW LESS AND LESS! . . . .     473  ALL SOUL NIGHT     75
    AND TWENTY MINUTES MORE OR LESS . . . . . . . .       501  VACILLATION        42
    AND FINDS THERE NOTHING TO MAKE ITS TERROR LESS . . .  618  BRONZE HEAD         6
    NAY, GRIEF IN FEEDING ON OLD GRIEF GROWS LESS. . .     659  ISLE STAT II 1     19
    THREE TIMES THE ROSES HAVE GROWN LESS AND LESS, . .    690  MOSADA 1            1
    THREE TIMES THE ROSES HAVE GROWN LESS AND LESS, . .    690  MOSADA 1            1
LESSER
    AND MANY A LESSER BELL SOUND THROUGH THE ROOM! . .     470  ALL SOUL NIGHT      2
    INTO SOME LESSER THING. . . . . . . . . . . .         517  HER ANXIETY         5
    A GREATER WITH A LESSER PANG ASSUAGE . . . . . .       537  HER VISION          5
    FIRST DREAMS, AND GOBLINS, AND THE LESSER SPRITES, .   722  WITCH VIVIEN       56
LESSON
    IT HAD NOT LEARNED ITS LESSON. . . . . . . . .        389  IMAGE PAST         14
LEST
    LEST THEY SHOULD LOOK UPON SOME DREADFUL SIGHT! . .     38  OISIN 2           142
    STOOD TIMIDLY.  LEST THEY SHOULD SEE SOME SIGHT . .     38  OISIN 2        V  141
    LEST NIAMH SHUDDER. FULL OF HOPE AND DREAD . . . .     41  OISIN 2           183
    CAST THE LOOSE BULK, LEST NIAM FEAR HIM DEAD! . . .    41  OISIN 2        V  183
    LEST ALL THY TOILING ONLY BREEDS . . . . . . . .      66  HAPPY SHEPHERD     25
    LEST I NO MORE HEAR COMMON THINGS THAT CRAVE! . . .   101  ROSE UPON ROOD     15
    "BUT LEST YOU ARE MY ENEMY, . . . . . . . . . .       263  MASK               11
    HE HOLDS HIM FROM DESIRE, ALL BUT STOPS HIS BREATHING LEST 559 MAGIC DRUM      6
    AS I MY WATCHING LEST YOU WAKE, . . . . . . . .       658  ISLE STAT I 3      95
    LEST ON THINE HEART THE STONY SEAL . . . . . . .      667  ISLE STAT II 3     41
    LEST HE MAY SOME GLAMOUR FOLD . . . . . . . . .       717  FAIRY DOCTOR       22
```

LEST (CONTINUED)
```
     LEST SOME GLAMOUR HE MAY FOLD  . . . . . . . .    717 FAIRY DOCTOR    V   22
     WHISPER LEST WE TOO MAY SADDEN,  . . . . . . .    737 IN FIRELIGHT        5
     BEND LOWER LEST YOUR BATTLE-AXES GLIMMER.  . . .  752 SHADOW WATER A    117
     BEND LOWER LEST YOUR BATTLE AXES GLIMMER.  . . .  752 SHADOW WATER A  V 117
LET
     NOR THY COMPANIONS. LET THEM REST,  . . . . . .    11 OISIN 1        V 130
     THE FENIANS.  LET THEIR DEER-HOUNDS SLEEP. . . .   11 OISIN 1        V 131
     LET US PART, ERE THE SEASON OF PASSION FORGET US,  79 FALLING LEAVES      7
     "ALTHOUGH OUR LOVE IS WANING, LET US STAND  . .    79 EPHEMERA            4
     "THOUGH OUR SAD LOVE IS FADING, LET US YET  . .    79 EPHEMERA        V   4
     IN BOSOM AND HAIR.  THEN HE: "LET US NOT MOURN     80 EPHEMERA        V  20
     "HE BADE ME LET ALL KNOW HE GIVES HIS NAME  . .   109 CUCHULAIN SEA      52
     BELOVED, LET YOUR EYES HALF CLOSE, AND YOUR HEART BEAT  154 BELOVED PEACE  9
     LET THE STARRY WINDS AND THE FLAME AND THE FLOOD  158 TO HIS HEART        5
     DIM POWERS OF DROWSY THOUGHT, LET HER NO LONGER BE  175 ELEMENT POWERS   13
     BUT LET A GENTLE SILENCE WROUGHT WITH MUSIC FLOW  175 ELEMENT POWERS   17
     GREAT RULERS OF THE STILLNESS, LET HER NO LONGER BE  175 ELEMENT POWERS V 13
     GREAT RULERS OF STILLNESS, LET HER NO LONGER BE   175 ELEMENT POWERS V 13
     BUT LET A GENTLE SILENCE ENWROUGHT WITH MUSIC FLOW  175 ELEMENT POWERS V 17
     OR LET ITS MEANING MIX INTO THE STRINGS.  . . .   180 QUEEN MAEVE         8
     LET RUSH AND BIRD CRY OUT THEIR FILL  . . . .     197 BAILE AILLINN     198
     "LET PEEWIT CALL AND CURLEW CRY WHERE THEY WILL,  203 WITHER BOUGHS       2
     THAT WOULD LET THE SPADE LIE,  . . . . . . .      215 HAPPY TOWNLAND     30
     AND LET THE DREAM GO BY.  IT'S NOT A DREAM,  . .   229 SHADOW WATER B    158
     LET GO MY HANDS!  WHY DO YOU CAST A SHADOW?  . .   235 SHADOW WATER B    283
     WHEN SHE FINDS OUT I WILL NOT LET HER GO--   . .   236 SHADOW WATER B    302
     THAT YOU'LL NOT LET ME GO?  I AM A QUEEN.  . .     236 SHADOW WATER B    304
     I WOULD NOT LET YOU SPEAK, FOR I WOULD KNOW   .    246 SHADOW WATER B    492
     HOW GREAT A WRONG IT IS TO LET ONE'S THOUGHT  .    246 SHADOW WATER B    514
     LET THE BIRDS SCATTER, FOR THE TREE IS BROKEN,    250 SHADOW WATER B    584
     YET OLD ROMANCE BEING KIND, LET HIM PREVAIL  . .  258 KING NO KING        5
     "O NO, MY DEAR, LET ALL THAT BE:  . . . . . .     263 MASK               13
     BUT LET THAT BE--THE GODS WERE STILL,  . . . .    271 GREY ROCK       V  16
     THAN LOVER'S MUSIC--LET THAT BE,  . . . . . .     276 GREY ROCK         130
     LET PAUDEENS PLAY AT PITCH AND TOSS,  . . . .     288 TO WEALTHY MAN     31
     BUT LET THEM BE, THEY'RE DEAD AND GONE,  . . .    290 SEPTEMBER 1913     31
     LET THESE CONTENT YOU AND BE GONE AGAIN:  . . .   292 TO A SHADE          8
     SHE NEED NOT BE TOO COMELY--LET IT PASS."  . . .  300 BEGGAR CRIED       10
     BUT LET HIM KEEP HIS GRAVE FOR ONCE  . . . . .    303 HOUR DAWN          38
     LET THERE BE NO FOOT SILENT IN THE ROOM,  . . .   311 MOUNTAIN TOMB   V   6
     SONG, LET THEM TAKE IT,  . . . . . . . . .        320 COAT                8
     LET THE YOUNG WISH.  BUT WHAT HAS BROUGHT YOU HERE?  339 SHEP GOATHERD   6
     I LET THEM STRAY.  I THOUGHT OF RHYME ALONE,  .   339 SHEP GOATHERD      11
     LET HIM BE HOODED OR CAGED  . . . . . . . .       349 HAWK                2
     I KNEW A PHOENIX IN MY YOUTH, SO LET THEM HAVE THEIR DAY.  353 HIS PHOENIX   8
     I KNEW A PHOENIX IN MY YOUTH, SO LET THEM HAVE THEIR DAY.  354 HIS PHOENIX  16
     I KNEW A PHOENIX IN MY YOUTH, SO LET THEM HAVE THEIR DAY.  354 HIS PHOENIX  24
     I KNEW A PHOENIX IN MY YOUTH, SO LET THEM HAVE THEIR DAY.  354 HIS PHOENIX  32
     AND LET YOU GO.  . . . . . . . . . . . .          359 TO A SQUIRREL       8
     AMID THE DREAMS OF YOUTH) LET HER COME FACE TO FACE,  366 HER COURAGE     3
     O! SOLOMON! LET US TRY AGAIN."  . . . . . . .     389 SOLOMON WITCH      44
     SO LET HER THINK OPINIONS ARE ACCURSED.  . . .    405 FOR DAUGHTER       58
     COME LET US MOCK AT THE GREAT  . . . . . . .      432 NINETEEN 19        93
     COME LET US MOCK AT THE WISE:  . . . . . . .      432 NINETEEN 19        98
     COME LET US MOCK AT THE GOOD  . . . . . . .       432 NINETEEN 19       103
     LET THE NEW FACES PLAY WHAT TRICKS THEY WILL  .    435 NEW FACES           5
     BEFORE THE INDIFFERENT BEAK COULD LET HER DROP?   441 LEDA AND SWAN      14
     LET THE CAGE BIRD AND THE CAGE BIRD MATE . . .    450 OWEN AHERNE        16
     O LET HER CHOOSE A YOUNG MAN NOW AND ALL FOR HIS  450 OWEN AHERNE        24
         WILD SAKE."
     AND LET ALL BASE AMBITION PASS,  . . . . . .      460 THREE MONUMENT      9
     AND LET IT FALL UNNOTICED TO THE FLOOR.  . . .    461 HARUN RASHID       15
     "LET ALL THINGS PASS AWAY."  . . . . . . . .      502 VACILLATION        61
     "LET ALL THINGS PASS AWAY."  . . . . . . . .      502 VACILLATION        66
     "LET ALL THINGS PASS AWAY."  . . . . . . . .      502 VACILLATION        71
     COME, LET ME SING INTO YOUR EAR:  . . . . . .     524 DANCING DAYS        1
     THAT FOLLOWED IF I LET THE KERCHIEF FALL:  . .    533 HER TRIUMPH         4
     THAT BIRD . . . LET HIM SING ON,  . . . . .       536 PARTING            12
     "LET OTHERS BOAST THEIR FILL," SAID I,  . . .     539 MEETING             7
     TO THIS BARE SOUL, LET ALL MEN JUDGE THAT CAN .   542 PARN FUNERAL 1     30
     WHAT MATTER?  HEAVE NO SIGH, LET NO TEAR DROP,    564 GYRES              11
     LET HER FINISH HER DANCE,  . . . . . . . .        568 SWEET DANCER       12
     LET HER FINISH HER DANCE.  . . . . . . . .        568 SWEET DANCER       13
     AND LET HIM THINK ME THERE,  . . . . . . . .      570 THREE BUSHES       23
     LET THE FOOLS RAGE, I SWERVED IN NAUGHT,  . . .   577 WHAT THEN          18
     AND LET THE NEIGHBOURS VOTE,  . . . . . . .       598 STONE CROSS         6
     ALL THAT IS FINISHED, LET IT FADE.  . . . . .     613 MARCH SONGS 1      10
     AND ALL THAT'S FINISHED, LET IT FADE.  . . . .    613 MARCH SONGS 1      20
     AND ALL THAT'S FINISHED, LET IT FADE.  . . . .    614 MARCH SONGS 1      30
     AMONG THOSE BIRD-LIKE THINGS CAME, AND LET FALL   634 CUCHULAIN COMF      8
     NOR LET THE MODISH PAINTER SHIRK  . . . . . .     638 BEN BULBEN         38
     SO LET US DANCE WHERE THE YELLOW LANCE  . . .     643 SONG FAERIES        7
     SO LET US DANCE ON FRINGED WAVES,  . . . . .      644 SONG FAERIES        9
     SOME CAST OF DIE, OR LET SOME ARROW GLANCE  . .   656 ISLE STAT I 3      40
     LET HIM BETWEEN US JUDGE, FOR HE CAN GAUGE  . .   660 ISLE STAT II 1     36
     IN ALL SUCH THINGS, PRAY LET THINE EARS BE TURNED, 660 ISLE STAT II 1    39
     HERE WHERE THE ROUND WAVES COME, HERE LET THEM BUILD,  663 ISLE STAT II 2  19
     A WHITE, DUMB THING OF TEARS, HERE LET IT STAND,  663 ISLE STAT II 2     21
     AND ONCE A-YEAR LET THE ARCADIANS COME,  . . .    663 ISLE STAT II 2     29
     OF HUMAN SORROW LET THEM MORALIZE:  . . . . .     663 ISLE STAT II 2     31
```

447

LET   (CONTINUED)
    AND LET THEM TELL SAD HISTORIES, TILL THEIR EYES • • • •   663 ISLE STAT II 2   32
    AND LET THE TALE BE MOURNFUL EACH ONE TELLS. • • • • •   663 ISLE STAT II 2   36
    O LET ME PASS! THE SPELLS FROM OFF THE HEART • • • • • • 668 ISLE STAT II 3   44
    O LET ME PASS! THAT FLOWER NONE • • • • • • •   668 ISLE STAT II 3   47
    FOR SUCH A CALL. LET THE WILD WORD BE CRIED • • • • •   669 ISLE STAT II 3   76
    BUT ART THOU HAPPY? LET ME GAZE ON THEE • • • • • •   671 ISLE STAT II 3   144
    BEFORE I AM TOO WEAK, FIERCE MORTAL, LET ME FLY, • • •   675 ISLE STAT II 3   245
    BEFORE I AM TOO WEAK, OH LET ME FLY. • • • • • • •   675 ISLE STAT II 3 V   245
    SO LET US DANCE WHERE THE YELLOW LANCE • • • • • •   676 ISLE STAT II 3   254
    SO LET US DANCE ON THE FRINGED WAVES, • • • • • •   676 ISLE STAT II 3   256
    OF THIS LAKE-NURTURED ISLE! LET THY KING BE • • • • •   679 ISLE STAT II 3   315
    THEN LET ME SEE THY FACE BEFORE I DIE. • • • • • •   684 SEEKER   66
    AH, LET US KISS EACH OTHER'S EYES, • • • • • • •   686 LIFE   15
    UPON MY KNEES I PRAY YOU, LET IT SLEEP, • • • • •   693 MOSADA 1   72
    THEM ALL, AND LET THEM FIND YOU IN THE VAPOUR. • • •   694 MOSADA 1   V 108A
    WE GATHERED. FERENCZ, DO NOT LET ME DIE. • • • • •   713 FERENCZ RENYI   V 96
    I SWEAR IT. LET EVERY MAN DRAW OUT HIS SWORD. • • •   758 SHADOW WATER A   230
    LET HIM WHO BREAKS IT • • • • • • • • • • • • •   770 BLOOD BOND   4
    LET THE SEA BEAR WITNESS, • • • • • • • • • • •   770 BLOOD BOND   7
    LET THE WIND BEAR WITNESS, • • • • • • • • • • •   770 BLOOD BOND   8
    LET THE EARTH BEAR WITNESS, • • • • • • • • • •   770 BLOOD BOND   9
    LET THE FIRE BEAR WITNESS, • • • • • • • • • • •   770 BLOOD BOND   10
    LET THE DEW BEAR WITNESS, • • • • • • • • • • •   770 BLOOD BOND   11
    LET THE STARS BEAR WITNESS! • • • • • • • • • • •   770 BLOOD BOND   12
    I'D LET THE WHOLE WORLD GO; • • • • • • • • • • •   782 HEART FRIGHT   9
LETHEAN
    NO LONGER IN LETHEAN FOLIAGE CAUGHT • • • • • • • •   500 VACILLATION   27
LET'S
    LET'S HOME; I'D GIVE SOME RUBIES TO A WOMAN. • • • •   248 SHADOW WATER B   537
    LET'S HOME AND SPEND IT IN OUR VILLAGES. • • • • •   248 SHADOW WATER B V 538A
    AY, BOY. LET'S SEE IF THAT SAME HERON'S DEAD. • • •   651 ISLE STAT I 1   169
    I COULD NOT GO. LET'S TALK, AND LET'S BE SAD, • • •   651 ISLE STAT I 2   7
    I COULD NOT GO. LET'S TALK, AND LET'S BE SAD, • • •   651 ISLE STAT I 2   7
    AND HEAVEN, AND HOLINESS. LET'S TALK AND GRIEVE, • • •   702 MOSADA 3   84
LETS
    THERE DREAMY TIME LETS FALL HIS SICKLE • • • • • • •   77 INDIAN TO LOVE V   5A
    AND LETS THE KIND WORM TAKE THE LOT! • • • • • • •   779 ACCURSED WHO   4
LET'ST
    "ASSASSIN, MY ASSASSIN! THOU WHO LET'ST ME DIE, • • • • 714 FERENCZ RENYI   106
LETTER
    AND FOR NO EAR BUT HIS. CARRY THIS LETTER • • • • •   461 HARUN RASHID   4
    FOR SHOULD YOU LEAVE MY LETTER THERE, A BOY'S • • • •   461 HARUN RASHID   13
    AT THE BOTTOM OF A LETTER, FIFTY MEN. • • • • • • •   790 DEDICATION   10
LETTERED
    HEALING FROM ITS LETTERED SLAB. THOSE SELF-SAME HANDS   503 VACILLATION   82
       PERCHANCE
    AND LAID THEM ON LOVE'S LETTERED TOMB! • • • • • • •   519 HER DREAM   4
    SAD HISTORIES ARE LETTERED ON THY CHEEK. • • • • • •   660 ISLE STAT II 1   52
LETTERS
    THEREON IN OGHAM LETTERS, "MANANNAN"; • • • • • • •   38 OISIN 2   128
    IN CHANGELESS OGHAM LETTERS WRIT-- • • • • • • • •   194 BAILE AILLINN   117
    THAT LIFE AND LETTERS SEEM • • • • • • • • • •   255 WOMAN HOMER   20
LEVEE
    AFAR FROM OUR LAWN AND OUR LEVEE, • • • • • • • • •   706 FAIRY PEDANT   1
LEVEL
    WAS NOT MORE LEVEL THAN THE SEA, • • • • • • • •   13 OISIN 1   157
    AN ISLE LAY LEVEL BEFORE US, WITH DRIPPING HAZEL AND OAK? 47 OISIN 3   10
    AN ISLE LAY LEVEL BEFORE US, DRIPPING WITH HAZEL AND OAK? 47 OISIN 3   V 10
    AND DANCE UPON THE LEVEL SHORE? • • • • • • • • •   125 GOES FERGUS   3
    WHO DANCED ON A LEVEL PLACE, • • • • • • • • • •   144 HOST OF AIR   14
    AND ALL THINGS AT ONE COMMON LEVEL LIE. • • • • • •   265 THESE CLOUDS   6
    BUT ACTUAL SHELLS OF ROSSES' LEVEL SHORE. • • • • •   494 AT ALGECIRAS   12
    SCATTERED ON THE LEVEL GRASS • • • • • • • • • •   530 DELPHIC ORACLE   6
LEVELLED
    THEN DREW HIS SWORD TO HOLD ITS LEVELLED POINT • • • •   277 TWO KINGS   14
    BUT DREW HIS SWORD, AND THOUGHT WITH LEVELLED POINT • • 277 TWO KINGS   V 14
    O WHAT IF LEVELLED LAWNS AND GRAVELLED WAYS • • • • •   418 ANCEST HOUSES   29
LEVELLING
    NOR THOUGHT OF THE LEVELLING WIND. • • • • • • • •   432 NINETEEN 19   97
    A LEVELLING, RANCOROUS, RATIONAL SORT OF MIND • • • •   486 SEVEN SAGES   11
LEV'RET'S
    THE BEATING OF A LEV'RET'S HEART; • • • • • • • • •   730 PRIEST FAIRY   69
LIAR
    LIAR AND FLATTERER OF THE WEAK, IN WHAT STRANGE CLIME • • 42 OISIN 2   V 198
LIBATIONS
    LIBATIONS, FROM THE HUNGARY OF THE WEST. • • • • • •   709 FERENCZ RENYI   5
LIBERAL
    FINE MANNERS, LIBERAL SPEECH, • • • • • • • • • •   506 REMORSE SPEECH   7
LIBERTY
    SERVED HUMAN LIBERTY. • • • • • • • • • • • • •   493 SWIFTS EPITAPH   6
    SORROW THAT GIVES FOR GUERDON LIBERTY, • • • • • •   686 DRAWING-ROOM   6
    SORROW, THAT GIVES FOR GUERDON LIBERTY, • • • • • •   734 QUATRAIN APHOR   6
LIBRARY
    FOR THE SAN MARCO LIBRARY, • • • • • • • • • •   288 TO WEALTHY MAN   24
LICE
    THEY WERE COMMINGLING LICE AND BLOOD. • • • • • • •   297 THREE BEGGARS   56
LICKED
    WHAT FROM THE FOREST CAME? WHAT BEAST HAS LICKED   560 MAGIC DRUM   6
       ITS YOUNG?

448

```
                                                        PAGE     TITLE            LINE
LICKS
     BUT HERE THE LIONESS LICKS HER SOFT CUB  . . . . . . .  688 NETTLESHIP          2
LIDLESS
     TO BREED THE LIDLESS EYE THAT LOVES THE SUN?  . . . . .  264 HOUSE SHAKEN        4
LIDS
     UPON DARK THRONES. BETWEEN THE LIDS OF ONE  . . . . .   31 OISIN 2            37
     HUGE FORMS OF STONE: BETWEEN THE LIDS OF ONE  . . . . .  31 OISIN 2          V 37
     HELPLESS, MEN LIFTING THE LIDS OF HIS WEARY             53 OISIN 3            92
        AND DEATH-MAKING EYE.
     HELPLESS, MEN LIFTING THE LIDS OF HIS WEARY             53 OISIN 3          V 92
        AND DEATH-POURING EYE.
     ARE BOWED IN SORROW UNDER PENDULOUS LIDS,  . . . . . .   79 EPHEMERA            2
     LIE NOW HALF HIDDEN UNDER PENDULOUS LIDS,  . . . . . .   79 EPHEMERA         V  2
     ARE BOWED IN SORROW UNDER THEIR TREMBLING LIDS,  . . .   79 EPHEMERA         V  2
LIE
     AND IN SOME GLOOMY BARROW LIE  . . . . . . . . . . .    19 OISIN 1           272
     AND IN SOME URN FUNEREAL LIE  . . . . . . . . . . . .   19 OISIN 1         V 272
     FOR HIS LAST DAYS TO LIE IN WAIT.  . . . . . . . . .    24 OISIN 1           363
     AND IN THE SHADOW OF MY HAIR LIE HID,  . . . . . . .    33 OISIN 2            66
     TO LIE UNTIL THE FOURTH MORN SAW EMERGE  . . . . . .    44 OISIN 2           220
     TO LIE THERE 'TILL THE FOURTH DAY SAW EMERGE  . . . .   44 OISIN 2         V 220
     TO LIE UNTIL THE FOURTH MORN SUN EMERGE  . . . . . .    44 OISIN 2         V 220
     . . . WHEN THE FALLEN ON FALLEN LIE ROLLED:  . . . .    52 OISIN 3            78
     . . . "WHERE WHITE CLOUDS LIE SPREAD  . . . . . . .     59 OISIN 3           178
     WHERE MEN LIE FROZEN IN THE GLIMMERING SNOW:  . . . .   73 ANASHU VIJAYA      51
     LIE NOW HALF HIDDEN UNDER PENDULOUS LIDS,  . . . . .    79 EPHEMERA         V  2
     I SAW THIS HARP ALL SONGLESS LIE,  . . . . . . . . .    85 MAD KING GOLL    V 55
     AND THE YOUNG LIE LONG AND DREAM IN THEIR BED  . . .   150 OLD MOTHER          5
     WHILE THE YOUNG LIE LONG AND DREAM IN THEIR BED  . .   150 OLD MOTHER       V  5
     BUT THE YOUNG LIE LONG AND DREAM IN THEIR BED  . . .   150 OLD MOTHER       V  5
     YOUR BREAST WILL NOT LIE BY THE BREAST  . . . . . .    165 CRY OF SEDGE        9
     YOUR BREAST WILL NOT LIE ON THE BREAST  . . . . . .    165 CRY OF SEDGE     V  9
     BY A SPILLED WINE-CUP LIE.  . . . . . . . . . . . .    168 BLESSED          V 32
     MAY NOT LIE ON THE BREAST NOR HIS LIPS ON THE HAIR  .  177 PAST GREATNESS      9
     WOULD NOT LIE ON THE BREAST, OR HIS LIPS ON THE HAIR,  177 PAST GREATNESS V  9
     THAT WOULD LET THE SPADE LIE,  . . . . . . . . . . .   215 HAPPY TOWNLAND     30
     THAT RUN BEFORE THE REAPING-HOOK AND LIE  . . . . .    218 WOODS OF COOLE     32
     THAT RUN BEFORE THE REAPING HOOK AND LIE  . . . . .    218 WOODS OF COOLE V  32
     THIS SWORD IS TO LIE BESIDE HIM IN THE GRAVE.  . . .   242 SHADOW WATER B    412
     AND ALL THINGS AT ONE COMMON LEVEL LIE.  . . . . . .   265 THESE CLOUDS        6
     WHAT'S THAT BUT TO LIE  . . . . . . . . . . . . . .    310 WITCH               2
     "ALTHOUGH I'D LIE LAPPED UP IN LINEN  . . . . . . .    331 ROUND TOWER         1
     TOO PERFECT AT THE FULL TO LIE IN A CRADLE,  . . . .   374 PHASES OF MOON     60
     DRINKING THE FOUL DITCH WHERE THEY LIE?  . . . . . .   397 POLIT PRISONER     12
     UNLESS THE HOLY WRITINGS LIE,  . . . . . . . . . . .   436 FOR MY SON         28
     SO LIKE A BIT OF STONE I LIE  . . . . . . . . . . .    452 HUMAN DIGNITY       7
     FIVE HUNDRED YEARS AGO, ABOUT IT LIE  . . . . . . .    478 SELF AND SOUL      26
     LIE BODIES OF THE VAMPIRES FULL OF BLOOD:  . . . . .   483 OIL AND BLOOD       5
     WHAT ARE ALL THOSE FISH THAT LIE GASPING ON THE STRAND?  485 THREE MOVEMENT    3
     BUT WERE I LEFT TO LIE ALONE  . . . . . . . . . . .    511 JANE AND JACK      13
     FOR THE HEART CANNOT LIE,  . . . . . . . . . . . . .   516 MANS SONG          14
     PROVE THAT I LIE.  . . . . . . . . . . . . . . . . .   517 HER ANXIETY         6
     PROVE THAT I LIE.  . . . . . . . . . . . . . . . . .   517 HER ANXIETY        12
     ALL THAT WAS SAID IN IRELAND IS A LIE  . . . . . . .   542 PARN FUNERAL 1     26
     UNTIL THE TOWN LIE BEATEN FLAT.  . . . . . . . . . .   565 LAPIS LAZULI        8
     "SO YOU MUST LIE BESIDE HIM  . . . . . . . . . . . .   570 THREE BUSHES       22
     AND I MUST LIE BETWEEN THE SHEETS  . . . . . . . . .   570 THREE BUSHES       40
     TO LIE BETWEEN YOUR FEET?  . . . . . . . . . . . . .   572 LADYS 2ND SONG      2
     FOR SOON WE LIE WHERE HE IS LAID,  . . . . . . . . .   586 PARNELLITES         5
     THOUGH DRUNKARDS LIE AND SNORE.  . . . . . . . . . .   592 DRUNK SOBRIETY      8
     SAID TO THE WOMAN ON HIS KNEES, "LIE STILL.  . . . .   609 IN TARAS HALLS      2
     TO MANY WOMEN I HAVE SAID, "LIE STILL,"  . . . . . .   609 IN TARAS HALLS      6
     I MUST LIE DOWN WHERE ALL THE LADDERS START,  . . .    630 CIRCUS ANIMALS     39
     I LIE AWAKE NIGHT AFTER NIGHT  . . . . . . . . . . .   632 MAN AND ECHO        9
     SLEEPLESS WOULD LIE DOWN AND DIE.  . . . . . . . . .   632 MAN AND ECHO       18
     LIE DOWN AND DIE.  THAT WERE TO SHIRK  . . . . . . .   632 MAN AND ECHO       19
     WHEN WE HALE MEN LIE STRETCHED IN SLUMBER  . . . . .   636 BLACK TOWER        23
     LIE STREWN THE YELLOW LEAVES--THE CLOTTED LEAVES.  .    684 SEEKER             69
     LIE STREWN THE CLOTTED LEAVES--THE DEAD OLD LEAVES.  .  684 SEEKER           V 69
     THOU'RT WELCOME.  LIE THERE CLOSE AGAINST MY FINGERS.  700 MOSADA 3           44
     THAT SICKENING NEAR THEIR MOTHERS LIE:  . . . . . .    717 FAIRY DOCTOR       16
     GIVE ME THE HELM: CALL HITHER THOSE WHO LIE  . . . .   751 SHADOW WATER A     91
     I SWEAR IT, THOUGH I GLADLY WOULD LIE DOWN  . . . . .  758 SHADOW WATER A    225
     THEY ARE GONE, THEY ARE GONE.  THE PROUD MAY LIE BY THE 777 SONG DEIRDRE 3     1
        PROUD.
     AND ALL MEN LIE THAT SAY THAT I  . . . . . . . . . .   789 SINGING HEAD        3
     THEY LIE THAT SAY, IN MOCKERY  . . . . . . . . . . .   789 SINGING HEAD        9
     THEN CLOSE YOUR EARS WITH DUST AND LIE  . . . . . .    791 REPRISALS          23
LIED
     THEIR CHILDREN'S CHILDREN SHALL SAY THEY HAVE LIED.  .  166 EVIL OF BELOV       6
LIES
     LIES FAR."  I MOUNTED, AND SHE BOUND ME  . . . . . .     9 OISIN 1         V 106
     FOR HE IS WEAK AND POOR AND BLIND, AND LIES  . . . .    42 OISIN 2           203
     BLIND AND NIGH DEAF, WITH WITHERED ARMS HE LIES  . .    42 OISIN 2         V 203
     TILL I SAW WHERE MAEVE LIES SLEEPING  . . . . . . .     60 OISIN 3           184
     BEFORE US LIES ETERNITY: OUR SOULS  . . . . . . . .     81 EPHEMERA           23
     THERE LIES A LEAFY ISLAND  . . . . . . . . . . . . .    86 STOLEN CHILD        3
     ONE BLIND HOUND ONLY LIES APART  . . . . . . . . . .    99 FOXHUNTER          41
     "I ONLY ASK WHAT WAY MY JOURNEY LIES,  . . . . . . .   108 CUCHULAIN SEA      31
     "GOD ONLY SEES WHAT DOOM FOR ME LIES STORED."  . . .   110 CUCHULAIN SEA   V  62
     BUT NOW LIES UNDER BOARDS.  . . . . . . . . . . . .    123 DREAM OF DEATH     12
```

LIES   (CONTINUED)
AND THE FRET LIES ON ME.   131 OLD PENSIONER   V   6
AND THE FRET LIES ON ME.   132 OLD PENSIONER   V   18
AND MY BREAST LIES UPON HIS BREAST.   151 HEART OF WOMAN   4
MY HEART UPON HIS WARM HEART LIES,   152 HEART OF WOMAN   11
AND YOU HAVE TOLD ME THAT THEIR JOURNEY LIES   231 SHADOW WATER B   205
WHO, WERE IT PROVED HE LIES,   291 TO A FRIEND   6
LIES ONE LONG SOUGHT   310 WITCH   7
MANY A SON AND DAUGHTER LIES   360 ALF POLLEXFEN   13
SHE LIES, HER LOVELY PITEOUS HEAD AMID DULL RED HAIR   362 HER COURTESY   2
BRING WHERE OUR BEAUTY LIES   362 DOLLS DRAWINGS   1
BY PEN AND PAPER LIES,   421 MY TABLE   3
BUT FEEL THE STRANGE HEART BEATING WHERE IT LIES?   441 LEDA AND SWAN   8
AND FEELS THE STRANGE HEART BEATING WHERE IT LIES!   441 LEDA AND SWAN   V   8
"YOU BUT IMAGINE LIES ALL DAY, O MURDERER," I REPLIED.   450 OWEN AHERNE   17
"AND ALL THOSE LIES HAVE BUT ONE END, POOR WRETCHES TO   450 OWEN AHERNE   18
    BETRAY!
AND SPEAK BUT LIES. CALL UP TO MEMORY   462 HARUN RASHID   V   30
THE BODY OF SAINT TERESA LIES UNDECAYED IN TOMB,   503 VACILLATION   80
LIES IN A CIRCLE ON THE GRASS! THEREIN   555 RIBH AT TOMB   26
AND NOW LIES SUNK IN SLEEP. WHAT CLIMBS THE STAIR?   579 DOR WELLESLEY   11
BUT NOW LIES SUNK IN SLEEP. WHAT CLIMBS THE STAIR?   579 DOR WELLESLEY   V   11
HE TELLS HIS LIES BY ROTE!   598 STONE CROSS   2
A JOURNALIST MAKES UP HIS LIES .   598 STONE CROSS   3
AS LIES DARK WATER IN A MURMUROUS GLADE,   650 ISLE STAT I 1   138
AND NOD TO ONE ANOTHER, LIES A GREEN,   653 ISLE STAT I 2   35
WHEN SHE IN A CAVERN LIES,   658 ISLE STAT I 3   86
LIES TORN AND ROTTING. THE FIERCE KESTREL BIRDS   675 ISLE STAT II 3   234
THE FAERY FLOWER LIES UPON THY LIPS.   677 ISLE STAT II 3   277
THE FAERY BLOSSOM LIES UPON THY LIPS.   677 ISLE STAT II 3   285
THE FAERY BLOSSOM LIES UPON THY LIPS!   678 ISLE STAT II 3   291
WHERE LIES THE LONG-LOST FOREST OF THE SPRITE,   682 SEEKER   23
THERE LIES THE LONG-LOST FOREST OF THE SPRITE,   682 SEEKER   V   23
ABOUT THE SEA. BEFORE HER LIES THAT YOUTH,   687 TWO TITANS   22
WHERE LIES A SHALLOP IN THE YELLOW REEDS.   702 MOSADA 3   77
SAFE ON THE BREAST OF GOMEZ LIES THY HEAD,   703 MOSADA 3   101
AND SEE HOW THICK THE DEW LIES ON MY FACE.   703 MOSADA 3   104
WHERE LIES THE COW AT PEACE BESIDE HER CALF,   715 FERENCZ RENYI   121
LIES A CHILLY FINGER TIP .   732 STREET DANCERS   19
LIES A CHUBBY FINGER-TIP.   732 STREET DANCERS   V 19
LOOK! THERE SHE LIES UNDER A FLAPPING SAIL.   751 SHADOW WATER A   90
A WOMAN LIES AMONG EMBROIDERIES.   752 SHADOW WATER A   120

LIETH
THE GOBLIN FLOWER LIETH ON THY LIPS.   678 ISLE STAT II 3   298

LIEUTENANT
A BROWN LIEUTENANT AND HIS MEN,   424 ROAD AT DOOR   6

LIFE   SEE DEATH-IN-LIFE
BUT NOW TWO THINGS DEVOUR MY LIFE!   24 OISIN 1   358
AND NOW HAVE FALLEN ON MY LIFE .   24 OISIN 1   V 358
UPON THE LIFE THAT FADES AND FLICKERS AND DIES,   29 OISIN 2   12
A JUBILANT LIFE AMONG THE LEAVES, RETURN.   35 OISIN 2   V 89A
. . . WHEN LIFE IN MY BODY HAS CEASED,   63 OISIN 3   222
AND LIFE THE SANDALS OF HER FLEETNESS,   77 INDIAN TO LOVE V   5B
AND LIFE IS OVER SAVE THE MURMUR AND THE SWEETNESS.   77 INDIAN TO LOVE V   5E
I RULED AND RULED MY LIFE WITHIN--   82 MAD KING GOLL   V   7
SHE BID ME TAKE LIFE EASY, AS THE GRASS GROWS ON THE WEIRS!   90 SALLEY GARDENS   7
I SEE MY LIFE GO DRIFTING LIKE A RIVER   104 FERGUS DRUID   31
I SEE MY LIFE GO DRIPPING LIKE A STREAM   104 FERGUS DRUID   V   31
TO IDLE LIFE AWAY, A COMMON HERD."   107 CUCHULAIN SEA   21
TO IDLE LIFE AWAY WITH FLOCKS AND HERDS."   107 CUCHULAIN SEA   V   21
THE FLAMING CIRCLE OF OUR LIFE.   135 TWO TREES   V   16
I AM NO MORE WITH LIFE AND DEATH,   152 HEART OF WOMAN   10
WHO HAD BEEN THE LOVER OF HER MIDDLE LIFE.   183 QUEEN MAEVE   72
"HOW MAY A MORTAL WHOSE LIFE GUTTERS OUT   184 QUEEN MAEVE   85
THAT ALL THIS LIFE CAN GIVE US IS   190 BAILE AILLINN   39
THAT ALL LIFE HAS TO GIVE US IS   190 BAILE AILLINN   V   39
THAT ALL LIFE HAD TO GIVE US IS   190 BAILE AILLINN   V   39
AWAKEN TO LIFE AGAIN.   215 HAPPY TOWNLAND   26
FOR I AM GETTING ON IN LIFE--TO SOMETHING   222 SHADOW WATER B   6
WHERE I AM RID OF LIFE--THE EVENTS OF THE WORLD--   227 SHADOW WATER B   121
WHEN THEY HAVE TWENTY YEARS! IN MIDDLE LIFE   229 SHADOW WATER B   156
OF THAT MORE POWERFUL LIFE? HIS WIFE KNOWS BETTER.   230 SHADOW WATER B   172
HAD THE WORLD'S TOTAL LIFE GATHERED UP, IT SEEMED,   231 SHADOW WATER B   194
YOU'D NEVER DOUBT THAT IT WAS LIFE THEY PROMISED   231 SHADOW WATER B   197
THEY THAT HAVE ALL THE WISDOM THAT'S IN LIFE,   235 SHADOW WATER B   293
HAVING THEIR LIFE IN HIM. THOUGH IT BE THE MOON   240 SHADOW WATER B   377
BUT IN SOME ISLAND WHERE THE LIFE OF THE WORLD   249 SHADOW WATER B   559
HAVE WE NOT EVERYTHING THAT LIFE CAN GIVE   249 SHADOW WATER B   570
THAT LIFE AND LETTERS SEEM   255 WOMAN HOMER   20
"WERE NOT ALL HER LIFE BUT STORM,   259 PEACE   4
THAT HAS MORE LIFE IN IT THAN DEATH,   271 GREY ROCK   8
I'D SAVED HIS LIFE, YET FOR THE SAKE   275 GREY ROCK   102
I'D SAVE HIS LIFE, YET FOR THE SAKE   275 GREY ROCK   V 102
AND LOOSEN ON US DREAMS THAT WASTE OUR LIFE,   281 TWO KINGS   107
THIS HUMAN LIFE BLOTTED FROM MEMORY,   285 TWO KINGS   198
CAN BLOT OUT OF MY MEMORY THIS LIFE   285 TWO KINGS   204
A POOR LIFE, DO WHAT HE CAN,   301 RUN PARADISE   11
I'D HAVE A MERRY LIFE ENOUGH   306 HOUR DAWN   85
FOR ALL LIFE LONGS FOR THE LAST DAY   306 HOUR DAWN   98
MY LIFE OF EVERY PLEASANT THOUGHT   307 HOUR DAWN   110
THE COMMON GOOD OF LIFE.   317 NIGHT COME   5

                                                                    PAGE   TITLE   LINE

LIFE   (CONTINUED)
     A PORTION OF MY MIND AND LIFE, AS IT WERE,   325 ROBERT GREGORY   42
     IN BALANCE WITH THIS LIFE, THIS DEATH.   328 IRISH AIRMAN   16
     HOW HARD A LIFE HER SERVANT LIVES,   336 YOUNG BEAUTY   14
     YOU SING AS ALWAYS OF THE NATURAL LIFE,   342 SHEP GOATHERD   75
     AND, THOUGH YOU HAVE PASSED THE BEST OF LIFE, STILL TRACE,   367 EGO DOMINUS   5
     BEING MOCKED BY GUIDO FOR HIS LECHEROUS LIFE,   369 EGO DOMINUS   33
     OUT OF NO TRAGIC WAR, LOVERS OF LIFE,   369 EGO DOMINUS   39
     PLANNED IN A GOVERNMENT OFFICE, SHORTEN HIS LIFE,   372 ON GOING HOUSE   15
     JUST TRUTH ENOUGH TO SHOW THAT HIS WHOLE LIFE   373 PHASES OF MOON   22
     FOR THERE'S NO HUMAN LIFE AT THE FULL OR THE DARK.   373 PHASES OF MOON   35
     BECAUSE YOU ARE FORGOTTEN, HALF OUT OF LIFE,   376 PHASES OF MOON   96
     O NOT SINCE LIFE BEGAN.   382 VISION ROBART   8
     THAT, IT MAY BE, HAD DANCED HER LIFE AWAY,   383 VISION ROBART   22
     THAT IT MAYBE HAD DANCED HER LIFE AWAY,   383 VISION ROBART   V 22
     AN IMAGE FROM A PAST LIFE   389 IMAGE PAST   T
     A SWEETHEART FROM ANOTHER LIFE FLOATS THERE   390 IMAGE PAST   22
     HELEN BEING CHOSEN FOUND LIFE FLAT AND DULL   404 FOR DAUGHTER   25
     DEATH AND LIFE WERE NOT   415 TOWER   148
     LIFE OVERFLOWS WITHOUT AMBITIOUS PAINS;   417 ANCEST HOUSES   3
     AND RAINS DOWN LIFE UNTIL THE BASIN SPILLS,   417 ANCEST HOUSES   4
     LIFE SCARCE CAN CAST A FRAGRANCE ON THE WIND,   422 MY DESCENDANTS   5
     BEFORE THAT BRIEF GLEAM OF ITS LIFE BE GONE,   430 NINETEEN 19   63
     WHAT MY LABORIOUS LIFE IMAGINED, EVEN   431 NINETEEN 19   82
     ENDURE WHAT LIFE GOD GIVES AND ASK NO LONGER SPAN;   459 FROM OEDIPUS   1
     I CELEBRATE THE SILENT KISS THAT ENDS SHORT LIFE OR LONG.   459 FROM OEDIPUS   9
     NEVER TO HAVE DRAWN THE BREATH OF LIFE,   459 FROM OEDIPUS   11
     NEVER TO HAVE DRUNK THE BREATH OF LIFE,   459 FROM OEDIPUS   V 11
     SO STRAINS TO LOOK BEYOND OUR LIFE, AN EYE   465 HARUN RASHID   87
     BEING ALL BRIMMED WITH LIFE?" "WERE IT BUT TRUE   465 HARUN RASHID   90
     I WOULD HAVE FOUND THE BEST THAT LIFE CAN GIVE,   465 HARUN RASHID   91
     MUST NEEDS BE IN THIS LIFE AND IN WHAT FOLLOWS   465 HARUN RASHID   95
     SO LONGS TO LOOK BEYOND OUR LIFE, AN EYE   465 HARUN RASHID   V 87
     BEING SO BRIMMED WITH LIFE. "IF THAT COULD BE   465 HARUN RASHID   V 90
     AND YET AGAIN, IF IT BE LIFE TO PITCH   479 SELF AND SOUL   58
     A SOMETHING INCOMPATIBLE WITH LIFE; AND POWER,   482 BLOOD AND MOON   50
     SEEMED ONCE MORE DEAR THAN LIFE; ANCESTRAL TREES,   491 COOLE BALLYLEE   34
     PERFECTION OF THE LIFE, OR OF THE WORK,   491 COOLE BALLYLEE V   40B
     PERFECTION OF THE LIFE, OR OF THE WORK,   495 CHOICE   2
     FOUND ALL THE PLEASURE THAT LIFE GAVE";   521 THREE THINGS   11
     BY MANIFOLD ILLUSION; BUT MAN'S LIFE IS THOUGHT,   563 MERU   3
     HER EIGHTIETH WINTER APPROACHING. "YESTERDAY HE THREATENED
          MY LIFE.   578 LOFTY THINGS   8
     OR DEMONSTRATE IN MY OWN LIFE   605 YOU CONTENT   21
     MORE DREAD THE LIFE THAT WE LIVE,   615 MARCH SONGS 2   15
     A MOUTHFUL HELD THE EXTREME OF LIFE AND DEATH.   619 BRONZE HEAD   14
     A MOUTHFUL HOLD THE EXTREME OF LIFE AND DEATH.   619 BRONZE HEAD   V 14
     "YOUR LIFE CAN GROW MUCH SWEETER IF YOU WILL   634 CUCHULAIN COMF   12
     ON LIFE, ON DEATH.   640 BEN BULBEN   93
     THE WARMTH OF LIFE IS CHILLING, AND THE SHADOWS GROW   675 ISLE STAT II 3   232
     LIFE.   686 LIFE   T
     OF OCEAN FAN THEE INTO LIFE, AND FOLD   688 TWO TITANS   56
     WILL HE NOT SPARE HER LIFE? HOW WOULD ONE MATTER   696 MOSADA 2   3
     IF PETER WOULD BUT ASK HER LIFE--WHO KNOWS?   696 MOSADA 2   17
     "NOW ANSWER, IF THIS LIFE BE DEAR TO THEE,   713 FERENCZ RENYI   V 83
     SO MEN IN LIFE AND I IN MAGIC PLAY;   722 WITCH VIVIEN   55
     LIFE   734 QUATRAIN APHOR V   T
     AND NEED NO MORE OF LIFE TILL THE WHITE WINGS   751 SHADOW WATER A   102
     WOULD END THIS PEACEFUL LIFE THAT ROTS THE BONES,   752 SHADOW WATER A   110
     AND WHILE SHE FADES AND LIFE WITHERS AWAY,   768 SHADOW WATER A   422
     HAD WOVEN HER OF WIND. LIFE WITHERS OUT   768 SHADOW WATER A V   423
     O, WHAT IS LIFE BUT A MOUTHFUL OF AIR?   788 HAWTHORN TREE   9
LIFE-IN-DEATH
     I CALL IT DEATH-IN-LIFE AND LIFE-IN-DEATH.   497 BYZANTIUM   16
LIFE-KEY
     OR DEATH THAT COMETH WITH THE NEXT LIFE-KEY?   724 KANVA ON SELF   18
LIFELESS
     NEIGHING ALONG THE LIFELESS WASTE;   13 OISIN 1   170
LIFE'S
     WHOSE LIPS HAD LIFE'S MOST PROSPEROUS GLOW?   10 OISIN 1   118
     AS 'TWERE ALL LIFE'S EPITOME.   327 ROBERT GREGORY   87
     THAT OUT OF LIFE'S OWN SELF-DELIGHT HAD SPRUNG   417 ANCEST HOUSES   11
     THAT OUT OF LIFE'S OWN SELF DELIGHT HAD SPRUNG   417 ANCEST HOUSES   V 11
     HERE AT LIFE'S END   575 ACRE OF GRASS   8
     NOR, GAZING FORTH WHERE LIFE'S SAD SICKLES REAP,   710 FERENCZ RENYI   31
LIFETIME
     THE REPUTATION OF HIS LIFETIME LOST   351 PEOPLE   5
LIFT
     BUT LIFT A MOURNFUL ULALU,   86 MAD KING GOLL   68
     AND LIFT AN ULULU FORLORN,   86 MAD KING GOLL   V 68
     AND ON THESE HANDS THAT MAY NOT LIFT THE SWORD,   103 FERGUS DRUID   24
     YOUNG MAN, LIFT UP YOUR RUSSET BROW,   125 GOES FERGUS   4
     AND LIFT YOUR TENDER EYELIDS, MAID,   125 GOES FERGUS   5
     LIFT UP BEFORE US WHEN THEY PASS,   135 TWO TREES   23
     LIFT UP BEFORE US AS THEY PASS,   135 TWO TREES   V 23
     AND THEY SIGH IF THE WIND BUT LIFT A TRESS;   151 OLD MOTHER   8
     AND THEY SIGH IF THE WIND BUT LIFT UP A TRESS;   151 OLD MOTHER   V 8
     YOU NEED BUT LIFT A PEARL-PALE HAND,   158 BELOVED RHYMES   7
     AND LIFT UP AN OLD HORN   215 HAPPY TOWNLAND   49
     THAT I WILL NEVER LIFT A HAND AGAINST YOU.   227 SHADOW WATER B   108
     TOO MANY YEARS TO LIFT A HAND AGAINST YOU.   227 SHADOW WATER B   111

451

LIFT   (CONTINUED)
   THAT LIFT US TO THE FLOWING, CHANGING WORLD . . . . . . 230 SHADOW WATER B   182
   O WHY DO YOU NOT LIFT YOUR EYES TO MINE? . . . . 246 SHADOW WATER B   498
   I LIFT THE GLASS TO MY MOUTH, ... 261 DRINKING SONG   5
   STAND UP AND LIFT YOUR HAND AND BLESS . . . . 379 SAINT HUNCH   1
   THAT WOULD NOT LIFT A HAND MAYBE . . . . 432 NINETEEN 19   109
   THAT WOULD NOT LIFT A HAND MAY BE . . . . 432 NINETEEN 19   V 109
   LIFT, EVERY MOTHER'S SON. . . . . 548 TO SAME TUNE 3 V   15
   LIFT, LIFT, LIFT UP THE TUNE. . . . . 548 TO SAME TUNE 3 V   16
   LIFT, LIFT, LIFT UP THE TUNE. . . . . 548 TO SAME TUNE 3 V   16
   LIFT, LIFT, LIFT UP THE TUNE. . . . . 548 TO SAME TUNE 3 V   16
   MARCH, MARCH, LIFT UP THE SONG! . . . . 549 TO SAME TUNE 3   26
   LIFT, LIFT, LIFT UP THE SONG. . . . . 549 TO SAME TUNE 3 V   26
   LIFT, LIFT, LIFT UP THE SONG. . . . . 549 TO SAME TUNE 3 V   26
   LIFT, LIFT, LIFT UP THE SONG. . . . . 549 TO SAME TUNE 3 V   26
   LIFT MY SOUL FROM RAYLESS NIGHT-- . . . . 648 ISLE STAT I 1   95
   I TRY TO LIFT MINE ARMS--THEY FALL AGAIN. . . . . . 701 MOSADA 3   56
   LIFT THEIR CHINS AND TOSS THEIR CURLS, ... 726 LOVERS QUARREL   23
   LIFT THEIR CHINS AND TURN AWAY. . . . . 726 LOVERS QUARREL   24
LIFTED
   LIFTED THE DOME, WHERE FACE IN CARVEN FACE . . . . .   39 OISIN 1   V 145
   HALF WAKENING, WE LIFTED OUR EYELIDS. . . . .   54 OISIN 3   100
   LORD OF THE CROZIERS, YOU EVEN HAD LIFTED YOUR HANDS AND   54 OISIN 3   110
    WEPT!
   HALF-WAKENING, WE LIFTED OUR EYELIDS, ...   54 OISIN 3   V 100
   LORD OF THE CROSIERS, THOU EVEN HADST LIFTED THY HANDS   54 OISIN 3   V 110
    AND WEPT!
   CAME AFTER THE HARD GAZE OF YOUTH, OR AN OLD MAN LIFTED   59 OISIN 3   170
    HIS HEAD!
   . . . OR WAS LIFTED AN OLD MAN'S MILD HEAD. . . . .   59 OISIN 3   V 170
   . . . THEY LIFTED AND SHOULDERED A SACK FULL OF SAND, . .   60 OISIN 3   V 185
   LIFTED THE CURTAIN OF HER SLEEPING-ROOM, ... 182 QUEEN MAEVE   63
   LIFTED THE CURTAIN OF HER SLEEPING ROOM, ... 182 QUEEN MAEVE   V 63
   TILL THAT BE TUMBLED THAT WAS LIFTED HIGH . . . . . 265 THESE CLOUDS   4
   ALL THOSE HAD LIFTED UP THE DIM . . . . 272 GREY ROCK   27
   HAND LIFTED UP THAT BLEST! . . . . 383 VISION ROBART   20
   FROM HAYNAU'S LIFTED FINGERS--TWO DRAW NIGH . . . . 714 FERENCZ RENYI   104
   WERE THEY BUT LIFTED UP. THE RED HOUND IS FLED. . . . 761 SHADOW WATER A   266
LIFTING   SEE NEVER-LIFTING
   HELPLESS, MEN LIFTING THE LIDS OF HIS WEARY . . . .   53 OISIN 3   92
    AND DEATH-MAKING EYE.
   HELPLESS, MEN LIFTING THE LIDS OF HIS WEARY . . . .   53 OISIN 3   V 92
    AND DEATH-POURING EYE.
   FOR REMEMBRANCE, LIFTING HER LEANNESS, ...   57 OISIN 3   152
   LIFTING HIS DELICATE FEET. . . . . 378 CAT AND MOON   10
LIFTS
   LIFTS SLOW HIS WINTRY HEAD! . . . .   99 FOXHUNTER   46
   AND LIFTS HIS DELICATE FEET. . . . . 378 CAT AND MOON   V 10
   AND LIFTS TO THE CHANGING MOON . . . . 379 CAT AND MOON   27
   A NEIGHBOURING CRICKET LIFTS HIS SHRILLY SHOUT . . . . 711 FERENCZ RENYI   45
   HAYNAU, THE MAN OF SYSTEM, LIFTS HIS HAND . . . . . 712 FERENCZ RENYI   62
   YON BAUBLE OF THE HEAVENS, HE LIFTS HIS HANDS, ... 715 FERENCZ RENYI   119
LIGHT   SEE STAR-LIGHT TORCH-LIGHT CANDLE-LIGHT HALF-LIGHT
   PIERCED WITH SOFT LIGHT THE SHALLOWING DEEPS. . . . .   13 OISIN 1   164
   LIKE DROPS OF FROZEN RAINBOW LIGHT, ...   14 OISIN 1   183
   HUNG, LIKE METEORS OF RED LIGHT, ...   21 OISIN 1   V 306
   UNDER THE GOLDEN EVENING LIGHT, ...   25 OISIN 1   385
   THE ISLE LOOMED LARGELY IN THE LIGHT . . . .   25 OISIN 1   V 385
   THE ODOROUS WEIGHT OF HIS CURLS OF LIGHT, ...   28 OISIN 1   V 423D
   THE MIST CLOSED ROUND US! PEARLY LIGHT . . . . . .   28 OISIN 1   V 427C
   I LAY, AS OVER SEA THE LIGHT HOOVES GLANCED . . . .   30 OISIN 2   V 19A
   AND SURGING PHOSPHORUS ALONE GAVE LIGHT . . . . . .   31 OISIN 2   33
   OF SURGING PHOSPHORUS ALONE GAVE LIGHT. . . . . . .   31 OISIN 2   V 33
   AND THROUGH THEIR EYES NO LIGHT OF MOON OR DAY . . . .   34 OISIN 2   77
   GOES DROPPING FROM HIS EYES A LANGUID LIGHT, ...   34 OISIN 2   V 81A
   AND CAME AGAIN, HOLDING A SECOND LIGHT . . . . . .   37 OISIN 2   124
   AWHILE, AND CAME AGAIN, A SECOND LIGHT . . . . . .   37 OISIN 2   V 124
   WITH A PALE LIGHT, I JOURNEYED ROUND THE HALL . . . .   39 OISIN 2   153
   WHILE HIGH FRAIL CLOUDLETS, FED WITH A GREEN LIGHT, . . .   40 OISIN 2   165
   DAWN PASSIONED, FED WITH A FAINT GREEN LIGHT, ...   40 OISIN 2   V 165
   LIGHT IS MAN'S LOVE, AND LIGHTER IS MAN'S RAGE! . . . .   45 OISIN 2   243
   CEASED ON OUR HANDS AND OUR FACES, ON HAZEL AND OAK LEAF,   48 OISIN 3   23
    THE LIGHT.
   SOUNDLESS SHALL BE THE FOOTFALL LIGHT . . . . . .   70 CLOAK BOAT   13
   SUDDEN AND LIGHT." . . . .   70 CLOAK BOAT   15
   MY SPIRIT ROCKED IN EVENING LIGHT, THE RUSHES ROUND MY   76 INDIAN ON GOD   2
    KNEES,
   HIS LANGUID TAIL ABOVE US, LIT WITH MYRIAD SPOTS OF LIGHT.   77 INDIAN ON GOD   20
   THE DIM GREY SANDS WITH LIGHT, ...   87 STOLEN CHILD   14
   A GREEN DROP IN THE SURGE, A GLEAM OF LIGHT . . . . 104 FERGUS DRUID   33
   GO THERE, AND LIGHT A CAMP-FIRE AT WOOD'S RIM! . . . . 108 CUCHULAIN SEA   35
   GO THERE, AND LIGHT A CAMP FIRE AT WOOD'S RIM! . . . . 108 CUCHULAIN SEA   V 35
   HAVE DOWERED THE STARS WITH MERRY LIGHT! . . . . . 134 TWO TREES   6
   TO LIGHT A MEASURE HERE AND THERE. . . . . 138 TO IRELAND   14
   THE LIGHT FALL OF HER FLYING FEET . . . . 138 TO IRELAND   V 11
   TO HELP HER LIGHT FOOT HERE AND THERE. . . . . . . 138 TO IRELAND   V 14
   LIVE BUT TO LIGHT YOUR PASSING FEET. . . . . 158 BELOVED RHYMES   12
   OF A QUIET AND LIGHT FOOTFALL. . . . . 159 CAP AND BELLS   8
   ON A FOOT-FALL HUSHED AND LIGHT, ... 159 CAP AND BELLS   V 8
   OF A FOOTFALL HUSHED AND LIGHT, ... 159 CAP AND BELLS   V 8
   OF A QUIET AND LIGHT FOOT-FALL! . . . . 159 CAP AND BELLS   V 8

	PAGE	TITLE		LINE
LIGHT (CONTINUED)				
AND THE GIRDLE OF LIGHT IS UNBOUND,	165	CRY OF SEDGE		8
AND HURLED IT FROM ITS PLACE AMID THE PEARLY LIGHT	174	ELEMENT POWERS	V	3
AS THE LIGHT ON THE SEA,	175	ELEMENT POWERS	V	14
AND LIGHT WERE PALING OUT OF THE WEST,	175	BELOVED DEAD	V	2
ENWROUGHT WITH GOLDEN AND SILVER LIGHT,	176	CLOTHS HEAVEN		2
OF NIGHT AND LIGHT AND THE HALF-LIGHT,	176	CLOTHS HEAVEN		4
OF NIGHT AND LIGHT AND THE HALF-LIGHT,	176	CLOTHS HEAVEN	V	4
OF NIGHT AND LIGHT AND THE HALF LIGHT,	176	CLOTHS HEAVEN	V	4
SHE FOLLOWED WITH LIGHT FOOTFALL IN THE MIDST,	186	QUEEN MAEVE		128
AND IN THE LIGHT BODIES OF BIRDS	190	BAILE AILLINN		44
AND AMID LEAFY LIGHT HE CRIED,	193	BAILE AILLINN	V	113
TALL, PROUD AND RUDDY, AND LIGHT WINGS	195	BAILE AILLINN		140
SCALE RUBBING SCALE WHERE LIGHT IS DIM	195	BAILE AILLINN		145
OF MORNING LIGHT IN A DIM SKY!	195	BAILE AILLINN		150
BUT LIGHT FROM THE PALE STARS, AND GLEAMS	196	BAILE AILLINN		173
AWAKEN WANDERINGS OF LIGHT AIR	197	BAILE AILLINN		185
WIND AND UNWIND THEIR DANCES WHEN THE LIGHT GROWS COOL	203	WITHER BOUGHS		13
WIND AND UNWIND DANCING WHEN THE LIGHT GROWS COOL	203	WITHER BOUGHS	V	13
LAND-UNDER-WAVE, WHERE OUT OF THE MOON'S LIGHT AND THE SUN'S	209	UNDER THE MOON		6
AND DO YOU GATHER ABOUT US WHEN PALE LIGHT	218	WOODS OF COOLE		37
EVEN THOUGH IT BE THE LIGHTEST OF LIGHT LOVE,	230	SHADOW WATER B		184
SHALL LIGHT UPON A PLACE IN THE WORLD'S CORE,	231	SHADOW WATER B		212
"HOW LIGHT WE ARE, NOW WE ARE CHANGED TO BIRDS!"	233	SHADOW WATER B		253
OUR HEART'S DESIRE NOW THAT WE ARE SO LIGHT."	233	SHADOW WATER B		255
THAT IN THE BLINDING LIGHT BEYOND THE GRAVE	258	KING NO KING		12
THE GREY ROCK AND THE WINDY LIGHT?	275	GREY ROCK		111
AND WHERE BEECH-TREES HAD MIXED A PALE GREEN LIGHT	277	TWO KINGS		5
BETWEEN THE PALE GREEN LIGHT OF THE BEECH LEAVES	277	TWO KINGS	V	5
WHERE CERTAIN BEECHES MIXED A PALE GREEN LIGHT	277	TWO KINGS	V	5
AND WHERE BEECH TREES HAD MIXED A PALE GREEN LIGHT	277	TWO KINGS	V	5
AND THE GROUND IVY'S BLUER LIGHT, A STAG	277	TWO KINGS	V	6
SHOWED THEIR FAINT LIGHT THROUGH THE UNSHUTTERED WINDOWS,	279	TWO KINGS		50
IN THE HALF LIGHT, AND RUNS TO ITS OWN DOOR	279	TWO KINGS	V	45C
AS ON THE BLUE LIGHT OF A SWORD, A MAN	283	TWO KINGS		148
AMONG THE STONES AND THORN-TREES, UNDER MORNING LIGHT!	291	PAUDEEN		3
AMONG THE STONES AND THORN TREES, UNDER MORNING LIGHT,	291	PAUDEEN	V	3
TILL EVEN I SLEEP LIGHT! BUT WHO	303	HOUR DAWN		34
SO THAT IT SEEMS EVEN I SLEEP LIGHT!	303	HOUR DAWN	V	34
TO JUDGE IF A LIGHT SLEEPING FOOL	304	HOUR DAWN	V	52
AND VANITY HER FOOTFALL LIGHT,	314	MEMORY YOUTH		12
RIDDLED WITH LIGHT. AH! WHEN THE GHOST BEGINS TO QUICKEN,	316	COLD HEAVEN		9
IF HEAD AND LIMB HAVE BEAUTY AND THE INSTEP'S HIGH AND LIGHT	354	HIS PHOENIX		21
THAT IS OUR MODERN HOPE, AND BY ITS LIGHT	368	EGO DOMINUS		11
AND THE LIGHT PROVES THAT HE IS READING STILL,	373	PHASES OF MOON		11
THE LONELY LIGHT THAT SAMUEL PALMER ENGRAVED,	373	PHASES OF MOON		17
BECAUSE, IT MAY BE, OF THE CANDLE LIGHT	373	PHASES OF MOON	V	14
WHEN ALL IS FED WITH LIGHT AND HEAVEN IS BARE,	375	PHASES OF MOON		74
BECAUSE ALL DARK, LIKE THOSE THAT ARE ALL LIGHT,	376	PHASES OF MOON		104
THE LIGHT IN THE TOWER WINDOW WAS PUT OUT,	377	PHASES OF MOON		139
THE PURE COLD LIGHT IN THE SKY	378	CAT AND MOON		7
I SAW BY THE MOON'S LIGHT	383	VISION ROBART		27
THAT DRAGON THROUGH THE FADING LIGHT,	385	ROBARTES DANCE		4
THOUGH SEVERAL, ARE A SINGLE LIGHT,	388	SOLOMON WITCH		29
FOR THE PROSAIC LIGHT OF DAY—	411	TOWER		46
WHEN THE HEADLONG LIGHT IS LOOSE,	414	TOWER		135
VALLEY, RIVER, AND ELMS, UNDER THE LIGHT OF A MOON	426	PHANTOM HATRED		3
VALLEY, RIVER, ELMS, UNDER THE LIGHT OF A MOON	426	PHANTOM HATRED	V	3
BUT THOSE THE CANDLES LIGHT ARE NOT AS THOSE	445	SCHOOL CHILDR		50
SINCE FIRST WE SAW THE LIGHT,	456	SUMMER SPRING		4
TAKE THIS LIGHT PARCHMENT, PASS THROUGH THE GREAT CHAMBER	461	HARUN RASHID	V	5
PICK OUT MY FEATURES IN SUCH LIGHT AND SHADE	466	HARUN RASHID		116
OR DID THE TORCH LIGHT OF THAT MYSTERY	466	HARUN RASHID	V	115
AND FEARING THAT MY LIGHT DISTURBED HER SLEEP	467	HARUN RASHID		130
AND WROTE BY CANDLE LIGHT! BUT HER FORM MOVED	467	HARUN RASHID	V	129
THE LIGHT OF EVENING, LISSADELL,	475	EVA GORE-BOOTH		1
CROSS THE NARROW STRAITS TO LIGHT	494	AT ALGECIRAS		4
CROSSES THE NARROW STRAITS TO LIGHT	494	AT ALGECIRAS	V	4
CROSS THOSE NARROW STRAITS TO LIGHT	494	AT ALGECIRAS	V	4
SHALL LEAP INTO THE LIGHT LOST	511	JANE AND JACK		11
WENT IN THE DAWNING LIGHT	512	JANE ON GOD		3
NATURE'S PURE UNCHANGING LIGHT?	529	TOM LUNATIC		6
THAT LIGHT IS FROM THE MOON.	536	PARTING		11
FOR THE INTERCOURSE OF ANGELS IS A LIGHT	555	RIBH AT TOMB		15
MADE AQUILINE, ARE OPEN TO THAT LIGHT.	555	RIBH AT TOMB		24
THOUGH SOMEWHAT BROKEN BY THE LEAVES, THAT LIGHT	555	RIBH AT TOMB		25
THAT IS A LIGHT MY JEALOUS SOUL HAS SENT.	558	RIBH CHRISTIAN		8
"HIS LIGHT HAD STRUCK ME BLIND	559	HE AND SHE		5
THE GREATER GROWS MY LIGHT	559	HE AND SHE		9
HECTOR IS DEAD AND THERE'S A LIGHT IN TROY!	564	GYRES		7
BUT A WILD OLD MAN IN THE LIGHT.	589	OLD WICKED MAN		38
AS THOUGH WITH MAGNANIMITY OF LIGHT,	618	BRONZE HEAD		9
I, THROUGH THE TERRIBLE NOVELTY OF LIGHT, STALK ON, STALK ON!	623	HIGH TALK		13
WHILE THE WORLD IS ROLL'D IN LIGHT.	646	ISLE STAT I 1		29
PASSETH THE MOON WITH HER SICKLE OF LIGHT,	648	ISLE STAT I 1		82
MUSIC OF MY SOUL AND LIGHT—	648	ISLE STAT I 1		97
SAD LADY OF THE DEEP, POURS DOWN HER LIGHT!	650	ISLE STAT I 1		127
GOES FLICKERING IN REVERBERATED LIGHT.	653	ISLE STAT I 2		53

453

	PAGE	TITLE		LINE

LIGHT (CONTINUED)
THE LIGHT IS DANCING O'ER THE KNOTTED TREES,　•　•　•　•　•　662 ISLE STAT II 2　　2
AND SEE AGAIN THE HAPPY WOODLAND LIGHT,　•　•　•　•　•　•　664 ISLE STAT II 2　　58
SOUNDLESS SHALL BE THE FOOTFALL LIGHT　•　•　•　•　•　•　•　666 ISLE STAT II 3　　13
SUDDEN AND LIGHT.　•　•　•　•　•　•　•　•　•　•　•　•　•　666 ISLE STAT II 3　　15
AS LIGHT OF TRIUMPH IN THY GOBLIN EYES--　•　•　•　•　•　674 ISLE STAT II 3　　199
THOSE TWAIN ARE DUST. WAKE! LIGHT AS A BEE SIPS　•　•　678 ISLE STAT II 3　　290
OF ASIAN RIVERS, ROLLING ON IN LIGHT.　•　•　•　•　•　•　682 SEEKER　　20
OF INDIA'S RIVERS, ROLLING ON IN LIGHT.　•　•　•　•　•　•　682 SEEKER　　V　20
TO LIGHTEST OF LIGHT THINGS ALL SANCTITY.　•　•　•　•　•　686 DRAWING-ROOM　　8
BRUISING THE DARKNESS WITH THEIR CRACKLING LIGHT!　•　•　687 TWO TITANS　　2
FROM FASTING--SEE, THE RED LIGHT SLANTING DOWN　•　•　•　697 MOSADA 2　　36
THE HONEY-HEARTED LEISURE OF THE LIGHT,　•　•　•　•　•　705 REMEMBRANCE　　7
OF HER HE LOVED FIXED ON HIM FULL OF LIGHT,　•　•　•　•　710 FERENCZ RENYI　　27
HIGHER AND HIGHER GOLD WITH EVENING LIGHT!　•　•　•　•　714 FERENCZ RENYI　　113
WITHOUT THERE OF A LITTLE, LIGHT OLD MAN!　•　•　•　•　•　720 WITCH VIVIEN　　13
THAT WATCH ME WITH THEIR SUPPLIANT LIGHT--　•　•　•　•　723 GIRLS SONG A　　10
BY A WINDOW'S FEEBLE LIGHT　•　•　•　•　•　•　•　•　•　•　731 STREET DANCERS　　3
SINGING TO THEIR LIGHT FOOTFALL.　•　•　•　•　•　•　•　•　732 STREET DANCERS　　30
DROPPING LIQUID RAINBOW LIGHT,　•　•　•　•　•　•　•　•　732 STREET DANCERS　　33
TO LIGHTEST OF ALL LIGHT THINGS SANCTITY.　•　•　•　•　734 QUATRAIN APHOR　　8
TO LIGHTEST OF LIGHT THINGS ALL SANCTITY.　•　•　•　•　734 QUATRAIN APHOR　V　8
A HURTING BEAM OF LIGHT,　•　•　•　•　•　•　•　•　•　•　741 EARL PAUL　　38
A HURTING GLEAM OF LIGHT,　•　•　•　•　•　•　•　•　•　741 EARL PAUL　　V　38
WHEN FLYING TO THE HEART OF LIGHT　•　•　•　•　•　•　742 DANAAN QUICK　　8
"HOW LIGHT WE ARE NOW WE ARE CHANGED TO BIRDS!"　•　•　•　753 SHADOW WATER A　　143
OUR HEARTS' DESIRE NOW THAT WE ARE SO LIGHT."　•　•　753 SHADOW WATER A　　145
WHILE THE WIND IS LIGHT. THE OAR CAN HARDLY MOVE HER,　•　754 SHADOW WATER A　　157
WHERE THE MOON MAKES A CLOUDY LIGHT IN THE MIST.　•　•　764 SHADOW WATER A　　329
THE LOVE OF ALL UNDER THE LIGHT OF THE SUN　•　•　•　765 SHADOW WATER A　　353
WITH LIGHT IMAGES OF CLAY　•　•　•　•　•　•　•　•　•　775 AGAINST WITCH　　12
ACCURSED WHO BRINGS TO LIGHT OF DAY　•　•　•　•　•　779 ACCURSED WHO　　1
DIMMED AT THREE-QUARTER LIGHT,　•　•　•　•　•　•　•　•　786 YOUR HEART　　32
DIMMED AT THREE QUARTER LIGHT　•　•　•　•　•　•　•　•　786 YOUR HEART　　V　32
LIGHTED
BUT OUR HEARTS ARE LIGHTED FROM THE FLAME IN THE EYES　•　•　207 HANRAHANS SONG　V　9
ITS OPEN LIGHTED DOORWAY AND ITS WINDOWS ALL ALIGHT,　•　•　581 CURSE CROMWELL　　26
AS THOUGH UPON A LIGHTED SCREEN,　•　•　•　•　•　•　•　626 OLD MEN BE MAD　　12
'LIGHTED
AND WHERE OUR FOOTFALL 'LIGHTED LAST THERE CAME　•　•　•　•　37 OISIN 2　　V　119
LIGHT-ENDAPPLED
O'ER THE GRASS LIGHT-ENDAPPLED　•　•　•　•　•　•　•　•　•　•　654 ISLE STAT I 2　　63
LIGHTENED
AT TIMES OUR SLUMBER WAS LIGHTENED.　•　•　•　•　•　•　53 OISIN 3　　97
LIGHTER
BUT THE TALE, THOUGH WORDS BE LIGHTER THAN AIR,　•　•　•　•　3 OISIN 1　　11
LIGHT IS MAN'S LOVE, AND LIGHTER IS MAN'S RAGE!　•　•　45 OISIN 2　　243
WITH WORDS LIGHTER THAN AIR,　•　•　•　•　•　•　•　•　162 ASKS FORGIVE　　2
TROD WITH A LIGHTER TREAD.　•　•　•　•　•　•　•　•　•　323 SWANS AT COOLE　　18
LIGHTEST
EVEN THOUGH IT BE THE LIGHTEST OF LIGHT LOVE,　•　•　•　•　230 SHADOW WATER B　　184
TO LIGHTEST OF LIGHT THINGS ALL SANCTITY.　•　•　•　•　•　686 DRAWING-ROOM　　8
TO LIGHTEST OF ALL LIGHT THINGS SANCTITY.　•　•　•　•　734 QUATRAIN APHOR　　8
TO LIGHTEST OF LIGHT THINGS ALL SANCTITY.　•　•　•　•　734 QUATRAIN APHOR　V　8
'LIGHTING
AMONG THEM 'LIGHTING FROM OUR STEED,　•　•　•　•　•　•　14 OISIN 1　　V　193
LIGHTLESS
AND IN HER EYES A LIGHTLESS STARE,　•　•　•　•　•　•　668 ISLE STAT II 3　　60
LIGHTLY
AND SANG WE LIGHTLY TO EACH BLOOM　•　•　•　•　•　•　•　21 OISIN 1　　V 306B
BRUSH LIGHTLY AS HAYMOUSE EARTH'S PEBBLES,　•　•　•　•　56 OISIN 3　　128
BRUSH LIGHTLY AS HAY MOUSE EARTH'S PEBBLES,　•　•　•　56 OISIN 3　　V　128
THEY WEIGHED SO LIGHTLY WHAT THEY GAVE.　•　•　•　•　•　•　290 SEPTEMBER 1913　　30
"O WORDS ARE LIGHTLY SPOKEN,"　•　•　•　•　•　•　•　•　396 ROSE TREE　　1
WITH THEIR MUSHROOMS LIGHTLY THREADED　•　•　•　•　•　705 DAWN-SONG　　13
O SHINING ONES, LIGHTLY WITH SONG PASS,　•　•　•　•　•　708 FAIRY PEDANT　　21
LIGHTNESS
AND LOSS OF YOUR LAUGH AND ITS LIGHTNESS--　•　•　•　•　•　708 FAIRY PEDANT　　33
LIGHTNING
ARE CHOKED WITH THUNDER, LIGHTNING, AND FIERCE WIND,　•　•　42 OISIN 2　　205
AND LIGHTNING FLASH FOR EVER? CEASE AND HEAR.　•　•　•　42 OISIN 2　　V　207
NOW WORDS THAT CALLED UP THE LIGHTNING　•　•　•　•　•　171 MAID QUIET　　7
FOR THE WORDS THAT CALLED UP THE LIGHTNING　•　•　•　•　171 MAID QUIET　　V　7
WITH LIGHTNING, YOU WENT FROM ME, AND I COULD FIND　•　•　257 RECONCILIATION　　4
"THAT SOME STREAM OF LIGHTNING　•　•　•　•　•　•　•　•　589 OLD WICKED MAN　　55
AN OLD GHOST'S THOUGHTS ARE LIGHTNING,　•　•　•　•　•　600 SPIRIT MEDIUM　　17
AND WHEN ONCE MORE THE LIGHTNING GENII PASSED,　•　•　•　687 TWO TITANS　　29
WHEN FLASH ON FLASH ONCE MORE THE LIGHTNING CAME,　•　•　•　688 TWO TITANS　　39
FLAMES THE SHUTTLE OF THE LIGHTNING ACROSS THE DRIVING
  SLEET,　718 PHANTOM SHIP　　1
HALF DIZZY WITH THE LIGHTNING THERE RUNS A GATHERING BAND--　718 PHANTOM SHIP　　9
NOW HALF DIZZY WITH THE LIGHTNING THERE RUNS A GATHERING
  BAND!　718 PHANTOM SHIP　　V　9
LIGHTNINGS
STABLING HIS UNLOOSED LIGHTNINGS IN THEIR STALL,　•　•　•　•　36 OISIN 2　　110
THE VISION OF A ROCK WHERE LIGHTNINGS WHIRL'D　•　•　•　687 TWO TITANS　　1
THE LIGHTNINGS PULSE--BEHOLD HER, AYE BEHOLD--　•　•　•　687 TWO TITANS　　11
LIGHT-OBLITERATING
THROUGH LIGHT-OBLITERATING GARDEN FOLIAGE WHAT MAGIC DRUM?　560 MAGIC DRUM　　4
LIGHTS
AROUND A SCEPTRE OF ALL LIGHTS,　•　•　•　•　•　•　•　•　18 OISIN 1　　V　254

		PAGE	TITLE	LINE

LIGHTS (CONTINUED)
```
        AND LIGHTS THE CURTAINED ROOM,  . . . . . . . . . .    89 ISLE IN WATER        10
        GOD LIGHTS THE STARS, HIS CANDLES,  . . . . . . . .    96 MOLL MAGEE           51
        AND THOUGH THE SEVEN LIGHTS BOWED IN THEIR DANCE AND WEPT,  174 ELEMENT POWERS   3
        AND LIGHTS WERE PALING OUT OF THE WEST,  . . . . . .   175 BELOVED DEAD          2
        WHILE LIGHTS WERE PALING ONE BY ONE. . . . . . . .    176 BELOVED DEAD         13
        WHO AMID LEAFY LIGHTS AND SHADES   . . . . . . . .    193 BAILE AILLINN       103
        THE EVERLASTING TAPER LIGHTS THE GLOOM:  . . . . . .  311 MOUNTAIN TOMB        10
        O'ER HER NEST THE LIGHTS ARE BLENDING:  . . . . . .   646 ISLE STAT I 1        36
        SUCH MAY I LOVE.  THE SHUDDERING FOREST LIGHTS   . . . 651 ISLE STAT I 1      165
        WITH STREAMING HAIR AS WANDERING LIGHTS . . . . . . . 667 ISLE STAT II 3       19
        THY FLICKERING HAND?  WHAT MEAN THE LIGHTS THAT RISE  . . 674 ISLE STAT II 3  198
        BUT NEVER, NEVER DANGLING LEAVE THE LIVER AND THE LIGHTS.  790 HEART SLEEVE      2
LIKE    SEE FLOWER-LIKE MOUSE-LIKE CANDLE-LIKE MOTH-LIKE BIRD-LIKE ANTAEUS-LIKE
        DANCE-LIKE
        MUST LIVE TO BE OLD LIKE THE WANDERING MOON. . . . . . .   3 OISIN 1         12
        AND LIKE A SUNSET WERE HER LIPS,  . . . . . . . . . .     3 OISIN 1         22
        THAT WAVERED LIKE THE SUMMER STREAMS,  . . . . . . .      4 OISIN 1         29
        AND WAVERED LIKE A SUMMER RILL,  . . . . . . . . . .      4 OISIN 1     V   29
        THAT ARE LIKE COLOURED ASIAN BIRDS  . . . . . . . .      7 OISIN 1         69
        AND THE DAYS PASS BY LIKE A WAYWARD TUNE,  . . . . .      8 OISIN 1         83
        HAVE A SPEED LIKE THE SPEED OF THE SALMON HERDS,  . . .   9 OISIN 1         98
        AND NOW A LADY RODE LIKE THE WIND . . . . . . . . .     12 OISIN 1        142
        BUT NOW THE MOON LIKE A WHITE ROSE SHONE   . . . . .    12 OISIN 1        152
        AND NOW A MAIDEN RODE LIKE THE WIND  . . . . . . . .    12 OISIN 1     V  142
        LIKE SOOTY FINGERS, MANY A TREE   . . . . . . . . .     13 OISIN 1        171
        OR CLUNG THEREON LIKE SWARMING BEES:  . . . . . . .     14 OISIN 1        181
        LIKE DROPS OF FROZEN RAINBOW LIGHT,  . . . . . . . .    14 OISIN 1        183
        AND LAUGHED LIKE MURMURS OF THE SEA:  . . . . . . .     15 OISIN 1        210
        LIKE TO A MERRY WANDERING ROUT . . . . . . . . . .      18 OISIN 1        253
        FOLDED LIKE A FROZEN FLY:  . . . . . . . . . . . .      19 OISIN 1        273
        LIKE CRIMSON METEORS HANG IN THE GLOOM,  . . . . . .    21 OISIN 1        306
        HUNG, LIKE METEORS OF RED LIGHT,  . . . . . . . . .     21 OISIN 1     V  306
        LIKE BUBBLES IN A FROZEN POND:  . . . . . . . . . .     22 OISIN 1        336
        IN MURMURS, LIKE A FRIGHTED BIRD.  . . . . . . . . .    25 OISIN 1        376
        SOME DANCED LIKE SHADOWS ON THE MOUNTAINS,  . . . . .   25 OISIN 1        388
        EACH FOREHEAD LIKE AN OBSCURE STAR  . . . . . . . .     26 OISIN 1        391
        LIKE DROPS OF HONEY CAME THEIR WORDS,  . . . . . . .    26 OISIN 1        398
        LIKE TULIPS IN THE AIR A-WINGING,  . . . . . . . . .    27 OISIN 1        417
        AND THE MOON LIKE A PALE ROSE WITHER AWAY."  . . . .    28 OISIN 1        427
        LIKE A BRIDE BENDING OVER HER MIRROR ADORNING,  . . .   28 OISIN 1     V 423E
        AND THEN AWAY, AWAY, LIKE WHIRLING FLAMES:  . . . . .   29 OISIN 2          2
        AND THEN AWAY, AWAY, LIKE SPIRAL FLAMES:  . . . . . .   29 OISIN 2     V    2
        YET SANG NO MORE AS WHEN, LIKE A BROWN BEE  . . . . .   30 OISIN 2         15
        BUT SANG NO MORE, AS WHEN, LIKE A BROWN BEE  . . . .    30 OISIN 2     V   15
        FANNED THE DELIGHTED AIR LIKE WINGS OF BIRDS:  . . .    32 OISIN 2         50
        A-MURMUR LIKE YOUNG PARTRIDGE: WITH LOUD HORN  . . .    32 OISIN 2         52
        FROM HIGH ABOVE, LIKE FEATHERS OF YOUNG BIRDS.  . .     32 OISIN 2     V   50
        "THEY MURMUR LIKE YOUNG PARTRIDGE IN THE MORN,  . . .   32 OISIN 2     V   51
        A LADY WITH SOFT EYES LIKE FUNERAL TAPERS,  . . . . .   33 OISIN 2         69
        DOWN ON US WITH HER EYES LIKE FUNERAL TAPERS,  . . .    33 OISIN 2     V   69
        A MAIDEN WITH SOFT EYES LIKE FUNERAL TAPERS,  . . . .   33 OISIN 2     V   69
        AS LIKE A RUDDY MOTH THEY WAVED AND FLUTTERED.  . . .   34 OISIN 2     V   72
        LIKE A SMALL RIVER, AND WHERE FEET TOUCHED CAME  . . .  37 OISIN 2        117
        GREY IN THE MIDST LIKE A SMALL RIVULET'S FLOW,  . . .   37 OISIN 2     V  117
        SCARED OF ITS GLITTERING LIKE A METEOR STAR.  . . . .   38 OISIN 2     V  137
        LIKE DRIFTS OF LEAVES, IMMOVABLE AND BRIGHT,  . . . .   40 OISIN 2        166
        LIKE WINGS OF KINGFISHERS! AND HE AROSE  . . . . . .    40 OISIN 2        169
        LIKE DRIFTS OF LAUREL LEAVES, IMMOVABLE AND BRIGHT  . . 40 OISIN 2     V  166
        LIKE ROTTED FLESH, AND STONE BY STONE MY HALL .  . . .  45 OISIN 2     V  236
        LIKE AN ARMY OF OLD MEN LONGING FOR REST FROM THE MOAN  48 OISIN 3         16
           OF THE SEAS.
        . . . A SOUND LIKE THE STIRRING OF FLIES.  . . . . . .  51 OISIN 3         58
        SOFTER THAN SNOW-FLAKES IN APRIL AND PIERCING THE MARROW 51 OISIN 3         68
           LIKE FLAME.
        THE MOIL OF MY CENTURIES FILLED ME: AND GONE LIKE       51 OISIN 3         70
           A SEA-COVERED STONE
        SOFTER THAN SNOWFLAKES IN APRIL, AND PIERCING THE MARROW 51 OISIN 3     V   68
           LIKE FLAME.
        A STARLING LIKE THEM THAT FORGATHERED 'NEATH A MOON . . . 54 OISIN 3       103
        "LIKE ME WERE SOME GALLEY FORSAKEN FAR OFF IN MERIDIAN    55 OISIN 3       117
           ISLE,
        "I WOULD DIE LIKE A SMALL WITHERED LEAF IN THE AUTUMN,    56 OISIN 3       131
           . . .
        LIKE AN ARMY OF OLD MEN LONGING FOR REST FROM THE MOAN    57 OISIN 3       144
           OF THE SEAS.
        WHEN THEY FROZE THE CLOTH ON MY BODY LIKE ARMOUR RIVETED  57 OISIN 3       151
           FAST,
        CAME, AND MY FOREHEAD FELL LOW, AND MY TEARS LIKE BERRIES 57 OISIN 3       154
           FELL DOWN:
        LIKE AN ARMY OF OLD MEN LOUNGING FOR REST FROM THE FOAM   57 OISIN 3     V 144
           OF THE SEAS.
        . . . LIKE THE ROARING OF WIND IN A WOOD.  . . . . . .   58 OISIN 3       168
        COMING FORTH FROM THE SEA LIKE THE MORNING . . . . . . . 58 OISIN 3     V 158
        . . . AND THEIR EYES THAT GLIMMER LIKE SILK.  . . . .    59 OISIN 3       176
        AND MY TEARS WERE LARGE LIKE TO BERRIES, AND I MURMURED, 59 OISIN 3     V 178
           . . .
        THE HEART IN ME LONGING TO LEAP LIKE A GRASSHOPPER INTO   60 OISIN 3       182
           HER HEART:
        I FELL ON THE PATH, AND THE HORSE WENT AWAY LIKE A SUMMER 60 OISIN 3       190
           FLY:
```

455

	PAGE	TITLE	LINE

LIKE (CONTINUED)

CONCEIVE A THING SO SAD AND SOFT, A GENTLE THING LIKE ME?	77	INDIAN ON GOD	16
LIKE SWARMING BEES, ONE WITH THE DOVE	78	INDIAN TO LOVE V	16
FELL LIKE FAINT METEORS IN THE GLOOM, AND ONCE	80	EPHEMERA	14
IT QUENCHED, WITH SOUND LIKE FALLING DEW,	86	MAD KING GOLL	66
YOU WAVES, THOUGH YOU DANCE BY MY FEET LIKE CHILDREN AT PLAY,	90	OLD FISHERMAN	1
YE WAVES, THOUGH YE DANCE 'FORE MY FEET LIKE CHILDREN AT PLAY,	90	OLD FISHERMAN V	1
THIS BODY TREMBLING LIKE A WIND-BLOWN REED,	103	FERGUS DRUID	25
I SEE MY LIFE GO DRIFTING LIKE A RIVER	104	FERGUS DRUID	31
I SEE MY LIFE GO DRIPPING LIKE A STREAM	104	FERGUS DRUID V	31
"WITH HIM IS ONE SWEET-THROATED LIKE A BIRD."	106	CUCHULAIN SEA	16
"WITH HIM IS ONE SWEET THROATED LIKE A BIRD,	106	CUCHULAIN SEA V	16
WHO HAS A LIKE VOW FROM THEIR TRIPLE DUN."	108	CUCHULAIN SEA	38
STARED LIKE THE SPRING UPON THE ANCIENT SKIES,	108	CUCHULAIN SEA	41
WHO HAD A LIKE VOW FROM OUR TRIPLE DUN."	109	CUCHULAIN SEA V	54
"YOUR HEAD A WHILE SEEMED LIKE A WOMAN'S HEAD	110	CUCHULAIN SEA	63
WHO DREAMED THAT BEAUTY PASSES LIKE A DREAM?	111	ROSE OF WORLD	1
LIKE THE PALE WATERS IN THEIR WINTRY RACE,	112	ROSE OF WORLD	8
DOOMED LIKE ODYSSEUS AND THE LABOURING SHIPS	120	SORROW OF LOVE	7
AND MIDNIGHT THERE ENFOLD THEM LIKE A FLEECE	128	DREAM OF FAERY	34
A GENTLE FEELING WRAPS THEM LIKE A FLEECE,	128	DREAM OF FAERY V	34
OF PASSIONATE MEN, LIKE BATS IN THE DEAD TREES;	136	TO SOME I TALK	5
AND, LIKE A STORM, CRY THE INEFFABLE NAME,	137	TO SOME I TALK	12
LIKE A CANDLE BURNT OUT,	142	MOODS	2
. . . REMADE, LIKE A CASKET OF GOLD	143	ROSE IN HEART	7
. . . RE-MADE LIKE A CASKET OF GOLD	143	ROSE IN HEART V	7
WERE GONE LIKE A DRIFTING SMOKE!	145	HOST OF AIR	40
AND STARS LIKE MOTHS WERE SHINING OUT,	149	WANDER AENGUS V	6
FOR HOURS WHEN ALL MUST FADE LIKE DEW,	156	FORGOT BEAUTY	20
THEY SET UP A NOISE LIKE CRICKETS,	161	CAP AND BELLS	33
AND CUMHAL SAW LIKE A DRIFTING SMOKE	167	BLESSED	13
LIKE THE SPARKS BLOWN OUT OF A SMITHY, AND DIE?	170	SECRET ROSE	30
THE POWERS, NOT KIND LIKE YOU, CAME WHERE GOD'S GARDEN BLOWS,	174	ELEMENT POWERS V	1
LIKE THE PALE CUP OF THE SEA,	175	ELEMENT POWERS	14
FOLK DANCE LIKE A WAVE OF THE SEA;	178	FIDDLER DOONEY	2
AND DANCE LIKE A WAVE OF THE SEA.	179	FIDDLER DOONEY	20
AND WISDOM THAT CAUGHT FIRE LIKE THE DRIED FLAX,	181	QUEEN MAEVE	28
FOR ALL THEIR BEAUTY'S LIKE A HOLLOW DREAM,	184	QUEEN MAEVE	88
FOR ALL THEIR BEAUTY, LIKE A HOLLOW DREAM"	184	QUEEN MAEVE V	89
ALTHOUGH THEIR BEAUTY'S LIKE A HOLLOW DREAM"	184	QUEEN MAEVE V	89
BODIES OF SHADOW AND BLIND EYES LIKE PEARLS,	185	QUEEN MAEVE	116
QUIET'S WILD HEART, LIKE DAILY MEAT;	196	BAILE AILLINN	178
LIKE THEM THAT ARE NO MORE ALIVE.	197	BAILE AILLINN	207
LIKE AN OLD PAUPER, IN ALL KINDS OF WEATHER;	205	ADAMS CURSE	9
OUR COURAGE BREAKS LIKE AN OLD TREE IN A BLACK WIND AND DIES,	207	HANRAHANS SONG	3
ANGERS THAT ARE LIKE NOISY CLOUDS HAVE SET OUR HEARTS ABEAT,	207	HANRAHANS SONG	8
LIKE TUFTED REEDS OUR COURAGE DROOPS IN A BLACK WIND AND DIES,	207	HANRAHANS SONG V	3
LIKE TATTERED CLOUDS OF THE WORLD, PASSIONS CALL AND OUR HEARTS BEAT;	207	HANRAHANS SONG V	8
ANGERS THAT ARE LIKE BUNDLED CLOUDS HAVE SET OUR HEARTS ABEAT,	207	HANRAHANS SONG V	8
LIKE HEAVY FLOODED WATERS OUR BODIES AND OUR BLOOD;	208	HANRAHANS SONG	13
LIKE HEAVY SWOLLEN WATERS ARE OUR BODIES AND OUR BLOOD;	208	HANRAHANS SONG V	13
THEY HAD HANDS LIKE CLAWS, AND THEIR KNEES	208	OLD MEN ADMIRE	4
WERE TWISTED LIKE THE OLD THORN-TREES	208	OLD MEN ADMIRE	5
LIKE THE WATERS."	208	OLD MEN ADMIRE	9
WERE TWISTED LIKE THE OLD THORN TREES	208	OLD MEN ADMIRE V	5
THEREIN ARE MANY QUEENS LIKE BRANWEN AND GUINEVERE;	209	UNDER THE MOON	11
LIKE AN OLD SONG.	211	O DO NOT LOVE	4
LIKE AN OLD SONG.	212	O DO NOT LOVE	12
LIKE PLOVERS THAT HAVE HEARD THE CALL.	213	BLESS PSALTER	13
QUEENS, THEIR EYES BLUE LIKE THE ICE,	214	HAPPY TOWNLAND	11
THEIR HEARTS WOULD BE LIKE A CUP	215	HAPPY TOWNLAND	31
FOR THEIR HEARTS WOULD BE LIKE A CUP	215	HAPPY TOWNLAND V	31
I HAD NOT EYES LIKE THOSE ENCHANTED EYES,	218	WOODS OF COOLE	17
HEAVY LIKE STONE, THEIR WISDOM BEING HALF SILENCE.	218	WOODS OF COOLE	26
LIKE A GREY GULL UPON THE BREAST OF EACH.	223	SHADOW WATER B	24
NO, NOR WITH A HUNDRED MEN LIKE YOU	225	SHADOW WATER B V	74
HAS SHE NOT SEEN HIM LYING LIKE A LOG,	230	SHADOW WATER B	173
LIKE CHARMED APPLES MADE OF CHRYSOPRASE,	231	SHADOW WATER B	214
SHE WILL BE LIKE A WILD CAT; FOR THESE QUEENS	232	SHADOW WATER B	233
ALONE AND WINGED. OUR LOVE SHALL BE LIKE THEIRS	250	SHADOW WATER B	581
TREMBLING IN THE BLUE HEAVENS LIKE A WHITE FAWN	251	SHADOW WATER B	611
WITH BEAUTY LIKE A TIGHTENED BOW, A KIND	256	NO SECOND TROY	8
THAT IS NOT NATURAL IN AN AGE LIKE THIS,	257	NO SECOND TROY	9
THAT WERE LIKE MEMORIES OF YOU—BUT NOW	257	RECONCILIATION	7
TILL THEY HAD CHANGED US TO LIKE STRENGTH?"	259	PEACE V	9
'TWERE POLITIC TO DO THE LIKE BY THESE;	262	TO A POET	3
THAT TURNS AND CHANGES LIKE HIS DRAUGHTY SEAS?	265	ABBEY THEATRE	12
FOR ONE THAT WAS LIKE WOMAN MADE	272	GREY ROCK	29
OF MEN AND WOMEN MADE LIKE THESE;	272	GREY ROCK	43
IT VANISHED LIKE A SHADOW, AND A CRY	278	TWO KINGS	38
LIKE THE EYES OF SOME GREAT KITE SCOURING THE WOODS,	283	TWO KINGS	150
I GAZED AT HIM LIKE GROUSE UPON A KITE;	283	TWO KINGS	152
THEY HAVE GONE ABOUT THE WORLD LIKE WIND,	289	SEPTEMBER 1913	11

LIKE (CONTINUED)

	PAGE	TITLE	LINE
AND LIKE A LAUGHING STRING	291	TO A FRIEND	11
LIKE GENTLE BLOOD, HAS BEEN DRIVEN FROM THE PLACE,	292	TO A SHADE	14
EVEN LIKE THESE TO RAIL AND SWEAT	294	HATED PLAYBOY	5
AND LIKE THESE TO RAIL AND SWEAT	294	HATED PLAYBOY V	5
SANG UNNOTICED LIKE A BIRD!	298	THREE HERMITS	7
SANG UNNOTICED LIKE A BIRD.	299	THREE HERMITS	32
TO TAKE MY FANCY LIKE THE WIND	301	RUN PARADISE	26
"I'D LIKE TO SLEEP TILL WINTER'S GONE	305	HOUR DAWN	60
LIKE SOME OLD RABBIT TO MY CLEFT	307	HOUR DAWN	105
LIKE SOME LAST COURTIER AT A GYPSY CAMPING-PLACE	314	FALLEN MAJESTY	3
LIKE SOME LAST COURTIER AT A GYPSY CAMPING PLACE	314	FALLEN MAJESTY V	3
THAT IS LIKE LAUGHTER, SPRANG AGAIN	318	APPOINTMENT	6
WITH ALL THEIR ANCIENT FACES LIKE RAIN-BEATEN STONES,	318	MAGI	4
PASSIONATE AND SIMPLE LIKE HIS HEART.	325	ROBERT GREGORY	32
COULD A BRACE OF BLACKBIRDS SING.	332	ROUND TOWER	24
LIKE AN OLD HORSE IN A POUND."	333	SOLOMON SHEBA	8
"LIKE THE SPECKLED BIRD THAT STEERS	341	SHEP GOATHERD	62
AND I THAT MADE LIKE MUSIC IN MY YOUTH	342	SHEP GOATHERD	76
AND LIVE LIKE SOLOMON	346	ON WOMAN	42
COURTESY AND PASSION INTO ONE LIKE THOSE	352	PEOPLE	17
HAS SET ME MUTTERING LIKE A FOOL.	356	BROKEN DREAMS	26
I THINK IT BETTER THAT IN TIMES LIKE THESE	359	WAR POEM	1
I THINK IT BETTER THAT AT TIMES LIKE THESE	359	WAR POEM V	1
OR, IT MAY BE, LIKE A BOY'S.	363	DOLLS DRAWINGS	9
BECAUSE THE PRIEST MUST HAVE LIKE EVERY DOG HIS DAY	364	DOLLS FACES	10
SHE IS PLAYING LIKE A CHILD	364	END OF DAY	1
AND LOOK MOST LIKE ME, BEING INDEED MY DOUBLE,	371	EGO DOMINUS	72
IS ALWAYS HAPPY LIKE A BIRD OR A BEAST!	373	PHASES OF MOON	38
BECAUSE ALL DARK, LIKE THOSE THAT ARE ALL LIGHT,	376	PHASES OF MOON	104
CRYING TO ONE ANOTHER LIKE THE BATS!	376	PHASES OF MOON	106
AND THE MOON SPUN ROUND LIKE A TOP,	378	CAT AND MOON	2
LIKE THE CLANGOUR OF A BELL.	382	SONG OF FOOL	9
LEARNED LIKE A MAN? PAUL VERONESE	386	ROBARTES DANCE	26
AND LEAD US TO THE LIKE—IF THEY	387	ROBARTES DANCE	47
BEFORE MY TIME, SEEM LIKE A VIVID MEMORY.	391	UNDER SATURN	10
LIKE ANY ROCK-BRED, SEA-BORNE BIRD!	397	POLIT PRISONER	18
I WOULD HAVE TOUCHED IT LIKE A CHILD	399	BREAK OF DAY	12
THAT ALL HER THOUGHTS MAY LIKE THE LINNET BE,	404	FOR DAUGHTER	42
O MAY SHE LIVE LIKE SOME GREEN LAUREL	405	FOR DAUGHTER	47
TREE, LIKE A SOOTY FINGER, STARTS FROM THE EARTH!	410	TOWER	19
PRIDE, LIKE THAT OF THE MORN,	414	TOWER	134
IN SOME LIKE CHAMBER, SHADOWING FORTH	419	MY HOUSE	15
CURVED LIKE NEW MOON, MOON-LUMINOUS,	421	MY TABLE	10
AND SEEMED UNCHANGING LIKE THE SWORD.	421	MY TABLE	21
CURVED LIKE NEW MOON, MOON LUMINOUS,	421	MY TABLE V	10
A MIST THAT IS LIKE BLOWN SNOW IS SWEEPING OVER ALL,	425	PHANTOM HATRED	2
TRANSPARENT LIKE THE WIND,	449	HERO GIRL FOOL	27
THOUGH NURTURED LIKE THE SAILING MOON	451	FIRST LOVE	1
LIKE THE MOON HER KINDNESS IS,	452	HUMAN DIGNITY	1
SO LIKE A BIT OF STONE I LIE	452	HUMAN DIGNITY	7
AND BODIES BROKEN LIKE A THORN	454	HIS MEMORIES	3
MY ARMS ARE LIKE THE TWISTED THORN	455	HIS MEMORIES	11
SOUNDS LIKE AN OLD SONG.	457	SECRETS OF OLD	6
THOUGH MARGERY IS LIKE A FISH	457	SECRETS OF OLD V	7
LIKE MEN WHO LIVE BY HABIT. EVERY DAY	463	HARUN RASHID	56
LIKE THIS PURE JET, NOW LOST AMID BLUE SKY,	464	HARUN RASHID	64
LIKE PASSION STIRS THE PEACOCK AND HIS MATE,	465	HARUN RASHID	100
STILL RAZOR-KEEN, STILL LIKE A LOOKING-GLASS	477	SELF AND SOUL	11
STILL RAZOR-KEEN, STILL LIKE A LOOKING GLASS	477	SELF AND SOUL V	11
ROSE LIKE THESE WALLS FROM THESE	480	BLOOD AND MOON	6
IS EVERY MODERN NATION LIKE THE TOWER,	482	BLOOD AND MOON	47
LIKE EVERYTHING THAT HAS THE STAIN OF BLOOD,	482	BLOOD AND MOON	51
IS EVERY NATION LIKE THE TOWER	482	BLOOD AND MOON V	47
LIKE MILK SPILT ON A STONE.	484	SPILT MILK	4
THEY CAME LIKE SWALLOWS AND LIKE SWALLOWS WENT,	489	COOLE PARK 29	17
THEY CAME LIKE SWALLOWS AND LIKE SWALLOWS WENT,	489	COOLE PARK 29	17
AND, LIKE THE SOUL, IT SAILS INTO THE SIGHT	490	COOLE BALLYLEE	19
LIKE SOME POOR ARAB TRIBESMAN AND HIS TENT.	491	COOLE BALLYLEE	40
SPOKE THESE, OR WORDS LIKE THESE.	496	MOHINI CHATTER	15
CAN LIKE THE COCKS OF HADES CROW,	498	BYZANTIUM	20
TARGETED, TROD LIKE SPRING.	504	QUARREL IN AGE	16
ALL THINGS HANG LIKE A DROP OF DEW	505	GRAT INSTRUCT	3
WHAT MADE ME LIVE LIKE THESE THAT SEEM	507	STREAM AND SUN	14
WHAT BIDS ME LIVE LIKE THESE THAT SEEM	507	STREAM AND SUN V	14
CRIED THAT WE LIVED LIKE BEAST AND BEAST!	508	JANE BISHOP	13
WRINKLED LIKE THE FOOT OF A GOOSE,	508	JANE BISHOP	16
THOUGH LIKE A ROAD	512	JANE ON GOD	20
LOVE IS LIKE THE LION'S TOOTH.	514	JANE GROWN OLD	7
LOVE IS LIKE THE LION'S TOOTH.	514	JANE GROWN OLD	14
LOVE IS LIKE THE LION'S TOOTH.	515	JANE GROWN OLD	21
ARE SOMEWHERE SLEEPING LIKE A TOP	525	DANCING DAYS	13
WE LIVED LIKE MEN THAT WATCH A PAINTED STAGE.	542	PARN FUNERAL 1	18
PITCH LIKE KING BILLY BOMB-BALLS IN	565	LAPIS LAZULI	7
HIS LONG LAMP-CHIMNEY SHAPED LIKE THE STEM	566	LAPIS LAZULI	33
HIS LONG LAMP CHIMNEY SHAPED LIKE THE STEM	566	LAPIS LAZULI V	33
LIKE A DUMB BEAST IN A SHOW,	572	LADYS 1ST SONG	2
HAS HAD A LIKE INHERITANCE,	584	GHOST ROG CASE	25
KEEP DANCING LIKE A WAVE,	592	DRUNK SOBRIETY	10
FOR THINGS LIKE THESE WHAT DECENT MAN	598	MODEL LAUREATE	22
THE ROARING TINKER IF YOU LIKE,	605	SONGS BURDEN 1	1

		PAGE	TITLE		LINE
LIKE	(CONTINUED)				
	LAY SIGHING LIKE THE REST.	612	NEWS ORACLE		12
	STOOD, TOOK DEATH LIKE A TUNE	613	MARCH SONGS 1		15
	LIKE A LONG-LEGGED FLY UPON THE STREAM	617	LONG-LEG FLY		9
	LIKE A LONG-LEGGED FLY UPON THE STREAM	617	LONG-LEG FLY		19
	LIKE A LONG-LEGGED FLY UPON THE STREAM	618	LONG-LEG FLY		29
	LIKE AN OLD JEW MAN.	620	JOHN KINSELLA		14
	WITH AN EYE LIKE A HAWK.	627	STATES HOLIDAY		32
	'TIS MORN! LIKE OLD MEN'S EYES THE STARS ARE PALE,	645	ISLE STAT I 1		4
	DRIFT AND FLOAT LIKE SILVER SHIPS!	647	ISLE STAT I 1		67
	REPLY LIKE MOANING OF IMPRISONED ELF!	652	ISLE STAT I 2		11
	THE SKIES MORE DIM, THOUGH BURNING LIKE A SHIELD,	656	ISLE STAT I 3		26
	AND THE WAVES BOWED BEFORE IT LIKE MOWN CORN,	657	ISLE STAT I 3		56
	FROM THE WOOD'S WAYS, THEN, LIKE A SILVER FLAME,	658	ISLE STAT II 1		6
	I LIKE YOU, AND, IN SOOTH I KNOW NOT WHY.	661	ISLE STAT II 1		64
	BEHOLD, HOW LIKE A SWARM OF FIERY BEES	662	ISLE STAT II 2		1
	DEEP IN HIS SOUL, LIKE RAIN UPON A SOIL	692	MOSADA 1		56
	NOT GOOD! BUT YOU ARE LIKE THE BUTTERFLIES.	693	MOSADA 1		65
	I HAD A SISTER LIKE HER ONCE, MY FRIEND.	696	MOSADA 2		11
	AND YON FEW STARS GROWN DIM, LIKE EYES OF LOVERS	700	MOSADA 3		33
	THIS DEATH IS HEAVY IN MY VEINS LIKE SLEEP.	701	MOSADA 3		57
	LIKE HAPPY THOUGHTS GROWN SAD IN EVIL DAYS.	703	MOSADA 3		116
	HE TURNS WHERE, HUNG LIKE DROPS OF DRIPPING GOLD,	710	FERENCZ RENYI		18
	HE TURNS WHERE, HUNG LIKE DROPS OF LIQUID GOLD,	710	FERENCZ RENYI	V	18
	LIKE SMALL BROWN MOTHS, A-TREMBLE. "RENYI SAY	713	FERENCZ RENYI		82
	LIKE SMALL BROWN MOTHS, A-TREMBLE CEASELESSLY.	713	FERENCZ RENYI	V	82
	HANG THE MIST-THREADS FOR A LITTLE WHILE LIKE COBWEBS IN THE AIR!	719	PHANTOM SHIP		29
	HANG THE MIST THREADS FOR A LITTLE WHILE LIKE COBWEBS IN THE AIR!	719	PHANTOM SHIP	V	29
	PUFFED LIKE PUFF-BALLS ON A TREE,	727	LOVERS QUARREL		37
	WHERE THE MOSS WAS SPREAD LIKE HIS OWN DOORMAT.	728	PRIEST FAIRY		8
	AND LIKE A SILVER TRUMPET RING.	736	SUMMER EVENING		4
	AND LIKE A SILVER TRUMPET RING.	737	SUMMER EVENING		20
	LIKE A GREY OWL MEN HARRY OUT	740	EARL PAUL		23
	WHEN SOMETHING THAT WAS BEARDED LIKE A GOAT	747	SHADOW WATER A		11
	ARE DOUBTFUL LIKE THESE PULLERS OF THE OAR!	748	SHADOW WATER A		30
	SHE WILL ANSWER NOW LIKE ANY WAITING WOMAN	757	SHADOW WATER A		193
	THAT I WOULD SHED LIKE TWILIGHT OVER YOU.	765	SHADOW WATER A		352
	HAVE FOUND IT LIKE THE FROTH UPON THE ALE.	767	SHADOW WATER A		387
	TREMBLING IN THE BLUE HEAVENS LIKE A WHITE FAWN	769	SHADOW WATER A		427
	LIKE BROTHER TO BROTHER,	769	BLOOD BOND		2
	LIKE SON TO FATHER	769	BLOOD BOND	V	2
	LIKE SON TO FATHER	770	BLOOD BOND		3
	COME RIDE LIKE THE MARCH WIND!	774	COME RIDE		6
	RUN LIKE THE MARCH WIND!	774	COME RIDE	V	6
	LIKE WINE THAT FILLS TO THE TOP	781	MY HEART BEAT		14
	A WOMAN'S BEAUTY IS LIKE A WHITE	784	WOMANS BEAUTY		1
	FRAIL BIRD, LIKE A WHITE SEA-BIRD ALONE	784	WOMANS BEAUTY		2
LIKED					
	BUT LIKED THE WAY HIS FINGER SMELT.	619	STICK INCENSE		4
LIKELIHOOD					
	OUT OF ALL LIKELIHOOD, OR REASON,	389	IMAGE PAST		9
LIKELY					
	NO LIKELY END COULD BRING THEM LOSS	328	IRISH AIRMAN		7
	THROW LIKELY COUPLES INTO BED	606	SONGS BURDEN 1		25
	SOME HAVE KNOWN A LIKELY LAD	625	OLD MEN BE MAD		2
LIKENESS					
	BUT NOT THE EXACT LIKENESS, THE SIMPLICITY OF A CHILD,	354	HIS PHOENIX		28
LILAC					
	OF LILAC O'ER THE PULSING WATER GLEAMS,	664	ISLE STAT II 2		48
LILIES					
	THE DEW-COLD LILIES LADIES BORE	156	FORGOT BEAUTY		11
	LILIES OF DEATH-PALE HOPE, ROSES OF PASSIONATE DREAM.	172	TRAV PASSION		8
	WHITE LILIES, AND HER SONG FLEW FORTH AFAR	693	MOSADA 3		85
LILY	SEE WATER-LILY				
	WHERE DAFFODIL AND LILY WAVE,	67	HAPPY SHEPHERD		46
	. . DEW-DABBLED, THE LILY AND ROSE!	122	WHITE BIRDS		5
	SOON FAR FROM THE ROSE AND THE LILY	122	WHITE BIRDS		11
	. . DEW DABBLED, THE LILY AND ROSE!	122	WHITE BIRDS	V	5
	NOW BATHING LILY LEAF AND FISH'S SCALE,	464	HARUN RASHID		65
	NOW BATHING LILY LEAF AND FISHES' SCALE,	464	HARUN RASHID	V	65
	AND THY NECK'S A POISED LILY!	647	ISLE STAT I 1		55
	THE LONG LILY BLOWS,	672	ISLE STAT II 3		165
	A LILY BLANCHED PLACE, SHE SAT AND SANG,	693	MOSADA 1	V	83
LILY-BLANCHED					
	A LILY-BLANCHED PLACE, SHE SAT AND SANG,	693	MOSADA 1		83
LIMB					
	THERE WAS NO LIMB OF MINE BUT FELL	7	OISIN 1		72
	NO LIMB OF ME THAT WAS NOT FALLEN,	7	OISIN 1	V	72
	WHILE A HUNDRED YOUTHS, MIGHTY OF LIMB,	8	OISIN 1		94
	--IT HAD SUCH DIGNITY OF LIMB--	254	HIS DREAM		11
	BRED THAT FIERCE TOOTH AND CLEANLY LIMB	318	APPOINTMENT		10
	IF HEAD AND LIMB HAVE BEAUTY AND THE INSTEP'S HIGH AND LIGHT	354	HIS PHOENIX		21
	THAT DREAM IS A NORM! AND SHOULD SOME LIMB OF THE DEVIL	372	ON GOING HOUSE		12
	DOWN LIMB AND BREAST OR DOWN THAT GLIMMERING BELLY	560	MAGIC DRUM		5
LIMBED	SEE GREAT-LIMBED LONG-LIMBED				
	AND YET HAD BEEN GREAT BODIED AND GREAT LIMBED,	181	QUEEN MAEVE	V	25
LIMBS					
	AND A HUNDRED YOUTHS, WHOSE LIMBS ARE STRUNG	9	OISIN 1	V	97

458

LIMBS (CONTINUED)   PAGE   TITLE   LINE
  AND OVER THE LIMBS AND THE VALLEY THE SLOW OWLS WANDERED
    AND CAME.   49 OISIN 3   41
  . . . THE LIMBS OF THE FENIANS ARE TOST: 62 OISIN 3   213
  WITH STILL AND STONY LIMBS AND OPEN EYES.   182 QUEEN MAEVE   46
  INTO THEIR SHINING LIMBS--I'VE HAD GREAT TEACHERS.   231 SHADOW WATER B   195
  TO GO--FOR HOPE WOULD GIVE HIS LIMBS THE POWER--   282 TWO KINGS   V 133A
  FOR HOPE WOULD GIVE HIS LIMBS THE POWER--AND AWAIT   283 TWO KINGS   136
  PUSH OUT HIS VIGOROUS LIMBS AND RUB HIS EYES,   284 TWO KINGS   162
  BY THESE WIRE-JOINTED JAWS AND LIMBS OF WOOD,   382 VISION ROBART   10
  ON LIMBS THAT HAD RUN WILD.   394 EASTER 1916   64
  STRETCH OUT YOUR LIMBS AND SLEEP A LONG SATURNIAN SLEEP: 442 BLACK CENTAUR   13
  SHE MOVED HER LIMBS CONFUSEDLY AS THOUGH   466 HARUN RASHID V 125A
  SO THAT I HAD THE LIMBS TO TRY   515 JANE GROWN OLD   19
  FROM THE LIMBS OF LEDA SANK   522 LULLABY   17
  FROM THE LIMBS OF HELEN SANK   522 LULLABY   V   17
  PRIMORDIAL MOTHERHOOD FORSAKE HIS LIMBS, THE CHILD   559 MAGIC DRUM   2
    NO LONGER REST,
  LIMBS A LOVE IN COMMON
  HER LIMBS ARE DELICATE AS AN EYELID,   573 LADYS 2ND SONG   17
  AND HER GIGANTIC LIMBS. THE WEARY THIRST   612 NEWS ORACLE   27
  HAD NOT ALL HIS LIMBS A STIR   687 TWO TITANS   16
  IN THE TUMULT OF THE LIMBS   772 SONG DEIRDRE 1   11
LIME   SEE QUICK-LIME   777 SONG DEIRDRE 2   7
  HUM IN THE LIME TREE FLOWERS: AND PUT AWAY   198 SEVEN WOODS   V   3
  NEITHER CATALPA-TREE NOR SCENTED LIME   435 NEW FACES   2
  NEITHER CATALPA TREE NOR SCENTED LIME   435 NEW FACES   V   2
  A SYCAMORE AND LIME TREE LOST IN NIGHT   488 COOLE PARK 29 V   3
LIMESTONE
  ON LIMESTONE QUARRIED NEAR THE SPOT   640 BEN BULBEN   90
LIME-TREE
  HUM IN THE LIME-TREE FLOWERS: AND PUT AWAY   198 SEVEN WOODS   3
  A SYCAMORE AND LIME-TREE LOST IN NIGHT   488 COOLE PARK 29   3
LIMP
  LIMP AS A WORM,   575 MAIDS 2ND SONG   4
LIMPED
  A RABBIT OLD AND LAME LIMPED DOWN THE PATH: 80 EPHEMERA   15
LIMPS
  SHE LIMPS ALONG IN AN AGED WHITENESS: 27 OISIN 1   415
  SHE LIMPS ALONG IN AN AGED WHITENESS.   28 OISIN 1   V 423
LINE
  BEFORE GOD WAS OR MY OLD LINE BEGAN: 29 OISIN 2   8
  THINGS DONE ERE GOD FIRST WAS OR MY OLD LINE BEGAN: 29 OISIN 2   V   8
  THERE WAS NO MIGHTIER SOUL OF HEBER'S LINE: 36 OISIN 2   95
  MY SOUL, ONCE GLORY OF ITS ANCIENT LINE,   36 OISIN 2   V 95
  I CRIED, "THOU ART SURELY A WARRIOR, FORGETTING HIS FAMOUS   51 OISIN 3   V 61
    LINE,
  I SAID: "A LINE WILL TAKE US HOURS MAYBE: 204 ADAMS CURSE   4
  TO THAT STERN COLOUR AND THAT DELICATE LINE   326 ROBERT GREGORY   67
  THE LONG FLOWING LINE,   355 PROPERTIUS   3
LINEAGE
  BUT TELL YOUR NAME AND LINEAGE TO HIM   108 CUCHULAIN SEA   36
  ANOTHER LINEAGE FEED THE CROW,   437 SONGS PLAY 1   10
LINEAMENTS
  THE LINEAMENTS, A HEART THAT LAUGHTER HAS MADE SWEET,   315 FALLEN MAJESTY   5
  THE LINEAMENTS, THE HEART THAT LAUGHTER HAS MADE SWEET,   315 FALLEN MAJESTY V   5
  OF HER UNBLEMISHED LINEAMENTS, A WHITENESS WITH NO STAIN,   353 HIS PHOENIX   3
  THE LINEAMENTS THAT PLEASE THEIR VIEW   387 ROBARTES DANCE   49
  SHOWS THROUGH OUR LINEAMENTS. MY CANDLE'S BRIGHT,   464 HARUN RASHID   70
  AND ANCIENT LINEAMENTS ARE BLOTTED OUT.   564 GYRES   4
  IRELAND'S HISTORY IN THEIR LINEAMENTS TRACE: 604 GALLERY REVIS   53
  THE LINEAMENTS OF A PLUMMET-MEASURED FACE.   611 STATUES   32
LINED
  AMID GREAT CHAMBERS AND LONG GALLERIES, LINED   418 ANCEST HOUSES   36
LINEN
  "ALTHOUGH I'D LIE LAPPED UP IN LINEN   331 ROUND TOWER   1
  BETWEEN THE PANTRY AND THE LINEN CHEST,   340 SHEP GOATHERD   36
  A BUNDLE OF LINEN. SHROUDS BY TWO AND THREE   634 CUCHULAIN COMF V 9
LINEN-CARRIER
  AND THEREUPON THAT LINEN-CARRIER SAID: 634 CUCHULAIN COMF   11
LINEN-CHEST
  BETWEEN THE PANTRY AND THE LINEN-CHEST,   340 SHEP GOATHERD   36
LINES   SEE FISHING-LINES
  THE LINES ARE NOT HEAVY, NOR HEAVY THE LONG NETS BROWN--   91 OLD FISHERMAN V 5
  WITH SHORE LINES IN THE SAY: 94 MOLL MAGEE   6
  INTRODUCTORY LINES   217 WOODS OF COOLE V T
  OF SUCH NOBLE LINES," I SAID: 259 PEACE   6
  EDIT AND ANNOTATE THE LINES   337 SCHOLARS   3
  LINES WRITTEN IN DEJECTION   343 DEJECTION   T
  THOSE TERRIBLE IMPLACABLE STRAIGHT LINES   467 HARUN RASHID   142
  THE INTELLECTUAL SWEETNESS OF THOSE LINES   489 COOLE PARK 29   23
  DO NOT BREAK UP THEIR LINES TO WEEP.   565 LAPIS LAZULI   15
  IN LEMON-TINTED LINES, SO BLAZE THE DAFFODILLS.   645 ISLE STAT I 1   19
  FROM DEATH'S LATE LANGUOR AS THESE LINES I READ   734 QUATRAIN APHOR   14
LINGER
  MAYBE THEY LINGER BY THE WAY.   212 BLESS PSALTER   8
  IS SHADOW, AND NOT LINGER WRETCHEDLY   230 SHADOW WATER B   180
  BUT WHAT'S THE MEANING? WHY DO YOU LINGER THERE?   234 SHADOW WATER B   271
  WHY LINGER? RUN TO YOUR DESIRE,   234 SHADOW WATER B   272
  AS THOUGH SHE HAD BEEN FORCED TO LINGER   390 IMAGE PAST   23
  TO MAKE IT LINGER HALF A DAY.   401 DEMON BEAST   42

LINGER   (CONTINUED)
    (SOMETHING MAY LINGER THERE THOUGH ALL ELSE DIE!)   •   •   •   618 BRONZE HEAD   5
    IN TROUBLE IS, THE DOE WILL LINGER NEAR.   •   •   •   •   •   713 FERENCZ RENYI   80
    I LINGER WHILE THE BIRDS ARE ON THE WING,   •   •   •   •   •   754 SHADOW WATER A V   157
LINGERED   SEE OVER-LINGERED
    HE HATH OVER LINGERED HIS WELCOME! THE DAYS,   •   •   •   •   27 OISIN 1   V 406
    SCARCELY A FEATHER LINGERED, THEN YOU SEEMED   •   •   •   •   102 FERGUS DRUID   4
    WEARY AND KIND ONE LINGERED BY HIS SEAT!   •   •   •   •   •   112 ROSE OF WORLD   13
    AND LINGERED IN THE HIDDEN DESOLATE PLACE   •   •   •   •   •   162 ASKS FORGIVE   15
    OR HAVE LINGERED AWHILE AND SAID   •   •   •   •   •   •   •   392 EASTER 1916   7
LINGERETH
    SHE ALONE, MY LADY, LINGERETH   •   •   •   •   •   •   •   •   646 ISLE STAT I 1   28
LINGERING
    SNATCHING THE HORN OF NIAMH, I BLEW A LONG LINGERING NOTE.   51 OISIN 3   57
    SNATCHING THE HORN OF NIAM, I BLEW FORTH A LINGERING NOTE!   51 OISIN 3   57
    SNATCHING THE HORN OF NIAM, I BLEW A LINGERING NOTE!   •   •   51 OISIN 3   V   57
    AND PRESSING ON, OR LINGERING SLOW WITH FEAR,   •   •   •   •   114 ROSE OF BATTLE V   5
    FOR THAT PALE BREAST AND LINGERING HAND   •   •   •   •   •   156 FORGOT BEAUTY   15
    FOR THAT DIM BROW AND LINGERING HAND   •   •   •   •   •   •   156 FORGOT BEAUTY   V   15
LINGERINGS
    WILD CRIES, GROWN SWEET WITH LULLS AND LINGERINGS LONG.   674 ISLE STAT II 3   222
LINGERS
    OR THE FLAME OF THE BLUE STAR THAT LINGERS   •   •   •   •   •   122 WHITE BIRDS   7
    AND THE WAN WAVE THAT LINGERS   •   •   •   •   •   •   •   •   672 ISLE STAT II 3   166
LINK
    IF FOLLY LINK WITH ELEGANCE   •   •   •   •   •   •   •   •   •   598 STONE CROSS   13
LINKED
    SWEPT ON THE DANCE'S LINKED FLOW,   •   •   •   •   •   •   •   20 OISIN 1   V 291
    ONCE MORE THE DANCE'S LINKED FLOW,   •   •   •   •   •   •   •   22 OISIN 1   V 323A
    LINKED BY A GOLD CHAIN EACH TO EACH,   •   •   •   •   •   •   194 BAILE AILLINN   136
LINKS
    IF FOLLY LINKS WITH ELEGANCE   •   •   •   •   •   •   •   •   •   598 STONE CROSS   V   13
LINNET
    THAT ALL HER THOUGHTS MAY LIKE THE LINNET BE,   •   •   •   •   404 FOR DAUGHTER   42
    CAN NEVER TEAR THE LINNET FROM THE LEAF.   •   •   •   •   •   405 FOR DAUGHTER   56
LINNET'S
    AND EVENING FULL OF THE LINNET'S WINGS.   •   •   •   •   •   •   117 ISLE INNISFREE   8
LINNETS'
    AND EVENING FULL OF THE LINNETS' WINGS.   •   •   •   •   •   •   117 ISLE INNISFREE V   8
LION
    "O FLAMING LION OF THE WORLD, O WHEN WILL YOU TURN TO YOUR   56 OISIN 3   129
        REST?"
    O FLAMING LION OF THE WORLD, O WHEN WILL YOU TURN TO YOUR   56 OISIN 3   136
        REST?"
    "OH, FLAMING LION OF THE WORLD, OH, WHEN WILT THOU TURN   56 OISIN 3   V 129
        TO THY REST?"
    AND IN THE FLAMING FORESTS COWER THE LION   •   •   •   •   •   73 ANASHU VIJAYA   52
    THEY SEE IN FLAMING FORESTS COWER THE LION   •   •   •   •   •   73 ANASHU VIJAYA V   52
    A DREAM THAT A LION HAD DREAMED   •   •   •   •   •   •   •   259 UNWORTH PRAISE   7
    HALF LION, HALF CHILD, IS AT PEACE.   •   •   •   •   •   •   260 UNWORTH PRAISE   20
    A SPHINX WITH WOMAN BREAST AND LION PAW,   •   •   •   •   •   383 VISION ROBART   18
    A SHAPE WITH LION BODY AND THE HEAD OF A MAN,   •   •   •   •   402 SECOND COMING   14
    THE LION AND THE HONEYCOMB, WHAT HAS SCRIPTURE SAID?   •   •   503 VACILLATION   88
    THE LION AND THE HONEY-COMB, WHAT HAS SCRIPTURE SAID?   •   •   503 VACILLATION   V   88
    THE LION AND THE VIRGIN,   •   •   •   •   •   •   •   •   •   601 THOSE IMAGES   11
    LION AND WOMAN AND THE LORD KNOWS WHAT.   •   •   •   •   •   629 CIRCUS ANIMALS   8
    THE LION, THE WORLD'S GREAT SOLITARY, BENDS   •   •   •   •   689 NETTLESHIP   5
LIONEL
    LIONEL JOHNSON COMES THE FIRST TO MIND,   •   •   •   •   •   •   324 ROBERT GREGORY   17
LIONESS
    AND LIONESS, WITH ALL THEIR WHIMPERING CUBS!   •   •   •   •   73 ANASHU VIJAYA   53
    BUT HERE THE LIONESS LICKS HER SOFT CUB   •   •   •   •   •   •   688 NETTLESHIP   2
LION'S
    LOVE IS LIKE THE LION'S TOOTH.   •   •   •   •   •   •   •   •   514 JANE GROWN OLD   7
    LOVE IS LIKE THE LION'S TOOTH.   •   •   •   •   •   •   •   •   514 JANE GROWN OLD   14
    LOVE IS LIKE THE LION'S TOOTH.   •   •   •   •   •   •   •   •   515 JANE GROWN OLD   21
    HE'LL SNAP HIS SWORD. RAISED IS THE LION'S PAW.   •   •   •   •   664 ISLE STAT II 2   63
LIONS
    BECAUSE PIEBALD PONIES, LED BEARS, CAGED LIONS, MAKE BUT   623 HIGH TALK   5
        POOR SHOWS,
    BRAVED LIONS FOR MY SAKE,   •   •   •   •   •   •   •   •   •   789 SINGING HEAD   2
LIP
    OF ONE LONG FINGER ON MY LIP.   •   •   •   •   •   •   •   •   12 OISIN 1   151
    MURMURING SOFTLY LIP TO LIP,   •   •   •   •   •   •   •   •   78 INDIAN TO LOVE   8
    MURMURING SOFTLY LIP TO LIP,   •   •   •   •   •   •   •   •   78 INDIAN TO LOVE   8
    THOUGH I'D MY FINGER ON MY LIP,   •   •   •   •   •   •   •   254 HIS DREAM   13
    STARED AT THE GODS WITH LAUGHING LIP.   •   •   •   •   •   •   276 GREY ROCK   123
    WHATEVER COULD RECALL THE LIP OF LOVER.   •   •   •   •   •   537 HER VISION   8
    HUSH! HUSH! HUSH! ON EVERY LIP   •   •   •   •   •   •   •   732 STREET DANCERS   18
LIPPED   SEE LAUGHTER-LIPPED LOOSE-LIPPED
    NO LOOSE LIPPED DEMAGOGUE HAD WON THE DAY,   •   •   •   •   542 PARN FUNERAL 2 V   3
LIPS   SEE FROTH-LIPS
    AND LIKE A SUNSET WERE HER LIPS,   •   •   •   •   •   •   •   3 OISIN 1   22
    WHOSE LIPS HAD LIFE'S MOST PROSPEROUS GLOW?   •   •   •   •   10 OISIN 1   118
    FROM ALL THEIR LIPS, AND ONCE THEY SANG   •   •   •   •   •   16 OISIN 1   226
    AND KISSED THE SCEPTRE WITH RED LIPS,   •   •   •   •   •   •   18 OISIN 1   258
    AND KISSED THE SCEPTRE WITH HOT LIPS,   •   •   •   •   •   •   18 OISIN 1   V 258
    HAPPY AS CHILDREN WITH UNWITHERING LIPS,   •   •   •   •   •   30 OISIN 2   V 148
    THE STREAM CHURNED, CHURNED, AND CHURNED---HIS LIPS APART,   31 OISIN 2   43
    •   •   •   AND CHURNED. HIS LIPS WERE ROLLED APART,   •   •   •   31 OISIN 2   V   43
    FLUTTER ALONG THE FROTH LIPS OF THE SEA,   •   •   •   •   •   33 OISIN 2   58

```
LIPS   (CONTINUED)                                              PAGE    TITLE              LINE
       AND SHORES THE FROTH LIPS WET!  . . . . . . . . . .       33 OISIN 2                  59
       FLUTTER ALONG THE FROTH LIPS OF THE SEA  . . . . . .      33 OISIN 2                  64
       SO PALE!  AND SOUNDS OF WONDER HER LIPS UTTERED, . . .    34 OISIN 2          V       71
       UPON THE LIPS OF SEA-GODS IN THEIR DAY! . . . . . . .     41 OISIN 2                 190
       AND NOW THE WARMTH OF SIGHS, AND AFTER THE QUIVER OF LIPS.  47 OISIN 3                 8
       HE, SHAKING THE FOLD OF HIS LIPS, . . . . . . . . . .     51 OISIN 3                  59
       HIS LIPS MOVED SLOWLY IN ANSWER, NO ANSWER OUT OF THEM    51 OISIN 3                  66
         CAME!
       HE, SHAKING THE FOLDS OF HIS LIPS . . . . . . . . . .     51 OISIN 3          V       59
       COMING OUT OF THE SEA AS THE DAWN COMES, A CHAUNT OF LOVE 58 OISIN 3                 158
         ON MY LIPS,
       . . . WITH RED LIPS MURMURING A SONG,  . . . . . . .      58 OISIN 3          V      158
       AND TO ITS LIPS THY STORY TELL,  . . . . . . . . . .      66 HAPPY SHEPHERD           37
       HE SPAKE ONCE MORE AND FONDLED WITH HIS LIPS . . . .      81 EPHEMERA           V    24A
       GLIMMERING IN HER DROOPED EYES, SAW HER LIPS MOVE . .     81 EPHEMERA           V    24D
       PARTED HER LIPS WITH A LOUD SUDDEN CRY. . . . . . . .    105 CUCHULAIN SEA             8
       FOR THESE RED LIPS, WITH ALL THEIR MOURNFUL PRIDE, .     111 ROSE OF WORLD             2
       OR COMES IN LAUGHTER FROM THE SEA'S SAD LIPS. . . . .    114 ROSE OF BATTLE           19
       A GIRL AROSE THAT HAD RED MOURNFUL LIPS  . . . . . .     120 SORROW OF LOVE            5
       AND THEN YOU CAME WITH THOSE RED MOURNFUL LIPS, . . .    120 SORROW OF LOVE  V         5
       AND MADE MY LIPS AND MUSIC WED, . . . . . . . . . . .    134 TWO TREES                11
       OUR ARMS ARE WAVING, OUR LIPS ARE APART! . . . . . .     140 HOSTING SIDHE             9
       "ARMS ARE A-WAVING AND LIPS APART . . . . . . . . . .    140 HOSTING SIDHE    V        9
       OUR ARMS ARE WEAVING, OUR LIPS ARE APART! . . . . . .    140 HOSTING SIDHE    V        9
       AND KISS HER LIPS AND TAKE HER HANDS! . . . . . . . .    150 WANDER AENGUS            20
       AND KISS HER LIPS AND TAKE HER HAND, . . . . . . . .     150 WANDER AENGUS    V       20
       AND HER RED LIPS SANG THEM A LOVE-SONG . . . . . . .     160 CAP AND BELLS            27
       HER RED LIPS SANG THEM A LOVE-SONG, . . . . . . . . .    160 CAP AND BELLS    V       27
       AND HER RED LIPS SANG THEM A LOVE SONG. . . . . . . .    160 CAP AND BELLS    V       27
       AND COVER YOUR LIPS WITH ODOROUS TWILIGHT AND SAY: . .   162 ASKS FORGIVE              5
       COVER YOUR LIPS WITH ROSE-HEAVY TWILIGHT, AND SAY! .     162 ASKS FORGIVE     V        5
       MAY NOT LIE ON THE BREAST NOR HIS LIPS ON THE HAIR .     177 PAST GREATNESS            9
       WOULD NOT LIE ON THE BREAST, OR HIS LIPS ON THE HAIR,    177 PAST GREATNESS   V        9
       BROKE FROM HIS PARTED LIPS AND BROKE AGAIN, . . . . .    182 QUEEN MAEVE              48
       THE PARTED LIPS REPLIED, "I SEEK YOUR HELP, . . . . .    183 QUEEN MAEVE              83
       COULD BUT AWAKEN SADLY UPON LIPS . . . . . . . . . .     185 QUEEN MAEVE             104
       A MURMUR OF SOFT WORDS AND MEETING LIPS. . . . . . .     187 QUEEN MAEVE             154
       FOR THEY, FOR ALL SMOOTH LIPS CAN SAY, . . . . . . .     202 NEVER GIVE ALL            9
       AND KISS MORE LIPS THAN LASTING PEACEABLE MEN. . . .     225 SHADOW WATER B           71
       WHAT THE WORLD'S MILLION LIPS ARE THIRSTING FOR . . .    229 SHADOW WATER B          161
       WITH SO RED LIPS, AND RUNNING ON SUCH FEET, . . . . .    231 SHADOW WATER B          199
       HE HAS STOOPED DOWN AND KISSED HER ON THE LIPS. . . .    232 SHADOW WATER B          230
       TO BE HIS BEDFELLOW?  UNTIL YOUR LIPS . . . . . . . .    237 SHADOW WATER B          335
       ALL THAT IS NOT THE MEETING OF OUR LIPS. . . . . . .     246 SHADOW WATER B          506
       MY FANCY, AND SET MY BOYISH LIPS TO SAY, . . . . . .     270 PARDON FATHERS           17
       HER EYES WERE COLD AND STEADY, HER LIPS TIGHT. . . .     279 TWO KINGS                64
       KNOWING THAT HE SHOULD FIND UPON HER LIPS  . . . . .     280 TWO KINGS                77
       "SPEAKING OF LOVE THROUGH OTHER LIPS AND LOOKING . .     283 TWO KINGS               155
       THAT WERE A DOUBLE HUNGER IN MY LIPS . . . . . . . .     285 TWO KINGS               206
       THAT WERE A DOUBLE HUNGER ON MY LIPS . . . . . . . .     285 TWO KINGS        V      206
       AND TOUCHED HER FOREHEAD WITH HIS LIPS AND SAID: . .     286 TWO KINGS        V    211B
       UPON THE LIPS OF COMMON MEN  . . . . . . . . . . . .     361 ALF POLLEXFEN            33
       THEIR SHROUDS ARE BLOODY AND THEIR LIPS ARE WET. . .     483 OIL AND BLOOD             6
       AND THE LIPS MORE SCARLET, . . . . . . . . . . . . .     532 BEFORE WORLD              3
       LIVE LIPS UPON A PLUMMET-MEASURED FACE. . . . . . . .    610 STATUES                   8
       BLOSSOMS OPEN DEWY LIPS! . . . . . . . . . . . . . .     647 ISLE STAT I 1            65
       IF ON HIS LIPS THE ENCHANTED FLOWER BE LAID! . . . .     668 ISLE STAT II 3           46
       MY LIPS, FAIR YOUTH.  IT SHALL BE AS YOU ASK. . . . .    669 ISLE STAT II 3           80
       LAUGHS NOT.  IT DWELLS ALONE ON MORTAL LIPS. . . . .     670 ISLE STAT II 3          100
       IS IN THY FACE, AND LIPS TOGETHER PRESSED! . . . . .     671 ISLE STAT II 3          139
       THE FAERY FLOWER LIES UPON THY LIPS. . . . . . . . .     677 ISLE STAT II 3          277
       THE FAERY BLOSSOM LIES UPON THY LIPS. . . . . . . . .    677 ISLE STAT II 3          285
       ENAMOURED OF THE WAVES' IMPETUOUS LIPS. . . . . . . .    677 ISLE STAT II 3          289
       THE FAERY BLOSSOM LIES UPON THY LIPS! . . . . . . . .    678 ISLE STAT II 3          291
       THE GOBLIN FLOWER LIETH ON THY LIPS. . . . . . . . .     678 ISLE STAT II 3          298
       THE FAERY BLOSSOM BROODS UPON THY LIPS. . . . . . . .    678 ISLE STAT II 3          306
       O BROTHER, LAY THY FLUTE UPON THY LIPS! . . . . . . .    681 SEEKER                    6
       TO DEATH.  HIS LIPS ARE GLUED, WITH QUIVERING TOUCH,     684 SEEKER           V       63
       WHAT, LOVER, DIE BEFORE OUR LIPS HAVE MET? . . . . .     685 SEEKER                   80
       AROUND THE TWITTER OF THE LIPS OF DUST . . . . . . .     685 DRAWING-ROOM              1
       "I LAUGHED UPON THE LIPS OF SOPHOCLES, . . . . . . .     686 LIFE                     17
       GATHERED ON HER OWN LIPS, OH YOUTH, AND FLING . . . .    688 TWO TITANS               53
       SLID CIRCLING DOWN AND SOFTLY TOUCHED MY LIPS . . . .    690 MOSADA 1                 21
       WITH POISONOUS LIPS, AND HE IS PINING SINCE? . . . .     696 MOSADA 2                  7
       YOU'RE PALE, MY LORD.  HIS LIPS ARE QUIVERING! . . .     704 MOSADA 3                127
       HE RUSHES, ROLLING FROM HIS LIPS A MADMAN'S LAUGH. .     715 FERENCZ RENYI           122
       THE GHOSTS WENT BY ME WITH THEIR LIPS APART  . . . .     734 QUATRAIN APHOR           13
       "I LAUGHED UPON THE LIPS OF SOPHOCLES, . . . . . . .     735 QUATRAIN APHOR           19
       "AROUND, THE TWITTER OF THE LIPS OF DUST . . . . . .     735 QUATRAIN APHOR           21
       AND LEAN YOUR LIPS DEVOUTLY TO THIS HARP, . . . . . .    762 SHADOW WATER A          287
       AND HEARD THE DEAD LIPS SING. . . . . . . . . . . .      790 SINGING HEAD             24
LIQUID
       OUR TREAD, AS ROSE AND FELL THE LIQUID TONES . . . .     33 OISIN 2          V      68B
       HE TURNS WHERE, HUNG LIKE DROPS OF LIQUID GOLD, . . .   710 FERENCZ RENYI    V       18
       DROPPING LIQUID RAINBOW LIGHT, . . . . . . . . . . .     732 STREET DANCERS           33
LIQUORICE
       AND THAT IS CURED BY A BOILED LIQUORICE ROOT. . . . .   227 SHADOW WATER B   V     116B
LISADILL
       AS HE WENT BY THE SANDS OF LISADILL  . . . . . . . .    127 DREAM OF FAERY   V       13
```

461

	PAGE	TITLE	LINE

LISS
AND HIM WHO DROVE THE GODS OUT OF THEIR LISS, • • • • • 170 SECRET ROSE 16

LISSADELL
HE WANDERED BY THE SANDS OF LISSADELL: • • • • • • 127 DREAM OF FAERY 13
THE LIGHT OF EVENING, LISSADELL, • • • • • • • • 475 EVA GORE-BOOTH 1

LISTEN
• • • SHALL LISTEN AND RISE UP AND WEEP: • • • • • 62 OISIN 3 206
BUT THE YOUNG QUEEN WOULD NOT LISTEN: • • • • • • 159 CAP AND BELLS 9
AND LISTEN TO ME FOR A WHILE. THE SAILORS • • • • • 226 SHADOW WATER B 92
AND LISTEN TO ME FOR AWHILE. THE SAILORS • • • • • 226 SHADOW WATER B V 92
LISTEN TO THAT LOW-LAUGHING STRING OF THE MOON • • • 243 SHADOW WATER B 432
THAT FLY INTO THE WEST? BUT LISTEN, LISTEN! • • • • 247 SHADOW WATER B 518
THAT FLY INTO THE WEST? BUT LISTEN, LISTEN! • • • • 247 SHADOW WATER B 518
IF YOU'LL BUT LISTEN CLOSELY TO THAT CRYING • • • • 247 SHADOW WATER B 520
AND LISTEN AT THE CORNERS HAS NOT COME! • • • • • 293 TO A SHADE 22
HOW COULD YOU DREAM THEY'D LISTEN • • • • • • • 395 SIXTEEN DEAD 13
WILL WONDERING LISTEN, AND THIS TALE SHALL EASE • • • 693 MOSADA 1 70
HANGS ON MY BREAST! LISTEN, WE SHALL BE SAFE. • • • 701 MOSADA 3 73

LISTENED
AS THOUGH ONE LISTENED THERE, AND HIS VOICE SANK • • • 180 QUEEN MAEVE 7
FOR YOU HAVE LISTENED TO ME PLAYING IT • • • • • 243 SHADOW WATER B 434

LISTENING
BUT NAUGHT THEY HEARD, FOR THEY ARE ALWAYS LISTENING, • • 68 SAD SHEPHERD 15
BUT NAUGHT THEY HEARD, FOR THEY ARE EVER LISTENING. • • 68 SAD SHEPHERD V 15
AND THEY WERE LISTENING THERE BEYOND THE SAIL. • • • 223 SHADOW WATER B 37
AND LISTENING TO THE CRY OF WIND AND WAVE • • • • 236 SHADOW WATER B 315
AND LISTENING TO THE CRY OF THE WIND AND WAVE • • • 236 SHADOW WATER B V 315
AN OATEN PIPE UNTO A LISTENING FAWN. • • • • • • 678 ISLE STAT II 3 301
AN OATEN PIPE UNTO A LISTENING FAUN, • • • • • • 678 ISLE STAT II 3 V 301
LISTENING, UPON THEIR SHADOWS STOOD. • • • • • • • 725 LEGEND 8

LISTENS
BUT THETIS' BELLY LISTENS. • • • • • • • • • 612 NEWS ORACLE 29

LISTLESS
AND ALL LISTLESS HOURS FEAR US, • • • • • • • • 21 OISIN 1 317

LIST'NING
IN LIST'NING SILENCE GAZING ON OUR GRIEF. • • • • • 702 MOSADA 3 87

LIT
SEE LAUGHTER-LIT A-LIT STAR-LIT
A GOLDEN CRESCENT LIT THE PLAIN, • • • • • • • 2 OISIN 1 V 788
THEN IN THAT HALL, LIT BY THE DIM SEA-SHINE, • • • 41 OISIN 2 187
THEN IN THAT HALL, LIT BY THE DIM SEA SHINE, • • • 41 OISIN 2 V 187
HIS LANGUID TAIL ABOVE US, LIT WITH MYRIAD SPOTS OF LIGHT. 77 INDIAN ON GOD 20
WHAT MEASURER TIME HAS LIT ABOVE, • • • • • • • 139 TO IRELAND 38
AND HAVING LIT UPON THIS WOMAN THERE, • • • • • • 248 SHADOW WATER B 542
AND HAVING LIT UPON THIS WOMAN HERE, • • • • • • 248 SHADOW WATER B V 542
TO HAVE LIT UPON AS CLEAN AND SWEET A TALE • • • • 258 KING NO KING 8
"WERE IT NOT THAT WHEN THE DAWN HAS LIT MY BED • • • 285 TWO KINGS 187
YET NEVER HAVE I LIT ON A FRIEND • • • • • • • 301 RUN PARADISE 25
WHERE EVERY DAY MY FOOTFALL SHOULD HAVE LIT • • • • 352 PEOPLE 8
AND WHEN SHE MEETS OUR GAZE HER EYES ARE LAUGHTER LIT • 362 HER COURTESY V 5
WE HAVE LIT UPON THE GENTLE, SENSITIVE MIND • • • • 368 EGO DOMINUS 12
ONE LASHED HER TAIL; HER EYES LIT BY THE MOON • • • 383 VISION ROBART 29
LIT UP THE DARK MAHOGANY AND THE WINE, • • • • • 410 TOWER 27
HAVE LIT UPON A WOMAN WHO SO SHARES • • • • • • 465 HARUN RASHID 85
HAD SO LIT UP THE WHOLE • • • • • • • • • • 472 ALL SOUL NIGHT 37
FLAMES THAT NO FAGGOT FEEDS, NOR STEEL HAS LIT, • • • 498 BYZANTIUM 26
SUDDENLY LIT UP • • • • • • • • • • • • 512 JANE ON GOD 16
"HAVE NO LIT CANDLES IN YOUR ROOM," • • • • • • 569 THREE BUSHES 8
WHERE NO LIT CANDLES ARE, • • • • • • • • • 570 THREE BUSHES V 25
THAT BROAD NOON HAS NEVER LIT, • • • • • • • • 632 MAN AND ECHO 4
HALF LIT, SO FLAPT THE WINGS ACROSS THE LAKE— • • • 659 ISLE STAT II 1 17
I LIT BY THE THING, 'TWAS A SHEPHERD-BOY, • • • • • 673 ISLE STAT II 3 180
HAVE LIT LONE TAPERS. NOW THE NIGHT WAS CAST, • • • 687 TWO TITANS 27
CASTLE DARGAN'S RUIN ALL LIT. • • • • • • • • 788 HAWTHORN TREE 3

LITERATURE
• • • HAVE JOINED THE AGITATION AGAINST IMMORAL LITERATURE 262 STUDENTS AGIT T
• • • AGITATION AGAINST IMMORAL LITERATURE • • • • • 262 STUDENTS AGIT V T

LITTER
SHOULDERED A LITTER WITH A WOUNDED MAN, • • • • • 537 HER VISION 14

LITTLE
MAID NIAM FROM A LITTLE TRUMP • • • • • • • • 14 OISIN 1 V 194
OUT OF A LITTLE SILVER TRUMP! • • • • • • • • 15 OISIN 1 196
AND MAKES THE LITTLE PLANETS RUN! • • • • • • • 18 OISIN 1 268
FOR JOY THE LITTLE PLANETS RUN • • • • • • • • 18 OISIN 1 V 267
AND STAY A LITTLE WHILE, AND BID THEM WEEP! • • • • 33 OISIN 2 60
A LITTLE RUNNEL MADE A BUBBLING STRAIN, • • • • • 39 OISIN 2 156
ROSE FROM A LITTLE RUNNEL ON WHOSE EDGE • • • • • 39 OISIN 2 V 157
THY FRETFUL WORDS A LITTLE WHILE, • • • • • • • 66 HAPPY SHEPHERD 40
A LITTLE FROM THE OTHER SHADES APART, • • • • • • 71 ANASHU VIJAYA 9
SIGH, O YOU LITTLE STARS! O SIGH AND SHAKE YOUR
    BLUE APPAREL! 72 ANASHU VIJAYA 18
SING, O YOU LITTLE STARS! O SING AND RAISE YOUR RAPTUROUS
    CAROL 72 ANASHU VIJAYA 20
SIGH, OH YE LITTLE STARS! OH, SIGH AND SHAKE YOUR BLUE
    APPAREL! 72 ANASHU VIJAYA V 18
SING, OH YE LITTLE STARS! OH, SING, AND RAISE YOUR
    RAPTUROUS CAROL 72 ANASHU VIJAYA V 20
I PASSED A LITTLE FURTHER ON AND HEARD A LOTUS TALK! • • 76 INDIAN ON GOD 9
A LITTLE WAY WITHIN THE GLOOM A ROEBUCK RAISED HIS EYES 76 INDIAN ON GOD 13
I PACED A LITTLE FURTHER ON AND HEARD A LOTUS TALK!— • • 76 INDIAN ON GOD V 9
I PASSED A LITTLE FURTHER ON AND HEARD A PEACOCK SAY! • • 77 INDIAN ON GOD 17
I PACED A LITTLE FURTHER AND I HEARD A PEACOCK SAY!— • • 77 INDIAN ON GOD V 17

	PAGE	TITLE		LINE

LITTLE (CONTINUED)

I PASSED A LITTLE FURTHER AND I HEARD A PEACOCK SAY:--	77	INDIAN ON GOD	V	17
THE LITTLE WAVES THAT WALKED IN EVENING WHITENESS,	81	EPHEMERA	V	24C
I CAME UPON A LITTLE TOWN	85	MAD KING GOLL		49
AS ONCE WITHIN A LITTLE TOWN	85	MAD KING GOLL	V	49
TIME WAS, AS IN A LITTLE TOWN,	85	MAD KING GOLL	V	49
ONCE, WHILE WITHIN A LITTLE TOWN	85	MAD KING GOLL	V	49
SHE PASSED THE SALLEY GARDENS WITH LITTLE SNOW-WHITE FEET.	90	SALLEY GARDENS		2
COME ROUND ME, LITTLE CHILDER:	94	MOLL MAGEE		1
YE LITTLE CHILDER DEAR,	95	MOLL MAGEE		18
THE LITTLE STRAWS WERE TURNIN' ROUND	95	MOLL MAGEE		31
SO NOW, YE LITTLE CHILDER,	96	MOLL MAGEE		53
A LITTLE SPACE FOR THE ROSE-BREATH TO FILL!	101	ROSE UPON ROOD		14
TAKE, IF YOU MUST, THIS LITTLE BAG OF DREAMS:	104	FERGUS DRUID		29
GOD'S BELL HAS CLAIMED THEM BY THE LITTLE CRY	114	ROSE OF BATTLE		23
WE SHALL NO LONGER HEAR THE LITTLE CRY	115	ROSE OF BATTLE		35
MURMUR, A LITTLE SADLY, HOW LOVE FLED	121	YOU ARE OLD		10
MURMUR, A LITTLE SAD, "FROM US FLED LOVE,	121	YOU ARE OLD	V	10
IT SEEMED THEY RAISED THEIR LITTLE SILVER HEADS,	126	DREAM OF FAERY		6
TOLD WHERE--AH, LITTLE, ALL-UNNEEDED VOICE!--	127	DREAM OF FAERY	V	30
AND ALL GREW FRIENDLY FOR A LITTLE WHILE.	129	BOOK STORIES		8
FOR ALL WHO HEARD IT DREAMED A LITTLE WHILE.	129	BOOK STORIES	V	8
AND RODE WITH LITTLE CARE.	133	FR GILLIGAN		28
OR ONLY GAZE A LITTLE WHILE:	135	TWO TREES		24
OVER THE LITTLE SILVER CORDS,	146	FISH		6
AND CAUGHT A LITTLE SILVER TROUT.	149	WANDER AENGUS		8
AND HOOKED A LITTLE SILVER TROUT.	149	WANDER AENGUS	V	8
O WHAT TO ME THE LITTLE ROOM	151	HEART OF WOMAN		1
A LITTLE STOLEN TRESS. I, TOO, AWAIT	170	SECRET ROSE		27
CALLED RATHER BAILE LITTLE LAND,	189	BAILE AILLINN	V	17
WHEN THEY HAD RIDDEN A LITTLE WAY	191	BAILE AILLINN		56
THEREFORE IT IS BUT LITTLE NEWS	194	BAILE AILLINN		124
AND LITTLE SHADOWS COME ABOUT HER EYES:	199	FOLLY COMFORT		3
AND THERE ARE LITTLE CREASES ABOUT HER EYES:	199	FOLLY COMFORT	V	3
THE LITTLE FOX HE MURMURED,	214	HAPPY TOWNLAND		13
BUT THE LITTLE RED FOX MURMURED,	214	HAPPY TOWNLAND		17
THE LITTLE FOX HE MURMURED,	215	HAPPY TOWNLAND		33
BUT THE LITTLE RED FOX MURMURED,	215	HAPPY TOWNLAND		37
AND BLOW A LITTLE NOISE	215	HAPPY TOWNLAND		43
THE LITTLE FOX HE MURMURED,	216	HAPPY TOWNLAND		53
BUT THE LITTLE RED FOX MURMURED,	216	HAPPY TOWNLAND		57
OR HURLED THE LITTLE STREETS UPON THE GREAT,	256	NO SECOND TROY		4
"WHILE I HAVE HIM AND YOU IT MATTERS LITTLE	280	TWO KINGS		85
BUT LITTLE TIME HAD THEY TO PRAY	289	SEPTEMBER 1913		12
OF A MOST RIDICULOUS LITTLE BIRD	314	MEMORY YOUTH		20
A LITTLE NEARER TO HIS THOUGHT.	324	ROBERT GREGORY		23
A DEAL I'D SWEAT AND LITTLE EARN	331	ROUND TOWER		2
"IF LITTLE PLANNED IS LITTLE SINNED	338	TOM OROUGHLEY		9
"IF LITTLE PLANNED IS LITTLE SINNED	338	TOM OROUGHLEY		9
BUT LITTLE NEED THE GRAVE DISTRESS.	338	TOM OROUGHLEY		10
"OH, LITTLE PLANNED IS LITTLE SINNED	338	TOM OROUGHLEY	V	9
"OH, LITTLE PLANNED IS LITTLE SINNED	338	TOM OROUGHLEY	V	9
AND LITTLE NEED THE GRAVE DISTRESS.	338	TOM OROUGHLEY	V	10
AND WHEN 'TWAS DONE SO LITTLE HAD I DONE	341	SHEP GOATHERD		59
GIVE HER A LITTLE GRACE,	367	HER CHRIS TREE		9
YET LITTLE PEACE HE HAD,	383	VISION ROBART		35
O LITTLE DID THEY CARE WHO DANCED BETWEEN,	383	VISION ROBART		37
AND LITTLE SHE BY WHOM HER DANCE WAS SEEN	383	VISION ROBART		38
SHE THAT BUT LITTLE PATIENCE KNEW,	397	POLIT PRISONER		1
BESIDE THE LITTLE LAKE	400	DEMON BEAST		23
PROSPER BUT LITTLE, HAS DRIED UP OF LATE,	405	FOR DAUGHTER		51
AND BROUGHT THEM IN A LITTLE COVERED DISH.	410	TOWER		32
THOUGHT THAT UNLESS A LITTLE POWDER BURNED	429	NINETEEN 19		21
THE WOMEN TAKE SO LITTLE STOCK	455	HIS MEMORIES		7
AND WAIT WAR'S MUSIC: PASS THE LITTLE GALLERY:	461	HARUN RASHID		8
GREAT HATRED, LITTLE ROOM,	506	REMORSE SPEECH		12
"BODES ME LITTLE GOOD."	539	MEETING		6
SWEETENS THE LITTLE HALF-WAY HOUSE	567	LAPIS LAZULI		48
SWEETEN THE LITTLE HALFWAY HOUSE	567	LAPIS LAZULI	V	48
THAT HAD SUCH LITTLE SENSE	585	ORAHILLY		11
AND THAT SHOULD MOTHER SEEK HER SON SHE'D HAVE BUT LITTLE LUCK	593	PILGRIM		12
OR SAD SEA-SHELLS WHERE LITTLE ECHOES SIT?	650	ISLE STAT I 1		149
SUCH QUESTS AS THESE, I TROW, NEED LITTLE WIT.	650	ISLE STAT I 1		150
THERE'S LITTLE I'D REFUSE THEE, DEAREST YOUTH.	669	ISLE STAT II 3		71
SWIFT LAKE. A VERY LITTLE THING THAT IS,	669	ISLE STAT II 3		78
SO BE THOU STILL, DEAR HEART, A LITTLE WHILE!	677	ISLE STAT II 3		283
THE PLAIN, A LITTLE FAIR-HAIRED MAID I LOVE.	679	ISLE STAT II 3		312
THERE DWELLS A LITTLE FAIR-HAIRED MAID I LOVE.	679	ISLE STAT II 3	V	312
WITH LITTLE VOICES SONGS OF FEARFUL THINGS.	682	SEEKER		31
A LITTLE WHILE AND--RED EVE DIES--	686	LIFE		13
WITH LITTLE CRIES OF JOY HE KISSED THE RAIN	688	TWO TITANS		33
AND FLOWERS AND LITTLE CHILDREN. SUDDENLY	688	TWO TITANS		36
SINKS, SHINING ON THE LITTLE CRUCIFIX	691	MOSADA 1		34
A-SHINING ON THE LITTLE CRUCIFIX	691	MOSADA 1	V	34
A LITTLE MOORISH GIRL? SMALL WORTH. MY SONG--	696	MOSADA 2		10
AS QUIET AS THE LITTLE RIVULETS	698	MOSADA 2		57
ABOVE THE FARM-HOUSE BY THE LITTLE LAKE	699	MOSADA 3		3
A LITTLE NEARER THOSE BRIGHT STARS. TELL ME,	701	MOSADA 3		59
YOU ARE WASTING AWAY, LITTLE FAIRY.	707	FAIRY PEDANT		12
WHILE I MURMUR A LITTLE AND PONDER	707	FAIRY PEDANT		14

	PAGE	TITLE		LINE
LITTLE (CONTINUED)				
YOU ARE WASTING AWAY, LITTLE FAIRY.	707	FAIRY PEDANT		20
YOU ARE WASTING AWAY, LITTLE FAIRY.	708	FAIRY PEDANT		28
SHE IS WASTING AWAY, LITTLE FAIRY.	708	FAIRY PEDANT		40
ABOLISHED BY A MIRE OF LITTLE THINGS,	711	FERENCZ RENYI		36
"A LITTLE WILL I LAY MY WEARY HEAD,	712	FERENCZ RENYI		75
BELOVED, HOW TWO LITTLE YEARS AGO	713	FERENCZ RENYI		89
SO LITTLE. AS THE MONTHS PASSED BY WE GREW	713	FERENCZ RENYI		93
A LITTLE BOY OUTSIDE THE SYCAMORE WOOD	715	DWELT SYCAMORE		1
A LITTLE BOY INSIDE THE SYCAMORE WOOD	715	DWELT SYCAMORE		5
A LITTLE WITHERED MAN, AND OLD.	716	FAIRY DOCTOR		4
THE LITTLE WITHERED MAN, AND OLD.	717	FAIRY DOCTOR		24
HANG THE MIST-THREADS FOR A LITTLE WHILE LIKE COBWEBS IN THE AIR:	719	PHANTOM SHIP		29
HANG THE MIST THREADS FOR A LITTLE WHILE LIKE COBWEBS IN THE AIR.	719	PHANTOM SHIP	V	29
SAVE, WITH THE LITTLE GOLDEN GREEDY CARP,	720	WITCH VIVIEN		2
WITHOUT THERE OF A LITTLE, LIGHT OLD MAN:	720	WITCH VIVIEN		13
THE PASSING OF THOSE LITTLE GRAINS IS SNOW	722	WITCH VIVIEN		48
AND LITTLE BOYS PLAYED PITCH AND TOSS.	725	LEGEND		4
"IF I WERE FREE TO DO AS LITTLE	731	PRIEST FAIRY		77
THE LITTLE OLD GLOVE OF A CHILD:	744	GLOVE CLOAK		9
AND WHEN YOU CAME TO SCORN OUR LITTLE WARS	749	SHADOW WATER A	V	34
I SHALL BE HOME NOW IN A LITTLE WHILE,	759	SHADOW WATER A		240
SHE WILL SAY SOMETHING IN A LITTLE WHILE,	760	SHADOW WATER A		248
HOW LITTLE AND REEDY A SOUND AWAKES A GOD	760	SHADOW WATER A		252
LITTLE-LAND				
CALLED RATHER BAILE LITTLE-LAND,	189	BAILE AILLINN		17
LIVE SEE RE-LIVE				
MUST LIVE TO BE OLD LIKE THE WANDERING MOON.	3	OISIN 1		12
"MY BROTHERS AND MY SISTERS LIVE AND THRIVE,	32	OISIN 2	V	50C
FORMS WITHOUT NUMBER! WHEN THE LIVE WEST FLASHED	41	OISIN 2	V	180
FOR NO LIVE CREATURES LIVED THERE, NO WEASELS MOVED IN THE DARK:	48	OISIN 3		19
FOR NO LIVE CREATURES LIVE THERE, NO WEASELS MOVE IN THE DARK:	56	OISIN 3		139
FOR NO LIVE CREATURES LIVE THERE, NO WEASELS MOVE IN THE DARK:	56	OISIN 3		139
NO LIVE MAN GOES THITHER.	62	OISIN 3	V	214
YOU LIVE, AND ON THE VILLAGE BORDER SHE,	74	ANASHU VIJAYA		62
YOU LIVE, AND ON THE BORDER OF THE VILLAGE SHE,	74	ANASHU VIJAYA	V	62
IN ALL POOR FOOLISH THINGS THAT LIVE A DAY,	101	ROSE UPON ROOD		11
OF THEIR SAD HEARTS, THAT MAY NOT LIVE NOR DIE.	114	ROSE OF BATTLE		24
OF OUR SAD HEARTS, THAT MAY NOT LIVE NOR DIE.	115	ROSE OF BATTLE		36
AND LIVE ALONE IN THE BEE-LOUD GLADE.	117	ISLE INNISFREE		4
AND TALKED OF THE DARK FOLK WHO LIVE IN SOULS	136	TO SOME I TALK		4
FOR THERE LIVE THE MYSTIC BROTHERHOOD	148	INTO TWILIGHT	V	10
LIVE BUT TO LIGHT YOUR PASSING FEET.	158	BELOVED RHYMES		12
BUT WITH THE BURNING, LIVE, UNSHAKEN VOICE	183	QUEEN MAEVE		75
THE NOTES THEY WAKEN SHALL LIVE ON	213	BLESS PSALTER		16
THE PROUD AND CARELESS NOTES LIVE ON,	213	BLESS PSALTER		19
THAT HAVE HAD DREAMS FOR FATHER, LIVE IN US.	252	SHADOW WATER B		619
AND BEEN CONTENT TO LIVE.	256	WORDS		16
WHY MUST I LIVE SOME THIRTY, FORTY YEARS,	285	TWO KINGS		199
FOR HE KNEW BETTER HOW TO LIVE.	288	TO WEALTHY MAN		30
AM I TO LIVE ON LEBEEN-LONE?"	295	THREE BEGGARS		5
DO, BUT AWAKE A HOPE TO LIVE	309	REALISTS		6
DO BUT WAKE THE HOPE TO LIVE	309	REALISTS	V	6
LIVE HE OR DIE	310	PEACOCK		7
SO CHANGED ME THAT I LIVE	315	FRIENDS		15
AND SOLID MEN, FOR ALL THEIR PASSION, LIVE	325	ROBERT GREGORY		37
IF I SHOULD LIVE AS LIVE THE NEIGHBOURS,"	331	ROUND TOWER		3
IF I SHOULD LIVE AS LIVE THE NEIGHBOURS,"	331	ROUND TOWER		3
IF I SHOULD LIVE AS LIVES THE NEIGHBOURS"	331	ROUND TOWER	V	3
AND LIVE LIKE SOLOMON	346	ON WOMAN		42
A DAPHNE AND A MARY WHO LIVE IN PRIVACY:	354	HIS PHOENIX		18
MERE IMAGES: CHOSEN THIS PLACE TO LIVE IN	373	PHASES OF MOON		13
LIVE IN UNCOMPOSITE BLESSEDNESS.	387	ROBARTES DANCE		46
MINUTE BY MINUTE THEY LIVE:	393	EASTER 1916		55
O MAY SHE LIVE LIKE SOME GREEN LAUREL	405	FOR DAUGHTER		47
AND LIVE AMONG THE ANCIENT HOLY MEN,	448	HERO GIRL FOOL	V	11A
LIKE MEN WHO LIVE BY HABIT. EVERY DAY	463	HARUN RASHID		56
I SAY THAT A DJIN SPOKE. A LIVE LONG HOUR	467	HARUN RASHID	V	136
WHAT MATTER IF I LIVE IT ALL ONCE MORE?	478	SELF AND SOUL		43
I AM CONTENT TO LIVE IT ALL AGAIN	479	SELF AND SOUL		57
WHAT MADE ME LIVE LIKE THESE THAT SEEM	507	STREAM AND SUN		14
WHAT BIDS ME LIVE LIKE THESE THAT SEEM	507	STREAM AND SUN	V	14
LIVE IN A HEAVENLY MANSION.	513	JANE TALK BISH		5
IN THAT FAITH I LIVE OR DIE.	529	TOM LUNATIC		18
LIVE LONE, ALONE WITH A SPECKLED SHIN?	551	SONGS REWRIT 1	V	8
HOW CAN SHE LIVE TILL IN HER BLOOD HE LIVE!	558	RIBH CHRISTIAN		24
HOW CAN SHE LIVE TILL IN HER BLOOD HE LIVE!	558	RIBH CHRISTIAN		24
BUT STORIES THAT LIVE LONGEST	587	PARNELLITES		29
"ALL MEN LIVE IN SUFFERING,	589	OLD WICKED MAN		46
AND DRUNK OR SOBER LIVE AT EASE	597	MODEL LAUREATE		13
FROM THOSE THEY LIVE AMONG,	607	SONGS BURDEN 2		13
LIVE LIPS UPON A PLUMMET-MEASURED FACE.	610	STATUES		8
MORE DREAD THE LIFE THAT WE LIVE,	615	MARCH SONGS 2		15
A VISION OF TERROR THAT IT MUST LIVE THROUGH	619	BRONZE HEAD		17
LIVE TO BEAR CHILDREN TO A DUNCE:	626	OLD MEN BE MAD		6
THERE LIVE HIS SISTER AND HIS MOTHER. HIGH	710	FERENCZ RENYI	V	25

LIVE   (CONTINUED)
    JOYS AND FEARS IN THEIR GREY FACES THAT THE LIVE EARTH   719 PHANTOM SHIP   26
        KNOWETH NOT.
    LIVE, FOR I SAW THEM DANCING THERE. . . . .   788 HAWTHORN TREE   12
LIVED   SEE LONG-LIVED
    NOR THE HIGH GODS WHO NEVER LIVED, MAY FIGHT . . . . .   34 OISIN 2   80
    FOR NO LIVE CREATURES LIVED THERE, NO WEASELS MOVED IN   48 OISIN 3   19
        THE DARK.
    SO LIVED I AND LIVED NOT, SO WROUGHT I AND WROUGHT NOT,   53 OISIN 3   95
    . . .
    SO LIVED I AND LIVED NOT, SO WROUGHT I AND WROUGHT NOT,   53 OISIN 3   95
    . . .
    THE LOVE I LIVED, THE DREAM I KNEW. . . . .   139 TO IRELAND   34
    HAS LOVER LIVED, BUT LONGED TO WIVE . . . .   197 BAILE AILLINN   206
    SEVEN OLD SISTERS WIND THE THREADS OF THE LONG LIVED ONES,   209 UNDER THE MOON V   7
    NONE BUT THE DEAD, OR THOSE THAT NEVER LIVED, ...   231 SHADOW WATER B   202
    WHEN HELEN LIVED . . . .   293 HELEN LIVED   T
    SHE LIVED IN STORM AND STRIFE, ...   317 NIGHT COME   1
    BUT LIVED AS 'TWERE A KING . . . .   317 NIGHT COME   6
    HER LABOURING MEN, AS THOUGH HER DARLING LIVED, ...   340 SHEP GOATHERD   38
    BETWEEN THE NIGHT AND MORNING. I MIGHT HAVE LIVED, . .   351 PEOPLE   6
    WAS: "YOU, THAT HAVE NOT LIVED IN THOUGHT BUT DEED, . . .   353 PEOPLE   30
    WHO HAVE LIVED IN JOY AND LAUGHED INTO THE FACE OF DEATH.   366 HER COURAGE   10
    WHO LIVED IN SHAMELESS JOY AND LAUGHED INTO THE FACE OF   366 HER COURAGE   V   10
        DEATH.
    THAT LIVED IN JOY AND LAUGHED INTO THE FACE OF DEATH. . .   366 HER COURAGE   V   10
    WHO HAVE LIVED IN JOY AND LAUGHED IN THE FACE OF DEATH.   366 HER COURAGE   V   10
    ONCE HE LIVED A SCHOOLMASTER . . . .   381 SONG OF FOOL   5
    BUT LIVED WHERE MOTLEY IS WORN. . . . .   392 EASTER 1916   14
    BEYOND THAT RIDGE LIVED MRS. FRENCH, AND ONCE . . . .   410 TOWER   25
    WHO'D LIVED SOMEWHERE UPON THAT ROCKY PLACE, SAY: . . .   410 TOWER   35
    NEVER TO HAVE LIVED IS BEST, ANCIENT WRITERS SAY: . . .   459 FROM OEDIPUS   10
    LIVED AT MY SIDE; THOUGHT TIME'S DISFIGURING TOUCH . . .   466 HARUN RASHID   110
    LIVED AT MY SIDE; THAT TIME'S DISFIGURING TOUCH . . .   466 HARUN RASHID   V   110
    A SPOT WHEREON THE FOUNDERS LIVED AND DIED . . . . .   491 COOLE BALLYLEE   33
    NO MAN HAS EVER LIVED THAT HAD ENOUGH . . . .   500 VACILLATION   25
    ALL LIVES THAT HAS LIVED: . . . .   504 QUARREL IN AGE   9
    EVERY THING THAT HAS LIVED . . . .   504 QUARREL IN AGE V   9
    CRIED THAT WE LIVED LIKE BEAST AND BEAST. . . . . .   508 JANE BISHOP   13
    WE LIVED LIKE MEN THAT WATCH A PAINTED STAGE. . . . .   542 PARN FUNERAL 1   18
    SEVENTY YEARS HAVE I LIVED: . . . .   567 FROM JAPANESE   2
    SEVENTY YEARS HAVE I LIVED . . . .   567 FROM JAPANESE   5
    SEVENTY YEARS HAVE I LIVED, ...   567 FROM JAPANESE   7
    THE CHAMBERMAID LIVED LONG, AND TOOK . . . .   571 THREE BUSHES   57
    HE THOUGHT THE SAME AND LIVED BY RULE, ...   576 WHAT THEN   3
    HONOUR HAD LIVED SO LONG, ALL LACKING FOUND. . . . .   603 GALLERY REVIS   35
    HONOUR HAD LIVED SO LONG, THEIR HEALTH I FOUND. . . .   603 GALLERY REVIS V   35
    KNOWS I HAVE LIVED SO LONG. . . . .   607 SONGS BURDEN 2   26
    I LIVED AMONG GREAT HOUSES, ...   626 STATES HOLIDAY   1
    WHO, DREAMING TO A WONDROUS AGE, LIVED ON, ...   692 MOSADA 1   52
    ANY THAT LIVED, AND I HAVE BROUGHT MY GALLEY . . . .   756 SHADOW WATER A V 191A
LIVELONG
    AND HAD THE LIVELONG SUMMER DAY TO SPEND. . . . . .   409 TOWER   10
    I SAY THAT A DJINN SPOKE. A LIVELONG HOUR . . . . .   467 HARUN RASHID   136
LIVE-LONG
    I SAY THAT A JINN SPOKE. A LIVE-LONG HOUR . . . . .   467 HARUN RASHID V   136
    DREAMING THE LIVE-LONG SUMMER IN THE SHADE, ...   650 ISLE STAT I 1   139
LIVELY
    WHAT LIVELY LAD MOST PLEASURED ME . . . .   538 LAST CONFESS   1
LIVER
    BUT NEVER, NEVER DANGLING LEAVE THE LIVER AND THE LIGHTS.   790 HEART SLEEVE   2
LIVERPOOL
    IN LONDON OR IN LIVERPOOL: . . . .   360 ALF POLLEXFEN   16
LIVERY
    THE ILL-BRED SON OF A LIVERY STABLE KEEPER— . . . .   370 EGO DOMINUS V   61
    THE ILL-BRED SON OF A LIVERY STABLE-KEEPER— . . . .   370 EGO DOMINUS V   61
LIVERY-STABLE
    THE COARSE-BRED SON OF A LIVERY-STABLE KEEPER— . . .   370 EGO DOMINUS   61
LIVES
    OUR LIVES HAVE KNOWN NO LAW NOR RULE: . . . . . .   22 OISIN 1 V   340
    IS AN UNDYING MOORFOWL, AND HE LIVES BEYOND THE SKY. . .   76 INDIAN ON GOD   7
    SHALL WARM THEIR LIVES AT MANY A RUSTLING FLAME." . . .   80 EPHEMERA V   12B
    LIVES ON THIS LONELY FACE. . . . .   112 ROSE OF WORLD   10
    IN THEIR LONG LIVES? WILL YOU BE OF OUR TROOP . . . .   225 SHADOW WATER B   72
    IN THEIR LONG LIVES? IF YOU'LL BE OF OUR TROOP . . . .   225 SHADOW WATER B V   72
    WE'LL OUT, FOR THE WORLD LIVES AS LONG AGO: . . . .   257 RECONCILIATION   8
    ALL THEIR LIVES THROUGH INTO SOME DRIFT OF WINGS. . .   265 ABBEY THEATRE   7
    "HE LIVES?" "HE LIVES AND IS A HEALTHY MAN." . . . .   280 TWO KINGS   84
    "HE LIVES?" "HE LIVES AND IS A HEALTHY MAN." . . . .   280 TWO KINGS   84
    IF I SHOULD LIVE AS LIVES THE NEIGHBOURS" . . . .   331 ROUND TOWER V   3
    HOW HARD A LIFE HER SERVANT LIVES, ...   336 YOUNG BEAUTY   14
    THAT LIVES IN MEMORY. . . . .   459 HIS WILDNESS   10
    ALL LIVES THAT HAS LIVED: . . . .   504 QUARREL IN AGE   9
    LIVES THAT LONELY THING . . . .   504 QUARREL IN AGE   14
    LIVES: THAT MUCH IS CERTAIN: . . . .   504 QUARREL IN AGE V   10
    IT HAD NOT TOUCHED OUR LIVES. BUT POPULAR RAGE, . .   542 PARN FUNERAL 1   20
    MANY TIMES MAN LIVES AND DIES . . . .   637 BEN BULBEN   13
    BEAT OUT THEIR LIVES LAMENTING O'ER THE SAND: . . .   652 ISLE STAT I 2   14
    FOR THERE THE GREAT ENCHANTRESS LIVES. AND THERE . .   653 ISLE STAT I 2   38
    FOR, AH, OUR LIVES WERE BUT TWO STARRY WORDS . . . .   675 ISLE STAT II 3   236
    UPON THEIR THRONES. THE LIVES OF MEN SHALL FLOW . .   698 MOSADA 2   56

```
                                                     PAGE    TITLE              LINE

LIVES   (CONTINUED)
     IN OTHER LIVES?  HAST THOU NOT QUAFFED OLD WINE  . . . .   724  KANVA ON SELF          12
     I THINK HE LIVES IN LOCHLANN.  NO, NOT THERE!  . . . .     760  SHADOW WATER A  V  254A
     THAT LIVES AMONG THE WOODS OF THE DARK HOUNDS.  . . . .    766  SHADOW WATER A        376
     ONE LIVES UNDER THE WAVES.  . . . . . . . . . . .          770  SPINNING SONG           2
     ONE LIVES IN THE HOUSE OF THE SUN,  . . . . . . .          771  SPINNING SONG           6
     AND ONE LIVES UNDER THE BOUGHS .  . . . . . . . .          771  SPINNING SONG           8
     "LIVES ALL HIS DAYS .  . . . . . . . . . . . .             780  WELL AND TREE           3
     THEIR BRIEF LIVES I NEVER KNEW.  . . . . . . . .           787  HUDDON DUDDON           5
LIVID
     AND THEREUPON I DREW THE LIVID CHOP .  . . . . . .          40  OISIN 2               178
     ONCE HELD BETWEEN MY ARMS, WITH LIVID CHOP  . . . .         40  OISIN 2         V     178
     I HELD A DRIPPING CORPSE, WITH LIVID CHOP  . . . .          40  OISIN 2         V     178
     AND I BUT HELD A CORPSE, WITH LIVID CHOP  . . . .           40  OISIN 2         V     178
LIVING     SEE EVER-LIVING HARD-LIVING OUT-LIVING
     THE ISLAND OF THE LIVING .  . . . . . . . . . .              1  OISIN 1         V       T
     MY DREAMS WERE LIVING.  NOW THE HOOF .  . . . . .           25  OISIN 1         V     382
     "NEITHER THE LIVING, NOR THE UNLABOURING DEAD,  . .         34  OISIN 2                79
     COME FROM THE ISLE OF THE LIVING."  "THEN GET YE  .        34  OISIN 2         V      79
     ISLES OF THE LIVING AND OF VICTORIES  . . . . . .           46  OISIN 2         V     247
     THIS WOULD I SAY, MOST WISE OF LIVING SOULS!  . . .        102  FERGUS DRUID            9
     THE POWERS WHOSE NAME AND SHAPE NO LIVING CREATURE KNOWS   174  ELEMENT POWERS          1
     IN COMFORTABLE SLEEP; ALL LIVING SLEPT  . . . . .          180  QUEEN MAEVE            15
     WHAT GOOD IS THERE IN THIS HARD WAY OF LIVING,  . .        225  SHADOW WATER B         69
     FOR NEITHER I NOR ANY LIVING MAN .  . . . . . . .          250  SHADOW WATER B        588
     NOR HAD THERE BEEN THE NOISE OF LIVING THING  . . .        279  TWO KINGS              54
     AND THERE HAD BEEN NO SOUND OF LIVING THING  . . .         279  TWO KINGS       V      54
     "IF HE BE LIVING STILL THE WHOLE WORLD'S MINE,  . .        280  TWO KINGS       V      85
     BUT IF NOT LIVING, HALF THE WORLD IS LOST."  . . .         280  TWO KINGS       V      86
     THAT DYING CHOSE THE LIVING WORLD FOR TEXT  . . . .        324  ROBERT GREGORY         26
     THE LIVING BEAUTY  . . . . . . . . . . . . .               333  LIVING BEAUTY           T
     THE LIVING BEAUTY IS FOR YOUNGER MEN,  . . . . .           334  LIVING BEAUTY           9
     THE LIVING MEN THAT I HATE,  . . . . . . . . .             347  FISHERMAN              13
     TO TROUBLE THE LIVING STREAM.  . . . . . . . .             393  EASTER 1916            44
     AND HELEN HAS ALL LIVING HEARTS BETRAYED.  . . . .         411  TOWER                  53
     SHOULD HEAR MY LIVING FEET, NOR WOULD I TREAD  . . .       435  NEW FACES               3
     THE LIVING SEEM MORE SHADOWY THAN THEY.  . . . . .         435  NEW FACES               8
     SHE STANDS BEFORE ME AS A LIVING CHILD.  . . . . .         444  SCHOOL CHILDR          24
     MIRACLE-BRED OUT OF THE LIVING STONE;  . . . . .           446  COLONUS PRAISE         13
     AND THAT NONE LIVING KNOWS.  . . . . . . . . .             455  HIS MEMORIES            6
     FARISTAH, AND NO LIVING EAR BUT HIS.  . . . . . .          461  HARUN RASHID    V       4
     NONE BUT THE LIVING MOCK,  . . . . . . . . . .             471  ALL SOUL NIGHT         17
     NO LIVING MAN CAN DRINK FROM THE WHOLE WINE.  . . .        474  ALL SOUL NIGHT         85
     WHEREAT THE LIVING MOCK,  . . . . . . . . . .             474  ALL SOUL NIGHT         87
     A LIVING MAN IS BLIND AND DRINKS HIS DROP.  . . . .        478  SELF AND SOUL          41
     A PROPERTY OF THE LIVING!  BUT NO STAIN  . . . . .         482  BLOOD AND MOON         52
     SAY THAT OF LIVING MEN I HATE  . . . . . . . .             539  MEETING                11
     AND NOW NONE LIVING CAN,  . . . . . . . . . .             571  THREE BUSHES           74
     AND TOM MAKE OUT A LIVING  . . . . . . . . . .            597  COLONEL MARTIN         70
     WHEN TOM MADE OUT A LIVING .  . . . . . . . .             597  COLONEL MARTIN  V      70
     HAZEL LAVERY LIVING AND DYING, THAT TALE  . . . . .       602  GALLERY REVIS          23
     LIVING, WIDE WINGED, ON THE WATERS FLOAT.  . . . .        657  ISLE STAT I 3          54
     AND LOUDLY TWICE THE LIVING WINGS FLAPT WIDE,  . . .      659  ISLE STAT II 1         12
     FROM WHOSE GREEN BANKS NO LIVING THING MAY ROVE,  .       664  ISLE STAT II 2         57
     THE ORB OF THE MOST INNER LIVING HEART  . . . . .         689  NETTLESHIP             15
     THE LIVING WOODS FOREGO THEIR CARE,  . . . . . .          736  SUMMER EVENING          1
     I LEFT HER LIVING, THINKING THAT I HAD FOUND  . . .       755  SHADOW WATER A        174
     THE FALLING BLOSSOMS, AND THE DEAD THE LIVING.  . .       756  SHADOW WATER A        182
     I WAIT YOUR WORDS AS THE DEAD WAIT THE LIVING.  . .       756  SHADOW WATER A  V     182
     LIVING OR DYING.  BID AIBRIC TO YOUR COUNTRY,  . . .      768  SHADOW WATER A        413
LIZARD
     A LIZARD CRAWLS--THE TWO MEN GAZE INTENT,  . . . .        711  FERENCZ RENYI          47
LIZARDS
     THE CHILD PURSUING LIZARDS IN THE GRASS,  . . . . .       686  LIFE                    1
     THE CHILD WHO CHASES LIZARDS IN THE GRASS,  . . . .       734  QUATRAIN APHOR          1
     THE CHILD PURSUING LIZARDS IN THE GRASS,  . . . . .       734  QUATRAIN APHOR  V       1
LO
     TO THE ISLAND OF FORGETFULNESS, FOR LO!  . . . . .         46  OISIN 2               246
     AND LO! MY ANCIENT BURDEN MAY DEPART.  . . . . . .         69  SAD SHEPHERD           24
     AND LO--MY HEAVY BURTHEN MAY DEPART!"  . . . . . .         69  SAD SHEPHERD    V      24
LOAD
     MAY PANTHERS END HIM.--HEAR, AND LOAD OUR KING  . .        71  ANASHU VIJAYA           6
     YOUTH'S DREAMY LOAD, TILL SHE  . . . . . . . .            315  FRIENDS                14
     OR SHIFT TIME'S FILTHY LOAD,  . . . . . . . . .           505  RESULT THOUGHT         15
LOADED
     NOT LOADED CENTURIES MIGHT VAPOUR.  RAN  . . . . .         38  OISIN 2         V     127
     WAS LOADED WITH THE MEMORY OF DAYS  . . . . . .            39  OISIN 2               150
     HE UNPACKS THE LOADED PERN .  . . . . . . . .            342  SHEP GOATHERD          97
     I LOSE!  THEY'RE LOADED DICE.  TIME ALWAYS PLAYS  .       721  WITCH VIVIEN           44
     WITH LOADED DICE.  ANOTHER CHANCE!  COME, FATHER!  .      721  WITCH VIVIEN           45
LOADS
     BUT UNDER HEAVY LOADS OF TRAMPLED CLAY  . . . . .         483  OIL AND BLOOD           4
LOADSTONE
     OR IMAGE, FROM BEYOND THE LOADSTONE MOUNTAIN,  . . .      371  ON GOING HOUSE         11
LOAM
     OUT OF THE FOREST LOAM,  . . . . . . . . . .             439  FRAGMENTS               8
LOCHLANN
     FROM HILLY LOCHLANN; BUT OUR SAIL HAS PASSED  . . .       749  SHADOW WATER A         44
     A GALLEY FROM THE LOCHLANN SEAS! HER FLAG  . . . .        751  SHADOW WATER A         98
     WHEN YOU ARE ABOARD THE LOCHLANN GALLEY, LASH  . . .      752  SHADOW WATER A        128
     ENDS ALL THINGS.  I HAVE SLAIN THE LOCHLANN KING.  .      754  SHADOW WATER A        163
```

LOCHLANN   (CONTINUED)

BESIDE A LOCHLANN WHARF, AND THOUGH SHE HAD SWORN	• • •	756 SHADOW WATER A		188
HAVE BID ME HOPE, SAIL TO THE LOCHLANN SHORE	• • •	756 SHADOW WATER A	V	184
IN SOUTHERN LOCHLANN. I WOULD NOT OBEY	• • •	756 SHADOW WATER A		191
I THINK HE LIVES IN LOCHLANN. NO, NOT THERE!	• • •	760 SHADOW WATER A	V	254A
SEEK AIBRIC ON THE LOCHLANN GALLEY, AND TELL HIM	• • •	767 SHADOW WATER A		401

LOCK

| MADE LOCK, STOCK AND BARREL | • • • | 415 TOWER | | 150 |

LOCKE

| LOCKE SANK INTO A SWOON! | • • • | 439 FRAGMENTS | | 1 |

LOCKED

| HORN LOCKED IN SWORD, THEY TUGGED AND STRUGGLED THERE | • • | 277 TWO KINGS | | 18 |
| THOUGH I HAVE LOCKED MY GATE ON THEM, | • • • | 607 SONGS BURDEN 2 | | 10 |

LOCKS

• • • THE OWLS HAD BUILDED THEIR NESTS IN THEIR LOCKS,	• •	49 OISIN 3		39
AND SING, AND SHAKE MY HEAVY LOCKS.	• • •	84 MAD KING GOLL		44
UNDER THE SHADOW OF STUPID STRAW-PALE LOCKS,	• • •	433 NINETEEN 19		127
THAT I HAD SHORN MY LOCKS AWAY	• • •	519 HER DREAM		3

LODGE

| CRIED FROM THE PORTER'S LODGE, AND WITH LONG CLAMOUR | • • | 181 QUEEN MAEVE | | 37 |

LOFTIER

| HUNG THE FRAIL LOFTIER CLOUDLETS. TURNED HE SLOW-- | • • | 40 OISIN 2 | V | 167 |
| HAD GIVEN THEIR CHILDREN'S CHILDREN LOFTIER THOUGHT, | • • | 292 TO A SHADE | | 12 |

LOFTY

AND MANY A PRINCE OF LOFTY NAME,	• • •	7 OISIN 1	V	63
AND MANY A MAN OF LOFTY NAME,	• • •	7 OISIN 1	V	63
"YOUR STRENGTH, THAT IS SO LOFTY AND FIERCE AND KIND,	• •	201 OLD MEMORY		3
ON NO LONG BENCH NOR LOFTY MILKING-SHED	• • •	341 SHEP GOATHERD		51
OF SORROWFUL, AUSTERE, SWEET, LOFTY PIPE TUNES.	• • •	341 SHEP GOATHERD		57
ON NO LONG BENCH NOR LOFTY MILKING SHED	• • •	341 SHEP GOATHERD	V	51
UPON SOME LOFTY ROCK TO STARE	• • •	397 POLIT PRISONER		21
THAT LOFTY WHITE STAG, LEAP	• • •	399 BREAK OF DAY		24
OR LOFTY SLOPE WHERE IT STILL SNOWS	• • •	567 LAPIS LAZULI		46
BEAUTIFUL LOFTY THINGS	• • •	577 LOFTY THINGS		T
BEAUTIFUL LOFTY THINGS: O'LEARY'S NOBLE HEAD!	• •	577 LOFTY THINGS		1
A BEAUTIFUL LOFTY THING, OR A THING	• • •	578 CRAZED GIRL		7
THE LOFTY INNOCENCE THAT IT HAS SLAIN,	• • •	614 MARCH SONGS 2		12

LOG

| HAS SHE NOT SEEN HIM LYING LIKE A LOG, | • • • | 230 SHADOW WATER B | | 173 |
| • • • A LOG BOOK OF THE SUN'S JOURNEY AND THE MOON'S, | • • | 480 BLOOD AND MOON | V | 14 |

LOG-BOOK

| • • • A LOG-BOOK OF THE SUN'S JOURNEY AND THE MOON'S! | • • | 480 BLOOD AND MOON | | 14 |

LOGIC

IN LOGIC AND IN NATURAL LAW	• • •	288 TO WEALTHY MAN		27
"THOUGH LOGIC CHOPPERS RULE THE TOWN,	• • •	337 TOM OROUGHLEY	V	1
AND IS THEIR LOGIC TO OUTWEIGH	• • •	395 SIXTEEN DEAD		11

LOGIC-CHOPPERS

| "THOUGH LOGIC-CHOPPERS RULE THE TOWN, | • • • | 337 TOM OROUGHLEY | | 1 |

LOIE

| WHEN LOIE FULLER'S CHINESE DANCERS ENWOUND | • • • | 430 NINETEEN 19 | | 49 |

LOIN

| THAT HAS NOT PASSED THROUGH ANY HUCKSTER'S LOIN, | • • • | 269 PARDON FATHERS | | 8 |

LOINS

A SHUDDER IN THE LOINS ENGENDERS THERE	• • •	441 LEDA AND SWAN		9
THE FLAGELLANT LASHES THOSE SUBMISSIVE LOINS	• • •	560 WHENCE COME		7
SPOILT WHAT OLD LOINS HAVE SENT?	• • •	604 YOU CONTENT		6

LOITERING

| WHILE THOSE DEAD MEN ARE LOITERING THERE | • • • | 395 SIXTEEN DEAD | | 5 |

LOLLARD

LEAD MY LOLLARD TO AND FRO,	• • •	97 FOXHUNTER		7
MY LOLLARD OLD AND DEAR.	• • •	97 FOXHUNTER	V	8
BROWN LOLLARD TREADS UPON THE LAWN,	• • •	98 FOXHUNTER		17
HIS LOLLARD LEAD THEY ROUND THE LAWN,	• • •	98 FOXHUNTER	V	17

LOLLING

| WERE LOLLING THEIR TONGUES, AND THE SILKEN HAIR | • • • | 2 OISIN 1 | V | 7S |

LOMAIR

BRAN, SGEOLAN, AND LOMAIR,	• • •	2 OISIN 1	V	7D
AND BRAN, SGEOLAN, AND LOMAIR	• • •	2 OISIN 1	V	7R
WITH BRAN, SCEOLAN, AND LOMAIR,	• • •	3 OISIN 1		15
AND BRAN, SCEOLAN, AND LOMAIR,	• • •	11 OISIN 1		125
I MUSED ON THE CHASE WITH THE FENIANS, AND BRAN, SCEOLAN, LOMAIR.		47 OISIN 3		5
WHEN THE FENIANS MADE FORAY AT MORNING WITH BRAN, SCEOLAN, LOMAIR.		54 OISIN 3		104
WHAT PLACE HAVE CAOILTE AND CONAN, AND BRAN, SCEOLAN, LOMAIR?		61 OISIN 3		195
WHAT PLACE HAVE CAOLTE AND FIN, AND BRAN, SGEOLAN, LOMAIR?		61 OISIN 3	V	195
I WILL GO TO CAOILTE, AND CONAN, AND BRAN, SCEOLAN, LOMAIR,		63 OISIN 3		223
TO FIN, CAOLTE, AND CONAN, AND BRAN, SGEOLAN, LOMAIR.	• •	63 OISIN 3	V	224

LONDON

IN LONDON OR IN LIVERPOOL!	• • •	360 ALF POLLEXFEN		16
IN A CROWDED LONDON SHOP,	• • •	501 VACILLATION		37
SINGING IN THIS LONDON STREET,	• • •	731 STREET DANCERS		1
LONDON STREETS HAVE HERITAGE,	• • •	733 STREET DANCERS		57

LONE   SEE LEBEEN-LONE

I MOUNTED, AND WE PASSED OVER THE LONE	• • •	45 OISIN 2		231
I MOUNTED, AND WE RODE ACROSS THE LONE	• • •	45 OISIN 2	V	231
WE SHALL MINGLE NO MORE, NOR OUR GAZES EMPTY THEIR SWEETNESS LONE		56 OISIN 3		132
BUT THE SAD DWELLER BY THE SEA-WAYS LONE	• • •	69 SAD SHEPHERD		26
BUT THE SAD DWELLER BY THE SEAWAYS LONE	• • •	69 SAD SHEPHERD	V	26

467

	PAGE	TITLE		LINE
LONE (CONTINUED)				
BY THE LONE BORDER OF THE LAKE ONCE MORE,	79	EPHEMERA		5
ON THE LONE BORDER OF THE LAKE ONCE MORE!	80	EPHEMERA		17
ON THE LONE BORDER OF THE SULLEN LAKE.	80	EPHEMERA	V	17
DID SHE IN TOUCHING THAT LONE WING	397	POLIT PRISONER		7
IS DRINKING HER HEALTH WHEN LONE, ALONE---	551	SONGS REWRIT 1	V	4
LIVE LONE, ALONE WITH A SPECKLED SHIN?	551	SONGS REWRIT 1	V	8
LONE, AND WANTING THEE, I WEEP;	647	ISLE STAT I 1		72
SOME SAY THAT ALL WHO TOUCH THE ISLAND LONE	653	ISLE STAT I 2		42
LONE REGENT OF THE WOODS, DEEP MUTTERING,	657	ISLE STAT I 3		49
WHO, SWIMMING, SOUGHT THE ISLAND LONE!	673	ISLE STAT II 3		181
BEHOLD THE LOVING LOVELESS FLOWER OF LONE WAYS,	674	ISLE STAT II 3		201
AND AIMLESS WANDERINGS THE WOODLANDS LONE,	674	ISLE STAT II 3		209
HAVE LIT LONE TAPERS. NOW THE NIGHT WAS CAST,	687	TWO TITANS		27
"I AM LONE LADY QUIETNESS, MY SWEET,	716	DWELT SYCAMORE		13
CLAMOUR OF THE LONE NIGHTJAR.	732	STREET DANCERS		21
LONELINESS				
IN ALL THEIR LONELINESS AND PAIN,	290	SEPTEMBER 1913		27
AND WHEN HE PLAYED IT WAS THEIR LONELINESS.	339	SHEP GOATHERD		24
THEIR BEAUTY DROPPED OUT OF THE LONELINESS	375	PHASES OF MOON		70
THE SOUL REMEMBERING ITS LONELINESS	375	PHASES OF MOON		88
MUCH BOISTEROUS COURAGE, BEFORE LONELINESS	473	ALL SOUL NIGHT		72
LOVE'S LONELINESS	518	LOVES LONENESS		T
IF EVER LOVER'S LONELINESS	518	LOVES LONENESS		3
OF CEASELESS LONELINESS AND HIGH REGRET	705	REMEMBRANCE		9
LONELY				
BUT WE IN A LONELY LAND ABIDE	22	OISIN 1		337
STOOD LONELY, WITH DIM EYEBALLS ON EACH SIDE,	34	OISIN 2	V	74
AND LONELY AND LONGING FOR NIAMH, I SHIVERED AND TURNED ME ABOUT,	60	OISIN 3		181
AND SHIVERING AND LONELY, AND LONGING FOR NIAM, I TURNED ME ABOUT,	60	OISIN 3	V	181
FOR LONELY TO MOVE 'MONG THE SOFT EYES	63	OISIN 3	V	222
A LONELY LAUGHTER, AND MAY KISS HIS HANDS TO ME IN SLEEP.	75	ANASHU VIJAYA		82
A LONELY LAUGHTER, THAT HE MAY KISS HANDS TO ME IN SLEEP.	75	ANASHU VIJAYA	V	82
HERE WE WILL MOOR OUR LONELY SHIP	78	INDIAN TO LOVE		6
THERE WE WILL MOOR OUR LONELY SHIP	78	INDIAN TO LOVE	V	6
SING IN THEIR HIGH AND LONELY MELODY.	101	ROSE UPON ROOD		8
LIVES ON THIS LONELY FACE.	112	ROSE OF WORLD		10
THE SAD, THE LONELY, THE INSATIABLE,	114	ROSE OF BATTLE		21
OLD SILENCE BIDS A LONELY FOLK REJOICE,	127	DREAM OF FAERY	V	31
AND GOD STANDS WINDING HIS LONELY HORN,	148	INTO TWILIGHT		13
DROWNING LOVE'S LONELY HOUR IN DEEP TWILIGHT OF REST,	154	BELOVED PEACE		11
BROOD HER HIGH LONELY MYSTERIES.	156	FORGOT BEAUTY		24
ON HER MOST LONELY MYSTERIES.	156	FORGOT BEAUTY	V	24
WITH THE LONELY, MAJESTICAL MULTITUDE.	158	TO HIS HEART		7
WITH THE LONELY, PROUD, WINGED MULTITUDE.	158	TO HIS HEART	V	7
AND I FELL ASLEEP UPON LONELY ECHTGE OF STREAMS.	203	WITHER BOUGHS		6
THAT ON THE LONELY HEIGHT WHERE ALL ARE IN GOD'S EYE,	291	PAUDEEN		6
A LONELY IMPULSE OF DELIGHT	328	IRISH AIRMAN		11
I MOURN FOR THAT MOST LONELY THING; AND YET GOD'S WILL BE DONE!	354	HIS PHOENIX		31
THE LONELY LIGHT THAT SAMUEL PALMER ENGRAVED,	373	PHASES OF MOON		17
TOO LONELY FOR THE TRAFFIC OF THE WORLD!	374	PHASES OF MOON		61
WITH ALL YOUTH'S LONELY WILDNESS STIRRED,	397	POLIT PRISONER		16
TO EXALT A LONELY MIND,	420	MY HOUSE		29
PARDONED, DRAGS OUT LONELY YEARS	475	EVA GORE-BOOTH		8
LIVES THAT LONELY THING	504	QUARREL IN AGE		14
A LONELY GHOST THE GHOST IS	511	JANE AND JACK		7
IN THIS LONELY PLACE.	617	LONG-LEG FLY		14
WHERE ALL NIGHT LONG THE LONELY MOON, THE WHITE	650	ISLE STAT I 1		126
BY DAY AND NIGHT A LONELY FOUNTAIN SINGS,	650	ISLE STAT I 1		130
WHO SITS IN LONELY SPLENDOUR, MAIL'D IN GOLD,	651	ISLE STAT I 1		163
DID HER LONELY WATCHING TAKE	658	ISLE STAT I 3		94
OF BEAMS A-FLICKER ON YON LONELY FIR,	661	ISLE STAT II 1		72
BETWEEN THE LONELY FOREST AND THE SAND.	663	ISLE STAT II 2		22
TWO LONELY SPIRITS WAIT,	680	LOVE AND DEATH		18
SHALL AWAKE WITH LONELY BLEAT,	726	LOVERS QUARREL		6
THE MAN IS GONE WHO FROM HIS LONELY STATION	738	MOURN THEN ON		7
HAS MADE IT BUT A LONELY THING.	781	HEART FRIGHT		4
LONG SEE DAY-LONG LIVE-LONG DADDY-LONG-LEGS				
WHOSE LONG WOOL WHITER THAN SEA-FROTH FLOWS,	8	OISIN 1		90
WHOSE LONG WOOL WHITER THAN SEA FROTH FLOWS,	8	OISIN 1	V	90
WHERE ARE YOU WITH YOUR LONG ROUGH HAIR?	11	OISIN 1		126
COMPANIONS LONG ACCURST AND DEAD,	11	OISIN 1		130
WHERE ARE YE WITH YOUR LONG ROUGH HAIR?	11	OISIN 1	V	126
OF ONE LONG FINGER ON MY LIP.	12	OISIN 1		151
BLEW ONE LONG NOTE. FROM OVER REED	14	OISIN 1	V	195
ERE LONG AN ANSWERING WHISPER FLEW,	15	OISIN 1	V	197
THEY LED US BY LONG AND SHADOWY WAYS	16	OISIN 1		221
THEY LEAD US BY LONG AND SHADOWY WAYS	16	OISIN 1	V	221
AND EACH ONE SAID, WITH A LONG, LONG SIGH,	17	OISIN 1		244
AND EACH ONE SAID, WITH A LONG, LONG SIGH,	17	OISIN 1		244
WITH ONE LONG GLANCE FOR GIRL AND BOY	19	OISIN 1		287
WITH ONE LONG GLANCE ON MAID AND BOY	19	OISIN 1	V	287
IN A LONG AND SHADOWY ROW,	20	OISIN 1	V	295
WE WENT A-FISHING IN LONG BOATS	23	OISIN 1		352
I LOVED AND SANG, AND IN LONG WASSAILS	23	OISIN 1	V	345C
LOOSED LONG AGO FROM HEAVEN'S GATE.	24	OISIN 1		362
AND THE LONG GREY GRASSES, WHOSE TENDEREST TOUCHES	27	OISIN 1	V	415B
FROM MACE AND SWORD AND POLE-AXE, LONG AGO	31	OISIN 2		30

LONG   (CONTINUED)

	PAGE	TITLE		LINE
STRETCHED HIS LONG ARM TO WHERE, A MISTY SMOTHER, • • •	31	OISIN 2		42
AND CLIMBED SO LONG, I THOUGHT THE LAST STEPS WERE • • •	32	OISIN 2		48
LOOK TO LONG FISHING-LINES, OR POINT AND PARE • • • • •	32	OISIN 2		55
LONG WHILE, ARE WHIPS OF STEEL." "IS HE SO DREAD?" • • •	35	OISIN 2	V	88
HOLDING THAT HORSE LONG SEEN NOT, NIAM STOOD. • • • • •	44	OISIN 2	V	230
WERE WE DAYS LONG OR HOURS LONG IN RIDING, • • • • • • •	47	OISIN 3		9
WERE WE DAYS LONG OR HOURS LONG IN RIDING. • • • • • • •	47	OISIN 3		9
LONG SIGHS AROSE IN OUR SPIRITS, BENEATH US BUBBLED THE GROUND.	48	OISIN 3		20
A VALLEY FLOWED DOWN FROM HIS HOOFS, AND THERE IN THE LONG GRASS LAY,	48	OISIN 3		26
• • • LONG WARLESS, GROWN WHITER THAN CURDS. • • • • •	49	OISIN 3		36
SO LONG WERE THEY SLEEPING. • • • • • • • • • • • •	49	OISIN 3		39
FILLING THE FIBROUS DIMNESS WITH LONG GENERATIONS OF EYES.	49	OISIN 3		40
SNATCHING THE HORN OF NIAMH, I BLEW A LONG LINGERING NOTE.	51	OISIN 3		57
IN A LONG IRON SLEEP, AS A FISH IN THE WATER GOES DUMB AS A STONE.	53	OISIN 3		96
NO MORE TO CRAWL ON THE SEAS WITH LONG OARS MILE AFTER MILE,	55	OISIN 3		119
LONG FLED THE FOAM-FLAKES AROUND ME, THE WINDS FLED OUT OF THE VAST,	57	OISIN 3		149
• • • "THE FENIANS A LONG TIME ARE DEAD." • • • • •	59	OISIN 3		172
• • • HE CRIED, "NO, THE GODS A LONG TIME ARE DEAD." • •	59	OISIN 3		180
• • • HE CRIED, "NAY, THE GODS A LONG TIME ARE DEAD." • •	59	OISIN 3	V	180
AUTUMN IS OVER THE LONG LEAVES THAT LOVE US, • • • • •	79	FALLING LEAVES		1
OF MY LONG SPEAR, WITH SCREAM AND LAUGH, • • • • • •	84	MAD KING GOLL	V	34
OF MY LONG SPEAR WITH SONG AND LAUGH • • • • • • • •	84	MAD KING GOLL	V	34
ORCHIL SHAKES OUT HER LONG DARK HAIR • • • • • • • •	85	MAD KING GOLL		62
THE LINES ARE NOT HEAVY, NOR HEAVY THE LONG NETS BROWN—	91	OLD FISHERMAN	V	5
THE WHOLE OF THE LONG DAY. • • • • • • • • • • •	94	MOLL MAGEE		8
HE SMOOTHS THE LONG BROWN NOSE. • • • • • • • • •	98	FOXHUNTER		20
BY GOD TO THE BRIGHT HEARTS OF THOSE LONG DEAD, • • • •	101	ROSE UPON ROOD		20
"I HAVE LONG WAITED, MOTHER, FOR THAT WORD! • • • •	107	CUCHULAIN SEA		22
"LONG HAVE I WAITED, MOTHER, FOR THOSE WORDS." • • • •	107	CUCHULAIN SEA	V	22
"I HAVE LONG WAITED, MOTHER, FOR THOSE WORDS! • • • •	107	CUCHULAIN SEA	V	22
OR DO YOU LONG FOR THE DIM SLEEPY GROUND, • • • • • •	109	CUCHULAIN SEA		60
AND THROUGH THE OTHER'S SHIELD HIS LONG BLADE BROKE, • •	110	CUCHULAIN SEA	V	66
AND WENT DOWN TO THE LONG SANDS ALONE, • • • • • • •	111	CUCHULAIN SEA	V	84
AND HE WENT DOWN TO THE LONG SANDS ALONE. • • • • • •	111	CUCHULAIN SEA	V	84
STOOD UP, AND CAME TO THE LONG SANDS ALONE! • • • • •	111	CUCHULAIN SEA	V	84
AND WAGE GOD'S BATTLES IN THE LONG GREY SHIPS. • • • •	114	ROSE OF BATTLE		20
OUR LONG SHIPS LOOSE THOUGHT-WOVEN SAILS AND WAIT, • •	115	ROSE OF BATTLE		31
AND THE LONG DEW-DROPPING HOURS OF THE NIGHT, • • • •	116	FAERY SONG		7
THE LONG HAIR IS ON HER FACE! • • • • • • • • • •	124	CATHLEEN PARA	V	10
THE LONG HAIR SHADOWS HER FACE! • • • • • • • • •	124	CATHLEEN PARA	V	10
AS IN THE OLD DAYS LONG GONE BY, • • • • • • • • •	131	OLD PENSIONER		15
OF THEIR LONG WINGS, THE FLASH OF THEIR WHITE FEET, • •	137	TO SOME I TALK		16
OF THEIR LONG WINGS, THE FLASH OF THEIR SWIFT FEET. • •	137	TO SOME I TALK	V	16
AND DREAMED OF THE LONG DIM HAIR • • • • • • • • •	144	HOST OF AIR		7
OF HER LONG DIM HAIR. • • • • • • • • • • • • •	145	HOST OF AIR		28
WERE DROWNED IN HER LONG DIM HAIR. • • • • • • • •	145	HOST OF AIR		36
AND WALK AMONG LONG DAPPLED GRASS, • • • • • • • •	150	WANDER AENGUS		21
AND THE YOUNG LIE LONG AND DREAM IN THEIR BED • • • •	150	OLD MOTHER		5
WHILE THE YOUNG LIE LONG AND DREAM IN THEIR BED • • • •	150	OLD MOTHER	V	5
BUT THE YOUNG LIE LONG AND DREAM IN THEIR BED • • • •	150	OLD MOTHER	V	5
I HEAR THE SHADOWY HORSES, THEIR LONG MANES A-SHAKE, • •	154	BELOVED PEACE		1
PASSION-DIMMED EYES AND LONG HEAVY HAIR • • • • • • •	155	REPROVE CURLEW		4
THAT HAS LONG FADED FROM THE WORLD! • • • • • • • •	155	FORGOT BEAUTY		3
THAT HAS LONG FADED IN THE WORLD! • • • • • • • • •	155	FORGOT BEAUTY	V	3
AND BIND UP YOUR LONG HAIR AND SIGH! • • • • • • • •	158	BELOVED RHYMES		8
IN A LONG AND STRAIGHT BLUE GARMENT • • • • • • • •	159	CAP AND BELLS	V	5
AND STILL MURMUR AND LONG! • • • • • • • • • • •	163	ASKS FORGIVE		18
O WOMEN, KNEELING BY YOUR ALTAR-RAILS LONG HENCE, • • •	173	SPEAKS HEARERS		1
O COLLEENS, KNEELING BY YOUR ALTAR RAILS LONG HENCE, • •	173	SPEAKS HEARERS	V	1
O, WOMEN, KNEELING BY YOUR ALTAR RAILS LONG HENCE, • • •	173	SPEAKS HEARERS	V	1
IN HER HIGH HOUSE AT CRUACHAN, THE LONG HEARTH, • • •	180	QUEEN MAEVE		11
CRIED FROM THE PORTER'S LODGE, AND WITH LONG CLAMOUR • •	181	QUEEN MAEVE		37
ONE THAT THE GENERATIONS HAD LONG WAITED • • • • • •	182	QUEEN MAEVE		66
WITH LONG WHITE BODIES CAME OUT OF THE AIR • • • • •	185	QUEEN MAEVE		118
WHEN THE LONG WARS FOR THE WHITE HORN • • • • • • •	189	BAILE AILLINN		14
HE HAD RAGGED LONG GRASS-COLOURED HAIR! • • • • • •	190	BAILE AILLINN		26
AWOKE THE HARP-STRINGS LONG AGO. • • • • • • • • •	190	BAILE AILLINN		37
HE HAD RAGGED, LONG GRASS-YELLOW HAIR! • • • • • • •	190	BAILE AILLINN	V	26
AWOKE THE HARP STRINGS LONG AGO. • • • • • • • • •	190	BAILE AILLINN	V	37
HAVE SUCH LONG MEMORIES THAT THEY STILL • • • • • • •	192	BAILE AILLINN		90
BUT THE GODS LONG AGO DECREED • • • • • • • • • •	194	BAILE AILLINN		119
AND THAT LONG FIGHTING AT THE FORD, • • • • • • • •	197	BAILE AILLINN		194
THE QUEENS THAT WERE IMAGINED LONG AGO, • • • • • •	201	OLD MEMORY		5
THROUGH THE LONG YEARS OF YOUTH, AND WHO WOULD HAVE THOUGHT	201	OLD MEMORY		7
THROUGH THE LONG DAYS OF YOUTH, AND WHO WOULD HAVE THOUGHT	201	OLD MEMORY	V	7
I LONG FOR YOUR MERRY AND TENDER AND PITIFUL WORDS, • • •	203	WITHER BOUGHS		3
SEVEN OLD SISTERS WIND THE THREADS OF THE LONG LIVED ONES.	209	UNDER THE MOON	V	7
O DO NOT LOVE TOO LONG • • • • • • • • • • • •	211	O DO NOT LOVE		T
DO NOT LOVE TOO LONG • • • • • • • • • • • • •	211	O DO NOT LOVE	V	T
SWEETHEART, DO NOT LOVE TOO LONG! • • • • • • • • •	211	O DO NOT LOVE		1
I LOVED LONG AND LONG, • • • • • • • • • • • •	211	O DO NOT LOVE		2
I LOVED LONG AND LONG, • • • • • • • • • • • •	211	O DO NOT LOVE		2
O DO NOT LOVE TOO LONG, • • • • • • • • • • • •	212	O DO NOT LOVE		10
SWEET WITH ALL MUSIC, OUT OF HIS LONG HAIR, • • • • •	219	HARP OF AENGUS		8
FOR LONG ENOUGH? AYE, LONG AND LONG ENOUGH. • • • • •	221	SHADOW WATER B		2

469

LONG (CONTINUED)

		PAGE	TITLE	LINE
FOR LONG ENOUGH? AYE, LONG AND LONG ENOUGH.	• • • •	221	SHADOW WATER B	2
FOR LONG ENOUGH? AYE, LONG AND LONG ENOUGH.	• • • •	221	SHADOW WATER B	2
AS THAT WILD AENGUS. LONG BEFORE HER DAY	• • • •	224	SHADOW WATER B	47
IN THEIR LONG LIVES? WILL YOU BE OF OUR TROOP	• • •	225	SHADOW WATER B	72
THIS LONG WHILE NOW! WE HAD NOT TURNED AGAINST HIM	• •	225	SHADOW WATER B V	68B
IN THEIR LONG LIVES? IF YOU'LL BE OF OUR TROOP	• • •	225	SHADOW WATER B V	72
I ALMOST LONG THAT IT WERE POSSIBLE!	• • • •	236	SHADOW WATER B	306
CRIED OUT THE WHOLE NIGHT LONG,	• • • •	254	HIS DREAM	16
WE'LL OUT, FOR THE WORLD LIVES AS LONG AGO!	• • •	257	RECONCILIATION	8
IN MOMENTARY ANGER LONG AGO!	• • • •	258	KING NO KING	10
THAT LONG TO GIVE THEMSELVES FOR WAGE,	• • • •	262	STUDENTS AGIT	2
"ALTHOUGH THE EVENT WAS LONG IN DOUBT,	• • • •	273	GREY ROCK	67
"A WEARY WOOING AND A LONG," HE SAID,	• • • •	283	TWO KINGS	154
HE HAD COUNTED, WHERE LONG YEARS AGO	• • • •	302	HOUR DAWN	7
HE COUNTED, WHERE LONG YEARS AGO	• • • •	302	HOUR DAWN V	7
BUT THE OTHER CRIED, "YOU LONG FOR SPRING	• • • •	306	HOUR DAWN V	91
LIES ONE LONG SOUGHT	• • • •	310	WITCH	7
WITH THE HOT BLOOD OF YOUTH, OF LOVE CROSSED LONG AGO!	• •	316	COLD HEAVEN	6
—SEEING THAT FAME HAS PERISHED THIS LONG WHILE,	• • •	321	REED WHISPERER	11
A LONG BLAST UPON THE HORN THAT BROUGHT	• • • •	324	ROBERT GREGORY	22
BUT THAT, LONG TRAVELLING, HE HAD COME	• • • •	325	ROBERT GREGORY	28
AND ALL DAY LONG I LOOK	• • • •	329	MEN IMPROVE	4
"ALL DAY LONG FROM MID-DAY	• • • •	332	SOLOMON SHEBA	3
ALL DAY LONG FROM SHADOWLESS NOON	• • • •	332	SOLOMON SHEBA	5
"ALL DAY LONG FROM MIDDAY	• • • •	332	SOLOMON SHEBA V	3
AND ALL DAY LONG WE HAVE FOUND	• • • •	333	SOLOMON SHEBA	22
ON NO LONG BENCH NOR LOFTY MILKING-SHED	• • • •	341	SHEP GOATHERD	51
ON NO LONG BENCH NOR LOFTY MILKING SHED	• • • •	341	SHEP GOATHERD V	51
TILL THAT IS THEIR LONG SHOUTING PLAYTIME!	• • • •	343	SHEP GOATHERD V	106
THE ROUND GREEN EYES AND THE LONG WAVERING BODIES	• •	343	DEJECTION	2
IT'S LONG SINCE I BEGAN	• • • •	347	FISHERMAN	6
I WILL TALK NO MORE OF BOOKS OR THE LONG WAR	• • •	351	HER PRAISE	11
THE LONG FLOWING LINE,	• • • •	355	PROPERTIUS	3
SINCE HE WHO HAD BEEN CONTENTED LONG,	• • • •	361	ALF POLLEXFEN	28
THAT THOSE THAT WE HAVE LOVED GOT THEIR LONG FINGERS	• •	375	PHASES OF MOON	66
SEEING THAT I, IGNORANT FOR SO LONG,	• • • •	384	VISION ROBART	66
WHO GRIPS HIS LONG SPEAR SO TO PUSH	• • • •	385	ROBARTES DANCE	3
WHEN THE LONG LOOKING-GLASS IS FULL,	• • • •	387	ROBARTES DANCE	50
TOO LONG A SACRIFICE	• • • •	394	EASTER 1916	57
WHEN LONG AGO I SAW HER RIDE	• • • •	397	POLIT PRISONER	13
THOUGH I HAD LONG PERNED IN THE GYRE,	• • • •	400	DEMON BEAST	5
FISH, FLESH, OR FOWL, COMMEND ALL SUMMER LONG	• • •	407	SAIL BYZANTIUM	5
FLOAT OUT UPON A LONG	• • • •	414	TOWER	142
AMID GREAT CHAMBERS AND LONG GALLERIES, LINED	• • •	418	ANCEST HOUSES	36
WHERE THROUGH LONG WARS AND SUDDEN NIGHT ALARMS	• • •	420	MY HOUSE	24
WHERE THROUGH LONG WARS AND SUDDEN NIGHT ALARUMS	• •	420	MY HOUSE V	24
THEIR LEGS LONG, DELICATE AND SLENDER, AQUAMARINE THEIR EYES,		426	PHANTOM HATRED	17
PUBLIC OPINION RIPENING FOR SO LONG	• • • •	428	NINETEEN 19	13
STRETCH OUT YOUR LIMBS AND SLEEP A LONG SATURNIAN SLEEP!		442	BLACK CENTAUR	13
I WALK THROUGH THE LONG SCHOOLROOM QUESTIONING!	• • •	443	SCHOOL CHILDR	1
BUT WHAT CARE I THAT LONG FOR A MAN'S LOVE?	• • •	448	HERO GIRL FOOL	17
IN THE LONG ECHOING STREET THE LAUGHING DANCERS THRONG,		459	FROM OEDIPUS	7
I CELEBRATE THE SILENT KISS THAT ENDS SHORT LIFE OR LONG.		459	FROM OEDIPUS	9
IN THE LONG ECHOING STREETS THE LAUGHING DANCERS THRONG,		459	FROM OEDIPUS V	7
I SAY THAT A DJIN SPOKE. A LIVE LONG HOUR	• • • •	467	HARUN RASHID V	136
AND TWO LONG GLASSES BRIMMED WITH MUSCATEL	• • •	470	ALL SOUL NIGHT	4
LONG PAST HIS PRIME REMEMBER THINGS THAT ARE	• • •	477	SELF AND SOUL	18
THOUGHTS LONG KNITTED INTO A SINGLE THOUGHT,	• • •	488	COOLE PARK 29	7
THINGS SAID OR DONE LONG YEARS AGO,	• • • •	501	VACILLATION	51
I TOILED LONG YEARS AND AT LENGTH	• • • •	505	RESULT THOUGHT	9
TOILED LONG YEARS AND AT LENGTH	• • • •	505	RESULT THOUGHT V	9
AFTER LONG SILENCE	• • • •	523	LONG SILENCE	T
SPEECH AFTER LONG SILENCE! IT IS RIGHT,	• • • •	523	LONG SILENCE	1
"THAT IS A LONG WAY OFF,	• • • •	526	AM OF IRELAND	11
I LONG FOR TRUTH, AND YET	• • • •	533	FIRST CONFESS	7
STOOD OR HAVE MARCHED THE NIGHT LONG	• • • •	546	TO SAME TUNE 2	15
OR HAVE MARCHED THE NIGHT LONG,	• • • •	546	TO SAME TUNE 2 V	15
CUCHULAIN THAT FOUGHT NIGHT LONG WITH THE FOAM,	• • •	549	SEVERED HEAD	9
THINGS THOUGHT TOO LONG CAN BE NO LONGER THOUGHT,	• •	564	GYRES	2
HIS LONG LAMP-CHIMNEY SHAPED LIKE THE STEM	• • •	566	LAPIS LAZULI	33
HIS LONG LAMP CHIMNEY SHAPED LIKE THE STEM	• • •	566	LAPIS LAZULI V	33
THE CHAMBERMAID LIVED LONG, AND TOOK	• • • •	571	THREE BUSHES	57
LONG LOOKED HE IN HER FACE,	• • • •	571	THREE BUSHES	67
FROM TIME LONG PASSED AWAY,	• • • •	589	OLD WICKED MAN	42
HONOUR HAD LIVED SO LONG, ALL LACKING FOUND.	• • •	603	GALLERY REVIS	35
HONOUR HAD LIVED SO LONG, THEIR HEALTH I FOUND.	• • •	603	GALLERY REVIS V	35
KNOWS I HAVE LIVED SO LONG.	• • • •	607	SONGS BURDEN 2	26
AS MY LONG PLANNED HALF SOLITUDE,	• • • •	624	APPARITIONS V	10
IF HE DIED LONG AGO	• • • •	635	BLACK TOWER	15
THOUGH GRAVE-DIGGERS' TOIL IS LONG,	• • • •	637	BEN BULBEN	21
THAT PALE, LONG VISAGED COMPANY	• • • •	637	BEN BULBEN V	7
SOMETHING DROPS FROM EYES LONG BLIND,	• • • •	638	BEN BULBEN	29
LONG YEARS AGO, A CHURCH STANDS NEAR.	• • • •	640	BEN BULBEN	87
WHERE ALL NIGHT LONG THE HEAVENS WEEP AND WEEP,	• •	649	ISLE STAT I 1	124
WHERE ALL NIGHT LONG THE LONELY MOON, THE WHITE	• •	650	ISLE STAT I 1	126
LONG ERE AN ARROW WHIZZED OR SWORD LEFT SHEATH	• •	650	ISLE STAT I 1	135
AND ELVISH WISDOM, AND LONG YEARS OF YOUTH	• • •	653	ISLE STAT I 2	47
LONG YEARS AGO, AND UNTO STONE CONGEALED.	• • •	656	ISLE STAT I 3	28
UNTO HER DOOR! FOR THIS, WHERE NOD THE LONG	• • •	660	ISLE STAT II 1	43

		PAGE	TITLE		LINE

LONG   (CONTINUED)
```
    A LONG, BROWN GRASSHOPPER OF MAIDS!  PEACE, SIR! • • •       661  ISLE STAT II 1        69
    A SHEPHERDESS LONG YEARS FORETOLD! • • • • • •               668  ISLE STAT II 3        49
    BUT, FOR A BOY, HOW LONG THINE HAIR HAS GROWN! • • • •       670  ISLE STAT II 3       104
    LONG CITRON COILS THAT HANG AROUND THEE, BLOWN • • •         670  ISLE STAT II 3       105
    THE LONG LILY BLOWS, • • • • • • • • • • •                   672  ISLE STAT II 3       165
    WILD CRIES, GROWN SWEET WITH LULLS AND LINGERINGS LONG•      674  ISLE STAT II 3       222
    MEETING LONG HENCE THE PHANTOM HERDSMAN, KING • •            675  ISLE STAT II 3       242
    HAVE I SLEPT LONG?  LONG YEARS.  WITH HUNGRY HEART •         677  ISLE STAT II 3       286
    HAVE I SLEPT LONG?  LONG YEARS.  WITH HUNGRY HEART •         677  ISLE STAT II 3       286
    SEAFARER, WAKE!  WAS MY SLEEP LONG?  LONG YEARS• • •         678  ISLE STAT II 3       292
    SEAFARER, WAKE!  WAS MY SLEEP LONG?  LONG YEARS• • •         678  ISLE STAT II 3       292
    HE IS LONG DEAD.  WAKE!  SOFT AS A BEE SIPS • • •            678  ISLE STAT II 3       297
    WAS MY SLEEP LONG, OH, YOUTH?  LONG, LONG AND DEEP• •        678  ISLE STAT II 3       299
    WAS MY SLEEP LONG, OH, YOUTH?  LONG, LONG AND DEEP• •        678  ISLE STAT II 3       299
    WAS MY SLEEP LONG, OH, YOUTH?  LONG, LONG AND DEEP• •        678  ISLE STAT II 3       299
    SLEEPER, AWAKE!  HOW LONG MY SLEEP?  UNNUMBERED • •          678  ISLE STAT II 3       307
    SHE IS LONG AGES DUST.  AH, WOE IS ME! • • • •               679  ISLE STAT II 3       313
    OR LONG ERE THIS HAD LOST THEIR RUDDY STAIN! • • •           687  TWO TITANS             8
    WORN WITH LONG STRUGGLES! AND THE WAVES HAVE SUNG • •        687  TWO TITANS            23
    LOW, LONG AND MUSICAL.  A DEW-DROP HUNG • • • • •            689  NETTLESHIP             9
    HIDING MY FACE, I CRIED LONG, BITTERLY• • • • • •            690  MOSADA 1              17
    DOWN THE LONG VALLEYS FROM MY PEOPLE'S TENTS, • • •          691  MOSADA 1              30
    FOR LONG THE BURTHEN OF THEIR TALKING GRIEFS• • • •          693  MOSADA 1              71
    HE WILL BE TALLER NOW--'TWAS LONG AGO• • • • •               699  MOSADA 3              15
    ERE LONG SHALL FALTER THROUGH THE NOISY SQUARE, • •          699  MOSADA 3              21
    SOFT AS A LONG DEAD FOOTSTEP WHISPERING THROUGH • •          699  MOSADA 3          V    5
    THE FOOT-WORN WAY IS LONG, AND IT GROWS DARK• • • •          702  MOSADA 3              92
    THE FOOTWORN WAY IS LONG, AND IT GROWS DARK• • • •           702  MOSADA 3          V   92
    MY MOTHER DREW FORTH FROM THE LONG GRASS • • • •             708  FAIRY PEDANT          23
    BUT SPEECHLESS, AND THE MAIDEN WITH LONG WAIL • • •          713  FERENCZ RENYI         85
    IN THE LONG GRASS--FOUR EYES DROOP LOW--A SEAT • •           716  DWELT SYCAMORE        11
    ALL THOSE LONG FORGOTTEN FISHERS, TILL IN THE EASTERN SKIES  719  PHANTOM SHIP      V   32
    GOLD UNTO GOLD, A GLEAM IN ITS LONG HAIR, • • • • •          720  WITCH VIVIEN           3
    LONG BEFORE THE MORNING FIRE • • • • • • • •                 727  LOVERS QUARREL        45
    A FULL HOUR LONG, WHEN ROSE A FEATHER • • • • •              728  PRIEST FAIRY          19
    "AND CUT NO WOOD THE WHOLE DAY LONG, • • • • •               731  PRIEST FAIRY          81
    LONG THOU FOR NOTHING, NEITHER SAD NOR GAY! • • •            734  QUATRAIN APHOR         9
    LONG THOU FOR NOTHING, NEITHER NIGHT NOR DAY! • • •          734  QUATRAIN APHOR        10
    NOT EVEN "I LONG TO SEE THY LONGING OVER," • • •             734  QUATRAIN APHOR        11
    WHERE LONG GREY GRASSES BOW AND BEND, • • • • •              736  SUMMER EVENING         6
    THROUGH THE LONG BITTER WAY• • • • • • • • •                 738  MOURN THEN ON          4
    GOD PLANTED HIM LONG AGO• • • • • • • • •                    743  WISDOM DREAMS          8
    AND MURMURED!  "O LONG GREY CLOAK, • • • • • •               744  GLOVE CLOAK           11
    I HAD KILLED HIM LONG AGO, BUT THAT THE FOOL • • • •         748  SHADOW WATER A        17
    AH, THEY HAVE PIERCED HIS HEART!  I HAVE SLEPT LONG!         761  SHADOW WATER A       270
    SWEET WITH ALL MUSIC, OUT OF HIS LONG HAIR, • • •            762  SHADOW WATER A       303
    I HAVE STOOD SO LONG BY A GAP IN THE WALL • • • •            788  HAWTHORN TREE         15
    I HAVE STOPPED SO LONG A GAP IN THE WALL • • • •             788  HAWTHORN TREE     V   15
```
LONG-ARMED
```
    HAD KISSED MY FATHER, LONG-ARMED FIN, • • • • • •             10  OISIN 1           V 112B
```
LONGED
```
    HAS LOVER LIVED, BUT LONGED TO WIVE • • • • • •              197  BAILE AILLINN        206
    SO BITTERLY, YOU'D DREAM THEY LONGED TO LOOK • • • •         265  ABBEY THEATRE          6
    THE SWEETNESS THAT ALL LONGED FOR NIGHT AND DAY, • •         418  ANCEST HOUSES         20
    WHOSE FOOTFALL I HAVE LONGED FOR, THREE SAD SUMMERS• •       692  MOSADA 1              45
```
LONGER
```
    "VEX THEM NO LONGER," NIAMH SAID, • • • • • •                 12  OISIN 1              148
    IT PASSETH AWAY, AND IS HEARD OF NO LONGER• • • •             26  OISIN 1           V 399B
    NO LONGER GLAD AS ON THAT MORNING, SPED • • • •               30  OISIN 2           V   16
    WE SHALL NO LONGER HEAR THE LITTLE CRY • • • ∘ • •           115  ROSE OF BATTLE        35
    AND CALL TO MY BELOVED AND ME!  "NO LONGER FLY • • •         173  SPEAKS HEARERS         7
    DIM POWERS OF DROWSY THOUGHT, LET HER NO LONGER BE •         175  ELEMENT POWERS        13
    GREAT RULERS OF THE STILLNESS, LET HER NO LONGER BE •        175  ELEMENT POWERS V      13
    GREAT RULERS OF STILLNESS, LET HER NO LONGER BE •            175  ELEMENT POWERS V      13
    FOR WE WILL GAZE UPON THIS WORLD NO LONGER• • • •            251  SHADOW WATER B       614
    FOR HE WILL GAZE UPON THIS WORLD NO LONGER• • • •            251  SHADOW WATER B V     614
    FOR WE WILL GAZE UPON THE WORLD NO LONGER• • • •             251  SHADOW WATER B V     614
    I WAS NO LONGER TERRIFIED--HIS VOICE • • • • •               284  TWO KINGS            171
    I AM NO LONGER FAINT • • • • • • • •                         335  SONG                   9
    YOUNG MEN NO LONGER SUDDENLY CATCH THEIR BREATH • •          355  BROKEN DREAMS          2
    ENDURE WHAT LIFE GOD GIVES AND ASK NO LONGER SPAN!           459  FROM OEDIPUS           1
    FOR INTELLECT NO LONGER KNOWS • • • • • •                    478  SELF AND SOUL         36
    NO LONGER IN LETHEAN FOLIAGE CAUGHT • • • •                  500  VACILLATION           27
    PRIMORDIAL MOTHERHOOD FORSAKE HIS LIMBS, THE CHILD           559  MAGIC DRUM             2
       NO LONGER REST,
    THINGS THOUGHT TOO LONG CAN BE NO LONGER THOUGHT,            564  GYRES                  2
    I'LL SEE HIM LONGER IF I STAND OUT HERE • • • •              703  MOSADA 3             113
    I AM SO YOUNG.  DOST THOU NO LONGER KNOW, • • • •            713  FERENCZ RENYI         88
    CEASE THE SAILS THEIR FLAPPING UPROAR, AND THE HULL NO       719  PHANTOM SHIP          18
       LONGER ROLLS•
    CEASE THE SAILS, THEIR FLAPPING UPROAR TO THE HULL           719  PHANTOM SHIP      V   18
       NO LONGER ROLLS•
    TILL HIS EDAINE, NO LONGER A GOLDEN FLY • • • •              757  SHADOW WATER A       210
    AND SHE, NO LONGER BLOWN AMONG THE WINDS, • • •              763  SHADOW WATER A       323
    FOR WE WILL GAZE UPON THIS WORLD NO LONGER• • • •            769  SHADOW WATER A       430
    UPON THIS WORLD NO LONGER.  THE HARP CRIES OUT• • • •        769  SHADOW WATER A V     430
```
LONGEST
```
    BUT STORIES THAT LIVE LONGEST • • • • • • • • •              587  PARNELLITES           29
```
LONGEVITY
```
    A SYMBOL OF LONGEVITY! • • • • • • • • • • •                 566  LAPIS LAZULI          40
```

                          PAGE   TITLE   LINE

LONG—FORGOTTEN
    THOSE WARRIORS OF A LONG—FORGOTTEN DAY, ...   30 OISIN 2   V 14A
    AND LONG—FORGOTTEN MURIAS, ... 196 BAILE AILLINN   163
LONG—HAIRED
    THE LONG—HAIRED WARRIORS, THE SPREAD FEAST: . . . . .   2 OISIN 1   V   7
LONGHI
    HER DOMINO, HER PANNIERED SKIRT COPIED FROM LONGHI: . . . 363 DOLLS FACES   7
LONGING   SEE DEATH—LONGING EVER—LONGING LOVE—LONGING
    LIKE AN ARMY OF OLD MEN LONGING FOR REST FROM THE MOAN   48 OISIN 3   16
      OF THE SEAS,
    LIKE AN ARMY OF OLD MEN LONGING FOR REST FROM THE MOAN   57 OISIN 3   144
      OF THE SEAS,
    AND LONELY AND LONGING FOR NIAMH, I SHIVERED AND TURNED   60 OISIN 3   181
      ME ABOUT,
    THE HEART IN ME LONGING TO LEAP LIKE A GRASSHOPPER INTO   60 OISIN 3   182
      HER HEART:
    AND SHIVERING AND LONELY, AND LONGING FOR NIAM, I TURNED   60 OISIN 3   V 181
      ME ABOUT,
    THAT MURMURING AND LONGING CAME . . . . 162 ASKS FORGIVE   8
    THAT LONGING AND MURMURING CAME . . . . 162 ASKS FORGIVE   V   8
    AND TROUBLE WITH A SIGH FOR ALL THINGS LONGING FOR REST 163 ASKS FORGIVE   23
    LOVES IN BRIEF LONGING AND DECEIVING HOPE . . . . . . 228 SHADOW WATER B 146
    LONGING TO KNEAD AND PULL IT INTO SHAPE . . . . 246 SHADOW WATER B 510
    AND YOU KNOW WELL HOW GREAT THE LONGING HAS BEEN, . . . 352 PEOPLE   7
    WHERE EVEN LONGING DROWNS UNDER ITS OWN EXCESS: . . . . 426 PHANTOM HATRED   22
    IS BUT ITS LONGING FOR THE TOMB. . . . . 434 WHEEL   8
    THE SOUTH WIND BROUGHT IT LONGING, AND THE EAST WIND 449 OWEN AHERNE   5
      DESPAIR,
    THE SOUTH WIND BROUGHT IT LONGING, AND THE EAST BROUGHT 449 OWEN AHERNE   V   5
      IN DESPAIR,
    THE SOUTH WIND BROUGHT IT LONGING, AND THE EAST BROUGHT 449 OWEN AHERNE   V   5
      IT DESPAIR,
    DELIGHT BECOMES DEATH—LONGING IF ALL LONGING ELSE BE VAIN. 459 FROM OEDIPUS   3
    DREAD HAS FOLLOWED LONGING, ... 519 LOVES LONENESS   11
    NINE NIGHTS I LAY IN LONGING SORE . . . . 551 SONGS REWRIT 1 V 13
    NINE NIGHTS I LAY AND IN LONGING SORE . . . . 551 SONGS REWRIT 1 V 13
    NOT EVEN "I LONG TO SEE THY LONGING OVER," . . . . . . 734 QUATRAIN APHOR   11
    AND TURN BRIEF LONGING AND DECEIVING HOPE . . . . . . 750 SHADOW WATER A   59
    THAN IN BRIEF LONGING AND DECEIVING HOPE . . . . 750 SHADOW WATER A   65
    IS BUT BRIEF LONGING, AND DECEIVING HOPE, ... 765 SHADOW WATER A 354
    WHEN LOVE LONGING IS BUT DROUGHT . . . . 777 SONG DEIRDRE 2 V 11
LONGINGS
    OF BIRDS EVEN, LONGINGS FOR AERY . . . . 708 FAIRY PEDANT   26
LONG—LEGGED
    THE LONG—LEGGED MOOR—HENS DIVE, ... 393 EASTER 1916   53
    WHERE LONG—LEGGED MOOR—HENS DIVE, ... 393 EASTER 1916   V 53
    OVER THEM FLIES A LONG—LEGGED BIRD, ... 566 LAPIS LAZULI   39
    LONG—LEGGED FLY . . . . 617 LONG—LEG FLY   T
    LIKE A LONG—LEGGED FLY UPON THE STREAM . . . . 617 LONG—LEG FLY   9
    LIKE A LONG—LEGGED FLY UPON THE STREAM . . . . 617 LONG—LEG FLY   19
    LIKE A LONG—LEGGED FLY UPON THE STREAM . . . . 618 LONG—LEG FLY   29
LONG—LIMBED
    AND THE JOY OF THE STREAMS WHERE LONG—LIMBED HERONS WADE: 674 ISLE STAT II 3 217
LONG—LIVED
    SEVEN OLD SISTERS WIND THE THREADS OF THE LONG—LIVED ONES, 209 UNDER THE MOON   7
LONG—LOST
    WHERE LIES THE LONG—LOST FOREST OF THE SPRITE, ... 682 SEEKER   23
    THERE LIES THE LONG—LOST FOREST OF THE SPRITE, ... 682 SEEKER   V 23
    SOFT AS THE WHISPERING OF A LONG—LOST FOOTSTEP . . . . 699 MOSADA 3   5
LONG—OARED
    REMEMBERING ITS LONG—OARED COMPANIONS. . . . . 55 OISIN 3   118
LONG—PLANNED
    AS MY LONG—PLANNED HALF SOLITUDE, ... 624 APPARITIONS   10
LONGS
    . . . AND HIS BELOVED, AND LONGS FOR THE END OF THE WORLD 153 CHANGE BELOVED   T
    THAT THE HEART LONGS FOR. WHAT IS LOVE ITSELF, ... 230 SHADOW WATER B 183
    FOR ALL LIFE LONGS FOR THE LAST DAY . . . . 306 HOUR DAWN   98
    SO LONGS TO LOOK BEYOND OUR LIFE, AN EYE . . . . . . 465 HARUN RASHID V 87
    AND BODILY TENDERNESS: AND HE WHO LONGS . . . . 750 SHADOW WATER A   66
    O! WHY IS LOVE SO CRAZY THAT IT LONGS . . . . 765 SHADOW WATER A 363
LONG—VISAGED
    THAT PALE, LONG—VISAGED COMPANY . . . . 637 BEN BULBEN   7
LONG—WARLESS
    . . . LONG—WARLESS, GROWN WHITER THAN CURDS. . . . . . 49 OISIN 3   V 36
LOOK
    THEREON DID SHE LOOK HAUGHTY AND SWEET: . . . .   6 OISIN 1   54
    LOOK TO LONG FISHING—LINES, OR POINT AND PARE . . . . . 32 OISIN 2   55
    LEST THEY SHOULD LOOK UPON SOME DREADFUL SIGHT: . . . . 38 OISIN 2   142
    LOOK ON MY THIN GREY HAIR AND HOLLOW CHEEKS . . . . . 103 FERGUS DRUID   23
    AND SLOWLY READ, AND DREAM OF THE SOFT LOOK . . . . . 121 YOU ARE OLD   3
    WITH "LOOK AT THAT OLD FELLOW THERE! . . . . 131 OLD PENSIONER V   3
    THERE'S NO MAN MAY LOOK UPON HER, NO MAN, ... 199 ARROW   3
    IN A WHITE BREAKING WAVE! THEY HAD THE LOOK . . . . . 223 SHADOW WATER B   34
    LOOK THERE! THERE IN THE MIST! A SHIP OF SPICE! . . . . 232 SHADOW WATER B 219
    THEY ARE TOO BUSY WITH EACH OTHER. LOOK! . . . . . . 232 SHADOW WATER B 229
    AND I WOULD HAVE YOU LOOK INTO MY FACE . . . . 238 SHADOW WATER B 349
    THAT I WOULD LOOK UPON FOR EVER? MY GRIEF! . . . . . 244 SHADOW WATER B 462
    WHY ARE YOU LOOKING AT THE SEA? LOOK THERE! . . . . . 246 SHADOW WATER B 516
    I TOO, I TOO. WHY DO YOU LOOK AWAY? . . . . 246 SHADOW WATER B V 507
    WHAT MORE HAVE YOU TO LOOK FOR ON THE SEAS? . . . . . 248 SHADOW WATER B 543
    OR LOOK UPON THEM. WERE THEY BUT LOWLIER . . . . . . 250 SHADOW WATER B 576

		PAGE	TITLE		LINE

LOOK   (CONTINUED)

WILL LOOK UPON HIS FACE AGAIN. GO WITH HIM,	250	SHADOW WATER B		589
I LOOK AT YOU, AND I SIGH.	261	DRINKING SONG		6
DEAR CRAOIBHIN AOIBHIN, LOOK INTO OUR CASE.	264	ABBEY THEATRE		1
SO BITTERLY, YOU'D DREAM THEY LONGED TO LOOK	265	ABBEY THEATRE		6
BUT NOW SHE HAD NO MILD AND NO KIND LOOK;	279	TWO KINGS	V	62D
SHE WOULD NOT LOOK IN ANY KNOWN MAN'S FACE	280	TWO KINGS		73
WOULD NEVER LOOK AGAIN ON KNOWN MAN'S FACE."	280	TWO KINGS		75
WILL NEVER LOOK AGAIN ON KNOWN MAN'S FACE."	280	TWO KINGS	V	75
SHALL MAKE HER LOOK UPON HER HANDIWORK,	282	TWO KINGS		115
LOOK UP IN THE SUN'S EYE AND GIVE	288	TO WEALTHY MAN		32
WHETHER TO LOOK UPON YOUR MONUMENT	292	TO A SHADE		2
AND SNORED, NO PHANTOM BY HIS LOOK.	303	HOUR DAWN		30
PLAINLY NO PHANTOM BY HIS LOOK;	303	HOUR DAWN	V	30
WITH SCARCE A PITYING LOOK?	315	FRIENDS		19
WHAT EAGLE LOOK STILL SHOWS,	316	FRIENDS		25
AND NOW THEIR BREATHLESS FACES SEEM TO LOOK	325	ROBERT GREGORY		43
AND THEIR BREATHLESS FACES SEEM TO LOOK	325	ROBERT GREGORY	V	43
AND ALL DAY LONG I LOOK	329	MEN IMPROVE		4
YET DID BUT LOOK, ROCKING THE GLITTERING COACH	344	DAWN	V	11
AND THAT PROUD LOOK AS THOUGH SHE HAD GAZED INTO THE BURNING SUN,	354	HIS PHOENIX		29
YET ALWAYS WHEN I LOOK DEATH IN THE FACE,	357	DEEP-SWORN VOW		3
AND SHE MAY LOOK FROM THE BED	366	HER CHRIS TREE		6
IMPULSIVE MEN THAT LOOK FOR HAPPINESS	369	EGO DOMINUS		40
AND LOOK MOST LIKE ME, BEING INDEED MY DOUBLE,	371	EGO DOMINUS		72
AND BOTH LOOK UP TO ME ALONE	380	SONGS FOOL 1		4
AS I LOOK UP TO PROVIDENCE.	380	SONGS FOOL 1		6
WITH A STARK, DENYING LOOK;	381	SONG OF FOOL		6
THE SOUL'S UNCHANGING LOOK;	422	MY TABLE		24
I LOOK UPON ONE CHILD OR T'OTHER THERE	443	SCHOOL CHILDR		18
I AM JEALOUS OF THE LOOK MEN TURN ON YOU	447	HERO GIRL FOOL	V	A
THEN PETER HAD A MURDERING LOOK,	457	SUMMER SPRING		9
THOUGH BUT A FEW LEARNED MEN SHALL LOOK WITHIN,	461	HARUN RASHID	V	18A
MY HEART MUST LOOK UPON A DAILY RUIN	464	HARUN RASHID	V	83
SO STRAINS TO LOOK BEYOND OUR LIFE, AN EYE	465	HARUN RASHID		87
SO LONGS TO LOOK BEYOND OUR LIFE, AN EYE	465	HARUN RASHID	V	87
EVERYTHING WE LOOK UPON IS BLEST.	479	SELF AND SOUL		72
I CANNOT LOOK THEREON,	501	VACILLATION		49
LOOK ON THAT FIRE, SALVATION WALKS WITHIN.	502	VACILLATION		76
WHAT IF I LOOK UPON A MAN	532	BEFORE WORLD		9
WHERE CAN SHE LOOK UNTIL HE MAKE THE SHOW!	558	RIBH CHRISTIAN		22
THE GYRES! THE GYRES! OLD ROCKY FACE, LOOK FORTH;	564	GYRES		1
WE THAT LOOK ON BUT LAUGH IN TRAGIC JOY.	564	GYRES		8
IF SOUL MAY LOOK AND BODY TOUCH,	573	LADYS 2ND SONG		19
HE FIXED A BITTER LOOK;	585	ORAHILLY		24
A GENTLE QUESTIONING LOOK THAT CANNOT HIDE	601	GALLERY REVIS		6
KEVIN O'HIGGINS, AND THAT LOOK HE WEARS,	601	GALLERY REVIS	V	5
WHERE MY FRIENDS' PORTRAITS HANG AND LOOK THEREON!	604	GALLERY REVIS		52
CALCULATIONS THAT LOOK BUT CASUAL FLESH, PUT DOWN	610	STATUES		11
CAN THERE BE MERCY IN THAT LOOK?	625	NATIVITY		12
FOR, LOOK YOU, SAD'S THE MURMUR OF THE BEES,	652	ISLE STAT I 2		9
YOUR WEEPING FITS! LOOK YOU, SO VERY STRAIT	659	ISLE STAT II 1		22
LOOK UP, LOOK UP, THY GOMEZ IS BY THEE.	701	MOSADA 3		68
LOOK UP, LOOK UP, THY GOMEZ IS BY THEE.	701	MOSADA 3		68
LOOK UP, LOOK UP, THY VALLENCE IS BY THEE.	701	MOSADA 3	V	68
LOOK UP, LOOK UP, THY VALLENCE IS BY THEE.	701	MOSADA 3	V	68
I KNEEL BY THEE--NO PARTING NOW--LOOK UP.	702	MOSADA 3		94
FOR NIGHT COMES FAST. LOOK DOWN ON ME, MY LOVE,	703	MOSADA 3		103
LOOK ON ME ONCE. WHY SINK YOUR EYELIDS THUS?	703	MOSADA 3		107
LOVE, WILL YOU DIE WHEN WE HAVE MET? ONE LOOK	703	MOSADA 3		109
LOOK ON ME ONCE. WHY SINK YOUR EYELIDS SO?	703	MOSADA 3	V	107
LOOK! THERE SHE LIES UNDER A FLAPPING SAIL.	751	SHADOW WATER A		90
AENGUS LOOKS ON YOU WHEN I LOOK! HE AWAITS	757	SHADOW WATER A		209
AENGUS LOOKS ON YOU WHEN I LOOK! HE WAITS	757	SHADOW WATER A	V	209
I AM CAUGHT IN WOVEN NETS OF ENCHANTMENT. LOOK!	762	SHADOW WATER A		293
IS LAUGHING THROUGH A MORTAL'S EYES. O LOOK!	763	SHADOW WATER A		324
THAT HAVE GONE THITHER TO LOOK FOR THE LOUD STREAMS.	765	SHADOW WATER A		348
LOOK ON THIS BODY AND THIS HEAVY HAIR;	767	SHADOW WATER A		397
SHOULD LOOK UPON HIS EYES WITH LOVE, IN THE END	768	SHADOW WATER A		409
SHOULD LOOK UPON HIS EYES WITH LOVE UNTO THE END	768	SHADOW WATER A	V	409

LOOKED

AS ANY RUDDY MOTH, LOOKED DOWN ON US;	34	OISIN 2		72
LOOKED DOWN ON ME; AND IN THE SELF-SAME PLACE	39	OISIN 2		146
I LOOKED ON MY COLD BABY	95	MOLL MAGEE		19
LOOKED DOWN ON YOU FROM HEAVEN'S DOOR-POST	112	ROSE OF PEACE		3
LOOKED DOWN ON YOU FROM HEAVEN'S DOOR-POSTS,	112	ROSE OF PEACE	V	3
SHE LOOKED IN MY HEART ONE DAY	152	LOSS OF LOVE		5
WHEN THEY HAVE BUT LOOKED UPON THEIR IMAGES--	210	RAGGED WOOD		3
WHEN THE SUN LOOKED OUT OF HIS GOLDEN HOOD,	210	RAGGED WOOD	V	3
WHEN THE SUN LOOKED OUT OF HIS GOLDEN HOOD?--	211	RAGGED WOOD		7
WHEN THEY HAVE BUT LOOKED UPON THEIR IMAGES,	211	RAGGED WOOD	V	7
UNTIL THE MOON HAD SET; AND WHEN I LOOKED	223	SHADOW WATER B		22
HAD YOU LOOKED ON THEM FACE TO FACE AS I DID,	231	SHADOW WATER B		198
FOOL! FOOL! ALTHOUGH YOU HAVE LOOKED INTO MY FACE	238	SHADOW WATER B		356
MY ENEMY? I LOOKED UPON THE MOON,	246	SHADOW WATER B		509
I HAVE LOOKED UPON THOSE BRILLIANT CREATURES,	322	SWANS AT COOLE		13
I HAVE LOOKED UPON THESE BRILLIANT CREATURES	322	SWANS AT COOLE	V	13
WHEN HAVE I LAST LOOKED ON	343	DEJECTION		1
THAT HAS LOOKED DOWN	344	DAWN		2
ALL DAY I'D LOOKED IN THE FACE	347	FISHERMAN		9

473

		PAGE	TITLE	LINE
LOOKED	(CONTINUED)			
THAT NEVER LOOKED UPON MAN WITH DESIRE,		358	PRESENCES	13
HAVE LOOKED INTO YOUR FACE?		367	HER CHRIS TREE	11
THAT I HAVE HANDLED LEAST, LEAST LOOKED UPON.		367	EGO DOMINUS	9
THE CREEPING CAT, LOOKED UP.		378	CAT AND MOON	4
. . . NEVER TO HAVE LOOKED INTO THE EYE OF DAY!		459	FROM OEDIPUS	11
. . . AT ALL NOR LOOKED INTO THE EYE OF DAY.		459	FROM OEDIPUS	V 11
WHEN IT HAS LOOKED IN GLORY FROM A CLOUD.		482	BLOOD AND MOON	54
THAT NEVER LOOKED OUT OF THE EYE OF A SAINT		486	SEVEN SAGES	12
I TURNED ABOUT AND LOOKED WHERE BRANCHES BREAK		490	COOLE BALLYLEE	15
I TURNED ABOUT AND LOOKED WHERE BRANCHES BROKE		490	COOLE BALLYLEE	V 15
TROY LOOKED ON HELEN, IT DIED AND ADORED!		547	TO SAME TUNE 3 V	4
MY LOVER LOOKED SO GAY"!		570	THREE BUSHES	32
LOOKED HALF ASLEEP ALL DAY.		570	THREE BUSHES	34
LONG LOOKED HE IN HER FACE,		571	THREE BUSHES	67
AND NEVER HAVE I LOOKED UPON .		595	COLONEL MARTIN	32
WHEREVER I HAD LOOKED I HAD LOOKED UPON .		602	GALLERY REVIS	19
WHEREVER I HAD LOOKED I HAD LOOKED UPON .		602	GALLERY REVIS	19
PLOTINUS CAME AND LOOKED ABOUT,		611	NEWS ORACLE	9
AS THOUGH A STERNER EYE LOOKED THROUGH HER EYE		619	BRONZE HEAD	23
AN OLD HORSE LOOKED ACROSS A FENCE,		725	LEGEND	27
THE PRIEST LOOKED NEITHER TO RIGHT NOR LEFT,		730	PRIEST FAIRY	49
AND LOOKED ON NO ONE THERE		741	EARL PAUL	34
AND LEAVE HER DREAMING. WHEN I LOOKED ON HER,		761	SHADOW WATER A V	258
THE MOMENT HE HAS LOOKED AT YOU,		786	YOUR HEART	18
LOOKING				
LOOKING ON HER, ALEEL, THE SWINEHERD, SAID!		106	CUCHULAIN SEA V	9
WHEN LOOKING ON THEIR SHAKEN HAIR,		135	TWO TREES	V 17
HE CHANGED ME SUDDENLY! I WAS LOOKING ANOTHER WAY!		153	CHANGE BELOVED	7
WHILE I WAS LOOKING THEY ROSE HURRIEDLY,		223	SHADOW WATER B	25
FOR YOU ARE LOOKING AT THE SEA. DO YOU NOT KNOW .		246	SHADOW WATER B	513
WHY ARE YOU LOOKING AT THE SEA? LOOK THERE!		246	SHADOW WATER B	516
"SPEAKING OF LOVE THROUGH OTHER LIPS AND LOOKING .		283	TWO KINGS	155
FROM STONE TO STONE. I AM LOOKING FOR STRAYED SHEEP!		339	SHEP GOATHERD	9
IN THEIR GREAT WINDOW LOOKING AT THE DAWN!		352	PEOPLE	15
STILL RAZOR-KEEN, STILL LIKE A LOOKING GLASS .		477	SELF AND SOUL V	11
I'M LOOKING FOR THE FACE I HAD .		532	BEFORE WORLD	7
GAVE WOMEN DREAMS AND DREAMS THEIR LOOKING GLASS.		610	STATUES	V 16
LOOKING-GLASS				
"BUT THERE'S A DEVIL IN A LOOKING-GLASS."		300	BEGGAR CRIED	12
IS WHAT YOUR LOOKING-GLASS CAN SHOW,		385	ROBARTES DANCE	15
WHEN THE LONG LOOKING-GLASS IS FULL,		387	ROBARTES DANCE	50
OR HERS BEFORE A LOOKING-GLASS, FOR SUCH,		403	FOR DAUGHTER	19
AT MY OWN IMAGE IN THE LOOKING-GLASS .		447	HERO GIRL FOOL V	1
STILL RAZOR-KEEN, STILL LIKE A LOOKING-GLASS .		477	SELF AND SOUL	11
GAVE WOMEN DREAMS AND DREAMS THEIR LOOKING-GLASS.		610	STATUES	16
LOOKS				
AND LOOKS UPON THE POOR.		96	MOLL MAGEE	52
BUT GATHER WITH YOUR SHININ' LOOKS		96	MOLL MAGEE	55
THAT THEY WOULD SIGH AND QUOTE WITH LEARNED LOOKS		205	ADAMS CURSE	25
LOOKS AT THE CRADLE AND BAWLS!		319	DOLLS	2
AND OF A RED-HAIRED YEATS WHOSE LOOKS, ALTHOUGH HE DIED		391	UNDER SATURN	9
I KNOW, ALTHOUGH WHEN LOOKS MEET		511	JANE AND JACK	1
CRAZY JANE GROWN OLD LOOKS AT THE DANCERS .		514	JANE GROWN OLD	T
BUT THE GOLDEN RACE LOOKS DIM,		530	DELPHIC ORACLE	4
MY LOVER LOOKS SO GAY."		570	THREE BUSHES V	32
THAT NOBODY LOOKS! HER FEET .		617	LONG-LEG FLY	16
NOT TO ALLOW HIS LOOKS TO TELL .		624	APPARITIONS	13
AENGUS LOOKS ON YOU WHEN I LOOK! HE AWAITS .		757	SHADOW WATER A	209
AMONG THE WINDS, LOOKS UNDER YOUR PALE EYELIDS.		757	SHADOW WATER A	211
AENGUS LOOKS ON YOU WHEN I LOOK! HE WAITS .		757	SHADOW WATER A V	209
LOOM				
OR WEAVER BENT AT HIS LOOM,		589	OLD WICKED MAN	51
AND ON THIS LOOM I WEAVE THY DESTINY."		716	DWELT SYCAMORE	14
LOOMED				
THE ISLE LOOMED LARGELY IN THE LIGHT .		25	OISIN 1	V 385
LOONY'D				
"A LOONY'D BOAST OF SUCH A LOVE,"		539	MEETING	13
LOOPED				
I AM LOOPED IN THE LOOPS OF HER HAIR.		268	BROWN PENNY	8
LOOPHOLE				
AS AT THE LOOPHOLE THERE .		415	TOWER	166
AND AT THE LOOPHOLE THERE,		415	TOWER	V 166
LOOPS				
I AM LOOPED IN THE LOOPS OF HER HAIR.		268	BROWN PENNY	8
LOOSE				
SHAKE THE LOOSE REINS! YOU SLAVES OF GOD,		22	OISIN 1	331
SHAKE THE LOOSE REINS! YE SLAVES OF GOD,		22	OISIN 1	V 331
AND HIS LOOSE BULK BE THROWN IN THE LOUD TIDE."		35	OISIN 2	91
CAST THE LOOSE BULK, LEST NIAM FEAR HIM DEAD!		41	OISIN 2	V 183
. . . HEAPED LOOSE WHERE THEY LAY.		48	OISIN 3	V 28
LAY LOOSE IN A PLACE OF SHADOW! WE DREW THE REINS BY HIS SIDE.		50	OISIN 3	44
OUR LONG SHIPS LOOSE THOUGHT-WOVEN SAILS AND WAIT,		115	ROSE OF BATTLE	31
"OH GOD IF HE GOT LOOSE!" AND THEN .		307	HOUR DAWN V	118
WHATEVER THEIR LOOSE FANTASY INVENT		398	LEADERS CROWD	4
WHATEVER THEIR LOOSE PHANTASY INVENT .		398	LEADERS CROWD V	4
WHEN THE HEADLONG LIGHT IS LOOSE,		414	TOWER	135
ARE BUT LOOSE THREAD, ARE BUT LOOSE THREAD!		449	HERO GIRL FOOL	23
ARE BUT LOOSE THREAD, ARE BUT LOOSE THREAD!		449	HERO GIRL FOOL	23
NO LOOSE LIPPED DEMAGOGUE HAD WON THE DAY,		542	PARN FUNERAL 2 V	3

474

		PAGE	TITLE	LINE

LOOSE   (CONTINUED)
NEITHER LOOSE IMAGINATION, ...   575 ACRE OF GRASS   9
. . . NIGHT SPLITS AND THE DAWN BREAKS LOOSE: . . . . .   623 HIGH TALK   12
NOW FLINGING LOOSE THE SLANTING SAIL, ...   742 DANAAN QUICK   3
LOOSED
LOOSED LONG AGO FROM HEAVEN'S GATE, ...   24 OISIN 1   362
MERE ANARCHY IS LOOSED UPON THE WORLD, ...   402 SECOND COMING   4
THE BLOOD-DIMMED TIDE IS LOOSED, AND EVERYWHERE . . . .   402 SECOND COMING   5
WHEN THE DARK HOUNDS WERE LOOSED. COME TO THE ALE. . . .   766 SHADOW WATER A   379
LOOSE-LIPPED
NO LOOSE-LIPPED DEMAGOGUE HAD WON THE DAY, ...   542 PARN FUNERAL 2   3
LOOSELY
. . . FLUNG LOOSELY ALONG THE DIM GROUND: . . . . . .   50 OISIN 3   45
LOOSEN
HALF CLOSE YOUR EYELIDS, LOOSEN YOUR HAIR, ...   166 EVIL OF BELOV   1
WE WILL BEND DOWN AND LOOSEN OUR HAIR OVER YOU, ...   172 TRAV PASSION   6
AND LOOSEN ON US DREAMS THAT WASTE OUR LIFE, ...   281 TWO KINGS   107
MERELY TO LOOSEN OUT A TRESS . . . .   390 IMAGE PAST   26
LOOSENED
HE SAT WITH TIGHTENED REIN AND LOOSENED MOUTH . . . .   277 TWO KINGS   10
OR IT MAY BE LOOSENED IN REPOSE, ...   386 ROBARTES DANCE   35
WITH LOOSENED HAIR OR FOREHEADS GRIEF-DISTRAUGHT, . . .   537 HER VISION   18
WITH LOOSENED HAIR OR FOREHEADS GRIEF DISTRAUGHT, . . .   537 HER VISION   V 18
LOOSENING
OF LOOSENING MASONRY, AND THERE . . . .   424 STARES NEST   2
MY WALL IS LOOSENING: HONEY-BEES, ...   424 STARES NEST   4
MY WALL IS LOOSENING, HONEY BEES . . . .   424 STARES NEST   V 4
THE FEATHERED GLORY FROM HER LOOSENING THIGHS? . . . .   441 LEDA AND SWAN   6
LOOSENS
THE HUNTSMAN LOOSENS ON THE MORN . . . .   98 FOXHUNTER   27
LORD
LORD OF THE CROZIERS, YOU EVEN HAD LIFTED YOUR HANDS AND   54 OISIN 3   110
    WEPT:
LORD OF THE CROSIERS, THOU EVEN HADST LIFTED THY HANDS   54 OISIN 3   V 110
    AND WEPT:
LORD, WHAT WOULD THEY SAY . . . .   337 SCHOLARS   11
LORD EDWARD AND WOLFE TONE, ...   395 SIXTEEN DEAD   16
IN HIS NOSTRILS, THE GREAT LORD OF CHOU . . . . .   502 VACILLATION   59
THE DEVOTEE PROFFERS A KNEE TO HIS LORD, ...   547 TO SAME TUNE 3   2
THE LORD HAVE MERCY UPON US- . . . .   572 LADYS 2ND SONG   7
THE LORD HAVE MERCY UPON US. . . . .   573 LADYS 2ND SONG   14
THE LORD HAVE MERCY UPON US. . . . .   573 LADYS 2ND SONG   21
THE DEVOTEE PROFFERS A KNEE TO HIS LORD, ...   614 MARCH SONGS 2   2
AM I A GREAT LORD CHANCELLOR . . . .   627 STATES HOLIDAY   14
LION AND WOMAN AND THE LORD KNOWS WHAT. . . . . .   629 CIRCUS ANIMALS   8
WAKING HE THANKS THE LORD THAT HE . . . .   633 MAN AND ECHO   27
"SEND WAR IN OUR TIME, O LORD!" . . . .   638 BEN BULBEN   26
SLEEPING LORD OF ARCHERY, ...   658 ISLE STAT I 3   81
SLEEPING LORD OF ARCHERY. . . . .   658 ISLE STAT I 3   96
WHY THESE NEW FEARS? THE SERVANT OF THE LORD, . . .   692 MOSADA 1   V 46
MY LORD, IF IT MUST BE, I PRAY DESCEND . . . . .   697 MOSADA 2   43
MY LORD, YOU CALLED? NOT I. THIS MAID IS DEAD. . . .   704 MOSADA 3   125
YOU'RE PALE, MY LORD. HIS LIPS ARE QUIVERING: . . .   704 MOSADA 3   127
LORD'S
THE FLAGRANT SIGNAL OF HER LORD'S RETURN, ...   645 ISLE STAT I 1   13
LORDS
TO LORDS AND LADIES OF BYZANTIUM . . . .   408 SAIL BYZANTIUM   31
SING THE LORDS AND LADIES GAY . . . .   640 BEN BULBEN   78
LORE
HAD FELT THE ISLAND BREEZE, MY LORE . . . .   668 ISLE STAT II 3   55
HAD LEFT THE ISLAND BREEZE, MY LORE . . . .   668 ISLE STAT II 3 V   55
LORN   SEE LOVE-LORN
LOSE
LOSE NATURAL KINDNESS AND MAYBE . . . .   404 FOR DAUGHTER   22
AND WHAT IF MY DESCENDANTS LOSE THE FLOWER . . . . .   423 MY DESCENDANTS   9
TO SHOW HOW VIOLENT GREAT HEARTS CAN LOSE . . . . .   463 HARUN RASHID   47
WHAT IF SHE LOSE HER IGNORANCE AND SO . . . . . .   468 HARUN RASHID   170
WERE SHE TO LOSE HER LOVE, BECAUSE SHE HAD LOST . . .   469 HARUN RASHID   175
HER CONFIDENCE IN MINE, OR EVEN LOSE . . . . . .   469 HARUN RASHID   176
LEAVES WHAT MAN WOULD LOSE. . . . .   620 JOHN KINSELLA   4
I LOSE! THEY'RE LOADED DICE. TIME ALWAYS PLAYS . .   721 WITCH VIVIEN   44
AND I MUST LOSE MORE TIME BECAUSE THESE FOOLS . . . .   754 SHADOW WATER A   158
LOSS
BUT HAVE NO SHARE IN LOSS OR VICTORY. . . . . .   104 FERGUS DRUID   V 38E
THE LOVER MOURNS FOR THE LOSS OF LOVE . . . . . .   152 LOSS OF LOVE   T
AEDH LAMENTS THE LOSS OF LOVE . . . .   152 LOSS OF LOVE   V T
YOUR OPEN HAND BUT SHOWS OUR LOSS, ...   288 TO WEALTHY MAN   29
NO LIKELY END COULD BRING THEM LOSS . . . . . .   328 IRISH AIRMAN   7
HAS PLUCKED A FLOWER AND SUNG HER LOSS: . . . . .   447 COLONUS PRAISE   22
AH! WOE FOR THE LOSS OF YOUR FACE, ...   708 FAIRY PEDANT   32
AND LOSS OF YOUR LAUGH AND ITS LIGHTNESS— . . . . .   708 FAIRY PEDANT   33
HE WHO MEASURES GAIN AND LOSS, ...   744 ROSY CROSS   1
HE WHO MEASURES GAIN AND LOSS, ...   744 ROSY CROSS   9
LOST   SEE LATE-LOST HALF-LOST LONG-LOST
HALF LOST IN VAPOUR, SHADOWS CALLED OUR NAMES, . . .   29 OISIN 2   V 3
AND THEN LOST NIAMH MURMURED, "LOVE, WE GO . . . .   46 OISIN 2   245
LOST NIAM MOURN AND SAY, "AH, LOVE, WE GO . . . .   46 OISIN 2   V 245B
NOR LOST IN THE STAR-FIRES AND ODOURS . . . . . .   56 OISIN 3   135
LATER A SOUND CAME, HALF LOST IN THE SOUND OF A SHORE FAR   57 OISIN 3   155
    AWAY,

475

	PAGE	TITLE		LINE

LOST   (CONTINUED)
BUT KNEEL AND WEAR OUT THE FLAGS AND PRAY FOR YOUR SOUL	63	OISIN 3		215
THAT IS LOST				
. . . FOR THY SOUL THAT IS LOST,	63	OISIN 3	V	215
KNEEL, USHEEN, WEAR OUT THE FLAGS AND PRAY FOR YOUR SOUL	63	OISIN 3	V	215
THAT IS LOST				
A THIN GREY MAN HALF LOST IN GATHERING NIGHT,	102	FERGUS DRUID		7
AND I DREAMED MY LOST LOVE CAME STEALTHILY OUT OF THE WOOD	163	VALLEY LOVERS		3
AND LOST THE WORLD AND EMER FOR A KISS,	170	SECRET ROSE		15
YOUR BEAUTY PERISH AND BE LOST	173	PLEADS FRIEND		7
AND YOUR HIGH BEAUTY FALL AND BE LOST	173	PLEADS FRIEND	V	7
TILL THE ATTORNEY FOR LOST SOULS CRY HER SWEET CRY,	173	SPEAKS HEARERS		6
OR BIRDS LOST IN THE ONE CLEAR SPACE	195	BAILE AILLINN		149
OR BIRDS LOST IN ONE CLEAR SPACE	195	BAILE AILLINN	V	149
FOR HE GAVE ALL HIS HEART AND LOST.	202	NEVER GIVE ALL		14
WE'D BETTER GO, FOR WE HAVE LOST THIS CHANCE.	226	SHADOW WATER B		80
FOR THEY'RE MY ONLY PILOTS. IF I LOST THEM	226	SHADOW WATER B		85
BROKEN-HEARTED, HAVING LOST HIS QUEEN	242	SHADOW WATER B		407
BROKENHEARTED, HAVING LOST HIS QUEEN .	242	SHADOW WATER B	V	407
WE'LL FIND SO GOOD A THING AS THAT WE HAVE LOST?	258	KING NO KING		13
TILL YOUR BAD MASTER BLENCHED AND ALL WAS LOST,	270	PARDON FATHERS	V	12
WHO HAD LOST SOME UNIMAGINABLE TREASURE .	278	TWO KINGS		40
WHAT MAN YOU HAVE LOST, WHAT EVIL YOU HAVE FOUND."	280	TWO KINGS		86
BUT IF NOT LIVING, HALF THE WORLD IS LOST."	280	TWO KINGS	V	86
THAT I MAY FIND THE SLEEP I HAVE LOST."	303	HOUR DAWN		39
I HAVE TO FIND THE SLEEP I HAVE LOST."	303	HOUR DAWN	V	39
LOVE LOST AS SOON AS WON,	312	CHILD DANCING		8
I HAVE NOT LOST DESIRE	335	SONG		13
AND CERTAIN LOST COMPANIONS OF MY OWN.	342	SHEP GOATHERD		78
ALL KNOWLEDGE LOST IN TRANCE	343	SHEP GOATHERD		111
THE REPUTATION OF HIS LIFETIME LOST	351	PEOPLE		5
AND LOST THE OLD NONCHALANCE OF THE HAND,	368	EGO DOMINUS		13
IN THINKING OF HIS LOST RENOWN.	379	SAINT HUNCH		3
IMAGINE THAT LOST LOVE, INSEPARABLE FROM MY THOUGHT	390	UNDER SATURN		2
IMAGINE THAT SOME LOST LOVE, UNASSAILABLE	390	UNDER SATURN	V	2
A GREY GULL LOST ITS FEAR AND FLEW	397	POLIT PRISONER		3
UPON A WOMAN WON OR WOMAN LOST?	413	TOWER		114
IF ON THE LOST, ADMIT YOU TURNED ASIDE	413	TOWER		115
IS LOST AMID THE LABYRINTH THAT HE HAS MADE	431	NINETEEN 19		70
AND I REMEMBER WILDNESS LOST	453	DEATH OF HARE		9
LIKE THIS PURE JET, NOW LOST AMID BLUE SKY,	464	HARUN RASHID		64
WERE SHE TO LOSE HER LOVE, BECAUSE SHE HAD LOST	469	HARUN RASHID		175
NOR DAZZLED BY THE EMBROIDERY, NOR LOST	470	HARUN RASHID		191
A SYCAMORE AND LIME-TREE LOST IN NIGHT	488	COOLE PARK 29		3
A SYCAMORE AND LIME TREE LOST IN NIGHT	488	COOLE PARK 29	V	3
SHALL LEAP INTO THE LIGHT LOST .	511	JANE AND JACK		11
WHERE FOR ITS MOMENT BOTH SEEM LOST, CONSUMED.	555	RIBH AT TOMB		16
ALL MEN HAVE AIMED AT, FOUND AND LOST,	566	LAPIS LAZULI		18
IF I LOST MY CHASTITY,	570	THREE BUSHES		20
HEROICALLY LOST, HEROICALLY FOUND.	578	CRAZED GIRL		8
WHAT WAS LOST	591	WHAT WAS LOST		T
I SING WHAT WAS LOST AND DREAD WHAT WAS WON,	591	WHAT WAS LOST		1
MY KING A LOST KING, AND LOST SOLDIERS MY MEN,	591	WHAT WAS LOST		3
MY KING A LOST KING, AND LOST SOLDIERS MY MEN,	591	WHAT WAS LOST		3
ITS GREAT BATTLE LOST,	617	LONG-LEG FLY		2
BUT HUSH, FOR I HAVE LOST THE THEME.	633	MAN AND ECHO		41
WHAT IS IT, FRIEND? HE LOST I' THE WOODS THE CHIEF	661	ISLE STAT II 1		60
THY PEACE. AH, NOW I'LL WAKE THESE SLEEPERS, LOST	677	ISLE STAT II 3		274
OR LONG ERE THIS HAD LOST THEIR RUDDY STAIN,	687	TWO TITANS		8
SOFT AS THE WHISPERING OF A LOST FOOTSTEP	699	MOSADA 3	V	5
WHEN MY LOST LOVER LEFT THESE ARMS. MY GOMEZ	701	MOSADA 3		51
WHEN MY LOST LOVER LEFT THESE ARMS. MY VALLENCE,	701	MOSADA 3	V	51
AND LOST AND FAR IN YONDER HILLS I KNOW,	713	FERENCZ RENYI		98
FOR OTHER STAKES WE PLAY. YOU LOST THE GLASS.	722	WITCH VIVIEN		50
I AM DULL TO-DAY, OR YOU WERE NOW ALL LOST.	722	WITCH VIVIEN		59
"THEY ARE LOST, THEY ARE LOST, EACH ONE," CRIED HE.	730	PRIEST FAIRY		58
"THEY ARE LOST, THEY ARE LOST, EACH ONE," CRIED HE.	730	PRIEST FAIRY		58
I SHALL FIND OUT IF I HAVE LOST MY WAY	753	SHADOW WATER A		137
I SHALL FIND OUT IF I HAVE LOST THE WAY	753	SHADOW WATER A	V	137
AND ONE SPINNER IS LOST.	771	SPINNING SONG		10
EMPTIED, RUINED, WRACKED, AND LOST,	776	AGAINST WITCH		27
MUSIC OF A LOST KINGDOM	782	GREY ROUND		2
A MAN IS LOST OF A SUDDEN,	783	GREY ROUND		9
MUSIC OF A LOST KINGDOM?	783	GREY ROUND		12

LOT
MEASURE THE LOT, FORGIVE MYSELF THE LOT,	479	SELF AND SOUL		67
MEASURE THE LOT, FORGIVE MYSELF THE LOT,	479	SELF AND SOUL		67
BLACKENS ALL OUR LOT?	534	CONSOLATION		10
THE LOT OF LOVE IS CHOSEN. I LEARNT THAT MUCH	534	CHOSEN		1
I CHOSE IT FOR MY LOT, IF QUESTIONED ON	535	CHOSEN		11
FOR I CAN PUT THE WHOLE LOT DOWN, AND ALL I HAVE TO SAY	593	PILGRIM		24
AND LETS THE KIND WORM TAKE THE LOT,	779	ACCURSED WHO		4

LOTUS
I PASSED A LITTLE FURTHER ON AND HEARD A LOTUS TALK,	76	INDIAN ON GOD		9
I PACED A LITTLE FURTHER ON AND HEARD A LOTUS TALK,--	76	INDIAN ON GOD	V	9
A LOTUS IN THEIR HANDS--YOUNG MOORISH GIRL	694	MOSADA 1		103

LOUD   SEE BEE-LOUD
A-MURMUR LIKE YOUNG PARTRIDGE, WITH LOUD HORN	32	OISIN 2		52
WHEN THEY AWAKE UPSPRINGING, WITH LOUD HORN	32	OISIN 2	V	52
AND HIS LOOSE BULK BE THROWN IN THE LOUD TIDE."	35	OISIN 2		91
OF THE LOUD CRASHING AND EARTH SHAKING FIGHT	38	OISIN 2	V	141

476

	PAGE	TITLE		LINE

LOUD (CONTINUED)

AND BY ME, IN SOFT RED RAIMENT, THE FENIANS MOVED IN LOUD STREAMS,	53	OISIN 3		93
HEARING HELL LOUD WITH A MURMUR, AS SHOUTING AND MOCKING WE SWEEP.	62	OISIN 3		208
AND MY LOUD BRAZEN BATTLE-CARS	83	MAD KING GOLL		18
AND WITH LOUD SINGING I RUSHED ON	83	MAD KING GOLL	V	31
PARTED HER LIPS WITH A LOUD SUDDEN CRY,	105	CUCHULAIN SEA		8
THAT HE MAY FIGHT THE WAVES OF THE LOUD SEA."	111	CUCHULAIN SEA	V	81
THAT HE MIGHT FIGHT THE WAVES OF THE LOUD SEA."	111	CUCHULAIN SEA	V	81
WHILE HUSHED FROM FEAR, OR LOUD WITH HOPE, A BAND	114	ROSE OF BATTLE		5
AND THE LOUD SONG OF THE EVER-SINGING LEAVES	120	SORROW OF LOVE	V	3
AND THE LOUD CHANTING OF THE UNQUIET LEAVES,	120	SORROW OF LOVE	V	11
AND THE LOUD CHAUNTING OF THE UNQUIET LEAVES,	120	SORROW OF LOVE	V	11
AND THE WHITE HUSH END ALL BUT THE LOUD BEAT	137	TO SOME I TALK		15
FROM MARBLE CITIES LOUD WITH TABORS OF OLD	162	ASKS FORGIVE		9
NOR GAVE LOUD SERVICE TO A CAUSE	273	GREY ROCK		57
WITH THE LOUD HOST BEFORE THE SEA,	276	GREY ROCK		128
THEY HAVE LOUD MUSIC, HOPE EVERY DAY RENEWED	398	LEADERS CROWD		11
THAT CRAFTY DEMON AND THAT LOUD BEAST	399	DEMON BEAST		2
NOW THAT THE LOUD BEAST RAN	400	DEMON BEAST		16
COME WITH LOUD CRY AND PANTING BREAST	412	TOWER		86
UPON CROAGH PATRICK SANG IT LOUD:	528	DANCER CRUACH	V	5
WHILE HIS LOUD SONG REPROVES	536	PARTING		7
I'LL QUENCH HIS SINGING WITH LOUD SONG--	647	ISLE STAT I 1		63
LOUD FOR THEE THE MORNING CRIETH,	648	ISLE STAT I 1		86
OH, CEASE YOUR SINGING! WILD AND SHRILL AND LOUD,	648	ISLE STAT I 1		99
BUT LOUD THE GRASSHOPPER THAT SITS BENEATH.	662	ISLE STAT II 2		8
A TITAN, WITH LOUD LAUGHTER,	680	LOVE AND DEATH		11
THAT HAVE GONE THITHER TO LOOK FOR THE LOUD STREAMS,	765	SHADOW WATER A		348
THOUGH WE WERE BIDDEN TO SING, CRY NOTHING LOUD.	778	SONG DEIRDRE 3		2
TO THE LOUD SANDS BEFORE DAY HAS BROKEN.	784	WOMANS BEAUTY		18

LOUD-CRASHING

OF THE LOUD-CRASHING AND EARTH-SHAKING FIGHT,	38	OISIN 2		141

LOUDER

SOUL CLAP ITS HANDS AND SING, AND LOUDER SING	407	SAIL BYZANTIUM		11
BUT LOUDER SANG THAT GHOST, "WHAT THEN?"	577	WHAT THEN		20

LOUDLY

AND HE CALLED LOUDLY TO THE STARS TO BEND	68	SAD SHEPHERD		5
AND LOUDLY TWICE THE LIVING WINGS FLAPT WIDE,	659	ISLE STAT II 1		12

LOUGH

WE RODE IN SADNESS ABOVE LOUGH LAEN,	2	OISIN 1	V	7H
ROUND LOUGH DERG'S HOLY ISLAND I WENT UPON THE STONES,	593	PILGRIM		6

LOUGHLAN

AND THOUGH THEY HAVE TO CROSS THE LOUGHLAN WATERS	282	TWO KINGS		113
AND THOUGH THEY HAVE TO CROSS THE LOUGHLAN SEAS	282	TWO KINGS	V	113

LOUNGING

LIKE AN ARMY OF OLD MEN LOUNGING FOR REST FROM THE FOAM OF THE SEAS.	57	OISIN 3	V	144

LOUR

I CAN SCOFF AND LOUR	510	JANE JUDGMENT		8

LOUT

I NEEDS MUST MARRY SOME POOR LOUT,"	273	GREY ROCK		47
I NEED MUST MARRY SOME POOR LOUT,"	273	GREY ROCK	V	47
WITH SKELPING HIS BIG BRAWLING LOUT,	301	RUN PARADISE		9
A DRUNKEN, VAINGLORIOUS LOUT.	393	EASTER 1916		32
A DRUNKEN, VAIN-GLORIOUS LOUT.	393	EASTER 1916	V	32
AND LEFT ME BUT A LOUT,	451	FIRST LOVE		14
DAN AND JERRY LOUT	520	HIS BARGAIN		5
A LOUT BEGETS A LOUT,	605	SONGS BURDEN 1		6
A LOUT BEGETS A LOUT,	605	SONGS BURDEN 1		6

LOVE   SEE TRUE-LOVE

AND LOVE, IN THE HOURS WHEN YOUTH HAS CEASED:	2	OISIN 1	V	7A
FOR LOVE OF USHEEN MY FEET RAN	6	OISIN 1	V	57
FOR LOVE OF OISIN FOAM WET FEET	6	OISIN 1	V	57
FOR LOVE OF OISIN FOAM-WET FEET	6	OISIN 1	V	57
INTO A DESPERATE GULPH OF LOVE!	7	OISIN 1		73
"GOOD REASON HAVE I FOR MY LOVE,"	7	OISIN 1	V	62
LOVE, TILL THE DANAAN POETS BROUGHT	7	OISIN 1	V	63
IN LOVE. I CRIED, "THEE WILL I WED,	7	OISIN 1	V	74
AND THE BLUSHES OF FIRST LOVE NEVER HAVE FLOWN:	8	OISIN 1		85
AND THE FLUSHES OF FIRST LOVE NEVER HAVE FLOWN:	8	OISIN 1	V	85
MUSIC AND LOVE AND SLEEP AWAIT,	9	OISIN 1		103
FOLDED IN LOVE THAT FEARS NO MORROW,	23	OISIN 1		341
FOR LOVE THEY FOLLOWED ONE AND ALL:	23	OISIN 1	V	345G
WHILE HIS HEART STILL DREAMS OF BATTLE AND LOVE	27	OISIN 1		406
YET LOVE AND KISS ON DIM SHORES FAR AWAY	29	OISIN 2		13
THEY LOVE AND KISS IN ISLANDS FAR AWAY,	29	OISIN 2		13
BUT LOVE AND KISS ON DIM SHORES FAR AWAY	29	OISIN 2	V	13
LIGHT IS MAN'S LOVE, AND LIGHTER IS MAN'S RAGE:	45	OISIN 2		243
AND THEN LOST NIAMH MURMURED, "LOVE, WE GO	46	OISIN 2		245
LOST NIAM MOURN AND SAY, "AH, LOVE, WE GO	46	OISIN 2	V	245B
. . . IN THE DIMNESS THEY LOVE GOING BY:	53	OISIN 3		98
COMING OUT OF THE SEA AS THE DAWN COMES, A CHAUNT OF LOVE ON MY LIPS,	58	OISIN 3		158
AND THEIR HOUND, AND THEIR HORSE, AND THEIR LOVE,	59	OISIN 3		176
THROUGH THE DEMON LOVE OF ITS YOUTH	63	OISIN 3		216
WHEN WANDERING IN THE FOREST, IF HE LOVE	71	ANASHU VIJAYA		3
BE PLENTIFUL.--AND IF HE LOVE ANOTHER,	71	ANASHU VIJAYA		5
AS IN THE WOODS HE WANDERS, IF HE LOVE	71	ANASHU VIJAYA	V	3
BE PLENTY.--IF HE GIVES ANOTHER LOVE,	71	ANASHU VIJAYA	V	5

477

LOVE   (CONTINUED)

	PAGE	TITLE		LINE
AMRITA, WHILE--AH ME! YOU LOVE ANOTHER,	74	ANASHU VIJAYA		58
I LOVED ANOTHER! NOW I LOVE NO OTHER.	74	ANASHU VIJAYA		60
VIJAYA, SWEAR TO HER LOVE NEVER MORE.	74	ANASHU VIJAYA		65
OF RED FLAMINGOES! AND MY LOVE, VIJAYA!	75	ANASHU VIJAYA		89
OF RED FLAMINGO! AND MY LOVE, VIJAYA,	75	ANASHU VIJAYA	V	89
THE INDIAN TO HIS LOVE	77	INDIAN TO LOVE		T
AND LOVE IS KINDLY AND DECEITLESS,	77	INDIAN TO LOVE	V	5D
WHILE OUR LOVE GROWS AN INDIAN STAR,	78	INDIAN TO LOVE		13
WHILE GROWS OUR LOVE AN INDIAN STAR,	78	INDIAN TO LOVE	V	13
AUTUMN IS OVER THE LONG LEAVES THAT LOVE US,	79	FALLING LEAVES		1
THE HOUR OF THE WANING OF LOVE HAS BESET US,	79	FALLING LEAVES		5
BECAUSE OUR LOVE IS WANING." AND THEN SHE!	79	EPHEMERA		3
"ALTHOUGH OUR LOVE IS WANING, LET US STAND	79	EPHEMERA		4
VEILED IN A DREAMY SORROW FOR THEIR LOVE	79	EPHEMERA	V	2A
"THOUGH OUR SAD LOVE IS FADING, LET US YET	79	EPHEMERA	V	4
HATE ON AND LOVE THROUGH UNREPINING HOURS.	80	EPHEMERA		22
ARE LOVE, AND A CONTINUAL FAREWELL."	81	EPHEMERA		24
DOWN BY THE SALLEY GARDENS MY LOVE AND I DID MEET!	90	SALLEY GARDENS		1
SHE BID ME TAKE LOVE EASY, AS THE LEAVES GROW ON THE TREE!	90	SALLEY GARDENS		3
IN A FIELD BY THE RIVER MY LOVE AND I DID STAND,	90	SALLEY GARDENS		5
SHE BID ME TAKE LOVE EASY, AS THE LEAVES GROW ON THE TREES!	90	SALLEY GARDENS	V	3
I FIND UNDER THE BOUGHS OF LOVE AND HATE,	101	ROSE UPON ROOD		10
FOR HIM WHO HEARS LOVE SING AND NEVER CEASE,	114	ROSE OF BATTLE		10
BUT GATHER ALL FOR WHOM NO LOVE HATH MADE	114	ROSE OF BATTLE		12
SILENCE AND LOVE!	116	FAERY SONG		6
THE PITY OF LOVE	119	PITY OF LOVE		T
IS HID IN THE HEART OF LOVE!	119	PITY OF LOVE		2
THREATEN THE HEAD THAT I LOVE.	119	PITY OF LOVE		8
ALL THREATEN THE HEAD THAT I LOVE.	119	PITY OF LOVE	V	8
THE SORROW OF LOVE	119	SORROW OF LOVE		T
AND LOVED YOUR BEAUTY WITH LOVE FALSE OR TRUE,	121	YOU ARE OLD		6
MURMUR, A LITTLE SADLY, HOW LOVE FLED	121	YOU ARE OLD		10
AND LOVED YOUR BEAUTY WILL LOVE FALSE OR TRUE!	121	YOU ARE OLD	V	6
MURMUR, A LITTLE SAD, "FROM US FLED LOVE.	121	YOU ARE OLD	V	10
SHE WAS MORE BEAUTIFUL THAN THY FIRST LOVE,	123	DREAM OF DEATH		11
WHERE PEOPLE LOVE BESIDE THE RAVELLED SEAS!	126	DREAM OF FAERY		9
WHERE PEOPLE LOVE BESIDE STAR-LADEN SEAS!	126	DREAM OF FAERY	V	9
THAT TALKED OF LOVE OR POLITICS!	131	OLD PENSIONER		5
THE LOVE I LIVED, THE DREAM I KNEW.	139	TO IRELAND		34
AND WE, OUR SINGING AND OUR LOVE,	139	TO IRELAND		37
NO PLACE FOR LOVE AND DREAM AT ALL!	139	TO IRELAND		43
THOUGH HOPE FALL FROM YOU AND LOVE DECAY,	148	INTO TWILIGHT		7
AND LOVE IS LESS KIND THAN THE GREY TWILIGHT,	148	INTO TWILIGHT		15
THOUGH HOPE FALL FROM THEE OR LOVE DECAY	148	INTO TWILIGHT	V	7
THE LOVER MOURNS FOR THE LOSS OF LOVE	152	LOSS OF LOVE		T
AEDH LAMENTS THE LOSS OF LOVE	152	LOSS OF LOVE	V	T
WOULD END IN LOVE IN THE END!	152	LOSS OF LOVE		4
MIGHT FADE IN LOVE IN THE END!	152	LOSS OF LOVE	V	4
TWO LOVE POEMS THE SHADOWY HORSES	154	BELOVED PEACE		T
AND HER RED LIPS SANG THEM A LOVE SONG.	160	CAP AND BELLS	V	27
AND THE QUIET OF LOVE IN HER FEET.	161	CAP AND BELLS		36
AND I DREAMED MY LOST LOVE CAME STEALTHILY OUT OF THE WOOD	163	VALLEY LOVERS		3
THE HOUR OF THY GREAT WIND OF LOVE AND HATE.	170	SECRET ROSE		28
ENCIRCLE HER I LOVE AND SING HER INTO PEACE,	174	ELEMENT POWERS		9
CRY OF HIS LOVE WITH THEIR PITIFUL CRIES,	177	PAST GREATNESS		12
AND THE MERRY LOVE THE FIDDLE,	179	FIDDLER DOONEY		15
AND THE MERRY LOVE TO DANCE!	179	FIDDLER DOONEY		16
FOR I AM AENGUS, AND I AM CROSSED IN LOVE."	183	QUEEN MAEVE		84
CAER, HIS BLUE-EYED DAUGHTER THAT I LOVE.	184	QUEEN MAEVE		96
CAER, HIS BLUE EYED DAUGHTER THAT I LOVE.	184	QUEEN MAEVE	V	96
THEIR LOVE WAS NEVER DROWNED IN CARE	189	BAILE AILLINN		8
NO COMMON LOVE IS TO OUR MIND,	190	BAILE AILLINN		34
TO MAKE THE SAVAGE HEART OF LOVE	193	BAILE AILLINN		109
OF THE EBB OF ALL THINGS TO MAKE LOVE	193	BAILE AILLINN	V	109
IN THE MID PLACE, BEING CRAZED BY LOVE.	195	BAILE AILLINN		143
AND TREMBLE WITH THEIR LOVE AND KISS.	196	BAILE AILLINN		169
ALL THE LOVE STORIES THAT THEY KNEW.	197	BAILE AILLINN		197
FOR WHEN WE HAVE BLAMED THE WIND WE CAN BLAME LOVE!	201	OLD MEMORY		10
NEVER GIVE ALL THE HEART, FOR LOVE	202	NEVER GIVE ALL		1
IF DEAF AND DUMB AND BLIND WITH LOVE?	202	NEVER GIVE ALL		12
THERE HAVE BEEN LOVERS WHO THOUGHT LOVE SHOULD BE	205	ADAMS CURSE		23
WE SAT GROWN QUIET AT THE NAME OF LOVE!	205	ADAMS CURSE		28
TO LOVE YOU IN THE OLD HIGH WAY OF LOVE!	206	ADAMS CURSE		36
TO LOVE YOU IN THE OLD HIGH WAY OF LOVE!	206	ADAMS CURSE		36
TO LOVE YOU IN THE OLD HIGHWAY OF LOVE!	206	ADAMS CURSE	V	36
TO LOVE YOU IN THE OLD HIGHWAY OF LOVE!	206	ADAMS CURSE	V	36
O DO NOT LOVE TOO LONG	211	O DO NOT LOVE		T
DO NOT LOVE TOO LONG	211	O DO NOT LOVE	V	T
SWEETHEART, DO NOT LOVE TOO LONG!	211	O DO NOT LOVE		1
O DO NOT LOVE TOO LONG,	212	O DO NOT LOVE		10
BECAUSE HER HANDS HAD BEEN MADE WILD BY LOVE.	219	HARP OF AENGUS		9
HAS HATED EVERY MAN THAT'S NOT IN LOVE,	224	SHADOW WATER B		51
AND ALL THE OTHERS! BUT IT MUST BE LOVE	228	SHADOW WATER B		139
FOR IT IS LOVE THAT I AM SEEKING FOR,	228	SHADOW WATER B		141
BUT HE THAT GETS THEIR LOVE AFTER THE FASHION	228	SHADOW WATER B		145
THE BED OF LOVE, THAT IN THE IMAGINATION	228	SHADOW WATER B		148
THAT THE HEART LONGS FOR. WHAT IS LOVE ITSELF,	230	SHADOW WATER B		183
EVEN THOUGH IT BE THE LIGHTEST OF LIGHT LOVE,	230	SHADOW WATER B		184
TO DEATH! FOR THEY THAT PROMISED TO ME LOVE	230	SHADOW WATER B		192
OR SOMEWHERE, I SHALL FIND THE LOVE THEY HAVE PROMISED.	231	SHADOW WATER B		208

LOVE   (CONTINUED)
 I SHALL HAVE LOVE IN THEIR IMMORTAL FASHION; . . . .   237 SHADOW WATER B   326
 AND YET YOU TALK OF LOVE. THE MOVEMENT OF TIME . . . .   237 SHADOW WATER B   338
 BECAUSE I HAVE AWAKENED HER TO LOVE . . . .   243 SHADOW WATER B   439
 THERE IS NOT ONE AMONG YOU THAT MADE LOVE . . . . . .   244 SHADOW WATER B   454
 FOR LOVE IS WAR, AND THERE IS HATRED IN IT; . . . . .   244 SHADOW WATER B   459
 IS IT THAT THOUGH YOUR EYES ARE FULL OF LOVE . . . . .   245 SHADOW WATER B   473
 WANDER A MOMENT WHEN ONE IS IN LOVE? . . . .   246 SHADOW WATER B   515
 ALONE AND WINGED. OUR LOVE SHALL BE LIKE THEIRS . . .   250 SHADOW WATER B   581
 AND LOVE COMES IN AT THE EYE; . . . .   261 DRINKING SONG   2
 LOVE OR DECEIT." . . . .   263 MASK   7
 TO FIND OUT IF I MIGHT LOVE. . . . .   268 BROWN PENNY   4
 "GO AND LOVE, GO AND LOVE, YOUNG MAN, ...   268 BROWN PENNY   5
 "GO AND LOVE, GO AND LOVE, YOUNG MAN, ...   268 BROWN PENNY   5
 O LOVE IS THE CROOKED THING, ...   268 BROWN PENNY   9
 FOR HE WOULD BE THINKING OF LOVE . . . .   268 BROWN PENNY   12
 HER LOVE, AND WOULD NOT HAVE ME DIE, ...   274 GREY ROCK   87
 WHY SHOULD THE FAITHFULLEST HEART MOST LOVE . . . . .   275 GREY ROCK   112
 WHY MUST THE LASTING LOVE WHAT PASSES, ...   275 GREY ROCK   114
 "SPEAKING OF LOVE THROUGH OTHER LIPS AND LOOKING . . .   283 TWO KINGS   155
 YOUR EMPTY BED." "HOW SHOULD I LOVE," I ANSWERED, . . .   285 TWO KINGS   186
 OR HOW SHOULD LOVE BE WORTH ITS PAINS WERE IT NOT . . .   285 TWO KINGS   190
 BEING WEARIED OUT, I LOVE IN MAN THE CHILD? . . . . .   285 TWO KINGS   192
 WHAT CAN THEY KNOW OF LOVE THAT DO NOT KNOW . . . . .   285 TWO KINGS   193
 AND FOR THE LOVE THAT YOU HAVE SHOWN YOUR KING, ...   286 TWO KINGS   V 212A
 TO MOCK AT EVERYTHING I LOVE . . . .   306 HOUR DAWN   83
 LOVE LOST AS SOON AS WON, ...   312 CHILD DANCING   8
 LOVE AND THE BIRD . . . .   313 MEMORY YOUTH   V   T
 I HAD THE WISDOM LOVE BRINGS FORTH; . . . .   313 MEMORY YOUTH   2
 I HAD THE WISDOM LOVE CAN BRING, ...   313 MEMORY YOUTH   V   2
 THAT EVEN THE BEST OF LOVE MUST DIE, ...   314 MEMORY YOUTH   17
 WERE IT NOT THAT LOVE UPON THE CRY . . . .   314 MEMORY YOUTH   19
 WITH THE HOT BLOOD OF YOUTH, OF LOVE CROSSED LONG AGO; . . 316 COLD HEAVEN   6
 THOSE THAT I GUARD I DO NOT LOVE; . . . . 328 IRISH AIRMAN   4
 IN THE NARROW THEME OF LOVE . . . .   333 SOLOMON SHEBA   7
 THERE'S NOT A THING BUT LOVE CAN MAKE . . . .   333 SOLOMON SHEBA   23
 IN THE ONE NARROW THEME OF LOVE . . . .   333 SOLOMON SHEBA   V   7
 RETURNED AND YET UNREQUITED LOVE. . . . . 358 PRESENCES   8
 FOR THOSE THAT LOVE THE WORLD SERVE IT IN ACTION, . . .   369 EGO DOMINUS   42
 NO ONE DENIES TO KEATS LOVE OF THE WORLD; . . . . . .   370 EGO DOMINUS   52
 FOR THOSE THAT LOVE ARE SAD. . . . .   383 VISION ROBART   36
 BY THE LAGOON YOU LOVE SO MUCH, ...   386 ROBARTES DANCE   29
 FOR THOUGH LOVE HAS A SPIDER'S EYE . . . .   388 SOLOMON WITCH   19
 IMAGINE THAT LOST LOVE, INSEPARABLE FROM MY THOUGHT . . . 390 UNDER SATURN   2
 IMAGINE THAT SOME LOST LOVE, UNASSAILABLE . . . . . .   390 UNDER SATURN   V   2
 AND WHAT IF EXCESS OF LOVE . . . .   394 EASTER 1916   72
 NOTHING THAT WE LOVE OVER-MUCH . . . . 399 BREAK OF DAY   17
 I MUST RECALL A MAN THAT NEITHER LOVE . . . .   412 TOWER   74
 OLD LECHER WITH A LOVE ON EVERY WIND, ...   413 TOWER   105
 AND MEMORIES OF LOVE, ... 415 TOWER   161
 SEEING THAT LOVE AND FRIENDSHIP ARE ENOUGH, ...   423 MY DESCENDANTS   20
 AND DECKED AND ALTERED IT FOR A GIRL'S LOVE, ...   423 MY DESCENDANTS   22
 THAN IN OUR LOVE! O HONEY-BEES, ...   425 STARES NEST   19
 MAN IS IN LOVE AND LOVES WHAT VANISHES, ... 429 NINETEEN 19   42
 TO BE IN LOVE AND LOVE WHAT VANISHES. . . . .   429 NINETEEN 19   V 42
 TO BE IN LOVE AND LOVE WHAT VANISHES. . . . .   429 NINETEEN 19   V 42
 WITH HUMAN LOVE. . . . .   436 FOR MY SON   32
 LOVE'S PLEASURE DRIVES HIS LOVE AWAY, ...   438 SONGS PLAY 2   11
 FOR ALL MEN LOVE YOUR WORTH! AND I MUST RAGE . . . . .   447 HERO GIRL FOOL   V   8
 BUT WHAT CARE I THAT LONG FOR A MAN'S LOVE? . . . . .   448 HERO GIRL FOOL   17
 A FAITHFUL LOVE, A FAITHFUL LOVE. . . . . 449 HERO GIRL FOOL   29
 A FAITHFUL LOVE, A FAITHFUL LOVE. . . . . 449 HERO GIRL FOOL   29
 A STRANGE THING SURELY THAT MY HEART, WHEN LOVE HAD COME   449 OWEN AHERNE   1
   UNSOUGHT
 IT FEARED TO GIVE ITS LOVE A HURT WITH ALL THE TEMPEST   450 OWEN AHERNE   7
   THERE;
 HER CHILDISH GRATITUDE FOR LOVE AND MATCH YOUR FIFTY YEARS? 450 OWEN AHERNE   23
 FIRST LOVE . . . .   451 FIRST LOVE   T
 A MAN YOUNG AND OLD FIRST LOVE . . . .   451 FIRST LOVE   V   T
 REMEMBERING THAT HER SHRIEK WAS LOVE . . . .   456 FRIENDS YOUTH   19
 FOR PEG AND MEG AND PARIS' LOVE . . . .   458 HIS WILDNESS   3
 YOU THINK THAT LOVE HAS SEASONS, AND YOU THINK . . . .   464 HARUN RASHID   75
 ITSELF AND NOT SOME OTHER SOUL." "THAT LOVE . . . . .   465 HARUN RASHID   94
 EVERY PHILOSOPHER SHOULD PRAISE THAT LOVE. . . . . . .   465 HARUN RASHID   97
 ITSELF AND NOT SOME OTHER SOUL. "SUCH LOVE . . . . .   465 HARUN RASHID   V 94
 PHILOSOPHERS SHOULD PRAISE LOVE THE MOST, ...   465 HARUN RASHID   V 97
 YET WAS IT LOVE OF ME, OR WAS IT LOVE . . . .   466 HARUN RASHID   112
 YET WAS IT LOVE OF ME, OR WAS IT LOVE . . . .   466 HARUN RASHID   112
 DREAM THAT I LOVE HER ONLY FOR THE VOICE, ...   469 HARUN RASHID   171
 WERE SHE TO LOSE HER LOVE, BECAUSE SHE HAD LOST . . . .   469 HARUN RASHID   175
 ITS FIRST SIMPLICITY, LOVE, VOICE AND ALL, ...   469 HARUN RASHID   177
 DREAM THAT I LOVE HER ONLY FOR THAT VOICE, ...   469 HARUN RASHID   V 171
 ITS FIRST SIMPLICITY, LOVE AND ALL, ...   469 HARUN RASHID   V 177
 FOR EVERY SEPARATE QUALITY OF LOVE! . . . .   469 HARUN RASHID   V 189A
 THAT'S CALLED PLATONIC LOVE, ...   471 ALL SOUL NIGHT   23
 ANODYNE FOR HIS LOVE. . . . . 471 ALL SOUL NIGHT   26
 EMBLEMATICAL OF LOVE AND WAR? . . . .   477 SELF AND SOUL   19
 LOVE YOU FOR YOURSELF ALONE . . . . 492 ANNE GREGORY   5
 MAY LOVE ME FOR MYSELF ALONE . . . .   492 ANNE GREGORY   11
 COULD LOVE YOU FOR YOURSELF ALONE . . . . 492 ANNE GREGORY   17
 THE THREEFOLD TERROR OF LOVE! A FALLEN FLARE . . . . .   499 MOTHER OF GOD   1

479

LOVE   (CONTINUED)

	PAGE	TITLE	LINE
THIS LOVE THAT MAKES MY HEART'S BLOOD STOP	499	MOTHER OF GOD	13
THE THREE-FOLD TERROR OF LOVE: A FALLEN FLARE	499	MOTHER OF GOD V	1
OF CHILDREN'S GRATITUDE OR WOMAN'S LOVE.	500	VACILLATION	26
"LOVE IS ALL	510	JANE JUDGMENT	1
WHAT TRUE LOVE BE?	510	JANE JUDGMENT	17
THE SOONER LOVE IS GONE,	511	JANE AND JACK	4
FOR LOVE IS BUT A SKEIN UNWOUND	511	JANE AND JACK	5
WHEN ON LOVE INTENT:	513	JANE TALK BISH	14
BUT LOVE HAS PITCHED HIS MANSION IN	513	JANE TALK BISH	15
LOVE IS LIKE THE LION'S TOOTH.	514	JANE GROWN OLD	7
LOVE IS LIKE THE LION'S TOOTH.	514	JANE GROWN OLD	14
LOVE IS LIKE THE LION'S TOOTH.	515	JANE GROWN OLD	21
ALL TRUE LOVE MUST DIE.	517	HER ANXIETY	3
LOVE IS NEARER DEATH.	517	HER ANXIETY	11
UNDYING LOVE TO BUY	517	HIS CONFIDENCE	1
FOR UNDYING LOVE?	518	HIS CONFIDENCE	6
LOVE LEAPS UPON ITS COURSE.	518	HIS CONFIDENCE	12
AND ALL THE CHOIR OF LOVE.	531	DELPHIC ORACLE	10
I'D HAVE HIM LOVE THE THING THAT WAS	532	BEFORE WORLD	15
BECAUSE I HAD FANCIED LOVE A CASUAL	533	HER TRIUMPH	2
THE LOT OF LOVE IS CHOSEN. I LEARNT THAT MUCH	534	CHOSEN	1
TOO OLD FOR A MAN'S LOVE I STOOD IN RAGE	536	HER VISION	3
TOO OLD FOR A MAN'S LOVE I STOOD AND RAGED	536	HER VISION V	1
"A LOONY'D BOAST OF SUCH A LOVE,"	539	MEETING	13
I WOULD THAT I DRANK WITH MY LOVE ON MY KNEE,	551	SONGS REWRIT 1	9
COULD I BUT DRINK, MY LOVE ON MY KNEE	551	SONGS REWRIT 1 V	9
O COULD I DRINK, MY LOVE ON MY KNEE,	551	SONGS REWRIT 1 V	9
THINKING TO MEET MY LOVE ONCE MORE	551	SONGS REWRIT 1 V	15
AND COULD BEGET OR BEAR THEMSELVES COULD THEY BUT LOVE AS HE.	556	RIBH PATRICK	12
RIBH CONSIDERS CHRISTIAN LOVE INSUFFICIENT	558	RIBH CHRISTIAN	T
WHY SHOULD I SEEK FOR LOVE OR STUDY IT?	558	RIBH CHRISTIAN	1
A LOVE THAT LACKS ITS PROPER FOOD:	569	THREE BUSHES	3
AND IF YOUR LOVE WERE GONE	569	THREE BUSHES	4
HOW COULD YOU SING THOSE SONGS OF LOVE?	569	THREE BUSHES	5
"I LOVE A MAN IN SECRET,	569	THREE BUSHES	15
I AM IN LOVE	572	LADYS 1ST SONG	7
HE SHALL LOVE MY SOUL AS THOUGH	572	LADYS 2ND SONG	8
HE SHALL LOVE YOUR BODY	572	LADYS 2ND SONG	10
LOVE CRAM LOVE'S TWO DIVISIONS	573	LADYS 2ND SONG	12
SOUL MUST LEARN A LOVE THAT IS	573	LADYS 2ND SONG	15
LIMBS A LOVE IN COMMON	573	LADYS 2ND SONG	17
BUT IN HONOUR SPLIT HIS LOVE	573	LADYS 3RD SONG	7
GOD'S LOVE HAS HIDDEN HIM	574	MAIDS 1ST SONG	7
"LOVE TO GIVE OR TO WITHHOLD	588	OLD WICKED MAN	21
A ROOF, GOOD CLOTHES, PASSION, LOVE PERHAPS,	609	IN TARAS HALLS	8
BUT NEVER ASKED FOR LOVE: SHOULD I ASK THAT,	609	IN TARAS HALLS	9
BUT BOYS AND GIRLS, PALE FROM THE IMAGINED LOVE	610	STATUES	4
AND THE GREAT WATER SIGHED FOR LOVE,	611	NEWS ORACLE	3
THERE SIGHED AMID HIS CHOIR OF LOVE	611	NEWS ORACLE	7
WHERE WADES THE CHOIR OF LOVE	612	NEWS ORACLE	22
LOVE HAS BLINDED HIM WITH TEARS:	612	NEWS ORACLE	28
WHERE WADE THE CHOIR OF LOVE	612	NEWS ORACLE V	22
BECAUSE WE LOVE BARE HILLS AND STUNTED TREES	621	HOUND VOICE	1
THIS DREAM ITSELF HAD ALL MY THOUGHT AND LOVE.	630	CIRCUS ANIMALS	24
PLAYERS AND PAINTED STAGE TOOK ALL MY LOVE,	630	CIRCUS ANIMALS	31
WINE OR LOVE DRUG HIM TO SLEEP,	633	MAN AND ECHO	26
WINE OR LOVE DRUGS HIM TO SLEEP,	633	MAN AND ECHO V	26
A QUENCHLESS GRIEVING OF LOVE MELODY.	645	ISLE STAT I 1	21
JOY AND LOVE ARE ONE EXISTENCE.	647	ISLE STAT I 1	71
LOVE AND SORROW, ONE EXISTENCE.	647	ISLE STAT I 1	73
LOVE FROM HEAVEN CAME OF YORE	648	ISLE STAT I 1	77
POOR RACE OF LEAFY ARCADY, YOUR LOVE	650	ISLE STAT I 1	145
TO PROVE HIS LOVE A KNIGHT WITH LANCE IN REST	651	ISLE STAT I 1	158
SUCH MAY I LOVE. THE SHUDDERING FOREST LIGHTS	651	ISLE STAT I 1	165
HER LOVE: TO HER WHO WEARS THAT BLOOM COMES TRUTH.	653	ISLE STAT I 2	46
TWO MEN WHO LOVE ONE MAID HAVE AMPLE CAUSE	659	ISLE STAT II 1	30
WE LOVE NASCHINA BOTH. WHOM LOVES SHE BEST?	660	ISLE STAT II 1	48
ALMINTOR WITH HER LOVE. WHO ART THOU?—SPEAK,	660	ISLE STAT II 1	50
FOR THIS THING FIGHT—WE LOVE ONE MAID? HER NAME?	661	ISLE STAT II 1	66
IF HER YE LOVE. AYE, COLIN, WE MUST FIGHT.	662	ISLE STAT II 1	76
NASCHINA'S GONE, DRAWN BY A THIRST OF LOVE,	664	ISLE STAT II 2	59
THE DIRGE OF HER YE LOVE. CEASE!—CEASE!	665	ISLE STAT II 2	74
LOVE STORM: AND STAINED WITH MIST THE NEW MOONS FLARE.	678	ISLE STAT II 3	294
LOVE STORM AND STAINED WITH MIST THE NEW MOON'S FLARE	678	ISLE STAT II 3 V	294
THE PLAIN, A LITTLE FAIR-HAIRED MAID I LOVE.	679	ISLE STAT II 3	312
THERE DWELLS A LITTLE FAIR-HAIRED MAID I LOVE.	679	ISLE STAT II 3 V	312
LOVE AND DEATH.	680	LOVE AND DEATH	T
AND THEY'LL ANSWER DEATH AND LOVE.	680	LOVE AND DEATH	16
ARE THE SPIRITS LOVE AND DEATH.	680	LOVE AND DEATH	32
OF LOVE FROM OUT A DREAMLESS RACE FOR STRIFE,	684	SEEKER	58
UNTOUCHED OF HUMAN JOY OR HUMAN LOVE?	684	SEEKER	65
OUR LOVE SHALL BE OF YESTERDAY,	686	LIFE	14
AND LAUGH OUR LOVE AWAY.	686	LIFE	16
AND, NODDING TO AND FRO, SANG SONGS OF LOVE,	688	TWO TITANS	35
THE SHADOWS PASS: BUT NOW, I LOVE MY RING.	700	MOSADA 3	27
AND OUT-SPREAD ARMS. BE NOT SO PALE, DEAR LOVE.	701	MOSADA 3	70
FOR NIGHT COMES FAST. LOOK DOWN ON ME, MY LOVE,	703	MOSADA 3	103
LOVE, WILL YOU DIE WHEN WE HAVE MET? ONE LOOK	703	MOSADA 3	109
POOR LOVE AND SORROW, WITH THEIR ARMS THROWN ROUND	703	MOSADA 3	119

		PAGE	TITLE	LINE

LOVE (CONTINUED)
SPEAK, FERENCZ, SPEAK. WE LOVE EACH OTHER. SEE,	713	FERENCZ RENYI		87
TO LOVE EACH OTHER. IN MY PRAYER-BOOK STILL	713	FERENCZ RENYI		94
TO LOVE EACH OTHER. IN MY PRAYER BOOK STILL	713	FERENCZ RENYI	V	94
AND THEN HIS HEART FILLS FULL OF LOVE,	716	FAIRY DOCTOR		11
AND THEN HIS HEART IS FULL OF LOVE,	716	FAIRY DOCTOR	V	11
LOVE SONG	717	LOVE SONG		T
MY LOVE, WE WILL GO, WE WILL GO, I AND YOU,	717	LOVE SONG		1
MY LOVE, WE WILL HEAR, I AND YOU, WE WILL HEAR,	717	LOVE SONG		4
SUCH WAR PLOTS, PEACE PLOTS, LOVE PLOTS—EVERY SIDE!	722	WITCH VIVIEN		66
FULL MOODY IS MY LOVE AND SAD,	723	GIRLS SONG A		1
MY LOVE HATH MANY AN EVIL MOOD,	723	GIRLS SONG A		5
MY LOVE HATH MANY A RUTHLESS MOOD,	723	GIRLS SONG A	V	5
SINGING A LOVE RHYME TO HIMSELF,	741	EARL PAUL		41
I DOUBT YOUR WISDOM, BUT DO NOT DOUBT MY LOVE.	748	SHADOW WATER A		31
THE GREATNESS OF MY LOVE. DID I NOT RULE	748	SHADOW WATER A	V	32
I THOUGHT SHE LOVED YOU, AND I THOUGHT HER LOVE	749	SHADOW WATER A		51
AND YET, THERE IS A LOVE THAT THE GODS LOVE,	749	SHADOW WATER A		56
THE FOOL FORETOLD ME I WOULD FIND THIS LOVE	750	SHADOW WATER A		62
FOR HAPPIER LOVE BUT FINDS UNHAPPINESS.	750	SHADOW WATER A		67
ARE BETTER THAN THE WOODS WHERE NO LOVE FADES	754	SHADOW WATER A		160
WHOSE SHADOW IS THE SLEEP THAT COMES WITH LOVE,	754	SHADOW WATER A		162
AND LURED ME HITHER, THAT YOU MIGHT BE MY LOVE.	757	SHADOW WATER A		208
WHEN SHE DREAMT FIRST OF LOVE, SHALL FLICKER OUT	760	SHADOW WATER A		257
AND TELL ME A LOVE STORY WHILE I DRINK.	760	SHADOW WATER A	V	250
WHEN SHE DREAMED FIRST OF LOVE, SHALL FLICKER OUT	760	SHADOW WATER A		257
FOR LOVE IS A-WEAVING WHEN A WOMAN'S HEART	761	SHADOW WATER A		262
BECAUSE HER HANDS HAD BEEN MADE WILD BY LOVE!	762	SHADOW WATER A		304
THAT MY TRUE LOVE WOULD COME IN A SHIP OF PEARL	763	SHADOW WATER A	V	315
WHERE TRUE LOVE WANDERS AMONG THE HOLY WOODS.	764	SHADOW WATER A	V	337
WHAT WERE TRUE LOVE AMONG THE RUSH OF HIS STREAMS?	764	SHADOW WATER A	V	338
THE LOVE I KNOW IS HIDDEN IN THESE HANDS	765	SHADOW WATER A		350
THE LOVE OF ALL UNDER THE LIGHT OF THE SUN	765	SHADOW WATER A		353
AND BODILY TENDERNESS! BUT LOVE IS MADE	765	SHADOW WATER A		355
THAT CAN CHANGE LOVE TO IMPERISHABLE FIRE?	765	SHADOW WATER A		360
O! WHY IS LOVE SO CRAZY THAT IT LONGS	765	SHADOW WATER A		363
THAT COMES WITH LOVE, COMES MURMURING OF AN HOUR	765	SHADOW WATER A		365
ALL THAT KNOW LOVE AMONG THE WINDS OF THE WORLD	767	SHADOW WATER A		386
IT MAY BE, AND HAVE GROWN WEARY OF LOVE.	767	SHADOW WATER A		390
BUT I AM NEW TO LOVE. GO AMONG THESE	767	SHADOW WATER A		391
THAT HAVE KNOWN LOVE AMONG THE WINDS OF THE WORLD	767	SHADOW WATER A		392
LOVE WAS NOT MADE FOR DARKNESS AND THE WINDS	767	SHADOW WATER A		394
FOR LOVE IS KIND AND HAPPY. O COME WITH ME!	767	SHADOW WATER A		396
HOW MANY HOURS TO DAYBREAK, BECAUSE LOVE	767	SHADOW WATER A		405
I THINK THAT THERE IS LOVE IN AIBRIC'S EYES.	768	SHADOW WATER A		407
SHOULD LOOK UPON HIS EYES WITH LOVE, IN THE END	768	SHADOW WATER A		409
MY LOVE SHAKES OUT HER HAIR UPON THE STREAMS	768	SHADOW WATER A		416
WHY HAVE YOU CLOVEN ME WITH A MORTAL LOVE?	768	SHADOW WATER A		419
SHOULD LOOK UPON HIS EYES WITH LOVE UNTO THE END	768	SHADOW WATER A	V	409
"LOVE WOULD BE A THING OF NAUGHT	772	SONG DEIRDRE 1		10
AT THE BURNING WHEEL OF LOVE	776	AGAINST WITCH		34
LOVE IS AN IMMODERATE THING	777	SONG DEIRDRE 2		1
WHAT'S THE MERIT IN LOVE PLAY,	777	SONG DEIRDRE 2	V	6
WHEN LOVE LONGING IS BUT DROUGHT	777	SONG DEIRDRE 2	V	11
INTO THE SECRET WILDERNESS OF THEIR LOVE.	778	SONG DEIRDRE 3		4
A MAN BUT WILL GIVE YOU HIS LOVE	786	YOUR HEART		17
AND LOVE WENCH WISDOM'S CRUEL FACE.	787	HUDDON DUDDON		10
AND LOVE WENCH—WISDOM'S CRUEL FACE.	787	HUDDON DUDDON	V	10
GAVE ALL THE LOVE THAT WOMEN KNOW!	789	SINGING HEAD		21

LOVED
"I LOVED NO MAN, THOUGH KINGS BESOUGHT,	7	OISIN 1		62
"I LOVED NO MAN, THOUGH CANNS BESOUGHT,	7	OISIN 1	V	62
I NE'ER LOVED ANY TILL SONG BROUGHT ME	7	OISIN 1	V	69
I LOVED AND SANG, AND IN LONG WASSAILS	23	OISIN 1	V	345C
IT WERE SAD TO GAZE ON THE BLESSED AND NO MAN I LOVED OF OLD THERE!	63	OISIN 3		221
IT WAS SAD TO GAZE ON THE BLESSED AND NO MAN I LOVED OF OLD THERE!	63	OISIN 3	V	221
I LOVED ANOTHER! NOW I LOVE NO OTHER.	74	ANASHU VIJAYA		60
AH, YOU WILL KNOW MY LOVED ONE BY HIS HUNTER'S ARROWS TRULY,	75	ANASHU VIJAYA		80
ALL LOVED HIM, ONLY THE SHONEEN,	92	FATHER OHART		13
NO WOMAN'S LOVED ME, NO MAN SOUGHT MY HELP.	103	FERGUS DRUID		26
THAT I LOVED ONCE." AGAIN THE FIGHTING SPED,	110	CUCHULAIN SEA		64
HOW MANY LOVED YOUR MOMENTS OF GLAD GRACE,	121	YOU ARE OLD		5
AND LOVED YOUR BEAUTY WITH LOVE FALSE OR TRUE,	121	YOU ARE OLD		6
BUT ONE MAN LOVED THE PILGRIM SOUL IN YOU,	121	YOU ARE OLD		7
AND LOVED THE SORROWS OF YOUR CHANGING FACE!	121	YOU ARE OLD		8
AND LOVED YOUR BEAUTY WILL LOVE FALSE OR TRUE!	121	YOU ARE OLD	V	6
AND MEN WHO LOVED THE CAUSE THAT NEVER DIES.	130	BOOK STORIES	V	24
AND YET THE BEAUTIES THAT I LOVED	131	OLD PENSIONER		15
A QUEEN WAS LOVED BY A JESTER,	159	CAP AND BELLS	V	1
WOULD NONE HAD EVER LOVED BUT YOU AND I!	210	RAGGED WOOD		4
O THAT NONE EVER LOVED BUT YOU AND I!	210	RAGGED WOOD	V	4
O THAT NONE EVER LOVED BUT YOU AND I!	211	RAGGED WOOD		8
NO ONE HAS EVER LOVED BUT YOU AND I.	211	RAGGED WOOD		12
I LOVED LONG AND LONG,	211	O DO NOT LOVE		2
FOR THAT BRIEF SIGHING. IF YOU HAD LOVED SOME WOMAN—	228	SHADOW WATER B		135
AND AS SOON FINISHED. ALL THAT EVER LOVED	229	SHADOW WATER B		151
HAVE LOVED THAT WAY—THERE IS NO OTHER WAY.	229	SHADOW WATER B		152
FOR GOLDEN-ARMED IOLLAN THAT I LOVED.	242	SHADOW WATER B		421

481

		PAGE	TITLE	LINE

LOVED   (CONTINUED)
BUT WHAT IS IT THAT MADE ME SAY I LOVED HIM? . . . . . 242 SHADOW WATER B 422
HAVE I NOT LOVED YOU FOR A THOUSAND YEARS? . . . . . . 244 SHADOW WATER B 463
I LOVED HIM; I WOULD COVER UP MY EARS, ... 246 SHADOW WATER B 494
DRAGON THAT LOVED THE WORLD AND HELD US TO IT, ... 251 SHADOW WATER B 598
HAVING LOVED GOD ONCE, BUT MAYBE . . . . 299 THREE HERMITS 26
THAT LOVED HIS LEARNING BETTER THAN MANKIND, ... 324 ROBERT GREGORY 18
WERE LOVED BY HIM; THE OLD STORM-BROKEN TREES . . . . 326 ROBERT GREGORY 50
ALL THOSE THAT MANHOOD TRIED, OR CHILDHOOD LOVED . . . 327 ROBERT GREGORY 91
THE DEAD MAN THAT I LOVED, ... 347 FISHERMAN 14
THE MOST EXALTED LADY LOVED BY A MAN. . . . . . . 369 EGO DOMINUS 37
THAT THOSE THAT WE HAVE LOVED GOT THEIR LONG FINGERS . . 375 PHASES OF MOON 66
BEING FIXED ON ALL THINGS LOVED, ALL THINGS UNLOVED, . . 383 VISION ROBART 34
LOVED THE LADY; AND IT'S PLAIN . . . . 385 ROBARTES DANCE 5
LOVED AND THOUGHT HIMSELF BELOVED, ... 404 FOR DAUGHTER 39
MY MIND, BECAUSE THE MINDS THAT I HAVE LOVED, ... 405 FOR DAUGHTER 49
THAT LOVED INFERIOR ART, ... 422 MY TABLE 27
HAVE LOVED INFERIOR ART, ... 422 MY TABLE V 27
I HAVE LOVED YOU BETTER THAN MY SOUL FOR ALL MY WORDS, . 442 BLACK CENTAUR 14
I HAVE RAGED AT MY OWN STRENGTH BECAUSE YOU HAVE LOVED IT. 448 HERO GIRL FOOL 9
THAT ONLY GOD HAS LOVED US FOR OURSELVES, ... 448 HERO GIRL FOOL 16
HOW SUCH A PAIR LOVED MANY YEARS . . . . 458 SECRETS OF OLD 15
HORTON'S THE FIRST I CALL. HE LOVED STRANGE THOUGHT . . 471 ALL SOUL NIGHT 21
WE LOVED EACH OTHER AND WERE IGNORANT. . . . . . . 523 LONG SILENCE 8
AND LOVED IN MISERY, ... 538 LAST CONFESS 4
THAT I LOVED BODILY. . . . . 538 LAST CONFESS 6
AND THOUGH IT LOVED IN MISERY . . . . 538 LAST CONFESS 21
EACH HATING WHAT THE OTHER LOVED, ... 539 MEETING 3
LOVED HIM WITH HER SOUL, ... 571 THREE BUSHES 55
THAT PARNELL LOVED A LASS. . . . . 586 PARNELLITES 16
AND PARNELL LOVED HIS COUNTRY, ... 587 PARNELLITES 31
AND PARNELL LOVED HIS LASS. . . . . 587 PARNELLITES 32
AND PARNELL LOVED A LASS. . . . . 587 PARNELLITES V 32
POETRY, MUSIC, I HAVE LOVED, AND YET . . . . 599 SPIRIT MEDIUM 1
"GOD I HAVE LOVED, BUT SHOULD I ASK RETURN . . . . . 609 IN TARAS HALLS 14
AND ONLY SHEEP HE LOVED OF ALL THE TROOP. . . . . . 661 ISLE STAT II 1 61
OF HER HE LOVED FIXED ON HIM FULL OF LIGHT, ... 710 FERENCZ RENYI 27
A FAIRY WHOM WE LOVED FULL WELL; . . . . 729 PRIEST FAIRY 44
AND, THOUGH YOU LOVED HER, GAVE HER UP TO ME? . . . . 749 SHADOW WATER A 50
I THOUGHT SHE LOVED YOU, AND I THOUGHT HER LOVE . . . 749 SHADOW WATER A 51
NO MAN NOR WOMAN HAS LOVED OTHERWISE . . . . . . 750 SHADOW WATER A 64
NO MAN OR WOMAN HAS LOVED OTHERWISE . . . . . . 750 SHADOW WATER A V 64
TO WANDER IN; YOU HAVE LOVED MANY WOMEN, ... 767 SHADOW WATER A 389
HE THAT HAS LOVED THE BEST . . . . 786 YOUR HEART 19
DANCED, LAUGHED, LOVED, FOUGHT THROUGH . . . . . . 787 HUDDON DUDDON 4
LOVE-DEW
BUT THE LOVE-DEW DIMS OUR EYES TILL THE DAY . . . . 28 OISIN 1 424
LOVE-DREAMS
AND THRO' THE ODOROUS AIR LOVE-DREAMS ARE WINGING-- . . 645 ISLE STAT I 1 5
LOVELESS
THAT HE'S A LOVELESS MAN; GAY BELLS BRING LAUGHTER . . 130 BOOK STORIES 18
DESCENDS INTO THE LOVELESS DUST. . . . . 540 FROM ANTIGONE 16
BEHOLD THE LOVING LOVELESS FLOWER OF LONE WAYS, . . . 674 ISLE STAT II 3 201
LOVELIER
AND LOVELIER THAN THE MOON UPON THE SEA; . . . . . 106 CUCHULAIN SEA V 16A
SHE IS NOT WISER NOR LOVELIER, ... 197 BAILE AILLINN 201
LOVELIEST
HAVE I NOT SEEN THE LOVELIEST WOMAN BORN . . . . . 405 FOR DAUGHTER 59
HAS FOUND THE LOVELIEST SPECTACLE THERE IS. . . . . 447 COLONUS PRAISE 24
LOVELINESS
MY HEART UPON THE LOVELINESS . . . . 155 FORGOT BEAUTY 2
BUILDING A SORROWFUL LOVELINESS . . . . 158 BELOVED RHYMES 5
A WOMAN OF SO SHINING LOVELINESS . . . . 170 SECRET ROSE 25
WROUGHT OF HIGH LAUGHTER, LOVELINESS AND EASE? . . . 264 HOUSE SHAKEN 12
IN THE FIRST LOVELINESS OF WOMANHOOD, ... 356 BROKEN DREAMS 24
OR ARROGANT LOVELINESS, ... 390 IMAGE PAST 25
OF THEIR OWN SWEETNESS, BODIES OF THEIR LOVELINESS. . . 426 PHANTOM HATRED 24
TRADITIONAL SANCTITY AND LOVELINESS; . . . . . . 491 COOLE BALLYLEE 42
THAT LOVELINESS? . . . . 784 WOMANS BEAUTY 14
THIS LOVELINESS? . . . . 785 WOMANS BEAUTY 28
LOVE-LONGING
WHEN LOVE-LONGING IS BUT DROUTH . . . . 777 SONG DEIRDRE 2 11
LOVELORN
A BOY'S LOVELORN INDIFFERENT HANDS MIGHT FIND . . . . 461 HARUN RASHID V 14
LOVE-LORN
THAT SAW YOUNG NIAMH HOVER WITH LOVE-LORN FACE . . . 162 ASKS FORGIVE 13
TO WHOM THE LOVE-LORN LADY KYTELER BROUGHT . . . . 433 NINETEEN 19 129
LOVE-LORN, INDIFFERENT HANDS MIGHT COME UPON IT . . . 461 HARUN RASHID 14
LOVELY
O LOVELY TO SEE IN ALL MEN'S SIGHT . . . . 69 CLOAK BOAT 3
WHO BEING LOVELY WAS SO WISE-- . . . . 193 BAILE AILLINN 98
FOR EVERYTHING THAT'S LOVELY IS . . . . 202 NEVER GIVE ALL 6
OR A WITTY LOVELY LADY." . . . . 299 THREE HERMITS 28
IN ALL LOVELY INTRICACIES OF A HOUSE . . . . . . 327 ROBERT GREGORY 74
ONE HAD A LOVELY FACE. . . . . 350 MEMORY 1
SHE LIES, HER LOVELY PITEOUS HEAD AMID DULL RED HAIR . 362 HER COURTESY 2
OF LOVELY, SATISFIED, INDIFFERENT EYES. . . . . . 375 PHASES OF MOON 83
AMID MOST LOVELY PLACES; SMITTEN AS THOUGH . . . . 389 IMAGE PAST 13
MANY INGENIOUS LOVELY THINGS ARE GONE . . . . . . 428 NINETEEN 19 1
MANY INGENUOUS LOVELY THINGS ARE GONE . . . . . . 428 NINETEEN 19 V 1
AND IS SO LOVELY THAT IT SETS TO RIGHT . . . . . . 490 COOLE BALLYLEE 21

```
LOVELY   (CONTINUED)                                  PAGE     TITLE          LINE
    THAT LOVELY LADY SAID,  . . . . . . . . . . . . .   569 THREE BUSHES        9
    AND A PROUD MAN'S A LOVELY MAN,  . . . . . . . . .   587 PARNELLITES        23
    OH, LOVELY TO SEE IN ALL MEN'S SIGHT . . . . . . .   666 ISLE STAT II 3      3
    WITH MANY A LOVELY FACE  . . . . . . . . . . . . .   740 EARL PAUL          30
    LOVELY LADIES DANCING IN IT. . . . . . . . . . . .   788 HAWTHORN TREE       4
    LOVELY LADY OR GALLANT MAN . . . . . . . . . . . .   788 HAWTHORN TREE       7
    YET ALL THE LOVELY THINGS THAT WERE  . . . . . . .   788 HAWTHORN TREE      11
    LOVELY LADY AND GALLANT MAN  . . . . . . . . . . .   788 HAWTHORN TREE  V    7
LOVE-MAKING
    . . . LOVE-MAKING OR PIERCING THE TEMPEST WITH SAILS. . .   53 OISIN 3      88
LOVE-PLAY
    WHAT'S THE MERIT IN LOVE-PLAY, . . . . . . . . . .   777 SONG DEIRDRE 2      6
LOVER       SEE HUNTER-LOVER GHOST-LOVER
    AND LOVER THERE BY LOVER BE AT PEACE. . . . . . . .   128 DREAM OF FAERY    35
    AND LOVER THERE BY LOVER BE AT PEACE. . . . . . . .   128 DREAM OF FAERY    35
    THE LOVER TELLS OF THE ROSE IN HIS HEART . . . . .   142 ROSE IN HEART      T
    THE LOVER MOURNS FOR THE LOSS OF LOVE  . . . . . .   152 LOSS OF LOVE       T
    THE LOVER ASKS FORGIVENESS BECAUSE OF HIS MANY MOODS . . 162 ASKS FORGIVE   T
    THE LOVER MOURNS BECAUSE OF HIS WANDERINGS . . . . .   171 MAID QUIET   V   T
    THE LOVER PLEADS WITH HIS FRIEND FOR OLD FRIENDS . . .   172 PLEADS FRIEND  T
    THE LOVER SPEAKS TO THE HEARERS OF HIS SONGS IN COMING DAYS  173 SPEAKS HEARERS  T
    A LOVER SPEAKS TO THE HEARERS OF HIS SONGS IN COMING DAYS  173 SPEAKS HEARERS V  T
    WHATEVER WOMAN'S LOVER HAD HIT HER FANCY. . . . . .   181 QUEEN MAEVE       24
    WHO HAD BEEN THE LOVER OF HER MIDDLE LIFE. . . . .   183 QUEEN MAEVE        72
    HAS LOVER LIVED, BUT LONGED TO WIVE . . . . . . . .   197 BAILE AILLINN     206
    AND THE WOOD-WOMAN, WHOSE LOVER WAS CHANGED TO A BLUE-EYED
        HAWK,                                            209 UNDER THE MOON     13
    AND THE WOOD WOMAN, WHOSE LOVER WAS CHANGED TO A BLUE-EYED
        HAWK,                                            209 UNDER THE MOON V   13
    AND KILLED A LOVER OR HUSBAND AT MY FEET-- . . . .   246 SHADOW WATER B    491
    UNWEARIED STILL, LOVER BY LOVER, . . . . . . . . .   323 SWANS AT COOLE     19
    UNWEARIED STILL, LOVER BY LOVER, . . . . . . . . .   323 SWANS AT COOLE     19
    HER LOVER THOUGHT, UPON THE GLASS. . . . . . . . .   385 ROBARTES DANCE     11
    FOR EVERY NERVE, AND TESTS A LOVER . . . . . . . .   388 SOLOMON WITCH      22
    A LOVER WITH A SPIDER'S EYE  . . . . . . . . . . .   388 SOLOMON WITCH  V   19
    FOR EVERY NERVE:  LOVER TESTS LOVER  . . . . . . .   388 SOLOMON WITCH  V   22
    FOR EVERY NERVE:  LOVER TESTS LOVER  . . . . . . .   388 SOLOMON WITCH  V   22
    THE LOVER SPEAKS . . . . . . . . . . . . . . . . .   449 OWEN AHERNE    V   T
    REJOICE AS LOVER SHOULD  . . . . . . . . . . . . .   453 DEATH OF HARE      4
    AND WHAT HAD DROWNED A LOVER ONCE  . . . . . . . .   457 SECRETS OF OLD     5
    THAT CHANGED A LOVER FOR A BULL. . . . . . . . . .   509 JANE REPROVED      6
    THAT LOVER OF A NIGHT  . . . . . . . . . . . . . .   512 JANE ON GOD        1
    I HAD WILD JACK FOR A LOVER: . . . . . . . . . . .   512 JANE ON GOD       19
    WHATEVER COULD RECALL THE LIP OF LOVER. . . . . . .   537 HER VISION         8
    FOR LOVER IN THE PAST: . . . . . . . . . . . . . .   539 MEETING           10
    SAID LADY ONCE TO LOVER: . . . . . . . . . . . . .   569 THREE BUSHES       1
    MY LOVER LOOKED SO GAY" . . . . . . . . . . . . . .   570 THREE BUSHES      32
    MY LOVER LOOKS SO GAY." . . . . . . . . . . . . . .   570 THREE BUSHES   V  32
    WHEN YOU AND MY TRUE LOVER MEET  . . . . . . . . .   573 LADYS 3RD SONG     1
    WOULD KEEP HIS LOVER WAITING, . . . . . . . . . . .   598 MODEL LAUREATE    23
    KEEP HIS LOVER WAITING?  . . . . . . . . . . . . .   598 MODEL LAUREATE    24
    LOVER, THE VOICE THAT SUMMONED THEE WAS MINE. . . .   685 SEEKER            77
    WHAT, LOVER, DIE BEFORE OUR LIPS HAVE MET? . . . .   685 SEEKER            80
    WHEN MY LOST LOVER LEFT THESE ARMS.  MY GOMEZ. . .   701 MOSADA 3          51
    WHEN MY LOST LOVER LEFT THESE ARMS.  MY VALLENCE, .   701 MOSADA 3       V  51
LOVER'S
    THAT TIME CAN NEVER MAR A LOVER'S VOWS . . . . . .   126 DREAM OF FAERY    10
    BECAUSE A LOVER'S HEART'S WORN OUT, . . . . . . . .   191 BAILE AILLINN     65
    THAN LOVER'S MUSIC--LET THAT BE, . . . . . . . . .   276 GREY ROCK        130
    OF BODY AND SOUL.  THE LOVER'S HEART KNOWS THAT. .   375 PHASES OF MOON    71
    BUT BEAR IN MIND YOUR LOVER'S WAGE . . . . . . . .   385 ROBARTES DANCE    14
    IF EVER LOVER'S LONELINESS . . . . . . . . . . . .   518 LOVES LONENESS     3
    THE LOVER'S SONG . . . . . . . . . . . . . . . . .   574 LOVERS SONG        T
    IN TERROR FLINGS HER AT HER LOVER'S FEET. . . . . .   713 FERENCZ RENYI  V  85
    FOR HURTS AND AILS AND LOVER'S MOAN-- . . . . . . .   717 FAIRY DOCTOR      18
    A LOVER'S QUARREL AMONG THE FAIRIES. . . . . . . .   726 LOVERS QUARREL     T
LOVERS
    AND HOW THOSE LOVERS NEVER TURN THEIR EYES . . . .    29 OISIN 2          11
    WHY SHOULD THOSE LOVERS THAT NO LOVERS MISS  . . .   128 DREAM OF FAERY    46
    WHY SHOULD THOSE LOVERS THAT NO LOVERS MISS  . . .   128 DREAM OF FAERY    46
    HE TELLS OF A VALLEY FULL OF LOVERS  . . . . . . .   163 VALLEY LOVERS      T
    THE VALLEY OF LOVERS . . . . . . . . . . . . . . .   163 VALLEY LOVERS  V   T
    AEDH TELLS OF A VALLEY FULL OF LOVERS  . . . . . .   163 VALLEY LOVERS  V   T
    FOR HAPPY LOVERS PASSED TWO BY TWO WHERE I STOOD: .   163 VALLEY LOVERS      2
    HANRAHAN SPEAKS TO THE LOVERS OF HIS SONGS IN COMING DAYS  173 SPEAKS HEARERS V  T
    UNTIL TWO LOVERS CAME OUT OF THE AIR . . . . . . .   187 QUEEN MAEVE      143
    THEN MAEVE: "O AENGUS, MASTER OF ALL LOVERS, . . .   187 QUEEN MAEVE      149
    THERE HAVE BEEN LOVERS WHO THOUGHT LOVE SHOULD BE .   205 ADAMS CURSE       23
    I WILL DRIVE ALL THOSE LOVERS OUT AND CRY-- . . . .   211 RAGGED WOOD       10
    I'LL HOLLO ALL THOSE LOVERS OUT AND CRY-- . . . . .   211 RAGGED WOOD    V  10
    BUT FAITHFUL LOVERS. . . . . . . . . . . . . . . .   220 HARP OF AENGUS    14
    'TWAS AENGUS AND EDAIN, THE WANDERING LOVERS, . . .   224 SHADOW WATER B    42
    TO WHOM ALL LOVERS PRAY.  BUT WHAT OF THAT? . . . .   224 SHADOW WATER B    43
    YET NEVER HAVE TWO LOVERS KISSED BUT THEY  . . . .   229 SHADOW WATER B   153
    AND THAT IS WHY THEIR LOVERS ARE AFRAID  . . . . .   245 SHADOW WATER B   481
    CAN LOVERS HAVE THAT KNOW THEIR HAPPINESS  . . . .   284 TWO KINGS        178
    ONE'S HAD HER FILL OF LOVERS, ANOTHER'S HAD BUT ONE, . . 354 HIS PHOENIX   19
    OUT OF NO TRAGIC WAR, LOVERS OF LIFE. . . . . . . .   369 EGO DOMINUS       39
    GREEKS WERE BUT LOVERS: ALL THAT COUNTRY ROUND . .   430 NINETEEN 19    V  43
    THAT EVEN LOVERS DROWN. . . . . . . . . . . . . . .   453 MERMAID            6
```

LOVERS   (CONTINUED)
    OF ALL ARABIA'S LOVERS I ALONE-- . . . .   470 HARUN RASHID   190
    "OLD LOVERS YET MAY HAVE . . . .   496 MOHINI CHATTER   17
    OLD LOVERS YET SHALL HAVE . . . .   496 MOHINI CHATTER V 17
    SUCH BODY LOVERS HAVE, ...   517 HER ANXIETY   7
    ALL OTHER LOVERS BEING ESTRANGED OR DEAD, ...   523 LONG SILENCE   2
    BIDS ALL TRUE LOVERS REST. . . . .   536 PARTING   6
    THOSE LOVERS, PURIFIED BY TRAGEDY, ...   555 RIBH AT TOMB   21
    LOVERS OF HORSES AND OF WOMEN, SHALL, ...   564 GYRES   19
    THE LOVERS AND THE DANCERS ARE BEATEN INTO THE CLAY, .   580 CURSE CROMWELL   3
    AND COME WITH LEARNED LOVERS OR WITH WHAT MEN YOU MAY, .   593 PILGRIM   23
    AND COME WITH LEARNED LOVERS OR WITH WHAT MAN YOU MAY, .   593 PILGRIM   V 23
    SHOULD KEEP THEIR LOVERS WAITING. . . . .   597 MODEL LAUREATE   7
    KEEP THEIR LOVERS WAITING? . . . .   597 MODEL LAUREATE   8
    AND KEEP THEIR LOVERS WAITING, ...   597 MODEL LAUREATE   15
    KEEP THEIR LOVERS WAITING. . . . .   597 MODEL LAUREATE   16
    AND DEAD AS ARE THE LOVERS OF OLD RIME . . . .   674 ISLE STAT II 3   204
    AND DEAD AS ARE THE LOVERS OF OLD RHYME . . . .   674 ISLE STAT II 3 V 204
    I'LL SING THE SONGS THE DUSKY LOVERS SING, ...   694 MOSADA 1   101
    AND YON FEW STARS GROWN DIM, LIKE EYES OF LOVERS . . .   700 MOSADA 3   33
    HE WATCHES OVER NONE BUT FAITHFUL LOVERS. . . . . . .   762 SHADOW WATER A   295
    BUT FAITHFUL LOVERS. SOMETHING GLITTERS THERE-- . . .   763 SHADOW WATER A V 309
    BUT FAITHFUL LOVERS. WHITHER HAVE YOU COME, ...   763 SHADOW WATER A V 309
    TO SNATCH ALIVE OUT OF THE STREAMS ALL LOVERS . . . .   765 SHADOW WATER A   347
    LOVERS, IF THEY MAY NOT LAUGH, ...   772 SONG DEIRDRE 1   15
    OF ALL THAT LOVERS SAID, ...   789 SINGING HEAD   10
LOVERS'
    BEFORE THEY DROWNED THEIR LOVERS' EYES . . . .   156 FORGOT BEAUTY V 10A
    AND UNDER LOVERS' EYELIDS. BEND YOUR HEAD . . . . .   762 SHADOW WATER A   286
LOVE'S
    OR LOVE'S FIRST TENDERNESS DIE IN OUR GAZE. . . . . .   27 OISIN 1   411
    OR LOVE'S FIRST TENDERNESS DIE IN OUR GAZE. . . . . .   27 OISIN 1 V 419D
    OR LOVE'S FIRST TENDERNESS DIE IN OUR GAZE." . . . . .   28 OISIN 1 V 427
    UPON LOVE'S BITTER MYSTERY! . . . .   125 GOES FERGUS   8
    DROWNING LOVE'S LONELY HOUR IN DEEP TWILIGHT OF REST, .   154 BELOVED PEACE   11
    WHERE LOVE'S TO GIVE AND TO SPARE! . . . .   214 HAPPY TOWNLAND V 4
    SUDDENLY HID LOVE'S MOON AWAY. . . . .   313 MEMORY YOUTH   7
    LOVE'S MOON WAS WITHERING AWAY. . . . .   313 MEMORY YOUTH V 7
    RHYMED OUT IN LOVE'S DESPAIR . . . .   337 SCHOLARS   5
    LOVE'S PLEASURE DRIVES HIS LOVE AWAY. . . . .   438 SONGS PLAY 2   11
    I RAN, I RAN, FROM MY LOVE'S SIDE BECAUSE MY HEART WENT   450 OWEN AHERNE   12
      MAD.
    A QUALITY OF WISDOM FROM HER LOVE'S . . . .   469 HARUN RASHID   180
    QUALITY OF WISDOM FROM LOVE'S QUALITY, ...   469 HARUN RASHID V 180
    I--LOVE'S SKEIN UPON THE GROUND, ...   511 JANE AND JACK   9
    LOVE'S LONELINESS . . . .   518 LOVES LONENESS   T
    AND LAID THEM ON LOVE'S LETTERED TOMB! . . . .   519 HER DREAM   4
    NO, NIGHT'S BIRD AND LOVE'S . . . .   536 PARTING   5
    I OFFER TO LOVE'S PLAY . . . .   536 PARTING   13
    AND, THOUGH LOVE'S BITTER-SWEET HAD ALL COME BACK, . .   537 HER VISION   27
    LOVE CRAM LOVE'S TWO DIVISIONS . . . .   573 LADYS 2ND SONG   12
LOVES
    WE SANG THE LOVES AND ANGERS WITHOUT SLEEP, ...   42 OISIN 2   194
    THE SPACIOUS LOVES, THE ANGER WITHOUT SLEEP . . . . .   42 OISIN 2 V 194
    AND THEIR HOUNDS, AND THEIR STEEDS, AND THEIR LOVES, . .   59 OISIN 3   176
    "THAT WE ARE TIRED, FOR OTHER LOVES AWAIT US! . . . .   80 EPHEMERA   21
    NO MAIDEN LOVES ME, NO MAN SEEKS MY HELP, ...   103 FERGUS DRUID V 26
    NO WOMAN LOVES ME, NO MAN SEEKS MY HELP, ...   103 FERGUS DRUID V 26
    WHO LOVES YOU, NO WHITE ARMS TO WRAP YOU ROUND, . . .   109 CUCHULAIN SEA   59
    THERE THE LOVES A CIRCLE GO. . . . .   135 TWO TREES   13
    WINGED LOVES BORNE ON IN GENTLE STRIFE. . . . .   135 TWO TREES V 14
    OF THE WOMAN THAT HE LOVES, UNTIL HE DIES. . . . . .   177 PAST GREATNESS   10
    VEERING, FLEETING, FICKLE, OUR LOVES AND ANGERS MEET! .   207 HANRAHANS SONG V 3
    LOVES IN BRIEF LONGING AND DECEIVING HOPE . . . . . .   228 SHADOW WATER B   146
    TO BREED THE LIDLESS EYE THAT LOVES THE SUN? . . . .   264 HOUSE SHAKEN   4
    TO CHANGE MY LOVES WHILE DANCING . . . .   330 BONE OF A HARE   7
    AND HEARTIER LOVES! THAT LAMP IS FROM THE TOMB. . . .   398 LEADERS CROWD   12
    THAN IN OUR LOVES! OH, HONEY-BEES . . . .   425 STARES NEST V 19
    MAN IS IN LOVE AND LOVES WHAT VANISHES, ...   429 NINETEEN 19   42
    AND NOT THEIR WORTH. GOD LOVES US FOR OUR WORTH! . .   448 HERO GIRL FOOL V 15
    CHANGE THEIR LOVES ABOUT. . . . .   520 HIS BARGAIN   6
    BECAUSE HE LOVES TOO MUCH. . . . .   588 OLD WICKED MAN   15
    WE LOVE NASCHINA BOTH. WHOM LOVES SHE BEST? . . . .   660 ISLE STAT II 1   48
    MY WORDS WERE ALL! "HERE NO LOVES WANE AND WITHER, . .   669 ISLE STAT II 3   84
    HE LOVES OUR BROTHER PETER IN HIS HEART. . . . . . .   696 MOSADA 2   16
LOVE-SICK
    THOUGH MY LOVE-SICK HEART IS RENDING, ...   646 ISLE STAT I 1   38
LOVE-SONG
    AND HER RED LIPS SANG THEM A LOVE-SONG . . . .   160 CAP AND BELLS   27
    HER RED LIPS SANG THEM A LOVE-SONG, ...   160 CAP AND BELLS V 27
LOVE-STORY
    AND TELL ME A LOVE-STORY WHILE I DRINK. . . . . . .   760 SHADOW WATER A   250
LOVE-TALES
    THE LOVE-TALES WROUGHT WITH SILKEN THREAD . . . . .   155 FORGOT BEAUTY   6
    THE LOVE-TALES WOVE WITH SILKEN THREAD . . . . . .   155 FORGOT BEAUTY V 6
LOVETH
    IT IS THE SHEPHERD GUARIMOND, WHO LOVETH WELL . . . .   661 ISLE STAT II 1   53
LOVE-WORN
    BEFORE HER LOVE-WORN HEART HAD BROKE, ...   194 BAILE AILLINN   127
LOVING
    AS, FULL OF LOVING FANTASY, ...   13 OISIN 1   158

LOVING (CONTINUED)

IF HE STOP LOVING ME,	569	THREE BUSHES	18
BEHOLD THE LOVING LOVELESS FLOWER OF LONE WAYS,	674	ISLE STAT II 3	201

LOW

"WHY, AS YE RIDE, DROOPS LOW EACH HEAD?	4	OISIN 1 V	32
AND THOSE ON GAVRA LYING LOW,	5	OISIN 1 V	41
WITH LAUGHTER LOW, AND TENDER, AND SWEET:	6	OISIN 1 V	54
AND WITH LOW MURMURS, WE RODE ON,	13	OISIN 1	159
TO THAT LOW LAUGHING WOODLAND RHYME,	14	OISIN 1	176
AND WITH LOW MURMURS PRAYED TO HIM,	18	OISIN 1	257
BENT LOW ABOVE EACH HOOKED KNEE,	26	OISIN 1 V	392
IN THE ROOTS OF THE GRASSES, THE SORRELS, I LAID MY BODY AS LOW:	52	OISIN 3	73
HOW THE SLOW, BLUE-EYED OXEN OF FINN LOW SADLY AT EVENING TIDE,	52	OISIN 3	84
CAME, AND MY FOREHEAD FELL LOW, AND MY TEARS LIKE BERRIES FELL DOWN:	57	OISIN 3	154
BENDING LOW HIS PIOUS HEAD,	82	MAD KING GOLL V	10
BENDING LOW HIS FADING HEAD,	82	MAD KING GOLL V	10
HIS EYELIDS DROOP, HIS HEAD FALLS LOW,	98	FOXHUNTER	13
HIS EYELIDS CLOSE, HIS HEAD DROOPS LOW,	98	FOXHUNTER	13
I HEAR LAKE WATER LAPPING WITH LOW SOUNDS BY THE SHORE:	117	ISLE INNISFREE	10
I HEAR LAKE WATER LAPPING WITH LOW SOUNDS ON THE SHORE:	117	ISLE INNISFREE	10
. . . HUNG LOW ON THE RIM OF THE SKY,	122	WHITE BIRDS	3
. . . HUNG LOW IN THE FALL OF THE DEW:	122	WHITE BIRDS	7
A-TELLING WITH THEIR LOW AND REEDY CRY	128	DREAM OF FAERY V	42
PROCLAIMING WITH A LOW AND REEDY CRY,	128	DREAM OF FAERY V	42
IN TWILIGHT SHAKEN WITH LOW SIGHS:	156	FORGOT BEAUTY	10B
HIS FACE BOWED LOW TO WEEP THE END	192	BAILE AILLINN	75
AND WITH LOW MURMURING LAUGHING SPEECH	195	BAILE AILLINN	137
THE HONEY-PALE MOON LAY LOW ON THE SLEEPY HILL,	203	WITHER BOUGHS	5
THE HONEY PALE MOON HUNG LOW ON THE SLEEPY HILL,	203	WITHER BOUGHS V	5
ON FINDING THAT HER VOICE IS SWEET AND LOW	205	ADAMS CURSE	17
IN FINDING THAT IT'S YOUNG AND MILD AND LOW,	205	ADAMS CURSE V	17
O TUFTED REEDS, BEND LOW AND LOW IN POOLS ON THE GREEN LAND,	206	HANRAHANS SONG V	1
O TUFTED REEDS, BEND LOW AND LOW IN POOLS ON THE GREEN LAND,	206	HANRAHANS SONG V	1
BUT WE HAVE ALL BENT LOW AND LOW AND KISSED THE QUIET FEET	207	HANRAHANS SONG	9
BUT WE HAVE ALL BENT LOW AND LOW AND KISSED THE QUIET FEET	207	HANRAHANS SONG	9
TO MAKE LOW LAUGHTER MORE THAN MEAT AND DRINK,	230	SHADOW WATER B	186
AND HE, WITH THAT LOW WHINNYING SOUND	318	APPOINTMENT	5
A PIERCED BOY, IMAGE OF A STAR LAID LOW.	541	PARN FUNERAL 1	12
A SLOW LOW NOTE AND AN IRON BELL.	549	SEVERED HEAD	7
A SLOW LOW NOTE AND AN IRON BELL.	550	SEVERED HEAD	14
A SLOW LOW NOTE AND AN IRON BELL.	550	SEVERED HEAD	21
OR STAY CONTENT ON THE LOW,	589	OLD WICKED MAN	49
THE WOMEN THAT I PICKED SPOKE SWEET AND LOW	622	HOUND VOICE	8
WHEN LOW THE SUN SANK DOWN IN CLOTTED FLAME	656	ISLE STAT I 3	30
HE WAS OUR ANCIENT GOD. IF I SPEAK LOW,	658	ISLE STAT I 3	78
LOW BOWED AND DUMB UPON THE SAND,	671	ISLE STAT II 3	130
FIERCE MORTAL, AND CROUCHED LOW BESIDE THE LAKE	675	ISLE STAT II 3 V	245A
A BEARDED WITCH, HER SLUGGISH HEAD LOW BENT	685	SEEKER	72
LOW, LONG AND MUSICAL. A DEW-DROP HUNG	689	NETTLESHIP	9
DOWN LOW THE HEAD OF HIS MAGNIFICENCE	689	NETTLESHIP V	6
BUT THIS ONE--THIS ONE. NOW HIS HEAD DROPS LOW,	711	FERENCZ RENYI	39
BENT LOW WITH TOIL AND HOARIEST YEARS. THE OTHER	711	FERENCZ RENYI	52
DROOPETH NOW HIS FOREHEAD LOW	711	FERENCZ RENYI V	39
IN THE LONG GRASS--FOUR EYES DROOP LOW--A SEAT	716	DWELT SYCAMORE	11
HIS MOODS BOW LOW HIS SOMBRE CREST,	723	GIRLS SONG A	2
I AM AFRAID OF HIS LOW LAUGHING HARP.	759	SHADOW WATER A V	239

LOWER

AND, AS THE SUN SANK EVER LOWER,	13	OISIN 1 V	170A
SPEAK LOWER, OR THEY'LL HEAR. THEY CANNOT HEAR:	232	SHADOW WATER B	228
BEND LOWER, O KING, THAT I MAY CROWN YOU WITH IT.	251	SHADOW WATER B	607
BEND LOWER, THAT I MAY COVER YOU WITH MY HAIR,	251	SHADOW WATER B	613
BEND LOWER LEST YOUR BATTLE-AXES GLIMMER,	752	SHADOW WATER A	117
BEND LOWER LEST YOUR BATTLE AXES GLIMMER,	752	SHADOW WATER A V	117
I CROWN YOU WITH THIS CROWN. BEND LOWER, O KING,	768	SHADOW WATER A	423
BEND LOWER, THAT I MAY COVER YOU WITH MY HAIR,	769	SHADOW WATER A	429

LOWERED

UPON KING EOCHAID'S FACE, WHO LOWERED HIS FACE	286	TWO KINGS V	211A

LOWING

HE'LL HEAR NO MORE THE LOWING	88	STOLEN CHILD	44

LOW-LAUGHING

LISTEN TO THAT LOW-LAUGHING STRING OF THE MOON	243	SHADOW WATER B	432
I AM AFRAID OF HIS LOW-LAUGHING HARP.	759	SHADOW WATER A	239

LOWLIER

OR LOOK UPON THEM. WERE THEY BUT LOWLIER	250	SHADOW WATER B	576

LOWLINESS

LEARNED IN BODILY LOWLINESS	513	JANE TALK BISH	11

LOWLY

LOWLY THE HEAD OF HIS MAGNIFICENCE	689	NETTLESHIP·	6

LOYAL

MY LANTERN IS TOO LOYAL NOT TO SHOW	464	HARUN RASHID	71

LUCK

OUR GIVER OF GOOD COUNSEL AND GOOD LUCK."	185	QUEEN MAEVE	102
HOW SHOULD THEIR LUCK RUN HIGH ENOUGH TO REACH	264	HOUSE SHAKEN	9
THOSE WINE-DRENCHED EYES, AND CURSE OUR LUCK	272	GREY ROCK	39
AND THOSE FIERCE EYES, AND CURSE OUR LUCK	272	GREY ROCK V	39
"IT'S CERTAIN THAT MY LUCK IS BROKEN,"	332	ROUND TOWER	25

		PAGE	TITLE		LINE

LUCK (CONTINUED)
WHEN MY LUCK CHANGED AND THEY DARED MEET MY FACE, . . .   352 PEOPLE   25
WHEN MY LUCK CHANGED AND THEY DARED TO MEET MY FACE, . .   352 PEOPLE   V   25
AND RUTH ST. DENIS HAD MORE CHARM ALTHOUGH SHE HAD POOR   353 HIS PHOENIX   10
    LUCK
IN LUCK OR OUT THE TOIL HAS LEFT ITS MARK: . . . .   491 COOLE BALLYLEE V   40F
IN LUCK OR OUT THE TOIL HAS LEFT ITS MARK: . . . .   495 CHOICE   6
AND THERE'S NO LUCK ABOUT A HOUSE . . . .   584 GHOST ROG CASE   27
AND THAT SHOULD MOTHER SEEK HER SON SHE'D HAVE BUT LITTLE   593 PILGRIM   12
    LUCK
OUR LUCK IS WITHERED AWAY, ...   783 GREY ROUND   18
LUCKIER
HOW SHOULD THE WORLD BE LUCKIER IF THIS HOUSE, ...   264 HOUSE SHAKEN   1
LUCKY
AND SHE'D HAD LUCKY EYES AND A HIGH HEART, ...   181 QUEEN MAEVE   27
IT IS LUCKY THAT THEIR STORY . . . .   215 HAPPY TOWNLAND   27
A LUCKY BATTLE, OR A WOMAN'S KISS . . . .   227 SHADOW WATER B   115
"MAYBE I SHALL BE LUCKY YET. . . . .   297 THREE BEGGARS   61
I HAVE A LUCKY WOODEN SHIN . . . .   302 HOUR DAWN   18
THAT WERE A LUCKY DEATH. . . . .   431 NINETEEN 19   77
"THAT WAS A LUCKY THOUGHT OF MINE, ...   570 THREE BUSHES   31
LUGAIDH'S
AILLINN, WHO WAS KING LUGAIDH'S HEIR. . . . .   189 BAILE AILLINN   7
LUGNAGALL
HE SLEPT UNDER THE HILL OF LUGNAGALL: . . . .   128 DREAM OF FAERY   37
LUG-WORM
A LUG-WORM WITH ITS GREY AND MUDDY MOUTH . . . . . .   127 DREAM OF FAERY   18
LUKA
KUSTA BEN LUKA IS MY NAME, I WRITE . . . .   460 HARUN RASHID   1
LUKE
OF OLD LUKE WADDING'S PORTRAIT SAID . . . .   400 DEMON BEAST   10
LULLABULLOO
LULLABULLOO, BULOO, BULOO, LULLABULLOO, BULLO. . . .   594 COLONEL MARTIN V   REF
LULLABULLOO, BULOO, BULOO, LULLABULLOO, BULLO. . . .   594 COLONEL MARTIN V   REF
LULLABY
AND SING IT LULLABY. . . . .   459 HIS WILDNESS   12
LULLABY . . . .   522 LULLABY   T
LULLED   SEE LAKE-LULLED
LULLED WEARINESS, AND SOFTLY ROUND . . . .   11 OISIN 1   137
LULLED WEARINESS: AND CLOSELY ROUND . . . .   11 OISIN 1   V 137
WHOSE DWELLING WAS A TREE-WRAPT ISLAND, LULLED . . .   693 MOSADA 1   79
LULLING
AND HOLLOW LULLING THE YOUNG WINDS WITH SONG. . . . .   675 ISLE STAT II 3   226
LULLS
WILD CRIES, GROWN SWEET WITH LULLS AND LINGERINGS LONG.   674 ISLE STAT II 3   222
LULLY
RAYMOND LULLY AND HIS WIFE PERNELLA . . . .   253 HIS DREAM   V   T
LUMBERING
THE CRY OF A CHILD BY THE ROADWAY, THE CREAK OF A LUMBERING 142 ROSE IN HEART   2
    CART,
LUMINOUS   SEE MOON-LUMINOUS
UNTIL A CURLEW CRIED AND IN THE LUMINOUS WIND . . . . .   291 PAUDEEN   4
CURVED LIKE NEW MOON, MOON LUMINOUS, ...   421 MY TABLE   V 10
ALTHOUGH THAT WESTERN CLOUD IS LUMINOUS, ...   488 COOLE PARK 29   4
LUNATIC
FOR EVERY HAND IS LUNATIC . . . .   451 FIRST LOVE   11
I THOUGHT HIM HALF A LUNATIC, HALF KNAVE. . . . . . .   473 ALL SOUL NIGHT   64
TOM THE LUNATIC . . . .   528 TOM LUNATIC   T
SANG OLD TOM THE LUNATIC . . . .   528 TOM LUNATIC   1
LUNGED
THROUGH MANY SHAPES: I LUNGED AT THE SMOOTH THROAT . . .   40 OISIN 2   175
TO MANY SHAPES: I LUNGED AT THE SMOOTH THROAT . . . . .   40 OISIN 2   V 175
SURGED UP IN PLUMY FIRE, I LUNGED AND DRAVE . . . . . .   41 OISIN 2   V 181
LUNGING
WITH SURGE OF PLUMY FIRE, LUNGING I DRAVE . . . . . .   41 OISIN 2   V 181
LURCHES
THERE LURCHES PAST, HIS GREAT EYES WITHOUT THOUGHT . .   433 NINETEEN 19   126
LURE
OUT OF MERE WANTONNESS TO LURE A SAIL . . . .   750 SHADOW WATER A   79
THEY LURE US TO THE STREAMS WHERE THE WORLD ENDS. . .   764 SHADOW WATER A   334
THESE MESSENGERS TO LURE MEN TO HIS PEACE, ...   764 SHADOW WATER A   336
LURED
. . . LURED FROM HIS LAIR IN THE MOULD: . . . . . .   53 OISIN 3   99
PLUNGE, LURED BY A SOFTENING EYE, ...   413 TOWER   110
ON TEARS AND LAUGHTER: THEY HAVE LURED YOU HITHER . .   757 SHADOW WATER A   207
AND LURED ME HITHER, THAT YOU MIGHT BE MY LOVE. . . .   757 SHADOW WATER A   208
LURES
THESE ARE THEIR LURES: BUT THEY HAVE SET THEIR HEARTS . . 757 SHADOW WATER A   206
LURID
FROM THE DEEP EARTH UNTO THE LURID SKY . . . .   662 ISLE STAT II 2   5
LURKS
JOY'S BROTHER, FEAR, LURKS IN EACH LEAFY WAY. . . . .   651 ISLE STAT I 1   156
LUSH
THAT STARING FURY AND THE BLIND LUSH LEAF . . . . . .   500 VACILLATION   17
LUST
YOU THINK IT HORRIBLE THAT LUST AND RAGE . . . . . .   591 SPUR   1
LUSTRE
AWAKEN, AWAKEN TO NEW-BORN LUSTRE: . . . .   646 ISLE STAT I 1   43
HURLS THEIR SWOONING LUSTRE UP. . . . .   647 ISLE STAT I 1   49
LUTE
WITH MINGLING HAIR, AND PLAY UPON ONE LUTE. . . . . .   71 ANASHU VIJAYA   10

486

LUTE   (CONTINUED)
    HERE'S A MONTENEGRIN LUTE, ... 627 STATES HOLIDAY 22
    ON A GIRL'S FORGOTTEN LUTE, ... 668 ISLE STAT II 3 66
    HEARD YOU? YOUR LUTE HUNG IN THE WINDOW SOUNDED! . . . 694 MOSADA 1 95
    HEARD YOU? YOUR LUTE UPON THE WALL HAS SOUNDED! . . . 694 MOSADA 1 V 95
LUTE-THRONGED
    WHEN THE FLAMING LUTE-THRONGED ANGELIC DOOR IS WIDE! . . 172 TRAV PASSION 1
LUXURIANT
    LUXURIANT SONG, WHY SHOULD YOU LEAVE THE LAMP . . . . 370 EGO DOMINUS 62
LUXURY
    SHUT OUT FROM ALL THE LUXURY OF THE WORLD, ... 370 EGO DOMINUS 60
LYING   SEE HALF-LYING
    AND ON THE HEROES LYING SLAIN . . . . 5 OISIN 1 42
    AND THOSE ON GAVRA LYING LOW, ... 5 OISIN 1 V 41
    TO ONE VAST FOOT, FROTH-SPLASHED, WITH CURVED TOES LYING 32 OISIN 2 V 46A
    BUT NOW THE LYING CLERICS MURDER SONG . . . . . 42 OISIN 2 196
    WERE YOU BUT LYING COLD AND DEAD, ... 175 BELOVED DEAD 1
    HAS SHE NOT SEEN HIM LYING LIKE A LOG, ... 230 SHADOW WATER B 173
    THROUGH ALL THE LYING DAYS OF MY YOUTH . . . . . . 261 COMING WISDOM 2
    SHE WOULD NOT HAVE US SAD BECAUSE SHE IS LYING THERE, . 362 HER COURTESY 4
    LYING ALONE ON A BED . . . . 552 SONGS REWRIT 2 V 10
    BUT HE'S A LYING HOUND! . . . . 636 BLACK TOWER 25
LYNX
    THAT I MYSELF COULD SHOOT A GREAT GREY LYNX. . . . . 650 ISLE STAT I 1 152
    HAVE THEY NE'ER SEEN THE EYES OF LYNX OR KINE, ... 672 ISLE STAT II 3 152
LYNX'S
    AND THE GREAT GREY LYNX'S SKIN! IN SOOTH, METHINKS . . . 650 ISLE STAT I 1 151
LYRIC
    A LYRIC FROM AN UNPUBLISHED PLAY . . . . 263 MASK V T
LYRICS
    LYRICS FROM "THE ISLAND OF STATUES" . . . . 646 ISLE STAT I 1 V T
MA
    WAKE, MA CUSHLA, SLEEPY-HEADED! . . . . 705 DAWN-SONG 9
MAC
    CAME BLANAID, MAC NESSA, TALL FERGUS WHO FEASTWARD OF OLD 53 OISIN 3 89
        TIME SLUNK,
    CAME BLANID, MAC NESSA, CUCHULIN! . . . . 53 OISIN 3 V 89
    CAME BLANID, MAC NESSA, AND FERGUS WHO FEASTWARD OF OLD 53 OISIN 3 V 89
        TIME SLUNK,
MACBRIDE
    MACDONAGH AND MACBRIDE . . . . 394 EASTER 1916 75
MACCARTAN
    FIRST I GREET MACCARTAN, REVOLUTIONARY LEADER. . . . . 790 DEDICATION 1
MACDONAGH
    MACDONAGH AND MACBRIDE . . . . 394 EASTER 1916 75
MACDONAGH'S
    MACDONAGH'S BONY THUMB? . . . . 395 SIXTEEN DEAD 12
MACE
    FROM MACE AND SWORD AND POLE-AXE, LONG AGO . . . . . 31 OISIN 2 30
    BY MACE AND SPEAR AND SWORD OF SEA-GODS, NAILS . . . . 31 OISIN 2 V 30A
MACGREGOR
    AND I CALL UP MACGREGOR FROM THE GRAVE, ... 473 ALL SOUL NIGHT 61
    I CALL MACGREGOR MATHERS FROM HIS GRAVE, ... 473 ALL SOUL NIGHT V 61
MACKEREL-CROWDED
    THE SALMON-FALLS, THE MACKEREL-CROWDED SEAS, ... 407 SAIL BYZANTIUM 4
    THE SALMON FALLS, THE MACKEREL-CROWDED SEAS, ... 407 SAIL BYZANTIUM V 4
MAD   SEE WHOLE-MAD
    A MAD SONG . . . . 149 WANDER AENGUS V T
    HAVE DRIVEN TRAVELLERS MAD FOR THEIR OWN SPORT. . . . 227 SHADOW WATER B 105
    MAY NOT HAVE DRIVEN YOU MAD FOR THEIR OWN SPORT? . . . 227 SHADOW WATER B V 105
    BRING MADNESS? QUEEN, I AM NOT MAD. YET SAY . . . . 236 SHADOW WATER B 316
    WOULD RISE AGAINST ME. NO, I AM NOT MAD-- . . . . 236 SHADOW WATER B 318
    THE EVER-LIVING HAVE MADE YOU MAD! BUT NO, ... 248 SHADOW WATER B 546
    WHEREON MAD FINGERS PLAY . . . . 291 TO A FRIEND 12
    UNTIL I AM DRIVEN MAD, ... 346 ON WOMAN 35
    EVEN TO EYES THAT BEAUTY HAD DRIVEN MAD, ... 390 IMAGE PAST 34
    FOR IF I TRIUMPH I MUST MAKE MEN MAD. . . . . . 411 TOWER 56
    IN THE MAD ABSTRACT DARK AND GROUND IT GRAIN BY GRAIN . 442 BLACK CENTAUR 8
    IT COULD NOT BEAR THAT BURDEN AND THEREFORE IT WENT MAD. 449 OWEN AHERNE 4
    IT FEARED THE HURT THAT SHE COULD GIVE AND THEREFORE IT 450 OWEN AHERNE 8
        WENT MAD.
    I RAN, I RAN, FROM MY LOVE'S SIDE BECAUSE MY HEART WENT 450 OWEN AHERNE 12
        MAD.
    . . . "YOU HAVE CALLED ME MAD," IT SAID, ... 450 OWEN AHERNE 13
    MAD AS THE MIST AND SNOW . . . . 523 MAD AS MIST T
    MAD AS THE MIST AND SNOW. . . . . 523 MAD AS MIST 6
    MAD AS THE MIST AND SNOW? . . . . 524 MAD AS MIST 12
    MAD AS THE MIST AND SNOW. . . . . 524 MAD AS MIST 18
    "BECAUSE I AM MAD ABOUT WOMEN . . . . 587 OLD WICKED MAN 1
    I AM MAD ABOUT THE HILLS," . . . . 587 OLD WICKED MAN 2
    WHY SHOULD NOT OLD MEN BE MAD? . . . . 625 OLD MEN BE MAD T
    WHY SHOULD NOT OLD MEN BE MAD? . . . . 625 OLD MEN BE MAD 1
    KNOW WHY AN OLD MAN SHOULD BE MAD. . . . . . . 626 OLD MEN BE MAD 20
    AND A MAN IS FIGHTING MAD! . . . . 638 BEN BULBEN 28
    I BID THEE STAY, RENOUNCING THY MAD QUEST." . . . . 669 ISLE STAT II 3 89
    AND ROARS, MAD WITH THE TOUCH OF THE UNKNOWN, ... 689 NETTLESHIP 7
    I WILL BURN HERESY FROM THIS MAD EARTH, ... 697 MOSADA 2 40
    GOD! THEY'RE MAD TO FLY SUCH CANVAS!" . . . . 718 PHANTOM SHIP 14
    AND ALL HER STARLIGHT IS WITH SORROW MAD, ... 738 YOU ARE SAD 3
MADAM
    CAN DISTURB GLOBE-TROTTING MADAM . . . . 638 BEN BULBEN 48

487

	PAGE	TITLE		LINE
MADDENED				
HAS MADDENED EVERY MOTHER'S SON"¡	290	SEPTEMBER 1913		29
MADDENED BY THAT SINEWY THIGH.	294	HATED PLAYBOY	V	6
AND CERTAIN MEN, BEING MADDENED BY THOSE RHYMES,	410	TOWER		41
MADE SEE RE—MADE				
THEIR CLOAKS MADE OUT OF YELLOW SILK,	15	OISIN 1		205
THEIR BRATTAS MADE OUT OF YELLOW SILK,	15	OISIN 1	V	205
AND MADE IN ALL THEIR DISTANT PARTS,	16	OISIN 1		228
WHERE TREES MADE SUDDEN CAVERN—GLOOMS	16	OISIN 1	V	224B
SINCE GOD MADE TIME AND DEATH AND SLEEP¡ THE OTHER	31	OISIN 2		41
AND A SAD MOUTH, THAT FEAR MADE TREMULOUS	34	OISIN 2		71
MADE THE WAY SLIPPERY, AND TIME ON TIME	37	OISIN 2		114
A DOME MADE OUT OF ENDLESS CARVEN JAGS,	38	OISIN 2		144
A LITTLE RUNNEL MADE A BUBBLING STRAIN,	39	OISIN 2		156
WHILE THE WOOD-PECKER MADE A MERRY DIN,	44	OISIN 2	V	228
ARE FACES ALIVE WITH SUCH BEAUTY MADE KNOWN TO THE SALT EYE OF MAN,	50	OISIN 3	V	51
ARE FACES ALIVE WITH SUCH BEAUTY MADE KNOWN TO THE SOFT EYE OF MAN,	50	OISIN 3	V	51
. . . MADE CONCHUBAR'S SWORD—BLADE OF OLD.	52	OISIN 3		80
THAT THE SPEAR-SHAFT IS MADE OUT OF ASHWOOD,	52	OISIN 3		82
. . . MADE ARMOUR FOR CONOR THE OLD.	52	OISIN 3	V	80
. . . MADE ARMOUR FOR CONHOR OF OLD.	52	OISIN 3	V	80
. . . MADE ARMOUR FOR MIDHIR OF OLD.	52	OISIN 3	V	80
THAT THE SPEARSHAFT IS MADE OUT OF ASHWOOD,	52	OISIN 3	V	82
WHEN THE FENIANS MADE FORAY AT MORNING WITH BRAN, SCEOLAN, LOMAIR.	54	OISIN 3		104
I SAW FROM A DISTANT SADDLE¡ FROM THE EARTH SHE MADE HER MOAN¡	56	OISIN 3		130
AND THE WINDS MADE THE SANDS ON THE SEA'S EDGE	57	OISIN 3		145
AS MY MIND MADE THE NAMES OF THE FENIANS.	57	OISIN 3		146
MUCH WONDERING TO SEE UPON ALL HANDS, OF WATTLES AND WOODWORK MADE,	58	OISIN 3		162
MUCH WONDERING TO SEE UPON ALL HANDS, OF WATTLES AND WOOD-WORK MADE,	58	OISIN 3	V	162
TO MIGHTY BRAHMA, HE WHO MADE YOU MANY AS THE SANDS,	72	ANASHU VIJAYA		21
WITHIN THE TEMPLE, DEVIOUS WALKING, MADE	72	ANASHU VIJAYA		32
TO MIGHTY BRAHMA--HE WHO MADE YE MANY AS THE SANDS,	72	ANASHU VIJAYA	V	21
TO MIGHTY BRAHMA, WHO HAS MADE YOU MANY AS THE SANDS,	72	ANASHU VIJAYA	V	21
WHO HOLDS THE WORLD BETWEEN HIS BILL AND MADE US STRONG OR WEAK	76	INDIAN ON GOD		6
WHO MADE THE WORLD AND RULETH IT, HE HANGETH ON A STALK,	76	INDIAN ON GOD		10
FOR I AM IN HIS IMAGE MADE, AND ALL THIS TINKLING TIDE	76	INDIAN ON GOD		11
WHO MADE THE GRASS AND MADE THE WORMS AND MADE MY FEATHERS GAY,	77	INDIAN ON GOD		18
WHO MADE THE GRASS AND MADE THE WORMS AND MADE MY FEATHERS GAY,	77	INDIAN ON GOD		18
WHO MADE THE GRASS AND MADE THE WORMS AND MADE MY FEATHERS GAY,	77	INDIAN ON GOD		18
HE MADE FOR HER AN ARMY CEASE TO BE."	106	CUCHULAIN SEA	V	16B
"MY FATHER," MADE HE, SMILING, ANSWER THEN,	107	CUCHULAIN SEA	V	25
FOR HE WHO MADE YOU BITTER MADE YOU WISE."	108	CUCHULAIN SEA		32
FOR HE WHO MADE YOU BITTER MADE YOU WISE."	108	CUCHULAIN SEA		32
FOR GOD WHO MADE YOU BITTER MADE YOU WISE."	108	CUCHULAIN SEA	V	32
FOR GOD WHO MADE YOU BITTER MADE YOU WISE."	108	CUCHULAIN SEA	V	32
AT LAST CUCHULAIN SPAKE, "SOME MAN HAS MADE	109	CUCHULAIN SEA		47
CUCHULAIN CRIED, "HAVE MADE AND KEEP THAT VOW."	109	CUCHULAIN SEA	V	56
HE MADE THE WORLD TO BE A GRASSY ROAD	112	ROSE OF WORLD		14
BUT GATHER ALL FOR WHOM NO LOVE HATH MADE	114	ROSE OF BATTLE		12
MADE YOU OF US, AND OF THE DIM GREY SEA.	115	ROSE OF BATTLE		30
AND A SMALL CABIN BUILD THERE, OF CLAY AND WATTLES MADE¡	117	ISLE INNISFREE		2
AND A SMALL CABIN BUILT THERE, OF CLAY AND WATTLES MADE¡	117	ISLE INNISFREE	V	2
A CROSS THEY HAD MADE OUT OF TWO BITS OF WOOD,	123	DREAM OF DEATH		7
BEFORE EARTH MADE OF HIM HER SLEEPY CARE¡	126	DREAM OF FAERY	V	4
"HE WHO HATH MADE THE NIGHT OF STARS	134	FR GILLIGAN		41
AND MADE MY LIPS AND MUSIC WED,	134	TWO TREES		11
MADE WHEN GOD SLEPT IN TIMES OF OLD,	135	TWO TREES		32
BEFORE GOD MADE THE ANGELIC CLAN,	138	TO IRELAND		8
MADE IRELAND'S HEART BEGIN TO BEAT¡	138	TO IRELAND		12
THAT HAS MADE FAT THE MURDEROUS MOTH¡	156	FORGOT BEAUTY		8
HE MADE HIS SOUL GO UPWARD	159	CAP AND BELLS	V	3
I MADE IT OUT OF A MOUTHFUL OF AIR,	166	EVIL OF BELOV		5
AT NEED, AND MADE HER BEAUTIFUL AND FIERCE,	181	QUEEN MAEVE		29
WITH BODIES MADE OUT OF SOFT FIRE. THE ONE,	187	QUEEN MAEVE		144
SOME GOD OR KING HAD MADE THE LAWS	194	BAILE AILLINN		131
OR THE TWO STRINGS THAT MADE ONE SOUND	195	BAILE AILLINN		155
BECAUSE THEY HAVE MADE SO GOOD A FRIEND.	195	BAILE AILLINN		159
MADE OF THE APPLE AND THE YEW,	197	BAILE AILLINN		196
MADE OUT OF A WILD THOUGHT, IS IN MY MARROW.	199	ARROW		2
HE THAT MADE THIS KNOWS ALL THE COST,	202	NEVER GIVE ALL		13
HAS MADE THEM SO HAPPY AND HOPELESS, SO DEAF AND SO BLIND	204	WITHER BOUGHS		20
I HAVE MADE THIS POEM FOR YOU, THAT MEN MAY READ IT	219	WOODS OF COOLE		41
AND SLEEPY BOUGHS, AND BOUGHS WHERE APPLES MADE	219	HARP OF AENGUS		5
BECAUSE HER HANDS HAD BEEN MADE WILD BY LOVE.	219	HARP OF AENGUS		9
HE MADE A HARP WITH DRUID APPLE—WOOD	220	HARP OF AENGUS		11
HE MADE A HARP WITH DRUID APPLE WOOD	220	HARP OF AENGUS	V	11
YOU HAVE TAKEN PAY AND MADE YOUR BARGAIN FOR IT.	225	SHADOW WATER B		68
THE MIND IS MADE UNCHANGING, FOR IT FINDS	227	SHADOW WATER B		101
I'LL SHOW YOU THAT I AM MADE DIFFERENTLY,	227	SHADOW WATER B		119
THEY HAVE MADE YOU FOLLOW THE MAN—HEADED BIRDS,	231	SHADOW WATER B		204
LIKE CHARMED APPLES MADE OF CHRYSOPRASE,	231	SHADOW WATER B		214

488

MADE   (CONTINUED)

		PAGE	TITLE		LINE
MADE OF DIM GOLD RAVE OUT IN SECRET TOMBS;		235	SHADOW WATER B		295
BUT WHAT IS IT THAT MADE ME SAY I LOVED HIM?		242	SHADOW WATER B		422
THERE IS NOT ONE AMONG YOU THAT MADE LOVE		244	SHADOW WATER B		454
THE EVER—LIVING HAVE MADE YOU MAD; BUT NO;		248	SHADOW WATER B		546
WHAT COULD HAVE MADE HER PEACEFUL WITH A MIND		256	NO SECOND TROY		6
THAT NOBLENESS MADE SIMPLE AS A FIRE,		256	NO SECOND TROY		7
BECAUSE WE HAVE MADE OUR ART OF COMMON THINGS,		265	ABBEY THEATRE		5
HAVE YOU MADE GREATNESS YOUR COMPANION,		265	THESE CLOUDS		9
THE SMOKY TORCHES MADE A GLARE		271	GREY ROCK		18
AND SMOKY TORCHES MADE A GLARE		271	GREY ROCK	V	18
NOW FROM THAT JUICE THAT MADE THEM WISE		272	GREY ROCK		26
FOR ONE THAT WAS LIKE WOMAN MADE		272	GREY ROCK		29
OF MEN AND WOMEN MADE LIKE THESE;		272	GREY ROCK		43
BUT FROM THE JUICE THAT MADE THEM WISE		272	GREY ROCK	V	26
BUT NEVER MADE A POORER SONG		273	GREY ROCK		55
THAT HAD MADE PRINTS UPON THE GROUND,		274	GREY ROCK		79
AND RENT HER CLOTHES AND MADE HER MOAN;		275	GREY ROCK		108
A CLUMP OF BEECH TREES MADE AN EMPTY SPACE		277	TWO KINGS	V	4A
NOR DOOR, NOR MOUTH, NOR SLIPPER MADE A NOISE;		279	TWO KINGS		51
SOME PASSION HAD MADE HER STONE. HEARING A FOOT		279	TWO KINGS		65
THAT MADE THE BODY SEEM AS IT WERE A STRING		284	TWO KINGS		176
AND GUIDOBALDO, WHEN HE MADE		287	TO WEALTHY MAN		14
UNLESS DESIRE HAD MADE THEM SO?"		295	THREE BEGGARS		18
OR IF THEY MADE A MOMENT'S STAY		297	THREE BEGGARS		52
I'VE STOOD AS I WERE MADE OF STONE		297	THREE BEGGARS		64
AND MADE A GOLDEN CRADLE		308	PLAYER QUEEN		3
AND MADE A GOLDEN GOWN,		308	PLAYER QUEEN		10
THAT HAS MADE A GREAT PEACOCK		310	PEACOCK		2
TILL PRIDE HAD MADE HER EYES GROW BRIGHT,		314	MEMORY YOUTH		10
AND PLEASURE MADE HER CHEEKS GROW RED,		314	MEMORY YOUTH		11
THE LINEAMENTS, A HEART THAT LAUGHTER HAS MADE SWEET,		315	FALLEN MAJESTY		5
THE LINEAMENTS, THE HEART THAT LAUGHTER HAS MADE SWEET,		315	FALLEN MAJESTY	V	5
I MADE MY SONG A COAT		320	COAT		1
THOSE UNDREAMT ACCIDENTS THAT HAVE MADE ME		321	REED WHISPERER		10
SINCE I FIRST MADE MY COUNT;		322	SWANS AT COOLE		8
WHAT MADE US DREAM THAT HE COULD COMB GREY HAIR?		327	ROBERT GREGORY		88
HAIR SPREAD ON THE WIND THEY MADE;		332	ROUND TOWER		22
HAIRS SPREAD ON THE WIND THEY MADE;		332	ROUND TOWER	V	22
AND I THAT MADE LIKE MUSIC IN MY YOUTH		342	SHEP GOATHERD		76
OF ALL THAT HE HAD MADE.		342	SHEP GOATHERD		99
AND TOOK THEIR TABLETS AND MADE SUMS—		344	DAWN	V	9
THAT MADE THEM STRETCH AND YAWN,		345	ON WOMAN		21
SHUDDER THAT MADE THEM ONE.		346	ON WOMAN		23
IN THE GREY STONE TOMB HE MADE.		360	ALF POLLEXFEN		5
(I HAVE NO SPEECH BUT SYMBOL, THE PAGAN SPEECH I MADE		365	HER COURAGE		2
THAT MADE HER DIARMUID DEAR, AND SOME OLD CARDINAL		366	HER COURAGE		6
AND THAT MADE HER DERMUID DEAR, AND SOME OLD CARDINAL		366	HER COURAGE	V	6
THAT HE HAS MADE THAT HOLLOW FACE OF HIS		368	EGO DOMINUS		20
OR WAS THE HUNGER THAT HAD MADE IT HOLLOW		368	EGO DOMINUS		23
YET SURELY THERE ARE MEN WHO HAVE MADE THEIR ART		369	EGO DOMINUS		38
AND MADE—BEING POOR, AILING AND IGNORANT;		370	EGO DOMINUS		59
WHAT MADE THAT SOUND? A RAT OR WATER—HEN		372	PHASES OF MOON		8
THEREON I MADE MY MOAN,		384	VISION ROBART		63
THE COMFORT THAT YOU MADE? ALTHOUGH MY WITS HAVE GONE		391	UNDER SATURN		5
IT MADE HIM HAPPIER TO KNOW		400	DEMON BEAST		14
FOR AIMLESS JOY HAD MADE ME STOP		400	DEMON BEAST		22
BEING MADE BEAUTIFUL OVERMUCH,		403	FOR DAUGHTER		20
FOR BEAUTY'S VERY SELF, HAS CHARM MADE WISE,		404	FOR DAUGHTER		37
STRANGE, BUT THE MAN WHO MADE THE SONG WAS BLIND;		411	TOWER		49
TILL MAN MADE UP THE WHOLE,		415	TOWER		149
MADE LOCK, STOCK AND BARREL		415	TOWER		150
BEING OF THAT METAL MADE		416	TOWER		178
THAT MADE A CATCH IN THE BREATH—		416	TOWER		191
HAS MADE THE VERY OWLS IN CIRCLES MOVE;		423	MY DESCENDANTS		18
OR EYES THAT RAGE HAS BRIGHTENED, ARMS IT HAS MADE LEAN,		427	PHANTOM HATRED		27
IT HAD BUT MADE US PINE THE MORE. THE ABSTRACT JOY,		427	PHANTOM HATRED		38
OF EYES THAT RAGE HAS BRIGHTENED, ARMS IT HAS MADE LEAN,		427	PHANTOM HATRED	V	27
AN ANCIENT IMAGE MADE OF OLIVE WOOD—		428	NINETEEN 19		6
TO BRIBE OR THREAT; HABITS THAT MADE OLD WRONG		428	NINETEEN 19		11
IS LOST AMID THE LABYRINTH THAT HE HAS MADE		431	NINETEEN 19		70
MADE ALL PLATONIC TOLERANCE VAIN		438	SONGS PLAY 2		7
MADE PLATO'S TOLERANCE IN VAIN,		438	SONGS PLAY 2	V	7
THE WEST WIND MADE IT PITIFUL, AND THE NORTH WIND AFRAID,		449	OWEN AHERNE		6
"BECAUSE I MADE YOU TURN AWAY AND RUN FROM THAT YOUNG CHILD;		450	OWEN AHERNE		14
THAT IT WAS MADE IN YOUR GREAT FATHER'S REIGN."		464	HARUN RASHID		72
HANDS UPON EITHER SHOULDER MADE HER MOVE,		466	HARUN RASHID	V	125B
WHAT'S BOWED YOUR SHOULDER AND MADE PALE YOUR CHEEK";		467	HARUN RASHID		133
MADE DRIVE THE ARABIAN HOST. THE VOICE GREW STILL,		467	HARUN RASHID	V	145
THAT MADE THE MAGNITUDE AND GLORY THERE		483	VERONIC NAPKIN		5
MADE MY ATTENTION STRAY.		507	STREAM AND SUN		5
WHAT MADE ME LIVE LIKE THESE THAT SEEM		507	STREAM AND SUN		14
MADE THE JOINTS OF HEAVEN CRACK;		509	JANE REPROVED		11
BEFORE THE WORLD WAS MADE."		516	MANS SONG		12
I MADE, AND MAY NOT BREAK IT		520	HIS BARGAIN		9
SOMETHING MADE THESE EYEBALLS WEARY		529	TOM LUNATIC		11
BEFORE THE WORLD WAS MADE		531	BEFORE WORLD		T
BEFORE THE WORLD WAS MADE.		532	BEFORE WORLD		8
BEFORE THE WORLD WAS MADE.		532	BEFORE WORLD		16
WHAT MADE THEM MOUNT AND WHAT MADE THEM COME,		549	SEVERED HEAD	V	8

489

MADE   (CONTINUED)
    WHAT MADE THEM MOUNT AND WHAT MADE THEM COME,   549 SEVERED HEAD   V   8
    MADE AQUILINE, ARE OPEN TO THAT LIGHT.   555 RIBH AT TOMB   24
    WHAT MASTER MADE THE LASH. WHENCE HAD THEY COME,   560 WHENCE COME   9
    MADE DRAPERIES THAT SEEMED TO RISE   566 LAPIS LAZULI   31
    SHE MADE A FULL CONFESSION.   571 THREE BUSHES   66
    PLEASURE HAS MADE HIM   574 MAIDS 1ST SONG   9
    WOUND, WOUND, AND SHE MADE IN HER TRIUMPH   578 CRAZED GIRL   11
    AND ALL MY FRIENDS WERE THERE AND MADE ME WELCOME TOO!   581 CURSE CROMWELL   27
    THAT SOME AMENDS BE MADE   582 ROGER CASEMENT   22
    O WHAT HAS MADE THAT SUDDEN NOISE?   583 GHOST ROG CASE   1
    THAT TRAGIC STORY MADE,   587 PARNELLITES   26
    WITH FLOPPING AND WITH FLAPPING IT MADE A GREAT DISPLAY,   593 PILGRIM   18
    WITH THEIR FLOPPING AND THEIR FLAPPING IT MADE A GREAT   593 PILGRIM   V   18
        DISPLAY
    WHEN TOM MADE OUT A LIVING   597 COLONEL MARTIN V   70
    NOR EVER MADE AN IRON RED   606 SONGS BURDEN 1   14
    WHAT MADE THE DRAPERY GLISTEN SO?   625 NATIVITY   3
    WHAT MADE THE CEILING WATERPROOF?   625 NATIVITY   5
    OR THE MAN THAT MADE THE MOTORS?   627 STATES HOLIDAY   20
    SING WHATEVER IS WELL MADE,   639 BEN BULBEN   69
    THE SHEPHERD PARIS FOR OENONE MADE,   650 ISLE STAT I 1   136
    MADE THEM OF FIRE AND CLAY.   680 LOVE AND DEATH   12
    WORN BY THE SOLSTICE FIERCE, AND MADE IT PURE.   692 MOSADA 1   57
    THAT SONG I'VE MADE. 'TIS OF AN IRISH TALE.   696 MOSADA 2   19
    THAT SONG I'VE MADE--IS OF A RUSSIAN TALE.   696 MOSADA 2   V   19
    IN SPACE, MADE EQUAL WITH A SIGH, WE MET.   705 REMEMBRANCE   14
    ON THE NOSE OF THE SLEEPER HE MADE IT PLAY;   729 PRIEST FAIRY   30
    AND MADE THE TYRANT BOW.   738 MOURN THEN ON   12
    AND MADE THEIR GLORY NAUGHT.   741 EARL PAUL   44
    AND MADE THE BRIGHT SPEAR BEND,   741 EARL PAUL   46
    BECAUSE A GOD HAS MADE HIM WISE WITH DREAMS;   748 SHADOW WATER A   26
    AND SLEEPY BOUGHS, AND BOUGHS WHERE APPLES MADE   762 SHADOW WATER A   300
    BECAUSE HER HANDS HAD BEEN MADE WILD BY LOVE;   762 SHADOW WATER A   304
    HE MADE A HARP WITH DRUID APPLE WOOD   763 SHADOW WATER A   306
    HE MADE A HARP WITH DRUID APPLE-WOOD   763 SHADOW WATER A V   306
    ALL DIES AMONG THOSE STREAMS. THE FOOL HAS MADE   764 SHADOW WATER A   335
    THE FOOL, WHO HAS MADE THE WISDOM THAT MEN WRITE   764 SHADOW WATER A   342
    MADE OF DIM GOLD, RAVE OUT IN SECRET TOMBS,   765 SHADOW WATER A   345
    AND BODILY TENDERNESS; BUT LOVE IS MADE   765 SHADOW WATER A   355
    LOVE WAS NOT MADE FOR DARKNESS AND THE WINDS   767 SHADOW WATER A   394
    HAS MADE MY FEET UNSTEADY, AND BLINDED ME.   767 SHADOW WATER A   406
    WHERE THE DEW IS MADE BEFORE DAWN;   771 SPINNING SONG   5
    THAT IS MADE OUT OF THE GREASE   776 AGAINST WITCH   24
    HAS MADE IT BUT A LONELY THING.   781 HEART FRIGHT   4
MADEST
    THOU CALLED'ST ME FORTH. AND HOW THOU MADEST ME   683 SEEKER   52
MADGE
    FOR THAT OLD MADGE COMES DOWN THE LANE,   456 FRIENDS YOUTH   5
    MADGE TELLS ME WHAT I DARED NOT THINK   457 SECRETS OF OLD   3
MADGE'S
    IF THROWN IN MADGE'S WAY,   457 SECRETS OF OLD   8
MADMAN'S
    HE RUSHES, ROLLING FROM HIS LIPS A MADMAN'S LAUGH.   715 FERENCZ RENYI   122
MADNESS
    THE MADNESS OF KING GOLL   81 MAD KING GOLL   T
    BRING MADNESS? QUEEN, I AM NOT MAD. YET SAY   236 SHADOW WATER B   316
MADONNA
    MADONNA FROM MY BREAST?   686 LIFE   12
MAEVE
    WHERE PASSIONATE MAEVE IS STONY-STILL;   3 OISIN 1   18
    TILL I SAW WHERE MAEVE LIES SLEEPING   60 OISIN 3   184
    THE OLD AGE OF QUEEN MAEVE   180 QUEEN MAEVE   T
    MAEVE THE GREAT QUEEN WAS PACING TO AND FRO,   180 QUEEN MAEVE   9
    MAEVE WALKED, YET WITH SLOW FOOTFALL, BEING OLD,   181 QUEEN MAEVE   43
    MAEVE WAITED, AND WHEN THAT EAR-PIERCING NOISE   182 QUEEN MAEVE   47
    MAEVE WALKED THROUGH THAT GREAT HALL, AND WITH A SIGH   182 QUEEN MAEVE   62
    AND WITH GLAD VOICE MAEVE ANSWERED HIM, "WHAT KING   183 QUEEN MAEVE   79
    AND WITH GLAD VOICE MAEVE ANSWERED "MANY A TIME   183 QUEEN MAEVE   V   79
    BUT MAEVE, AND NOT WITH A SLOW FEEBLE FOOT,   185 QUEEN MAEVE   107
    TILL MAEVE CALLED OUT, "THESE ARE BUT COMMON MEN.   186 QUEEN MAEVE   122
    TO MAEVE AND TO MAEVE'S HOUSEHOLD, OWING ALL   187 QUEEN MAEVE   147
    THEN MAEVE: "O AENGUS, MASTER OF ALL LOVERS,   187 QUEEN MAEVE   149
    AND THROWN THE THUNDER ON THE STONES FOR ALL THAT MAEVE   207 HANRAHANS SONG   7
        CAN SAY.
    FROM MAEVE AND ALL THAT JUGGLING PLAIN,   307 HOUR DAWN   120
MAEVE'S
    TO MAEVE AND TO MAEVE'S HOUSEHOLD, OWING ALL   187 QUEEN MAEVE   147
    QUEEN MAEVE'S NINE MAINES HAD BEEN NURSED,   302 HOUR DAWN   8
    WHAT ONE OF MAEVE'S NINE BRAWLING SONS   303 HOUR DAWN   36
    HAS ONE OF MAEVE'S NINE BRAWLING SONS   303 HOUR DAWN   V   36
MAGAI
    BETWEEN THE WOOD OF DURAS AND MAGAI   276 TWO KINGS   V   G
MAGEE
    THE BALLAD OF MOLL MAGEE   94 MOLL MAGEE   T
    BUT PITY MOLL MAGEE.   94 MOLL MAGEE   4
    AND PITY MOLL MAGEE.   96 MOLL MAGEE   56
MAGH
    HE SAID, "HIGH QUEEN OF CRUACHAN AND MAGH AI,   183 QUEEN MAEVE   77
MAGI
    OF THE CROWNED MAGI; AND THE KING WHOSE EYES   169 SECRET ROSE   9

490

	PAGE	TITLE		LINE
MAGI (CONTINUED)				
OF THE CROWNED MAGI: AND THE HOUND OF CU	169	SECRET ROSE	V	9
OF THE CROWNED MAGI: AND THE KINGS WHOSE EYES	169	SECRET ROSE	V	9
THE MAGI	318	MAGI		T
MAGIC				
WERE'T NOT THAT THERE IS MAGIC IN HIS HARP, ...	222	SHADOW WATER B		16
THAT THERE IS MAGIC IN THAT HARP OF HIS, ...	222	SHADOW WATER B	V	16
A MAGIC THAT CAN CALL A DEMON UP, ...	238	SHADOW WATER B		344
I WILL END ALL YOUR MAGIC ON THE INSTANT.	242	SHADOW WATER B		411
BY MAGIC STRINGS, I'LL MAKE THIS ANSWER TO IT:	243	SHADOW WATER B		440
MY MAGIC STRINGS, I'LL MAKE THIS ANSWER TO IT:	243	SHADOW WATER B	V	440
IF YOU HAD TAKEN ME BY MAGIC SPELLS, ...	245	SHADOW WATER B		490
WHAT MAGIC DRUM?	559	MAGIC DRUM		T
THROUGH LIGHT-OBLITERATING GARDEN FOLIAGE WHAT MAGIC DRUM?	560	MAGIC DRUM		4
TAKEN IN MAGIC, IN THE CHURCH'S NAME	694	MOSADA 1		104
WITH PITILESS MAGIC HAS BOUND YOU--	708	FAIRY PEDANT		31
SO MEN IN LIFE AND I IN MAGIC PLAY:	722	WITCH VIVIEN		55
MAGICAL				
CHAUNT IN HIS EAR DELUSIONS MAGICAL, ...	111	CUCHULAIN SEA		80
GO, CAST ON HIM DELUSIONS MAGICAL.	111	CUCHULAIN SEA	V	80
THE MAGICAL POWERS TO AND FRO.	138	TO IRELAND	V	24
MAGICAL SHAPES. BY THE HELP OF AN IMAGE	367	EGO DOMINUS		7
OBEDIENT TO SOME HIDDEN MAGICAL BREATH.	382	VISION ROBART		13
MAGICAL UNICORNS BEAR LADIES ON THEIR BACKS.	426	PHANTOM HATRED		18
MAGICIAN				
OBEYS. SOME FIERCE MAGICIAN FLIES OR WALKS	720	WITCH VIVIEN		9
MAGNANIMITIES				
THEIR MAGNANIMITIES OF SOUND, ...	404	FOR DAUGHTER		44
MAGNANIMITY				
THE STRENGTH THAT GIVES OUR BLOOD AND STATE MAGNANIMITY	481	BLOOD AND MOON		29
. . .				
AS THOUGH WITH MAGNANIMITY OF LIGHT, ...	618	BRONZE HEAD		9
MAGNIFICENCE				
MONUMENTS OF ITS OWN MAGNIFICENCE:	407	SAIL BYZANTIUM		14
LOWLY THE HEAD OF HIS MAGNIFICENCE	689	NETTLESHIP		6
DOWN LOW THE HEAD OF HIS MAGNIFICENCE	689	NETTLESHIP	V	6
MAGNIFIED				
MY MEMORIES HAD MAGNIFIED	399	BREAK OF DAY		10
MAGNIFY				
CONSIDER MOST TO MAGNIFY, OR TO BLESS, ...	418	ANCEST HOUSES		39
MAGNITUDE				
THAT MADE THE MAGNITUDE AND GLORY THERE	483	VERONIC NAPKIN		5
MAGNUS				
OF MAGNUS ANNUS AT THE SPRING, ...	437	SONGS PLAY 1		7
MAHOGANY				
LIT UP THE DARK MAHOGANY AND THE WINE, ...	410	TOWER		27
MAHRAJAS				
OF RAJAS AND MAHRAJAS BEYOND NUMBER?	724	KANVA ON SELF		6
MAID SEE WAITING-MAID SERVING-MAID				
AND NOW A MAID, ON A SWIFT BROWN STEED	12	OISIN 1	V	142
MAID NIAM FROM A LITTLE TRUMP	14	OISIN 1	V	194
AND KNELT THEM, EVERY MAID AND MAN, ...	15	OISIN 1	V	214
THEY HUSHED THEM, EVERY MAN AND MAID.	17	OISIN 1	V	235
WITH ONE LONG GLANCE ON MAID AND BOY	19	OISIN 1	V	287
AROSE FROM EVERY MAID AND BOY, ...	20	OISIN 1	V	289
HE SPAKE TO THE YOUNG MAN, "IS THERE NO MAID	109	CUCHULAIN SEA		58
THEN CONCHUBAR SENT THAT SWEET-THROATED MAID, ...	110	CUCHULAIN SEA		72
THEN CONCOBAR SENT THAT SWEET THROATED MAID	110	CUCHULAIN SEA	V	72
AND LIFT YOUR TENDER EYELIDS, MAID, ...	125	GOES FERGUS		5
MAID QUIET	171	MAID QUIET		T
WHERE HAS MAID QUIET GONE TO, ...	171	MAID QUIET		1
I NEVER HAVE SEEN MAID QUIET	171	MAID QUIET		1
NO WAITING MAID SHOULD EVER SPREAD	194	BAILE AILLINN	V	120
A SERVING MAID AND A SERVING MAN, ...	301	RUN PARADISE	V	13
AND EVERY MAN AND MAID AND BOY	337	TOM OROUGHLEY		2
WHETHER TO MAID OR HAG!	525	DANCING DAYS		22
"I AM SORRY," SAID THE MAID.	595	COLONEL MARTIN		29
TWO MEN WHO LOVE ONE MAID HAVE AMPLE CAUSE	659	ISLE STAT II 1		30
FOR THIS THING FIGHT--WE LOVE ONE MAID? HER NAME? . .	661	ISLE STAT II 1		66
THE PLAIN, A LITTLE FAIR-HAIRED MAID I LOVE.	679	ISLE STAT II 3		312
THERE DWELLS A LITTLE FAIR-HAIRED MAID I LOVE.	679	ISLE STAT II 3	V	312
MY LORD, YOU CALLED? NOT I. THIS MAID IS DEAD. . . .	704	MOSADA 3		125
THEN EACH WIFE AND MAID AND MOTHER CALLS BY NAME	719	PHANTOM SHIP		24
SOME DROWNED ONE.				
DO NOT FEAR US, EARTHLY MAID!	726	LOVERS QUARREL		1
TEASING EVERY WILFUL MAID.	727	LOVERS QUARREL		28
MAIDEN				
A MAIDEN, ON A SLENDER STEED, ...	2	OISIN 1	V	7V
"O PLEASANT MAIDEN," ANSWERED FINN, ...	5	OISIN 1	V	40
NOW, PLEASANT MAIDEN, TELL TO ME	5	OISIN 1	V	43
OF THE YOUNG. "YOUNG MAIDEN, WHAT MAY BRING	5	OISIN 1	V	50
AND NOW A MAIDEN RODE LIKE THE WIND	12	OISIN 1	V	142
AND ONCE A MAIDEN BY MY SIDE	16	OISIN 1	V	231
FULL MANY MORE, WHEN PEERED A MAIDEN SWEET	33	OISIN 2	V	68F
A MAIDEN WITH SOFT EYES LIKE FUNERAL TAPERS, ...	33	OISIN 2	V	69
OH MAIDEN." "ARE YE SPIRITS OF THE SEA, ...	34	OISIN 2	V	78B
THAT MAIDEN FOUND A RING HUNG ON THE WALL, ...	37	OISIN 2	V	120
AND AH, YOU PROUD MAIDEN, YOU ARE NOT SO FAIR WHEN HIS OAR	91	OLD FISHERMAN		9
PROUD MAIDEN, YE ARE NOT SO FAIR, WHEN HIS OAR . . .	91	OLD FISHERMAN	V	9
NO MAIDEN LOVES ME, NO MAN SEEKS MY HELP, ...	103	FERGUS DRUID	V	26
MAIDEN, COME FORTH! THE WOODS KEEP WATCH FOR THEE! . . .	645	ISLE STAT I 1		1

491

MAIDEN   (CONTINUED)
    SLOW WATERS, AND THE BOAT AND MAIDEN SINK . . . . . . 663 ISLE STAT II 2   39
    THAT MAIDEN BRING THEY. WHEN THE TALL RED DEER . . . . 713 FERENCZ RENYI   79
    BUT SPEECHLESS, AND THE MAIDEN WITH LONG WAIL . . . . . 713 FERENCZ RENYI   85
    WHITE, RENYI SILENT STANDS; THAT MAIDEN SWEET . . . . . 713 FERENCZ RENYI V 84
    OF MOSS, A MAIDEN WEAVING. SINGETH SHE! . . . . 716 DWELT SYCAMORE   12
    AND, MAIDEN, BE THOU MIRTHFUL TOO, ... 736 SUMMER EVENING   13
MAIDEN'S
    AS SOME DEAD MAIDEN'S SINGING IN A DREAM. . . . . . . 654 ISLE STAT I 2   59
MAIDENS
    AND FEET OF MAIDENS DANCING IN TUNE, ... 3 OISIN 1   V   9
    AND A HUNDRED MAIDENS WISE AND YOUNG, ... 8 OISIN 1   V   94
    AND A HUNDRED MAIDENS, MERRY AS BIRDS, ... 9 OISIN 1   V   96
    OF YOUTHS AND MAIDENS HAND IN HAND, ... 15 OISIN 1   V 202
    OF MEN AND MAIDENS, HAND IN HAND, ... 15 OISIN 1   V 202
    AND MEN AND MAIDENS KNELT THEM THERE . . . . 18 OISIN 1   V 255
    AND, AH, YE PROUD MAIDENS, YE ARE NOT SO FAIR, WHEN HIS OAR 91 OLD FISHERMAN V   9
MAIDS   SEE WAITING-MAIDS
    WHERE AILLINN RODE WITH WAITING MAIDS . . . . 193 BAILE AILLINN V 102
    A LONG, BROWN GRASSHOPPER OF MAIDS! PEACE, SIR! . . . 661 ISLE STAT II 1   69
    A FASHION WITH US MOORISH MAIDS, BEGOT . . . . 700 MOSADA 3   25
MAIL
    OR CARRY THE RINGED MAIL UPON MY BACK, ... 463 HARUN RASHID   58
    A COAT OF GILDED MAIL. . . . . 740 EARL PAUL   16
    WITH A CLANG OF HIS DIM MAIL, ... 742 EARL PAUL   66
MAIL'D
    WHO SITS IN LONELY SPLENDOUR, MAIL'D IN GOLD, ... 651 ISLE STAT I 1   163
MAILED
    ERE FALL OF EVENING, MY MAILED HOST, ... 83 MAD KING GOLL V   19
    I DREW AT EVENING MY MAILED MEN, ... 83 MAD KING GOLL V   19
MAIMED
    MAIMED US AT THE START. . . . . 506 REMORSE SPEECH   13
MAINE
    NOT I, NOR MAINE THERE, NOR DUACH'S SON. . . . . . . 748 SHADOW WATER A   22
    EOCHA AND MAINE ARE ALWAYS QUARRELLING. . . . . . . 766 SHADOW WATER A   371
MAINES
    THE CHILDREN OF THE MAINES OUT OF SLEEP, ... 184 QUEEN MAEVE   92
    QUEEN MAEVE'S NINE MAINES HAD BEEN NURSED, ... 302 HOUR DAWN   8
MAINES'
    THE MAINES' CHILDREN DROPPED THEIR SPADES, AND STOOD . . 185 QUEEN MAEVE   120
    THE MAINES' CHILDREN HAVE NOT DROPPED THEIR SPADES . . 186 QUEEN MAEVE   123
MAINLY
    MAINLY BECAUSE OF WHAT WE ONLY KNOW . . . . 634 CUCHULAIN COMF   14
MAIVE
    WHERE PASSIONATE MAIVE IS STONY STILL! . . . . 3 OISIN 1   V   18
    O TATTERED CLOUDS OF THE WORLD, CALL FROM THE HIGH CAIRN 207 HANRAHANS SONG V   6
    OF MAIVE,
MAJESTIC
    HIS MAJESTIC MOTHER SAT . . . . 440 WISDOM   11
MAJESTICAL
    WITH THE LONELY, MAJESTICAL MULTITUDE. . . . . 158 TO HIS HEART   7
    WITH THE PROUD, MAJESTICAL MULTITUDE. . . . . 158 TO HIS HEART   V   7
    WHERE RISE THE WALLS MAJESTICAL ABOVE . . . . 679 ISLE STAT II 3   311
MAJESTY
    THE MAJESTY THAT SHUTS HIS BURNING EYE! . . . . 265 THESE CLOUDS   2
    THE MAJESTY THAT SHUTS HIS BURNING EYE. . . . . 265 THESE CLOUDS   12
    WHO HAD UNNATURAL MAJESTY, AND EYES . . . . 283 TWO KINGS   149
    AND THE GAUNT HOUSES PUT ON MAJESTY! . . . . 292 TO A SHADE   7
    FALLEN MAJESTY . . . . 314 FALLEN MAJESTY   T
    BABBLING OF FALLEN MAJESTY, RECORDS WHAT'S GONE. . . . . 314 FALLEN MAJESTY   4
MAJOR
    IN MEMORY OF MAJOR ROBERT GREGORY . . . . 323 ROBERT GREGORY   T
MAKE
    YET WILL I MAKE ALL PLAIN FOR THEE. . . . . 2 OISIN 1   V   7B
    "AND I WILL MAKE A THOUSAND SONGS, ... 7 OISIN 1   75
    I BELLOW TO THE WINDS WHEN STORMS MAKE MOAN, ... 45 OISIN 2   V 239D
    AND MORE COMELY THAN MAN CAN MAKE THEM . . . . 49 OISIN 3   V   32
    MORE COMELY THAN MAN MAY MAKE THEM, INLAID WITH SILVER . 49 OISIN 3   V   29
    AND GOLD,
    MAKE CLEAN AS A BROOM CLEANS, ... 62 OISIN 3   211
    "WHAT DO YOU MAKE SO FAIR AND BRIGHT?" . . . . 69 CLOAK BOAT   1
    "I MAKE THE CLOAK OF SORROW! . . . . 69 CLOAK BOAT   2
    MAKE THE HILLS REPLY." . . . . 98 FOXHUNTER   26
    AND MAKE THE HILLS REPLY." . . . . 98 FOXHUNTER   26
    MAKE THE HILLS REPLY." . . . . 99 FOXHUNTER   34
    AND MAKE THE HILLS REPLY." . . . . 99 FOXHUNTER   V   34
    AND SOFTLY MAKE A ROSY PEACE, ... 113 ROSE OF PEACE   15
    AND WITH THE CLASHING OF THEIR SWORD-BLADES MAKE . . . 137 TO SOME I TALK   13
    AND WITH THE CLANGING OF THEIR SWORD-BLADES MAKE . . . 137 TO SOME I TALK V   13
    AND WITH THE CLASHING OF THEIR SWORD BLADES MAKE . . . 137 TO SOME I TALK V   13
    IN DRUID VAPOUR AND MAKE THE TORCHES DIM! . . . . . . 169 SECRET ROSE   11
    TO MAKE THE SAVAGE HEART OF LOVE . . . . 193 BAILE AILLINN   109
    OF THE EBB OF ALL THINGS TO MAKE LOVE . . . . 193 BAILE AILLINN V 109
    MAKE THEIR FAINT THUNDER, AND THE GARDEN BEES . . . . . 198 SEVEN WOODS   2
    TIME CAN BUT MAKE IT EASIER TO BE WISE . . . . 200 FOLLY COMFORT   4
    TIME CAN BUT MAKE HER BEAUTY OVER AGAIN! . . . . . . 200 FOLLY COMFORT   8
    THE WATERS OF SLEEP CAN MAKE A CHATTERING TONGUE . . . 218 WOODS OF COOLE   25
    THESE DOZEN WEEKS. AND I HAD THOUGHT TO MAKE . . . . 222 SHADOW WATER B   4
    TO MAKE AN END WHILE HE IS SLEEPING THERE. . . . . . 222 SHADOW WATER B V   14
    TO MAKE AN END OF FORGAEL WHILE HE SLEEPS. . . . . . 225 SHADOW WATER B   65
    TO MAKE LOW LAUGHTER MORE THAN MEAT AND DRINK, ... 230 SHADOW WATER B   186

MAKE   (CONTINUED)
    TO MAKE HER FAST WHILE WE ARE PLUNDERING HER. . . . . .   232 SHADOW WATER B   225
    BY MAGIC STRINGS, I'LL MAKE THIS ANSWER TO IT! . . . . .   243 SHADOW WATER B   440
    AND YET YOU MAKE A CLAMOUR OF REPROACH. . . . . . .   243 SHADOW WATER B   444
    MY MAGIC STRINGS, I'LL MAKE THIS ANSWER TO IT! . . . . .   243 SHADOW WATER B V   440
    WAS DONE TO MAKE IT PLAIN! . . . .   256 WORDS   8
    NOTHING TO MAKE A SONG ABOUT BUT KINGS, ...   257 RECONCILIATION   5
    "O NO, MY DEAR, YOU MAKE SO BOLD . . . .   263 MASK   3
    "I BID THEM MAKE HIS BED UNDER THIS ROOF . . . .   280 TWO KINGS   87
    THAT MAKE THE HEART AKIN TO THE DUMB STONE." . . . . .   281 TWO KINGS   94
    SHALL MAKE HER LOOK UPON HER HANDIWORK, ...   282 TWO KINGS   115
    IMAGINES BEST TO MAKE IT THRIVE. . . . .   287 TO WEALTHY MAN   8
    AND WHAT COULD MAKE THEIR MUSCLES TAUT . . . .   295 THREE BEGGARS   17
    "AND MAKE MY SOUL BEFORE MY PATE IS BARE." . . . . . .   299 BEGGAR CRIED   4
    REMINDED HIM THAT HE COULD MAKE, ...   302 HOUR DAWN   13
    TO MAKE A CLATTER IN THE HOLE . . . .   304 HOUR DAWN   V   54
    THE FORD WHERE DRINKING CATTLE MAKE A STIR . . . . . .   326 ROBERT GREGORY   53
    THERE'S NOT A THING BUT LOVE CAN MAKE . . . .   333 SOLOMON SHEBA   23
    COULD MAKE ME WISH FOR ANYTHING THIS DAY, ...   338 SHEP GOATHERD   3
    AND MAKE THE DAYLIGHT SWEET ONCE MORE! BUT WHEN . . . .   339 SHEP GOATHERD   13
    SOME MEDICABLE HERB TO MAKE OUR GRIEF . . . .   342 SHEP GOATHERD   86
    OR WHO HAVE FOUND A PAINTER TO MAKE THEM SO FOR PAY . . .   353 HIS PHOENIX   6
    THERE'LL BE THAT CROWD TO MAKE MEN WILD THROUGH ALL THE   354 HIS PHOENIX   V   25
        CENTURIES,
    AND MAY BE THERE'LL BE SOME YOUNG BELLE WALK OUT TO MAKE   354 HIS PHOENIX   V   26
        MEN WILD
    AND MAYBE THERE'LL BE SOME YOUNG BELLE WALK OUT TO MAKE   354 HIS PHOENIX   V   26
        MEN WILD
    SO GREAT HER PORTION IN THAT PEACE YOU MAKE . . . . .   356 BROKEN DREAMS   12
    BUT IMAGES TO MAKE ME FONDER? . . . .   390 IMAGE PAST   35
    BECAUSE I HAVE NO OTHER YOUTH, CAN MAKE ME PINE! . . . .   391 UNDER SATURN   3
    BEING A PORTION OF MY YOUTH, CAN MAKE ME PINE . . . . .   391 UNDER SATURN   V   3
    CAN MAKE A STONE OF THE HEART. . . . .   394 EASTER 1916   58
    "TO MAKE THE GREEN COME OUT AGAIN . . . .   396 ROSE TREE   9
    CAN MAKE A RIGHT ROSE TREE." . . . .   396 ROSE TREE   18
    TO MAKE IT LINGER HALF A DAY. . . . .   401 DEMON BEAST   42
    BEAUTY TO MAKE A STRANGER'S EYE DISTRAUGHT, ...   403 FOR DAUGHTER   18
    BUT SUCH A FORM AS GRECIAN GOLDSMITHS MAKE . . . . . .   408 SAIL BYZANTIUM   27
    FOR IF I TRIUMPH I MUST MAKE MEN MAD. . . . . . .   411 TOWER   56
    NOW SHALL I MAKE MY SOUL, ...   416 TOWER   181
    THAT WE MIGHT MAKE IT WHOLE! . . . .   457 SUMMER SPRING   8
    WE THREE MAKE UP A SOLITUDE! . . . .   457 SECRETS OF OLD   9
    FOR INTELLECT WOULD MAKE US PROUD . . . .   460 THREE MONUMENT   10
    THAT MAKE A MAN'S SOUL OR A WOMAN'S SOUL . . . . . .   465 HARUN RASHID   93
    MAKE HUMAN INTERCOURSE GROW LESS AND LESS! . . . . . .   473 ALL SOUL NIGHT   75
    IF I MAKE THE LASHES DARK . . . .   531 BEFORE WORLD   1
    THE KING THAT COULD MAKE HIS PEOPLE STARE, ...   550 SEVERED HEAD   19
    WHERE CAN SHE LOOK UNTIL HE MAKE THE SHOW! . . . . . .   558 RIBH CHRISTIAN   22
    WASH! MAKE YOUR BODY SWEET! . . . .   572 LADYS 2ND SONG   4
    CAN MAKE THE TRUTH KNOWN. . . . .   575 ACRE OF GRASS   12
    THAT CAN MAKE A CAT LAUGH, OR . . . .   589 OLD WICKED MAN   39
    AND TOM MAKE OUT A LIVING . . . .   597 COLONEL MARTIN   70
    THAT MAKE THE MUSES SING. . . . .   601 THOSE IMAGES   16
    I SCRUB ITS FLOORS AND MAKE MY BED, ...   607 SONGS BURDEN 2   5
    BRACE ME AND MAKE ME STRONG! . . . .   607 SONGS BURDEN 2   24
    DIGGERS AND CARPENTERS MAKE GRAVE AND COFFIN! . . . . .   609 IN TARAS HALLS   17
    WITH NO MORE SOUND THAN THE MICE MAKE . . . .   618 LONG-LEG FLY   27
    AND FINDS THERE NOTHING TO MAKE ITS TERROR LESS . . . .   618 BRONZE HEAD   6
    BECAUSE PIEBALD PONIES, LED BEARS, CAGED LIONS, MAKE BUT   623 HIGH TALK   5
        POOR SHOWS,
    WOULD NOT MAKE HIM A MAN. . . . .   628 JANE MOUNTAIN   4
    "OBEY OUR ANCIENT RULE AND MAKE A SHROUD! . . . . . .   634 CUCHULAIN COMF   13
    MAKE HIM FILL THE CRADLES RIGHT. . . . .   638 BEN BULBEN   41
    ALAS! I MAKE YOU SADDER, SHEPHERDESS. . . . .   659 ISLE STAT II 1   18
    MAKE MOAN AND CRY. WITHIN YON SUNLESS VALLEY, ...   682 SEEKER   26
    TO MAKE US GLAD WITH WONDER AS WE SAT . . . .   683 SEEKER   41
    AND FOR HIM MAKE ME WISE AND BRIGHT. . . . .   723 GIRLS SONG A   12
    AND WHOM WILL YOU MAKE LEADER? WHO WILL MAKE . . . . .   748 SHADOW WATER A   20
    AND WHOM WILL YOU MAKE LEADER? WHO WILL MAKE . . . . .   748 SHADOW WATER A   20
    MAKE GALLEYS OUT OF WIND THAT CHANGE TO WIND . . . . .   751 SHADOW WATER A   105
    BECAUSE THESE WATERS MAKE ALL WOMEN ONE. . . . . . .   757 SHADOW WATER A   194
    THEY WOULD MAKE A PRINCE DECAY . . . .   775 AGAINST WITCH   11
MAKER
    THE MAKER OF THE STARS AND WORLDS . . . .   724 LEGEND   1
    THE MAKER OF THE STARS AND WORLDS . . . .   725 LEGEND   29
MAKER'S   SEE DOLL-MAKER'S
MAKES
    AND MAKES THE INFANT FERNS UNWRAP, ...   18 OISIN 1   265
    AND MAKES THE LITTLE PLANETS RUN! . . . .   18 OISIN 1   268
    "'TIS JOY MAKES SWIM THE SAPPY TIDE, ...   18 OISIN 1   V   261
    WHO HOLDS THE WORLD BETWEEN HIS BILL AND MAKES US STRONG   76 INDIAN ON GOD V   6
        OR WEAK
    A DANAAN FRUITAGE MAKES A SHOWER OF MOONS, ...   127 DREAM OF FAERY V   22
    THAT MAKES ME FEAR TO RAISE A HAND AGAINST HIM, ...   222 SHADOW WATER B V   16A
    BUT THE REALITY THAT MAKES OUR PASSION . . . .   229 SHADOW WATER B   159
    DELIGHT MAKES ALL OF THE ONE MIND, ...   266 GALWAY RACES   2
    WHAT MAKES YOUR HEART BEAT SO! . . . .   336 YOUNG GIRL   3
    A CRAZY JUICE THAT MAKES THE PULSES BEAT . . . . . .   384 VISION ROBART   54
    MAN MAKES A SUPERHUMAN . . . .   415 TOWER   164
    MAN MAKES A SUPERMAN, ...   415 TOWER   V   164
    IT MAKES MY PASSION STRONGER BUT TO THINK . . . . . .   465 HARUN RASHID   99

MAKES (CONTINUED)
    THIS LOVE THAT MAKES MY HEART'S BLOOD STOP . . . . . .   499 MOTHER OF GOD   13
    AND MAKES MY HAIR STAND UP? . . . .   499 MOTHER OF GOD V 15
    MY BODY MAKES NO MOAN . . . .   512 JANE ON GOD   22
    YOU ASK WHAT MAKES ME SIGH, OLD FRIEND, ...   524 MAD AS MIST   13
    WHAT MAKES ME SHUDDER SO? . . . .   524 MAD AS MIST   14
    FROM ALL THAT MAKES A WISE OLD MAN . . . .   553 PRAYER OLD AGE   5
    A JOURNALIST MAKES UP HIS LIES . . . .   598 STONE CROSS   3
    MAKES NO DEMAND. . . . .   600 SPIRIT MEDIUM   22
    MAKES ME SWEET MUSIC . . . .   627 STATES HOLIDAY   24
    THE RATTLE OF THOSE ARMS MAKES US AFRAID. . . . . .   634 CUCHULAIN COMF   15
    SO SMALL MAKES ONE GROW WEAK AND TOTTERING! . . . .   700 MOSADA 3   35
    OWLS THERE BE WHOM AGE MAKES NUMB." . . . .   727 LOVERS QUARREL   35
    THAT THE RED RUST MAKES DIM." . . . .   740 EARL PAUL   20
    THE WHITE FOOL MAKES AT MORNING OUT OF FOAM; . . .   761 SHADOW WATER A 261
    WHERE THE MOON MAKES A CLOUDY LIGHT IN THE MIST. . .   764 SHADOW WATER A 329
    WHAT MAKES HER HEART BEAT THUS; . . . .   785 YOUR HEART   V   1
    WHAT MAKES YOUR HEART SO BEAT? . . . .   786 YOUR HEART   27
MAKE-UP
    FOR PAINTED FORMS OR BOXES OF MAKE-UP . . . . . .   564 GYRES   13
MAKING   SEE LOVE-MAKING DEATH-MAKING PEACE-MAKING
    MAKING A WORLD ABOUT HER IN THE AIR, ...   37 OISIN 2   122
    MAKING A WORLD ABOUT HER, PASSED FROM SIGHT . . . .   37 OISIN 2   V 123
    MAKING WAY FROM THE KINDLING SURGES, I RODE ON A   58 OISIN 3   161
      BRIDLE-PATH
    . . . THEY WILL RISE, MAKING CLOUDS WITH THEIR BREATH, . .   61 OISIN 3   202
    THEN FEAST, MAKING CONVERSE OF WARS, ...   62 OISIN 3   212
    THEN FEAST, MAKING CONVERSE OF EIRE, OF WARS, . . .   62 OISIN 3   V 212
    THOUGH LADS ARE MAKING PIKES AGAIN . . . .   131 OLD PENSIONER   7
    MAKING ALL ONE O'ER ROCK AND SEA AND SKIES! . . . .   687 TWO TITANS   28
    NOW MAKING BUSY WITH THE OAR, ...   742 DANAAN QUICK   2
MALACHI
    MALACHI STILT-JACK AM I, WHATEVER I LEARNED HAS RUN WILD,   623 HIGH TALK   9
    ALL METAPHOR, MALACHI, STILTS AND ALL. A BARNACLE GOOSE   623 HIGH TALK   11
MALEDICTION
    AND SANG MY MALEDICTION WITH THE REST. . . . . . .   537 HER VISION   24
MALICIOUS
    THERE ARE MALICIOUS THINGS, ALTHOUGH . . . .   435 FOR MY SON   V 10
    THE MIRROR OF MALICIOUS EYES . . . .   479 SELF AND SOUL   52
    BLENCHED BY THAT MALICIOUS DREAM . . . .   488 CRAZED MOON   16
    AND COCKED A MALICIOUS EYE, ...   527 AM OF IRELAND   25
MALIGN
    OF HIS DEATH AND CHANGE MALIGN. . . . .   648 ISLE STAT I 1   80
MALL
    THE MALL AND EADES'S GRAMMAR SCHOOL, ...   360 ALF POLLEXFEN   15
MALLET
    THAT WITH A MALLET OR A CHISEL MODELLED THESE . . . .   610 STATUES   10
MAN   SEE SERVING-MAN TRAVELLING-MAN FANCY-MAN JOURNEY-MAN BEGGAR-MAN
    BEEN SPOKEN OF WITH ANY MAN; . . . .   6 OISIN 1   56
    OF OISIN, THE YOUNG MAN, MY SON? . . . .   6 OISIN 1   V   60
    BY THIS YOUNG MAN, USHEEN MY SON?" . . . .   6 OISIN 1   V   60
    PRINCESS, BY THIS YOUNG MAN, MY SON?" . . . . . .   6 OISIN 1   V   61
    ON THIS YOUNG MAN, OISIN, MY SON?" . . . .   6 OISIN 1   V   61
    "I LOVED NO MAN, THOUGH KINGS BESOUGHT, ...   7 OISIN 1   V   62
    "I LOVED NO MAN, THOUGH CANNS BESOUGHT, ...   7 OISIN 1   V   62
    AND MANY A MAN OF LOFTY NAME, ...   7 OISIN 1   V   63
    AND A BEAUTIFUL YOUNG MAN FOLLOWED BEHIND . . . .   12 OISIN 1   144
    A BEAUTIFUL YOUNG MAN FOLLOWED BEHIND. . . . . . .   12 OISIN 1   V 145
    AND KNELT THERE, EVERY GIRL AND MAN, ...   15 OISIN 1   214
    AND KNELT THEM, EVERY MAID AND MAN, ...   15 OISIN 1   V 214
    A BEAUTIFUL YOUNG MAN DREAMED WITHIN . . . . . .   17 OISIN 1   248
    THEY HUSHED THEM, EVERY MAN AND MAID. . . . . . .   17 OISIN 1   V 235
    THERE WAS A WONDROUS YOUNG MAN SITTING. . . . . .   18 OISIN 1   V 252
    WITH A CLEAR VOICE THE YOUNG MAN CRIED, ...   18 OISIN 1   V 260
    "AN OLD MAN STIRS THE FIRE TO A BLAZE, ...   26 OISIN 1   400
    NOW, MAN OF CROZIERS, SHADOWS CALLED OUR NAMES . . .   29 OISIN 2   1
    AND HER BRIGHT BODY, SANG OF FAERY AND MAN . . . .   29 OISIN 2   7
    NOW, MAN OF CROSIERS, PHANTOMS DREW AROUND . . . .   29 OISIN 2   V   1
    AND HER BRIGHT BODY—NOW OF FAY AND MAN; . . . . .   29 OISIN 2   V   7
    AND TELL ME THAT YOU FOUND A MAN UNBID; . . . . .   33 OISIN 2   67
    AND MORE COMELY THAN MAN CAN MAKE THEM . . . . .   49 OISIN 3   32
    MORE COMELY THAN MAN MAY MAKE THEM, INLAID WITH SILVER   49 OISIN 3   V   29
      AND GOLD,
    HAVE FACES ALIVE WITH SUCH BEAUTY BEEN KNOWN TO THE SALT   50 OISIN 3   51
      EYE OF MAN,
    ARE FACES ALIVE WITH SUCH BEAUTY MADE KNOWN TO THE SALT   50 OISIN 3   V   51
      EYE OF MAN,
    ARE FACES ALIVE WITH SUCH BEAUTY MADE KNOWN TO THE SOFT   50 OISIN 3   V   51
      EYE OF MAN,
    AND, MAN OF THE MANY WHITE CROZIERS, A CENTURY THERE I   52 OISIN 3   77
      FORGOT
    AND, MAN OF THE MANY WHITE CROZIERS, A CENTURY THERE I   52 OISIN 3   81
      FORGOT
    -BUT IN DREAMS, MILD MAN OF THE CROZIERS, ...   53 OISIN 3   85
    SO WATCHED I WHEN, MAN OF THE CROZIERS, ...   54 OISIN 3   101
    THAT ONCE MORE MOVED IN MY BOSOM THE ANCIENT SADNESS OF   54 OISIN 3   107
      MAN,
    CAME AFTER THE HARD GAZE OF YOUTH, OR AN OLD MAN LIFTED   59 OISIN 3   170
      HIS HEAD;
    THE REST YOU HAVE HEARD OF, O CROZIERED MAN; . . . .   60 OISIN 3   189
    A CREEPING OLD MAN, FULL OF SLEEP, ...   60 OISIN 3   192

	PAGE	TITLE		LINE
MAN   (CONTINUED)
. . . AN OLD MAN SURROUNDED WITH DREAMS. . . . . 61 OISIN 3   196
NO LIVE MAN GOES THITHER. . . . . 62 OISIN 3   V 214
. . . AND NO MAN MAY WAR WITH THE STRONG SPIRITS WAGE: . . 62 OISIN 3   V 214
IT WERE SAD TO GAZE ON THE BLESSED AND NO MAN I LOVED OF
    OLD THERE: 63 OISIN 3   221
IT WAS SAD TO GAZE ON THE BLESSED AND NO MAN I LOVED OF
    OLD THERE: 63 OISIN 3   V 221
THERE WAS A MAN WHOM SORROW NAMED HIS FRIEND. . . . . 67 SAD SHEPHERD   1
AND THEN THE MAN WHOM SORROW NAMED HIS FRIEND . . . . 68 SAD SHEPHERD   8
AND THEN THE MAN WHOM SORROW NAMED HIS FRIEND . . . . 68 SAD SHEPHERD   17
THEN CRIED THE MAN WHOM SORROW NAMED HIS FRIEND: . . . 68 SAD SHEPHERD   V   8
FROM GIRL AND BOY AND MAN AND BEAST: . . . . 82 MAD KING GOLL   V   6
AND EVERY MUMBLING OLD MAN SAID, ... 82 MAD KING GOLL   V   9
AND EVERY WHISPERING OLD MAN SAID, ... 82 MAD KING GOLL   V   9
"THIS YOUNG MAN BRINGS THE AGE OF GOLD." . . . . . . 82 MAD KING GOLL   V 11
FOR HE WAS A MAN OF BOOKS. . . . . 93 FATHER OHART   24
MY MAN WAS A POOR FISHER . . . . 94 MOLL MAGEE   5
MY MAN GREW RED AND PALE, ... 95 MOLL MAGEE   22
SHE SAYS MY MAN WILL SURELY COME, ... 96 MOLL MAGEE   41
A THIN GREY MAN HALF LOST IN GATHERING NIGHT. . . . . 102 FERGUS DRUID   7
A THIN, GREY MAN, HALF-LOST IN GATHERING NIGHT. . . . 102 FERGUS DRUID   V 7
NO WOMAN'S LOVED ME, NO MAN SOUGHT MY HELP. . . . . . 103 FERGUS DRUID   26
NO MAIDEN LOVES ME, NO MAN SEEKS MY HELP, ... 103 FERGUS DRUID   V 26
NO WOMAN LOVES ME, NO MAN SEEKS MY HELP, ... 103 FERGUS DRUID   V 26
A MAN CAME SLOWLY FROM THE SETTING SUN, ... 105 CUCHULAIN SEA   1
"NO MAN ALIVE, NO MAN AMONG THE DEAD, ... 106 CUCHULAIN SEA   10
"NO MAN ALIVE, NO MAN AMONG THE DEAD, ... 106 CUCHULAIN SEA   10
BUT WHEREFORE NOW?" "THERE IS A MAN TO DIE: . . . . 107 CUCHULAIN SEA   23
"BUT YOU HAVE GROWN TO BE THE TALLER MAN." . . . . . 107 CUCHULAIN SEA   27
"HE IS THE MIGHTIEST MAN IN SHIP OR DUN." . . . . . . 107 CUCHULAIN SEA   28
SOME FEASTING MAN THAT THE SAME OATH HAS BOUND. . . . 108 CUCHULAIN SEA   38
SOME FEATING MAN THAT THE SAME OATH HAS BOUND." . . . 108 CUCHULAIN SEA V 38
AT LAST CUCHULAIN SPAKE, "SOME MAN HAS MADE . . . . . 109 CUCHULAIN SEA   47
SEEK OUT WHAT MAN HE IS." ONE WENT AND CAME. . . . . 109 CUCHULAIN SEA   51
SOME FEASTING MAN THAT THE SAME OATH HAS BOUND." . . . 109 CUCHULAIN SEA   54
CUCHULAIN CRIED, "I AM THE ONLY MAN . . . . 109 CUCHULAIN SEA   55
HE SPAKE TO THE YOUNG MAN, "IS THERE NO MAID . . . . 109 CUCHULAIN SEA   58
AT LAST CUCHULAIN SPAKE, "A YOUNG MAN STRAYS . . . . 109 CUCHULAIN SEA V 47
"SOME FEATING MAN THAT THE SAME OATH HAS BOUND." . . . 109 CUCHULAIN SEA V 54
BUT ONE MAN LOVED THE PILGRIM SOUL IN YOU, ... 121 YOU ARE OLD   7
MAN HAD NO MORE TO DO--- . . . . 123 DREAM OF DEATH V 8
YOUNG MAN, LIFT UP YOUR RUSSET BROW, ... 125 GOES FERGUS   4
THE MAN WHO DREAMED OF FAERYLAND . . . . 126 DREAM OF FAERY   T
A MAN WHO DREAMED OF FAIRYLAND . . . . 126 DREAM OF FAERY V   T
BUT WHEN A MAN POURED FISH INTO A PILE, ... 126 DREAM OF FAERY   5
NOW THAT THE EARTH HAD TAKEN MAN AND ALL: . . . . . . 128 DREAM OF FAERY   40
THE MAN HAS FOUND NO COMFORT IN THE GRAVE. . . . . . 128 DREAM OF FAERY   48
NOW THAT OLD EARTH HAD TAKEN MAN AND ALL: . . . . . . 128 DREAM OF FAERY   40
THAT COUNTRY WHERE A MAN CAN BE SO CROSSED: . . . . . 130 BOOK STORIES   16
THAT HE'S A LOVELESS MAN: GAY BELLS BRING LAUGHTER . . 130 BOOK STORIES   18
ANOTHER POOR MAN SENT FOR HIM, ... 132 FR GILLIGAN   7
"MAVRONE, MAVRONE! THE MAN HAS DIED . . . . 133 FR GILLIGAN   25
"AND IS THE POOR MAN DEAD?" HE CRIED. . . . . 133 FR GILLIGAN   33
"OCHONE, OCHONE! THE MAN HAS DIED, ... 133 FR GILLIGAN   V 25
THAT GOD GIVES UNTO MAN IN SLEEP. . . . . 138 TO IRELAND   V 22
MAN EVER JOURNEYS ON WITH THEM . . . . 139 TO IRELAND   29
AND A YOUNG MAN BROUGHT HIM RED WINE . . . . 144 HOST OF AIR   19
THE HANDSOMEST YOUNG MAN THERE, ... 145 HOST OF AIR   34
THE DESIRE OF MAN AND OF WOMAN . . . . 153 CHANGE BELOVED V   T
A MAN WITH A HAZEL WAND CAME WITHOUT SOUND: . . . . . 153 CHANGE BELOVED V   6
A MAN WITH A WAND OF HAZEL CAME WITHOUT SOUND: . . . . 153 CHANGE BELOVED V   6
I BECAME A MAN, A HATER OF THE WIND, ... 177 PAST GREATNESS   7
THEY FOUND AN OLD MAN RUNNING THERE: . . . . 190 BAILE AILLINN   25
AN OLD MAN CAUGHT THE HORSE'S HEAD . . . . 191 BAILE AILLINN   57
A YOUNG MAN CRIED AND KISSED HER HAND, ... 191 BAILE AILLINN   60
REMEMBER DEIRDRE AND HER MAN: . . . . 192 BAILE AILLINN   91
THAT OLD MAN CLIMBED: THE DAY GREW DIM: . . . . 194 BAILE AILLINN   134
FOR THIS YOUNG GIRL AND THIS YOUNG MAN . . . . 195 BAILE AILLINN   157
THERE'S NO MAN MAY LOOK UPON HER, NO MAN, ... 199 ARROW   3
THERE'S NO MAN MAY LOOK UPON HER, NO MAN, ... 199 ARROW   3
AN OLD MAN PLAYS THE BAGPIPES . . . . 214 HAPPY TOWNLAND   9
A BEAUTIFUL YOUNG MAN AND GIRL CAME UP . . . . 223 SHADOW WATER B   33
HAS HATED EVERY MAN THAT'S NOT IN LOVE, ... 224 SHADOW WATER B   51
THERE'S NOT A MAN BUT WILL BE GLAD OF IT . . . . . . 225 SHADOW WATER B   66
HAS BEAUTIFUL WOMEN TO PLEASE EVERY MAN. . . . . . . 228 SHADOW WATER B   144
THAT EVERY MAN SHOULD CARRY HIS OWN SOUL . . . . . . 235 SHADOW WATER B   299
WE'LL PUT THIS MAN TO DEATH. I PROMISE IT. . . . . . 238 SHADOW WATER B   363
WHEN I HAVE SAID FAREWELL TO THIS MAN HERE, ... 250 SHADOW WATER B   587
FOR NEITHER I NOR ANY LIVING MAN . . . . 250 SHADOW WATER B   588
IF ANY MAN DREW NEAR . . . . 254 WOMAN HOMER   1
"GO AND LOVE, GO AND LOVE, YOUNG MAN, ... 268 BROWN PENNY   5
YOU MOST OF ALL, SILENT AND FIERCE OLD MAN, ... 270 PARDON FATHERS   15
"COME OUT AND DIG FOR A DEAD MAN, ... 272 GREY ROCK   32
THE SHOUTING OF AN UNSEEN MAN: . . . . 274 GREY ROCK   76
WHERE BY OLD THORN-TREES THAT MAN STOOD: . . . . . . 274 GREY ROCK   80
THEREON A YOUNG MAN MET HIS EYE, ... 274 GREY ROCK   85
NO MAN SHOULD SEE TO DO ME HURT: . . . . 274 GREY ROCK   91
WHERE BY OLD THORN TREES THAT MAN STOOD: . . . . . . 274 GREY ROCK   V 80
"HE LIVES?" "HE LIVES AND IS A HEALTHY MAN." . . . . 280 TWO KINGS   84
WHAT MAN YOU HAVE LOST, WHAT EVIL YOU HAVE FOUND." . . 280 TWO KINGS   86

495

MAN   (CONTINUED)
AS ON THE BLUE LIGHT OF A SWORD, A MAN . . . .   283 TWO KINGS   148
BEING WEARIED OUT, I LOVE IN MAN THE CHILD? . . . . .   285 TWO KINGS   192
GIVING HIS HAND TO THAT MAN AND TO THIS, ...   286 TWO KINGS   V 218A
TO A WEALTHY MAN WHO PROMISED A SECOND SUBSCRIPTION . . .   287 TO WEALTHY MAN   T
FOR THEY ARE AT THEIR OLD TRICKS YET. A MAN . . . . .   292 TO A SHADE   9
WHOM MAN OR DEVIL CANNOT TIRE, ...   295 THREE BEGGARS   16
ONE OF YOU THREE IS A RICH MAN, ...   295 THREE BEGGARS   21
A SERVING MAID AND A SERVING MAN, ...   301 RUN PARADISE   V 13
A ONE-LEGGED, ONE-ARMED, ONE-EYED MAN . . . .   302 HOUR DAWN   V 1
BUT I'LL HAVE NO MAN CALL ME GHOST." . . . .   304 HOUR DAWN   41
"IT'S PLAIN THAT YOU ARE NO RIGHT MAN . . . .   306 HOUR DAWN   82
AND THERE'S NO MAN BUT COCKS HIS EAR . . . .   306 HOUR DAWN   99
THERE'S NOT A MAN CAN REPORT . . . .   319 DOLLS   8
THE MAN AND THE WOMAN BRING . . . .   319 DOLLS   10
AND THAT ENQUIRING MAN JOHN SYNGE COMES NEXT, ...   324 ROBERT GREGORY   25
OUR SIDNEY AND OUR PERFECT MAN, ...   325 ROBERT GREGORY   47
NOR PUBLIC MAN, NOR ANGRY CROWDS, ...   328 IRISH AIRMAN   V 10
NOR PUBLIC MAN, NOR CHEERING CROWDS, ...   328 IRISH AIRMAN   V 10
"THERE'S NOT A MAN OR WOMAN . . . .   333 SOLOMON SHEBA   19
ALL KNOW THE MAN THEIR NEIGHBOUR KNOWS. . . . .   337 SCHOLARS   10
AND EVERY MAN AND MAID AND BOY . . . .   337 TOM OROUGHLEY   2
NO SETTLED MAN. AND NOW THAT HE IS GONE . . . . . .   341 SHEP GOATHERD   55
HE CAME, BUT MAN IS A FOOL." . . . .   341 SHEP GOATHERD   74
I HEARD HIM FIRST, BUT MAN IS A FOOL." . . . .   341 SHEP GOATHERD   V 74
HEARING IT NOW HAVE SIGHED FOR THAT YOUNG MAN . . . .   342 SHEP GOATHERD   77
A MAN MAY FIND IN NO MAN . . . .   345 ON WOMAN   3
A MAN MAY FIND IN NO MAN . . . .   345 ON WOMAN   3
THE FRECKLED MAN WHO GOES . . . .   347 FISHERMAN   2
THIS WISE AND SIMPLE MAN. . . . .   347 FISHERMAN   8
THE DEAD MAN THAT I LOVED, ...   347 FISHERMAN   14
THE CRAVEN MAN IN HIS SEAT, ...   347 FISHERMAN   15
THE WITTY MAN AND HIS JOKE . . . .   347 FISHERMAN   19
THE CLEVER MAN WHO CRIES . . . .   347 FISHERMAN   21
IMAGINING A MAN, ...   348 FISHERMAN   28
A MAN WHO DOES NOT EXIST, ...   348 FISHERMAN   35
A MAN WHO IS BUT A DREAM! . . . .   348 FISHERMAN   36
AS A MAN DOES WHO HAS PUBLISHED A NEW BOOK, ...   350 HER PRAISE   3
A MAN CONFUSEDLY IN A HALF DREAM . . . .   351 HER PRAISE   8
A MAN—SO VAGUELY THAT HE SEEMED TO DREAM— . . . . .   351 HER PRAISE   V 8
A YOUNG MAN WHEN THE OLD MEN ARE DONE TALKING . . . .   356 BROKEN DREAMS   16
WILL SAY TO AN OLD MAN, "TELL ME OF THAT LADY . . . .   356 BROKEN DREAMS   17
THAT NEVER LOOKED UPON MAN WITH DESIRE, ...   358 PRESENCES   13
OR AN OLD MAN UPON A WINTER'S NIGHT. . . . .   359 WAR POEM   6
UPON A MELANCHOLY MAN . . . .   360 ALF POLLEXFEN   11
A HUMOROUS, UNAMBITIOUS MAN. . . . .   361 ALF POLLEXFEN   25
LAMENTING THAT A MAN SHOULD DIE! . . . .   361 ALF POLLEXFEN   38
THE MAN THAT LAPO AND THAT GUIDO KNEW? . . . .   368 EGO DOMINUS   26
THE MOST EXALTED LADY LOVED BY A MAN. . . . .   369 EGO DOMINUS   37
AN OLD MAN COCKED HIS EAR UPON A BRIDGE! . . . . . .   372 PHASES OF MOON   1
WERE DISTANT STILL. AN OLD MAN COCKED HIS EAR. . . .   372 PHASES OF MOON   7
WERE DISTANT. AN OLD MAN COCKED HIS EAR. . . . . .   372 PHASES OF MOON   V 7
THE CRADLES THAT A MAN MUST NEEDS BE ROCKED IN! . . .   373 PHASES OF MOON   34
BUT SUMMONS TO ADVENTURE AND THE MAN . . . .   373 PHASES OF MOON   37
AHERNE LAUGHED, THINKING OF THE MAN WITHIN, ...   375 PHASES OF MOON   85
REFORMER, MERCHANT, STATESMAN, LEARNED MAN, ...   376 PHASES OF MOON   98
BUT TAKE ME FOR SOME DRUNKEN COUNTRY MAN! . . . . . .   377 PHASES OF MOON   V 130
A MAN THAT FINDS GREAT BITTERNESS . . . .   379 SAINT HUNCH   2
UNDER THIS HUMP. GOD TRIES EACH MAN . . . .   379 SAINT HUNCH   5
THE PARTICULAR IS POUNDED TILL IT IS MAN. . . . . . .   382 VISION ROBART   6
LEARNED LIKE A MAN? PAUL VERONESE . . . .   386 ROBARTES DANCE   26
GIVE MAN HIS THOUGHT OR HIS MERE BODY? . . . .   386 ROBARTES DANCE   40
YOU HEARD THAT LABOURING MAN WHO HAD SERVED MY PEOPLE.   391 UNDER SATURN   11
   HE SAID
THIS MAN HAD KEPT A SCHOOL . . . .   392 EASTER 1916   24
THIS MAN HAD MANAGED A SCHOOL . . . .   392 EASTER 1916   V 24
THIS OTHER MAN I HAD DREAMED . . . .   393 EASTER 1916   31
A SHAPE WITH LION BODY AND THE HEAD OF A MAN, ...   402 SECOND COMING   14
YET CHOSE A BANDY-LEGGED SMITH FOR MAN. . . . . . .   404 FOR DAUGHTER   29
AND MANY A POOR MAN THAT HAS ROVED, ...   404 FOR DAUGHTER   38
AN AGED MAN IS BUT A PALTRY THING, ...   407 SAIL BYZANTIUM   9
A SERVING MAN THAT COULD DIVINE . . . .   410 TOWER   V 28
STRANGE, BUT THE MAN WHO MADE THE SONG WAS BLIND! . .   411 TOWER   49
WITH HOMER THAT WAS A BLIND MAN, ...   411 TOWER   52
I MUST RECALL A MAN THAT NEITHER LOVE . . . .   412 TOWER   74
COME OLD, NECESSITOUS, HALF-MOUNTED MAN! . . . . . .   412 TOWER   90
THE RED MAN THE JUGGLER SENT . . . .   412 TOWER   92
THE MAN DROWNED IN A BOG'S MIRE, ...   413 TOWER   95
TILL MAN MADE UP THE WHOLE, ...   415 TOWER   149
MAN MAKES A SUPERHUMAN . . . .   415 TOWER   164
MAN MAKES A SUPERMAN, ...   415 TOWER   V 164
SOME VIOLENT BITTER MAN, SOME POWERFUL MAN . . . . .   418 ANCEST HOUSES   17
SOME VIOLENT BITTER MAN, SOME POWERFUL MAN . . . . .   418 ANCEST HOUSES   17
AND LEAVE A WOMAN AND A MAN BEHIND . . . .   422 MY DESCENDANTS   3
TO LEAVE A WOMAN AND A MAN BEHIND . . . .   422 MY DESCENDANTS   V 3
A HEAVILY-BUILT FALSTAFFIAN MAN, ...   423 ROAD AT DOOR   2
A HEAVILY BUILT FALSTAFFIAN MAN, ...   423 ROAD AT DOOR   V 2
A MAN IS KILLED, OR A HOUSE BURNED, ...   425 STARES NEST   8
SUFFICE THE AGEING MAN AS ONCE THE GROWING BOY. . . .   427 PHANTOM HATRED   40
MAN IS IN LOVE AND LOVES WHAT VANISHES, ...   429 NINETEEN 19   42
A MAN IN HIS OWN SECRET MEDITATION . . . .   431 NINETEEN 19   69

MAN   (CONTINUED)

		PAGE	TITLE	LINE
A WOMAN AND A MAN,		436	FOR MY SON	27
EVERYTHING THAT MAN ESTEEMS		438	SONGS PLAY 2	9
A SIXTY-YEAR-OLD SMILING PUBLIC MAN.		443	SCHOOL CHILDR	8
A SIXTY YEAR OLD SMILING PUBLIC MAN.		443	SCHOOL CHILDR V	8
O LET HER CHOOSE A YOUNG MAN NOW AND ALL FOR HIS WILD SAKE."		450	OWEN AHERNE	24
A MAN YOUNG AND OLD FIRST LOVE		451	FIRST LOVE V	T
A CRAZY MAN THAT FOUND A CUP,		454	EMPTY CUP	1
AND WAS A PUSHING MAN		456	FRIENDS YOUTH	14
HOW SUCH A MAN PLEASED WOMEN MOST		458	SECRETS OF OLD	13
HOW SUCH A MAN HAD PLEASURED MOST		458	SECRETS OF OLD V	13
FOR THAT IS NATURAL TO A MAN		459	HIS WILDNESS	9
CEASE TO REMEMBER THE DELIGHTS OF YOUTH, TRAVEL-WEARIED AGED MAN:		459	FROM OEDIPUS	2
THE PARCHMENT WILL DISCLOSE TO SOME LEARNED MAN		461	HARUN RASHID	20
SHE SEEMED THE LEARNED MAN AND I THE CHILD:		467	HARUN RASHID	137
CAN HEAR THE ARMED MAN SPEAK.		470	HARUN RASHID	193
THAT STORMS ARE SHAKING, HEAR THE ARMED MAN SPEAK.		470	HARUN RASHID V	193
NO LIVING MAN CAN DRINK FROM THE WHOLE WINE.		474	ALL SOUL NIGHT	85
A MAN AWAITS HIS END		476	DEATH	3
A GREAT MAN IN HIS PRIDE		476	DEATH	7
MAN HAS CREATED DEATH.		476	DEATH	12
WHY SHOULD THE IMAGINATION OF A MAN		477	SELF AND SOUL	17
THAT MAN IS STRICKEN DEAF AND DUMB AND BLIND,		478	SELF AND SOUL	35
A LIVING MAN IS BLIND AND DRINKS HIS DROP.		478	SELF AND SOUL	41
THAT MAN IS DEAF AND DRUNK AND BLIND		478	SELF AND SOUL V	35
WHAT MATTER IF A BLIND MAN DRINK HIS DROP?		478	SELF AND SOUL V	41
OF BOYHOOD CHANGING INTO MAN:		479	SELF AND SOUL	46
THE UNFINISHED MAN AND HIS PAIN		479	SELF AND SOUL	47
THE FINISHED MAN AMONG HIS ENEMIES?--		479	SELF AND SOUL	49
A BLIND MAN BATTERING BLIND MEN:		479	SELF AND SOUL	60
THE FOLLY THAT MAN DOES		479	SELF AND SOUL	62
FOR ALL HIS TIMID HEART, THERE THAT SLOW MAN,		489	COOLE PARK 29	12
THAT MEDITATIVE MAN, JOHN SYNGE, AND THOSE,		489	COOLE PARK 29	13
AND IN THE MORNING'S GONE, NO MAN KNOWS WHY:		490	COOLE BALLYLEE	20
MAN SHIFTS ABOUT--ALL THAT GREAT GLORY SPENT--		491	COOLE BALLYLEE V	39
THE INTELLECT OF MAN IS FORCED TO CHOOSE		491	COOLE BALLYLEE V	40A
THE MIND OF MAN OR ELEVATE A RHYME:		492	COOLE BALLYLEE	45
"NEVER SHALL A YOUNG MAN,		492	ANNE GREGORY	1
"I HEARD AN OLD RELIGIOUS MAN		492	ANNE GREGORY	13
THE INTELLECT OF MAN IS FORCED TO CHOOSE		495	CHOICE	1
ALL THAT MAN IS,		497	BYZANTIUM	6
BEFORE ME FLOATS AN IMAGE, MAN OR SHADE,		497	BYZANTIUM	9
SHADE MORE THAN MAN, MORE IMAGE THAN A SHADE:		497	BYZANTIUM	10
MAN RUNS HIS COURSE:		499	VACILLATION	2
ALL WOMEN DOTE UPON AN IDLE MAN		500	VACILLATION	23
NO MAN HAS EVER LIVED THAT HAD ENOUGH		500	VACILLATION	25
I SAT, A SOLITARY MAN,		501	VACILLATION	36
ISAIAH'S COAL, WHAT MORE CAN MAN DESIRE?		502	VACILLATION	74
EZEKIEL'S COAL, WHAT MORE CAN MAN DESIRE?		502	VACILLATION V	74
DID I BECOME A CHRISTIAN MAN AND CHOOSE FOR MY BELIEF		503	VACILLATION	85
SENSE THAN A COMMON MAN?		507	STREAM AND SUN	10
THE SOLID MAN AND THE COXCOMB.		508	JANE BISHOP	7
THE SOLID MAN AND THE COXCOMB.		508	JANE BISHOP	14
THE SOLID MAN AND THE COXCOMB.		508	JANE BISHOP	21
THE SOLID MAN AND THE COXCOMB.		509	JANE BISHOP	28
MY FANCY ON A MAN,		515	GIRLS SONG B	3
SAW I AN OLD MAN YOUNG		515	GIRLS SONG B	11
OR YOUNG MAN OLD?		515	GIRLS SONG B	12
OR A YOUNG MAN OLD?		515	GIRLS SONG B V	12
"A MAN IF I BUT HELD HIM SO		521	THREE THINGS	9
FACE TO FACE MY RIGHTFUL MAN		521	THREE THINGS	16
A MAN MAY PUT PRETENCE AWAY		525	DANCING DAYS	19
ONE MAN, ONE MAN ALONE		526	AM OF IRELAND	6
ONE MAN, ONE MAN ALONE		526	AM OF IRELAND	6
ONE SOLITARY MAN		526	AM OF IRELAND	8
ONE MAN, AND ONE MAN ALONE		526	AM OF IRELAND V	6
ONE MAN, AND ONE MAN ALONE		526	AM OF IRELAND V	6
BIRD, BEAST, FISH OR MAN,		529	TOM LUNATIC	14
BEING MENTIONED WITH A MAN		531	FATHER CHILD	4
WHAT IF I LOOK UPON A MAN		532	BEFORE WORLD	9
WHERE MAN IS COMFORTED.		534	CONSOLATION	6
MY UTMOST PLEASURE WITH A MAN		535	CHOSEN	12
SHOULDERED A LITTER WITH A WOUNDED MAN,		537	HER VISION	14
THAT SUCH AS I HAD SUCH A MAN		539	MEETING	9
SUCH A MAN THE MOST."		539	MEETING	12
THE RICH MAN AND HIS AFFAIRS,		540	FROM ANTIGONE	3
WHETHER IT BE AN ANIMAL OR A MAN.		542	PARN FUNERAL 1	31
"ON, ON, MY DARLING MAN".		545	TO SAME TUNE 1	16
"WHO'D CARE TO DIG 'EM," SAID THE OLD, OLD MAN,		548	TO SAME TUNE 3	7
TIME I WERE BURIED," SAID THE OLD, OLD MAN.		548	TO SAME TUNE 3	10
"WHO'D CARE TO DIG 'EM," SAID THE OLD, OLD MAN,		548	TO SAME TUNE 3	17
TIME I WERE BURIED," SAID THE OLD, OLD MAN.		548	TO SAME TUNE 3	20
"WHO'D CARE TO DIG 'EM," SAID THE OLD, OLD MAN,		549	TO SAME TUNE 3	27
TIME I WERE BURIED," SAID THE OLD, OLD MAN.		549	TO SAME TUNE 3	30
SADDLE AND RIDE, I HEARD A MAN SAY,		549	SEVERED HEAD	1
IMAGES RIDE, I HEARD A MAN SAY,		549	SEVERED HEAD V	1
THAT SEEMED BUT A WILD WENCHING MAN:		550	SEVERED HEAD	16
WHAT IS THE GOOD OF A MAN AND HE		551	SONGS REWRIT 1	7
WHAT IS THE GOOD OF A MAN IF HE		551	SONGS REWRIT 1 V	7

MAN   (CONTINUED)
        OR ANYTHING ELSE BUT A MAN . . . .   552 SONGS REWRIT 2 V   9
        FROM ALL THAT MAKES A WISE OLD MAN . . . .   553 PRAYER OLD AGE   5
        A FOOLISH, PASSIONATE MAN. . . . .   553 PRAYER OLD AGE   12
        AN ABSTRACT GREEK ABSURDITY HAS CRAZED THE MAN-- . . 556 RIBH PATRICK   1
        . . . MAN, WOMAN, CHILD (A DAUGHTER OR A SON), . .   556 RIBH PATRICK   2
        AS MAN, AS BEAST, AS AN EPHEMERAL FLY BEGETS, GODHEAD 556 RIBH PATRICK   5
           BEGETS GODHEAD,
        ABSTRACTIONS OF THE GREEK PHILOSOPHY HAVE CRAZED THE MAN, 556 RIBH PATRICK V 1
        WHY DO I HATE MAN, WOMAN OR EVENT? . . . . . .   558 RIBH CHRISTIAN   7
        A PASSION-DRIVEN EXULTANT MAN SINGS OUT . . . .   560 WHENCE COME   5
        THE FOUR AGES OF MAN . . . .   561 FOUR AGES MAN   T
        SEVENTY YEARS MAN AND BOY, ...   567 FROM JAPANESE   8
        NO RAGGED BEGGAR MAN, ...   567 FROM JAPANESE V   6
        I SHOULD BE BLAMED, YOUNG MAN. . . . .   569 THREE BUSHES   6
        "I LOVE A MAN IN SECRET, ...   569 THREE BUSHES   15
        DID EVER MAN RIDE SUCH A RACE? . . . .   570 THREE BUSHES   47
        AND O HE WAS A GOOD MAN . . . .   571 THREE BUSHES   68
        BESIDE HER LADY'S MAN, ...   571 THREE BUSHES   72
        WHAT SORT OF MAN IS COMING . . . .   572 LADYS 2ND SONG   1
        HE MUST GROW A FAMOUS MAN . . . .   576 WHAT THEN   2
        AND WHETHER A MAN BE RICH OR POOR . . . . . .   582 ROGER CASEMENT V   19
        FOUND MANY A FAMOUS MAN THERE, ...   584 GHOST ROG CASE   35
        BUT FOR WHAT SOME TRAVELLING MAN . . . .   585 ORAHILLY   21
        AND PRAISE OUR CHOSEN MAN, ...   586 PARNELLITES   2
        EVERY MAN THAT SINGS A SONG . . . .   586 PARNELLITES   19
        FOR PARNELL WAS A PROUD MAN, ...   587 PARNELLITES   21
        AND A PROUD MAN'S A LOVELY MAN, ...   587 PARNELLITES   23
        THE WILD OLD WICKED MAN . . . .   587 OLD WICKED MAN   T
        SAID THAT WILD OLD WICKED MAN . . . .   587 OLD WICKED MAN   3
        FROM THE OLD MAN IN THE SKIES. . . . .   588 OLD WICKED MAN   8
        I HAVE WHAT NO YOUNG MAN CAN HAVE . . . . . .   588 OLD WICKED MAN   14
        THEN SAID SHE TO THAT WILD OLD MAN, ...   588 OLD WICKED MAN   19
        I GAVE IT ALL TO AN OLDER MAN, ...   588 OLD WICKED MAN   23
        THAT OLD MAN IN THE SKIES. . . . .   588 OLD WICKED MAN   24
        "A YOUNG MAN IN THE DARK AM I, ...   589 OLD WICKED MAN   37
        BUT A WILD OLD MAN IN THE LIGHT, ...   589 OLD WICKED MAN   38
        FROM THE OLD MAN IN THE SKIES . . . .   589 OLD WICKED MAN   56
        NO RIGHT-TAUGHT MAN DENIES. . . . .   590 OLD WICKED MAN   58
        BUT A COARSE OLD MAN AM I, ...   590 OLD WICKED MAN   59
        NO RIGHT TAUGHT MAN DENIES. . . . .   590 OLD WICKED MAN V   58
        PARNELL CAME DOWN THE ROAD, HE SAID TO A CHEERING MAN, 590 PARNELL   1
        THAT I MAY STAY A SOBER MAN . . . .   591 DRUNK SOBRIETY   3
        A DEAD MAN IN HIS GRAVE. . . . .   592 DRUNK SOBRIETY   12
        A DRUNKARD IS A DEAD MAN, ...   592 DRUNK SOBRIETY   15
        AND THERE I FOUND AN OLD MAN, AND THOUGH I PRAYED ALL DAY 593 PILGRIM   8
        AND THAT OLD MAN BESIDE ME, NOTHING WOULD HE SAY . . . 593 PILGRIM   9
        AND COME WITH LEARNED LOVERS OR WITH WHAT MAN YOU MAY, 593 PILGRIM V   23
        "O WHAT'S A WIFELESS MAN?" SAID HE, ...   594 COLONEL MARTIN   5
        AND O HE WAS A CLEVER MAN, ...   595 COLONEL MARTIN   39
        HIS WIFE HE FOUND AND THE RICH MAN . . . . . .   595 COLONEL MARTIN   43
        THE COLONEL SAID TO TOM HIS MAN, ...   596 COLONEL MARTIN   50
        A MAN WITH A PISTOL STOOD, ...   596 COLONEL MARTIN   56
        AND THE RICH MAN HAD PAID THEM WELL . . . . .   596 COLONEL MARTIN   57
        THAT THEY COULD NEVER SHOOT A MAN . . . . . .   596 COLONEL MARTIN   61
        FOR THINGS LIKE THESE WHAT DECENT MAN . . . .   598 MODEL LAUREATE   22
        A STATESMAN IS AN EASY MAN, ...   598 STONE CROSS   1
        SAID THE MAN IN THE GOLDEN BREASTPLATE . . . .   598 STONE CROSS   7
        NO MAN CAN KNOW A HAPPY MAN . . . .   598 STONE CROSS   11
        NO MAN CAN KNOW A HAPPY MAN . . . .   598 STONE CROSS   11
        NO MAN KNOWS WHICH IS WHICH, ...   599 STONE CROSS   14
        SAID THE MAN IN THE GOLDEN BREASTPLATE . . . .   599 STONE CROSS   15
        SAID THE MAN IN THE GOLDEN BREASTPLATE . . . .   599 STONE CROSS   23
        SAID THE OLD MAN IN THE GOLDEN BREASTPLATE . .   599 STONE CROSS V   23
        AND HERE'S JOHN SYNGE HIMSELF, THAT ROOTED MAN, .   603 GALLERY REVIS   48
        AND HERE'S JOHN SYNGE, A MEDITATIVE MAN, . . .   603 GALLERY REVIS V   48
        A GOOD MAN ON A HORSE . . . .   604 YOU CONTENT   12
        SANDYMOUNT CORBETS, THAT NOTABLE MAN . . . .   604 YOU CONTENT   13
        BEST PLEASE A WANDERING MAN. . . . .   606 SONGS BURDEN 1   17
        PRAISE EVERY MAN THAT CAME AGAIN, ...   608 SONGS BURDEN 3   7
        PRAISE EVERY MAN THAT FELL. . . . .   608 SONGS BURDEN 3   8
        WHO WAS THE FIRST MAN SHOT THAT DAY? . . . . .   608 SONGS BURDEN 3   10
        A MAN I PRAISE THAT ONCE IN TARA'S HALLS . . .   609 IN TARAS HALLS   1
        I SHALL BE OLD INDEED." THEREON THE MAN . . .   609 IN TARAS HALLS   10
        AND NO MAN KNOWS WHAT TREADS THE GRASS. . . .   614 MARCH SONGS 2   10
        AND NO MAN KNOWS WHAT TREADS THE GRASS. . . .   615 MARCH SONGS 2   20
        AND NO MAN KNOWS WHAT TREADS THE GRASS. . . .   615 MARCH SONGS 2   30
        "ON, ON, MY DARLING MAN." . . . .   616 MARCH SONGS 3   16
        "OH, ON, MY DARLING MAN." . . . .   616 MARCH SONGS 3 V   16
        FOR DEATH WHO TAKES WHAT MAN WOULD KEEP, . . .   620 JOHN KINSELLA   3
        LEAVES WHAT MAN WOULD LOSE. . . . .   620 JOHN KINSELLA   4
        NONE OTHER KNOWS WHAT PLEASURES MAN . . . . .   620 JOHN KINSELLA   9
        LIKE AN OLD JEW MAN, ...   620 JOHN KINSELLA   14
        TO KEEP THE SOUL OF MAN ALIVE, ...   620 JOHN KINSELLA   19
        NO MAN GROWS OLD, NO GIRL GROWS COLD, ...   621 JOHN KINSELLA   31
        OR SEEM PLAUSIBLE TO A MAN OF SENSE. . . . . .   624 APPARITIONS   4
        WHEN A MAN GROWS OLD HIS JOY . . . .   624 APPARITIONS   17
        NOT A MAN BUT DELACROIX. . . . .   625 NATIVITY   4
        KNOW WHY AN OLD MAN SHOULD BE MAD. . . . . . .   626 OLD MEN BE MAD   20
        OR THE MAN THAT MADE THE MOTORS? . . . . . .   627 STATES HOLIDAY   20
        WOULD NOT MAKE HIM A MAN. . . . .   628 JANE MOUNTAIN   4

498

```
                                                  PAGE    TITLE            LINE
MAN   (CONTINUED)
      HER VIOLENT MAN . . . . . . . . . . . .      628  JANE MOUNTAIN        16
      MAYBE AT LAST, BEING BUT A BROKEN MAN, . . . .  629  CIRCUS ANIMALS      3
      AND WHEN THE FOOL AND BLIND MAN STOLE THE BREAD  630  CIRCUS ANIMALS     25
      YET HERE'S A TRAVELLED MAN THAT KNOWS  . . . .  631  POLITICS            5
      THE MAN AND THE ECHO . . . . . . . . . .      632  MAN AND ECHO         T
      MAN AND THE ECHO . . . . . . . . . . .        632  MAN AND ECHO    V    T
      WHILE MAN CAN STILL HIS BODY KEEP  . . . . .   633  MAN AND ECHO        25
      A MAN THAT HAD SIX MORTAL WOUNDS, A MAN . . .  634  CUCHULAIN COMF       1
      A MAN THAT HAD SIX MORTAL WOUNDS, A MAN . . .  634  CUCHULAIN COMF       1
      CAME CREEPING UP BECAUSE THE MAN WAS STILL.    634  CUCHULAIN COMF      10
      ALL MUST TOGETHER DO." THAT DONE, THE MAN . .  634  CUCHULAIN COMF      17
      MANY TIMES MAN LIVES AND DIES  . . . . . .     637  BEN BULBEN          13
      WHETHER MAN DIE IN HIS BED . . . . . . . .     637  BEN BULBEN          17
      IS THE WORST MAN HAS TO FEAR. . . . . . .      637  BEN BULBEN          20
      AND A MAN IS FIGHTING MAD, . . . . . . .       638  BEN BULBEN          28
      EVEN THE WISEST MAN GROWS TENSE  . . . . .     638  BEN BULBEN          33
      BRING THE SOUL OF MAN TO GOD, . . . . . .      638  BEN BULBEN          40
      A MAN HAS THE FIELDS OF HEAVEN, . . . . .      643  SONG FAERIES         1
      A MAN HAS A HOPE FOR HEAVEN, . . . . . .       643  SONG FAERIES    V    1
      MORE GRIEF IS MINE.  NO MAN SHALL EVER STOOP . 661  ISLE STAT II 1      62
      A MAN WHO BY A DEAD MAN STOOD. . . . . . .     671  ISLE STAT II 3     124
      A MAN WHO BY A DEAD MAN STOOD. . . . . . .     671  ISLE STAT II 3     124
      A MAN HAS A HOPE FOR HEAVEN, . . . . . .       676  ISLE STAT II 3     248
      DOTH STILL THE MAN WHOM EACH STERN ROVER FEARS, 678  ISLE STAT II 3     295
      TWO SPIRIT THINGS A MAN HATH FOR HIS FRIENDS:  686  DRAWING-ROOM         5
      THE DARK STILL MAN, HAS COME AND SAYS 'TIS SIN. 692  MOSADA 1           47
      HE WAS A MAN MOST LEARNED AND MOST MILD,       692  MOSADA 1           51
      ALONG THE SEA: AND MANY A MAN GREW HUSHED . .  693  MOSADA 1           86
      FAMOUS, A MAN OF RULES, A VICTOR.  STANDS . .  709  FERENCZ RENYI        9
      HAYNAU, THE MAN OF SYSTEM, LIFTS HIS HAND . .  712  FERENCZ RENYI       62
      A LITTLE WITHERED MAN, AND OLD. . . . . .      716  FAIRY DOCTOR         4
      THE MAN WHOSE HOUR OF DEATH DRAWS NIGH, . .    716  FAIRY DOCTOR         6
      THE LITTLE WITHERED MAN, AND OLD. . . . .      717  FAIRY DOCTOR        24
      WITHOUT THERE OF A LITTLE, LIGHT OLD MAN:      720  WITCH VIVIEN        13
      THERE STOOD A MAN, OF MEN THE LEAST--          729  PRIEST FAIRY        24
      "MAN OF WISDOM, FROM THY SLEEPING  . . . .     729  PRIEST FAIRY        39
      "MAN OF WISDOM, DOST THOU KNOW . . . . .       729  PRIEST FAIRY        47
      TWO SPIRIT-THINGS A MAN HATH FOR HIS FRIENDS-- 734  QUATRAIN APHOR       5
      TWO SPIRIT THINGS A MAN HATH FOR HIS FRIENDS:  734  QUATRAIN APHOR  V    5
      THE MAN IS GONE WHO GUIDED YE, UNWEARY, . .    738  MOURN THEN ON        3
      THE MAN IS GONE WHO FROM HIS LONELY STATION    738  MOURN THEN ON        7
      AND HER DIM WAVE BIDS MAN BE NO MORE GLAD, .   738  YOU ARE SAD         11
      BUT WOULD TURN HOME AGAIN.  NO MAN HAD DOUBTS . 749  SHADOW WATER A      38
      NO MAN NOR WOMAN HAS LOVED OTHERWISE . . .     750  SHADOW WATER A      64
      NO MAN OR WOMAN HAS LOVED OTHERWISE  . . .     750  SHADOW WATER A  V   64
      AND NO MAN KILL ME: FOR SOME WIND HAS BLOWN    751  SHADOW WATER A      97
      THE TIDE NARROWS BETWEEN, AND ONE OLD MAN .    752  SHADOW WATER A     118
      BEYOND THE SAIL A MAN WITH A RED CROWN  . .    752  SHADOW WATER A     126
      I SWEAR IT.  LET EVERY MAN DRAW OUT HIS SWORD. 758  SHADOW WATER A     230
      TO CRY HIS FOLDING CRY.  THERE IS SOME MAN .   760  SHADOW WATER A  V  253
      BUT HER GOOD MAN ANSWERED HER  . . . . .       772  SONG DEIRDRE 1  V    9
      NAMES WHEREBY A MAN HAS KNOWN  . . . . .       775  AGAINST WITCH        5
      BUT THE MAN IS THRICE FORLORN, . . . . .       776  AGAINST WITCH       26
      BUT THE MAN IS TWICE FORLORN, . . . . .        776  AGAINST WITCH   V   26
      AND I MET WITH A MAN THAT WAS NO RIGHT MAN .   779  GOING THE ROAD       3
      AND I MET WITH A MAN THAT WAS NO RIGHT MAN .   779  GOING THE ROAD       3
      "THE MAN THAT I PRAISE," . . . . . . . .       780  WELL AND TREE        1
      "THE MAN THAT I PRAISE," . . . . . . . .       780  WELL AND TREE        9
      A MAN IS LOST OF A SUDDEN, . . . . . . .       783  GREY ROUND           9
      WHAT BONDS NO MAN COULD UNBIND, . . . . .      785  WOMANS BEAUTY       22
      A MAN BUT WILL GIVE YOU HIS LOVE . . . . .     786  YOUR HEART          17
      WHAT MAN IS AT YOUR SIDE? . . . . . . .        786  YOUR HEART          28
      IS THERE NO MAN AT YOUR SIDE?  . . . . .       786  YOUR HEART      V   28
      LOVELY LADY OR GALLANT MAN . . . . . . .       788  HAWTHORN TREE        7
      LOVELY LADY AND GALLANT MAN . . . . . .        788  HAWTHORN TREE   V    7
      NOW A NOTABLE MAN ON STAGE AND ON SCREEN:      790  DEDICATION           8
      CAN GHOST OR MAN BE SATISFIED? . . . . .       791  REPRISALS            4
MANACLE
      MANACLE HIS SOUL UPON THE RED SEA BOTTOM.      372  ON GOING HOUSE      16
MANAGE
      MANAGE THE TALK UNTIL HER NAME COME ROUND.     351  HER PRAISE          14
      MANAGE TO TALK UNTIL HER NAME COME ROUND. .    351  HER PRAISE      V   14
MANAGED
      THIS MAN HAD MANAGED A SCHOOL  . . . . .       392  EASTER 1916     V   24
MANAGEMENT
      THEATRE BUSINESS, MANAGEMENT OF MEN. . . .     260  FASC DIFFICULT      11
MANANAN
      DEEP SUNKEN ON THE BLADE'S LENGTH, "MANANAN:"   38  OISIN 2         V  128
      THE DRUID SWORD OF MANANAN, HE GREW  . . .      40  OISIN 2         V  174
      AND TELL HOW MANANAN SACKED MURIAS  . . .      766  SHADOW WATER A     377
MANANAN'S
      AND MANANAN'S DARK TOWER, STONE BY STONE,       45  OISIN 2         V  236
MANANNAN
      THEREON IN OGHAM LETTERS, "MANANNAN":           38  OISIN 2            128
      AND WHEN HE KNEW THE SWORD OF MANANNAN          40  OISIN 2            173
      ALL MANNIONS COME FROM MANANNAN, . . . .       606  SONGS BURDEN 1      10
MANANNAN'S
      AND MANANNAN'S DARK TOWER, STONE AFTER STONE,   45  OISIN 2            236
MAN-AT-ARMS
      TWO MEN HAVE FOUNDED HERE.  A MAN-AT-ARMS .    420  MY HOUSE            21
```

499

MAN-AT-ARMS (CONTINUED)
   TWO MEN HAVE FOUND IT HERE. A MAN-AT-ARMS • • • • • •   420 MY HOUSE   V   21
MANCINI'S
   MANCINI'S PORTRAIT OF AUGUSTA GREGORY, • • • • • • • •   602 GALLERY REVIS   25
MANE
   AND 'TWEEN HIS EARS, ABOVE HIS MANE, • • • • • • • •   2 OISIN 1   V 7AA
   ON DELICATE SENSITIVE EAR OR TOSSING MANE, • • • • • •   433 NINETEEN 19   115
MANES
   I HEAR THE SHADOWY HORSES, THEIR LONG MANES A-SHAKE, • •   154 BELOVED PEACE   1
   AND HIDING THEIR TOSSING MANES AND THEIR TUMULTUOUS FEET.   154 BELOVED PEACE   12
   AND HIDE THEIR TOSSING MANES AND THEIR TUMULTUOUS FEET.   154 BELOVED PEACE   V   12
MANGAN
   WITH DAVIS, MANGAN, FERGUSON, • • • • • • • • •   138 TO IRELAND   18
MAN-HEADED
   HAS EVER COME BUT THOSE MAN-HEADED BIRDS, • • • • •   226 SHADOW WATER B   99
   THEY HAVE MADE YOU FOLLOW THE MAN-HEADED BIRDS, • • •   231 SHADOW WATER B   204
   THEY HAVE BADE YOU FOLLOW THE MAN-HEADED BIRDS, • • •   231 SHADOW WATER B V 204
MANHOOD
   POUR WINE AND DANCE IF MANHOOD STILL HAVE PRIDE, • • •   311 MOUNTAIN TOMB   1
   ALL THOSE THAT MANHOOD TRIED, OR CHILDHOOD LOVED • • •   327 ROBERT GREGORY   91
   WHAT MANHOOD LED THE DANCE! • • • • • • • • •   488 CRAZED MOON   12
MANIFOLD
   BY MANIFOLD ILLUSION! BUT MAN'S LIFE IS THOUGHT, • • • •   563 MERU   3
MANKIND
   AND WHISPERED TO MANKIND. • • • • • • • • •   133 FR GILLIGAN   20
   POUR WINE AND DANCE, IF MANKIND STILL HAVE PRIDE, • • •   311 MOUNTAIN TOMB V   1
   THAT LOVED HIS LEARNING BETTER THAN MANKIND, • • • •   324 ROBERT GREGORY   18
   WITH THE MINUTE PARTICULARS OF MANKIND? • • • • • •   384 VISION ROBART   42
   MANKIND INANIMATE PHANTASY. • • • • • • • • •   406 IN TIME OF WAR   5
   MANKIND INANIMATE FANTASY. • • • • • • • • •   406 IN TIME OF WAR V   5
   WHAT IF THOSE THINGS THE GREATEST OF MANKIND • • • •   418 ANCEST HOUSES   38
   TO AFFLICT MANKIND, BUT NOW • • • • • • • •   431 NINETEEN 19   86
   AND SO REMEMBERS THAT WHEN ALL MANKIND • • • • •   447 COLONUS PRAISE   26
   • • • ALL ENTANGLEMENTS OF MANKIND GROW, • • • •   459 FROM OEDIPUS   5
   • • • HAD DRAGGED HIM DOWN INTO MANKIND. • • • •   481 BLOOD AND MOON   20
   "HEAR, GENTLEMEN, LADIES, AND ALL MANKIND! • • • •   544 TO SAME TUNE 1   2
   WHERE ARE THE CAPTAINS THAT GOVERN MANKIND? • • • •   548 TO SAME TUNE 3   22
   FROM EVERY THOUGHT OF GOD MANKIND HAS HAD. • • • •   558 RIBH CHRISTIAN   15
   FORGOTTEN ELSE BY MANKIND, • • • • • • • •   576 ACRE OF GRASS   23
   WHERE ARE THE CAPTAINS THAT GOVERN MANKIND? • • • •   615 MARCH SONGS 2   22
   "HEAR, GENTLEMEN, LADIES, AND ALL MANKIND! • • • •   615 MARCH SONGS 3   2
   PROFANE PERFECTION OF MANKIND. • • • • • • • •   639 BEN BULBEN   52
   AT CHANCES AND AT MOMENTS WITH MANKIND. • • • • •   721 WITCH VIVIEN   35
MAN-KIND
   OF GOD-KIND AND MAN-KIND. • • • • • • • •   770 BLOOD BOND   6
MANLY
   THERE ONE THAT RUFFLED IN A MANLY POSE • • • • •   489 COOLE PARK 29   11
MANNA
   AND--MERCY IS THE MANNA OF THE WORLD. • • • • • •   697 MOSADA 2   41
MANNED
   AND MANNED AN ARGOSY AND SAILING DIED. • • • • •   693 MOSADA 1   89
MANNER
   ALL MANNER OF BLESSED SOULS, • • • • • • • •   167 BLESSED   14
   ALL MANNER OF BLESSEDEST SOULS, • • • • • • •   167 BLESSED   V   14
   HE HAS FOUND, AFTER THE MANNER OF HIS KIND, • • • •   373 PHASES OF MOON   12
MANNERS
   FINE MANNERS, LIBERAL SPEECH, • • • • • • • •   506 REMORSE SPEECH   7
MANNION
   BUT MANNION IS MY NAME, • • • • • • • • •   605 SONGS BURDEN 1   2
MANNIONS
   ALL MANNIONS COME FROM MANANNAN, • • • • • • •   606 SONGS BURDEN 1   10
MAN-PICKER
   MAN-PICKER NIAMH LEANT AND SIGHED • • • • • •   611 NEWS ORACLE   5
MAN'S
   FOR NO MAN'S CRY SHALL EVER MOUNT SO FAR! • • • •   36 OISIN 2   108
   NOR NO MAN'S CRY SHALL EVER MOUNT SO FAR! • • • •   36 OISIN 2   V 108
   LIGHT IS MAN'S LOVE, AND LIGHTER IS MAN'S RAGE! • • •   45 OISIN 2   243
   LIGHT IS MAN'S LOVE, AND LIGHTER IS MAN'S RAGE! • • •   45 OISIN 2   243
   IN MIDST OF AN OLD MAN'S BOSOM! OWLS RUFFLING AND PACING   50 OISIN 3   47
     AROUND
   IN THE MIDST OF AN OLD MAN'S BOSOM! OWLS RUFFLING   50 OISIN 3   V   47
     AND PACING AROUND
   • • • OR WAS LIFTED AN OLD MAN'S MILD HEAD. • • • •   59 OISIN 3   V 170
   IN EACH MAN'S EARS OF SORROW-- • • • • • • • •   70 CLOAK BOAT   V   14
   AND NOW THE OLD MAN'S DREAMS ARE GONE, • • • • •   98 FOXHUNTER   19
   FIRE IS IN THE OLD MAN'S EYES, • • • • • • • •   98 FOXHUNTER   29
   A FIRE IS IN THE OLD MAN'S EYES, • • • • • • •   98 FOXHUNTER   V   29
   COME NEAR, THAT NO MORE BLINDED BY MAN'S FATE, • • •   101 ROSE UPON ROOD   9
   AND GOD WOULD BID MAN'S WARFARE CEASE, • • • •   113 ROSE OF PEACE V   13
   HAD BLOTTED OUT MAN'S IMAGE AND HIS CRY. • • • •   120 SORROW OF LOVE   4
   COULD BUT COMPOSE MAN'S IMAGE AND HIS CRY. • • • •   120 SORROW OF LOVE   12
   THE SICK MAN'S WIFE OPENED THE DOOR! • • • •   133 FR GILLIGAN   31
   THEY HUDDLE FROM MAN'S PONDERING MIND, • • •   138 TO IRELAND   V   26
   AND NOT WITH HIS OWN VOICE OR A MAN'S VOICE, • • •   183 QUEEN MAEVE   74
   BUT WITH A MAN'S HEAD, OR A FAIR WOMAN'S, • • • •   233 SHADOW WATER B   245
   THE YOUNG MAN'S SONG • • • • • • • • •   268 BROWN PENNY   V   T
   SHE WOULD NOT LOOK IN ANY KNOWN MAN'S FACE • • •   280 TWO KINGS   73
   WOULD NEVER LOOK AGAIN ON KNOWN MAN'S FACE." • • •   280 TWO KINGS   75
   WILL NEVER LOOK AGAIN ON KNOWN MAN'S FACE." • • •   280 TWO KINGS   V   75
   END IN A BEAUTIFUL MAN'S OR WOMAN'S BODY. • • •   374 PHASES OF MOON   64
   CAUGHT BY AN OLD MAN'S JUGGLERIES • • • • •   411 TOWER   60

	PAGE	TITLE		LINE
MAN'S (CONTINUED)				
SURELY AMONG A RICH MAN'S FLOWERING LAWNS,	417	ANCEST HOUSES		1
IN PITY FOR MAN'S DARKENING THOUGHT	438	SONGS PLAY 2		1
MAN'S OWN RESINOUS HEART HAS FED.	438	SONGS PLAY 2		16
O SELF-BORN MOCKERS OF MAN'S ENTERPRISE;	445	SCHOOL CHILDR		56
BUT WHAT CARE I THAT LONG FOR A MAN'S LOVE?	448	HERO GIRL FOOL		17
THAT MAKE A MAN'S SOUL OR A WOMAN'S SOUL	465	HARUN RASHID		93
IS A MAN'S MOCKERY OF THE CHANGELESS SOUL."	465	HARUN RASHID		102
INTO THE FROG-SPAWN OF A BLIND MAN'S DITCH,	479	SELF AND SOUL		59
FROM MAN'S BLOOD-SODDEN HEART ARE SPRUNG	502	VACILLATION		67
YOUNG MAN'S SONG	516	MANS SONG		T
FOR A MAN'S ATTENTION	533	FIRST CONFESS		10
TOO OLD FOR A MAN'S LOVE I STOOD IN RAGE	536	HER VISION		3
TOO OLD FOR A MAN'S LOVE I STOOD AND RAGED	536	HER VISION	V	1
BY MANIFOLD ILLUSION; BUT MAN'S LIFE IS THOUGHT,	563	MERU		3
GRANT ME AN OLD MAN'S FRENZY,	576	ACRE OF GRASS		13
AN OLD MAN'S EAGLE MIND.	576	ACRE OF GRASS		24
AND A PROUD MAN'S A LOVELY MAN,	587	PARNELLITES		23
WHEN AN OLD MAN'S BLOOD GROWS COLD?	588	OLD WICKED MAN		13
A DRUNKEN MAN'S PRAISE OF SOBRIETY	591	DRUNK SOBRIETY		T
IN A YOUNG MAN'S BED."	594	COLONEL MARTIN		17
THE COLONEL KNOCKED ON THE RICH MAN'S DOOR,	595	COLONEL MARTIN		28
THE COLONEL KNOCKED ON A RICH MAN'S DOOR,	595	COLONEL MARTIN	V	28
THINK WHERE MAN'S GLORY MOST BEGINS AND ENDS,	604	GALLERY REVIS		54
AS THAT WHICH CLEANS MAN'S DIRTY SLATE.	633	MAN AND ECHO		24
OR WHISPER THAT A MAN'S A FOOL	635	BLACK TOWER		12
IN EACH MAN'S EARS OF SORROW,	666	ISLE STAT II 3		14
THERE WAS SOME TALKING OF MAN'S GOD,	725	LEGEND		19
GROWS YOUNG AND A MAN'S HEART GROWS OLD IN A TWINKLING.	761	SHADOW WATER A		263
I HAVE MET IN A MAN'S HOUSE	785	YOUR HEART		3
MANSION				
OF THAT OLD GEORGIAN MANSION, MIX	475	EVA GORE-BOOTH		16
A HEAVENLY MANSION, RAGING IN THE DARK,	491	COOLE BALLYLEE	V	40D
A HEAVENLY MANSION, RAGING IN THE DARK.	495	CHOICE		4
LIVE IN A HEAVENLY MANSION,	513	JANE TALK BISH		5
BUT LOVE HAS PITCHED HIS MANSION IN	513	JANE TALK BISH		15
THE BARRED WOODPECKER'S MANSION IS AND DEEP,	659	ISLE STAT II 1		23
AND WHO WILL THROW HIS MANSION DOWN	671	ISLE STAT II 3		135
AND THROUGH THE MANSION OF THE SPIRIT ROVE	681	SEEKER		2
HER HANGING MANSION. GIVE TO ME, I PRAY,	698	MOSADA 2		52
MANSIONS				
MANSIONS OF MEMORIES AND MELLOW THOUGHTS	721	WITCH VIVIEN		21
MANTEGNA'S				
A THOUGHTLESS IMAGE OF MANTEGNA'S THOUGHT--	537	HER VISION		20
MANTLING				
AT THE MANTLING OF THE BLOOD.	453	DEATH OF HARE		6
OR MANTLING OF THE BLOOD.	453	DEATH OF HARE	V	6
MANUSCRIPT				
AND NOW HE SEEKS IN BOOK OR MANUSCRIPT	373	PHASES OF MOON		19
MANY				
OF MANY A FIGURED EMBROIDERY;	4	OISIN 1		27
THAT MANY A PEACEFUL MOMENT HAD,	4	OISIN 1		35
OF MANY A FIGURED CREATURE STRANGE,	4	OISIN 1	V	27
OF PRINCES THERE IS MANY A ONE."	6	OISIN 1	V	61
AND MANY A PRINCE OF LOFTY NAME;	7	OISIN 1	V	63
AND MANY A MAN OF LOFTY NAME,	7	OISIN 1	V	63
FULL MANY BOWING KINGS BESOUGHT ME,	7	OISIN 1	V	67
AND MANY PRINCES OF HIGH NAME.	7	OISIN 1	V	68
AND MANY A MILE IS THE FAERY STATE,	9	OISIN 1	V	103
AND BID ME STAY, WITH MANY A TEAR;	10	OISIN 1		113
WHERE MANY A TRUMPET-TWISTED SHELL	13	OISIN 1		160
LIKE SOOTY FINGERS, MANY A TREE	13	OISIN 1		171
WE RODE ON MURMURING. MANY A SHELL	13	OISIN 1	V	159
AND ON THE SHORES WERE MANY BOATS	14	OISIN 1		188
AND TRIMMED WITH MANY A CRIMSON FEATHER;	15	OISIN 1		206
TRIMMED ROUND WITH MANY A CRIMSON FEATHER;	15	OISIN 1	V	206
OF MANY A SLAUGHTERED FOREST ROVER.	17	OISIN 1	V	249A
SAVE ONLY MANY TIMES MY NAME.	25	OISIN 1		375
SHONE MANY TIMES AMONG THE GLIMMERING FLOWERS	30	OISIN 2		21
AND SHIVERED, KNOWING THE ISLE OF MANY FEARS,	30	OISIN 2		25
BURST FROM A GREAT DOOR MARRED BY MANY A BLOW	31	OISIN 2		29
OF MANY THOUSAND STEPS. SAT EITHER SIDE,	31	OISIN 2	V	35
FULL MANY MORE, WHEN PEERED A MAIDEN SWEET	33	OISIN 2	V	68F
THROUGH MANY SHAPES; I LUNGED AT THE SMOOTH THROAT	40	OISIN 2		175
THE DEAD GOD'S SWORD, TO MANY FORMS HE GREW,	40	OISIN 2	V	175
TO MANY SHAPES; I LUNGED AT THE SMOOTH THROAT	40	OISIN 2	V	175
AND MANY PATER NOSTERS SAID SINCE DAWN,	43	OISIN 2	V	208D
FIN, CONAN, OSCAR, MANY MORE, THE TIDE	44	OISIN 2	V	228A
IN ONE WAS A BRANCH SOFT-SHINING WITH BELLS MORE MANY THAN SIGHS	50	OISIN 3		46
IN REALMS WHERE THE HANDSOME WERE MANY,	50	OISIN 3		50
IN A REALM WHERE THE HANDSOME ARE MANY,	50	OISIN 3	V	50
IN REALMS WHERE THE HANDSOME ARE MANY,	50	OISIN 3	V	50
AND, MAN OF THE MANY WHITE CROZIERS, A CENTURY THERE I FORGOT	52	OISIN 3		77
AND, MAN OF THE MANY WHITE CROZIERS, A CENTURY THERE I FORGOT	52	OISIN 3		81
ON CREVROE OR BROAD KNOCKFEFIN, WITH MANY OF OLD THEY FEAST	59	OISIN 3		179
ON CREVROE OR ON BROAD KNOCKFEFIN, WITH MANY OF OLD THEY FAST	59	OISIN 3	V	179
OF ALL THE MANY CHANGING THINGS	65	HAPPY SHEPHERD		7

	PAGE	TITLE		LINE
MANY (CONTINUED)				
TO MIGHTY BRAHMA, HE WHO MADE YOU MANY AS THE SANDS,	72	ANASHU VIJAYA		21
TO MIGHTY BRAHMA--HE WHO MADE YE MANY AS THE SANDS,	72	ANASHU VIJAYA	V	21
TO MIGHTY BRAHMA, WHO HAS MADE YOU MANY AS THE SANDS,	72	ANASHU VIJAYA	V	21
WITH ALL YOUR WHIRLING HAIR, AND DROP MANY AN AZURE TEAR.	73	ANASHU VIJAYA		46
WITH ALL OUR WHIRLING HAIR, AND DROP MANY AN AZURE TEAR.	73	ANASHU VIJAYA	V	46
SHALL WARM THEIR LIVES AT MANY A RUSTLING FLAME."	80	EPHEMERA	V	128
MANY A LANDSMAN, MANY A SEAMAN.	82	MAD KING GOLL	V	4
MANY A LANDSMAN, MANY A SEAMAN.	82	MAD KING GOLL	V	4
THESE HANDS WON MANY A TORQUE OF GOLD.	83	MAD KING GOLL	V	23
THESE HANDS SLEW MANY WARRIORS BOLD--	83	MAD KING GOLL	V	23
THESE HANDS SLEW MANY ROBBERS BOLD--	83	MAD KING GOLL	V	23
THESE HANDS SLEW MANY A SEAMAN BOLD.	83	MAD KING GOLL	V	23
MY SORROW! FOR MANY A CREAK GAVE THE CREEL IN THE CART	91	OLD FISHERMAN		6
AH WOE! FULL MANY A CREAK GAVE THE CREEL IN THE CART	91	OLD FISHERMAN	V	6
AH ME! FULL MANY A CREAK GAVE THE CREEL IN THE CART	91	OLD FISHERMAN	V	6
AND NOW MOVES MANY A PLEASANT TONGUE	98	FOXHUNTER		21
AND MOVES THERE MANY A PLEASANT TONGUE,	98	FOXHUNTER	V	23
FROM CHANGE TO CHANGE! I HAVE BEEN MANY THINGS--	104	FERGUS DRUID		32
"NAY, HE IS OLD AND SAD WITH MANY WARS,	107	CUCHULAIN SEA	V	29
"BUT HE IS OLD AND SAD WITH MANY WARS."	107	CUCHULAIN SEA	V	30
HOW MANY LOVED YOUR MOMENTS OF GLAD GRACE,	121	YOU ARE OLD		5
I AM HAUNTED BY NUMBERLESS ISLANDS, AND MANY A DANAAN SHORE,	122	WHITE BIRDS		9
THERE WAS A GREEN BRANCH HUNG WITH MANY A BELL	129	BOOK STORIES		1
AH, EXILES, WANDERING OVER MANY SEAS,	129	BOOK STORIES	V	9
AH, EXILES, WANDERING OVER MANY LANDS,	130	BOOK STORIES	V	17
TO THOSE WITH WHOM I HAVE TALKED MANY TIMES,	136	TO SOME I TALK	V	2
AND MANY A SWEET THING SAID,	144	HOST OF AIR		18
AND BLAME YOU WITH MANY BITTER WORDS.	146	FISH		8
THE DOORS OF HELL AND BLOW THERE MANY A WHIMPERING GHOST!	147	UNAPPEAS HOST		10
THROUGH MANY A SACRED CORRIDOR	156	FORGOT BEAUTY		12
THE LOVER ASKS FORGIVENESS BECAUSE OF HIS MANY MOODS	162	ASKS FORGIVE		T
MICHAEL ROBARTES ASKS FORGIVENESS BECAUSE OF HIS MANY MOODS	162	ASKS FORGIVE	V	T
AND WONDERING WHO OF THE MANY CHANGING SIDHE	181	QUEEN MAEVE	V	41
TO MANY THOUSAND EYES, AND TO HER OWN	182	QUEEN MAEVE		65
AND WITH GLAD VOICE MAEVE ANSWERED "MANY A TIME	183	QUEEN MAEVE	V	79
FRIEND OF THESE MANY YEARS, YOU TOO HAD STOOD	186	QUEEN MAEVE		130
FRIEND OF THESE MANY YEARS, YOU TO HAVE STOOD	186	QUEEN MAEVE	V	130
WITH THE FIRST KINGS OF MANY PILLARED CRUACHAN	187	QUEEN MAEVE		151
TO MANY PASTURED MUIRTHEMNE,	189	BAILE AILLINN	V	21
AFTER THE DEATHS OF MANY MEN,	197	BAILE AILLINN		193
THERE'S MANY A ONE SHALL FIND OUT ALL HEARTACHE	205	ADAMS CURSE		16
THEREIN ARE MANY QUEENS LIKE BRANWEN AND GUINEVERE!	209	UNDER THE MOON		11
THERE'S MANY A STRONG FARMER	213	HAPPY TOWNLAND		1
WHERE MANY HUNDRED SQUIRRELS ARE AS HAPPY	217	WOODS OF COOLE		5
FLEW WESTWARD! AND MANY A TIME SINCE THEN	223	SHADOW WATER B		27
THESE MANY DAYS! AND YET THERE MUST BE MANY	226	SHADOW WATER B		89
THESE MANY DAYS! AND YET THERE MUST BE MANY	226	SHADOW WATER B		89
TOO MANY YEARS TO LIFT A HAND AGAINST YOU.	227	SHADOW WATER B		111
THOUGH LEAVES ARE MANY, THE ROOT IS ONE!	261	COMING WISDOM		1
WEARY OF MANY QUESTIONS! "THERE ARE THINGS	281	TWO KINGS		93
AND MANY A DARLING WIT'S GROWN DULL	301	RUN PARADISE		18
MANY TIMES TROUBLED YEARS,	315	FRIENDS	V	7
THEY WERE MY CLOSE COMPANIONS MANY A YEAR,	325	ROBERT GREGORY		41
WHERE MANY A KING HAS GONE	330	BONE OF A HARE		2
AND MANY A KING'S DAUGHTER,	330	BONE OF A HARE		3
THOUGH I HAVE MANY WORDS,	334	SONG		7
MANY A SON AND DAUGHTER LIES	360	ALF POLLEXFEN		13
THAT SO MANY LANDS HAD KNOWN,	360	ALF POLLEXFEN		18
THROUGHOUT SO MANY VARYING CENTURIES	371	ON GOING HOUSE		8
SHUDDERS IN MANY CRADLES! ALL IS CHANGED,	375	PHASES OF MOON		89
SO MANY TIMES CHILDISH DELIGHT.	399	BREAK OF DAY		11
YET MANY, THAT HAVE PLAYED THE FOOL	404	FOR DAUGHTER		36
AND MANY A POOR MAN THAT HAS ROVED,	404	FOR DAUGHTER		38
WONDER HOW MANY TIMES I COULD HAVE PROVED MY WORTH	427	PHANTOM HATRED		34
MANY INGENIOUS LOVELY THINGS ARE GONE	428	NINETEEN 19		1
WE TOO HAD MANY PRETTY TOYS WHEN YOUNG!	428	NINETEEN 19		9
MANY INGENUOUS LOVELY THINGS ARE GONE	428	NINETEEN 19	V	1
I HAVE ATTEMPTED MANY THINGS	451	FIRST LOVE		9
HOW SUCH A PAIR LOVED MANY YEARS	458	SECRETS OF OLD		15
AND MANY A LESSER BELL SOUND THROUGH THE ROOM!	470	ALL SOUL NIGHT		2
MANY A TIME I THINK TO SEEK	475	EVA GORE-BOOTH		14
MANY TIMES HE DIED,	476	DEATH		5
MANY TIMES ROSE AGAIN.	476	DEATH		6
HOW MANY YEARS AGO	524	MAD AS MIST		10
THEIR EYES MID MANY WRINKLES, THEIR EYES,	567	LAPIS LAZULI		55
FOUND MANY A FAMOUS MAN THERE!	584	GHOST ROG CASE		35
AND I HAVE MANY MORE,	586	PARNELLITES		10
TO MANY WOMEN I HAVE SAID, "LIE STILL,"	609	IN TARAS HALLS		6
AND EMPTIED MANY A CAN!	620	JOHN KINSELLA		16
SO MANY YEARS COMPANIONED BY A HOUND,	621	HOUND VOICE		4
MANY TIMES MAN LIVES AND DIES	637	BEN BULBEN		13
BY MANY SOUGHT, AND 'TIS A FOREST TALE,	653	ISLE STAT I 2		40
I PASSED BY MANY CAVES OF DRIPPING STONE,	657	ISLE STAT I 3		47
TWO CAME, HIS NAME AND MINE ON MANY A TREE	662	ISLE STAT II 2		10
AND THAT WAS STRANGE! BUT THIS IS MANY A WORLD	664	ISLE STAT II 2		60
AND WHEN THOU HAST THESE THINGS FOR MANY AGES FELT,	674	ISLE STAT II 3		214
THOUGH SAD IS MANY A SPIRIT	680	LOVE AND DEATH		23
THE SULLEN WOOD. BUT MANY WOODS I SEE	682	SEEKER		24
THEN HAS THIS ONE BEEN SINNED FULL MANY TIMES.	692	MOSADA 1		49

502

MANY   (CONTINUED)
ALONG THE SEA; AND MANY A MAN GREW HUSHED . . . . . . 693 MOSADA 1   86
WHEN THERE ARE MANY? EBREMAR WILL STAMP . . . . . . 696 MOSADA 2   4
THE AUSTRIAN HAYNAU HE, IN MANY LANDS . . . . 709 FERENCZ RENYI   8
AND MANY A HERB AND MANY A SPELL . . . . 717 FAIRY DOCTOR   17
AND MANY A HERB AND MANY A SPELL . . . . 717 FAIRY DOCTOR   17
AND MANY HERBS AND MANY A SPELL . . . . 717 FAIRY DOCTOR   V 17
AND MANY HERBS AND MANY A SPELL . . . . 717 FAIRY DOCTOR   V 17
THEN GIVE ME TRIUMPH IN MY MANY PLOTS. . . . . . . 722 WITCH VIVIEN   51
MY LOVE HATH MANY AN EVIL MOOD, ... 723 GIRLS SONG A   5
MY LOVE HATH MANY A RUTHLESS MOOD, ... 723 GIRLS SONG A   V 5
AND MANY A PURPLE GILLYFLOWER EATEN, ... 729 PRIEST FAIRY   35
WITH MANY A LOVELY FACE . . . . 740 EARL PAUL   30
HOW MANY MOONS HAVE DIED FROM THE FULL MOON . . . . 747 SHADOW WATER A   10
WHO MIGHT HAVE FLOCKS AND HERDS AND MANY THRALLS, . . 757 SHADOW WATER A 216
TO WANDER IN; YOU HAVE LOVED MANY WOMEN, ... 767 SHADOW WATER A 389
HOW MANY HOURS TO DAYBREAK, BECAUSE LOVE . . . . . 767 SHADOW WATER A 405
OR, FOR MANY SHAPES THEY HAVE, ... 775 AGAINST WITCH   14
AND MANY A NIGHT IT SEEMS . . . . 781 MY HEART BEAT   9
HOW MANY CENTURIES SPENT . . . . 784 WOMANS BEAUTY   7
OF MANY A TRAGIC TOMB! . . . . 785 YOUR HEART   10
OF MANY A TRAGIC TOMB! . . . . 786 YOUR HEART   23
OF MANY A TRAGIC TOMB! . . . . 786 YOUR HEART   36
MANY-CHANGING
AND WONDERING WHO OF THE MANY-CHANGING SIDHE . . . . 181 QUEEN MAEVE   41
WHO OF THE WANDERING MANY-CHANGING ONES . . . . . 182 QUEEN MAEVE   51
SHE TOLD THEM OF THE MANY-CHANGING ONES! . . . . 185 QUEEN MAEVE   112
MANY-COLOURED
THE MANY-COLOURED DANCERS RUSHED, ... 21 OISIN 1   V 322
MANY-FOLDED
AND HATH HER HOME BY MANY-FOLDED DELLS. . . . . . 657 ISLE STAT I 3   46
MANY-HEADED
THE MANY-HEADED FOAM AT SALAMIS. . . . . . 610 STATUES   14
ONE IMAGE CROSSED THE MANY-HEADED, SAT . . . . 610 STATUES   17
MANY-MINDED
AND MANY-MINDED HOMER WERE . . . . 524 MAD AS MIST   17
MANY-PASTURED
TO MANY-PASTURED MUIRTHEMNE, ... 189 BAILE AILLINN   21
MANY-PILLARED
WITH THE FIRST KINGS OF MANY-PILLARED CRUACHAN. . . . 187 QUEEN MAEVE   151
MANY-SORROWED
THE WILLOW OF THE MANY-SORROWED WORLD. . . . . . 130 BOOK STORIES   V 16
MANY-TIMES-TROUBLED
MANY-TIMES-TROUBLED YEARS, ... 315 FRIENDS   7
MAPS
WHERE THE MAPS ARE SPREAD, ... 617 LONG-LEG FLY   6
MAR
THAT TIME CAN NEVER MAR A LOVER'S VOWS . . . . 126 DREAM OF FAERY   10
HOW TIME MAY NEVER MAR THEIR FAERY VOWS . . . 126 DREAM OF FAERY V 10
FOR TRIUMPH CAN BUT MAR OUR SOLITUDE. . . . . 431 NINETEEN 19   78
SHEPHERD, TO MAR THE MORNING HAST THOU COME? . . . 646 ISLE STAT I 1   30
MARBLE
PAINTING WITH SHADOW ALL THE MARBLE STEPS! . . . 72 ANASHU VIJAYA   30
FROM MARBLE CITIES LOUD WITH TABORS OF OLD . . . 162 ASKS FORGIVE   9
A WEATHER-WORN, MARBLE TRITON . . . . . . 329 MEN IMPROVE   2
A WEATHER-WORN, MARBLE TRITON . . . . . . 329 MEN IMPROVE   17
IN BRONZE, OR THAT IN DAZZLING MARBLE APPEARS, . . 334 LIVING BEAUTY   5
FOR ALL ITS BRONZE AND MARBLE, 'S BUT A MOUSE. . . 418 ANCEST HOUSES   24
BUT KEEP A MARBLE OR A BRONZE REPOSE. . . . . 445 SCHOOL CHILDR   52
SAT DOWN UPON THE FOUNTAIN'S MARBLE EDGE, . . . 463 HARUN RASHID   43
OLD MARBLE HEADS, OLD PICTURES EVERYWHERE! . . . 491 COOLE BALLYLEE   28
ON THE MARBLE TABLE-TOP. . . . . 501 VACILLATION   39
UNDER A MARBLE FLAG? . . . . 525 DANCING DAYS   14
FROM MARBLE OF A BROKEN SEPULCHRE, ... 565 GYRES   20
WHO HANDLED MARBLE AS IF IT WERE BRONZE, . . . 566 LAPIS LAZULI   30
IN MARBLE OR IN BRONZE, LACKED CHARACTER. . . . 610 STATUES   3
NO MARBLE, NO CONVENTIONAL PHRASE! . . . . . 640 BEN BULBEN   89
AND ONE ARM POINTING THUS, IN MARBLE WHITE. . . . 663 ISLE STAT II 2   28
THAT FROM THE MILK-WHITE MARBLE . . . . . . 680 LOVE AND DEATH   3
MARBLES
MARBLES OF THE DANCING FLOOR . . . . . . 498 BYZANTIUM   36
MARCH
. . . AND MARCH ON AS OXEN MOVE OVER YOUNG GRASS! . . 62 OISIN 3   211
COLD AS THE MARCH WIND HIS EYES. . . . . . 531 FATHER CHILD   8
COME MARCH, SINGING THIS SONG, ... 544 TO SAME TUNE 1 V REF
MARCH, MARCH—HOW DOES IT RUN?— . . . . . . 548 TO SAME TUNE 3   15
MARCH, MARCH—HOW DOES IT RUN?— . . . . . . 548 TO SAME TUNE 3   15
MARCH, MARCH, LIFT UP THE SONG! . . . . . . 549 TO SAME TUNE 3   26
MARCH, MARCH, LIFT UP THE SONG! . . . . . . 549 TO SAME TUNE 3   26
MARCH WIND, AND ANY OLD TUNE, ... 615 MARCH SONGS 2   25
MARCH, MARCH, AND HOW DOES IT RUN? . . . . . 615 MARCH SONGS 2   26
MARCH, MARCH, AND HOW DOES IT RUN? . . . . . 615 MARCH SONGS 2   26
AS BLOSSOMS, WHEN THE WINDS OF MARCH . . . . 671 ISLE STAT II 3 127
COME RIDE LIKE THE MARCH WIND! . . . . . . 774 COME RIDE   6
RUN LIKE THE MARCH WIND! . . . . . . 774 COME RIDE   V 6
RED BIRD OF MARCH, BEGIN TO CROW! . . . . . 782 HEART FRIGHT   5
RED BIRD OF MARCH, BEGIN TO CROW! . . . . . 782 HEART FRIGHT   12
RED BIRD OF MARCH, BEGIN TO CROW! . . . . . 782 HEART FRIGHT   19
THE STRONG MARCH BIRDS A-CROW. . . . . . 783 GREY ROUND   26
MARCHED
STOOD OR HAVE MARCHED THE NIGHT LONG . . . . . 546 TO SAME TUNE 2   15

MARCHED   (CONTINUED)
    OR HAVE MARCHED THE NIGHT LONG, ...   546 TO SAME TUNE 2 V   15
MARCHES
    WHAT MARCHES THROUGH THE MOUNTAIN PASS? . . . . . .   614 MARCH SONGS 2   7
    WHAT MARCHES DOWN THE MOUNTAIN PASS? . . . .   615 MARCH SONGS 2   17
    WHAT MARCHES DOWN THE MOUNTAIN PASS? . . . .   615 MARCH SONGS 2   27
MARCHING
    TAKE TO THE ROADS AND GO MARCHING ALONG. . . . . .   548 TO SAME TUNE 3   14
    O MARCHING WIND, O A BLAST OF THE WIND, ...   548 TO SAME TUNE 3   24
    MARCHING, MARCHING ALONG. . . . .   549 TO SAME TUNE 3   25
    MARCHING, MARCHING ALONG. . . . .   549 TO SAME TUNE 3   25
    THREE MARCHING SONGS . . . .   613 MARCH SONGS 1   T
    A BLAST OF THE WIND, O A MARCHING WIND, ...   615 MARCH SONGS 2   24
    A BLAST OF WIND, O A MARCHING WIND, ...   615 MARCH SONGS 2 V   24
MARCO
    FOR THE SAN MARCO LIBRARY, ...   288 TO WEALTHY MAN   24
MARE
    MARE OR STALLION, COCK OR HEN, ...   529 TOM LUNATIC   15
    MOUNTED THE MARE OF TIME, ...   529 TOM CRUACHAN   5
    SOME BACK A MARE THROWN FROM A THOROUGHBRED, . . .   547 TO SAME TUNE 3   3
    SOME BACK A MARE THROWN FROM A THOROUGH-BRED, . . .   547 TO SAME TUNE 3 V   3
    SOME BACK A MARE THROWN FROM A THOROUGHBRED, . . .   614 MARCH SONGS 2   3
MAREOTIC
    OR BY THE MAREOTIC SEA . . . .   401 DEMON BEAST   45
    ROUND THE MAREOTIC LAKE . . . .   636 BEN BULBEN   2
MARGARET
    THERE'S MARGARET AND MARJORIE AND DOROTHY AND NAN, . . .   354 HIS PHOENIX   17
MARGE
    IN ENDLESS DARK, AND BY THE WEEDY MARGE . . . . .   682 SEEKER   19
    ITS PAVEN LENGTH TOWARDS THE RIVER'S MARGE . . . .   702 MOSADA 3   76
MARGERY
    THOUGH MARGERY IS STRICKEN DUMB . . . .   457 SECRETS OF OLD   7
    THOUGH MARGERY IS LIKE A FISH . . . .   457 SECRETS OF OLD V   7
MARGIN
    YOUR HOOVES HAVE STAMPED AT THE BLACK MARGIN OF THE WOOD,   442 BLACK CENTAUR 1
MARIE
    "AVE MARIE," MUTTERED HE . . . .   730 PRIEST FAIRY   51
MARIGOLDS
    AND UNDER HER HOOFS THE MARIGOLDS BEATEN. . . . .   729 PRIEST FAIRY   36
MARINERS
    THE MARINERS OF NIGHT ABOVE, ...   139 TO IRELAND   V   38
    MARINERS, ROUGH HARVESTERS: . . . .   540 FROM ANTIGONE   5
    MARINERS, WILD HARVESTERS: . . . .   540 FROM ANTIGONE V   5
MARJORIE
    THERE'S MARGARET AND MARJORIE AND DOROTHY AND NAN, . . .   354 HIS PHOENIX   17
MARK
    IN LUCK OR OUT THE TOIL HAS LEFT ITS MARK: . . . .   491 COOLE BALLYLEE V 40F
    IN LUCK OR OUT THE TOIL HAS LEFT ITS MARK: . . . .   495 CHOICE   6
    MARK AND DIGEST MY TALE, CARRY IT AFAR . . . . .   554 RIBH AT TOMB   3
    I CHOOSE ANOTHER MARK, ...   588 OLD WICKED MAN   29
MARKED
    HAS MARKED A DISTANT OBJECT DOWN, ...   337 TOM OROUGHLEY   3
    AND THERE MARKED OUT THOSE EMBLEMS ON THE SAND . .   468 HARUN RASHID   156
    AND THERE MARKED OUT EMBLEMS ON THE SAND . . . .   468 HARUN RASHID   V 156
    BEFORE I HAD MARKED HIM ON HIS NORTHERN WAY, . . .   535 CHOSEN   8
    "THOSE SIX FEET MARKED IN CHALK? . . . .   548 TO SAME TUNE 3   8
    "THOSE SIX FEET MARKED IN CHALK? . . . .   548 TO SAME TUNE 3   18
    "THOSE SIX FEET MARKED IN CHALK? . . . .   549 TO SAME TUNE 3   28
MARKET
    HIS MUMMERS TO THE MARKET PLACE, ...   287 TO WEALTHY MAN V   10
    SAT UNDERNEATH THE MARKET CROSS, ...   724 LEGEND   2
MARKET-PLACE
    HIS MUMMERS TO THE MARKET-PLACE, ...   287 TO WEALTHY MAN   10
MARKETS
    FROM MARKETS AND FROM FAIRS . . . .   420 MY HOUSE   19
MARKIEWICZ
    IN MEMORY OF EVA GORE-BOOTH AND CON MARKIEWICZ . . . .   475 EVA GORE-BOOTH T
MARKS
    THE NETTED MARKS OF CRAWLING SCALES SEA-SPRUNG . . .   37 OISIN 2   V 115
    UPON THE STAR THAT MARKS THE HIDDEN POLE: . . . . .   477 SELF AND SOUL   5
MARMALADE
    THE STRUGGLE OF THE FLY IN MARMALADE. . . . . . .   369 EGO DOMINUS   45
MARRED
    BURST FROM A GREAT DOOR MARRED BY MANY A BLOW . . .   31 OISIN 2   29
    BASALTIC PILLARS MARRED WITH HEW AND HACK . . . . .   31 OISIN 2   V   30
MARRIAGE
    WHEN THEY HAD COME TO THE MARRIAGE BED: . . . . .   193 BAILE AILLINN V 106
    BAILE AND AILLINN'S MARRIAGE BED, ...   194 BAILE AILLINN V 121
    AND KEEP TO THE ONE WEARY MARRIAGE BED. . . . . .   224 SHADOW WATER B V   55
    AND THE HIGH FAME THAT COME TO THEM IN MARRIAGE, . .   232 SHADOW WATER B   235
    AND ALL THAT MURMURING IS BUT A MARRIAGE SONG: . .   244 SHADOW WATER B V 452
    THAT PACKED HIS MARRIAGE DAY . . . .   317 NIGHT COME   7
    THROUGH TOO MUCH PLAY, OR MARRIAGE WITH A FOOL? . .   423 MY DESCENDANTS   12
MARRIAGE-BED
    WHEN THEY HAD COME TO THE MARRIAGE-BED: . . . . .   193 BAILE AILLINN   106
    BAILE AND AILLINN'S MARRIAGE-BED, ...   194 BAILE AILLINN   121
    AND KEEP TO THE ONE WEARY MARRIAGE-BED. . . . . .   224 SHADOW WATER B   55
MARRIAGE-DAY
    THAT PACKED HIS MARRIAGE-DAY . . . .   317 NIGHT COME   V   7
MARRIAGES
    MARRIAGES, ALLIANCES AND FAMILIES, ...   491 COOLE BALLYLEE   36

	PAGE	TITLE		LINE

MARRIAGE-SONG
  AND ALL THAT MURMURING'S BUT A MARRIAGE-SONG: 244 SHADOW WATER B   452
MARRIED   SEE NEW-MARRIED
  OUR MARRIED VOICES WILDLY TROLLED.   85 MAD KING GOLL   59
  OUR MARRIED VOICE WILDLY TROLLED.   85 MAD KING GOLL V 59
  AND THEY MARRIED BEYOND THEIR PLACE.   92 FATHER OHART   8
  MY MARRIED SISTER PUT INTO MY CARE   276 TWO KINGS V E
  THAT SHE MIGHT BE THAT SPRIGHTLY GIRL WHO HAD MARRIED WITH A BIRD: 353 HIS PHOENIX V 4
  BY SOME NEW MARRIED BRIDE I TAKE   535 CHOSEN V 13
  "HAS MARRIED AND STAYS   780 WELL AND TREE   11
MARROW
  SOFTER THAN SNOW-FLAKES IN APRIL AND PIERCING THE MARROW LIKE FLAME.   51 OISIN 3   68
  SOFTER THAN SNOWFLAKES IN APRIL, AND PIERCING THE MARROW LIKE FLAME.   51 OISIN 3 V 68
  MADE OUT OF A WILD THOUGHT, IS IN MY MARROW.   199 ARROW   2
  BETTER GO DOWN UPON YOUR MARROW BONES   204 ADAMS CURSE V 7
  TO BURN US TO THE MARROW IF WE STRIKE.   239 SHADOW WATER B   372
  YOU HAVE DRIED THE MARROW FROM THE BONE?   289 SEPTEMBER 1913   5
  THINKS IN A MARROW BONE: 553 PRAYER OLD AGE V 4
  THINGS HID IN THEIR MARROW BONES   589 OLD WICKED MAN V 41
  I PRAYED AT ALL THE STATIONS UPON MY MARROW BONES,   593 PILGRIM V 7
MARROW-BONE
  THINKS IN A MARROW-BONE: 553 PRAYER OLD AGE   4
MARROWBONES
  THINGS HID IN THEIR MARROWBONES   589 OLD WICKED MAN V 41
MARROW-BONES
  BETTER GO DOWN UPON YOUR MARROW-BONES   204 ADAMS CURSE   7
  THINGS HID IN THEIR MARROW-BONES   589 OLD WICKED MAN   41
  I PRAYED AT ALL THE STATIONS UPON MY MARROW-BONES,   593 PILGRIM   7
MARRY
  BEING FORBID TO MARRY ON EARTH,   189 BAILE AILLINN   11
  I NEEDS MUST MARRY SOME POOR LOUT,"   273 GREY ROCK   47
  I NEED MUST MARRY SOME POOR LOUT."   273 GREY ROCK V 47
  "AND THOUGH I'D MARRY WITH A COMELY LASS,   300 BEGGAR CRIED   9
  AT THE OLD BITTER WORLD WHERE THEY MARRY IN CHURCHES,   330 BONE OF A HARE   13
  AT ALL WHO MARRY IN CHURCHES,   330 BONE OF A HARE   15
MARS
  ON BREAST OF MARS THE GODDESS SIGHED.   562 CONJUNCTIONS   4
MARSH
  WITH HIS SNIPE MARSH AND HIS TROUT.   92 FATHER OHART V 4
  CLOGGED IN A MARSH WHERE THE SLOW MARSH CLAY CLINGS,   711 FERENCZ RENYI   35
  CLOGGED IN A MARSH WHERE THE SLOW MARSH CLAY CLINGS,   711 FERENCZ RENYI   35
MARSHY
  IN BARREN HILLS AND MARSHY LAND,   150 WANDER AENGUS V 18
MART
  SORDID SORROWS OF THE MART,   733 STREET DANCERS   59
MARTEN-CAT
  AND MARTEN-CAT, AND BORDERS THAT OLD WOOD   218 WOODS OF COOLE   14
MARTIN
  AND MARTIN CAT, AND BORDERS THAT OLD WOOD   218 WOODS OF COOLE V 14
  COLONEL MARTIN   594 COLONEL MARTIN   T
MARTIN'S   SEE HONEY-MARTS
  BEYOND OLD MARTIN'S BYRE   95 MOLL MAGEE   34
  BEYOND OLD MARTIN'S WOOD,   95 MOLL MAGEE V 34
MARTS
  FROM BEES AMONG THEIR HONEY MARTS,   16 OISIN 1 V 229
  WITH BOOM OF BEES IN HONEY MARTS,   16 OISIN 1 V 229
MARTYRS
  THE MARTYRS CALL THE WORLD." AND THEREUPON   205 ADAMS CURSE   14
  THE MARTYRS CALL THE WORLD." THAT WOMAN THEN   205 ADAMS CURSE V 14
MARVEL
  SHALL WITHER THAT OLD MARVEL, FOR   447 COLONUS PRAISE   15
  THAT DAY BY DAY I STUDY AND MARVEL AT,   468 HARUN RASHID   157
MARVELLOUS
  TORE FROM THE CLOUDS HIS MARVELLOUS MOON.   314 MEMORY YOUTH   21
  THREW UP IN THE AIR HIS MARVELLOUS MOON.   314 MEMORY YOUTH V 21
  THE MARVELLOUS STAG OF ARTHUR,   399 BREAK OF DAY   23
  AS IF SOME MARVELLOUS EMPTY SEA-SHELL FLUNG   417 ANCEST HOUSES   13
  A MARVELLOUS ACCOMPLISHMENT,   421 MY TABLE   17
  BECAUSE I HAVE A MARVELLOUS THING TO SAY,   471 ALL SOUL NIGHT   15
  A CERTAIN MARVELLOUS THING   471 ALL SOUL NIGHT   16
  I NEVER KNEW AN EVE SO MARVELLOUS STILL.   702 MOSADA 3   88
MARY
  DID THE KISS OF MOTHER MARY,   124 CATHLEEN PARA   9
  HERS THE KISS OF MOTHER MARY,   124 CATHLEEN PARA V 9
  O'SULLIVAN RUA TO MARY LAVELL   155 FORGOT BEAUTY V T
  O'SULLIVAN THE RED TO MARY LAVELL.   157 POET BELOVED   T
  TWO POEMS BY O'SULLIVAN THE RED CONCERNING MARY LAVELL.   157 POET BELOVED V T
  A DAPHNE AND A MARY WHO LIVE IN PRIVACY: 354 HIS PHOENIX   18
  FOUR POEMS CRACKED MARY AND THE BISHOP   507 JANE BISHOP V T
  CRACKED MARY REPROVED   509 JANE REPROVED V T
  CRACKED MARY AND THE DANCERS   514 JANE GROWN OLD V T
  JOHN KINSELLA'S LAMENT FOR MRS. MARY MOORE   620 JOHN KINSELLA   T
  BUT MY DEAR MARY MOORE,   620 JOHN KINSELLA   8
MARY'S
  IS COMELIER THAN CANDLES AT MOTHER MARY'S FEET.   147 UNAPPEAS HOST   12
  BY THE DOOR OF MARY'S GARDEN   680 LOVE AND DEATH   31
MASCULINE
  RECALL THAT MASCULINE TRINITY.   556 RIBH PATRICK   2

505

		PAGE	TITLE	LINE
MASK				
	THE MASK	263	MASK	T
	"PUT OFF THAT MASK OF BURNING GOLD	263	MASK	1
	"IT WAS THE MASK ENGAGED YOUR MIND, ...	263	MASK	8
	A HOUSE, A SWORD, A SHIP, A MASK.	788	BRAVEST ASK	2
MASKER'S				
	IN MASKER'S CLOAK AND HOOD, ...	539	MEETING	2
MASONRY				
	MAY BUILD IN THE CRACKED MASONRY AND CRY	423	MY DESCENDANTS	15
	OF LOOSENING MASONRY, AND THERE	424	STARES NEST	2
MASONS				
	AND MASONS DROVE FROM MILES AWAY	360	ALF POLLEXFEN	9
MASS				
	THEY HAD A PRIEST SAY MASS, AND EVEN THE JAPANESE, . . .	363	DOLLS FACES	2
	AND TOOK A MASS OF SHADOWS FOR ITS MEAT, ...	444	SCHOOL CHILDR V	28
MASSACRE				
	AND WONDERED WHAT WAS LEFT FOR MASSACRE TO SAVE. . . .	619	BRONZE HEAD	28
MASSED				
	BUT WE OLD MEN ARE MASSED AGAINST THE WORLD. . . .	486	SEVEN SAGES	14
MAST				
	WHAT ARE YOU CALLING OUT ABOVE THE MAST?	243	SHADOW WATER B	437
	HE HOVERS ABOVE THE MAST AND WAITS HIS KIND:	753	SHADOW WATER A	135
	HE, DISGUISED AS A SAILOR BEFORE THE MAST, ...	790	DEDICATION	2
MASTER				
	"BUT IF YOUR MASTER COMES HOME TRIUMPHING	106	CUCHULAIN SEA	12
	MASTER OF THE STILL STARS AND OF THE FLAMING DOOR. . . .	161	BLACK PIG	8
	THEN MAEVE: "O AENGUS, MASTER OF ALL LOVERS, . . .	187	QUEEN MAEVE	149
	AND HE MY MASTER FROM MY CHILDHOOD UP!	225	SHADOW WATER B	77
	EVEN IF FORGAEL HAD NOT BEEN MY MASTER	225	SHADOW WATER B V	76
	BEING AS DOUBTFUL? I HAVE CALLED YOU MASTER	227	SHADOW WATER B	110
	TILL YOUR BAD MASTER BLENCHED AND ALL WAS LOST! . . .	270	PARDON FATHERS V	12
	AN ANCIENT BANKRUPT MASTER OF THIS HOUSE.	412	TOWER	80
	ON MASTER WORK OF INTELLECT OR HAND, ...	429	NINETEEN 19 V	37
	TILL MEDITATION MASTER ALL ITS PARTS, ...	474	ALL SOUL NIGHT	92
	CUT OUT HIS HEART. SOME MASTER OF DESIGN	541	PARN FUNERAL 1	14
	THEIR SCHOOL A CROWD, HIS MASTER SOLITUDE:	543	PARN FUNERAL 2	10
	THEIR SCHOOL THE CROWD, HIS MASTER SOLITUDE. . . .	543	PARN FUNERAL 2 V	10
	WHAT CAN SHE TAKE UNTIL HER MASTER GIVE!	558	RIBH CHRISTIAN	21
	WHAT MASTER MADE THE LASH. WHENCE HAD THEY COME, . . .	560	WHENCE COME	9
	OUR MASTER CAESAR IS IN THE TENT	617	LONG-LEG FLY	5
	THEY WILL HAVE FOR MASTER NONE	776	AGAINST WITCH V	39
	THEN FARRELL, STEEL KING, MASTER OF MEN, ...	790	DEDICATION	5
MASTERED				
	TILL TOES MASTERED A SWEET MEASURE, ...	331	ROUND TOWER	15
	MOUTH MASTERED A SWEET SOUND, ...	331	ROUND TOWER	16
	SO MASTERED BY THE BRUTE BLOOD OF THE AIR, ...	441	LEDA AND SWAN	12
	I MOCKED, BEING CRAZY, BUT YOU MASTERED IT	533	HER TRIUMPH	8
MASTERFUL				
	HATH COME A SEA-KING MASTERFUL, ...	82	MAD KING GOLL V	15
	SOUTHWARD A SEA-KING MASTERFUL	82	MAD KING GOLL V	15
	COMES A SEA-KING MASTERFUL	82	MAD KING GOLL V	15
	WOMEN CAN FIND." WITH A MOST MASTERFUL VOICE, . . .	284	TWO KINGS	175
	BUT MASTERFUL HEAVEN HAD INTERVENED TO SAVE IT. . . .	630	CIRCUS ANIMALS	20
	THOSE MASTERFUL IMAGES BECAUSE COMPLETE	630	CIRCUS ANIMALS	33
MASTERING				
	UTTERING, MASTERING IT, ...	480	BLOOD AND MOON	5
MASTER'S				
	IN HONOUR SOON BY HIS MASTER'S SIDE	26	OISIN 1	V 399C
	BUT WHEN THE MASTER'S BURIED MICE CAN PLAY, ...	418	ANCEST HOUSES	22
	THEIR SCHOOL A CROWD, HIS MASTER'S SOLITUDE:	543	PARN FUNERAL 2 V	10
MASTERS SEE SINGING-MASTERS				
	THE MIGHTIER MASTERS OF A MIGHTIER RACE!	38	OISIN 2	133
	ROOTED IN FOAM AND CLOUDS. THERE MIGHTIER MASTERS MET . .	38	OISIN 2	V 132
	NONE WAR ON THE MASTERS OF HELL, ...	62	OISIN 3	214
	A MYSTICAL PRAYER TO THE MASTERS OF THE ELEMENTS, . . .	174	ELEMENT POWERS V	T
	O MASTERS OF THE GLITTERING TOWN!	212	BLESS PSALTER	3
	AND BY THE IMITATION OF GREAT MASTERS.	370	EGO DOMINUS	66
	AND BE THE SINGING MASTERS OF MY SOUL.	408	SAIL BYZANTIUM V	20
	AND EDDY TO EDDY. MASTERS OF OUR DREAMS, ...	768	SHADOW WATER A	418
	THEY WILL HAVE FOR MASTERS NONE	776	AGAINST WITCH	39
MASTER-WORK				
	ON MASTER-WORK OF INTELLECT OR HAND, ...	429	NINETEEN 19	37
MASTERY				
	RIGHT MASTERY OF NATURAL THINGS, ...	401	DEMON BEAST	37
	ATHENIAN INTELLECT ITS MASTERY, ...	446	COLONUS PRAISE	11
MASTHEAD				
	THEY HOVER OVER THE MASTHEAD AWHILE	233	SHADOW WATER B	246
	CIRCLING AND CIRCLING OVER THE MASTHEAD?	234	SHADOW WATER B	266
MAST-HEAD				
	HE, THOUGH BUT A LANDSMAN, WENT TO THE MAST-HEAD: . . .	790	DEDICATION	4
MAT				
	STRETCHED UP ON TWO LEGS FROM THE MAT, ...	381	SONGS FOOL 2	7
	SITTING ON A WARM SMOOTH MAT	726	LOVERS QUARREL	11
MATCH				
	DARE MATCH IN LEARNING WITH US TWO, ...	333	SOLOMON SHEBA	21
	HER CHILDISH GRATITUDE FOR LOVE AND MATCH YOUR FIFTY YEARS?	450	OWEN AHERNE	23
	ARISE AND BID ME STRIKE A MATCH	476	EVA GORE-BOOTH	26
	BID ME STRIKE A MATCH AND BLOW.	476	EVA GORE-BOOTH	32
MATCHING				
	OF THE MATCHING OF RIBBONS FOR BOSOM AND HEAD, . . .	151	OLD MOTHER	6
	OF THE MATCHING OF RIBBONS THE BLUE AND THE RED, . . .	151	OLD MOTHER	V 6

506

		PAGE	TITLE	LINE

MATCHING (CONTINUED)
    MATCHING OUR BROKEN-HEARTED WIT AGAINST HER WIT, ...   362 HER COURTESY   7
MATE
    HOW COULD SHE MATE WITH FIFTY YEARS THAT WAS SO WILDLY   450 OWEN AHERNE   15
      BRED?
    LET THE CAGE BIRD AND THE CAGE BIRD MATE . . . .   450 OWEN AHERNE   16
    . . . AND THE WILD BIRD MATE IN THE WILD." . . . . . .   450 OWEN AHERNE   16
    LIKE PASSION STIRS THE PEACOCK AND HIS MATE, ...   465 HARUN RASHID   100
    KNOW HIS WORK OR CHOOSE HIS MATE. . . . .   638 BEN BULBEN   36
    AMONG THE WHIMPERING GHOSTS. MATE THUS. ALREADY? . . .   722 WITCH VIVIEN   68
MATERNAL
    ON THE MATERNAL MIDNIGHT OF MY BREAST . . . .   535 CHOSEN   7
MATHEMATICAL
    CAST BUT DEAD LEAVES TO MATHEMATICAL EQUALITY, ...   481 BLOOD AND MOON   24
    CASTS BUT DEAD LEAVES TO MATHEMATICAL EQUALITY, ...   481 BLOOD AND MOON V   24
MATHERS
    I CALL MACGREGOR MATHERS FROM HIS GRAVE, ...   473 ALL SOUL NIGHT V   61
MATTER
    TOWARDS THE COUNTRY OF THE DEAD. WHAT MATTER . . . . .   231 SHADOW WATER B   206
    IF THERE BE HALF A HUNDRED MORE, WHAT MATTER? . . . . .   245 SHADOW WATER B   476
    WHAT MATTER, SO THERE IS BUT FIRE . . . .   263 MASK   14
    "IF YOU HAD BROACHED A MATTER . . . .   333 SOLOMON SHEBA   11
    AND THERE ARE--BUT NO MATTER IF THERE ARE SCORES BESIDE,   354 HIS PHOENIX   15
    WHAT MATTER THAT NO CANNON HAD BEEN TURNED . . . . . .   429 NINETEEN 19   19
    BE MIMICRY?" "WHAT MATTER IF OUR SOULS . . . .   464 HARUN RASHID   66
    BUT NAMES ARE NOTHING. WHAT MATTER HOW IT BE, ...   473 ALL SOUL NIGHT   81
    WHAT MATTER IF THE DITCHES ARE IMPURE? . . . .   478 SELF AND SOUL   42
    WHAT MATTER IF I LIVE IT ALL ONCE MORE? . . . .   478 SELF AND SOUL   43
    WHAT MATTER IF A BLIND MAN DRINK HIS DROP? . . . . . .   478 SELF AND SOUL V   41
    HALF DEAD AT THE TOP? NO MATTER WHAT I SAID, ...   482 BLOOD AND MOON   48
    FOR NO MATTER WHAT IS SAID . . . .   514 JANE GROWN OLD   12
    WHAT MATTER? FOR I KNOW . . . .   518 HIS CONFIDENCE   9
    WHAT MATTER IF THE KNAVE . . . .   525 DANCING DAYS   10
    WHAT MATTER FOR THE SCENE, THE SCENE ONCE GONE, ...   542 PARN FUNERAL 1   19
    NO MATTER WHAT HAPPENS AND WHO TAKES THE FALL, ...   545 TO SAME TUNE 1 V   22
    NO MATTER WHAT HAPPENS OR WHO TAKES THE FALL, ...   545 TO SAME TUNE 1 V   22
    HERE IS FRESH MATTER, POET, ...   553 CHURCH STATE   1
    MATTER FOR OLD AGE MEET, ...   553 CHURCH STATE   2
    WHAT MATTER THAT YOU UNDERSTOOD NO WORD! . . . . . .   557 RIBH ECSTASY   1
    WHAT MATTER THOUGH NUMB NIGHTMARE RIDE ON TOP, ...   564 GYRES   9
    WHAT MATTER? HEAVE NO SIGH, LET NO TEAR DROP, ...   564 GYRES   11
    WHAT MATTER? OUT OF CAVERN COMES A VOICE, ...   564 GYRES   15
    WHAT MATTER? THOSE THAT ROCKY FACE HOLDS DEAR, ...   564 GYRES   18
    WHAT MATTER? OUT OF CAVERN COME A VOICE . . . . . .   564 GYRES V   15
    WHAT MATTER, WE ARE BUT WOMEN. . . . .   572 LADYS 2ND SONG   3
    NO MATTER WHAT DISASTER OCCURRED . . . .   578 CRAZED GIRL   9
    NO MATTER WHAT THE NAMES THEY WEAR! . . . .   582 ROGER CASEMENT V   17
    NO MATTER WHAT HAPPENS AND WHO TAKES THE FALL, ...   616 MARCH SONGS 3   22
    SOME THINK IT A MATTER OF COURSE THAT CHANCE . . . . .   626 OLD MEN BE MAD   9
    SOME THINK IT MATTER OF COURSE THAT CHANCE . . . . . .   626 OLD MEN BE MAD V   9
    WILL HE NOT SPARE HER LIFE? HOW WOULD ONE MATTER . . .   696 MOSADA 2   3
MATTERS
    WHAT MATTERS WERE AFOOT AMONG THE SIDHE, ...   182 QUEEN MAEVE   61
    ARE DUST ON THE MOTH'S WING, THAT NOTHING MATTERS . . .   235 SHADOW WATER B   297
    "WHILE I HAVE HIM AND YOU IT MATTERS LITTLE . . . . .   280 TWO KINGS   85
MATTOCK
    AND A SMALL AND A FEEBLE POPULACE STOOPING WITH MATTOCK   58 OISIN 3   164
      AND SPADE,
    AND A SMALL AND A FEEBLE RACE STOOPING WITH MATTOCK AND   58 OISIN 3   V 164
      SPADE.
    AND A SMALL AND FEEBLE RACE STOOPING WITH MATTOCK   58 OISIN 3   V 164
      AND SPADE.
MATTRESS
    ON GRASSY MATTRESS I HAD LAID ME, ...   387 SOLOMON WITCH   3
MAUD
    THE BLINDS DRAWN UP", MAUD GONNE AT HOWTH STATION WAITING   578 LOFTY THINGS   10
      A TRAIN,
MAULED
    THEY MAULED AND BIT THE WHOLE NIGHT THROUGH, ...   297 THREE BEGGARS   48
    THEY MAULED AND BIT TILL THE DAY SHONE, ...   297 THREE BEGGARS   49
    THEY MAULED AND BIT THROUGH ALL THAT DAY . . . . . .   297 THREE BEGGARS   50
    THEY'D MAULED AND BITTEN THE NIGHT THROUGH, ...   297 THREE BEGGARS V   48
MAUNDERING
    MAUNDERING HERE, AND MAUNDERING THERE, ...   451 FIRST LOVE   15
    MAUNDERING HERE, AND MAUNDERING THERE, ...   451 FIRST LOVE   15
MAURYA
    TILL MAURYA OF THE WOUNDED HEART CRY A SWEET CRY, . . .   173 SPEAKS HEARERS V   6
MAURYA'S
    IS COMELIER THAN CANDLES BEFORE MAURYA'S FEET. . . . .   147 UNAPPEAS HOST V   12
MAVRONE
    "MAVRONE, MAVRONE! THE MAN HAS DIED . . . .   133 FR GILLIGAN   25
    "MAVRONE, MAVRONE! THE MAN HAS DIED . . . .   133 FR GILLIGAN   25
MAXIMS
    AND YET UPON THESE MAXIMS MEDITATE, ...   500 VACILLATION   22
MAYBE
    MAYBE YOU HAVE NOT HEARD OF US, YOU HAVE COME FORTH SO   75 ANASHU VIJAYA   78
      NEWLY,
    I SAID, "A LINE WILL TAKE US HOURS MAYBE, ...   204 ADAMS CURSE   4
    MAYBE THEY LINGER BY THE WAY. . . . .   212 BLESS PSALTER   8
    MAYBE IT IS BUT NATURAL TO DOUBT ME. . . . .   227 SHADOW WATER B   112
    ANOTHER ANSWERS, "MAYBE WE SHALL FIND . . . .   233 SHADOW WATER B   254

507

PAGE   TITLE   LINE

MAYBE (CONTINUED)
    MAYBE YOUR IMAGES HAVE STOOD,   273 GREY ROCK   50
    "MAYBE I SHALL BE LUCKY YET,   297 THREE BEGGARS   61
    AND MAYBE I SHALL TAKE A TROUT   297 THREE BEGGARS   67
    HAVING LOVED GOD ONCE, BUT MAYBE   299 THREE HERMITS   26
    OR MAYBE TO MIDSUMMER DAY,"   305 HOUR DAWN   58
    MAYBE THE WEATHER WAS ACCURSED   305 HOUR DAWN   65
    I'LL SAY AND MAYBE DREAM I HAVE DRAWN CONTENT,   333 LIVING BEAUTY   V   1
    THAT MAYBE "I AM SORRY" IN PLAIN PROSE   341 SHEP GOATHERD   60
    MAYBE A TWELVEMONTH SINCE   348 FISHERMAN   25
    POEM MAYBE AS COLD   348 FISHERMAN   39
    MAYBE A TWELVE-MONTH SINCE   348 FISHERMAN   V 25
    THERE IS A QUEEN IN CHINA, OR MAYBE IT'S IN SPAIN,   353 HIS PHOENIX   1
    AND MAYBE THERE'LL BE SOME YOUNG BELLE WALK OUT TO MAKE   354 HIS PHOENIX   V 26
      MEN WILD
    BUT MAYBE SOME OLD GAFFER MUTTERS A BLESSING   355 BROKEN DREAMS   4
    FEATURES, OR MAYBE SHOWING   363 DOLLS DRAWINGS   4
    MAYBE THE MOON MAY LEARN,   378 CAT AND MOON   14
    THAT IT MAYBE HAD DANCED HER LIFE AWAY,   383 VISION ROBART   V 22
    MAYBE THE BRIDE-BED BRINGS DESPAIR,   388 SOLOMON WITCH   25
    MAYBE AN IMAGE IS TOO STRONG   388 SOLOMON WITCH   36
    OR MAYBE IS NOT STRONG ENOUGH."   388 SOLOMON WITCH   37
    "MAYBE A BREATH OF POLITIC WORDS   396 ROSE TREE   3
    OR MAYBE BUT A WIND THAT BLOWS   396 ROSE TREE   5
    LOSE NATURAL KINDNESS AND MAYBE   404 FOR DAUGHTER   22
    AND MAYBE THE GREAT-GRANDSON OF THAT HOUSE,   418 ANCEST HOUSES   23
    THAT WOULD NOT LIFT A HAND MAYBE   432 NINETEEN 19   109
    WHEN MAYBE THRICE IN EVERY MOON HER MOUTH   468 HARUN RASHID   162
    FOR MAYBE ALL THAT HEAR   474 ALL SOUL NIGHT   89
    AND MAYBE WE ARE ALL THE SAME   570 THREE BUSHES   24
    AND MAYBE WE ARE ALL THE SAME   570 THREE BUSHES   26
    OR MAYBE SUBSTANCE CAN BE COMPOSITE,   619 BRONZE HEAD   12
    MAYBE AT LAST, BEING BUT A BROKEN MAN,   629 CIRCUS ANIMALS   3
    AND MAYBE WHAT THEY SAY IS TRUE   631 POLITICS   9
    SOME DAY YOU'LL BUY THEM, MAYBE. NEVER! NEVER?   721 WITCH VIVIEN   24
    MAYBE NOW IN SOME FAR LANE,   731 STREET DANCERS   14
    MAYBE IN SOME ISLE OF ISLES,   732 STREET DANCERS   27
    MAYBE NOW A BEDOUIN'S BROOD,   732 STREET DANCERS   40
    AND THE OTHER ANSWERS, "MAYBE WE SHALL FIND   753 SHADOW WATER A   144
    OR MAYBE AN AGATE CUP.   781 MY HEART BEAT   16
    MAYBE I SHALL NOT DIE AT ALL.   788 HAWTHORN TREE   16
MAYHAP
    MAYHAP 'TWERE BETTER THAT ASIDE I THROW   656 ISLE STAT I 3   38
    ONCE MORE THOSE SHEPHERDS COME. MAYHAP SOME MIRTH   664 ISLE STAT II 2   49
MAYO
    IN MUSCULAR YOUTH WELL KNOWN TO MAYO MEN   325 ROBERT GREGORY   34
    IN MUSCULAR YOUTH WELLKNOWN TO MAYO MEN   325 ROBERT GREGORY V   34
MAYOR
    THE MAYOR CAME, LEANING HIS DEAF EAR—   725 LEGEND   13
MAY-TREASURE
    ALL THE HEALING EARTH MAY-TREASURE,   733 STREET DANCERS   63
MCTAGGART
    PROFOUND MCTAGGART THOUGHT SO, AND IN A BREATH   619 BRONZE HEAD   13
MEAD
    AS THOUGH HE HELD AN EARTHLY MEAD   2 OISIN 1   V 7X
    WE PASSED IN SILENCE O'ER THE MEAD,   25 OISIN 1   V 376A
MEADOW
    BY LAKES AND MEADOW LANDS AND LAWNS AFAR,   32 OISIN 2   V 50F
    LEAP IN THE MEADOW. ON THE MISTY STAIRS   44 OISIN 2   V 229
    WEAK, IN THE MIDST OF THE MEADOW.   54 OISIN 3   102
    OR ELSE AT MEADOW OR AT GRAZING OVERLOOKS   340 SHEP GOATHERD   37
MEADOW-MICE
    AND GAZE ON THE MEADOW-MICE WARY,   707 FAIRY PEDANT   18
MEADOWS
    AMONG THE WINDY MEADOWS OF THE DAWN."   234 SHADOW WATER B   264
    ON HIS YELLOW LEGS THROUGH OUR MEADOWS,   341 SHEP GOATHERD   65
    UPON HIS YELLOW LEGS THROUGH OUR MEADOWS,   341 SHEP GOATHERD V   65
    THROUGH GOD-FORSAKEN MEADOWS! MRS. FRENCH,   412 TOWER   93
    AMONG THE WINDY MEADOWS OF THE DAWN."   754 SHADOW WATER A   153
    WE WILL FIND OUT VALLEYS AND WOODS AND MEADOWS   767 SHADOW WATER A   388
    OR AMONG WINDS THAT MOVE IN THE MEADOWS AND WOODS.   768 SHADOW WATER A V   413
MEADOW-SAFFRONS
    WHERE THE MEADOW-SAFFRONS BLOW,   680 LOVE AND DEATH   6
MEAGRE
    FROM MEAGRE GIRLHOOD'S PUTTING ON   356 BROKEN DREAMS   9
MEAL
    AND SLEEPY HAVING HAD THEIR MEAL!   271 GREY ROCK   V 17
    TILL HIS MORNING MEAL COME ROUND!   435 FOR MY SON   4
MEAN
    MEAN ROOF-TREES WERE THE STURDIER FOR ITS FALL,   264 HOUSE SHAKEN   8
    YOU MEAN THEY ARGUED. PUT IT SO!   385 ROBARTES DANCE   13
    HERE'S THE GIST OF WHAT THEY MEAN.   637 BEN BULBEN   12
    THY FLICKERING HAND? WHAT MEAN THE LIGHTS THAT RISE   674 ISLE STAT II 3   198
MEANING
    OR LET ITS MEANING MIX INTO THE STRINGS.   180 QUEEN MAEVE   8
    A MEANING IN THAT CIRCLING OVERHEAD?   234 SHADOW WATER B   270
    BUT WHAT'S THE MEANING? WHY DO YOU LINGER THERE?   234 SHADOW WATER B   271
    THEY CANNOT HEAR MY VOICE! BUT WHAT'S THE MEANING?   234 SHADOW WATER B   275
    THAT CANNOT BE THE MEANING OF THE BIRDS.   235 SHADOW WATER B   278
    THE MEANING OF THAT MONSTROUS DAY. THEN SHE!   280 TWO KINGS   78
    DAY AFTER DAY, YET NEVER FIND THE MEANING.   377 PHASES OF MOON   135

		PAGE	TITLE	LINE

MEANING   (CONTINUED)
    WHAT'S THE MEANING OF ALL SONG?   . . . .   502 VACILLATION   70
MEANINGLESS
    OR POLITE MEANINGLESS WORDS, ...   392 EASTER 1916   6
    POLITE MEANINGLESS WORDS, ...   392 EASTER 1916   8
MEANS
    BY ANY OTHER MEANS. YOU CALL IT PASSION, ...   244 SHADOW WATER B   455
    IT'S PLAIN THE BIBLE MEANS   . . . .   345 ON WOMAN   10
MEANT
    AND THAT DEAR WORDS MEANT NOTHING?" BUT ENOUGH, ...   201 OLD MEMORY   9
    THAT THINK SWORD-STROKES WERE BETTER MEANT . . . . . .   276 GREY ROCK   129
    THAT THINK SWORD STROKES WERE BETTER MEANT . . . . . .   276 GREY ROCK   V   129
    WHAT ROBERT BROWNING MEANT . . . .   605 YOU CONTENT   22
MEASURE
    WHO WHEN THEY DANCE TO A FITFUL MEASURE . . . .   9 OISIN 1   97
    IN A VIGOUR MORE THAN MORTAL MEASURE, ...   9 OISIN 1   V   98
    THE MEASURE OF HER FLYING FEET . . . .   138 TO IRELAND   11
    TO LIGHT A MEASURE HERE AND THERE: . . . .   138 TO IRELAND   14
    WORTH KNITTING TO A MEASURE OF SWEET SOUND?   . . . .   181 QUEEN MAEVE   33
    OUTRUN THE MEASURE. I'D TELL OF THAT GREAT QUEEN   . . .   187 QUEEN MAEVE   141
    THAT WEIGH AND MEASURE ALL IN THESE WASTE SEAS--   . . .   235 SHADOW WATER B   292
    AND MEASURE OUT A COURSE AND BRING US HOME, ...   238 SHADOW WATER B   362
    THERE IS NO MEASURE THAT IT WOULD NOT BURST.   . . . .   245 SHADOW WATER B   484
    HAVE BEEN THE MEASURE OF THAT CARE." BUT EOCHAID,   . .   276 TWO KINGS   V   H
    TILL TOES MASTERED A SWEET MEASURE, ...   331 ROUND TOWER   15
    I'D DANCE A MEASURE ON HIS GRAVE."   . . . .   338 TOM OROUGHLEY   16
    FOR RHYME CAN BEAT A MEASURE OUT OF TROUBLE   . . . .   339 SHEP GOATHERD   12
    MEASURE THE LOT: FORGIVE MYSELF THE LOT!   . . . . .   479 SELF AND SOUL   67
    AND MEASURE OUT THE WAYS OF CHIVALRY.   . . . . . .   660 ISLE STAT II 1   37
    NAY, GIVE IT ME, AND I WILL SOUND A MEASURE: . . . .   681 SEEKER   9
    AND MEASURE THE MINDS OF THE FLOWERS, ...   707 FAIRY PEDANT   17
    AS THOUGH THEY'D VOWED TO MEASURE ALL ITS WAYS.   . . .   711 FERENCZ RENYI   48
    WOULD THEY FOOT SO FLEET A MEASURE?   . . . .   731 STREET DANCERS   12
    WOULD THEY FOOT SO FLEET A MEASURE?   . . . .   732 STREET DANCERS   25
    WOULD THEY FOOT SO FLEET A MEASURE?   . . . .   732 STREET DANCERS   38
    WOULD THEY FOOT SO FLEET A MEASURE?   . . . .   733 STREET DANCERS   51
    WOULD THEY FOOT SO FLEET A MEASURE?   . . . .   733 STREET DANCERS   64
    WERE HIS MEASURE RUNNING DRY.   . . . .   772 SONG DEIRDRE 1   14
MEASURED   SEE PLUMMET-MEASURED
    UPON A MEASURED QUIETUDE.   . . . .   138 TO IRELAND   16
    YET HE WHO TREADS IN MEASURED WAYS   . . . .   138 TO IRELAND   27
    YOU HAVE MEASURED OUT THE ROAD THAT THE SOUL TREADS . .   342 SHEP GOATHERD   80
MEASURELESS
    A MEASURELESS CONSUMMATION THAT HE DREAMED.   . . . .   324 ROBERT GREGORY   24
MEASUREMENT
    WHAT CALCULATION, NUMBER, MEASUREMENT, REPLIED?   . . .   611 STATUES   27
    MEASUREMENT BEGAN OUR MIGHT: . . . .   638 BEN BULBEN   42
    IN TOILS OF MEASUREMENT   . . . .   784 WOMANS BEAUTY   9
    IN TOIL OF MEASUREMENT   . . . .   784 WOMANS BEAUTY   V   9
MEASURER
    WHAT MEASURER TIME HAS LIT ABOVE, ...   139 TO IRELAND   38
MEASURES
    HE WHO MEASURES GAIN AND LOSS, ...   744 ROSY CROSS   1
    HE WHO MEASURES GAIN AND LOSS, ...   744 ROSY CROSS   9
    WERE HIS MEASURES RUNNING DRY.   . . . .   772 SONG DEIRDRE 1 V   14
MEASURING
    ON THAT OLD QUEEN MEASURING A TOWN   . . . .   344 DAWN   3
    ON THE OLD QUEEN MEASURING A TOWN . . . .   344 DAWN   V   3
MEAT
    THOSE TWO CAME CARRYING WINE AND MEAT AND BREAD,   . . .   41 OISIN 2   184
    QUIET'S WILD HEART, LIKE DAILY MEAT: . . . . . .   196 BAILE AILLINN   178
    TO MAKE LOW LAUGHTER MORE THAN MEAT AND DRINK,   . . .   230 SHADOW WATER B   186
    FOR ALL WERE FULL OF WINE AND MEAT.   . . . .   271 GREY ROCK   17
    TO TAKE THE ROSES FOR HIS MEAT.   . . . .   382 SONG OF FOOL   12
    AND YET IN FLYING FLING INTO MY MEAT   . . . . . .   384 VISION ROBART   53
    A CRAZY SALAD WITH THEIR MEAT   . . . .   404 FOR DAUGHTER   31
    AND TOOK A MESS OF SHADOWS FOR ITS MEAT?   . . . . .   444 SCHOOL CHILDR   28
    AND TOOK A MASS OF SHADOWS FOR ITS MEAT, ...   444 SCHOOL CHILDR   V   28
    AND MEAT TO THE ASLAUGA SHEE.   . . . .   743 DANAAN QUICK   17
    AND TASTE WITH ME THE FAERIES' MEAT, ...   743 DANAAN QUICK   26
MECHANICAL
    AND NEVER STOOP TO A MECHANICAL   . . . .   417 ANCEST HOUSES   7
MEDDLE
    OR MEDDLE WITH OUR GIVE AND TAKE   . . . .   395 SIXTEEN DEAD   17
MEDDLING
    HE HAS HAD ENOUGH OF MEDDLING WHO CAN PLEASE   . . . .   359 WAR POEM   4
MEDIAEVAL
    MY MEDIAEVAL KNEES LACK HEALTH UNTIL THEY BEND,   . . .   603 GALLERY REVIS   33
MEDIAN
    WHAT MEDIAN, PERSIAN, BABYLONIAN, ...   420 MY HOUSE   V   20D
MEDIATION
    A MEDIATION IN TIME OF WAR . . . .   406 IN TIME OF WAR V   T
MEDICABLE
    SOME MEDICABLE HERB TO MAKE OUR GRIEF   . . . . . .   342 SHEP GOATHERD   86
MEDICINE
    FOR MEDICINE." THEREON HE CRIED ALOUD, ...   281 TWO KINGS   98
MEDITATE
    I MEDITATE UPON A SWALLOW'S FLIGHT, ...   488 COOLE PARK 29   1
    AND YET UPON THESE MAXIMS MEDITATE: . . . . . .   500 VACILLATION   22
    TO MEDITATE ON.   . . . .   628 JANE MOUNTAIN   6
    AS THOUGH TO MEDITATE ON WOUNDS AND BLOOD.   . . . .   634 CUCHULAIN COMF   6

509

	PAGE	TITLE		LINE

MEDITATION
THE MEDITATION OF THE OLD FISHERMAN • • • • • • • • 90 OLD FISHERMAN T
A MEDITATION IN TIME OF WAR • • • • • • • • • • • 406 IN TIME OF WAR T
A MAN IN HIS OWN SECRET MEDITATION • • • • • • • • 431 NINETEEN 19 69
TILL MEDITATION MASTER ALL ITS PARTS. • • • • • • • 474 ALL SOUL NIGHT 92
AT ALGECIRAS--A MEDITATION UPON DEATH • • • • • • • 493 AT ALGECIRAS T
A MEDITATION WRITTEN DURING SICKNESS AT ALGECIRAS • • 493 AT ALGECIRAS V T
FOR ANTIQUARIAN MEDITATION. AY, • • • • • • • • • 721 WITCH VIVIEN 38
MEDITATIONS
MEDITATIONS IN TIME OF CIVIL WAR ANCESTRAL HOUSES • • • 417 ANCEST HOUSES V T
FOR MEDITATIONS UPON UNKNOWN THOUGHT • • • • • • • 473 ALL SOUL NIGHT 74
MEDITATIONS UPON DEATH • • • • • • • • • • • • • 493 AT ALGECIRAS V T
MEDITATIVE
THE MEDITATIVE CRITIC: ALL ARE ON THEIR TOES, • • • • 363 DOLLS FACES 8
THAT MEDITATIVE MAN, JOHN SYNGE, AND THOSE • • • • • 489 COOLE PARK 29 13
AND HERE'S JOHN SYNGE, A MEDITATIVE MAN, • • • • • • 603 GALLERY REVIS V 48
MEDIUM
THE SPIRIT MEDIUM • • • • • • • • • • • • • • • 599 SPIRIT MEDIUM T
MEDIUM'S
OUT OF A MEDIUM'S MOUTH, • • • • • • • • • • • • 439 FRAGMENTS 6
MEEK
OR HAST THOU NEVER SEEN, WITH VISAGE MEEK, • • • • • 672 ISLE STAT II 3 156
MEET
AND WHERE THE WOOD AND WATERS MEET • • • • • • • • 14 OISIN 1 193
AND WHERE THE WOODS AND WATERS MEET • • • • • • • • 14 OISIN 1 V 193
DOWN BY THE SALLEY GARDENS MY LOVE AND I DID MEET: • • 90 SALLEY GARDENS 1
AND CRIED WITH ANGRY VOICE, "IT IS NOT MEET • • • • 107 CUCHULAIN SEA 20
AND CRIED OUT TO HIM, "SON IT IS NOT MEET • • • • • 107 CUCHULAIN SEA V 20
AND CALLED OUT TO HIM, "SON IT IS NOT MEET • • • • • 107 CUCHULAIN SEA V 20
THAT YOU COME HERE TO MEET THIS ANCIENT SWORD?" • • • 109 CUCHULAIN SEA V 61
MAY SURELY MEET THEIR ANCIENT GAZE. • • • • • • • • 139 TO IRELAND V 28
VEERING, FLEETING, FICKLE, OUR LOVES AND ANGERS MEET! • 207 HANRAHANS SONG V 3
BY THE WOOD'S EDGE WHERE ONLY EQUALS MEET, • • • • • 321 REED WHISPERER V 8
ALWAYS WE'D HAVE THE NEW FRIEND MEET THE OLD • • • • 324 ROBERT GREGORY 9
SO PERILOUS THAT HALF THE ASTONISHED MEET • • • • • 326 ROBERT GREGORY 61
I KNOW THAT I SHALL MEET MY FATE • • • • • • • • • 328 IRISH AIRMAN 1
WHEN MY LUCK CHANGED AND THEY DARED MEET MY FACE, • • 352 PEOPLE 25
WHEN MY LUCK CHANGED AND THEY DARED TO MEET MY FACE, • 352 PEOPLE V 25
SUDDENLY I MEET YOUR FACE. • • • • • • • • • • • 357 DEEP-SWORN VOW 6
WHEN TWO CLOSE KINDRED MEET, • • • • • • • • • • 378 CAT AND MOON 12
UNDER BEN BULBEN TO THE MEET, • • • • • • • • • • 397 POLIT PRISONER 14
BIRTH-HOUR AND DEATH-HOUR MEET, • • • • • • • • • 496 MOHINI CHATTER 26
I KNOW, ALTHOUGH WHEN LOOKS MEET • • • • • • • • • 511 JANE AND JACK 1
THINKING TO MEET MY LOVE ONCE MORE • • • • • • • • 551 SONGS REWRIT 1 V 15
MATTER FOR OLD AGE MEET: • • • • • • • • • • • • 553 CHURCH STATE 2
IF JUPITER AND SATURN MEET, • • • • • • • • • • • 562 CONJUNCTIONS 1
WHEN YOU AND MY TRUE LOVER-MEET • • • • • • • • • 573 LADYS 3RD SONG 1
NOW HER SHEEP ALL BROWSING MEET • • • • • • • • • 646 ISLE STAT I 1 22
BENDING HER FACE O'ER HIS, SHE WATCHES MEET • • • • • 688 TWO TITANS 45
YET SOMEWHERE IN THE FOOTSORE WORLD WE MEET, • • • • 691 MOSADA 1 23
WE MEET--WE TWO, HOW MERRY ALL THESE ARE • • • • • • 691 MOSADA 1 31
WE MEET AT LAST, THE MINISTERING STARS • • • • • • • 701 MOSADA 3 52
MEETING
A MURMUR OF SOFT WORDS AND MEETING LIPS. • • • • • • 187 QUEEN MAEVE 154
ALL THAT IS NOT THE MEETING OF OUR LIPS. • • • • • 246 SHADOW WATER B 506
MEETING • • • • • • • • • • • • • • • • • • • 539 MEETING T
MEETING LONG HENCE THE PHANTOM HERDSMAN, KING • • • • 675 ISLE STAT II 3 242
MEETINGS
THEY HOLD THEIR PUBLIC MEETINGS WHERE • • • • • • • 460 THREE MONUMENT 1
MEET'S
THE MEET'S UPON THE MOUNTAIN-SIDE. • • • • • • • • 549 SEVERED HEAD 6
THE MEET'S UPON THE MOUNTAIN SIDE. • • • • • • • • 549 SEVERED HEAD V 6
MEETS
FOR HORSEMANSHIP AT MEETS OR AT RACECOURSES, • • • • 325 ROBERT GREGORY 35
IN MUSCULAR YOUTH, AT MEETS OR AT RACECOURSES, • • • 325 ROBERT GREGORY V 35
FOR HORSEMANSHIP AT MEETS OR AT RACE-COURSES, • • • • 325 ROBERT GREGORY V 35
AND WHEN SHE MEETS OUR GAZE HER EYES ARE LAUGHTER-LIT. • 362 HER COURTESY 5
AND WHEN SHE MEETS OUR GAZE HER EYES ARE LAUGHTER LIT • 362 HER COURTESY V 5
WHERE EVERYTHING THAT MEETS THE EYE. • • • • • • • 639 BEN BULBEN 56
MEG
FOR PEG AND MEG AND PARIS' LOVE • • • • • • • • • 458 HIS WILDNESS 3
MELANCHOLY
TO WANDER BY THEIR MELANCHOLY MINDS. • • • • • • • 72 ANASHU VIJAYA 33
A MELANCHOLY THAT A CUP OF WINE, • • • • • • • • • 227 SHADOW WATER B 114
UPON A MELANCHOLY MAN ; • • • • • • • • • • • • 360 ALF POLLEXFEN 11
BUT A SUDDEN MELANCHOLY • • • • • • • • • • • • 667 ISLE STAT II 3 30
MELLOW
MANSIONS OF MEMORIES AND MELLOW THOUGHTS • • • • • 721 WITCH VIVIEN 21
TO THOSE YOUR "MELLOW" WARES HAVE WEARIED OUT. • • • 721 WITCH VIVIEN 27
MELODIES
ONE ASKS FOR MOURNFUL MELODIES: • • • • • • • • • 567 LAPIS LAZULI 53
MELODIOUS
REWORDING IN MELODIOUS GUILE • • • • • • • • • • 66 HAPPY SHEPHERD 39
REWARDING IN MELODIOUS GUILE • • • • • • • • • • 66 HAPPY SHEPHERD V 39
MELODY
SING IN THEIR HIGH AND LONELY MELODY. • • • • • • • 101 ROSE UPON ROOD 8
HAS GIVEN THE WAVES THEIR MELODY, • • • • • • • • 134 TWO TREES 10
HARRIED, AND BURKE'S GREAT MELODY AGAINST IT. • • • • 487 SEVEN SAGES 16
A QUENCHLESS GRIEVING OF LOVE MELODY. • • • • • • • 645 ISLE STAT I 1 21
MELT
MELT DOWN, AS IT WERE WAX IN THE SUN'S RAYS: • • • • 428 NINETEEN 19 12

		PAGE	TITLE		LINE

MELT (CONTINUED)
    SAINT JOSEPH THOUGHT THE WORLD WOULD MELT • • • • • • • 619 STICK INCENSE 3
MELTED
    THE SINGING MELTED IN THE NIGHT; • • • • • • • • • • 28 OISIN 1 V 427A
    MELTED AND FLOWED; AND IN THE SELF-SAME PLACE • • • • • 39 OISIN 2 V 146
MELTING
    DREAMING OF HER OWN MELTING HUES, • • • • • • • • • 13 OISIN 1 162
    AND DREAMS OF HER OWN MELTING HUES, • • • • • • • • • 13 OISIN 1 V 162
MEMORIAM
    IN MEMORIAM • • • • • • • • • • • • • • • • 737 MOURN THEN ON V T
MEMORIES
    WERE THE MEMORIES OF THE WHOLE OF MY SORROW • • • • • • 52 OISIN 3 71
    • • • AND THE MEMORIES OF THE WHOLE OF MY MIRTH, • • • 52 OISIN 3 71
    SPEAK, YOU TOO ARE OLD WITH YOUR MEMORIES, • • • • • 61 OISIN 3 196
    SPEAK, THOU TOO ART OLD WITH THY MEMORIES, • • • • 61 OISIN 3 V 196
    GAY BELLS OR SAD, THEY BRING YOU MEMORIES • • • • • 130 BOOK STORIES 21
    THEY BRING YOU MEMORIES OF OLD VILLAGE FACES, • • • • • 130 BOOK STORIES V 22
    HAVE SUCH LONG MEMORIES THAT THEY STILL • • • • • • • 192 BAILE AILLINN 90
    THAT WERE LIKE MEMORIES OF YOU--BUT NOW • • • • • • 257 RECONCILIATION 7
    VANISHED, AND LEFT BUT MEMORIES, THAT SHOULD BE OUT OF 316 COLD HEAVEN 5
        SEASON
    VAGUE MEMORIES, NOTHING BUT MEMORIES. • • • • • • • 356 BROKEN DREAMS 15
    VAGUE MEMORIES, NOTHING BUT MEMORIES. • • • • • • • 356 BROKEN DREAMS 15
    VAGUE MEMORIES, NOTHING BUT MEMORIES, • • • • • • • 356 BROKEN DREAMS 20
    VAGUE MEMORIES, NOTHING BUT MEMORIES. • • • • • • • 356 BROKEN DREAMS 20
    VAGUE MEMORIES, NOTHING BUT MEMORIES. • • • • • • • 357 BROKEN DREAMS 41
    VAGUE MEMORIES, NOTHING BUT MEMORIES. • • • • • • • 357 BROKEN DREAMS 41
    BY CHILDISH MEMORIES OF AN OLD CROSS POLLEXFEN, • • • • 391 UNDER SATURN 7
    MY MEMORIES HAD MAGNIFIED • • • • • • • • • • 399 BREAK OF DAY 10
    IMAGES AND MEMORIES • • • • • • • • • • • • 410 TOWER 22
    FOR I NEED ALL HIS MIGHTY MEMORIES. • • • • • • • 413 TOWER 104
    AND MEMORIES OF LOVE, • • • • • • • • • • • 415 TOWER 161
    MEMORIES OF THE WORDS OF WOMEN, • • • • • • • • 415 TOWER 162
    HIS MEMORIES • • • • • • • • • • • • • • 454 HIS MEMORIES T
    MEMORIES OF THE TALK • • • • • • • • • • • 607 SONGS BURDEN 2 22
    MANSIONS OF MEMORIES AND MELLOW THOUGHTS • • • • • 721 WITCH VIVIEN 21
MEMORY
    IN BROODING MEMORY, NOR WEEP. • • • • • • • • 11 OISIN 1 V 131B
    IN SOME DIM MEMORY OR ANCIENT MOOD, • • • • • • 36 OISIN 2 99
    WRAPT ROUND IN SOME DIM MEMORY, IT SEEMED-- • • • • 36 OISIN 2 V 99
    WAS LOADED WITH THE MEMORY OF DAYS • • • • • • 39 OISIN 2 150
    'TIS OVER; FAR WITH MEMORY I SWAY AND ROCK. • • • • 43 OISIN 2 V 212
    AND TURNED THE FARMER'S MEMORY FROM HIS CATTLE, • • • • 129 BOOK STORIES 6
    ARE IN MY MEMORY; • • • • • • • • • • • 132 OLD PENSIONER 16
    WE HOLD, BECAUSE OUR MEMORY IS • • • • • • • • 192 BAILE AILLINN 85
    OLD MEMORY • • • • • • • • • • • • • • 201 OLD MEMORY T
    AWAKENS AN OLD MEMORY, AND SAY, • • • • • • • 201 OLD MEMORY 2
    WHERE WINGS HAVE MEMORY OF WINGS, AND ALL • • • • • 264 HOUSE SHAKEN 6
    A HUNDRED-YEAR-OLD MEMORY TO THE POOR; • • • • • 269 PARDON FATHERS 6
    IN·DAYS YOU HAVE NOT KEPT IN MEMORY, • • • • • • 284 TWO KINGS 168
    HAD HALF AWAKENED SOME OLD MEMORY-- • • • • • • 284 TWO KINGS 172
    HAD HALF WAKENED SOME OLD MEMORY, • • • • • • • 284 TWO KINGS V 172
    THIS HUMAN LIFE BLOTTED FROM MEMORY, • • • • • • 285 TWO KINGS 198
    CAN BLOT OUT OF MY MEMORY THIS LIFE • • • • • • 285 TWO KINGS 204
    A MEMORY OF YOUTH • • • • • • • • • • • 313 MEMORY YOUTH T
    IN MEMORY OF MAJOR ROBERT GREGORY • • • • • • • 323 ROBERT GREGORY T
    IN MEMORY OF ROBERT GREGORY • • • • • • • • • 323 ROBERT GREGORY V T
    MEMORY • • • • • • • • • • • • • • • 350 MEMORY T
    IN MEMORY OF ALFRED POLLEXFEN • • • • • • • • 360 ALF POLLEXFEN T
    IN MEMORY • • • • • • • • • • • • • • 360 ALF POLLEXFEN V T
    WHO CARRIED IN THEIR MEMORY • • • • • • • • • 361 ALF POLLEXFEN 34
    IS MEMORY OR FOREKNOWLEDGE OF THE HOUR • • • • • 375 PHASES OF MOON 73
    BEFORE MY TIME, SEEM LIKE A VIVID MEMORY. • • • • 391 UNDER SATURN 10
    WHOSE IMAGES, IN THE GREAT MEMORY STORED, • • • • 412 TOWER 85
    AND THAT IF MEMORY RECUR, THE SUN'S • • • • • • 414 TOWER 119
    THAT LIVES IN MEMORY. • • • • • • • • • • 459 HIS WILDNESS 10
    EVEN FROM THAT DELIGHT MEMORY TREASURES SO, • • • • 459 FROM OEDIPUS 4
    AND SPEAK BUT LIES. CALL UP TO MEMORY • • • • 462 HARUN RASHID V 30
    IN MEMORY OF EVA GORE-BOOTH AND CON MARKIEWICZ • • • • 475 EVA GORE-BOOTH T
    A MOMENT'S MEMORY TO THAT LAURELLED HEAD. • • • • 489 COOLE PARK 29 32
    OR GARDENS RICH IN MEMORY GLORIFIED • • • • • 491 COOLE BALLYLEE 35
    MOCK AT THE MEMORY OF BOTH O'NEILLS, • • • • • 546 TO SAME TUNE 2 24
    MOCK AT THE MEMORY OF· BOTH O'NEILLS, • • • • • 614 MARCH SONGS 1 24
    TO ENGROSS THE PRESENT AND DOMINATE MEMORY. • • • • 630 CIRCUS ANIMALS 30
    AND THY MEMORY I KEEP, • • • • • • • • • 647 ISLE STAT I 1 59
    HIS MEMORY NOW IS A TALL PILLAR, BURNING • • • • 738 MOURN THEN ON 15
    OUT OF MEMORY AND MIND. • • • • • • • • • 775 AGAINST WITCH 10
    A MEMORY, EVEN TO THE DEAD, • • • • • • • • 791 REPRISALS 8
MEN   SEE FIGHTING-MEN
    THE BAD OLD DAYS. THOU WERT, MEN SING, • • • • • 2 OISIN 1 V 3
    CRIED FIN; AND CRIED SHE, "MEN OF FAME, • • • • • 5 OISIN 1 V 45
    ALL MEN, AND STRONGER OF HIS HANDS, • • • • • • 7 OISIN 1 V 63
    WHERE MEN HAVE HEAPED NO BURIAL-MOUNDS, • • • • • 8 OISIN 1 82
    WHERE MEN HAVE HEAPED NO BURIAL MOUNDS, • • • • • 8 OISIN 1 V 82
    OF MEN AND LADIES, HAND IN HAND, • • • • • • • 15 OISIN 1 202
    OF MEN AND MAIDENS, HAND IN HAND, • • • • • • • 15 OISIN 1 V 202
    AND MEN AND LADIES KNELT THEM THERE • • • • • • 18 OISIN 1 255
    AND MEN AND MAIDENS KNELT THEM THERE • • • • • • 18 OISIN 1 V 255
    O'ER MEN WHO SLEEP, AND WAKE, AND DIE, • • • • • 22 OISIN 1 V 340B
    WITH ALL THE ANCIENT SORROW OF MEN"; • • • • • 25 OISIN 1 381
    WHO WEDDED MEN WITH RINGS OF DRUID GOLD; • • • • • 29 OISIN 2 10

MEN (CONTINUED)

	PAGE	TITLE		LINE
THE SADDEST OF ALL MEN."	33	OISIN 2		68
"FOR ALL MEN FLEE THE DEMONS"; BUT MOVED NOT	36	OISIN 2		93
TO RULE MORE MIGHTY MEN, AND TO THE WORLD	38	OISIN 2	V	133
WAR ON THE MIGHTIEST MEN UNDER THE SKIES,	45	OISIN 2		241
LIKE AN ARMY OF OLD MEN LONGING FOR REST FROM THE MOAN OF THE SEAS.	48	OISIN 3		16
AND EACH OF THE HUGE WHITE CREATURES WAS HUGER THAN FOURSCORE MEN;	49	OISIN 3		33
AND EACH OF THE HUGE WHITE CREATURES WAS HUGER THAN FOUR-SCORE MEN;	49	OISIN 3	V	33
HELPLESS, MEN LIFTING THE LIDS OF HIS WEARY AND DEATH-MAKING EYE.	53	OISIN 3		92
HELPLESS, MEN LIFTING THE LIDS OF HIS WEARY AND DEATH-POURING EYE.	53	OISIN 3	V	92
. . . AND MOVE WHERE THE OLD MEN AND YOUNG	55	OISIN 3		114
. . . AND SEE WHAT THE MORTAL MEN DO.	55	OISIN 3	V	125
LIKE AN ARMY OF OLD MEN LONGING FOR REST FROM THE MOAN OF THE SEAS.	57	OISIN 3		144
LIKE AN ARMY OF OLD MEN LOUNGING FOR REST FROM THE FOAM OF THE SEAS.	57	OISIN 3	V	144
. . . AND I KNEW HOW MEN SORROW AND PASS,	59	OISIN 3		175
. . . AND I KNEW HOW MEN PASS,	59	OISIN 3	V	175
WITH A SOB FOR MEN WAXING SO WEAKLY,	60	OISIN 3		188
HOW THE MEN OF THE SAND-SACK SHOWED ME A CHURCH	61	OISIN 3		193
HOW THE MEN OF THE SAND-SACK LED ME TO SHAUL,	61	OISIN 3	V	193
NO LEARNING FROM THE STARRY MEN,	66	HAPPY SHEPHERD		28
WHERE MEN LIE FROZEN IN THE GLIMMERING SNOW;	73	ANASHU VIJAYA		51
FIELDS FATTENING SLOW, MEN WISE IN JOY,	82	MAD KING GOLL	V	6
I CALLED MY BATTLE-BREAKING MEN	83	MAD KING GOLL		17
AROUND ME SHONE KEEN EYES OF MEN;	83	MAD KING GOLL		30
I DREW AT EVENING MY MAILED MEN,	83	MAD KING GOLL	V	19
AND SHONE AROUND THE EYES OF MEN;	83	MAD KING GOLL	V	30
AND LEARN TO CHAUNT A TONGUE MEN DO NOT KNOW.	101	ROSE UPON ROOD		21
AND LEARN TO CHANT A TONGUE MEN DO NOT KNOW.	101	ROSE UPON ROOD	V	21
"STILL TREADS THE WORLD AMID HIS ARMED MEN."	107	CUCHULAIN SEA	V	26
AMONG THOSE FEASTING MEN CUCHULAIN DWELT,	108	CUCHULAIN SEA		39
"THE DOOMS OF MEN ARE IN GOD'S HIDDEN PLACE."	110	CUCHULAIN SEA		62
THEN CONCHUBAR, THE SUBTLEST OF ALL MEN,	110	CUCHULAIN SEA		75
"THE DOOMS OF MEN ARE IN GOD'S HIDDEN HOARD."	110	CUCHULAIN SEA	V	62
REST FAR FROM MEN.	116	FAERY SONG		10
AND MEN WHO LOVED THE CAUSE THAT NEVER DIES.	130	BOOK STORIES	V	24
OF PASSIONATE MEN, LIKE BATS IN THE DEAD TREES;	136	TO SOME I TALK		5
AND HE SAW YOUNG MEN AND YOUNG GIRLS	144	HOST OF AIR		13
TO OLD MEN PLAYING AT CARDS.	144	HOST OF AIR		23
HE PLAYED WITH THE MERRY OLD MEN.	145	HOST OF AIR		29
OLD MEN AND YOUNG MEN AND YOUNG GIRLS	145	HOST OF AIR		39
OLD MEN AND YOUNG MEN AND YOUNG GIRLS	145	HOST OF AIR		39
BUT THE OLD MEN AND DANCERS WERE GONE,	145	HOST OF AIR	V	39
I CRIED IN MY DREAM, O WOMEN, BID THE YOUNG MEN LAY	163	VALLEY LOVERS		5
AND I CRIED IN MY DREAM "O WOMEN, BID THE YOUNG MEN LAY	163	VALLEY LOVERS	V	5
WOMEN AND CHILDREN, YOUNG MEN WITH BOOKS,	167	BLESSED		15
AND OLD MEN WITH CROZIERS AND STOLES.	167	BLESSED		16
CHILDREN AND WOMEN AND TONSURED YOUNG MEN,	167	BLESSED	V	15
MEN HAVE NAMED BEAUTY. THY GREAT LEAVES ENFOLD	169	SECRET ROSE		7
MEN HAVE NAMED BEAUTY. YOUR HEAVY LEAVES ENFOLD	169	SECRET ROSE	V	7
MEN HAVE NAMED BEAUTY. YOUR GREAT LEAVES ENFOLD	169	SECRET ROSE	V	7
THAT MEN THRESHED CORN AT MIDNIGHT BY A TRESS,	170	SECRET ROSE		26
TILL MAEVE CALLED OUT, "THESE ARE BUT COMMON MEN.	186	QUEEN MAEVE		122
OF HARPERS AND YOUNG MEN; AND THEY	189	BAILE AILLINN		19
AND OLD AND YOUNG MEN RODE WITH HER;	191	BAILE AILLINN		51
AND LEATHER-COATED MEN WITH SLINGS	193	BAILE AILLINN	V	111
AFTER THE DEATHS OF MANY MEN,	197	BAILE AILLINN		193
THE OLD MEN ADMIRING THEMSELVES IN THE WATER	208	OLD MEN ADMIRE		T
I HEARD THE OLD, OLD MEN SAY,	208	OLD MEN ADMIRE		1
I HEARD THE OLD, OLD MEN SAY,	208	OLD MEN ADMIRE		7
IS NOT KNOWN AMONG MEN.	215	HAPPY TOWNLAND		28
ON WET ROADS WHERE MEN WALK,	215	HAPPY TOWNLAND		48
YET DREAMED THAT BEINGS HAPPIER THAN MEN	218	WOODS OF COOLE		18
I HAVE MADE THIS POEM FOR YOU, THAT MEN MAY READ IT	219	WOODS OF COOLE		41
AS MEN IN THE OLD TIMES, BEFORE THE HARPS BEGAN,	219	WOODS OF COOLE		43
AS MEN IN THE OLD TIMES, BEFORE THE HARP BEGAN,	219	WOODS OF COOLE	V	43
PEACEABLE MEN THAT SHUT THE WIND AWAY,	224	SHADOW WATER B		54
AND KISS MORE LIPS THAN LASTING PEACEABLE MEN	225	SHADOW WATER B		71
NO, NOR WITH A HUNDRED MEN LIKE YOU	225	SHADOW WATER B	V	74
WHEN SHE FINDS OUT WE HAVE BETTER MEN ABOARD	232	SHADOW WATER B		231
ARMED MEN HAVE COME UPON US! O I AM SLAIN!	233	SHADOW WATER B		241
ARMED MEN HAVE COME UPON US! O I AM SLAIN!	233	SHADOW WATER B		243
MEN RAN UPON THE SHORE.	253	HIS DREAM	V	4
HAVE TAUGHT TO IGNORANT MEN MOST VIOLENT WAYS,	256	NO SECOND TROY		3
THEATRE BUSINESS, MANAGEMENT OF MEN.	260	FASC DIFFICULT		11
THE GIFTS THAT GOVERN MEN, AND AFTER THESE	264	HOUSE SHAKEN		10
OR IS THERE NONE, MOST POPULAR OF MEN,	265	ABBEY THEATRE		13
AND WE FIND HEARTENERS AMONG MEN	266	GALWAY RACES		15
AND FIND HEARTENERS AMONG MEN	266	GALWAY RACES	V	15
FOR HE IS THE WORST OF ALL DEAD MEN."	272	GREY ROCK		36
OF MEN AND WOMEN MADE LIKE THESE;	272	GREY ROCK		43
WHY ARE THE GODS BY MEN BETRAYED?	275	GREY ROCK		115
HE HAD OUTRIDDEN HIS WAR-WASTED MEN	277	TWO KINGS		3
HE HAD OUT-RIDDEN HIS WAR-WASTED MEN	277	TWO KINGS	V	3
THE FIGHTING MEN AND SERVANTS OF THIS HOUSE,	280	TWO KINGS	V	70

PAGE TITLE   LINE

MEN (CONTINUED)

	PAGE	TITLE		LINE
MY MEN, WHETHER IT PLEASE HER OR DISPLEASE,	281	TWO KINGS		112
AND TAKE HER IN THE MIDDLE OF ARMED MEN,	282	TWO KINGS		114
HAPPINESS TO CHILDREN AND TO MEN."	282	TWO KINGS		121
JOSTLED AND SHOUTED THOSE WAR-WASTED MEN,	286	TWO KINGS		216
FOR MEN WERE BORN TO PRAY AND SAVE!	289	SEPTEMBER 1913		6
WHEN GREY GULLS FLIT ABOUT INSTEAD OF MEN,	292	TO A SHADE		6
WHEN GREY GULLS FLY ABOUT INSTEAD OF MEN,	292	TO A SHADE	V	6
THAT MEN DESERT,	293	HELEN LIVED		2
OF THE MEN AND WOMEN OF TROY,	293	HELEN LIVED		11
DO MEN WHO LEAST DESIRE GET MOST,	295	THREE BEGGARS		13
THAT THE SHADES OF HOLY MEN	298	THREE HERMITS		17
POOR MEN HAVE GROWN TO BE RICH MEN,	301	RUN PARADISE		15
POOR MEN HAVE GROWN TO BE RICH MEN,	301	RUN PARADISE		15
AND RICH MEN GROWN TO BE POOR AGAIN,	301	RUN PARADISE		16
WHAT CAN BOOKS OF MEN THAT WIVE	309	REALISTS		2
IN MUSCULAR YOUTH WELL KNOWN TO MAYO MEN	325	ROBERT GREGORY		34
IN MUSCULAR YOUTH WELLKNOWN TO MAYO MEN,	325	ROBERT GREGORY	V	34
AND SOLID MEN, FOR ALL THEIR PASSION, LIVE	325	ROBERT GREGORY		37
WELL KNOWN FOR HORSEMANSHIP TO CONNACHT MEN	325	ROBERT GREGORY	V	34
NOR PUBLIC MEN, NOR CHEERING CROWDS,	328	IRISH AIRMAN		10
MEN IMPROVE WITH THE YEARS	329	MEN IMPROVE		T
FOR MEN IMPROVE WITH THE YEARS;	329	MEN IMPROVE		11
THE LIVING BEAUTY IS FOR YOUNGER MEN;	334	LIVING BEAUTY		9
THAT YOUNG MEN, TOSSING ON THEIR BEDS,	337	SCHOLARS		4
HER LABOURING MEN, AS THOUGH HER DARLING LIVED,	340	SHEP GOATHERD		38
OR ON THE WITHERED MEN THAT SAW	344	DAWN		5
THE LIVING MEN THAT I HATE,	347	FISHERMAN		13
THE YOUNG MEN EVERY NIGHT APPLAUD THEIR GABY'S LAUGHING EYE,	353	HIS PHOENIX		9
AND WHO CAN SAY BUT SOME YOUNG BELLE MAY WALK AND TALK MEN WILD	354	HIS PHOENIX		26
THERE'LL BE THAT CROWD TO MAKE MEN WILD THROUGH ALL THE CENTURIES,	354	HIS PHOENIX	V	25
AND MAY BE THERE'LL BE SOME YOUNG BELLE WALK OUT TO MAKE MEN WILD	354	HIS PHOENIX	V	26
AND MAYBE THERE'LL BE SOME YOUNG BELLE WALK OUT TO MAKE MEN WILD	354	HIS PHOENIX	V	26
YOUNG MEN NO LONGER SUDDENLY CATCH THEIR BREATH	355	BROKEN DREAMS		2
A YOUNG MAN WHEN THE OLD MEN ARE DONE TALKING	356	BROKEN DREAMS		16
UPON THE LIPS OF COMMON MEN	361	ALF POLLEXFEN		33
YET SURELY THERE ARE MEN WHO HAVE MADE THEIR ART	369	EGO DOMINUS		38
IMPULSIVE MEN THAT LOOK FOR HAPPINESS	369	EGO DOMINUS		40
THOSE MEN THAT IN THEIR WRITINGS ARE MOST WISE	370	EGO DOMINUS		68
WOULD CARRY IT AWAY TO BLASPHEMOUS MEN.	371	EGO DOMINUS		79
ARE MET ON THE WASTE HILLS BY COUNTRY MEN	375	PHASES OF MOON	V	76
MEN THAT DO ALL BY RULE,	380	SONGS FOOL 1		14
SIXTEEN DEAD MEN	395	SIXTEEN DEAD		T
THE SIXTEEN MEN WERE SHOT,	395	SIXTEEN DEAD		2
WHILE THOSE DEAD MEN ARE LOITERING THERE	395	SIXTEEN DEAD		5
THAT IS NO COUNTRY FOR OLD MEN. THE YOUNG	407	SAIL BYZANTIUM		1
AND CERTAIN MEN, BEING MADDENED BY THOSE RHYMES,	410	TOWER		41
FOR IF I TRIUMPH I MUST MAKE MEN MAD.	411	TOWER		56
ROUGH MEN AT ARMS, CROSS-GARTERED TO THE KNEES	412	TOWER	V	82
AND CERTAIN MEN AT ARMS THERE WERE	412	TOWER	V	84
DID ALL OLD MEN AND WOMEN, RICH AND POOR,	413	TOWER		97
I CHOOSE UPSTANDING MEN	414	TOWER		122
TO YOUNG UPSTANDING MEN	416	TOWER		174
BITTER AND VIOLENT MEN, MIGHT REAR IN STONE	418	ANCEST HOUSES		19
TWO MEN HAVE FOUNDED HERE. A MAN-AT-ARMS	420	MY HOUSE		21
TWO MEN HAVE FOUND IT HERE. A MAN-AT-ARMS	420	MY HOUSE	V	21
OUR LEARNED MEN HAVE URGED	421	MY TABLE		15
MEN AND THEIR BUSINESS TOOK	421	MY TABLE		23
A BROWN LIEUTENANT AND HIS MEN,	424	ROAD AT DOOR		6
ALL MEN ARE DANCERS AND THEIR TREAD	430	NINETEEN 19		57
I AM JEALOUS OF THE LOOK MEN TURN ON YOU	447	HERO GIRL FOOL	V	A
FOR ALL MEN LOVE YOUR WORTH; AND I MUST RAGE	447	HERO GIRL FOOL	V	B
THAT MEN HAVE REVERENCE FOR THEIR HOLINESS	448	HERO GIRL FOOL		14
ALL MEN HAVE PRAISED MY STRENGTH BUT NOT MY WORTH.	448	HERO GIRL FOOL		9
AND LIVE AMONG THE ANCIENT HOLY MEN,	448	HERO GIRL FOOL	V	11A
THOUGH BUT A FEW LEARNED MEN SHALL LOOK WITHIN,	461	HARUN RASHID	V	18A
LIKE MEN WHO LIVE BY HABIT. EVERY DAY	463	HARUN RASHID		56
CONFRONTING MURDEROUS MEN	476	DEATH		8
A BLIND MAN BATTERING BLIND MEN;	479	SELF AND SOUL		60
BODIES OF HOLY MEN AND WOMEN EXUDE	483	OIL AND BLOOD		2
MORE WOMEN BORN THAN MEN."	485	STATISTICS		4
BUT WE OLD MEN ARE MASSED AGAINST THE WORLD.	486	SEVEN SAGES		14
BUT WE OLD MEN ARE OUT AGAINST THE WORLD.	486	SEVEN SAGES	V	14
IMPETUOUS MEN, SHAWE-TAYLOR AND HUGH LANE,	489	COOLE PARK 29		14
GREAT ROOMS WHERE TRAVELLED MEN AND CHILDREN FOUND	491	COOLE BALLYLEE		29
THAT YOUNG MEN IN DESPAIR	492	ANNE GREGORY		10
MEN DANCE ON DEATHLESS FEET."	496	MOHINI CHATTER		28
THAT ARE NOT SUITED FOR SUCH MEN AS COME	501	VACILLATION		33
AND CRIED TO BATTLE-WEARY MEN,	502	VACILLATION		65
MEN COME, MEN GO,	512	JANE ON GOD		5
MEN COME, MEN GO.	512	JANE ON GOD		5
THAT MEN PASS OVER	512	JANE ON GOD		21
MEN HAVE PASSED OVER	512	JANE ON GOD	V	21
AMONG BIRDS OR BEASTS OR MEN	528	DANCER CRUACH		2
THOUGH FANTASTIC MEN SUPPOSE	530	OLD TOM AGAIN		4
OF ALL GOOD MEN AND WOMEN,	531	FATHER CHILD		3

513

		PAGE	TITLE	LINE

MEN   (CONTINUED)

	PAGE	TITLE	LINE
IMAGINING MEN. IMAGINING THAT I COULD	537	HER VISION	4
SAY THAT OF LIVING MEN I HATE	539	MEETING	11
WE LIVED LIKE MEN THAT WATCH A PAINTED STAGE.	542	PARN FUNERAL 1	18
TO THIS BARE SOUL, LET ALL MEN JUDGE THAT CAN	542	PARN FUNERAL 1	30
GOD GUARD ME FROM THOSE THOUGHTS MEN THINK	553	PRAYER OLD AGE	1
ALL MEN HAVE AIMED AT, FOUND AND LOST!	566	LAPIS LAZULI	18
IF STRANGE MEN COME FROM THE HOUSE	568	SWEET DANCER	8
DID EVER MEN HEAR SUCH A SONG?	570	THREE BUSHES	45
AND THE TALL MEN AND THE SWORDSMEN AND THE HORSEMEN, WHERE ARE THEY?	580	CURSE CROMWELL	4
DRAW ROUND, BELOVED AND BITTER MEN,	584	GHOST ROG CASE	37
KEEPING ALL THE KERRY MEN	585	ORAHILLY	14
"ALL MEN LIVE IN SUFFERING,	589	OLD WICKED MAN	46
MY KING A LOST KING, AND LOST SOLDIERS MY MEN!	591	WHAT WAS LOST	3
AND ALL DEAD MEN ARE DRUNK.	592	DRUNK SOBRIETY	16
AND COME WITH LEARNED LOVERS OR WITH WHAT MEN YOU MAY,	593	PILGRIM	23
AND ALL MEN HEARD THEM SWEAR	596	COLONEL MARTIN	60
THAT MEN AND WOMEN OF ALL SORTS	597	MODEL LAUREATE	3
PUTS ALL MEN IN A FRIGHT,	597	MODEL LAUREATE	12
THE MUSE IS MUTE WHEN PUBLIC MEN	597	MODEL LAUREATE	17
APPROVED PATTERNS OF WOMEN OR OF MEN	602	GALLERY REVIS	31
HALF LEGENDARY MEN.	605	YOU CONTENT	16
HALF-LEGENDARY MEN.	605	YOU CONTENT V	16
OF HENWIVES AND OF QUEER OLD MEN	607	SONGS BURDEN 2	23
OF HEN WIVES AND OF QUEER OLD MEN	607	SONGS BURDEN 2 V	23
NO! GREATER THAN PYTHAGORAS, FOR THE MEN	610	STATUES	9
WHERE MEN FORGIVE IF THE BELLY GAIN?	615	MARCH SONGS 2	14
AND MEN RECALL THAT FACE,	617	LONG-LEG FLY	12
WHY SHOULD NOT OLD MEN BE MAD?	625	OLD MEN BE MAD	T
WHY SHOULD NOT OLD MEN BE MAD?	625	OLD MEN BE MAD	1
SHOULD STARVE GOOD MEN AND BAD ADVANCE,	626	OLD MEN BE MAD	10
YOUNG MEN KNOW NOTHING OF THIS SORT,	626	OLD MEN BE MAD	16
OBSERVANT OLD MEN KNOW IT WELL!	626	OLD MEN BE MAD	17
CERTAIN MEN THE ENGLISH SHOT?	632	MAN AND ECHO	12
SAY THAT THE MEN OF THE OLD BLACK TOWER,	635	BLACK TOWER	1
THAT ALL ARE OATH-BOUND MEN!	635	BLACK TOWER	5
WHEN WE HALE MEN LIE STRETCHED IN SLUMBER	636	BLACK TOWER	23
THEY BUT THRUST THEIR BURIED MEN	637	BEN BULBEN	23
WHOM MEN HAVE NAMED ARCADIA'S SWEETEST TONGUE.	649	ISLE STAT I 1	109
HERE, WHERE MEN KNOW THE GRACIOUS WOODLAND JOYS,	651	ISLE STAT I 1	154
SUCH MEN, SUCH HEARTS. BUT, UNCOUTH HUNTER, THOU	651	ISLE STAT I 1	167
ABOVE THESE MEN WHOSE MOUTHS WERE SEALED	656	ISLE STAT I 3	27
TWO MEN WHO LOVE ONE MAID HAVE AMPLE CAUSE	659	ISLE STAT II 1	30
NO, NO! WHEN THAT SHALL BE, THEN MEN MAY CALL	662	ISLE STAT II 1	79
TO WATCH THEE PASS? YET DEEPER THAN MEN KNOW	672	ISLE STAT II 3	158
A COWARD IN THE FIELD! AND ALL MEN CRIED!	684	SEEKER	53
I SOUGHT THEE NOT. MEN CALL ME INFAMY.	685	SEEKER	75
THAT ALL MEN EVERMORE MAY HUMBLY BOW	688	TWO TITANS	49
AND DYING MEN--AND YET--BUT NO, FAREWELL.	698	MOSADA 2	49
UPON THEIR THRONES. THE LIVES OF MEN SHALL FLOW	698	MOSADA 2	56
THE MEN ARE BUSY IN THE GLIMMERING SQUARE.	699	MOSADA 3	16
SEARCHED THE UNSEARCHABLE--WHY GOOD MEN WEEP!	710	FERENCZ RENYI	32
A LIZARD CRAWLS--THE TWO MEN GAZE INTENT,	711	FERENCZ RENYI	47
AND THE FISHER MEN AND WOMEN FROM THE DRIPPING HARBOUR WALL	718	PHANTOM SHIP	11
WHERE DWELL THE MINDS OF OLD MEN HAVING PEACE,	721	WITCH VIVIEN	22
SO MEN IN LIFE AND I IN MAGIC PLAY!	722	WITCH VIVIEN	55
AND THE OLD MEN WERE WALKING, WALKING,	725	LEGEND	3
ARE PRAYERS OF PATIENT MEN AND GOOD."	725	LEGEND	6
THE BOYS, THE WOMEN, AND OLD MEN,	725	LEGEND	7
AND SENT THE OLD MEN ON THEIR WAY,	725	LEGEND	23
AT THE HOUSE OF WEARY MEN	727	LOVERS QUARREL	51
THERE STOOD A MAN, OF MEN THE LEAST--	729	PRIEST FAIRY	24
FOR ALL GOOD MEN NOW FALLEN ILL,	736	IN CHURCH	5
FOR MERRY MEN THAT WEEP,	736	IN CHURCH	6
AND COMMON MEN THAT SLEEP.	736	IN CHURCH	8
MEN CRY "BRING PAUL, SHIELD BREAKER,	740	EARL PAUL	11
LIKE A GREY OWL MEN HARRY OUT	740	EARL PAUL	23
MEN CRY! "BRING PAUL, SHIELD-BREAKER,	740	EARL PAUL V	11
THAT ARE A POISON TO ALL MEN	743	DANAAN QUICK	16
FORGAEL, SEEK OUT CONTENT, WHERE OTHER MEN	750	SHADOW WATER A	71
I HAVE GOOD PILOTS, AIBRIC. WHEN MEN DIE	750	SHADOW WATER A	81
BEST PLEASES YOU. ARMED MEN HAVE COME UPON US.	752	SHADOW WATER A	131
ARMED MEN HAVE COME UPON US. O! I AM SLAIN!	753	SHADOW WATER A	133
THESE MESSENGERS TO LURE MEN TO HIS PEACE,	764	SHADOW WATER A	336
THE FOOL, WHO HAS MADE THE WISDOM THAT MEN WRITE	764	SHADOW WATER A	342
I HAVE COMMANDED MEN IN DREAMS. BELOVED,	766	SHADOW WATER A	381
SO WORTHY AMONG MEN. I FOLLOW YOU,	768	SHADOW WATER A V	412
HARD-LIVING MEN AND MEN OF THOUGHT	787	HUDDON DUDDON	13
HARD-LIVING MEN AND MEN OF THOUGHT	787	HUDDON DUDDON	13
AND ALL MEN LIE THAT SAY THAT I	789	SINGING HEAD	3
THEN FARRELL, STEEL KING, MASTER OF MEN,	790	DEDICATION	5
AT THE BOTTOM OF A LETTER, FIFTY MEN.	790	DEDICATION	10
MEN THAT REVERE YOUR FATHER YET	791	REPRISALS	17
AND SUCKLE CHILDREN NOW? ARMED MEN	791	REPRISALS	20

MEN-AT-ARMS

	PAGE	TITLE	LINE
ROUGH MEN-AT-ARMS, CROSS-GARTERED TO THE KNEES	412	TOWER	82
AND CERTAIN MEN-AT-ARMS THERE WERE	412	TOWER	84
MEN-AT-ARMS TREAD!	512	JANE ON GOD	8

MEND

	PAGE	TITLE	LINE
AND THEN I MUST MEND AND BAKE AND SWEEP	150	OLD MOTHER V	3

514

	PAGE	TITLE		LINE
MEND (CONTINUED)				
O BUT WE DREAMED TO MEND • • • • • • • •	431	NINETEEN 19		84
MEN'S				
"MEN'S HEARTS OF OLD WERE DROPS OF FLAME • • •\ • • •	19	OISIN 1		276
O LOVELY TO SEE IN ALL MEN'S SIGHT • • • • • • •	69	CLOAK BOAT		3
IN ALL MEN'S SIGHT•" • • • • • • • • • • • •	69	CLOAK BOAT		5
IN ALL MEN'S EARS OF SORROW• • • • • • • • •	70	CLOAK BOAT		14
AMID MEN'S SOULS, THAT WAVER AND GIVE PLACE • • •	112	ROSE OF WORLD		7
AMID MEN'S SOULS THAT DAY BY DAY GIVE PLACE, • • • •	112	ROSE OF WORLD	V	7
TO SEE MEN'S SOULS BARTERED AND BOUGHT• • • • • •	136	TWO TREES	V	36
AND ALL MEN'S HEARTS MUST BURN AND BEAT• • • • •	158	BELOVED RHYMES		9
AND EVEN OLD MEN'S EYES GREW DIM, THIS HAND ALONE, • •	314	FALLEN MAJESTY		2
DELIGHT MEN'S EYES WHEN I AWAKE SOME DAY • • • • •	323	SWANS AT COOLE		29
THOUGH SHE HAD YOUNG MEN'S PRAISE AND OLD MEN'S BLAME, • •	351	HER PRAISE		17
THOUGH SHE HAD YOUNG MEN'S PRAISE AND OLD MEN'S BLAME, • •	351	HER PRAISE		17
BE BUT THE BREAKERS OF MEN'S HEARTS OR ENGINES OF DELIGHT•	354	HIS PHOENIX		23
FOR ALL MEN'S THOUGHTS GREW CLEAR • • • • • • •	400	DEMON BEAST		19
FOR ALL MEN'S THOUGHT GREW CLEAR • • • • • • •	400	DEMON BEAST	V	19
A NUN AT LEAST HAS ALL MEN'S REVERENCE • • • • •	448	HERO GIRL FOOL		12
FOR THEY AT LEAST HAVE ALL MEN'S REVERENCE • • • •	448	HERO GIRL FOOL	V	12
'TIS MORN• LIKE OLD MEN'S EYES THE STARS ARE PALE, • •	645	ISLE STAT I 1		4
OH, LOVELY TO SEE IN ALL MEN'S SIGHT • • • • • •	666	ISLE STAT II 3		3
IN ALL MEN'S SIGHT• • • • • • • • • • • • •	666	ISLE STAT II 3		5
A ROVER I, WHO COME FROM WHERE MEN'S EARS • • • • •	678	ISLE STAT II 3		293
ON THE DROWNED MEN'S HANDS AND FACES, ON THE SPARS AND ON THE SAILS•	719	PHANTOM SHIP		22
THAN OLD MEN'S ANY DAY, AS MERLIN FOUND• • • • • •	721	WITCH VIVIEN		47
MENTAL				
A BODILY OR MENTAL FURNITURE• • • • • • • • •	558	RIBH CHRISTIAN		20
MENTIONED				
BEING MENTIONED WITH A MAN • • • • • • • • •	531	FATHER CHILD		4
MERCHANT				
IT CHARMED AWAY THE MERCHANT FROM HIS GUILE, • • • •	129	BOOK STORIES		5
BEFORE THE MERCHANT AND THE CLERK • • • • • • •	266	GALWAY RACES		8
OLD DUBLIN MERCHANT "FREE OF TEN AND FOUR" • • • •	269	PARDON FATHERS		3
MERCHANT AND SCHOLAR WHO HAVE LEFT ME BLOOD • • • •	269	PARDON FATHERS		7
OLD DUBLIN MERCHANT "FREE OF THE TEN AND FOUR" • • •	269	PARDON FATHERS	V	3
OLD MERCHANT SKIPPER THAT LEAPED OVERBOARD • • • •	270	PARDON FATHERS		13
YOU MERCHANT SKIPPER THAT LEAPED OVERBOARD • • • •	270	PARDON FATHERS	V	13
AND MERCHANT SKIPPER THAT LEAPED OVERBOARD • • • •	270	PARDON FATHERS	V	13
REFORMER, MERCHANT, STATESMAN, LEARNED MAN, • • • •	376	PHASES OF MOON		98
MERCHANTS				
IN HIS OWN HOUSE OR 'MONG THE MERCHANTS GREY, • • • •	693	MOSADA 1		87
MERCY				
THE LORD HAVE MERCY UPON US• • • • • • • • •	572	LADYS 2ND SONG		7
THE LORD HAVE MERCY UPON US• • • • • • • • •	573	LADYS 2ND SONG		14
THE LORD HAVE MERCY UPON US• • • • • • • • •	573	LADYS 2ND SONG		21
CAN THERE BE MERCY IN THAT LOOK? • • • • • • •	625	NATIVITY		12
AND——MERCY IS THE MANNA OF THE WORLD• • • • • • •	697	MOSADA 2		41
MERE				
OR HOPES THAT IN MERE HOPING FLICKER AND CEASE• • • •	162	ASKS FORGIVE		3
AND HOPES THAT IN MERE HOPING FLICKER AND CEASE• • • •	162	ASKS FORGIVE	V	3
MERE BONE AND MUSCLE THROWN ASIDE, • • • • • • •	273	GREY ROCK		51
AND LEFT MERE SLEEP. HE'LL WAKE WHEN THE SUN WAKES, • •	284	TWO KINGS		161
OR MERE COMPANIONS OF MY YOUTH, • • • • • • •	324	ROBERT GREGORY		7
MERE IMAGES• CHOSEN THIS PLACE TO LIVE IN • • • • •	373	PHASES OF MOON		13
FOR WHAT MERE BOOK CAN GRANT A KNOWLEDGE • • • • •	386	ROBARTES DANCE		20
GIVE MAN HIS THOUGHT OR HIS MERE BODY? • • • • •	386	ROBARTES DANCE		40
AND THAT MERE GROWING OLD, THAT BRINGS • • • • • •	401	DEMON BEAST		38
MERE ANARCHY IS LOOSED UPON THE WORLD, • • • • •	402	SECOND COMING		4
MERE DREAMS, MERE DREAMS• YET HOMER HAD NOT SUNG • • •	417	ANCEST HOUSES		9
MERE DREAMS, MERE DREAMS• YET HOMER HAD NOT SUNG • • •	417	ANCEST HOUSES		9
MOCKED ME WITH PRAISE OF MY MERE OPPOSITE• • • • •	448	HERO GIRL FOOL		4
MOCK ME WITH PRAISE OF MY MERE OPPOSITE• • • • •	448	HERO GIRL FOOL	V	4
AND I MERE SHADE AT LAST • • • • • • • • •	449	HERO GIRL FOOL		25
WHERE FASHION OR MERE FANTASY DECREES • • • • • •	491	COOLE BALLYLEE		38
ALL MERE COMPLEXITIES, • • • • • • • • • •	497	BYZANTIUM		7
THE FALLING HAWTHORN BLOOM• BY MERE AND BROOK • • •	677	ISLE STAT II 3		279
BY HEATH OR HOLLOW OR RUSHY MERE, • • • • • • •	716	FAIRY DOCTOR		10
OUT OF MERE WANTONNESS TO LURE A SAIL • • • • • •	750	SHADOW WATER A		79
OR IN MERE WOMAN'S CRUELTY • • • • • • • • •	789	SINGING HEAD		11
MERELY				
"WOULD IT WERE ANYTHING BUT MERELY VOICE!" • • • • •	258	KING NO KING		1
MERELY FOR STUMBLING ON THIS HOLE • • • • • • •	304	HOUR DAWN		54
THAT MERELY STOOD, ROCKING THE GLITTERING COACH • • •	344	DAWN		11
BY MERELY WALKING IN A ROOM, • • • • • • • •	356	BROKEN DREAMS		13
MERELY TO LOOSEN OUT A TRESS • • • • • • • •	390	IMAGE PAST		26
MERGE				
SO DID THEIR ROSES MERGE• • • • • • • • • •	571	THREE BUSHES		62
MERIDIAN				
"LIKE ME WERE SOME GALLEY FORSAKEN FAR OFF IN MERIDIAN ISLE,	55	OISIN 3		117
MERIT				
WHAT'S THE MERIT IN LOVE-PLAY, • • • • • • • •	777	SONG DEIRDRE 2		6
WHAT'S THE MERIT IN LOVE PLAY• • • • • • • •	777	SONG DEIRDRE 2	V	6
MERLIN				
YET WHITER BEARD HAVE YOU THAN MERLIN HAD• • • • •	721	WITCH VIVIEN		30
THAN OLD MEN'S ANY DAY, AS MERLIN FOUND• • • • • •	721	WITCH VIVIEN		47
MERMAID				
THE MERMAID • • • • • • • • • • • • •	452	MERMAID		T
A MERMAID FOUND A SWIMMING LAD, • • • • • • • •	452	MERMAID		1

515

	PAGE	TITLE	LINE

MERMAID   (CONTINUED)
A MERMAID, NOT A PUNK! . . . .   592 DRUNK SOBRIETY   14
MERRIMENT
NOR BUT IN MERRIMENT BEGIN A CHASE, ...   405 FOR DAUGHTER   45
NOR BUT IN MERRIMENT A QUARREL. . . . .   405 FOR DAUGHTER   46
MERRY
THOSE MERRY COUPLES DANCING IN TUNE, ...   3 OISIN 1   9
AND A HUNDRED LADIES, MERRY AS BIRDS, ...   9 OISIN 1   96
AND A HUNDRED MAIDENS, MERRY AS BIRDS, ...   9 OISIN 1   V   96
AND NIAMH BLEW THREE MERRY NOTES . . . .   14 OISIN 1   195
A SORROW WRAPPED EACH MERRY FACE, ...   17 OISIN 1   235
LIKE TO A MERRY WANDERING ROUT . . . .   18 OISIN 1   253
BUT ONLY KIND AND MERRY BREATH, ...   19 OISIN 1   285
WHILE THE WOOD-PECKER MADE A MERRY DIN, ...   44 OISIN 2   V   228
THE MERRY LAMBS AND THE COMPLACENT KINE, . . .   75 ANASHU VIJAYA   86
THE MERRY LAMBS AND ALL THE KINE COMPLACENT, . .   75 ANASHU VIJAYA   V   86
AS MERRY AS A BIRD." . . . .   133 FR GILLIGAN   38
HAVE DOWERED THE STARS WITH MERRY LIGHT! . . . .   134 TWO TREES   6
AWAY FROM THE MERRY BANDS . . . .   144 HOST OF AIR   22
HE PLAYED WITH THE MERRY OLD MEN . . . . . .   145 HOST OF AIR   29
AWAY FROM THE MERRY DANCE. . . . .   145 HOST OF AIR   32
FOR THE GOOD ARE ALWAYS THE MERRY, ...   178 FIDDLER DOONEY   13
AND THE MERRY LOVE THE FIDDLE, ...   179 FIDDLER DOONEY   15
AND THE MERRY LOVE TO DANCE! . . . .   179 FIDDLER DOONEY   16
I LONG FOR YOUR MERRY AND TENDER AND PITIFUL WORDS, . .   203 WITHER BOUGHS   3
HOW HAVE I WRONGED HER NOW THAT SHE IS MERRY? . . .   244 SHADOW WATER B   448
AND THEREON, MERRY AS A BIRD . . . .   296 THREE BEGGARS   25
A CURSING ROGUE WITH A MERRY FACE, ...   302 HOUR DAWN   1
I'D HAVE A MERRY LIFE ENOUGH . . . .   306 HOUR DAWN   85
WE MEET--WE TWO. HOW MERRY ALL THESE ARE . .   691 MOSADA 1   31
HO! HO! HO! THE MERRY BLADE!-- . . . .   727 LOVERS QUARREL   26
IF THESE MERRY ONES SHOULD KNOW, ...   731 STREET DANCERS   9
IF THESE MERRY ONES SHOULD KNOW, ...   732 STREET DANCERS   22
IF THESE MERRY ONES SHOULD KNOW, ...   732 STREET DANCERS   35
IF THESE MERRY ONES SHOULD KNOW, ...   733 STREET DANCERS   48
IF THESE MERRY ONES SHOULD KNOW, ...   733 STREET DANCERS   61
FOR MERRY MEN THAT WEEP, ...   736 IN CHURCH   6
MERU
MERU . . . .   563 MERU   T
HERMITS UPON MOUNT MERU OR EVEREST, ...   563 MERU   9
MESH
FOR NEITHER I NOR YOU CAN BREAK A MESH . . . .   238 SHADOW WATER B   351
AND KNITTED MESH TO MESH, WE GROW IMMORTAL! . .   252 SHADOW WATER B   616
AND KNITTED MESH TO MESH, WE GROW IMMORTAL! . .   252 SHADOW WATER B   616
AND KNITTING MESH TO MESH, WE GROW IMMORTAL! . .   252 SHADOW WATER B V   616
AND KNITTING MESH TO MESH, WE GROW IMMORTAL! . .   252 SHADOW WATER B V   616
MESS
AND TOOK A MESS OF SHADOWS FOR ITS MEAT? . . . .   444 SCHOOL CHILDR   28
MESSAGE
YOUR RAVING OF A MESSAGE AND A HARP . . . .   237 SHADOW WATER B   331
IS IT YOUR MESSAGE, STARS, THAT WHEN DEATH COMES . . .   701 MOSADA 3   60
MESSAGES
IF IT BE NOT THAT HEARING MESSAGES . . . . .   236 SHADOW WATER B   319
THAT WERE CLEAR MESSAGES FROM THE EVER-LIVING, ...   243 SHADOW WATER B   442
MESSENGER
HE STOOD A MESSENGER. IN APRIL'S PRIME . . . . .   690 MOSADA 1   6
MESSENGERS
IF I REFUSED THE MESSENGERS AND PILOTS . . . . .   249 SHADOW WATER B   572
THESE MESSENGERS TO LURE MEN TO HIS PEACE, ...   764 SHADOW WATER A   336
MET
WHEN AMBLING DOWN THE VALE WE MET . . . . . .   2 OISIN 1   V   7U
ROOTED IN FOAM AND CLOUDS. THERE MIGHTIER MASTERS MET . .   38 OISIN 2   V   132
WHEN HEAVEN AND HELL ARE MET, ...   112 ROSE OF PEACE   2
WHEN THEY FOR WAR ARE MET, ...   112 ROSE OF PEACE   V   2
WHO MET FAND WALKING AMONG FLAMING DEW . . . .   169 SECRET ROSE   13
THEREON A YOUNG MAN MET HIS EYE, ...   274 GREY ROCK   85
AGAINST THE STAG. WHEN HORN AND STEEL WERE MET . . .   277 TWO KINGS   15
AS THOUGH A STAG AND UNICORN WERE MET . . . .   277 TWO KINGS   19
TO STAY THE STAG'S NEXT RUSH. WHEN SWORD MET HORN . . .   277 TWO KINGS   V   15
THE STRONG THIGH AND THE AGILE THIGH WERE MET, . . .   278 TWO KINGS   28
EUNUCHS RAN THROUGH HELL AND MET . . . . . .   294 HATED PLAYBOY   2
O WOULD THAT WE HAD MET . . . .   329 MEN IMPROVE   14
NEVER UNTIL THIS MOMENT HAVE WE MET . . . . .   339 SHEP GOATHERD   7
ARE MET ON THE WASTE HILLS BY COUNTRYMEN . . . .   375 PHASES OF MOON   76
ARE MET ON THE WASTE HILLS BY COUNTRY MEN . . . .   375 PHASES OF MOON V   76
I HAVE MET THEM AT CLOSE OF DAY . . . . . .   391 EASTER 1916   1
I MET THE BISHOP ON THE ROAD . . . .   513 JANE TALK BISH   1
"IS THAT MORNING WHEN I MET . . . .   521 THREE THINGS   15
"THAT I HAVE MET WITH SUCH," SAID HE, ...   539 MEETING   5
BUT OF THE DEATH HE MET . . . .   585 ORAHILLY   29
THE COLONEL MET A PEDLAR, ...   595 COLONEL MARTIN   19
I MET HER ALL BUT FIFTY YEARS AGO . . . . . .   602 GALLERY REVIS   15
WHAT, LOVER, DIE BEFORE OUR LIPS HAVE MET? . . .   685 SEEKER   80
LOVE, WILL YOU DIE WHEN WE HAVE MET? ONE LOOK . .   703 MOSADA 3   109
IN SPACE, MADE EQUAL WITH A SIGH, WE MET. . . .   705 REMEMBRANCE   14
THE DIM SPEAR MET THE BRIGHT SPEAR, ...   741 EARL PAUL   45
THE DIM SPEAR MET THE BRIGHT SPEAR . . . . .   741 EARL PAUL   V   49
AND I MET WITH A MAN THAT WAS NO RIGHT MAN . . .   779 GOING THE ROAD   3
I HAVE MET IN A MAN'S HOUSE . . . .   785 YOUR HEART   3
METAL   SEE ROAD-METAL.
AS THOUGH IT DRAGGED ROAD METAL. MY CURSE ON PLAYS . . .   260 FASC DIFFICULT V   8

516

			PAGE	TITLE		LINE

METAL   (CONTINUED)
ON METAL GOBAN'D HAMMERED AT, ...   271 GREY ROCK   19
ALL WORK IN METAL OR IN WOOD, ...   327 ROBERT GREGORY   76
BEING OF THAT METAL MADE . . . .   416 TOWER   178
IN GLORY OF CHANGELESS METAL . . . .   498 BYZANTIUM   22
METAPHOR
NOT SUCH AS ARE IN NEWTON'S METAPHOR, ... 494 AT ALGECIRAS   11
ALL METAPHOR, MALACHI, STILTS AND ALL. A BARNACLE GOOSE 623 HIGH TALK   11
METEOR
SCARED OF ITS GLITTERING LIKE A METEOR STAR, ... 38 OISIN 2   V 137
A METEOR OF THE BURNING HEART, ...   78 INDIAN TO LOVE   14
WE TIRE OF THE FLAME OF THE METEOR, BEFORE IT CAN FADE 122 WHITE BIRDS   2
    AND FLEE;
AH, DREAM NOT OF THEM, MY BELOVED, THE FLAME OF THE METEOR 122 WHITE BIRDS   6
    THAT GOES,
FOR WE TIRE OF THE FLAME OF THE METEOR BEFORE IT CAN PASS 122 WHITE BIRDS V   2
    BY AND FLEE
WE TIRE OF THE FLAME OF THE METEOR, BEFORE IT CAN PASS 122 WHITE BIRDS   V   2
    BY AND FLEE;
METEORS
LIKE CRIMSON METEORS HANG IN THE GLOOM, ...   21 OISIN 1   306
HUNG, LIKE METEORS OF RED LIGHT, ...   21 OISIN 1   V   306
THE IMAGED METEORS HAD FLASHED AND RUN . . . . . .   31 OISIN 2   38
THE IMAGED METEORS HAD SHONE AND RUN, ...   31 OISIN 2   V   38
FELL LIKE FAINT METEORS IN THE GLOOM, AND ONCE . . . 80 EPHEMERA   14
METHINKS
AND THE GREAT GREY LYNX'S SKIN! IN SOOTH, METHINKS . . 650 ISLE STAT I 1   151
METTLESOME
AND OUR WINGED METTLESOME HORSE. . . . .   392 EASTER 1916   V   25
MEW   SEE SEA-MEW
MIAU-D
HOWLED, MIAU-D, BARKED, BRAYED, BELLED, YELLED, CRIED, 387 SOLOMON WITCH   8
    CROWED,
MICE   SEE MEADOW-MICE
THE FLIES BELOW THE LEAVES, AND THE YOUNG MICE . . . 75 ANASHU VIJAYA   87
AND OVER THE MICE IN THE BARLEY SHEAVES! . . . . . . 79 FALLING LEAVES   2
OR SEE THE BROWN MICE BOB . . . .   88 STOLEN CHILD   48
OR MICE IN THE ONE WHEATEN SHEAF . . . . 195 BAILE AILLINN   147
FROM HUMAN THOUGHT, AS HARES AND MICE AND CONEYS . . 218 WOODS OF COOLE   31
BUT WHEN THE MASTER'S BURIED MICE CAN PLAY, ... 418 ANCEST HOUSES   22
WITH NO MORE SOUND THAN THE MICE MAKE . . . . 618 LONG-LEG FLY   27
AH! HOW LARGE MICE USED TO BE . . . .   727 LOVERS QUARREL   39
MICHAEL
IF MICHAEL, LEADER OF GOD'S HOST . . . . 112 ROSE OF PEACE   1
IF MICHAEL, LEADER OF GOD'S HOSTS . . . . 112 ROSE OF PEACE   V   1
MICHAEL ROBARTES BIDS HIS BELOVED BE AT PEACE . . . 154 BELOVED PEACE   V   T
MICHAEL ROBARTES REMEMBERS FORGOTTEN BEAUTY . . . . 155 FORGOT BEAUTY   V   T
MICHAEL ROBARTES ASKS FORGIVENESS BECAUSE OF HIS MANY MOODS 162 ASKS FORGIVE V T
. . . MICHAEL, GABRIEL, AND RAPHAEL . . . . 174 ELEMENT POWERS V   T
MICHAEL WILL UNHOOK HIS TRUMPET . . . . 215 HAPPY TOWNLAND   41
COULD TRUMPETER MICHAEL BE SO BRAVE?" . . . . 338 TOM OROUGHLEY   13
THAT MICHAEL ROBARTES LEFT, YOU WALK IN THE MOON, . . 367 EGO DOMINUS   4
THE DOUBLE VISION OF MICHAEL ROBARTES . . . . 382 VISION ROBART   T
MICHAEL ROBARTES AND THE DANCER . . . . 385 ROBARTES DANCE   T
WHILE MICHAEL ANGELO'S SISTINE ROOF, ... 386 ROBARTES DANCE   32
THAT MY MICHAEL MAY SLEEP SOUND, ... 435 FOR MY SON   2
A MIND MICHAEL ANGELO KNEW . . . . 576 ACRE OF GRASS   19
MICHAEL ANGELO. . . . .   618 LONG-LEG FLY   26
MICHAEL ANGELO LEFT A PROOF . . . .   638 BEN BULBEN   45
MICHAELANGELO
MICHAELANGELO LEFT A PROOF . . . . 638 BEN BULBEN   V 45
MICHAEL'S
TO KNOW WHEN MICHAEL'S TRUMPET CRIES . . . . 307 HOUR DAWN   100
MICHELOZZO'S
TO MICHELOZZO'S LATEST PLAN . . . .   288 TO WEALTHY MAN   23
MID
THEIR EYES MID MANY WRINKLES, THEIR EYES, ... 567 LAPIS LAZULI   55
SO! MID THE WILLOW-GLADE YOU PAUSE AT LAST. . . . . . 651 ISLE STAT I 2   2
MID BUBBLING LEAVES A WANDERING SONG-RAPT BIRD . . . 672 ISLE STAT II 3   154
MID BABBLING LEAVES A WANDERING SONG-RAPT BIRD . . . 672 ISLE STAT II 3 V 154
'MID
BUT TO BE 'MID THE SHOOTING OF FLIES . . . .   55 OISIN 3   V 120
'MID CLANGING SPACE A MOMENT HEARD . . . .   65 HAPPY SHEPHERD V 20
AND THEY WILL WAR, 'MID WONDROUS ELFIN-SIGHTS! . . . . 651 ISLE STAT I 1   164
THOU KNOWEST THIS, AND HOW FROM 'MID THE DANCE . . . 683 SEEKER   51
MIDDAY
"ALL DAY LONG FROM MIDDAY . . . . 332 SOLOMON SHEBA   V   3
MID-DAY
"ALL DAY LONG FROM MID-DAY . . . . 332 SOLOMON SHEBA   3
MIDDLE
WITH CHAIN SEA-ROTTED, ROUND HER MIDDLE TIED, ... 34 OISIN 2   V 75
WHO HAD BEEN THE LOVER OF HER MIDDLE LIFE. . . . . . 183 QUEEN MAEVE   72
TO MIDDLE NIGHT, THEY DUG INTO THE HILL. . . . . . . 185 QUEEN MAEVE   114
AS MIDDLE NIGHT GREAT CATS WITH SILVER CLAWS, ... 185 QUEEN MAEVE   115
WHEN THEY HAVE TWENTY YEARS! IN MIDDLE LIFE . . . . 229 SHADOW WATER B   156
WESTWARD OF TARA. WHERE IN THE MIDDLE WOOD . . . . . 277 TWO KINGS   V   4
AND TAKE HER IN THE MIDDLE OF ARMED MEN, ... 282 TWO KINGS   114
I CAME ON A GREAT HOUSE IN THE MIDDLE OF THE NIGHT, . . 581 CURSE CROMWELL   25
FIND IN MIDDLE AIR . . . .   601 THOSE IMAGES   13
DREAMER OF THE MIDDLE AGES. EMPTY EYEBALLS KNEW . . . 610 STATUES   20
OF MIDDLE AGE. "HIS SISTER HERE AND MOTHER." . . . . 711 FERENCZ RENYI   53

517

	PAGE	TITLE		LINE

MIDDLE-AGE
RESTRAINING RECKLESS MIDDLE-AGE? • • • • • • • • • • 262 STUDENTS AGIT 4
MIDDLE-AGES
DREAMER OF THE MIDDLE-AGES. EMPTY EYE-BALLS KNEW • • 610 STATUES V 20
MIDDLETON
AND OF A MIDDLETON, WHOSE NAME YOU NEVER HEARD, • • • • 391 UNDER SATURN 8
THE SMUGGLER MIDDLETON, BUTLERS FAR BACK, • • • • • • 605 YOU CONTENT 15
MY NAME IS HENRY MIDDLETON, • • • • • • • • • • 606 SONGS BURDEN 2 1
MIDHER'S
EDAINE CAME OUT OF MIDHER'S HILL, AND LAY • • • • 762 SHADOW WATER A 296
WHEN MIDHER'S WIFE HAD CHANGED HER TO A FLY • • • • 763 SHADOW WATER A 305
MIDHIR
• • • MADE ARMOUR FOR MIDHIR OF OLD • • • • • • • • 52 OISIN 3 V 80
MIDHIR'S
THAT EDAIN, MIDHIR'S WIFE, HAD WOVE • • • • • • 195 BAILE AILLINN 142
EDAIN CAME OUT OF MIDHIR'S HILL, AND LAY • • • • 219 HARP OF AENGUS 1
WHEN MIDHIR'S WIFE HAD CHANGED HER TO A FLY, • • • • 220 HARP OF AENGUS 10
MIDNIGHT
THAT LACKEY THE WORN MOON IN MIDNIGHT HOURS, • • • • 41 OISIN 2 V 185A
FOR HE HAS WROUGHT MIDNIGHT AND DAWN AND DAY• • • • • 43 OISIN 2 208
• • • TILL STARLIGHT AND MIDNIGHT PART.• • • • • • 60 OISIN 3 184
AND MIDNIGHT THERE ENFOLD THEM LIKE A FLEECE • • • • 128 DREAM OF FAERY 34
THAT MEN THRESHED CORN AT MIDNIGHT BY A TRESS, • • • • 170 SECRET ROSE 26
AT THE MOST QUIET MIDNIGHT IS TO BE STRICKEN, • • • • 236 SHADOW WATER B 321
ONCE, WHEN MIDNIGHT SMOTE THE AIR, • • • • • • • 294 HATED PLAYBOY 1
THE STATELY MIDNIGHT THROUGH UNTIL THEY STOOD • • • • 352 PEOPLE 14
THE LAST STROKE OF MIDNIGHT DIES.• • • • • • 357 BROKEN DREAMS 37
HAVE SEEN HIS MIDNIGHT CANDLE GLIMMERING.• • • • • 420 MY HOUSE 20
HAD SEEN HIS MIDNIGHT CANDLE GLIMMERING • • • • • 420 MY HOUSE V 20
NOR BLEAR-EYED WISDOM OUT OF MIDNIGHT OIL.• • • • 446 SCHOOL CHILDR 60
IS BUT A PAYMENT FOR THAT MIDNIGHT VOICE • • • • 469 HARUN RASHID 173
ALL, ALL THOSE GYRES AND CUBES AND MIDNIGHT THINGS • • 469 HARUN RASHID 184
THOSE CONES AND CUBES AND GYRES, THOSE MIDNIGHT THINGS, 469 HARUN RASHID V 184
MIDNIGHT HAS COME, AND THE GREAT CHRIST CHURCH BELL • • 470 ALL SOUL NIGHT 1
FOR IT IS NOW MIDNIGHT; • • • • • • • • • 470 ALL SOUL NIGHT V 3
IN THE RICH MIDNIGHT OF THE GARDEN TREES • • • • 494 AT ALGECIRAS 5
IN THE RICH MIDNIGHT OF THE GARDEN TREE • • • • 494 AT ALGECIRAS V 5
AT MIDNIGHT ON THE EMPEROR'S PAVEMENT FLIT • • • • 498 BYZANTIUM 25
THAT I, MIDNIGHT UPON THE STROKE, • • • • • • • 507 JANE BISHOP 2
ON THE MATERNAL MIDNIGHT OF MY BREAST • • • • • 535 CHOSEN 7
AT WINE-DARK MIDNIGHT IN THE SACRED WOOD, • • • • 536 HER VISION 2
AT STROKE OF MIDNIGHT SOUL CANNOT ENDURE • • • • 558 RIBH CHRISTIAN 19
AT STROKE OF MIDNIGHT GOD SHALL WIN. • • • • • 561 FOUR AGES MAN 8
"THAT I AT MIDNIGHT BY THE CLOCK • • • • • • 569 THREE BUSHES 10
AT MIDNIGHT TO MY ROOM, • • • • • • • • 570 THREE BUSHES 39
MIDNIGHT, AN OLD HOUSE • • • • • • • • • 575 ACRE OF GRASS 5
STRETCH TOWARDS THE MOONLESS MIDNIGHT OF THE TREES, • • 579 DOR WELLESLEY 1
AND PRESSED AT MIDNIGHT IN SOME PUBLIC PLACE • • • 610 STATUES 7
CRIES A VOICE AT ROARING MIDNIGHT BESIDE THE MOONLESS DEEP. 718 PHANTOM SHIP 8
SAY WHAT RINGER RINGS AT MIDNIGHT: FOR, IN THE BELFRY HIGH, 718 PHANTOM SHIP 15
FOR NOON AND MIDNIGHT FROM EACH OTHER BORROW, • • • • • 735 QUATRAIN APHOR 26
MIDNIGHT'S
THERE MIDNIGHT'S ALL A GLIMMER, AND NOON A PURPLE GLOW, 117 ISLE INNISFREE 7
MIDNIGHTS
BUT NO DOGS BARKED, AND MIDNIGHTS CHIMED, • • • • • 570 THREE BUSHES 29
AND NO DOGS BARKED THROUGH MIDNIGHTS CHIMED • • • • 570 THREE BUSHES V 29
MIDST
GREY IN THE MIDST LIKE A SMALL RIVULET'S FLOW, • • • 37 OISIN 2 V 117
IN MIDST OF AN OLD MAN'S BOSOM; OWLS RUFFLING AND PACING 50 OISIN 3 47
  AROUND
IN THE MIDST OF AN OLD MAN'S BOSOM: OWLS RUFFLING 50 OISIN 3 V 47
  AND PACING AROUND
• • • HER BROW ON THE MIDST OF MY BREAST: • • • • • 52 OISIN 3 74
SAD NIAM CAME NEAR ME, AND LAID HER BROWS ON THE MIDST 52 OISIN 3 V 74
  OF MY BREAST
AND PEARL-PALE NEAVE LAY BY ME, HER BROW ON THE MIDST OF 52 OISIN 3 74
  MY BREAST:
WEAK, IN THE MIDST OF THE MEADOW, • • • • • • • 54 OISIN 3 102
• • • FROM HIS MILES IN THE MIDST OF THE AIR, • • • • 54 OISIN 3 103
SHE FOLLOWED WITH LIGHT FOOTFALL IN THE MIDST, • • • 186 QUEEN MAEVE 128
AND SAW WHERE IN THE MIDST OF THE GREAT HALL • • • • 279 TWO KINGS 60
AND IN THE MIDST KING EOCHAID'S BROTHER STOOD, • • • • 286 TWO KINGS 217
THE STONE'S IN THE MIDST OF ALL. • • • • • • 393 EASTER 1916 56
MIDSUMMER
OR MAYBE TO MIDSUMMER DAY," • • • • • • • • 305 HOUR DAWN 58
MIEN
(HOW GLAD WAS HER MIEN!), • • • • • • • • 654 ISLE STAT I 2 72
MIGHT
I'D PUT AWAY THE FOOLISH MIGHT OF A KING, • • • • 103 FERGUS DRUID V 21A
ONE MOMENT HAS NO MIGHT UPON THE MOMENT • • • • • 237 SHADOW WATER B 340
"WHY ARE THEY FAITHLESS WHEN THEIR MIGHT • • • • 275 GREY ROCK 109
THE HANDS THAT GATHERED UP THE MIGHT OF THE WORLD, • • 278 TWO KINGS 29
WHEREIN THE GAZING HEART DOUBLES HER MIGHT. • • • • 326 ROBERT GREGORY 69
EXHAUST HIS GLORY AND HIS MIGHT: • • • • • • 438 SONGS PLAY 2 14
MIGHT OF THE CHURCH AND THE STATE, • • • • • 554 CHURCH STATE 3
HE FOUGHT THE MIGHT OF ENGLAND • • • • • • 586 PARNELLITES 11
WE KNOW WHAT RASCAL MIGHT HAS DEFILED, • • • • 614 MARCH SONGS 2 11
MEASUREMENT BEGAN OUR MIGHT: • • • • • • 638 BEN BULBEN 42
SUSTAINS HIS SOUL IN COURAGE OR IN MIGHT. • • • • 650 ISLE STAT I 1 144
WHERE THEIR SINEWY MIGHT IS STRUNG • • • • • 658 ISLE STAT I 3 88

518

```
                                          PAGE    TITLE              LINE
MIGHTIER
   NO MIGHTIER CREATURES BAY AT THE MOON:  . . . . . . .    8 OISIN 1               87
   THERE WAS NO MIGHTIER SOUL OF HEBER'S LINE:  . . . . .   36 OISIN 2               95
   THE MIGHTIER MASTERS OF A MIGHTIER RACE:  . . . . . .    38 OISIN 2              133
   THE MIGHTIER MASTERS OF A MIGHTIER RACE:  . . . . . .    38 OISIN 2              133
   ROOTED IN FOAM AND CLOUDS.  THERE MIGHTIER MASTERS MET . .  38 OISIN 2         V 132
   FOR I AM MIGHTIER NOW BY FAR THAN THEE, . . . . . . .   673 ISLE STAT II 3       193
   AND SAID IT WAS MIGHTIER THAN THE SUN AND MOON, . . . .  762 SHADOW WATER A       289
MIGHTIEST
   WAR ON THE MIGHTIEST MEN UNDER THE SKIES, . . . . . .    45 OISIN 2              241
   "HE IS THE MIGHTIEST MAN IN SHIP OR DUN." . . . . . .   107 CUCHULAIN SEA  V  28
   THE MIGHTIEST OF THE PRINCES OF THE WORLD  . . . . . .  462 HARUN RASHID         41
   AMONG THE QUEENS, AND CHOSE THE MIGHTIEST  . . . . . .  757 SHADOW WATER A       213
MIGHTY
   "I AM NEAVE, A CHILD OF THE MIGHTY SHEE,  . . . . . .     5 OISIN 1         V  48
   WHILE A HUNDRED YOUTHS, MIGHTY OF LIMB,  . . . . . . .    8 OISIN 1              94
   CAME SWIMMING SADLY DOWN THE MIGHTY STAIR. . . . . . .   32 OISIN 2         V 50B
   TO RULE MORE MIGHTY MEN, AND TO THE WORLD  . . . . . .   38 OISIN 2         V 133
   BURIED AND MIGHTY,  WHEN THROUGH THE GREAT DOOR  . . .   39 OISIN 2              151
   BURIED AND MIGHTY,  THENCE I JOURNEYED NOT  . . . . . .   39 OISIN 2         V 151
   THEIR MIGHTY AND NAKED AND GLEAMING BODIES . . . . . . .  48 OISIN 3         V  28
   DARK BALOR, AS OLD AS A FOREST, CAR-BORNE, HIS MIGHTY HEAD  53 OISIN 3             91
      SUNK
   CAME BALOR, AS OLD AS A FOREST, CAR BORNE, HIS MIGHTY HEAD  53 OISIN 3          V  91
      SUNK
   BY MIGHTY BRAHMA'S EVER-RUSTLING ROBE, . . . . . . .     71 ANASHU VIJAYA        14
   BY MIGHTY BRAHMA'S EVER RUSTLING ROBE, . . . . . . .     71 ANASHU VIJAYA   V  14
   TO MIGHTY BRAHMA, HE WHO MADE YOU MANY AS THE SANDS, . .  72 ANASHU VIJAYA        21
   TO MIGHTY BRAHMA--HE WHO MADE YE MANY AS THE SANDS, . .   72 ANASHU VIJAYA   V  21
   TO MIGHTY BRAHMA, WHO HAS MADE YOU MANY AS THE SANDS, . . 72 ANASHU VIJAYA   V  21
   HAS SLAIN SO MIGHTY ARMIES, SO GREAT KINGS, . . . . .   106 CUCHULAIN SEA   V 10A
   "CUCHULAIN I, MIGHTY CUCHULAIN'S SON."  . . . . . . .   110 CUCHULAIN SEA        68
   "I AM FINMOLE, MIGHTY CUCHULAIN'S SON."  . . . . . . .   110 CUCHULAIN SEA   V  68
   WHAT POWER THAT IS MORE MIGHTY THAN DESIRE, . . . . .   234 SHADOW WATER B       267
   THAT IS MORE MIGHTY THAN THE SUN AND MOON, . . . . . .  237 SHADOW WATER B       328
   MORE MIGHTY THAN THE STARS HALF TROUBLED ME, . . . . .  237 SHADOW WATER B       332
   FOR I NEED ALL HIS MIGHTY MEMORIES. . . . . . . . .     413 TOWER                104
   NO HONOUR LEAVE ITS MIGHTY MONUMENT. . . . . . . . .    429 NINETEEN 19           38
   TO MIGHTY PARIS WHEN HE FOUND  . . . . . . . .         522 LULLABY                4
   ROUNDS A MIGHTY SCENE, . . . . . . . . . .             599 STONE CROSS           22
   I AND THAT MIGHTY KING A SUDDEN BLOW . . . . . . .     757 SHADOW WATER A       195
   HAVE CALLED HIM MIGHTY.  I WILL FOLLOW YOU  . . . . .   768 SHADOW WATER A       412
MILCH
   CAN CALL THE MILCH COWS . . . . . . . . . . . .        780 WELL AND TREE          5
MILCH-COWS
   CAN CALL THE MILCH-COWS . . . . . . . . . . . .        780 WELL AND TREE   V      5
MILD
   ON A MORNING MISTY AND MILD AND FAIR. . . . . . . .      2 OISIN 1         V  7E
   HIS MISTRESS WAS MORE MILD AND FAIR . . . . . . . .      3 OISIN 1         V 7DD
   HUNG FROM THE MORNING STAR: WHEN THESE MILD WORDS . . .  32 OISIN 2              49
   BUT IN DREAMS, MILD MAN OF THE CROZIERS, . . . . . .     53 OISIN 3              85
   . . . GROWN MILD WITH MYSTERIOUS THOUGHT, . . . . . .    55 OISIN 3             121
   . . . OR WAS LIFTED AN OLD MAN'S MILD HEAD. . . . . .    59 OISIN 3         V 170
   AND WITH A RULE SERENE AND MILD . . . . . . . . .       82 MAD KING GOLL   V   6
   PEACE-MAKING, MILD, A KINGLY BOY, . . . . . . . .       82 MAD KING GOLL   V   8
   AND THAT MILD WOMAN OF THE SOUTH, . . . . . . . .      189 BAILE AILLINN         6
   THAT BEAUTIFUL MILD WOMAN, YOUR CLOSE FRIEND, . . . .   204 ADAMS CURSE           2
   THAT BEAUTIFUL MILD WOMAN FOR WHOSE SAKE  . . . . .     205 ADAMS CURSE          15
   MURMURED WITH HER YOUNG VOICE FOR WHOSE MILD SAKE . . . 205 ADAMS CURSE     V  15
   IN FINDING THAT IT'S YOUNG AND MILD AND LOW. . . . . .  205 ADAMS CURSE     V  17
   HAVE SEEN IMMORTAL, MILD, PROUD SHADOWS WALK: . . . .   217 WOODS OF COOLE       12
   HOW SHALL I NAME YOU, IMMORTAL, MILD, PROUD SHADOWS?  . 218 WOODS OF COOLE       27
   A KIND MILD WOMAN HAD SHE BEEN, WHO POURED  . . . . .   279 TWO KINGS       V 62A
   BUT NOW SHE HAD NO MILD AND NO KIND LOOK: . . . . . .   279 TWO KINGS       V 62D
   TILL THE YELLOW EYE HAS GROWN MILD, . . . . . . . .     349 HAWK                  3
   HE WAS A MAN MOST LEARNED AND MOST MILD, . . . . . .    692 MOSADA 1             51
   ABOVE, THE WOODS WHERE WITH THE SOFT MILD EYE . . . .   710 FERENCZ RENYI        26
   HOW "THE ONLY GOOD IS MUSING MILD, . . . . . . . .      728 PRIEST FAIRY         13
   OF SOME MILD WOMAN, OR IN CHILDREN'S WAYS. . . . . .    750 SHADOW WATER A       74
MILE
   AND MANY A MILE IS THE FAERY STATE, . . . . . . . .      9 OISIN 1         V 103
   NO MORE TO CRAWL ON THE SEAS WITH LONG OARS MILE AFTER   55 OISIN 3             119
      MILE,
   NO MORE TO CRAWL ON THE SEAS WITH LONG OARS MILE AFTER   55 OISIN 3             119
      MILE,
   RUN FOR A MILE UNDIMMED IN HEAVEN'S FACE  . . . . . .   490 COOLE BALLYLEE        3
   AND FOUND.  'TIS WELL!--ANOTHER MILE OF WAY  . . . .    651 ISLE STAT I 2         6
MILES
   . . . FROM HIS MILES IN THE MIDST OF THE AIR, . . . .    54 OISIN 3             103
   AND MASONS DROVE FROM MILES AWAY  . . . . . . . .      360 ALF POLLEXFEN         9
   IN THE SOUTH SEA'S AZURE MILES, . . . . . . . . .      732 STREET DANCERS       28
   IN THE SOUTH SEAS' AZURE MILES, . . . . . . . . .      732 STREET DANCERS  V  28
MILK
   AND OIL AND WINE AND HONEY AND MILK, . . . . . . . .     8 OISIN 1              92
   AND HONEY, AND OIL, AND WINE, AND MILK, . . . . . . .    8 OISIN 1         V  92
   THEIR BROWS WERE WHITE AS FRAGRANT MILK, . . . . . .    15 OISIN 1             204
   THEIR BROWS WERE WHITE AS THE FRAGRANT MILK . . . . .    15 OISIN 1         V 204
   . . . HE SAD AS A CHILD WITHOUT MILK: . . . . . . .     59 OISIN 3             174
   THAT IS TO AGE WHAT MILK IS TO A CHILD? . . . . . . .   469 HARUN RASHID        174
   SPILT MILK  . . . . . . . . . . . . . . .             484 SPILT MILK            T
   LIKE MILK SPILT ON A STONE. . . . . . . . . . .        484 SPILT MILK            4
```

519

		PAGE	TITLE	LINE

MILK   (CONTINUED)
```
                                                         PAGE    TITLE            LINE
    THIS FALLEN STAR MY MILK SUSTAINS,  . . . . . . .    499 MOTHER OF GOD          12
    DRINKING JOY AS IT WERE MILK UPON HIS BREAST. . . . . . . .  559 MAGIC DRUM      3
    OR SUCKED SUCH MILK AS HE. . . . . . . . . . . .    584 GHOST ROG CASE         26
MILKING
    ON NO LONG BENCH NOR LOFTY MILKING SHED . . . . . .  341 SHEP GOATHERD  V       51
MILKING-PLACE
    THE MILKING-PLACE, THE SHELTERED FARM? . . . . . .   151 HEART OF WOMAN V        6
MILKING-SHED
    ON NO LONG BENCH NOR LOFTY MILKING-SHED . . . . . .  341 SHEP GOATHERD          51
MILK-PALE
    AND AT HIS CRY THERE CAME NO MILK-PALE FACE . . . .   38 OISIN 2              134
MILK-WHITE
    WHEELS BY MILK-WHITE ASSES DRAWN . . . . . . . . .   502 VACILLATION            62
    AS THE CANKER-WORM ON A MILK-WHITE ROSE: . . . . .   673 ISLE STAT II 3        177
    THAT FROM THE MILK-WHITE MARBLE . . . . . . . .      680 LOVE AND DEATH          3
MILKY
    OF MILKY BRIGHTNESS TO AND FRO . . . . . . . . .      22 OISIN 1              328
    FLED FOAM UNDERNEATH US, AND ROUND US, A WANDERING AND     47 OISIN 3           1
        MILKY SMOKE,
    FLED FOAM UNDERNEATH US, AND ROUND US, A WANDERING AND     47 OISIN 3          12
        MILKY SMOKE.
    FLED FOAM UNDERNEATH US, AND AROUND US, A WANDERING AND    47 OISIN 3      V    1
        MILKY SMOKE,
    FLED FOAM UNDERNEATH ME, AND ROUND ME, A WANDERING AND     57 OISIN 3        148
        MILKY SMOKE.
    THE BRILLIANT MOON AND ALL THE MILKY SKY, . . . . .  119 SORROW OF LOVE          2
MILL
    WITH OLD MILL BOARDS AND SEA-GREEN SLATES, . . . .   406 CARVED STONE           2
    NOR THE MILL OF THE MIND . . . . . . . . . . .      575 ACRE OF GRASS         10
MILLION
    WHILE ROUND THE SHORE A MILLION STOOD  . . . . .     14 OISIN 1              182
    WHAT THE WORLD'S MILLION LIPS ARE THIRSTING FOR  . . . .   229 SHADOW WATER B  161
MILLION-FOOTED
    FAR FLEETER THAN THE MILLION-FOOTED SEA.  . . . .    670 ISLE STAT II 3       108
MILLIONS
    WHERE WHITE DEWDROPS IN MILLIONS FALL: . . . . . .   16 OISIN 1          V   222
    THEY SLOWLY INTO MILLIONS GREW, . . . . . . . .     133 FR GILLIGAN           17
MILTON'S
    FROM THE FAR TOWER WHERE MILTON'S PLATONIST . . . .  373 PHASES OF MOON         15
MIMIC
    MIMICKING WHAT THEY HEARD, AS CHILDREN MIMIC: . . . . .   487 SEVEN SAGES       25
MIMICKING
    MIMICKING WHAT THEY HEARD, AS CHILDREN MIMIC: . . . . .   487 SEVEN SAGES       25
MIMICRY
    A MIMICRY OF YOUTH. CAN POET'S THOUGHT . . . . . .   463 HARUN RASHID          62
    A MIMICRY OF YOUTH. AN ARTIST'S THOUGHT, . . . . .   463 HARUN RASHID   V      62
    BE MIMICRY?" "WHAT MATTER IF OUR SOULS . . . . .    464 HARUN RASHID          66
    CAN BE NO MIMICRY. "WHAT IF OUR SOULS . . . . . .   464 HARUN RASHID   V      66
MINARET
    SINKS DOWN AT LAST WITH YONDER MINARET, . . . . . .  691 MOSADA 1        V     36
MIND
    WITH A HEAVY HEART AND A WANDERING MIND, . . . . .    2 OISIN 1                2
    "HOW COMES IT, PRINCESS, THAT YOUR MIND . . . . .    6 OISIN 1         V    59A
    WRAPPED IN THE THINGS OF THE UNHUMAN MIND, . . . .   36 OISIN 2              98
    ROLLED IN THE THINGS OF THE UNHUMAN MIND, . . . .    36 OISIN 2         V    98
    WE TRAMPLED TO AND FRO.  WHEN HIS MIND KNEW . . . .  40 OISIN 2         V   173
    FOR GOD HAS HEARD, AND SPEAKS HIS ANGRY MIND: . . .  42 OISIN 2             206
    DARKEN: HEAVEN IS ANGRY.  CEASE!  UNTO MY MIND,  . . 42 OISIN 2         V   205
    AS MY MIND MADE THE NAMES OF THE FENIANS. . . . . .  57 OISIN 3             146
    ANOTHER FILLS YOUR MIND.  MY MOTHER'S NAME. . . . .  71 ANASHU VIJAYA        16
    SOME OTHER FILLS YOUR MIND.  MY MOTHER'S NAME. . . .  71 ANASHU VIJAYA  V     16
    HIS MIND RAN ALL ON MONEY CARES AND FEARS, . . . .  127 DREAM OF FAERY        14
    THAT HURRY FROM UNMEASURED MIND . . . . . . . .     138 TO IRELAND            25
    THEY HUDDLE FROM MAN'S PONDERING MIND, . . . . . .  138 TO IRELAND     V      26
    AND HOW YOU HAVE LEAPED TIMES OUT OF MIND . . . .   146 FISH                  5
    BECAUSE YOUR CRYING BRINGS TO MY MIND  . . . . .    155 REPROVE CURLEW        3
    AMONG MY LEAVES IN TIMES OUT OF MIND: . . . . . .   177 PAST GREATNESS        5
    NO COMMON LOVE IS TO OUR MIND, . . . . . . . . .    190 BAILE AILLINN         34
    THAT OUT OF SIGHT IS OUT OF MIND. . . . . . . .     192 BAILE AILLINN         87
    IT MIGHT CALL UP A NEW AGE, CALLING TO MIND . . . . .  201 OLD MEMORY          4
    FOR THE ROADS ARE UNENDING, AND THERE IS NO PLACE TO MY   203 WITHER BOUGHS     4
        MIND."
    I WOULD BE OF YOUR MIND: BUT WHEN HE PLAYS IT . . . .  222 SHADOW WATER B     17
    IF WE WERE OF ONE MIND I'D DO IT.  WERE'T NOT . . . . .  222 SHADOW WATER B V  15
    THE MIND IS MADE UNCHANGING, FOR IT FINDS . . . . .  227 SHADOW WATER B      101
    IF YOU WILL GIVE ME ALL YOUR MIND AWHILE-- . . . .  227 SHADOW WATER B       117
    THE IMMORTAL MOCKERS HAVE CAST INTO HIS MIND, . . . .  249 SHADOW WATER B    567
    WHAT COULD HAVE MADE HER PEACEFUL WITH A MIND . . . .  256 NO SECOND TROY      6
    "IT WAS THE MASK ENGAGED YOUR MIND, . . . . . .     263 MASK                  8
    TIME OUT OF MIND, BECAME TOO RUINOUS . . . . . .    264 HOUSE SHAKEN          3
    DELIGHT MAKES ALL OF THE ONE MIND. . . . . . . .    266 GALWAY RACES          2
    AND FOR NINE DAYS MY MIND WENT WHIRLING ROUND . . . .  282 TWO KINGS        127
    I PRAISED HER BODY AND HER MIND . . . . . . . .     314 MEMORY YOUTH          9
    MIND AND DELIGHTED MIND: . . . . . . . . . . .      315 FRIENDS               9
    MIND AND DELIGHTED MIND: . . . . . . . . . . .      315 FRIENDS               9
    FOR ALL THAT COME INTO MY MIND ARE DEAD. . . . . .  324 ROBERT GREGORY       16
    LIONEL JOHNSON COMES THE FIRST TO MIND . . . . .    324 ROBERT GREGORY       17
    A PORTION OF MY MIND AND LIFE, AS IT WERE . . . .   325 ROBERT GREGORY       42
    AND YET HIS MIND OUTRAN THE HORSES' FEET. . . . .   326 ROBERT GREGORY       64
    THAT SHAKES THE SHUTTER, TO HAVE BROUGHT TO MIND . . . .  327 ROBERT GREGORY  90
```

520

MIND (CONTINUED)   PAGE   TITLE   LINE
I BALANCED ALL, BROUGHT ALL TO MIND, ...   328   IRISH AIRMAN   13
THROUGH VICTORIES OF THE MIND, ...   343   SHEP GOATHERD   108
THAT GIVES UP ALL HER MIND, ...   345   ON WOMAN   2
YELLOW-EYED HAWK OF THE MIND, ...   349   HAWK   14
OF THE ANALYTIC MIND, CAN NEITHER CLOSE   353   PEOPLE   33
THE EYE OF THE MIND NOR KEEP MY TONGUE FROM SPEECH." . .   353   PEOPLE   34
I WAS ABASHED, AND NOW THEY COME TO MIND   353   PEOPLE   36
AND SMOOTH OUT STAIN AND BLEMISH WITH THE ELEGANCE OF HIS   353   HIS PHOENIX   7
    MIND:
THE BALLOON OF THE MIND   358   BALLOON MIND   T
BRING THE BALLOON OF THE MIND   358   BALLOON MIND   2
WE HAVE LIT UPON THE GENTLE, SENSITIVE MIND   368   EGO DOMINUS   12
HIS ART IS HAPPY, BUT WHO KNOWS HIS MIND?   370   EGO DOMINUS   54
AS WITH THE CAT-O'-NINE-TAILS OF THE MIND, ...   374   PHASES OF MOON   42
AND YET THEY SPEAK WHAT'S BLOWN INTO THE MIND: 376   PHASES OF MOON   110
DEFORMITY OF BODY AND OF MIND.   377   PHASES OF MOON   123
BEFORE SHE HAD SETTLED HER MIND   381   SONGS FOOL 2   8
FOR WHAT BUT EYE AND EAR SILENCE THE MIND   384   VISION ROBART   41
MIND MOVED YET SEEMED TO STOP   384   VISION ROBART   43
BUT BEAR IN MIND YOUR LOVER'S WAGE   385   ROBARTES DANCE   14
RECALL THE YEARS BEFORE HER MIND   397   POLIT PRISONER   8
BECAUSE OF THE GREAT GLOOM THAT IS IN MY MIND.   403   FOR DAUGHTER   8
MY MIND, BECAUSE THE MINDS THAT I HAVE LOVED, ...   405   FOR DAUGHTER   49
IF THERE'S NO HATRED IN A MIND   405   FOR DAUGHTER   54
BECAUSE OF HER OPINIONATED MIND   405   FOR DAUGHTER   61
BRING UP OUT OF THAT DEEP CONSIDERING MIND   413   TOWER   106
TO EXALT A LONELY MIND, ...   420   MY HOUSE   29
MIND FROM MIND HAS CAUGHT: 420   MY HOUSE   V 20G
MIND FROM MIND HAS CAUGHT: 420   MY HOUSE   V 20G
HAVING INHERITED A VIGOROUS MIND   422   MY DESCENDANTS   1
AS VIGOROUS OF MIND, AND YET IT SEEMS   422   MY DESCENDANTS   4
FRENZIES BEWILDER, REVERIES PERTURB THE MIND   426   PHANTOM HATRED   7
WHETHER HEALTH, WEALTH OR PEACE OF MIND WERE SPENT . .   429   NINETEEN 19   36
THAT HAD SUCH BURDENS ON THE MIND   432   NINETEEN 19   94
HER PRESENT IMAGE FLOATS INTO THE MIND--   444   SCHOOL CHILDR   25
BECAUSE THIS COUNTRY HAS A PIOUS MIND   447   COLONUS PRAISE   25
I CAN EXCHANGE OPINION WITH ANY NEIGHBOURING MIND, . .   450   OWEN AHERNE   9
"SPEAK ALL YOUR MIND," MY HEART SANG OUT, ...   450   OWEN AHERNE   21
. . . "SPEAK ALL YOUR MIND; WHO CARES, ...   450   OWEN AHERNE   21
NOR THOUGHT OUT OF HER MIND OR MINE BEGOT, ...   467   HARUN RASHID   140
NOR THOUGHT OUT OF HER MIND OR OUT OF MINE   467   HARUN RASHID   V 140
THE BEAUTY OF A WOMAN'S MIND OR BODY   469   HARUN RASHID   V 187
I NEED SOME MIND THAT, IF THE CANNON SOUND   471   ALL SOUL NIGHT   11
AND WHAT IF MIND SEEM CHANGED, ...   473   ALL SOUL NIGHT   66
AND IT SEEM CHANGED WITH THE MIND, ...   473   ALL SOUL NIGHT   67
AND WHAT IF MIND SEEMED CHANGE   473   ALL SOUL NIGHT V   66
AND IT SEEMED CHANGED WITH THE MIND, ...   473   ALL SOUL NIGHT V   67
PICTURES OF THE MIND, RECALL   475   EVA GORE-BOOTH   17
SET ALL YOUR MIND UPON THE STEEP ASCENT, ...   477   SELF AND SOUL   2
AND FALLS INTO THE BASIN OF THE MIND   478   SELF AND SOUL   34
GOLDSMITH DELIBERATELY SIPPING AT THE HONEY-POT OF HIS   481   BLOOD AND MOON   21
    MIND,
MUST VANISH ON THE INSTANT IF THE MIND BUT CHANGE   481   BLOOD AND MOON   27
    ITS THEME:
GOLDSMITH DELIBERATELY SIPPING AT THE HONEY POT OF HIS   481   BLOOD AND MOON V   21
    MIND:
A LEVELLING, RANCOROUS, RATIONAL SORT OF MIND   486   SEVEN SAGES   11
THE MIND OF MAN OR ELEVATE A RHYME: 492   COOLE BALLYLEE   45
DID AN OLDER MIND COMMEND--   494   AT ALGECIRAS   10
BUT GOOD STRONG BLOWS ARE DELIGHTS TO THE MIND." . .   544   TO SAME TUNE 1   4
IN THE MIND ALONE: 553   PRAYER OLD AGE   2
. . . DAMPED BY THE BODY OR THE MIND, ...   556   RIBH PATRICK   8
OF EVERYTHING THAT IS NOT MIND OR SENSE.   558   RIBH CHRISTIAN   6
THEN HE STRUGGLED WITH THE MIND: 561   FOUR AGES MAN   5
ON MIND, ON NEST, ...   574   LOVERS SONG   5
NOR THE MILL OF THE MIND   575   ACRE OF GRASS   10
A MIND MICHAEL ANGELO KNEW   576   ACRE OF GRASS   19
AN OLD MAN'S EAGLE MIND.   576   ACRE OF GRASS   24
KEEPS PARNELL IN HIS MIND.   586   PARNELLITES   20
O MIND YOUR FEET, O MIND YOUR FEET, ...   592   DRUNK SOBRIETY   9
O MIND YOUR FEET, O MIND YOUR FEET, ...   592   DRUNK SOBRIETY   9
THE CAVERN OF THE MIND?   600   THOSE IMAGES   2
THAT IRELAND'S MIND BE GREATER, ...   608   SONGS BURDEN 3   21
HOW CAN THE MIND FORGIVE?   615   MARCH SONGS 2   16
BUT GOOD STRONG BLOWS ARE DELIGHTS TO THE MIND." . .   616   MARCH SONGS 3   4
HIS MIND MOVES UPON SILENCE.   617   LONG-LEG FLY   10
HER MIND MOVES UPON SILENCE.   617   LONG-LEG FLY   20
HIS MIND MOVES UPON SILENCE.   618   LONG-LEG FLY   30
OF AN UNBROKEN HAPPY MIND, ...   626   OLD MEN BE MAD   14
AND MIND AND BODY SHRANK.   626   STATES HOLIDAY   4
GREW IN PURE MIND, BUT OUT OF WHAT BEGAN?   630   CIRCUS ANIMALS   34
BACK IN THE HUMAN MIND AGAIN.   637   BEN BULBEN   24
HE COMPLETES HIS PARTIAL MIND, ...   638   BEN BULBEN   30
BEFORE THE SECRET WORKING MIND: 639   BEN BULBEN   51
CAST YOUR MIND ON OTHER DAYS   640   BEN BULBEN   81
OH, LEARNED IS EACH MONK'S-HOOD'S MIND, ...   655   ISLE STAT I 3   8
IN THE FAR WORLD WILL VANISH FROM THY MIND, ...   670   ISLE STAT II 3   93
HE DIGS HIS CABBAGES. HE BRINGS TO MIND   696   MOSADA 2   18
OH, HUSH THE WANDERING MUSIC OF THY MIND.   703   MOSADA 3   106
CLOSELY ROUND US, BODY AND MIND--   717   FAIRY DOCTOR   23

521

		PAGE	TITLE	LINE

MIND (CONTINUED)
    TO MIND HIS COWS AND SWINE BY THE RED LAKE.   752 SHADOW WATER A   112
    AND STABLING TO YOUR MIND.   774 COME RIDE   8
    OUT OF MEMORY AND MIND.   775 AGAINST WITCH   10
    THE LABYRINTH OF THE MIND,   785 WOMANS BEAUTY   24
MINDED   SEE MANY-MINDED
    A NEIGHBOUR MINDED HER BY DAY,   94 MOLL MAGEE   15
    I MINDED HER TILL MORN.   94 MOLL MAGEE   16
MINDFUL
    BUT, THE BIRD IN MY FINGERS, I MOUNTED, MINDFUL ONLY TO 54 OISIN 3   V   111
        LAUNCH
MIND'S
    NOW AS AT ALL TIMES I CAN SEE IN THE MIND'S EYE,   318 MAGI   1
    MORE PLAIN TO THE MIND'S EYE THAN ANY FACE   368 EGO DOMINUS   21
    CAUGHT UP IN CONTEMPLATION, THE MIND'S EYE   375 PHASES OF MOON   79
    ON THE GREY ROCK OF CASHEL THE MIND'S EYE   382 VISION ROBART   1
    ALTHOUGH I SAW IT ALL IN THE MIND'S EYE   383 VISION ROBART   25
    MONSTROUS FAMILIAR IMAGES SWIM TO THE MIND'S EYE.   426 PHANTOM HATRED   8
    WOUND IN MIND'S PONDERING   471 ALL SOUL NIGHT   13
    BUT THINK THAT HIS MIND'S EYE,   471 ALL SOUL NIGHT   33
    WOUND IN MIND'S WANDERING   474 ALL SOUL NIGHT   99
    MIND'S BREAD GROW SWEET,   554 CHURCH STATE   6
    "HOW FEW THE MIND'S INTEMPERANCE RULE!   725 LEGEND   10
MINDS
    FOR THEIR DIM MINDS WERE WITH THE ANCIENT THINGS,   34 OISIN 2   77
    TO WANDER BY THEIR MELANCHOLY MINDS.   72 ANASHU VIJAYA   33
    MY MIND, BECAUSE THE MINDS THAT I HAVE LOVED,   405 FOR DAUGHTER   49
    HAVE CLOSED THE LADIES' EYES, THEIR MINDS ARE BUT A POOL 426 PHANTOM HATRED   21
    THAT SEEMS UNNATURAL TO ARABIAN MINDS,   464 HARUN RASHID   79
    FROM FOUR GREAT MINDS THAT HATED WHIGGERY.   486 SEVEN SAGES   7
    OUR MINDS ARE AT THEIR BEST THIS NIGHT,   523 MAD AS MIST   3
    AND MEASURE THE MINDS OF THE FLOWERS,   707 FAIRY PEDANT   17
    WHERE DWELL THE MINDS OF OLD MEN HAVING PEACE,   721 WITCH VIVIEN   22
MINE
    AND THE WHITE BODY THAT LAY BY MINE!   3 OISIN 1   10
    THERE WAS NO LIMB OF MINE BUT FELL   7 OISIN 1   72
    WITH HOPE, MINE ENEMY. AS HE BY NIGHT   34 OISIN 2   V   81
    BURNING BETWEEN HER FINGERS, AND IN MINE   37 OISIN 2   125
    AND MINE OWN WORDS RE-ECHOING SHALL SEND   68 SAD SHEPHERD   V   20
    AND MINE OWN TALE AGAIN FOR ME SHALL SING,   68 SAD SHEPHERD   V   22
    AND MINE OWN WHISPERING WORDS BE COMFORTING,   68 SAD SHEPHERD   V   23
    "YOUR EYES THAT ONCE WERE NEVER WEARY OF MINE   79 EPHEMERA   1
    MINE WAS A CHAIR OF SKINS AND GOLD,   81 MAD KING GOLL   V   1
    MINE WAS THE THRONE IN EMAN'S HALL,   81 MAD KING GOLL   V   2
    MINE WERE CLAN MORNA'S TRIBES UNTOLD,   81 MAD KING GOLL   V   3
    AND MINE WAS EVERY TROPHIED WALL,   82 MAD KING GOLL   V   4
    OF ONE WHO IS NO FRIEND TO ME OR TO MINE,   184 QUEEN MAEVE   V   94A
    AND BEAT THE BULWARK OF YOUR SHIP ON MINE,   236 SHADOW WATER B   312
    O WHY DO YOU NOT LIFT YOUR EYES TO MINE?   246 SHADOW WATER B   498
    . . . CERTAIN BAD POETS, IMITATORS OF HIS AND MINE   262 TO A POET   T
    . . . CERTAIN BAD POETS, IMITATORS OF HIS AND OF MINE 262 TO A POET   V   T
    NOTHING BUT THAT TO PROVE YOUR BLOOD AND MINE.   270 PARDON FATHERS   22
    THE MORAL'S YOURS BECAUSE IT'S MINE.   271 GREY ROCK   11
    "IF HE BE LIVING STILL THE WHOLE WORLD'S MINE,   280 TWO KINGS   V   85
    NOR AN UNLAUGHING MOUTH, BUT MINE THAT MOURNS,   285 TWO KINGS   184
    THAT DEEP-SWORN VOW HAVE BEEN FRIENDS OF MINE!   357 DEEP-SWORN VOW   2
    THAT DEEP SWORN VOW, HAVE BEEN FRIENDS OF MINE,   357 DEEP-SWORN VOW V   2
    TRUE SONG, THOUGH SPEECH! "MINE AUTHOR SUNG IT ME." 373 PHASES OF MOON   30
    NOT HIS, NOT MINE." WHO UNDERSTOOD   387 SOLOMON WITCH   6
    NOT HIS, NOT MINE." AND HE THAT KNEW   387 SOLOMON WITCH   V   6
    BEING DEAR AS MINE ARE DEAR.   400 DEMON BEAST   20
    THESE STONES REMAIN THEIR MONUMENT AND MINE.   423 MY DESCENDANTS   24
    AND IF HER EYE SHOULD NOT GROW BRIGHT FOR MINE   464 HARUN RASHID   81
    NOR THOUGHT OUT OF HER MIND OR MINE BEGOT.   467 HARUN RASHID   140
    NOR THOUGHT OUT OF HER MIND OR OUT OF MINE   467 HARUN RASHID   V 140
    HER CONFIDENCE IN MINE, OR EVEN LOSE .   469 HARUN RASHID   176
    BUT MINE SAW STELLA ONCE. WHENCE CAME OUR THOUGHT? 486 SEVEN SAGES   6
    MINE SAW STELLA ONCE. WHENCE CAME OUR THOUGHT?   486 SEVEN SAGES   V   6
    MINE SAW STELLA ONCE. WHEN CAME OUR THOUGHT?   486 SEVEN SAGES   V   6
    MINE MUST WALK WHEN DEAD.   511 JANE AND JACK   18
    MINE WOULD WALK, BEING DEAD.   511 JANE AND JACK   V   18
    HALF TURNED AND FIXED A GLAZING EYE ON MINE,   537 HER VISION   26
    "THAT WAS A LUCKY THOUGHT OF MINE,   570 THREE BUSHES   31
    AND MINE WERE BUT FIFTEEN FOOT, NO MODERN STALKS   623 HIGH TALK   3
        UPON HIGHER.
    DID THAT PLAY OF MINE SEND OUT   632 MAN AND ECHO   11
    DID WORDS OF MINE PUT TOO GREAT STRAIN   632 MAN AND ECHO   13
    UPON THE WIND, AND GUIDE MINE ARROW'S COURSE.   657 ISLE STAT I 3   62
    I'LL SEND MINE ARROW, NOW MY ONE RESOURCE!   657 ISLE STAT I 3   64
    WITHIN MINE HEART! AND NAUGHT BUT SORROW NOW   659 ISLE STAT II 1   26
    MORE GRIEF IS MINE. NO MAN SHALL EVER STOOP   661 ISLE STAT II 1   62
    TWO CAME, HIS NAME AND MINE ON MANY A TREE   662 ISLE STAT II 2   10
    IN SAND HIS NAME AND MINE I'VE ALSO READ.   662 ISLE STAT II 2   12
    TO MINE, AND HE IS SLOWLY SUCKING FORTH   684 SEEKER   V   63A
    MINE HEART-STRINGS ARE ALL BROKEN SAVING ONE,   684 SEEKER   V   69B
    LOVER, THE VOICE THAT SUMMONED THEE WAS MINE.   685 SEEKER   77
    WANDER AWAY FROM MINE?   686 LIFE   8
    I TRY TO LIFT MINE ARMS--THEY FALL AGAIN.   701 MOSADA 3   56
    MINE WHERE WATERS BROOD AND TOSS!   744 ROSY CROSS   7
    AGAINST MY FACE AND EYES. MINE TOO ARE BEATEN.   759 SHADOW WATER A V   233

	PAGE	TITLE	LINE

MINGLE
    WE SHALL MINGLE NO MORE, NOR OUR GAZES EMPTY THEIR   56 OISIN 3   132
      SWEETNESS LONE
MINGLED
    WHO SIGH WITH MINGLED SORROW AND CONTENT, ...   136 TO SOME I TALK   7
    TILL THE DAWN BREAK UPON THOSE MINGLED SEAS. . . . . .   494 AT ALGECIRAS   6
MINGLES
    THEIR HAIR MINGLES ON SOME STRINGED INSTRUMENT, ...   752 SHADOW WATER A   123
MINGLING
    MINGLING OF SWORD AND WAR-AXE, WHILE THE DAY   40 OISIN 2   V 171
    WITH MINGLING HAIR, AND PLAY UPON ONE LUTE. . . . . .   71 ANASHU VIJAYA   10
    MINGLING HANDS AND MINGLING GLANCES . . . .   87 STOLEN CHILD   18
    MINGLING HANDS AND MINGLING GLANCES . . . .   87 STOLEN CHILD   18
    AND LANGUORS THAT AWAKE IN MINGLING HANDS . . . . .   765 SHADOW WATER A   367
    AND MINGLING HAIR FALL FROM THE FIERY BOUGHS, ...   765 SHADOW WATER A   368
    ALL THAT MINGLING OF OUR BREATH, ...   777 SONG DEIRDRE 2   10
MINION
    OH FAMOUS DYING MINION OF THE SUN, ...   673 ISLE STAT II 3   197
MINIONS
    OF THE HAPPY FLOWER MINIONS. . . . .   667 ISLE STAT II 3   29
'MINISHED
    WITH 'MINISHED BEAUTY, MULTIPLIED COMMONPLACE, ...   472 ALL SOUL NIGHT   45
MINISTER
    BY BOSKY JUNE I SWEAR, AND BY THE BEE, HER MINISTER. . .   661 ISLE STAT II 1   74
MINISTERING
    WE MEET AT LAST, THE MINISTERING STARS . . . . . .   701 MOSADA 3   52
MINNALOUSHE
    BLACK MINNALOUSHE STARED AT THE MOON, ...   378 CAT AND MOON   5
    MINNALOUSHE RUNS IN THE GRASS . . . .   378 CAT AND MOON   9
    DO YOU DANCE, MINNALOUSHE, DO YOU DANCE? . . . . . .   378 CAT AND MOON   11
    MINNALOUSHE CREEPS THROUGH THE GRASS . . . .   378 CAT AND MOON   17
    DOES MINNALOUSHE KNOW THAT HIS PUPILS . . . . . .   379 CAT AND MOON   21
    MINNALOUSHE CREEPS THROUGH THE GRASS . . . .   379 CAT AND MOON   25
MINNOWED
    HE RUFFLES WITH HIS BILL THE MINNOWED STREAMS. . . . .   73 ANASHU VIJAYA   37
MINOS
    PLATO THERE AND MINOS PASS, ...   531 DELPHIC ORACLE   8
MINSTREL-WORD
    AS FLAMING MINSTREL-WORD UPON HIS CREST. . . . . .   679 ISLE STAT II 3   317
MINUTE
    BUT O, IN A MINUTE SHE CHANGED— . . . .   212 O DO NOT LOVE   9
    AND I WILL HEAR THEM TALKING IN A MINUTE. . . . . .   233 SHADOW WATER B   250
    HIS NAME WILL COME INTO OUR THOUGHTS IN A MINUTE. . . .   241 SHADOW WATER B   391
    I HAD NOT WAKED A SINGLE MINUTE, ...   305 HOUR DAWN   72
    WITH THE MINUTE PARTICULARS OF MANKIND? . . . . .   384 VISION ROBART   42
    AND THE MOON IS WILDER EVERY MINUTE. . . . . . .   389 SOLOMON WITCH   43
    MINUTE BY MINUTE THEY CHANGE; . . . .   393 EASTER 1916   48
    MINUTE BY MINUTE THEY CHANGE; . . . .   393 EASTER 1916   48
    CHANGES MINUTE BY MINUTE; . . . .   393 EASTER 1916   50
    CHANGES MINUTE BY MINUTE; . . . .   393 EASTER 1916   50
    MINUTE BY MINUTE THEY LIVE; . . . .   393 EASTER 1916   55
    MINUTE BY MINUTE THEY LIVE; . . . .   393 EASTER 1916   55
    MINUTE BY MINUTE CHANGE. . . . .   393 EASTER 1916   V 48
    MINUTE BY MINUTE CHANGE. . . . .   393 EASTER 1916   V 48
    THOSE DEEDS WERE BEST THAT GAVE THE MINUTE WINGS . . .   533 HER TRIUMPH   5
MINUTES
    FOR CERTAIN MINUTES AT THE LEAST . . . .   399 DEMON BEAST   1
    AND TWENTY MINUTES MORE OR LESS . . . .   501 VACILLATION   42
    FOR TWENTY MINUTES IN SOME STUDIO. . . . . . .   602 GALLERY REVIS   16
    OH, WOULD THE BUSY MINUTES MIGHT FOLD UP . . . . .   702 MOSADA 3   97
MIRACLE
    MIRACLE, ECSTASY, THE IMPOSSIBLE HOPE, ...   227 SHADOW WATER B   102
    THAT SEEMED SHEER MIRACLE TO THE MULTITUDE, ...   428 NINETEEN 19   2
    MIRACLE HAD ITS PLAYTIME WHERE . . . .   440 WISDOM   8
    MIRACLE, BIRD OR GOLDEN HANDIWORK, ...   497 BYZANTIUM   17
    MORE MIRACLE THAN BIRD OR HANDIWORK, ...   497 BYZANTIUM   18
    MIRACLE, BIRD OR GOLDEN HANDY-WORK . . . .   497 BYZANTIUM   V 17
    MORE MIRACLE THAN BIRD OR HANDY-WORK . . . . . .   497 BYZANTIUM   V 18
    THE MIRACLE THAT GAVE THEM SUCH A DEATH . . . . .   555 RIBH AT TOMB   10
MIRACLE-BRED
    MIRACLE-BRED OUT OF THE LIVING STONE; . . . . . .   446 COLONUS PRAISE   13
MIRACLES
    ACCEPT THE MIRACLES OF THE SAINTS AND HONOUR SANCTITY? . .   503 VACILLATION   79
    COURAGEOUS MIRACLES! THE SUNLIGHT SHONE . . . . . .   649 ISLE STAT I 1   113
MIRACLE-WORKING
    WITH A MIRACLE-WORKING JUICE . . . .   776 AGAINST WITCH   23
MIRACULOUS
    A SWEET, MIRACULOUS, TERRIFYING SOUND. . . . . . .   277 TWO KINGS   17
    IMMENSE MIRACULOUS HOUSE . . . .   472 ALL SOUL NIGHT   38
    MIRACULOUS OIL, ODOUR OF VIOLET. . . . .   483 OIL AND BLOOD   3
    BATHED IN MIRACULOUS OIL, SWEET ODOURS FROM IT COME, . .   503 VACILLATION   81
    AND A MIRACULOUS STRANGE BIRD SHRIEKS AT US . . . . .   534 HER TRIUMPH   12
    AND BOTH ADRIFT ON THE MIRACULOUS STREAM . . . . .   535 CHOSEN   16
MIRE
    WAS DIM WITH MIRE OF A MORTAL SHORE, ...   15 OISIN 1   208
    WAS DIM WITH THE MIRE OF A MORTAL SHORE, ...   15 OISIN 1   V 208
    AND TRAMPLED IN THE BUBBLING MIRE. . . . . . .   83 MAD KING GOLL   26
    AND TRAMPLED ON THE BUBBLING MIRE. . . . . . .   83 MAD KING GOLL   V 26
    TOILED WITH EMPOUNDED CATTLE THROUGH THE MIRE, ...   276 TWO KINGS   V 2
    THAT WITH EMPOUNDED CATTLE TROD THE MIRE, ...   277 TWO KINGS   4
    TILL ALL THE PLACE WAS BEATEN INTO MIRE. . . . . .   278 TWO KINGS   27

		PAGE	TITLE		LINE

MIRE (CONTINUED)

BUT FOR THE TRODDEN MIRE, THE POOL OF BLOOD, • • • • • • 278 TWO KINGS 44
THE MAN DROWNED IN A BOG'S MIRE, • • • • • • • • • 413 TOWER 95
THE FURY AND THE MIRE OF HUMAN VEINS. • • • • • • • 497 BYZANTIUM 8
AND ALL COMPLEXITIES OF MIRE OR BLOOD. • • • • • • • 498 BYZANTIUM 24
ASTRADDLE ON THE DOLPHIN'S MIRE AND BLOOD, • • • • • 498 BYZANTIUM 33
A STRADDLE ON THE DOLPHIN'S MIRE AND BLOOD • • • • • 498 BYZANTIUM V 33
THAT THING ALL BLOOD AND MIRE, THAT BEAST-TORN WRECK, • • 537 HER VISION 25
AND BLOOD AND MIRE THE SENSITIVE BODY STAIN? • • • • 564 GYRES 10
ABOLISHED BY A MIRE OF LITTLE THINGS, • • • • • • • 711 FERENCZ RENYI 36

MIRROR

LIKE A BRIDE BENDING OVER HER MIRROR ADORNING, • • • • 28 OISIN 1 V 423E
BREATHE ON THE BURNISHED MIRROR OF THE WORLD • • • • 228 SHADOW WATER B 132
NOT IN ITS IMAGE ON THE MIRROR! WHILE • • • • • • • 230 SHADOW WATER B 189
YOU MAY, THAT MIRROR FOR A SCHOOL, • • • • • • • • 335 YOUNG BEAUTY 7
MIRROR RESEMBLING DREAMS. • • • • • • • • • • 415 TOWER V 165
SATISFIED IF A TROUBLED MIRROR SHOW IT, • • • • • • 430 NINETEEN 19 62
CONTENTED THAT A TROUBLED MIRROR SHOW IT, • • • • • 430 NINETEEN 19 V 62
THE MIRROR OF MALICIOUS EYES • • • • • • • • • • 479 SELF AND SOUL 52
AND ALL THE RANT'S A MIRROR OF MY MOOD! • • • • • • 490 COOLE BALLYLEE 13
AND ALL THE RANT A MIRROR OF MY MOOD! • • • • • • • 490 COOLE BALLYLEE V 13
FROM MIRROR AFTER MIRROR, • • • • • • • • • • • 532 BEFORE WORLD 5
FROM MIRROR AFTER MIRROR, • • • • • • • • • • • 532 BEFORE WORLD 5
THE MIRROR SCALED SERPENT IS MULTIPLICITY, • • • • • 556 RIBH PATRICK V 10
MIRROR ON MIRROR MIRRORED IS ALL THE SHOW. • • • • • 610 STATUES 22
MIRROR ON MIRROR MIRRORED IS ALL THE SHOW. • • • • • 610 STATUES 22
BREATHE ON THE BURNISHED MIRROR OF THE WORLD • • • • 750 SHADOW WATER A 69

MIRRORED

MIRRORED IN STREAMS THAT NEITHER HAIL NOR RAIN • • • • 184 QUEEN MAEVE 89
MIRRORED IN WATERS THAT NOR HAIL NOR RAIN • • • • • 184 QUEEN MAEVE V 89
MIRROR ON MIRROR MIRRORED IS ALL THE SHOW. • • • • • 610 STATUES 22
AS FIGURES MOVING MIRRORED IN A GLASS, • • • • • • 676 ISLE STAT II 3 270

MIRROR-RESEMBLING

MIRROR-RESEMBLING DREAM. • • • • • • • • • • • 415 TOWER 165

MIRRORS

MIRRORS A STILL SKY! • • • • • • • • • • • • 322 SWANS AT COOLE 4

MIRROR-SCALED

THE MIRROR-SCALED SERPENT IS MULTIPLICITY, • • • • • 556 RIBH PATRICK 10

MIRTH

• • • AND THE MEMORIES OF THE WHOLE OF MY MIRTH, • • • 52 OISIN 3 71
HIS SHOUTING DAYS WITH MIRTH WERE CROWNED! • • • • • 67 HAPPY SHEPHERD 50
OR SIGHS AMID THE WANDERING STARRY MIRTH, • • • • • 114 ROSE OF BATTLE 18
ONE WITH HER ARE MIRTH AND DUTY! • • • • • • • 124 CATHLEEN PARA V 5
THEY BLOSSOMED TO IMMORTAL MIRTH. • • • • • • • 189 BAILE AILLINN 12
ONCE MORE THOSE SHEPHERDS COME. MAYHAP SOME MIRTH • • 664 ISLE STAT II 2 49
IN THEIR DAYS OF YOUTHFUL MIRTH! • • • • • • • 727 LOVERS QUARREL 40
FAR AWAY THE STARRY MIRTH • • • • • • • • • 731 STREET DANCERS 7
OTHER PEOPLE'S MIRTH AND PLEASURE, • • • • • • • 732 STREET DANCERS 24
OTHER PEOPLE'S MIRTH AND PLEASURE, • • • • • • • 732 STREET DANCERS 37
OTHER'S PEOPLE'S MIRTH AND PLEASURE, • • • • • • 733 STREET DANCERS 50
OTHERS KNOW THE STARRY MIRTH! • • • • • • • • 733 STREET DANCERS 54
AND HER OLD WIND THAT NO MIRTH EVER HAD, • • • • • 738 YOU ARE SAD 7

MIRTHFUL

WITH MIRTHFUL SONGS BEFORE THE DAWN. • • • • • • 67 HAPPY SHEPHERD 49
WITH MIRTHFUL SONGS TILL RISE THE DAWN. • • • • • 67 HAPPY SHEPHERD V 49
AND, MAIDEN, BE THOU MIRTHFUL TOO, • • • • • • • 736 SUMMER EVENING 13
AND PIERCED THE MIRTHFUL BREAST, • • • • • • • 741 EARL PAUL 50

MISCALCULATE

I TRAP YOU. CHECK. I DO MISCALCULATE. • • • • • • 722 WITCH VIVIEN 58

MISCHIEF

WHATEVER MISCHIEF SEEMED • • • • • • • • • • 431 NINETEEN 19 85
WHAT EVER MISCHIEF SEEMED • • • • • • • • • • 431 NINETEEN 19 V 85

MISCHIEVOUS

"OF PLASTER SAINTS"! HIS BEAUTIFUL MISCHIEVOUS HEAD THROWN 577 LOFTY THINGS 4
BACK.

MISER

SOME OLD MISER TELLS HIS STORE! • • • • • • • • 647 ISLE STAT I 1 58
OLD MISER HOARDS OF GRIEF TO TELL AND TELL! • • • • 661 ISLE STAT II 1 55

MISERABLE

ONCE MORE HOW ON THAT MISERABLE DAY • • • • • • • 658 ISLE STAT II 1 4

MISERIES

THROUGH MISERIES UNHUMAN EVER ON • • • • • • • 684 SEEKER 59
TILL THEIR FIERCE MISERIES WITHIN HIS EYES • • • • • 687 TWO TITANS 26

MISERRIMUS

MISERRIMUS • • • • • • • • • • • • • 67 SAD SHEPHERD V T

MISERY

OF SOME INHUMAN MISERY • • • • • • • • • • • 85 MAD KING GOLL 58
OF SOME UNHUMAN MISERY • • • • • • • • • • • 85 MAD KING GOLL V 58
WITH MISERY, OR THAT SHE WOULD OF LATE • • • • • • 256 NO SECOND TROY 2
CONTENT TO TRACE THAT MISERY TO ITS SOURCE, • • • • 479 SELF AND SOUL V 65
AND LOVED IN MISERY, • • • • • • • • • • • 538 LAST CONFESS 4
AND THOUGH IT LOVED IN MISERY • • • • • • • • 538 LAST CONFESS 21

MISREPRESENT

SOME ANCIENT FAMOUS AUTHORS MISREPRESENT, • • • • • 579 DOR WELLESLEY 15

MISS

THAT I SHALL MISS YOU • • • • • • • • • • • 118 CRADLE SONG 11
AH! HOW I SHALL MISS YOU, • • • • • • • • • • 118 CRADLE SONG V 11
AH, HOW SHALL I MISS YOU, • • • • • • • • • • 118 CRADLE SONG V 11
WHY SHOULD THOSE LOVERS THAT NO LOVERS MISS • • • • 128 DREAM OF FAERY 46
AND NO ONE ANY LEAF-CROWNED DANCER MISS • • • • • 128 DREAM OF FAERY V 46
I SENT AN ARROW. AND I SAW YOU MISS! • • • • • • 649 ISLE STAT I 1 115

524

MISS'D
    NAY, NAY, I MISS'D HIM NOT; HIS DAYS • • • • • • • •   649 ISLE STAT I 1   117
MISSHAPEN
    THE WRONG OF THE THINGS MISSHAPEN IS WRONG TOO GREAT TO   143 ROSE IN HEART V   5
      BE TOLD;
MIST
    THE MIST CLOSED ROUND US; PEARLY LIGHT • • • • • • •   28 OISIN 1   V 427C
    CAME NOW THE SLIDING OF TEARS AND SWEEPING OF MIST COLD   47 OISIN 3   V   7
      HAIR,
    THE PHANTOM, BEAUTY, IN A MIST OF TEARS; • • • • •   73 ANASHU VIJAYA   55
    LOOK THERE! THERE IN THE MIST! A SHIP OF SPICE! • • • •   232 SHADOW WATER B   219
    THE MIST HAS COVERED THE HEAVENS, AND YOU AND I • • •   251 SHADOW WATER B   604
    IN THE BROKEN MIST • • • • • • • • • • • • • •   349 HAWK   11
    A MIST THAT IS LIKE BLOWN SNOW IS SWEEPING OVER ALL, • •   425 PHANTOM HATRED   2
    AND THOSE WHITE GLIMMERING FRAGMENTS OF THE MIST SWEEP BY.   426 PHANTOM HATRED   6
    MAD AS THE MIST AND SNOW • • • • • • • • • • • •   523 MAD AS MIST   T
    MAD AS THE MIST AND SNOW. • • • • • • • • • • •   523 MAD AS MIST   6
    MAD AS THE MIST AND SNOW? • • • • • • • • • • • •   524 MAD AS MIST   12
    MAD AS THE MIST AND SNOW. • • • • • • • • • • • •   524 MAD AS MIST   18
    WITH CLINGING MIST, EACH STAR-FOUGHT WANDERER CAME • • •   656 ISLE STAT I 3   33
    LOVE STORM; AND STAINED WITH MIST THE NEW MOONS FLARE. • •   678 ISLE STAT II 3   294
    LOVE STORM AND STAINED WITH MIST THE NEW MOON'S FLARE • •   678 ISLE STAT II 3 V   294
    HANG THE MIST THREADS FOR A LITTLE WHILE LIKE COBWEBS IN   719 PHANTOM SHIP   V   29
      THE AIR,
    WHERE THE MOON MAKES A CLOUDY LIGHT IN THE MIST. • • • •   764 SHADOW WATER A   329
MISTAKE
    NOW THAT YOUR TONGUE CANNOT PERSUADE THE CHILD TILL SHE   450 OWEN AHERNE   22
      MISTAKE
MIST-COLD
    CAME NOW THE SLIDING OF TEARS AND SWEEPING OF MIST-COLD   47 OISIN 3   7
      HAIR,
    CAME NOW THE SLIDING OF TEARS AND SWEEPING OF MIST-COLD   47 OISIN 3   V   7
      AIR,
MIST-COVERED
    AND NOW FLED BY, MIST-COVERED, WITHOUT SOUND, • • • •   29 OISIN 2   3
MIST-DROPS
    THE MIST-DROPS HUNG ON THE FRAGRANT TREES, • • • • • •   2 OISIN 1   V   7F
MISTOOK
    BUT THEY MISTOOK THE BRIGHTNESS OF THE MOON • • • • •   411 TOWER   45
MISTRESS
    HIS MISTRESS WAS MORE MILD AND FAIR • • • • • • • •   3 OISIN 1   V   7DD
    "MY MISTRESS CANNOT SEE THESE THINGS, • • • • • • •   595 COLONEL MARTIN   30
    "TAKE ALL TO YOUR MISTRESS," • • • • • • • • • •   595 COLONEL MARTIN   34
MISTS
    AWAY FROM ME WHERE MISTS OF EVENING DRINK • • • • • •   663 ISLE STAT II 2   40
    HE FADES AMONG THE MISTS; HOW FAST THEY COME, • • • • •   703 MOSADA 3   117
MIST-THREADS
    HANG THE MIST-THREADS FOR A LITTLE WHILE LIKE COBWEBS IN   719 PHANTOM SHIP   29
      THE AIR;
MISTY
    ON A MORNING MISTY AND MILD AND FAIR. • • • • • • •   2 OISIN 1   V   7E
    CLOSED IN THE MISTY AIR PROFOUND. • • • • • • • • •   10 OISIN 1   V 114D
    THAT HAS DRUNK FULL, SHE CROSSED THE MISTY SEA • • • •   30 OISIN 2   16
    STRETCHED HIS LONG ARM TO WHERE, A MISTY SMOTHER, • • •   31 OISIN 2   42
    OF EVERY FOAMDROP ON ITS MISTY WAY. • • • • • • • •   32 OISIN 2   45
    AND STOOD WITHIN; CLOTHED IN A MISTY RAY • • • • • •   36 OISIN 2   104
    AND STOOD WITHIN THE HALL. A MISTY RAY • • • • • •   36 OISIN 2   V   104
    FEEBLER AND FEEBLER SHONE THE MISTY GLARE. • • • • • •   37 OISIN 2   V   121
    OF MISTY DAWN; WHEN, CIRCLING ROUND THE HALL, • • • • •   39 OISIN 2   V   153
    LEAP IN THE MEADOW. ON THE MISTY STAIRS • • • • • •   44 OISIN 2   V   229
    I PACE REMEMBERING. FROM MY MISTY THRONE • • • • • •   45 OISIN 2   V 239C
    UPON THE MISTY BORDER OF THE WOOD, • • • • • • • •   251 SHADOW WATER B   612
    AMONG THESE MISTY WATERS. TWO! NOW FOUR! • • • • •   753 SHADOW WATER A   138
    UPON THE MISTY BORDER OF THE WOOD,— • • • • • • • •   769 SHADOW WATER A   428
MITCHEL'S
    YOU THAT MITCHEL'S PRAYER HAVE HEARD, • • • • • • •   638 BEN BULBEN   25
MIX
    OR LET ITS MEANING MIX INTO THE STRINGS. • • • • • •   180 QUEEN MAEVE   8
    COULD WE BUT MIX OURSELVES INTO A DREAM, • • • • • •   230 SHADOW WATER B   188
    I MIGHT HAVE HAD NO FRIEND THAT COULD NOT MIX • • • • •   352 PEOPLE   16
    OF THAT OLD GEORGIAN MANSION, MIX • • • • • • • •   475 EVA GORE-BOOTH   16
    THAT I WOULD MIX WITH YOURS, AND IN THIS HAIR • • • • •   765 SHADOW WATER A   351
MIXED   SEE UN-MIXED
    SURLY AND DISTANT, MIXED INSEPARABLY • • • • • • • •   45 OISIN 2   233
    RISING AND FALLING, MIXED INSEPARABLY, • • • • • • •   45 OISIN 2   V   233
    AND MIXED WITH THE SOUND OF THAT ROARER • • • • • • •   60 OISIN 3   V   184
    MY BREATH IS MIXED INTO HIS BREATH. • • • • • • • •   152 HEART OF WOMAN   12
    AND WHERE BEECH-TREES HAD MIXED A PALE GREEN LIGHT • • •   277 TWO KINGS   5
    WHERE CERTAIN BEECHES MIXED A PALE GREEN LIGHT • • • •   277 TWO KINGS   V   5
    AND WHERE BEECH TREES HAD MIXED A PALE GREEN LIGHT • • •   277 TWO KINGS   V   5
    TWO THOUGHTS WERE SO MIXED UP I COULD NOT TELL • • • •   471 ALL SOUL NIGHT   31
MOAN
    I BELLOW TO THE WINDS WHEN STORMS MAKE MOAN, • • • • •   45 OISIN 2   V 239D
    LIKE AN ARMY OF OLD MEN LONGING FOR REST FROM THE MOAN   48 OISIN 3   16
      OF THE SEAS.
    I SAW FROM A DISTANT SADDLE; FROM THE EARTH SHE MADE HER   56 OISIN 3   130
      MOAN!
    LIKE AN ARMY OF OLD MEN LONGING FOR REST FROM THE MOAN   57 OISIN 3   144
      OF THE SEAS.
    CHANGED ALL HE SANG TO INARTICULATE MOAN • • • • • •   69 SAD SHEPHERD   27
    CHANGED ALL HIS WORDS TO INARTICULATE MOAN • • • • • •   69 SAD SHEPHERD   V   27

	PAGE	TITLE	LINE

MOAN   (CONTINUED)
IN THREE DAYS' TIME HE STOOD UP WITH A MOAN, ...   111 CUCHULAIN SEA V   83
IN THREE DAYS' TIME, CUCHULAIN WITH A MOAN . . . .   111 CUCHULAIN SEA V   83
AND RENT HER CLOTHES AND MADE HER MOAN: . . . .   275 GREY ROCK   108
BUT THE SECOND MOCKED HIS MOAN: . . . .   299 THREE HERMITS   24
THEREON I MADE MY MOAN, ...   384 VISION ROBART   63
MY BODY MAKES NO MOAN . . . .   512 JANE ON GOD   22
AS AN HURT LEOPARD FILLS WITH CEASELESS MOAN, ...   674 ISLE STAT II 3   208
AS A HURT LEOPARD FILLS WITH CEASELESS MOAN   . . . .   674 ISLE STAT II 3 V 208
MAKE MOAN AND CRY, WITHIN YON SUNLESS VALLEY, ...   682 SEEKER   26
AND WHO WILL MOAN IN THE UNDER PIT, ...   716 FAIRY DOCTOR   7
FOR HURTS AND AILS AND LOVER'S MOAN--   . . . . . .   717 FAIRY DOCTOR   18
MOANED
THAN DOVES THAT MOANED ROUND EMAN'S HALL   . . . . .   3 OISIN 1   V 7EE
TO WHERE SHE MOANED UPON THE GROUND, ...   275 GREY ROCK   119
MOANED THE OTHER, "THEY ARE THROWN   . . . .   299 THREE HERMITS   22
MY BODY HAS NOT MOANED   . . . .   512 JANE ON GOD   V 22
MOANING
REPLY LIKE MOANING OF IMPRISONED ELF: . . . . . .   652 ISLE STAT I 2   11
MOANS
THAT MOANS AND SIGHS A HUNDRED DAYS: . . . .   78 INDIAN TO LOVE   17
AND THERE TO ITS OWN HEART FOR EVER MOANS.   . . . . .   650 ISLE STAT I 1   131
MOB
ARE THE MOB THAT HOWLS AT THE DOOR: . . . .   554 CHURCH STATE   10
MOBILE
THE PRIMUM MOBILE THAT FASHIONED US   . . . .   423 MY DESCENDANTS   17
MOBS
THEIR MOBS PUT UNDER THEIR FEET.   . . . .   554 CHURCH STATE   4
THE MOBS OF STARS IN GOLD AND GREEN AND BLUE, ...   663 ISLE STAT II 2   43
MOCHARABUIEE
MY BROTHER IN MOCHARABUIEE.   . . . .   178 FIDDLER DOONEY   4
MOCK
THEN MOCK AT DEATH AND TIME WITH GLANCES   . . . . .   19 OISIN 1   274
WHILE THOSE SAME HUNDREDS MOCK ANOTHER DAY   . . . . .   265 ABBEY THEATRE   4
BUT WHEN THEY MOCK US, THAT WE MOCK AGAIN?   . . . . .   265 ABBEY THEATRE   14
BUT WHEN THEY MOCK US, THAT WE MOCK AGAIN?   . . . . .   265 ABBEY THEATRE   14
AND MOCK HIM TO HIS FACE AND THEN   . . . .   272 GREY ROCK   34
TO MOCK AT EVERYTHING I LOVE   . . . .   306 HOUR DAWN   83
I MOCK PLOTINUS' THOUGHT   . . . .   415 TOWER   146
COME LET US MOCK AT THE GREAT   . . . .   432 NINETEEN 19   93
COME LET US MOCK AT THE WISE: . . . .   432 NINETEEN 19   98
COME LET US MOCK AT THE GOOD   . . . .   432 NINETEEN 19   103
MOCK MOCKERS AFTER THAT   . . . .   432 NINETEEN 19   108
MOCK ME WITH PRAISE OF MY MERE OPPOSITE: . . . . .   448 HERO GIRL FOOL V   4
NONE BUT THE LIVING MOCK, ...   471 ALL SOUL NIGHT   17
WHEREAT THE LIVING MOCK, ...   474 ALL SOUL NIGHT   87
THOSE THAT COME AFTER SHALL MOCK AT O'DONNELL, ...   546 TO SAME TUNE 2   23
MOCK AT THE MEMORY OF BOTH O'NEILLS, ...   546 TO SAME TUNE 2   24
THOSE THAT COME AFTER SHALL MOCK O'DONNELL, ...   546 TO SAME TUNE 2 V 23
MOCK EMMET, MOCK PARNELL: . . . .   547 TO SAME TUNE 2   25
MOCK EMMET, MOCK PARNELL: . . . .   547 TO SAME TUNE 2   25
THOSE THAT COME AFTER SHALL MOCK AT O'DONNELL, ...   614 MARCH SONGS 1   23
MOCK AT THE MEMORY OF BOTH O'NEILLS, ...   614 MARCH SONGS 1   24
MOCK EMMET, MOCK PARNELL, ...   614 MARCH SONGS 1   25
MOCK EMMET, MOCK PARNELL, ...   614 MARCH SONGS 1   25
I MOCK AT ALL SO BURNING OUT.   . . . .   787 HUDDON DUDDON   15
BUT HOW THEY MOCK US BURNING OUT.   . . . .   787 HUDDON DUDDON V 15
MOCKED
WE MOCKED AT TIME AND FATE AND CHANCE   . . . . . .   20 OISIN 1   291
BUT THE SECOND MOCKED HIS MOAN: . . . .   299 THREE HERMITS   24
BEING MOCKED BY GUIDO FOR HIS LECHEROUS LIFE, ...   369 EGO DOMINUS   33
MOCKED ME WITH PRAISE OF MY MERE OPPOSITE: . . . . .   448 HERO GIRL FOOL   4
I MOCKED, BEING CRAZY, BUT YOU MASTERED IT   . . . . .   533 HER TRIUMPH   8
HEROIC REVERIE MOCKED BY CLOWN AND KNAVE, ...   619 BRONZE HEAD   27
MOCKERS   SEE BE-MOCKERS
HE MUSED UPON HIS MOCKERS: WITHOUT FAIL   . . . . .   127 DREAM OF FAERY   26
THE IMMORTAL MOCKERS HAVE CAST INTO HIS MIND, ...   249 SHADOW WATER B   567
MOCK MOCKERS AFTER THAT   . . . .   432 NINETEEN 19   108
O SELF-BORN MOCKERS OF MAN'S ENTERPRISE: . . . . .   445 SCHOOL CHILDR   56
MOCKERY
IF RAILING AND REPROACH AND MOCKERY   . . . . . .   243 SHADOW WATER B   438
TRAFFIC IN MOCKERY.   . . . .   432 NINETEEN 19   112
IS A MAN'S MOCKERY OF THE CHANGELESS SOUL."   . . . .   465 HARUN RASHID   102
IN MOCKERY I HAVE SET   . . . .   480 BLOOD AND MOON   8
IN MOCKERY OF A TIME   . . . .   480 BLOOD AND MOON   11
WHAT GAVE THAT ROAR OF MOCKERY, ...   583 GHOST ROG CASE   7
THEY LIE THAT SAY, IN MOCKERY   . . . .   789 SINGING HEAD   9
MOCKING
HEARING HELL LOUD WITH A MURMUR, AS SHOUTING AND MOCKING   62 OISIN 3   208
WE SWEEP.
OF A MOCKING TALE OR A GIBE . . . .   392 EASTER 1916   10
WHEN MOCKING MUSES CHOSE THE COUNTRY WENCH.   . . . .   413 TOWER   96
MOCKING WITH PATIENT LAUGHTER ALL THE NIGHT   . . . .   657 ISLE STAT I 3   52
MOCKS
AND MOCKS RETURNING VICTORY, HE PASSED   . . . . .   279 TWO KINGS   58
MODEL
A MODEL FOR THE LAUREATE . . . .   597 MODEL LAUREATE   T
MODELLED
A NEW MODELLED DOLL, OR DRAWING, ...   362 DOLLS DRAWINGS   2
THAT WITH A MALLET OR A CHISEL MODELLED THESE . . . . .   610 STATUES   10

	PAGE	TITLE	LINE

MODERN
THAT IS OUR MODERN HOPE, AND BY ITS LIGHT • • • • • • 368 EGO DOMINUS 11
IN THE BEST MODERN WAY—THE CHILDREN'S EYES • • • • 443 SCHOOL CHILDR 6
IS EVERY MODERN NATION LIKE THE TOWER, • • • • • • 482 BLOOD AND MOON 47
ETERNALISED THE BODY OF A MODERN SAINT THAT ONCE • • • • 503 VACILLATION 83
APPLAUD A MODERN THRONE! • • • • • • • • • 597 MODEL LAUREATE 18
WE THREE ALONE IN MODERN TIMES HAD BROUGHT • • • • 603 GALLERY REVIS 45
BUT THROWN UPON THIS FILTHY MODERN TIDE • • • • • • 611 STATUES 29
AND MINE WERE BUT FIFTEEN FOOT, NO MODERN STALKS 623 HIGH TALK 3
UPON HIGHER,
SCOFF THEY AT THE MODERN EARTH— • • • • • • • 727 LOVERS QUARREL 38
MODISH
NOR LET THE MODISH PAINTER SHIRK • • • • • • • • 638 BEN BULBEN 38
MOHINI
MOHINI CHATTERJEE • • • • • • • • • • 495 MOHINI CHATTER T
MOHINI CHATTERJEE • • • • • • • • • • 496 MOHINI CHATTER 14
MOIDERED
AND MOIDERED IN THAT SNARE • • • • • • • • • 783 GREY ROUND 8
MOIL
THE MOIL OF MY CENTURIES FILLED ME! AND GONE LIKE 51 OISIN 3 70
A SEA-COVERED STONE
MOIST
DROPS ON HIS BOSOM, SOMBRE, MOIST AND SLOW. • • • • • 711 FERENCZ RENYI 40
UPON HIS BOSOM, SOMBRE, MOIST AND SLOW. • • • • • • 711 FERENCZ RENYI V 40
MOISTENED
ABOUNDING FOLIAGE MOISTENED WITH THE DEW! • • • • • 500 VACILLATION 13
MOISTURE
A MOUTH THAT HAS NO MOISTURE AND NO BREATH • • • • • 497 BYZANTIUM 13
MOLAY
"VENGEANCE FOR JACQUES MOLAY." IN CLOUD-PALE RAGS, OR 426 PHANTOM HATRED 10
IN LACE,
FOR VENGEANCE ON THE MURDERERS OF JACQUES MOLAY. • • • • 426 PHANTOM HATRED 16
"VENGENCE FOR JACQUES MOLAY." IN CLOUD PALE RAGS, OR IN 426 PHANTOM HATRED V 10
LACE,
MOLE
BEYOND EAGLE OR MOLE, • • • • • • • • • • • 784 WOMANS BEAUTY 10
MOLL
THE BALLAD OF MOLL MAGEE • • • • • • • • • 94 MOLL MAGEE T
BUT PITY MOLL MAGEE. • • • • • • • • • • 94 MOLL MAGEE 4
AND PITY MOLL MAGEE. • • • • • • • • • • 96 MOLL MAGEE 56
I COULD GIVE ALL MY HEART TO THAT RED MOLL • • • • • • 222 SHADOW WATER B 9
FOR THAT RED MOLL THAT HAD BUT THE ONE EYE. • • • • • 222 SHADOW WATER B V 10
MOMENT
THAT MANY A PEACEFUL MOMENT HAD, • • • • • • • 4 OISIN 1 35
IN CLANGING SPACE A MOMENT HEARD, • • • • • • • 65 HAPPY SHEPHERD 20
'MID CLANGING SPACE A MOMENT HEARD • • • • • • 65 HAPPY SHEPHERD V 20
DYING AT EVERY MOMENT IN THE WORLD, • • • • • • 226 SHADOW WATER B 90
THAT NONE MIGHT TAKE YOU FROM ME. FOR A MOMENT • • • 237 SHADOW WATER B 330
ONE MOMENT HAS NO MIGHT UPON THE MOMENT • • • • • 237 SHADOW WATER B 340
ONE MOMENT HAS NO MIGHT UPON THE MOMENT • • • • • 237 SHADOW WATER B 340
WANDER A MOMENT WHEN ONE IS IN LOVE? • • • • • • 246 SHADOW WATER B 515
NEVER UNTIL THIS MOMENT HAVE WE MET • • • • • • 339 SHEP GOATHERD 7
UPON A MOMENT, AND SO STRETCHED IT OUT • • • • • • 384 VISION ROBART 46
ALL THAT TO THIS MOMENT CHARMED YOU? • • • • • • 390 IMAGE PAST 21
ENDURES A MOMENT OR A DAY. • • • • • • • • 438 SONGS PLAY 2 10
WHERE FOR ITS MOMENT BOTH SEEM LOST, CONSUMED. • • • • 555 RIBH AT TOMB 16
SHOUTED A MOMENT 'TWEEN THE EARTH AND SKY. • • • • 675 ISLE STAT II 3 237
I HAVE BEEN WAITING YOU. A MOMENT SINCE • • • • • 763 SHADOW WATER A 313
IT PASSED BUT A MOMENT AGO. • • • • • • • • 781 MY HEART BEAT 3
IT PASSED BY A MOMENT AGO. • • • • • • • • 781 MY HEART BEAT V 3
THE MOMENT HE HAS LOOKED AT YOU, • • • • • • • 786 YOUR HEART 18
MOMENTARY
A MOMENTARY GLEAM OF PHOSPHORUS FLAME. • • • • • 37 OISIN 2 118
A MOMENTARY GLIMMER OF VAGUE PHOSPHORUS FLAME. • • • 37 OISIN 2 V 120
IN MOMENTARY ANGER LONG AGO! • • • • • • • • 258 KING NO KING 10
MOMENTARY THOUGHTS • • • • • • • • • • 260 FASC DIFFICULT V T
THEIR MOMENTARY CRIES BEFORE IT IS DAWN, • • • • • 371 EGO DOMINUS 78
IN MOMENTARY WONDER STARE UPON • • • • • • • 443 SCHOOL CHILDR 7
NOISE! AND A FLASH, A MOMENTARY BLOT. • • • • • • 714 FERENCZ RENYI 110
NOISE! UPROAR! AND A MOMENTARY BLOT. • • • • • • 714 FERENCZ RENYI V 110
MOMENT'S
YET IF IT DOES NOT SEEM A MOMENT'S THOUGHT, • • • • 204 ADAMS CURSE 5
OR IF THEY MADE A MOMENT'S STAY • • • • • • • 297 THREE BEGGARS 52
A MOMENT'S MEMORY TO THAT LAURELLED HEAD. • • • • • 489 COOLE PARK 29 32
MOMENTS
THE MOMENTS PASS AND PASS! • • • • • • • • 99 FOXHUNTER 44
HOW MANY LOVED YOUR MOMENTS OF GLAD GRACE, • • • • 121 YOU ARE OLD 5
THE MOMENTS PASSED AS AT A PLAY! • • • • • • • 313 MEMORY YOUTH 1
AT CHANCES AND AT MOMENTS WITH MANKIND. • • • • • 721 WITCH VIVIEN 35
MONEY
AND GAVE ME MONEY, AND BADE ME GO • • • • • • 95 MOLL MAGEE 23
HIS MIND RAN ALL ON MONEY CARES AND FEARS, • • • • 127 DREAM OF FAERY 14
LAND FOR YOUR CHILDREN OR MONEY IN A POT." • • • • 228 SHADOW WATER B 125
MONEY IS GOOD AND A GIRL MIGHT BE BETTER, • • • • • 544 TO SAME TUNE 1 3
MONEY I HAD, AND IT WENT IN THE NIGHT, • • • • • 544 TO SAME TUNE 1 12
"MONEY IS GOOD AND A GIRL MIGHT BE BETTER, • • • • 545 TO SAME TUNE 1 21
SUFFICIENT MONEY FOR HIS NEED, • • • • • • • 577 WHAT THEN 8
MONEY IS GOOD AND A GIRL MIGHT BE BETTER, • • • • • 616 MARCH SONGS 3 3
MONEY I HAD, AND IT WENT IN THE NIGHT, • • • • • 616 MARCH SONGS 3 12
"MONEY IS GOOD AND A GIRL MIGHT BE BETTER, • • • • 616 MARCH SONGS 3 21
THEIR MONEY SPENT, THEIR WINE GONE SOUR, • • • • • 635 BLACK TOWER 3

527

PAGE   TITLE   LINE

MONEY'S
  MY MONEY'S ALL USED UP, ...   96 MOLL MAGEE   38
  BUT THERE'S NO GOOD COMPLAINING, FOR MONEY'S RANT IS ON.   580 CURSE CROMWELL   10
'MONG
  FOR LONELY TO MOVE 'MONG THE SOFT EYES . . . .   63 OISIN 3   V   222
  WALKING GHOSTLY 'MONG THE DEW, ...   67 HAPPY SHEPHERD V   52
  'MONG THE FEET OF ANGELS SEVEN . . . .   125 CATHLEEN PARA   13
  AND 'MONG THE STUNTED ASH-TREES' DROOPING RINGS, . . .   650 ISLE STAT I 1   128
  FORSWEARS HIS WANDERING 'MONG THE PINE, ...   686 LIFE   6
  SINCE 'MONG MY PEOPLE, TENTED ON THE HILLS, ...   690 MOSADA 1   4
  IN HIS OWN HOUSE OR 'MONG THE MERCHANTS GREY, ...   693 MOSADA 1   87
  BUT NO, IN THIS WARM WEATHER, 'MONG THE HILLS, . . .   699 MOSADA 3   9
  NESTED 'MONG THE VAPOURS BROWN. . . . .   731 STREET DANCERS   6
MONGAN
  MONGAN LAMENTS THE CHANGE THAT HAS COME UPON HIM AND HIS 153 CHANGE BELOVED V   T
    BELOVED
  SONG OF MONGAN . . . .   177 PAST GREATNESS V   T
  MONGAN THINKS OF HIS PAST GREATNESS . . . .   177 PAST GREATNESS V   T
MONK
  WHY THESE NEW FEARS? THE GREAT MONK EBREMAR, ...   692 MOSADA 1   46
MONKEY
  WITH A MONKEY ON A CHAIN, ...   627 STATES HOLIDAY   36
MONK'S-HOOD
  OF THE MONK'S-HOOD HOW THEY SHAKE, ...   655 ISLE STAT I 3   2
MONK'S-HOOD'S
  OH, LEARNED IS EACH MONK'S-HOOD'S MIND, ...   655 ISLE STAT I 3   8
MONKS
  THE HOLINESS OF MONKS, AND AFTER . . . .   640 BEN BULBEN   76
  THE HOLINESS OF THE MONKS, AND AFTER . . . . . .   640 BEN BULBEN   V   76
MONOTONE
  AND DRIFTING GREYNESS, WHILE THIS MONOTONE, ...   45 OISIN 2   232
  AND DRIFTING GREYNESS. CAME THIS MONOTONE . . . .   45 OISIN 2   V   232
  I HEARD THE DEATHFUL MONOTONE, ...   673 ISLE STAT II 3   183
MONSTROUS
  UNDER THE STARLIGHT AND SHADOW, A MONSTROUS SLUMBERING   48 OISIN 3   27
    FOLK,
  FROM HIS HOOVES IN THE HEAVY GRASSES, WITH MONSTROUS   48 OISIN 3   V   27
    SLUMBERING FOLK,
  CAME SOUND FROM THOSE MONSTROUS SLEEPERS, ...   51 OISIN 3   58
  HE IS A MONSTROUS PEACOCK, AND HE WAVETH ALL THE NIGHT .   77 INDIAN ON GOD   19
  THE MEANING OF THAT MONSTROUS DAY. THEN SHE: . . . .   280 TWO KINGS   78
  THE MONSTROUS CRYING OF WIND? . . . .   312 CHILD DANCING   12
  ALL I HAD RHYMED OF THAT MONSTROUS THING . . . . .   358 PRESENCES   7
  ALL I HAVE RHYMED OF THAT MONSTROUS THING . . . . .   358 PRESENCES   V   7
  MONSTROUS FAMILIAR IMAGES SWIM TO THE MIND'S EYE. . .   426 PHANTOM HATRED   8
MONTASHIGI
  MONTASHIGI, THIRD OF HIS FAMILY, FASHIONED IT . . . .   478 SELF AND SOUL   25
  MONTASHIGI OF OSAFUME FASHIONED IT . . . .   478 SELF AND SOUL   25
MONTENEGRIN
  HERE'S A MONTENEGRIN LUTE, ...   627 STATES HOLIDAY   22
MONTH   SEE TWELVE-MONTH
  MORE STILL THAN THEY HAD BEEN FOR A GOOD MONTH, ... 182 QUEEN MAEVE   54
MONTHS
  AND WONDER WHAT HAS AILED HIM THESE TWELVE MONTHS." . . 284 TWO KINGS   163
  SO LITTLE. AS THE MONTHS PASSED BY WE GREW . . . .   713 FERENCZ RENYI   93
MONTHS'
  OUTRODE HIS TROOP THAT AFTER TWELVE MONTHS' WAR . . .   276 TWO KINGS   V   1
MONUMENT
  WHETHER TO LOOK UPON YOUR MONUMENT . . . . . .   292 TO A SHADE   2
  THESE STONES REMAIN THEIR MONUMENT AND MINE. . . . .   423 MY DESCENDANTS   24
  NO HONOUR LEAVE ITS MIGHTY MONUMENT, ...   429 NINETEEN 19   38
  TO LEAVE SOME MONUMENT BEHIND, ...   432 NINETEEN 19   96
MONUMENTS
  MONUMENTS OF UNAGEING INTELLECT. . . . .   407 SAIL BYZANTIUM   8
  MONUMENTS OF ITS OWN MAGNIFICENCE: . . . . . .   407 SAIL BYZANTIUM   14
  THE THREE MONUMENTS . . . .   460 THREE MONUMENT   T
  HIS GLORY AND HIS MONUMENTS ARE GONE. . . . . . .   563 MERU   14
MOOD
  AND PONDERED IN A SOFT VAIN MOOD . . . .   14 OISIN 1   184
  IN SOME DIM MEMORY OR ANCIENT MOOD, ...   36 OISIN 2   99
  WITH NO RETURNING GLANCE, IN WORDLESS MOOD . . . . .   44 OISIN 2   V 230A
  THEY WERE OF NO WORDY MOOD: . . . .   65 HAPPY SHEPHERD V 13A
  ARE GAY WITH HIS MOOD. . . . .   118 CRADLE SONG   8
  GROW SWEET WITH HIS MOOD. . . . .   118 CRADLE SONG   V   8
  GROW GAY WITH HIS MOOD. . . . .   118 CRADLE SONG   V   8
  THE TALE DROVE HIS FINE ANGRY MOOD AWAY. . . . . .   128 DREAM OF FAERY   36
  AND ALL THE RANT'S A MIRROR OF MY MOOD: . . . . .   490 COOLE BALLYLEE   13
  AND ALL THE RANT A MIRROR OF MY MOOD: . . . . .   490 COOLE BALLYLEE V   13
  I SAW HIS JOVIAL MOOD BRING ONCE A SMILE . . . . .   696 MOSADA 2   14
  AND FREE—'TWILL THIEVE AWAY WITH SLEEPY MOOD . . . .   700 MOSADA 3   30
  TROTTED BESIDE HIM IN A PLAYFUL MOOD. . . . . . .   715 DWELT SYCAMORE   4
  AND THE CUCKOO UNSEEN IN HIS FESTIVAL MOOD: . . . .   717 LOVE SONG   7
  MY LOVE HATH MANY AN EVIL MOOD, ...   723 GIRLS SONG A   5
  MY LOVE HATH MANY A RUTHLESS MOOD, ...   723 GIRLS SONG A   V   5
  LAUGHING GOES IN WILDEST MOOD, ...   732 STREET DANCERS   41
MOODS
  THE MOODS . . . .   142 MOODS   T
  OF THE FIRE-BORN MOODS . . . .   142 MOODS   6
  THE LOVER ASKS FORGIVENESS BECAUSE OF HIS MANY MOODS . . 162 ASKS FORGIVE   T
  MICHAEL ROBARTES ASKS FORGIVENESS BECAUSE OF HIS MANY MOODS 162 ASKS FORGIVE V   T
  HIS MOODS BOW LOW HIS SOMBRE CREST, ...   723 GIRLS SONG A   2

528

MOODY

FULL MOODY IS MY LOVE AND SAD, • • • • • • • • • 723 GIRLS SONG A   1

MOON

MUST LIVE TO BE OLD LIKE THE WANDERING MOON. • • • • 3 OISIN 1   12
AND SLEEP DROWN SUN AND MOON AND STAR." • • • • • • 5 OISIN 1   V   49
NO MIGHTIER CREATURES BAY AT THE MOON: • • • • • • 8 OISIN 1   87
WHERE I WOULD BE WHEN THE WHITE MOON CLIMBS, • • • • 9 OISIN 1   104
BUT NOW THE MOON LIKE A WHITE ROSE SHONE • • • • • 12 OISIN 1   152
SLEEP THERE TILL THE MOON AND THE STARS DIE!" • • • 17 OISIN 1   246
IT FELL, OR FROM THE TWISTED MOON, • • • • • • • 19 OISIN 1   V   278
AND THE PALE BLOSSOM OF THE MOON, • • • • • • • 20 OISIN 1   288
AND THE THIN CRESCENT OF THE MOON, • • • • • • • 20 OISIN 1   V   288
AND THE MOON LIKE A PALE ROSE WITHER AWAY." • • • 28 OISIN 1   427
AT LAST THE MOON AND STARS SHONE, AND A FLIGHT • • 31 OISIN 2   V   34
AND THROUGH THEIR EYES NO LIGHT OF MOON OR DAY • • 34 OISIN 2   77
THAT LACKEY THE WORN MOON IN MIDNIGHT HOURS, • • • 41 OISIN 2   V 185A
AND THE MOON GOAD THE WATERS NIGHT AND DAY, • • • 45 OISIN 2   238
"BUT TILL THE MOON HAS TAKEN ALL, I WAGE • • • • 45 OISIN 2   240
A STARLING LIKE THEM THAT FORGATHERED 'NEATH A MOON • • 54 OISIN 3   103
THAT SLUMBERED IN THE HARVEST MOON, • • • • • • 85 MAD KING GOLL   50
THAT SLUMBERED 'NEATH THE HARVEST MOON, • • • • • 85 MAD KING GOLL   V   50
TILL THE MOON HAS TAKEN FLIGHT: • • • • • • • 87 STOLEN CHILD   19
AND LOVELIER THAN THE MOON UPON THE SEA: • • • • 106 CUCHULAIN SEA   V 16A
OR IN THE SUN AND MOON, OR ON THE EARTH, • • • • 114 ROSE OF BATTLE   17
THE BRILLIANT MOON AND ALL THE MILKY SKY, • • • • 119 SORROW OF LOVE   2
THE FULL ROUND MOON AND THE STAR-LADEN SKY, • • • 119 SORROW OF LOVE V   2
A CLIMBING MOON UPON AN EMPTY SKY, • • • • • • 120 SORROW OF LOVE   10
THE CRUMBLING MOON, THE WHITE STARS IN THE SKY, • • 120 SORROW OF LOVE V   10
THE CURD-PALE MOON, THE WHITE STARS IN THE SKY, • • 120 SORROW OF LOVE V   10
IT SEEMED THE SUN AND MOON WERE IN THE FRUIT! • • 127 DREAM OF FAERY   23
AH, FAERIES, DANCING UNDER THE MOON, • • • • • 139 TO IRELAND   31
OF THE PALE TIDE WHEN THE MOON HAS SET, • • • • 146 FISH   2
OF SUN AND MOON AND HOLLOW AND WOOD • • • • • 148 INTO TWILIGHT   11
AND THE CHANGING MOON WORK OUT THEIR WILL. • • • 148 INTO TWILIGHT   V   12
THE SILVER APPLES OF THE MOON, • • • • • • • 150 WANDER AENGUS   23
AND HAD ROOTED THE SUN AND MOON AND STARS OUT OF THE SKY 153 CHANGE BELOVED   11
AND ROOTED THE SUN AND MOON AND STARS OUT OF THE SKY, • 153 CHANGE BELOVED V   11
WHEN WINDS HAVE GATHERED AND SUN AND MOON BURNED DIM • • 175 ELEMENT POWERS   15
ABOUT THE STARS AND MOON AND SUN• • • • • • • 176 BELOVED DEAD   10
ABOVE THE STARS AND MOON AND SUN: • • • • • • 176 BELOVED DEAD   V   10
OR APPLES OF THE SUN AND MOON. • • • • • • • 196 BAILE AILLINN   176
I CRIED WHEN THE MOON WAS MURMURING TO THE BIRDS' • 203 WITHER BOUGHS   1
THE HONEY-PALE MOON LAY LOW ON THE SLEEPY HILL, • • 203 WITHER BOUGHS   5
I KNOW WHERE A DIM MOON DRIFTS, WHERE THE DANAAN KIND • 203 WITHER BOUGHS   12
THE HONEY PALE MOON HUNG LOW ON THE SLEEPY HILL, • • 203 WITHER BOUGHS   V   5
A MOON, WORN AS IF IT HAD BEEN A SHELL • • • • 206 ADAMS CURSE   31
AS WEARY-HEARTED AS THAT HOLLOW MOON. • • • • • 206 ADAMS CURSE   38
A MOON--MOON WORN AS IF IT HAD BEEN A SHELL • • • 206 ADAMS CURSE   V   31
A MOON--MOON WORN AS IF IT HAD BEEN A SHELL • • • 206 ADAMS CURSE   V   31
AS WEARY HEARTED AS THAT HOLLOW MOON. • • • • • 206 ADAMS CURSE   V   38
UNDER THE MOON • 209 UNDER THE MOON   T
OF THE HUNTER'S MOON, THAT HUNG BETWEEN THE NIGHT AND THE 210 UNDER THE MOON   18
DAY,
OF THE THIRD MOON, THAT HUNG BETWEEN THE NIGHT AND THE DAY, 210 UNDER THE MOON V   18
I WILL DRIVE OUT THE DEER AND MOON AND CRY-- • • • 211 RAGGED WOOD   V   10
THE MOON PLUCKED AT MY REIN: • • • • • • • 214 HAPPY TOWNLAND   16
THE MOON PLUCKED AT MY REIN: • • • • • • • 215 HAPPY TOWNLAND   36
THE MOON PLUCKED AT MY REIN: • • • • • • • 216 HAPPY TOWNLAND   56
AND ALL THE ALE RAN OUT AT THE NEW MOON: • • • • 222 SHADOW WATER B V   11
AT THE FULL MOON? HE PLAYED ALL THROUGH THE NIGHT. • • 223 SHADOW WATER B   21
UNTIL THE MOON HAD SET: AND WHEN I LOOKED • • • 223 SHADOW WATER B   22
AS THOSE THAT CAN OUTLIVE THE MOON HAVE KNOWN IT, • 230 SHADOW WATER B   193
AS THOSE THAT CAN OUTLIVE THE MOON HAVE SHOWN IT, • 230 SHADOW WATER B V   193
UNTIL THE OVERBURTHENED MOON IS DEAD. • • • • • 231 SHADOW WATER B   218
FROM LASTING WATCHERS, THAT OUTLIVE THE MOON, • • 236 SHADOW WATER B   320
THAT IS MORE MIGHTY THAN THE SUN AND MOON, • • • 237 SHADOW WATER B   328
HE HAS PUT A SUDDEN DARKNESS OVER THE MOON. • • • 239 SHADOW WATER B   367
HE HAS CAUGHT THE CRESCENT MOON OUT OF THE SKY, • • 239 SHADOW WATER B   370
HAVING THEIR LIFE IN HIM. THOUGH IT BE THE MOON • • 240 SHADOW WATER B   377
LISTEN TO THAT LOW-LAUGHING STRING OF THE MOON • • 243 SHADOW WATER B   432
THAT I SHOULD KEEN HIM FROM THE FULL OF THE MOON • • 243 SHADOW WATER B   446
IN HAPPY DANCES UNDER A WINDY MOON, • • • • • 245 SHADOW WATER B   470
AM I TO FEAR THE WAVES, OR IS THE MOON • • • • 246 SHADOW WATER B   508
MY ENEMY? I LOOKED UPON THE MOON, • • • • • 246 SHADOW WATER B   509
WHERE NO CHILD'S BORN BUT TO OUTLIVE THE MOON." • • 247 SHADOW WATER B   531
SING ON: SOMEWHERE AT SOME NEW MOON, • • • • • 266 GALWAY RACES   10
BUT SOME DAY AND AT SOME NEW MOON, • • • • • 266 GALWAY RACES   V   10
SING ON: SOMETIME, AND AT SOME NEW MOON, • • • 266 GALWAY RACES   V   10
AND THE SHADOWS EATEN THE MOON. • • • • • • 268 BROWN PENNY   14
AMONG THE AFRICAN MOUNTAINS OF THE MOON, • • • • 277 TWO KINGS   20
IN AFRICA ON MOUNTAIN OF THE MOON, • • • • • 277 TWO KINGS   V   20
THE FRENZY OF THE BEGGARS' MOON • • • • • • 296 THREE BEGGARS   43
THE FRENZY OF THE BEGGAR'S MOON • • • • • • 296 THREE BEGGARS   V   43
SUDDENLY HID LOVE'S MOON AWAY. • • • • • • • 313 MEMORY YOUTH   7
LOVE'S MOON WAS WITHERING AWAY. • • • • • • 313 MEMORY YOUTH   V   7
TORE FROM THE CLOUDS HIS MARVELLOUS MOON. • • • • 314 MEMORY YOUTH   21
THREW UP IN THE AIR HIS MARVELLOUS MOON. • • • • 314 MEMORY YOUTH   V   21
OF SUN AND MOON THAT A GOOD HOUR • • • • • • 331 ROUND TOWER   11
OF THE DARK LEOPARDS OF THE MOON? • • • • • • 343 DEJECTION   3
BANISHED HEROIC MOTHER MOON AND VANISHED, • • • • 344 DEJECTION   9
HEROIC MOTHER MOON HAS VANISHED, • • • • • • 344 DEJECTION   V   9

		PAGE	TITLE	LINE
MOON (CONTINUED)				
THE STARS FADE OUT WHERE THE MOON COMES,		344	DAWN	8
THE PESTLE OF THE MOON		346	ON WOMAN	30
OR KEEP US ALL AWAKE WITH BAYING AT THE MOON,		364	DOLLS FACES	11
THAT MICHAEL ROBARTES LEFT, YOU WALK IN THE MOON,		367	EGO DOMINUS	4
THE PHASES OF THE MOON		372	PHASES OF MOON	T
. . . I. THE WHEEL AND THE PHASES OF THE MOON		372	PHASES OF MOON V	T
DESPITE A DWINDLING AND LATE-RISEN MOON,		372	PHASES OF MOON	6
DESPITE A DWINDLING AND LATE RISEN MOON,		372	PHASES OF MOON V	6
SING ME THE CHANGES OF THE MOON ONCE MORE:		373	PHASES OF MOON	29
TWENTY-AND-EIGHT THE PHASES OF THE MOON,		373	PHASES OF MOON	31
BUT WHILE THE MOON IS ROUNDING TOWARDS THE FULL		373	PHASES OF MOON	39
BEFORE THE FULL MOON, HELPLESS AS A WORM.		374	PHASES OF MOON	49
THE THIRTEENTH MOON BUT SETS THE SOUL AT WAR		374	PHASES OF MOON	50
UNDER THE FRENZY OF THE FOURTEENTH MOON,		374	PHASES OF MOON	53
AND AFTER THAT THE CRUMBLING OF THE MOON.		375	PHASES OF MOON	87
UNDER THE THREE LAST CRESCENTS OF THE MOON,		377	PHASES OF MOON	133
THE CAT AND THE MOON		378	CAT AND MOON	T
AND THE MOON SPUN ROUND LIKE A TOP,		378	CAT AND MOON	2
AND THE NEAREST KIN OF THE MOON,		378	CAT AND MOON	3
BLACK MINNALOUSHE STARED AT THE MOON,		378	CAT AND MOON	5
MAYBE THE MOON MAY LEARN,		378	CAT AND MOON	14
THE SACRED MOON OVERHEAD		379	CAT AND MOON	19
AND LIFTS TO THE CHANGING MOON		379	CAT AND MOON	27
WHEN THE OLD MOON IS VANISHED FROM THE SKY		382	VISION ROBART	3
WHEN THE OLD MOON IS VANISHING FROM THE SKY		382	VISION ROBART V	3
ONE LASHED HER TAIL: HER EYES LIT BY THE MOON		383	VISION ROBART	29
OF THE DARK MOON AND THE FULL,		384	VISION ROBART	60
"LAST NIGHT, WHERE UNDER THE WILD MOON		387	SOLOMON WITCH	2
THEREFORE A BLESSED MOON LAST NIGHT		388	SOLOMON WITCH	31
AND THE MOON IS WILDER EVERY MINUTE.		389	SOLOMON WITCH	43
BUT THEY MISTOOK THE BRIGHTNESS OF THE MOON		411	TOWER	45
O MAY THE MOON AND SUNLIGHT SEEM		411	TOWER	54
AYE, SUN AND MOON AND STAR, ALL,		415	TOWER	152
CURVED LIKE NEW MOON, MOON-LUMINOUS,		421	MY TABLE	10
NO MOON: ONLY AN ACHING HEART		421	MY TABLE	13
CURVED LIKE NEW MOON, MOON LUMINOUS,		421	MY TABLE V	10
CURVED LIKE NEW MOON, MOON LUMINOUS,		421	MY TABLE V	10
VALLEY, RIVER, AND ELMS, UNDER THE LIGHT OF A MOON		426	PHANTOM HATRED	3
VALLEY, RIVER, ELMS, UNDER THE LIGHT OF A MOON		426	PHANTOM HATRED V	3
THE INNUMERABLE CLANGING WINGS THAT HAVE PUT OUT THE MOON.		427	PHANTOM HATRED	32
PROTECTED FROM THE CIRCLE OF THE MOON		428	NINETEEN 19	3
ABOVE THE MURDEROUS TREACHERY OF THE MOON,		428	NINETEEN 19 V	3
THOUGH NURTURED LIKE THE SAILING MOON		451	FIRST LOVE	1
THAT TRAVELS ON THE MOON.		451	FIRST LOVE	12
WHEN THE MOON SAILS OUT.		451	FIRST LOVE	18
LIKE THE MOON HER KINDNESS IS,		452	HUMAN DIGNITY	1
IMAGINING MOON ACCURSED,		454	EMPTY CUP V	4
WHEN THE FULL MOON SWAM TO ITS GREATEST HEIGHT		468	HARUN RASHID	151
WHEN MAYBE THRICE IN EVERY MONTH HER MOUTH		468	HARUN RASHID	162
WHEREVER THE ORBIT OF THE MOON CAN REACH,		472	ALL SOUL NIGHT	55
BLOOD AND THE MOON		480	BLOOD AND MOON	T
THE PURITY OF THE UNCLOUDED MOON		482	BLOOD AND MOON	31
AND CLAMOUR IN DRUNKEN FRENZY FOR THE MOON.		482	BLOOD AND MOON	42
CAN COME UPON THE VISAGE OF THE MOON		482	BLOOD AND MOON	53
THE CRAZED MOON		487	CRAZED MOON	T
THE MOON IS STAGGERING IN THE SKY:		487	CRAZED MOON	2
FLY-CATCHERS OF THE MOON,		488	CRAZED MOON	13
OR, BY THE MOON EMBITTERED, SCORN ALOUD		498	BYZANTIUM	21
WHERE THE GAUDY MOON IS HUNG.		502	VACILLATION	69
THE MOON IN A SILVER BAG.		525	DANCING DAYS	8
THE MOON IN A SILVER BAG.		525	DANCING DAYS	16
THE MOON IN A SILVER BAG.		525	DANCING DAYS	24
THAT LIGHT IS FROM THE MOON.		536	PARTING	11
AS THE MOON SIDLES UP		559	HE AND SHE	1
AS TRIPS THE SCARED MOON		559	HE AND SHE	3
SHE SINGS AS THE MOON SINGS:		559	HE AND SHE	7
AS TRIPS THE SACRED MOON		559	HE AND SHE V	3
BUT A GREAT DANE THAT CANNOT BAY THE MOON		579	DOR WELLESLEY	10
BUT HE TOOK DOWN THE MOON		616	MARCH SONGS 3	8
BUT HE TOOK DOWN THE MOON		616	MARCH SONGS 3	18
BUT HE TOOK DOWN THE MOON		616	MARCH SONGS 3	28
PASSETH THE MOON WITH HER SICKLE OF LIGHT,		648	ISLE STAT I 1	82
WHERE ALL NIGHT LONG THE LONELY MOON, THE WHITE		650	ISLE STAT I 1	126
YONDER THE SICKLE OF THE MOON SAILS ON,		688	NETTLESHIP	1
GONE THE STARS AND GONE THE WHITE MOON,		718	PHANTOM SHIP	3
HIDE WHERE HE WILL, IN WAVE OR WRINKLED MOON,		720	WITCH VIVIEN	8
FROM THE DISTAFF OF THE MOON.		743	WISDOM DREAMS	4
HOW MANY MOONS HAVE DIED FROM THE FULL MOON		747	SHADOW WATER A	10
BE PATIENT YET A WHILE: FOR THIS NINTH MOON,		748	SHADOW WATER A	23
BEING THE MOON OF BIRTH, MAY END OUR DOUBT.		748	SHADOW WATER A	24
BE PATIENT YET AWHILE: FOR THIS NINTH MOON,		748	SHADOW WATER A V	23
I WILL SWEAR BY SUN AND MOON TO PARDON ALL		756	SHADOW WATER A	183
BY SUN AND MOON AND A HUNDRED GODS AS WELL,		756	SHADOW WATER A	189
AND WILL YOU SWEAR IT BY THE SUN AND MOON?		758	SHADOW WATER A	229
AND SAID IT WAS MIGHTIER THAN THE SUN AND MOON,		762	SHADOW WATER A	289
IN HAPPY DANCES, UNDER A WINDY MOON!		763	SHADOW WATER A	318
WHERE THE MOON MAKES A CLOUDY LIGHT IN THE MIST.		764	SHADOW WATER A	329
HAVE FALLEN AND MY SUN AND MOON GONE OUT.		767	SHADOW WATER A V	405
AND ONE IN THE HOUSE OF THE MOON,		771	SPINNING SONG	7

		PAGE	TITLE		LINE

MOON—ACCURSED
    IMAGINING, MOON—ACCURSED, ... 454 EMPTY CUP 4
MOONBEAMS
    THE RAINS ARE FROM HIS DRIPPING WING, THE MOONBEAMS FROM 76 INDIAN ON GOD 8
        HIS EYE.
MOONEEN
    AT MOONEEN HE HAD LEAPED A PLACE . . . . 326 ROBERT GREGORY 60
MOONLESS
    FROM MOONLESS PLACE TO PLACE. . . . . 379 CAT AND MOON V 18
    WERE SOME DEAR CHEEK. UPON A MOONLESS NIGHT . . . . . 466 HARUN RASHID 127
    WERE SOME DEAR FACE. UPON A MOONLESS NIGHT . . . . . 466 HARUN RASHID V 127
    STRETCH TOWARDS THE MOONLESS MIDNIGHT OF THE TREES, . . 579 DOR WELLESLEY 1
    CRIES A VOICE AT ROARING MIDNIGHT BESIDE THE MOONLESS DEEP. 718 PHANTOM SHIP 8
MOONLIGHT
    WHERE THE WAVE OF MOONLIGHT GLOSSES . . . . 87 STOLEN CHILD 13
    UNDER THE BLESSED MOONLIGHT, ... 94 MOLL MAGEE 11
    HOME IN THE BLESSED MOONLIGHT . . . . 94 MOLL MAGEE V 11
    FROM MOONLIGHT PLACE TO PLACE. . . . . 379 CAT AND MOON V 18
    OR WINTRY MOONLIGHT SINK THE FIELD . . . . 501 VACILLATION 47
    THERE IN THE TOMB DROPS THE FAINT MOONLIGHT, ... 636 BLACK TOWER 17
    WHOSE BEARD A MOONLIGHT RIVER IS, WHOSE BROW . . . . . 657 ISLE STAT I 3 73
MOONLIT
    OF MOONLIT STEPS GLIMMERED; AND LEFT AND RIGHT . . . 31 OISIN 2 35
    AND FACE THAT SEEMED WROUGHT OUT OF MOONLIT VAPOURS, . . 33 OISIN 2 70
    HER FACE SEEMED FASHIONED ALL OF MOONLIT VAPOURS, . . . 33 OISIN 2 V 70
    FROM MOONLIT PLACE TO PLACE, ... 379 CAT AND MOON 18
    THAT OTHER'S MOONLIT EYEBALLS NEVER MOVED, ... 383 VISION ROBART 33
    AND SEEM TO CLING UPON THE MOONLIT SKIES, ... 482 BLOOD AND MOON 44
    A STARLIT OR A MOONLIT DOME DISDAINS . . . . 497 BYZANTIUM 5
    A STARLIGHT OR A MOONLIT DOME DISTAINS . . . . . . 497 BYZANTIUM V 5
MOON—LUMINOUS
    CURVED LIKE NEW MOON, MOON—LUMINOUS, ... 421 MY TABLE 10
MOON'S
    OUT OF THE MOON'S PALE TWISTED SHELL; . . . . 19 OISIN 1 279
    LAND—UNDER—WAVE, WHERE OUT OF THE MOON'S LIGHT AND THE 209 UNDER THE MOON 6
        SUN'S
    THE FULL AND THE MOON'S DARK AND ALL THE CRESCENTS, . . 373 PHASES OF MOON 32
    WHEN THE MOON'S FULL THOSE CREATURES OF THE FULL . . . 375 PHASES OF MOON 75
    I SAW BY THE MOON'S LIGHT . . . . 383 VISION ROBART 27
    AND WHEN THE MOON'S POT—BELLIED . . . . 455 FRIENDS YOUTH 3
    . . . A LOG—BOOK OF THE SUN'S JOURNEY AND THE MOON'S; . 480 BLOOD AND MOON 14
    . . . A LOG BOOK OF THE SUN'S JOURNEY AND THE MOON'S, . 480 BLOOD AND MOON V 14
    THIN IS THE MOON'S HORN; . . . . 519 LOVES LONENESS 8
    LOVE STORM AND STAINED WITH MIST THE NEW MOON'S FLARE . 678 ISLE STAT II 3 V 294
    COME AWAY WHILE THE MOON'S IN THE WOODLAND, ... 707 FAIRY PEDANT 9
    COME AWAY WHILE THE MOON'S IN THE WOODLAND, ... 708 FAIRY PEDANT 37
    DANCING ON THE MOON'S BROAD STAIN, ... 731 STREET DANCERS 15
    WHEN MOON'S ROUND IS FINISHED . . . . 786 YOUR HEART 33
MOONS
    A DANAAN FRUITAGE MAKES A SHOWER OF MOONS, ... 127 DREAM OF FAERY V 22
    AND DRUID MOONS, AND MURMURING OF BOUGHS, ... 219 HARP OF AENGUS 4
    LOVE STORM; AND STAINED WITH MIST THE NEW MOONS FLARE. . 678 ISLE STAT II 3 294
    HOW MANY MOONS HAVE DIED FROM THE FULL MOON . . . . 747 SHADOW WATER A 10
    NINE MOONS. AND FROM THE HARPING OF THE FOOL? . . . 747 SHADOW WATER A 14
    THREE MOONS. IT WERE BEST TO KILL HIM, AND CHOOSE OUT . 748 SHADOW WATER A 15
    AND DRUID MOONS, AND MURMURING OF BOUGHS, ... 762 SHADOW WATER A 299
MOONSHINE
    FLICKERING UNDER THE WHITE MOONSHINE? . . . . 646 ISLE STAT I 1 33
MOON—STRUCK
    MOON—STRUCK BY THE DESPAIRING . . . . 487 CRAZED MOON 3
MOON—WHITE
    ARE CHANGED FOR EVER INTO MOON—WHITE STONE. . . . . 653 ISLE STAT I 2 43
MOONY
    DANCING IN SOME MOONY PLACE, ... 647 ISLE STAT I 1 54
    AND CALM, ROBED ALL IN RAIMENT MOONY WHITE. . . . . 693 MOSADA 1 77
MOOR
    HERE WE WILL MOOR OUR LONELY SHIP . . . . 78 INDIAN TO LOVE 6
    THERE WE WILL MOOR OUR LONELY SHIP . . . . 78 INDIAN TO LOVE V 6
    OTTERS BELOW AND MOOR HENS ON THE TOP; . . . . . . 490 COOLE BALLYLEE V 2
    THE STAR—TAUGHT MOOR, SAID THUS IT WAS DECREED . . . 691 MOSADA 1 25
    AND IMPORTUNE WITH WEIGHTY WORDS THIS MOOR, ... 698 MOSADA 2 45
MOOR—COCKS
    AND HENS TO MOOR—COCKS CALL; . . . . 393 EASTER 1916 54
MOORE
    JOHN KINSELLA'S LAMENT FOR MRS. MARY MOORE . . . . . 620 JOHN KINSELLA T
    BUT MY DEAR MARY MOORE, ... 620 JOHN KINSELLA 8
    ON GEORGE MOORE; . . . . 792 GEORGE MOORE T
    MOORE ONCE HAD VISITS FROM THE MUSE . . . . 792 GEORGE MOORE 1
MOORED
    COVER YOUR EARS; FOR ONCE WE HAD MOORED OUR GALLEY . . 756 SHADOW WATER A 187
MOORFOWL
    MY SPIRIT ROCKED IN SLEEP AND SIGHS; AND SAW THE MOORFOWL 76 INDIAN ON GOD 3
        PACE
    IS AN UNDYING MOORFOWL, AND HE LIVES BEYOND THE SKY. . . 76 INDIAN ON GOD 7
    AS THE MOORFOWL AND THE HARE, ... 706 DAWN—SONG 28
MOOR—HEN
    THE MOOR—HEN GUIDES UPON THE STREAM, ... 424 ROAD AT DOOR 12
MOOR—HENS
    THE LONG—LEGGED MOOR—HENS DIVE, ... 393 EASTER 1916 53
    WHERE LONG—LEGGED MOOR—HENS DIVE, ... 393 EASTER 1916 V 53
    OTTERS BELOW AND MOOR—HENS ON THE TOP, ... 490 COOLE BALLYLEE 2

531

			PAGE	TITLE	LINE

MOORISH
A LOTUS IN THEIR HANDS--YOUNG MOORISH GIRL . . . . . . 694 MOSADA 1   103
A LITTLE MOORISH GIRL? SMALL WORTH. MY SONG-- . . . . 696 MOSADA 2   10
I WILL NOT HEAR! THE MOORISH GIRL MUST DIE. . . . . . 697 MOSADA 2   39
A FASHION WITH US MOORISH MAIDS, BEGOT . . . . . . 700 MOSADA 3   25
YOUNG MOORISH GIRL, THY FINAL HOUR IS HERE! . . . . . 701 MOSADA 3   63

MOORS
FROM POISON! FOR YOU CANNOT TRUST THESE MOORS. . . . . 704 MOSADA 3   126
I ALWAYS SAID YOU COULD NOT TRUST THESE MOORS. . . . . 704 MOSADA 3   V 134A

MOPING
MOPING FOR ONE VOYAGE MORE. . . . . 361 ALF POLLEXFEN   22

MORALISE
THAT IT MAY MORALISE . . . . 421 MY TABLE   4

MORALIST
SOME MORALIST OR MYTHOLOGICAL POET . . . . 430 NINETEEN 19   59

MORALIZE
OF HUMAN SORROW LET THEM MORALIZE! . . . . 663 ISLE STAT II 2   31

MORAL'S
THE MORAL'S YOURS BECAUSE IT'S MINE. . . . . 271 GREY ROCK   11

MORE
THE STAG WE CHASED WAS NOT MORE SAD, ... 2 OISIN 1   V 7J
HIS MISTRESS WAS MORE MILD AND FAIR . . . . 3 OISIN 1   V 7DD
THE HORNLESS DEER IS NOT MORE SAD . . . . 4 OISIN 1   34
MORE SLEEK THAN ANY GRANARY MOUSE, ... 4 OISIN 1   36
THE STAG YE CHASE IS NOT MORE SAD, ... 4 OISIN 1   V 35
IN A VIGOUR MORE THAN MORTAL MEASURE, ... 9 OISIN 1   V 98
WAS NOT MORE LEVEL THAN THE SEA, ... 13 OISIN 1   157
ONCE MORE THE DANCE'S LINKED FLOW, ... 22 OISIN 1   V 323A
AND ONCE MORE SADDLED THE WHITE STEED, ... 25 OISIN 1   V 378
THE HUMAN SADNESS DAWNS ONCE MORE!" . . . . 25 OISIN 1   V 381
"GAZE NO MORE ON THE PHANTOMS," NIAMH SAID, ... 29 OISIN 2   5
ONCE MORE--THE YOUTH AND LADY, DEER AND HOUND! . . . . 29 OISIN 2   V 2
YET SANG NO MORE AS WHEN, LIKE A BROWN BEE . . . . . 30 OISIN 2   15
BUT SANG NO MORE, AS WHEN, LIKE A BROWN BEE . . . . . 30 OISIN 2   V 15
FULL MANY MORE, WHEN PEERED A MAIDEN SWEET . . . . . 33 OISIN 2   V 68F
ONCE MORE UNTO YOUR FLOWERS, FOR NONE MAY FIGHT, . . . 34 OISIN 2   V 80
TO RULE MORE MIGHTY MEN, AND TO THE WORLD . . . . . 38 OISIN 2   V 133
AND WHEN THE SUN ONCE MORE IN SAFFRON STEPT, ... 41 OISIN 2   192
BUT WHEN THE SUN ONCE MORE IN SAFFRON STEPT, ... 41 OISIN 2   192
AND ONCE MORE TO A DAY-LONG BATTLE FELL, ... 43 OISIN 2   218
GOD SHAKES THE WORLD WITH RESTLESS HANDS. MORE NEAR . . 43 OISIN 2   V 208
AND WE ONCE MORE UNTO OUR FIGHTING FELL. . . . . . 43 OISIN 2   V 218
FIN, CONAN, OSCAR, MANY MORE, THE TIDE . . . . . . 44 OISIN 2   V 228A
AND MORE COMELY THAN MAN CAN MAKE THEM . . . . . . 49 OISIN 3   32
MORE COMELY THAN MAN MAY MAKE THEM, INLAID WITH SILVER 49 OISIN 3   V 29
  AND GOLD,
IN ONE WAS A BRANCH SOFT-SHINING WITH BELLS MORE MANY THAN 50 OISIN 3   46
  SIGHS
WRAPT IN THE WAVE OF THAT MUSIC, WITH WEARINESS MORE THAN 51 OISIN 3   69
  OF EARTH,
THAT ONCE MORE MOVED IN MY BOSOM THE ANCIENT SADNESS OF 54 OISIN 3   107
  MAN,
NO MORE TO CRAWL ON THE SEAS WITH LONG OARS MILE AFTER 55 OISIN 3   119
  MILE,
. . . YOU WILL COME NO MORE TO MY SIDE. . . . . . 56 OISIN 3   128
WE SHALL MINGLE NO MORE, NOR OUR GAZES EMPTY THEIR 56 OISIN 3   132
  SWEETNESS LONE
. . . NO MORE SHALT THOU BE BY MY SIDE. . . . . . 56 OISIN 3   V 128
I WILL PRAY NO MORE WITH THE SMOOTH STONES! . . . 63 OISIN 3   V 221
VIJAYA, SWEAR TO HER LOVE NEVER MORE. . . . . . . 74 ANASHU VIJAYA   65
AND SLEEK YOUNG JOY IS NO MORE FICKLE, ... 77 INDIAN TO LOVE V 5C
BY THE LONE BORDER OF THE LAKE ONCE MORE, ... 79 EPHEMERA   5
STAND BY THE BORDER OF THE LAKE ONCE MORE, ... 79 EPHEMERA   V 5
ON THE LONE BORDER OF THE LAKE ONCE MORE! . . . . . 80 EPHEMERA   17
HE SPAKE ONCE MORE AND FONDLED WITH HIS LIPS . . . . 81 EPHEMERA   V 24A
FOR THE WORLD'S MORE FULL OF WEEPING THAN YOU CAN 87 STOLEN CHILD   12
  UNDERSTAND.
FOR THE WORLD'S MORE FULL OF WEEPING THAN YOU CAN 87 STOLEN CHILD   27
  UNDERSTAND.
FOR THE WORLD'S MORE FULL OF WEEPING THAN YOU CAN 88 STOLEN CHILD   41
  UNDERSTAND.
HE'LL HEAR NO MORE THE LOWING . . . . 88 STOLEN CHILD   44
FROM A WORLD MORE FULL OF WEEPING THAN HE CAN UNDERSTAND. 89 STOLEN CHILD   53
FOR THE WORLD'S MORE FULL OF WEEPING THAN HE CAN UNDERSTAND 89 STOLEN CHILD   V 53
. . . THE WAVES WERE MORE GAY, ... 91 OLD FISHERMAN   3
TO SEE THE WORLD ONCE MORE. . . . . 97 FOXHUNTER   4
COME NEAR, THAT NO MORE BLINDED BY MAN'S FATE, . . . 101 ROSE UPON ROOD   9
LEST I NO MORE HEAR COMMON THINGS THAT CRAVE! . . . 101 ROSE UPON ROOD   15
WHAT WOULD YOU, FERGUS? BE NO MORE A KING, ... 103 FERGUS DRUID   21
WHAT WOULD YOU? I WOULD BE NO MORE A KING, ... 103 FERGUS DRUID   V 21
BUT NOW I HAVE NO NEED TO WATCH IT MORE. . . . . . 105 CUCHULAIN SEA   5
BUT NOW MY YEARS OF WATCHING ARE NO MORE." . . . . 105 CUCHULAIN SEA   V 5
THEREON HE SHOOK THE MORE AND CAST HIM DOWN . . . . 106 CUCHULAIN SEA   14
MORE MOURNFUL THAN THE DEPTH OF STARRY SKIES, . . . 108 CUCHULAIN SEA   V 42
"I PUT YOU FROM YOUR PAIN. I CAN NO MORE." . . . . 110 CUCHULAIN SEA   69
FOR THREE DAYS MORE IN DREADFUL QUIETUDE, ... 110 CUCHULAIN SEA   78
MORE FLEETING THAN THE SEA'S FOAM-FICKLE FACE, . . . 112 ROSE OF WORLD V 8
MORE FLEETING THAN THE SEA'S FOAM FICKLE FACE, . . . 112 ROSE OF WORLD V 8
BROODING NO MORE UPON GOD'S WARS . . . . 113 ROSE OF PEACE   5
WHO HAVE SOUGHT MORE THAN IS IN RAIN OR DEW . . . . 114 ROSE OF BATTLE   16

MORE (CONTINUED)

	PAGE	TITLE		LINE
WHERE TIME WOULD SURELY FORGET US, AND SORROW COME NEAR US NO MORE:	122	WHITE BIRDS		10
WHERE SURELY TIME WOULD FORGET US AND SORROW COME NEAR US NO MORE:	122	WHITE BIRDS	V	10
SHE WAS MORE BEAUTIFUL THAN THY FIRST LOVE,	123	DREAM OF DEATH		11
MAN HAD NO MORE TO DO—	123	DREAM OF DEATH	V	8
AND BROOD ON HOPES AND FEAR NO MORE.	125	GOES FERGUS		6
AND NO MORE TURN ASIDE AND BROOD	125	GOES FERGUS		7
AND BROOD ON HOPES AND FEARS NO MORE.	125	GOES FERGUS	V	6
AND AT THAT SINGING HE WAS NO MORE WISE.	127	DREAM OF FAERY		24
WHEN THE MOTHS CAME ONCE MORE,	133	FR GILLIGAN		22
WHEN MOTHS CAME ONCE MORE,	133	FR GILLIGAN	V	22
GAZE NO MORE IN THE BITTER GLASS	135	TWO TREES		21
GAZE NO MORE IN THE BITTER GLASS.	136	TWO TREES		40
MY RHYMES MORE THAN THEIR RHYMING TELL	138	TO IRELAND		20
"AND BROOD NO MORE WHERE THE FIRE IS BRIGHT	140	HOSTING SIDHE	V	5
FLAME UNDER FLAME, TILL TIME BE NO MORE:	141	EVERLAST VOICE		4
I AM NO MORE WITH LIFE AND DEATH,	152	HEART OF WOMAN		10
O CURLEW, CRY NO MORE IN THE AIR,	155	REPROVE CURLEW		1
COME FROM A MORE DREAM-HEAVY LAND,	156	FORGOT BEAUTY		16
A MORE DREAM-HEAVY HOUR THAN THIS:	156	FORGOT BEAUTY		17
AND WITH HEART MORE OLD THAN THE HORN	157	POET BELOVED		5
AND WITH THE HEART MORE OLD THAN THE HORN	157	POET BELOVED	V	5
WHEN THE OWLS CALLED OUT NO MORE:	159	CAP AND BELLS		14
WHEN THE BATS CRIED OUT NO MORE:	159	CAP AND BELLS	V	14
O, WHEN SHALL SORROW WANDER NO MORE IN THE LAND	174	ELEMENT POWERS	V	5
BUT THAT GREAT QUEEN, WHO MORE THAN HALF THE NIGHT	180	QUEEN MAEVE		16
MORE STILL THAN THEY HAD BEEN FOR A GOOD MONTH,	182	QUEEN MAEVE		54
AND YOU ARE MORE HIGH OF HEART THAN SHE,	197	BAILE AILLINN		202
LIKE THEM THAT ARE NO MORE ALIVE.	197	BAILE AILLINN		207
BURNS BUT MORE CLEARLY. O SHE HAD NOT THESE WAYS	200	FOLLY COMFORT		11
IT ALL, AND MORE THAN IT ALL, WOULD COME TO NAUGHT,	201	OLD MEMORY		8
OR, IF THERE NEEDS BE MORE, BE NOTHING SAID	201	OLD MEMORY		11
IT ALL, MORE THAN IT ALL, WOULD COME TO NAUGHT,	201	OLD MEMORY	V	8
AND MORE I MAY NOT WRITE OF, FOR THEY THAT CLEAVE	218	WOODS OF COOLE		24
AND WINDS AND PONDS COVER MORE QUIET WOODS,	218	WOODS OF COOLE		34
MORE SHINING WINDS, MORE STAR-GLIMMERING PONDS?	218	WOODS OF COOLE		35
MORE SHINING WINDS, MORE STAR-GLIMMERING PONDS?	218	WOODS OF COOLE		35
AND MORE I MAY NOT WRITE OF, FOR THEY THAT CLEAVE	218	WOODS OF COOLE	V	24
UNLESS WE DRAIN MORE FLAGONS IN A YEAR	225	SHADOW WATER B		70
AND KISS MORE LIPS THAN LASTING PEACEABLE MEN	225	SHADOW WATER B		71
MORE RICHES THAN THEY EVER HOPED TO FIND?	226	SHADOW WATER B		94
WHY SHOULD YOU BE MORE FAITHFUL THAN THE REST,	227	SHADOW WATER B		109
IS NO MORE THAN A WINE-CUP IN THE TASTING,	229	SHADOW WATER B		150
IS NO MORE THAN A WINE CUP IN THE TASTING,	229	SHADOW WATER B	V	150
OF THAT MORE POWERFUL LIFE? HIS WIFE KNOWS BETTER.	230	SHADOW WATER B		172
TO MAKE LOW LAUGHTER MORE THAN MEAT AND DRINK,	230	SHADOW WATER B		186
CARE MORE ABOUT THE KEGS OF SILVER AND GOLD	232	SHADOW WATER B		234
WHAT POWER THAT IS MORE MIGHTY THAN DESIRE	234	SHADOW WATER B		267
ALTHOUGH YOU ARE MORE BEAUTIFUL THAN ANY,	236	SHADOW WATER B		305
THAT IS MORE MIGHTY THAN THE SUN AND MOON,	237	SHADOW WATER B		328
MORE MIGHTY THAN THE STARS HALF TROUBLED ME,	237	SHADOW WATER B		332
IF THERE BE HALF A HUNDRED MORE, WHAT MATTER?	245	SHADOW WATER B		476
WHAT MORE HAVE YOU TO LOOK FOR ON THE SEAS?	248	SHADOW WATER B		543
AND IF THAT HAPPINESS BE MORE THAN DREAMS,	248	SHADOW WATER B		554
MORE THAN THE FROTH, THE FEATHER, THE DUST-WHIRL,	248	SHADOW WATER B		555
MORE THAN THE FROTH, THE FEATHER, THE DUSTWHIRL,	248	SHADOW WATER B	V	555
THAT BALANCED WITH A WORD IS MORE THAN NOISE:	258	KING NO KING		4
AND THESE THINGS CAME, SO MUCH THE MORE THEREBY	265	THESE CLOUDS		8
THAT HAS MORE LIFE IN IT THAN DEATH,	271	GREY ROCK		8
NO MORE REMEMBERING WHAT HAD BEEN,	276	GREY ROCK		122
MORE HANDS IN HEIGHT THAN ANY STAG IN THE WORLD	277	TWO KINGS		9
AND I BUT ASKED THE MORE, TILL HE CRIED OUT,	281	TWO KINGS		92
BUT ASKED THE MORE UNTIL HE SPOKE THESE WORDS,	281	TWO KINGS	V	92A
A FARMER HAS MORE DIGNITY."	296	THREE BEGGARS		37
KIND EYES SHOULD BE MORE LEARN'D?	312	TWO YEAR LATER		2
THAT SEEMED AS THOUGH ICE BURNED AND WAS BUT THE MORE ICE,	316	COLD HEAVEN		2
AND ALL THEIR EYES STILL FIXED, HOPING TO FIND ONCE MORE,	318	MAGI		6
FOR THERE'S MORE ENTERPRISE	320	COAT		9
BEING MORE INDIFFERENT TO OUR SOLITUDE	334	LIVING BEAUTY		7
I THOUGHT NO MORE WAS NEEDED	334	SONG		1
MORE THAN ANOTHER	336	YOUNG GIRL		2
AND MAKE THE DAYLIGHT SWEET ONCE MORE: BUT WHEN	339	SHEP GOATHERD		13
BUT GROWS MORE GENTLE WHEN HE SPEAKS HER NAME,	340	SHEP GOATHERD		29
I WILL TALK NO MORE OF BOOKS OR THE LONG WAR	351	HER PRAISE		11
AND RUTH ST. DENIS HAD MORE CHARM ALTHOUGH SHE HAD POOR LUCK:	353	HIS PHOENIX		10
YOU ARE MORE BEAUTIFUL THAN ANY ONE,	356	BROKEN DREAMS		27
YOU WERE MORE BEAUTIFUL THAN ANY ONE,	356	BROKEN DREAMS	V	27
YOU ARE MORE BEAUTIFUL THAN ANYONE	356	BROKEN DREAMS	V	27
MOPING FOR ONE VOYAGE MORE.	361	ALF POLLEXFEN		22
MORE PLAIN TO THE MIND'S EYE THAN ANY FACE	368	EGO DOMINUS		21
SING ME THE CHANGES OF THE MOON ONCE MORE:	373	PHASES OF MOON		29
THE FIRST THIN CRESCENT IS WHEELED ROUND ONCE MORE.	377	PHASES OF MOON		116
WHAT VOICE MORE SWEET THAN HERS	392	EASTER 1916		21
BEING NO MORE DEMONIAC	400	DEMON BEAST		30
AND TWICE A THOUSAND MORE	401	DEMON BEAST		47
ONCE MORE THE STORM IS HOWLING, AND HALF HID	403	FOR DAUGHTER		1
AS TO A DOG'S TAIL? NEVER HAD I MORE	409	TOWER		4
THAT MORE EXPECTED THE IMPOSSIBLE—	409	TOWER		7

MORE (CONTINUED)

	PAGE	TITLE		LINE
AS UPON A DOG'S TAIL. NEVER HAD I MORE	409	TOWER	V	4
AND MOUNTS MORE DIZZY HIGH THE MORE IT RAINS	417	ANCEST HOUSES		5
AND MOUNTS MORE DIZZY HIGH THE MORE IT RAINS	417	ANCEST HOUSES		5
BUT THAT HE FOUND MORE SUBSTANCE THERE THAN DREAMS,	417	ANCEST HOUSES	V	10
AN ANCIENT BRIDGE, AND A MORE ANCIENT TOWER,	419	MY HOUSE		1
MORE SUBSTANCE IN OUR ENMITIES	425	STARES NEST		18
IT HAD BUT MADE US PINE THE MORE. THE ABSTRACT JOY,	427	PHANTOM HATRED		38
WHAT MORE IS THERE TO SAY? THAT COUNTRY ROUND	430	NINETEEN 19		43
THE LIVING SEEM MORE SHADOWY THAN THEY.	435	NEW FACES		8
WITH SIXTY OR MORE WINTERS ON ITS HEAD,	444	SCHOOL CHILDR		38
IF YOU ARE NO MORE STRENGTH THAN I AM BEAUTY	448	HERO GIRL FOOL		10
BUT O! MY HEART COULD BEAR NO MORE WHEN THE UPLAND CAUGHT THE WIND!	450	OWEN AHERNE		11
MORE SONGS OF AN OLD COUNTRYMAN	454	HIS MEMORIES	V	T
CAN SHAKE MORE BLOSSOM FROM AUTUMNAL CHILL	465	HARUN RASHID		104
THAT BRINGS MORE BLOSSOM TO AUTUMNAL CHILL	465	HARUN RASHID	V	104
GAVE BUT MORE REASON FOR A WOMAN'S CARE.	466	HARUN RASHID		111
AND MAY HAVE GROWN MORE ARROGANT BEING A GHOST.	473	ALL SOUL NIGHT		80
A CHARTER TO COMMIT THE CRIME ONCE MORE.	478	SELF AND SOUL		32
WHAT MATTER IF I LIVE IT ALL ONCE MORE?	478	SELF AND SOUL		43
MORE BLESSED STILL THIS TOWER!	480	BLOOD AND MOON		2
THOUGH THE GREAT SONG RETURN NO MORE	485	NINETEENTH CEN		1
MORE WOMEN BORN THAN MEN."	485	STATISTICS		4
SEEMED ONCE MORE DEAR THAN LIFE! ANCESTRAL TREES,	491	COOLE BALLYLEE		34
HOPING MORE SUBSTANTIAL JOY	494	AT ALGECIRAS		9
HOPING A MORE SUBSTANTIAL JOY	494	AT ALGECIRAS	V	9
SHADE MORE THAN MAN, MORE IMAGE THAN A SHADE!	497	BYZANTIUM		10
SHADE MORE THAN MAN, MORE IMAGE THAN A SHADE!	497	BYZANTIUM		10
MORE MIRACLE THAN BIRD OR HANDIWORK,	497	BYZANTIUM		18
MORE MIRACLE THAN BIRD OR HANDY-WORK,	497	BYZANTIUM	V	18
AND TWENTY MINUTES MORE OR LESS	501	VACILLATION		42
ISAIAH'S COAL, WHAT MORE CAN MAN DESIRE?	502	VACILLATION		74
EZEKIEL'S COAL, WHAT MORE CAN MAN DESIRE?	502	VACILLATION	V	74
BETTER CONDUCT MYSELF OR HAVE MORE	507	STREAM AND SUN		9
THE MORE I LEAVE THE DOOR UNLATCHED	511	JANE AND JACK		3
AND THE EYES MORE BRIGHT	531	BEFORE WORLD		2
AND THE LIPS MORE SCARLET,	532	BEFORE WORLD		3
HAD EVEN O'DUFFY--BUT I NAME NO MORE--	543	PARN FUNERAL 2		9
NO MORE SANG HE, FOR HIS THROAT WAS TOO SMALL!	545	TO SAME TUNE 1		24
HE SAID NO MORE FOR HIS THROAT WAS TOO SMALL.	545	TO SAME TUNE 1	V	24
MUCH I TALK, MORE I WALK!	548	TO SAME TUNE 3		9
MUCH I TALK, MORE I WALK!	548	TO SAME TUNE 3		19
MUCH I TALK, MORE I WALK!	549	TO SAME TUNE 3		29
THINKING TO MEET MY LOVE ONCE MORE	551	SONGS REWRIT 1	V	15
WANDER IN DREAMS NO MORE!	554	CHURCH STATE		8
A GREATER, A MORE GRACIOUS TIME HAS GONE!	564	GYRES		12
WHICH IS THE MORE BLEST?	573	LADYS 2ND SONG		20
AND I HAVE MANY MORE.	586	PARNELLITES		10
HURRAH FOR REVOLUTION AND MORE CANNON-SHOT!	590	GREAT DAY		1
HURRAH FOR REVOLUTION AND MORE CANNON SHOT!	590	GREAT DAY	V	1
THEY SAY IT IS MORE HUMAN	599	STONE CROSS		19
MORE DREAD THE LIFE THAT WE LIVE,	615	MARCH SONGS 2		15
NO MORE SANG HE, FOR HIS THROAT WAS TOO SMALL!	616	MARCH SONGS 3		24
WITH NO MORE SOUND THAN THE MICE MAKE	618	LONG-LEG FLY		27
STUMBLING UPON THE BLOOD-DARK TRACK ONCE MORE,	622	HOUND VOICE		18
GROWS MORE DEEP DAY AFTER DAY,	624	APPARITIONS		18
BUT BODY GONE HE SLEEPS NO MORE.	633	MAN AND ECHO		29
OH, MORE DARK THY GLEAMING HAIR IS	647	ISLE STAT I 1		51
AND THINE EYES MORE BRIGHT THAN FAERY'S,	647	ISLE STAT I 1		53
THE SKIES MORE DIM, THOUGH BURNING LIKE A SHIELD,	656	ISLE STAT I 3		26
NO MORE A-ROVING SHALT THOU SEE	658	ISLE STAT I 3		82
ONCE MORE HOW ON THAT MISERABLE DAY	658	ISLE STAT II 1		4
WE'VE TALKED AND TALKED, AND NOT A WHIT MORE RARE	659	ISLE STAT II 1		21
WITH THEIR UNHUMAN SORROWS. CEASE! NO MORE!	661	ISLE STAT II 1		58
MORE GRIEF IS MINE. NO MAN SHALL EVER STOOP	661	ISLE STAT II 1		62
IS NOT MORE FAIR AND JOYOUS THAN SHE IS	661	ISLE STAT II 1		71
ANTONIO, IF I RETURN NO MORE,	663	ISLE STAT II 2		17
ONCE MORE THOSE SHEPHERDS COME. MAYHAP SOME MIRTH	664	ISLE STAT II 2		49
MORE WONDERFUL! AND WE HAVE SWORDS. O NIGHT	664	ISLE STAT II 2		61
HAD DRIVEN HER FORTH, FOR EVER MORE	668	ISLE STAT II 3		56
YET EVER MORE, THROUGH ALL THY DAYS OF RUTH,	674	ISLE STAT II 3		206
AND NEVER ANY MORE THE WIDE-EYED BANDS	674	ISLE STAT II 3		218
MORE DARK BENEATH THE POPLARS, WHERE YON OWL	675	ISLE STAT II 3		233
BY THEE SPELL-BOUND? THOU SHALT KNOW MORE!	675	ISLE STAT II 3		241
IGNOBLE JOY, AND MORE IGNOBLE PAIN	687	TWO TITANS		12
AND WHEN ONCE MORE THE LIGHTNING GENII PASSED,	687	TWO TITANS		29
WHEN FLASH ON FLASH ONCE MORE THE LIGHTNING CAME,	688	TWO TITANS		39
NO MORE! TAKE ME INSTEAD OF HER, GREAT SIRS,	695	MOSADA 1		114
EVER MORE TO SPEAK A WORD	697	MOSADA 2		32
OH, CAN MY KISSES BRING A FLUSH NO MORE	701	MOSADA 3		71
'TIS LATE, WAIT ONE MORE DAY! BELOW THE HILLS	702	MOSADA 3		91
THERE IS NO LEAVE-TAKING. I GO NO MORE.	702	MOSADA 3		100
THERE IS NO LEAVE TAKING. I GO NO MORE.	702	MOSADA 3	V	100
OF TRAITOR EVER MORE IS ON OUR NAME."	712	FERENCZ RENYI	V	61
CLOSE AND MORE CLOSE—I FEEL HIM IN MY HEART—	720	WITCH VIVIEN		11
A BIRD WALK ON THE DOORSTEP. CHECK ONCE MORE.	722	WITCH VIVIEN		64
THE FAIRIES' HERALD SPAKE ONCE MORE!	730	PRIEST FAIRY		53
AND JOY, IN GROWING DEEPER AND MORE DEEP,	735	QUATRAIN APHOR		27
AND DREAD NO MORE FOUL AUTUMN'S WING,	737	SUMMER EVENING		18
AND HER DIM WAVE BIDS MAN BE NO MORE GLAD,	738	YOU ARE SAD		11

534

		PAGE	TITLE		LINE

MORE   (CONTINUED)
AND SAID: "I WILL SEE HER NO MORE." . . . .   744 GLOVE CLOAK   6
AND NEED NO MORE OF LIFE TILL THE WHITE WINGS . . . . .   751 SHADOW WATER A   102
AND I MUST LOSE MORE TIME BECAUSE THESE FOOLS . . . . .   754 SHADOW WATER A   158
AND MORE, IF YOU WILL WAR AGAINST THE DANES . . . . . .   756 SHADOW WATER A V   190
TILL HIS EDAINE, NO MORE A SILVER FLY . . . . . .   757 SHADOW WATER A V   210
BESEECHING HANDS AND MORE BESEECHING EYES? . . . . . .   763 SHADOW WATER A V   312
A HIGH, GREY CAIRN. WHAT MORE IS TO BE SAID? . . . . .   778 SONG DEIRDRE 3   5
MORN
THAN THE HORNLESS DEER WE CHASED THAT MORN, ...   2 OISIN 1   V   7P
I CHASED AT MORN THE FLYING DEER, ...   10 OISIN 1   121
AND "WAKEN, COURTIERS OF THE MORN!" . . . .   18 OISIN 1   262
"MY BROTHERS SPRING OUT OF THEIR BEDS AT MORN, ...   32 OISIN 2   51
"THEY MURMUR LIKE YOUNG PARTRIDGE IN THE MORN, ...   32 OISIN 2   V   51
WE FEASTED FOR THREE DAYS. ON THE FOURTH MORN . . . . .   43 OISIN 2   214
THREE DAYS WE FEASTED, WHEN ON THE FOURTH MORN . . . . .   43 OISIN 2   V 214
TO LIE UNTIL THE FOURTH MORN SAW EMERGE . . . . . .   44 OISIN 2   220
TO LIE UNTIL THE FOURTH MORN SUN EMERGE . . . . . .   44 OISIN 2   V 220
I MINDED HER TILL MORN. . . . .   94 MOLL MAGEE   16
WHEN THE MORN GREW FROSTY AND CLEAR. . . . .   95 MOLL MAGEE   20
THE HUNTSMAN LOOSENS ON THE MORN . . . .   98 FOXHUNTER   27
SIGH, HEART, AGAIN IN THE DEW OF THE MORN. . . . . . .   147 INTO TWILIGHT   4
AND HOPE IS LESS DEAR THAN THE DEW OF THE MORN. . . . .   148 INTO TWILIGHT   16
IT TALKED, ERE THE MORN GREW WHITE. . . . .   159 CAP AND BELLS   V   6
IT TALKED BEFORE MORN WAS WHITE, ...   159 CAP AND BELLS   V   6
AND AS SOON AS THE MORN HAD WHITENED, ...   160 CAP AND BELLS   V   23
IN THE GREY REEDS THAT NIGHT AND MORN . . . . . .   190 BAILE AILLINN   42
EVENING AND MORN, THE STEEP STREET OF URBINO . . . . .   352 PEOPLE   V   12
PRIDE, LIKE THAT OF THE MORN. . . . .   414 TOWER   134
AND WHEN I WAKE TOWARDS MORN I DREAD MYSELF, ...   448 HERO GIRL FOOL   5
CATCHING SMALL BIRDS IN THE DEW OF THE MORN . . . . .   636 BLACK TOWER   22
'TIS MORN! THY SHEEP ARE WANDERING DOWN THE VALE— . . .   645 ISLE STAT I 1   3
'TIS MORN! LIKE OLD MEN'S EYES THE STARS ARE PALE, . . .   645 ISLE STAT I 1   4
'TIS MORN, AND FROM THE DEW-DRENCH'D WOOD I'VE SPED . .   645 ISLE STAT I 1   6
COME FORTH! THE MORN IS FAIR! AS FROM THE PYRE . . . .   645 ISLE STAT I 1   8
HUNDRED-THROATED MORN IS SINGING . . . .   647 ISLE STAT I 1   70
FROM MORN THE TWAIN UNTIL THE EVENING PALES . . . . .   651 ISLE STAT I 1   161
EACH CAME ONE MORN, WITH WELCOMING OF SONG, ...   660 ISLE STAT II 1   42
UNTIL THIS MORN. AS ADDER'S BACK . . . .   667 ISLE STAT II 3   22
UNTIL THIS MORN. THE SKY WITH WRACK . . . .   667 ISLE STAT II 3 V   22
AT MORN, AND WITH HER FEET EACH COBWEB RENDS, ...   670 ISLE STAT II 3   99
MORNA'S
MINE WERE CLAN MORNA'S TRIBES UNTOLD, ...   81 MAD KING GOLL   V   3
MORN-BEWILDERED
MORN-BEWILDERED, AND THE CUP . . . .   646 ISLE STAT I 1   47
MORNIN'
BLOWIN' HER MORNIN' FIRE. . . . .   95 MOLL MAGEE   36
IN THE FROSTY MORNIN' CLEAR, ...   95 MOLL MAGEE   V   20
A-BLOWIN' OF HER MORNIN' FIRE, ...   95 MOLL MAGEE   V   35
MORNING
ON A MORNING MISTY AND MILD AND FAIR. . . . .   2 OISIN 1   V   7E
THAT FROM THE SAFFRON MORNING CAME, ...   19 OISIN 1   277
AND THE STARS SHALL ARISE AND SAY IN THE MORNING, . . .   28 OISIN 1   V 423G
OR HOURS PASSED BY, YET HOLD THE MORNING RAYS . . . . .   30 OISIN 2   20
NO LONGER GLAD AS ON THAT MORNING, SPED . . . . . .   30 OISIN 2   V   16
YET DIMLY DEEM I THAT THE MORNING RAYS . . . . . .   30 OISIN 2   V   20
HUNG FROM THE MORNING STAR! WHEN THESE MILD WORDS . . .   32 OISIN 2   49
WHEN THE FENIANS MADE FORAY AT MORNING WITH BRAN, SCEOLAN,   54 OISIN 3   104
    LOMAIR.
TILL, FATTENING THE WINDS OF THE MORNING, AN ODOUR . . .   57 OISIN 3   153
    OF NEW-MOWN HAY
COMING FORTH FROM THE SEA LIKE THE MORNING . . . . . .   58 OISIN 3   V 158
AND UNDER THE BLINK O' THE MORNING STAR, ...   83 MAD KING GOLL   V   20
DROPPING FROM THE VEILS OF THE MORNING TO WHERE THE CRICKET   117 ISLE INNISFREE   6
    SINGS!
AND SANG WHAT GOLD MORNING OR EVENING SHEDS . . . . .   126 DREAM OF FAERY   7
A RAPTUROUS MUSIC, TILL THE MORNING BREAK . . . . . .   137 TO SOME I TALK   14
CONTINUAL MUSIC TILL THE MORNING BREAK, ...   137 TO SOME I TALK   14
THE EAST HER HIDDEN JOY BEFORE THE MORNING BREAK, . . .   154 BELOVED PEACE   4
AND WHEN THE MORNING WHITENED . . . .   160 CAP AND BELLS   23
OF MORNING LIGHT IN A DIM SKY! . . . .   195 BAILE AILLINN   150
OUT OF THE RUNNING STREAM, O MORNING STAR, ...   251 SHADOW WATER B   610
AMONG THE STONES AND THORN-TREES, UNDER MORNING LIGHT! .   291 PAUDEEN   3
AMONG THE STONES AND THORN TREES, UNDER MORNING LIGHT, .   291 PAUDEEN   V   3
BETWEEN THE NIGHT AND MORNING. I MIGHT HAVE LIVED, . . .   351 PEOPLE   6
EVENING AND MORNING, THE STEEP STREET OF URBINO . . . .   352 PEOPLE   12
THAT NIGHT AND MORNING I MAY THRASH . . . .   379 SAINT HUNCH   9
THAT EVERY MORNING ROSE AGAIN" . . . .   385 ROBARTES DANCE   7
HIS "MORNING" AND HIS "NIGHT" DISCLOSE . . . . . .   386 ROBARTES DANCE   33
SCARCE SPREAD A GLORY TO THE MORNING BEAMS, ...   422 MY DESCENDANTS   6
TILL HIS MORNING MEAL COME ROUND! . . . .   435 FOR MY SON   4
THE MORNING STARS TO SING, ...   436 FOR MY SON   19
UNTIL THE MORNING BREAK AS ON A DARK BREAST. . . . . .   494 AT ALGECIRAS   V   6
"IS THAT MORNING WHEN I MET! . . . .   521 THREE THINGS   15
AND NIGHT AND MORNING SING! . . . .   627 STATES HOLIDAY   12
SHEPHERD, TO MAR THE MORNING HAST THOU COME? . . . . .   646 ISLE STAT I 1   30
LOUD FOR THEE THE MORNING CRIETH, ...   648 ISLE STAT I 1   86
FAR THE MORNING VAPOURS SHATTER, ...   648 ISLE STAT I 1   89
SHEPHERDS, I CAME THIS MORNING TO YOUR LAND . . . . .   682 SEEKER   15
WE'LL FLY FROM THIS BEFORE THE MORNING STAR. . . . . .   702 MOSADA 3   74
FOR YOUR FEET THE MORNING PRAYETH! . . . .   706 DAWN-SONG   25

PAGE   TITLE   LINE

MORNING   (CONTINUED)
    WHILE THE MORNING STAR DECAYETH . . . . 706 DAWN-SONG   29
    CAME OLIVE FIRES OF MORNING AND ON THE DARKNESS FED, . . 719 PHANTOM SHIP   33
    CAME THE OLIVE FIRE OF MORNING, AND ON THE DARKNESS FED, 719 PHANTOM SHIP V 33
    LONG BEFORE THE MORNING FIRE . . . . 727 LOVERS QUARREL 45
    THE WHITE FOOL MAKES AT MORNING OUT OF FOAM; . . . . . 761 SHADOW WATER A 261
    OUT OF A RUNNING STREAM, O MORNING STAR . . . . 769 SHADOW WATER A 426
MORNING'S
    ALL DREAD AFAR TILL MORNING'S BACK, ... 435 FOR MY SON   6
    AND IN THE MORNING'S GONE, NO MAN KNOWS WHY; . . . . . 490 COOLE BALLYLEE 20
    AND TROUBLED EYES CAME MORNING'S FIRST-BORN GLOW; . . . 648 ISLE STAT I 1 103
MORNINGS
    BUT FOR THOSE MORNINGS WHEN I FIND . . . . 306 HOUR DAWN   76
    I FADE, AND SHALL NOT SEE THE MORNINGS WAKE, ... 674 ISLE STAT II 3 223
MORNS
    AND TILL A HUNDRED MORNS HAD FLOWERED RED . . . . . . 170 SECRET ROSE   17
MOROCCAN
    OF THE MOROCCAN FLOCKS AND HERDS . . . . 493 AT ALGECIRAS   3
    OF A MOROCCAN FLOCK OR HERD, ... 493 AT ALGECIRAS V 3
MORROW   SEE TO-MORROW
    AND THINGS THAT FEAR THE DAWN OF THE MORROW . . . . . 20 OISIN 1   302
    AND WE FEAR NO DAWNING MORROW, ... 21 OISIN 1   318
    AND WE NEVER FEAR THE MORROW . . . . 21 OISIN 1 V 318
    FOLDED IN LOVE THAT FEARS NO MORROW, ... 23 OISIN 1   341
    OR TIRED ON ANY DAWNING MORROW, ... 23 OISIN 1 V 341
    AND PLANNING, PLOTTING ALWAYS THAT SOME MORROW . . . . 129 BOOK STORIES 10
MORTAL
    YOUR MORTAL SHORES TILL TIME IS DONE!" . . . . 6 OISIN 1 V 59
    IN A VIGOUR MORE THAN MORTAL MEASURE; . . . . 9 OISIN 1 V 98
    OR HAVE THEY BREATHED THE MORTAL AIR?" . . . . 12 OISIN 1 V 147
    WAS DIM WITH MIRE OF A MORTAL SHORE, ... 15 OISIN 1   208
    WAS DIM WITH THE MIRE OF A MORTAL SHORE, ... 15 OISIN 1 V 208
    TAKING THE MORTAL WARRIORS BY THE HANDS; . . . . . . 29 OISIN 2 V 10B
    FOR NEVER MORTAL CRY SO FAR HATH SENT. . . . . 36 OISIN 2 V 108
    . . . AND SEE WHAT THE MORTAL MEN DO, ... 55 OISIN 3 V 125
    AND HEAVY MORTAL HOPES THAT TOIL AND PASS! . . . . . 101 ROSE UPON ROOD 18
    "NOT ANY GOD ALIVE NOR MORTAL DEAD, ... 106 CUCHULAIN SEA V 10
    EMPTY YOUR HEART OF ITS MORTAL DREAM. . . . . 140 HOSTING SIDHE   5
    FILLING THY HEART WITH A MORTAL DREAM, ... 140 HOSTING SIDHE V 6
    WHEN AN IMMORTAL PASSION BREATHES IN MORTAL CLAY; . . . 172 TRAV PASSION   2
    THAT WORK TOO DIFFICULT FOR MORTAL HANDS . . . . . . 182 QUEEN MAEVE 67
    "HOW MAY A MORTAL WHOSE LIFE GUTTERS OUT . . . . . . 184 QUEEN MAEVE 85
    AND WITH A GROAN, AS IF THE MORTAL BREATH . . . . . 185 QUEEN MAEVE 103
    HE DREADS THE WEIGHT OF MORTAL HOURS. . . . . 212 BLESS PSALTER 11
    NO MORTAL CAN. YES! IF THEY GIVE US HELP. . . . . . 229 SHADOW WATER B 165
    FOR EVERY TATTER IN ITS MORTAL DRESS, ... 407 SAIL BYZANTIUM 12
    A MAN THAT HAD SIX MORTAL WOUNDS, A MAN . . . . . . 634 CUCHULAIN COMF 1
    LAUGHS NOT. IT DWELLS ALONE ON MORTAL LIPS! . . . . 670 ISLE STAT II 3 100
    BEFORE I AM TOO WEAK, FIERCE MORTAL, LET ME FLY, . . 675 ISLE STAT II 3 245
    FIERCE MORTAL, AND CROUCHED LOW BESIDE THE LAKE . . . 675 ISLE STAT II 3 V 245A
    THEIR DREAD OF AUTUMN'S MORTAL WING, ... 736 SUMMER EVENING 2
    WHY HAVE YOU CLOVEN ME WITH A MORTAL LOVE? . . . . . 768 SHADOW WATER A 419
MORTAL'S
    BEYOND A MORTAL'S YEARS. I WAIT THE SONG . . . . . 653 ISLE STAT I 2 48
    HIS WELL-BELOVED THROUGH A MORTAL'S EYES; . . . . . 763 SHADOW WATER A 322
    IS LAUGHING THROUGH A MORTAL'S EYES. O LOOK! . . . 763 SHADOW WATER A 324
MORTALS
    "THEN GO THROUGH THE LANDS IN THE SADDLE AND SEE WHAT THE 55 OISIN 3   125
        MORTALS DO,
    HOW WE ALONE OF MORTALS ARE . . . . 78 INDIAN TO LOVE 11
MOSADA
    MOSADA. . . . . 689 MOSADA 1   T
    MOSADA, IT IS THEN SO MUCH THE WORSE! . . . . 692 MOSADA 1 V 41A
    FROM THE UNDYING WORM. SHE SLEEPS--MOSADA-- . . . . 701 MOSADA 3   65
    FROM DATELESS PAIN. SHE SLEEPS--MOSADA--THOU-- . . . 701 MOSADA 3 V 65
    MOSADA! OH, MOSADA! . . . . 704 MOSADA 3 V 124A
    MOSADA! OH, MOSADA! . . . . 704 MOSADA 3 V 124A
MOSAIC   SEE GLASS-MOSAIC
    AS IN THE GOLD MOSAIC OF A WALL, ... 408 SAIL BYZANTIUM 18
MOSCOW
    TO MOSCOW OR TO ROME. . . . . 600 THOSE IMAGES   6
MOSS
    BY WOODS OF MOSS, BY LAWNS OF CLOVER, ... 25 OISIN 1 V 377
    OF MOSS, A MAIDEN WEAVING. SINGETH SHE! . . . . . 716 DWELT SYCAMORE 12
    WHERE THE MOSS WAS SPREAD LIKE HIS OWN DOORMAT. . . . 728 PRIEST FAIRY   8
    IN A WOOD OF DEW AND MOSS, ... 744 ROSY CROSS   5
MOSSY
    TO PRISONS GO, AND MOSSY RUIN REST . . . . 709 FERENCZ RENYI 2
    TO PRISON GO, AND MOSSY RUIN REST . . . . 709 FERENCZ RENYI V 2
MOST
    WHOSE LIPS HAD LIFE'S MOST PROSPEROUS GLOW? . . . . 10 OISIN 1   118
    THE THINGS THAT MOST OF ALL I HATE! . . . . 24 OISIN 1   359
    THAT WAS MOST DISTANT FROM THE DOOR! GREEN SLIME . . 37 OISIN 2   113
    MOST DISTANT STRODE WE. ON THE FLOOR LAY SLIME, . . 37 OISIN 2 V 113
    CRIED OUT, DIM SEA, HEAR MY MOST PITEOUS STORY! . . 68 SAD SHEPHERD   9
    HID IN THE EARTH'S MOST HIDDEN PART. . . . . 78 INDIAN TO LOVE V 12
    IN MY MOST SECRET SPIRIT GREW . . . . 83 MAD KING GOLL 27
    THIS WOULD I SAY, MOST WISE OF LIVING SOULS! . . . 102 FERGUS DRUID 9
    ON HER MOST LONELY MYSTERIES. . . . . 156 FORGOT BEAUTY V 24
    IT HAD GROWN MOST WISE WITH THINKING . . . . 159 CAP AND BELLS V 7
    FAR-OFF, MOST SECRET, AND INVIOLATE ROSE, ... 169 SECRET ROSE   1

536

		PAGE	TITLE		LINE
MOST	(CONTINUED)				
	FAR OFF, MOST SECRET, AND INVIOLATE ROSE,	169	SECRET ROSE	V	1
	FAR-OFF, MOST SECRET, AND INVIOLATE ROSE?	170	SECRET ROSE		32
	FAR OFF, MOST SECRET, AND INVIOLATE ROSE?	170	SECRET ROSE	V	32
	BUT THINK ABOUT OLD FRIENDS THE MOST!	173	PLEADS FRIEND		5
	BUT THINK OF YOUR OLD FRIENDS THE MOST!	173	PLEADS FRIEND	V	5
	WITH SPEEDY FEET AND A MOST THANKFUL HEART!	185	QUEEN MAEVE		100
	AT THE MOST QUIET MIDNIGHT IS TO BE STRICKEN.	236	SHADOW WATER B		321
	IF SOMETHING THAT'S MOST FABULOUS WERE TRUE--	245	SHADOW WATER B		489
	HAVE TAUGHT TO IGNORANT MEN MOST VIOLENT WAYS,	256	NO SECOND TROY		3
	BEING HIGH AND SOLITARY AND MOST STERN?	257	NO SECOND TROY		10
	OR IS THERE NONE, MOST POPULAR OF MEN,	265	ABBEY THEATRE		13
	YOU MOST OF ALL, SILENT AND FIERCE OLD MAN,	270	PARDON FATHERS		15
	DOWSON AND JOHNSON MOST I PRAISE--	273	GREY ROCK		62
	HE CLAIMED HIS COUNTRY'S NEED WAS MOST,	275	GREY ROCK		101
	WHY SHOULD THE FAITHFULLEST HEART MOST LOVE	275	GREY ROCK		112
	WOMEN CAN FIND." WITH A MOST MASTERFUL VOICE,	284	TWO KINGS		175
	WOMEN CAN FIND." WITH A MOST BURNING VOICE	284	TWO KINGS	V	175
	THAT IS MOST DIFFICULT.	291	TO A FRIEND		16
	DO MEN WHO LEAST DESIRE GET MOST,	295	THREE BEGGARS		13
	OR GET THE MOST WHO MOST DESIRE?"	295	THREE BEGGARS		14
	OR GET THE MOST WHO MOST DESIRE?"	295	THREE BEGGARS		14
	A BEGGAR SAID, "THEY GET THE MOST	295	THREE BEGGARS		15
	INTO SOME MOST FEARFUL SHAPE."	299	THREE HERMITS		23
	OF A MOST RIDICULOUS LITTLE BIRD	314	MEMORY YOUTH		20
	IN A MOST DESOLATE STONY PLACE,	325	ROBERT GREGORY		30
	MOST COURTEOUS TO SLOW AGE AND HASTY YOUTH,	339	SHEP GOATHERD		19
	ALL THE WILD WITCHES, THOSE MOST NOBLE LADIES,	343	DEJECTION		4
	WHERE WHO HAS SERVED THE MOST IS MOST DEFAMED,	351	PEOPLE		4
	WHERE WHO HAS SERVED THE MOST IS MOST DEFAMED,	351	PEOPLE		4
	I MOURN FOR THAT MOST LONELY THING; AND YET GOD'S WILL BE DONE!	354	HIS PHOENIX		31
	MOST OUT OF REACH? AND IS THAT SPECTRAL IMAGE	368	EGO DOMINUS		25
	THE MOST EXALTED LADY LOVED BY A MAN.	369	EGO DOMINUS		37
	THOSE MEN THAT IN THEIR WRITINGS ARE MOST WISE	370	EGO DOMINUS		68
	AND LOOK MOST LIKE ME, BEING INDEED MY DOUBLE,	371	EGO DOMINUS		72
	THE MOST UNLIKE, BEING MY ANTI-SELF,	371	EGO DOMINUS		74
	HE FOLLOWS WHATEVER WHIM'S MOST DIFFICULT	374	PHASES OF MOON		40
	CHOOSING WHATEVER TASK'S MOST DIFFICULT	376	PHASES OF MOON		91
	BUT MOST TO ALCIBIADES.	380	SAINT HUNCH		16
	AMID MOST LOVELY PLACES; SMITTEN AS THOUGH	389	IMAGE PAST		13
	HE HAD DONE MOST BITTER WRONG	393	EASTER 1916		33
	THAT MOST RESPECTED LADY'S EVERY WISH,	410	TOWER		29
	DOES THE IMAGINATION DWELL THE MOST	413	TOWER		113
	CONSIDER MOST TO MAGNIFY, OR TO BLESS,	418	ANCEST HOUSES		39
	SOUL'S BEAUTY BEING MOST ADORED,	421	MY TABLE		22
	FOR THE MOST RICH INHERITOR,	422	MY TABLE		25
	AND I, THAT COUNT MYSELF MOST PROSPEROUS,	423	MY DESCENDANTS		19
	OF SOME MOST HAUGHTY DEED OR THOUGHT	436	FOR MY SON		13
	HOW SUCH A MAN PLEASED WOMEN MOST	458	SECRETS OF OLD		13
	HOW SUCH A MAN HAD PLEASURED MOST	458	SECRETS OF OLD	V	13
	OUR MOST RENOWNED PATRIOTS STAND,	460	THREE MONUMENT		2
	PHILOSOPHERS SHOULD PRAISE THAT LOVE THE MOST,	465	HARUN RASHID	V	97
	OLD FELLOW-STUDENT, WHOSE MOST PATIENT EAR	468	HARUN RASHID		167
	OLD FELLOW STUDENT, WHOSE MOST PATIENT EAR	468	HARUN RASHID	V	167
	WHETHER OF HER OR GOD HE THOUGHT THE MOST,	471	ALL SOUL NIGHT		32
	OR INTO THAT MOST FECUND DITCH OF ALL,	479	SELF AND SOUL		61
	THE BOOK OF THE PEOPLE; WHATEVER MOST CAN BLESS	492	COOLE BALLYLEE		44
	WHAT SEEMS MOST WELCOME IN THE TOMB--PLAY A PREDESTINED PART.	503	VACILLATION		86
	THAT THE MOST COULD PLEASURE YOU,	525	DANCING DAYS		11
	WHAT MOST COULD SHAKE HIS SOUL!	529	TOM CRUACHAN		3
	WHAT MOST CAN SHAKE HIS SOUL!	529	TOM CRUACHAN	V	3
	WHAT LIVELY LAD MOST PLEASURED ME	538	LAST CONFESS		1
	SUCH A MAN THE MOST."	539	MEETING		12
	A MOST ASTONISHING THING--	567	FROM JAPANESE		1
	OF THAT MOST SENSUOUS SILENCE OF THE NIGHT	579	DOR WELLESLEY		6
	TO THIS MOST GALLANT GENTLEMAN	582	ROGER CASEMENT		23
	DO MOST EXCITE MY SPLEEN,	599	STONE CROSS		18
	THINK WHERE MAN'S GLORY MOST BEGINS AND ENDS,	604	GALLERY REVIS		54
	MOVE MOST GENTLY IF MOVE YOU MUST	617	LONG-LEG FLY		13
	YET A MOST GENTLE WOMAN; WHO CAN TELL	618	BRONZE HEAD		10
	SADNESS, SOUL OF JOY MOST DEEP,	647	ISLE STAT I 1		74
	OF FLIGHT ARE DONE. MOST FAIR OF ALL WHO GRAZE	649	ISLE STAT I 1		118
	NASCHINA, HAIL! MOST FAIR OF ALL WHO GRAZE	649	ISLE STAT I 1		120
	OR SOME SMALL BEAST MOST WONDERFULLY FURR'D,	650	ISLE STAT I 1		148
	OH, BOY, I'M BOUND ON A MOST FEARFUL QUEST;	653	ISLE STAT I 2		31
	THIS BLOSSOM IS MOST NEAR. STATUE! OH, THOU	657	ISLE STAT I 3		72
	YEA, NOBLE AND MOST KNIGHTLY HATH IT BEEN.	679	ISLE STAT II 3		320
	THE ORB OF THE MOST INNER LIVING HEART	689	NETTLESHIP		15
	HE WAS A MAN MOST LEARNED AND MOST MILD,	692	MOSADA 1		51
	HE WAS A MAN MOST LEARNED AND MOST MILD,	692	MOSADA 1		51
	THE PROUDEST OR MOST COY OF SPIRIT THINGS,	720	WITCH VIVIEN		7
	WANDERS AND WAILS BEFORE MY HEART MOST TRUE	738	YOU ARE SAD		8
	THAT THEY FOLLOW, FOR AT MOST	776	AGAINST WITCH		28
MOTH					
	AS ANY RUDDY MOTH, LOOKED DOWN ON US;	34	OISIN 2		72
	AS LIKE A RUDDY MOTH THEY WAVED AND FLUTTERED.	34	OISIN 2	V	72
	THAT HAS MADE FAT THE MURDEROUS MOTH;	156	FORGOT BEAUTY		8
	AT THE MOTH HOUR AND HID IT IN HER BOSOM.	199	ARROW	V	6
	WHAT BRUSHES FLY AND MOTH ASIDE?	625	NATIVITY		7

537

	PAGE	TITLE		LINE
MOTHER SEE FOSTER-MOTHER				
"MY FATHER AND MY MOTHER ARE	5	OISIN 1		46
"I HAVE LONG WAITED, MOTHER, FOR THAT WORD:	107	CUCHULAIN SEA		22
"LONG HAVE I WAITED, MOTHER, FOR THOSE WORDS, ...	107	CUCHULAIN SEA	V	22
"I HAVE LONG WAITED, MOTHER, FOR THOSE WORDS:	107	CUCHULAIN SEA	V	22
DID THE KISS OF MOTHER MARY	124	CATHLEEN PARA		9
HERS THE KISS OF MOTHER MARY, ...	124	CATHLEEN PARA	V	9
IS COMELIER THAN CANDLES AT MOTHER MARY'S FEET. . . .	147	UNAPPEAS HOST		12
YOUR MOTHER EIRE IS ALWAYS YOUNG, ...	148	INTO TWILIGHT		5
THY MOTHER ERI IS ALWAYS YOUNG, ...	148	INTO TWILIGHT	V	5
THE SONG OF THE OLD MOTHER	150	OLD MOTHER		T
"PRAISE GOD AND GOD'S MOTHER," DATHI SAID, ...	167	BLESSED		17
"FOR GOD AND GOD'S MOTHER HAVE SENT	167	BLESSED		18
O WHERE IS OUR MOTHER OF PEACE	171	MAID QUIET	V	1
AND OUR MOTHER OF PEACE HAS FORGOT ME	171	MAID QUIET	V	7
FASHIONED TO BE THE MOTHER OF STRONG CHILDREN: . . .	181	QUEEN MAEVE		26
THE ALE CUP IS MY FATHER AND MY MOTHER.	222	SHADOW WATER B	V	11B
MY MOTHER TOLD ME THAT THERE IS NOT ONE	224	SHADOW WATER B		45
MY MOTHER DANDLED ME AND SANG, ...	308	PLAYER QUEEN		1
"HE WENT AWAY," MY MOTHER SANG, ...	308	PLAYER QUEEN		5
"WHEN SHE WAS GOT," MY MOTHER SANG, ...	308	PLAYER QUEEN		13
SUFFER AS YOUR MOTHER SUFFERED, ...	313	TWO YEAR LATER		9
I HAD MY SHARE OF MOTHER WIT:	313	MEMORY YOUTH	V	3
NOT EVEN YOUR OWN MOTHER	336	YOUNG GIRL		4
UNDER HIS FINGERS. I HAD IT FROM HIS MOTHER, ...	339	SHEP GOATHERD		26
MAY BE A QUIET THOUGHT TO WIFE AND MOTHER, ...	343	SHEP GOATHERD		118
BANISHED HEROIC MOTHER MOON AND VANISHED, ...	344	DEJECTION		9
HEROIC MOTHER MOON HAS VANISHED, ...	344	DEJECTION	V	9
AS A MOTHER NAMES HER CHILD	394	EASTER 1916		62
THE MOTHER BIRD WILL REST	415	TOWER		170
THE MOTHER BIRDS BRING GRUBS AND FLIES.	424	STARES NEST		3
CAN LEAVE THE MOTHER, MURDERED AT HER DOOR, ...	429	NINETEEN 19		27
THAT HIS MOTHER MAY NOT LACK	435	FOR MY SON		7
HIS MAJESTIC MOTHER SAT	440	WISDOM		11
WHAT YOUTHFUL MOTHER, A SHAPE UPON HER LAP	444	SCHOOL CHILDR		33
WHERE THE GREAT MOTHER, MOURNING FOR HER DAUGHTER . . .	447	COLONUS PRAISE		19
THE MOTHER OF GOD	499	MOTHER OF GOD		T
THAT WOMAN, THE GREAT MOTHER IMAGING, ...	541	PARN FUNERAL 1		13
RECALL HIS TRINITY. A FATHER, MOTHER, CHILD (A DAUGHTER OR A SON),	556	RIBH PATRICK	V	2
CAN TOUCH BY MOTHER WIT	589	OLD WICKED MAN		40
AND THAT SHOULD MOTHER SEEK HER SON SHE'D HAVE BUT LITTLE LUCK	593	PILGRIM		12
FOR MOTHER EVE'S WINNING	654	ISLE STAT I 2		61
BUT A MOTHER PANTHER NEVER	658	ISLE STAT I 3		92
DOWN TO THE MOTHER OF THE FOILED AND DEAD.	688	TWO TITANS		50
MY MOTHER DREW FORTH FROM THE LONG GRASS	708	FAIRY PEDANT		23
THERE LIVE HIS SISTER AND HIS MOTHER. HIGH	710	FERENCZ RENYI	V	25
OF MIDDLE AGE. "HIS SISTER HERE AND MOTHER."	711	FERENCZ RENYI		53
THAT ANCIENT MOTHER CRIES, "SPEAK NOT, MY SON. . . .	711	FERENCZ RENYI		56
HUSH'D THE FISHERS, TILL A MOTHER CALLS BY NAME HER DROWNED SON:	719	PHANTOM SHIP		23
THEN EACH WIFE AND MAID AND MOTHER CALLS BY NAME SOME DROWNED ONE.	719	PHANTOM SHIP		24
BY THE SLOW HEAVING OCEAN--MUMBLING MOTHER OF THE DEAD.	719	PHANTOM SHIP		34
PRAYED BESIDE THE OCEAN, THE OLD MUMBLING MOTHER OF THE DEAD.	719	PHANTOM SHIP	V	34
SHE PRAYS FOR FATHER, MOTHER DEAR, ...	735	IN CHURCH		1
HER PRAYER FOR FATHER, MOTHER DEAR, ...	736	IN CHURCH		13
THE MOTHER OF THE STARS WEEPS TOO, ...	738	YOU ARE SAD		2
THE MOTHER OF THE WIND MOURNS TOO, ...	738	YOU ARE SAD		6
THE MOTHER OF THE WAVE SIGHS TOO, ...	738	YOU ARE SAD		10
I SAT BESIDE MY FOSTER MOTHER, AND NOW	762	SHADOW WATER A	V	292
MY FOSTER MOTHER SANG IN AN OLD RHYME	763	SHADOW WATER A	V	314
MOTHERHOOD				
PRIMORDIAL MOTHERHOOD FORSAKE HIS LIMBS, THE CHILD NO LONGER REST,	559	MAGIC DRUM		2
MOTHER-OF-PEARL				
WITH THE DELICATE MOTHER-OF-PEARL, ...	509	JANE REPROVED		10
MOTHER'S SEE FOSTER-MOTHER'S				
ANOTHER FILLS YOUR MIND. MY MOTHER'S NAME.	71	ANASHU VIJAYA		16
SOME OTHER FILLS YOUR MIND. MY MOTHER'S NAME. . . .	71	ANASHU VIJAYA	V	16
O WHAT TO ME MY MOTHER'S CARE, ...	151	HEART OF WOMAN		5
THERE WAS NO MOTHER'S SON BUT SAID, ...	253	HIS DREAM		6
HAS MADDENED EVERY MOTHER'S SON"!	290	SEPTEMBER 1913		29
HE DREAMS HIMSELF HIS MOTHER'S PRIDE, ...	343	SHEP GOATHERD		110
DROVE HORROR FROM HIS MOTHER'S BREAST.	440	WISDOM		20
THAT ANIMATE A MOTHER'S REVERIES, ...	445	SCHOOL CHILDR		51
PERCHED IN SOME WINDOW OF HER MOTHER'S HOUSE	466	HARUN RASHID		106
I CARRY FROM MY MOTHER'S WOMB	506	REMORSE SPEECH		14
IN MY MOTHER'S WOMB.	511	JANE AND JACK		12
LIFT, EVERY MOTHER'S SON, ...	548	TO SAME TUNE 3	V	15
MY FOSTER MOTHER'S GARDEN IN THE SOUTH	758	SHADOW WATER A	V	227
MOTHERS				
BOTH NUNS AND MOTHERS WORSHIP IMAGES, ...	445	SCHOOL CHILDR		49
THAT SICKENING NEAR THEIR MOTHERS LIE:	717	FAIRY DOCTOR		16
MOTHER-WIT				
I HAD MY SHARE OF MOTHER-WIT, ...	313	MEMORY YOUTH		3
MOTH-HOUR				
AT THE MOTH-HOUR OF EVE, ...	132	FR GILLIGAN		6
AND THE MOTH-HOUR WENT FROM THE FIELDS, ...	133	FR GILLIGAN		15

		PAGE	TITLE	LINE

MOTH-LIKE
  AND MOTH-LIKE STARS WERE FLICKERING OUT, ...   149 WANDER AENGUS   6
  GENTLY SHOOK THEIR MOTH-LIKE WINGS: 667 ISLE STAT II 3   26
MOTH'S
  ARE DUST ON THE MOTH'S WING: THAT NOTHING MATTERS . . .   235 SHADOW WATER B   297
  THAT HAVE BUILT ALL ARE DUST ON A MOTH'S WING. . . . .   757 SHADOW WATER A   205
MOTHS   SEE NIGHT-MOTHS
  THAT FEED WHITE MOTHS BY SOME DE DANAAN SHRINE: . . . .   41 OISIN 2   186
  FEEDING WHITE MOTHS AROUND SOME EASTERN SHRINE, ...   41 OISIN 2   V 186
  WHEN THE MOTHS CAME ONCE MORE, ...   133 FR GILLIGAN   22
  WHEN MOTHS CAME ONCE MORE, ...   133 FR GILLIGAN   V   22
  AND WHEN WHITE MOTHS WERE ON THE WING, ...   149 WANDER AENGUS   5
  AND STARS LIKE MOTHS WERE SHINING OUT, ...   149 WANDER AENGUS V   6
  THE MOTHS ARE WHEN THEY ARE BURNED? . . . .   313 TWO YEAR LATER   4
  A COUPLE OF NIGHT MOTHS ARE ON THE WING, ...   482 BLOOD AND MOON   46
  AS MOTHS WITH BROKEN WINGS, AND AS WE SIT . . . . .   671 ISLE STAT II 3   142
  LIKE SMALL BROWN MOTHS, A-TREMBLE. "RENYI SAY . . .   713 FERENCZ RENYI   82
  LIKE SMALL BROWN MOTHS, A-TREMBLE CEASELESSLY. . . . .   713 FERENCZ RENYI   V 82
MOTION
  WHAT MOTION OF THE SUN OR STREAM . . . .   507 STREAM AND SUN   11
MOTIONED
  SHE MOTIONED HIM AFAR, AND ROSE AND SPOKE: . . . . .   280 TWO KINGS   68
MOTIONLESS
  THEIR MOTIONLESS EYEBALLS OF SPIRITS . . . .   55 OISIN 3   121
  WITH MOTIONLESS HEAD ERECT. . . . .   383 VISION ROBART   32
MOTIONS
  THROUGH INTRICATE MOTIONS RAN . . . .   506 STREAM AND SUN   1
MOTLEY
  BUT LIVED WHERE MOTLEY IS WORN: . . . .   392 EASTER 1916   14
MOTORS
  OR THE MAN THAT MADE THE MOTORS? . . . .   627 STATES HOLIDAY   20
MOULD
  . . . LURED FROM HIS LAIR IN THE MOULD: . . . . . .   53 OISIN 3   99
  THE HEAVY STEPS OF THE PLOUGHMAN, SPLASHING THE WINTRY   143 ROSE IN HEART   3
    MOULD,
  THE HEAVY STEPS OF THE PLOUGHMAN SPLASHING THE WINTER   143 ROSE IN HEART V   3
    MOULD,
  FROM BEAUTY THAT IS CAST OUT OF A MOULD . . . . . .   334 LIVING BEAUTY   4
  FAILURE FOR GLORY DOWN ON THEE, AND MOULD . . . . .   688 TWO TITANS   54
MOULDED
  IN MOULDED PLASTER OR IN CARVEN STONE? . . . .   327 ROBERT GREGORY   77
  HIS BODY MOULDED FROM WITHIN HIS BODY . . . .   374 PHASES OF MOON   43
  HAS MOULDED THE HARD YEARS. . . . .   738 MOURN THEN ON   8
MOULDERING
  AMONG THE MOULDERING OF ANCIENT WOODS . . . .   74 ANASHU VIJAYA   61
  THAT SHAKES A MOULDERING COBWEB FROM THE RAFTER: . . .   130 BOOK STORIES   19
  AND SHAKE A MOULDERING COBWEB FROM THE RAFTER, ...   130 BOOK STORIES   V   19
MOULDING
  MOULDING IT OF DUST OR SAND, ...   600 SPIRIT MEDIUM   14
MOUND   SEE BURIAL-MOUND
  AND RAISED ABOVE HER MOUND . . . .   123 DREAM OF DEATH   6
  A BOY OF TWENTY YEARS:--A MOUND AND STONE . . . . .   276 TWO KINGS   V   F
  AND SHOULD HE DIE TO HEAP HIS BURIAL MOUND . . . . .   280 TWO KINGS   V   82
  THAN MOUND AND STONE THAT KEEP ALL VIRTUE IN, ...   281 TWO KINGS   106
  WHEN NETTLES WAVE UPON A SHAPELESS MOUND   . . . . .   489 COOLE PARK 29   27
  A MOUND OF REFUSE OR THE SWEEPINGS OF A STREET, . . .   630 CIRCUS ANIMALS   35
  A MOUND OF REFUSE OR THE SWEEPINGS OF THE STREET, . .   630 CIRCUS ANIMALS V   35
MOUND'S
  THAT THE IMMEDICABLE MOUND'S BEYOND . . . .   282 TWO KINGS   129
MOUNDS   SEE BURIAL-MOUNDS
  AND PASSING THE FIRBOLGS' BURIAL MOUNDS, ...   3 OISIN 1   V   16
  WHERE MEN HAVE HEAPED NO BURIAL MOUNDS, ...   8 OISIN 1   V   82
MOUNT
  "O OISIN, MOUNT BY ME AND RIDE . . . .   8 OISIN 1   80
  MOUNT MY WHITE STEED, FOR THE FAIRY STATE . . . . .   9 OISIN 1   V 103
  FOR NO MAN'S CRY SHALL EVER MOUNT SO FAR: . . . . .   36 OISIN 2   108
  NOR NO MAN'S CRY SHALL EVER MOUNT SO FAR: . . . . .   36 OISIN 2   V 108
  ALL SUDDENLY MOUNT . . . .   322 SWANS AT COOLE   10
  O BID ME MOUNT AND SAIL UP THERE . . . .   458 HIS WILDNESS   1
  WHAT MADE THEM MOUNT AND WHAT MADE THEM COME, ...   549 SEVERED HEAD   V   8
  HERMITS UPON MOUNT MERU OR EVEREST, ...   563 MERU   9
  HE THAT'S MOUNTING UP MUST ON HIS NEIGHBOUR MOUNT, . .   580 CURSE CROMWELL   11
  HER HEART MOUNT UP ON HIGH: . . . .   608 SONGS BURDEN 3   22
  AS FAIR AS ANY THAT ON IDA'S MOUNT . . . .   650 ISLE STAT I 1   134
MOUNTAIN
  AND THERE AT THE FOOT OF THE MOUNTAIN, ...   60 OISIN 3   185
  A MURMURING A MOUNTAIN TUNE, ...   85 MAD KING GOLL V   52
  MURMURING A MOUNTAIN TUNE, ...   85 MAD KING GOLL V   52
  HAD COME THROUGH THE MOUNTAIN SIDE, ...   171 MAID QUIET   V   4B
  AND TRAMPLED THE MOUNTAIN AWAY, ...   171 MAID QUIET   V   4C
  HAD HAMMERED OUT ON MOUNTAIN TOP . . . .   271 GREY ROCK   23
  IN AFRICA ON MOUNTAIN OF THE MOON, ...   277 TWO KINGS   V   20
  THE MOUNTAIN TOMB . . . .   311 MOUNTAIN TOMB   T
  THE CATARACT SMOKES UPON THE MOUNTAIN SIDE, ...   311 MOUNTAIN TOMB   3
  THE CATARACT SMOKES ON THE MOUNTAIN SIDE. . . . . .   311 MOUNTAIN TOMB V   3
  HAD SOUNDED BETTER TO YOUR MOUNTAIN FANCY, ...   341 SHEP GOATHERD   61
  THEY SAY THAT ON YOUR BARREN MOUNTAIN RIDGE . . . .   342 SHEP GOATHERD   79
  TO KNOW THE MOUNTAIN AND THE VALLEY HAVE GRIEVED . . .   343 SHEP GOATHERD   117
  TO KNOW THE MOUNTAIN AND THE VALLEY GRIEVE . . . . .   343 SHEP GOATHERD V 117
  BECAUSE THE MOUNTAIN GRASS . . . .   350 MEMORY   4
  WHERE THE MOUNTAIN HARE HAS LAIN. . . . .   350 MEMORY   6

539

		PAGE	TITLE		LINE
MOUNTAIN	(CONTINUED)				
OR IMAGE, FROM BEYOND THE LOADSTONE MOUNTAIN,		371	ON GOING HOUSE		11
FROM MOUNTAIN STEEP TO STEEP.		399	BREAK OF DAY		25
THAT CLIMB THE MOUNTAIN SIDE,		416	TOWER	V	175
CRIED, CASTING OFF THE MOUNTAIN SNOW,		502	VACILLATION		60
THE MOUNTAIN THROWS A SHADOW,		519	LOVES LONENESS		7
FROM MOUNTAIN CREST TO CREST.		536	PARTING		10
THE MEET'S UPON THE MOUNTAIN SIDE.		549	SEVERED HEAD	V	6
THERE, ON THE MOUNTAIN AND THE SKY,		567	LAPIS LAZULI		51
FROM MOUNTAIN TO MOUNTAIN RIDE THE FIERCE HORSEMEN.		605	SONGS BURDEN 1		9
FROM MOUNTAIN TO MOUNTAIN RIDE THE FIERCE HORSEMEN.		605	SONGS BURDEN 1		9
FROM MOUNTAIN TO MOUNTAIN RIDE THE FIERCE HORSEMEN.		606	SONGS BURDEN 1		18
FROM MOUNTAIN TO MOUNTAIN RIDE THE FIERCE HORSEMEN.		606	SONGS BURDEN 1		18
FROM MOUNTAIN TO MOUNTAIN RIDE THE FIERCE HORSEMEN.		606	SONGS BURDEN 1		27
FROM MOUNTAIN TO MOUNTAIN RIDE THE FIERCE HORSEMEN.		606	SONGS BURDEN 1		27
FROM MOUNTAIN TO MOUNTAIN RIDE THE FIERCE HORSEMEN.		607	SONGS BURDEN 2		9
FROM MOUNTAIN TO MOUNTAIN RIDE THE FIERCE HORSEMEN.		607	SONGS BURDEN 2		9
FROM MOUNTAIN TO MOUNTAIN RIDE THE FIERCE HORSEMEN.		607	SONGS BURDEN 2		18
FROM MOUNTAIN TO MOUNTAIN RIDE THE FIERCE HORSEMEN.		607	SONGS BURDEN 2		18
FROM MOUNTAIN TO MOUNTAIN RIDE THE FIERCE HORSEMEN.		607	SONGS BURDEN 2		27
FROM MOUNTAIN TO MOUNTAIN RIDE THE FIERCE HORSEMEN.		607	SONGS BURDEN 2		27
FROM MOUNTAIN TO MOUNTAIN RIDE THE FIERCE HORSEMEN.		608	SONGS BURDEN 3		9
FROM MOUNTAIN TO MOUNTAIN RIDE THE FIERCE HORSEMEN.		608	SONGS BURDEN 3		9
FROM MOUNTAIN TO MOUNTAIN RIDE THE FIERCE HORSEMEN.		608	SONGS BURDEN 3		18
FROM MOUNTAIN TO MOUNTAIN RIDE THE FIERCE HORSEMEN.		608	SONGS BURDEN 3		18
FROM MOUNTAIN TO MOUNTAIN RIDE THE FIERCE HORSEMEN.		608	SONGS BURDEN 3		27
FROM MOUNTAIN TO MOUNTAIN RIDE THE FIERCE HORSEMEN.		608	SONGS BURDEN 3		27
DOWN THE MOUNTAIN WALLS		612	NEWS ORACLE		30
WHAT MARCHES THROUGH THE MOUNTAIN PASS?		614	MARCH SONGS 2		7
WHAT MARCHES DOWN THE MOUNTAIN PASS?		615	MARCH SONGS 2		17
WHAT MARCHES DOWN THE MOUNTAIN PASS?		615	MARCH SONGS 2		27
CRAZY JANE ON THE MOUNTAIN		628	JANE MOUNTAIN		T
LAST NIGHT I LAY ON THE MOUNTAIN,		628	JANE MOUNTAIN		11
OLD BONES UPON THE MOUNTAIN SHAKE.		635	BLACK TOWER		10
OLD BONES UPON THE MOUNTAIN SHAKE.		636	BLACK TOWER		20
OLD BONES UPON THE MOUNTAIN SHAKE.		636	BLACK TOWER		30
IN AUTUMN, WHEN FAR DOWN THE MOUNTAIN SLOPES		690	MOSADA 1		12
WHERE HOMES ONCE WHITENED VALE AND MOUNTAIN CREST!		709	FERENCZ RENYI		3
OR YONDER MOUNTAIN. WHERE? THOU SHALT BE FREE--		710	FERENCZ RENYI	V	15
THE MOUNTAIN OF THE GODS, THE UNAPPEASABLE GODS		764	SHADOW WATER A		332
AMONG HIGH MOUNTAINS, AND THE MOUNTAIN ROBBERS		768	SHADOW WATER A		411
OR GO BESIDE HIM TO HIS MOUNTAIN WARS.		768	SHADOW WATER A		414
MOUNTAINOUS					
WHERE GODS ARE BROODING IN A MOUNTAINOUS PLACE		757	SHADOW WATER A		198
MOUNTAIN'S					
FIRST TROD ON THE MOUNTAIN'S HEAD		488	CRAZED MOON		9
UPON THE MOUNTAIN'S BROW. YONDER HE TREADS		703	MOSADA 3		114
MOUNTAINS					
SOME DANCED LIKE SHADOWS ON THE MOUNTAINS,		25	OISIN 1		388
THEIR HAIR ALONG THE MOUNTAINS ROLLED AND FILLED		74	ANASHU VIJAYA		71
WOLF-BREEDING MOUNTAINS, GALLERIED EMAN,		81	MAD KING GOLL	V	2
AND PACED UPON THE MOUNTAINS OVERHEAD		121	YOU ARE OLD		11
HE PACED UPON THE MOUNTAINS FAR ABOVE,		121	YOU ARE OLD	V	11
AND THE MOUNTAINS AND WOODS		142	MOODS		3
THE MOUNTAINS AND WOODS		142	MOODS	V	3
AND TRAMPLED THE MOUNTAINS AWAY,		171	MAID QUIET	V	4C
AMONG THE AFRICAN MOUNTAINS OF THE MOON,		277	TWO KINGS		20
AND ALONG THE MOUNTAINS PASS,		705	DAWN-SONG		12
OR YONDER MOUNTAINS. WHERE? THOU SHALT BE FREE--		710	FERENCZ RENYI		15
YE ON THE BROAD HIGH MOUNTAINS OF OLD ERI,		737	MOURN THEN ON		1
AMONG HIGH MOUNTAINS, AND THE MOUNTAIN ROBBERS		768	SHADOW WATER A		411
MOUNTAIN-SIDE					
CLIMBING THE MOUNTAIN-SIDE,		416	TOWER		175
THE MEET'S UPON THE MOUNTAIN-SIDE.		549	SEVERED HEAD		6
MOUNTAIN-TOP					
I DRAGGED FROM GOBAN'S MOUNTAIN-TOP		304	HOUR DAWN		50
MOUNTED	SEE HALF-MOUNTED BELL-MOUNTED				
AND THEN I MOUNTED AND SHE BOUND ME		9	OISIN 1		106
LIES FAR." I MOUNTED, AND SHE BOUND ME		9	OISIN 1	V	106
WE MOUNTED ON THE STAIR, THE WHITE STEED TYING,		32	OISIN 2	V	46
HALF IN THE UNVESSELLED SEA. WE'D MOUNTED FAR:		32	OISIN 2	V	47
THEN, MOUNTED ON A HERON, O'ER THE DEEP		33	OISIN 2	V	64
SOBBED INTO SILENCE. WE HAD MOUNTED FEET		33	OISIN 2	V	68E
I MOUNTED, AND WE PASSED OVER THE LONE		45	OISIN 2		231
I MOUNTED, AND WE RODE ACROSS THE LONE		45	OISIN 2	V	231
BUT, THE BIRD IN MY FINGERS, I MOUNTED,		54	OISIN 3		111
BUT, THE BIRD IN MY FINGERS, I MOUNTED, MINDFUL ONLY TO LAUNCH		54	OISIN 3	V	111
WHEN THEY HAVE MOUNTED UP,		415	TOWER		169
THOUGH MOUNTED IN THAT SADDLE HOMER RODE		492	COOLE BALLYLEE		47
MOUNTED THE MARE OF TIME,		529	TOM CRUACHAN		5
MOUNTING					
AT SUDDEN THUNDER OF THE MOUNTING SWAN		490	COOLE BALLYLEE		14
HE THAT'S MOUNTING UP MUST ON HIS NEIGHBOUR MOUNT,		580	CURSE CROMWELL		11
MOUNTS					
AND MOUNTS MORE DIZZY HIGH THE MORE IT RAINS		417	ANCEST HOUSES		5
THAT JUGGLING NATURE MOUNTS, HER COIL IN THEIR EMBRACES TWINED.		556	RIBH PATRICK		9
MOURN					
BOAST NOT, NOR MOURN WITH DROOPING HEAD		11	OISIN 1		129
LOST NIAM MOURN AND SAY, "AH, LOVE, WE GO		46	OISIN 2	V	245B

MOURN   (CONTINUED)
    IN BOSOM AND HAIR. "AH, DO NOT MOURN," HE SAID, ...   80 EPHEMERA   20
    IN BOSOM AND HAIR. THEN HE: "LET US NOT MOURN . . . .   80 EPHEMERA   V   20
    I MOURN FOR THAT MOST LONELY THING; AND YET GOD'S WILL   354 HIS PHOENIX   31
        BE DONE!
    MOURN--AND THEN ONWARD! . . . .   737 MOURN THEN ON   T
    MOURN ALL THE NIGHT AND DAY, ...   737 MOURN THEN ON   2
    MOURN YE ON GRASS-GREEN PLAINS OF ERI FATED, ...   738 MOURN THEN ON   9
    MOURN--AND THEN ONWARD, THERE IS NO RETURNING . . . . .   738 MOURN THEN ON   13
MOURNFUL
    MOURNFUL, AND GATHERED ON THE SANDS; . . . . . .   10 OISIN 1   V 111B
    HEARING AEDH TOUCH THE MOURNFUL STRINGS OF GOLD." . .   35 OISIN 2   87
    BACCHANT AND MOURNFUL, PASSING TO AND FRO . . . . .   39 OISIN 2   161
    CEASE, CEASE, O MOURNFUL, LAUGHING FENIAN HORN! . . .   43 OISIN 2   213
    AH, CEASE, THOU MOURNFUL, LAUGHING FENIAN HORN! . . .   43 OISIN 2   V 213
    AH, CEASE, YOU MOURNFUL, LAUGHING FENIAN HORN! . . .   43 OISIN 2   V 213
    IMMEDIATE, MOURNFUL, WHITE WITH SUDDEN CARES, ...   44 OISIN 2   V 229A
    WATCHED ME WITH MOURNFUL WONDER OUT OF THE WELLS OF HIS   51 OISIN 3   60
        EYES.
    BUT LIFT A MOURNFUL ULALU, ...   86 MAD KING GOLL   68
    THE BLIND HOUND WITH A MOURNFUL DIN . . . . . .   99 FOXHUNTER   45
    THE OLDEST HOUND WITH MOURNFUL DIN, ...   99 FOXHUNTER   V 45
    STARED ON THE MOURNFUL WONDER OF HIS EYES, ...   108 CUCHULAIN SEA   41
    MORE MOURNFUL THAN THE DEPTH OF STARRY SKIES, ...   108 CUCHULAIN SEA V 42
    UPON THE MOURNFUL WONDER OF HIS EYES, ...   108 CUCHULAIN SEA V 42
    FOR THESE RED LIPS, WITH ALL THEIR MOURNFUL PRIDE, . .   111 ROSE OF WORLD   2
    MOURNFUL THAT NO NEW WONDER MAY BETIDE, ...   111 ROSE OF WORLD   3
    A GIRL AROSE THAT HAD RED MOURNFUL LIPS . . . . .   120 SORROW OF LOVE   5
    AND THEN YOU CAME WITH THOSE RED MOURNFUL LIPS, . . .   120 SORROW OF LOVE V   5
    AND GAZED UPON THE MOURNFUL STARS ABOVE, ...   123 DREAM OF DEATH V 11
    AND HEARD THE MOURNFUL BREEZE, ...   123 DREAM OF DEATH V 12
    CARRY ALL THAT MOURNFUL BEAUTY . . . .   124 CATHLEEN PARA   7
    I HEAR THE HARP-STRING PRAISE THEM, OR HEAR THEIR MOURNFUL   210 UNDER THE MOON 16
        TALK.
    I HEAR THE HARP STRINGS PRAISE THEM, OR HEAR THEIR MOURNFUL   210 UNDER THE MOON V 16
        TALK.
    I HEAR THE HARPSTRING PRAISE THEM OR HEAR THEIR MOURNFUL   210 UNDER THE MOON V 16
        TALK.
    I HEAR THE HARP STRING PRAISE THEM OR HEAR THEIR MOURNFUL   210 UNDER THE MOON V 16
        TALK.
    SO MOURNFUL THAT IT SEEMED THE CRY OF ONE . . . . .   278 TWO KINGS   39
    ONE ASKS FOR MOURNFUL MELODIES; . . . .   567 LAPIS LAZULI   53
    AND LET THE TALE BE MOURNFUL EACH ONE TELLS. . . . .   663 ISLE STAT II 2 36
    NOW THEIR SONGS ARE MOURNFUL WHOLLY . . . . . .   667 ISLE STAT II 3 32
    HUNG ON HIS DOUBLET--DEAR AND MOURNFUL CHILD, ...   691 MOSADA 1   35
    TO THE EVER-LONGING AND MOURNFUL SPIRIT SAY. . . . .   734 QUATRAIN APHOR 12
    MOURNFUL UNDER MOURNFUL STARS. . . . .   737 IN FIRELIGHT   4
    MOURNFUL UNDER MOURNFUL STARS. . . . .   737 IN FIRELIGHT   4
    (AH, MOURNFUL DANAAN QUICKEN TREE!) . . . . . .   742 DANAAN QUICK   6
    (AH, MOURNFUL DANAAN QUICKEN TREE!) . . . . . .   743 DANAAN QUICK   12
    (AH, MOURNFUL DANAAN QUICKEN TREE!) . . . . . .   743 DANAAN QUICK   18
    (AH, MOURNFUL DANAAN QUICKEN TREE!) . . . . . .   743 DANAAN QUICK   24
    (AH, MOURNFUL DANAAN QUICKEN TREE!) . . . . . .   743 DANAAN QUICK   30
MOURNING
    WHERE THE GREAT MOTHER, MOURNING FOR HER DAUGHTER . . .   447 COLONUS PRAISE 19
MOURNS
    THE LOVER MOURNS FOR THE LOSS OF LOVE . . . . . .   152 LOSS OF LOVE   T
    HE MOURNS FOR THE CHANGE THAT HAS COME UPON HIM . . . .   153 CHANGE BELOVED   T
    THE LOVER MOURNS BECAUSE OF HIS WANDERINGS . . . . .   171 MAID QUIET   V   T
    NOR AN UNLAUGHING MOUTH, BUT MINE THAT MOURNS, ...   285 TWO KINGS   184
    THE MOTHER OF THE WIND MOURNS TOO, ...   738 YOU ARE SAD   6
MOURTEEN
    MY BROTHER MOURTEEN IS WORN OUT . . . .   301 RUN PARADISE   8
MOUSE   SEE FIELD-MOUSE
    SLEEK AS ANY GRANARY MOUSE . . . .   2 OISIN 1   V   7M
    MORE SLEEK THAN ANY GRANARY MOUSE, ...   4 OISIN 1   36
    SLEEK AS ANY GRANARY MOUSE, ...   4 OISIN 1   V 37
    AND "A WEARINESS SOON IS MY SPEED," SAYS THE MOUSE, . .   27 OISIN 1   V 417
    AND "MY SPEED IS A WEARINESS," FALTERS THE MOUSE, . .   28 OISIN 1   421
    BRUSH LIGHTLY AS HAY MOUSE EARTH'S PEBBLES, ...   56 OISIN 3   V 128
    THE FIELD MOUSE RUNNING BY ME IN THE GRASS, ...   101 ROSE UPON ROOD V 17
    FOR ALL ITS BRONZE AND MARBLE, 'S BUT A MOUSE. . . . .   418 ANCEST HOUSES 24
    WHERE NOTHING STIRS BUT A MOUSE. . . . .   575 ACRE OF GRASS   6
    A MOUSE FROM HIS SLEEPING, ...   672 ISLE STAT II 3 172
MOUSE-GREY
    WHERE MOUSE-GREY WATERS ARE FLOWING, ...   119 PITY OF LOVE   7
    THE MOUSE-GREY WATERS ON FLOWING, ...   119 PITY OF LOVE   V 5
MOUSELIKE
    NOW OLD AND MOUSELIKE. FOR AN ANSWERING SIGN . . . .   36 OISIN 2   V 96
MOUSE-LIKE
    NOW IT IS OLD AND MOUSE-LIKE. FOR A SIGN . . . . .   36 OISIN 2   96
MOUSETAIL
    COME YOU, COLTSFOOT, MOUSETAIL, COME! . . . . . .   727 LOVERS QUARREL 33
MOUTH   SEE HONEY-MOUTH CAVE-MOUTH
    AND A SAD MOUTH, THAT FEAR MADE TREMULOUS . . . . .   34 OISIN 2   71
    WENT THE LAUGHTER OF SCORN FROM MY MOUTH . . .   58 OISIN 3   168
    AND IN FOLDS ROUND HIS EYES AND HIS MOUTH, ...   59 OISIN 3   174
    A LUG-WORM WITH ITS GREY AND MUDDY MOUTH . . . . .   127 DREAM OF FAERY 18
    WITH A BLINK IN HIS EYES AT THE CAVE MOUTH, ...   166 BLESSED   V 3
    BAILE, WHO HAD THE HONEY MOUTH! . . . .   189 BAILE AILLINN V 5
    YOUNG BAILE HONEY MOUTH, WHOM SOME . . . . . .   189 BAILE AILLINN V 16

		PAGE	TITLE		LINE

MOUTH   (CONTINUED)

I RUN TO BAILE HONEY MOUTH	191	BAILE AILLINN	V	48
AND NOW THAT HONEY MOUTH IS LAID	192	BAILE AILLINN	V	80
WINE COMES IN AT THE MOUTH	261	DRINKING SONG		1
I LIFT THE GLASS TO MY MOUTH,	261	DRINKING SONG		5
HE SAT WITH TIGHTENED REIN AND LOOSENED MOUTH	277	TWO KINGS		10
NOR DOOR, NOR MOUTH, NOR SLIPPER MADE A NOISE,	279	TWO KINGS		51
NOR AN UNLAUGHING MOUTH, BUT MINE THAT MOURNS,	285	TWO KINGS		184
YOUR ENEMY, AN OLD FOUL MOUTH, HAD SET	292	TO A SHADE		17
AN OLD FOUL MOUTH THAT ONCE CRIED OUT ON YOU	292	TO A SHADE		17
AN OLD FOUL MOUTH THAT SLANDERED YOU HAD SET	292	TO A SHADE	V	17
HELL MOUTH LAY OPEN NEAR THAT PLACE,	303	HOUR DAWN		25
BUT THE HELL MOUTH AT CRUACHAN	303	HOUR DAWN	V	24
I SHOULD NOT BE TOO DOWN IN THE MOUTH	306	HOUR DAWN		88
FROM THE HELL MOUTH AT CRUACHAN	307	HOUR DAWN	V	120
NOR MOUTH FROM KISSING, NOR FROM WINE UNWET:	311	MOUNTAIN TOMB		7
NOR MOUTH WITH KISSING NOR WITH WINE UNWET.	311	MOUNTAIN TOMB	V	7
NOR MOUTH WITH KISSING NOR WITH THE WINE UNWET.	311	MOUNTAIN TOMB	V	7
MOUTH MASTERED A SWEET SOUND,	331	ROUND TOWER		16
A POET'S MOUTH BE SILENT, FOR IN TRUTH	359	WAR POEM		2
A POET KEEP HIS MOUTH SHUT, FOR IN TRUTH	359	WAR POEM	V	2
OUT OF THE MOUTH OF PLENTY'S HORN,	405	FOR DAUGHTER		60
OUT OF A MEDIUM'S MOUTH,	439	FRAGMENTS		6
HARDLY DARED TO WET HIS MOUTH	454	EMPTY CUP		3
THE WILD STAG AND THE DOE: THAT MOUTH TO MOUTH	465	HARUN RASHID		101
THE WILD STAG AND THE DOE: THAT MOUTH TO MOUTH	465	HARUN RASHID		101
WHEN MAYBE THRICE IN EVERY MOON HER MOUTH	468	HARUN RASHID		162
A MOUTH THAT HAS NO MOISTURE AND NO BREATH	497	BYZANTIUM		13
. . . MOVE HIS MOUTH AND SINEWY TONGUE.	560	MAGIC DRUM		5
AND PART HIS FOAMING MOUTH WITH EAGER EYE--	688	TWO TITANS		46
WITH OPEN MOUTH AND BEATING HEART.	729	PRIEST FAIRY		32
HEART ON HEART, OR MOUTH ON MOUTH,	777	SONG DEIRDRE 2		9
HEART ON HEART, OR MOUTH ON MOUTH,	777	SONG DEIRDRE 2		9

MOUTHFUL

I MADE IT OUT OF A MOUTHFUL OF AIR,	166	EVIL OF BELOV		5
THAT ANOTHER MOUTHFUL	454	EMPTY CUP		5
A MOUTHFUL HELD THE EXTREME OF LIFE AND DEATH.	619	BRONZE HEAD		14
A MOUTHFUL HOLD THE EXTREME OF LIFE AND DEATH.	619	BRONZE HEAD	V	14
O, WHAT IS LIFE BUT A MOUTHFUL OF AIR?	788	HAWTHORN TREE		9

MOUTHS

THE MOUTHS THAT SPEAK, THE NOTES AND STRINGS,	212	BLESS PSALTER		2
AND BLEW YOU HITHER: AND THEIR MOUTHS HAVE PROMISED	237	SHADOW WATER B		325
AMONG THOSE MOUTHS THAT SING THEIR SWEETHEARTS' PRAISE,	285	TWO KINGS		185
WE POETS KEEP OUR MOUTHS SHUT, FOR IN TRUTH	359	WAR POEM	V	2
BREATHLESS MOUTHS MAY SUMMON:	497	BYZANTIUM		14
ABOVE THESE MEN WHOSE MOUTHS WERE SEALED	656	ISLE STAT I 3		27

MOVE

. . . AND MOVE WHERE THE OLD MEN AND YOUNG	55	OISIN 3		114
FOR NO LIVE CREATURES LIVE THERE, NO WEASELS MOVE IN THE DARK:	56	OISIN 3		139
WATCHING THE BLESSED ONES MOVE FAR OFF, AND THE SMILE ON GOD'S FACE,	61	OISIN 3		199
. . . AND MARCH ON AS OXEN MOVE OVER YOUNG GRASS:	62	OISIN 3		211
FOR LONELY TO MOVE 'MONG THE SOFT EYES	63	OISIN 3	V	222
GLIMMERING IN HER DROOPED EYES, SAW HER LIPS MOVE	81	EPHEMERA	V	24D
HIS FINGERS MOVE AND SWAY,	98	FOXHUNTER		30
THE STARS OF GOD WHERE THEY MOVE,	119	PITY OF LOVE	V	4
THE VERSES THAT COULD MOVE THEM ON THE DAY	257	RECONCILIATION		2
HAS MADE THE VERY OWLS IN CIRCLES MOVE:	423	MY DESCENDANTS		18
THE EXTRAVAGANCE OF SPRING: OR MOVE A HAND	466	HARUN RASHID		125
HANDS UPON EITHER SHOULDER MADE HER MOVE,	466	HARUN RASHID	V	125B
. . . MOVE HIS MOUTH AND SINEWY TONGUE.	560	MAGIC DRUM		5
HIS NUMBERS, THOUGH THEY MOVED OR SEEMED TO MOVE	610	STATUES		2
MOVE MOST GENTLY IF MOVE YOU MUST	617	LONG-LEG FLY		13
MOVE MOST GENTLY IF MOVE YOU MUST	617	LONG-LEG FLY		13
WILL MOVE THE FAINT FAR THUNDER-SOUND, AS THOUGH	699	MOSADA 3	V	10
YOU MOVE IN ANOTHER DOMINION	707	FAIRY PEDANT		5
HE SEES THE FAIRY HOSTING MOVE	716	FAIRY DOCTOR		9
WHILE THE WIND IS LIGHT. THE OAR CAN HARDLY MOVE HER,	754	SHADOW WATER A		157
OR AMONG WINDS THAT MOVE IN THE MEADOWS AND WOODS.	768	SHADOW WATER A	V	413

MOVED

THE IMMORTALS MOVED AMONG THE FOUNTAINS	25	OISIN 1		386
THE FAIRIES MOVED AMONG THE FOUNTAINS,	25	OISIN 1	V	386
"FOR ALL MEN FLEE THE DEMONS": BUT MOVED NOT	36	OISIN 2		93
THE FLOWERS STILL GREW THERE. MOVED BEYOND HIM THE SEA'S WASTE:	39	OISIN 2	V	163
FOR NO LIVE CREATURES LIVED THERE, NO WEASELS MOVED IN THE DARK:	48	OISIN 3		19
HIS LIPS MOVED SLOWLY IN ANSWER, NO ANSWER OUT OF THEM CAME:	51	OISIN 3		66
SQUARE LEAVES OF THE IVY MOVED OVER US, BINDING US DOWN TO OUR REST.	52	OISIN 3		76
MOVED ROUND ME, OF SEAMEN OR LANDSMEN, ALL WHO ARE WINTER TALES:	53	OISIN 3		86
OR MOVED AS THEY MOVED ONCE,	53	OISIN 3		88
OR MOVED AS THEY MOVED ONCE,	53	OISIN 3		88
AND BY ME, IN SOFT RED RAIMENT, THE FENIANS MOVED IN LOUD STREAMS,	53	OISIN 3		93
THAT ONCE MORE MOVED IN MY BOSOM THE ANCIENT SADNESS OF MAN,	54	OISIN 3		107
THAT HAPPIER BREATH HAD MOVED, HER HUSBAND TURNED	185	QUEEN MAEVE		105

542

| | | PAGE | TITLE | LINE |

MOVED   (CONTINUED)

	PAGE	TITLE	LINE
MOVED ROUND ME IN THE SHADOWS, AND AT NIGHT	218	WOODS OF COOLE	19
MOVED ROUND ME IN THE VOICES AND THE FIRES,	218	WOODS OF COOLE	23
THAT OTHER'S MOONLIT EYEBALLS NEVER MOVED,	383	VISION ROBART	33
MIND MOVED YET SEEMED TO STOP	384	VISION ROBART	43
SHE MOVED HER LIMBS CONFUSEDLY AS THOUGH	466	HARUN RASHID	V 125A
AND WROTE BY CANDLE-LIGHT; BUT HER FORM MOVED,	467	HARUN RASHID	129
AND WROTE BY CANDLE LIGHT; BUT HER FORM MOVED	467	HARUN RASHID	V 129
HIS NUMBERS, THOUGH THEY MOVED OR SEEMED TO MOVE	610	STATUES	2
A WRIGGLING THING ON THE WHITE LAKE MOVED,	673	ISLE STAT II 3	176

MOVEMENT

	PAGE	TITLE	LINE
BECOME ONE MOVEMENT, ENERGY, DELIGHT,	231	SHADOW WATER B	217
AND YET YOU TALK OF LOVE. THE MOVEMENT OF TIME	237	SHADOW WATER B	338
OR BODILY MOVEMENT DID I DARE,	514	JANE GROWN OLD	5

MOVEMENTS

	PAGE	TITLE	LINE
THREE MOVEMENTS	485	THREE MOVEMENT	T

MOVES

	PAGE	TITLE	LINE
FOR THERE MOVES ALIVE IN YOUR FINGERS	55	OISIN 3	124
SHE MOVES IN THE FIRELIGHT	89	ISLE IN WATER	3
AND NOW MOVES MANY A PLEASANT TONGUE	98	FOXHUNTER	21
AND MOVES THERE MANY A PLEASANT TONGUE,	98	FOXHUNTER	V 23
HIS MIND MOVES UPON SILENCE.	617	LONG-LEG FLY	10
HER MIND MOVES UPON SILENCE.	617	LONG-LEG FLY	20
HIS HAND MOVES TO AND FRO.	618	LONG-LEG FLY	28
HIS MIND MOVES UPON SILENCE.	618	LONG-LEG FLY	30
HER SPIRIT. AS SHE MOVES, THE FOAM-GLOBES BURST	687	TWO TITANS	14
RE-SHINING IN HIS EYES. SO EVER MOVES	689	NETTLESHIP	12
WHERE MOVES THERE ANY BEAUTIFUL AS I,	720	WITCH VIVIEN	1
CHECK. AH! HOW BRIGHT YOUR EYES. HOW SWIFT YOUR MOVES.	722	WITCH VIVIEN	61

MOVETH

	PAGE	TITLE	LINE
FOR MOVETH ALIVE IN THY FINGERS THE FLUTTERING SADNESS OF EARTH.	55	OISIN 3	V 124
THAT DREAMS. SHE MOVETH, FEELING IN HER BRAIN	687	TWO TITANS	10

MOVIN'

	PAGE	TITLE	LINE
BUT ALWAYS, AS I'M MOVIN' ROUND,	96	MOLL MAGEE	43

MOVING   SEE EVER-MOVING

	PAGE	TITLE	LINE
A WEASEL MOVING ON FROM STONE TO STONE,	102	FERGUS DRUID	5
IS MOVING ITS SLOW THIGHS, WHILE ALL ABOUT IT	402	SECOND COMING	16
AN IMAGE OF THE MOVING HEAVENS.	480	BLOOD AND MOON	14
ALL STATELY WOMEN MOVING TO A SONG	537	HER VISION	17
THAT OF OLD WERT MOVING EVER,	658	ISLE STAT I 3	91
AS FIGURES MOVING MIRRORED IN A GLASS,	676	ISLE STAT II 3	270
WAS MOVING. BLEEDING NOW, HIS GRASP UNLOCKS,	688	TWO TITANS	42
BEYOND WHERE THE WATERS ARE MOVING,	739	WHERE BOOKS GO	7
MOVING THERE AND WALKING;	785	YOUR HEART	5

MOWN   SEE NEW-MOWN

	PAGE	TITLE	LINE
ON THE LEAF-SOWN, NEW MOWN, SMOOTH	568	SWEET DANCER	V 2
AND THE WAVES BOWED BEFORE IT LIKE MOWN CORN,	657	ISLE STAT I 3	56

MR

	PAGE	TITLE	LINE
AND "MR. ALFRED" BE AGAIN	361	ALF POLLEXFEN	32
ON MR. NETTLESHIP'S PICTURE AT THE ROYAL HIBERNIAN ACADEMY.	688	NETTLESHIP	T

MRS

	PAGE	TITLE	LINE
BEYOND THAT RIDGE LIVED MRS. FRENCH, AND ONCE	410	TOWER	25
THROUGH GOD-FORSAKEN MEADOWS; MRS. FRENCH,	412	TOWER	93
JOHN KINSELLA'S LAMENT FOR MRS. MARY MOORE	620	JOHN KINSELLA	T

MUCH   SEE OVER-MUCH

	PAGE	TITLE	LINE
AND YET, OF YORE, MUCH PEACE HE HAD	2	OISIN 1	V 7K
AND YET, OF YORE, MUCH PEACE HE HAD,	4	OISIN 1	V 36
SO MUCH REMAINED THAT ON THE EVENING STAR	32	OISIN 2	V 48
MUCH WONDERING TO SEE UPON ALL HANDS, OF WATTLES AND WOODWORK MADE,	58	OISIN 3	162
MUCH WONDERING TO SEE UPON ALL HANDS, OF WATTLES AND WOOD-WORK MADE,	58	OISIN 3	V 162
SINCE ADAM'S FALL BUT NEEDS MUCH LABOURING.	205	ADAMS CURSE	22
SO MUCH COMPOUNDED OF HIGH COURTESY	205	ADAMS CURSE	24
WE WERE SO MUCH AT ONE. I SHALL FIND A WOMAN,	212	O DO NOT LOVE	8
THAT MUCH IS CERTAIN. I SHALL FIND A WOMAN,	231	SHADOW WATER B	209
SO MUCH STERNNESS AND SUCH CHARM."	259	PEACE	V 8
AND THESE THINGS CAME, SO MUCH THE MORE THEREBY	265	THESE CLOUDS	8
CALLED CRUACHAN, AND IT WAS AS MUCH	302	HOUR DAWN	4
CURSING THE WIND. IT WAS AS MUCH	302	HOUR DAWN	V 4
THOUGH COURTEOUS TO THE WORST; MUCH FALLING HE	324	ROBERT GREGORY	19
MUCH TOO SOLEMN SEEMED;	342	SHEP GOATHERD	91
MUCH TOO SOLEMN AND RESERVED.	342	SHEP GOATHERD	94
BY THE LAGOON YOU LOVE SO MUCH,	386	ROBARTES DANCE	29
FROM CHILDHOOD ON, HAD NOW SO MUCH	397	POLIT PRISONER	2
AND LATER HAD MUCH TROUBLE FROM A FOOL,	404	FOR DAUGHTER	26
THROUGH TOO MUCH BUSINESS WITH THE PASSING HOUR,	423	MY DESCENDANTS	11
THROUGH TOO MUCH PLAY, OR MARRIAGE WITH A FOOL?	423	MY DESCENDANTS	12
MUCH DID I RAGE WHEN YOUNG,	434	YOUTH AND AGE	1
IN AFTER TIME THEY WILL SPEAK MUCH OF ME	462	HARUN RASHID	29
BEFORE THAT END MUCH HAD SHE RAVELLED OUT	472	ALL SOUL NIGHT	51
HE HAD MUCH INDUSTRY AT SETTING OUT,	473	ALL SOUL NIGHT	71
MUCH BOISTEROUS COURAGE, BEFORE LONELINESS	473	ALL SOUL NIGHT	72
CRAZED THROUGH MUCH CHILD-BEARING	487	CRAZED MOON	1
MUCH ON THE GREAT QUESTIONER;	494	AT ALGECIRAS	16
MUST WE PART, VON HUEGEL, THOUGH MUCH ALIKE, FOR WE	503	VACILLATION	78
SO MUCH IS CERTAIN;	504	QUARREL IN AGE	10
LIVES; THAT MUCH IS CERTAIN;	504	QUARREL IN AGE	V 10
NOR SO MUCH AS PARISH PRIEST,	508	JANE BISHOP	11
AND MUCH SAID HE AND I.	513	JANE TALK BISH	2

543

MUCH   (CONTINUED)

	PAGE	TITLE		LINE
THE LOT OF LOVE IS CHOSEN. I LEARNT THAT MUCH	534	CHOSEN		1
BEAST GAVE BEAST AS MUCH.	538	LAST CONFESS		12
MUCH I TALK, MORE I WALK:	548	TO SAME TUNE 3		9
MUCH I TALK, MORE I WALK:	548	TO SAME TUNE 3		19
MUCH I TALK, MORE I WALK:	549	TO SAME TUNE 3		29
BECAUSE HE LOVES TOO MUCH.	588	OLD WICKED MAN		15
THAT I DO MUCH ADORE:	592	DRUNK SOBRIETY		6
"I KEPT HER MUCH IN THE COUNTRY	594	COLONEL MARTIN		10
AND SHE WAS MUCH ALONE,	594	COLONEL MARTIN		11
"YOUR LIFE CAN GROW MUCH SWEETER IF YOU WILL	634	CUCHULAIN COMF		12
O'ER MUCH I'VE TALKED! I SHALL BE SILENT SOON.	657	ISLE STAT I 3		75
GRIEF NEEDS MUCH FEEDING THEN. OF HIM I SWEAR	659	ISLE STAT II 1		20
MOSADA, IT IS THEN SO MUCH THE WORSE:	692	MOSADA 1	V	41A
THE VAPOUR IS MUCH THICKER. GOD! THE STAKE!	695	MOSADA 1		112
A SAINT OF MUNSTER, WHEN MUCH FASTING, SAW	696	MOSADA 2		20
SO MUCH OF WEALTH AS MAY BEFIT THEIR RANK!	756	SHADOW WATER A	V	186
AND A STRONG GALLEY. I GIVE YOU ALL AS MUCH.	758	SHADOW WATER A		222
THERE'S SO MUCH TO THINK ABOUT .	772	SONG DEIRDRE 1		7

MUCH-TOIL

	PAGE	TITLE		LINE
OR WEEDING OR PLOUGHING WITH FACES A-SHINING WITH MUCH-TOIL WET:	58	OISIN 3		165

MUCK

	PAGE	TITLE		LINE
WHAT'S EQUALITY?--MUCK IN THE YARD:	547	TO SAME TUNE 3	V	4

MUD

	PAGE	TITLE		LINE
MY WORKS ARE ALL STAMPED DOWN INTO THE SULTRY MUD.	442	BLACK CENTAUR		3

MUDDY

	PAGE	TITLE		LINE
A LUG-WORM WITH ITS GREY AND MUDDY MOUTH	127	DREAM OF FAERY		18

MUFFLED   SEE SLOW-MUFFLED CLOUD-O'ER-MUFFLED O'ER-MUFFLED

	PAGE	TITLE		LINE
THE PATH O'ER MUFFLED WITH THE LEAVES--DEAD LEAVES,	703	MOSADA 3	V	115

MUIRTHEMNE

	PAGE	TITLE		LINE
TO MANY-PASTURED MUIRTHEMNE,	189	BAILE AILLINN		21
TO MANY PASTURED MUIRTHEMNE,	189	BAILE AILLINN	V	21
IN MUIRTHEMNE, AND OVER IT	194	BAILE AILLINN		116

MULE-BACK

	PAGE	TITLE		LINE
CAMEL-BACK, HORSE-BACK, ASS-BACK, MULE-BACK,	566	LAPIS LAZULI		26

MULTIPLICITY

	PAGE	TITLE		LINE
THE MIRROR-SCALED SERPENT IS MULTIPLICITY,	556	RIBH PATRICK		10
THE MIRROR SCALED SERPENT IS MULTIPLICITY,	556	RIBH PATRICK	V	10

MULTIPLIED

	PAGE	TITLE		LINE
WITH 'MINISHED BEAUTY, MULTIPLIED COMMONPLACE:	472	ALL SOUL NIGHT		45
DIMINISHED BEAUTY, MULTIPLIED COMMONPLACE:	472	ALL SOUL NIGHT	V	45

MULTITUDE

	PAGE	TITLE		LINE
AND THE GREY TIDE, THE RED BRANCH MULTITUDE	108	CUCHULAIN SEA	V	38B
AND OF THE EMBATTLED FLAMING MULTITUDE	137	TO SOME I TALK		10
AND OF THE PROUD EMBATTLED MULTITUDE	137	TO SOME I TALK	V	10
WITH THE LONELY, MAJESTICAL MULTITUDE.	158	TO HIS HEART		7
WITH THE LONELY, PROUD, WINGED MULTITUDE.	158	TO HIS HEART	V	7
WITH THE PROUD, MAJESTICAL MULTITUDE.	158	TO HIS HEART	V	7
GIVE PLACE TO AN INDIFFERENT MULTITUDE, GIVE PLACE	427	PHANTOM HATRED		28
THAT SEEMED SHEER MIRACLE TO THE MULTITUDE,	428	NINETEEN 19		2
A MURMURING FAERY MULTITUDE,	742	DANAAN QUICK		7

MULTITUDINOUS

	PAGE	TITLE		LINE
WINDOWLESS, PILLARLESS, MULTITUDINOUS HOME	39	OISIN 2		148

MUMBLING

	PAGE	TITLE		LINE
AND EVERY MUMBLING OLD MAN SAID,	82	MAD KING GOLL	V	9
AND TRAILING CRIMSON VANS, A MUMBLING BROOD,	687	TWO TITANS		20
BY THE SLOW HEAVING OCEAN--MUMBLING MOTHER OF THE DEAD.	719	PHANTOM SHIP		34
PRAYED BESIDE THE OCEAN, THE OLD MUMBLING MOTHER OF THE DEAD.	719	PHANTOM SHIP	V	34

MUMMERS

	PAGE	TITLE		LINE
HIS MUMMERS TO THE MARKET-PLACE,	287	TO WEALTHY MAN		10
HIS MUMMERS TO THE MARKET PLACE,	287	TO WEALTHY MAN	V	10

MUMMIES

	PAGE	TITLE		LINE
AS MUMMIES IN THE MUMMY-CLOTH ARE WOUND:	471	ALL SOUL NIGHT		14
AS MUMMIES IN THE MUMMY CLOTH ARE WOUND:	471	ALL SOUL NIGHT	V	14
AS MUMMIES IN THE MUMMY-CLOTH ARE WOUND.	474	ALL SOUL NIGHT		100
AS MUMMIES IN THE MUMMY CLOTH ARE WOUND.	474	ALL SOUL NIGHT	V	100

MUMMY

	PAGE	TITLE		LINE
BECAUSE OF SOME GREEN WING, GATHERED OLD MUMMY WHEAT	442	BLACK CENTAUR		7
AS MUMMIES IN THE MUMMY CLOTH ARE WOUND:	471	ALL SOUL NIGHT	V	14
I HAVE MUMMY TRUTHS TO TELL	474	ALL SOUL NIGHT		86
AS MUMMIES IN THE MUMMY CLOTH ARE WOUND.	474	ALL SOUL NIGHT	V	100
FOR HADES' BOBBIN BOUND IN MUMMY CLOTH	497	BYZANTIUM		11
HAD SCOOPED OUT PHARAOH'S MUMMY. I--THOUGH HEART MIGHT FIND RELIEF	503	VACILLATION		84
WHAT A CROP OF MUMMY WHEAT!	562	CONJUNCTIONS		2

MUMMY-CLOTH

	PAGE	TITLE		LINE
AS MUMMIES IN THE MUMMY-CLOTH ARE WOUND:	471	ALL SOUL NIGHT		14
AS MUMMIES IN THE MUMMY-CLOTH ARE WOUND.	474	ALL SOUL NIGHT		100
FOR HADES' BOBBIN BOUND IN MUMMY-CLOTH	497	BYZANTIUM		11

MUMMY-DEAD

	PAGE	TITLE		LINE
EVERYTHING ELSE WITHERED AND MUMMY-DEAD.	618	BRONZE HEAD		3

MUNDI

	PAGE	TITLE		LINE
ROSA MUNDI	111	ROSE OF WORLD	V	T
WHEN A VAST IMAGE OUT OF SPIRITUS MUNDI	402	SECOND COMING		12

MUNICIPAL

	PAGE	TITLE		LINE
. . . TO THE DUBLIN MUNICIPAL GALLERY IF IT WERE PROVED	287	TO WEALTHY MAN		T
THE MUNICIPAL GALLERY REVISITED	601	GALLERY REVIS		T
THE MUNICIPAL GALLERY RE-VISITED	601	GALLERY REVIS	V	T

MUNSTER
    ON MUNSTER GRASS AND CONNEMARA SKIES. . . . .   130 BOOK STORIES   24
    ON MUNSTER GRASS, OR CONNEMARA SKIES. . . . .   130 BOOK STORIES   V 24
    A SAINT OF MUNSTER, WHEN MUCH FASTING, SAW . . . . . .   696 MOSADA 2   20
MURAL
    . . . AND THE LEAVES OF THE MURAL GLEN, ...   49 OISIN 3   35
    WATCHED HER THOSE SEAMLESS FACES FROM THE VALLEY'S MURAL   55 OISIN 3   V 122
        GIRTH
MURDER
    BUT NOW THE LYING CLERICS MURDER SONG . . . .   42 OISIN 2   196
    WHO HAVE PLANNED HIS MURDER, FOR THEY KNOW . . . . . .   436 FOR MY SON   12
    MAY MURDER THEM IN PASSING BY . . . .   791 REPRISALS   21
MURDERED
    AND PROUD AS PRIAM MURDERED WITH HIS PEERS; . . . . .   120 SORROW OF LOVE   8
    CAN LEAVE THE MOTHER, MURDERED AT HER DOOR, ...   429 NINETEEN 19   27
    IT CAN BE MURDERED WITH A SPOT OF INK. . . . .   491 COOLE BALLYLEE   24
    WHEN STRANGERS MURDERED EMMET, FITZGERALD, TONE, . . .   541 PARN FUNERAL 1   17
MURDERER
    "YOU BUT IMAGINE LIES ALL DAY, O MURDERER," I REPLIED. . .   450 OWEN AHERNE   17
MURDERERS
    "VENGEANCE UPON THE MURDERERS," THE CRY GOES UP, . . .   426 PHANTOM HATRED   9
    FOR VENGEANCE ON THE MURDERERS OF JACQUES MOLAY. . . .   426 PHANTOM HATRED   16
MURDERING
    THEN PETER HAD A MURDERING LOOK, ...   457 SUMMER SPRING   9
    ARE MURDERING YOUR TENANTS THERE. . . . .   791 REPRISALS   16
MURDEROUS
    THAT HAS MADE FAT THE MURDEROUS MOTH; . . . .   156 FORGOT BEAUTY   8
    OUT OF THE MURDEROUS INNOCENCE OF THE SEA. . . . . . .   403 FOR DAUGHTER   16
    ABOVE THE MURDEROUS TREACHERY OF THE MOON, ...   428 NINETEEN 19   V 3
    I KNEW THAT HORSE-PLAY, KNEW IT FOR A MURDEROUS THING. .   442 BLACK CENTAUR   4
    I KNEW THAT HORSE PLAY, KNEW IT FOR A MURDEROUS THING. .   442 BLACK CENTAUR V 4
    IN BEAUTY'S MURDEROUS BROOD, ...   451 FIRST LOVE   2
    CONFRONTING MURDEROUS MEN . . . .   476 DEATH   8
    THE MURDEROUS STEALTH OF DAY. . . . .   536 PARTING   8
    NOTHING BUT CROMWELL'S HOUSE AND CROMWELL'S MURDEROUS CREW,   580 CURSE CROMWELL   2
MURDER'S
    AND WHEN AT LAST THAT MURDER'S OVER . . . .   388 SOLOMON WITCH   24
MURIAS
    AND LONG-FORGOTTEN MURIAS, ...   196 BAILE AILLINN   163
    FROM MURMURING MURIAS; ON CUPS-- . . . .   271 GREY ROCK   V 22
    AND TELL HOW MANANAN SACKED MURIAS . . . .   766 SHADOW WATER A   377
MURMUR   SEE A-MURMUR
    MUST MURMUR AT LAST, "UNJUST, UNJUST"; . . . .   28 OISIN 1   420
    "THEY MURMUR LIKE YOUNG PARTRIDGE IN THE MORN, ...   32 OISIN 2   V 51
    FROM SLEEPER UNTO SLEEPER MURMUR YOU. . . . .   33 OISIN 2   V 60
    HEARING HELL LOUD WITH A MURMUR, AS SHOUTING AND MOCKING   62 OISIN 3   208
        WE SWEEP.
    AND LIFE IS OVER SAVE THE MURMUR AND THE SWEETNESS. . .   77 INDIAN TO LOVE V 5E
    AND ALL IS OVER SAVE THE MURMUR AND THE SWEETNESS. . .   77 INDIAN TO LOVE V 5E
    MURMUR, A LITTLE SADLY, HOW LOVE FLED . . . .   121 YOU ARE OLD   10
    MURMUR, A LITTLE SAD, "FROM US FLED LOVE. . . . . . .   121 YOU ARE OLD   V 10
    AH, WHEREFORE MURMUR YE . . . .   131 OLD PENSIONER   V 14
    AND STILL MURMUR AND LONG! . . . .   163 ASKS FORGIVE   18
    AND YOU WOULD MURMUR TENDER WORDS, ...   175 BELOVED DEAD   5
    A MURMUR OF SOFT WORDS AND MEETING LIPS. . . . . . .   187 QUEEN MAEVE   154
    TO MURMUR NAME UPON NAME, ...   394 EASTER 1916   61
    AND MURMUR IT WITH BATED BREATH, AS THOUGH . . . . .   398 LEADERS CROWD   5
    FOR, LOOK YOU, SAD'S THE MURMUR OF THE BEES, ...   652 ISLE STAT I 2   9
    I HEAR THE MURMUR AS THEY RAISE THE BEAMS . . . . . .   699 MOSADA 3   17
    WHILE I MURMUR A LITTLE AND PONDER . . . .   707 FAIRY PEDANT   14
    WHILE THEY MURMUR, "AFTER THIS . . . .   776 AGAINST WITCH   30
MURMURED
    AND MURMURED SNATCHES OF DELIGHT; . . . .   14 OISIN 1   187
    AND THEN LOST NIAMH MURMURED, "LOVE, WE GO . . . . .   46 OISIN 2   245
    AS SHE MURMURED, "O WANDERING OISIN, ...   55 OISIN 3   123
    . . . I MURMURED, "IN OLD AGE THEY CEASED"; . . . . .   59 OISIN 3   177
    AND MY TEARS WERE LARGER THAN BERRIES, AND I MURMURED,   59 OISIN 3   178
        . . .
    AND MY TEARS WERE LARGE LIKE TO BERRIES, AND I MURMURED,   59 OISIN 3   V - 178
        . . .
    MURMURED WITH HER YOUNG VOICE FOR WHOSE MILD SAKE . . .   205 ADAMS CURSE   V 15
    THE LITTLE FOX HE MURMURED, ...   214 HAPPY TOWNLAND   13
    BUT THE LITTLE RED FOX MURMURED, ...   214 HAPPY TOWNLAND   17
    THE LITTLE FOX HE MURMURED, ...   215 HAPPY TOWNLAND   33
    BUT THE LITTLE RED FOX MURMURED, ...   215 HAPPY TOWNLAND   37
    THE LITTLE FOX HE MURMURED, ...   216 HAPPY TOWNLAND   53
    BUT THE LITTLE RED FOX MURMURED, ...   216 HAPPY TOWNLAND   57
    AND MURMURED "MAY GOD CURSE THE NIGHT . . . .   303 HOUR DAWN   V 32B
    WHO HAD MURMURED OF GIORGIONE AT HIS LATEST BREATH-- . .   366 HER COURAGE   8
    MURMURED THE WISDOM OF THE DESERT DJINNS, ...   468 HARUN RASHID   163
    HAS MURMURED WISDOM OF THE DESERT DJINNS, ...   468 HARUN RASHID   V 163
    A PEERING HARE'S!" AND YET I MURMURED NOT, ...   684 SEEKER   56
    THE BISHOP MURMURED, "ATHEIST! . . . .   725 LEGEND   21
    AND MURMURED; "O LONG GREY CLOAK, ...   744 GLOVE CLOAK   11
MURMURING
    AND A HUNDRED ROBES OF MURMURING SILK, ...   8 OISIN 1   88
    WE RODE ON MURMURING. MANY A SHELL . . . .   13 OISIN 1   V 159
    THE MURMURING BIRDS IN SOLEMN POMP . . . .   20 OISIN 1   V 293
    OF MURMURING OCEAN, AND BEHIND US . . . .   25 OISIN 1   V 384
    . . . WITH RED LIPS MURMURING A SONG, ...   58 OISIN 3   V 158
    PIERCING THE TWILIGHT WITH THEIR MURMURING BARBS. . . .   72 ANASHU VIJAYA   28

		PAGE	TITLE	LINE

MURMURING   (CONTINUED)
```
    MURMURING SOFTLY LIP TO LIP,                           78  INDIAN TO LOVE         8
    MURMURING HOW FAR AWAY ARE THE UNQUIET LANDS!          78  INDIAN TO LOVE        10
    MURMURING HOW FAR AWAY ARE ALL EARTH'S FEVERISH LANDS. 78  INDIAN TO LOVE     V  10
    MURMURING GENTLY HOW FAR OFF ARE THE UNQUIET LANDS!    78  INDIAN TO LOVE     V  10
    MURMURING, TO A FITFUL TUNE,                           85  MAD KING GOLL      V  52
    A MURMURING A MOUNTAIN TUNE,                           85  MAD KING GOLL      V  52
    MURMURING A MOUNTAIN TUNE,                             85  MAD KING GOLL      V  52
    IN THE WHITE BORDER OF THE MURMURING SEA!             103  FERGUS DRUID          19
    AND FROM ITS MURMURING GREENNESS, CALM OF FAERY,      129  BOOK STORIES           3
    THE ROAD-SIDE TREES KEEP MURMURING--                  131  OLD PENSIONER      V  13
    MURMURING A WIZARD SONG FOR THEE.                     134  TWO TREES             12
    THAT MURMURING AND LONGING CAME                       162  ASKS FORGIVE           8
    THAT LONGING AND MURMURING CAME                       162  ASKS FORGIVE       V   8
    AND DRUNK UP THE MURMURING TIDE!                      171  MAID QUIET         V  4D
    AND WITH LOW MURMURING LAUGHING SPEECH                195  BAILE AILLINN        137
    I CRIED WHEN THE MOON WAS MURMURING TO THE BIRDS!     203  WITHER BOUGHS          1
    AND DRUID MOONS, AND MURMURING OF BOUGHS,             219  HARP OF AENGUS         4
    AND ALL THAT MURMURING IS BUT A MARRIAGE SONG!        244  SHADOW WATER B     V 452
    FROM MURMURING MURIAS! ON CUPS--                      271  GREY ROCK          V  22
    AND WANDERED MURMURING EVERYWHERE, "MY CHILD, MY CHILD!" 619  BRONZE HEAD        21
    A MURMURING FAERY MULTITUDE,                          742  DANAAN QUICK           7
    AND DRUID MOONS, AND MURMURING OF BOUGHS,             762  SHADOW WATER A       299
    THAT COMES WITH LOVE, COMES MURMURING OF AN HOUR      765  SHADOW WATER A       365
```
MURMURING'S
```
    AND ALL THAT MURMURING'S BUT A MARRIAGE-SONG!         244  SHADOW WATER B       452
```
MURMUROUS
```
    DROPPING! A MURMUROUS DROPPING! OLD SILENCE AND THAT ONE  48  OISIN 3           18
        SOUND!
    WHERE EVER IS MURMUROUS DROPPING, OLD SILENCE AND THAT    56  OISIN 3          138
        ONE SOUND!
    AS LIES DARK WATER IN A MURMUROUS GLADE,             650  ISLE STAT I 1        138
```
MURMURS
```
    AND WITH LOW MURMURS, WE RODE ON,                     13  OISIN 1              159
    AND LAUGHED LIKE MURMURS OF THE SEA!                  15  OISIN 1              210
    AND WITH LOW MURMURS PRAYED TO HIM,                   18  OISIN 1              257
    IN MURMURS, LIKE A FRIGHTED BIRD,                     25  OISIN 1              376
    MY BELL BRANCH MURMURS!  THE GAY BELLS BRING LAUGHTER, 130  BOOK STORIES      V  18
    SEVEN ODOURS, SEVEN MURMURS, SEVEN WOODS.            218  WOODS OF COOLE        16
    SHE MURMURS INTO HIS EAR,                            319  DOLLS                 17
    AND THEN NEW MURMURS CAME NEW UTTERING               657  ISLE STAT I 3         50
    ALONE AMONG THE MURMURS OF THE DAWN,                 702  MOSADA 3              81
    MURMURS OF HER CHILDREN TALKING--                    705  DAWN-SONG              6
    WITH CRIES AND MURMURS.  SUDDENLY HE FLINGS          714  FERENCZ RENYI        101
    AMONG THE MURMURS OF THE BEES,                       728  PRIEST FAIRY          18
    AND A STRING MURMURS AS THOUGH TIME WERE DEAD        752  SHADOW WATER A       124
    THAT MURMURS WITH HOLY WOODS, AND WIN THEIR HELP     757  SHADOW WATER A       199
```
MURROUGH
```
    MURROUGH, THE KING OF IRELAND'S SON,                 274  GREY ROCK             71
    AND BEING THANKFUL MURROUGH FOUND,                   274  GREY ROCK             77
```
MUSCATEL
```
    AND TWO LONG GLASSES BRIMMED WITH MUSCATEL           470  ALL SOUL NIGHT         4
    THE FUME OF MUSCATEL                                 473  ALL SOUL NIGHT        83
```
MUSCLE
```
    MERE BONE AND MUSCLE THROWN ASIDE,                   273  GREY ROCK             51
    THERE IS NO MUSCLE IN THE ARM! AND AFTER,            374  PHASES OF MOON        52
    SHARP THEIR SPADES, THEIR MUSCLE STRONG,             637  BEN BULBEN         V  22
```
MUSCLES
```
    AND WHAT COULD MAKE THEIR MUSCLES TAUT               295  THREE BEGGARS         17
    SHARP THEIR SPADES, THEIR MUSCLES STRONG,            637  BEN BULBEN            22
```
MUSCULAR
```
    IN MUSCULAR YOUTH WELL KNOWN TO MAYO MEN             325  ROBERT GREGORY        34
    IN MUSCULAR YOUTH WELLKNOWN TO MAYO MEN              325  ROBERT GREGORY        34
    IN MUSCULAR YOUTH, AT MEETS OR AT RACECOURSES,       325  ROBERT GREGORY     V  35
```
MUSE
```
    THEN MUSE THEY ON THE HOUSEHOLD WOOL INTENT,          32  OISIN 2            V  55
    THAT WE MAY MUSE IN THE STARLIGHT AND TALK OF THE BATTLES  51  OISIN 3          63
        OF OLD!
    IT SEEMS THAT I MUST BID THE MUSE GO PACK,          409  TOWER                 11
    THE MUSE IS MUTE WHEN PUBLIC MEN                    597  MODEL LAUREATE        17
    GHOSTS OF HER VANISHED GLORIES, MUSE AND STALK      687  TWO TITANS            21
    REMEMBERING THEE, I MUSE, WHILE FADES IN FLIGHT     705  REMEMBRANCE            6
    MOORE ONCE HAD VISITS FROM THE MUSE                 792  GEORGE MOORE           1
```
MUSED
```
    I MUSED ON THE CHASE WITH THE FENIANS, AND BRAN, SCEOLAN, 47  OISIN 3           5
        LOMAIR,
    I SAT AND MUSED AND DRANK SWEET WINE!                82  MAD KING GOLL         13
    HE MUSED BESIDE THE WELL OF SCANAVIN,               127  DREAM OF FAERY        25
    HE MUSED UPON HIS MOCKERS! WITHOUT FAIL             127  DREAM OF FAERY        26
```
MUSES
```
    WHEN MOCKING MUSES CHOSE THE COUNTRY WENCH.         413  TOWER                 96
    AND THEN DID ALL THE MUSES SING                     437  SONGS PLAY 1           6
    WHAT A STAR SANG AND CARELESS MUSES HEARD!          445  SCHOOL CHILDR         47
    THAT NOBLE BLADE THE MUSES BUCKLED ON,              489  COOLE PARK 29         10
    AND WE AND ALL THE MUSES ARE THINGS OF NO ACCOUNT.  580  CURSE CROMWELL        12
    CALL THE MUSES HOME.                                600  THOSE IMAGES           8
    THAT MAKE THE MUSES SING.                           601  THOSE IMAGES          16
```
MUSES'
```
    YOU KEPT THE MUSES' STERNER LAWS,                   273  GREY ROCK             59
```
MUSHROOMS
```
    GATHERING MUSHROOMS IN THE DEW.                     705  DAWN-SONG              8
```

	PAGE	TITLE	LINE

MUSHROOMS   (CONTINUED)

WITH THEIR MUSHROOMS LIGHTLY THREADED . . . . 705 DAWN-SONG 13
GATHERING MUSHROOMS IN THE DEW. . . . . 705 DAWN-SONG 16
GATHERING MUSHROOMS IN THE DEW. . . . . 706 DAWN-SONG 24
GATHERING MUSHROOMS IN THE DEW. . . . . 706 DAWN-SONG 32

MUSIC

MUSIC AND LOVE AND SLEEP AWAIT, ... 9 OISIN 1 103
THE HORSE TOWARDS THE MUSIC RACED, ... 13 OISIN 1 169
THE STEED TOWARDS THE MUSIC RACED, ... 13 OISIN 1 V 169
TO THE MUSIC OF THE GOLDEN RHYME . . . . 14 OISIN 1 V 176
ROLLED ROUND WITH MUSIC OF THE SIGHING SPRAY; . . . . . . 30 OISIN 2 14
OF KNITTED MUSIC. OFT THE FOND REPINING . . . . 33 OISIN 2 V 68C
AND NEVER FIND, THOUGH YE IN MUSIC SPEAK. . . . . 42 OISIN 2 V 201
WRAPT IN THE WAVE OF THAT MUSIC, WITH WEARINESS MORE THAN 51 OISIN 3 69
OF EARTH,
AND WHEN THE WANDERING MUSIC DIES . . . . 99 FOXHUNTER 31
PUT THAT MUSIC IN HER FACE? . . . . 124 CATHLEEN PARA 10
AND MADE MY LIPS AND MUSIC WED, ... 134 TWO TREES 11
A RAPTUROUS MUSIC, TILL THE MORNING BREAK . . . . . . 137 TO SOME I TALK 14
CONTINUAL MUSIC TILL THE MORNING BREAK, ... 137 TO SOME I TALK V 14
BUT LET A GENTLE SILENCE WROUGHT WITH MUSIC FLOW . . . . 175 ELEMENT POWERS 17
BUT LET A GENTLE SILENCE ENWROUGHT WITH MUSIC FLOW . . . 175 ELEMENT POWERS V 17
AS THOUGH THEIR MUSIC WERE ENOUGH . . . . 193 BAILE AILLINN 108
A MUSIC THAT HAD THOUGHT ENOUGH . . . . 193 BAILE AILLINN V 108
SWEET WITH ALL MUSIC, OUT OF HIS LONG HAIR, ... 219 HARP OF AENGUS 8
THAN LOVER'S MUSIC--LET THAT BE, ... 276 GREY ROCK 130
BUT WITH A VOICE THAT HAD UNNATURAL MUSIC, ... 283 TWO KINGS 153
AND I THAT MADE LIKE MUSIC IN MY YOUTH . . . . 342 SHEP GOATHERD 76
THEY HAVE LOUD MUSIC, HOPE EVERY DAY RENEWED . . . . . 398 LEADERS CROWD 11
CAUGHT IN THAT SENSUAL MUSIC ALL NEGLECT . . . . . . 407 SAIL BYZANTIUM 7
MUSIC HAD DRIVEN THEIR WITS ASTRAY-- . . . . 411 TOWER 47
NOR MUSIC NOR AN ENEMY'S CLIPPED EAR . . . . 412 TOWER 75
O BODY SWAYED TO MUSIC, O BRIGHTENING GLANCE, ... 446 SCHOOL CHILDR 63
O BODY SWAYED TO MUSIC BRIGHTENING GLANCE . . . . . . 446 SCHOOL CHILDR V 63
AND WAIT WAR'S MUSIC; PASS THE LITTLE GALLERY; . . . . . 461 HARUN RASHID 8
MY GREAT-GRANDFATHER'S FATHER TALKED OF MUSIC, ... 486 SEVEN SAGES 4
MY GREAT-GRANDFATHER'S FATHER TALKED OF MUSIC AND PAINTING, 486 SEVEN SAGES V 4
WORDS FOR MUSIC PERHAPS . . . . 507 JANE BISHOP V T
A SONG FOR MUSIC . . . . 524 DANCING DAYS V T
AND HEAVENLY MUSIC IF THEY GAVE IT WIT; . . . . 533 HER TRIUMPH 6
AND DEAFENING MUSIC SHOOK THE LEAVES; A TROOP . . . . . 537 HER VISION 13
THAT CRAZED GIRL IMPROVISING HER MUSIC, ... 578 CRAZED GIRL 1
SHE STOOD IN DESPERATE MUSIC WOUND, ... 578 CRAZED GIRL 10
BUT ACTORS LACKING MUSIC . . . . 599 STONE CROSS 17
POETRY, MUSIC, I HAVE LOVED, AND YET . . . . 599 SPIRIT MEDIUM 1
POETRY AND MUSIC I HAVE BANISHED, ... 600 SPIRIT MEDIUM 19
INTOLERABLE MUSIC FALLS. . . . . 612 NEWS ORACLE 32
MAKES ME SWEET MUSIC . . . . 627 STATES HOLIDAY 24
COME FORTH; COME FORTH, MY MUSIC FLOWS FOR THEE, ... 645 ISLE STAT I 1 20
MUSIC OF MY SOUL AND LIGHT-- . . . . 648 ISLE STAT I 1 97
I, AS MUSIC THAT GROWS MUTE, ... 668 ISLE STAT II 3 65
WILD INDOLENCE AND MUSIC HAVE NO DATE. . . . . 686 LIFE 20
FOR THAT'S THE SWEETEST MUSIC FOR SAD SOULS. . . . . . 702 MOSADA 3 85
OH, HUSH THE WANDERING MUSIC OF THY MIND. . . . . . . 703 MOSADA 3 106
WILD INDOLENCE AND MUSIC HAVE NO DATE, ... 735 QUATRAIN APHOR 18
AND HEARD THE MUSIC IN THE WIND, AND SAW . . . . . . 747 SHADOW WATER A 5
WAS FORGAEL'S COURAGE THAT THE MUSIC KILLED. . . . . . 747 SHADOW WATER A 9
TAUGHT ME WISE MUSIC, AND GAVE ME THIS OLD HARP; . . . . 750 SHADOW WATER A 76
SWEET WITH ALL MUSIC, OUT OF HIS LONG HAIR, ... 762 SHADOW WATER A 303
MUSIC OF A LOST KINGDOM . . . . 782 GREY ROUND 2
A WANDERING AIRY MUSIC; . . . . 783 GREY ROUND 7
MUSIC OF A LOST KINGDOM? . . . . 783 GREY ROUND 12
A WANDERING AIRY MUSIC; . . . . 783 GREY ROUND 17

MUSICAL

SHALL BLOW INTO RUIN OUR MUSICAL DAYS, ... 28 OISIN 1 V 425
CARRIES A MUSICAL INSTRUMENT, ... 566 LAPIS LAZULI 42
LOW, LONG AND MUSICAL. A DEW-DROP HUNG . . . . 689 NETTLESHIP 9

MUSING

THE LADIES CLOSE THEIR MUSING EYES. NO PROPHECIES, . . . 426 PHANTOM HATRED 19
HOW "THE ONLY GOOD IS MUSING MILD, ... 728 PRIEST FAIRY 13

MUSINGLY

MUSINGLY WANDERED THE VILLAGE PRIEST. . . . . 728 PRIEST FAIRY 3

MUTE

THE MUSE IS MUTE WHEN PUBLIC MEN . . . . 597 MODEL LAUREATE 17
I, AS MUSIC THAT GROWS MUTE, ... 668 ISLE STAT II 3 65

MUTTER

BECAUSE I MUTTER AS I GO; . . . . 94 MOLL MAGEE 3
WHEN IN RAGGED VAPOUR THEY MUTTER NIGHT AND DAY, ... 206 HANRAHANS SONG V 2
MUTTER SUCH THINGS AS THEY AWAKE FROM TRANCE. . . . . . 229 SHADOW WATER B 163
AND IF SHE HEAR HIM MUTTER OF WILD RIDERS, ... 230 SHADOW WATER B 175
I'D STAND AND MUTTER THERE UNTIL HE CAUGHT . . . . . . 377 PHASES OF MOON 131

MUTTERED

MUTTERED THE OLD CRANE OF GORT. . . . . 295 THREE BEGGARS 6
SEEMED SO ON PURPOSE, MUTTERED JAFFER'S FRIENDS, ... 462 HARUN RASHID 37
THEN CERTAIN SHROUDS THAT MUTTERED HEAD TO HEAD . . . . 634 CUCHULAIN COMF 4
"AVE MARIE," MUTTERED HE . . . . 730 PRIEST FAIRY 51

MUTTERING

WHEN SHE KNOWS THAT. WHAT IS IT THAT YOU ARE MUTTERING-- 236 SHADOW WATER B 303
THE ONE DISASTROUS ZODIAC, MUTTERING . . . . 282 TWO KINGS 128
FIRST WAS MUTTERING A PRAYER. . . . . 298 THREE HERMITS 3
HAS SET ME MUTTERING LIKE A FOOL. . . . . 356 BROKEN DREAMS 26

                                                              PAGE   TITLE   LINE

MUTTERING   (CONTINUED)
        LONE REGENT OF THE WOODS, DEEP MUTTERING, ...   657 ISLE STAT I 3   49
MUTTERS
        ONE LEANS AND MUTTERS BY THE WALL-- . . . .   212 BLESS PSALTER   10
        BUT MAYBE SOME OLD GAFFER MUTTERS A BLESSING . . . . .   355 BROKEN DREAMS   4
MYRIAD
        HIS LANGUID TAIL ABOVE US, LIT WITH MYRIAD SPOTS OF LIGHT. 77 INDIAN ON GOD   20
        AND ALL THE BURDEN OF HER MYRIAD YEARS. . . . .   120 SORROW OF LOVE V   8
        AND ALL THE TROUBLE OF HER MYRIAD YEARS. . . . . . .   120 SORROW OF LOVE V   8
        A MYRIAD HEADS HAVE LAIN." " . . . .   496 MOHINI CHATTER   11
        HAVE NOT A MYRIAD SWAYED BELOW STRANGE TREES . . . . .   724 KANVA ON SELF   11
MYRIADS
        WHERE DROPS OF DEW IN MYRIADS FALL, ...   16 OISIN 1   222
        OF MYRIADS OF BELOVEDS, AND ON THINE . . . .   724 KANVA ON SELF   10
MYRRH
        AND COVERS AWAY THE SMOKE OF MYRRH AND FRANKINCENSE; . . 173 SPEAKS HEARERS   4
MYSTERIES   SEE HEART-MYSTERIES
        BROOD HER HIGH LONELY MYSTERIES. . . . .   156 FORGOT BEAUTY   24
        ON HER MOST LONELY MYSTERIES. . . . .   156 FORGOT BEAUTY V   24
        YOUR THIRST FOR THOSE OLD CRABBED MYSTERIES, ...   465 HARUN RASHID   86
        HEART MYSTERIES THERE, AND YET WHEN ALL IS SAID . . . . 630 CIRCUS ANIMALS V   27
MYSTERIOUS
        . . . GROWN MILD WITH MYSTERIOUS THOUGHT, ...   55 OISIN 3   121
        MYSTERIOUS, BEAUTIFUL; . . . .   323 SWANS AT COOLE   26
        IN THAT MYSTERIOUS, ALWAYS BRIMMING LAKE . . . . . .   356 BROKEN DREAMS   32
        I CALL TO THE MYSTERIOUS ONE WHO YET . . . .   371 EGO DOMINUS   70
        AN IMAGE OF MYSTERIOUS WISDOM WON BY TOIL; . . . . . .   373 PHASES OF MOON   18
        COMPANIONSHIP IN THOSE MYSTERIOUS THINGS . . . .   465 HARUN RASHID   92
MYSTERY
        ON THEIR VAST FACES MYSTERY AND DREAMS; . . . .   74 ANASHU VIJAYA   70
        THE DRUIDS TOOK THEM TO THEIR MYSTERY, ...   111 CUCHULAIN SEA   82
        TO THESE OLD NIGHT SHALL ALL HER MYSTERY TELL; . . . .   114 ROSE OF BATTLE   22
        UPON LOVE'S BITTER MYSTERY; . . . .   125 GOES FERGUS   8
        THE UNCONTROLLABLE MYSTERY ON THE BESTIAL FLOOR. . . .   318 MAGI   8
        A MYSTERY THAT ELSE HAD FOUND NO CHRONICLER . . . . .   461 HARUN RASHID   21
        OF THE STARK MYSTERY THAT HAS DAZED MY SIGHT, ...   466 HARUN RASHID   113
        OR DID THE TORCHLIGHT OF THAT MYSTERY . . . .   466 HARUN RASHID   115
        OF THAT STARK MYSTERY WHERE I AM PLUNGED . . . . . .   466 HARUN RASHID   V   113
        OR DID THE TORCH LIGHT OF THAT MYSTERY . . . .   466 HARUN RASHID   V   115
        OR DID THE TORCH-LIGHT OF THAT MYSTERY . . . .   466 HARUN RASHID   V   115
        AND NOW MY UTMOST MYSTERY IS OUT. . . . .   469 HARUN RASHID   187
        THAT OPENS HER MYSTERY AND FRIGHT. . . . .   624 APPARITIONS   22
        GLAD, SIMPLE--NAY, HE SOUGHT NOT MYSTERY, ...   710 FERENCZ RENYI   30
MYSTIC
        FOR THERE LIVE THE MYSTIC BROTHERHOOD . . . .   148 INTO TWILIGHT V   10
MYSTICAL
        FOR THERE THE MYSTICAL BROTHERHOOD . . . .   148 INTO TWILIGHT   10
        A MYSTICAL PRAYER TO THE MASTERS OF THE ELEMENTS, . . . 174 ELEMENT POWERS V   T
MYTHOLOGICAL
        SOME MORALIST OR MYTHOLOGICAL POET . . . .   430 NINETEEN 19   59
MYTHOLOGIES
        OUT OF OLD MYTHOLOGIES . . . .   320 COAT   3
NA   SEE KYLE-NA-INO KYLE-NA-NO PAIRC-NA-LEE CLOOTH-NA-BARE PAIRC-NA-TARAV
                 PAIRC-NA-CARRAIG
NAIL
        AND PAID YOU ON THE NAIL. TAKE UP THAT ROPE . . . . .   232 SHADOW WATER B   224
        STARED AT THE WINE-DARK NAIL, OR DARK THAT RAN . . . .   537 HER VISION   10
NAILED
        AND THEY HAD NAILED THE BOARDS ABOVE HER FACE, ...   123 DREAM OF DEATH   3
        AND AFTER NAILED UPON THE NIGHT . . . .   519 HER DREAM   7
NAIL-PIERCED
        THE KNOTTED SCOURGE, THE NAIL-PIERCED HANDS, THE WOUNDED 172 TRAV PASSION   V   4
              SIDE,
NAILS
        BY MACE AND SPEAR AND SWORD OF SEA-GODS, NAILS . . . .   31 OISIN 2   V   30A
        GOLDEN THE NAILS OF HIS BIRD-CLAWS, ...   50 OISIN 3   45
        I CRIED, "COME OUT OF THE SHADOW, KING OF THE NAILS OF   51 OISIN 3   61
              GOLD!
        I CRIED, "COME OUT OF THE SHADOW, CANN OF THE NAILS OF   51 OISIN 3   V   61
              GOLD!
        AND DIRTY NAILS OF CARPENTERS. . . . .   440 WISDOM   V   7
        'TIS THOU, FOR THEY'VE GROWN BLUE AROUND THE NAILS.. .   700 MOSADA 3   46
        ARMLETS OF GOLD OR SHIELDS WITH GOLDEN NAILS . . . . .   749 SHADOW WATER A   43
NAISI
        OR ULADH WHEN NAISI HAD HUNG A SAIL UPON THE WIND; . .   209 UNDER THE MOON V   4
NAKED
        THEIR NAKED AND GLEAMING BODIES POURED OUT AND HEAPED IN 48 OISIN 3   28
              THE WAY.
        THEIR MIGHTY AND NAKED AND GLEAMING BODIES . . . . .   48 OISIN 3   V   28
        OUT NAKED ON THE ROADS, AS THE BOOKS SAY, AND STRICKEN . 316 COLD HEAVEN   11
        IN WALKING NAKED. . . . .   320 COAT   10
        "NAKED I LAY, ...   510 JANE JUDGMENT   11
        NAKED AND HIDDEN AWAY, ...   510 JANE JUDGMENT   13
        NAKED TO NAKED GOES, ...   538 LAST CONFESS   16
        NAKED TO NAKED GOES, ...   538 LAST CONFESS   16
        BEAT DOWN UPON THEIR NAKED BODIES, KNOW . . . .   563 MERU   12
NAME
        AENGUS AND EDAIN, MY OWN NAME . . . .   5 OISIN 1   47
        THY NAME, THY KIN, AND THY COUNTRY," . . . .   5 OISIN 1   V   44
        AENGUS AND EDAIN, AND MY NAME . . . .   5 OISIN 1   V   47

```
                                              PAGE    TITLE           LINE
NAME  (CONTINUED)
    YE WORN DEED-DOERS, AND MY NAME  . . . . . . . . . .      5 OISIN 1      V   48
    RHYME THAT RHYMED UPON OISIN'S NAME, . . . . . . . .      7 OISIN 1          64
    AND SET YOUR NAME ALL NAMES ABOVE, . . . . . . . . .      7 OISIN 1          76
    AND MANY A PRINCE OF LOFTY NAME, . . . . . . . . . .      7 OISIN 1      V   63
    AND MANY A MAN OF LOFTY NAME, . . . . . . . . . . .      7 OISIN 1      V   63
    "RHYME, THAT RHYMED TO USHEEN'S NAME, . . . . . . .      7 OISIN 1      V   64
    AND MANY PRINCES OF HIGH NAME. . . . . . . . . . . .      7 OISIN 1      V   68
    SAVE ONLY MANY TIMES MY NAME. . . . . . . . . . . .     25 OISIN 1         375
    THAT SEA-GOD'S NAME, WHO IN A DEEP CONTENT  . . . .     38 OISIN 2         129
    THAT SEA GOD'S NAME, WHO IN A DEEP CONTENT  . . . .     38 OISIN 2      V  129
    HOLDING THAT HORSE, AND SADLY CALLED MY NAME: . . . .     44 OISIN 2         230
    A GOOD NAME IS GOODLY TO HEAR OF, AND A GOOD NAME SURELY 51 OISIN 3      V   63
      IS THINE.
    A GOOD NAME IS GOODLY TO HEAR OF, AND A GOOD NAME SURELY 51 OISIN 3      V   63
      IS THINE.
    AND THE NAME OF THE DEMON WHOSE HAMMER . . . . . . .     52 OISIN 3          80
    ANOTHER FILLS YOUR MIND.  MY MOTHER'S NAME. . . . .     71 ANASHU VIJAYA     16
    SOME OTHER FILLS YOUR MIND.  MY MOTHER'S NAME. . . .     71 ANASHU VIJAYA V   16
    BUT TELL YOUR NAME AND LINEAGE TO HIM  . . . . . . .    108 CUCHULAIN SEA     36
    BUT TELL ALONE YOUR NAME AND HOUSE TO HIM  . . . . .    108 CUCHULAIN SEA V   36
    "HE BADE ME LET ALL KNOW HE GIVES HIS NAME  . . . .    109 CUCHULAIN SEA     52
    THE CARS OF BATTLE AND HIS OWN NAME CRIED: . . . . .    111 CUCHULAIN SEA     85
    AND, LIKE A STORM, CRY THE INEFFABLE NAME, . . . . .    137 TO SOME I TALK    12
    AND SOME ONE CALLED ME BY MY NAME: . . . . . . . . .    149 WANDER AENGUS     12
    AND SOMEONE CALLED ME BY MY NAME. . . . . . . . . .    149 WANDER AENGUS V   12
    WHO CALLED ME BY MY NAME AND RAN  . . . . . . . . .    150 WANDER AENGUS     15
    THAT CALLED ME BY MY NAME AND RAN  . . . . . . . . .    150 WANDER AENGUS V   15
    THE POWERS WHOSE NAME AND SHAPE NO LIVING CREATURE KNOWS 174 ELEMENT POWERS   1
    TO THAT HIGH HILL THE HERDSMEN NAME  . . . . . . . .    194 BAILE AILLINN    129
    WE SAT GROWN QUIET AT THE NAME OF LOVE: . . . . . .    205 ADAMS CURSE       28
    HOW SHALL I NAME YOU, IMMORTAL, MILD, PROUD SHADOWS?  .  218 WOODS OF COOLE    27
    WHAT NAME TO CALL HIM BY?  COME TO HIS SHIP, . . . .    240 SHADOW WATER B   390
    HIS NAME WILL COME INTO OUR THOUGHTS IN A MINUTE. . .    241 SHADOW WATER B   391
    WHAT NAME HAD THAT DEAD KING?  ARTHUR OF BRITAIN?  .    242 SHADOW WATER B   404
    BY THE SWEET NAME OF DEATH. . . . . . . . . . . . .    254 HIS DREAM         12
    BY THE SWEET NAME OF DEATH. . . . . . . . . . . . .    254 HIS DREAM         20
    AND CARVE HIS NAME IN OGHAM."  EOCHAID SAID, . . . .    280 TWO KINGS         83
    I'LL NAME THE FRIENDS THAT CANNOT SUP WITH US  . . .    323 ROBERT GREGORY     2
    BUT GROWS MORE GENTLE WHEN HE SPEAKS HER NAME, . . .    340 SHEP GOATHERD     29
    BUT PUT NO NAME AND LEAVE THEM AT HER DOOR. . . . .    343 SHEP GOATHERD    116
    AS THOUGH SOME OTHER NAME RAN IN HIS HEAD. . . . . .    351 HER PRAISE         9
    MANAGE THE TALK UNTIL HER NAME COME ROUND. . . . . .    351 HER PRAISE        14
    IF THERE BE RAGS ENOUGH HE WILL KNOW HER NAME  . . .    351 HER PRAISE        15
    OF SOME STRANGE WOMAN'S NAME THAT RAN IN HIS HEAD. .    351 HER PRAISE     V   9
    MANAGE TO TALK UNTIL HER NAME COME ROUND. . . . . .    351 HER PRAISE     V  14
    AND CALLED HER NAME, SHE HAD HEARD, . . . . . . . .    381 SONGS FOOL 2      11
    AND OF A MIDDLETON, WHOSE NAME YOU NEVER HEARD, . . .    391 UNDER SATURN       8
    TO MURMUR NAME UPON NAME, . . . . . . . . . . . . .    394 EASTER 1916       61
    TO MURMUR NAME UPON NAME, . . . . . . . . . . . . .    394 EASTER 1916       61
    CEREMONY'S A NAME FOR THE RICH HORN, . . . . . . . .    406 FOR DAUGHTER      79
    KUSTA BEN LUKA IS MY NAME, I WRITE  . . . . . . . .    460 HARUN RASHID       1
    HOW IN THE NAME OF HEAVEN CAN HE ESCAPE  . . . . . .    479 SELF AND SOUL     50
    WHERE NONE HAS REIGNED THAT LACKED A NAME AND FAME  .    491 COOLE BALLYLEE    31
    WHATEVER'S WRITTEN IN WHAT POETS NAME  . . . . . . .    492 COOLE BALLYLEE    43
    ALL THAT IS WRITTEN IN WHAT POETS NAME . . . . . . .    492 COOLE BALLYLEE V  43
    HAD EVEN O'DUFFY--BUT I NAME NO MORE--  . . . . . .    543 PARN FUNERAL 2     9
    INTO ONE NAME: . . . . . . . . . . . . . . . . . .    572 LADYS 1ST SONG     6
    AND BLACKENED HIS GOOD NAME. . . . . . . . . . . . .    582 ROGER CASEMENT     8
    SING A "THE" BEFORE HIS NAME: . . . . . . . . . . .    584 ORAHILLY           3
    BUT MANNION IS MY NAME, . . . . . . . . . . . . . .    605 SONGS BURDEN 1     2
    MY NAME IS HENRY MIDDLETON, . . . . . . . . . . . .    606 SONGS BURDEN 1     1
    GIVE TONGUE, PROCLAIM THEIR HIDDEN NAME--"HOUND VOICE."  622 HOUND VOICE        7
    AND IN THAT TERROR'S NAME OBEYED THE CALL, . . . . .    622 HOUND VOICE       12
    THE COUNTESS CATHLEEN WAS THE NAME I GAVE IT: . . . .    629 CIRCUS ANIMALS    18
    WE SAW THE DOLOROUS LAKE: AND THEN THY NAME  . . . .    659 ISLE STAT II 1     7
    FOR THIS THING FIGHT--WE LOVE ONE MAID?  HER NAME?  .    661 ISLE STAT II 1    66
    TWO CAME, HIS NAME AND MINE ON MANY A TREE  . . . .    662 ISLE STAT II 2    10
    IN SAND HIS NAME AND MINE I'VE ALSO READ. . . . . .    662 ISLE STAT II 2    12
    HERE, FACING TO THE LAKE, AND NO NAME GILD: . . . .    663 ISLE STAT II 2    20
    TAKEN IN MAGIC, IN THE CHURCH'S NAME . . . . . . . .    694 MOSADA 1         104
    THY NAME IS?"  "RENYI."  "OF?"  "THIS VILLAGE."  "GOOD!  709 FERENCZ RENYI    13
    THY NAME IS?"  "FERENCZ RENYI."  "OF?"  "THIS VILLAGE."  709 FERENCZ RENYI V  13
      "GOOD!
    OF TRAITOR EVERMORE IS ON OUR NAME." . . . . . . . .    712 FERENCZ RENYI    61
    OF' TRAITOR EVER MORE IS ON OUR NAME." . . . . . . .    712 FERENCZ RENYI V  61
    HUSH'D THE FISHERS, TILL A MOTHER CALLS BY NAME HER DROWNED 719 PHANTOM SHIP   23
      SON:
    THEN EACH WIFE AND MAID AND MOTHER CALLS BY NAME    719 PHANTOM SHIP      24
      SOME DROWNED ONE.
NAMED
    AND NAMED HIM BY SWEET NAMES.  A FOAMING TIDE  . . .     30 OISIN 2          27
    THERE WAS A MAN WHOM SORROW NAMED HIS FRIEND, . . .     67 SAD SHEPHERD       1
    AND THEN THE MAN WHOM SORROW NAMED HIS FRIEND  . . .     68 SAD SHEPHERD       8
    AND THEN THE MAN WHOM SORROW NAMED HIS FRIEND  . . .     68 SAD SHEPHERD      17
    THEN CRIED THE MAN WHOM SORROW NAMED HIS FRIEND: . .     68 SAD SHEPHERD   V   8
    FAR, FAR AWAY.  I NAMED HIM AFTER YOU. . . . . . . .     72 ANASHU VIJAYA     35
    FAR, FAR AWAY.  I'VE NAMED HIM AFTER YOU. . . . . .     72 ANASHU VIJAYA V   35
    MEN HAVE NAMED BEAUTY.  THY GREAT LEAVES ENFOLD  . .    169 SECRET ROSE        7
    MEN HAVE NAMED BEAUTY.  YOUR HEAVY LEAVES ENFOLD  .    169 SECRET ROSE    V   7
    MEN HAVE NAMED BEAUTY.  YOUR GREAT LEAVES ENFOLD  .    169 SECRET ROSE    V   7
```

549

		PAGE	TITLE		LINE

NAMED (CONTINUED)
| IF THESE HAVE NAMED IT RIGHT | · · · · · · · | 500 | VACILLATION | V | 9 |
| WHOM MEN HAVE NAMED ARCADIA'S SWEETEST TONGUE. | · · · · · | 649 | ISLE STAT I 1 | | 109 |

NAMES
AND SET YOUR NAME ALL NAMES ABOVE,	· · · · · ·	7	OISIN 1		76
NOW, MAN OF CROZIERS, SHADOWS CALLED OUR NAMES	· · · ·	29	OISIN 2		1
HALF LOST IN VAPOUR, SHADOWS CALLED OUR NAMES,	· · · ·	29	OISIN 2	V	3
AND NAMED HIM BY SWEET NAMES. A FOAMING TIDE.	· · · ·	30	OISIN 2		27
AND CALLED HIM SWEETEST NAMES AND SOOTHED HIS FEARS.	· ·	30	OISIN 2	V	27
AND EVEN THE NAMES OF HIS FATHERS, AND EVEN THE WORKS OF HIS HANDS?		51	OISIN 3	V	62
AND THE NAMES OF THE DEMONS WHOSE HAMMERS	· · · · · ·	52	OISIN 3	V	80
AS MY MIND MADE THE NAMES OF THE FENIANS.	· · · · ·	57	OISIN 3		146
THE NAMES THAT STILLED YOUR CHILDISH PLAY,	· · · · ·	289	SEPTEMBER 1913		10
AS A MOTHER NAMES HER CHILD	· · · · · · ·	394	EASTER 1916		62
BUT NAMES ARE NOTHING. WHAT MATTER WHO IT BE,	· · · ·	473	ALL SOUL NIGHT		81
BUT NAMES ARE NOTHING. I CARE NOT WHO IT BE.	· · · ·	473	ALL SOUL NIGHT	V	81
THAT HAS THE WORST OF ALL BAD NAMES!	· · · · · ·	531	FATHER CHILD		5
NO MATTER WHAT THE NAMES THEY WEAR!	· · · · · ·	582	ROGER CASEMENT	V	17
NAMES AFTER ME, LADY--I COME. FORGIVE,	· · · · ·	695	MOSADA 1		117
OF THE GREAT WARRIORS WHOSE NAMES HAVE SUNG	· · · · ·	698	MOSADA 2		60
AND UNFORGOTTEN NAMES, AND THE COLD STARS	· · · · ·	757	SHADOW WATER A		204
NAMES WHEREBY A MAN HAS KNOWN	· · · · · ·	775	AGAINST WITCH		5
THEN THOSE OTHERS THAT ARE BUT NAMES OR NAMES	· · · ·	790	DEDICATION		9
THEN THOSE OTHERS THAT ARE BUT NAMES OR NAMES	· · · ·	790	DEDICATION		9

NAMING
| NAMING IT WITH ECSTATIC BREATH, | · · · · · · · | 254 | HIS DREAM | | 18 |

NAN
AND OUR POOR KATE OR NAN IS LESS	· · · · · ·	190	BAILE AILLINN		35
AND WHEN WE WALK WITH KATE OR NAN	· · · · ·	192	BAILE AILLINN		92
THERE'S MARGARET AND MARJORIE AND DOROTHY AND NAN,	· ·	354	HIS PHOENIX		17

NAOISE
| WHO KNOW THE WAY THAT NAOISE WENT? | · · · · · · | 193 | BAILE AILLINN | | 96 |
| NOR ULADH, WHEN NAOISE HAD THROWN A SAIL UPON THE WIND; | | 209 | UNDER THE MOON | | 4 |

NAPE
| BY THE DARK WEBS, HER NAPE CAUGHT IN HIS BILL, | · · · · | 441 | LEDA AND SWAN | | 3 |

NAPKIN
| VERONICA'S NAPKIN | · · · · · · · · · | 483 | VERONIC NAPKIN | | T |
| A PATTERN ON A NAPKIN DIPPED IN BLOOD. | · · · · · · | 483 | VERONIC NAPKIN | | 8 |

NAPS
| IN THEIR DOWNY CAPS, AND STARTLE THE NAPS | · · · · · | 644 | SONG FAERIES | | 11 |
| IN THEIR DOWNY CAPS, AND STARTLE THE NAPS | · · · · · | 676 | ISLE STAT II 3 | | 258 |

NARCISSUS
| WHERE GOLDEN CROCUS AND NARCISSUS BLOOM, | · · · · · · | 447 | COLONUS PRAISE | | 18 |

NARROW
AND TOSS AND TURN IN NARROW CAVES!	· · · · · ·	19	OISIN 1		281
AND HEAR THE NARROW GRAVES CALLING MY CHILD AND ME.	· · ·	147	UNAPPEAS HOST		6
SHE BUILDS HER NEST UPON A NARROW LEDGE	· · · · ·	285	TWO KINGS		194
CLIMB UP THE NARROW WINDING STAIR TO BED!	· · · · ·	324	ROBERT GREGORY		5
IN THE NARROW THEME OF LOVE	· · · · · · · ·	333	SOLOMON SHEBA		7
ARE BUT A NARROW POUND."	· · · · · · · ·	333	SOLOMON SHEBA		16
THE WORLD A NARROW POUND."	· · · · · · ·	333	SOLOMON SHEBA		24
IN THE ONE NARROW THEME OF LOVE	· · · · · · ·	333	SOLOMON SHEBA	V	7
INTO ITS NARROW SHED.	· · · · · · · · ·	358	BALLOON MIND		4
AS NARROW NATURES WOULD	· · · · · · · ·	365	HER RACE		2
OR SHOD IN IRON, CLIMBED THE NARROW STAIRS,	· · · · ·	412	TOWER		83
CROSS THE NARROW STRAITS TO LIGHT	· · · · ·	494	AT ALGECIRAS		4
CROSSES THE NARROW STRAITS TO LIGHT	· · · · ·	494	AT ALGECIRAS	V	4
CROSS THOSE NARROW STRAITS TO LIGHT	· · · · ·	494	AT ALGECIRAS	V	4
IN THE NARROW PASS!	· · · · · · · · ·	512	JANE ON GOD		11
THE WOMEN-SLINGERS ON THE NARROW BRIDGE,	· · · · ·	749	SHADOW WATER A		41
A CAPTIVE WOMAN FROM THE NARROW BRIDGE,	· · · · ·	749	SHADOW WATER A		49
THE WOMEN SLINGERS ON THE NARROW BRIDGE,	· · · · ·	749	SHADOW WATER A	V	41

NARROWS
| THE TIDE NARROWS BETWEEN, AND ONE OLD MAN | · · · · · | 752 | SHADOW WATER A | | 118 |

NASCHINA
TO WELCOME THEE, NASCHINA, WITH SWEET SINGING.	· · · ·	645	ISLE STAT I 1		7
THEIR SHEEP IN ARCADY, NASCHINA, HAIL!	· · · · ·	649	ISLE STAT I 1		119
NASCHINA, HAIL! MOST FAIR OF ALL WHO GRAZE	· · · ·	649	ISLE STAT I 1		120
THEIR SHEEP IN ARCADY, NASCHINA, HAIL!	· · · · ·	649	ISLE STAT I 1		121
NASCHINA, HAIL! I'D DRIVE THY WOOLLY SHEEP,	· · · ·	649	ISLE STAT I 1		122
NASCHINA, WHEREFORE ARE YOUR EYES SO BRIGHT	· · · ·	650	ISLE STAT I 1		141
OH STAY, NASCHINA, STAY!	· · · · · · · ·	650	ISLE STAT I 1		153
WE LOVE NASCHINA BOTH. WHOM LOVES SHE BEST?	· · · ·	660	ISLE STAT II 1		48
NASCHINA. OH, I KNOW HER WELL--A LAME,	· · · · ·	661	ISLE STAT II 1		67
THE OTTERS DREAMING LAY. NASCHINA! AY!	· · · · ·	677	ISLE STAT II 3	V	280

NASCHINA'S
| NASCHINA'S GONE, DRAWN BY A THIRST OF LOVE, | · · · · · | 664 | ISLE STAT II 2 | | 59 |
| AND OF NASCHINA'S NOW THEY TELL--REND! REND! | · · · · | 665 | ISLE STAT II 2 | | 69 |

NATION
AH, WORLD-WIDE NATION, ALWAYS GROWING SORROW,	· · · ·	130	BOOK STORIES	V	11
AH, WORLDWIDE NATION, ALWAYS GROWING SORROW!	· · · ·	130	BOOK STORIES	V	11
IS EVERY MODERN NATION LIKE THE TOWER,	· · · · ·	482	BLOOD AND MOON		47
IS EVERY NATION LIKE THE TOWER ·	· · · · · ·	482	BLOOD AND MOON	V	47
'TWAS EVENING, AND THE CRICKET NATION SANG	· · · · ·	690	MOSADA 1		18
ONCE IN THY NATION NONE SHALL KNOW THAT I	· · · ·	702	MOSADA 3		82
AMONG THY NATION NONE SHALL KNOW THAT I	· · · ·	702	MOSADA 3	V	82
THEREFORE, O NATION OF THE BLEEDING BREAST,	· · · · ·	709	FERENCZ RENYI		4
YE BY THE WAVES THAT CLOSE IN OUR SAD NATION,	· · · ·	738	MOURN THEN ON		5

NATIONAL
| HALF DRESSED IN NATIONAL UNIFORM, | · · · · · · | 424 | ROAD AT DOOR | | 7 |

		PAGE	TITLE		LINE
NATIONS					
	AND DROWNED THE TREASURES OF NINE CONQUERED NATIONS,	235	SHADOW WATER B		287
	GREAT NATIONS BLOSSOM ABOVE!	547	TO SAME TUNE 3		5
	HISTORIC NATIONS GROW	547	TO SAME TUNE 3	V	5
	WHEN NATIONS ARE EMPTY UP THERE AT THE TOP,	548	TO SAME TUNE 3		11
	GREAT NATIONS BLOSSOM ABOVE!	614	MARCH SONGS 2		5
	BOWING NATIONS, PLUMED WARS—	737	IN FIRELIGHT		10
NATIVITY					
	A NATIVITY	625	NATIVITY		T
	THAT WHEN THE STARS OF OUR NATIVITY	691	MOSADA 1		28
	OF OUR NATIVITY HANG SIDE BY SIDE,	701	MOSADA 3		53
NATURAL					
	MAYBE IT IS BUT NATURAL TO DOUBT ME.	227	SHADOW WATER B		112
	THERE'S NOBODY IS NATURAL BUT A ROBBER,	233	SHADOW WATER B		237
	THAT IS NOT NATURAL IN AN AGE LIKE THIS,	257	NO SECOND TROY		9
	SPONTANEOUS JOY AND NATURAL CONTENT	260	FASC DIFFICULT		3
	IN LOGIC AND IN NATURAL LAW	288	TO WEALTHY MAN		27
	YOU SING AS ALWAYS OF THE NATURAL LIFE,	342	SHEP GOATHERD		75
	WHEN IT HAS VANISHED FROM OUR NATURAL EYES!	342	SHEP GOATHERD		81
	CAN HAVE THE PURITY OF A NATURAL FORCE,	353	PEOPLE		31
	THAT EVERY NATURAL VICTORY	401	DEMON BEAST		34
	RIGHT MASTERY OF NATURAL THINGS,	401	DEMON BEAST		37
	LOSE NATURAL KINDNESS AND MAYBE	404	FOR DAUGHTER		22
	MY BODILY FORM FROM ANY NATURAL THING,	408	SAIL BYZANTIUM		26
	THROUGH NATURAL DECLENSION OF THE SOUL,	423	MY DESCENDANTS		10
	FOR THAT IS NATURAL TO A MAN	459	HIS WILDNESS		9
	A DOZEN NIGHTS OF NATURAL SLEEP, AND THEN	468	HARUN RASHID		150
	THAT'S HOW ALL NATURAL OR SUPERNATURAL STORIES RUN.	556	RIBH PATRICK		3
	NATURAL AND SUPERNATURAL WITH THE SELF-SAME RING ARE WED.	556	RIBH PATRICK		4
NATURE					
	FROM THE BOOK OF KAURI THE INDIAN— SECTION V. ON THE	76	INDIAN ON GOD	V	T
	NATURE OF GOD				
	DREAM, UNTIL GOD BURN NATURE WITH A KISS?	128	DREAM OF FAERY		47
	UNTIL HE BURN UP NATURE WITH A KISS!—	128	DREAM OF FAERY	V	47
	THAT IT CAN TAKE WHAT FORM COOK NATURE FANCIES	377	PHASES OF MOON		115
	THAT IT CAN TAKE WHAT FORM COOK NATURE FANCY	377	PHASES OF MOON	V	115
	SO SENSITIVE HIS NATURE SEEMED,	392	EASTER 1916		29
	COULD ROUSE MY WHOLE NATURE.	400	DEMON BEAST		32
	ONCE OUT OF NATURE I SHALL NEVER TAKE	408	SAIL BYZANTIUM		25
	PLATO THOUGHT NATURE BUT A SPUME THAT PLAYS	445	SCHOOL CHILDR		41
	THAT JUGGLING NATURE MOUNTS, HER COIL IN THEIR EMBRACES	556	RIBH PATRICK		9
	TWINED.				
	THE SAGE, WHO DEEP IN CENTRAL NATURE DELVES,	686	LIFE		2
	THE SAGE WHO DEEP IN CENTRAL NATURE DELVES,	734	QUATRAIN APHOR		2
NATURE'D					
	FOR NATURE'D PULLED HER TRAGIC BUSKIN ON	490	COOLE BALLYLEE	V	12
NATURE'S					
	GREAT WORKS CONSTRUCTED THERE IN NATURE'S SPITE	488	COOLE PARK 29		5
	FOR NATURE'S PULLED HER TRAGIC BUSKIN ON	490	COOLE BALLYLEE		12
	FOR NATURE'S PULLED HER TRAGIC BUCKSKIN ON	490	COOLE BALLYLEE	V	12
	NATURE'S PURE UNCHANGING LIGHT?	529	TOM LUNATIC		6
NATURES					
	AS NARROW NATURES WOULD	365	HER RACE		2
	BY QUIET NATURES UNDERSTOOD	405	FOR DAUGHTER		63
	TOLD, AND IT SEEMED THAT OUR TWO NATURES BLENT	443	SCHOOL CHILDR		13
NAUGHT					
	. . . THE STRENGTH OF THE BELL-BRANCH IS NAUGHT,	55	OISIN 3		123
	BUT NAUGHT THEY HEARD, FOR THEY ARE ALWAYS LISTENING,	68	SAD SHEPHERD		15
	BUT NAUGHT THEY HEARD, FOR THEY ARE EVER LISTENING,	68	SAD SHEPHERD	V	15
	TILL THERE BE NAUGHT BUT THRONE ON THRONE	156	FORGOT BEAUTY	V	21
	IT ALL, AND MORE THAN IT ALL, WOULD COME TO NAUGHT,	201	OLD MEMORY		8
	IT ALL, MORE THAN IT ALL, WOULD COME TO NAUGHT,	201	OLD MEMORY	V	8
	OUR STITCHING AND UNSTITCHING HAS BEEN NAUGHT.	204	ADAMS CURSE		6
	THEY CLOSED THEIR BLOOD-SHOT EYES FOR NAUGHT.	296	THREE BEGGARS	V	44
	WE HAVE NAUGHT FOR DEATH BUT TOYS.	363	DOLLS DRAWINGS		11
	LET THE FOOLS RAGE, I SWERVED IN NAUGHT,	577	WHAT THEN		18
	KNOW'ST NAUGHT OF THIS. AND, UNCOUTH HUNTER, NOW—	651	ISLE STAT I 1		168
	WITHIN MINE HEART; AND NAUGHT BUT SORROW NOW	659	ISLE STAT II 1		26
	AND MADE THEIR GLORY NAUGHT.	741	EARL PAUL		44
	"LOVE WOULD BE A THING OF NAUGHT	772	SONG DEIRDRE 1		10
	ON NAUGHT HAS SET STORE	780	WELL AND TREE		13
NAY					
	YOUNG WARRIOR." "NAY," I ANSWERED! "MY HANDS BURN	35	OISIN 2	V	89B
	. . . HE CRIED, "NAY, THE GODS A LONG TIME ARE DEAD."	59	OISIN 3	V	180
	AND ENTER, AND NONE SAYETH "NAY"	62	OISIN 3	V	210
	HAIL! HAIL, MY ANASHUYA. NAY! BE STILL.	71	ANASHU VIJAYA	V	11
	FAREWELL, VIJAYA. NAY, NO WORD, NO WORD!	75	ANASHU VIJAYA		83
	"NAY, YOU ARE TALLER THAN CUCHULAIN, SON."	107	CUCHULAIN SEA	V	27
	"NAY, HE IS OLD AND SAD WITH MANY WARS,	107	CUCHULAIN SEA	V	29
	NAY, NAY, I MISS'D HIM NOT; HIS DAYS	649	ISLE STAT I 1		117
	NAY, NAY, I MISS'D HIM NOT; HIS DAYS	649	ISLE STAT I 1		117
	NAY, NAY, ALMINTOR, YONDER SONG IS GLAD.	652	ISLE STAT I 2		23
	NAY, NAY, ALMINTOR, YONDER SONG IS GLAD.	652	ISLE STAT I 2		23
	THE LAKE-EMBOSOMED ISLE. NAY, THIS MY QUEST	657	ISLE STAT I 3		60
	NAY, GRIEF IN FEEDING ON OLD GRIEF GROWS LESS.	659	ISLE STAT II 1		19
	I'D KILL HER IF SHE WERE. NAY, DO NOT FEAR!	669	ISLE STAT II 3		69
	NAY, HE IS GONE. WAKE! WAKE! AS A BEE SIPS	678	ISLE STAT II 3		305
	NAY, GIVE IT ME, AND I WILL SOUND A MEASURE!	681	SEEKER		9
	NAY HERE, I'LL LAY ME DOWN WHERE I CAN WATCH	700	MOSADA 3		39
	GLAD, SIMPLE—NAY, HE SOUGHT NOT MYSTERY,	710	FERENCZ RENYI		30
	WE GATHERED. FERENCZ, NAY, I MUST NOT DIE!	713	FERENCZ RENYI		96

551

		PAGE	TITLE		LINE

NAY (CONTINUED)
BESIDE THE WILLOW. NAY, TO YONDER STAR, ... 715 FERENCZ RENYI 118
BENEATH THE WILLOW--NAY, TO YONDER STAR, ... 715 FERENCZ RENYI V 118
NAY, RISE AND FLATTER HER WITH GOLDEN RHYME, ... 724 KANVA ON SELF 19
NEAR
CAOILTE, CONAN, AND FINN CAME NEAR, ... 10 OISIN 1 111
NEAR BY, THE FENIANS SAW, AND KNEW . . . . 10 OISIN 1 V 111
FOR NEITHER DEATH NOR CHANGE COMES NEAR US, ... 21 OISIN 1 316
FOR CHANGE AND DEATH THEY COME NOT NEAR US, ... 21 OISIN 1 V 316
GOD SHAKES THE WORLD WITH RESTLESS HANDS. MORE NEAR . . 43 OISIN 2 V 208
SAD NIAM CAME NEAR ME, AND LAID HER BROWS ON THE MIDST 52 OISIN 3 V 74
OF MY BREAST
AMRITA. DRAW YOU NEAR, AND 'NEATH YON PILLAR . . . . 71 ANASHU VIJAYA V 13A
WITH HORSEMEN HURRYING NEAR AND FAR, ... 83 MAD KING GOLL V 18
AND HARES RUN NEAR ME GROWING BOLD. . . . . . . 84 MAD KING GOLL V 47
BRING MY BROWN HUNTER NEAR. . . . . 97 FOXHUNTER V 6
THE HUNTSMAN NEAR HIM STANDS. . . . . 98 FOXHUNTER 24
THE HUNTSMAN NEAR HIM STANDS. . . . . 98 FOXHUNTER V 22
COME NEAR ME, WHILE I SING THE ANCIENT WAYS! . . . . 100 ROSE UPON ROOD 2
COME NEAR, THAT NO MORE BLINDED BY MAN'S FATE, . . . 101 ROSE UPON ROOD 9
COME NEAR, COME NEAR, COME NEAR--AH, LEAVE ME STILL . . 101 ROSE UPON ROOD 13
COME NEAR, COME NEAR, COME NEAR--AH, LEAVE ME STILL . . 101 ROSE UPON ROOD 13
COME NEAR, COME NEAR, COME NEAR--AH, LEAVE ME STILL . . 101 ROSE UPON ROOD 13
COME NEAR! I WOULD, BEFORE MY TIME TO GO, ... 101 ROSE UPON ROOD 22
NEAR TO CUCHULLIN, ROUND A QUICKEN TREE, ... 111 CUCHULAIN SEA V 81A
THE THRONGS WITH BLOWN WET HAIR ARE GATHERING NEAR. . . 114 ROSE OF BATTLE V 6
WHERE TIME WOULD SURELY FORGET US, AND SORROW COME NEAR 122 WHITE BIRDS 10
US NO MORE!
WHERE SURELY TIME WOULD FORGET US AND SORROW COME NEAR 122 WHITE BIRDS V 10
US NO MORE!
NEAR NO ACCUSTOMED HAND! . . . . 123 DREAM OF DEATH 2
BELIEVED THERE WAS SOME OTHER NEAR AT HAND, ... 229 SHADOW WATER B 154
IF ANY MAN DREW NEAR . . . . 254 WOMAN HOMER 1
"WE RIDE BUT SLOWLY THOUGH SO NEAR OUR HOME," . . . . 276 TWO KINGS V A
"THOUGH THE DOOR OF DEATH IS NEAR . . . . 298 THREE HERMITS 8
HELL MOUTH LAY OPEN NEAR THAT PLACE, ... 303 HOUR DAWN 25
"NIGHT GROWS UNEASY NEAR THE DAWN . . . . 303 HOUR DAWN 33
THAT'S GROWN UNEASY NEAR THE DAWN . . . . 303 HOUR DAWN V 33
WAS BURIED NEAR THE ASTROLOGER, ... 361 ALF POLLEXFEN 26
UPON THE OPEN ROAD, NEAR TO THE SLIGO QUAY-- . . . . 391 UNDER SATURN 12
TO SOME WHO ARE NEAR MY HEART, ... 393 EASTER 1916 34
"FAIR AND FOUL ARE NEAR OF KIN, ... 513 JANE TALK BISH 7
LONG YEARS AGO, A CHURCH STANDS NEAR, ... 640 BEN BULBEN 87
ON LIMESTONE QUARRIED NEAR THE SPOT . . . . 640 BEN BULBEN 90
SOME BARBAROUS, UN-FAERY THING DRAW NEAR. . . . . . 656 ISLE STAT I 3 21
THIS BLOSSOM IS MOST NEAR. STATUE! OH, THOU . . . . 657 ISLE STAT I 3 72
AND PONDER IT IF THEY WILL)! THEN NEAR AT HAND . . . 659 ISLE STAT II 1 10
THE BOAT DRAWS NEAR AND NEAR. YOU HEED ME NOT! . . . 663 ISLE STAT II 2 23
THE BOAT DRAWS NEAR AND NEAR. YOU HEED ME NOT! . . . 663 ISLE STAT II 2 23
AND ALL HIS VEINS HAD NEAR RUN DRY, ... 670 ISLE STAT II 3 119
THOU WILT NOT SPEAK, AND I WITH AGE AM NEAR . . . . 684 SEEKER 62
TOO LATE, TOO LATE, FOR I AM NEAR TO DEATH. . . . . 701 MOSADA 3 55
I SAW A GIRL AFRAID TO BE TOO NEAR, ... 712 FERENCZ RENYI 68
IN TROUBLE IS, THE DOE WILL LINGER NEAR. . . . . . 713 FERENCZ RENYI 80
THAT SICKENING NEAR THEIR MOTHERS LIE! . . . . . . 717 FAIRY DOCTOR 16
AND DEATH, OH MY FAIR ONE, WILL NEVER COME NEAR . . . 717 LOVE SONG 8
NEAR BY, BUT IN THE SHADOW OF THE SAIL, ... 752 SHADOW WATER A 121
NEARER
AND EVER NEARER, NEARER GREW! . . . . 15 OISIN 1 200
AND EVER NEARER, NEARER GREW! . . . . 15 OISIN 1 200
NEARER THE CASTLE CAME WE. A VAST TIDE, ... 31 OISIN 2 V 27A
A LITTLE NEARER TO HIS THOUGHT . . . . 324 ROBERT GREGORY 23
ARE NEARER TO THE SURFACE OF THE BODY . . . . . . 464 HARUN RASHID 67
LOVE IS NEARER DEATH. . . . . 517 HER ANXIETY 11
A LITTLE NEARER THOSE BRIGHT STARS. TELL ME, ... 701 MOSADA 3 59
NODS BY THE HELM, AND NEARER TO THE SAIL . . . . . 752 SHADOW WATER A 119
IF I GO NEARER TO THE WINDWARD SIDE, ... 753 SHADOW WATER A 140
NEAREST
MY CHAIR WAS NEAREST TO THE FIRE . . . . 131 OLD PENSIONER 3
AND THE NEAREST KIN OF THE MOON, ... 378 CAT AND MOON 3
TOOK UP THE NEAREST AND BEGAN TO SEW. . . . . . . 634 CUCHULAIN COMF 18
NEARLY
THEY HAVE FLOWN AWAY TOGETHER. WE ARE NEARLY . . . . 754 SHADOW WATER A 154
NEAT
TO CUT AND SEW, BE NEAT IN EVERYTHING . . . . . . 443 SCHOOL CHILDR 5
'NEATH
LAY 'NEATH US! OF ITS HOLLOW COOL . . . . 17 OISIN 1 V 241
I SAW NOT WHO! 'NEATH OTHER SKIES . . . . 25 OISIN 1 V 381A
AT EMAN, 'NEATH THE BEECH TREES, ON EACH SIDE, . . . 44 OISIN 2 V 228
A STARLING LIKE THEM THAT FORGATHERED 'NEATH A MOON . . . 54 OISIN 3 103
. . . THEY LAY 'NEATH THE SAND-SACK AT LENGTH . . . 60 OISIN 3 V 186
AMRITA. DRAW YOU NEAR, AND 'NEATH YON PILLAR . . . 71 ANASHU VIJAYA V 13A
THAT SLUMBERED 'NEATH THE HARVEST MOON, ... 85 MAD KING GOLL V 50
AND 'NEATH IT SIT, AND OF THE WOVEN SUM . . . . . 663 ISLE STAT II 2 30
ARE 'NEATH ITS PROW, AND CRUSHING SHELLS. . . . . . 663 ISLE STAT II 2 35
TRAILING AND SHINING 'NEATH THE FLICKERING GLARE. . . . 688 TWO TITANS 32
YOURSELF INTO THE DUNGEON 'NEATH OUR FEET . . . . . 697 MOSADA 2 44
A SCORE OF YARDS OFF 'NEATH A WILLOW, SHOT. . . . . 712 FERENCZ RENYI 65
NO TASTE HAVE I FOR SLUMBER 'NEATH AN OAK. . . . . 721 WITCH VIVIEN 31
NEAVE
"I AM NEAVE, A CHILD OF THE MIGHTY SHEE, ... 5 OISIN 1 V 48

552

```
                                                        PAGE    TITLE           LINE
NEAVE  (CONTINUED)
    FOR NEAVE SANG CONTINUALLY . . . . . . . .       11 OISIN 1         V  134
    AND PEARL-PALE NEAVE LAY BY ME, HER BROW ON THE MIDST OF   52 OISIN 3    V   74
        MY BREAST:
    O, HAD YOU SEEN BEAUTIFUL NEAVE WAIL TO HERSELF AND BLANCH,  54 OISIN 3  V  109
NECESSITOUS
    COME OLD, NECESSITOUS, HALF-MOUNTED MAN:  . . . . . .    412 TOWER            90
NECK
    AND HIS NECK AND HIS BREAST AND HIS ARMS   . . . . .    145 HOST OF AIR      35
    OF SILVER HANGING ROUND LAME COLA'S NECK-- . . . . .    691 MOSADA 1     V   35
    UP WITH THE NECK AND CLAP THE WING,  . . . . . . .      782 HEART FRIGHT      6
    UP WITH THE NECK AND CLAP THE WING,  . . . . . . .      782 HEART FRIGHT     13
    UP WITH THE NECK AND CLAP THE WING,  . . . . . . .      782 HEART FRIGHT     20
    STRETCH NECK AND CLAP THE WING,  . . . . . . . .       783 GREY ROUND       27
NECKLACE
    UPON MY NECKLACE. BUT THE GOBLIN QUEEN . . . . . .      676 ISLE STAT II 3  267
NECK'S
    AND THY NECK'S A POISED LILY:  . . . . . . . . .       647 ISLE STAT I 1    55
NECKS
    EACH OTHER'S NECKS, AND WHISPERING AS THEY GO,  . . . .  703 MOSADA 3       120
NEED
    BUT NOW I HAVE NO NEED TO WATCH IT MORE."  . . . . .    105 CUCHULAIN SEA     5
    TO HELP ME IN MY NEED.  . . . . . . . . . .            134 FR GILLIGAN      44
    YOU NEED BUT LIFT A PEARL-PALE HAND,  . . . . . .       158 BELOVED RHYMES    7
    AT NEED, AND MADE HER BEAUTIFUL AND FIERCE,  . . . .    181 QUEEN MAEVE      29
    AND I WOULD HAVE YOUR HELP IN MY GREAT NEED,  . . . .    184 QUEEN MAEVE      98
    ALL THAT YOU NEED IS PATIENCE."  HEART CRIES, "NO,  . . . 200 FOLLY COMFORT    6
    PATIENCE IS ALL THAT YOU HAVE NEED OF."  NO,  . . . .   200 FOLLY COMFORT V   6
    NO NEED TO DROWN, FOR, IF YOU WILL PARDON US  . . . .   238 SHADOW WATER B  361
    QUEEN, GIVE IT ME.  NO, I HAVE NEED OF IT.  . . . .     241 SHADOW WATER B  399
    WHY DO YOU NEED A SWORD?  BUT YOU MAY KEEP IT.  . . . .  241 SHADOW WATER B  400
    NOW THAT HE'S DEAD I HAVE NO NEED OF IT,  . . . . .     241 SHADOW WATER B  401
    I NEED MUST MARRY SOME POOR LOUT,"  . . . . . .        273 GREY ROCK     V   47
    HE CLAIMED HIS COUNTRY'S NEED WAS MOST,  . . . . .      275 GREY ROCK       101
    SIGHING REPLIED:  "WHAT NEED HAVE WE FOR HASTE  . . . .  276 TWO KINGS    V    C
    WHAT NEED YOU, BEING COME TO SENSE,  . . . . . .       289 SEPTEMBER 1913    1
    SHE NEED NOT BE TOO COMELY--LET IT PASS,"  . . . . .    300 BEGGAR CRIED     10
    AND ALL THAT I NEED DO IS TO WISH  . . . . . .         300 RUN PARADISE      4
    WHAT NEED HAVE YOU TO CARE  . . . . . . . .            312 CHILD DANCING     2
    WHAT NEED HAVE YOU TO DREAD  . . . . . . . .           312 CHILD DANCING    11
    WHAT NEED THAT YOU SHOULD DREAD  . . . . . . .         312 CHILD DANCING V  11
    WHO COMES AT NEED, ALTHOUGH NOT NOW AS ONCE  . . . .    320 REED WHISPERER    2
    BUT LITTLE NEED THE GRAVE DISTRESS.  . . . . . .       338 TOM OROUGHLEY    10
    AND LITTLE NEED THE GRAVE DISTRESS.  . . . . . .       338 TOM OROUGHLEY V  10
    FOR I NEED ALL HIS MIGHTY MEMORIES.  . . . . . .       413 TOWER           104
    AND HAVE NO NEED OF CRUELTY TO KEEP  . . . . . .       448 HERO GIRL FOOL V 12A
    OR THOSE WHO NEED HIS BOUNTY OR HIS LAW,  . . . . .     462 HARUN RASHID  V 25A
    THE HEART NEED SUFFER NO DEFEAT: BUT I  . . . . .      464 HARUN RASHID     77
    I NEED SOME MIND THAT, IF THE CANNON SOUND  . . . .     471 ALL SOUL NIGHT   11
    I NEED NO OTHER THING,  . . . . . . . . .             474 ALL SOUL NIGHT   98
    ALTHOUGH THEIR CHILDREN NEED A RICH ESTATE:  . . . .    500 VACILLATION      24
    OF BAILE AND AILLINN YOU NEED NOT SPEAK,  . . . . .     555 RIBH AT TOMB      6
    SUFFICIENT MONEY FOR HIS NEED,  . . . . . . .          577 WHAT THEN         8
    BUT HE HAS NEED OF ALL THAT STRENGTH  . . . . . .      624 APPARITIONS      20
    SUCH QUESTS AS THESE, I TROW, NEED LITTLE WIT.  . . . .  650 ISLE STAT I 1   150
    NO NEED TO BIND MY HANDS.  WHERE ARE YE, SIRS?  . . . .  695 MOSADA 1        110
    THIS HEATHEN HORDE AWAY.  YOU NEED NOT HOPE:  . . . .   696 MOSADA 2          5
    I DO NOT NEED YOUR SCYTHE.  MAY THAT BRING PEACE  . . . . 721 WITCH VIVIEN    26
    AND NEED NO MORE OF LIFE TILL THE WHITE WINGS . . . .   751 SHADOW WATER A  102
NEEDED
    I THOUGHT NO MORE WAS NEEDED  . . . . . . . .          334 SONG              1
NEEDLE
    AND GRANIA, WALKING AND SMILING, SEWED WITH HER NEEDLE   53 OISIN 3          94
        OF BONE.
    AND ALL THE WHILE HER NEEDLE PULLED  . . . . . . .      308 PLAYER QUEEN      7
    INSTEAD OF THREAD AND NEEDLE  . . . . . . . .          595 COLONEL MARTIN   23
NEEDLE'S
    STOOD IN THE CIRCUIT OF A NEEDLE'S EYE.  . . . . .      483 VERONIC NAPKIN    6
    A NEEDLE'S EYE  . . . . . . . . . . .                  562 NEEDLES EYE       T
    CAME OUT OF A NEEDLE'S EYE:  . . . . . . . .           562 NEEDLES EYE       2
    FROM NEEDLE'S EYE STILL GOAD IT ON.  . . . . . .       562 NEEDLES EYE       4
NEEDLES
    BUT SLENDER NEEDLES OF BONE:  . . . . . . . .          488 CRAZED MOON      15
NEEDLES'
    "WE THREAD THE NEEDLES' EYES, AND ALL WE DO  . . . .    634 CUCHULAIN COMF   16
NEEDLESS
    WAS IT NEEDLESS DEATH AFTER ALL?  . . . . . . .        394 EASTER 1916      67
NEEDS
    AND I MUST NEEDS ENDURE AND HATE AND WEEP,  . . . . .    35 OISIN 2          85
    FOR SHE NEEDS NOT HER SAD BEAUTY--  . . . . . .        124 CATHLEEN PARA V   7
    OR, IF THERE NEEDS BE MORE, BE NOTHING SAID  . . . .    201 OLD MEMORY       11
    SINCE ADAM'S FALL BUT NEEDS MUCH LABOURING.  . . . .    205 ADAMS CURSE      22
    THE SEEMING NEEDS OF MY FOOL-DRIVEN LAND:  . . . . .    267 ALL TEMPT ME      3
    I NEEDS MUST MARRY SOME POOR LOUT,"  . . . . . .       273 GREY ROCK        47
    THE CRADLES THAT A MAN MUST NEEDS BE ROCKED IN:  . . . . 373 PHASES OF MOON  34
    "IT NEEDS TO BE BUT WATERED,"  . . . . . . . .         396 ROSE TREE         7
    AND NEEDS NO CRUELTY.  I HAVE HEARD ONE SAY  . . . .    448 HERO GIRL FOOL   13
    MUST NEEDS NEGLECT, I CANNOT HIDE THE TRUTH  . . . .    462 HARUN RASHID     26
    MUST NEEDS NEGLECT, BUT CANNOT HIDE THE TRUTH,  . . . .  462 HARUN RASHID  V  26
    MUST NEEDS BE IN THIS LIFE AND IN WHAT FOLLOWS  . . . .  465 HARUN RASHID     95
```

		PAGE	TITLE	LINE

NEEDS (CONTINUED)
AND FAIR NEEDS FOUL," I CRIED. . . . . 513 JANE TALK BISH 8
AND GIVEN EVERYTHING A WOMAN NEEDS, ... 609 IN TARAS HALLS 7
LACK NOTHING THAT A SOLDIER NEEDS, ... 635 BLACK TOWER 4
GRIEF NEEDS MUCH FEEDING THEN. OF HIM I SWEAR . . . . 659 ISLE STAT II 1 20

NE'ER
"NOT SO, GREAT KING! FOR I HAVE NE'ER . . . . 6 OISIN 1 V 55
I NE'ER LOVED ANY TILL SONG BROUGHT ME . . . . 7 OISIN 1 V 69
HAVE THEY NE'ER SEEN THE EYES OF LYNX OR KINE, . . . 672 ISLE STAT II 3 152

NEGLECT
CAUGHT IN THAT SENSUAL MUSIC ALL NEGLECT . . . . . . 407 SAIL BYZANTIUM 7
MUST NEEDS NEGLECT, I CANNOT HIDE THE TRUTH . . . . . 462 HARUN RASHID 26
MUST NEEDS NEGLECT, BUT CANNOT HIDE THE TRUTH, . . . 462 HARUN RASHID V 26

NEIGH
ARMOURED HORSES NEIGH . . . . 512 JANE ON GOD 9

NEIGHBOUR
A NEIGHBOUR MINDED HER BY DAY, ... 94 MOLL MAGEE 15
NO NEIGHBOUR COULD I SEE. . . . . 95 MOLL MAGEE 28
I SAW A KINDLY NEIGHBOUR . . . . 95 MOLL MAGEE 35
I SAW A NEIGHBOUR GOOD. . . . . 95 MOLL MAGEE V 36
ALL KNOW THE MAN THEIR NEIGHBOUR KNOWS. . . . . . . 337 SCHOLARS 10
THERE'S NOT A NEIGHBOUR LEFT TO SAY . . . . 412 TOWER 78
AWAY FROM NEIGHBOUR OR FRIEND, ... 472 ALL SOUL NIGHT 47
HE THAT'S MOUNTING UP MUST ON HIS NEIGHBOUR MOUNT, . . 580 CURSE CROMWELL 11

NEIGHBOURING
FROM SOMEWHERE IN THE NEIGHBOURING COTTAGES. . . . . 411 TOWER 59
I CAN EXCHANGE OPINION WITH ANY NEIGHBOURING MIND, . . 450 OWEN AHERNE 9
A NEIGHBOURING CRICKET LIFTS HIS SHRILLY SHOUT . . . 711 FERENCZ RENYI 45
OUT OF A NEIGHBOURING BUNCH OF HEATHER; . . . . . . 728 PRIEST FAIRY 20

NEIGHBOURLY
ALL NEIGHBOURLY CONTENT AND EASY TALK ARE GONE, . . . 580 CURSE CROMWELL 9

NEIGHBOUR'S
FOR AN OLD NEIGHBOUR'S FRIENDSHIP CHOSE THE HOUSE . . 423 MY DESCENDANTS 21

NEIGHBOURS
IF I SHOULD LIVE AS LIVE THE NEIGHBOURS," . . . . . 331 ROUND TOWER 3
IF I SHOULD LIVE AS LIVES THE NEIGHBOURS" . . . . . 331 ROUND TOWER V 3
THE RHETORICIAN WOULD DECEIVE HIS NEIGHBOURS, ... 369 EGO DOMINUS 46
AND LET THE NEIGHBOURS VOTE, ... 598 STONE CROSS 6
THAT IF THEIR NEIGHBOURS FIGURED PLAIN, ... 626 OLD MEN BE MAD 11

NEIGHBOURS'
NOR IN HIS NEIGHBOURS' EYES? . . . . 291 TO A FRIEND 8

NEIGHED
HE SHOOK HIMSELF AND NEIGHED THREE TIMES! . . . . . 10 OISIN 1 110
AND NEIGHED THREE TIMES. WHEN, WONDERING . . . . . 10 OISIN 1 V 110A

NEIGHING
NEIGHING ALONG THE LIFELESS WASTE! . . . . 13 OISIN 1 170

NERVE
FOR EVERY NERVE, AND TESTS A LOVER . . . . 388 SOLOMON WITCH 22
FOR EVERY NERVE! LOVER TESTS LOVER . . . . 388 SOLOMON WITCH V 22

NERVELESS
HIS TOOTHLESS HOUND AT HIS NERVELESS FEET, ... 26 OISIN 1 V 400
I BURST THE CHAIN! STILL EARLESS, NERVELESS, BLIND, . . 36 OISIN 2 97
STILL EARLESS, NERVELESS, BLIND, THE EAGLES STOOD. . . 36 OISIN 2 100
STILL EARLESS, NERVELESS, BLIND, THE EAGLES DREAMED. . 36 OISIN 2 V 100

NESSA
CAME BLANAID, MAC NESSA, TALL FERGUS WHO FEASTWARD OF OLD   53 OISIN 3 89
  TIME SLUNK,
CAME BLANID, MAC NESSA, CUCHULIN! . . . . 53 OISIN 3 V 89
CAME BLANID, MAC NESSA, AND FERGUS WHO FEASTWARD OF OLD   53 OISIN 3 V 89
  TIME SLUNK,

NESSA'S
AND OF THAT FAMOUS FERGUS, NESSA'S HUSBAND, ... 183 QUEEN MAEVE 71

NEST
. . . WHO SLEEPS ON HER NEST, ... 56 OISIN 3 134
SHE BUILDS HER NEST UPON A NARROW LEDGE . . . . . . 285 TWO KINGS 194
BUT THE RIGHT TWIGS FOR AN EAGLE'S NEST! . . . . . . 288 TO WEALTHY MAN 36
WHEN FIRST IT SPRANG OUT OF THE NEST . . . . 397 POLIT PRISONER 20
AND SO WARM HER WILD NEST. . . . . 415 TOWER 172
THE STARE'S NEST BY MY WINDOW . . . . 424 STARES NEST T
THE JAY'S NEST BY MY WINDOW . . . . 424 STARES NEST V T
ON MIND, ON NEST, ... 574 LOVERS SONG 5
O'ER HER NEST THE LIGHTS ARE BLENDING! . . . . . . 646 ISLE STAT I 1 36
AS ALIEN AS A CUCKOO IN A ROBIN'S NEST, ... 671 ISLE STAT II 3 138
ALIEN AS CUCKOO IN A ROBIN'S NEST, ... 671 ISLE STAT II 3 V 138

NESTED
NESTED 'MONG THE VAPOURS BROWN. . . . . 731 STREET DANCERS 6

NESTLE
THE BIRDS THAT NESTLE IN THE LEAVES ARE SAD, ... 652 ISLE STAT I 2 15
WHERE SPICE-ISLES NESTLE ON THE STAR-TROD SEAS, . . . 682 SEEKER 17

NESTLES
THAT NESTLES ALONE IN THE WHISTLING WIND, ... 657 ISLE STAT I 3 68

NESTS
. . . THE OWLS HAD BUILDED THEIR NESTS IN THEIR LOCKS, . . 49 OISIN 3 39
FROM YEAR TO YEAR BY THE UNNUMBERED NESTS . . . . . 74 ANASHU VIJAYA 72

NET
. . . CROZIERED ONE, CAUGHT IN YOUR NET! . . . . . 58 OISIN 3 167
. . . CROSIERED ONE, CAUGHT IN THY NET— . . . . . 58 OISIN 3 V 167
. . . CROZIERED ONE, CAUGHT IN THEIR NET! . . . . . 58 OISIN 3 V 167
ABOUT THE CASTING OUT OF MY NET, ... 146 FISH 4
I THINK THAT HE HAS FORGAEL IN HIS NET, ... 224 SHADOW WATER B 56
AND DRAGS HIM THROUGH THE SEA. WELL, NET OR NONE, . . 224 SHADOW WATER B 57

NET (CONTINUED)
    BOTH YOU AND I ARE TAKEN IN THE NET. . . . .   237 SHADOW WATER B   323
    OF THE GREAT GOLDEN NET THAT IS ABOUT US. . . . . .   238 SHADOW WATER B   352
    YOU CANNOT LEAP OUT OF THE GOLDEN NET. . . . . . .   238 SHADOW WATER B   360
    FLASHES AS IF IT WERE A NET OF HERRINGS. . . . . .   248 SHADOW WATER B   536
    BELOVED, HAVING DRAGGED THE NET ABOUT US, ...   252 SHADOW WATER B   615
    SHE WOULD WEAVE A NET TO TAKE US. SHE MIGHT KEEP FAITH! 756 SHADOW WATER A   190
    OR THAN THE SHIVERING CASTING NET OF THE STARS. . .   762 SHADOW WATER A V 290
    O! I WOULD BREAK THIS NET THE GODS HAVE WOVEN . . .   765 SHADOW WATER A   361
NETS
    WHO PACED IN THE EVE BY THE NETS ON THE PEBBLY SHORE, . .   91 OLD FISHERMAN   11
    THE LINES ARE NOT HEAVY, NOR HEAVY THE LONG NETS BROWN--   91 OLD FISHERMAN V   5
    COME CLEAR OF THE NETS OF WRONG AND RIGHT; . . . . .   147 INTO TWILIGHT   2
    COME CLEAR OFF THE NETS OF WRONG AND RIGHT! . . . .   147 INTO TWILIGHT   V   2
    THE NETS OF DAY AND NIGHT. . . . .   175 ELEMENT POWERS   12
    ROMANTIC FISH SWAM IN NETS COMING TO THE HAND! . . .   485 THREE MOVEMENT   2
    I AM CAUGHT IN WOVEN NETS OF ENCHANTMENT. LOOK! . .   762 SHADOW WATER A   293
    THE GODS WEAVE NETS, AND TAKE US IN THEIR NETS, . .   764 SHADOW WATER A   339
    THE GODS WEAVE NETS, AND TAKE US IN THEIR NETS, . .   764 SHADOW WATER A   339
    THE NETS THE GODS HAVE WOVEN AND OUR OWN HEARTS, . .   766 SHADOW WATER A   383
    THE GODS HATE HAPPINESS, AND WEAVE THEIR NETS . . .   767 SHADOW WATER A   399
NETTED
    THE NETTED MARKS OF CRAWLING SCALES SEA-SPRUNG . . . .   37 OISIN 2   V 115
NETTLES
    WHEN NETTLES WAVE UPON A SHAPELESS MOUND . . . . . .   489 COOLE PARK 29   27
NETTLESHIP'S
    ON MR. NETTLESHIP'S PICTURE AT THE ROYAL HIBERNIAN ACADEMY. 688 NETTLESHIP   T
NEVER
    A SWIFTER CREATURE NEVER WAS BORN, ...   2 OISIN 1   V 7Q
    WHERE BROKEN FAITH HAS NEVER BEEN KNOWN, ...   8 OISIN 1   84
    AND THE BLUSHES OF FIRST LOVE NEVER HAVE FLOWN; . .   8 OISIN 1   85
    TO SHORES WHERE DYING HAS NEVER BEEN KNOWN, ...   8 OISIN 1   V 84
    AND THE FLUSHES OF FIRST LOVE NEVER HAVE FLOWN; . .   8 OISIN 1   V 85
    AND KISSED, AS THEY WOULD NEVER CEASE, ...   16 OISIN 1   215
    "A SADDER CREATURE NEVER STEPT . . . .   17 OISIN 1   238
    BUT NEVER, NEVER ON OUR GRAVES, ...   21 OISIN 1   313
    BUT NEVER, NEVER ON OUR GRAVES, ...   21 OISIN 1   313
    NEVER, NEVER ON OUR GRAVES, ...   21 OISIN 1   V 313
    NEVER, NEVER ON OUR GRAVES, ...   21 OISIN 1   V 313
    AND WE NEVER FEAR THE MORROW . . . .   21 OISIN 1   V 318
    "BUT NEVER WITH US WHERE THE WILD FOWL CHASES . . .   27 OISIN 1   V 408
    "BUT NEVER THE YEARS IN THE ISLE'S SOFT PLACES . .   27 OISIN 1   V 419A
    "BUT NEVER THE YEARS IN OUR ISLE'S SOFT PLACES . .   28 OISIN 1   V 424
    AND HOW THOSE LOVERS NEVER TURN THEIR EYES . . . .   29 OISIN 2   11
    HOW SUCH A WARRIOR NEVER TURNED HIS GAZE . . . . .   29 OISIN 2   V 11
    AS THOUGH UNTO HIS NEVER SLUMBERING HEART . . . . .   32 OISIN 2   V 44
    AS THOUGH HE TOLD HIS NEVER SLUMBERING HEART . . .   32 OISIN 2   V 44
    NOR THE HIGH GODS WHO NEVER LIVED, MAY FIGHT . . .   34 OISIN 2   80
    FOR NEVER MORTAL CRY SO FAR HATH SENT. . . . . . .   36 OISIN 2   V 108
    AND NEVER FIND, THOUGH YE IN MUSIC SPEAK. . . . . .   42 OISIN 2   V 201
    AND NEVER A SONG SANG NIAMH, AND OVER MY FINGER-TIPS .   47 OISIN 3   6
    . . . THE SPITTLE ON HIS BEARD NEVER DRY, ...   53 OISIN 3   90
    . . . WITH THE SPITTLE ON HIS BEARD NEVER DRY. . .   60 OISIN 3   192
    VIJAYA, SWEAR TO HER LOVE NEVER MORE. . . . . . .   74 ANASHU VIJAYA   65
    WHO PACED THE UNFORGIVING HOUND. . . . .   75 ANASHU VIJAYA   75
    WHO NEVER HEARD THE UNFORGIVING HOUND. . . . . .   75 ANASHU VIJAYA V 75
    MAY NEVER RESTLESS FAY WITH FIDGET FINGER . . . .   75 ANASHU VIJAYA V 90
    "YOUR EYES THAT ONCE WERE NEVER WEARY OF MINE . .   79 EPHEMERA   1
    WHEN I WAS A BOY WITH NEVER A CRACK IN MY HEART. .   91 OLD FISHERMAN   4
    WHEN I WAS A BOY WITH NEVER A CRACK IN MY HEART. .   91 OLD FISHERMAN   8
    WHEN I WAS A BOY WITH NEVER A CRACK IN MY HEART. .   91 OLD FISHERMAN   12
    TO DO AND DO AND DO AND NEVER DREAM. . . . . . .   103 FERGUS DRUID   V 28
    TURN IF YOU MAY FROM BATTLES NEVER DONE, ...   114 ROSE OF BATTLE   7
    FOR HIM WHO HEARS LOVE SING AND NEVER CEASE, . . .   114 ROSE OF BATTLE   10
    "FROM THE GREY SHIPS AND BATTLES NEVER WON. . . . .   114 ROSE OF BATTLE V   8
    HAS AWAKED IN OUR HEARTS, MY BELOVED, A SADNESS THAT NEVER
        MAY DIE. . . . .   122 WHITE BIRDS   V   4
    THAT TIME CAN NEVER MAR A LOVER'S VOWS . . . . . .   126 DREAM OF FAERY   10
    HOW TIME MAY NEVER MAR THEIR FAERY VOWS . . . . .   126 DREAM OF FAERY V 10
    AND MEN WHO LOVED THE CAUSE THAT NEVER DIES. . . .   130 BOOK STORIES   V 24
    HE RODE NOW AS HE NEVER RODE, ...   133 FR GILLIGAN   29
    BECAUSE THEIR BLOSSOMING DREAMS HAVE NEVER BENT . .   136 TO SOME I TALK   8
    AND NEVER WAS PIPING SO SAD, ...   144 HOST OF AIR   11
    AND NEVER WAS PIPING SO GAY, ...   144 HOST OF AIR   12
    AND NEVER WAS PIPING SO SAD, ...   145 HOST OF AIR   43
    AND NEVER WAS PIPING SO GAY, ...   145 HOST OF AIR   44
    BY A GREY SHORE WHERE THE WIND NEVER BLEW, ...   170 SECRET ROSE   14
    I NEVER HAVE SEEN MAID QUIET . . . .   171 MAID QUIET   V   1
    OF THOSE THAT, IT MAY BE, CAN NEVER AGE. . . . . .   183 QUEEN MAEVE   76
    OF THOSE THAT IT MAY BE SHALL NEVER FADE. . . . .   183 QUEEN MAEVE   V 76
    BY RIVERS WHERE THE RAIN HAS NEVER DIMMED . . . .   184 QUEEN MAEVE   V 87
    THEIR LOVE WAS NEVER DROWNED IN CARE . . . . . .   189 BAILE AILLINN   8
    THOSE OTHER TWO; FOR NEVER YET . . . .   197 BAILE AILLINN   205
    NEVER GIVE ALL THE HEART . . . .   202 NEVER GIVE ALL   T
    NEVER GIVE ALL THE HEART, FOR LOVE . . . .   202 NEVER GIVE ALL   1
    CERTAIN, AND THEY NEVER DREAM . . . .   202 NEVER GIVE ALL   4
    O NEVER GIVE THE HEART OUTRIGHT, ...   202 NEVER GIVE ALL   8
    ALTHOUGH WE NEVER HEARD OF IT AT SCHOOL . . . . .   205 ADAMS CURSE   V 19
    WILL NEVER FIND US THERE . . . .   213 HAPPY TOWNLAND V   2
    YOU'RE CERTAIN OF IT? I NEVER WAKE FROM SLEEP . .   226 SHADOW WATER B   83
    I'D NEVER COME UPON THE HAPPINESS . . . .   226 SHADOW WATER B   87
    THAT I WILL NEVER LIFT A HAND AGAINST YOU. . . . .   227 SHADOW WATER B   108

555

NEVER   (CONTINUED)

	PAGE	TITLE		LINE
YOU'VE NEVER KNOWN, I'D LAY A WAGER ON IT,	227	SHADOW WATER B		113
THAT NEVER DID A HAND'S TURN? AIBRIC! AIBRIC!	228	SHADOW WATER B		130
YET NEVER HAVE TWO LOVERS KISSED BUT THEY	229	SHADOW WATER B		153
YOU'D NEVER DOUBT THAT IT WAS LIFE THEY PROMISED	231	SHADOW WATER B		197
NONE BUT THE DEAD, OR THOSE THAT NEVER LIVED,	231	SHADOW WATER B		202
I NEVER HAVE BEEN GOLDEN-ARMED IOLLAN.	244	SHADOW WATER B		464
I'LL NEVER GIVE ANOTHER THOUGHT TO IT!	245	SHADOW WATER B		477
THAT YOU MAY NEVER HEAR THE CRY OF THE BIRDS,	250	SHADOW WATER B		575
BUT NEVER MADE A POORER SONG	273	GREY ROCK		55
WOULD NEVER LOOK AGAIN ON KNOWN MAN'S FACE."	280	TWO KINGS		75
WILL NEVER LOOK AGAIN ON KNOWN MAN'S FACE."	280	TWO KINGS	V	75
"NEVER WILL I BELIEVE THERE IS ANY CHANGE	285	TWO KINGS		203
YET NEVER HAVE I LIT ON A FRIEND	301	RUN PARADISE		25
AND NEVER COULD HAVE RESTED IN THE TOMB	325	ROBERT GREGORY		27
NEVER UNTIL THIS MOMENT HAVE WE MET	339	SHEP GOATHERD		7
YET NEVER COULD, ALTHOUGH	345	ON WOMAN		13
YET NEVER HAVE I, NOW NOR ANY TIME,	352	PEOPLE		28
THAT NEVER LOOKED UPON MAN WITH DESIRE,	358	PRESENCES		13
HE NEVER FOUND HIS REST ASHORE,	361	ALF POLLEXFEN		21
WHAT HE SHALL NEVER FIND. WHY SHOULD NOT YOU	373	PHASES OF MOON		20
AND NEVER WROTE A BOOK, YOUR THOUGHT IS CLEAR.	376	PHASES OF MOON		97
THAT THE WILL NEVER FIND! I'D PLAY A PART!	377	PHASES OF MOON		128
HE WOULD NEVER KNOW ME AFTER ALL THESE YEARS	377	PHASES OF MOON		129
DAY AFTER DAY, YET NEVER FIND THE MEANING.	377	PHASES OF MOON		135
WE NEVER THOUGHT TO ENQUIRE	381	SONGS FOOL 2		3
UNDER BLANK EYES AND FINGERS NEVER STILL	382	VISION ROBART		5
THAT OTHER'S MOONLIT EYEBALLS NEVER MOVED,	383	VISION ROBART		33
WHO NEVER GAVE THE BURNING TOWN A THOUGHT!	384	VISION ROBART		57
AND NEVER CREW AGAIN TILL NOW,	388	SOLOMON WITCH		12
NEVER UNTIL THIS NIGHT HAVE I BEEN STIRRED.	389	IMAGE PAST		1
MY EYES SHOULD NEVER REST?	389	IMAGE PAST		18
AND OF A MIDDLETON, WHOSE NAME YOU NEVER HEARD,	391	UNDER SATURN		8
NEVER TO LEAVE THAT VALLEY HIS FATHERS CALLED THEIR HOME.	391	UNDER SATURN		16
THAT NEVER YET HAD FREEMAN	401	DEMON BEAST		36
THAT CHOOSES RIGHT, AND NEVER FIND A FRIEND.	404	FOR DAUGHTER		24
CAN NEVER TEAR THE LINNET FROM THE LEAF.	405	FOR DAUGHTER		56
ONCE OUT OF NATURE I SHALL NEVER TAKE	408	SAIL BYZANTIUM		25
AS TO A DOG'S TAIL? NEVER HAD I MORE	409	TOWER		4
AS UPON A DOG'S TAIL. NEVER HAD I MORE	409	TOWER	V	4
AND NEVER STOOP TO A MECHANICAL	417	ANCEST HOUSES		7
THEY NEVER SAW HOW SEASONS RUN,	432	NINETEEN 19		101
NOAH'S FRESHET NEVER REACHED.	440	WISDOM		15
WHERE SEVEN EPHESIAN TOPERS SLEPT AND NEVER KNEW	442	BLACK CENTAUR		11
AND I THOUGH NEVER OF LEDAEAN KIND	444	SCHOOL CHILDR		29
NEVER TO HAVE LIVED IS BEST, ANCIENT WRITERS SAY!	459	FROM OEDIPUS		10
NEVER TO HAVE DRAWN THE BREATH OF LIFE,	459	FROM OEDIPUS		11
. . . NEVER TO HAVE LOOKED INTO THE EYE OF DAY!	459	FROM OEDIPUS		11
NEVER TO HAVE DRUNK THE BREATH OF LIFE,	459	FROM OEDIPUS	V	11
MY HEART COULD NEVER TURN FROM DAILY RUIN,	464	HARUN RASHID		83
THAT NEVER KNEW THAT STRAIN WOULD SCARCE SEEM BRIGHT,	465	HARUN RASHID		88
ON OLD DRY FAGGOTS THAT COULD NEVER PLEASE.	466	HARUN RASHID		124
AND TOLD HIM SO, BUT FRIENDSHIP NEVER ENDS!	473	ALL SOUL NIGHT		65
THAT NEVER LOOKED OUT OF THE EYE OF A SAINT	486	SEVEN SAGES		12
BUT NEVER SAW THE TREFOIL STAINED WITH BLOOD,	487	SEVEN SAGES		19
"NEVER SHALL A YOUNG MAN,	492	ANNE GREGORY		1
SO NEVER HANG YOUR HEART UPON	509	JANE REPROVED		12
HAD I NEVER THOUGHT	534	CONSOLATION		8
"BUT NEVER DARE TO BOAST	539	MEETING		8
TO THOSE THAT NEVER SAW THIS TONSURED HEAD	555	RIBH AT TOMB		4
SENTENCES THAT HE HAS NEVER THOUGHT!	560	WHENCE COME		6
AND NEVER HAVE I DANCED FOR JOY.	567	FROM JAPANESE		9
ALL THE OLYMPIANS! A THING NEVER KNOWN AGAIN.	578	LOFTY THINGS		12
IT NEVER CROSSED THE SEA BECAUSE	583	GHOST ROG CASE		3
CAN NEVER CLOSE THOSE EYES."	588	OLD WICKED MAN		26
BUT I NEVER STOPPED TO QUESTION, WHAT COULD THE BOATMAN SAY	593	PILGRIM		19
AND NEVER HAVE I LOOKED UPON	595	COLONEL MARTIN		32
THAT THEY COULD NEVER SHOOT A MAN	596	COLONEL MARTIN		61
"I NEVER THOUGHT OF THAT, SIR."	596	COLONEL MARTIN		66
I NEVER BADE YOU GO	600	THOSE IMAGES		5
DEEP-ROOTED THINGS," BUT NEVER FORESAW ITS END,	603	GALLERY REVIS		37
WHAT DEEP ROOTS ARE," AND NEVER FORESAW THE END	603	GALLERY REVIS	V	37
HE NEVER LAY BEHIND FOUR WALLS	606	SONGS BURDEN 1		12
BUT NEVER ASKED FOR LOVE! SHOULD I ASK THAT,	609	IN TARAS HALLS		9
BUT NEVER SAID A THING,	627	STATES HOLIDAY		10
THAT BROAD NOON HAS NEVER LIT,	632	MAN AND ECHO		4
AND NEVER GET THE ANSWERS RIGHT.	632	MAN AND ECHO		10
OF THE SONGS THAT NEVER SLEEP.	647	ISLE STAT I 1		76
THAT FLOWER I SEEK. THOU NEVER WILT RETURN.	653	ISLE STAT I 2		44
BUT A MOTHER PANTHER NEVER	658	ISLE STAT I 3		92
TO YONDER ISLE, WHERE NEVER SAIL WAS FURLED,	664	ISLE STAT II 2		56
AND NEVER HEARD OF GRIEF OR CARE	667	ISLE STAT II 3		21
AND EVEN SHE SHALL NEVER HOLD	668	ISLE STAT II 3		50
OR AUGHT REMOTE! OR HAST THOU NEVER HEARD	672	ISLE STAT II 3		153
OR HAST THOU NEVER SEEN, WITH VISAGE MEEK,	672	ISLE STAT II 3		156
AND NEVER ANY MORE THE WIDE-EYED BANDS	674	ISLE STAT II 3		218
A GREY-HAIRED YOUTH, WHOSE CHEEKS HAD NEVER FOUND,	687	TWO TITANS		7
WITH WONDERFUL WHITE SANDS, WHERE NEVER YET	693	MOSADA 1		81
WITH WONDERFUL WHITE SAND, WHERE NEVER YET	693	MOSADA 1	V	81
I NEVER KNEW AN EVE SO MARVELLOUS STILL.	702	MOSADA 3		88
THEIR THIEVING WINGS THAT WE MIGHT NEVER PART.	702	MOSADA 3		98

NEVER (CONTINUED)
    I NEVER KNEW A NIGHT SO HONEY-SWEET. . . . . 702 MOSADA 3   99
    I NEVER KNEW A NIGHT SO HONEY-SWEET. . . . . 702 MOSADA 3   V 99
    I NEVER KNEW A NIGHT SO DEW-BEDROWNED. . . . . 703 MOSADA 3   105
    I NEVER KNEW A NIGHT SO BITTER COLD. . . . . 704 MOSADA 3   124
    AND DEATH, OH MY FAIR ONE, WILL NEVER COME NEAR . . . . 717 LOVE SONG   8
    NEVER STORM AROSE SO SWIFTLY; SCARCE THE CHILDREN WERE 718 PHANTOM SHIP   4
        IN BED,
    SOME DAY YOU'LL BUY THEM, MAYBE. NEVER! NEVER? . . . . 721 WITCH VIVIEN   24
    SOME DAY YOU'LL BUY THEM, MAYBE. NEVER! NEVER? . . . . 721 WITCH VIVIEN   24
    AND NEVER REST IN THEIR FLIGHT, ... 739 WHERE BOOKS GO   4
    HIS FACE HAS NEVER GLADDENED SINCE HE CAME . . . . . . 747 SHADOW WATER A   1
    AND WILL YOU SWEAR NEVER TO BE AVENGED . . . . 758 SHADOW WATER A 223
    BODIES THAT CAN NEVER TIRE . . . . 776 AGAINST WITCH   20
    AND CAN NEVER BE CONTENT . . . . 777 SONG DEIRDRE 2   2
    THEIR BRIEF LIVES I NEVER KNEW. . . . . 787 HUDDON DUDDON   5
    BUT NEVER STOOD BEFORE A STAKE . . . . 790 SINGING HEAD   23
    BUT NEVER, NEVER DANGLING LEAVE THE LIVER AND THE LIGHTS. 790 HEART SLEEVE   2
    BUT NEVER, NEVER DANGLING LEAVE THE LIVER AND THE LIGHTS. 790 HEART SLEEVE   2
NEVER-ANXIOUS
    AND ALWAYS NEVER-ANXIOUS SLEEP; . . . . 8 OISIN 1   93
NEVER-LIFTING
    IN THE NEVER-LIFTING DARK. . . . . 658 ISLE STAT I 3 89
NEVER-SLUMBERING
    AS THOUGH HE TOLD HIS NEVER-SLUMBERING HEART . . . . . 32 OISIN 2   44
NEW   SEE BRAND-NEW
    BLOSSOM IN SOME NEW CRIMSON FLOWER, ... 16 OISIN 1   224
    WE SAW, SOME NEW, SOME PRINTED WHEN THE PLACE WAS YOUNG, 37 OISIN 2   V 116
    HIS NEW HEALED SHAPE! AND FOR A HUNDRED YEARS . . . . 44 OISIN 2   V 221
    NEW DREAMS, NEW DREAMS; THERE IS NO TRUTH . . . . . . 66 HAPPY SHEPHERD 26
    NEW DREAMS, NEW DREAMS; THERE IS NO TRUTH . . . . . . 66 HAPPY SHEPHERD 26
    I HAVE FORGIVEN, O NEW STAR! . . . . 75 ANASHU VIJAYA   77
    ARE WITH NEW SORROW WRUNG! . . . . 99 FOXHUNTER   38
    AND THROUGH THAT NEW BLADE'S GUARD THE OLD BLADE BROKE, 110 CUCHULAIN SEA 66
    MOURNFUL THAT NO NEW WONDER MAY BETIDE, ... 111 ROSE OF WORLD   3
    GIVE TO THESE CHILDREN, NEW FROM THE WORLD, ... 116 FAERY SONG   5
    GIVE TO THESE CHILDREN, NEW FROM THE WORLD, ... 116 FAERY SONG   9
    SHINING BRIGHT AS A NEW LANCE! . . . . 125 CATHLEEN PARA V 14
    THE SINGING SHOOK HIM OUT OF HIS NEW EASE. . . . . . . 126 DREAM OF FAERY 12
    A HONIED RINGING! UNDER THE NEW SKIES . . . . 130 BOOK STORIES V 21
    AND NEW FRIENDS BUSY WITH YOUR PRAISE, ... 173 PLEADS FRIEND   3
    AND OF NEW FRIENDS ARE GLAD WITH YOUR PRAISE. . . . . 173 PLEADS FRIEND V 3
    TARA UPROOTED, AND NEW COMMONNESS . . . . 198 SEVEN WOODS   6
    IT MIGHT CALL UP A NEW AGE, CALLING TO MIND . . . . . 201 OLD MEMORY   4
    AND ALL THE ALE RAN OUT AT THE NEW MOON! . . . . . . 222 SHADOW WATER B V 11
    THAT HAS THE HEADY FLAVOUR OF NEW WINE, ... 240 SHADOW WATER B 374
    ON HEARING THAT THE STUDENTS OF OUR NEW UNIVERSITY . . 262 STUDENTS AGIT   T
    WE'LL KEEP THE SECRET—A NEW TRICK TO PLEASE. . . . . 265 ABBEY THEATRE 10
    SING ON! SOMEWHERE AT SOME NEW MOON, ... 266 GALWAY RACES   10
    BUT SOME DAY AND AT SOME NEW MOON . . . . 266 GALWAY RACES V 10
    SING ON! SOMETIME, AND AT SOME NEW MOON . . . . 266 GALWAY RACES V 10
    OF A NEW FRIEND HE HAS TURNED A GHOST. . . . . 275 GREY ROCK   103
    THAT SOME NEW DAY MAY BREED THE BEST . . . . 288 TO WEALTHY MAN 34
    ALWAYS WE'D HAVE THE NEW FRIEND MEET THE OLD . . . . . 324 ROBERT GREGORY 9
    NEW WELCOME AND OLD WISDOM AT HER FIRE . . . . 340 SHEP GOATHERD 32
    AS A MAN DOES WHO HAS PUBLISHED A NEW BOOK, ... 350 HER PRAISE   3
    OR A YOUNG GIRL DRESSED OUT IN HER NEW GOWN, ... 350 HER PRAISE   4
    A WOMAN SPOKE OF SOME NEW TALE SHE HAD READ, ... 350 HER PRAISE   7
    A NEW MODELLED DOLL, OR DRAWING, ... 362 DOLLS DRAWINGS 2
    A NEW DANCE TURN. . . . . 378 CAT AND MOON   16
    A NEW DANCE TUNE. . . . . 378 CAT AND MOON V 16
    AND NEW DANCE TURN. . . . . 378 CAT AND MOON V 16
    HAS TAKEN A NEW PHASE. . . . . 379 CAT AND MOON   20
    AND THE NEW STILL HIDES HER HORN. . . . . 382 VISION ROBART   4
    FOR THOSE NEW COMRADES THEY HAVE FOUND, ... 395 SIXTEEN DEAD   15
    CURVED LIKE NEW MOON, MOON-LUMINOUS, ... 421 MY TABLE   10
    CURVED LIKE NEW MOON, MOON LUMINOUS, ... 421 MY TABLE V 10
    WHIRLS OUT NEW RIGHT AND WRONG, ... 430 NINETEEN 19   55
    THE NEW FACES . . . . 435 NEW FACES   T
    LET THE NEW FACES PLAY WHAT TRICKS THEY WILL . . . . . 435 NEW FACES   5
    ARE BUT A NEW EXPRESSION OF HER BODY . . . . 469 HARUN RASHID 185
    BY SOME NEW MARRIED BRIDE I TAKE . . . . 535 CHOSEN V 13
    ON THE LEAF-SOWN, NEW MOWN, SMOOTH . . . . 568 SWEET DANCER V 2
    BUT THAT IS NOTHING NEW. . . . . 581 ROGER CASEMENT 4
    AND THAT IS SOMETHING NEW! . . . . 582 ROGER CASEMENT 12
    BECAUSE OF THOSE NEW DEAD . . . . 599 SPIRIT MEDIUM   2
    BUT EVEN AT THE STARTING-POST, ALL SLEEK AND NEW, . . 619 BRONZE HEAD   15
    A NEW DAY'S TROOP OF WASP AND BEE . . . . 646 ISLE STAT I 1 44
    AND THEN NEW MURMURS CAME NEW UTTERING . . . . 657 ISLE STAT I 3 50
    AND THEN NEW MURMURS CAME NEW UTTERING . . . . 657 ISLE STAT I 3 50
    AND NOT TOO CLEAR, HOW WILL THE NEW GOD KNOW . . . . . 658 ISLE STAT I 3 79
    LOVE STORM! AND STAINED WITH MIST THE NEW MOONS FLARE. 678 ISLE STAT II 3 294
    LOVE STORM AND STAINED WITH MIST THE NEW MOON'S FLARE . 678 ISLE STAT II 3 V 294
    WHY THESE NEW FEARS? THE GREAT MONK EBREMAR, ... 692 MOSADA 1   46
    WHY THESE NEW FEARS? THE SERVANT OF THE LORD, ... 692 MOSADA 1 V 46
    WILL YOU NOT HEAR MY LAST NEW SONG? HUSH! HUSH! . . . 695 MOSADA 2   1
    A STRANGER NEW ARISEN WAIT . . . . 696 MOSADA 2 V 22
    FLOATING FROM YON BARRED WINDOW. NEW COMER, ... 700 MOSADA 3   43
    BUT I AM NEW TO LOVE. GO AMONG THESE . . . . 767 SHADOW WATER A 391
NEW-BORN
    AWAKEN, AWAKEN TO NEW-BORN LUSTRE; . . . . 646 ISLE STAT I 1 43

557

```
                                                            PAGE      TITLE            LINE
NEW-COMER
     FLOATING FROM YON BARRED WINDOW.  SMALL NEW-COMER, . . .   700 MOSADA 3             43
NEW-FANGLED
     OF THEIR TALL, NEW-FANGLED QUEEN. . . . . . . . . .        727 LOVERS QUARREL       48
NEW-HEALED
     HIS NEW-HEALED SHAPE: AND FOR A HUNDRED YEARS . . . . .     44 OISIN 2             221
NEWLY
     MAYBE YOU HAVE NOT HEARD OF US, YOU HAVE COME FORTH SO      75 ANASHU VIJAYA        78
        NEWLY,
     AS WHEN NEWLY GROWN TO BE A WOMAN,  . . . . . . . .        199 ARROW                 4
NEW-MARRIED
     BY SOME NEW-MARRIED BRIDE, I TAKE . . . . . . . . .        535 CHOSEN               13
     WHERE MAY NEW-MARRIED WOMEN SIT  . . . . . . . . .         791 REPRISALS            19
NEW-MOWN
     TILL, FATTENING THE WINDS OF THE MORNING, AN ODOUR          57 OISIN 3             153
        OF NEW-MOWN HAY
     AN ODOUR OF THE NEW-MOWN HAY . . . . . . . . . .           502 VACILLATION          58
     ON THE LEAF-SOWN, NEW-MOWN, SMOOTH . . . . . . . .         568 SWEET DANCER          2
NEWS
     AND THEY HAVE NEWS OF DEIRDRE'S EYES,  . . . . . . .       193 BAILE AILLINN        97
     THEREFORE IT IS BUT LITTLE NEWS  . . . . . . . . .         194 BAILE AILLINN       124
     WHEN I FIRST HEARD THE NEWS?  AH, THERE IT IS!  . . .      241 SHADOW WATER B      398
     BROUGHT THE BARE NEWS.  HE HAD THROWN THE CROOK AWAY . .   339 SHEP GOATHERD        21
     PULL DOWN ESTABLISHED HONOUR: HAWK FOR NEWS . . . .        398 LEADERS CROWD         3
     AND WHEN THE STORY'S FINISHED, WHAT'S THE NEWS? . . .      491 COOLE BALLYLEE V    40E
     WHEN ALL THAT STORY'S FINISHED, WHAT'S THE NEWS? . . .     495 CHOICE                5
     NEWS FOR THE DELPHIC ORACLE . . . . . . . . . .            611 NEWS ORACLE           T
NEWT
     HUGS AND PETS AND PATS YON NEWT, . . . . . . . . .         727 LOVERS QUARREL       27
NEWTON'S
     NOT SUCH AS ARE IN NEWTON'S METAPHOR, . . . . . . .        494 AT ALGECIRAS         11
NEW-TORN
     CUT OUT OUR RHYMES ON STRIPS OF NEW-TORN BARK . . . .      343 SHEP GOATHERD       115
NEW-WASHED
     . . . FOR WHITER THAN NEW-WASHED FLEECE . . . . . .         47 OISIN 3             11
NEXT
     AND ALL THAT NIGHT, AND ALL THROUGH THE NEXT DAY . . .     185 QUEEN MAEVE         113
     TO STAY THE STAG'S NEXT RUSH.  WHEN SWORD MET HORN . .     277 TWO KINGS         V  15
     AND THAT ENQUIRING MAN JOHN SYNGE COMES NEXT, . . . .      324 ROBERT GREGORY       25
     OF THAT OR THE NEXT WINTER WOULD BE DEATH. . . . . .       471 ALL SOUL NIGHT       30
     ON FLORENCE EMERY I CALL THE NEXT, . . . . . . . .         472 ALL SOUL NIGHT       41
     BECAUSE THIS AGE AND THE NEXT AGE  . . . . . . . .         598 STONE CROSS           9
     OR DEATH THAT COMETH WITH THE NEXT LIFE-KEY? . . . .       724 KANVA ON SELF        18
NIAM
     IS NIAM, DAUGHTER OF THE KING . . . . . . . . . .            5 OISIN 1           V  49
     YOUNG NIAM, AND THOU SHALT BE CALLEN . . . . . . .           7 OISIN 1           V  75
     SANG NIAM, AND THEIR DEWY SHOWERS . . . . . . . .           11 OISIN 1           V 135
     SAID NIAM, AS SHE LAID THE TIP . . . . . . . . .            12 OISIN 1           V 150
     MAID NIAM FROM A LITTLE TRUMP . . . . . . . . . .           14 OISIN 1           V 194
     BUT NIAM, WITH A SAD DISTRESS . . . . . . . . . .           15 OISIN 1           V 211
     THEN SOFTLY TO ME NIAM CAME, . . . . . . . . . .            25 OISIN 1           V 373
     AND NOW SANG NIAM, SWAYING HER BRIGHT HEAD . . . . .        29 OISIN 2           V   6
     SO SANG YOUNG NIAM, SWAYING HER BRIGHT HEAD, . . . .        30 OISIN 2           V  15
     BUT NIAM WITH HER HANDS CARESSED HIS EARS, . . . . .        30 OISIN 2           V  26
     AND THUS, MY LATE-LOST NIAM, DIDST THOU SAY: . . . .        34 OISIN 2           V  78
     SAID NIAM.  "AY, AND HUGE.  WHEN YE HAVE LED . . . .        35 OISIN 2           V  89
     TO FLY A SPIRIT," NIAM WEEPING SAID. . . . . . . .          35 OISIN 2           V  92
     THE STRANGER WATCHED THE SWORD: BUT NIAM FAR, . . . .       38 OISIN 2           V 136
     CAST THE LOOSE BULK, LEST NIAM FEAR HIM DEAD: . . . .       41 OISIN 2           V 183
     HOLDING THAT HORSE LONG SEEN NOT, NIAM STOOD. . . . .       44 OISIN 2           V 230
     LOST NIAM MOURN AND SAY, "AH, LOVE, WE GO  . . . . .        46 OISIN 2           V 245B
     YE HAVE NO POWER." "AND, NIAM, SAY, OF THESE . . . . .      46 OISIN 2           V 248
     SNATCHING THE HORN OF NIAM, I BLEW FORTH A LINGERING NOTE:  51 OISIN 3           V  57
     SNATCHING THE HORN OF NIAM, I BLEW A LINGERING NOTE: . .    51 OISIN 3           V  57
     SAD NIAM CAME NEAR ME, AND LAID HER BROWS ON THE MIDST      52 OISIN 3           V  74
        OF MY BREAST
     OH, HADST THOU SEEN BEAUTIFUL NIAM WAIL TO HERSELF AND      54 OISIN 3           V 109
        BLANCH,
     AND SOFTLY COME TO THY NIAM OVER THE TOPS OF THE TIDE: . .  52 OISIN 3           V 126
     BUT WEEP FOR THY NIAM, OH OISIN, WEEP: FOR IF ONLY THY SHOE 55 OISIN 3           V 127
     AND SHIVERING AND LONELY, AND LONGING FOR NIAM, I TURNED    60 OISIN 3           V 181
        ME ABOUT,
     AND FAND, AND NIAM, AND LABAN, WHO COULD CHANGE TO AN OTTER 209 UNDER THE MOON V  12
        OR FAWN,
     WHERE NIAM HEADS THE REVELRY. . . . . . . . . . .          743 DANAAN QUICK         29
NIAMH
     NIAMH, AND MY COUNTRY FAR  . . . . . . . . . .               5 OISIN 1              48
     IS NIAMH, AND MY LAND WHERE TIDE . . . . . . . .             5 OISIN 1           V  48
     AND NIAMH BE WITH YOU FOR A WIFE." . . . . . . .             9 OISIN 1             101
     AND NIAMH SANG CONTINUALLY . . . . . . . . . .              11 OISIN 1             134
     "VEX THEM NO LONGER," NIAMH SAID, . . . . . . . .           12 OISIN 1             148
     AND NIAMH BLEW THREE MERRY NOTES . . . . . . . .            14 OISIN 1             195
     BUT NIAMH WITH A SWIFT DISTRESS  . . . . . . . .            15 OISIN 1             211
     THE GENTLE NIAMH WAS MY WIFE: . . . . . . . . .             24 OISIN 1             357
     THEREON YOUNG NIAMH SOFTLY CAME  . . . . . . . .            25 OISIN 1             373
     "GAZE NO MORE ON THE PHANTOMS," NIAMH SAID, . . . .         29 OISIN 2               5
     NOR CEASED UNTIL WHITE NIAMH STROKED HIS EARS . . .         30 OISIN 2              26
     "I BRING DELIVERANCE," PEARL-PALE NIAMH SAID. . . . .       34 OISIN 2              78
     "FLEE FROM HIM," PEARL-PALE NIAMH WEEPING CRIED, . . .      35 OISIN 2              92
     BUT ONLY EXULTANT FACES.  NIAMH STOOD  . . . . . .          38 OISIN 2             136
     LEST NIAMH SHUDDER.  FULL OF HOPE AND DREAD . . . . .       41 OISIN 2             183
```

558

		PAGE	TITLE	LINE
NIAMH (CONTINUED)				
OUTCRY OF BATS. AND THEN YOUNG NIAMH CAME • • • • •		44	OISIN 2	229
THE HARE LEAPED IN THE GRASS. YOUNG NIAMH CAME • • • •		44	OISIN 2	V 229
AND THEN LOST NIAMH MURMURED, "LOVE, WE GO • • • • •		46	OISIN 2	245
AND NEVER A SONG SANG NIAMH, AND OVER MY FINGER-TIPS • •		47	OISIN 3	6
SNATCHING THE HORN OF NIAMH, I BLEW A LONG LINGERING NOTE.		51	OISIN 3	57
AND THE PEARL-PALE NIAMH LAY BY ME, • • • • • • •		52	OISIN 3	74
O HAD YOU SEEN BEAUTIFUL NIAMH GROW WHITE AS THE WATERS ARE WHITE,		54	OISIN 3	109
I CRIED, "O NIAMH! O WHITE ONE! IF ONLY A TWELVE-HOURED DAY,		55	OISIN 3	113
AND SOFTLY COME TO YOUR NIAMH OVER THE TOPS OF THE TIDE;		55	OISIN 3	126
BUT WEEP FOR YOUR NIAMH, O OISIN, WEEP; FOR IF ONLY YOUR SHOE		55	OISIN 3	127
AND LONELY AND LONGING FOR NIAMH, I SHIVERED AND TURNED ME ABOUT,		60	OISIN 3	181
AND NIAMH CALLING AWAY, COME AWAY! • • • • • ▬ • •		140	HOSTING SIDHE	4
AND NIAMH CALLING AWAY, COME AWAY. • • • • • • • •		141	HOSTING SIDHE	16
THAT SAW YOUNG NIAMH HOVER WITH LOVE-LORN FACE • • • •		162	ASKS FORGIVE	13
AND NIAMH AND LABAN AND FAND, WHO COULD CHANGE TO AN OTTER OR FAWN,		209	UNDER THE MOON	12
NIAMH THAT RODE ON IT! LAD AND LASS • • • • • • • •		550	SEVERED HEAD	11
MAN-PICKER NIAMH LEANT AND SIGHED • • • • • • • • •		611	NEWS ORACLE	5
NIAM'S				
IN NIAM'S HAIR--WHEN ROSE A WORLD OF TOWERS • • • • •		30	OISIN 2	V 22
NIETZSCHE				
HECTOR IS IN THE DUST, NIETZSCHE IS BORN, • • • • • •		374	PHASES OF MOON	46
NIGH SEE WELL-NIGH				
AND NOW STILL SAD OUR TROOP DREW NIGH • • • • • • •		17	OISIN 1	V 247
AND NIGH UNTO HIM EACH ONE DREW, • • • • • • • • •		18	OISIN 1	V 257
BLIND AND NIGH DEAF, WITH WITHERED ARMS HE LIES • • • •		42	OISIN 2	V 203
THEN HE SANG SOFTLY NIGH THE PEARLY RIM; • • • • • •		69	SAD SHEPHERD	25
THEN SANG HE SOFTLY NIGH THE PEARLY RIM; • • • • • •		69	SAD SHEPHERD	V 25
AND SHOREWARD WAVES, WE NIGH HAVE FOUGHT! WAVES BRING • •		660	ISLE STAT II 1	44
AND YONDER HUDDLING BLACKNESS DRAWETH NIGH-- • • • • •		663	ISLE STAT II 2	15
WELL NIGH IMMORTAL IN THIS CHARMED CLIME, • • • • • •		674	ISLE STAT II 3	202
WHY NOT? HE IS HER OWN! AND CROUCHING NIGH • • • • •		688	TWO TITANS	44
WHERE IS OUR BROTHER PETER? WHEN YOU'RE NIGH, • • • •		696	MOSADA 2	12
FROM HAYNAU'S LIFTED FINGERS--TWO DRAW NIGH • • • • • •		714	FERENCZ RENYI	104
THE MAN WHOSE HOUR OF DEATH DRAWS NIGH, • • • • • • •		716	FAIRY DOCTOR	6
NIGH OF HIS WITS BY FEAR BEREFT. • • • • • • • • •		730	PRIEST FAIRY	50
NIGHEST				
THE NIGHEST BLOSSOM WHERE IT FALLS I'LL TAKE. • • • • •		657	ISLE STAT I 3	65
NIGHT SEE TO-NIGHT				
DAMASK ROSES IN THE NIGHT, • • • • • • • • • • •		21	OISIN 1	V 306A
BY RIVERS AND THE WOODS' OLD NIGHT; • • • • • • • •		25	OISIN 1	387
THE RIVERS, AND THE WOOD'S OLD NIGHT. • • • • • • •		25	OISIN 1	V 387
THAT SCARES WITH HIS BUSTLE THE DELICATE NIGHT, • • • •		28	OISIN 1	V 423B
THE SINGING MELTED IN THE NIGHT! • • • • • • • • •		28	OISIN 1	V 427A
JABBER AND SCREAM ABOUT HIM IN THE NIGHT! • • • • • •		34	OISIN 2	82
WITH HOPE, MINE ENEMY. AS HE BY NIGHT • • • • • • •		34	OISIN 2	V 81
GAVE TO HIGH NOON AND NOON TO NIGHT GAVE WAY; • • • • •		40	OISIN 2	172
AMID THE SHADES OF NIGHT, HE CHANGED AND RAN • • • • •		40	OISIN 2	174
AND THE MOON GOAD THE WATERS NIGHT AND DAY, • • • • • •		45	OISIN 2	238
AND THE EARS OF THE HORSE WENT SINKING AWAY IN THE HOLLOW NIGHT,		48	OISIN 3	21
• • • "THE FENIANS HUNT WOLVES IN THE NIGHT, • • • • •		59	OISIN 3	171
O SWIFT ON THE SEAS ALL DAY AND NIGHT • • • • • • •		70	CLOAK BOAT	8
ALL DAY AND NIGHT." • • • • • • • • • • • • • •		70	CLOAK BOAT	10
HE IS A MONSTROUS PEACOCK, AND HE WAVETH ALL THE NIGHT • •		77	INDIAN ON GOD	19
HOW I HAVE FOLLOWED, NIGHT AND DAY, • • • • • • • •		85	MAD KING GOLL	53
WE FOOT IT ALL THE NIGHT, • • • • • • • • • • •		87	STOLEN CHILD	16
A THIN GREY MAN HALF LOST IN GATHERING NIGHT. • • • • •		102	FERGUS DRUID	7
A THIN, GREY MAN, HALF-LOST IN GATHERING NIGHT. • • • •		102	FERGUS DRUID	V 7
TO THESE OLD NIGHT SHALL ALL HER MYSTERY TELL; • • • •		114	ROSE OF BATTLE	22
AND THE LONG DEW-DROPPING HOURS OF THE NIGHT; • • • • •		116	FAERY SONG	7
I WILL ARISE AND GO NOW, FOR ALWAYS NIGHT AND DAY • • • •		117	ISLE INNISFREE	9
WHEN EARTHY NIGHT HAD DRUNK HIS BODY IN; • • • • • •		127	DREAM OF FAERY	28
WAS WEARY NIGHT AND DAY! • • • • • • • • • • •		132	FR GILLIGAN	2
"HE WHO HATH MADE THE NIGHT OF STARS • • • • • • •		134	FR GILLIGAN	41
HAS PLANTED QUIET IN THE NIGHT; • • • • • • • • •		134	TWO TREES	8
THAT THE STORMY NIGHT RECEIVES; • • • • • • • • •		135	TWO TREES	26
WHILE THE NIGHT GREW, ABOVE THE FADING COALS, • • • • •		136	TO SOME I TALK V	3
THE MARINERS OF NIGHT ABOVE, • • • • • • • • • •		139	TO IRELAND	V 38
THE HOST IS RUSHING 'TWIXT NIGHT AND DAY, • • • • • •		141	HOSTING SIDHE	13
AT THE COMING OF NIGHT TIDE; • • • • • • • • • •		144	HOST OF AIR	V 6
UNDER MY FEET THAT THEY FOLLOW YOU NIGHT AND DAY. • • • •		153	CHANGE BELOVED	5
UNDER MY FEET, THAT I FOLLOW YOU, NIGHT AND DAY. • • • •		153	CHANGE BELOVED V	5
THE NORTH UNFOLDS ABOVE THEM CLINGING, CREEPING NIGHT, • •		154	BELOVED PEACE	3
THE NORTH UNROLLS ABOVE THEM CLINGING, CREEPING NIGHT, • •		154	BELOVED PEACE	V 3
SHE ROSE IN HER PALE NIGHT GOWN, • • • • • • • • •		159	CAP AND BELLS	V 10
THE NIGHT SMELLED RICH WITH JUNE, • • • • • • • •		160	CAP AND BELLS	V 28
O WINDS, OLDER THAN CHANGING OF NIGHT AND DAY, • • • •		162	ASKS FORGIVE	7
O WINDS, ELDER THAN CHANGING OF NIGHT AND DAY, • • • •		162	ASKS FORGIVE	V 7
"O BLESSEDNESS COMES IN THE NIGHT AND THE DAY • • • • •		168	BLESSED	33
INTO THE BLINDING NIGHT.-- • • • • • • • • • • •		174	ELEMENT POWERS V	4
THE NETS OF DAY AND NIGHT. • • • • • • • • • • •		175	ELEMENT POWERS	12
OF NIGHT AND LIGHT AND THE HALF-LIGHT, • • • • • • •		176	CLOTHS HEAVEN	4
OF NIGHT AND LIGHT AND THE HALF LIGHT, • • • • • • •		176	CLOTHS HEAVEN V	4
BUT THAT GREAT QUEEN, WHO MORE THAN HALF THE NIGHT • • •		180	QUEEN MAEVE	16
WHEN NIGHT WAS AT ITS DEEPEST, A WILD GOOSE • • • • •		181	QUEEN MAEVE	36

NIGHT (CONTINUED)

	PAGE	TITLE	LINE
AND ALL THAT NIGHT, AND ALL THROUGH THE NEXT DAY	185	QUEEN MAEVE	113
TO MIDDLE NIGHT, THEY DUG INTO THE HILL.	185	QUEEN MAEVE	114
AS MIDDLE NIGHT GREAT CATS WITH SILVER CLAWS,	185	QUEEN MAEVE	115
IN THE GREY REEDS THAT NIGHT AND MORN	190	BAILE AILLINN	42
WHO WHEN NIGHT THICKENS ARE AFLOAT	196	BAILE AILLINN	179
WHEN IN RAGGED VAPOUR THEY MUTTER NIGHT AND DAY,	206	HANRAHANS SONG V	2
TO FIND IT WHEN NIGHT FALLS LAID ON A GOLDEN BIER.	209	UNDER THE MOON	10
OF THE HUNTER'S MOON, THAT HUNG BETWEEN THE NIGHT AND THE DAY,	210	UNDER THE MOON	18
OF THE THIRD MOON, THAT HUNG BETWEEN THE NIGHT AND THE DAY,	210	UNDER THE MOON V	18
MOVED ROUND ME IN THE SHADOWS, AND AT NIGHT	218	WOODS OF COOLE	19
AT THE FULL MOON? HE PLAYED ALL THROUGH THE NIGHT.	223	SHADOW WATER B	21
I SAW THEM ON THAT NIGHT AS WELL AS YOU.	223	SHADOW WATER B	29
THE OTHER NIGHT, WHILE HE WAS PLAYING IT.	223	SHADOW WATER B	32
I SAW THEM, TOO, ONE NIGHT. FORGAEL WAS PLAYING,	223	SHADOW WATER B	36
THAT HE HAS BEEN ALL NIGHT UPON THE HILLS.	229	SHADOW WATER B	168
BUT MY BELOVED--THAT NIGHT AND DAY HAD PERISHED,	246	SHADOW WATER B	504
CRIED OUT THE WHOLE NIGHT LONG.	254	HIS DREAM	16
'TWAS ROUNDLY SPOKE, BUT WHEN NIGHT CAME	275	GREY ROCK	95
AND WOULD BE NO HARSH FRIEND. WHEN NIGHT HAD DEEPENED,	283	TWO KINGS	138
I WAITED TILL THE NIGHT WAS ON THE TURN,	283	TWO KINGS	144
THEY MAULED AND BIT THE WHOLE NIGHT THROUGH;	297	THREE BEGGARS	48
AND TILL ANOTHER NIGHT HAD GONE,	297	THREE BEGGARS	51
THEY'D MAULED AND BITTEN THE NIGHT THROUGH,	297	THREE BEGGARS V	48
"NIGHT GROWS UNEASY NEAR THE DAWN	303	HOUR DAWN	33
AND MURMURED "MAY GOD CURSE THE NIGHT	303	HOUR DAWN V	32B
THAT THE NIGHT COME.	317	NIGHT COME	T
THAT THE NIGHT COME.	317	NIGHT COME	12
THIS NIGHT CAN SET US QUARRELLING,	324	ROBERT GREGORY	15
BETWEEN THE NIGHT AND MORNING. I MIGHT HAVE LIVED,	351	PEOPLE	6
THE YOUNG MEN EVERY NIGHT APPLAUD THEIR GABY'S LAUGHING EYE,	353	HIS PHOENIX	9
THIS NIGHT HAS BEEN SO STRANGE THAT IT SEEMED	358	PRESENCES	1
OR AN OLD MAN UPON A WINTER'S NIGHT.	359	WAR POEM	6
THAT NIGHT AND MORNING I MAY THRASH	379	SAINT HUNCH	9
NOW AT ITS FIFTEENTH NIGHT.	383	VISION ROBART	28
HIS "MORNING" AND HIS "NIGHT" DISCLOSE	386	ROBARTES DANCE	33
"LAST NIGHT, WHERE UNDER THE WILD MOON	387	SOLOMON WITCH	2
THEREFORE A BLESSED MOON LAST NIGHT	388	SOLOMON WITCH	31
"THE NIGHT HAS FALLEN; NOT A SOUND	389	SOLOMON WITCH	38
NEVER UNTIL THIS NIGHT COULD I HAVE BEEN STIRRED.	389	IMAGE PAST	1
THAT ANY NIGHT COULD BRING	390	IMAGE PAST	32
OF THE HOVERING THING NIGHT BROUGHT ME.	390	IMAGE PAST	42
NO, NO, NOT NIGHT BUT DEATH;	394	EASTER 1916	66
THAT PLAGUE ME DAY AND NIGHT.	399	DEMON BEAST	3
THE SWEETNESS THAT ALL LONGED FOR NIGHT AND DAY,	418	ANCEST HOUSES	20
WHERE THROUGH LONG WARS AND SUDDEN NIGHT ALARMS	420	MY HOUSE	24
WHERE THROUGH LONG WARS AND SUDDEN NIGHT ALARUMS	420	MY HOUSE V	24
LAST NIGHT THEY TRUNDLED DOWN THE ROAD	425	STARES NEST	13
THE NIGHT CAN SWEAT WITH TERROR AS BEFORE	429	NINETEEN 19	29
THOSE WINDS THAT CLAMOUR OF APPROACHING NIGHT.	431	NINETEEN 19	68
IN THE OLD ROOMS; NIGHT CAN OUTBALANCE DAY,	435	NEW FACES	6
WHATEVER FLAMES UPON THE NIGHT	438	SONGS PLAY 2	15
OUT OF DARK NIGHT WHERE LAY	439	FRAGMENTS	9
SUMMER AND WINTER, DAY AND NIGHT,	447	COLONUS PRAISE	31
AND TALKED AWAY THE NIGHT,	456	SUMMER SPRING	2
WERE SOME DEAR CHEEK. UPON A MOONLESS NIGHT	466	HARUN RASHID	127
WERE SOME DEAR FACE. UPON A MOONLESS NIGHT	466	HARUN RASHID V	127
ALL SOULS' NIGHT	470	ALL SOUL NIGHT	T
AND IT IS ALL SOULS' NIGHT,	470	ALL SOUL NIGHT	3
IT IS ALL SOULS' NIGHT AND THE GREAT CHRIST CHURCH BELL	470	ALL SOUL NIGHT V	1
THINK OF ANCESTRAL NIGHT THAT CAN,	478	SELF AND SOUL	20
EMBLEMATICAL OF THE NIGHT.	478	SELF AND SOUL	30
A COUPLE OF NIGHT MOTHS ARE ON THE WING,	482	BLOOD AND MOON V	46
A SYCAMORE AND LIME-TREE LOST IN NIGHT	488	COOLE PARK 29	3
A SYCAMORE AND LIME TREE LOST IN NIGHT	488	COOLE PARK 29 V	3
EVERY NIGHT IN BED,	495	MOHINI CHATTER	4
NIGHT RESONANCE RECEDES, NIGHT-WALKERS' SONG	497	BYZANTIUM	3
OF DAY AND NIGHT;	500	VACILLATION	6
THOSE BRANCHES OF THE NIGHT AND DAY	502	VACILLATION	68
WANDERS OUT INTO THE NIGHT	508	JANE BISHOP	25
PASSING ON THE ROAD THAT NIGHT,	511	JANE AND JACK	17
THAT LOVER OF A NIGHT	512	JANE ON GOD	1
AND AFTER NAILED UPON THE NIGHT	519	HER DREAM	7
THAT FIRST NIGHT IN HELEN'S ARMS.	522	LULLABY V	6
THE CURTAINS DRAWN UPON UNFRIENDLY NIGHT,	523	LONG SILENCE	4
OUR MINDS ARE AT THEIR BEST THIS NIGHT,	523	MAD AS MIST	3
"AND THE NIGHT GROWS ROUGH."	526	AM OF IRELAND	13
IF EMPTY NIGHT REPLIES?	533	FIRST CONFESS	18
WHILE NIGHT SHUTS THE EYES	535	PARTING	2
MONEY I HAD, AND IT WENT IN THE NIGHT,	544	TO SAME TUNE 1	12
STOOD OR HAVE MARCHED THE NIGHT LONG	546	TO SAME TUNE 2	15
OR HAVE MARCHED THE NIGHT LONG,	546	TO SAME TUNE 2 V	15
CUCHULAIN THAT FOUGHT NIGHT LONG WITH THE FOAM,	549	SEVERED HEAD	9
TO-MORROW NIGHT I WILL BREAK DOWN THE DOOR.	551	SONGS REWRIT 1	6
TO-MORROW NIGHT I WILL BREAK DOWN THE DOOR.	551	SONGS REWRIT 1	12
TO-MORROW NIGHT I WILL BREAK DOWN THE DOOR.	551	SONGS REWRIT 1	18
TOMORROW NIGHT I WILL BREAK DOWN THE DOOR.	551	SONGS REWRIT 1 V	REF
TO-MORROW NIGHT I WILL BREAK IN THE DOOR.	551	SONGS REWRIT 1 V	REF
BECAUSE YOU HAVE FOUND ME IN THE PITCH-DARK NIGHT	554	RIBH AT TOMB	1

NIGHT   (CONTINUED)
BECAUSE YOU HAVE IT IN THE PITCH DARK NIGHT . . . . .   554 RIBH AT TOMB   V   1
BECAUSE YOU HAVE FOUND ME IN THE PITCH DARK NIGHT . . .   554 RIBH AT TOMB   V   1
CAVERNED IN NIGHT UNDER THE DRIFTED SNOW. . . . . . .   563 MERU   10
THAT DAY BRINGS ROUND THE NIGHT, THAT BEFORE DAWN . . .   563 MERU   13
AND AT NIGHT TIME WOULD SHE SAY, ...   570 THREE BUSHES   V   30
STRANGE NIGHT HAS COME; . . . .   574 MAIDS 1ST SONG   6
OF THAT MOST SENSUOUS SILENCE OF THE NIGHT . . . . . .   579 DOR WELLESLEY   6
I CAME ON A GREAT HOUSE IN THE MIDDLE OF THE NIGHT, . .   581 CURSE CROMWELL   25
HAD TRAVELLED HALF THE NIGHT. . . . .   585 ORAHILLY   17
THEIR ROBBERY BY NIGHT! . . . .   607 SONGS BURDEN 2   15
MONEY I HAD, AND IT WENT IN THE NIGHT, ...   616 MARCH SONGS 3   12
FAR UP IN THE STRETCHES OF NIGHT; . . . .   623 HIGH TALK   12
. . . NIGHT SPLITS AND THE DAWN BREAKS LOOSE; . . . .   623 HIGH TALK   12
WHERE I CAN SIT UP HALF THE NIGHT . . . .   624 APPARITIONS   11
BECAUSE OF THE INCREASING NIGHT . . . .   624 APPARITIONS   21
AND NIGHT AND MORNING SING! . . . .   627 STATES HOLIDAY   12
LAST NIGHT I LAY ON THE MOUNTAIN, ...   628 JANE MOUNTAIN   11
I LIE AWAKE NIGHT AFTER NIGHT . . . .   632 MAN AND ECHO   9
I LIE AWAKE NIGHT AFTER NIGHT . . . .   632 MAN AND ECHO   9
AND SINKS AT LAST INTO THE NIGHT. . . . .   633 MAN AND ECHO   36
INTO THE NIGHT. O ROCKY VOICE, ...   633 MAN AND ECHO   37
SHALL WE IN THAT GREAT NIGHT REJOICE? . . . .   633 MAN AND ECHO   38
ITS JOY OR NIGHT SEEM BUT A DREAM; . . . .   633 MAN AND ECHO   42
ITS JOY OR NIGHT SEEMS BUT A DREAM. . . . .   633 MAN AND ECHO   V   42
WEARY OF REAPING THE BARREN NIGHT . . . .   648 ISLE STAT I 1   84
LIFT MY SOUL FROM RAYLESS NIGHT-- . . . .   648 ISLE STAT I 1   95
STRICKEN ALL THE NIGHT IS PAST-- . . . .   648 ISLE STAT I 1   96
WHERE ALL NIGHT LONG THE HEAVENS WEEP AND WEEP, . . .   649 ISLE STAT I 1   124
WHERE ALL NIGHT LONG THE LONELY MOON, THE WHITE . . .   650 ISLE STAT I 1   126
BY DAY AND NIGHT A LONELY FOUNTAIN SINGS, ...   650 ISLE STAT I 1   130
THERE! THERE! DOST THOU NOT SEE? I SEE THE NIGHT, . .   653 ISLE STAT I 2   54
MOCKING WITH PATIENT LAUGHTER ALL THE NIGHT . . . .   657 ISLE STAT I 3   52
ONE HAND BROW-SHADING, FAR ACROSS THE NIGHT, ...   663 ISLE STAT II 2   27
MORE WONDERFUL! AND WE HAVE SWORDS. O NIGHT . . . .   664 ISLE STAT II 2   61
CAST ON THE SOUND, ON, ON. THIS NIGHT OF GRAVES, . .   665 ISLE STAT II 2   71
O SWIFT ON THE SEAS ALL DAY AND NIGHT . . . . . .   666 ISLE STAT II 3   8
ALL DAY AND NIGHT. . . . .   666 ISLE STAT II 3   10
IT IS, YET SHALL IT FAIL THEE DAY AND NIGHT . . . .   674 ISLE STAT II 3   211
WEARY OF WATCHING ROUND THE FIRE AT NIGHT. . . . . .   683 SEEKER   42
BEAT ON IT WITH THEIR HAMMERS DAY AND NIGHT. . . . .   687 TWO TITANS   4
HAVE LIT LONE TAPERS. NOW THE NIGHT WAS CAST, . . .   687 TWO TITANS   27
THIS EVE, TO-MORROW, OR TO-MORROW NIGHT . . . . . .   699 MOSADA 3   2
THE BURGHERS OF THE NIGHT FADE ONE BY ONE. . . . .   700 MOSADA 3   40
OH, ALLAH! IT WAS THUS THEY SHONE THAT NIGHT . . . .   701 MOSADA 3   50
I NEVER KNEW A NIGHT SO HONEY-SWEET. . . . .   702 MOSADA 3   99
I NEVER KNEW A NIGHT SO HONEY SWEET. . . . .   702 MOSADA 3   V   99
FOR NIGHT COMES FAST. LOOK DOWN ON ME, MY LOVE, . .   703 MOSADA 3   103
I NEVER KNEW A NIGHT SO DEW-BEDROWNED. . . . . . .   703 MOSADA 3   105
I NEVER KNEW A NIGHT SO BITTER COLD. . . . .   704 MOSADA 3   124
OF RHYME; REMEMBERING THEE, THIS CRESCENT NIGHT, . .   704 REMEMBRANCE   2
BENEATH THE FLAMING EYEBALLS OF THE NIGHT, ...   723 KANVA ON SELF   4
LONG THOU FOR NOTHING, NEITHER NIGHT NOR DAY; . . .   734 QUATRAIN APHOR   10
MOURN ALL THE NIGHT AND DAY, ...   737 MOURN THEN ON   2
AND SING TO YOU IN THE NIGHT, ...   739 WHERE BOOKS GO   6
TILL DAY AND NIGHT TIME END. . . . .   741 EARL PAUL   48
WITH CREATURES OF OUR HEAVY NIGHT, ...   743 DANAAN QUICK   10
I HAVE SPUN IN THE HOUSE THIS NIGHT! . . . .   771 SPINNING SONG   13
AND MANY A NIGHT IT SEEMS . . . .   781 MY HEART BEAT   9
THE BITTER SWEETNESS OF THE NIGHT . . . .   781 HEART FRIGHT   3
BECAUSE THE NIGHT WINDS BLOW . . . .   782 HEART FRIGHT   16
I HAVE HEARD IN THE NIGHT AIR . . . .   783 GREY ROUND   6
BUT NOW THE NIGHT IS GONE. . . . .   783 GREY ROUND   24
AT DAYBREAK AFTER STORMY NIGHT . . . .   784 WOMANS BEAUTY   3
NIGHT-COLOURED
WHERE BANNERS OF THE CALIPHS HANG, NIGHT-COLOURED . . .   461 HARUN RASHID   6
NIGHT-DARK
IN THE CONFUSION OF ITS NIGHT-DARK FOLDS, ...   470 HARUN RASHID   192
NIGHTFALL
TOWARDS NIGHTFALL UPON CERTAIN SET APART . . . . .   325 ROBERT GREGORY   29
TOWARDS NIGHTFALL UPON A RACE . . . .   325 ROBERT GREGORY   31
TOWARDS NIGHTFALL UPON A PLACE . . . .   325 ROBERT GREGORY   V   31
"BEFORE NIGHTFALL I'LL PICK A POCKET . . . . . .   332 ROUND TOWER   27
WHAT IS IT BUT NIGHTFALL? . . . .   394 EASTER 1916   65
NIGHT-GOWN
SHE ROSE IN HER PALE NIGHT-GOWN; . . . .   159 CAP AND BELLS   10
NIGHTINGALE
THE NIGHTINGALE THAT DEAFENS DAYLIGHT THERE, ...   446 COLONUS PRAISE   3
NIGHTINGALE'S
A PIECE OF A NIGHTINGALE'S EGG, ...   708 FAIRY PEDANT   24
NIGHTJAR
CLAMOUR OF THE LONE NIGHTJAR. . . . .   732 STREET DANCERS   21
NIGHTLY
AND HEAR AMID THE GARDEN'S NIGHTLY PEACE," . . . . .   300 BEGGAR CRIED   18
NIGHTLY, AND STARTLED BY THAT SOUND . . . . . .   326 ROBERT GREGORY   54
I TOLD HIM THAT NIGHTLY FROM SIX TO SEVEN I SAT AT THIS   578 LOFTY THINGS   9
   TABLE,
NIGHTMARE
WERE VEXED TO NIGHTMARE BY A ROCKING CRADLE, ...   402 SECOND COMING   20
NOW DAYS ARE DRAGON-RIDDEN, THE NIGHTMARE . . . . .   429 NINETEEN 19   25
NOW DAYS ARE DRAGON RIDDEN, THE NIGHTMARE . . . . .   429 NINETEEN 19   V   25

NIGHTMARE   (CONTINUED)
    WHAT MATTER THOUGH NUMB NIGHTMARE RIDE ON TOP, ...   564 GYRES   9
NIGHT-MOTHS
    A COUPLE OF NIGHT-MOTHS ARE ON THE WING. . . . .   482 BLOOD AND MOON   46
NIGHT'S
    AND FILLS WITH STARS NIGHT'S PURPLE CUP, ...   18 OISIN 1   262
    I WEEP--I WEEP BECAUSE BARE NIGHT'S ABOVE, ... 246 SHADOW WATER B   499
    BUT BRILLIANT AS THE NIGHT'S EMBROIDERY, ...   461 HARUN RASHID   7
    OR THE DAY'S VANITY, THE NIGHT'S REMORSE. . . . . 491 COOLE BALLYLEE V   40H
    OR THE DAY'S VANITY, THE NIGHT'S REMORSE. . . . . 495 CHOICE   8
    NIGHT'S RESONANCE RECEDES, NIGHT-WALKERS SONG . . . . . . 497 BYZANTIUM   V   3
    ALL NIGHT'S FATHOMLESS WISDOM COME, ... 519 HER DREAM   2
    NO, NIGHT'S BIRD AND LOVE'S . . . . 536 PARTING   5
NIGHTS
    IT'S CERTAIN I'D SLEEP EASIER O' NIGHTS . . . . 224 SHADOW WATER B   59
    THAT GIRL MY UNREMEMBERING NIGHTS HOLD FAST . . . . 384 VISION ROBART   50
    HER NIGHTS IN ARGUMENT . . . . 392 EASTER 1916   19
    A DOZEN NIGHTS OF NATURAL SLEEP, AND THEN . . . . 468 HARUN RASHID   150
    ALONE AND ALONE NINE NIGHTS I LAY . . . . 551 SONGS REWRIT 1   13
    NINE NIGHTS I LAY IN LONGING SORE . . . . 551 SONGS REWRIT 1 V   13
    NINE NIGHTS I LAY AND IN LONGING SORE . . . . 551 SONGS REWRIT 1 V   13
    UPON CLEAR NIGHTS THEY LEAVE THE UPPER AIR . . . . 750 SHADOW WATER A   87
NIGHT-TIDE
    AT THE COMING OF NIGHT-TIDE, ... 144 HOST OF AIR   6
NIGHT-VESTED
    THROUGH THIS NIGHT-VESTED PLACE THE RED BEAMS BREAK. . . . 662 ISLE STAT II 2   4
NIGHT-WALKERS
    NIGHT'S RESONANCE RECEDES, NIGHT-WALKERS SONG . . . . . . 497 BYZANTIUM   V   3
NIGHT-WALKERS'
    NIGHT RESONANCE RECEDES, NIGHT-WALKERS' SONG . . . . . . 497 BYZANTIUM   3
NIGHT-WANDERING
    WHAT ROGUE IS NIGHT-WANDERING? . . . . 781 MY HEART BEAT   5
NIMBLE   SEE OVER-NIMBLE
NINE   SEE FORTY-NINE NINETEEN-TWENTY-NINE CAT-O'-NINE-TAILS
    AND SUNKEN SHAPE, A NINE DAYS' CORPSE SEA-DASHED-- . . .   40 OISIN 2   V   179
    NINE BEAN-ROWS WILL I HAVE THERE, A HIVE FOR THE HONEY-BEE,   117 ISLE INNISFREE   3
    NINE BEAN ROWS WILL I HAVE THERE, A HIVE FOR THE HONEY BEE,   117 ISLE INNISFREE V   3
    I'D GIVE THE PROFIT OF NINE VOYAGES . . . . 222 SHADOW WATER B V   9
    AND DROWNED THE TREASURES OF NINE CONQUERED NATIONS, . . . 235 SHADOW WATER B   287
    THEY GAVE ME THAT OLD HARP OF THE NINE SPELLS . . . . . . 237 SHADOW WATER B V   327
    NINE SWORDS WITH HANDLES OF RHINOCEROS HORN . . . . 239 SHADOW WATER B   368
    AND FOR NINE DAYS HE HAD FOOD FROM OTHER HANDS, ... 282 TWO KINGS   126
    AND FOR NINE DAYS MY MIND WENT WHIRLING ROUND . . . . . . 282 TWO KINGS   127
    BUT WHEN NINE DAYS HAD GONE I STOOD AGAIN . . . . 282 TWO KINGS   131
    QUEEN MAEVE'S NINE MAINES HAD BEEN NURSED, ... 302 HOUR DAWN   8
    WHAT ONE OF MAEVE'S NINE BRAWLING SONS . . . . 303 HOUR DAWN   36
    HAS ONE OF MAEVE'S NINE BRAWLING SONS . . . . 303 HOUR DAWN   V   36
    MY SLEEP WERE NOW NINE CENTURIES . . . . 306 HOUR DAWN   75
    ARE NINE AND FIFTY SWANS. . . . . 322 SWANS AT COOLE V   6
    AFTER NINE YEARS, I SINK MY HEAD ABASHED. . . . . 353 PEOPLE   37
    FROM NINETEEN HUNDRED NINE OR TEN, PAVLOVA'S HAD THE CRY,   354 HIS PHOENIX   11
    ALONE AND ALONE NINE NIGHTS I LAY . . . . 551 SONGS REWRIT 1   13
    NINE NIGHTS I LAY IN LONGING SORE . . . . 551 SONGS REWRIT 1 V   13
    NINE NIGHTS I LAY AND IN LONGING SORE . . . . 551 SONGS REWRIT 1 V   13
    NINE BOOKS OR NINE HATS . . . . 628 JANE MOUNTAIN   3
    NINE BOOKS OR NINE HATS . . . . 628 JANE MOUNTAIN   3
    NINE MOONS. AND FROM THE HARPING OF THE FOOL? . . . . . 747 SHADOW WATER A   14
    HE HAS HEARD ME AND NOT YOU. NINE DAYS AGO . . . . . . 752 SHADOW WATER A   113
    FOR THESE NINE YEARS? O ARROW UPON ARROW! . . . . 761 SHADOW WATER A   268
NINE-AND-FIFTY
    ARE NINE-AND-FIFTY SWANS. . . . . 322 SWANS AT COOLE   6
NINETEEN
    FROM NINETEEN HUNDRED NINE OR TEN, PAVLOVA'S HAD THE CRY,   354 HIS PHOENIX   11
    NINETEEN HUNDRED AND NINETEEN . . . . 428 NINETEEN 19   T
    NINETEEN HUNDRED AND NINETEEN . . . . 428 NINETEEN 19   T
    COME PRAISE NINETEEN SIXTEEN, ... 608 SONGS BURDEN 3 V   2
    SOME NINETEEN GERMAN PLANES, THEY SAY, ... 791 REPRISALS   1
NINETEEN-SEVEN
    . . . OF THE WESTERN WORLD", [NINETEEN-SEVEN] . . . . . 294 HATED PLAYBOY   T
NINETEEN-SIXTEEN
    EASTER [NINETEEN-SIXTEEN] . . . . 391 EASTER 1916   T
    COME PRAISE NINETEEN-SIXTEEN, ... 608 SONGS BURDEN 3   2
NINETEENTH
    THE NINETEENTH AUTUMN HAS COME UPON ME . . . . 322 SWANS AT COOLE   7
    THE NINETEENTH CENTURY AND AFTER . . . . 485 NINETEENTH CEN   T
NINETEEN-THIRTEEN
    SEPTEMBER [NINETEEN-THIRTEEN] . . . . 289 SEPTEMBER 1913   T
NINETEEN-THIRTY-ONE
    COOLE PARK AND BALLYLEE, [NINETEEN-THIRTY-ONE] . . . . . 490 COOLE BALLYLEE   T
    COOLE AND BALLYLEE, [NINETEEN-THIRTY-ONE] . . . . 490 COOLE BALLYLEE V   T
NINETEEN-THIRTY-TWO
    COOLE PARK AND BALLYLEE [NINETEEN-THIRTY-TWO] . . . . . . 490 COOLE BALLYLEE V   T
NINETEEN-TWENTY-NINE
    COOLE PARK, [NINETEEN-TWENTY-NINE] . . . . 488 COOLE PARK 29   T
NINETY
    NOR HEARD THIS VOICE THAT NINETY YEARS HAVE CRACKED. . . . 555 RIBH AT TOMB   5
NINETY-FOUR
    FOR HE'D DIED AT NINETY-FOUR. . . . .   93 FATHER OHART   28
NINEVEH
    THE CROWNS OF NINEVEH. . . . . 439 FRAGMENTS   10
    WHERE BABYLON OR NINEVEH . . . . 502 VACILLATION   63

```
                                                    PAGE     TITLE        LINE
NINTH
    BE PATIENT YET A WHILE: FOR THIS NINTH MOON,  .  .  .  .  .   748 SHADOW WATER A      23
    BE PATIENT YET AWHILE: FOR THIS NINTH MOON,   .  .  .  .  .   748 SHADOW WATER A V    23
NOAH'S
    NOAH'S FRESHET NEVER REACHED.  .  .  .  .  .  .  .  .  .  .   440 WISDOM              15
NOBLE
    BUT WHERE ARE YOUR NOBLE KITH AND KIN,  .  .  .  .  .  .  .     5 OISIN 1             44
    OF NOBLE OISIN AND HIS FAME,  .  .  .  .  .  .  .  .  .  .      7 OISIN 1       V     66
    IN WAR, THE NOBLE FENIANS STEPT.  .  .  .  .  .  .  .  .  .    24 OISIN 1       V    372
    TALL AND NOBLE BUT WITH FACE AND BOSOM  .  .  .  .  .  .  .   199 ARROW                5
    OF SUCH NOBLE LINES," I SAID,  .  .  .  .  .  .  .  .  .  .   259 PEACE                6
    ALL THE WILD WITCHES, THOSE MOST NOBLE LADIES,  .  .  .  .   343 DEJECTION            4
    SHE MIGHT, SO NOBLE FROM HEAD  .  .  .  .  .  .  .  .  .  .   355 PROPERTIUS           1
    THAT NOBLE BLADE THE MUSES BUCKLED ON,  .  .  .  .  .  .  .   489 COOLE PARK 29       10
    IN NOBLE RAGE REPLIED  .  .  .  .  .  .  .  .  .  .  .  .  .   516 MANS SONG            5
    THE WORKMAN, NOBLE AND SAINT, AND ALL THINGS RUN  .  .  .  .  565 GYRES               23
    WITH EVERY NOBLE BEAST.  .  .  .  .  .  .  .  .  .  .  .  .   573 LADYS 2ND SONG      18
    WITH EVERY NOBLE BREAST.  .  .  .  .  .  .  .  .  .  .  .  .   573 LADYS 2ND SONG V    18
    BEAUTIFUL LOFTY THINGS: O'LEARY'S NOBLE HEAD:  .  .  .  .  .   577 LOFTY THINGS         1
    DREAM OF THE NOBLE AND THE BEGGAR-MAN.  .  .  .  .  .  .  .   603 GALLERY REVIS       47
    DREAM OF THE NOBLE AND THE BEGGARMAN.  .  .  .  .  .  .  .   603 GALLERY REVIS V      47
    O, MY ALMINTOR, NOBLE WAS THY QUEST:  .  .  .  .  .  .  .  .   679 ISLE STAT II 3     319
    YEA, NOBLE AND MOST KNIGHTLY HATH IT BEEN.  .  .  .  .  .  .   679 ISLE STAT II 3     320
NOBLENESS
    BECAUSE OF THAT GREAT NOBLENESS OF HERS  .  .  .  .  .  .  .   200 FOLLY COMFORT        9
    THAT NOBLENESS MADE SIMPLE AS A FIRE,  .  .  .  .  .  .  .  .   256 NO SECOND TROY      7
    "YOUR STRENGTH AND NOBLENESS WILL PASS AWAY"?  .  .  .  .  .   285 TWO KINGS          189
NOBLY
    THAT HE MIGHT BE NOBLY BREECHED  .  .  .  .  .  .  .  .  .  .   440 WISDOM              13
NOBODY
    THERE'S NOBODY IS NATURAL BUT A ROBBER,  .  .  .  .  .  .  .   233 SHADOW WATER B     237
    THERE IS NOBODY WISE ENOUGH.  .  .  .  .  .  .  .  .  .  .  .   268 BROWN PENNY         10
    THAT NOBODY CAN BUY OR BIND:  .  .  .  .  .  .  .  .  .  .  .   301 RUN PARADISE        27
    IF THEY HAVE SINNED NOBODY KNOWS:  .  .  .  .  .  .  .  .  .   337 SCHOLARS      V     10
    A NOBODY IN A GREAT THRONG,  .  .  .  .  .  .  .  .  .  .  .   361 ALF POLLEXFEN       29
    THAT NOBODY LOOKS: HER FEET  .  .  .  .  .  .  .  .  .  .  .   617 LONG-LEG FLY        16
    NOBODY KNOWS WHAT MAY BEFALL,  .  .  .  .  .  .  .  .  .  .   788 HAWTHORN TREE       13
NOD
    I HAVE PASSED WITH A NOD OF THE HEAD  .  .  .  .  .  .  .  .   392 EASTER 1916          5
    WHAT HEADS SHAKE OR NOD?  .  .  .  .  .  .  .  .  .  .  .  .   505 RESULT THOUGHT      18
    AND NOD TO ONE ANOTHER, LIES A GREEN,  .  .  .  .  .  .  .  .   653 ISLE STAT I 2       35
    UNTO HER DOOR: FOR THIS, WHERE NOD THE LONG  .  .  .  .  .   660 ISLE STAT II 1      43
    SOON WILL THE CHURCHMEN NOD ABOVE THE CROWD.  .  .  .  .  .   699 MOSADA 3            19
    NOD TO THE IRON SHOES OF TIME,  .  .  .  .  .  .  .  .  .  .   736 SUMMER EVENING      11
NODDED
    ONCE, WHILE HE NODDED ON A CHAIR,  .  .  .  .  .  .  .  .  .   132 FR GILLIGAN          5
    NODDED UPON THE WALL,  .  .  .  .  .  .  .  .  .  .  .  .  .   400 DEMON BEAST         12
    HE THOUGHT WISE THINGS AS HIS GREY HEAD NODDED.  .  .  .  .   728 PRIEST FAIRY        12
NODDING
    AND NODDING BY THE FIRE, TAKE DOWN THIS BOOK,  .  .  .  .  .   120 YOU ARE OLD          2
    NODDING HER RUSSET HOOD?  .  .  .  .  .  .  .  .  .  .  .  .   171 MAID QUIET           2
    NODDING HER PURPLE HOOD?  .  .  .  .  .  .  .  .  .  .  .  .   171 MAID QUIET    V      2
    NODDING ALONE AND APART,  .  .  .  .  .  .  .  .  .  .  .  .   171 MAID QUIET    V      6
    NODDING BY THE FLICKERING LAKE,  .  .  .  .  .  .  .  .  .  .   655 ISLE STAT I 3        3
    AND, NODDING TO AND FRO, SANG SONGS OF LOVE,  .  .  .  .  .   688 TWO TITANS          35
NODS
    AND HE NODS A DRUNKEN HEAD.  .  .  .  .  .  .  .  .  .  .  .   168 BLESSED             32
    NODS BY THE HELM, AND NEARER TO THE SAIL  .  .  .  .  .  .   752 SHADOW WATER A     119
NOISE
    THEY SET UP A NOISE LIKE CRICKETS,  .  .  .  .  .  .  .  .  .   161 CAP AND BELLS       33
    MAEVE WAITED, AND WHEN THAT EAR-PIERCING NOISE  .  .  .  .   182 QUEEN MAEVE         47
    AND BLOW A LITTLE NOISE  .  .  .  .  .  .  .  .  .  .  .  .  .   215 HAPPY TOWNLAND      43
    THAT BALANCED WITH A WORD IS MORE THAN NOISE:  .  .  .  .  .   258 KING NO KING        4
    NOR DOOR, NOR MOUTH, NOR SLIPPER MADE A NOISE,  .  .  .  .   279 TWO KINGS           51
    FROM WELL-SIDE OR FROM PLOUGH-LAND, WAS THERE NOISE:  .  .   279 TWO KINGS           53
    NOR HAD THERE BEEN THE NOISE OF LIVING THING  .  .  .  .  .   279 TWO KINGS           54
    FROM WELL SIDE OR FROM PLOUGH LAND, WAS THEIR NOISE:  .  .   279 TWO KINGS     V     53
    FROM WELLSIDE OR FROM PLOUGHLAND, WAS THERE NOISE:  .  .  .   279 TWO KINGS     V     53
    O WHAT HAS MADE THAT SUDDEN NOISE?  .  .  .  .  .  .  .  .  .   583 GHOST ROG CASE       1
    BUT YONDER THING, YON IDLE NOISE, YON CROW,  .  .  .  .  .   648 ISLE STAT I 1      104
    NOISE: AND A FLASH, A MOMENTARY BLOT.  .  .  .  .  .  .  .  .   714 FERENCZ RENYI      110
    NOISE: UPROAR: AND A MOMENTARY BLOT.  .  .  .  .  .  .  .  .   714 FERENCZ RENYI V    110
NOISY
    BE THOUGHT AN IDLER BY THE NOISY SET  .  .  .  .  .  .  .  .   205 ADAMS CURSE         12
    ANGERS THAT ARE LIKE NOISY CLOUDS HAVE SET OUR HEARTS        207 HANRAHANS SONG       8
        ABEAT:
    OR NOISY, INSOLENT SPORT,  .  .  .  .  .  .  .  .  .  .  .  .   293 HELEN LIVED          4
    A NOISY AND FILTHY THING."  .  .  .  .  .  .  .  .  .  .  .  .   319 DOLLS               12
    ERE LONG SHALL FALTER THROUGH THE NOISY SQUARE,  .  .  .  .   699 MOSADA 3            21
    THE NOISY WORLD DIVIDES.  HOW SOON A DEED  .  .  .  .  .  .   700 MOSADA 3            34
NONCHALANCE
    AND LOST THE OLD NONCHALANCE OF THE HAND:  .  .  .  .  .  .   368 EGO DOMINUS         13
NONE
    OF SOME FORGOTTEN FIEND.  NOW NONE ASSAILS  .  .  .  .  .  .    31 OISIN 2       V    30B
    ONCE MORE UNTO YOUR FLOWERS: FOR NONE MAY FIGHT,  .  .  .  .    34 OISIN 2       V     80
    NONE MAY BEGUILE HIM, AND HIS PASSIONS COLD  .  .  .  .  .    35 OISIN 2       V    83A
    IS THE ISLAND OF CONTENT?"  "NONE KNOW," SHE SAID:  .  .  .    46 OISIN 2            249
    WHICH IS THE ISLE OF YOUTH?"  "NONE KNOW," SHE SAID,  .  .    46 OISIN 2       V    249
    AND ENTER, AND NONE SAYETH "NO"  .  .  .  .  .  .  .  .  .  .    62 OISIN 3            210
    NONE WAR ON THE MASTERS OF HELL,  .  .  .  .  .  .  .  .  .    62 OISIN 3            214
    AND ENTER, AND NONE SAYETH "NAY"  .  .  .  .  .  .  .  .  .  .    62 OISIN 3       V    210
```

563

		PAGE	TITLE		LINE

NONE   (CONTINUED)

THAT NONE MAY FEEL THE POWER OF SQUALL AND WAVE,	128	DREAM OF FAERY	V	45
TO SOME STRINGED INSTRUMENT NONE THERE HAD SEEN,	180	QUEEN MAEVE		4
BEFORE HIS EYES, HE HAS TEARS FOR NONE,	192	BAILE AILLINN		82
FROM THE HOLY ORCHARDS, WHERE THERE IS NONE	196	BAILE AILLINN		174
WOULD NONE HAD EVER LOVED BUT YOU AND I!	210	RAGGED WOOD		4
O THAT NONE EVER LOVED BUT YOU AND I!	210	RAGGED WOOD	V	4
O THAT NONE EVER LOVED BUT YOU AND I!	211	RAGGED WOOD		8
AND FROM THAT HOUR HE HAS WATCHED OVER NONE	220	HARP OF AENGUS		13
AND DRAGS HIM THROUGH THE SEA. WELL, NET OR NONE,	224	SHADOW WATER B		57
WE JOINED HIM FOR HIS PAY, BUT HAVE HAD NONE	225	SHADOW WATER B	V	68A
NONE BUT THE DEAD, OR THOSE THAT NEVER LIVED,	231	SHADOW WATER B		202
THAT NONE MIGHT TAKE YOU FROM ME. FOR A MOMENT	237	SHADOW WATER B		330
THERE IS NONE TO TAKE HIS SIDE. I AM ON HIS SIDE.	239	SHADOW WATER B		364
OR IS THERE NONE, MOST POPULAR OF MEN,	265	ABBEY THEATRE		13
I KNEW A WOMAN NONE COULD PLEASE,	272	GREY ROCK		41
I KNOW A WOMAN NONE COULD PLEASE,	272	GREY ROCK	V	41
AND WHISPERING THAT NONE BUT HE SHOULD HEAR,	281	TWO KINGS		110
NONE CLOSED HIS BLOOD-SHOT EYES BUT SOUGHT	296	THREE BEGGARS		44
WHAT NONE CAN UNDERSTAND,	315	FRIENDS		12
WHAT NONE CAN HAVE AND THRIVE,	315	FRIENDS		13
THE GENTLENESS NONE THERE HAD EVER KNOWN!	418	ANCEST HOUSES		21
KNOWING THAT NONE COULD PASS HEAVEN'S DOOR	422	MY TABLE		26
KNOWING THAT NONE WHO PASS HEAVEN'S DOOR	422	MY TABLE	V	26
KNOWING THAT NONE CAN PASS HEAVEN'S DOOR	422	MY TABLE	V	26
NONE DARED ADMIT, IF SUCH A THOUGHT WERE HIS,	430	NINETEEN 19		44
AND THERE IS NONE SO FIT TO KEEP A WATCH AND KEEP	442	BLACK CENTAUR		15
AND THAT NONE LIVING KNOWS.	455	HIS MEMORIES		6
FOR NONE ALIVE TO-DAY	458	SECRETS OF OLD		10
FOR NONE ALIVE TODAY	458	SECRETS OF OLD	V	10
WERE I BUT THERE AND NONE TO HEAR	458	HIS WILDNESS		7
THAT NONE MIGHT KNOW THAT HE WAS CONSCIENCE-STRUCK--	462	HARUN RASHID		38
THAT NONE MIGHT KNOW THAT HE WAS CONSCIENCE STRUCK,	462	HARUN RASHID	V	38
BUT I BEING NONE CAN PRAISE ITS OPPOSITE.	465	HARUN RASHID		98
NONE BUT THE LIVING MOCK,	471	ALL SOUL NIGHT		17
AND WE THAT HAVE SHED NONE MUST GATHER THERE	482	BLOOD AND MOON		41
WHERE NONE HAS REIGNED THAT LACKED A NAME AND FAME	491	COOLE BALLYLEE		31
NONE SO OLD AS HE AND I!	508	JANE BISHOP	V	6
WHAT NONE OTHER KNOWS,	538	LAST CONFESS		18
NONE SHARED OUR GUILT! NOR DID WE PLAY A PART	542	PARN FUNERAL 1		22
SURMOUNT THEIR BONES! BUT SPEAK WHAT NONE HAVE HEARD.	555	RIBH AT TOMB		9
SURMOUNTS THEIR BONES! BUT SPEAK WHAT NONE HAVE HEARD.	555	RIBH AT TOMB	V	9
"NONE CAN RELY UPON	569	THREE BUSHES		2
AND NOW NONE LIVING CAN,	571	THREE BUSHES		74
THAT NONE OF ANOTHER BREED	583	GHOST ROG CASE		24
WHERE NONE GAINSAY THEIR RIGHT,	597	MODEL LAUREATE		14
NONE OTHER KNOWS WHAT PLEASURES MAN	620	JOHN KINSELLA		9
AND UNDERSTOOD, WHAT NONE HAVE UNDERSTOOD,	622	HOUND VOICE		13
WITH TEARS? I WEARY OF YE. THERE IS NONE	650	ISLE STAT I 1		142
O LET ME PASS! THAT FLOWER NONE	668	ISLE STAT II 3		47
AND NONE THERE IS! IF SUCH THERE WERE,	668	ISLE STAT II 3		53
YOURSELF. NONE BUT THE INNOCENT CAN SEE.	692	MOSADA 1		59
ONCE IN THY NATION NONE SHALL KNOW THAT I	702	MOSADA 3		82
AMONG THY NATION NONE SHALL KNOW THAT I	702	MOSADA 3	V	82
AND--NO! I'LL NONE OF THESE, OLD FATHER WRINKLES.	721	WITCH VIVIEN		23
NONE SHOULD ESCAPE MY SWORD! I WOULD SEND ALL	752	SHADOW WATER A		111
I PROMISED HIM THAT NONE SHOULD ESCAPE MY SWORD	752	SHADOW WATER A		114
HE WATCHES OVER NONE BUT FAITHFUL LOVERS.	762	SHADOW WATER A		295
AND FROM THAT HOUR HE HAS WATCHED OVER NONE	763	SHADOW WATER A		308
AND NONE KNOWS WHEREFORE! BUT THE HEART'S DESIRE	764	SHADOW WATER A		340
I WILL FOLLOW YOU. I WILL HAVE NONE OF YOU.	768	SHADOW WATER A		415
THAT WOULD BE HAPPIEST, FOR THERE IS NONE	768	SHADOW WATER A	V	410
THE WOMEN NONE CAN KISS AND THRIVE,	775	AGAINST WITCH		8
WOMEN! THAT NONE CAN KISS AND THRIVE,	775	AGAINST WITCH	V	8
THEY WILL HAVE FOR MASTERS NONE	776	AGAINST WITCH		39
THEY WILL HAVE FOR MASTER NONE	776	AGAINST WITCH	V	39

NONSENSICAL

SPEAKING TO A DRUNKEN AUDIENCE HIGH NONSENSICAL WORDS!	577	LOFTY THINGS		6

NOOK

HE CRAWLED INTO THAT PLEASANT NOOK.	303	HOUR DAWN		32

NOON

SAVE DEER TOWARDS NOON THAT WATER SOUGHT.	17	OISIN 1	V	243
THEY CHASE AT NOON THE DEER.	32	OISIN 2	V	53
GAVE TO HIGH NOON AND NOON TO NIGHT GAVE WAY!	40	OISIN 2		172
GAVE TO HIGH NOON AND NOON TO NIGHT GAVE WAY!	40	OISIN 2		172
GAVE TO THE NOON, AND NOON TO EVE GAVE WAY,	40	OISIN 2		172
GAVE TO THE NOON, AND NOON TO EVE GAVE WAY,	40	OISIN 2	V	172
THERE MIDNIGHT'S ALL A GLIMMER, AND NOON A PURPLE GLOW,	117	ISLE INNISFREE		7
SLEEP BEFORE THE THIRD NOON SOUNDS."	295	THREE BEGGARS		24
SANG THROUGH THEIR TEETH FROM NOON TO NOON!	296	THREE BEGGARS		41
SANG THROUGH THEIR TEETH FROM NOON TO NOON!	296	THREE BEGGARS		41
ALL DAY LONG FROM SHADOWLESS NOON	332	SOLOMON SHEBA		5
NOON UPON THE CLOCK,	525	DANCING DAYS		18
THAT BROAD NOON HAS NEVER LIT.	632	MAN AND ECHO		4
NOON WRAPT THE TREES IN VEILS OF VIOLET WEATHER,	715	DWELT SYCAMORE		7
NOON WRAPPED THE WOODS IN VEILS OF VIOLET WEATHER!	715	DWELT SYCAMORE	V	7
THE HEART OF NOON FOLDS SILENCE AND FOLDS SLEEP,	735	QUATRAIN APHOR		25
FOR NOON AND MIDNIGHT FROM EACH OTHER BORROW,	735	QUATRAIN APHOR		26
HITHER AND THITHER AND SAY AT THE HIGH NOON	767	SHADOW WATER A		404

NO-ONE

IN THE LAND THAT NO-ONE KNOWS.	774	COME RIDE	V	17

564

	PAGE	TITLE		LINE

NOONTIDE
THEY CHASE THE NOONTIDE DEER; . . . .   32 OISIN 2   53
NOON-TIDE
THEY CHASE THE NOON-TIDE DEER; . . . .   32 OISIN 2   V   53
NOOSE
WHILE THERE'S A ROPE TO RUN INTO A NOOSE . . . . . 238 SHADOW WATER B   347
GUNSHOT OR A NOOSE, ...   620 JOHN KINSELLA   2
NORM
WE TAKE IT FOR THE NORM; YET SHOULD I DREAM . . . . 371 ON GOING HOUSE   9
THAT DREAM IS A NORM; AND SHOULD SOME LIMB OF THE DEVIL   372 ON GOING HOUSE   12
NORMAN
UPON THE NORMAN UPLAND OR IN THAT POPLAR SHADE, . . 449 OWEN AHERNE   2
TO THROW THE NORMAN KNIGHT." " . . . .   740 EARL PAUL   12
STOOD THERE THE NORMAN KNIGHT. . . . .   741 EARL PAUL   40
NORMANDY
FOR A KNIGHT, COME FROM NORMANDY . . . .   740 EARL PAUL   7
NORTH
THE ICICLES THAT FAMISH ALL THE NORTH, ...   73 ANASHU VIJAYA   50
SANG THAT SOMEWHERE TO NORTH OR WEST OR SOUTH . . . 127 DREAM OF FAERY   19
SANG HOW SOMEWHERE TO NORTH OR EAST OR SOUTH . . . 127 DREAM OF FAERY V 19
SANG HOW SOMEWHERE TO NORTH OR WEST OR SOUTH . . . 127 DREAM OF FAERY V 19
FOR THEY WILL RIDE THE NORTH WHEN THE GER-EAGLE FLIES, . 146 UNAPPEAS HOST   3
THE NORTH UNFOLDS ABOVE THEM CLINGING, CREEPING NIGHT, . 154 BELOVED PEACE   3
THE NORTH UNROLLS ABOVE THEM CLINGING, CREEPING NIGHT,   154 BELOVED PEACE V 3
NOR THE COLD NORTH HAS TROUBLED?" HE REPLIED, . . . 184 QUEEN MAEVE   90
THE NORTH WIND TUMBLES TO AND FRO . . . .   191 BAILE AILLINN   45
THAT NORTH WIND TUMBLES TO AND FRO . . . .   191 BAILE AILLINN V   45
THE RIDER FROM THE NORTH . . . .   213 HAPPY TOWNLAND V   T
STRAYING TOO FAR INTO THE NORTH OR SOUTH, ...   226 SHADOW WATER B   86
A CLOUD BLOWN FROM THE CUT-THROAT NORTH . . . . .   313 MEMORY YOUTH   6
THE WEST WIND MADE IT PITIFUL, AND THE NORTH WIND AFRAID.   449 OWEN AHERNE   6
WHEREON THE BLEAK NORTH BLOWS, ...   454 HIS MEMORIES   4
AND WHEN YOU CAME, THE NORTH UNDER YOUR SAILS, . .   749 SHADOW WATER A   34
WHEN WE ROWED NORTH, SINGING ABOVE THE OARS, . . .   749 SHADOW WATER A   39
TO CONQUER AMONG THE COUNTRIES OF THE NORTH. . . .   757 SHADOW WATER A   200
NORTHERN
"HE DRIVES AWAY THE NORTHERN COLD." . . . .   82 MAD KING GOLL   11
UPON THE NORTHERN UPLAND OR IN THAT POPLAR SHADE, . 449 OWEN AHERNE   V 2
BEFORE I HAD MARKED HIM ON HIS NORTHERN WAY, . . .   535 CHOSEN   8
AND PASSED THE NORTHERN HEBRIDES, AND TOOK . . . .   749 SHADOW WATER A V 42
NORTHUMBERLAND
"AND ALL DOWN FROM NORTHUMBERLAND . . . .   740 EARL PAUL   9
NOSE
THRUSTING HIS NOSE TO MY SHOULDER; HE KNEW IN HIS BOSOM   54 OISIN 3   106
DEEP
HE SMOOTHS THE LONG BROWN NOSE. . . . .   98 FOXHUNTER   20
SHALL DIP HIS NOSE INTO MY LADLE . . . .   304 HOUR DAWN   53
DIPPING HIS NOSE INTO MY LADLE . . . .   304 HOUR DAWN   V 53
WITH FACE AND NOSE PRESSED TO A SWEET-SHOP WINDOW, . 370 EGO DOMINUS   56
WITH FACE AND NOSE PRESSED TO A SWEETSHOP WINDOW. .   370 EGO DOMINUS   V 56
FIRST THAT SEA-RIDER OISIN LED BY THE NOSE . . . .   629 CIRCUS ANIMALS   10
AND RUBBED ALONG THE RAIL HIS NOSE. . . . .   725 LEGEND   28
ON THE NOSE OF THE SLEEPER HE MADE IT PLAY; . . .   729 PRIEST FAIRY   30
NOSTERS
AND MANY PATER NOSTERS SAID SINCE DAWN. . . . . .   43 OISIN 2   V 208D
NOSTRIL
THE COLD BLOWN SPRAY IN MY NOSTRIL. . . . .   399 BREAK OF DAY   20
NOSTRILS
IN HIS NOSTRILS, THE GREAT LORD OF CHOU . . . . .   502 VACILLATION   59
NOTABLE
SANDYMOUNT CORBETS, THAT NOTABLE MAN . . . .   604 YOU CONTENT   13
NOW A NOTABLE MAN ON STAGE AND ON SCREEN; . . . .   790 DEDICATION   8
NOTE
BLEW ONE LONG NOTE. FROM OVER REED . . . .   14 OISIN 1   V 195
SNATCHING THE HORN OF NIAMH, I BLEW A LONG LINGERING NOTE.   51 OISIN 3   57
SNATCHING THE HORN OF NIAM, I BLEW FORTH A LINGERING NOTE;   51 OISIN 3   57
SNATCHING THE HORN OF NIAM, I BLEW A LINGERING NOTE;   51 OISIN 3   V 57
THE HORN'S SWEET NOTE AND THE TOOTH OF THE HOUND. .   380 SONGS FOOL 1   12
THE HORN'S SWEET NOTE AND THE TOOTH OF THE HOUND. .   381 SONGS FOOL 2   14
A SLOW LOW NOTE AND AN IRON BELL. . . . .   549 SEVERED HEAD   7
A SLOW LOW NOTE AND AN IRON BELL. . . . .   550 SEVERED HEAD   14
A SLOW LOW NOTE AND AN IRON BELL. . . . .   550 SEVERED HEAD   21
NOT A SAD NOTE WILL I SING. . . . .   646 ISLE STAT I 1   39
NOTES   SEE BELL-NOTES
AND NIAMH BLEW THREE MERRY NOTES . . . .   14 OISIN 1   195
THE MOUTHS THAT SPEAK, THE NOTES AND STRINGS, . .   212 BLESS PSALTER   2
THE NOTES THEY WAKEN SHALL LIVE ON . . . .   213 BLESS PSALTER   16
THE PROUD AND CARELESS NOTES LIVE ON, ...   213 BLESS PSALTER   19
NOTHING
BUT NOW I HAVE GROWN NOTHING, KNOWING ALL. . . . .   104 FERGUS DRUID   38
BUT NOW I HAVE GROWN NOTHING, BEING ALL; . . . .   104 FERGUS DRUID   V 38
HE HAD FALLEN ASLEEP, AND, THOUGH HE HAD DREAMED NOTHING,   182 QUEEN MAEVE   55
THOUGH NOTHING TROUBLES THE GREAT STREAMS . . . .   196 BAILE AILLINN   172
AND THAT DEAR WORDS MEANT NOTHING?" BUT ENOUGH, .   201 OLD MEMORY   9
OR, IF THERE NEEDS BE MORE, BE NOTHING SAID . . .   201 OLD MEMORY   11
OR CRY ABOUT ONE'S EARS. NOTHING TO FEAR. . . . .   222 SHADOW WATER B   19
BUT THERE WERE OTHERS. I HAVE SEEN NOTHING PASS. .   226 SHADOW WATER B   82
WHERE NO SHIP SAILS, WHERE NOTHING THAT'S ALIVE . . 226 SHADOW WATER B   98
THAT NOTHING CAN AMEND IT BUT THESE WATERS, . . .   227 SHADOW WATER B   120
I'VE NOTHING TO COMPLAIN OF BUT HEARTBURN, ...   227 SHADOW WATER B V 116A
ARE DUST ON THE MOTH'S WING; THAT NOTHING MATTERS . . . 235 SHADOW WATER B 297

```
                                                              PAGE    TITLE              LINE
NOTHING   (CONTINUED)
    UPON HIS SHOULDERS.  YOU'VE NOTHING BUT WILD WORDS,  . . .    235  SHADOW WATER B       300
    THERE'S NOTHING IN THE WORLD THAT'S WORTH A FEAR.  . . .      238  SHADOW WATER B       353
    HAVE BURIED NOTHING BUT MY GOLDEN ARMS. . . . . . . .         243  SHADOW WATER B       431
    I WEEP BECAUSE I'VE NOTHING FOR YOUR EYES . . . . . .         246  SHADOW WATER B       496
    I WOULD THAT THERE WAS NOTHING IN THE WORLD . . . . .         246  SHADOW WATER B       503
    THE CRAZY NOTHING THAT I THINK IT IS, . . . . . . . .         248  SHADOW WATER B       556
    BUT HARRY US WITH HOPES THAT COME TO NOTHING, . . . .         250  SHADOW WATER B       579
    NOTHING TO MAKE A SONG ABOUT BUT KINGS, . . . . . . .         257  RECONCILIATION         5
    NOW NOTHING BUT COMES READIER TO THE HAND . . . . . .         267  ALL TEMPT ME           4
    I HAVE NO CHILD, I HAVE NOTHING BUT A BOOK, . . . . .         270  PARDON FATHERS        21
    NOTHING BUT THAT TO PROVE YOUR BLOOD AND MINE. . . . .        270  PARDON FATHERS        22
    "WHAT IS THIS TROUBLE?"  HE WOULD ANSWER NOTHING,  . .        281  TWO KINGS             90
    TO A FRIEND WHOSE WORK HAS COME TO NOTHING . . . . . .        290  TO A FRIEND            T
    AND THERE BE NOTHING BUT GOD LEFT! . . . . . . . . .          307  HOUR DAWN            103
    NOTHING BUT DARKNESS OVERHEAD. . . . . . . . . . . .          314  MEMORY YOUTH          14
    THERE'S NOTHING OF HIM LEFT BUT HALF A SCORE . . . . .        341  SHEP GOATHERD         56
    I HAVE NOTHING BUT THE EMBITTERED SUN! . . . . . . . .        344  DEJECTION              8
    AND I HAVE NOTHING BUT HARSH SUN! . . . . . . . . . .         344  DEJECTION        V     8
    VAGUE MEMORIES, NOTHING BUT MEMORIES. . . . . . . . .         356  BROKEN DREAMS         15
    VAGUE MEMORIES, NOTHING BUT MEMORIES. . . . . . . . .         356  BROKEN DREAMS         20
    VAGUE MEMORIES, NOTHING BUT MEMORIES. . . . . . . . .         357  BROKEN DREAMS         41
    OWN NOTHING BUT THEIR BLIND, STUPEFIED HEARTS. . . . .        370  EGO DOMINUS           69
    MAY HANDLE NOTHING AND SET EYES ON NOTHING . . . . . .        371  ON GOING HOUSE         6
    MAY HANDLE NOTHING AND SET EYES ON NOTHING . . . . . .        371  ON GOING HOUSE         6
    THERE CAN BE NOTHING SOLIDER TILL I DIE! . . . . . . .        383  VISION ROBART         26
    THERE'S NOTHING BUT OUR OWN RED BLOOD . . . . . . . .         396  ROSE TREE             17
    NOTHING THAT WE LOVE OVER-MUCH . . . . . . . . . . .          399  BREAK OF DAY          17
    THAT NOTHING STRANGE! THE TRAGEDY BEGAN . . . . . . .         411  TOWER                 51
    PLUNGES TOWARDS NOTHING, ARMS AND FINGERS SPREADING WIDE      426  PHANTOM HATRED        13
    FOR THE EMBRACE OF NOTHING! AND I, MY WITS ASTRAY  . . .      426  PHANTOM HATRED        14
    NOTHING BUT STILLNESS CAN REMAIN WHEN HEARTS ARE FULL  .      426  PHANTOM HATRED        23
    NOTHING BUT GRIP OF CLAW, AND THE EYE'S COMPLACENCY,  .       427  PHANTOM HATRED        31
    AND AFTER THAT THERE'S NOTHING GOOD . . . . . . . . .         434  WHEEL                  5
    FROM NOTHING EVERY DAY, AND TEACH . . . . . . . . . .         436  FOR MY SON            18
    OUT OF NOTHING IT CAME. . . . . . . . . . . . . . .           439  FRAGMENTS              7
    NOTHING COULD BRING HIM, WHEN HIS LADY DIED, . . . . .        471  ALL SOUL NIGHT        25
    BUT NAMES ARE NOTHING.  WHAT MATTER WHO IT BE, . . . .        473  ALL SOUL NIGHT        81
    BUT NAMES ARE NOTHING.  I CARE NOT WHO IT BE. . . . .         473  ALL SOUL NIGHT V      81
    NOTHING CAN STAY MY GLANCE . . . . . . . . . . . . .          474  ALL SOUL NIGHT        93
    "PRAY FOR NOTHING, SAY . . . . . . . . . . . . . . .          495  MOHINI CHATTER         3
    NOTHING SAID OR DONE CAN REACH . . . . . . . . . . .          506  REMORSE SPEECH         9
    FOR NOTHING CAN BE SOLE OR WHOLE . . . . . . . . . .          513  JANE TALK BISH        17
    NOTHING BUT DISSEMBLING, . . . . . . . . . . . . . .          532  FIRST CONFESS          5
    NOTHING BUT COQUETRY. . . . . . . . . . . . . . . .           532  FIRST CONFESS          6
    LEAVE NOTHING BUT THE NOTHINGS THAT BELONG . . . . . .        542  PARN FUNERAL 1        29
    WHAT HAPPENS A TREE THAT HAS NOTHING WITHIN IT? . . .         548  TO SAME TUNE 3        23
    WHAT HAPPENS TO A TREE THAT HAS NOTHING WITHIN IT? . .        548  TO SAME TUNE 3 V      23
    OR ANY RICH, DARK NOTHING DISINTER . . . . . . . . .          565  GYRES                 22
    THAT IF NOTHING DRASTIC IS DONE . . . . . . . . . .           565  LAPIS LAZULI           5
    THAT IF NOTHING DRASTIC CAN BE DONE . . . . . . . .           565  LAPIS LAZULI   V       5
    WHERE NOTHING STIRS BUT A MOUSE. . . . . . . . . . .          575  ACRE OF GRASS          6
    NOTHING THAT COMMON WOMEN PONDER ON . . . . . . . . .         579  DOR WELLESLEY         12
    NOTHING BUT CROMWELL'S HOUSE AND CROMWELL'S MURDEROUS CREW,   580  CURSE CROMWELL         2
    BUT THAT IS NOTHING NEW. . . . . . . . . . . . . . .          581  ROGER CASEMENT         4
    AND THAT OLD MAN BESIDE ME, NOTHING WOULD HE SAY . . .        593  PILGRIM                9
    WHAT IF THERE'S NOTHING UP THERE AT THE TOP? . . . . .        615  MARCH SONGS 2         21
    WHAT TEARS DOWN A TREE THAT HAS NOTHING WITHIN IT? . .        615  MARCH SONGS 2         23
    WHAT TEARS DOWN A TREE HAS NOTHING WITHIN IT? . . . .         615  MARCH SONGS 2 V       23
    HIS EYES FIXED UPON NOTHING, . . . . . . . . . . . .          617  LONG-LEG FLY           7
    AND FINDS THERE NOTHING TO MAKE ITS TERROR LESS . . .         618  BRONZE HEAD            6
    BUT NOTHING SATISFIED THE FOOL . . . . . . . . . . .          620  JOHN KINSELLA          7
    PROCESSIONS THAT LACK HIGH STILTS HAVE NOTHING THAT CATCHES   622  HIGH TALK              1
        THE EYE.
    I HAVE FOUND NOTHING HALF SO GOOD . . . . . . . . .           624  APPARITIONS            9
    YOUNG MEN KNOW NOTHING OF THIS SORT, . . . . . . . .          626  OLD MEN BE MAD        16
    LACK NOTHING THAT A SOLDIER NEEDS, . . . . . . . . .          635  BLACK TOWER            4
    FADED AND VANISHED, NOTHING NOW IS SEEN. . . . . . .          676  ISLE STAT II 3       268
    LONG THOU FOR NOTHING, NEITHER SAD NOR GAY! . . . . .         734  QUATRAIN APHOR         9
    LONG THOU FOR NOTHING, NEITHER NIGHT NOR DAY! . . . .         734  QUATRAIN APHOR        10
    I HAVE FOUND NOTHING BUT THESE EMPTY WATERS! . . . .          757  SHADOW WATER A       201
    THOUGH WE WERE BIDDEN TO SING, CRY NOTHING LOUD. . . .        778  SONG DEIRDRE 3         2
NOTHINGNESS
    EVEN A HALF-HOUR'S NOTHINGNESS, . . . . . . . . . .           305  HOUR DAWN             70
    EVEN A HALF HOUR'S NOTHINGNESS, . . . . . . . . . .           305  HOUR DAWN      V      70
NOTHINGS
    LEAVE NOTHING BUT THE NOTHINGS THAT BELONG . . . . . .        542  PARN FUNERAL 1        29
NOTORIETY
    NOTORIETY . . . . . . . . . . . . . . . . . . . .            320  REED WHISPERER V       T
NOTORIOUS
    NOTORIOUS, TILL ALL MY PRICELESS THINGS . . . . . . .        321  REED WHISPERER        13
NOUGHT
    BRING THAT TO NOUGHT. . . . . . . . . . . . . . . .           436  FOR MY SON            16
    BURN THEIR BODIES UP FOR NOUGHT, . . . . . . . . . .          787  HUDDON DUDDON         14
NOURISH
    WOULD NOURISH HIS WHIM. . . . . . . . . . . . . . .           310  PEACOCK                6
    FROM MY OLD FATHERS, I MUST NOURISH DREAMS . . . . . .        422  MY DESCENDANTS         2
    NOURISH THE PANTHERS IN DIM SOLITUDES! . . . . . . .         657  ISLE STAT I 3         44
NOVELIST
    THE DEDICATION TO A BOOK OF STORIES SELECTED FROM THE IRISH   129  BOOK STORIES           T
        NOVELISTS
```

	PAGE	TITLE		LINE
NOVELS				
HE NOW GETS NOVELS AT HIS EASE. • • • • • • • • •	792	GEORGE MOORE		4
NOVELTY				
I, THROUGH THE TERRIBLE NOVELTY OF LIGHT, STALK ON, STALK ON:	623	HIGH TALK		13
NOWHERE				
IF JOY WERE NOWHERE ON THE EARTH • • • • • • • •	18	OISIN 1	V	269
• • • FOR NOWHERE IN ANY CLANN • • • • • • • • • •	50	OISIN 3	V	49
NOWISE				
THEN NOWISE WORSHIP DUSTY DEEDS, • • • • • • • • •	65	HAPPY SHEPHERD		22
NOYES				
COME ALFRED NOYES AND ALL THE TROUP • • • • • • •	582	ROGER CASEMENT	V	17
NUMB				
WHAT MATTER THOUGH NUMB NIGHTMARE RIDE ON TOP, • • •	564	GYRES		9
OWLS THERE BE WHOM AGE MAKES NUMB: • • • • • • • •	727	LOVERS QUARREL		35
NUMBER				
FORMS WITHOUT NUMBER! WHEN THE LIVE WEST FLASHED • • •	41	OISIN 2	V	180
YET I NUMBER HIM IN THE SONG: • • • • • • • • • •	393	EASTER 1916		35
WHAT CALCULATION, NUMBER, MEASUREMENT, REPLIED? • • •	611	STATUES		27
AND NUMBER THEIR DAYS AND THEIR HOURS-- • • • • • •	707	FAIRY PEDANT		19
OF RAJAS AND MAHRAJAS BEYOND NUMBER? • • • • • • • •	724	KANVA ON SELF		6
NUMBERLESS				
I DREW OUT OF THE NUMBERLESS • • • • • • • • • • •	24	OISIN 1	V	365
I AM HAUNTED BY NUMBERLESS ISLANDS, AND MANY A DANAAN SHORE,	122	WHITE BIRDS		9
THE BOOKS OF MY NUMBERLESS DREAMS, • • • • • • • •	157	POET BELOVED		2
WHITE WOMAN WITH NUMBERLESS DREAMS, • • • • • • • •	157	POET BELOVED		7
AND SOUGHT THROUGH LANDS AND ISLANDS NUMBERLESS YEARS, • •	170	SECRET ROSE		23
NUMBERS				
HIS NUMBERS, THOUGH THEY MOVED OR SEEMED TO MOVE • • •	610	STATUES		2
HE NUMBERS. HE A BROWN FARM-HOUSE SEES, • • • • •	710	FERENCZ RENYI		22
HE NUMBERS. HE, WITH FLOWERING CURRANT TREES, • • •	710	FERENCZ RENYI	V	22
NUN				
A KIND OLD NUN IN A WHITE HOOD REPLIES: • • • • • •	443	SCHOOL CHILDR		2
I HAD BETTER FIND A CONVENT AND TURN NUN: • • • • •	448	HERO GIRL FOOL		11
A NUN AT LEAST HAS ALL MEN'S REVERENCE • • • • • • •	448	HERO GIRL FOOL		12
NUNS				
BOTH NUNS AND MOTHERS WORSHIP IMAGES, • • • • • • •	445	SCHOOL CHILDR		49
NURSE				
BEING ALL ALONE I'D NURSE A STONE • • • • • • • • •	459	HIS WILDNESS		11
NURSED				
QUEEN MAEVE'S NINE MAINES HAD BEEN NURSED, • • • • •	302	HOUR DAWN		8
NURTURED SEE WOOD-NURTURED ROCK-NURTURED LAKE-NURTURED				
THE DRUID, GREY, WOOD NURTURED, QUIET EYED, • • • • •	101	ROSE UPON ROOD	V	4
THOUGH NURTURED LIKE THE SAILING MOON • • • • • • •	451	FIRST LOVE		1
NUT				
AH! IT DWELT WITHIN THE TWILIGHT AS THE WORM WITHIN THE NUT.	718	PHANTOM SHIP		6
NY SEE KATHLEEN-NY-HOOLIHAN				
NYMPH				
SLIM ADOLESCENCE THAT A NYMPH HAS STRIPPED, • • • • •	612	NEWS ORACLE		25
NYMPHS SEE SEA-NYMPHS				
SEA NYMPHS IN THEIR PEARLY WAGGONS, • • • • • • • •	309	REALISTS	V	5
FLASH FISHLIKE: NYMPHS AND SATYRS • • • • • • • • •	612	NEWS ORACLE		35
OAK				
AN ISLE LAY LEVEL BEFORE US, WITH DRIPPING HAZEL AND OAK?	47	OISIN 3		10
AN ISLE LAY LEVEL BEFORE US, DRIPPING WITH HAZEL AND OAK?	47	OISIN 3	V	10
CEASED ON OUR HANDS AND OUR FACES, ON HAZEL AND OAK LEAF, THE LIGHT,	48	OISIN 3		23
• • • FOR, CUMBROUS WITH STEMS OF THE HAZEL AND OAK, •	48	OISIN 3		25
OF HOLLIES, AND HAZELS, AND OAK TREES, A VALLEY WAS SLOPING AWAY	48	OISIN 3	V	26
• • • FAR FROM THE HAZEL AND OAK, • • • • • • • • •	57	OISIN 3		146
GREEN OAK AND POPLAR TREE! • • • • • • • • • • • •	132	OLD PENSIONER	V	16
O HEAVY SWOLLEN WATERS, BRIM THE FALL OF THE OAK TREES,	207	HANRAHANS SONG	V	11
TILL OAK AND HAZEL CEASED AND BEECH BEGAN, • • • • •	283	TWO KINGS	V	139A
BRING ME TO THE BLASTED OAK • • • • • • • • • • •	507	JANE BISHOP		1
AND BIDS ME TO THE OAK, FOR HE • • • • • • • • • •	508	JANE BISHOP		23
SET ME BY THAT OAK, FOR HE • • • • • • • • • • • •	508	JANE BISHOP	V	22
AND BIDS ME TO THAT OAK, FOR HE, • • • • • • • • •	508	JANE BISHOP	V	23
UNDER OAK AND BEECHEN BOUGH, • • • • • • • • • • •	522	LULLABY		11
UNDER OAK AND BEECHES BOUGH, • • • • • • • • • • •	522	LULLABY	V	11
NO TASTE HAVE I FOR SLUMBER 'NEATH AN OAK. • • • • •	721	WITCH VIVIEN		31
OAKEN				
TO THE SCENTED OAKEN PRESS. • • • • • • • • • • •	124	CATHLEEN PARA		8
THOU HAST FORGOTTEN. ON THE OAKEN STOOL • • • • • •	713	FERENCZ RENYI		91
OAK-TREE				
AND UNDER A SHADY OAK-TREE SAT, • • • • • • • • •	728	PRIEST FAIRY		7
OAR SEE STEERING-OAR				
AND AH, YOU PROUD MAIDEN, YOU ARE NOT SO FAIR WHEN HIS OAR	91	OLD FISHERMAN		9
PROUD MAIDEN, YE ARE NOT SO FAIR, WHEN HIS OAR • • •	91	OLD FISHERMAN	V	9
AND, AH, YE PROUD MAIDENS, YE ARE NOT SO FAIR, WHEN HIS OAR	91	OLD FISHERMAN	V	9
OR ON THE UNPEOPLED WAVES WITH KINGS TO PULL AT THE OAR,	210	UNDER THE MOON		15
I HELD A PAINTED STEERING OAR, • • • • • • • • • •	253	HIS DREAM		2
THE BUTT END OF A STEERING OAR, • • • • • • • • •	253	HIS DREAM	V	2
POSEIDON GAVE IT BIT AND OAR, • • • • • • • • • • •	447	COLONUS PRAISE		28
OF THAT OAR AND OF THAT BIT: • • • • • • • • • • •	447	COLONUS PRAISE		30
NOW MAKING BUSY WITH THE OAR, • • • • • • • • • • •	742	DANAAN QUICK		2
ARE DOUBTFUL LIKE THESE PULLERS OF THE OAR! • • • • •	748	SHADOW WATER A		30
WHILE THE WIND IS LIGHT. THE OAR CAN HARDLY MOVE HER, • •	754	SHADOW WATER A		157
BE PULLERS OF THE OAR UNTIL YOU DIE? • • • • • • •	757	SHADOW WATER A		217

	PAGE	TITLE		LINE
OAR (CONTINUED)				
THERE--THERE--BY THE OAR. THE CROWN OF A FAR COUNTRY . . .	763	SHADOW WATER A		310
OARED SEE LONG-OARED				
OARING				
THEY WALK ON SHORES UNSEEN OF OARING GALLEYS, ...	30	OISIN 2	V	14D
OARS				
NO MORE TO CRAWL ON THE SEAS WITH LONG OARS MILE AFTER	55	OISIN 3		119
MILE,				
AND NOT THE BANKS OF OARS THAT SWAM UPON	610	STATUES		13
WHEN WE ROWED NORTH, SINGING ABOVE THE OARS, ...	749	SHADOW WATER A		39
HAVE FOUND DELIGHT, IN THE RESOUNDING OARS, ...	750	SHADOW WATER A		72
OATEN				
AN OATEN PIPE UNTO A LISTENING FAWN, ...	678	ISLE STAT II 3		301
AN OATEN PIPE UNTO A LISTENING FAUN, ...	678	ISLE STAT II 3	V	301
OATH				
DREAD OATH, WHO DWELL ON SACRED HIMALAY, ...	74	ANASHU VIJAYA		67
SOME FEASTING MAN THAT THE SAME OATH HAS BOUND."	108	CUCHULAIN SEA		38
SOME FEATING MAN THAT THE SAME OATH HAS BOUND."	108	CUCHULAIN SEA	V	38
SOME FEATING MAN THAT THE SAME OATH HAS BOUND."	109	CUCHULAIN SEA		54
"SOME FEATING MAN THAT THE SAME OATH HAS BOUND."	109	CUCHULAIN SEA	V	54
OATH-BOUND				
THAT ALL ARE OATH-BOUND MEN!	635	BLACK TOWER		5
STAND WE ON GUARD OATH-BOUND!	636	BLACK TOWER		26
OATMEAL				
ROUND AND ROUND THE OATMEAL CHEST.	88	STOLEN CHILD	V	49
OATMEAL-CHEST				
ROUND AND ROUND THE OATMEAL-CHEST.	88	STOLEN CHILD		49
OBEDIENCE				
AT THE PERFECTION OF ONE'S OWN OBEDIENCE!	376	PHASES OF MOON		109
OBEDIENT				
THEMSELVES OBEDIENT, ...	382	VISION ROBART		11
OBEDIENT TO SOME HIDDEN MAGICAL BREATH.	382	VISION ROBART		13
OBEY				
SHALL FOLLOW YOUR HORN AND OBEY YOUR WHIM, ...	9	OISIN 1		99
QUEEN OF HIGH CRUACHAN." "I OBEY YOUR WILL	184	QUEEN MAEVE		99
I HAVE DONE RIGHT. WHAT COULD I BUT OBEY?	243	SHADOW WATER B		443
AND WORDS OBEY MY CALL"	256	WORDS		12
TRIUMPH THAT WE OBEY.	382	VISION ROBART		16
"OBEY OUR ANCIENT RULE AND MAKE A SHROUD!	634	CUCHULAIN COMF		13
IN SOUTHERN LOCHLANN. I WOULD NOT OBEY	756	SHADOW WATER A	V	191
I KNOW HE WILL OBEY YOU! AND IF YOUR EYES	768	SHADOW WATER A		408
OBEYED				
WHERE THOSE THAT HAVE OBEYED THE HOLY LAW	356	BROKEN DREAMS		33
WHERE EVERY FOOT OBEYED HER GLANCE!	488	CRAZED MOON		11
WHERE VERY FOOT OBEYED HER GLANCE!	488	CRAZED MOON	V	11
TILL TRUTH OBEYED HIS CALL!	576	ACRE OF GRASS		18
AND IN THAT TERROR'S NAME OBEYED THE CALL, ...	622	HOUND VOICE		12
OBEYING				
AND BID THEM WANDER OBEYING YOUR WILL, ...	141	EVERLAST VOICE		3
OBEYS				
OBEYS. SOME FIERCE MAGICIAN FLIES OR WALKS	720	WITCH VIVIEN		9
OBJECT				
HAS MARKED A DISTANT OBJECT DOWN, ...	337	TOM OROUGHLEY		3
BUT HE'D OBJECT TO THE HOST, ...	473	ALL SOUL NIGHT		77
OBLITERATING SEE LIGHT-OBLITERATING				
OBSCURE				
EACH FOREHEAD LIKE AN OBSCURE STAR	26	OISIN 1		391
INDIGNANT AT THE FUMBLING WITS, THE OBSCURE SPITE . . .	291	PAUDEEN		1
OUT OF THE OBSCURE DARK OF THE RICH STREAMS, ...	417	ANCEST HOUSES		14
OBSCURITY				
CRAWLED FROM OBSCURITY, AND SET UPON ME	352	PEOPLE		26
OBSERVANT				
OBSERVANT OLD MEN KNOW IT WELL:	626	OLD MEN BE MAD		17
OBSTACLE				
MY CHILD SLEEPS ON. THERE IS NO OBSTACLE	403	FOR DAUGHTER		3
O'BYRNES				
WHERE THE O'BYRNES AND BYRNES ARE BURIED, ...	331	ROUND TOWER		9
OCCUPIED				
WHAT GREAT HARUN AL-RASHID, OCCUPIED	462	HARUN RASHID		24
BELOVED HAROUN EL RASHID, OCCUPIED	462	HARUN RASHID	V	24
OCCURRED				
NO MATTER WHAT DISASTER OCCURRED	578	CRAZED GIRL		9
OCEAN				
OF MURMURING OCEAN, AND BEHIND US	25	OISIN 1	V	384
OF OCEAN FAN THEE INTO LIFE, AND FOLD	688	TWO TITANS		56
BY THE SLOW HEAVING OCEAN--MUMBLING MOTHER OF THE DEAD.	719	PHANTOM SHIP		34
PRAYED BESIDE THE OCEAN, THE OLD MUMBLING MOTHER OF THE	719	PHANTOM SHIP	V	34
DEAD.				
OCEAN'S				
A VAPOURY FOOTFALL ON THE OCEAN'S SLEEPY BLAZE.	78	INDIAN TO LOVE	V	20
HIDING AWAY THE OCEAN'S YELPING FLOCKS.	688	TWO TITANS		38
OCHONE				
"OCHONE, OCHONE! THE MAN HAS DIED, ...	133	FR GILLIGAN	V	25
"OCHONE, OCHONE! THE MAN HAS DIED, ...	133	FR GILLIGAN	V	25
OCTOBER				
UNDER THE OCTOBER TWILIGHT THE WATER	322	SWANS AT COOLE		3
OCTOBER LAST I FOUND IT TOO	454	EMPTY CUP		7
ODDS				
AND WHAT'S THE ODDS IF SUCH AS THESE	597	MODEL LAUREATE		5
TALKED OF ODDS AND ENDS.	627	STATES HOLIDAY		8

O'DONNELL
    DOWN TO THE TUNE OF O'DONNELL ABU. . . . .   544 TO SAME TUNE 1   10
    DOWN TO THE TUNE OF O'DONNELL ABU. . . . .   545 TO SAME TUNE 1   20
    DOWN TO THE TUNE OF O'DONNELL ABU. . . . .   545 TO SAME TUNE 1   30
    THOSE THAT COME AFTER SHALL MOCK AT O'DONNELL, ...   546 TO SAME TUNE 2   23
    DOWN TO THE TUNE OF O'DONNELL ABU. . . . .   546 TO SAME TUNE 2 V REF
    THOSE THAT COME AFTER SHALL MOCK O'DONNELL, ...   546 TO SAME TUNE 2 V   23
    DOWN TO THE TUNE OF O'DONNELL ABU. . . . .   548 TO SAME TUNE 3 V REF
    THOSE THAT COME AFTER SHALL MOCK AT O'DONNELL, . . .   614 MARCH SONGS 1   23
ODOROUS
    THE ODOROUS WEIGHT OF HIS CURLS OF LIGHT, ...   28 OISIN 1   V 423D
    AND COVER YOUR LIPS WITH ODOROUS TWILIGHT AND SAY, . .   162 ASKS FORGIVE   5
    THE ODOROUS TWILIGHT THERE. . . . .   163 ASKS FORGIVE   24
    AND THRO' THE ODOROUS AIR LOVE-DREAMS ARE WINGING-- . .   645 ISLE STAT I 1   5
    AND CLINGING WITH THE DEW OF ODOROUS SHOWERS. . . . .   704 REMEMBRANCE   4
ODOUR
    TILL, FATTENING THE WINDS OF THE MORNING, AN ODOUR   57 OISIN 3   153
       OF NEW-MOWN HAY
    AND SHEDS FAINT ODOUR THROUGH THE AIR: . . . . . .   85 MAD KING GOLL V   64
    ODOUR OF BLOOD WHEN CHRIST WAS SLAIN . . . .   438 SONGS PLAY 2   6
    ODOUR OF BLOOD ON THE ANCESTRAL STAIR! . . . . . .   482 BLOOD AND MOON   40
    MIRACULOUS OIL, ODOUR OF VIOLET. . . . .   483 OIL AND BLOOD   3
    AN ODOUR OF THE NEW-MOWN HAY . . . .   502 VACILLATION   58
ODOUR-LADEN
    WHERE TIME IS DROWNED IN ODOUR-LADEN WINDS . . . . .   219 HARP OF AENGUS   3
    DREAMING IN THEIR SOFT ODOUR-LADEN SLEEP: . . . . .   650 ISLE STAT I 1   125
    WHERE TIME IS DROWNED IN ODOUR-LADEN WINDS . . . . .   762 SHADOW WATER A   298
ODOURS
    NOR LOST IN THE STAR-FIRES AND ODOURS . . .   56 OISIN 3   135
    AND SHEDS FAINT ODOURS THROUGH THE AIR! . . . . . .   85 MAD KING GOLL   64
    SEVEN ODOURS, SEVEN MURMURS, SEVEN WOODS. . . . . .   218 WOODS OF COOLE   16
    BATHED IN MIRACULOUS OIL, SWEET ODOURS FROM IT COME, . .   503 VACILLATION   81
O'DRISCOLL
    O'DRISCOLL DROVE WITH A SONG . . . .   143 HOST OF AIR   1
    O'DRISCOLL SCATTERED THE CARDS . . . .   145 HOST OF AIR   37
    O'DRISCOLL GOT UP FROM THE GRASS, ...   145 HOST OF AIR   V 37
O'DUFFY
    HAD EVEN O'DUFFY--BUT I NAME NO MORE--   543 PARN FUNERAL 2   9
ODYSSEUS
    DOOMED LIKE ODYSSEUS AND THE LABOURING SHIPS . . . . .   120 SORROW OF LOVE   7
OEDIPUS
    FROM "OEDIPUS AT COLONUS" . . . .   459 FROM OEDIPUS   T
OEDIPUS'
    AND YET I WEEP--OEDIPUS' CHILD . . . .   540 FROM ANTIGONE   15
OENONE
    OENONE SAW THE FIRES OF TROIA LEAP, ...   645 ISLE STAT I 1   17
    THE SHEPHERD PARIS FOR OENONE MADE, ...   650 ISLE STAT I 1   136
O'ER   SEE CLOUD-O'ER-MUFFLED
    A STORMY SUNSET O'ER DOOMED SHIPS. . . . .   3 OISIN 1   V 23
    TO PEAK AND PINE O'ER OISIN'S FAME." . . . .   7 OISIN 1   V 70
    ON, ON, WE GALLOPED O'ER THE SEA. . . . .   11 OISIN 1   V 132
    O'ER MEN WHO SLEEP, AND WAKE, AND DIE, ...   22 OISIN 1   V 340B
    WE PASSED IN SILENCE O'ER THE MEAD. . . . .   25 OISIN 1   V 376A
    AND SHAKES O'ER THE WIDTH OF THE SEA-WORLD BORDER . .   28 OISIN 1   V 423C
    THEN, MOUNTED ON A HERON, O'ER THE DEEP . . . . . .   33 OISIN 2   V 64
    REMEMBERING HOW I PACED IN DAYS GONE O'ER, ...   44 OISIN 2   V 227
    . . . AND O'ER YOUR CAR HEADS PEER . . . .   73 ANASHU VIJAYA V 45
    I RULED O'ER ALL MY FAIR DOMINIONS. . . . .   82 MAD KING GOLL V 7
    O'ER HILL AND HEATH AND SPONGY FEN, ...   83 MAD KING GOLL V 32
    O'ER HER NEST THE LIGHTS ARE BLENDING! . . . . . .   646 ISLE STAT I 1   36
    SEE, I TELL THY BEAUTIES O'ER, ...   647 ISLE STAT I 1   56
    SINGING O'ER AND O'ER AND O'ER . . . .   648 ISLE STAT I 1   79
    SINGING O'ER AND O'ER AND O'ER . . . .   648 ISLE STAT I 1   79
    SINGING O'ER AND O'ER AND O'ER . . . .   648 ISLE STAT I 1   79
    TO WELCOME THEE, WHEN O'ER THE OWLET'S WINGS . . . .   648 ISLE STAT I 1   102
    BEAT OUT THEIR LIVES LAMENTING O'ER THE SAND! . . . .   652 ISLE STAT I 2   14
    O'ER THE GRASS LIGHT-ENDAPPLED. . . . .   654 ISLE STAT I 2   63
    O'ER THE GREEN EDEN-SOD. . . . .   654 ISLE STAT I 2   65
    O'ER THE GREEN EDEN-SOD, ...   654 ISLE STAT I 2   75
    O'ER THE LAKE THIS VERY DAY. . . . .   656 ISLE STAT I 3   17
    O'ER MUCH I'VE TALKED! I SHALL BE SILENT SOON, . . .   657 ISLE STAT I 3   75
    WATCHING O'ER HER AWFUL YOUNG, ...   658 ISLE STAT I 3   87
    O'ER HER YOUNG SO EAGERLY . . . .   658 ISLE STAT I 3   93
    YOUNG GUARIMOND HE TELLS THEM O'ER AND O'ER, ...   661 ISLE STAT II 1   56
    YOUNG GUARIMOND HE TELLS THEM O'ER AND O'ER, ...   661 ISLE STAT II 1   56
    THE LIGHT IS DANCING O'ER THE KNOTTED TREES, ...   662 ISLE STAT II 2   2
    THE FAERY THING FLEW WITH HER O'ER THE GRAY . . . .   663 ISLE STAT II 2   38
    OF SWORD-BLUE WAVES OF CALM! WHILE O'ER HEAD BLINK . .   663 ISLE STAT II 2   42
    O'ER GRIEF. THE WORLD DRINKS SORROW FROM THE BEAMS . .   664 ISLE STAT II 2   46
    OF LILAC O'ER THE PULSING WATER GLEAMS, ...   664 ISLE STAT II 2   48
    TILL HIS LAST WRETCHEDNESS WAS O'ER AND DONE." . . .   664 ISLE STAT II 2   54
    THE SKY WAS BANDED O'ER WITH WRACK. . . . .   667 ISLE STAT II 3   23
    BEFORE A DEATH. O'ER WAVE AND BANK . . . .   673 ISLE STAT II 3   185
    MY DREAMS O'ER THOUGHTS OF PLENTY, AS THE RED- . . .   681 SEEKER   V 3
    MAKING ALL ONE O'ER ROCK AND SEA AND SKIES: . . . .   687 TWO TITANS   28
    BENDING HER FACE O'ER HIS, SHE WATCHES MEET . . . .   688 TWO TITANS   45
    POURS UP AND FLOATS IN FRAGRANCE O'ER MY HEAD . . . .   691 MOSADA 1   V 40
    THE PATH O'ER MUFFLED WITH THE LEAVES--DEAD LEAVES, . .   703 MOSADA 3   V 115
    WHILE O'ER THE BUDS, AND O'ER THE GRASS-BLADES, BRIGHT . .   704 REMEMBRANCE   3
    WHILE O'ER THE BUDS, AND O'ER THE GRASS-BLADES, BRIGHT . .   704 REMEMBRANCE   3

O'ER   (CONTINUED)
    AND HANGING O'ER THE HUSH OF WILLOW BOWERS, ...   705 REMEMBRANCE   8
    AND HANG O'ER THE HISTORIED STONE! . . . .   707 FAIRY PEDANT   6
    AND FOLLOWING O'ER THE FIELDS AND PASTURE LANDS, . . .   715 FERENCZ RENYI   V 120
    HANGS O'ER ALL THE WOODED EARTH. . . . .   731 STREET DANCERS   8
O'ER-APPLED
    WHEN THE TREE WAS O'ER-APPLED . . . .   654 ISLE STAT I 2   60
O'ER-MUFFLED
    THE PATH O'ER-MUFFLED WITH THE LEAVES--DEAD LEAVES, . . 703 MOSADA 3   115
O'ERWORN
    THESE NOW O'ERWORN AND WITHERED HANDS, ...   23 OISIN 1   V 348
OFF   SEE FAR-OFF
    "LIKE ME WERE SOME GALLEY FORSAKEN FAR OFF IN MERIDIAN   55 OISIN 3   117
       ISLE,
    WATCHING THE BLESSED ONES MOVE FAR OFF, AND THE SMILE ON 61 OISIN 3   199
       GOD'S FACE,
    NOW CUFF HIM OFF. HE'S OFF! A KISS FOR YOU, ...   73 ANASHU VIJAYA   39
    NOW CUFF HIM OFF. HE'S OFF! A KISS FOR YOU, ...   73 ANASHU VIJAYA   39
    MURMURING GENTLY HOW FAR OFF ARE THE UNQUIET LANDS! . .   78 INDIAN TO LOVE   V   10
    FAR OFF BY FURTHEST ROSSES . . . .   87 STOLEN CHILD   15
    DIE OFF THE FEEBLE SOUNDS! . . . .   99 FOXHUNTER   V   42
    COME CLEAR OFF THE NETS OF WRONG AND RIGHT! . . . .   147 INTO TWILIGHT   V   2
    AND WAVED IT OFF ON THE AIR. . . . .   160 CAP AND BELLS   20
    FAR OFF, MOST SECRET, AND INVIOLATE ROSE, ...   169 SECRET ROSE   V   1
    FAR OFF, MOST SECRET, AND INVIOLATE ROSE? . . . . .   170 SECRET ROSE   V   32
    WILL OVERTHROW HIS SHADOWS AND CARRY OFF . . . . .   184 QUEEN MAEVE   95
    "ANOTHER'S HURRIED OFF," CRIED HE. . . . . . .   193 BAILE AILLINN   113
    HE CARRIED EDAIN OFF FROM A KING'S HOUSE, ...   224 SHADOW WATER B   48
    HOW ARE WE BETTER OFF THAN SEAGHAN THE FOOL, ...   228 SHADOW WATER B   129
    WE HAVE BEEN NO BETTER OFF THAN SEAGHAN THE FOOL, . .   228 SHADOW WATER B V   129
    "PUT OFF THAT MASK OF BURNING GOLD . . . .   263 MASK   1
    BEFORE HIM OR BEHIND, BUT THAT FAR OFF . . . . . .   279 TWO KINGS   55
    "TIME TO PUT OFF THE WORLD AND GO SOMEWHERE . . . .   299 BEGGAR CRIED   1
    WERE NOT OUR BEDS FAR OFF I'D RING THE BELL, ...   377 PHASES OF MOON   124
    SHOOK OFF THE WATER FROM HIS BACK! . . . .   400 DEMON BEAST   29
    OR HURRIED THEM OFF ON ITS OWN FURIOUS PATH! . . . .   430 NINETEEN 19   53
    WHERE WE SHOULD CAST OFF BODY AND TRADE . . . . .   431 NINETEEN 19   73
    I'D TEAR IT OFF AND THROW IT IN THE FIRE." . . . . .   462 HARUN RASHID   34
    THAT IF THE SPRING BEAR OFF WHAT THE SPRING GAVE . .   464 HARUN RASHID   76
    CRIED, CASTING OFF THE MOUNTAIN SNOW, ...   502 VACILLATION   60
    "THAT IS A LONG WAY OFF, ...   526 AM OF IRELAND   11
    BUT WHEN THIS SOUL, ITS BODY OFF, ...   538 LAST CONFESS   15
    SOMEWHERE OFF HENRY STREET! . . . .   585 ORAHILLY   31
    COULD CRAZY JANE PUT OFF OLD AGE . . . .   606 SONGS BURDEN 1   19
    EUROPE PUT OFF THAT FOAM WHEN PHIDIAS . . . . . .   610 STATUES   15
    THEY PITCH THEIR BURDENS OFF. . . . .   612 NEWS ORACLE   24
    O LET ME PASS! THE SPELLS FROM OFF THE HEART . . . .   668 ISLE STAT II 3   44
    FAR OFF IN DROWSY VALLEYS . . . .   680 LOVE AND DEATH   5
    HEARING THE FAR OFF SINGING GUILE AND GROANED, . . .   693 MOSADA 1   V   88
    CAST OFF THY HERESIES, AND SAVE THY SOUL . . . . .   701 MOSADA 3   64
    WAVES OFF THE FLIES, AND WARMS HIM IN THE SHINE. . . .   709 FERENCZ RENYI   7
    A SCORE OF YARDS OFF 'NEATH A WILLOW, SHOT. . . . .   712 FERENCZ RENYI   65
    HER OFF AND TURNS AWAY. SHE THROWS . . . . . .   714 FERENCZ RENYI   V 102
    AND DROVE THE BOYS AND WOMEN OFF. . . . . . .   725 LEGEND   24
    HIS HEAD FROM OFF HIS BODY . . . .   789 SINGING HEAD   5
OFFENDED
    TO MY OFFENDED HEART . . . .   516 MANS SONG   17
OFFER
    I, PRIESTESS OF THIS TEMPLE, OFFER UP . . . . .   71 ANASHU VIJAYA   12
    I, PRIESTESS OF THIS TEMPLE, OFFER UP . . . . .   75 ANASHU VIJAYA   84
    I OFFER TO LOVE'S PLAY . . . .   536 PARTING   13
OFFERED
    O YOU WILL TAKE WHATEVER'S OFFERED . . . .   313 TWO YEAR LATER   7
OFFERS
    SHE OFFERS GREAT REWARDS IF WE TURN EAST . . . . .   755 SHADOW WATER A   169
OFFICE
    PLANNED IN A GOVERNMENT OFFICE, SHORTEN HIS LIFE, . .   372 ON GOING HOUSE   15
    THAT OFFICE FOOLS HAVE RUN. . . . .   598 MODEL LAUREATE   20
    THAT FOUGHT IN THE POST OFFICE . . . .   608 SONGS BURDEN 3   5
    WHAT STALKED THROUGH THE POST OFFICE? WHAT INTELLECT, . . 611 STATUES   26
OFFICER
    COMMANDING OFFICER THAT TORE . . . .   627 STATES HOLIDAY   16
OFT
    OF KNITTED MUSIC. OFT THE FOND REPINING . . . .   33 OISIN 2   V 68C
    FLOWED ON ANEW, AND OFT, ANEW DECLINING, ...   33 OISIN 2   V 68D
OFTEN
    "PASSION HAS OFTEN WORN OUR WANDERING HEARTS." . . . .   80 EPHEMERA   12
    "OFTEN HAS PASSION WORN OUR WANDERING HEARTS, ...   80 EPHEMERA   V   12
    I HAVE OFTEN HEARD HIM SINGING TO AND FRO, ...   109 CUCHULAIN SEA   49
    I HAVE OFTEN HEARD THE SWEET SOUND OF HIS BOW. . . .   109 CUCHULAIN SEA   50
    I OFTEN HEAR HIM SINGING TO AND FRO, ...   109 CUCHULAIN SEA   V   49
    I OFTEN HEAR THE SWEET SOUND OF HIS BOW. . . . . .   109 CUCHULAIN SEA   V   50
    YOU SAY, AS I HAVE OFTEN GIVEN TONGUE . . . . .   262 TO A POET   1
    HE HAD OFTEN PLAYED HIS PIPES AMONG MY HILLS, . . .   339 SHEP GOATHERD   23
    AND OFTEN THOSE FIRST DAYS I SAW HER STARE . . . .   466 HARUN RASHID   122
    OFTEN AT EVENING WHEN A BOY . . . .   494 AT ALGECIRAS   7
    OFTEN HE HAD BENT DOWN SOME BOUGH ALL BRIGHT . . . .   710 FERENCZ RENYI   28
    WHY THOSE WHO DO GOOD OFTEN BE NOT GOOD, ...   710 FERENCZ RENYI   33
    OFTEN HE HAD BENT DOWN SOME BOUGH ALL BRIGHT WITH BERRIES! 710 FERENCZ RENYI V   28
OGHAM
    THEREON IN OGHAM LETTERS, "MANANNAN"! . . . .   38 OISIN 2   128

		PAGE	TITLE		LINE
OGHAM	(CONTINUED)				
	IN CHANGELESS OGHAM LETTERS WRIT-- • • • • • • • •	194	BAILE AILLINN		117
	AND CARVE HIS NAME IN OGHAM." EOCHAID SAID, • • • • •	280	TWO KINGS		83
O'GRADY					
	STANDISH O'GRADY SUPPORTING HIMSELF BETWEEN THE TABLES • •	577	LOFTY THINGS		5
O'HART					
	THE BALLAD OF FATHER O'HART • • • • • • • • • • • •	91	FATHER OHART		T
	FATHER O'HART • • • • • • • • • • • • • • • • • • •	91	FATHER OHART	V	T
	GOOD FATHER JOHN O'HART • • • • • • • • • • • • • •	91	FATHER OHART		1
O'HIGGINS					
	O'HIGGINS ITS SOLE STATESMAN HAD NOT DIED• • • • • • •	543	PARN FUNERAL 2		8
	KEVIN O'HIGGINS, AND THAT LOOK HE WEARS, • • • • • •	601	GALLERY REVIS	V	5
O'HIGGINS'					
	KEVIN O'HIGGINS' COUNTENANCE THAT WEARS • • • • • • •	601	GALLERY REVIS		5
OHONE					
	AND HAS NOT YET BEEN WAKED. OHONE! O! O! O! • • • • •	241	SHADOW WATER B		393
OIL					
	AND OIL AND WINE AND HONEY AND MILK, • • • • • • • •	8	OISIN 1		92
	AND HONEY, AND OIL, AND WINE, AND MILK, • • • • • • •	8	OISIN 1	V	92
	I BADE, BECAUSE THE WICK AND OIL ARE SPENT • • • • • •	333	LIVING BEAUTY		1
	THE WICK OF YOUTH BEING BURNED AND THE OIL SPENT, • • •	334	LIVING BEAUTY	V	3
	WHEN OIL AND WICK ARE BURNED IN ONE! • • • • • • • • •	388	SOLOMON WITCH		30
	NOR BLEAR-EYED WISDOM OUT OF MIDNIGHT OIL• • • • • • •	446	SCHOOL CHILDR		60
	OIL AND BLOOD • • • • • • • • • • • • • • • • • • •	483	OIL AND BLOOD		T
	MIRACULOUS OIL, ODOUR OF VIOLET• • • • • • • • • • •	483	OIL AND BLOOD		3
	BATHED IN MIRACULOUS OIL, SWEET ODOURS FROM IT COME, • •	503	VACILLATION		81
OILY					
	WE RODE ACROSS THE OILY SEA, • • • • • • • • • • • •	10	OISIN 1	V	114
OISIN					
	THE WANDERINGS OF OISIN • • • • • • • • • • • • • • •	1	OISIN 1		T
	THE WANDERINGS OF OISIN AND HOW A DEMON TRAPPED HIM • • •	1	OISIN 1	V	T
	OISIN, TELL ME THE FAMOUS STORY • • • • • • • • • • •	2	OISIN 1	V	1
	OISIN, THOU ART HALF HEATHEN STILL! • • • • • • • • •	4	OISIN 1	V	31
	FOR LOVE OF OISIN FOAM WET FEET • • • • • • • • • • •	6	OISIN 1	V	57
	FOR LOVE OF OISIN FOAM-WET FEET • • • • • • • • • • •	6	OISIN 1	V	57
	OF OISIN, THE YOUNG MAN, MY SON? • • • • • • • • • • •	6	OISIN 1	V	60
	ON THIS YOUNG MAN, OISIN, MY SON?" • • • • • • • • • •	6	OISIN 1	V	61
	OF NOBLE OISIN AND HIS FAME, • • • • • • • • • • • •	7	OISIN 1	V	66
	"O OISIN, MOUNT BY ME AND RIDE • • • • • • • • • • •	8	OISIN 1		80
	"OISIN, THOU MUST AWAY WITH ME • • • • • • • • • • •	8	OISIN 1	V	80
	BARD OISIN, BOAST NOT OF THY DEEDS • • • • • • • • •	11	OISIN 1	V	129
	HOPELESS FOR EVER! ANCIENT OISIN KNOWS, • • • • • • • •	42	OISIN 2		202
	AY, OISIN KNOWS, FOR HE IS OF THE WEAK, • • • • • • •	42	OISIN 2	V	202
	YOUR QUESTIONER, OISIN, IS WORTHY, HE COMES FROM THE FENIAN LANDS."	51	OISIN 3		64
	WORTHY'S THY QUESTIONER, OISIN, HE FROM THE FENIAN LANDS."	51	OISIN 3	V	64
	AS SHE MURMURED, "O WANDERING OISIN, • • • • • • • •	55	OISIN 3		123
	BUT WEEP FOR YOUR NIAMH, O OISIN, WEEP! FOR IF ONLY YOUR SHOE	55	OISIN 3		127
	BUT WEEP FOR THY NIAM, OH OISIN, WEEP! FOR IF ONLY THY SHOE	55	OISIN 3	V	127
	BY OISIN ON THE GRASS! • • • • • • • • • • • • • • •	611	NEWS ORACLE		6
	FIRST THAT SEA-RIDER OISIN LED BY THE NOSE • • • • • •	629	CIRCUS ANIMALS		10
OISIN'S					
	RHYME THAT RHYMED UPON OISIN'S NAME, • • • • • • • •	7	OISIN 1		64
	TO PEAK AND PINE O'ER OISIN'S FAME." • • • • • • • •	7	OISIN 1	V	70
	FOR THESE WERE ANCIENT OISIN'S FATE • • • • • • • • •	24	OISIN 1		361
OLD	SEE SIXTY-YEAR-OLD HUNDRED-YEAR-OLD WORLD-OLD				
	THE BAD OLD DAYS. THOU WERT, MEN SING, • • • • • • •	2	OISIN 1	V	3
	MUST LIVE TO BE OLD LIKE THE WANDERING MOON. • • • • •	3	OISIN 1		12
	"MEN'S HEARTS OF OLD WERE DROPS OF FLAME." • • • • • •	19	OISIN 1		276
	IN OTHER YEARS FROM SOME OLD STAR • • • • • • • • • •	19	OISIN 1	V	277
	OF GRIEVOUS TIME ON HIS OLD CRUTCHES, • • • • • • • •	23	OISIN 1	V	341B
	FOR WE KNEW WELL THE OLD WAS OVER. • • • • • • • • •	25	OISIN 1		379
	BY RIVERS AND THE WOODS' OLD NIGHT! • • • • • • • • •	25	OISIN 1		387
	FOR WELL WE KNEW THE OLD WAS OVER, • • • • • • • • •	25	OISIN 1	V	379
	THE RIVERS, AND THE WOOD'S OLD NIGHT. • • • • • • • •	25	OISIN 1	V	387
	"AN OLD MAN STIRS THE FIRE TO A BLAZE, • • • • • • •	26	OISIN 1		400
	WATCHED THE OLD SUN THAT IN SEA-WAYS • • • • • • • •	26	OISIN 1	V	394
	AND THE CRY OF THE HOUNDS ON THE HILLS OF OLD. • • • •	27	OISIN 1		407
	THE HARE GROWS OLD AS SHE PLAYS IN THE SUN • • • • • •	27	OISIN 1		412
	"OLD GROWS THE HARE AS SHE PLAYS IN THE SUN, • • • • •	28	OISIN 1	V	420
	BEFORE GOD WAS OR MY OLD LINE BEGAN! • • • • • • • •	29	OISIN 2		8
	WARS SHADOWY, VAST, EXULTANT! FAERIES OF OLD • • • • •	29	OISIN 2		9
	THINGS DONE ERE GOD FIRST WAS OR MY OLD LINE BEGAN! • •	29	OISIN 2	V	8
	ON THE OLD SORROWS OF HIS HUMAN DAYS. • • • • • • • •	29	OISIN 2	V	12
	THAT OLD, SEA-WEEDY, SQUARED, THREE HUNDRED FEET • • • •	31	OISIN 2	V	30C
	TO TWO OLD EAGLES, FULL OF ANCIENT PRIDE, • • • • • •	34	OISIN 2		74
	NOW IT IS OLD AND MOUSE-LIKE. FOR A SIGN • • • • • •	36	OISIN 2		96
	NOW OLD AND MOUSELIKE. FOR AN ANSWERING SIGN • • • • •	36	OISIN 2	V	96
	PATRICK, BEFORE THY CRAFT DIES EACH OLD SONG, • • • • •	42	OISIN 2	V	196
	OLD AND REMEMBERING, WHAT AVAILS THE WIND • • • • • •	42	OISIN 2	V	206
	LIKE AN ARMY OF OLD MEN LONGING FOR REST FROM THE MOAN OF THE SEAS.	48	OISIN 3		16
	DROPPING: A MURMUROUS DROPPING: OLD SILENCE AND THAT ONE SOUND:	48	OISIN 3		18
	AND DEW-BLANCHED HORNS, IN WHOSE HOLLOW A CHILD OF THREE YEARS OLD	49	OISIN 3		30
	AND DEW-BLANCHED HORNS, IN WHOSE HOLLOWS A CHILD OF THREE YEARS OLD	49	OISIN 3	V	31
	IN MIDST OF AN OLD MAN'S BOSOM: OWLS RUFFLING AND PACING AROUND	50	OISIN 3		47

571

	PAGE	TITLE		LINE
OLD (CONTINUED)				
IN THE MIDST OF AN OLD MAN'S BOSOM: OWLS RUFFLING AND PACING AROUND	50	OISIN 3	V	47
THAT WE MAY MUSE IN THE STARLIGHT AND TALK OF THE BATTLES OF OLD:	51	OISIN 3		63
. . . MADE CONCHUBAR'S SWORD-BLADE OF OLD.	52	OISIN 3		80
. . . MADE ARMOUR FOR CONOR THE OLD.	52	OISIN 3	V	80
. . . MADE ARMOUR FOR CONHOR OF OLD.	52	OISIN 3	V	80
. . . MADE ARMOUR FOR MIDHIR OF OLD	52	OISIN 3	V	80
CAME BLANAID, MAC NESSA, TALL FERGUS WHO FEASTWARD OF OLD TIME SLUNK,	53	OISIN 3		89
DARK BALOR, AS OLD AS A FOREST, CAR-BORNE, HIS MIGHTY HEAD SUNK	53	OISIN 3		91
CAME BLANID, MAC NESSA, AND FERGUS WHO FEASTWARD OF OLD TIME SLUNK,	53	OISIN 3	V	89
CAME CAR-BORNE BALOR, AS OLD AS A FOREST, HIS VAST FACE SUNK	53	OISIN 3	V	91
CAME BALOR, AS OLD AS A FOREST, CAR BORNE, HIS MIGHTY HEAD SUNK	53	OISIN 3	V	91
. . . AND MOVE WHERE THE OLD MEN AND YOUNG	55	OISIN 3		114
WHERE EVER IS MURMUROUS DROPPING, OLD SILENCE AND THAT ONE SOUND:	56	OISIN 3		138
LIKE AN ARMY OF OLD MEN LONGING FOR REST FROM THE MOAN OF THE SEAS.	57	OISIN 3		144
LIKE AN ARMY OF OLD MEN LOUNGING FOR REST FROM THE FOAM OF THE SEAS.	57	OISIN 3	V	144
CAME AFTER THE HARD GAZE OF YOUTH, OR AN OLD MAN LIFTED HIS HEAD:	59	OISIN 3		170
. . . I MURMURED, "IN OLD AGE THEY CEASED":	59	OISIN 3		177
ON CREVROE OR BROAD KNOCKFEFIN, WITH MANY OF OLD THEY FEAST	59	OISIN 3		179
. . . OR WAS LIFTED AN OLD MAN'S MILD HEAD.	59	OISIN 3	V	170
ON CREVROE OR ON BROAD KNOCKFEFIN, WITH MANY OF OLD THEY FAST	59	OISIN 3	V	179
I TURNED AND RODE TO THE WESTWARD, AND FOLLOWED THE SEA'S OLD SHOUT	60	OISIN 3		183
. . . A SOB FOR THE FENIANS' OLD STRENGTH.	60	OISIN 3		188
A CREEPING OLD MAN, FULL OF SLEEP, ...	60	OISIN 3		192
AND RODE ON TILL OVER THE WORLD'S RIM FLOATED THE SEA'S OLD SHOUT,	60	OISIN 3	V	183
SPEAK, YOU TOO ARE OLD WITH YOUR MEMORIES, ...	61	OISIN 3		196
. . . AN OLD MAN SURROUNDED WITH DREAMS.	61	OISIN 3		196
THE WAR-SONGS THAT ROUSED THEM OF OLD:	61	OISIN 3		202
SPEAK, THOU TOO ART OLD WITH THY MEMORIES, ...	61	OISIN 3	V	196
. . . AND OF OLD WOUNDS, AND TURN TO OUR REST.	62	OISIN 3		212
. . . AND OF OLD WOUNDS AND REST.	62	OISIN 3	V	212
AH ME! TO BE SHAKEN WITH COUGHING AND BROKEN WITH OLD AGE AND PAIN,	63	OISIN 3		217
IT WERE SAD TO GAZE ON THE BLESSED AND NO MAN I LOVED OF OLD THERE:	63	OISIN 3		221
AH ME! TO BE OLD WITHOUT SUCCOUR, A SHOW UNTO CHILDREN, A STAIN,	63	OISIN 3	V	217
IT WAS SAD TO GAZE ON THE BLESSED AND NO MAN I LOVED OF OLD THERE:	63	OISIN 3	V	221
OF OLD THE WORLD ON DREAMING FED:	64	HAPPY SHEPHERD		3
THE KINGS OF THE OLD TIME ARE DEAD:	65	HAPPY SHEPHERD		17
TO THE OLD CRACKED TUNE THAT CHRONOS SINGS, ...	65	HAPPY SHEPHERD	V	9
WHERE ARE NOW THE OLD KINGS HOARY?	65	HAPPY SHEPHERD	V	13
THE KINGS OF THE OLD TIME ARE FLED.	65	HAPPY SHEPHERD	V	17
MY SONGS OF OLD EARTH'S DREAMY YOUTH:	67	HAPPY SHEPHERD		54
THE SEA SWEPT ON AND CRIED HER OLD CRY STILL, ...	68	SAD SHEPHERD		10
"OH SEA, OLD SEA: HEAR THOU MY PITEOUS STORY!"	68	SAD SHEPHERD	V	9
SEE HOW THE SACRED OLD FLAMINGOES COME, ...	72	ANASHU VIJAYA		29
THE VAN OF WANDERING QUIET: ERE YOU BE TOO CALM AND OLD,	73	ANASHU VIJAYA		43
THE VAN OF WANDERING QUIET: ERE YE BE TOO CALM AND OLD,	73	ANASHU VIJAYA	V	43
WITH HER OLD FATHER THE BLIND WOOD-CUTTER:	74	ANASHU VIJAYA		63
WHO STILL WERE OLD WHEN THE GREAT SEA WAS YOUNG:	74	ANASHU VIJAYA		69
THE DAUGHTER OF THE GREY OLD WOOD-CUTTER, ...	74	ANASHU VIJAYA	V	63
IS OUR FIRST KISS, AND AH, HOW OLD MY HEART!"	80	EPHEMERA		9
A RABBIT OLD AND LAME LIMPED DOWN THE PATH:	80	EPHEMERA		15
I WAS A WISE YOUNG KING OF OLD:	81	MAD KING GOLL	V	1
. . . THE BEECH LEAVES OLD:	82	MAD KING GOLL	V	12
AND EVERY MUMBLING OLD MAN SAID, ...	82	MAD KING GOLL	V	9
AND EVERY WHISPERING OLD MAN SAID, ...	82	MAD KING GOLL	V	9
. . . THE BEECH-LEAVES OLD.	82	MAD KING GOLL	V	REF
. . . THE BEECH LEAVES OLD.	83	MAD KING GOLL		24
. . . THE BEECH LEAVES OLD.	84	MAD KING GOLL		36
. . . THE BEECH LEAVES OLD.	84	MAD KING GOLL		48
AND SAW WHERE THIS OLD TYMPAN LAY	85	MAD KING GOLL		55
. . . THE BEECH LEAVES OLD.	85	MAD KING GOLL		60
. . . THE BEECH LEAVES OLD.	86	MAD KING GOLL		72
AN OLD SONG RE-SUNG	90	SALLEY GARDENS	V	T
THE MEDITATION OF THE OLD FISHERMAN	90	OLD FISHERMAN		T
THE HERRING ARE NOT IN THE TIDES AS THEY WERE OF OLD: . .	91	OLD FISHERMAN		5
THE YOUNG BIRDS AND OLD BIRDS	93	FATHER OHART		33
WHO DIG OLD CUSTOMS UP.	93	FATHER OHART		40
BEYOND OLD MARTIN'S BYRE	95	MOLL MAGEE		34
BEYOND OLD MARTIN'S WOOD, ...	95	MOLL MAGEE	V	34
THE BALLAD OF THE OLD FOX-HUNTER	97	FOXHUNTER	V	T
THE BALLAD OF THE OLD FOXHUNTER	97	FOXHUNTER	V	T
MY LOLLARD OLD AND DEAR.	97	FOXHUNTER	V	8
HIS OLD EYES CLOUD WITH DREAMS:	98	FOXHUNTER		14

572

OLD (CONTINUED)

	PAGE	TITLE		LINE
AND NOW THE OLD MAN'S DREAMS ARE GONE,	98	FOXHUNTER		19
FIRE IS IN THE OLD MAN'S EYES,	98	FOXHUNTER		29
A FIRE IS IN THE OLD MAN'S EYES,	98	FOXHUNTER	V	29
THE OLD HOUNDS AND THE YOUNG.	99	FOXHUNTER	V	40
ARE OLD AND PUPPY HOUNDS!	99	FOXHUNTER	V	44
AND THINE OWN SADNESS, WHEREOF STARS, GROWN OLD	101	ROSE UPON ROOD		6
SING OF OLD EIRE AND THE ANCIENT WAYS!	101	ROSE UPON ROOD		23
AN OLD SLAVE GRINDING AT A HEAVY QUERN,	104	FERGUS DRUID		35
"NAY, HE IS OLD AND SAD WITH MANY WARS,	107	CUCHULAIN SEA	V	29
"BUT HE IS OLD AND SAD WITH MANY WARS."	107	CUCHULAIN SEA	V	30
FEASTED, AND WITH THEM OLD CUCHULAIN DWELT,	108	CUCHULAIN SEA	V	39
AND THROUGH THAT NEW BLADE'S GUARD THE OLD BLADE BROKE,	110	CUCHULAIN SEA		66
TO THESE OLD NIGHT SHALL ALL HER MYSTERY TELL!	114	ROSE OF BATTLE		22
WE WHO ARE OLD, OLD AND GAY,	116	FAERY SONG		1
WE WHO ARE OLD, OLD AND GAY,	116	FAERY SONG		1
O SO OLD!	116	FAERY SONG		2
US WHO ARE OLD, OLD AND GAY,	116	FAERY SONG		13
US WHO ARE OLD, OLD AND GAY,	116	FAERY SONG		13
O SO OLD!	116	FAERY SONG		14
AND THE OLD PLANETS SEVEN	118	CRADLE SONG	V	7
THE OLD PLANETS SEVEN	118	CRADLE SONG	V	7
HAD HID AWAY EARTH'S OLD AND WEARY CRY.	120	SORROW OF LOVE	V	4
ARE SHAKEN WITH EARTH'S OLD AND WEARY CRY.	120	SORROW OF LOVE	V	12
WHEN YOU ARE OLD	120	YOU ARE OLD		T
WHEN YOU ARE OLD AND GREY AND FULL OF SLEEP,	120	YOU ARE OLD		1
FULL OF EARTH'S OLD TIMID GRACE.	124	CATHLEEN PARA		12
OLD SILENCE BIDS ITS CHOSEN RACE REJOICE,	127	DREAM OF FAERY		31
OLD SILENCE BIDS A LONELY FOLK REJOICE,	127	DREAM OF FAERY	V	31
NOW THAT OLD EARTH HAD TAKEN MAN AND ALL!	128	DREAM OF FAERY	V	40
AN OLD POEM RE-WRITTEN	129	BOOK STORIES	V	T
OF HALF-FORGOTTEN INNOCENT OLD PLACES!	130	BOOK STORIES		22
I TORE IT FROM THE GREEN BOUGHS OF OLD ERI,	130	BOOK STORIES	V	15
THEY BRING YOU MEMORIES OF OLD VILLAGE FACES,	130	BOOK STORIES	V	22
CABINS GONE NOW, OLD WELL-SIDES, OLD DEAR PLACES,	130	BOOK STORIES	V	23
CABINS GONE NOW, OLD WELL-SIDES, OLD DEAR PLACES,	130	BOOK STORIES	V	23
THE LAMENTATION OF THE OLD PENSIONER	131	OLD PENSIONER		T
THE OLD PENSIONER	131	OLD PENSIONER	V	T
WITH "LOOK AT THAT OLD FELLOW THERE;	131	OLD PENSIONER	V	3
AS IN THE OLD DAYS LONG GONE BY,	131	OLD PENSIONER	V	15
THE OLD PRIEST PETER GILLIGAN	132	FR GILLIGAN		1
THE OLD PRIEST PETER GILLIGAN	133	FR GILLIGAN		23
THE OLD PRIEST PETER GILLIGAN	133	FR GILLIGAN		35
THE OLD PRIEST PETER GILLIGAN	133	FR GILLIGAN		39
MADE WHEN GOD SLEPT IN TIMES OF OLD.	135	TWO TREES		32
OF THE DIM WISDOMS OLD AND DEEP,	138	TO IRELAND	V	21
HAVE YOU NOT HEARD THAT OUR HEARTS ARE OLD,	141	EVERLAST VOICE		5
BUT, KINDLY OLD ROUT	142	MOODS	V	5
ALL THINGS UNCOMELY AND BROKEN, ALL THINGS WORN OUT AND OLD,	142	ROSE IN HEART		1
ALL THINGS UNCOMELY AND BROKEN, ALL THINGS WORN AND OLD,	142	ROSE IN HEART	V	1
TO OLD MEN PLAYING AT CARDS	144	HOST OF AIR		23
HE PLAYED WITH THE MERRY OLD MEN	145	HOST OF AIR		29
OLD MEN AND YOUNG MEN AND YOUNG GIRLS	145	HOST OF AIR		39
BUT THE OLD MEN AND DANCERS WERE GONE,	145	HOST OF AIR	V	39
OLD WOMEN WERE KEENING THE DEAD!	145	HOST OF AIR	V	40D
THOUGH I AM OLD WITH WANDERING	150	WANDER AENGUS		17
THE SONG OF THE OLD MOTHER	150	OLD MOTHER		T
WHILE I MUST WORK BECAUSE I AM OLD,	151	OLD MOTHER		9
AND I MUST WORK BECAUSE I AM OLD.	151	OLD MOTHER	V	10
AND DREAMED THAT THE OLD DESPAIR	152	LOSS OF LOVE		3
THE ROSES THAT OF OLD TIME WERE	156	FORGOT BEAUTY		9
AND WITH HEART MORE OLD THAN THE HORN	157	POET BELOVED		5
AND WITH THE HEART MORE OLD THAN THE HORN	157	POET BELOVED	V	5
OUT OF THE BATTLES OF OLD TIMES.	158	BELOVED RHYMES		6
OUT OF THE OLD DAYS	158	TO HIS HEART	V	T
REMEMBER THE WISDOM OUT OF THE OLD DAYS!	158	TO HIS HEART		2
FROM MARBLE CITIES LOUD WITH TABORS OF OLD	162	ASKS FORGIVE		9
AND OLD MEN WITH CROZIERS AND STOLES.	167	BLESSED		16
THE LOVER PLEADS WITH HIS FRIEND FOR OLD FRIENDS	172	PLEADS FRIEND		T
THE POET PLEADS WITH HIS FRIEND FOR OLD FRIENDS	172	PLEADS FRIEND	V	T
BUT THINK ABOUT OLD FRIENDS THE MOST!	173	PLEADS FRIEND		5
BUT THINK OF YOUR OLD FRIENDS THE MOST!	173	PLEADS FRIEND	V	5
THAT MY OLD CARE MAY CEASE!	174	ELEMENT POWERS		10
HE WILL SMILE ON THE THREE OLD SPIRITS,	178	FIDDLER DOONEY		11
THE OLD AGE OF QUEEN MAEVE	180	QUEEN MAEVE		T
THOUGH NOW IN HER OLD AGE, IN HER YOUNG AGE	180	QUEEN MAEVE		18
SHE HAD BEEN BEAUTIFUL IN THAT OLD WAY	180	QUEEN MAEVE		19
HAD COME AS IN THE OLD TIMES TO COUNSEL HER,	181	QUEEN MAEVE		42
MAEVE WALKED, YET WITH SLOW FOOTFALL, BEING OLD,	181	QUEEN MAEVE		43
HAD COME, AS IN OLD TIMES, TO COUNSEL HER,	181	QUEEN MAEVE	V	42
AS IN THE OLD DAYS WHEN THEY WOULD COME AND GO	183	QUEEN MAEVE		81
TILL IT DIED OUT WHERE AN OLD THORN-TREE STOOD.	186	QUEEN MAEVE		129
AND WHEN I'VE HEARD HOW THEY GREW OLD AND DIED,	186	QUEEN MAEVE		136
"SHE WILL GROW OLD AND DIE, AND SHE HAS WEPT!"	186	QUEEN MAEVE		138
TILL IT DIED OUT WHERE AN OLD THORN TREE STOOD.	186	QUEEN MAEVE	V	129
BECAUSE THEIR BODIES HAD GROWN OLD.	189	BAILE AILLINN		10
THEY FOUND AN OLD MAN RUNNING THERE!	190	BAILE AILLINN		25
AND OLD AND YOUNG MEN RODE WITH HER!	191	BAILE AILLINN		51
AN OLD MAN CAUGHT THE HORSE'S HEAD	191	BAILE AILLINN		57
NOW HAD THAT OLD GAUNT CRAFTY ONE,	193	BAILE AILLINN		100

	PAGE	TITLE		LINE
OLD (CONTINUED)				
IN OLD TIMES AMONG THE CLOUDS OF THE AIR.	194	BAILE AILLINN		133
THAT OLD MAN CLIMBED; THE DAY GREW DIM;	194	BAILE AILLINN		134
AND POETS FOUND, OLD WRITERS SAY,	197	BAILE AILLINN		187
THE UNAVAILING OUTCRIES AND THE OLD BITTERNESS	198	SEVEN WOODS		4
I COULD WEEP THAT THE OLD IS OUT OF SEASON.	199	ARROW		8
OLD MEMORY	201	OLD MEMORY		T
AWAKENS AN OLD MEMORY, AND SAY,	201	OLD MEMORY		2
LIKE AN OLD PAUPER, IN ALL KINDS OF WEATHER;	205	ADAMS CURSE		9
PRECEDENTS OUT OF BEAUTIFUL OLD BOOKS;	205	ADAMS CURSE		26
TO LOVE YOU IN THE OLD HIGH WAY OF LOVE;	206	ADAMS CURSE		36
TO LOVE YOU IN THE OLD HIGHWAY OF LOVE;	206	ADAMS CURSE	V	36
THE OLD BROWN THORN-TREES BREAK IN TWO HIGH OVER CUMMEN STRAND,	206	HANRAHANS SONG		1
THE OLD BROWN THORN TREES BREAK IN TWO HIGH OVER CUMANN'S STRAND,	206	HANRAHANS SONG	V	1
OUR COURAGE BREAKS LIKE AN OLD TREE IN A BLACK WIND AND DIES,	207	HANRAHANS SONG		3
THE OLD MEN ADMIRING THEMSELVES IN THE WATER	208	OLD MEN ADMIRE		T
I HEARD THE OLD, OLD MEN SAY,	208	OLD MEN ADMIRE		1
I HEARD THE OLD, OLD MEN SAY,	208	OLD MEN ADMIRE		1
WERE TWISTED LIKE THE OLD THORN-TREES	208	OLD MEN ADMIRE		5
I HEARD THE OLD, OLD MEN SAY,	208	OLD MEN ADMIRE		7
I HEARD THE OLD, OLD MEN SAY,	208	OLD MEN ADMIRE		7
WERE TWISTED LIKE THE OLD THORN TREES	208	OLD MEN ADMIRE	V	5
SEVEN OLD SISTERS WIND THE THREADS OF THE LONG-LIVED ONES,	209	UNDER THE MOON		7
OR LANDS THAT SEEMED TOO OLD TO BE BURDENS ON THE HEART,	209	UNDER THE MOON	V	5
SEVEN OLD SISTERS WIND THE THREADS OF THE LONG LIVED ONES,	209	UNDER THE MOON	V	7
EVEN IN AN OLD STORY, IS A BURDEN NOT TO BE BORNE.	210	UNDER THE MOON		20
LIKE AN OLD SONG.	211	O DO NOT LOVE		4
LIKE AN OLD SONG.	212	O DO NOT LOVE		12
O DEATH'S OLD BONY FINGER	213	HAPPY TOWNLAND	V	1
AN OLD MAN PLAYS THE BAGPIPES	214	HAPPY TOWNLAND		9
AND LIFT UP AN OLD HORN	215	HAPPY TOWNLAND		49
WHERE OLD AGE CANNOT FIND THEM; PAIRC-NA-LEE,	217	WOODS OF COOLE		7
AND MARTEN-CAT, AND BORDERS THAT OLD WOOD	218	WOODS OF COOLE		14
AND MARTIN CAT, AND BORDERS THAT OLD WOOD	218	WOODS OF COOLE	V	14
AS MEN IN THE OLD TIMES, BEFORE THE HARPS BEGAN,	219	WOODS OF COOLE		43
AS MEN IN THE OLD TIMES, BEFORE THE HARP BEGAN,	219	WOODS OF COOLE	V	43
WHAT DO YOU CALL IT?--THAT OLD PROMISE-BREAKER,	228	SHADOW WATER B		122
BECAUSE OF THAT OLD DRAUGHT UNDER THE DOOR,	228	SHADOW WATER B		127
AND FOR THIS END THEY GAVE ME MY OLD HARP	237	SHADOW WATER B		327
THEY GAVE ME THAT OLD HARP OF THE NINE SPELLS	237	SHADOW WATER B	V	327
AND THAT OLD HARP AWAKENS OF ITSELF	252	SHADOW WATER B		617
YET OLD ROMANCE BEING KIND, LET HIM PREVAIL	258	KING NO KING		5
BEFORE WE GROW OLD AND DIE.	261	DRINKING SONG		4
AND THEN, "I AM OLD ENOUGH";	268	BROWN PENNY		2
PARDON, OLD FATHERS, IF YOU STILL REMAIN	269	PARDON FATHERS		1
OLD DUBLIN MERCHANT "FREE OF TEN AND FOUR",	269	PARDON FATHERS		3
OLD COUNTRY SCHOLAR, ROBERT EMMET'S FRIEND,	269	PARDON FATHERS		5
OLD DUBLIN MERCHANT "FREE OF THE TEN AND FOUR"	269	PARDON FATHERS	V	3
OLD MERCHANT SKIPPER THAT LEAPED OVERBOARD	270	PARDON FATHERS		13
YOU MOST OF ALL, SILENT AND FIERCE OLD MAN,	270	PARDON FATHERS		15
OLD BUTLERS WHEN YOU TOOK TO HORSE AND STOOD	270	PARDON FATHERS	V	10
HERE'S AN OLD STORY I'VE REMADE,	270	GREY ROCK		3
HERE'S AN OLD STORY I'VE RE-MADE,	270	GREY ROCK	V	3
OLD WHOLESOME GOBAN HAD NO SAY;	271	GREY ROCK		10
ON OLD DEEP SILVER ROLLING THERE	271	GREY ROCK		20
OF OLD STRINGED INSTRUMENTS, HUNG THERE	271	GREY ROCK	V	20
OLD GOBAN HAMMERED THEM AND WROUGHT THEM,	271	GREY ROCK	V	23
WHERE BY OLD THORN-TREES THAT MAN STOOD;	274	GREY ROCK		80
WHERE BY OLD THORN TREES THAT MAN STOOD;	274	GREY ROCK	V	80
TO AN OLD EMPTY WOODMAN'S HOUSE THAT'S HIDDEN	282	TWO KINGS		134
FOUND THAT HOUSE, A SPUTTERING TORCH WITHIN,	283	TWO KINGS		140
HAD HALF AWAKENED SOME OLD MEMORY--	284	TWO KINGS		172
HAD HALF WAKENED SOME OLD MEMORY,	284	TWO KINGS	V	172
OF OUR OLD PAUDEEN IN HIS SHOP, I STUMBLED BLIND	291	PAUDEEN		2
FOR THEY ARE AT THEIR OLD TRICKS YET. A MAN	292	TO A SHADE		9
YOUR ENEMY, AN OLD FOUL MOUTH, HAD SET	292	TO A SHADE		17
AN OLD FOUL MOUTH THAT ONCE CRIED OUT ON YOU	292	TO A SHADE	V	17
AN OLD FOUL MOUTH THAT SLANDERED YOU HAD SET	292	TO A SHADE	V	17
MUTTERED THE OLD CRANE OF GORT.	295	THREE BEGGARS		6
AND THERE TO THREE OLD BEGGARS SAID,	295	THREE BEGGARS		10
WITH HIS OLD THOUGHTS, KING GUAIRE WENT	296	THREE BEGGARS		26
"THOUGH I AM OLD I SHALL PERSUADE	296	THREE BEGGARS		30
AND WHEN OLD GUAIRE CAME AND STOOD	297	THREE BEGGARS		54
THREE OLD HERMITS TOOK THE AIR	298	THREE HERMITS		1
NOW IT HAS FILLED AN OLD SOCK FULL;	301	RUN PARADISE		20
THE WIND IS OLD AND STILL AT PLAY	301	RUN PARADISE		22
A PAIR OF LAPWINGS, ONE OLD SHEEP,	302	HOUR DAWN		9
I HAD BEEN HURT," THE OLD BEGGAR THOUGHT	302	HOUR DAWN	V	19
AND STUFFED WITH ALL THAT'S OLD AND BAD;	303	HOUR DAWN		25
THAT'S STUFFED WITH ALL THAT'S OLD AND BAD;	303	HOUR DAWN	V	25
LIKE SOME OLD RABBIT TO MY CLEFT	307	HOUR DAWN		105
BUT I AM OLD AND YOU ARE YOUNG,	313	TWO YEAR LATER		11
AND EVEN OLD MEN'S EYES GREW DIM, THIS HAND ALONE,	314	FALLEN MAJESTY		2
OUT OF OLD MYTHOLOGIES	320	COAT		3
THEIR HEARTS HAVE NOT GROWN OLD;	323	SWANS AT COOLE		22
ALWAYS WE'D HAVE THE NEW FRIEND MEET THE OLD	324	ROBERT GREGORY		9
AND THEN I THINK OF OLD GEORGE POLLEXFEN,	325	ROBERT GREGORY		33
OUT OF SOME OLD PICTURE-BOOK;	325	ROBERT GREGORY		44

574

OLD (CONTINUED)

	PAGE	TITLE		LINE
OUT OF SOME OLD PICTURE BOOK:	325	ROBERT GREGORY	V	44
WERE LOVED BY HIM: THE OLD STORM-BROKEN TREES	326	ROBERT GREGORY		50
BUT I GROW OLD AMONG DREAMS,	329	MEN IMPROVE		16
AT THE OLD BITTER WORLD WHERE THEY MARRY IN CHURCHES,	330	BONE OF A HARE		13
UPON A GREY OLD BATTERED TOMBSTONE	331	ROUND TOWER		7
UPON THE GREY OLD BATTERED TOMBSTONE	331	ROUND TOWER	V	7
LIKE AN OLD HORSE IN A POUND."	333	SOLOMON SHEBA		8
THAN 'TWERE AN APPARITION. O HEART, WE ARE OLD:	334	LIVING BEAUTY		8
THAT THE HEART GROWS OLD?	334	SONG		6
THAT THE HEART GROWS OLD?	335	SONG		12
THAT THE HEART GROWS OLD?	335	SONG		18
WITH OLD EZEKIEL'S CHERUBIM	336	YOUNG BEAUTY		11
OLD, LEARNED, RESPECTABLE BALD HEADS	337	SCHOLARS		2
BEING OLD, BUT THAT THE OLD ALONE MIGHT DIE,	339	SHEP GOATHERD		4
BEING OLD, BUT THAT THE OLD ALONE MIGHT DIE,	339	SHEP GOATHERD		4
NEW WELCOME AND OLD WISDOM AT HER FIRE	340	SHEP GOATHERD		32
OLD GOATHERDS AND OLD GOATS, IF IN ALL ELSE	340	SHEP GOATHERD		46
OLD GOATHERDS AND OLD GOATS, IF IN ALL ELSE	340	SHEP GOATHERD		46
AT SOME OLD WINDING WHITETHORN ROOT	342	SHEP GOATHERD		101
WHEN I HAVE SHUT THESE EWES AND THIS OLD RAM	343	SHEP GOATHERD		113
ON THAT OLD QUEEN MEASURING A TOWN	344	DAWN		3
ON THE OLD QUEEN MEASURING A TOWN	344	DAWN	V	3
NOW I AM GROWING OLD,	346	ON WOMAN		28
AND CRIED, "BEFORE I AM OLD	348	FISHERMAN		37
THE OLD COOK ENRAGED,	349	HAWK		5
AND BE WELL PLEASED REMEMBERING IT, FOR IN THE OLD DAYS,	351	HER PRAISE		16
THOUGH SHE HAD YOUNG MEN'S PRAISE AND OLD MEN'S BLAME,	351	HER PRAISE		17
AMONG THE POOR BOTH OLD AND YOUNG GAVE HER PRAISE.	351	HER PRAISE		18
BUT MAYBE SOME OLD GAFFER MUTTERS A BLESSING	355	BROKEN DREAMS		4
A YOUNG MAN WHEN THE OLD MEN ARE DONE TALKING	356	BROKEN DREAMS		16
WILL SAY TO AN OLD MAN, "TELL ME OF THAT LADY	356	BROKEN DREAMS		17
FOR OLD SAKE'S SAKE.	357	BROKEN DREAMS		36
OR AN OLD MAN UPON A WINTER'S NIGHT.	359	WAR POEM		6
SINCE OLD WILLIAM POLLEXFEN	360	ALF POLLEXFEN		2
WITH THE OLD KINDNESS, THE OLD DISTINGUISHED GRACE,	362	HER COURTESY		1
WITH THE OLD KINDNESS, THE OLD DISTINGUISHED GRACE,	362	HER COURTESY		1
--PEDANT IN PASSION, LEARNED IN OLD COURTESIES,	363	DOLLS FACES		4
THAT MADE HER DIARMUID DEAR, AND SOME OLD CARDINAL	366	HER COURAGE		6
AND THAT MADE HER DERMUID DEAR, AND SOME OLD CARDINAL	366	HER COURAGE	V	6
UNDER YOUR OLD WIND-BEATEN TOWER, WHERE STILL	367	EGO DOMINUS		2
AND LOST THE OLD NONCHALANCE OF THE HAND:	368	EGO DOMINUS		13
AN OLD MAN COCKED HIS EAR UPON A BRIDGE:	372	PHASES OF MOON		1
WERE DISTANT STILL. AN OLD MAN COCKED HIS EAR.	372	PHASES OF MOON		7
WERE DISTANT. AN OLD MAN COCKED HIS EAR.	372	PHASES OF MOON	V	7
WHEN THE OLD MOON IS VANISHED FROM THE SKY	382	VISION ROBART		3
WHEN THE OLD MOON IS VANISHING FROM THE SKY	382	VISION ROBART	V	3
BY CHILDISH MEMORIES OF AN OLD CROSS POLLEXFEN,	391	UNDER SATURN		7
OF OLD LUKE WADDING'S PORTRAIT SAID	400	DEMON BEAST		10
AND THAT MERE GROWING OLD, THAT BRINGS	401	DEMON BEAST		38
FOR AN OLD BELLOWS FULL OF ANGRY WIND?	405	FOR DAUGHTER		64
WHILE ON THAT OLD GREY STONE I SAT	406	IN TIME OF WAR		2
UNDER THE OLD WIND-BROKEN TREE,	406	IN TIME OF WAR		3
WITH OLD MILL BOARDS AND SEA-GREEN SLATES,	406	CARVED STONE		2
THAT IS NO COUNTRY FOR OLD MEN. THE YOUNG	407	SAIL BYZANTIUM		1
CAUGHT BY AN OLD MAN'S JUGGLERIES	411	TOWER		60
GOOD FELLOWS SHUFFLED CARDS IN AN OLD BAWN:	411	TOWER		65
COME OLD, NECESSITOUS, HALF-MOUNTED MAN:	412	TOWER		90
DID ALL OLD MEN AND WOMEN, RICH AND POOR,	413	TOWER		97
AS I DO NOW AGAINST OLD AGE?	413	TOWER		100
OLD LECHER WITH A LOVE ON EVERY WIND,	413	TOWER		105
WITH DELICATE FEET UPON OLD TERRACES,	418	ANCEST HOUSES		26
OLD RAGGED ELMS, OLD THORNS INNUMERABLE,	419	MY HOUSE		5
OLD RAGGED ELMS, OLD THORNS INNUMERABLE,	419	MY HOUSE		5
FROM MY OLD FATHERS, I MUST NOURISH DREAMS	422	MY DESCENDANTS		2
FOR AN OLD NEIGHBOUR'S FRIENDSHIP CHOSE THE HOUSE	423	MY DESCENDANTS		21
TO BRIBE OR THREAT: HABITS THAT MADE OLD WRONG	428	NINETEEN 19		11
WHIRLS IN THE OLD INSTEAD:	430	NINETEEN 19		56
THEY FIXED OLD ACHING EYES,	432	NINETEEN 19		100
IF YOU, THAT HAVE GROWN OLD, WERE THE FIRST DEAD,	435	NEW FACES		1
IN THE OLD ROOMS: NIGHT CAN OUTBALANCE DAY,	435	NEW FACES		6
BECAUSE OF SOME GREEN WING, GATHERED OLD MUMMY WHEAT	442	BLACK CENTAUR		7
A KIND OLD NUN IN A WHITE HOOD REPLIES:	443	SCHOOL CHILDR		2
A SIXTY YEAR OLD SMILING PUBLIC MAN.	443	SCHOOL CHILDR	V	8
THERE IS A COMFORTABLE KIND OF OLD SCARECROW.	444	SCHOOL CHILDR		32
OLD CLOTHES UPON OLD STICKS TO SCARE A BIRD.	445	SCHOOL CHILDR		48
OLD CLOTHES UPON OLD STICKS TO SCARE A BIRD.	445	SCHOOL CHILDR		48
SHALL WITHER THAT OLD MARVEL, FOR	447	COLONUS PRAISE		15
A MAN YOUNG AND OLD FIRST LOVE	451	FIRST LOVE	V	T
TWO SONGS FROM THE OLD COUNTRYMAN	454	EMPTY CUP	V	T
THE OLD COUNTRYMAN	454	EMPTY CUP	V	T
MORE SONGS OF AN OLD COUNTRYMAN	454	HIS MEMORIES	V	T
FOR THAT OLD MADGE COMES DOWN THE LANE,	456	FRIENDS YOUTH		5
WE SAT UNDER AN OLD THORN-TREE,	456	SUMMER SPRING		1
THE SECRETS OF THE OLD	457	SECRETS OF OLD		T
I HAVE OLD WOMEN'S SECRETS NOW	457	SECRETS OF OLD		1
SOUNDS LIKE AN OLD SONG.	457	SECRETS OF OLD		6
AS THAT OLD WANDERING BEGGAR AND THESE GOD-HATED CHILDREN KNOW.	459	FROM OEDIPUS		6
THE THREE OLD RASCALS LAUGH ALOUD.	460	THREE MONUMENT		12
"BUT SUCH AS YOU AND I DO NOT SEEM OLD	463	HARUN RASHID		55

D (CONTINUED)

	PAGE	TITLE	LINE
YOUR THIRST FOR THOSE OLD CRABBED MYSTERIES,	465	HARUN RASHID	86
ON OLD DRY WRITING IN A LEARNED TONGUE,	466	HARUN RASHID	123
ON OLD DRY FAGGOTS THAT COULD NEVER PLEASE	466	HARUN RASHID	124
OLD FELLOW-STUDENT, WHOSE MOST PATIENT EAR	468	HARUN RASHID	167
OLD FELLOW STUDENT, WHOSE MOST PATIENT EAR	468	HARUN RASHID V	167
WHEN WITHERED OLD AND SKELETON-GAUNT,	475	EVA GORE-BOOTH	12
OF THAT OLD GEORGIAN MANSION, MIX	475	EVA GORE-BOOTH	16
THAT FLOWERING, SILKEN, OLD EMBROIDERY, TORN	477	SELF AND SOUL	13
A STORM-BEATEN OLD WATCH-TOWER,	484	SYMBOLS	1
A STORM-BEATEN OLD WATCH TOWER,	484	SYMBOLS V	1
BUT WE OLD MEN ARE MASSED AGAINST THE WORLD.	486	SEVEN SAGES	14
BUT WE OLD MEN ARE OUT AGAINST THE WORLD.	486	SEVEN SAGES V	14
OLD MARBLE HEADS, OLD PICTURES EVERYWHERE;	491	COOLE BALLYLEE	28
OLD MARBLE HEADS, OLD PICTURES EVERYWHERE;	491	COOLE BALLYLEE	28
THAT OLD PERPLEXITY AN EMPTY PURSE,	491	COOLE BALLYLEE V	40G
"I HEARD AN OLD RELIGIOUS MAN	492	ANNE GREGORY	13
THAT OLD PERPLEXITY AN EMPTY PURSE,	495	CHOICE	7
"OLD LOVERS YET MAY HAVE	496	MOHINI CHATTER	17
THE OLD TROOPS PARADE,	496	MOHINI CHATTER	22
OLD LOVERS YET SHALL HAVE	496	MOHINI CHATTER	17
QUARREL IN OLD AGE	503	QUARREL IN AGE	T
THAT HAD FORGIVEN OLD AGE.	504	QUARREL IN AGE	8
OLD SAGES WERE NOT DECEIVED!	504	QUARREL IN AGE	11
YET HE, AN OLD BOOK IN HIS FIST;	508	JANE BISHOP	12
NONE SO OLD AS HE AND I:	508	JANE BISHOP V	6
CRAZY JANE GROWN OLD LOOKS AT THE DANCERS	514	JANE GROWN OLD	T
SAW I AN OLD MAN YOUNG	515	GIRLS SONG B	11
OR YOUNG MAN OLD?	515	GIRLS SONG B	12
OR A YOUNG MAN OLD?	515	GIRLS SONG B V	12
OLD FATHERS, GREAT-GRANDFATHERS,	518	LOVES LONENESS	1
OLD FATHERS, GREAT GRANDFATHERS,	518	LOVES LONENESS V	1
YOU ASK WHAT MAKES ME SIGH, OLD FRIEND,	524	MAD AS MIST	13
SANG OLD TOM THE LUNATIC	528	TOM LUNATIC	1
OLD TOM AT CRUACHAN	529	TOM CRUACHAN V	T
OLD TOM AGAIN	530	OLD TOM AGAIN	T
A WOMAN YOUNG AND OLD I FATHER AND CHILD	531	FATHER CHILD V	T
TOO OLD FOR A MAN'S LOVE I STOOD IN RAGE	536	HER VISION	3
TOO OLD FOR A MAN'S LOVE I STOOD AND RAGED	536	HER VISION V	1
HIDDEN BY OLD AGE AWHILE	539	MEETING	1
"WHO'D CARE TO DIG 'EM," SAID THE OLD, OLD MAN,	548	TO SAME TUNE 3	7
"WHO'D CARE TO DIG 'EM," SAID THE OLD, OLD MAN,	548	TO SAME TUNE 3	7
TIME I WERE BURIED," SAID THE OLD, OLD MAN.	548	TO SAME TUNE 3	10
TIME I WERE BURIED," SAID THE OLD, OLD MAN.	548	TO SAME TUNE 3	10
O ANY OLD WORDS TO A TUNE.	548	TO SAME TUNE 3	16
"WHO'D CARE TO DIG 'EM," SAID THE OLD, OLD MAN,	548	TO SAME TUNE 3	17
"WHO'D CARE TO DIG 'EM," SAID THE OLD, OLD MAN,	548	TO SAME TUNE 3	17
TIME I WERE BURIED," SAID THE OLD, OLD MAN.	548	TO SAME TUNE 3	20
TIME I WERE BURIED," SAID THE OLD, OLD MAN.	548	TO SAME TUNE 3	20
"WHO'D CARE TO DIG 'EM," SAID THE OLD, OLD MAN,	549	TO SAME TUNE 3	27
"WHO'D CARE TO DIG 'EM," SAID THE OLD, OLD MAN,	549	TO SAME TUNE 3	27
TIME I WERE BURIED," SAID THE OLD, OLD MAN.	549	TO SAME TUNE 3	30
TIME I WERE BURIED," SAID THE OLD, OLD MAN.	549	TO SAME TUNE 3	30
I WOULD THAT I WERE AN OLD BEGGAR	552	SONGS REWRIT 2	1
O WOULD THAT I WERE AN OLD BEGGAR	552	SONGS REWRIT 2 V	1
A PRAYER FOR OLD AGE	553	PRAYER OLD AGE	T
OLD AGE	553	PRAYER OLD AGE V	T
FROM ALL THAT MAKES A WISE OLD MAN	553	PRAYER OLD AGE	5
THAT I MAY SEEM, THOUGH I DIE OLD,	553	PRAYER OLD AGE	11
MATTER FOR OLD AGE MEET;	553	CHURCH STATE	2
THE GYRES! THE GYRES! OLD ROCKY FACE, LOOK FORTH!	564	GYRES	1
OLD CIVILISATIONS PUT TO THE SWORD.	566	LAPIS LAZULI	27
WHEN SHE WAS OLD AND DYING,	571	THREE BUSHES	64
MIDNIGHT, AN OLD HOUSE	575	ACRE OF GRASS	5
GRANT ME AN OLD MAN'S FRENZY,	576	ACRE OF GRASS	13
AN OLD MAN'S EAGLE MIND.	576	ACRE OF GRASS	24
A SMALL OLD HOUSE, WIFE, DAUGHTER, SON,	577	WHAT THEN	12
"THE WORK IS DONE," GROWN OLD HE THOUGHT,	577	WHAT THEN	16
AND THEY BUT FAMOUS OLD UPHOLSTERIES	579	DOR WELLESLEY	3
AND THERE IS AN OLD BEGGAR WANDERING IN HIS PRIDE--	580	CURSE CROMWELL	5
AS THE FOX IN THE OLD FABLE DESTROYED THE SPARTAN BOY'S,	580	CURSE CROMWELL	18
BUT I WOKE IN AN OLD RUIN THAT THE WINDS HOWLED THROUGH!	581	CURSE CROMWELL	28
BUT THIS IS NOT THE OLD SEA	583	GHOST ROG CASE	5
NOR THIS THE OLD SEASHORE.	583	GHOST ROG CASE	6
THE WILD OLD WICKED MAN	587	OLD WICKED MAN	T
SAID THAT WILD OLD WICKED MAN	587	OLD WICKED MAN	3
FROM THE OLD MAN IN THE SKIES.	588	OLD WICKED MAN	8
WHEN AN OLD MAN'S BLOOD GROWS COLD?	588	OLD WICKED MAN	13
THEN SAID SHE TO THAT WILD OLD MAN,	588	OLD WICKED MAN	19
THAT OLD MAN IN THE SKIES.	588	OLD WICKED MAN	24
BUT A WILD OLD MAN IN THE LIGHT,	589	OLD WICKED MAN	38
FROM THE OLD MAN IN THE SKIES	589	OLD WICKED MAN	56
BUT A COARSE OLD MAN AM I,	590	OLD WICKED MAN	59
SHOULD DANCE ATTENTION UPON MY OLD AGE!	591	SPUR	2
SHOULD DANCE ATTENDANCE UPON MY OLD AGE!	591	SPUR V	2
AND THERE I FOUND AN OLD MAN, AND THOUGH I PRAYED ALL DAY	593	PILGRIM	8
AND THAT OLD MAN BESIDE ME, NOTHING WOULD HE SAY	593	PILGRIM	9
THE OLD STONE CROSS	598	STONE CROSS	T
UNDER THE OLD STONE CROSS.	598	STONE CROSS	8
UNDER THE OLD STONE CROSS.	599	STONE CROSS	16
UNDER THE OLD STONE CROSS.	599	STONE CROSS	24

		PAGE	TITLE		LINE
OLD	(CONTINUED)				
SAID THE OLD MAN IN THE GOLDEN BREASTPLATE • • • • •		599	STONE CROSS	V	23
AN OLD GHOST'S THOUGHTS ARE LIGHTNING, • • • • • •		600	SPIRIT MEDIUM		17
SPOILT WHAT OLD LOINS HAVE SENT? • • • • • •		604	YOU CONTENT		6
SET UP THE OLD STONE CROSS, • • • • • • • • •		604	YOU CONTENT		10
OLD WILLIAM POLLEXFEN, • • • • • • • • •		604	YOU CONTENT		14
BY AN OLD HUNTER TALKING WITH GODS! • • • • • •		605	YOU CONTENT		23
COULD CRAZY JANE PUT OFF OLD AGE • • • • • • •		606	SONGS BURDEN 1		19
COULD THAT OLD GOD RISE UP AGAIN • • • • • • •		606	SONGS BURDEN 1		21
HAVE KEYS TO MY OLD GATE. • • • • • • • •		607	SONGS BURDEN 2		8
OF HENWIVES AND OF QUEER OLD MEN • • • • • •		607	SONGS BURDEN 2		23
OF HEN WIVES AND OF QUEER OLD MEN • • • • •		607	SONGS BURDEN 2	V	23
THAT THE ADVENTURE OF OLD AGE BEGINS. • • • • •		609	IN TARAS HALLS		5
I SHALL BE OLD INDEED." THEREON THE MAN • • • •		609	IN TARAS HALLS		10
BUT TIME AMENDS OLD WRONG, • • • • • • • •		613	MARCH SONGS 1		9
ON AN OLD TAMBOURINE. • • • • • • • • • •		613	MARCH SONGS 1		16
BUT TIME AMENDS OLD WRONG, • • • • • • • •		613	MARCH SONGS 1		19
BUT TIME AMENDS OLD WRONG, • • • • • • • •		614	MARCH SONGS 1		29
MARCH WIND, AND ANY OLD TUNE, • • • • • • •		615	MARCH SONGS 2		25
ROBBERS HAD TAKEN HIS OLD TAMBOURINE. • • • •		616	MARCH SONGS 3		7
ROBBERS HAD TAKEN HIS OLD TAMBOURINE. • • • •		616	MARCH SONGS 3		10
ROBBERS HAD TAKEN HIS OLD TAMBOURINE. • • • •		616	MARCH SONGS 3		17
ROBBERS HAD TAKEN HIS OLD TAMBOURINE. • • • •		616	MARCH SONGS 3		20
ROBBERS HAD TAKEN HIS OLD TAMBOURINE. • • • •		616	MARCH SONGS 3		27
ROBBERS HAD TAKEN HIS OLD TAMBOURINE. • • • •		616	MARCH SONGS 3		30
NOW MY OLD BAWD IS DEAD? • • • • • • • • •		620	JOHN KINSELLA		12
LIKE AN OLD JEW MAN, • • • • • • • • •		620	JOHN KINSELLA		14
AND BEING OLD SHE PUT A SKIN • • • • • • •		621	JOHN KINSELLA		21
NOW MY OLD BAWD IS DEAD? • • • • • • •		621	JOHN KINSELLA		24
NO MAN GROWS OLD, NO GIRL GROWS COLD, • • • • •		621	JOHN KINSELLA		31
NOW MY OLD BAWD IS DEAD? • • • • • • • •		621	JOHN KINSELLA		36
THAT PATCHING OLD HEELS THEY MAY SHRIEK, I TAKE TO CHISEL AND PLANE.		623	HIGH TALK		8
WHEN A MAN GROWS OLD HIS JOY • • • • • • •		624	APPARITIONS		17
WHY SHOULD NOT OLD MEN BE MAD? • • • • • • •		625	OLD MEN BE MAD		T
WHY SHOULD NOT OLD MEN BE MAD? • • • • • • •		625	OLD MEN BE MAD		1
OBSERVANT OLD MEN KNOW IT WELL; • • • • • •		626	OLD MEN BE MAD		17
AND WHEN THEY KNOW WHAT OLD BOOKS TELL, • • • •		626	OLD MEN BE MAD		18
KNOW WHY AN OLD MAN SHOULD BE MAD. • • • • •		626	OLD MEN BE MAD		20
AND ITS OLD SOLE STRING • • • • • • • •		627	STATES HOLIDAY		23
WITH OLD PATCHED SHOES, • • • • • • • •		627	STATES HOLIDAY		30
WITH AN OLD FOUL TUNE. • • • • • • • • •		627	STATES HOLIDAY		38
WINTER AND SUMMER TILL OLD AGE BEGAN • • • • •		629	CIRCUS ANIMALS		5
WHAT CAN I BUT ENUMERATE OLD THEMES? • • • • •		629	CIRCUS ANIMALS		9
THAT MIGHT ADORN OLD SONGS OR COURTLY SHOWS; • • •		629	CIRCUS ANIMALS		14
OLD KETTLES, OLD BOTTLES, AND A BROKEN CAN, • • •		630	CIRCUS ANIMALS		36
OLD KETTLES, OLD BOTTLES, AND A BROKEN CAN, • • •		630	CIRCUS ANIMALS		36
OLD IRON, OLD BONES, OLD RAGS, THAT RAVING SLUT • •		630	CIRCUS ANIMALS		37
OLD IRON, OLD BONES, OLD RAGS, THAT RAVING SLUT • •		630	CIRCUS ANIMALS		37
OLD IRON, OLD BONES, OLD RAGS, THAT RAVING SLUT • •		630	CIRCUS ANIMALS		37
NOW THAT I AM OLD AND ILL, • • • • • • • •		632	MAN AND ECHO		7
SAY THAT THE MEN OF THE OLD BLACK TOWER, • • • •		635	BLACK TOWER		1
OLD BONES UPON THE MOUNTAIN SHAKE. • • • • •		635	BLACK TOWER		10
OLD BONES UPON THE MOUNTAIN SHAKE. • • • • •		636	BLACK TOWER		20
THE TOWER'S OLD COOK MUST CLIMB AND CLAMBER • • •		636	BLACK TOWER		21
OLD BONES UPON THE MOUNTAIN SHAKE. • • • • •		636	BLACK TOWER		30
AS A LEAF THAT IS OLD, AND WITHERED, AND COLD, • •		643	SONG FAERIES		3
AS A LEAF THAT IS OLD, AND WITHERED, AND COLD, • •		644	SONG FAERIES		15
'TIS MORN; LIKE OLD MEN'S EYES THE STARS ARE PALE, •		645	ISLE STAT I 1		4
SOME OLD MISER TELLS HIS STORE; • • • • • •		647	ISLE STAT I 1		58
SINGING OF ARMS AND BATTLES SOME OLD STAVE, • • •		650	ISLE STAT I 1		137
WILL STRUGGLE. OR HE'LL SEEK ENCHANTER OLD, • • •		651	ISLE STAT I 1		162
IS STONE! OLD SLEEPER! THIS SAME AFTERNOON • • •		657	ISLE STAT I 3		74
THAT OF OLD WERT MOVING EVER, • • • • • • •		658	ISLE STAT I 3		91
NAY, GRIEF IN FEEDING ON OLD GRIEF GROWS LESS. • •		659	ISLE STAT II 1		19
OLD MISER HOARDS OF GRIEF TO TELL AND TELL! • • •		661	ISLE STAT II 1		55
AND DEAD AS ARE THE LOVERS OF OLD RIME • • • •		674	ISLE STAT II 3		204
AND DEAD AS ARE THE LOVERS OF OLD RHYME • • • •		674	ISLE STAT II 3	V	204
AS A LEAF THAT IS OLD, AND WITHERED, AND COLD, • •		676	ISLE STAT II 3		250
AS A LEAF THAT IS OLD, AND WITHERED, AND COLD, • •		676	ISLE STAT II 3		262
OLD WARRIOR, WAKE! FOR SOFT AS A BEE SIPS, • • •		677	ISLE STAT II 3		284
LIE STREWN THE CLOTTED LEAVES—THE DEAD OLD LEAVES. •		684	SEEKER	V	69
THROUGH HIS SAD SOUL FOR EVER OLD AND YOUNG, • • •		687	TWO TITANS		25
IN CREVICED ROCKS, AND LAUGHED TO THE OLD SEA, • •		688	TWO TITANS		34
NOR HEEDS THE OLD, DIM PROTEST AND THE CRY • • •		689	NETTLESHIP		14
WHERE SAT OLD SUMMER FADING INTO SONG, • • • •		690	MOSADA 1	V	18
SHALL SEE A THING TO TALK ON WHEN YOU'RE OLD, • •		693	MOSADA 1		67
HER DREAMS ARE TALKING WITH OLD YEARS. AWAKE, • •		702	MOSADA 3		89
HALF ASLEEP THE OLD COW CROPS, • • • • • •		706	DAWN-SONG		20
THE SPIRIT OF YOUNG RENYI HAS GROWN OLD. • • • •		710	FERENCZ RENYI		17
IF THESE BE PRECIOUS." "I AM OLD AND WEAK," • • •		711	FERENCZ RENYI		55
FOR I AM OLD AND WEAK." AND AT HER SIDE • • • •		712	FERENCZ RENYI		59
A LITTLE WITHERED MAN, AND OLD. • • • • • •		716	FAIRY DOCTOR		4
THE LITTLE WITHERED MAN, AND OLD. • • • • • •		717	FAIRY DOCTOR		24
SCARCE THE OLD AND WIZEN HOUSES HAD THEIR DOORS AND WINDOWS SHUT.		718	PHANTOM SHIP		5
SCARCE THE OLD AND WIZENED HOUSES HAD THEIR DOORS AND WINDOWS SHUT.		718	PHANTOM SHIP	V	5
PRAYED BESIDE THE OCEAN, THE OLD MUMBLING MOTHER OF THE DEAD.		719	PHANTOM SHIP	V	34
WITHOUT THERE OF A LITTLE, LIGHT OLD MAN; • • • •		720	WITCH VIVIEN		13

		PAGE	TITLE		LINE
OLD (CONTINUED)					
WHERE DWELL THE MINDS OF OLD MEN HAVING PEACE,		721	WITCH VIVIEN		22
AND--NO! I'LL NONE OF THESE, OLD FATHER WRINKLES.		721	WITCH VIVIEN		23
I'LL PLAY YOU FOR YOUR OLD HOUR-GLASS. YOU SEE		721	WITCH VIVIEN		36
THAN OLD MEN'S ANY DAY, AS MERLIN FOUND.		721	WITCH VIVIEN		47
UPON MY SOUL, OLD TIME. NO! THUS IT STANDS.		721	WITCH VIVIEN		49
CHANCE, AND NOT SKILL, HAS FAVOURED YOU, OLD FATHER!		722	WITCH VIVIEN		60
IN OTHER LIVES? HAST THOU NOT QUAFFED OLD WINE		724	KANVA ON SELF		12
AND THE OLD MEN WERE WALKING, WALKING,		725	LEGEND		3
THE BOYS, THE WOMEN, AND OLD MEN,		725	LEGEND		7
THE WORLD GROWS OLD AND PLAYS THE FOOL."		725	LEGEND		12
AND SENT THE OLD MEN ON THEIR WAY,		725	LEGEND		23
AN OLD HORSE LOOKED ACROSS A FENCE.		725	LEGEND		27
AND OUR SLAVES BE AS OF OLD.		727	LOVERS QUARREL		56
FROM WHERE THE OLD IVY CRAWLS ROUND THE OLD STEEPLE,		728	PRIEST FAIRY		6
FROM WHERE THE OLD IVY CRAWLS ROUND THE OLD STEEPLE,		728	PRIEST FAIRY		6
YE ON THE BROAD HIGH MOUNTAINS OF OLD ERI,		737	MOURN THEN ON		1
AND HER OLD WIND THAT NO MIRTH EVER HAD,		738	YOU ARE SAD		7
"GO BRING ME MY OLD ARMOUR		740	EARL PAUL		19
THE LITTLE OLD GLOVE OF A CHILD!		744	GLOVE CLOAK		9
TAUGHT ME WISE MUSIC, AND GAVE ME THIS OLD HARP!		750	SHADOW WATER A		76
THE TIDE NARROWS BETWEEN, AND ONE OLD MAN		752	SHADOW WATER A		118
HAS BLOSSOMED, AND I GROW AS OLD AS TIME.		756	SHADOW WATER A		179
AND I AM OLD AS TIME, BECAUSE I KNOW		756	SHADOW WATER A	V	179
I GREW AS OLD AS TIME, AND SHE GROWS YOUNG		761	SHADOW WATER A		259
GROWS YOUNG AND A MAN'S HEART GROWS OLD IN A TWINKLING.		761	SHADOW WATER A		263
MY FOSTER-MOTHER SANG IN AN OLD RHYME		763	SHADOW WATER A		314
MY FOSTER MOTHER SANG IN AN OLD RHYME		763	SHADOW WATER A	V	314
AND ALL THE WISDOM THAT OLD IMAGES,		764	SHADOW WATER A		344
AND ONE IN THE OLD GRAY HOUSE		771	SPINNING SONG		4
LEAPS AND TIME'S OLD LANTHORN DIMS.		777	SONG DEIRDRE 2		5
BY AN OLD HEARTH, AND HE		780	WELL AND TREE		12
HAVE NOT OLD WRITERS SAID		781	MY HEART BEAT		6
THEN THAT OLD ABBEY ACTOR, DUDLEY DIGGES,		790	DEDICATION		7
OLDEN					
WEAVING OLDEN DANCES,		87	STOLEN CHILD		17
OLDER					
O WINDS, OLDER THAN CHANGING OF NIGHT AND DAY,		162	ASKS FORGIVE		7
THE OLDER IS CONDEMNED TO DEATH,		475	EVA GORE-BOOTH		7
DID AN OLDER MIND COMMEND--		494	AT ALGECIRAS		10
RIBH PREFERS AN OLDER THEOLOGY		556	RIBH PATRICK	V	T
I GAVE IT ALL TO AN OLDER MAN!		588	OLD WICKED MAN		23
OLDEST					
THE OLDEST HOUND WITH MOURNFUL DIN,		99	FOXHUNTER	V	45
BUT THE OLDEST OF ALL THE DOLLS,		319	DOLLS		4
O'LEARY					
IT'S WITH O'LEARY IN THE GRAVE.		289	SEPTEMBER 1913		8
IT'S WITH O'LEARY IN THE GRAVE.		289	SEPTEMBER 1913		16
IT'S WITH O'LEARY IN THE GRAVE.		290	SEPTEMBER 1913		24
THEY'RE WITH O'LEARY IN THE GRAVE.		290	SEPTEMBER 1913		32
"HUDDON AND DUDDON AND DANIEL O'LEARY,		529	TOM LUNATIC		7
HUDDON, DUDDON AND DANIEL O'LEARY		787	HUDDON DUDDON		1
HUDDON, DUDDON AND DANIEL O'LEARY		787	HUDDON DUDDON		6
HUDDON, DUDDON AND DANIEL O'LEARY		787	HUDDON DUDDON		11
O'LEARY'S					
BEAUTIFUL LOFTY THINGS! O'LEARY'S NOBLE HEAD!		577	LOFTY THINGS		1
OLIVE					
AN ANCIENT IMAGE MADE OF OLIVE WOOD--		428	NINETEEN 19		6
EVEN THE GREY-LEAVED OLIVE TREE		446	COLONUS PRAISE	V	12
GLITTERING AMONG GREY-LEAVED OLIVE TREES,		447	COLONUS PRAISE	V	21
CAME OLIVE FIRES OF MORNING AND ON THE DARKNESS FED,		719	PHANTOM SHIP		33
CAME THE OLIVE FIRE OF MORNING, AND ON THE DARKNESS FED,		719	PHANTOM SHIP	V	33
OLIVER					
A POT-HOUSE BENCH WITH OLIVER GOLDSMITH ONCE.		486	SEVEN SAGES		3
OLIVER GOLDSMITH SANG WHAT HE HAD SEEN,		487	SEVEN SAGES		17
OLIVE-TREE					
EVEN THE GREY-LEAVED OLIVE-TREE		446	COLONUS PRAISE		12
OLIVE-TREES					
GLITTERING AMONG GREY-LEAVED OLIVE-TREES,		447	COLONUS PRAISE		21
OLLAVE					
AND EVERY ANCIENT OLLAVE SAID,		82	MAD KING GOLL		9
OLYMPIANS					
ALL THE OLYMPIANS! A THING NEVER KNOWN AGAIN.		578	LOFTY THINGS		12
OLYMPUS					
NOR ON OLYMPUS LEAPED FROM CLOUD TO CLOUD,		260	FASC DIFFICULT		6
NOR ON AN OLYMPUS LEAPED FROM CLOUD TO CLOUD,		260	FASC DIFFICULT	V	6
OMEN					
AN OMEN! AN OMEN!		681	SEEKER		11
AN OMEN! AN OMEN!		681	SEEKER		11
ONCE					
AND ONCE A SUDDEN LAUGHTER SPRANG		16	OISIN 1		225
FROM ALL THEIR LIPS, AND ONCE THEY SANG		16	OISIN 1		226
AND ONCE A LADY BY MY SIDE		16	OISIN 1		231
AND ONCE A MAIDEN BY MY SIDE		16	OISIN 1	V	231
ONCE MORE THE DANCE'S LINKED FLOW,		22	OISIN 1	V	323A
WHEN ONCE BESIDE THE SHORE I STOOD,		24	OISIN 1	V	364
AND ONCE MORE SADDLED THE WHITE STEED,		25	OISIN 1	V	378
THE HUMAN SADNESS DAWNS ONCE MORE!"		25	OISIN 1	V	381
ONCE MORE--THE YOUTH AND LADY, DEER AND HOUND!		29	OISIN 2	V	2
ONCE MORE UNTO YOUR FLOWERS, FOR NONE MAY FIGHT,		34	OISIN 2	V	80

ONCE   (CONTINUED)

	PAGE	TITLE		LINE
MY SOUL, ONCE GLORY OF ITS ANCIENT LINE,	36	OISIN 2	V	95
SEA-GOD, THAT ONCE, TO GIVE HIS SLAVES CONTENT,	38	OISIN 2	V	129
EVADING, TURNING; ONCE DID I HEW AND HEW	40	OISIN 2	V	176
ONCE HELD BETWEEN MY ARMS, WITH LIVID CHOP	40	OISIN 2	V	178
AND WHEN THE SUN ONCE MORE IN SAFFRON STEPT,	41	OISIN 2		192
BUT WHEN THE SUN ONCE MORE IN SAFFRON STEPT,	41	OISIN 2	V	192
AND ONCE MORE TO A DAY-LONG BATTLE FELL,	43	OISIN 2		218
AND WE ONCE MORE UNTO OUR FIGHTING FELL.	43	OISIN 2	V	218
OR MOVED AS THEY MOVED ONCE,	53	OISIN 3		88
THAT ONCE MORE MOVED IN MY BOSOM THE ANCIENT SADNESS OF MAN,	54	OISIN 3		107
IF I WERE AS I ONCE WAS,	58	OISIN 3		157
SOUGHT ONCE AGAIN THE SHORE, AND FOUND A SHELL,	68	SAD SHEPHERD		18
SOUGHT ONCE AGAIN THE SHORE, AND CHOSE A SHELL	68	SAD SHEPHERD	V	18
"YOUR EYES THAT ONCE WERE NEVER WEARY OF MINE	79	EPHEMERA		1
BY THE LONE BORDER OF THE LAKE ONCE MORE,	79	EPHEMERA		5
STAND BY THE BORDER OF THE LAKE ONCE MORE,	79	EPHEMERA	V	5
FELL LIKE FAINT METEORS IN THE GLOOM, AND ONCE	80	EPHEMERA		14
ON THE LONE BORDER OF THE LAKE ONCE MORE!	80	EPHEMERA		17
HE SPAKE ONCE MORE AND FONDLED WITH HIS LIPS	81	EPHEMERA	V	24A
AS ONCE WITHIN A LITTLE TOWN	85	MAD KING GOLL	V	49
ONCE, WHILE WITHIN A LITTLE TOWN	85	MAD KING GOLL	V	49
TO SEE THE WORLD ONCE MORE.	97	FOXHUNTER		4
THAT I LOVED ONCE." AGAIN THE FIGHTING SPED,	110	CUCHULAIN SEA		64
YOUR EYES HAD ONCE, AND OF THEIR SHADOWS DEEP;	121	YOU ARE OLD		4
ONCE, WHILE HE NODDED ON A CHAIR,	132	FR GILLIGAN		5
WHEN THE MOTHS CAME ONCE MORE,	133	FR GILLIGAN		22
WHEN MOTHS CAME ONCE MORE,	133	FR GILLIGAN	V	22
AND ONCE, WHEN THE OWLS GREW STILL,	159	CAP AND BELLS	V	2
WE, TOO, HAD GOOD ATTENDANCE ONCE,	266	GALWAY RACES		5
AN OLD FOUL MOUTH THAT ONCE CRIED OUT ON YOU	292	TO A SHADE	V	17
ONCE, WHEN MIDNIGHT SMOTE THE AIR,	294	HATED PLAYBOY		1
HAVING LOVED GOD ONCE, BUT MAYBE	299	THREE HERMITS		26
BUT LET HIM KEEP HIS GRAVE FOR ONCE	303	HOUR DAWN		38
ALTHOUGH CROWDS GATHERED ONCE IF SHE BUT SHOWED HER FACE,	314	FALLEN MAJESTY		1
WHEREON A THING ONCE WALKED THAT SEEMED A BURNING CLOUD.	315	FALLEN MAJESTY		8
ONCE WALKED A THING THAT SEEMED, AS IT WERE, A BURNING CLOUD.	315	FALLEN MAJESTY	V	8
AND ALL THEIR EYES STILL FIXED, HOPING TO FIND ONCE MORE,	318	MAGI		6
WHO COMES AT NEED, ALTHOUGH NOT NOW AS ONCE	320	REED WHISPERER		2
AND MAKE THE DAYLIGHT SWEET ONCE MORE; BUT WHEN	339	SHEP GOATHERD		13
TO FIND WHAT ONCE I HAD	346	ON WOMAN		33
AND KNOW WHAT ONCE I HAVE KNOWN,	346	ON WOMAN		34
SING ME THE CHANGES OF THE MOON ONCE MORE!	373	PHASES OF MOON		29
FIXED UPON IMAGES THAT ONCE WERE THOUGHT;	375	PHASES OF MOON		80
THE FIRST THIN CRESCENT IS WHEELED ROUND ONCE MORE.	377	PHASES OF MOON		116
THE BURNING BOW THAT ONCE COULD SHOOT AN ARROW	377	PHASES OF MOON		119
ONCE HE LIVED A SCHOOLMASTER	381	SONG OF FOOL		5
ONCE MORE THE STORM IS HOWLING, AND HALF HID	403	FOR DAUGHTER		1
WHEN ALL IS RUIN ONCE AGAIN.	406	CARVED STONE		6
ONCE OUT OF NATURE I SHALL NEVER TAKE	408	SAIL BYZANTIUM		25
BEYOND THAT RIDGE LIVED MRS. FRENCH, AND ONCE	410	TOWER		25
OR ANYTHING CALLED CONSCIENCE ONCE;	413	TOWER		118
SUFFICE THE AGEING MAN AS ONCE THE GROWING BOY.	427	PHANTOM HATRED		40
HAD PRETTY PLUMAGE ONCE—ENOUGH OF THAT,	444	SCHOOL CHILDR		30
AND WHAT HAD DROWNED A LOVER ONCE	457	SECRETS OF OLD		5
TO ABD AL-RABBAN; FELLOW-ROYSTERER ONCE,	460	HARUN RASHID		2
TO ABD-AL-RABBAN; FELLOW ROYSTERER ONCE,	460	HARUN RASHID	V	2
AND ONCE AGAIN SHE ROSE AND SWEPT THE HOUSE	468	HARUN RASHID		159
A CHARTER TO COMMIT THE CRIME ONCE MORE.	478	SELF AND SOUL		32
WHAT MATTER IF I LIVE IT ALL ONCE MORE?	478	SELF AND SOUL		43
. . . THOUGHT'S CROWNED POWERS HE CALLED THEM ONCE.	480	BLOOD AND MOON		15
A POT-HOUSE BENCH WITH OLIVER GOLDSMITH ONCE.	486	SEVEN SAGES		3
BUT MINE SAW STELLA ONCE. WHENCE CAME OUR THOUGHT?	486	SEVEN SAGES		6
MINE SAW STELLA ONCE. WHENCE CAME OUR THOUGHT?	486	SEVEN SAGES		6
MINE SAW STELLA ONCE. WHEN CAME OUR THOUGHT?	486	SEVEN SAGES	V	6
SEEMED ONCE MORE DEAR THAN LIFE; ANCESTRAL TREES,	491	COOLE BALLYLEE		34
ETERNALISED THE BODY OF A MODERN SAINT THAT ONCE	503	VACILLATION		83
WHAT MATTER FOR THE SCENE, THE SCENE ONCE GONE;	542	PARN FUNERAL 1		19
THINKING TO MEET MY LOVE ONCE MORE	551	SONGS REWRIT 1	V	15
TRANSFIGURED TO PURE SUBSTANCE WHAT HAD ONCE	555	RIBH AT TOMB		11
AND ALL THE DROP-SCENES DROP AT ONCE	566	LAPIS LAZULI		22
AND ALL THE DROP SCENES DROP AT ONCE	566	LAPIS LAZULI	V	22
SAID LADY ONCE TO LOVER,	569	THREE BUSHES		1
A MAN I PRAISE THAT ONCE IN TARA'S HALLS	609	IN TARAS HALLS		1
NO DARK TOMB-HAUNTER ONCE; HER FORM ALL FULL	618	BRONZE HEAD		8
STUMBLING UPON THE BLOOD-DARK TRACK ONCE MORE,	622	HOUND VOICE		18
A GIRL THAT KNEW ALL DANTE ONCE	626	OLD MEN BE MAD		5
ONCE MORE HOW ON THAT MISERABLE DAY	658	ISLE STAT II 1		4
FOUGHT ONCE FOR SELF-SAME REASON ON THE HEM	660	ISLE STAT II 1		32
AND ONCE A-YEAR LET THE ARCADIANS COME,	663	ISLE STAT II 2		29
ONCE MORE THOSE SHEPHERDS COME. MAYHAP SOME MIRTH	664	ISLE STAT II 2		49
AND WHEN ONCE MORE THE LIGHTNING GENII PASSED,	687	TWO TITANS		29
WHEN FLASH ON FLASH ONCE MORE THE LIGHTNING CAME,	688	TWO TITANS		39
SHE WAS A GREAT ENCHANTRESS ONCE OF YORE,	693	MOSADA 1		78
AH! NOW I'M EASTERN-HEARTED ONCE AGAIN,	694	MOSADA 1		99
I HAD A SISTER LIKE HER ONCE, MY FRIEND.	696	MOSADA 2		11
I SAW HIS JOVIAL MOOD BRING ONCE A SMILE	696	MOSADA 2		14
A POISON DROP. A TOY, A FANCY ONCE,	700	MOSADA 3		24

579

```
                                                          PAGE    TITLE           LINE

ONCE   (CONTINUED)
    A POISON DROP.  THE TOY OF FANCY ONCE,  . . . . . . .  700 MOSADA 3        V  24
    ONCE IN THY NATION NONE SHALL KNOW THAT I  . . . . . .  702 MOSADA 3           82
    LOOK ON ME ONCE.  WHY SINK YOUR EYELIDS THUS? . . . .  703 MOSADA 3          107
    LOOK ON ME ONCE.  WHY SINK YOUR EYELIDS SO? . . . . .  703 MOSADA 3        V 107
    WHERE HOMES ONCE WHITENED VALE AND MOUNTAIN CREST: . .  709 FERENCZ RENYI       3
    A BIRD WALK ON THE DOORSTEP.  CHECK ONCE MORE. . . . .  722 WITCH VIVIEN       64
    THE FAIRIES' HERALD SPAKE ONCE MORE. . . . . . . . . .  730 PRIEST FAIRY       53
    COVER YOUR EARS! FOR ONCE WE HAD MOORED OUR GALLEY . .  756 SHADOW WATER A    187
    MOORE ONCE HAD VISITS FROM THE MUSE  . . . . . . . . .  792 GEORGE MOORE        1
ONE       SEE NO-ONE NINETEEN-THIRTY-ONE
    THEN DID YOU ANSWER, PEARL-PALE ONE, . . . . . . . . .    6 OISIN 1        V  53
    BEEN SPOKEN OF WITH ANY ONE. . . . . . . . . . . . . .    6 OISIN 1        V  56
    OF PRINCES THERE IS MANY A ONE." . . . . . . . . . . .    6 OISIN 1        V  61
    SHALL KNEEL AND PRAISE YOU, ONE BY ONE,  . . . . . . .    8 OISIN 1           78
    SHALL KNEEL AND PRAISE YOU, ONE BY ONE,  . . . . . . .    8 OISIN 1           78
    ALL PEARLY WHITE, SAVE ONE RED EAR!  . . . . . . . . .   12 OISIN 1          141
    OF ONE LONG FINGER ON MY LIP.  . . . . . . . . . . . .   12 OISIN 1          151
    BLEW ONE LONG NOTE.  FROM OVER REED  . . . . . . . . .   14 OISIN 1        V 195
    UNTIL ONE CAME, A TEARFUL BOY: . . . . . . . . . . . .   17 OISIN 1          237
    AND EACH ONE SAID, WITH A LONG, LONG SIGH, . . . . . .   17 OISIN 1          244
    ONE HAND UPHELD HIS BEARDLESS CHIN,  . . . . . . . . .   17 OISIN 1          250
    AND ONE A SCEPTRE FLASHING OUT . . . . . . . . . . . .   17 OISIN 1          251
    AND ONE CAME CLOSE, A TEARFUL BOY  . . . . . . . . . .   17 OISIN 1        V 237
    ONE HAND BENEATH HIS BEARDLESS CHIN, . . . . . . . . .   17 OISIN 1        V 251
    AND NIGH UNTO HIM EACH ONE DREW, . . . . . . . . . . .   18 OISIN 1        V 257
    WITH ONE LONG GLANCE FOR GIRL AND BOY  . . . . . . . .   19 OISIN 1          287
    WITH ONE LONG GLANCE ON MAID AND BOY . . . . . . . . .   19 OISIN 1        V 287
    EACH ONE WOVEN TO THE OTHER, . . . . . . . . . . . . .   22 OISIN 1          334
    EACH ONE WOVEN TO HIS BROTHER  . . . . . . . . . . . .   22 OISIN 1          335
    FOR LOVE THEY FOLLOWED ONE AND ALL!  . . . . . . . . .   23 OISIN 1        V 345G
    WHEN ONE DAY BY THE TIDE I STOOD,  . . . . . . . . . .   24 OISIN 1          364
    WHEN ONE DAY BY THE SHORE I STOOD, . . . . . . . . . .   24 OISIN 1        V 364
    I HEARD ONE SAY, "HIS EYES GROW DIM  . . . . . . . . .   25 OISIN 1          380
    I HEARD ONE SAY, "WITHIN HIS EYES  . . . . . . . . . .   25 OISIN 1        V 380
    AS THEY GAZE AT EACH OTHER, "OH, WHERE IS THAT GREAT ONE?"  28 OISIN 1      V 423H
    UPON DARK THRONES.  BETWEEN THE LIDS OF ONE  . . . . .   31 OISIN 2           37
    HUGE FORMS OF STONE! BETWEEN THE LIDS OF ONE . . . . .   31 OISIN 2        V  37
    TO ONE VAST FOOT, FROTH-SPLASHED, WITH CURVED TOES LYING   32 OISIN 2      V 46A
    AND ONE WHOM YOU WILL GO TO WITHOUT TELLING, . . . . .   33 OISIN 2        V  67
    AND TELL ME HOW YOU CAME TO ONE UNBID, . . . . . . . .   33 OISIN 2        V  67
    MY ANGRY KING-REMEMBERING SOUL ONE JOT.  . . . . . . .   36 OISIN 2           94
    NOR SHOOK MY FIRM AND SPACIOUS SOUL ONE JOT! . . . . .   36 OISIN 2        V  94
    MY ANGRY, KING REMEMBERING SOUL ONE JOT! . . . . . . .   36 OISIN 2        V  94
    "EACH ONE A HORSEHAIR SHIRT HATH ON, . . . . . . . . .   43 OISIN 2        V 208C
    DROPPING! A MURMUROUS DROPPING! OLD SILENCE AND THAT ONE   48 OISIN 3         18
       SOUND!
    . . . AND THE WHOLE OF THE WORLD WAS ONE. . . . . . .   48 OISIN 3           24
    IN ONE WAS A BRANCH SOFT-SHINING WITH BELLS MORE MANY THAN 50 OISIN 3         46
       SIGHS
    I CRIED, "O NIAMH!  O WHITE ONE! IF ONLY A TWELVE-HOURED  55 OISIN 3        113
       DAY,
    WHERE EVER IS MURMUROUS DROPPING, OLD SILENCE AND THAT   56 OISIN 3          138
       ONE SOUND!
    . . . CROZIERED ONE, CAUGHT IN YOUR NET! . . . . . . .   58 OISIN 3          167
    . . . CROZIERED ONE, CAUGHT IN THY NET-- . . . . . . .   58 OISIN 3        V 167
    . . . CROZIERED ONE, CAUGHT IN THEIR NET!  . . . . . .   58 OISIN 3        V 167
    THE REST THOU HAST HEARD OF, THOU CROSIERED ONE-- . . .   60 OISIN 3        V 189
    WITH MINGLING HAIR, AND PLAY UPON ONE LUTE.  . . . . .   71 ANASHU VIJAYA      10
    YON TALL ONE EYES MY SUPPER! CHASE HIM AWAY, . . . . .   72 ANASHU VIJAYA      34
    YON TALL ONE EYES MY SUPPER! SWIFTLY CHASE HIM . . . .   72 ANASHU VIJAYA   V  34
    AH, YOU WILL KNOW MY LOVED ONE BY HIS HUNTER'S ARROWS    75 ANASHU VIJAYA      80
       TRULY,
    ONE WITH THE TIDE THAT GLEAMS, THE WINGS THAT GLEAM AND  78 INDIAN TO LOVE     15
       DART,
    ONE WITH THE WAVES THAT SOFTLY ROUND US LAUGH AND DART.  78 INDIAN TO LOVE V   15
    ONE WITH THE GLIMMERING TIDE,  . . . . . . . . . . . .   78 INDIAN TO LOVE V   15
    LIKE SWARMING BEES, ONE WITH THE DOVE  . . . . . . . .   78 INDIAN TO LOVE V   16
    ONE WITH THE LEAVES! ONE WITH THE DOVE . . . . . . . .   78 INDIAN TO LOVE V   16
    ONE WITH THE LEAVES! ONE WITH THE DOVE . . . . . . . .   78 INDIAN TO LOVE V   16
    THE GREY WOLF KNOWS ME! BY ONE EAR . . . . . . . . . .   84 MAD KING GOLL      45
    THE WILD BOAR KNOWS ME, BY ONE EAR . . . . . . . . . .   84 MAD KING GOLL  V   45
    SHY ONE, SHY ONE, . . . . . . . . . . . . . . . . . .   89 ISLE IN WATER       1
    SHY ONE, SHY ONE, . . . . . . . . . . . . . . . . . .   89 ISLE IN WATER       1
    SHY ONE OF MY HEART, . . . . . . . . . . . . . . . . .   89 ISLE IN WATER       2
    BUT IF WHEN ANY ONE DIED,  . . . . . . . . . . . . . .   92 FATHER OHART   V   21
    ONE STAR SHONE FAINT AND GREEN,  . . . . . . . . . . .   95 MOLL MAGEE         30
    "AND OF MY SERVANTS SOME ONE GO, . . . . . . . . . . .   97 FOXHUNTER      V    5
    AND SOME ONE FROM THE STABLE BRING . . . . . . . . . .   97 FOXHUNTER      V    5
    AND SOME ONE FROM THE STABLES BRING  . . . . . . . . .   97 FOXHUNTER      V    5
    ONE BLIND HOUND ONLY LIES APART  . . . . . . . . . . .   99 FOXHUNTER          41
    "WITH HIM IS ONE SWEET-THROATED LIKE A BIRD." . . . . .  106 CUCHULAIN SEA      16
    "WITH HIM IS ONE SWEET THROATED LIKE A BIRD,  . . . . .  106 CUCHULAIN SEA  V   16
    WHOSE BLADE COMPELS, AND BID THEM SEND YOU ONE  . . . .  108 CUCHULAIN SEA      37
    AND HIS YOUNG DEAR ONE CLOSE BESIDE HIM KNELT, . . . .  108 CUCHULAIN SEA  V   40
    SEEK OUT WHAT MAN HE IS."  ONE WENT AND CAME. . . . . .  109 CUCHULAIN SEA      51
    AT THE SWORD POINT, AND BADE ME BRING HIM ONE  . . . .  109 CUCHULAIN SEA  V   53
    TROY PASSED AWAY IN ONE HIGH FUNERAL GLEAM, . . . . . .  111 ROSE OF WORLD       4
    WEARY AND KIND ONE LINGERED BY HIS SEAT! . . . . . . .  112 ROSE OF WORLD      13
    WEARY AND KIND ONE STOOD BESIDE HIS SEAT!  . . . . . .  112 ROSE OF WORLD  V   13
    I CALL, AS THEY GO BY ME ONE BY ONE, . . . . . . . . .  114 ROSE OF BATTLE      8
```

ONE   (CONTINUED)

	PAGE	TITLE		LINE
I CALL, AS THEY GO BY ME ONE BY ONE,	114	ROSE OF BATTLE		8
"TURN IF YE MAY," I CALL OUT TO EACH ONE,	114	ROSE OF BATTLE	V	7
BUT ONE MAN LOVED THE PILGRIM SOUL IN YOU,	121	YOU ARE OLD		7
I DREAMED THAT ONE HAD DIED IN A STRANGE PLACE	123	DREAM OF DEATH		1
ONE WITH HER ARE MIRTH AND DUTY;	124	CATHLEEN PARA	V	5
BUT ONE SMALL KNOT-GRASS GROWING BY THE POOL	127	DREAM OF FAERY		29
BUT ONE SMALL KNOT-GRASS GROWING BY THE RIM	127	DREAM OF FAERY		29
AND NO ONE ANY LEAF-CROWNED DANCER MISS	128	DREAM OF FAERY	V	46
WHEN NO ONE TURNED TO SEE	131	OLD PENSIONER	V	2
SENT ONE OF HIS GREAT ANGELS DOWN	134	FR GILLIGAN		43
NOR MAY I LESS BE COUNTED ONE	138	TO IRELAND		17
WHAT ONE IN THE ROUT	142	MOODS		5
UNTIL ONE BORE BRIDGET HIS BRIDE	145	HOST OF AIR		31
AND SOME ONE CALLED ME BY MY NAME;	149	WANDER AENGUS		12
SHE LOOKED IN MY HEART ONE DAY	152	LOSS OF LOVE		5
I HAVE BEEN CHANGED TO A HOUND WITH ONE RED EAR;	153	CHANGE BELOVED		2
TO HER RIGHT HAND CAME THE RED ONE,	160	CAP AND BELLS		31
AND ONE HAS SEEN IN THE REDNESS OF WINE	168	BLESSED		35
WHILE LIGHTS WERE PALING ONE BY ONE.	176	BELOVED DEAD		13
WHILE LIGHTS WERE PALING ONE BY ONE.	176	BELOVED DEAD		13
WHILE BIRDS GREW SILENT ONE BY ONE.	176	BELOVED DEAD		13
WHILE BIRDS GREW SILENT ONE BY ONE.	176	BELOVED DEAD	V	13
KNOWING ONE, OUT OF ALL THINGS, ALONE, THAT HIS HEAD	177	PAST GREATNESS		8
AS THOUGH ONE LISTENED THERE, AND HIS VOICE SANK	180	QUEEN MAEVE		7
ONE THAT THE GENERATIONS HAD LONG WAITED	182	QUEEN MAEVE		66
OF ONE WHO IS NO FRIEND TO ME OR TO MINE,	184	QUEEN MAEVE	V	94A
WITH BODIES MADE OUT OF SOFT FIRE. THE ONE,	187	QUEEN MAEVE		144
"O LADY, WED WITH ONE OF US";	191	BAILE AILLINN		61
NOW HAD THAT OLD GAUNT CRAFTY ONE,	193	BAILE AILLINN		100
OR MICE IN THE ONE WHEATEN SHEAF	195	BAILE AILLINN		147
OR BIRDS LOST IN THE ONE CLEAR SPACE	195	BAILE AILLINN		149
OR, IT MAY BE, THE EYELIDS OF ONE EYE,	195	BAILE AILLINN		151
OR THE DOOR-PILLARS OF ONE HOUSE,	195	BAILE AILLINN		152
THAT HAVE ONE SHADOW ON THE GROUND;	195	BAILE AILLINN		154
OR THE TWO STRINGS THAT MADE ONE SOUND	195	BAILE AILLINN		155
OR BIRDS LOST IN ONE CLEAR SPACE	195	BAILE AILLINN	V	149
OR THE DOOR PILLARS OF ONE HOUSE,	195	BAILE AILLINN	V	152
ONE THAT IS EVER KIND SAID YESTERDAY;	199	FOLLY COMFORT		1
WE SAT TOGETHER AT ONE SUMMER'S END,	204	ADAMS CURSE		1
THERE'S MANY A ONE SHALL FIND OUT ALL HEARTACHE	205	ADAMS CURSE		16
"THERE IS ONE THING THAT ALL WE WOMEN KNOW	205	ADAMS CURSE	V	18
I HAD A THOUGHT FOR NO ONE BUT YOUR EARS;	206	ADAMS CURSE	V	34
AND ONE BY ONE WE DROP AWAY."	208	OLD MEN ADMIRE		3
AND ONE BY ONE WE DROP AWAY."	208	OLD MEN ADMIRE		3
WHERE ONE FOUND LANCELOT CRAZED AND HID HIM FOR A WHILE;	209	UNDER THE MOON		3
AND WOOD-OF-WONDERS, WHERE ONE KILLS AN OX AT DAWN,	209	UNDER THE MOON		9
WHERE ONE FOUND LANCELOT CRAZED, AND HID HIM FOR AWHILE,	209	UNDER THE MOON	V	3
NO ONE HAS EVER LOVED BUT YOU AND I,	211	RAGGED WOOD		12
WE WERE SO MUCH AT ONE.	212	O DO NOT LOVE		8
ONE GATHERS UP HIS PURPLE GOWN;	212	BLESS PSALTER		9
ONE LEANS AND MUTTERS BY THE WALL--	212	BLESS PSALTER		10
O KINSMEN OF THE THREE IN ONE,	213	BLESS PSALTER		14
AND WHEN ONE CHANGED HER TO A SILVER FLY,	220	HARP OF AENGUS	V	10
THAT HAD BUT THE ONE EYE. CAN NO BEWITCHMENT	222	SHADOW WATER B		10
FOR THAT RED MOLL THAT HAD BUT THE ONE EYE.	222	SHADOW WATER B	V	10
IF WE WERE OF ONE MIND I'D DO IT. WERE'T NOT	222	SHADOW WATER B	V	15
I SAW THEM, TOO, ONE NIGHT. FORGAEL WAS PLAYING,	223	SHADOW WATER B		36
MY MOTHER TOLD ME THAT THERE IS NOT ONE	224	SHADOW WATER B		45
AND KEEP TO THE ONE WEARY MARRIAGE-BED.	224	SHADOW WATER B		55
AND KEEP TO THE ONE WEARY MARRIAGE BED.	224	SHADOW WATER B	V	55
WHEN IT IS OVER, NOR ONE TO GRUMBLE AT US.	225	SHADOW WATER B		67
BE OF YOUR TROOP! AIBRIC BE ONE OF YOU	225	SHADOW WATER B		75
ONE OF THE EVER-LIVING, AS I THINK--	231	SHADOW WATER B		210
ONE OF THE LAUGHING PEOPLE--AND SHE AND I	231	SHADOW WATER B		211
BECOME ONE MOVEMENT, ENERGY, DELIGHT,	231	SHADOW WATER B		217
AND WHERE THERE IS ONE WOMAN THERE'LL BE OTHERS.	232	SHADOW WATER B		227
ONE--AND ONE--A COUPLE--FIVE TOGETHER!	233	SHADOW WATER B		249
ONE--AND ONE--A COUPLE--FIVE TOGETHER;	233	SHADOW WATER B		249
NOW I CAN HEAR. THERE'S ONE OF THEM THAT SAYS,	233	SHADOW WATER B		252
AND THEN ONE ASKS ANOTHER HOW HE DIED,	234	SHADOW WATER B		256
THEY WOULD NOT SEND ME ONE THAT CASTS A SHADOW.	235	SHADOW WATER B		285
IS SHAKEN IN THESE SEAS, AND WHAT ONE DOES	237	SHADOW WATER B		339
ONE MOMENT HAS NO MIGHT UPON THE MOMENT	237	SHADOW WATER B		340
THERE IS NOT ONE AMONG YOU THAT MADE LOVE	244	SHADOW WATER B		454
WANDER A MOMENT WHEN ONE IS IN LOVE?	246	SHADOW WATER B		515
YOU'LL HEAR THEM CALLING OUT TO ONE ANOTHER	247	SHADOW WATER B		521
HAD RUN INTO ONE FOUNTAIN. SPEAK TO HIM.	249	SHADOW WATER B		561
IN HAVING ONE ANOTHER? HOW COULD I REST	249	SHADOW WATER B		571
THOUGH LEAVES ARE MANY, THE ROOT IS ONE;	261	COMING WISDOM		1
WHERE PASSION AND PRECISION HAVE BEEN ONE	264	HOUSE SHAKEN		2
AND ALL THINGS AT ONE COMMON LEVEL LIE.	265	THESE CLOUDS		6
DELIGHT MAKES ALL OF THE ONE MIND,	266	GALWAY RACES		2
ONE TIME IT WAS A WOMAN'S FACE, OR WORSE--	267	ALL TEMPT ME		2
THAT ONE BELIEVED HE HAD A SWORD UPSTAIRS;	267	ALL TEMPT ME		8
ONE CANNOT BEGIN IT TOO SOON.	268	BROWN PENNY		16
FOR ONE THAT WAS LIKE WOMAN MADE	272	GREY ROCK		29
SO MOURNFUL THAT IT SEEMED THE CRY OF ONE	278	TWO KINGS		39
FOR I WOULD HAVE YOUR JUDGMENT UPON ONE	280	TWO KINGS		71
ALWAYS IN HIS ONE SEAT, AND BID ME CARE HIM	280	TWO KINGS		80

E   (CONTINUED)

	PAGE	TITLE	LINE
THE ONE DISASTROUS ZODIAC, MUTTERING	282	TWO KINGS	128
BEING HONOUR BRED, WITH ONE	291	TO A FRIEND	5
ONE OF YOU THREE IS A RICH MAN,	295	THREE BEGGARS	21
"AND IF I WIN," ONE BEGGAR SAID,	296	THREE BEGGARS	29
ONE TO ANOTHER SIGHED AND CRIED:	296	THREE BEGGARS	38
ONE BEGGAR CRIED: "YOU'RE SHAMMING SLEEP,"	297	THREE BEGGARS V	45
AS THE ONE STURDY LEG COULD DO	302	HOUR DAWN	5
A PAIR OF LAPWINGS, ONE OLD SHEEP,	302	HOUR DAWN	9
WHAT ONE OF MAEVE'S NINE BRAWLING SONS	303	HOUR DAWN	36
HAS ONE OF MAEVE'S NINE BRAWLING SONS	303	HOUR DAWN V	36
AND WHEN AT ONE YEAR'S END I FOUND	305	HOUR DAWN	71
LIES ONE LONG SOUGHT	310	WITCH	7
HAS NO ONE SAID THOSE DARING	312	TWO YEAR LATER	1
ONE BECAUSE NO THOUGHT,	315	FRIENDS	4
AND ONE BECAUSE HER HAND	315	FRIENDS	10
ONE THAT NO PASSING THOUGHT,	315	FRIENDS V	4
HOW COULD I PRAISE THAT ONE?	316	FRIENDS	20
HOW SHOULD I PRAISE THAT ONE?	316	FRIENDS V	20
AS THOUGH HE HAD BUT THAT ONE TRADE ALONE.	327	ROBERT GREGORY	80
THE ENTIRE COMBUSTIBLE WORLD IN ONE SMALL ROOM	327	ROBERT GREGORY	82
ALL THE COMBUSTIBLE WORLD IN ONE SMALL ROOM	327	ROBERT GREGORY V	82
WE HAVE TALKED IN THE ONE PLACE,	332	SOLOMON SHEBA	4
IN THE ONE NARROW THEME OF LOVE	333	SOLOMON SHEBA V	7
SHUDDER THAT MADE THEM ONE.	346	ON WOMAN	23
AND ALL BECAUSE OF SOME ONE	346	ON WOMAN	40
I SHALL HAVE WRITTEN HIM ONE	348	FISHERMAN	38
ONE HAD A LOVELY FACE,	350	MEMORY	1
COURTESY AND PASSION INTO ONE LIKE THOSE	352	PEOPLE	17
I MIGHT HAVE USED THE ONE SUBSTANTIAL RIGHT	352	PEOPLE	19
ONE'S HAD HER FILL OF LOVERS, ANOTHER'S HAD BUT ONE,	354	HIS PHOENIX	19
YOU ARE MORE BEAUTIFUL THAN ANY ONE,	356	BROKEN DREAMS	27
YOU WERE MORE BEAUTIFUL THAN ANY ONE,	356	BROKEN DREAMS V	27
ALL DAY IN THE ONE CHAIR	357	BROKEN DREAMS	38
ONE IS A HARLOT, AND ONE A CHILD	358	PRESENCES	12
ONE IS A HARLOT, AND ONE A CHILD	358	PRESENCES	12
AND ONE, IT MAY BE, A QUEEN.	358	PRESENCES	14
MOPING FOR ONE VOYAGE MORE.	361	ALF POLLEXFEN	22
SHOWS HER THAT SOME ONE SOON	364	END OF DAY	5
NO ONE DENIES TO KEATS LOVE OF THE WORLD:	370	EGO DOMINUS	52
I CALL TO THE MYSTERIOUS ONE WHO YET	371	EGO DOMINUS	70
CRYING TO ONE ANOTHER LIKE THE BATS:	376	PHASES OF MOON	106
ONE LASHED HER TAIL: HER EYES LIT BY THE MOON	383	VISION ROBART	29
CHANCE BEING AT ONE WITH CHOICE AT LAST,	388	SOLOMON WITCH	14
WHEN OIL AND WICK ARE BURNED IN ONE:	388	SOLOMON WITCH	30
HEARTS WITH ONE PURPOSE ALONE	393	EASTER 1916	41
BUT GREGORY'S WOOD AND ONE BARE HILL	403	FOR DAUGHTER	4
BUT GREGORY'S WOODS AND ONE BARE HILL	403	FOR DAUGHTER V	4
ROOTED IN ONE DEAR PERPETUAL PLACE.	405	FOR DAUGHTER	48
FOR ONE THROB OF THE ARTERY,	406	IN TIME OF WAR	1
I KNEW THAT ONE IS ANIMATE,	406	IN TIME OF WAR	4
IN ONE ANOTHER'S ARMS, BIRDS IN THE TREES	407	SAIL BYZANTIUM	2
AND ONE WAS DROWNED IN THE GREAT BOG OF CLOONE.	411	TOWER	48
ONE INEXTRICABLE BEAM,	411	TOWER	55
THAT ALL BUT THE ONE CARD BECAME	411	TOWER	68
ONE HEARS THE RUMBLE OF IT FAR BELOW	420	MY HOUSE V	20B
HAS BUT ONE COMFORT LEFT: ALL TRIUMPH WOULD	429	NINETEEN 19	39
INTO THE YOLK AND WHITE OF THE ONE SHELL.	443	SCHOOL CHILDR	16
I LOOK UPON ONE CHILD OR T'OTHER THERE	443	SCHOOL CHILDR	18
AND NEEDS NO CRUELTY. I HAVE HEARD ONE SAY	448	HERO GIRL FOOL	13
"AND ALL THOSE LIES HAVE BUT ONE END, POOR WRETCHES TO BETRAY:	450	OWEN AHERNE	18
AND FELL THE ONE IN T'OTHER'S ARMS	457	SUMMER SPRING	7
AND SUCH A PAIR BUT ONE,	458	SECRETS OF OLD	16
ONE AMONG THE BIRDS OF THE AIR,	460	THREE MONUMENT	3
ONE HAND AMID THE GOLDFISH IN THE POOL:	463	HARUN RASHID	44
TWO CONTEMPLATING PASSIONS CHOSE ONE THEME	466	HARUN RASHID	117
AND I ALONE, ONE IN TEN THOUSAND YEARS,	470	HARUN RASHID V	190
ONE DEAR HOPE HAD HE.	471	ALL SOUL NIGHT	28
WHEN UPWARD TURNED, ON ONE SOLE IMAGE FELL:	471	ALL SOUL NIGHT	34
WHEN UPWARD TURNED ON ONE SOUL IMAGE FELL,	471	ALL SOUL NIGHT V	34
BEAUTIFUL, ONE A GAZELLE.	475	EVA GORE-BOOTH	4
ONE OR THE OTHER OUT AND SPEAK	475	EVA GORE-BOOTH	15
BEAUTIFUL, ONE A GAZELLE.	475	EVA GORE-BOOTH	20
THERE ONE THAT RUFFLED IN A MANLY POSE	489	COOLE PARK 29	11
ONE DEAR BRILLIANT WOMAN:	504	RESULT THOUGHT	2
ERE THE ONE OR T'OTHER DIE,	508	JANE BISHOP V	5
ONE MAN, ONE MAN ALONE	526	AM OF IRELAND	6
ONE MAN, ONE MAN ALONE	526	AM OF IRELAND	6
ONE SOLITARY MAN	526	AM OF IRELAND	8
ONE MAN, AND ONE MAN ALONE	526	AM OF IRELAND V	6
ONE MAN, AND ONE MAN ALONE	526	AM OF IRELAND V	6
ONE THAT IS PERFECT OR AT PEACE,	528	DANCER CRUACH	3
THE REST I PASS, ONE SENTENCE I UNSAY.	542	PARN FUNERAL 2	1
I PASS THE REST--ONE SENTENCE I UNSAY--	542	PARN FUNERAL 2 V	1
THERE ALL THE GYRES CONVERGE IN ONE,	557	THERE	3
AND ALL IT KNOWS IS THAT ONE WORD "REJOICE!"	564	GYRES	16
ONE ASKS FOR MOURNFUL MELODIES:	567	LAPIS LAZULI	53
INTO ONE NAME!	572	LADYS 1ST SONG	6
NO BOOKS UPON THE KNEE, AND NO ONE THERE	579	DOR WELLESLEY	9
BUT COPY SOME ONE ACTION,	600	SPIRIT MEDIUM	13

		PAGE	TITLE		LINE
ONE	(CONTINUED)				
	THREE SONGS TO THE ONE BURDEN • • • • • • • • •	605	SONGS BURDEN 1		T
	ONE IMAGE CROSSED THE MANY-HEADED, SAT • • • • •	610	STATUES		17
	THAT ALL'S ARRANGED IN ONE CLEAR VIEW, • • • • • •	633	MAN AND ECHO		31
	ONE ANOTHER IN THIS PLACE? • • • • • • • • •	633	MAN AND ECHO		40
	JOY AND LOVE ARE ONE EXISTENCE. • • • • • • • •	647	ISLE STAT I 1		71
	LOVE AND SORROW, ONE EXISTENCE, • • • • • • • •	647	ISLE STAT I 1		73
	I HEAR THE WHOLE SKY'S SORROW IN ONE VOICE. • • •	652	ISLE STAT I 2		22
	AND NOD TO ONE ANOTHER, LIES A GREEN, • • • • •	653	ISLE STAT I 2		35
	I'LL SEND MINE ARROW, NOW MY ONE RESOURCE: • • • •	657	ISLE STAT I 3		64
	TWO MEN WHO LOVE ONE MAID HAVE AMPLE CAUSE • • • •	659	ISLE STAT II 1		30
	EACH CAME ONE MORN, WITH WELCOMING OF SONG, • • •	660	ISLE STAT II 1		42
	FOR THIS THING FIGHT--WE LOVE ONE MAID? HER NAME? •	661	ISLE STAT II 1		66
	EACH ONE AT GAZE FOR AYE UPON HIS WHIRLING THRONE. •	662	ISLE STAT II 1		81
	ONE HAND BROW-SHADING, FAR ACROSS THE NIGHT, • • •	663	ISLE STAT II 2		27
	AND ONE ARM POINTING THUS, IN MARBLE WHITE. • • •	663	ISLE STAT II 2		28
	AND LET THE TALE BE MOURNFUL EACH ONE TELLS. • • •	663	ISLE STAT II 2		36
	I'LL HAVE. OH, ABSENT ONE 'TIS NOT FOR DEARTH • •	664	ISLE STAT II 2		50
	WHO SEEK MAY FIND, SAVE ONLY ONE, • • • • • • •	668	ISLE STAT II 3		48
	THAT ONE SHALL DIE, UNLESS ONE DIE FOR HER. • • •	669	ISLE STAT II 3		74
	THAT ONE SHALL DIE, UNLESS ONE DIE FOR HER. • • •	669	ISLE STAT II 3		74
	AND ONE ALONE OF ALL WOULD HARK. • • • • • • •	671	ISLE STAT II 3		123
	A SCARLET BLOOM. WHY RAISEST THOU, PALE ONE, • • •	673	ISLE STAT II 3		196
	IF ONE SHOULD RISE BESIDE THEE, • • • • • • •	680	LOVE AND DEATH		27
	THY GARMENTS' HEM, THOU VISIONARY ONE! • • • • •	684	SEEKER		71
	MINE HEART-STRINGS ARE ALL BROKEN SAVING ONE, • • •	684	SEEKER	V	69B
	THY GARMENT'S HEM, THOU VISIONARY ONE! • • • • •	684	SEEKER	V	71
	TO ONE ANOTHER WITH A COILING CHAIN: • • • • • •	687	TWO TITANS		6
	MAKING ALL ONE O'ER ROCK AND SEA AND SKIES: • • •	687	TWO TITANS		28
	THEN HAS THIS ONE BEEN SINNED FULL MANY TIMES. • •	692	MOSADA 1		49
	I AM: ONE SHOULDER TURNED AWRY--WHY THEN • • • •	692	MOSADA 1		61
	ONE SHOULDER TWISTED, AND THE CHILDREN CRY • • • •	695	MOSADA 1		116
	WILL HE NOT SPARE HER LIFE? HOW WOULD ONE MATTER • •	696	MOSADA 2		3
	SO SMALL MAKES ONE GROW WEAK AND TOTTERING! • • •	700	MOSADA 3		35
	THE BURGHERS OF THE NIGHT FADE ONE BY ONE. • • • •	700	MOSADA 3		40
	THE BURGHERS OF THE NIGHT FADE ONE BY ONE. • • • •	700	MOSADA 3		40
	BE ONE? I THINK ALL'S FINISHED NOW AND SEALED. • •	701	MOSADA 3		62
	'TIS LATE, WAIT ONE MORE DAY: BELOW THE HILLS • •	702	MOSADA 3		91
	UNHAPPY ONE. GO NOT, GO NOT, GO NOT: • • • • •	703	MOSADA 3		102
	LOVE, WILL YOU DIE WHEN WE HAVE MET? ONE LOOK • •	703	MOSADA 3		109
	BEFORE HIM ONE WELL GUARDED, WITH BOUND HANDS: • •	709	FERENCZ RENYI		10
	UNTUNED BY THEIR OWN STRIVING. IF ONE SUCH • • •	711	FERENCZ RENYI		37
	BUT THIS ONE--THIS ONE. NOW HIS HEAD DROPS LOW, • •	711	FERENCZ RENYI		39
	BUT THIS ONE--THIS ONE. NOW HIS HEAD DROPS LOW, • •	711	FERENCZ RENYI		39
	TWO WOMEN, WITHERED ONE AND SMALL AND THIN, • • •	711	FERENCZ RENYI		51
	I'M WEAK, AND BY THE HANDS SHALL HOLD EACH ONE • •	712	FERENCZ RENYI		57
	I'M WEAK, AND BY THE HAND SHALL HOLD EACH ONE • •	712	FERENCZ RENYI	V	57
	THE YOUNG ONE WITH THE OTHERS." RENYI'S PALE • •	713	FERENCZ RENYI		84
	AND SOFT, ONE GLIMMERING STAR. RENYI HAS CAST • •	714	FERENCZ RENYI		115
	AND SOFT, ONE GLIMMERING STAR--WITH POWER VAST: • •	714	FERENCZ RENYI	V	115
	A KID, HELD BY ONE SOFT WHITE EAR FOR TETHER, • •	715	DWELT SYCAMORE		3
	AND DEATH, OH MY FAIR ONE, WILL NEVER COME NEAR • •	717	LOVE SONG		8
	THEN EACH WIFE AND MAID AND MOTHER CALLS BY NAME	719	PHANTOM SHIP		24
	SOME DROWNED ONE.				
	WHAT ROSEATE FINGERS! NO: NOR IS THERE ONE • • •	720	WITCH VIVIEN		5
	SOME GREAT ONE. NO: I HEAR THE WAVERING STEPS • •	720	WITCH VIVIEN		12
	I DREAMT SOME GREAT ONE. AH, MY BEAUTIFUL, • • •	720	WITCH VIVIEN		14
	LEAD THEY ONE WITH FOOLISH CARE, • • • • • • •	727	LOVERS QUARREL		29
	ONE WHOSE BREATHING SHAKES THE AIR, • • • • • •	727	LOVERS QUARREL		31
	ONE WHOSE FOOTFALL SHAKES THE GROUND. • • • • •	727	LOVERS QUARREL		32
	AND COME KNEELING ON ONE KNEE, • • • • • • • •	727	LOVERS QUARREL		53
	"THEY ARE LOST, THEY ARE LOST, EACH ONE," CRIED HE. •	730	PRIEST FAIRY		58
	AND LOOKED ON NO ONE THERE • • • • • • • • •	741	EARL PAUL		34
	WISDOM AND DREAMS ARE ONE, • • • • • • • • •	743	WISDOM DREAMS		5
	YET ONE JOY HAVE I, HID CLOSE, • • • • • • • •	744	ROSY CROSS		8
	AND GAZE ON ONE ANOTHER THROUGH OUR EYES, • • • •	749	SHADOW WATER A		58
	WHEN ONE HAS LEAPT ON BOARD. NO, FOR I HAVE HOPE •	751	SHADOW WATER A		106
	THE TIDE NARROWS BETWEEN, AND ONE OLD MAN • • • •	752	SHADOW WATER A		118
	A BOY AND GIRL HOLD ONE ANOTHER'S HANDS: • • • •	752	SHADOW WATER A		122
	TWO HOVER THERE TOGETHER, AND ONE SAYS, • • • • •	753	SHADOW WATER A		142
	AND THEN ONE ASKS ANOTHER HOW HE DIED, • • • • •	753	SHADOW WATER A		146
	BECAUSE THESE WATERS MAKE ALL WOMEN ONE. • • • •	757	SHADOW WATER A		194
	WITH ONE YOU HAVE KILLED AND DIE: FOR WHEN I LEFT •	758	SHADOW WATER A		226
	IN ONE ANOTHER'S ARMS. AENGUS HAS SEEN • • • •	763	SHADOW WATER A		321
	AND WHEN ONE CHANGED HER TO A SILVER FLY, • • • •	763	SHADOW WATER A	V	305
	ONE LIVES UNDER THE WAVES, • • • • • • • • •	770	SPINNING SONG		2
	AND ONE WHERE THE WINDS ARE WOVE, • • • • • •	771	SPINNING SONG		3
	AND ONE IN THE OLD GRAY HOUSE • • • • • • • •	771	SPINNING SONG		4
	ONE LIVES IN THE HOUSE OF THE SUN, • • • • • •	771	SPINNING SONG		6
	AND ONE IN THE HOUSE OF THE MOON, • • • • • •	771	SPINNING SONG		7
	AND ONE LIVES UNDER THE BOUGHS, • • • • • • •	771	SPINNING SONG		8
	AND ONE SPINNER IS LOST. • • • • • • • • • •	771	SPINNING SONG		10
	THAT HAVE ONE ANOTHER'S EYES? • • • • • • • •	773	SONG DEIRDRE 1		24
	IN THE LAND THAT NO ONE KNOWS. • • • • • • • •	774	COME RIDE		17
	I WAS GOING THE ROAD ONE DAY • • • • • • • •	779	GOING THE ROAD		1
	SOME ONE SHOULD STAY AT HER SIDE. • • • • • • •	786	YOUR HEART	V	28
ONE-ARMED					
	A ONE-LEGGED, ONE-ARMED, ONE-EYED MAN • • • • •	302	HOUR DAWN	V	1
ONE-EYED					
	A ONE-LEGGED, ONE-ARMED, ONE-EYED MAN • • • • • •	302	HOUR DAWN	V	1

```
                                                            PAGE    TITLE          LINE
O'NEILLS
    MOCK AT THE MEMORY OF BOTH O'NEILLS, . . . . . . . .    546 TO SAME TUNE 2      24
    MOCK AT THE MEMORY OF BOTH O'NEILLS, . . . . . . . .    614 MARCH SONGS 1       24
ONE-LEGGED
    A ONE-LEGGED, ONE-ARMED, ONE-EYED MAN  . . . . . . .    302 HOUR DAWN       V   1
ONE'S
    I HAD A THOUGHT FOR NO ONE'S BUT YOUR EARS!  . . . .    206 ADAMS CURSE         34
    STRANGE CREATURES FLUTTER UP BEFORE ONE'S EYES,  . .    222 SHADOW WATER B      18
    OR CRY ABOUT ONE'S EARS.  NOTHING TO FEAR. . . . . .    222 SHADOW WATER B      19
    HOW GREAT A WRONG IT IS TO LET ONE'S THOUGHT  . . . .   246 SHADOW WATER B     514
    ONE'S HAD HER FILL OF LOVERS, ANOTHER'S HAD BUT ONE, .  354 HIS PHOENIX         19
    AT THE PERFECTION OF ONE'S OWN OBEDIENCE!  . . . . . .  376 PHASES OF MOON     109
    I, TOO, WILL FOLLOW FOR THIS EVIL-STARRED ONE'S SAKE .  655 ISLE STAT I 2       84
ONES
    "WHO ARE THE RIDING ONES?" I SAID. . . . . . . . .      12 OISIN 1         V 146
    WATCHING THE BLESSED ONES MOVE FAR OFF, AND THE SMILE ON 61 OISIN 3           199
        GOD'S FACE,
    . . . OF BEST ONES A SAD THING WERE--  . . . . . . .    63 OISIN 3         V 222
    WHO OF THE WANDERING MANY-CHANGING ONES . . . . . . .  182 QUEEN MAEVE         51
    SHE TOLD THEM OF THE MANY-CHANGING ONES!  . . . . . .  185 QUEEN MAEVE        112
    SEVEN OLD SISTERS WIND THE THREADS OF THE LONG-LIVED ONES, 209 UNDER THE MOON    7
    SEVEN OLD SISTERS WIND THE THREADS OF THE LONG LIVED ONES, 209 UNDER THE MOON V  7
    POURED OUT WINE FOR THE HIGH INVISIBLE ONES. . . . .   219 WOODS OF COOLE      44
    WITHHOLDS THEM NOW?  HAVE THE EVER-LIVING ONES  . . .  234 SHADOW WATER B     269
    THAT THE SHAPE-CHANGERS, THE EVER-LAUGHING ONES, . . . 249 SHADOW WATER B     566
    IN THEIR STIFF, PAINTED CLOTHES, THE PALE UNSATISFIED ONES 318 MAGI              2
    AH! CRUEL ONES, LEAVE ME ALONE NOW  . . . . . . . .    707 FAIRY PEDANT        13
    AH! CRUEL ONES, LEAVE ME ALONE . . . . . . . . . .     707 FAIRY PEDANT    V   13
    O SHINING ONES, LIGHTLY WITH SONG PASS,  . . . . . .   708 FAIRY PEDANT        21
    AND THEN THE GREAT ONES COME, AND LAST THE KING. . . . 722 WITCH VIVIEN        54
    YONDER FOOLISH ONES WILL TIRE  . . . . . . . . . .     727 LOVERS QUARREL      47
    IF THESE MERRY ONES SHOULD KNOW, . . . . . . . . .     731 STREET DANCERS       9
    IF THESE MERRY ONES SHOULD KNOW, . . . . . . . . .     732 STREET DANCERS      22
    IF THESE MERRY ONES SHOULD KNOW, . . . . . . . . .     732 STREET DANCERS      35
    IF THESE MERRY ONES SHOULD KNOW, . . . . . . . . .     733 STREET DANCERS      48
    IF THESE MERRY ONES SHOULD KNOW, . . . . . . . . .     733 STREET DANCERS      61
ONION
    WHAT TH' ONION SELLERS THOUGHT OR DID  . . . . . . .   287 TO WEALTHY MAN V    11
ONION-SELLERS
    WHAT TH' ONION-SELLERS THOUGHT OR DID  . . . . . . .   287 TO WEALTHY MAN      11
ONLIE
    HUGH LANE, "ONLIE BEGETTER" OF ALL THESE!  . . . . .   602 GALLERY REVIS       22
ONLY
    "YOU ONLY WILL I WED," I CRIED,  . . . . . . . . .       7 OISIN 1            74
    BUT ONLY KIND AND MERRY BREATH,  . . . . . . . . .      19 OISIN 1           285
    WE ONLY KNOW THAT WE WERE GLAD . . . . . . . . . .      22 OISIN 1         V 340D
    SAVE ONLY MANY TIMES MY NAME,  . . . . . . . . . .      25 OISIN 1           375
    BUT ONLY EXULTANT FACES.  NIAMH STOOD  . . . . . . .    38 OISIN 2           136
    BUT, THE BIRD IN MY FINGERS, I MOUNTED, MINDFUL ONLY TO  54 OISIN 3         V 111
        LAUNCH
    I CRIED, "O NIAMH!  O WHITE ONE! IF ONLY A TWELVE-HOURED 55 OISIN 3           113
        DAY,
    BUT WEEP FOR YOUR NIAMH, O OISIN, WEEP! FOR IF ONLY YOUR 55 OISIN 3           127
        SHOE
    BUT WEEP FOR THY NIAM, OH OISIN, WEEP! FOR IF ONLY THY SHOE 55 OISIN 3       V 127
    "IN THE ISLES OF THE FARTHEST SEAS WHERE ONLY THE SPIRITS 56 OISIN 3         133
        COME.
    ONLY A SUDDEN FLAMING WORD, . . . . . . . . . . .      65 HAPPY SHEPHERD      19
    LEST ALL THY TOILING ONLY BREEDS . . . . . . . . .     66 HAPPY SHEPHERD      25
    ALL LOVED HIM, ONLY THE SHONEEN  . . . . . . . . .     92 FATHER OHART        13
    ONE BLIND HOUND ONLY LIES APART  . . . . . . . . .     99 FOXHUNTER           41
    "I ONLY ASK WHAT WAY MY JOURNEY LIES,  . . . . . . .  108 CUCHULAIN SEA       31
    CUCHULAIN CRIED, "I AM THE ONLY MAN  . . . . . . . .  109 CUCHULAIN SEA       55
    "I ONLY OF THE RED BRANCH HOSTED NOW," . . . . . . .  109 CUCHULAIN SEA   V  55
    "GOD ONLY SEES WHAT DOOM FOR ME LIES STORED." . . . . 110 CUCHULAIN SEA   V  62
    WERE WE ONLY WHITE BIRDS, MY BELOVED,  . . . . . .    122 WHITE BIRDS         12
    OR ONLY GAZE A LITTLE WHILE! . . . . . . . . . . .    135 TWO TREES           24
    WHERE ONLY BODY'S LAID ASLEEP. . . . . . . . . . .    138 TO IRELAND          22
    OR ONLY TO THE WATER IN THE WEST!  . . . . . . . .    155 REPROVE CURLEW       2
    OR ONLY TO WATERS IN THE WEST! . . . . . . . . . .    155 REPROVE CURLEW V     2
    OR ONLY TO THE WATERS IN THE WEST! . . . . . . . .    155 REPROVE CURLEW V     2
    THAT ONLY GOD'S EYES DID NOT CLOSE!  . . . . . . .    156 FORGOT BEAUTY       14
    THAT ONLY THE GODS' EYES DID NOT CLOSE! . . . . . .   156 FORGOT BEAUTY   V   14
    BUT I, BEING POOR, HAVE ONLY MY DREAMS!  . . . . .    176 CLOTHS HEAVEN        6
    I ONLY KNOW THAT ALL WE KNOW COMES FROM YOU, . . .    218 WOODS OF COOLE      28
    FOR THEY'RE MY ONLY PILOTS.  IF I LOST THEM  . . .    226 SHADOW WATER B      85
    THE ONLY RICHES THAT HAVE HIT MY FANCY.  . . . . .    226 SHADOW WATER B      96
    "ONLY THE WASTEFUL VIRTUES EARN THE SUN"!  . . . .    270 PARDON FATHERS      18
    THAT ONLY GODS MAY BUY OF HIM.  . . . . . . . . .     272 GREY ROCK           25
    IN HIS FULL HANDS WHAT, HAD THEY ONLY KNOWN, . . .    292 TO A SHADE          11
    FOR ONLY RUBBISH COMES MY WAY. . . . . . . . . . .    295 THREE BEGGARS        4
    "WHY, BEER IS ONLY BEER."  "BUT SAY  . . . . . . .    305 HOUR DAWN           56
    BY THE WOOD'S EDGE WHERE ONLY EQUALS MEET,  . . . .   321 REED WHISPERER V     8
    NO MOON! ONLY AN ACHING HEART  . . . . . . . . . .    421 MY TABLE            13
    THAT ONLY GOD HAS LOVED US FOR OURSELVES,  . . . .    448 HERO GIRL FOOL      16
    OR BRIGHTEN ONLY FOR SOME YOUNGER EYE, . . . . . .    464 HARUN RASHID        82
    DREAM THAT I LOVE HER ONLY FOR THE VOICE, . . . . .   469 HARUN RASHID       171
    DREAM THAT I LOVE HER ONLY FOR THAT VOICE, . . . .    469 HARUN RASHID    V  171
    ONLY THE DEAD CAN BE FORGIVEN!  . . . . . . . . .     478 SELF AND SOUL       39
    THAT ONLY GOD, MY DEAR,  . . . . . . . . . . . .      492 ANNE GREGORY        16
    MAINLY BECAUSE OF WHAT WE ONLY KNOW  . . . . . . .    634 CUCHULAIN COMF      14
```

		PAGE	TITLE	LINE

ONLY (CONTINUED)

WITH ONLY BED AND BEDSTEAD THERE, ... 639 BEN BULBEN 61
WE MUST GET SWORDS. IS'T THE ONLY WAY? OH, SEE, . . . 660 ISLE STAT II 1 34
AND ONLY SHEEP HE LOVED OF ALL THE TROOP. . . . . 661 ISLE STAT II 1 61
WHO SEEK MAY FIND, SAVE ONLY ONE, ... 668 ISLE STAT II 3 48
TILL THOU REMEMBEREST ONLY HOW THE SEA . . . . 670 ISLE STAT II 3 94
SHE WAS MY ONLY FRIEND! I'M LAME, YOU KNOW-- . . . . . 695 MOSADA 1 115
TWO ONLY NOW THEY ARE, TWO SIDE BY SIDE. . . . . 700 MOSADA 3 49
HALF HID. HE BRINGS THE PEASANT'S ONLY KIN, ... 711 FERENCZ RENYI 50
HOW "THE ONLY GOOD IS MUSING MILD, ... 728 PRIEST FAIRY 13
AND THAT DREAM ONLY SHINE BEFORE HER FEET. . . . . . . 761 SHADOW WATER A 258

ONSET

CRY AT THE ONSET OF THEIR SEXUAL JOY . . . . 560 WHENCE COME 2
CRY AT THE ONSET OF THE SEXUAL JOY . . . . 560 WHENCE COME V 2

ONWARD

THEN ONWARD IN THE WINDING THICKET . . . . 20 OISIN 1 V 304
MOURN--AND THEN ONWARD! . . . . 737 MOURN THEN ON T
MOURN--AND THEN ONWARD, THERE IS NO RETURNING . . . . 738 MOURN THEN ON 13

ONYX

ALL WISDOM SHUT INTO HIS ONYX EYES, ... 311 MOUNTAIN TOMB 11
ALL WISDOM SHUT INTO ITS ONYX EYES. . . . . 311 MOUNTAIN TOMB V 11

OOZY   SEE FOAM-OOZY

WHERE CYPRESS IS AND OOZY PINE, ... 670 ISLE STAT II 3 110

OPAL

OF OPAL AND RUBY AND PALE CHRYSOLITE . . . . 219 HARP OF AENGUS 6
OF OPAL AND RUBY AND PALE CHRYSOLITE . . . . 762 SHADOW WATER A 301

OPEN   SEE WIDE-OPEN

HALF OPEN HIS EYES WERE, AND HELD ME, ... 51 OISIN 3 65
WITH STILL AND STONY LIMBS AND OPEN EYES. . . . . 182 QUEEN MAEVE 46
YOUR OPEN HAND BUT SHOWS OUR LOSS, ... 288 TO WEALTHY MAN 29
HELL MOUTH LAY OPEN NEAR THAT PLACE, ... 303 HOUR DAWN 25
A LAMP BURNS ON BESIDE THE OPEN BOOK . . . . 367 EGO DOMINUS 3
A LAMP BURNS ON ABOVE THE OPEN BOOK . . . . 367 EGO DOMINUS V 3
BURNING ALONE BESIDE AN OPEN BOOK, ... 370 EGO DOMINUS 63
UPON THE OPEN ROAD, NEAR TO THE SLIGO QUAY-- . . . . . 391 UNDER SATURN 12
A GREY STONE FIREPLACE WITH AN OPEN HEARTH, ... 419 MY HOUSE 12
A GREY STONE FIRE-PLACE WITH AN OPEN HEARTH, ... 419 MY HOUSE V 12
GREAT WINDOWS OPEN TO THE SOUTH, ... 475 EVA GORE-BOOTH 2
AN OPEN BOOK AND EMPTY CUP . . . . 501 VACILLATION 38
AND HERE IS TULLY'S OPEN PAGE. . . . . 524 MAD AS MIST 9
WITH OPEN BOOK YOU ASK ME WHAT I DO. . . . . 554 RIBH AT TOMB 2
MADE AQUILINE, ARE OPEN TO THAT LIGHT. . . . . 555 RIBH AT TOMB 24
ITS OPEN LIGHTED DOORWAY AND ITS WINDOWS ALL ALIGHT, . 581 CURSE CROMWELL 26
THEIR WOUNDS OPEN AGAIN. . . . . 612 NEWS ORACLE 16
BLOSSOMS OPEN DEWY LIPS! . . . . 647 ISLE STAT I 1 65
THEN HE SHOUTED, "OPEN WIDE . . . . 697 MOSADA 2 24
AND HE SHOUTED OPEN WIDE . . . . 697 MOSADA 2 V 24
THE STRANGER SHOUTED, "OPEN WIDE . . . . 697 MOSADA 2 V 24
THE BISHOP CAME WITH OPEN BOOK, ... 725 LEGEND 17
WITH OPEN MOUTH AND BEATING HEART. . . . . 729 PRIEST FAIRY 32
ARE SHOT AT ON THE OPEN PLAIN. . . . . 791 REPRISALS 18

OPENED

THE BIRDS, FOR HE OPENED THEIR CAGES . . . . 92 FATHER OHART 17
THE SICK MAN'S WIFE OPENED THE DOOR. . . . . 133 FR GILLIGAN 31
SHE OPENED HER DOOR AND HER WINDOW, ... 160 CAP AND BELLS 29
THAT HEAVENS HAD OPENED. GYRES RUN ON! . . . . 639 BEN BULBEN 62

OPEN-EYED

PROUD, OPEN-EYED AND LAUGHING TO THE TOMB. . . . . . . 501 VACILLATION 34

OPEN-HANDEDNESS

AND FOR HIS OPEN-HANDEDNESS, DISGRACE! . . . . 292 TO A SHADE 16

OPENIN'

WHEN, OPENIN' WIDE HIS DOOR, ... 96 MOLL MAGEE 50

OPENS

THAT OPENS HER MYSTERY AND FRIGHT. . . . . 624 APPARITIONS 22

OPHELIA

THAT'S OPHELIA, THAT CORDELIA! . . . . 565 LAPIS LAZULI 11

OPINION

OPINION IS NOT WORTH A RUSH! . . . . 385 ROBARTES DANCE 1
PUBLIC OPINION RIPENING FOR SO LONG . . . . 428 NINETEEN 19 13
I CAN EXCHANGE OPINION WITH ANY NEIGHBOURING MIND, . . 450 OWEN AHERNE 9

OPINIONATED

BECAUSE OF HER OPINIONATED MIND . . . . 405 FOR DAUGHTER 61

OPINIONS

SO LET HER THINK OPINIONS ARE ACCURSED. . . . . 405 FOR DAUGHTER 58

OPOPONAX

NO! BUT OPOPONAX AND CINNAMON. . . . . 232 SHADOW WATER B 222

OPPOSITE

I CALL TO MY OWN OPPOSITE, SUMMON ALL . . . . 367 EGO DOMINUS 8
I THINK HE FASHIONED FROM HIS OPPOSITE . . . . 368 EGO DOMINUS 27
MOCKED ME WITH PRAISE OF MY MERE OPPOSITE! . . . . . . 448 HERO GIRL FOOL 4
MOCK ME WITH PRAISE OF MY MERE OPPOSITE! . . . . 448 HERO GIRL FOOL V 4
BUT I BEING NONE CAN PRAISE ITS OPPOSITE. . . . . 465 HARUN RASHID 98

OPPOSITION

BY OPPOSITION, SQUARE AND TRINE! . . . . 325 ROBERT GREGORY 39

OPPRESSED

BEING BY THE WORLD OPPRESSED, ... 434 YOUTH AND AGE 2

OPTIC

WHO FOLLOW WITH THE OPTIC GLASS . . . . 66 HAPPY SHEPHERD 29

ORACLE

THE DELPHIC ORACLE UPON PLOTINUS . . . . 530 DELPHIC ORACLE T
NEWS FOR THE DELPHIC ORACLE . . . . 611 NEWS ORACLE T

		PAGE	TITLE	LINE
O'RAHILLY				
	THE O'RAHILLY	584	ORAHILLY	T
	SING OF THE O'RAHILLY,	584	ORAHILLY	1
	SING OF THE O'RAHILLY,	585	ORAHILLY	10
	"HERE DIED THE O'RAHILLY.	585	ORAHILLY	34
ORB				
	THE ORB OF THE MOST INNER LIVING HEART	689	NETTLESHIP	15
ORBIT				
	WHEREVER THE ORBIT OF THE MOON CAN REACH,	472	ALL SOUL NIGHT	55
ORCHARD-CIRCLED				
	TO THE ORCHARD-CIRCLED FARM!	727	LOVERS QUARREL	50
ORCHARDS				
	FROM THE HOLY ORCHARDS, WHERE THERE IS NONE	196	BAILE AILLINN	174
ORCHIL				
	ORCHIL SHAKES OUT HER LONG DARK HAIR	85	MAD KING GOLL	62
ORDER				
	SHOOT ON HIM SHAFTS OF QUIETNESS, AND ORDER HIM TO KEEP	75	ANASHU VIJAYA	V 81
	... HAVE JOINED THE ANCIENT ORDER OF HIBERNIANS AND THE	262	STUDENTS AGIT	V T
	WHEN ORDER HAS WEAKENED OR FACTION IS STRONG,	548	TO SAME TUNE 3	12
ORIGINAL				
	WHAT THEME HAD HOMER BUT ORIGINAL SIN?	502	VACILLATION	77
ORION				
	TOLD HIM, THAT WHEN ORION ROSE, AND ALL	282	TWO KINGS	V 132A
ORMOLU				
	AUGUSTA GREGORY SEATED AT HER GREAT ORMOLU TABLE,	577	LOFTY THINGS	7
ORMONDES				
	WELCOME, AND THE ORMONDES ALL	400	DEMON BEAST	11
ORNAMENTAL				
	AMID THE ORNAMENTAL BRONZE AND STONE	428	NINETEEN 19	5
ORO				
	ORO, ORO!	551	SONGS REWRIT 1	5
	ORO, ORO!	551	SONGS REWRIT 1	5
	ORO, ORO!	551	SONGS REWRIT 1	11
	ORO, ORO!	551	SONGS REWRIT 1	11
	ORO, ORO!	551	SONGS REWRIT 1	17
	ORO, ORO!	551	SONGS REWRIT 1	17
O'ROUGHLEY				
	TOM O'ROUGHLEY	337	TOM OROUGHLEY	T
	OR SO DID TOM O'ROUGHLEY SAY	338	TOM OROUGHLEY	5
OSAFUME				
	MONTASHIGI OF OSAFUME FASHIONED IT	478	SELF AND SOUL	V 25
OSCAR				
	FIN, CONAN, OSCAR, MANY MORE, THE TIDE	44	OISIN 2	V 228A
	NO OSCAR RULED THE TABLE,	626	STATES HOLIDAY	5
OSCAR'S				
	WE THOUGHT ON OSCAR'S PENCILLED URN.	2	OISIN 1	V 70
	"WE THINK ON OSCAR'S PENCILLED URN,	5	OISIN 1	41
OSIER				
	... THE SHIELD OUT OF OSIER AND HIDE!	52	OISIN 3	82
OSPREY				
	NOR SORROW WITH HER OSPREY CLAW.	19	OISIN 1	V 285
	OR THE GREY WANDERING OSPREY SORROW."	20	OISIN 1	303
	OR THE WILD GREY OSPREY SORROW,"	20	OISIN 1	V 303
	NOR THE GREY WANDERING OSPREY SORROW."	21	OISIN 1	319
	OR THE WILD GREY OSPREY SORROW."	21	OISIN 1	V 319
	NOR THE GREY WANDERING OSPREY SORROW."	23	OISIN 1	342
	OR FEAR THE WILD GREY OSPREY SORROW."	23	OISIN 1	V 342D
	THE OSPREY OF SORROW GOES AFTER AND CLUTCHES,	27	OISIN 1	V 415D
O'SULLIVAN				
	WINDLE-STRAWS I. O'SULLIVAN RUA TO THE CURLEW	155	REPROVE CURLEW	V T
	O'SULLIVAN RUA TO MARY LAVELL	155	FORGOT BEAUTY	V T
	O'SULLIVAN THE RED TO MARY LAVELL.	157	POET BELOVED	V T
	TWO POEMS BY O'SULLIVAN THE RED CONCERNING MARY LAVELL.	157	POET BELOVED	V T
	O'SULLIVAN RUA TO THE SECRET ROSE	169	SECRET ROSE	V T
	O'SULLIVAN THE RED UPON HIS WANDERINGS	171	MAID QUIET	V T
OTHERWISE				
	NO MAN NOR WOMAN HAS LOVED OTHERWISE	750	SHADOW WATER A	64
	NO MAN OR WOMAN HAS LOVED OTHERWISE	750	SHADOW WATER A	64
OTTER				
	I SAT ON CUSHIONED OTTER SKIN!	81	MAD KING GOLL	V 1
	CHAIRED IN THE CUSHIONED OTTER SKIN,	82	MAD KING GOLL	V 5
	AND NIAMH AND LABAN AND FAND, WHO COULD CHANGE TO AN OTTER OR FAWN,	209	UNDER THE MOON	12
	AND FAND, AND NIAM, AND LABAN, WHO COULD CHANGE TO AN OTTER OR FAWN,	209	UNDER THE MOON	V 12
	SPLASHED, OR AN OTTER SLID INTO THE STREAM.	372	PHASES OF MOON	9
OTTERS				
	WE LAY ON SKINS OF OTTERS, AND DRANK WINE,	41	OISIN 2	188
	AND THEN ON HEAPED-UP SKINS OF OTTERS SLEPT.	41	OISIN 2	191
	OTTERS BELOW AND MOOR-HENS ON THE TOP,	490	COOLE BALLYLEE	2
	OTTERS BELOW AND MOOR HENS ON THE TOP,	490	COOLE BALLYLEE	V 2
	THE OTTERS DREAMING LAY. AYE!	677	ISLE STAT II 3	280
	THE OTTERS DREAMING LAY. NASCHINA! AY!	677	ISLE STAT II 3	V 280
OTTER-SKIN				
	I SAT ON CUSHIONED OTTER-SKIN!	81	MAD KING GOLL	1
	CHAIRED IN A CUSHIONED OTTER-SKIN.	82	MAD KING GOLL	V 5
OUGHT				
	IS FROM THE OUGHT, OR KNOWER FROM THE KNOWN--	478	SELF AND SOUL	37
OUNCE				
	IT CANNOT GROW BY AN INCH OR AN OUNCE.	566	LAPIS LAZULI	24

586

OUSEL   PAGE TITLE   LINE

AND THE SALMON BEHOLD, AND THE OUSEL TOO, ... 717 LOVE SONG 3

OUT

BUT WE RODE OUT FROM THE HUMAN LANDS. . . . . 10 OISIN 1 114
ROSE EVER OUT OF THE WARM SEA! . . . . 13 OISIN 1 172
OUT OF A LITTLE SILVER TRUMP! . . . . 15 OISIN 1 196
AND FROM THE WOODS RUSHED OUT A BAND . . . . 15 OISIN 1 201
THEIR CLOAKS MADE OUT OF YELLOW SILK, ... 15 OISIN 1 205
THEIR BRATTAS MADE OUT OF YELLOW SILK, ... 15 OISIN 1 205
AND ONE A SCEPTRE FLASHING OUT . . . . 15 OISIN 1 V 205
OUT OF THE MOON'S PALE TWISTED SHELL! . . . . 17 OISIN 1 251
AND SWEPT OUT OF THE WATTLED HALL . . . . 19 OISIN 1 279
I DREW OUT OF THE NUMBERLESS . . . . 20 OISIN 1 292
AND WRAPPED IN DREAMS RODE OUT AGAIN . . . . 24 OISIN 1 365
"MY BROTHERS SPRING OUT OF THEIR BEDS AT MORN, ... 25 OISIN 1 V 382
AND FACE THAT SEEMED WROUGHT OUT OF MOONLIT VAPOURS, . . 32 OISIN 2 51
PASSED UNDER THE DIM DOORWAY, OUT OF SIGHT, ... 33 OISIN 2 70
PASSED UNDER A DIM DOORWAY, OUT OF SIGHT, ... 37 OISIN 2 123
OUT OF THE SEVENFOLD SEAS, BUILT THE DARK HALL . . . . 37 OISIN 2 V 123
A DOME MADE OUT OF ENDLESS CARVEN JAGS, ... 38 OISIN 2 131
OUT OF THE SEVEN-FOLD SEAS, BUILT THE DARK HALL . . . 38 OISIN 2 144
AND HEALED MY WOUNDS WITH UNGUENTS OUT OF FLOWERS . . . 38 OISIN 2 V 131
ROLLING HIS FLAGRANT WHEEL OUT OF THE DEEP, ... 41 OISIN 2 185
THEIR NAKED AND GLEAMING BODIES POURED OUT AND HEAPED IN 42 OISIN 2 193
 THE WAY.   48 OISIN 3 28
WATCHED ME WITH MOURNFUL WONDER OUT OF THE WELLS OF HIS 51 OISIN 3 60
 EYES.
I CRIED, "COME OUT OF THE SHADOW, KING OF THE NAILS OF 51 OISIN 3 61
 GOLD!
HIS LIPS MOVED SLOWLY IN ANSWER, NO ANSWER OUT OF THEM 51 OISIN 3 66
 CAME!
I CRIED, "COME OUT OF THE SHADOW, CANN OF THE NAILS OF 51 OISIN 3 V 61
 GOLD!
THAT THE SPEAR-SHAFT IS MADE OUT OF ASHWOOD, ... 52 OISIN 3 82
. . . THE SHIELD OUT OF OSIER AND HIDE! . . . . 52 OISIN 3 82
THAT THE SPEARSHAFT IS MADE OUT OF ASHWOOD, ... 52 OISIN 3 V 82
I AWOKE! THE STRANGE HORSE WITHOUT SUMMONS OUT OF 54 OISIN 3 105
 THE DISTANCE RAN,
LONG FLED THE FOAM-FLAKES AROUND ME, THE WINDS FLED OUT 57 OISIN 3 149
 OF THE VAST,
COMING OUT OF THE SEA AS THE DAWN COMES, A CHAUNT OF LOVE 58 OISIN 3 158
 ON MY LIPS,
AND I RODE AND I RODE, AND I CRIED OUT, ... 59 OISIN 3 171
AND THE DREAMS OF THE ISLANDS WENT OUT OF ME, ... 59 OISIN 3 175
WE WILL TEAR OUT THE FLAMING STONES, AND BATTER THE GATEWAY 62 OISIN 3 V 209
 OF BRASS
WE WILL TEAR OUT THE RED FLAMING STONES, ... 62 OISIN 3 209
WE WILL TEAR THE RED FLAMING STONES OUT, ... 62 OISIN 3 V 209
BUT KNEEL AND WEAR OUT THE FLAGS AND PRAY FOR YOUR SOUL 63 OISIN 3 215
 THAT IS LOST
AS A HAY-COCK OUT ON THE FLOOD, OR A WOLF SUCKED UNDER 63 OISIN 3 220
 A WEIR.
BUT WEEP YOU AND KNEEL! WEAR OUT THE FLAGS! . . . . . 63 OISIN 3 V 215
KNEEL, USHEEN, WEAR OUT THE FLAGS AND PRAY FOR YOUR SOUL 63 OISIN 3 V 215
 THAT IS LOST
CRIED OUT, DIM SEA, HEAR MY MOST PITEOUS STORY! . . . . 68 SAD SHEPHERD 9
THEY PINE AWAY AND YELLOW AND WEAR OUT . . . . 81 EPHEMERA V 24H
ORCHIL SHAKES OUT HER LONG DARK HAIR . . . . 85 MAD KING GOLL 62
LEANING SOFTLY OUT . . . . 88 STOLEN CHILD 35
IN PENAL DAYS RODE OUT . . . . 91 FATHER OHART 2
HE DROVE ME OUT AND SHUT THE DOOR, ... 95 MOLL MAGEE 25
AND STRETCHING OUT HER ARMS, RED WITH THE DYE, ... 105 CUCHULAIN SEA V 7
MY FATHER STANDS." "AGED, WORN OUT WITH WARS . . . . 107 CUCHULAIN SEA 29
AND CRIED OUT TO HIM, "SON IT IS NOT MEET . . . . . . 107 CUCHULAIN SEA V 20
AND CALLED OUT TO HIM, "SON IT IS NOT MEET . . . . . . 107 CUCHULAIN SEA V 20
SEEK OUT WHAT MAN HE IS." ONE WENT AND CAME. . . . . 109 CUCHULAIN SEA 51
HE WOULD GO WEAVE OUT OF THE STARS . . . . 113 ROSE OF PEACE 7
"TURN IF YE MAY," I CALL OUT TO EACH ONE, ... 114 ROSE OF BATTLE V 7
HAD BLOTTED OUT MAN'S IMAGE AND HIS CRY. . . . . . . 120 SORROW OF LOVE 4
. . . BUOYED OUT ON THE FOAM OF THE SEA! . . . . . . 122 WHITE BIRDS 12
A CROSS THEY HAD MADE OUT OF TWO BITS OF WOOD, ... 123 DREAM OF DEATH 7
THE SINGING SHOOK HIM OUT OF HIS NEW EASE. . . . . . . 126 DREAM OF FAERY 12
OF HOW GOD LEANS HIS HANDS OUT OF THE SKY, ... 128 DREAM OF FAERY V 43
THAT GOD HAD LEANED HIS HANDS OUT OF THE SKY, ... 128 DREAM OF FAERY V 43
THAT GOD HAD LEANT HIS HANDS OUT OF THE SKY, ... 128 DREAM OF FAERY V 43
HE ROUSED HIS HORSE OUT OF ITS SLEEP, ... 133 FR GILLIGAN 27
WHILE I WROUGHT OUT THESE FITFUL DANAAN RHYMES, ... 136 TO SOME I TALK 1
WHILE STILL I MAY I WRITE OUT TRUE . . . . 139 TO IRELAND V 33
LIKE A CANDLE BURNT OUT, ... 142 MOODS 2
ALL THINGS UNCOMELY AND BROKEN, ALL THINGS WORN OUT AND 142 ROSE IN HEART 1
 OLD,
AND OUT OF HIS DREAM AWOKE! . . . . 145 HOST OF AIR 38
ABOUT THE CASTING OUT OF MY NET, ... 146 FISH 4
AND HOW YOU HAVE LEAPED TIMES OUT OF MIND . . . . . . 146 FISH 5
AND RIVER AND STREAM WORK OUT THEIR WILL! . . . . . . 148 INTO TWILIGHT 12
AND LAUGH OUT THEIR WHIMSEY AND WORK OUT THEIR WILL. . . 148 INTO TWILIGHT V 12
AND LAUGH OUT THEIR WHIMSEY AND WORK OUT THEIR WILL. . . 148 INTO TWILIGHT V 12
LAUGH OUT THEIR WHIMSEY AND WORK OUT THEIR WILL. . . . 148 INTO TWILIGHT V 12
LAUGH OUT THEIR WHIMSEY AND WORK OUT THEIR WILL. . . . 148 INTO TWILIGHT V 12
AND THE CHANGING MOON WORK OUT THEIR WILL. . . . . . . 148 INTO TWILIGHT V 12
I WENT OUT TO THE HAZEL WOOD, ... 149 WANDER AENGUS 1
AND MOTH-LIKE STARS WERE FLICKERING OUT, ... 149 WANDER AENGUS 6

	PAGE	TITLE	LINE

OUT   (CONTINUED)

AND STARS LIKE MOTHS WERE SHINING OUT,	149	WANDER AENGUS V	6
I WILL FIND OUT WHERE SHE HAS GONE,	150	WANDER AENGUS	19
I WILL FIND OUT WHERE SHE IS GONE	150	WANDER AENGUS V	19
HE BADE ME OUT INTO THE GLOOM,	151	HEART OF WOMAN	3
AND HAD ROOTED THE SUN AND MOON AND STARS OUT OF THE SKY	153	CHANGE BELOVED	11
AND ROOTED THE SUN AND MOON AND STARS OUT OF THE SKY,	153	CHANGE BELOVED V	11
THAT WAS SHAKEN OUT OVER MY BREAST!	155	REPROVE CURLEW	5
IT WORKED AT THEM, DAY OUT, DAY IN,	158	BELOVED RHYMES	4
OUT OF THE BATTLES OF OLD TIMES.	158	BELOVED RHYMES	6
OUT OF THE OLD DAYS	158	TO HIS HEART V	T
REMEMBER THE WISDOM OUT OF THE OLD DAYS!	158	TO HIS HEART	2
WHEN THE OWLS CALLED OUT NO MORE!	159	CAP AND BELLS	14
WHEN THE BATS CRIED OUT NO MORE!	159	CAP AND BELLS V	14
TILL STARS GREW OUT OF THE AIR.	160	CAP AND BELLS	28
AND WAVED IT OUT ON THE AIR.	160	CAP AND BELLS V	20
THE STARS GREW OUT OF THE AIR.	160	CAP AND BELLS V	28
AND I DREAMED MY LOST LOVE CAME STEALTHILY OUT OF THE WOOD	163	VALLEY LOVERS	3
I MADE IT OUT OF A MOUTHFUL OF AIR,	166	EVIL OF BELOV	5
CUMHAL CALLED OUT, BENDING HIS HEAD,	166	BLESSED	1
"I CAN BRING YOU SALMON OUT OF THE STREAMS	167	BLESSED	9
AND HERON OUT OF THE SKIES."	167	BLESSED	10
CUMHAL CALLED OUT, BOWING HIS HEAD,	167	BLESSED V	4A
"THE ROSE THAT MUST DROP, OUT OF SWEET LEAVES,	168	BLESSED V	37
AND HIM WHO DROVE THE GODS OUT OF THEIR LISS,	170	SECRET ROSE	16
LIKE THE SPARKS BLOWN OUT OF A SMITHY, AND DIE?	170	SECRET ROSE	30
UNFOLD YOUR FLAMING WINGS AND COVER OUT OF SIGHT	175	ELEMENT POWERS	11
OUT OF THEIR WHIRLING CARS,	175	ELEMENT POWERS V	16
AND LIGHTS WERE PALING OUT OF THE WEST,	175	BELOVED DEAD	2
AND LIGHT WERE PALING OUT OF THE WEST,	175	BELOVED DEAD V	2
AMONG MY LEAVES IN TIMES OUT OF MIND!	177	PAST GREATNESS	5
KNOWING ONE, OUT OF ALL THINGS, ALONE, THAT HIS HEAD	177	PAST GREATNESS	8
SUDDENLY AILELL SPOKE OUT OF HIS SLEEP,	183	QUEEN MAEVE	73
"HOW MAY A MORTAL WHOSE LIFE GUTTERS OUT	184	QUEEN MAEVE	85
THE CHILDREN OF THE MAINES OUT OF SLEEP,	184	QUEEN MAEVE	92
CAME UP OUT OF THE HOLE, AND RED-EARED HOUNDS	185	QUEEN MAEVE	117
WITH LONG WHITE BODIES CAME OUT OF THE AIR	185	QUEEN MAEVE	118
TILL MAEVE CALLED OUT, "THESE ARE BUT COMMON MEN.	186	QUEEN MAEVE	122
TILL IT DIED OUT WHERE AN OLD THORN-TREE STOOD.	186	QUEEN MAEVE	129
AND WHEN I'D WRITE IT OUT ANEW, THE WORDS,	186	QUEEN MAEVE	139
TILL IT DIED OUT WHERE AN OLD THORN TREE STOOD.	186	QUEEN MAEVE V	129
UNTIL TWO LOVERS CAME OUT OF THE AIR	187	QUEEN MAEVE	143
WITH BODIES MADE OUT OF SOFT FIRE. THE ONE,	187	QUEEN MAEVE	144
BUT OUT OF THE DARK AIR OVER HER HEAD THERE CAME	187	QUEEN MAEVE	153
RODE OUT OF EMAIN WITH A BAND	189	BAILE AILLINN	18
THAT ALL THINGS FELL OUT HAPPILY,	189	BAILE AILLINN	22
HE HAD KNEES THAT STUCK OUT OF HIS HOSE!	190	BAILE AILLINN	27
BECAUSE A LOVER'S HEART'S WORN OUT,	191	BAILE AILLINN	65
THAT OUT OF SIGHT IS OUT OF MIND.	192	BAILE AILLINN	87
THAT OUT OF SIGHT IS OUT OF MIND.	192	BAILE AILLINN	87
"HE IS WELL OUT OF WIND AND WAVE,	193	BAILE AILLINN V	114
FAR OUT UNDER A WINDLESS SKY;	197	BAILE AILLINN	181
LET RUSH AND BIRD CRY OUT THEIR FILL	197	BAILE AILLINN	198
MADE OUT OF A WILD THOUGHT, IS IN MY MARROW.	199	ARROW	2
I COULD WEEP THAT THE OLD IS OUT OF SEASON.	199	ARROW	8
THAT IT FADES OUT FROM KISS TO KISS!	202	NEVER GIVE ALL	5
AND THEIR SECRET SMILE, OUT OF THE DEPTHS OF THE LAKE!	203	WITHER BOUGHS	11
AND THEIR SECRET SMILE, OUT OF THE DEEPS OF THE LAKE!	203	WITHER BOUGHS V	11
THERE'S MANY A ONE SHALL FIND OUT ALL HEARTACHE	205	ADAMS CURSE	16
PRECEDENTS OUT OF BEAUTIFUL OLD BOOKS!	205	ADAMS CURSE	26
UNDER THE BITTER BLACK WINDS BLOWING OUT OF THE LEFT HAND!	206	HANRAHANS SONG V	2
BUT WE HAVE HIDDEN IN OUR HEARTS THE FLAME OUT OF THE EYES	207	HANRAHANS SONG	4
FOR THE WET WINDS ARE BLOWING OUT OF THE CLINGING AIR!	207	HANRAHANS SONG	12
WHEN THE RAIN IS PELTING OUT OF THE WINTRY AIR!	207	HANRAHANS SONG	12
FOR THE GREY WINDS ARE BLOWING UP, OUT OF THE CLINGING SEAS!	207	HANRAHANS SONG V	12
LAND-UNDER-WAVE, WHERE OUT OF THE MOON'S LIGHT AND THE SUN'S	209	UNDER THE MOON	6
A QUEEN-WOMAN DRESSED OUT IN SILVER, CRY	210	RAGGED WOOD V	2
WHEN THE SUN LOOKED OUT OF HIS GOLDEN HOOD,	210	RAGGED WOOD V	3
WHEN THE SUN LOOKED OUT OF HIS GOLDEN HOOD?--	211	RAGGED WOOD	7
I WILL DRIVE ALL THOSE LOVERS OUT AND CRY--	211	RAGGED WOOD	10
I WILL DRIVE OUT THE DEER AND MOON AND CRY--	211	RAGGED WOOD V	10
I'LL HOLLO ALL THOSE LOVERS OUT AND CRY--	211	RAGGED WOOD V	10
AND GREW TO BE OUT OF FASHION	211	O DO NOT LOVE	3
OR YOU WILL GROW OUT OF FASHION	212	O DO NOT LOVE	11
IS EDEN OUT OF TIME AND OUT OF SPACE?	218	WOODS OF COOLE	36
IS EDEN OUT OF TIME AND OUT OF SPACE?	218	WOODS OF COOLE	36
POURED OUT WINE FOR THE HIGH INVISIBLE ONES.	219	WOODS OF COOLE	44
EDAIN CAME OUT OF MIDHIR'S HILL, AND LAY	219	HARP OF AENGUS	1
SWEET WITH ALL MUSIC, OUT OF HIS LONG HAIR,	219	HARP OF AENGUS	8
AND ALL THE ALE RAN OUT AT THE NEW MOON!	222	SHADOW WATER B V	11
HE COULD NOT SEE THEM, BUT I HELD OUT MY HANDS	223	SHADOW WATER B	38
IF YOU WILL DRAW THAT SWORD OUT OF ITS SCABBARD	225	SHADOW WATER B	78
AND THEN SMOOTH OUT WITH IVORY HANDS AND SIGH,	228	SHADOW WATER B	133
AS THEY HAVE KNOWN IT. NOW THE SECRET'S OUT!	228	SHADOW WATER B	140
AENGUS AND EDAIN RAN UP OUT OF THE WAVE--	231	SHADOW WATER B	196
WHEN SHE FINDS OUT WE HAVE BETTER MEN ABOARD	232	SHADOW WATER B	231
MADE OF DIM GOLD RAVE OUT IN SECRET TOMBS!	235	SHADOW WATER B	295
WHEN SHE FINDS OUT I WILL NOT LET HER GO--	236	SHADOW WATER B	302
IT HAD WASHED AMONG THE STARS AND PUT THEM OUT,	236	SHADOW WATER B	311
YOU CANNOT LEAP OUT OF THE GOLDEN NET.	238	SHADOW WATER B	360

AND MEASURE OUT A COURSE AND BRING US HOME, ... 238 SHADOW WATER B 362
HE HAS CAUGHT THE CRESCENT MOON OUT OF THE SKY, . . . 239 SHADOW WATER B 370
WHERE IS MY SWORD THAT FELL OUT OF MY HAND . . . . . 241 SHADOW WATER B 397
IT WAS SO GIVEN OUT, BUT I WILL PROVE . . . . 243 SHADOW WATER B 429
WHAT ARE YOU CALLING OUT ABOVE THE MAST? . . . . . . 243 SHADOW WATER B 437
WHY, IT'S A WONDER OUT OF RECKONING . . . . 243 SHADOW WATER B 445
OUT OF ALL RECKONING. IS IT NOT TRUE . . . . 244 SHADOW WATER B 467
YOU'LL HEAR THEM CALLING OUT TO ONE ANOTHER . . . . 247 SHADOW WATER B 521
THEY'RE CRYING OUT, COULD YOU BUT HEAR THEIR WORDS, . 247 SHADOW WATER B 529
WITH ALL THOSE SIGHTS AND ALL THAT CRYING OUT? . . . 249 SHADOW WATER B 573
OUT OF THE RUNNING STREAM, O MORNING STAR, ... 251 SHADOW WATER B 610
CRIED OUT UPON THAT THING BENEATH . . . . 254 HIS DREAM 10
CRIED OUT THE WHOLE NIGHT LONG, ... 254 HIS DREAM 16
WE'LL OUT, FOR THE WORLD LIVES AS LONG AGO; . . . . 257 RECONCILIATION 8
HAS DRIED THE SAP OUT OF MY VEINS, AND RENT . . . . 260 FASC DIFFICULT 2
OUT OF MY HEART. THERE'S SOMETHING AILS OUR COLT . . 260 FASC DIFFICULT 4
I'LL FIND THE STABLE AND PULL OUT THE BOLT. . . . . 260 FASC DIFFICULT 13
TIME OUT OF MIND, BECAME TOO RUINOUS . . . . 264 HOUSE SHAKEN 3
OUT YONDER, WHERE THE RACE COURSE IS, ... 266 GALWAY RACES V 1
TO FIND OUT IF I MIGHT LOVE. . . . . 268 BROWN PENNY 4
TO FIND OUT ALL THAT IS IN IT, ... 268 BROWN PENNY 11
OR TRADING OUT OF GALWAY INTO SPAIN; . . . . 269 PARDON FATHERS 4
HAD HAMMERED OUT ON MOUNTAIN TOP . . . . 271 GREY ROCK 23
"COME OUT AND DIG FOR A DEAD MAN" . . . . 272 GREY ROCK 32
HAD RAVELLED HER OWN STORY OUT, ... 272 GREY ROCK 45
"THE DANISH TROOP WAS DRIVEN OUT . . . . 273 GREY ROCK 65
A SQUIRREL WHINNIED AND A BIRD SCREAMED OUT; . . . . 278 TWO KINGS 34
"I HAVE SENT OUT INTO THE FIELDS AND WOODS . . . . . 280 TWO KINGS V 69
AND I BUT ASKED THE MORE, TILL HE CRIED OUT, ... 281 TWO KINGS 92
AND I, THAT I MIGHT FIND AND STUB IT OUT, ... 281 TWO KINGS V 92
AND AT THOSE WORDS I ROSE AND I WENT OUT . . . . . . 282 TWO KINGS 125
AND STRETCHED OUT SLEEPING ON A PILE OF SKINS . . . 283 TWO KINGS 141
TO SHAKE HIM OUT OF SLEEP, I COULD NOT ROUSE HIM. . 283 TWO KINGS 143
WENT OUT. AMONG THE IVY-COVERED ROCKS, ... 283 TWO KINGS 147
SUCKED UP THE PASSION OUT OF HIM AGAIN . . . . 284 TWO KINGS 160
PUSH OUT HIS VIGOROUS LIMBS AND RUB HIS EYES, . . . 284 TWO KINGS 162
BEING WEARIED OUT, I LOVE IN MAN THE CHILD? . . . . 285 TWO KINGS 192
CAN BLOT OUT OF MY MEMORY THIS LIFE . . . . 285 TWO KINGS 204
AND RIDDEN OUT TO WELCOME THEM, AND NOW, ... 286 TWO KINGS V 218
AND WHEN THEY DROVE OUT COSIMO, ... 288 TO WEALTHY MAN 20
NOW ALL THE TRUTH IS OUT, ... 290 TO A FRIEND 1
TO DRINK OF THAT SALT BREATH OUT OF THE SEA . . . . 292 TO A SHADE 5
AN OLD FOUL MOUTH THAT ONCE CRIED OUT ON YOU . . . . 292 TO A SHADE V 17
CAN RAVEL OUT WHAT'S IN MY HEAD. . . . . 295 THREE BEGGARS 12
MY BROTHER MOURTEEN IS WORN OUT . . . . 301 RUN PARADISE 8
WOULD HAVE HIS FILL OUT OF MY LADLE . . . . 304 HOUR DAWN V 53
AND DRANK AND YAWNED AND STRETCHED HIM OUT, ... 307 HOUR DAWN 108
AND TUMBLE OUT YOUR HAIR . . . . 312 CHILD DANCING 4
I HAVE FOUND OUT HOW DESPAIRING . . . . 313 TWO YEAR LATER V 3
VANISHED, AND LEFT BUT MEMORIES, THAT SHOULD BE OUT OF 316 COLD HEAVEN 5
    SEASON
AND I TOOK ALL THE BLAME OUT OF ALL SENSE AND REASON, . 316 COLD HEAVEN 7
OUT NAKED ON THE ROADS, AS THE BOOKS SAY, AND STRICKEN 316 COLD HEAVEN 11
BEING OUT OF HEART WITH GOVERNMENT . . . . 317 APPOINTMENT 1
BEING OUT OF HEART AT GOVERNMENT . . . . 317 APPOINTMENT V 1
OUT OF OLD MYTHOLOGIES . . . . 320 COAT 3
AND THERE IS SALT TO LENGTHEN OUT THE SMART . . . . 324 ROBERT GREGORY 11
OUT OF SOME OLD PICTURE-BOOK; . . . . 325 ROBERT GREGORY 44
OUT OF SOME OLD PICTURE BOOK; . . . . 325 ROBERT GREGORY V 44
THE BARE CHIMNEY IS GONE BLACK OUT . . . . 327 ROBERT GREGORY 84
I AM WORN OUT WITH DREAMS; . . . . 329 MEN IMPROVE 1
FROM BEAUTY THAT IS CAST OUT OF A MOULD . . . . . . 334 LIVING BEAUTY 4
RHYMED OUT IN LOVE'S DESPAIR . . . . 337 SCHOLARS 5
WEAR OUT THE CARPET WITH THEIR SHOES . . . . 337 SCHOLARS V 8
FOR RHYME CAN BEAT A MEASURE OUT OF TROUBLE . . . . 339 SHEP GOATHERD 12
YOU HAVE MEASURED OUT THE ROAD THAT THE SOUL TREADS . 342 SHEP GOATHERD 80
CUT OUR RHYMES ON STRIPS OF NEW-TORN BARK . . . . . 343 SHEP GOATHERD 115
THE STARS FADE OUT WHERE THE MOON COMES, ... 344 DAWN 8
OR A YOUNG GIRL DRESSED OUT IN HER NEW GOWN, ... 350 HER PRAISE 4
AND SMOOTH OUT STAIN AND BLEMISH WITH THE ELEGANCE OF HIS 353 HIS PHOENIX 7
    MIND;
AND FLINGS HERSELF OUT OF THE ROOM WHEN JULIET WOULD BE 354 HIS PHOENIX 13
    BRIDE
THEY CAN SPREAD OUT WHAT SAIL THEY PLEASE FOR ALL I HAVE 354 HIS PHOENIX 22
    TO SAY,
AND FLINGS HERSELF OUT OF THE ROOM WHEN JULIET WOULD BE 354 HIS PHOENIX V 13
    A BRIDE
AND MAY BE THERE'LL BE SOME YOUNG BELLE WALK OUT TO MAKE 354 HIS PHOENIX V 26
    MEN WILD
AND MAYBE THERE'LL BE SOME YOUNG BELLE WALK OUT TO MAKE 354 HIS PHOENIX V 26
    MEN WILD
MOST OUT OF REACH? AND IS THAT SPECTRAL IMAGE . . . 368 EGO DOMINUS 25
DERIDED AND DERIDING, DRIVEN OUT . . . . 369 EGO DOMINUS 34
OUT OF NO TRAGIC WAR, LOVERS OF LIFE, ... 369 EGO DOMINUS 39
SHUT OUT FROM ALL THE LUXURY OF THE WORLD, ... 370 EGO DOMINUS 60
THEIR CONNEMARA CLOTH WORN OUT OF SHAPE; . . . . . . 372 PHASES OF MOON 4
SING OUT THE SONG; SING TO THE END, AND SING . . . . 374 PHASES OF MOON 56
BODY AND SOUL CAST OUT AND CAST AWAY . . . . 374 PHASES OF MOON 62
THEIR BEAUTY DROPPED OUT OF THE LONELINESS . . . . . 375 PHASES OF MOON 70
BECAUSE YOU ARE FORGOTTEN, HALF OUT OF LIFE, ... 376 PHASES OF MOON 96

	PAGE	TITLE	LINE
OUT (CONTINUED)			
OUT OF THE UP AND DOWN, THE WAGON-WHEEL	377	PHASES OF MOON	120
OUT OF THAT RAVING TIDE--IS DRAWN BETWIXT	377	PHASES OF MOON	122
AUSTERITY, A PLACE SET OUT FOR WISDOM	377	PHASES OF MOON	127
AND THEN I'D STAGGER OUT. HE'D CRACK HIS WITS	377	PHASES OF MOON	134
THE LIGHT IN THE TOWER WINDOW WAS PUT OUT.	377	PHASES OF MOON	139
OUT OF THE UP AND DOWN, THE WAGON WHEEL	377	PHASES OF MOON V	120
I START OUT OF MY SLEEP TO THINK	380	SONGS FOOL 1	7
UPON A MOMENT, AND SO STRETCHED IT OUT	384	VISION ROBART	46
I SUDDENLY CRIED OUT IN A STRANGE TONGUE	387	SOLOMON WITCH	5
HE THAT CROWED OUT ETERNITY	388	SOLOMON WITCH	17
TO FIND OUT SOME APPROPRIATE PAIN--	388	SOLOMON WITCH	20
WILL FIND OUT SOME APPROPRIATE PAIN,	388	SOLOMON WITCH V	20
OUT OF ALL LIKELIHOOD, OR REASON,	389	IMAGE PAST	9
MERELY TO LOOSEN OUT A TRESS	390	IMAGE PAST	26
NO, NO, NOT SAID, BUT CRIED IT OUT--"YOU HAVE COME AGAIN,	391	UNDER SATURN	13
I WRITE IT OUT IN A VERSE--	394	EASTER 1916	74
"TO MAKE THE GREEN COME OUT AGAIN	396	ROSE TREE	9
WHEN FIRST IT SPRANG OUT OF THE NEST	397	POLIT PRISONER	20
CRIED OUT THE HOLLOWS OF THE SEA.	397	POLIT PRISONER	24
RAN OUT OF MY SIGHT!	399	DEMON BEAST	4
THAN THAT I MAY FIND OUT A WAY	401	DEMON BEAST	41
THE SECOND COMING! HARDLY ARE THOSE WORDS OUT	402	SECOND COMING	11
WHEN A VAST IMAGE OUT OF SPIRITUS MUNDI	402	SECOND COMING	12
OUT OF THE MURDEROUS INNOCENCE OF THE SEA.	403	FOR DAUGHTER	16
WHILE THAT GREAT QUEEN, THAT ROSE OUT OF THE SPRAY,	404	FOR DAUGHTER	27
OUT OF THE MOUTH OF PLENTY'S HORN,	405	FOR DAUGHTER	60
ONCE OUT OF NATURE I SHALL NEVER TAKE	408	SAIL BYZANTIUM	25
I THOUGHT IT ALL OUT TWENTY YEARS AGO!	411	TOWER	64
BRING UP OUT OF THAT DEEP CONSIDERING MIND	413	TOWER	106
FROM A GREAT LABYRINTH OUT OF PRIDE,	413	TOWER	116
FROM SOME GREAT LABYRINTH OUT OF PRIDE,	413	TOWER V	116
UNDER ECLIPSE AND THE DAY BLOTTED OUT.	414	TOWER	120
FLOAT OUT UPON A LONG	414	TOWER	142
OUT OF HIS BITTER SOUL,	415	TOWER	151
THAT OUT OF LIFE'S OWN SELF-DELIGHT HAD SPRUNG	417	ANCEST HOUSES	11
OUT OF THE OBSCURE DARK OF THE RICH STREAMS,	417	ANCEST HOUSES	14
THAT OUT OF LIFE'S OWN SELF DELIGHT HAD SPRUNG	417	ANCEST HOUSES V	11
MY DAYS OUT OF THEIR AIMLESSNESS.	421	MY TABLE	5
A GLITTERING SWORD OUT OF THE EAST. A PUFF OF WIND	426	PHANTOM HATRED	5
REMEMBERED OUT OF BABYLONIAN ALMANACS,	426	PHANTOM HATRED	20
THE INNUMERABLE CLANGING WINGS THAT HAVE PUT OUT THE MOON.	427	PHANTOM HATRED	32
THAT THE WORST ROGUES AND RASCALS HAD DIED OUT.	428	NINETEEN 19	16
WHIRLS OUT NEW RIGHT AND WRONG,	430	NINETEEN 19	55
THE BREAST THRUST OUT IN PRIDE,	430	NINETEEN 19	66
TO BAR THAT FOUL STORM OUT, FOR WE	432	NINETEEN 19	111
AND TEAR THE HEART OUT OF HIS SIDE,	437	SONGS PLAY 1	3
OUT OF THE FABULOUS DARKNESS CALLED.	437	SONGS PLAY 1	16
OUT OF HIS SIDE.	439	FRAGMENTS	4
OUT OF A MEDIUM'S MOUTH,	439	FRAGMENTS	6
OUT OF NOTHING IT CAME,	439	FRAGMENTS	7
OUT OF THE FOREST LOAM,	439	FRAGMENTS	8
OUT OF DARK NIGHT WHERE LAY	439	FRAGMENTS	9
I BRING FULL-FLAVOURED WINE OUT OF A BARREL FOUND	442	BLACK CENTAUR	10
STRETCH OUT YOUR LIMBS AND SLEEP A LONG SATURNIAN SLEEP!	442	BLACK CENTAUR	13
I BRING FULL FLAVOURED WINE OUT OF A BARREL FOUND	442	BLACK CENTAUR V	10
NOR BEAUTY BORN OUT OF ITS OWN DESPAIR,	445	SCHOOL CHILDR	59
NOR BLEAR-EYED WISDOM OUT OF MIDNIGHT OIL.	446	SCHOOL CHILDR	60
MIRACLE-BRED OUT OF THE LIVING STONE!	446	COLONUS PRAISE	13
I WILL FIND OUT SOME CAVERN IN THE HILLS	448	HERO GIRL FOOL V	11
SHOULD FIND NO BURDEN BUT ITSELF AND YET SHOULD BE WORN	449	OWEN AHERNE	3
OUT.			
THE HEART BEHIND ITS RIB LAUGHED OUT.	450	OWEN AHERNE	13
"SPEAK ALL YOUR MIND," MY HEART SANG OUT,	450	OWEN AHERNE	21
WHEN THE MOON SAILS OUT.	451	FIRST LOVE	18
I HAVE POINTED OUT THE YELLING PACK,	453	DEATH OF HARE	1
O WHAT A BURSTING OUT THERE WAS,	457	SUMMER SPRING	13
PICK OUT MY FEATURES IN SUCH LIGHT AND SHADE	466	HARUN RASHID	116
NOR THOUGHT OUT OF HER MIND OR MINE BEGOT,	467	HARUN RASHID	140
NOR THOUGHT OUT OF HER MIND OR OUT OF MINE	467	HARUN RASHID V	140
NOR THOUGHT OUT OF HER MIND OR OUT OF MINE	467	HARUN RASHID V	140
AND THERE MARKED OUT THOSE EMBLEMS ON THE SAND	468	HARUN RASHID	156
AND THERE MARKED OUT EMBLEMS ON THE SAND	468	HARUN RASHID V	156
AND NOW MY UTMOST MYSTERY IS OUT.	469	HARUN RASHID	187
OUT OF TEN THOUSAND WINTERS, I ALONE--	470	HARUN RASHID V	190
BEFORE THAT END MUCH HAD SHE RAVELLED OUT	472	ALL SOUL NIGHT	51
HE HAD MUCH INDUSTRY AT SETTING OUT,	473	ALL SOUL NIGHT	71
PARDONED, DRAGS OUT LONELY YEARS	475	EVA GORE-BOOTH	8
ONE OR THE OTHER OUT AND SPEAK	475	EVA GORE-BOOTH	15
WHEN SUCH AS I CAST OUT REMORSE	479	SELF AND SOUL	68
ROSE OUT OF THE RACE	480	BLOOD AND MOON	4
OR OUT OF ABSTRACT HATRED, AND SHED BLOOD,	482	BLOOD AND MOON	38
MUST RAMBLE, AND THIN OUT	484	SPILT MILK	3
THAT NEVER LOOKED OUT OF THE EYE OF A SAINT	486	SEVEN SAGES	12
OR OUT OF DRUNKARD'S EYE. ALL'S WHIGGERY NOW,	486	SEVEN SAGES	13
OR OUT OF A DRUNKARD'S EYE. ALL'S WHIGGERY NOW,	486	SEVEN SAGES V	13
BUT WE OLD MEN ARE OUT AGAINST THE WORLD.	486	SEVEN SAGES V	14
OR OUT OF FOLLY INTO FOLLY CAME.	491	COOLE BALLYLEE	32
IN LUCK OR OUT THE TOIL HAS LEFT ITS MARK!	491	COOLE BALLYLEE V	40F
IN LUCK OR OUT THE TOIL HAS LEFT ITS MARK!	495	CHOICE	6
A RIVERY FIELD SPREAD OUT BELOW,	502	VACILLATION	57

		PAGE	TITLE	LINE
OUT (CONTINUED)

	PAGE	TITLE	LINE
SEEK OUT REALITY, LEAVE THINGS THAT SEEM.	502	VACILLATION	72
HAD SCOOPED OUT PHARAOH'S MUMMY. I--THOUGH HEART MIGHT FIND RELIEF	503	VACILLATION	84
BUT I HAVE STRAIGHTENED OUT	505	RESULT THOUGHT	7
OUT OF IRELAND HAVE WE COME.	506	REMORSE SPEECH	11
WANDERS OUT INTO THE NIGHT	508	JANE BISHOP	25
MAY CALL A CURSE OUT OF THE SKY	508	JANE BISHOP V	4
I WENT OUT ALONE	515	GIRLS SONG B	1
THAT OUT OF ROCK, ...	518	HIS CONFIDENCE	10
OUT OF A DESOLATE SOURCE, ...	518	HIS CONFIDENCE	11
BUT SOMETHING BORE THEM OUT OF SIGHT	519	HER DREAM	5
I THOUGHT IT OUT THIS VERY DAY, ...	525	DANCING DAYS	17
"COME OUT OF CHARITY, ...	526	AM OF IRELAND	4
"COME OUT OF CHARITY, ...	527	AM OF IRELAND	17
"COME OUT OF CHARITY, ...	527	AM OF IRELAND	30
THINGS OUT OF PERFECTION SAIL, ...	530	OLD TOM AGAIN	1
THAT STEPPED OUT OF THEIR CLOTHES.	538	LAST CONFESS	14
HEAVEN AND EARTH OUT OF THEIR PLACES, ...	540	FROM ANTIGONE	8
CUT OUT HIS HEART. SOME MASTER OF DESIGN	541	PARN FUNERAL 1	14
BRED OUT OF THE CONTAGION OF THE THRONG, ...	542	PARN FUNERAL 1	27
HE DID IT OUT OF PRIDE.	545	TO SAME TUNE 1	26
TIME FOR US ALL TO PICK OUT A GOOD TUNE, ...	548	TO SAME TUNE 3	13
OUT OF BEN BULBEN AND KNOCKNAREA, ...	549	SEVERED HEAD	2
OUT OF THE GRAVE. SADDLE AND RIDE	549	SEVERED HEAD V	4
I HAD THOUGHT TO HAVE CALLED HER OUT TO THE DOOR, ...	551	SONGS REWRIT 1 V	15
I PRAY--FOR FASHION'S WORD IS OUT	553	PRAYER OLD AGE	9
THOSE AMOROUS CRIES THAT OUT OF QUIET COME	557	RIBH ECSTASY	7
A PASSION-DRIVEN EXULTANT MAN SINGS OUT	560	WHENCE COME	5
CAME OUT OF A NEEDLE'S EYE	562	NEEDLES EYE	2
AND ANCIENT LINEAMENTS ARE BLOTTED OUT.	564	GYRES	4
WHAT MATTER? OUT OF CAVERN COMES A VOICE, ...	564	GYRES	15
WHAT MATTER? OUT OF CAVERN COME A VOICE	564	GYRES V	15
AEROPLANE AND ZEPPELIN WILL COME OUT, ...	565	LAPIS LAZULI	6
BLACK OUT; HEAVEN BLAZING INTO THE HEAD!	566	LAPIS LAZULI	19
ESCAPED OUT OF HER CROWD, ...	568	SWEET DANCER	5
OR OUT OF HER BLACK CLOUD.	568	SWEET DANCER	6
OUT OF ALL HARM, ...	574	MAIDS 1ST SONG	8
"THIS LAND OF SAINTS," AND THEN AS THE APPLAUSE DIED OUT,	577	LOFTY THINGS	3
AND WHEN I PAY ATTENTION I MUST OUT AND WALK	581	CURSE CROMWELL	29
THEY GAVE IT OUT TO ALL THE WORLD, ...	582	ROGER CASEMENT	11
AND COPIED OUT WHAT I COULD READ	584	GHOST ROG CASE	33
HE WROTE OUT THAT WORD HIMSELF.	585	ORAHILLY	7
OUT OF THAT CRAZY FIGHT!	585	ORAHILLY	15
CAN BURN OUT THAT SUFFERING	589	OLD WICKED MAN	57
SOME TWENTY FEET FROM TIP TO TIP HAD IT STRETCHED RIGHTLY OUT.	593	PILGRIM	17
SOME TWENTY FEET FROM TIP TO TIP HAD ITS WINGS STRETCHED RIGHTLY OUT,	593	PILGRIM V	17
THE COLONEL WENT OUT SAILING, ...	594	COLONEL MARTIN	1
THE COLONEL WENT OUT SAILING.	594	COLONEL MARTIN	9
THE COLONEL WENT OUT SAILING.	594	COLONEL MARTIN	18
THE COLONEL WENT OUT SAILING.	595	COLONEL MARTIN	27
THE COLONEL WENT OUT SAILING.	595	COLONEL MARTIN	36
THE COLONEL WENT OUT SAILING.	596	COLONEL MARTIN	45
THE COLONEL WENT OUT SAILING.	596	COLONEL MARTIN	54
THE COLONEL WENT OUT SAILING.	596	COLONEL MARTIN	63
AND TOM MAKE OUT A LIVING	597	COLONEL MARTIN	70
THE COLONEL WENT OUT SAILING.	597	COLONEL MARTIN	72
WHEN TOM MADE OUT A LIVING	597	COLONEL MARTIN V	70
(AN IMAGE OUT OF SPENSER AND THE COMMON TONGUE). . . .	603	GALLERY REVIS	40
AND OUT AND LAY OUR LEADERSHIP	606	SONGS BURDEN 1	23
BUT HAD GONE OUT TO DIE	608	SONGS BURDEN 3	20
AND RATTLED OUT A TUNE!	616	MARCH SONGS 3	9
AND RATTLED OUT A TUNE!	616	MARCH SONGS 3	19
HE DID IT OUT OF PRIDE.	616	MARCH SONGS 3	26
AND RATTLED OUT A TUNE!	616	MARCH SONGS 3	29
KEEP THOSE CHILDREN OUT.	618	LONG-LEG FLY	24
IMAGINATION TO THAT PITCH WHERE IT CASTS OUT	619	BRONZE HEAD	19
THEN CLEANING OUT AND BANDAGING OF WOUNDS, ...	622	HOUND VOICE	20
WHAT HURRIES OUT THE KNAVE AND DOLT?	625	NATIVITY	9
RICHES DROVE OUT RANK.	626	STATES HOLIDAY	2
BASE DROVE OUT THE BETTER BLOOD, ...	626	STATES HOLIDAY	3
WITH A HAT OUT OF FASHION, ...	627	STATES HOLIDAY	29
I LAY STRETCHED OUT IN THE DIRT	628	JANE MOUNTAIN	21
AND THEN A COUNTER-TRUTH FILLED OUT ITS PLAY, ...	629	CIRCUS ANIMALS	17
GREW IN PURE MIND, BUT OUT OF WHAT BEGAN?	630	CIRCUS ANIMALS	34
DID THAT PLAY OF MINE SEND OUT	632	MAN AND ECHO	11
OUT OF INTELLECT AND SIGHT	633	MAN AND ECHO	35
DROPPING OUT OF SKY OR ROCK, ...	633	MAN AND ECHO	44
A STRICKEN RABBIT IS CRYING OUT, ...	633	MAN AND ECHO	45
EYES STARED OUT OF THE BRANCHES AND WERE GONE.	634	CUCHULAIN COMF	3
ALL OUT OF SHAPE FROM TOE TO TOP, ...	639	BEN BULBEN	71
BEAT OUT THEIR LIVES LAMENTING O'ER THE SAND;	652	ISLE STAT I 2	14
OUT OF THE AIR. AND WHEN? WHEN THE SUN GOES DOWN . .	652	ISLE STAT I 2	29
AND MEASURE OUT THE WAYS OF CHIVALRY.	660	ISLE STAT II 1	37
OF LOVE FROM OUT A DREAMLESS RACE FOR STRIFE, ...	684	SEEKER	58
FAR OUT UPON THE WATER WORLD AND RINGED	693	MOSADA 1	80
I'LL SEE HIM LONGER IF I STAND OUT HERE	703	MOSADA 3	113
HAS FLICKERED AND GONE OUT. I AM NOT WELL.	704	MOSADA 3	129
REMEMBERING THEE, I SEARCH OUT THESE FAINT FLOWERS . . .	704	REMEMBRANCE	1

591

		PAGE	TITLE	LINE

OUT   (CONTINUED)

HE WHISPERS TO A SOLDIER, WHO GOES OUT-- . . . .   711 FERENCZ RENYI   44
THEN THE STARS GROW OUT OF HEAVEN WITH THEIR COUNTENANCES   719 PHANTOM SHIP   30
    FAIR.
TO THOSE YOUR "MELLOW" WARES HAVE WEARIED OUT.   721 WITCH VIVIEN   27
OUT OF A NEIGHBOURING BUNCH OF HEATHER; . . . .   728 PRIEST FAIRY   20
MUST SPREAD OUT THEIR WINGS UNTIRING, ...   739 WHERE BOOKS GO   3
LIKE A GREY OWL MEN HARRY OUT . . . .   740 EARL PAUL   23
CAST OUT ALL HOPE, CAST OUT ALL FEAR, ...   743 DANAAN QUICK   25
CAST OUT ALL HOPE, CAST OUT ALL FEAR, ...   743 DANAAN QUICK   25
BUT WEAVING IT OUT OF THREADS . . . .   743 WISDOM DREAMS   3
OUT OF THAT ISLAND WHERE THE FOOL OF THE WOOD . . . . .   747 SHADOW WATER A   2
HIS HEART'S DESIRE WHERE THE WORLD DWINDLES OUT? . . .   747 SHADOW WATER A   13
THREE MOONS. IT WERE BEST TO KILL HIM, AND CHOOSE OUT   748 SHADOW WATER A   15
TIME AND THE WORLD AND ALL THINGS DWINDLE OUT. . . . .   749 SHADOW WATER A   47
AND THEN SMOOTH OUT WITH IVORY HANDS AND SIGH. . . . .   750 SHADOW WATER A   70
FORGAEL, SEEK OUT CONTENT, WHERE OTHER MEN . . . .   750 SHADOW WATER A   71
THE FOOL THAT CAME OUT OF THE WINTRY WOOD . . . . .   750 SHADOW WATER A   75
OUT OF MERE WANTONNESS TO LURE A SAIL . . . . . .   750 SHADOW WATER A   79
THEY ARE CHANGED AND AS GREY BIRDS FLY OUT TO SEA, . . .   750 SHADOW WATER A   82
MAKE GALLEYS OUT OF WIND THAT CHANGE TO WIND . . . .   751 SHADOW WATER A   105
NOW RUSH UPON HER AND FIND OUT WHAT PREY . . . . .   752 SHADOW WATER A   130
I SHALL FIND OUT IF I HAVE LOST MY WAY . . . . . .   753 SHADOW WATER A   137
I SHALL FIND OUT IF I HAVE LOST THE WAY . . . . .   753 SHADOW WATER A V   137
AND SHE CRIES OUT, "I HAVE FLED TO MY BELOVED . . . .   754 SHADOW WATER A   151
THIS BLADE OUT OF MY HAND AND DIED OF A SUDDEN. . . . .   755 SHADOW WATER A   168
SHE CAUGHT THIS BLADE OUT OF MY BELT AND DIED. . . . .   755 SHADOW WATER A V   168
I SWEAR IT. LET EVERY MAN DRAW OUT HIS SWORD. . . . .   758 SHADOW WATER A   230
STRIKE QUICKLY; IT WILL FADE OUT WHEN YOU STRIKE. . . .   759 SHADOW WATER A   238
WHEN SHE DREAMT FIRST OF LOVE, SHALL FLICKER OUT . . .   760 SHADOW WATER A   257
WHEN SHE DREAMED FIRST OF LOVE, SHALL FLICKER OUT . . .   760 SHADOW WATER A V   257
THE WHITE FOOL MAKES AT MORNING OUT OF FOAM; . . . .   761 SHADOW WATER A   261
I WILL DRINK OUT OF THE STREAM. THE STREAM IS GONE! .   761 SHADOW WATER A   273
BREATHED OUT A DRUID VAPOUR, AND CRUMBLED AWAY . . .   761 SHADOW WATER A   279
EDAINE CAME OUT OF MIDHER'S HILL, AND LAY . . . . .   762 SHADOW WATER A   296
SWEET WITH ALL MUSIC, OUT OF HIS LONG HAIR, ...   762 SHADOW WATER A   303
MADE OF DIM GOLD, RAVE OUT IN SECRET TOMBS. . . . .   765 SHADOW WATER A   345
TO SNATCH ALIVE OUT OF THE STREAMS ALL LOVERS . . . .   765 SHADOW WATER A   347
WE WILL FIND OUT VALLEYS AND WOODS AND MEADOWS . . .   767 SHADOW WATER A   388
OUT OF THEIR HATRED. MY BELOVED, FAREWELL. . . . .   767 SHADOW WATER A   400
HAVE FALLEN AND MY SUN AND MOON GONE OUT. . . . . .   767 SHADOW WATER A V   405
MY LOVE SHAKES OUT HER HAIR UPON THE STREAMS . . . .   768 SHADOW WATER A   416
HAD WOVEN HER OF WIND. LIFE WITHERS OUT . . . .   768 SHADOW WATER A V   423
OUT OF A RUNNING STREAM, O MORNING STAR . . . .   769 SHADOW WATER A   426
THE HARP-STRINGS HAVE BEGUN TO CRY OUT TO THE EAGLES.   769 SHADOW WATER A   431
UPON THIS WORLD NO LONGER. THE HARP CRIES OUT. . . .   769 SHADOW WATER A V   430
IT HAS BEGUN TO CRY OUT TO THE EAGLES. . . . . .   769 SHADOW WATER A V   431
OR THE GANNETS CALLING OUT . . . .   772 SONG DEIRDRE 1   5
BORN OUT OF IMMODERATE THOUGHT; . . . .   772 SONG DEIRDRE 1   12
MAY THIS FIRE HAVE DRIVEN OUT . . . .   775 AGAINST WITCH   1
OUT OF MEMORY AND MIND. . . . .   775 AGAINST WITCH   10
MAY THIS FLAME HAVE DRIVEN OUT . . . .   775 AGAINST WITCH V   1
THAT IS MADE OUT OF THE GREASE . . . .   776 AGAINST WITCH   24
THAT DIES OUT BEFORE 'TIS DAY, ...   777 SONG DEIRDRE 2   8
CRIES OUT THE EMPTY WELL. . . . .   780 WELL AND TREE   2
CRIES OUT THE LEAFLESS TREE, ...   780 WELL AND TREE   10
THE DREAMING BONES CRY OUT . . . .   782 HEART FRIGHT   15
THE WINDS OUT OF CLARE-GALWAY . . . .   783 GREY ROUND   4
THE STARS ARE OUT OF SIGHT. . . . .   786 YOUR HEART   34
I MOCK AT ALL SO BURNING OUT. . . . .   787 HUDDON DUDDON   15
BUT HOW THEY MOCK US BURNING OUT. . . . .   787 HUDDON DUDDON V   15

OUTBALANCE

IN THE OLD ROOMS; NIGHT CAN OUTBALANCE DAY, ...   435 NEW FACES   6

OUT-BURN

AS ARGIVE CLYTEMNESTRA SAW OUT-BURN . . . . . .   645 ISLE STAT I 1   12

OUTCRIES

THE UNAVAILING OUTCRIES AND THE OLD BITTERNESS . . .   198 SEVEN WOODS   4

OUTCRY

OUTCRY OF BATS. AND THEN YOUNG NIAMH CAME . . . .   44 OISIN 2   229

OUTDANCED

SO SHE HAD OUTDANCED THOUGHT. . . . .   383 VISION ROBART   39

OUTER

THE GLASS OF OUTER WEARINESS, ...   135 TWO TREES   31
TO THAT SMALL CHAMBER BY THE OUTER GATE. . . . .   181 QUEEN MAEVE   44
THE FLAMING CIRCLE OF THE OUTER LAW, ...   689 NETTLESHIP   13
AND PASSED THE OUTER HEBRIDES, AND TOOK . . . .   749 SHADOW WATER A   42

OUTGREW

BUT OUTGREW THAT SCHOOL, ...   506 REMORSE SPEECH   2

OUTLANDISH

A CERTAIN POET IN OUTLANDISH CLOTHES . . . . . .   180 QUEEN MAEVE   1
IN SOME OUTLANDISH COAT BESIDE . . . .   303 HOUR DAWN   V   28
IN THAT OUTLANDISH GEAR, ...   526 AM OF IRELAND   7

OUTLAWED

AND TOADS AND EVERY OUTLAWED THING . . . . . .   85 MAD KING GOLL   V   61

OUTLAWS

THE SONG OF OUTLAWS AND THEIR FEAR; . . . . .   85 MAD KING GOLL   V   64

OUTLIVE

AS THOSE THAT CAN OUTLIVE THE MOON HAVE KNOWN IT,   230 SHADOW WATER B   193
AS THOSE THAT CAN OUTLIVE THE MOON HAVE SHOWN IT,   230 SHADOW WATER B V   193
FROM LASTING WATCHERS, THAT OUTLIVE THE MOON, . . .   236 SHADOW WATER B   320
WHERE NO CHILD'S BORN BUT TO OUTLIVE THE MOON." . . .   247 SHADOW WATER B   531

OUTLIVE   (CONTINUED)
    WE THOUGHT IT WOULD OUTLIVE ALL FUTURE DAYS. . . . . .   428 NINETEEN 19   14
    THOU SHALT OUTLIVE THINE AMOROUS HAPPY TIME, ...   674 ISLE STAT II 3   203
OUTLIVEST
    WHY THOU OUTLIVEST, BLIND AND HOARY, ...   2 OISIN 1   V   2
OUT-LIVING
    IN DAY OUT-LIVING BATTLE, ON THE BREAST . . . .   750 SHADOW WATER A   73
OUTRAGEOUS
    AND THE OUTRAGEOUS CANNON, ...   317 NIGHT COME   10
    BUT AS THE OUTRAGEOUS STARS INCLINE . . . .   325 ROBERT GREGORY   38
    THE OUTRAGEOUS WAR SHALL FADE; . . . .   342 SHEP GOATHERD   100
OUTRAN
    AND YET HIS MIND OUTRAN THE HORSES' FEET. . . . . . .   326 ROBERT GREGORY   64
OUTRIDDEN
    HE HAD OUTRIDDEN HIS WAR-WASTED MEN . . . .   277 TWO KINGS   3
OUT-RIDDEN
    HE HAD OUT-RIDDEN HIS WAR-WASTED MEN . . . .   277 TWO KINGS   V   3
OUTRIGHT
    O NEVER GIVE THE HEART OUTRIGHT, ...   202 NEVER GIVE ALL   8
OUTRODE
    OUTRODE HIS TROOP THAT AFTER TWELVE MONTHS' WAR . . . .   276 TWO KINGS   V   1
OUTRUN
    OUTRUN THE MEASURE. I'D TELL OF THAT GREAT QUEEN . . .   187 QUEEN MAEVE   141
OUT-SCREAMS
    OUT-SCREAMS THE WHOLE SHELF; "ALTHOUGH . . . .   319 DOLLS   7
OUTSIDE
    THAT EVERYTHING OUTSIDE US IS . . . .   523 MAD AS MIST   5
    A LITTLE BOY OUTSIDE THE SYCAMORE WOOD . . . .   715 DWELT SYCAMORE   1
OUT-SPREAD
    AND OUT-SPREAD ARMS. BE NOT SO PALE, DEAR LOVE. . . . .   701 MOSADA 3   70
OUTWEIGH
    AND IS THEIR LOGIC TO OUTWEIGH . . . .   395 SIXTEEN DEAD   11
OUTWEIGHED
    OUTWEIGHED ALL OTHER YEARS, YOU SAID, ...   791 REPRISALS   6
OUTWORN
    THESE NOW OUTWORN AND WITHERED HANDS . . . .   23 OISIN 1   349
    OUTWORN HEART IN A TIME OUTWORN, ...   147 INTO TWILIGHT V 1
    OUTWORN HEART IN A TIME OUTWORN, ...   147 INTO TWILIGHT V 1
OUT-WORN
    OUT-WORN HEART, IN A TIME OUT-WORN, ...   147 INTO TWILIGHT   1
    OUT-WORN HEART, IN A TIME OUT-WORN, ...   147 INTO TWILIGHT   1
OVEN
    AND AFTER BAKED IT SLOWLY IN AN OVEN; BUT NOW . . . . .   442 BLACK CENTAUR   9
OVER
    OVER THE GLOSSY SEA." "O, WILD . . . . . .   6 OISIN 1   V 58
    WE GALLOPED OVER THE GLOSSY SEA; . . . .   11 OISIN 1   132
    HURRIED AWAY, AND OVER HER RAISED . . . .   12 OISIN 1   V 142B
    BLEW ONE LONG NOTE. FROM OVER REED . . . .   14 OISIN 1   V 195
    OVER THE BARE AND WOODY LAND, ...   15 OISIN 1   198
    AND, WEEPING OVER THE WHITE STRINGS, HURLED . . . . .   17 OISIN 1   241
    A FIRWOOD HOUSE, ALL COVERED OVER . . . .   17 OISIN 1   V 248
    AND BENDING OVER THEM SOFTLY SAID, ...   21 OISIN 1   307
    BENDING OVER THEM IN THE DANCE, ...   21 OISIN 1   308
    FOR WE KNEW WELL THE OLD WAS OVER. . . . .   25 OISIN 1   379
    OVER THE GLIMMERING PURPLE SEA. . . . .   25 OISIN 1   384
    FOR WELL WE KNEW THE OLD WAS OVER, ...   25 OISIN 1   V 379
    HE HATH OVER LINGERED HIS WELCOME; THE DAYS, ...   27 OISIN 1   V 406
    LIKE A BRIDE BENDING OVER HER MIRROR ADORNING, ...   28 OISIN 1   V 423E
    THE ISLE WAS OVER NOW AND GONE; . . . .   28 OISIN 1   V 427B
    I LAY, AS OVER SEA THE LIGHT HOOVES GLANCED . . . . .   30 OISIN 2   V 19A
    DARK STATUES GLIMMERED OVER THE PALE TIDE . . . . .   31 OISIN 2   36
    "IS HE SO DREADFUL?" "BE NOT OVER BOLD, ...   35 OISIN 2   V 88
    'TIS OVER; FAR WITH MEMORY I SWAY AND ROCK. . . . .   43 OISIN 2   V 212
    I MOUNTED, AND WE PASSED OVER THE LONE . . . . . .   45 OISIN 2   231
    AND NEVER A SONG SANG NIAMH, AND OVER MY FINGER-TIPS . .   47 OISIN 3   6
    GREY SAND ON THE GREEN OF THE GRASSES AND OVER THE DRIPPING   48 OISIN 3   14
        TREES,
    GREY SANDS ON THE GREEN OF THE GRASSES AND OVER THE   48 OISIN 3   V 14
        DRIPPING TREES,
    AND OVER THE LIMBS AND THE VALLEY THE SLOW OWLS WANDERED   49 OISIN 3   41
        AND CAME,
    SQUARE LEAVES OF THE IVY MOVED OVER US, BINDING US DOWN   52 OISIN 3   76
        TO OUR REST.
    AND SOFTLY COME TO YOUR NIAMH OVER THE TOPS OF THE TIDE;   55 OISIN 3   126
    AND SOFTLY COME TO THY NIAM OVER THE TOPS OF THE TIDE; . .   52 OISIN 3   V 126
    IN A REVERIE FORGETFUL OF ALL THINGS, OVER THE BUBBLING   56 OISIN 3   140
        GROUND.
    IN REVERIE FORGETFUL OF ALL THINGS, OVER THE BUBBLING   56 OISIN 3   V 140
        GROUND.
    GREY SAND ON THE GREEN OF THE GRASSES AND OVER THE DRIPPING   57 OISIN 3   142
        TREES,
    GREY SANDS ON THE GREEN OF THE GRASSES AND OVER THE   57 OISIN 3   V 142
        DRIPPING TREES,
    AND RODE ON TILL OVER THE WORLD'S RIM FLOATED THE SEA'S   60 OISIN 3   V 183
        OLD SHOUT,
    . . . AND MARCH ON AS OXEN MOVE OVER YOUNG GRASS; . . .   62 OISIN 3   211
    AND OVER IS THEIR ANTIQUE JOY; . . . .   64 HAPPY SHEPHERD   2
    AND LIFE IS OVER SAVE THE MURMUR AND THE SWEETNESS. . . .   77 INDIAN TO LOVE V 5E
    AND ALL IS OVER SAVE THE MURMUR AND THE SWEETNESS. . . .   77 INDIAN TO LOVE V 5E
    AUTUMN IS OVER THE LONG LEAVES THAT LOVE US, ...   79 FALLING LEAVES   1
    AND OVER THE MICE IN THE BARLEY SHEAVES; . . . . . .   79 FALLING LEAVES   2

OVER (CONTINUED)

AUTUMN WAS OVER HIM; AND NOW THEY STOOD	80	EPHEMERA	16
OVER THE HEATH AND SPONGY FEN,	83	MAD KING GOLL V	32
OVER THE YOUNG STREAMS.	88	STOLEN CHILD	37
HE BADE THEM GIVE OVER THEIR KEENING;	93	FATHER OHART	23
OVER THE DOOR-STEP INTO THE AIR,	97	FOXHUNTER V	3
ALL THE HEAVY DAYS ARE OVER;	124	CATHLEEN PARA	1
AH, EXILES WANDERING OVER LANDS AND SEAS,	129	BOOK STORIES	9
AH, EXILES, WANDERING OVER MANY SEAS,	129	BOOK STORIES V	9
AH, EXILES, WANDERING OVER MANY LANDS,	130	BOOK STORIES V	17
AND OVER THE GRAVE OF CLOOTH-NA-BARE;	140	HOSTING SIDHE	2
OVER THE LITTLE SILVER CORDS,	146	FISH	6
DESOLATE WINDS THAT CRY OVER THE WANDERING SEA;	147	UNAPPEAS HOST	7
AND THEIR DAY GOES OVER IN IDLENESS,	151	OLD MOTHER	7
OVER MY HEART, AND YOUR HAIR FALL OVER MY BREAST,	154	BELOVED PEACE	10
OVER MY HEART, AND YOUR HAIR FALL OVER MY BREAST,	154	BELOVED PEACE	10
OVER MY HEART, AND YOUR HAIR FALL ABOUT MY BREAST	154	BELOVED PEACE V	10
THAT WAS SHAKEN OUT OVER MY BREAST!	155	REPROVE CURLEW	5
THRONE OVER THRONE WHERE IN HALF SLEEP,	156	FORGOT BEAUTY	22
COVER OVER AND HIDE, FOR HE HAS NO PART	158	TO HIS HEART	6
WE WILL BEND DOWN AND LOOSEN OUR HAIR OVER YOU,	172	TRAV PASSION	6
A WALL BEHIND HIS BACK, OVER HIS HEAD	180	QUEEN MAEVE	5
SHE COULD HAVE CALLED OVER THE RIM OF THE WORLD	181	QUEEN MAEVE	23
OVER THE WHITE-HORNED BULL AND THE BROWN BULL.	182	QUEEN MAEVE	58
BUT OUT OF THE DARK AIR OVER HER HEAD THERE CAME	187	QUEEN MAEVE	153
IN MUIRTHEMNE, AND OVER IT	194	BAILE AILLINN	116
WERE HOVERING OVER THE HARP-STRINGS	195	BAILE AILLINN	141
WERE HOVERING OVER THE HARP STRINGS	195	BAILE AILLINN V	141
WHILE OVER THEM BIRDS OF AENGUS FLY,	197	BAILE AILLINN	182
AND OVER THE TILLER AND THE PROW,	197	BAILE AILLINN	183
A CLOUDY QUIVER OVER PAIRC-NA-LEE.	198	SEVEN WOODS	14
TIME CAN BUT MAKE HER BEAUTY OVER AGAIN!	200	FOLLY COMFORT	8
THE OLD BROWN THORN-TREES BREAK IN TWO HIGH OVER CUMMEN STRAND,	206	HANRAHANS SONG	1
THE OLD BROWN THORN TREES BREAK IN TWO HIGH OVER CUMANN'S STRAND,	206	HANRAHANS SONG V	1
THE WIND HAS BUNDLED UP THE CLOUDS HIGH OVER KNOCKNAREA,	207	HANRAHANS SONG	6
THE WINDS HAVE BUNDLED UP THE CLOUDS HIGH OVER KNOCKNAREA	207	HANRAHANS SONG V	6
OVER THE RAMPARTS AND THE TOWERS,	212	BLESS PSALTER	6
RIVERS ARE RUNNING OVER	214	HAPPY TOWNLAND	7
WHERE RIVERS ARE RUNNING OVER	214	HAPPY TOWNLAND V	7
AND FROM THAT HOUR HE HAS WATCHED OVER NONE	220	HARP OF AENGUS	13
WHEN IT IS OVER, NOR ONE TO GRUMBLE AT US.	225	SHADOW WATER B	67
THEY HOVER OVER THE MASTHEAD AWHILE	233	SHADOW WATER B	246
CIRCLING AND CIRCLING OVER THE MASTHEAD?	234	SHADOW WATER B	266
HE HAS PUT A SUDDEN DARKNESS OVER THE MOON.	239	SHADOW WATER B	367
THEY HAVE BEEN CIRCLING OVER OUR HEADS IN THE AIR,	247	SHADOW WATER B	525
THROUGH BUSH THEY PLUNGED AND OVER IVIED ROOT,	278	TWO KINGS	32
I GROPED MY WAY THROUGH BOUGHS, AND OVER ROOTS,	283	TWO KINGS V	139
AS I CAME OVER WINDY GAP	300	RUN PARADISE	1
THEY TOPPLED OVER. "WERE IT NOT	302	HOUR DAWN	17
CONFUSION OF THE DEATH-BED OVER, IS IT SENT	316	COLD HEAVEN	10
AND LAUGH OVER THE UNTROUBLED WATER	330	BONE OF A HARE	14
WHEN HER SON'S TURN WAS OVER. SING YOUR SONG.	340	SHEP GOATHERD	42
HOVERING OVER THE WOOD	349	HAWK	10
OVER SOME SILKEN DRESS	363	DOLLS DRAWINGS	7
AND WHEN AT LAST THAT MURDER'S OVER	388	SOLOMON WITCH	24
COWARDICE, OVER SOME SILLY SUBTLE THOUGHT	413	TOWER V	117
A MIST THAT IS LIKE BLOWN SNOW IS SWEEPING OVER ALL,	425	PHANTOM HATRED	2
OVER THE BLACKENED EARTH	496	MOHINI CHATTER	21
THAT MEN PASS OVER	512	JANE ON GOD	21
MEN HAVE PASSED OVER	512	JANE ON GOD V	21
OVER THEM FLIES A LONG-LEGGED BIRD,	566	LAPIS LAZULI	39
I WALK IN A BATTLE FOUGHT OVER AGAIN,	591	WHAT WAS LOST	2
WHO QUARRELS OVER HALFPENNIES	621	JOHN KINSELLA	33
WHO QUARRELS OVER HALF-PENNIES	621	JOHN KINSELLA V	33
AND OUR LAUGHTER OVER AND DONE!	643	SONG FAERIES	6
OVER THE LAKE THE WATER-FLOWERS	647	ISLE STAT I 1	66
OVER THEM CRIMSON VAPOURS WINGING.	648	ISLE STAT I 1	92
BUT WHENCE, AND WHEN? OVER THE WILLOWS SERE	652	ISLE STAT I 2	28
OVER THE CROWN OF THE WILLOWS BROWN.	653	ISLE STAT I 2	30
OVER THE CROWN OF THE WILLOWS BROWN.	653	ISLE STAT I 2	51
OF THINE CRY OVER WOLD AND WATER WHITE,	669	ISLE STAT II 3	73
AND OUR LAUGHTER OVER AND DONE!	676	ISLE STAT II 3	253
A CREEPING HORROR IS ALL OVER ME.	681	SEEKER	12
OVER HER SPOTTED FLESH AND FLYING HAIR	687	TWO TITANS	15
AND OVER TILLAGE FIELDS AND PASTURE LANDS	715	FERENCZ RENYI	120
OVER THE SORREL-COVERED WOLD—	716	FAIRY DOCTOR	2
OVER THE BEADS OF HIS ROSARY.	730	PRIEST FAIRY	52
NOT EVEN "I LONG TO SEE THY LONGING OVER,"	734	QUATRAIN APHOR	11
THE YEARS THAT HAVE GONE OVER HER FROM THE HOUR	760	SHADOW WATER A	256
SHOOK THE PALE APPLE-BLOSSOM OVER IT;	761	SHADOW WATER A	275
SHOOK THE PALE APPLE BLOSSOM OVER IT;	761	SHADOW WATER A	275
O, AENGUS OF THE HERDS, WATCH OVER ME!	762	SHADOW WATER A	291
HE WATCHES OVER NONE BUT FAITHFUL LOVERS.	762	SHADOW WATER A	295
AND FROM THAT HOUR HE HAS WATCHED OVER NONE	763	SHADOW WATER A	308
THAT I WOULD SHED LIKE TWILIGHT OVER YOU,	765	SHADOW WATER A	352
AND TELL ITS STORY OVER THEIR BROWN ALE.	767	SHADOW WATER A	393
IN THE TOWER OVER HEAD,	772	SONG DEIRDRE 1 V	3
TO THE TOWER OVER HEAD,	772	SONG DEIRDRE 1 V	3

OVERBOARD
    OLD MERCHANT SKIPPER THAT LEAPED OVERBOARD . . . . . .   270 PARDON FATHERS   13
    YOU MERCHANT SKIPPER THAT LEAPED OVERBOARD . . . . . .   270 PARDON FATHERS V   13
    AND MERCHANT SKIPPER THAT LEAPED OVERBOARD . . . . . .   270 PARDON FATHERS V   13
OVER-BOLD
    "IS HE SO DREADFUL?" "BE NOT OVER-BOLD, ...   35 OISIN 2   88
OVERBURTHENED
    UNTIL THE OVERBURTHENED MOON IS DEAD. . . . . . .   231 SHADOW WATER B   218
OVERCOME
    TILL GERMANY'S OVERCOME! . . . .   395 SIXTEEN DEAD   8
    OVERCOME--O BITTER SWEETNESS, ...   540 FROM ANTIGONE   1
    OVERCOME GODS UPON PARNASSUS! . . . .   540 FROM ANTIGONE   6
    OVERCOME THE EMPYREAN! HURL . . . .   540 FROM ANTIGONE   7
    WOULD OVERCOME YOUR SORROW AND YOUR DREAMS. . . . . .   749 SHADOW WATER A   52
OVERFLOW
    THEY OVERFLOW THE HILLS, ...   781 MY HEART BEAT   12
OVERFLOWED
    THE YELLOW POOL HAS OVERFLOWED HIGH UP ON CLOOTH-NA-BARE,   207 HANRAHANS SONG   11
    THE YELLOW POOL HAS OVERFLOWED HIGH UPON CLOOTH-NA-BARE,   207 HANRAHANS SONG V   11
OVERFLOWS
    LIFE OVERFLOWS WITHOUT AMBITIOUS PAINS! . . . . . .   417 ANCEST HOUSES   3
    SUCH FULLNESS IN THAT QUARTER OVERFLOWS . . . . . .   478 SELF AND SOUL   33
OVERHEAD
    THE DARKNESS COMES. A CLOUD HANGS OVERHEAD-- . . . . .   43 OISIN 2   V 208A
    AND PACED UPON THE MOUNTAINS OVERHEAD . . . . . .   121 YOU ARE OLD   11
    FROM A BOUGH OVERHEAD, ...   215 HAPPY TOWNLAND   42
    I'VE HEARD A RUSTLING OVERHEAD IN THE WIND. . . . .   223 SHADOW WATER B   28
    A MEANING IN THAT CIRCLING OVERHEAD? . . . .   234 SHADOW WATER B   270
    NOR GAVE GOD THANKS TILL OVERHEAD . . . .   307 HOUR DAWN   121
    AND GAVE GOD THANKS THAT OVERHEAD . . . .   307 HOUR DAWN   V 121
    NOTHING BUT DARKNESS OVERHEAD. . . . .   314 MEMORY YOUTH   14
    THE SACRED MOON OVERHEAD . . . .   379 CAT AND MOON   19
    TO THE TOWER OVERHEAD, ...   772 SONG DEIRDRE 1   3
OVER-LINGERED
    HE HAS OVER-LINGERED HIS WELCOME! THE DAYS, ...   26 OISIN 1   402
OVERLOOKS
    OR ELSE AT MEADOW OR AT GRAZING OVERLOOKS . . . . .   340 SHEP GOATHERD   37
OVERMUCH
    BEING MADE BEAUTIFUL OVERMUCH, ...   403 FOR DAUGHTER   20
OVER-MUCH
    NOTHING THAT WE LOVE OVER-MUCH . . . .   399 BREAK OF DAY   17
OVER-NIMBLE
    THOU HAST AN OVER-NIMBLE TONGUE. THY GRIEF, ...   661 ISLE STAT II 1   59
OVERPOWER
    AND OVERPOWER THE CREW WHILE YET ASLEEP! . . . . .   233 SHADOW WATER B   240
OVERSEA
    THOUSANDS OF LEAGUES OVERSEA, ...   341 SHEP GOATHERD   63
OVER-SEA
    FOR ALL HER WANDERINGS OVER-SEA! . . . .   197 BAILE AILLINN   203
OVER-SUBTLE
    COWARDICE, SOME SILLY OVER-SUBTLE THOUGHT . . . . .   413 TOWER   117
OVERTHREW
    WOULD THAT THE STORM THAT OVERTHREW MY SHIPS, ...   235 SHADOW WATER B   286
    AND HARRIED ALBAN TOWNS, AND OVERTHREW . . . . . .   749 SHADOW WATER A   40
OVERTHROW
    WILL OVERTHROW HIS SHADOWS AND CARRY OFF . . . . .   184 QUEEN MAEVE   95
OVERTHROWN
    THAT ALL BE OVERTHROWN. . . . .   45 OISIN 2   239
    ARE OVERTHROWN BY A WOMAN'S GAZE . . . .   164 PERFECT BEAUTY   4
    STILL OVERTHROWN BY A WOMAN'S GAZE, ...   164 PERFECT BEAUTY V   4
    THAT THEY, TIME OVERTHROWN, ...   384 VISION ROBART   47
    HAS TWELVE KNIGHTS OVERTHROWN! . . . .   740 EARL PAUL   8
    FOR HE HAD OVERTHROWN TWELVE KNIGHTS . . . . . .   741 EARL PAUL   43
    AND EVIL FORTUNE HAVE OVERTHROWN SAILED HITHER . . .   757 SHADOW WATER A   196
OVERTURNED
    AND OVERTURNED THE DEMON WITH A SOUND . . . . .   762 SHADOW WATER A   283
OWEN
    OWEN AHERNE AND HIS DANCERS . . . .   449 OWEN AHERNE   T
OWING
    TO MAEVE AND TO MAEVE'S HOUSEHOLD, OWING ALL . . . .   187 QUEEN MAEVE   147
    IN OWING THEM THE BRIDE-BED THAT GIVES PEACE." . . .   187 QUEEN MAEVE   148
OWL
    BECOME A ROOFLESS RUIN THAT THE OWL . . . .   423 MY DESCENDANTS   14
    OR DARK BETWIXT THE POLECAT AND THE OWL, ...   565 GYRES   21
    UP THERE SOME HAWK OR OWL HAS STRUCK, ...   633 MAN AND ECHO   43
    WHERE IS THE OWL THAT LATELY FLEW . . . .   646 ISLE STAT I 1   32
    AN OWL, WHO IN AN ALDER TREE . . . .   670 ISLE STAT II 3   115
    MORE DARK BENEATH THE POPLARS, WHERE YON OWL . . .   675 ISLE STAT II 3   233
    LIKE A GREY OWL MEN HARRY OUT . . . .   740 EARL PAUL   23
OWLET'S
    TO WELCOME THEE, WHEN O'ER THE OWLET'S WINGS . . . .   648 ISLE STAT I 1   102
OWLETS
    SHE SLEEPS WITH OWLETS TWO AND TWO, ...   646 ISLE STAT I 1   34
OWLS
    . . . THE OWLS HAD BUILDED THEIR NESTS IN THEIR LOCKS, . .   49 OISIN 3   39
    AND OVER THE LIMBS AND THE VALLEY THE SLOW OWLS WANDERED   49 OISIN 3   41
        AND CAME,
    IN MIDST OF AN OLD MAN'S BOSOM! OWLS RUFFLING AND PACING   50 OISIN 3   47
        AROUND
    IN THE MIDST OF AN OLD MAN'S BOSOM! OWLS RUFFLING   50 OISIN 3   V   47
        AND PACING AROUND

	PAGE	TITLE		LINE
OWLS (CONTINUED)				
WHEN BRUSHED WITH THE WINGS OF THE OWLS,	53	OISIN 3		98
WHEN OWLS BEGAN TO CALL:	159	CAP AND BELLS		6
WHEN THE OWLS CALLED OUT NO MORE:	159	CAP AND BELLS		14
AND ONCE, WHEN THE OWLS GREW STILL,	159	CAP AND BELLS	V	2
HAS MADE THE VERY OWLS IN CIRCLES MOVE:	423	MY DESCENDANTS		18
AND SHOUT AT THE WISEST OWLS	644	SONG FAERIES		10
HE WROTE IT ON THE SANDS (THE OWLS MAY READ	659	ISLE STAT II 1		9
AND SHOUT AT THE WISEST OWLS	676	ISLE STAT II 3		257
OWLS THERE BE WHOM AGE MAKES NUMB:	727	LOVERS QUARREL		35
AMONG GREAT TREES, AND IN THE WINGS OF OWLS,	762	SHADOW WATER A		285
OWN				
IN HIS OWN LEAFY FOREST HOUSE,	2	OISIN 1	V	7L
IN HIS OWN LEAFY FOREST HOUSE	4	OISIN 1		37
AENGUS AND EDAIN, MY OWN NAME	5	OISIN 1		47
TO MY OWN KINGDOM IN THE SEA--	8	OISIN 1	V	80A
DREAMING OF HER OWN MELTING HUES,	13	OISIN 1		162
AND DREAMS OF HER OWN MELTING HUES,	13	OISIN 1	V	162
ON THEIR OWN SELVES IN THE WATERS WHITE,	14	OISIN 1	V	185
CRAZED WITH ITS OWN INTERMINABLE SOUND,	30	OISIN 2	V	23A
SAVING IN THINE OWN HEART. SEEK, THEN,	66	HAPPY SHEPHERD		27
THE DEWDROPS, FOR THE SOUND OF THEIR OWN DROPPING.	68	SAD SHEPHERD		16
TILL MY OWN WORDS, RE-ECHOING, SHALL SEND	68	SAD SHEPHERD		20
AND MY OWN TALE AGAIN FOR ME SHALL SING,	68	SAD SHEPHERD		22
AND MY OWN WHISPERING WORDS BE COMFORTING,	68	SAD SHEPHERD		23
THE DEW DROPS, FOR THE SOUND OF THEIR OWN DROPPING--	68	SAD SHEPHERD	V	16
AND MINE OWN WORDS RE-ECHOING SHALL SEND	68	SAD SHEPHERD	V	20
AND MINE OWN TALE AGAIN FOR ME SHALL SING,	68	SAD SHEPHERD	V	22
AND MINE OWN WHISPERING WORDS BE COMFORTING,	68	SAD SHEPHERD	V	23
RAGING AT HIS OWN IMAGE IN THE ENAMELLED SEA.	77	INDIAN TO LOVE		5
RAGES AT HIS OWN IMAGE IN THE ENAMELLED SEA	77	INDIAN TO LOVE	V	5
RAGING AT HIS OWN IMAGE IN THE DIM ENAMELLED SEA	77	INDIAN TO LOVE	V	5
TO HIS OWN ICE!" I GATHERED ROUND ME,	83	MAD KING GOLL	V	18
AND HIS OWN SNIPE AND TROUT.	92	FATHER OHART		4
TO MY OWN PLACE, KINSALE.	95	MOLL MAGEE		24
AND THINE OWN SADNESS, WHEREOF STARS, GROWN OLD	101	ROSE UPON ROOD		6
WITH HIS OWN FINGERS TOUCHED THE BRAZEN STRINGS.	109	CUCHULAIN SEA		46
WITH HIS OWN FINGER TOUCHED THE BRAZEN STRINGS	109	CUCHULAIN SEA	V	46
THE CARS OF BATTLE AND HIS OWN NAME CRIED:	111	CUCHULAIN SEA		85
FOR I MUST OWN	118	CRADLE SONG		10
MY ARMS ROUND MY OWN:	118	CRADLE SONG	V	10
WITH ARMS ROUND MY OWN,	118	CRADLE SONG	V	10
MY PIGEON, MY OWN;	118	CRADLE SONG	V	10
WHEN HER OWN PEOPLE RULED THIS TRAGIC EIRE:	129	BOOK STORIES		2
WHEN HER OWN PEOPLE RULED IN WAVE-WORN ERI,	129	BOOK STORIES	V	2
BELOVED, GAZE IN THINE OWN HEART,	134	TWO TREES		1
BELOVED, GAZE IN THINE OWN HEART.	135	TWO TREES		20
AS IF THERE WERE NO TALE BUT YOUR OWN TALE	181	QUEEN MAEVE		32
TO MANY THOUSAND EYES; AND TO HER OWN	182	QUEEN MAEVE		65
AND NOT WITH HIS OWN VOICE OR A MAN'S VOICE,	183	QUEEN MAEVE		74
WITH SOMEBODY IN YOUR OWN LAND."	191	BAILE AILLINN		59
BY ITS OWN BLIND IMAGINING,	191	BAILE AILLINN		67
THEIR OWN THOUGHT FROM THE OTHER'S,	212	O DO NOT LOVE		7
HAVE DRIVEN TRAVELLERS MAD FOR THEIR OWN SPORT.	227	SHADOW WATER B		105
MAY NOT HAVE DRIVEN YOU MAD FOR THEIR OWN SPORT?	227	SHADOW WATER B	V	105
THAT EVERY MAN SHOULD CARRY HIS OWN SOUL	235	SHADOW WATER B		299
TO WIN A WOMAN IN HER OWN DESPITE,	244	SHADOW WATER B		458
BETTER THAN MY OWN HANDS. I HAVE DECEIVED YOU	244	SHADOW WATER B		466
TO WIN A WOMAN IS IN HER OWN DESPITE,	244	SHADOW WATER B	V	458
WE WOULD RETURN TO OUR OWN COUNTRY, FORGAEL,	248	SHADOW WATER B		539
THAT HER OWN STRANGENESS PERPLEXED:	260	UNWORTH PRAISE		14
HAD RAVELLED HER OWN STORY OUT,	272	GREY ROCK		45
IN THE HALF LIGHT, AND RUNS TO ITS OWN DOOR	279	TWO KINGS	V	45C
AND CARRIED HIM HIS FOOD WITH MY OWN HANDS,	280	TWO KINGS		88
WERE NEITHER SHAMED IN HIS OWN	291	TO A FRIEND		7
OF YOUR OWN PASSIONATE SERVING KIND WHO HAD BROUGHT	292	TO A SHADE		10
OF YOUR OWN PASSIONATE SERVING KIND WHO HAS BROUGHT	292	TO A SHADE	V	10
SO WITH A LAUGH AT HIS OWN FEAR	303	HOUR DAWN		31
HAS TIRED OF HIS OWN COMPANY?	303	HOUR DAWN		35
GROWN TIRED OF HIS OWN COMPANY?	303	HOUR DAWN	V	37
NOT EVEN YOUR OWN MOTHER	336	YOUNG GIRL		4
AND HIS OWN FLOCK WAS BROWSING AT THE DOOR.	340	SHEP GOATHERD		27
AND CERTAIN LOST COMPANIONS OF MY OWN.	342	SHEP GOATHERD		78
TO HIS OWN DAYSPRING,	342	SHEP GOATHERD		96
BECAUSE IT IS NOT HER OWN.	345	ON WOMAN		8
TO WRITE FOR MY OWN RACE	347	FISHERMAN		11
"FOR ALL THAT I HAVE DONE AT MY OWN CHARGE?	351	PEOPLE		2
I CALL TO MY OWN OPPOSITE, SUMMON ALL	367	EGO DOMINUS		8
OWN NOTHING BUT THEIR BLIND, STUPEFIED HEARTS.	370	EGO DOMINUS		69
IN ITS OWN BEING, AND WHEN THAT WAR'S BEGUN	374	PHASES OF MOON		51
OR FROM SOME BLOODY WHIP IN THEIR OWN HANDS.	375	PHASES OF MOON		68
AT THE PERFECTION OF ONE'S OWN OBEDIENCE:	376	PHASES OF MOON		109
WHEN HAD I MY OWN WILL?	382	VISION ROBART		7
THERE'S NOTHING BUT OUR OWN RED BLOOD	396	ROSE TREE		17
AND THAT ITS OWN SWEET WILL IS HEAVEN'S WILL;	405	FOR DAUGHTER		69
MONUMENTS OF ITS OWN MAGNIFICENCE:	407	SAIL BYZANTIUM		14
THAT OUT OF LIFE'S OWN SELF-DELIGHT HAD SPRUNG	417	ANCEST HOUSES		11
THAT OUT OF LIFE'S OWN SELF DELIGHT HAD SPRUNG	417	ANCEST HOUSES	V	11
WHERE EVEN LONGING DROWNS UNDER ITS OWN EXCESS:	426	PHANTOM HATRED		22
OF THEIR OWN SWEETNESS, BODIES OF THEIR LOVELINESS.	426	PHANTOM HATRED		24
TO CRAWL IN HER OWN BLOOD, AND GO SCOT-FREE:	429	NINETEEN 19		28

596

	PAGE	TITLE	LINE

OWN   (CONTINUED)
OR HURRIED THEM OFF ON ITS OWN FURIOUS PATH♦ • • • • •	430	NINETEEN 19	53
A MAN IN HIS OWN SECRET MEDITATION • • • • • • • • • •	431	NINETEEN 19	69
MAN'S OWN RESINOUS HEART HAS FED• • • • • • • • • •	438	SONGS PLAY 2	16
NOR BEAUTY BORN OUT OF ITS OWN DESPAIR♦ • • • • • • •	445	SCHOOL CHILDR	59
I RAGE AT MY OWN IMAGE IN THE GLASS • • • • • • • • •	447	HERO GIRL FOOL	1
AT MY OWN IMAGE IN THE LOOKING-GLASS • • • • • • • •	447	HERO GIRL FOOL V	1
I HAVE RAGED AT MY OWN STRENGTH BECAUSE YOU HAVE LOVED IT•	448	HERO GIRL FOOL	9
PICKED HIM FOR HER OWN• • • • • • • • • • •	452	MERMAID	2
THE SOUL'S OWN YOUTH AND NOT THE BODY'S YOUTH • • • • •	464	HARUN RASHID	69
AND SINK INTO ITS OWN DELIGHT AT LAST♦ • • • • • • •	473	ALL SOUL NIGHT	60
BROUGHT FACE TO FACE WITH HIS OWN CLUMSINESS♦ • • • • •	479	SELF AND SOUL	48
• • • OF ITS OWN DESIRE♦ • • • • • • • • • • •	481	BLOOD AND MOON	29
AND EVERYTHING THAT YOUR OWN HANDS HAVE WROUGHT♦ • • • •	501	VACILLATION	31
AND GIVE HIS OWN AND TAKE HIS OWN • • • • • • • • •	538	LAST CONFESS	19
AND GIVE HIS OWN AND TAKE HIS OWN • • • • • • • • •	538	LAST CONFESS	19
AND RULE IN HIS OWN RIGHT♦ • • • • • • • • • •	538	LAST CONFESS	20
ALL HAPPINESS IN ITS OWN CAUSE OR GROUND• • • • • • •	557	RIBH ECSTASY	4
FOR THAT'S A PASSION IN MY OWN CONTROL♦ • • • • • • •	558	RIBH CHRISTIAN	4
ON THEIR OWN FEET THEY CAME♦ OR ON SHIPBOARD♦ • • • • •	566	LAPIS LAZULI	25
THEY HAVE SCHOOLING OF THEIR OWN♦ BUT I PASS THEIR SCHOOLING BY♦	580	CURSE CROMWELL	13
AND WANT HE DID♦ FOR MY OWN GRAND-DAD • • • • • •	596	COLONEL MARTIN	68
OR DEMONSTRATE IN MY OWN LIFE • • • • • • • •	605	YOU CONTENT	21
HYSTERICA PASSIO OF ITS OWN EMPTINESS? • • • • • • • •	618	BRONZE HEAD	7
HYSTERICO-PASSIO OF ITS OWN EMPTINESS? • • • • • • • •	618	BRONZE HEAD V	7
I THOUGHT MY DEAR MUST HER OWN SOUL DESTROY♦ • • • • •	630	CIRCUS ANIMALS	21
WHO♦ WHEN HIS OWN RIGHT KING'S SOLDIER♦ • • • • •	635	BLACK TOWER	13
AND THERE TO ITS OWN HEART FOR EVER MOANS• • • • • • •	650	ISLE STAT I 1	131
WHY NOT? HE IS HER OWN♦ AND CROUCHING NIGH • • • • •	688	TWO TITANS	44
GATHERED ON HER OWN LIPS♦ OH YOUTH♦ AND FLING • • • • •	688	TWO TITANS	53
IN HIS OWN HOUSE OR 'MONG THE MERCHANTS GREY♦ • • • • •	693	MOSADA 1	87
ALONE WITH OUR OWN WHISPERS AND REPLIES— • • • • • •	702	MOSADA 3	80
UNTUNED BY THEIR OWN STRIVING. IF ONE SUCH • • • • •	711	FERENCZ RENYI	37
GLAMOURED BY FAIRIES FOR THEIR OWN• • • • • • • • •	717	FAIRY DOCTOR	20
TO HIS OWN HOUSE DID HIM BETAKE♦ • • • • • • • •	725	LEGEND	30
WHERE THE MOSS WAS SPREAD LIKE HIS OWN DOORMAT• • • • •	728	PRIEST FAIRY	8
AND THOU CANST DWELL IN THINE OWN HOME♦ • • • • • • •	739	EARL PAUL	3
GO BRING ME MY OWN ARMOUR • • • • • • • • •	740	EARL PAUL V	19
THEN GO TO HIS OWN LAND♦ • • • • • • • • • •	741	EARL PAUL	58
AND CAME AND DWELT IN HIS OWN HOUSE♦ • • • • • • •	742	EARL PAUL	67
TO DROWN IN ITS OWN IMAGE? EVEN THAT SLEEP • • • • •	765	SHADOW WATER A	364
THE NETS THE GODS HAVE WOVEN AND OUR OWN HEARTS♦ • • •	766	SHADOW WATER A	383
YOUR OWN THOUGHT WILL HAVE DIED • • • • • • • • •	786	YOUR HEART	30
HER OWN THOUGHT WILL HAVE DIED • • • • • • • • •	786	YOUR HEART V	30

OX
| AND WOOD-OF-WONDERS♦ WHERE ONE KILLS AN OX AT DAWN♦ • • | 209 | UNDER THE MOON | 9 |

OXEN
HOW THE SLOW♦ BLUE-EYED OXEN OF FINN LOW SADLY AT EVENING TIDE.	52	OISIN 3	84
• • • AND MARCH ON AS OXEN MOVE OVER YOUNG GRASS♦ • • •	62	OISIN 3	211
AND TO GIVE WEALTH OF OXEN AND SHEEP TO ALL♦ • • • • •	756	SHADOW WATER A	184
A HUNDRED OXEN AND A HUNDRED SHEEP♦ • • • • • • • •	756	SHADOW WATER A V	189

PACE
I PACE REMEMBERING. FROM MY MISTY THRONE • • • • • • •	45	OISIN 2	V 239C
MY SPIRIT ROCKED IN SLEEP AND SIGHS♦ AND SAW THE MOORFOWL PACE	76	INDIAN ON GOD	3
OR PACE AND WEEP IN WOODS FORLORN♦ • • • • • • • •	86	MAD KING GOLL V	68
AND PACE THE WOODS♦ AND DRIVE MY CHARIOT-WHEELS • • • •	103	FERGUS DRUID	18
AND PACE THE WOODS♦ AND DRIVE MY CHARIOT WHEELS • • • •	103	FERGUS DRUID V	18
HELP THEM THAT PACE♦ HAND IN UNWITHERING HAND♦ • • • •	184	QUEEN MAEVE	86
SO THAT HIS PLAUTUS SET THE PACE • • • • • • • • •	287	TO WEALTHY MAN	12
SO THAT HIS PLUTARCH SET THE PACE • • • • • • • • •	287	TO WEALTHY MAN V	12
OR ESSERKELLY PLAIN♦ FEW KEPT HIS PACE♦ • • • • • • •	326	ROBERT GREGORY	59
AND ESERKELLY PLAINS♦ FEW KEPT HIS PACE♦ • • • • • • •	326	ROBERT GREGORY V	59
OR ESERKELLY PLAINS♦ FEW KEPT HIS PACE♦ • • • • • • •	326	ROBERT GREGORY V	59
THEY HAD KEPT A STEADY PACE AS THOUGH THEIR BEDS♦ • • •	372	PHASES OF MOON	5
I PACE UPON THE BATTLEMENTS AND STARE • • • • • • •	409	TOWER	17
THAT DESPAIR AND KEEP THE PACE • • • • • • • • •	787	HUDDON DUDDON	9

PACED
BENEATH HAD PACED CONTENT♦ WE HELD OUR WAY • • • • •	36	OISIN 2	103
BASALTIC♦ MIGHT HAVE PACED. WE HELD OUR WAY • • • • •	36	OISIN 2	V 103
REMEMBERING HOW I PACED IN DAYS GONE O'ER• • • • • • •	44	OISIN 2	V 227
I PACED A LITTLE FURTHER ON AND HEARD A LOTUS TALK♦— • •	76	INDIAN ON GOD	V 9
I PACED A LITTLE FURTHER AND I HEARD A PEACOCK SAY♦— • •	77	INDIAN ON GOD	V 17
PENSIVE THEY PACED ALONG THE FADED LEAVES♦ • • • • •	80	EPHEMERA	10
WHO PACED IN THE EVE BY THE NETS ON THE PEBBLY SHORE♦ • •	91	OLD FISHERMAN	11
AND PACED UPON THE MOUNTAINS OVERHEAD • • • • • • •	121	YOU ARE OLD	11
HE PACED UPON THE MOUNTAINS FAR ABOVE♦ • • • • • • •	121	YOU ARE OLD V	11
HAD PACED FROM DOOR TO FIRE AND FIRE TO DOOR• • • • • •	180	QUEEN MAEVE	17
THROUGH SHEER BEWILDERMENT? SHE HAD NOT PACED • • • •	466	HARUN RASHID	118

PACES
| THAT SPRING FIVE PACES IN THEIR BOUNDS♦ • • • • • • • | 8 | OISIN 1 | V 86A |

PACING
IN MIDST OF AN OLD MAN'S BOSOM♦ OWLS RUFFLING AND PACING AROUND	50	OISIN 3	47
• • • AND PACING THE SHORES OF THE WANDERING SEAS♦ • • •	50	OISIN 3	55
IN THE MIDST OF AN OLD MAN'S BOSOM♦ OWLS RUFFLING AND PACING AROUND	50	OISIN 3	V 47
• • • AND PACING THE SHORES OF THE SEVEN SEAS♦ • • • •	50	OISIN 3	V 55
AND♦ EVER PACING ON THE VERGE OF THINGS♦ • • • • • •	73	ANASHU VIJAYA	54

		PAGE	TITLE		LINE
PACING	(CONTINUED)				
	MAEVE THE GREAT QUEEN WAS PACING TO AND FRO,	180	QUEEN MAEVE		9
	AND HARPERS, PACING WITH HIGH HEAD	193	BAILE AILLINN		107
	PACING WITH HALF-CLOSED EYELIDS IN A SUNNY SPOT	366	HER COURAGE		7
	THE PACING TO AND FRO ON POLISHED FLOORS	418	ANCEST HOUSES		35
PACK					
	THE PACK UPON HIM. GO, UNQUIET WANDERER,	292	TO A SHADE		18
	HERDING THE PACK. UNQUIET WANDERER	292	TO A SHADE	V	18
	IT SEEMS THAT I MUST BID THE MUSE GO PACK,	409	TOWER		11
	A PACK OF HOUNDS AND NOT A PACK OF CARDS,	411	TOWER		69
	A PACK OF HOUNDS AND NOT A PACK OF CARDS,	411	TOWER		69
	I HAVE POINTED OUT THE YELLING PACK,	453	DEATH OF HARE		1
	PUT JEWELRY IN THE PACK,	595	COLONEL MARTIN		24
PACKED					
	THAT PACKED HIS MARRIAGE DAY	317	NIGHT COME		7
	THAT PACKED HIS MARRIAGE-DAY	317	NIGHT COME	V	7
PADDLE					
	THEY PADDLE IN THE COLD	323	SWANS AT COOLE		20
	AND PADDLE TO THE WRIST	356	BROKEN DREAMS		31
	PADDLE AND ARE PERFECT. LEAVE UNCHANGED	357	BROKEN DREAMS		34
PADDLED					
	BUT TROD THE ROAD, OR PADDLED BY THE SHORE,	447	COLONUS PRAISE	V	27
PADDLER'S					
	SOMETHING OF EVERY PADDLER'S HERITAGE--	444	SCHOOL CHILDR		21
PAGAN					
	(I HAVE NO SPEECH BUT SYMBOL, THE PAGAN SPEECH I MADE	365	HER COURAGE		2
	SAINT GEORGE OR ELSE A PAGAN PERSEUS:	533	HER TRIUMPH		10
PAGE					
	TRAILS ALL ABOUT THE WRITTEN PAGE.	138	TO IRELAND		9
	A CANDLE AND WRITTEN PAGE.	419	MY HOUSE		13
	THE HALF-IMAGINED, THE HALF-WRITTEN PAGE:	431	NINETEEN 19		83
	THE HALF IMAGINED, THE HALF WRITTEN PAGE.	431	NINETEEN 19	V	83
	AS IF THAT WRITING OR THE FIGURED PAGE	466	HARUN RASHID		126
	AS THOUGH THE WRITTEN OR THE PICTURED PAGE	466	HARUN RASHID	V	126
	AND HERE IS TULLY'S OPEN PAGE.	524	MAD AS MIST		9
	YON IS THE HUNTER'S, SIR ALMINTOR'S, PAGE:	660	ISLE STAT II 1		35
	SIR PAGE, ALMINTOR'S FRIEND, AND THEREFORE LEARNED	660	ISLE STAT II 1		38
	BEING ALMINTOR'S PAGE. NOW JUDGE YOU HERE.	660	ISLE STAT II 1		47
PAGES					
	I TURN THE PAGES OF MY HOLY BOOK.	555	RIBH AT TOMB		27
PAID					
	AND PAID YOU ON THE NAIL. TAKE UP THAT ROPE	232	SHADOW WATER B		224
	(I WONDER IF THE BUILDER HAS BEEN PAID)	292	TO A SHADE		3
	THEY ARE NEITHER PAID NOR PRAISED.	473	ALL SOUL NIGHT		76
	THEY ARE NEITHER PAID OR PRAISED.	473	ALL SOUL NIGHT	V	76
	AND THE RICH MAN HAD PAID THEM WELL	596	COLONEL MARTIN		57
PAIN					
	AH ME! TO BE SHAKEN WITH COUGHING AND BROKEN WITH OLD AGE AND PAIN,	63	OISIN 3		217
	THE PAIN OF WOUNDS, THE LABOUR OF THE SPEAR,	104	FERGUS DRUID	V	38D
	"I PUT YOU FROM YOUR PAIN. I CAN NO MORE."	110	CUCHULAIN SEA		69
	IN ALL THEIR LONELINESS AND PAIN,	290	SEPTEMBER 1913		27
	OF ALL 'TWAS PAIN OR JOY TO LEARN,	342	SHEP GOATHERD		98
	TO FIND OUT SOME APPROPRIATE PAIN--	388	SOLOMON WITCH		20
	WILL FIND OUT SOME APPROPRIATE PAIN,	388	SOLOMON WITCH	V	20
	THE UNFINISHED MAN AND HIS PAIN	479	SELF AND SOUL		47
	FOR CHILDREN BORN OF HER PAIN.	487	CRAZED MOON		6
	A GUERDON OF DEEP-ROOTED PAIN,	668	ISLE STAT II 3		59
	IGNOBLE JOY, AND MORE IGNOBLE PAIN	687	TWO TITANS		12
	FROM DATELESS PAIN. SHE SLEEPS--MOSADA--THOU--	701	MOSADA 3	V	65
PAINS					
	OR HOW SHOULD LOVE BE WORTH ITS PAINS WERE IT NOT	285	TWO KINGS		190
	AND INSULT HEAPED UPON HIM FOR HIS PAINS,	292	TO A SHADE		15
	"FOR ALL MY PAINS ON LEBEEN-LONE?"	295	THREE BEGGARS		7
	LIFE OVERFLOWS WITHOUT AMBITIOUS PAINS,	417	ANCEST HOUSES		3
	WHAT IS THIS FLESH I PURCHASED WITH MY PAINS,	499	MOTHER OF GOD		11
PAINT					
	WOULD NOT PAINTERS PAINT A FORM	259	PEACE		5
	AND SHOULD THEY PAINT OR WRITE, STILL IT IS ACTION:	369	EGO DOMINUS		44
	AND SHOULD THEY PAINT OR WRITE STILL IS IT ACTION,	369	EGO DOMINUS	V	44
	QUATTROCENTO PUT IN PAINT	639	BEN BULBEN		53
	QUATTRO-CENTO PUT IN PAINT	639	BEN BULBEN	V	53
PAINTED					
	AND, AS THEY SANG, THE PAINTED BIRDS	26	OISIN 1		396
	GREY TRUTH IS NOW HER PAINTED TOY!	65	HAPPY SHEPHERD		4
	CAME TO THE THRESHOLD OF THE PAINTED HOUSE	185	QUEEN MAEVE		108
	THERE ON THE HIGH AND PAINTED STERN	253	HIS DREAM	V	1
	I HELD A PAINTED STEERING OAR,	253	HIS DREAM	V	2
	UPON A PAINTED BED?"	253	HIS DREAM	V	8
	AND FISH AND CROWD AND PAINTED SHIP,	254	HIS DREAM	V	15
	ON PAINTED PILLARS, ON A DEAL	271	GREY ROCK	V	19
	UNTIL HE CAME BEFORE THE PAINTED WALL,	279	TWO KINGS		47
	IN THEIR STIFF, PAINTED CLOTHES, THE PALE UNSATISFIED ONES	318	MAGI		2
	SINBAD THE SAILOR'S BROUGHT A PAINTED CHEST,	371	ON GOING HOUSE		10
	ANOTHER ARGO'S PAINTED PROW,	437	SONGS PLAY 1		11
	WHEN PAINTED PANEL, STATUARY,	440	WISDOM		2
	UPON A PAINTED WALL.	452	HUMAN DIGNITY		6
	WE LIVED LIKE MEN THAT WATCH A PAINTED STAGE.	542	PARN FUNERAL 1		18
	UPON A PAINTED STAGE WHEN WE DEVOURED HIS HEART.	542	PARN FUNERAL 1		23
	FOR PAINTED FORMS OR BOXES OF MAKE-UP	564	GYRES		13
	OR FROM THE PAINTED SCENE	608	SONGS BURDEN 3		4

598

		PAGE	TITLE		LINE

PAINTED   (CONTINUED)
```
  BEFORE THE PAINTED SCENE.  . . . . . . . .        608 SONGS BURDEN 3        17
  PLAYERS AND PAINTED STAGE TOOK ALL MY LOVE,       630 CIRCUS ANIMALS        31
  A-FLUTTERING THE PAINTED POPULACE OF LAKE . . . . 675 ISLE STAT II 3       224
  FROM THE GREAT PAINTED WINDOW WRAPS HIS BROW, . . 697 MOSADA 2              37
PAINTER
  WE DREAMED THAT A GREAT PAINTER HAD BEEN BORN     326 ROBERT GREGORY        65
  OR WHO HAVE FOUND A PAINTER TO MAKE THEM SO FOR PAY . . 353 HIS PHOENIX      6
  NOR LET THE MODISH PAINTER SHIRK . . . . . . .    638 BEN BULBEN            38
PAINTER'S
  THE PAINTER'S BRUSH CONSUMES HIS DREAMS:  . . . . 438 SONGS PLAY 2         12
  IT SEEMED A QUATTROCENTO PAINTER'S THRONG, . . . . 537 HER VISION          19
  IT SEEMED A QUATTRO-CENTO PAINTER'S THRONG . . . . 537 HER VISION     V    19
PAINTERS
  WOULD NOT PAINTERS PAINT A FORM  . . . . . . .    259 PEACE                 5
PAINTING
  PAINTING WITH SHADOW ALL THE MARBLE STEPS!  . . .  72 ANASHU VIJAYA        30
  IN PAINTING OR IN POTTERY, WENT  . . . . . . . .  421 MY TABLE             18
  MY GREAT-GRANDFATHER'S FATHER TALKED OF MUSIC AND PAINTING, 486 SEVEN SAGES V 4
PAINTINGS
  PAINTINGS OF THE DOLPHIN-DRAWN . . . . . . . .    309 REALISTS              4
  PAINTINGS OF THE DOLPHIN DRAWN:  . . . . . . .    309 REALISTS       V      4
PAINTS
  AND FOR THE PEEWIT PAINTS HIS CAP,  . . . . . .    18 OISIN 1            266
PAIR
  A PAIR OF LAPWINGS, ONE OLD SHEEP,  . . . . . .   302 HOUR DAWN             9
  HOW SUCH A PAIR LOVED MANY YEARS . . . . . . . .  458 SECRETS OF OLD       15
  AND SUCH A PAIR BUT ONE,  . . . . . . . . . .    458 SECRETS OF OLD       16
  WHAT IF MY GREAT-GRANDDAD HAD A PAIR THAT WERE TWENTY FOOT 622 HIGH TALK    2
     HIGH,
  POOR EARTH-ENKINDLED PAIR,  . . . . . . . . .    680 LOVE AND DEATH       22
PAIRC-NA-CARRAIG
  DIM PAIRC-NA-CARRAIG, WHERE THE WILD BEES FLING . 217 WOODS OF COOLE        9
PAIRC-NA-LEE
  A CLOUDY QUIVER OVER PAIRC-NA-LEE.  . . . . . .   198 SEVEN WOODS          14
  WHERE OLD AGE CANNOT FIND THEM; PAIRC-NA-LEE, . . 217 WOODS OF COOLE        7
PAIRC-NA-TARAV
  DIM PAIRC-NA-TARAV, WHERE ENCHANTED EYES  . . .   217 WOODS OF COOLE       11
PAISTIN
  MY PAISTIN FINN IS MY SOLE DESIRE,  . . . . . .   550 SONGS REWRIT 1        1
  MY PRETTY PAISTIN IS MY HEART'S DESIRE, . . . . . 550 SONGS REWRIT 1 V      1
PALACES
  OUR SUDDEN PALACES IN THE STILL AIR . . . . . .   284 TWO KINGS           180
  WANDERING IN SULTRY PALACES OF IND, . . . . . .   694 MOSADA 1            102
PALACE-YARD
  THE PALACE-YARD AND RIVER-SIDE . . . . . . . .    295 THREE BEGGARS         9
  FROM RIVER-SIDE AND PALACE-YARD  . . . . . . .    296 THREE BEGGARS        27
PALATE
  CAN GIVE HIS SHARPENED PALATE ECSTASY . . . . .   474 ALL SOUL NIGHT       84
  GIVE TO HIS SHARPENED PALATE ECSTACY  . . . . .   474 ALL SOUL NIGHT V     84
PALATES
  WHILE OUR GROSS PALATES DRINK FROM THE WHOLE WINE, . . . 471 ALL SOUL NIGHT 10
PALE     SEE STRAW-PALE CLOUD-PALE FOAM-PALE PEARL-PALE CURD-PALE MILK-PALE DEATH-PALE
                   HONEY-PALE
  AND IT WAS BOUND WITH A PEARL PALE SHELL  . . .     4 OISIN 1        V     28
  IN THE PALE WEST, AND THE SUN'S RIM SANK, . . . .  12 OISIN 1            153
  OUT OF THE MOON'S PALE TWISTED SHELL: . . . . .    19 OISIN 1            279
  AND THE PALE BLOSSOM OF THE MOON, . . . . . . .    20 OISIN 1            288
  WITH HOOFS OF THE PALE FINDRINNY  . . . . . . .    25 OISIN 1            383
  OR SAT IN DREAMS ON THE PALE STRAND, . . . . . .   25 OISIN 1            390
  AND THE MOON LIKE A PALE ROSE WITHER AWAY." . .    28 OISIN 1            427
  DARK STATUES GLIMMERED OVER THE PALE TIDE . . .    31 OISIN 2             36
  SO PALE! AND SOUNDS OF WONDER HER LIPS UTTERED, .  34 OISIN 2        V    71
  WITH A PALE LIGHT, I JOURNEYED ROUND THE HALL . .  39 OISIN 2            153
  FROM THEIR PALE THRONES AND COMFORT HIM, BUT THEY  68 SAD SHEPHERD         6
  MY MAN GREW RED AND PALE,  . . . . . . . . .      95 MOLL MAGEE           22
  MY HUSBAND STOOD UP PALE,  . . . . . . . . .      95 MOLL MAGEE       V   22
  WHY ARE YOU PALE AND SHAKE FROM FOOT TO CROWN?"   106 CUCHULAIN SEA   V   13
  LIKE THE PALE WATERS IN THEIR WINTRY RACE, . . .  112 ROSE OF WORLD        8
  TO SMILE ON THE PALE DAWN: AND GATHER YOU . . .   114 ROSE OF BATTLE      15
  OUR CHEEKS ARE PALE, OUR HAIR IS UNBOUND, . . .   140 HOSTING SIDHE        7
  OF THE PALE TIDE WHEN THE MOON HAS SET, . . . .   146 FISH                 2
  PALE BROWS, STILL HANDS AND DIM HAIR, . . . . .   152 LOSS OF LOVE         1
  PALE BROW, STILL HANDS, AND DIM HAIR, . . . . .   152 LOSS OF LOVE    V    1
  THE WEST WEEPS IN PALE DEW AND SIGHS PASSING AWAY, 154 BELOVED PEACE       5
  FOR THAT PALE BREAST AND LINGERING HAND . . . .   156 FORGOT BEAUTY       15
  I HEAR PALE BEAUTY SIGHING TOO, . . . . . . .     156 FORGOT BEAUTY   V   19
  THAT IS BRIMMED FROM THE PALE FIRE OF TIME! . .   157 POET BELOVED         6
  SHE ROSE IN HER PALE NIGHT-GOWN! . . . . . . .    159 CAP AND BELLS       10
  SHE ROSE IN HER PALE NIGHT GOWN, . . . . . . .    159 CAP AND BELLS   V   10
  AND COVER THE PALE BLOSSOMS OF YOUR BREAST . . .  163 ASKS FORGIVE        21
  THEN COVER THE PALE BLOSSOM OF YOUR BREAST . . .  163 ASKS FORGIVE    V   21
  AMONG PALE EYELIDS, HEAVY WITH THE SLEEP  . . .   169 SECRET ROSE          6
  I WOULD THE PALE DEER HAD COME . . . . . . . .    171 MAID QUIET      V   4A
  LIKE THE PALE CUP OF THE SEA, . . . . . . . .     175 ELEMENT POWERS      14
  BUT LIGHT FROM THE PALE STARS, AND GLEAMS . . .   196 BAILE AILLINN      173
  BLOSSOM PALE, SHE PULLED DOWN THE PALE BLOSSOM    199 ARROW           V    5
  BLOSSOM PALE, SHE PULLED DOWN THE PALE BLOSSOM    199 ARROW           V    5
  ON THE ISLAND LAWNS, THEIR FEET WHERE THE PALE FOAM GLEAMS. 203 WITHER BOUGHS 14
  THE HONEY PALE MOON HUNG LOW ON THE SLEEPY HILL, . . . 203 WITHER BOUGHS V 5
  PALE SILVER-PROUD QUEEN-WOMAN OF THE SKY, . . . . 211 RAGGED WOOD          6
```

599

PALE   (CONTINUED)
    AND DO YOU GATHER ABOUT US WHEN PALE LIGHT . . . . . . 218 WOODS OF COOLE   37
    OF OPAL AND RUBY AND PALE CHRYSOLITE . . . . 219 HARP OF AENGUS   6
    AND WHERE BEECH-TREES HAD MIXED A PALE GREEN LIGHT . . . 277 TWO KINGS   5
    BETWEEN THE PALE GREEN LIGHT OF THE BEECH LEAVES . . . . 277 TWO KINGS   5
    WHERE CERTAIN BEECHES MIXED A PALE GREEN LIGHT . . . . 277 TWO KINGS   V 5
    AND WHERE BEECH TREES HAD MIXED A PALE GREEN LIGHT . . . 277 TWO KINGS   V 5
    IN THEIR STIFF, PAINTED CLOTHES, THE PALE UNSATISFIED ONES 318 MAGI   2
    "VENGENCE FOR JACQUES MOLAY." IN CLOUD PALE RAGS, OR IN   426 PHANTOM HATRED V 10
        LACE,
    THE CLOUD PALE UNICORNS, THE EYES OF AQUAMARINE, ... 427 PHANTOM HATRED V 25
    WHAT'S BOWED YOUR SHOULDER AND MADE PALE YOUR CHEEK": . . 467 HARUN RASHID   133
    THE HERON-BILLED PALE CATTLE-BIRDS . . . . 493 AT ALGECIRAS   1
    THE HERON-BILLED PALE CATTLE BIRD, ... 493 AT ALGECIRAS   V 1
    THE HERON-BILLED PALE CATTLE BIRDS, ... 493 AT ALGECIRAS   V 1
    BUT BOYS AND GIRLS, PALE FROM THE IMAGINED LOVE . . . . 610 STATUES   4
    THAT PALE, LONG-VISAGED COMPANY . . . . 637 BEN BULBEN   7
    THAT PALE, LONG VISAGED COMPANY . . . . 637 BEN BULBEN   V 7
    'TIS MORN! LIKE OLD MEN'S EYES THE STARS ARE PALE, . . 645 ISLE STAT I 1   4
    I'D BE ALONE. WE TWO, BY THAT PALE FOUNT, ... 650 ISLE STAT I 1   132
    THE PALE ANEMONES. WE'VE SOUGHT ALL DAY, ... 651 ISLE STAT I 2   5
    A SCARLET BLOOM. WHY RAISEST THOU, PALE ONE, ... 673 ISLE STAT II 3 196
    THE VISION. YOU ARE PALE AND WEEPING. CHILD, ... 693 MOSADA 1   73
    I'M NOT OF THAT PALE COMPANY WHOSE FEET . . . . 699 MOSADA 3   20
    AND OUT-SPREAD ARMS. BE NOT SO PALE, DEAR LOVE. . . . 701 MOSADA 3   70
    YOU'RE PALE, MY LORD. HIS LIPS ARE QUIVERING: . . . . 704 MOSADA 3   127
    A PEASANT PALE AND PRETTY, HER EYES FOR FEAR, ... 713 FERENCZ RENYI   81
    THE YOUNG ONE WITH THE OTHERS." RENYI'S PALE . . . . 713 FERENCZ RENYI   84
    A PEASANT, PALE AND PRETTY, HER EYES FROM FEAR, . . . 713 FERENCZ RENYI V 81
    "PRAY FOR THE SOULS IN PURGATORY," THE PALE PRIEST   719 PHANTOM SHIP   31
        TREMBLING CRIES.
    AMONG THE WINDS, LOOKS UNDER YOUR PALE EYELIDS. . . . 757 SHADOW WATER A 211
    SHOOK THE PALE APPLE-BLOSSOM OVER IT: . . . . 761 SHADOW WATER A 275
    AND THE PALE BLOSSOM: BUT I WOKE INSTEAD . . . . . . 761 SHADOW WATER A 281
    SHOOK THE PALE APPLE BLOSSOM OVER IT: . . . . 761 SHADOW WATER A V 275
    OF OPAL AND RUBY AND PALE CHRYSOLITE . . . . 762 SHADOW WATER A 301
    THE PALE HOUND AND THE DEER WANDER FOR EVER . . . . . 764 SHADOW WATER A 330
    IS THIS POOR BODY THAT REDDENS AND GROWS PALE. . . . . 764 SHADOW WATER A 341
    THE PALE HOUND AND THE DEER WANDER FOREVER . . . . . 764 SHADOW WATER A V 330
    A FRAGILE, EXQUISITE, PALE SHELL, ... 784 WOMANS BEAUTY   16
PALED
    AND AT THESE WORDS HE PALED, AS SHE HAD PALED, ... 280 TWO KINGS   76
    AND AT THESE WORDS HE PALED, AS SHE HAD PALED, ... 280 TWO KINGS   76
PALE-FACED
    PALE-FACED, ALONE UPON A BENCH, EDAIN . . . . 279 TWO KINGS   61
    PALE-FACED, ALONE UPON A BENCH, HIS WIFE . . . . . . 279 TWO KINGS   V 61
PALENESS
    UPON THE PALENESS OF A FINGER. . . . . 390 IMAGE PAST   28
    A FEARFUL PALENESS CREEPS ACROSS HER BREAST . . . . . 701 MOSADA 3   69
PALES
    FROM MORN THE TWAIN UNTIL THE EVENING PALES . . . . . 651 ISLE STAT I 1   161
PALETTE
    THEY ARE SICK OF THE PALETTE AND FIDDLE-BOW, ... 565 LAPIS LAZULI   2
PALING
    AND LIGHTS WERE PALING OUT OF THE WEST, ... 175 BELOVED DEAD   2
    AND LIGHT WERE PALING OUT OF THE WEST, ... 175 BELOVED DEAD   V 2
    WHILE LIGHTS WERE PALING ONE BY ONE. . . . . 176 BELOVED DEAD   13
PALLAS
    AT PALLAS ATHENE'S SIDE, ... 355 PROPERTIUS   6
    PALLAS ATHENE IN THAT STRAIGHT BACK AND ARROGANT HEAD! . . 578 LOFTY THINGS   11
PALLOR
    PROPPED UPON PILLOWS, ROUGE ON THE PALLOR OF HER FACE. . . 362 HER COURTESY   3
PALM
    CROWDED WITH BITTER FACES, THE WOUNDS IN PALM AND SIDE, 172 TRAV PASSION   4
    OF A SLENDER PALM, STOOD BUT A DAY: . . . . 566 LAPIS LAZULI   34
    ERE YONDER PALM COMMENCED HIS THOUSAND YEARS? . . . . 724 KANVA ON SELF   14
PALMER
    THE LONELY LIGHT THAT SAMUEL PALMER ENGRAVED, ... 373 PHASES OF MOON   17
PALMER'S
    PALMER'S PHRASE, BUT AFTER THAT . . . . 639 BEN BULBEN   66
PALM-STEMS
    PAST THE SPEARS AND PALM-STEMS DRY, ... 733 STREET DANCERS   42
PALTRY
    AN AGED MAN IS BUT A PALTRY THING, ... 407 SAIL BYZANTIUM   9
PAN
    NOR SOLDERED POT OR PAN: . . . . 606 SONGS BURDEN 1   15
    OH! GRACIOUS PAN, TAKE NOW THY SERVANT'S PART. . . . . 657 ISLE STAT I 3   77
    AS HERE I CAME I SAW GOD PAN. HE PLAYED . . . . . . 678 ISLE STAT II 3 300
PANE
    BECAUSE WOMEN IN THE UPPER STOREYS DEMAND A FACE AT THE   623 HIGH TALK   7
        PANE,
PANEL
    WHEN PAINTED PANEL, STATUARY, ... 440 WISDOM   2
PANG
    A COMPENSATION FOR THE PANG OF HIS BIRTH, ... 444 SCHOOL CHILDR   39
    A GREATER WITH A LESSER PANG ASSUAGE . . . . 537 HER VISION   5
PANIC
    STRICKEN WITH PANIC FROM THE ATTACK, ... 274 GREY ROCK   75
    IN FURY AND IN PANIC FLED . . . . 307 HOUR DAWN   V 119
PANNIERED
    HER DOMINO, HER PANNIERED SKIRT COPIED FROM LONGHI: . . . 363 DOLLS FACES   7

600

		PAGE	TITLE		LINE

PAN'S
    FROM WHERE PAN'S CAVERN IS • • • • • • • • • • • • 612 NEWS ORACLE   31
PANSY'S
    THAN THE PEEPING PANSY'S FACE, • • • • • • • • • • • 647 ISLE STAT I 1   52
PANT
    INNUMERABLE, SINGING, EXULTANT: THE CLAY UNDERNEATH THEM   61 OISIN 3   203
        SHALL PANT,
PANTHER
    THE PANTHER WITH HER YELLOW HIDE, • • • • • • • • • • 658 ISLE STAT I 3   83
    BUT A MOTHER PANTHER NEVER • • • • • • • • • • • • 658 ISLE STAT I 3   92
PANTHER-KITTENS
    OF THE PIED PANTHER-KITTENS FROM MY HANDS • • • • • • 674 ISLE STAT II 3   219
PANTHERS
    MAY PANTHERS END HIM.--HEAR, AND LOAD OUR KING • • • •   71 ANASHU VIJAYA   6
    NOURISH THE PANTHERS IN DIM SOLITUDES: • • • • • • • 657 ISLE STAT I 3   44
    OF DESERT-CAVES THE RED-EYED PANTHERS ROVE • • • • • • 681 SEEKER   4
    EYED PANTHERS IN THEIR DESERT CAVERNS ROVE • • • • • • 681 SEEKER   V   4
PANTING
    AND, GATHERED IN A PANTING BAND, • • • • • • • • • •   22 OISIN 1   324
    COME WITH LOUD CRY AND PANTING BREAST • • • • • • • • 412 TOWER   86
PANTRY
    BETWEEN THE PANTRY AND THE LINEN-CHEST, • • • • • • • 340 SHEP GOATHERD   36
    BETWEEN THE PANTRY AND THE LINEN CHEST, • • • • • • • 340 SHEP GOATHERD V   36
PAPER
    AND HANGING ITS PAPER FLOWERS FROM POST TO POST, • • • • 198 SEVEN WOODS   8
    BY PEN AND PAPER LIES, • • • • • • • • • • • • • 421 MY TABLE   3
PARABLE
    OR ELSE, TO ALTER PLATO'S PARABLE, • • • • • • • • • 443 SCHOOL CHILDR   15
PARADE
    THE OLD TROOPS PARADE, • • • • • • • • • • • • • 496 MOHINI CHATTER   22
PARADIGM
    UPON A GHOSTLY PARADIGM OF THINGS: • • • • • • • • • 445 SCHOOL CHILDR   42
PARADISE
    THE COUNTESS CATHLEEN IN PARADISE • • • • • • • • • • 124 CATHLEEN PARA   T
    RUNNING TO PARADISE • • • • • • • • • • • • • • 300 RUN PARADISE   T
    FOR I AM RUNNING TO PARADISE: • • • • • • • • • • 300 RUN PARADISE   3
    AND I AM RUNNING TO PARADISE: • • • • • • • • • • 301 RUN PARADISE   10
    AND I AM RUNNING TO PARADISE: • • • • • • • • • • 301 RUN PARADISE   17
    FOR I AM RUNNING TO PARADISE: • • • • • • • • • • 301 RUN PARADISE   24
    WHILE I AM RUNNING TO PARADISE. • • • • • • • • • • 301 RUN PARADISE   V REF
    TRANSLUNAR PARADISE. • • • • • • • • • • • • • 415 TOWER   156
    THE FINAL PARADISE. • • • • • • • • • • • • • • 415 TOWER   V 156
    AWAY IN THE GREEN PARADISE, • • • • • • • • • • • 654 ISLE STAT I 2   70
PARADISE'S
    'FORE PARADISE'S GATE. • • • • • • • • • • • • • 680 LOVE AND DEATH   20
PARAGON
    BY HOMER'S PARAGON • • • • • • • • • • • • • • 384 VISION ROBART   56
PARASITE
    THAT FEED ON SOME FOUL PARASITE • • • • • • • • • • 493 AT ALGECIRAS   2
    THAT FEEDS ON SOME FOUL PARASITE • • • • • • • • • • 493 AT ALGECIRAS V   2
PARCHED
    "WHEN ALL THE WELLS ARE PARCHED AWAY? • • • • • • • • 396 ROSE TREE   15
PARCHMENT
    THE PARCHMENT WILL DISCLOSE TO SOME LEARNED MAN • • • • 461 HARUN RASHID   20
    TAKE THIS LIGHT PARCHMENT, PASS THROUGH THE GREAT CHAMBER 461 HARUN RASHID V   5
    IF YOU SHOULD HIDE MY PARCHMENT IN THAT BOOK • • • • • 461 HARUN RASHID V   13
PARDON
    NO NEED TO DROWN, FOR, IF YOU WILL PARDON US • • • • • 238 SHADOW WATER B   361
    PARDON, OLD FATHERS, IF YOU STILL REMAIN • • • • • • 269 PARDON FATHERS   1
    PARDON, AND YOU THAT DID NOT WEIGH THE COST, • • • • • 269 PARDON FATHERS V   9
    PARDON THAT FOR A BARREN PASSION'S SAKE, • • • • • • 270 PARDON FATHERS   19
    PARDON, GREAT ENEMY, • • • • • • • • • • • • • 366 HER CHRIS TREE   1
    UNTIL IT PARDON ME. • • • • • • • • • • • • • 516 MANS SONG   18
    SO THEY ESCAPE FROM HELL. BUT, PARDON ME, • • • • • 704 MOSADA 3   132
    AND JOHN WILL PARDON THEE, • • • • • • • • • • • 739 EARL PAUL   2
    I WILL SWEAR BY SUN AND MOON TO PARDON ALL • • • • • 756 SHADOW WATER A   183
PARDONED
    PARDONED, DRAGS OUT LONELY YEARS • • • • • • • • • • 475 EVA GORE-BOOTH   8
    SAYING "EARL PAUL IS PARDONED • • • • • • • • • • • 741 EARL PAUL   55
PARE
    LOOK TO LONG FISHING-LINES, OR POINT AND PARE • • • • •   32 OISIN 2   55
PARENTS
    AY, AY. SWEAR BY THE PARENTS OF THE GODS, • • • • •   74 ANASHU VIJAYA   66
    SWEAR! BY THE PARENTS OF THE GODS, I SWEAR. • • • • •   75 ANASHU VIJAYA   76
PARIS
    TO MIGHTY PARIS WHEN HE FOUND • • • • • • • • • • 522 LULLABY   4
    WHAT WERE THEY WHEN PARIS FOUND • • • • • • • • • • 522 LULLABY   V   4
    IN COUNTRY SHAWL OR PARIS CLOAK, HAD PUT MY WITS ASTRAY, 592 PILGRIM   3
    THE SHEPHERD PARIS FOR OENONE MADE, • • • • • • • • 650 ISLE STAT I 1   136
PARIS'
    FOR PEG AND MEG AND PARIS' LOVE • • • • • • • • • • 458 HIS WILDNESS   3
PARISH
    NOR SO MUCH AS PARISH PRIEST, • • • • • • • • • • 508 JANE BISHOP   11
PARK
    COOLE PARK, [NINETEEN-TWENTY-NINE] • • • • • • • • • 488 COOLE PARK 29   T
    COOLE PARK • • • • • • • • • • • • • • • • 488 COOLE PARK 29 V   T
    COOLE PARK AND BALLYLEE, [NINETEEN-THIRTY-ONE] • • • • 490 COOLE BALLYLEE   T
    COOLE PARK AND BALLYLEE [NINETEEN-THIRTY-TWO] • • • • 490 COOLE BALLYLEE V   T
PARLIAMENT
    INTO A PLOUGHSHARE? PARLIAMENT AND KING • • • • • • 429 NINETEEN 19   20
    JOHN BULL HAS STOOD FOR PARLIAMENT, • • • • • • • • 583 GHOST ROG CASE   11

601

	PAGE	TITLE	LINE
PARLIAMENT (CONTINUED)			
NOR LAW NOR PARLIAMENT TAKE HEED.	791	REPRISALS	22
PARMENIDES			
PAUSE AT THE TREATISE OF PARMENIDES	461	HARUN RASHID	16
FROM THE GREAT TREATISE OF PARMENIDES:	469	HARUN RASHID	183
PARNASSUS			
OVERCOME GODS UPON PARNASSUS:	540	FROM ANTIGONE	6
PARNELL			
MOCK EMMET, MOCK PARNELL!	547	TO SAME TUNE 2	25
THAT PARNELL LOVED A LASS.	586	PARNELLITES	16
KEEPS PARNELL IN HIS MIND.	586	PARNELLITES	20
FOR PARNELL WAS A PROUD MAN.	587	PARNELLITES	21
AND PARNELL LOVED HIS COUNTRY,	587	PARNELLITES	31
AND PARNELL LOVED HIS LASS.	587	PARNELLITES	32
AND PARNELL LOVED A LASS.	587	PARNELLITES V	32
PARNELL	590	PARNELL	T
PARNELL CAME DOWN THE ROAD, HE SAID TO A CHEERING MAN:	590	PARNELL	1
MOCK EMMET, MOCK PARNELL,	614	MARCH SONGS 1	25
PARNELLITE			
A PARNELLITE AT PARNELL'S FUNERAL	541	PARN FUNERAL 1 V	T
PARNELLITES			
COME GATHER ROUND ME, PARNELLITES	586	PARNELLITES	T
COME GATHER ROUND ME, PARNELLITES,	586	PARNELLITES	1
PARNELL'S			
PARNELL'S FUNERAL	541	PARN FUNERAL 1	T
A PARNELLITE AT PARNELL'S FUNERAL	541	PARN FUNERAL 1 V	T
HAD DE VALERA EATEN PARNELL'S HEART	542	PARN FUNERAL 2	2
HAD COSGRAVE EATEN PARNELL'S HEART, THE LAND'S	543	PARN FUNERAL 2	5
PARROT			
A PARROT SWAYS UPON A TREE,	77	INDIAN TO LOVE	4
A PARROT SWAYING ON A TREE	77	INDIAN TO LOVE V	4
PARROTS			
EVEN WHERE HORRIBLE GREEN PARROTS CALL AND SWING.	442	BLACK CENTAUR	2
EVEN WHERE THE HORRIBLE GREEN PARROTS CALL AND SWING.	442	BLACK CENTAUR V	2
PART			
AS THOUGH HIS HOUR WERE COME. WE SOUGHT THE PART	37	OISIN 2	112
AS THOUGH HIS HOUR WERE ON HIM. TO THE PART	37	OISIN 2 V	112
. . . TILL STARLIGHT AND MIDNIGHT PART.	60	OISIN 3	184
HID IN THE EARTH'S MOST HIDDEN PART,	78	INDIAN TO LOVE V	12
LET US PART, ERE THE SEASON OF PASSION FORGET US,	79	FALLING LEAVES	7
COVER OVER AND HIDE, FOR HE HAS NO PART	158	TO HIS HEART	6
. . . WHEN A PART OF THE CONSTELLATIONS OF HEAVEN	177	PAST GREATNESS	T
AND FOR A DOZEN HOURS HAVE BEEN A PART	230	SHADOW WATER B	171
BEING BUT A PART OF ANCIENT CEREMONY--	321	REED WHISPERER	12
THAT HE WILL NEVER FIND: I'D PLAY A PART:	377	PHASES OF MOON	128
HE, TOO, HAS RESIGNED HIS PART	393	EASTER 1916	36
THAT IS HEAVEN'S PART, OUR PART	394	EASTER 1916	60
THAT IS HEAVEN'S PART, OUR PART	394	EASTER 1916	60
MUST WE PART, VON HUEGEL, THOUGH MUCH ALIKE, FOR WE	503	VACILLATION	78
WHAT SEEMS MOST WELCOME IN THE TOMB--PLAY A PREDESTINED PART.	503	VACILLATION	86
WOULD TRANSFORM THE PART,	506	REMORSE SPEECH	3
NONE SHARED OUR GUILT: NOR DID WE PLAY A PART	542	PARN FUNERAL 1	22
IF WORTHY THEIR PROMINENT PART IN THE PLAY,	565	LAPIS LAZULI	14
THROW IT IN EVERY PART."	596	COLONEL MARTIN	53
SHE THINKS, PART WOMAN, THREE PARTS A CHILD,	617	LONG-LEG FLY	15
OH! GRACIOUS PAN, TAKE NOW THY SERVANT'S PART.	657	ISLE STAT I 3	77
AND PART HIS FOAMING MOUTH WITH EAGER EYE--	688	TWO TITANS	46
THEIR THIEVING WINGS THAT WE MIGHT NEVER PART.	702	MOSADA 3	98
IN THE GREEN HILL'S INMOST PART.	726	LOVERS QUARREL	12
PARTED			
PARTED HER LIPS WITH A LOUD SUDDEN CRY.	105	CUCHULAIN SEA	8
BROKE FROM HIS PARTED LIPS AND BROKE AGAIN,	182	QUEEN MAEVE	48
THE PARTED LIPS REPLIED, "I SEEK YOUR HELP,	183	QUEEN MAEVE	83
PARTIAL			
HE COMPLETES HIS PARTIAL MIND,	638	BEN BULBEN	30
PARTICULAR			
THE PARTICULAR IS POUNDED TILL IT IS MAN.	382	VISION ROBART	6
PARTICULAR QUALITY. THE SIGNS AND SHAPES:	469	HARUN RASHID	181
PARTICULARS			
WITH THE MINUTE PARTICULARS OF MANKIND?	384	VISION ROBART	42
PARTING			
IT SPEEDS THE PARTING GUEST.	434	YOUTH AND AGE	4
PARTING	535	PARTING	T
A BRIEF PARTING FROM THOSE DEAR	637	BEN BULBEN	19
I KNEEL BY THEE--NO PARTING NOW--LOOK UP.	702	MOSADA 3	94
PARTLY			
BOOK I WHAT THE CALIPH PARTLY LEARNED	372	PHASES OF MOON V	T
PARTRIDGE			
A-MURMUR LIKE YOUNG PARTRIDGE: WITH LOUD HORN	32	OISIN 2	52
"THEY MURMUR LIKE YOUNG PARTRIDGE IN THE MORN,	32	OISIN 2 V	51
PARTS			
AND MADE IN ALL THEIR DISTANT PARTS,	16	OISIN 1	228
AND ROSE FROM ALL THEIR DISTANT PARTS,	16	OISIN 1 V	228
TILL MEDITATION MASTER ALL ITS PARTS,	474	ALL SOUL NIGHT	92
SHE THINKS, PART WOMAN, THREE PARTS A CHILD,	617	LONG-LEG FLY	15
PARTY			
THE BISHOPS AND THE PARTY	587	PARNELLITES	25
PASS			
AND THE DAYS PASS BY LIKE A WAYWARD TUNE,	8	OISIN 1	83
. . . AND I KNEW HOW MEN SORROW AND PASS,	59	OISIN 3	175

	PAGE	TITLE		LINE
PASS (CONTINUED)				
. . . AND I KNEW HOW MEN PASS, ...	59	OISIN 3	V	175
THE WHIRLING WAYS OF STARS THAT PASS--	66	HAPPY SHEPHERD		30
AMRITA. THIS SAME EVE SHE WATCHED ME PASS.	74	ANASHU VIJAYA	V	64
THAT I MAY CONTENTED PASS	97	FOXHUNTER		11
AND I ON THIS STRANGE ROAD WILL PASS	97	FOXHUNTER	V	11
THE MOMENTS PASS AND PASS;	99	FOXHUNTER		44
THE MOMENTS PASS AND PASS;	99	FOXHUNTER		44
AND HEAVY MORTAL HOPES THAT TOIL AND PASS;	101	ROSE UPON ROOD		18
FOR WE TIRE OF THE FLAME OF THE METEOR BEFORE IT CAN PASS BY AND FLEE	122	WHITE BIRDS	V	2
WE TIRE OF THE FLAME OF THE METEOR, BEFORE IT CAN PASS BY AND FLEE;	122	WHITE BIRDS	V	2
LIFT UP BEFORE US WHEN THEY PASS, ...	135	TWO TREES		23
LIFT UP BEFORE US AS THEY PASS, ...	135	TWO TREES	V	23
YOU PASS NOT AWAY.	142	MOODS	V	7
THEY KNOW ALL WONDERS, FOR THEY PASS	196	BAILE AILLINN		160
BUT THERE WERE OTHERS. I HAVE SEEN NOTHING PASS. . . .	226	SHADOW WATER B		82
IF HE COULD PASS HER BY	255	WOMAN HOMER		6
"YOUR STRENGTH AND NOBLENESS WILL PASS AWAY"?	285	TWO KINGS		189
PASS THE DOOR OF BIRTH AGAIN, ...	298	THREE HERMITS		19
SHE NEED NOT BE TOO COMELY--LET IT PASS,"	300	BEGGAR CRIED		10
BUT THE HOUR WHEN YOU SHALL PASS AWAY	306	HOUR DAWN		96
GROWS COMELIER. ELEVEN PASS, AND THEN	374	PHASES OF MOON		44
WILL PASS FROM CHANGE TO CHANGE, ...	379	CAT AND MOON		22
COULD THE IMPOSSIBLE COME TO PASS	385	ROBARTES DANCE		9
KNOWING THAT NONE COULD PASS HEAVEN'S DOOR	422	MY TABLE		26
KNOWING THAT NONE WHO PASS HEAVEN'S DOOR	422	MY TABLE	V	26
KNOWING THAT NONE CAN PASS HEAVEN'S DOOR	422	MY TABLE	V	26
AND WHEN I PASS A COMPLIMENT	453	DEATH OF HARE		3
AND WAIT WAR'S MUSIC; PASS THE LITTLE GALLERY; . . .	461	HARUN RASHID		8
PASS BOOKS OF LEARNING FROM BYZANTIUM	461	HARUN RASHID		9
TAKE THIS LIGHT PARCHMENT, PASS THROUGH THE GREAT CHAMBER	461	HARUN RASHID	V	5
"LET ALL THINGS PASS AWAY."	502	VACILLATION		61
"LET ALL THINGS PASS AWAY."	502	VACILLATION		66
"LET ALL THINGS PASS AWAY."	502	VACILLATION		71
THEY BROUGHT TO PASS;	505	GRAT INSTRUCT		2
IN THE NARROW PASS;	512	JANE ON GOD		11
THAT MEN PASS OVER	512	JANE ON GOD		21
PLATO THERE AND MINOS PASS, ...	531	DELPHIC ORACLE		8
THE REST I PASS, ONE SENTENCE I UNSAY.	542	PARN FUNERAL 2		1
I PASS THE REST--ONE SENTENCE I UNSAY--	542	PARN FUNERAL 2	V	1
THEY HAVE SCHOOLING OF THEIR OWN, BUT I PASS THEIR SCHOOLING BY,	580	CURSE CROMWELL		13
AND PASS THE BOTTLE ROUND.	586	PARNELLITES		8
HE BROUGHT IT ALL TO PASS;	586	PARNELLITES		14
SO PASS THE BOTTLE ROUND.	587	PARNELLITES		24
WHAT MARCHES THROUGH THE MOUNTAIN PASS?	614	MARCH SONGS 2		7
WHAT MARCHES DOWN THE MOUNTAIN PASS?	615	MARCH SONGS 2		17
WHAT MARCHES DOWN THE MOUNTAIN PASS?	615	MARCH SONGS 2		27
HORSEMAN, PASS BY!	640	BEN BULBEN		94
O LET ME PASS! THE SPELLS FROM OFF THE HEART	668	ISLE STAT II 3		44
O LET ME PASS! THAT FLOWER NONE	668	ISLE STAT II 3		47
PASS AWAY--	668	ISLE STAT II 3		67
TO WATCH THEE PASS? YET DEEPER THAN MEN KNOW . . .	672	ISLE STAT II 3		158
THEY MAY NOT PASS THE PORTAL, ...	680	LOVE AND DEATH		21
TO PASS AND LEAVE THEM THERE	680	LOVE AND DEATH		24
THE PREACHER WATCHING FOR THE EVIL HOUR TO PASS, . .	686	LIFE		3
I SAW HIM SIGH AND TURN AND PASS AWAY;	690	MOSADA 1		14
CIRCLING THE BRAIN? MY BROTHERS WILL PASS DOWN . . .	699	MOSADA 3		6
CIRCLING THE BRAIN? MY BROTHERS NOW PASS DOWN . . .	699	MOSADA 3	·V	6
THE SHADOWS PASS; BUT NOW, I LOVE MY RING, ...	700	MOSADA 3		27
'TWILL PASS. I'LL SEE THE OTHER PRISONERS NOW, . . .	704	MOSADA 3		130
AND ALONG THE MOUNTAINS PASS, ...	705	DAWN-SONG		12
O SHINING ONES, LIGHTLY WITH SONG PASS, ...	708	FAIRY PEDANT		21
TALKING HOURS SWIFTLY PASS!	727	LOVERS QUARREL		44
THE PREACHER WATCHING FOR THE ILL HOUR TO PASS-- . .	734	QUATRAIN APHOR		3
THE PREACHER WATCHING FOR THE EVIL HOUR TO PASS, . .	734	QUATRAIN APHOR	V	3
IT WERE BETTER TO PASS BY, BECAUSE THE GODS	751	SHADOW WATER A		104
AMONG THE WINDS AND WATERS; AND WHEN THEY PASS . .	764	SHADOW WATER A		331
DID NOT A SHADOW PASS?	781	MY HEART BEAT		2
PASSAGE				
HAD WATCHED MY DAILY PASSAGE TO AND FRO;	466	HARUN RASHID		107
PASSAGES				
WHEN ALL THOSE ROOMS AND PASSAGES ARE GONE, ...	489	COOLE PARK 29		26
PASSED				
I KNOW NOT IF DAYS PASSED OR HOURS, ...	11	OISIN 1		133
PASSED BY US, CHASED BY A PHANTOM HOUND	11	OISIN 1		140
I KNEW NOT IF DAYS PASSED OR HOURS, ...	11	OISIN 1	V	133
PASSED BY US, CHASED OF A PHANTOM HOUND	11	OISIN 1	V	140
WE PASSED THE PORTALS, AND WITHIN, ...	17	OISIN 1	V	250
PASSED A-TIPTOE UP AND DOWN	20	OISIN 1	V	294
WE PASSED BY WOODS, AND LAWNS OF CLOVER, ...	25	OISIN 1		377
WE PASSED IN SILENCE O'ER THE MEAD, ...	25	OISIN 1	V	376A
OR HOURS PASSED BY, YET HOLD THE MORNING RAYS . . .	30	OISIN 2		20
PASSED UNDER THE DIM DOORWAY, OUT OF SIGHT, ...	37	OISIN 2		123
MAKING A WORLD ABOUT HER, PASSED FROM SIGHT	37	OISIN 2	V	123
PASSED UNDER A DIM DOORWAY, OUT OF SIGHT, ...	37	OISIN 2	V	123
I MOUNTED, AND WE PASSED OVER THE LONE	45	OISIN 2		231
I PASSED ALONG THE WATER'S EDGE BELOW THE HUMID TREES, . .	76	INDIAN ON GOD		1
I PASSED A LITTLE FURTHER ON AND HEARD A LOTUS TALK! . .	76	INDIAN ON GOD		9

603

                                                       PAGE   TITLE   LINE

PASSED   (CONTINUED)
    I PASSED A LITTLE FURTHER ON AND HEARD A PEACOCK SAY: . .   77 INDIAN ON GOD   17
    I PASSED A LITTLE FURTHER AND I HEARD A PEACOCK SAY:-- .   77 INDIAN ON GOD   V   17
    AND PASSED A-TIPTOE UP AND DOWN, ...   85 MAD KING GOLL   51
    I PASSED A TIP-TOE UP AND DOWN, ...   85 MAD KING GOLL   V   51
    I PASSED A-TIPTOE UP AND DOWN, ...   85 MAD KING GOLL   V   51
    WHEN MY HAND PASSED FROM WIRE TO WIRE . . . .   86 MAD KING GOLL   65
    SHE PASSED THE SALLEY GARDENS WITH LITTLE SNOW-WHITE FEET.   90 SALLEY GARDENS   2
    TROY PASSED AWAY IN ONE HIGH FUNERAL GLEAM, ...   111 ROSE OF WORLD   4
    A SONG INTO THE AIR, AND SINGING PASSED . . . . . .   114 ROSE OF BATTLE   14
    BUT WHILE HE PASSED BEFORE A PLASHY PLACE, ...   127 DREAM OF FAERY   17
    FOR HAPPY LOVERS PASSED TWO BY TWO WHERE I STOOD. . .   163 VALLEY LOVERS   2
    I PASSED MY BROTHER AND COUSIN: . . . .   178 FIDDLER DOONEY   5
    FOR ALTHOUGH YEARS HAD PASSED AWAY . . . .   192 BAILE AILLINN   77
    HAVE THE BIRDS PASSED US? I COULD HEAR YOUR VOICE, . .   226 SHADOW WATER B   81
    BUT THAT I AM AFRAID THEY MAY HAVE PASSED, ...   226 SHADOW WATER B   84
    THAT HAS NOT PASSED THROUGH ANY HUCKSTER'S LOIN, . . .   269 PARDON FATHERS   8
    BUT THE STAG STOOPED AND RAN AT HIM, AND PASSED, . . .   277 TWO KINGS   12
    AND RAN AT HIM, AND PASSED, AND AS IT PASSED . . . . .   277 TWO KINGS   V 12A
    AND RAN AT HIM, AND PASSED, AND AS IT PASSED . . . . .   277 TWO KINGS   V 12A
    AND MOCKS RETURNING VICTORY, HE PASSED . . . .   279 TWO KINGS   58
    AND SO THE WEEKS PASSED BY. BUT WHEN I SAID, ...   280 TWO KINGS   89
    THE MOMENTS PASSED AS AT A PLAY: . . . .   313 MEMORY YOUTH   1
    AND, THOUGH YOU HAVE PASSED THE BEST OF LIFE, STILL TRACE,   367 EGO DOMINUS   5
    I HAVE PASSED WITH A NOD OF THE HEAD . . . .   392 EASTER 1916   5
    WHO TROD UPON THESE ROCKS OR PASSED THIS DOOR, ...   413 TOWER   98
    WHEN ALEXANDER'S EMPIRE PASSED, THEY SLEPT SO SOUND. . .   442 BLACK CENTAUR   12
    SO GREAT ITS FAME. WHEN FITTING TIME HAS PASSED . . .   461 HARUN RASHID   19
    IN CHILDISH IGNORANCE OF ALL THAT PASSED. . . . . . .   468 HARUN RASHID   149
    IN CHILDISH IGNORANCE OF ALL THAT PASSED. . . . . . .   468 HARUN RASHID   160
    SEVEN CENTURIES HAVE PASSED AND IT IS PURE, ...   482 BLOOD AND MOON   33
    MEN HAVE PASSED OVER . . . .   512 JANE ON GOD   V   21
    THROUGH JONATHAN SWIFT'S DARK GROVE HE PASSED, AND THERE   543 PARN FUNERAL 2   11
    FROM TIME LONG PASSED AWAY, ...   589 OLD WICKED MAN   42
    I PASSED BY MANY CAVES OF DRIPPING STONE, ...   657 ISLE STAT I 3   47
    HE PASSED ACROSS THE LAKE. WHEN WE TWO CAME . . . .   658 ISLE STAT II 1   5
    THEY PASSED A-TIP-TOE EVERYWHERE, ...   667 ISLE STAT II 3   20
    THEY PASSED A-TIPTOE EVERYWHERE, ...   667 ISLE STAT II 3 V   20
    THE SINGING SHEPHERDS, TOO, HAVE PASSED AWAY. . . . .   676 ISLE STAT II 3   271
    AND WHEN ONCE MORE THE LIGHTNING GENII PASSED, ...   687 TWO TITANS   29
    DRAW STAR TO STAR, AS ON THAT EVE HE PASSED . . . . .   691 MOSADA 1   29
    SO LITTLE. AS THE MONTHS PASSED BY WE GREW . . . . .   713 FERENCZ RENYI   93
    DEEP IN THE WOODLAND PASSED THEY. THE SIX FEET . . . .   716 DWELT SYCAMORE   9
    SLOW THE CHAPEL BELL IS TOLLING AS THOUGH THE DEAD PASSED   718 PHANTOM SHIP   16
        BY.
    AND PASSED THE OUTER HEBRIDES, AND TOOK . . . . . .   749 SHADOW WATER A   42
    FROM HILLY LOCHLANN: BUT OUR SAIL HAS PASSED . . . .   749 SHADOW WATER A   44
    AND PASSED THE NORTHERN HEBRIDES, AND TOOK . . . . .   749 SHADOW WATER A V   42
    IT PASSED BUT A MOMENT AGO. . . . .   781 MY HEART BEAT   3
    IT PASSED BY A MOMENT AGO. . . . .   781 MY HEART BEAT   V   3
PASSES
    WHO DREAMED THAT BEAUTY PASSES LIKE A DREAM? . . . .   111 ROSE OF WORLD   1
    WHY MUST THE LASTING LOVE WHAT PASSES, ...   275 GREY ROCK   114
    IT IS OF GOD AND PASSES HUMAN WIT. . . . .   558 RIBH CHRISTIAN   2
PASSETH
    IT PASSETH AWAY, AND IS HEARD OF NO LONGER. . . . . .   26 OISIN 1   V 399B
    PASSETH THE MOON WITH HER SICKLE OF LIGHT, ...   648 ISLE STAT I 1   82
PASSING
    AND PASSING THE FIRBOLGS' BURIAL-MOUNDS, ...   3 OISIN 1   16
    AND PASSING THE FIRBOLGS' BURIAL MOUNDS, ...   3 OISIN 1   V   16
    BACCHANT AND MOURNFUL, PASSING TO AND FRO . . . . . .   39 OISIN 2   161
    WE AND THE LABOURING WORLD ARE PASSING BY: . . . . .   112 ROSE OF WORLD   6
    UNDER THE PASSING STARS, FOAM OF THE SKY, ...   112 ROSE OF WORLD   9
    ARE PASSING ON TO WHERE MAY BE, ...   139 TO IRELAND   41
    THE WEST WEEPS IN PALE DEW AND SIGHS PASSING AWAY, . .   154 BELOVED PEACE   5
    LIVE BUT TO LIGHT YOUR PASSING FEET. . . . .   158 BELOVED RHYMES   12
    ONE THAT NO PASSING THOUGHT, ...   315 FRIENDS   V   4
    ARE BUT A POST THE PASSING DOGS DEFILE. . . . . . .   321 REED WHISPERER   14
    WHEN YOU ARE PASSING: . . . .   355 BROKEN DREAMS   3
    OF WHAT IS PAST, OR PASSING, OR TO COME. . . . . . .   408 SAIL BYZANTIUM   32
    THROUGH TOO MUCH BUSINESS WITH THE PASSING HOUR, . . .   423 MY DESCENDANTS   11
    TO PASSING BIRD, BUT I AM DUMB . . . .   452 HUMAN DIGNITY   11
    PASSING ON THE ROAD THAT NIGHT, ...   511 JANE AND JACK   17
    FOR PASSING ROUND THE BOTTLE WITH GIRLS IN RAGS OR SILK,   592 PILGRIM   2
    FOR PASSING ROUND THE BOTTLE WITH GIRLS IN RAG OR SILK,   592 PILGRIM   V   2
    FROM ANY PASSING WRETCH: . . . .   598 STONE CROSS   12
    THE BRAIN. MY BROTHERS WILL BE PASSING DOWN . . . .   699 MOSADA 3   V   6
    THE PASSING OF THOSE LITTLE GRAINS IS SNOW . . . . .   722 WITCH VIVIEN   48
    A GREY PROFESSOR PASSING CRIED, ...   725 LEGEND   9
    A PASSING WORD. . . . .   786 YOUR HEART   13
    A PASSING WORD. . . . .   786 YOUR HEART   26
    A PASSING WORD. . . . .   786 YOUR HEART   39
    MAY MURDER THEM IN PASSING BY . . . .   791 REPRISALS   21
PASSIO   SEE HYSTERICO-PASSIO
    HYSTERICA PASSIO DRAGGED THIS QUARRY DOWN. . . . . .   542 PARN FUNERAL 1   21
    HYSTERICA PASSIO OF ITS OWN EMPTINESS? . . . .   618 BRONZE HEAD   7
PASSION
    LET US PART, ERE THE SEASON OF PASSION FORGET US, . .   79 FALLING LEAVES   7
    WHEN THE POOR TIRED CHILD, PASSION, FALLS ASLEEP. . . .   80 EPHEMERA   7
    "PASSION HAS OFTEN WORN OUR WANDERING HEARTS." . . . .   80 EPHEMERA   12
    "OFTEN HAS PASSION WORN OUR WANDERING HEARTS, ...   80 EPHEMERA   V   12

```
                                                           PAGE      TITLE            LINE

PASSION   (CONTINUED)
    WHITE WOMAN THAT PASSION HAS WORN . . . . . . . . . .    157  POET BELOVED          3
    THE TRAVAIL OF PASSION . . . . . . . . . . . . . .       172  TRAV PASSION          T
    WHEN AN IMMORTAL PASSION BREATHES IN MORTAL CLAY;  . .   172  TRAV PASSION          2
    BUT THE REALITY THAT MAKES OUR PASSION . . . . . .       229  SHADOW WATER B      159
    WHERE PASSION GROWS TO BE A CHANGELESS THING, . . . .    231  SHADOW WATER B      213
    BY ANY OTHER MEANS.  YOU CALL IT PASSION, . . . . .      244  SHADOW WATER B      455
    WHERE PASSION AND PRECISION HAVE BEEN ONE . . . . .      264  HOUSE SHAKEN          2
    PRETENDING THAT THERE CAN BE PASSION . . . . .          271  GREY ROCK             7
    AND TREMBLING WITH HER PASSION SAID, . . . . . .        272  GREY ROCK            31
    SOME PASSION HAD MADE HER STONE.  HEARING A FOOT . .     279  TWO KINGS            65
    THAT PUT A PASSION IN THE SLEEPER THERE, . . . . .       284  TWO KINGS           157
    SUCKED UP THE PASSION OUT OF HIM AGAIN . . . . . .       284  TWO KINGS           160
    THEY'VE THE PASSION TO ESCAPE." . . . . . . . .         299  THREE HERMITS        21
    PASSION OR CONQUEST, WANDER WHERE THEY WILL, . . .       323  SWANS AT COOLE       23
    AND SOLID MEN, FOR ALL THEIR PASSION, LIVE . . . .       325  ROBERT GREGORY       37
    COURTESY AND PASSION INTO ONE LIKE THOSE . . . . .       352  PEOPLE               17
    WITH ALL A WOMAN'S PASSION, A CHILD'S IMPERIOUS WAY,     354  HIS PHOENIX          14
    THE POET STUBBORN WITH HIS PASSION SANG US . . . .       356  BROKEN DREAMS        18
    WE HAVE GIVEN THE WORLD OUR PASSION, . . . . . .        363  DOLLS DRAWINGS       10
    --PEDANT IN PASSION, LEARNED IN OLD COURTESIES, . .      363  DOLLS FACES           4
    A SUFFERING PASSION AND A LABOURING THOUGHT? . . .       420  MY HOUSE       V   20J
    THAT PASSION, PIETY OR AFFECTION KNOWS, . . . . .        445  SCHOOL CHILDR        54
    IT MAKES MY PASSION STRONGER BUT TO THINK . . . .        465  HARUN RASHID         99
    LIKE PASSION STIRS THE PEACOCK AND HIS MATE, . . .       465  HARUN RASHID        100
    AND THAT TO SUCH A PITCH OF PASSION WROUGHT . . . .      471  ALL SOUL NIGHT       24
    HOW COULD PASSION RUN SO DEEP . . . . . . . .           534  CONSOLATION           7
    TO THINK HIS PASSION SUCH . . . . . . . . . .           538  LAST CONFESS          8
    WHEN THE CONFLAGRATION OF THEIR PASSION SINKS, . . .     556  RIBH PATRICK          8
    FOR THAT'S A PASSION IN MY OWN CONTROL, . . . . .        558  RIBH CHRISTIAN        4
    ETERNITY IS PASSION, GIRL OR BOY . . . . . . .          560  WHENCE COME           1
    A ROOF, GOOD CLOTHES, PASSION, LOVE PERHAPS, . . .       609  IN TARAS HALLS        8
    THAT PASSION COULD BRING CHARACTER ENOUGH, . . . .       610  STATUES               6
    WHERE DREAM-FED PASSION IS AND PEACE ENCLOSES, . . .     669  ISLE STAT II 3       85
    THEIR PASSION AND THEIR RESTLESSNESS AND RUTH . . .      687  TWO TITANS           24
PASSIONATE
    WHERE PASSIONATE MAEVE IS STONY-STILL; . . . . . .         3  OISIN 1              18
    WHERE PASSIONATE MAIVE IS STONY STILL; . . . . . .         3  OISIN 1         V    18
    HUNG IN THE PASSIONATE DAWN.  HE SLOWLY TURNED;  . .      40  OISIN 2             167
    . . . AND ITS GODLESS AND PASSIONATE AGE. . . . .        63  OISIN 3             216
    OF PASSIONATE MEN, LIKE BATS IN THE DEAD TREES; . .     136  TO SOME I TALK        5
    I BRING YOU MY PASSIONATE RHYME. . . . . . . .          157  POET BELOVED          8
    LILIES OF DEATH-PALE HOPE, ROSES OF PASSIONATE DREAM.    172  TRAV PASSION          8
    TO PASSIONATE WOMEN IF IT SEEM . . . . . . . .          202  NEVER GIVE ALL        3
    AENGUS AND EDAIN, THOSE PASSIONATE WANDERERS, . . .      228  SHADOW WATER B      138
    OF YOUR OWN PASSIONATE SERVING KIND WHO HAD BROUGHT .    292  TO A SHADE           10
    OF YOUR OWN PASSIONATE SERVING KIND WHO HAS BROUGHT .    292  TO A SHADE      V    10
    PASSIONATE AND SIMPLE LIKE HIS HEART. . . . . .         325  ROBERT GREGORY       32
    BE PASSIONATE, NOT BOUNTIFUL . . . . . . . .           335  YOUNG BEAUTY          8
    AND PASSIONATE AS THE DAWN." . . . . . . . .           348  FISHERMAN            40
    BUT WHAT THE GREAT AND PASSIONATE HAVE USED . . . .      371  ON GOING HOUSE        7
    ARE FULL OF PASSIONATE INTENSITY. . . . . . .          402  SECOND COMING         8
    EXCITED, PASSIONATE, FANTASTICAL . . . . . . .         409  TOWER                 5
    HEARD ALL THE ANXIETY OF MY PASSIONATE YOUTH, . . .      468  HARUN RASHID        168
    A FOOLISH, PASSIONATE MAN. . . . . . . . . .           553  PRAYER OLD AGE       12
    SO PASSIONATE IS A SHADE, . . . . . . . . . .          781  MY HEART BEAT        13
PASSION-DIMMED
    PASSION-DIMMED EYES AND LONG HEAVY HAIR . . . . .       155  REPROVE CURLEW        4
PASSION-DRIVEN
    A PASSION-DRIVEN EXULTANT MAN SINGS OUT . . . . .       560  WHENCE COME           5
PASSIONED
    DAWN PASSIONED, FED WITH A FAINT GREEN LIGHT, . . .      40  OISIN 2         V   165
PASSION'S
    PARDON THAT FOR A BARREN PASSION'S SAKE, . . . . .      270  PARDON FATHERS       19
    AYE, THOUGH ALL PASSION'S IN THE GLANCE-- . . . .       388  SOLOMON WITCH        21
PASSIONS
    NONE MAY BEGUILE HIM, AND HIS PASSIONS COLD  . . . .     35  OISIN 2         V   83A
    YET WEARY WITH PASSIONS THAT FADED . . . . . .          50  OISIN 3              52
    LIKE TATTERED CLOUDS OF THE WORLD, PASSIONS CALL AND OUR 207  HANRAHANS SONG V      8
        HEARTS BEAT;
    TWO CONTEMPLATING PASSIONS CHOSE ONE THEME . . . . .     466  HARUN RASHID        117
    COMPLETENESS OF THEIR PASSIONS WON; . . . . . .         637  BEN BULBEN            9
    OF ANCIENT PASSIONS AND OF ANCIENT FEARS? . . . .       724  KANVA ON SELF        16
PAST
    IN DREARY DANCING PAST US WHIRLED, . . . . . . .         65  HAPPY SHEPHERD        8
    A SONG INTO THE AIR, AND SINGING PAST . . . . .         114  ROSE OF BATTLE V     14
    HE THINKS OF HIS PAST GREATNESS . . . . . . .          177  PAST GREATNESS        T
    MONGAN THINKS OF HIS PAST GREATNESS . . . . .          177  PAST GREATNESS V      T
    OR CLIMBED AMONG THE IMAGES OF THE PAST-- . . . .       352  PEOPLE               10
    AN IMAGE FROM A PAST LIFE . . . . . . . . .            389  IMAGE PAST            T
    YOUTH'S BITTERNESS BEING PAST, . . . . . . . .         389  IMAGE PAST           11
    OF WHAT IS PAST, OR PASSING, OR TO COME. . . . .        408  SAIL BYZANTIUM       32
    THERE LURCHES PAST, HIS GREAT EYES WITHOUT THOUGHT .     433  NINETEEN 19         126
    PROTECTING, TILL THE DANGER PAST, . . . . . .          436  FOR MY SON           31
    WHEN ALEXANDER'S EMPIRE PAST, THEY SLEPT SO SOUND. .     442  BLACK CENTAUR  V     12
    WHEN CRADLE AND SPOOL ARE PAST . . . . . . .           449  HERO GIRL FOOL       24
    HAD HEARD IMPOSSIBLE HISTORY OF MY PAST; . . . .        466  HARUN RASHID        108
    LONG PAST HIS PRIME REMEMBER THINGS THAT ARE . . .      477  SELF AND SOUL        18
    FOR LOVER IN THE PAST; . . . . . . . . . .             539  MEETING              10
    ALL THAT GREAT PAST TO A TROUBLE OF FOOLS; . . . .      546  TO SAME TUNE 2       22
```

	PAGE	TITLE		LINE

PAST   (CONTINUED)

HOW SOUL MAY WALK WHEN ALL SUCH THINGS ARE PAST, ... 558 RIBH CHRISTIAN   11
ALL THAT GREAT PAST TO A TROUBLE OF FOOLS; . . . . . . 614 MARCH SONGS 1   22
STRICKEN ALL THE NIGHT IS PAST-- . . . . 648 ISLE STAT I 1   96
PAST THE SPEARS AND PALM-STEMS DRY, ... 733 STREET DANCERS   42
PAST THE CAMEL'S DREAMING EYE. . . . . 733 STREET DANCERS   43

PASTERN

WHOSE CAREFUL PASTERN PRESSED THE SOD . . . . 2 OISIN 1   V   7W

PASTURE

TO PLOUGH OR PASTURE LAND, MIGHT SEE ME THERE . . . . . 283 TWO KINGS   V 146
AND OVER TILLAGE FIELDS AND PASTURE LANDS . . . . . 715 FERENCZ RENYI   120
AND FOLLOWING O'ER THE FIELDS AND PASTURE LANDS, ... 715 FERENCZ RENYI   V 120
BY THE PASTURE WHERE THE LAMBS . . . . 726 LOVERS QUARREL   5

PASTURED   SEE MANY-PASTURED

TO MANY PASTURED MUIRTHEMNE, ... 189 BAILE AILLINN V   21

PASTURE-LAND

TO PLOUGH OR PASTURE-LAND, MIGHT SEE ME THERE, ... 283 TWO KINGS   146
OF PASTURE-LAND AND PLOUGH-LAND AMONG THE HILLS? . . . . 748 SHADOW WATER A   33

PATCH

SOME ROGUE OF THE WORLD STOLE THEM TO PATCH UP A FENCE 623 HIGH TALK   4
  OR A FIRE.
MY THOUGHTS, AND YONDER BRIGHTENING PATCH OF SKY . . . . 700 MOSADA 3   31

PATCHED

WITH OLD PATCHED SHOES, ... 627 STATES HOLIDAY   30

PATCHING

THAT PATCHING OLD HEELS THEY MAY SHRIEK, I TAKE TO CHISEL 623 HIGH TALK   8
  AND PLANE.

PATE

"AND MAKE MY SOUL BEFORE MY PATE IS BARE." . . . . . . 299 BEGGAR CRIED   4

PATED   SEE GREEN-PATED CRACK-PATED

PATER

AND MANY PATER NOSTERS SAID SINCE DAWN. . . . . 43 OISIN 2   V 208D
HE HAD LEARNT FROM PATER, AND TO ROUND HIS TALE . . . . 373 PHASES OF MOON   27

PATH   SEE BRIDLE-PATH

FOR ALL YOUR CROZIERS, THEY HAVE LEFT THE PATH . . . . 42 OISIN 2   200
I FELL ON THE PATH, AND THE HORSE WENT AWAY LIKE A SUMMER 60 OISIN 3   190
  FLY;
A RABBIT OLD AND LAME LIMPED DOWN THE PATH; . . . . . 80 EPHEMERA   15
I HAVE BEEN IN THE PATH OF STONES AND THE WOOD OF THORNS, 153 CHANGE BELOVED   3
I KNOW OF THE LEAFY PATH THAT THE WITCHES TAKE, ... 203 WITHER BOUGHS V   9
BECAUSE IT STOOD UPON HIS PATH AND SEEMED . . . . . 277 TWO KINGS   8
STOOD ON MY PATH. TREMBLING FROM HEAD TO FOOT . . . . 283 TWO KINGS   151
STOOD ON MY PATH. TREMBLING FROM HAND TO FOOT . . . . 283 TWO KINGS   V 151
HAVE FOUND THE PATH MY GOATS' FEET CANNOT FIND. . . . . 342 SHEP GOATHERD   84
HAVE FOUND THE PATH MY GOAT'S FEET CANNOT FIND. . . . . 342 SHEP GOATHERD   V   84
OR HURRIED THEM OFF ON ITS OWN FURIOUS PATH; . . . . . 430 NINETEEN 19   53
MAY UNWIND THE WINDING PATH; . . . . 497 BYZANTIUM   12
THE PATH O'ER-MUFFLED WITH THE LEAVES--DEAD LEAVES, . . . 703 MOSADA 3   115
THE PATH O'ER MUFFLED WITH THE LEAVES--DEAD LEAVES, . . . 703 MOSADA 3   V 115
WEASEL WARMS HIM ON THE PATH, ... 705 DAWN-SONG   19
WHISPERING ALONG THE SUNNY PATH; . . . . 725 LEGEND   18
A PATH AMONG THESE WAVES AND WEIGH THE WIND? . . . . . 748 SHADOW WATER A   21

PATHS

I KNOW OF THE LEAFY PATHS THAT THE WITCHES TAKE . . . . 203 WITHER BOUGHS   9
WHERE HAZEL AND ASH AND PRIVET BLIND THE PATHS; . . . . 217 WOODS OF COOLE   8
NOR ON THE ANCIENT BEATEN PATHS, THAT WOUND . . . . . 279 TWO KINGS   52
THE WOODLAND PATHS ARE DRY, ... 322 SWANS AT COOLE   2
CANNOT ENDURE TO THINK YOU TREAD THESE PATHS, ... 463 HARUN RASHID   52
THE GARDEN PATHS, NOR COUNTED UP THE ROOMS, ... 466 HARUN RASHID   119

PATHWAY

ON OUR DARK PATHWAY, TILL A COUNTLESS FLIGHT . . . . . 31 OISIN 2   34
A WHITEBEARD STOOD HUSHED ON THE PATHWAY, ... 59 OISIN 3   173
BUT PRONE ON THE PATHWAY, PRONE STRUGGLING, ... 60 OISIN 3   V 186
AND ON MY PATHWAY STOOD . . . . 451 FIRST LOVE   4
THERE THY WANDERING PATHWAY GOES, ... 744 ROSY CROSS   6

PATIENCE

AWAITING IN PATIENCE THE STRAW-DEATH, ... 58 OISIN 3   167
ALL THAT YOU NEED IS PATIENCE." HEART CRIES, "NO, . . . 200 FOLLY COMFORT   6
PATIENCE IS ALL THAT YOU HAVE NEED OF." NO, ... 200 FOLLY COMFORT V   6
SHE THAT BUT LITTLE PATIENCE KNEW, ... 397 POLIT PRISONER   1

PATIENT

AND SO BE PATIENT; BE WISE AND PATIENT FRIEND." . . . . 200 FOLLY COMFORT V   6
AND SO BE PATIENT; BE WISE AND PATIENT FRIEND." . . . . 200 FOLLY COMFORT V   6
OLD FELLOW-STUDENT, WHOSE MOST PATIENT EAR . . . . . 468 HARUN RASHID   167
OLD FELLOW STUDENT, WHOSE MOST PATIENT EAR . . . . . 468 HARUN RASHID   V 167
MOCKING WITH PATIENT LAUGHTER ALL THE NIGHT . . . . . 657 ISLE STAT I 3   52
WITH PATIENT BEAUTY YONDER ATTIC BUST . . . . 685 DRAWING-ROOM   3
THAT RUSTLES IN THE REEDS WITH PATIENT PUSHES, ... 699 MOSADA 3   4
THAT'S RUSTLING IN THE REEDS WITH PATIENT PUSHES, . . . 699 MOSADA 3   V   4
ARE PRAYERS OF PATIENT MEN AND GOOD." . . . . 725 LEGEND   6
WITH PATIENT BEAUTY YONDER ATTIC BUST . . . . 735 QUATRAIN APHOR   23
BE PATIENT YET A WHILE; FOR THIS NINTH MOON, ... 748 SHADOW WATER A   23
BE PATIENT YET AWHILE; FOR THIS NINTH MOON, ... 748 SHADOW WATER A V   23

PATRICK   SEE CRO-PATRICK

O PATRICK, BY YOUR BRAZEN BELL, ... 7 OISIN 1   71
THERE WAS, OH PATRICK, BY THY HEAD, ... 7 OISIN 1   V   71
AND, PATRICK! BY YOUR BEARD, THEY WEPT, ... 17 OISIN 1   236
OH, PATRICK, BY THY BEARD, THEY WEPT, ... 17 OISIN 1   V 236
O PATRICK! FOR A HUNDRED YEARS . . . . 23 OISIN 1   343
O PATRICK! FOR A HUNDRED YEARS . . . . 23 OISIN 1   346
O PATRICK! FOR A HUNDRED YEARS . . . . 23 OISIN 1   351

		PAGE	TITLE		LINE

PATRICK   (CONTINUED)
    O PATRICK! FOR A HUNDRED YEARS . . . . 23 OISIN 1   356
    OH, PATRICK, ON THAT WOODY SHORE . . . . 23 OISIN 1   V   343
    OH, PATRICK, THERE A HUNDRED SEASONS . . . . 23 OISIN 1   V 345B
    OH, PATRICK, THERE A HUNDRED YEARS, ... 23 OISIN 1   346
    PATRICK, BEFORE THY CRAFT DIES EACH OLD SONG. . . . . 42 OISIN 2   V   196
    UPON CROAGH PATRICK SANG IT LOUD; . . . . 528 DANCER CRUACH V   5
    RIBH DENOUNCES PATRICK . . . . 556 RIBH PATRICK   T
    FOR PATRICK PEARSE HAD SAID . . . . 608 SONGS BURDEN 3   24
PATRIOTS
    OUR MOST RENOWNED PATRIOTS STAND, ... 460 THREE MONUMENT   2
PATS
    HUGS AND PETS AND PATS YON NEWT, ... 727 LOVERS QUARREL   27
PATTERN
    AND PUT HIS PATTERN ROUND THEIR TOPS . . . . 272 GREY ROCK   V   24
    A PATTERN ON A NAPKIN DIPPED IN BLOOD. . . . . 483 VERONIC NAPKIN   8
PATTERNS
    APPROVED PATTERNS OF WOMEN OR OF MEN . . . . 602 GALLERY REVIS   31
    THROUGH THEIR ANCESTRAL PATTERNS DANCE, ... 612 NEWS ORACLE   19
PAUDEEN
    PAUDEEN . . . . 291 PAUDEEN   T
    OF OUR OLD PAUDEEN IN HIS SHOP, I STUMBLED BLIND . . . 291 PAUDEEN   2
PAUDEEN'S
    UNTIL ENOUGH OF PAUDEEN'S PENCE . . . . 287 TO WEALTHY MAN   2
PAUDEENS
    LET PAUDEENS PLAY AT PITCH AND TOSS, ... 288 TO WEALTHY MAN   31
    LEAVE PAUDEENS TO THEIR PITCH AND TOSS; . . . . 288 TO WEALTHY MAN V   31
PAUL
    LEARNED LIKE A MAN? PAUL VERONESE . . . . 386 ROBARTES DANCE   26
    THE BALLAD OF EARL PAUL . . . . 739 EARL PAUL   T
    MEN CRY "BRING PAUL, SHIELD BREAKER, ... 740 EARL PAUL   11
    EARL PAUL STOOD ON THE BED OF STRAW, ... 740 EARL PAUL   17
    WHEN PAUL RODE FROM THE TOWN . . . . 740 EARL PAUL   21
    EARL PAUL CAME WHERE THE KING SAT, ... 740 EARL PAUL   29
    MEN CRY: "BRING PAUL, SHIELD-BREAKER, ... 740 EARL PAUL   V   11
    SAYING "EARL PAUL IS PARDONED . . . . 741 EARL PAUL   55
PAUPER
    LIKE AN OLD PAUPER, IN ALL KINDS OF WEATHER; . . . . . 205 ADAMS CURSE   9
PAUSE
    AND PAUSE AT LAST, I WAS ABOUT TO SAY, ... 461 HARUN RASHID   11
    PAUSE AT THE TREATISE OF PARMENIDES . . . . 461 HARUN RASHID   16
    SO! MID THE WILLOW-GLADE YOU PAUSE AT LAST. . . . . . 651 ISLE STAT I 2   2
    OF WAR. OF YORE, TWO SHEPHERDS, WHERE WE PAUSE, . . . 659 ISLE STAT II 1   31
    HUSH! HUSH! THEY PAUSE AND POINT . . . . 732 STREET DANCERS   31
    HUSH! HUSH! HUSH! THEY PAUSE THEM WHERE . . . . 733 STREET DANCERS   44
PAUSED
    HE SHIVERING PAUSED, AND RAISED HIS HEAD AND SCREAMED. . 30 OISIN 2   V   25
    I PAUSED--THE STARS ABOVE ME FLASHED, ... 83 MAD KING GOLL   V   29
    I PAUSED--THE STARS ABOVE ME SHONE . . . . 83 MAD KING GOLL   V   29
    I PAUSED--AND FAR AWAY I DASHED . . . . 83 MAD KING GOLL   V   31
    I PAUSED--AND FAR AWAY RUSHED ON, ... 83 MAD KING GOLL   V   31
    DEEP IN THE WOODLAND PAUSED THEY, THE SIX FEET . . . . 716 DWELT SYCAMORE   9
PAVEMENT
    WHILE I STAND ON THE ROADWAY, OR ON THE PAVEMENT GREY, . 117 ISLE INNISFREE V   11
    AND SCRUB A KITCHEN PAVEMENT, OR BREAK STONES . . . . 204 ADAMS CURSE   8
    AT MIDNIGHT ON THE EMPEROR'S PAVEMENT FLIT . . . . . 498 BYZANTIUM   25
PAVEMENTS
    WHILE I STAND ON THE ROADWAY, OR ON THE PAVEMENTS GREY, 117 ISLE INNISFREE   11
PAVEN
    ITS PAVEN LENGTH TOWARDS THE RIVER'S MARGE . . . . . 702 MOSADA 3   76
PAVLOVA'S
    FROM NINETEEN HUNDRED NINE OR TEN, PAVLOVA'S HAD THE CRY, 354 HIS PHOENIX   11
PAW
    A SPHINX WITH WOMAN BREAST AND LION PAW, ... 383 VISION ROBART   18
    HE'LL SNAP HIS SWORD. RAISED IS THE LION'S PAW. . . . 664 ISLE STAT II 2   63
PAWNS
    THUS PLAY WE FIRST WITH PAWNS, POOR THINGS AND WEAK; . . 722 WITCH VIVIEN   53
PAY
    YOU HAVE TAKEN PAY AND MADE YOUR BARGAIN FOR IT. . . . 225 SHADOW WATER B   68
    SILENCE! FOR YOU HAVE TAKEN FORGAEL'S PAY. . . . . . 225 SHADOW WATER B V   68
    WE JOINED HIM FOR HIS PAY, BUT HAVE HAD NONE . . . . 225 SHADOW WATER B V   68A
    AND PAY BUT A KISS FOR A KISS. . . . . 330 BONE OF A HARE   8
    WE CANNOT PAY ITS TRIBUTE OF WILD TEARS. . . . . . . 334 LIVING BEAUTY   10
    OR WHO HAVE FOUND A PAINTER TO MAKE THEM SO FOR PAY . . 353 HIS PHOENIX   6
    CAN PAY THE POET FOR A VERSE AND HEAR THE FIDDLE SOUND, 581 CURSE CROMWELL   21
    AND WHEN I PAY ATTENTION I MUST OUT AND WALK . . . . 581 CURSE CROMWELL   29
    HE TAKES THE DEVIL'S PAY. . . . . 582 ROGER CASEMENT V   20
    AND ALL MUST PAY HIM HEED, ... 583 GHOST ROG CASE   22
PAYMENT
    IS BUT A PAYMENT FOR THAT MIDNIGHT VOICE . . . . . . 469 HARUN RASHID   173
    WHAT PAYMENT WERE ENOUGH . . . . 518 HIS CONFIDENCE   5
PAYMENTS
    WHAT PAYMENTS WERE ENOUGH . . . . 518 HIS CONFIDENCE V   5
PEACE
    AND YET, OF YORE, MUCH PEACE HE HAD . . . . 2 OISIN 1   V   7K
    AND YET, OF YORE, MUCH PEACE HE HAD, ... 4 OISIN 1   V   36
    BID THEM AWAY AND HOLD THEIR PEACE; . . . . 15 OISIN 1   212
    . . . WHEN, ROLLED IN A GRISLY PEACE, ... 47 OISIN 3   9
    FOR THY YOUTH WITHOUT PEACE, AND THY YEARS WITH THE DEMONS, 63 OISIN 3   V   216
    . . .
    SEND PEACE ON ALL THE LANDS AND FLICKERING CORN.-- . . 71 ANASHU VIJAYA   1

607

	PAGE	TITLE		LINE
PEACE (CONTINUED)				
THAT WORD OF THE SOUL'S PEACE--"ETERNITY."	81	EPHEMERA	V	24B
CRIED A HERALD, "PEACE WITH THINE"	82	MAD KING GOLL	V	14
SING PEACE INTO HIS BREAST,	88	STOLEN CHILD		47
AND HE SAID WITH A SMILE, "HAVE PEACE NOW";	92	FATHER OHART		19
THE ROSE OF PEACE	112	ROSE OF PEACE		T
THE PEACE OF THE ROSE	112	ROSE OF PEACE	V	T
AND SOFTLY MAKE A ROSY PEACE,	113	ROSE OF PEACE		15
A PEACE OF HEAVEN WITH HELL.	113	ROSE OF PEACE		16
DANGER NO REFUGE HOLDS, AND WAR NO PEACE,	114	ROSE OF BATTLE		9
AND I SHALL HAVE SOME PEACE THERE, FOR PEACE COMES DROPPING SLOW,	117	ISLE INNISFREE		5
AND I SHALL HAVE SOME PEACE THERE, FOR PEACE COMES DROPPING SLOW,	117	ISLE INNISFREE		5
AND LOVER THERE BY LOVER BE AT PEACE.	128	DREAM OF FAERY		35
AND ALL THEIR TROUBLE DIES INTO ITS PEACE;--	128	DREAM OF FAERY	V	35
"I HAVE NO REST, NOR JOY, NOR PEACE,	132	FR GILLIGAN		9
HE BIDS HIS BELOVED BE AT PEACE	154	BELOVED PEACE		T
MICHAEL ROBARTES BIDS HIS BELOVED BE AT PEACE	154	BELOVED PEACE	V	T
IF THIS IMPORTUNATE HEART TROUBLE YOUR PEACE	162	ASKS FORGIVE		1
O WHERE IS OUR MOTHER OF PEACE	171	MAID QUIET	V	1
AND OUR MOTHER OF PEACE HAS FORGOT ME	171	MAID QUIET	V	7
ENCIRCLE HER I LOVE AND SING HER INTO PEACE,	174	ELEMENT POWERS		9
IN OWING THEM THE BRIDE-BED THAT GIVES PEACE."	187	QUEEN MAEVE		148
AND FLYING TOWARDS THEIR PEACE. PUT BY THESE THOUGHTS,	226	SHADOW WATER B		91
HAD SEEMED TO BE THE GIVER OF ALL PEACE,	228	SHADOW WATER B		149
PEACE	258	PEACE		T
AH, BUT PEACE THAT COMES AT LENGTH,	259	PEACE		10
O HEART, BE AT PEACE, BECAUSE	259	UNWORTH PRAISE		1
HALF LION, HALF CHILD, IS AT PEACE.	260	UNWORTH PRAISE		20
DELIGHT IN ART WHOSE END IS PEACE,	288	TO WEALTHY MAN		26
AND HEAR AMID THE GARDEN'S NIGHTLY PEACE,"	300	BEGGAR CRIED		18
I CANNOT FIND THE PEACE OF HOME	332	ROUND TOWER		29
SO GREAT HER PORTION IN THAT PEACE YOU MAKE	356	BROKEN DREAMS		12
YET LITTLE PEACE HE HAD,	383	VISION ROBART		35
I HAVE PREPARED MY PEACE	415	TOWER		157
WHETHER HEALTH, WEALTH OR PEACE OF MIND WERE SPENT	429	NINETEEN 19		36
IT DROPPED THE REINS OF PEACE AND WAR	437	SONGS PLAY 1		14
NOR ACCIDENT OF PEACE NOR WAR	446	COLONUS PRAISE		14
UNCHANGING AND AT PEACE, AND IT IS RIGHT	465	HARUN RASHID		96
IT SEEMS I MUST BUY KNOWLEDGE WITH MY PEACE.	468	HARUN RASHID		169
ONE THAT IS PERFECT OR AT PEACE,	528	DANCER CRUACH		3
INNOCENCE AND PEACE DEPART.	561	FOUR AGES MAN		4
UNDER A RULE, UNDER THE SEMBLANCE OF PEACE	563	MERU		2
LAUGHS ALOUD, HIS HEART AT PEACE.	638	BEN BULBEN		32
PEACE, PEACE, THE EARTH'S A-QUAKE. I HEAR	656	ISLE STAT I 3		20
PEACE, PEACE, THE EARTH'S A-QUAKE. I HEAR	656	ISLE STAT I 3		20
A LONG, BROWN GRASSHOPPER OF MAIDS! PEACE, SIR!	661	ISLE STAT II 1		69
WHERE DREAM-FED PASSION IS AND PEACE ENCLOSES,	669	ISLE STAT II 3		85
THOU'LT TEACH ME LAUGHING, AND I'LL TEACH THEE PEACE,	670	ISLE STAT II 3		101
FOR PEACE AND LAUGHTER HAVE BEEN SELDOM FRIENDS.	670	ISLE STAT II 3		103
BUT ART THOU HAPPY? YOUTH, I AM AT PEACE.	672	ISLE STAT II 3		150
THESE ARE AT PEACE.	672	ISLE STAT II 3		159
THY PEACE. AH, NOW I'LL WAKE THESE SLEEPERS, LOST	677	ISLE STAT II 3		274
AND PEACE BE WITH YOU, PEACE AND WEALTH OF DAYS.	682	SEEKER		28
AND PEACE BE WITH YOU, PEACE AND WEALTH OF DAYS.	682	SEEKER		28
WHERE LIES THE COW AT PEACE BESIDE HER CALF,	715	FERENCZ RENYI		121
WHERE DWELL THE MINDS OF OLD MEN HAVING PEACE,	721	WITCH VIVIEN		22
I DO NOT NEED YOUR SCYTHE. MAY THAT BRING PEACE	721	WITCH VIVIEN		26
SUCH WAR PLOTS, PEACE PLOTS, LOVE PLOTS--EVERY SIDE!	722	WITCH VIVIEN		66
PEACE OF YOUTH AND PEACE OF AGE,	733	STREET DANCERS		46
PEACE OF YOUTH AND PEACE OF AGE,	733	STREET DANCERS		46
ARE WISER WITCHCRAFT, FOR OUR PEACE AWAKES	763	SHADOW WATER A		320
THESE MESSENGERS TO LURE MEN TO HIS PEACE,	764	SHADOW WATER A		336
PEACEABLE				
PEACEABLE MEN THAT SHUT THE WIND AWAY,	224	SHADOW WATER B		54
AND KISS MORE LIPS THAN LASTING PEACEABLE MEN	225	SHADOW WATER B		71
PEACEFUL				
THAT MANY A PEACEFUL MOMENT HAD, --	4	OISIN 1		35
"HE BRINGS THE PEACEFUL AGE OF GOLD"--	82	MAD KING GOLL	V	11
WHAT COULD HAVE MADE HER PEACEFUL WITH A MIND	256	NO SECOND TROY		6
WOULD END THIS PEACEFUL LIFE THAT ROTS THE BONES,	752	SHADOW WATER A		110
PEACE-MAKING				
PEACE-MAKING, MILD, A KINGLY BOY.	82	MAD KING GOLL	V	8
PEACHES				
AND THRICE THE PEACHES FLUSHED UPON THE WALLS,	690	MOSADA 1		2
PEACOCK				
I PASSED A LITTLE FURTHER ON AND HEARD A PEACOCK SAY:	77	INDIAN ON GOD		17
HE IS A MONSTROUS PEACOCK, AND HE WAVETH ALL THE NIGHT	77	INDIAN ON GOD		19
I PACED A LITTLE FURTHER AND I HEARD A PEACOCK SAY:--	77	INDIAN ON GOD		17
I PASSED A LITTLE FURTHER AND I HEARD A PEACOCK SAY:--	77	INDIAN ON GOD	V	17
THE PEACOCK	310	PEACOCK		T
THAT HAS MADE A GREAT PEACOCK	310	PEACOCK		2
O WHAT IF GARDENS WHERE THE PEACOCK STRAYS	418	ANCEST HOUSES		25
JUNO'S PEACOCK SCREAMED.	422	MY TABLE		32
BRONZED PEACOCK FEATHERS, RED COMBS OF HER COCKS.	433	NINETEEN 19		130
I'D HAVE A PEACOCK CRY,	458	HIS WILDNESS		8
LIKE PASSION STIRS THE PEACOCK AND HIS MATE,	465	HARUN RASHID		100
TORTOISESHELL BUTTERFLIES, PEACOCK BUTTERFLIES,	482	BLOOD AND MOON		45
PEACOCKS				
SHRIEKS, "I AM KING OF THE PEACOCKS,"	456	FRIENDS YOUTH		15

PEAHENS
    THE PEAHENS DANCE ON A SMOOTH LAWN, ...   77 INDIAN TO LOVE   3
PEA-HENS
    THE PEA-HENS DANCE, IN CRIMSON FEATHER . . . .   77 INDIAN TO LOVE V   3
PEAK
    TO PEAK AND PINE O'ER OISIN'S FAME." . . . .   7 OISIN 1   V 70
    AND PEAK AND PINE WE KNOW NOT WHY, ...   22 OISIN 1   V 340C
    ON THE FAR GOLDEN PEAK: ENORMOUS SHAPES, ...   74 ANASHU VIJAYA   68
PEALED
    FROM THE HILLS OF EARTH HAVE PEALED . . . . 705 DAWN-SONG   5
PEAR
    A PEAR TREE BROKEN BY THE STORM. . . . . 424 ROAD AT DOOR V 10
PEARL   SEE MOTHER-OF-PEARL
    AND IT WAS BOUND WITH A PEARL PALE SHELL . . . . .   4 OISIN 1   V 28
    OF SEA-SPRUNG PEARL, AND QUEENS OF FAIRY LANDS . . .   29 OISIN 2   V 10A
    WHO COME WITH THEIR CROWNS OF PEARL AND THEIR SPINDLES 203 WITHER BOUGHS   10
        OF WOOL,
    ROLLING A BLIND PEARL EYE, ... 552 SONGS REWRIT 2   2
    THAT MY TRUE-LOVE WOULD COME IN A SHIP OF PEARL . . . 763 SHADOW WATER A V 315
    THAT MY TRUE LOVE WOULD COME IN A SHIP OF PEARL . . . 763 SHADOW WATER A V 315
PEARL-PALE
    A PEARL-PALE, HIGH-BORN LADY, WHO RODE . . . . . .   3 OISIN 1   20
    AND IT WAS BOUND WITH A PEARL-PALE SHELL . . . . .   4 OISIN 1   28
    THEN DID YOU ANSWER, PEARL-PALE ONE, ...   6 OISIN 1   V 53
    HER PEARL-PALE HAND AND THE HEM OF HER DRESS. . . .   16 OISIN 1   216
    "I BRING DELIVERANCE," PEARL-PALE NIAMH SAID. . . .   34 OISIN 2   78
    "FLEE FROM HIM," PEARL-PALE NIAMH WEEPING CRIED, . .   35 OISIN 2   92
    AND THE PEARL-PALE NIAMH LAY BY ME, ...   52 OISIN 3   74
    AND PEARL-PALE NEAVE LAY BY ME, HER BROW ON THE MIDST OF 52 OISIN 3   V 74
        MY BREAST:
    YOU NEED BUT LIFT A PEARL-PALE HAND, ... 158 BELOVED RHYMES   7
PEARLS
    BODIES OF SHADOW AND BLIND EYES LIKE PEARLS, . . . 185 QUEEN MAEVE   116
    ANCESTRAL PEARLS ALL PITCHED INTO A STY, ... 619 BRONZE HEAD   26
PEARLY
    AND PEARLY WHITE HIS WELL-GROOMED HAIR. . . . . . .   3 OISIN 1   V 7CC
    ALL PEARLY WHITE, SAVE ONE RED EAR: . . . .   12 OISIN 1   141
    AND SIGHING LAID THE PEARLY TIP . . . .   12 OISIN 1   150
    THE MIST CLOSED ROUND US: PEARLY LIGHT . . . . . .   28 OISIN 1   V 427C
    AND DIE A PEARLY BROTHERHOOD, ...   66 HAPPY SHEPHERD   42
    THEIR SADNESS THROUGH A HOLLOW, PEARLY HEART: . . .   68 SAD SHEPHERD   21
    THEN HE SANG SOFTLY NIGH THE PEARLY RIM: . . . . .   69 SAD SHEPHERD   25
    THEN SANG HE SOFTLY NIGH THE PEARLY RIM: . . . . .   69 SAD SHEPHERD V 25
    AND HURLED IT FROM ITS PLACE AMID THE PEARLY LIGHT . . 174 ELEMENT POWERS V   3
    SEA-NYMPHS IN THEIR PEARLY WAGONS, ... 309 REALISTS   5
    SEA NYMPHS IN THEIR PEARLY WAGGONS, ... 309 REALISTS   V 5
PEARSE
    AND CONNOLLY AND PEARSE . . . . 394 EASTER 1916   76
    NOW PEARSE IS DEAF AND DUMB? . . . . 395 SIXTEEN DEAD   10
    SAID PEARSE TO CONNOLLY, ... 396 ROSE TREE   2
    SAID PEARSE TO CONNOLLY, ... 396 ROSE TREE   14
    HE TOLD PEARSE AND CONNOLLY . . . . 585 ORAHILLY   12
    THEN ON PEARSE AND CONNOLLY . . . . 585 ORAHILLY   23
    FOR PATRICK PEARSE HAD SAID . . . . 608 SONGS BURDEN 3   24
    WHEN PEARSE SUMMONED CUCHULAIN TO HIS SIDE, ... 611 STATUES   25
PEAR-TREE
    A PEAR-TREE BROKEN BY THE STORM. . . . . 424 ROAD AT DOOR   10
PEASANT
    TWO POEMS CONCERNING PEASANT VISIONARIES A CRADLE SONG 146 UNAPPEAS HOST V T
    A PEASANT GIRL COMMENDED BY A SONG, ... 410 TOWER   34
    BY SOME PEASANT GOSPELLER: . . . . 440 WISDOM   5
    THROUGH THE PEASANT GOSPELLERS' . . . . 440 WISDOM   V   5
    WHEN SOME PEASANT GOSPELLER . . . . 440 WISDOM   V   5
    THIS SULLEN PEASANT SPOILS THE GOOD SUNSHINE, . . . 711 FERENCZ RENYI   42
    THIS SULLEN PEASANT SPOILS THE GOOD RED WINE. . . . 711 FERENCZ RENYI   43
    THE SOLDIER THUS, AND HAYNAU--"PEASANT, SPEAK . . . 711 FERENCZ RENYI   54
    THIS SULLEN PEASANT CHILLS THE GOOD SUNSHINE, . . . 711 FERENCZ RENYI V 42
    THIS SULLEN PEASANT SOURS THE GOOD RED WINE. . . . 711 FERENCZ RENYI V 43
    A PEASANT PALE AND PRETTY, HER EYES FOR FEAR, . . . 713 FERENCZ RENYI   81
    A PEASANT YOUNG AND FAIR, HER EYES FOR FEAR . . . 713 FERENCZ RENYI V 81
    A PEASANT, PALE AND PRETTY, HER EYES FROM FEAR, . . 713 FERENCZ RENYI V 81
PEASANTRY
    SING THE PEASANTRY, AND THEN . . . . 639 BEN BULBEN   74
PEASANT'S
    WERE WE NOT BORN IN THE PEASANT'S COT . . . . . . 615 MARCH SONGS 2   13
    WE WERE NOT BORN IN THE PEASANT'S COT . . . . . . 615 MARCH SONGS 2 V 13
    HALF HID. HE BRINGS THE PEASANT'S ONLY KIN, . . . 711 FERENCZ RENYI   50
PEASANTS
    THE PEASANTS OF THAT LAND, ... 123 DREAM OF DEATH   4
PEBBLE
    AS A GRASS SEED CRUSHED BY A PEBBLE, AS A WOLF SUCKED UNDER 63 OISIN 3   V 220
        A WEIR.
PEBBLES
    BRUSH LIGHTLY AS HAYMOUSE EARTH'S PEBBLES, ...   56 OISIN 3   128
    BRUSH LIGHTLY AS HAY MOUSE EARTH'S PEBBLES, . . .   56 OISIN 3   V 128
    THE RATTLE OF PEBBLES ON THE SHORE . . . . 485 NINETEENTH CEN   3
PEBBLY
    WHO PACED IN THE EVE BY THE NETS ON THE PEBBLY SHORE, . . 91 OLD FISHERMAN   11
    ALONG THE PEBBLY STREET. . . . .   94 MOLL MAGEE   12
PECKER   SEE WOOD-PECKER

		PAGE	TITLE	LINE

PEDANT
--PEDANT IN PASSION, LEARNED IN OLD COURTESIES, ... 363 DOLLS FACES 4
THE FAIRY PEDANT. . . . . 706 FAIRY PEDANT T
PEDANTIC
FROM THEIR PEDANTIC BABYLON . . . . 344 DAWN 6
PEDANTRY
THOUGH PEDANTRY DENIES, ... 345 ON WOMAN 9
PEDDLED
PEDDLED IN THE THOROUGHFARES. . . . . 406 FOR DAUGHTER 76
PEDESTALLED
FOG-DRIPPING, PEDESTALLED ABOVE THE TIDE, ... 31 OISIN 2 V 36
PEDLAR
THE COLONEL MET A PEDLAR, ... 595 COLONEL MARTIN 19
PEELED
AND CUT AND PEELED A HAZEL WAND, ... 149 WANDER AENGUS 3
AND CUT AND PEELED A HAZEL ROD . . . . 149 WANDER AENGUS V 3
PEEP
AND STARS BEGAN TO PEEP. . . . . 133 FR GILLIGAN 16
TILL STARS ARE BEGINNING TO BLINK AND PEEP; . . . . . 150 OLD MOTHER 4
PEEPING
THAN THE PEEPING PANSY'S FACE, ... 647 ISLE STAT I 1 52
PEER
. . . AND FROM YOUR CARHEADS PEER, ... 73 ANASHU VIJAYA 45
. . . AND O'ER YOUR CAR HEADS PEER . . . . 73 ANASHU VIJAYA V 45
PEERED
FULL MANY MORE, WHEN PEERED A MAIDEN SWEET . . . . . . 33 OISIN 2 V 68F
WHO PEERED ABOUT ON EVERY SIDE; . . . . 193 BAILE AILLINN V 112
PEERING
PEERING AND FLYING TO AND FRO, ... 136 TWO TREES V 35
A PEERING HARE'S!" AND YET I MURMURED NOT, ... 684 SEEKER 56
PEERS
OR WRESTLE WITH THEIR PEERS IN DEWY VALLEYS. . . . . . 30 OISIN 2 V 14E
AND PROUD AS PRIAM MURDERED WITH HIS PEERS; . . . . . 120 SORROW OF LOVE 8
PEEWIT
AND FOR THE PEEWIT PAINTS HIS CAP, ... 18 OISIN 1 266
"LET PEEWIT CALL AND CURLEW CRY WHERE THEY WILL, . . . 203 WITHER BOUGHS 2
I KNOW, AND THE CURLEW AND PEEWIT ON ECHTGE OF STREAMS. 204 WITHER BOUGHS 22
AND THE CURLEW AND PEEWIT KNOW ON ECHTGE OF STREAMS. . 204 WITHER BOUGHS V 22
PEG
FOR PEG AND MEG AND PARIS' LOVE . . . . 458 HIS WILDNESS 3
PELEUS
PELEUS ON THETIS STARES. . . . . 612 NEWS ORACLE 26
PELTING
WHEN THE RAIN IS PELTING OUT OF THE WINTRY AIR; . . . . 207 HANRAHANS SONG V 12
PEN
WHETHER WE HAVE CHOSEN CHISEL, PEN OR BRUSH, ... 368 EGO DOMINUS 14
HIS SLEEPLESS CANDLE AND LABORIOUS PEN. . . . . 375 PHASES OF MOON 86
BY PEN AND PAPER LIES, ... 421 MY TABLE 3
PENAL
IN PENAL DAYS RODE OUT . . . . 91 FATHER OHART 2
PENANCE
AND PENANCE IS THE PLAY, ... 364 END OF DAY 2
OR SING A PENANCE ON THE ROAD; . . . . 529 TOM LUNATIC 10
PENCE
UNTIL ENOUGH OF PAUDEEN'S PENCE . . . . 287 TO WEALTHY MAN 2
AND ADD THE HALFPENCE TO THE PENCE . . . . 289 SEPTEMBER 1913 3
PENCILLED
WE THOUGHT ON OSCAR'S PENCILLED URN. . . . . 2 OISIN 1 V 70
"WE THINK ON OSCAR'S PENCILLED URN, ... 5 OISIN 1 41
PENDULOUS
ARE BOWED IN SORROW UNDER PENDULOUS LIDS, ... 79 EPHEMERA 2
LIE NOW HALF HIDDEN UNDER PENDULOUS LIDS, ... 79 EPHEMERA V 2
PENETRATION
AND PENETRATION OF THEIR EYES. WHERE YONDER BLOTCH . . 664 ISLE STAT II 2 47
PENITENCE
AND IMPORTUNE THEIR SOULS TO PENITENCE, ... 704 MOSADA 3 131
PENITENTIAL
AMID THE HOVERING, PITEOUS, PENITENTIAL THRONG." . . . 173 SPEAKS HEARERS 8
PENNIES   SEE HALF-PENNIES
WITH A BAG FULL OF PENNIES, ... 627 STATES HOLIDAY 35
PENNON
WITH BANNERET AND PENNON, ... 317 NIGHT COME 8
PENNY
I HAD NOT GIVEN A PENNY FOR A SONG . . . . 267 ALL TEMPT ME 6
BROWN PENNY . . . . 268 BROWN PENNY T
WHEREFORE I THREW A PENNY . . . . 268 BROWN PENNY 3
AH, PENNY, BROWN PENNY, BROWN PENNY, ... 268 BROWN PENNY 7
AH, PENNY, BROWN PENNY, BROWN PENNY, ... 268 BROWN PENNY 7
AH, PENNY, BROWN PENNY, BROWN PENNY, ... 268 BROWN PENNY 7
AH, PENNY, BROWN PENNY, BROWN PENNY, ... 268 BROWN PENNY 15
AH, PENNY, BROWN PENNY, BROWN PENNY, ... 268 BROWN PENNY 15
AH, PENNY, BROWN PENNY, BROWN PENNY, ... 268 BROWN PENNY 15
PENSEROSO'S
IL PENSEROSO'S PLATONIST TOILED ON . . . . 419 MY HOUSE 14
PENSIONER
THE LAMENTATION OF THE OLD PENSIONER . . . . 131 OLD PENSIONER T
THE OLD PENSIONER . . . . 131 OLD PENSIONER V T
PENSIVE
OF PENSIVE LAUGHTER, UNHUMAN SOUND, ... 11 OISIN 1 136
PENSIVE THEY PACED ALONG THE FADED LEAVES, ... 80 EPHEMERA 10

610

```
                                                    PAGE    TITLE           LINE
PENSIVELY
    PENSIVELY APART.  . . . . . . . . . . . . . . .  89 ISLE IN WATER          4
PEOPLE
    AMONG UNDYING PEOPLE HAS RUN  . . . . . . . . .   6 OISIN 1         V     60
    OF THE HIGH PEOPLE OF SORACA NOR IN GLAMOUR BY DEMONS  50 OISIN 3      V     50
        FLUNG,
    PEOPLE CAME INTO COLOONEY:  . . . . . . . . . .  93 FATHER OHART         27
    I FEAST AMID MY PEOPLE ON THE HILL,  . . . . . . 103 FERGUS DRUID        17
    WHERE PEOPLE LOVE BESIDE THE RAVELLED SEAS:  . . 126 DREAM OF FAERY       9
    WHERE PEOPLE LOVE BESIDE STAR-LADEN SEAS:  . . . 126 DREAM OF FAERY V     9
    WHEN HER OWN PEOPLE RULED THIS TRAGIC EIRE:  . . 129 BOOK STORIES         2
    WHEN HER OWN PEOPLE RULED IN WAVE-WORN ERI,  . . 129 BOOK STORIES    V    2
    FOR PEOPLE DIE AND DIE",  . . . . . . . . . . . 132 FR GILLIGAN         10
    THE PEOPLE OF COMING DAYS WILL KNOW  . . . . . . 146 FISH                 3
    TALKED OF HIS COUNTRY AND ITS PEOPLE, SANG  . . 180 QUEEN MAEVE          3
    ONE OF THE LAUGHING PEOPLE--AND SHE AND I  . . . 231 SHADOW WATER B     211
    PROTECT ME NOW, GODS THAT MY PEOPLE SWEAR BY.  . 241 SHADOW WATER B     396
    . . . THE PEOPLE WANTED PICTURES  . . . . . . . 287 TO WEALTHY MAN       T
    ALL THINK WHAT OTHER PEOPLE THINK:  . . . . . . 337 SCHOLARS             9
    THE PEOPLE  . . . . . . . . . . . . . . . . . . 351 PEOPLE               T
    TO WHERE THE DUCHESS AND HER PEOPLE TALKED  . . 352 PEOPLE              13
    COMPLAINED OF THE PEOPLE."  ALL I COULD REPLY .  352 PEOPLE              29
    YOU HEARD THAT LABOURING MAN WHO HAD SERVED MY PEOPLE.  391 UNDER SATURN      11
        HE SAID
    THE PRIDE OF PEOPLE THAT WERE  . . . . . . . . . 414 TOWER              128
    THE PEOPLE OF BURKE AND OF GRATTAN  . . . . . . 414 TOWER              132
    THE BOOK OF THE PEOPLE: WHATEVER MOST CAN BLESS  492 COOLE BALLYLEE      44
    THE KING THAT COULD MAKE HIS PEOPLE STARE,  . . 550 SEVERED HEAD        19
    PYTHAGORAS PLANNED IT.  WHY DID THE PEOPLE STARE? 610 STATUES             1
    PREPARED A REST FOR THE PEOPLE OF GOD,  . . . . 639 BEN BULBEN          65
    BY A PEOPLE SADLY GAY:  . . . . . . . . . . . . 680 LOVE AND DEATH      10
    SINCE 'MONG MY PEOPLE, TENTED ON THE HILLS,  . . 690 MOSADA 1             4
    FOR I AND ALL MY PEOPLE WERE ACCURST  . . . . . 690 MOSADA 1            15
    THE PLACE WAS EMPTY NOW OF PEOPLE.  . . . . . . 725 LEGEND              25
    HE CAME TO THE HOME OF THE FOREST PEOPLE  . . . 728 PRIEST FAIRY         5
    THE PEOPLE CRIED "SHIELD-BREAKER!"  . . . . . . 741 EARL PAUL           53
    AND BRING HER TO HER KINGDOM AND HER PEOPLE.  . 755 SHADOW WATER A     170
    AND BRING ME TO MY PEOPLE.  I PROMISED THESE  . 756 SHADOW WATER A V   185
    FOR THOSE AMONG YOUR PEOPLE THAT ARE DEAD?  . . 758 SHADOW WATER A     224
    THAT I WOULD BID MY PEOPLE PUT TO DEATH.  . . . 760 SHADOW WATER A V   254
PEOPLED
    IF HE HAD BROUGHT US AMONG PEOPLED SEAS,  . . . 225 SHADOW WATER B V   68C
    TOWARD PEOPLED TARA, NOR STOOD TO DRAW HIS BREATH 279 TWO KINGS          46
    ON PEOPLED TARA, NOR STOOD TO DRAW HIS BREATH .  279 TWO KINGS       V   46
    TOWARDS PEOPLED TARA, NOR STOOD TO DRAW HIS BREATH  279 TWO KINGS       46
PEOPLE'S
    THE WISDOM OF THE PEOPLE'S GONE,  . . . . . . . 607 SONGS BURDEN 2      16
    DOWN THE LONG VALLEYS FROM MY PEOPLE'S TENTS,  . 691 MOSADA 1            30
    OTHER PEOPLE'S MIRTH AND PLEASURE,  . . . . . . 732 STREET DANCERS      24
    OTHER PEOPLE'S MIRTH AND PLEASURE,  . . . . . . 732 STREET DANCERS      37
    OTHER'S PEOPLE'S MIRTH AND PLEASURE,  . . . . . 733 STREET DANCERS      50
PERCH
    THERE'S NOT A PILOT ON THE PERCH  . . . . . . . 607 SONGS BURDEN 2      25
PERCHANCE
    AND YET IT LACK ALL GLORY: AND PERCHANCE  . . . 429 NINETEEN 19         23
    HEALING FROM ITS LETTERED SLAB.  THOSE SELF-SAME HANDS  503 VACILLATION    82
        PERCHANCE
PERCHED
    PERCHED IN SOME WINDOW OF HER MOTHER'S HOUSE  . 466 HARUN RASHID       106
PERCHES
    AGED AND WISE, THEY SEEK THEIR WONTED PERCHES .  72 ANASHU VIJAYA       31
    AND PERCHES ON A STONE:  . . . . . . . . . . . 456 FRIENDS YOUTH       16
PERCHING
    OR PERCHING ON THE TENTS, A-WEARY STILL  . . . 690 MOSADA 1             8
PERFECT
    HE TELLS OF THE PERFECT BEAUTY .  . . . . . . . 164 PERFECT BEAUTY       T
    AEDH TELLS OF THE PERFECT BEAUTY  . . . . . . . 164 PERFECT BEAUTY V     T
    TO BUILD A PERFECT BEAUTY IN RHYME  . . . . . . 164 PERFECT BEAUTY       3
    TO BUILD THE PERFECT BEAUTY IN RHYME,  . . . . 164 PERFECT BEAUTY V     3
    OUR SIDNEY AND OUR PERFECT MAN,  . . . . . . . 325 ROBERT GREGORY      47
    PADDLE AND ARE PERFECT.  LEAVE UNCHANGED  . . . 357 BROKEN DREAMS       34
    TOO PERFECT AT THE FULL TO LIE IN A CRADLE,  . 374 PHASES OF MOON      60
    FOR SEPARATE, PERFECT, AND IMMOVABLE .  . . . . 375 PHASES OF MOON      81
    MUST KEEP THAT PERFECT, AS THEY KEEP HER SONG,  461 HARUN RASHID       18
    ONE THAT IS PERFECT OR AT PEACE,  . . . . . . . 528 DANCER CRUACH        3
PERFECTED
    FOR PERFECTED, COMPLETED, AND IMMOVABLE . . . . 375 PHASES OF MOON V    81
PERFECTION
    AT THE PERFECTION OF ONE'S OWN OBEDIENCE:  . . . 376 PHASES OF MOON     109
    BODY PERFECTION BROUGHT,  . . . . . . . . . . . 383 VISION ROBART       40
    PERFECTION OF THE LIFE, OR OF THE WORK,  . . . . 491 COOLE BALLYLEE V   40B
    PERFECTION OF THE LIFE, OR OF THE WORK,  . . . . 495 CHOICE               2
    THINGS OUT OF PERFECTION SAIL,  . . . . . . . . 530 OLD TOM AGAIN        1
    SOMETHING TO PERFECTION BROUGHT":  . . . . . . . 577 WHAT THEN           19
    PROFANE PERFECTION OF MANKIND.  . . . . . . . . 639 BEN BULBEN          52
PERFECTLY
    AND ALL HE DID DONE PERFECTLY  . . . . . . . . . 327 ROBERT GREGORY      79
PERFORM
    ALL PERFORM THEIR TRAGIC PLAY,  . . . . . . . . 565 LAPIS LAZULI         9
PERFUME
    THAT IT MAY DROP FAINT PERFUME, AND BE HEAVY WITH DEW, . . 172 TRAV PASSION    7
```

611

PERHAPS
    WORDS FOR MUSIC PERHAPS . . . .   507 JANE BISHOP   V   T
    A ROOF, GOOD CLOTHES, PASSION, LOVE PERHAPS, ...   609 IN TARAS HALLS   8
PERILOUS
    SO PERILOUS THAT HALF THE ASTONISHED MEET . . . . . .   326 ROBERT GREGORY   61
PERILS
    ALL BUT THE PERILS OF THE WOODLAND FLIGHT FORGOT, . . .   366 HER COURAGE   V   5
PERISH
    YOUR BEAUTY PERISH AND BE LOST . . . .   173 PLEADS FRIEND   7
    THE HAUGHTY IMAGES, THAT CANNOT PERISH . . . .   184 QUEEN MAEVE   V   88
PERISHED
    BUT MY BELOVED--THAT NIGHT AND DAY HAD PERISHED, ...   246 SHADOW WATER B   504
    HAD PERISHED THERE, BUT THE DANES RAN, ...   274 GREY ROCK   74
    --SEEING THAT FAME HAS PERISHED THIS LONG WHILE, ...   321 REED WHISPERER   11
PERISHING
    OF UNKNOWN PERISHING ARMIES BEAT ABOUT MY EARS. . . . .   161 BLACK PIG   4
PERJURER
    A PERJURER STOOD READY . . . .   582 ROGER CASEMENT   9
PERJURER'S
    DESERT THE PERJURER'S SIDE, ...   582 ROGER CASEMENT   20
PERMANENT
    MY PERMANENT OR IMPERMANENT IMAGES, ...   602 GALLERY REVIS   20
PERMIT
    PERMIT FOUL YEARS TO WEAR . . . .   472 ALL SOUL NIGHT   49
PERN
    HE UNPACKS THE LOADED PERN . . . .   342 SHEP GOATHERD   97
PERNE
    COME FROM THE HOLY FIRE, PERNE IN A GYRE, ...   408 SAIL BYZANTIUM   19
PERNED
    THOUGH I HAD LONG PERNED IN THE GYRE, ...   400 DEMON BEAST   5
PERNELLA
    RAYMOND LULLY AND HIS WIFE PERNELLA . . . .   253 HIS DREAM   V   T
PERNING
    NOW GYRING DOWN AND PERNING THERE . . . .   400 DEMON BEAST   26
    PERNING IN A BAND, ...   599 SPIRIT MEDIUM   6
PERPETUAL
    ROOTED IN ONE DEAR PERPETUAL PLACE. . . . .   405 FOR DAUGHTER   48
PERPLEXED
    THAT HER OWN STRANGENESS PERPLEXED, ...   260 UNWORTH PRAISE   14
    MY WRETCHED DRAGON IS PERPLEXED. . . . .   386 ROBARTES DANCE   41
    PERPLEXED HER FANTASY AND PLANNED HER CARE? . . . . .   466 HARUN RASHID   114
    PERPLEXED HER PHANTASY AND PLANNED HER CARE? . . . .   466 HARUN RASHID   V 114
PERPLEXITY
    THAT OLD PERPLEXITY AN EMPTY PURSE, ...   491 COOLE BALLYLEE   V 40G
    THAT OLD PERPLEXITY AN EMPTY PURSE, ...   495 CHOICE   7
PERSECUTION
    HE FLED THE PERSECUTION OF HER GLORY . . . .   68 SAD SHEPHERD   12
    AND FROM THE PERSECUTION OF HER GLORY . . . .   68 SAD SHEPHERD   V   12
PERSEUS
    SAINT GEORGE OR ELSE A PAGAN PERSEUS, ...   533 HER TRIUMPH   10
PERSIAN
    WHAT MEDIAN, PERSIAN, BABYLONIAN, ...   420 MY HOUSE   V 20D
    WITH PERSIAN EMBASSY OR GRECIAN WAR, ...   462 HARUN RASHID   25
    WITH PERSIAN WARS OR GREEK AMBASSADORS . . . .   462 HARUN RASHID   V   25
PERSISTENCE
    WITH UNFALTERING PERSISTENCE, ...   647 ISLE STAT I 1   69
    IS THE BURTHEN AND PERSISTENCE . . . .   647 ISLE STAT I 1   75
PERSONAE
    IGNORANT WHAT DRAMATIS PERSONAE SPAKE, ...   560 WHENCE COME   4
PERSONS
    I PUT THREE PERSONS IN THEIR PLACE . . . .   787 HUDDON DUDDON   8
PERSUADE
    "THOUGH I AM OLD I SHALL PERSUADE . . . .   296 THREE BEGGARS   30
    NOW THAT YOUR TONGUE CANNOT PERSUADE THE CHILD TILL SHE   450 OWEN AHERNE   22
        MISTAKE
PERTURB
    FRENZIES BEWILDER, REVERIES PERTURB THE MIND, ...   426 PHANTOM HATRED   7
PERU
    ON THRONES FROM CHINA TO PERU . . . .   597 MODEL LAUREATE   1
PERVERSE
    PERVERSE CREATURE OF CHANCE, ...   346 ON WOMAN   41
PESTLE
    THE PESTLE OF THE MOON . . . .   346 ON WOMAN   30
PETAL
    UNLESS A PETAL HIT THE GROUND, ...   389 SOLOMON WITCH   40
    COMMON BIRD OR PETAL . . . .   498 BYZANTIUM   23
PETALS
    IS BUT A SLIDING DROP OF RAIN BETWEEN HIS PETALS WIDE. . .   76 INDIAN ON GOD   12
    IS BUT A SLIDING DROP OF RAIN WITHIN HIS PETALS WIDE." . .   76 INDIAN ON GOD   V   12
    BUT THE TORN PETALS STREW THE GARDEN PLOT, ...   422 MY DESCENDANTS   7
    WHEN THE TORN PETALS STREW THE GARDEN PLOT, ...   422 MY DESCENDANTS   V   7
PETER
    THE OLD PRIEST PETER GILLIGAN . . . .   132 FR GILLIGAN   1
    THE OLD PRIEST PETER GILLIGAN . . . .   133 FR GILLIGAN   23
    THE OLD PRIEST PETER GILLIGAN . . . .   133 FR GILLIGAN   35
    THE OLD PRIEST PETER GILLIGAN . . . .   133 FR GILLIGAN   39
    TO PETER SITTING IN STATE, ...   178 FIDDLER DOONEY   10
    AND PETER THAT HAD GREAT AFFAIRS . . . .   456 FRIENDS YOUTH   13
    THEN PETER HAD A MURDERING LOOK, ...   457 SUMMER SPRING   9
    WHERE IS OUR BROTHER PETER? WHEN YOU'RE NIGH, ...   696 MOSADA 2   12
    HE LOVES OUR BROTHER PETER IN HIS HEART. . . . . . .   696 MOSADA 2   16

612

PETER (CONTINUED)
 IF PETER WOULD BUT ASK HER LIFE--WHO KNOWS? 696 MOSADA 2 17
 THIS VISION OF PETER AND THE BURNING GATE. 696 MOSADA 2 21
 OF HOLY PETER OF THE BURNING GATE! 696 MOSADA 2 V 20
 THY SACRED DOOR!" BUT PETER CRIED, 697 MOSADA 2 25
 ANSWERED PETER: "ENTER IN, 697 MOSADA 2 30
PETER'S
 BY THE DOOR OF PETER'S GATE, 696 MOSADA 2 23
 BESIDE THE DOOR OF PETER'S GATE. 696 MOSADA 2 V 23
PETRONIUS
 THINKING OF SAINTS AND OF PETRONIUS ARBITER. 362 HER COURTESY 8
PETS
 HUGS AND PETS AND PATS YON NEWT, 727 LOVERS QUARREL 27
PEWS
 THE SUNLIGHT FLICKERING ON THE PEWS, 736 IN CHURCH 9
PHANTASY
 WHATEVER THEIR LOOSE PHANTASY INVENT 398 LEADERS CROWD V 4
 MANKIND INANIMATE PHANTASY. 406 IN TIME OF WAR 5
 AND SPEAK BUT PHANTASY. RECALL THE YEAR 462 HARUN RASHID V 30
 PERPLEXED HER PHANTASY AND PLANNED HER CARE? 466 HARUN RASHID V 114
PHANTOM
 PASSED BY US, CHASED BY A PHANTOM HOUND 11 OISIN 1 140
 PASSED BY US, CHASED BY A PHANTOM HOUND. 11 OISIN 1 V 140
 THE PHANTOM, BEAUTY, IN A MIST OF TEARS: 73 ANASHU VIJAYA 55
 AND SNORED, NO PHANTOM BY HIS LOOK. 303 HOUR DAWN 30
 PLAINLY NO PHANTOM BY HIS LOOK: 303 HOUR DAWN V 30
 MEETING LONG HENCE THE PHANTOM HERDSMAN, KING 675 ISLE STAT II 3 242
 THUS BECKON TO OUR AID A PHANTOM FAIR 693 MOSADA 1 76
 THE PHANTOM SHIP. 718 PHANTOM SHIP T
 A LEGEND OF THE PHANTOM SHIP. 718 PHANTOM SHIP V T
 STANDS EACH GREY AND SILENT PHANTOM ON THE SAME REGARDLESS 719 PHANTOM SHIP 25
  SPOT--
PHANTOMS
 OR ARE YOU PHANTOMS WHITE AS SNOW, 10 OISIN 1 117
 OR ARE YE PHANTOMS WHITE AS SNOW, 10 OISIN 1 V 117
 "FRET NOT WITH SPEECH THE PHANTOMS DREAD," 12 OISIN 1 V 148
 "GAZE NO MORE ON THE PHANTOMS," NIAMH SAID, 29 OISIN 2 5
 NOW, MAN OF CROSIERS, PHANTOMS DREW AROUND 29 OISIN 2 V 1
 "THESE FORMS?" "VEX NOT WITH SPEECH THE PHANTOMS DREAD." 29 OISIN 2 V 5
 I SEE PHANTOMS OF HATRED AND OF THE HEART'S 425 PHANTOM HATRED T
 THE PHANTOMS OF HER FADED PLEASURES WALK: 687 TWO TITANS 19
 THE PHANTOMS COME; HA! HA! THEY COME, THEY COME! 694 MOSADA 1 97
 THE PHANTOMS COME; THEY COME, THEY COME, THEY COME! 694 MOSADA 1 V 97
PHARAOH'S
 HAD SCOOPED OUT PHARAOH'S MUMMY. I--THOUGH HEART MIGHT 503 VACILLATION 84
  FIND RELIEF
PHASE
 HAS TAKEN A NEW PHASE. 379 CAT AND MOON 20
PHASES
 THE PHASES OF THE MOON 372 PHASES OF MOON T
 . . . I. THE WHEEL AND THE PHASES OF THE MOON 372 PHASES OF MOON V T
 TWENTY-AND-EIGHT THE PHASES OF THE MOON, 373 PHASES OF MOON 31
PHIDIAS
 EUROPE PUT OFF THAT FOAM WHEN PHIDIAS 610 STATUES 15
 FORMS THAT GENTLER PHIDIAS WROUGHT. 638 BEN BULBEN 44
PHIDIAS'
 AND GONE ARE PHIDIAS' FAMOUS IVORIES 428 NINETEEN 19 7
 AND GONE ARE PHIDIAS' CARVEN IVORIES 428 NINETEEN 19 V 7
PHILOSOPHER
 EVERY PHILOSOPHER SHOULD PRAISE THAT LOVE. 465 HARUN RASHID 97
PHILOSOPHERS
 PHILOSOPHERS SHOULD PRAISE THAT LOVE THE MOST, 465 HARUN RASHID V 97
PHILOSOPHY
 WE PIECED OUR THOUGHTS INTO PHILOSOPHY, 429 NINETEEN 19 30
 ABSTRACTIONS OF THE GREEK PHILOSOPHY HAVE CRAZED THE MAN, 556 RIBH PATRICK V 1
PHOENIX
 WHERE THE LAST PHOENIX DIED, 162 ASKS FORGIVE 16
 THE PHOENIX 351 PEOPLE V T
 THEREON MY PHOENIX ANSWERED IN REPROOF, 352 PEOPLE 22
 HIS PHOENIX 353 HIS PHOENIX T
 I KNEW A PHOENIX IN MY YOUTH, SO LET THEM HAVE THEIR DAY. 353 HIS PHOENIX 8
 I KNEW A PHOENIX IN MY YOUTH, SO LET THEM HAVE THEIR DAY. 354 HIS PHOENIX 16
 I KNEW A PHOENIX IN MY YOUTH, SO LET THEM HAVE THEIR DAY. 354 HIS PHOENIX 24
 I KNEW A PHOENIX IN MY YOUTH, SO LET THEM HAVE THEIR DAY. 354 HIS PHOENIX 32
PHOSPHORUS
 AND SURGING PHOSPHORUS ALONE GAVE LIGHT 31 OISIN 2 33
 OF SURGING PHOSPHORUS ALONE GAVE LIGHT. 31 OISIN 2 V 33
 A MOMENTARY GLEAM OF PHOSPHORUS FLAME. 37 OISIN 2 118
 A MOMENTARY GLIMMER OF VAGUE PHOSPHORUS FLAME. 37 OISIN 2 V 120
PHRASE
 --BEN JONSON'S PHRASE--AND FIND WHEN JUNE IS COME 321 REED WHISPERER 6
 BEN JONSON'S PHRASE--AND STILL MAY TURN MY FEET 321 REED WHISPERER V 6
 PALMER'S PHRASE, BUT AFTER THAT 639 BEN BULBEN 66
 NO MARBLE, NO CONVENTIONAL PHRASE: 640 BEN BULBEN 89
PHRASING
 HAVE DONE THIS PHRASING, AND SAY WHY, IN SOOTH, 652 ISLE STAT I 2 25
PICK
 "BEFORE NIGHTFALL I'LL PICK A POCKET 332 ROUND TOWER 27
 ANOTHER BOASTS, "I PICK AND CHOOSE AND HAVE BUT TWO OR 354 HIS PHOENIX 20
  THREE."
 PICK OUT MY FEATURES IN SUCH LIGHT AND SHADE 466 HARUN RASHID 116

	PAGE	TITLE		LINE

PICK   (CONTINUED)
    TIME FOR US ALL TO PICK OUT A GOOD TUNE, ...   548 TO SAME TUNE 3   13
PICKED
    PICKED HIM FOR HER OWN, ...   452 MERMAID   2
    PICKED UP ON A STREET. . . . .   617 LONG-LEG FLY   18
    PICKED UP ON THE STREET. . . . .   617 LONG-LEG FLY   V 18
    THE WOMEN THAT I PICKED SPOKE SWEET AND LOW . . . .   622 HOUND VOICE   8
    WE PICKED EACH OTHER FROM AFAR AND KNEW . . . . . .   622 HOUND VOICE   10
    SO I HAVE PICKED A BETTER TRADE . . . .   6_7 STATES HOLIDAY   11
PICKER   SEE MAN-PICKER
PICTURE
    OUT OF SOME OLD PICTURE BOOK; . . . .   325 ROBERT GREGORY V   44
    ON A PICTURE OF A BLACK CENTAUR BY EDMUND DULAC . . .   442 BLACK CENTAUR V   T
    SUGGESTED BY A PICTURE OF A BLACK CENTAUR . . . . .   442 BLACK CENTAUR V   T
    THOSE BODIES FROM A PICTURE OR A COIN . . . .   537 HER VISION   28
    PICTURE AND BOOK REMAIN, ...   575 ACRE OF GRASS   1
    ON MR. NETTLESHIP'S PICTURE AT THE ROYAL HIBERNIAN ACADEMY.   688 NETTLESHIP   T
PICTURE-BOOK
    OUT OF SOME OLD PICTURE-BOOK; . . . .   325 ROBERT GREGORY   44
PICTURED
    A PICTURED BEAUTY, ...   329 MEN IMPROVE   7
    AT ALL THAT IS NOT PICTURED THERE. . . . .   385 ROBARTES DANCE   17
    AS THOUGH THE WRITTEN OR THE PICTURED PAGE . . . . .   466 HARUN RASHID   V 126
    PICTURED, WHERE WANDER THE BELOVED FEET . . . . . .   692 MOSADA 1   44
PICTURES
    . . . THE PEOPLE WANTED PICTURES . . . .   287 TO WEALTHY MAN   T
    AND ASKED ABOUT THE PICTURES OR THE TEXT; . . . . .   466 HARUN RASHID   121
    AND ASKED ABOUT THESE PICTURES OR THOSE OTHERS; . . .   466 HARUN RASHID   V 121
    PICTURES OF THE MIND, RECALL . . . .   475 EVA GORE-BOOTH   17
    OLD MARBLE HEADS, OLD PICTURES EVERYWHERE; . . . . .   491 COOLE BALLYLEE   28
PIEBALD
    BECAUSE PIEBALD PONIES, LED BEARS, CAGED LIONS, MAKE BUT   623 HIGH TALK   5
        POOR SHOWS,
PIECE   SEE ALTAR-PIECE
    A PIECE OF A NIGHTINGALE'S EGG, ...   708 FAIRY PEDANT   24
PIECED
    WE PIECED OUR THOUGHTS INTO PHILOSOPHY, ...   429 NINETEEN 19   30
PIECES
    AND DEMONS BE BROKEN IN PIECES, AND TRAMPLED BENEATH THEM   61 OISIN 3   204
        IN DEATH.
    AND DEMONS, ALL BROKEN IN PIECES, BE TRAMPLED BENEATH THEM   61 OISIN 3   V 204
        IN DEATH.
PIED
    OF THE PIED PANTHER-KITTENS FROM MY HANDS . . . . .   674 ISLE STAT II 3   219
PIERCE
    AND PIERCE THE DEEP WOOD'S WOVEN SHADE, ...   125 GOES FERGUS   2
    AND PIERCE IT THROUGH WITH A GIMLET, AND STARE . . .   330 BONE OF A HARE   12
    THAT CAN PIERCE THE CLOUDS, ...   576 ACRE OF GRASS   20
    WORDS I HAVE THAT CAN PIERCE THE HEART, ...   588 OLD WICKED MAN   16
PIERCED   SEE NAIL-PIERCED
    PIERCED WITH SOFT LIGHT THE SHALLOWING DEEPS. . . . .   13 OISIN 1   164
    "THIS DEMON SHALL BE PIERCED AND DROP AND DIE, . . .   35 OISIN 2   V 90
    PIERCED BY MY GLAD SINGING THROUGH, ...   67 HAPPY SHEPHERD   53
    AND PIERCED HIM. "SPEAK BEFORE YOUR BREATH IS DONE." .   110 CUCHULAIN SEA   67
    SAW THE PIERCED HANDS AND ROOD OF ELDER RISE . . . .   169 SECRET ROSE   10
    AND SAYS, "A SWORD-BLADE PIERCED ME IN MY SLEEP." . .   234 SHADOW WATER B   257
    AND SAYS: "A SWORD BLADE PIERCED ME IN MY SLEEP." . .   234 SHADOW WATER B V 257
    BUTTED BELOW THE SINGLE AND SO PIERCED . . . . . .   278 TWO KINGS   22
    THAT PIERCED MY BODY THROUGH? . . . .   507 STREAM AND SUN   13
    RECALL THE CRETAN BARB THAT PIERCED A STAR? . . . .   541 PARN FUNERAL 1   7
    A PIERCED BOY, IMAGE OF A STAR LAID LOW. . . . . .   541 PARN FUNERAL 1   12
    PIERCED THROUGH, CHATTERING FROM HABIT IN THE SUN, . .   664 ISLE STAT II 2   53
    AND PIERCED THE MIRTHFUL BREAST, ...   741 EARL PAUL   50
    AND SAYS, "A SWORD-BLADE PIERCED ME IN MY SLEEP." . .   753 SHADOW WATER A   147
    AND SAYS: "A SWORD BLADE PIERCED ME IN MY SLEEP." . .   753 SHADOW WATER A V 147
    AH, THEY HAVE PIERCED HIS HEART! I HAVE SLEPT LONG; . .   761 SHADOW WATER A   270
PIERCING   SEE EAR-PIERCING
    SOFTER THAN SNOW-FLAKES IN APRIL AND PIERCING THE MARROW   51 OISIN 3   68
        LIKE FLAME.
    SOFTER THAN SNOWFLAKES IN APRIL, AND PIERCING THE MARROW   51 OISIN 3   V 68
        LIKE FLAME.
    . . . LOVE-MAKING OR PIERCING THE TEMPEST WITH SAILS. . .   53 OISIN 3   88
    FORTH, PIERCING THE DISTANCE-- . . . .   54 OISIN 3   V 112
    PIERCING THE TWILIGHT WITH THEIR MURMURING BARBS. . .   72 ANASHU VIJAYA   28
    PIERCING THE QUIVERING WATERS THROUGH AND THROUGH, . .   664 ISLE STAT II 2   44
PIETY
    THAT PASSION, PIETY OR AFFECTION KNOWS, ...   445 SCHOOL CHILDR   54
PIG
    THE VALLEY OF THE BLACK PIG . . . .   161 BLACK PIG   T
    THAT THIS PRAGMATICAL, PREPOSTEROUS PIG OF A WORLD, . .   481 BLOOD AND MOON   26
PIGEON
    WERE THE WINDS LESS SOFT THAN THE BREATH OF A PIGEON . .   56 OISIN 3   134
    MY PIGEON, MY OWN; . . . .   118 CRADLE SONG   V 10
PIGEONS
    I HAVE HEARD THE PIGEONS OF THE SEVEN WOODS . . . .   198 SEVEN WOODS   1
    AMONG PIGEONS AND BEES, WHILE THAT GREAT ARCHER, . . .   198 SEVEN WOODS   12
PIKES
    THOUGH LADS ARE MAKING PIKES AGAIN . . . .   131 OLD PENSIONER   7
PILE
    MY SOUL, MY PREY, AND THIS MY HEAPED PILE. . . . . .   45 OISIN 2   V 239B
    BUT WHEN A MAN POURED FISH INTO A PILE, ...   126 DREAM OF FAERY   5

```
                                                    PAGE      TITLE           LINE
PILE    (CONTINUED)
    AND STRETCHED OUT SLEEPING ON A PILE OF SKINS  • • • • •  283 TWO KINGS        141
PILED       SEE CLAY-PILED
PILED-UP
    BESIDE THE PILED-UP HUNTING SPEARS,  • • • • • • • • •    23 OISIN 1          348
    BESIDE THE PILED-UP HUNTING-SPEARS,  • • • • • • • • •    23 OISIN 1       V  349
PILFERERS
    "THE DRUNKARDS, PILFERERS OF PUBLIC FUNDS,  • • • • • •   352 PEOPLE           23
PILGRIM
    BUT ONE MAN LOVED THE PILGRIM SOUL IN YOU,  • • • • • •   121 YOU ARE OLD        7
    THE PILGRIM  • • • • • • • • • • • • • • • • • •         592 PILGRIM           T
    COMPANIONING THE RIVER'S PILGRIM TORCH.  • • • • • •      703 MOSADA 3         112
PILGRIMS
    AN AMBUSH! PILGRIMS AT THE WATER-SIDE!  • • • • • • •     601 GALLERY REVIS      2
    AN AMBUSH! PILGRIMS AT THE WATER SIDE!  • • • • • • •     601 GALLERY REVIS  V   2
PILIN'      SEE A-PILIN'
    PILIN' THE WOOD OR PILIN' THE TURF,  • • • • • • • • •    96 MOLL MAGEE         45
    PILIN' THE WOOD OR PILIN' THE TURF,  • • • • • • • • •    96 MOLL MAGEE         45
    A-PILIN' WOOD OR PILIN' TURF,  • • • • • • • • • • •      96 MOLL MAGEE      V  45
PILLAR
    • • • AND HEAVING THE PILLAR OF HIS THROAT,  • • • • •    51 OISIN 3           59
    AMRITA.  DRAW YOU NEAR, AND 'NEATH YON PILLAR • • • •     71 ANASHU VIJAYA  V 13A
    AND RAISE HIS PILLAR STONE."  KING EOCHAID SAID,  • • •   280 TWO KINGS      V  83
    HIS MEMORY NOW IS A TALL PILLAR, BURNING  • • • • • •     738 MOURN THEN ON      15
PILLARED    SEE MANY-PILLARED
    UNTIL THE PILLARED DARK BEGAN TO STIR  • • • • • • •      185 QUEEN MAEVE       110
    WITH THE FIRST KINGS OF MANY PILLARED CRUACHAN  • • • •   187 QUEEN MAEVE    V 151
PILLARLESS
    WINDOWLESS, PILLARLESS, MULTITUDINOUS HOME • • • • • •    39 OISIN 2          148
PILLARS     SEE DOOR-PILLARS
    THE SEAWEED-COVERED PILLARS! AND THE GREEN • • • • • •    31 OISIN 2           32
    BASALTIC PILLARS MARRED WITH HEW AND HACK • • • • • •     31 OISIN 2        V  30
    MY PILLARS TOWARDS THEIR FALL. • • • • • • • • • •        44 OISIN 2        V 239
    THE BRAZEN PILLARS OF HIS DOOR, • • • • • • • • • •       192 BAILE AILLINN     74
    OR THE DOOR PILLARS OF ONE HOUSE, • • • • • • • • •       195 BAILE AILLINN  V 152
    AND STRIKE THE GOLDEN PILLARS WITH MY HANDS. • • • •      246 SHADOW WATER B   502
    ON PAINTED PILLARS, ON A DEAL • • • • • • • • • •         271 GREY ROCK      V  19
    BETWEEN THE PILLARS WITH A BEATING HEART • • • • • •      279 TWO KINGS         59
PILLOWS
    PROPPED UPON PILLOWS, ROUGE ON THE PALLOR OF HER FACE. • •  362 HER COURTESY      3
PILOT
    THE PILOT STAR AND THE CROOKED PLOUGH • • • • • • •       177 PAST GREATNESS     4
    THERE'S NOT A PILOT ON THE PERCH • • • • • •             607 SONGS BURDEN 2    25
    GO PILOT THE COURSE OF HIS ARROW'S DECEIT! • • • • •      657 ISLE STAT I 3     69
    AMONG THE WATERS THAT NO PILOT KNOWS. • • • • • • •       750 SHADOW WATER A    80
PILOTS
    WHAT KNOW THE PILOTS OF THE STARS OF TEARS? • • • • •     73 ANASHU VIJAYA     47
    FOR THEY'RE MY ONLY PILOTS.  IF I LOST THEM • • • • •     226 SHADOW WATER B    85
    WE HAVE TO FOLLOW, FOR THEY ARE OUR PILOTS! • • • •       247 SHADOW WATER B   527
    THAT I HAVE THE BEST OF PILOTS.  SHADOWS, ILLUSIONS, • •  249 SHADOW WATER B   565
    IF I REFUSED THE MESSENGERS AND PILOTS • • • • • •        249 SHADOW WATER B   572
    I HAVE GOOD PILOTS, AIBRIC.  WHEN MEN DIE • • • • •       750 SHADOW WATER A    81
PIN     SEE DOOR-PIN
    FASTEN YOUR HAIR WITH A GOLDEN PIN, • • • • • • • •       157 BELOVED RHYMES     1
    ROCK-NURTURED AOIFE TOOK A PIN, • • • • • • • • •         274 GREY ROCK         88
    WITH THE PIN OF A BROOCH, • • • • • • • • • • •           344 DAWN               4
PINCHES
    AND PINCHES AMONG HAIL AND SNOW? • • • • • • • •          191 BAILE AILLINN     46
PINCHING
    IN PINCHING WAYS I TOIL AND TURN." • • • • • • • •        19 OISIN 1        V 282
PINE
    TO PEAK AND PINE O'ER OISIN'S FAME." • • • • • • •        7 OISIN 1        V  70
    AND PEAK AND PINE WE KNOW NOT WHY, • • • • • • • •        22 OISIN 1        V 340C
    THEY PINE AWAY AND YELLOW AND WEAR OUT, • • • • • •       81 EPHEMERA       V 24H
    AND AH, THEY KNOW NOT, AS THEY PINE AND CEASE, • • •      81 EPHEMERA       V 24I
    BECAUSE I HAVE NO OTHER YOUTH, CAN MAKE ME PINE! • •      391 UNDER SATURN       3
    BEING A PORTION OF MY YOUTH, CAN MAKE ME PINE . . •       391 UNDER SATURN   V   3
    IT HAD BUT MADE US PINE THE MORE.  THE ABSTRACT JOY, •    427 PHANTOM HATRED    38
    WHERE CYPRESS IS AND OOZY PINE, • • • • • • • • •         670 ISLE STAT II 3   110
    FORSWEARS HIS WANDERING 'MONG THE PINE, • • • • •         686 LIFE               6
    HEARING THE HARPERS PLAY, THE PINE WOOD CRACKLE, • • •    759 SHADOW WATER A V 241
PINE-WOOD
    HEARING THE HARPERS PLAY, THE PINE-WOOD CRACKLE, • • • •  759 SHADOW WATER A   241
PINING
    WITH POISONOUS LIPS, AND HE IS PINING SINCE? • • • •      696 MOSADA 2           7
    FOR ALL SAVE HIM WHO PINING FELL, • • • • • • • •         717 FAIRY DOCTOR      19
    FOR ALL SAVE HE WHO PINING FELL, • • • • • • • •          717 FAIRY DOCTOR   V  19
PINION
    UNPRUNED IS YOUR BEAUTIFUL PINION • • • • • • • •         707 FAIRY PEDANT       7
PINIONS
    THE HORNS AND SHIELDS AND WILD SWAN'S PINIONS! • • • •    82 MAD KING GOLL  V   5
    FROM THE EVER-MOVING PINIONS • • • • • • • • •           667 ISLE STAT II 3    28
    DID I ON QUIVERING PINIONS HASTE, • • • • • • • •         670 ISLE STAT II 3   111
PINNACLE
    FROM YONDER PINNACLE ABOVE THE LAKE • • • • • • • •       657 ISLE STAT I 3     63
PIN'S
    PROMISED THAT FOR A PIN'S SAKE • • • • • • • • •          274 GREY ROCK         90
PIOUS
    BENDING LOW HIS PIOUS HEAD, • • • • • • • • •             82 MAD KING GOLL  V  10
    BECAUSE THIS COUNTRY HAS A PIOUS MIND • • • • • • •       447 COLONUS PRAISE    25
    AND KNOW YOU NOT SHE KISSED THAT PIOUS CHILD • • •        696 MOSADA 2           6
```

PAGE   TITLE   LINE

PIPE
     OF SORROWFUL, AUSTERE, SWEET, LOFTY PIPE TUNES. • • • • •   341 SHEP GOATHERD   57
     AN OATEN PIPE UNTO A LISTENING FAWN, • • • • • • • • •   678 ISLE STAT II 3   301
     AN OATEN PIPE UNTO A LISTENING FAUN, • • • • • • • • •   678 ISLE STAT II 3 V   301
PIPER
     A PIPER PIPING AWAY, • • • • • • • • • • • • • • • •   144 HOST OF AIR   10
     A PIPER PIPING AWAY, • • • • • • • • • • • • • • • •   145 HOST OF AIR   42
PIPES
     THE PLAYING UPON PIPES AND THE DANCING, • • • • • • •   330 BONE OF A HARE   5
     HE HAD OFTEN PLAYED HIS PIPES AMONG MY HILLS, • • • • •   339 SHEP GOATHERD   23
PIPING
     A PIPER PIPING AWAY, • • • • • • • • • • • • • • • •   144 HOST OF AIR   10
     AND NEVER WAS PIPING SO SAD, • • • • • • • • • • • •   144 HOST OF AIR   11
     AND NEVER WAS PIPING SO GAY. • • • • • • • • • • • •   144 HOST OF AIR   12
     A PIPER PIPING AWAY, • • • • • • • • • • • • • • • •   145 HOST OF AIR   42
     AND NEVER WAS PIPING SO SAD, • • • • • • • • • • • •   145 HOST OF AIR   43
     AND NEVER WAS PIPING SO GAY. • • • • • • • • • • • •   145 HOST OF AIR   44
PIRATES
     CRYING, THE PIRATES DROVE HIS SWINE • • • • • • • • •   82 MAD KING GOLL   15
     FELL ON THE PIRATES BY THE DEEP, • • • • • • • • • •   83 MAD KING GOLL   21
     FELL ON THE PIRATES BY THE DEEP, • • • • • • • • • •   83 MAD KING GOLL   V   21
PISTOL
     A MAN WITH A PISTOL STOOD, • • • • • • • • • • • • •   596 COLONEL MARTIN   56
PISTOLS
     BUT THEY THREW DOWN THEIR PISTOLS • • • • • • • • • •   596 COLONEL MARTIN   59
PIT
     HURL HELMETS, CROWNS, AND SWORDS INTO THE PIT. • • • •   257 RECONCILIATION   10
     THOSE FROM THE PIT AND GALLERY • • • • • • • • • • •   608 SONGS BURDEN 3   3
     AT THE BOTTOM OF A PIT • • • • • • • • • • • • • • •   632 MAN AND ECHO   3
     AND WHO WILL MOAN IN THE UNDER PIT, • • • • • • • • •   716 FAIRY DOCTOR   7
PITCH
     TO SUCH A PITCH MY THOUGHT • • • • • • • • • • • • •   255 WOMAN HOMER   11
     LET PAUDEENS PLAY AT PITCH AND TOSS, • • • • • • • •   288 TO WEALTHY MAN   31
     LEAVE PAUDEENS TO THEIR PITCH AND TOSS! • • • • • • •   288 TO WEALTHY MAN V   31
     TO SUCH A PITCH OF FOLLY I AM BROUGHT. • • • • • • •   384 VISION ROBART   58
     AND THAT TO SUCH A PITCH OF PASSION WROUGHT • • • • •   471 ALL SOUL NIGHT   24
     AND YET AGAIN, IF IT BE LIFE TO PITCH • • • • • • • •   479 SELF AND SOUL   58
     BECAUSE YOU HAVE IT IN THE PITCH DARK NIGHT • • • •   554 RIBH AT TOMB   V   1
     BECAUSE YOU HAVE FOUND ME IN THE PITCH DARK NIGHT • •   554 RIBH AT TOMB   V   1
     HERE IN THE PITCH DARK ATMOSPHERE ABOVE • • • • • • •   555 RIBH AT TOMB   V   17
     PITCH LIKE KING BILLY BOMB-BALLS IN • • • • • • • • •   565 LAPIS LAZULI   7
     THEIR DRINK, THEIR PITCH AND TOSS BY DAY, • • • • • •   607 SONGS BURDEN 2 V   14
     THEY PITCH THEIR BURDENS OFF. • • • • • • • • • • • •   612 NEWS ORACLE   24
     IMAGINATION TO THAT PITCH WHERE IT CASTS OUT • • • • •   619 BRONZE HEAD   19
     AND LITTLE BOYS PLAYED PITCH AND TOSS. • • • • • • •   725 LEGEND   4
PITCH-AND-TOSS
     THEIR DRINK, THEIR PITCH-AND-TOSS BY DAY, • • • • • •   607 SONGS BURDEN 2   14
PITCH-DARK
     BECAUSE YOU HAVE FOUND ME IN THE PITCH-DARK NIGHT • •   554 RIBH AT TOMB   1
     HERE IN THE PITCH-DARK ATMOSPHERE ABOVE • • • • • • •   555 RIBH AT TOMB   17
PITCHED   SEE HIGH-PITCHED
     BUT LOVE HAS PITCHED HIS MANSION IN • • • • • • • • •   513 JANE TALK BISH   15
     ANCESTRAL PEARLS ALL PITCHED INTO A STY, • • • • • • •   619 BRONZE HEAD   26
PITCHES
     THAT PITCHES COMMON THINGS ABOUT. THERE STOOD • • • •   428 NINETEEN 19   4
PITEOUS
     CRIED OUT, DIM SEA, HEAR MY MOST PITEOUS STORY! • • •   68 SAD SHEPHERD   9
     "OH SEA, OLD SEA, HEAR THOU MY PITEOUS STORY!" • • • •   68 SAD SHEPHERD   V   9
     O PITEOUS HEARTS, CHANGING TILL CHANGE BE DEAD • • • •   163 ASKS FORGIVE   19
     AMID THE HOVERING, PITEOUS, PENITENTIAL THRONG." • • •   173 SPEAKS HEARERS   8
     AND WHEN NO FACE GREW PITEOUS • • • • • • • • • • •   191 BAILE AILLINN   62
     SHE LIES, HER LOVELY PITEOUS HEAD AMID DULL RED HAIR • •   362 HER COURTESY   2
PITIFUL
     CRY OF HIS LOVE WITH THEIR PITIFUL CRIES. • • • • • •   177 PAST GREATNESS V   12
     I LONG FOR YOUR MERRY AND TENDER AND PITIFUL WORDS, • •   203 WITHER BOUGHS   3
     THE WEST WIND MADE IT PITIFUL, AND THE NORTH WIND AFRAID.   449 OWEN AHERNE   6
PITILESS
     A GAZE BLANK AND PITILESS AS THE SUN, • • • • • • •   402 SECOND COMING   15
     THY SOUL SHALL BE, THOUGH PITILESS AND BRIGHT • • • •   674 ISLE STAT II 3   210
     THE SOUL OF THE PITILESS PLACE • • • • • • • • • • •   708 FAIRY PEDANT   30
     WITH PITILESS MAGIC HAS BOUND YOU-- • • • • • • • • •   708 FAIRY PEDANT   31
     THE HEART OF THE PITILESS PLACE • • • • • • • • • • •   708 FAIRY PEDANT   V   30
PITRI'S
     AND MAY NO RESTLESS PITRI'S FIDGET FINGER • • • • • •   75 ANASHU VIJAYA   V   90
PITTANCE
     WHETHER FOR DAILY PITTANCE OR IN BLIND FEAR • • • • •   482 BLOOD AND MOON   37
PITY
     BUT PITY MOLL MAGEE. • • • • • • • • • • • • • • • •   94 MOLL MAGEE   4
     AND PITY MOLL MAGEE. • • • • • • • • • • • • • • • •   96 MOLL MAGEE   56
     THE PITY OF LOVE • • • • • • • • • • • • • • • • • •   119 PITY OF LOVE   T
     A PITY BEYOND ALL TELLING • • • • • • • • • • • • • •   119 PITY OF LOVE   1
     HAD PITY ON THE LEAST OF THINGS • • • • • • • • • • •   134 FR GILLIGAN   47
     OUR QUESTIONING, BEYOND OUR PITY EVEN. • • • • • • •   282 TWO KINGS   130
     QUESTION OF OURS, BEYOND OUR PITY EVEN. • • • • • • •   282 TWO KINGS   V   130
     PITY, AN ACHING HEAD, • • • • • • • • • • • • • • • •   346 ON WOMAN   38
     NOR HATE OF WHAT'S TO COME, NOR PITY FOR WHAT'S GONE, • •   427 PHANTOM HATRED   30
     IN PITY FOR MAN'S DARKENING THOUGHT • • • • • • • • •   438 SONGS PLAY 2   1
     I PITY ALL THE YOUNG, • • • • • • • • • • • • • • •   607 SONGS BURDEN 2   11
     PITY THESE WEEPING EYES! I WILL FOLLOW YOU. • • • • •   768 SHADOW WATER A   420
PITY-CRAZED
     SHE, PITY-CRAZED, HAD GIVEN HER SOUL AWAY, • • • • • •   629 CIRCUS ANIMALS   19

616

PITYIN'
   AND STILL, WITH PITYIN', SCORNIN' EYE, ... 96 MOLL MAGEE 39
PITYING
   WITH SCARCE A PITYING LOOK? . . . . 315 FRIENDS 19
   UNLESS SOME PITYING GOD SHALL SUCCOUR ME . . . . 656 ISLE STAT I 3 36
PLACE   SEE DANCING-PLACE CAMPING-PLACE FIRE-PLACE SHADOW-PLACE THRESHING-PLACE
      MARKET-PLACE
   IT DOWN IN A LEAF-HID, HOLLOW PLACE . . . . 17 OISIN 1 242
   WE SAW, SOME NEW, SOME PRINTED WHEN THE PLACE WAS YOUNG, . . 37 OISIN 2 V 116
   LOOKED DOWN ON ME; AND IN THE SELF-SAME PLACE . . . . . 39 OISIN 2 146
   MELTED AND FLOWED; AND IN THE SELF-SAME PLACE . . . . . 39 OISIN 2 V 146
   AND THEY WHO TO A FAR-OFF PLACE HAD FLED, ... 41 OISIN 2 V 184
   NOW IN A PLACE OF STAR-FIRE, AND NOW IN A SHADOW-PLACE 49 OISIN 3 42
      WIDE;
   NOW IN A PLACE OF STAR-FIRE, AND NOW IN A SHADOW PLACE 49 OISIN 3 V 42
      WIDE;
   NOW IN A PLACE OF STAR-FIRE, AND NOW IN A SHADOW PLACE 49 OISIN 3 V 42
      WIDE;
   LAY LOOSE IN A PLACE OF SHADOW; WE DREW THE REINS BY HIS 50 OISIN 3 44
      SIDE.
   WHILE IN THIS PLACE AND THAT PLACE, ... 58 OISIN 3 166
   WHILE IN THIS PLACE AND THAT PLACE, ... 58 OISIN 3 166
   AND IN THIS PLACE AND THAT PLACE, ... 58 OISIN 3 166
   AND IN THIS PLACE AND THAT PLACE, ... 58 OISIN 3 V 166
   SORRY PLACE, WHERE FOR SWING OF THE WAR-AXE IN MY DIM EYES 61 OISIN 3 194
   . . .
   WHAT PLACE HAVE CAOILTE AND CONAN, AND BRAN, SCEOLAN, 61 OISIN 3 195
      LOMAIR?
   . . . ON THE BURNING STONES IS THEIR PLACE; . . . . . 61 OISIN 3 197
   WHAT PLACE HAVE CAOLTE AND FIN, AND BRAN, SGEOLAN, LOMAIR? 61 OISIN 3 V 195
   AND THEY MARRIED BEYOND THEIR PLACE. . . . . 92 FATHER OHART 8
   TO MY OWN PLACE, KINSALE. . . . . 95 MOLL MAGEE 24
   SERVANTS ROUND HIS CUSHIONED PLACE . . . . 99 FOXHUNTER 37
   THE SERVANTS ROUND HIS CUSHIONED PLACE . . . . 99 FOXHUNTER V 37
   "THE DOOMS OF MEN ARE IN GOD'S HIDDEN PLACE." . . . . 110 CUCHULAIN SEA 62
   AMID MEN'S SOULS, THAT WAVER AND GIVE PLACE . . . . . 112 ROSE OF WORLD 7
   AMID MEN'S SOULS THAT DAY BY DAY GIVE PLACE, ... 112 ROSE OF WORLD V 7
   I DREAMED THAT ONE HAD DIED IN A STRANGE PLACE . . . . 123 DREAM OF DEATH 1
   BUT WHILE HE PASSED BEFORE A PLASHY PLACE, ... 127 DREAM OF FAERY 17
   NO PLACE FOR LOVE AND DREAM AT ALL; . . . . 139 TO IRELAND 43
   WHO DANCED ON A LEVEL PLACE, ... 144 HOST OF AIR 14
   AND LINGERED IN THE HIDDEN DESOLATE PLACE . . . . . . 162 ASKS FORGIVE 15
   FROM GULLEON'S PLACE OF PRIDE, ... 171 MAID QUIET V 48
   AND HURLED IT FROM ITS PLACE BEFORE HIS FOOTSTOOL WHITE, 174 ELEMENT POWERS V 3
   AND HURLED IT FROM ITS PLACE AMID THE PEARLY LIGHT . . 174 ELEMENT POWERS V 3
   THEIR BODICES IN SOME DIM PLACE . . . . 193 BAILE AILLINN 105
   IN THE HID PLACE, BEING CRAZED BY LOVE. . . . . 195 BAILE AILLINN 143
   FORGOTTEN AT THE THRESHING PLACE; . . . . 195 BAILE AILLINN 148
   FOR THE ROADS ARE UNENDING, AND THERE IS NO PLACE TO MY 203 WITHER BOUGHS 4
      MIND."
   SHALL LIGHT UPON A PLACE IN THE WORLD'S CORE, ... 231 SHADOW WATER B 212
   WHERE DO YOU COME FROM? WHO BROUGHT YOU TO THIS PLACE? 235 SHADOW WATER B 284
   TO SOME SURE COUNTRY, SOME FAMILIAR PLACE. . . . . . 249 SHADOW WATER B 569
   THAT IF WE HOLD THAT FLIGHT THEY'LL LEAVE THE PLACE, . . 265 ABBEY THEATRE 3
   TILL ALL THE PLACE WAS BEATEN INTO MIRE. . . . . . . 278 TWO KINGS 27
   HIS MUMMERS TO THE MARKET PLACE, ... 287 TO WEALTHY MAN V 10
   AMID A PLACE OF STONE, ... 291 TO A FRIEND 13
   LIKE GENTLE BLOOD, HAS BEEN DRIVEN FROM THE PLACE, . . 292 TO A SHADE 14
   STUMBLED UPON THAT WINDY PLACE . . . . 302 HOUR DAWN 3
   HELL MOUTH LAY OPEN NEAR THAT PLACE, ... 303 HOUR DAWN 25
   BEING CERTAIN IT WAS NO RIGHT PLACE . . . . 303 HOUR DAWN V 23
   LIKE SOME LAST COURTIER AT A GYPSY CAMPING PLACE . . . 314 FALLEN MAJESTY V 3
   EVIL OF THIS PLACE. . . . . 319 DOLLS 9
   IN A MOST DESOLATE STONY PLACE, ... 325 ROBERT GREGORY 30
   TOWARDS NIGHTFALL UPON A PLACE . . . . 325 ROBERT GREGORY V 31
   AT MOONEEN HE HAD LEAPED A PLACE . . . . 326 ROBERT GREGORY 60
   WE HAVE TALKED IN THE ONE PLACE, ... 332 SOLOMON SHEBA 4
   I HAD DRIVEN EVERY RHYME INTO ITS PLACE . . . . 339 SHEP GOATHERD 14
   TO A GREY PLACE ON A HILL . . . . 347 FISHERMAN 3
   CLIMBING UP TO A PLACE . . . . 348 FISHERMAN 31
   MERE IMAGES; CHOSEN THIS PLACE TO LIVE IN . . . . . . 373 PHASES OF MOON 13
   AUSTERITY, A PLACE SET OUT FOR WISDOM . . . . 377 PHASES OF MOON 127
   FROM MOONLIT PLACE TO PLACE, ... 379 CAT AND MOON 18
   FROM MOONLIT PLACE TO PLACE, ... 379 CAT AND MOON 18
   FROM MOONLESS PLACE TO PLACE. . . . . 379 CAT AND MOON V 18
   FROM MOONLESS PLACE TO PLACE. . . . . 379 CAT AND MOON V 18
   FROM MOONLIGHT PLACE TO PLACE, ... 379 CAT AND MOON V 18
   FROM MOONLIGHT PLACE TO PLACE, ... 379 CAT AND MOON V 18
   ROOTED IN ONE DEAR PERPETUAL PLACE. . . . . 405 FOR DAUGHTER 48
   WHO'D LIVED SOMEWHERE UPON THAT ROCKY PLACE, ... 410 TOWER 35
   GIVE PLACE TO AN INDIFFERENT MULTITUDE, GIVE PLACE . . 427 PHANTOM HATRED 28
   GIVE PLACE TO AN INDIFFERENT MULTITUDE, GIVE PLACE . . 427 PHANTOM HATRED 28
   AND THEREUPON A COLLOQUY TOOK PLACE . . . . 463 HARUN RASHID 45
   THAT THEREUPON A COLLOQUY TOOK PLACE . . . . 463 HARUN RASHID V 45
   BLESSED BE THIS PLACE, ... 480 BLOOD AND MOON 1
   RUN UNDERGROUND, RISE IN A ROCKY PLACE . . . . 490 COOLE BALLYLEE 5
   THE PLACE OF EXCREMENT; . . . . 513 JANE TALK BISH 16
   ALL KNOW THAT ALL THE DEAD IN THE WORLD ABOUT THAT PLACE 593 PILGRIM 11
      ARE STUCK,
   THIS BOOK OR THAT, COME TO THIS HALLOWED PLACE . . . . 604 GALLERY REVIS 51
   AND PRESSED AT MIDNIGHT IN SOME PUBLIC PLACE . . . . 610 STATUES 7

	PAGE	TITLE	LINE

PLACE   (CONTINUED)

IN THIS LONELY PLACE. • • • • • • • •	617	LONG-LEG FLY	14
ONE ANOTHER IN THIS PLACE? • • • • • • •	633	MAN AND ECHO	40
DANCING IN SOME MOONY PLACE• • • • • • •	647	ISLE STAT I 1	54
HERE IS THE PLACE, THE CLIFF-ENCIRCLED WOOD; • • • •	651	ISLE STAT I 2	3
THROUGH THIS NIGHT-VESTED PLACE THE RED BEAMS BREAK. • • •	662	ISLE STAT II 2	4
LEAD ME, I PRAY THEE, TO THE STATUED PLACE! • • • •	667	ISLE STAT II 3	37
WE TURNED AROUND THE PLACE ALWAY, • • • • • •	667	ISLE STAT II 3	40
TO PLACE A KISS OF FIRE ON THE DIM BROW • • • • •	688	TWO TITANS	47
A LILY-BLANCHED PLACE, SHE SAT AND SANG, • • • •	693	MOSADA 1	83
A LILY BLANCHED PLACE, SHE SAT AND SANG, • • • •	693	MOSADA 1 V	83
THE SOUL OF THE PITILESS PLACE • • • • • • •	708	FAIRY PEDANT	30
THE HEART OF THE PITILESS PLACE • • • • • • •	708	FAIRY PEDANT V	30
ENCLOSE A QUIET PLACE OF BEDS BOX-BORDERED, BEES, • • •	710	FERENCZ RENYI	24
THE PLACE WAS EMPTY NOW OF PEOPLE. • • • • • •	725	LEGEND	25
AN EVENING PRESENCE FILLS THE PLACE. • • • • • •	736	SUMMER EVENING	16
BEFORE A SANDED PLACE! • • • • • • • • •	740	EARL PAUL	32
WHERE GODS ARE BROODING IN A MOUNTAINOUS PLACE • • •	757	SHADOW WATER A	198
I PUT THREE PERSONS IN THEIR PLACE • • • • • •	787	HUDDON DUDDON	8

PLACES

"BUT WE ARE APART IN THE GRASSY PLACES, • • • • •	27	OISIN 1	408
"BUT NEVER THE YEARS IN THE ISLE'S SOFT PLACES • • •	27	OISIN 1	V 419A
"BUT NEVER THE YEARS IN OUR ISLE'S SOFT PLACES • • •	28	OISIN 1	V 424
OF HALF-FORGOTTEN INNOCENT OLD PLACES! • • • • •	130	BOOK STORIES	22
CABINS GONE NOW, OLD WELL-SIDES, OLD DEAR PLACES, • •	130	BOOK STORIES	V 23
AMID MOST LOVELY PLACES! SMITTEN AS THOUGH • • •	389	IMAGE PAST	13
HEAVEN AND EARTH OUT OF THEIR PLACES, • • • • •	540	FROM ANTIGONE	8
THE BEGGARS HAVE CHANGED PLACES, BUT THE LASH GOES ON. • •	590	GREAT DAY	4
IN WASTE PLACES OF THE SKY, • • • • • • •	772	SONG DEIRDRE 1	6

PLACID

WITH BERRIES. PLACID AS A HOMEWARD BEE, • • • •	710	FERENCZ RENYI	29
WATCHED OF PLACID POPLAR-TREES • • • • • • •	732	STREET DANCERS	16
WATCHED OF PLACID POPLAR TREES, • • • • • •	732	STREET DANCERS V	16
SORROW-WORN, YET PLACID BROWED. • • • • • •	733	STREET DANCERS V	56

PLACID-BROWED

SORROW-WORN, YET PLACID-BROWED. • • • • • •	733	STREET DANCERS	56

PLAGUE

THAT PLAGUE ME DAY AND NIGHT • • • • • • •	399	DEMON BEAST	3
THEY WERE NOT SUCH A PLAGUE WHEN I WAS YOUNG! • • • •	591	SPUR	3

PLAGUED

AND ARE PLAGUED BY CROWDS, UNTIL • • • • • •	298	THREE HERMITS	20

PLAIN

YET WILL I MAKE ALL PLAIN FOR THEE. • • • • •	2	OISIN 1	V 7B
A GOLDEN CRESCENT LIT THE PLAIN. • • • • • •	2	OISIN 1	V 7BB
ON GABHRA'S RAVEN-COVERED PLAIN! • • • • • •	5	OISIN 1	43
STROKED THE YOUNG WINDS AS THEY ROLLED ON THE PLAIN, • •	27	OISIN 1	V 415C
THE LEAST OF DOORS! BEYOND ON A DIM PLAIN • • • •	39	OISIN 2	155
THE LEAST OF DOORS! BEYOND THE DOOR A PLAIN, • • • •	39	OISIN 2	V 155
BARKING. ALONG THE HERBLESS PLAIN, WITH BLOWS • • •	40	OISIN 2	V 170
A KING OF THE GREAT PLAIN WOULD SPEAK WITH YOU." • • •	183	QUEEN MAEVE	78
KINGS OF THE GREAT PLAIN HAVE COME AND GONE • • • •	183	QUEEN MAEVE	V 81
WHERE WILD BEES HIVE ON THE GREAT PLAIN. • • • • •	194	BAILE AILLINN	123
TO TELL THEM A PLAIN STORY. THAT'S NOT THE STORY! • •	245	SHADOW WATER B	482
WAS DONE TO MAKE IT PLAIN! • • • • • • •	256	WORDS	8
SO IT'S PLAIN TO BE DISCERNED • • • • • • •	298	THREE HERMITS	16
"IT'S PLAIN THAT YOU ARE NO RIGHT MAN • • • • •	306	HOUR DAWN	82
FROM MAEVE AND ALL THAT JUGGLING PLAIN, • • • • •	307	HOUR DAWN	120
OR ESSERKELLY PLAIN! FEW KEPT HIS PACE! • • • • •	326	ROBERT GREGORY	59
THAT MAYBE "I AM SORRY" IN PLAIN PROSE • • • • •	341	SHEP GOATHERD	60
IT'S PLAIN THE BIBLE MEANS • • • • • • • •	345	ON WOMAN	10
MORE PLAIN TO THE MIND'S EYE THAN ANY FACE • • • •	368	EGO DOMINUS	21
LOVED THE LADY; AND IT'S PLAIN • • • • • • •	385	ROBARTES DANCE	5
O PLAIN AS PLAIN CAN BE • • • • • • • • •	396	ROSE TREE	16
O PLAIN AS PLAIN CAN BE • • • • • • • • •	396	ROSE TREE	16
DANCED ON CRUACHAN'S WINDY PLAIN, • • • • • •	528	DANCER CRUACH	4
DANCED IT ON CRUACHAN'S WINDY PLAIN, • • • • •	528	DANCER CRUACH V	4
ON CRUACHAN'S PLAIN SLEPT HE • • • • • • •	529	TOM CRUACHAN	1
THAT IF THEIR NEIGHBOURS FIGURED PLAIN, • • • • •	626	OLD MEN BE MAD	11
THE PLAIN, A LITTLE FAIR-HAIRED MAID I LOVE. • • • •	679	ISLE STAT II 3	312
PLAIN TO BE UNDERSTOOD. • • • • • • • • •	785	YOUR HEART	2
ARE SHOT AT ON THE OPEN PLAIN. • • • • • • •	791	REPRISALS	18

'PLAINING

CURES FOR CALVES WITH 'PLAINING THROAT, • • • • •	717	FAIRY DOCTOR	15
CURES FOR CALF WITH 'PLAINING THROAT, • • • • •	717	FAIRY DOCTOR V	15

PLAINLY

PLAINLY NO PHANTOM BY HIS LOOK! • • • • • •	303	HOUR DAWN V	30

PLAIN'S

AND NOT A HOUSE TO THE PLAIN'S EDGE. • • • • •	302	HOUR DAWN	10

PLAINS

ALONG THE BLOOD-BEDABBLED PLAINS, • • • • • •	24	OISIN 1	371
REMEMBERING HOW ALONG THE PLAINS, • • • • • •	24	OISIN 1	V 370
AND WE RODE ON THE PLAINS OF THE SEA'S EDGE! • • • •	48	OISIN 3	13
AND I RODE BY THE PLAINS OF THE SEA'S EDGE, • • • •	56	OISIN 3	141
AND ESERKELLY PLAINS, FEW KEPT HIS PACE! • • • • •	326	ROBERT GREGORY V	59
OR ESERKELLY PLAINS, FEW KEPT HIS PACE! • • • • •	326	ROBERT GREGORY	59
MOURN YE ON GRASS-GREEN PLAINS OF ERI FATED, • • • •	738	MOURN THEN ON	9

PLAITED

OUR HEARTS ENDURE THE SCOURGE, THE PLAITED THORNS, THE WAY	172	TRAV PASSION	3
OUR HEARTS ENDURE THE PLAITED THORN, THE CROWDED WAY, • •	172	TRAV PASSION V	3

PLAN

TO MICHELOZZO'S LATEST PLAN • • • • • • • •	288	TO WEALTHY MAN	23

PLAN   (CONTINUED)
    "I HAD NO BETTER PLAN AT FIRST. . . . .   305 HOUR DAWN   63
    ACCORDING TO A DIFFERENT PLAN. . . . .   379 SAINT HUNCH   6
    1 UNDERSTOOD HIS PLAN. . . . .   400 DEMON BEAST   15
    "ACCORDING TO MY BOYISH PLAN! . . . .   577 WHAT THEN   17
PLANE
    THAT PATCHING OLD HEELS THEY MAY SHRIEK, I TAKE TO CHISEL 623 HIGH TALK   8
        AND PLANE.
PLANES
    SOME NINETEEN GERMAN PLANES, THEY SAY, ...   791 REPRISALS   1
PLANETS
    AND MAKES THE LITTLE PLANETS RUN! . . . .   18 OISIN 1   268
    FOR JOY THE LITTLE PLANETS RUN . . . .   18 OISIN 1   V 267
    OF PLANETS WATCHING, WATCHING THE RACE OF HARES . . . . 44 OISIN 2   V 228B
    AND THE OLD PLANETS SEVEN . . . .   118 CRADLE SONG   V   7
    THE OLD PLANETS SEVEN . . . .   118 CRADLE SONG   V   7
    WITH PLANETS IN HIS CARE, ...   134 FR GILLIGAN   46
    THE CARELESS PLANETS IN THEIR COURSES, ...   344 DAWN   7
    THERE ALL THE PLANETS DROP IN THE SUN. . . . . . .   557 THERE   4
PLANNED   SEE LONG-PLANNED
    "IF LITTLE PLANNED IS LITTLE SINNED . . . .   338 TOM OROUGHLEY   9
    "OH, LITTLE PLANNED IS LITTLE SINNED . . . .   338 TOM OROUGHLEY   V   9
    PLANNED IN A GOVERNMENT OFFICE, SHORTEN HIS LIFE, . . . 372 ON GOING HOUSE   15
    AND PLANNED TO BRING THE WORLD UNDER A RULE, ...   429 NINETEEN 19   31
    WHO HAVE PLANNED HIS MURDER, FOR THEY KNOW . . . . .   436 FOR MY SON   12
    PERPLEXED HER FANTASY AND PLANNED HER CARE? . . . . .   466 HARUN RASHID   114
    PERPLEXED HER PHANTASY AND PLANNED HER CARE? . . . .   466 HARUN RASHID   V 114
    THAT STIRRED HER FANTASY AND PLANNED HER CARE, . . .   466 HARUN RASHID   V 114
    PYTHAGORAS PLANNED IT. WHY DID THE PEOPLE STARE? . . . 610 STATUES   1
    AS MY LONG PLANNED HALF SOLITUDE, ...   624 APPARITIONS   V 10
PLANNING
    AND PLANNING, PLOTTING ALWAYS THAT SOME MORROW . . .   129 BOOK STORIES   10
PLANS
    THEY HAVE IT THAT THE PLANS OF KINGS AND QUEENS . . . . 235 SHADOW WATER B   296
PLANTED
    AND PLANTED CYPRESS ROUND! . . . .   123 DREAM OF DEATH   8
    AND WONDERING PLANTED BY HER SOLITUDE . . . . . .   123 DREAM OF DEATH V   5
    HAS PLANTED QUIET IN THE NIGHT! . . . .   134 TWO TREES   8
    PLANTED ON HIS KNEES, ...   333 SOLOMON SHEBA   10
    AMID THE RUSTLE OF HIS PLANTED HILLS, ...   417 ANCEST HOUSES   2
    PLANTED ON THE STAR-LIT GOLDEN BOUGH, ...   497 BYZANTIUM   19
    PLANTED ON THE STARLIT GOLDEN BOUGH, ...   497 BYZANTIUM   V 19
    AND THERE TWO BUSHES PLANTED . . . .   571 THREE BUSHES   59
    GOD PLANTED HIM LONG AGO. . . . .   743 WISDOM DREAMS   8
    PLANTED IN THE RUNNING WAVE! . . . .   775 AGAINST WITCH   13
PLANTS
    AMONG THE PLANTS! THE FLOWERY SILENCE FELL . . . . .   692 MOSADA 1   55
PLASHES
    AND A HORSE PLASHES WITHIN IT! . . . .   393 EASTER 1916   52
PLASHY
    BUT WHILE HE PASSED BEFORE A PLASHY PLACE, ...   127 DREAM OF FAERY   17
PLASTER
    IN MOULDED PLASTER OR IN CARVEN STONE? . . . . . .   327 ROBERT GREGORY   77
    "OF PLASTER SAINTS"! HIS BEAUTIFUL MISCHIEVOUS HEAD THROWN 577 LOFTY THINGS   4
        BACK.
PLATE
    I COOK AND CHANGE MY PLATE, ...   607 SONGS BURDEN 2   6
PLATO
    CHOOSE PLATO AND PLOTINUS FOR A FRIEND . . . . . .   409 TOWER   12
    PLATO THOUGHT NATURE BUT A SPUME THAT PLAYS . . . .   445 SCHOOL CHILDR   41
    PLATO STANDS BELOW, ...   524 MAD AS MIST   8
    PLATO THERE AND MINOS PASS, ...   531 DELPHIC ORACLE   8
PLATONIC
    SO THE PLATONIC YEAR . . . .   430 NINETEEN 19   54
    MADE ALL PLATONIC TOLERANCE VAIN . . . .   438 SONGS PLAY 2   7
    THAT'S CALLED PLATONIC LOVE, ...   471 ALL SOUL NIGHT   23
PLATONIST
    FROM THE FAR TOWER WHERE MILTON'S PLATONIST . . . .   373 PHASES OF MOON   15
    IL PENSEROSO'S PLATONIST TOILED ON . . . .   419 MY HOUSE   14
    SOME PLATONIST AFFIRMS THAT IN THE STATION . . . . .   431 NINETEEN 19   72
PLATONISTS
    "THOSE PLATONISTS ARE A CURSE," HE SAID, ...   485 STATISTICS   1
PLATO'S
    AND CRY IN PLATO'S TEETH, ...   415 TOWER   147
    MADE PLATO'S TOLERANCE IN VAIN, ...   438 SONGS PLAY 2   V   7
    OR ELSE, TO ALTER PLATO'S PARABLE, ...   443 SCHOOL CHILDR   15
    WHO TALKS OF PLATO'S SPINDLE! . . . .   520 HIS BARGAIN   1
    "WHAT THEN?" SANG PLATO'S GHOST. "WHAT THEN?" . . . . 576 WHAT THEN   5
    "WHAT THEN?" SANG PLATO'S GHOST. "WHAT THEN?" . . .   577 WHAT THEN   10
    "WHAT THEN?" SANG PLATO'S GHOST. "WHAT THEN?" . . . . 577 WHAT THEN   15
PLAUSIBLE
    OR SEEM PLAUSIBLE TO A MAN OF SENSE, ...   624 APPARITIONS   4
PLAUTUS
    SO THAT HIS PLAUTUS SET THE PACE . . . .   287 TO WEALTHY MAN   12
PLAY   SEE HORSE-PLAY LOVE-PLAY
    IN THE FENIANS' DWELLINGS OF WATTLE LEAN ON THE CHESSBOARDS 55 OISIN 3   115
        AND PLAY,
    WITH MINGLING HAIR, AND PLAY UPON ONE LUTE. . . . . .   71 ANASHU VIJAYA   10
    YOU WAVES, THOUGH YOU DANCE BY MY FEET LIKE CHILDREN AT 90 OLD FISHERMAN   1
        PLAY,

	PAGE	TITLE	LINE

PLAY   (CONTINUED)

YE WAVES, THOUGH YE DANCE 'FORE MY FEET LIKE CHILDREN AT PLAY, — 90 OLD FISHERMAN V 1
WHEN I PLAY ON MY FIDDLE IN DOONEY, — 178 FIDDLER DOONEY 1
HAVE GIVEN THEIR HEARTS UP TO THE PLAY, — 202 NEVER GIVE ALL 10
AND WHO COULD PLAY IT WELL ENOUGH — 202 NEVER GIVE ALL 11
AND WHO CAN PLAY IT WELL ENOUGH — 202 NEVER GIVE ALL V 11
HURRY TO BLESS THE HANDS THAT PLAY, — 212 BLESS PSALTER 1
O KINSMEN, BLESS THE HANDS THAT PLAY. — 213 BLESS PSALTER 15
A LYRIC FROM AN UNPUBLISHED PLAY — 263 MASK V T
LET PAUDEENS PLAY AT PITCH AND TOSS, — 288 TO WEALTHY MAN 31
THE NAMES THAT STILLED YOUR CHILDISH PLAY, — 289 SEPTEMBER 1913 10
WHEREON MAD FINGERS PLAY — 291 TO A FRIEND 12
THE ATTACK ON THE "PLAY BOY" — 294 HATED PLAYBOY V T
THE WIND IS OLD AND STILL AT PLAY — 301 RUN PARADISE 22
THE PLAYER QUEEN SONG FROM AN UNFINISHED PLAY — 308 PLAYER QUEEN V T
THE MOMENTS PASSED AS AT A PLAY! — 313 MEMORY YOUTH 1
COME PLAY WITH ME! — 359 TO A SQUIRREL 1
AND PENANCE IS THE PLAY, — 364 END OF DAY 2
THOUGH PLAY IS BUT HALF DONE-- — 364 END OF DAY 7
"COME IN AND LEAVE THE PLAY." — 364 END OF DAY 8
THOUGH PLAY IS BUT HALF-DONE-- — 364 END OF DAY V 7
THAT HE WILL NEVER FIND! I'D PLAY A PART! — 377 PHASES OF MOON 128
AND RIGHT BETWEEN THESE TWO A GIRL AT PLAY — 383 VISION ROBART 21
BUT WHEN THE MASTER'S BURIED MICE CAN PLAY, — 418 ANCEST HOUSES 22
THROUGH TOO MUCH PLAY, OR MARRIAGE WITH A FOOL? — 423 MY DESCENDANTS 12
THE FINEST PLAY UNDER THE SUN. — 424 ROAD AT DOOR 5
WHETHER TO PLAY, OR TO RIDE — 431 NINETEEN 19 67
LET THE NEW FACES PLAY WHAT TRICKS THEY WILL — 435 NEW FACES 5
TWO SONGS FROM A PLAY — 437 SONGS PLAY 1 T
AS THOUGH GOD'S DEATH WERE BUT A PLAY. — 437 SONGS PLAY 1 8
I KNEW THAT HORSE PLAY, KNEW IT FOR A MURDEROUS THING. — 442 BLACK CENTAUR V 4
WHAT SEEMS MOST WELCOME IN THE TOMB--PLAY A PREDESTINED PART. — 503 VACILLATION 86
I OFFER TO LOVE'S PLAY — 536 PARTING 13
NONE SHARED OUR GUILT! NOR DID WE PLAY A PART — 542 PARN FUNERAL 1 22
ALL PERFORM THEIR TRAGIC PLAY, — 565 LAPIS LAZULI 9
IF WORTHY THEIR PROMINENT PART IN THE PLAY, — 565 LAPIS LAZULI 14
ACCOMPLISHED FINGERS BEGIN TO PLAY. — 567 LAPIS LAZULI 54
AND THEN A COUNTER-TRUTH FILLED OUT ITS PLAY, — 629 CIRCUS ANIMALS 17
DID THAT PLAY OF MINE SEND OUT — 632 MAN AND ECHO 11
I'LL PLAY YOU FOR YOUR OLD HOUR-GLASS. YOU SEE — 721 WITCH VIVIEN 36
FOR OTHER STAKES WE PLAY. YOU LOST THE GLASS. — 722 WITCH VIVIEN 50
THUS PLAY WE FIRST WITH PAWNS, POOR THINGS AND WEAK; — 722 WITCH VIVIEN 53
SO MEN IN LIFE AND I IN MAGIC PLAY; — 722 WITCH VIVIEN 55
ON THE NOSE OF THE SLEEPER HE MADE IT PLAY; — 729 PRIEST FAIRY 30
AND PLAY WITH HIS IMMORTAL HATE. — 736 SUMMER EVENING 12
HEARING THE HARPERS PLAY, THE PINE-WOOD CRACKLE, — 759 SHADOW WATER A 241
HEARING THE HARPERS PLAY, THE PINE WOOD CRACKLE, — 759 SHADOW WATER A V 241
CHORUS FOR A PLAY — 771 SONG DEIRDRE 1 V T
WHAT'S THE MERIT IN LOVE PLAY, — 777 SONG DEIRDRE 2 V 6
THOSE CRAZY FINGERS PLAY — 783 GREY ROUND 16

PLAYBOY

ON THOSE THAT HATED "THE PLAYBOY — 294 HATED PLAYBOY T
ON THOSE WHO DISLIKE THE PLAYBOY — 294 HATED PLAYBOY V T
THE ATTACK ON "THE PLAYBOY OF THE WESTERN WORLD" — 294 HATED PLAYBOY V T

PLAY-BOY

ON THOSE THAT HATED "THE PLAY-BOY — 294 HATED PLAYBOY T

PLAYED

HE SAT AND PLAYED IN A DREAM — 145 HOST OF AIR 27
HE PLAYED WITH THE MERRY OLD MEN — 145 HOST OF AIR 29
HE SAT DOWN AND PLAYED IN A DREAM — 145 HOST OF AIR V 27
WHERE I HAVE LAUGHED AND SPUN AND PLAYED? — 151 HEART OF WOMAN V 2
AT THE FULL MOON? HE PLAYED ALL THROUGH THE NIGHT. — 223 SHADOW WATER B 21
AS WHEN I ALSO PLAYED THE FOOL." — 306 HOUR DAWN 79
HE HAD OFTEN PLAYED HIS PIPES AMONG MY HILLS, — 339 SHEP GOATHERD 23
AND WHEN HE PLAYED IT WAS THEIR LONELINESS, — 339 SHEP GOATHERD 24
YET MANY, THAT HAVE PLAYED THE FOOL — 404 FOR DAUGHTER 36
SOLIDER ARISTOTLE PLAYED THE TAWS — 445 SCHOOL CHILDR 43
GREAT EUROPA PLAYED THE FOOL — 509 JANE REPROVED 5
WHEN SHE, AND THOUGH SOME SAID SHE PLAYED — 514 JANE GROWN OLD 8
THAT SAT SO STILL AND PLAYED AT THE CHESS? — 550 SEVERED HEAD 12
AS HERE I CAME I SAW GOD PAN. HE PLAYED — 678 ISLE STAT II 3 300
AND LITTLE BOYS PLAYED PITCH AND TOSS. — 725 LEGEND 4
PLAYED ON HIS HARP. AND I WOULD BE AS SAD — 747 SHADOW WATER A 3

PLAYER

A SONG FROM "THE PLAYER QUEEN" — 308 PLAYER QUEEN T
THE PLAYER QUEEN SONG FROM AN UNFINISHED PLAY — 308 PLAYER QUEEN V T
AND THERE'S A PLAYER IN THE STATES WHO GATHERS UP HER CLOAK — 354 HIS PHOENIX 12
AND THERE'S THE PLAYER IN THE STATES WHO GATHERS UP HER CLOAK — 354 HIS PHOENIX V 12
THE PLAYER CONNOLLY, — 608 SONGS BURDEN 3 11
THEY SAY YOU ARE A GAMBLER AND A PLAYER — 721 WITCH VIVIEN 34

PLAYERS

THE PLAYERS ASK FOR A BLESSING ON THE PSALTERIES AND ON THEMSELVES — 212 BLESS PSALTER T
THE PLAYERS ASK FOR A BLESSING ON THE PSALTERIES AND THEMSELVES — 212 BLESS PSALTER V T
COME GATHER ROUND ME, PLAYERS ALL! — 608 SONGS BURDEN 3 1
PLAYERS AND PAINTED STAGE TOOK ALL MY LOVE, — 630 CIRCUS ANIMALS 31
BUT WOMEN AND JUGGLERS AND PLAYERS ON THE HARP. — 752 SHADOW WATER A 115

620

		PAGE	TITLE	LINE

PLAYFUL
TROTTED BESIDE HIM IN A PLAYFUL MOOD. • • • • • • • 715 DWELT SYCAMORE 4
PLAYING
TO OLD MEN PLAYING AT CARDS • • • • • • • • • 144 HOST OF AIR 23
THE OTHER NIGHT, WHILE HE WAS PLAYING IT, • • • • 223 SHADOW WATER B 32
I SAW THEM, TOO, ONE NIGHT. FORGAEL WAS PLAYING, • • 223 SHADOW WATER B 36
FOR YOU HAVE LISTENED TO ME PLAYING IT • • • • • 243 SHADOW WATER B 434
THE PLAYING UPON PIPES AND THE DANCING, • • • • • 330 BONE OF A HARE 5
SHE IS PLAYING LIKE A CHILD • • • • • • • • • 364 END OF DAY 1
WHERE THE SHAKING LEAF WITH THE BEAM WAS PLAYING, • • 728 PRIEST FAIRY 2
FROM PLAYING HURLEY IN THE WOOD • • • • • • • 743 DANAAN QUICK 9
PLAYS
THE HARE GROWS OLD AS SHE PLAYS IN THE SUN • • • • 27 OISIN 1 412
"OLD GROWS THE HARE AS SHE PLAYS IN THE SUN, • • • • 28 OISIN 1 V 420
AN OLD MAN PLAYS THE BAGPIPES • • • • • • • 214 HAPPY TOWNLAND 9
I WOULD BE OF YOUR MIND: BUT WHEN HE PLAYS IT • • • 222 SHADOW WATER B 17
AS THOUGH IT DRAGGED ROAD-METAL. MY CURSE ON PLAYS • • 260 FASC DIFFICULT 8
AS THOUGH IT DRAGGED ROAD METAL. MY CURSE ON PLAYS • • 260 FASC DIFFICULT V 8
PLATO THOUGHT NATURE BUT A SPUME THAT PLAYS • • • • 445 SCHOOL CHILDR 41
AND HE PLAYS TUNES BETWEEN YOUR FEET, • • • • • 573 LADYS 3RD SONG 2
I LOSE! THEY'RE LOADED DICE. TIME ALWAYS PLAYS • • • 721 WITCH VIVIEN 44
THE WORLD GROWS OLD AND PLAYS THE FOOL." • • • • • 725 LEGEND 12
PLAYTIME
TILL DAYTIME, PLAYTIME SEEM THE SAME: • • • • • 343 SHEP GOATHERD 106
TILL THAT IS THEIR LONG SHOUTING PLAYTIME: • • • • 343 SHEP GOATHERD V 106
MIRACLE HAD ITS PLAYTIME WHERE • • • • • • • 440 WISDOM 8
PLEADS
THE LOVER PLEADS WITH HIS FRIEND FOR OLD FRIENDS • • • 172 PLEADS FRIEND T
THE POET PLEADS WITH HIS FRIEND FOR OLD FRIENDS • • • 172 PLEADS FRIEND V T
THE POET PLEADS WITH THE ELEMENTAL POWERS • • • • • 174 ELEMENT POWERS T
AODH PLEADS WITH THE ELEMENTAL POWERS • • • • • • 174 ELEMENT POWERS V T
PLEASANT
"O PLEASANT WOMAN," ANSWERED FINN, • • • • • • 5 OISIN 1 40
"O PLEASANT MAIDEN," ANSWERED FINN, • • • • • • 5 OISIN 1 V 40
NOW, PLEASANT MAIDEN, TELL TO ME • • • • • • 5 OISIN 1 V 43
AND SWEETER OF VOICE THAN THE PLEASANT BIRDS, • • • • 9 OISIN 1 V 95
AND NOW MOVES MANY A PLEASANT TONGUE • • • • • • 98 FOXHUNTER 21
AND MOVES THERE MANY A PLEASANT TONGUE, • • • • • 98 FOXHUNTER V 23
HE CRAWLED INTO THAT PLEASANT NOOK• • • • • • • 303 HOUR DAWN 32
MY LIFE OF EVERY PLEASANT THOUGHT • • • • • • • 307 HOUR DAWN 110
PLEASE
AND I WOULD PLEASE THE HAPLESS FAUN, • • • • • • 67 HAPPY SHEPHERD 47
HAS BEAUTIFUL WOMEN TO PLEASE EVERY MAN. • • • • • 228 SHADOW WATER B 144
WE'LL KEEP THE SECRET—A NEW TRICK TO PLEASE• • • • • 265 ABBEY THEATRE 10
IMAGINING 'TWOULD BETTER PLEASE • • • • • • • 271 GREY ROCK 4
I KNEW A WOMAN NONE COULD PLEASE, • • • • • • 272 GREY ROCK 41
I KNOW A WOMAN NONE COULD PLEASE, • • • • • • 272 GREY ROCK V 41
MY MEN, WHETHER IT PLEASE HER OR DISPLEASE, • • • • 281 TWO KINGS 112
"SAY WHAT YOU PLEASE, BUT FROM DAYBREAK • • • • • 304 HOUR DAWN 42
"SAY WHAT YOU PLEASE, BUT FROM DAY-BREAK • • • • • 304 HOUR DAWN V 42
THAT MIGHT THE LEARNED PLEASE, • • • • • • • 333 SOLOMON SHEBA 12
THEY CAN SPREAD OUT WHAT SAIL THEY PLEASE FOR ALL I HAVE 354 HIS PHOENIX 22
    TO SAY,
HE HAS HAD ENOUGH OF MEDDLING WHO CAN PLEASE • • • • 359 WAR POEM 4
PLEASE A FANTASTIC HEAD• • • • • • • • • 366 HER CHRIS TREE 8
THE LINEAMENTS THAT PLEASE THEIR VIEW • • • • • • 387 ROBARTES DANCE 49
TO PLEASE A COMPANION • • • • • • • • • 392 EASTER 1916 11
ON OLD DRY FAGGOTS THAT COULD NEVER PLEASE • • • • 466 HARUN RASHID 124
BEST PLEASE A WANDERING MAN• • • • • • • • 606 SONGS BURDEN 1 17
ACH, CALL ME WHAT YOU PLEASE! • • • • • • • 627 STATES HOLIDAY 21
PLEASED
PLEASED TO HAVE FILLED THE EYES • • • • • • • 329 MEN IMPROVE 8
AND BE WELL PLEASED REMEMBERING IT, FOR IN THE OLD DAYS, 351 HER PRAISE 16
AND CHOSEN WHAT SCENERY HAD PLEASED ME BEST." • • • • 352 PEOPLE 21
HOW SUCH A MAN PLEASED WOMEN MOST • • • • • • • 458 SECRETS OF OLD 13
PLEASES
BEST PLEASES YOU. ARMED MEN HAVE COME UPON US• • • • 752 SHADOW WATER A 131
PLEASING
NO PLEASING HABIT ENDS, • • • • • • • • • 621 JOHN KINSELLA 30
PLEASURE
OF WAR, AND THE CHASE, AND HUNTING, AND PLEASURE: • • 26 OISIN 1 V 403
PLEASURE ITSELF CAN BRING NO WEARINESS, • • • • • 284 TWO KINGS 181
GAVE ME SUCH PLEASURE I'D FORGO • • • • 305 HOUR DAWN 69
AND PLEASURE MADE HER CHEEKS GROW RED, • • • • • 314 MEMORY YOUTH 11
PLEASURE THAT COMES WITH SLEEP, • • • • • • • 345 ON WOMAN 22
SHRIEK WITH PLEASURE IF WE SHOW • • • • • • • 431 NINETEEN 19 91
LOVE'S PLEASURE DRIVES HIS LOVE AWAY, • • • • • 438 SONGS PLAY 2 11
THE BODY IS NOT BRUISED TO PLEASURE SOUL, • • • • 445 SCHOOL CHILDR 58
AND DID SUCH PLEASURE TAKE— • • • • • • • 455 HIS MEMORIES 14
WHETHER OF PLEASURE OR OF REST, • • • • • • • 521 THREE THINGS 4
FOUND ALL THE PLEASURE THAT LIFE GAVE": • • • • • 521 THREE THINGS 11
THAT THE MOST COULD PLEASURE YOU, • • • • • • 525 DANCING DAYS 11
MY UTMOST PLEASURE WITH A MAN • • • • • • • 535 CHOSEN 12
BUT HAD GREAT PLEASURE WITH A LAD • • • • • • 538 LAST CONFESS 5
PLEASURE HAS MADE HIM • • • • • • • • • 574 MAIDS 1ST SONG 9
FROM PLEASURE OF THE BED, • • • • • • • • 575 MAIDS 2ND SONG 1
OTHER PEOPLE'S MIRTH AND PLEASURE, • • • • • • 732 STREET DANCERS 24
OTHER PEOPLE'S MIRTH AND PLEASURE, • • • • • • 732 STREET DANCERS 37
OTHER'S PEOPLE'S MIRTH AND PLEASURE, • • • • • • 733 STREET DANCERS 50
PLEASURED
HOW SUCH A MAN HAD PLEASURED MOST • • • • • • • 458 SECRETS OF OLD V 13

```
                                                      PAGE      TITLE          LINE
PLEASURED   (CONTINUED)
    WHAT LIVELY LAD MOST PLEASURED ME . . . . . . . .  538 LAST CONFESS          1
PLEASURES
    AND CALLED THE PLEASURES EVIL . . . . . . . . . .  365 HER RACE              3
    NONE OTHER KNOWS WHAT PLEASURES MAN . . . . . . .  620 JOHN KINSELLA         9
    THE PHANTOMS OF HER FADED PLEASURES WALK! . . . .  687 TWO TITANS           19
PLEDGE
    HAVE BEEN DEFEATED BY THAT PLEDGE YOU GAVE . . . .  258 KING NO KING          9
PLENTIFUL
    BE PLENTIFUL.--AND IF HE LOVE ANOTHER, . . . . . .  71 ANASHU VIJAYA          5
PLENTY
    BE PLENTY.--IF HE GIVES ANOTHER LOVE, . . . . . .   71 ANASHU VIJAYA   V      5
    WHEREBY THE HORN OF PLENTY IS UNDONE. . . . . . .  404 FOR DAUGHTER          32
    MY DREAMS ROUND THOUGHTS OF PLENTY, AS IN GLOOM . 681 SEEKER                 3
    MY DREAMS O'ER THOUGHTS OF PLENTY, AS THE RED- . . 681 SEEKER          V      3
PLENTY'S
    OUT OF THE MOUTH OF PLENTY'S HORN, . . . . . . . . 405 FOR DAUGHTER         60
PLODDED
    AND AS THE TIME TO DARKNESS PLODDED . . . . . . .  728 PRIEST FAIRY         11
PLOT    SEE DEWY-PLOT
    HOW THE FALCONER FOLLOWS THE FALCON IN THE WEEDS OF THE   52 OISIN 3        79
        HERON'S PLOT,
    DO YOU, TOO, DOUBT ME? HAVE YOU JOINED THEIR PLOT? . . 227 SHADOW WATER B  106
    BUT THE TORN PETALS STREW THE GARDEN PLOT! . . . .  422 MY DESCENDANTS       7
    WHEN THE TORN PETALS STREW THE GARDEN PLOT! . . .  422 MY DESCENDANTS V      7
    GRASS PLOT OF THE GARDEN! . . . . . . . . . . . .  568 SWEET DANCER          3
    WITH QUIET SHADE ITS EVER DEWY PLOT. . . . . . . . 714 FERENCZ RENYI  V    109
PLOTINUS
    CHOOSE PLATO AND PLOTINUS FOR A FRIEND . . . . . . 409 TOWER                12
    THE DELPHIC ORACLE UPON PLOTINUS . . . . . . . . . 530 DELPHIC ORACLE        T
    BEHOLD THAT GREAT PLOTINUS SWIM, . . . . . . . . . 530 DELPHIC ORACLE        1
    PLOTINUS CAME AND LOOKED ABOUT, . . . . . . . . .  611 NEWS ORACLE           9
PLOTINUS'
    I MOCK PLOTINUS' THOUGHT . . . . . . . . . . . . . 415 TOWER               146
PLOTS
    THEN GIVE ME TRIUMPH IN MY MANY PLOTS. . . . . . . 722 WITCH VIVIEN         51
    DEFEAT IS DEATH.  SHOULD MY PLOTS FAIL I'D DIE. . . 722 WITCH VIVIEN        52
    I MUST BE CAREFUL NOW.  I HAVE SUCH PLOTS-- . . .  722 WITCH VIVIEN         65
    SUCH WAR PLOTS, PEACE PLOTS, LOVE PLOTS--EVERY SIDE! . 722 WITCH VIVIEN     66
    SUCH WAR PLOTS, PEACE PLOTS, LOVE PLOTS--EVERY SIDE! . 722 WITCH VIVIEN     66
    SUCH WAR PLOTS, PEACE PLOTS, LOVE PLOTS--EVERY SIDE! . 722 WITCH VIVIEN     66
PLOTTING
    AND PLANNING, PLOTTING ALWAYS THAT SOME MORROW . . . 129 BOOK STORIES       10
    ARE PLOTTING FOR YOUR DEATH. HAVE I NOT GIVEN . . . 226 SHADOW WATER B      93
PLOUGH
    THE PILOT STAR AND THE CROOKED PLOUGH . . . . . .  177 PAST GREATNESS        4
    FROM WELL SIDE OR FROM PLOUGH LAND, WAS THEIR NOISE! . 279 TWO KINGS   V    53
    TO PLOUGH OR PASTURE-LAND, MIGHT SEE ME THERE, . . 283 TWO KINGS          146
    TO PLOUGH OR PASTURE LAND, MIGHT SEE ME THERE . .  283 TWO KINGS     V    146
    THE GOLDEN PLOUGH AND HARROW AND SPOKE ALOUD . . . 609 IN TARAS HALLS       12
PLOUGHED
    BETWEEN TWO FURROWS UPON THE PLOUGHED LAND! . . .  784 WOMANS BEAUTY         4
    BETWEEN DARK FURROWS UPON THE PLOUGHED LAND, . . . 784 WOMANS BEAUTY         6
PLOUGHING
    OR WEEDING OR PLOUGHING WITH FACES A-SHINING WITH MUCH-TOIL   58 OISIN 3    165
        WET!
PLOUGHLAND
    FROM WELLSIDE OR FROM PLOUGHLAND, WAS THERE NOISE! . . 279 TWO KINGS    V   53
PLOUGH-LAND
    FROM WELL-SIDE OR FROM PLOUGH-LAND, WAS THERE NOISE! . . 279 TWO KINGS      53
    OF PASTURE-LAND AND PLOUGH-LAND AMONG THE HILLS? . . . 748 SHADOW WATER A   33
PLOUGHMAN
    THE HEAVY STEPS OF THE PLOUGHMAN, SPLASHING THE WINTRY   143 ROSE IN HEART   3
        MOULD!
    THE HEAVY STEPS OF THE PLOUGHMAN SPLASHING THE WINTER   143 ROSE IN HEART V 3
        MOULD,
PLOUGHSHARE
    INTO A PLOUGHSHARE? PARLIAMENT AND KING . . . . .  429 NINETEEN 19          20
PLOVER'S
    AND HIS HAIR WAS AS DARK AS A PLOVER'S EYE. . . .  729 PRIEST FAIRY         46
PLOVERS
    LIKE PLOVERS THAT HAVE HEARD THE CALL. . . . . . . 213 BLESS PSALTER        13
PLUCK
    SHALL THEY TURN WROTH OR PLUCK THE WINGS OF TIME? . .  42 OISIN 2      V   199
    AND PLUCK TILL TIME AND TIMES ARE DONE . . . . .   150 WANDER AENGUS        22
    "O DO NOT PLUCK AT HIS REIN, . . . . . . . . . .   214 HAPPY TOWNLAND       18
    "O DO NOT PLUCK AT HIS REIN, . . . . . . . . . .   215 HAPPY TOWNLAND       38
    "O DO NOT PLUCK AT HIS REIN, . . . . . . . . . .   216 HAPPY TOWNLAND       58
    GO PLUCK ATHENE BY THE HAIR! . . . . . . . . . .   386 ROBARTES DANCE       19
PLUCKED
    THE MOON PLUCKED AT MY REIN! . . . . . . . . . .   214 HAPPY TOWNLAND       16
    THE MOON PLUCKED AT MY REIN! . . . . . . . . . .   215 HAPPY TOWNLAND       36
    THE MOON PLUCKED AT MY REIN! . . . . . . . . . .   216 HAPPY TOWNLAND       56
    IT WAS THEIR HANDS THAT PLUCKED THE WINDS AWAKE . . 237 SHADOW WATER B     324
    SING, FOR IT MAY BE THAT YOUR THOUGHTS HAVE PLUCKED . . 342 SHEP GOATHERD   85
    HAS PLUCKED A FLOWER AND SUNG HER LOSS! . . . . .  447 COLONUS PRAISE       22
    ALL MY FINE FEATHERS WOULD BE PLUCKED AWAY . . . . 469 HARUN RASHID        178
    PLUCKED BITTER WISDOM THAT ENRICHED HIS BLOOD. . . 543 PARN FUNERAL 2       12
    WHEN THEY HAVE PLUCKED A ROSE THERE, . . . . . . . 571 THREE BUSHES         75
    I PLUCKED HER BACKWARDS BY HER DRESS OF GREEN. . . 676 ISLE STAT II 3      264
    AND PLUCKED SMALL FRUITS ON INNISFREE. . . . . . . 742 DANAAN QUICK          5
```

622

	PAGE	TITLE	LINE

PLUCKS
THAT PLUCKS THE TREES FOR BREAD? . . . . 621 JOHN KINSELLA 34
PLUM
THOUGH DOUBTLESS PLUM OR CHERRY-BRANCH . . . . 567 LAPIS LAZULI 47
GROUNDS WHERE PLUM AND CABBAGE GREW, ... 577 WHAT THEN 13
PLUMAGE
HAD PRETTY PLUMAGE ONCE--ENOUGH OF THAT, ... 444 SCHOOL CHILDR 30
PLUME
IRVING AND HIS PLUME OF PRIDE. . . . . 625 NATIVITY 8
PLUMED
DREAMING OF FLASHING FLIGHT AND OF THE PLUMED WAVE. . . . 650 ISLE STAT I 1 140
BOWING NATIONS, PLUMED WARS-- . . . . 737 IN FIRELIGHT 10
AND PLUMED HEADS ABOUT HIM, ... 740 EARL PAUL 31
PLUMELESS
E'EN THOUGH HIS WINGS WERE PLUMELESS STUMPS, ... 670 ISLE STAT II 3 118
PLUMES
BY ROOTS THAT JOINED ABOVE OUR PLUMES-- . . . . . . 16 OISIN 1 V 224C
AND, SHAKING THE PLUMES OF THE GRASSES . . . . . . 49 OISIN 3 35
PLUMMET-MEASURED
LIVE LIPS UPON A PLUMMET-MEASURED FACE. . . . . . . 610 STATUES 8
THE LINEAMENTS OF A PLUMMET-MEASURED FACE. . . . . . 611 STATUES 32
PLUMY
HAD SURGED UP IN A PLUMY FIRE, I DRAVE . . . . . . 41 OISIN 2 181
WITH SURGE OF PLUMY FIRE, LUNGING I DRAVE . . . . . 41 OISIN 2 V 181
SURGED UP IN PLUMY FIRE, I LUNGED AND DRAVE . . . . 41 OISIN 2 V 181
PLUNDERING
TO MAKE HER FAST WHILE WE ARE PLUNDERING HER. . . . . 232 SHADOW WATER B 225
PLUNGE
THE HORSES OF DISASTER PLUNGE IN THE HEAVY CLAY! . . . 154 BELOVED PEACE 8
THE HORSES OF DISASTER PLUNGE IN THE DESOLATE CLAY. . . 154 BELOVED PEACE V 8
PLUNGE, LURED BY A SOFTENING EYE, ... 413 TOWER 110
UNTIL IT PLUNGE INTO THE SUN! . . . . 472 ALL SOUL NIGHT 56
AND THE BRUTE DOLPHINS PLUNGE . . . . 612 NEWS ORACLE 20
PLUNGED
THROUGH BUSH THEY PLUNGED AND OVER IVIED ROOT, ... 278 TWO KINGS 32
THAT PLUNGED IN STREAM AGAIN . . . . 419 MY HOUSE V 9
OF THAT STARK MYSTERY WHERE I AM PLUNGED . . . . . 466 HARUN RASHID V 113
UNTIL IT PLUNGED INTO THE SUN! . . . . 472 ALL SOUL NIGHT V 56
PLUNGES
PLUNGES TOWARDS NOTHING, ARMS AND FINGERS SPREADING WIDE 426 PHANTOM HATRED 13
PLUNGING
LAUGHED; AND PLUNGING DOWN . . . . 453 MERMAID 4
PLUTARCH
SO THAT HIS PLUTARCH SET THE PACE . . . . 287 TO WEALTHY MAN V 12
PLUTO
BOOK IV THE GATES OF PLUTO I. THE FOOL BY THE ROADSIDE 447 HERO GIRL FOOL V T
POCKET
"BEFORE NIGHTFALL I'LL PICK A POCKET . . . . 332 ROUND TOWER 27
PODS SEE SEED-PODS
SEED PODS AND FLOWERS THAT ARE NOT ALL WILD POPPY. . . 342 SHEP GOATHERD V 88
POEM
AN OLD POEM RE-WRITTEN . . . . 129 BOOK STORIES V T
INTRODUCTION TO A DRAMATIC POEM . . . . 217 WOODS OF COOLE V T
I HAVE MADE THIS POEM FOR YOU, THAT MEN MAY READ IT . . 219 WOODS OF COOLE 41
POEM MAYBE AS COLD . . . . 348 FISHERMAN 39
POEM MAY BE AS COLD . . . . 348 FISHERMAN V 39
ON BEING ASKED FOR A WAR POEM . . . . 359 WAR POEM T
POEMS
TWO POEMS CONCERNING PEASANT VISIONARIES A CRADLE SONG 146 UNAPPEAS HOST V T
TWO LOVE POEMS THE SHADOWY HORSES . . . . 154 BELOVED PEACE V T
TWO POEMS BY O'SULLIVAN THE RED CONCERNING MARY LAVELL. 157 POET BELOVED V T
SEVEN POEMS I UPON A DYING LADY . . . . 362 HER COURTESY V T
FOUR POEMS CRACKED MARY AND THE BISHOP . . . . . 507 JANE BISHOP V T
EIGHT POEMS CRAZY JANE AND THE BISHOP . . . . . 507 JANE BISHOP V T
SEVEN POEMS GIRL'S SONG . . . . 515 GIRLS SONG B V T
POET
A POET TO HIS BELOVED . . . . 157 POET BELOVED T
THE POET PLEADS WITH HIS FRIEND FOR OLD FRIENDS . . . . 172 PLEADS FRIEND V T
THE POET PLEADS WITH THE ELEMENTAL POWERS . . . . . 174 ELEMENT POWERS T
A CERTAIN POET IN OUTLANDISH CLOTHES . . . . 180 QUEEN MAEVE 1
TO A POET, WHO WOULD HAVE ME PRAISE . . . . . . 262 TO A POET T
DID NOT THE POET SING IT WITH SUCH AIRS . . . . . 267 ALL TEMPT ME 7
DID NOT THE POET CARRY HIM WITH AN AIR . . . . . . 267 ALL TEMPT ME V 7
TO A POET OR A KING . . . . 299 THREE HERMITS 27
THE POET STUBBORN WITH HIS PASSION SANG US . . . . . 356 BROKEN DREAMS 18
A POET KEEP HIS MOUTH SHUT, FOR IN TRUTH . . . . . 359 WAR POEM V 2
I, THE POET WILLIAM YEATS, ... 406 CARVED STONE 1
SOME MORALIST OR MYTHOLOGICAL POET . . . . 430 NINETEEN 19 59
HERE, TRAVELLER, SCHOLAR, POET, TAKE YOUR STAND . . . 489 COOLE PARK 29 25
HERE IS FRESH MATTER, POET, ... 553 CHURCH STATE 1
CAN PAY THE POET FOR A VERSE AND HEAR THE FIDDLE SOUND, 581 CURSE CROMWELL 21
POET AND SCULPTOR, DO THE WORK, ... 638 BEN BULBEN 37
POETRY
AND YOU AND I, AND TALKED OF POETRY. . . . . 204 ADAMS CURSE 3
HER POETRY, DANCING UPON THE SHORE, ... 578 CRAZED GIRL 2
POETRY, MUSIC, I HAVE LOVED, AND YET . . . . 599 SPIRIT MEDIUM 1
POETRY AND MUSIC I HAVE BANISHED, ... 600 SPIRIT MEDIUM 19
POET'S
A POET'S MOUTH BE SILENT, FOR IN TRUTH . . . . . . 359 WAR POEM 2
POET'S IMAGININGS . . . . 415 TOWER 160
A MIMICRY OF YOUTH. CAN POET'S THOUGHT . . . . . . 463 HARUN RASHID 62

623

POETS
    HAVE KNOWN THREE CENTURIES, POETS SING,   2 OISIN 1   3
    UNTIL THE DANAAN POETS BROUGHT   7 OISIN 1   63
    LOVE, TILL THE DANAAN POETS BROUGHT   7 OISIN 1   63
    UNTIL THE DANAAN POETS CAME,   7 OISIN 1   V   64
    THE POETS LABOURING ALL THEIR DAYS   164 PERFECT BEAUTY   2
    WE POETS LABOUR ALL OUR DAYS,   164 PERFECT BEAUTY V   2
    AND POETS FOUND, OLD WRITERS SAY,   197 BAILE AILLINN   187
    . . . CERTAIN BAD POETS, IMITATORS OF HIS AND MINE   262 TO A POET   T
    . . . CERTAIN BAD POETS, IMITATORS OF HIS AND OF MINE 262 TO A POET   T
    POETS WITH WHOM I LEARNED MY TRADE,   270 GREY ROCK   1
    WE POETS KEEP OUR MOUTHS SHUT, FOR IN TRUTH   359 WAR POEM   V   2
    FOR SCHOLARS AND FOR POETS AFTER US,   488 COOLE PARK 29   6
    WHATEVER'S WRITTEN IN WHAT POETS NAME   492 COOLE BALLYLEE   43
    ALL THAT IS WRITTEN IN WHAT POETS NAME   492 COOLE BALLYLEE V   43
    OF POETS THAT ARE ALWAYS GAY,   565 LAPIS LAZULI   3
    POETS AND WITS ABOUT HIM DREW,   577 WHAT THEN   14
    THE POETS HAVE IMAGINED, TERRIBLE AND GAY."   602 GALLERY REVIS   12
    IRISH POETS, LEARN YOUR TRADE,   639 BEN BULBEN   68
POIGNANT
    IMAGE OF POIGNANT RECOLLECTION.   389 IMAGE PAST   7
POINT   SEE SWORD-POINT COMPASS-POINT
    LOOK TO LONG FISHING-LINES, OR POINT AND PARE   32 OISIN 2   55
    AT THE SWORD POINT, AND BADE ME BRING HIM ONE   109 CUCHULAIN SEA V   53
    AT THE SWORD POINT, AND WAITS TILL WE HAVE FOUND   109 CUCHULAIN SEA V   53
    THEN DREW HIS SWORD TO HOLD ITS LEVELLED POINT   277 TWO KINGS   14
    BUT DREW HIS SWORD, AND THOUGHT WITH LEVELLED POINT   277 TWO KINGS   V   14
    OR THAT THE WIND WOULD SHIFT A POINT,   306 HOUR DAWN   92
    THAT SEEMED TO WHIRL UPON A COMPASS POINT,   489 COOLE PARK 29 V   21
    HUSH! HUSH! HUSH! THEY PAUSE AND POINT   732 STREET DANCERS   31
POINTED
    I HAVE POINTED OUT THE YELLING PACK,   453 DEATH OF HARE   1
    AND THEN A POINTED FACE WAS SEEN   728 PRIEST FAIRY   21
    BENEATH A POINTED CAP OF GREEN: 728 PRIEST FAIRY   22
POINTING
    AND ONE ARM POINTING THUS, IN MARBLE WHITE.   663 ISLE STAT II 2   28
POINTS
    THE WAVES IN YONDER LAKE WHERE POINTS MY HAND   652 ISLE STAT I 2   13
POISED
    AND THY NECK'S A POISED LILY!   647 ISLE STAT I 1   55
POISON
    A POISON DROP. A TOY, A FANCY ONCE,   700 MOSADA 3   24
    A POISON DROP. THE TOY OF FANCY ONCE,   700 MOSADA 3   V   24
    FROM POISON! FOR YOU CANNOT TRUST THESE MOORS.   704 MOSADA 3   126
    THAT ARE A POISON TO ALL MEN   743 DANAAN QUICK   16
POISONOUS
    WITH POISONOUS LIPS, AND HE IS PINING SINCE?   696 MOSADA 2   7
POKED
    I POKED ABOUT A VILLAGE CHURCH   584 GHOST ROG CASE   31
POLAR
    THE POLAR DRAGON SLEPT,   174 ELEMENT POWERS   4
    AND WHERE THE POLAR WINDS AND WATERS WRESTLE   682 SEEKER   18
POLE   SEE TENT-POLE
    UPON THE STAR THAT MARKS THE HIDDEN POLE: 477 SELF AND SOUL   5
    THE POLE-STAR AND THE SILENCE OF THE POLE.   477 SELF AND SOUL V   8
    SOME FOUND A DIFFERENT POLE, AND WHERE IT STOOD   483 VERONIC NAPKIN   7
    TENT POLE OF EDEN: THE TENT'S DRAPERY: 483 VERONIC NAPKIN V   2
POLE-AXE
    FROM MACE AND SWORD AND POLE-AXE, LONG AGO   31 OISIN 2   30
POLECAT
    OR DARK BETWIXT THE POLECAT AND THE OWL,   565 GYRES   21
POLES
    . . . CEASE THE WINDS, AND ON THEIR POLES   719 PHANTOM SHIP   17
POLE-STAR
    THE POLE-STAR AND THE SILENCE OF THE POLE.   477 SELF AND SOUL V   8
POLISHED
    THE POSTS OF POLISHED YEW, CIRCLED WITH BRONZE,   279 TWO KINGS   48
    THE PACING TO AND FRO ON POLISHED FLOORS   418 ANCEST HOUSES   35
POLITE
    OR POLITE MEANINGLESS WORDS,   392 EASTER 1916   6
    POLITE MEANINGLESS WORDS,   392 EASTER 1916   8
POLITIC
    'TWERE POLITIC TO DO THE LIKE BY THESE: 262 TO A POET   3
    "MAYBE A BREATH OF POLITIC WORDS   396 ROSE TREE   3
POLITICAL
    ON A POLITICAL PRISONER   397 POLIT PRISONER   T
POLITICIAN
    AND THERE'S A POLITICIAN   631 POLITICS   7
POLITICIANS
    "SOME POLITICIANS IDLE WORDS   396 ROSE TREE   V   3
POLITICS
    THAT TALKED OF LOVE OR POLITICS,   131 OLD PENSIONER   5
    IN ART OR POLITICS: 431 NINETEEN 19   71
    AN IMAGE OF SUCH POLITICS.   475 EVA GORE-BOOTH   13
    POLITICS   631 POLITICS   T
    OR ON SPANISH POLITICS?   631 POLITICS   4
POLLEXFEN
    AND THEN I THINK OF OLD GEORGE POLLEXFEN,   325 ROBERT GREGORY   33
    IN MEMORY OF ALFRED POLLEXFEN   360 ALF POLLEXFEN   T
    SINCE OLD WILLIAM POLLEXFEN   360 ALF POLLEXFEN   2
    BY CHILDISH MEMORIES OF AN OLD CROSS POLLEXFEN,   391 UNDER SATURN   7

624

		PAGE	TITLE	LINE

POLLEXFEN   (CONTINUED)
OLD WILLIAM POLLEXFEN, ...   604 YOU CONTENT   14
POMP
THE MURMURING BIRDS IN SOLEMN POMP   . . . .   20 OISIN 1   V   293
POND
LIKE BUBBLES IN A FROZEN POND: . . . .   22 OISIN 1   336
FROM POND AND FALLEN TREE--ME SING   . . . .   85 MAD KING GOLL   V   63
SHAN-WALLA, WHERE A WILLOW-BORDERED POND   . . . . .   217 WOODS OF COOLE   2
SHANWALLA, WHERE A WILLOW BORDERED POND   . . . . . .   217 WOODS OF COOLE V   2
PONDER
NOTHING THAT COMMON WOMEN PONDER ON   . . . . . .   579 DOR WELLESLEY   12
AND PONDER IT IF THEY WILL:: THEN NEAR AT HAND   . . . .   659 ISLE STAT II 1   10
WHILE I MURMUR A LITTLE AND PONDER   . . . .   707 FAIRY PEDANT   14
PONDERABLE
IS PONDERABLE TO OUR TOUCH. . . . .   399 BREAK OF DAY   18
PONDERED
AND PONDERED IN A SOFT VAIN MOOD   . . . . . .   14 OISIN 1   184
AND PONDERED ON THE GLORY OF HIS DAYS: . . . . . .   108 CUCHULAIN SEA   43
AND PONDERED ON THE WONDER OF HIS DAYS, ...   108 CUCHULAIN SEA   V   43
"I HAVE CAP AND BELLS," HE PONDERED, ...   160 CAP AND BELLS   21
"I'VE CAP AND BELL," HE PONDERED, ...   160 CAP AND BELLS   V   21
PONDERING
THEY HUDDLE FROM MAN'S PONDERING MIND, ...   138 TO IRELAND   V   26
IMAGINING AND PONDERING   . . . .   193 BAILE AILLINN   111
AND HARPERS PONDERING WITH BOWED HEAD   . . . . . .   193 BAILE AILLINN   V   107
WOUND IN MIND'S PONDERING   . . . .   471 ALL SOUL NIGHT   13
PONDERS
BECAUSE, TO HIM WHO PONDERS WELL, ...   138 TO IRELAND   19
PONDS
AND WINDS AND PONDS COVER MORE QUIET WOODS, ...   218 WOODS OF COOLE   34
MORE SHINING WINDS, MORE STAR-GLIMMERING PONDS?   . . . .   218 WOODS OF COOLE   35
PONIES
BECAUSE PIEBALD PONIES, LED BEARS, CAGED LIONS, MAKE BUT   623 HIGH TALK   5
POOR SHOWS,
PONY
QUIET THE DOG, TETHER THE PONY   . . . .   617 LONG-LEG FLY   3
POOL   SEE RINSING-POOL
THE HARP AWAY. A DOLOROUS POOL   . . . . . .   17 OISIN 1   V   240
BUT ONE SMALL KNOT-GRASS GROWING BY THE POOL   . . . . .   127 DREAM OF FAERY   29
THE YELLOW POOL HAS OVERFLOWED HIGH UP ON CLOOTH-NA-BARE,   207 HANRAHANS SONG   11
THE YELLOW POOL HAS OVERFLOWED HIGH UPON CLOOTH-NA-BARE,   207 HANRAHANS SONG V   11
BUT FOR THE TRODDEN MIRE, THE POOL OF BLOOD, ...   278 TWO KINGS   44
BY WHAT LAKE'S EDGE OR POOL   . . . .   323 SWANS AT COOLE   28
TO HIS SHAPE AT THE RINSING POOL   . . . .   341 SHEP GOATHERD   V   70
WHERE THE SHEEP ARE THROWN IN THE POOL, ...   341 SHEP GOATHERD   V   71
HAVE CLOSED THE LADIES' EYES, THEIR MINDS ARE BUT A POOL   426 PHANTOM HATRED   21
ONE HAND AMID THE GOLDFISH IN THE POOL: . . . . . .   463 HARUN RASHID   44
THEY WERE SITTING ROUND A POOL, ...   667 ISLE STAT II 3   24
AND THEY WERE SITTING ROUND A POOL.   . . . . . .   667 ISLE STAT II 3 V   24
I DREW MY SWORD TO FLING IT IN A POOL,--   . . . . .   747 SHADOW WATER A   7
POOLS
--FROM POOLS AND ROTTING LEAVES--ME SING   . . . . . .   85 MAD KING GOLL   V   63
IN POOLS AMONG THE RUSHES   . . . .   88 STOLEN CHILD   30
IN SHADOWY POOLS, WHEN ARMIES FLED: . . . . . .   155 FORGOT BEAUTY   5
O TUFTED REEDS, BEND LOW AND LOW IN POOLS ON THE GREEN   206 HANRAHANS SONG V   1
LAND,
I HAD WOVEN OF THE SLEEP THAT IS IN POOLS   . . . . .   762 SHADOW WATER A   284
POOR
FOR HE IS WEAK AND POOR AND BLIND, AND LIES   . . . . .   42 OISIN 2   203
WHEN THE POOR TIRED CHILD, PASSION, FALLS ASLEEP.   . . . .   80 EPHEMERA   7
MY MAN WAS A POOR FISHER   . . . .   94 MOLL MAGEE   5
MY HUSBAND WAS A FISHER POOR   . . . .   94 MOLL MAGEE   V   5
AND LOOKS UPON THE POOR.   . . . .   96 MOLL MAGEE   52
IN ALL POOR FOOLISH THINGS THAT LIVE A DAY, ...   101 ROSE UPON ROOD   11
ANOTHER POOR MAN SENT FOR HIM, ...   132 FR GILLIGAN   7
"AND IS THE POOR MAN DEAD?" HE CRIED.   . . . . . .   133 FR GILLIGAN   33
I BADE MY HEART BUILD THESE POOR RHYMES: . . . . .   158 BELOVED RHYMES   3
BUT I, BEING POOR, HAVE ONLY MY DREAMS: . . . . .   176 CLOTHS HEAVEN   6
AND OUR POOR KATE OR NAN IS LESS   . . . .   190 BAILE AILLINN   35
I MIGHT HAVE THROWN POOR WORDS AWAY   . . . . . .   256 WORDS   15
A HUNDRED-YEAR-OLD MEMORY TO THE POOR: . . . . .   269 PARDON FATHERS   6
I NEEDS MUST MARRY SOME POOR LOUT,"   . . . . . .   273 GREY ROCK   47
I NEED MUST MARRY SOME POOR LOUT,"   . . . . . .   273 GREY ROCK   V   47
A POOR LIFE, DO WHAT HE CAN, ...   301 RUN PARADISE   11
POOR MEN HAVE GROWN TO BE RICH MEN, ...   301 RUN PARADISE   15
AND RICH MEN GROWN TO BE POOR AGAIN, ...   301 RUN PARADISE   16
MY COUNTRYMEN KILTARTAN'S POOR, ...   328 IRISH AIRMAN   6
AMONG THE POOR BOTH OLD AND YOUNG GAVE HER PRAISE.   . . .   351 HER PRAISE   18
AND RUTH ST. DENIS HAD MORE CHARM ALTHOUGH SHE HAD POOR   353 HIS PHOENIX   10
LUCK:
AND MADE--BEING POOR, AILING AND IGNORANT, ...   370 EGO DOMINUS   59
NOT A POOR FOOL UNDERSTANDS.   . . . .   381 SONG OF FOOL   4
AND MANY A POOR MAN THAT HAS ROVED, ...   404 FOR DAUGHTER   38
DID ALL OLD MEN AND WOMEN, RICH AND POOR, ...   413 TOWER   97
"AND ALL THOSE LIES HAVE BUT ONE END, POOR WRETCHES TO   450 OWEN AHERNE   18
BETRAY:
LIKE SOME POOR ARAB TRIBESMAN AND HIS TENT.   . . . .   491 COOLE BALLYLEE   40
AND WHETHER A MAN BE RICH OR POOR   . . . . . .   582 ROGER CASEMENT V   19
AND SAVED THE IRISH POOR, ...   586 PARNELLITES   12
DID ALL THAT FOR THE POOR.   . . . .   596 COLONEL MARTIN   62

625

		PAGE	TITLE	LINE

POOR (CONTINUED)

BECAUSE PIEBALD PONIES, LED BEARS, CAGED LIONS, MAKE BUT POOR SHOWS, 623 HIGH TALK 5
ON MY POOR BRAIN YOUR BUSY TUMULTS CROWD. 648 ISLE STAT I 1 100
POOR RACE OF LEAFY ARCADY, YOUR LOVE 650 ISLE STAT I 1 145
POOR SAD WOOD-RHAPSODISTS. NOT SO! THEY'RE GLAD. 652 ISLE STAT I 2 16
SLEW THEE, POOR SIBYL! COMRADES THOU AND I! 675 ISLE STAT II 3 235
POOR EARTH-ENKINDLED PAIR, 680 LOVE AND DEATH 22
POOR LOVE AND SORROW, WITH THEIR ARMS THROWN ROUND 703 MOSADA 3 119
THUS PLAY WE FIRST WITH PAWNS, POOR THINGS AND WEAK! 722 WITCH VIVIEN 53
THERE WAS SOME TALKING OF THE POOR— 725 LEGEND 14
IS THIS POOR BODY THAT REDDENS AND GROWS PALE. 764 SHADOW WATER A 341

POORER

BUT NEVER MADE A POORER SONG 273 GREY ROCK 55

POPE'S

SHUT THE DOOR OF THE POPE'S CHAPEL, 618 LONG-LEG FLY 23

POPINJAY

AND HEAR, AND JUDGE. MY POPINJAY, WHAT NOW? 660 ISLE STAT II 1 40
SAY THEN,—"A POPINJAY BEFORE GRIEF'S SHAFT 664 ISLE STAT II 2 52

POPLAR

GREEN OAK AND POPLAR TREE! 132 OLD PENSIONER V 16
UPON THE NORMAN UPLAND OR IN THAT POPLAR SHADE, 449 OWEN AHERNE 2
UPON THE NORTHERN UPLAND OR IN THAT POPLAR SHADE, 449 OWEN AHERNE V 2
WATCHED OF PLACID POPLAR TREES, 732 STREET DANCERS V 16

POPLARS

THE POPLARS GAZE ACROSS THE WATERS GREY, 653 ISLE STAT I 2 34
MORE DARK BENEATH THE POPLARS, WHERE YON OWL 675 ISLE STAT II 3 233

POPLAR-TREES

WATCHED OF PLACID POPLAR-TREES 732 STREET DANCERS 16

POPPIES

FOR FAIR ARE POPPIES ON THE BROW! 67 HAPPY SHEPHERD 56
WEARY, WITH ALL HIS POPPIES GATHERED ROUND HIM. 72 ANASHU VIJAYA 25
QUITE SOON THE CORNFIELD, WHERE THE POPPIES GROW, 699 MOSADA 3 7
ALONG THE CORNFIELD, WHERE THE POPPIES GROW, 699 MOSADA 3 V 7
GOES HIS POPPIES NOW A-HAWKING! 705 DAWN-SONG 4

POPPY

SEED-PODS AND FLOWERS THAT ARE NOT ALL WILD POPPY. 342 SHEP GOATHERD 88
SEED PODS AND FLOWERS THAT ARE NOT ALL WILD POPPY. 342 SHEP GOATHERD V 88

POPPY-HUNG

IN THE POPPY-HUNG HOUSE OF THE TWILIGHT FLUTED! 8 OISIN 1 V 83

POPULACE

AND A SMALL AND A FEEBLE POPULACE STOOPING WITH MATTOCK AND SPADE, 58 OISIN 3 164
A-FLUTTERING THE PAINTED POPULACE OF LAKE 675 ISLE STAT II 3 224

POPULAR

OR IS THERE NONE, MOST POPULAR OF MEN, 265 ABBEY THEATRE 13
GROW RICH, POPULAR AND FULL OF INFLUENCE, 369 EGO DOMINUS 43
HER THOUGHT SOME POPULAR ENMITY! 397 POLIT PRISONER 10
FOR THOUGHT SOME POPULAR ENMITY. 397 POLIT PRISONER V 10
AND ALL THE POPULAR STATESMEN SAY 460 THREE MONUMENT 5
IT HAD NOT TOUCHED OUR LIVES. BUT POPULAR RAGE, 542 PARN FUNERAL 1 20
DISTRUSTFUL OF THAT POPULAR EYE 624 APPARITIONS 5

POPULOUS

AND BRING US INTO POPULOUS SEAS AGAIN? 225 SHADOW WATER B 74

PORTAL

THEY MAY NOT PASS THE PORTAL, 680 LOVE AND DEATH 21

PORTALS

WE PASSED THE PORTALS, AND WITHIN, 17 OISIN 1 V 250

PORTER

THE PORTER SLEPT, ALTHOUGH HE SAT UPRIGHT 182 QUEEN MAEVE 45

PORTER-DRINKERS'

PORTER-DRINKERS' RANDY LAUGHTER! 640 BEN BULBEN 77

PORTER'S

CRIED FROM THE PORTER'S LODGE, AND WITH LONG CLAMOUR 181 QUEEN MAEVE 37

PORTION

THAT OUR SUFFICIENT PORTION OF THE WORLD 282 TWO KINGS 119
A PORTION OF MY MIND AND LIFE, AS IT WERE, 325 ROBERT GREGORY 42
SO GREAT HER PORTION IN THAT PEACE YOU MAKE 356 BROKEN DREAMS 12
WHAT PORTION IN THE WORLD CAN THE ARTIST HAVE 369 EGO DOMINUS 49
BEING A PORTION OF MY YOUTH, CAN MAKE ME PINE 391 UNDER SATURN V 3

PORTIONING

DID GOD IN PORTIONING WINE AND BREAD 386 ROBARTES DANCE 39

PORTIONS

THAT I MYSELF FOR PORTIONS OF THE YEAR 371 ON GOING HOUSE 5

PORTLY

PORTLY GREEN-PATED BIRD 400 DEMON BEAST 28

PORTRAIT

OF OLD LUKE WADDING'S PORTRAIT SAID 400 DEMON BEAST 10
THERE WAS NO PORTRAIT IN THE GALLERY 400 DEMON BEAST 17
BEFORE A WOMAN'S PORTRAIT SUDDENLY I STAND, 602 GALLERY REVIS 13
MANCINI'S PORTRAIT OF AUGUSTA GREGORY, 602 GALLERY REVIS 25
A GREAT EBULLIENT PORTRAIT CERTAINLY! 602 GALLERY REVIS 27
AN EBULLIENT GREAT PORTRAIT CERTAINLY! 602 GALLERY REVIS V 27

PORTRAITS

WITH FAMOUS PORTRAITS OF OUR ANCESTORS! 418 ANCEST HOUSES 37
WHERE MY FRIENDS' PORTRAITS HANG AND LOOK THEREON! 604 GALLERY REVIS 52

POSE

THERE ONE THAT RUFFLED IN A MANLY POSE 489 COOLE PARK 29 11

POSEIDON

POSEIDON GAVE IT BIT AND OAR, 447 COLONUS PRAISE 28

	PAGE	TITLE	LINE

POSSESSED
   IT IS POSSESSED. A PROPHESYING VOICE. • • • • • • •   681 SEEKER   8
POSSESSION
   AS OTHERS WILL, WHEN FIRST THEY TAKE POSSESSION, • • • •   341 SHEP GOATHERD   52
POSSIBLE
   I ALMOST LONG THAT IT WERE POSSIBLE; • • • • • • • •   236 SHADOW WATER B   306
POST   SEE DOOR-POST STARTING-POST
   AND HANGING ITS PAPER FLOWERS FROM POST TO POST, • • • •   198 SEVEN WOODS   8
   AND HANGING ITS PAPER FLOWERS FROM POST TO POST, • • • •   198 SEVEN WOODS   8
   ARE BUT A POST THE PASSING DOGS DEFILE. • • • • • • •   321 REED WHISPERER   14
   THE POST AND GARDEN-BOY ALONE • • • • • • • • •   607 SONGS BURDEN 2   7
   THAT FOUGHT IN THE POST OFFICE • • • • • • • • •   608 SONGS BURDEN 3   5
   WHAT STALKED THROUGH THE POST OFFICE? WHAT INTELLECT, • •   611 STATUES   26
   TO A DISTANT POST; • • • • • • • • • • • • •   617 LONG-LEG FLY   4
POSTS   SEE DOOR-POSTS
   THE POSTS OF POLISHED YEW, CIRCLED WITH BRONZE, • • • •   279 TWO KINGS   48
POT   SEE HONEY-POT
   LAND FOR YOUR CHILDREN OR MONEY IN A POT." • • • • • •   228 SHADOW WATER B   125
   TO STIR THE BOILING POT? • • • • • • • • • • • •   395 SIXTEEN DEAD   6
   GOLDSMITH DELIBERATELY SIPPING AT THE HONEY POT OF HIS   481 BLOOD AND MOON V   21
    MIND;
   NOR SOLDERED POT OR PAN; • • • • • • • • • • •   606 SONGS BURDEN 1   15
POT-BELLIED
   AND WHEN THE MOON'S POT-BELLIED • • • • • • • •   455 FRIENDS YOUTH   3
POT-HOUSE
   A POT-HOUSE BENCH WITH OLIVER GOLDSMITH ONCE. • • • •   486 SEVEN SAGES   3
POTION'S
   WHEN, THE POTION'S WORK BEING DONE, • • • • • • •   522 LULLABY   9
POTTERY
   IN PAINTING OR IN POTTERY, WENT • • • • • • • • •   421 MY TABLE   18
POUND
   LIKE AN OLD HORSE IN A POUND." • • • • • • • • •   333 SOLOMON SHEBA   8
   ARE BUT A NARROW POUND." • • • • • • • • • • •   333 SOLOMON SHEBA   16
   THE WORLD A NARROW POUND." • • • • • • • • • • •   333 SOLOMON SHEBA   24
POUNDED
   THE PARTICULAR IS POUNDED TILL IT IS MAN. • • • • • •   382 VISION ROBART   6
POUNDS
   FOR HE SHALL HAVE A THOUSAND POUNDS • • • • • • • •   295 THREE BEGGARS   22
   THAT POUNDS UP ALL ANEW • • • • • • • • • • • •   346 ON WOMAN   31
POUR
   HER BEAUTY AS THE CONSTELLATIONS POUR • • • • • • •   279 TWO KINGS   V 62B
   POUR WINE AND DANCE IF MANHOOD STILL HAVE PRIDE, • • •   311 MOUNTAIN TOMB   1
   POUR WINE AND DANCE, IF MANKIND STILL HAVE PRIDE, • • •   311 MOUNTAIN TOMB V   1
   AND POUR UPON THE WORLD! AH! WELL-A-DAY! • • • • •   703 MOSADA 3   118
   AND POUR UPON THE WORLD! AH! WELL A DAY! • • • • •   703 MOSADA 3   V 118
POURED
   THEIR NAKED AND GLEAMING BODIES POURED OUT AND HEAPED IN   48 OISIN 3   28
    THE WAY.
   BUT WHEN A MAN POURED FISH INTO A PILE, • • • • • •   126 DREAM OF FAERY   5
   POURED OUT WINE FOR THE HIGH INVISIBLE ONES. • • • •   219 WOODS OF COOLE   44
   A KIND MILD WOMAN HAD SHE BEEN, WHO POURED • • • • •   279 TWO KINGS   V 62A
POURING   SEE DEATH-POURING
   THE SOUTH IS POURING DOWN ROSES OF CRIMSON FIRE! • • • •   154 BELOVED PEACE   6
   THAT FROM THE FIRE IS EVER POURING UP • • • • • • •   683 SEEKER   37
POURS
   POURS ROUND HIS SLEEPY STREAMS. • • • • • • • • •   98 FOXHUNTER   V 16
   POURS ROUND IN SLEEPY STREAMS. • • • • • • • • • •   98 FOXHUNTER   V 16
   SAD LADY OF THE DEEP, POURS DOWN HER LIGHT; • • • • •   650 ISLE STAT I 1   127
   POURS UP AND FLOATS IN FRAGRANCE ROUND MY HEAD • • • •   691 MOSADA 1   40
   POURS UP AND FLOATS IN FRAGRANCE O'ER MY HEAD • • • • •   691 MOSADA 1   V 40
POWDER
   THOUGHT THAT UNLESS A LITTLE POWDER BURNED • • • • • •   429 NINETEEN 19   21
POWER
   ARE EMPTY OF ALL POWER." "AND WHICH OF THESE • • • •   46 OISIN 2   248
   YE HAVE NO POWER." "AND, NIAM, SAY, OF THESE • • • •   46 OISIN 2   V 248
   THAT NONE MAY FEEL THE POWER OF SQUALL AND WAVE, • • • •   128 DREAM OF FAERY V   45
   BUT THE HORSE-BOYS SLEPT ON; AS THOUGH SOME POWER • • •   181 QUEEN MAEVE   39
   BECAUSE EARTH, CRAZY FOR ITS BROKEN POWER, • • • • •   186 QUEEN MAEVE   124
   WHAT POWER THAT IS MORE MIGHTY THAN DESIRE • • • • •   234 SHADOW WATER B   267
   TO GO--FOR HOPE WOULD GIVE HIS LIMBS THE POWER-- • • •   282 TWO KINGS   V 133A
   FOR HOPE WOULD GIVE HIS LIMBS THE POWER--AND AWAIT • • •   283 TWO KINGS   136
   DID SHE PUT ON HIS KNOWLEDGE WITH HIS POWER • • • • •   441 LEDA AND SWAN   13
   A BLOODY, ARROGANT POWER • • • • • • • • • • •   480 BLOOD AND MOON   3
   A SOMETHING INCOMPATIBLE WITH LIFE; AND POWER, • • • •   482 BLOOD AND MOON   50
   AND SOFT, ONE GLIMMERING STAR--WITH POWER VAST; • • •   714 FERENCZ RENYI   V 115
   OF EQUAL POWER IN SPELLS AND SECRET RITES. • • • • •   720 WITCH VIVIEN   6
   FOR GOD GIVES POWER TO THE SAD • • • • • • • • •   741 EARL PAUL   47
   FOR GOD GIVES POWER TO THE SAD • • • • • • • • •   741 EARL PAUL   51
   PUT ALL YOUR POWER ON THE THREAD • • • • • • • • •   771 SPINNING SONG   12
POWERFUL   SEE ALL-POWERFUL
   OF THAT MORE POWERFUL LIFE? HIS WIFE KNOWS BETTER. • •   230 SHADOW WATER B   172
   SOME VIOLENT BITTER MAN, SOME POWERFUL MAN • • • • •   418 ANCEST HOUSES   17
   BY THE WEBBED TOES, AND THAT ALL POWERFUL BILL • • • •   441 LEDA AND SWAN   V 3
   A POWERFUL EMBLEM UP, • • • • • • • • • • • •   480 BLOOD AND MOON   9
   AND YET A WOMAN'S POWERFUL CHARACTER • • • • • • •   489 COOLE PARK 29   18
POWERLESS
   IN WHAT LAND DO THE POWERLESS TURN THE BEAK • • • • •   42 OISIN 2   198
POWERS
   THE MAGICAL POWERS TO AND FRO. • • • • • • • • • •   138 TO IRELAND   V 24
   THE POET PLEADS WITH THE ELEMENTAL POWERS • • • • • •   174 ELEMENT POWERS   T
   AODH PLEADS WITH THE ELEMENTAL POWERS • • • • • • •   174 ELEMENT POWERS V   T

	PAGE	TITLE		LINE
POWERS (CONTINUED)				
THE POWERS WHOSE NAME AND SHAPE NO LIVING CREATURE KNOWS	174	ELEMENT POWERS		1
GREAT POWERS OF FALLING WAVE AND WIND AND WINDY FIRE, • •	174	ELEMENT POWERS		7
THE POWERS, NOT KIND LIKE YOU, CAME WHERE GOD'S GARDEN BLOWS,	174	ELEMENT POWERS	V	1
YOU GREAT ANGELIC POWERS OF WIND, AND WAVE, AND FIRE, • •	174	ELEMENT POWERS	V	7
GREAT ELEMENTAL POWERS OF WIND, AND WAVE, AND FIRE, • •	174	ELEMENT POWERS	V	7
DIM POWERS OF DROWSY THOUGHT, LET HER NO LONGER BE • •	175	ELEMENT POWERS		13
• • • THOUGHT'S CROWNED POWERS HE CALLED THEM ONCE. • • •	480	BLOOD AND MOON		15
GRATITUDE TO THE UNKNOWN POWERS • • • • • • • • •	505	GRAT INSTRUCT	V	T
PRACTICE				
PRACTICE A TINKER SHUFFLE • • • • • • • • • • •	617	LONG-LEG FLY		17
PRACTISE				
HE'LL PRACTISE ON THE SHEPHERD'S FLUTE, • • • • • • •	343	SHEP GOATHERD		102
PRACTISED				
AS HE THAT PRACTISED OR THAT UNDERSTOOD • • • • • •	327	ROBERT GREGORY		75
PRAGMATICAL				
THAT THIS PRAGMATICAL, PREPOSTEROUS PIG OF A WORLD, • • •	481	BLOOD AND MOON		26
PRAISE				
SHALL KNEEL AND PRAISE YOU, ONE BY ONE, • • • • • • •	8	OISIN 1		78
AND PRAISE THEE IN MY WESTERN HALL." • • • • • • •	8	OISIN 1	V	79
AND ALL AROUND THE HARP-STRING TOLD HIS PRAISE, • • • •	109	CUCHULAIN SEA		44
AND ALL AROUND THE HARPSTRING TOLD HIS PRAISE, • • •	109	CUCHULAIN SEA	V	44
AND ALL AROUND THE HARP STRING TOLD HIS PRAISE, • • •	109	CUCHULAIN SEA	V	44
AND WHITE STARS TELL YOUR PRAISE, • • • • • • • •	113	ROSE OF PEACE		10
"PRAISE GOD AND GOD'S MOTHER," DATHI SAID, • • • • •	167	BLESSED		17
AND NEW FRIENDS BUSY WITH YOUR PRAISE, • • • • • •	173	PLEADS FRIEND		3
AND OF NEW FRIENDS ARE GLAD WITH YOUR PRAISE, • • •	173	PLEADS FRIEND	V	3
WHY DO YOU PRAISE ANOTHER, PRAISING HER, • • • • • •	181	QUEEN MAEVE		31
WHAT WERE OUR PRAISE TO THEM? THEY EAT • • • • •	196	BAILE AILLINN		177
I HEAR THE HARP-STRING PRAISE THEM, OR HEAR THEIR MOURNFUL TALK.	210	UNDER THE MOON		16
I HEAR THE HARP STRINGS PRAISE THEM, OR HEAR THEIR MOURNFUL TALK.	210	UNDER THE MOON	V	16
I HEAR THE HARPSTRING PRAISE THEM OR HEAR THEIR MOURNFUL TALK.	210	UNDER THE MOON	V	16
I HEAR THE HARP STRING PRAISE THEM OR HEAR THEIR MOURNFUL TALK.	210	UNDER THE MOON	V	16
THEIR HEADS BEING TURNED WITH PRAISE AND FLATTERY! • • •	245	SHADOW WATER B		480
AGAINST UNWORTHY PRAISE • • • • • • • • • • •	259	UNWORTH PRAISE		T
WHAT, STILL YOU WOULD HAVE THEIR PRAISE! • • • • •	259	UNWORTH PRAISE		11
TO A POET, WHO WOULD HAVE ME PRAISE • • • • • • •	262	TO A POET		T
IN PRAISE OF WHAT ANOTHER'S SAID OR SUNG, • • • • •	262	TO A POET		2
BUT HAVE YOU KNOWN A DOG TO PRAISE HIS FLEAS? • • •	262	TO A POET	V	4
DOWSON AND JOHNSON MOST I PRAISE-- • • • • • • •	273	GREY ROCK		62
AMONG THOSE MOUTHS THAT SING THEIR SWEETHEARTS' PRAISE,	285	TWO KINGS		185
AND THOUGH I HAD HER PRAISE FOR IT, • • • • • • •	313	MEMORY YOUTH		5
YET WE, FOR ALL THAT PRAISE, COULD FIND • • • • •	314	MEMORY YOUTH		13
NOW MUST I THESE THREE PRAISE-- • • • • • • • •	315	FRIENDS		1
HOW COULD I PRAISE THAT ONE? • • • • • • • • •	316	FRIENDS		20
HOW SHOULD I PRAISE THAT ONE? • • • • • • • • •	316	FRIENDS	V	20
YET PRAISE THE WINTERS GONE! • • • • • • • • •	336	YOUNG BEAUTY		15
HER PRAISE • • • • • • • • • • • • • • • •	350	HER PRAISE		T
UNTIL HER PRAISE SHOULD BE THE UPPERMOST THEME, • • • •	350	HER PRAISE		6
THOUGH SHE HAD YOUNG MEN'S PRAISE AND OLD MEN'S BLAME, •	351	HER PRAISE		17
AMONG THE POOR BOTH OLD AND YOUNG GAVE HER PRAISE. • •	351	HER PRAISE		18
A LAW INDIFFERENT TO BLAME OR PRAISE, • • • • • •	428	NINETEEN 19		10
COLONUS' PRAISE • • • • • • • • • • • • • •	446	COLONUS PRAISE		T
COME PRAISE COLONUS' HORSES, AND COME PRAISE • • • •	446	COLONUS PRAISE		1
COME PRAISE COLONUS' HORSES, AND COME PRAISE • • • •	446	COLONUS PRAISE		1
THAT'S SO UNLIKE MYSELF THAT WHEN YOU PRAISE IT • • •	447	HERO GIRL FOOL		2
MOCKED ME WITH PRAISE OF MY MERE OPPOSITE! • • • •	448	HERO GIRL FOOL		4
IT IS AS THOUGH YOU PRAISE ANOTHER, OR EVEN • • • •	448	HERO GIRL FOOL	V	3
MOCK ME WITH PRAISE OF MY MERE OPPOSITE! • • • • •	448	HERO GIRL FOOL	V	4
EVERY PHILOSOPHER SHOULD PRAISE THAT LOVE. • • • • •	465	HARUN RASHID		97
BUT I BEING NONE CAN PRAISE ITS OPPOSITE. • • • • •	465	HARUN RASHID		98
PHILOSOPHERS SHOULD PRAISE THAT LOVE THE MOST, • • •	465	HARUN RASHID	V	97
THAT EVERY GIFT AND EVERY WORD OF PRAISE • • • • •	469	HARUN RASHID		172
AND PRAISE OUR CHOSEN MAN! • • • • • • • • • •	586	PARNELLITES		2
A DRUNKEN MAN'S PRAISE OF SOBRIETY • • • • • • •	591	DRUNK SOBRIETY		T
COME PRAISE NINETEEN-SIXTEEN, • • • • • • • • •	608	SONGS BURDEN 3		2
PRAISE EVERY MAN THAT CAME AGAIN, • • • • • • • •	608	SONGS BURDEN 3		7
PRAISE EVERY MAN THAT FELL. • • • • • • • • • •	608	SONGS BURDEN 3		8
COME PRAISE NINETEEN SIXTEEN, • • • • • • • • •	608	SONGS BURDEN 3	V	2
A MAN I PRAISE THAT ONCE IN TARA'S HALLS • • • • •	609	IN TARAS HALLS		1
AND PRAISE A WAR AMONG THE ENDLESS SEAS, • • • • •	749	SHADOW WATER A	V	35
THE PRAISE OF DEIRDRE • • • • • • • • • • •	771	SONG DEIRDRE 1	V	T
PRAISE THE BEAUTIFUL AND STRONG! • • • • • • • •	773	SONG DEIRDRE 1		19
PRAISE THE REDNESS OF THE YEW! • • • • • • • •	773	SONG DEIRDRE 1		20
PRAISE THE BLOSSOMING APPLE-STEM. • • • • • • • •	773	SONG DEIRDRE 1		21
WHAT IS ALL OUR PRAISE TO THEM • • • • • • • •	773	SONG DEIRDRE 1		23
PRAISE THE BLOSSOMING APPLE STEM! • • • • • • • •	773	SONG DEIRDRE 1	V	21
"THE MAN THAT I PRAISE," • • • • • • • • • •	780	WELL AND TREE		1
WHO BUT AN IDIOT WOULD PRAISE • • • • • • • •	780	WELL AND TREE		7
"THE MAN THAT I PRAISE," • • • • • • • • • •	780	WELL AND TREE		9
WHO BUT AN IDIOT WOULD PRAISE • • • • • • • •	780	WELL AND TREE		15
FOR PRAISE OF CLOWN OR KING, • • • • • • • • •	789	SINGING HEAD		20
PRAISED				
BUT WAS THERE EVER DOG THAT PRAISED HIS FLEAS? • • • •	262	TO A POET		4
BUT WHERE'S THE WILD DOG THAT HAS PRAISED HIS FLEAS? • •	262	TO A POET	V	4
PRAISED THEIR GREAT VICTORIES AND GAVE THEM JOY • • •	286	TWO KINGS	V	218B

	PAGE	TITLE	LINE
PRAISED (CONTINUED)			
I PRAISED HER BODY AND HER MIND • • • • • • • • •	314	MEMORY YOUTH	9
MAY GOD BE PRAISED FOR WOMAN • • • • • • • • •	345	ON WOMAN	1
SHE IS FOREMOST OF THOSE THAT I WOULD HEAR PRAISED• • •	350	HER PRAISE	1
SHE IS FOREMOST OF THOSE THAT I WOULD HEAR PRAISED• • •	351	HER PRAISE	10
AND PRAISED THE COLOUR OF HER FACE• • • • • • • •	410	TOWER	36
IT IS AS THOUGH YOU PRAISED ANOTHER, OR EVEN • • • •	448	HERO GIRL FOOL	3
ALL MEN HAVE PRAISED MY STRENGTH BUT NOT MY WORTH• • •	448	HERO GIRL FOOL V	9
THEY ARE NEITHER PAID NOR PRAISED• • • • • • • •	473	ALL SOUL NIGHT	76
THEY ARE NEITHER PAID OR PRAISED• • • • • • • • •	473	ALL SOUL NIGHT V	76
THAT CAN BE PRAISED OF ALL! • • • • • • • • • •	553	PRAYER OLD AGE	6
AND PRAISED YOUR WAR AMONG THE ENDLESS SEAS, • • • •	749	SHADOW WATER A	35
PRAISES			
WHOM BRAHMA, TOUCHING WITH HIS FINGER, PRAISES, FOR YOU HOLD	73	ANASHU VIJAYA	42
WHOM BRAHMA, TOUCHING WITH HIS FINGER, PRAISES, FOR YE HOLD	73	ANASHU VIJAYA V	42
COUNT ALL THE PRAISES DUE • • • • • • • • •	345	ON WOMAN	15
AND BIRTHDAYS AND HOLIDAYS SUCH PRAISES CAN BE HEARD • •	353	HIS PHOENIX	2
PRAISING			
WHY DO YOU PRAISE ANOTHER, PRAISING HER, • • • • •	181	QUEEN MAEVE	31
AND HAD THE GREATER JOY IN PRAISING HER, • • • • •	410	TOWER	37
PRANCE			
THE GUARDSMEN'S DROWSY CHARGERS WOULD NOT PRANCE• • • •	429	NINETEEN 19	24
PRANCED			
BELLOWED AND PRANCED IN THE ROUND TOWER! • • • • • •	331	ROUND TOWER	12
UNTIL THEY PRANCED UPON THE TOP• • • • • • • • •	331	ROUND TOWER	18
PRANCING			
PRANCING ROUND AND PRANCING UP • • • • • • • • •	331	ROUND TOWER	17
PRANCING ROUND AND PRANCING UP • • • • • • • • •	331	ROUND TOWER	17
PRAY			
GO CAST YOUR BODY ON THE STONES AND PRAY, • • • • •	42	OISIN 2	207
BUT KNEEL AND WEAR OUT THE FLAGS AND PRAY FOR YOUR SOUL THAT IS LOST	63	OISIN 3	215
KNEEL, USHEEN, WEAR OUT THE FLAGS AND PRAY FOR YOUR SOUL THAT IS LOST	63	OISIN 3 V	215
I WILL PRAY NO MORE WITH THE SMOOTH STONES! • • • •	63	OISIN 3 V	221
PRAYERS FOR THE LAND• PRAY ON, AND I WILL WAIT YOU, • •	71	ANASHU VIJAYA V	13
HE IS A GENTLE ROEBUCK! FOR HOW ELSE, I PRAY, COULD HE • •	76	INDIAN ON GOD	15
AND LEARN TO PRAY WHEN YOU PRAY• • • • • • • •	167	BLESSED	8
AND LEARN TO PRAY WHEN YOU PRAY• • • • • • • •	167	BLESSED	8
BEND DOWN AND PRAY FOR ALL THAT SIN I WOVE IN SONG, • • •	173	SPEAKS HEARERS	5
BEND DOWN AND PRAY FOR THE GREAT SIN I WOVE IN SONG, • •	173	SPEAKS HEARERS V	5
TO WHOM ALL LOVERS PRAY• BUT WHAT OF THAT? • • • •	224	SHADOW WATER B	43
FOR MEN WERE BORN TO PRAY AND SAVE! • • • • • • •	289	SEPTEMBER 1913	6
BUT LITTLE TIME HAD THEY TO PRAY • • • • • • • •	289	SEPTEMBER 1913	12
FALL ASLEEP WHEN I SHOULD PRAY•" • • • • • • •	298	THREE HERMITS	12
BUT PRAY TO GOD THAT HE EASE • • • • • • • •	380	SONGS FOOL 1	17
I ASKED IF I SHOULD PRAY, • • • • • • • • • •	495	MOHINI CHATTER	1
"PRAY FOR NOTHING, SAY • • • • • • • • • •	495	MOHINI CHATTER	3
PRAY THAT HEAVEN PROTECT US • • • • • • • • •	518	LOVES LONENESS	5
PRAY I WILL AND SING I MUST, • • • • • • • • •	540	FROM ANTIGONE	14
I PRAY—FOR FASHION'S WORD IS OUT • • • • • • •	553	PRAYER OLD AGE	9
IN ALL SUCH THINGS, PRAY LET THINE EARS BE TURNED, • • •	660	ISLE STAT II 1	39
LEAD ME, I PRAY THEE, TO THE STATUED PLACE! • • • •	667	ISLE STAT II 3	37
UPON MY KNEES I PRAY YOU, LET IT SLEEP, • • • • •	693	MOSADA 1	72
MY LORD, IF IT MUST BE, I PRAY DESCEND • • • • • •	697	MOSADA 2	43
HER HANGING MANSION• GIVE TO ME, I PRAY, • • • • •	698	MOSADA 2	52
AH! LEAVE ME, I PRAY YOU AND BEG• • • • • • • •	708	FAIRY PEDANT	22
"PRAY FOR THE SOULS IN PURGATORY," THE PALE PRIEST TREMBLING CRIES•	719	PHANTOM SHIP	31
I PRAY THAT I EVER BE WEAVING • • • • • • • • •	743	WISDOM DREAMS	1
PRAYED			
AND WITH LOW MURMURS PRAYED TO HIM, • • • • • • •	18	OISIN 1	257
HE PRAYED AND FELL ASLEEP! • • • • • • • • •	132	FR GILLIGAN	14
HE KNELT, PRAYED, FELL ASLEEP! • • • • • • • •	132	FR GILLIGAN V	14
AND THEN, GROWN WEARY, PRAYED AND CURSED • • • • •	307	HOUR DAWN	117
AND PRAYED AND CURSED AND CURSED AND FLED • • • • •	307	HOUR DAWN	119
AND CURSED AND PRAYED, AND PRAYED AND CURSED • • • •	307	HOUR DAWN V	117
AND CURSED AND PRAYED, AND PRAYED AND CURSED • • • •	307	HOUR DAWN V	117
AND FOR AN HOUR I HAVE WALKED AND PRAYED • • • • •	403	FOR DAUGHTER	7
I HAVE WALKED AND PRAYED FOR THIS YOUNG CHILD AN HOUR • •	403	FOR DAUGHTER	9
I PRAYED AT ALL THE STATIONS UPON MY MARROW-BONES, • • •	593	PILGRIM	7
AND THERE I FOUND AN OLD MAN, AND THOUGH I PRAYED ALL DAY	593	PILGRIM	8
I PRAYED AT ALL THE STATIONS UPON MY MARROW BONES, • • •	593	PILGRIM V	7
PRAYED THOSE FORGOTTEN FISHERS, TILL IN THE EASTERN SKIES	719	PHANTOM SHIP	32
PRAYED BESIDE THE OCEAN, THE OLD MUMBLING MOTHER OF THE DEAD•	719	PHANTOM SHIP V	34
PRAYER			
THAT WAS BRIMMED UP WITH PRAYER AND REST! • • • • •	151	HEART OF WOMAN	2
WHEN SONGS I WOVE FOR MY BELOVED HIDE THE PRAYER, • • •	173	SPEAKS HEARERS	2
WHEN SONG I WOVE FOR MY BELOVED HIDES THE PRAYER, • • •	173	SPEAKS HEARERS V	2
A MYSTICAL PRAYER TO THE MASTERS OF THE ELEMENTS, • • •	174	ELEMENT POWERS V	T
THEY READ IN THEIR BOOKS OF PRAYER! • • • • • • •	178	FIDDLER DOONEY	6
THEY READ IN A BOOK OF PRAYER, • • • • • • • •	178	FIDDLER DOONEY V	6
AND PRAYER TO SHIVERING PRAYER, UNTIL • • • • • •	289	SEPTEMBER 1913	4
AND PRAYER TO SHIVERING PRAYER, UNTIL • • • • • •	289	SEPTEMBER 1913	4
FIRST WAS MUTTERING A PRAYER, • • • • • • • •	298	THREE HERMITS	3
BECAUSE IT WAS YOUR PRAYER • • • • • • • • •	355	BROKEN DREAMS	5
A PRAYER ON GOING INTO MY HOUSE • • • • • • • •	371	ON GOING HOUSE	T
A PRAYER FOR MY DAUGHTER • • • • • • • • • •	403	FOR DAUGHTER	T
A PRAYER FOR MY SON • • • • • • • • • • •	435	FOR MY SON	T

629

```
                                                      PAGE    TITLE              LINE
PRAYER   (CONTINUED)
      A PRAYER FOR OLD AGE . . . . . . . . . . . . . .  553 PRAYER OLD AGE       T
      AND PRAYER COMES ROUND AGAIN-- . . . . . . . . .  553 PRAYER OLD AGE      10
      BY WATER, HERB AND SOLITARY PRAYER . . . . . . .  555 RIBH AT TOMB        23
      YOU THAT MITCHEL'S PRAYER HAVE HEARD, . . . . . . 638 BEN BULBEN          25
      TO LOVE EACH OTHER.  IN MY PRAYER BOOK STILL . .  713 FERENCZ RENYI   V   94
      THEY SEEM TO JOIN HER PRAYER-- . . . . . . . . .  736 IN CHURCH           12
      HER PRAYER FOR FATHER, MOTHER DEAR, . . . . . . . 736 IN CHURCH           13
      A PRAYER FOR EVERY FALLING TEAR . . . . . . . . . 736 IN CHURCH           15
PRAYER-BOOK
      TO LOVE EACH OTHER.  IN MY PRAYER-BOOK STILL . . . 713 FERENCZ RENYI      94
PRAYERS
      FASTING AND PRAYERS.  TELL ON.  YES, YES, . . . .  24 OISIN 1            360
      FASTING AND PRAYERS.  TELL ON.  AY, AY! . . . . .  24 OISIN 1         V  360
      PRAYERS FOR THE LAND.  I WILL WAIT HERE, AMRITA. .  71 ANASHU VIJAYA      13
      PRAYERS FOR THE LAND.  PRAY ON, AND I WILL WAIT YOU,  71 ANASHU VIJAYA V  13
      PRAYERS FOR THE LAND.  O BRAHMA, GUARD IN SLEEP . .  75 ANASHU VIJAYA     85
      AND LEARN THE PRAYERS THAT YOU SAY. . . . . . . . 167 BLESSED         V    8
      ARE PRAYERS OF PATIENT MEN AND GOOD." . . . . . . 725 LEGEND               6
PRAYETH
      FOR YOUR FEET THE MORNING PRAYETH! . . . . . . . 706 DAWN-SONG           25
PRAYING
      . . . AND PRAYING, AND WROTH WITH THE BELLS, . . .  58 OISIN 3           159
PRAYS
      SHE PRAYS FOR FATHER, MOTHER DEAR, . . . . . . . 735 IN CHURCH            1
      SHE PRAYS FOR EVERY FALLING TEAR . . . . . . . . 735 IN CHURCH            3
PREACHER
      THE PREACHER WATCHING FOR THE EVIL HOUR TO PASS, . . 686 LIFE             3
      THE PREACHER WATCHING FOR THE ILL HOUR TO PASS-- . . 734 QUATRAIN APHOR   3
      THE PREACHER WATCHING FOR THE EVIL HOUR TO PASS, . . 734 QUATRAIN APHOR V 3
PRECEDENTS
      PRECEDENTS OUT OF BEAUTIFUL OLD BOOKS! . . . . . . 205 ADAMS CURSE       26
PRECIOUS
      BUT FRUIT THAT IS OF PRECIOUS STONE, . . . . . . 196 BAILE AILLINN      175
      TREASURE ON TREASURE.  BOXES OF PRECIOUS SPICE. . . 247 SHADOW WATER B   533
      TREASURE AND TREASURE.  BOXES OF PRECIOUS SPICE. . . 247 SHADOW WATER B V 533
      THUS DO I BURN THESE PRECIOUS HERBS, WHOSE SMOKE . . 691 MOSADA 1        39
      IF THESE BE PRECIOUS."  "I AM OLD AND WEAK," . . .  711 FERENCZ RENYI    55
PRECIPICE
      ABOVE A WINDY PRECIPICE?"  THEN HE: . . . . . . . 285 TWO KINGS         195
PRECISION
      WHERE PASSION AND PRECISION HAVE BEEN ONE . . . . 264 HOUSE SHAKEN        2
PREDESTINED
      WHEN HER SOUL FLIES TO THE PREDESTINED DANCING-PLACE . . 365 HER COURAGE  1
      WHAT SEEMS MOST WELCOME IN THE TOMB--PLAY A PREDESTINED   503 VACILLATION 86
          PART.
      ACCOMPLISHED HIS PREDESTINED WILL, . . . . . . . 522 LULLABY           16
PREFERRED
      PREFERRED TO TEACH A SCHOOL . . . . . . . . . . . 472 ALL SOUL NIGHT    46
PREFERS
      RIBH PREFERS AN OLDER THEOLOGY . . . . . . . . . 556 RIBH PATRICK    V    T
PRELUDE
      HOW SPED THY QUEST?  THIS PRELUDE WE'LL NOT HEAR IT. . . 673 ISLE STAT II 3 174
PREPARATION
      BEGIN THE PREPARATION FOR YOUR DEATH . . . . . . 500 VACILLATION        28
PREPARED
      I HAVE PREPARED MY PEACE . . . . . . . . . . . . 415 TOWER             157
      PREPARED A REST FOR THE PEOPLE OF GOD, . . . . . 639 BEN BULBEN         65
PREPOSTEROUS
      THAT THIS PRAGMATICAL, PREPOSTEROUS PIG OF A WORLD, . . . 481 BLOOD AND MOON 26
PRESENCE
      NOR HAD FORGOT THE STRANGENESS OF MY PRESENCE . . . . 466 HARUN RASHID V 119A
      AN EVENING PRESENCE FILLS THE PLACE. . . . . . . 736 SUMMER EVENING    16
PRESENCES
      PRESENCES . . . . . . . . . . . . . . . . . . . 358 PRESENCES            T
      AND YET THEY TOO BREAK HEARTS--O PRESENCES . . . 445 SCHOOL CHILDR      53
PRESENT
      THOUGHTS UPON THE PRESENT STATE OF THE WORLD . . . 428 NINETEEN 19    V    T
      HER PRESENT IMAGE FLOATS INTO THE MIND-- . . . . 444 SCHOOL CHILDR      25
      TO ENGROSS THE PRESENT AND DOMINATE MEMORY. . . . 630 CIRCUS ANIMALS    30
PRESS
      TO THE SCENTED OAKEN PRESS. . . . . . . . . . . . 124 CATHLEEN PARA      8
      I KISS MY WAILING CHILD AND PRESS IT TO MY BREAST, . . 147 UNAPPEAS HOST   5
      WHEN MY ARMS WRAP YOU ROUND I PRESS . . . . . . . 155 FORGOT BEAUTY      1
      WORK AT THE CIDER PRESS. . . . . . . . . . . . . 774 COME RIDE         12
      WHAT WOUNDS, WHAT BLOODY PRESS, . . . . . . . . . 785 WOMANS BEAUTY     26
PRESSED
      WHOSE CAREFUL PASTERN PRESSED THE SOD . . . . . .   2 OISIN 1        V   7W
      PRESSED ON THE EVER-TREMBLING ROOF . . . . . . .  25 OISIN 1        V  383
      MY HANDS WERE PRESSED TO VANISHED SUDDENLY. . . . 286 TWO KINGS        208
      WITH FACE AND NOSE PRESSED TO A SWEET-SHOP WINDOW, . . 370 EGO DOMINUS   56
      WITH FACE AND NOSE PRESSED TO A SWEETSHOP WINDOW. . . 370 EGO DOMINUS V 56
      THE BIRD DESCENDS, AND HER FRAIL THIGHS ARE PRESSED . . 441 LEDA AND SWAN V 2
      PRESSED HER BODY TO HIS BODY, . . . . . . . . . . 453 MERMAID            3
      AND PRESSED AT MIDNIGHT IN SOME PUBLIC PLACE . . . 610 STATUES           7
      IS IN THY FACE, AND LIPS TOGETHER PRESSED! . . . 671 ISLE STAT II 3    139
PRESSING
      AND PRESSING ON, OR LINGERING SLOW WITH FEAR, . . . 114 ROSE OF BATTLE V  5
PRETENCE
      A PRETENCE OF WIT." . . . . . . . . . . . . . . . 349 HAWK              18
      A MAN MAY PUT PRETENCE AWAY . . . . . . . . . . . 525 DANCING DAYS      19
```

630

		PAGE	TITLE	LINE

PRETENDING
PRETENDING THAT THERE CAN BE PASSION . . . . 271 GREY ROCK 7
PRETTY
A PRETTY GIRL TO SHARE MY BED"; . . . . 296 THREE BEGGARS 31
ON PRETTY THINGS THAT MAY . . . . 366 HER CHRIS TREE 7
WE TOO HAD MANY PRETTY TOYS WHEN YOUNG; . . . . 428 NINETEEN 19 9
HAD PRETTY PLUMAGE ONCE--ENOUGH OF THAT, ... 444 SCHOOL CHILDR 30
MY PRETTY PAISTIN IS MY HEART'S DESIRE. . . . . . 550 SONGS REWRIT 1 V 1
COME SWISH AROUND, MY PRETTY PUNK, ... 591 DRUNK SOBRIETY 1
NO UPS AND DOWNS, MY PRETTY, ... 592 DRUNK SOBRIETY 13
WHAT SHALL I DO FOR PRETTY GIRLS . . . . 620 JOHN KINSELLA 11
WHAT SHALL I DO FOR PRETTY GIRLS . . . . 621 JOHN KINSELLA 23
WHAT SHALL I DO FOR PRETTY GIRLS . . . . 621 JOHN KINSELLA 35
MY PRETTY CHILD, SINCE HE HAS GONE, OH SAY . . . . 658 ISLE STAT II 1 3
A PEASANT PALE AND PRETTY, HER EYES FOR FEAR, . . . 713 FERENCZ RENYI 81
A PEASANT, PALE AND PRETTY, HER EYES FROM FEAR, . . . 713 FERENCZ RENYI V 81
PREVAIL
YET OLD ROMANCE BEING KIND, LET HIM PREVAIL . . . . 258 KING NO KING 5
PREY
MY SOUL, MY PREY, AND THIS MY HEAPED PILE. . . . . 45 OISIN 2 V 239B
THE STRONGEST OF THE WORLD, TO SNATCH MY PREY, . . . 45 OISIN 2 V 241
AND NOT A GLOOMY BIRD OF PREY. . . . . 338 TOM OROUGHLEY 8
NOW RUSH UPON HER AND FIND OUT WHAT PREY . . . . 752 SHADOW WATER A 130
PRIAM
AND PROUD AS PRIAM MURDERED WITH HIS PEERS; . . . . 120 SORROW OF LOVE 8
PRICELESS
NOTORIOUS, TILL ALL MY PRICELESS THINGS . . . . . 321 REED WHISPERER 13
PRIDE
AND TOLD THE PURPLE DEEPS THEIR PRIDE, ... 14 OISIN 1 186
"SWIFT ARE THE YEARS OF A WARRIOR'S PRIDE; . . . . 26 OISIN 1 V 399A
TO TWO OLD EAGLES, FULL OF ANCIENT PRIDE, ... 34 OISIN 2 74
TO EAGLES TWAIN THAT, FULL OF ANCIENT PRIDE, . . . 34 OISIN 2 V 73
FOR THESE RED LIPS, WITH ALL THEIR MOURNFUL PRIDE, . . 111 ROSE OF WORLD 2
LEAVE THE BODY'S COLOURED PRIDE . . . . 124 CATHLEEN PARA 2
AND DREAM ABOUT THE GREAT AND THEIR PRIDE; . . . . 166 EVIL OF BELOV 2
BUT WEIGH THIS SONG WITH THE GREAT AND THEIR PRIDE; . . 166 EVIL OF BELOV 4
FROM GULLEON'S PLACE OF PRIDE, ... 171 MAID QUIET V 4B
WHERE, WHERE BUT HERE HAVE PRIDE AND TRUTH, . . . 262 STUDENTS AGIT 1
THAT THINGS IT WERE A PRIDE TO GIVE . . . . . . 287 TO WEALTHY MAN 6
THAT IDLENESS HAD BORNE TO PRIDE, ... 296 THREE BEGGARS 40
WITH THE PRIDE OF HIS EYE? . . . . 310 PEACOCK 3
FOR THE PRIDE OF HIS EYE. . . . . 311 PEACOCK 11
POUR WINE AND DANCE IF MANHOOD STILL HAVE PRIDE, . . 311 MOUNTAIN TOMB 1
POUR WINE AND DANCE, IF MANKIND STILL HAVE PRIDE, . . 311 MOUNTAIN TOMB V 1
TILL PRIDE HAD MADE HER EYES GROW BRIGHT, ... 314 MEMORY YOUTH 10
HE DREAMS HIMSELF HIS MOTHER'S PRIDE, ... 343 SHEP GOATHERD 110
TO BE THE GARDEN'S PRIDE." . . . . 396 ROSE TREE 12
FROM A GREAT LABYRINTH OUT OF PRIDE, ... 413 TOWER 116
FROM SOME GREAT LABYRINTH OUT OF PRIDE, ... 413 TOWER V 116
THEY SHALL INHERIT MY PRIDE, ... 414 TOWER 127
THE PRIDE OF PEOPLE THAT WERE . . . . 414 TOWER 128
PRIDE, LIKE THAT OF THE MORN, ... 414 TOWER 134
I LEAVE BOTH FAITH AND PRIDE . . . . 416 TOWER 173
THE BREAST THRUST OUT IN PRIDE . . . . 430 NINETEEN 19 66
AND THAT HE SHRIEKS FROM PRIDE. . . . . 456 FRIENDS YOUTH 20
AND PRIDE BRING IN IMPURITY! . . . . 460 THREE MONUMENT 11
AND KNEW THAT SWEET EXTREMITY OF PRIDE . . . . . 471 ALL SOUL NIGHT 22
A GREAT MAN IN HIS PRIDE . . . . 476 DEATH 7
WHEN SHE IN ALL HER VIRGINAL PRIDE . . . . . . 488 CRAZED MOON 8
FOUND PRIDE ESTABLISHED IN HUMILITY, ... 489 COOLE PARK 29 15
AND IN THE HEART'S PRIDE. . . . . 513 JANE TALK BISH 12
HE DID IT OUT OF PRIDE. . . . . 545 TO SAME TUNE 1 26
THE SOLDIER TAKES PRIDE . . . . 547 TO SAME TUNE 3 V T
THE SOLDIER TAKES PRIDE IN SALUTING HIS CAPTAIN, . . 547 TO SAME TUNE 3 1
SOLDIERS TAKE PRIDE IN SALUTING THEIR CAPTAIN, . . . 547 TO SAME TUNE 3 V 1
SOLDIERS TAKE PRIDE IN SALUTING THEIR CAPTAIN, . . . 548 TO SAME TUNE 3 21
AND THERE IS AN OLD BEGGAR WANDERING IN HIS PRIDE-- . . 580 CURSE CROMWELL 5
GUARDED; GRIFFITH STARING IN HYSTERICAL PRIDE; . . . 601 GALLERY REVIS 4
OF ALL THAT PRIDE AND THAT HUMILITY? . . . . . . 602 GALLERY REVIS 29
THE SOLDIER TAKES PRIDE IN SALUTING HIS CAPTAIN, . . 614 MARCH SONGS 2 1
HE DID IT OUT OF PRIDE. . . . . 616 MARCH SONGS 3 26
IRVING AND HIS PLUME OF PRIDE, ... 625 NATIVITY 8
OF THE FORESTS ALL THE PRIDE, ... 658 ISLE STAT I 3 84
PRIEST
THE PRIEST OF COLOONY . . . . 91 FATHER OHART V T
THE OLD PRIEST PETER GILLIGAN . . . . 132 FR GILLIGAN 1
THE OLD PRIEST PETER GILLIGAN . . . . 133 FR GILLIGAN 23
THE OLD PRIEST PETER GILLIGAN . . . . 133 FR GILLIGAN 35
THE OLD PRIEST PETER GILLIGAN . . . . 133 FR GILLIGAN 39
MY COUSIN IS PRIEST IN KILVARNET, ... 178 FIDDLER DOONEY V 3
MY BROTHER IS PRIEST OF KILBARNET, ... 178 FIDDLER DOONEY V 3
MY BROTHER IS PRIEST IN KILVARNET, ... 178 FIDDLER DOONEY V 3
THEY HAD A PRIEST SAY MASS, AND EVEN THE JAPANESE, . . 363 DOLLS FACES 2
BECAUSE THE PRIEST MUST HAVE LIKE EVERY DOG HIS DAY . . 364 DOLLS FACES 10
NOR SO MUCH AS PARISH PRIEST; . . . . 508 JANE BISHOP 11
THE PRIEST CAME WHERE SHE WAS; . . . . 571 THREE BUSHES 65
"PRAY FOR THE SOULS IN PURGATORY," THE PALE PRIEST 719 PHANTOM SHIP 31
  TREMBLING CRIES.
THE PRIEST AND THE FAIRY. . . . . 728 PRIEST FAIRY T
MUSINGLY WANDERED THE VILLAGE PRIEST. . . . . . 728 PRIEST FAIRY 3
AND STRAIGHT BEFORE THE SLEEPING PRIEST . . . . . 729 PRIEST FAIRY 23

631

PRIEST   (CONTINUED)
    NOW, WHAT HAS A FAIRY TO DO WITH A PRIEST • • • • • •   729 PRIEST FAIRY   27
    THE PRIEST LOOKED NEITHER TO RIGHT NOR LEFT, • • • • • •   730 PRIEST FAIRY   49
PRIESTESS
    I, PRIESTESS OF THIS TEMPLE, OFFER UP • • • • • • •   71 ANASHU VIJAYA   12
    I, PRIESTESS OF THIS TEMPLE, OFFER UP • • • • • . • •   75 ANASHU VIJAYA   84
PRIEST'S
    THOUGH NOT FOR THE PRIEST'S EAR, • • • • • • • • •   620 JOHN KINSELLA   18
PRIESTS
    THE PRIESTS HAVE GOT A BOOK THAT SAYS • • • • • •   621 JOHN KINSELLA   25
PRIME
    LONG PAST HIS PRIME REMEMBER THINGS THAT ARE • • • •   477 SELF AND SOUL   18
    HE STOOD A MESSENGER. IN APRIL'S PRIME • • • • • •   690 MOSADA 1   6
PRIMORDIAL
    PRIMORDIAL MOTHERHOOD FORSAKE HIS LIMBS, THE CHILD   559 MAGIC DRUM   2
       NO LONGER REST,
PRIMUM
    THE PRIMUM MOBILE THAT FASHIONED US • • • • • • • •   423 MY DESCENDANTS   17
PRINCE
    AND MANY A PRINCE OF LOFTY NAME, • • • • • • • •   7 OISIN 1   V   63
    SAT LATE, OR SHELLEY'S VISIONARY PRINCE• • • • • •   373 PHASES OF MOON   16
    "GREAT PRINCE, FORGIVE THE FREEDOM OF MY SPEECH! • • •   464 HARUN RASHID   74
    THEY WOULD MAKE A PRINCE DECAY • • • • • • • • •   775 AGAINST WITCH   11
PRINCE'S
    WENT WE TO FIND THEIR PRINCE'S HALL-- • • • • • • •   16 OISIN 1   V   217
PRINCES
    OF PRINCES THERE IS MANY A ONE." • • • • • • • •   6 OISIN 1   V   61
    AND MANY PRINCES OF HIGH NAME. • • • • • • • •   7 OISIN 1   V   68
    THE MIGHTIEST OF THE PRINCES OF THE WORLD • • • • • •   462 HARUN RASHID   41
PRINCESS
    YOUNG PRINCESS, WHY WERT THOU BEGUILED • • • • • •   6 OISIN 1   V   59
    YOUNG PRINCESS, WHEN WERE YOU BEGUILED • • • • • •   6 OISIN 1   V   59
    "HOW COMES IT, PRINCESS, THAT YOUR MIND • • • • • •   6 OISIN 1   V   59A
    PRINCESS, BY THIS YOUNG MAN, MY SON?" • • • • • • •   6 OISIN 1   V   61
PRINCIPLES
    I HAVE PRINCIPLES TO PROVE ME RIGHT. • • • • • • • •   386 ROBARTES DANCE   42
PRINTED
    WE SAW, SOME NEW, SOME PRINTED WHEN THE PLACE WAS YOUNG,   37 OISIN 2   V   116
PRINTS
    SHOWED PRINTS OF SEA-BORN SCALES, WHILE DOWN THROUGH IT   37 OISIN 2   115
    THAT HAD MADE PRINTS UPON THE GROUND, • • • • • • •   274 GREY ROCK   79
PRISON
    IN THE PRISON OF MY HANDS, • • • • • • • • •   381 SONG OF FOOL   2
    TO PRISON GO, AND MOSSY RUIN REST • • • • • • • • •   709 FERENCZ RENYI   V   2
PRISONER
    ON A POLITICAL PRISONER • • • • • • • • • • • •   397 POLIT PRISONER   T
PRISONERS
    'TWILL PASS. I'LL SEE THE OTHER PRISONERS NOW, • • • •   704 MOSADA 3   130
PRISONS
    TO PRISONS GO, AND MOSSY RUIN REST • • • • • • • •   709 FERENCZ RENYI   2
PRIVACY
    A DAPHNE AND A MARY WHO LIVE IN PRIVACY! • • • • • •   354 HIS PHOENIX   18
PRIVET
    WHERE HAZEL AND ASH AND PRIVET BLIND THE PATHS! • • • •   217 WOODS OF COOLE   8
PROCESSIONS
    PROCESSIONS THAT LACK HIGH STILTS HAVE NOTHING THAT CATCHES   622 HIGH TALK   1
       THE EYE.
PROCLAIM
    PROCLAIM WITH THAT UNWEARIED, REEDY CRY • • • • • •   128 DREAM OF FAERY   42
    MIGHT PROCLAIM A HOLIDAY! • • • • • • • • • • •   432 NINETEEN 19   106
    GIVE TONGUE, PROCLAIM THEIR HIDDEN NAME--"HOUND VOICE."   622 HOUND VOICE   7
PROCLAIMED
    I EVERYWHERE PROCLAIMED THERE IS • • • • • • • •   528 DANCER CRUACH   V   1
    PROCLAIMED BOTH GOOD AND GREAT! • • • • • • • • •   597 MODEL LAUREATE   4
PROCLAIMING
    PROCLAIMING WITH A LOW AND REEDY CRY, • • • • • •   128 DREAM OF FAERY   V   42
    I, PROCLAIMING THAT THERE IS • • • • • • • •   528 DANCER CRUACH   1
    ACCLAIMING, PROCLAIMING, DECLAIMING HIM. • • • • •   528 DANCER CRUACH   8
PRODIGIES
    OF WONDERS! EVE OF PRODIGIES! DRAW! DRAW! • • • • • •   664 ISLE STAT II 2   62
PRODUCTS
    BASE-BORN PRODUCTS OF BASE BEDS. • • • • • • • • •   639 BEN BULBEN   73
PROFANE
    PROFANE PERFECTION OF MANKIND. • • • • • • • • •   639 BEN BULBEN   52
PROFESSOR
    A GREY PROFESSOR PASSING CRIED, • • • • • • • • •   725 LEGEND   9
PROFFERING
    PROFFERING ITS SACRED LAUREL CROWNS, • • • • • • •   612 NEWS ORACLE   23
PROFFERS
    THE DEVOTEE PROFFERS A KNEE TO HIS LORD, • • • • • •   547 TO SAME TUNE 3   2
    THE DEVOTEE PROFFERS A KNEE TO HIS LORD, • • • • • •   614 MARCH SONGS 2   2
PROFIT
    I'D GIVE THE PROFIT OF NINE VOYAGES • • • • • • •   222 SHADOW WATER B   V   9
PROFOUND
    CLOSED IN THE MISTY AIR PROFOUND. • • • • • • • •   10 OISIN 1   V   114D
    PROFOUND MCTAGGART THOUGHT SO, AND IN A BREATH • • •   619 BRONZE HEAD   13
PROLONG
    YOUTH TO PROLONG • • • • • • • • • • • • • •   334 SONG   2
PROMINENT
    IF WORTHY THEIR PROMINENT PART IN THE PLAY, • • • • •   565 LAPIS LAZULI   14

PROMISE
WE'LL PUT THIS MAN TO DEATH. I PROMISE IT. . . . . . 238 SHADOW WATER B 363
I PROMISE YOU A HUNDRED DRINKING BOWLS, ... 756 SHADOW WATER A V 187
PROMISE-BREAKER
WHAT DO YOU CALL IT?--THAT OLD PROMISE-BREAKER, ... 228 SHADOW WATER B 122
PROMISED
THAT HAS BEEN PROMISED ME. I HAVE NOT SEEN THEM . . . . 226 SHADOW WATER B 88
TO DEATH! FOR THEY THAT PROMISED TO ME LOVE . . . . . 230 SHADOW WATER B 192
YOU'D NEVER DOUBT THAT IT WAS LIFE THEY PROMISED . . . . 231 SHADOW WATER B 197
OR SOMEWHERE, I SHALL FIND THE LOVE THEY HAVE PROMISED. 231 SHADOW WATER B 208
AND BLEW YOU HITHER! AND THEIR MOUTHS HAVE PROMISED . . . 237 SHADOW WATER B 325
THAT IS NOT TRUE, FOR HE HAS PROMISED ME . . . . . . 248 SHADOW WATER B 552
PROMISED THAT FOR A PIN'S SAKE . . . . 274 GREY ROCK 90
I'D PROMISED HIM TWO HUNDRED YEARS, ... 275 GREY ROCK 98
FOR THAT SHE PROMISED, AND FOR THAT REFUSED." . . . . 286 TWO KINGS 213
FOR THAT YOU PROMISED, AND FOR THAT REFUSED." . . . . 286 TWO KINGS V 213
TO A WEALTHY MAN WHO PROMISED A SECOND SUBSCRIPTION . . . 287 TO WEALTHY MAN T
THE BIBLE PROMISED US, ... 472 ALL SOUL NIGHT 39
I PROMISED HIM THAT NONE SHOULD ESCAPE MY SWORD . . . . 752 SHADOW WATER A 114
HE HAS HEARD ME BECAUSE I PROMISED ALL. . . . . . . 752 SHADOW WATER A 116
AND BRING ME TO MY PEOPLE. I PROMISED THESE . . . . . 756 SHADOW WATER A V 185
PRONE
BUT PRONE ON THE PATHWAY, PRONE STRUGGLING, ... 60 OISIN 3 V 186
BUT PRONE ON THE PATHWAY, PRONE STRUGGLING, ... 60 OISIN 3 V 186
PROOF
FOR PROUD, SOFT, CEREMONIOUS PROOF . . . . 386 ROBARTES DANCE 30
BUT O! AMBITIOUS HEART, HAD SUCH A PROOF DRAWN FORTH . . 427 PHANTOM HATRED 36
MICHAEL ANGELO LEFT A PROOF . . . . 638 BEN BULBEN 45
MICHAELANGELO LEFT A PROOF . . . . 638 BEN BULBEN V 45
PROOF THAT THERE'S A PURPOSE SET . . . . 639 BEN BULBEN 50
PROPER
A LOVE THAT LACKS ITS PROPER FOOD! . . . . 569 THREE BUSHES 3
PROPER TO MY BREAST, ... 573 LADYS 2ND SONG 16
CLIMB TO OUR PROPER DARK, THAT WE MAY TRACE . . . . . 611 STATUES 31
PROPERTIUS
A THOUGHT FROM PROPERTIUS . . . . 355 PROPERTIUS T
PROPERTY
FOR WISDOM IS THE PROPERTY OF THE DEAD, ... 482 BLOOD AND MOON 49
A PROPERTY OF THE LIVING! BUT NO STAIN . . . . . . 482 BLOOD AND MOON 52
PROPHECIES
BEING TOO HIGH, THEIR HEADY PROPHECIES . . . . 250 SHADOW WATER B 578
THE LADIES CLOSE THEIR MUSING EYES. NO PROPHECIES, . . . 426 PHANTOM HATRED 19
PROPHESYING
AND ALL THAT PROPHESYING IMAGES . . . . 235 SHADOW WATER B 294
IT IS POSSESSED. A PROPHESYING VOICE. . . . . . . 681 SEEKER 8
AND ALL THAT PROPHESYING IMAGES . . . . 764 SHADOW WATER A V 344
PROPINQUITY
HAD SHATTERED HER SOUL. PROPINQUITY HAD BROUGHT . . . . 619 BRONZE HEAD 18
PROPPED
PROPPED UPON PILLOWS, ROUGE ON THE PALLOR OF HER FACE. . . 362 HER COURTESY 3
PROPPED UPON MY TWO KNEES, ... 628 JANE MOUNTAIN 19
PROPS
"THE PROPS," SAID HE, "OF STARS AND WORLDS . . . . . . 725 LEGEND 5
PROSAIC
FOR THE PROSAIC LIGHT OF DAY-- . . . . 411 TOWER 46
PROSE
THAT MAYBE "I AM SORRY" IN PLAIN PROSE . . . . 341 SHEP GOATHERD 60
THERE HYDE BEFORE HE HAD BEATEN INTO PROSE . . . . . 489 COOLE PARK 29 9
PROSPER
PROSPER BUT LITTLE, HAS DRIED UP OF LATE, ... 405 FOR DAUGHTER 51
PROSPEROUS
WHOSE LIPS HAD LIFE'S MOST PROSPEROUS GLOW? . . . . . 10 OISIN 1 118
AND I, THAT COUNT MYSELF MOST PROSPEROUS, ... 423 MY DESCENDANTS 19
PROTECT
PROTECT ME NOW, GODS THAT MY PEOPLE SWEAR BY. . . . . 241 SHADOW WATER B 396
CAN, TATTERED, STILL PROTECT, FADED ADORN. . . . . . 477 SELF AND SOUL 16
PRAY THAT HEAVEN PROTECT US . . . . 518 LOVES LONENESS 5
THAT PROTECT YOUR BLOOD. . . . . 518 LOVES LONENESS 6
PROTECTED
PROTECTED FROM THE CIRCLE OF THE MOON . . . . 428 NINETEEN 19 3
PROTECTING
PROTECTING, TILL THE DANGER PAST, ... 436 FOR MY SON 31
BUT NOT FROM HER PROTECTING CARE. . . . . 522 LULLABY 18
PROTEST
NOR HEEDS THE OLD, DIM PROTEST AND THE CRY . . . . . 689 NETTLESHIP 14
PROTEUS
IS THERE A BRIDLE FOR THIS PROTEUS . . . . 265 ABBEY THEATRE 11
PROUD   SEE SILVER-PROUD
AND FLOATING-HAIRED AND PROUD IN STRIFE! . . . . . . 9 OISIN 1 V 99
UNLANGUID AS THE BIRDS, IN PROUD COMPANIONSHIPS! . . . . 30 OISIN 2 V 14C
AND AH, YOU PROUD MAIDEN, YOU ARE NOT SO FAIR WHEN HIS OAR 91 OLD FISHERMAN 9
IS HEARD ON THE WATER, AS THEY WERE, THE PROUD AND APART, 91 OLD FISHERMAN 10
PROUD MAIDEN, YE ARE NOT SO FAIR, WHEN HIS OAR . . . . 91 OLD FISHERMAN V 9
AND, AH, YE PROUD MAIDENS, YE ARE NOT SO FAIR, WHEN HIS OAR 91 OLD FISHERMAN V 9
RED ROSE, PROUD ROSE, SAD ROSE OF ALL MY DAYS! . . . . 100 ROSE UPON ROOD 1
RED ROSE, PROUD ROSE, SAD ROSE OF ALL MY DAYS. . . . . 101 ROSE UPON ROOD 24
WHAT WOULD YOU, KING OF THE PROUD RED BRANCH KINGS? . . . 102 FERGUS DRUID 8
WHAT WOULD YOU, KING OF THE PROUD RED BRANCH KINGS? . . . 102 FERGUS DRUID 15
A KING AND PROUD! AND THAT IS MY DESPAIR. . . . . . 103 FERGUS DRUID 16
WHAT WOULD YOU, KING OF THE PROUD RED BRANCH KINGS? . . . 103 FERGUS DRUID V 21
AND PROUD AS PRIAM MURDERED WITH HIS PEERS! . . . . . 120 SORROW OF LOVE 8

PROUD   (CONTINUED)
     AND OF THE PROUD EMBATTLED MULTITUDE . . . . 137 TO SOME I TALK V   10
     WITH THE LONELY, PROUD, WINGED MULTITUDE. . . . . . . 158 TO HIS HEART   V   7
     WITH THE PROUD, MAJESTICAL MULTITUDE. . . . . 158 TO HIS HEART   V   7
     AND THE PROUD DREAMING KING WHO FLUNG THE CROWN . . . 170 SECRET ROSE   19
     BE NOT UNKIND OR PROUD. . . . . 173 PLEADS FRIEND   4
     THAT'S ALL BUT GONE! FOR THE PROUD HEART IS GONE, . . 181 QUEEN MAEVE   20
     TALL, PROUD AND RUDDY, AND LIGHT WINGS . . . . 195 BAILE AILLINN   140
     THE PROUD AND CARELESS NOTES LIVE ON, ... 213 BLESS PSALTER   19
     HAVE SEEN IMMORTAL, MILD, PROUD SHADOWS WALK; . . . . 217 WOODS OF COOLE   12
     HOW SHALL I NAME YOU, IMMORTAL, MILD, PROUD SHADOWS? . 218 WOODS OF COOLE   27
     FOR I HAVE HEARD THAT HE WAS PROUD AND LAUGHING, . . 242 SHADOW WATER B   415
     WOMEN ARE HARD AND PROUD AND STUBBORN-HEARTED, . . . 245 SHADOW WATER B   479
     BECAUSE WE ARE NOT PROUD, IMPERISHABLE, ... 250 SHADOW WATER B   580
     AND TROD SO SWEETLY PROUD . . . . 255 WOMAN HOMER   17
     BETWEEN THE PROUD AND THE PROUD. . . . . 259 UNWORTH PRAISE   10
     BETWEEN THE PROUD AND THE PROUD. . . . . 259 UNWORTH PRAISE   10
     AND COPY THEIR PROUD STEADY GAZE. . . . . 273 GREY ROCK   64
     SHE'LL NOT BE PROUD, KNOWING WITHIN HER HEART . . . . 282 TWO KINGS   118
     FOR WHAT PROUD DEATH MAY BRING . . . . 317 NIGHT COME   3
     WHERE THE PROUD, WAYWARD SQUIRREL WENT, ... 317 APPOINTMENT   3
     NOW I HAVE LEARNT TO BE PROUD . . . . 349 HAWK   9
     AND THAT PROUD LOOK AS THOUGH SHE HAD GAZED INTO   354 HIS PHOENIX   29
         THE BURNING SUN,
     FOR PROUD, SOFT, CEREMONIOUS PROOF . . . . 386 ROBARTES DANCE   30
     AND THE PROUD STONES OF GREECE, ... 415 TOWER   159
     FOR INTELLECT WOULD MAKE US PROUD . . . . 460 THREE MONUMENT   10
     A PROUD WOMAN NOT KINDRED OF HIS SOUL. . . . . 479 SELF AND SOUL   64
     PROUD, OPEN-EYED AND LAUGHING TO THE TOMB. . . . . . 501 VACILLATION   34
     "A WOMAN CAN BE PROUD AND STIFF . . . . 513 JANE TALK BISH   13
     HIS PROUD HEART HE LEFT BEHIND. . . . . 561 FOUR AGES MAN   6
     THE PROUD FURIES EACH WITH HER TORCH ON HIGH. . . . . 579 DOR WELLESLEY   16
     FOR PARNELL WAS A PROUD MAN, ... 587 PARNELLITES   21
     AND A PROUD MAN'S A LOVELY MAN, ... 587 PARNELLITES   23
     THEY ARE GONE, THEY ARE GONE. THE PROUD MAY LIE BY THE 777 SONG DEIRDRE 3   1
         PROUD.
     THEY ARE GONE, THEY ARE GONE. THE PROUD MAY LIE BY THE 777 SONG DEIRDRE 3   1
         PROUD.
     MY RASCAL HEART IS PROUD . . . . 782 HEART FRIGHT   10
PROUDER
     NO PROUDER TROD THE GROUND, ... 587 PARNELLITES   22
PROUDEST
     THE PROUDEST OR MOST COY OF SPIRIT THINGS, ... 720 WITCH VIVIEN   7
PROUDLY
     PROUDLY IN HIS SAFFRON WALKING; . . . . 705 DAWN-SONG   2
PROVE
     IT WAS SO GIVEN OUT, BUT I WILL PROVE . . . . 243 SHADOW WATER B   429
     NOTHING BUT THAT TO PROVE YOUR BLOOD AND MINE. . . . 270 PARDON FATHERS   22
     AND PROVE OF ALL IMAGINABLE THINGS . . . . 371 EGO DOMINUS   73
     AND PROVE IF ALL IMAGINABLE THINGS . . . . 371 EGO DOMINUS   V   73
     I HAVE PRINCIPLES TO PROVE ME RIGHT. . . . . 386 ROBARTES DANCE   42
     THAT HE HAD FOUND A TEXT TO PROVE . . . . 492 ANNE GREGORY   15
     PROVE THAT I LIE. . . . . 517 HER ANXIETY   6
     PROVE THAT I LIE. . . . . 517 HER ANXIETY   12
     TO PROVE THEIR FORGERY TRUE! . . . . 582 ROGER CASEMENT   10
     FOR HISTORIES ARE THERE TO PROVE . . . . 583 GHOST ROG CASE   23
     COMPLEXION AND FORM PROVE SUPERHUMAN, ... 637 BEN BULBEN   6
     TO PROVE WHAT CAN YE DO? WHAT THINGS ABOVE . . . . . 650 ISLE STAT I 1   146
     TO PROVE HIS LOVE A KNIGHT WITH LANCE IN REST . . . . 651 ISLE STAT I 1   158
     SHALL NOT SO HOPELESS PROVE! SOME GOD MAY REST . . . 657 ISLE STAT I 3   61
PROVED
     . . . TO THE DUBLIN MUNICIPAL GALLERY IF IT WERE PROVED 287 TO WEALTHY MAN   T
     . . .
     WHO, WERE IT PROVED HE LIES, ... 291 TO A FRIEND   6
     WONDER HOW MANY TIMES I COULD HAVE PROVED MY WORTH . . 427 PHANTOM HATRED   34
     AND HAUGHTIER-HEADED BURKE THAT PROVED THE STATE A TREE, 481 BLOOD AND MOON   22
     AND GOD-APPOINTED BERKELEY THAT PROVED ALL THINGS A DREAM, 481 BLOOD AND MOON   25
     AND HAUGHTIER HEADED BURKE THAT PROVED THE STATE A TREE 481 BLOOD AND MOON V   22
PROVES
     AND THE LIGHT PROVES THAT HE IS READING STILL. . . . . 373 PHASES OF MOON   11
     BECAUSE IT PROVES THAT THINGS BOTH CAN AND CANNOT BE! . . 580 CURSE CROMWELL   19
PROVIDENCE
     AND THAT WOULD BE AGAINST GOD'S PROVIDENCE. . . . . . 339 SHEP GOATHERD   5
     AS I LOOK UP TO PROVIDENCE. . . . . 380 SONGS FOOL 1   6
PROW
     AND OVER THE TILLER AND THE PROW, ... 197 BAILE AILLINN   183
     ANOTHER ARGO'S PAINTED PROW . . . . 437 SONGS PLAY 1   11
     THE BOAT'S PROW GRATED ON THE SHALLOW SAND, ... 659 ISLE STAT II 1   11
     CURVING BENEATH THE PROW! AS SOME WILD DRAKE . . . . 659 ISLE STAT II 1   16
     ARE 'NEATH ITS PROW, AND CRUSHING SHELLS. . . . . . . 663 ISLE STAT II 2   35
PROWS
     AND CARVEN FIGURES ON THEIR PROWS . . . . 14 OISIN 1   190
     AND CARVEN FIGURES ON THEIR PROWS . . . . 23 OISIN 1   354
PRUDENT
     AND HE HAD KNOWN AT LAST SOME PRUDENT YEARS . . . . . 127 DREAM OF FAERY   15
PSALTERIES
     THE PLAYERS ASK FOR A BLESSING ON THE PSALTERIES AND ON 212 BLESS PSALTER   T
         THEMSELVES
     THE PLAYERS ASK FOR A BLESSING ON THE PSALTERIES   212 BLESS PSALTER   V   T
         AND THEMSELVES

	PAGE	TITLE		LINE
PUBERTY				
THAT GIRLS AT PUBERTY MAY FIND • • • • • • • • • •	617	LONG-LEG FLY		21
PUBLIC				
NOR PUBLIC MEN, NOR CHEERING CROWDS, • • • • • • •	328	IRISH AIRMAN		10
NOR PUBLIC MAN, NOR ANGRY CROWDS, • • • • • • • •	328	IRISH AIRMAN	V	10
NOR PUBLIC MAN, NOR CHEERING CROWDS, • • • • • • •	328	IRISH AIRMAN	V	10
"THE DRUNKARDS, PILFERERS OF PUBLIC FUNDS, • • • • •	352	PEOPLE		23
WHETHER IN PUBLIC OR IN SECRET RAGE • • • • • • •	413	TOWER		99
PUBLIC OPINION RIPENING FOR SO LONG • • • • • • •	428	NINETEEN 19		13
A SIXTY-YEAR-OLD SMILING PUBLIC MAN, • • • • • • •	443	SCHOOL CHILDR		8
A SIXTY YEAR OLD SMILING PUBLIC MAN, • • • • • • •	443	SCHOOL CHILDR	V	8
THEY HOLD THEIR PUBLIC MEETINGS WHERE • • • • • •	460	THREE MONUMENT		1
COME SPEAK YOUR BIT IN PUBLIC • • • • • • • • •	582	ROGER CASEMENT		21
NOW I AM IN THE PUBLIC HOUSE AND LEAN UPON THE WALL,	593	PILGRIM	V	21
THE MUSE IS MUTE WHEN PUBLIC MEN • • • • • • • •	597	MODEL LAUREATE		17
AND PRESSED AT MIDNIGHT IN SOME PUBLIC PLACE • • • •	610	STATUES		7
PUBLIC-HOUSE				
NOW I AM IN THE PUBLIC-HOUSE AND LEAN UPON THE WALL, • •	593	PILGRIM		21
PUBLISHED				
TO HAVE PUBLISHED ALL TO BE A WORLD'S DELIGHT, • • •	327	ROBERT GREGORY		72
AS A MAN DOES WHO HAS PUBLISHED A NEW BOOK, • • • •	350	HER PRAISE		3
PUDDLE				
HE HAD PUDDLE WATER IN HIS SHOES; • • • • • • • •	190	BAILE AILLINN	V	28
PUDDLE-WATER				
HE HAD PUDDLE-WATER IN HIS SHOES; • • • • • • • •	190	BAILE AILLINN		28
PUFF				
A GLITTERING SWORD OUT OF THE EAST. A PUFF OF WIND • •	426	PHANTOM HATRED		5
PUFF-BALLS				
PUFFED LIKE PUFF-BALLS ON A TREE, • • • • • • • •	727	LOVERS QUARREL		37
PUFFED				
• • • GONE AND PUFFED AWAY AND DEAD, • • • • • •	718	PHANTOM SHIP		3
PUFFED LIKE PUFF-BALLS ON A TREE, • • • • • • • •	727	LOVERS QUARREL		37
PULL				
OR ON THE UNPEOPLED WAVES WITH KINGS TO PULL AT THE OAR,	210	UNDER THE MOON		15
LONGING TO KNEAD AND PULL IT INTO SHAPE • • • • • •	246	SHADOW WATER B		510
I'LL FIND THE STABLE AND PULL OUT THE BOLT, • • • •	260	FASC DIFFICULT		13
PULL DOWN THE BLINDS, BRING FIDDLE AND CLARIONET • • •	311	MOUNTAIN TOMB		5
BEING CAUGHT BETWEEN THE PULL • • • • • • • • •	384	VISION ROBART		59
PULL DOWN ESTABLISHED HONOUR; HAWK FOR NEWS • • • •	398	LEADERS CROWD		3
BRIGHTNESS THAT I PULL BACK • • • • • • • • • •	533	FIRST CONFESS		13
THERE ARE SEVEN THAT PULL THE THREAD. • • • • • •	770	SPINNING SONG		1
PULLED				
HAVE PULLED THE IMMORTAL ROSE; • • • • • • • • •	174	ELEMENT POWERS		2
BLOSSOM PALE, SHE PULLED DOWN THE PALE BLOSSOM • • •	199	ARROW	V	5
AND ALL THE WHILE HER NEEDLE PULLED • • • • • • •	308	PLAYER QUEEN		7
SHE PULLED THE THREAD AND BIT THE THREAD • • • • •	308	PLAYER QUEEN		9
HOW SINEW THAT HAS BEEN PULLED TIGHT, • • • • • •	386	ROBARTES DANCE		34
FOR NATURE'S PULLED HER TRAGIC BUSKIN ON • • • • •	490	COOLE BALLYLEE		12
FOR NATURE'S PULLED HER TRAGIC BUCKSKIN ON • • • • •	490	COOLE BALLYLEE	V	12
FOR NATURE'D PULLED HER TRAGIC BUSKIN ON • • • • •	490	COOLE BALLYLEE	V	12
PULLERS				
ARE DOUBTFUL LIKE THESE PULLERS OF THE OAR; • • • •	748	SHADOW WATER A		30
BE PULLERS OF THE OAR UNTIL YOU DIE? • • • • • •	757	SHADOW WATER A		217
PULSE				
THE LIGHTNINGS PULSE--BEHOLD HER, AYE BEHOLD-- • • •	687	TWO TITANS		11
PULSES				
THAT FAN THE PULSES OF DELIGHTED AIR, • • • • • •	32	OISIN 2	V	50A
A CRAZY JUICE THAT MAKES THE PULSES BEAT • • • • •	384	VISION ROBART		54
PULSING				
OF LILAC O'ER THE PULSING WATER GLEAMS, • • • • • •	664	ISLE STAT II 2		48
PUMMELLED				
BUT MIGHT HAVE PUMMELLED AT A STONE • • • • • • •	307	HOUR DAWN		114
PUMMELLING				
HE GAVE HIM A GREAT PUMMELLING, • • • • • • • • •	307	HOUR DAWN		113
PUNISHMENT				
I ASK A FITTING PUNISHMENT FOR ALL • • • • • • •	235	SHADOW WATER B		290
BY THE INJUSTICE OF THE SKIES FOR PUNISHMENT? • • • •	316	COLD HEAVEN		12
PUNK				
COME SWISH AROUND, MY PRETTY PUNK, • • • • • • •	591	DRUNK SOBRIETY		1
A MERMAID, NOT A PUNK; • • • • • • • • • • •	592	DRUNK SOBRIETY		14
PUNY				
WITH FIERY SONG I'LL DROWN YON PUNY VOICE, • • • • •	648	ISLE STAT I 1		81
PUPILS				
DOES MINNALOUSHE KNOW THAT HIS PUPILS • • • • • • •	379	CAT AND MOON		21
PUPPY				
ARE OLD AND PUPPY HOUNDS; • • • • • • • • • •	99	FOXHUNTER	V	44
PURCHASED				
WHAT IS THIS FLESH I PURCHASED WITH MY PAINS, • • • •	499	MOTHER OF GOD		11
PURE				
BUT PURE AS A TALL CANDLE BEFORE THE TRINITY • • • •	208	HANRAHANS SONG V		14
AN AIMLESS JOY IS A PURE JOY," • • • • • • • •	338	TOM OROUGHLEY		4
THE PURE COLD LIGHT IN THE SKY • • • • • • • • •	378	CAT AND MOON		7
LIKE THIS PURE JET, NOW LOST AMID BLUE SKY, • • • •	464	HARUN RASHID		64
SEVEN CENTURIES HAVE PASSED AND IT IS PURE, • • • •	482	BLOOD AND MOON		33
SO ARROGANTLY PURE, A CHILD MIGHT THINK • • • • • •	491	COOLE BALLYLEE		23
NATURE'S PURE UNCHANGING LIGHT? • • • • • • • •	529	TOM LUNATIC		6
O BUT HEART'S WINE SHALL RUN PURE, • • • • • • •	554	CHURCH STATE		5
TRANSFIGURED TO PURE SUBSTANCE WHAT HAD ONCE • • • •	555	RIBH AT TOMB		11
GREW IN PURE MIND, BUT OUT OF WHAT BEGAN? • • • • •	630	CIRCUS ANIMALS		34
WORN BY THE SOLSTICE FIERCE, AND MADE IT PURE, • • •	692	MOSADA 1		57

PAGE   TITLE   LINE

PUREBRED
   THAT COULD HAVE SHOWN HOW PUREBRED HORSES • • • • •   325 ROBERT GREGORY V   36
PURE-BRED
   THAT COULD HAVE SHOWN HOW PURE-BRED HORSES • • • • •   325 ROBERT GREGORY   36
PURER
   BUT PURER THAN A TALL CANDLE BEFORE THE HOLY ROOD • • •   208 HANRAHANS SONG   14
   BUT PURER THAN A TALL CANDLE BEFORE THE BLESSED ROOD •   208 HANRAHANS SONG V   14
PURGATORY
   BECAUSE THE FIRES OF PURGATORY HAVE ATE THEIR SHAPES AWAY!   593 PILGRIM   13
   "PRAY FOR THE SOULS IN PURGATORY," THE PALE PRIEST   719 PHANTOM SHIP   31
     TREMBLING CRIES•
PURIFIED
   THOSE LOVERS, PURIFIED BY TRAGEDY, • • • • • • • •   555 RIBH AT TOMB   21
PURITY
   CAN HAVE THE PURITY OF A NATURAL FORCE, • • • • • • •   353 PEOPLE   31
   THAT PURITY BUILT UP THE STATE • • • • • • • • • • •   460 THREE MONUMENT   6
   THE PURITY OF THE UNCLOUDED MOON • • • • • • • • • •   482 BLOOD AND MOON   31
PURPLE
   AND TOLD THE PURPLE DEEPS THEIR PRIDE, • • • • • •   14 OISIN 1   186
   AND FILLS WITH STARS NIGHT'S PURPLE CUP, • • • • • •   18 OISIN 1   262
   OVER THE GLIMMERING PURPLE SEA. • • • • • • • • • •   25 OISIN 1   384
   ALL EMPTIED OF PURPLE HOURS AS A BEGGAR'S CLOAK IN THE   63 OISIN 3   219
     RAIN,
   OF PURPLE AND OF HEAVY GOLD! • • • • • • • • • •   81 MAD KING GOLL V   3
   THERE MIDNIGHT'S ALL A GLIMMER, AND NOON A PURPLE GLOW,   117 ISLE INNISFREE   7
   "HE WHO IS WRAPPED IN PURPLE ROBES, • • • • • •   134 FR GILLIGAN   45
   FROM BATTLE-BANNERS, FOLD UPON PURPLE FOLD, • • • •   162 ASKS FORGIVE   11
   FROM BATTLE BANNERS FOLD UPON PURPLE FOLD, • • • •   162 ASKS FORGIVE V   11
   NODDING HER PURPLE HOOD? • • • • • • • • • • • •   171 MAID QUIET V   2
   UNDER HER PURPLE HOOD. • • • • • • • • • • • •   171 MAID QUIET V   8
   ONE GATHERS UP HIS PURPLE GOWN! • • • • • • • • •   212 BLESS PSALTER   9
   THIS GREAT PURPLE BUTTERFLY, • • • • • • • • • •   381 SONG OF FOOL   1
   STITCHING AT A PURPLE HOARDED • • • • • • • • • •   440 WISDOM   12
   WRITTEN IN GOLD UPON A PURPLE STAIN, • • • • • • •   461 HARUN RASHID   10
   HEART'S PURPLE--AND ALL THESE I SET • • • • • • •   478 SELF AND SOUL   28
   THY WITHERED FOE, AND WITH THE PURPLE WING • • • •   688 TWO TITANS   55
   WITH PURPLE SANDALS SWEEP THE GRAVE-EYED HOURS--   705 REMEMBRANCE   5
   CREEPING ALONG THE HEAVENS' PURPLE CUP, • • • • •   714 FERENCZ RENYI   112
   AND MANY A PURPLE GILLYFLOWER EATEN, • • • • • •   729 PRIEST FAIRY   35
PURPOSE
   HIS PURPOSE DRIFTS AND DIES." • • • • • • • • •   45 OISIN 2   244
   HIS PURPOSE DRIFTS AWAY." • • • • • • • • • • •   45 OISIN 2 V   244
   YOU DO NOT SEE MY PURPOSE. I SHALL HAVE GONE • • •   238 SHADOW WATER B   357
   YOU DID NOT SEE MY PURPOSE. I SHALL HAVE GONE • • •   238 SHADOW WATER B V   357
   HEARTS WITH ONE PURPOSE ALONE • • • • • • • • • •   393 EASTER 1916   41
   THEIR PURPOSE IN THE LABYRINTH OF THE WIND! • • • •   433 NINETEEN 19   121
   SEEMED SO ON PURPOSE, MUTTERED JAFFER'S FRIENDS, • •   462 HARUN RASHID   37
   PROOF THAT THERE'S A PURPOSE SET • • • • • • • • •   639 BEN BULBEN   50
PURR
   THOUGH YOU GLOW AND YOU GLANCE, THOUGH YOU PURR AND YOU   90 OLD FISHERMAN   2
     DART!
   THOUGH YE GLOW AND YE GLANCE, THOUGH YE PURR AND YE DART,   90 OLD FISHERMAN V   2
PURSE
   THAT YOU MIGHT HAVE A HEAVIER PURSE, • • • • • • •   273 GREY ROCK   56
   THAT OLD PERPLEXITY AN EMPTY PURSE, • • • • • • •   491 COOLE BALLYLEE V   40G
   THAT OLD PERPLEXITY AN EMPTY PURSE, • • • • • • •   495 CHOICE   7
PURSES
   GAVE THEIR BODIES, EMPTIED PURSES • • • • • • • •   789 SINGING HEAD   19
PURSUE
   PURSUES THE THOUGHTS THAT I PURSUE, • • • • • • • •   633 MAN AND ECHO   32
PURSUES
   PURSUES THE THOUGHTS THAT I PURSUE, • • • • • • • •   633 MAN AND ECHO   32
PURSUING
   THE CHILD PURSUING LIZARDS IN THE GRASS, • • • • • •   686 LIFE   1
   THE CHILD PURSUING LIZARDS IN THE GRASS, • • • • • •   734 QUATRAIN APHOR V   1
   WHAT PURSUING OR FLEEING, • • • • • • • • • •   785 WOMANS BEAUTY   25
PUSH
   PUSH OUT HIS VIGOROUS LIMBS AND RUB HIS EYES, • • • •   284 TWO KINGS   162
   WHO GRIPS HIS LONG SPEAR SO TO PUSH • • • • • • •   385 ROBARTES DANCE   3
   HOW CAN THOSE TERRIFIED VAGUE FINGERS PUSH • • • • •   441 LEDA AND SWAN   5
PUSHED
   AND PUSHED THE LATCHES DOWN. • • • • • • • • • •   159 CAP AND BELLS   12
   AND PUSHED THE BRASS BOLT DOWN. • • • • • • • •   159 CAP AND BELLS V   12
   BUT THE OTHER PUSHED HIS HAND ASIDE, • • • • • • •   304 HOUR DAWN V   48
PUSHES
   THAT RUSTLES IN THE REEDS WITH PATIENT PUSHES, • • •   699 MOSADA 3   4
   THAT'S RUSTLING IN THE REEDS WITH PATIENT PUSHES, • •   699 MOSADA 3 V   4
PUSHING
   AND PUSHING IT INTO MY SHIRT, • • • • • • • • •   274 GREY ROCK   89
   AND WAS A PUSHING MAN • • • • • • • • • • • •   456 FRIENDS YOUTH   14
PUT
   PUT THE STAFF IN MY HANDS! • • • • • • •   61 OISIN 3   201
   "PUT THE CHAIR UPON THE GRASS! • • • • • • • • •   97 FOXHUNTER   9
   I'D PUT AWAY THE FOOLISH MIGHT OF A KING, • •   103 FERGUS DRUID V 21A
   "I PUT YOU FROM YOUR PAIN. I CAN NO MORE." • •   110 CUCHULAIN SEA   69
   PUT THAT MUSIC IN HER FACE? • • • • • • • • •   124 CATHLEEN PARA   10
   AND PUT A BERRY ON A THREAD! • • • • • • • •   149 WANDER AENGUS V   4
   YOU PUT SUCH FOLLY IN OUR HEADS • • • • • • •   190 BAILE AILLINN   32
   WHO WAS IT PUT SO GREAT A SCORN • • • • • •   190 BAILE AILLINN   41
   THAT PUT THIS HURRY IN MY SHOES." • • • • • • •   194 BAILE AILLINN   125
   HUM IN THE LIME-TREE FLOWERS! AND PUT AWAY • • • •   198 SEVEN WOODS   3

636

PUT   (CONTINUED)
    HUM IN THE LIME TREE FLOWERS: AND PUT AWAY . . . . . .   198 SEVEN WOODS   V   3
    AND FLYING TOWARDS THEIR PEACE. PUT BY THESE THOUGHTS,   226 SHADOW WATER B   91
    BUT IF I WERE TO PUT YOU ON THAT SHIP, ...   236 SHADOW WATER B   307
    IT HAD WASHED AMONG THE STARS AND PUT THEM OUT, ...   236 SHADOW WATER B   311
    I CAN PUT FEAR AWAY AS A QUEEN SHOULD. . . . .   238 SHADOW WATER B   355
    WE'LL PUT THIS MAN TO DEATH. I PROMISE IT. . . . . .   238 SHADOW WATER B   363
    HE HAS PUT A SUDDEN DARKNESS OVER THE MOON. . . . . .   239 SHADOW WATER B   367
    IT WAS THAT HARPER PUT IT IN MY THOUGHTS, ...   243 SHADOW WATER B   423
    WHEN WE HAVE PUT THEIR CHANGELESS IMAGE ON. . . . . .   250 SHADOW WATER B   582
    WHO CANNOT PUT ME FROM HIS SIGHT FOR EVER. . . . . .   251 SHADOW WATER B   601
    FORGAEL, BECAUSE YOU CANNOT PUT ME FROM YOU. . . . .   251 SHADOW WATER B   603
    "PUT OFF THAT MASK OF BURNING GOLD . . . .   263 MASK   1
    AND PUT HIS PATTERN ROUND THEIR TOPS . . . .   272 GREY ROCK   V   24
    MY MARRIED SISTER PUT INTO MY CARE . . . .   276 TWO KINGS   V   E
    SAID, "IF A WOMAN HAS PUT THIS ON YOU, ...   281 TWO KINGS   111
    THAT PUT A PASSION IN THE SLEEPER THERE, ...   284 TWO KINGS   157
    BEFORE YOU'LL PUT YOUR GUINEAS DOWN, ...   287 TO WEALTHY MAN   5
    BEFORE YOU'VE PUT YOUR GUINEAS DOWN, ...   287 TO WEALTHY MAN V   5
    AND THE GAUNT HOUSES PUT ON MAJESTY: . . . .   292 TO A SHADE   7
    "TIME TO PUT OFF THE WORLD AND GO SOMEWHERE . . . . .   299 BEGGAR CRIED   1
    YOU HAVE PUT THE THOUGHT IN RHYME. I WORKED ALL DAY, . .   341 SHEP GOATHERD   58
    OR PUT HIS HEART INTO SOME GAME . . . .   343 SHEP GOATHERD   105
    BUT PUT NO NAME AND LEAVE THEM AT HER DOOR. . . . . .   343 SHEP GOATHERD   116
    HEAVEN HAS PUT AWAY THE STROKE OF HER DOOM, ...   356 BROKEN DREAMS   11
    THE LIGHT IN THE TOWER WINDOW WAS PUT OUT. . . . . .   377 PHASES OF MOON   139
    YOU MEAN THEY ARGUED. PUT IT SO: . . . .   385 ROBARTES DANCE   13
    MAY I NOT PUT MYSELF TO COLLEGE? . . . .   385 ROBARTES DANCE   18
    THE INNUMERABLE CLANGING WINGS THAT HAVE PUT OUT THE MOON.   427 PHANTOM HATRED   32
    DID SHE PUT ON HIS KNOWLEDGE WITH HIS POWER . . . . .   441 LEDA AND SWAN   13
    AND PUT ALL TROY TO WRECK-- . . . .   455 HIS MEMORIES   16
    AND PUT ALL TROY TO WRACK-- . . . .   455 HIS MEMORIES   V   16
    AND PUT THAT CRACK IN IT, ...   455 FRIENDS YOUTH   2
    WHEN OUR BELOVED CALIPH PUT TO DEATH . . . .   462 HARUN RASHID   31
    PUT HER IN A RAGE. . . . .   504 QUARREL IN AGE   6
    A MAN MAY PUT PRETENCE AWAY . . . .   525 DANCING DAYS   19
    "WHAT CHANGE HAS PUT MY THOUGHTS ASTRAY . . . . . .   529 TOM LUNATIC   3
    THEIR MOBS PUT UNDER THEIR FEET. . . . .   554 CHURCH STATE   4
    OLD CIVILISATIONS PUT TO THE SWORD. . . . .   566 LAPIS LAZULI   27
    BUT WHEN HIS HORSE HAD PUT ITS HOOF . . . .   571 THREE BUSHES   50
    IN COUNTRY SHAWL OR PARIS CLOAK, HAD PUT MY WITS ASTRAY, .   592 PILGRIM   3
    FOR I CAN PUT THE WHOLE LOT DOWN, AND ALL I HAVE TO SAY   593 PILGRIM   24
    PUT JEWELRY IN THE PACK, ...   595 COLONEL MARTIN   24
    HAVE I, THAT PUT IT INTO WORDS, ...   604 YOU CONTENT   5
    COULD CRAZY JANE PUT OFF OLD AGE . . . .   606 SONGS BURDEN 1   19
    CALCULATIONS THAT LOOK BUT CASUAL FLESH, PUT DOWN . . .   610 STATUES   11
    EUROPE PUT OFF THAT FOAM WHEN PHIDIAS . . . .   610 STATUES   15
    AND BEING OLD SHE PUT A SKIN . . . .   621 JOHN KINSELLA   21
    DID WORDS OF MINE PUT TOO GREAT STRAIN . . . . . .   632 MAN AND ECHO   13
    QUATTROCENTO PUT IN PAINT . . . .   639 BEN BULBEN   53
    QUATTRO-CENTO PUT IN PAINT . . . .   639 BEN BULBEN   V   53
    THAT I WOULD BID MY PEOPLE PUT TO DEATH. . . . . .   760 SHADOW WATER A V   254
    PUT ALL YOUR POWER ON THE THREAD . . . .   771 SPINNING SONG   12
    THE SHAPE-CHANGERS THAT CAN PUT . . . .   775 AGAINST WITCH   2
    THE SHAPE CHANGERS THAT CAN PUT . . . .   775 AGAINST WITCH   V   2
    I PUT THREE PERSONS IN THEIR PLACE . . . .   787 HUDDON DUDDON   8
PUTS
    AND NOW THAT TIME PUTS WATER IN MY BLOOD, ...   222 SHADOW WATER B V 11A
    AND SOMEBODY PUTS HIS HAND IN THE DISH . . . . . .   301 RUN PARADISE   5
    PUTS ALL MEN IN A FRIGHT, ...   597 MODEL LAUREATE   12
PUTTING
    FROM MEAGRE GIRLHOOD'S PUTTING ON . . . .   356 BROKEN DREAMS   9
PYRE
    COME FORTH: THE MORN IS FAIR: AS FROM THE PYRE . . .   645 ISLE STAT I 1   8
    TENDER AND FEARLESS ON HER FUNERAL PYRE: . . . . .   688 NETTLESHIP   3
PYTHAGORAS
    WORLD-FAMOUS GOLDEN-THIGHED PYTHAGORAS . . . . . .   445 SCHOOL CHILDR   45
    WORLD-FAMOUS GOLDEN THIGHED PYTHAGORAS . . . . . .   445 SCHOOL CHILDR   V   45
    THERE STATELY PYTHAGORAS . . . .   531 DELPHIC ORACLE   9
    PYTHAGORAS PLANNED IT. WHY DID THE PEOPLE STARE? . . .   610 STATUES   1
    NO: GREATER THAN PYTHAGORAS, FOR THE MEN . . . . .   610 STATUES   9
    TALL PYTHAGORAS. . . . .   611 NEWS ORACLE   8
QUAFFED
    OF WOLVES, OF BOREAL BEARS, WE QUAFFED THE WINE . . .   41 OISIN 2   V 188
    IN OTHER LIVES? HAST THOU NOT QUAFFED OLD WINE . . .   724 KANVA ON SELF   12
QUAKE   SEE A-QUAKE
QUAKING
    WITH QUAKING JOINTS AND TERROR-STRICKEN FACES, . . .   185 QUEEN MAEVE   121
    WITH QUAKING JOINTS AND TERROR STRUCKEN FACES, . . .   185 QUEEN MAEVE   V 121
    WITH QUAKING JOINTS AND TERROR-STRUCKEN FACES, . . .   185 QUEEN MAEVE   V 121
QUALITY
    A QUALITY OF WISDOM FROM HER LOVE'S . . . .   469 HARUN RASHID   180
    PARTICULAR QUALITY. THE SIGNS AND SHAPES: . . . . .   469 HARUN RASHID   181
    QUALITY OF WISDOM FROM LOVE'S QUALITY, ...   469 HARUN RASHID   V 180
    QUALITY OF WISDOM FROM LOVE'S QUALITY, ...   469 HARUN RASHID   V 180
    FOR EVERY SEPARATE QUALITY OF LOVE: . . . .   469 HARUN RASHID   V 189A
QUARREL
    THE QUARREL OF THE SPARROWS IN THE EAVES, ...   119 SORROW OF LOVE V   1
    NOR BUT IN MERRIMENT A QUARREL. . . . .   405 FOR DAUGHTER   46
    QUARREL IN OLD AGE . . . .   503 QUARREL IN AGE   T
    A LOVER'S QUARREL AMONG THE FAIRIES. . . . .   726 LOVERS QUARREL   T

		PAGE	TITLE	LINE
QUARREL	(CONTINUED)			
	WE WILL NOT QUARREL, NOW THAT ALL IS WELL,	766	SHADOW WATER A	373
QUARRELLING				
	THIS NIGHT CAN SET US QUARRELLING,	324	ROBERT GREGORY	15
	THEY ARE ALWAYS QUARRELLING. GIVE ME YOUR SWORDS.	766	SHADOW WATER A	370
	EOCHA AND MAINE ARE ALWAYS QUARRELLING.	766	SHADOW WATER A	371
	ALE SETS THEM QUARRELLING. GIVE ME YOUR SWORDS.	766	SHADOW WATER A	372
	GIVE ME YOUR SWORDS. THEY ARE ALWAYS QUARRELLING.	766	SHADOW WATER A V	370
QUARRELS				
	AND QUARRELS ARE BLOWN UP UPON THAT HEAD!	324	ROBERT GREGORY	13
	NOR QUARRELS WITH A THOUGHT	345	ON WOMAN	7
	WHO QUARRELS OVER HALFPENNIES	621	JOHN KINSELLA	33
	WHO QUARRELS OVER HALF-PENNIES	621	JOHN KINSELLA V	33
QUARRIED				
	ON LIMESTONE QUARRIED NEAR THE SPOT	640	BEN BULBEN	90
QUARRY				
	HYSTERICA PASSIO DRAGGED THIS QUARRY DOWN.	542	PARN FUNERAL 1	21
QUARTER	SEE THREE-QUARTER			
	AND EVERY WINDY QUARTER HOWL	405	FOR DAUGHTER	71
	FROM EVERY QUARTER OF THE WORLD, CAN STAY	471	ALL SOUL NIGHT	12
	THAT QUARTER WHERE ALL THOUGHT IS DONE!	477	SELF AND SOUL	7
	SUCH FULLNESS IN THAT QUARTER OVERFLOWS	478	SELF AND SOUL	33
	A QUARTER OF THE HEAVENS FROM OUR RIGHT WAY.	754	SHADOW WATER A	155
	DIMMED AT THREE QUARTER LIGHT	786	YOUR HEART V	32
QUATRAINS				
	QUATRAINS AND APHORISMS.	734	QUATRAIN APHOR	T
QUATTROCENTO				
	DID QUATTROCENTO FINGER FASHION IT	444	SCHOOL CHILDR	26
	IT SEEMED A QUATTROCENTO PAINTER'S THRONG,	537	HER VISION	19
	QUATTROCENTO PUT IN PAINT	639	BEN BULBEN	53
QUATTRO-CENTO				
	IT SEEMED A QUATTRO-CENTO PAINTER'S THRONG	537	HER VISION V	19
	QUATTRO-CENTO PUT IN PAINT	639	BEN BULBEN V	53
QUAY				
	UPON THE OPEN ROAD, NEAR TO THE SLIGO QUAY—	391	UNDER SATURN	12
QUEEN				
	BUT THE YOUNG QUEEN WOULD NOT LISTEN:	159	CAP AND BELLS	9
	A QUEEN WAS LOVED BY A JESTER,	159	CAP AND BELLS V	1
	A QUEEN WAS BELOVED BY A JESTER,	159	CAP AND BELLS V	1
	THE OLD AGE OF QUEEN MAEVE	180	QUEEN MAEVE	T
	MAEVE THE GREAT QUEEN WAS PACING TO AND FRO,	180	QUEEN MAEVE	9
	BUT THAT GREAT QUEEN, WHO MORE THAN HALF THE NIGHT	180	QUEEN MAEVE	16
	HAVE I NOT BID YOU TELL OF THAT GREAT QUEEN	181	QUEEN MAEVE	34
	HE SAID, "HIGH QUEEN OF CRUACHAN AND MAGH AI,	183	QUEEN MAEVE	77
	HE SAID "QUEEN OF UNSHELTERED CRUACHAN,	183	QUEEN MAEVE V	77
	QUEEN OF HIGH CRUACHAN." "I OBEY YOUR WILL	184	QUEEN MAEVE	99
	OUTRUN THE MEASURE. I'D TELL OF THAT GREAT QUEEN	187	QUEEN MAEVE	141
	A KING AND A QUEEN ARE WANDERING THERE, AND THE SOUND	204	WITHER BOUGHS	19
	THERE IS A KING AND QUEEN UPON HER DECK,	232	SHADOW WATER B	226
	BUT HAVE NOT BITTEN YET. I AM A QUEEN,	235	SHADOW WATER B	280
	THAT YOU'LL NOT LET ME GO? I AM A QUEEN.	236	SHADOW WATER B	304
	BRING MADNESS? QUEEN, I AM NOT MAD. YET SAY	236	SHADOW WATER B	316
	I CAN PUT FEAR AWAY AS A QUEEN SHOULD.	238	SHADOW WATER B	355
	QUEEN, GIVE IT ME. NO, I HAVE NEED OF IT.	241	SHADOW WATER B	399
	BROKEN-HEARTED, HAVING LOST HIS QUEEN	242	SHADOW WATER B	407
	BROKENHEARTED, HAVING LOST HIS QUEEN	242	SHADOW WATER B V	407
	WESTWARD OF TARA. HURRYING TO HIS QUEEN	276	TWO KINGS	2
	HAVING NO THOUGHT BUT FOR HIS QUEEN EDAIN,	276	TWO KINGS V	I
	QUEEN MAEVE'S NINE MAINES HAD BEEN NURSED.	302	HOUR DAWN	8
	A SONG FROM "THE PLAYER QUEEN"	308	PLAYER QUEEN	T
	THE PLAYER QUEEN SONG FROM AN UNFINISHED PLAY	308	PLAYER QUEEN V	T
	ON THAT OLD QUEEN MEASURING A TOWN	344	DAWN	3
	ON THE OLD QUEEN MEASURING A TOWN	344	DAWN V	3
	THERE IS A QUEEN IN CHINA	353	HIS PHOENIX V	T
	THERE IS A QUEEN IN CHINA, OR MAYBE IT'S IN SPAIN,	353	HIS PHOENIX	1
	THERE IS A QUEEN IN CHINA, OR MAY BE IT'S IN SPAIN,	353	HIS PHOENIX V	1
	AND ONE, IT MAY BE, A QUEEN.	358	PRESENCES	14
	WHILE THAT GREAT QUEEN, THAT ROSE OUT OF THE SPRAY,	404	FOR DAUGHTER	27
	OF SAD QUEEN DIDO SHONE THE LAPPING FIRE	645	ISLE STAT I 1	9
	IS WORN AS THOUGH WITH FIRE. OH, GOBLIN QUEEN,	667	ISLE STAT II 3	36
	UPON MY NECKLACE. BUT THE GOBLIN QUEEN	676	ISLE STAT II 3	267
	OF THESE STAR-SHUDDERING SKIES, YOU ARE THE QUEEN.	679	ISLE STAT II 3	323
	OF THEIR TALL, NEW-FANGLED QUEEN.	727	LOVERS QUARREL	48
	"OF OUR GREAT QUEEN IS EVER HEARD	729	PRIEST FAIRY	41
	AND THEN THE FAY QUEEN SOBBED APART,	730	PRIEST FAIRY	70
	I HAVE BROUGHT HIS CROWN. AND I HAVE BROUGHT HIS QUEEN.	755	SHADOW WATER A	166
	WE BRING YOU THIS GREAT QUEEN.	755	SHADOW WATER A V	166
	THE GODS HOLD WATCH ABOUT THE WORDS OF A QUEEN.	756	SHADOW WATER A	191
	ALL THAT TIME KNOWS. SPEAK TO ME, QUEEN. O SPEAK!	756	SHADOW WATER A V	180
	IS IT YOUR WILL THAT I, WHO AM A QUEEN	757	SHADOW WATER A	212
	I CEASED TO BE A WOMAN, BEING A QUEEN.	758	SHADOW WATER A	228
	OF GOLDEN-ARMED IOLAN AND THE QUEEN	766	SHADOW WATER A	375
	OF GOLDEN ARMED AOLAN AND THE QUEEN	766	SHADOW WATER A V	375
	QUEEN EDAINE	771	SONG DEIRDRE 1 V	T
	"WHY IS IT," QUEEN EDAIN SAID,	771	SONG DEIRDRE 1	1
QUEENS				
	WEDDING THE QUEENS OF EARTHLY LANDS WITH RINGS	29	OISIN 2 V	10
	OF SEA-SPRUNG PEARL, AND QUEENS OF FAIRY LANDS	29	OISIN 2 V	10A
	QUEENS WROUGHT WITH GLIMMERING HANDS!	162	ASKS FORGIVE	12
	FOR THERE IS NO HIGH STORY ABOUT QUEENS	186	QUEEN MAEVE	134
	THE QUEENS THAT WERE IMAGINED LONG AGO,	201	OLD MEMORY	5

638

	PAGE	TITLE		LINE
QUEENS (CONTINUED)				
THEREIN ARE MANY QUEENS LIKE BRANWEN AND GUINEVERE;	209	UNDER THE MOON		11
QUEENS, THEIR EYES BLUE LIKE THE ICE,	214	HAPPY TOWNLAND		11
SHE WILL BE LIKE A WILD CAT; FOR THESE QUEENS	232	SHADOW WATER B		233
THEY HAVE IT THAT THE PLANS OF KINGS AND QUEENS	235	SHADOW WATER B		296
WHILE TALKING WITH HIS QUEENS,	345	ON WOMAN		12
AMONG THE QUEENS, AND CHOSE THE MIGHTIEST	757	SHADOW WATER A		213
QUEEN-WOMAN				
A QUEEN-WOMAN DRESSED OUT IN SILVER, CRY	210	RAGGED WOOD	V	2
PALE SILVER-PROUD QUEEN-WOMAN OF THE SKY,	211	RAGGED WOOD		6
QUEER				
OF HENWIVES AND OF QUEER OLD MEN	607	SONGS BURDEN 2		23
OF HEN WIVES AND OF QUEER OLD MEN	607	SONGS BURDEN 2	V	23
QUENCH				
THAT SHE MAY QUENCH THE RICK SHE HAS FIRED; AND THOUGH	282	TWO KINGS		116
I'LL QUENCH HIS SINGING WITH LOUD SONG—	647	ISLE STAT I 1		63
QUENCHED				
IT QUENCHED, WITH SOUND LIKE FALLING DEW,	86	MAD KING GOLL		66
QUENCHLESS				
WITH QUENCHLESS GAZE AND FLUTTERING HAIR.	12	OISIN 1		145
AND WITH QUENCHLESS EYES AND FLUTTERING HAIR	12	OISIN 1	V	144
A QUENCHLESS GRIEVING OF LOVE MELODY.	645	ISLE STAT I 1		21
QUERN				
AN OLD SLAVE GRINDING AT A HEAVY QUERN,	104	FERGUS DRUID		35
QUEST				
WILL CIRCLE ROUND THE WORLD UPON A QUEST,	651	ISLE STAT I 1		159
OH, BOY, I'M BOUND ON A MOST FEARFUL QUEST;	653	ISLE STAT I 2		31
THE LAKE-EMBOSOMED ISLE. NAY, THIS MY QUEST	657	ISLE STAT I 3		60
I BID THEE STAY, RENOUNCING THY MAD QUEST."	669	ISLE STAT II 3		89
HOW SPED THY QUEST? THIS PRELUDE WE'LL NOT HEAR IT.	673	ISLE STAT II 3		174
O, MY ALMINTOR, NOBLE WAS THY QUEST;	679	ISLE STAT II 3		319
QUESTION				
"DAY AFTER DAY YOU QUESTION ME, AND I,	281	TWO KINGS		99
QUESTION OF OURS, BEYOND OUR PITY EVEN.	282	TWO KINGS	V	130
FOR I WOULD ASK A QUESTION OF THEM ALL.	410	TOWER		24
AS I WOULD QUESTION ALL, COME ALL WHO CAN;	412	TOWER		89
WHAT HE CAN QUESTION, WHAT IF QUESTIONED I	494	AT ALGECIRAS		17
WHAT HE MAY QUESTION, WHAT IF QUESTIONED I	494	AT ALGECIRAS	V	17
BUT I NEVER STOPPED TO QUESTION, WHAT COULD THE BOATMAN SAY	593	PILGRIM		19
TURNS INTO A QUESTION TILL	632	MAN AND ECHO		8
TO QUESTION HER—OH NO, I DID NOT FEAR,	676	ISLE STAT II 3		265
WHERE SHALL I LAY ME DOWN? THAT QUESTION IS	700	MOSADA 3		36
A WEIGHTY QUESTION, FOR IT IS THE LAST.	700	MOSADA 3		37
QUESTIONED				
WHAT HE CAN QUESTION, WHAT IF QUESTIONED I	494	AT ALGECIRAS		17
WHAT HE MAY QUESTION, WHAT IF QUESTIONED I	494	AT ALGECIRAS	V	17
I CHOSE IT FOR MY LOT! IF QUESTIONED ON	535	CHOSEN		11
I SWEAR TO GOD I QUESTIONED THEM, AND ALL THEY HAD TO SAY	593	PILGRIM		14
I SWEAR TO GOD I QUESTIONED THEM ALL AND ALL THEY HAD TO SAY	593	PILGRIM	V	14
QUESTIONER				
YOUR QUESTIONER, OISIN, IS WORTHY, HE COMES FROM THE FENIAN LANDS."	51	OISIN 3		64
WORTHY'S THY QUESTIONER, OISIN, HE FROM THE FENIAN LANDS."	51	OISIN 3	V	64
MUCH ON THE GREAT QUESTIONER;	494	AT ALGECIRAS		16
QUESTIONING				
OUR QUESTIONING, BEYOND OUR PITY EVEN.	282	TWO KINGS		130
I WALK THROUGH THE LONG SCHOOLROOM QUESTIONING;	443	SCHOOL CHILDR		1
WHY THOSE QUESTIONING EYES	533	FIRST CONFESS		15
A GENTLE QUESTIONING LOOK THAT CANNOT HIDE	601	GALLERY REVIS		6
QUESTIONS				
WEARY OF MANY QUESTIONS; "THERE ARE THINGS	281	TWO KINGS		93
QUESTS				
SUCH QUESTS AS THESE, I TROW, NEED LITTLE WIT.	650	ISLE STAT I 1		150
QUICK				
AND MAY SOME DREADFUL ILL BEFALL HER QUICK!	74	ANASHU VIJAYA	V	59
BLUE-EYED, AND A QUICK RUNNER ON BARE FEET,	242	SHADOW WATER B		416
QUICKEN				
NEAR TO CUCHULLIN, ROUND A QUICKEN TREE,	111	CUCHULAIN SEA	V	81A
AND TEN BY TEN UNDER A QUICKEN TREE,	111	CUCHULAIN SEA	V	81A
TALL WANDS OF ALDER AND WHITE QUICKEN WANDS.	111	CUCHULAIN SEA	V	82A
UNDER THE WOVEN ROOFS OF QUICKEN BOUGHS;—	126	DREAM OF FAERY	V	11
RIDDLED WITH LIGHT. AH! WHEN THE GHOST BEGINS TO QUICKEN,	316	COLD HEAVEN		9
OF THE TARN WHERE YOUNG WAVES QUICKEN	647	ISLE STAT I 1		48
THE DANAAN QUICKEN TREE	742	DANAAN QUICK		T
(AH, MOURNFUL DANAAN QUICKEN TREE!)	742	DANAAN QUICK		6
(AH, MOURNFUL DANAAN QUICKEN TREE!)	743	DANAAN QUICK		12
(AH, MOURNFUL DANAAN QUICKEN TREE!)	743	DANAAN QUICK		18
(AH, MOURNFUL DANAAN QUICKEN TREE!)	743	DANAAN QUICK		24
(AH, MOURNFUL DANAAN QUICKEN TREE!)	743	DANAAN QUICK		30
QUICKLIME				
THAT IS IN QUICKLIME LAID.	582	ROGER CASEMENT		24
QUICK-LIME				
THAT IS IN THE QUICK-LIME LAID.	582	ROGER CASEMENT	V	24
QUICKLY				
THE SECOND BEST'S A GAY GOODNIGHT AND QUICKLY TURN AWAY.	459	FROM OEDIPUS		12
STRIKE QUICKLY; IT WILL FADE OUT WHEN YOU STRIKE.	759	SHADOW WATER A		238
THERE! THERE! THEY HAVE GONE QUICKLY, FOR ALREADY	764	SHADOW WATER A		326
QUIET				
AND LAID YOU ON THE GATES OF EVENING WITH HIS QUIET HANDS.	72	ANASHU VIJAYA		22
AND LAID YE ON THE GATES OF EVENING WITH HIS QUIET HANDS.	72	ANASHU VIJAYA	V	22

```
                                                              PAGE      TITLE        LINE
QUIET   (CONTINUED)
    THE VAN OF WANDERING QUIET! ERE YOU BE TOO CALM AND OLD,    73  ANASHU VIJAYA     43
    THE VAN OF WANDERING QUIET! ERE YE BE TOO CALM AND OLD,     73  ANASHU VIJAYA  V  43
    HID UNDER QUIET BOUGHS APART, . . . . . .                   78  INDIAN TO LOVE    12
    HID UNDER QUIET BOWS APART, . . . . . . .                   78  INDIAN TO LOVE V  12
    THE DRUID, GREY, WOOD NURTURED, QUIET EYED, . . . . .      101  ROSE UPON ROOD V   4
    BESIDE HER CLEAN-SWEPT HEARTH, HER QUIET SHADE!           114  ROSE OF BATTLE V  11
    BESIDES HER CLEAN SWEPT HEARTH, HER QUIET SHADE!          114  ROSE OF BATTLE V  11
    HAS PLANTED QUIET IN THE NIGHT; . . . . . . .             134  TWO TREES          8
    OF A QUIET AND LIGHT FOOTFALL; . . . . . . . .           159  CAP AND BELLS      8
    OF A QUIET AND LIGHT FOOT-FALL! . . . . . . .            159  CAP AND BELLS  V   8
    AND THE QUIET OF LOVE IN HER FEET. . . . . . .           161  CAP AND BELLS     36
    MAID QUIET . . . . . . . . . . . . . .                   171  MAID QUIET         T
    WHERE HAS MAID QUIET GONE TO, . . . . . . . .            171  MAID QUIET         1
    I NEVER HAVE SEEN MAID QUIET . . . . . . . .             171  MAID QUIET     V   1
    I AM CONTENTED, FOR I KNOW THAT QUIET . . . . . .        198  SEVEN WOODS       10
    WE SAT GROWN QUIET AT THE NAME OF LOVE; . . . . . .      205  ADAMS CURSE       28
    BUT WE HAVE ALL BENT LOW AND LOW AND KISSED THE QUIET FEET 207  HANRAHANS SONG     9
    BUT WE BEND TOGETHER AND KISS THE QUIET FEET . . . . .   207  HANRAHANS SONG V   4
    AND WINDS AND PONDS COVER MORE QUIET WOODS, . . . . .    218  WOODS OF COOLE    34
    AND THE GREEN QUIET, HAVE UPLIFTED THE HEART? . . . .    219  WOODS OF COOLE    40
    AT THE MOST QUIET MIDNIGHT IS TO BE STRICKEN. . . . .    236  SHADOW WATER B   321
    MAY BE A QUIET THOUGHT TO WIFE AND MOTHER, . . . . .     343  SHEP GOATHERD    118
    QUIET LANDS OR UNQUIET SEAS . . . . . . . .             360  ALF POLLEXFEN     19
    BY QUIET NATURES UNDERSTOOD . . . . . . . . .           405  FOR DAUGHTER      63
    THOSE AMOROUS CRIES THAT OUT OF QUIET COME . . . .      557  RIBH ECSTASY       7
    MY TEMPTATION IS QUIET. . . . . . . . .                575  ACRE OF GRASS      7
    QUIET THE DOG, TETHER THE PONY . . . . . . .           617  LONG-LEG FLY       3
    ALL THINGS ARE QUIET IN THE EVE'S WIDE EYE. . . . .     662  ISLE STAT II 2     6
    AND ALL WAS QUIET ROUND ME SPREAD, . . . . . .         670  ISLE STAT II 3   112
    AS QUIET AS THE CLAY-COLD DEAD. . . . . . . .          670  ISLE STAT II 3   113
    AS QUIET AS THE LITTLE RIVULETS . . . . . .           698  MOSADA 2          57
    ENCLOSE A QUIET PLACE OF BEDS BOX-BORDERED, BEES, . .  710  FERENCZ RENYI     24
    WITH QUIET SHADE ITS EVER DEWY-PLOT. . . . . .        714  FERENCZ RENYI    109
    WITH QUIET SHADE ITS EVER DEWY SPOT, . . . . .        714  FERENCZ RENYI V  109
    WITH QUIET SHADE ITS EVER DEWY PLOT. . . . . .        714  FERENCZ RENYI V  109
QUIET-EYED
    THE DRUID, GREY, WOOD-NURTURED, QUIET-EYED, . . . . .  101  ROSE UPON ROOD     4
QUIETNESS
    SHOOT ON HIM SHAFTS OF QUIETNESS, THAT HE MAY EVER KEEP 75  ANASHU VIJAYA     81
    SHOOT ON HIM SHAFTS OF QUIETNESS, AND ORDER HIM TO KEEP 75  ANASHU VIJAYA V   81
    "I AM LONE LADY QUIETNESS, MY SWEET, . . . . . . .    716  DWELT SYCAMORE    13
QUIET'S
    QUIET'S WILD HEART, LIKE DAILY MEAT! . . . . . . .    196  BAILE AILLINN    178
QUIETUDE
    FOR THREE DAYS MORE IN DREADFUL QUIETUDE, . . . . .   110  CUCHULAIN SEA     78
    UPON A MEASURED QUIETUDE. . . . . . . . . .          138  TO IRELAND        16
    UPON HER HOLY QUIETUDE. . . . . . . . . .           138  TO IRELAND    V   16
QUINTO-CENTO
    WHAT QUINTO-CENTO FINGER FASHIONED IT, . . . . . .   444  SCHOOL CHILDR V   26
QUIRE
    WITH YOUR HARMONIOUS QUIRE, . . . . . . . .         174  ELEMENT POWERS V   8
QUIRES
    AND A FAR SOUND OF FEATHERY QUIRES! . . . . . . .     13  OISIN 1          166
QUITE
    QUITE SOON THE CORNFIELD, WHERE THE POPPIES GROW, . . 699  MOSADA 3           7
QUIVER
    AND NOW THE WARMTH OF SIGHS, AND AFTER THE QUIVER OF LIPS. 47  OISIN 3         8
    . . . AND THE QUIVER OF STRETCHED BOWSTRINGS, . . . .  62  OISIN 3          207
    A CLOUDY QUIVER OVER PAIRC-NA-LEE. . . . . . .       198  SEVEN WOODS       14
QUIVERING
    IN A RED AND QUIVERING GARMENT . . . . . . . .      160  CAP AND BELLS     15
    IN A GARMENT RED AND QUIVERING, . . . . . . .       160  CAP AND BELLS V   15
    THE QUIVERING HALF-CLOSED EYELIDS, THE RAGS OF CLOUD OR 427  PHANTOM HATRED   26
        OF LACE.
    DOTH NOT YON BIRD, YON QUIVERING BIRD, REJOICE? . . .  652  ISLE STAT I 2   21
    PIERCING THE QUIVERING WATERS THROUGH AND THROUGH, . .  664  ISLE STAT II 2  44
    DID I ON QUIVERING PINIONS HASTE. . . . . . .         670  ISLE STAT II 3  111
    WAS BROKEN IN HIS QUIVERING HAND. . . . . . .         671  ISLE STAT II 3  126
    HIS BODY SHAKE?  AY, QUIVERING AS YON SMOKE . . . .   683  SEEKER           36
    TO DEATH.  HIS LIPS ARE GLUED, WITH QUIVERING TOUCH,  . .  684  SEEKER     V   63
    YOU'RE PALE, MY LORD.  HIS LIPS ARE QUIVERING;  . .   704  MOSADA 3        127
    AND SEIZE HER, AND THUS FLOATS HER QUIVERING CRY!  . .  714  FERENCZ RENYI  105
QUOTE
    THAT THEY WOULD SIGH AND QUOTE WITH LEARNED LOOKS  . . .  205  ADAMS CURSE   25
RABBAN     SEE ABD-AL-RABBAN AL-RABBAN
RABBIT
    A RABBIT OLD AND LAME LIMPED DOWN THE PATH;  . . . . .  80  EPHEMERA         15
    AND SHY AS A RABBIT, . . . . . . . . . .              89  ISLE IN WATER     13
    LIKE SOME OLD RABBIT TO MY CLEFT . . . . . . .       307  HOUR DAWN        105
    INTO A RABBIT HOLE . . . . . . . . . .               571  THREE BUSHES V    51
    A STRICKEN RABBIT IS CRYING OUT, . . . . . . .       633  MAN AND ECHO      45
RABBIT-HOLE
    INTO A RABBIT-HOLE . . . . . . . . . .               571  THREE BUSHES      51
RACE
    THE MIGHTIER MASTERS OF A MIGHTIER RACE!  . . . . . .  38  OISIN 2          133
    OF PLANETS WATCHING, WATCHING THE RACE OF HARES . . . .  44  OISIN 2     V 228B
    "LAST OF MY RACE, THREE THINGS I RULE ALONE-- . . . .  45  OISIN 2     V 239A
    AND A SMALL AND A FEEBLE RACE STOOPING WITH MATTOCK AND  58  OISIN 3     V  164
        SPADE.
```

640

RACE   (CONTINUED)   PAGE   TITLE   LINE
  AND A SMALL AND FEEBLE RACE STOOPING WITH MATTOCK
    AND SPADE.   58 OISIN 3   V 164
  SLEIVEENS WERE ALL HIS RACE:
  LIKE THE PALE WATERS IN THEIR WINTRY RACE,   92 FATHER OHART   6
  THERE DWELT A GAY, EXULTING, GENTLE RACE   112 ROSE OF WORLD   8
  OLD SILENCE BIDS ITS CHOSEN RACE REJOICE,   127 DREAM OF FAERY   20
  AND THEREFORE, FRIEND, IF YOUR GREAT RACE WERE RUN   127 DREAM OF FAERY   31
  OUT YONDER, WHERE THE RACE COURSE IS,   265 THESE CLOUDS   7
  CRYING ALOUD AS THE RACE COURSE IS,   266 GALWAY RACES   V   1
  TOWARDS NIGHTFALL UPON A RACE   266 GALWAY RACES   V   14
  HE RODE A RACE WITHOUT A BIT?   325 ROBERT GREGORY   31
  TO WRITE FOR MY OWN RACE   326 ROBERT GREGORY   63
  HER RACE   347 FISHERMAN   11
  UNRECKONABLE RACE: 365 HER RACE   T
  ROSE OUT OF THE RACE   365 HER RACE   8
  UNDER MY WINDOW-LEDGE THE WATERS RACE,   480 BLOOD AND MOON   4
  BUT THE GOLDEN RACE LOOKS DIM,   490 COOLE BALLYLEE   1
  DID EVER MAN RIDE SUCH A RACE?   530 DELPHIC ORACLE   4
  THAT OF RACE AND THAT OF SOUL,   570 THREE BUSHES   47
  POOR RACE OF LEAFY ARCADY, YOUR LOVE   637 BEN BULBEN   15
  OF LOVE FROM OUT A DREAMLESS RACE FOR STRIFE,   650 ISLE STAT I 1   145
  IN TRUTH, AN EVIL RACE. WHY STRIVE FOR HER,   684 SEEKER   58
  LAY DOWN THE BURDEN OF THY RACE,   696 MOSADA 2   9
  "I ASK THAT I AND ALL MY RACE,"   736 SUMMER EVENING   14
  "MAY STAND BEFORE THY RACE AND THEE   742 EARL PAUL   61
RACECOURSE   742 EARL PAUL   63
  CRYING ALOUD AS THE RACECOURSE IS   266 GALWAY RACES   14
  THERE WHERE THE RACECOURSE IS   266 GALWAY RACES   V   1
RACE-COURSE
  CRYING ALOUD AS THE RACE-COURSE IS,   266 GALWAY RACES   V   14
RACECOURSES
  FOR HORSEMANSHIP AT MEETS OR AT RACECOURSES,   325 ROBERT GREGORY   35
  IN MUSCULAR YOUTH, AT MEETS OR AT RACECOURSES,   325 ROBERT GREGORY   35
RACE-COURSES
  FOR HORSEMANSHIP AT MEETS OR AT RACE-COURSES,   325 ROBERT GREGORY V   35
RACED
  THE HORSE TOWARDS THE MUSIC RACED,   13 OISIN 1   169
  THE STEED TOWARDS THE MUSIC RACED,   13 OISIN 1   V 169
RACES
  AT GALWAY RACES   266 GALWAY RACES   T
  GALWAY RACES   266 GALWAY RACES   V   T
RACHLIN
  . . . FROM RACHLIN TO BERA OF SHIPS.   58 OISIN 3   160
RACK
  THEN THEY AND THEIR WISDOM WENT TO RACK: 566 LAPIS LAZULI   28
RADDLED
  AND RAISING ARMS ALL RADDLED WITH THE DYE,   105 CUCHULAIN SEA   7
  SHE SMOTE WITH RADDLED FIST, AND WHERE HER SON   106 CUCHULAIN SEA   18
RADDLING
  TO EMER, RADDLING RAIMENT IN HER DUN,   105 CUCHULAIN SEA   2
RADICAL
  THE SOUL RECOVERS RADICAL INNOCENCE   405 FOR DAUGHTER   66
RAFTER
  THAT SHAKES A MOULDERING COBWEB FROM THE RAFTER: 130 BOOK STORIES   19
  LEAPING TO SHAKE A COBWEB FROM THE RAFTER!   130 BOOK STORIES   V   19
  AND SHAKE A MOULDERING COBWEB FROM THE RAFTER,   130 BOOK STORIES   V   19
RAFTERY'S
  THEN DARKENING THROUGH "DARK" RAFTERY'S "CELLAR" DROP, 490 COOLE BALLYLEE   4
RAG
  IN AS FOUL A RAG: 525 DANCING DAYS   6
  CONSUMING ITS RAG AND BONE,   575 ACRE OF GRASS   11
  FOR PASSING ROUND THE BOTTLE WITH GIRLS IN RAG OR SILK, 592 PILGRIM   2
  SO COME IN RAG OR COME IN SILK, IN CLOAK OR COUNTRY SHAWL, 593 PILGRIM   V   22
  IN THE FOUL RAG AND BONE SHOP OF THE HEART.   630 CIRCUS ANIMALS V   40
RAG-AND-BONE
  IN THE FOUL RAG-AND-BONE SHOP OF THE HEART.   630 CIRCUS ANIMALS   40
RAGE   SEE WAR-RAGE
  KINGFISHER COLOUR GREW WITH RAGE. HE ROSE   40 OISIN 2   V 169
  LIGHT IS MAN'S LOVE, AND LIGHTER IS MAN'S RAGE: 45 OISIN 2   243
  . . . WHO COULD BREAK UP THE WORLD IN THEIR RAGE: 62 OISIN 3   214
  BUT NOW THE WAR RAGE IN CUCHULAIN WOKE,   110 CUCHULAIN SEA   V 65
  AND CRAZY RASCALS RAGE THEIR FILL   131 OLD PENSIONER   9
  WHEN TIME BEGAN TO RANT AND RAGE   138 TO IRELAND   10
  TO RANT AND RAGE IN FLOOD AND WIND: 138 TO IRELAND   26
  THE BEGGAR IN A RAGE BEGAN   306 HOUR DAWN   80
  AND THAT HE WILL TURN GREEN WITH RAGE   385 ROBARTES DANCE   16
  WHETHER IN PUBLIC OR IN SECRET RAGE   413 TOWER   99
  HOW THE DAEMONIC RAGE   419 MY HOUSE   16
  HOW THE DEMONIC RAGE   419 MY HOUSE   V   16
  THE RAGE DRIVEN, RAGE TORMENTED, AND RAGE HUNGRY TROOP, 426 PHANTOM HATRED V 11
  THE RAGE DRIVEN, RAGE TORMENTED, AND RAGE HUNGRY TROOP, 426 PHANTOM HATRED V 11
  THE RAGE DRIVEN, RAGE TORMENTED, AND RAGE HUNGRY TROOP, 426 PHANTOM HATRED V 11
  OR EYES THAT RAGE HAS BRIGHTENED, ARMS IT HAS MADE LEAN, 426 PHANTOM HATRED V 27
  OF EYES THAT RAGE HAS BRIGHTENED, ARMS IT HAS MADE LEAN, 427 PHANTOM HATRED V 27
  THAT IMAGE CAN BRING WILDNESS, BRING A RAGE   431 NINETEEN 19   80
  MUCH DID I RAGE WHEN YOUNG,   434 YOUTH AND AGE   1
  AND THINKING OF THAT FIT OF GRIEF OR RAGE   443 SCHOOL CHILDR   17
  I RAGE AT MY OWN IMAGE IN THE GLASS   447 HERO GIRL FOOL   1
  FOR ALL MEN LOVE YOUR WORTH: AND I MUST RAGE   447 HERO GIRL FOOL V   B
  PUT HER IN A RAGE.   504 QUARREL IN AGE   6

	PAGE	TITLE	LINE

RAGE (CONTINUED)
IN NOBLE RAGE REPLIED . . . . 516 MANS SONG 5
TOO OLD FOR A MAN'S LOVE I STOOD IN RAGE . . . . . 536 HER VISION 3
HE IN HIS RAGE DECLARED, ... 539 MEETING 14
IT HAD NOT TOUCHED OUR LIVES. BUT POPULAR RAGE, . . 542 PARN FUNERAL 1 20
LET THE FOOLS RAGE, I SWERVED IN NAUGHT, ... 577 WHAT THEN 18
YOU THINK IT HORRIBLE THAT LUST AND RAGE . . . . 591 SPUR 1
AND FILL ME WITH THY RAGE, THAT I MAY BRUISE . . 698 MOSADA 2 54
RAGED
I HAVE RAGED AT MY OWN STRENGTH BECAUSE YOU HAVE LOVED IT. 448 HERO GIRL FOOL 9
TOO OLD FOR A MAN'S LOVE I STOOD AND RAGED . . . . 536 HER VISION V 1
RAGE-DRIVEN
THE RAGE-DRIVEN, RAGE-TORMENTED, AND RAGE-HUNGRY TROOP, 426 PHANTOM HATRED 11
RAGE-HUNGRY
THE RAGE-DRIVEN, RAGE-TORMENTED, AND RAGE-HUNGRY TROOP, 426 PHANTOM HATRED 11
RAGES
RAGES AT HIS OWN IMAGE IN THE ENAMELLED SEA . . . . 77 INDIAN TO LOVE V 5
THOUGH HAMLET RAMBLES AND LEAR RAGES, ... 566 LAPIS LAZULI 21
RAGE-TORMENTED
THE RAGE-DRIVEN, RAGE-TORMENTED, AND RAGE-HUNGRY TROOP, 426 PHANTOM HATRED 11
RAGGED
AND SHAKE THEIR RAGGED WINGS! ALAS! . . . . . . 136 TWO TREES 38
HE HAD RAGGED LONG GRASS-COLOURED HAIR; . . . . 190 BAILE AILLINN 26
HE HAD RAGGED, LONG GRASS-YELLOW HAIR; . . . . 190 BAILE AILLINN V 26
WHEN IN RAGGED VAPOUR THEY MUTTER NIGHT AND DAY, . 206 HANRAHANS SONG V 2
THE RAGGED WOOD . . . . 210 RAGGED WOOD T
I HEARD UNDER A RAGGED HOLLOW WOOD, ... 210 RAGGED WOOD V 1
O HURRY TO THE RAGGED WOOD, FOR THERE . . . . 211 RAGGED WOOD 9
AFTER A RAGGED HAT IN BISCAY BAY; . . . . . . 270 PARDON FATHERS 14
OLD RAGGED ELMS, OLD THORNS INNUMERABLE, . . . 419 MY HOUSE 5
UNDER THE RAGGED THORN? . . . . 519 LOVES LONENESS 10
NO RAGGED BEGGAR-MAN, ... 567 FROM JAPANESE 6
NO RAGGED BEGGAR MAN, ... 567 FROM JAPANESE V 6
A GREAT BLACK RAGGED BIRD APPEARED WHEN I WAS IN THE BOAT; 593 PILGRIM 16
WITH A RAGGED BANDIT CLOAK, ... 627 STATES HOLIDAY 31
GAZE ON TILL RAGGED TIME HIMSELF DECAY. . . . . 672 ISLE STAT II 3 148
ARE TWO RAGGED CHILDREN BRIGHT— . . . . . . 731 STREET DANCERS 4
RAGING
RAGING AT HIS OWN IMAGE IN THE ENAMELLED SEA. . . 77 INDIAN TO LOVE 5
RAGING AT HIS OWN IMAGE IN THE DIM ENAMELLED SEA . 77 INDIAN TO LOVE V 5
A HEAVENLY MANSION, RAGING IN THE DARK. . . . . 491 COOLE BALLYLEE V 40D
A HEAVENLY MANSION, RAGING IN THE DARK. . . . 495 CHOICE 4
RAVENING, RAGING, AND UPROOTING THAT HE MAY COME . 563 MERU 6
MY FATHER UPON THE ABBEY STAGE, BEFORE HIM A RAGING CROWD; 577 LOFTY THINGS 2
RAGS
. . . SAILS TURNING TO THREADBARE RAGS; . . . . 55 OISIN 3 118
. . . SAILS TURNING TO THREAD-BARE RAGS; . . . 55 OISIN 3 V 118
WHILE HE'D RUMMAGED RAGS AND HAIR, ... 299 THREE HERMITS 29
A BUNDLE OF RAGS UPON A CRUTCH, ... 302 HOUR DAWN 2
IF THERE BE RAGS ENOUGH HE WILL KNOW HER NAME . . 351 HER PRAISE 15
"VENGEANCE FOR JACQUES MOLAY." IN CLOUD—PALE RAGS, OR
IN LACE, 426 PHANTOM HATRED 10
"VENGENCE FOR JACQUES MOLAY." IN CLOUD PALE RAGS, OR IN
LACE, 426 PHANTOM HATRED V 10
THE QUIVERING HALF-CLOSED EYELIDS, THE RAGS OF CLOUD OR
OF LACE, 427 PHANTOM HATRED 26
FOR PASSING ROUND THE BOTTLE WITH GIRLS IN RAGS OR SILK, 592 PILGRIM 2
SO COME IN RAGS OR COME IN SILK, IN CLOAK OR COUNTRY SHAWL, 593 PILGRIM 22
OLD IRON, OLD BONES, OLD RAGS, THAT RAVING SLUT . . . 630 CIRCUS ANIMALS 37
RAIL
EVEN LIKE THESE TO RAIL AND SWEAT . . . . . . 294 HATED PLAYBOY 5
AND LIKE THESE TO RAIL AND SWEAT . . . . . . 294 HATED PLAYBOY V 5
THEY SAT UPON THEIR HEELS TO RAIL, ... 297 THREE BEGGARS 53
OR SAT UPON THEIR HEELS TO RAIL . . . . . . 297 THREE BEGGARS V 53
AND RUBBED ALONG THE RAIL HIS NOSE. . . . . . 725 LEGEND 28
RAILING
IF RAILING AND REPROACH AND MOCKERY . . . . . 243 SHADOW WATER B 438
RAILS   SEE ALTAR-RAILS
O COLLEENS, KNEELING BY YOUR ALTAR RAILS LONG HENCE, . 173 SPEAKS HEARERS V 1
O, WOMEN, KNEELING BY YOUR ALTAR RAILS LONG HENCE, . 173 SPEAKS HEARERS V 1
AND THE GHASTLY GHOST-FLAMES GLIMMER ALL ALONG THE TAFFRAIL
RAILS 719 PHANTOM SHIP 21
AND THE GHASTLY GHOST FLAMES GLIMMER ALONG THE TAFFREL
RAILS, 719 PHANTOM SHIP V 21
RAIMENT
AND BY ME, IN SOFT RED RAIMENT, THE FENIANS MOVED IN LOUD
STREAMS; 53 OISIN 3 93
TO EMER, RADDLING RAIMENT IN HER DUN, ... 105 CUCHULAIN SEA 2
AND CALM, ROBED ALL IN RAIMENT MOONY WHITE. . . . 693 MOSADA 1 77
RAIN
ALL EMPTIED OF PURPLE HOURS AS A BEGGAR'S CLOAK IN THE
RAIN, 63 OISIN 3 219
IS BUT A SLIDING DROP OF RAIN BETWEEN HIS PETALS WIDE. . 76 INDIAN ON GOD 12
IS BUT A SLIDING DROP OF RAIN WITHIN HIS PETALS WIDE." . 76 INDIAN ON GOD V 12
WHO HAVE SOUGHT MORE THAN IS IN RAIN OR DEW . . . 114 ROSE OF BATTLE 16
ALTHOUGH I SHELTER FROM THE RAIN . . . . . . 131 OLD PENSIONER 1
MIRRORED IN STREAMS THAT NEITHER HAIL NOR RAIN . . 184 QUEEN MAEVE 89
BY RIVERS WHERE THE RAIN HAS NEVER DIMMED . . . 184 QUEEN MAEVE V 87
BY RIVERS WHERE NOR RAIN NOR HAIL HAS DIMMED . . 184 QUEEN MAEVE V 87
MIRRORED IN WATERS THAT NOR HAIL NOR RAIN . . . 184 QUEEN MAEVE V 89
WHEN THE RAIN IS PELTING OUT OF THE WINTRY AIR; . . 207 HANRAHANS SONG V 12

642

	PAGE	TITLE		LINE

RAIN (CONTINUED)
THE SOUND OF THE RAIN OR SOUND . . . . 419 MY HOUSE 6
OF THE FOUL WEATHER, HAIL AND RAIN, ... 424 ROAD AT DOOR 9
BETWEEN TWO BUSHES UNDER THE RAIN; . . . . 551 SONGS REWRIT 1 14
WITH LITTLE CRIES OF JOY HE KISSED THE RAIN . . . . . . 688 TWO TITANS 33
DEEP IN HIS SOUL, LIKE RAIN UPON A SOIL . . . . 692 MOSADA 1 56
RAIN-BEATEN
WITH ALL THEIR ANCIENT FACES LIKE RAIN-BEATEN STONES, . . 318 MAGI 4
RAINBOW
LIKE DROPS OF FROZEN RAINBOW LIGHT, ... 14 OISIN 1 183
DROPPING LIQUID RAINBOW LIGHT, ... 732 STREET DANCERS 33
RAINLESS
AT EVENING IN THEIR RAINLESS LANDS." . . . . 7 OISIN 1 70
AT EVENING IN THEIR RAINLESS LANDS. . . . . 7 OISIN 1 V 66
RAINS
THE RAINS ARE FROM HIS DRIPPING WING, THE MOONBEAMS FROM 76 INDIAN ON GOD 8
HIS EYE.
AND RAINS DOWN LIFE UNTIL THE BASIN SPILLS, ... 417 ANCEST HOUSES 4
AND MOUNTS MORE DIZZY HIGH THE MORE IT RAINS . . . . . 417 ANCEST HOUSES 5
RAISE
THAT RAISE THEIR HEADS AND WANDER SINGING, ... 27 OISIN 1 419
SING, O YOU LITTLE STARS! O SING AND RAISE YOUR RAPTUROUS 72 ANASHU VIJAYA 20
CAROL
SING, OH YE LITTLE STARS! OH, SING, AND RAISE YOUR 72 ANASHU VIJAYA V 20
RAPTUROUS CAROL
SING, TILL YOU RAISE YOUR HANDS AND SIGH, ... 73 ANASHU VIJAYA 45
SING, TILL YE RAISE YOUR HANDS AND SIGH, ... 73 ANASHU VIJAYA V 45
THAT MAKES ME FEAR TO RAISE A HAND AGAINST HIM, ... 222 SHADOW WATER B V 16A
HOW CAN WE RAISE THE KEEN THAT DO NOT KNOW . . . . . . 240 SHADOW WATER B 389
AND RAISE HIS PILLAR STONE." KING EOCHAID SAID, ... 280 TWO KINGS V 83
DRAW ROUND AND RAISE A SHOUT; . . . . 584 GHOST ROG CASE 38
THEN BID THEM RAISE MY STATUE ON THE SHORE; . . . . . 663 ISLE STAT II 2 18
GO UP AND DOWN, AND RAISE THEIR HEADS AND SING . . . . 682 SEEKER 30
MY ECHOING HEART. NOW RAISE THY VOICE AND SPEAK! . . . 683 SEEKER 47
I HEAR THE MURMUR AS THEY RAISE THE BEAMS . . . . . . 699 MOSADA 3 17
RAISE THE DOOR-PIN WITH ALARM, ... 727 LOVERS QUARREL 52
TO RAISE INTO BEING . . . . 784 WOMANS BEAUTY 13
RAISED   SEE UP-RAISED
AND WEPT, AND RAISED THEIR LAMENTING HANDS, ... 10 OISIN 1 112
THEY WEPT, AND RAISED LAMENTING HANDS. . . . . 10 OISIN 1 V 112
HURRIED AWAY, AND OVER HER RAISED . . . . 12 OISIN 1 V 142B
IN OUR RAISED EYES THERE FLASHED A GLOW . . . . 22 OISIN 1 327
HE SHIVERING PAUSED, AND RAISED HIS HEAD AND SCREAMED. . 30 OISIN 2 V 25
A LITTLE WAY WITHIN THE GLOOM A ROEBUCK RAISED HIS EYES 76 INDIAN ON GOD 13
AND RAISED ABOVE HER MOUND . . . . 123 DREAM OF DEATH 6
IT SEEMED THEY RAISED THEIR LITTLE SILVER HEADS, . . . 126 DREAM OF FAERY 6
THAT RAISED THEIR HANDS AGAINST HIM. THERE ARE SOME . 235 SHADOW WATER B 291
AND WITH THAT CRY I HAVE RAISED MY CRY. . . . . 361 ALF POLLEXFEN 39
OR RANK, RAISED FROM A COMMON . . . . 365 HER RACE 7
THE AVENGING LEAF THOSE FIELDS RAISED UP AGAINST IT. . 487 SEVEN SAGES 20
THE ARCADIANS BRING, AND BID THE STONE BE RAISED . . . 663 ISLE STAT II 2 25
HE'LL SNAP HIS SWORD. RAISED IS THE LION'S PAW. . . . 664 ISLE STAT II 2 63
THE SHEPHERD RAISED HIS ARMS AND SANK, ... 673 ISLE STAT II 3 187
RAISEST
A SCARLET BLOOM. WHY RAISEST THOU, PALE ONE, ... 673 ISLE STAT II 3 196
RAISING
AND RAISING ARMS ALL RADDLED WITH THE DYE, ... 105 CUCHULAIN SEA 7
RAJA'S
HAST THOU NOT KNOWN A RAJA'S DREAMLESS SLUMBER? . . . 724 KANVA ON SELF 8
RAJAS
OF RAJAS AND MAHRAJAS BEYOND NUMBER? . . . . 724 KANVA ON SELF 6
RAM
WHEN I HAVE SHUT THESE EWES AND THIS OLD RAM . . . . 343 SHEP GOATHERD 113
THE TRIVIAL DAYS AND RAM THEM WITH THE SUN, ... 500 VACILLATION 21
RAMBLE
MUST RAMBLE, AND THIN OUT . . . . 484 SPILT MILK 3
RAMBLED
OF ALL THAT RAMBLED THERE . . . . 526 AM OF IRELAND 9
RAMBLES
THOUGH HAMLET RAMBLES AND LEAR RAGES, ... 566 LAPIS LAZULI 21
RAMBLING
THAT RAMBLING JAILBIRD BILLY SAID; . . . . 332 ROUND TOWER 26
IN RAMBLING TALK WITH AN IMAGE OF AIR; . . . . 357 BROKEN DREAMS 40
AND BRING BEAUTY'S BLIND RAMBLING CELEBRANT; . . . . 412 TOWER 91
SAID THE RAMBLING, SHAMBLING TRAVELLING-MAN; . . . . 788 HAWTHORN TREE 2
SAID THE RAMBLING, SHAMBLING TRAVELLING-MAN; . . . . 788 HAWTHORN TREE 10
RAMMED
AS THOUGH TO DRAW THEM CLOSER YET. RAMMED FULL . . . 579 DOR WELLESLEY 5
RAMPARTS
OVER THE RAMPARTS AND THE TOWERS, ... 212 BLESS PSALTER 6
RAMPARTS AT YOUR EAR, ... 492 ANNE GREGORY 4
RAN
RAN THROUGH THE FOAM AND RAN TO THIS . . . . 6 OISIN 1 58
RAN THROUGH THE FOAM AND RAN TO THIS . . . . 6 OISIN 1 58
FOR LOVE OF USHEEN MY FEET RAN . . . . 6 OISIN 1 V 57
AND WHEN THEY HEARD HER VOICE THEY RAN . . . . 15 OISIN 1 213
NO CENTURIES COULD DIM, AND A WORD RAN . . . . 38 OISIN 2 127
NOT LOADED CENTURIES MIGHT VAPOUR. RAN . . . . 38 OISIN 2 V 127
AMID THE SHADES OF NIGHT, HE CHANGED AND RAN . . . . 40 OISIN 2 174
I AWOKE! THE STRANGE HORSE WITHOUT SUMMONS OUT OF 54 OISIN 3 105
THE DISTANCE RAN,

643

		PAGE	TITLE	LINE

RAN   (CONTINUED)
HIS MIND RAN ALL ON MONEY CARES AND FEARS, ...   127 DREAM OF FAERY   14
AND HE RAN TO THE DOOR OF HIS HOUSE! . . . .   145 HOST OF AIR   V 40C
WHO CALLED ME BY MY NAME AND RAN . . . .   150 WANDER AENGUS   15
THAT CALLED ME BY MY NAME AND RAN . . . .   150 WANDER AENGUS   V   15
SUDDENLY, AND RAN AT THEM AND HARRIED THEM. . . . . .   185 QUEEN MAEVE   119
AND WHEN THE UPROAR RAN ALONG THE GRASS . . . .   186 QUEEN MAEVE   127
HE RAN AND LAUGHED UNTIL HE CAME . . . .   194 BAILE AILLINN   128
WHERE THAT WISE HARPER'S FINGER RAN. . . . .   195 BAILE AILLINN   156
WHERE THAT WISE HARPER'S FINGERS RAN. . . . .   195 BAILE AILLINN   V 156
AND ALL THE ALE RAN OUT AT THE NEW MOON! . . . . . .   222 SHADOW WATER B   V   11
AENGUS AND EDAIN RAN UP OUT OF THE WAVE-- . . . . . .   231 SHADOW WATER B   196
MEN RAN UPON THE SHORE. . . . .   253 HIS DREAM   V   4
BEFORE THEIR SLEEPY EYELIDS RAN . . . .   272 GREY ROCK   30
AND AFTER, WHEN HER BLOOD RAN WILD, ...   272 GREY ROCK   44
HAD PERISHED THERE, BUT THE DANES RAN, ...   274 GREY ROCK   74
BUT THE STAG STOOPED AND RAN AT HIM, AND PASSED, . .   277 TWO KINGS   12
AND RAN AT HIM, AND PASSED, AND AS IT PASSED . . . .   277 TWO KINGS   V 12A
THE DISEMBOWELLED HORSE. KING EOCHAID RAN . . . . .   278 TWO KINGS   45
HE RAN TOWARDS THE HOUSE HIS FATHERS BUILT . . . . .   279 TWO KINGS   V 45E
BUT THAT SWEET-SOUNDING VOICE RAN ON! "WOMAN, . . .   284 TWO KINGS   165
INDIFFERENT HOW THE RANCOUR RAN, ...   288 TO WEALTHY MAN   21
EUNUCHS RAN THROUGH HELL AND MET . . . .   294 HATED PLAYBOY   2
AS THOUGH SOME OTHER NAME RAN IN HIS HEAD. . . . . .   351 HER PRAISE   9
OF SOME STRANGE WOMAN'S NAME THAT RAN IN HIS HEAD. .   351 HER PRAISE   V   9
THEY RAN FROM CRADLE TO CRADLE TILL AT LAST . . . .   375 PHASES OF MOON   69
RAN OUT OF MY SIGHT! . . . .   399 DEMON BEAST   4
NOW THAT THE LOUD BEAST RAN . . . .   400 DEMON BEAST   16
RAN AND WITH THE GARDEN SHEARS . . . .   410 TOWER   30
AND THROUGH THE CENTURIES RAN . . . .   421 MY TABLE   20
AND WHEN THROUGH ALL THE TOWN THERE RAN . . . . . .   436 FOR MY SON   25
I RAN, I RAN, FROM MY LOVE'S SIDE BECAUSE MY HEART WENT   450 OWEN AHERNE   12
   MAD.
I RAN, I RAN, FROM MY LOVE'S SIDE BECAUSE MY HEART WENT   450 OWEN AHERNE   12
   MAD.
WHAT STIR RAN THROUGH THE COUNTRYSIDE . . . .   488 CRAZED MOON   10
THROUGH INTRICATE MOTIONS RAN . . . .   506 STREAM AND SUN   1
OR BUT TO FIND IF WITHERED VEIN RAN BLOOD, ...   537 HER VISION   6
STARED AT THE WINE-DARK NAIL, OR DARK THAT RAN . . .   537 HER VISION   10
HE RAN ON AHEAD, ...   595 COLONEL MARTIN   42
THAT ON TWO WHEELS RAN . . . .   628 JANE MOUNTAIN   14
MY HEART RAN WILD WHEN IT HEARD . . . .   783 GREY ROUND   21
RANCOROUS
A LEVELLING, RANCOROUS, RATIONAL SORT OF MIND . . . .   486 SEVEN SAGES   11
RANCOUR
INDIFFERENT HOW THE RANCOUR RAN, ...   288 TO WEALTHY MAN   21
NO CIVIL RANCOUR TORN THE LAND APART. . . . .   542 PARN FUNERAL 2   4
RANDY
PORTER-DRINKERS' RANDY LAUGHTER! . . . .   640 BEN BULBEN   77
RANG
TOGETHER, WHILE THE DARK WOODS RANG, ...   16 OISIN 1   227
RANGE
AND BIRDS THAT ON THE SEVEN SEAS RANGE. . . . . . .   4 OISIN 1   V 27A
FROM CRESCENT TO ROUND THEY RANGE? . . . .   379 CAT AND MOON   24
THE RIDER, THE BIRDS THAT RANGE . . . .   393 EASTER 1916   46
RANGED
FROM DREAM TO DREAM AND RHYME TO RHYME I HAVE RANGED . .   357 BROKEN DREAMS   39
RANGER
HOW CAME THIS RANGER . . . .   574 MAIDS 1ST SONG   1
RANK
AND CLOUDS ARRAYED THEIR RANK ON RANK . . . .   12 OISIN 1   154
AND CLOUDS ARRAYED THEIR RANK ON RANK . . . .   12 OISIN 1   154
THE CLOUDS ARRAYED THEM RANK ON RANK . . . .   12 OISIN 1   V 154
THE CLOUDS ARRAYED THEM RANK ON RANK . . . .   12 OISIN 1   V 154
OR RANK, RAISED FROM A COMMON . . . .   365 HER RACE   7
RICHES DROVE OUT RANK, ...   626 STATES HOLIDAY   2
SO MUCH OF WEALTH AS MAY BEFIT THEIR RANK! . . . . .   756 SHADOW WATER A   V 186
RANKED
OF SOLDIERS RANKED IS ON A GRASSY SPOT, ...   712 FERENCZ RENYI   64
RANKING
RANKING HIS DRUIDS ROUND HIM TEN BY TEN, ...   110 CUCHULAIN SEA   76
RANKS
AND BROKE THE HEAVING RANKS OF BATTLE! . . . .   10 OISIN 1   124
AND HUSHED IN SLEEP THE ROARING RANKS OF BATTLE! . .   129 BOOK STORIES   7
RANN
BALLAD AND STORY, RANN AND SONG! . . . .   137 TO IRELAND   4
RANT
WHEN TIME BEGAN TO RANT AND RAGE . . . .   138 TO IRELAND   10
TO RANT AND RAGE IN FLOOD AND WIND! . . . .   138 TO IRELAND   26
AND ALL THE RANT A MIRROR OF MY MOOD! . . . .   490 COOLE BALLYLEE   V   13
BUT THERE'S NO GOOD COMPLAINING, FOR MONEY'S RANT IS ON.   580 CURSE CROMWELL   10
RANTED
I RANTED TO THE KNAVE AND FOOL, ...   506 REMORSE SPEECH   1
RANTING
A ROARING, RANTING JOURNEYMAN. . . . .   509 JANE REPROVED   13
A ROARING RANTING JOURNEY-MAN. . . . .   509 JANE REPROVED   V   13
HIS ROARING AND HIS RANTING . . . .   606 SONGS BURDEN 1   16
AND RANTING TIME RENEW. . . . .   606 SONGS BURDEN 1   20
BUT WHERE THAT ROARING, RANTING CREW . . . .   787 HUDDON DUDDON   3
RANT'S
AND ALL THE RANT'S A MIRROR OF MY MOOD! . . . . . .   490 COOLE BALLYLEE   13

644

RAPHAEL
   . . . MICHAEL, GABRIEL, AND RAPHAEL . . . .   174 ELEMENT POWERS V   T
RAPIER
   A STAR-LIT RAPIER, HALF BLOOD-DARK, ...   671 ISLE STAT II 3   125
RAPT   SEE SONG-RAPT
RAPTUROUS
   SING, O YOU LITTLE STARS! O SING AND RAISE YOUR RAPTUROUS   72 ANASHU VIJAYA   20
     CAROL
   SING, OH YE LITTLE STARS! OH, SING, AND RAISE YOUR   72 ANASHU VIJAYA V   20
     RAPTUROUS CAROL
   A RAPTUROUS MUSIC, TILL THE MORNING BREAK . . . . . .   137 TO SOME I TALK   14
RARE
   CLEAR FLUTED THEN THAT GOBLIN RARE-- . . . .   6 OISIN 1   V   54
   WE'VE TALKED AND TALKED, AND NOT A WHIT MORE RARE . . .   659 ISLE STAT II 1   21
   THEN 'GAN TO SPEAK THAT GOBLIN RARE, ...   729 PRIEST FAIRY   37
RASCAL
   TRANSFORM THESE RASCAL BILLOWS INTO WOMEN . . . . . .   222 SHADOW WATER B   11
   FOOL, RASCAL, KNAVE, ...   496 MOHINI CHATTER   8
   WE KNOW WHAT RASCAL MIGHT HAS DEFILED, ...   614 MARCH SONGS 2   11
   MY RASCAL HEART IS PROUD . . . .   782 HEART FRIGHT   10
RASCALLY
   BUT A THIEVING RASCALLY CUR-- . . . .   552 SONGS REWRIT 2   7
RASCALS
   AND CRAZY RASCALS RAGE THEIR FILL . . . .   131 OLD PENSIONER   9
   THAT THE WORST ROGUES AND RASCALS HAD DIED OUT. . . .   428 NINETEEN 19   16
   THE THREE OLD RASCALS LAUGH ALOUD . . . .   460 THREE MONUMENT   12
   OF RASCALS BLACK AND WHITE . . . .   597 MODEL LAUREATE   10
RASCHID   SEE AL-RASCHID
RASHID   SEE AL-RASHID
   BELOVED HAROUN EL RASHID, OCCUPIED . . . .   462 HARUN RASHID V   24
   THAT YEAR WHEN GREAT HAROUN EL RASHID KILLED . . . .   462 HARUN RASHID V   31
RAT
   WHAT MADE THAT SOUND? A RAT OR WATER-HEN . . . . .   372 PHASES OF MOON   8
RATH
   . . . AND GUARDLESS THE SACRED CAIRN AND THE RATH, . . .   58 OISIN 3   163
   IN THE FAIRY-HAUNTED RATH, ...   706 DAWN-SONG   21
RATHER
   CALLED RATHER BAILE LITTLE-LAND, ...   189 BAILE AILLINN   17
   CALLED RATHER BAILE LITTLE LAND, ...   189 BAILE AILLINN V   17
RATIONAL
   A LEVELLING, RANCOROUS, RATIONAL SORT OF MIND . . . .   486 SEVEN SAGES   11
RATS   SEE WATER-RATS
   THE DROWSY WATER RATS! . . . .   87 STOLEN CHILD V   5
   SAVING THE RHYME RATS HEAR BEFORE THEY DIE. . . . .   542 PARN FUNERAL 1   28
RATTLE
   AND HEARD THE FOEMEN'S BUCKLERS RATTLE, ...   10 OISIN 1   123
   AND HEARD THE FOEMAN'S BUCKLERS RATTLE, ...   10 OISIN 1   V 123
   THE RATTLE OF PEBBLES ON THE SHORE . . . .   485 NINETEENTH CEN   3
   THE RATTLE OF THOSE ARMS MAKES US AFRAID. . . . . .   634 CUCHULAIN COMF   15
RATTLED
   AND RATTLED OUT A TUNE! . . . .   616 MARCH SONGS 3   9
   AND RATTLED OUT A TUNE! . . . .   616 MARCH SONGS 3   19
   AND RATTLED OUT A TUNE! . . . .   616 MARCH SONGS 3   29
RAVE
   TRICKLING ALONG THE EARTH, I RAVE! . . . .   19 OISIN 1   V 281
   AND SHAKE DOWN THUNDER ON THE STONES BECAUSE THE RED WINDS 207 HANRAHANS SONG V 7
     RAVE!
   MADE OF DIM GOLD RAVE OUT IN SECRET TOMBS! . . . . .   235 SHADOW WATER B   295
   MADE OF DIM GOLD, RAVE OUT IN SECRET TOMBS, ...   765 SHADOW WATER A   345
RAVEL
   CAN RAVEL OUT WHAT'S IN MY HEAD. . . . .   295 THREE BEGGARS   12
RAVELLED
   WHERE PEOPLE LOVE BESIDE THE RAVELLED SEAS! . . . .   126 DREAM OF FAERY   9
   WHATEVER RAVELLED WATERS RISE AND FALL . . . . . .   127 DREAM OF FAERY   32
   HAD RAVELLED HER OWN STORY OUT, ...   272 GREY ROCK   45
   BEFORE THAT END MUCH HAD SHE RAVELLED OUT . . . . .   472 ALL SOUL NIGHT   51
RAVEN
   FIRST AS A RAVEN ON WHOSE ANCIENT WINGS . . . . . .   102 FERGUS DRUID   3
   HER RAVEN FLUTTERS. ROB HIM OF HIS FOOD . . . . . .   751 SHADOW WATER A   100
RAVEN-COVERED
   ON GABHRA'S RAVEN-COVERED PLAIN! . . . .   5 OISIN 1   43
RAVENING
   OF RAVENING SORROW, OR THE HAND OF WRATH? . . . . .   42 OISIN 2   199
   RAVENING THROUGH CENTURY AFTER CENTURY, ...   563 MERU   5
   RAVENING, RAGING, AND UPROOTING THAT HE MAY COME . . .   563 MERU   6
RAVENS
   WHERE ROUND AND ROUND THE RAVENS GO. . . . .   5 OISIN 1   V   42
   AND NOW THE DAYLIGHT-DARKENING RAVENS FLOCK. . . . .   43 OISIN 2   212
   ALL IS DONE NOW--I SEE THE RAVENS FLOCK-- . . . . .   43 OISIN 2   V 212
   THE RAVENS OF UNRESTING THOUGHT! . . . .   136 TWO TREES   34
RAVING
   AND THEN ARISE, AND RAVING SLAY US ALL. . . . . .   110 CUCHULAIN SEA   79
   YOUR RAVING OF A MESSAGE AND A HARP . . . .   237 SHADOW WATER B   331
   BUT ALL THAT'S RAVING. WHO IS THERE CAN COMPEL . . .   237 SHADOW WATER B   333
   OUT OF THAT RAVING TIDE--IS DRAWN BETWIXT . . . .   377 PHASES OF MOON   122
   BUT A RAVING AUTUMN SHEARS . . . .   475 EVA GORE-BOOTH   5
   OLD IRON, OLD BONES, OLD RAGS, THAT RAVING SLUT . . .   630 CIRCUS ANIMALS   37
RAY
   AND STOOD WITHIN! CLOTHED IN A MISTY RAY . . . . .   36 OISIN 2   104
   AND STOOD WITHIN THE HALL. A MISTY RAY . . . . . .   36 OISIN 2   V 104

RAYLESS
    LIFT MY SOUL FROM RAYLESS NIGHT-- . . . . 648 ISLE STAT I 1   95
RAYMOND
    RAYMOND LULLY AND HIS WIFE PERNELLA . . . . 253 HIS DREAM   V   T
RAYS
    OR HOURS PASSED BY, YET HOLD THE MORNING RAYS . . . . . 30 OISIN 2   20
    YET DIMLY DEEM I THAT THE MORNING RAYS . . . . 30 OISIN 2   V   20
    MELT DOWN, AS IT WERE WAX IN THE SUN'S RAYS; . . . . . 428 NINETEEN 19   12
    RETURNS THAT SOLDIER IN THE EVENING RAYS . . . . . . 711 FERENCZ RENYI   49
RAZOR-KEEN
    STILL RAZOR-KEEN, STILL LIKE A LOOKING-GLASS . . . . . 477 SELF AND SOUL   11
    STILL RAZOR-KEEN, STILL LIKE A LOOKING GLASS . . . . . 477 SELF AND SOUL V 11
REACH
    HOW SHOULD THEIR LUCK RUN HIGH ENOUGH TO REACH . . . . 264 HOUSE SHAKEN   9
    MOST OUT OF REACH? AND IS THAT SPECTRAL IMAGE . . . . 368 EGO DOMINUS   25
    LAST REACH OF GLITTERING STREAM . . . . 414 TOWER   143
    WHEREVER THE ORBIT OF THE MOON CAN REACH, ... 472 ALL SOUL NIGHT 55
    MAY REND WHAT COMES IN REACH. . . . . 488 CRAZED MOON   18
    NOTHING SAID OR DONE CAN REACH . . . . 506 REMORSE SPEECH   9
    AS THOUGH THAT HAND COULD REACH TO WHERE THEY STAND, . . 579 DOR WELLESLEY   2
    AH ME! I CANNOT REACH THEM--HERE AND THERE . . . . . 694 MOSADA 1   93
    THE BURTHEN OF THY TRUTH. REACH DOWN THY HANDS . . . . 698 MOSADA 2   53
REACHED
    NOAH'S FRESHET NEVER REACHED. . . . . 440 WISDOM   15
REACHES
    THE GLITTERING REACHES OF THE FLOODED LAKE. . . . . . 490 COOLE BALLYLEE 16
READ   SEE HALF-READ
    AND SLOWLY READ, AND DREAM OF THE SOFT LOOK . . . . . 121 YOU ARE OLD   3
    THEY READ IN THEIR BOOKS OF PRAYER; . . . . 178 FIDDLER DOONEY 6
    I READ IN MY BOOK OF SONGS . . . . 178 FIDDLER DOONEY 7
    THEY READ IN A BOOK OF PRAYER, ... 178 FIDDLER DOONEY V 6
    I READ IN A BOOK OF SONGS . . . . 178 FIDDLER DOONEY V 7
    I HAVE MADE THIS POEM FOR YOU, THAT MEN MAY READ IT . . 219 WOODS OF COOLE 41
    BEFORE THEY READ OF FORGAEL AND DECTORA, ... 219 WOODS OF COOLE 42
    A WOMAN SPOKE OF SOME NEW TALE SHE HAD READ, ... 350 HER PRAISE   7
    CLIMBED UP MY CREAKING STAIR. THEY HAD READ . . . . . 358 PRESENCES   6
    THE HALF READ WISDOM OF DAEMONIC IMAGES, ... 427 PHANTOM HATRED V 39
    HE WHO CAN READ THE SIGNS NOR SINK UNMANNED . . . . . 429 NINETEEN 19   33
    OF ALL THE UNCOUNTED BOOKS THAT I HAVE READ, ... 467 HARUN RASHID   139
    EVERYTHING HE WROTE WAS READ, ... 577 WHAT THEN   6
    AND COPIED OUT WHAT I COULD READ . . . . 584 GHOST ROG CASE 33
    THAT HAS READ AND THOUGHT. . . . . 631 POLITICS   8
    THAT HAS BOTH READ AND THOUGHT, ... 631 POLITICS   V 8
    HE WROTE IT ON THE SANDS (THE OWLS MAY READ . . . . . 659 ISLE STAT II 1 9
    IN SAND HIS NAME AND MINE I'VE ALSO READ. . . . . . . 662 ISLE STAT II 2 12
    FROM DEATH'S LATE LANGUOR AS THESE LINES I READ . . . . 734 QUATRAIN APHOR 14
READIER
    NOW NOTHING BUT COMES READIER TO THE HAND . . . . . . 267 ALL TEMPT ME   4
READING
    READING SOME ENTANGLED STORY; . . . . 65 HAPPY SHEPHERD 16
    AND THE LIGHT PROVES THAT HE IS READING STILL. . . . . 373 PHASES OF MOON 11
    TO STUDY READING BOOKS AND HISTORY . . . . 443 SCHOOL CHILDR V 4
    TO STUDY READING BOOKS AND HISTORIES, ... 443 SCHOOL CHILDR V 4
READING-BOOKS
    TO STUDY READING-BOOKS AND HISTORY, ... 443 SCHOOL CHILDR   4
READY
    THAN A STRONG BODY AND A READY HAND. . . . . 232 SHADOW WATER B 236
    A PERJURER STOOD READY . . . . 582 ROGER CASEMENT 9
    IN COIL ON COIL OF AZURE. ALL IS READY. . . . . . . 691 MOSADA 1   41
REAL
    AND FINDS A REAL IMAGE THERE; . . . . 388 SOLOMON WITCH   27
REALISTS
    THE REALISTS . . . . 309 REALISTS   T
REALITY
    BUT THE REALITY THAT MAKES OUR PASSION . . . . 229 SHADOW WATER B 159
    AND THE REALITY; . . . . 347 FISHERMAN   12
    IS BUT A VISION OF REALITY. . . . . 369 EGO DOMINUS   48
    SEEK OUT REALITY, LEAVE THINGS THAT SEEM. . . . . . . 502 VACILLATION   72
    INTO THE DESOLATION OF REALITY; . . . . 563 MERU   7
REALM
    IN A REALM WHERE THE HANDSOME ARE MANY, ... 50 OISIN 3   V 50
REALMS
    IN REALMS WHERE THE HANDSOME WERE MANY, ... 50 OISIN 3   50
    IN REALMS WHERE THE HANDSOME ARE MANY. . . . . 50 OISIN 3   V 50
REAP
    NOR, GAZING FORTH WHERE LIFE'S SAD SICKLES REAP, ... 710 FERENCZ RENYI   31
REAPING
    THAT RUN BEFORE THE REAPING HOOK AND LIE . . . . . . 218 WOODS OF COOLE V 32
    WEARY OF REAPING THE BARREN NIGHT . . . . 648 ISLE STAT I 1   84
REAPING-HOOK
    THAT RUN BEFORE THE REAPING-HOOK AND LIE . . . . . . 218 WOODS OF COOLE 32
REAR
    BITTER AND VIOLENT MEN, MIGHT REAR IN STONE . . . . . 418 ANCEST HOUSES   19
    THE RED SQUIRREL SHALL REAR HER YOUNG WHERE THOU . . . 674 ISLE STAT II 3 215
        HAST DWELT--
REASON
    "GOOD REASON HAVE I FOR MY LOVE," . . . . 7 OISIN 1   V 62
    THE REASON OF THE TREMBLING TREES; . . . . 14 OISIN 1   179
    THIS BEAUTY'S KINDER, YET FOR A REASON . . . . 199 ARROW   7
    I HAVE GOOD REASON FOR THAT THOUGHT. AND NOW . . . . . 238 SHADOW WATER B 354
    AND I TOOK ALL THE BLAME OUT OF ALL SENSE AND REASON, . . 316 COLD HEAVEN   7

	PAGE	TITLE		LINE

REASON   (CONTINUED)
```
        A REASON FOR KEEPING SILENT . . . . . . . . . . .    359 WAR POEM          V    T
        OUT OF ALL LIKELIHOOD, OR REASON, . . . . . . . .    389 IMAGE PAST             9
        AND FOR THAT REASON AM I CRAZED . . . . . . . . .    454 EMPTY CUP               9
        HIS VIZIR JAFFER FOR AN UNKNOWN REASON . . . . . .    462 HARUN RASHID          32
        GAVE BUT MORE REASON FOR A WOMAN'S CARE. . . . . .    466 HARUN RASHID         111
        AND HERE'S A COGENT REASON, . . . . . . . . . . .    586 PARNELLITES            9
        AND HERE'S ANOTHER REASON, . . . . . . . . . . .     586 PARNELLITES           15
        AND HERE'S A FINAL REASON, . . . . . . . . . . .     586 PARNELLITES           17
        FOR REASON OF THE STATE . . . . . . . . . . . . .    597 MODEL LAUREATE         6
        FOUGHT ONCE FOR SELF-SAME REASON ON THE HEM . . . .   660 ISLE STAT II 1        32
REBEL
        HIDING THE REBEL WORMS IN YONDER WOOD, . . . . . .    709 FERENCZ RENYI     V   14
REBELLION
        GRANDFATHER SAID IN THE GREAT REBELLION! . . . . .    544 TO SAME TUNE 1 V       1
REBELS
        HIDING THE REBELS WORM IN YONDER WOOD . . . . . .     709 FERENCZ RENYI         14
        HIDING THE REBELS SWARM IN YONDER WOOD . . . . . .    709 FERENCZ RENYI     V   14
        WHERE WORM THE REBELS, OR MY BULLETS LAY . . . . .    713 FERENCZ RENYI         83
        WHERE IN THE WOODS OR HILLS THE REBELS BE?" . . . .   713 FERENCZ RENYI     V  83A
RECALL
        RECALL THE YEARS BEFORE HER MIND . . . . . . . . .    397 POLIT PRISONER         8
        I MUST RECALL A MAN THAT NEITHER LOVE . . . . . .     412 TOWER                 74
        AND SPEAK BUT FANTASY.  RECALL THE YEAR . . . . .     462 HARUN RASHID          30
        AND SPEAK BUT PHANTASY.  RECALL THE YEAR . . . . .    462 HARUN RASHID      V   30
        PICTURES OF THE MIND, RECALL  . . . . . . . . . .    475 EVA GORE-BOOTH        17
        WHATEVER COULD RECALL THE LIP OF LOVER. . . . . .     537 HER VISION             8
        RECALL THE CRETAN BARB THAT PIERCED A STAR? . . . .   541 PARN FUNERAL 1         7
        RECALL THAT MASCULINE TRINITY. . . . . . . . . . .   556 RIBH PATRICK           2
        RECALL HIS TRINITY.  A FATHER, MOTHER, CHILD (A DAUGHTER   556 RIBH PATRICK  V   2
            OR A SON),
        FOR I WOULD NOT RECALL . . . . . . . . . . . . .     599 SPIRIT MEDIUM         10
        AND MEN RECALL THAT FACE, . . . . . . . . . . . .    617 LONG-LEG FLY          12
RECALLED
        BUT SOMETHING IS RECALLED, . . . . . . . . . . .     501 VACILLATION           55
RECEDE
        THE UNPURGED IMAGES OF DAY RECEDE; . . . . . . . .    497 BYZANTIUM              1
RECEDES
        NIGHT RESONANCE RECEDES, NIGHT-WALKERS' SONG . . .    497 BYZANTIUM              3
        NIGHT'S RESONANCE RECEDES, NIGHT-WALKERS SONG . . .   497 BYZANTIUM         V    3
RECEDING
        UNDER THE RECEDING WAVE. . . . . . . . . . . . .     485 NINETEENTH CEN         4
RECEIVES
        THAT THE STORMY NIGHT RECEIVES, . . . . . . . . .    135 TWO TREES             26
RECENT
        ON A RECENT GOVERNMENT APPOINTMENT IN IRELAND . . .   317 APPOINTMENT       V    T
RECKLESS
        RESTRAINING RECKLESS MIDDLE-AGE? . . . . . . . . .    262 STUDENTS AGIT          4
RECKON
        IMAGINATION CANNOT RECKON IT. . . . . . . . . . .    248 SHADOW WATER B       541
RECKONED
        WHEN ALL THOUGHTS AND DEEDS ARE RECKONED, . . . .     298 THREE HERMITS         15
        THAT WERE ALL HIS BIRTHDAYS RECKONED . . . . . .     342 SHEP GOATHERD         90
        RECKONED UP EVERY UNFOREKNOWN, UNSEEING . . . . .     413 TOWER                109
RECKONING
        WHY, IT'S A WONDER OUT OF RECKONING . . . . . . .     243 SHADOW WATER B       445
        OUT OF ALL RECKONING.  IS IT NOT TRUE . . . . . .    244 SHADOW WATER B       467
RECLINES
        THERE ON THAT SCAFFOLDING RECLINES . . . . . . .     618 LONG-LEG FLY          25
RECOGNIZE
        RECOGNIZE THE FIVE . . . . . . . . . . . . . . .     601 THOSE IMAGES          15
RECOLLECT
        AND YOU WILL RECOLLECT MY FACE AND VOICE, . . . .     243 SHADOW WATER B       433
RECOLLECTION
        IMAGE OF POIGNANT RECOLLECTION. . . . . . . . . .    389 IMAGE PAST             7
        AS RECOLLECTION OR THE DRUG DECIDE, . . . . . . .    444 SCHOOL CHILDR         36
RECONCILIATION
        RECONCILIATION . . . . . . . . . . . . . . . . .     257 RECONCILIATION         T
RECORD
        THESE, THESE REMAIN, BUT I RECORD WHAT'S GONE.  A CROWD   315 FALLEN MAJESTY    6
RECORDS
        BABBLING OF FALLEN MAJESTY, RECORDS WHAT'S GONE. . .  314 FALLEN MAJESTY         4
RECOVER
        I COULD RECOVER IF I SHRIEKED . . . . . . . . . .    452 HUMAN DIGNITY          9
        I COULD RECOVER IF I SHRIEK . . . . . . . . . . .    452 HUMAN DIGNITY     V    9
RECOVERED
        RECOVERED HIM UPON THE BED OF DEATH. . . . . . . .    355 BROKEN DREAMS          6
RECOVERING
        MY HEART RECOVERING WITH COVERED EYES; . . . . . .   602 GALLERY REVIS         18
RECOVERS
        THE SOUL RECOVERS RADICAL INNOCENCE . . . . . . .     405 FOR DAUGHTER          66
RECTOR
        THAT RED-HEADED RECTOR IN COUNTY DOWN, . . . . . .    604 YOU CONTENT           11
        AN ANCESTOR WAS RECTOR THERE . . . . . . . . . .     640 BEN BULBEN            86
RECUR
        AND THAT IF MEMORY RECUR, THE SUN'S . . . . . . .    414 TOWER                119
RED     SEE BLOOD-RED
        THE RED SUN FALLS AND THE WORLD GROWS DIM." . . .      9 OISIN 1              105
        YOU GO NOT WHERE THE RED DEER FEEDS, . . . . . . .    11 OISIN 1              127
        YE GO NOT WHERE THE RED DEER FEEDS, . . . . . . .     11 OISIN 1           V  127
        ALL PEARLY WHITE, SAVE ONE RED EAR; . . . . . . .     12 OISIN 1              141
```

		PAGE	TITLE		LINE
RED	(CONTINUED)				
	WILD FLAMES OF RED AND GOLD AND BLUE,	18	OISIN 1		252
	AND KISSED THE SCEPTRE WITH RED LIPS,	18	OISIN 1		258
	WILD FLAMES OF RED AND CREAMY WHITES,	18	OISIN 1	V	255
	HUNG, LIKE METEORS OF RED LIGHT,	21	OISIN 1	V	306
	CAME BY ME THE KINGS OF THE RED BRANCH,	53	OISIN 3		87
	AND BY ME, IN SOFT RED RAIMENT, THE FENIANS MOVED IN LOUD STREAMS,	53	OISIN 3		93
	CAME BY ME THE CANNS OF THE RED BRANCH	53	OISIN 3	V	87
	. . . WITH RED LIPS MURMURING A SONG,	58	OISIN 3	V	158
	WE WILL TEAR OUT THE RED FLAMING STONES,	62	OISIN 3	V	209
	WE WILL TEAR THE RED FLAMING STONES OUT,	62	OISIN 3	V	209
	ON THE RED FLAMING STONES WITHOUT REFUGE	62	OISIN 3	V	213
	OF RED FLAMINGOES; AND MY LOVE, VIJAYA!	75	ANASHU VIJAYA		89
	OF RED FLAMINGO! AND MY LOVE, VIJAYA,	75	ANASHU VIJAYA	V	89
	MY MAN GREW RED AND PALE,	95	MOLL MAGEE		22
	RED ROSE, PROUD ROSE, SAD ROSE OF ALL MY DAYS!	100	ROSE UPON ROOD		1
	RED ROSE, PROUD ROSE, SAD ROSE OF ALL MY DAYS.	101	ROSE UPON ROOD		24
	WHAT WOULD YOU, KING OF THE PROUD RED BRANCH KINGS?	102	FERGUS DRUID		8
	WHAT WOULD YOU, KING OF THE PROUD RED BRANCH KINGS?	102	FERGUS DRUID		15
	WHAT WOULD YOU, KING OF THE PROUD RED BRANCH KINGS?	103	FERGUS DRUID	V	21
	AND STRETCHING OUT HER ARMS, RED WITH THE DYE,	105	CUCHULAIN SEA	V	7
	"THE RED BRANCH CAMP IN A GREAT COMPANY	108	CUCHULAIN SEA		33
	"THE RED BRANCH KINGS A TIRELESS BANQUET KEEP,	108	CUCHULAIN SEA	V	33
	"THE RED BRANCH GATHER A GREAT COMPANY	108	CUCHULAIN SEA	V	33
	AND THE GREY TIDE, THE RED BRANCH MULTITUDE	108	CUCHULAIN SEA	V	38B
	AND CONCHUBAR, THE RED BRANCH KING OF KINGS,	109	CUCHULAIN SEA		45
	"I ONLY OF THE RED BRANCH HOSTED NOW."	109	CUCHULAIN SEA	V	55
	FOR THESE RED LIPS, WITH ALL THEIR MOURNFUL PRIDE,	111	ROSE OF WORLD		2
	A GIRL AROSE THAT HAD RED MOURNFUL LIPS	120	SORROW OF LOVE		5
	AND THEN YOU CAME WITH THOSE RED MOURNFUL LIPS,	120	SORROW OF LOVE	V	5
	BECAUSE THE RED ROSE BORDERED HEM	137	TO IRELAND	V	6
	AFTER THE RED ROSE BORDERED HEM.	139	TO IRELAND	V	30
	AFTER THE RED ROSE BORDERED HEM.	139	TO IRELAND	V	48
	AND A YOUNG MAN BROUGHT HIM RED WINE	144	HOST OF AIR		19
	OF THE MATCHING OF RIBBONS THE BLUE AND THE RED,	151	OLD MOTHER	V	6
	I HAVE BEEN CHANGED TO A HOUND WITH ONE RED EAR!	153	CHANGE BELOVED		2
	O'SULLIVAN THE RED TO MARY LAVELL.	157	POET BELOVED	V	T
	TWO POEMS BY O'SULLIVAN THE RED CONCERNING MARY LAVELL.	157	POET BELOVED	V	T
	IN A RED AND QUIVERING GARMENT	160	CAP AND BELLS		15
	AND HER RED LIPS SANG THEM A LOVE-SONG	160	CAP AND BELLS		27
	TO HER RIGHT HAND CAME THE RED ONE,	160	CAP AND BELLS		31
	IN A GARMENT RED AND QUIVERING,	160	CAP AND BELLS	V	15
	HER RED LIPS SANG THEM A LOVE-SONG,	160	CAP AND BELLS	V	27
	AND HER RED LIPS SANG THEM A LOVE SONG.	160	CAP AND BELLS	V	27
	AND TILL A HUNDRED MORNS HAD FLOWERED RED	170	SECRET ROSE		17
	O'SULLIVAN THE RED UPON HIS WANDERINGS	171	MAID QUIET	V	T
	RED HANRAHAN'S SONG ABOUT IRELAND	206	HANRAHANS SONG		T
	THE SONG OF RED HANRAHAN	206	HANRAHANS SONG	V	T
	AND SHAKE DOWN THUNDER ON THE STONES BECAUSE THE RED WINDS RAVE!	207	HANRAHANS SONG	V	7
	WITH RED BEER AND BROWN BEER.	214	HAPPY TOWNLAND		8
	BUT THE LITTLE RED FOX MURMURED,	214	HAPPY TOWNLAND		17
	BUT THE LITTLE RED FOX MURMURED,	215	HAPPY TOWNLAND		37
	BUT THE LITTLE RED FOX MURMURED,	216	HAPPY TOWNLAND		57
	I COULD GIVE ALL MY HEART TO THAT RED MOLL	222	SHADOW WATER B		9
	FOR THAT RED MOLL THAT HAD BUT THE ONE EYE.	222	SHADOW WATER B	V	10
	WITH SO RED LIPS, AND RUNNING ON SUCH FEET,	231	SHADOW WATER B		199
	AND PLEASURE MADE HER CHEEKS GROW RED,	314	MEMORY YOUTH		11
	SHE LIES, HER LOVELY PITEOUS HEAD AMID DULL RED HAIR	362	HER COURTESY		2
	OF DULL RED HAIR WAS FLOWING	363	DOLLS DRAWINGS		6
	WHO HAD SEEMED TO GLIDE TO SOME INTRIGUE IN HER RED SHOES,	363	DOLLS FACES		6
	NO RED AND WHITE OF A FACE,	365	HER RACE		6
	MANACLE HIS SOUL UPON THE RED SEA BOTTOM.	372	ON GOING HOUSE		16
	THERE'S NOTHING BUT OUR OWN RED BLOOD	396	ROSE TREE		17
	THE RED MAN THE JUGGLER SENT	412	TOWER		92
	BRONZED PEACOCK FEATHERS, RED COMBS OF HER COCKS.	433	NINETEEN 19		130
	BUT THE DARK CHANGED TO RED, AND TORCHES SHONE,	537	HER VISION		12
	NOR EVER MADE AN IRON RED	606	SONGS BURDEN 1		14
	THE EVENING GLEAMS ARE GREEN AND GOLD AND RED	656	ISLE STAT I 3		22
	DULL-WITTED THING, WITH FACE RED SQUIRREL-BROWN.	661	ISLE STAT II 1		68
	THROUGH THIS NIGHT-VESTED PLACE THE RED BEAMS BREAK.	662	ISLE STAT II 2		4
	THE RED SQUIRREL SHALL REAR HER YOUNG WHERE THOU HAST DWELT—	674	ISLE STAT II 3		215
	MY DREAMS O'ER THOUGHTS OF PLENTY, AS THE RED—	681	SEEKER	V	3
	A LITTLE WHILE AND—RED EVE DIES—	686	LIFE		13
	FROM FASTING—SEE, THE RED LIGHT SLANTING DOWN	697	MOSADA 2		36
	AH! WOE FOR YOUR SLIPPERS OF RED.	708	FAIRY PEDANT		36
	THIS SULLEN PEASANT SPOILS THE GOOD RED WINE.	711	FERENCZ RENYI		43
	THIS SULLEN PEASANT SOURS THE GOOD RED WINE.	711	FERENCZ RENYI	V	43
	AMONG THE GOLD, THE AMBER, AND THE RED."	712	FERENCZ RENYI		76
	AMONG THE BLUE, THE AMBER AND THE RED."	712	FERENCZ RENYI	V	76
	THAT MAIDEN BRING THEY. WHEN THE TALL RED DEER	713	FERENCZ RENYI		79
	A TOSSING LAUGH BETWEEN THEIR RED ABIDES!	735	QUATRAIN APHOR		22
	THAT THE RED RUST MAKES DIM."	740	EARL PAUL		20
	A RED HOUND RUNNING FROM A SILVER ARROW.	747	SHADOW WATER A		6
	I HAVE FORGOTTEN WHEREFORE. THE RED HOUND	747	SHADOW WATER A		8
	I SWORE BUT YESTERDAY IF THE RED GOD	751	SHADOW WATER A		109
	TO MIND HIS COWS AND SWINE BY THE RED LAKE.	752	SHADOW WATER A		112
	BEYOND THE SAIL A MAN WITH A RED CROWN	752	SHADOW WATER A		126
	WERE THEY BUT LIFTED UP. THE RED HOUND IS FLED.	761	SHADOW WATER A		266

648

		PAGE	TITLE		LINE
RED	(CONTINUED)				
	A HOUND THAT HAD LAIN IN THE RED RUSHES	761	SHADOW WATER A		278
	RED BIRD OF MARCH, BEGIN TO CROW!	782	HEART FRIGHT		5
	RED COCK, AND CROW!	782	HEART FRIGHT		7
	RED BIRD OF MARCH, BEGIN TO CROW!	782	HEART FRIGHT		12
	RED COCK, AND CROW!	782	HEART FRIGHT		14
	RED BIRD OF MARCH, BEGIN TO CROW!	782	HEART FRIGHT		19
	RED COCK, AND CROW!	782	HEART FRIGHT		21
	RED COCKS, AND CROW!	783	GREY ROUND		28
REDDENS					
	IS THIS POOR BODY THAT REDDENS AND GROWS PALE.	764	SHADOW WATER A		341
REDDEST					
	AND OF REDDEST STOLEN CHERRIES.	87	STOLEN CHILD		8
RED-EARED					
	CAME UP OUT OF THE HOLE, AND RED-EARED HOUNDS	185	QUEEN MAEVE		117
	A RED-EARED HOUND FOLLOWS A HORNLESS DEER.	764	SHADOW WATER A		325
RED-EYED					
	OF DESERT-CAVES THE RED-EYED PANTHERS ROVE	681	SEEKER		4
	EYED PANTHERS IN THEIR DESERT CAVERNS ROVE	681	SEEKER	V	4
RED-HAIRED					
	HE HAD SEEN A RED-HAIRED JOLLY LAD	303	HOUR DAWN	V	27
	AND OF A RED-HAIRED YEATS WHOSE LOOKS, ALTHOUGH HE DIED	391	UNDER SATURN		9
RED-HEAD					
	YOUNG RED-HEAD STRETCHED HIMSELF TO YAWN	303	HOUR DAWN	V	32A
RED-HEADED					
	THAT RED-HEADED RECTOR IN COUNTY DOWN,	604	YOU CONTENT		11
REDNESS					
	AND ONE HAS SEEN IN THE REDNESS OF WINE	168	BLESSED		35
	A TOSSING LAUGH BETWEEN THEIR REDNESS 'BIDES--	685	DRAWING-ROOM		2
	A TOSSING LAUGH BETWEEN THEIR REDNESS 'BIDES--	735	QUATRAIN APHOR	V	22
	PRAISE THE REDNESS OF THE YEW!	773	SONG DEIRDRE 1		20
RED-ROSE-BORDERED					
	BECAUSE THE RED-ROSE-BORDERED HEM	137	TO IRELAND		6
	AFTER THE RED-ROSE-BORDERED HEM.	139	TO IRELAND		30
	AFTER THE RED-ROSE-BORDERED HEM.	139	TO IRELAND		48
RE-ECHOING					
	TILL MY OWN WORDS, RE-ECHOING, SHALL SEND	68	SAD SHEPHERD		20
	AND MINE OWN WORDS RE-ECHOING SHALL SEND	68	SAD SHEPHERD	V	20
REED					
	BLEW ONE LONG NOTE. FROM OVER REED	14	OISIN 1	V	195
	THIS BODY TREMBLING LIKE A WIND-BLOWN REED.	103	FERGUS DRUID		25
	SOFT AS THE RUSTLE OF A REED FROM CLOYNE	487	SEVEN SAGES		22
REEDS					
	AND WHISPER, "THE INNUMERABLE REEDS	81	EPHEMERA	V	24E
	FROM THE TALL AND THE TUFTED REEDS	143	HOST OF AIR		3
	AND HE SAW HOW THE REEDS GREW DARK	144	HOST OF AIR		5
	IN THE GREY REEDS THAT NIGHT AND MORN	190	BAILE AILLINN		42
	O TUFTED REEDS, BEND LOW AND LOW IN POOLS ON THE GREEN LAND,	206	HANRAHANS SONG	V	1
	LIKE TUFTED REEDS OUR COURAGE DROOPS IN A BLACK WIND AND DIES!	207	HANRAHANS SONG	V	3
	THAT RUSTLES IN THE REEDS WITH PATIENT PUSHES,	699	MOSADA 3		4
	THAT'S RUSTLING IN THE REEDS WITH PATIENT PUSHES,	699	MOSADA 3	V	4
	WHERE LIES A SHALLOP IN THE YELLOW REEDS.	702	MOSADA 3		77
REED-THROATED					
	WHILE I, FROM THAT REED-THROATED WHISPERER	320	REED WHISPERER		1
REEDY					
	PROCLAIM WITH THAT UNWEARIED, REEDY CRY	128	DREAM OF FAERY		42
	A-TELLING WITH THEIR LOW AND REEDY CRY	128	DREAM OF FAERY		42
	PROCLAIMING WITH A LOW AND REEDY CRY,	128	DREAM OF FAERY	V	42
	HOW LITTLE AND REEDY A SOUND AWAKES A GOD	760	SHADOW WATER A		252
REEL					
	REEL SHADOWS OF THE INDIGNANT DESERT BIRDS.	402	SECOND COMING		17
REELED					
	RENDING THE HORSE'S FLANK. KING EOCHAID REELED,	277	TWO KINGS		13
	RIPPED THROUGH THE HORSE'S FLANKS. KING EOCHAID REELED,	277	TWO KINGS	V	13
	FROM THE WAVES THE SUN HATH REELED,	705	DAWN-SONG		1
REELING					
	ON THAT WOMAN'S REELING BRAIN?	632	MAN AND ECHO		14
REFLECTION					
	THE ELABORATE STARLIGHT THROWS A REFLECTION	389	IMAGE PAST		2
REFLECTIONS					
	THE ELABORATE STAR-LIGHT HAS THROWN REFLECTIONS	389	IMAGE PAST	V	2
REFORM					
	OR RUN WHERE LADS REFORM OUR DAYTIME	343	SHEP GOATHERD	V	105
REFORMER					
	REFORMER, MERCHANT, STATESMAN, LEARNED MAN,	376	PHASES OF MOON		98
REFUGE					
	ON THE FLAMING STONES, WITHOUT REFUGE,	62	OISIN 3		213
	ON THE RED FLAMING STONES WITHOUT REFUGE	62	OISIN 3	V	213
	DANGER NO REFUGE HOLDS, AND WAR NO PEACE,	114	ROSE OF BATTLE		9
REFUSE					
	THAT GAVE, THOUGH FREE TO REFUSE--	414	TOWER		133
	AND IF IT TAKE THE SECOND MUST REFUSE	491	COOLE BALLYLEE	V	40C
	AND IF IT TAKE THE SECOND MUST REFUSE	495	CHOICE		3
	A MOUND OF REFUSE OR THE SWEEPINGS OF A STREET,	630	CIRCUS ANIMALS		35
	A MOUND OF REFUSE OR THE SWEEPINGS OF THE STREET,	630	CIRCUS ANIMALS		35
	THERE'S LITTLE I'D REFUSE THEE, DEAREST YOUTH.	669	ISLE STAT II 3		71
	BUT FEARING THAT SHE WOULD REFUSE	792	GEORGE MOORE		2
REFUSED					
	IF I REFUSED THE MESSENGERS AND PILOTS	249	SHADOW WATER B		572

		PAGE	TITLE		LINE

REFUSED (CONTINUED)
    FOR THAT SHE PROMISED, AND FOR THAT REFUSED. • • • • • 286 TWO KINGS 213
    FOR THAT YOU PROMISED, AND FOR THAT REFUSED." • • • • 286 TWO KINGS V 213
    BOOK II WHAT THE CALIPH REFUSED TO LEARN • • • • • • 460 HARUN RASHID V T
REGARDLESS
    STANDS EACH GREY AND SILENT PHANTOM ON THE SAME REGARDLESS 719 PHANTOM SHIP 25
        SPOT--
REGENT
    LONE REGENT OF THE WOODS, DEEP MUTTERING, • • • • • • 657 ISLE STAT I 3 49
REGRET
    OF CEASELESS LONELINESS AND HIGH REGRET • • • • • • • 705 REMEMBRANCE 9
REIGN
    THAT IT WAS MADE IN YOUR GREAT FATHER'S REIGN." • • • • 464 HARUN RASHID 72
REIGNED
    WHERE NONE HAS REIGNED THAT LACKED A NAME AND FAME • • • 491 COOLE BALLYLEE 31
REIN
    FOR GOLD HIS HOOVES AND SILK HIS REIN, • • • • • • • 2 OISIN 1 V 72
    THE MOON PLUCKED AT MY REIN; • • • • • • • • • • 214 HAPPY TOWNLAND 16
    "O DO NOT PLUCK AT HIS REIN, • • • • • • • • • • 214 HAPPY TOWNLAND 18
    THE MOON PLUCKED AT MY REIN; • • • • • • • • • • 215 HAPPY TOWNLAND 36
    "O DO NOT PLUCK AT HIS REIN, • • • • • • • • • • 215 HAPPY TOWNLAND 38
    THE MOON PLUCKED AT MY REIN; • • • • • • • • • • 216 HAPPY TOWNLAND 56
    "O DO NOT PLUCK AT HIS REIN, • • • • • • • • • • 216 HAPPY TOWNLAND 58
    HE SAT WITH TIGHTENED REIN AND LOOSENED MOUTH • • • • 277 TWO KINGS 10
    HE SAT WITH TIGHTENED REIN AMAZED, HIS HORSE • • • • 277 TWO KINGS V 10
    ROSE; SOME CONQUEROR DREW REIN • • • • • • • • • 502 VACILLATION 64
REINS
    SHAKE THE LOOSE REINS; YOU SLAVES OF GOD, • • • • • 22 OISIN 1 331
    SHAKE THE LOOSE REINS; YE SLAVES OF GOD, • • • • • • 22 OISIN 1 V 331
    LAY LOOSE IN A PLACE OF SHADOW; WE DREW THE REINS BY HIS 50 OISIN 3 44
    SIDE.
    IT DROPPED THE REINS OF PEACE AND WAR • • • • • • 437 SONGS PLAY 1 14
REITERANT
    REITERANT. A BIRD GOES BY THE TENT, • • • • • • • 711 FERENCZ RENYI 46
    REITERANT. A BOY GOES BY THE TENT, • • • • • • • 711 FERENCZ RENYI V 46
REJOICE
    OLD SILENCE BIDS ITS CHOSEN RACE REJOICE, • • • • • 127 DREAM OF FAERY 31
    OLD SILENCE BIDS A LONELY FOLK REJOICE, • • • • • • 127 DREAM OF FAERY V 31
    REJOICE AS LOVER SHOULD • • • • • • • • • • • 453 DEATH OF HARE 4
    AND ALL IT KNOWS IS THAT ONE WORD "REJOICE!" • • • • 564 GYRES 16
    SHALL WE IN THAT GREAT NIGHT REJOICE? • • • • • • 633 MAN AND ECHO 38
    DOTH NOT YON BIRD, YON QUIVERING BIRD, REJOICE? • • • 652 ISLE STAT I 2 21
RELEASE
    AND SHIRK IT IN VAIN. THERE IS NO RELEASE • • • • • 632 MAN AND ECHO 21
RELIED
    THAT ON A STICK RELIED • • • • • • • • • • • 515 GIRLS SONG B 6
RELIEF
    HAD SCOOPED OUT PHARAOH'S MUMMY. I--THOUGH HEART MIGHT 503 VACILLATION 84
    FIND RELIEF
RELIGIOUS
    BECAUSE TO-DAY IS SOME RELIGIOUS FESTIVAL • • • • • 363 DOLLS FACES 1
    "I HEARD AN OLD RELIGIOUS MAN • • • • • • • • • 492 ANNE GREGORY 13
    IN THAT RELIGIOUS GLOOM; • • • • • • • • • • • 584 GHOST ROG CASE 34
RELIVE
    THESE INNOCENTS RELIVE THEIR DEATH, • • • • • • • 612 NEWS ORACLE V 15
RE-LIVE
    THOSE INNOCENTS RE-LIVE THEIR DEATH, • • • • • • • 612 NEWS ORACLE 15
RELY
    "NONE CAN RELY UPON • • • • • • • • • • • • 569 THREE BUSHES 2
REMADE
    . . . REMADE, LIKE A CASKET OF GOLD • • • • • • • 143 ROSE IN HEART 7
    HERE'S AN OLD STORY I'VE REMADE, • • • • • • • • 270 GREY ROCK 3
RE-MADE
    . . . RE-MADE LIKE A CASKET OF GOLD • • • • • • • 143 ROSE IN HEART V 7
    HERE'S AN OLD STORY I'VE RE-MADE, • • • • • • • • 270 GREY ROCK V 3
REMAIN
    PARDON, OLD FATHERS, IF YOU STILL REMAIN • • • • • • 269 PARDON FATHERS 1
    THESE, THESE REMAIN, BUT I RECORD WHAT'S GONE. A CROWD 315 FALLEN MAJESTY 6
    AND ON MY HEIRS, IF ALL REMAIN UNSPOILED, • • • • • 371 ON GOING HOUSE 2
    AND MAY THESE CHARACTERS REMAIN • • • • • • • • 406 CARVED STONE 5
    THESE STONES REMAIN THEIR MONUMENT AND MINE. • • • • 423 MY DESCENDANTS 24
    NOTHING BUT STILLNESS CAN REMAIN WHEN HEARTS ARE FULL • 426 PHANTOM HATRED 23
    ALL THINGS REMAIN IN GOD. • • • • • • • • • • 512 JANE ON GOD 6
    ALL THINGS REMAIN IN GOD. • • • • • • • • • • 512 JANE ON GOD 12
    ALL THINGS REMAIN IN GOD. • • • • • • • • • • 512 JANE ON GOD 18
    ALL THINGS REMAIN IN GOD. • • • • • • • • • • 512 JANE ON GOD 24
    WENCHING, DRINKING, STILL REMAIN • • • • • • • • 529 TOM LUNATIC 9
    PICTURE AND BOOK REMAIN, • • • • • • • • • • • 575 ACRE OF GRASS 1
REMAINED
    SO MUCH REMAINED THAT ON THE EVENING STAR • • • • • 32 OISIN 2 V 48
REMAINS
    BRIGHTNESS REMAINS; A BRIGHTER STAR SHOOTS DOWN; • • • 541 PARN FUNERAL 1 4
    WHAT REMAINS TO SING ABOUT • • • • • • • • • • 585 ORAHILLY 28
REMAKE
    MYSELF MUST I REMAKE • • • • • • • • • • • • 576 ACRE OF GRASS 14
    MYSELF I MUST REMAKE • • • • • • • • • • • • 576 ACRE OF GRASS V 14
    WHEN EVER I REMAKE A SONG, • • • • • • • • • • 778 FRIENDS WRONG 2
    IT IS MYSELF THAT I REMAKE. • • • • • • • • • • 778 FRIENDS WRONG 4
REMBRANDT
    "GREATEST SINCE REMBRANDT," ACCORDING TO JOHN SYNGE; • • 602 GALLERY REVIS 26

650

REMEDY
    NOR FIND A REMEDY." "BUT WHAT IF I . . . .   464 HARUN RASHID   84
    AND FIND NO REMEDY. "BUT WHAT IF I . . . .   464 HARUN RASHID   V   84
REMEMBER
    SAD TO REMEMBER, SICK WITH YEARS, ...   2 OISIN 1   5
    REMEMBER THE WISDOM OUT OF THE OLD DAYS! . . . . .   158 TO HIS HEART   2
    HE COULD REMEMBER WHEN HE HAD HAD FINE DREAMS. . .   182 QUEEN MAEVE   56
    REMEMBER DEIRDRE AND HER MAN! . . . .   192 BAILE AILLINN   91
    DO YOU REMEMBER WHEN WE SANK THAT GALLEY . . . . .   223 SHADOW WATER B   20
    NO, NO--NOT ARTHUR. I REMEMBER NOW. . . . .   242 SHADOW WATER B   405
    I HALF REMEMBER. IT HAS BEEN IN MY DREAMS. . . . .   251 SHADOW WATER B   606
    REMEMBER HIS DELIBERATE HAPPINESS. . . . .   370 EGO DOMINUS   53
    AND I REMEMBER WILDNESS LOST . . . .   453 DEATH OF HARE   9
    CEASE TO REMEMBER THE DELIGHTS OF YOUTH, TRAVEL-WEARIED   459 FROM OEDIPUS   2
        AGED MAN!
    LONG PAST HIS PRIME REMEMBER THINGS THAT ARE . . .   477 SELF AND SOUL   18
    WHAT DID WE REMEMBER . . . .   519 LOVES LONENESS   9
    REMEMBER ALL THOSE RENOWNED GENERATIONS, ...   613 MARCH SONGS 1   1
    REMEMBER ALL THOSE RENOWNED GENERATIONS, ...   613 MARCH SONGS 1   11
    REMEMBER ALL THAT HAVE SUNK IN THEIR BLOOD, ...   613 MARCH SONGS 1   12
    REMEMBER ALL THAT HAVE DIED ON THE SCAFFOLD, . . .   613 MARCH SONGS 1   13
    REMEMBER ALL THAT HAVE FLED, THAT HAVE STOOD, . . .   613 MARCH SONGS 1   14
    REMEMBER ALL THESE RENOWNED GENERATIONS, ...   613 MARCH SONGS 1   V   11
    DO YOU REMEMBER, AIBRIC, HOW YOU BORE . . . . . .   749 SHADOW WATER A   48
REMEMBERED
    SOME FEW REMEMBERED STILL WHEN I WAS YOUNG . . . . .   410 TOWER   33
    REMEMBERED OUT OF BABYLONIAN ALMANACS, ...   426 PHANTOM HATRED   20
REMEMBEREST
    TILL THOU REMEMBEREST ONLY HOW THE SEA . . . . . .   670 ISLE STAT II 3   94
REMEMBERING   SEE KING-REMEMBERING
    'TIS SAD REMEMBERING, SICK WITH YEARS, ...   2 OISIN 1   V   5
    REMEMBERING HOW THE FENIANS STEPT . . . .   24 OISIN 1   370
    REMEMBERING HOW ALONG THE PLAINS, ...   24 OISIN 1   V 370
    SMOTE ON THEIR BRAINS THAT DWELT REMEMBERING AYE. .   34 OISIN 2   V 77A
    MY ANGRY, KING REMEMBERING SOUL ONE JOT! . . . . .   36 OISIN 2   V   94
    OLD AND REMEMBERING, WHAT AVAILS THE WIND . . . . .   42 OISIN 2   V 206
    REMEMBERING HOW I HAD STOOD BY WHITE-HAIRED FINN .   44 OISIN 2   227
    REMEMBERING HOW I PACED IN DAYS GONE O'ER, ...   44 OISIN 2   V 227
    REMEMBERING HOW I STOOD BY WHITE-HAIRED FINN . . .   44 OISIN 2   V 227
    I PACE REMEMBERING. FROM MY MISTY THRONE . . . . .   45 OISIN 2   V 239C
    . . . REMEMBERING ALONE THAT DELIGHT . . . .   54 OISIN 3   111
    REMEMBERING ITS LONG-OARED COMPANIONS, ...   55 OISIN 3   118
    FOR MY REMEMBERING HOUR IS DONE! . . . .   86 MAD KING GOLL   V   69
    REMEMBERING ALL THAT SHAKEN HAIR . . . .   135 TWO TREES   17
    OR REMEMBERING HERS THEY WILL FIND NO OTHER FACE FAIR .   163 VALLEY LOVERS   7
    OR, REMEMBERING HERS, THEY WILL HOLD NO OTHER FACE FAIR 163 VALLEY LOVERS V   7
    REMEMBERING THAT SHE TOO HAD SEEMED DIVINE . . . .   182 QUEEN MAEVE   64
    REMEMBERING THAT THE BEST I HAVE DONE . . . . . .   256 WORDS   7
    NO MORE REMEMBERING WHAT HAD BEEN, ...   276 GREY ROCK   122
    REMEMBERING WHAT SHE HAD, ...   316 FRIENDS   24
    REMEMBERING KINDNESS DONE, AND HOW CAN I, ...   340 SHEP GOATHERD   30
    AND BE WELL PLEASED REMEMBERING IT, FOR IN THE OLD DAYS, 351 HER PRAISE   16
    THE SOUL REMEMBERING ITS LONELINESS . . . .   375 PHASES OF MOON   88
    REMEMBERING THAT, IF WALKED SHE THERE, ...   410 TOWER   38
    REMEMBERING THAT HER SHRIEK WAS LOVE . . . .   456 FRIENDS YOUTH   19
    REMEMBERING A WOMAN'S BEAUTY, ...   552 SONGS REWRIT 2 V   11
    REMEMBERING THEE, I SEARCH OUT THESE FAINT FLOWERS . .   704 REMEMBRANCE   1
    OF RHYME; REMEMBERING THEE, THIS CRESCENT NIGHT, . . 704 REMEMBRANCE   2
    REMEMBERING THEE, I MUSE, WHILE FADES IN FLIGHT . .   705 REMEMBRANCE   6
    I HAVE BEGUN REMEMBERING MY DREAMS. . . . .   766 SHADOW WATER A   380
    REMEMBERING AND REMEMBERING. . . . .   782 HEART FRIGHT   11
    REMEMBERING AND REMEMBERING. . . . .   782 HEART FRIGHT   11
REMEMBERS
    HE REMEMBERS FORGOTTEN BEAUTY . . . .   155 FORGOT BEAUTY   T
    MICHAEL ROBARTES REMEMBERS FORGOTTEN BEAUTY . . .   155 FORGOT BEAUTY   V   T
    AND SO REMEMBERS THAT WHEN ALL MANKIND . . . . . .   447 COLONUS PRAISE   26
REMEMBRANCE
    FOR REMEMBRANCE, LIFTING HER LEANNESS, ...   57 OISIN 3   152
    . . . ALONE WITH REMEMBRANCE AND FEAR! . . . . . .   63 OISIN 3   218
    WITHOUT LAUGHTER, A COUGHING, ALONE WITH REMEMBRANCE AND   63 OISIN 3   V 218
        FEAR!
    REMEMBRANCE. . . . .   704 REMEMBRANCE   T
REMINDED
    REMINDED HIM THAT HE COULD MAKE, ...   302 HOUR DAWN   13
REMORSE
    WHEN SUCH AS I CAST OUT REMORSE . . . .   479 SELF AND SOUL   68
    OR THE DAY'S VANITY, THE NIGHT'S REMORSE. . . . .   491 COOLE BALLYLEE V   40H
    OR THE DAY'S VANITY, THE NIGHT'S REMORSE. . . . .   495 CHOICE   8
    THE HEART REMORSE. . . . .   500 VACILLATION   8
    REMORSE FOR INTEMPERATE SPEECH . . . .   506 REMORSE SPEECH   T
    A SOUL INCAPABLE OF REMORSE OR REST! . . . .   601 GALLERY REVIS   7
REMOTE
    OR AUGHT REMOTE! OR HAST THOU NEVER HEARD . . . .   672 ISLE STAT II 3   153
    REMOTE FROM ALL THE HARD EARTH TROUBLES, ...   731 PRIEST FAIRY   80
REND
    MAY REND WHAT COMES IN REACH. . . . .   488 CRAZED MOON   18
    AND OF NASCHINA'S NOW THEY TELL--RENDI RENDI . . .   665 ISLE STAT II 2   69
    AND OF NASCHINA'S NOW THEY TELL--RENDI RENDI . . .   665 ISLE STAT II 2   69
RENDING
    RENDING THE HORSE'S FLANK. KING EOCHAID REELED, .   277 TWO KINGS   13
    THOUGH MY LOVE-SICK HEART IS RENDING, ...   646 ISLE STAT I 1   38

RENDS
AT MORN, AND WITH HER FEET EACH COBWEB RENDS, ... 670 ISLE STAT II 3   99
RENEW
SO DID SHE YOUR STRENGTH RENEW, ... 259 UNWORTH PRAISE   6
AND HALF AND HALF CONSUME WHAT THEY RENEW, ... 500 VACILLATION   15
AND RANTING TIME RENEW, ... 606 SONGS BURDEN 1   20
SOME FEW HALF WAKE AND HALF RENEW THEIR CHOICE, ... 622 HOUND VOICE   6
RENEWED
BUT IN THE GRAVE ALL, ALL, SHALL BE RENEWED. . . . . . 356 BROKEN DREAMS   21
THEY HAVE LOUD MUSIC, HOPE EVERY DAY RENEWED . . . . . 398 LEADERS CROWD   11
RENOUNCE
RENOUNCE THAT DRUDGERY, ... 600 THOSE IMAGES   7
RENOUNCING
I BID THEE STAY, RENOUNCING THY MAD QUEST." . . . . . 669 ISLE STAT II 3   89
RENOWN
IN THINKING OF HIS LOST RENOWN. . . . . 379 SAINT HUNCH   3
ALL THE RENOWN THAT FELL. . . . . 547 TO SAME TUNE 2   26
ALL THE RENOWN THAT FELL. . . . . 614 MARCH SONGS 1   26
RENOWNED
OUR MOST RENOWNED PATRIOTS STAND, ... 460 THREE MONUMENT   2
JUSTIFY ALL THOSE RENOWNED GENERATIONS; . . . . . . 545 TO SAME TUNE 2   1
JUSTIFY ALL THOSE RENOWNED GENERATIONS, ... 546 TO SAME TUNE 2   11
REMEMBER ALL THOSE RENOWNED GENERATIONS, ... 613 MARCH SONGS 1   1
REMEMBER ALL THOSE RENOWNED GENERATIONS, ... 613 MARCH SONGS 1   11
REMEMBER ALL THESE RENOWNED GENERATIONS, ... 613 MARCH SONGS 1 V 11
RENT
HAS CLOVEN AND RENT THEIR HEARTS IN TWAIN, ... 66 HAPPY SHEPHERD   33
HAS TORN AND RENT THEIR HEARTS IN TWAIN, ... 66 HAPPY SHEPHERD V 33
HAS DRIED THE SAP OUT OF MY VEINS, AND RENT . . . . . 260 FASC DIFFICULT   2
AND RENT HER CLOTHES AND MADE HER MOAN: . . . . . . 275 GREY ROCK   108
THAT HAS NOT BEEN RENT." . . . . 513 JANE TALK BISH   18
RENYI
HOW FERENCZ RENYI KEPT SILENT. . . . . 709 FERENCZ RENYI   T
THY NAME IS?" "RENYI." "OF?" "THIS VILLAGE." "GOOD! . . 709 FERENCZ RENYI   13
THY NAME IS?" "FERENCZ RENYI." "OF?" "THIS VILLAGE." . . 709 FERENCZ RENYI V 13
   "GOOD!
THE SPIRIT OF YOUNG RENYI HAS GROWN OLD. . . . . . 710 FERENCZ RENYI   17
LIKE SMALL BROWN MOTHS, A-TREMBLE. "RENYI SAY . . . . 713 FERENCZ RENYI   82
WHITE, RENYI SILENT STANDS; THAT MAIDEN SWEET . . . . 713 FERENCZ RENYI V 84
I CURSE THEE--CURSE THEE!" RENYI SILENT STANDS, ... 714 FERENCZ RENYI   107
AND SOFT, ONE GLIMMERING STAR. RENYI HAS CAST . . . . 714 FERENCZ RENYI   115
YOUNG FERENCZ RENYI BURSTS HIS BONDS--AT LAST, ... 714 FERENCZ RENYI V 116
RENYI'S
THE YOUNG ONE WITH THE OTHERS." RENYI'S PALE . . . . 713 FERENCZ RENYI   84
REPENTANCE
REPENTANCE KEEPS MY HEART IMPURE: . . . . 507 STREAM AND SUN   6
REPINING
OF KNITTED MUSIC. OFT THE FOND REPINING . . . . . 33 OISIN 2 V 68C
REPLIED
THAT WANES." "AH, WISTFUL VOICE," REPLIED THE OTHER, . . 79 EPHEMERA V   3
WHILE SLOWLY HE WHOSE HAND HELD HERS REPLIED: . . . . 80 EPHEMERA   11
THE PARTED LIPS REPLIED, "I SEEK YOUR HELP, ... 183 QUEEN MAEVE   83
NOR THE COLD NORTH HAS TROUBLED?" HE REPLIED, ... 184 QUEEN MAEVE   90
REPLIED: "TO BE BORN WOMAN IS TO KNOW-- . . . . . 205 ADAMS CURSE   18
SIGHING REPLIED: "WHAT NEED HAVE WE FOR HASTE . . . . 276 TWO KINGS V   C
THEN I REPLIED, "ALTHOUGH YOU HIDE A SECRET, ... 281 TWO KINGS   95
THEREON REPLIED: "A COCKEREL . . . . 387 SOLOMON WITCH   9
JAMES CONNOLLY REPLIED: . . . . 396 ROSE TREE   8
"YOU BUT IMAGINE LIES ALL DAY, O MURDERER," I REPLIED. . 450 OWEN AHERNE   17
IN NOBLE RAGE REPLIED . . . . 516 MANS SONG   5
WHAT CALCULATION, NUMBER, MEASUREMENT, REPLIED? . . . . 611 STATUES   27
REPLIES
A KIND OLD NUN IN A WHITE HOOD REPLIES: . . . . . 443 SCHOOL CHILDR   2
THE HEART REPLIES . . . . 449 OWEN AHERNE V   T
AND THEREUPON REPLIES . . . . 531 FATHER CHILD   6
IF EMPTY NIGHT REPLIES? . . . . 533 FIRST CONFESS   18
ALONE WITH OUR OWN WHISPERS AND REPLIES-- . . . . . 702 MOSADA 3   80
REPLY
MAKE THE HILLS REPLY." . . . . 98 FOXHUNTER   26
AND MAKE THE HILLS REPLY." . . . . 98 FOXHUNTER V   26
MAKE THE HILLS REPLY." . . . . 99 FOXHUNTER   34
AND MAKE THE HILLS REPLY." . . . . 99 FOXHUNTER V   34
COMPLAINED OF THE PEOPLE." ALL I COULD REPLY . . . . 352 PEOPLE   29
CAN WITH A FITTING CONFIDENCE REPLY. . . . . . . 494 AT ALGECIRAS   18
REPLY LIKE MOANING OF IMPRISONED ELF: . . . . . . 652 ISLE STAT I 2   11
REPORT
THERE'S NOT A MAN CAN REPORT . . . . 319 DOLLS   8
ABASHED BY THAT REPORT, ... 516 MANS SONG   13
REPOSE
OR IT MAY BE LOOSENED IN REPOSE, ... 386 ROBARTES DANCE   35
BUT KEEP A MARBLE OR A BRONZE REPOSE. . . . . . . 445 SCHOOL CHILDR   52
VAIN GAIETY, VAIN BATTLE, VAIN REPOSE, ... 629 CIRCUS ANIMALS   12
REPRISALS
REPRISALS . . . . 791 REPRISALS   T
REPROACH
IF RAILING AND REPROACH AND MOCKERY . . . . . . 243 SHADOW WATER B   438
AND YET YOU MAKE A CLAMOUR OF REPROACH. . . . . . 243 SHADOW WATER B   444
BUT IF IT BE REPROACH, I ANSWER THIS: . . . . . . 244 SHADOW WATER B   453
REPROOF
THEREON MY PHOENIX ANSWERED IN REPROOF, ... 352 PEOPLE   22
TOLD OF A HARSH REPROOF, OR TRIVIAL EVENT . . . . . 443 SCHOOL CHILDR   11

652

REPROVED
    THIS WAY WERE ALL REPROVED . . . . 93 FATHER OHART   39
    CRAZY JANE REPROVED . . . . 509 JANE REPROVED   T
    CRACKED MARY REPROVED . . . . 509 JANE REPROVED V   T
REPROVES
    HE REPROVES THE CURLEW . . . . 155 REPROVE CURLEW   T
    HANRAHAN REPROVES THE CURLEW . . . . 155 REPROVE CURLEW V   T
    WHILE HIS LOUD SONG REPROVES . . . . 536 PARTING   7
REPUTATION
    THE REPUTATION OF HIS LIFETIME LOST . . . . 351 PEOPLE   5
REPUTE
    AND I AM IN NO GOOD REPUTE . . . . 276 GREY ROCK   127
RESEMBLE
    RESEMBLE FORMS THAT ARE OR SEEM . . . . 639 BEN BULBEN   58
RESEMBLING   SEE MIRROR-RESEMBLING
    MIRROR RESEMBLING DREAMS. . . . . 415 TOWER V   165
RESERVED
    MUCH TOO SOLEMN AND RESERVED. . . . . 342 SHEP GOATHERD   94
RE-SHINING
    IN BUSY FLAKES, RE-SHINING FROM THE LAKE, ... 662 ISLE STAT II 2   3
    RE-SHINING IN HIS EYES. SO EVER MOVES . . . . 689 NETTLESHIP   12
RESIGNED
    HE, TOO, HAS RESIGNED HIS PART . . . . 393 EASTER 1916   36
RESINOUS
    MAN'S OWN RESINOUS HEART HAS FED. . . . . 438 SONGS PLAY 2   16
RESOLVED
    BECOME OUR CAPTAIN, AIBRIC. I AM RESOLVED . . . . . 225 SHADOW WATER B   64
    ANTONIO! WE HAVE RESOLVED TO FIGHT. . . . . . . 664 ISLE STAT II 2   55
RESONANCE
    NIGHT RESONANCE RECEDES, NIGHT-WALKERS' SONG . . . 497 BYZANTIUM   3
    NIGHT'S RESONANCE RECEDES, NIGHT-WALKERS SONG . . . . 497 BYZANTIUM V   3
RESOUNDED
    THE HORN RESOUNDED AS THOUGH IT HAD BEEN SILVER, ... 277 TWO KINGS   16
RESOUNDING
    HAVE FOUND DELIGHT, IN THE RESOUNDING OARS, ... 750 SHADOW WATER A   72
RESOUNDS
    THAT TREMBLES AND RESOUNDS WITH HYMNS TO THEE, ... 684 SEEKER V   69C
RESOURCE
    I'LL SEND MINE ARROW, NOW MY ONE RESOURCE; . . . . . 657 ISLE STAT I 3   64
RESPECT
    EARNING RESPECT, HAVE NO STRANGE FRIEND; . . . . . . 337 SCHOLARS V   9
RESPECTABLE
    OLD, LEARNED, RESPECTABLE BALD HEADS . . . . 337 SCHOLARS   2
RESPECTED
    "AND THERE I'LL GROW RESPECTED AT MY EASE, ... 300 BEGGAR CRIED   17
    THAT MOST RESPECTED LADY'S EVERY WISH, ... 410 TOWER   29
RESPONSIBILITIES
    MY GREAT RESPONSIBILITIES? . . . . 380 SONGS FOOL 1   18
RESPONSIBILITY
    RESPONSIBILITY SO WEIGHS ME DOWN. . . . . 501 VACILLATION   50
REST
    NOR THY COMPANIONS. LET THEM REST. . . . . 11 OISIN 1 V 130
    LIKE AN ARMY OF OLD MEN LONGING FOR REST FROM THE MOAN
        OF THE SEAS. . . . . 48 OISIN 3   16
    SQUARE LEAVES OF THE IVY MOVED OVER US, BINDING US DOWN
        TO OUR REST. . . . . 52 OISIN 3   76
    "O FLAMING LION OF THE WORLD, O WHEN WILL YOU TURN TO YOUR
        REST?" . . . . 56 OISIN 3   129
    O FLAMING LION OF THE WORLD, O WHEN WILL YOU TURN TO YOUR
        REST?" . . . . 56 OISIN 3   136
    "OH, FLAMING LION OF THE WORLD, OH, WHEN WILT THOU TURN
        TO THY REST?" . . . . 56 OISIN 3 V 129
    LIKE AN ARMY OF OLD MEN LONGING FOR REST FROM THE MOAN
        OF THE SEAS. . . . . 57 OISIN 3   144
    LIKE AN ARMY OF OLD MEN LOUNGING FOR REST FROM THE FOAM
        OF THE SEAS. . . . . 57 OISIN 3 V 144
    THE REST YOU HAVE HEARD OF, O CROZIERED MAN: . . . . . . 60 OISIN 3   189
    THE REST THOU HAST HEARD OF, THOU CROSIERED ONE-- . . . 60 OISIN 3 V 189
    . . . AND OF OLD WOUNDS, AND TURN TO OUR REST. . . . . 62 OISIN 3   212
    . . . AND OF OLD WOUNDS AND REST. . . . . 62 OISIN 3 V 212
    REST FAR FROM MEN. . . . . 116 FAERY SONG   10
    "I HAVE NO REST, NOR JOY, NOR PEACE, ... 132 FR GILLIGAN   9
    THAT WAS BRIMMED UP WITH PRAYER AND REST: . . . . . . 151 HEART OF WOMAN   2
    AND LAY IN THE DARKNESS, GRUNTING, AND TURNING TO HIS REST. 153 CHANGE BELOVED   12
    DROWNING LOVE'S LONELY HOUR IN DEEP TWILIGHT OF REST, . . 154 BELOVED PEACE   11
    AND TROUBLE WITH A SIGH FOR ALL THINGS LONGING FOR REST . 163 ASKS FORGIVE   23
    AND TROUBLE WITH SIGHS FOR ALL HEARTS WITHOUT REST . . 163 ASKS FORGIVE V   23
    WHY SHOULD YOU BE MORE FAITHFUL THAN THE REST, ... 227 SHADOW WATER B   109
    IN HAVING ONE ANOTHER? HOW COULD I REST . . . . . . 249 SHADOW WATER B   571
    HAD GIVEN BUT AS THE REST . . . . 293 HELEN LIVED   10
    WHO DRAWS A BUCKET WITH THE REST . . . . 335 YOUNG BEAUTY   5
    HE NEVER FOUND HIS REST ASHORE, ... 361 ALF POLLEXFEN   21
    A BUDDHA, HAND AT REST, ... 383 VISION ROBART   19
    AND MAY THE DEVIL TAKE THE REST. . . . . 386 ROBARTES DANCE   24
    MY EYES SHOULD NEVER REST? . . . . 389 IMAGE PAST   18
    TO BREAK UPON A SLEEPER'S REST . . . . 412 TOWER   87
    THE MOTHER BIRD WILL REST . . . . 415 TOWER   170
    AND SHE CAN GET NO REST . . . . 456 FRIENDS YOUTH   8
    SWIFT HAS SAILED INTO HIS REST; . . . . 493 SWIFTS EPITAPH   1
    "JONATHAN SWIFT'S AT REST! . . . . 493 SWIFTS EPITAPH V   1
    SWIFT HAD SAILED INTO HIS REST; . . . . 493 SWIFTS EPITAPH V   1

		PAGE	TITLE		LINE

REST   (CONTINUED)
   IN ALGECIRAS GARDENS, AND THERE REST . . . . 494 AT ALGECIRAS V 5
   THAT HE MIGHT SET AT REST . . . . 496 MOHINI CHATTER 12
   THINKING TO SET AT REST . . . . 496 MOHINI CHATTER V 12
   WHETHER OF PLEASURE OR OF REST. . . . . 521 THREE THINGS 4
   OR FOUND A SUBTERRANEAN REST . . . . 535 CHOSEN 6
   BIDS ALL TRUE LOVERS REST. . . . . 536 PARTING 6
   AND SANG MY MALEDICTION WITH THE REST. . . . . 537 HER VISION 24
   THE REST I PASS, ONE SENTENCE I UNSAY. . . . . 542 PARN FUNERAL 2 1
   I PASS THE REST--ONE SENTENCE I UNSAY-- . . . . 542 PARN FUNERAL 2 V 1
   PRIMORDIAL MOTHERHOOD FORSAKE HIS LIMBS, THE CHILD
     NO LONGER REST, 559 MAGIC DRUM 2
   NOW SINKS THE SAME REST . . . . 574 LOVERS SONG 4
   NOW SUNK IN REST, ... 574 MAIDS 1ST SONG 2
   DO NOT THE REST WITHHOLD. . . . . 588 OLD WICKED MAN 11
   A SOUL INCAPABLE OF REMORSE OR REST: . . . . 601 GALLERY REVIS 7
   LAY SIGHING LIKE THE REST. . . . . 612 NEWS ORACLE 12
   PREPARED A REST FOR THE PEOPLE OF GOD, ... 639 BEN BULBEN 65
   TO PROVE HIS LOVE A KNIGHT WITH LANCE IN REST . . . . 651 ISLE STAT I 1 158
   SHALL NOT SO HOPELESS PROVE: SOME GOD MAY REST . . . 657 ISLE STAT I 3 61
   WILT ROAM AWAY FROM THIS RICH ISLAND REST? . . . . . 669 ISLE STAT II 3 88
   EVE-SOOTHED IN SOME FAR LEAFY REST, ... 686 LIFE 10
   TO PRISONS GO, AND MOSSY RUIN REST . . . . 709 FERENCZ RENYI 2
   TO PRISON GO, AND MOSSY RUIN REST . . . . 709 FERENCZ RENYI V 2
   COME, FATHER. LADY, I NOR REST NOR SIT. . . . . . . 720 WITCH VIVIEN 18
   AND NEVER REST IN THEIR FLIGHT, ... 739 WHERE BOOKS GO 4
   TILL ALL THINGS ARE AT REST. . . . . 741 EARL PAUL 52
RESTED
   I THOUGHT THE END HAD RESTED, WHEN THESE WORDS . . . 32 OISIN 2 V 49
   AND NEVER COULD HAVE RESTED IN THE TOMB . . . . . . 325 ROBERT GREGORY 27
RESTLESS
   GOD SHAKES THE WORLD WITH RESTLESS HANDS. MORE NEAR . 43 OISIN 2 V 208
   YET STILL SHE TURNS HER RESTLESS HEAD: . . . . 65 HAPPY SHEPHERD 5
   AND MAY NO RESTLESS FAY WITH FIDGET FINGER . . . . . 75 ANASHU VIJAYA 90
   MAY NEVER RESTLESS FAY WITH FIDGET FINGER . . . . . . 75 ANASHU VIJAYA V 90
   AND MAY NO RESTLESS PITRI'S FIDGET FINGER . . . . . . 75 ANASHU VIJAYA V 90
   "CHOOSE!" RESTLESS HAYNAU'S FINGERS TAPPING GO. . . . 711 FERENCZ RENYI 41
RESTLESS-FOOTED
   WHERE GOES TO GAZE THE RESTLESS-FOOTED STAR . . . . . 32 OISIN 2 V 50G
RESTLESSNESS
   THEIR PASSION AND THEIR RESTLESSNESS AND RUTH . . . . 687 TWO TITANS 24
RESTORED
   RESTORED THIS TOWER FOR MY WIFE GEORGE: . . . . 406 CARVED STONE 4
RESTRAINING
   RESTRAINING RECKLESS MIDDLE-AGE? . . . . 262 STUDENTS AGIT 4
RESULTS
   THE RESULTS OF THOUGHT . . . . 504 RESULT THOUGHT T
RESUME
   AND MUST THE COMMON ROUND OF DAY RESUME. . . . . . . 557 RIBH ECSTASY 8
RE-SUNG
   AN OLD SONG RE-SUNG . . . . 90 SALLEY GARDENS V T
RETIRING
   HERE GROW THAT SHY, RETIRING SISTERHOOD, ... 651 ISLE STAT I 2 4
RETURN
   RETURN WHEN YOU ARE WEARY, ... 33 OISIN 2 V 65
   A JUBILANT LIFE AMONG THE LEAVES, RETURN, ... 35 OISIN 2 V 89A
   WE WOULD RETURN TO OUR OWN COUNTRY, FORGAEL, ... 248 SHADOW WATER B 539
   YOU MUST RETURN, WHETHER YOU WOULD OR NO, ... 285 TWO KINGS 197
   OF THEIR RETURN TO THAT ANCESTRAL HOUSE. . . . . . . 286 TWO KINGS V 218C
   THOUGH THE GREAT SONG RETURN NO MORE . . . . 485 NINETEENTH CEN 1
   "GOD I HAVE LOVED, BUT SHOULD I ASK RETURN . . . . . 609 IN TARAS HALLS 14
   THE FLAGRANT SIGNAL OF MY LORD'S RETURN, ... 645 ISLE STAT I 1 13
   THAT FLOWER I SEEK. THOU NEVER WILT RETURN. . . . . 653 ISLE STAT I 2 44
   MY SHEPHERD GARMENTS, AND RETURN ANON. . . . . 659 ISLE STAT II 1 29
   ANTONIO, IF I RETURN NO MORE. . . . . 663 ISLE STAT II 2 17
RETURNED
   RETURNED AND YET UNREQUITED LOVE. . . . . 358 PRESENCES 8
   HERODIAS' DAUGHTERS HAVE RETURNED AGAIN, ... 433 NINETEEN 19 118
RETURNING
   WITH NO RETURNING GLANCE, IN WORDLESS MOOD . . . . . 44 OISIN 2 V 230A
   AND MOCKS RETURNING VICTORY, HE PASSED . . . . 279 TWO KINGS 58
   AWAITS RETURNING SPRING. . . . . 517 HER ANXIETY 2
   MOURN--AND THEN ONWARD, THERE IS NO RETURNING . . . . 738 MOURN THEN ON 13
RETURNS
   RETURNS THAT SOLDIER IN THE EVENING RAYS . . . . . . 711 FERENCZ RENYI 49
REVEALING   SEE HEART-REVEALING
REVEL
   WHERE REVEL OF FOX-GLOVE IS AND REVEL OF ROSES." . . . 669 ISLE STAT II 3 86
   WHERE REVEL OF FOX-GLOVE IS AND REVEL OF ROSES." . . . 669 ISLE STAT II 3 86
   WHERE REVEL OF FOXGLOVE IS AND REVEL OF ROSES." . . . 669 ISLE STAT II 3 V 86
   WHERE REVEL OF FOXGLOVE IS AND REVEL OF ROSES." . . . 669 ISLE STAT II 3 V 86
REVELATION
   SURELY SOME REVELATION IS AT HAND: . . . . 402 SECOND COMING 9
REVELRY
   AND THERE WE HUSHED THE REVELRY: . . . . 20 OISIN 1 295
   IN A SAD REVELRY HE SANG AND SWUNG . . . . 39 OISIN 2 160
   AND SILENCE HOLDING REVELRY AND FEAST: . . . . 705 REMEMBRANCE 12
   WHERE NIAM HEADS THE REVELRY. . . . . 743 DANAAN QUICK 29
REVERBERATED
   GOES FLICKERING IN REVERBERATED LIGHT. . . . . 653 ISLE STAT I 2 53

		PAGE	TITLE	LINE

REVERE
  MEN THAT REVERE YOUR FATHER YET . . . .   791 REPRISALS   17
REVERENCE
  A NUN AT LEAST HAS ALL MEN'S REVERENCE . . . . . .   448 HERO GIRL FOOL   12
  THAT MEN HAVE REVERENCE FOR THEIR HOLINESS . . . .   448 HERO GIRL FOOL   14
  FOR THEY AT LEAST HAVE ALL MEN'S REVERENCE . . . .   448 HERO GIRL FOOL V   12
REVERENT
  I BRING YOU WITH REVERENT HANDS . . . .   157 POET BELOVED   1
REVERIE
  IN A REVERIE FORGETFUL OF ALL THINGS, OVER THE BUBBLING   56 OISIN 3   140
    GROUND.
  IN REVERIE FORGETFUL OF ALL THINGS, OVER THE BUBBLING   56 OISIN 3   V   140
    GROUND.
  TROUBLING THE ENDLESS REVERIE. . . . .   65 HAPPY SHEPHERD   21
  IN THE UNIVERSE'S REVERIE. . . . .   65 HAPPY SHEPHERD V   21
  IN SOLEMN REVERIE ROSE TO HEAR . . . .   85 MAD KING GOLL   V   62
  IMAGINING IN EXCITED REVERIE . . . .   403 FOR DAUGHTER   13
  IN REVERIE, OR IN VISION, SAW . . . .   420 MY HOUSE   V   20E
  TO BRAZEN HAWKS. NOR SELF-DELIGHTING REVERIE,   427 PHANTOM HATRED   29
  HEROIC REVERIE MOCKED BY CLOWN AND KNAVE, ... 619 BRONZE HEAD   27
REVERIES
  I TOO HAVE RHYMED MY REVERIES, BUT YOUTH . . . . .   340 SHEP GOATHERD   43
  FRENZIES BEWILDER, REVERIES PERTURB THE MIND; . . . 426 PHANTOM HATRED   7
  THAT ANIMATE A MOTHER'S REVERIES. . . . .   445 SCHOOL CHILDR   51
REVERSAL
  AN AGE IS THE REVERSAL OF AN AGE! . . . .   541 PARN FUNERAL 1   16
REVISITED
  IF YOU HAVE REVISITED THE TOWN, THIN SHADE, ... 292 TO A SHADE   1
  THE MUNICIPAL GALLERY REVISITED . . . .   601 GALLERY REVIS   T
RE-VISITED
  THE MUNICIPAL GALLERY RE-VISITED . . . .   601 GALLERY REVIS   V   T
REVOLUTION
  HURRAH FOR REVOLUTION AND MORE CANNON-SHOT! . . . . 590 GREAT DAY   1
  HURRAH FOR REVOLUTION AND CANNON COME AGAIN! . . .   590 GREAT DAY   3
  HURRAH FOR REVOLUTION AND MORE CANNON SHOT! . . . . 590 GREAT DAY   V   1
  IRELAND AFTER THE REVOLUTION IV . . . .   628 JANE MOUNTAIN   V   T
REVOLUTIONARY
  A REVOLUTIONARY SOLDIER KNEELING TO BE BLESSED; . . 601 GALLERY REVIS   8
  FIRST I GREET MACCARTAN, REVOLUTIONARY LEADER. . .   790 DEDICATION   1
REWARD
  THE STRANGE REWARD OF ALL THAT DISCIPLINE. . . . .   374 PHASES OF MOON   57
  O BITTER REWARD . . . .   785 YOUR HEART   9
  O BITTER REWARD . . . .   786 YOUR HEART   22
  O BITTER REWARD . . . .   786 YOUR HEART   35
REWARDED
  HAD BEEN REWARDE' THUS . . . .   384 VISION ROBART   67
REWARDING
  REWARDING IN ME_DIOUS GUILE . . . .   66 HAPPY SHEPHERD V   39
REWARDS
  SHE OFFERS GREAT REWARDS IF WE TURN EAST . . . . .   755 SHADOW WATER A   169
REWORDING
  REWORDING IN MELODIOUS GUILE . . . .   66 HAPPY SHEPHERD   39
REWRITTEN
  TWO SONGS REWRITTEN FOR THE TUNE'S SAKE . . . . .   550 SONGS REWRIT 1   T
RE-WRITTEN
  AN OLD POEM RE-WRITTEN . . . .   129 BOOK STORIES   V   T
RHADAMANTHUS
  BLAND RHADAMANTHUS BECKONS HIM, ...   530 DELPHIC ORACLE   3
RHAPSODISTS   SEE WOOD-RHAPSODISTS
RHAPSODY
  ALL RHAPSODY HATH SORROW FOR ITS SOUL. . . . . .   652 ISLE STAT I 2   17
RHETORICIAN
  THE RHETORICIAN WOULD DECEIVE HIS NEIGHBOURS, . . . 369 EGO DOMINUS   46
RHINOCEROS
  NINE SWORDS WITH HANDLES OF RHINOCEROS HORN . . . . 239 SHADOW WATER B   368
RHYME
  RHYME THAT RHYMED UPON OISIN'S NAME, ...   7 OISIN 1   64
  "RHYME, THAT RHYMED TO USHEEN'S NAME, ...   7 OISIN 1   V   64
  TO THAT LOW LAUGHING WOODLAND RHYME. . . . . . .   14 OISIN 1   176
  TO THE MUSIC OF THE GOLDEN RHYME. . . . .   14 OISIN 1   V   176
  I BRING YOU MY PASSIONATE RHYME. . . . .   157 POET BELOVED   8
  TO BUILD A PERFECT BEAUTY IN RHYME. . . . .   164 PERFECT BEAUTY   3
  TO BUILD THE PERFECT BEAUTY IN RHYME, ...   164 PERFECT BEAUTY V   3
  INTRODUCTORY RHYME . . . .   269 PARDON FATHERS V   T
  CLOSING RHYME . . . .   320 REED WHISPERER V   T
  I LET THEM STRAY. I THOUGHT OF RHYME ALONE, . . .   339 SHEP GOATHERD   11
  FOR RHYME CAN BEAT A MEASURE OUT OF TROUBLE . . .   339 SHEP GOATHERD   12
  I HAD DRIVEN EVERY RHYME INTO ITS PLACE . . . . .   339 SHEP GOATHERD   14
  YOU HAVE PUT THE THOUGHT IN RHYME. I WORKED ALL DAY, 341 SHEP GOATHERD   58
  FROM DREAM TO DREAM AND RHYME TO RHYME I HAVE RANGED 357 BROKEN DREAMS   39
  FROM DREAM TO DREAM AND RHYME TO RHYME I HAVE RANGED 357 BROKEN DREAMS   39
  THAN SOULS THAT START NO GAME AND TURN NO RHYME! . . 464 HARUN RASHID   68
  AND SING IT RHYME UPON RHYME . . . .   480 BLOOD AND MOON   10
  AND SING IT RHYME UPON RHYME . . . .   480 BLOOD AND MOON   10
  THE MIND OF MAN OR ELEVATE A RHYME! . . . .   492 COOLE BALLYLEE   45
  THAT MUST SING IN A RHYME . . . .   529 TOM CRUACHAN   2
  SAVING THE RHYME RATS HEAR BEFORE THEY DIE. . . . . 542 PARN FUNERAL 1   28
  AND DEAD AS ARE THE LOVERS OF OLD RHYME . . . . .   674 ISLE STAT II 3 V   204
  OF RHYME: REMEMBERING THEE, THIS CRESCENT NIGHT, . . 704 REMEMBRANCE   2
  NAY, RISE AND FLATTER HER WITH GOLDEN RHYME, ... 724 KANVA ON SELF   19
  SINGING A LOVE RHYME TO HIMSELF, ...   741 EARL PAUL   41

	PAGE	TITLE		LINE

RHYME (CONTINUED)
```
      THAT CROWN WAS IN MY DREAMS--NO, NO--IN A RHYME.  . . . .    763 SHADOW WATER A      311
      MY FOSTER-MOTHER SANG IN AN OLD RHYME   . . . . . . .       763 SHADOW WATER A      314
      MY FOSTER MOTHER SANG IN AN OLD RHYME   . . . . . . .       763 SHADOW WATER A  V   314
RHYMED
      RHYME THAT RHYMED UPON OISIN'S NAME, . . . . . . . . .        7 OISIN 1             64
      "RHYME, THAT RHYMED TO USHEEN'S NAME,  . . . . . . . .        7 OISIN 1         V   64
      RHYMED OUT IN LOVE'S DESPAIR . . . . . . . . . . . .        337 SCHOLARS             5
      I TOO HAVE RHYMED MY REVERIES, BUT YOUTH  . . . . . .       340 SHEP GOATHERD       43
      ALL I HAD RHYMED OF THAT MONSTROUS THING  . . . . . .       358 PRESENCES            7
      ALL I HAVE RHYMED OF THAT MONSTROUS THING . . . . . .       358 PRESENCES       V    7
RHYMER
      OR ANYTHING ELSE BUT A RHYMER  . . . . . . . . . . .       552 SONGS REWRIT 2       9
RHYMER'S
      I HAVE AS HEALTHY FLESH AND BLOOD AS ANY RHYMER'S HAD, . .  450 OWEN AHERNE         10
RHYMES
      WHILE I WROUGHT OUT THESE FITFUL DANAAN RHYMES,  . . . .    136 TO SOME I TALK       1
      I DEDICATE THESE FITFUL DANAAN RHYMES  . . . . . . . .     136 TO SOME I TALK  V    1
      MY RHYMES MORE THAN THEIR RHYMING TELL  . . . . . . .      138 TO IRELAND          20
      I CAST MY HEART INTO MY RHYMES,  . . . . . . . . . .       139 TO IRELAND          45
      HE GIVES HIS BELOVED CERTAIN RHYMES  . . . . . . . . .     157 BELOVED RHYMES       T
      AEDH GIVES HIS BELOVED CERTAIN RHYMES  . . . . . . . .     157 BELOVED RHYMES  V    T
      I BADE MY HEART BUILD THESE POOR RHYMES!  . . . . . .      158 BELOVED RHYMES       3
      INTRODUCTORY RHYMES  . . . . . . . . . . . . . . .        217 WOODS OF COOLE  V    T
      INTRODUCTORY RHYMES  . . . . . . . . . . . . . . .        269 PARDON FATHERS  V    T
      CLOSING RHYMES . . . . . . . . . . . . . . . . . .        320 REED WHISPERER  V    T
      CUT OUT OUR RHYMES ON STRIPS OF NEW-TORN BARK  . . . .     343 SHEP GOATHERD      115
      AND CERTAIN MEN, BEING MADDENED BY THOSE RHYMES, . . .     410 TOWER               41
      BUT RHYMES FOR A BEAUTIFUL LADY,  . . . . . . . . .        552 SONGS REWRIT 2      11
RHYMING
      MY RHYMES MORE THAN THEIR RHYMING TELL  . . . . . . .      138 TO IRELAND          20
      HE RHYMING ALONE IN HIS BED. . . . . . . . . . . .        552 SONGS REWRIT 2      12
RHYTHM
      TO THE RHYTHM OF THEIR FEET, . . . . . . . . . . . .      731 STREET DANCERS       2
RIB
      THE HEART BEHIND ITS RIB LAUGHED OUT. . . . . . . .       450 OWEN AHERNE         13
RIBBON
      A SHINING WEB, A FLOATING RIBBON OF CLOTH, . . . . . .     430 NINETEEN 19         50
RIBBONS
      OF THE MATCHING OF RIBBONS FOR BOSOM AND HEAD,  . . . .    151 OLD MOTHER           6
      OF THE MATCHING OF RIBBONS THE BLUE AND THE RED, . . .     151 OLD MOTHER      V    6
RIBH
      RIBH AT THE TOMB OF BAILE AND AILLINN  . . . . . . .      554 RIBH AT TOMB         T
      RIBH DENOUNCES PATRICK . . . . . . . . . . . . . .        556 RIBH PATRICK         T
      RIBH PREFERS AN OLDER THEOLOGY . . . . . . . . . .        556 RIBH PATRICK    V    T
      RIBH IN ECSTASY  . . . . . . . . . . . . . . . . .        557 RIBH ECSTASY         T
      RIBH CONSIDERS CHRISTIAN LOVE INSUFFICIENT  . . . . .     558 RIBH CHRISTIAN       T
RICE
      VIJAYA, I HAVE BROUGHT MY EVENING RICE!  . . . . . .       72 ANASHU VIJAYA       23
      AH! THERE HE SNAPS MY RICE.  I TOLD YOU SO. . . . . .      73 ANASHU VIJAYA       38
      BECAUSE YOU SAVED MY RICE.  HAVE YOU NO THANKS?  . . .     73 ANASHU VIJAYA       40
      FOR SPRING RICE HAD TO WHISPER IT, . . . . . . . .       582 ROGER CASEMENT      13
RICH
      THE NIGHT SMELLED RICH WITH JUNE.  . . . . . . . .       160 CAP AND BELLS   V   28
      ONE OF YOU THREE IS A RICH MAN, . . . . . . . . . .      295 THREE BEGGARS       21
      "NOR SHOULD SHE BE TOO RICH, BECAUSE THE RICH  . . .     300 BEGGAR CRIED        13
      "NOR SHOULD SHE BE TOO RICH, BECAUSE THE RICH  . . .     300 BEGGAR CRIED        13
      POOR MEN HAVE GROWN TO BE RICH MEN, . . . . . . . .      301 RUN PARADISE        15
      AND RICH MEN GROWN TO BE POOR AGAIN, . . . . . . . .     301 RUN PARADISE        16
      TOIL AND GROW RICH, . . . . . . . . . . . . . . .        310 WITCH                1
      GROW RICH, POPULAR AND FULL OF INFLUENCE, . . . . .      369 EGO DOMINUS         43
      CEREMONY'S A NAME FOR THE RICH HORN, . . . . . . . .     406 FOR DAUGHTER        79
      DID ALL OLD MEN AND WOMEN, RICH AND POOR, . . . . .      413 TOWER               97
      SURELY AMONG A RICH MAN'S FLOWERING LAWNS, . . . . .     417 ANCEST HOUSES        1
      OUT OF THE OBSCURE DARK OF THE RICH STREAMS,  . . . .    417 ANCEST HOUSES       14
      SHADOWS THE INHERITED GLORY OF THE RICH. . . . . . .     418 ANCEST HOUSES       16
      FOR THE MOST RICH INHERITOR, . . . . . . . . . . .       422 MY TABLE            25
      OR GARDENS RICH IN MEMORY GLORIFIED  . . . . . . .       491 COOLE BALLYLEE      35
      IN THE RICH MIDNIGHT OF THE GARDEN TREES  . . . . .      494 AT ALGECIRAS         5
      IN THE RICH MIDNIGHT OF THE GARDEN TREE  . . . . . .     494 AT ALGECIRAS    V    5
      ALTHOUGH THEIR CHILDREN NEED A RICH ESTATE;  . . . .     500 VACILLATION         24
      DRY TIMBER UNDER THAT RICH FOLIAGE,  . . . . . . .       536 HER VISION           1
      THE RICH MAN AND HIS AFFAIRS, . . . . . . . . . . .      540 FROM ANTIGONE        3
      RICH FOLIAGE THAT THE STARLIGHT GLITTERED THROUGH,  . .   541 PARN FUNERAL 1       8
      OR ANY RICH, DARK NOTHING DISINTER  . . . . . . . .      565 GYRES               22
      AND WHETHER A MAN BE RICH OR POOR  . . . . . . . .       582 ROGER CASEMENT  V   19
      THE COLONEL KNOCKED ON THE RICH MAN'S DOOR,  . . . .     595 COLONEL MARTIN      28
      HIS WIFE HE FOUND AND THE RICH MAN  . . . . . . . .      595 COLONEL MARTIN      43
      THE COLONEL KNOCKED ON A RICH MAN'S DOOR.  . . . . .     595 COLONEL MARTIN      28
      AND THE RICH MAN HAD PAID THEM WELL  . . . . . . .       596 COLONEL MARTIN      57
      THOUGH RICH ON EVERY SHORE . . . . . . . . . . . .       606 SONGS BURDEN 1      11
      WILT ROAM AWAY FROM THIS RICH ISLAND REST?  . . . .      669 ISLE STAT II 3      88
RICHES
      MORE RICHES THAN THEY EVER HOPED TO FIND?  . . . . .      226 SHADOW WATER B      94
      THE ONLY RICHES THAT HAVE HIT MY FANCY. . . . . . .      226 SHADOW WATER B      96
      WHAT RICHES CAN YOU FIND IN THIS WASTE SEA  . . . . .     226 SHADOW WATER B      97
      WHAT'S RICHES TO HIM . . . . . . . . . . . . . .         310 PEACOCK              1
      RICHES DROVE OUT RANK, . . . . . . . . . . . . . .       626 STATES HOLIDAY       2
RICHNESS
      THEIR RICHNESS THROUGH THE SUMMER AND THE SPRING; . . .   279 TWO KINGS       V   62C
```

```
RICK                                                           PAGE      TITLE            LINE
        THAT SHE MAY QUENCH THE RICK SHE HAS FIRED, AND THOUGH  .   .  282 TWO KINGS          116
RID
        WHERE I AM RID OF LIFE--THE EVENTS OF THE WORLD--
        TO RID ME OF THE DEVIL IN MY SHOES," .   .   .   .   .   .  227 SHADOW WATER B     121
RIDDEN      SEE DRAGON-RIDDEN OUT-RIDDEN                          299 BEGGAR CRIED         6
        WHEN THEY HAD RIDDEN A LITTLE WAY
        AND RIDDEN OUT TO WELCOME THEM, AND NOW,    .   .   .   .  191 BAILE AILLINN        56
        AND RIDDEN TOWARDS IT, BEING IGNORANT.  .   .   .   .   .  286 TWO KINGS      V    218
        SHE HAD RIDDEN WELL TO HOUNDS.  .   .   .   .   .   .   .  286 TWO KINGS      V    218
        NOW DAYS ARE DRAGON RIDDEN, THE NIGHTMARE  .   .   .   .  392 EASTER 1916    V     23
RIDDLED                                                           429 NINETEEN 19    V     25
        RIDDLED WITH LIGHT.  AH! WHEN THE GHOST BEGINS TO QUICKEN, 316 COLD HEAVEN         9
RIDE
        "WHY, AS YE RIDE, DROOPS LOW EACH HEAD?  .   .   .   .   .    4 OISIN 1        V     32
        AND FROM WHAT COUNTRY DO YOU RIDE?  .   .   .   .   .   .    5 OISIN 1              45
        AND INTO WHAT COUNTRY DO YOU RIDE?"  .   .   .   .   .   .    5 OISIN 1        V     45
        "O OISIN, MOUNT BY ME AND RIDE  .   .   .   .   .   .   .    8 OISIN 1              80
        FOR THEY WILL RIDE THE NORTH WHEN THE GER-EAGLE FLIES,  .  146 UNAPPEAS HOST        3
        FOR THEY WILL RIDE THE WINDS WHEN THE GIER-EAGLE FLIES  .  146 UNAPPEAS HOST  V     3
        THAT RIDE UPON HORSES.  .   .   .   .   .   .   .   .   .  266 GALWAY RACES        16
        "WE RIDE BUT SLOWLY THOUGH SO NEAR OUR HOME,"  .   .   .  276 TWO KINGS      V     A
        WHEN WITH THE GALWAY FOXHOUNDS HE WOULD RIDE  .   .   .   .  326 ROBERT GREGORY      57
        ON A FANTASTIC RIDE, MY HORSE'S FLANKS ARE SPURRED .   .  391 UNDER SATURN         6
        ON A FANTASTIC RIDE I SWEAR MY HORSE'S FLANKS WERE SPURRED 391 UNDER SATURN   V     6
        WHEN LONG AGO I SAW HER RIDE  .   .   .   .   .   .   .   .  397 POLIT PRISONER      13
        WHETHER TO PLAY, OR TO RIDE  .   .   .   .   .   .   .   .  431 NINETEEN 19         67
        I RIDE WITH FALCON TO THE RIVER'S EDGE  .   .   .   .   .  463 HARUN RASHID        57
        I RIDE WITH FALCON TO THE WATER'S EDGE  .   .   .   .   .  463 HARUN RASHID   V     57
        SADDLE AND RIDE, I HEARD A MAN SAY,  .   .   .   .   .   .  549 SEVERED HEAD         1
        ALL THOSE TRAGIC CHARACTERS RIDE  .   .   .   .   .   .   .  549 SEVERED HEAD         4
        IMAGES RIDE, I HEARD A MAN SAY,  .   .   .   .   .   .   .  549 SEVERED HEAD   V     1
        OUT OF THE GRAVE.  SADDLE AND RIDE  .   .   .   .   .   .  549 SEVERED HEAD   V     4
        WHAT MATTER THOUGH NUMB NIGHTMARE RIDE ON TOP,  .   .   .  564 GYRES               9
        DID EVER MAN RIDE SUCH A RACE?  .   .   .   .   .   .   .  570 THREE BUSHES        47
        FROM MOUNTAIN TO MOUNTAIN RIDE THE FIERCE HORSEMEN.  .   .  605 SONGS BURDEN 1       9
        FROM MOUNTAIN TO MOUNTAIN RIDE THE FIERCE HORSEMEN.  .   .  606 SONGS BURDEN 1      18
        FROM MOUNTAIN TO MOUNTAIN RIDE THE FIERCE HORSEMEN.  .   .  606 SONGS BURDEN 1      27
        FROM MOUNTAIN TO MOUNTAIN RIDE THE FIERCE HORSEMEN.  .   .  607 SONGS BURDEN 2       9
        FROM MOUNTAIN TO MOUNTAIN RIDE THE FIERCE HORSEMEN.  .   .  607 SONGS BURDEN 2      18
        FROM MOUNTAIN TO MOUNTAIN RIDE THE FIERCE HORSEMEN.  .   .  607 SONGS BURDEN 2      27
        FROM MOUNTAIN TO MOUNTAIN RIDE THE FIERCE HORSEMEN.  .   .  608 SONGS BURDEN 3       9
        FROM MOUNTAIN TO MOUNTAIN RIDE THE FIERCE HORSEMEN.  .   .  608 SONGS BURDEN 3      18
        BUT WHAT CARED I THAT SET HIM ON TO RIDE,  .   .   .   .  608 SONGS BURDEN 3      27
        NOW THEY RIDE THE WINTRY DAWN  .   .   .   .   .   .   .   .  629 CIRCUS ANIMALS      15
        COME RIDE AND RIDE TO THE GARDEN,  .   .   .   .   .   .   .  637 BEN BULBEN          10
        COME RIDE AND RIDE TO THE GARDEN,  .   .   .   .   .   .   .  773 COME RIDE            1
        COME RIDE AND RIDE WITH A WILL!  .   .   .   .   .   .   .  773 COME RIDE            1
        COME RIDE AND RIDE WITH A WILL!  .   .   .   .   .   .   .  773 COME RIDE            2
        COME RIDE AND RIDE TO THE GARDEN,  .   .   .   .   .   .   .  773 COME RIDE            5
        COME RIDE AND RIDE TO THE GARDEN,  .   .   .   .   .   .   .  774 COME RIDE            5
        COME RIDE LIKE THE MARCH WIND!  .   .   .   .   .   .   .  774 COME RIDE            6
        COME RIDE AND RIDE TO THE GARDEN,  .   .   .   .   .   .   .  774 COME RIDE           13
        COME RIDE AND RIDE TO THE GARDEN,  .   .   .   .   .   .   .  774 COME RIDE           13
        COME RIDE AND RIDE TO THE GARDEN,  .   .   .   .   .   .   .  774 COME RIDE           18
        COME RIDE AND RIDE TO THE GARDEN,  .   .   .   .   .   .   .  774 COME RIDE           18
RIDER       SEE SEA-RIDER
        THE RIDER FROM THE NORTH  .   .   .   .   .   .   .   .   .  213 HAPPY TOWNLAND V     T
        THE RIDER, THE BIRDS THAT RANGE  .   .   .   .   .   .   .  393 EASTER 1916         46
RIDERLESS
        BUT ALL IS CHANGED, THAT HIGH HORSE RIDERLESS,
        BUT FASHION'S CHANGED, THAT HIGH-HORSE RIDERLESS .   .   .  492 COOLE BALLYLEE      46
RIDERS                                                            492 COOLE BALLYLEE V     46
        AND IF SHE HEAR HIM MUTTER OF WILD RIDERS,  .   .   .   .  230 SHADOW WATER B     175
        THE RIDERS UPON THE GALLOPING HORSES,  .   .   .   .   .  266 GALWAY RACES         3
        THE RIDERS UPON THE SWIFT HORSES,  .   .   .   .   .   .   .  266 GALWAY RACES         3
        RIDERS UPON THE SWIFT HORSES,  .   .   .   .   .   .   .   .  266 GALWAY RACES   V     3
        THE RIDERS AND THE GALLOPING HORSES,  .   .   .   .   .   .  266 GALWAY RACES   V     3
        SOME FEW HAVE HANDSOME RIDERS, ARE GARLANDED  .   .   .   .  432 NINETEEN 19        114
RIDES
        RIDES UPON SLEEP: A DRUNKEN SOLDIERY  .   .   .   .   .   .  429 NINETEEN 19         26
RIDGE
        "AND BREAKS THE RIDGE OF BATTLE WITH HIS HANDS."  .   .   .  107 CUCHULAIN SEA  V     26
        IN THE LAST RIDGE OF THE BARLEY?  DO OUR WOODS  .   .   .  218 WOODS OF COOLE      33
        THEY SAY THAT ON YOUR BARREN MOUNTAIN RIDGE  .   .   .   .  342 SHEP GOATHERD       79
        LESS BITTER.  THEY HAVE BROUGHT ME FROM THAT RIDGE  .   .  342 SHEP GOATHERD       87
        BEYOND THAT RIDGE LIVED MRS. FRENCH, AND ONCE  .   .   .  410 TOWER               25
        HALF RUNNING, DROPPED AT THE FIRST RIDGE OF THE DESERT  .  468 HARUN RASHID       155
RIDICULOUS
        OF A MOST RIDICULOUS LITTLE BIRD  .   .   .   .   .   .   .  314 MEMORY YOUTH        20
RIDING      SEE HARD-RIDING
        "WHO ARE THE RIDING ONES?" I SAID.  .   .   .   .   .   .   .   12 OISIN 1        V    146
        WERE WE DAYS LONG OR HOURS LONG IN RIDING,  .   .   .   .   47 OISIN 3              9
        THE HOST IS RIDING FROM KNOCKNAREA  .   .   .   .   .   .  140 HOSTING SIDHE        1
        THAT WE ARE RIDING TO:  .   .   .   .   .   .   .   .   .   .  214 HAPPY TOWNLAND      4
        HE IS RIDING TO THE TOWNLAND  .   .   .   .   .   .   .   .  214 HAPPY TOWNLAND     19
        THAT WE WERE RIDING TO:  .   .   .   .   .   .   .   .   .  214 HAPPY TOWNLAND V     4
        HE IS RIDING TO THE TOWNLAND  .   .   .   .   .   .   .   .  215 HAPPY TOWNLAND     39
        HE IS RIDING TO THE TOWNLAND  .   .   .   .   .   .   .   .  216 HAPPY TOWNLAND     59
        RIDING TO HURLEY, OR IN THE BATTLE-HOST  .   .   .   .   .  229 SHADOW WATER B     169
```

			PAGE	TITLE		LINE

RIDING (CONTINUED)
UPON GREAT JUAN RIDING BY: · · · · · · · · · · · · 294 HATED PLAYBOY 4
AT GREAT JUAN RIDING BY: · · · · · · · · · · · 294 HATED PLAYBOY V 4
AND ALL ALONE COMES RIDING THERE · · · · · · · 550 SEVERED HEAD 18

RIFLE
OR THE RIFLE KNOCKS HIM DEAD, · · · · · · · · 637 BEN BULBEN 18
OR THE RIFLE KNOCK HIM DEAD, · · · · · · · · 637 BEN BULBEN V 18

RIGHT
OF MOONLIT STEPS GLIMMERED: AND LEFT AND RIGHT · 31 OISIN 2 35
COME CLEAR OF THE NETS OF WRONG AND RIGHT: · · 147 INTO TWILIGHT 2
COME CLEAR OFF THE NETS OF WRONG AND RIGHT: · · 147 INTO TWILIGHT V 2
TO HER RIGHT HAND CAME THE RED ONE, · · · · · 160 CAP AND BELLS 31
NO, NO, DO NOT SAY THAT. YOU KNOW RIGHT WELL · 227 SHADOW WATER B 107
BUT IT WAS SUDDEN. YOU ARE IN THE RIGHT: · · · 240 SHADOW WATER B 383
I HAVE DONE RIGHT. WHAT COULD I BUT OBEY? · · 243 SHADOW WATER B 443
AND THEREFORE EARNED THE RIGHT—AND YET · · · 273 GREY ROCK 61
BUT THE RIGHT TWIGS FOR AN EAGLE'S NEST: · · · 288 TO WEALTHY MAN 36
WHEN CLOSE TO HIS RIGHT HAND A HEAP · · · · · 302 HOUR DAWN 11
BEING CERTAIN IT WAS NO RIGHT ROCK · · · · · 303 HOUR DAWN 23
BEING CERTAIN IT WAS NO RIGHT PLACE · · · · 303 HOUR DAWN V 23
"IT'S PLAIN THAT YOU ARE NO RIGHT MAN · · · 306 HOUR DAWN 82
THE SHEEP HAD GONE FROM THEIRS. I KNOW RIGHT WELL 339 SHEP GOATHERD 15
I MIGHT HAVE USED THE ONE SUBSTANTIAL RIGHT · · 352 PEOPLE 19
WE HAVE NO GIFT TO SET A STATESMAN RIGHT: · · 359 WAR POEM 3
AND RIGHT BETWEEN THESE TWO A GIRL AT PLAY · · 383 VISION ROBART 21
CAN RULE BY SUPERNATURAL RIGHT. · · · · · · 386 ROBARTES DANCE 36
I HAVE PRINCIPLES TO PROVE ME RIGHT. · · · · 386 ROBARTES DANCE 42
CAN MAKE A RIGHT ROSE TREE." · · · · · · · 396 ROSE TREE 18
RIGHT MASTERY OF NATURAL THINGS, · · · · · 401 DEMON BEAST 37
THAT CHOOSES RIGHT, AND NEVER FIND A FRIEND. · 404 FOR DAUGHTER 24
ROSE FROM THE TABLE AND DECLARED IT RIGHT · · 410 TOWER 43
WHIRLS OUT NEW RIGHT AND WRONG, · · · · · · 430 NINETEEN 19 55
UNCHANGING AND AT PEACE, AND IT IS RIGHT · · 465 HARUN RASHID 96
FOR IT IS A GHOST'S RIGHT, · · · · · · · · 470 ALL SOUL NIGHT 6
WITH A COMMON WRONG OR RIGHT. · · · · · · 476 EVA GORE-BOOTH 23
AND CLAIM AS BY A SOLDIER'S RIGHT . · · · · 478 SELF AND SOUL 31
AND IS SO LOVELY THAT IT SETS TO RIGHT · · · 490 COOLE BALLYLEE 21
BUT IF THESE BE RIGHT · · · · · · · · · 500 VACILLATION 9
IF THESE HAVE NAMED IT RIGHT · · · · · · · 500 VACILLATION V 9
SPEECH AFTER LONG SILENCE: IT IS RIGHT, · · · 523 LONG SILENCE 1
OR ASK IF ALL BE RIGHT · · · · · · · · · 532 BEFORE WORLD 4
AND RULE IN HIS OWN RIGHT: · · · · · · · · 538 LAST CONFESS 20
DO NOT DENY HIS RIGHT: · · · · · · · · · 584 ORAHILLY 2
NO RIGHT TAUGHT MAN DENIES. · · · · · · · 590 OLD WICKED MAN V 58
THAT RULE BECAUSE A STRONG RIGHT ARM · · · 597 MODEL LAUREATE 11
WHERE NONE GAINSAY THEIR RIGHT, · · · · · 597 MODEL LAUREATE 14
HERE AT RIGHT OF THE ENTRANCE THIS BRONZE HEAD, 618 BRONZE HEAD 1
WHICH OF HER FORMS HAS SHOWN HER SUBSTANCE RIGHT? 618 BRONZE HEAD 11
AND NEVER GET THE ANSWERS RIGHT. · · · · · 632 MAN AND ECHO 10
WHO, WHEN HIS OWN RIGHT KING'S FORGOTTEN, · · 635 BLACK TOWER 13
MAKE HIM FILL THE CRADLES RIGHT. · · · · · 638 BEN BULBEN 41
THE PRIEST LOOKED NEITHER TO RIGHT NOR LEFT, · 730 PRIEST FAIRY 49
SITTING ON MY RIGHT HAND." · · · · · · · · 741 EARL PAUL 60
A QUARTER OF THE HEAVENS FROM OUR RIGHT WAY. · 754 SHADOW WATER A 155
AND I MET WITH A MAN THAT WAS NO RIGHT MAN · · 779 GOING THE ROAD 3

RIGHTFUL
FACE TO FACE MY RIGHTFUL MAN · · · · · · · 521 THREE THINGS 16

RIGHTLY
SOME TWENTY FEET FROM TIP TO TIP HAD IT STRETCHED RIGHTLY 593 PILGRIM 17
OUT,
SOME TWENTY FEET FROM TIP TO TIP HAD ITS WINGS STRETCHED 593 PILGRIM V 17
RIGHTLY OUT,

RIGHT-TAUGHT
NO RIGHT-TAUGHT MAN DENIES. · · · · · · · 590 OLD WICKED MAN 58

RILL
AND WAVERED LIKE A SUMMER RILL, · · · · · 4 OISIN 1 V 29

RILLS
AND LAUGH'D, SO, SO ALONG THE BUBBLING RILLS · · 645 ISLE STAT I 1 18

RIM
IN THE PALE WEST, AND THE SUN'S RIM SANK, · · 12 OISIN 1 153
NOW IN THE SEA THE SUN'S RIM SANK, · · · · 12 OISIN 1 V 153
AND RODE ON TILL OVER THE WORLD'S RIM FLOATED THE SEA'S 60 OISIN 3 V 183
OLD SHOUT,
THEN HE SANG SOFTLY NIGH THE PEARLY RIM: · · · 69 SAD SHEPHERD 25
THEN SANG HE SOFTLY NIGH THE PEARLY RIM: · · · 69 SAD SHEPHERD V 25
BETWEEN WOOD'S RIM AND THE HORSES OF THE SEA. · 108 CUCHULAIN SEA 34
GO THERE, AND LIGHT A CAMP-FIRE AT WOOD'S RIM: · 108 CUCHULAIN SEA 35
GO THERE AND DWELL ON THE GREEN FOREST RIM. · 108 CUCHULAIN SEA V 35
GO THERE, AND CAMP UPON THE FOREST'S RIM: · 108 CUCHULAIN SEA V 35
GO THERE, AND LIGHT A CAMP FIRE AT WOOD'S RIM: · 108 CUCHULAIN SEA V 35
· · · HUNG LOW ON THE RIM OF THE SKY, · · 122 WHITE BIRDS 3
BUT ONE SMALL KNOT-GRASS GROWING BY THE RIM · 127 DREAM OF FAERY V 29
ABOVE ITS CLOUDY RIM: · · · · · · · · · 175 ELEMENT POWERS 16
SHE COULD HAVE CALLED OVER THE RIM OF THE WORLD · 181 QUEEN MAEVE 23

RIME
AND DEAD AS ARE THE LOVERS OF OLD RIME · · · 674 ISLE STAT II 3 204

RING
THAT WOMAN FOUND A RING HUNG ON THE WALL, · · 37 OISIN 2 120
AND IN THE RING A TORCH, AND WITH ITS FLARE · · 37 OISIN 2 121
THAT MAIDEN FOUND A RING HUNG ON THE WALL, · · 37 OISIN 2 V 120
OR GENTLY IN A RING. · · · · · · · · · 97 FOXHUNTER 8

	PAGE	TITLE	LINE

RING (CONTINUED)
   AND LEAD HIM GENTLY IN A RING, ...   97 FOXHUNTER   V   7
   UPON THE WHARVES OF SORROW, AND HEARD RING . . . . . .   115 ROSE OF BATTLE   27
   WHO KNOW IT ALL RING AT HIS DOOR, AND SPEAK . . . . .   373 PHASES OF MOON   21
   WERE NOT OUR BEDS FAR OFF I'D RING THE BELL, ...   377 PHASES OF MOON   124
   AND WHEN ABOUNDING HEDGES RING . . . .   434 WHEEL   3
   NATURAL AND SUPERNATURAL WITH THE SELF-SAME RING ARE WED.   556 RIBH PATRICK   4
   BINDS, AS WITHIN A GIRDLE OR A RING, ...   657 ISLE STAT I 3   59
   UNTIL WE DIE WITHIN THE CHARMED RING . . . .   679 ISLE STAT II 3   322
   AND NOT COME THENCE; FOR HERE IN THIS SMALL RING-- . . .   699 MOSADA 3   22
   THE SHADOWS PASS; BUT NOW, I LOVE MY RING, ...   700 MOSADA 3   27
   AND LIKE A SILVER TRUMPET RING. . . . .   736 SUMMER EVENING   4
   AND LIKE A SILVER TRUMPET RING. . . . .   737 SUMMER EVENING   20
RINGDOVE'S
   FOLLOWED A RINGDOVE'S ASH-GREY GLEAM OF FEATHER. . . . .   715 DWELT SYCAMORE   6
RING-DOVE'S
   FOLLOWED THE RING-DOVE'S ASH-GREY GLEAM OF FEATHER. . .   715 DWELT SYCAMORE   V   6
RINGED   SEE BRONZE-RINGED
   OR CARRY THE RINGED MAIL UPON MY BACK, ...   463 HARUN RASHID   58
   FAR OUT UPON THE WATER WORLD AND RINGED . . . .   693 MOSADA 1   80
   RINGED ROUND AND FONDLED, A BROWN FARM HOUSE SEES. . . .   710 FERENCZ RENYI   V   23
   HIS GARDEN RINGED WITH JESSAMINE, ...   729 PRIEST FAIRY   34
RINGER
   SAY WHAT RINGER RINGS AT MIDNIGHT; FOR, IN THE BELFRY HIGH,   718 PHANTOM SHIP   15
RINGING
   AMONG THE RINGING HALLS A SHOUT . . . .   20 OISIN 1   V   288
   A HONIED RINGING! UNDER THE NEW SKIES . . . .   130 BOOK STORIES   V   21
   EVER RINGING, RINGING, RINGING, ...   647 ISLE STAT I 1   68
   EVER RINGING, RINGING, RINGING, ...   647 ISLE STAT I 1   68
   EVER RINGING, RINGING, RINGING, ...   647 ISLE STAT I 1   68
   ALL THE WORLD IS RINGING, RINGING; . . . .   648 ISLE STAT I 1   93
   ALL THE WORLD IS RINGING, RINGING; . . . .   648 ISLE STAT I 1   93
RINGS   SEE DRAGON-RINGS
   WHO WEDDED MEN WITH RINGS OF DRUID GOLD; . . . . . .   29 OISIN 2   10
   WEDDING THE QUEENS OF EARTHLY LANDS WITH RINGS . . . .   29 OISIN 2   V   10
   HIS HEAVY RINGS UNCOILED FROM GLIMMERING DEEP TO DEEP; . .   174 ELEMENT POWERS   5
   AND SCATTER WHEELING IN GREAT BROKEN RINGS . . . . . .   322 SWANS AT COOLE   11
   A BLIND HERMIT RINGS THE HOUR. . . . .   484 SYMBOLS   2
   AND THEN YOU STOOD AMONG THE DRAGON RINGS. . . . . . .   533 HER TRIUMPH   V   7
   AND 'MONG THE STUNTED ASH-TREES' DROOPING RINGS, . . .   650 ISLE STAT I 1   128
   AT THEIR FEET THE WAVES IN RINGS . . . .   667 ISLE STAT II 3   25
   SAY WHAT RINGER RINGS AT MIDNIGHT; FOR, IN THE BELFRY HIGH,   718 PHANTOM SHIP   15
RINSING
   TO HIS SHAPE AT THE RINSING POOL . . . .   341 SHEP GOATHERD   V   70
RINSING-POOL
   TO HIS SHAPE AT THE RINSING-POOL . . . .   341 SHEP GOATHERD   70
R.I.P.
   R.I.P." WRIT IN BLOOD. . . . .   585 ORAHILLY   35
RIPENED
   WHAT WHOLESOME SUN HAS RIPENED IS WHOLESOME FOOD TO EAT,   442 BLACK CENTAUR   5
RIPENING
   PUBLIC OPINION RIPENING FOR SO LONG . . . .   428 NINETEEN 19   13
RIPPED
   RIPPED THROUGH THE HORSE'S FLANKS. KING EOCHAID REELED,   277 TWO KINGS   V   13
RISE
   . . . THEY WILL RISE, MAKING CLOUDS WITH THEIR BREATH, . .   61 OISIN 3   202
   . . . SHALL LISTEN AND RISE UP AND WEEP; . . . . . .   62 OISIN 3   206
   WITH MIRTHFUL SONGS TILL RISE THE DAWN. . . . . . .   67 HAPPY SHEPHERD V   49
   ABOVE THE TIDE OF HOURS, RISE ON THE AIR, ...   114 ROSE OF BATTLE V   3
   WHATEVER RAVELLED WATERS RISE AND FALL . . . .   127 DREAM OF FAERY   32
   WHO RISE, WING ABOVE WING, FLAME ABOVE FLAME, ...   137 TO SOME I TALK   11
   I RISE IN THE DAWN, AND I KNEEL AND BLOW . . . . . .   150 OLD MOTHER   1
   I RISE AT THE DAWN, AND I KNEEL AND BLOW . . . . . .   150 OLD MOTHER   V   1
   HE BADE HIS SOUL RISE UPWARD . . . .   159 CAP AND BELLS   3
   SAW THE PIERCED HANDS AND ROOD OF ELDER RISE . . . . .   169 SECRET ROSE   10
   TIME'S BITTER FLOOD WILL RISE, ...   173 PLEADS FRIEND   6
   NOR WOULD YOU RISE AND HASTEN AWAY, ...   176 BELOVED DEAD   7
   WOULD RISE OF A SUDDEN, OR A WAVE SO HUGE . . . . . .   236 SHADOW WATER B   310
   WOULD RISE AGAINST ME. NO, I AM NOT MAD-- . . . . . .   236 SHADOW WATER B   318
   THAT, BEING DEAD, WE RISE, ...   415 TOWER   154
   ANOTHER TROY MUST RISE AND SET, ...   437 SONGS PLAY 1   9
   WHEN THOUGHTS RISE UP UNBID . . . .   473 ALL SOUL NIGHT   68
   RUN UNDERGROUND, RISE IN A ROCKY PLACE . . . .   490 COOLE BALLYLEE   5
   RISE AS KINDRED SHOULD. . . . .   518 LOVES LONENESS   2
   MADE DRAPERIES THAT SEEMED TO RISE . . . .   566 LAPIS LAZULI   31
   COULD THAT OLD GOD RISE UP AGAIN . . . .   606 SONGS BURDEN 1   21
   WHEN THE WINTRY VAPOURS RISE. . . . .   643 SONG FAERIES   4
   WHEN THE WINTRY VAPOURS RISE. . . . .   644 SONG FAERIES   16
   THY FLICKERING HAND? WHAT MEAN THE LIGHTS THAT RISE . . .   674 ISLE STAT II 3   198
   WHEN THE WINTRY VAPOURS RISE. . . . .   676 ISLE STAT II 3   251
   WHEN THE WINTRY VAPOURS RISE. . . . .   676 ISLE STAT II 3   263
   WHERE RISE THE WALLS MAJESTICAL ABOVE . . . .   679 ISLE STAT II 3   311
   IF ONE SHOULD RISE BESIDE THEE, ...   680 LOVE AND DEATH   27
   AND NOW AND THEN A BUBBLE RISE. I HEAR . . . . . .   722 WITCH VIVIEN   63
   NAY, RISE AND FLATTER HER WITH GOLDEN RHYME, ...   724 KANVA ON SELF   19
   TO THE FIDDLE'S RISE AND FALL. . . . .   726 LOVERS QUARREL   20
   YET RISE FROM YOUR ITALIAN TOMB, ...   791 REPRISALS   10
RISEN   SEE LATE-RISEN
   DESPITE A DWINDLING AND LATE RISEN MOON, ...   372 PHASES OF MOON V   6
RISES
   RISES, AND SHOWERS ABROAD HIS FRAGRANT ARROWS, ...   72 ANASHU VIJAYA   27

	PAGE	TITLE		LINE

RISES (CONTINUED)
THE RIVER RISES, AND IT SINKS AGAIN: • • • • • • • • 420 MY HOUSE V 20A
AND COLA, SEEING, KNOWS THE SIGN AND RISES. • • • • • 691 MOSADA 1 V 38

RISING
RISING AND FALLING, MIXED INSEPARABLY, • • • • • • • • 45 OISIN 2 V 233
FEET TO THE RISING AND SETTING MAY RUN, • • • • • • 591 WHAT WAS LOST 4
WAKE! THE HERON, RISING, HATH • • • • • • • • • • • 705 DAWN-SONG 17
KINGDOMS RISING, KINGDOMS FALLING, • • • • • • • • • 737 IN FIRELIGHT 9

RITES
OF EQUAL POWER IN SPELLS AND SECRET RITES. • • • • • 720 WITCH VIVIEN 6

RIVER
AND RIVER, FERN AND FLOWERY CLUMP, • • • • • • • • 15 OISIN 1 V 196
LIKE A SMALL RIVER, AND WHERE FEET TOUCHED CAME • • • 37 OISIN 2 117
IN A FIELD BY THE RIVER MY LOVE AND I DID STAND, • • • 90 SALLEY GARDENS 5
I SEE MY LIFE GO DRIFTING LIKE A RIVER • • • • • • • 104 FERGUS DRUID 31
AND RIVER AND STREAM WORK OUT THEIR WILL: • • • • • • 148 INTO TWILIGHT 12
THE RIVER IMAGING THE FLASHING SKIES, • • • • • • • 390 IMAGE PAST 20
THE RIVER RISES, AND IT SINKS AGAIN: • • • • • • • • 420 MY HOUSE V 20A
VALLEY, RIVER, AND ELMS, UNDER THE LIGHT OF A MOON • • 426 PHANTOM HATRED 3
VALLEY, RIVER, ELMS, UNDER THE LIGHT OF A MOON • • • 426 PHANTOM HATRED V 3
ON THE RUDDY RIVER SEDGE, • • • • • • • • • • • • 646 ISLE STAT I 25
WHOSE BEARD A MOONLIGHT RIVER IS, WHOSE BROW • • • • 657 ISLE STAT I 3 73

RIVER'S
I RIDE WITH FALCON TO THE RIVER'S EDGE • • • • • • 463 HARUN RASHID 57
ITS PAVEN LENGTH TOWARDS THE RIVER'S MARGE • • • • • 702 MOSADA 3 76
AFAR ALONG THE FLEET WHITE RIVER'S FACE-- • • • • • 702 MOSADA 3 79
COMPANIONING THE RIVER'S PILGRIM TORCH. • • • • • • 703 MOSADA 3 112

RIVERS
BY RIVERS AND THE WOODS' OLD NIGHT: • • • • • • • • 25 OISIN 1 387
THE RIVERS, AND THE WOOD'S OLD NIGHT. • • • • • • • 25 OISIN 1 V 387
"I AM FROM THOSE RIVERS AND I BID YOU CALL • • • • • 184 QUEEN MAEVE 91
BY RIVERS WHERE THE RAIN HAS NEVER DIMMED • • • • • 184 QUEEN MAEVE V 87
BY RIVERS WHERE NOR RAIN NOR HAIL HAS DIMMED • • • • 184 QUEEN MAEVE 87
"I COME FROM THE UNDIMMED RIVERS TO BID YOU CALL • • 184 QUEEN MAEVE V 91
"I AM FROM THE UNDIMMED RIVERS, I BID YOU CALL • • • 184 QUEEN MAEVE V 91
"I AM FROM THOSE RIVERS AND WOULD HAVE YOU CALL • • • 184 QUEEN MAEVE V 91
RIVERS ARE RUNNING OVER • • • • • • • • • • • • 214 HAPPY TOWNLAND 7
WHERE RIVERS ARE RUNNING OVER • • • • • • • • • 214 HAPPY TOWNLAND V 7
IN THE HEART OF THE DAWN THE RIVERS ARE SINGING, • • 648 ISLE STAT I 1 91
OF ASIAN RIVERS, ROLLING ON IN LIGHT. • • • • • • 682 SEEKER 20
OF INDIA'S RIVERS, ROLLING ON IN LIGHT. • • • • • 682 SEEKER V 20

RIVER-SIDE
THE PALACE-YARD AND RIVER-SIDE • • • • • • • • • 295 THREE BEGGARS 9
FROM RIVER-SIDE AND PALACE-YARD • • • • • • • • • 296 THREE BEGGARS 27

RIVERY
FROM ROLLING VALE AND RIVERY GLEN: • • • • • • • • 83 MAD KING GOLL 19
FROM ROLLING VALLEY AND RIVERY GLEN, • • • • • • • 83 MAD KING GOLL V 17
A RIVERY FIELD SPREAD OUT BELOW, • • • • • • • • 502 VACILLATION 57

RIVETED
WHEN THEY FROZE THE CLOTH ON MY BODY LIKE ARMOUR RIVETED 57 OISIN 3 151
FAST,

RIVULET'S
GREY IN THE MIDST LIKE A SMALL RIVULET'S FLOW, • • • • 37 OISIN 2 V 117

RIVULETS
AS QUIET AS THE LITTLE RIVULETS • • • • • • • • • 698 MOSADA 2 57

ROAD
AND I ON THIS STRANGE ROAD WILL PASS • • • • • • • 97 FOXHUNTER V 11
GO WATCH THE ROAD BETWEEN THE WOOD AND TIDE, • • • • 105 CUCHULAIN SEA 4
HE MADE THE WORLD TO BE A GRASSY ROAD • • • • • • 112 ROSE OF WORLD 14
BUT NOW THAT THEY HAVE TAKEN TO THE ROAD • • • • • 247 SHADOW WATER B 526
YET SHE, SINGING UPON HER ROAD, • • • • • • • • 260 UNWORTH PRAISE 19
AS THOUGH IT DRAGGED ROAD METAL. MY CURSE ON PLAYS • 260 FASC DIFFICULT V 8
THAT CAST THEIR SHADOWS UPON ROAD AND BRIDGE: • • • 326 ROBERT GREGORY 51
YOU HAVE MEASURED OUT THE ROAD THAT THE SOUL TREADS • 342 SHEP GOATHERD 80
THAT SHADES THE ROAD, OR SETTING UP A COTTAGE • • • 372 ON GOING HOUSE 14
HAD TROD THE UNEVEN ROAD. THEIR BOOTS WERE SOILED, • 372 PHASES OF MOON 3
UPON THE OPEN ROAD, NEAR TO THE SLIGO QUAY-- • • • 391 UNDER SATURN 12
THE HORSE THAT COMES FROM THE ROAD, • • • • • • • 393 EASTER 1916 45
THE ROAD AT MY DOOR • • • • • • • • • • • • 423 ROAD AT DOOR T
LAST NIGHT THEY TRUNDLED DOWN THE ROAD • • • • • • 425 STARES NEST 13
BUT TROD THE ROAD, OR SPLASHED ABOUT THE SHORE, • • 447 COLONUS PRAISE 27
BUT TROD THE ROAD, OR PADDLED BY THE SHORE, • • • • 447 COLONUS PRAISE V 27
PASSING ON THE ROAD THAT NIGHT, • • • • • • • • 511 JANE AND JACK 17
THOUGH LIKE A ROAD • • • • • • • • • • • • 512 JANE ON GOD 20
I MET THE BISHOP ON THE ROAD • • • • • • • • • 513 JANE TALK BISH 1
OR SING A PENANCE ON THE ROAD: • • • • • • • • 529 TOM LUNATIC 10
WHETHER THEY TAKE THE UPPER ROAD • • • • • • • • 589 OLD WICKED MAN 48
PARNELL CAME DOWN THE ROAD, HE SAID TO A CHEERING MAN: • • 590 PARNELL 1
BY THE ROAD AN ANCIENT CROSS. • • • • • • • • • 640 BEN BULBEN 88
I WAS GOING THE ROAD ONE DAY • • • • • • • • • 779 GOING THE ROAD 1

ROAD-METAL
AS THOUGH IT DRAGGED ROAD-METAL. MY CURSE ON PLAYS • • 260 FASC DIFFICULT 8

ROADS
FOR THE ROADS ARE UNENDING, AND THERE IS NO PLACE TO MY 203 WITHER BOUGHS 4
MIND."
ON WET ROADS WHERE MEN WALK, • • • • • • • • • 215 HAPPY TOWNLAND 48
OUT NAKED ON THE ROADS, AS THE BOOKS SAY, AND STRICKEN • • 316 COLD HEAVEN 11
AND WHEN YOU HAVE SPOKEN TAKE THE ROADS AGAIN? • • • 373 PHASES OF MOON 25
VIOLENCE UPON THE ROADS: VIOLENCE OF HORSES: • • • • 432 NINETEEN 19 113
ROADS FULL OF BEGGARS, CATTLE IN THE FIELDS, • • • • 487 SEVEN SAGES 18
WHAT SCHOOLING HAD THESE FOUR? THEY WALKED THE ROADS • • 487 SEVEN SAGES 24

ROADS (CONTINUED)   PAGE   TITLE   LINE
  TAKE TO THE ROADS AND GO MARCHING ALONG. . . . .   548 TO SAME TUNE 3   14
  ROUND US THE WHITE ROADS ARE ENDLESS, ...   737 IN FIRELIGHT   3
  WAR-LADEN GALLEYS, AND ARMIES ON WHITE ROADS, ...   757 SHADOW WATER A   203
  WAR-LADEN GALLEYS, AND ARMIES ON WHITE ROADS, ...   757 SHADOW WATER A V   203
ROADSIDE
  BOOK IV THE GATES OF PLUTO I. THE FOOL BY THE ROADSIDE   447 HERO GIRL FOOL V   T
ROAD-SIDE
  THE ROAD-SIDE TREES KEEP MURMURING--   131 OLD PENSIONER V   13
ROADWAY
  WHILE I STAND ON THE ROADWAY, OR ON THE PAVEMENTS GREY,   117 ISLE INNISFREE   11
  WHILE I STAND ON THE ROADWAY, OR ON THE PAVEMENT GREY, .   117 ISLE INNISFREE V   11
  THE CRY OF A CHILD BY THE ROADWAY, THE CREAK OF A LUMBERING   142 ROSE IN HEART   2
     CART,
ROAM
  WILT ROAM AWAY FROM THIS RICH ISLAND REST? . . . .   669 ISLE STAT II 3   88
  AND WHEREFORE SHOULD THY BRIGHT BROW ROAM . . . .   686 LIFE   11
ROAR
  FOR WIND OR WATER'S ROAR? . . .   312 CHILD DANCING   3
  WHAT GAVE THAT ROAR OF MOCKERY, ...   583 GHOST ROG CASE   7
  THAT ROAR IN THE SEA'S ROAR? . . . .   583 GHOST ROG CASE   8
  THAT ROAR IN THE SEA'S ROAR? . . . .   583 GHOST ROG CASE   8
  THEY SHAKE WHEN THE WINDS ROAR, ...   635 BLACK TOWER   9
  THEY SHAKE WHEN THE WINDS ROAR, ...   636 BLACK TOWER   19
  THEY SHAKE WHEN THE WINDS ROAR, ...   636 BLACK TOWER   29
  AND HEARS THE ROAR OF THE STREAMS WHERE, DRUIDS SAY, . .   749 SHADOW WATER A   46
ROARER
  AND MIXED WITH THE SOUND OF THAT ROARER . . . .   60 OISIN 3   V   184
ROARING
  A FIR-TREE ROARING IN ITS LEAFLESS TOP; . . . .   40 OISIN 2   177
  A FIR TREE ROARING IN ITS LEAFLESS TOP, ...   40 OISIN 2   V   177
  . . . WITH ROARING OF LAUGHTER AND SONGS, ...   53 OISIN 3   87
  AND HUSHED IN SLEEP THE ROARING RANKS OF BATTLE; . . .   58 OISIN 3   168
  A ROARING, RANTING JOURNEYMAN. . . . .   129 BOOK STORIES   7
  A ROARING RANTING JOURNEY-MAN. . . . .   509 JANE REPROVED   13
  ALL THE STREAM THAT'S ROARING BY . . . .   509 JANE REPROVED V   13
  THE ROARING TINKER IF YOU LIKE, ...   562 NEEDLES EYE   1
  HIS ROARING AND HIS RANTING . . . .   605 SONGS BURDEN 1   1
  CRIES A VOICE AT ROARING MIDNIGHT BESIDE THE MOONLESS DEEP.   606 SONGS BURDEN 1   16
  BUT WHERE THAT ROARING, RANTING CREW . . . .   718 PHANTOM SHIP   8
ROARS   787 HUDDON DUDDON   3
  AND ROARS, MAD WITH THE TOUCH OF THE UNKNOWN, ...   689 NETTLESHIP   7
ROASTING
  ROASTING BERRIES STEAM AND SHAKE-- . . . .   727 LOVERS QUARREL   43
ROB
  THE OTHER SHOUTED, "YOU WOULD ROB . . . . . .   307 HOUR DAWN   109
  HER RAVEN FLUTTERS. ROB HIM OF HIS FOOD . . . . . .   751 SHADOW WATER A   100
ROBARTES
  MICHAEL ROBARTES BIDS HIS BELOVED BE AT PEACE . . . .   154 BELOVED PEACE V   T
  MICHAEL ROBARTES REMEMBERS FORGOTTEN BEAUTY . . . . .   155 FORGOT BEAUTY V   T
  MICHAEL ROBARTES ASKS FORGIVENESS BECAUSE OF HIS MANY MOODS   162 ASKS FORGIVE   V   T
  THAT MICHAEL ROBARTES LEFT, YOU WALK IN THE MOON, . .   367 EGO DOMINUS   4
  THE DOUBLE VISION OF MICHAEL ROBARTES . . . .   382 VISION ROBART   T
  MICHAEL ROBARTES AND THE DANCER . . . .   385 ROBARTES DANCE   T
ROBBED
  WAS ROBBED BEFORE EARTH GAVE THE WHEAT; . . . . . .   196 BAILE AILLINN   166
ROBBER
  THERE'S NOBODY IS NATURAL BUT A ROBBER, ...   233 SHADOW WATER B   237
ROBBERS
  FELL ON THE ROBBERS BY THE DEEP. . .   83 MAD KING GOLL V   21
  THESE HANDS SLEW MANY ROBBERS BOLD-- . . .   83 MAD KING GOLL V   23
  ROBBERS HAD TAKEN HIS OLD TAMBOURINE, ...   616 MARCH SONGS 3   7
  ROBBERS HAD TAKEN HIS OLD TAMBOURINE. . . . .   616 MARCH SONGS 3   10
  ROBBERS HAD TAKEN HIS OLD TAMBOURINE. . . . .   616 MARCH SONGS 3   17
  ROBBERS HAD TAKEN HIS OLD TAMBOURINE. . . . .   616 MARCH SONGS 3   20
  ROBBERS HAD TAKEN HIS OLD TAMBOURINE. . . . .   616 MARCH SONGS 3   27
  A HORN! SOME TROOP OF ROBBERS WINDING GOES . . . . .   616 MARCH SONGS 3   30
  AMONG HIGH MOUNTAINS, AND THE MOUNTAIN ROBBERS . . .   649 ISLE STAT I 1   110
                                                                768 SHADOW WATER A   411
ROBBERY
  THAT HAS LESS UPS AND DOWNS THAN ROBBERY. . . . . .   222 SHADOW WATER B   7
  THEIR ROBBERY BY NIGHT; . . . .   607 SONGS BURDEN 2   15
ROBE
  BY MIGHTY BRAHMA'S EVER-RUSTLING ROBE, ...   71 ANASHU VIJAYA   14
  STAND YOU. BY BRAHMA'S EVER-RUSTLING ROBE, ...   71 ANASHU VIJAYA   14
  BY MIGHTY BRAHMA'S EVER RUSTLING ROBE, ...   71 ANASHU VIJAYA V   14
ROBED
  AND CALM, ROBED ALL IN RAIMENT MOONY WHITE. . . . .   693 MOSADA 1   77
ROBERT
  OLD COUNTRY SCHOLAR, ROBERT EMMET'S FRIEND, ...   269 PARDON FATHERS   5
  AND COUNTRY SCHOLAR, ROBERT EMMET'S FRIEND, ...   269 PARDON FATHERS V   5
  AND ROBERT EMMET AND WOLFE TONE, ...   290 SEPTEMBER 1913   21
  IN MEMORY OF MAJOR ROBERT GREGORY . . . .   323 ROBERT GREGORY   T
  IN MEMORY OF ROBERT GREGORY . . . .   323 ROBERT GREGORY V   T
  THAT INSOLENT FIEND ROBERT ARTISSON . . . .   433 NINETEEN 19   128
  WHAT ROBERT BROWNING MEANT . . . .   605 YOU CONTENT   22
ROBES
  AND A HUNDRED ROBES OF MURMURING SILK, ...   8 OISIN 1   88
  AND A HUNDRED ROBES OF THE SOFTEST SILK, ...   8 OISIN 1   88
  THEIR ROBES WERE ALL OF YELLOW SILK . . . .   15 OISIN 1   V   205

661

                                                      PAGE   TITLE   LINE

ROBES   (CONTINUED)   134 FR GILLIGAN   45
    "HE WHO IS WRAPPED IN PURPLE ROBES, ...
ROBIN'S   671 ISLE STAT II 3   138
    AS ALIEN AS A CUCKOO IN A ROBIN'S NEST, ... 671 ISLE STAT II 3 V   138
    ALIEN AS CUCKOO IN A ROBIN'S NEST, ...
ROCK   SEE THREE-ROCK   43 OISIN 2   V   212
    'TIS OVER! FAR WITH MEMORY I SWAY AND ROCK. . . . . 270 GREY ROCK   T
    THE GREY ROCK . . . .   275 GREY ROCK   111
    THE GREY ROCK AND THE WINDY LIGHT?   303 HOUR DAWN   21
    A DARK DEEP HOLLOW IN THE ROCK.   303 HOUR DAWN   23
    BEING CERTAIN IT WAS NO RIGHT ROCK   310 PEACOCK   5
    AND DESOLATE THREE ROCK   311 PEACOCK   V   8
    BETWEEN ROCK AND WET HEATHER,   326 ROBERT GREGORY   66
    TO COLD CLARE ROCK AND GALWAY ROCK AND THORN,   326 ROBERT GREGORY   66
    TO COLD CLARE ROCK AND GALWAY ROCK AND THORN,   382 VISION ROBART   1
    ON THE GREY ROCK OF CASHEL THE MIND'S EYE   383 VISION ROBART   17
    ON THE GREY ROCK OF CASHEL I SUDDENLY SAW   397 POLIT PRISONER   21
    UPON SOME LOFTY ROCK TO STARE   518 HIS CONFIDENCE   10
    THAT OUT OF ROCK,   633 MAN AND ECHO   44
    DROPPING OUT OF SKY OR ROCK,   673 ISLE STAT II 3   195
    I SEE WITHIN A CLOVEN ROCK DISPART   687 TWO TITANS   1
    THE VISION OF A ROCK WHERE LIGHTNINGS WHIRL'D   687 TWO TITANS   5
    TWO FIGURES CROUCHING ON THE BLACK ROCK, BOUND   687 TWO TITANS   28
    MAKING ALL ONE O'ER ROCK AND SEA AND SKIES!
ROCK-BORN   276 GREY ROCK   125
    TO THAT ROCK-BORN, ROCK-WANDERING FOOT, ...
ROCK-BRED   397 POLIT PRISONER   18
    LIKE ANY ROCK-BRED, SEA-BORNE BIRD!
ROCKED   76 INDIAN ON GOD   2
    MY SPIRIT ROCKED IN EVENING LIGHT, THE RUSHES ROUND MY
       KNEES,   76 INDIAN ON GOD   3
    MY SPIRIT ROCKED IN SLEEP AND SIGHS, AND SAW THE MOORFOWL
       PACE   76 INDIAN ON GOD   V   2
    MY SPIRIT ROCKED IN EVENING'S HUSH, THE RUSHES ROUND MY
       KNEES,   316 COLD HEAVEN   8
    UNTIL I CRIED AND TREMBLED AND ROCKED TO AND FRO,   373 PHASES OF MOON   34
    THE CRADLES THAT A MAN MUST NEEDS BE ROCKED IN!
ROCKING   344 DAWN   11
    THAT MERELY STOOD, ROCKING THE GLITTERING COACH   344 DAWN   V   11
    YET DID BUT LOOK, ROCKING THE GLITTERING COACH   402 SECOND COMING   20
    WERE VEXED TO NIGHTMARE BY A ROCKING CRADLE,
ROCK-NURTURED   274 GREY ROCK   88
    ROCK-NURTURED AOIFE TOOK A PIN, ...
ROCK'S   303 HOUR DAWN   V   21
    A DARK DEEP HOLE IN THE ROCK'S FACE,
ROCKS   84 MAD KING GOLL   42
    THE CORMORANTS SHIVER ON THEIR ROCKS!   102 FERGUS DRUID   1
    THIS WHOLE DAY HAVE I FOLLOWED IN THE ROCKS,   102 FERGUS DRUID   V   1
    THE WHOLE DAY HAVE I FOLLOWED IN THE ROCKS.   283 TWO KINGS   147
    WENT OUT. AMONG THE IVY-COVERED ROCKS,   311 PEACOCK   8
    AMID WET ROCKS AND HEATHER,   413 TOWER   98
    WHO TROD UPON THESE ROCKS OR PASSED THIS DOOR,   687 TWO TITANS   30
    STREWING UPON THE ROCKS THEIR STEEL-BLUE HAIR,   688 TWO TITANS   34
    IN CREVICED ROCKS, AND LAUGHED TO THE OLD SEA,   688 TWO TITANS   40
    THE YOUTH HAD FLUNG HIS ARMS AROUND THE ROCKS,
ROCK-WANDERING   276 GREY ROCK   125
    TO THAT ROCK-BORN, ROCK-WANDERING FOOT, ...
ROCKY   83 MAD KING GOLL   32
    BY ROCKY SHORE AND RUSHY FEN!   86 STOLEN CHILD   1
    WHERE DIPS THE ROCKY HIGHLAND   133 FR GILLIGAN   30
    BY ROCKY LANE AND FEN!   302 HOUR DAWN   12
    OF GREY STONES AND A ROCKY LEDGE   410 TOWER   35
    WHO'D LIVED SOMEWHERE UPON THAT ROCKY PLACE,   420 MY HOUSE   V 20C
    UNDER ITS ROCKY HOLE.   490 COOLE BALLYLEE   5
    RUN UNDERGROUND, RISE IN A ROCKY PLACE   499 MOTHER OF GOD   9
    OR ROCKY CISTERN WHERE WE TREAD THE CLOTHES   564 GYRES   1
    THE GYRES! THE GYRES! OLD ROCKY FACE, LOOK FORTH!   564 GYRES   18
    WHAT MATTER? THOSE THAT ROCKY FACE HOLDS DEAR,   633 MAN AND ECHO   37
    INTO THE NIGHT. O ROCKY VOICE,
ROD   22 OISIN 1   332
    HE RULES YOU WITH AN IRON ROD,   149 WANDER AENGUS   V   3
    AND CUT AND PEELED A HAZEL ROD,   409 TOWER   8
    NO, NOT IN BOYHOOD WHEN WITH ROD AND FLY,   575 MAIDS 2ND SONG   3
    HIS ROD AND ITS BUTTING HEAD
RODE   2 OISIN 1   V 7C
    WE RODE IN SORROW, WITH STRONG HOUNDS THREE,   2 OISIN 1   V 7H
    WE RODE IN SADNESS ABOVE LOUGH LAEN,   3 OISIN 1   20
    A PEARL-PALE, HIGH-BORN LADY, WHO RODE   9 OISIN 1   V 101A
    WE RODE BEYOND THE FURZE AND HEATHER,   10 OISIN 1   114
    BUT WE RODE OUT FROM THE HUMAN LANDS.   10 OISIN 1   V 114
    WE RODE ACROSS THE OILY SEA.   12 OISIN 1   142
    AND NOW A LADY RODE LIKE THE WIND   12 OISIN 1   V 142
    AND NOW A MAIDEN RODE LIKE THE WIND   13 OISIN 1   159
    AND WITH LOW MURMURS, WE RODE ON,   13 OISIN 1   V 159
    WE RODE ON MURMURING. MANY A SHELL   25 OISIN 1   382
    AND WRAPPED IN DREAMS RODE OUT AGAIN   25 OISIN 1   V 379A
    AND RODE AND STOOD BESIDE THE SHORE.   31 OISIN 2   31
    WHEN GODS AND GIANTS WARRED. WE RODE BETWEEN   45 OISIN 2   V 231
    I MOUNTED, AND WE RODE ACROSS THE LONE   48 OISIN 3   13
    AND WE RODE ON THE PLAINS OF THE SEA'S EDGE!

	PAGE	TITLE		LINE

RODE   (CONTINUED)

THE WAILING GREW DISTANT; I RODE BY THE WOODS OF THE WRINKLING BARK,	56	OISIN 3		137
AND I RODE BY THE PLAINS OF THE SEA'S EDGE,	56	OISIN 3		141
I RODE AWAY ON THE SURGES, WHERE, HIGH AS THE SADDLE-BOW,	57	OISIN 3		147
I RODE AWAY ON THE SURGES, WHERE HIGH AS THE SADDLE BOW	57	OISIN 3	V	147
I RODE AWAY ON THE SURGES, WHERE, HIGH AS THE SADDLEBOW,	57	OISIN 3	V	147
MAKING WAY FROM THE KINDLING SURGES, I RODE ON A BRIDLE-PATH	58	OISIN 3		161
AND I RODE AND I RODE, AND I CRIED OUT,	59	OISIN 3		171
AND I RODE AND I RODE, AND I CRIED OUT,	59	OISIN 3		171
I TURNED AND RODE TO THE WESTWARD, AND FOLLOWED THE SEA'S OLD SHOUT	60	OISIN 3		183
AND RODE ON TILL OVER THE WORLD'S RIM FLOATED THE SEA'S OLD SHOUT,	60	OISIN 3	V	183
IN PENAL DAYS RODE OUT	91	FATHER OHART		2
AND RODE WITH LITTLE CARE.	133	FR GILLIGAN		28
HE RODE NOW AS HE NEVER RODE,	133	FR GILLIGAN		29
HE RODE NOW AS HE NEVER RODE,	133	FR GILLIGAN		29
RODE OUT OF EMAIN WITH A BAND	189	BAILE AILLINN		18
RODE FROM THE COUNTRY OF HER KIN,	191	BAILE AILLINN		50
AND OLD AND YOUNG MEN RODE WITH HER;	191	BAILE AILLINN		51
WHERE AILLINN RODE WITH WAITING-MAIDS,	193	BAILE AILLINN		102
WHERE AILLINN RODE WITH WAITING MAIDS	193	BAILE AILLINN	V	102
I WAS YOUR HUSBAND WHEN YOU RODE THE AIR,	284	TWO KINGS		166
HE RODE A RACE WITHOUT A BIT?	326	ROBERT GREGORY		63
SHE RODE TO HARRIERS?	392	EASTER 1916		23
AND RODE OUR WINGED HORSE;	392	EASTER 1916		25
THOUGH MOUNTED IN THAT SADDLE HOMER RODE	492	COOLE BALLYLEE		47
NIAMH THAT RODE ON IT; LAD AND LASS	550	SEVERED HEAD		11
NO, NOT UNTIL HE RODE.	571	THREE BUSHES		48
WHEN PAUL RODE FROM THE TOWN	740	EARL PAUL		21

RODY

BRING RODY AND HIS HOUNDS,	97	FOXHUNTER		10
"HUNTSMAN RODY, BLOW THE HORN,	98	FOXHUNTER		25
"NOW HUNTSMAN RODY, BLOW THY HORN,	98	FOXHUNTER	V	REF
"MY HUNTSMAN RODY, BLOW THE HORN,	98	FOXHUNTER	V	REF
"HUNTSMAN RODY, BLOW THE HORN,	99	FOXHUNTER		33

ROE

ROE COULD RUN OR DOE COULD LEAP	522	LULLABY		10
ROE COULD LEAP OR DOE COULD RUN;	522	LULLABY		12
STAG COULD RUN AND ROE COULD LEAP	522	LULLABY	V	10
STAG COULD LEAP AND ROE COULD RUN.	522	LULLABY	V	12

ROEBUCK

| A LITTLE WAY WITHIN THE GLOOM A ROEBUCK RAISED HIS EYES | 76 | INDIAN ON GOD | | 13 |
| HE IS A GENTLE ROEBUCK; FOR HOW ELSE, I PRAY, COULD HE | 76 | INDIAN ON GOD | | 15 |

ROGER

ROGER CASEMENT	581	ROGER CASEMENT		T
I SAY THAT ROGER CASEMENT	581	ROGER CASEMENT		1
THE GHOST OF ROGER CASEMENT	583	GHOST ROG CASE		T
THE GHOST OF ROGER CASEMENT	583	GHOST ROG CASE		9
THE GHOST OF ROGER CASEMENT	583	GHOST ROG CASE		19
THE GHOST OF ROGER CASEMENT	584	GHOST ROG CASE		29
THE GHOST OF ROGER CASEMENT	584	GHOST ROG CASE		39

ROGUE

A CURSING ROGUE WITH A MERRY FACE,	302	HOUR DAWN		1
THAT GREAT ROGUE ALCIBIADES.	379	SAINT HUNCH		12
SOME ROGUE OF THE WORLD STOLE THEM TO PATCH UP A FENCE OR A FIRE.	623	HIGH TALK		4
WHAT ROGUE IS NIGHT-WANDERING?	781	MY HEART BEAT		5

ROGUES

| THAT THE WORST ROGUES AND RASCALS HAD DIED OUT. | 428 | NINETEEN 19 | | 16 |

ROLL'D

| WHILE THE WORLD IS ROLL'D IN LIGHT. | 646 | ISLE STAT I 1 | | 29 |

ROLLED

STROKED THE YOUNG WINDS AS THEY ROLLED ON THE PLAIN,	27	OISIN 1	V	415C
ROLLED ROUND WITH MUSIC OF THE SIGHING SPRAY;	30	OISIN 2		14
AND BLACKNESS IN THE DARK. THE SEA ROLLED ROUND,	30	OISIN 2	V	23
. . . AND CHURNED. HIS LIPS WERE ROLLED APART,	31	OISIN 2	V	43
ROLLED IN THE THINGS OF THE UNHUMAN MIND,	36	OISIN 2	V	98
. . . WHEN, ROLLED IN A GRISLY PEACE,	47	OISIN 3		9
. . . WHEN THE FALLEN ON FALLEN LIE ROLLED;	52	OISIN 3		78
THEIR HAIR ALONG THE MOUNTAINS ROLLED AND FILLED	74	ANASHU VIJAYA		71
AND RUSHES WAVED AND WATERS ROLLED.	84	MAD KING GOLL		35
AND SONG THAT DOWN THE VALLEYS ROLLED--	84	MAD KING GOLL		35
AND SONG THAT DOWN THE VALLEYS ROLLED--	84	MAD KING GOLL	V	35
THAT DOWN THE ECHOING VALLEYS ROLLED.	84	MAD KING GOLL	V	35
IN ALL HIS EVENING VAPOURS ROLLED--	86	MAD KING GOLL	V	71
IS ROLLED AS VERDANT SMOKE; O THOU WHOSE FACE	667	ISLE STAT II 3		35
HAS ROLLED AWAY THE STARS AND DRIED THE SEA	671	ISLE STAT II 3		146

ROLLING

BUT WE, OH ROLLING STARS, ARE FREE.	22	OISIN 1	V	337
ROLLING HIS FLAGRANT WHEEL OUT OF THE DEEP,	42	OISIN 2		193
ROLLING HIS WHEEL, WE SANG BESIDE THE DEEP.	42	OISIN 2	V	193
ROLLING ALONG IN DREAMS FROM HILL TO HILL.	68	SAD SHEPHERD		11
FROM ROLLING VALE AND RIVERY GLEN;	83	MAD KING GOLL		19
FROM ROLLING VALLEY AND RIVERY GLEN,	83	MAD KING GOLL	V	17
ON OLD DEEP SILVER ROLLING THERE	271	GREY ROCK		20
ROLLING A BLIND PEARL EYE.	552	SONGS REWRIT 2		2
WITH ROLLING FIRE, BEYOND THE HIGH TREES TURBANED	656	ISLE STAT I 3		32
YOU MUST BE GONE; THE ROLLING GRAINS OF SAND	663	ISLE STAT II 2		34

	PAGE	TITLE		LINE

ROLLING (CONTINUED)
OF ASIAN RIVERS, ROLLING ON IN LIGHT. . . . . 682 SEEKER 20
OF INDIA'S RIVERS, ROLLING ON IN LIGHT. . . . . 682 SEEKER V 20
HE RUSHES, ROLLING FROM HIS LIPS A MADMAN'S LAUGH. . . 715 FERENCZ RENYI 122
ROLLS
AND ROLLS ALONG THE UNWIELDY SUN, ... 18 OISIN 1 267
ROUND US, AND ROLLS THE UNWIELDY SUN. . . . . 18 OISIN 1 V 268
CEASE THE SAILS THEIR FLAPPING UPROAR, AND THE HULL NO 719 PHANTOM SHIP 18
LONGER ROLLS.
CEASE THE SAILS, THEIR FLAPPING UPROAR TO THE HULL 719 PHANTOM SHIP V 18
NO LONGER ROLLS.
ROLLS ALONG THE SEA SANDS WHITE. . . . . 732 STREET DANCERS 34
ROLLS ALONG THE SEA-SANDS WHITE. . . . . 732 STREET DANCERS V 34
ROLLY
IS FOL DE ROL DE ROLLY O. . . . . 592 PILGRIM 5
BUT FOL DE ROL DE ROLLY O. . . . . 593 PILGRIM 10
WAS FOL DE ROL DE ROLLY O. . . . . 593 PILGRIM 15
BUT FOL DE ROL DE ROLLY O. . . . . 593 PILGRIM 20
IS FOL DE ROL DE ROLLY O. . . . . 593 PILGRIM 25
ROMAN
A ROMAN CAESAR IS HELD DOWN . . . . 379 SAINT HUNCH 4
THE ROMAN EMPIRE STOOD APPALLED! . . . . 437 SONGS PLAY 1 13
ON ROMAN OR ON RUSSIAN . . . . 631 POLITICS 3
ROMANCE
YET OLD ROMANCE BEING KIND, LET HIM PREVAIL . . . . . 258 KING NO KING 5
ROMANCE IN IRELAND . . . . 289 SEPTEMBER 1913 V T
ROMANTIC
ROMANTIC IRELAND . . . . 289 SEPTEMBER 1913 V T
ROMANTIC IRELAND'S DEAD AND GONE, ... 289 SEPTEMBER 1913 7
ROMANTIC IRELAND'S DEAD AND GONE, ... 289 SEPTEMBER 1913 15
ROMANTIC IRELAND'S DEAD AND GONE, ... 290 SEPTEMBER 1913 23
ROMANTIC FISH SWAM IN NETS COMING TO THE HAND! . . . . 485 THREE MOVEMENT 2
ROMANTICS
WE WERE THE LAST ROMANTICS--CHOSE FOR THEME . . . . . 491 COOLE BALLYLEE 41
ROME
THE HAND AND LASH THAT BEAT DOWN FRIGID ROME? . . . . 560 WHENCE COME 10
EGYPT AND GREECE, GOOD-BYE, AND GOOD-BYE, ROME! . . . 563 MERU 8
TO MOSCOW OR TO ROME. . . . . 600 THOSE IMAGES 6
ROMP
WE HUSHED THE SINGING AND THE ROMP, ... 20 OISIN 1 V 296
ROOD
WORD BE-MOCKERS?--BY THE ROOD, ... 65 HAPPY SHEPHERD 12
WORD BEMOCKERS?--BY THE ROOD . . . . 65 HAPPY SHEPHERD V 12
TO THE ROSE UPON THE ROOD OF TIME . . . . 100 ROSE UPON ROOD T
SAW THE PIERCED HANDS AND ROOD OF ELDER RISE . . . . 169 SECRET ROSE 10
BUT PURER THAN A TALL CANDLE BEFORE THE HOLY ROOD . . 208 HANRAHANS SONG 14
BUT PURER THAN A TALL CANDLE BEFORE THE BLESSED ROOD . 208 HANRAHANS SONG V 14
ROOF
PRESSED ON THE EVER-TREMBLING ROOF . . . . 25 OISIN 1 V 383
AND THE ROOF FALLS IN OF HIS TUNNELLED HOUSE. . . . . 27 OISIN 1 V 419
AND THE ROOF FALLS IN OF HIS TUNNELLED HOUSE. . . . . 28 OISIN 1 423
TWO WALLS, A ROOF, A FLOOD! THERE TREMBLING GREEN . . 31 OISIN 2 V 32
UNDER THE ROOF, AND WITH A STRAINING THROAT . . . . . 36 OISIN 2 106
UNDER THAT WOVEN CHANGELESS ROOF OF BOUGHS! . . . . 126 DREAM OF FAERY 11
AND NOT A ROOF OF IVORY AND GOLD. . . . . 246 SHADOW WATER B 500
I WOULD GROW JEALOUS OF THE IVORY ROOF, ... 246 SHADOW WATER B 501
"I BID THEM MAKE HIS BED UNDER THIS ROOF . . . . . . 280 TWO KINGS 87
AT KYLE-NA-NO UNDER THAT ANCIENT ROOF . . . . 321 REED WHISPERER 7
TO KYLE-NA-INO AND TO THAT ANCIENT ROOF . . . . . . 321 REED WHISPERER V 7
STARING UPON A BEDOUIN'S HORSE-HAIR ROOF . . . . . . 368 EGO DOMINUS 29
WHILE MICHAEL ANGELO'S SISTINE ROOF, ... 386 ROBARTES DANCE 32
THE BROKEN WALL, THE BURNING ROOF AND TOWER . . . . . 441 LEDA AND SWAN 10
A ROOF, GOOD CLOTHES, PASSION, LOVE PERHAPS, ... 609 IN TARAS HALLS 8
LANDOR'S TARPAULIN ON THE ROOF. . . . . 625 NATIVITY 6
ON THE SISTINE CHAPEL ROOF, ... 638 BEN BULBEN 46
ROOFLESS
BECOME A ROOFLESS RUIN THAT THE OWL . . . . 423 MY DESCENDANTS 14
ROOF-LEVELLING
WHEREBY THE HAYSTACK- AND ROOF-LEVELLING WIND, ... 403 FOR DAUGHTER 5
ROOFS
UNDER THE WOVEN ROOFS OF QUICKEN BOUGHS!-- . . . . . 126 DREAM OF FAERY V 11
ROOF-TIMBERS
STAND UNDER THE ROUGH ROOF-TIMBERS OF THE HALL . . . . 377 PHASES OF MOON 125
ROOF-TREES
MEAN ROOF-TREES WERE THE STURDIER FOR ITS FALL, . . . 264 HOUSE SHAKEN 8
ROOK
SUDDENLY I SAW THE COLD AND ROOK DELIGHTING HEAVEN . . 316 COLD HEAVEN V 1
ROOK-DELIGHTING
SUDDENLY I SAW THE COLD AND ROOK-DELIGHTING HEAVEN . . 316 COLD HEAVEN 1
ROOKS
CAME KEENERS HOARSER THAN ROOKS, ... 92 FATHER OHART 22
ROOM SEE SLEEPING-ROOM DRAWING-ROOM
AND LIGHTS THE CURTAINED ROOM, ... 89 ISLE IN WATER 10
O WHAT TO ME THE LITTLE ROOM . . . . 151 HEART OF WOMAN 1
"O, WHAT TO ME THE FIRELIT ROOM, ... 151 HEART OF WOMAN V 1
LIFTED THE CURTAIN OF HER SLEEPING ROOM, ... 182 QUEEN MAEVE V 63
IF WE BUT SAW IN DREAMS THAT ROOM, ... 272 GREY ROCK 38
THAT THERE BE NO FOOT SILENT IN THE ROOM . . . . . . 311 MOUNTAIN TOMB 6
LET THERE BE NO FOOT SILENT IN THE ROOM, ... 311 MOUNTAIN TOMB V 6
THE ENTIRE COMBUSTIBLE WORLD IN ONE SMALL ROOM . . . . 327 ROBERT GREGORY 82
ALL THE COMBUSTIBLE WORLD IN ONE SMALL ROOM . . . . . 327 ROBERT GREGORY V 82

		PAGE	TITLE	LINE

ROOM   (CONTINUED)

    AND FLINGS HERSELF OUT OF THE ROOM WHEN JULIET WOULD BE   354 HIS PHOENIX   13
       BRIDE
    AND FLINGS HERSELF OUT OF THE ROOM WHEN JULIET WOULD BE   354 HIS PHOENIX   V   13
       A BRIDE
    BY MERELY WALKING IN A ROOM. . . . .   356 BROKEN DREAMS   13
    HE WALKED THAT ROOM AND ISSUED THENCE . . . . .   438 SONGS PLAY 2   2
    AND MANY A LESSER BELL SOUND THROUGH THE ROOM; . . .   470 ALL SOUL NIGHT   2
    WINGS BEATING ABOUT THE ROOM; . . . .   499 MOTHER OF GOD   3
    GREAT HATRED, LITTLE ROOM, ...   506 REMORSE SPEECH   12
    "HAVE NO LIT CANDLES IN YOUR ROOM," . . . .   569 THREE BUSHES   8
    AT MIDNIGHT TO MY ROOM, ...   570 THREE BUSHES   39
    AND FOUND AN EMPTY ROOM. . . . .   594 COLONEL MARTIN   8

ROOMFUL

    BEFORE THAT ROOMFUL OR AS GOOD. . . . .   273 GREY ROCK   52

ROOMS

    IN THE OLD ROOMS; NIGHT CAN OUTBALANCE DAY, ...   435 NEW FACES   6
    THE GARDEN PATHS, NOR COUNTED UP THE ROOMS, ...   466 HARUN RASHID   119
    WHEN ALL THOSE ROOMS AND PASSAGES ARE GONE, ...   489 COOLE PARK 29   26
    GREAT ROOMS WHERE TRAVELLED MEN AND CHILDREN FOUND . .   491 COOLE BALLYLEE   29

ROOT

    THE SURETY OF ITS HIDDEN ROOT . . . .   134 TWO TREES   7
    AND THAT IS CURED BY A BOILED LIQUORICE ROOT. . . .   227 SHADOW WATER B V 116B
    THOUGH LEAVES ARE MANY, THE ROOT IS ONE; . . . . .   261 COMING WISDOM   1
    THROUGH BUSH THEY PLUNGED AND OVER IVIED ROOT, . . .   278 TWO KINGS   32
    WHILE UP FROM MY HEART'S ROOT . . . .   316 FRIENDS   26
    I TOOK A BROKEN ROOT TO FLING . . . .   317 APPOINTMENT   2
    AT SOME OLD WINDING WHITETHORN ROOT . . . .   342 SHEP GOATHERD   101
    AND SAPLINGS ROOT AMONG THE BROKEN STONE . . . . .   489 COOLE PARK 29   28
    SEEMED SPRUNG FROM BUT A SINGLE ROOT . . . .   571 THREE BUSHES   61
    OF ROOT, SHOOT, BLOSSOM OR CLAY . . . .   600 SPIRIT MEDIUM   21
    FOR IF SEVERED FROM THE ROOT . . . .   668 ISLE STAT II 3   61
    AND THEREON GREW A TENDER ROOT, ...   743 DANAAN QUICK   13

ROOTED   SEE GREAT-ROOTED DEEP-ROOTED

    ROOTED IN FOAM AND CLOUDS, AND CRIED TO ALL . . . . .   38 OISIN 2   132
    ROOTED IN FOAM AND CLOUDS. THERE MIGHTIER MASTERS MET .   38 OISIN 2   V   132
    AND HAD ROOTED THE SUN AND MOON AND STARS OUT OF THE SKY .   153 CHANGE BELOVED   11
    AND ROOTED THE SUN AND MOON AND STARS OUT OF THE SKY, .   153 CHANGE BELOVED V   11
    ROOTED IN ONE DEAR PERPETUAL PLACE. . . . .   405 FOR DAUGHTER   48
    O CHESTNUT TREE, GREAT ROOTED BLOSSOMER, ...   446 SCHOOL CHILDR V   61
    AND HERE'S JOHN SYNGE HIMSELF, THAT ROOTED MAN, . . .   603 GALLERY REVIS   48

ROOTS

    BY ROOTS THAT JOINED ABOVE OUR PLUMES-- . . . . . .   16 OISIN 1   V 224C
    IN THE ROOTS OF THE GRASSES, THE SORRELS, I LAID MY BODY   52 OISIN 3   73
       AS LOW:
    IN THE TREE ROOTS, AND ALL THE SACRED FLOCKS . . . .   75 ANASHU VIJAYA   88
    IN THE TREE ROOTS, AND ALL THY SACRED FLOCKS . . . .   75 ANASHU VIJAYA V   88
    ROOTS HALF HIDDEN UNDER SNOWS, ...   135 TWO TREES   27
    AND ROOTS HALF HIDDEN UNDER SNOWS . . . .   135 TWO TREES   V   27
    THE ROOTS OF THE WORLD. SHADOWS BEFORE NOW . . . . .   227 SHADOW WATER B   104
    THE ROOTS OF THE WORLD. WHO KNOWS THAT SHADOWS . . .   227 SHADOW WATER B V 104
    I GROPED MY WAY THROUGH BOUGHS, AND OVER ROOTS, . . .   283 TWO KINGS   V   139
    KNOW WHERE ITS ROOTS BEGAN. . . . .   571 THREE BUSHES   76
    WHAT DEEP ROOTS ARE," AND NEVER FORESAW THE END . . .   603 GALLERY REVIS V   37
    THE ROOTS OF THE ROSES. . . . .   672 ISLE STAT II 3   169

ROPE

    AND PAID YOU ON THE NAIL. TAKE UP THAT ROPE . . . .   232 SHADOW WATER B   224
    WHILE THERE'S A ROPE TO RUN INTO A NOOSE . . . . .   238 SHADOW WATER B   347
    AND I WILL FOLLOW YOU AND CUT THE ROPE . . . . . .   250 SHADOW WATER B   586
    AND CUT THE ROPE, FOR I GO ON WITH FORGAEL. . . . .   250 SHADOW WATER B   592
    FAREWELL! FAREWELL! THE SWORD IS IN THE ROPE-- . . .   251 SHADOW WATER B   595
    FOR WHOM THE HANGMAN'S ROPE WAS SPUN. . . . .   289 SEPTEMBER 1913   13
    BUT A GOOD STRONG CAUSE"--THE ROPE GAVE A JERK THERE, .   545 TO SAME TUNE 1   23
    BUT A GOOD STRONG CAUSE"--THE ROPE GAVE A JERK THERE, .   616 MARCH SONGS 3   23
    I HAD THROWN IT DOWN BEHIND THIS COIL OF ROPE. . . .   759 SHADOW WATER A   245
    I HAVE CUT THE ROPE THAT BOUND THIS GALLEY TO OURS, . .   768 SHADOW WATER A   421

ROPE'S

    THE ROPE'S IN TWO--IT FALLS INTO THE SEA, ...   251 SHADOW WATER B   596

ROPES

    "BRING THE ROPES NOW! STAND YE BY NOW! . . . .   718 PHANTOM SHIP   13

ROSA

    ROSA MUNDI . . . .   111 ROSE OF WORLD V   T

ROSARY

    OVER THE BEADS OF HIS ROSARY. . . . .   730 PRIEST FAIRY   52
    THE FATHER DROPT HIS ROSARY-- . . . .   730 PRIEST FAIRY   57

ROSE (NOUN)   SEE RED-ROSE-BORDERED

    BUT NOW THE MOON LIKE A WHITE ROSE SHONE . . . . . .   12 OISIN 1   152
    AND THE MOON LIKE A PALE ROSE WITHER AWAY." . . . .   28 OISIN 1   427
    TO THE ROSE UPON THE ROOD OF TIME . . . .   100 ROSE UPON ROOD   T
    RED ROSE, PROUD ROSE, SAD ROSE OF ALL MY DAYS! . . .   100 ROSE UPON ROOD   1
    RED ROSE, PROUD ROSE, SAD ROSE OF ALL MY DAYS! . . .   100 ROSE UPON ROOD   1
    RED ROSE, PROUD ROSE, SAD ROSE OF ALL MY DAYS! . . .   100 ROSE UPON ROOD   1
    RED ROSE, PROUD ROSE, SAD ROSE OF ALL MY DAYS. . . .   101 ROSE UPON ROOD   24
    RED ROSE, PROUD ROSE, SAD ROSE OF ALL MY DAYS. . . .   101 ROSE UPON ROOD   24
    RED ROSE, PROUD ROSE, SAD ROSE OF ALL MY DAYS. . . .   101 ROSE UPON ROOD   24
    THE ROSE OF THE WORLD . . . .   111 ROSE OF WORLD   T
    THE ROSE OF PEACE . . . .   112 ROSE OF PEACE   T
    THE PEACE OF THE ROSE . . . .   112 ROSE OF PEACE V   T
    THE ROSE OF BATTLE . . . .   113 ROSE OF BATTLE   T
    ROSE OF ALL ROSES, ROSE OF ALL THE WORLD! . . . . .   113 ROSE OF BATTLE   1
    ROSE OF ALL ROSES, ROSE OF ALL THE WORLD! . . . . .   113 ROSE OF BATTLE   1

665

	PAGE	TITLE	LINE
ROSE (CONTINUED)			
ROSE OF ALL ROSES, ROSE OF ALL THE WORLD!	115	ROSE OF BATTLE	25
ROSE OF ALL ROSES, ROSE OF ALL THE WORLD!	115	ROSE OF BATTLE	25
. . . DEW-DABBLED, THE LILY AND ROSE!	122	WHITE BIRDS	5
SOON FAR FROM THE ROSE AND THE LILY . . .	122	WHITE BIRDS	11
. . . DEW DABBLED, THE LILY AND ROSE!	122	WHITE BIRDS V	5
AND HOW, WHEN FADES THE SEA-STREWN ROSE OF DAY,	128	DREAM OF FAERY V	33
BECAUSE THE RED ROSE BORDERED HEM	137	TO IRELAND V	6
AFTER THE RED ROSE BORDERED HEM.	139	TO IRELAND V	30
AFTER THE RED ROSE BORDERED HEM.	139	TO IRELAND V	48
THE LOVER TELLS OF THE ROSE IN HIS HEART	142	ROSE IN HEART	T
THE ROSE IN MY HEART .	142	ROSE IN HEART V	T
AEDH TELLS OF THE ROSE IN HIS HEART	142	ROSE IN HEART V	T
ARE WRONGING YOUR IMAGE THAT BLOSSOMS A ROSE	143	ROSE IN HEART	4
FOR MY DREAMS OF YOUR IMAGE THAT BLOSSOMS A ROSE	143	ROSE IN HEART	8
CRUMPLE THE ROSE IN YOUR HAIR!	162	ASKS FORGIVE	4
CRUSH THE ROSE IN YOUR HAIR,	162	ASKS FORGIVE V	4
THE INCORRUPTIBLE ROSE,	168	BLESSED	36
"THE ROSE THAT MUST DROP, OUT OF SWEET LEAVES,	168	BLESSED V	37
THE SECRET ROSE .	169	SECRET ROSE	T
O'SULLIVAN RUA TO THE SECRET ROSE	169	SECRET ROSE V	T
TO THE SECRET ROSE .	169	SECRET ROSE V	T
FAR-OFF, MOST SECRET, AND INVIOLATE ROSE,	169	SECRET ROSE	1
FAR OFF, MOST SECRET, AND INVIOLATE ROSE,	169	SECRET ROSE V	1
FAR-OFF, MOST SECRET, AND INVIOLATE ROSE?	170	SECRET ROSE	32
FAR OFF, MOST SECRET, AND INVIOLATE ROSE?	170	SECRET ROSE V	32
HAVE PULLED THE IMMORTAL ROSE!	174	ELEMENT POWERS	2
AND STOLE THE CRIMSON ROSE,	174	ELEMENT POWERS V	2
OF THE ROSE IN ITS DOOM.	175	ELEMENT POWERS V	12
BRING ROSES IF THE ROSE BE YET IN BLOOM!	311	MOUNTAIN TOMB	2
THE ROSE TREE .	396	ROSE TREE	T
HAS WITHERED OUR ROSE TREE!	396	ROSE TREE	4
CAN MAKE A RIGHT ROSE TREE."	396	ROSE TREE	18
HAVE WITHERED OUR ROSE TREE!	396	ROSE TREE V	4
WHERE THE SYMBOLIC ROSE CAN BREAK IN FLOWER,	419	MY HOUSE	4
WHEN THEY HAVE PLUCKED A ROSE THERE, . . .	571	THREE BUSHES	75
AS THE CANKER-WORM ON A MILK-WHITE ROSE!	673	ISLE STAT II 3	177
WHEN HE GAVE TO THEE THE ROSE,	744	ROSY CROSS	2
WHEN HE GAVE TO THEE THE ROSE,	744	ROSY CROSS	10
ROSE (VERB)			
AS HER SOFT BOSOM ROSE AND FELL.	4	OISIN 1	30
ROSE EVER OUT OF THE WARM SEA!	13	OISIN 1	172
ROSE EVER FROM THE SEA'S WARM FLOOR,	13	OISIN 1 V	172
AND ROSE FROM ALL THEIR DISTANT PARTS,	16	OISIN 1 V	228
ROSE IN THE DARKNESS, AND THE WHITE SURF GLEAMED	30	OISIN 2	23
IN NIAM'S HAIR--WHEN ROSE A WORLD OF TOWERS	30	OISIN 2 V	22
OUR TREAD, AS ROSE AND FELL THE LIQUID TONES	33	OISIN 2 V	68B
ROSE FROM A LITTLE RUNNEL ON WHOSE EDGE	39	OISIN 2 V	157
KINGFISHER COLOUR GREW WITH RAGE. HE ROSE	40	OISIN 2 V	169
. . . AND I ROSE, AND WALKED ON THE EARTH,	60	OISIN 3	191
WITH EYES OF SADNESS ROSE TO HEAR,	85	MAD KING GOLL V	62
IN SOLEMN REVERIE ROSE TO HEAR	85	MAD KING GOLL V	62
WHERE SUCH GREY CLOUDS OF INCENSE ROSE	156	FORGOT BEAUTY	13
WHERE A SO SLEEPY INCENSE ROSE	156	FORGOT BEAUTY V	13
IT ROSE IN A STRAIGHT BLUE GARMENT,	159	CAP AND BELLS	5
SHE ROSE IN HER PALE NIGHT-GOWN!	159	CAP AND BELLS	10
SHE ROSE IN HER PALE NIGHT GOWN,	159	CAP AND BELLS V	10
WHEN SHE ROSE UP TO DEPART?	171	MAID QUIET	6
WASHED BY TIME'S WATERS AS THEY ROSE AND FELL	206	ADAMS CURSE	32
WHILE I WAS LOOKING THEY ROSE HURRIEDLY,	223	SHADOW WATER B	25
SHE MOTIONED HIM AFAR, AND ROSE AND SPOKE!	280	TWO KINGS	68
AND AT THOSE WORDS I ROSE AND I WENT OUT	282	TWO KINGS	125
TOLD HIM, THAT WHEN ORION ROSE, AND ALL	282	TWO KINGS V	132A
ROSE ROUND THE WALLS, AND THROUGH THE BRONZE-RINGED DOOR	286	TWO KINGS	215
SHOULD BE SO SIMPLE--A BAT ROSE FROM THE HAZELS	377	PHASES OF MOON	137
THAT EVERY MORNING ROSE AGAIN	385	ROBARTES DANCE	7
WHILE THAT GREAT QUEEN, THAT ROSE OUT OF THE SPRAY,	404	FOR DAUGHTER	27
ROSE FROM THE TABLE AND DECLARED IT RIGHT	410	TOWER	43
HANRAHAN ROSE IN FRENZY THERE	412	TOWER	71
I ROSE THAT I MIGHT SCREEN IT WITH A CLOTH.	467	HARUN RASHID	131
BUT WOKE AT THE FIRST GLEAM OF DAY, ROSE UP	467	HARUN RASHID	147
SHE ROSE, AND WITH HER EYES SHUT FAST IN SLEEP	468	HARUN RASHID	152
AND ONCE AGAIN SHE ROSE AND SWEPT THE HOUSE	468	HARUN RASHID	159
MANY TIMES ROSE AGAIN.	467	DEATH	6
ROSE OUT OF THE RACE	480	BLOOD AND MOON	4
ROSE LIKE THESE WALLS FROM THESE	480	BLOOD AND MOON	6
ROSE! SOME CONQUEROR DREW REIN	502	VACILLATION	64
HE ROSE THE LATCH AND WENT UPSTAIRS	594	COLONEL MARTIN	7
I ROSE, I ROSE	672	ISLE STAT II 3	161
I ROSE, I ROSE	672	ISLE STAT II 3	161
I ROSE, I ROSE	672	ISLE STAT II 3	163
I ROSE, I ROSE	672	ISLE STAT II 3	163
JUST NOW MY SOUL ROSE UP AND TOUCHED IT, FAR	705	REMEMBRANCE	13
A FULL HOUR LONG, WHEN ROSE A FEATHER	728	PRIEST FAIRY	19
THREE SPANS HIGH AS HE ROSE TO HIS FEET,	729	PRIEST FAIRY	25
AND JOHN ROSE UP AND STOOD,	741	EARL PAUL	54
ROSEATE			
WHAT ROSEATE FINGERS! NO! NOR IS THERE ONE	720	WITCH VIVIEN	5
WHAT ROSEATE FINGERS! HA, HA! HA, HA, HA!	720	WITCH VIVIEN	15
ROSE-BREATH			
A LITTLE SPACE FOR THE ROSE-BREATH TO FILL!	101	ROSE UPON ROOD	14

ROSE-HEAVY
      COVER YOUR LIPS WITH ROSE-HEAVY TWILIGHT, AND SAY: . . .   162 ASKS FORGIVE   V   5
      THE ROSE-HEAVY TWILIGHT THERE. . . . . 163 ASKS FORGIVE   V   24
ROSE'S
      AS WE KISSED EACH ROSE'S HEAD: . . . .   21 OISIN 1   V 307
ROSES
      THE DAMASK ROSES, BLOOM ON BLOOM, ...   21 OISIN 1   305
      FALL THE LEAVES OF OTHER ROSES, ...   21 OISIN 1   311
      SHALL FALL THE LEAVES OF DAMASK ROSES. . . . . . .   21 OISIN 1   315
      DAMASK ROSES IN THE NIGHT, ...   21 OISIN 1   V 306A
      ROSE OF ALL ROSES, ROSE OF ALL THE WORLD: . . . .   113 ROSE OF BATTLE   1
      ROSE OF ALL ROSES, ROSE OF ALL THE WORLD: . . . .   115 ROSE OF BATTLE   25
      THE SOUTH IS POURING DOWN ROSES OF CRIMSON FIRE: .   154 BELOVED PEACE   6
      THE SOUTH WOULD COVER THEM WITH ROSES OF CRIMSON FIRE: 154 BELOVED PEACE   V   6
      THE ROSES THAT OF OLD TIME WERE . . . .   156 FORGOT BEAUTY   9
      LILIES OF DEATH-PALE HOPE, ROSES OF PASSIONATE DREAM.   172 TRAV PASSION   8
      BRING ROSES IF THE ROSE BE YET IN BLOOM: . . . . .   311 MOUNTAIN TOMB   2
      TO TAKE THE ROSES FOR HIS MEAT. . . . .   382 SONG OF FOOL   12
      SO DID THEIR ROSES MERGE. . . . .   571 THREE BUSHES   62
      WHERE REVEL OF FOX-GLOVE IS AND REVEL OF ROSES." .   669 ISLE STAT II 3   86
      WHERE REVEL OF FOXGLOVE IS AND REVEL OF ROSES." . .   669 ISLE STAT II 3   V 86
      THE ROOTS OF THE ROSES. . . . .   672 ISLE STAT II 3   169
      THREE TIMES THE ROSES HAVE GROWN LESS AND LESS, . .   690 MOSADA 1   1
      TENDING THE ROSES ROUND HIS LATTICE DOOR. . . . .   692 MOSADA 1   53
      WHERE THE ROSES IN SCARLET ARE HEAVY . . . .   707 FAIRY PEDANT   3
      THOUGH TENDEREST ROSES WERE ROUND YOU, ...   708 FAIRY PEDANT   29
ROSE-TREE
      AND SET A ROSE-TREE ON HER GRAVE, ...   571 THREE BUSHES   73
ROSICROSS
      OUR FATHER ROSICROSS IS IN HIS TOMB. . . . .   311 MOUNTAIN TOMB   4
      OUR FATHER ROSICROSS IS IN HIS TOMB. . . . .   311 MOUNTAIN TOMB   8
      OUR FATHER ROSICROSS SLEEPS IN HIS TOMB. . . . . .   311 MOUNTAIN TOMB   12
ROSNAREE
      MY COUSIN OF ROSNAREE. . . . .   178 FIDDLER DOONEY V   4
      MY COUSIN IN ROSNAREE. . . . .   178 FIDDLER DOONEY V   4
ROSSES
      FAR OFF BY FURTHEST ROSSES . . . .   87 STOLEN CHILD   15
ROSSES'
      BUT ACTUAL SHELLS OF ROSSES' LEVEL SHORE. . . . .   494 AT ALGECIRAS   12
      BUT TURN FROM ROSSES' CRAWLING TIDE, ...   549 SEVERED HEAD   5
ROSY
      AND SOFTLY MAKE A ROSY PEACE, ...   113 ROSE OF PEACE   15
      A SONG OF THE ROSY CROSS . . . .   744 ROSY CROSS   T
ROT
      BUT FAME AND VIRTUE ROT. . . . .   584 GHOST ROG CASE   36
ROTE
      HE TELLS HIS LIES BY ROTE: . . . .   598 STONE CROSS   2
ROTS
      WOULD END THIS PEACEFUL LIFE THAT ROTS THE BONES, . .   752 SHADOW WATER A   110
ROTTED   SEE SEA-ROTTED
      LIKE ROTTED FLESH, AND STONE BY STONE MY HALL . . .   45 OISIN 2   V 236
ROTTING
      --FROM POOLS AND ROTTING LEAVES--ME SING . . . . .   85 MAD KING GOLL   V   63
      LIES TORN AND ROTTING. THE FIERCE KESTREL BIRDS . . . 675 ISLE STAT II 3   234
ROUGE
      PROPPED UPON PILLOWS, ROUGE ON THE PALLOR OF HER FACE. . 362 HER COURTESY   3
ROUGH
      WHERE ARE YOU WITH YOUR LONG ROUGH HAIR? . . . . .   11 OISIN 1   126
      WHERE ARE YE WITH YOUR LONG ROUGH HAIR? . . . . . .   11 OISIN 1   V 126
      STAND UNDER THE ROUGH ROOF-TIMBERS OF THE HALL . . .   377 PHASES OF MOON   125
      AND WHAT ROUGH BEAST, ITS HOUR COME ROUND AT LAST, . . 402 SECOND COMING   21
      ROUGH MEN-AT-ARMS, CROSS-GARTERED TO THE KNEES . . .   412 TOWER   82
      ROUGH MEN AT ARMS, CROSS-GARTERED TO THE KNEES . . .   412 TOWER   V 82
      HURRIED THROUGH THE SMOOTH AND ROUGH . . . .   436 FOR MY SON   29
      HAVE BORNE YOU THROUGH THE SMOOTH AND ROUGH . . . .   436 FOR MY SON   V 29
      "AND THE NIGHT GROWS ROUGH." . . . .   526 AM OF IRELAND   13
      MARINERS, ROUGH HARVESTERS: . . . .   540 FROM ANTIGONE   5
ROUND
      THAN DOVES THAT MOANED ROUND EMAN'S HALL . . . . .   3 OISIN 1   V 7EE
      WHERE ROUND AND ROUND THE RAVENS GO. . . . .   5 OISIN 1   V 42
      WHERE ROUND AND ROUND THE RAVENS GO. . . . .   5 OISIN 1   V 42
      AND FAR BEHIND US, SLOWLY ROUND . . . .   10 OISIN 1   V 114B
      LULLED WEARINESS, AND SOFTLY ROUND . . . .   11 OISIN 1   137
      LULLED WEARINESS: AND CLOSELY ROUND . . . .   11 OISIN 1   V 137
      IN SILENCE ROUND HIS CRIMSON BALL. . . . .   12 OISIN 1   V 155
      WHEN ROUND US SUDDENLY THERE CAME . . . .   13 OISIN 1   V 165
      OF THE GREAT ROUND SUN, FROM HIS CENTRAL FIRES. . .   13 OISIN 1   V 168
      ROUND EVERY BRANCH THE SONG-BIRDS FLEW, ...   14 OISIN 1   180
      WHILE ROUND THE SHORE A MILLION STOOD . . . .   14 OISIN 1   182
      FOR ROUND EACH BRANCH THE SONG-BIRDS FLEW, ...   14 OISIN 1   V 180
      TRIMMED ROUND WITH MANY A CRIMSON FEATHER: . . . .   15 OISIN 1   V 206
      ROUND US, AND ROLLS THE UNWIELDY SUN. . . . .   18 OISIN 1   V 268
      THE MIST CLOSED ROUND US: PEARLY LIGHT . . . . . .   28 OISIN 1   V 427C
      ROLLED ROUND WITH MUSIC OF THE SIGHING SPRAY: . . .   30 OISIN 2   14
      AND BLACKNESS IN THE DARK. THE SEA ROLLED ROUND, . .   30 OISIN 2   V 23
      WITH CHAIN SEA-ROTTED, ROUND HER MIDDLE TIED, . . .   34 OISIN 2   V 75
      WRAPT ROUND IN SOME DIM MEMORY, IT SEEMED-- . . . .   36 OISIN 2   V 99
      CLOTHING HIM ROUND, I SAW A SEAGULL FLOAT . . . . .   36 OISIN 2   V 105
      WITH A PALE LIGHT, I JOURNEYED ROUND THE HALL . . .   39 OISIN 2   153
      OF MISTY DAWN: WHEN, CIRCLING ROUND THE HALL, . . .   39 OISIN 2   V 153
      HUNG ROUND WITH SLIME, AND WHISPERING IN HIS HAIR, . . 43 OISIN 2   V 216

		PAGE	TITLE		LINE
ROUND	(CONTINUED)				
FLED FOAM UNDERNEATH US, AND ROUND US, A WANDERING AND MILKY SMOKE,		47	OISIN 3		1
FLED FOAM UNDERNEATH US, AND ROUND US, A WANDERING AND MILKY SMOKE,		47	OISIN 3		12
COULD SLEEP ON A COUCH OF RUSHES--ROUND AND ABOUT THEM LAID.		49	OISIN 3	V	32
MOVED ROUND ME, OF SEAMEN OR LANDSMEN, ALL WHO ARE WINTER TALES;		53	OISIN 3		86
FLED FOAM UNDERNEATH ME, AND ROUND ME, A WANDERING AND MILKY SMOKE.		57	OISIN 3		148
AND IN FOLDS ROUND HIS EYES AND HIS MOUTH,		59	OISIN 3		174
WEARY, WITH ALL HIS POPPIES GATHERED ROUND HIM.		72	ANASHU VIJAYA		25
WHILE WE ALONE HAVE ROUND US WOVEN WOODS,		73	ANASHU VIJAYA		56
OF AWELESS BIRDS, AND ROUND THEIR STIRLESS FEET		74	ANASHU VIJAYA		73
MY SPIRIT ROCKED IN EVENING LIGHT, THE RUSHES ROUND MY KNEES,		76	INDIAN ON GOD		2
EACH OTHER ROUND IN CIRCLES, AND HEARD THE ELDEST SPEAK;		76	INDIAN ON GOD		5
MY SPIRIT ROCKED IN EVENING'S HUSH, THE RUSHES ROUND MY KNEES,		76	INDIAN ON GOD	V	2
EACH OTHER ROUND IN CIRCLES; AND I HEARD THE ELDEST SPEAK;--		76	INDIAN ON GOD	V	5
ONE WITH THE WAVES THAT SOFTLY ROUND US LAUGH AND DART.		78	INDIAN TO LOVE	V	15
THE WOODS WERE ROUND THEM, AND THE YELLOW LEAVES		80	EPHEMERA		13
THEY WILL NOT HUSH, THE LEAVES A-FLUTTER ROUND ME,		82	MAD KING GOLL		12
(THEY WILL NOT HUSH, THE LEAVES THAT ROUND ME FLUTTER--		82	MAD KING GOLL	V	REF
THEY WILL NOT HUSH, THE LEAVES A-FLUTTER ROUND ME,		83	MAD KING GOLL		24
TO HIS OWN ICE!" I GATHERED ROUND ME,		83	MAD KING GOLL	V	18
THEY WILL NOT HUSH, THE LEAVES A-FLUTTER ROUND ME,		84	MAD KING GOLL		36
THEY WILL NOT HUSH, THE LEAVES A-FLUTTER ROUND ME,		84	MAD KING GOLL		48
THEY WILL NOT HUSH, THE LEAVES A-FLUTTER ROUND ME,		85	MAD KING GOLL		60
THEY WILL NOT HUSH, THE LEAVES A-FLUTTER ROUND ME,		86	MAD KING GOLL		72
ROUND AND ROUND THE OATMEAL-CHEST.		88	STOLEN CHILD		49
ROUND AND ROUND THE OATMEAL-CHEST.		88	STOLEN CHILD		49
ROUND AND ROUND THE OATMEAL CHEST.		88	STOLEN CHILD	V	49
ROUND AND ROUND THE OATMEAL CHEST.		88	STOLEN CHILD	V	49
AND THE WORLD ROUND KNOCKNASHEE		93	FATHER OHART		31
COME ROUND ME, LITTLE CHILDER;		94	MOLL MAGEE		1
THE LITTLE STRAWS WERE TURNIN' ROUND		95	MOLL MAGEE		31
BUT ALWAYS, AS I'M MOVIN' ROUND,		96	MOLL MAGEE		43
POURS ROUND HIS SLEEPY STREAMS.		98	FOXHUNTER	V	16
POURS ROUND IN SLEEPY STREAMS.		98	FOXHUNTER	V	16
HIS LOLLARD LEAD THEY ROUND THE LAWN,		98	FOXHUNTER		17
SERVANTS ROUND HIS CUSHIONED PLACE		99	FOXHUNTER		37
THE SERVANTS ROUND HIS CUSHIONED PLACE		99	FOXHUNTER	V	37
WHO CAST ROUND FERGUS DREAMS, AND RUIN UNTOLD;		101	ROSE UPON ROOD		5
UNLOOSE THE CORD, AND THEY WILL WRAP YOU ROUND.		104	FERGUS DRUID		30
WHO LOVES YOU, NO WHITE ARMS TO WRAP YOU ROUND,		109	CUCHULAIN SEA		59
RANKING HIS DRUIDS ROUND HIM TEN BY TEN,		110	CUCHULAIN SEA		76
NEAR TO CUCHULLIN, ROUND A QUICKEN TREE,		111	CUCHULAIN SEA	V	81A
MY ARMS ROUND MY OWN!		118	CRADLE SONG	V	10
WITH ARMS ROUND MY OWN,		118	CRADLE SONG	V	10
THE FULL ROUND MOON AND THE STAR-LADEN SKY,		119	SORROW OF LOVE	V	2
AND PLANTED CYPRESS ROUND;		123	DREAM OF DEATH		8
FOR ROUND ABOUT MY TABLE GO		138	TO IRELAND	V	23
THE WINDS AWAKEN, THE LEAVES WHIRL ROUND,		140	HOSTING SIDHE		6
WHEN MY ARMS WRAP YOU ROUND I PRESS		155	FORGOT BEAUTY		1
THAT KEEPS THE STARS IN THEIR ROUND,		165	CRY OF SEDGE		5
I KNOW OF THE SLEEPY COUNTRY, WHERE SWANS FLY ROUND		204	WITHER BOUGHS		17
MOVED ROUND ME IN THE SHADOWS, AND AT NIGHT		218	WOODS OF COOLE		19
MOVED ROUND ME IN THE VOICES AND THE FIRES,		218	WOODS OF COOLE		23
A GOOD ROUND SUM UPON THIS CRUISE, AND TURN--		222	SHADOW WATER B		5
I SWEAR BEFORE THE DAWN COMES ROUND AGAIN		260	FASC DIFFICULT		12
WHEN CUPS WENT ROUND AT CLOSE OF DAY--		271	GREY ROCK		12
AND PUT HIS PATTERN ROUND THEIR TOPS		272	GREY ROCK	V	24
AND FOR NINE DAYS MY MIND WENT WHIRLING ROUND		282	TWO KINGS		127
ROSE ROUND THE WALLS, AND THROUGH THE BRONZE-RINGED DOOR		286	TWO KINGS		215
ROUND ABOUT HELL'S GATE TO STARE		294	HATED PLAYBOY	V	3
UNDER THE ROUND TOWER		331	ROUND TOWER		T
BELLOWED AND PRANCED IN THE ROUND TOWER;		331	ROUND TOWER		12
BELLOWING UP AND BELLOWING ROUND,		331	ROUND TOWER		14
PRANCING ROUND AND PRANCING UP		331	ROUND TOWER		17
WE HAVE GONE ROUND AND ROUND		332	SOLOMON SHEBA		6
WE HAVE GONE ROUND AND ROUND		332	SOLOMON SHEBA		6
THE ROUND GREEN EYES AND THE LONG WAVERING BODIES		343	DEJECTION		2
MANAGE THE TALK UNTIL HER NAME COME ROUND.		351	HER PRAISE		14
MANAGE TO TALK UNTIL HER NAME COME ROUND.		351	HER PRAISE	V	14
HE HAD LEARNT FROM PATER, AND TO ROUND HIS TALE		373	PHASES OF MOON		27
THE FIRST THIN CRESCENT IS WHEELED ROUND ONCE MORE.		377	PHASES OF MOON		116
AND CIRCLED ROUND HIM WITH ITS SQUEAKY CRY,		377	PHASES OF MOON		138
AND THE MOON SPUN ROUND LIKE A TOP,		378	CAT AND MOON		2
AND THAT FROM ROUND TO CRESCENT,		379	CAT AND MOON		23
FROM CRESCENT TO ROUND THEY RANGE?		379	CAT AND MOON		24
AND WHAT ROUGH BEAST, ITS HOUR COME ROUND AT LAST,		402	SECOND COMING		21
AND HAVE NO BUSINESS BUT DISPENSING ROUND		404	FOR DAUGHTER		43
WHAT MORE IS THERE TO SAY? THAT COUNTRY ROUND		430	NINETEEN 19		43
HAD FALLEN AMONG DANCERS, HAD WHIRLED THEM ROUND		430	NINETEEN 19		52
GREEKS WERE BUT LOVERS; ALL THAT COUNTRY ROUND		430	NINETEEN 19	V	43
BUT WEARIED RUNNING ROUND AND ROUND IN THEIR COURSES		433	NINETEEN 19		116
BUT WEARIED RUNNING ROUND AND ROUND IN THEIR COURSES		433	NINETEEN 19		116

ROUND (CONTINUED)　　　　　　　　　　　　　　　PAGE　TITLE　LINE

	PAGE	TITLE		LINE
BUT, WEARY RUNNING ROUND AND ROUND IN THEIR COURSES,	433	NINETEEN 19	V	116
BUT, WEARY RUNNING ROUND AND ROUND IN THEIR COURSES,	433	NINETEEN 19	V	116
TILL HIS MORNING MEAL COME ROUND;	435	FOR MY SON		4
FROM SOME COURT-LADY'S DRESS AND ROUND	477	SELF AND SOUL		14
FROM SOME COURT-LADIES' DRESS AND ROUND	477	SELF AND SOUL	V	14
TO ROUND THAT SHELL'S ELABORATE WHORL,	509	JANE REPROVED		8
WHAT SET IT WHIRLING ROUND?	520	HIS BARGAIN		2
AND PRAYER COMES ROUND AGAIN--	553	PRAYER OLD AGE		10
AND MUST THE COMMON ROUND OF DAY RESUME.	557	RIBH ECSTASY		8
THAT DAY BRINGS ROUND THE NIGHT, THAT BEFORE DAWN	563	MERU		13
I TURN ROUND	572	LADYS 1ST SONG		1
DRAW ROUND, BELOVED AND BITTER MEN,	584	GHOST ROG CASE		37
DRAW ROUND AND RAISE A SHOUT;	584	GHOST ROG CASE		38
COME GATHER ROUND ME, PARNELLITES,	586	PARNELLITES		T
COME GATHER ROUND ME, PARNELLITES,	586	PARNELLITES		1
AND PASS THE BOTTLE ROUND.	586	PARNELLITES		8
SO PASS THE BOTTLE ROUND.	587	PARNELLITES		24
FOR PASSING ROUND THE BOTTLE WITH GIRLS IN RAGS OR SILK,	592	PILGRIM		2
FOR PASSING ROUND THE BOTTLE WITH GIRLS IN RAG OR SILK,	592	PILGRIM	V	2
ROUND LOUGH DERG'S HOLY ISLAND I WENT UPON THE STONES,	593	PILGRIM		6
COME GATHER ROUND ME, PLAYERS ALL;	608	SONGS BURDEN 3		1
OR ROUND THE CITY HALL.	608	SONGS BURDEN 3		6
UNDER THE TROPIC SHADE, GREW ROUND AND SLOW,	610	STATUES		18
HUMAN, SUPERHUMAN, A BIRD'S ROUND EYE,	618	BRONZE HEAD		2
HUMAN, SUPER-HUMAN, A BIRD'S ROUND EYE,	618	BRONZE HEAD	V	2
ROUND THE MAREOTIC LAKE	636	BEN BULBEN		2
SLEEPILY CLOSE HER ROUND BRIGHT EYNE,	646	ISLE STAT I 1		35
HANG ON THE SIDE OF THE ROUND GRAPE-CLUSTER;	646	ISLE STAT I 1		45
WITH SINGING SWEET AS E'ER ROUND LAKE-LULLED ISLE	649	ISLE STAT I 1		106
WILL CIRCLE ROUND THE WORLD UPON A QUEST,	651	ISLE STAT I 1		159
AND I SANG ROUND THE TREE	654	ISLE STAT I 2		66
AND I SANG ROUND THE TREE,	654	ISLE STAT I 2		76
AND I SANG ROUND THE TREE,	655	ISLE STAT I 2		80
HERE WHERE THE ROUND WAVES COME, HERE LET THEM BUILD,	663	ISLE STAT II 2		19
THE SPINNING STARS--THE TOILING SEA--WHIRL ROUND	665	ISLE STAT II 2		72
THEY WERE SITTING ROUND A POOL,	667	ISLE STAT II 3		24
AND THEY WERE SITTING ROUND A POOL.	667	ISLE STAT II 3	V	24
HAS FENCED US ROUND FOR ALL ETERNITY.	670	ISLE STAT II 3		95
AND ALL WAS QUIET ROUND ME SPREAD,	670	ISLE STAT II 3		112
MY DREAMS ROUND THOUGHTS OF PLENTY, AS IN GLOOM	681	SEEKER		3
AND ROVE UNCEASING ROUND THEIR DREADFUL BROOD.	681	SEEKER		5
WEARY OF WATCHING ROUND THE FIRE AT NIGHT,	683	SEEKER		42
AS ROUND HER, SLOW ON FEET THAT HAVE NO BLOOD,	687	TWO TITANS		18
FOR EVER ROUND THY WAKING AND THY SLEEP	688	TWO TITANS		57
NOR TREMBLE TO ITS FALL. THE FIRE SWEEPS ROUND	689	NETTLESHIP		11
POURS UP AND FLOATS IN FRAGRANCE ROUND MY HEAD	691	MOSADA 1		40
OF SILVER HANGING ROUND LAME COLA'S NECK--	691	MOSADA 1	V	35
TENDING THE ROSES ROUND HIS LATTICE DOOR.	692	MOSADA 1		53
AND, WHILE THEY GATHER ROUND MY BECKONING ARMS,	694	MOSADA 1		100
FOR YE ARE HID WITH VAPOUR. ROUND THE STAKE	695	MOSADA 1		111
FOR YE ARE HID WITH VAPOURS? ROUND THE STAKE	695	MOSADA 1	V	111
POOR LOVE AND SORROW, WITH THEIR ARMS THROWN ROUND	703	MOSADA 3		119
THOUGH TENDEREST ROSES WERE ROUND YOU,	708	FAIRY PEDANT		29
RINGED ROUND AND FONDLED, A BROWN FARM HOUSE SEES.	710	FERENCZ RENYI	V	23
CLOSELY ROUND US, BODY AND MIND--	717	FAIRY DOCTOR		23
ROUND SHE COMES IN STAYS BEFORE THEM;	719	PHANTOM SHIP		17
FROM WHERE THE OLD IVY CRAWLS ROUND THE OLD STEEPLE,	728	PRIEST FAIRY		6
ROUND US THE WHITE ROADS ARE ENDLESS,	737	IN FIRELIGHT		3
ROUND US HERDS OF SHADOWS STEAL--	737	IN FIRELIGHT		6
AND GATHER ROUND HIM, THAT NO GOD MAY KNOW	758	SHADOW WATER A	V	231
AT THE GREY ROUND OF THE HILL	782	GREY ROUND		1
WHEN MOON'S ROUND IS FINISHED	786	YOUR HEART		33

ROUNDING

	PAGE	TITLE	LINE
BUT WHILE THE MOON IS ROUNDING TOWARDS THE FULL	373	PHASES OF MOON	39

ROUNDLY

	PAGE	TITLE	LINE
'TWAS ROUNDLY SPOKE, BUT WHEN NIGHT CAME	275	GREY ROCK	95

ROUNDS

	PAGE	TITLE	LINE
ROUNDS A MIGHTY SCENE,	599	STONE CROSS	22
... SEE, SHE ROUNDS THE HARBOUR CLEAR.	718	PHANTOM SHIP	13

ROUSE

	PAGE	TITLE	LINE
TO SHAKE HIM OUT OF SLEEP, I COULD NOT ROUSE HIM.	283	TWO KINGS	143
COULD ROUSE MY WHOLE NATURE.	400	DEMON BEAST	32

ROUSED

	PAGE	TITLE	LINE
THE WAR-SONGS THAT ROUSED THEM OF OLD;	61	OISIN 3	202
HE ROUSED HIS HORSE OUT OF ITS SLEEP,	133	FR GILLIGAN	27
I HAVE ROUSED THEE, FOR THE WEEPING	729	PRIEST FAIRY	40

ROUT

	PAGE	TITLE		LINE
LIKE TO A MERRY WANDERING ROUT	18	OISIN 1		253
AND THROUGH THE DOORS, A RUSTLING ROUT,	20	OISIN 1	V	290
WHAT ONE IN THE ROUT	142	MOODS		5
BUT, KINDLY OLD ROUT	142	MOODS	V	5
WITH EQUAL COURAGE IN THAT WHIRLING ROUT;	186	QUEEN MAEVE		131

ROVE

	PAGE	TITLE		LINE
HOW WHEN WE DIE OUR SHADES WILL ROVE,	78	INDIAN TO LOVE		18
HOW WHEN WE DIE OUR SHADES MAY ROVE,	78	INDIAN TO LOVE	V	18
IS FROM THE HOLY SHADES THAT ROVE	275	GREY ROCK		110
OUR SHADOWS ROVE THE GARDEN GRAVEL STILL,	435	NEW FACES		7
FROM WHOSE GREEN BANKS NO LIVING THING MAY ROVE,	664	ISLE STAT II 2		57
DOTH STILL THE WANDERER ROVE? WITH ALL HIS SHIPS	677	ISLE STAT II 3		287
AND THROUGH THE MANSION OF THE SPIRIT ROVE	681	SEEKER		2

669

		PAGE	TITLE	LINE

ROVE   (CONTINUED)
OF DESERT-CAVES THE RED-EYED PANTHERS ROVE . . . . . .   681 SEEKER   4
AND ROVE UNCEASING ROUND THEIR DREADFUL BROOD. . . . .   681 SEEKER   5
EYED PANTHERS IN THEIR DESERT CAVERNS ROVE . . . . . .   681 SEEKER   V   4
ROVED
AND MANY A POOR MAN THAT HAS ROVED, ...   404 FOR DAUGHTER   38
ROVER
OF MANY A SLAUGHTERED FOREST ROVER. . . . .   17 OISIN 1   V 249A
SAILETH THE ROVER SORROW, ...   70 CLOAK BOAT   9
SAILETH THE ROVER SORROW, ...   666 ISLE STAT II 3   9
A ROVER I, WHO COME FROM WHERE MEN'S EARS . . . . .   678 ISLE STAT II 3   293
DOTH STILL THE MAN WHOM EACH STERN ROVER FEARS, . . .   678 ISLE STAT II 3   ˚295
ROVING   SEE A-ROVING
ROW
IN A LONG AND SHADOWY ROW, ...   20 OISIN 1   V 295
AND LAYS THEM IN A ROW. . . . .   89 ISLE IN WATER   6
THE ARCHANGELS STAND IN A ROW THERE . . . .   774 COME RIDE   9
ROWAN
YELLOW THE LEAVES OF THE ROWAN ABOVE US, ...   79 FALLING LEAVES   3
ROWBOAT
ROWER BENT IN HIS ROWBOAT . . . .   589 OLD WICKED MAN V   50
ROW-BOAT
ROWER BENT IN HIS ROW-BOAT . . . .   589 OLD WICKED MAN   50
ROWED
WHEN WE ROWED NORTH, SINGING ABOVE THE OARS, ...   749 SHADOW WATER A   39
ROWER
ROWER BENT IN HIS ROW-BOAT . . . .   589 OLD WICKED MAN   50
ROWER BENT IN HIS ROWBOAT . . . .   589 OLD WICKED MAN V   50
ROWERS'
UPON THE ROWERS' BENCHES UNDERNEATH, ...   751 SHADOW WATER A   92
ROWS   SEE BEAN-ROWS
NINE BEAN ROWS WILL I HAVE THERE, A HIVE FOR THE HONEY BEE,   117 ISLE INNISFREE V   3
ROXBOROUGH
FROM CASTLE TAYLOR TO THE ROXBOROUGH SIDE . . . . . .   326 ROBERT GREGORY   58
ROYAL
ON MR. NETTLESHIP'S PICTURE AT THE ROYAL HIBERNIAN ACADEMY.   688 NETTLESHIP   T
ROYSTERER   SEE FELLOW-ROYSTERER
TO ABD-AL-RABBAN: FELLOW ROYSTERER ONCE . . . . . .   460 HARUN RASHID   V   2
RUA
WINDLE-STRAWS I. O'SULLIVAN RUA TO THE CURLEW . . . .   155 REPROVE CURLEW V   T
O'SULLIVAN RUA TO MARY LAVELL . . . .   155 FORGOT BEAUTY V   T
O'SULLIVAN RUA TO THE SECRET ROSE . . . .   169 SECRET ROSE   V   T
RUB
PUSH OUT HIS VIGOROUS LIMBS AND RUB HIS EYES, ...   284 TWO KINGS   162
IF I SHOULD RUB AN EYE, ...   384 VISION ROBART   52
RUBBED
AND RUBBED ALONG THE RAIL HIS NOSE. . . . .   725 LEGEND   28
RUBBING
SCALE RUBBING SCALE WHERE LIGHT IS DIM . . . .   195 BAILE AILLINN   145
RUBBISH
FOR ONLY RUBBISH COMES MY WAY. . . . .   295 THREE BEGGARS   4
AND SEEN THE RUBBISH RUN ABOUT, ...   297 THREE BEGGARS   65
AND SEEN THE RUBBISH RUNABOUT, ...   297 THREE BEGGARS V   65
FAIL, AND THAT HISTORY TURNS INTO RUBBISH, ...   546 TO SAME TUNE 2   21
FAIL, AND THAT HISTORY TURNS INTO RUBBISH, ...   614 MARCH SONGS 1   21
RUBIES
LET'S HOME: I'D GIVE SOME RUBIES TO A WOMAN. . . . .   248 SHADOW WATER B   537
RUBY
ACROSS YOUR WANDERING RUBY CARS . . . .   22 OISIN 1   330
THE ANCIENT BEARDS, THE HELMS OF RUBY AND GOLD . . .   169 SECRET ROSE   8
OF OPAL AND RUBY AND PALE CHRYSOLITE . . . .   219 HARP OF AENGUS   6
DRAGONS WITH EYES OF RUBY. THE WHOLE SHIP . . . . .   248 SHADOW WATER B   535
OF OPAL AND RUBY AND PALE CHRYSOLITE . . . .   762 SHADOW WATER A   301
AND CHRYSOPRASE AND RUBY AND SARDONYX. . . . .   765 SHADOW WATER A   358
RUDDY
WITH HOOFS OF THE RUDDY FINDRINNY . . . .   25 OISIN 1   V 383
AS ANY RUDDY MOTH, LOOKED DOWN ON US: . . . . . .   34 OISIN 2   72
AS LIKE A RUDDY MOTH THEY WAVED AND FLUTTERED. . . .   34 OISIN 2   V 72
TALL, PROUD AND RUDDY, AND LIGHT WINGS . . . .   195 BAILE AILLINN   140
ON THE RUDDY RIVER SEDGE, ...   646 ISLE STAT I 1   25
OR LONG ERE THIS HAD LOST THEIR RUDDY STAIN: . . . .   687 TWO TITANS   8
AND THEREON GREW THE RUDDY FRUIT . . . .   743 DANAAN QUICK   15
RUEFUL
HIS RUEFUL SPIRIT FLUTTERED BY. . . . .   673 ISLE STAT II 3   188
RUFFIAN'S
AND WHEN THAT ANCIENT RUFFIAN'S TURN WAS ON . . . . .   411 TOWER   66
RUFFLED
THERE ONE THAT RUFFLED IN A MANLY POSE . . . .   489 COOLE PARK 29   11
RUFFLES
HE RUFFLES WITH HIS BILL THE MINNOWED STREAMS. . . .   73 ANASHU VIJAYA   37
RUFFLING
IN MIDST OF AN OLD MAN'S BOSOM: OWLS RUFFLING AND PACING   50 OISIN 3   47
  AROUND
IN THE MIDST OF AN OLD MAN'S BOSOM: OWLS RUFFLING   50 OISIN 3   V 47
  AND PACING AROUND
RUIN
WILL SCATTER IN RUIN THE LEAST OF OUR DAYS, ...   27 OISIN 1   V 419B
SHALL BLOW INTO RUIN OUR MUSICAL DAYS, ...   28 OISIN 1   V 425
WHO CAST ROUND FERGUS DREAMS, AND RUIN UNTOLD: . . .   101 ROSE UPON ROOD   5
WHEN ALL IS RUIN ONCE AGAIN. . . . .   406 CARVED STONE   6
FROM RUIN OR FROM ANCIENT TREES, ...   410 TOWER   23

```
                                                   PAGE      TITLE          LINE
RUIN  (CONTINUED)
    BEFORE THAT RUIN CAME, FOR CENTURIES,  . . . . . . .  412 TOWER            81
    BECOME A ROOFLESS RUIN THAT THE OWL . . . . . . . .   423 MY DESCENDANTS   14
    MY HEART COULD NEVER TURN FROM DAILY RUIN, . . . . .  464 HARUN RASHID     83
    MY HEART MUST LOOK UPON A DAILY RUIN . . . . . . .    464 HARUN RASHID   V 83
    RUIN, WRECK AND WRACK; . . . . . . . . . . . .        505 RESULT THOUGHT    8
    BUT I WOKE IN AN OLD RUIN THAT THE WINDS HOWLED THROUGH; 581 CURSE CROMWELL 28
    THAT WITH THEIR FIERY RUIN FILL THE HALL, . . . . .   683 SEEKER           45
    TO PRISONS GO, AND MOSSY RUIN REST . . . . . . .      709 FERENCZ RENYI     2
    TO PRISON GO, AND MOSSY RUIN REST . . . . . . .       709 FERENCZ RENYI  V  2
    RUIN ON A GREAT KING'S HOUSE . . . . . . . .          775 AGAINST WITCH     3
    CASTLE DARGAN'S RUIN ALL LIT, . . . . . . . .         788 HAWTHORN TREE     3
RUINED
    IN CORMAC'S RUINED HOUSE. . . . . . . . . .           384 VISION ROBART    68
    EMPTIED, RUINED, WRACKED, AND LOST, . . . . . . .     776 AGAINST WITCH    27
RUINOUS
    TIME OUT OF MIND, BECAME TOO RUINOUS . . . . . . .    264 HOUSE SHAKEN      3
    UNINHABITED, RUINOUS, . . . . . . . . . .             512 JANE ON GOD      15
    UNTIL ALL BE RUINOUS. . . . . . . . . . .             775 AGAINST WITCH     4
RULE
    BUT HERE THERE IS NOR LAW NOR RULE, . . . . . . .      19 OISIN 1         282
    WITH HEARTS THAT KNOW NOR LAW NOR RULE, . . . . .      22 OISIN 1         339
    OUR LIVES HAVE KNOWN NO LAW NOR RULE; . . . . . .      22 OISIN 1       V 340
    TO RULE MORE MIGHTY MEN, AND TO THE WORLD . . . . .    38 OISIN 2       V 133
    "LAST OF MY RACE, THREE THINGS I RULE ALONE-- . . .    45 OISIN 2       V 239A
    AND WITH A RULE SERENE AND MILD . . . . . . .         82 MAD KING GOLL  V  6
    "THOUGH LOGIC-CHOPPERS RULE THE TOWN, . . . . .      337 TOM OROUGHLEY     1
    "THOUGH LOGIC CHOPPERS RULE THE TOWN, . . . . .      337 TOM OROUGHLEY  V  1
    MEN THAT DO ALL BY RULE, . . . . . . . . .           380 SONGS FOOL 1     14
    CAN RULE BY SUPERNATURAL RIGHT . . . . . . .         386 ROBARTES DANCE   36
    AND PLANNED TO BRING THE WORLD UNDER A RULE, . . .   429 NINETEEN 19      31
    FIT AUDIENCE FOUND, BUT CANNOT RULE . . . . .        506 REMORSE SPEECH    4
    AND RULE IN HIS OWN RIGHT; . . . . . . . .           538 LAST CONFESS     20
    UNDER A RULE, UNDER THE SEMBLANCE OF PEACE . . . .   563 MERU              2
    HE THOUGHT THE SAME AND LIVED BY RULE, . . . . .     576 WHAT THEN         3
    THAT RULE BECAUSE A STRONG RIGHT ARM . . . . .       597 MODEL LAUREATE   11
    "OBEY OUR ANCIENT RULE AND MAKE A SHROUD; . . . .    634 CUCHULAIN COMF   13
    CARES WHAT KING SETS UP HIS RULE. . . . . . .        635 BLACK TOWER      14
    THE AUSTERE ARTHUR, RULE FROM UTHER'S CHAIR? . . .   678 ISLE STAT II 3  296
    AND RULE THE SHADOWS OF THE EVE AND DAWN? . . . .    678 ISLE STAT II 3  304
    "HOW FEW THE MIND'S INTEMPERANCE RULE! . . . . .     725 LEGEND           10
    THE GREATNESS OF MY LOVE. DID I NOT RULE . . . . .   748 SHADOW WATER A V 32
    AND RULE TOGETHER UNDER A CANOPY. . . . . . .        767 SHADOW WATER A  385
RULED
    I RULED O'ER ALL MY FAIR DOMINIONS, . . . . . .       82 MAD KING GOLL  V  7
    I RULED AND RULED MY LIFE WITHIN-- . . . . . .        82 MAD KING GOLL  V  7
    I RULED AND RULED MY LIFE WITHIN-- . . . . . .        82 MAD KING GOLL  V  7
    WHEN HER OWN PEOPLE RULED THIS TRAGIC EIRE; . . . .  129 BOOK STORIES      2
    WHEN HER OWN PEOPLE RULED IN WAVE-WORN ERI, . . . .  129 BOOK STORIES   V  2
    NO OSCAR RULED THE TABLE, . . . . . . . .            626 STATES HOLIDAY    5
    HAST THOU NOT RULED AMONG THE GILDED WALLS? . . . .  724 KANVA ON SELF     7
RULERS
    GREAT RULERS OF THE STILLNESS, LET HER NO LONGER BE . . 175 ELEMENT POWERS V 13
    GREAT RULERS OF STILLNESS, LET HER NO LONGER BE . . .  175 ELEMENT POWERS V 13
RULES
    HE RULES YOU WITH AN IRON ROD, . . . . . . . .        22 OISIN 1         332
    FOR FERGUS RULES THE BRAZEN CARS, . . . . . . .      126 GOES FERGUS       9
    AND RULES THE SHADOWS OF THE WOOD, . . . . . .       126 GOES FERGUS      10
    FAMOUS, A MAN OF RULES, A VICTOR. STANDS . . . . .   709 FERENCZ RENYI     9
RULETH
    WHO MADE THE WORLD AND RULETH IT, HE HANGETH ON A STALK,  76 INDIAN ON GOD  10
RUMBLE
    ONE HEARS THE RUMBLE OF IT FAR BELOW . . . . . . .   420 MY HOUSE       V 20B
RUMMAGED
    SECOND RUMMAGED FOR A FLEA; . . . . . . .            298 THREE HERMITS     4
    WHILE HE'D RUMMAGED RAGS AND HAIR, . . . . . . .     299 THREE HERMITS    29
RUMOROUS
    WANDERING OF YORE IN FORESTS RUMOROUS, . . . . . .   723 KANVA ON SELF     3
RUMOUR
    A RUMOUR OF DELIGHTED HEARTS. . . . . . . .           16 OISIN 1         230
    VAST GREENNESS, WHERE ETERNAL RUMOUR DWELLS, . . . .  657 ISLE STAT I 3   45
RUN
    THAT YOU THROUGH ALL THAT FOAM SHOULD RUN?" . . . .     6 OISIN 1         61
    AMONG UNDYING PEOPLE HAS RUN . . . . . . .             6 OISIN 1       V 60
    AND MAKES THE LITTLE PLANETS RUN; . . . . . .         18 OISIN 1         268
    FOR JOY THE LITTLE PLANETS RUN . . . . . . .          18 OISIN 1       V 267
    THE IMAGED METEORS HAD FLASHED AND RUN . . . . .      31 OISIN 2          38
    THE IMAGED METEORS HAD SHONE AND RUN, . . . . .       31 OISIN 2       V 38
    THE HARES RUN BY ME GROWING BOLD. . . . . . .         84 MAD KING GOLL    47
    AND HARES RUN NEAR ME GROWING BOLD. . . . . .         84 MAD KING GOLL  V 47
    BEFORE MY THOUGHTS BEGIN TO RUN . . . . . . .        189 BAILE AILLINN     3
    I RUN TO BAILE HONEY-MOUTH, . . . . . . . .          191 BAILE AILLINN    48
    I RUN TO BAILE HONEY MOUTH . . . . . . . .           191 BAILE AILLINN  V 48
    GATHERING HIS CLOAK ABOUT HIM, RUN . . . . . .       193 BAILE AILLINN   101
    THAT RUN BEFORE THE REAPING-HOOK AND LIE . . . .     218 WOODS OF COOLE   32
    THAT RUN BEFORE THE REAPING HOOK AND LIE . . . .     218 WOODS OF COOLE V 32
    UPON ITS BANDY LEGS. RUN AT THEM NOW, . . . . .      233 SHADOW WATER B  239
    COMES CRYING, "I HAVE RUN UPON THE SWORD. . . . .    234 SHADOW WATER B  261
    WHY LINGER? RUN TO YOUR DESIRE; . . . . . .          234 SHADOW WATER B  272
    WHY DO YOU NOT RUN TO YOUR DESIRE, . . . . .         234 SHADOW WATER B V 272
    WHILE THERE'S A ROPE TO RUN INTO A NOOSE . . . . .   238 SHADOW WATER B  347
```

	PAGE	TITLE	LINE

RUN   (CONTINUED)
BUT IT IS TRUE. WHY DID THEY RUN UPON HIM, ...   243 SHADOW WATER B   424
HAD RUN INTO ONE FOUNTAIN. SPEAK TO HIM. . . . . . .   249 SHADOW WATER B   561
HOW SHOULD THEIR LUCK RUN HIGH ENOUGH TO REACH . . . .   264 HOUSE SHAKEN   9
AND THEREFORE, FRIEND, IF YOUR GREAT RACE WERE RUN . . .   265 THESE CLOUDS   7
TILL THE STARS HAD RUN AWAY . . . .   268 BROWN PENNY   13
IS NOT THAT HOW GOOD STORIES RUN?-- . . . .   271 GREY ROCK   13
AND SEEN THE RUBBISH RUN ABOUT. . . . .   297 THREE BEGGARS   65
TREMBLED AND GASPED AND SHOULD HAVE RUN . . . . . .   303 HOUR DAWN   V 22
HE GAVE A GASP AND THOUGHT TO RUN, ...   303 HOUR DAWN   V 22
OR RUN WHERE LADS REFORM OUR DAYTIME . . . .   343 SHEP GOATHERD   V 105
AND I AM AFRAID THAT YOU WILL RUN . . . .   356 BROKEN DREAMS   30
I AM AFRAID THAT YOU WILL RUN . . . .   356 BROKEN DREAMS   V 30
WHY SHOULD YOU RUN . . . .   359 TO A SQUIRREL   2
THE HARE MAY RUN TILL IT'S FOUND . . . .   380 SONGS FOOL 1   11
ON LIMBS THAT HAD RUN WILD. . . . .   394 EASTER 1916   64
THEY NEVER SAW HOW SEASONS RUN, ...   432 NINETEEN 19   101
FROM CRADLE RUN TO GRAVE . . . .   449 HERO GIRL FOOL   19
FROM GRAVE TO CRADLE RUN INSTEAD; . . . .   449 HERO GIRL FOOL   20
"BECAUSE I MADE YOU TURN AWAY AND RUN FROM THAT YOUNG   450 OWEN AHERNE   14
    CHILD:
AND THEN I LAUGH TILL TEARS RUN DOWN . . . .   456 FRIENDS YOUTH   17
UNTIL THAT GLANCE RUN IN THE WORLD'S DESPITE . . . .   474 ALL SOUL NIGHT   94
RUN TILL ALL THE SAGES KNOW. . . . .   476 EVA GORE-BOOTH   29
RUN FOR A MILE UNDIMMED IN HEAVEN'S FACE . . . . .   490 COOLE BALLYLEE   3
RUN UNDERGROUND, RISE IN A ROCKY PLACE . . . . . .   490 COOLE BALLYLEE   5
SPREAD TO A LAKE AND RUN INTO A HOLE. . . . . . .   490 COOLE BALLYLEE   V   7
BID IMAGINATION RUN . . . .   494 AT ALGECIRAS   15
WHEN THE LAST THREAD HAS RUN, ...   520 HIS BARGAIN   10
WHEN THE LAZY THREAD HAS RUN-- . . . .   520 HIS BARGAIN   V 10
ROE COULD RUN OR DOE COULD LEAP . . . .   522 LULLABY   10
ROE COULD LEAP OR DOE COULD RUN: . . . .   522 LULLABY   12
STAG COULD RUN AND ROE LEAP . . . .   522 LULLABY   V 10
STAG COULD LEAP AND ROE COULD RUN. . . . .   522 LULLABY   V 12
ALL THAT COULD RUN OR LEAP OR SWIM . . . .   528 DANCER CRUACH   6
ALL THAT RUN OR LEAP CR SWIM . . . .   528 DANCER CRUACH   V   6
HOW COULD PASSION RUN SO DEEP . . . .   534 CONSOLATION   7
WHAT SHUDDERS RUN THROUGH ALL THAT ANIMAL BLOOD? . . .   541 PARN FUNERAL 1   5
MARCH, MARCH--HOW DOES IT RUN?-- . . . .   548 TO SAME TUNE 3   15
O BUT HEART'S WINE SHALL RUN PURE, ...   554 CHURCH STATE   5
WINE SHALL RUN THICK TO THE END. . . . .   554 CHURCH STATE   11
THAT'S HOW ALL NATURAL OR SUPERNATURAL STORIES RUN. . . .   556 RIBH PATRICK   3
BUT ALL THAT RUN IN COUPLES, ON EARTH, IN FLOOD OR AIR,   556 RIBH PATRICK   11
      . . .
THE WORKMAN, NOBLE AND SAINT, AND ALL THINGS RUN . . .   565 GYRES   23
FEET TO THE RISING AND SETTING MAY RUN, ...   591 WHAT WAS LOST   4
THAT OFFICE FOOLS HAVE RUN, ...   598 MODEL LAUREATE   20
MARCH, MARCH, AND HOW DOES IT RUN? . . . .   615 MARCH SONGS 2   26
ON GANGLING STOCKS GROWN GREAT, GREAT STOCKS RUN DRY, . .   619 BRONZE HEAD   25
MALACHI STILT-JACK AM I, WHATEVER I LEARNED HAS RUN WILD,   623 HIGH TALK   9
THAT HEAVENS HAD OPENED. GYRES RUN ON: . . . . . .   639 BEN BULBEN   62
AND ALL HIS VEINS HAD NEAR RUN DRY, ...   670 ISLE STAT II 3   119
RUN LIKE THE MARCH WIND: . . . .   774 COME RIDE   V   6
RUNABOUT
AND SEEN THE RUBBISH RUNABOUT, ...   297 THREE BEGGARS   V 65
RUNNEL
A LITTLE RUNNEL MADE A BUBBLING STRAIN, ...   39 OISIN 2   156
ROSE FROM A LITTLE RUNNEL ON WHOSE EDGE . . . . . .   39 OISIN 2   V 157
RUNNEL'S
AND ON THE RUNNEL'S STONY AND BARE EDGE . . . . . .   39 OISIN 2   157
HIS HAND ALONG THE RUNNEL'S SIDE, AS THOUGH . . . .   39 OISIN 2   162
RUNNER
THAT RUNNER SAID: "I AM FROM THE SOUTH: . . . . . .   191 BAILE AILLINN   47
BLUE-EYED, AND A QUICK RUNNER ON BARE FEET, ...   242 SHADOW WATER B   416
RUNNERS
HAD SENT NO RUNNERS TO AND FRO . . . .   288 TO WEALTHY MAN   18
RUNNING
THE FIELD-MOUSE RUNNING BY ME IN THE GRASS, ...   101 ROSE UPON ROOD   17
THE FIELD MOUSE RUNNING BY ME IN THE GRASS, ...   101 ROSE UPON ROOD   V 17
THEY FOUND AN OLD MAN RUNNING THERE: . . . .   190 BAILE AILLINN   25
RIVERS ARE RUNNING OVER . . . .   214 HAPPY TOWNLAND   7
WHERE RIVERS ARE RUNNING OVER . . . .   214 HAPPY TOWNLAND   V   7
WITH SO RED LIPS, AND RUNNING ON SUCH FEET, ...   231 SHADOW WATER B   199
OUT OF THE RUNNING STREAM, O MORNING STAR, ...   251 SHADOW WATER B   610
AND AFTER RUNNING AT THE BRIM . . . .   254 HIS DREAM   9
AND RUNNING CROWD AND GAUDY SHIP . . . .   254 HIS DREAM   15
RUNNING TO PARADISE . . . .   300 RUN PARADISE   T
FOR I AM RUNNING TO PARADISE: . . . .   300 RUN PARADISE   3
AND I AM RUNNING TO PARADISE: . . . .   301 RUN PARADISE   10
AND I AM RUNNING TO PARADISE: . . . .   301 RUN PARADISE   17
FOR I AM RUNNING TO PARADISE: . . . .   301 RUN PARADISE   24
WHILE I AM RUNNING TO PARADISE. . . . .   301 RUN PARADISE   V REF
THAT SAW THE SURGES RUNNING BY, ...   338 TOM OROUGHLEY   6
BUT WEARIED RUNNING ROUND AND ROUND IN THEIR COURSES . .   433 NINETEEN 19   116
BUT, WEARY RUNNING ROUND AND ROUND IN THEIR COURSES, . .   433 NINETEEN 19   V 116
HALF RUNNING, DROPPED AT THE FIRST RIDGE OF THE DESERT . .   468 HARUN RASHID   155
A RED HOUND RUNNING FROM A SILVER ARROW. . . . . .   747 SHADOW WATER A   6
OUT OF A RUNNING STREAM, O MORNING STAR . . . . . .   769 SHADOW WATER A   426
WERE HIS MEASURE RUNNING DRY . . . .   772 SONG DEIRDRE 1   14
WERE HIS MEASURES RUNNING DRY. . . . .   772 SONG DEIRDRE 1   V 14
PLANTED IN THE RUNNING WAVE: . . . .   775 AGAINST WITCH   13

RUNS
    THE HARE RUNS BY ME GROWING BOLD--   • • • • • • •   84 MAD KING GOLL V   47
    THAT FROM THOSE FINGERS GLITTERING SUMMER RUNS • • • • 128 DREAM OF FAERY   44
    IN THE HALF LIGHT, AND RUNS TO ITS OWN DOOR • • • • 279 TWO KINGS   V 45C
    AND RUNS OR A WHILE HALF-FLIES • • • • • • •   341 SHEP GOATHERD   64
    AND RUNS FOR A WHILE OR A WHILE HALF-FLIES • • • • 341 SHEP GOATHERD V   64
    MINNALOUSHE RUNS IN THE GRASS • • • • • • • •   378 CAT AND MOON   9
    MAN RUNS HIS COURSE: • • • • • • • • •   499 VACILLATION   2
    AND TIME RUNS ON," CRIED SHE. • • • • • • •   526 AM OF IRELAND   3
    AND TIME RUNS ON," HE SAID. • • • • • • • •   526 AM OF IRELAND   12
    AND TIME RUNS ON," CRIED SHE. • • • • • • •   527 AM OF IRELAND   16
    "BUT TIME RUNS ON, RUNS ON." • • • • • • • •   527 AM OF IRELAND   26
    "BUT TIME RUNS ON, RUNS ON." • • • • • • • •   527 AM OF IRELAND   26
    AND TIME RUNS ON," CRIED SHE. • • • • • • •   527 AM OF IRELAND   29
    HALF DIZZY WITH THE LIGHTNING THERE RUNS A GATHERING BAND-- 718 PHANTOM SHIP   9
    NOW HALF DIZZY WITH THE LIGHTNING THERE RUNS A GATHERING   718 PHANTOM SHIP V   9
        BAND:
    WHERE THE WORLD ENDS, OR RUNS FROM WIND TO WIND • • • 768 SHADOW WATER A   417
    RUNS, RUNS AND IS SUDDENLY STILL. • • • • • • •   783 GREY ROUND   3
    RUNS, RUNS AND IS SUDDENLY STILL. • • • • • • •   783 GREY ROUND   3
RURY'S
    BAILE, THAT WAS OF RURY'S SEED. • • • • • • •   194 BAILE AILLINN   118
RUSH
    I BECAME A RUSH THAT HORSES TREAD: • • • • •   177 PAST GREATNESS   6
    NOR THE GREY RUSH WHEN THE WIND IS HIGH, • • • • 189 BAILE AILLINN   2
    NOR THE GREY RUSH WHEN WIND IS HIGH • • • • • 189 BAILE AILLINN V   2
    BUT THE GREY RUSH UNDER THE WIND • • • • • •   192 BAILE AILLINN   88
    LET RUSH AND BIRD CRY OUT THEIR FILL • • • • • 197 BAILE AILLINN   198
    BUT I'D HAVE BIRD AND RUSH FORGET • • • • • • 197 BAILE AILLINN   204
    BUT I'D HAVE BIRDS AND RUSH FORGET • • • • • 197 BAILE AILLINN V 204
    TO STAY THE STAG'S NEXT RUSH. WHEN SWORD MET HORN • 277 TWO KINGS   V   15
    OPINION IS NOT WORTH A RUSH: • • • • • • •   385 ROBARTES DANCE   1
    AND HOW CAN BODY, LAID IN THAT WHITE RUSH, • • • 441 LEDA AND SWAN   7
    A RUSH, A SUDDEN WHEEL, AND HOVERING STILL • • • 441 LEDA AND SWAN V   1
    ALL THE STRETCHED BODY'S LAID ON THE WHITE RUSH • • 441 LEDA AND SWAN V   7
    NOW RUSH UPON HER AND FIND OUT WHAT PREY • • • 752 SHADOW WATER A   130
    WHAT WERE TRUE-LOVE AMONG THE RUSH OF HIS STREAMS? • • 764 SHADOW WATER A   338
    WHAT WERE TRUE LOVE AMONG THE RUSH OF HIS STREAMS? • • 764 SHADOW WATER A V 338
RUSHED
    AND FROM THE WOODS RUSHED OUT A BAND • • • • •   15 OISIN 1   201
    AND FROM THE WOODS THERE RUSHED A BAND • • • •   15 OISIN 1   V 201
    THE MANY-COLOURED DANCERS RUSHED, • • • • • •   21 OISIN 1   V 322
    I PAUSED--AND FAR AWAY RUSHED ON, • • • • • •   83 MAD KING GOLL V   31
    AND WITH LOUD SINGING I RUSHED ON • • • • • •   83 MAD KING GOLL V   31
RUSHES
    COULD SLEEP ON A COUCH OF RUSHES, AND ALL INWROUGHT AND   49 OISIN 3   31
        INLAID,
    COULD SLEEP ON A BED OF RUSHES, AND ALL INWROUGHT   49 OISIN 3   V   31
        AND INLAID,
    COULD SLEEP ON A COUCH OF RUSHES--ROUND AND ABOUT THEM   49 OISIN 3   V   32
        LAID,
    BUT TO BE AMID SHOOTING OF FLIES AND FLOWERING OF RUSHES   55 OISIN 3   120
        AND FLAGS."
    . . . AND THE FLOWERING OF RUSHES AND FLAGS." • • • •   55 OISIN 3   V 120
    MY SPIRIT ROCKED IN EVENING LIGHT, THE RUSHES ROUND MY   76 INDIAN ON GOD   2
        KNEES,
    MY SPIRIT ROCKED IN EVENING'S HUSH, THE RUSHES ROUND MY   76 INDIAN ON GOD V   2
        KNEES,
    AND RUSHES WAVED AND WATERS ROLLED. • • • • •   84 MAD KING GOLL   35
    IN POOLS AMONG THE RUSHES • • • • • • • •   88 STOLEN CHILD   30
    ALTHOUGH THE RUSHES AND THE FOWL OF THE AIR • • • 177 PAST GREATNESS V   11
    WHERE THE TIRED HORSE-BOYS LAY UPON THE RUSHES, • • 180 QUEEN MAEVE   13
    AMONG WHAT RUSHES WILL THEY BUILD, • • • • • 323 SWANS AT COOLE   27
    HE RUSHES, ROLLING FROM HIS LIPS A MADMAN'S LAUGH. • • 715 FERENCZ RENYI   122
    A HOUND THAT HAD LAIN IN THE RED RUSHES • • • • 761 SHADOW WATER A   278
RUSHING
    AND IF ANY GAZE ON OUR RUSHING BAND, • • • • • 141 HOSTING SIDHE   10
    THE HOST IS RUSHING 'TWIXT NIGHT AND DAY, • • • 141 HOSTING SIDHE   13
    OH, HEART! HER DIRGE! WITH RUSHING ARMS THE WAVES • • 665 ISLE STAT II 2   70
RUSHY
    BY ROCKY SHORE AND RUSHY FEN: • • • • • • •   83 MAD KING GOLL   32
    O WANDERING BIRDS AND RUSHY BEDS, • • • • • • 190 BAILE AILLINN   31
    BY HEATH OR HOLLOW OR RUSHY MERE, • • • • • • 716 FAIRY DOCTOR   10
RUSSET
    YOUNG MAN, LIFT UP YOUR RUSSET BROW, • • • • • 125 GOES FERGUS   4
    NODDING HER RUSSET HOOD? • • • • • • • • • 171 MAID QUIET   4
    OF THE DREAD WOODS: ALONG THEIR RUSSET FLOOR • • • 675 ISLE STAT II 3   243
RUSSIA
    A SAINT OF RUSSIA IN A VISION SAW • • • • • • 696 MOSADA 2)   V   21
RUSSIAN
    ON ROMAN OR ON RUSSIAN • • • • • • • • •   631 POLITICS   3
    THAT SONG I'VE MADE--IS OF A RUSSIAN TALE • • • • 696 MOSADA 2   V   19
RUST
    IS NOT THY BODY BUT THE GARNERED RUST • • • • 724 KANVA ON SELF   15
    THAT THE RED RUST MAKES DIM." • • • • • • • 740 EARL PAUL   20
RUSTED   SEE WAVE-RUSTED
RUSTLE
    IN RUSTLE OF LACE OR SILKEN STUFF, • • • • • • 358 PRESENCES   5
    AMID THE RUSTLE OF HIS PLANTED HILLS, • • • • • 417 ANCEST HOUSES   2
    SOFT AS THE RUSTLE OF A REED FROM CLOYNE • • • • 487 SEVEN SAGES   22

	PAGE	TITLE		LINE

RUSTLED
BUT SOMETHING RUSTLED ON THE FLOOR, • • • • • • • •   149 WANDER AENGUS   11
BUT SOMETHING RUSTLED ON THE STOOL, • • • • • • • •   149 WANDER AENGUS   V 11
RUSTLES
THAT RUSTLES IN THE REEDS WITH PATIENT PUSHES, • • • •   699 MOSADA 3   4
RUSTLING   SEE EVER-RUSTLING
AND THROUGH THE DOORS, A RUSTLING ROUT, • • • • • •   20 OISIN 1   V 290
BY MIGHTY BRAHMA'S EVER RUSTLING ROBE, • • • • • • •   71 ANASHU VIJAYA V 14
SHALL WARM THEIR LIVES AT MANY A RUSTLING FLAME." • •   80 EPHEMERA   V 12B
I'VE HEARD A RUSTLING OVERHEAD IN THE WIND, • • • •   223 SHADOW WATER B   28
THAT'S RUSTLING IN THE REEDS WITH PATIENT PUSHES, • •   699 MOSADA 3   V   4
FROM THE RUSTLING OF OUR FEET. • • • • • • • • • •   726 LOVERS QUARREL   8
RUTH
TILL THEY SHALL SINGING FADE IN RUTH • • • • • • • •   66 HAPPY SHEPHERD   41
FOR RUTH AND JOY HAVE BROTHERHOOD, • • • • • • • • •   66 HAPPY SHEPHERD V 42
AND RUTH ST. DENIS HAD MORE CHARM ALTHOUGH SHE HAD POOR   353 HIS PHOENIX   10
  LUCK.
ALMINTOR, THOU HAST GROWN SO FULL OF RUTH, • • • • •   652 ISLE STAT I 2   26
YET EVER MORE, THROUGH ALL THY DAYS OF RUTH, • • • •   674 ISLE STAT II 3   206
YET EVERMORE, THROUGH ALL THY DAYS OF RUTH, • • • •   674 ISLE STAT II 3 V 206
THEIR PASSION AND THEIR RESTLESSNESS AND RUTH • • • •   687 TWO TITANS   24
AS THOUGH HIS DAYS WERE FULL OF RUTH. • • • • • • •   731 PRIEST FAIRY   76
RUTHLESS
MY LOVE HATH MANY A RUTHLESS MOOD, • • • • • • • •   723 GIRLS SONG A   V   5
SACK   SEE SAND-SACK
• • • TWO CARRIED A SACK FULL OF SAND, • • • • • • •   60 OISIN 3   185
• • • THEY LIFTED AND SHOULDERED A SACK FULL OF SAND, • •   60 OISIN 3   V 185
HAVE CHANGED THEIR SILK FOR SACK. • • • • • • • • •   458 HIS WILDNESS   6
THAT SLEPT UPON THE SACK? • • • • • • • • • • • •   627 STATES HOLIDAY   15
SACKED
AND TELL HOW MANANAN SACKED MURIAS • • • • • • • •   766 SHADOW WATER A   377
SACRED
• • • AND GUARDLESS THE SACRED CAIRN AND THE RATH, • • •   58 OISIN 3   163
SEE HOW THE SACRED OLD FLAMINGOES COME, • • • • • •   72 ANASHU VIJAYA   29
DREAD OATH, WHO DWELL ON SACRED HIMALAY, • • • • • •   74 ANASHU VIJAYA   67
IN THE TREE ROOTS, AND ALL THE SACRED FLOCKS • • • •   75 ANASHU VIJAYA   88
IN THE TREE ROOTS, AND ALL THY SACRED FLOCKS • • • •   75 ANASHU VIJAYA V 88
THROUGH MANY A SACRED CORRIDOR • • • • • • • • • •   156 FORGOT BEAUTY   12
TO HOLD THE SACRED STUFF HE BREWS • • • • • • • • •   272 GREY ROCK   24
THAT SACRED GOBAN BREWED," HE CRIED • • • • • • • •   304 HOUR DAWN   V 50
THE SACRED MOON OVERHEAD • • • • • • • • • • • • •   379 CAT AND MOON   19
AND ALL HIS SACRED COMPANY • • • • • • • • • • • •   386 ROBARTES DANCE   27
IN THE FORBIDDEN SACRED GROVE • • • • • • • • • • •   389 SOLOMON WITCH   39
AT WINE-DARK MIDNIGHT IN THE SACRED WOOD, • • • • •   536 HER VISION   2
A BEAUTIFUL SEATED BOY; A SACRED BOW; • • • • • • •   541 PARN FUNERAL 1   10
AS TRIPS THE SACRED MOON • • • • • • • • • • • • •   559 HE AND SHE   V   3
WHAT SACRED DRAMA THROUGH HER BODY HEAVED • • • • •   560 WHENCE COME   11
"A LAUGHING, CRYING, SACRED SONG, • • • • • • • • •   570 THREE BUSHES   43
WENT TO THE SACRED HOUSE AND STOOD BETWEEN • • • • •   609 IN TARAS HALLS   11
PROFFERING ITS SACRED LAUREL CROWNS, • • • • • • •   612 NEWS ORACLE   23
FOR GUIDING OF THE GODS.   THE SACRED BLOOM • • • • •   656 ISLE STAT I 3   41
THY SACRED DOOR!" BUT PETER CRIED, • • • • • • • •   697 MOSADA 2   25
SACRIFICE
TOO LONG A SACRIFICE • • • • • • • • • • • • • •   394 EASTER 1916   57
WHAT IS THIS SACRIFICE? CAN SOMEONE THERE • • • • •   541 PARN FUNERAL 1   6
SAD
SAD TO REMEMBER, SICK WITH YEARS, • • • • • • • •   2 OISIN 1   5
'TIS SAD REMEMBERING, SICK WITH YEARS, • • • • • •   2 OISIN 1   V   5
THE STAG WE CHASED WAS NOT MORE SAD, • • • • • • •   2 OISIN 1   V 7J
THE HORNLESS DEER IS NOT MORE SAD • • • • • • • • •   4 OISIN 1   34
THE STAG YE CHASE IS NOT MORE SAD, • • • • • • • •   4 OISIN 1   V 35
BUT NIAM, WITH A SAD DISTRESS, • • • • • • • • • •   15 OISIN 1   V 211
AND NOW, STILL SAD, WE CAME TO WHERE • • • • • • •   17 OISIN 1   247
AND NOW STILL SAD OUR TROOP DREW NIGH • • • • • • •   17 OISIN 1   V 247
THEN, WARRIOR, WHY SO SAD AND STERN, • • • • • • •   19 OISIN 1   V 286
AND THINGS THAT HAVE GROWN SAD ARE WICKED, • • • • •   20 OISIN 1   301
EVERYTHING THAT'S SAD IS WICKED-- • • • • • • • • •   20 OISIN 1   V 301
AFORETIME, AND SHALL NOT GROW SAD • • • • • • • •   22 OISIN 1   V 340E
AND A SAD MOUTH, THAT FEAR MADE TREMULOUS • • • • •   34 OISIN 2   71
IN A SAD REVELRY HE SANG AND SWUNG • • • • • • • •   39 OISIN 2   160
SAD NIAM CAME NEAR ME, AND LAID HER BROWS ON THE MIDST   52 OISIN 3   V 74
  OF MY BREAST
• • • CAME FERGUS WHO FEASTWARD SAD SLUNK, • • • • •   53 OISIN 3   V 89
• • • HE SAD AS A CHILD WITHOUT MILK! • • • • • • •   59 OISIN 3   174
IT WERE SAD TO GAZE ON THE BLESSED AND NO MAN I LOVED OF   63 OISIN 3   221
  OLD THERE!
IT WAS SAD TO GAZE ON THE BLESSED AND NO MAN I LOVED OF   63 OISIN 3   V 221
  OLD THERE!
• • • OF BEST ONES A SAD THING WERE-- • • • • • • •   63 OISIN 3   V 222
THE SAD SHEPHERD • • • • • • • • • • • • • • • •   67 SAD SHEPHERD   T
BUT THE SAD DWELLER BY THE SEA-WAYS LONE • • • • •   69 SAD SHEPHERD   26
BUT THE SAD DWELLER BY THE SEAWAYS LONE • • • • • •   69 SAD SHEPHERD   V 26
A SAD, SAD THOUGHT WENT BY ME SLOWLY! • • • • • • •   72 ANASHU VIJAYA   17
A SAD, SAD THOUGHT WENT BY ME SLOWLY! • • • • • • •   72 ANASHU VIJAYA   17
THE SAD, SAD THOUGHT HAS GONE FROM ME NOW WHOLLY! •   72 ANASHU VIJAYA   19
THE SAD, SAD THOUGHT HAS GONE FROM ME NOW WHOLLY! •   72 ANASHU VIJAYA   19
CONCEIVE A THING SO SAD AND SOFT, A GENTLE THING LIKE ME?   77 INDIAN ON GOD   16
AND WEARY AND WORN ARE OUR SAD SOULS NOW! • • • • •   79 FALLING LEAVES   6
"THOUGH OUR SAD LOVE IS FADING, LET US YET • • • •   79 EPHEMERA   V   4
CAME FLYING, HEAVY AND SAD! • • • • • • • • • • •   93 FATHER OHART   34
RED ROSE, PROUD ROSE, SAD ROSE OF ALL MY DAYS! • • •   100 ROSE UPON ROOD   1

674

		PAGE	TITLE		LINE
SAD	(CONTINUED)				
	RED ROSE, PROUD ROSE, SAD ROSE OF ALL MY DAYS.	101	ROSE UPON ROOD		24
	"NAY, HE IS OLD AND SAD WITH MANY WARS.	107	CUCHULAIN SEA	V	29
	"BUT HE IS OLD AND SAD WITH MANY WARS."	107	CUCHULAIN SEA	V	30
	OR COMES IN LAUGHTER FROM THE SEA'S SAD LIPS,	114	ROSE OF BATTLE		19
	THE SAD, THE LONELY, THE INSATIABLE,	114	ROSE OF BATTLE		21
	OF THEIR SAD HEARTS, THAT MAY NOT LIVE NOR DIE.	114	ROSE OF BATTLE		24
	BEAUTY GROWN SAD WITH ITS ETERNITY	115	ROSE OF BATTLE		29
	OF OUR SAD HEARTS, THAT MAY NOT LIVE NOR DIE.	115	ROSE OF BATTLE		36
	MURMUR, A LITTLE SAD, "FROM US FLED LOVE,	121	YOU ARE OLD	V	10
	FOR SHE NEEDS NOT HER SAD BEAUTY—	124	CATHLEEN PARA	V	7
	GAY BELLS OR SAD, THEY BRING YOU MEMORIES	130	BOOK STORIES		21
	THE SAD BELLS BOW THE FOREHEAD ON THE HANDS.	130	BOOK STORIES	V	20
	AND NEVER WAS PIPING SO SAD,	144	HOST OF AIR		11
	WITH A SAD AND A GAY FACE.	144	HOST OF AIR		16
	AND NEVER WAS PIPING SO SAD,	145	HOST OF AIR		43
	CUMHAL THE KING, BEING ANGRY AND SAD,	166	BLESSED	V	1
	THE SAD SHEPHERD	338	SHEP GOATHERD	V	T
	SHE WOULD NOT HAVE US SAD BECAUSE SHE IS LYING THERE,	362	HER COURTESY		4
	FOR THOSE THAT LOVE ARE SAD.	383	VISION ROBART		36
	OF SAD QUEEN DIDO SHONE THE LAPPING FIRE	645	ISLE STAT I 1		9
	NOT A SAD NOTE WILL I SING.	646	ISLE STAT I 1		39
	SAD LADY OF THE DEEP, POURS DOWN HER LIGHT,	650	ISLE STAT I 1		127
	OR SAD SEA-SHELLS WHERE LITTLE ECHOES SIT?	650	ISLE STAT I 1		149
	I COULD NOT GO. LET'S TALK, AND LET'S BE SAD,	651	ISLE STAT I 2		7
	THE BIRDS THAT NESTLE IN THE LEAVES ARE SAD,	652	ISLE STAT I 2		15
	POOR SAD WOOD-RHAPSODISTS. NOT SO! THEY'RE GLAD.	652	ISLE STAT I 2		16
	'TIS BEAUTIFUL, AND THEREFORE IT IS SAD.	652	ISLE STAT I 2		24
	SAD FAERY TONES. 'TIS THUS THEY EVER SEEM,	654	ISLE STAT I 2		58
	SAD HISTORIES ARE LETTERED ON THY CHEEK.	660	ISLE STAT II 1		52
	AND LET THEM TELL SAD HISTORIES, TILL THEIR EYES	663	ISLE STAT II 2		32
	OF MY SAD HUNTER-FRIEND WILL ALL DEPART	668	ISLE STAT II 3		45
	SAD LADY, CEASE!	672	ISLE STAT II 3		160
	I SAW HIM FROM SAD DIDO'S SHORES DEPART,	677	ISLE STAT II 3		288
	THOUGH SAD IS MANY A SPIRIT	680	LOVE AND DEATH		23
	THROUGH HIS SAD SOUL FOR EVER OLD AND YOUNG,	687	TWO TITANS		25
	OF HIS SAD GOD! AND DOWN AMONG THE GRASS	690	MOSADA 1		16
	WHOSE FOOTFALL I HAVE LONGED FOR, THREE SAD SUMMERS.	692	MOSADA 1		45
	TO SAINTED EBREMAR'S SAD EYES. I THINK	696	MOSADA 2		15
	FOR THAT'S THE SWEETEST MUSIC FOR SAD SOULS.	702	MOSADA 3		85
	LIKE HAPPY THOUGHTS GROWN SAD IN EVIL DAYS.	703	MOSADA 3		116
	NOR, GAZING FORTH WHERE LIFE'S SAD SICKLES REAP,	710	FERENCZ RENYI		31
	FULL MOODY IS MY LOVE AND SAD,	723	GIRLS SONG A		1
	AND ALL THE SAD FAY CHIVALRY	730	PRIEST FAIRY		71
	LONG THOU FOR NOTHING, NEITHER SAD NOR GAY:	734	QUATRAIN APHOR		9
	YE BY THE WAVES THAT CLOSE IN OUR SAD NATION,	738	MOURN THEN ON		5
	WHEN YOU ARE SAD,	738	YOU ARE SAD		T
	WHEN YOU ARE SAD,	738	YOU ARE SAD		1
	WHEN YOU ARE SAD,	738	YOU ARE SAD		5
	WHEN YOU ARE SAD,	738	YOU ARE SAD		9
	TILL THEY COME WHERE YOUR SAD, SAD HEART IS,	739	WHERE BOOKS GO		5
	TILL THEY COME WHERE YOUR SAD, SAD HEART IS,	739	WHERE BOOKS GO		5
	FOR GOD GIVES POWER TO THE SAD	741	EARL PAUL		47
	FOR GOD GIVES POWER TO THE SAD	741	EARL PAUL		51
	PLAYED ON HIS HARP. AND I WOULD BE AS SAD	747	SHADOW WATER A		3
SADDEN					
	WHISPER LEST WE TOO MAY SADDEN,	737	IN FIRELIGHT		5
SADDER					
	"A SADDER CREATURE NEVER STEPT	17	OISIN 1		238
	ALAS! I MAKE YOU SADDER, SHEPHERDESS.	659	ISLE STAT II 1		18
SADDEST					
	"O SADDEST HARP IN ALL THE WORLD,	17	OISIN 1		245
	"THE SADDEST HARP IN ALL THE WORLD!"	17	OISIN 1	V	246
	THE SADDEST OF ALL MEN."	33	OISIN 2		68
	AND YET THE SADDEST CHIMES ARE BEST ENJOYED.	130	BOOK STORIES		20
SADDLE					
	ON HORSE AND SEA AND SADDLE SHONE.	28	OISIN 1	V	427D
	HIGH AS THE SADDLE GIRTH, COVERING AWAY FROM OUR GLANCES THE TIDE:	47	OISIN 3	V	2
	"THEN GO THROUGH THE LANDS IN THE SADDLE AND SEE WHAT THE MORTALS DO,	55	OISIN 3		125
	I SAW FROM A DISTANT SADDLE: FROM THE EARTH SHE MADE HER MOAN:	56	OISIN 3		130
	I RODE AWAY ON THE SURGES, WHERE HIGH AS THE SADDLE BOW	57	OISIN 3	V	147
	LEANING DOWN FROM THE GEM-STUDDED SADDLE,	60	OISIN 3		187
	LEANING FORTH FROM THE GEM-STUDDED SADDLE,	60	OISIN 3	V	187
	THOUGH MOUNTED IN THAT SADDLE HOMER RODE	492	COOLE BALLYLEE		47
	SADDLE AND RIDE, I HEARD A MAN SAY,	549	SEVERED HEAD		1
	OUT OF THE GRAVE. SADDLE AND RIDE	549	SEVERED HEAD	V	4
SADDLEBOW					
	I RODE AWAY ON THE SURGES, WHERE, HIGH AS THE SADDLEBOW,	57	OISIN 3	V	147
SADDLE-BOW					
	I RODE AWAY ON THE SURGES, WHERE, HIGH AS THE SADDLE-BOW,	57	OISIN 3		147
SADDLED					
	AND ONCE MORE SADDLED THE WHITE STEED,	25	OISIN 1	V	378
SADDLE-GIRTH					
	HIGH AS THE SADDLE-GIRTH, COVERING AWAY FROM OUR GLANCES THE TIDE:	47	OISIN 3		2
SADLY					
	CAME SWIMMING SADLY DOWN THE MIGHTY STAIR.	32	OISIN 2	V	50B
	HOLDING THAT HORSE, AND SADLY CALLED MY NAME:	44	OISIN 2		230

675

		PAGE	TITLE		LINE
SADLY	**(CONTINUED)**				
	HOW THE SLOW, BLUE-EYED OXEN OF FINN LOW SADLY AT EVENING TIDE.	52	OISIN 3		84
	MURMUR, A LITTLE SADLY, HOW LOVE FLED	121	YOU ARE OLD		10
	COULD BUT AWAKEN SADLY UPON LIPS	185	QUEEN MAEVE		104
	YON WIND GOES SADLY, AND THE GRASS AND TREES	652	ISLE STAT I 2		10
	THE WHOLE WORLD'S SADLY TALKING TO ITSELF.	652	ISLE STAT I 2		12
	BY A PEOPLE SADLY GAY!	680	LOVE AND DEATH		10
	NOW SADLY, NOW UNEARTHLY GAY.	716	FAIRY DOCTOR		3
SADNESS					
	WE RODE IN SADNESS ABOVE LOUGH LAEN.	2	OISIN 1	V	7H
	MY HUMAN SADNESS FAY ARMS WOUND.	11	OISIN 1	V	138
	THE HUMAN SADNESS DAWNS ONCE MORE!"	25	OISIN 1	V	381
	THAT ONCE MORE MOVED IN MY BOSOM THE ANCIENT SADNESS OF MAN,	54	OISIN 3		107
	. . . THE FLUTTERING SADNESS OF EARTH.	55	OISIN 3		124
	FOR MOVETH ALIVE IN THY FINGERS THE FLUTTERING SADNESS OF EARTH.	55	OISIN 3	V	124
	THEIR SADNESS THROUGH A HOLLOW, PEARLY HEART!	68	SAD SHEPHERD		21
	THEIR SADNESS THROUGH THE HOLLOWS OF ITS HEART,	68	SAD SHEPHERD	V	21
	FLASHES THE FIRE OF SADNESS, FOR THEY SEE	73	ANASHU VIJAYA		49
	WITH EYES OF SADNESS CAME TO HEAR	85	MAD KING GOLL	V	62
	WITH EYES OF SADNESS ROSE TO HEAR,	85	MAD KING GOLL	V	62
	AND THINE OWN SADNESS, WHEREOF STARS, GROWN OLD	101	ROSE UPON ROOD		6
	HAS AWAKED IN OUR HEARTS, MY BELOVED, A SADNESS THAT MAY NOT DIE.	122	WHITE BIRDS		4
	HAS AWAKED IN OUR HEARTS, MY BELOVED, A SADNESS THAT NEVER MAY DIE.	122	WHITE BIRDS	V	4
	SADNESS, SOUL OF JOY MOST DEEP,	647	ISLE STAT I 1		74
SAD'S					
	FOR, LOOK YOU, SAD'S THE MURMUR OF THE BEES,	652	ISLE STAT I 2		9
SAEVA					
	SAEVA INDIGNATIO AND THE LABOURER'S HIRE,	481	BLOOD AND MOON		28
SAFE					
	THE HOUSE WHERE I WAS SAFE AND WARM!	151	HEART OF WOMAN		6
	THE HOME WHERE I WAS SAFE AND WARM?	151	HEART OF WOMAN	V	6
	HANGS ON MY BREAST! LISTEN, WE SHALL BE SAFE.	701	MOSADA 3		73
	SAFE ON THE BREAST OF GOMEZ LIES THY HEAD,	703	MOSADA 3		101
	SAFE ON THE BREAST OF VALLENCE IS THY HEAD	703	MOSADA 3	V	101
	SAFE ON THE BREAST OF GOMEZ IS THY HEAD,	703	MOSADA 3	V	101
SAFER					
	AWAY, AWAY! YOU ARE SAFER IN THE TOMB.	293	TO A SHADE		24
SAFETY					
	(ALL FIND SAFETY IN THE TOMB.)	508	JANE BISHOP		3
	(ALL FIND SAFETY IN THE TOMB.)	508	JANE BISHOP		10
	(ALL FIND SAFETY IN THE TOMB.)	508	JANE BISHOP		17
	(ALL FIND SAFETY IN THE TOMB.)	508	JANE BISHOP		24
	BECAUSE THERE IS SAFETY IN DERISION	624	APPARITIONS		1
SAFFRON					
	THAT FROM THE SAFFRON MORNING CAME,	19	OISIN 1		277
	WATCHED WHERE THE SUN IN A SAFFRON BLAZE	26	OISIN 1		394
	HALF SLUMBERED WITH HIS SAFFRON BLAZE!	26	OISIN 1	V	395
	AND WHEN THE SUN ONCE MORE IN SAFFRON STEPT,	41	OISIN 2		192
	AND WHEN THE SUN IN ALL HIS FLAGRANT SAFFRON STEPT,	41	OISIN 2	V	192
	BUT WHEN THE SUN ONCE MORE IN SAFFRON STEPT,	41	OISIN 2	V	192
	PROUDLY IN HIS SAFFRON WALKING!	705	DAWN-SONG		2
SAFFRONS	**SEE MEADOW-SAFFRONS**				
SAGE					
	THE SAGE, WHO DEEP IN CENTRAL NATURE DELVES,	686	LIFE		2
	THOUGHTLESS JOY AND SORROW SAGE.	733	STREET DANCERS		47
	THOUGHTLESS JOYS AND SORROWS SAGE.	733	STREET DANCERS	V	47
	THE SAGE WHO DEEP IN CENTRAL NATURE DELVES,	734	QUATRAIN APHOR		2
SAGES					
	O SAGES STANDING IN GOD'S HOLY FIRE	408	SAIL BYZANTIUM		17
	RUN TILL ALL THE SAGES KNOW.	476	EVA GORE-BOOTH		29
	THE SEVEN SAGES	486	SEVEN SAGES		T
	OR, AS GREAT SAGES SAY,	496	MOHINI CHATTER		27
	OLD SAGES WERE NOT DECEIVED!	504	QUARREL IN AGE		11
	IN WHAT THE SAGES SAID!	534	CONSOLATION		2
	TILL I HAVE TOLD THE SAGES	534	CONSOLATION		5
	SWEAR BY WHAT THE SAGES SPOKE	636	BEN BULBEN		1
SAID					
	"WHY DO YOU WIND NO HORN?" SHE SAID,	4	OISIN 1		32
	WHY DO YE SOUND NO HORN?" SHE SAID.	4	OISIN 1		33
	WHY DO YOU WIND NO HORN?" SHE SAID.	4	OISIN 1	V	33
	SHE SAID, WITH LAUGHTER TENDER AND SWEET!	6	OISIN 1	V	54
	SHE SAID: "FOR HE IS FAIR ABOVE	7	OISIN 1	V	62A
	"VEX THEM NO LONGER," NIAMH SAID.	12	OISIN 1		148
	"WHO ARE THE RIDING ONES?" I SAID.	12	OISIN 1	V	146
	SAID NIAM, AS SHE LAID THE TIP	12	OISIN 1	V	150
	AND EACH ONE SAID, WITH A LONG, LONG SIGH,	17	OISIN 1		244
	AND BENDING OVER THEM SOFTLY SAID,	21	OISIN 1		307
	"GAZE NO MORE ON THE PHANTOMS," NIAMH SAID.	29	OISIN 2		5
	"I BRING DELIVERANCE," PEARL-PALE NIAMH SAID.	34	OISIN 2		78
	SAID NIAM. "AY, AND HUGE, WHEN YE HAVE LED	35	OISIN 2	V	89
	TO FLY A SPIRIT," NIAM WEEPING SAID.	35	OISIN 2	V	92
	AND MANY PATER NOSTERS SAID SINCE DAWN.	43	OISIN 2	V	208D
	IS THE ISLAND OF CONTENT?" "NONE KNOW," SHE SAID!	46	OISIN 2		249
	WHICH IS THE ISLE OF YOUTH?" "NONE KNOW," SHE SAID,	46	OISIN 2	V	249
	BY THE STAMMERING SCHOOLBOY SAID,	65	HAPPY SHEPHERD		15

676

	PAGE	TITLE		LINE
SAID (CONTINUED)				
BRIMFUL OF STARLIGHT, AND HE SAID: THE STAMPER OF THE SKIES.	76	INDIAN ON GOD		14
IN BOSOM AND HAIR. "AH, DO NOT MOURN," HE SAID.	80	EPHEMERA		20
AND EVERY ANCIENT OLLAVE SAID,	82	MAD KING GOLL		9
AND EVERY WHISPERING DRUID SAID,	82	MAD KING GOLL	V	9
AND EVERY MUMBLING OLD MAN SAID,	82	MAD KING GOLL	V	9
AND EVERY WHISPERING OLD MAN SAID,	82	MAD KING GOLL	V	9
AND HE SAID WITH A SMILE, "HAVE PEACE NOW":	92	FATHER OHART		19
BUT SEEK ALONE TO HEAR THE STRANGE THINGS SAID	101	ROSE UPON ROOD		19
AND SAID, "I AM THAT SWINEHERD WHOM YOU BID	105	CUCHULAIN SEA		3
AND SAID, CASTING ASIDE HIS DRAGGLED HAIR,	105	CUCHULAIN SEA	V	3
THAT SWINEHERD STARED UPON HER FACE AND SAID,	106	CUCHULAIN SEA		9
LOOKING ON HER, ALEEL, THE SWINEHERD, SAID:	106	CUCHULAIN SEA	V	9
AND MANY A SWEET THING SAID,	144	HOST OF AIR		18
AND CUMHAL SAID, BENDING HIS KNEES,	167	BLESSED		5
"PRAISE GOD AND GOD'S MOTHER," DATHI SAID,	167	BLESSED		17
"AND WHICH IS THE BLESSEDEST," CUMHAL SAID,	167	BLESSED		21
"AND WHO IS THE BLESSEDEST," CUMHAL SAID,	167	BLESSED	V	21
"MY EYES ARE BLINKING," DATHI SAID,	168	BLESSED		25
HE SAID, "HIGH QUEEN OF CRUACHAN AND MAGH AI,	183	QUEEN MAEVE		77
HE SAID "QUEEN OF UNSHELTERED CRUACHAN,	183	QUEEN MAEVE	V	77
OR FELL INTO UNHAPPINESS, I'VE SAID,	186	QUEEN MAEVE		137
SAID, "AENGUS AND HIS SWEETHEART GIVE THEIR THANKS	187	QUEEN MAEVE		146
AND THERE, FOR ALL THAT FOOLS HAD SAID,	190	BAILE AILLINN		23
THAT RUNNER SAID: "I AM FROM THE SOUTH:	191	BAILE AILLINN		47
ONE THAT IS EVER KIND SAID YESTERDAY:	199	FOLLY COMFORT		1
OR, IF THERE NEEDS BE MORE, BE NOTHING SAID	201	OLD MEMORY		11
I SAID: "A LINE WILL TAKE US HOURS MAYBE:	204	ADAMS CURSE		4
I SAID: "IT'S CERTAIN THERE IS NO FINE THING	205	ADAMS CURSE		21
WHEN I HAVE SAID FAREWELL TO THIS MAN HERE,	250	SHADOW WATER B		587
THERE WAS NO MOTHER'S SON BUT SAID,	253	HIS DREAM		6
OF SUCH NOBLE LINES," I SAID,	259	PEACE		6
IN PRAISE OF WHAT ANOTHER'S SAID OR SUNG,	262	TO A POET		2
AND TREMBLING WITH HER PASSION SAID,	272	GREY ROCK		31
AND SAID, "IN TWO OR IN THREE YEARS	272	GREY ROCK		46
AND HAVING SAID IT, BURST IN TEARS.	273	GREY ROCK		48
BETWEEN THE DAWN AND DUSK," SHE SAID:	273	GREY ROCK		66
WHO SAID, "BECAUSE SHE HELD ME IN	274	GREY ROCK		86
AND WHEN FOR ALL I'D DONE OR SAID--	275	GREY ROCK		99
KING EOCHAID SAID, AND HE THAT BORE HIS SHIELD	276	TWO KINGS	V	8
AND CARVE HIS NAME IN OGHAM." EOCHAID SAID,	280	TWO KINGS		83
AND SO THE WEEKS PASSED BY. BUT WHEN I SAID,	280	TWO KINGS		89
AND RAISE HIS PILLAR STONE." KING EOCHAID SAID,	280	TWO KINGS	V	83
SAID, "IF A WOMAN HAS PUT THIS ON YOU,	281	TWO KINGS		111
"A WEARY WOOING AND A LONG," HE SAID,	283	TWO KINGS		154
AND TOUCHED HER FOREHEAD WITH HIS LIPS AND SAID:	286	TWO KINGS	V	211B
AND THERE TO THREE OLD BEGGARS SAID,	295	THREE BEGGARS		10
A BEGGAR SAID, "THEY GET THE MOST	295	THREE BEGGARS		15
"AND IF I WIN," ONE BEGGAR SAID,	296	THREE BEGGARS		29
ANOTHER SAID: "AND I WILL TRADE	296	THREE BEGGARS	V	32
NOW THEY ARE SILENT," SAID THE CRANE.	297	THREE BEGGARS		62
BECAUSE AN ANCIENT HISTORY SAID	303	HOUR DAWN		24
FOR ANYTHING YOU DID OR SAID	306	HOUR DAWN		89
HAS NO ONE SAID THOSE DARING	312	TWO YEAR LATER		1
BELIEVING EVERY WORD I SAID,	314	MEMORY YOUTH		8
WE KNEW, THOUGH SHE'D NOT SAID A WORD,	314	MEMORY YOUTH		16
AND KNEW, THOUGH SHE'D NOT SAID A WORD,	314	MEMORY YOUTH	V	16
THAT RAMBLING JAILBIRD BILLY SAID:	332	ROUND TOWER		26
SAID SOLOMON TO SHEBA	333	SOLOMON SHEBA	V	17
OR SOMETHING OF THAT SORT HE SAID,	338	TOM OROUGHLEY		14
"WHAT HAVE I EARNED FOR ALL THAT WORK," I SAID,	351	PEOPLE		1
SAID I WAS DEAD: AND DEAD I CHOOSE TO BE.	373	PHASES OF MOON		28
SAID I WAS DEAD: AND DEAD I CHOSE TO BE.	373	PHASES OF MOON	V	28
YET BE BUT SINEW. I HAVE HEARD SAID	386	ROBARTES DANCE		37
WHATEVER HAS BEEN SAID, SIGHED, SUNG,	387	SOLOMON WITCH		7
YOU HEARD THAT LABOURING MAN WHO HAD SERVED MY PEOPLE. HE SAID	391	UNDER SATURN		11
NO, NO, NOT SAID, BUT CRIED IT OUT--"YOU HAVE COME AGAIN,	391	UNDER SATURN		13
OR HAVE LINGERED AWHILE AND SAID	392	EASTER 1916		7
FOR ALL THAT IS DONE AND SAID.	394	EASTER 1916		69
FOR ALL SHE HAD DONE AND SAID.	394	EASTER 1916	V	69
SAID PEARSE TO CONNOLLY,	396	ROSE TREE		2
SAID PEARSE TO CONNOLLY,	396	ROSE TREE		14
OF OLD LUKE WADDING'S PORTRAIT SAID	400	DEMON BEAST		10
. . . "YOU HAVE CALLED ME MAD," IT SAID,	450	OWEN AHERNE		13
TOLD ALL THAT HAD BEEN SAID OR DONE	456	SUMMER SPRING		3
HALF DEAD AT THE TOP? NO MATTER WHAT I SAID,	482	BLOOD AND MOON		48
"THOSE PLATONISTS ARE A CURSE," HE SAID,	485	STATISTICS		1
BUT THE BRAHMIN SAID:	495	MOHINI CHATTER		2
THINGS SAID OR DONE LONG YEARS AGO,	501	VACILLATION		51
THE LION AND THE HONEYCOMB, WHAT HAS SCRIPTURE SAID?	503	VACILLATION		88
THE LION AND THE HONEY-COMB, WHAT HAS SCRIPTURE SAID?	503	VACILLATION	V	88
NOTHING SAID OR DONE CAN REACH	506	REMORSE SPEECH		9
COXCOMB WAS THE LEAST HE SAID:	508	JANE BISHOP		6
AND THAT IS WHAT JANE SAID.	510	JANE JUDGMENT		5
"THAT'S CERTAINLY THE CASE," SAID HE.	510	JANE JUDGMENT		10
AND THAT IS WHAT JANE SAID.	510	JANE JUDGMENT		15
"THAT'S CERTAINLY THE CASE," SAID HE.	510	JANE JUDGMENT		20
"THAT'S CERTAINLY THE CASE," SAID SHE.	510	JANE JUDGMENT	V	10
AND MUCH SAID HE AND I.	513	JANE TALK BISH		2

	PAGE	TITLE	LINE

SAID   (CONTINUED)

WHEN SHE, AND THOUGH SOME SAID SHE PLAYED	514	JANE GROWN OLD	8
I SAID THAT SHE HAD DANCED HEART'S TRUTH,	514	JANE GROWN OLD	9
FOR NO MATTER WHAT IS SAID	514	JANE GROWN OLD	12
AND TIME RUNS ON," HE SAID,	526	AM OF IRELAND	12
IN WHAT THE SAGES SAID!	534	CONSOLATION	2
"THAT I HAVE MET WITH SUCH," SAID HE,	539	MEETING	5
"LET OTHERS BOAST THEIR FILL," SAID I,	539	MEETING	7
ALL THAT WAS SAID IN IRELAND IS A LIE	542	PARN FUNERAL 1	26
GRANDFATHER SAID IN THE GREAT REBELLION!	544	TO SAME TUNE 1 V	1
HE SAID NO MORE FOR HIS THROAT WAS TOO SMALL.	545	TO SAME TUNE 1 V	24
"DROWN ALL THE DOGS," SAID THE FIERCE YOUNG WOMAN,	546	TO SAME TUNE 2	7
DROWN ALL THE DOGS," SAID THE FIERCE YOUNG WOMAN.	546	TO SAME TUNE 2	10
"DROWN ALL THE DOGS," SAID THE FIERCE YOUNG WOMAN,	546	TO SAME TUNE 2	17
DROWN ALL THE DOGS," SAID THE FIERCE YOUNG WOMAN.	546	TO SAME TUNE 2	20
"DROWN ALL THE DOGS," SAID THE FIERCE YOUNG WOMAN,	547	TO SAME TUNE 2	27
DROWN ALL THE DOGS," SAID THE FIERCE YOUNG WOMAN.	547	TO SAME TUNE 2	30
"WHO'D CARE TO DIG 'EM," SAID THE OLD, OLD MAN,	548	TO SAME TUNE 3	7
TIME I WERE BURIED," SAID THE OLD, OLD MAN.	548	TO SAME TUNE 3	10
"WHO'D CARE TO DIG 'EM," SAID THE OLD, OLD MAN,	548	TO SAME TUNE 3	17
TIME I WERE BURIED," SAID THE OLD, OLD MAN.	548	TO SAME TUNE 3	20
"WHO'D CARE TO DIG 'EM," SAID THE OLD, OLD MAN,	549	TO SAME TUNE 3	27
TIME I WERE BURIED," SAID THE OLD, OLD MAN.	549	TO SAME TUNE 3	30
FOR THINGS BELOW ARE COPIES, THE GREAT SMARAGDINE TABLET SAID.	556	RIBH PATRICK	6
SAID LADY ONCE TO LOVER,	569	THREE BUSHES	1
THAT LOVELY LADY SAID,	569	THREE BUSHES	9
DEAR CHAMBERMAID," SAID SHE.	569	THREE BUSHES	16
"NO, NOT ANOTHER SONG," SAID HE,	570	THREE BUSHES	36
A LECHING SONG," THEY SAID.	570	THREE BUSHES	44
SAID THAT WILD OLD WICKED MAN	587	OLD WICKED MAN	3
THEN SAID SHE TO THAT WILD OLD MAN,	588	OLD WICKED MAN	19
PARNELL CAME DOWN THE ROAD, HE SAID TO A CHEERING MAN!	590	PARNELL	1
"O WHAT'S A WIFELESS MAN?" SAID HE,	594	COLONEL MARTIN	5
AND THOUGH SHE MAY BE THERE," HE SAID,	594	COLONEL MARTIN	12
FOR WHO CAN SAY?" HE SAID.	594	COLONEL MARTIN	15
"I AM SORRY," SAID THE MAID,	595	COLONEL MARTIN	29
THE COLONEL SAID TO TOM HIS MAN,	596	COLONEL MARTIN	50
YOU HAD THREE KEGS" SAID HE.	596	COLONEL MARTIN	65
SAID THE MAN IN THE GOLDEN BREASTPLATE	598	STONE CROSS	7
SAID THE MAN IN THE GOLDEN BREASTPLATE	599	STONE CROSS	15
SAID THE MAN IN THE GOLDEN BREASTPLATE	599	STONE CROSS	23
SAID THE OLD MAN IN THE GOLDEN BREASTPLATE	599	STONE CROSS V	23
ALL THAT WE DID, ALL THAT WE SAID OR SANG	603	GALLERY REVIS	42
FOR PATRICK PEARSE HAD SAID	608	SONGS BURDEN 3	24
SAID TO THE WOMAN ON HIS KNEES, "LIE STILL.	609	IN TARAS HALLS	2
TO MANY WOMEN I HAVE SAID, "LIE STILL,"	609	IN TARAS HALLS	6
BE STILL, BE STILL, WHAT CAN BE SAID?	613	MARCH SONGS 1	7
BE STILL, BE STILL, WHAT CAN BE SAID?	613	MARCH SONGS 1	17
BE STILL, BE STILL, WHAT CAN BE SAID?	614	MARCH SONGS 1	27
ON EVERYTHING SHE SAID.	621	JOHN KINSELLA	22
BUT NEVER SAID A THING,	627	STATES HOLIDAY	10
(SAID CRAZY JANE)	628	JANE MOUNTAIN	2
(SAID CRAZY JANE)	628	JANE MOUNTAIN	12
HEART-MYSTERIES THERE, AND YET WHEN ALL IS SAID	630	CIRCUS ANIMALS	27
HEART MYSTERIES THERE, AND YET WHEN ALL IS SAID	630	CIRCUS ANIMALS V	27
ALL THAT I HAVE SAID AND DONE,	632	MAN AND ECHO	6
AND THEREUPON THAT LINEN-CARRIER SAID!	634	CUCHULAIN COMF	11
KNOW THAT WHEN ALL WORDS ARE SAID	638	BEN BULBEN	27
THE STAR-TAUGHT MOOR, SAID THUS IT WAS DECREED	691	MOSADA 1	25
THEY SAID I'D BURN IN HELL UNLESS I TOLD.	694	MOSADA 1	108
YE SAID THAT YE WOULD FRIGHT HER FROM HER SIN--	695	MOSADA 1	113
I ALWAYS SAID YOU COULD NOT TRUST THESE MOORS.	704	MOSADA 3 V	134A
"ON THIS EMBROIDERED CLOUD," THE SUN HATH SAID,	712	FERENCZ RENYI	74
"THE PROPS," SAID HE, "OF STARS AND WORLDS	725	LEGEND	5
BECAUSE OF THE THING HIS TONGUE HAD SAID.	730	PRIEST FAIRY	60
AND SAID, "YON BITTERN CRIES, IN TRUTH,	731	PRIEST FAIRY	75
THE EARL OF KINSALE SAID.	742	EARL PAUL	62
AND SAID! "SHE HAS FOOLED ME ENOUGH,"	744	GLOVE CLOAK	3
AND SAID! "I WILL SEE HER NO MORE,"	744	GLOVE CLOAK	6
WHO SAID WE HAD A SKIN OF YELLOW ALE?	759	SHADOW WATER A	243
I SAID THE ALE WAS BROWN. I HAVE FOUND THE ALE,	759	SHADOW WATER A	244
AND SAID IT WAS MIGHTIER THAN THE SUN AND MOON,	762	SHADOW WATER A	289
"WHY IS IT," QUEEN EDAIN SAID,	771	SONG DEIRDRE 1	1
A HIGH, GREY CAIRN. WHAT MORE IS TO BE SAID?	778	SONG DEIRDRE 3	5
"GIVE ME YOUR WIFE," SAID HE,	779	GOING THE ROAD	5
HAVE NOT OLD WRITERS SAID	781	MY HEART BEAT	6
SAID THE RAMBLING, SHAMBLING TRAVELLING-MAN!	788	HAWTHORN TREE	2
SAID THE WICKED, CROOKED, HAWTHORN TREE!	788	HAWTHORN TREE	6
SAID THE RAMBLING, SHAMBLING TRAVELLING-MAN!	788	HAWTHORN TREE	10
SAID THE WICKED, CROOKED, HAWTHORN TREE.	788	HAWTHORN TREE	14
OF ALL THAT LOVERS SAID,	789	SINGING HEAD	10
OUTWEIGHED ALL OTHER YEARS, YOU SAID,	791	REPRISALS	6

SAIL

NOR ULADH, WHEN NAOISE HAD THROWN A SAIL UPON THE WIND!	209	UNDER THE MOON	4
OR ULADH WHEN NAISI HAD HUNG A SAIL UPON THE WIND!	209	UNDER THE MOON V	4
AND THEY WERE LISTENING THERE BEYOND THE SAIL.	223	SHADOW WATER B	37
AND YOU HAD SPREAD A SAIL FOR HOME, A WIND	236	SHADOW WATER B	309
WOULD I COULD CAST A SAIL ON THE WATER	330	BONE OF A HARE	1
THEY CAN SPREAD OUT WHAT SAIL THEY PLEASE FOR ALL I HAVE TO SAY,	354	HIS PHOENIX	22

SAIL   (CONTINUED)
O BID ME MOUNT AND SAIL UP THERE . . . .   458 HIS WILDNESS   1
THINGS OUT OF PERFECTION SAIL, ...   530 OLD TOM AGAIN   1
TO YONDER ISLE, WHERE NEVER SAIL WAS FURLED, . . .   664 ISLE STAT II 2   56
AWAKE, AWAKE, AND WE WILL SAIL AFAR, ...   702 MOSADA 3   78
NOW FLINGING LOOSE THE SLANTING SAIL, ...   742 DANAAN QUICK   3
FROM HILLY LOCHLANN; BUT OUR SAIL HAS PASSED . . .   749 SHADOW WATER A   44
OUT OF MERE WANTONNESS TO LURE A SAIL . . . . . .   750 SHADOW WATER A   79
LOOK! THERE SHE LIES UNDER A FLAPPING SAIL. . . .   751 SHADOW WATER A   90
AND BID THEM HIDE IN SHADOW OF THE SAIL, ...   751 SHADOW WATER A   93
NODS BY THE HELM, AND NEARER TO THE SAIL . . . .   752 SHADOW WATER A   119
NEAR BY, BUT IN THE SHADOW OF THE SAIL, ...   752 SHADOW WATER A   121
BEYOND THE SAIL A MAN WITH A RED CROWN . . . . .   752 SHADOW WATER A   126
BULWARK TO BULWARK, AND SQUARE HER SAIL BY OURS. .   752 SHADOW WATER A   129
HAVE BID ME HOPE, SAIL TO THE LOCHLANN SHORE . . .   756 SHADOW WATER A V 184
UNDER A SILKEN SAIL AND SILVER YARD, ...   763 SHADOW WATER A   316
SAILED
AND THEREFORE I HAVE SAILED THE SEAS AND COME . .   408 SAIL BYZANTIUM   15
AND THEREFORE HAVE I SAILED THE SEAS AND COME . .   408 SAIL BYZANTIUM V   15
SWIFT HAS SAILED INTO HIS REST; . . . .   493 SWIFTS EPITAPH   1
SWIFT HAD SAILED INTO HIS REST; . . . .   493 SWIFTS EPITAPH V   1
AND EVIL FORTUNE HAVE OVERTHROWN SAILED HITHER . .   757 SHADOW WATER A   196
SAILETH
SAILETH THE ROVER SORROW, ...   70 CLOAK BOAT   9
SAILETH THE ROVER SORROW, ...   666 ISLE STAT II 3   9
SAILING
THE SAILING SEVEN . . . .   118 CRADLE SONG   7
SAILING TO BYZANTIUM . . . .   407 SAIL BYZANTIUM   T
THOUGH NURTURED LIKE THE SAILING MOON . . . . .   451 FIRST LOVE   1
THE COLONEL WENT OUT SAILING, ...   594 COLONEL MARTIN   1
AND HE CAME SAILING HOME. . . . .   594 COLONEL MARTIN   6
THE COLONEL WENT OUT SAILING. . . . .   594 COLONEL MARTIN   9
THE COLONEL WENT OUT SAILING. . . . .   594 COLONEL MARTIN   18
THE COLONEL WENT OUT SAILING. . . . .   595 COLONEL MARTIN   27
THE COLONEL WENT OUT SAILING. . . . .   595 COLONEL MARTIN   36
THE COLONEL WENT OUT SAILING. . . . .   596 COLONEL MARTIN   45
THE COLONEL WENT OUT SAILING. . . . .   596 COLONEL MARTIN   54
THE COLONEL WENT OUT SAILING. . . . .   596 COLONEL MARTIN   63
THE COLONEL WENT OUT SAILING. . . . .   597 COLONEL MARTIN   72
AND MANNED AN ARGOSY AND SAILING DIED. . . . . .   693 MOSADA 1   89
SAILOR
FOR, AS DRIFT FROM A SAILOR SLOW DROWNING . . . .   48 OISIN 3   22
BUT WHERE IS LAID THE SAILOR JOHN . . . .   360 ALF POLLEXFEN   17
WHERE HAVE THEY LAID THE SAILOR JOHN? . . . . .   361 ALF POLLEXFEN   23
HE, DISGUISED AS A SAILOR BEFORE THE MAST, . . .   790 DEDICATION   2
SAILOR'S
SINBAD THE SAILOR'S BROUGHT A PAINTED CHEST, . .   371 ON GOING HOUSE   10
SAILORS
AND LISTEN TO ME FOR A WHILE. THE SAILORS . . .   226 SHADOW WATER B   92
AND LISTEN TO ME FOR AWHILE. THE SAILORS . . .   226 SHADOW WATER B V   92
WITH SAILORS THAT WERE SWORN TO DO YOUR WILL, . .   236 SHADOW WATER B   308
I CARE NOT WHAT THE SAILORS SAY; . . . . . .   509 JANE REPROVED   1
WE WILL GO CALL THESE SAILORS, AND ESCAPE . . .   766 SHADOW WATER A   382
SAILS
. . . LOVE-MAKING OR PIERCING THE TEMPEST WITH SAILS. . .   53 OISIN 3   88
. . . SAILS TURNING TO THREADBARE RAGS; . . . . .   55 OISIN 3   118
. . . SAILS TURNING TO THREAD-BARE RAGS; . . . .   55 OISIN 3   V 118
"WHAT DO YOU BUILD WITH SAILS FOR FLIGHT?" . . .   69 CLOAK BOAT   6
THE TALL THOUGHT-WOVEN SAILS, THAT FLAP UNFURLED .   113 ROSE OF BATTLE   2
OUR LONG SHIPS LOOSE THOUGHT-WOVEN SAILS AND WAIT .   115 ROSE OF BATTLE   31
WHERE NO SHIP SAILS, WHERE NOTHING THAT'S ALIVE .   226 SHADOW WATER B   98
WHEN THE MOON SAILS OUT . . . .   451 FIRST LOVE   18
AND, LIKE THE SOUL, IT SAILS INTO THE SIGHT . .   490 COOLE BALLYLEE   19
AND FAR AWAY THE HERON SAILS; I WIS. . . . . .   649 ISLE STAT I 1   116
WHAT DO YOU BUILD WITH SAILS FOR FLIGHT? . . . .   666 ISLE STAT II 3   6
YONDER THE SICKLE OF THE MOON SAILS ON, ...   688 NETTLESHIP   1
CEASE THE SAILS THEIR FLAPPING UPROAR, AND THE HULL NO
LONGER ROLLS. . . . .   719 PHANTOM SHIP   18
ON THE DROWNED MEN'S HANDS AND FACES, ON THE SPARS AND
ON THE SAILS. . . . .   719 PHANTOM SHIP   22
CEASE THE SAILS, THEIR FLAPPING UPROAR TO THE HULL
NO LONGER ROLLS. . . . .   719 PHANTOM SHIP   V   18
AND WHEN YOU CAME, THE NORTH UNDER YOUR SAILS, . .   749 SHADOW WATER A   34
BUT THESE WASTE WATERS AND WIND-BEATEN SAILS . .   763 SHADOW WATER A   319
SAINT
SAINT, DO YOU WEEP? I HEAR AMID THE THUNDER . .   43 OISIN 2   209
SAINT, DOST THOU WEEP? I HEAR AMID THE THUNDER . .   43 OISIN 2   V 209
HUNCHBACK AND SAINT AND FOOL ARE THE LAST CRESCENTS. .   377 PHASES OF MOON   118
"HUNCHBACK AND SAINT AND FOOL," AND THAT THEY CAME .   377 PHASES OF MOON   132
THE SAINT AND THE HUNCHBACK . . . .   379 SAINT HUNCH   T
THAT NEVER LOOKED OUT OF THE EYE OF A SAINT . .   486 SEVEN SAGES   12
THE BODY OF SAINT TERESA LIES UNDECAYED IN TOMB, .   503 VACILLATION   80
ETERNALISED THE BODY OF A MODERN SAINT THAT ONCE .   503 VACILLATION   83
SAINT GEORGE OR ELSE A PAGAN PERSEUS; . . . . .   533 HER TRIUMPH   10
THE WORKMAN, NOBLE AND SAINT, AND ALL THINGS RUN .   565 GYRES   23
SAINT JOSEPH THOUGHT THE WORLD WOULD MELT . . .   619 STICK INCENSE   3
ON BACKGROUNDS FOR A GOD OR SAINT . . . . . .   639 BEN BULBEN   54
A SAINT OF MUNSTER, WHEN MUCH FASTING, SAW . . .   696 MOSADA 2   20
A SAINT OF RUSSIA IN A VISION SAW . . . . . .   696 MOSADA 2   V   21
SAINTED
TO SAINTED EBREMAR'S SAD EYES. I THINK . . . . .   696 MOSADA 2   15

	PAGE	TITLE	LINE
SAINT'S			
I WOULD LEAVE NO SAINT'S HEAD ON HIS BODY	58	OISIN 3	160
SAINTS			
THINKING OF SAINTS AND OF PETRONIUS ARBITER.	362	HER COURTESY	8
ACCEPT THE MIRACLES OF THE SAINTS AND HONOUR SANCTITY?	503	VACILLATION	79
"THIS LAND OF SAINTS," AND THEN AS THE APPLAUSE DIED OUT,	577	LOFTY THINGS	3
"OF PLASTER SAINTS"; HIS BEAUTIFUL MISCHIEVOUS HEAD THROWN BACK.	577	LOFTY THINGS	4
SAKE			
THAT BEAUTIFUL MILD WOMAN FOR WHOSE SAKE	205	ADAMS CURSE	15
MURMURED WITH HER YOUNG VOICE FOR WHOSE MILD SAKE	205	ADAMS CURSE V	15
I'LL DO IT FOR HIS SAKE. NO. TAKE THIS SWORD	250	SHADOW WATER B	591
BEING FOR A WOMAN'S SAKE.	259	UNWORTH PRAISE	4
PARDON THAT FOR A BARREN PASSION'S SAKE,	270	PARDON FATHERS	19
PROMISED THAT FOR A PIN'S SAKE	274	GREY ROCK	90
I'D SAVED HIS LIFE, YET FOR THE SAKE	275	GREY ROCK	102
I'D SAVE HIS LIFE, YET FOR THE SAKE	275	GREY ROCK V	102
BEING WAKEFUL FOR HER SAKE,	316	FRIENDS	23
FOR YOUR SOLE SAKE—THAT ALL HEART'S ACHE HAVE KNOWN,	355	BROKEN DREAMS	7
BUT FOR YOUR SAKE—THAT ALL HEART'S ACHE HAVE KNOWN,	355	BROKEN DREAMS V	7
BURDENSOME BEAUTY—FOR YOUR SOLE SAKE	356	BROKEN DREAMS	10
BURDENSOME BEAUTY—BUT FOR YOUR SAKE	356	BROKEN DREAMS V	10
FOR OLD SAKE'S SAKE.	357	BROKEN DREAMS	36
O LET HER CHOOSE A YOUNG MAN NOW AND ALL FOR HIS WILD SAKE."	450	OWEN AHERNE	24
TWO SONGS REWRITTEN FOR THE TUNE'S SAKE	550	SONGS REWRIT 1	T
FOR THE SONG'S SAKE A FOOL?	553	PRAYER OLD AGE	8
I, TOO, WILL FOLLOW FOR THIS EVIL-STARRED ONE'S SAKE	655	ISLE STAT I 2	84
BRAVED LIONS FOR MY SAKE,	789	SINGING HEAD	2
SAKE'S			
FOR OLD SAKE'S SAKE.	357	BROKEN DREAMS	36
SALAD			
A CRAZY SALAD WITH THEIR MEAT	404	FOR DAUGHTER	31
SALAMIS			
THE MANY-HEADED FOAM AT SALAMIS.	610	STATUES	14
SALE			
THAT CARRIED THE FISH FOR THE SALE IN THE FAR-AWAY TOWN,	91	OLD FISHERMAN V	7
SALIVA			
ABOVE, SALIVA DRIPPING FROM HIS JAWS,	689	NETTLESHIP	4
SALLEY			
DOWN BY THE SALLEY GARDENS	90	SALLEY GARDENS	T
DOWN BY THE SALLEY GARDENS MY LOVE AND I DID MEET;	90	SALLEY GARDENS	1
SHE PASSED THE SALLEY GARDENS WITH LITTLE SNOW-WHITE FEET.	90	SALLEY GARDENS	2
SALMON			
HAVE A SPEED LIKE THE SPEED OF THE SALMON HERDS,	9	OISIN 1	98
AND SWIFTER THAN THE SALMON HERDS;	9	OISIN 1 V	96
"I CAN BRING YOU SALMON OUT OF THE STREAMS	167	BLESSED	9
THE SALMON FALLS, THE MACKEREL-CROWDED SEAS,	407	SAIL BYZANTIUM V	4
AND THE SALMON BEHOLD, AND THE OUSEL TOO,	717	LOVE SONG	3
SALMON-FALLS			
THE SALMON-FALLS, THE MACKEREL-CROWDED SEAS,	407	SAIL BYZANTIUM	4
SALMON-SHOALED			
AND STREAMS, WIDE-WATERING, SALMON-SHOALED,	81	MAD KING GOLL V	3
SALT			
HAVE FACES ALIVE WITH SUCH BEAUTY BEEN KNOWN TO THE SALT EYE OF MAN,	50	OISIN 3	51
ARE FACES ALIVE WITH SUCH BEAUTY MADE KNOWN TO THE SALT EYE OF MAN,	50	OISIN 3 V	51
TO DRINK OF THAT SALT BREATH OUT OF THE SEA	292	TO A SHADE	5
THE TIME FOR YOU TO TASTE OF THAT SALT BREATH	293	TO A SHADE	21
THAT THE SALT DROPS HAVE WET;	312	CHILD DANCING	5
AND THERE IS SALT TO LENGTHEN OUT THE SMART	324	ROBERT GREGORY	11
SALT BLOOD BLOCKS HIS EYES,	530	DELPHIC ORACLE	5
THE SALT FLAKES ON HIS BREAST,	612	NEWS ORACLE V	10
SALTED			
TO THROW ME A BIT OF SALTED FISH!	301	RUN PARADISE	6
SALT-FLAKES			
THE SALT-FLAKES ON HIS BREAST,	612	NEWS ORACLE	10
SALTIN'			
MY WORK WAS SALTIN' HERRINGS	94	MOLL MAGEE	7
AND SOMETIMES FROM THE SALTIN' SHED	94	MOLL MAGEE	9
TIMES FROM THE SALTIN' SHED,	94	MOLL MAGEE V	9
SALUTING			
THE SOLDIER TAKES PRIDE IN SALUTING HIS CAPTAIN,	547	TO SAME TUNE 3	1
SOLDIERS TAKE PRIDE IN SALUTING THEIR CAPTAIN,	547	TO SAME TUNE 3 V	1
SOLDIERS TAKE PRIDE IN SALUTING THEIR CAPTAIN,	548	TO SAME TUNE 3	21
THE SOLDIER TAKES PRIDE IN SALUTING HIS CAPTAIN,	614	MARCH SONGS 2	1
SALVATION			
LOOK ON THAT FIRE, SALVATION WALKS WITHIN.	502	VACILLATION	76
SAME SEE SELF-SAME			
AMRITA. THIS SAME EVE SHE WATCHED ME PASS.	74	ANASHU VIJAYA V	64
SOME FEASTING MAN THAT THE SAME OATH HAS BOUND."	108	CUCHULAIN SEA	38
SOME FEATING MAN THAT THE SAME OATH HAS BOUND."	108	CUCHULAIN SEA V	38
SOME FEASTING MAN THAT THE SAME OATH HAS BOUND."	109	CUCHULAIN SEA	54
"SOME FEATING MAN THAT THE SAME OATH HAS BOUND."	109	CUCHULAIN SEA V	54
THEY HAVE GONE DOWN UNDER THE SAME WHITE STARS,	115	ROSE OF BATTLE	34
WHILE THOSE SAME HUNDREDS MOCK ANOTHER DAY	265	ABBEY THEATRE	4
TILL DAYTIME, PLAYTIME SEEM THE SAME;	343	SHEP GOATHERD	106
BUT IS THE SAME FOR ALL	452	HUMAN DIGNITY	4
GAME-BIRD, NOR WOMAN DOES THE SAME THING TWICE;	463	HARUN RASHID	60
GAME BIRD, OR WOMAN DOES THE SAME THING TWICE;	463	HARUN RASHID V	60

680

SAME (CONTINUED)

	PAGE	TITLE		LINE
GAMEBIRD, NOR WOMAN DOES THE SAME THING TWICE,	463	HARUN RASHID	V	60
THAT IN THE SAME CALAMITY	540	FROM ANTIGONE		9
THREE SONGS TO THE SAME TUNE	543	TO SAME TUNE 1		T
THREE SONGS TO THE SAME TUNE SECOND SONG	544	TO SAME TUNE 1	V	T
AND MAYBE WE ARE ALL THE SAME	570	THREE BUSHES		24
AND MAYBE WE ARE ALL THE SAME	570	THREE BUSHES		26
NOW SINKS THE SAME REST	574	LOVERS SONG		4
HE THOUGHT THE SAME AND LIVED BY RULE,	576	WHAT THEN		3
THEY ALWAYS BEAT ON THE SAME SMALL STONE.	591	WHAT WAS LOST		5
AY, BOY. LET'S SEE IF THAT SAME HERON'S DEAD.	651	ISLE STAT I 1		169
IS STONE: OLD SLEEPER: THIS SAME AFTERNOON	657	ISLE STAT I 3		74
STANDS EACH GREY AND SILENT PHANTOM ON THE SAME REGARDLESS SPOT—	719	PHANTOM SHIP		25

SAMUEL

	PAGE	TITLE		LINE
THE LONELY LIGHT THAT SAMUEL PALMER ENGRAVED,	373	PHASES OF MOON		17

SAN

	PAGE	TITLE		LINE
FOR THE SAN MARCO LIBRARY,	288	TO WEALTHY MAN		24

SANCTITY

	PAGE	TITLE		LINE
BROODED UPON SANCTITY	324	ROBERT GREGORY		20
TRADITIONAL SANCTITY AND LOVELINESS:	491	COOLE BALLYLEE		42
ACCEPT THE MIRACLES OF THE SAINTS AND HONOUR SANCTITY?	503	VACILLATION		79
TO LIGHTEST OF LIGHT THINGS ALL SANCTITY.	686	DRAWING-ROOM		8
TO LIGHTEST OF ALL LIGHT THINGS SANCTITY.	734	QUATRAIN APHOR		8
TO LIGHTEST OF LIGHT THINGS ALL SANCTITY.	734	QUATRAIN APHOR	V	8

SAND

	PAGE	TITLE		LINE
GREY SAND ON THE GREEN OF THE GRASSES AND OVER THE DRIPPING TREES,	48	OISIN 3		14
GREY SAND ON THE GREEN OF THE GRASSES AND OVER THE DRIPPING TREES,	57	OISIN 3		142
• • • THE STRONG HOOFS CRUSHING THE SAND AND THE SHELLS,	58	OISIN 3		157
• • • TWO CARRIED A SACK FULL OF SAND,	60	OISIN 3		185
• • • THEY LIFTED AND SHOULDERED A SACK FULL OF SAND,	60	OISIN 3	V	185
AND CANDLE-LIKE FOAM ON THE DIM SAND,	158	BELOVED RHYMES		10
ON THE GREY SAND BESIDE THE SHALLOW STREAM	367	EGO DOMINUS		1
AND TRACE THESE CHARACTERS UPON THE SAND?	370	EGO DOMINUS	V	64
SHALL WALK THE WET SAND BY THE WATER'S EDGE,	371	EGO DOMINUS	V	71
TROUBLES MY SIGHT: A WASTE OF DESERT SAND:	402	SECOND COMING	V	13
AND THERE MARKED OUT THOSE EMBLEMS ON THE SAND	468	HARUN RASHID		156
AND THERE MARKED OUT EMBLEMS ON THE SAND	468	HARUN RASHID	V	156
MOULDING IT OF DUST OR SAND,	600	SPIRIT MEDIUM		14
BEAT OUT THEIR LIVES LAMENTING O'ER THE SAND:	652	ISLE STAT I 2		14
IT BORE ME SOFTLY WHERE THE SHALLOW SAND	657	ISLE STAT I 3		58
THE BOAT'S PROW GRATED ON THE SHALLOW SAND,	659	ISLE STAT II 1		11
IN SAND HIS NAME AND MINE I'VE ALSO READ.	662	ISLE STAT II 2		12
BETWEEN THE LONELY FOREST AND THE SAND.	663	ISLE STAT II 2		22
YOU MUST BE GONE: THE ROLLING GRAINS OF SAND	663	ISLE STAT II 2		34
LOW BOWED AND DUMB UPON THE SAND.	671	ISLE STAT II 3		130
WITH WONDERFUL WHITE SAND, WHERE NEVER YET	693	MOSADA 1	V	81

SANDALLED   SEE SILVER-SANDALLED

	PAGE	TITLE		LINE
IN DANCING SILVER SANDALLED ON THE SEA,	101	ROSE UPON ROOD	V	7

SANDALS

	PAGE	TITLE		LINE
THE SANDALS THESE OF SORROW:	70	CLOAK BOAT	V	12
AND LIFE THE SANDALS OF HER FLEETNESS,	77	INDIAN TO LOVE	V	58
AND HOW THE WINGED SANDALS DART,	135	TWO TREES		18
THE SANDALS THESE OF SORROW.	666	ISLE STAT II 3		12
WITH PURPLE SANDALS SWEEP THE GRAVE-EYED HOURS—	705	REMEMBRANCE		5

SANDALWOOD

	PAGE	TITLE		LINE
BUT FOR THE AMBERGRIS AND SANDALWOOD.	232	SHADOW WATER B		221

SANDED

	PAGE	TITLE		LINE
BEFORE A SANDED PLACE:	740	EARL PAUL		32

SANDS   SEE SEA-SANDS

	PAGE	TITLE		LINE
MOURNFUL, AND GATHERED ON THE SANDS:	10	OISIN 1	V	111B
AT EVENING ON THE GLIMMERING SANDS,	23	OISIN 1		347
GREY SANDS ON THE GREEN OF THE GRASSES AND OVER THE DRIPPING TREES,	48	OISIN 3	V	14
AND THE WINDS MADE THE SANDS ON THE SEA'S EDGE	57	OISIN 3		145
GREY SANDS ON THE GREEN OF THE GRASSES AND OVER THE DRIPPING TREES,	57	OISIN 3	V	142
• • • THE GOLD HOOVES CRUSHING THE SANDS AND THE SHELLS	58	OISIN 3	V	157
• • • THE STRONG HOOFS CRUSHING THE SANDS AND THE SHELLS	58	OISIN 3	V	157
AND HUMMING SANDS, WHERE WINDY SURGES WEND:	68	SAD SHEPHERD		4
TO MIGHTY BRAHMA, HE WHO MADE YOU MANY AS THE SANDS,	72	ANASHU VIJAYA		21
TO MIGHTY BRAHMA—HE WHO MADE YE MANY AS THE SANDS,	72	ANASHU VIJAYA		21
TO MIGHTY BRAHMA, WHO HAS MADE YOU MANY AS THE SANDS,	72	ANASHU VIJAYA	V	21
ALONG THE GRASS, ALONG THE SANDS,	78	INDIAN TO LOVE		9
THE DIM GREY SANDS WITH LIGHT,	87	STOLEN CHILD		14
AND WENT DOWN TO THE LONG SANDS ALONE,	111	CUCHULAIN SEA	V	84
AND HE WENT DOWN TO THE LONG SANDS ALONE,	111	CUCHULAIN SEA	V	84
STOOD UP, AND CAME TO THE LONG SANDS ALONE:	111	CUCHULAIN SEA	V	84
HE WANDERED BY THE SANDS OF LISADELL:	127	DREAM OF FAERY		13
AS HE WENT BY THE SANDS OF LISADILL	127	DREAM OF FAERY	V	13
AS THE TIDE WEARS THE DOVE-GREY SANDS,	157	POET BELOVED		4
AS THE TIDE HAS THE DOVE-GREY SANDS,	157	POET BELOVED	V	4
AND TRACE THESE CHARACTERS UPON THE SANDS?	370	EGO DOMINUS		64
SHALL WALK THE WET SANDS BY THE EDGE OF THE STREAM	371	EGO DOMINUS		71
TROUBLES MY SIGHT: SOMEWHERE IN SANDS OF THE DESERT	402	SECOND COMING		13
HE WROTE IT ON THE SANDS (THE OWLS MAY READ	659	ISLE STAT II 1		9
WITH WONDERFUL WHITE SANDS, WHERE NEVER YET	693	MOSADA 1		81
ROLLS ALONG THE SEA SANDS WHITE.	732	STREET DANCERS		34
TO THE LOUD SANDS BEFORE DAY HAS BROKEN.	784	WOMANS BEAUTY		18

681

	PAGE	TITLE		LINE
SAND-SACK				
. . . THEY LAY 'NEATH THE SAND-SACK AT LENGTH	60	OISIN 3	V	186
HOW THE MEN OF THE SAND-SACK SHOWED ME A CHURCH	61	OISIN 3		193
HOW THE MEN OF THE SAND-SACK LED ME TO SHAUL, ...	61	OISIN 3	V	193
SANDY				
COME, BESIDE A SANDY LAKE, ...	727	LOVERS QUARREL		41
SANDYMOUNT				
SANDYMOUNT CORBETS, THAT NOTABLE MAN	604	YOU CONTENT		13
SANG				
AND NIAMH SANG CONTINUALLY	11	OISIN 1		134
FOR NEAVE SANG CONTINUALLY	11	OISIN 1	V	134
SANG NIAM, AND THEIR DEWY SHOWERS	11	OISIN 1	V	135
FROM ALL THEIR LIPS, AND ONCE THEY SANG	16	OISIN 1		226
AND WHILE THEY SANG, A SINGER LAID	16	OISIN 1	V	231
BUT WHEN I SANG OF HUMAN JOY	17	OISIN 1		234
AND WHEN I SANG OF HUMAN JOY	17	OISIN 1	V	234
SANG, "GOD IS JOY AND JOY IS GOD, ...	20	OISIN 1		300
AND SANG WE LIGHTLY TO EACH BLOOM	21	OISIN 1	V	306B
SANG WE SOFTLY IN THE DANCE, ...	21	OISIN 1	V	308
SANG WE SOFTLY, "ON THE DEAD, ...	21	OISIN 1	V	310
AND SANG UNTO THE STARRY BROODS	22	OISIN 1		326
I LOVED AND SANG, AND IN LONG WASSAILS	23	OISIN 1	V	345C
AND SANG, AND WITH A DREAMY GAZE	26	OISIN 1		393
AND, AS THEY SANG, THE PAINTED BIRDS	26	OISIN 1		396
AND HER BRIGHT BODY, SANG OF FAERY AND MAN	29	OISIN 2		7
AND NOW SANG NIAM, SWAYING HER BRIGHT HEAD	29	OISIN 2	V	6
YET SANG NO MORE AS WHEN, LIKE A BROWN BEE	30	OISIN 2		15
SO SANG YOUNG NIAM, SWAYING HER BRIGHT HEAD, ...	30	OISIN 2	V	15
BUT SANG NO MORE, AS WHEN, LIKE A BROWN BEE	30	OISIN 2	V	15
IN A SAD REVELRY HE SANG AND SWUNG	39	OISIN 2		160
WE SANG THE LOVES AND ANGERS WITHOUT SLEEP, ...	42	OISIN 2		194
ROLLING HIS WHEEL, WE SANG BESIDE THE DEEP	42	OISIN 2	V	193
AND NEVER A SONG SANG NIAMH, AND OVER MY FINGER-TIPS . .	47	OISIN 3		6
THEN HE SANG SOFTLY NIGH THE PEARLY RIM;	69	SAD SHEPHERD		25
CHANGED ALL HE SANG TO INARTICULATE MOAN	69	SAD SHEPHERD		27
THEN SANG HE SOFTLY NIGH THE PEARLY RIM;	69	SAD SHEPHERD	V	25
I SANG HOW, WHEN DAY'S TOIL IS DONE, ...	85	MAD KING GOLL		61
AND AS I SANG MY SOUL WAS FREE	86	MAD KING GOLL	V	65
MY SINGING SANG ME FEVER FREE, ...	86	MAD KING GOLL	V	65
MY SINGING SANG ME FEVER-FREE;	86	MAD KING GOLL	V	65
AND SANG WHAT GOLD MORNING OR EVENING SHEDS	126	DREAM OF FAERY		7
AND SANG HOW DAY A DRUID TWILIGHT SHEDS	126	DREAM OF FAERY	V	7
SANG THAT SOMEWHERE TO NORTH OR WEST OR SOUTH	127	DREAM OF FAERY		19
SANG WHERE--UNNECESSARY CRUEL VOICE--	127	DREAM OF FAERY		30
SANG HOW SOMEWHERE TO NORTH OR EAST OR SOUTH	127	DREAM OF FAERY	V	19
SANG HOW SOMEWHERE TO NORTH OR WEST OR SOUTH	127	DREAM OF FAERY	V	19
THAT SANG, TO SWEETEN IRELAND'S WRONG, ...	137	TO IRELAND		3
WHO SANG TO SWEETEN IRELAND'S WRONG, ...	137	TO IRELAND	V	3
HE HEARD WHILE HE SANG AND DREAMED	144	HOST OF AIR		9
IT SANG TO HER THROUGH THE DOOR.	160	CAP AND BELLS		16
AND HER RED LIPS SANG THEM A LOVE-SONG	160	CAP AND BELLS		27
HER RED LIPS SANG THEM A LOVE-SONG	160	CAP AND BELLS	V	27
AND HER RED LIPS SANG THEM A LOVE SONG, ...	160	CAP AND BELLS	V	27
TALKED OF HIS COUNTRY AND ITS PEOPLE, SANG	180	QUEEN MAEVE		3
THEY SANG A DROWSY SONG, OR SNORED, ...	271	GREY ROCK		16
AND SANG A DROWSY SONG, OR SNORED, ...	271	GREY ROCK	V	16
SANG THROUGH THEIR TEETH FROM NOON TO NOON;	296	THREE BEGGARS		41
SANG UNNOTICED LIKE A BIRD;	298	THREE HERMITS		7
SANG UNNOTICED LIKE A BIRD.	299	THREE HERMITS		32
MY MOTHER DANDLED ME AND SANG, ...	308	PLAYER QUEEN		1
"HE WENT AWAY," MY MOTHER SANG, ...	308	PLAYER QUEEN		5
"WHEN SHE WAS GOT," MY MOTHER SANG, ...	308	PLAYER QUEEN		13
SANG TILL STARS BEGAN TO FADE;	332	ROUND TOWER		20
SANG SOLOMON TO SHEBA, ...	332	SOLOMON SHEBA		1
TO SOLOMON SANG SHEBA, ...	333	SOLOMON SHEBA		9
SANG SOLOMON TO SHEBA, ...	333	SOLOMON SHEBA		17
THE POET STUBBORN WITH HIS PASSION SANG US	356	BROKEN DREAMS		18
WHAT A STAR SANG AND CARELESS MUSES HEARD;	445	SCHOOL CHILDR		47
"SPEAK ALL YOUR MIND," MY HEART SANG OUT, ...	450	OWEN AHERNE		21
AND SWEPT THE HOUSE AND SANG ABOUT HER WORK	468	HARUN RASHID		148
OLIVER GOLDSMITH SANG WHAT HE HAD SEEN, ...	487	SEVEN SAGES		17
SANG A BONE UPON THE SHORE;	521	THREE THINGS		2
SANG A BONE UPON THE SHORE;	521	THREE THINGS		8
SANG A BONE UPON THE SHORE, ...	521	THREE THINGS		14
UPON CRO-PATRICK SANG ALOUD;	528	DANCER CRUACH		5
UPON CROAGH PATRICK SANG IT LOUD;	528	DANCER CRUACH	V	5
SANG OLD TOM THE LUNATIC	528	TOM LUNATIC		1
SANG OF THE BEAST THAT GAVE THE FATAL WOUND.	537	HER VISION		16
AND SANG MY MALEDICTION WITH THE REST.	537	HER VISION		24
GRANDFATHER SANG IT UNDER THE GALLOWS;	544	TO SAME TUNE 1		1
HE SANG IT FROM HIS HEART.	544	TO SAME TUNE 1		6
NO MORE SANG HE, FOR HIS THROAT WAS TOO SMALL; . . .	545	TO SAME TUNE 1		24
DOUBTLESS I SPOKE OR SANG WHAT I HAD HEARD	557	RIBH ECSTASY		2
"WHAT THEN?" SANG PLATO'S GHOST. "WHAT THEN?" . .	576	WHAT THEN		5
"WHAT THEN?" SANG PLATO'S GHOST. "WHAT THEN?" . .	577	WHAT THEN		10
"WHAT THEN?" SANG PLATO'S GHOST. "WHAT THEN?" . .	577	WHAT THEN		15
BUT LOUDER SANG THAT GHOST, "WHAT THEN?"	577	WHAT THEN		20
BUT SANG, "O SEA-STARVED, HUNGRY SEA."	578	CRAZED GIRL		14
ALL THAT WE DID, ALL THAT WE SAID OR SANG	603	GALLERY REVIS		42
MY FATHER SANG THAT SONG, ...	613	MARCH SONGS 1		8
MY FATHER SANG THAT SONG, ...	613	MARCH SONGS 1		18

682

		PAGE	TITLE		LINE

SANG   (CONTINUED)
MY FATHER SANG THAT SONG,	614 MARCH SONGS 1		28
GRANDFATHER SANG IT UNDER THE GALLOWS!	615 MARCH SONGS 3		1
HE SANG IT FROM HIS HEART.	616 MARCH SONGS 3		6
NO MORE SANG HE, FOR HIS THROAT WAS TOO SMALL!	616 MARCH SONGS 3		24
THEY SANG, BUT HAD NOR HUMAN TUNES NOR WORDS,	635 CUCHULAIN COMF		23
AND I SANG ROUND THE TREE	654 ISLE STAT I 2		66
AND I SANG ROUND THE TREE,	654 ISLE STAT I 2		76
AND I SANG ROUND THE TREE,	655 ISLE STAT I 2		80
AND, NODDING TO AND FRO, SANG SONGS OF LOVE,	688 TWO TITANS		35
'TWAS EVENING, AND THE CRICKET NATION SANG	690 MOSADA 1		18
A LILY-BLANCHED PLACE, SHE SAT AND SANG,	693 MOSADA 1		83
A LILY BLANCHED PLACE, SHE SAT AND SANG,	693 MOSADA 1	V	83
IN THE FAR ISLE SHE SANG HERSELF ASLEEP,	694 MOSADA 1		90
MY FOSTER-MOTHER SANG IN AN OLD RHYME	763 SHADOW WATER A		314
MY FOSTER MOTHER SANG IN AN OLD RHYME	763 SHADOW WATER A	V	314

SANK
FOR THE SPARKLING HOOVES THEY SANK NOT IN!	10 OISIN 1	V	114A
IN THE PALE WEST, AND THE SUN'S RIM SANK,	12 OISIN 1		153
NOW IN THE SEA THE SUN'S RIM SANK,	12 OISIN 1	V	153
AND, AS THE SUN SANK EVER LOWER,	13 OISIN 1	V	170A
AS THOUGH ONE LISTENED THERE, AND HIS VOICE SANK	180 QUEEN MAEVE		7
DO YOU REMEMBER WHEN WE SANK THAT GALLEY	223 SHADOW WATER B		20
FOR CERTAINLY HE SANK INTO HIS GRAVE	370 EGO DOMINUS		57
LOCKE SANK INTO A SWOON!	439 FRAGMENTS		1
FROM THE LIMBS OF LEDA SANK	522 LULLABY		17
FROM THE LIMBS OF HELEN SANK	522 LULLABY	V	17
SCARCE SANK HE FROM THE WEST	535 CHOSEN		5
WHEN LOW THE SUN SANK DOWN IN CLOTTED FLAME	656 ISLE STAT I 3		30
THE SHEPHERD RAISED HIS ARMS AND SANK,	673 ISLE STAT II 3		187

SAP
| UNTIL THE SAP OF SUMMER HAD GROWN WEARY! | 130 BOOK STORIES | | 14 |
| HAS DRIED THE SAP OUT OF MY VEINS, AND RENT | 260 FASC DIFFICULT | | 2 |

SAPLINGS
| AND SAPLINGS ROOT AMONG THE BROKEN STONE, | 489 COOLE PARK 29 | | 28 |

SAPPHO'S
| AT THE GREAT BOOK OF SAPPHO'S SONG! BUT NO, | 461 HARUN RASHID | | 12 |

SAPPING
| SORROWS SAPPING BRAIN AND HEART. | 733 STREET DANCERS | | 60 |

SAPPY
| "'TIS JOY MAKES SWIM THE SAPPY TIDE, | 18 OISIN 1 | V | 261 |

SARDONYX
| AND CHRYSOPRASE AND RUBY AND SARDONYX. | 765 SHADOW WATER A | | 358 |

SAT
OR SAT IN DREAMS ON THE PALE STRAND,	25 OISIN 1		390
AND OTHERS SAT THEM BY THE SEA,	25 OISIN 1	V	390
OF MANY THOUSAND STEPS. SAT EITHER SIDE,	31 OISIN 2	V	35
HE HAD SAT DOWN AND SIGHED WITH CUMBERED HEART,	37 OISIN 2		111
I SAT ON CUSHIONED OTTER-SKIN!	81 MAD KING GOLL		1
I SAT ON CUSHIONED OTTER-SKIN!	81 MAD KING GOLL	V	1
I SAT AND MUSED AND DRANK SWEET WINE!	82 MAD KING GOLL		13
YOUNG SUBTLE CONCHUBAR SAT CLOSE BY ME	102 FERGUS DRUID		10
HE SAT AND PLAYED IN A DREAM	145 HOST OF AIR		27
HE SAT DOWN AND PLAYED IN A DREAM	145 HOST OF AIR	V	27
THE PORTER SLEPT, ALTHOUGH HE SAT UPRIGHT	182 QUEEN MAEVE		45
WHERE THE HOUND OF ULADH SAT BEFORE	192 BAILE AILLINN		73
WE SAT TOGETHER AT ONE SUMMER'S END,	204 ADAMS CURSE		1
WE SAT GROWN QUIET AT THE NAME OF LOVE!	205 ADAMS CURSE		28
HE SAT WITH TIGHTENED REIN AND LOOSENED MOUTH	277 TWO KINGS		10
HE SAT WITH TIGHTENED REIN AMAZED, HIS HORSE	277 TWO KINGS	V	10
SAT UPRIGHT WITH A SWORD BEFORE HER FEET.	279 TWO KINGS		62
"YOU BROUGHT ME WHERE YOUR BROTHER ARDAN SAT	280 TWO KINGS		79
THEY SAT UPON THEIR HEELS TO RAIL,	297 THREE BEGGARS		53
OR SAT UPON THEIR HEELS TO RAIL	297 THREE BEGGARS	V	53
WE SAT AS SILENT AS A STONE,	314 MEMORY YOUTH		15
I SAT AS SILENT AS A STONE	314 MEMORY YOUTH	V	15
LAST EVENING? THAT I, WHO HAD SAT	349 HAWK		15
SAT LATE, OR SHELLEY'S VISIONARY PRINCE!	373 PHASES OF MOON		16
WHILE ON THAT OLD GREY STONE I SAT	406 IN TIME OF WAR		2
HIS MAJESTIC MOTHER SAT	440 WISDOM		11
WE SAT UNDER AN OLD THORN-TREE	456 SUMMER SPRING		1
SAT DOWN UPON THE FOUNTAIN'S MARBLE EDGE,	463 HARUN RASHID		43
I SAT WHERE I COULD WATCH HER SLEEPING FORM,	467 HARUN RASHID		128
I SAT, A SOLITARY MAN,	501 VACILLATION		36
I SAT AND CRIED.	515 GIRLS SONG B		8
THAT SAT SO STILL AND PLAYED AT THE CHESS?	550 SEVERED HEAD		12
I TOLD HIM THAT NIGHTLY FROM SIX TO SEVEN I SAT AT THIS TABLE,	578 LOFTY THINGS		9
ALL SORTS OF KINGS HAVE SAT	597 MODEL LAUREATE		2
ONE IMAGE CROSSED THE MANY-HEADED, SAT	610 STATUES		17
GREAT-BLADDERED EMER SAT,	628 JANE MOUNTAIN		15
CUCHULAIN SAT AT HER SIDE!	628 JANE MOUNTAIN		17
GREAT BLADDERED EMER SAT,	628 JANE MOUNTAIN	V	15
HE SAT, AND THEN I HEARD THE WHITE LAKE SING,	659 ISLE STAT II 1		15
FILLED THEM AS THEY SAT TOGETHER!	667 ISLE STAT II 3		31
TO MAKE US GLAD WITH WONDER AS WE SAT	683 SEEKER		41
WHERE SAT OLD SUMMER FADING INTO SONG,	690 MOSADA 1	V	18
A LILY-BLANCHED PLACE, SHE SAT AND SANG,	693 MOSADA 1		83
A LILY BLANCHED PLACE, SHE SAT AND SANG,	693 MOSADA 1	V	83
I SAT ME DOWN BESIDE THEE, AND I KNEW	713 FERENCZ RENYI		92
HAST THOU NOT SAT OF YORE UPON THE KNEES	724 KANVA ON SELF		9

683

SAT   (CONTINUED)
    SAT UNDERNEATH THE MARKET CROSS, ...   724 LEGEND   2
    AND UNDER A SHADY OAK-TREE SAT, ...   728 PRIEST FAIRY   7
    EARL PAUL CAME WHERE THE KING SAT, ...   740 EARL PAUL   29
    I SAT BESIDE MY FOSTER-MOTHER, AND NOW . . . . . .   762 SHADOW WATER A   292
    I SAT BESIDE MY FOSTER MOTHER, AND NOW . . . . . .   762 SHADOW WATER A V   292
SATIN
    ALL THAT SILK AND SATIN GEAR! . . . .   525 DANCING DAYS   3
SATISFACTION
    AND ASK FOR SATISFACTION UPON THESE . . . .   235 SHADOW WATER B   281
    BRINGS SUCH SATISFACTION . . . .   533 FIRST CONFESS   11
SATISFIED
    WHAT WOMAN'S SATISFIED, ...   334 SONG   8
    OF LOVELY, SATISFIED, INDIFFERENT EYES. . . . . . .   375 PHASES OF MOON   83
    I AM SATISFIED WITH THAT, ...   430 NINETEEN 19   61
    SATISFIED IF A TROUBLED MIRROR SHOW IT, ...   430 NINETEEN 19   62
    AND EVERY BRIDE'S AMBITION SATISFIED. . . . .   491 COOLE BALLYLEE   37
    THAT THEY BE SATISFIED-- . . . .   496 MOHINI CHATTER   20
    IMAGINATION HAD BEEN SATISFIED, ...   543 PARN FUNERAL 2   6
    NOR SATISFIED CONSCIENCE, BUT THAT GREAT FAMILY . .   579 DOR WELLESLEY   14
    BUT NOTHING SATISFIED THE FOOL . . . .   620 JOHN KINSELLA   7
    I MUST BE SATISFIED WITH MY HEART, ALTHOUGH . . . .   629 CIRCUS ANIMALS   4
    CAN GHOST OR MAN BE SATISFIED? . . . .   791 REPRISALS   4
SATISFY
    SATISFY AMBITION, ANIMATE . . . .   500 VACILLATION   20
    SATISFY AMBITION, OR ANIMATE . . . .   500 VACILLATION   V   20
SATO'S
    WHERE SATO'S GIFT, A CHANGELESS SWORD, ...   421 MY TABLE   2
    WHEN IT WAS FORGED. IN SATO'S HOUSE, ...   421 MY TABLE   9
    IS SATO'S ANCIENT BLADE, STILL AS IT WAS, ...   477 SELF AND SOUL   10
    IS SATO'S ANCIENT SWORD, STILL AS IT WAS, ...   477 SELF AND SOUL V   10
SATURATED   SEE BLOOD-SATURATED
    THERE, ON BLOOD SATURATED GROUND, HAVE STOOD . . .   482 BLOOD AND MOON V   35
SATURN
    UNDER SATURN . . . .   390 UNDER SATURN   T
    IF JUPITER AND SATURN MEET, ...   562 CONJUNCTIONS   1
SATURNIAN
    STRETCH OUT YOUR LIMBS AND SLEEP A LONG SATURNIAN SLEEP!   442 BLACK CENTAUR   13
SATURNINE
    DO NOT BECAUSE THIS DAY I HAVE GROWN SATURNINE . . . 390 UNDER SATURN   1
SATYRS
    FLASH FISHLIKE! NYMPHS AND SATYRS . . . .   612 NEWS ORACLE   35
SAVAGE
    TO MAKE THE SAVAGE HEART OF LOVE . . . .   193 BAILE AILLINN   109
    SAVAGE INDIGNATION THERE . . . .   493 SWIFTS EPITAPH   2
    DANCE THE SAVAGE CHILDREN SMALL, ...   732 STREET DANCERS   29
SAVAGELY
    AND HAD BEEN SAVAGELY UNDONE . . . .   314 MEMORY YOUTH   18
SAVE
    ALL PEARLY WHITE, SAVE ONE RED EAR! . . . .   12 OISIN 1   141
    SAVE DEER TOWARDS NOON THAT WATER SOUGHT. . . . . .   17 OISIN 1   V   243
    SAVE ONLY MANY TIMES MY NAME, ...   25 OISIN 1   375
    AND LIFE IS OVER SAVE THE MURMUR AND THE SWEETNESS. .   77 INDIAN TO LOVE V   5E
    AND ALL IS OVER SAVE THE MURMUR AND THE SWEETNESS. .   77 INDIAN TO LOVE V   5E
    SAVE BY AN EVIL CHANCE, ...   178 FIDDLER DOONEY   14
    I'D SAVE HIS LIFE, YET FOR THE SAKE . . . .   275 GREY ROCK   V   102
    FOR MEN WERE BORN TO PRAY AND SAVE! . . . .   289 SEPTEMBER 1913   6
    AND WHAT, GOD HELP US, COULD THEY SAVE? . . . . .   289 SEPTEMBER 1913   14
    AND WONDERED WHAT WAS LEFT FOR MASSACRE TO SAVE. . . 619 BRONZE HEAD   28
    BUT MASTERFUL HEAVEN HAD INTERVENED TO SAVE IT. . .   630 CIRCUS ANIMALS   20
    WHO SEEK MAY FIND, SAVE ONLY ONE, ...   668 ISLE STAT II 3   48
    THE FLOWER, SAVE SOME THING BE FOUND . . . . . .   668 ISLE STAT II 3   51
    THAT SHE FORSWEAR HER HERESIES AND SAVE . . . . .   698 MOSADA 2   46
    CAST OFF THY HERESIES, AND SAVE THY SOUL . . . . .   701 MOSADA 3   64
    FLINGS HER BEFORE HIM. "SAVE THYSELF AND ME. . . .   713 FERENCZ RENYI   86
    "AH, FERENCZ, SPEAK AND SAVE THYSELF AND ME! . . .   713 FERENCZ RENYI V   86
    FOR ALL SAVE HIM WHO PINING FELL, ...   717 FAIRY DOCTOR   19
    FOR ALL SAVE HE WHO PINING FELL, ...   717 FAIRY DOCTOR   V   19
    SAVE, WITH THE LITTLE GOLDEN GREEDY CARP, ... 720 WITCH VIVIEN   2
SAVED
    BECAUSE YOU SAVED MY RICE. HAVE YOU NO THANKS? . .   73 ANASHU VIJAYA   40
    I'D SAVED HIS LIFE, YET FOR THE SAKE . . . .   275 GREY ROCK   102
    AND SAVED THE IRISH POOR, ...   586 PARNELLITES   12
SAVES
    BUT SAVES US FROM A DREAM. AND WHAT OF THOSE . . .   376 PHASES OF MOON   102
SAVING
    SAVING IN THINE OWN HEART. SEEK, THEN, ...   66 HAPPY SHEPHERD   27
    SAVING THE RHYME RATS HEAR BEFORE THEY DIE. . . .   542 PARN FUNERAL 1   28
    SAVING A GREEN FROG DEAD UPON THE GRASS. . . . . .   676 ISLE STAT II 3   269
    MINE HEART-STRINGS ARE ALL BROKEN SAVING ONE, . . . 684 SEEKER   V   69B
SAW
    NEAR BY, THE FENIANS SAW, AND KNEW . . . .   10 OISIN 1   V   111
    AND WHEN THEY SAW THE CLOAK I WORE . . . .   15 OISIN 1   207
    AND WHEN THEY SAW MY EARTHLY DRESS, ...   15 OISIN 1   V   207
    AND WHEN THEY SAW THAT THE BRATTA I WORE . . . . .   15 OISIN 1   V   207
    I SAW NOT WHO! 'NEATH OTHER SKIES . . . .   25 OISIN 1   V 381A
    AND WHEN THE WHITE STEED SAW WHAT BLACKNESS GLEAMED,   30 OISIN 2   V   24
    I SAW A FOAM-WHITE SEAGULL DRIFT AND FLOAT . . . .   36 OISIN 2   105
    CLOTHING HIM ROUND, I SAW A SEAGULL FLOAT . . . . .   36 OISIN 2   V   105
    WE SAW, SOME NEW, SOME PRINTED WHEN THE PLACE WAS YOUNG, 37 OISIN 2   V   116
    TO LIE UNTIL THE FOURTH MORN SAW EMERGE . . . . . .   44 OISIN 2   220

SAW   (CONTINUED)

		PAGE	TITLE		LINE
TO LIE THERE 'TILL THE FOURTH DAY SAW EMERGE		44	OISIN 2	V	220
THE IMMORTAL DESIRE OF IMMORTALS WE SAW IN THEIR FACES, AND SIGHED.		47	OISIN 3		4
AND WE STOOD ON A SEA'S EDGE WE SAW NOT;		47	OISIN 3		11
I SAW HOW THOSE SLUMBERERS, GROWN WEARY,		50	OISIN 3		54
I SAW FROM A DISTANT SADDLE; FROM THE EARTH SHE MADE HER MOAN;		56	OISIN 3		130
TILL I SAW WHERE MAEVE LIES SLEEPING		60	OISIN 3		184
I SAW HER STANDING IN HER DOOR BUT NOW.		74	ANASHU VIJAYA		64
MY SPIRIT ROCKED IN SLEEP AND SIGHS; AND SAW THE MOORFOWL PACE		76	INDIAN ON GOD		3
ALL DRIPPING ON A GRASSY SLOPE, AND SAW THEM CEASE TO CHASE		76	INDIAN ON GOD		4
TURNING, HE SAW THAT SHE HAD THRUST DEAD LEAVES		80	EPHEMERA		18
GLIMMERING IN HER DROOPED EYES, SAW HER LIPS MOVE		81	EPHEMERA	V	240
AND SAW WHERE THIS OLD TYMPAN LAY		85	MAD KING GOLL		55
I SAW THIS HARP ALL SONGLESS LIE,		85	MAD KING GOLL	V	55
I SAW A KINDLY NEIGHBOUR		95	MOLL MAGEE		35
I SAW A NEIGHBOUR GOOD.		95	MOLL MAGEE	V	36
AND HE SAW HOW THE REEDS GREW DARK		144	HOST OF AIR		5
AND HE SAW YOUNG MEN AND YOUNG GIRLS		144	HOST OF AIR		13
AND SAW YOUR IMAGE WAS THERE;		152	LOSS OF LOVE		6
THAT SAW YOUNG NIAMH HOVER WITH LOVE-LORN FACE		162	ASKS FORGIVE		13
AND CUMHAL SAW LIKE A DRIFTING SMOKE.		167	BLESSED		13
SAW THE PIERCED HANDS AND ROOD OF ELDER RISE		169	SECRET ROSE		10
SHE SAW HER HUSBAND AILELL SLEEPING THERE,		183	QUEEN MAEVE		69
WE SAW THE LAST EMBERS OF DAYLIGHT DIE,		205	ADAMS CURSE		29
I SAW THEM ON THAT NIGHT AS WELL AS YOU.		223	SHADOW WATER B		29
I SAW THEM, TOO, ONE NIGHT. FORGAEL WAS PLAYING.		223	SHADOW WATER B		36
I SAW A FLAGON OF BROWN ALE ABOARD HER.		240	SHADOW WATER B		388
AND SAW WHEREVER I COULD TURN		253	HIS DREAM		3
IF WE BUT SAW IN DREAMS THAT ROOM,		272	GREY ROCK		38
WITH THE GROUND-IVY'S BLUE, HE SAW A STAG		277	TWO KINGS		6
HE THOUGHT TO HAVE GIVEN HIS HORSE THE SPUR, BUT SAW		277	TWO KINGS	V	48
AND SAW WHERE IN THE MIDST OF THE GREAT HALL		279	TWO KINGS		60
AND THEREON SAW, WHERE STONES HAD BEEN		302	HOUR DAWN	V	20
AND SAW A FLAKE OF THE YELLOW FOAM		309	PLAYER QUEEN		15
I SAW A FLAKE OF YELLOW FOAM		309	PLAYER QUEEN	V	15
SUDDENLY I SAW THE COLD AND ROCK-DELIGHTING HEAVEN		316	COLD HEAVEN		1
SUDDENLY I SAW THE COLD AND ROCK DELIGHTING HEAVEN		316	COLD HEAVEN	V	1
I SAW, BEFORE I HAD WELL FINISHED,		322	SWANS AT COOLE		9
THAT SAW THE SURGES RUNNING BY,		338	TOM OROUGHLEY		6
OR ON THE WITHERED MEN THAT SAW		344	DAWN		5
THAT SAW THE WICKS GROW YELLOW IN THE DAWN;		352	PEOPLE		18
ON THE GREY ROCK OF CASHEL I SUDDENLY SAW		383	VISION ROBART		17
ALTHOUGH I SAW IT ALL IN THE MIND'S EYE		383	VISION ROBART		25
I SAW BY THE MOON'S LIGHT		383	VISION ROBART		27
WHEN LONG AGO I SAW HER RIDE		397	POLIT PRISONER		13
I SAW MY FREEDOM WON		400	DEMON BEAST		7
IN REVERIE, OR IN VISION, SAW		420	MY HOUSE	V	20E
THEY NEVER SAW HOW SEASONS RUN,		432	NINETEEN 19		101
I SAW A STARING VIRGIN STAND		437	SONGS PLAY 1		1
I SAW THAT STARING, VIRGIN STAND		437	SONGS PLAY 1	V	1
SINCE FIRST WE SAW THE LIGHT,		456	SUMMER SPRING		4
AND OFTEN THOSE FIRST DAYS I SAW HER STARE		466	HARUN RASHID		122
AND SAW HER SITTING UPRIGHT ON THE BED;		467	HARUN RASHID		134
I SAW HER SITTING UPRIGHT ON THE BED,		467	HARUN RASHID	V	134
BUT MINE SAW STELLA ONCE. WHENCE CAME OUR THOUGHT?		486	SEVEN SAGES		6
MINE SAW STELLA ONCE. WHENCE CAME OUR THOUGHT?		486	SEVEN SAGES	V	6
MINE SAW STELLA ONCE. WHEN CAME OUR THOUGHT?		486	SEVEN SAGES	V	6
BUT NEVER SAW THE TREFOIL STAINED WITH BLOOD,		487	SEVEN SAGES		19
SAW I AN OLD MAN YOUNG		515	GIRLS SONG B		11
NO WITHERED CRONE I SAW		516	MANS SONG		11
THAT BLINKED AND SAW THEM IN A SHROUD.		529	TOM LUNATIC		12
NOR SAW MY BODY FALL NOR HEARD IT SHRIEK,		537	HER VISION		29
TO THOSE THAT NEVER SAW THIS TONSURED HEAD		555	RIBH AT TOMB		4
FOR IF I SAW MYSELF CREEP IN		569	THREE BUSHES		12
HIS LADY SAW IT ALL		571	THREE BUSHES		53
AND WANT HE DID FOR MY GRAND-DAD SAW		596	COLONEL MARTIN	V	68
SAW THE STORY'S END.		597	COLONEL MARTIN		69
SAW THAT THE GRAVE WAS DEEP, THE COFFIN SOUND,		609	IN TARAS HALLS		18
I SAW THE WILDNESS IN HER AND I THOUGHT		619	BRONZE HEAD		16
AS ARGIVE CLYTEMNESTRA SAW OUT-BURN		645	ISLE STAT I 1		12
OENONE SAW THE FIRES OF TROIA LEAP,		645	ISLE STAT I 1		17
I SENT AN ARROW. AND I SAW YOU MISS;		649	ISLE STAT I 1		115
I SAW HER AS YOU NOW ARISE;		654	ISLE STAT I 2		73
OF THOSE VAST WOODS; AND THEN I SAW THE BOAT,		657	ISLE STAT I 3		53
WE SAW THE DOLOROUS LAKE; AND THEN THY NAME		659	ISLE STAT II 2		7
AND, BOY, SAW YOU, WHEN THROUGH THE FOREST WE		662	ISLE STAT II 2		9
I SAW HIM FROM SAD DIDO'S SHORES DEPART,		677	ISLE STAT II 3		288
AS HERE I CAME I SAW GOD PAN. HE PLAYED		678	ISLE STAT II 3		300
BEFORE THE WIND. SAW YOU HIS EYES A-GLITTER?		683	SEEKER		35
I SAW HIM STAGGER WITH THE CLANKING CHAIN,		687	TWO TITANS		31
ALONG THE VELVET VALE I SAW HIM COME--		690	MOSADA 1		10
I SAW HIM SIGH AND TURN AND PASS AWAY;		690	MOSADA 1		14
I SAW HIS JOVIAL MOOD BRING ONCE A SMILE		696	MOSADA 2		14
A SAINT OF MUNSTER, WHEN MUCH FASTING, SAW		696	MOSADA 2		20
I SAW A STRANGER TAP AND WAIT		696	MOSADA 2		22
A SAINT OF RUSSIA IN A VISION SAW		696	MOSADA 2	V	21
A WEAK, THIN CHILD, WHEN LAST I SAW HIM THERE.		699	MOSADA 3		14
I SAW A GIRL AFRAID TO BE TOO NEAR,		712	FERENCZ RENYI		68

685

		PAGE	TITLE	LINE

SAW (CONTINUED)
SAW ON THE WOOD'S EDGE GLEAM AN ASH-GREY FEATHER;	715 DWELT SYCAMORE	2
I SAW HER GLITTER AND GLEAM;	744 GLOVE CLOAK	1
AND HEARD THE MUSIC IN THE WIND, AND SAW	747 SHADOW WATER A	5
O, BUT I SAW A SOLEMN SIGHT;	788 HAWTHORN TREE	1
LIVE, FOR I SAW THEM DANCING THERE.	788 HAWTHORN TREE	12

SAWDUST
| SWEPT THE SAWDUST FROM THE FLOOR | 440 WISDOM | 6 |

SAY
I HEARD ONE SAY, "HIS EYES GROW DIM	25 OISIN 1	380
I HEARD ONE SAY, "WITHIN HIS EYES	25 OISIN 1 V	380
AND THE STARS SHALL ARISE AND SAY IN THE MORNING,	28 OISIN 1 V	423G
SAY HOW HE WEEPS IN ERI."	33 OISIN 1 V	68
AND THUS, MY LATE-LOST NIAM, DIDST THOU SAY:	34 OISIN 2 V	78
LOST NIAM MOURN AND SAY, "AH, LOVE, WE GO	46 OISIN 2 V	245B
YE HAVE NO POWER." "AND, NIAM, SAY, OF THESE	46 OISIN 2	248
I PASSED A LITTLE FURTHER ON AND HEARD A PEACOCK SAY:	77 INDIAN ON GOD	17
I PACED A LITTLE FURTHER AND I HEARD A PEACOCK SAY:--	77 INDIAN ON GOD	17
I PASSED A LITTLE FURTHER AND I HEARD A PEACOCK SAY:--	77 INDIAN ON GOD V	17
WITH SHORE LINES IN THE SAY;	94 MOLL MAGEE	6
THEY HEAR HIM FEEBLY SAY,	99 FOXHUNTER	32
THIS WOULD I SAY, MOST WISE OF LIVING SOULS:	102 FERGUS DRUID	9
AND COVER YOUR LIPS WITH ODOROUS TWILIGHT AND SAY:	162 ASKS FORGIVE	5
COVER YOUR LIPS WITH ROSE-HEAVY TWILIGHT, AND SAY:	162 ASKS FORGIVE V	5
THEIR CHILDREN'S CHILDREN SHALL SAY THEY HAVE LIED.	166 EVIL OF BELOV	6
AND LEARN THE PRAYERS THAT YOU SAY.	167 BLESSED V	8
AND SHOOK HIM WIDE AWAKE, AND BID HIM SAY	182 QUEEN MAEVE	50
HAD TROUBLED HIS SLEEP. BUT ALL HE HAD TO SAY	182 QUEEN MAEVE	52
AND POETS FOUND, OLD WRITERS SAY	197 BAILE AILLINN	187
AWAKENS AN OLD MEMORY, AND SAY:	201 OLD MEMORY	2
FOR THEY, FOR ALL SMOOTH LIPS CAN SAY,	202 NEVER GIVE ALL	9
AND THROWN THE THUNDER ON THE STONES FOR ALL THAT MAEVE	207 HANRAHANS SONG	7
CAN SAY.	208 OLD MEN ADMIRE	1
I HEARD THE OLD, OLD MEN SAY,	208 OLD MEN ADMIRE	7
I HEARD THE OLD, OLD MEN SAY,	225 SHADOW WATER B V	75
WHEN FORGAEL'S IN THE OTHER SCALE. I'D SAY IT	227 SHADOW WATER B	107
NO, NO, DO NOT SAY THAT. YOU KNOW RIGHT WELL	228 SHADOW WATER B	136
YOU SAY THAT ALSO? YOU HAVE HEARD THE VOICES,	228 SHADOW WATER B	137
FOR THAT IS WHAT THEY SAY--ALL, ALL THE SHADOWS--	236 SHADOW WATER B	316
BRING MADNESS? QUEEN, I AM NOT MAD. YET SAY	236 SHADOW WATER B V	317
AND YET YOU SAY THE WATER AND THE WIND	242 SHADOW WATER B	422
BUT WHAT IS IT THAT MADE ME SAY I LOVED HIM?	244 SHADOW WATER B	460
AND IF YOU SAY THAT SHE CAME WILLINGLY--	244 SHADOW WATER B V	460
AND YOU SAY THAT SHE CAME WILLINGLY--	255 WOMAN HOMER	12
THAT COMING TIME CAN SAY,	256 WORDS	13
THAT HAD SHE DONE SO WHO CAN SAY	262 TO A POET	1
YOU SAY, AS I HAVE OFTEN GIVEN TONGUE	265 ABBEY THEATRE	2
WHEN WE ARE HIGH AND AIRY HUNDREDS SAY	267 ALL TEMPT ME V	8
AS THOUGH TO SAY "IT IS THE SWORD ELSEWHERE,"	270 PARDON FATHERS	17
MY FANCY, AND SET MY BOYISH LIPS TO SAY,	271 GREY ROCK	10
OLD WHOLESOME GOBAN HAD NO SAY!	271 GREY ROCK V	10
THE BOW-LEGGED GOBAN HAD NO SAY:	304 HOUR DAWN	42
"SAY WHAT YOU PLEASE, BUT FROM DAYBREAK	304 HOUR DAWN V	42
"SAY WHAT YOU PLEASE, BUT FROM DAY-BREAK	304 HOUR DAWN V	51
"I'LL HAVE MY SAY, TILL I AM ABLE	305 HOUR DAWN	56
"WHY, BEER IS ONLY BEER." "BUT SAY	305 HOUR DAWN V	56
YOU'VE BUT TO DRINK THE BEER AND SAY	305 HOUR DAWN V	56
IF YOU BUT DRINK THAT BEER AND SAY	313 MEMORY YOUTH	4
AND YET FOR ALL THAT I COULD SAY,	316 COLD HEAVEN	11
OUT NAKED ON THE ROADS, AS THE BOOKS SAY, AND STRICKEN	333 LIVING BEAUTY V	1
I'LL SAY AND MAYBE DREAM I HAVE DRAWN CONTENT,	337 SCHOLARS	11
LORD, WHAT WOULD THEY SAY	338 TOM OROUGHLEY	5
OR SO DID TOM O'ROUGHLEY SAY	342 SHEP GOATHERD	79
THEY SAY THAT ON YOUR BARREN MOUNTAIN RIDGE	345 ON WOMAN	14
THEY SAY HE COUNTED GRASS.	354 HIS PHOENIX	22
THEY CAN SPREAD OUT WHAT SAIL THEY PLEASE FOR ALL I HAVE		
TO SAY,	354 HIS PHOENIX	26
AND WHO CAN SAY BUT SOME YOUNG BELLE MAY WALK AND TALK		
MEN WILD	356 BROKEN DREAMS	17
WILL SAY TO AN OLD MAN, "TELL ME OF THAT LADY	363 DOLLS FACES	2
THEY HAD A PRIEST SAY MASS, AND EVEN THE JAPANESE;	364 END OF DAY	6
WILL COME FROM THE HOUSE, AND SAY--	387 ROBARTES DANCE	52
THEY SAY SUCH DIFFERENT THINGS AT SCHOOL.	395 SIXTEEN DEAD	7
YOU SAY THAT WE SHOULD STILL THE LAND	412 TOWER	78
THERE'S NOT A NEIGHBOUR LEFT TO SAY.	430 NINETEEN 19	43
WHAT MORE IS THERE TO SAY? THAT COUNTRY ROUND	448 HERO GIRL FOOL	13
AND NEEDS NO CRUELTY. I HAVE HEARD ONE SAY	448 HERO GIRL FOOL	15
AND NOT THEMSELVES. SAY ON AND SAY	448 HERO GIRL FOOL	15
AND NOT THEMSELVES. SAY ON AND SAY	448 HERO GIRL FOOL V	13
WHAT NO DECEPTION WON. I HAVE HEARD THEM SAY	455 HIS MEMORIES	8
IN WHAT I DO OR SAY	458 SECRETS OF OLD	12
OR SAY THE THINGS WE SAY:	458 SECRETS OF OLD	12
OR SAY THE THINGS WE SAY:	459 FROM OEDIPUS	10
NEVER TO HAVE LIVED IS BEST, ANCIENT WRITERS SAY:	460 THREE MONUMENT	5
AND ALL THE POPULAR STATESMEN SAY	461 HARUN RASHID	11
AND PAUSE AT LAST, I WAS ABOUT TO SAY,	467 HARUN RASHID	136
I SAY THAT A DJINN SPOKE. A LIVELONG HOUR	467 HARUN RASHID V	136
I SAY THAT A DJIN SPOKE. A LIVE LONG HOUR	467 HARUN RASHID V	136
I SAY THAT A JINN SPOKE. A LIVE-LONG HOUR	471 ALL SOUL NIGHT	15
BECAUSE I HAVE A MARVELLOUS THING TO SAY,	478 SELF AND SOUL	38
THAT IS TO SAY, ASCENDS TO HEAVEN:		

686

```
                                                          PAGE      TITLE            LINE
SAY   (CONTINUED)
     "PRAY FOR NOTHING, SAY  . . . . . . . . . . . . .   495  MOHINI CHATTER        3
     OR, AS GREAT SAGES SAY, . . . . . . . . . . . . .   496  MOHINI CHATTER       27
     OR THINGS I DID NOT DO OR SAY . . . . . . . . . .   501  VACILLATION          52
     BUT THOUGHT THAT I MIGHT SAY OR DO, . . . . . . .   501  VACILLATION          53
     I CARE NOT WHAT THE SAILORS SAY. . . . . . . . .    509  JANE REPROVED         1
     SHE HEARS ME STRIKE THE BOARD AND SAY . . . . . .   531  FATHER CHILD          1
     SAY THAT OF LIVING MEN I HATE . . . . . . . . . .   539  MEETING              11
     SADDLE AND RIDE, I HEARD A MAN SAY, . . . . . . .   549  SEVERED HEAD          1
     IMAGES RIDE, I HEARD A MAN SAY, . . . . . . . .     549  SEVERED HEAD     V    1
     I HAVE HEARD THAT HYSTERICAL WOMEN SAY . . . . .    565  LAPIS LAZULI          1
     TO LEAD HER AWAY, DO NOT SAY  . . . . . . . . . .   568  SWEET DANCER          9
     AND THROUGH THE CHIME SHE'D SAY, . . . . . . . .    570  THREE BUSHES         30
     AND AT NIGHT TIME WOULD SHE SAY, . . . . . . . .    570  THREE BUSHES     V   30
     WHAT IS THERE LEFT TO SAY? . . . . . . . . . . .    580  CURSE CROMWELL        8
     WHAT IS THERE LEFT TO SAY? . . . . . . . . . . .    580  CURSE CROMWELL       16
     WHAT IS THERE LEFT TO SAY? . . . . . . . . . . .    581  CURSE CROMWELL       24
     WHAT IS THERE LEFT TO SAY? . . . . . . . . . . .    581  CURSE CROMWELL       32
     I SAY THAT ROGER CASEMENT . . . . . . . . . . . .   581  ROGER CASEMENT        1
     FOR HE KNOWS HOW TO SAY, . . . . . . . . . . . .    583  GHOST ROG CASE       14
     AND WHAT'S THE GOOD OF WOMEN, FOR ALL THAT THEY CAN SAY  592  PILGRIM          4
     AND THAT OLD MAN BESIDE ME, NOTHING WOULD HE SAY . . .   593  PILGRIM          9
     I SWEAR TO GOD I QUESTIONED THEM, AND ALL THEY HAD TO SAY  593  PILGRIM       14
     BUT I NEVER STOPPED TO QUESTION, WHAT COULD THE BOATMAN SAY  593  PILGRIM     19
     FOR I CAN PUT THE WHOLE LOT DOWN, AND ALL I HAVE TO SAY  593  PILGRIM         24
     I SWEAR TO GOD I QUESTIONED THEM ALL AND ALL THEY HAD TO  593  PILGRIM    V   14
       SAY
     FOR WHO CAN SAY?" HE SAID. . . . . . . . . . . .    594  COLONEL MARTIN       15
     THEY SAY IT IS MORE HUMAN . . . . . . . . . . . .   599  STONE CROSS          19
     BLESSING THE TRICOLOUR. "THIS IS NOT," I SAY, . .   601  GALLERY REVIS        10
     AND SAY MY GLORY WAS I HAD SUCH FRIENDS. . . . .    604  GALLERY REVIS        55
     AND MAYBE WHAT THEY SAY IS TRUE . . . . . . . . .   631  POLITICS              9
     SAY THAT THE MEN OF THE OLD BLACK TOWER, . . . .    635  BLACK TOWER           1
     HAVE DONE THIS PHRASING, AND SAY WHY, IN SOOTH, .   652  ISLE STAT I 2        25
     SOME SAY THAT ALL WHO TOUCH THE ISLAND LONE . . .   653  ISLE STAT I 2        42
     MY PRETTY CHILD, SINCE HE HAS GONE, OH SAY . . .    658  ISLE STAT II 1        3
     OF GRIEF. AND IF THEY SAY, "ANTONIO LAUGHED," . .   664  ISLE STAT II 2       51
     SAY THEN,--"A POPINJAY BEFORE GRIEF'S SHAFT . . .   664  ISLE STAT II 2       52
     SHE WILL SAY WITH BATED BREATH, . . . . . . . . .   680  LOVE AND DEATH       30
     THEY SAY THE WISH ITSELF IS HALF THE SIN: . . . .   692  MOSADA 1             48
     THEY SAY I AM ALL UGLINESS: LAME-FOOTED . . . . .   692  MOSADA 1             60
     SO SHE MUST BURN, YOU SAY? SHE MUST IN TRUTH. . .   696  MOSADA 2              2
     LIKE SMALL BROWN MOTHS, A-TREMBLE. "RENYI SAY . .   713  FERENCZ RENYI        82
     SAY WHAT RINGER RINGS AT MIDNIGHT: FOR, IN THE BELFRY HIGH,  718  PHANTOM SHIP  15
     THEY SAY YOU ARE A GAMBLER AND A PLAYER . . . . .   721  WITCH VIVIEN         34
     "SAY AND THRICE ANIGH THY DOOR . . . . . . . . .    730  PRIEST FAIRY         54
     TO THE EVER-LONGING AND MOURNFUL SPIRIT SAY. . .    734  QUATRAIN APHOR       12
     AND HEARS THE ROAR OF THE STREAMS WHERE, DRUIDS SAY, .   749  SHADOW WATER A   46
     SHE WILL SAY SOMETHING IN A LITTLE WHILE, . . . .   760  SHADOW WATER A      248
     WHY DID YOU SAY THAT I HAVE FOLLOWED HIM . . . .    761  SHADOW WATER A      267
     HITHER AND THITHER AND SAY AT THE HIGH NOON . . .   767  SHADOW WATER A      404
     AND ALL MEN LIE THAT SAY THAT I . . . . . . . . .   789  SINGING HEAD          3
     THEY LIE THAT SAY, IN MOCKERY . . . . . . . . . .   789  SINGING HEAD          9
     SOME NINETEEN GERMAN PLANES, THEY SAY, . . . . .    791  REPRISALS             1
SAYETH
     AND ENTER, AND NONE SAYETH "NO" . . . . . . . . .    62  OISIN 3             210
     AND ENTER, AND NONE SAYETH "NAY" . . . . . . . .     62  OISIN 3          V  210
SAYING
     SAYING ALL THINGS WERE WELL: . . . . . . . . . :    113  ROSE OF PEACE        14
     BUT YOU WERE SAYING THERE IS SOMEBODY . . . . . .   240  SHADOW WATER B      380
     YOU KNOW THE SAYING, "CHANGE THE BRIDE WITH SPRING," .  463  HARUN RASHID      50
     SAYING "EARL PAUL IS PARDONED . . . . . . . . .     741  EARL PAUL            55
SAYS
     AND "A WEARINESS SOON IS MY SPEED," SAYS THE MOUSE, . .  27  OISIN 1     V  417
     SHE SAYS MY MAN WILL SURELY COME, . . . . . . . .    96  MOLL MAGEE          41
     SHE SAYS MY HUSBAND SURE WILL COME . . . . . . .     96  MOLL MAGEE       V   41
     NOW I CAN HEAR. THERE'S ONE OF THEM THAT SAYS, .    233  SHADOW WATER B      252
     AND SAYS, "A SWORD-BLADE PIERCED ME IN MY SLEEP." .  234  SHADOW WATER B     257
     AND SAYS: "A SWORD BLADE PIERCED ME IN MY SLEEP." .  234  SHADOW WATER B V   257
     WHAT SAYS THE CLOCK IN THE GREAT CLOCK TOWER? . .   549  SEVERED HEAD          3
     WHAT SAYS THE CLOCK IN THE GREAT CLOCK TOWER? . .   550  SEVERED HEAD         10
     WHAT SAYS THE CLOCK IN THE GREAT CLOCK TOWER? . .   550  SEVERED HEAD         17
     THE PRIESTS HAVE GOT A BOOK THAT SAYS . . . . . .   621  JOHN KINSELLA        25
     HE SAYS 'TWAS HE, AND 'TWAS NO OTHER, . . . . . .   656  ISLE STAT I 3        15
     THE DARK STILL MAN, HAS COME AND SAYS 'TIS SIN. .   692  MOSADA 1             47
     TWO HOVER THERE TOGETHER, AND ONE SAYS, . . . .     753  SHADOW WATER A      142
     AND SAYS, "A SWORD-BLADE PIERCED ME IN MY SLEEP." .  753  SHADOW WATER A     147
     AND SAYS, "A SWORD BLADE PIERCED ME IN MY SLEEP." .  753  SHADOW WATER A V   147
SCABBARD
     IF YOU WILL DRAW THAT SWORD OUT OF ITS SCABBARD . .  225  SHADOW WATER B      78
     THE WOODEN SCABBARD BOUND AND WOUND, . . . . . .    477  SELF AND SOUL        15
SCAFFOLD
     JUSTIFY ALL THAT HAVE DIED ON THE SCAFFOLD, . . .   546  TO SAME TUNE 2       13
     REMEMBER ALL THAT HAVE DIED ON THE SCAFFOLD, . .    613  MARCH SONGS 1        13
SCAFFOLDING
     THERE ON THAT SCAFFOLDING RECLINES . . . . . . .    618  LONG-LEG FLY         25
SCALE
     SCALE RUBBING SCALE WHERE LIGHT IS DIM . . . . .    195  BAILE AILLINN       145
     SCALE RUBBING SCALE WHERE LIGHT IS DIM . . . . .    195  BAILE AILLINN       145
     AND FORGAEL IN THE OTHER SCALE: KILL FORGAEL, . .   225  SHADOW WATER B       76
     WHEN FORGAEL'S IN THE OTHER SCALE. I'D SAY IT . .   225  SHADOW WATER B V     75
```

687

		PAGE	TITLE		LINE

SCALE (CONTINUED)
    THOUGHT, IN THAT SCALE OF HIS! . . . .   267 FRIEND ILLNESS   2
    NOW BATHING LILY LEAF AND FISH'S SCALE, ...   464 HARUN RASHID   65
    NOW BATHING LILY LEAF AND FISHES' SCALE, ...   464 HARUN RASHID   V   65
SCALED   SEE MIRROR-SCALED
    THE MIRROR SCALED SERPENT IS MULTIPLICITY, ...   556 RIBH PATRICK   V   10
SCALES   SEE DRAGON-SCALES
    SHOWED PRINTS OF SEA-BORN SCALES, WHILE DOWN THROUGH IT   37 OISIN 2   115
    THE NETTED MARKS OF CRAWLING SCALES SEA-SPRUNG . . . .   37 OISIN 2   V   115
SCANAVIN
    HE MUSED BESIDE THE WELL OF SCANAVIN, ...   127 DREAM OF FAERY   25
SCARCE
    SCARCE WORTHY OF A HOOF GOLD-SHOD. . . . .   2 OISIN 1   V   7Y
    SCARCE LEFT A WHITENING FEATHER, GREY AND SERE! . . . .   34 OISIN 2   V   76A
    THAT SCARCE COULD BATHE A STAR, ...   88 STOLEN CHILD   31
    I SCARCE COULD DRAG MY FEET, ...   94 MOLL MAGEE   10
    THEN SEEING THAT HE SCARCE HAD SPOKE . . . .   194 BAILE AILLINN   126
    WITH SCARCE A PITYING LOOK? . . . .   315 FRIENDS   19
    WHERE MY GOATS BROWSE ON THE SCARCE GRASS OR LEAP . . .   339 SHEP GOATHERD   8
    LIFE SCARCE CAN CAST A FRAGRANCE ON THE WIND, ...   422 MY DESCENDANTS   5
    SCARCE SPREAD A GLORY TO THE MORNING BEAMS, ...   422 MY DESCENDANTS   6
    THAT NEVER KNEW THAT STRAIN WOULD SCARCE SEEM BRIGHT, . .   465 HARUN RASHID   88
    SCARCE DID HE MY BODY TOUCH, ...   535 CHOSEN   4
    SCARCE SANK HE FROM THE WEST . . . .   535 CHOSEN   5
    I SLEPT, 'TWAS SULTRY, AND SCARCE CIRCLING SHOOK . . . .   677 ISLE STAT II 3   278
    NEVER STORM AROSE SO SWIFTLY! SCARCE THE CHILDREN WERE   718 PHANTOM SHIP   4
      IN BED,
    SCARCE THE OLD AND WIZEN HOUSES HAD THEIR DOORS AND WINDOWS   718 PHANTOM SHIP   5
      SHUT.
    SCARCE THE OLD AND WIZENED HOUSES HAD THEIR DOORS   718 PHANTOM SHIP   V   5
      AND WINDOWS SHUT.
SCARCELY
    SCARCELY A FEATHER LINGERED, THEN YOU SEEMED . . . . .   102 FERGUS DRUID   4
    HAD SCARCELY ACCUSTOMED OUR EARS . . . .   341 SHEP GOATHERD   67
    HAD SCARCELY ACCUSTOMED OUR EYES . . . .   341 SHEP GOATHERD   69
    WILL SCARCELY FIND FOR HIM A BROKEN CRUST . . . .   373 PHASES OF MOON   23
    THAT WILL BE LATER, DAY IS SCARCELY DAWNING. . . . . .   699 MOSADA 3   12
SCARE
    OLD CLOTHES UPON OLD STICKS TO SCARE A BIRD. . . . . .   445 SCHOOL CHILDR   48
SCARECROW
    THERE IS A COMFORTABLE KIND OF OLD SCARECROW. . . . . .   444 SCHOOL CHILDR   32
SCARED
    SCARED OF ITS GLITTERING LIKE A METEOR STAR, ...   38 OISIN 2   V   137
    SCARED BY THE SPLASHING OF A DOZEN COWS! . . . .   419 MY HOUSE   10
    SCARED BY THE SPLASHING OF A HUNDRED COWS, ...   419 MY HOUSE   V   10
    AS TRIPS THE SCARED MOON . . . .   559 HE AND SHE   3
SCARES
    THAT SCARES WITH HIS BUSTLE THE DELICATE NIGHT, ...   28 OISIN 1   V   423B
SCARLET
    AND THE LIPS MORE SCARLET, ...   532 BEFORE WORLD   3
    A SCARLET BLOOM. WHY RAISEST THOU, PALE ONE, ...   673 ISLE STAT II 3   196
    WHERE THE ROSES IN SCARLET ARE HEAVY . . . .   707 FAIRY PEDANT   3
SCARRED
    AMONG WHIMS NOT IMPOSSIBLE, AND THOUGH SCARRED, ...   374 PHASES OF MOON   41
SCATTER
    WILL SCATTER IN RUIN THE LEAST OF OUR DAYS, ...   27 OISIN 1   V   419B
    LET THE BIRDS SCATTER, FOR THE TREE IS BROKEN, ...   250 SHADOW WATER B   584
    AND SCATTER WHEELING IN GREAT BROKEN RINGS . . . . . .   322 SWANS AT COOLE   11
    TO SCATTER THE ACACIA SPRAY . . . .   360 ALF POLLEXFEN   10
    AS THE LEAVES IN AUTUMN SCATTER. . . . .   648 ISLE STAT I 1   90
    AND AWAY IN THE WOODS WE WILL SCATTER THE DEW! . . . .   717 LOVE SONG   2
SCATTERED   SEE STORM-SCATTERED
    O'DRISCOLL SCATTERED THE CARDS . . . .   145 HOST OF AIR   37
    AND SCATTERED THE CARDS WITH A CRY, ...   145 HOST OF AIR   V   38
    AND ALL THE BIRDS ARE SCATTERED. O! O! O! O! . . . . .   241 SHADOW WATER B   395
    AND ALL THE BIRDS ARE SCATTERED--O! O! O! . . . . . .   251 SHADOW WATER B   594
    SCATTERED ON THE LEVEL GRASS . . . .   530 DELPHIC ORACLE   6
SCENE
    AS THOUGH MY SORROW WERE A SCENE . . . .   452 HUMAN DIGNITY   5
    A SCENE WELL SET AND EXCELLENT COMPANY. . . . .   489 COOLE PARK 29   16
    AND HALF IS HALF AND YET IS ALL THE SCENE! . . . . . .   500 VACILLATION   14
    WHAT MATTER FOR THE SCENE, THE SCENE ONCE GONE! . . . .   542 PARN FUNERAL 1   19
    WHAT MATTER FOR THE SCENE, THE SCENE ONCE GONE! . . . .   542 PARN FUNERAL 1   19
    YET THEY, SHOULD THE LAST SCENE BE THERE, ...   565 LAPIS LAZULI   12
    ON ALL THE TRAGIC SCENE THEY STARE. . . . .   567 LAPIS LAZULI   52
    ROUNDS A MIGHTY SCENE. . . . .   599 STONE CROSS   22
    OR FROM THE PAINTED SCENE . . . .   608 SONGS BURDEN 3   4
    BEFORE THE PAINTED SCENE. . . . .   608 SONGS BURDEN 3   17
    WHERE BEN BULBEN SETS THE SCENE. . . . .   637 BEN BULBEN   11
SCENERY
    AND CHOSEN WHAT SCENERY HAD PLEASED ME BEST." . . . . .   352 PEOPLE   21
SCENES   SEE DROP-SCENES
    AND ALL THE DROP SCENES DROP AT ONCE . . . .   566 LAPIS LAZULI   V   22
SCENT
    O SCENT OF THE BROKEN APPLES! . . . .   774 COME RIDE   14
SCENTED
    TO THE SCENTED OAKEN PRESS. . . . .   124 CATHLEEN PARA   8
    NEITHER CATALPA-TREE NOR SCENTED LIME . . . .   435 NEW FACES   2
    NEITHER CATALPA TREE NOR SCENTED LIME . . . .   435 NEW FACES   V   2
SCENTS
    THE SUMMERS FLING THEIR SCENTS? AH, SUBTILE AND SLOW, . .   675 ISLE STAT II 3   231

	PAGE	TITLE	LINE

SCEOLAN
  WITH BRAN, SCEOLAN, AND LOMAIR, ... 3 OISIN 1 — 15
  AND BRAN, SCEOLAN, AND LOMAIR, ... 11 OISIN 1 — 125
  I MUSED ON THE CHASE WITH THE FENIANS, AND BRAN, SCEOLAN,
    LOMAIR, — 47 OISIN 3 — 5
  WHEN THE FENIANS MADE FORAY AT MORNING WITH BRAN, SCEOLAN,
    LOMAIR, — 54 OISIN 3 — 104
  WHAT PLACE HAVE CAOILTE AND CONAN, AND BRAN, SCEOLAN,
    LOMAIR? — 61 OISIN 3 — 195
  I WILL GO TO CAOILTE, AND CONAN, AND BRAN, SCEOLAN, LOMAIR,
     — 63 OISIN 3 — 223

SCEPTRE
  AND ONE A SCEPTRE FLASHING OUT .... 17 OISIN 1 — 251
  AND KISSED THE SCEPTRE WITH RED LIPS, ... 18 OISIN 1 — 258
  HE HELD THAT FLASHING SCEPTRE UP. .... 18 OISIN 1 — 260
  AROUND A SCEPTRE OF ALL LIGHTS, ... 18 OISIN 1 — 254 V
  AND KISSED THE SCEPTRE WITH HOT LIPS, ... 18 OISIN 1 V 258

SCHOLAR
  OLD COUNTRY SCHOLAR, ROBERT EMMET'S FRIEND, ... 269 PARDON FATHERS — 5
  MERCHANT AND SCHOLAR WHO HAVE LEFT ME BLOOD .... 269 PARDON FATHERS — 7
  AND COUNTRY SCHOLAR, ROBERT EMMET'S FRIEND, ... 269 PARDON FATHERS V 5
  SOLDIER, SCHOLAR, HORSEMAN, HE, ... 327 ROBERT GREGORY — 70
  SOLDIER, SCHOLAR, HORSEMAN, HE, ... 327 ROBERT GREGORY — 78
  HERE, TRAVELLER, SCHOLAR, POET, TAKE YOUR STAND . 327 ROBERT GREGORY — 86
   — 489 COOLE PARK 29 — 25

SCHOLARLY
  OF ALL THAT SCHOLARLY GENERATIONS HAD HELD DEAR; .. 603 GALLERY REVIS V 37A

SCHOLARS
  THE SCHOLARS .... 337 SCHOLARS — T
  A STRING OF SCHOLARS WENT IN FEAR .... 381 SONG OF FOOL — 7
  FOR SCHOLARS AND FOR POETS AFTER US, ... 488 COOLE PARK 29 — 6

SCHOOL
  ALTHOUGH THEY DO NOT TALK OF IT AT SCHOOL-- ... 205 ADAMS CURSE — 19
  ALTHOUGH WE NEVER HEARD OF IT AT SCHOOL. ..... 205 ADAMS CURSE V 19
  THAT GRAMMAR SCHOOL OF COURTESIES .... 288 TO WEALTHY MAN — 15
  THAT TOSSED A BARE HEEL WHEN AT SCHOOL, ... 301 RUN PARADISE — 19
  YOU MAY, THAT MIRROR FOR A SCHOOL, ... 335 YOUNG BEAUTY — 7
  THE MALL AND EADES'S GRAMMAR SCHOOL, ... 360 ALF POLLEXFEN — 15
  I SEE A SCHOOL BOY WHEN I THINK OF HIM ..... 370 EGO DOMINUS V 55
  THEY SAY SUCH DIFFERENT THINGS AT SCHOOL. .... 387 ROBARTES DANCE — 52
  THIS MAN HAD KEPT A SCHOOL .... 392 EASTER 1916 — 24
  THIS MAN HAD MANAGED A SCHOOL .... 392 EASTER 1916 V 24
  NOR IS THERE SINGING SCHOOL BUT STUDYING .... 407 SAIL BYZANTIUM — 13
  AND THERE'S NO SINGING SCHOOL BUT STUDYING ... 407 SAIL BYZANTIUM V 13
  IN A LEARNED SCHOOL .... 416 TOWER — 183
  AMONG SCHOOL CHILDREN .... 443 SCHOOL CHILDR — T
  PREFERRED TO TEACH A SCHOOL .... 472 ALL SOUL NIGHT — 46
  BUT OUTGREW THAT SCHOOL, ... 506 REMORSE SPEECH — 2
  THEIR SCHOOL A CROWD, HIS MASTER SOLITUDE; ... 543 PARN FUNERAL 2 — 10
  THEIR SCHOOL THE CROWD, HIS MASTER SOLITUDE, .. 543 PARN FUNERAL 2 — 10
  THEIR SCHOOL A CROWD, HIS MASTER'S SOLITUDE; .. 543 PARN FUNERAL 2 V 10
  HIS CHOSEN COMRADES THOUGHT AT SCHOOL ..... 543 PARN FUNERAL 2 V 10
  I CAME THE FIRST TIME TO THY VILLAGE SCHOOL? .. 576 WHAT THEN — 1
   — 713 FERENCZ RENYI — 90

SCHOOLBOY
  BY THE STAMMERING SCHOOLBOY SAID, ... 65 HAPPY SHEPHERD — 15
  I SEE A SCHOOLBOY WHEN I THINK OF HIM, ... 370 EGO DOMINUS — 55

SCHOOLCHILDREN
  AMONG SCHOOLCHILDREN .... 443 SCHOOL CHILDR V T

SCHOOLING
  WHAT SCHOOLING HAD THESE FOUR? THEY WALKED THE ROADS .. 487 SEVEN SAGES — 24
  THEY HAVE SCHOOLING OF THEIR OWN, BUT I PASS THEIR
    SCHOOLING BY, — 580 CURSE CROMWELL — 13
  THEY HAVE SCHOOLING OF THEIR OWN, BUT I PASS THEIR
    SCHOOLING BY, — 580 CURSE CROMWELL — 13

SCHOOLMASTER
  ONCE HE LIVED A SCHOOLMASTER .... 381 SONG OF FOOL — 5
  SCHOOLMASTER HE, A DREAMER, FIDDLER, FIRST ... 709 FERENCZ RENYI — 11

SCHOOLMASTERS
  OF BANKERS, SCHOOLMASTERS, AND CLERGYMEN .... 205 ADAMS CURSE — 13

SCHOOLROOM
  I WALK THROUGH THE LONG SCHOOLROOM QUESTIONING; .. 443 SCHOOL CHILDR — 1

SCOFF
  I CAN SCOFF AND LOUR .... 510 JANE JUDGMENT — 8
  HOW SINFULLY THE WICKED SCOFF!" .... 725 LEGEND — 22
  SCOFF THEY AT THE MODERN EARTH-- ...... 727 LOVERS QUARREL — 38

SCOLD
  AND SCOLD FOR AN HOUR." .... 510 JANE JUDGMENT — 9
  WHILE WE SHAKE OUR HEADS AND SCOLD ..... 727 LOVERS QUARREL — 54

SCONCE
  WHEN EVERY SILVER CANDLESTICK OR SCONCE .... 410 TOWER — 26

SCOOPED
  HAD SCOOPED OUT PHARAOH'S MUMMY. I--THOUGH HEART MIGHT
    FIND RELIEF — 503 VACILLATION — 84

SCORE   SEE FOUR-SCORE
  WHEN, WEEPING SCORE BY SCORE, ... 93 FATHER OHART — 26
  WHEN, WEEPING SCORE BY SCORE, ... 93 FATHER OHART — 26
  SENT FOR HIS DRUIDS TWENTY SCORE AND TEN, ... 110 CUCHULAIN SEA V 76
  THERE'S NOTHING OF HIM LEFT BUT HALF A SCORE .. 341 SHEP GOATHERD — 56
  AND THERE'S A SCORE OF DUCHESSES, SURPASSING WOMANKIND, 353 HIS PHOENIX — 5
  AND THERE'S A SCORE OF DUCHESSES, SURPASSING WOMAN-KIND, 353 HIS PHOENIX V 5
  OR ELSE BY TOASTING HER A SCORE OF TIMES, ... 410 TOWER — 42
  GATHERED A SCORE OF HORSE AND SPENT HIS DAYS .. 420 MY HOUSE — 22

SCORE   (CONTINUED)
HIS DWINDLING SCORE AND HE SEEMED CASTAWAYS . . . . .   420 MY HOUSE   25
HIS DWINDLING SCORE AND HE SEEMED CAST-A-WAYS . . . . .   420 MY HOUSE   V   25
AND WRITERS BY THE SCORE. . . . .   582 ROGER CASEMENT   16
SO WHEN I TAKE ON HALF A SCORE . . . .   605 SONGS BURDEN 1   7
MY COUSINS BY THE SCORE. . . . .   620 JOHN KINSELLA   6
A SCORE OF YARDS OFF 'NEATH A WILLOW, SHOT. . . . . .   712 FERENCZ RENYI   65
DID I NOT FOLLOW WITH A SCORE OF SHIPS? . . . . . .   749 SHADOW WATER A   36

SCORES
AND THERE ARE--BUT NO MATTER IF THERE ARE SCORES BESIDE: 354 HIS PHOENIX   15

SCORN
WENT THE LAUGHTER OF SCORN FROM MY MOUTH . . . .   58 OISIN 3   168
WHO WAS IT PUT SO GREAT A SCORN . . . .   190 BAILE AILLINN   41
IN SCORN OF THIS AUDIENCE, ...   348 FISHERMAN   27
IF BUT IMAGINATION SCORN THE EARTH . . . .   478 SELF AND SOUL   21
OR, BY THE MOON EMBITTERED, SCORN ALOUD . . . . .   498 BYZANTIUM   21
SCORN THE SORT NOW GROWING UP . . . .   639 BEN BULBEN   70
AND WHEN YOU CAME TO SCORN OUR LITTLE WARS . . . . .   749 SHADOW WATER A V   34

SCORNIN'
AND STILL, WITH PITYIN', SCORNIN' EYE, ...   96 MOLL MAGEE   39

SCOT-FREE
TO CRAWL IN HER OWN BLOOD, AND GO SCOT-FREE: . . . . .   429 NINETEEN 19   28

SCOURGE
OUR HEARTS ENDURE THE SCOURGE, THE PLAITED THORNS, THE WAY   172 TRAV PASSION   3
THE KNOTTED SCOURGE, THE NAIL-PIERCED HANDS, THE WOUNDED   172 TRAV PASSION V   4
SIDE,

SCOURING
LIKE THE EYES OF SOME GREAT KITE SCOURING THE WOODS, . .   283 TWO KINGS   150

SCOWL
SHE CAN, THOUGH EVERY FACE SHOULD SCOWL . . . . . .   405 FOR DAUGHTER   70

SCRATCH
IS TO SCRATCH YOUR HEAD . . . .   359 TO A SQUIRREL   7

SCREAM
JABBER AND SCREAM ABOUT HIM IN THE NIGHT: . . . .   34 OISIN 2   82
JABBER AND SCREAM, YET HE, FOR ALL HIS BOLD . . . .   34 OISIN 2   V   82
OF MY LONG SPEAR, WITH SCREAM AND LAUGH. . . . .   84 MAD KING GOLL   V   34
AND THEREUPON THERE COMES THAT SCREAM . . . . .   389 IMAGE PAST   5
AND HEARD THE SEA-WIND SCREAM UPON THE TOWER, . . .   403 FOR DAUGHTER   10
AND UNDER THE ARCHES OF THE BRIDGE, AND SCREAM . . .   403 FOR DAUGHTER   11
THE DAWS CHATTER AND SCREAM, ...   415 TOWER   167
AS THOUGH TO STRANGLE HER, NO SCREAM . . . . . .   514 JANE GROWN OLD   4
CLIMB ON A WAGONETTE TO SCREAM. . . . .   626 OLD MEN BE MAD   8
NOW A SCREAM FROM ALL THOSE FISHERS, FOR THERE ON DECK   719 PHANTOM SHIP   19
THERE BE

SCREAMED
ABOUT THEM: AND THE HORSE OF FAERY SCREAMED . . . . .   30 OISIN 2   24
HE SHIVERING PAUSED, AND RAISED HIS HEAD AND SCREAMED. .   30 OISIN 2   V   25
A SQUIRREL WHINNIED AND A BIRD SCREAMED OUT: . . . .   278 TWO KINGS   34
JUNO'S PEACOCK SCREAMED. . . . .   422 MY TABLE   32

SCREAMS   SEE OUT-SCREAMS

SCREEN
I ROSE THAT I MIGHT SCREEN IT WITH A CLOTH. . . . .   467 HARUN RASHID   131
AS THOUGH UPON A LIGHTED SCREEN, ...   626 OLD MEN BE MAD   12
NOW A NOTABLE MAN ON STAGE AND ON SCREEN: . . . .   790 DEDICATION   8

SCRIPTURE
THE LION AND THE HONEYCOMB, WHAT HAS SCRIPTURE SAID? . .   503 VACILLATION   88
THE LION AND THE HONEY-COMB, WHAT HAS SCRIPTURE SAID? . . 503 VACILLATION V   88

SCRUB
AND THEN I MUST SCRUB AND BAKE AND SWEEP . . . . .   150 OLD MOTHER   3
AND SCRUB A KITCHEN PAVEMENT, OR BREAK STONES . . . .   204 ADAMS CURSE   8
I SCRUB ITS FLOORS AND MAKE MY BED, ...   607 SONGS BURDEN 2   5

SCULLION
THE SCULLION GONE WILD." . . . .   349 HAWK   6

SCULPTOR
POET AND SCULPTOR, DO THE WORK, ...   638 BEN BULBEN   37

SCYTHE
I DO NOT NEED YOUR SCYTHE. MAY THAT BRING PEACE . . . .   721 WITCH VIVIEN   26

SEA   SEE HUMMING-SEA OVER-SEA
AND FOUND ON THE DOVE-GREY EDGE OF THE SEA . . . .   3 OISIN 1   19
THY WANDERING STEPS ACROSS THE SEA? . . . .   5 OISIN 1   V   51
ACROSS THE GLOSSY SEA." "OH, WILD . . . .   6 OISIN 1   V   58
OVER THE GLOSSY SEA." "O, WILD . . . .   6 OISIN 1   V   58
TO MY OWN KINGDOM IN THE SEA-- . . . .   8 OISIN 1   V   80A
WHOSE LONG WOOL WHITER THAN SEA FROTH FLOWS, ...   8 OISIN 1   V   90
AND STOOD BESIDE THE SEA TOGETHER: . . . .   9 OISIN 1   V   101B
WE RODE ACROSS THE OILY SEA, ...   10 OISIN 1   V   114
WE GALLOPED OVER THE GLOSSY SEA: . . . .   11 OISIN 1   132
ON, ON, WE GALLOPED O'ER THE SEA. . . . .   11 OISIN 1   V   132
NOW IN THE SEA THE SUN'S RIM SANK, ...   12 OISIN 1   V   153
WAS NOT MORE LEVEL THAN THE SEA, ...   13 OISIN 1   157
ROSE EVER OUT OF THE WARM SEA: . . . .   13 OISIN 1   172
AND LAUGHED LIKE MURMURS OF THE SEA: . . . . . .   15 OISIN 1   210
AMONG THE FOAMDROPS OF THE SEA, ...   20 OISIN 1   294
BESIDE THE SEA, WHERE, HUSHED AND SLOW, ...   20 OISIN 1   V   292
WHISPERED TO THE SEA WHOSE FLOW . . . .   20 OISIN 1   V   298
THE EVER-WINDING WAKEFUL SEA, ...   22 OISIN 1   V   338
OVER THE GLIMMERING PURPLE SEA, ...   25 OISIN 1   384
AND OTHERS SAT THEM BY THE SEA, ...   25 OISIN 1   V   390
WAS SLUMBERING HALF IN THE SEA WAYS: . . . . . .   26 OISIN 1   V   395
WHEN GOD SHALL COME FROM THE SEA WITH A SIGH . . . .   28 OISIN 1   425
ON HORSE AND SEA AND SADDLE SHONE. . . . .   28 OISIN 1   V   427D

SEA   (CONTINUED)   PAGE   TITLE   LINE

THAT HAS DRUNK FULL, SHE CROSSED THE MISTY SEA . . . .   30 OISIN 2   16
I LAY, AS OVER SEA THE LIGHT HOOVES GLANCED . . . . .   30 OISIN 2   V 19A
AND BLACKNESS IN THE DARK. THE SEA ROLLED ROUND, . . .   30 OISIN 2   V   23
HALF IN THE UNVESSELLED SEA, WE CLIMBED THE STAIR . . .   32 OISIN 2   47
HALF IN THE UNVESSELLED SEA. WE'D MOUNTED FAR, ...   32 OISIN 2   V   47
HALF IN THE UNVESSELLED SEA, WE CLIMBED THE STAIRS . .   32 OISIN 2   V   47
FLUTTER ALONG THE FROTH LIPS OF THE SEA, ...   33 OISIN 2   58
FLUTTER ALONG THE FROTH LIPS OF THE SEA . . . .   33 OISIN 2   64
FLUTTER ALONG THE FROTH-LIPS OF THE SEA, ...   33 OISIN 2   V   58
OH MAIDEN." "ARE YE SPIRITS OF THE SEA, ...   34 OISIN 2   V 78B
THAT SEA GOD'S NAME, WHO IN A DEEP CONTENT . . . . . .   38 OISIN 2   V 129
THEN IN THAT HALL, LIT BY THE DIM SEA SHINE, ...   41 OISIN 2   V 187
BREWED BY THE SEA GODS, FROM HUGE CUPS THAT LAY . . . .   41 OISIN 2   V 189
I FOUND, DROPPING SEA FOAM ON THE WIDE STAIR, ...   43 OISIN 2   V 215
INTO THE CLANGOUR OF THE WIND AND SEA. . . . .   45 OISIN 2   234
SURLY AND DISTANT, WITH THE WINDS AND SEA:-- . . . . .   45 OISIN 2   V 234
GATHER SEA SLIME AND FALL THE SEAWARD WAY. . . . . . .   45 OISIN 2   V 237
COMING OUT OF THE SEA AS THE DAWN COMES, A CHAUNT OF LOVE   58 OISIN 3   158
   ON MY LIPS,
COMING FORTH FROM THE SEA LIKE THE MORNING . . . . . .   58 OISIN 3   V 158
GO GATHER BY THE HUMMING SEA . . . .   66 HAPPY SHEPHERD   35
CRIED OUT, DIM SEA, HEAR MY MOST PITEOUS STORY! . . . .   68 SAD SHEPHERD   9
THE SEA SWEPT ON AND CRIED HER OLD CRY STILL, ...   68 SAD SHEPHERD   10
"OH SEA, OLD SEA, HEAR THOU MY PITEOUS STORY!" . . . .   68 SAD SHEPHERD   9
"OH SEA, OLD SEA, HEAR THOU MY PITEOUS STORY!" . . . .   68 SAD SHEPHERD   V   9
WHO STILL WERE OLD WHEN THE GREAT SEA WAS YOUNG; . . .   74 ANASHU VIJAYA   69
RAGING AT HIS OWN IMAGE IN THE ENAMELLED SEA. . . . . .   77 INDIAN TO LOVE   5
RAGES AT HIS OWN IMAGE IN THE ENAMELLED SEA . . . . .   77 INDIAN TO LOVE   5
RAGING AT HIS OWN IMAGE IN THE DIM ENAMELLED SEA . . .   77 INDIAN TO LOVE V   5
WHIPS TO THE SEA THE COWS AND SWINE." . . . .   82 MAD KING GOLL V   16
AND I MUST WAIL BESIDE THE SEA . . . .   86 MAD KING GOLL V   67
I MUST AWAY BY WOOD AND SEA . . . .   86 MAD KING GOLL   67
IN DANCING SILVER-SANDALLED ON THE SEA, ...   101 ROSE UPON ROOD   7
IN DANCING SILVER SANDALLED ON THE SEA, ...   101 ROSE UPON ROOD V   7
IN THE WHITE BORDER OF THE MURMURING SEA; . . . . . .   103 FERGUS DRUID   19
CUCHULAIN'S FIGHT WITH THE SEA . . . .   105 CUCHULAIN SEA   T
GO DWELL UPON THE SEA CLIFFS, VAPOUR HID, ...   105 CUCHULAIN SEA V   4
GO DWELL UPON THE SEA CLIFFS, VAPOUR-HID, ...   105 CUCHULAIN SEA V   4
AND LOVELIER THAN THE MOON UPON THE SEA; . . . . . .   106 CUCHULAIN SEA V   16A
BETWEEN WOOD'S RIM AND THE HORSES OF THE SEA. . . . .   108 CUCHULAIN SEA   34
BETWEEN THE GAME AND THE HORSES OF THE SEA. . . . . .   108 CUCHULAIN SEA V   34
THAT HE MAY FIGHT THE HORSES OF THE SEA." . . . . . .   111 CUCHULAIN SEA   81
STARED ON THE HORSES OF THE SEA, AND HEARD . . . . .   111 CUCHULAIN SEA   84
THAT HE MAY FIGHT THE WAVES OF THE LOUD SEA." . . . .   111 CUCHULAIN SEA   81
THAT HE MIGHT FIGHT THE WAVES OF THE LOUD SEA." . . .   111 CUCHULAIN SEA V   81
MADE YOU OF US, AND OF THE DIM GREY SEA. . . . .   115 ROSE OF BATTLE   30
I WOULD THAT WE WERE, MY BELOVED, WHITE BIRDS ON THE FOAM   121 WHITE BIRDS   1
   OF THE SEA!
O WOULD THAT WE WERE, MY BELOVED, WHITE BIRDS ON THE FOAM   121 WHITE BIRDS   V   1
   OF THE SEA,
. . . BUOYED OUT ON THE FOAM OF THE SEA! . . . . . .   122 WHITE BIRDS   12
AND THE WHITE BREAST OF THE DIM SEA . . . .   126 GOES FERGUS   11
DESOLATE WINDS THAT CRY OVER THE WANDERING SEA! . . .   147 UNAPPEAS HOST   7
LIKE THE PALE CUP OF THE SEA, ...   175 ELEMENT POWERS   14
AS THE LIGHT ON THE SEA, ...   175 ELEMENT POWERS V   14
FOLK DANCE LIKE A WAVE OF THE SEA! . . . .   178 FIDDLER DOONEY   2
AND DANCE LIKE A WAVE OF THE SEA. . . . .   179 FIDDLER DOONEY   20
AND DRAGS HIM THROUGH THE SEA. WELL, NET OR NONE, . .   224 SHADOW WATER B   57
WHAT RICHES CAN YOU FIND IN THIS WASTE SEA . . . . .   226 SHADOW WATER B   97
WRUNG FROM THE COLD WOMEN OF THE SEA-- . . . .   237 SHADOW WATER B   343
FOR YOU ARE LOOKING AT THE SEA. DO YOU NOT KNOW . .   246 SHADOW WATER B   513
WHY ARE YOU LOOKING AT THE SEA? LOOK THERE! . . . .   246 SHADOW WATER B   516
THE ROPE'S IN TWO--IT FALLS INTO THE SEA, ...   251 SHADOW WATER B   596
CRYING AMID THE GLITTERING SEA, ...   254 HIS DREAM   17
WITH THE LOUD HOST BEFORE THE SEA, ...   276 GREY ROCK   128
WHITER THAN CURDS, ITS EYES THE TINT OF THE SEA. . .   277 TWO KINGS   7
TO DRINK OF THAT SALT BREATH OUT OF THE SEA . . . . .   292 TO A SHADE   5
BY A COLD AND DESOLATE SEA, ...   298 THREE HERMITS   2
AND FIND MY HEALTH AGAIN IN THE SEA AIR," . . . . .   299 BEGGAR CRIED   2
SEA NYMPHS IN THEIR PEARLY WAGGONS, ...   309 REALISTS   V   5
AND DIED IN THE GREAT WAR BEYOND THE SEA. . . . . . .   339 SHEP GOATHERD   22
A VISIONARY WHITE SEA BIRD . . . .   361 ALF POLLEXFEN V   37
MANACLE HIS SOUL UPON THE RED SEA BOTTOM. . . . . . .   372 ON GOING HOUSE   16
ACROSS THE BITTER SEA." . . . .   396 ROSE TREE   6
CRIED OUT THE HOLLOWS OF THE SEA. . . . .   397 POLIT PRISONER   24
OR BY THE MAREOTIC SEA . . . .   401 DEMON BEAST   45
OUT OF THE MURDEROUS INNOCENCE OF THE SEA. . . . . .   403 FOR DAUGHTER   16
OF HORSES AND HORSES OF THE SEA, WHITE HORSES. . . .   447 COLONUS PRAISE   32
SHAKESPEAREAN FISH SWAM THE SEA, FAR AWAY FROM LAND!   485 THREE MOVEMENT   1
THAT DOLPHIN-TORN, THAT GONG-TORMENTED SEA. . . . . .   498 BYZANTIUM   40
AND NOW WE STARE ASTONISHED AT THE SEA, ...   534 HER TRIUMPH   11
BUT SANG, "O SEA-STARVED, HUNGRY SEA." . . . .   578 CRAZED GIRL   14
"O SEA--STARVED, HUNGRY SEA." . . . .   578 CRAZED GIRL   V   14
"O SEA--STARVED, HUNGRY SEA." . . . .   578 CRAZED GIRL   V   14
IT NEVER CROSSED THE SEA BECAUSE . . . .   583 GHOST ROG CASE   3
JOHN BULL AND THE SEA ARE FRIENDS; . . . .   583 GHOST ROG CASE   4
BUT THIS IS NOT THE OLD SEA . . . .   583 GHOST ROG CASE   5
SMILING AT THE SEA, ...   605 YOU CONTENT   20
CUCHULAIN FOUGHT THE UNGOVERNABLE SEA! . . . .   630 CIRCUS ANIMALS   26
THE WOOD AND THE VALLEY AND SEA . . . .   646 ISLE STAT ! 1   42

691

		PAGE	TITLE		LINE

SEA   (CONTINUED)
AND THE DESOLATE SHUDDERING SEA. . . . . 648 ISLE STAT I 1   85
THE SPINNING STARS--THE TOILING SEA--WHIRL ROUND . . . 665 ISLE STAT II 2   72
TILL THOU REMEMBEREST ONLY HOW THE SEA . . . . 670 ISLE STAT II 3   94
FAR FLEETER THAN THE MILLION-FOOTED SEA. . . . . . . 670 ISLE STAT II 3   108
HAS ROLLED AWAY THE STARS AND DRIED THE SEA . . . . . 671 ISLE STAT II 3   146
ABOUT THE SEA. BEFORE HER LIES THAT YOUTH, ... 687 TWO TITANS   22
MAKING ALL ONE O'ER ROCK AND SEA AND SKIES, ... 687 TWO TITANS   28
IN CREVICED ROCKS, AND LAUGHED IN THE OLD SEA, ... 688 TWO TITANS   34
ALONG THE SEA, AND MANY A MAN GREW HUSHED . . . . . . 693 MOSADA 1   86
AYE AND SHAKES IN SEA GREEN WAVERINGS, ALONG THE FISHERS' 718 PHANTOM SHIP V   2
   STREET.
ALL THE DROWNED THAT EVER WERE DROWNED FROM THAT VILLAGE 719 PHANTOM SHIP   20
   BY THE SEA.
ROLLS ALONG THE SEA SANDS WHITE. . . . . 732 STREET DANCERS   34
ON THE CLIFF BY THE SEA, ... 739 EARL PAUL   4
THEY ARE CHANGED AND AS GREY BIRDS FLY OUT TO SEA, . . . 750 SHADOW WATER A   82
LEANS ON HIS ELBOWS, GAZING AT THE SEA. . . . . 752 SHADOW WATER A   127
LET THE SEA BEAR WITNESS. . . . . 770 BLOOD BOND   7
SEA-BIRD
A VISIONARY WHITE SEA-BIRD . . . . 361 ALF POLLEXFEN   37
FRAIL BIRD, LIKE A WHITE SEA-BIRD ALONE . . . . 784 WOMANS BEAUTY   2
SEA-BORN
SHOWED PRINTS OF SEA-BORN SCALES, WHILE DOWN THROUGH IT   37 OISIN 2   115
SEA-BORNE
LIKE ANY ROCK-BRED, SEA-BORNE BIRD; . . . . 397 POLIT PRISONER   18
SEA-BORNE, OR BALANCED ON THE AIR . . . . 397 POLIT PRISONER   19
SEA-COVERED
THE MOIL OF MY CENTURIES FILLED ME; AND GONE LIKE   51 OISIN 3   70
   A SEA-COVERED STONE
SEA-DASHED
AND SUNKEN SHAPE, A NINE DAYS' CORPSE SEA-DASHED-- . . . 40 OISIN 2   V 179
SEAFARER
SEAFARER, WAKE! WAS MY SLEEP LONG? LONG YEARS. . . . . 678 ISLE STAT II 3   292
SEAFARERS
HE DOES NOT HATE SEAFARERS AS HE HATES . . . . 224 SHADOW WATER B   53
SEA-FOAM
I FOUND, DROPPING SEA-FOAM ON THE WIDE STAIR, ... 43 OISIN 2   215
SEA-FROTH
WHOSE LONG WOOL WHITER THAN SEA-FROTH FLOWS, ...   8 OISIN 1   90
SEAGHAN
HOW ARE WE BETTER OFF THAN SEAGHAN THE FOOL, ... 228 SHADOW WATER B   129
WE HAVE BEEN NO BETTER OFF THAN SEAGHAN THE FOOL, . . . 228 SHADOW WATER B V 129
SEA-GOD
SEA-GOD, THAT ONCE, TO GIVE HIS SLAVES CONTENT, ... 38 OISIN 2   V 129
SEA-GOD'S
THAT SEA-GOD'S NAME, WHO IN A DEEP CONTENT . . . . . . 38 OISIN 2   129
SEA-GODS
BY MACE AND SPEAR AND SWORD OF SEA-GODS, NAILS . . . . . 31 OISIN 2   V 30A
BREWED BY THE SEA-GODS, FROM HUGE CUPS THAT LAY . . . . 41 OISIN 2   189
UPON THE LIPS OF SEA-GODS IN THEIR DAY; . . . . 41 OISIN 2   190
BREWED OF THE SEA-GODS, FROM HUGE CUPS THAT LAY . . . . 41 OISIN 2   V 189
SEA-GREEN
AND STARED INTO THE SEA-GREEN EYE, AND SO . . . . . . 278 TWO KINGS   25
AND STARED INTO THE SEA-GREEN EYES, AND SO . . . . . . 278 TWO KINGS   V 25
WITH OLD MILL BOARDS AND SEA-GREEN SLATES, ... 406 CARVED STONE   2
AY, AND SHAKES IN SEA-GREEN WAVERINGS ALONG THE FISHERS' 718 PHANTOM SHIP   2
   STREET;
SEAGULL
I SAW A FOAM-WHITE SEAGULL DRIFT AND FLOAT . . . . . . 36 OISIN 2   105
CLOTHING HIM ROUND, I SAW A SEAGULL FLOAT . . . . . . 36 OISIN 2   V 105
SEA-HORSES
THOSE GREAT SEA-HORSES BARE THEIR TEETH AND LAUGH AT THE 623 HIGH TALK   14
   DAWN.
SEA-KING
HATH COME A SEA-KING MASTERFUL, ... 82 MAD KING GOLL V 15
SOUTHWARD A SEA-KING MASTERFUL . . . . 82 MAD KING GOLL V 15
COMES A SEA-KING MASTERFUL . . . . 82 MAD KING GOLL V 15
SEAL
THAT WAXEN SEAL, THAT SIGNATURE, ... 598 MODEL LAUREATE   21
LEST ON THINE HEART THE STONY SEAL . . . . 667 ISLE STAT II 3   41
SEALED
ABOVE THESE MEN WHOSE MOUTHS WERE SEALED . . . . . . 656 ISLE STAT I 3   27
BE ONE? I THINK ALL'S FINISHED NOW AND SEALED. . . . . 701 MOSADA 3   62
SEALING
WITH DEW, AS THOUGH 'TWERE SEALING THEM FOR DEATH. . . . 691 MOSADA 1   22
SEAMAN
MANY A LANDSMAN, MANY A SEAMAN. . . . . 82 MAD KING GOLL V   4
THESE HANDS SLEW MANY A SEAMAN BOLD. . . . . 83 MAD KING GOLL V 23
SEAMEN
MOVED ROUND ME, OF SEAMEN OR LANDSMEN, ALL WHO ARE WINTER 53 OISIN 3   86
   TALES;
THE HEARTS OF THE WORLD-TROUBLING SEAMEN, ... 82 MAD KING GOLL   4
SEAMEW
"I HEARD A SEAMEW CRY, ... 308 PLAYER QUEEN V 14
SEA-MEW
"I HEARD A SEA-MEW CRY, ... 308 PLAYER QUEEN   14
SEAMLESS
WATCHED HER THOSE SEAMLESS FACES FROM THE VALLEY'S   55 OISIN 3   122
   GLIMMERING GIRTH;

		PAGE	TITLE		LINE
SEAMLESS (CONTINUED)					
WATCHED HER THOSE SEAMLESS FACES FROM THE VALLEY'S MURAL GIRTH		55	OISIN 3	V	122
SEA-NYMPHS					
SEA-NYMPHS IN THEIR PEARLY WAGONS • • • • • • • •		309	REALISTS		5
SEARCH					
YONDER'S THE ISLE IN SEARCH WHEREOF WE CAME: • • • •		662	ISLE STAT II 2		13
REMEMBERING THEE, I SEARCH OUT THESE FAINT FLOWERS • • •		704	REMEMBRANCE		1
SEARCHED					
SEARCHED THE UNSEARCHABLE--WHY GOOD MEN WEEP: • • • •		710	FERENCZ RENYI		32
SEA-RIDER					
FIRST THAT SEA-RIDER OISIN LED BY THE NOSE • • • • • •		629	CIRCUS ANIMALS		10
SEA-ROTTED					
WITH CHAIN SEA-ROTTED, ROUND HER MIDDLE TIED, • • • • •		34	OISIN 2	V	75
SEA'S					
ROSE EVER FROM THE SEA'S WARM FLOOR, • • • • • • • •		13	OISIN 1	V	172
THE FLOWERS STILL GREW THERE: FAR ON THE SEA'S WASTE • •		39	OISIN 2		163
THE FLOWERS STILL GREW THERE. MOVED BEYOND HIM THE SEA'S WASTE:		39	OISIN 2	V	163
AND WE STOOD ON A SEA'S EDGE WE SAW NOT: • • • • • •		47	OISIN 3		11
AND WE RODE ON THE PLAINS OF THE SEA'S EDGE: • • • • •		48	OISIN 3		13
• • • THE SEA'S EDGE BARREN AND GREY, • • • • • • •		48	OISIN 3		13
• • • THE SOUND OF THE SEA'S VAGUE DRUM? • • • • • •		48	OISIN 3		13
AND I RODE BY THE PLAINS OF THE SEA'S EDGE, • • • • •		56	OISIN 3		135
AND THE WINDS MADE THE SANDS ON THE SEA'S EDGE • • • •		56	OISIN 3		141
I TURNED AND RODE TO THE WESTWARD, AND FOLLOWED THE SEA'S OLD SHOUT		57	OISIN 3		145
AND RODE ON TILL OVER THE WORLD'S RIM FLOATED THE SEA'S OLD SHOUT,		60	OISIN 3		183
MORE FLEETING THAN THE SEA'S FOAM-FICKLE FACE, • • • •		60	OISIN 3	V	183
MORE FLEETING THAN THE SEA'S FOAM FICKLE FACE, • • • •		112	ROSE OF WORLD	V	8
OR COMES IN LAUGHTER FROM THE SEA'S SAD LIPS, • • • •		112	ROSE OF WORLD	V	8
THAT ROAR IN THE SEA'S ROAR? • • • • • • • • • •		114	ROSE OF BATTLE		19
AS THE SEA'S FURROWS ON A SEA-TOST SHELL, • • • • • •		583	GHOST ROG CASE		8
IN THE SOUTH SEA'S AZURE MILES, • • • • • • • •		660	ISLE STAT II 1		51
SEAS		732	STREET DANCERS		28
AND BIRDS THAT ON THE SEVEN SEAS RANGE. • • • • • • •		4	OISIN 1	V	27A
AND THE GENTLE WAVES OF THE SUMMER SEAS; • • • • • •		27	OISIN 1		418
FOR HE IS STRONG AND CRAFTY AS THE SEAS • • • • • •		35	OISIN 2		83
OUT OF THE SEVENFOLD SEAS, BUILT THE DARK HALL • • • •		38	OISIN 2		131
FROM THE WHOLE SEVEN SEAS, THOSE TOWERS SET • • • • •		38	OISIN 2	V	131
OUT OF THE SEVEN-FOLD SEAS, BUILT THE DARK HALL • • • •		38	OISIN 2	V	131
LIKE AN ARMY OF OLD MEN LONGING FOR REST FROM THE MOAN OF THE SEAS.		48	OISIN 3		16
• • • WHEN THE SEVENFOLD SEAS WERE YOUNG. • • • • •		50	OISIN 3		52
• • • AND PACING THE SHORES OF THE WANDERING SEAS, • •		50	OISIN 3		55
• • • WHEN THE SEVEN-FOLD SEAS WERE YOUNG: • • • • •		50	OISIN 3	V	52
• • • AND PACING THE SHORES OF THE SEVEN SEAS, • • • •		50	OISIN 3	V	55
NO MORE TO CRAWL ON THE SEAS WITH LONG OARS MILE AFTER MILE.		55	OISIN 3		119
"IN THE ISLES OF THE FARTHEST SEAS WHERE ONLY THE SPIRITS COME.		56	OISIN 3		133
LIKE AN ARMY OF OLD MEN LONGING FOR REST FROM THE MOAN OF THE SEAS.		57	OISIN 3		144
LIKE AN ARMY OF OLD MEN LOUNGING FOR REST FROM THE FOAM OF THE SEAS.		57	OISIN 3		144
O SWIFT ON THE SEAS ALL DAY AND NIGHT • • •		70	CLOAK BOAT		8
WHERE PEOPLE LOVE BESIDE THE RAVELLED SEAS: • • • •		126	DREAM OF FAERY		9
WHERE PEOPLE LOVE BESIDE STAR-LADEN SEAS: • • • • •		126	DREAM OF FAERY	V	9
AH, EXILES WANDERING OVER LANDS AND SEAS, • • • • •		129	BOOK STORIES		9
AH, EXILES, WANDERING OVER MANY SEAS, • • • • • •		129	BOOK STORIES	V	9
FOR THE GREY WINDS ARE BLOWING UP, OUT OF THE CLINGING SEAS!		207	HANRAHANS SONG	V	12
HAS HE NOT LED US INTO THESE WASTE SEAS • • • • •		221	SHADOW WATER B		1
AND BRING US INTO POPULOUS SEAS AGAIN? • • • • • •		225	SHADOW WATER B		74
IF HE HAD BROUGHT US AMONG PEOPLED SEAS, • • • • •		225	SHADOW WATER B	V	68C
THAT WEIGH AND MEASURE ALL IN THESE WASTE SEAS-- • •		235	SHADOW WATER B		292
AS NOW. DOES WANDERING IN THESE DESOLATE SEAS • • •		236	SHADOW WATER B		314
IS SHAKEN IN THESE SEAS, AND WHAT ONE DOES • • • •		237	SHADOW WATER B		339
WHAT MORE HAVE YOU TO LOOK FOR ON THE SEAS? • • • •		248	SHADOW WATER B		543
THAT TURNS AND CHANGES LIKE HIS DRAUGHTY SEAS? • • •		265	ABBEY THEATRE		12
AND THOUGH THEY HAVE TO CROSS THE LOUGHLAN SEAS • • •		282	TWO KINGS	V	113
QUIET LANDS OR UNQUIET SEAS • • • • • • • • •		360	ALF POLLEXFEN		19
THAT HAVE THE FRENZY OF OUR WESTERN SEAS. • • • • •		384	VISION ROBART		62
THE SALMON-FALLS, THE MACKEREL-CROWDED SEAS; • • • •		407	SAIL BYZANTIUM		4
THE SALMON FALLS, THE MACKEREL-CROWDED SEAS; • • • •		407	SAIL BYZANTIUM	V	4
AND THEREFORE I HAVE SAILED THE SEAS AND COME • • • •		408	SAIL BYZANTIUM		15
AND THEREFORE HAVE I SAILED THE SEAS AND COME • • • •		408	SAIL BYZANTIUM	V	15
TILL THE DAWN BREAK UPON THOSE MINGLED SEAS. • • • •		494	AT ALGECIRAS		6
BUFFETED BY SUCH SEAS!		530	DELPHIC ORACLE		2
O SWIFT ON THE SEAS ALL DAY AND NIGHT • • • •		666	ISLE STAT II 3		8
WHERE SPICE-ISLES NESTLE ON THE STAR-TROD SEAS, • • •		682	SEEKER		17
FROM WASTE SEAS CROSS'D, YET EVER GARRULOUS) • • • •		690	MOSADA 1		9
HER SOUL FROM SEAS OF ENDLESS FLAME IN HELL. • • • •		698	MOSADA 2		47
WHERE A SHELL THE SEAS ANOINT, • • • • •		732	STREET DANCERS		32
AND PRAISED YOUR WAR AMONG THE ENDLESS SEAS, • • • •		749	SHADOW WATER A		35
AND PRAISE A WAR AMONG THE ENDLESS SEAS, • • • • •		749	SHADOW WATER A	V	35
A GALLEY FROM THE LOCHLANN SEAS: HER FLAG • • • •		751	SHADOW WATER A		98
SEAS!					
IN THE SOUTH SEAS' AZURE MILES, • • • • • • • • •		732	STREET DANCERS	V	28

693

                                                        PAGE   TITLE   LINE

SEA-SANDS
    ROLLS ALONG THE SEA-SANDS WHITE.   732 STREET DANCERS   V   34
SEA-SHELL
    FOR BROOCH 'TWAS BOUND WITH A BRIGHT SEA-SHELL,   4 OISIN 1   V   28
    AS IF SOME MARVELLOUS EMPTY SEA-SHELL FLUNG   417 ANCEST HOUSES   13
SEA-SHELLS
    OR SAD SEA-SHELLS WHERE LITTLE ECHOES SIT?   650 ISLE STAT I 1   149
SEASHINE
    THE SEASHINE ON OUR FACES, WE OUR WAY   41 OISIN 2   V 184B
SEA-SHINE
    THEN IN THAT HALL, LIT BY THE DIM SEA-SHINE,   41 OISIN 2   187
SEASHORE
    NOR THIS THE OLD SEASHORE.   583 GHOST ROG CASE   6
    GIRLS DOWN ON THE SEASHORE   588 OLD WICKED MAN   30
SEA-SLIME
    GATHER SEA-SLIME AND FALL THE SEAWARD WAY,   45 OISIN 2   237
    GATHERS SEA-SLIME AND GOES THE SEAWARD WAY,   45 OISIN 2   V   237
SEASON
    LET US PART, ERE THE SEASON OF PASSION FORGET US,   79 FALLING LEAVES   7
    I COULD WEEP THAT THE OLD IS OUT OF SEASON.   199 ARROW   8
    VANISHED, AND LEFT BUT MEMORIES, THAT SHOULD BE OUT OF 316 COLD HEAVEN   5
      SEASON
    "AND YET THE JASMINE SEASON WARMS OUR BLOOD."   464 HARUN RASHID   73
    AS THOUGH THEIR SEASON HAD NO DATE,   736 SUMMER EVENING   10
SEASONS
    OH, PATRICK, THERE A HUNDRED SEASONS   23 OISIN 1   V 345B
    A HUNDRED SEASONS, FOR A SOUND OF TEARS   30 OISIN 2   V   18
    THEY NEVER SAW HOW SEASONS RUN,   432 NINETEEN 19   101
    YOU THINK THAT LOVE HAS SEASONS, AND YOU THINK   464 HARUN RASHID   75
    HAVE I NOT SEEN A THOUSAND SEASONS EBB AND FLOW   675 ISLE STAT II 3   229
SEA-SPRUNG
    OF SEA-SPRUNG PEARL, AND QUEENS OF FAIRY LANDS   29 OISIN 2   V   10A
    THE NETTED MARKS OF CRAWLING SCALES SEA-SPRUNG   37 OISIN 2   V   115
SEA-STARVED
    BUT SANG, "O SEA-STARVED, HUNGRY SEA."   578 CRAZED GIRL   14
SEA-STREWN
    AND HOW, WHEN FADES THE SEA-STREWN ROSE OF DAY,   128 DREAM OF FAERY   V   33
SEAT
    DESERTED ON A DOORWAY SEAT,   85 MAD KING GOLL   56
    DESERTED IN A DOORWAY SEAT,   85 MAD KING GOLL   V   56
    WEARY AND KIND ONE LINGERED BY HIS SEAT!   112 ROSE OF WORLD   13
    WEARY AND KIND ONE STOOD BESIDE HIS SEAT!   112 ROSE OF WORLD   V   13
    THE HILL SEAT OF LAIGHEN, BECAUSE   194 BAILE AILLINN   130
    ALWAYS IN HIS ONE SEAT, AND BID ME CARE HIM   280 TWO KINGS   80
    THE CRAVEN MAN IN HIS SEAT,   347 FISHERMAN   15
    IN DAMASK CLOTHED AND ON A SEAT   440 WISDOM   9
    IN THE LONG GRASS—FOUR EYES DROOP LOW—A SEAT   716 DWELT SYCAMORE   11
SEATED
    A BEAUTIFUL SEATED BOY! A SACRED BOW!   541 PARN FUNERAL 1   10
    DELIGHT TO IMAGINE THEM SEATED THERE!   567 LAPIS LAZULI   50
    AUGUSTA GREGORY SEATED AT HER GREAT ORMOLU TABLE,   577 LOFTY THINGS   7
    COME HERE. BE SEATED NOW! I'D BUY OF YOU.   720 WITCH VIVIEN   17
SEA-TOST
    AS THE SEA'S FURROWS ON A SEA-TOST SHELL,   660 ISLE STAT II 1   51
SEATS
    TO BUILD THE CIRCLING SEATS, WHERE HIGH IN AIR   699 MOSADA 3   18
    BEFORE WE TAKE OUR SEATS ABOVE THE CROWD.   704 MOSADA 3   134
SEAWARD
    GATHER SEA-SLIME AND FALL THE SEAWARD WAY,   45 OISIN 2   237
    GATHERS SEA-SLIME AND GOES THE SEAWARD WAY,   45 OISIN 2   V   237
    GATHER SEA SLIME AND FALL THE SEAWARD WAY,   45 OISIN 2   V   237
SEAWAYS
    BUT THE SAD DWELLER BY THE SEAWAYS LONE   69 SAD SHEPHERD   V   26
SEA-WAYS
    WAS SLUMBERING HALF IN THE SEA-WAYS!   26 OISIN 1   395
    WATCHED THE OLD SUN THAT IN SEA-WAYS   26 OISIN 1   V   394
    BUT THE SAD DWELLER BY THE SEA-WAYS LONE   69 SAD SHEPHERD   26
SEAWEED
    FROM THE SEAWEED ON THE STRAND.   597 COLONEL MARTIN   71
SEA-WEED
    FROM THE SEA-WEED ON THE STRAND.   597 COLONEL MARTIN   V   71
SEAWEED-COVERED
    THE SEAWEED-COVERED PILLARS! AND THE GREEN   31 OISIN 2   32
SEA-WEEDY
    THAT OLD, SEA-WEEDY, SQUARED, THREE HUNDRED FEET   31 OISIN 2   V   30C
SEA-WIND
    AND HEARD THE SEA-WIND SCREAM UPON THE TOWER,   403 FOR DAUGHTER   10
    WHEN SEA-WIND SWEPT THE CORNER, STANDS!   566 LAPIS LAZULI   32
SEA-WORLD
    AND SHAKES O'ER THE WIDTH OF THE SEA-WORLD BORDER   28 OISIN 1   V 423C
SEA-WORN
    A SEA-WORN WAIF CAME FLOATING BY.   24 OISIN 1   V   365
    "MY FATHER DWELLS AMONG THE SEA-WORN BANDS,   107 CUCHULAIN SEA   V   25
SECOND
    AND CAME AGAIN, HOLDING A SECOND LIGHT   37 OISIN 2   124
    AWHILE, AND CAME AGAIN, A SECOND LIGHT   37 OISIN 2   V   124
    NO SECOND TROY   256 NO SECOND TROY   T
    TO A WEALTHY MAN WHO PROMISED A SECOND SUBSCRIPTION 287 TO WEALTHY MAN   T
    THE SECOND: "I SHALL LEARN A TRADE"!   296 THREE BEGGARS   32
    THE SECOND: "I HAVE THOUGHT AGAIN!   296 THREE BEGGARS   36
    AND WHEN THE SECOND TWILIGHT BROUGHT   296 THREE BEGGARS   42

		PAGE	TITLE		LINE
SECOND (CONTINUED)					
ABOUT A FARM," THE SECOND CRIED.		296	THREE BEGGARS	V	38
SECOND RUMMAGED FOR A FLEA;		298	THREE HERMITS		4
SO THE FIRST, BUT NOW THE SECOND!		298	THREE HERMITS		13
BUT THE SECOND MOCKED HIS MOAN!		299	THREE HERMITS		24
WHAT'S DYING BUT A SECOND WIND?		338	TOM OROUGHLEY		11
"HE GROWS YOUNGER EVERY SECOND		342	SHEP GOATHERD		89
THE SECOND COMING		401	SECOND COMING		T
SURELY THE SECOND COMING IS AT HAND.		402	SECOND COMING		10
THE SECOND COMING! HARDLY ARE THOSE WORDS OUT .		402	SECOND COMING		11
THE SECOND BEST'S A GAY GOODNIGHT AND QUICKLY TURN AWAY.		459	FROM OEDIPUS		12
AND IF IT TAKE THE SECOND MUST REFUSE		491	COOLE BALLYLEE	V	40C
AND IF IT TAKE THE SECOND MUST REFUSE		495	CHOICE		3
THREE SONGS TO THE SAME TUNE SECOND SONG		544	TO SAME TUNE 1	V	T
THE LADY'S SECOND SONG		572	LADYS 2ND SONG		T
THE CHAMBERMAID'S SECOND SONG		575	MAIDS 2ND SONG		T
TILL CERTAIN SECOND THOUGHTS HAVE COME		791	REPRISALS		12
SECOND-BEST					
I CHOOSE THE SECOND-BEST, ...		590	OLD WICKED MAN		60
SECRET					
SNATCHING THE BIRD IN SECRET! NOR KNEW I, EMBOSOMED APART,		57	OISIN 3		150
IN MY MOST SECRET SPIRIT GREW		83	MAD KING GOLL		27
THE EAST TELLS ALL HER SECRET JOY BEFORE DAYBREAK, . .		154	BELOVED PEACE	V	4
THE SECRET ROSE		169	SECRET ROSE		T
O'SULLIVAN RUA TO THE SECRET ROSE		169	SECRET ROSE	V	T
TO THE SECRET ROSE		169	SECRET ROSE	V	T
FAR-OFF, MOST SECRET, AND INVIOLATE ROSE, ...		169	SECRET ROSE		1
FAR OFF, MOST SECRET, AND INVIOLATE ROSE, ...		169	SECRET ROSE	V	1
FAR-OFF, MOST SECRET, AND INVIOLATE ROSE?		170	SECRET ROSE		32
FAR OFF, MOST SECRET, AND INVIOLATE ROSE?		170	SECRET ROSE	V	32
AND THEIR SECRET SMILE, OUT OF THE DEPTHS OF THE LAKE! . .		203	WITHER BOUGHS		11
AND THEIR SECRET SMILE, OUT OF THE DEEPS OF THE LAKE! .		203	WITHER BOUGHS	V	11
THEY'LL FLY UPON THAT SECRET WAY OF THEIRS.		233	SHADOW WATER B		248
MADE OF DIM GOLD RAVE OUT IN SECRET TOMBS!		235	SHADOW WATER B		295
A SECRET BETWEEN YOU TWO, ...		259	UNWORTH PRAISE		9
WE'LL KEEP THE SECRET--A NEW TRICK TO PLEASE. . . .		265	ABBEY THEATRE		10
THEN I REPLIED, "ALTHOUGH YOU HIDE A SECRET, . . .		281	TWO KINGS		95
BE SECRET AND TAKE DEFEAT		290	TO A FRIEND		2
BE SECRET AND EXULT, ...		291	TO A FRIEND		14
BUT GUAIRE LAUGHED WITH SECRET THOUGHT, ...		295	THREE BEGGARS		19
THAT ARE OUR SECRET DISCIPLINE		326	ROBERT GREGORY		68
WHETHER IN PUBLIC OR IN SECRET RAGE		413	TOWER		99
A MAN IN HIS OWN SECRET MEDITATION		431	NINETEEN 19		69
ADORNING EVERY SECRET TRACK		509	JANE REPROVED		9
"I LOVE A MAN IN SECRET, ...		569	THREE BUSHES		15
AND SHOUT A SECRET TO THE STONE.		632	MAN AND ECHO		5
BEFORE THE SECRET WORKING MIND!		639	BEN BULBEN		51
IN THE DEEP CENTRES OF THE SECRET WOODS.		661	ISLE STAT II 1		54
DEAR HEART, THERE IS A SECRET WAY THAT LEADS . . .		702	MOSADA 3		75
HE KNOWS BY SIGNS OF SECRET WIT		716	FAIRY DOCTOR		5
OF EQUAL POWER IN SPELLS AND SECRET RITES.		720	WITCH VIVIEN		6
MADE OF DIM GOLD, RAVE OUT IN SECRET TOMBS, ...		765	SHADOW WATER A		345
INTO THE SECRET WILDERNESS OF THEIR LOVE.		778	SONG DEIRDRE 3		4
SECRET'S					
AS THEY HAVE KNOWN IT. NOW THE SECRET'S OUT!		228	SHADOW WATER B		140
SECRETS					
WITH THE SECRETS OF GOD IN HIS EYES.		167	BLESSED		12
"WITH THE SECRETS OF GOD HALF BLIND, ...		168	BLESSED		26
THE SECRETS OF THE OLD		457	SECRETS OF OLD		T
I HAVE OLD WOMEN'S SECRETS NOW		457	SECRETS OF OLD		1
SECT					
WE IRISH, BORN INTO THAT ANCIENT SECT		611	STATUES		28
SECTION					
FROM THE BOOK OF KAURI THE INDIAN-- SECTION V. ON THE		76	INDIAN ON GOD	V	T
NATURE OF GOD					
SEDENTARY					
A STYLE IS FOUND BY SEDENTARY TOIL		370	EGO DOMINUS		65
THIS SEDENTARY TRADE.		416	TOWER		180
THE SEDENTARY TRADE.		416	TOWER	V	180
THE SEDENTARY SOUL		784	WOMANS BEAUTY		8
SEDGE					
A DUSKY DEMON DRY AS A WITHERED SEDGE		39	OISIN 2		158
A DUSK DEMON, DRY AS A WITHERED SEDGE, ...		39	OISIN 2	V	158
A HUSKY DEMON, DRY AS A WITHERED SEDGE		39	OISIN 2	V	158
HE HEARS THE CRY OF THE SEDGE		165	CRY OF SEDGE		T
AEDH HEARS THE CRY OF THE SEDGE		165	CRY OF SEDGE	V	T
WHERE WIND CRIES IN THE SEDGE!		165	CRY OF SEDGE		3
ON THE RUDDY RIVER SEDGE, ...		646	ISLE STAT I 1		25
SEDGY					
AND SEDGY STREAM, AND IN EACH BABBLING BRAKE		675	ISLE STAT II 3		225
SEE					
STOOD TIMIDLY. LEST THEY SHOULD SEE SOME SIGHT		38	OISIN 2	V	141
ALL IS DONE NOW--I SEE THE RAVENS FLOCK--		43	OISIN 2	V	212
"THEN GO THROUGH THE LANDS IN THE SADDLE AND SEE WHAT THE		55	OISIN 3		125
MORTALS DO,					
. . . AND SEE WHAT THE MORTAL MEN DO, ...		55	OISIN 3	V	125
MUCH WONDERING TO SEE UPON ALL HANDS, OF WATTLES		58	OISIN 3		162
AND WOODWORK MADE,					
MUCH WONDERING TO SEE UPON ALL HANDS, OF WATTLES		58	OISIN 3	V	162
AND WOOD-WORK MADE,					
O LOVELY TO SEE IN ALL MEN'S SIGHT		69	CLOAK BOAT		3

695

		PAGE	TITLE		LINE
SEE	**(CONTINUED)**				
SEE HOW THE SACRED OLD FLAMINGOES COME,		72	ANASHU VIJAYA		29
FLASHES THE FIRE OF SADNESS, FOR THEY SEE		73	ANASHU VIJAYA		49
THEY SEE IN FLAMING FORESTS COWER THE LION		73	ANASHU VIJAYA	V	52
OR SEE THE BROWN MICE BOB		88	STOLEN CHILD		48
NO NEIGHBOUR COULD I SEE.		95	MOLL MAGEE		28
TO SEE THE WORLD ONCE MORE.		97	FOXHUNTER		4
I SEE MY LIFE GO DRIFTING LIKE A RIVER		104	FERGUS DRUID		31
I SEE MY LIFE GO DRIPPING LIKE A STREAM		104	FERGUS DRUID	V	31
TO SEE YOU SO GOOD!		118	CRADLE SONG		6
WHEN NO ONE TURNED TO SEE		131	OLD PENSIONER	V	2
TO SEE MEN'S SOULS BARTERED AND BOUGHT.		136	TWO TREES	V	36
BUT I CAN SEE WHERE THE WIND GOES		168	BLESSED		27
I SEE THE BLESSEDEST SOUL IN THE WORLD		168	BLESSED		31
BUT WHERE IT COULD SEE HER EVERY DAY.		191	BAILE AILLINN		55
IF HE COULD SEE THE TOWNLAND		214	HAPPY TOWNLAND		3
WHERE THE DEAD DRIFTED, I COULD SEE A BIRD		223	SHADOW WATER B		23
HE COULD NOT SEE THEM, BUT I HELD OUT MY HANDS		223	SHADOW WATER B		38
YOU DO NOT SEE MY PURPOSE. I SHALL HAVE GONE		238	SHADOW WATER B		357
YOU DID NOT SEE MY PURPOSE. I SHALL HAVE GONE		238	SHADOW WATER B	V	357
NO MAN SHOULD SEE TO DO ME HURT!		274	GREY ROCK		91
TO PLOUGH OR PASTURE—LAND, MIGHT SEE ME THERE,		283	TWO KINGS		146
TO PLOUGH OR PASTURE LAND, MIGHT SEE ME THERE,		283	TWO KINGS	V	146
NOW AS AT ALL TIMES I CAN SEE IN THE MIND'S EYE,		318	MAGI		1
ALTHOUGH I CAN SEE HIM STILL,		347	FISHERMAN		1
THE CERTAINTY THAT I SHALL SEE THAT LADY		356	BROKEN DREAMS		22
I SEE A SCHOOLBOY WHEN I THINK OF HIM,		370	EGO DOMINUS		55
I SEE A SCHOOL BOY WHEN I THINK OF HIM		370	EGO DOMINUS	V	55
I SEE PHANTOMS OF HATRED AND OF THE HEART'S		425	PHANTOM HATRED		T
WOULD THINK HER SON, DID SHE BUT SEE THAT SHAPE		444	SCHOOL CHILDR		37
FOR HE CANNOT SEE MY LADY		552	SONGS REWRIT 2		3
"MY MISTRESS CANNOT SEE THESE THINGS,		595	COLONEL MARTIN		30
SEE, I TELL THY BEAUTIES O'ER,		647	ISLE STAT I 1		56
AY, BOY. LET'S SEE IF THAT SAME HERON'S DEAD.		651	ISLE STAT I 1		169
SEE, YONDER SINKS THE SUN, YONDER A SHADE		653	ISLE STAT I 2		52
THERE! THERE! DOST THOU NOT SEE? I SEE THE NIGHT,		653	ISLE STAT I 2		54
THERE! THERE! DOST THOU NOT SEE? I SEE THE NIGHT,		653	ISLE STAT I 2		54
SEE! OH, SEE! THE DEW-DROWNED BUNCHES		655	ISLE STAT I 3		1
SEE! OH, SEE! THE DEW-DROWNED BUNCHES		655	ISLE STAT I 3		1
NO MORE A-ROVING SHALT THOU SEE		658	ISLE STAT I 3		82
CAN ENTER THERE. SEE! SEE! ABOVE YON BROW		659	ISLE STAT II 1		27
CAN ENTER THERE. SEE! SEE! ABOVE YON BROW		659	ISLE STAT II 1		27
WE MUST GET SWORDS. IS'T THE ONLY WAY? OH, SEE,		660	ISLE STAT II 1		34
TO SEE THEM DROWNED BY THOSE VAST SOLITUDES,		661	ISLE STAT II 1		57
AND SEE AGAIN THE HAPPY WOODLAND LIGHT,		664	ISLE STAT II 2		58
OH, LOVELY TO SEE IN ALL MEN'S SIGHT		666	ISLE STAT II 3		3
'TIS BUT TO SEE IF ANYTHING WILL STIR		669	ISLE STAT II 3		75
I SEE WITHIN A CLOVEN ROCK DISPART		673	ISLE STAT II 3		195
I FADE, AND SHALL NOT SEE THE MORNINGS WAKE,		674	ISLE STAT II 3		223
THE SULLEN WOOD. BUT MANY WOODS I SEE		682	SEEKER		24
THEN LET ME SEE THY FACE BEFORE I DIE.		684	SEEKER		66
NO SIN TO SEE IN COIL ON COIL OF AZURE		692	MOSADA 1		43
YOURSELF. NONE BUT THE INNOCENT CAN SEE.		692	MOSADA 1		59
THAT YOU SHALL SEE ON YONDER GLOWING CLOUD		692	MOSADA 1	V	43
I CANNOT SEE. THE BEETLES, AND THE BATS,		693	MOSADA 1		63
I CANNOT SEE! I CANNOT SEE! BUT YOU		693	MOSADA 1		66
I CANNOT SEE! I CANNOT SEE! BUT YOU		693	MOSADA 1		66
SHALL SEE A THING TO TALK ON WHEN YOU'RE OLD,		693	MOSADA 1		67
BE NOT AFRAID, YOU'LL SEE NO FEARFUL THING.		693	MOSADA 1		74
FROM FASTING—SEE, THE RED LIGHT SLANTING DOWN		697	MOSADA 2		36
AND SEE HOW THICK THE DEW LIES ON MY FACE.		703	MOSADA 3		104
I'LL SEE HIM LONGER IF I STAND OUT HERE		703	MOSADA 3		113
'TWILL PASS. I'LL SEE THE OTHER PRISONERS NOW,		704	MOSADA 3		130
YOUR HOOD IS THREADBARE—SEE THAT IT BE CHANGED		704	MOSADA 3		133
SPEAK, FERENCZ, SPEAK. WE LOVE EACH OTHER. SEE,		713	FERENCZ RENYI		87
SEE THE DARKNESS SLOW DISGORGING A VESSEL BLIND WITH SQUALL.		718	PHANTOM SHIP		12
. . . SEE, SHE ROUNDS THE HARBOUR CLEAR.		718	PHANTOM SHIP		13
I'LL PLAY YOU FOR YOUR OLD HOUR-GLASS. YOU SEE		721	WITCH VIVIEN		36
YONDER SEE THE FAIRY GIRLS		726	LOVERS QUARREL		21
SEE YOU, BROTHER, CRANBERRY FRUIT—		727	LOVERS QUARREL		25
"EVERY SUMMER WILT THOU SEE		730	PRIEST FAIRY		55
NOT EVEN "I LONG TO SEE THY LONGING OVER,"		734	QUATRAIN APHOR		11
WHEN HUNDREDS STOOD ABOUT TO SEE		740	EARL PAUL		27
AND SAID: "I WILL SEE HER NO MORE,"		744	GLOVE CLOAK		6
SEED					
AS A GRASS SEED CRUSHED BY A PEBBLE, AS A WOLF SUCKED UNDER A WEIR.		63	OISIN 3	V	220
TILL THE SEED OF THE FIRE FLICKER AND GLOW;		150	OLD MOTHER		2
AND THE SEED OF THE FIRE GETS FEEBLE AND COLD.		151	OLD MOTHER		10
BUT THE SEED OF THE FIRE GETS FEEBLE AND COLD,		151	OLD MOTHER	V	9
BAILE, THAT WAS OF RURY'S SEED.		194	BAILE AILLINN		118
SEED PODS AND FLOWERS THAT ARE NOT ALL WILD POPPY.		342	SHEP GOATHERD	V	88
FOR THE WOMB THE SEED SIGHS.		574	LOVERS SONG		3
FIERCE THRUST! A TARDY BLOSSOM HAD THE SEED,		665	ISLE STAT II 2		65
SEED-PODS					
SEED-PODS AND FLOWERS THAT ARE NOT ALL WILD POPPY.		342	SHEP GOATHERD		88
SEEDS					
AND WAKES THE SLUGGARD SEEDS OF CORN,		18	OISIN 1		263
CRIES TO THE SLUGGARD SEEDS OF CORN,		18	OISIN 1	V	263

		PAGE	TITLE	LINE

SEEING
AND ALL FOLK SEEING HIM BOW DOWN, ... 113 ROSE OF PEACE 9
THEN SEEING THAT HE SCARCE HAD SPOKE . . . . 194 BAILE AILLINN 126
SEEING, KING'S SON, WHAT WOUNDS YOU HAVE." . . . . . 275 GREY ROCK 94
"SEEING THAT WHEN YOU COME TO THE DEATHBED . . . . . 285 TWO KINGS 196
"SEEING THAT WHEN YOU COME TO THE DEATH-BED . . . . . 285 TWO KINGS V 196
--SEEING THAT FAME HAS PERISHED THIS LONG WHILE, . . . 321 REED WHISPERER 11
I HAD THOUGHT, SEEING HOW BITTER IS THAT WIND . . . . 327 ROBERT GREGORY 89
SEEING THAT TIME HAS FROZEN UP THE BLOOD . . . . . . 333 LIVING BEAUTY V 2
SEEING THAT I, IGNORANT FOR SO LONG, ... 384 VISION ROBART 66
SEEING THAT LOVE AND FRIENDSHIP ARE ENOUGH, ... 423 MY DESCENDANTS 20
AND COLA, SEEING, KNOWS THE SIGN AND COMES. . . . . 691 MOSADA 1 38
AND COLA, SEEING, KNOWS THE SIGN AND RISES. . . . . 691 MOSADA 1 V 38
BEYOND HEARING OR SEEING, ... 784 WOMANS BEAUTY 11

SEEK
HOPELESS FOR EVER, THEY ALONE SHALL SEEK . . . . . 42 OISIN 2 V 200
NOR SEEK, FOR THIS IS ALSO SOOTH, ... 65 HAPPY SHEPHERD 23
SAVING IN THINE OWN HEART. SEEK, THEN, ... 66 HAPPY SHEPHERD 27
SEEK, THEN, FOR THIS IS ALSO SOOTH, ... 66 HAPPY SHEPHERD 31
AGED AND WISE, THEY SEEK THEIR WONTED PERCHES . . . 72 ANASHU VIJAYA 31
WE SEEK FOR SLUMBERING TROUT . . . . 88 STOLEN CHILD 32
BUT SEEK ALONE TO HEAR THE STRANGE THINGS SAID . . 101 ROSE UPON ROOD 19
SEEK OUT WHAT MAN HE IS." ONE WENT AND CAME. . . . 109 CUCHULAIN SEA 51
THE PARTED LIPS REPLIED, "I SEEK YOUR HELP, ... 183 QUEEN MAEVE 83
AND NOW THEY WILL NOT FOLLOW, WHILE I SEEK . . . . 226 SHADOW WATER B 95
BECAUSE I SEEK AN IMAGE, NOT A BOOK. . . . . 370 EGO DOMINUS 67
ALL THAT I SEEK; AND WHISPER IT AS THOUGH . . . . . 371 EGO DOMINUS 76
MANY A TIME I THINK TO SEEK . . . . 475 EVA GORE-BOOTH 14
SEEK OUT REALITY, LEAVE THINGS THAT SEEM. . . . . . 502 VACILLATION 72
WHY SHOULD I SEEK FOR LOVE OR STUDY IT? . . . . . . 558 RIBH CHRISTIAN 1
AND THAT SHOULD MOTHER SEEK HER SON SHE'D HAVE BUT LITTLE 593 PILGRIM 12
    LUCK
SEEK THOSE IMAGES . . . . 601 THOSE IMAGES 9
WILL STRUGGLE. OR HE'LL SEEK ENCHANTER OLD, ... 651 ISLE STAT I 1 162
HOW THEY WHO SEEK ARE EVER DOOMED TO FAIL. . . . . 653 ISLE STAT I 2 41
THAT FLOWER I SEEK. THOU NEVER WILT RETURN. . . . . 653 ISLE STAT I 2 44
TO SEEK NOT HOPELESS HAVE I CROSSED THE GLOOM, . . . 656 ISLE STAT I 3 42
I, AS A SHEPHERD DRESSED, WILL SEEK AND SEEK . . . . 658 ISLE STAT II 1 1
I, AS A SHEPHERD DRESSED, WILL SEEK AND SEEK . . . . 658 ISLE STAT II 1 1
WHO SEEK MAY FIND, SAVE ONLY ONE, ... 668 ISLE STAT II 3 48
SEEK NOT THAT WOOD, FOR THERE THE GOBLIN SNAKES . . 682 SEEKER 29
"OR SEEK WHERE SWEETEST WATER BUBBLES, ... 731 PRIEST FAIRY 79
WALKED ON THE WATERS AND BID FORGAEL SEEK . . . . . 747 SHADOW WATER A 12
FORGAEL, SEEK OUT CONTENT, WHERE OTHER MEN . . . . 750 SHADOW WATER A 56
SEEK AIBRIC ON THE LOCHLANN GALLEY, AND TELL HIM . . 767 SHADOW WATER A 401

SEEKER
AN EPILOGUE TO "THE ISLAND OF STATUES" AND "THE SEEKER" 64 HAPPY SHEPHERD V T
THE SEEKER. . . . . 681 SEEKER T

SEEKING
FOR IT IS LOVE THAT I AM SEEKING FOR, ... 228 SHADOW WATER B 141

SEEKS
NO MAIDEN LOVES ME, NO MAN SEEKS MY HELP, ... 103 FERGUS DRUID V 26
NO WOMAN LOVES ME, NO MAN SEEKS MY HELP, ... 103 FERGUS DRUID V 26
AND NOW HE SEEKS IN BOOK OR MANUSCRIPT . . . . . . 373 PHASES OF MOON 19

SEEM
HOW FAR AWAY THE STARS SEEM, AND HOW FAR . . . . . 80 EPHEMERA 8
THOUGH NOW IT SEEM IMPOSSIBLE, AND SO . . . . . . 200 FOLLY COMFORT 5
WILL HARDLY SEEM WORTH THINKING OF . . . . 202 NEVER GIVE ALL 2
TO PASSIONATE WOMEN IF IT SEEM . . . . 202 NEVER GIVE ALL 3
YET IF IT DOES NOT SEEM A MOMENT'S THOUGHT, ... 204 ADAMS CURSE 5
NOR LANDS THAT SEEM TOO DIM TO BE BURDENS ON THE HEART! 209 UNDER THE MOON 5
THAT LIFE AND LETTERS SEEM . . . . 255 WOMAN HOMER 20
THAT MADE THE BODY SEEM AS IT WERE A STRING . . . . 284 TWO KINGS 176
IF BUT I DO NOT SEEM TO CARE." . . . . 297 THREE BEGGARS 68
AND WE ARE HURT IF EITHER FRIEND SEEM COLD, ... 324 ROBERT GREGORY 10
AND NOW THEIR BREATHLESS FACES SEEM TO LOOK . . . . 325 ROBERT GREGORY 43
AND THEIR BREATHLESS FACES SEEM TO LOOK . . . . . . 325 ROBERT GREGORY V 43
TILL DAYTIME, PLAYTIME SEEM THE SAME; . . . . . . 343 SHEP GOATHERD 106
BEFORE MY TIME, SEEM LIKE A VIVID MEMORY. . . . . . 391 UNDER SATURN 10
THROUGH SUMMER AND WINTER SEEM . . . . 393 EASTER 1916 42
O MAY THE MOON AND SUNLIGHT SEEM . . . . 411 TOWER 54
SEEM BUT THE CLOUDS OF THE SKY . . . . 416 TOWER 192
THE LIVING SEEM MORE SHADOWY THAN THEY. . . . . . . 435 NEW FACES 8
"BUT SUCH AS YOU AND I DO NOT SEEM OLD . . . . . . 463 HARUN RASHID 55
THAT NEVER KNEW THAT STRAIN WOULD SCARCE SEEM BRIGHT, 465 HARUN RASHID 88
AND YET HERSELF CAN SEEM YOUTH'S VERY FOUNTAIN, . . 465 HARUN RASHID 89
AND WHAT IF MIND SEEM CHANGED, ... 473 ALL SOUL NIGHT 66
AND IT SEEM CHANGED WITH THE MIND, ... 473 ALL SOUL NIGHT 67
. . . ITS FARROW THAT SO SOLID SEEM, ... 481 BLOOD AND MOON 26
AND SEEM TO CLING UPON THE MOONLIT SKIES, ... 482 BLOOD AND MOON 44
OUR HANDS ARE BLENCHED, OUR FINGERS SEEM . . . . . 488 CRAZED MOON 14
SEEK OUT REALITY, LEAVE THINGS THAT SEEM. . . . . . 502 VACILLATION 72
WHAT MADE ME LIVE LIKE THESE THAT SEEM . . . . . . 507 STREAM AND SUN 14
WHAT BIDS ME LIVE LIKE THESE THAT SEEM . . . . . . 507 STREAM AND SUN V 14
SEEM TO DIE OR DIED THEY BOTH? . . . . 514 JANE GROWN OLD V 16
AND I SEEM TO KNOW . . . . 523 MAD AS MIST 4
WHERE HIS HEART MY HEART DID SEEM . . . . 535 CHOSEN 15
O WHAT AM I THAT I SHOULD NOT SEEM . . . . 553 PRAYER OLD AGE 7
THAT I MAY SEEM, THOUGH I DIE OLD, ... 553 PRAYER OLD AGE 11
WHERE FOR ITS MOMENT BOTH SEEM LOST, CONSUMED. . . . 555 RIBH AT TOMB 16
OR SEEM PLAUSIBLE TO A MAN OF SENSE, ... 624 APPARITIONS 4

697

		PAGE	TITLE	LINE

SEEM   (CONTINUED)

ITS JOY OR NIGHT SEEM BUT A DREAM;	633 MAN AND ECHO	42
RESEMBLE FORMS THAT ARE OR SEEM	639 BEN BULBEN	58
SAD FAERY TONES. 'TIS THUS THEY EVER SEEM,	654 ISLE STAT I 2	58
THEY SEEM TO JOIN HER PRAYER--	736 IN CHURCH	12
OR CROWD BEHIND THE BULWARK, THAT WE SEEM	751 SHADOW WATER A	94
AND ALL SEEM WELL ENOUGH,	786 YOUR HEART	15

SEEMED

IT SEEMED TO BLOW FROM THE DYING FLAME,	13 OISIN 1		167
THEY SEEMED TO SING IN THE SMOULDERING FIRES.	13 OISIN 1		168
IT SEEMED TO FALL FROM THE VERY FLAME	13 OISIN 1	V	167
HE SEEMED THE WATCHER FOR A SIGN. THE OTHER	31 OISIN 2		41
AND FACE THAT SEEMED WROUGHT OUT OF MOONLIT VAPOURS,	33 OISIN 2		70
HER FACE SEEMED FASHIONED ALL OF MOONLIT VAPOURS,	33 OISIN 2	V	70
WRAPT ROUND IN SOME DIM MEMORY, IT SEEMED--	36 OISIN 2	V	99
SCARCELY A FEATHER LINGERED, THEN YOU SEEMED	102 FERGUS DRUID		4
TO HIM SEEMED EASY, SO I LAID THE CROWN	102 FERGUS DRUID		13
"YOUR HEAD A WHILE SEEMED LIKE A WOMAN'S HEAD	110 CUCHULAIN SEA		63
AND SEEMED THE GREATNESS OF THE WORLD IN TEARS,	120 SORROW OF LOVE		6
IT SEEMED THEY RAISED THEIR LITTLE SILVER HEADS,	126 DREAM OF FAERY		6
IT SEEMED THE SUN AND MOON WERE IN THE FRUIT!	127 DREAM OF FAERY		23
REMEMBERING THAT SHE TOO HAD SEEMED DIVINE	182 QUEEN MAEVE		64
THAT IT HAD ALL SEEMED HAPPY, AND YET WE'D GROWN	206 ADAMS CURSE		37
OR LANDS THAT SEEMED TOO OLD TO BE BURDENS ON THE HEART,	209 UNDER THE MOON	V	5
HAD SEEMED TO BE THE GIVER OF ALL PEACE,	228 SHADOW WATER B		149
HAD THE WORLD'S TOTAL LIFE GATHERED UP, IT SEEMED,	231 SHADOW WATER B		194
ENOUGH IF THE WORK HAS SEEMED,	259 UNWORTH PRAISE		5
BECAUSE IT STOOD UPON HIS PATH AND SEEMED	277 TWO KINGS		8
SO MOURNFUL THAT IT SEEMED THE CRY OF ONE	278 TWO KINGS		39
TILL ALL HAD SEEMED A SHADOW OR A VISION	278 TWO KINGS		43
AND SHE SEEMED HAPPY AS A KING,	313 MEMORY YOUTH	V	6
WHEREON A THING ONCE WALKED THAT SEEMED A BURNING CLOUD.	315 FALLEN MAJESTY		8
ONCE WALKED A THING THAT SEEMED, AS IT WERE, A BURNING CLOUD.	315 FALLEN MAJESTY	V	8
THAT SEEMED AS THOUGH ICE BURNED AND WAS BUT THE MORE ICE,	316 COLD HEAVEN		2
TILL ALL HIS GREEK AND LATIN LEARNING SEEMED	324 ROBERT GREGORY		21
THE YEARS TO COME SEEMED WASTE OF BREATH,	328 IRISH AIRMAN		14
MUCH TOO SOLEMN SEEMED;	342 SHEP GOATHERD		91
A MAN--SO VAGUELY THAT HE SEEMED TO DREAM--	351 HER PRAISE	V	8
THIS NIGHT HAS BEEN SO STRANGE THAT IT SEEMED	358 PRESENCES		1
VEHEMENT AND WITTY SHE HAD SEEMED--: THE VENETIAN LADY	363 DOLLS FACES		5
WHO HAD SEEMED TO GLIDE TO SOME INTRIGUE IN HER RED SHOES,	363 DOLLS FACES		6
AND THEN HE LAUGHED TO THINK THAT WHAT SEEMED HARD	377 PHASES OF MOON		136
FOR NOW BEING DEAD IT SEEMED	383 VISION ROBART		23
MIND MOVED YET SEEMED TO STOP	384 VISION ROBART		43
SO SENSITIVE HIS NATURE SEEMED,	392 EASTER 1916		29
SHE SEEMED TO HAVE GROWN CLEAN AND SWEET	397 POLIT PRISONER		17
HIS DWINDLING SCORE AND HE SEEMED CASTAWAYS	420 MY HOUSE		25
HIS DWINDLING SCORE AND HE SEEMED CAST-A-WAYS	420 MY HOUSE	V	25
AND SEEMED UNCHANGING LIKE THE SWORD.	421 MY TABLE		21
HAD WAKING WITS! IT SEEMED	422 MY TABLE		31
THAT SEEMED SHEER MIRACLE TO THE MULTITUDE,	428 NINETEEN 19		2
IT SEEMED THAT A DRAGON OF AIR	430 NINETEEN 19		51
WHATEVER MISCHIEF SEEMED	431 NINETEEN 19	V	85
WHAT EVER MISCHIEF SEEMED	431 NINETEEN 19		85
TOLD, AND IT SEEMED THAT OUR TWO NATURES BLENT	443 SCHOOL CHILDR		13
FOR IT SEEMED THAT HE AND SHE	457 SUMMER SPRING		10
SEEMED FOR A WHILE TO HAVE GROWN YOUNG AGAIN;	462 HARUN RASHID		36
SEEMED SO ON PURPOSE, MUTTERED JAFFER'S FRIENDS,	462 HARUN RASHID		37
SHE SEEMED THE LEARNED MAN AND I THE CHILD;	467 HARUN RASHID		137
IT SEEMED A GOLD-FISH SWIMMING IN A BOWL,	472 ALL SOUL NIGHT		40
AND WHAT IF MIND SEEMED CHANGE	473 ALL SOUL NIGHT	V	66
AND IT SEEMED CHANGED WITH THE MIND.	473 ALL SOUL NIGHT	V	67
THAT SEEMED TO WHIRL UPON A COMPASS-POINT,	489 COOLE PARK 29		21
THAT SEEMED TO WHIRL UPON A COMPASS POINT,	489 COOLE PARK 29	V	21
SEEMED ONCE MORE DEAR THAN LIFE; ANCESTRAL TREES,	491 COOLE BALLYLEE		34
IT SEEMED, SO GREAT MY HAPPINESS,	501 VACILLATION		43
AND ALL MY HEART SEEMED GAY!	507 STREAM AND SUN		3
SEEMED TO DIE OR DIED THEY BOTH?	514 JANE GROWN OLD		16
AND SEEMED TO STAND ALTHOUGH IN BED I LAY.	535 CHOSEN		9
IT SEEMED A QUATTROCENTO PAINTER'S THRONG,	537 HER VISION		19
IT SEEMED A QUATTRO-CENTO PAINTER'S THRONG	537 HER VISION	V	19
THAT SEEMED BUT A WILD WENCHING MAN;	550 SEVERED HEAD		16
MADE DRAPERIES THAT SEEMED TO RISE	566 LAPIS LAZULI		31
SEEMED SPRUNG FROM BUT A SINGLE ROOT	571 THREE BUSHES		61
HIS NUMBERS, THOUGH THEY MOVED OR SEEMED TO MOVE	610 STATUES		2
A SHROUD THAT SEEMED TO HAVE AUTHORITY	634 CUCHULAIN COMF		7

SEEMING

THE SEEMING NEEDS OF MY FOOL-DRIVEN LAND;	267 ALL TEMPT ME		3

SEEMS

THOUGH NOW IT SEEMS IMPOSSIBLE, AND SO	200 FOLLY COMFORT	V	5
YET NOW IT SEEMS AN IDLE TRADE ENOUGH."	205 ADAMS CURSE		27
"WHO IS THE FRIEND THAT SEEMS BUT AIR	274 GREY ROCK		83
"IF THAT BE TRUE AS IT SEEMS TRUE,	295 THREE BEGGARS		20
SO THAT IT SEEMS EVEN I SLEEP LIGHT;	303 HOUR DAWN	V	34
IT SEEMS THAT I MUST BID THE MUSE GO PACK,	409 TOWER		11
THE ABOUNDING GLITTERING JET; THOUGH NOW IT SEEMS	417 ANCEST HOUSES		12
AS VIGOROUS OF MIND, AND YET IT SEEMS	422 MY DESCENDANTS		4
THAT SEEMS UNLIKE ITSELF, THAT SEEMS UNCHANGEABLE,	426 PHANTOM HATRED		4
THAT SEEMS UNLIKE ITSELF, THAT SEEMS UNCHANGEABLE,	426 PHANTOM HATRED		4
THAT SEEMS UNNATURAL TO ARABIAN MINDS,	464 HARUN RASHID		79

698

		PAGE	TITLE	LINE

SEEMS   (CONTINUED)
```
    IT SEEMS ENOUGH THAT I AM THERE; AND YET,  . . . . .     468 HARUN RASHID         166
    IT SEEMS I MUST BUY KNOWLEDGE WITH MY PEACE. . . . . .    468 HARUN RASHID         169
    SOME VAGUE UTOPIA--AND SHE SEEMS, . . . . . . . . .       475 EVA GORE-BOOTH        11
    BUT SEEMS A CONCENTRATION OF THE SKY; . . . . . . . .     490 COOLE BALLYLEE        18
    WHAT SEEMS MOST WELCOME IN THE TOMB--PLAY A PREDESTINED   503 VACILLATION           86
        PART.
    SEEMS A WATER-COURSE OR AN AVALANCHE, . . . . . . .       567 LAPIS LAZULI          45
    THEMES OF THE EMBITTERED HEART, OR SO IT SEEMS, . . . .   629 CIRCUS ANIMALS        13
    AND ALL SEEMS EVIL UNTIL I . . . . . . . . . . . .       632 MAN AND ECHO          17
    ITS JOY OR NIGHT SEEMS BUT A DREAM. . . . . . . . .       633 MAN AND ECHO     V    42
    IT SEEMS TO FONDLE, WITH A FINGER BRIGHT  . . . . . .     714 FERENCZ RENYI        114
    MY WAY IS WEST.  SHE SEEMS BOTH YOUNG AND SHAPELY; . . .  755 SHADOW WATER A       171
    AND MANY A NIGHT IT SEEMS . . . . . . . . . . . .        781 MY HEART BEAT          9
SEEN
    HOLDING THAT HORSE LONG SEEN NOT, NIAM STOOD. . . . .      44 OISIN 2          V   230
    O HAD YOU SEEN BEAUTIFUL NIAMH GROW WHITE AS THE WATERS    54 OISIN 3              109
        ARE WHITE,
    OH, HADST THOU SEEN BEAUTIFUL NIAM WAIL TO HERSELF AND     54 OISIN 3          V   109
        BLANCH,
    O, HAD YOU SEEN BEAUTIFUL NEAVE WAIL TO HERSELF AND BLANCH, 54 OISIN 3         V   109
    AND ONE HAS SEEN IN THE REDNESS OF WINE . . . . . .      168 BLESSED               35
    AND HAVE SEEN THE BLESSEDEST SOUL IN THE WORLD, . . . .  168 BLESSED          V    31
    I NEVER HAVE SEEN MAID QUIET . . . . . . . . . . .      171 MAID QUIET       V     1
    TO SOME STRINGED INSTRUMENT NONE THERE HAD SEEN, . . . . 180 QUEEN MAEVE           4
    HAVE SEEN IMMORTAL, MILD, PROUD SHADOWS WALK; . . . .    217 WOODS OF COOLE       12
    BUT THERE WERE OTHERS.  I HAVE SEEN NOTHING PASS. . . .  226 SHADOW WATER B       82
    THAT HAS BEEN PROMISED ME.  I HAVE NOT SEEN THEM . . .   226 SHADOW WATER B       88
    HAS SHE NOT SEEN HIM LYING LIKE A LOG, . . . . . . .     230 SHADOW WATER B      173
    NOW I HAVE SEEN IT WEIGHED  . . . . . . . . . . .       267 FRIEND ILLNESS        6
    WHO HAS SEEN A GARDEN IMAGE OR TWISTED TREE . . . . .    279 TWO KINGS        V  45B
    AND SEEN THE RUBBISH RUN ABOUT, . . . . . . . . .       297 THREE BEGGARS        65
    AND SEEN THE RUBBISH RUNABOUT, . . . . . . . . . .      297 THREE BEGGARS    V   65
    HE HAD SEEN A RED-HAIRED JOLLY LAD  . . . . . . . .      303 HOUR DAWN        V   27
    WHO HAD SEEN, BEING KEPT FOR SHOW, . . . . . . . .      319 DOLLS                 5
    BUT SUCH AS I HAVE SEEN UPON HER FACE . . . . . . .      340 SHEP GOATHERD        40
    ARE LEARNED IN WAITING.  YOU CANNOT BUT HAVE SEEN  . .   340 SHEP GOATHERD        48
    AND LITTLE SHE BY WHOM HER DANCE WAS SEEN . . . . .      383 VISION ROBART        38
    I KNEW THAT I HAD SEEN, HAD SEEN AT LAST  . . . . .      384 VISION ROBART        49
    I KNEW THAT I HAD SEEN, HAD SEEN AT LAST  . . . . .      384 VISION ROBART        49
    HAVE I NOT SEEN THE LOVELIEST WOMAN BORN  . . . . .      405 FOR DAUGHTER         59
    HAVE SEEN HIS MIDNIGHT CANDLE GLIMMERING. . . . . .      420 MY HOUSE             20
    HAD SEEN HIS MIDNIGHT CANDLE GLIMMERING . . . . . .      420 MY HOUSE         V   20
    IF YOU HAVE SEEN THAT IMAGE AND NOT THE WOMAN. . . .     448 HERO GIRL FOOL        8
    IF YOU HAVE SEEN THAT IMAGE AND NOT MY WORTH. . . .      448 HERO GIRL FOOL V      8
    OLIVER GOLDSMITH SANG WHAT HE HAD SEEN, . . . . . .      487 SEVEN SAGES          17
    FIFTEEN APPARITIONS HAVE I SEEN; . . . . . . . . .      624 APPARITIONS           7
    FIFTEEN APPARITIONS HAVE I SEEN; . . . . . . . . .      624 APPARITIONS          15
    FIFTEEN APPARITIONS HAVE I SEEN; . . . . . . . . .      624 APPARITIONS          23
    'TIS CLEAR THAT YOU HAVE SEEN HER NOT.  THE CROWN  . .   661 ISLE STAT II 1       70
    HAVE THEY NE'ER SEEN THE EYES OF LYNX OR KINE, . . .    672 ISLE STAT II 3      152
    OR HAST THOU NEVER SEEN, WITH VISAGE MEEK, . . . . .    672 ISLE STAT II 3      156
    HAVE I NOT SEEN A THOUSAND SEASONS EBB AND FLOW  . .    675 ISLE STAT II 3      229
    THE TIDE OF STARS?  HAVE I NOT SEEN A THOUSAND YEARS .  675 ISLE STAT II 3      230
    FADED AND VANISHED, NOTHING NOW IS SEEN, . . . . .     676 ISLE STAT II 3      268
    WE, TOO, HAVE SEEN OUR BRAVEST AND OUR BEST . . . .    709 FERENCZ RENYI         1
    AND THEN A POINTED FACE WAS SEEN  . . . . . . . .      728 PRIEST FAIRY         21
    FOR I HAVE SEEN A SHIP HID IN THE FOG. . . . . . .     751 SHADOW WATER A       89
    IN ONE ANOTHER'S ARMS.  AENGUS HAS SEEN . . . . .      763 SHADOW WATER A      321
SEER
    SEER OF VISIONS!  NOW EVE FALLS ASLEEP, . . . . . .    691 MOSADA 1             36
SEES
    "GOD ONLY SEES WHAT DOOM FOR ME LIES STORED." . . . .  110 CUCHULAIN SEA    V   62
    FOR ALL THINGS THE DELIGHTED EYE NOW SEES . . . . .    326 ROBERT GREGORY       49
    HE NUMBERS.  HE A BROWN FARM-HOUSE SEES, . . . . .     710 FERENCZ RENYI        22
    RINGED ROUND AND FONDLED, A BROWN FARM HOUSE SEES. . . 710 FERENCZ RENYI    V   23
    HE SEES THE FAIRY HOSTING MOVE  . . . . . . . . .      716 FAIRY DOCTOR          9
SEIZE
    AND SEIZE HER, AND THUS FLOATS HER QUIVERING CRY; . .   714 FERENCZ RENYI       105
SEIZED
    KING EOCHAID SEIZED THE HORNS IN HIS STRONG HANDS  . . 278 TWO KINGS            24
    EOCHAID SEIZED BOTH THE HORNS IN HIS STRONG HANDS  . . 278 TWO KINGS        V   24
    THEREON HE SEIZED ME IN HIS ARMS, BUT I . . . . . .    285 TWO KINGS           201
SELDOM
    FOR PEACE AND LAUGHTER HAVE BEEN SELDOM FRIENDS. . . . 670 ISLE STAT II 3      103
SELECTED
    THE DEDICATION TO A BOOK OF STORIES SELECTED FROM THE IRISH 129 BOOK STORIES    T
        NOVELISTS
SELF       SEE ANTI-SELF
    FOR BEAUTY'S VERY SELF, HAS CHARM MADE WISE, . . . .   404 FOR DAUGHTER         37
    THAT OUT OF LIFE'S OWN SELF DELIGHT HAD SPRUNG . . .   417 ANCEST HOUSES    V   11
    A DIALOGUE OF SELF AND SOUL . . . . . . . . . .        477 SELF AND SOUL         T
    MY BETTER SELF DISOWNS, . . . . . . . . . . . .        533 FIRST CONFESS         9
SELF-ACCUSED
    WHO IS SELF-ACCUSED.  IF SHE BE INNOCENT  . . . . .    280 TWO KINGS            72
SELF-AFFRIGHTING
    SELF-APPEASING, SELF-AFFRIGHTING, . . . . . . . .      405 FOR DAUGHTER         68
SELF-APPEASING
    SELF-APPEASING, SELF-AFFRIGHTING, . . . . . . . .      405 FOR DAUGHTER         68
SELF-BEGOTTEN
    THE SELF-SOWN, SELF-BEGOTTEN SHAPE THAT GIVES . . . .  446 COLONUS PRAISE       10
```

		PAGE	TITLE		LINE

SELF—BEGOTTEN   (CONTINUED)
   NOR SHALL THE SELF-BEGOTTEN FAIL . . . . 530 OLD TOM AGAIN   3
SELF—BORN
   O SELF-BORN MOCKERS OF MAN'S ENTERPRISE: . . . . . 445 SCHOOL CHILDR   56
   SELF-BORN, HIGH-BORN, AND SOLITARY TRUTHS. . . . . 467 HARUN RASHID   141
   BEGOT: SELF-BORN, HIGH-BORN, AND SOLITARY. . . . . 467 HARUN RASHID   V 141
   SELF-BORN, BORN ANEW? . . . . 507 STREAM AND SUN   15
SELF—DELIGHT
   THAT OUT OF LIFE'S OWN SELF-DELIGHT HAD SPRUNG . . . 417 ANCEST HOUSES   11
SELF—DELIGHTING
   AND LEARNS AT LAST THAT IT IS SELF-DELIGHTING, . . . 405 FOR DAUGHTER   67
   TO BRAZEN HAWKS. NOR SELF-DELIGHTING REVERIE, . . . 427 PHANTOM HATRED   29
SELFSAME
   BUT NOT THAT SELFSAME EXCELLENCE AGAIN. . . . . . . 602 GALLERY REVIS   32
SELF—SAME
   LOOKED DOWN ON ME: AND IN THE SELF-SAME PLACE . . .   39 OISIN 2   146
   MELTED AND FLOWED: AND IN THE SELF-SAME PLACE . . .   39 OISIN 2   V 146
   FROM SELF-SAME DOLT AND KNAVE: . . . . 260 UNWORTH PRAISE   17
   HEALING FROM ITS LETTERED SLAB. THOSE SELF-SAME HANDS 503 VACILLATION   82
    PERCHANCE
   NATURAL AND SUPERNATURAL WITH THE SELF-SAME RING ARE WED. 556 RIBH PATRICK   4
   BUT NOT THAT SELF-SAME EXCELLENCE AGAIN. . . . . . 602 GALLERY REVIS V   32
   FOUGHT ONCE FOR SELF-SAME REASON ON THE HEM . . . . 660 ISLE STAT II 1   32
SELF—SOWN
   THE SELF-SOWN, SELF-BEGOTTEN SHAPE THAT GIVES . . . 446 COLONUS PRAISE   10
SELL
   THE SISTER: "SELL THY COUNTRY, AND THE SHAME . . . 712 FERENCZ RENYI   60
   I'D BUY YOUR GLASS. MY GLASS I WILL NOT SELL. . . . 721 WITCH VIVIEN   28
SELLERS   SEE ONION-SELLERS
   WHAT TH' ONION SELLERS THOUGHT OR DID . . . . 287 TO WEALTHY MAN V   11
SELLING
   THE FOLK WHO ARE BUYING AND SELLING, ... 119 PITY OF LOVE   3
SELVES
   ON THEIR OWN SELVES IN THE WATERS WHITE: . . . . .   14 OISIN 1   V 185
   ALL THESE ARE SOULS THAT FLY FROM THEIR DREAD SELVES. 686 LIFE   4
   ALL THESE ARE SOULS WHO FLY FROM THEIR DREAD SELVES. . 734 QUATRAIN APHOR   4
   ALL THESE ARE SOULS THAT FLY FROM THEIR DREAD SELVES. 734 QUATRAIN APHOR V   4
SEMBLANCE
   UNDER A RULE, UNDER THE SEMBLANCE OF PEACE . . . . . 563 MERU   2
SEMELE'S
   SEMELE'S LAD A GAY COMPANION. . . . . 446 COLONUS PRAISE   8
SEND
   TILL MY OWN WORDS, RE-ECHOING, SHALL SEND . . . . .   68 SAD SHEPHERD   20
   AND MINE OWN WORDS RE-ECHOING SHALL SEND . . . . .   68 SAD SHEPHERD   V   20
   SEND PEACE ON ALL THE LANDS AND FLICKERING CORN.—   71 ANASHU VIJAYA   1
   WHOSE BLADE COMPELS, AND BID THEM SEND YOU ONE . . . 108 CUCHULAIN SEA V   37
   "I WILL SEND THEM TO HER AND DIE": . . . . 160 CAP AND BELLS   22
   THEY WOULD NOT SEND ME ONE THAT CASTS A SHADOW. . . 235 SHADOW WATER B   285
   SPEAK IT, THAT I MAY SEND THROUGH THE WIDE WORLD . . 281 TWO KINGS   97
   AND SEND IMAGINATION FORTH . . . . 410 TOWER   20
   DID THAT PLAY OF MINE SEND OUT . . . . 632 MAN AND ECHO   11
   "SEND WAR IN OUR TIME, O LORD!" . . . . 638 BEN BULBEN   26
   I'LL SEND MINE ARROW: NOW MY ONE RESOURCE: . . . . 657 ISLE STAT I 3   64
   THE BLESSED GOD WAS GOOD TO SEND US SUCH, ... 683 SEEKER   40
   NONE SHOULD ESCAPE MY SWORD: I WOULD SEND ALL . . . 752 SHADOW WATER A   111
   HAS TOLD ME THAT THE UNDYING SEND THEIR EAGLES . . . 765 SHADOW WATER A   346
   TO GARRET OR CELLAR A WHEEL I SEND, ... 787 GARRET CELLAR   1
SENNACHIES
   . . . FAR SUNG BY THE SENNACHIES. . . . .   50 OISIN 3   53
   . . . FAR SUNG OF THE SENNACHIES. . . . .   50 OISIN 3   V   53
SENSE
   AND GET INTO THEIR WORLD THAT TO THE SENSE . . . . 230 SHADOW WATER B   179
   AND THERE, IN JUGGLERIES OF SIGHT AND SENSE, . . . 231 SHADOW WATER B   216
   WHAT NEED YOU, BEING COME TO SENSE, ... 289 SEPTEMBER 1913   1
   AND I TOOK ALL THE BLAME OUT OF ALL SENSE AND REASON, 316 COLD HEAVEN   7
   AND CHILDHOOD A DELIGHT FOR EVERY SENSE, ... 418 ANCEST HOUSES   31
   SENSE THAN A COMMON MAN? . . . . 507 STREAM AND SUN   10
   OF EVERYTHING THAT IS NOT MIND OR SENSE. . . . . . 558 RIBH CHRISTIAN   6
   THAT HAD SUCH LITTLE SENSE . . . . 585 ORAHILLY   11
   OR SEEM PLAUSIBLE TO A MAN OF SENSE, ... 624 APPARITIONS   4
SENSELESS
   BECAUSE OF ALL THAT SENSELESS TUMULT, ALL BUT CRIED . . 426 PHANTOM HATRED   15
SENSES
   HIS SENSES AND HIS HEART UNSATISFIED, ... 370 EGO DOMINUS   58
SENSITIVE
   WE HAVE LIT UPON THE GENTLE, SENSITIVE MIND . . . . 368 EGO DOMINUS   12
   SO SENSITIVE HIS NATURE SEEMED, ... 392 EASTER 1916   29
   ON DELICATE SENSITIVE EAR OR TOSSING MANE, ... 433 NINETEEN 19   115
   AND BLOOD AND MIRE THE SENSITIVE BODY STAIN? . . . 564 GYRES   10
SENSUAL
   CAUGHT IN THAT SENSUAL MUSIC ALL NEGLECT . . . . . 407 SAIL BYZANTIUM   7
SENSUALITY
   AND ALL THE SENSUALITY OF THE SHADE-- . . . . . . 489 COOLE PARK 29   31
SENSUOUS
   OF THAT MOST SENSUOUS SILENCE OF THE NIGHT . . . . 579 DOR WELLESLEY   6
SENT
   FOR NEVER MORTAL CRY SO FAR HATH SENT. . . . . . .   36 OISIN 2   V 108
   SPRANG DRIPPING, AND: WITH CAPTIVE DEMONS SENT . .   38 OISIN 2   130
   THEN CONCHUBAR SENT THAT SWEET-THROATED MAID, . . . 110 CUCHULAIN SEA   72
   THEN CONCOBAR SENT THAT SWEET THROATED MAID . . . . 110 CUCHULAIN SEA V   72
   SENT FOR HIS DRUIDS TWENTY SCORE AND TEN, ... 110 CUCHULAIN SEA V   76

700

```
                                                      PAGE      TITLE        LINE
SENT    (CONTINUED)
    ANOTHER POOR MAN SENT FOR HIM,  . . . . . . . . .  132 FR GILLIGAN          7
    SENT ONE OF HIS GREAT ANGELS DOWN . . . . . . . .  134 FR GILLIGAN         43
    "FOR GOD AND GOD'S MOTHER HAVE SENT  . . . . . .   167 BLESSED             18
    "I HAVE SENT AMONG THE FIELDS OR TO THE WOODS . . .  280 TWO KINGS         69
    "I HAVE SENT OUT INTO THE FIELDS AND WOODS . . . .  280 TWO KINGS        V  69
    HAD SENT NO RUNNERS TO AND FRO . . . . . . . . .   288 TO WEALTHY MAN      18
    CONFUSION OF THE DEATH-BED OVER, IS IT SENT . . .  316 COLD HEAVEN         10
    THE RED MAN THE JUGGLER SENT  . . . . . . . . . .  412 TOWER               92
    THAT IS A LIGHT MY JEALOUS SOUL HAS SENT. . . . .  558 RIBH CHRISTIAN       8
    SPOILT WHAT OLD LOINS HAVE SENT? . . . . . . . .   604 YOU CONTENT          6
    I SENT AN ARROW.  AND I SAW YOU MISS; . . . . . .  649 ISLE STAT I 1      115
    AND SENT THE OLD MEN ON THEIR WAY. . . . . . . .   725 LEGEND              23
SENTENCE
    THE REST I PASS, ONE SENTENCE I UNSAY. . . . . . .  542 PARN FUNERAL 2      1
    I PASS THE REST—ONE SENTENCE I UNSAY—. . . . . .   542 PARN FUNERAL 2   V  1
SENTENCES
    IN BROKEN SENTENCES. MY SOUL HAD FOUND . . . . . .  557 RIBH ECSTASY        3
    SENTENCES THAT HE HAS NEVER THOUGHT; . . . . . . .  560 WHENCE COME         6
SENTIMENTALIST
    THE SENTIMENTALIST HIMSELF; WHILE ART  . . . . . .  369 EGO DOMINUS        47
SENTINELS
    THE AGELESS SENTINELS WHO HOLD THEIR WATCH . . . .  664 ISLE STAT II 2     45
SENTRIES
    BEYOND THE GATEWAY—BY THE SENTRIES NOW—  . . . . .  720 WITCH VIVIEN       10
SEPARATE
    FOR SEPARATE, PERFECT, AND IMMOVABLE . . . . . . .  375 PHASES OF MOON     81
    UNDER IT ARMED WISDOM STANDS, A SEPARATE WISDOM . .  469 HARUN RASHID   V 189
    FOR EVERY SEPARATE QUALITY OF LOVE; . . . . . . .  469 HARUN RASHID   V 189A
SEPTEMBER
    SEPTEMBER [NINETEEN-THIRTEEN] . . . . . . . . . .  289 SEPTEMBER 1913      T
SEPULCHRE
    WHO SOUGHT THEE IN THE HOLY SEPULCHRE, . . . . . .  169 SECRET ROSE         3
    WHO SOUGHT THEE AT THE HOLY SEPULCHRE, . . . . . .  169 SECRET ROSE    V    3
    FROM MARBLE OF A BROKEN SEPULCHRE, . . . . . . . .  565 GYRES              20
SERAPHS
    OF SERAPHS, BROODING, EACH ALONE, . . . . . . . .  156 FORGOT BEAUTY  V   22
SERE
    SCARCE LEFT A WHITENING FEATHER, GREY AND SERE; . .  34 OISIN 2        V  76A
    BUT WHENCE, AND WHEN?  OVER THE WILLOWS SERE . . .  652 ISLE STAT I 2      28
SERENE
    AND WITH A RULE SERENE AND MILD . . . . . . . . .   82 MAD KING GOLL  V    6
    SERENE. THEY'RE LED AWAY, AND WHERE A BAND . . .   712 FERENCZ RENYI      63
SERPENT    SEE WATER-SERPENT
    THE MIRROR-SCALED SERPENT IS MULTIPLICITY, . . . .  556 RIBH PATRICK       10
    THE MIRROR SCALED SERPENT IS MULTIPLICITY, . . . .  556 RIBH PATRICK   V   10
    A CONTRAPUNTAL SERPENT HISS, . . . . . . . . . .   573 LADYS 3RD SONG     10
SERPENT-TAILS
    THERE ALL THE SERPENT-TAILS ARE BIT, . . . . . . .  557 THERE               2
SERVANT
    HOW HARD A LIFE HER SERVANT LIVES, . . . . . . . .  336 YOUNG BEAUTY       14
    IT WOULD BE THE WORLD'S SERVANT, AND AS IT SERVES, .  376 PHASES OF MOON   90
    THAT I AM STILL THEIR SERVANT THOUGH ALL ARE UNDERGROUND.  581 CURSE CROMWELL  22
    SOME GOBLIN, MY SERVANT, ON WINGS THAT ARE FLEET, .  657 ISLE STAT I 3     67
    WHY THESE NEW FEARS?  THE SERVANT OF THE LORD, . .  692 MOSADA 1       V   46
SERVANT'S
    OH! GRACIOUS PAN, TAKE NOW THY SERVANT'S PART. . .  657 ISLE STAT I 3     77
SERVANTS
    "AND OF MY SERVANTS SOME ONE GO, . . . . . . . .   97 FOXHUNTER      V    5
    SERVANTS ROUND HIS CUSHIONED PLACE . . . . . . . .  99 FOXHUNTER          37
    THE SERVANTS BEAR THE BODY IN; . . . . . . . . .   99 FOXHUNTER          47
    THE SERVANTS ROUND HIS CUSHIONED PLACE . . . . . .  99 FOXHUNTER      V   37
    THEN TO HER SERVANTS, "BEAT HIM FROM THE DOOR . .  106 CUCHULAIN SEA  V  17A
    THE FIGHTING-MEN AND SERVANTS OF THIS HOUSE, . . .  280 TWO KINGS         70
    THE FIGHTING MEN AND SERVANTS OF THIS HOUSE, . . .  280 TWO KINGS      V   70
    THE SERVANTS OF YOUR ENEMY, . . . . . . . . . .   436 FOR MY SON         26
    I SPEAK ALONE WITH SERVANTS OF THE CROSS . . . . .  698 MOSADA 2           48
SERVE
    FOR THOSE THAT LOVE THE WORLD SERVE IT IN ACTION, .  369 EGO DOMINUS       42
    IF YOU WOULD SERVE ME, AS YOUR WORD AND VOICE . . .  756 SHADOW WATER A V 183
SERVED
    OR THE AMBITIONS THAT HE SERVED, . . . . . . . .   342 SHEP GOATHERD      93
    WHERE WHO HAS SERVED THE MOST IS MOST DEFAMED, . .  351 PEOPLE              4
    THOSE I HAD SERVED AND SOME THAT I HAD FED; . . .  352 PEOPLE             27
    YOU HEARD THAT LABOURING MAN WHO HAD SERVED MY PEOPLE.  391 UNDER SATURN   11
        HE SAID
    SERVED HUMAN LIBERTY. . . . . . . . . . . . . .   493 SWIFTS EPITAPH      6
    HIS FATHERS SERVED THEIR FATHERS BEFORE CHRIST WAS  580 CURSE CROMWELL      6
        CRUCIFIED.
    UPON THE CAUSE YOU SERVED, THAT WE  . . . . . . .  791 REPRISALS          13
SERVES
    IT WOULD BE THE WORLD'S SERVANT, AND AS IT SERVES, .  376 PHASES OF MOON   90
SERVICE
    NOR GAVE LOUD SERVICE TO A CAUSE . . . . . . . .   273 GREY ROCK          57
    OR LEAVE SOME SERVICE ALL UNDONE, . . . . . . . .  743 DANAAN QUICK       21
SERVILE
    THAT THE LAST SERVILE CRESCENT HAS SET FREE? . . .  376 PHASES OF MOON    103
    OR SERVILE SHAPE, AT OTHERS' BECK AND CALL. . . .  417 ANCEST HOUSES       8
SERVING
    OF YOUR OWN PASSIONATE SERVING KIND WHO HAD BROUGHT . .  292 TO A SHADE     10
    OF YOUR OWN PASSIONATE SERVING KIND WHO HAS BROUGHT . .  292 TO A SHADE  V  10
```

	PAGE	TITLE		LINE
SERVING (CONTINUED)				
A SERVING MAID AND A SERVING MAN,	301	RUN PARADISE	V	13
A SERVING MAID AND A SERVING MAN,	301	RUN PARADISE	V	13
A SERVING MAN THAT COULD DIVINE	410	TOWER	V	28
SERVING-MAID				
A SERVING-MAID AND A SERVING-MAN,	301	RUN PARADISE		13
SERVING-MAN				
A SERVING-MAID AND A SERVING-MAN,	301	RUN PARADISE		13
A SERVING-MAN, THAT COULD DIVINE	410	TOWER		28
THE THIRD, DOUBTLESS A SERVING-MAN,	566	LAPIS LAZULI		41
SET				
AND SET YOUR NAME ALL NAMES ABOVE,	7	OISIN 1		76
AND THE FIXED STARS HAD DAWNED AND SHONE AND SET,	31	OISIN 2		40
FOR CENTURIES, AND STARS HAD DAWNED AND SET.	31	OISIN 2	V	40
FROM THE WHOLE SEVEN SEAS, THOSE TOWERS SET	38	OISIN 2	V	131
MAY SET A STONE UPON ANCESTRAL SORROW!	130	BOOK STORIES		11
OF THE PALE TIDE WHEN THE MOON HAS SET.	146	FISH		2
THEY SET UP A NOISE LIKE CRICKETS,	161	CAP AND BELLS		33
AND SET THEM DIGGING UNDER BUAL'S HILL.	184	QUEEN MAEVE		93
AND SET THEM DIGGING INTO ANBUAL'S HILL.	184	QUEEN MAEVE	V	93
AND SET THEM DIGGING IN THE WEST OF THE HILL.	184	QUEEN MAEVE	V	93
BE THOUGHT AN IDLER BY THE NOISY SET	205	ADAMS CURSE		12
ANGERS THAT ARE LIKE NOISY CLOUDS HAVE SET OUR HEARTS ABEAT!	207	HANRAHANS SONG		8
ANGERS THAT ARE LIKE BUNDLED CLOUDS HAVE SET OUR HEARTS ABEAT!	207	HANRAHANS SONG	V	8
UNTIL THE MOON HAD SET! AND WHEN I LOOKED	223	SHADOW WATER B		22
THAT SET HIM TO THE FANCY. ALL WOULD BE WELL	230	SHADOW WATER B		177
THOUGH IT BUT SET US SIGHING? FELLOW-WANDERER,	230	SHADOW WATER B		187
THOUGH IT BUT SET US SIGHING. FELLOW WANDERER	230	SHADOW WATER B	V	187
AND SET YOU DREAMING. HOW CAN WE HAVE A WAKE	240	SHADOW WATER B		386
THAT HAVE TO BE SET UP IN FIFTY WAYS,	260	FASC DIFFICULT		9
AND AFTER SET YOUR HEART TO BEAT,	263	MASK		9
MY FANCY, AND SET MY BOYISH LIPS TO SAY,	270	PARDON FATHERS		17
AND CAME INTO A WOOD AS THE SUN SET	277	TWO KINGS	V	3
SO THAT HIS PLAUTUS SET THE PACE	287	TO WEALTHY MAN		12
SO THAT HIS PLUTARCH SET THE PACE	287	TO WEALTHY MAN	V	12
HE GAVE THE HOURS THEY HAD SET FREE	288	TO WEALTHY MAN		22
YOUR ENEMY, AN OLD FOUL MOUTH, HAD SET	292	TO A SHADE		17
AN OLD FOUL MOUTH THAT SLANDERED YOU HAD SET	292	TO A SHADE	V	17
THIS NIGHT CAN SET US QUARRELLING,	324	ROBERT GREGORY		15
TOWARDS NIGHTFALL UPON CERTAIN SET APART	325	ROBERT GREGORY		29
THE TOWER SET ON THE STREAM'S EDGE,	326	ROBERT GREGORY		52
THE TOWER SET BY THE STREAM'S EDGE,	326	ROBERT GREGORY	V	52
SET ALL HER BLOOD ASTIR	336	YOUNG GIRL		10
SET CARPENTERS TO WORK ON NO WIDE TABLE,	340	SHEP GOATHERD		50
CRAWLED FROM OBSCURITY, AND SET UPON ME	352	PEOPLE		26
HAS SET ME MUTTERING LIKE A FOOL.	356	BROKEN DREAMS		26
WE HAVE NO GIFT TO SET A STATESMAN RIGHT!	359	WAR POEM		3
HE SET HIS CHISEL TO THE HARDEST STONE.	369	EGO DOMINUS		32
MAY HANDLE NOTHING AND SET EYES ON NOTHING	371	ON GOING HOUSE		6
THAT THE LAST SERVILE CRESCENT HAS SET FREE?	376	PHASES OF MOON		103
AUSTERITY, A PLACE SET OUT FOR WISDOM	377	PHASES OF MOON		127
IT HAD SET DOWN AMONG ITS LAWS!	399	BREAK OF DAY		16
OR SET UPON A GOLDEN BOUGH TO SING	408	SAIL BYZANTIUM		30
A COMPANY OF FRIENDS, A CONSCIENCE SET AT EASE,	427	PHANTOM HATRED		37
ANOTHER TROY MUST RISE AND SET,	437	SONGS PLAY 1		9
AM SET DOWN STANDING IN THE WOOD	453	DEATH OF HARE		11
SET ALL YOUR MIND UPON THE STEEP ASCENT,	477	SELF AND SOUL		2
HEART'S PURPLE--AND ALL THESE I SET	478	SELF AND SOUL		28
IN MOCKERY I HAVE SET	480	BLOOD AND MOON		8
A SCENE WELL SET AND EXCELLENT COMPANY.	489	COOLE PARK 29		16
WHAT KNOWLEDGE OR ITS LACK HAD SET AWRY,	490	COOLE BALLYLEE		22
WHAT KNOWLEDGE OR ITS LACK HAS SET AWRY,	490	COOLE BALLYLEE	V	22
AND SET SUCH COLOUR THERE,	492	ANNE GREGORY		8
THAT HE MIGHT SET AT REST	496	MOHINI CHATTER		12
THINKING TO SET AT REST	496	MOHINI CHATTER	V	12
SET ME BY THAT OAK, FOR HE	508	JANE BISHOP	V	22
WHAT SET IT WHIRLING ROUND?	520	HIS BARGAIN		2
AND BROKE THE CHAIN AND SET MY ANKLES FREE,	533	HER TRIUMPH		9
AND SET A ROSE-TREE ON HER GRAVE,	571	THREE BUSHES		73
SET UP THE OLD STONE CROSS,	604	YOU CONTENT		10
A SMALL FORGOTTEN HOUSE THAT'S SET	606	SONGS BURDEN 2		3
BUT WHAT CARED I THAT SET HIM ON TO RIDE,	629	CIRCUS ANIMALS		15
SPOKE AND SET THE COCKS A-CROW.	637	BEN BULBEN		4
PROOF THAT THERE'S A PURPOSE SET	639	BEN BULBEN		50
AND BLAME THE SNARE THEY SET FOR ME.	743	DANAAN QUICK		23
THESE ARE THEIR LURES, BUT THEY HAVE SET THEIR HEARTS	757	SHADOW WATER A		206
ON NAUGHT HAS SET STORE	780	WELL AND TREE		13
AND SET IT ON A STAKE.	789	SINGING HEAD		6
SETS				
THE THIRTEENTH MOON BUT SETS THE SOUL AT WAR	374	PHASES OF MOON		50
AND IS SO LOVELY THAT IT SETS TO RIGHT	490	COOLE BALLYLEE		21
CARES WHAT KING SETS UP HIS RULE.	635	BLACK TOWER		14
WHERE BEN BULBEN SETS THE SCENE.	637	BEN BULBEN		11
ALE SETS THEM QUARRELLING. GIVE ME YOUR SWORDS.	766	SHADOW WATER A		372
WHAT SETS IT BEATING SO?	781	HEART FRIGHT		2
SETTING				
WHEN WE ARE DEAD, BEYOND THE SETTING SUNS,	71	ANASHU VIJAYA		8
A MAN CAME SLOWLY FROM THE SETTING SUN,	105	CUCHULAIN SEA		1
THAT SHADES THE ROAD, OR SETTING UP A COTTAGE	372	ON GOING HOUSE		14

SETTING   (CONTINUED)
    OR THE UNCERTAINTY OF HIS SETTING FORTH? . . . . . .   444 SCHOOL CHILDR   40
    HE HAD MUCH INDUSTRY AT SETTING OUT. . . . . . .   473 ALL SOUL NIGHT   71
    FEET TO THE RISING AND SETTING MAY RUN, ...   591 WHAT WAS LOST   4
SETTLED
    NOW THAT WE'RE ALMOST SETTLED IN OUR HOUSE . . . . .   323 ROBERT GREGORY   1
    NOW THAT WE'VE ALMOST SETTLED IN OUR HOUSE . . . . .   323 ROBERT GREGORY V   1
    NO SETTLED MAN. AND NOW THAT HE IS GONE . . .   341 SHEP GOATHERD   55
    BEFORE SHE HAD SETTLED HER MIND . . . . . .   381 SONGS FOOL 2   8
    IMPROVISATION, OR A SETTLED GAME . . . . . .   533 HER TRIUMPH   3
    AND WERE THE LAST TO CHOOSE THE SETTLED GROUND, . . .   621 HOUND VOICE   2
SETTLES
    BUT NOW WIND DROPS, DUST SETTLES, THEREUPON . . . . .   433 NINETEEN 19   125
SEVEN   SEE NINETEEN-SEVEN
    AND BIRDS THAT ON THE SEVEN SEAS RANGE. . . . . . .   4 OISIN 1   V 27A
    THAT SPRANG UNDER THE SEVEN HAZEL TREES, ...   35 OISIN 2   84
    FROM THE WHOLE SEVEN SEAS, THOSE TOWERS SET . . . .   38 OISIN 2   V 131
    . . . AND PACING THE SHORES OF THE SEVEN SEAS, . . .   50 OISIN 3   V 55
    THE SAILING SEVEN . . . .   118 CRADLE SONG   7
    AND THE OLD PLANETS SEVEN . . . . . .   118 CRADLE SONG   V 7
    THE OLD PLANETS SEVEN . . . .   118 CRADLE SONG   V 7
    THE SHINING SEVEN . . . .   118 CRADLE SONG   V 7
    'MONG THE FEET OF ANGELS SEVEN . . . . . .   125 CATHLEEN PARA   13
    WITH WHITE FEET OF ANGELS SEVEN . . . . .   125 CATHLEEN PARA   V 13
    AND HER GUIDES ARE ANGELS SEVEN, ...   125 CATHLEEN PARA   V 15
    AND THOUGH THE SEVEN LIGHTS BOWED IN THEIR DANCE AND WEPT,   174 ELEMENT POWERS   3
    IN THE SEVEN WOODS . . . .   198 SEVEN WOODS   T
    I HAVE HEARD THE PIGEONS OF THE SEVEN WOODS . . .   198 SEVEN WOODS   1
    SEVEN OLD SISTERS WIND THE THREADS OF THE LONG-LIVED ONES,   209 UNDER THE MOON   7
    SEVEN OLD SISTERS WIND THE THREADS OF THE LONG LIVED ONES,   209 UNDER THE MOON V   7
    I WALKED AMONG THE SEVEN WOODS OF COOLE; . . . . .   217 WOODS OF COOLE   1
    SEVEN ODOURS, SEVEN MURMURS, SEVEN WOODS. . . . .   218 WOODS OF COOLE   16
    SEVEN ODOURS, SEVEN MURMURS, SEVEN WOODS. . . . .   218 WOODS OF COOLE   16
    SEVEN ODOURS, SEVEN MURMURS, SEVEN WOODS. . . . .   218 WOODS OF COOLE   16
    AWAKE UNSLEEPING FIRES; AND WOVE SEVEN STRINGS, . . .   219 HARP OF AENGUS   7
    SEVEN POEMS I UPON A DYING LADY . . . . .   362 HER COURTESY   V T
    WE, WHO SEVEN YEARS AGO . . . .   431 NINETEEN 19   89
    WHERE SEVEN EPHESIAN TOPERS SLEPT AND NEVER KNEW . .   442 BLACK CENTAUR   11
    EVEN TO-DAY, AFTER SOME SEVEN YEARS . . . . .   468 HARUN RASHID   161
    EVEN TODAY, AFTER SOME SEVEN YEARS . . . . .   468 HARUN RASHID   V 161
    SEVEN CENTURIES HAVE PASSED AND IT IS PURE, ...   482 BLOOD AND MOON   33
    THE SEVEN SAGES . . . .   486 SEVEN SAGES   T
    SEVEN POEMS GIRL'S SONG . . . . . .   515 GIRLS SONG B   V T
    I TOLD HIM THAT NIGHTLY FROM SIX TO SEVEN I SAT AT THIS   578 LOFTY THINGS   9
       TABLE,
    THROUGH SEVEN HEROIC CENTURIES; . . . . .   640 BEN BULBEN   80
    ARE DYING TOO. THEY WERE FULL SEVEN STARS; . . .   700 MOSADA 3   48
    AWAKE UNSLEEPING FIRES; AND WOVE SEVEN STRINGS, . . .   762 SHADOW WATER A   302
    THERE ARE SEVEN THAT PULL THE THREAD. . . . .   770 SPINNING SONG   1
    HOLIEST, HOLIEST SEVEN, ...   771 SPINNING SONG   11
SEVENFOLD
    OUT OF THE SEVENFOLD SEAS, BUILT THE DARK HALL . . .   38 OISIN 2   131
    . . . WHEN THE SEVENFOLD SEAS WERE YOUNG. . . .   50 OISIN 3   52
SEVEN-FOLD
    OUT OF THE SEVEN-FOLD SEAS, BUILT THE DARK HALL . . .   38 OISIN 2   V 131
    . . . WHEN THE SEVEN-FOLD SEAS WERE YOUNG; . . .   50 OISIN 3   V 52
SEVENTY
    SEVENTY YEARS HAVE I LIVED; . . . . . .   567 FROM JAPANESE   2
    SEVENTY YEARS HAVE I LIVED . . . . . .   567 FROM JAPANESE   5
    SEVENTY YEARS HAVE I LIVED, ...   567 FROM JAPANESE   7
    SEVENTY YEARS MAN AND BOY, ...   567 FROM JAPANESE   8
SEVERAL
    THOUGH SEVERAL, ARE A SINGLE LIGHT, ...   388 SOLOMON WITCH   29
SEVERED
    ALTERNATIVE SONG FOR THE SEVERED HEAD IN . . .   549 SEVERED HEAD   T
    FOR IF SEVERED FROM THE ROOT . . . . . .   668 ISLE STAT II 3   61
SEW
    TO CUT AND SEW, BE NEAT IN EVERYTHING . . . .   443 SCHOOL CHILDR   5
    TOOK UP THE NEAREST AND BEGAN TO SEW. . . . .   634 CUCHULAIN COMF   18
SEWED
    AND GRANIA, WALKING AND SMILING, SEWED WITH HER NEEDLE   53 OISIN 3   94
       OF BONE.
SEWN   SEE GOLD-SEWN
SEXUAL
    GODHEAD ON GODHEAD IN SEXUAL SPASM BEGOT . . .   557 RIBH ECSTASY   5
    CRY AT THE ONSET OF THEIR SEXUAL JOY . . . . .   560 WHENCE COME   2
    CRY AT THE ONSET OF THE SEXUAL JOY . . . . .   560 WHENCE COME   V 2
SGEOLAN
    BRAN, SGEOLAN, AND LOMAIR; . . . . . .   2 OISIN 1   V 7D
    AND BRAN, SGEOLAN, AND LOMAIR. . . . . .   2 OISIN 1   V 7R
    WHAT PLACE HAVE CAOLTE AND FIN, AND BRAN, SGEOLAN, LOMAIR?   61 OISIN 3   V 195
    TO FIN, CAOLTE, AND CONAN, AND BRAN, SGEOLAN, LOMAIR. . .   63 OISIN 3   V 224
SHADE
    SIDLED THEIR BODIES AGAINST HIM, FILLING THE SHADE WITH   50 OISIN 3   48
       THEIR EYES.
    HIS EVENING FIRE AMID THE LEAFY SHADE. . . . . .   109 CUCHULAIN SEA   48
    AFTER SHORT FIGHTING IN THE LEAFY SHADE. . . . .   109 CUCHULAIN SEA   57
    BESIDE HER CLEAN-SWEPT HEARTH, HER QUIET SHADE; . . .   114 ROSE OF BATTLE   11
    BESIDES HER CLEAN SWEPT HEARTH, HER QUIET SHADE; . . .   114 ROSE OF BATTLE V   11
    AND PIERCE THE DEEP WOOD'S WOVEN SHADE, ...   125 GOES FERGUS   2
    AND GOD COVERED THE WORLD WITH SHADE, ...   133 FR GILLIGAN   19

	PAGE	TITLE		LINE

SHADE (CONTINUED)

TO A SHADE
IF YOU HAVE REVISITED THE TOWN, THIN SHADE, ... 292 TO A SHADE   T
AMID THAT FIRST ASTONISHMENT, WITH GRANIA'S SHADE, . . . 292 TO A SHADE   1
WHILE WONDERING STILL TO BE A SHADE, WITH GRANIA'S SHADE, 366 HER COURAGE   4
WHILE WONDERING STILL TO BE A SHADE, WITH GRANIA'S SHADE, 366 HER COURAGE   V   4
AND I MERE SHADE AT LAST . . . . 366 HER COURAGE   V   4
UPON THE NORMAN UPLAND OR IN THAT POPLAR SHADE, ... 449 HERO GIRL FOOL   25
UPON THE NORTHERN UPLAND OR IN THAT POPLAR SHADE, . . . 449 OWEN AHERNE   2
PICK OUT MY FEATURES IN SUCH LIGHT AND SHADE . . . . . 449 OWEN AHERNE   V   2
AND ALL THE SENSUALITY OF THE SHADE-- . . . . 466 HARUN RASHID   116
BEFORE ME FLOATS AN IMAGE, MAN OR SHADE, ... 489 COOLE PARK 29   31
SHADE MORE THAN MAN, MORE IMAGE THAN A SHADE! . . . . 497 BYZANTIUM   9
SHADE MORE THAN MAN, MORE IMAGE THAN A SHADE! . . . . 497 BYZANTIUM   10
UNFRIENDLY LAMPLIGHT HID UNDER ITS SHADE, ... 497 BYZANTIUM   10
UNDER THE TROPIC SHADE, GREW ROUND AND SLOW, ... 523 LONG SILENCE   3
DREAMING THE LIVE-LONG SUMMER IN THE SHADE, ... 610 STATUES   18
HERE IN THE SHADE. WHY? WHY? FOR WHAT IS GLAD? . . . 650 ISLE STAT I 1   139
SEE, YONDER SINKS THE SUN, YONDER A SHADE . . . . . . 652 ISLE STAT I 2   8
AH, WOE IS ME! I GO FROM SUN AND SHADE, ... 653 ISLE STAT I 2   52
DOTH HE STILL DWELL WITHIN THE WOODY SHADE, ... 674 ISLE STAT II 3   216
WITH QUIET SHADE ITS EVER DEWY-PLOT. . . . . 678 ISLE STAT II 3   303
WITH QUIET SHADE ITS EVER DEWY SPOT, ... 714 FERENCZ RENYI   109
WITH QUIET SHADE ITS EVER DEWY PLOT. . . . . 714 FERENCZ RENYI   V   109
SO PASSIONATE IS A SHADE, ... 714 FERENCZ RENYI   V   109
                                                    781 MY HEART BEAT   13

SHADED
FROM THE GREEN SHADED HOLLOW . . . . 655 ISLE STAT I 2   82

SHADES
AMID THE SHADES OF NIGHT, HE CHANGED AND RAN . . . . 40 OISIN 2   174
A LITTLE FROM THE OTHER SHADES APART, ... 71 ANASHU VIJAYA   9
HOW WHEN WE DIE OUR SHADES WILL ROVE . . . . 78 INDIAN TO LOVE   18
HOW WHEN WE DIE OUR SHADES MAY ROVE, ... 78 INDIAN TO LOVE   V   18
WHO AMID LEAFY LIGHTS AND SHADES . . . . 193 BAILE AILLINN   103
IS FROM THE HOLY SHADES THAT ROVE . . . . 275 GREY ROCK   110
THAT THE SHADES OF HOLY MEN . . . . 298 THREE HERMITS   17
THAT SHADES THE ROAD, OR SETTING UP A COTTAGE . . . . 372 ON GOING HOUSE   14
AMONG THE DEEPENING SHADES. . . . . 416 TOWER   195

SHADING   SEE BROW-SHADING

SHADOW
HIS SHADOW ALONG IN THE EVENING BLAZE, ... 27 OISIN 1   V   409
AND IN THE SHADOW OF MY HAIR LIE HID, ... 33 OISIN 2   66
UNDER THE STARLIGHT AND SHADOW, A MONSTROUS SLUMBERING 48 OISIN 3   27
  FOLK,
NOW IN A PLACE OF STAR-FIRE, AND NOW IN A SHADOW PLACE 49 OISIN 3   V   42
  WIDE!
LAY LOOSE IN A PLACE OF SHADOW! WE DREW THE REINS BY HIS 50 OISIN 3   44
  SIDE.
I CRIED, "COME OUT OF THE SHADOW, KING OF THE NAILS OF 51 OISIN 3   61
  GOLD!
I CRIED, "COME OUT OF THE SHADOW, CANN OF THE NAILS OF 51 OISIN 3   V   61
  GOLD!
PAINTING WITH SHADOW ALL THE MARBLE STEPS! . . . . . 72 ANASHU VIJAYA   30
BODIES OF SHADOW AND BLIND EYES LIKE PEARLS, ... 185 QUEEN MAEVE   116
THAT HAVE ONE SHADOW ON THE GROUND! . . . . 195 BAILE AILLINN   154
O SHE WAS BUT A SHADOW, AND SLIPPED FROM ME. . . . . 223 SHADOW WATER B   40
A SHADOW DOES NOT CARRY SWORD OR SPEAR. . . . . . . 224 SHADOW WATER B   44
AS A LAMP SHADOW--NO--NO LAMP, THE SUN. . . . . . . 229 SHADOW WATER B   160
IS SHADOW, AND NOT LINGER WRETCHEDLY . . . . 230 SHADOW WATER B   180
LET GO MY HANDS! WHY DO YOU CAST A SHADOW? . . . . . 235 SHADOW WATER B   283
THEY WOULD NOT SEND ME ONE THAT CASTS A SHADOW. . . . 235 SHADOW WATER B   285
IT VANISHED LIKE A SHADOW, AND A CRY . . . . 278 TWO KINGS   38
TILL ALL HAD SEEMED A SHADOW OR A VISION . . . . . . 278 TWO KINGS   43
IN THE GREEN SHADOW OF FERRARA WALL! . . . . 352 PEOPLE   9
IN THE GREEN SHADOW ON FERRARA WALL! . . . . 352 PEOPLE   V   9
WE ARE ON THE BRIDGE! THAT SHADOW IS THE TOWER, . . . 372 PHASES OF MOON   10
A SHADOW OF CLOUD ON THE STREAM . . . . 393 EASTER 1916   49
UNDER THE SHADOW OF STUPID STRAW-PALE LOCKS, ... 433 NINETEEN 19   127
THE MOUNTAIN THROWS A SHADOW, ... 519 LOVES LONENESS   7
GODHEAD. SOME SHADOW FELL. MY SOUL FORGOT . . . . . 557 RIBH ECSTASY   6
BENEATH THE SHELTERING SHADOW OF THY CHURCH! . . . . 698 MOSADA 2   58
WHERE SHADOW OF CHERRY, AND SHADOW OF APPLE TREES, . . 710 FERENCZ RENYI   23
WHERE SHADOW OF CHERRY, AND SHADOW OF APPLE TREES, . . 710 FERENCZ RENYI   23
AND EVERY FLOWER ABOVE ITS SHADOW SITS, ... 712 FERENCZ RENYI   73
AND EVERY FLOWER ABOVE A SHADOW SITS. . . . . 712 FERENCZ RENYI   V   73
AND BID THEM HIDE IN SHADOW OF THE SAIL, ... 751 SHADOW WATER A   93
NEAR BY, BUT IN THE SHADOW OF THE SAIL, ... 752 SHADOW WATER A   121
OR A GOD HID THEM UNDER THE SHADOW OF WINGS, ... 752 SHADOW WATER A   125
WHOSE SHADOW IS THE SLEEP THAT COMES WITH LOVE, . . . 754 SHADOW WATER A   162
THE GRASS AND THE BLUE SHADOW ON THE STREAM . . . . 761 SHADOW WATER A   280
DID NOT A SHADOW PASS? . . . . 781 MY HEART BEAT   2

SHADOWED
"HE SHADOWED IN A GLASS . . . . 255 WOMAN HOMER   13

SHADOWING
IN SOME LIKE CHAMBER, SHADOWING FORTH . . . . 419 MY HOUSE   15

SHADOWLESS
ALL DAY LONG FROM SHADOWLESS NOON . . . . 332 SOLOMON SHEBA   5

SHADOW-PLACE
NOW IN A PLACE OF STAR-FIRE, AND NOW IN A SHADOW-PLACE 49 OISIN 3   42
  WIDE!

SHADOWS
UPON THEIR SHADOWS IN THE TIDE, ... 14 OISIN 1   185

704

		PAGE	TITLE		LINE
SHADOWS (CONTINUED)					
SOME DANCED LIKE SHADOWS ON THE MOUNTAINS.		25	OISIN 1		388
NOW, MAN OF CROZIERS, SHADOWS CALLED OUR NAMES		29	OISIN 2		1
HALF LOST IN VAPOUR, SHADOWS CALLED OUR NAMES,		29	OISIN 2	V	3
UNDER THE DEEPEST SHADOWS OF THE HALL		37	OISIN 2		119
UNDER THE SHADOWS TILL THE TUMULTS DIED		38	OISIN 2		140
YOUR EYES HAD ONCE, AND OF THEIR SHADOWS DEEP!		121	YOU ARE OLD		4
THE LONG HAIR SHADOWS HER FACE!		124	CATHLEEN PARA	V	10
AND RULES THE SHADOWS OF THE WOOD.		126	GOES FERGUS		10
OF THE FAR-WANDERING SHADOWS HAS COME TO ME		183	QUEEN MAEVE		80
OF THE FAR WANDERING SHADOWS HAS COME TO ME,		183	QUEEN MAEVE	V	80
WE SHADOWS, WHILE THEY UPROOT HIS EARTHY HOUSE,		184	QUEEN MAEVE		94
WILL OVERTHROW HIS SHADOWS AND CARRY OFF		184	QUEEN MAEVE		95
WE SHADOWS, WHILE THEY UPROOT THE EARTHY HOUSE		184	QUEEN MAEVE	V	94
WITH HOLY SHADOWS." HER HIGH HEART WAS GLAD,		186	QUEEN MAEVE		126
AND LITTLE SHADOWS COME ABOUT HER EYES!		199	FOLLY COMFORT		3
HAVE SEEN IMMORTAL, MILD, PROUD SHADOWS WALK!		217	WOODS OF COOLE		12
MOVED ROUND ME IN THE SHADOWS, AND AT NIGHT		218	WOODS OF COOLE		19
HOW SHALL I NAME YOU, IMMORTAL, MILD, PROUD SHADOWS?		218	WOODS OF COOLE		27
THE ROOTS OF THE WORLD. SHADOWS BEFORE NOW		227	SHADOW WATER B		104
THE ROOTS OF THE WORLD. WHO KNOWS THAT SHADOWS		227	SHADOW WATER B	V	104
FOR THAT IS WHAT THEY SAY—ALL, ALL THE SHADOWS—		228	SHADOW WATER B		137
THAT I HAVE THE BEST OF PILOTS. SHADOWS, ILLUSIONS,		249	SHADOW WATER B		565
AND THE SHADOWS EATEN THE MOON.		268	BROWN PENNY		14
SHADOWS AND SHOWS THAT CAN BUT TURN THE BRAIN."		281	TWO KINGS		108
THAT CAST THEIR SHADOWS UPON ROAD AND BRIDGE!		326	ROBERT GREGORY		51
OUR SHADOWS ON THE GROUND		333	SOLOMON SHEBA		14
AMONG THE EVENING SHADOWS.		341	SHEP GOATHERD		71
TO HIS SHAPE IN THE LENGTHENING SHADOWS,		341	SHEP GOATHERD	V	70
REEL SHADOWS OF THE INDIGNANT DESERT BIRDS.		402	SECOND COMING		17
WIND SHADOWS OF THE INDIGNANT DESERT BIRDS.		402	SECOND COMING	V	17
SHADOWS THE INHERITED GLORY OF THE RICH.		418	ANCEST HOUSES		16
OUR SHADOWS ROVE THE GARDEN GRAVEL STILL,		435	NEW FACES		7
AND TOOK A MESS OF SHADOWS FOR ITS MEAT?		444	SCHOOL CHILDR		28
AND TOOK A MASS OF SHADOWS FOR ITS MEAT,		444	SCHOOL CHILDR	V	28
DEAR SHADOWS, NOW YOU KNOW IT ALL,		476	EVA GORE-BOOTH		21
BACK THE SHADOWS CREEP AGHAST—		648	ISLE STAT I 1		98
THE WARMTH OF LIFE IS CHILLING, AND THE SHADOWS GROW		675	ISLE STAT II 3		232
AND RULE THE SHADOWS OF THE EVE AND DAWN?		678	ISLE STAT II 3		304
THE SHADOWS PASS! BUT NOW, I LOVE MY RING,		700	MOSADA 3		27
ENFOLDEN IN THE SHADOWS OF THE EAST,		705	REMEMBRANCE		11
LISTENING, UPON THEIR SHADOWS STOOD.		725	LEGEND		8
ROUND US HERDS OF SHADOWS STEAL—		737	IN FIRELIGHT		6
CARE NOT IF BEYOND THE SHADOWS		737	IN FIRELIGHT		7
SHADOWY					
THEY LED US BY LONG AND SHADOWY WAYS		16	OISIN 1		221
THEY LEAD US BY LONG AND SHADOWY WAYS		16	OISIN 1	V	221
IN A LONG AND SHADOWY ROW,		20	OISIN 1	V	295
WARS SHADOWY, VAST, EXULTANT! FAERIES OF OLD		29	OISIN 2		9
WARS SHADOWY, VAST, EXULTANT! FAIRY KINGS		29	OISIN 2	V	9
WHERE SHADOWY FACE FLOWED INTO SHADOWY FACE,		39	OISIN 2		145
WHERE SHADOWY FACE FLOWED INTO SHADOWY FACE,		39	OISIN 2		145
AND THE SHADOWY HAZEL GROVE		119	PITY OF LOVE		6
THE SHADOWY BLOSSOM OF MY HAIR		152	HEART OF WOMAN		7
TWO LOVE POEMS THE SHADOWY HORSES		154	BELOVED PEACE	V	T
I HEAR THE SHADOWY HORSES, THEIR LONG MANES A-SHAKE,		154	BELOVED PEACE		1
IN SHADOWY POOLS, WHEN ARMIES FLED!		155	FORGOT BEAUTY		5
WITH YOUR DIM SHADOWY HAIR,		163	ASKS FORGIVE	V	22
DEDICATION TO THE "SHADOWY WATERS"		217	WOODS OF COOLE	V	T
THE SHADOWY WATERS		221	SHADOW WATER B		T
THE LIVING SEEM MORE SHADOWY THAN THEY.		435	NEW FACES		8
FROM THE SHADOWY HOLLOW		654	ISLE STAT I 2		56
FROM THE SHADOWY HOLLOW		654	ISLE STAT I 2		78
IN SHADOWY DIMNESS. TO BE FAIR AS THEE		670	ISLE STAT II 3		106
FROM HERE, ALONG THE SHADOWY WAY THAT WINDS		703	MOSADA 3		111
THE SHADOWY WATERS		745	SHADOW WATER A		T
SHADY SEE A-SHAKE					
I FIND NO HAPPINESS IN SHADY BRYCELINDE		209	UNDER THE MOON	V	1
SHADY KYLE-DORTHA! SUNNIER KYLE-NA-NO,		217	WOODS OF COOLE		4
AND UNDER A SHADY OAK-TREE SAT,		728	PRIEST FAIRY		7
SHAFT SEE SPEAR-SHAFT					
HAS FLUNG ITS ARROWY SHAFT UPON THE FLOOR.		482	BLOOD AND MOON		32
HAD FLUNG ITS ARROWY SHAFT UPON THE FLOOR,		482	BLOOD AND MOON	V	32
AROUND THE FEATHERY TIP. UNTO THE SHAFT		657	ISLE STAT I 3		71
SAY THEN,—"A POPINJAY BEFORE GRIEF'S SHAFT		664	ISLE STAT II 2		52
SHAFTS					
SHOOT ON HIM SHAFTS OF QUIETNESS, THAT HE MAY EVER KEEP		75	ANASHU VIJAYA		81
SHOOT ON HIM SHAFTS OF QUIETNESS, AND ORDER HIM TO KEEP		75	ANASHU VIJAYA	V	81
SHAGGY SEE A-SHAKE					
WITH ANTLERS AND THE SHAGGY SKIN		17	OISIN 1	V	249
SHAKE SEE A-SHAKE					
SHAKE THE LOOSE REINS! YOU SLAVES OF GOD,		22	OISIN 1		331
SHAKE THE LOOSE REINS! YE SLAVES OF GOD,		22	OISIN 1	V	331
AND SHAKE THEIR COVERLET.		33	OISIN 2		62
AND SHAKE THEIR COVERLET'S HEM,		33	OISIN 2	V	62
SIGH, O YOU LITTLE STARS! O SIGH AND SHAKE YOUR BLUE APPAREL!		72	ANASHU VIJAYA		18
SIGH, OH YE LITTLE STARS! OH, SIGH AND SHAKE YOUR BLUE APPAREL!		72	ANASHU VIJAYA	V	18
AND SING, AND SHAKE MY HEAVY LOCKS.		84	MAD KING GOLL		44
WHY MUST YOU BLENCH AND SHAKE FROM FOOT TO CROWN?"		106	CUCHULAIN SEA		13

		PAGE	TITLE		LINE
SHAKE	(CONTINUED)				
	WHY ARE YOU PALE AND SHAKE FROM FOOT TO CROWN?"	106	CUCHULAIN SEA	V	13
	LEAPING TO SHAKE A COBWEB FROM THE RAFTER:	130	BOOK STORIES	V	19
	AND SHAKE A MOULDERING COBWEB FROM THE RAFTER,	130	BOOK STORIES	V	19
	AND SHAKE THEIR RAGGED WINGS: ALAS!	136	TWO TREES		38
	AND WHEN THEY SHAKE THEIR WINGS--ALAS!	136	TWO TREES	V	38
	AND SHAKE DOWN THUNDER ON THE STONES BECAUSE THE RED WINDS RAVE!	207	HANRAHANS SONG	V	7
	TO SHAKE THEIR WICKED SIDES AT YOUTH	262	STUDENTS AGIT		3
	TO SHAKE HIM OUT OF SLEEP, I COULD NOT ROUSE HIM.	283	TWO KINGS		143
	I SHAKE FROM HEAD TO FOOT.	316	FRIENDS		28
	AND SHAKE THE BLOSSOM FROM THE BUD	396	ROSE TREE		11
	CAN SHAKE MORE BLOSSOM FROM AUTUMNAL CHILL	465	HARUN RASHID		104
	WHAT HEADS SHAKE OR NOD?	505	RESULT THOUGHT		18
	WHAT MOST COULD SHAKE HIS SOUL!	529	TOM CRUACHAN		3
	WHAT MOST CAN SHAKE HIS SOUL!	529	TOM CRUACHAN	V	3
	SHAKE THE DEAD IN THEIR SHROUDS!	576	ACRE OF GRASS		22
	THEY SHAKE WHEN THE WINDS ROAR,	635	BLACK TOWER		9
	OLD BONES UPON THE MOUNTAIN SHAKE.	635	BLACK TOWER		10
	THEY SHAKE WHEN THE WINDS ROAR,	636	BLACK TOWER		19
	OLD BONES UPON THE MOUNTAIN SHAKE.	636	BLACK TOWER		20
	THEY SHAKE WHEN THE WINDS ROAR,	636	BLACK TOWER		29
	OLD BONES UPON THE MOUNTAIN SHAKE.	636	BLACK TOWER		30
	OF THE MONK'S-HOOD HOW THEY SHAKE,	655	ISLE STAT I 3		2
	WILL HE HAVE HAPPINESS? GREAT SOBS HER BEING SHAKE.	676	ISLE STAT II 3		247
	HIS BODY SHAKE? AY, QUIVERING AS YON SMOKE	683	SEEKER		36
	THE HEATHEN. YEA, AND SHAKE THE SULLEN KINGS	698	MOSADA 2		55
	ROASTING BERRIES STEAM AND SHAKE--	727	LOVERS QUARREL		43
	WHILE WE SHAKE OUR HEADS AND SCOLD	727	LOVERS QUARREL		54
	AND SHAKE THEIR BIRDS UPON THE AIR,	736	SUMMER EVENING		3
	AND SHAKE THEIR BIRDS UPON THE AIR,	737	SUMMER EVENING		19
SHAKEN					
	AH ME! TO BE SHAKEN WITH COUGHING AND BROKEN WITH OLD AGE AND PAIN,	63	OISIN 3		217
	ARE SHAKEN WITH EARTH'S OLD AND WEARY CRY.	120	SORROW OF LOVE	V	12
	REMEMBERING ALL THAT SHAKEN HAIR	135	TWO TREES		17
	WHEN LOOKING ON THEIR SHAKEN HAIR,	135	TWO TREES	V	17
	IN SHAKEN BOUGHS, IN TIDE ON THE SHORE?	141	EVERLAST VOICE		7
	O HEART THE WINDS HAVE SHAKEN, THE UNAPPEASABLE HOST	147	UNAPPEAS HOST		11
	AND HEART THE WINDS HAVE SHAKEN! THE UNAPPEASABLE HOST	147	UNAPPEAS HOST	V	11
	AND HEAR THE WINDS HAVE SHAKEN, THE UNAPPEASABLE HOST	147	UNAPPEAS HOST	V	11
	THAT WAS SHAKEN OUT OVER MY BREAST.	155	REPROVE CURLEW		5
	IN TWILIGHT SHAKEN WITH LOW SIGHS!	156	FORGOT BEAUTY	V	10B
	IS SHAKEN IN THESE SEAS, AND WHAT ONE DOES	237	SHADOW WATER B		339
	WHAT WOULD HAVE SHAKEN FROM THE SIEVE?	256	WORDS		14
	UPON A HOUSE SHAKEN BY THE LAND AGITATION	264	HOUSE SHAKEN		T
SHAKES					
	AND BENDS TO THE FIRE AND SHAKES WITH THE COLD	26	OISIN 1		405
	AND SHAKES O'ER THE WIDTH OF THE SEA-WORLD BORDER	28	OISIN 1	V	423C
	GOD SHAKES THE WORLD WITH RESTLESS HANDS. MORE NEAR	43	OISIN 2	V	208
	ORCHIL SHAKES OUT HER LONG DARK HAIR	85	MAD KING GOLL		62
	THAT SHAKES A MOULDERING COBWEB FROM THE RAFTER!	130	BOOK STORIES		19
	THAT SHAKES THE SHUTTER, TO HAVE BROUGHT TO MIND	327	ROBERT GREGORY		90
	NOT AS HE SHAKES THE FOREST! BUT A CRY	689	NETTLESHIP		8
	AY, AND SHAKES IN SEA-GREEN WAVERINGS ALONG THE FISHERS' STREET!	718	PHANTOM SHIP		2
	AYE AND SHAKES IN SEA GREEN WAVERINGS, ALONG THE FISHERS' STREET.	718	PHANTOM SHIP	V	2
	ONE WHOSE BREATHING SHAKES THE AIR,	727	LOVERS QUARREL		31
	ONE WHOSE FOOTFALL SHAKES THE GROUND.	727	LOVERS QUARREL		32
	MY LOVE SHAKES OUT HER HAIR UPON THE STREAMS	768	SHADOW WATER A		416
SHAKESPEAREAN					
	SHAKESPEAREAN FISH SWAM THE SEA, FAR AWAY FROM LAND!	485	THREE MOVEMENT		1
SHAKING	SEE EARTH-SHAKING				
	OF THE LOUD CRASHING AND EARTH SHAKING FIGHT	38	OISIN 2	V	141
	SHAKING AND WAVING, VAPOUR VAPOUR CHASED,	39	OISIN 2		164
	SHAKING AND WAVING, VAPOURS VAPOURS CHASED;	39	OISIN 2	V	164
	AND, SHAKING THE PLUMES OF THE GRASSES	49	OISIN 3		35
	HE, SHAKING THE FOLD OF HIS LIPS,	51	OISIN 3		59
	HE, SHAKING THE FOLDS OF HIS LIPS	51	OISIN 3	V	59
	HEARING THE SHAKING OF SHIELDS	62	OISIN 3		207
	THE SHAKING OF ITS LEAFY HEAD	134	TWO TREES		9
	THROUGH THE SHAKING TREE	359	TO A SQUIRREL		3
	THAT STORMS ARE SHAKING, HEAR THE ARMED MAN SPEAK.	470	HARUN RASHID	V	193
	WHERE THE SHAKING LEAF WITH THE BEAM WAS PLAYING,	728	PRIEST FAIRY		2
SHALLOP					
	WHERE LIES A SHALLOP IN THE YELLOW REEDS.	702	MOSADA 3		77
SHALLOW					
	ON THE GREY SAND BESIDE THE SHALLOW STREAM	367	EGO DOMINUS		1
	FROM SHALLOW WITS: WHO KNOWS NO WORK CAN STAND,	429	NINETEEN 19		35
	IT BORE ME SOFTLY WHERE THE SHALLOW SAND	657	ISLE STAT I 3		58
	THE BOAT'S PROW GRATED ON THE SHALLOW SAND,	659	ISLE STAT II 1		11
	WHAT SHALLOW THOUGHTS ABOUT DEEP THINGS!	725	LEGEND		11
SHALLOWING					
	PIERCED WITH SOFT LIGHT THE SHALLOWING DEEPS.	13	OISIN 1		164
SHAMBLING					
	SAID THE RAMBLING, SHAMBLING TRAVELLING-MAN!	788	HAWTHORN TREE		2
	SAID THE RAMBLING, SHAMBLING TRAVELLING-MAN!	788	HAWTHORN TREE		10
SHAME					
	IT BRINGS NO SHAME UPON A HUMAN HEAD	35	OISIN 2	V	90A
	THE FORTUNE THAT HAD BEEN MY SHAME	274	GREY ROCK		93

706

		PAGE	TITLE	LINE

SHAME   (CONTINUED)
AND THAT IS MY SHAME. . . . . 572 LADYS 1ST SONG   8
AND THINK IT IS NO SHAME. . . . . 605 SONGS, BURDEN 1   4
THE SISTER: "SELL THY COUNTRY, AND THE SHAME . . . . 712 FERENCZ RENYI   60
SHAMED
WERE NEITHER SHAMED IN HIS OWN . . . . 291 TO A FRIEND   7
SHAMELESS
WHO LIVED IN SHAMELESS JOY AND LAUGHED INTO THE FACE OF   366 HER COURAGE   V 10
DEATH.
SHAMMING
ONE BEGGAR CRIED: "YOU'RE SHAMMING SLEEP," . . . . . 297 THREE BEGGARS V 45
SHANWALLA
SHANWALLA, WHERE A WILLOW BORDERED POND . . . . 217 WOODS OF COOLE V   2
SHAN-WALLA
SHAN-WALLA, WHERE A WILLOW-BORDERED POND . . . . . . 217 WOODS OF COOLE   2
SHAPE
AND SUNKEN SHAPE, A NINE DAYS' CORPSE SEA-DASHED-- . . .   40 OISIN 2   V 179
AND SUNKEN SHAPE, AGAINST MY FACE AND BREAST, ...   40 OISIN 2   V 179
AND DRIPPING AND SUNKEN SHAPE, TO FACE AND BREAST, . . .   40 OISIN 2   V 179
HIS NEW-HEALED SHAPE: AND FOR A HUNDRED YEARS . . . .   44 OISIN 2   221
HIS HEALED SHAPE: AND FOR A HUNDRED YEARS . . . . .   44 OISIN 2   V 221
HIS NEW HEALED SHAPE: AND FOR A HUNDRED YEARS . . . .   44 OISIN 2   V 221
AND YOU HAVE CHANGED AND FLOWED FROM SHAPE TO SHAPE, . . 102 FERGUS DRUID   2
AND YOU HAVE CHANGED AND FLOWED FROM SHAPE TO SHAPE, . . 102 FERGUS DRUID   2
AND NOW AT LAST YOU WEAR A HUMAN SHAPE, ... 102 FERGUS DRUID   6
AND NOW AT LAST YOU TAKE ON HUMAN SHAPE-- . . . . . 102 FERGUS DRUID   V   6
THE POWERS WHOSE NAME AND SHAPE NO LIVING CREATURE KNOWS 174 ELEMENT POWERS   1
LONGING TO KNEAD AND PULL IT INTO SHAPE . . . . . . 246 SHADOW WATER B   510
FOR WHAT IS DOUBLY BRIEF." AND NOW THE SHAPE . . . . 285 TWO KINGS   207
FOR WHAT IS DOUBLY BRIEF." "BUT NOW THE SHAPE, . . . 285 TWO KINGS   V 207
INTO SOME MOST FEARFUL SHAPE." . . . . 299 THREE HERMITS   23
TO HIS SHAPE AT THE RINSING-POOL . . . . 341 SHEP GOATHERD   70
TO HIS SHAPE IN THE LENGTHENING SHADOWS, ... 341 SHEP GOATHERD V 70
TO HIS SHAPE AT THE RINSING POOL . . . . 341 SHEP GOATHERD V 70
THEIR CONNEMARA CLOTH WORN OUT OF SHAPE: . . . . . 372 PHASES OF MOON   4
A SHAPE WITH LION BODY AND THE HEAD OF A MAN, ... 402 SECOND COMING   14
AS THOUGH TO CHOOSE WHATEVER SHAPE IT WILLS . . . . 417 ANCEST HOUSES   6
OR SERVILE SHAPE, AT OTHERS' BECK AND CALL. . . . . 417 ANCEST HOUSES   8
WHAT YOUTHFUL MOTHER, A SHAPE UPON HER LAP . . . . . 444 SCHOOL CHILDR   33
WOULD THINK HER SON, DID SHE BUT SEE THAT SHAPE . . . 444 SCHOOL CHILDR   37
THE SELF-SOWN, SELF-BEGOTTEN SHAPE THAT GIVES . . . . 446 COLONUS PRAISE   10
THAT DEFILING AND DISFIGURED SHAPE . . . . 479 SELF AND SOUL   51
HE THINKS THAT SHAPE MUST BE HIS SHAPE? . . . . . . 479 SELF AND SOUL   54
HE THINKS THAT SHAPE MUST BE HIS SHAPE? . . . . . . 479 SELF AND SOUL   54
ALL OUT OF SHAPE FROM TOE TO TOP, ... 639 BEN BULBEN   71
THE SHAPE CHANGERS THAT CAN PUT . . . . 775 AGAINST WITCH V   2
SHAPE-CHANGERS
THAT THE SHAPE-CHANGERS, THE EVER-LAUGHING ONES, . . . 249 SHADOW WATER B   566
THE SHAPE-CHANGERS THAT CAN PUT . . . . 775 AGAINST WITCH   2
SHAPED
HIS LONG LAMP-CHIMNEY SHAPED LIKE THE STEM . . . . . 566 LAPIS LAZULI   33
HIS LONG LAMP CHIMNEY SHAPED LIKE THE STEM . . . . . 566 LAPIS LAZULI   V 33
SHAPELESS
WHEN NETTLES WAVE UPON A SHAPELESS MOUND . . . . . 489 COOLE PARK 29   27
SHAPELY
AND ALL THE SHAPELY BODY NO TITTLE GONE ASTRAY. . . . 354 HIS PHOENIX   30
TO GREAT SHAPELY KNEES . . . . 355 PROPERTIUS   2
MY WAY IS WEST. SHE SEEMS BOTH YOUNG AND SHAPELY: . . 755 SHADOW WATER A   171
SHAPES
THROUGH MANY SHAPES: I LUNGED AT THE SMOOTH THROAT . . .   40 OISIN 2   175
TO MANY SHAPES: I LUNGED AT THE SMOOTH THROAT . . . .   40 OISIN 2   V 175
ON THE FAR GOLDEN PEAK: ENORMOUS SHAPES, ...   74 ANASHU VIJAYA   68
MAGICAL SHAPES. BY THE HELP OF AN IMAGE . . . . . 367 EGO DOMINUS   7
PARTICULAR QUALITY. THE SIGNS AND SHAPES: . . . . . 469 HARUN RASHID   181
BECAUSE THE FIRES OF PURGATORY HAVE ATE THEIR SHAPES AWAY: 593 PILGRIM   13
OR, FOR MANY SHAPES THEY HAVE, ... 775 AGAINST WITCH   14
SHARE
BUT HAVE NO SHARE IN LOSS OR VICTORY. . . . . . . 104 FERGUS DRUID   V 38E
FOR GOD HAS BID THEM SHARE AN EQUAL FATE: . . . . . 115 ROSE OF BATTLE   32
O MY SHARE OF THE WORLD, O YELLOW HAIR! . . . . . . 211 RAGGED WOOD   11
AND TAKE THE CAPTAIN'S SHARE OF EVERYTHING . . . . . 225 SHADOW WATER B   73
YOU'LL HAVE THE CAPTAIN'S SHARE OF EVERYTHING. . . . 225 SHADOW WATER B V 67A
A PRETTY GIRL TO SHARE MY BED": . . . . 296 THREE BEGGARS   31
I HAD MY SHARE OF MOTHER-WIT, ... 313 MEMORY YOUTH   3
I HAD MY SHARE OF MOTHER WIT: . . . . 313 MEMORY YOUTH   V   3
COULD SHARE IN THAT DISCOURTESY OF DEATH. . . . . . 325 ROBERT GREGORY   48
IN SOMETHING THAT ALL OTHERS UNDERSTAND OR SHARE: . . . 427 PHANTOM HATRED   35
FOR EVEN DAUGHTERS OF THE SWAN CAN SHARE . . . . . 444 SCHOOL CHILDR   20
. . . SHARE GOD THAT IS BUT THREE: . . . . 556 RIBH PATRICK   11
I WILL NOT SHARE YOUR SIN. THIS IS NO SIN. . . . . 692 MOSADA 1   42
I WILL NOT SHARE YOUR SIN. IT IS NO SIN. . . . . . 692 MOSADA 1   V 42
SHARED
IN GRATTAN'S HOUSE. MY GREAT-GRANDFATHER SHARED . . . 486 SEVEN SAGES   2
NONE SHARED OUR GUILT: NOR DID WE PLAY A PART . . . . 542 PARN FUNERAL 1   22
SHARED THE BYZANTINE CROWN? . . . . 789 SINGING HEAD   14
SHARES
HAVE LIT UPON A WOMAN WHO SO SHARES . . . . . . 465 HARUN RASHID   85
SHARP
SHARP THEIR SPADES, THEIR MUSCLES STRONG, ... 637 BEN BULBEN   22
SHARP THEIR SPADES, THEIR MUSCLE STRONG, ... 637 BEN BULBEN   V 22

		PAGE	TITLE		LINE
SHARPENED					
BEING SHARPENED BY HIS DEATH,		471	ALL SOUL NIGHT		8
CAN GIVE HIS SHARPENED PALATE ECSTASY		474	ALL SOUL NIGHT		84
GIVE TO HIS SHARPENED PALATE ECSTACY		474	ALL SOUL NIGHT	V	84
SHATTER					
FAR THE MORNING VAPOURS SHATTER,		648	ISLE STAT I 1		89
SHATTERED					
HAD SHATTERED HER SOUL. PROPINQUITY HAD BROUGHT		619	BRONZE HEAD		18
THE DARKNESS OF THE WHIRLWIND SHATTERED DEEP.		688	TWO TITANS		58
SHAUL					
HOW THE MEN OF THE SAND-SACK LED ME TO SHAUL,		61	OISIN 3	V	193
SHAVINGS					
DREAM OF SHAVINGS ON A FLOOR		440	WISDOM	V	6
SHAWE-TAYLOR					
IMPETUOUS MEN, SHAWE-TAYLOR AND HUGH LANE,		489	COOLE PARK 29		14
SHAWL					
IN COUNTRY SHAWL OR PARIS CLOAK, HAD PUT MY WITS ASTRAY,		592	PILGRIM		3
SO COME IN RAGS OR COME IN SILK, IN CLOAK OR COUNTRY SHAWL,		593	PILGRIM		22
SO COME IN RAG OR COME IN SILK, IN CLOAK OR COUNTRY SHAWL,		593	PILGRIM	V	22
SHEAF					
OR MICE IN THE ONE WHEATEN SHEAF		195	BAILE AILLINN		147
SHEARS					
RAN AND WITH THE GARDEN SHEARS		410	TOWER		30
BUT A RAVING AUTUMN SHEARS		475	EVA GORE-BOOTH		5
SHEATH					
COVERS ITS WOODEN SHEATH.		421	MY TABLE		7
LONG ERE AN ARROW WHIZZED OR SWORD LEFT SHEATH		650	ISLE STAT I 1		135
SHEAVES					
AND OVER THE MICE IN THE BARLEY SHEAVES!		79	FALLING LEAVES		2
AND ALL THE SHEAVES TO BIND.		312	CHILD DANCING		10
SHEBA					
SOLOMON TO SHEBA		332	SOLOMON SHEBA		T
SANG SOLOMON TO SHEBA,		332	SOLOMON SHEBA		1
TO SOLOMON SANG SHEBA,		333	SOLOMON SHEBA		9
SANG SOLOMON TO SHEBA,		333	SOLOMON SHEBA		17
SAID SOLOMON TO SHEBA,		333	SOLOMON SHEBA	V	17
WHEN SHEBA WAS HIS LASS,		345	ON WOMAN		16
THAT SHEBA LED A DANCE.		346	ON WOMAN		43
GAVE SHEBA TO HER SOLOMON."		388	SOLOMON WITCH		32
SHED SEE MILKING-SHED					
AND SOMETIMES FROM THE SALTIN' SHED		94	MOLL MAGEE		9
TIMES FROM THE SALTIN' SHED		94	MOLL MAGEE	V	9
AND THESE IMMORTAL EYES SHED TEARS--		275	GREY ROCK		100
FOR THIS THAT ALL THAT BLOOD WAS SHED,		290	SEPTEMBER 1913		19
ON NO LONG BENCH NOR LOFTY MILKING SHED		341	SHEP GOATHERD	V	51
INTO ITS NARROW SHED.		358	BALLOON MIND		4
OR OUT OF ABSTRACT HATRED, AND SHED BLOOD,		482	BLOOD AND MOON		38
AND WE THAT HAVE SHED NONE MUST GATHER THERE		482	BLOOD AND MOON		41
MUST IRELAND'S BLOOD BE SHED.		608	SONGS BURDEN 3		26
THAT I WOULD SHED LIKE TWILIGHT OVER YOU.		765	SHADOW WATER A		352
SHEDS					
AND SHEDS FAINT ODOURS THROUGH THE AIR!		85	MAD KING GOLL		64
AND SHEDS FAINT ODOUR THROUGH THE AIR!		85	MAD KING GOLL	V	64
AND SANG WHAT GOLD MORNING OR EVENING SHEDS		126	DREAM OF FAERY		7
AND SANG HOW DAY A DRUID TWILIGHT SHEDS		126	DREAM OF FAERY	V	7
SHEE					
"I AM NEAVE, A CHILD OF THE MIGHTY SHEE,		5	OISIN 1	V	48
AND MEAT TO THE ASLAUGA SHEE.		743	DANAAN QUICK		17
SHEEN					
SMALL ISLAND, WHERE THE FULL SOFT SHEEN		653	ISLE STAT I 2		36
SHEEP					
AND A HUNDRED CALVES AND A HUNDRED SHEEP		8	OISIN 1		89
A PAIR OF LAPWINGS, ONE OLD SHEEP,		302	HOUR DAWN		9
AND THE SHEEP BLEATING AT THE WIND		306	HOUR DAWN		78
FROM STONE TO STONE. I AM LOOKING FOR STRAYED SHEEP!		339	SHEP GOATHERD		9
THE SHEEP HAD GONE FROM THEIRS. I KNOW RIGHT WELL		339	SHEP GOATHERD		15
WHERE THE SHEEP ARE THROWN IN THE POOL,		341	SHEP GOATHERD	V	71
'TIS MORN! THY SHEEP ARE WANDERING DOWN THE VALE--		645	ISLE STAT I 1		3
NOW HER SHEEP ALL BROWSING MEET		646	ISLE STAT I 1		22
THEIR SHEEP IN ARCADY, NASCHINA, HAIL!		649	ISLE STAT I 1		119
THEIR SHEEP IN ARCADY, NASCHINA, HAIL!		649	ISLE STAT I 1		121
NASCHINA, HAIL! I'D DRIVE THY WOOLLY SHEEP,		649	ISLE STAT I 1		122
AND ONLY SHEEP HE LOVED OF ALL THE TROOP,		661	ISLE STAT II 1		61
HEAVY WITH WOOL THE SHEEP ARE GATHERED IN,		681	SEEKER		1
ARE ALL THINGS WELL WITH YOU AND WITH YOUR SHEEP?		682	SEEKER		13
AND TO GIVE WEALTH OF OXEN AND SHEEP TO ALL!		756	SHADOW WATER A		184
A HUNDRED OXEN AND A HUNDRED SHEEP,		756	SHADOW WATER A	V	189
GIVE ME A HUNDRED SHEEP. GIVE ME A HOUSE		758	SHADOW WATER A		220
SHEEP-GUIDING					
SHEEP-GUIDING, OR THE BRINGING SOME STRANGE BIRD,		650	ISLE STAT I 1		147
SHEER					
THAT SEEMED SHEER MIRACLE TO THE MULTITUDE,		428	NINETEEN 19		2
THROUGH SHEER BEWILDERMENT? SHE HAD NOT PACED		466	HARUN RASHID		118
SHEET SEE WINDING-SHEET					
I CAN STREW THE SHEET.		572	LADYS 2ND SONG		6
THE WHITE WAVES WRAP IT IN A SHEET OF FLAME,		662	ISLE STAT II 2		14
SHEETS					
AND I MUST LIE BETWEEN THE SHEETS		570	THREE BUSHES		40
SHELF					
OUT-SCREAMS THE WHOLE SHELF! "ALTHOUGH		319	DOLLS		7

	PAGE	TITLE		LINE
SHELL SEE SEA-SHELL				
AND IT WAS BOUND WITH A PEARL-PALE SHELL	4	OISIN 1		28
AND IT WAS BOUND WITH A PEARL PALE SHELL	4	OISIN 1	V	28
WHERE MANY A TRUMPET-TWISTED SHELL	13	OISIN 1		160
WE RODE ON MURMURING, MANY A SHELL	13	OISIN 1	V	159
OUT OF THE MOON'S PALE TWISTED SHELL:	19	OISIN 1		279
. . . WAKING WHITE AS A SHELL	54	OISIN 3		103
SOME TWISTED, ECHO-HARBOURING SHELL,	66	HAPPY SHEPHERD		36
SOUGHT ONCE AGAIN THE SHORE, AND FOUND A SHELL,	68	SAD SHEPHERD		18
SOUGHT ONCE AGAIN THE SHORE, AND CHOSE A SHELL	68	SAD SHEPHERD	V	18
A MOON, WORN AS IF IT HAD BEEN A SHELL	206	ADAMS CURSE		31
A MOON--MOON WORN AS IF IT HAD BEEN A SHELL	206	ADAMS CURSE	V	31
INTO THE YOLK AND WHITE OF THE ONE SHELL.	443	SCHOOL CHILDR		16
AS THE SEA'S FURROWS ON A SEA-TOST SHELL,	660	ISLE STAT II 1		51
WHERE A SHELL THE SEAS ANOINT,	732	STREET DANCERS		32
A FRAGILE, EXQUISITE, PALE SHELL,	784	WOMANS BEAUTY		16
SHELLEY				
AND SHELLEY HAD HIS TOWERS,	480	BLOOD AND MOON		15
SHELLEY'S				
SAT LATE, OR SHELLEY'S VISIONARY PRINCE:	373	PHASES OF MOON		16
SHELL'S				
TO ROUND THAT SHELL'S ELABORATE WHORL,	509	JANE REPROVED		8
SHELLS SEE SEA-SHELLS				
. . . THE STRONG HOOFS CRUSHING THE SAND AND THE SHELLS,	58	OISIN 3		157
. . . THE GOLD HOOVES CRUSHING THE SANDS AND THE SHELLS	58	OISIN 3	V	157
. . . THE STRONG HOOFS CRUSHING THE SAND AND THE SHELLS	58	OISIN 3	V	157
BUT ACTUAL SHELLS OF ROSSES' LEVEL SHORE.	494	AT ALGECIRAS		12
ARE 'NEATH ITS PROW, AND CRUSHING SHELLS.	663	ISLE STAT II 2		35
SHELTER				
BETWEEN THE LAVISH SHELTER OF A WOOD	108	CUCHULAIN SEA	V	38A
ALTHOUGH I SHELTER FROM THE RAIN	131	OLD PENSIONER		1
FOR HE WILL SHELTER YOU AND BRING YOU HOME.	250	SHADOW WATER B		590
A SHELTER TILL THE DAYLIGHT BROKE.	302	HOUR DAWN		15
AND THERE IS SHELTER UNDER IT,	509	JANE BISHOP		26
THEY LEFT THEIR HOMESTEADS TO SHELTER THE FOXES,	546	TO SAME TUNE 2	V	3
SHELTERED SEE CLIFF-SHELTERED				
THE MILKING-PLACE, THE SHELTERED FARM?	151	HEART OF WOMAN	V	6
A FARMHOUSE THAT IS SHELTERED BY ITS WALL,	419	MY HOUSE		2
A FARM-HOUSE THAT IS SHELTERED BY ITS WALL,	419	MY HOUSE	V	2
FLED TO FAR COUNTRIES, OR SHELTERED THEMSELVES	546	TO SAME TUNE 2		4
FLED TO FAR COUNTRIES, OR SHELTERED THEMSELVES	613	MARCH SONGS 1		4
WELL SHELTERED FROM THE WINDS, AND FRUITFUL FIELDS,	758	SHADOW WATER A		221
SHELTERING				
SOME BEGGAR SHELTERING FROM THE WIND, AND THERE	351	HER PRAISE		13
BENEATH THE SHELTERING SHADOW OF THY CHURCH:	698	MOSADA 2		58
SHEPHERD				
THE SONG OF THE HAPPY SHEPHERD	64	HAPPY SHEPHERD		T
THE SAD SHEPHERD	67	SAD SHEPHERD		T
SHEPHERD AND GOATHERD	338	SHEP GOATHERD		T
THE SAD SHEPHERD	338	SHEP GOATHERD	V	T
WHAT TURNED SO GOOD A SHEPHERD FROM HIS CHARGE.	339	SHEP GOATHERD		16
HOW DOES SHE BEAR HER GRIEF? THERE IS NOT A SHEPHERD	340	SHEP GOATHERD		28
WATCHING OUR SHEPHERD SPORTS AT HARVEST-TIME	340	SHEP GOATHERD		41
COURT HIS SHEPHERD LASS,	343	SHEP GOATHERD		104
FOR SHEPHERD LADS IN GALILEE: AND GRANT	371	ON GOING HOUSE		4
SHEPHERD, TO MAR THE MORNING HAST THOU COME?	646	ISLE STAT I 1		30
HEAR ME, AND, SHEPHERD, HEARING ME, GROW DUMB.	646	ISLE STAT I 1		31
YON SHEPHERD--CAME YOUR SPIRIT TO BEGUILE	648	ISLE STAT I 1		105
SING SUMMER WAVES. BUT YONDER SHEPHERD VILE,	649	ISLE STAT I 1		107
THE SHEPHERD PARIS FOR OENONE MADE,	650	ISLE STAT I 1		136
I, AS A SHEPHERD DRESSED, WILL SEEK AND SEEK	658	ISLE STAT II 1		1
MY SHEPHERD GARMENTS, AND RETURN ANON.	659	ISLE STAT II 1		29
IT IS THE SHEPHERD GUARIMOND, WHO LOVETH WELL	661	ISLE STAT II 1		53
NOW, JUDGE, MUST SHEPHERD THERNOT THERE AND I	661	ISLE STAT II 1		65
E'EN THEN, BEFORE HER SHEPHERD HAIR	668	ISLE STAT II 3		54
FAIR SHEPHERD, AS WE WANDERED HITHER,	669	ISLE STAT II 3		83
THE SHEPHERD RAISED HIS ARMS AND SANK,	673	ISLE STAT II 3		187
NO SHEPHERD FOOT HAS EVER DARED ITS DEPTHS.	682	SEEKER		32
SHEPHERD-BOY				
I LIT BY THE THING, 'TWAS A SHEPHERD-BOY,	673	ISLE STAT II 3		180
SHEPHERDESS				
ALAS! I MAKE YOU SADDER, SHEPHERDESS.	659	ISLE STAT II 1		18
A SHEPHERDESS LONG YEARS FORETOLD:	668	ISLE STAT II 3		49
THAT SHEPHERDESS: ARISE, AND BRING TO ME,	673	ISLE STAT II 3		191
SHEPHERD'S				
HE'LL PRACTISE ON THE SHEPHERD'S FLUTE,	343	SHEP GOATHERD		102
SHEPHERDS				
FLY! FLY! SO THESE BRAVE SHEPHERDS BOTH ARE GONE!	649	ISLE STAT I 1		112
OF HILL TWO SHEPHERDS COME. FAREWELL! I'LL DON	659	ISLE STAT II 1		28
OF WAR. OF YORE, TWO SHEPHERDS, WHERE WE PAUSE,	659	ISLE STAT II 1		31
ONCE MORE THOSE SHEPHERDS COME. MAYHAP SOME MIRTH	664	ISLE STAT II 2		49
THE SINGING SHEPHERDS, TOO, HAVE PASSED AWAY.	676	ISLE STAT II 3		271
SHEPHERDS, I CAME THIS MORNING TO YOUR LAND	682	SEEKER		15
BETWEEN THE HORNED HILLS--SHEPHERDS, FAREWELL!	682	SEEKER		27
SHEPHERDS, FAREWELL! HE SOON WILL BE--ASHES	682	SEEKER		34
SHEPHERDS'				
THAT HE MIGHT LEARN THE SHEPHERDS' WILL.	288	TO WEALTHY MAN		19
THE SHEPHERDS' CONTEST OF SONG	646	ISLE STAT I 1	V	T
SHIELD				
AH, FENIANS, WITH THE SHIELD AND BOW?	10	OISIN 1		116

709

	PAGE	TITLE		LINE

SHIELD (CONTINUED)
AND BY THEM WERE ARROW AND WAR-AXE, ARROW AND SHIELD AND BLADE: 49 OISIN 3   29
WERE ARROW AND SHIELD AND WAR-AXE, ARROW AND SPEAR AND BLADE,   49 OISIN 3   V   30
. . . THE SHIELD OUT OF OSIER AND HIDE: 52 OISIN 3   82
AND THROUGH THE OTHER'S SHIELD HIS LONG BLADE BROKE,   110 CUCHULAIN SEA   V   66
KING EOCHAID SAID, AND HE THAT BORE HIS SHIELD   276 TWO KINGS   V   8
THE SKIES MORE DIM, THOUGH BURNING LIKE A SHIELD,   656 ISLE STAT I 3   26
"SHIELD BREAKER, BREAK A SHIELD TO-DAY,   739 EARL PAUL   1
"SHIELD BREAKER, BREAK A SHIELD TO-DAY,   739 EARL PAUL   1
SHIELD-BREAKER, BREAK A SHIELD TO-DAY,   739 EARL PAUL   V   1
MEN CRY "BRING PAUL, SHIELD BREAKER,   740 EARL PAUL   11
"SHIELD BREAKER, GREAT SHIELD BREAKER,"   740 EARL PAUL   25
"SHIELD BREAKER, GREAT SHIELD BREAKER,"   740 EARL PAUL   25
WITH SHIELD AND ARMOUR WROUGHT WITH GOLD,   741 EARL PAUL   37
THE DIM SPEAR BREAKS THE BRIGHT SHIELD   741 EARL PAUL   49

SHIELD-BREAKER
SHIELD-BREAKER, BREAK A SHIELD TO-DAY,   739 EARL PAUL   V   1
MEN CRY: "BRING PAUL, SHIELD-BREAKER,   740 EARL PAUL   V   11
THOUGH THE GLAD CRY "SHIELD-BREAKER,"   741 EARL PAUL   35
THE PEOPLE CRIED "SHIELD-BREAKER!"   741 EARL PAUL   53

SHIELDS
HEARING THE SHAKING OF SHIELDS   62 OISIN 3   207
THE HORNS AND SHIELDS AND WILD SWAN'S PINIONS: 82 MAD KING GOLL   V   5
SHOOK THE ALE-HORNS AND SHIELDS UPON THEIR HOOKS: 181 QUEEN MAEVE   38
SHOOK THE ALE HORNS AND SHIELDS UPON THEIR HOOKS: 181 QUEEN MAEVE   38
ARMLETS OF GOLD OR SHIELDS WITH GOLDEN NAILS   749 SHADOW WATER A   43
AND TO GIVE YOU BESIDES A HUNDRED SHIELDS,   756 SHADOW WATER A   185
A HUNDRED SHIELDS OF BRASS, A HUNDRED SWORDS,   756 SHADOW WATER A   V   188

SHIFT
OR THAT THE WIND WOULD SHIFT A POINT,   306 HOUR DAWN   92
WE SHIFT ABOUT—ALL THAT GREAT GLORY SPENT—   491 COOLE BALLYLEE   39
OR SHIFT TIME'S FILTHY LOAD,   505 RESULT THOUGHT   15

SHIFTED
IF HE BUT SHIFTED A FEW STONES,   302 HOUR DAWN   14

SHIFTS
MAN SHIFTS ABOUT—ALL THAT GREAT GLORY SPENT—   491 COOLE BALLYLEE   V   39

SHIN
I HAVE A LUCKY WOODEN SHIN   302 HOUR DAWN   18
ALONE AND ALONE, WITH A SPECKLED SHIN?   551 SONGS REWRIT 1   8
DRINKING ALONE WITH A SPECKLED SHIN?   551 SONGS REWRIT 1   V   8
LIVE LONE, ALONE WITH A SPECKLED SHIN?   551 SONGS REWRIT 1   V   8

SHINE   SEE SEA-SHINE
LAID IT AND SIGHED: I HELD A SWORD WHOSE SHINE   37 OISIN 2   126
LAID IT AND SIGHED—A SWORD WHOSE WIZARD SHINE   37 OISIN 2   V   126
THEN IN THAT HALL, LIT BY THE DIM SEA SHINE,   41 OISIN 2   V   187
DOWN TO THEIR FEET THE STARS THAT SHINE ALONE,   662 ISLE STAT II 1   80
SHINE DULL UNMOVING EYES. WHAT THING ART THOU?   685 SEEKER   74
WAVES OFF THE FLIES, AND WARMS HIM IN THE SHINE.   709 FERENCZ RENYI   7
AND THAT DREAM ONLY SHINE BEFORE HER FEET.   761 SHADOW WATER A   258

SHININ'
BUT GATHER WITH YOUR SHININ' LOOKS   96 MOLL MAGEE   55

SHINING   SEE A-SHINING SOFT-SHINING CLEAR-SHINING RE-SHINING
THE SHINING SEVEN   118 CRADLE SONG   V   7
SHINING BRIGHT AS A NEW LANCE!   125 CATHLEEN PARA   V   14
DEW EVER SHINING AND TWILIGHT GREY: 148 INTO TWILIGHT   6
AND STARS LIKE MOTHS WERE SHINING OUT,   149 WANDER AENGUS   V   6
A WOMAN OF SO SHINING LOVELINESS   170 SECRET ROSE   25
THOUGH YOU ARE IN YOUR SHINING DAYS,   172 PLEADS FRIEND   1
ALTHOUGH YOU ARE IN YOUR SHINING DAYS,   172 PLEADS FRIEND   V   1
MORE SHINING WINDS, MORE STAR-GLIMMERING PONDS?   218 WOODS OF COOLE   35
SHINING ON WATER AND FALLEN AMONG LEAVES,   218 WOODS OF COOLE   38
INTO THEIR SHINING LIMBS—I'VE HAD GREAT TEACHERS.   231 SHADOW WATER B   195
AND HAVING SUCH WIDE-OPEN, SHINING EYES,   231 SHADOW WATER B   200
A SHINING WEB, A FLOATING RIBBON OF CLOTH,   430 NINETEEN 19   50
EACH SHINING CLEAR AS SOME UNBAFFLED STAR!   656 ISLE STAT I 3   25
TRAILING AND SHINING 'NEATH THE FLICKERING GLARE.   688 TWO TITANS   32
SINKS, SHINING ON THE LITTLE CRUCIFIX   691 MOSADA 1   34
O SHINING ONES, LIGHTLY WITH SONG PASS,   708 FAIRY PEDANT   21

SHIP
HERE WE WILL MOOR OUR LONELY SHIP   78 INDIAN TO LOVE   6
THERE WE WILL MOOR OUR LONELY SHIP   78 INDIAN TO LOVE   V   6
"HE IS THE MIGHTIEST MAN IN SHIP OR DUN."   107 CUCHULAIN SEA   V   28
WE HAVE NOT COME UPON A SHORE OR SHIP   222 SHADOW WATER B   3
WHERE NO SHIP SAILS, WHERE NOTHING THAT'S ALIVE   226 SHADOW WATER B   98
LOOK THERE! THERE IN THE MIST! A SHIP OF SPICE!   232 SHADOW WATER B   219
BUT IF I WERE TO PUT YOU ON THAT SHIP,   236 SHADOW WATER B   307
AND BEAT THE BULWARK OF YOUR SHIP ON MINE,   236 SHADOW WATER B   312
UPON THAT OTHER SHIP WE ARE TO WAKE.   240 SHADOW WATER B   381
WHAT NAME TO CALL HIM BY? COME TO HIS SHIP.   240 SHADOW WATER B   390
BUT DESOLATE WATERS AND A BATTERED SHIP.   246 SHADOW WATER B   497
DRAGONS WITH EYES OF RUBY. THE WHOLE SHIP   248 SHADOW WATER B   535
AND THERE'S NO HELP IN WORDS. TO THE OTHER SHIP,   250 SHADOW WATER B   585
AND RUNNING CROWD AND GAUDY SHIP   254 HIS DREAM   15
AND FISH AND CROWD AND PAINTED SHIP,   254 HIS DREAM   V   15
AND FISH AND CROWD AND GAUDY SHIP   254 HIS DREAM   V   15
THE FAERY SHIP THAT SWIMS ATHWART THE SKY.   663 ISLE STAT II 2   16
THE PHANTOM SHIP   718 PHANTOM SHIP   T
A LEGEND OF THE PHANTOM SHIP.   718 PHANTOM SHIP   V   T
FOR I HAVE SEEN A SHIP HID IN THE FOG.   751 SHADOW WATER A   89

SHIP   (CONTINUED)
      THAT MY TRUE-LOVE WOULD COME IN A SHIP OF PEARL • • • •   763 SHADOW WATER A   315
      THAT MY TRUE LOVE WOULD COME IN A SHIP OF PEARL • • • •   763 SHADOW WATER A V   315
      A HOUSE, A SWORD, A SHIP, A MASK• • • • • • • • • • • •   788 BRAVEST ASK   2
SHIPBOARD
      ON THEIR OWN FEET THEY CAME, OR ON SHIPBOARD, • • • • •   566 LAPIS LAZULI   25
SHIPS
      A STORMY SUNSET ON DOOMED SHIPS; • • • • • • • • • • •   3 OISIN 1   23
      A STORMY SUNSET O'ER DOOMED SHIPS, • • • • • • • • • •   3 OISIN 1   V 23
      • • • FROM RACHLIN TO BERA OF SHIPS. • • • • • • • •   58 OISIN 3   160
      AND WAGE GOD'S BATTLES IN THE LONG GREY SHIPS. • • • •   114 ROSE OF BATTLE   20
      "FROM THE GREY SHIPS AND BATTLES NEVER WON• • • • • •   114 ROSE OF BATTLE V   8
      OUR LONG SHIPS LOOSE THOUGHT-WOVEN SAILS AND WAIT, • •   115 ROSE OF BATTLE   31
      DOOMED LIKE ODYSSEUS AND THE LABOURING SHIPS • • • • •   120 SORROW OF LOVE   7
      AND ALL THE SORROWS OF HER LABOURING SHIPS, • • • • •   120 SORROW OF LOVE V   7
      AND ALL THE TROUBLE OF HER LABOURING SHIPS, • • • • •   120 SORROW OF LOVE V   7
      WOULD THAT THE STORM THAT OVERTHREW MY SHIPS, • • • •   235 SHADOW WATER B   286
      UNTO THE WANDERER'S SHIPS, OR AS DAY FILLS • • • • •   645 ISLE STAT I 1   10
      DRIFT AND FLOAT LIKE SILVER SHIPS, • • • • • • • • •   647 ISLE STAT I 1   67
      DOTH STILL THE WANDERER ROVE? WITH ALL HIS SHIPS • •   677 ISLE STAT II 3   287
      WERE FURLED THE WINGS OF SHIPS. THERE IN A DELL, • •   693 MOSADA 1   82
      DID I NOT FOLLOW WITH A SCORE OF SHIPS? • • • • • •   749 SHADOW WATER A   36
SHIRK
      LIE DOWN AND DIE. THAT WERE TO SHIRK • • • • • • •   632 MAN AND ECHO   19
      AND SHIRK IT IN VAIN. THERE IS NO RELEASE • • • • •   632 MAN AND ECHO   21
      NOR LET THE MODISH PAINTER SHIRK • • • • • • • • • •   638 BEN BULBEN   38
SHIRT
      "EACH ONE A HORSEHAIR SHIRT HATH ON, • • • • • • • •   43 OISIN 2   V 208C
      AND PUSHING IT INTO MY SHIRT, • • • • • • • • • • •   274 GREY ROCK   89
      "IF BUT THE SHIRT UPON MY BODY KNEW IT • • • • • •   462 HARUN RASHID   33
SHIVER
      THE CORMORANTS SHIVER ON THEIR ROCKS; • • • • • • •   84 MAD KING GOLL   42
      SHIVER UNDER THE LASH, STRAIN, SWEAT AND JOLT • • • •   260 FASC DIFFICULT   7
SHIVERED
      AND SHIVERED, KNOWING THE ISLE OF MANY FEARS, • • • •   30 OISIN 2   25
      AND LONELY AND LONGING FOR NIAMH, I SHIVERED AND TURNED   60 OISIN 3   181
          ME ABOUT,
SHIVERING
      HE SHIVERING PAUSED, AND RAISED HIS HEAD AND SCREAMED• •   30 OISIN 2   V 25
      AND SHIVERING AND LONELY, AND LONGING FOR NIAM, I TURNED   60 OISIN 3   V 181
          ME ABOUT,
      OR THAN THE SHIVERING CASTING-NET OF THE STARS. • • •   237 SHADOW WATER B   329
      AND PRAYER TO SHIVERING PRAYER, UNTIL • • • • • •   289 SEPTEMBER 1913   4
      AND I LEFT SHIVERING. THE VOICE HAS DRAWN • • • • •   469 HARUN RASHID   179
      SHIVERING CLOSER TO THEIR DAMS • • • • • • • • •   726 LOVERS QUARREL   7
      OR THAN THE SHIVERING CASTING-NET OF THE STARS. • •   762 SHADOW WATER A   290
      OR THAN THE SHIVERING CASTING NET OF THE STARS. • •   762 SHADOW WATER A V   290
SHIVERS
      ALL CREATION SHIVERS • • • • • • • • • • • • • • •   559 HE AND SHE   11
SHOALED   SEE SALMON-SHOALED
SHOCK
      LAUGHTER AND CRIES. THE ARMIES CLASH AND SHOCK, • • • •   43 OISIN 2   211
      OF ARMOUR--LAUGHTER AND CRIES--THE ARMIES' SHOCK. • •   43 OISIN 2   V 211
SHOD   SEE GOLD-SHOD
      OR SHOD IN IRON, CLIMBED THE NARROW STAIRS, • • • • •   412 TOWER   83
      TO HIM WITH THUNDER SHOD, • • • • • • • • • • • • •   735 IN CHURCH   2
      TO HIM WITH THUNDER SHOD, • • • • • • • • • • • • •   736 IN CHURCH   14
SHOE
      BUT WEEP FOR YOUR NIAMH, O OISIN, WEEP; FOR IF ONLY YOUR   55 OISIN 3   127
          SHOE
      BUT WEEP FOR THY NIAM, OH OISIN, WEEP; FOR IF ONLY THY SHOE 55 OISIN 3   V 127
SHOED   SEE SILVER-SHOED
SHOES
      THE CLOAK, THE BOAT, AND THE SHOES • • • • • • • • •   69 CLOAK BOAT   T
      "I WEAVE THE SHOES OF SORROW; • • • • • • • • • • •   70 CLOAK BOAT   12
      AND HE WORE SMALL HOLES IN HIS SHOES, • • • • • • •   92 FATHER OHART   11
      HE HAD PUDDLE-WATER IN HIS SHOES; • • • • • • • • •   190 BAILE AILLINN   28
      HE HAD PUDDLE WATER IN HIS SHOES; • • • • • • • •   190 BAILE AILLINN V   28
      THAT PUT THIS HURRY IN MY SHOES." • • • • • • • •   194 BAILE AILLINN   125
      OR CREAKY SHOES. AND AT THE END OF ALL • • • • • •   228 SHADOW WATER B   128
      TO RID ME OF THE DEVIL IN MY SHOES," • • • • • • •   299 BEGGAR CRIED   6
      ALL WEAR THE CARPET WITH THEIR SHOES; • • • • • • •   337 SCHOLARS   8
      WEAR OUT THE CARPET WITH THEIR SHOES • • • • • • •   337 SCHOLARS   V   8
      WHO HAD SEEMED TO GLIDE TO SOME INTRIGUE IN HER RED SHOES, 363 DOLLS FACES   6
      WITH OLD PATCHED SHOES, • • • • • • • • • • • • • •   627 STATES HOLIDAY   30
      NOD TO THE IRON SHOES OF TIME, • • • • • • • • • •   736 SUMMER EVENING   11
      O SHUFFLING OF HOLY SHOES! • • • • • • • • • • • •   774 COME RIDE   15
SHONE
      BUT NOW THE MOON LIKE A WHITE ROSE SHONE • • • • • •   12 OISIN 1   152
      ON HORSE AND SEA AND SADDLE SHONE. • • • • • • • •   28 OISIN 1   V 427D
      SHONE MANY TIMES AMONG THE GLIMMERING FLOWERS • • •   30 OISIN 2   21
      AND THE FIXED STARS HAD DAWNED AND SHONE AND SET, • •   31 OISIN 2   40
      AT LAST THE MOON AND STARS SHONE, AND A FLIGHT • • •   31 OISIN 2   V 34
      THE IMAGED METEORS HAD SHONE AND RUN. • • • • • •   31 OISIN 2   V 38
      FEEBLER AND FEEBLER SHONE THE MISTY GLARE. • • • •   37 OISIN 2   V 121
      WITH BOWED HEAD; TREMBLING WHEN THE WHITE BLADE SHONE, • • 38 OISIN 2   137
      I STOOD; KEEN STARS ABOVE ME SHONE, • • • • • • •   83 MAD KING GOLL   29
      AROUND ME SHONE KEEN EYES OF MEN; • • • • • • • •   83 MAD KING GOLL   30
      I PAUSED--THE STARS ABOVE ME SHONE • • • • • • •   83 MAD KING GOLL   V 29
      AND SHONE AROUND THE EYES OF MEN; • • • • • • • •   83 MAD KING GOLL   V 30
      ONE STAR SHONE FAINT AND GREEN, • • • • • • • • •   95 MOLL MAGEE   30

SHONE   (CONTINUED)
    THEY MAULED AND BIT TILL THE DAY SHONE: . . . .   297 THREE BEGGARS   49
    TRUTH FLOURISHES WHERE THE STUDENT'S LAMP HAS SHONE,   398 LEADERS CROWD   8
    THAT SHONE BEFORE THESE EYES . . . .   504 QUARREL IN AGE   15
    BUT THE DARK CHANGED TO RED, AND TORCHES SHONE, ...   537 HER VISION   12
    OF SAD QUEEN DIDO SHONE THE LAPPING FIRE . . . .   645 ISLE STAT I 1   9
    COURAGEOUS MIRACLES! THE SUNLIGHT SHONE . . . .   649 ISLE STAT I 1   113
    OF ALL ON WHOM ARCADIAN SUNS HAVE SHONE . . . .   650 ISLE STAT I 1   143
    OH, ALLAH! IT WAS THUS THEY SHONE THAT NIGHT . . . . .   701 MOSADA 3   50
    THE FLAME THAT SHONE WITHIN HIS EYES BUT NOW . . . . .   704 MOSADA 3   128
SHONEEN
    TO A SHONEEN WHO HAD FREE LANDS . . . .   92 FATHER OHART   3
    ALL LOVED HIM, ONLY THE SHONEEN, ...   92 FATHER OHART   13
    TO A SHONEEN IN HIS FREELANDS, ...   92 FATHER OHART   V   3
SHOOK
    HE SHOOK HIMSELF AND NEIGHED THREE TIMES! . . . . . .   10 OISIN 1   110
    HE SHOOK HIMSELF FOR TRAVELLING. . . . .   10 OISIN 1   V   110
    NOR SHOOK MY FIRM AND SPACIOUS SOUL ONE JOT! . . . . .   36 OISIN 2   V   94
    AND SHOOK AT INVER AMERGIN . . . .   81 MAD KING GOLL   3
    THEREON HE SHOOK THE MORE AND CAST HIM DOWN . . . . .   106 CUCHULAIN SEA   14
    THE SINGING SHOOK HIM OUT OF HIS NEW EASE. . . . . .   126 DREAM OF FAERY   12
    AND LEAVES SHOOK IN THE WIND! . . . .   133 FR GILLIGAN   18
    SHOOK THE ALE-HORNS AND SHIELDS UPON THEIR HOOKS! . .   181 QUEEN MAEVE   38
    SHOOK THE ALE HORNS AND SHIELDS UPON THEIR HOOKS! . .   181 QUEEN MAEVE   V   38
    AND SHOOK HIM WIDE AWAKE, AND BID HIM SAY . . . . .   182 QUEEN MAEVE   50
    AND SHOOK WITH HATE AND FEAR. . . . .   254 WOMAN HOMER   4
    SHOOK OFF THE WATER FROM HIS BACK! . . . .   400 DEMON BEAST   29
    AND DEAFENING MUSIC SHOOK THE LEAVES: A TROOP . . . .   537 HER VISION   13
    GENTLY SHOOK THEIR MOTH-LIKE WINGS! . . . .   667 ISLE STAT II 3   26
    I SLEPT, 'TWAS SULTRY, AND SCARCE CIRCLING SHOOK . .   677 ISLE STAT II 3   278
    SHOOK THE PALE APPLE-BLOSSOM OVER IT! . . . .   761 SHADOW WATER A   275
    SHOOK THE PALE APPLE BLOSSOM OVER IT! . . . .   761 SHADOW WATER A V   275
SHOOT
    SHOOT ON HIM SHAFTS OF QUIETNESS, THAT HE MAY EVER KEEP   75 ANASHU VIJAYA   81
    SHOOT ON HIM SHAFTS OF QUIETNESS, AND ORDER HIM TO KEEP   75 ANASHU VIJAYA   V   81
    WHO BUT AWAITS HIS HOUR TO SHOOT, STILL HANGS . . . .   198 SEVEN WOODS   13
    THE BURNING BOW THAT ONCE COULD SHOOT AN ARROW . . .   377 PHASES OF MOON   119
    TO SHOOT THE COLONEL DEAD! . . . .   596 COLONEL MARTIN   58
    THAT THEY COULD NEVER SHOOT A MAN . . . .   596 COLONEL MARTIN   61
    OF ROOT, SHOOT, BLOSSOM OR CLAY . . . .   600 SPIRIT MEDIUM   21
    THAT I MYSELF COULD SHOOT A GREAT GREY LYNX. . . . .   650 ISLE STAT I 1   152
SHOOTING
    BUT TO BE AMID SHOOTING OF FLIES AND FLOWERING OF RUSHES   55 OISIN 3   120
        AND FLAGS."
    BUT TO BE 'MID THE SHOOTING OF FLIES . . . .   55 OISIN 3   V   120
SHOOTS
    BRIGHTNESS REMAINS! A BRIGHTER STAR SHOOTS DOWN! . . .   541 PARN FUNERAL 1   4
    OF THE BARLEY SHOOTS IN THE SUN. . . . .   643 SONG FAERIES   8
    OF THE BARLEY SHOOTS IN THE SUN. . . . .   676 ISLE STAT II 3   255
SHOP   SEE SWEET-SHOP
    OF OUR OLD PAUDEEN IN HIS SHOP, I STUMBLED BLIND . . .   291 PAUDEEN   2
    IN A CROWDED LONDON SHOP, ...   501 VACILLATION   37
    WHILE ON THE SHOP AND STREET I GAZED . . . .   501 VACILLATION   40
    IN A GALWAY SHOP, ...   595 COLONEL MARTIN   22
    IN THE FOUL RAG-AND-BONE SHOP OF THE HEART. . . . .   630 CIRCUS ANIMALS   40
    IN THE FOUL RAG AND BONE SHOP OF THE HEART. . . . .   630 CIRCUS ANIMALS V   40
SHORE
    TO THIS DIM SHORE THOSE GENTLE FEET? . . . .   5 OISIN 1   V   51
    TO THIS DIM SHORE ON FOAM WET FEET? . . . .   5 OISIN 1   V   51
    TO THIS DIM SHORE ON FOAM-WET FEET? . . . .   5 OISIN 1   V   51
    WE CANTERED TO THE SHORE, AND KNEW . . . .   14 OISIN 1   178
    WHILE ROUND THE SHORE A MILLION STOOD . . . .   14 OISIN 1   182
    WAS DIM WITH MIRE OF A MORTAL SHORE, ...   15 OISIN 1   208
    WAS DIM WITH THE MIRE OF A MORTAL SHORE, ...   15 OISIN 1   V   208
    I CHASED UPON THAT WOODY SHORE . . . .   23 OISIN 1   344
    OH, PATRICK, ON THAT WOODY SHORE . . . .   23 OISIN 1   V   343
    WHEN ONCE BESIDE THE SHORE I STOOD, ...   24 OISIN 1   V   364
    WHEN ONE DAY BY THE SHORE I STOOD, ...   24 OISIN 1   V   364
    AND RODE AND STOOD BESIDE THE SHORE. . . . .   25 OISIN 1   V 379A
    LATER A SOUND CAME, HALF LOST IN THE SOUND OF A SHORE FAR   57 OISIN 3   155
        AWAY,
    SOUGHT ONCE AGAIN THE SHORE, AND FOUND A SHELL, . . .   68 SAD SHEPHERD   18
    SOUGHT ONCE AGAIN THE SHORE, AND CHOSE A SHELL . . .   68 SAD SHEPHERD   V   18
    AND SING FROM SHORE TO SHORE, AND EVERY YEAR . . . .   81 EPHEMERA   V 24G
    AND SING FROM SHORE TO SHORE, AND EVERY YEAR . . . .   81 EPHEMERA   V 24G
    BY ROCKY SHORE AND RUSHY FEN! . . . .   83 MAD KING GOLL   32
    WHO PACED IN THE EVE BY THE NETS ON THE PEBBLY SHORE,   91 OLD FISHERMAN   11
    WITH SHORE LINES IN THE SAY! . . . .   94 MOLL MAGEE   6
    I HEAR LAKE WATER LAPPING WITH LOW SOUNDS BY THE SHORE!   117 ISLE INNISFREE   10
    I HEAR LAKE WATER LAPPING WITH LOW SOUNDS ON THE SHORE!   117 ISLE INNISFREE V   10
    I AM HAUNTED BY NUMBERLESS ISLANDS, AND MANY A DANAAN   122 WHITE BIRDS   9
        SHORE,
    AND DANCE UPON THE LEVEL SHORE? . . . .   125 GOES FERGUS   3
    IN SHAKEN BOUGHS, IN TIDE ON THE SHORE? . . . . . .   141 EVERLAST VOICE   7
    WE WHO STILL LABOUR BY THE CROMLECH ON THE SHORE, . .   161 BLACK PIG   5
    WE, WHO ARE LABOURING BY THE CROMLECH ON THE SHORE, .   161 BLACK PIG   V   5
    BY A GREY SHORE WHERE THE WIND NEVER BLEW. . . . . .   170 SECRET ROSE   14
    AND WHETHER I GO IN MY DREAMS BY WOODLAND, OR DUN,   210 UNDER THE MOON   14
        OR SHORE,
    WE HAVE NOT COME UPON A SHORE OR SHIP . . . .   222 SHADOW WATER B   3
    A CROWD UPON A SHORE. . . . .   253 HIS DREAM   4

SHORE   (CONTINUED)

MEN RAN UPON THE SHORE.	253	HIS DREAM	V	4
I, THOUGH UPRIGHT ON THE SHORE,	298	THREE HERMITS		11
TO A CHILD DANCING UPON THE SHORE	312	CHILD DANCING	V	T
DANCE THERE UPON THE SHORE!	312	CHILD DANCING		1
THE FIRST TIME ON THIS SHORE,	323	SWANS AT COOLE		16
STARVED UPON THE SHORE	401	DEMON BEAST		48
BUT TROD THE ROAD, OR SPLASHED ABOUT THE SHORE,	447	COLONUS PRAISE		27
BUT TROD THE ROAD, OR PADDLED BY THE SHORE,	447	COLONUS PRAISE	V	27
THE RATTLE OF PEBBLES ON THE SHORE	485	NINETEENTH CEN		3
BUT ACTUAL SHELLS OF ROSSES' LEVEL SHORE.	494	AT ALGECIRAS		12
SANG A BONE UPON THE SHORE!	521	THREE THINGS		2
SANG A BONE UPON THE SHORE!	521	THREE THINGS		8
SANG A BONE UPON THE SHORE,	521	THREE THINGS		14
BUILDING-YARD AND STORMY SHORE,	530	OLD TOM AGAIN		5
BUILDING YARD AND STORMY SHORE,	530	OLD TOM AGAIN	V	5
HER POETRY, DANCING UPON THE SHORE,	578	CRAZED GIRL		2
THOUGH RICH ON EVERY SHORE	606	SONGS BURDEN 1		11
THEN STUMBLING TO THE KILL BESIDE THE SHORE!	622	HOUND VOICE		19
THAT STUMBLING TO THE KILL BESIDE THE SHORE!	622	HOUND VOICE	V	19
BUT WINDS COME UP FROM THE SHORE!	635	BLACK TOWER		8
BUT WINDS COMES UP FROM THE SHORE!	636	BLACK TOWER		18
BUT WINDS COMES UP FROM THE SHORE!	636	BLACK TOWER		28
BUT WINDS COME UP FROM THE SHORE!	636	BLACK TOWER	V	REF
THEN BID THEM RAISE MY STATUE ON THE SHORE!	663	ISLE STAT II 2		18
TO WANDER BY THE BUBBLING SHORE,	668	ISLE STAT II 3		57
I HURRIED FROM THE WOODY SHORE,	742	DANAAN QUICK		4
HAVE BID ME HOPE, SAIL TO THE LOCHLANN SHORE	756	SHADOW WATER A	V	184

SHORES

WASHES THE SHORES WHERE YE ABIDE,	5	OISIN 1	V	47
YOUR MORTAL SHORES TILL TIME IS DONE!"	6	OISIN 1	V	59
TO SHORES BY THE WASH OF THE TREMULOUS TIDE,	8	OISIN 1		81
TO SHORES WHERE DYING HAS NEVER BEEN KNOWN,	8	OISIN 1	V	84
AND ON THE SHORES WERE MANY BOATS	14	OISIN 1		188
YET LOVE AND KISS ON DIM SHORES FAR AWAY	29	OISIN 2		13
BUT LOVE AND KISS ON DIM SHORES FAR AWAY	29	OISIN 2	V	13
THEY WALK ON SHORES UNSEEN OF OARING GALLEYS,	30	OISIN 2	V	14D
AND SHORES THE FROTH LIPS WET!	33	OISIN 2		59
. . . AND PACING THE SHORES OF THE WANDERING SEAS,	50	OISIN 3		55
. . . AND PACING THE SHORES OF THE SEVEN SEAS,	50	OISIN 3	V	55
I SAW HIM FROM SAD DIDO'S SHORES DEPART,	677	ISLE STAT II 3		288

SHOREWARD

AND SHOREWARD WAVES, WE NIGH HAVE FOUGHT! WAVES BRING	660	ISLE STAT II 1		44

SHORE-WEEDS

. . . AND LATER THE SHORE-WEEDS BROWN.	57	OISIN 3		156

SHORN

THAT I HAD SHORN MY LOCKS AWAY	519	HER DREAM		3

SHORT

AFTER SHORT FIGHTING IN THE LEAFY SHADE,	109	CUCHULAIN SEA		57
I CELEBRATE THE SILENT KISS THAT ENDS SHORT LIFE OR LONG.	459	FROM OEDIPUS		9

SHORTEN

PLANNED IN A GOVERNMENT OFFICE, SHORTEN HIS LIFE,	372	ON GOING HOUSE		15

SHOT   SEE EAR-SHOT BLOOD-SHOT CANNON-SHOT

THE SIXTEEN MEN WERE SHOT,	395	SIXTEEN DEAD		2
OR EYELID SHOT THE GLEAM	507	STREAM AND SUN		4
HURRAH FOR REVOLUTION AND MORE CANNON SHOT!	590	GREAT DAY	V	1
WHO WAS THE FIRST MAN SHOT THAT DAY?	608	SONGS BURDEN 3		10
ANOTHER STAR HAS SHOT AN EAR.	625	NATIVITY		2
CERTAIN MEN THE ENGLISH SHOT?	632	MAN AND ECHO		12
A SCORE OF YARDS OFF 'NEATH A WILLOW, SHOT.	712	FERENCZ RENYI		65
ARE SHOT AT ON THE OPEN PLAIN.	791	REPRISALS		18

SHOULDER

THRUSTING HIS NOSE TO MY SHOULDER! HE KNEW IN HIS BOSOM DEEP	54	OISIN 3		106
AND ON MY LEANING SHOULDER SHE LAID HER SNOW-WHITE HAND.	90	SALLEY GARDENS		6
HEAD UPON SHOULDER LEANT!	319	DOLLS		18
AND CHILDREN WHEN THEY SPRING UP SHOULDER HIGH.	343	SHEP GOATHERD	V	119
AND START--I AT YOUR SHOULDER--	390	IMAGE PAST		30
HANDS UPON EITHER SHOULDER MADE HER MOVE,	466	HARUN RASHID	V	125B
WHAT'S BOWED YOUR SHOULDER AND MADE PALE YOUR CHEEK"!	467	HARUN RASHID		133
BELLY, SHOULDER, BUM,	612	NEWS ORACLE		34
I AM! ONE SHOULDER TURNED AWRY--WHY THEN	692	MOSADA 1		61
ONE SHOULDER TWISTED, AND THE CHILDREN CRY	695	MOSADA 1		116

SHOULDERED

. . . THEY LIFTED AND SHOULDERED A SACK FULL OF SAND,	60	OISIN 3	V	185
NOT DOUBTING TO HAVE LAUGHED IT AWAY.	277	TWO KINGS	V	11A
SHOULDERED A LITTER WITH A WOUNDED MAN,	537	HER VISION		14

SHOULDER-HIGH

AND CHILDREN WHEN THEY SPRING UP SHOULDER-HIGH.	343	SHEP GOATHERD		119

SHOULDERS

SHE LAID A HAND ON EITHER OF HIS SHOULDERS,	182	QUEEN MAEVE		49
UPON HIS SHOULDERS. YOU'VE NOTHING BUT WILD WORDS,	235	SHADOW WATER B		300
ABOVE THE CLOUDY SHOULDERS OF THE HORSES!	344	DAWN		12

SHOUT

AMONG THE RINGING HALLS A SHOUT	20	OISIN 1	V	288
I TURNED AND RODE TO THE WESTWARD, AND FOLLOWED THE SEA'S OLD SHOUT	60	OISIN 3		183
AND RODE ON TILL OVER THE WORLD'S RIM FLOATED THE SEA'S OLD SHOUT,	60	OISIN 3	V	183
DRAW ROUND AND RAISE A SHOUT!	584	GHOST ROG CASE		38
AND SHOUT A SECRET TO THE STONE.	632	MAN AND ECHO		5

```
                                                           PAGE      TITLE          LINE
SHOUT   (CONTINUED)
     AND SHOUT AT THE WISEST OWLS . . . . . . . . . . .    644 SONG FAERIES          10
     AND SHOUT AT THE WISEST OWLS . . . . . . . . . . .    676 ISLE STAT II 3       257
     A NEIGHBOURING CRICKET LIFTS HIS SHRILLY SHOUT  . . . 711 FERENCZ RENYI         45
SHOUTED
     SHOUTED, AND HAILED HIM: HE HUNG THERE A STAR,  . . .  36 OISIN 2              107
     SHOUTED AND HAILED HIM.  STILL HE HUNG CONTENT, . . .  36 OISIN 2            V 107
     SHOUTED.  WITH FIRE OF HAIR ABOUT HER SWIRLED,  . . .  38 OISIN 2              134
     JOSTLED AND SHOUTED THOSE WAR-WASTED MEN, . . . . . . 286 TWO KINGS            216
     ALL SHOUTED TILL THEIR ANGER GREW . . . . . . . . . . 297 THREE BEGGARS         46
     THE OTHER SHOUTED, "YOU WOULD ROB . . . . . . . . . . 307 HOUR DAWN            109
     SHOUTED A MOMENT 'TWEEN THE EARTH AND SKY . . . . . . 675 ISLE STAT II 3       237
     THEN HE SHOUTED, "OPEN WIDE . . . . . . . . . . . . . 697 MOSADA 2              24
     AND HE SHOUTED OPEN WIDE  . . . . . . . . . . . . . . 697 MOSADA 2           V  24
     THE STRANGER SHOUTED, "OPEN WIDE  . . . . . . . . . . 697 MOSADA 2           V  24
SHOUTING
     HEARING HELL LOUD WITH A MURMUR, AS SHOUTING AND MOCKING 62 OISIN 3           208
        WE SWEEP,
     HIS SHOUTING DAYS WITH MIRTH WERE CROWNED: . . . . . . 67 HAPPY SHEPHERD        50
     BUT SLOWLY, AS I SHOUTING SLEW  . . . . . . . . . . .  83 MAD KING GOLL         25
     WITH SHOUTING AND THE CLANG OF UNHOOKED ARMS. . . . . 185 QUEEN MAEVE          111
     THE SHOUTING OF AN UNSEEN MAN:  . . . . . . . . . . . 274 GREY ROCK             76
     TILL THAT IS THEIR LONG SHOUTING PLAYTIME:  . . . . . 343 SHEP GOATHERD      V 106
     WITH SHOUTING AND SINGING.  . . . . . . . . . . . . . 672 ISLE STAT II 3       173
SHOVE
     ALL HIS BODY CAN BUT SHOVE  . . . . . . . . . . . . . 776 AGAINST WITCH         33
SHOW
     WITHOUT LAUGHTER, A SHOW UNTO CHILDREN, . . . . . . .  63 OISIN 3              218
     AH ME! TO BE OLD WITHOUT SUCCOUR, A SHOW UNTO CHILDREN, 63 OISIN 3           V 217
        A STAIN,
     CASTS UP A SHOW AND THE WINDS ANSWER IT . . . . . . . 186 QUEEN MAEVE          125
     I'LL SHOW YOU THAT I AM MADE DIFFERENTLY, . . . . . . 227 SHADOW WATER B       119
     THAT COULD SHOW WHAT HOMER'S AGE  . . . . . . . . . . 258 PEACE                  2
     WHO HAD SEEN, BEING KEPT FOR SHOW,  . . . . . . . . . 319 DOLLS                  5
     IS HOT TO SHOW WHATEVER IT HAS FOUND,  . . . . . . .  340 SHEP GOATHERD         44
     JUST TRUTH ENOUGH TO SHOW THAT HIS WHOLE LIFE . . . . 373 PHASES OF MOON        22
     IS WHAT YOUR LOOKING-GLASS CAN SHOW,  . . . . . . . . 385 ROBARTES DANCE        15
     SATISFIED IF A TROUBLED MIRROR SHOW IT, . . . . . . . 430 NINETEEN 19           62
     CONTENTED THAT A TROUBLED MIRROR SHOW IT, . . . . . . 430 NINETEEN 19        V  62
     SHRIEK WITH PLEASURE IF WE SHOW . . . . . . . . . . . 431 NINETEEN 19           91
     BETTER TO SMILE ON ALL THAT SMILE, AND SHOW . . . . . 444 SCHOOL CHILDR         31
     TO SHOW HOW VIOLENT GREAT HEARTS CAN LOSE . . . . . . 463 HARUN RASHID          47
     MY LANTERN IS TOO LOYAL NOT TO SHOW . . . . . . . . . 464 HARUN RASHID          71
     CAN BUT SHOW THAT HEAVEN YAWNS: . . . . . . . . . . . 509 JANE REPROVED          4
     SHE WOULD AS BRAVELY SHOW . . . . . . . . . . . . . . 516 MANS SONG              9
     DISCOVER IMPURITIES, CAN SHOW AT LAST . . . . . . . . 558 RIBH CHRISTIAN        10
     WHERE CAN SHE LOOK UNTIL HE MAKE THE SHOW:  . . . . . 558 RIBH CHRISTIAN        22
     LIKE A DUMB BEAST IN A SHOW,  . . . . . . . . . . . . 572 LADYS 1ST SONG         2
     BUT WHERE IS THE BRUSH THAT COULD SHOW ANYTHING . . . 602 GALLERY REVIS         28
     MIRROR ON MIRROR MIRRORED IS ALL THE SHOW.  . . . . . 610 STATUES               22
     MY CIRCUS ANIMALS WERE ALL ON SHOW, . . . . . . . . . 629 CIRCUS ANIMALS         6
SHOWED
     AND SHOWED THEIR EYES WITH TEARDROPS DIM, . . . . . .  18 OISIN 2              256
     SHOWED PRINTS OF SEA-BORN SCALES, WHILE DOWN THROUGH IT 37 OISIN 2            115
     HOW THE MEN OF THE SAND-SACK SHOWED ME A CHURCH . . .  61 OISIN 3              193
     FLICKERING WITH ASH AND HAZEL, BUT HALF SHOWED  . . . 180 QUEEN MAEVE           12
     SHOWED THEIR FAINT LIGHT THROUGH THE UNSHUTTERED WINDOWS, 279 TWO KINGS        50
     ALTHOUGH CROWDS GATHERED ONCE IF SHE BUT SHOWED HER FACE, 314 FALLEN MAJESTY    1
SHOWER
     A DANAAN FRUITAGE MAKES A SHOWER OF MOONS,  . . . . . 127 DREAM OF FAERY     V  22
     OR THAT OF THE SUDDEN SHOWER  . . . . . . . . . . . . 414 TOWER                137
SHOWERED
     SHOWERED AWAY THE KEEN DEW DROPS: . . . . . . . . . . 705 DAWN-SONG             18
SHOWERS
     DANAAN SONGS, AND THEIR DEWY SHOWERS  . . . . . . . .  11 OISIN 1              135
     SANG NIAM, AND THEIR DEWY SHOWERS . . . . . . . . . .  11 OISIN 1            V 135
     RISES, AND SHOWERS ABROAD HIS FRAGRANT ARROWS,  . . .  72 ANASHU VIJAYA         27
     AND CLINGING WITH THE DEW OF ODOROUS SHOWERS, . . . . 704 REMEMBRANCE            4
SHOWING
     FEATURES, OR MAYBE SHOWING  . . . . . . . . . . . . . 363 DOLLS DRAWINGS         4
     FEATURES, OR MAY BE SHOWING . . . . . . . . . . . . . 363 DOLLS DRAWINGS     V   4
SHOWN
     AS THOSE THAT CAN OUTLIVE THE MOON HAVE SHOWN IT, . . 230 SHADOW WATER B     V 193
     AND SHOWN MY HUSBAND SLEEPING THERE, I HAVE SIGHED, . 285 TWO KINGS            188
     AND FOR THE LOVE THAT YOU HAVE SHOWN YOUR KING, . . . 286 TWO KINGS          V 212A
     THAT COULD HAVE SHOWN HOW PURE-BRED HORSES  . . . . . 325 ROBERT GREGORY        36
     THAT COULD HAVE SHOWN HOW PUREBRED HORSES . . . . . . 325 ROBERT GREGORY     V  36
     "WHAT CAN BE SHOWN? . . . . . . . . . . . . . . . . . 510 JANE JUDGMENT         16
     ALL COULD BE KNOWN OR SHOWN . . . . . . . . . . . . . 510 JANE JUDGMENT         18
     WHICH OF HER FORMS HAS SHOWN HER SUBSTANCE RIGHT? . . 618 BRONZE HEAD           11
SHOWS
     SHADOWS AND SHOWS THAT CAN BUT TURN THE BRAIN." . . . 281 TWO KINGS            108
     YOUR OPEN HAND BUT SHOWS OUR LOSS, . . . . . . . . .  288 TO WEALTHY MAN        29
     WHAT EAGLE LOOK STILL SHOWS,  . . . . . . . . . . . . 316 FRIENDS               25
     SHOWS HER THAT SOME ONE SOON  . . . . . . . . . . . . 364 END OF DAY             5
     SHOWS HER THAT SOMEONE SOON . . . . . . . . . . . . . 364 END OF DAY         V   5
     BEING BUT HOLY SHOWS, . . . . . . . . . . . . . . . . 454 HIS MEMORIES           2
     SHOWS THROUGH OUR LINEAMENTS.  MY CANDLE'S BRIGHT,  . 464 HARUN RASHID          70
     HAD I NOT FOUND CONTENT AMONG THE SHOWS . . . . . . . 499 MOTHER OF GOD          6
     BECAUSE PIEBALD PONIES, LED BEARS, CAGED LIONS, MAKE BUT 623 HIGH TALK          5
        POOR SHOWS,
```

714

	PAGE	TITLE	LINE

SHOWS   (CONTINUED)
THAT MIGHT ADORN OLD SONGS OR COURTLY SHOWS;   • • • • •   629 CIRCUS ANIMALS   14
SHOWY
AND A GREAT ARMY BUT A SHOWY THING;   • • • • • • • •   429 NINETEEN 19   18
SHRANK
AND MIND AND BODY SHRANK.   • • • • • • • • • • •   626 STATES HOLIDAY   4
HE SHRANK BEFORE MY VOICE, AND STOOD • • • • • • • •   671 ISLE STAT II 3   129
SHRIEK
SHRIEK WITH PLEASURE IF WE SHOW   • • • • • • • • •   431 NINETEEN 19   91
AND THAT MUST SLEEP, SHRIEK, STRUGGLE TO ESCAPE • • • •   444 SCHOOL CHILDR   35
I COULD RECOVER IF I SHRIEK • • • • • • • • • •   452 HUMAN DIGNITY   V   9
"STRIKE ME IF I SHRIEK." • • • • • • • • • • • •   455 HIS MEMORIES   18
REMEMBERING THAT HER SHRIEK WAS LOVE • • • • • • • •   456 FRIENDS YOUTH   19
NOR SAW MY BODY FALL NOR HEARD IT SHRIEK, • • • • • •   537 HER VISION   29
THAT PATCHING OLD HEELS THEY MAY SHRIEK, I TAKE TO CHISEL   623 HIGH TALK   8
    AND PLANE.
SHRIEKED
AND DUG ITS CLAWS AND SHRIEKED AND FOUGHT. • • • • • •   385 ROBARTES DANCE   8
WIND SHRIEKED--AND WHERE ARE THEY? • • • • • • • •   432 NINETEEN 19   107
I COULD RECOVER IF I SHRIEKED • • • • • • • • • •   452 HUMAN DIGNITY   9
SHRIEKS
SHRIEKS, "I AM KING OF THE PEACOCKS," • • • • • • •   456 FRIENDS YOUTH   15
AND THAT HE SHRIEKS FROM PRIDE. • • • • • • • • •   456 FRIENDS YOUTH   20
AND A MIRACULOUS STRANGE BIRD SHRIEKS AT US. • • • • •   534 HER TRIUMPH   12
SHRILL
UNTIL HER VOICE GREW SHRILL. • • • • • • • • • •   392 EASTER 1916   20
THAT WOMAN A WHILE WOULD BE SHRILL • • • • • • • •   392 EASTER 1916   V   17
OH, CEASE YOUR SINGING! WILD AND SHRILL AND LOUD, • •   648 ISLE STAT I 1   99
SHRILLY
O! LAY THE SHRILLY TRUMPET DOWN, • • • • • • • •   212 BLESS PSALTER   4
A NEIGHBOURING CRICKET LIFTS HIS SHRILLY SHOUT • • • •   711 FERENCZ RENYI   45
SHRINE
THAT FEED WHITE MOTHS BY SOME DE DANAAN SHRINE; • • • •   41 OISIN 2   186
FEEDING WHITE MOTHS AROUND SOME EASTERN SHRINE, • • • •   41 OISIN 2   V   186
SHROUD
"WHAT IS THE FIGURE IN A SHROUD • • • • • • • •   253 HIS DREAM   7
THAT BLINKED AND SAW THEM IN A SHROUD. • • • • • • •   529 TOM LUNATIC   12
A SHROUD THAT SEEMED TO HAVE AUTHORITY • • • • • • •   634 CUCHULAIN COMF   7
"OBEY OUR ANCIENT RULE AND MAKE A SHROUD; • • • • • •   634 CUCHULAIN COMF   13
THEY WILL WRAP THEM IN THE SHROUD, • • • • • • • •   733 STREET DANCERS   55
SHROUDS
THEIR SHROUDS ARE BLOODY AND THEIR LIPS ARE WET. • • •   483 OIL AND BLOOD   6
SHAKE THE DEAD IN THEIR SHROUDS; • • • • • • • • •   576 ACRE OF GRASS   22
THEN CERTAIN SHROUDS THAT MUTTERED HEAD TO HEAD • • • •   634 CUCHULAIN COMF   4
A BUNDLE OF LINEN. SHROUDS BY TWO AND THREE • • • •   634 CUCHULAIN COMF   9
SHRUNKEN
AND I AM SHRUNKEN TO SKIN AND BONE, • • • • • • • •   550 SONGS REWRIT 1   2
YET I AM SHRUNKEN TO SKIN AND BONE • • • • • • • •   550 SONGS REWRIT 1 V   2
YET AM I SHRUNKEN TO SKIN AND BONE, • • • • • • • •   550 SONGS REWRIT 1 V   2
BUT I AM SHRUNKEN TO SKIN AND BONE, • • • • • • • •   550 SONGS REWRIT 1 V   2
THOUGH I AM SHRUNKEN TO BONE AND SKIN, • • • • • • •   551 SONGS REWRIT 1 V   8
SHUDDER
LEST NIAMH SHUDDER. FULL OF HOPE AND DREAD • • • • •   41 OISIN 2   183
SHUDDER THAT MADE THEM ONE. • • • • • • • • • •   346 ON WOMAN   23
WHO SHUDDER AND HURRY BY; BODY AND SOUL • • • • • •   375 PHASES OF MOON   77
A SHUDDER IN THE LOINS ENGENDERS THERE • • • • • • •   441 LEDA AND SWAN   9
WHAT MAKES ME SHUDDER SO? • • • • • • • • • •   524 MAD AS MIST   14
I SHUDDER AND I SIGH TO THINK • • • • • • • • •   524 MAD AS MIST   15
SHUDDERED
IT SHUDDERED IN THE WATER; • • • • • • • • • •   345 ON WOMAN   19
SHUDDERING   SEE STAR-SHUDDERING
AND THE DESOLATE SHUDDERING SEA. • • • • • • • •   648 ISLE STAT I 1   85
SUCH MAY I LOVE. THE SHUDDERING FOREST LIGHTS • • •   651 ISLE STAT I 1   165
SHUDDERS
SHUDDERS IN MANY CRADLES; ALL IS CHANGED, • • • • • •   375 PHASES OF MOON   89
WHAT SHUDDERS RUN THROUGH ALL THAT ANIMAL BLOOD? • • • •   541 PARN FUNERAL 1   5
SHUFFLE
ALL SHUFFLE THERE; ALL COUGH IN INK; • • • • • • • •   337 SCHOLARS   7
TO SHUFFLE, GRUNT AND GROAN, • • • • • • • • •   599 STONE CROSS   20
PRACTICE A TINKER SHUFFLE • • • • • • • • • •   617 LONG-LEG FLY   17
SHUFFLED
GOOD FELLOWS SHUFFLED CARDS IN AN OLD BAWN; • • • • •   411 TOWER   65
SHUFFLING
O SHUFFLING OF HOLY SHOES! • • • • • • • • • •   774 COME RIDE   15
SHUN
WHAT CAN THEY DO BUT SHUN ME • • • • • • • • • •   533 FIRST CONFESS   17
SHUT
HE DROVE ME OUT AND SHUT THE DOOR, • • • • • • • •   95 MOLL MAGEE   25
THE WINDOWS AND THE DOORS WERE SHUT, • • • • • • •   95 MOLL MAGEE   29
HE DROVE ME FORTH AND SHUT THE DOOR, • • • • • • •   95 MOLL MAGEE   V   25
PEACEABLE MEN THAT SHUT THE WIND AWAY, • • • • • • •   224 SHADOW WATER B   54
ALL WISDOM SHUT INTO HIS ONYX EYES. • • • • • • •   311 MOUNTAIN TOMB   11
ALL WISDOM SHUT INTO ITS ONYX EYES. • • • • • • •   311 MOUNTAIN TOMB   V   11
HAD SHUT THEIR EYES; AND WHERE WAS IT • • • • • •   326 ROBERT GREGORY   62
WHEN I HAVE SHUT THESE EWES AND THIS OLD RAM • • • •   343 SHEP GOATHERD   113
WE POETS KEEP OUR MOUTHS SHUT, FOR IN TRUTH • • • •   359 WAR POEM   V   2
A POET KEEP HIS MOUTH SHUT, FOR IN TRUTH • • • • •   359 WAR POEM   V   2
SHUT OUT FROM ALL THE LUXURY OF THE WORLD, • • • • •   370 EGO DOMINUS   60
AND WHETHER THE DOOR WERE SHUT. • • • • • • • •   381 SONGS FOOL 2   5
I TURN AWAY AND SHUT THE DOOR, AND ON THE STAIR • • • •   427 PHANTOM HATRED   33
SHE ROSE, AND WITH HER EYES SHUT FAST IN SLEEP • • • •   468 HARUN RASHID   152

715

	PAGE	TITLE	LINE

SHUT   (CONTINUED)
SHUT THE DOOR OF THE POPE'S CHAPEL, ...   618 LONG-LEG FLY   23
SCARCE THE OLD AND WIZEN HOUSES HAD THEIR DOORS AND WINDOWS   718 PHANTOM SHIP   5
SHUT.
SCARCE THE OLD AND WIZENED HOUSES HAD THEIR DOORS   718 PHANTOM SHIP   V   5
AND WINDOWS SHUT.
THE HARVEST'S IN! THE GRANARY DOORS ARE SHUT! . . . . . .   755 SHADOW WATER A   177
ALTHOUGH THE DOOR BE SHUT . . . .   786 YOUR HEART   14
SHUTS
THE MAJESTY THAT SHUTS HIS BURNING EYE! . . . .   265 THESE CLOUDS   2
THE MAJESTY THAT SHUTS HIS BURNING EYE. . . . .   265 THESE CLOUDS   12
WHILE NIGHT SHUTS THE EYES . . . .   535 PARTING   2
SHUTTER
THAT SHAKES THE SHUTTER, TO HAVE BROUGHT TO MIND . . . .   327 ROBERT GREGORY   90
BOLT AND BAR THE SHUTTER, ...   523 MAD AS MIST   1
SHUTTLE
FLAMES THE SHUTTLE OF THE LIGHTNING ACROSS THE DRIVING   718 PHANTOM SHIP   1
SLEET,
SHY
SHY ONE, SHY ONE, ...   89 ISLE IN WATER   1
SHY ONE, SHY ONE, ...   89 ISLE IN WATER   1
SHY ONE OF MY HEART, ...   89 ISLE IN WATER   2
SHY IN THE DOORWAY . . . .   89 ISLE IN WATER   11
AND SHY IN THE GLOOM! . . . .   89 ISLE IN WATER   12
AND SHY AS A RABBIT, ...   89 ISLE IN WATER   13
HELPFUL AND SHY. . . . .   89 ISLE IN WATER   14
HERE GROW THAT SHY, RETIRING SISTERHOOD, ...   651 ISLE STAT I 2   4
SIBYL
SLEW THEE, POOR SIBYL! COMRADES THOU AND I! . . . . .   675 ISLE STAT II 3   235
A SIBYL, WITH FIERCE FACE AS OF A HOUND . . . .   687 TWO TITANS   9
SIBYLLINE
SWIFT BEATING ON HIS BREAST IN SIBYLLINE FRENZY BLIND . .   481 BLOOD AND MOON   19
SIBYL'S
AND IN THE SIBYL'S EYES A LANGUID FLAME . . . .   688 TWO TITANS   41
SICILIAN
STAMPED BOY AND TREE UPON SICILIAN COIN. . . . . . .   541 PARN FUNERAL 1   15
SICK   SEE LOVE-SICK
SAD TO REMEMBER, SICK WITH YEARS, ...   2 OISIN 1   5
'TIS SAD REMEMBERING, SICK WITH YEARS, ...   2 OISIN 1   V   5
BUT O, SICK CHILDREN OF THE WORLD, ...   65 HAPPY SHEPHERD   6
THE SICK MAN'S WIFE OPENED THE DOOR! . . . .   133 FR GILLIGAN   31
SICK OF HIS GRAVE HAS WAKENED ME? . . . .   303 HOUR DAWN   37
CONSUME MY HEART AWAY! SICK WITH DESIRE . . . .   408 SAIL BYZANTIUM   21
AND SICK OF SOLITUDE . . . .   432 NINETEEN 19   105
THEY ARE SICK OF THE PALETTE AND FIDDLE-BOW, ...   565 LAPIS LAZULI   2
SICKEN
BLENCHING ON HIGH THE DULL STARS SICKEN . . . .   646 ISLE STAT I 1   46
SICKENING
THAT SICKENING NEAR THEIR MOTHERS LIE! . . . .   717 FAIRY DOCTOR   16
SICKLE
THERE DREAMY TIME LETS FALL HIS SICKLE . . . .   77 INDIAN TO LOVE V   5A
PASSETH THE MOON WITH HER SICKLE OF LIGHT, ...   648 ISLE STAT I 1   82
YONDER THE SICKLE OF THE MOON SAILS ON, ...   688 NETTLESHIP   1
SICKLES
AND THRICE THE CORN AROUND THE SICKLES FLAMED, ...   690 MOSADA 1   3
NOR, GAZING FORTH WHERE LIFE'S SAD SICKLES REAP, ...   710 FERENCZ RENYI   31
SICKNESS
SICKNESS BROUGHT ME THIS . . . .   267 FRIEND ILLNESS   1
OR SICKNESS BREAK HER WILL . . . .   365 HER RACE   10
A MEDITATION WRITTEN DURING SICKNESS AT ALGECIRAS . . .   493 AT ALGECIRAS   V   T
SIDE   SEE CRADLE-SIDE MOUNTAIN-SIDE COUNTRY-SIDE HILL-SIDE ROAD-SIDE
RIVER-SIDE WATER-SIDE
AND ONCE A LADY BY MY SIDE . . . .   16 OISIN 1   231
AND ONCE A MAIDEN BY MY SIDE . . . .   16 OISIN 1   V   231
IN HONOUR SOON BY HIS MASTER'S SIDE . . . .   26 OISIN 1   V 399C
OF MANY THOUSAND STEPS. SAT EITHER SIDE, ...   31 OISIN 2   V   35
THAT WITH DIM EYEBALLS STOOD ON EITHER SIDE. . . . . .   34 OISIN 2   75
STOOD LONELY, WITH DIM EYEBALLS ON EACH SIDE, ...   34 OISIN 2   V   74
HIS HAND ALONG THE RUNNEL'S SIDE, AS THOUGH . . . . .   39 OISIN 2   162
AT EMAN, 'NEATH THE BEECH TREES, ON EACH SIDE, ...   44 OISIN 2   V   228
LAY LOOSE IN A PLACE OF SHADOW! WE DREW THE REINS BY HIS   50 OISIN 3   44
SIDE.
. . . YOU WILL COME NO MORE TO MY SIDE. . . . . . .   56 OISIN 3   128
. . . NO MORE SHALT THOU BE BY MY SIDE. . . . . . .   56 OISIN 3   V   128
OF THE CALVES ON THE WARM HILL SIDE, ...   88 STOLEN CHILD   V   45
WITH THE FEET LAID SIDE BY SIDE. . . . .   124 CATHLEEN PARA   4
WITH THE FEET LAID SIDE BY SIDE. . . . .   124 CATHLEEN PARA   4
HAD COME THROUGH THE MOUNTAIN SIDE, ...   171 MAID QUIET   V   4B
CROWDED WITH BITTER FACES, THE WOUNDS IN PALM AND SIDE,   172 TRAV PASSION   4
THE KNOTTED SCOURGE, THE NAIL-PIERCED HANDS, THE WOUNDED   172 TRAV PASSION   4
SIDE,
ABOUT THE WINDY WATER SIDE . . . .   192 BAILE AILLINN   V   93
WHO PEERED ABOUT ON EVERY SIDE! . . . .   193 BAILE AILLINN   V   112
TO THE OTHER SIDE, AND HIGHER IN THE AIR. . . . . . .   234 SHADOW WATER B   259
THERE IS NONE TO TAKE HIS SIDE. I AM ON HIS SIDE. . . .   239 SHADOW WATER B   364
THERE IS NONE TO TAKE HIS SIDE. I AM ON HIS SIDE. . . .   239 SHADOW WATER B   364
HER HANDS ON EITHER SIDE HAD GRIPPED THE BENCH. . . . .   279 TWO KINGS   63
FROM WELL SIDE OR FROM PLOUGH LAND, WAS THEIR NOISE! . .   279 TWO KINGS   V   53
THE CATARACT SMOKES UPON THE MOUNTAIN SIDE. . . . . .   311 MOUNTAIN TOMB   3
THE CATARACT SMOKES ON THE MOUNTAIN SIDE. . . . . . .   311 MOUNTAIN TOMB   V   3
AND ALL THEIR HELMS OF SILVER HOVERING SIDE BY SIDE, . .   318 MAGI   5

716

SIDE   (CONTINUED)
    AND ALL THEIR HELMS OF SILVER HOVERING SIDE BY SIDE, • •   318 MAGI   5
    FROM CASTLE TAYLOR TO THE ROXBOROUGH SIDE • • • • •   326 ROBERT GREGORY   58
    BECAUSE AT HER SIDE? • • • • • • • • • • • • •   335 SONG   10
    TILL, CLAMBERING AT THE CRADLE SIDE, • • • • • • •   343 SHEP GOATHERD   V   109
    AT PALLAS ATHENE'S SIDE, • • • • • • • • • • • •   355 PROPERTIUS   6
    AND SPREAD ON EVERY SIDE, • • • • • • • • • • •   396 ROSE TREE   10
    UPON BEN BULBEN SIDE • • • • • • • • • • • •   398 BREAK OF DAY   6
    DROP THEIR CAST AT THE SIDE • • • • • • • • • •   414 TOWER   125
    THAT CLIMB THE MOUNTAIN SIDE, • • • • • • • • •   416 TOWER   V   175
    AND TEAR THE HEART OUT OF HIS SIDE, • • • • • • •   437 SONGS PLAY 1   3
    OUT OF HIS SIDE. • • • • • • • • • • • • • •   439 FRAGMENTS   4
    I RAN, I RAN, FROM MY LOVE'S SIDE BECAUSE MY HEART WENT   450 OWEN AHERNE   12
        MAD.
    I DID NOT FIND IN ANY CAGE THE WOMAN AT MY SIDE. • • •   450 OWEN AHERNE   19
    AND THE HEART THUMPS AT MY SIDE, • • • • • • • •   456 FRIENDS YOUTH   18
    LIVED AT MY SIDE: THOUGHT TIME'S DISFIGURING TOUCH • •   466 HARUN RASHID   110
    LIVED AT MY SIDE: THAT TIME'S DISFIGURING TOUCH • • •   466 HARUN RASHID   V   110
    THE HEART IN MY SIDE, • • • • • • • • • • • •   516 MANS SONG   3
    THE MEET'S UPON THE MOUNTAIN SIDE. • • • • • • •   549 SEVERED HEAD   V   6
    DESERT THE PERJURER'S SIDE: • • • • • • • • • •   582 ROGER CASEMENT   20
    AN AMBUSH: PILGRIMS AT THE WATER SIDE: • • • • • •   601 GALLERY REVIS   V   2
    WHEN PEARSE SUMMONED CUCHULAIN TO HIS SIDE, • • • •   611 STATUES   25
    CUCHULAIN SAT AT HER SIDE: • • • • • • • • • •   628 JANE MOUNTAIN   17
    HANG ON THE SIDE OF THE ROUND GRAPE-CLUSTER: • • • •   646 ISLE STAT I 1   45
    BRIGHT ON A GRASS BLADE'S UNDER SIDE, MIGHT HEAR, • •   689 NETTLESHIP   10
    BUT NOW I WAVE HER HITHER TO MY SIDE. • • • • • •   694 MOSADA 1   91
    AT LAST. BUT NOW I WAVE HER TO MY SIDE. • • • • •   694 MOSADA 1   V   91
    TWO ONLY NOW THEY ARE, TWO SIDE BY SIDE. • • • • •   700 MOSADA 3   49
    TWO ONLY NOW THEY ARE, TWO SIDE BY SIDE. • • • • •   700 MOSADA 3   49
    OF OUR NATIVITY HANG SIDE BY SIDE, • • • • • • •   701 MOSADA 3   53
    OF OUR NATIVITY HANG SIDE BY SIDE, • • • • • • •   701 MOSADA 3   53
    FOR I AM OLD AND WEAK." AND AT HER SIDE • • • • •   712 FERENCZ RENYI   59
    SUCH WAR PLOTS, PEACE PLOTS, LOVE PLOTS--EVERY SIDE: 722 WITCH VIVIEN   66
    IF I GO NEARER TO THE WINDWARD SIDE, • • • • • • •   753 SHADOW WATER A   140
    TO THE OTHER SIDE AND HIGHER IN THE AIR. • • • • •   753 SHADOW WATER A   149
    IN THE WASTE AIR. I WILL WANDER BY HIS SIDE • • • •   754 SHADOW WATER A   152
    TILL THE SIDE OF HATE COMES UP. • • • • • • • •   776 AGAINST WITCH   35
    WHAT MAN IS AT YOUR SIDE? • • • • • • • • • •   786 YOUR HEART   28
    SOME ONE SHOULD STAY AT HER SIDE. • • • • • • •   786 YOUR HEART   V   28
    IS THERE NO MAN AT YOUR SIDE? • • • • • • • •   786 YOUR HEART   V   28
SIDES   SEE WELL-SIDES
    TO SHAKE THEIR WICKED SIDES AT YOUTH • • • • • •   262 STUDENTS AGIT   3
    STRANGE DRAPERIES DID ALL THE SIDES ADORN, • • • • •   657 ISLE STAT I 3   55
SIDHE
    THE HOSTING OF THE SIDHE • • • • • • • • • • •   140 HOSTING SIDHE   T
    AND WONDERING WHO OF THE MANY-CHANGING SIDHE • • • •   181 QUEEN MAEVE   41
    AND WONDERING WHO OF THE MANY CHANGING SIDHE • • • •   181 QUEEN MAEVE   V   41
    WHAT MATTERS WERE AFOOT AMONG THE SIDHE, • • • • •   182 QUEEN MAEVE   61
SIDLE
    MUST SHE SIDLE UP, • • • • • • • • • • • • •   559 HE AND SHE   2
SIDLED
    SIDLED THEIR BODIES AGAINST HIM, FILLING THE SHADE WITH   50 OISIN 3   48
        THEIR EYES.
SIDLES
    AS THE MOON SIDLES UP • • • • • • • • • • • •   559 HE AND SHE   1
SIDNEY
    OUR SIDNEY AND OUR PERFECT MAN, • • • • • • • •   325 ROBERT GREGORY   47
SIEVE
    WHAT WOULD HAVE SHAKEN FROM THE SIEVE? • • • • • •   256 WORDS   14
SIGH
    AND EACH ONE SAID, WITH A LONG, LONG SIGH, • • • •   17 OISIN 1   244
    GROWN DESOLATE, WHISPER AND SIGH TO EACH OTHER: • • •   26 OISIN 1   403
    GROWN DESOLATE, WHISPER AND SIGH TO EACH OTHER. • • •   27 OISIN 1   V   407
    AND THEY CEASE WITH A SIGH OF "UNJUST! UNJUST!" • • •   27 OISIN 1   V   416
    WHEN GOD SHALL COME FROM THE SEA WITH A SIGH • • • •   28 OISIN 1   425
    O SIGH, O FLUTTERING SIGH, BE KIND TO ME: • • • • •   33 OISIN 2   57
    O SIGH, O FLUTTERING SIGH, BE KIND TO ME: • • • • •   33 OISIN 2   57
    "OH, SIGH, AWAKE AND GO YOU FORTH FOR ME: • • • • •   33 OISIN 2   V   57
    • • • AND GAZED ON THE GRASS WITH A SIGH. • • • •   54 OISIN 3   100
    SIGH, O YOU LITTLE STARS! O SIGH AND SHAKE YOUR   72 ANASHU VIJAYA   18
        BLUE APPAREL!
    SIGH, O YOU LITTLE STARS! O SIGH AND SHAKE YOUR   72 ANASHU VIJAYA   18
        BLUE APPAREL!
    SIGH, OH YE LITTLE STARS! OH, SIGH AND SHAKE YOUR BLUE   72 ANASHU VIJAYA   V   18
        APPAREL!
    SIGH, OH YE LITTLE STARS! OH, SIGH AND SHAKE YOUR BLUE   72 ANASHU VIJAYA   V   18
        APPAREL!
    SING, TILL YOU RAISE YOUR HANDS AND SIGH, • • • •   73 ANASHU VIJAYA   45
    SING, TILL YE RAISE YOUR HANDS AND SIGH, • • • •   73 ANASHU VIJAYA   V   45
    I CAN BUT WEEP AND SIGH." • • • • • • • • • •   99 FOXHUNTER   36
    I SIGH THAT KISS YOU, • • • • • • • • • • • •   118 CRADLE SONG   9
    WHO SIGH WITH MINGLED SORROW AND CONTENT, • • • • •   136 TO SOME I TALK   7
    SIGH, HEART, AGAIN IN THE DEW OF THE MORN. • • • • •   147 INTO TWILIGHT   4
    AND THEY SIGH IF THE WIND BUT LIFT A TRESS: • • • •   151 OLD MOTHER   8
    AND THEY SIGH IF THE WIND BUT LIFT UP A TRESS: • • •   151 OLD MOTHER   V   8
    AND WHEN YOU SIGH FROM KISS TO KISS • • • • • •   156 FORGOT BEAUTY   18
    AND BIND UP YOUR LONG HAIR AND SIGH: • • • • • •   158 BELOVED RHYMES   8
    AND TROUBLE WITH A SIGH FOR ALL THINGS LONGING FOR REST   163 ASKS FORGIVE   23
    MAEVE WALKED THROUGH THAT GREAT HALL, AND WITH A SIGH • •   182 QUEEN MAEVE   62
    THAT THEY WOULD SIGH AND QUOTE WITH LEARNED LOOKS • •   205 ADAMS CURSE   25

717

		PAGE	TITLE		LINE

SIGH (CONTINUED)

THE DELICATE-STEPPING STAG AND HIS LADY SIGH,	210	RAGGED WOOD		2
FOR THERE THE TALL DEER AND HIS LEMAN SIGH .	210	RAGGED WOOD	V	2
THE DELICATE STEPPING STAG AND HIS LADY SIGH	210	RAGGED WOOD	V	2
AND THEN SMOOTH OUT WITH IVORY HANDS AND SIGH,	228	SHADOW WATER B		133
I LOOK AT YOU, AND I SIGH.	261	DRINKING SONG		6
ALTHOUGH IT BE FOR CHILDREN THAT YOU SIGH!	265	THESE CLOUDS		10
OR BY A TOUCH OR A SIGH,	413	TOWER		111
THAT THEY TOUCH OR SIGH.	517	HER ANXIETY		9
YOU ASK WHAT MAKES ME SIGH, OLD FRIEND,	524	MAD AS MIST		13
I SHUDDER AND I SIGH TO THINK	524	MAD AS MIST		15
WHAT MATTER? HEAVE NO SIGH, LET NO TEAR DROP,	564	GYRES		11
BUT HEAVED A SIGH IF THE CHAMBERMAID	570	THREE BUSHES		33
ALL THE LABOURING HEAVENS SIGH.	573	LADYS 3RD SONG		12
WHAT'S LEFT TO SIGH FOR?	574	MAIDS 1ST SONG		5
I SAW HIM SIGH AND TURN AND PASS AWAY!	690	MOSADA 1		14
IN SPACE, MADE EQUAL WITH A SIGH, WE MET.	705	REMEMBRANCE		14
AND THEN SMOOTH OUT WITH IVORY HANDS AND SIGH.	750	SHADOW WATER A		70
OR GIVE BUT A SIGH AND A WORD,	786	YOUR HEART		12
OR GIVE BUT A SIGH AND A WORD,	786	YOUR HEART		25
OR GIVE BUT A SIGH AND A WORD,	786	YOUR HEART		38

SIGHED

THEN SHE SIGHED GENTLY, "IT GROWS LATE.	9	OISIN 1		102
THEN SIGHED SHE SOFTLY, "LATE! 'TIS LATE!	9	OISIN 1	V	102
HE HAD SAT DOWN AND SIGHED WITH CUMBERED HEART,	37	OISIN 2		111
LAID IT AND SIGHED! I HELD A SWORD WHOSE SHINE	37	OISIN 2		126
LAID IT AND SIGHED---A SWORD WHOSE WIZARD SHINE	37	OISIN 2	V	126
THE IMMORTAL DESIRE OF IMMORTALS WE SAW IN THEIR FACES, AND SIGHED.	47	OISIN 3		4
SIGHED, "YOU, EVEN YOU YOURSELF, COULD WORK THE CURE!"	282	TWO KINGS		124
AND SHOWN MY HUSBAND SLEEPING THERE, I HAVE SIGHED,	285	TWO KINGS		188
ONE TO ANOTHER SIGHED AND CRIED!	296	THREE BEGGARS		38
HEARING IT NOW HAVE SIGHED FOR THAT YOUNG MAN	342	SHEP GOATHERD		77
WHATEVER HAS BEEN SAID, SIGHED, SUNG,	387	SOLOMON WITCH		7
ON BREAST OF MARS THE GODDESS SIGHED.	562	CONJUNCTIONS		4
IN ANCIENT TOMBS I SIGHED, BUT NOT AGAIN!	564	GYRES		14
AND THE GREAT WATER SIGHED FOR LOVE,	611	NEWS ORACLE		3
AND THE WIND SIGHED TOO.	611	NEWS ORACLE		4
MAN-PICKER NIAMH LEANT AND SIGHED	611	NEWS ORACLE		5
THERE SIGHED AMID HIS CHOIR OF LOVE	611	NEWS ORACLE		7

SIGHING

AND SIGHING BOWED HER GENTLE HEAD,	12	OISIN 1		149
AND SIGHING LAID THE PEARLY TIP	12	OISIN 1		150
ROLLED ROUND WITH MUSIC OF THE SIGHING SPRAY!	30	OISIN 2		14
I HEAR WHITE BEAUTY SIGHING, TOO,	156	FORGOT BEAUTY		19
I HEAR PALE BEAUTY SIGHING TOO,	156	FORGOT BEAUTY	V	19
FOR THAT BRIEF SIGHING. IF YOU HAD LOVED SOME WOMAN--	228	SHADOW WATER B		135
THOUGH IT BUT SET US SIGHING? FELLOW-WANDERER,	230	SHADOW WATER B		187
THOUGH IT BUT SET US SIGHING. FELLOW WANDERER	230	SHADOW WATER B	V	187
SIGHING REPLIED! "WHAT NEED HAVE WE FOR HASTE	276	TWO KINGS	V	C
LAY SIGHING LIKE THE REST.	612	NEWS ORACLE		12

SIGHS

AND NOW THE WARMTH OF SIGHS, AND AFTER THE QUIVER OF LIPS,	47	OISIN 3		8
LONG SIGHS AROSE IN OUR SPIRITS, BENEATH US BUBBLED THE GROUND.	48	OISIN 3		20
IN ONE WAS A BRANCH SOFT-SHINING WITH BELLS MORE MANY THAN SIGHS	50	OISIN 3		46
MY SPIRIT ROCKED IN SLEEP AND SIGHS! AND SAW THE MOORFOWL PACE	76	INDIAN ON GOD		3
THAT MOANS AND SIGHS A HUNDRED DAYS!	78	INDIAN TO LOVE		17
OR SIGHS AMID THE WANDERING, STARRY MIRTH,	114	ROSE OF BATTLE		18
THE WEST WEEPS IN PALE DEW AND SIGHS PASSING AWAY,	154	BELOVED PEACE		5
IN TWILIGHT SHAKEN WITH LOW SIGHS!	156	FORGOT BEAUTY	V	10B
AND TROUBLE WITH SIGHS FOR ALL HEARTS OWN REST	163	ASKS FORGIVE	V	23
I DREAMED THAT I STOOD IN A VALLEY, AND AMID SIGHS,	163	VALLEY LOVERS		1
AND SOULS AS IF THEY WERE BUT SIGHS,	307	HOUR DAWN		102
BIRD SIGHS FOR THE AIR,	574	LOVERS SONG		1
FOR THE WOMB THE SEED SIGHS.	574	LOVERS SONG		3
THE MOTHER OF THE WAVE SIGHS TOO,	738	YOU ARE SAD		10
FROM ITS FIRST SIGHS AND LAUGHTER, BEFORE THE SLEEP,	754	SHADOW WATER A		161

SIGHT

PASSED UNDER THE DIM DOORWAY, OUT OF SIGHT,	37	OISIN 2		123
MAKING A WORLD ABOUT HER, PASSED FROM SIGHT	37	OISIN 2		123
PASSED UNDER A DIM DOORWAY, OUT OF SIGHT,	37	OISIN 2	V	123
LEST THEY SHOULD LOOK UPON SOME DREADFUL SIGHT!	38	OISIN 2		142
STOOD TIMIDLY. LEST THEY SHOULD SEE SOME SIGHT	38	OISIN 2	V	141
O LOVELY TO SEE IN ALL MEN'S SIGHT	69	CLOAK BOAT		3
IN ALL MEN'S SIGHT."	69	CLOAK BOAT		5
UNFOLD YOUR FLAMING WINGS AND COVER OUT OF SIGHT	175	ELEMENT POWERS		11
THAT OUT OF SIGHT IS OUT OF MIND.	192	BAILE AILLINN		87
AND THERE, IN JUGGLERIES OF SIGHT AND SENSE,	231	SHADOW WATER B		216
WHO CANNOT PUT ME FROM HIS SIGHT FOR EVER.	251	SHADOW WATER B		601
WHEN, THE EARS BEING DEAFENED, THE SIGHT OF THE EYES BLIND	257	RECONCILIATION		3
THAT ALL MUST COME TO SIGHT AND TOUCH!	386	ROBARTES DANCE		31
NOR ANY HUMAN SIGHT WITHIN IT	389	SOLOMON WITCH		41
RAN OUT OF MY SIGHT!	399	DEMON BEAST		4
TROUBLES MY SIGHT! SOMEWHERE IN SANDS OF THE DESERT	402	SECOND COMING		13
TROUBLES MY SIGHT! A WASTE OF DESERT SAND!	402	SECOND COMING	V	13
TO TEST THEIR FANCY BY THEIR SIGHT!	410	TOWER		44
OF THE STARK MYSTERY THAT HAS DAZED MY SIGHT,	466	HARUN RASHID		113
AND, LIKE THE SOUL, IT SAILS INTO THE SIGHT	490	COOLE BALLYLEE		19

718

| | PAGE | TITLE | | LINE |

SIGHT   (CONTINUED)
```
    ANOTHER CAME IN SIGHT . . . . . . . . . . . . .    515 GIRLS SONG B          5
    BUT SOMETHING BORE THEM OUT OF SIGHT . . . . . .    519 HER DREAM            5
    AND EYES THAT HAD SO KEEN A SIGHT? . . . . . .      529 TOM LUNATIC          4
    OUT OF INTELLECT AND SIGHT . . . . . . . .          633 MAN AND ECHO        35
    OH, LOVELY TO SEE IN ALL MEN'S SIGHT . . . . .      666 ISLE STAT II 3       3
    IN ALL MEN'S SIGHT. . . . . . . . . . . .           666 ISLE STAT II 3       5
    THE FAIRY VANISHED FROM HIS SIGHT, . . . . . .      730 PRIEST FAIRY        62
    THE STARS ARE OUT OF SIGHT. . . . . . . . . .       786 YOUR HEART          34
    O, BUT I SAW A SOLEMN SIGHT! . . . . . . . .        788 HAWTHORN TREE        1
SIGHTS      SEE ELFIN-SIGHTS
    WITH ALL THOSE SIGHTS AND ALL THAT CRYING OUT?  . . . .  249 SHADOW WATER B     573
    THE HEART WELL WORN UPON THE SLEEVE MAY BE THE BEST OF   790 HEART SLEEVE        1
        SIGHTS,
SIGN
    HE SEEMED THE WATCHER FOR A SIGN. THE OTHER . . . . .     31 OISIN 2         V   41
    NOW IT IS OLD AND MOUSE-LIKE. FOR A SIGN . . . . .        36 OISIN 2             96
    NOW OLD AND MOUSELIKE. FOR AN ANSWERING SIGN . . . . .    36 OISIN 2         V   96
    AS A TOKEN AND A SIGN, . . . . . . . . . . . .          648 ISLE STAT I 1       78
    AND COLA, SEEING, KNOWS THE SIGN AND COMES. . . . . .    691 MOSADA 1            38
    AND COLA, SEEING, KNOWS THE SIGN AND RISES. . . . . .    691 MOSADA 1        V   38
SIGNAL
    THE FLAGRANT SIGNAL OF HER LORD'S RETURN, . . . . . .    645 ISLE STAT I 1        6
    HER ARMS AROUND HIS FEET. THE SIGNAL GOES . . . . . .    714 FERENCZ RENYI      103
SIGNATURE
    THAT WAXEN SEAL, THAT SIGNATURE, . . . . . . . . .       598 MODEL LAUREATE      21
SIGNS
    HE WHO CAN READ THE SIGNS NOR SINK UNMANNED . . . . .    429 NINETEEN 19         33
    PARTICULAR QUALITY. THE SIGNS AND SHAPES! . . . . .      469 HARUN RASHID       181
    HE KNOWS BY SIGNS OF SECRET WIT . . . . . . . .         716 FAIRY DOCTOR         5
SILENCE
    IN SILENCE ROUND HIS CRIMSON BALL. . . . . . . .         12 OISIN 1         V  155
    THAT IN IMMORTAL SILENCE SLEEPS . . . . . . . .          13 OISIN 1            161
    WE PASSED IN SILENCE O'ER THE MEAD, . . . . . . .        25 OISIN 1         V 376A
    SOBBED INTO SILENCE. WE HAD MOUNTED FEET . . . . .       33 OISIN 2         V  68E
    DROPPING: A MURMUROUS DROPPING: OLD SILENCE AND THAT ONE  48 OISIN 3            18
        SOUND:
    WHERE EVER IS MURMUROUS DROPPING, OLD SILENCE AND THAT   56 OISIN 3           138
        ONE SOUND:
    GATHERED IN SILENCE, DEWY AS HER EYES, . . . . . . .     80 EPHEMERA           19
    I WENT AWAY IN SILENCE, . . . . . . . . . .             95 MOLL MAGEE          27
    I WENT AWAY IN SILENCE! . . . . . . . . . .             95 MOLL MAGEE          33
    A WOVEN SILENCE, OR BUT CAME TO CAST . . . . . .       114 ROSE OF BATTLE      13
    SILENCE AND LOVE! . . . . . . . . . . . . .            116 FAERY SONG           6
    OLD SILENCE BIDS ITS CHOSEN RACE REJOICE, . . . . .    127 DREAM OF FAERY      31
    OLD SILENCE BIDS A LONELY FOLK REJOICE. . . . . .      127 DREAM OF FAERY V    31
    BUT LET A GENTLE SILENCE WROUGHT WITH MUSIC FLOW . .   175 ELEMENT POWERS      17
    BUT LET A GENTLE SILENCE ENWROUGHT WITH MUSIC FLOW . . 175 ELEMENT POWERS V    17
    WHO STOOD AMID A SILENCE BY THE THORN . . . . .        187 QUEEN MAEVE        142
    HEAVY LIKE STONE, THEIR WISDOM BEING HALF SILENCE. . . 218 WOODS OF COOLE      26
    SILENCE! FOR YOU HAVE TAKEN FORGAEL'S PAY. . . . .     225 SHADOW WATER B V    68
    KNOWING THAT SILENCE BRINGS NO GOOD TO KINGS, . . . .  279 TWO KINGS           57
    FOR WHAT BUT EYE AND EAR SILENCE THE MIND . . . . .    384 VISION ROBART       41
    TO SILENCE THE ENVY IN MY THOUGHT! . . . . . .         424 ROAD AT DOOR        13
    THE POLE-STAR AND THE SILENCE OF THE POLE. . . . .     477 SELF AND SOUL  V     8
    AFTER LONG SILENCE . . . . . . . . . . .               523 LONG SILENCE         T
    SPEECH AFTER LONG SILENCE! IT IS RIGHT. . . . .        523 LONG SILENCE         1
    OF THAT MOST SENSUOUS SILENCE OF THE NIGHT . . . .     579 DOR WELLESLEY        6
    HIS MIND MOVES UPON SILENCE. . . . . . . .             617 LONG-LEG FLY        10
    HER MIND MOVES UPON SILENCE. . . . . . . .             617 LONG-LEG FLY        20
    HIS MIND MOVES UPON SILENCE. . . . . . . .             618 LONG-LEG FLY        30
    I'LL SILENCE THIS DULL SINGER— . . . . . . .           647 ISLE STAT I 1       50
    OF EVENING AND GLAD SILENCE DWELLETH AYE, . . . .      653 ISLE STAT I 2       37
    IN SILENCE, THAT FAMED FLOWER OF WIZARDRY, . . . .     673 ISLE STAT II 3     192
    AMONG THE PLANTS: THE FLOWERY SILENCE FELL . . . .     692 MOSADA 1            55
    IN LIST'NING SILENCE GAZING ON OUR GRIEF. . . . .      702 MOSADA 3            87
    AND SILENCE HOLDING REVELRY AND FEAST: . . . . .       705 REMEMBRANCE         12
    SILENCE! THOU SHALT BE DEAD!" NOW SUDDENLY . . . .     710 FERENCZ RENYI       16
    THE HEART OF NOON FOLDS SILENCE AND FOLDS SLEEP, . .   735 QUATRAIN APHOR      25
    BUT OUR SILENCE HAD BEEN WISE. . . . . . . .           773 SONG DEIRDRE 1      22
    YET OUR SILENCE HAD BEEN WISE! . . . . . . .           773 SONG DEIRDRE 1 V    22
SILENT
    WHILE BIRDS GREW SILENT ONE BY ONE. . . . . . .        176 BELOVED DEAD   V    13
    YOU MOST OF ALL, SILENT AND FIERCE OLD MAN, . . . .    270 PARDON FATHERS      15
    BUT FINDING HIM STILL SILENT I STOOPED DOWN . . . .    281 TWO KINGS          109
    NOW THEY ARE SILENT," SAID THE CRANE. . . . . .        297 THREE BEGGARS       62
    THAT THERE BE NO FOOT SILENT IN THE ROOM . . . .       311 MOUNTAIN TOMB        6
    LET THERE BE NO FOOT SILENT IN THE ROOM, . . . .       311 MOUNTAIN TOMB  V     6
    WE SAT AS SILENT AS A STONE. . . . . . . .             314 MEMORY YOUTH        15
    I SAT AS SILENT AS A STONE . . . . . . . .             314 MEMORY YOUTH   V    15
    A REASON FOR KEEPING SILENT . . . . . . . .            359 WAR POEM       V     T
    A POET'S MOUTH BE SILENT, FOR IN TRUTH . . . . .       359 WAR POEM             2
    I CELEBRATE THE SILENT KISS THAT ENDS SHORT LIFE OR LONG. 459 FROM OEDIPUS      9
    I AM NOT DUMB: I'D SOONER SILENT WAIT . . . . .        646 ISLE STAT I 1       40
    O'ER MUCH I'VE TALKED: I SHALL BE SILENT SOON, . . .   657 ISLE STAT I 3       75
    IF WRONG MY CHOICE, AS SILENT AS THOU ART. . . .       657 ISLE STAT I 3       76
    BUT WHY ART THOU SO SILENT? DID'ST THOU HEAR . . .     670 ISLE STAT II 3      96
    AND WHY SO SILENT? I WOULD HAVE THEE SPEAK. . . .      671 ISLE STAT II 3     140
    TO THEIR FARM WORK! HOW SILENT ALL WILL BE! . . .      699 MOSADA 3             8
    TO THEIR FARM-WORK! HOW SILENT ALL WILL BE. . . .      699 MOSADA 3       V     8
    HOW FERENCZ RENYI KEPT SILENT. . . . . . . .           709 FERENCZ RENYI        T
```

719

		PAGE	TITLE		LINE
SILENT	**(CONTINUED)**				
	WHITE, RENYI SILENT STANDS; THAT MAIDEN SWEET • • • •	713	FERENCZ RENYI	V	84
	I CURSE THEE—CURSE THEE!" RENYI SILENT STANDS, • • • •	714	FERENCZ RENYI		107
	STANDS EACH GREY AND SILENT PHANTOM ON THE SAME REGARDLESS	719	PHANTOM SHIP		25
	SPOT—				
	TO CRY HIS FOLDING CRY! NO, NO, BE SILENT, • • • • •	760	SHADOW WATER A		253
SILK					
	FOR GOLD HIS HOOVES AND SILK HIS REIN, • • • • • •	2	OISIN 1	V	7Z
	AND A HUNDRED ROBES OF MURMURING SILK, • • • • • • •	8	OISIN 1		88
	AND A HUNDRED ROBES OF THE SOFTEST SILK, • • • • • •	8	OISIN 1	V	88
	THEIR CLOAKS MADE OUT OF YELLOW SILK, • • • • • • • •	15	OISIN 1		205
	THEIR ROBES WERE ALL OF YELLOW SILK • • • • • • • •	15	OISIN 1	V	205
	THEIR BRATTAS MADE OUT OF YELLOW SILK, • • • • • • •	15	OISIN 1	V	205
	• • • AND THEIR EYES THAT GLIMMER LIKE SILK. • • • •	59	OISIN 3		176
	• • • AND THEIR YOUTH, AND THEIR EYES SOFT AS SILK. • •	59	OISIN 3	V	176
	SHE MAY HAVE WORN SILK CLOTHES, OR WORN A CROWN, • • •	282	TWO KINGS		117
	HAVE CHANGED THEIR SILK FOR SACK. • • • • • • • • •	458	HIS WILDNESS		6
	TWO GIRLS IN SILK KIMONOS, BOTH • • • • • • • • •	475	EVA GORE-BOOTH		3
	TWO GIRLS IN SILK KIMONOS, BOTH • • • • • • • • •	475	EVA GORE-BOOTH		19
	GOLD-SEWN SILK ON THE SWORD-BLADE, • • • • • • • •	484	SYMBOLS		5
	GOLD-SOWN SILK ON THE SWORD BLADE! • • • • • • • •	484	SYMBOLS	V	5
	ALL THAT SILK AND SATIN GEAR! • • • • • • • • • •	525	DANCING DAYS		3
	FOR PASSING ROUND THE BOTTLE WITH GIRLS IN RAGS OR SILK,	592	PILGRIM		2
	FOR PASSING ROUND THE BOTTLE WITH GIRLS IN RAG OR SILK,	592	PILGRIM	V	2
	SO COME IN RAGS OR COME IN SILK, IN CLOAK OR COUNTRY SHAWL,	593	PILGRIM		22
	SO COME IN RAG OR COME IN SILK, IN CLOAK OR COUNTRY SHAWL,	593	PILGRIM	V	22
SILKEN					
	WERE LOLLING THEIR TONGUES, AND THE SILKEN HAIR • • • •	2	OISIN 1	V	7S
	HIS HEART HUNG ALL UPON A SILKEN DRESS, • • • • • •	126	DREAM OF FAERY		2
	THE LOVE-TALES WROUGHT WITH SILKEN THREAD • • • • • •	155	FORGOT BEAUTY		6
	THE LOVE-TALES WOVE WITH SILKEN THREAD • • • • • • •	155	FORGOT BEAUTY	V	6
	IN RUSTLE OF LACE OR SILKEN STUFF, • • • • • • • •	358	PRESENCES		5
	OVER SOME SILKEN DRESS • • • • • • • • • • • •	363	DOLLS DRAWINGS		7
	FOR SILKEN CLOTHES AND STATELY WALK, • • • • • •	422	MY TABLE		30
	THAT FLOWERING, SILKEN, OLD EMBROIDERY, TORN • • • • •	477	SELF AND SOUL		13
	UNDER A SILKEN SAIL AND SILVER YARD, • • • • • • •	763	SHADOW WATER A		316
SILL	**SEE WINDOW-SILL**				
	AND STAND ON HER WINDOW SILL. • • • • • • • • •	159	CAP AND BELLS	V	4
SILLY					
	COWARDICE, SOME SILLY OVER-SUBTLE THOUGHT • • • • • •	413	TOWER		117
	COWARDICE, OVER SOME SILLY SUBTLE THOUGHT • • • • • •	413	TOWER	V	117
SILVER					
	AND GATHERED IN A SILVER CINCTURE! • • • • • • •	3	OISIN 1	V	24A
	OUT OF A LITTLE SILVER TRUMP! • • • • • • • • •	15	OISIN 1		196
	A HARP OF SILVER IN MY HANDS, • • • • • • • • •	16	OISIN 1	V	232
	AND TOUCH THE LAUGHING SILVER STRING! • • • • • • •	17	OISIN 1		233
	AND CAUGHT THE SILVER HARP AWAY, • • • • • • • •	17	OISIN 1	V	240
	THEREIN THE SILVER HARP HE HURLED, • • • • • • • •	17	OISIN 1	V	244
	OR DROPS OF SILVER JOY THAT FELL • • • • • • • •	19	OISIN 1		278
	• • • WITH BRONZE AND SILVER AND GOLD. • • • • • •	49	OISIN 3		32
	MORE COMELY THAN MAN MAY MAKE THEM, INLAID WITH SILVER	49	OISIN 3	V	29
	AND GOLD,				
	• • • WHEN THE SUN WAS ON SILVER OR GOLD! • • • • •	53	OISIN 3		97
	IN DANCING SILVER SANDALLED ON THE SEA, • • • • • •	101	ROSE UPON ROOD	V	7
	IT SEEMED THEY RAISED THEIR LITTLE SILVER HEADS, • • •	126	DREAM OF FAERY		6
	UNDER THE GOLDEN OR THE SILVER SKIES! • • • • • •	127	DREAM OF FAERY		21
	OR STORMY SILVER FRET THE GOLD OF DAY, • • • • • •	128	DREAM OF FAERY		33
	OVER THE LITTLE SILVER CORDS, • • • • • • • • •	146	FISH		6
	AND CAUGHT A LITTLE SILVER TROUT. • • • • • • • •	149	WANDER AENGUS		8
	AND HOOKED A LITTLE SILVER TROUT. • • • • • • • •	149	WANDER AENGUS	V	8
	THE SILVER APPLES OF THE MOON, • • • • • • • • •	150	WANDER AENGUS		23
	ENWROUGHT WITH GOLDEN AND SILVER LIGHT, • • • • • •	176	CLOTHS HEAVEN		2
	AS MIDDLE NIGHT GREAT CATS WITH SILVER CLAWS, • • • •	185	QUEEN MAEVE		115
	A QUEEN-WOMAN DRESSED OUT IN SILVER, CRY • • • • •	210	RAGGED WOOD	V	2
	IN A GOLDEN AND SILVER WOOD! • • • • • • • • •	214	HAPPY TOWNLAND		10
	IN A GOLD AND SILVER WOOD! • • • • • • • • • •	214	HAPPY TOWNLAND	V	10
	FROM GOLDEN AND SILVER BOUGHS! • • • • • • • • •	215	HAPPY TOWNLAND		24
	OF HAMMERED SILVER, AND DRINK • • • • • • • • •	215	HAPPY TOWNLAND		50
	FROM THE GOLDEN AND SILVER BOUGHS. • • • • • • •	215	HAPPY TOWNLAND	V	24
	AND WHEN ONE CHANGED HER TO A SILVER FLY, • • • • •	220	HARP OF AENGUS	V	10
	CARE MORE ABOUT THE KEGS OF SILVER AND GOLD • • • •	232	SHADOW WATER B		234
	O SILVER FISH THAT MY TWO HANDS HAVE TAKEN • • • • •	251	SHADOW WATER B		609
	ON OLD DEEP SILVER ROLLING THERE • • • • • • • •	271	GREY ROCK		20
	THE HORN RESOUNDED AS THOUGH IT HAD BEEN SILVER, • • •	277	TWO KINGS		16
	THE GOLD AND SILVER THREAD. • • • • • • • • • •	308	PLAYER QUEEN		8
	AND ALL THEIR HELMS OF SILVER HOVERING SIDE BY SIDE, • •	318	MAGI		5
	OF GOLDEN KING AND SILVER LADY, • • • • • • • •	331	ROUND TOWER		13
	WHEN EVERY SILVER CANDLESTICK OR SCONCE • • • • • •	410	TOWER		26
	GET ALL THE GOLD AND SILVER THAT YOU CAN, • • • • •	500	VACILLATION		19
	THE MOON IN A SILVER BAG. • • • • • • • • • •	525	DANCING DAYS		8
	THE MOON IN A SILVER BAG. • • • • • • • • • •	525	DANCING DAYS		16
	THE MOON IN A SILVER BAG. • • • • • • • • • •	525	DANCING DAYS		24
	THERE THE SILVER DEW, • • • • • • • • • • •	611	NEWS ORACLE		2
	DRIFT AND FLOAT LIKE SILVER SHIPS! • • • • • • •	647	ISLE STAT I 1		67
	FROM THE WOOD'S WAYS, THEN, LIKE A SILVER FLAME, • • •	658	ISLE STAT II 1		6
	OF SILVER HANGING ROUND LAME COLA'S NECK— • • • • •	691	MOSADA 1	V	35
	AND LIKE A SILVER TRUMPET RING. • • • • • • • •	736	SUMMER EVENING	V	4
	AND LIKE A SILVER TRUMPET RING. • • • • • • • •	737	SUMMER EVENING		20
	A RED HOUND RUNNING FROM A SILVER ARROW. • • • • •	747	SHADOW WATER A		6
	HAD I NOT GOLD AND SILVER, AND ENOUGH • • • • • •	748	SHADOW WATER A		32
	TILL HIS EDAINE, NO MORE A SILVER FLY • • • • • •	757	SHADOW WATER A	V	210

	PAGE	TITLE	LINE

SILVER   (CONTINUED)
A WHITE BIRD HAS TORN ME WITH HIS SILVER CLAWS. • • • • •   759 SHADOW WATER A   234
MY EYES ARE TROUBLED BY THE SILVER ARROWS: • • • • •   761 SHADOW WATER A   269
UNDER A SILKEN SAIL AND SILVER YARD, • • • • • •   763 SHADOW WATER A   316
AND WHEN ONE CHANGED HER TO A SILVER FLY, • • • • •   763 SHADOW WATER A V 305
O SILVER FISH THAT MY TWO HANDS HAVE TAKEN • • • •   769 SHADOW WATER A   425
SILVER-PROUD
PALE SILVER-PROUD QUEEN-WOMAN OF THE SKY, • • • • •   211 RAGGED WOOD   6
SILVER-SANDALLED
IN DANCING SILVER-SANDALLED ON THE SEA, • • • • • •   101 ROSE UPON ROOD   7
SILVER-SHOED
OR HAVE YOU HEARD THAT SLIDING SILVER-SHOED • • • •   211 RAGGED WOOD   5
SIMPLE
THAT NOBLENESS MADE SIMPLE AS A FIRE, • • • • •   256 NO SECOND TROY   7
PASSIONATE AND SIMPLE LIKE HIS HEART. • • • • •   325 ROBERT GREGORY   32
THIS WISE AND SIMPLE MAN. • • • • • • • •   347 FISHERMAN   8
NO TABLE OR CHAIR OR STOOL NOT SIMPLE ENOUGH • • •   371 ON GOING HOUSE   3
SHOULD BE SO SIMPLE--A BAT ROSE FROM THE HAZELS • •   377 PHASES OF MOON   137
GLAD, SIMPLE--NAY, HE SOUGHT NOT MYSTERY, • • • • •   710 FERENCZ RENYI   30
SIMPLEST
TO TELL YOUR SIMPLEST WANT, AND KNOWN, • • • • •   436 FOR MY SON   21
TO TELL YOUR SIMPLEST WANT, AND KNOW, • • • • •   436 FOR MY SON V 21
SIMPLICITY
BUT NOT THE EXACT LIKENESS, THE SIMPLICITY OF A CHILD, • •   354 HIS PHOENIX   28
ITS FIRST SIMPLICITY, LOVE, VOICE AND ALL, • • • • •   469 HARUN RASHID   177
ITS FIRST SIMPLICITY, LOVE AND ALL, • • • • • •   469 HARUN RASHID V 177
STRUCK DUMB IN THE SIMPLICITY OF FIRE! • • • • •   502 VACILLATION   75
SIN
BEND DOWN AND PRAY FOR ALL THAT SIN I WOVE IN SONG, • • •   173 SPEAKS HEARERS   5
BEND DOWN AND PRAY FOR THE GREAT SIN I WOVE IN SONG, • •   173 SPEAKS HEARERS V 5
COUNT EVERY SIN OF ACTION OR OF THOUGHT: • • • •   479 SELF AND SOUL V 66
WHAT THEME HAD HOMER BUT ORIGINAL SIN? • • • • •   502 VACILLATION   77
BUT FOR ADAM'S SIN • • • • • • • • •   621 JOHN KINSELLA   26
I WILL NOT SHARE YOUR SIN. THIS IS NO SIN. • • • •   692 MOSADA 1   42
I WILL NOT SHARE YOUR SIN. THIS IS NO SIN. • • • •   692 MOSADA 1   42
NO SIN TO SEE IN COIL ON COIL OF AZURE• • • • •   692 MOSADA 1   43
THE DARK STILL MAN, HAS COME AND SAYS 'TIS SIN. • • •   692 MOSADA 1   47
THEY SAY THE WISH ITSELF IS HALF THE SIN: • • • •   692 MOSADA 1   48
YET 'TIS NO SIN: MY FATHER TAUGHT IT ME. • • • •   692 MOSADA 1   50
WOULD HE TEACH ANY SIN? GAZE IN THE CLOUD • • • •   692 MOSADA 1   58
I WILL NOT SHARE YOUR SIN. IT IS NO SIN. • • • •   692 MOSADA 1 V 42
I WILL NOT SHARE YOUR SIN. IT IS NO SIN. • • • •   692 MOSADA 1 V 42
YE SAID THAT YE WOULD FRIGHT HER FROM HER SIN--- • • •   695 MOSADA 1   113
FRIEND: BUT 'TWERE A DEADLY SIN • • • • • •   697 MOSADA 2   31
THE WAGES OF SIN IS DEATH. NO USE. NO GOOD• • • •   697 MOSADA 2   42
THE WAGE OF SIN IS DEATH. NO USE. NO USE. • • •   697 MOSADA 2 V 42
SINAI'S
FROM DEATH, AND WOUNDS, OR ON SINAI'S TOP, • • • •   375 PHASES OF MOON   67
SINBAD
SINBAD THE SAILOR'S BROUGHT A PAINTED CHEST, • • • •   371 ON GOING HOUSE   10
SINCE
SINCE GOD MADE TIME AND DEATH AND SLEEP: THE OTHER • • •   31 OISIN 2   41
AND MANY PATER NOSTERS SAID SINCE DAWN. • • • • •   43 OISIN 2 V 208D
• • • NO, NOT SINCE THE WORLD BEGAN, • • • • •   50 OISIN 3   49
SINCE ADAM'S FALL BUT NEEDS MUCH LABOURING. • • • •   205 ADAMS CURSE   22
FLEW WESTWARD: AND MANY A TIME SINCE THEN • • • • •   223 SHADOW WATER B   27
BUT, DEAR, CLING CLOSE TO ME: SINCE YOU WERE GONE, • • •   257 RECONCILIATION   11
SINCE, TAVERN COMRADES, YOU HAVE DIED, • • • • •   273 GREY ROCK   49
AND THE WORLD'S ALTERED SINCE YOU DIED, • • • • •   276 GREY ROCK   126
SINCE I FIRST MADE MY COUNT: • • • • • • •   322 SWANS AT COOLE   8
ALL'S CHANGED SINCE I, HEARING AT TWILIGHT, • • • •   322 SWANS AT COOLE   15
MY DAILY THOUGHTS SINCE THE FIRST STUPOR OF YOUTH • • •   342 SHEP GOATHERD   83
IT'S LONG SINCE I BEGAN • • • • • • • •   347 FISHERMAN   6
MAYBE A TWELVEMONTH SINCE • • • • • • •   348 FISHERMAN   25
MAYBE A TWELVE-MONTH SINCE • • • • • • •   348 FISHERMAN V 25
MAY BE A TWELVEMONTH SINCE • • • • • • •   348 FISHERMAN V 25
SINCE OLD WILLIAM POLLEXFEN • • • • • • •   360 ALF POLLEXFEN   2
SINCE HE WHO HAD BEEN CONTENTED LONG, • • • • •   361 ALF POLLEXFEN   28
O NOT SINCE LIFE BEGAN. • • • • • • • •   382 VISION ROBART   8
BUT SINCE I LAID A HAND THEREON • • • • • •   451 FIRST LOVE   7
SINCE FIRST WE SAW THE LIGHT, • • • • • • •   456 SUMMER SPRING   4
(FOR SINCE THE HORIZON'S BOUGHT STRANGE DOGS ARE STILL) • •   579 DOR WELLESLEY   7
"GREATEST SINCE REMBRANDT," ACCORDING TO JOHN SYNGE: • •   602 GALLERY REVIS   26
MY PRETTY CHILD, SINCE HE HAS GONE, OH SAY • • • •   658 ISLE STAT II 1   3
SINCE 'MONG MY PEOPLE, TENTED ON THE HILLS, • • • •   690 MOSADA 1   4
WITH POISONOUS LIPS, AND HE IS PINING SINCE? • • • •   696 MOSADA 2   7
HIS FACE HAS NEVER GLADDENED SINCE HE CAME • • • •   747 SHADOW WATER A   1
I HAVE BEEN WAITING YOU. A MOMENT SINCE • • • •   763 SHADOW WATER A   313
SINEW
HOW SINEW THAT HAS BEEN PULLED TIGHT, • • • • •   386 ROBARTES DANCE   34
YET BE BUT SINEW. I HAVE HEARD SAID • • • • •   386 ROBARTES DANCE   37
BEEN BONE AND SINEW: WHEN SUCH BODIES JOIN • • • •   555 RIBH AT TOMB   12
SINEWY
BUT WHEN AT LAST HE FORCED THOSE SINEWY FLANKS • • •   278 TWO KINGS   35
STARING UPON HIS SINEWY THIGH. • • • • • • •   294 HATED PLAYBOY   6
MADDENED BY THAT SINEWY THIGH. • • • • • •   294 HATED PLAYBOY V 6
STARING ON HIS SINEWY THIGH. • • • • • • •   294 HATED PLAYBOY V 6
• • • MOVE HIS MOUTH AND SINEWY TONGUE. • • • •   560 MAGIC DRUM   5
WHERE THEIR SINEWY MIGHT IS STRUNG • • • • •   658 ISLE STAT I 3   88
WHEN HIS SINEWY WINGS TOGETHER CLOSE. • • • • •   673 ISLE STAT II 3   179

721

	PAGE	TITLE		LINE
SINFULLY				
HOW SINFULLY THE WICKED SCOFF!"	725	LEGEND		22
SING				
HAVE KNOWN THREE CENTURIES, POETS SING, ...	2	OISIN 1		3
THE BAD OLD DAYS. THOU WERT, MEN SING, ...	2	OISIN 1	V	3
THEY SEEMED TO SING IN THE SMOULDERING FIRES.	13	OISIN 1		168
GAVE ME A HARP, AND BID ME SING, ...	16	OISIN 1		232
GAVE ME A HARP, AND BADE ME SING, ...	16	OISIN 1	V	232
AND BADE ME SING OF EARTHLY LANDS!	17	OISIN 1	V	233
SING, THEN, FOR THIS IS ALSO SOOTH.	66	HAPPY SHEPHERD		44
AMONG THEMSELVES LAUGH ON AND SING ALWAY!	68	SAD SHEPHERD		7
AND MY OWN TALE AGAIN FOR ME SHALL SING, ...	68	SAD SHEPHERD		22
AND MINE OWN TALE AGAIN FOR ME SHALL SING, ...	68	SAD SHEPHERD	V	22
SING, O YOU LITTLE STARS! O SING AND RAISE YOUR RAPTUROUS CAROL	72	ANASHU VIJAYA		20
SING, O YOU LITTLE STARS! O SING AND RAISE YOUR RAPTUROUS CAROL	72	ANASHU VIJAYA		20
SING, OH YE LITTLE STARS! OH, SING, AND RAISE YOUR RAPTUROUS CAROL	72	ANASHU VIJAYA	V	20
SING, OH YE LITTLE STARS! OH, SING, AND RAISE YOUR RAPTUROUS CAROL	72	ANASHU VIJAYA	V	20
SING YOU OF HER, O FIRST FEW STARS, ...	73	ANASHU VIJAYA		41
SING, TURNING IN YOUR CARS, ...	73	ANASHU VIJAYA		44
SING, TILL YOU RAISE YOUR HANDS AND SIGH, ...	73	ANASHU VIJAYA		45
SING YE OF HER, OH FIRST FEW STARS, ...	73	ANASHU VIJAYA	V	41
SING, TILL YE RAISE YOUR HANDS AND SIGH, ...	73	ANASHU VIJAYA	V	45
AND SING FROM SHORE TO SHORE, AND EVERY YEAR	81	EPHEMERA	V	24G
AND SING, AND SHAKE MY HEAVY LOCKS.	84	MAD KING GOLL		44
FROM POND AND FALLEN TREE--ME SING	85	MAD KING GOLL	V	63
--FROM POOLS AND ROTTING LEAVES--ME SING	85	MAD KING GOLL	V	63
SING PEACE INTO HIS BREAST, ...	88	STOLEN CHILD		47
COME NEAR ME, WHILE I SING THE ANCIENT WAYS!	100	ROSE UPON ROOD		2
SING IN THEIR HIGH AND LONELY MELODY.	101	ROSE UPON ROOD		8
SING OF OLD EIRE AND THE ANCIENT WAYS!	101	ROSE UPON ROOD		23
FOR HIM WHO HEARS LOVE SING AND NEVER CEASE, ...	114	ROSE OF BATTLE		10
ENCIRCLE HER I LOVE AND SING HER INTO PEACE, ...	174	ELEMENT POWERS		9
COUPLED WITH GOLDEN CHAINS, AND SING AS THEY FLY. . . .	204	WITHER BOUGHS		18
SING ON! SOMEWHERE AT SOME NEW MOON, ...	266	GALWAY RACES		10
SING ON! SOMETIME, AND AT SOME NEW MOON	266	GALWAY RACES	V	10
DID NOT THE POET SING IT WITH SUCH AIRS	267	ALL TEMPT ME		7
AMONG THOSE MOUTHS THAT SING THEIR SWEETHEARTS' PRAISE,	285	TWO KINGS		185
COULD LIKE A BRACE OF BLACKBIRDS SING.	332	ROUND TOWER		24
WHEN HER SON'S TURN WAS OVER. SING YOUR SONG. . . .	340	SHEP GOATHERD		42
YOU SING AS ALWAYS OF THE NATURAL LIFE, ...	342	SHEP GOATHERD		75
SING, FOR IT MAY BE THAT YOUR THOUGHTS HAVE PLUCKED . .	342	SHEP GOATHERD		85
AND SING WHEN THEY HAVE FOUND IT. NO, NOT SING, . . .	369	EGO DOMINUS		41
AND SING WHEN THEY HAVE FOUND IT. NO, NOT SING, . . .	369	EGO DOMINUS		41
SING ME THE CHANGES OF THE MOON ONCE MORE!	373	PHASES OF MOON		29
SING OUT THE SONG! SING TO THE END, AND SING	374	PHASES OF MOON		56
SING OUT THE SONG! SING TO THE END, AND SING	374	PHASES OF MOON		56
SING OUT THE SONG! SING TO THE END, AND SING	374	PHASES OF MOON		56
SOUL CLAP ITS HANDS AND SING, AND LOUDER SING	407	SAIL BYZANTIUM		11
SOUL CLAP ITS HANDS AND SING, AND LOUDER SING	407	SAIL BYZANTIUM		11
OR SET UPON A GOLDEN BOUGH TO SING	408	SAIL BYZANTIUM		30
AND THERE SING HIS LAST SONG.	414	TOWER		144
AND WHEN ABOUNDING HEDGES SING	434	WHEEL	V	3
THE MORNING STARS TO SING, ...	436	FOR MY SON		19
AND THEN DID ALL THE MUSES SING	437	SONGS PLAY 1		6
THE CHILDREN LEARN TO CIPHER AND TO SING, ...	443	SCHOOL CHILDR		3
AND SING IT LULLABY.	459	HIS WILDNESS		12
WE MUST LAUGH AND WE MUST SING, ...	479	SELF AND SOUL		70
AND SING IT RHYME UPON RHYME	480	BLOOD AND MOON		10
TO SING A SONG OR TWO, ...	515	GIRLS SONG B		2
COME, LET ME SING INTO YOUR EAR!	524	DANCING DAYS		1
CURSE AS YOU MAY I SING IT THROUGH!	525	DANCING DAYS		9
MAY SING, AND SING UNTIL HE DROP, ...	525	DANCING DAYS		21
MAY SING, AND SING UNTIL HE DROP, ...	525	DANCING DAYS		21
OR SING A PENANCE ON THE ROAD!	529	TOM LUNATIC		10
THAT MUST SING IN A RHYME	529	TOM CRUACHAN		2
THAT BIRD . . . LET HIM SING ON, ...	536	PARTING		12
PRAY I WILL AND SING I MUST, ...	540	FROM ANTIGONE		14
HOW COULD YOU SING THOSE SONGS OF LOVE?	569	THREE BUSHES		5
I AM CONTENT TO STAND AND SING	582	ROGER CASEMENT	V	21
SING OF THE O'RAHILLY, ...	584	ORAHILLY		1
SING A "THE" BEFORE HIS NAME!	584	ORAHILLY		3
SING OF THE O'RAHILLY	585	ORAHILLY		10
WHAT REMAINS TO SING ABOUT	585	ORAHILLY		28
I SING WHAT WAS LOST AND DREAD WHAT WAS WON, ...	591	WHAT WAS LOST		1
THAT MAKE THE MUSES SING.	601	THOSE IMAGES		16
AND NIGHT AND MORNING SING!	627	STATES HOLIDAY		12
AND I DELIGHT TO SING!	627	STATES HOLIDAY		25
"NOW MUST WE SING AND SING THE BEST WE CAN, ...	634	CUCHULAIN COMF		19
"NOW MUST WE SING AND SING THE BEST WE CAN, ...	634	CUCHULAIN COMF		19
SING WHATEVER IS WELL MADE, ...	639	BEN BULBEN		69
SING THE PEASANTRY, AND THEN	639	BEN BULBEN		74
SING THE LORDS AND LADIES GAY	640	BEN BULBEN		78
NOT A SAD NOTE WILL I SING.	646	ISLE STAT I 1		39
SING SUMMER WAVES. BUT YONDER SHEPHERD VILE, ...	649	ISLE STAT I 1		107
AS I SING NOW TO THEE!	654	ISLE STAT I 2		67
AS I SING NOW TO THEE!	654	ISLE STAT I 2		77
AS I SING NOW TO THEE!	655	ISLE STAT I 2		81

		PAGE	TITLE	LINE

SING   (CONTINUED)
HE SAT, AND THEN I HEARD THE WHITE LAKE SING, ... 659 ISLE STAT II 1   15
GO UP AND DOWN, AND RAISE THEIR HEADS AND SING   . . . . 682 SEEKER   30
I'LL SING THE SONGS THE DUSKY LOVERS SING, ... 694 MOSADA 1   101
I'LL SING THE SONGS THE DUSKY LOVERS SING, ... 694 MOSADA 1   101
CHILDREN SING IN TWOS AND THREES. . . . . 732 STREET DANCERS   17
AND SING TO YOU IN THE NIGHT, ... 739 WHERE BOOKS GO   6
THOUGH WE WERE BIDDEN TO SING, CRY NOTHING LOUD. . . . 778 SONG DEIRDRE 3   2
HE SWORE TO SING MY BEAUTY . . . . 789 SINGING HEAD   7
AND HEARD THE DEAD LIPS SING. . . . . 790 SINGING HEAD   24
SINGE
AN AGONY OF FLAME THAT CANNOT SINGE A SLEEVE. . . . . . 498 BYZANTIUM   32
SINGER   SEE BALLAD-SINGER
AND WHILE THEY SANG, A SINGER LAID . . . . 16 OISIN 1   V 231
WHAT, BE A SINGER BORN AND LACK A THEME? . . . . 502 VACILLATION   73
AS THOUGH SOME BALLAD SINGER HAD SUNG IT ALL. . . . . . 602 GALLERY REVIS V 24
I'LL SILENCE THIS DULL SINGER-- . . . . 647 ISLE STAT I 1   50
SINGETH
OF MOSS, A MAIDEN WEAVING. SINGETH SHE: . . . . 716 DWELT SYCAMORE   12
SINGING   SEE EVER-SINGING
AND SINGING, SINGING ALL TOGETHER: . . . . 15 OISIN 1   203
AND SINGING, SINGING ALL TOGETHER: . . . . 15 OISIN 1   203
AND SINGING, SINGING ALTOGETHER: . . . . 15 OISIN 1   203
AND SINGING, SINGING ALTOGETHER: . . . . 15 OISIN 1   V 203
WE HUSHED THE SINGING AND THE ROMP, ... 20 OISIN 1   V 296
THAT RAISE THEIR HEADS AND WANDER SINGING, ... 27 OISIN 1   419
THE SINGING MELTED IN THE NIGHT: . . . . 28 OISIN 1   V 427A
FLOATED IN ALL HER SINGING. HALF ENTRANCED . . . . . . 30 OISIN 2   V 19
INNUMERABLE, SINGING, EXULTANT: THE CLAY UNDERNEATH THEM   61 OISIN 3   203
    SHALL PANT,
TILL THEY SHALL SINGING FADE IN RUTH . . . . 66 HAPPY SHEPHERD   41
PIERCED BY MY GLAD SINGING THROUGH, ... 67 HAPPY SHEPHERD   53
AND WITH LOUD SINGING I RUSHED ON . . . . 83 MAD KING GOLL V 31
MY SINGING SANG ME FEVER FREE, ... 86 MAD KING GOLL V 65
MY SINGING SANG ME FEVER-FREE: . . . . 86 MAD KING GOLL V 65
MY SINGING FADES, THE STRINGS ARE TORN, ... 86 MAD KING GOLL V 66
I HAVE OFTEN HEARD HIM SINGING TO AND FRO, ... 109 CUCHULAIN SEA   49
I OFTEN HEAR HIM SINGING TO AND FRO, ... 109 CUCHULAIN SEA V 49
A SONG INTO THE AIR, AND SINGING PASSED . . . . 114 ROSE OF BATTLE 14
A SONG INTO THE AIR, AND SINGING PAST . . . . 114 ROSE OF BATTLE V 14
THE SINGING SHOOK HIM OUT OF HIS NEW EASE. . . . . . . 126 DREAM OF FAERY 12
AND AT THAT SINGING HE WAS NO MORE WISE. . . . . 127 DREAM OF FAERY 24
AND WE, OUR SINGING AND OUR LOVE, ... 139 TO IRELAND   37
ARE SINGING ABOUT THE WOOD?" . . . . 167 BLESSED   24
YET SHE, SINGING UPON HER ROAD, ... 260 UNWORTH PRAISE 19
NOR IS THERE SINGING SCHOOL BUT STUDYING . . . . 407 SAIL BYZANTIUM 13
AND THERE'S NO SINGING SCHOOL BUT STUDYING . . . . . . 407 SAIL BYZANTIUM V 13
AND BE THE SINGING MASTERS OF MY SOUL. . . . . 408 SAIL BYZANTIUM V 20
WITH SINGING HUSH AND HUSH-A-BYE; . . . . 456 FRIENDS YOUTH   9
NOR KNEW, DRUNKEN WITH SINGING AS WITH WINE, ... 537 HER VISION   30
COME MARCH, SINGING THIS SONG, ... 544 TO SAME TUNE 1 V REF
SINGING, SINGING A SONG. . . . . 546 TO SAME TUNE 2 16
SINGING, SINGING A SONG. . . . . 546 TO SAME TUNE 2 16
TO WELCOME THEE, NASCHINA, WITH SWEET SINGING. . . . . 645 ISLE STAT I 1   7
BY THE SINGING WATERS' EDGE, ... 646 ISLE STAT I 1   23
I'LL QUENCH HIS SINGING WITH LOUD SONG-- . . . . 647 ISLE STAT I 1   63
HUNDRED-THROATED MORN IS SINGING, ... 647 ISLE STAT I 1   70
SINGING O'ER AND O'ER AND O'ER . . . . 648 ISLE STAT I 1   79
IN THE HEART OF THE DAWN THE RIVERS ARE SINGING, . . . 648 ISLE STAT I 1   91
ALL THE WORLD IS SINGING, SINGING. . . . . 648 ISLE STAT I 1   94
ALL THE WORLD IS SINGING, SINGING. . . . . 648 ISLE STAT I 1   94
OH, CEASE YOUR SINGING! WILD AND SHRILL AND LOUD, . . . 648 ISLE STAT I 1   99
I FAIN HAD BEEN THE FIRST OF SINGING THINGS   . . . . 648 ISLE STAT I 1 101
WITH SINGING SWEET AS E'ER ROUND LAKE-LULLED ISLE . . . 649 ISLE STAT I 1 106
SINGING OF ARMS AND BATTLES SOME OLD STAVE. . . . . . 650 ISLE STAT I 1 137
AS SOME DEAD MAIDEN'S SINGING IN A DREAM. . . . . . . 654 ISLE STAT I 2   59
WITH SHOUTING AND SINGING. . . . . 672 ISLE STAT II 3 173
THE SINGING SHEPHERDS, TOO, HAVE PASSED AWAY. . . . . . 676 ISLE STAT II 3 271
AND IN HER SINGING WOVE AROUND HER HEAD . . . . 693 MOSADA 1   84
HEARING THE FAR-OFF SINGING GUILE, AND GROANED, ... 693 MOSADA 1   88
HEARING THE FAR OFF SINGING GUILE AND GROANED, ... 693 MOSADA 1   V 88
HE'D SLEPT AMONG THE SINGING TREES, ... 728 PRIEST FAIRY   17
SINGING IN THIS LONDON STREET, ... 731 STREET DANCERS   1
SINGING TO THEIR LIGHT FOOTFALL. . . . . 732 STREET DANCERS 30
SINGING A LOVE RHYME TO HIMSELF, ... 741 EARL PAUL   41
WHEN WE ROWED NORTH, SINGING ABOVE THE OARS, ... 749 SHADOW WATER A 39
THE SINGING HEAD AND THE LADY . . . . 789 SINGING HEAD V T
SINGING-MASTERS
AND BE THE SINGING-MASTERS OF MY SOUL. . . . . 408 SAIL BYZANTIUM 20
SINGLE
BUTTED BELOW THE SINGLE AND SO PIERCED . . . . 278 TWO KINGS   22
A SINGLE SOUL THAT LACKS A SWEET CRYSTALLINE CRY. . . . 291 PAUDEEN   8
THREE TIMES IN A SINGLE DAY . . . . 298 THREE HERMITS   10
I HAD NOT WAKED A SINGLE MINUTE, ... 305 HOUR DAWN   72
THOUGH SEVERAL, ARE A SINGLE LIGHT. . . . . 388 SOLOMON WITCH   29
BUT COULD NOT CAST A SINGLE JET THEREON. . . . . 482 BLOOD AND MOON 39
THOUGHTS LONG KNITTED INTO A SINGLE THOUGHT, ... 488 COOLE PARK 29   7
SEEMED SPRUNG FROM BUT A SINGLE ROOT . . . . 571 THREE BUSHES   61
NO SINGLE STORY WOULD THEY FIND . . . . 626 OLD MEN BE MAD 13
SINGLED
KNOWING THAT THOU HADST SINGLED ME WITH WORD . . . . . 684 SEEKER   57

```
                                                      PAGE    TITLE          LINE
SINGS
     TO THE CRACKED TUNE THAT CHRONOS SINGS,  . . . . . . . .    65 HAPPY SHEPHERD      9
     TO THE OLD CRACKED TUNE THAT CHRONOS SINGS,  . . . . . .    65 HAPPY SHEPHERD V    9
     DROPPING FROM THE VEILS OF THE MORNING TO WHERE THE CRICKET 117 ISLE INNISFREE     6
        SINGS!
     BUT SINGS ON!  . . . . . . . . . . . . . . . . . . . . .   512 JANE ON GOD        23
     HE THAT SINGS A LASTING SONG  . . . . . . . . . . . . .    553 PRAYER OLD AGE      3
     SHE SINGS AS THE MOON SINGS!  . . . . . . . . . . . . .    559 HE AND SHE          7
     SHE SINGS AS THE MOON SINGS!  . . . . . . . . . . . . .    559 HE AND SHE          7
     A PASSION-DRIVEN EXULTANT MAN SINGS OUT . . . . . . . .    560 WHENCE COME         5
     EVERY MAN THAT SINGS A SONG . . . . . . . . . . . . . .    586 PARNELLITES        19
     BY DAY AND NIGHT A LONELY FOUNTAIN SINGS,  . . . . . . .   650 ISLE STAT I 1     130
     THE WATER-SERPENT SINGS HIS HEART . . . . . . . . . . .    673 ISLE STAT II 3    184
     SINGS THE YOUNG WISTFUL SPIRIT OF A STAR  . . . . . . .    705 REMEMBRANCE        10
SINK
     AFTER NINE YEARS, I SINK MY HEAD ABASHED. . . . . . . .    353 PEOPLE             37
     HE WHO CAN READ THE SIGNS NOR SINK UNMANNED . . . . . .    429 NINETEEN 19        33
     AND SINK INTO ITS OWN DELIGHT AT LAST.  . . . . . . . .    473 ALL SOUL NIGHT     60
     OR WINTRY MOONLIGHT SINK THE FIELD  . . . . . . . . . .    501 VACILLATION        47
     HEART-SMITTEN WITH EMOTION I SINK DOWN. . . . . . . . .    602 GALLERY REVIS      17
     HEART SMITTEN WITH EMOTION, I SINK DOWN,  . . . . . . .    602 GALLERY REVIS V    17
     THAT CIVILISATION MAY NOT SINK, . . . . . . . . . . . .    617 LONG-LEG FLY        1
     SLOW WATERS, AND THE BOAT AND MAIDEN SINK . . . . . . .    663 ISLE STAT II 2     39
     LOOK ON ME ONCE.  WHY SINK YOUR EYELIDS THUS? . . . . .    703 MOSADA 3          107
     LOOK ON ME ONCE.  WHY SINK YOUR EYELIDS SO? . . . . . .    703 MOSADA 3       V  107
SINKING
     AND THE EARS OF THE HORSE WENT SINKING AWAY IN THE HOLLOW   48 OISIN 3            21
        NIGHT,
     ABOVE A SINKING FIRE, A TALE THAT SHE . . . . . . . . .    443 SCHOOL CHILDR      10
     ABOVE A SINKING FIRE, SOME TALE THAT SHE  . . . . . . .    443 SCHOOL CHILDR V    10
     MY SINKING BRAIN!--CEASE!--CEASE!  HEARD YE YON SOUND? .    665 ISLE STAT II 2     73
SINKS
     THE GREY CAIRN ON THE HILL, WHEN DAY SINKS DROWNED IN DEW,  161 BLACK PIG           6
     THE RIVER RISES, AND IT SINKS AGAIN,  . . . . . . . . .    420 MY HOUSE       V  20A
     WHEN THE CONFLAGRATION OF THEIR PASSION SINKS,  . . . .    556 RIBH PATRICK        8
     NOW SINKS THE SAME REST . . . . . . . . . . . . . . . .    574 LOVERS SONG         4
     AND SINKS AT LAST INTO THE NIGHT. . . . . . . . . . . .    633 MAN AND ECHO       36
     SEE, YONDER SINKS THE SUN, YONDER A SHADE . . . . . . .    653 ISLE STAT I 2      52
     SINKS, SHINING ON THE LITTLE CRUCIFIX . . . . . . . . .    691 MOSADA 1           34
     SINKS DOWN AT LAST WITH YONDER MINARET, . . . . . . . .    691 MOSADA 1       V   36
     A WOMAN IN MY ARMS, SHE SINKS AWAY  . . . . . . . . . .    749 SHADOW WATER A     54
SINNED
     IF THEY HAVE SINNED NOBODY KNOWS! . . . . . . . . . . .    337 SCHOLARS       V   10
     "IF LITTLE PLANNED IS LITTLE SINNED . . . . . . . . . .    338 TOM OROUGHLEY       9
     "OH, LITTLE PLANNED IS LITTLE SINNED  . . . . . . . . .    338 TOM OROUGHLEY V     9
     THEN HAS THIS ONE BEEN SINNED FULL MANY TIMES.  . . . .    692 MOSADA 1           49
SINNING
     I WAS AT HER SINNING. . . . . . . . . . . . . . . . . .    654 ISLE STAT I 2      62
     TELLS ALL HIS SINNING IN THEIR EARS.  . . . . . . . . .    655 ISLE STAT I 3      14
     TELLS ALL HER SINNING IN THEIR EARS.  . . . . . . . . .    655 ISLE STAT I 3  V   14
SINS
     BALD HEADS FORGETFUL OF THEIR SINS, . . . . . . . . . .    337 SCHOLARS            1
SIPPING
     GOLDSMITH DELIBERATELY SIPPING AT THE HONEY-POT OF HIS     481 BLOOD AND MOON     21
        MIND,
     GOLDSMITH DELIBERATELY SIPPING AT THE HONEY POT OF HIS     481 BLOOD AND MOON V   21
        MIND!
SIPS
     O WAKE! WAKE! WAKE! FOR SOFT AS A BEE SIPS  . . . . . .    677 ISLE STAT II 3    276
     OLD WARRIOR, WAKE! FOR SOFT AS A BEE SIPS,  . . . . . .    677 ISLE STAT II 3    284
     THOSE TWAIN ARE DUST.  WAKE!  LIGHT AS A BEE SIPS . . .    678 ISLE STAT II 3    290
     HE IS LONG DEAD.  WAKE! SOFT AS A BEE SIPS  . . . . . .    678 ISLE STAT II 3    297
     NAY, HE IS GONE.  WAKE! WAKE! AS A BEE SIPS . . . . . .    678 ISLE STAT II 3    305
     BEFORE HIS TENT THE GENERAL SIPS HIS WINE,  . . . . . .    709 FERENCZ RENYI       6
SIR
     "I NEVER THOUGHT OF THAT, SIR." . . . . . . . . . . . .    596 COLONEL MARTIN     66
     YON IS THE HUNTER'S, SIR ALMINTOR'S, PAGE! . . . . . .     660 ISLE STAT II 1     35
     SIR PAGE, ALMINTOR'S FRIEND, AND THEREFORE LEARNED  . .    660 ISLE STAT II 1     38
     A LONG, BROWN GRASSHOPPER OF MAIDS!  PEACE, SIR!  . . .    661 ISLE STAT II 1     69
SIRS
     NO NEED TO BIND MY HANDS.  WHERE ARE YE, SIRS?  . . . .    695 MOSADA 1          110
     NO MORE! TAKE ME INSTEAD OF HER, GREAT SIRS.  . . . . .    695 MOSADA 1          114
SISTER
     MY MARRIED SISTER PUT INTO MY CARE  . . . . . . . . . .    276 TWO KINGS      V    E
     HE MIGHT HAVE HAD MY SISTER,  . . . . . . . . . . . . .    620 JOHN KINSELLA      5
     I HAD A SISTER LIKE HER ONCE, MY FRIEND.  . . . . . . .    696 MOSADA 2          11
     O SISTER OF SORROWFUL GAZE! . . . . . . . . . . . . . .    706 FAIRY PEDANT        2
     THERE LIVE HIS SISTER AND HIS MOTHER.  HIGH  . . . . .     710 FERENCZ RENYI V    25
     OF MIDDLE AGE.  "HIS SISTER HERE AND MOTHER." . . . . .    711 FERENCZ RENYI      53
     THE SISTER!  "SELL THY COUNTRY, AND THE SHAME . . . . .    712 FERENCZ RENYI      60
     WALKS IN THE VESTURE OF HER SISTER SORROW.  . . . . . .    735 QUATRAIN APHOR     28
SISTERHOOD
     HERE GROW THAT SHY, RETIRING SISTERHOOD,  . . . . . . .    651 ISLE STAT I 2       4
SISTER'S
     AUGUSTA GREGORY'S SON! HER SISTER'S SON,  . . . . . . .    602 GALLERY REVIS      21
SISTERS
     "MY BROTHERS AND MY SISTERS LIVE AND THRIVE,  . . . . .     32 OISIN 2        V  50C
     SEVEN OLD SISTERS WIND THE THREADS OF THE LONG-LIVED ONES,  209 UNDER THE MOON      7
     SEVEN OLD SISTERS WIND THE THREADS OF THE LONG LIVED ONES,  209 UNDER THE MOON V    7
SISTINE
     WHILE MICHAEL ANGELO'S SISTINE ROOF,  . . . . . . . . .    386 ROBARTES DANCE     32
```

724

	PAGE	TITLE	LINE

SISTINE   (CONTINUED)
ON THE SISTINE CHAPEL ROOF, ...   638 BEN BULBEN   46
SIT
I HUNGER TO BUILD THEM ANEW AND SIT ON A GREEN KNOLL APART,   143 ROSE IN HEART   6
WHERE I CAN SIT UP HALF THE NIGHT . . . .   624 APPARITIONS   11
OR SAD SEA-SHELLS WHERE LITTLE ECHOES SIT? . . . . .   650 ISLE STAT I 1   149
AND 'NEATH IT SIT, AND OF THE WOVEN SUM . . . . . .   663 ISLE STAT II 2   30
AS MOTHS WITH BROKEN WINGS, AND AS WE SIT . . . . .   671 ISLE STAT II 3   142
BY THOSE WAN STARS THAT SIT IN COMPANY . . . .   691 MOSADA 1   26
COME, FATHER. LADY, I NOR REST NOR SIT. . . . . . .   720 WITCH VIVIEN   18
WHERE MAY NEW-MARRIED WOMEN SIT . . . .   791 REPRISALS   19
SITS
SITS A YOUNGER AND A STRONGER. . . . .   26 OISIN 1   V 399D
WHO SITS IN LONELY SPLENDOUR, MAIL'D IN GOLD, . . .   651 ISLE STAT I 1   163
BUT LOUD THE GRASSHOPPER THAT SITS BENEATH. . . . .   662 ISLE STAT II 2   8
AND EVERY FLOWER ABOVE ITS SHADOW SITS. . . . . . .   712 FERENCZ RENYI   73
AND EVERY FLOWER ABOVE A SHADOW SITS. . . . .   712 FERENCZ RENYI V   73
SITTING
THERE WAS A WONDROUS YOUNG MAN SITTING. . . . . . .   18 OISIN 1   V 252
A KING SITTING UPON A CHAIR OF GOLD-- . . . .   104 FERGUS DRUID   36
TO PETER SITTING IN STATE, ...   178 FIDDLER DOONEY   10
THE GODS WERE SITTING AT THE BOARD . . . .   271 GREY ROCK   14
AND SAW HER SITTING UPRIGHT ON THE BED, ...   467 HARUN RASHID   134
I SAW HER SITTING UPRIGHT ON THE BED, ...   467 HARUN RASHID V   134
THEY WERE SITTING ROUND A POOL, ...   667 ISLE STAT II 3   24
AND THEY WERE SITTING ROUND A POOL. . . . .   667 ISLE STAT II 3 V   24
AND ALL THE ELDERS SITTING IN THE SUN . . . .   693 MOSADA 1   69
SITTING ON A WARM SMOOTH MAT . . . .   726 LOVERS QUARREL   11
SITTING ON MY RIGHT HAND." . . . .   741 EARL PAUL   60
SIX   SEE FIVE-SIX FOUR-SIX THREE-SIX
"THOSE SIX FEET MARKED IN CHALK? . . . .   548 TO SAME TUNE 3   8
"THOSE SIX FEET MARKED IN CHALK? . . . .   548 TO SAME TUNE 3   18
"THOSE SIX FEET MARKED IN CHALK? . . . .   549 TO SAME TUNE 3   28
I TOLD HIM THAT NIGHTLY FROM SIX TO SEVEN I SAT AT THIS   578 LOFTY THINGS   9
TABLE,
I SOUGHT IT DAILY FOR SIX WEEKS OR SO. . . . . . .   629 CIRCUS ANIMALS   2
A MAN THAT HAD SIX MORTAL WOUNDS, A MAN . . . . . .   634 CUCHULAIN COMF   1
DEEP IN THE WOODLAND PAUSED THEY, THE SIX FEET . . .   716 DWELT SYCAMORE   9
DEEP IN THE WOODLAND PASSED THEY. THE SIX FEET . . .   716 DWELT SYCAMORE V   9
WHO IS SIX FEET HIGH IN HIS SOCKS AT LEAST? . . . .   729 PRIEST FAIRY   28
SIX THAT ARE DEATHLESS, ...   770 BLOOD BOND   13
SIX HOLY CREATURES, ...   770 BLOOD BOND   14
SIX-AND-TWENTY
TWENTY-AND-EIGHT, AND YET BUT SIX-AND-TWENTY . . . .   373 PHASES OF MOON   33
SIXES
DOUBLE SIXES! . . . .   721 WITCH VIVIEN   43
SIXTEEN   SEE NINETEEN-SIXTEEN
SIXTEEN DEAD MEN . . . .   395 SIXTEEN DEAD   T
THE SIXTEEN MEN WERE SHOT, ...   395 SIXTEEN DEAD   2
COME PRAISE NINETEEN SIXTEEN, ...   608 SONGS BURDEN 3 V   2
SIXTY
A SIXTY YEAR OLD SMILING PUBLIC MAN. . . . .   443 SCHOOL CHILDR V   8
WITH SIXTY OR MORE WINTERS ON ITS HEAD, ...   444 SCHOOL CHILDR   38
SIXTY-YEAR-OLD
A SIXTY-YEAR-OLD SMILING PUBLIC MAN. . . . .   443 SCHOOL CHILDR   8
SKEIN
FOR LOVE IS BUT A SKEIN UNWOUND . . . .   511 JANE AND JACK   5
I--LOVE'S SKEIN UPON THE GROUND, ...   511 JANE AND JACK   9
THE SKEIN SO BOUND US GHOST TO GHOST . . . .   511 JANE AND JACK   15
SKELETON-GAUNT
WHEN WITHERED OLD AND SKELETON-GAUNT, ...   475 EVA GORE-BOOTH   12
SKELPING
WITH SKELPING HIS BIG BRAWLING LOUT, ...   301 RUN PARADISE   9
SKIES
I SAW NOT WHO! 'NEATH OTHER SKIES . . . .   25 OISIN 1   V 381A
ON THE ANVIL OF THE WORLD. BE STILL! THE SKIES . . .   42 OISIN 2   204
UPON THE ANVIL OF THE WORLD. THE SKIES . . . . . .   42 OISIN 2   V 204
WAR ON THE MIGHTIEST MEN UNDER THE SKIES, ...   45 OISIN 2   241
. . . NOR GO FROM HIS DEW-CUMBERED SKIES . . . . .   49 OISIN 3   38
BRIMFUL OF STARLIGHT, AND HE SAID! THE STAMPER OF   76 INDIAN ON GOD   14
THE SKIES,
EVEN AS SPRING UPON THE ANCIENT SKIES, ...   108 CUCHULAIN SEA   42
STARED LIKE THE SPRING UPON THE ANCIENT SKIES, . . .   108 CUCHULAIN SEA V   41
MORE MOURNFUL THAN THE DEPTH OF STARRY SKIES, . . .   108 CUCHULAIN SEA V   42
UNDER THE GOLDEN OR THE SILVER SKIES! . . . . . .   127 DREAM OF FAERY   21
AND HOW BENEATH THOSE THREE TIMES BLESSED SKIES . . .   127 DREAM OF FAERY V   21
ON MUNSTER GRASS AND CONNEMARA SKIES. . . . . . .   130 BOOK STORIES   24
A HONIED RINGING! UNDER THE NEW SKIES . . . . . .   130 BOOK STORIES V   21
ON MUNSTER GRASS, OR CONNEMARA SKIES. . . . . . .   130 BOOK STORIES V   24
AND BY THE UNLABOURING BROOD OF THE SKIES! . . . .   164 PERFECT BEAUTY   5
AND HERON OUT OF THE SKIES." . . . .   167 BLESSED   10
BY THE INJUSTICE OF THE SKIES FOR PUNISHMENT? . . .   316 COLD HEAVEN   12
BORN UNDER THE SKIES . . . .   333 SOLOMON SHEBA   20
FAR FROM THE CUSTOMARY SKIES, ...   360 ALF POLLEXFEN   14
THE RIVER IMAGING THE FLASHING SKIES, ...   390 IMAGE PAST   20
AND SEEM TO CLING UPON THE MOONLIT SKIES, ...   482 BLOOD AND MOON   44
FROM THE OLD MAN IN THE SKIES. . . . .   588 OLD WICKED MAN   8
THAT OLD MAN IN THE SKIES. . . . .   588 OLD WICKED MAN   24
FROM THE OLD MAN IN THE SKIES . . . .   589 OLD WICKED MAN   56
THE SKIES MORE DIM, THOUGH BURNING LIKE A SHIELD, . .   656 ISLE STAT I 3   26
OF THESE STAR-SHUDDERING SKIES, YOU ARE THE QUEEN. . .   679 ISLE STAT II 3   323

725

	PAGE	TITLE	LINE

SKIES   (CONTINUED)
MAKING ALL ONE O'ER ROCK AND SEA AND SKIES! . . . . . . 687 TWO TITANS   28
PRAYED THOSE FORGOTTEN FISHERS, TILL IN THE EASTERN SKIES 719 PHANTOM SHIP   32
ALL THOSE LONG FORGOTTEN FISHERS, TILL IN THE EASTERN SKIES 719 PHANTOM SHIP   V 32
UNTO THE WHITE SKIES. . . . . 740 EARL PAUL   24

SKILL
HE LACKED THOSE YEARS THAT GO WITH SKILL, ... 608 SONGS BURDEN 3   14
CHANCE, AND NOT SKILL, HAS FAVOURED YOU, OLD FATHER! . . 722 WITCH VIVIEN   60
CHANCE HATH A SKILL! . . . . 722 WITCH VIVIEN   69

SKIN   SEE OTTER-SKIN
A HOUSE OF WATTLES, CLAY, AND SKIN! . . . . 17 OISIN 1   249
WITH ANTLERS AND THE SHAGGY SKIN . . . . 17 OISIN 1   V 249
THEY HEALED MY WOUNDS! AND ON THE SKIN SUPINE . . . . 41 OISIN 2   V 187
I SAT ON CUSHIONED OTTER SKIN! . . . . 81 MAD KING GOLL   V   1
CHAIRED IN THE CUSHIONED OTTER SKIN, ... 82 MAD KING GOLL   V   5
SUDDENLY DRENCHED HER TO THE SKIN! . . . . 275 GREY ROCK   120
THE BISHOP HAS A SKIN, GOD KNOWS, ... 508 JANE BISHOP   15
AND I AM SHRUNKEN TO SKIN AND BONE, ... 550 SONGS REWRIT 1   2
YET I AM SHRUNKEN TO SKIN AND BONE, ... 550 SONGS REWRIT 1 V   2
YET AM I SHRUNKEN TO SKIN AND BONE, ... 550 SONGS REWRIT 1 V   2
BUT I AM SHRUNKEN TO SKIN AND BONE, ... 550 SONGS REWRIT 1 V   2
THOUGH I AM SHRUNKEN TO BONE AND SKIN, ... 551 SONGS REWRIT 1 V   8
AND BEING OLD SHE PUT A SKIN . . . . 621 JOHN KINSELLA   21
AND THE GREAT GREY LYNX'S SKIN! IN SOOTH, METHINKS . . 650 ISLE STAT I 1   151
WHO SAID WE HAD A SKIN OF YELLOW ALE? . . . . . . 759 SHADOW WATER A   243

SKINS
WE LAY ON SKINS OF OTTERS, AND DRANK WINE, ... 41 OISIN 2   188
AND THEN ON HEAPED-UP SKINS OF OTTERS SLEPT. . . . . 41 OISIN 2   191
AND ON THE SKINS OF WOLVES AND BEARS WE SLEPT! . . . . 41 OISIN 2   191
MINE WAS A CHAIR OF SKINS AND GOLD, ... 81 MAD KING GOLL   V   1
ON DAPPLED SKINS IN A GLASS BOAT, ... 196 BAILE AILLINN   180
AND STRETCHED OUT SLEEPING ON A PILE OF SKINS . . . 283 TWO KINGS   141
AMONG DARK SKINS, AND THERE . . . . 472 ALL SOUL NIGHT   48

SKIPPER
OLD MERCHANT SKIPPER THAT LEAPED OVERBOARD . . . . . 270 PARDON FATHERS   13
YOU MERCHANT SKIPPER THAT LEAPED OVERBOARD . . . . . 270 PARDON FATHERS V   13
AND MERCHANT SKIPPER THAT LEAPED OVERBOARD . . . . . 270 PARDON FATHERS V   13

SKIRT
HER DOMINO, HER PANNIERED SKIRT COPIED FROM LONGHI! . 363 DOLLS FACES   7

SKY
THAT KEPT DIM WATERS FROM THE SKY! . . . . 17 OISIN 1   243
AND BID THE STARS DROP DOWN FROM THE SKY, ... 28 OISIN 1   426
IS AN UNDYING MOORFOWL, AND HE LIVES BEYOND THE SKY. . 76 INDIAN ON GOD   7
YOU HAVE THE HEAVIEST ARM UNDER THE SKY." . . . . . 107 CUCHULAIN SEA   24
UNDER THE PASSING STARS, FOAM OF THE SKY, ... 112 ROSE OF WORLD   9
THE BRILLIANT MOON AND ALL THE MILKY SKY, ... 119 SORROW OF LOVE   2
THE FULL ROUND MOON AND THE STAR-LADEN SKY, ... 119 SORROW OF LOVE V   2
A CLIMBING MOON UPON AN EMPTY SKY, ... 120 SORROW OF LOVE   10
THE CRUMBLING MOON, THE WHITE STARS IN THE SKY, . . 120 SORROW OF LOVE V   10
THE CURD-PALE MOON, THE WHITE STARS IN THE SKY, . . 120 SORROW OF LOVE V   10
. . . HUNG LOW ON THE RIM OF THE SKY, ... 122 WHITE BIRDS   3
THAT GOD HAS LAID HIS FINGERS ON THE SKY, ... 128 DREAM OF FAERY   43
OF HOW GOD LEANS HIS HANDS OUT OF THE SKY, ... 128 DREAM OF FAERY V   43
THAT GOD HAD LEANED HIS HANDS OUT OF THE SKY, . . . 128 DREAM OF FAERY V   43
THAT GOD HAD LEANT HIS HANDS OUT OF THE SKY, . . . 128 DREAM OF FAERY V   43
WITH THE EARTH AND THE SKY AND THE WATER, ... 143 ROSE IN HEART   7
AS A CLOUD FADED INTO THE SKY. . . . . 145 HOST OF AIR   V 40
AND HAD ROOTED THE SUN AND MOON AND STARS OUT OF THE SKY 153 CHANGE BELOVED   11
AND ROOTED THE SUN AND MOON AND STARS OUT OF THE SKY, 153 CHANGE BELOVED V   11
AND STARS CLIMBING THE DEW-DROPPING SKY, ... 158 BELOVED RHYMES   11
WHEN SHALL THE STARS BE BLOWN ABOUT THE SKY, . . . 170 SECRET ROSE   29
OF MORNING LIGHT IN A DIM SKY! . . . . 195 BAILE AILLINN   150
FAR OUT UNDER A WINDLESS SKY! . . . . 197 BAILE AILLINN   181
AND IN THE TREMBLING BLUE-GREEN OF THE SKY . . . . 206 ADAMS CURSE   30
PALE SILVER-PROUD QUEEN-WOMAN OF THE SKY, ... 211 RAGGED WOOD   6
HE HAS CAUGHT THE CRESCENT MOON OUT OF THE SKY, . . 239 SHADOW WATER B   370
APPEAR AND DISAPPEAR IN THE BLUE DEPTH OF THE SKY . 318 MAGI   3
APPEAR AND DISAPPEAR IN THE BLUE DEPTHS OF THE SKY . 318 MAGI   V   3
MIRRORS A STILL SKY! . . . . 322 SWANS AT COOLE   4
THE PURE COLD LIGHT IN THE SKY . . . . 378 CAT AND MOON   7
WHEN THE OLD MOON IS VANISHED FROM THE SKY . . . . . 382 VISION ROBART   3
WHEN THE OLD MOON IS VANISHING FROM THE SKY . . . . 382 VISION ROBART V   3
SEEM BUT THE CLOUDS OF THE SKY . . . . 416 TOWER   192
HER DESOLATION INTO THE DESOLATE SKY. . . . . 423 MY DESCENDANTS   16
LIKE THIS PURE JET, NOW LOST AMID BLUE SKY, ... 464 HARUN RASHID   64
THE MOON IS STAGGERING IN THE SKY! . . . . 487 CRAZED MOON   2
BUT SEEMS A CONCENTRATION OF THE SKY! . . . . . . 490 COOLE BALLYLEE   18
CLOUDY LEAFAGE OF THE SKY, ... 501 VACILLATION   46
MAY CALL A CURSE OUT OF THE SKY . . . . 508 JANE BISHOP   V   4
BANNERS CHOKE THE SKY! . . . . 512 JANE ON GOD   7
ABOUT THE SKY! WHERE THAT IS CLEAR OF CLOUD . . . . 541 PARN FUNERAL 1   3
THERE, ON THE MOUNTAIN AND THE SKY, ... 567 LAPIS LAZULI   51
WHAT GREAT TOMB-HAUNTER SWEEPS THE DISTANT SKY . . 618 BRONZE HEAD   4
DROPPING OUT OF SKY OR ROCK, ... 633 MAN AND ECHO   44
FLOWERS AND GRASS AND CLOUDLESS SKY, ... 639 BEN BULBEN   57
THE BRAZEN SKY, SO BLAZE THE DAFFODILLS! . . . . . 645 ISLE STAT I 1   11
FROM THE DEEP EARTH UNTO THE LURID SKY . . . . . . 662 ISLE STAT II 2   5
THE FAERY SHIP THAT SWIMS ATHWART THE SKY. . . . . . 663 ISLE STAT II 2   16
THE SKY WAS BANDED O'ER WITH WRACK . . . . 667 ISLE STAT II 3   23
UNTIL THIS MORN. THE SKY WITH WRACK . . . . 667 ISLE STAT II 3 V   22
SHOUTED A MOMENT 'TWEEN THE EARTH AND SKY. . . . . . 675 ISLE STAT II 3   237

	PAGE	TITLE	LINE

SKY   (CONTINUED)
    MY THOUGHTS, AND YONDER BRIGHTENING PATCH OF SKY . . . .   700 MOSADA 3   31
    AND WHO FOREGATHER IN THE SKY. . . . .   716 FAIRY DOCTOR   8
    IN WASTE PLACES OF THE SKY, ...   772 SONG DEIRDRE 1   6
SKY'S
    I HEAR THE WHOLE SKY'S SORROW IN ONE VOICE. . . . . .   652 ISLE STAT I 2   22
SLAB
    HEALING FROM ITS LETTERED SLAB. THOSE SELF-SAME HANDS   503 VACILLATION   82
      PERCHANCE
SLAIN
    AND ON THE HEROES LYING SLAIN . . . .   5 OISIN 1   42
    BY AGE'S WEARINESS ARE SLAIN, ...   27 OISIN 1   V 415A
    HAS SLAIN SO MIGHTY ARMIES, SO GREAT KINGS, ...   106 CUCHULAIN SEA   V 10A
    ARMED MEN HAVE COME UPON US! O I AM SLAIN! . . . . .   233 SHADOW WATER B   241
    ARMED MEN HAVE COME UPON US! O I AM SLAIN! . . . . .   233 SHADOW WATER B   243
    WHO HAVE SLAIN MY HUSBAND AND LAID HANDS UPON ME. . .   235 SHADOW WATER B   282
    ODOUR OF BLOOD WHEN CHRIST WAS SLAIN . . . .   438 SONGS PLAY 2   6
    THE LOFTY INNOCENCE THAT IT HAS SLAIN, ...   614 MARCH SONGS 2   12
    CONVICTED COWARDS ALL, BY KINDRED SLAIN . . . .   634 CUCHULAIN COMF   21
    ARMED MEN HAVE COME UPON US. O! I AM SLAIN! . . . .   753 SHADOW WATER A   133
    ENDS ALL THINGS. I HAVE SLAIN THE LOCHLANN KING. . .   754 SHADOW WATER A   163
SLANDER
    EARNED SLANDER, INGRATITUDE, ...   260 UNWORTH PRAISE   16
SLANDERED
    AN OLD FOUL MOUTH THAT SLANDERED YOU HAD SET . . . .   292 TO A SHADE   V   17
SLANDEROUS
    AH, SWEET TO ME NOW WERE EVEN BALD CONAN'S SLANDEROUS   55 OISIN 3   116
      TONGUE!
    BURNING IN FIRES OF A SLANDEROUS TONGUE. . . . . . .   148 INTO TWILIGHT   8
SLANTING
    FROM FASTING--SEE, THE RED LIGHT SLANTING DOWN . . .   697 MOSADA 2   36
    NOW FLINGING LOOSE THE SLANTING SAIL, ...   742 DANAAN QUICK   3
SLATE
    AS THAT WHICH CLEANS MAN'S DIRTY SLATE. . . . .   633 MAN AND ECHO   24
SLATE-COLOURED
    LAY HIDDEN IN THE SMALL SLATE-COLOURED THING! . . . .   104 FERGUS DRUID   40
    TAKE THEN THIS SMALL SLATE-COLOURED BAG OF DREAMS! . .   104 FERGUS DRUID   V   29
    LAY HIDDEN IN THE SMALL SLATE-COLOURED BAG! . . . . .   104 FERGUS DRUID   V   40
SLATES
    WITH OLD MILL BOARDS AND SEA-GREEN SLATES, ...   406 CARVED STONE   2
SLAUGHTERED
    OF MANY A SLAUGHTERED FOREST ROVER. . . . .   17 OISIN 1   V 249A
SLAVE
    TO ALL THINGS CRIED! "I AM A SLAVE! . . . .   19 OISIN 1   V 280
    AN OLD SLAVE GRINDING AT A HEAVY QUERN, ...   104 FERGUS DRUID   35
    I HAVE BEEN A SLAVE, ...   495 MOHINI CHATTER   6
    A SLAVE BOWS DOWN TO A SLAVE. . . . .   547 TO SAME TUNE 3   6
    A SLAVE BOWS DOWN TO A SLAVE. . . . .   547 TO SAME TUNE 3   6
    A SLAVE BOWS DOWN TO A SLAVE. . . . .   614 MARCH SONGS 2   6
    A SLAVE BOWS DOWN TO A SLAVE. . . . .   614 MARCH SONGS 2   6
    AND AS A SLAVE BEEN WAKEFUL IN THE HALLS . . . . . .   724 KANVA ON SELF   5
SLAVES
    BUT NOW HEARTS CRY THAT HEARTS ARE SLAVES, ...   19 OISIN 1   280
    SHAKE THE LOOSE REINS! YOU SLAVES OF GOD, ...   22 OISIN 1   331
    SHAKE THE LOOSE REINS! YE SLAVES OF GOD, ...   22 OISIN 1   V 331
    SEA-GOD, THAT ONCE, TO GIVE HIS SLAVES CONTENT, . . .   38 OISIN 2   V 129
    NEITHER TO SLAVES THAT WERE SPAT ON, ...   414 TOWER   130
    AND OUR SLAVES BE AS OF OLD. . . . .   727 LOVERS QUARREL   56
SLAY
    AND THEN ARISE, AND RAVING SLAY US ALL. . . . .   110 CUCHULAIN SEA   79
SLEEK
    SLEEK AS ANY GRANARY MOUSE . . . .   2 OISIN 1   V   7M
    MORE SLEEK THAN ANY GRANARY MOUSE, ...   4 OISIN 1   36
    SLEEK AS ANY GRANARY MOUSE, ...   4 OISIN 1   V   37
    AND SLEEK YOUNG JOY IS NO MORE FICKLE, ...   77 INDIAN TO LOVE V   5C
    BUT EVEN AT THE STARTING-POST, ALL SLEEK AND NEW, . .   619 BRONZE HEAD   15
SLEEP
    AND SLEEP DROWN SUN AND MOON AND STAR." . . . . . .   5 OISIN 1   V   49
    AND ALWAYS NEVER-ANXIOUS SLEEP! . . . .   8 OISIN 1   93
    MUSIC AND LOVE AND SLEEP AWAIT, ...   9 OISIN 1   103
    THE FENIANS. LET THEIR DEER-HOUNDS SLEEP. . . . . .   11 OISIN 1   V 131
    SLEEP THERE TILL THE MOON AND THE STARS DIE!" . . . .   17 OISIN 1   246
    O'ER MEN WHO SLEEP, AND WAKE, AND DIE, ...   22 OISIN 1   V 340B
    MAY SLEEP IN THE END WITH THE WHOLE OF HIS FATE DONE,   28 OISIN 1   V 423F
    SINCE GOD MADE TIME AND DEATH AND SLEEP! THE OTHER .   31 OISIN 2   41
    AH, TOUCH THEIR BLUE-VEINED EYELIDS IF THEY SLEEP, .   33 OISIN 2   61
    AH, TOUCH THEIR BLUE VEINED EYELIDS IF THEY SLEEP, .   33 OISIN 2   V   61
    WE SANG THE LOVES AND ANGERS WITHOUT SLEEP, ...   42 OISIN 2   194
    THE SPACIOUS LOVES, THE ANGER WITHOUT SLEEP . . . . .   42 OISIN 2   V 194
    COULD SLEEP ON A COUCH OF RUSHES, AND ALL INWROUGHT AND   49 OISIN 3   31
      INLAID,
    COULD SLEEP ON A BED OF RUSHES, AND ALL INWROUGHT . .   49 OISIN 3   V   31
      AND INLAID,
    COULD SLEEP ON A COUCH OF RUSHES--ROUND AND ABOUT THEM   49 OISIN 3   V   32
      LAID,
    . . . AND FED OF UNHUMAN SLEEP. . . . .   51 OISIN 3   56
    IN A LONG IRON SLEEP, AS A FISH IN THE WATER GOES DUMB   53 OISIN 3   96
      AS A STONE.
    . . . THEIR DIMNESS, THEIR DEWS DROPPING SLEEP. . . .   54 OISIN 3   108
    SO SLEEP THEE BY DAYTIME." A VOICE CRIED, ...   59 OISIN 3   172
    SO SLEEP THEY BY DAYTIME." A VOICE CRIED, ...   59 OISIN 3   V 172

		PAGE	TITLE		LINE
SLEEP (CONTINUED)					
A CREEPING OLD MAN, FULL OF SLEEP,		60	OISIN 3		192
A LONELY LAUGHTER, AND MAY KISS HIS HANDS TO ME IN SLEEP.		75	ANASHU VIJAYA		82
PRAYERS FOR THE LAND. O BRAHMA, GUARD IN SLEEP		75	ANASHU VIJAYA		85
AN INNER LAUGHTER, AND MAY KISS HIS HANDS TO ME IN SLEEP.		75	ANASHU VIJAYA	V	82
A LONELY LAUGHTER, THAT HE MAY KISS HANDS TO ME IN SLEEP.		75	ANASHU VIJAYA	V	82
MY SPIRIT ROCKED IN SLEEP AND SIGHS; AND SAW THE MOORFOWL PACE		76	INDIAN ON GOD		3
AND HURLED THEM IN THE GULPH OF SLEEP;		83	MAD KING GOLL		22
AND THEY INHERIT THE GREAT SLEEP.		83	MAD KING GOLL	V	22
AND IS ANXIOUS IN ITS SLEEP.		87	STOLEN CHILD		23
WHEN YOU ARE OLD AND GREY AND FULL OF SLEEP,		120	YOU ARE OLD		1
AND MIGHT HAVE KNOWN AT LAST UNHAUNTED SLEEP		128	DREAM OF FAERY		38
AND HUSHED IN SLEEP THE ROARING RANKS OF BATTLE!		129	BOOK STORIES		7
HE ROUSED HIS HORSE OUT OF ITS SLEEP,		133	FR GILLIGAN		27
THAT GOD GIVES UNTO MAN IN SLEEP.		138	TO IRELAND	V	22
O VANITY OF SLEEP, HOPE, DREAM, ENDLESS DESIRE,		154	BELOVED PEACE		7
THRONE OVER THRONE WHERE IN HALF SLEEP,		156	FORGOT BEAUTY		22
IS DROPPING SLEEP, UNTIL GOD BURN TIME,		164	PERFECT BEAUTY		7
OF YOUR BELOVED IN SLEEP.		165	CRY OF SEDGE		10
AMONG PALE EYELIDS, HEAVY WITH THE SLEEP		169	SECRET ROSE		6
WHEN WILL HE WAKE FROM SLEEP?		174	ELEMENT POWERS		6
IN COMFORTABLE SLEEP; ALL LIVING SLEPT		180	QUEEN MAEVE		15
HAD TROUBLED HIS SLEEP. BUT ALL HE HAD TO SAY		182	QUEEN MAEVE		52
SHE TURNED AWAY; HE TURNED AGAIN TO SLEEP		182	QUEEN MAEVE		59
SUDDENLY AILELL SPOKE OUT OF HIS SLEEP,		183	QUEEN MAEVE		73
THE CHILDREN OF THE MAINES OUT OF SLEEP,		184	QUEEN MAEVE		92
FACE DOWNWARD, TOSSING IN A TROUBLED SLEEP;		185	QUEEN MAEVE		106
THE WATERS OF SLEEP CAN MAKE A CHATTERING TONGUE		218	WOODS OF COOLE		25
IT'S CERTAIN I'D SLEEP EASIER O' NIGHTS		224	SHADOW WATER B		59
YOU'RE CERTAIN OF IT? I NEVER WAKE FROM SLEEP		226	SHADOW WATER B		83
WAKE ALL BELOW! WHY HAVE YOU BROKEN OUR SLEEP?		233	SHADOW WATER B		242
AND SAYS, "A SWORD-BLADE PIERCED ME IN MY SLEEP."		234	SHADOW WATER B		257
AND SAYS: "A SWORD BLADE PIERCED ME IN MY SLEEP."		234	SHADOW WATER B	V	257
TO SHAKE HIM OUT OF SLEEP, I COULD NOT ROUSE HIM.		283	TWO KINGS		143
AND LEFT MERE SLEEP. HE'LL WAKE WHEN THE SUN WAKES,		284	TWO KINGS		161
SLEEP BEFORE THE THIRD NOON SOUNDS."		295	THREE BEGGARS		24
TO KEEP HIS FELLOWS FROM THEIR SLEEP;		297	THREE BEGGARS		45
ONE BEGGAR CRIED: "YOU'RE SHAMMING SLEEP,"		297	THREE BEGGARS	V	45
TILL EVEN I SLEEP LIGHT; BUT WHO		303	HOUR DAWN		34
THAT I MAY FIND THE SLEEP I HAVE LOST."		303	HOUR DAWN		39
SO THAT IT SEEMS EVEN I SLEEP LIGHT;		303	HOUR DAWN	V	34
I HAVE TO FIND THE SLEEP I HAVE LOST."		303	HOUR DAWN	V	39
"WHAT CARE I IF YOU SLEEP OR WAKE?		304	HOUR DAWN		40
I'LL SLEEP ANOTHER CENTURY."		304	HOUR DAWN		43
"AND I WILL TALK BEFORE I SLEEP		304	HOUR DAWN		44
"I'LL SLEEP UNTIL THE WINTER'S GONE,		305	HOUR DAWN		57
AND DRINK, AND YOU WILL SLEEP THAT LENGTH."		305	HOUR DAWN		59
"I'D LIKE TO SLEEP TILL WINTER'S GONE		305	HOUR DAWN		60
YOU WILL SLEEP THAT LENGTH; AND AT THE FIRST		305	HOUR DAWN	V	59
I'LL SLEEP AWAY ALL TIME WITHIN IT;		306	HOUR DAWN		74
MY SLEEP WERE NOW NINE CENTURIES		306	HOUR DAWN		75
AND SLEEP AWAY ALL TIME WITHIN IT.		306	HOUR DAWN	V	74
AND WAIT HIM IN A DRUNKEN SLEEP."		307	HOUR DAWN		106
PLEASURE THAT COMES WITH SLEEP,		345	ON WOMAN		22
SLEEP DRIVEN FROM MY BED,		346	ON WOMAN		36
WHEN I CLAMBER TO THE HEIGHTS OF SLEEP,		357	DEEP-SWORN VOW		4
AND SLEEP THERE!		380	SONGS FOOL 1		3
I START OUT OF MY SLEEP TO THINK		380	SONGS FOOL 1		7
HAD I BUT AWAKENED FROM SLEEP		381	SONGS FOOL 2		10
WHEN SLEEP AT LAST HAS COME		394	EASTER 1916		63
HAD WATCHED IN BITTERER SLEEP		399	BREAK OF DAY		22
THAT TWENTY CENTURIES OF STONY SLEEP		402	SECOND COMING		19
THAT THIRTY CENTURIES OF STONY SLEEP		402	SECOND COMING	V	19
RIDES UPON SLEEP; A DRUNKEN SOLDIERY		429	NINETEEN 19		26
THAT MY MICHAEL MAY SLEEP SOUND,		435	FOR MY SON		2
HER FILL OF SLEEP.		435	FOR MY SON		8
STRETCH OUT YOUR LIMBS AND SLEEP A LONG SATURNIAN SLEEP;		442	BLACK CENTAUR		13
STRETCH OUT YOUR LIMBS AND SLEEP A LONG SATURNIAN SLEEP;		442	BLACK CENTAUR		13
AND THAT MUST SLEEP, SHRIEK, STRUGGLE TO ESCAPE		444	SCHOOL CHILDR		35
AND MY SLEEP IS GONE.		454	EMPTY CUP		10
AND FEARING THAT MY LIGHT DISTURBED HER SLEEP		467	HARUN RASHID		130
A DOZEN NIGHTS OF NATURAL SLEEP, AND THEN		468	HARUN RASHID		150
SHE ROSE, AND WITH HER EYES SHUT FAST IN SLEEP		468	HARUN RASHID		152
BELOVED, MAY YOUR SLEEP BE SOUND		522	LULLABY		1
SLEEP UPON A GOLDEN BED		522	LULLABY		5
SLEEP, BELOVED, SUCH A SLEEP		522	LULLABY		7
SLEEP, BELOVED, SUCH A SLEEP		522	LULLABY		7
SUCH A SLEEP AND SOUND AS FELL		522	LULLABY		13
BELOVED SUCH A SLEEP AS FELL		522	LULLABY	V	13
AND NOW LIES SUNK IN SLEEP. WHAT CLIMBS THE STAIR?		579	DOR WELLESLEY		11
BUT NOW LIES SUNK IN SLEEP. WHAT CLIMBS THE STAIR?		579	DOR WELLESLEY	V	11
WINE OR LOVE DRUG HIM TO SLEEP,		633	MAN AND ECHO		26
WINE OR LOVE DRUGS HIM TO SLEEP,		633	MAN AND ECHO	V	26
OF THE SONGS THAT NEVER SLEEP.		647	ISLE STAT I 1		76
DREAMING IN THEIR SOFT ODOUR-LADEN SLEEP!		650	ISLE STAT I 1		125
SEAFARER, WAKE! WAS MY SLEEP LONG? LONG YEARS.		678	ISLE STAT II 3		292
WAS MY SLEEP LONG, OH, YOUTH? LONG, LONG AND DEEP.		678	ISLE STAT II 3		299
SLEEPER, AWAKE! HOW LONG MY SLEEP? UNNUMBERED		678	ISLE STAT II 3		307
THE YEARS OF GOBLIN SLEEP. AH! WHILE I SLUMBERED,		679	ISLE STAT II 3		308
FOR EVER ROUND THY WAKING AND THY SLEEP		688	TWO TITANS		57

		PAGE	TITLE	LINE
SLEEP (CONTINUED)				
UPON MY KNEES I PRAY YOU, LET IT SLEEP,		693	MOSADA 1	72
THE WORLD WERE DREAMING IN ITS SUMMER SLEEP;		699	MOSADA 3	11
THIS DEATH IS HEAVY IN MY VEINS LIKE SLEEP.		701	MOSADA 3	57
SLEEP IN SOME FAR OTHER FIELD		705	DAWN-SONG	3
"WAKEN, WAKEN, SLEEPY FISHERS! NO HOUR IS THIS FOR SLEEP,"		718	PHANTOM SHIP	7
THE HEART OF NOON FOLDS SILENCE AND FOLDS SLEEP,		735	QUATRAIN APHOR	25
AND COMMON MEN THAT SLEEP.		736	IN CHURCH	8
WHEN AENGUS AND HIS EDAINE WAKE FROM SLEEP		749	SHADOW WATER A	57
WAKE ALL BELOW. WHY HAVE YOU BROKEN OUR SLEEP?		753	SHADOW WATER A	132
AND SAYS, "A SWORD-BLADE PIERCED ME IN MY SLEEP."		753	SHADOW WATER A	147
AND SAYS, "A SWORD BLADE PIERCED ME IN MY SLEEP."		753	SHADOW WATER A V	147
FROM ITS FIRST SIGHS AND LAUGHTER, BEFORE THE SLEEP,		754	SHADOW WATER A	161
WHOSE SHADOW IS THE SLEEP THAT COMES WITH LOVE,		754	SHADOW WATER A	162
I HAD WOVEN OF THE SLEEP THAT IS IN POOLS		762	SHADOW WATER A	284
TO DROWN IN ITS OWN IMAGE? EVEN THAT SLEEP		765	SHADOW WATER A	364
SLEEPER				
FROM SLEEPER UNTO SLEEPER MURMUR YOU.		33	OISIN 2 V	60
FROM SLEEPER UNTO SLEEPER MURMUR YOU.		33	OISIN 2 V	60
THAT PUT A PASSION IN THE SLEEPER THERE,		284	TWO KINGS	157
HAD NOT THE SLEEPER STARTED UP.		304	HOUR DAWN	48
FOR ALL THE SLEEPER KNEW OR CARED!		307	HOUR DAWN	115
IS STONE! OLD SLEEPER! THIS SAME AFTERNOON .		657	ISLE STAT I 3	74
SLEEPER, AWAKE! HOW LONG MY SLEEP? UNNUMBERED		678	ISLE STAT II 3	307
ON THE NOSE OF THE SLEEPER HE MADE IT PLAY!		729	PRIEST FAIRY	30
THE SLEEPER AWOKE WITH A SUDDEN START,		729	PRIEST FAIRY	31
SLEEPER'S				
INTO THE SLEEPER'S TUB OF BEER		304	HOUR DAWN	47
TO BREAK UPON A SLEEPER'S REST		412	TOWER	87
SLEEPERS				
AND MY GAZE WAS THRONGED WITH THE SLEEPERS;		50	OISIN 3	49
CAME SOUND FROM THOSE MONSTROUS SLEEPERS,		51	OISIN 3	58
WHEN SLEEPERS WAKE AND YET STILL DREAM,		639	BEN BULBEN	59
THY PEACE. AH, NOW I'LL WAKE THESE SLEEPERS, LOST		677	ISLE STAT II 3	274
BEHOLD THE HAPLESS SLEEPERS STANDING BY.		677	ISLE STAT II 3	281
SLEEPILY				
SLEEPILY CLOSE HER ROUND BRIGHT EYNE!		646	ISLE STAT I 1	35
SLEEPING				
SO LONG WERE THEY SLEEPING,		49	OISIN 3	39
TILL I SAW WHERE MAEVE LIES SLEEPING		60	OISIN 3	184
TROUBLE HIS SLEEPING! GIVE HIM DREAMS OF ME.		75	ANASHU VIJAYA	91
LIFTED THE CURTAIN OF HER SLEEPING ROOM,		182	QUEEN MAEVE V	63
SHE SAW HER HUSBAND AILELL SLEEPING THERE,		183	QUEEN MAEVE	69
TO MAKE AN END WHILE HE IS SLEEPING THERE.		222	SHADOW WATER B V	14
WE'LL LEARN THAT SLEEPING IS NOT DEATH,		266	GALWAY RACES	11
AND STRETCHED OUT SLEEPING ON A PILE OF SKINS		283	TWO KINGS	141
AND SHOWN MY HUSBAND SLEEPING THERE, I HAVE SIGHED,		285	TWO KINGS	188
TO JUDGE IF A LIGHT SLEEPING FOOL		304	HOUR DAWN V	52
I SAT WHERE I COULD WATCH HER SLEEPING FORM,		467	HARUN RASHID	128
ARE SOMEWHERE SLEEPING LIKE A TOP		525	DANCING DAYS	13
SLEEPING LORD OF ARCHERY,		658	ISLE STAT I 3	81
SLEEPING LORD OF ARCHERY.		658	ISLE STAT I 3	96
A MOUSE FROM HIS SLEEPING,		672	ISLE STAT II 3	172
AND STRAIGHT BEFORE THE SLEEPING PRIEST		729	PRIEST FAIRY	23
"MAN OF WISDOM, FROM THY SLEEPING		729	PRIEST FAIRY	39
SLEEPING-ROOM				
LIFTED THE CURTAIN OF HER SLEEPING-ROOM,		182	QUEEN MAEVE	63
SLEEPLESS				
HIS SLEEPLESS CANDLE AND LABORIOUS PEN.		375	PHASES OF MOON	86
SLEEPLESS WOULD LIE DOWN AND DIE.		632	MAN AND ECHO	18
SLEEP'S				
AND I GAZED ON THE BELL-BRANCH, SLEEP'S FOREBEAR,		50	OISIN 3	53
SLEEPS				
THAT IN IMMORTAL SILENCE SLEEPS		13	OISIN 1	161
. . . WHO SLEEPS ON HER NEST,		56	OISIN 3	134
A WEARY WOMAN SLEEPS SO HARD!		95	MOLL MAGEE	21
TO TAKE HIM WHILE HE SLEEPS AND CARRY HIM		222	SHADOW WATER B	14
TO MAKE AN END OF FORGAEL WHILE HE SLEEPS.		225	SHADOW WATER B	65
OUR FATHER ROSICROSS SLEEPS IN HIS TOMB.		311	MOUNTAIN TOMB	12
MY CHILD SLEEPS ON. THERE IS NO OBSTACLE		403	FOR DAUGHTER	3
THAT SLEEPS UNDER THE CANOPY!		528	TOM LUNATIC	2
BUT BODY GONE HE SLEEPS NO MORE,		633	MAN AND ECHO	29
SHE SLEEPS WITH OWLETS TWO AND TWO,		646	ISLE STAT I 1	34
FROM THE UNDYING WORM. SHE SLEEPS—MOSADA—		701	MOSADA 3	65
OH, GOD!—AWAKE! THOU SHALT NOT DIE. SHE SLEEPS,		701	MOSADA 3	66
FROM DATELESS PAIN. SHE SLEEPS—MOSADA—THOU—		701	MOSADA 3 V	65
SLEEPY				
BURIED UNDER THE SLEEPY GROUND,		67	HAPPY SHEPHERD	48
(WHO'S BURIED IN THE SLEEPY GROUND),		67	HAPPY SHEPHERD V	48
THE HOUR WHEN KAMA, FULL OF SLEEPY LAUGHTER,		72	ANASHU VIJAYA	26
A VAPOURY FOOTFALL ON THE OCEAN'S SLEEPY BLAZE.		78	INDIAN TO LOVE V	20
FALLS IN SLEEPY STREAMS.		98	FOXHUNTER	16
POURS ROUND HIS SLEEPY STREAMS.		98	FOXHUNTER V	16
POURS ROUND IN SLEEPY STREAMS.		98	FOXHUNTER V	16
OR DO YOU LONG FOR THE DIM SLEEPY GROUND,		109	CUCHULAIN SEA	60
BEFORE EARTH MADE OF HIM HER SLEEPY CARE!		126	DREAM OF FAERY V	4
WHERE A SO SLEEPY INCENSE ROSE		156	FORGOT BEAUTY V	13
UNDER A CAIRN OF SLEEPY STONE		192	BAILE AILLINN	81
THE HONEY-PALE MOON LAY LOW ON THE SLEEPY HILL,		203	WITHER BOUGHS	5
THE HONEY PALE MOON HUNG LOW ON THE SLEEPY HILL,		203	WITHER BOUGHS V	5
I KNOW OF THE SLEEPY COUNTRY, WHERE SWANS FLY ROUND		204	WITHER BOUGHS	17

729

		PAGE	TITLE		LINE
SLEEPY	(CONTINUED)				
	AND SLEEPY BOUGHS, AND BOUGHS WHERE APPLES MADE	219	HARP OF AENGUS		5
	AND SLEEPY HAVING HAD THEIR MEAL'	271	GREY ROCK	V	17
	BEFORE THEIR SLEEPY EYELIDS RAN	272	GREY ROCK		30
	OR A BIRD'S SLEEPY CRY	416	TOWER		194
	AND FREE—'TWILL THIEVE AWAY WITH SLEEPY MOOD	700	MOSADA 3		30
	"WAKEN, WAKEN, SLEEPY FISHERS! NO HOUR IS THIS FOR SLEEP,"	718	PHANTOM SHIP		7
	AND SLEEPY BOUGHS, AND BOUGHS WHERE APPLES MADE	762	SHADOW WATER A		300
SLEEPY-HEADED					
	WAKE, MA CUSHLA, SLEEPY-HEADED!	705	DAWN-SONG		9
SLEET					
	IT DIED AFAR. GREY SLEET THOSE TOWERS HID	46	OISIN 2	V	245
	FLAMES THE SHUTTLE OF THE LIGHTNING ACROSS THE DRIVING SLEET,	718	PHANTOM SHIP		1
SLEEVE					
	BUT BRIDGET DREW HIM BY THE SLEEVE	144	HOST OF AIR		21
	AN AGONY OF FLAME THAT CANNOT SINGE A SLEEVE.	498	BYZANTIUM		32
	THE HEART WELL WORN UPON THE SLEEVE MAY BE THE BEST OF SIGHTS,	790	HEART SLEEVE		1
SLEIVEENS					
	SLEIVEENS WERE ALL HIS RACE!	92	FATHER OHART		6
SLENDER					
	A MAIDEN, ON A SLENDER STEED, ...	2	OISIN 1	V	7V
	THEIR LEGS LONG, DELICATE AND SLENDER, AQUAMARINE THEIR EYES,	426	PHANTOM HATRED		17
	"I HAVE BROUGHT A SLENDER BRIDE INTO THE HOUSE!	463	HARUN RASHID		49
	BUT SLENDER NEEDLES OF BONE!	488	CRAZED MOON		15
	OF A SLENDER PALM, STOOD BUT A DAY!	566	LAPIS LAZULI		34
SLEPT					
	AND THEN ON HEAPED-UP SKINS OF OTTERS SLEPT.	41	OISIN 2		191
	AND ON THE SKINS OF WOLVES AND BEARS WE SLEPT!	41	OISIN 2	V	191
	HE SLEPT UNDER THE HILL OF LUGNAGALL!	128	DREAM OF FAERY		37
	WHILE I SLEPT ON THE CHAIR"!	133	FR GILLIGAN		26
	MADE WHEN GOD SLEPT IN TIMES OF OLD.	135	TWO TREES		32
	THE POLAR DRAGON SLEPT, ...	174	ELEMENT POWERS		4
	IN COMFORTABLE SLEEP! ALL LIVING SLEPT	180	QUEEN MAEVE		15
	BUT THE HORSE-BOYS SLEPT ON, AS THOUGH SOME POWER . . .	181	QUEEN MAEVE		39
	THE PORTER SLEPT, ALTHOUGH HE SAT UPRIGHT	182	QUEEN MAEVE		45
	WHERE HER GRANDCHILDREN SLEPT, AND CRIED ALOUD, ...	185	QUEEN MAEVE		109
	WHERE HER GRAND-CHILDREN SLEPT, AND CRIED ALOUD	185	QUEEN MAEVE	V	109
	I BADE HIM GO WHEN ALL HIS HOUSEHOLD SLEPT	282	TWO KINGS		133
	SO SLEPT FOR HALF A YEAR OR SO!	305	HOUR DAWN		67
	AND SLEPT FOR HALF A YEAR OR SO!	305	HOUR DAWN	V	67
	I SLEPT ON MY THREE-LEGGED STOOL BY THE FIRE, ...	381	SONGS FOOL 2		1
	THE SPECKLED CAT SLEPT ON MY KNEE!	381	SONGS FOOL 2		2
	WHERE SEVEN EPHESIAN TOPERS SLEPT AND NEVER KNEW	442	BLACK CENTAUR		11
	WHEN ALEXANDER'S EMPIRE PASSED, THEY SLEPT SO SOUND. . .	442	BLACK CENTAUR		12
	WHEN ALEXANDER'S EMPIRE PAST, THEY SLEPT SO SOUND. . .	442	BLACK CENTAUR	V	12
	AND SHE LAY DOWN UPON HER BED AND SLEPT, ...	467	HARUN RASHID		146
	ON CRUACHAN'S PLAIN SLEPT HE	529	TOM CRUACHAN		1
	THAT SLEPT UPON THE SACK?	627	STATES HOLIDAY		15
	I SLEPT, 'TWAS SULTRY, AND SCARCE CIRCLING SHOOK . . .	677	ISLE STAT II 3		278
	HAVE I SLEPT LONG? LONG YEARS. WITH HUNGRY HEART . . .	677	ISLE STAT II 3		286
	HE'D SLEPT AMONG THE SINGING TREES, ...	728	PRIEST FAIRY		17
	AH, THEY HAVE PIERCED HIS HEART! I HAVE SLEPT LONG! . .	761	SHADOW WATER A		270
SLEUTH					
	OF SLEUTH WOOD IN THE LAKE, ...	86	STOLEN CHILD		2
SLEUTH-HOUNDS					
	HIS SLEUTH-HOUNDS FOLLOW EVERY FAERY THING.	675	ISLE STAT II 3		244
SLEW					
	AND SLEW THE BADGER AND THE DEER, ...	23	OISIN 1	V	345
	BUT SLOWLY, AS I SHOUTING SLEW	83	MAD KING GOLL		25
	THESE HANDS SLEW MANY WARRIORS BOLD—	83	MAD KING GOLL	V	23
	THESE HANDS SLEW MANY ROBBERS BOLD—	83	MAD KING GOLL	V	23
	THESE HANDS SLEW MANY A SEAMAN BOLD, ...	83	MAD KING GOLL	V	23
	SLEW THEE, POOR SIBYL! COMRADES THOU AND I!	675	ISLE STAT II 3		235
SLID					
	SPLASHED, OR AN OTTER SLID INTO THE STREAM.	372	PHASES OF MOON		9
	SLID CIRCLING DOWN AND SOFTLY TOUCHED MY LIPS	690	MOSADA 1		21
SLIDES					
	A HORSE-HOOF SLIDES ON THE BRIM, ...	393	EASTER 1916		51
SLIDING					
	CAME NOW THE SLIDING OF TEARS AND SWEEPING OF MIST-COLD HAIR,	47	OISIN 3		7
	CAME NOW THE SLIDING OF TEARS AND SWEEPING OF MIST-COLD AIR,	47	OISIN 3	V	7
	CAME NOW THE SLIDING OF TEARS AND SWEEPING OF MIST COLD HAIR,	47	OISIN 3	V	7
	IS BUT A SLIDING DROP OF RAIN BETWEEN HIS PETALS WIDE. . .	76	INDIAN ON GOD		12
	IS BUT A SLIDING DROP OF RAIN WITHIN HIS PETALS WIDE." . .	76	INDIAN ON GOD	V	12
	OR HAVE YOU HEARD THAT SLIDING SILVER-SHOED	211	RAGGED WOOD		5
SLIEVENAMON					
	IN THEIR GREAT HOUSE AT SLIEVENAMON.	271	GREY ROCK		15
	IF BOOKS SPEAK TRUTH, IN SLIEVENAMON—	271	GREY ROCK	V	15
SLIGHT					
	AND THAT A SLIGHT COMPANIONABLE GHOST, ...	472	ALL SOUL NIGHT		35
SLIGO					
	THAT CARRIED THE TAKE TO SLIGO TOWN TO BE SOLD, ...	91	OLD FISHERMAN		7
	I BOUGHT AT THE SLIGO FAIR.	178	FIDDLER DOONEY		8
	UPON THE OPEN ROAD, NEAR TO THE SLIGO QUAY—	391	UNDER SATURN		12
	HE THAT IN SLIGO AT DRUMCLIFF	604	YOU CONTENT		9

730

		PAGE	TITLE		LINE
SLIM					
SLIM ADOLESCENCE THAT A NYMPH HAS STRIPPED, ...		612	NEWS ORACLE		25
SLIME	SEE SEA-SLIME				
THAT WAS MOST DISTANT FROM THE DOOR: GREEN SLIME . . .		37	OISIN 2		113
MOST DISTANT STRODE WE. ON THE FLOOR LAY SLIME, . . .		37	OISIN 2	V	113
AND HUNG WITH SLIME, AND WHISPERING IN HIS HAIR, . . .		43	OISIN 2		216
HUNG ROUND WITH SLIME, AND WHISPERING IN HIS HAIR, . . .		43	OISIN 2	V	216
GATHER SEA SLIME AND FALL THE SEAWARD WAY, ...		45	OISIN 2	V	237
SLIMY					
AND THRUST THE TORCH BETWEEN THE SLIMY FLAGS.		38	OISIN 2		143
SLINGERS	SEE WOMEN-SLINGERS				
THE WOMEN SLINGERS ON THE NARROW BRIDGE, ...		749	SHADOW WATER A	V	41
SLINGS					
AND LEATHER-COATED MEN WITH SLINGS		193	BAILE AILLINN	V	111
SLIPPED					
O SHE WAS BUT A SHADOW, AND SLIPPED FROM ME.		223	SHADOW WATER B		40
SLIPPER					
NOR DOOR, NOR MOUTH, NOR SLIPPER MADE A NOISE, ...		279	TWO KINGS		51
SLIPPERED					
WHERE SLIPPERED CONTEMPLATION FINDS HIS EASE		418	ANCEST HOUSES		30
SLIPPERS					
FOR HE HIS SLIPPERS WORE.		595	COLONEL MARTIN		40
AH! WOE FOR YOUR SLIPPERS OF RED.		708	FAIRY PEDANT		36
SLIPPERY					
MADE THE WAY SLIPPERY, AND TIME ON TIME		37	OISIN 2		114
GREENISH AND SLIPPERY. TIME AFTER TIME		37	OISIN 2	V	114
SLOE-BERRIES					
AND FIGHT FOR THE BLACK SLOE-BERRIES, ...		644	SONG FAERIES		13
AND FIGHT FOR THE BLACK SLOE-BERRIES, ...		676	ISLE STAT II 3		260
SLOPE					
ALL DRIPPING ON A GRASSY SLOPE, AND SAW THEM CEASE TO CHASE		76	INDIAN ON GOD		4
OR LOFTY SLOPE WHERE IT STILL SNOWS		567	LAPIS LAZULI		46
SLOPES					
IN AUTUMN, WHEN FAR DOWN THE MOUNTAIN SLOPES		690	MOSADA 1		12
SLOPING					
O YOU, WITH WHOM IN SLOPING VALLEYS, ...		10	OISIN 1		119
OH YE WITH WHOM, IN SLOPING VALLEYS		10	OISIN 1	V	119
THAT SLOPING GREEN DE DANAAN SOD		20	OISIN 1		299
EAT AWAY THE SLOPING SOD, ...		20	OISIN 1	V	299
OF HOLLIES, AND HAZELS, AND OAK TREES, A VALLEY WAS SLOPING AWAY		48	OISIN 3	V	26
SLOUCHES					
SLOUCHES TOWARDS BETHLEHEM TO BE BORN?		402	SECOND COMING		22
SLOW					
BESIDE THE SEA, WHERE, HUSHED AND SLOW, ...		20	OISIN 1	V	292
HUNG THE FRAIL LOFTIER CLOUDLETS. TURNED HE SLOW-- . . .		40	OISIN 2	V	167
FOR, AS DRIFT FROM A SAILOR SLOW DROWNING		48	OISIN 3		22
AND OVER THE LIMBS AND THE VALLEY THE SLOW OWLS WANDERED AND CAME,		49	OISIN 3		41
. . . SLOW DROPPING A SOUND IN FAINT STREAMS		51	OISIN 3		67
HOW THE SLOW, BLUE-EYED OXEN OF FINN LOW SADLY AT EVENING TIDE.		52	OISIN 3		84
WENT WALKING WITH SLOW STEPS ALONG THE GLEAMING		68	SAD SHEPHERD		3
FIELDS FATTENING SLOW, MEN WISE IN JOY, ...		82	MAD KING GOLL	V	6
LIFTS SLOW HIS WINTRY HEAD!		99	FOXHUNTER		46
AND PRESSING ON, OR LINGERING SLOW WITH FEAR, ...		114	ROSE OF BATTLE	V	5
AND I SHALL HAVE SOME PEACE THERE, FOR PEACE COMES DROPPING SLOW,		117	ISLE INNISFREE		5
MAEVE WALKED, YET WITH SLOW FOOTFALL, BEING OLD, ...		181	QUEEN MAEVE		43
BUT MAEVE, AND NOT WITH A SLOW FEEBLE FOOT, ...		185	QUEEN MAEVE		107
WITH A SLOW SMILE AND WITHOUT SOUND, ...		275	GREY ROCK		117
MOST COURTEOUS TO SLOW AGE AND HASTY YOUTH, ...		339	SHEP GOATHERD		19
IS MOVING ITS SLOW THIGHS, WHILE ALL ABOUT IT		402	SECOND COMING		16
SLOW DECAY OF BLOOD, ...		416	TOWER		185
FOR ALL HIS TIMID HEART, THERE THAT SLOW MAN, ...		489	COOLE PARK 29		12
A SLOW LOW NOTE AND AN IRON BELL.		549	SEVERED HEAD		7
A SLOW LOW NOTE AND AN IRON BELL.		550	SEVERED HEAD		14
A SLOW LOW NOTE AND AN IRON BELL.		550	SEVERED HEAD		21
UNDER THE TROPIC SHADE, GREW ROUND AND SLOW, ...		610	STATUES		18
THAT DIETH SLOW WITH SUNSICK DOOM.		655	ISLE STAT I 3		12
SLOW WATERS, AND THE BOAT AND MAIDEN SINK		663	ISLE STAT II 2		39
THE SUMMERS FLING THEIR SCENTS? AH, SUBTLE AND SLOW, . .		675	ISLE STAT II 3		231
IN THEIR COILING CALM AND SLOW.		680	LOVE AND DEATH		8
AS ROUND HER, SLOW ON FEET THAT HAVE NO BLOOD, ...		687	TWO TITANS		18
CLOGGED IN A MARSH WHERE THE SLOW MARSH CLAY CLINGS, . .		711	FERENCZ RENYI		35
DROPS ON HIS BOSOM, SOMBRE, MOIST AND SLOW.		711	FERENCZ RENYI		40
UPON HIS BOSOM, SOMBRE, MOIST AND SLOW.		711	FERENCZ RENYI	V	40
SEE THE DARKNESS SLOW DISGORGING A VESSEL BLIND WITH SQUALL.		718	PHANTOM SHIP		12
SLOW THE CHAPEL BELL IS TOLLING AS THOUGH THE DEAD PASSED BY.		718	PHANTOM SHIP		16
BY THE SLOW HEAVING OCEAN--MUMBLING MOTHER OF THE DEAD.		719	PHANTOM SHIP		34
SLOW-FOOTING					
DEEP-EYED, SLOW-FOOTING DOWN THE EMPTY GLADE.		653	ISLE STAT I 2		55
SLOWLY					
AND FAR BEHIND US, SLOWLY ROUND		10	OISIN 1	V	114B
HUNG IN THE PASSIONATE DAWN. HE SLOWLY TURNED:		40	OISIN 2		167
HIS LIPS MOVED SLOWLY IN ANSWER, NO ANSWER OUT OF THEM CAME!		51	OISIN 3		66
A SAD, SAD THOUGHT WENT BY ME SLOWLY:		72	ANASHU VIJAYA		17
WHILE SLOWLY HE WHOSE HAND HELD HERS REPLIED:		80	EPHEMERA		11

		PAGE	TITLE		LINE

SLOWLY   (CONTINUED)
```
        WHILE SLOWLY ANSWERED HE WHOSE HAND HELD HERS--   . . . . .      80 EPHEMERA        V   11
        BUT SLOWLY, AS I SHOUTING SLEW  . . . . . . . . . . .            83 MAD KING GOLL       25
        AND LEAD HIM SLOWLY TO AND FRO,  . . . . . . . . .               97 FOXHUNTER       V    7
        AND SLOWLY UP AND DOWN.  . . . . . . . . . . . . . .             97 FOXHUNTER       V    8
        A MAN CAME SLOWLY FROM THE SETTING SUN,  . . . . . .            105 CUCHULAIN SEA        1
        AND SLOWLY READ, AND DREAM OF THE SOFT LOOK  . . . . .          121 YOU ARE OLD          3
        THEY SLOWLY INTO MILLIONS GREW,  . . . . . . . . . .           133 FR GILLIGAN        17
        THE DEWS DROP SLOWLY AND DREAMS GATHER: UNKNOWN SPEARS  . .    161 BLACK PIG            1
        THE DEW DROPS SLOWLY: THE DREAMS GATHER: UNKNOWN SPEARS       161 BLACK PIG       V    1
        "WE RIDE BUT SLOWLY THOUGH SO NEAR OUR HOME,"  . . . . .      276 TWO KINGS       V    A
        WHAT IS THERE BUT THE SLOWLY FADING WEST,  . . . . . .        390 IMAGE PAST          19
        AND AFTER BAKED IT SLOWLY IN AN OVEN: BUT NOW  . . . .        442 BLACK CENTAUR        9
        SLOWLY, SLOWLY FADETH SHE,  . . . . . . . . . . . .           648 ISLE STAT I 1      83
        SLOWLY, SLOWLY FADETH SHE,  . . . . . . . . . . . .           648 ISLE STAT I 1      83
        TO MINE, AND HE IS SLOWLY SUCKING FORTH  . . . . . .          684 SEEKER          V  63A
        AS SLOWLY AUTUMN CLIMBED THE GOLDEN THRONE  . . . . .         690 MOSADA 1        V   1A
SLOW-MUFFLED
        CARVED: HERE, BEYOND THE LAKE'S SLOW-MUFFLED TREAD,  . . .    662 ISLE STAT II 2      11
SLUGGARD
        AND WAKES THE SLUGGARD SEEDS OF CORN,  . . . . . . .          18 OISIN 1            263
        CRIES TO THE SLUGGARD SEEDS OF CORN,  . . . . . . . .         18 OISIN 1         V  263
SLUGGISH
        HAVING GROWN SLUGGISH AND CONTEMPLATIVE.  . . . . . .        325 ROBERT GREGORY      40
        A BEARDED WITCH, HER SLUGGISH HEAD LOW BENT  . . . . .       685 SEEKER              72
SLUMBER
        IF THEY STILL SLUMBER, TOUCH THEIR EYELIDS BLUE,  . . . .     33 OISIN 2         V   61
        AT TIMES OUR SLUMBER WAS LIGHTENED,  . . . . . . . .          53 OISIN 3             97
        OF TWILIGHT AND SLUMBER WERE GONE, AND THAT HOOFS            54 OISIN 3            112
            IMPATIENTLY STEPT,
        OUR VOICES CARRY: AND THOUGH SLUMBER BOUND,  . . . . .      622 HOUND VOICE     V    5
        WHEN WE HALE MEN LIE STRETCHED IN SLUMBER  . . . . . .      636 BLACK TOWER         23
        NO TASTE HAVE I FOR SLUMBER 'NEATH AN OAK.  . . . . . .     721 WITCH VIVIEN        31
        AND HE SHALL SLUMBER ON MY BREAST.  . . . . . . . .         723 GIRLS SONG A         4
        HAST THOU NOT KNOWN A RAJA'S DREAMLESS SLUMBER?  . . . .    724 KANVA ON SELF        8
SLUMBER-BOUND
        OUR VOICES CARRY: AND THOUGH SLUMBER-BOUND,  . . . . .      622 HOUND VOICE          5
SLUMBERED
        HALF SLUMBERED WITH HIS SAFFRON BLAZE:  . . . . . . .        26 OISIN 1         V  395
        THAT SLUMBERED IN THE HARVEST MOON,  . . . . . . . .         85 MAD KING GOLL       50
        THAT SLUMBERED 'NEATH THE HARVEST MOON,  . . . . . . .       85 MAD KING GOLL   V   50
        THE YEARS OF GOBLIN SLEEP. AH! WHILE I SLUMBERED,  . . .    679 ISLE STAT II 3     308
SLUMBERERS
        I SAW HOW THOSE SLUMBERERS, GROWN WEARY,  . . . . . . .      50 OISIN 3             54
SLUMBERING       SEE NEVER-SLUMBERING
        WAS SLUMBERING HALF IN THE SEA-WAYS:  . . . . . . . .        26 OISIN 1            395
        WAS SLUMBERING HALF IN THE SEA WAYS:  . . . . . . . .        26 OISIN 1         V  395
        AS THOUGH UNTO HIS NEVER SLUMBERING HEART  . . . . . .       32 OISIN 2             44
        AS THOUGH HE TOLD HIS NEVER SLUMBERING HEART  . . . . .      32 OISIN 2         V   44
        UNDER THE STARLIGHT AND SHADOW, A MONSTROUS SLUMBERING       48 OISIN 3             27
            FOLK,
        FROM HIS HOOVES IN THE HEAVY GRASSES, WITH MONSTROUS         48 OISIN 3         V   27
            SLUMBERING FOLK,
        WE SEEK FOR SLUMBERING TROUT  . . . . . . . . . . .          88 STOLEN CHILD        32
SLUNK
        CAME BLANAID, MAC NESSA, TALL FERGUS WHO FEASTWARD OF OLD    53 OISIN 3             89
            TIME SLUNK,
        . . . CAME FERGUS WHO FEASTWARD SAD SLUNK,  . . . . . .      53 OISIN 3         V   89
        CAME BLANID, MAC NESSA, AND FERGUS WHO FEASTWARD OF OLD      53 OISIN 3         V   89
            TIME SLUNK,
SLUT
        OLD IRON, OLD BONES, OLD RAGS, THAT RAVING SLUT  . . . .    630 CIRCUS ANIMALS      37
SLY
        WHETHER IT BE BOLD OR SLY.  . . . . . . . . . . . .         624 APPARITIONS          6
SMALL
        LIKE A SMALL RIVER, AND WHERE FEET TOUCHED CAME  . . . .     37 OISIN 2            117
        GREY IN THE MIDST LIKE A SMALL RIVULET'S FLOW,  . . . .      37 OISIN 2         V  117
        "I WOULD DIE LIKE A SMALL WITHERED LEAF IN THE AUTUMN,       56 OISIN 3            131
            . . .
        AND A SMALL AND A FEEBLE POPULACE STOOPING WITH MATTOCK      58 OISIN 3            164
            AND SPADE,
        AND A SMALL AND A FEEBLE RACE STOOPING WITH MATTOCK AND      58 OISIN 3         V  164
            SPADE.
        AND A SMALL AND FEEBLE RACE STOOPING WITH MATTOCK            58 OISIN 3         V  164
            AND SPADE.
        I THROW DOWN THE CHAIN OF SMALL STONES!  . . . . . . .       63 OISIN 3            222
        AND HE WORE SMALL HOLES IN HIS SHOES,  . . . . . . .         92 FATHER OHART        11
        THE WEAK WORM HIDING DOWN IN ITS SMALL CAVE,  . . . . .     101 ROSE UPON ROOD      16
        LAY HIDDEN IN THE SMALL SLATE-COLOURED THING!  . . . .      104 FERGUS DRUID        40
        TAKE THEN THIS SMALL SLATE-COLOURED BAG OF DREAMS!  . . .   104 FERGUS DRUID    V   29
        LAY HIDDEN IN THE SMALL SLATE-COLOURED BAG!  . . . . .      104 FERGUS DRUID    V   40
        AND A SMALL CABIN BUILD THERE, OF CLAY AND WATTLES MADE:    117 ISLE INNISFREE       2
        AND A SMALL CABIN BUILT THERE, OF CLAY AND WATTLES MADE:    117 ISLE INNISFREE V     2
        BUT ONE SMALL KNOT-GRASS GROWING BY THE POOL  . . . . .     127 DREAM OF FAERY      29
        BUT ONE SMALL KNOT-GRASS GROWING BY THE RIM  . . . . .      127 DREAM OF FAERY V    29
        TO THAT SMALL CHAMBER BY THE OUTER GATE.  . . . . . .       181 QUEEN MAEVE         44
        THE ENTIRE COMBUSTIBLE WORLD IN ONE SMALL ROOM  . . . .     327 ROBERT GREGORY      82
        ALL THE COMBUSTIBLE WORLD IN ONE SMALL ROOM  . . . . .      327 ROBERT GREGORY V    82
        YOUR SMALL HANDS WERE NOT BEAUTIFUL,  . . . . . . . .       356 BROKEN DREAMS       29
        AWAIT THE HOUR OF WAR, ENTER THE SMALL,  . . . . . . .      461 HARUN RASHID    V    8
        NO MORE SANG HE, FOR HIS THROAT WAS TOO SMALL:  . . . .     545 TO SAME TUNE 1      24
```

732

		PAGE	TITLE		LINE

SMALL   (CONTINUED)
    HE SAID NO MORE FOR HIS THROAT WAS TOO SMALL. • • • • • • 545 TO SAME TUNE 1 V 24
    A SMALL OLD HOUSE, WIFE, DAUGHTER, SON, • • • • • • • 577 WHAT THEN   12
    THEY ALWAYS BEAT ON THE SAME SMALL STONE. • • • • • • 591 WHAT WAS LOST   5
    I HAVE A SMALL DEMESNE, • • • • • • • • • • • • • 606 SONGS BURDEN 2   2
    A SMALL FORGOTTEN HOUSE THAT'S SET • • • • • • 606 SONGS BURDEN 2   3
    NO MORE SANG HE, FOR HIS THROAT WAS TOO SMALL! • • • • • 616 MARCH SONGS 3   24
    CATCHING SMALL BIRDS IN THE DEW OF THE MORN • • • • • 636 BLACK TOWER   22
    OR SOME SMALL BEAST MOST WONDERFULLY FURR'D. • • • • • 650 ISLE STAT I 1 148
    SMALL ISLAND, WHERE THE FULL SOFT SHEEN • • • • • • 653 ISLE STAT I 2   36
    A LITTLE MOORISH GIRL? SMALL WORTH. MY SONG-- • • • 696 MOSADA 2   10
    AND HASSAN WILL BE WITH THEM--HE WAS SO SMALL, • • • 699 MOSADA 3   13
    AND NOT COME THENCE! FOR HERE IN THIS SMALL RING-- • • 699 MOSADA 3   22
    HASSAN IS WITH THEM TOO--HE WAS SO SMALL, • • • • • 699 MOSADA 3   V 13
    SO SMALL MAKES ONE GROW WEAK AND TOTTERING! • • • • 700 MOSADA 3   35
    FLOATING FROM YON BARRED WINDOW. SMALL NEW-COMER, • • • 700 MOSADA 3   43
    TWO WOMEN, WITHERED ONE AND SMALL AND THIN, • • • • 711 FERENCZ RENYI   51
    LIKE SMALL BROWN MOTHS, A-TREMBLE. "RENYI SAY • • • 713 FERENCZ RENYI   82
    LIKE SMALL BROWN MOTHS, A-TREMBLE CEASELESSLY. • • • 713 FERENCZ RENYI V 82
    AND WE ARE SO VERY SMALL! • • • • • • • • • • 726 LOVERS QUARREL 18
    DANCE THE SAVAGE CHILDREN SMALL, • • • • • • • • 732 STREET DANCERS 29
    AND PLUCKED SMALL FRUITS ON INNISFREE. • • • • • • 742 DANAAN QUICK   5
    WHEN SOMETHING FOLDED AND SMALL • • • • • • • • 744 GLOVE CLOAK   7
SMALLEST
    BEYOND THE LAKE, WHOSE SMALLEST WAVE WAS BURDENED • • • 656 ISLE STAT I 3   31
    THE BREATHING OF THE SMALLEST BIRD, • • • • • • • 730 PRIEST FAIRY   68
SMARAGDINE
    FOR THINGS BELOW ARE COPIES, THE GREAT SMARAGDINE TABLET   556 RIBH PATRICK   6
        SAID.
SMART
    AND THERE IS SALT TO LENGTHEN OUT THE SMART • • • • • 324 ROBERT GREGORY 11
SMELLED
    THE NIGHT SMELLED RICH WITH JUNE. • • • • • • • • 160 CAP AND BELLS V 28
SMELT
    BUT LIKED THE WAY HIS FINGER SMELT. • • • • • • • 619 STICK INCENSE   4
SMILE
    WATCHING THE BLESSED ONES MOVE FAR OFF, AND THE SMILE ON   61 OISIN 3   199
        GOD'S FACE,
    THE HOUR WHEN KAMA, WITH A SUMPTUOUS SMILE, • • • • 72 ANASHU VIJAYA V 26
    AND HE SAID WITH A SMILE, "HAVE PEACE NOW"! • • • • 92 FATHER OHART   19
    TO SMILE ON THE PALE DAWN! AND GATHER YOU • • • • 114 ROSE OF BATTLE 15
    TO SMILE UPON HER STARS! AND GATHER YOU, • • • • 114 ROSE OF BATTLE V 15
    HE WILL SMILE ON THE THREE OLD SPIRITS, • • • • • 178 FIDDLER DOONEY 11
    AND THEIR SECRET SMILE, OUT OF THE DEPTHS OF THE LAKE! • 203 WITHER BOUGHS   11
    AND THEIR SECRET SMILE, OUT OF THE DEEPS OF THE LAKE! • 203 WITHER BOUGHS V 11
    WITH A SLOW SMILE AND WITHOUT SOUND, • • • • • • 275 GREY ROCK   117
    BETTER TO SMILE ON ALL THAT SMILE, AND SHOW • • • • 444 SCHOOL CHILDR   31
    BETTER TO SMILE ON ALL THAT SMILE, AND SHOW • • • • 444 SCHOOL CHILDR   31
    SOON WILT THOU SMILE, FOR HERE THE WINDS ARE WEAK • • 671 ISLE STAT II 3 141
    I SAW HIS JOVIAL MOOD BRING ONCE A SMILE • • • • • 696 MOSADA 2   14
SMILED
    BUT DATHI FOLDED HIS HANDS AND SMILED • • • • • • 167 BLESSED   11
    AND EVEN STRAFFORD SMILED AS THOUGH • • • • • • • 400 DEMON BEAST   13
    AND EVEN STAFFORD SMILED AS THOUGH • • • • • • • 400 DEMON BEAST   V 13
    SHE SMILED AND THAT TRANSFIGURED ME • • • • • • • 451 FIRST LOVE   13
SMILES
    GOD SMILES IN HIGH HEAVEN • • • • • • • • • • 118 CRADLE SONG   V   5
    IN THE DEEP ALCOVES DIMNESS SMILES AND HIDES. • • • • 685 DRAWING-ROOM   4
    SHE SMILES--IS HAPPY WITH HER WANDERING GRIEFS. • • • 702 MOSADA 3   95
    IN THE DEEP ALCOVE'S DIMNESS SMILES AND HIDES." • • • 735 QUATRAIN APHOR 24
    IN THE DEEP ALCOVES DIMNESS SMILES AND HIDES. • • • 735 QUATRAIN APHOR V 24
SMILING
    AND GRANIA, WALKING AND SMILING, SEWED WITH HER NEEDLE   53 OISIN 3   94
        OF BONE.
    "MY FATHER," MADE HE, SMILING, ANSWER THEN, • • • • 107 CUCHULAIN SEA V 25
    A SIXTY-YEAR-OLD SMILING PUBLIC MAN. • • • • • • 443 SCHOOL CHILDR   8
    A SIXTY YEAR OLD SMILING PUBLIC MAN. • • • • • • 443 SCHOOL CHILDR V   8
    SMILING AT THE SEA, • • • • • • • • • • • • 605 YOU CONTENT   20
    AND SMILING FROM SWEET THOUGHT, • • • • • • • • 741 EARL PAUL   42
SMITH
    YET CHOSE A BANDY-LEGGED SMITH FOR MAN. • • • • • • 404 FOR DAUGHTER   29
SMITHIES
    SPIRIT AFTER SPIRIT! THE SMITHIES BREAK THE FLOOD, • • • 498 BYZANTIUM   34
    THE GOLDEN SMITHIES OF THE EMPEROR! • • • • • • • 498 BYZANTIUM   35
SMITHY
    LIKE THE SPARKS BLOWN OUT OF A SMITHY, AND DIE? • • • 170 SECRET ROSE   30
    WHEN FROM THE SMITHY FIRE • • • • • • • • • • 345 ON WOMAN   18
    AND SMITHY WORK FROM THE GORT FORGE, • • • • • • 406 CARVED STONE   3
SMITTEN   SEE SUN-SMITTEN FAIRY-SMITTEN HEART-SMITTEN
    AN IMAGE OF MY HEART THAT IS SMITTEN THROUGH • • • • 389 IMAGE PAST   8
    AMID MOST LOVELY PLACES! SMITTEN AS THOUGH • • • • • 389 IMAGE PAST   13
    HEART SMITTEN WITH EMOTION, I SINK DOWN, • • • • • 602 GALLERY REVIS V 17
SMOKE
    FLED FOAM UNDERNEATH US, AND ROUND US, A WANDERING AND   47 OISIN 3   1
        MILKY SMOKE,
    FLED FOAM UNDERNEATH US, AND ROUND US, A WANDERING AND   47 OISIN 3   12
        MILKY SMOKE.
    FLED FOAM UNDERNEATH US, AND AROUND US, A WANDERING AND   47 OISIN 3   V   1
        MILKY SMOKE,
    • • • DULL WITH THE SMOKE OF THEIR DREAMS! • • • • • 51 OISIN 3   65

733

		PAGE	TITLE	LINE

SMOKE   (CONTINUED)
FLED FOAM UNDERNEATH ME, AND ROUND ME, A WANDERING AND   57 OISIN 3   148
   MILKY SMOKE.
WERE GONE LIKE A DRIFTING SMOKE! . . . .   145 HOST OF AIR   40
AND CUMHAL SAW LIKE A DRIFTING SMOKE . . . .   167 BLESSED   13
AND SMOKE FROM THIS DEAD HEART DRIFTS THROUGH THE VIOLET   173 SPEAKS HEARERS   3
   AIR
AND COVERS AWAY THE SMOKE OF MYRRH AND FRANKINCENSE: . .   173 SPEAKS HEARERS   4
IS ROLLED AS VERDANT SMOKE! O THOU WHOSE FACE . . .   667 ISLE STAT II 3   35
HIS BODY SHAKE? AY, QUIVERING AS YON SMOKE . . . . .   683 SEEKER   36
THUS DO I BURN THESE PRECIOUS HERBS, WHOSE SMOKE . . .   691 MOSADA 1   39
SO ENDS A BRAIN——A WORLD! THE SMOKE GOES UP, ...   714 FERENCZ RENYI   111
OF FIRE. SO ENDS A BRAIN——A WORLD! THE SMOKE FLOATS UP,   714 FERENCZ RENYI   V   111
AS A WREATH OF SMOKE IN WIND-BLOWN FLIGHT . . . . . .   730 PRIEST FAIRY   61
SMOKES
THE CATARACT SMOKES UPON THE MOUNTAIN SIDE, ...   311 MOUNTAIN TOMB   3
THE CATARACT SMOKES ON THE MOUNTAIN SIDE. . . . . . .   311 MOUNTAIN TOMB   V   3
SMOKING
AND LEAVE NO SMOKING WICK BEHIND, ...   306 HOUR DAWN   97
WHAT HAS TURNED TO SMOKING WICK . . . .   529 TOM LUNATIC   5
SMOKY
THE SMOKY TORCHES MADE A GLARE . . . .   271 GREY ROCK   18
AND SMOKY TORCHES MADE A GLARE . . . .   271 GREY ROCK   V   18
SMOOTH
THROUGH MANY SHAPES: I LUNGED AT THE SMOOTH THROAT . . .   40 OISIN 2   175
TO MANY SHAPES: I LUNGED AT THE SMOOTH THROAT . . . .   40 OISIN 2   V   175
I WILL PRAY NO MORE WITH THE SMOOTH STONES! . . .   63 OISIN 3   V   221
THE PEAHENS DANCE ON A SMOOTH LAWN, ...   77 INDIAN TO LOVE   3
AND WHERE HER SON, FINMOLE, ON THE SMOOTH GRASS . . .   106 CUCHULAIN SEA V   18
FOR THEY, FOR ALL SMOOTH LIPS CAN SAY, ...   202 NEVER GIVE ALL   9
AND THEN SMOOTH OUT WITH IVORY HANDS AND SIGH, ...   228 SHADOW WATER B   133
AND SMOOTH OUT STAIN AND BLEMISH WITH THE ELEGANCE OF HIS   353 HIS PHOENIX   7
   MIND!
HURRIED THROUGH THE SMOOTH AND ROUGH . . . .   436 FOR MY SON   29
HAVE BORNE YOU THROUGH THE SMOOTH AND ROUGH . . . . .   436 FOR MY SON   V   29
ON THE LEAF-SOWN, NEW-MOWN, SMOOTH . . . .   568 SWEET DANCER   2
ON THE LEAF-SOWN, NEW MOWN, SMOOTH . . . .   568 SWEET DANCER   V   2
SITTING ON A WARM SMOOTH MAT . . . .   726 LOVERS QUARREL   11
AND THEN SMOOTH OUT WITH IVORY HANDS AND SIGH. . . . .   750 SHADOW WATER A   70
SMOOTHS
HE SMOOTHS THE LONG BROWN NOSE. . . . .   98 FOXHUNTER   20
SMOTE
SMOTE ON THEIR BRAINS THAT DWELT REMEMBERING AYE. . . .   34 OISIN 2   V   77A
OF A GREAT EEL! IT CHANGED, AND I BUT SMOTE . . . .   40 OISIN 2   176
SHE SMOTE WITH RADDLED FIST, AND WHERE HER SON . . . .   106 CUCHULAIN SEA   18
ONCE, WHEN MIDNIGHT SMOTE THE AIR, ...   294 HATED PLAYBOY   1
OR SMOTE UPON THE STRING AND TO THE SOUND . . . . . .   537 HER VISION   15
SMOTHER
STRETCHED HIS LONG ARM TO WHERE, A MISTY SMOTHER, . . .   31 OISIN 2   42
SMOULDERING
THEY SEEMED TO SING IN THE SMOULDERING FIRES. . . . . .   13 OISIN 1   168
SMUGGLER
THE SMUGGLER MIDDLETON, BUTLERS FAR BACK, ...   605 YOU CONTENT   15
SNAKES
SEEK NOT THAT WOOD, FOR THERE THE GOBLIN SNAKES . . . .   682 SEEKER   29
SNAP
HE'LL SNAP HIS SWORD. RAISED IS THE LION'S PAW. . . . .   664 ISLE STAT II 2   63
SNAPS
AH! THERE HE SNAPS MY RICE. I TOLD YOU SO. . . . . .   73 ANASHU VIJAYA   38
SNARE
AND BLAME THE SNARE THEY SET FOR ME. . . . .   743 DANAAN QUICK   23
AND MOIDERED IN THAT SNARE . . . .   783 GREY ROUND   8
IN THAT SWEET WANDERING SNARE. . . . .   783 GREY ROUND   10
SNATCH
THE STRONGEST OF THE WORLD, TO SNATCH MY PREY, ...   45 OISIN 2   V   241
TO SNATCH ALIVE OUT OF THE STREAMS ALL LOVERS . . . .   765 SHADOW WATER A   347
SNATCHED
FROM THEE I SNATCHED IT! E'EN THE FAY THAT TRIPS . . .   670 ISLE STAT II 3   98
SNATCHES
AND MURMURED SNATCHES OF DELIGHT: . . . .   14 OISIN 1   187
SNATCHING
SNATCHING THE HORN OF NIAMH, I BLEW A LONG LINGERING NOTE.   51 OISIN 3   57
SNATCHING THE HORN OF NIAM, I BLEW FORTH A LINGERING NOTE!   51 OISIN 3   57
SNATCHING THE HORN OF NIAM, I BLEW A LINGERING NOTE! . .   51 OISIN 3   V   57
SNATCHING THE BIRD IN SECRET! NOR KNEW I, EMBOSOMED APART,   57 OISIN 3   150
SNICKED
SHE SNICKED THE BRASS BOLTS DOWN. . . . .   159 CAP AND BELLS V   12
SNIFF
OR ELSE THEY STAND AND SNIFF THE WIND, ...   136 TWO TREES   37
SNIPE
AND HIS OWN SNIPE AND TROUT. . . . .   92 FATHER OHART   4
WITH HIS SNIPE MARSH AND HIS TROUT. . . . .   92 FATHER OHART   V   4
SNORE
THOUGH DRUNKARDS LIE AND SNORE. . . . .   592 DRUNK SOBRIETY   8
SNORED
THEY SANG A DROWSY SONG, OR SNORED, ...   271 GREY ROCK   16
AND SANG A DROWSY SONG, OR SNORED, ...   271 GREY ROCK   V   16
FELL DOWN UPON THE DUST AND SNORED. . . . .   297 THREE BEGGARS   60
AND SNORED, NO PHANTOM BY HIS LOOK. . . . .   303 HOUR DAWN   30
SNOW
OR ARE YOU PHANTOMS WHITE AS SNOW, ...   10 OISIN 1   117

734

		PAGE	TITLE		LINE

SNOW   (CONTINUED)
```
      OR ARE YE PHANTOMS WHITE AS SNOW,  . . . . . .        10 OISIN 1      V  117
      A DEMON'S LEISURE.  EYES FIRST WHITE AS SNOW, . . . .  40 OISIN 2      V  168
      WHERE MEN LIE FROZEN IN THE GLIMMERING SNOW! . . . .   73 ANASHU VIJAYA    51
      AND PINCHES AMONG HAIL AND SNOW?  . . . . . . . .     191 BAILE AILLINN    46
      A MIST THAT IS LIKE BLOWN SNOW IS SWEEPING OVER ALL,  425 PHANTOM HATRED    2
      CRIED, CASTING OFF THE MOUNTAIN SNOW,  . . . . .      502 VACILLATION      60
      MAD AS THE MIST AND SNOW . . . . . . . . . .         523 MAD AS MIST       T
      MAD AS THE MIST AND SNOW. . . . . . . . . . .        523 MAD AS MIST       6
      MAD AS THE MIST AND SNOW. . . . . . . . . . .        524 MAD AS MIST      12
      MAD AS THE MIST AND SNOW? . . . . . . . . . .        524 MAD AS MIST      18
      MAD AS THE MIST AND SNOW. . . . . . . . . . .        524 MAD AS MIST      18
      CAVERNED IN NIGHT UNDER THE DRIFTED SNOW, . . . .     563 MERU             10
      OR WHERE THAT SNOW AND WINTER'S DREADFUL BLAST . . .  563 MERU             11
      THE PASSING OF THOSE LITTLE GRAINS IS SNOW . . . .    722 WITCH VIVIEN     48
SNOWFLAKES
      SOFTER THAN SNOWFLAKES IN APRIL, AND PIERCING THE MARROW   51 OISIN 3   V   68
        LIKE FLAME.
SNOW-FLAKES
      SOFTER THAN SNOW-FLAKES IN APRIL AND PIERCING THE MARROW   51 OISIN 3       68
        LIKE FLAME.
SNOWS
      AND WANDER IN THE STORMS AND CLINGING SNOWS, . . . .  42 OISIN 2         201
      ROOTS HALF HIDDEN UNDER SNOWS. . . . . . . . .       135 TWO TREES        27
      AND ROOTS HALF HIDDEN UNDER SNOWS . . . . . . .      135 TWO TREES     V  27
      IN THE COLD SNOWS OF A DREAM. . . . . . . . .        424 ROAD AT DOOR     15
      OR LOFTY SLOPE WHERE IT STILL SNOWS . . . . . .      567 LAPIS LAZULI     46
SNOW-WHITE
      SHE PASSED THE SALLEY GARDENS WITH LITTLE SNOW-WHITE FEET.  90 SALLEY GARDENS   2
      AND ON MY LEANING SHOULDER SHE LAID HER SNOW-WHITE HAND.    90 SALLEY GARDENS   6
SNUG
      AND SNUG IT IN A FEATHER BED. . . . . . . . .        332 ROUND TOWER      28
      AND SNUG IT IN A FEATHER-BED, . . . . . . . .        332 ROUND TOWER   V  28
SOB
      WITH A SOB FOR MEN WAXING SO WEAKLY, . . . . .        60 OISIN 3         188
      . . . A SOB FOR THE FENIANS' OLD STRENGTH. . . . .    60 OISIN 3         188
SOBBED
      SOBBED INTO SILENCE.  WE HAD MOUNTED FEET . . . .     33 OISIN 2      V  68E
      AND THEN THE FAY QUEEN SOBBED APART, . . . . .       730 PRIEST FAIRY     70
SOBER
      AND DROVE HIM DRUNK OR SOBER THROUGH THE DAWN . . .  411 TOWER            58
      THOUGH NOT FOR SOBER EAR! . . . . . . . . . .        471 ALL SOUL NIGHT   18
      THOUGH NOT FOR SOBER EAR, . . . . . . . . . .        474 ALL SOUL NIGHT   88
      THAT I MAY STAY A SOBER MAN . . . . . . . . .        591 DRUNK SOBRIETY    3
      AND DRUNK OR SOBER LIVE AT EASE . . . . . . .        597 MODEL LAUREATE   13
SOBRIETY
      A DRUNKEN MAN'S PRAISE OF SOBRIETY  . . . . . .      591 DRUNK SOBRIETY    T
      SOBRIETY IS A JEWEL . . . . . . . . . . . .          592 DRUNK SOBRIETY    5
SOBS
      WILL HE HAVE HAPPINESS?  GREAT SOBS HER BEING SHAKE. .  676 ISLE STAT II 3  247
SOCIAL
      A HELEN OF SOCIAL WELFARE DREAM, . . . . . . .       626 OLD MEN BE MAD    7
SOCK
      NOW IT HAS FILLED AN OLD SOCK FULL! . . . . . .      301 RUN PARADISE     20
SOCKS
      WHO IS SIX FEET HIGH IN HIS SOCKS AT LEAST? . . . .  729 PRIEST FAIRY     28
SOD       SEE EDEN-SOD
      WHOSE CAREFUL PASTERN PRESSED THE SOD . . . . .        2 OISIN 1      V  7W
      THAT SLOPING GREEN DE DANAAN SOD . . . . . .          20 OISIN 1         299
      EAT AWAY THE SLOPING SOD, . . . . . . . . .           20 OISIN 1      V  299
      AND YOU HAVE GROWN TO BE A BURNING SOD . . . .       245 SHADOW WATER B  487
      THIS SOD HAS BOUND US . . . . . . . . . . .          769 BLOOD BOND        1
SODDEN        SEE BLOOD-SODDEN
SODS
      OR UNDER GREEN SODS LAY. . . . . . . . . . .         132 FR GILLIGAN       4
SOFT
      HER EYES WERE SOFT AS DEWDROPS HANGING  . . . . .      3 OISIN 1      V  7HH
      AS HER SOFT BOSOM ROSE AND FELL. . . . . . . .         4 OISIN 1          30
      PIERCED WITH SOFT LIGHT THE SHALLOWING DEEPS. . . .   13 OISIN 1         164
      AND PONDERED IN A SOFT VAIN MOOD  . . . . . . .       14 OISIN 1         184
      "BUT NEVER THE YEARS IN THE ISLE'S SOFT PLACES  . . . 27 OISIN 1      V 419A
      "BUT NEVER THE YEARS IN OUR ISLE'S SOFT PLACES  . . . 28 OISIN 1    \ V  424
      A LADY WITH SOFT EYES LIKE FUNERAL TAPERS, . . . .    33 OISIN 2          69
      A MAIDEN WITH SOFT EYES LIKE FUNERAL TAPERS, . . . .  33 OISIN 2      V   69
      . . . HIS KNEES IN THE SOFT STAR-FLAME, . . . . .     50 OISIN 3          43
      ARE FACES ALIVE WITH SUCH BEAUTY MADE KNOWN TO THE SOFT 50 OISIN 3     V   51
        EYE OF MAN,
      AND BY ME, IN SOFT RED RAIMENT, THE FENIANS MOVED IN LOUD  53 OISIN 3     93
        STREAMS,
      WERE THE WINDS LESS SOFT THAN THE BREATH OF A PIGEON . . .  56 OISIN 3   134
      . . . AND THEIR YOUTH, AND THEIR EYES SOFT AS SILK. . .  59 OISIN 3   V 176
      FOR LONELY TO MOVE 'MONG THE SOFT EYES . . . . .      63 OISIN 3      V  222
      "WHAT DO YOU WEAVE SO SOFT AND BRIGHT?" . . . . .     69 CLOAK BOAT    V    1
      CONCEIVE A THING SO SAD AND SOFT, A GENTLE THING LIKE ME?  77 INDIAN ON GOD 16
      IN VAIN HER ARMS, IN VAIN HER SOFT WHITE BREAST. . . 110 CUCHULAIN SEA    74
      AND SLOWLY READ, AND DREAM OF THE SOFT LOOK . . . .  121 YOU ARE OLD       3
      WHERE HER SOFT FOOTSTEPS GO. . . . . . . . .         175 ELEMENT POWERS V 18
      BUT SOFT BEAUTY AND INDOLENT DESIRE. . . . . .       181 QUEEN MAEVE      22
      WITH BODIES MADE OUT OF SOFT FIRE.  THE ONE, . . . . 187 QUEEN MAEVE     144
      A MURMUR OF SOFT WORDS AND MEETING LIPS. . . . .     187 QUEEN MAEVE     154
      FOR PROUD, SOFT, CEREMONIOUS PROOF  . . . . . .      386 ROBARTES DANCE   30
      SOFT AS THE RUSTLE OF A REED FROM CLOYNE . . . .     487 SEVEN SAGES      22
```

735

```
                                                              PAGE      TITLE           LINE
SOFT  (CONTINUED)
      INHABITANT OF THE SOFT CHEEK OF A GIRL--   . . . .      540 FROM ANTIGONE         2
      DREAMING IN THEIR SOFT ODOUR-LADEN SLEEP;  . . . . .    650 ISLE STAT I 1       125
      SMALL ISLAND, WHERE THE FULL SOFT SHEEN .  . . . . .    653 ISLE STAT I 2        36
      O WAKE! WAKE! WAKE! FOR SOFT AS A BEE SIPS . . . . .    677 ISLE STAT II 3      276
      OLD WARRIOR, WAKE! FOR SOFT AS A BEE SIPS, . . . . .    677 ISLE STAT II 3      284
      HE IS LONG DEAD.  WAKE! SOFT AS A BEE SIPS . . . . .    678 ISLE STAT II 3      297
      I GO AS SOFT AS FOLLY! I AM FATE."  . . . .            686 LIFE                 18
      BUT HERE THE LIONESS LICKS HER SOFT CUB .  . . . .     688 NETTLESHIP            2
      SOFT AS THE WHISPERING OF A LONG-LOST FOOTSTEP . . .    699 MOSADA 3             5
      SOFT AS A LONG DEAD FOOTSTEP WHISPERING THROUGH . . .   699 MOSADA 3        V    5
      SOFT AS THE WHISPERING OF A LOST FOOTSTEP . . . . .     699 MOSADA 3        V    5
      ABOVE, THE WOODS WHERE WITH THE SOFT MILD EYE .  . .    710 FERENCZ RENYI        26
      AND SOFT, ONE GLIMMERING STAR. RENYI HAS CAST . . .     714 FERENCZ RENYI       115
      AND SOFT, ONE GLIMMERING STAR--WITH POWER VAST! . .     714 FERENCZ RENYI   V   115
      A KID! HELD BY ONE SOFT WHITE EAR FOR TETHER, . . .     715 DWELT SYCAMORE        3
      ILL WORDS FOR ALL THINGS SOFT AND FAIR, . . . . .      723 GIRLS SONG A          6
      I GO AS SOFT AS FOLLY! I AM FATE."  . . . . .          735 QUATRAIN APHOR       20
      AND BODILY TENDERNESS TO THE SOFT FIRE  . . . . .      750 SHADOW WATER A       60
SOFTENING
      PLUNGE, LURED BY A SOFTENING EYE, . . . . . . . .      413 TOWER               110
SOFTER
      SOFTER THAN SNOW-FLAKES IN APRIL AND PIERCING THE MARROW 51 OISIN 3            68
         LIKE FLAME.
      SOFTER THAN SNOWFLAKES IN APRIL, AND PIERCING THE MARROW 51 OISIN 3         V  68
         LIKE FLAME.
SOFTEST
      AND A HUNDRED ROBES OF THE SOFTEST SILK, . . . . .       8 OISIN 1         V   88
SOFTLY
      THEN SIGHED SHE SOFTLY, "LATE! 'TIS LATE! . . . . .      9 OISIN 1         V  102
      LULLED WEARINESS, AND SOFTLY ROUND  . . . . . . .       11 OISIN 1            137
      AND BENDING OVER THEM SOFTLY SAID, . . . . . . .        21 OISIN 1            307
      SANG WE SOFTLY IN THE DANCE, . . . . . . . . . .        21 OISIN 1            308
      SANG WE SOFTLY, "ON THE DEAD, . . . . . . . . . .       21 OISIN 1         V  310
      THEREON YOUNG NIAMH SOFTLY CAME . . . . . . . .         25 OISIN 1            373
      THEN SOFTLY TO ME NIAM CAME, . . . . . . . . . .        25 OISIN 1         V  373
      AND SOFTLY COME TO YOUR NIAMH OVER THE TOPS OF THE TIDE! 55 OISIN 3          126
      AND SOFTLY COME TO THY NIAM OVER THE TOPS OF THE TIDE! . 52 OISIN 3       V  126
      THEN HE SANG SOFTLY NIGH THE PEARLY RIM! . . . . .      69 SAD SHEPHERD        25
      THEN SANG HE SOFTLY NIGH THE PEARLY RIM! . . . . .      69 SAD SHEPHERD    V   25
      MURMURING SOFTLY LIP TO LIP, . . . . . . . . . .        78 INDIAN TO LOVE       8
      ONE WITH THE WAVES THAT SOFTLY ROUND US LAUGH AND DART.  78 INDIAN TO LOVE  V   15
      LEANING SOFTLY OUT . . . . . . . . . . . . . .          88 STOLEN CHILD        35
      AND SOFTLY MAKE A ROSY PEACE, . . . . . . . . .        113 ROSE OF PEACE        15
      TREAD SOFTLY BECAUSE YOU TREAD ON MY DREAMS. . . .      176 CLOTHS HEAVEN        8
      IT BORE ME SOFTLY WHERE THE SHALLOW SAND . . . . .      657 ISLE STAT I 3       58
      SLID CIRCLING DOWN AND SOFTLY TOUCHED MY LIPS . . .     690 MOSADA 1            21
      THEN THE STRANGER SOFTLY CREW-- . . . . . . . .        697 MOSADA 2            28
SOFTNESS
      OR THE SOFTNESS OF YOUTH BE GONE FROM OUR FACES, . .     27 OISIN 1           410
      WILL THE SOFTNESS OF YOUTH BE GONE FROM OUR FACES, . .   27 OISIN 1        V  410
      OR THE SOFTNESS OF YOUTH BE GONE FROM OUR FACES, . .     27 OISIN 1        V 419C
      OR THE SOFTNESS OF YOUTH BE GONE FROM OUR FACES, . .     28 OISIN 1        V  426
      AND A SOFTNESS CAME FROM THE STARLIGHT . . . . .        52 OISIN 3            72
      AND FEEL THE SOFTNESS OF EACH OTHER'S HAND, . . . .     74 ANASHU VIJAYA       57
      AND FEEL THE SOFTNESS OF EACH OTHER'S HANDS, . . . .    74 ANASHU VIJAYA   V   57
SOFT-SHINING
      IN ONE WAS A BRANCH SOFT-SHINING WITH BELLS MORE MANY THAN 50 OISIN 3        46
         SIGHS
SOIL
      MUST COME FROM CONTACT WITH THE SOIL, FROM THAT . . .   603 GALLERY REVIS       43
      DEEP IN HIS SOUL, LIKE RAIN UPON A SOIL . . . . .      692 MOSADA 1            56
SOILED
      HAD TROD THE UNEVEN ROAD. THEIR BOOTS WERE SOILED, . .  372 PHASES OF MOON       3
SOLD
      THAT CARRIED THE TAKE TO SLIGO TOWN TO BE SOLD, . . .    91 OLD FISHERMAN        7
      AND HIM WHO SOLD TILLAGE, AND HOUSE, AND GOODS, . . .   170 SECRET ROSE         22
      A HUSBAND THAT HAD SOLD HIS WIFE . . . . . . . .       587 PARNELLITES         27
      A HUSBAND WHO HAD SOLD HIS WIFE . . . . . . . .        587 PARNELLITES     V   27
      THOSE CHEERS THAT CAN BE BOUGHT OR SOLD, . . . . .     598 MODEL LAUREATE      19
      CRAMM'D ALL HER YOUTH! AND HATES HAVE BOUGHT AND SOLD . 687 TWO TITANS          13
SOLDERED
      NOR SOLDERED POT OR PAN! . . . . . . . . . . .         606 SONGS BURDEN 1      15
SOLDIER
      SOLDIER, SCHOLAR, HORSEMAN, HE, . . . . . . . .        327 ROBERT GREGORY      70
      SOLDIER, SCHOLAR, HORSEMAN, HE, . . . . . . . .        327 ROBERT GREGORY      78
      SOLDIER, SCHOLAR, HORSEMAN, HE, . . . . . . . .        327 ROBERT GREGORY      86
      THAT DEAD YOUNG SOLDIER IN HIS BLOOD! . . . . . .      425 STARES NEST         14
      SOLDIER, ASSASSIN, EXECUTIONER, . . . . . . . .        482 BLOOD AND MOON      36
      THE SOLDIER TAKES PRIDE . . . . . . . . . . .          547 TO SAME TUNE 3 V     T
      THE SOLDIER TAKES PRIDE IN SALUTING HIS CAPTAIN, . .    547 TO SAME TUNE 3       1
      A REVOLUTIONARY SOLDIER KNEELING TO BE BLESSED! . .     601 GALLERY REVIS        8
      THE SOLDIER TAKES PRIDE IN SALUTING HIS CAPTAIN, . .    614 MARCH SONGS 2        1
      LACK NOTHING THAT A SOLDIER NEEDS, . . . . . . .       635 BLACK TOWER          4
      HE WHISPERS TO A SOLDIER, WHO GOES OUT-- . . . .       711 FERENCZ RENYI       44
      RETURNS THAT SOLDIER IN THE EVENING RAYS . . . . .     711 FERENCZ RENYI       49
      THE SOLDIER THUS; AND HAYNAU--"PEASANT, SPEAK . . .     711 FERENCZ RENYI       54
      A SOLDIER ANSWERS:  "BY THE CAMP'S FAR END . . . .     712 FERENCZ RENYI       67
SOLDIER'S
      THE HERALD'S CRY, THE SOLDIER'S TREAD . . . . . .      438 SONGS PLAY 2        13
      AND CLAIM AS BY A SOLDIER'S RIGHT . . . . . . .        478 SELF AND SOUL       31
```

	PAGE	TITLE		LINE

SOLDIERS
```
    SOLDIERS THAT GAVE, WHATEVER DIE WAS CAST!            269 PARDON FATHERS        9
    TRADERS OR SOLDIERS WHO HAVE LEFT ME BLOOD            269 PARDON FATHERS     V  7
    SOLDIERS TAKE PRIDE IN SALUTING THEIR CAPTAIN,        547 TO SAME TUNE 3   V  1
    SOLDIERS TAKE PRIDE IN SALUTING THEIR CAPTAIN,        548 TO SAME TUNE 3       21
    MY KING A LOST KING, AND LOST SOLDIERS MY MEN!        591 WHAT WAS LOST         3
    OF SOLDIERS RANKED IS ON A GRASSY SPOT,               712 FERENCZ RENYI        64
    OF SOLDIERS DRAWN IS ON A GRASSY SPOT,                712 FERENCZ RENYI     V  64
```
SOLDIERY
```
    RIDES UPON SLEEP! A DRUNKEN SOLDIERY                  429 NINETEEN 19          26
    THE EMPEROR'S DRUNKEN SOLDIERY ARE ABED!             497 BYZANTIUM              2
    THE EMPEROR'S DRUNKEN SOLDIERY ARE A-BED!            497 BYZANTIUM          V  2
    HALF-DRUNK OR WHOLE-MAD SOLDIERY                      791 REPRISALS            15
```
SOLE   SEE FOOT-SOLE
```
    FOR YOUR SOLE SAKE--THAT ALL HEART'S ACHE HAVE KNOWN, 355 BROKEN DREAMS         7
    BURDENSOME BEAUTY--FOR YOUR SOLE SAKE                 356 BROKEN DREAMS        10
    WHEN UPWARD TURNED, ON ONE SOLE IMAGE FELL!          471 ALL SOUL NIGHT        34
    FOR NOTHING CAN BE SOLE OR WHOLE                      513 JANE TALK BISH       17
    O'HIGGINS ITS SOLE STATESMAN HAD NOT DIED.           543 PARN FUNERAL 2        8
    MY PAISTIN FINN IS MY SOLE DESIRE,                    550 SONGS REWRIT 1        1
    EVERYTHING DOWN TO THAT SOLE TEST AGAIN,             603 GALLERY REVIS         46
    AND ITS OLD SOLE STRING                               627 STATES HOLIDAY       23
```
SOLEMN
```
    THE MURMURING BIRDS IN SOLEMN POMP                     20 OISIN 1          V 293
    IN SOLEMN REVERIE ROSE TO HEAR                         85 MAD KING GOLL    V  62
    MUCH TOO SOLEMN SEEMED!                               342 SHEP GOATHERD        91
    MUCH TOO SOLEMN AND RESERVED.                         342 SHEP GOATHERD        94
    O, BUT I SAW A SOLEMN SIGHT!                          788 HAWTHORN TREE         1
```
SOLEMN-EYED
```
    THE SOLEMN-EYED!                                       88 STOLEN CHILD         43
```
SOLID
```
    THERE IS A SOLID DIGNITY                              296 THREE BEGGARS    V  37
    AND SOLID MEN, FOR ALL THEIR PASSION, LIVE           325 ROBERT GREGORY       37
    . . . ITS FARROW THAT SO SOLID SEEM,                 481 BLOOD AND MOON       26
    THE SOLID MAN AND THE COXCOMB.                        508 JANE BISHOP           7
    THE SOLID MAN AND THE COXCOMB.                        508 JANE BISHOP          14
    THE SOLID MAN AND THE COXCOMB.                        508 JANE BISHOP          21
    THE SOLID MAN AND THE COXCOMB.                        509 JANE BISHOP          28
```
SOLIDER
```
    THERE CAN BE NOTHING SOLIDER TILL I DIE!             383 VISION ROBART        26
    SOLIDER ARISTOTLE PLAYED THE TAWS                     445 SCHOOL CHILDR        43
```
SOLITARY
```
    BEING HIGH AND SOLITARY AND MOST STERN?              257 NO SECOND TROY       10
    COMPARES THE SOLITARY SOUL TO A SWAN!                430 NINETEEN 19          60
    SELF-BORN, HIGH-BORN, AND SOLITARY TRUTHS,          467 HARUN RASHID        141
    BEGOT! SELF-BORN, HIGH-BORN, AND SOLITARY.          467 HARUN RASHID     V 141
    I SAT, A SOLITARY MAN,                                501 VACILLATION          36
    ONE SOLITARY MAN                                      526 AM OF IRELAND         8
    BY WATER, HERB AND SOLITARY PRAYER                   555 RIBH AT TOMB         23
    OF SOLITARY BEDS, KNEW WHAT THEY WERE,               610 STATUES               5
    THE LION, THE WORLD'S GREAT SOLITARY, BENDS          689 NETTLESHIP            5
    THE SOLITARY FAIRY                                    706 FAIRY PEDANT     V  T
```
SOLITUDE
```
    WONDERING TO LAY HER IN THAT SOLITUDE,               123 DREAM OF DEATH        5
    AND WONDERING PLANTED BY HER SOLITUDE                123 DREAM OF DEATH   V  5
    BEING MORE INDIFFERENT TO OUR SOLITUDE               334 LIVING BEAUTY         7
    IMAGES CAN BREAK THE SOLITUDE                         375 PHASES OF MOON       82
    AND THERE ALONE, THAT HAVE NO SOLITUDE?             398 LEADERS CROWD         9
    BUT BREAK UPON HIS GHOSTLY SOLITUDE.                 429 NINETEEN 19          40
    FOR TRIUMPH CAN BUT MAR OUR SOLITUDE.                431 NINETEEN 19          78
    AND SICK OF SOLITUDE                                  432 NINETEEN 19         105
    GROWN TIRED OF THEIR SOLITUDE,                        432 NINETEEN 19     V 105
    WE THREE MAKE UP A SOLITUDE!                         457 SECRETS OF OLD        9
    THEIR SCHOOL A CROWD, HIS MASTER SOLITUDE!          543 PARN FUNERAL 2       10
    THEIR SCHOOL THE CROWD, HIS MASTER SOLITUDE,        543 PARN FUNERAL 2 V    10
    THEIR SCHOOL A CROWD, HIS MASTER'S SOLITUDE!        543 PARN FUNERAL 2 V    10
    AS MY LONG-PLANNED HALF SOLITUDE,                    624 APPARITIONS          10
    AS MY LONG PLANNED HALF SOLITUDE,                    624 APPARITIONS      V  10
    A STATUE OF SOLITUDE,                                 785 YOUR HEART            4
```
SOLITUDES
```
    THE EVER-SUMMERED SOLITUDES!                          21 OISIN 1             321
    THE EVER SUMMERED SOLITUDES!                          21 OISIN 1          V 321
    OR IN AUTUMNAL SOLITUDES                               84 MAD KING GOLL        39
    OR IN THE AUTUMN SOLITUDES                             84 MAD KING GOLL    V  39
    NOURISH THE PANTHERS IN DIM SOLITUDES!              657 ISLE STAT I 3        44
    TO SEE THEM DROWNED BY THOSE VAST SOLITUDES,        661 ISLE STAT II 1       57
```
SOLOMON
```
    SOLOMON TO SHEBA                                      332 SOLOMON SHEBA         T
    SANG SOLOMON TO SHEBA,                                332 SOLOMON SHEBA         1
    TO SOLOMON SANG SHEBA,                                333 SOLOMON SHEBA         9
    SANG SOLOMON TO SHEBA,                                333 SOLOMON SHEBA        17
    SAID SOLOMON TO SHEBA,                                333 SOLOMON SHEBA    V  17
    THAT SOLOMON GREW WISE                                345 ON WOMAN             11
    AND LIVE LIKE SOLOMON                                 346 ON WOMAN             42
    SOLOMON AND THE WITCH                                 387 SOLOMON WITCH         T
    WITHIN MY ARMS GREAT SOLOMON,                         387 SOLOMON WITCH         4
    GAVE SHEBA TO HER SOLOMON."                           388 SOLOMON WITCH        32
    O! SOLOMON! LET US TRY AGAIN."                       389 SOLOMON WITCH        44
```
SOLSTICE
```
    WORN BY THE SOLSTICE FIERCE, AND MADE IT PURE.       692 MOSADA 1             57
```

```
                                                    PAGE    TITLE          LINE
SOMBRE
     DROPS ON HIS BOSOM, SOMBRE, MOIST AND SLOW.         711  FERENCZ RENYI        40
     UPON HIS BOSOM, SOMBRE, MOIST AND SLOW.             711  FERENCZ RENYI    V   40
     HIS MOODS BOW LOW HIS SOMBRE CREST.                 723  GIRLS SONG A          2
SOME
     BLOSSOM IN SOME NEW CRIMSON FLOWER,                  16  OISIN 1             224
     AND IN SOME GLOOMY BARROW LIE                        19  OISIN 1             272
     AND IN SOME URN FUNEREAL LIE                         19  OISIN 1          V  272
     IN OTHER YEARS FROM SOME OLD STAR                    19  OISIN 1          V  277
     FROM SOME DEAD WARRIOR'S BROKEN LANCE!               24  OISIN 1             367
     IT WAS OF SOME DEAD WARRIOR'S LANCE.                 24  OISIN 1             367
     SOME DANCED LIKE SHADOWS ON THE MOUNTAINS,           25  OISIN 1             388
     SOME WANDERED EVER HAND IN HAND!                     25  OISIN 1             389
     OF SOME FORGOTTEN FIEND.  NOW NONE ASSAILS           31  OISIN 2          V  30B
     IN SOME DIM MEMORY OR ANCIENT MOOD,                  36  OISIN 2              99
     WRAPT ROUND IN SOME DIM MEMORY, IT SEEMED--          36  OISIN 2          V   99
     WE SAW, SOME NEW, SOME PRINTED WHEN THE PLACE WAS YOUNG,  37  OISIN 2             116
     WE SAW, SOME NEW, SOME PRINTED WHEN THE PLACE WAS YOUNG,  37  OISIN 2          V  116
     LEST THEY SHOULD LOOK UPON SOME DREADFUL SIGHT!      38  OISIN 2             142
     STOOD TIMIDLY.  LEST THEY SHOULD SEE SOME SIGHT      38  OISIN 2          V  141
     THAT FEED WHITE MOTHS BY SOME DE DANAAN SHRINE!      41  OISIN 2             186
     FEEDING WHITE MOTHS AROUND SOME EASTERN SHRINE,      41  OISIN 2          V  186
     "LIKE ME WERE SOME GALLEY FORSAKEN FAR OFF IN MERIDIAN   55  OISIN 3             117
       ISLE,
     READING SOME ENTANGLED STORY!                       65  HAPPY SHEPHERD       16
     SOME TWISTED, ECHO-HARBOURING SHELL,                 66  HAPPY SHEPHERD       36
     THEIR HEARING, AND SOME COMFORT GIVE, BUT THEY       68  SAD SHEPHERD     V    6
     SOME OTHER FILLS YOUR MIND.  MY MOTHER'S NAME.       71  ANASHU VIJAYA    V   16
     AND MAY SOME SUDDEN DREADFUL ILL BEFALL HER!         74  ANASHU VIJAYA        59
     AND MAY SOME DREADFUL ILL BEFALL HER QUICK!          74  ANASHU VIJAYA    V   59
     OF SOME INHUMAN MISERY                               85  MAD KING GOLL        58
     OF SOME UNHUMAN MISERY                               85  MAD KING GOLL    V   58
     "AND OF MY SERVANTS SOME ONE GO,                     97  FOXHUNTER        V    5
     AND SOME ONE FROM THE STABLE BRING                   97  FOXHUNTER        V    5
     AND SOME ONE FROM THE STABLES BRING                  97  FOXHUNTER             5
     SOME FEASTING MAN THAT THE SAME OATH HAS BOUND."    108  CUCHULAIN SEA        38
     SOME FEATING MAN THAT THE SAME OATH HAS BOUND."     108  CUCHULAIN SEA    V   38
     AT LAST CUCHULAIN SPAKE, "SOME MAN HAS MADE         109  CUCHULAIN SEA        47
     SOME FEASTING MAN THAT THE SAME OATH HAS BOUND."    109  CUCHULAIN SEA        54
     "SOME FEATING MAN THAT THE SAME OATH HAS BOUND."    109  CUCHULAIN SEA    V   54
     AND I SHALL HAVE SOME PEACE THERE, FOR PEACE COMES DROPPING  117  ISLE INNISFREE        5
       SLOW,
     AND HE HAD KNOWN AT LAST SOME TENDERNESS,           126  DREAM OF FAERY        3
     AND HE HAD KNOWN AT LAST SOME PRUDENT YEARS         127  DREAM OF FAERY       15
     AND PLANNING, PLOTTING ALWAYS THAT SOME MORROW      129  BOOK STORIES         10
     FOR SOME CONSPIRACY,                                131  OLD PENSIONER         8
     TO SOME I HAVE TALKED WITH BY THE FIRE              136  TO SOME I TALK        T
     AND SOME ONE CALLED ME BY MY NAME!                  149  WANDER AENGUS        12
     GATHERED A CROWD IN SOME BYZANTINE LANE,            180  QUEEN MAEVE           2
     TO SOME STRINGED INSTRUMENT NONE THERE HAD SEEN,    180  QUEEN MAEVE           4
     WHO HAS BEEN BURIED SOME TWO THOUSAND YEARS?        181  QUEEN MAEVE          35
     BUT THE HORSE-BOYS SLEPT ON, AS THOUGH SOME POWER   181  QUEEN MAEVE          39
     YOUNG BAILE HONEY-MOUTH, WHOM SOME                  189  BAILE AILLINN        16
     YOUNG BAILE HONEY MOUTH, WHOM SOME                  189  BAILE AILLINN    V   16
     THEIR BODICES IN SOME DIM PLACE                     193  BAILE AILLINN       105
     SOME GOD OR KING HAD MADE THE LAWS                  194  BAILE AILLINN       131
     THEY COME WHERE SOME HUGE WATCHER IS,               196  BAILE AILLINN       168
     FOR THAT BRIEF SIGHING.  IF YOU HAD LOVED SOME WOMAN--  228  SHADOW WATER B      135
     BELIEVED THERE WAS SOME OTHER NEAR AT HAND,         229  SHADOW WATER B      154
     THAT RAISED THEIR HANDS AGAINST HIM.  THERE ARE SOME  235  SHADOW WATER B      291
     SOME OTHER WOMAN HAS A CLAIM ON YOU,                245  SHADOW WATER B      474
     LET'S HOME; I'D GIVE SOME RUBIES TO A WOMAN.        248  SHADOW WATER B      537
     BUT IN SOME ISLAND WHERE THE LIFE OF THE WORLD      249  SHADOW WATER B      559
     TO SOME SURE COUNTRY, SOME FAMILIAR PLACE.          249  SHADOW WATER B      569
     TO SOME SURE COUNTRY, SOME FAMILIAR PLACE,          249  SHADOW WATER B      569
     SOME MAY HAVE BLAMED YOU THAT YOU TOOK AWAY         257  RECONCILIATION        1
     ALL THEIR LIVES THROUGH INTO SOME DRIFT OF WINGS.   265  ABBEY THEATRE         7
     SING ON: SOMEWHERE AT SOME NEW MOON,                266  GALWAY RACES         10
     BUT SOME DAY AND AT SOME NEW MOON                   266  GALWAY RACES         10
     BUT SOME DAY AND AT SOME NEW MOON                   266  GALWAY RACES     V   10
     SING ON:  SOMETIME, AND AT SOME NEW MOON            266  GALWAY RACES     V   10
     OR ON SOME STILL UNEMPTIED CUP                      271  GREY ROCK            21
     SOMEWHERE WITHIN SOME HOLLOW HILL,                  271  GREY ROCK        V   14
     I NEEDS MUST MARRY SOME POOR LOUT,"                 273  GREY ROCK            47
     'TWAS WINE OR WOMEN, OR SOME CURSE--                273  GREY ROCK            54
     I NEED MUST MARRY SOME POOR LOUT,"                  273  GREY ROCK        V   47
     WHO HAD LOST SOME UNIMAGINABLE TREASURE             278  TWO KINGS            40
     SOME PASSION HAD MADE HER STONE.  HEARING A FOOT    279  TWO KINGS            65
     THEN FEARING THAT SOME LABOURER, ON HIS WAY         283  TWO KINGS           145
     LIKE THE EYES OF SOME GREAT KITE SCOURING THE WOODS,  283  TWO KINGS           150
     HAD HALF AWAKENED SOME OLD MEMORY--                 284  TWO KINGS           172
     HAD HALF WAKENED SOME OLD MEMORY,                   284  TWO KINGS        V  172
     WHY MUST I LIVE SOME THIRTY, FORTY YEARS,           285  TWO KINGS           199
     TO BE "SOME SORT OF EVIDENCE",                      287  TO WEALTHY MAN        4
     THAT SOME NEW DAY MAY BREED THE BEST                288  TO WEALTHY MAN       34
     YOU'D CRY, "SOME WOMAN'S YELLOW HAIR                290  SEPTEMBER 1913       28
     FOR SOME TRIVIAL AFFAIR                             293  HELEN LIVED           3
     INTO SOME MOST FEARFUL SHAPE."                      299  THREE HERMITS        23
     IN SOME OUTLANDISH COAT BESIDE                      303  HOUR DAWN        V   28
     LIKE SOME OLD RABBIT TO MY CLEFT                    307  HOUR DAWN           105
     LIKE SOME LAST COURTIER AT A GYPSY CAMPING-PLACE    314  FALLEN MAJESTY        3
```

		PAGE	TITLE		LINE

SOME   (CONTINUED)

	PAGE	TITLE		LINE
LIKE SOME LAST COURTIER AT A GYPSY CAMPING PLACE	314	FALLEN MAJESTY	V	3
DELIGHT MEN'S EYES WHEN I AWAKE SOME DAY	323	SWANS AT COOLE		29
AND HAVING TALKED TO SOME LATE HOUR	324	ROBERT GREGORY		4
OUT OF SOME OLD PICTURE-BOOK!	325	ROBERT GREGORY		44
OUT OF SOME OLD PICTURE BOOK!	325	ROBERT GREGORY	V	44
SOME BURN DAMP FAGGOTS, OTHERS MAY CONSUME	327	ROBERT GREGORY		81
WITH SOME APPROPRIATE COMMENTARY ON EACH;	328	ROBERT GREGORY		93
SOME MEDICABLE HERB TO MAKE OUR GRIEF	342	SHEP GOATHERD		86
AT SOME OLD WINDING WHITETHORN ROOT	342	SHEP GOATHERD		101
OR PUT HIS HEART INTO SOME GAME	343	SHEP GOATHERD		105
AND ALL BECAUSE OF SOME ONE	346	ON WOMAN		40
A WOMAN SPOKE OF SOME NEW TALE SHE HAD READ,	350	HER PRAISE		7
AS THOUGH SOME OTHER NAME RAN IN HIS HEAD.	351	HER PRAISE		9
SOME BEGGAR SHELTERING FROM THE WIND, AND THERE	351	HER PRAISE		13
OF SOME STRANGE WOMAN'S NAME THAT RAN IN HIS HEAD.	351	HER PRAISE	V	9
THOSE I HAD SERVED AND SOME THAT I HAD FED!	352	PEOPLE		27
AND WHO CAN SAY BUT SOME YOUNG BELLE MAY WALK AND TALK MEN WILD	354	HIS PHOENIX		26
AND MAY BE THERE'LL BE SOME YOUNG BELLE WALK OUT TO MAKE MEN WILD	354	HIS PHOENIX	V	26
AND MAYBE THERE'LL BE SOME YOUNG BELLE WALK OUT TO MAKE MEN WILD	354	HIS PHOENIX	V	26
BUT MAYBE SOME OLD GAFFER MUTTERS A BLESSING	355	BROKEN DREAMS		4
OVER SOME SILKEN DRESS	363	DOLLS DRAWINGS		7
BECAUSE TO-DAY IS SOME RELIGIOUS FESTIVAL	363	DOLLS FACES		1
WHO HAD SEEMED TO GLIDE TO SOME INTRIGUE IN HER RED SHOES,	363	DOLLS FACES		6
SHOWS HER THAT SOME ONE SOON	364	END OF DAY		5
THAT MADE HER DIARMUID DEAR, AND SOME OLD CARDINAL	366	HER COURAGE		6
AND THAT MADE HER DERMUID DEAR, AND SOME OLD CARDINAL	366	HER COURAGE	V	6
THAT DREAM IS A NORM; AND SHOULD SOME LIMB OF THE DEVIL	372	ON GOING HOUSE		12
OR FROM SOME BLOODY WHIP IN THEIR OWN HANDS.	375	PHASES OF MOON		68
BUT TAKE ME FOR SOME DRUNKEN COUNTRYMAN!	377	PHASES OF MOON		130
BUT TAKE ME FOR SOME DRUNKEN COUNTRY MAN!	377	PHASES OF MOON	V	130
SOME DAY I MAY FORGET!	380	SONGS FOOL 1		8
OBEDIENT TO SOME HIDDEN MAGICAL BREATH.	382	VISION ROBART		13
TO FIND OUT SOME APPROPRIATE PAIN--	388	SOLOMON WITCH		20
WILL FIND OUT SOME APPROPRIATE PAIN,	388	SOLOMON WITCH	V	20
IMAGINE THAT SOME LOST LOVE, UNASSAILABLE	390	UNDER SATURN	V	2
TO SOME WHO ARE NEAR MY HEART,	393	EASTER 1916		34
"SOME POLITICIANS IDLE WORDS	396	ROSE TREE	V	3
HER THOUGHT SOME POPULAR ENMITY!	397	POLIT PRISONER		10
UPON SOME LOFTY ROCK TO STARE	397	POLIT PRISONER		21
FOR THOUGHT SOME POPULAR ENMITY,	397	POLIT PRISONER	V	10
SURELY SOME REVELATION IS AT HAND;	402	SECOND COMING		9
O MAY SHE LIVE LIKE SOME GREEN LAUREL	405	FOR DAUGHTER		47
SOME FEW REMEMBERED STILL WHEN I WAS YOUNG	410	TOWER		33
COWARDICE, SOME SILLY OVER-SUBTLE THOUGHT	413	TOWER		117
FROM SOME GREAT LABYRINTH OUT OF PRIDE,	413	TOWER		116
COWARDICE, OVER SOME SILLY SUBTLE THOUGHT	413	TOWER	V	117
AS IF SOME MARVELLOUS EMPTY SEA-SHELL FLUNG	417	ANCEST HOUSES		13
SOME VIOLENT BITTER MAN, SOME POWERFUL MAN	418	ANCEST HOUSES		17
SOME VIOLENT BITTER MAN; SOME POWERFUL MAN	418	ANCEST HOUSES		17
IN SOME LIKE CHAMBER, SHADOWING FORTH	419	MY HOUSE		15
SOME FOURTEEN DAYS OF CIVIL WAR;	425	STARES NEST		12
INTO THE HALF-DECEIT OF SOME INTOXICANT	429	NINETEEN 19		34
SOME MORALIST OR MYTHOLOGICAL POET	430	NINETEEN 19		59
SOME PLATONIST AFFIRMS THAT IN THE STATION	431	NINETEEN 19		72
TO LEAVE SOME MONUMENT BEHIND,	432	NINETEEN 19		96
SOME FEW HAVE HANDSOME RIDERS, ARE GARLANDED	432	NINETEEN 19		114
UPON SOME BRAND-NEW HAPPY DAY!	432	NINETEEN 19	V	106
AND SHOULD SOME CRAZY HAND DARE TOUCH A DAUGHTER	433	NINETEEN 19		122
SOME THERE ARE, FOR I AVOW	435	FOR MY SON		10
OF SOME MOST HAUGHTY DEED OR THOUGHT	436	FOR MY SON		13
BY SOME PEASANT GOSPELLER!	440	WISDOM		5
WHEN SOME PEASANT GOSPELLER	440	WISDOM		5
BECAUSE OF SOME GREEN WING, GATHERED OLD MUMMY WHEAT	442	BLACK CENTAUR		7
THAT CHANGED SOME CHILDISH DAY TO TRAGEDY--	443	SCHOOL CHILDR		12
ABOVE A SINKING FIRE, SOME TALE THAT SHE	443	SCHOOL CHILDR		10
I WILL FIND OUT SOME CAVERN IN THE HILLS	448	HERO GIRL FOOL	V	11
ARE GONE AWAY, AND SOME THAT STAY	458	HIS WILDNESS		5
THE PARCHMENT WILL DISCLOSE TO SOME LEARNED MAN	461	HARUN RASHID		20
OR BRIGHTEN ONLY FOR SOME YOUNGER EYE,	464	HARUN RASHID		82
ITSELF AND NOT SOME OTHER SOUL." "THAT LOVE	465	HARUN RASHID		94
ITSELF AND NOT SOME OTHER SOUL. "SUCH LOVE	465	HARUN RASHID	V	94
PERCHED IN SOME WINDOW OF HER MOTHER'S HOUSE	466	HARUN RASHID		106
IMAGINED SOME IMPOSSIBLE HISTORY	466	HARUN RASHID		109
WERE SOME DEAR CHEEK. UPON A MOONLESS NIGHT	466	HARUN RASHID		127
WERE SOME DEAR FACE. UPON A MOONLESS NIGHT	466	HARUN RASHID	V	127
OR WAS IT SHE THAT SPOKE OR SOME GREAT DJINN?	467	HARUN RASHID		135
EVEN TO-DAY, AFTER SOME SEVEN YEARS	468	HARUN RASHID		161
EVEN TODAY, AFTER SOME SEVEN YEARS	468	HARUN RASHID	V	161
I NEED SOME MIND THAT, IF THE CANNON SOUND	471	ALL SOUL NIGHT		11
BY SOME LEARNED INDIAN	472	ALL SOUL NIGHT		53
SOME VAGUE UTOPIA--AND SHE SEEMS,	475	EVA GORE-BOOTH		11
FROM SOME COURT-LADY'S DRESS AND ROUND	477	SELF AND SOUL		14
FROM SOME COURT-LADIES' DRESS AND ROUND	477	SELF AND SOUL	V	14
SOME FOUND A DIFFERENT POLE, AND WHERE IT STOOD	483	VERONIC NAPKIN		7
LIKE SOME POOR ARAB TRIBESMAN AND HIS TENT.	491	COOLE BALLYLEE		40
THAT FEED ON SOME FOUL PARASITE	493	AT ALGECIRAS		2
THAT FEEDS ON SOME FOUL PARASITE	493	AT ALGECIRAS	V	2

739

SOME   (CONTINUED)
    ROSE! SOME CONQUEROR DREW REIN . . . .   502 VACILLATION   64
    SOME STUPID THING THAT I HAD DONE . . . .   507 STREAM AND SUN   4
    NOT IN SOME FOUL STY." . . . .   513 JANE TALK BISH   6
    WHEN SHE, AND THOUGH SOME SAID SHE PLAYED . . . . . .   514 JANE GROWN OLD   8
    INTO SOME LESSER THING. . . . .   517 HER ANXIETY   5
    BY SOME NEW-MARRIED BRIDE, I TAKE . . . .   535 CHOSEN   13
    BY SOME NEW MARRIED BRIDE I TAKE . . . .   535 CHOSEN   V   13
    CUT OUT HIS HEART. SOME MASTER OF DESIGN . . . . . .   541 PARN FUNERAL 1   14
    SOME BACK A MARE THROWN FROM A THOROUGHBRED, ...   547 TO SAME TUNE 3   3
    SOME TAKE DELIGHT IN ADORNING A WOMAN. . . . .   547 TO SAME TUNE 3 V   3
    SOME BACK A MARE THROWN FROM A THOROUGH-BRED, ...   547 TO SAME TUNE 3 V   3
    GODHEAD. SOME SHADOW FELL. MY SOUL FORGOT . . . . .   557 RIBH ECSTASY   6
    SOME ANCIENT FAMOUS AUTHORS MISREPRESENT, ...   579 DOR WELLESLEY   15
    THAT SOME AMENDS BE MADE . . . .   582 ROGER CASEMENT   22
    BUT FOR WHAT SOME TRAVELLING MAN . . . .   585 ORAHILLY   21
    "THAT SOME STREAM OF LIGHTNING . . . .   589 OLD WICKED MAN   55
    I FASTED FOR SOME FORTY DAYS ON BREAD AND BUTTERMILK, . . 592 PILGRIM   1
    SOME TWENTY FEET FROM TIP TO TIP HAD IT STRETCHED RIGHTLY 593 PILGRIM   17
        OUT,
    SOME TWENTY FEET FROM TIP TO TIP HAD ITS WINGS STRETCHED   593 PILGRIM   V   17
        RIGHTLY OUT,
    SOME BOAST OF BEGGAR-KINGS AND KINGS . . . .   597 MODEL LAUREATE   5
    SOME THAT BEING UNBEGOTTEN . . . .   600 SPIRIT MEDIUM   11
    BUT COPY SOME ONE ACTION. . . . .   600 SPIRIT MEDIUM   13
    FOR TWENTY MINUTES IN SOME STUDIO. . . . .   602 GALLERY REVIS   16
    AS THOUGH SOME BALLAD-SINGER HAD SUNG IT ALL! . . . .   602 GALLERY REVIS   24
    AS THOUGH SOME BALLAD SINGER HAD SUNG IT ALL. . . . .   602 GALLERY REVIS V   24
    IN SOME GOOD COMPANY, ...   605 YOU CONTENT   18
    SOME HAD NO THOUGHT OF VICTORY . . . .   608 SONGS BURDEN 3   19
    AND PRESSED AT MIDNIGHT IN SOME PUBLIC PLACE . . . .   610 STATUES   7
    UNTIL, IN SOME CLIFF-SHELTERED BAY . . . .   612 NEWS ORACLE   21
    SOME BACK A MARE THROWN FROM A THOROUGHBRED, ...   614 MARCH SONGS 2   3
    SOME FEW HALF WAKE AND HALF RENEW THEIR CHOICE, . . .   622 HOUND VOICE   6
    SOME DAY WE SHALL GET UP BEFORE THE DAWN . . . . . .   622 HOUND VOICE   15
    SOME ROGUE OF THE WORLD STOLE THEM TO PATCH UP A FENCE   623 HIGH TALK   4
        OR A FIRE.
    WITH SOME FRIEND THAT HAS THE WIT . . . .   624 APPARITIONS   12
    WITH SOME FRIEND WHO HAS THE WIT . . . .   624 APPARITIONS   V   12
    SOME HAVE KNOWN A LIKELY LAD . . . .   625 OLD MEN BE MAD   2
    SOME THINK IT A MATTER OF COURSE THAT CHANCE . . . . .   626 OLD MEN BE MAD   9
    SOME THINK IT MATTER OF COURSE THAT CHANCE . . . . .   626 OLD MEN BE MAD V   9
    SOME KNEW WHAT AILED THE WORLD . . . .   627 STATES HOLIDAY   9
    A KING HAD SOME BEAUTIFUL COUSINS, ...   628 JANE MOUNTAIN   7
    UP THERE SOME HAWK OR OWL HAS STRUCK, ...   633 MAN AND ECHO   43
    WITH SOME SORT OF VIOLENCE . . . .   638 BEN BULBEN   34
    DANCING IN SOME MOONY PLACE. . . . .   647 ISLE STAT I 1   54
    SOME OLD MISER TELLS HIS STORE! . . . .   647 ISLE STAT I 1   58
    A HORN! SOME TROOP OF ROBBERS WINDING GOES . . . . .   649 ISLE STAT I 1   110
    SINGING OF ARMS AND BATTLES SOME OLD STAVE, ...   650 ISLE STAT I 1   137
    SHEEP-GUIDING, OR THE BRINGING SOME STRANGE BIRD, . .   650 ISLE STAT I 1   147
    OR SOME SMALL BEAST MOST WONDERFULLY FURR'D, ...   650 ISLE STAT I 1   148
    SOME SAY THAT ALL WHO TOUCH THE ISLAND LONE . . . . .   653 ISLE STAT I 2   42
    AS SOME DEAD MAIDEN'S SINGING IN A DREAM. . . . . .   654 ISLE STAT I 2   59
    SOME BARBAROUS, UN-FAERY THING DRAW NEAR. . . . . . .   656 ISLE STAT I 3   21
    EACH SHINING CLEAR AS SOME UNBAFFLED STAR! . . . . .   656 ISLE STAT I 3   25
    UNLESS SOME PITYING GOD SHALL SUCCOUR ME . . . . . .   656 ISLE STAT I 3   36
    IN THIS MY CHOICE. SOME GOD MIGHT HELP! IF SO . . .   656 ISLE STAT I 3   37
    SOME CAST OF DIE, OR LET SOME ARROW GLANCE . . . . .   656 ISLE STAT I 3   40
    SOME CAST OF DIE, OR LET SOME ARROW GLANCE . . . . .   656 ISLE STAT I 3   40
    SHALL NOT SO HOPELESS PROVE! SOME GOD MAY REST . . .   657 ISLE STAT I 3   61
    SOME GOBLIN, MY SERVANT, ON WINGS THAT ARE FLEET, . .   657 ISLE STAT I 3   67
    CURVING BENEATH THE PROW! AS SOME WILD DRAKE . . . .   659 ISLE STAT II 1   16
    ONCE MORE THOSE SHEPHERDS COME. MAYHAP SOME MIRTH . .   664 ISLE STAT II 2   49
    THE FLOWER, SAVE SOME THING BE FOUND . . . .   668 ISLE STAT II 3   51
    IT IS MY WHIM! BID SOME ATTENDANT SPRITE . . . . . .   669 ISLE STAT II 3   72
    AND CROUCH IN SOME FAR STILLNESS OF THE ISLE, AND DIE. . 675 ISLE STAT II 3   246
    EVE-SOOTHED IN SOME FAR LEAFY REST, ...   686 LIFE   10
    SLEEP IN SOME FAR OTHER FIELD . . . .   705 DAWN-SONG   3
    OFTEN HE HAD BENT DOWN SOME BOUGH ALL BRIGHT . . . . .   710 FERENCZ RENYI   28
    OFTEN HE HAD BENT DOWN SOME BOUGH ALL BRIGHT WITH BERRIES! 710 FERENCZ RENYI V   28
    LEST HE MAY SOME GLAMOUR FOLD . . . .   717 FAIRY DOCTOR   22
    LEST SOME GLAMOUR HE MAY FOLD . . . .   717 FAIRY DOCTOR V   22
    THEN EACH WIFE AND MAID AND MOTHER CALLS BY NAME   719 PHANTOM SHIP   24
        SOME DROWNED ONE.
    OBEYS. SOME FIERCE MAGICIAN FLIES OR WALKS . . . . .   720 WITCH VIVIEN   9
    SOME GREAT ONE. NO! I HEAR THE WAVERING STEPS . . .   720 WITCH VIVIEN   12
    I DREAMT SOME GREAT ONE. AH, MY BEAUTIFUL, ...   720 WITCH VIVIEN   14
    SOME DAY YOU'LL BUY THEM, MAYBE. NEVER! NEVER? . . .   721 WITCH VIVIEN   24
    THERE WAS SOME TALKING OF THE POOR-- . . . .   725 LEGEND   14
    THERE WAS SOME TALKING OF MAN'S GOD, ...   725 LEGEND   19
    HE'D FIND FOR THIS SOME HOLY TEXT. . . . .   728 PRIEST FAIRY   16
    MAYBE NOW IN SOME FAR LANE. . . . .   731 STREET DANCERS   14
    MAYBE IN SOME ISLE OF ISLES, ...   732 STREET DANCERS   27
    OR LEAVE SOME SERVICE ALL UNDONE, ...   743 DANAAN QUICK   21
    OF SOME MILD WOMAN, OR IN CHILDREN'S WAYS. . . . . .   750 SHADOW WATER A   74
    AND NO MAN KILL ME! FOR SOME WIND HAS BLOWN . . . . .   751 SHADOW WATER A   97
    THEIR HAIR MINGLES ON SOME STRINGED INSTRUMENT, . . .   752 SHADOW WATER A   123
    WITH SOME YOU HAVE KILLED AND DIE! FOR WHEN I LEFT . .   758 SHADOW WATER A V 226
    TO CRY HIS FOLDING CRY. THERE IS SOME MAN . . . . .   760 SHADOW WATER A V 253
    AND, HURRYING HOMEWARD, FALL UPON SOME LAND . . . . .   767 SHADOW WATER A   384

SOME   (CONTINUED)
    WHERE SOME LAUGHING ELEMENT . . . .   777 SONG DEIRDRE 2   4
    SOME ONE SHOULD STAY AT HER SIDE. . . . .   786 YOUR HEART   V   28
    SOME NINETEEN GERMAN PLANES, THEY SAY, ...   791 REPRISALS   1
SOMEBODY
    FOR SOMEBODY HID HATRED AND HOPE AND DESIRE AND FEAR . .   153 CHANGE BELOVED   4
    WITH SOMEBODY IN YOUR OWN LAND." . . . .   191 BAILE AILLINN   59
    THAT SOMEBODY HAD DRUNK DRY. . . . .   215 HAPPY TOWNLAND   32
    BUT YOU WERE SAYING THERE IS SOMEBODY . . . . .   240 SHADOW WATER B   380
    THERE'S SOMEBODY I'D GIVE THE AMETHYST EYES TO.   248 SHADOW WATER B   538
    AND SOMEBODY PUTS HIS HAND IN THE DISH . . . . .   301 RUN PARADISE   5
    FROM SOMEBODY THAT TOILS FROM CHAIR TO CHAIR; . . 491 COOLE BALLYLEE   26
    FOR I AM CERTAIN SOMEBODY IS DEAD. . . . . . .   760 SHADOW WATER A   254
SOMEHOW
    SOMEWHERE OR SOMEHOW THAT I HAVE FORGOT, ...   258 KING NO KING   6
SOMEONE
    AND SOMEONE CALLED ME BY MY NAME. . . . .   149 WANDER AENGUS V   12
    SHOWS HER THAT SOMEONE SOON . . . .   364 END OF DAY   V   5
    WHAT IS THIS SACRIFICE? CAN SOMEONE THERE . . . . 541 PARN FUNERAL 1   6
SOMETHING
    BUT SOMETHING RUSTLED ON THE FLOOR, ...   149 WANDER AENGUS   11
    BUT SOMETHING RUSTLED ON THE STOOL, ...   149 WANDER AENGUS V   11
    BECAUSE OF SOMETHING TOLD UNDER THE FAMISHED HORN 210 UNDER THE MOON   17
    BECAUSE OF SOMETHING I HEARD OF UNDER THE THIN HORN . . 210 UNDER THE MOON V 17
    FOR I AM GETTING ON IN LIFE--TO SOMETHING . . . . 222 SHADOW WATER B   6
    IF SOMETHING THAT'S MOST FABULOUS WERE TRUE-- . . 245 SHADOW WATER B   489
    OUT OF MY HEART. THERE'S SOMETHING AILS OUR COLT   260 FASC DIFFICULT   4
    OR SOMETHING OF THAT SORT HE SAID, ...   338 TOM OROUGHLEY   14
    SOMETHING HAS TROUBLED ME AND IN MY TROUBLE . .   339 SHEP GOATHERD   10
    IN SOMETHING THAT ALL OTHERS UNDERSTAND OR SHARE; 427 PHANTOM HATRED   35
    SOMETHING OF EVERY PADDLER'S HERITAGE-- . . . .   444 SCHOOL CHILDR   21
    A SOMETHING INCOMPATIBLE WITH LIFE; AND POWER,   482 BLOOD AND MOON   50
    BUT SOMETHING IS RECALLED, ...   501 VACILLATION   55
    BUT SOMETHING BORE THEM OUT OF SIGHT . . . . . .   519 HER DREAM   5
    SOMETHING MADE THESE EYEBALLS WEARY . . . . . .   529 TOM LUNATIC   11
    SOMETHING TO PERFECTION BROUGHT"! . . . .   577 WHAT THEN   19
    AND THAT IS SOMETHING NEW! . . . .   582 ROGER CASEMENT   12
    (SOMETHING MAY LINGER THERE THOUGH ALL ELSE DIE!) 609 IN TARAS HALLS   4
    I HAVE FOUND SOMETHING WORSE . . . .   618 BRONZE HEAD   5
    SOMETHING DROPS FROM EYES LONG BLIND, ...   628 JANE MOUNTAIN   5
    WHEN SOMETHING FOLDED AND SMALL . . . .   638 BEN BULBEN   29
    WHEN SOMETHING THAT WAS BEARDED LIKE A GOAT . .   744 GLOVE CLOAK   7
    WHEN SOMETHING, HALF A LAMB AND HALF A GOAT, . .   747 SHADOW WATER A   11
    SHE WILL SAY SOMETHING IN A LITTLE WHILE, . . .   747 SHADOW WATER A V   11
    BUT FAITHFUL LOVERS. SOMETHING GLITTERS THERE--   760 SHADOW WATER A   248
                                                       763 SHADOW WATER A   309
SOMETIME
    SING ON! SOMETIME, AND AT SOME NEW MOON . . . .   266 GALWAY RACES   V   10
SOMETIMES
    AND SOMETIMES FROM THE SALTIN' SHED . . . . . .   94 MOLL MAGEE   9
    AND SOMETIMES I AM SURE SHE KNOWS . . . .   96 MOLL MAGEE   49
    WHY THEY WHO WILL THE HIGHEST SOMETIMES BROOD,   711 FERENCZ RENYI   34
SOMEWHAT
    THOUGH SOMEWHAT BROKEN BY THE LEAVES, THAT LIGHT   555 RIBH AT TOMB   25
SOMEWHERE
    "YET SOMEWHERE UNDER STARLIGHT OR THE SUN . . .   107 CUCHULAIN SEA   28
    "NO, SOMEWHERE UNDER DAYLIGHT OR THE STARS . . .   107 CUCHULAIN SEA V   25
    SANG THAT SOMEWHERE TO NORTH OR WEST OR SOUTH .   127 DREAM OF FAERY   19
    SANG HOW SOMEWHERE TO NORTH OR EAST OR SOUTH . .   127 DREAM OF FAERY V   19
    SANG HOW SOMEWHERE TO NORTH OR WEST OR SOUTH . .   127 DREAM OF FAERY V   19
    MUST BE SUBSTANTIAL SOMEWHERE. I HAVE HEARD THE DRUIDS 229 SHADOW WATER B 162
    OR SOMEWHERE, I SHALL FIND THE LOVE THEY HAVE PROMISED. 231 SHADOW WATER B 208
    SOMEWHERE OR SOMEHOW THAT I HAVE FORGOT. . . . .   258 KING NO KING   6
    SING ON! SOMEWHERE AT SOME NEW MOON, ...   266 GALWAY RACES   10
    SOMEWHERE IN EAR-SHOT FOR THE STORY'S END, . . .   269 PARDON FATHERS   2
    SOMEWHERE WITHIN SOME HOLLOW HILL. . . . . . .   271 GREY ROCK   V   14
    WHO'S BURROWING SOMEWHERE IN THE GROUND, ...   272 GREY ROCK   33
    IT'S CERTAIN THERE ARE TROUT SOMEWHERE . . . . .   297 THREE BEGGARS   66
    "TIME TO PUT OFF THE WORLD AND GO SOMEWHERE . .   299 BEGGAR CRIED   1
    SOMEWHERE AMONG THE CLOUDS ABOVE; . . . .   328 IRISH AIRMAN   2
    TROUBLES MY SIGHT; SOMEWHERE IN SANDS OF THE DESERT   402 SECOND COMING   13
    WHO'D LIVED SOMEWHERE UPON THAT ROCKY PLACE, . .   410 TOWER   35
    FROM SOMEWHERE IN THE NEIGHBOURING COTTAGES. . .   411 TOWER   59
    ON OUR UNCERTAINTY! SOMEWHERE . . . .   425 STARES NEST   7
    SOMEWHERE BEYOND THE CURTAIN . . . .   504 QUARREL IN AGE   12
    ARE SOMEWHERE SLEEPING LIKE A TOP . . . .   525 DANCING DAYS   13
    SOMEWHERE OFF HENRY STREET! . . . .   585 ORAHILLY   31
    YET SOMEWHERE IN THE FOOTSORE WORLD WE MEET, . .   691 MOSADA 1   23
SON
    THAT I MIGHT HAVE YOUR SON TO KISS." . . . . .   6 OISIN 1   59
    "WERE THERE NO BETTER THAN MY SON . . . .   6 OISIN 1   60
    OF OISIN, THE YOUNG MAN, MY SON?" . . . .   6 OISIN 1   V   60
    BY THIS YOUNG MAN, USHEEN MY SON?" . . . . . .   6 OISIN 1   V   60
    PRINCESS, BY THIS YOUNG MAN, MY SON?" . . . . .   6 OISIN 1   V   61
    ON THIS YOUNG MAN, OISIN, MY SON?" . . . . . .   6 OISIN 1   V   61
    SHE SMOTE WITH RADDLED FIST, AND WHERE HER SON   106 CUCHULAIN SEA   18
    AND WHERE HER SON, FINMOLE, ON THE SMOOTH GRASS   106 CUCHULAIN SEA V   18
    AND CRIED OUT TO HIM, "SON IT IS NOT MEET . . .   107 CUCHULAIN SEA   20
    AND CALLED OUT TO HIM, "SON IT IS NOT MEET . . .   107 CUCHULAIN SEA V   20
    "NAY, YOU ARE TALLER THAN CUCHULAIN, SON." . . .   107 CUCHULAIN SEA V   27
    "CUCHULAIN I, MIGHTY CUCHULAIN'S SON." . . . . .   110 CUCHULAIN SEA   68

	PAGE	TITLE		LINE
SON (CONTINUED)				
"I AM FINMOLE, MIGHTY CUCHULAIN'S SON."	110	CUCHULAIN SEA	V	68
ON THE HEIR OF ULADH, BUAN'S SON,	189	BAILE AILLINN		4
THERE WAS NO MOTHER'S SON BUT SAID,	253	HIS DREAM		6
MURROUGH, THE KING OF IRELAND'S SON,	274	GREY ROCK		71
SEEING, KING'S SON, WHAT WOUNDS YOU HAVE."	275	GREY ROCK		94
FOR HE AND THE KING'S SON WERE DEAD.	275	GREY ROCK		97
HAS MADDENED EVERY MOTHER'S SON"	290	SEPTEMBER 1913		29
BUT NOT THAT MY DEAR FRIEND'S DEAR SON,	325	ROBERT GREGORY		46
HIS SON GEORGE, THE ASTROLOGER;	360	ALF POLLEXFEN		8
MANY A SON AND DAUGHTER LIES	360	ALF POLLEXFEN		13
AND YESTERDAY THE YOUNGEST SON,	361	ALF POLLEXFEN		24
THE COARSE-BRED SON OF A LIVERY-STABLE KEEPER--	370	EGO DOMINUS		61
THE ILL-BRED SON OF A LIVERY STABLE KEEPER--	370	EGO DOMINUS	V	61
THE ILL-BRED SON OF A LIVERY STABLE-KEEPER--	370	EGO DOMINUS	V	61
FROM FATHER UNTO SON	421	MY TABLE		19
A PRAYER FOR MY SON	435	FOR MY SON		T
WOULD THINK HER SON, DID SHE BUT SEE THAT SHAPE	444	SCHOOL CHILDR		37
LIFT, EVERY MOTHER'S SON,	548	TO SAME TUNE 3	V	15
. . . MAN, WOMAN, CHILD (A DAUGHTER OR A SON),	556	RIBH PATRICK		2
RECALL HIS TRINITY. A FATHER, MOTHER, CHILD (A DAUGHTER OR A SON)	556	RIBH PATRICK	V	2
A SMALL OLD HOUSE, WIFE, DAUGHTER, SON,	577	WHAT THEN		12
AND THAT SHOULD MOTHER SEEK HER SON SHE'D HAVE BUT LITTLE LUCK	593	PILGRIM		12
AUGUSTA GREGORY'S SON! HER SISTER'S SON,	602	GALLERY REVIS		21
AUGUSTA GREGORY'S SON! HER SISTER'S SON,	602	GALLERY REVIS		21
I CALL ON THOSE THAT CALL ME SON,	604	YOU CONTENT		1
NO, NO, MY SON, NOT YET!	614	MARCH SONGS 2		8
NO, NO, MY SON, NOT YET!	615	MARCH SONGS 2		18
NO, NO, MY SON, NOT YET!	615	MARCH SONGS 2		28
THAT ANCIENT MOTHER CRIES, "SPEAK NOT, MY SON.	711	FERENCZ RENYI		56
HUSH'D THE FISHERS, TILL A MOTHER CALLS BY NAME HER DROWNED SON;	719	PHANTOM SHIP		23
NOT I, NOR MAINE THERE, NOR DUACH'S SON.	748	SHADOW WATER A		22
LIKE SON TO FATHER.	769	BLOOD BOND	V	2
LIKE SON TO FATHER.	770	BLOOD BOND		3
SONG SEE LOVE-SONG MARRIAGE-SONG DAWN-SONG				
I NE'ER LOVED ANY TILL SONG BROUGHT ME	7	OISIN 1	V	69
AS THUS OUR SONG AROSE! "YOU STARS,	22	OISIN 1		329
AS THUS OUR SONG AROSE! "YE STARS,	22	OISIN 1	V	329
TROUBLED HER SONG. I DO NOT KNOW IF DAYS	30	OISIN 2		19
BUT NOW THE LYING CLERICS MURDER SONG	42	OISIN 2		196
PATRICK, BEFORE THY CRAFT DIES EACH OLD SONG.	42	OISIN 2		196
AND NEVER A SONG SANG NIAMH, AND OVER MY FINGER-TIPS	47	OISIN 3		6
. . . WITH RED LIPS MURMURING A SONG,	58	OISIN 3	V	158
THE SONG OF THE HAPPY SHEPHERD	64	HAPPY SHEPHERD		T
SONG OF THE LAST ARCADIAN	64	HAPPY SHEPHERD	V	T
AN INDIAN SONG	77	INDIAN TO LOVE	V	T
OF MY LONG SPEAR WITH SONG AND LAUGH	84	MAD KING GOLL	V	34
AND SONG THAT DOWN THE VALLEYS ROLLED--	84	MAD KING GOLL	V	35
AND SONG THAT DOWN THE VALLEY ROLLED--	84	MAD KING GOLL	V	35
THE SONG OF OUTLAWS AND THEIR FEAR!	85	MAD KING GOLL	V	64
AN OLD SONG RE-SUNG	90	SALLEY GARDENS	V	T
A SONG INTO THE AIR, AND SINGING PASSED	114	ROSE OF BATTLE		14
A SONG INTO THE AIR, AND SINGING PAST	114	ROSE OF BATTLE	V	14
A FAERY SONG	115	FAERY SONG		T
A CRADLE SONG	118	CRADLE SONG		T
AND THE LOUD SONG OF THE EVER-SINGING LEAVES	120	SORROW OF LOVE	V	3
SONG	124	CATHLEEN PARA	V	T
MURMURING A WIZARD SONG FOR THEE.	134	TWO TREES		12
BALLAD AND STORY, RANN AND SONG!	137	TO IRELAND		4
O'DRISCOLL DROVE WITH A SONG	143	HOST OF AIR		1
TWO POEMS CONCERNING PEASANT VISIONARIES A CRADLE SONG	146	UNAPPEAS HOST	V	T
THE SONG OF WANDERING AENGUS	149	WANDER AENGUS		T
A MAD SONG	149	WANDER AENGUS	V	T
THE SONG OF THE OLD MOTHER	150	OLD MOTHER		T
AND HER RED LIPS SANG THEM A LOVE SONG.	160	CAP AND BELLS	V	27
IN A TUMULTUOUS SONG"!	163	ASKS FORGIVE		20
BUT WEIGH THIS SONG WITH THE GREAT AND THEIR PRIDE!	166	EVIL OF BELOV		4
SONG	172	PLEADS FRIEND	V	T
BEND DOWN AND PRAY FOR ALL THAT SIN I WOVE IN SONG,	173	SPEAKS HEARERS		5
WHEN SONG I WOVE FOR MY BELOVED HIDES THE PRAYER,	173	SPEAKS HEARERS	V	2
BEND DOWN AND PRAY FOR THE GREAT SIN I WOVE IN SONG,	173	SPEAKS HEARERS	V	5
SONG OF MONGAN	177	PAST GREATNESS	V	T
RED HANRAHAN'S SONG ABOUT IRELAND	206	HANRAHANS SONG		T
THE SONG OF RED HANRAHAN	206	HANRAHANS SONG	V	T
LIKE AN OLD SONG.	211	O DO NOT LOVE		4
LIKE AN OLD SONG.	212	O DO NOT LOVE		12
AND ALL THAT MURMURING IS BUT A MARRIAGE SONG!	244	SHADOW WATER B	V	452
WHAT COULD I BUT TAKE UP THE SONG?	254	HIS DREAM		14
NOTHING TO MAKE A SONG ABOUT BUT KINGS,	257	RECONCILIATION		5
A DRINKING SONG	261	DRINKING SONG		T
I HAD NOT GIVEN A PENNY FOR A SONG	267	ALL TEMPT ME		6
THE YOUNG MAN'S SONG	268	BROWN PENNY	V	T
THEY SANG A DROWSY SONG, OR SNORED,	271	GREY ROCK		16
AND SANG A DROWSY SONG, OR SNORED,	271	GREY ROCK	V	16
BUT NEVER MADE A POORER SONG	273	GREY ROCK		55
A SONG FROM "THE PLAYER QUEEN"	308	PLAYER QUEEN		T
THE PLAYER QUEEN SONG FROM AN UNFINISHED PLAY	308	PLAYER QUEEN	V	T
I MADE MY SONG A COAT	320	COAT		1

742

SONG (CONTINUED)

	PAGE	TITLE		LINE
SONG, LET THEM TAKE IT,	320	COAT		8
A SONG	334	SONG		T
WHEN HER SON'S TURN WAS OVER. SING YOUR SONG.	340	SHEP GOATHERD		42
LUXURIANT SONG. WHY SHOULD YOU LEAVE THE LAMP	370	EGO DOMINUS		62
TRUE SONG, THOUGH SPEECH: "MINE AUTHOR SUNG IT ME."	373	PHASES OF MOON		30
SING OUT THE SONG; SING TO THE END, AND SING	374	PHASES OF MOON		56
HAVE YOU NOT ALWAYS KNOWN IT? THE SONG WILL HAVE IT	374	PHASES OF MOON		65
ANOTHER SONG OF A FOOL	381	SONG OF FOOL		T
AND AFTER THAT ARRANGED IT IN A SONG	384	VISION ROBART		65
YET I NUMBER HIM IN THE SONG:	393	EASTER 1916		35
OR CALUMNY A SONG. HOW CAN THEY KNOW	398	LEADERS CROWD		7
—THOSE DYING GENERATIONS—AT THEIR SONG,	407	SAIL BYZANTIUM		3
A PEASANT GIRL COMMENDED BY A SONG,	410	TOWER		34
SO GREAT A GLORY DID THE SONG CONFER.	410	TOWER		40
STRANGE, BUT THE MAN WHO MADE THE SONG WAS BLIND:	411	TOWER		49
AND THERE SING HIS LAST SONG.	414	TOWER		144
SOUNDS LIKE AN OLD SONG.	457	SECRETS OF OLD		6
. . . THROUGH TORCHLIGHT AND TUMULTUOUS SONG:	459	FROM OEDIPUS		8
. . . THROUGH TORCH-LIGHT AND TUMULTUOUS SONG:	459	FROM OEDIPUS	V	8
AT THE GREAT BOOK OF SAPPHO'S SONG: BUT NO,	461	HARUN RASHID		12
MUST KEEP THAT PERFECT, AS THEY KEEP HER SONG,	461	HARUN RASHID		18
THOUGH THE GREAT SONG RETURN NO MORE	485	NINETEENTH CEN		1
NIGHT RESONANCE RECEDES, NIGHT-WALKERS' SONG	497	BYZANTIUM		3
NIGHT'S RESONANCE RECEDES, NIGHT-WALKERS SONG	497	BYZANTIUM	V	3
WHAT'S THE MEANING OF ALL SONG?	502	VACILLATION		70
GIRL'S SONG	515	GIRLS SONG B		T
SEVEN POEMS GIRL'S SONG	515	GIRLS SONG B	V	T
TO SING A SONG OR TWO,	515	GIRLS SONG B		2
AND THAT WAS ALL MY SONG—	515	GIRLS SONG B		9
YOUNG MAN'S SONG	516	MANS SONG		T
UPON THE SUPREME THEME OF ART AND SONG:	523	LONG SILENCE		6
A SONG FOR MUSIC	524	DANCING DAYS	V	T
THAT SONG ANNOUNCES DAWN.	536	PARTING		4
WHILE HIS LOUD SONG REPROVES	536	PARTING		7
ALL STATELY WOMEN MOVING TO A SONG	537	HER VISION		17
THREE SONGS TO THE SAME TUNE SECOND SONG	544	TO SAME TUNE 1	V	T
COME MARCH, SINGING THIS SONG,	544	TO SAME TUNE 1	V	REF
FIRST SONG	545	TO SAME TUNE 2	V	T
SINGING, SINGING A SONG.	546	TO SAME TUNE 2		16
THIRD SONG	547	TO SAME TUNE 3	V	T
MARCH, MARCH, LIFT UP THE SONG:	549	TO SAME TUNE 3	V	26
LIFT, LIFT, LIFT UP THE SONG.	549	TO SAME TUNE 3	V	26
ALTERNATIVE SONG FOR THE SEVERED HEAD IN	549	SEVERED HEAD		T
HE THAT SINGS A LASTING SONG	553	PRAYER OLD AGE		3
THAT WERE A COWARDLY SONG,	554	CHURCH STATE		7
"NO, NOT ANOTHER SONG," SAID HE,	570	THREE BUSHES		36
"A LAUGHING, CRYING, SACRED SONG,	570	THREE BUSHES		43
A LECHING SONG," THEY SAID.	570	THREE BUSHES		44
DID EVER MEN HEAR SUCH A SONG?	570	THREE BUSHES		45
THE LADY'S FIRST SONG	572	LADYS 1ST SONG		T
THE LADY'S SECOND SONG	572	LADYS 2ND SONG		T
THE LADY'S THIRD SONG	573	LADYS 3RD SONG		T
THE LOVER'S SONG	574	LOVERS SONG		T
THE CHAMBERMAID'S FIRST SONG	574	MAIDS 1ST SONG		T
THE CHAMBERMAID'S SECOND SONG	575	MAIDS 2ND SONG		T
EVERY MAN THAT SINGS A SONG	586	PARNELLITES		19
WHAT ELSE HAVE I TO SPUR ME INTO SONG?	591	SPUR		4
MY FATHER SANG THAT SONG,	613	MARCH SONGS 1		8
MY FATHER SANG THAT SONG,	613	MARCH SONGS 1		18
MY FATHER SANG THAT SONG,	614	MARCH SONGS 1		28
SONG OF THE FAERIES	643	SONG FAERIES	V	T
THE SHEPHERDS' CONTEST OF SONG	646	ISLE STAT I 1	V	T
I'LL QUENCH HIS SINGING WITH LOUD SONG—	647	ISLE STAT I 1		63
WITH FIERY SONG I'LL DROWN YON PUNY VOICE.	648	ISLE STAT I 1		81
YON EAGER LARK, THAT FILLS WITH SONG THE WHOLE	652	ISLE STAT I 2		18
IS SORROW IN HIS SONG, OR ANY CARE?	652	ISLE STAT I 2		20
NAY, NAY, ALMINTOR, YONDER SONG IS GLAD.	652	ISLE STAT I 2		23
AND WHEREFORE HAVE WE COME? A SONG TO HEAR.	652	ISLE STAT I 2		27
BEYOND A MORTAL'S YEARS. I WAIT THE SONG	653	ISLE STAT I 2		48
WITH THAT SONG LEADING WHERE HARMONIC WOODS	657	ISLE STAT I 3		43
IN SONG, FROM GOBLIN WATERS SWAYING WHITE,	657	ISLE STAT I 3		51
EACH CAME ONE MORN, WITH WELCOMING OF SONG,	660	ISLE STAT II 1		42
HAVE CLOTHED THEIR TONGUES WITH SONG OF SONGLESS DAYS?	666	ISLE STAT II 3		17
AND HOLLOW LULLING THE YOUNG WINDS WITH SONG.	675	ISLE STAT II 3		226
WHERE SAT OLD SUMMER FADING INTO SONG,	690	MOSADA 1	V	1B
WHITE LILIES, AND HER SONG FLEW FORTH AFAR	693	MOSADA 1		85
WILL YOU NOT HEAR MY LAST NEW SONG? HUSH, HUSH!	695	MOSADA 2		1
YOU'RE FULL OF WORDINESS. COME, HEAR MY SONG.	696	MOSADA 2		8
A LITTLE MOORISH GIRL? SMALL WORTH. MY SONG—	696	MOSADA 2		10
THAT SONG I'VE MADE. 'TIS OF AN IRISH TALE.	696	MOSADA 2		19
THAT SONG I'VE MADE—IS OF A RUSSIAN TALE	696	MOSADA 2	V	19
O SHINING ONES, LIGHTLY WITH SONG PASS,	708	FAIRY PEDANT		21
LOVE SONG	717	LOVE SONG		T
GIRL'S SONG	723	GIRLS SONG A	V	T
I'D GLAD FOLKS' HEARTS WITH BLITHER SONG."	731	PRIEST FAIRY		82
A SONG OF THE ROSY CROSS	744	ROSY CROSS		T
SPINNING SONG.	770	SPINNING SONG		T
BUT IS EDAIN WORTH A SONG	773	SONG DEIRDRE 1		17
WHEN EVER I REMAKE A SONG,	778	FRIENDS WRONG		2

743

		PAGE	TITLE		LINE
SONG-BIRDS					
	ROUND EVERY BRANCH THE SONG-BIRDS FLEW, ...	14	OISIN 1		180
	FOR ROUND EACH BRANCH THE SONG-BIRDS FLEW, ...	14	OISIN 1	V	180
SONGLESS					
	I SAW THIS HARP ALL SONGLESS LIE, ...	85	MAD KING GOLL	V	55
	HAVE CLOTHED THEIR TONGUES WITH SONG OF SONGLESS DAYS? . .	666	ISLE STAT II 3		17
SONG-RAPT					
	MID BUBBLING LEAVES A WANDERING SONG-RAPT BIRD	672	ISLE STAT II 3		154
	MID BABBLING LEAVES A WANDERING SONG-RAPT BIRD	672	ISLE STAT II 3	V	154
SONG'S					
	BUT THE ESCAPE; THE SONG'S NOT FINISHED YET.	377	PHASES OF MOON		117
	FOR THE SONG'S SAKE A FOOL?	553	PRAYER OLD AGE		8
SONGS SEE WAR-SONGS					
	"AND I WILL MAKE A THOUSAND SONGS, ...	7	OISIN 1		75
	BELOVED IN A THOUSAND SONGS.	7	OISIN 1	V	76
	DANAAN SONGS, AND THEIR DEWY SHOWERS	11	OISIN 1		135
	FOR FAIRY SONGS CONTINUALLY	11	OISIN 1	V	134
	HELD TO THE TOWERS WITH BOASTING SONGS AND GAY. . . .	41	OISIN 2	V	184C
	. . . WITH ROARING OF LAUGHTER AND SONGS, ...	53	OISIN 3		87
	WITH MIRTHFUL SONGS BEFORE THE DAWN.	67	HAPPY SHEPHERD		49
	MY SONGS OF OLD EARTH'S DREAMY YOUTH!	67	HAPPY SHEPHERD		54
	WITH MIRTHFUL SONGS TILL RISE THE DAWN.	67	HAPPY SHEPHERD	V	49
	AODH TO DECTORA THREE SONGS	152	LOSS OF LOVE	V	T
	THE LOVER SPEAKS TO THE HEARERS OF HIS SONGS IN COMING DAYS	173	SPEAKS HEARERS		T
	HANRAHAN SPEAKS TO THE LOVERS OF HIS SONGS IN COMING DAYS	173	SPEAKS HEARERS	V	T
	A LOVER SPEAKS TO THE HEARERS OF HIS SONGS IN COMING DAYS	173	SPEAKS HEARERS	V	T
	WHEN SONGS I WOVE FOR MY BELOVED HIDE THE PRAYER, . . .	173	SPEAKS HEARERS		2
	I READ IN MY BOOK OF SONGS	178	FIDDLER DOONEY		7
	I READ IN A BOOK OF SONGS	178	FIDDLER DOONEY	V	7
	TWO SONGS OF A FOOL	380	SONGS FOOL 1		T
	TWO SONGS FROM A PLAY	437	SONGS PLAY 1		T
	FOUR SONGS FROM THE YOUNG COUNTRYMAN	451	FIRST LOVE	V	T
	TWO SONGS FROM THE OLD COUNTRYMAN	454	EMPTY CUP	V	T
	MORE SONGS OF AN OLD COUNTRYMAN	454	HIS MEMORIES	V	T
	THREE SONGS TO THE SAME TUNE	543	TO SAME TUNE 1		T
	THREE SONGS TO THE SAME TUNE SECOND SONG	544	TO SAME TUNE 1	V	T
	TWO SONGS REWRITTEN FOR THE TUNE'S SAKE	550	SONGS REWRIT 1		T
	SUPERNATURAL SONGS	554	RIBH AT TOMB		T
	HOW COULD YOU SING THOSE SONGS OF LOVE?	569	THREE BUSHES		5
	THREE SONGS TO THE ONE BURDEN	605	SONGS BURDEN 1		T
	THREE MARCHING SONGS	613	MARCH SONGS 1		T
	THAT MIGHT ADORN OLD SONGS OR COURTLY SHOWS;	629	CIRCUS ANIMALS		14
	OF THE SONGS THAT NEVER SLEEP.	647	ISLE STAT I 1		76
	I WEARY OF YOUR SONGS AND HUNTER'S TOYS.	651	ISLE STAT I 1		157
	NOW THEIR SONGS ARE MOURNFUL WHOLLY	667	ISLE STAT II 3		32
	WITH LITTLE VOICES SONGS OF FEARFUL THINGS, ...	682	SEEKER		31
	AND, NODDING TO AND FRO, SANG SONGS OF LOVE, ...	688	TWO TITANS		35
	I'LL SING THE SONGS THE DUSKY LOVERS SING, ...	694	MOSADA 1		101
	SONGS FROM DEIRDRE	771	SONG DEIRDRE 1	V	T
SON'S					
	WHEN HER SON'S TURN WAS OVER. SING YOUR SONG.	340	SHEP GOATHERD		42
SONS					
	WHAT ONE OF MAEVE'S NINE BRAWLING SONS	303	HOUR DAWN		36
	HAS ONE OF MAEVE'S NINE BRAWLING SONS	303	HOUR DAWN	V	36
SOON					
	DRIPPED ON THE EARTH; BUT SOON, AH! SOON, ...	19	OISIN 1	V	279
	DRIPPED ON THE EARTH; BUT SOON, AH! SOON, ...	19	OISIN 1	V	279
	IN HONOUR SOON BY HIS MASTER'S SIDE	26	OISIN 1	V	399C
	AND "A WEARINESS SOON IS MY SPEED," SAYS THE MOUSE, . . .	27	OISIN 1	V	417
	SOON FAR FROM THE ROSE AND THE LILY	122	WHITE BIRDS		11
	AND AS SOON AS THE MORN HAD WHITENED, ...	160	CAP AND BELLS	V	23
	HOW COULD WE BE SO SOON CONTENT, ...	193	BAILE AILLINN		95
	AND AS SOON FINISHED. ALL THAT EVER LOVED	229	SHADOW WATER B		151
	ONE CANNOT BEGIN IT TOO SOON.	268	BROWN PENNY		16
	LOVE LOST AS SOON AS WON, ...	312	CHILD DANCING		8
	SOON TOPPLES DOWN THE HILL.	335	YOUNG BEAUTY		6
	SHOWS HER THAT SOME ONE SOON	364	END OF DAY		5
	SHOWS HER THAT SOMEONE SOON	364	END OF DAY	V	5
	BUT SOON A TEAR-DROP STARTED UP, ...	400	DEMON BEAST		21
	THOSE VEINS MUST SOON BE DRY!	513	JANE TALK BISH		4
	FOR SOON WE LIE WHERE HE IS LAID, ...	586	PARNELLITES		5
	AND THIS BROUGHT FORTH A DREAM AND SOON ENOUGH	630	CIRCUS ANIMALS		23
	SOON SHALL OUR WINGS BE STILLED, ...	643	SONG FAERIES		5
	O'ER MUCH I'VE TALKED; I SHALL BE SILENT SOON, ...	657	ISLE STAT I 3		75
	SOON WILT THOU SMILE, FOR HERE THE WINDS ARE WEAK . . .	671	ISLE STAT II 3		141
	SOON SHALL OUR WINGS BE STILLED, ...	676	ISLE STAT II 3		252
	SHEPHERDS, FAREWELL! HE SOON WILL BE--ASHES	682	SEEKER		34
	BUT SOON MY WANDERING SHALL BE DONE I KNOW.	682	SEEKER	V	21
	QUITE SOON THE CORNFIELD, WHERE THE POPPIES GROW, . . .	699	MOSADA 3		7
	SOON WILL THE CHURCHMEN NOD ABOVE THE CROWD.	699	MOSADA 3		19
	THE NOISY WORLD DIVIDES. HOW SOON A DEED	700	MOSADA 3		34
	OF MY DEAD CHILDREN SOON, WHATE'ER BETIDE, ...	712	FERENCZ RENYI		58
	I HAVE FORGOT IT ALL. HOW SOON DREAMS FADE!	761	SHADOW WATER A		272
SOONER					
	THEY'D SOONER LEAVE THEIR COSSETING	455	HIS MEMORIES		9
	THE SOONER LOVE IS GONE, ...	511	JANE AND JACK		4
	I AM NOT DUMB! I'D SOONER SILENT WAIT	646	ISLE STAT I 1		40
SOOT					
	I COUNT THOSE FEATHERED BALLS OF SOOT	424	ROAD AT DOOR		11
SOOTH					
	NOR SEEK, FOR THIS IS ALSO SOOTH, ...	65	HAPPY SHEPHERD		23

SOOTH   (CONTINUED)
    SEEK, THEN, FOR THIS IS ALSO SOOTH, ...   66 HAPPY SHEPHERD   31
    SING, THEN, FOR THIS IS ALSO SOOTH. . . . .   66 HAPPY SHEPHERD   44
    DREAM, DREAM, FOR THIS IS ALSO SOOTH. . . . .   67 HAPPY SHEPHERD   57
    AND THE GREAT GREY LYNX'S SKIN! IN SOOTH, METHINKS . . 650 ISLE STAT I 1   151
    HAVE DONE THIS PHRASING, AND SAY WHY, IN SOOTH, ... 652 ISLE STAT I 2   25
    I LIKE YOU, AND, IN SOOTH I KNOW NOT WHY. . . . . . . 661 ISLE STAT II 1   64
SOOTHE
    THAT I MAY SOOTHE THAT HAPLESS FAUN . . . .   67 HAPPY SHEPHERD V   47
SOOTHED   SEE EVE-SOOTHED
    AND CALLED HIM SWEETEST NAMES AND SOOTHED HIS FEARS. . . 30 OISIN 2   V   27
SOOTY
    LIKE SOOTY FINGERS, MANY A TREE . . . .   13 OISIN 1   171
    TREE, LIKE A SOOTY FINGER, STARTS FROM THE EARTH; . . . 410 TOWER   19
SOPHOCLES
    "I LAUGHED UPON THE LIPS OF SOPHOCLES, ...   686 LIFE   17
    "I LAUGHED UPON THE LIPS OF SOPHOCLES, ...   735 QUATRAIN APHOR   19
SORACA
    OF THE HIGH PEOPLE OF SORACA NOR IN GLAMOUR BY DEMONS   50 OISIN 3   V   50
        FLUNG,
SORDID
    SORDID SORROWS OF THE MART, ...   733 STREET DANCERS   59
SORE
    A BEECH-BOUGH TO ME, AND MY HEART GREW SORE, ...   44 OISIN 2   226
    A BEECH BOUGH TO ME, AND MY HEART GREW SORE, ...   44 OISIN 2   V   226
    AND NOW MY HEART IS SORE. . . . .   322 SWANS AT COOLE   14
    NINE NIGHTS I LAY IN LONGING SORE . . . .   551 SONGS REWRIT 1 V   13
    NINE NIGHTS I LAY AND IN LONGING SORE . . . .   551 SONGS REWRIT 1 V   13
    HIS BONDS AWAY, SORE STRUGGLING.   NOW AT LAST . . . . 714 FERENCZ RENYI   116
SORREL-COVERED
    OVER THE SORREL-COVERED WOLD-- . . . .   716 FAIRY DOCTOR   2
SORRELS
    IN THE ROOTS OF THE GRASSES, THE SORRELS, I LAID MY BODY   52 OISIN 3   73
        AS LOW;
SORROW
    WE RODE IN SORROW, WITH STRONG HOUNDS THREE, ...   2 OISIN 1   V   7C
    MY HUMAN SORROW HER WHITE ARMS WOUND. . . . .   11 OISIN 1   138
    A SORROW WRAPPED EACH MERRY FACE, ...   17 OISIN 1   235
    NOR SORROW WITH HER OSPREY CLAW. . . . .   19 OISIN 1   V   285
    OR THE GREY WANDERING OSPREY SORROW." . . . .   20 OISIN 1   303
    OR THE WILD GREY OSPREY SORROW," . . . .   20 OISIN 1   V   303
    NOR THE GREY WANDERING OSPREY SORROW." . . . .   21 OISIN 1   319
    OR THE WILD GREY OSPREY SORROW." . . . .   21 OISIN 1   V   319
    NOR THE GREY WANDERING OSPREY SORROW." . . . .   23 OISIN 1   342
    OR FEAR THE WILD GREY OSPREY SORROW." . . . .   23 OISIN 1   V   342
    WITH ALL THE ANCIENT SORROW OF MEN"! . . . .   25 OISIN 1   381
    THE OSPREY OF SORROW GOES AFTER AND CLUTCHES, ...   27 OISIN 1   V 415D
    OF RAVENING SORROW, OR THE HAND OF WRATH? . . . . .   42 OISIN 2   199
    WERE THE MEMORIES OF THE WHOLE OF MY SORROW . . . .   52 OISIN 3   71
    . . . AND I KNEW HOW MEN SORROW AND PASS, ...   59 OISIN 3   175
    THERE .WAS A MAN WHOM SORROW NAMED HIS FRIEND, ...   67 SAD SHEPHERD   1
    AND HE, OF HIS HIGH COMRADE SORROW DREAMING, ...   67 SAD SHEPHERD   2
    AND HE, OF HIS HIGH KINSMAN SORROW DREAMING, ...   67 SAD SHEPHERD V   2
    AND THEN THE MAN WHOM SORROW NAMED HIS FRIEND . . . .   68 SAD SHEPHERD   8
    AND THEN THE MAN WHOM SORROW NAMED HIS FRIEND . . . .   68 SAD SHEPHERD   17
    THEN CRIED THE MAN WHOM SORROW NAMED HIS FRIEND! . . .   68 SAD SHEPHERD V   8
    "I MAKE THE CLOAK OF SORROW! . . . .   69 CLOAK BOAT   2
    SHALL BE THE CLOAK OF SORROW, ...   69 CLOAK BOAT   4
    THE CLOAK I WEAVE OF SORROW! . . . .   69 CLOAK BOAT   V   2
    "I BUILD A BOAT FOR SORROW! . . . .   70 CLOAK BOAT   7
    SAILETH THE ROVER SORROW, ...   70 CLOAK BOAT   9
    "I WEAVE THE SHOES OF SORROW! . . . .   70 CLOAK BOAT   12
    IN ALL MEN'S EARS OF SORROW, ...   70 CLOAK BOAT   14
    A BOAT I BUILD FOR SORROW! . . . .   70 CLOAK BOAT   V   7
    THE SANDALS THESE OF SORROW! . . . .   70 CLOAK BOAT   V   12
    IN EACH MAN'S EARS OF SORROW-- . . . .   70 CLOAK BOAT   V   14
    WHO IS AMRITA? SORROW OF ALL SORROWS! . . . . . .   71 ANASHU VIJAYA   15
    ARE BOWED IN SORROW UNDER PENDULOUS LIDS, ...   79 EPHEMERA   2
    ARE BOWED IN SORROW UNDER THEIR TREMBLING LIDS, . . .   79 EPHEMERA   V   2
    VEILED IN A DREAMY SORROW FOR THEIR LOVE . . . . .   79 EPHEMERA   V   2A
    MY SORROW! FOR MANY A CREAK GAVE THE CREEL IN THE CART . .   91 OLD FISHERMAN   6
    ARE WITH NEW SORROW WRUNG! . . . .   99 FOXHUNTER   38
    UPON HIS HEAD TO CAST AWAY MY SORROW. . . . .   102 FERGUS DRUID   14
    AH! DRUID, DRUID, HOW GREAT WEBS OF SORROW . . . .   104 FERGUS DRUID   39
    UPON THE WHARVES OF SORROW, AND HEARD RING . . . . .   115 ROSE OF BATTLE   27
    THE SORROW OF LOVE . . . .   119 SORROW OF LOVE   T
    WHERE TIME WOULD SURELY FORGET US, AND SORROW COME NEAR   122 WHITE BIRDS   10
        US NO MORE!
    WHERE SURELY TIME WOULD FORGET US AND SORROW COME NEAR   122 WHITE BIRDS   V   10
        US NO MORE!
    MAY SET A STONE UPON ANCESTRAL SORROW! . . . .   130 BOOK STORIES   11
    AH, WORLD-WIDE NATION, ALWAYS GROWING SORROW, ...   130 BOOK STORIES V   11
    AH, WORLDWIDE NATION, ALWAYS GROWING SORROW! . . . .   130 BOOK STORIES V   11
    WHO SIGH WITH MINGLED SORROW AND CONTENT, ...   136 TO SOME I TALK   7
    AND SORROW AWAY, AND CALLING BARD AND CLOWN . . . .   170 SECRET ROSE   20
    O, WHEN SHALL SORROW WANDER NO MORE IN THE LAND . . .   174 ELEMENT POWERS V   5
    AND BLEW ME HITHER TO MY LASTING SORROW, ...   235 SHADOW WATER B   288
    YOU HAD ENOUGH OF SORROW BEFORE DEATH-- . . . . . .   293 TO A SHADE   23
    AS THOUGH MY SORROW WERE A SCENE . . . .   452 HUMAN DIGNITY   5
    STRONG DRINK I HAD, AND IT BROUGHT ME TO SORROW, . . .   544 TO SAME TUNE 1   13
    STRONG DRINK I HAD, AND IT BROUGHT ME TO SORROW, . . .   616 MARCH SONGS 3   13

745

	PAGE	TITLE		LINE

SORROW   (CONTINUED)
LOVE AND SORROW, ONE EXISTENCE,   647 ISLE STAT I 1   73
ALL RHAPSODY HATH SORROW FOR ITS SOUL.   652 ISLE STAT I 2   17
IS SORROW IN HIS SONG, OR ANY CARE?   652 ISLE STAT I 2   20
I HEAR THE WHOLE SKY'S SORROW IN ONE VOICE.   652 ISLE STAT I 2   22
AYE, VERY LATELY, SORROW CAME TO WEEP   659 ISLE STAT II 1   25
WITHIN MINE HEART; AND NAUGHT BUT SORROW NOW   659 ISLE STAT II 1   26
OF HUMAN SORROW LET THEM MORALIZE;   663 ISLE STAT II 2   31
O'ER GRIEF. THE WORLD DRINKS SORROW FROM THE BEAMS   664 ISLE STAT II 2   46
THE CLOAK I WEAVE OF SORROW,   666 ISLE STAT II 3   2
SHALL BE THE CLOAK OF SORROW,   666 ISLE STAT II 3   4
A BOAT I BUILD FOR SORROW.   666 ISLE STAT II 3   7
SAILETH THE ROVER SORROW,   666 ISLE STAT II 3   9
THE SANDALS THESE OF SORROW.   666 ISLE STAT II 3   12
IN EACH MAN'S EARS OF SORROW,   666 ISLE STAT II 3   14
SORROW THAT GIVES FOR GUERDON LIBERTY,   686 DRAWING-ROOM   6
POOR LOVE AND SORROW, WITH THEIR ARMS THROWN ROUND   703 MOSADA 3   119
HAST THOU NOT KNOWN ALL SORROW AND DELIGHT   723 KANVA ON SELF   2
THOUGHTLESS JOY AND SORROW SAGE.   733 STREET DANCERS   47
SORROW, THAT GIVES FOR GUERDON LIBERTY,   734 QUATRAIN APHOR   6
WALKS IN THE VESTURE OF HER SISTER SORROW.   735 QUATRAIN APHOR   28
AND ALL HER STARLIGHT IS WITH SORROW MAD,   738 YOU ARE SAD   3
AND STOOD IN MY SORROW APART,   744 GLOVE CLOAK   2
WOULD OVERCOME YOUR SORROW AND YOUR DREAMS.   749 SHADOW WATER A   52
SORROWED   SEE MANY-SORROWED
SORROWFUL
EARTH'S ALIENS. WHY SO SORROWFUL? OUR SOULS   80 EPHEMERA   V   12A
BUILDING A SORROWFUL LOVELINESS   158 BELOVED RHYMES   5
OF SORROWFUL, AUSTERE, SWEET, LOFTY PIPE TUNES.   341 SHEP GOATHERD   57
O SISTER OF SORROWFUL GAZE!   706 FAIRY PEDANT   2
SORROWING
GROW GENTLE WITHOUT SORROWING,   193 BAILE AILLINN   110
SORROWINGS
GROW GENTLE WITHOUT SORROWINGS!   193 BAILE AILLINN   V 110
SORROWS
ON THE OLD SORROWS OF HIS HUMAN DAYS.   29 OISIN 2   V   12
WHO IS AMRITA? SORROW OF ALL SORROWS!   71 ANASHU VIJAYA   15
THE SORROWS OF THE WORLD BOW DOWN MY HEAD,   104 FERGUS DRUID   V 38A
AND ALL THE SORROWS OF HER LABOURING SHIPS,   120 SORROW OF LOVE V   7
AND LOVED THE SORROWS OF YOUR CHANGING FACE;   121 YOU ARE OLD   8
WITH THEIR UNHUMAN SORROWS. CEASE! NO MORE!   661 ISLE STAT II 1   58
BLINDER SORROWS, HARDER WAGE--   733 STREET DANCERS   58
SORDID SORROWS OF THE MART.   733 STREET DANCERS   59
SORROWS SAPPING BRAIN AND HEART.   733 STREET DANCERS   60
THOUGHTLESS JOYS AND SORROWS SAGE.   733 STREET DANCERS V   47
SORROW-WORN
SORROW-WORN, YET PLACID-BROWED.   733 STREET DANCERS   56
SORROW-WORN, YET PLACID BROWED.   733 STREET DANCERS V   56
SORRY
SORRY PLACE, WHERE FOR SWING OF THE WAR-AXE IN MY DIM EYES   61 OISIN 3   194
 . . .
SHE MAY NOT BE TOO SORRY IN THE END.   232 SHADOW WATER B   232
THAT MAYBE "I AM SORRY" IN PLAIN PROSE   341 SHEP GOATHERD   60
"I AM SORRY," SAID THE MAID,   595 COLONEL MARTIN   29
WITHOUT MY GLASS I'D BE A SORRY CLOWN.   721 WITCH VIVIEN   29
SORT
TO BE "SOME SORT OF EVIDENCE",   287 TO WEALTHY MAN   4
GENERATIONS OF HIS SORT,   319 DOLLS   6
WITH EVERY SORT OF COMPANY,   335 YOUNG BEAUTY   2
OR SOMETHING OF THAT SORT HE SAID,   338 TOM OROUGHLEY   14
THE SORT OF BEAUTY THAT I HAVE APPROVED,   405 FOR DAUGHTER   50
A SORT OF BATTERED KETTLE AT THE HEEL,   409 TOWER   16
A LEVELLING, RANCOROUS, RATIONAL SORT OF MIND   486 SEVEN SAGES   11
A SORT OF BESOM THAT CAN CLEAR THE SOUL   558 RIBH CHRISTIAN   5
WHAT SORT OF MAN IS COMING   572 LADYS 2ND SONG   1
AND I BEAT UP THE COMMON SORT   605 SONGS BURDEN 1   3
YOUNG MEN KNOW NOTHING OF THIS SORT,   626 OLD MEN BE MAD   16
WITH ANY SORT OF CLOTHES,   627 STATES HOLIDAY   28
WITH SOME SORT OF VIOLENCE   638 BEN BULBEN   34
SCORN THE SORT NOW GROWING UP   639 BEN BULBEN   70
SORTS
ALL SORTS OF KINGS HAVE SAT   597 MODEL LAUREATE   2
THAT MEN AND WOMEN OF ALL SORTS   597 MODEL LAUREATE   3
SOUGHT
SAVE DEER TOWARDS NOON THAT WATER SOUGHT.   17 OISIN 1   V 243
AS THOUGH HIS HOUR WERE COME. WE SOUGHT THE PART   37 OISIN 2   112
SOUGHT ONCE AGAIN THE SHORE, AND FOUND A SHELL,   68 SAD SHEPHERD   18
SOUGHT ONCE AGAIN THE SHORE, AND CHOSE A SHELL   68 SAD SHEPHERD   V   18
NO WOMAN'S LOVED ME, NO MAN SOUGHT MY HELP.   103 FERGUS DRUID   26
WHO HAVE SOUGHT MORE THAN IS IN RAIN OR DEW   114 ROSE OF BATTLE   16
WHO SOUGHT THEE IN THE HOLY SEPULCHRE,   169 SECRET ROSE   3
WHO SOUGHT THEE AT THE HOLY SEPULCHRE,   169 SECRET ROSE   V   3
AND SOUGHT THROUGH LANDS AND ISLANDS NUMBERLESS YEARS,   170 SECRET ROSE   23
NONE CLOSED HIS BLOOD-SHOT EYES BUT SOUGHT   296 THREE BEGGARS   44
LIES ONE LONG SOUGHT   310 WITCH   7
IT SOUGHT ITSELF AND AFTERWARDS THE WORLD.   376 PHASES OF MOON   95
I SOUGHT MY BETTERS; THOUGH IN EACH   506 REMORSE SPEECH   6
I SOUGHT A THEME AND SOUGHT FOR IT IN VAIN,   629 CIRCUS ANIMALS   1
I SOUGHT A THEME AND SOUGHT FOR IT IN VAIN,   629 CIRCUS ANIMALS   1
I SOUGHT IT DAILY FOR SIX WEEKS OR SO.   629 CIRCUS ANIMALS   2
THE PALE ANEMONES. WE'VE SOUGHT ALL DAY,   651 ISLE STAT I 2   5

	PAGE	TITLE	LINE

SOUGHT   (CONTINUED)

BY MANY SOUGHT, AND 'TIS A FOREST TALE,	653 ISLE STAT I 2	40
WHO, SWIMMING, SOUGHT THE ISLAND LONE!	673 ISLE STAT II 3	181
I SOUGHT THEE NOT. MEN CALL ME INFAMY.	685 SEEKER	75
I KNOW NOT WHAT I AM. I SOUGHT THEE NOT.	685 SEEKER	76
IN EVERY DANCE, BY CHILDREN SOUGHT. "ACCURST,	709 FERENCZ RENYI	12
GLAD, SIMPLE--NAY, HE SOUGHT NOT MYSTERY,	710 FERENCZ RENYI	30

SOUL

"THE SOUL IS A DROP OF JOY AFAR,	19 OISIN 1 V	276
THE SOUL IS FREE, AND FINDS NO FLAW,	19 OISIN 1 V	284
MY ANGRY KING-REMEMBERING SOUL ONE JOT.	36 OISIN 2	94
THERE WAS NO MIGHTIER SOUL OF HEBER'S LINE!	36 OISIN 2	95
THEY STIRRED MY SPACIOUS SOUL IN ME NO JOT--	36 OISIN 2	94
NOR SHOOK MY FIRM AND SPACIOUS SOUL ONE JOT!	36 OISIN 2 V	94
MY ANGRY, KING REMEMBERING SOUL ONE JOT!	36 OISIN 2 V	94
MY SOUL, ONCE GLORY OF ITS ANCIENT LINE,	36 OISIN 2 V	95
"I HEAR MY SOUL DROP DOWN INTO DECAY,	45 OISIN 2	235
"AGE AFTER AGE I FEEL MY SOUL DECAY	45 OISIN 2 V	235
MY SOUL, MY PREY, AND THIS MY HEAPED PILE.	45 OISIN 2 V	239B
BUT KNEEL AND WEAR OUT THE FLAGS AND PRAY FOR YOUR SOUL THAT IS LOST	63 OISIN 3	215
. . . FOR THY SOUL THAT IS LOST,	63 OISIN 3 V	215
KNEEL, USHEEN, WEAR OUT THE FLAGS AND PRAY FOR YOUR SOUL THAT IS LOST	63 OISIN 3 V	215
AND AS I SANG MY SOUL WAS FREE	86 MAD KING GOLL V	65
BUT ONE MAN LOVED THE PILGRIM SOUL ·IN YOU,	121 YOU ARE OLD	7
HE BADE HIS SOUL RISE UPWARD	159 CAP AND BELLS	3
HE MADE HIS SOUL GO UPWARD	159 CAP AND BELLS V	3
AND THE HEART AND THE SOUL CAME THROUGH,	160 CAP AND BELLS	30
THE HEART AND THE SOUL CAME THROUGH!	160 CAP AND BELLS V	30
I SEE THE BLESSEDEST SOUL IN THE WORLD	168 BLESSED	31
AND HAVE SEEN THE BLESSEDEST SOUL IN THE WORLD,	168 BLESSED V	31
THAT EVERY MAN SHOULD CARRY HIS OWN SOUL	235 SHADOW WATER B	299
YOUR SOUL SHALL GIVE THE KISS. I AM NOT AFRAID,	238 SHADOW WATER B	346
WHEN NEITHER SOUL NOR BODY HAS BEEN CROSSED.	258 KING NO KING	16
AGAINST A SOUL?	267 FRIEND ILLNESS	7
A SINGLE SOUL THAT LACKS A SWEET CRYSTALLINE CRY.	291 PAUDEEN	8
"AND MAKE MY SOUL BEFORE MY PATE IS BARE."	299 BEGGAR CRIED	4
HER SOUL HAD SUCH DESIRE	317 NIGHT COME	2
YOU HAVE MEASURED OUT THE ROAD THAT THE SOUL TREADS	342 SHEP GOATHERD	80
WHEN HER SOUL FLIES TO THE PREDESTINED DANCING-PLACE	365 HER COURAGE	1
MANACLE HIS SOUL UPON THE RED SEA BOTTOM,	372 ON GOING HOUSE	16
THE THIRTEENTH MOON BUT SETS THE SOUL AT WAR	374 PHASES OF MOON	50
THE SOUL BEGINS TO TREMBLE INTO STILLNESS,	374 PHASES OF MOON	54
ALL THOUGHT BECOMES AN IMAGE AND THE SOUL	374 PHASES OF MOON	58
BECOMES A BODY! THAT BODY AND THAT SOUL	374 PHASES OF MOON	59
BODY AND SOUL CAST OUT AND CAST AWAY	374 PHASES OF MOON	62
BEYOND THE VISIBLE WORLD. ALL DREAMS OF THE SOUL	374 PHASES OF MOON	63
OF BODY AND SOUL. THE LOVER'S HEART KNOWS THAT.	375 PHASES OF MOON	71
WHO SHUDDER AND HURRY BY! BODY AND SOUL	375 PHASES OF MOON	77
THE SOUL REMEMBERING ITS LONELINESS	375 PHASES OF MOON	88
UPON THE BODY AND UPON THE SOUL	376 PHASES OF MOON	93
THE SOUL RECOVERS RADICAL INNOCENCE	405 FOR DAUGHTER	66
SOUL CLAP ITS HANDS AND SING, AND LOUDER SING	407 SAIL BYZANTIUM	11
AND BE THE SINGING-MASTERS OF MY SOUL.	408 SAIL BYZANTIUM	20
AND BE THE SINGING MASTERS OF MY SOUL.	408 SAIL BYZANTIUM V	20
OUT OF HIS BITTER SOUL,	415 TOWER	151
NOW SHALL I MAKE MY SOUL,	416 TOWER	181
SYMBOLS OF THE SOUL.	420 MY HOUSE V	20F
THROUGH NATURAL DECLENSION OF THE SOUL,	423 MY DESCENDANTS	10
COMPARES THE SOLITARY SOUL TO A SWAN!	430 NINETEEN 19	60
I HAVE LOVED YOU BETTER THAN MY SOUL FOR ALL MY WORDS,	442 BLACK CENTAUR	14
THE BODY IS NOT BRUISED TO PLEASURE SOUL,	445 SCHOOL CHILDR	58
KNEW THAT WE'D HALVED A SOUL	457 SUMMER SPRING	6
THAT MAKE A MAN'S SOUL OR A WOMAN'S SOUL	465 HARUN RASHID	93
THAT MAKE A MAN'S SOUL OR A WOMAN'S SOUL	465 HARUN RASHID	93
ITSELF AND NOT SOME OTHER SOUL." "THAT LOVE	465 HARUN RASHID	94
IS A MAN'S MOCKERY OF THE CHANGELESS SOUL."	465 HARUN RASHID	102
ITSELF AND NOT SOME OTHER SOUL. "SUCH LOVE	465 HARUN RASHID V	94
WHEN UPWARD TURNED ON ONE SOUL IMAGE FELL,	471 ALL SOUL NIGHT V	34
A DIALOGUE OF SELF AND SOUL	477 SELF AND SOUL	T
WHO CAN DISTINGUISH DARKNESS FROM THE SOUL?	477 SELF AND SOUL	8
A PROUD WOMAN NOT KINDRED OF HIS SOUL,	479 SELF AND SOUL	64
WHAT'S WATER BUT THE GENERATED SOUL?	490 COOLE BALLYLEE	8
AND, LIKE THE SOUL, IT SAILS INTO THE SIGHT	490 COOLE BALLYLEE	19
BODY AND SOUL"!	510 JANE JUDGMENT	4
WHAT MOST COULD SHAKE HIS SOUL!	529 TOM CRUACHAN	3
WHAT MOST CAN SHAKE HIS SOUL!	529 TOM CRUACHAN V	3
I ANSWER THAT I GAVE MY SOUL	538 LAST CONFESS	3
HE FANCIED THAT I GAVE A SOUL	538 LAST CONFESS	9
BUT WHEN THIS SOUL, ITS BODY OFF,	538 LAST CONFESS	15
TO THIS BARE SOUL, LET ALL MEN JUDGE THAT CAN	542 PARN FUNERAL 1	30
DEFENDING IRELAND'S SOUL.	546 TO SAME TUNE 2	6
IN BROKEN SENTENCES. MY SOUL HAD FOUND	557 RIBH ECSTASY	3
GODHEAD. SOME SHADOW FELL. MY SOUL FORGOT	557 RIBH ECSTASY	6
A SORT OF BESOM THAT CAN CLEAR THE SOUL	558 RIBH CHRISTIAN	5
THAT IS A LIGHT MY JEALOUS SOUL HAS SENT.	558 RIBH CHRISTIAN	8
HOW SOUL MAY WALK WHEN ALL SUCH THINGS ARE PAST,	558 RIBH CHRISTIAN	11
HOW SOUL COULD WALK BEFORE SUCH THINGS BEGAN.	558 RIBH CHRISTIAN	12
THEN MY DELIVERED SOUL HERSELF SHALL LEARN	558 RIBH CHRISTIAN	13
HATRED OF GOD MAY BRING THE SOUL TO GOD.	558 RIBH CHRISTIAN	18

	PAGE	TITLE	LINE
SOUL (CONTINUED)			
AT STROKE OF MIDNIGHT SOUL CANNOT ENDURE • • • • •	558	RIBH CHRISTIAN	19
HOW SOUL HAS WALKED BEFORE SUCH THINGS BEGAN. • • •	558	RIBH CHRISTIAN V	12
CONDUCT AND WORK GROW COARSE, AND COARSE THE SOUL, • •	564	GYRES	17
LOVED HIM WITH HER SOUL. • • • • • • • • • • •	571	THREE BUSHES	55
WHAT HURTS THE SOUL • • • • • • • • • • • • •	572	LADYS 1ST SONG	9
MY SOUL ADORES, • • • • • • • • • • • • • •	572	LADYS 1ST SONG	10
HE SHALL LOVE MY SOUL AS THOUGH • • • • • • • •	572	LADYS 2ND SONG	8
UNTROUBLED BY THE SOUL, • • • • • • • • • • •	573	LADYS 2ND SONG	11
SOUL MUST LEARN A LOVE THAT IS • • • • • • • •	573	LADYS 2ND SONG	15
IF SOUL MAY LOOK AND BODY TOUCH, • • • • • • •	573	LADYS 2ND SONG	19
SPEAK NO EVIL OF THE SOUL, • • • • • • • • •	573	LADYS 3RD SONG	3
HER SOUL IN DIVISION FROM ITSELF • • • • • • •	578	CRAZED GIRL	3
THAT COME INTO MY SOUL AND ESCAPE • • • • • • •	599	SPIRIT MEDIUM	3
A SOUL INCAPABLE OF REMORSE OR REST! • • • • • •	601	GALLERY REVIS	7
DEFENDING IRELAND'S SOUL. • • • • • • • • • •	613	MARCH SONGS 1	6
HAD SHATTERED HER SOUL. PROPINQUITY HAD BROUGHT • • •	619	BRONZE HEAD	18
TO KEEP THE SOUL OF MAN ALIVE, • • • • • • • •	620	JOHN KINSELLA	19
WHAT HOUR OF TERROR COMES TO TEST THE SOUL, • • • •	622	HOUND VOICE	11
SHE, PITY-CRAZED, HAD GIVEN HER SOUL AWAY, • • • •	629	CIRCUS ANIMALS	19
I THOUGHT MY DEAR MUST HER OWN SOUL DESTROY, • • • •	630	CIRCUS ANIMALS	21
THEN STANDS IN JUDGMENT ON HIS SOUL, • • • • • • •	633	MAN AND ECHO	33
THAT OF RACE AND THAT OF SOUL, • • • • • • • •	637	BEN BULBEN	15
BRING THE SOUL OF MAN TO GOD, • • • • • • • • •	638	BEN BULBEN	40
SADNESS, SOUL OF JOY MOST DEEP, • • • • • • • •	647	ISLE STAT I 1	74
AND MY SOUL IN WAITING DIETH, • • • • • • • • •	648	ISLE STAT I 1	87
LIFT MY SOUL FROM RAYLESS NIGHT— • • • • • • • •	648	ISLE STAT I 1	95
MUSIC OF MY SOUL AND LIGHT— • • • • • • • • • •	648	ISLE STAT I 1	97
SUSTAINS HIS SOUL IN COURAGE OR IN MIGHT. • • • • •	650	ISLE STAT I 1	144
ALL RHAPSODY HATH SORROW FOR ITS SOUL. • • • • • •	652	ISLE STAT I 2	17
THY SOUL SHALL BE, THOUGH PITILESS AND BRIGHT • • •	674	ISLE STAT II 3	210
MY SOUL. HIS DARKNESS AND HIS CHILL I FEEL. • • •	684	SEEKER V	63B
THROUGH HIS SAD SOUL FOR EVER OLD AND YOUNG, • • • •	687	TWO TITANS	25
DEEP IN HIS SOUL, LIKE RAIN UPON A SOIL • • • • •	692	MOSADA 1	56
HER SOUL FROM SEAS OF ENDLESS FLAME IN HELL. • • • •	698	MOSADA 2	47
MY SOUL SHALL TOUCH WITH HIS, AND THE TWO FLAMES • • •	701	MOSADA 3	61
CAST OFF THY HERESIES, AND SAVE THY SOUL • • • • •	701	MOSADA 3	64
JUST NOW MY SOUL ROSE UP AND TOUCHED IT, FAR • • • •	705	REMEMBRANCE	13
THE SOUL OF THE PITILESS PLACE • • • • • • • •	708	FAIRY PEDANT	30
UPON MY SOUL, OLD TIME. NO! THUS IT STANDS. • • • •	722	WITCH VIVIEN	49
THE SOUL UPON THE ASHES OF THE HEART." • • • • •	735	QUATRAIN APHOR	16
THE SEDENTARY SOUL • • • • • • • • • • • • • •	784	WOMANS BEAUTY	8
SOULED SEE SUBTLE-SOULED			
SOULLESS			
BUT SOULLESS A FAIRY DIES, • • • • • • • • • •	643	SONG FAERIES	2
FOR SOULLESS A FAIRY DIES, • • • • • • • • • •	644	SONG FAERIES	14
BUT SOULLESS A FAERY DIES, • • • • • • • • • •	676	ISLE STAT II 3	249
FOR SOULLESS A FAERY DIES, • • • • • • • • • •	676	ISLE STAT II 3	261
SOUL'S			
THAT WORD OF THE SOUL'S PEACE--"ETERNITY." • • • •	81	EPHEMERA V	24B
SOUL'S BEAUTY BEING MOST ADORED, • • • • • • • •	421	MY TABLE	22
THE SOUL'S UNCHANGING LOOK! • • • • • • • • • •	422	MY TABLE	24
THE SOUL'S OWN YOUTH AND NOT THE BODY'S YOUTH • • • •	464	HARUN RASHID	69
ON THE SOUL'S JOURNEY. HOW IT IS WHIRLED ABOUT, • • •	472	ALL NIGHT	54
THOUGHT IS A GARMENT AND THE SOUL'S A BRIDE • • • •	558	RIBH CHRISTIAN	16
GARDENS WHERE A SOUL'S AT EASE! • • • • • • • •	639	BEN BULBEN	55
SOULS			
AND WEARY AND WORN ARE OUR SAD SOULS NOW! • • • • •	79	FALLING LEAVES	6
EARTH'S ALIENS. WHY SO SORROWFUL? OUR SOULS • • • •	80	EPHEMERA V	12A
BEFORE US LIES ETERNITY! OUR SOULS • • • • • • •	81	EPHEMERA	23
THIS WOULD I SAY, MOST WISE OF LIVING SOULS! • • • •	102	FERGUS DRUID	9
AMID MEN'S SOULS, THAT WAVER AND GIVE PLACE • • • •	112	ROSE OF WORLD	7
AMID MEN'S SOULS THAT DAY BY DAY GIVE PLACE, • • • •	112	ROSE OF WORLD V	7
THE SOULS OF THE DEAD. • • • • • • • • • • • •	118	CRADLE SONG V	4
FOR SOULS WHO TIRE AND BLEED, • • • • • • • • •	134	FR GILLIGAN	42
TO SEE MEN'S SOULS BARTERED AND BOUGHT. • • • • •	136	TWO TREES V	36
AND TALKED OF THE DARK FOLK WHO LIVE IN SOULS • • • •	136	TO SOME I TALK	4
OF THAT DARK FOLK WHO GATHER IN THE SOULS • • • • •	136	TO SOME I TALK V	4
ALL MANNER OF BLESSED SOULS, • • • • • • • • •	167	BLESSED	14
THE BLESSEDEST SOULS THAT WALK IN THE WORLD • • • •	167	BLESSED	19
ALL MANNER OF BLESSEDEST SOULS, • • • • • • • •	167	BLESSED V	14
TILL THE ATTORNEY FOR LOST SOULS CRY HER SWEET CRY, • •	173	SPEAKS HEARERS	6
DARK AND DULL AND EARTHY OUR SOULS AND BODIES BE! • •	208	HANRAHANS SONG V	13
AND SOULS AS IF THEY WERE BUT SIGHS, • • • • • •	307	HOUR DAWN	102
THAT BLEST SOULS ARE NOT COMPOSITE, • • • • • • •	387	ROBARTES DANCE	44
BE MIMICRY?" "WHAT MATTER IF OUR SOULS • • • • •	464	HARUN RASHID	66
THAN SOULS THAT START NO GAME AND TURN NO RHYME! • • •	464	HARUN RASHID	6o
CAN BE NO MIMICRY. "WHAT IF OUR SOULS • • • • •	464	HARUN RASHID V	66
ALL THESE ARE SOULS THAT FLY FROM THEIR DREAD SELVES. • •	686	LIFE	4
FOR THAT'S THE SWEETEST MUSIC FOR SAD SOULS. • • • •	702	MOSADA 3	85
AND IMPORTUNE THEIR SOULS TO PENITENCE, • • • • • •	704	MOSADA 3	131
"PRAY FOR THE SOULS IN PURGATORY," THE PALE PRIEST	719	PHANTOM SHIP	31
TREMBLING CRIES.			
WHERE THE SOULS OF FAIRIES GO?" • • • • • • • •	729	PRIEST FAIRY	48
ALL THESE ARE SOULS WHO FLY FROM THEIR DREAD SELVES. • •	734	QUATRAIN APHOR	4
ALL THESE ARE SOULS THAT FLY FROM THEIR DREAD SELVES. V	734	QUATRAIN APHOR V	4
SOULS'			
ALL SOULS' NIGHT • • • • • • • • • • • • • •	470	ALL SOUL NIGHT	T
AND IT IS ALL SOULS' NIGHT, • • • • • • • • • •	470	ALL SOUL NIGHT	3
IT IS ALL SOULS' NIGHT AND THE GREAT CHRIST CHURCH BELL	470	ALL SOUL NIGHT V	1

748

		PAGE	TITLE		LINE
SOUND	SEE THUNDER-SOUND				
WHY DO YE SOUND NO HORN?" SHE SAID.		4	OISIN 1	V	33
OF PENSIVE LAUGHTER, UNHUMAN SOUND,		11	OISIN 1		136
AND A FAR SOUND OF FEATHERY QUIRES:		13	OISIN 1		166
A FAR VAGUE SOUND OF FEATHERY CHOIRS.		13	OISIN 1	V	166
AND NOW FLED BY, MIST-COVERED, WITHOUT SOUND,		29	OISIN 2		3
A HUNDRED SEASONS: FOR A SOUND OF TEARS		30	OISIN 2	V	18
CRAZED WITH ITS OWN INTERMINABLE SOUND,		30	OISIN 2	V	23A
DROPPING: A MURMUROUS DROPPING: OLD SILENCE AND THAT ONE SOUND:		48	OISIN 3		18
CAME SOUND FROM THOSE MONSTROUS SLEEPERS,		51	OISIN 3		58
. . . A SOUND LIKE THE STIRRING OF FLIES.		51	OISIN 3		58
. . . SLOW DROPPING A SOUND IN FAINT STREAMS		51	OISIN 3		67
. . . THE SOUND OF THE SEA'S VAGUE DRUM?		56	OISIN 3		135
WHERE EVER IS MURMUROUS DROPPING, OLD SILENCE AND THAT ONE SOUND:		56	OISIN 3		138
LATER A SOUND CAME, HALF LOST IN THE SOUND OF A SHORE FAR AWAY,		57	OISIN 3		155
LATER A SOUND CAME, HALF LOST IN THE SOUND OF A SHORE FAR AWAY,		57	OISIN 3		155
AND MIXED WITH THE SOUND OF THAT ROARER		60	OISIN 3	V	184
. . . THE SOUND OF TWO STUMBLING APART.		60	OISIN 3	V	184
THE DEWDROPS, FOR THE SOUND OF THEIR OWN DROPPING.		68	SAD SHEPHERD		16
THE DEW DROPS, FOR THE SOUND OF THEIR OWN DROPPING--		68	SAD SHEPHERD	V	16
IT QUENCHED, WITH SOUND LIKE FALLING DEW,		86	MAD KING GOLL		66
I HAVE OFTEN HEARD THE SWEET SOUND OF HIS BOW.		109	CUCHULAIN SEA		50
I OFTEN HEAR THE SWEET SOUND OF HIS BOW.		109	CUCHULAIN SEA	V	50
A MAN WITH A HAZEL WAND CAME WITHOUT SOUND:		153	CHANGE BELOVED		6
A MAN WITH A WAND OF HAZEL CAME WITHOUT SOUND		153	CHANGE BELOVED	V	6
WORTH KNITTING TO A MEASURE OF SWEET SOUND?		181	QUEEN MAEVE		33
OR THE TWO STRINGS THAT MADE ONE SOUND		195	BAILE AILLINN		155
A KING AND A QUEEN ARE WANDERING THERE, AND THE SOUND		204	WITHER BOUGHS		19
YOU HAVE A DRUID CRAFT OF WICKED SOUND		237	SHADOW WATER B		342
YOU HAVE A DRUID CRAFT, WICKED SOUND		237	SHADOW WATER B	V	342
WITH A SLOW SMILE AND WITHOUT SOUND,		275	GREY ROCK		117
A SWEET, MIRACULOUS, TERRIFYING SOUND.		277	TWO KINGS		17
AND THERE HAD BEEN NO SOUND OF LIVING THING		279	TWO KINGS	V	54
THERE CANNOT BE, CONFUSION OF OUR SOUND FORGOT,		291	PAUDEEN		7
AND HE, WITH THAT LOW WHINNYING SOUND		318	APPOINTMENT		5
NIGHTLY, AND STARTLED BY THAT SOUND		326	ROBERT GREGORY		54
MOUTH MASTERED A SWEET SOUND,		331	ROUND TOWER		16
WHAT MADE THAT SOUND? A RAT OR WATER-HEN		372	PHASES OF MOON		8
"THE NIGHT HAS FALLEN: NOT A SOUND		389	SOLOMON WITCH		38
THEIR MAGNANIMITIES OF SOUND,		404	FOR DAUGHTER		44
THE SOUND OF THE RAIN OR SOUND		419	MY HOUSE		6
THE SOUND OF THE RAIN OR SOUND		419	MY HOUSE		6
THAT MY MICHAEL MAY SLEEP SOUND,		435	FOR MY SON		2
WHEN ALEXANDER'S EMPIRE PASSED, THEY SLEPT SO SOUND.		442	BLACK CENTAUR		12
WHEN ALEXANDER'S EMPIRE PAST, THEY SLEPT SO SOUND.		442	BLACK CENTAUR	V	12
DIZZY WITH HARMONIOUS SOUND,		446	COLONUS PRAISE		7
AND MANY A LESSER BELL SOUND THROUGH THE ROOM:		470	ALL SOUL NIGHT		2
I NEED SOME MIND THAT, IF THE CANNON SOUND		471	ALL SOUL NIGHT		11
SOUND OF A STICK UPON THE FLOOR, A SOUND		491	COOLE BALLYLEE		25
SOUND OF A STICK UPON THE FLOOR, A SOUND		491	COOLE BALLYLEE		25
BELOVED, MAY YOUR SLEEP BE SOUND		522	LULLABY		1
SUCH A SLEEP AND SOUND AS FELL		522	LULLABY		13
OR SMOTE UPON THE STRING AND TO THE SOUND		537	HER VISION		15
NO COMMON INTELLIGIBLE SOUND		578	CRAZED GIRL		13
CAN PAY THE POET FOR A VERSE AND HEAR THE FIDDLE SOUND,		581	CURSE CROMWELL		21
SAW THAT THE GRAVE WAS DEEP, THE COFFIN SOUND,		609	IN TARAS HALLS		18
WITH NO MORE SOUND THAN THE MICE MAKE		618	LONG-LEG FLY		27
THAT HAD A SOUND FLY-FISHER'S WRIST		625	OLD MEN BE MAD		3
THAT HAD A SOUND FLY FISHER'S WRIST		625	OLD MEN BE MAD	V	3
CAST ON THE SOUND, ON, ON. THIS NIGHT OF GRAVES,		665	ISLE STAT II 2		71
MY SINKING BRAIN!--CEASE!--CEASE! HEARD YE YON SOUND?		665	ISLE STAT II 2		73
NAY, GIVE IT ME, AND I WILL SOUND A MEASURE!		681	SEEKER		9
DEAFENING US WITH IDLE SOUND--		727	LOVERS QUARREL		30
HOW LITTLE AND REEDY A SOUND AWAKES A GOD		760	SHADOW WATER A		252
AND OVERTURNED THE DEMON WITH A SOUND		762	SHADOW WATER A		283
SOUNDED					
HAD SOUNDED BETTER TO YOUR MOUNTAIN FANCY.		341	SHEP GOATHERD		61
THAT COGNOMEN SOUNDED BEST		440	WISDOM		18
HEARD YOU? YOUR LUTE HUNG IN THE WINDOW SOUNDED!		694	MOSADA 1		95
HEARD YOU? YOUR LUTE UPON THE WALL HAS SOUNDED!		694	MOSADA 1	V	95
SOUNDING	SEE SWEET-SOUNDING				
SOUNDLESS					
SOUNDLESS SHALL BE THE FOOTFALL LIGHT		70	CLOAK BOAT		13
SOUNDLESS SHALL BE THE FOOTFALL LIGHT		666	ISLE STAT II 3		13
SOUNDS					
SO PALE! AND SOUNDS OF WONDER HER LIPS UTTERED,		34	OISIN 2	V	71
DIE OFF THE FEEBLE SOUNDS!		99	FOXHUNTER	V	42
I HEAR LAKE WATER LAPPING WITH LOW SOUNDS BY THE SHORE:		117	ISLE INNISFREE		10
I HEAR LAKE WATER LAPPING WITH LOW SOUNDS ON THE SHORE:		117	ISLE INNISFREE	V	10
FOR TO ARTICULATE SWEET SOUNDS TOGETHER		205	ADAMS CURSE		10
SLEEP BEFORE THE THIRD NOON SOUNDS."		295	THREE BEGGARS		24
ALL SOUNDS BY BIRD OR ANGEL SUNG		387	SOLOMON WITCH	V	7
SOUNDS LIKE AN OLD SONG.		457	SECRETS OF OLD		6
SOUR					
"TAKE THE SOUR		510	JANE JUDGMENT		6
BREAD TASTE SOUR.		554	CHURCH STATE		12
THEIR MONEY SPENT, THEIR WINE GONE SOUR,		635	BLACK TOWER		3

749

	PAGE	TITLE		LINE
SOURCE				
I AM CONTENT TO FOLLOW TO ITS SOURCE	479	SELF AND SOUL		65
CONTENT TO TRACE THAT MISERY TO ITS SOURCE, ...	479	SELF AND SOUL	V	65
OUT OF A DESOLATE SOURCE, ...	518	HIS CONFIDENCE		11
SOURS				
THIS SULLEN PEASANT SOURS THE GOOD RED WINE.	711	FERENCZ RENYI	V	43
SOUTH				
SANG THAT SOMEWHERE TO NORTH OR WEST OR SOUTH	127	DREAM OF FAERY		19
SANG HOW SOMEWHERE TO NORTH OR EAST OR SOUTH	127	DREAM OF FAERY	V	19
SANG HOW SOMEWHERE TO NORTH OR WEST OR SOUTH	127	DREAM OF FAERY	V	19
THE SOUTH IS POURING DOWN ROSES OF CRIMSON FIRE! . . .	154	BELOVED PEACE		6
THE SOUTH WOULD COVER THEM WITH ROSES OF CRIMSON FIRE!	154	BELOVED PEACE	V	6
AND THAT MILD WOMAN OF THE SOUTH, ...	189	BAILE AILLINN		6
THAT RUNNER SAID! "I AM FROM THE SOUTH!	191	BAILE AILLINN		47
AND HURRYING TO THE SOUTH HE CAME	194	BAILE AILLINN	V	128
STRAYING TOO FAR INTO THE NORTH OR SOUTH, ...	226	SHADOW WATER B		86
IF BUT THIS WIND WERE IN THE SOUTH."	306	HOUR DAWN		90
NEITHER THE SPRING NOR THE SOUTH WIND	306	HOUR DAWN		95
HE AND HIS FRIEND, THEIR FACES TO THE SOUTH, ...	372	PHASES OF MOON		2
THE SOUTH WIND BROUGHT IT LONGING, AND THE EAST WIND DESPAIR,	449	OWEN AHERNE		5
THE SOUTH WIND BROUGHT IT LONGING, AND THE EAST BROUGHT IN DESPAIR,	449	OWEN AHERNE	V	5
THE SOUTH WIND BROUGHT IT LONGING, AND THE EAST BROUGHT IT DESPAIR,	449	OWEN AHERNE	V	5
GREAT WINDOWS OPEN TO THE SOUTH, ...	475	EVA GORE-BOOTH		2
THE SOUTH BREEZE NOW IN DYING FEARS	655	ISLE STAT I 3		13
IN THE SOUTH SEA'S AZURE MILES, ...	732	STREET DANCERS		28
IN THE SOUTH SEAS' AZURE MILES, ...	732	STREET DANCERS	V	28
MY FOSTER-MOTHER'S GARDEN IN THE SOUTH	758	SHADOW WATER A		227
MY FOSTER MOTHER'S GARDEN IN THE SOUTH	758	SHADOW WATER A	V	227
SOUTHERN				
OH WANDERER IN THE SOUTHERN WEATHER, ...	77	INDIAN TO LOVE	V	1
IN SOUTHERN LOCHLANN. I WOULD NOT OBEY	756	SHADOW WATER A	V	191
SOUTHWARD				
SOUTHWARD A SEA-KING MASTERFUL	82	MAD KING GOLL	V	15
SOWN SEE SELF-SOWN GOLD-SOWN LEAF-SOWN				
SPACE				
IN CLANGING SPACE A MOMENT HEARD, ...	65	HAPPY SHEPHERD		20
'MID CLANGING SPACE A MOMENT HEARD	65	HAPPY SHEPHERD	V	20
WITH ALL YOUR WHIRLING HAIR, AND DROP THROUGH SPACE AN AZURE TEAR,	73	ANASHU VIJAYA	V	46
A LITTLE SPACE FOR THE ROSE-BREATH TO FILL!	101	ROSE UPON ROOD		14
OR BIRDS LOST IN THE ONE CLEAR SPACE	195	BAILE AILLINN		149
OR BIRDS LOST IN ONE CLEAR SPACE	195	BAILE AILLINN	V	149
IS EDEN OUT OF TIME AND OUT OF SPACE?	218	WOODS OF COOLE		36
A CLUMP OF BEECH TREES MADE AN EMPTY SPACE	277	TWO KINGS	V	4A
IN SPACE, MADE EQUAL WITH A SIGH, WE MET.	705	REMEMBRANCE		14
SPACIOUS				
THEY STIRRED MY SPACIOUS SOUL IN ME NO JOT—	36	OISIN 2	V	94
NOR SHOOK MY FIRM AND SPACIOUS SOUL ONE JOT!	36	OISIN 2	V	94
THE SPACIOUS LOVES, THE ANGER WITHOUT SLEEP	42	OISIN 2	V	194
THE WOOD WAS SO SPACIOUS ABOVE THEM, ...	49	OISIN 3		37
SO SPACIOUS THE WOOD WAS ABOVE THEM, ...	49	OISIN 3	V	37
. . . THOUGH SPACIOUS HIS LANDS WERE AND STRONG. . . .	58	OISIN 3	V	160
SPADE				
AND A SMALL AND A FEEBLE POPULACE STOOPING WITH MATTOCK AND SPADE,	58	OISIN 3		164
AND A SMALL AND A FEEBLE RACE STOOPING WITH MATTOCK AND SPADE.	58	OISIN 3	V	164
AND A SMALL AND FEEBLE RACE STOOPING WITH MATTOCK AND SPADE.	58	OISIN 3	V	164
THAT WOULD LET THE SPADE LIE, ...	215	HAPPY TOWNLAND		30
I CALL FOR SPADE AND HORSE AND HOUND	275	GREY ROCK		105
I BEND MY BODY TO THE SPADE	599	SPIRIT MEDIUM		7
I BEND MY BODY TO THE SPADE	600	SPIRIT MEDIUM		15
I BEND MY BODY TO THE SPADE	600	SPIRIT MEDIUM		23
ITS BOREDOM OF THE DESK OR OF THE SPADE, BECAUSE . . .	621	HOUND VOICE		3
SPADES				
THE MAINES' CHILDREN DROPPED THEIR SPADES, AND STOOD . .	185	QUEEN MAEVE		120
THE MAINES' CHILDREN HAVE NOT DROPPED THEIR SPADES . .	186	QUEEN MAEVE		123
SHARP THEIR SPADES, THEIR MUSCLES STRONG, ...	637	BEN BULBEN		22
SHARP THEIR SPADES, THEIR MUSCLE STRONG, ...	637	BEN BULBEN	V	22
SPAIN				
OR TRADING OUT OF GALWAY INTO SPAIN!	269	PARDON FATHERS		4
THERE IS A QUEEN IN CHINA, OR MAYBE IT'S IN SPAIN, . . .	353	HIS PHOENIX		1
THERE IS A QUEEN IN CHINA, OR MAY BE IT'S IN SPAIN, . . .	353	HIS PHOENIX	V	1
SPAKE				
AND CAUGHT MY HANDS, BUT SPAKE NO WORD	25	OISIN 1		374
AND CAUGHT MY HANDS AND SPAKE NO WORD	25	OISIN 1	V	374
HE SPAKE ONCE MORE AND FONDLED WITH HIS LIPS	81	EPHEMERA	V	24A
WITH THONGS OF LEATHER." AS SHE SPAKE IT WAS!	106	CUCHULAIN SEA	V	17B
AT LAST CUCHULAIN SPAKE, "SOME MAN HAS MADE	109	CUCHULAIN SEA		47
HE SPAKE TO THE YOUNG MAN, "IS THERE NO MAID	109	CUCHULAIN SEA		58
AT LAST CUCHULAIN SPAKE, "A YOUNG MAN STRAYS	109	CUCHULAIN SEA	V	47
SPAKE THUS! "CUCHULAIN WILL DWELL THERE AND BROOD . . .	110	CUCHULAIN SEA		77
MY BODY SPAKE, NOT I!"	132	FR GILLIGAN		12
FOR ANY GENTLE THING SHE SPAKE, ...	191	BAILE AILLINN		63
IGNORANT WHAT DRAMATIS PERSONAE SPAKE!	560	WHENCE COME		4
THE FAIRIES' HERALD SPAKE ONCE MORE!	730	PRIEST FAIRY		53
THUS SPAKE THE TOWN JAILOR	740	EARL PAUL		13

750

	PAGE	TITLE	LINE
SPAN			
ENDURE WHAT LIFE GOD GIVES AND ASK NO LONGER SPAN▪ • • •	459	FROM OEDIPUS	1
SPANISH			
OR ON SPANISH POLITICS? • • • • • • • • • • • •	631	POLITICS	4
SPANS			
THREE SPANS HIGH AS HE ROSE TO HIS FEET▪ • • • • •	729	PRIEST FAIRY	25
SPARE			
WHERE LOVE'S TO GIVE AND TO SPARE▪ • • • • • • •	214	HAPPY TOWNLAND V	4
WILL HE NOT SPARE HER LIFE? HOW WOULD ONE MATTER • • •	696	MOSADA 2	3
SPARED			
I WOULD HAVE SPARED HER HANDMAID▪ BUT SHE CAUGHT • • •	755	SHADOW WATER A	167
I SPARED HER HANDMAID▪ TOO▪ BUT HALF WAY HITHER • • • •	755	SHADOW WATER A V	167
SPARKLING			
FOR THE SPARKLING HOOVES THEY SANK NOT IN▪ • • • • •	10	OISIN 1	V 114A
SPARKS			
LIKE THE SPARKS BLOWN OUT OF A SMITHY▪ AND DIE? • • • •	170	SECRET ROSE	30
SPARROW			
THE BRAWLING OF A SPARROW IN THE EAVES▪ • • • • • •	119	SORROW OF LOVE	1
UPON THE TIME OF SPARROW CHIRP▪ • • • • • • • • •	133	FR GILLIGAN V	21
SPARROW—CHIRP			
UPON THE TIME OF SPARROW—CHIRP • • • • • • • • •	133	FR GILLIGAN	21
SPARROWS			
THE QUARREL OF THE SPARROWS IN THE EAVES▪ • • • • •	119	SORROW OF LOVE V	1
AND NOW THE SPARROWS WARRING IN THE EAVES▪ • • • • •	120	SORROW OF LOVE V	9
LARGER SPARROWS OF THE TOWN▪ • • • • • • • • • •	731	STREET DANCERS	5
SPARS			
ON THE DROWNED MEN'S HANDS AND FACES▪ ON THE SPARS AND ON THE SAILS▪	719	PHANTOM SHIP	22
SPARTAN			
AS THE FOX IN THE OLD FABLE DESTROYED THE SPARTAN BOY'S▪	580	CURSE CROMWELL	18
SPASM			
GODHEAD ON GODHEAD IN SEXUAL SPASM BEGOT • • • • • •	557	RIBH ECSTASY	5
SPAT			
NEITHER TO SLAVES THAT WERE SPAT ON▪ • • • • • • •	414	TOWER	130
NOR TO THE TYRANTS THAT SPAT▪ • • • • • • • • • •	414	TOWER	131
SPAWN SEE FROG—SPAWN			
SPAWNING			
AND BY ITS FORMLESS SPAWNING FURY WRECKED▪ • • • • •	611	STATUES	30
SPEAK			
AND NEVER FIND▪ THOUGH YE IN MUSIC SPEAK▪ • • • • •	42	OISIN 2	V 201
SPEAK▪ YOU TOO ARE OLD WITH YOUR MEMORIES▪ • • • • •	61	OISIN 3	196
SPEAK▪ THOU TOO ART OLD WITH THY MEMORIES▪ • • • • •	61	OISIN 3	V 196
EACH OTHER ROUND IN CIRCLES▪ AND HEARD THE ELDEST SPEAK▪	76	INDIAN ON GOD	5
EACH OTHER ROUND IN CIRCLES▪ AND I HEARD THE ELDEST SPEAK▪——	76	INDIAN ON GOD V	5
AND PIERCED HIM▪ "SPEAK BEFORE YOUR BREATH IS DONE▪" • •	110	CUCHULAIN SEA	67
A KING OF THE GREAT PLAIN WOULD SPEAK WITH YOU▪" • •	183	QUEEN MAEVE	78
THE MOUTHS THAT SPEAK▪ THE NOTES AND STRINGS▪ • • • •	212	BLESS PSALTER	2
WITH THE EVER—LIVING▪ WHAT IF HE SPEAK THE TRUTH▪ • •	229	SHADOW WATER B	170
SPEAK LOWER▪ OR THEY'LL HEAR▪ THEY CANNOT HEAR▪ • • •	232	SHADOW WATER B	228
NO▪ NO▪ NOR HALF A THOUGHT▪ BUT DO NOT SPEAK▪ • • • •	245	SHADOW WATER B	478
I WOULD NOT LET YOU SPEAK▪ FOR I WOULD KNOW • • • •	246	SHADOW WATER B	492
HAD RUN INTO ONE FOUNTAIN▪ SPEAK TO HIM▪ • • • • • •	249	SHADOW WATER B	561
SPEAK——HE WILL NOT DENY IT▪ IS THAT TRUE? • • • • •	249	SHADOW WATER B	563
IF BOOKS SPEAK TRUTH▪ IN SLIEVENAMON—— • • • • • •	271	GREY ROCK V	15
SPEAK IT▪ THAT I MAY SEND THROUGH THE WIDE WORLD • • •	281	TWO KINGS	97
WHERE I MAY SPEAK TO YOU ALONE▪ MY CRAFT • • • • •	284	TWO KINGS	159
SO WE SPEAK A DIFFERENT TONGUE▪ • • • • • • • • •	313	TWO YEAR LATER	6
AND I SPEAK A BARBAROUS TONGUE▪ • • • • • • • • •	313	TWO YEAR LATER	12
TILL WINTER BLASTS WERE GONE▪ BUT SPEAK OF HER • • •	340	SHEP GOATHERD	33
WHO KNOW IT ALL RING AT HIS DOOR▪ AND SPEAK • • • •	373	PHASES OF MOON	21
AND YET THEY SPEAK WHAT'S BLOWN INTO THE MIND▪ • • •	376	PHASES OF MOON	110
"SPEAK ALL YOUR MIND▪" MY HEART SANG OUT▪ • • • • •	450	OWEN AHERNE	21
• • • "SPEAK ALL YOUR MIND▪ WHO CARES▪ • • • • • •	450	OWEN AHERNE	21
IN AFTER TIME THEY WILL SPEAK MUCH OF ME • • • • •	462	HARUN RASHID	29
AND SPEAK BUT FANTASY▪ RECALL THE YEAR • • • • •	462	HARUN RASHID	30
AND SPEAK BUT PHANTASY▪ RECALL THE YEAR • • • • •	462	HARUN RASHID V	30
AND SPEAK BUT LIES▪ CALL UP TO MEMORY • • • • •	462	HARUN RASHID V	30
CAN HEAR THE ARMED MAN SPEAK▪ • • • • • • • • •	470	HARUN RASHID	193
THAT STORMS ARE SHAKING▪ HEAR THE ARMED MAN SPEAK▪ • •	470	HARUN RASHID V	193
ONE OR THE OTHER OUT AND SPEAK • • • • • • • • •	475	EVA GORE—BOOTH	15
OF BAILE AND AILLINN YOU NEED NOT SPEAK▪ • • • • •	555	RIBH AT TOMB	6
SURMOUNT THEIR BONES▪ BUT SPEAK WHAT NONE HAVE HEARD▪ • •	555	RIBH AT TOMB	9
SURMOUNTS THEIR BONES▪ BUT SPEAK WHAT NONE HAVE HEARD▪ • •	555	RIBH AT TOMB V	9
SPEAK NO EVIL OF THE SOUL▪ • • • • • • • • • •	573	LADYS 3RD SONG	3
COME SPEAK YOUR BIT IN PUBLIC • • • • • • • • •	582	ROGER CASEMENT	21
HE WAS OUR ANCIENT GOD▪ IF I SPEAK LOW▪ • • • • •	658	ISLE STAT I 3	78
ALMINTOR WITH HER LOVE▪ WHO ART THOU?——SPEAK▪ • • •	660	ISLE STAT II 1	50
AND WHY SO SILENT? I WOULD HAVE THEE SPEAK▪ • • •	671	ISLE STAT II 3	140
I KNOW NOT OF THE THINGS YOU SPEAK▪ BUT WHAT • • •	675	ISLE STAT II 3	239
MY ECHOING HEART▪ NOW RAISE THY VOICE AND SPEAK▪ • • •	683	SEEKER	47
TO JOYS UNHUMAN▪ AND TO THEE——SPEAK▪ SPEAK▪ • • •	684	SEEKER	60
TO JOYS UNHUMAN▪ AND TO THEE——SPEAK▪ SPEAK▪ • • •	684	SEEKER	60
THOU WILT NOT SPEAK▪ AND I WITH AGE AM NEAR • • •	684	SEEKER	62
THOU WILT NOT SPEAK▪ OH CRUEL ART THOU YET▪ • • •	684	SEEKER V	69A
HE IS NOT FAR▪ I'D HAVE HIM SPEAK FOR HER▪ • • •	696	MOSADA 2	13
EVER MORE TO SPEAK A WORD • • • • • • • • • •	697	MOSADA 2	32
I SPEAK ALONE WITH SERVANTS OF THE CROSS • • • •	698	MOSADA 2	48
THE SOLDIER THUS▪ AND HAYNAU——"PEASANT▪ SPEAK • • •	711	FERENCZ RENYI	54
THAT ANCIENT MOTHER CRIES▪ "SPEAK NOT▪ MY SON▪ • • •	711	FERENCZ RENYI	56
SPEAK▪ FERENCZ▪ SPEAK▪ WE LOVE EACH OTHER▪ SEE▪ • • •	713	FERENCZ RENYI	87

751

		PAGE	TITLE		LINE

SPEAK   (CONTINUED)
    SPEAK, FERENCZ, SPEAK. WE LOVE EACH OTHER. SEE, • • •   713 FERENCZ RENYI   87
    "AH, FERENCZ, SPEAK AND SAVE THYSELF AND ME! • • • • •   713 FERENCZ RENYI   V   86
    THEN 'GAN TO SPEAK THAT GOBLIN RARE, • • • • • • •   729 PRIEST FAIRY   37
    FOR I HAVE ALL HIS GARDEN WISDOM. O SPEAK! • • • • •   756 SHADOW WATER A   180
    ALL THAT TIME KNOWS. SPEAK TO ME, QUEEN. O SPEAK! • • •   756 SHADOW WATER A   180
    ALL THAT TIME KNOWS. SPEAK TO ME, QUEEN. O SPEAK! • • •   756 SHADOW WATER A   V   180
SPEAKERS
    AND THEN THE SPEAKERS GOT IT • • • • • • • • • •   582 ROGER CASEMENT   13
SPEAKING
    TOWARDS THE HOUR FOR SPEAKING OF THE DEAD? • • • • •   276 TWO KINGS   V   D
    THE SPEAKING OF IT COULD BE NO GREAT WRONG, • • • • •   281 TWO KINGS   104
    AND SPEAKING WHAT HE WOULD NOT THOUGH HE WOULD, • • • •   282 TWO KINGS   123
    "SPEAKING OF LOVE THROUGH OTHER LIPS AND LOOKING • • • •   283 TWO KINGS   155
    SPEAKING TO A DRUNKEN AUDIENCE HIGH NONSENSICAL WORDS! • •   577 LOFTY THINGS   6
SPEAKS
    FOR GOD HAS HEARD, AND SPEAKS HIS ANGRY MIND! • • • • •   42 OISIN 2   206
    THE LOVER SPEAKS TO THE HEARERS OF HIS SONGS IN COMING DAYS   173 SPEAKS HEARERS   T
    HANRAHAN SPEAKS TO THE LOVERS OF HIS SONGS IN COMING DAYS   173 SPEAKS HEARERS   V   T
    A LOVER SPEAKS TO THE HEARERS OF HIS SONGS IN COMING DAYS   173 SPEAKS HEARERS   V   T
    BUT GROWS MORE GENTLE WHEN HE SPEAKS HER NAME, • • • •   340 SHEP GOATHERD   29
    THE LOVER SPEAKS • • • • • • • • • • • • •   449 OWEN AHERNE   V   T
SPEAR   SEE HUNTING-SPEAR
    WITH WHOM I HURLED THE HURRYING SPEAR, • • • • • •   10 OISIN 1   122
    BY MACE AND SPEAR AND SWORD OF SEA-GODS, NAILS • • • •   31 OISIN 2   V   30A
    AN ASHEN HUNTING SPEAR. • • • • • • • • • • •   32 OISIN 2   56
    OR CARVE A DREADFUL SPEAR. • • • • • • • • • •   32 OISIN 2   V   56
    A LARCH-WOOD HUNTING SPEAR. • • • • • • • • • •   32 OISIN 2   V   56
    AN ASH-WOOD HUNTING SPEAR. • • • • • • • • • •   32 OISIN 2   V   56
    WERE ARROW AND SHIELD AND WAR-AXE, ARROW AND SPEAR AND   49 OISIN 3   V   30
      BLADE,
    OF MY LONG SPEAR, WITH SCREAM AND LAUGH, • • • • •   84 MAD KING GOLL   V   34
    OF MY LONG SPEAR WITH SONG AND LAUGH • • • • •   84 MAD KING GOLL   V   34
    THE PAIN OF WOUNDS, THE LABOUR OF THE SPEAR, • • • •   104 FERGUS DRUID   V   38D
    CAULDRON AND SPEAR AND STONE AND SWORD, • • • • • •   196 BAILE AILLINN   165
    A SHADOW DOES NOT CARRY SWORD OR SPEAR. • • • • •   224 SHADOW WATER B   44
    WHO GRIPS HIS LONG SPEAR SO TO PUSH • • • • • •   385 ROBARTES DANCE   3
    THE DIM SPEAR MET THE BRIGHT SPEAR, • • • • • •   741 EARL PAUL   45
    THE DIM SPEAR MET THE BRIGHT SPEAR, • • • • • •   741 EARL PAUL   45
    AND MADE THE BRIGHT SPEAR BEND, • • • • • • •   741 EARL PAUL   46
    THE DIM SPEAR BREAKS THE BRIGHT SHIELD • • • • • •   741 EARL PAUL   49
    THE DIM SPEAR MET THE BRIGHT SPEAR • • • • • •   741 EARL PAUL   V   49
    THE DIM SPEAR MET THE BRIGHT SPEAR • • • • • •   741 EARL PAUL   V   49
SPEAR-GRASS
    AS DANCE UPON THE SPEAR-GRASS BRITTLE, • • • • • •   731 PRIEST FAIRY   78
SPEARHEAD'S
    HOW THE HAMMERS SPRING ON THE ANVIL, ON THE SPEARHEAD'S   52 OISIN 3   83
      BURNING SPOT!
SPEAR-HEAD'S
    • • • ON THE SPEAR-HEAD'S BURNING SPOT! • • • • •   52 OISIN 3   V   83
SPEARS   SEE HUNTING-SPEARS
    THE SWIFT INNUMERABLE SPEARS, • • • • • • • •   2 OISIN 1   6
    AND A HUNDRED SPEARS AND A HUNDRED BOWS, • • • • •   8 OISIN 1   91
    BESIDE THE PILED-UP HUNTING SPEARS, • • • • • •   23 OISIN 1   348
    THE DEWS DROP SLOWLY AND DREAMS GATHER! UNKNOWN SPEARS • •   161 BLACK PIG   1
    THE DEW DROPS SLOWLY! THE DREAMS GATHER! UNKNOWN SPEARS •   161 BLACK PIG   V   1
    OR AS THE CHANGING SPEARS FLUNG BY THE GOLDEN STARS • •   175 ELEMENT POWERS   V   15
    PAST THE SPEARS AND PALM-STEMS DRY, • • • • • • •   733 STREET DANCERS   42
SPEARSHAFT
    THAT THE SPEARSHAFT IS MADE OUT OF ASHWOOD, • • • • • •   52 OISIN 3   82
SPEAR-SHAFT
    THAT THE SPEAR-SHAFT IS MADE OUT OF ASHWOOD, • • • • •   52 OISIN 3   82
SPECKLED
    "LIKE THE SPECKLED BIRD THAT STEERS • • • • • • •   341 SHEP GOATHERD   62
    A SPECKLED CAT AND A TAME HARE • • • • • • •   380 SONGS FOOL 1   1
    THE SPECKLED CAT SLEPT ON MY KNEE! • • • • • •   381 SONGS FOOL 2   2
    ALONE AND ALONE, WITH A SPECKLED SHIN? • • • • •   551 SONGS REWRIT 1   8
    DRINKING ALONE WITH A SPECKLED SHIN? • • • • • •   551 SONGS REWRIT 1   V   8
    LIVE LONE, ALONE WITH A SPECKLED SHIN? • • • • •   551 SONGS REWRIT 1   V   8
SPECTACLE
    BECAUSE THE DAILY SPECTACLE THAT STIRRED • • • • •   270 PARDON FATHERS   16
    BECAUSE YOU WERE THE SPECTACLE THAT STIRRED • • • •   270 PARDON FATHERS   V   16
    HAS FOUND THE LOVELIEST SPECTACLE THERE IS. • • • • •   447 COLONUS PRAISE   24
SPECTRAL
    MOST OUT OF REACH? AND IS THAT SPECTRAL IMAGE • • • •   368 EGO DOMINUS   25
SPED
    NO LONGER GLAD AS ON THAT MORNING, SPED • • • • •   30 OISIN 2   V   16
    THAT I LOVED ONCE." AGAIN THE FIGHTING SPED, • • • •   110 CUCHULAIN SEA   64
    'TIS MORN, AND FROM THE DEW-DRENCH'D WOOD I'VE SPED • •   645 ISLE STAT I 1   6
    HOW SPED THY QUEST? THIS PRELUDE WE'LL NOT HEAR IT. • •   673 ISLE STAT II 3   174
SPEECH
    "FRET NOT WITH SPEECH THE PHANTOMS DREAD," • • • • •   12 OISIN 1   V   148
    "THESE FORMS?" "VEX NOT WITH SPEECH THE PHANTOMS DREAD."   29 OISIN 2   V   5
    AND WITH LOW MURMURING LAUGHING SPEECH • • • • •   195 BAILE AILLINN   137
    THE HOURLY KINDNESS, THE DAY'S COMMON SPEECH, • • • •   258 KING NO KING   14
    TO GRADUAL TIME'S LAST GIFT, A WRITTEN SPEECH • • • •   264 HOUSE SHAKEN   11
    "AND CANNOT HAVE A HUMOROUS HAPPY SPEECH." • • • • •   300 BEGGAR CRIED   16
    OF THAT LATE DEATH TOOK ALL MY HEART FOR SPEECH. • • •   328 ROBERT GREGORY   96
    TO HIS SPEECH AT THE BREAK OF DAY, • • • • • •   341 SHEP GOATHERD   68
    THE EYE OF THE MIND NOR KEEP MY TONGUE FROM SPEECH." • •   353 PEOPLE   34
    HER SPEECH A WICKED TALE THAT WE MAY VIE WITH HER, • •   362 HER COURTESY   6

752

	PAGE	TITLE		LINE
SPEECH (CONTINUED)				
(I HAVE NO SPEECH BUT SYMBOL, THE PAGAN SPEECH I MADE	365	HER COURAGE		2
(I HAVE NO SPEECH BUT SYMBOL, THE PAGAN SPEECH I MADE	365	HER COURAGE		2
TRUE SONG, THOUGH SPEECH: "MINE AUTHOR SUNG IT ME."	373	PHASES OF MOON		30
YOU HAVE LACKED ARTICULATE SPEECH	436	FOR MY SON		20
THAT SPEECH WAS ALL THAT THE TOWN KNEW, BUT HE	462	HARUN RASHID		35
THAT SPEECH WAS ALL THAT THE COURT KNOW, BUT HE	462	HARUN RASHID	V	35
"GREAT PRINCE, FORGIVE THE FREEDOM OF MY SPEECH:	464	HARUN RASHID		74
FROM A DISCOURSE IN FIGURATIVE SPEECH	472	ALL SOUL NIGHT		52
REMORSE FOR INTEMPERATE SPEECH	506	REMORSE SPEECH		T
FINE MANNERS, LIBERAL SPEECH,	506	REMORSE SPEECH		7
SPEECH AFTER LONG SILENCE: IT IS RIGHT,	523	LONG SILENCE		1
SPEECHLESS				
BUT SPEECHLESS, AND THE MAIDEN WITH LONG WAIL	713	FERENCZ RENYI		85
SPEED				
HAVE A SPEED LIKE THE SPEED OF THE SALMON HERDS,	9	OISIN 1		98
HAVE A SPEED LIKE THE SPEED OF THE SALMON HERDS,	9	OISIN 1		98
AND FOLLOWING HER AT A HEADLONG SPEED	12	OISIN 1	V	144
AND "A WEARINESS SOON IS MY SPEED," SAYS THE MOUSE,	27	OISIN 1	V	417
AND "MY SPEED IS A WEARINESS," FALTERS THE MOUSE,	28	OISIN 1		421
AND HOOF AND HORN THAT HAD SUCKED IN THEIR SPEED	278	TWO KINGS		30
SPEEDS				
IT SPEEDS THE PARTING GUEST.	434	YOUTH AND AGE		4
SPEEDY				
AND BECAUSE I WENT BY THEM SO HUGH AND SO SPEEDY WITH EYES SO BRIGHT,	59	OISIN 3		169
AND BEFORE I WENT BY THEM SO HUGE AND SO SPEEDY WITH EYES SO BRIGHT,	59	OISIN 3	V	169
WITH SPEEDY FEET AND A MOST THANKFUL HEART:	185	QUEEN MAEVE		100
SPELL				
HE HAS FLUNG A DRUID SPELL UPON THE AIR,	240	SHADOW WATER B		385
AND MANY A HERB AND MANY A SPELL	717	FAIRY DOCTOR		17
AND MANY HERBS AND MANY A SPELL	717	FAIRY DOCTOR	V	17
OR THEY'D HURL A SPELL AT HIM,	775	AGAINST WITCH		18
SPELL-BOUND				
BY THEE SPELL-BOUND? THOU SHALT KNOW MORE:	675	ISLE STAT II 3		241
SPELLS				
THEY GAVE ME THAT OLD HARP OF THE NINE SPELLS	237	SHADOW WATER B	V	327
FOR ALL HIS SPELLS WILL VANISH WHEN HE DIES,	240	SHADOW WATER B		376
THROUGH WICKED SPELLS. THAT IS NOT ALL THE TALE,	242	SHADOW WATER B		408
IF YOU HAD TAKEN ME BY MAGIC SPELLS,	245	SHADOW WATER B		490
O LET ME PASS: THE SPELLS FROM OFF THE HEART	668	ISLE STAT II 3		44
OF EQUAL POWER IN SPELLS AND SECRET RITES.	720	WITCH VIVIEN		6
SPEND				
LET'S HOME AND SPEND IT IN OUR VILLAGES.	248	SHADOW WATER B	V	538A
AND HAD THE LIVELONG SUMMER DAY TO SPEND.	409	TOWER		10
SPENSER				
(AN IMAGE OUT OF SPENSER AND THE COMMON TONGUE).	603	GALLERY REVIS		40
SPENT				
OR HAPPIER-THOUGHTED WHEN THE DAY IS SPENT	292	TO A SHADE		4
OR HAPPIER THOUGHTED WHEN THE DAY IS SPENT	292	TO A SHADE	V	4
I BADE, BECAUSE THE WICK AND OIL ARE SPENT	333	LIVING BEAUTY		1
THE WICK OF YOUTH BEING BURNED AND THE OIL SPENT,	334	LIVING BEAUTY	V	3
THAT WOMAN'S DAYS WERE SPENT	392	EASTER 1916		17
ALL THAT SHE GOT SHE SPENT,	392	EASTER 1916	V	20
GATHERED A SCORE OF HORSE AND SPENT HIS DAYS	420	MY HOUSE		22
WHETHER HEALTH, WEALTH OR PEACE OF MIND WERE SPENT	429	NINETEEN 19		36
WE SHIFT ABOUT--ALL THAT GREAT GLORY SPENT--	491	COOLE BALLYLEE		39
MAN SHIFTS ABOUT--ALL THAT GREAT GLORY SPENT--	491	COOLE BALLYLEE	V	39
THEIR MONEY SPENT, THEIR WINE GONE SOUR,	635	BLACK TOWER		3
HOW MANY CENTURIES SPENT	784	WOMANS BEAUTY		7
SPHERE				
INTO A SPHERE FROM YOUTHFUL SYMPATHY,	443	SCHOOL CHILDR		14
THE ZODIAC IS CHANGED INTO A SPHERE.	535	CHOSEN		18
SPHINX				
A SPHINX WITH WOMAN BREAST AND LION PAW,	383	VISION ROBART		18
SPICE				
LOOK THERE! THERE IN THE MIST! A SHIP OF SPICE!	232	SHADOW WATER B		419
TREASURE ON TREASURE. BOXES OF PRECIOUS SPICE.	247	SHADOW WATER B		533
TREASURE AND TREASURE. BOXES OF PRECIOUS SPICE.	247	SHADOW WATER B	V	533
SPICE-ISLES				
WHERE SPICE-ISLES NESTLE ON THE STAR-TROD SEAS,	682	SEEKER		17
SPIDER				
NOT THERE, FOR THERE A SPIDER WEAVES HER WEB.	700	MOSADA 3		38
SPIDER'S				
FOR THOUGH LOVE HAS A SPIDER'S EYE	388	SOLOMON WITCH		19
A LOVER WITH A SPIDER'S EYE	388	SOLOMON WITCH	V	19
SPIDERS				
AND SPIDERS ARE MY FRIENDS: I'M THEIRS, AND THEY ARE	693	MOSADA 1		64
SPIES				
OF THE HOUSEHOLD SPIES:	536	PARTING		3
SPILLED				
BY A SPILLED WINE-CUP LIE.	168	BLESSED	V	32
SPILLS				
AND RAINS DOWN LIFE UNTIL THE BASIN SPILLS,	417	ANCEST HOUSES		4
SPILT				
SPILT MILK	484	SPILT MILK		T
LIKE MILK SPILT ON A STONE.	484	SPILT MILK		4
SPINDLE				
WHO TALKS OF PLATO'S SPINDLE:	520	HIS BARGAIN		1

SPINDLES
    WHO COME WITH THEIR CROWNS OF PEARL AND THEIR SPINDLES   203 WITHER BOUGHS   10
        OF WOOL,
SPINE
    THROUGH HEART AND SPINE, AND CAST HIM IN THE WAVE . . .   41 OISIN 2   182
    THROUGH HEART AND DEMON SPINE, AND IN THE WAVE . . .   41 OISIN 2   V 182
SPINNER
    AND ONE SPINNER IS LOST. . . . .   771 SPINNING SONG   10
SPINNING
    SPINNING AT ALL TIMES ERI'S GOOD TO-MORROW, . . .   129 BOOK STORIES   V 10
    THE SPINNING STARS--THE TOILING SEA--WHIRL ROUND . .   665 ISLE STAT II 2   72
    SPINNING SONG. . . . .   770 SPINNING SONG   T
SPINNING-JENNY
    GOD TOOK THE SPINNING-JENNY . . . .   439 FRAGMENTS   3
SPINNING-TOP
    AS 'TWERE A SPINNING-TOP. . . . .   384 VISION ROBART   44
SPIRAL
    AND THEN AWAY, AWAY, LIKE SPIRAL FLAMES; . . . .   29 OISIN 2   V 2
SPIRED
    DID NOT THE WORMS THAT SPIRED ABOUT HIS BONES . . .   128 DREAM OF FAERY   41
    WERE NOT THE WORMS THAT SPIRED ABOUT HIS BONES . . .   128 DREAM OF FAERY V 41
SPIRING
    GYRING, SPIRING TO AND FRO . . . .   135 TWO TREES   15
    THIS WINDING, GYRING, SPIRING TREADMILL OF A STAIR . . .   480 BLOOD AND MOON   17
SPIRIT
    TO FLY A SPIRIT," NIAM WEEPING SAID. . . . .   35 OISIN 2   V 92
    MY SPIRIT ROCKED IN EVENING LIGHT, THE RUSHES ROUND MY   76 INDIAN ON GOD   2
        KNEES,
    MY SPIRIT ROCKED IN SLEEP AND SIGHS; AND SAW THE MOORFOWL   76 INDIAN ON GOD   3
        PACE
    MY SPIRIT ROCKED IN EVENING'S HUSH, THE RUSHES ROUND MY   76 INDIAN ON GOD V 2
        KNEES,
    IN MY MOST SECRET SPIRIT GREW . . . .   83 MAD KING GOLL   27
    A DREAM OF A BLESSED SPIRIT . . . .   124 CATHLEEN PARA V T
    SPIRIT AFTER SPIRIT! THE SMITHIES BREAK THE FLOOD, . .   498 BYZANTIUM   34
    SPIRIT AFTER SPIRIT! THE SMITHIES BREAK THE FLOOD, . .   498 BYZANTIUM   34
    HIS SPIRIT THAT HAS FLED . . . .   575 MAIDS 2ND SONG   5
    THE SPIRIT MEDIUM . . . .   599 SPIRIT MEDIUM   T
    YON SHEPHERD--CAME YOUR SPIRIT TO BEGUILE . . . .   648 ISLE STAT I 1   105
    I' FAITH THOU EVER WAST A WORDY SPIRIT! . . . .   673 ISLE STAT II 3   175
    HIS RUEFUL SPIRIT FLUTTERED BY. . . . .   673 ISLE STAT II 3   188
    THOUGH SAD IS MANY A SPIRIT . . . .   680 LOVE AND DEATH   23
    AND THROUGH THE MANSION OF THE SPIRIT ROVE . . .   681 SEEKER   2
    STAR-ENVIOUS. HE WAS A SPIRIT, BROTHER. . . .   683 SEEKER   39
    TWO SPIRIT THINGS A MAN HATH FOR HIS FRIENDS! . .   686 DRAWING-ROOM   5
    HER SPIRIT. AS SHE MOVES, THE FOAM-GLOBES BURST .   687 TWO TITANS   14
    SINGS THE YOUNG WISTFUL SPIRIT OF A STAR . . .   705 REMEMBRANCE   10
    WILD WISDOMS OF SPIRIT AND TONGUE. . . . .   708 FAIRY PEDANT   27
    THE SPIRIT OF YOUNG RENYI HAS GROWN OLD. . . .   710 FERENCZ RENYI   17
    THE PROUDEST OR MOST COY OF SPIRIT THINGS, . .   720 WITCH VIVIEN   7
    TO THE EVER-LONGING AND MOURNFUL SPIRIT SAY. . . .   734 QUATRAIN APHOR   12
    TWO SPIRIT THINGS A MAN HATH FOR HIS FRIENDS! . .   734 QUATRAIN APHOR V 5
SPIRITS
    OH MAIDEN." "ARE YE SPIRITS OF THE SEA, ...   34 OISIN 2   V 7&8
    LONG SIGHS AROSE IN OUR SPIRITS, BENEATH US BUBBLED THE   48 OISIN 3   20
        GROUND.
    THEIR MOTIONLESS EYEBALLS OF SPIRITS . . . . . .   55 OISIN 3   121
    "IN THE ISLES OF THE FARTHEST SEAS WHERE ONLY THE SPIRITS   56 OISIN 3   133
        COME.
    . . . AND NO MAN MAY WAR WITH THE STRONG SPIRITS WAGE! .   62 OISIN 3   V 214
    HE WILL SMILE ON THE THREE OLD SPIRITS, ...   178 FIDDLER DOONEY   11
    COULD NOT AMEND. I HAVE GOOD SPIRITS ENOUGH. . .   227 SHADOW WATER B   116
    HAS CALLED UP THE COLD SPIRITS THAT ARE BORN . . .   382 VISION ROBART   2
    WHERE BLOOD-BEGOTTEN SPIRITS COME . . . . .   498 BYZANTIUM   28
    WHERE BLOOD BEGOTTEN SPIRITS COME . . . . .   498 BYZANTIUM   V 28
    FORTH! FORTH! O SPIRITS, YE HAVE HEARD YOUR TASK! .   669 ISLE STAT II 3   81
    TWO LONELY SPIRITS WAIT. . . . .   680 LOVE AND DEATH   18
    ARE THE SPIRITS LOVE AND DEATH. . . . . .   680 LOVE AND DEATH   32
    THE SPIRITS STOLE, AND GAVE HIM IN ITS STEAD . .   684 SEEKER   55
    WILD SPIRITS OF WISDOM AND TONGUE. . . . . .   708 FAIRY PEDANT   V 27
SPIRIT-THINGS
    TWO SPIRIT-THINGS A MAN HATH FOR HIS FRIENDS-- . .   734 QUATRAIN APHOR   5
SPIRITUAL
    THE SPIRITUAL INTELLECT'S GREAT WORK, ...   632 MAN AND ECHO   20
SPIRITUALISED
    EYES SPIRITUALISED BY DEATH CAN JUDGE, . . .   604 YOU CONTENT   7
SPIRITUS
    WHEN A VAST IMAGE OUT OF SPIRITUS MUNDI . . .   402 SECOND COMING   12
SPIT
    I SPIT INTO THE FACE OF TIME . . . . . .   132 OLD PENSIONER   17
    FOR LARDER AND SPIT ARE BARE, ...   349 HAWK   4
    BUT SHOULD THAT OTHER COME, I SPIT! . . . .   509 JANE BISHOP   27
SPITE
    INDIGNANT AT THE FUMBLING WITS, THE OBSCURE SPITE .   291 PAUDEEN   1
    THE DAILY SPITE OF THIS UNMANNERLY TOWN, . . .   351 PEOPLE   3
    GREAT WORKS CONSTRUCTED THERE IN NATURE'S SPITE . .   488 COOLE PARK 29   5
SPITTLE
    . . . THE SPITTLE ON HIS BEARD NEVER DRY, ...   53 OISIN 3   90
    . . . WITH THE SPITTLE ON HIS BEARD NEVER DRY. . . .   60 OISIN 3   192
SPLASH
    HOW STILL IT IS! I HEAR THE CARP GO SPLASH, ...   722 WITCH VIVIEN   62

SPLASHED   SEE FROTH-SPLASHED
    SPLASHED ALL WITH CLAY AND JOURNEY DULL, ... 82 MAD KING GOLL V 13
    SPLASHED, OR AN OTTER SLID INTO THE STREAM. . . . . . 372 PHASES OF MOON 9
    HE SPLASHED WHERE AN ABSURD . . . . 400 DEMON BEAST 27
    BUT TROD THE ROAD, OR SPLASHED ABOUT THE SHORE, ... 447 COLONUS PRAISE 27
SPLASHING
    THE HEAVY STEPS OF THE PLOUGHMAN, SPLASHING THE WINTRY 143 ROSE IN HEART 3
        MOULD,
    THE HEAVY STEPS OF THE PLOUGHMAN SPLASHING THE WINTER 143 ROSE IN HEART V 3
        MOULD,
    SCARED BY THE SPLASHING OF A DOZEN COWS! . . . . 419 MY HOUSE 10
    SCARED BY THE SPLASHING OF A HUNDRED COWS. . . . . . . 419 MY HOUSE V 10
SPLEEN
    DO MOST EXCITE MY SPLEEN, ... 599 STONE CROSS 18
SPLENDOUR
    AND HORRIBLE SPLENDOUR OF DESIRE! . . . . 411 TOWER 63
    WHO SITS IN LONELY SPLENDOUR, MAIL'D IN GOLD, ... 651 ISLE STAT I 1 163
SPLIT
    BUT IN HONOUR SPLIT HIS LOVE . . . . 573 LADYS 3RD SONG 7
SPLITS
    . . . NIGHT SPLITS AND THE DAWN BREAKS LOOSE! . . . . . 623 HIGH TALK 12
SPOIL
    OR BEEN FIT SPOIL FOR A CENTAUR . . . . 355 PROPERTIUS 7
SPOILS
    THIS SULLEN PEASANT SPOILS THE GOOD SUNSHINE, ... 711 FERENCZ RENYI 42
    THIS SULLEN PEASANT SPOILS THE GOOD RED WINE. . . . . . 711 FERENCZ RENYI 43
SPOILT
    SPOILT WHAT OLD LOINS HAVE SENT? . . . . 604 YOU CONTENT 6
SPOKE
    SUDDENLY AILELL SPOKE OUT OF HIS SLEEP, ... 183 QUEEN MAEVE 73
    THEN SEEING THAT HE SCARCE HAD SPOKE . . . . 194 BAILE AILLINN 126
    HE HAD BUT GAZED ON THORN-TREES, SPOKE, ... 274 GREY ROCK 82
    HE HAD BUT GAZED ON THORN TREES, SPOKE! . . . . . . 274 GREY ROCK V 82
    'TWAS ROUNDLY SPOKE, BUT WHEN NIGHT CAME . . . . . . 275 GREY ROCK 95
    SHE MOTIONED HIM AFAR, AND ROSE AND SPOKE! . . . . . 280 TWO KINGS 68
    BUT ASKED THE MORE UNTIL HE SPOKE THESE WORDS, ... 281 TWO KINGS V 92A
    A WOMAN SPOKE OF SOME NEW TALE SHE HAD READ, ... 350 HER PRAISE 7
    OR WAS IT SHE THAT SPOKE OR SOME GREAT DJINN? . . . . 467 HARUN RASHID 135
    I SAY THAT A DJINN SPOKE. A LIVELONG HOUR . . . . . 467 HARUN RASHID 136
    I SAY THAT A DJIN SPOKE. A LIVE LONG HOUR . . . . . 467 HARUN RASHID V 136
    I SAY THAT A JINN SPOKE. A LIVE-LONG HOUR . . . . . 467 HARUN RASHID V 136
    MY GREAT-GRANDFATHER SPOKE TO EDMUND BURKE . . . . . 486 SEVEN SAGES 1
    SPOKE THESE, OR WORDS LIKE THESE. . . . . 496 MOHINI CHATTER 15
    DOUBTLESS I SPOKE OR SANG WHAT I HAD HEARD . . . . . 557 RIBH ECSTASY 2
    HE SPOKE WITH TURK AND JEW, ... 594 COLONEL MARTIN 2
    THE GOLDEN PLOUGH AND HARROW AND SPOKE ALOUD . . . . . 609 IN TARAS HALLS 12
    THE WOMEN THAT I PICKED SPOKE SWEET AND LOW . . . . . 622 HOUND VOICE 8
    SWEAR BY WHAT THE SAGES SPOKE . . . . 636 BEN BULBEN 1
    SPOKE AND SET THE COCKS A-CROW. . . . . 637 BEN BULBEN 4
SPOKEN
    BEEN SPOKEN OF WITH ANY MAN! . . . . 6 OISIN 1 56
    BEEN SPOKEN OF WITH ANY ONE, ... 6 OISIN 1 V 56
    BEEN SPOKEN OF WITH ANYONE! . . . . 6 OISIN 1 V 56
    HE THINKS OF THOSE WHO HAVE SPOKEN EVIL OF HIS BELOVED . 166 EVIL OF BELOV T
    AEDH THINKS OF THOSE WHO HAVE SPOKEN EVIL OF HIS BELOVED 166 EVIL OF BELOV V T
    THEY HAVE SPOKEN AGAINST YOU EVERYWHERE, ... 166 EVIL OF BELOV 3
    AND WHEN YOU HAVE SPOKEN TAKE THE ROADS AGAIN? . . . 373 PHASES OF MOON 25
    "O WORDS ARE LIGHTLY SPOKEN," . . . . 396 ROSE TREE 1
    HAD SPOKEN OF THEIR CHILDISH DAYS . . . . 457 SUMMER SPRING 11
    HAS SPOKEN THE WISDOM OF THE DESERT DJINS, ... 468 HARUN RASHID V 163
    COULD MY SPOKEN WORDS HAVE CHECKED . . . . 632 MAN AND ECHO 15
    AND SPOKEN IN THE COUNCIL, AND HEARD TALES . . . . . 748 SHADOW WATER A 28
SPONGE
    THE VINEGAR-HEAVY SPONGE, THE FLOWERS BY KEDRON STREAM! 172 TRAV PASSION 5
    THE HISSOP-HEAVY SPONGE, THE FLOWERS BY KIDRON STREAM! . 172 TRAV PASSION V 5
SPONGY
    O'ER HILL AND HEATH AND SPONGY FEN, ... 83 MAD KING GOLL V 32
    OVER THE HEATH AND SPONGY FEN, ... 83 MAD KING GOLL V 32
SPONTANEOUS
    SPONTANEOUS JOY AND NATURAL CONTENT . . . . 260 FASC DIFFICULT 3
SPOOL
    HAS WOUND UPON A SPOOL . . . . 449 HERO GIRL FOOL 22
    WHEN CRADLE AND SPOOL ARE PAST . . . . 449 HERO GIRL FOOL 24
SPORT
    HAVE DRIVEN TRAVELLERS MAD FOR THEIR OWN SPORT. . . . 227 SHADOW WATER B 105
    MAY NOT HAVE DRIVEN YOU MAD FOR THEIR OWN SPORT? . . . 227 SHADOW WATER B V 105
    OR NOISY, INSOLENT SPORT, ... 293 HELEN LIVED 4
    HE THAT WAS BEST IN EVERY COUNTRY SPORT . . . . . . 339 SHEP GOATHERD 17
    TURN HATRED INTO SPORT, ... 506 REMORSE SPEECH 8
SPORTS
    WATCHING OUR SHEPHERD SPORTS AT HARVEST-TIME . . . . . 340 SHEP GOATHERD 41
SPOT
    HOW THE HAMMERS SPRING ON THE ANVIL, ON THE SPEARHEAD'S 52 OISIN 3 83
        BURNING SPOT!
    . . . ON THE SPEAR-HEAD'S BURNING SPOT! . . . . . . 52 OISIN 3 V 83
    PACING WITH HALF-CLOSED EYELIDS IN A SUNNY SPOT . . . 366 HER COURAGE 7
    IN THIS TUMULTUOUS SPOT, ... 420 MY HOUSE 23
    IT CAN BE MURDERED WITH A SPOT OF INK. . . . . . . 491 COOLE BALLYLEE 24
    A SPOT WHEREON THE FOUNDERS LIVED AND DIED . . . . . 491 COOLE BALLYLEE 33
    THAT IS AN AIRY SPOT, ... 614 MARCH SONGS 2 9
    THAT IS AN AIRY SPOT, ... 615 MARCH SONGS 2 19

	PAGE	TITLE		LINE
SPOT (CONTINUED)				
THAT IS AN AIRY SPOT,	615	MARCH SONGS 2		29
ON LIMESTONE QUARRIED NEAR THE SPOT	640	BEN BULBEN		90
AND WHEN THE SUMMER'S DEEP, THEN TO THIS SPOT	663	ISLE STAT II 2		24
OF HIM ON YONDER BRAZEN-GATED SPOT,	675	ISLE STAT II 3		240
OF SOLDIERS RANKED IS ON A GRASSY SPOT,	712	FERENCZ RENYI		64
OF SOLDIERS DRAWN IS ON A GRASSY SPOT,	712	FERENCZ RENYI	V	64
WITH QUIET SHADE ITS EVER DEWY SPOT,	714	FERENCZ RENYI	V	109
STANDS EACH GREY AND SILENT PHANTOM ON THE SAME REGARDLESS SPOT--	719	PHANTOM SHIP		25
SPOTS				
HIS LANGUID TAIL ABOVE US, LIT WITH MYRIAD SPOTS OF LIGHT.	77	INDIAN ON GOD		20
SPOTTED				
OVER HER SPOTTED FLESH AND FLYING HAIR	687	TWO TITANS		15
SPRANG				
AND ONCE A SUDDEN LAUGHTER SPRANG	16	OISIN 1		225
SPRANG FROM A GATEWAY WALLED AROUND WITH BLACK	31	OISIN 2	V	29
THAT SPRANG UNDER THE SEVEN HAZEL TREES,	35	OISIN 2		84
SPRANG DRIPPING, AND, WITH CAPTIVE DEMONS SENT	38	OISIN 2		130
THAT IS LIKE LAUGHTER, SPRANG AGAIN	318	APPOINTMENT		6
WHEN FIRST IT SPRANG OUT OF THE NEST	397	POLIT PRISONER		20
A FRENZIED CROWD, AND WHERE THE BRANCHES SPRANG	541	PARN FUNERAL 1		9
SPRAY				
ROLLED ROUND WITH MUSIC OF THE SIGHING SPRAY,	30	OISIN 2		14
TO SCATTER THE ACACIA SPRAY	360	ALF POLLEXFEN		10
THE COLD BLOWN SPRAY IN MY NOSTRIL,	399	BREAK OF DAY		20
WHILE THAT GREAT QUEEN, THAT ROSE OUT OF THE SPRAY,	404	FOR DAUGHTER		27
SPRAY-DABBLED				
WITH BLOWN, SPRAY-DABBLED HAIR GATHER AT HAND.	114	ROSE OF BATTLE		6
SPREAD SEE OUT-SPREAD				
THE LONG-HAIRED WARRIORS, THE SPREAD FEAST,	2	OISIN 1	V	7
. . . "WHERE WHITE CLOUDS LIE SPREAD	59	OISIN 3		178
I WOULD SPREAD THE CLOTHS UNDER YOUR FEET,	176	CLOTHS HEAVEN		5
I HAVE SPREAD MY DREAMS UNDER YOUR FEET,	176	CLOTHS HEAVEN		7
NO WAITING-MAID SHOULD EVER SPREAD	194	BAILE AILLINN		120
NO WAITING MAID SHOULD EVER SPREAD	194	BAILE AILLINN	V	120
WHEN THE SUPPER HAS BEEN SPREAD.	215	HAPPY TOWNLAND		44
AND YOU HAD SPREAD A SAIL FOR HOME, A WIND	236	SHADOW WATER B		309
IT WAS IN ALL HIS BATTLES. I WILL SPREAD MY HAIR,	242	SHADOW WATER B		413
WAS IT FOR THIS THE WILD GEESE SPREAD	290	SEPTEMBER 1913		17
HAIR SPREAD ON THE WIND THEY MADE,	332	ROUND TOWER		22
HAIRS SPREAD ON THE WIND THEY MADE,	332	ROUND TOWER	V	22
THEY CAN SPREAD OUT WHAT SAIL THEY PLEASE FOR ALL I HAVE TO SAY,	354	HIS PHOENIX		22
AND SPREAD ON EVERY SIDE,	396	ROSE TREE		10
SCARCE SPREAD A GLORY TO THE MORNING BEAMS,	422	MY DESCENDANTS		6
THE WINGS HALF SPREAD FOR FLIGHT,	430	NINETEEN 19		65
BEFORE SHE HAD SPREAD A BOOK UPON HER KNEES	466	HARUN RASHID		120
THEY ARE SPREAD WIDE THAT EACH	488	CRAZED MOON		17
THEY ATE SPREAD WIDE THAT EACH	488	CRAZED MOON	V	17
SPREAD TO A LAKE AND DROP INTO A HOLE.	490	COOLE BALLYLEE		7
SPREAD TO A LAKE AND RUN INTO A HOLE.	490	COOLE BALLYLEE	V	7
A RIVERY FIELD SPREAD OUT BELOW,	502	VACILLATION		57
WHERE THE MAPS ARE SPREAD,	617	LONG-LEG FLY		6
AND ALL WAS QUIET ROUND ME SPREAD,	670	ISLE STAT II 3		112
WHERE THE MOSS WAS SPREAD LIKE HIS OWN DOORMAT.	728	PRIEST FAIRY		8
MUST SPREAD OUT THEIR WINGS UNTIRING.	739	WHERE BOOKS GO		3
SPREADING				
AND CUSTOM FOR THE SPREADING LAUREL TREE.	406	FOR DAUGHTER		80
PLUNGES TOWARDS NOTHING, ARMS AND FINGERS SPREADING WIDE	426	PHANTOM HATRED		13
SPRIGHTLY				
THAT SHE MIGHT BE THAT SPRIGHTLY GIRL TRODDEN BY A BIRD,	353	HIS PHOENIX		4
THAT SHE MIGHT BE THAT SPRIGHTLY GIRL WHO HAD MARRIED WITH A BIRD,	353	HIS PHOENIX	V	4
THAT SHE MIGHT BE THAT SPRIGHTLY GIRL WHO WAS TRODDEN BY A BIRD,	353	HIS PHOENIX	V	4
SPRIGHTS				
THEY ARE THE FLOWERS' GUARDIAN SPRIGHTS,	666	ISLE STAT II 3		18
SPRING				
THAT SPRING FIVE PACES IN THEIR BOUNDS,	8	OISIN 1	V	86A
"MY BROTHERS SPRING OUT OF THEIR BEDS AT MORN,	32	OISIN 2		51
HOW THE HAMMERS SPRING ON THE ANVIL, ON THE SPEARHEAD'S BURNING SPOT,	52	OISIN 3		83
EVEN AS SPRING UPON THE ANCIENT SKIES,	108	CUCHULAIN SEA		42
STARED LIKE THE SPRING UPON THE ANCIENT SKIES,	108	CUCHULAIN SEA	V	41
THEIR RICHNESS THROUGH THE SUMMER AND THE SPRING,	279	TWO KINGS	V	62C
"YOU CRY ALOUD, O WOULD 'TWERE SPRING	306	HOUR DAWN		91
NEITHER THE SPRING NOR THE SOUTH WIND	306	HOUR DAWN		95
BUT THE OTHER CRIED, "YOU LONG FOR SPRING	306	HOUR DAWN	V	91
TAKING DELIGHT THAT HE COULD SPRING,	317	APPOINTMENT		4
AND CHILDREN WHEN THEY SPRING UP SHOULDER-HIGH.	343	SHEP GOATHERD		119
AND CHILDREN WHEN THEY SPRING UP SHOULDER-HIGH.	343	SHEP GOATHERD	V	119
THROUGH WINTER-TIME WE CALL ON SPRING,	434	WHEEL		1
AND THROUGH THE SPRING ON SUMMER CALL,	434	WHEEL		2
OF MAGNUS ANNUS AT THE SPRING,	437	SONGS PLAY 1		7
SUMMER AND SPRING	456	SUMMER SPRING		T
AND SHE HAD ALL THE SPRING,	457	SUMMER SPRING		16
YOU KNOW THE SAYING, "CHANGE THE BRIDE WITH SPRING,"	463	HARUN RASHID		50
THAT IF THE SPRING BEAR OFF WHAT THE SPRING GAVE	464	HARUN RASHID		76
THAT IF THE SPRING BEAR OFF WHAT THE SPRING GAVE	464	HARUN RASHID		76
THE EXTRAVAGANCE OF SPRING, OR MOVE A HAND .	466	HARUN RASHID		125

756

		PAGE	TITLE	LINE

SPRING   (CONTINUED)
THE EXTRAVAGANCE OF SPRING; OR CERTAIN TIMES • • • • • 466 HARUN RASHID   V   125
TARGETED, TROD LIKE SPRING. • • • • • • • • • • 504 QUARREL IN AGE   16
AWAITS RETURNING SPRING. • • • • • • • • • • • 517 HER ANXIETY   2
(HURRAH FOR THE FLOWERS OF SPRING, • • • • • • • • 567 FROM JAPANESE   3
FOR SPRING IS HERE AGAIN.) • • • • • • • • • • 567 FROM JAPANESE   4
FOR SPRING RICE HAD TO WHISPER IT, • • • • • • • 582 ROGER CASEMENT   13
THAT DIZZY DREAMS CAN SPRING • • • • • • • • • 781 MY HEART BEAT   7
SPRINGING
GO ASK THE SPRINGING FLOWERS, • • • • • • • • • 680 LOVE AND DEATH   13
SPRINGS
THAT SPRINGS FROM BODY AND IN BODY FALLS • • • • • 463 HARUN RASHID   63
SPRINGTIME
THAN ALL MY BURSTING SPRINGTIME KNEW. A GIRL • • • • 466 HARUN RASHID   105
FOR IN MY FIRST HARD SPRINGTIME WE WERE FRIENDS, • • • 473 ALL SOUL NIGHT   62
SPRING-TIME
BECAUSE THE SPRING-TIME HAS NOT COME— • • • • • • 434 WHEEL   6
FOR IN MY FIRST HARD SPRING-TIME WE WERE FRIENDS, • • • 473 ALL SOUL NIGHT   V   62
SPRITE
IT IS MY WHIM! BID SOME ATTENDANT SPRITE • • • • • 669 ISLE STAT II 3   72
WHERE LIES THE LONG-LOST FOREST OF THE SPRITE, • • • • 682 SEEKER   23
THERE LIES THE LONG-LOST FOREST OF THE SPRITE, • • • 682 SEEKER   V   23
SPRITES
FIRST DREAMS, AND GOBLINS, AND THE LESSER SPRITES, • • • 722 WITCH VIVIEN   56
SPRUNG   SEE SEA-SPRUNG
THAT OUT OF LIFE'S OWN SELF-DELIGHT HAD SPRUNG • • • 417 ANCEST HOUSES   11
THAT OUT OF LIFE'S OWN SELF DELIGHT HAD SPRUNG • • • 417 ANCEST HOUSES   V   11
FROM MAN'S BLOOD-SODDEN HEART ARE SPRUNG • • • • • 502 VACILLATION   67
SEEMED SPRUNG FROM BUT A SINGLE ROOT • • • • • • 571 THREE BUSHES   61
SPUME
PLATO THOUGHT NATURE BUT A SPUME THAT PLAYS • • • • 445 SCHOOL CHILDR   41
SPUN
WHERE I HAVE LAUGHED AND SPUN AND PLAYED? • • • • • 151 HEART OF WOMAN V   2
FOR WHOM THE HANGMAN'S ROPE WAS SPUN, • • • • • • 289 SEPTEMBER 1913   13
AND THE MOON SPUN ROUND LIKE A TOP, • • • • • • 378 CAT AND MOON   2
I HAVE SPUN IN THE HOUSE THIS NIGHT! • • • • • • 771 SPINNING SONG   13
SPUR
UPON HIS TREMBLING HORSE, THEN DROVE THE SPUR! • • • 277 TWO KINGS   11
HE THOUGHT TO HAVE GIVEN HIS HORSE THE SPUR, BUT SAW • • 277 TWO KINGS   V   48
TREMBLING BENEATH HIM, AND THEN DROVE THE SPUR • • • 277 TWO KINGS   V   11
THE SPUR • • • • • • • • • • • • • • • 591 SPUR   T
WHAT ELSE HAVE I TO SPUR ME INTO SONG? • • • • • • 591 SPUR   4
SPURRED
ON A FANTASTIC RIDE, MY HORSE'S FLANKS ARE SPURRED • • • 391 UNDER SATURN   6
ON A FANTASTIC RIDE I SWEAR MY HORSE'S FLANKS WERE SPURRED 391 UNDER SATURN   V   6
SPUTTERING
FOUND THAT OLD HOUSE, A SPUTTERING TORCH WITHIN, • • • 283 TWO KINGS   140
AND FOUND THE HOUSE, A SPUTTERING TORCH WITHIN, • • • 283 TWO KINGS   V   140
SPY
AND WHEN THE FOLK THERE SPY ME, • • • • • • • 179 FIDDLER DOONEY   17
AND THE FOLK THERE WHEN THEY SPY ME • • • • • • 179 FIDDLER DOONEY V   17
AND WHEN THE FOLKS THERE SPY ME, • • • • • • • 179 FIDDLER DOONEY V   17
SPYING
THAT HIDES US FROM ALL HUMAN SPYING, • • • • • • 22 OISIN 1   V 338A
SQUALL
THAT NONE MAY FEEL THE POWER OF SQUALL AND WAVE, • • • 128 DREAM OF FAERY V   45
SEE THE DARKNESS SLOW DISGORGING A VESSEL BLIND WITH   718 PHANTOM SHIP   12
SQUALL.
SQUANDERER
THE WRINKLED SQUANDERER OF HUMAN WEALTH. • • • • • 720 WITCH VIVIEN   16
SQUARE
SQUARE LEAVES OF THE IVY MOVED OVER US, BINDING US DOWN   52 OISIN 3   76
TO OUR REST.
BY OPPOSITION, SQUARE AND TRINE! • • • • • • • 325 ROBERT GREGORY   39
THE MEN ARE BUSY IN THE GLIMMERING SQUARE. • • • • 699 MOSADA 3   16
ERE LONG SHALL FALTER THROUGH THE NOISY SQUARE, • • • 699 MOSADA 3   21
BULWARK TO BULWARK, AND SQUARE HER SAIL BY OURS. • • • 752 SHADOW WATER A   129
SQUARED
THAT OLD, SEA-WEEDY, SQUARED, THREE HUNDRED FEET • • • 31 OISIN 2   V 30C
SQUEAKY
AND CIRCLED ROUND HIM WITH ITS SQUEAKY CRY, • • • • 377 PHASES OF MOON   138
SQUIRREL
A SQUIRREL WHINNIED AND A BIRD SCREAMED OUT! • • • • 278 TWO KINGS   34
WHERE THE PROUD, WAYWARD SQUIRREL WENT, • • • • • 317 APPOINTMENT   3
TO A SQUIRREL AT KYLE-NA-NO • • • • • • • • 359 TO A SQUIRREL   T
THERE WHERE YONDER SQUIRREL CRUNCHES • • • • • • 655 ISLE STAT I 3   4
THE RED SQUIRREL SHALL REAR HER YOUNG WHERE THOU   674 ISLE STAT II 3   215
HAST DWELT—
THE VERY SQUIRREL DIES THAT ENTERS THERE. • • • • 682 SEEKER   33
THE VERY SQUIRREL DIES THAT ENTERS IT. • • • • • 682 SEEKER   V   33
THE SQUIRREL YONDER, HUSHED AND WISE, • • • • • • 686 LIFE   5
SQUIRREL-BROWN
DULL-WITTED THING, WITH FACE RED SQUIRREL-BROWN. • • • 661 ISLE STAT II 1   68
SQUIRREL'S
ALTHOUGH HE HAD A SQUIRREL'S EYE. • • • • • • • 190 BAILE AILLINN   30
SQUIRRELS
WHERE MANY HUNDRED SQUIRRELS ARE AS HAPPY • • • • • 217 WOODS OF COOLE   5
ST.
AND RUTH ST. DENIS HAD MORE CHARM ALTHOUGH SHE HAD POOR   353 HIS PHOENIX   10
LUCK!
BECAUSE ST. JOSEPH'S IMAGE HANGETH HERE • • • • • 676 ISLE STAT II 3   266

757

	PAGE	TITLE		LINE
STABLE SEE LIVERY-STABLE				
"TO STABLE AND TO KENNEL GO!	97	FOXHUNTER		5
AND SOME ONE FROM THE STABLE BRING	97	FOXHUNTER	V	5
I'LL FIND THE STABLE AND PULL OUT THE BOLT.	260	FASC DIFFICULT		13
THE ILL-BRED SON OF A LIVERY STABLE KEEPER—	370	EGO DOMINUS	V	61
STABLE-KEEPER				
THE ILL-BRED SON OF A LIVERY STABLE-KEEPER—	370	EGO DOMINUS	V	61
STABLES				
AND SOME ONE FROM THE STABLES BRING	97	FOXHUNTER	V	5
STABLING				
STABLING HIS UNLOOSED LIGHTNINGS IN THEIR STALL, ...	36	OISIN 2		110
AND STABLING TO YOUR MIND.	774	COME RIDE		8
STAFF				
OF DREAMY FOAM A STAFF OF WOOD	24	OISIN 1		366
I DREW IT FORTH! THE STAFF OF WOOD, ...	24	OISIN 1	V	366
WHITE FLOWERS OF THE FOAM A STAFF OF WOOD	24	OISIN 1		366
PUT THE STAFF IN MY HANDS!	61	OISIN 3		201
AND CRUMPLED IN MY HANDS THE STAFF	84	MAD KING GOLL	V	33
AND BROKE BETWEEN MY HANDS THE STAFF	84	MAD KING GOLL	V	33
STAFFORD				
AND EVEN STAFFORD SMILED AS THOUGH	400	DEMON BEAST	V	13
STAG				
THE STAG WE CHASED WAS NOT MORE SAD, ...	2	OISIN 1	V	7J
THE STAG YE CHASE IS NOT MORE SAD, ...	4	OISIN 1	V	35
THE DELICATE-STEPPING STAG AND HIS LADY SIGH, ...	210	RAGGED WOOD		2
THE DELICATE STEPPING STAG AND HIS LADY SIGH	210	RAGGED WOOD	V	2
WITH THE GROUND-IVY'S BLUE, HE SAW A STAG	277	TWO KINGS		6
MORE HANDS IN HEIGHT THAN ANY STAG IN THE WORLD . .	277	TWO KINGS		9
BUT THE STAG STOOPED AND RAN AT HIM, AND PASSED, . .	277	TWO KINGS		12
AGAINST THE STAG. WHEN HORN AND STEEL WERE MET . .	277	TWO KINGS		15
AS THOUGH A STAG AND UNICORN WERE MET	277	TWO KINGS		19
AND THE GROUND IVY'S BLUER LIGHT, A STAG	277	TWO KINGS	V	6
BUT THE STAG STOOPED ITS HEAVY BRANCHING HORNS, . .	277	TWO KINGS	V	12
THE MARVELLOUS STAG OF ARTHUR, ...	399	BREAK OF DAY		23
THAT LOFTY WHITE STAG, LEAP	399	BREAK OF DAY		24
THE WILD STAG AND THE DOE! THAT MOUTH TO MOUTH . .	465	HARUN RASHID		101
STAG COULD RUN AND ROE LEAP	522	LULLABY	V	10
STAG COULD LEAP AND ROE COULD RUN.	522	LULLABY	V	12
STAGE				
WE LIVED LIKE MEN THAT WATCH A PAINTED STAGE.	542	PARN FUNERAL 1		18
UPON A PAINTED STAGE WHEN WE DEVOURED HIS HEART, . . .	542	PARN FUNERAL 1		23
THE GREAT STAGE CURTAIN ABOUT TO DROP, ...	565	LAPIS LAZULI		13
MY FATHER UPON THE ABBEY STAGE, BEFORE HIM A RAGING CROWD!	577	LOFTY THINGS		2
PLAYERS AND PAINTED STAGE TOOK ALL MY LOVE, ...	630	CIRCUS ANIMALS		31
NOW A NOTABLE MAN ON STAGE AND ON SCREEN!	790	DEDICATION		8
STAGES				
UPON A HUNDRED THOUSAND STAGES, ...	566	LAPIS LAZULI		23
STAGGER				
AND THEN I'D STAGGER OUT. HE'D CRACK HIS WITS . . .	377	PHASES OF MOON		134
I SAW HIM STAGGER WITH THE CLANKING CHAIN, ...	687	TWO TITANS		31
STAGGERED				
I STAGGERED, BUT A BEECH-TREE STAYED MY FALL, ...	286	TWO KINGS		209
I STAGGERED, BUT A BEECH TREE STAYED MY FALL, ...	286	TWO KINGS	V	209
STAGGERING				
THEY BORE IT WITH STAGGERING AND SWEATING, ...	60	OISIN 3		186
WITH SWEATING, WITH STAGGERING.	60	OISIN 3	V	185
ABOVE THE STAGGERING GIRL, HER THIGHS CARESSED . . .	441	LEDA AND SWAN		2
THE MOON IS STAGGERING IN THE SKY!	487	CRAZED MOON		2
STAGGERING WITH LANGUID EYE.	717	FAIRY DOCTOR	V	16
STAG'S				
TO STAY THE STAG'S NEXT RUSH. WHEN SWORD MET HORN . . .	277	TWO KINGS	V	15
STAID				
WITH HEAD BOWED ON HIS KNEES, CUCHULLIN STAID, ...	110	CUCHULAIN SEA	V	71
STAIN				
AH ME! TO BE OLD WITHOUT SUCCOUR, A SHOW UNTO CHILDREN,	63	OISIN 3	V	217
A STAIN,				
OF HER UNBLEMISHED LINEAMENTS, A WHITENESS WITH NO STAIN,	353	HIS PHOENIX		3
AND SMOOTH OUT STAIN AND BLEMISH WITH THE ELEGANCE OF HIS	353	HIS PHOENIX		7
MIND!				
WRITTEN IN GOLD UPON A PURPLE STAIN, ...	461	HARUN RASHID		10
THE BLOOD OF INNOCENCE HAS LEFT NO STAIN.	482	BLOOD AND MOON		34
LIKE EVERYTHING THAT HAS THE STAIN OF BLOOD, ...	482	BLOOD AND MOON		51
A PROPERTY OF THE LIVING! BUT NO STAIN	482	BLOOD AND MOON		52
AND BLOOD AND MIRE THE SENSITIVE BODY STAIN?	564	GYRES		10
OR LONG ERE THIS HAD LOST THEIR RUDDY STAIN!	687	TWO TITANS		8
DANCING ON THE MOON'S BROAD STAIN, ...	731	STREET DANCERS		15
STAINED SEE WINE-STAINED				
BUT NEVER SAW THE TREFOIL STAINED WITH BLOOD, ...	487	SEVEN SAGES		19
LOVE STORM! AND STAINED WITH MIST THE NEW MOONS FLARE. . .	678	ISLE STAT II 3		294
LOVE STORM AND STAINED WITH MIST THE NEW MOON'S FLARE . .	678	ISLE STAT II 3	V	294
STAINING				
IRRATIONAL STREAMS OF BLOOD ARE STAINING EARTH!	564	GYRES		5
STAINS				
I TURNED IT IN MY HANDS! THE STAINS	24	OISIN 1		368
STAIR				
HALF IN THE UNVESSELLED SEA, WE CLIMBED THE STAIR . . .	32	OISIN 2		47
WE MOUNTED ON THE STAIR, THE WHITE STEED TYING, . . .	32	OISIN 2	V	46
CAME SWIMMING SADLY DOWN THE MIGHTY STAIR.	32	OISIN 2	V	50B
AND THEN WE CLIMBED THE STAIR TO A HIGH DOOR!	36	OISIN 2		101
AND UP THE STAIR WE TOILED TO A HIGH DOOR, ...	36	OISIN 2	V	101
I FOUND, DROPPING SEA-FOAM ON THE WIDE STAIR, ...	43	OISIN 2		215

758

STAIR   (CONTINUED)
I FOUND, FOAM—OOZY ON THE VASTY STAIR,   43 OISIN 2   V 215
I FOUND, DROPPING SEA FOAM ON THE WIDE STAIR,   43 OISIN 2   V 215
I STOOD UPON THE STAIR! THE SURGES BORE   44 OISIN 2   225
CLIMB UP THE NARROW WINDING STAIR TO BED!   324 ROBERT GREGORY   5
CLIMBED UP MY CREAKING STAIR. THEY HAD READ   358 PRESENCES   6
TO CLIMB THAT STAIR AND EAT THAT BITTER BREAD, 369 EGO DOMINUS   35
A WINDING STAIR, A CHAMBER ARCHED WITH STONE, 419 MY HOUSE   11
MAY THIS LABORIOUS STAIR AND THIS STARK TOWER 423 MY DESCENDANTS   13
I TURN AWAY AND SHUT THE DOOR, AND ON THE STAIR 427 PHANTOM HATRED   33
I SUMMON TO THE WINDING ANCIENT STAIR!   477 SELF AND SOUL   1
I SUMMON TO THE WINDY ANCIENT STAIR!   477 SELF AND SOUL   V   1
THIS WINDING, GYRING, SPIRING TREADMILL OF A STAIR 480 BLOOD AND MOON 17
. . . IS MY ANCESTRAL STAIR!   480 BLOOD AND MOON   17
ODOUR OF BLOOD ON THE ANCESTRAL STAIR!   482 BLOOD AND MOON   40
AND NOW LIES SUNK IN SLEEP. WHAT CLIMBS THE STAIR? 579 DOR WELLESLEY 11
BUT NOW LIES SUNK IN SLEEP. WHAT CLIMBS THE STAIR? 579 DOR WELLESLEY V 11
AND BOTH CLIMBED UP THE STAIR,   595 COLONEL MARTIN   38
AND WHEN THEY CAME TO THE TOP STAIR   595 COLONEL MARTIN   41
"IF I DO BUT CLIMB THE STAIR   771 SONG DEIRDRE 1   2
STAIRS
HALF IN THE UNVESSELLED SEA, WE CLIMBED THE STAIRS 32 OISIN 2   V 47
LEAP IN THE MEADOW. ON THE MISTY STAIRS   44 OISIN 2   V 229
OR SHOD IN IRON, CLIMBED THE NARROW STAIRS,   412 TOWER   83
STAKE
FOR YE ARE HID WITH VAPOUR. ROUND THE STAKE   695 MOSADA 1   111
THE VAPOUR IS MUCH THICKER. GOD! THE STAKE!   695 MOSADA 1   112
FOR YE ARE HID WITH VAPOURS? ROUND THE STAKE 695 MOSADA 1   V 111
SHOULD KNOW WHAT ISSUE IS AT STAKE!   778 FRIENDS WRONG   3
AND SET IT ON A STAKE.   789 SINGING HEAD   6
BUT NEVER STOOD BEFORE A STAKE   790 SINGING HEAD   23
STAKES
FOR OTHER STAKES WE PLAY. YOU LOST THE GLASS. 722 WITCH VIVIEN   50
STALK
WHO MADE THE WORLD AND RULETH IT, HE HANGETH ON A STALK, 76 INDIAN ON GOD 10
I, THROUGH THE TERRIBLE NOVELTY OF LIGHT, STALK ON, STALK 623 HIGH TALK 13
   ON!
I, THROUGH THE TERRIBLE NOVELTY OF LIGHT, STALK ON, STALK 623 HIGH TALK 13
   ON!
GHOSTS OF HER VANISHED GLORIES, MUSE AND STALK 687 TWO TITANS   21
STALKED
WHAT STALKED THROUGH THE POST OFFICE? WHAT INTELLECT, 611 STATUES   26
STALKS
AND MINE WERE BUT FIFTEEN FOOT, NO MODERN STALKS 623 HIGH TALK   3
   UPON HIGHER,
STALL
STABLING HIS UNLOOSED LIGHTNINGS IN THEIR STALL, 36 OISIN 2   110
STALLION
MARE OR STALLION, COCK OR HEN,   529 TOM LUNATIC   15
"THE STALLION ETERNITY   529 TOM CRUACHAN   4
STAMMERING
BY THE STAMMERING SCHOOLBOY SAID,   65 HAPPY SHEPHERD   15
STAMP
WHEN THERE ARE MANY? EBREMAR WILL STAMP   696 MOSADA 2   4
STAMPED
YOUR HOOVES HAVE STAMPED AT THE BLACK MARGIN OF THE WOOD, 442 BLACK CENTAUR 1
MY WORKS ARE ALL STAMPED DOWN INTO THE SULTRY MUD. 442 BLACK CENTAUR   3
STAMPED BOY AND TREE UPON SICILIAN COIN.   541 PARN FUNERAL 1   15
STAMPER
BRIMFUL OF STARLIGHT, AND HE SAID! THE STAMPER OF 76 INDIAN ON GOD   14
   THE SKIES,
STAND
WITH WISDOM HOUR BY HOUR.—MAY WE TWO STAND,   71 ANASHU VIJAYA   7
WITH WISDOM HOUR BY HOUR.—MAY WE TOO STAND,   71 ANASHU VIJAYA   V   7
STAND YOU. BY BRAHMA'S EVER-RUSTLING ROBE,   71 ANASHU VIJAYA   V 14
"ALTHOUGH OUR LOVE IS WANING, LET US STAND   79 EPHEMERA   4
STAND BY THE BORDER OF THE LAKE ONCE MORE,   79 EPHEMERA   V   5
IN A FIELD BY THE RIVER MY LOVE AND I DID STAND, 90 SALLEY GARDENS   5
WHILE I STAND ON THE ROADWAY, OR ON THE PAVEMENTS GREY, 117 ISLE INNISFREE 11
WHILE I STAND ON THE ROADWAY, OR ON THE PAVEMENT GREY,   117 ISLE INNISFREE V 11
OR ELSE THEY STAND AND SNIFF THE WIND,   136 TWO TREES   37
AND STAND ON HER WINDOW-SILL.   159 CAP AND BELLS   4
AND STAND ON HER WINDOW SILL.   159 CAP AND BELLS   V   4
STAND UNDER THE ROUGH ROOF-TIMBERS OF THE HALL 377 PHASES OF MOON   125
I'D STAND AND MUTTER THERE UNTIL HE CAUGHT   377 PHASES OF MOON   131
STAND UP AND LIFT YOUR HAND AND BLESS   379 SAINT HUNCH   1
STAND AT MY DOOR, AND I COMPLAIN   424 ROAD AT DOOR   8
FROM SHALLOW WITS! WHO KNOWS NO WORK CAN STAND, 429 NINETEEN 19   35
BID A STRONG GHOST STAND AT THE HEAD   435 FOR MY SON   1
I SAW A STARING VIRGIN STAND   437 SONGS PLAY 1   1
I SAW THAT STARING, VIRGIN STAND   437 SONGS PLAY 1   V   1
OUR MOST RENOWNED PATRIOTS STAND,   460 THREE MONUMENT   2
HERE, TRAVELLER, SCHOLAR, POET, TAKE YOUR STAND 489 COOLE PARK 29   25
AND BIDS MY HAIR STAND UP?   499 MOTHER OF GOD   15
AND MAKES MY HAIR STAND UP?   499 MOTHER OF GOD   V 15
AND SEEMED TO STAND ALTHOUGH IN BED I LAY.   535 CHOSEN   9
AS THOUGH THAT HAND COULD REACH TO WHERE THEY STAND, 579 DOR WELLESLEY 2
I AM CONTENT TO STAND AND SING   582 ROGER CASEMENT   V 21
STAND UPRIGHT ON YOUR LEGS AWHILE,   586 PARNELLITES   3
STAND UPRIGHT WHILE YOU CAN,   586 PARNELLITES   4
BEFORE A WOMAN'S PORTRAIT SUDDENLY I STAND,   602 GALLERY REVIS   13

			PAGE	TITLE		LINE
STAND	(CONTINUED)					
THERE IN THE TOMB STAND THE DEAD UPRIGHT,	. . . .	635	BLACK TOWER		7
STAND WE ON GUARD OATH-BOUND!	. . . .	636	BLACK TOWER		26
A WHITE, DUMB THING OF TEARS, HERE LET IT STAND,	. .	663	ISLE STAT II 2		21
I'LL SEE HIM LONGER IF I STAND OUT HERE	. . . . .	703	MOSADA 3		113
"BRING THE ROPES NOW! STAND YE BY NOW!	. . . . .	718	PHANTOM SHIP		13
"MAY STAND BEFORE THY RACE AND THEE	. . . . .	742	EARL PAUL		63
THE ARCHANGELS STAND IN A ROW THERE	. . . .	774	COME RIDE		9
STANDEST						
NO! THOU STANDEST STILL AND STARK,	. . . .	658	ISLE STAT I 3		90
STANDING						
I SAW HER STANDING IN HER DOOR BUT NOW,	. . . . .	74	ANASHU VIJAYA		64
WHY ARE YOU STANDING WITH YOUR EYES UPON ME?	. .	234	SHADOW WATER B		276
LEANING OR STANDING OR WALKING .	. . . . .	356	BROKEN DREAMS		23
AND, STANDING BY THESE CHARACTERS, DISCLOSE	. . . .	371	EGO DOMINUS		75
O SAGES STANDING IN GOD'S HOLY FIRE	. . . .	408	SAIL BYZANTIUM		17
AM SET DOWN STANDING IN THE WOOD	. . . .	453	DEATH OF HARE		11
THERE, STANDING ON THE CART,	. . . .	544	TO SAME TUNE 1		5
THERE, STANDING ON THE CART,	. . . .	616	MARCH SONGS 3		5
HOW CAN I, THAT GIRL STANDING THERE,	. . . . .	631	POLITICS		1
AS I AM STANDING NOW--AS THOUGH I GAZED,	. . . .	663	ISLE STAT II 2		26
BEHOLD THE HAPLESS SLEEPERS STANDING BY.	. . . . .	677	ISLE STAT II 3		281
STANDISH						
STANDISH O'GRADY SUPPORTING HIMSELF BETWEEN THE TABLES	. .	577	LOFTY THINGS		5
STANDS						
THE HUNTSMAN NEAR HIM STANDS,	. . . .	98	FOXHUNTER		24
THE HUNTSMAN NEAR HIM STANDS,	. . . .	98	FOXHUNTER	V	22
MY FATHER STANDS AMID HIS BATTLE-CARS."	. . . . .	107	CUCHULAIN SEA		26
MY FATHER STANDS." "AGED, WORN OUT WITH WARS	. . .	107	CUCHULAIN SEA		29
MY FATHER STANDS AMID HIS BATTLE CARS."	. . . . .	107	CUCHULAIN SEA	V	26
AND GOD STANDS WINDING HIS LONELY HORN,	. . . . .	148	INTO TWILIGHT		13
SHE STANDS BEFORE ME AS A LIVING CHILD.	. . . . .	444	SCHOOL CHILDR		24
UNDER IT WISDOM STANDS, AND I ALONE--	. . . . .	469	HARUN RASHID		189
UNDER IT ARMED WISDOM STANDS, A SEPARATE WISDOM	. . . .	469	HARUN RASHID	V	189
HORACE THERE BY HOMER STANDS,	. . . .	524	MAD AS MIST		7
PLATO STANDS BELOW,	. . . .	524	MAD AS MIST		8
"WHATEVER STANDS IN FIELD OR FLOOD,	. . . . .	529	TOM LUNATIC		13
STANDS IN GOD'S UNCHANGING EYE	. . . . . .	529	TOM LUNATIC		16
WHEN SEA-WIND SWEPT THE CORNER, STANDS!	. . . .	566	LAPIS LAZULI		32
WHAT ON THE THRESHOLD STANDS?	. . . . . .	583	GHOST ROG CASE		2
THEN STANDS IN JUDGMENT ON HIS SOUL,	. . . . .	633	MAN AND ECHO		33
FOR AN INSTANT STANDS AT EASE,	. . . . . .	638	BEN BULBEN		31
LONG YEARS AGO, A CHURCH STANDS NEAR,	. . . . .	640	BEN BULBEN		87
FAMOUS, A MAN OF RULES, A VICTOR. STANDS	. . . .	709	FERENCZ RENYI		9
WHITE, RENYI SILENT STANDS! THAT MAIDEN SWEET	. . .	713	FERENCZ RENYI	V	84
I CURSE THEE--CURSE THEE!" RENYI SILENT STANDS,	. . . .	714	FERENCZ RENYI		107
STANDS EACH GREY AND SILENT PHANTOM ON THE SAME REGARDLESS SPOT--		719	PHANTOM SHIP		25
UPON MY SOUL, OLD TIME. NO! THUS IT STANDS.	. . . .	722	WITCH VIVIEN		49
STAR	SEE POLE-STAR					
AND SLEEP DROWN SUN AND MOON AND STAR."	. . . . .	5	OISIN 1	V	49
IN OTHER YEARS FROM SOME OLD STAR .	. . . . .	19	OISIN 1	V	277
EACH FOREHEAD LIKE AN OBSCURE STAR	. . . . . .	26	OISIN 1		391
HUNG FROM THE MORNING STAR! WHEN THESE MILD WORDS	. .	32	OISIN 2		49
SO MUCH REMAINED THAT ON THE EVENING STAR .	. . .	32	OISIN 2	V	48
WHERE GOES TO GAZE THE RESTLESS-FOOTED STAR	. . .	32	OISIN 2	V	50G
WHEN THE EARLIEST DEW-WASHED STAR FROM EVE HATH LEANT,	. .	32	OISIN 2	V	54
SHOUTED, AND HAILED HIM! HE HUNG THERE A STAR,	. . .	36	OISIN 2		107
SCARED OF ITS GLITTERING LIKE A METEOR STAR,	. . .	38	OISIN 2	V	137
I HAVE FORGIVEN, O NEW STAR!	. . . . . .	75	ANASHU VIJAYA		77
WHILE OUR LOVE GROWS AN INDIAN STAR,	. . . . .	78	INDIAN TO LOVE		13
WHILE GROWS OUR LOVE AN INDIAN STAR,	. . . . .	78	INDIAN TO LOVE	V	13
AND UNDER THE BLINK O' THE MORNING STAR,	. . . .	83	MAD KING GOLL	V	20
THAT SCARCE COULD BATHE A STAR,	. . . . .	88	STOLEN CHILD		31
ONE STAR SHONE FAINT AND GREEN,	. . . . . .	95	MOLL MAGEE		30
AND THE FLAME OF THE BLUE STAR OF TWILIGHT,	. . .	122	WHITE BIRDS		3
OR THE FLAME OF THE BLUE STAR THAT LINGERS	. . . .	122	WHITE BIRDS		7
FOR THE WINDS THAT AWAKENED THE STAR,	. . . . .	171	MAID QUIET	V	3
THE PILOT STAR AND THE CROOKED PLOUGH	. . . . .	177	PAST GREATNESS		4
OUT OF THE RUNNING STREAM, O MORNING STAR,	. . . . .	251	SHADOW WATER B		610
AYE, SUN AND MOON AND STAR, ALL,	. . . . .	415	TOWER		152
WHEN THAT FIERCE VIRGIN AND HER STAR	. . . . .	437	SONGS PLAY 1		15
WHEN THE FIERCE VIRGIN AND HER STAR	. . . . .	437	SONGS PLAY 1	V	15
WHAT A STAR SANG AND CARELESS MUSES HEARD!	. . .	445	SCHOOL CHILDR		47
UPON THE STAR THAT MARKS THE HIDDEN POLE!	. . . .	477	SELF AND SOUL		5
THIS FALLEN STAR MY MILK SUSTAINS,	. . . . .	499	MOTHER OF GOD		12
BRIGHTNESS REMAINS! A BRIGHTER STAR SHOOTS DOWN!	. .	541	PARN FUNERAL 1		4
RECALL THE CRETAN BARB THAT PIERCED A STAR?	. . .	541	PARN FUNERAL 1		7
A PIERCED BOY, IMAGE OF A STAR LAID LOW.	. . . .	541	PARN FUNERAL 1		12
ANOTHER STAR HAS SHOT AN EAR.	. . . . .	625	NATIVITY		2
EACH SHINING CLEAR AS SOME UNBAFFLED STAR!	. . . .	656	ISLE STAT I 3		25
DRAW STAR TO STAR, AS ON THAT EVE HE PASSED	. . . .	691	MOSADA 1		29
DRAW STAR TO STAR, AS ON THAT EVE HE PASSED	. . . .	691	MOSADA 1		29
WE'LL FLY FROM THIS BEFORE THE MORNING STAR.	. . .	702	MOSADA 3		74
SINGS THE YOUNG WISTFUL SPIRIT OF A STAR	. . . .	705	REMEMBRANCE		10
WHILE THE MORNING STAR DECAYETH	. . . . . .	706	DAWN-SONG		29
AND SOFT, ONE GLIMMERING STAR. RENYI HAS CAST	. . .	714	FERENCZ RENYI		115
AND SOFT, ONE GLIMMERING STAR--WITH POWER VAST!	. . .	714	FERENCZ RENYI	V	115
BESIDE THE WILLOW. NAY, TO YONDER STAR,	. . . .	715	FERENCZ RENYI		118
BENEATH THE WILLOW--NAY, TO YONDER STAR,	. . . .	715	FERENCZ RENYI	V	118
OUT OF A RUNNING STREAM, O MORNING STAR .	. . . .	769	SHADOW WATER A		426

760

	PAGE	TITLE		LINE

STAR-BANE
NO WORD OF THEIRS--THE COLD STAR-BANE   66 HAPPY SHEPHERD   32

STARE
ON EVERY CROWDED STREET TO STARE   294 HATED PLAYBOY   3
ROUND ABOUT HELL'S GATE TO STARE   294 HATED PLAYBOY V   3
AND PIERCE IT THROUGH WITH A GIMLET, AND STARE   330 BONE OF A HARE   12
UPON SOME LOFTY ROCK TO STARE   397 POLIT PRISONER   21
I PACE UPON THE BATTLEMENTS AND STARE   409 TOWER   17
COME BUILD IN THE EMPTY HOUSE OF THE STARE.   424 STARES NEST   5
COME BUILD IN THE EMPTY HOUSE OF THE STARE.   425 STARES NEST   10
COME BUILD IN THE EMPTY HOUSE OF THE STARE.   425 STARES NEST   15
COME BUILD IN THE EMPTY HOUSE OF THE STARE.   425 STARES NEST   20
IN MOMENTARY WONDER STARE UPON   443 SCHOOL CHILDR   7
AND OFTEN THOSE FIRST DAYS I SAW HER STARE   466 HARUN RASHID   122
AND NOW WE STARE ASTONISHED AT THE SEA,   534 HER TRIUMPH   11
THE KING THAT COULD MAKE HIS PEOPLE STARE,   550 SEVERED HEAD   19
ON ALL THE TRAGIC SCENE THEY STARE.   567 LAPIS LAZULI   52
PYTHAGORAS PLANNED IT. WHY DID THE PEOPLE STARE?   610 STATUES   1
AND IN HER EYES A LIGHTLESS STARE,   668 ISLE STAT II 3   60
UNQUENCHABLE STILL GLOWS IN HER DULL STARE,   687 TWO TITANS   17

STARED
THAT SWINEHERD STARED UPON HER FACE AND SAID,   106 CUCHULAIN SEA   9
STARED ON THE MOURNFUL WONDER OF HIS EYES,   108 CUCHULAIN SEA   41
STARED LIKE THE SPRING UPON THE ANCIENT SKIES,   108 CUCHULAIN SEA V   41
STARED ON THE HORSES OF THE SEA, AND HEARD   111 CUCHULAIN SEA   84
STARED AT THE GODS WITH LAUGHING LIP.   276 GREY ROCK   123
AND STARED INTO THE SEA-GREEN EYE, AND SO   278 TWO KINGS   25
AND STARED INTO THE SEA-GREEN EYES, AND SO   278 TWO KINGS V   25
WITH BLOOD-SHOT EYES UPON HIM STARED.   297 THREE BEGGARS   58
BLACK MINNALOUSHE STARED AT THE MOON,   378 CAT AND MOON   5
STARED AT THE WINE-DARK NAIL, OR DARK THAT RAN   537 HER VISION   10
I STARED UPON HIS BLOOD-BEDABBLED BREAST   537 HER VISION   23
I STARED UPON MY BLOOD-BEDABBLED BREAST   537 HER VISION V   23
EYES STARED OUT OF THE BRANCHES AND WERE GONE.   634 CUCHULAIN COMF   3

STAR-ENVIOUS
STAR-ENVIOUS. HE WAS A SPIRIT, BROTHER.   683 SEEKER   39

STARE'S
THE STARE'S NEST BY MY WINDOW   424 STARES NEST   T

STARES
THE GREAT GREY-EYED ATHENE STARES THEREON.   447 COLONUS PRAISE   16
PELEUS ON THETIS STARES.   612 NEWS ORACLE   26

STAR-FIRE
NOW IN A PLACE OF STAR-FIRE, AND NOW IN A SHADOW-PLACE   49 OISIN 3   42
WIDE,
NOW IN A PLACE OF STAR-FIRE, AND NOW IN A SHADOW PLACE   49 OISIN 3   V   42
WIDE,

STAR-FIRES
NOR LOST IN THE STAR-FIRES AND ODOURS   56 OISIN 3   135

STAR-FLAME
. . . HIS KNEES IN THE SOFT STAR-FLAME,   50 OISIN 3   43

STAR-FOUGHT
WITH CLINGING MIST, EACH STAR-FOUGHT WANDERER CAME   656 ISLE STAT I 3   33

STAR-GLIMMERING
MORE SHINING WINDS, MORE STAR-GLIMMERING PONDS?   218 WOODS OF COOLE   35

STARING
STARING UPON HIS SINEWY THIGH.   294 HATED PLAYBOY   6
STARING ON HIS SINEWY THIGH.   294 HATED PLAYBOY V   6
STARING UPON A BEDOUIN'S HORSE-HAIR ROOF   368 EGO DOMINUS   29
I SAW A STARING VIRGIN STAND   437 SONGS PLAY 1   1
I SAW THAT STARING, VIRGIN STAND   437 SONGS PLAY 1 V   1
THAT STARING FURY AND THE BLIND LUSH LEAF   500 VACILLATION   17
GUARDED, GRIFFITH STARING IN HYSTERICAL PRIDE,   601 GALLERY REVIS   4
STILL STARING AT THEIR FLOWERS,   680 LOVE AND DEATH   25

STARK
BESIDE THE CASTLE DOOR, WHERE ALL IS STARK   377 PHASES OF MOON   126
WITH A STARK, DENYING LOOK,   381 SONG OF FOOL   6
MAY THIS LABORIOUS STAIR AND THIS STARK TOWER   423 MY DESCENDANTS   13
OF THE STARK MYSTERY THAT HAS DAZED MY SIGHT,   466 HARUN RASHID   113
OF THAT STARK MYSTERY WHERE I AM PLUNGED   466 HARUN RASHID V   113
FORMS A STARK EGYPTIAN THOUGHT,   638 BEN BULBEN   43
NO, THOU STANDEST STILL AND STARK,   658 ISLE STAT I 3   90

STAR-LADEN
THE FULL ROUND MOON AND THE STAR-LADEN SKY,   119 SORROW OF LOVE V   2
WHERE PEOPLE LOVE BESIDE STAR-LADEN SEAS,   126 DREAM OF FAERY V   9

STARLIGHT
UNDER THE STARLIGHT AND SHADOW, A MONSTROUS SLUMBERING   48 OISIN 3   27
FOLK,
THAT WE MAY MUSE IN THE STARLIGHT AND TALK OF THE BATTLES   51 OISIN 3   63
OF OLD,
AND A SOFTNESS CAME FROM THE STARLIGHT   52 OISIN 3   72
. . . TILL STARLIGHT AND MIDNIGHT PART.   60 OISIN 3   184
BRIMFUL OF STARLIGHT, AND HE SAID, THE STAMPER OF   76 INDIAN ON GOD   14
THE SKIES,
AND STARLIGHT GLEAMED, AND CLOUDS FLEW HIGH,   84 MAD KING GOLL   34
"YET SOMEWHERE UNDER STARLIGHT OR THE SUN   107 CUCHULAIN SEA   28
THE ELABORATE STARLIGHT THROWS A REFLECTION   389 IMAGE PAST   2
THE BABYLONIAN STARLIGHT BROUGHT   438 SONGS PLAY 2   4
A STARLIGHT OR A MOONLIT DOME DISTAINS   497 BYZANTIUM V   5
RICH FOLIAGE THAT THE STARLIGHT GLITTERED THROUGH,   541 PARN FUNERAL 1   8
AND ALL HER STARLIGHT IS WITH SORROW MAD,   738 YOU ARE SAD   3

	PAGE	TITLE	LINE

STAR-LIGHT
THE ELABORATE STAR-LIGHT HAS THROWN REFLECTIONS • • • • • 389 IMAGE PAST V 2
THE BABYLONIAN STAR-LIGHT DROUGHT • • • • • • • • • 438 SONGS PLAY 2 V 4
STARLING
A STARLING LIKE THEM THAT FORGATHERED 'NEATH A MOON • • • 54 OISIN 3 103
STARLIT
UPON THE BREATHLESS STARLIT AIR, • • • • • • • • • • 477 SELF AND SOUL 4
A STARLIT OR A MOONLIT DOME DISDAINS • • • • • • • • 497 BYZANTIUM 5
PLANTED ON THE STARLIT GOLDEN BOUGH, • • • • • • • • 497 BYZANTIUM V 19
STAR-LIT
PLANTED ON THE STAR-LIT GOLDEN BOUGH, • • • • • • • 497 BYZANTIUM 19
A STAR-LIT RAPIER, HALF BLOOD-DARK, • • • • • • • • 671 ISLE STAT II 3 125
STARN
ABOUT THE STARN AND BROKE IN DAYS AND YEARS. • • • • • 206 ADAMS CURSE V 33
STARRED   SEE EVIL-STARRED
THAT CALLS. O EVIL STARRED! IT COMES ALONG • • • • • 653 ISLE STAT I 2 49
STARRY
AND SANG UNTO THE STARRY BROODS. • • • • • • • • • 22 OISIN 1 326
NO LEARNING FROM THE STARRY MEN, • • • • • • • • • 66 HAPPY SHEPHERD 28
MORE MOURNFUL THAN THE DEPTH OF STARRY SKIES, • • • • • 108 CUCHULAIN SEA V 42
OR SIGHS AMID THE WANDERING, STARRY MIRTH, • • • • • • 114 ROSE OF BATTLE 18
AND STILL THE STARRY CANDLES FLARE • • • • • • • 138 TO IRELAND V 13
AND THE WINDS THAT BLOW THROUGH THE STARRY WAYS, • • • • 158 TO HIS HEART 4
LET THE STARRY WINDS AND THE FLAME AND THE FLOOD • • • • 158 TO HIS HEART 5
AND THE WINDS BLOWING THROUGH THE STARRY WAYS, • • • • • 158 TO HIS HEART V 4
UPON THE STARRY BRINK. • • • • • • • • • 216 HAPPY TOWNLAND 52
AMONG THE STARRY EDDIES OF HER HAIR • • • • • 390 IMAGE PAST 27
IN STARRY TOWERS OF BABYLON • • • • • • • • • • 440 WISDOM 14
FOR, AH, OUR LIVES WERE BUT TWO STARRY WORDS • • • • • 675 ISLE STAT II 3 236
FAR AWAY THE STARRY MIRTH • • • • • • • • • • 731 STREET DANCERS 7
OTHERS KNOW THE STARRY MIRTH! • • • • • • • • • • 733 STREET DANCERS 54
STORM DARKENED OR STARRY BRIGHT. • • • • • • • • • 739 WHERE BOOKS GO 8
STARS
WHEN THE STARS ARE TO WANE AND THE WORLD BE DONE. • • • • 16 OISIN 1 220
SLEEP THERE TILL THE MOON AND THE STARS DIE!" • • • • • 17 OISIN 1 246
AND FILLS WITH STARS NIGHT'S PURPLE CUP, • • • • • • 18 OISIN 1 262
AS THUS OUR SONG AROSE! "YOU STARS, • • • • • • • • 22 OISIN 1 329
AS THUS OUR SONG AROSE! "YE STARS, • • • • • • • • 22 OISIN 1 V 329
BUT WE, OH ROLLING STARS, ARE FREE. • • • • • • • • 22 OISIN 1 V 337
AND BID THE STARS DROP DOWN FROM THE SKY, • • • • • • 28 OISIN 1 426
AND THE STARS SHALL ARISE AND SAY IN THE MORNING, • • • • 28 OISIN 1 V 423G
AND THE FIXED STARS HAD DAWNED AND SHONE AND SET, • • • • 31 OISIN 2 40
AT LAST THE MOON AND STARS SHONE, AND A FLIGHT • • • • • 31 OISIN 2 V 34
FOR CENTURIES, AND STARS HAD DAWNED AND SET. • • • • • 31 OISIN 2 V 40
AND WHEN THE DEW-DROWNED STARS HANG IN THE AIR • • • • • 32 OISIN 2 54
AND THE STARS WERE BLOTTED ABOVE US, • • • • • • • • 48 OISIN 3 24
• • • THAT HE WHO HAS STARS FOR HIS FLOCKS • • • • • 49 OISIN 3 37
• • • THAT HE WHO HAD STARS FOR HIS FLOCKS • • • • • 49 OISIN 3 V 37
THE WHIRLING WAYS OF STARS THAT PASS• • • • • • • • 66 HAPPY SHEPHERD 30
AND HE CALLED LOUDLY TO THE STARS TO BEND • • • • • 68 SAD SHEPHERD 5
HE CALLED ALOUD TO ALL THE STARS TO LEND • • • • • • 68 SAD SHEPHERD V 5
SIGH, O YOU LITTLE STARS! O SIGH AND SHAKE YOUR 72 ANASHU VIJAYA 18
  BLUE APPAREL!
SING, O YOU LITTLE STARS! O SING AND RAISE YOUR RAPTUROUS 72 ANASHU VIJAYA 20
  CAROL
SIGH, OH YE LITTLE STARS! OH, SIGH AND SHAKE YOUR BLUE 72 ANASHU VIJAYA V 18
  APPAREL!
SING, OH YE LITTLE STARS! OH, SING, AND RAISE YOUR 72 ANASHU VIJAYA V 20
  RAPTUROUS CAROL
SING YOU OF HER, O FIRST FEW STARS, • • • • • • • 73 ANASHU VIJAYA 41
WHAT KNOW THE PILOTS OF THE STARS OF TEARS? • • • • • 73 ANASHU VIJAYA 47
SING YE OF HER, OH FIRST FEW STARS, • • • • • • • 73 ANASHU VIJAYA V 41
HOW FAR AWAY THE STARS SEEM, AND HOW FAR • • • • • • 80 EPHEMERA 8
AND UNDER THE BLINKING OF THE STARS • • • • • • • 83 MAD KING GOLL 20
I STOOD! KEEN STARS ABOVE ME SHONE, • • • • • • • 83 MAD KING GOLL 29
I PAUSED--THE STARS ABOVE ME FLASHED, • • • • • • 83 MAD KING GOLL V 29
I PAUSED--THE STARS ABOVE ME SHONE • • • • • • • 83 MAD KING GOLL V 29
GOD LIGHTS THE STARS, HIS CANDLES, • • • • • • • • 96 MOLL MAGEE 51
AND THINE OWN SADNESS, WHEREOF STARS, GROWN OLD • • • • 101 ROSE UPON ROOD 6
"WHETHER UNDER ITS DAYLIGHT OR ITS STARS • • • • • • 107 CUCHULAIN SEA 25
"NO, SOMEWHERE UNDER DAYLIGHT OR THE STARS • • • • • 107 CUCHULAIN SEA V 25
"WHETHER UNDER ITS DAYLIGHT OR THE STARS • • • • • 107 CUCHULAIN SEA V 25
UNDER THE PASSING STARS, FOAM OF THE SKY, • • • • • 112 ROSE OF WORLD 9
HE WOULD GO WEAVE OUT OF THE STARS • • • • • • • 113 ROSE OF PEACE 7
AND WHITE STARS TELL YOUR PRAISE. • • • • • • • 113 ROSE OF PEACE 10
TO SMILE UPON HER STARS! AND GATHER YOU, • • • • • 114 ROSE OF BATTLE V 15
THEY HAVE GONE DOWN UNDER THE SAME WHITE STARS, • • • 115 ROSE OF BATTLE 34
AND THE STARS ABOVE! • • • • • • • • 116 FAERY SONG 8
THE STARS OF GOD WHERE THEY MOVE, • • • • • • • 119 PITY OF LOVE V 4
THE CRUMBLING MOON, THE WHITE STARS IN THE SKY, • • • 120 SORROW OF LOVE V 10
THE CURD-PALE MOON, THE WHITE STARS IN THE SKY, • • • 120 SORROW OF LOVE V 10
AND HID HIS FACE AMID A CROWD OF STARS. • • • • • 121 YOU ARE OLD 12
AND LEFT HER TO THE INDIFFERENT STARS ABOVE • • • • 123 DREAM OF DEATH 9
AND GAZED UPON THE MOURNFUL STARS ABOVE • • • • • 123 DREAM OF DEATH V 11
WHILE YOUNG STARS ABOUT HER DANCE. • • • • • • 125 CATHLEEN PARA V 16
AND ALL DISHEVELLED WANDERING STARS. • • • • • • 126 GOES FERGUS 12
AND STARS BEGAN TO PEEP. • • • • • • • • 133 FR GILLIGAN 16
"HE WHO HATH MADE THE NIGHT OF STARS • • • • • • 134 FR GILLIGAN 41
HAVE DOWERED THE STARS WITH MERRY LIGHT! • • • • 134 TWO TREES 6
AND MOTH-LIKE STARS WERE FLICKERING OUT, • • • • • 149 WANDER AENGUS 6
AND STARS LIKE MOTHS WERE SHINING OUT, • • • • • • 149 WANDER AENGUS V 6

762

	PAGE	TITLE	LINE
STARS (CONTINUED)			
TILL STARS ARE BEGINNING TO BLINK AND PEEP¡	150	OLD MOTHER	4
AND HAD ROOTED THE SUN AND MOON AND STARS OUT OF THE SKY	153	CHANGE BELOVED	11
AND ROOTED THE SUN AND MOON AND STARS OUT OF THE SKY,	153	CHANGE BELOVED V	11
AND STARS CLIMBING THE DEW-DROPPING SKY,	158	BELOVED RHYMES	11
TILL STARS GREW OUT OF THE AIR.	160	CAP AND BELLS	28
THE STARS GREW OUT OF THE AIR.	160	CAP AND BELLS V	28
MASTER OF THE STILL STARS AND OF THE FLAMING DOOR.	161	BLACK PIG	8
BEFORE THE UNLABOURING STARS AND YOU.	164	PERFECT BEAUTY	8
BEFORE UNLABOURING STARS AND YOU.	164	PERFECT BEAUTY V	8
THAT KEEPS THE STARS IN THEIR ROUND,	165	CRY OF SEDGE	5
WHEN SHALL THE STARS BE BLOWN ABOUT THE SKY,	170	SECRET ROSE	29
THE WINDS THAT AWAKENED THE STARS	171	MAID QUIET	3
FOR THE WINDS THAT AWAKENED THE STARS	171	MAID QUIET V	3
OR AS THE CHANGING SPEARS FLUNG BY THE GOLDEN STARS	175	ELEMENT POWERS V	15
ABOUT THE STARS AND MOON AND SUN¡	176	BELOVED DEAD	10
ABOVE THE STARS AND MOON AND SUN¡	176	BELOVED DEAD V	10
BUT LIGHT FROM THE PALE STARS, AND GLEAMS	196	BAILE AILLINN	173
ABOUT THE STARS AND BROKE IN DAYS AND YEARS.	206	ADAMS CURSE	33
JUDGE OF THE STARS, AND FIND A COURSE FOR US?	224	SHADOW WATER B	61
FOR HE CAN JUDGE THE STARS AS WELL AS FORGAEL.	225	SHADOW WATER B	63
IT HAD WASHED AMONG THE STARS AND PUT THEM OUT,	236	SHADOW WATER B	311
OR THAN THE SHIVERING CASTING-NET OF THE STARS,	237	SHADOW WATER B	329
MORE MIGHTY THAN THE STARS HALF TROUBLED ME,	237	SHADOW WATER B	332
TILL THE STARS HAD RUN AWAY	268	BROWN PENNY	13
BUT AS THE OUTRAGEOUS STARS INCLINE	325	ROBERT GREGORY	38
SANG TILL STARS BEGAN TO FADE.	332	ROUND TOWER	20
THE STARS FADE OUT WHERE THE MOON COMES,	344	DAWN	8
THE MORNING STARS TO SING,	436	FOR MY SON	19
THAN THE HEAVENLY CIRCUIT OF ITS STARS	451	FIRST LOVE	17
THAN HEAVENLY CIRCUIT OF ITS STARS	451	FIRST LOVE V	17
'TIS MORN¡ LIKE OLD MEN'S EYES THE STARS ARE PALE,	645	ISLE STAT I 1	4
BLENCHING ON HIGH THE DULL STARS SICKEN	646	ISLE STAT I 1	46
DOWN TO THEIR FEET THE STARS THAT SHINE ALONE,	662	ISLE STAT II 1	80
THE MOBS OF STARS IN GOLD AND GREEN AND BLUE,	663	ISLE STAT II 2	43
THE SPINNING STARS—THE TOILING SEA—WHIRL ROUND	665	ISLE STAT II 2	72
HAS ROLLED AWAY THE STARS AND DRIED THE SEA	671	ISLE STAT II 3	146
THE TIDE OF STARS? HAVE I NOT SEEN A THOUSAND YEARS	675	ISLE STAT II 3	230
BY THOSE WAN STARS THAT SIT IN COMPANY	691	MOSADA 1	26
THAT WHEN THE STARS OF OUR NATIVITY	691	MOSADA 1	28
AND YON FEW STARS GROWN DIM, LIKE EYES OF LOVERS	700	MOSADA 3	33
MY BLOSSOM, I AM DYING, AND THE STARS	700	MOSADA 3	47
ARE DYING TOO. THEY WERE FULL SEVEN STARS¡	700	MOSADA 3	48
WE MEET AT LAST, THE MINISTERING STARS	701	MOSADA 3	52
A LITTLE NEARER THOSE BRIGHT STARS. TELL ME,	701	MOSADA 3	59
IS IT YOUR MESSAGE, STARS, THAT WHEN DEATH COMES	701	MOSADA 3	60
GONE THE STARS AND GONE THE WHITE MOON,	718	PHANTOM SHIP	3
THEN THE STARS GROW OUT OF HEAVEN WITH THEIR COUNTENANCES FAIR.	719	PHANTOM SHIP	30
THE MAKER OF THE STARS AND WORLDS	724	LEGEND	1
"THE PROPS," SAID HE, "OF STARS AND WORLDS"	725	LEGEND	5
THE MAKER OF THE STARS AND WORLDS	725	LEGEND	29
MOURNFUL UNDER MOURNFUL STARS.	737	IN FIRELIGHT	4
THE MOTHER OF THE STARS WEEPS TOO,	738	YOU ARE SAD	2
AND UNFORGOTTEN NAMES, AND THE COLD STARS	757	SHADOW WATER A	204
THE STARS WOULD HURL THEIR CROWNS AMONG THE FOAM	761	SHADOW WATER A	265
OR THAN THE SHIVERING CASTING-NET OF THE STARS.	762	SHADOW WATER A	290
OR THAN THE SHIVERING CASTING-NET OF THE STARS.	762	SHADOW WATER A V	290
AMID THE DARKNESS, NOW THAT ALL MY STARS	767	SHADOW WATER A V	404
LET THE STARS BEAR WITNESS¡	770	BLOOD BOND	12
THE STARS ARE OUT OF SIGHT.	786	YOUR HEART	34
STAR-SHUDDERING			
OF THESE STAR-SHUDDERING SKIES, YOU ARE THE QUEEN.	679	ISLE STAT II 3	323
START			
FROM JOY THE HOLY BRANCHES START,	134	TWO TREES	3
I START OUT OF MY SLEEP TO THINK	380	SONGS FOOL 1	7
AND START—I AT YOUR SHOULDER—	390	IMAGE PAST	30
THAN SOULS THAT START NO GAME AND TURN NO RHYME¡	464	HARUN RASHID	68
MAIMED US AT THE START.	506	REMORSE SPEECH	13
A FINISH WORTHY OF THE START.	626	OLD MEN BE MAD	15
I MUST LIE DOWN WHERE ALL THE LADDERS START,	630	CIRCUS ANIMALS	39
THE SLEEPER AWOKE WITH A SUDDEN START,	729	PRIEST FAIRY	31
I FELT A SUDDEN TEAR START,	744	GLOVE CLOAK	10
STAR-TAUGHT			
THE STAR-TAUGHT MOOR, SAID THUS IT WAS DECREED	691	MOSADA 1	25
STARTED			
SHE STARTED AND THEN KNEW WHOSE FOOT IT WAS¡	280	TWO KINGS	66
HAD NOT THE SLEEPER STARTED UP.	304	HOUR DAWN	48
BUT SOON A TEAR-DROP STARTED UP,	400	DEMON BEAST	21
STAR-THROBBING			
THE HEAVENS ALL STAR-THROBBING ARE A-LIT.	671	ISLE STAT II 3	143
THE HEAVENS ALL STAR-THROBBING ARE ALIT.	671	ISLE STAT II 3 V	143
STARTING-POST			
BUT EVEN AT THE STARTING-POST, ALL SLEEK AND NEW,	619	BRONZE HEAD	15
STARTLE			
IN THEIR DOWNY CAPS, AND STARTLE THE NAPS	644	SONG FAERIES	11
IN THEIR DOWNY CAPS, AND STARTLE THE NAPS	676	ISLE STAT II 3	258
STARTLED			
A CURLEW ANSWERED, AND I WAS STARTLED BY THE THOUGHT	291	PAUDEEN V	5
NIGHTLY, AND STARTLED BY THAT SOUND	326	ROBERT GREGORY	54

763

		PAGE	TITLE		LINE

STAR-TROD
    WHERE SPICE-ISLES NESTLE ON THE STAR-TROD SEAS, ...   682 SEEKER   17
STARTS
    TREE, LIKE A SOOTY FINGER, STARTS FROM THE EARTH; . . .   410 TOWER   19
STARVE   SEE SEA-STARVED
    SHOULD STARVE GOOD MEN AND BAD ADVANCE, ...   626 OLD MEN BE MAD   10
STARVED   SEE SEA-STARVED
    STARVED UPON THE SHORE . . . .   401 DEMON BEAST   48
    "O SEA--STARVED, HUNGRY SEA." . . . .   578 CRAZED GIRL   V   14
    I, STARVED FOR THE BOSOM OF HIS FAERY BRIDE? . . . . .   629 CIRCUS ANIMALS   16
STATE
    MOUNT MY WHITE STEED, FOR THE FAIRY STATE . . . . . .   9 OISIN 1   V   103
    AND MANY A MILE IS THE FAERY STATE, ...   9 OISIN 1   V   103
    TO PETER SITTING IN STATE, ...   178 FIDDLER DOONEY   10
    BOUND NEITHER TO CAUSE NOR TO STATE, ...   414 TOWER   129
    THOUGHTS UPON THE PRESENT STATE OF THE WORLD . . . . .   428 NINETEEN 19   V   T
    AN IMAGE OF ITS STATE; . . . .   430 NINETEEN 19   64
    THAT PURITY BUILT UP THE STATE . . . .   460 THREE MONUMENT   6
    WITH THE GREAT TOIL AND CEREMONY OF STATE, ...   462 HARUN RASHID   V   25
    AND HAUGHTIER-HEADED BURKE THAT PROVED THE STATE A TREE,   481 BLOOD AND MOON   22
    THE STRENGTH THAT GIVES OUR BLOOD AND STATE MAGNANIMITY   481 BLOOD AND MOON   29
    . . .
    AND HAUGHTIER HEADED BURKE THAT PROVED THE STATE A TREE   481 BLOOD AND MOON V   22
    CHURCH AND STATE . . . .   553 CHURCH STATE   T
    MIGHT OF THE CHURCH AND THE STATE, ...   554 CHURCH STATE   3
    WHAT IF THE CHURCH AND THE STATE . . . .   554 CHURCH STATE   9
    FOR REASON OF THE STATE . . . .   597 MODEL LAUREATE   6
STATELY
    THE STATELY MIDNIGHT THROUGH UNTIL THEY STOOD . . . .   352 PEOPLE   14
    FOR SILKEN CLOTHES AND STATELY WALK, ...   422 MY TABLE   30
    HAD TURNED HIS STATELY HEAD. . . . .   526 AM OF IRELAND   10
    THERE STATELY PYTHAGORAS . . . .   531 DELPHIC ORACLE   9
    ALL STATELY WOMEN MOVING TO A SONG . . . .   537 HER VISION   17
STATES
    AND THERE'S A PLAYER IN THE STATES WHO GATHERS UP HER CLOAK   354 HIS PHOENIX   12
    AND THERE'S THE PLAYER IN THE STATES WHO GATHERS UP HER   354 HIS PHOENIX   V   12
        CLOAK
STATESMAN
    WE HAVE NO GIFT TO SET A STATESMAN RIGHT; . . . . . .   359 WAR POEM   3
    REFORMER, MERCHANT, STATESMAN, LEARNED MAN, ...   376 PHASES OF MOON   98
    O'HIGGINS ITS SOLE STATESMAN HAD NOT DIED. . . . . . .   543 PARN FUNERAL 2   8
    A STATESMAN IS AN EASY MAN, ...   598 STONE CROSS   1
STATESMAN'S
    THE STATESMAN'S HOLIDAY . . . .   626 STATES HOLIDAY   T
STATESMEN
    AND ALL THE POPULAR STATESMEN SAY . . . .   460 THREE MONUMENT   5
STATION
    SOME PLATONIST AFFIRMS THAT IN THE STATION . . . . . .   431 NINETEEN 19   72
    THE BLINDS DRAWN UP"; MAUD GONNE AT HOWTH STATION WAITING   578 LOFTY THINGS   10
        A TRAIN,
    THE MAN IS GONE WHO FROM HIS LONELY STATION . . . . .   738 MOURN THEN ON   7
STATIONS
    I PRAYED AT ALL THE STATIONS UPON MY MARROW-BONES, . .   593 PILGRIM   7
    I PRAYED AT ALL THE STATIONS UPON MY MARROW BONES, . .   593 PILGRIM   V   7
STATISTICS
    STATISTICS . . . .   485 STATISTICS   T
STATUARY
    WHEN PAINTED PANEL, STATUARY, ...   440 WISDOM   2
STATUE
    THIS BLOSSOM IS MOST NEAR. STATUE! OH, THOU . . . .   657 ISLE STAT I 3   72
    THEN BID THEM RAISE MY STATUE ON THE SHORE; . . . . .   663 ISLE STAT II 2   18
    A STATUE OF SOLITUDE, ...   785 YOUR HEART   4
    MAY TURN FROM A STATUE . . . .   786 YOUR HEART   20
STATUED
    LEAD ME, I PRAY THEE, TO THE STATUED PLACE! . . . . .   667 ISLE STAT II 3   37
STATUES
    DARK STATUES GLIMMERED OVER THE PALE TIDE . . . . . .   31 OISIN 2   36
    AN EPILOGUE TO "THE ISLAND OF STATUES" AND "THE SEEKER"   64 HAPPY SHEPHERD V   T
    THE STATUES . . . .   610 STATUES   T
    THE ISLAND OF STATUES. . . . .   644 ISLE STAT I 1   T
    LYRICS FROM "THE ISLAND OF STATUES" . . . .   646 ISLE STAT I 1   V   T
    ISLAND OF STATUES A FRAGMENT . . . .   666 ISLE STAT II 3 V   T
STAVE
    SINGING OF ARMS AND BATTLES SOME OLD STAVE, ...   650 ISLE STAT I 1   137
STAY
    AND BID ME STAY, WITH MANY A TEAR; . . . .   10 OISIN 1   113
    AND STAY A LITTLE WHILE, AND BID THEM WEEP; . . . . .   33 OISIN 2   60
    THAT YOU STAY IDLING HERE WITH FLOCKS AND HERDS." . .   107 CUCHULAIN SEA V   21
    THAT YOU STAY IDLING HERE WITH FLOCK AND HERDS." . . .   107 CUCHULAIN SEA V   21
    TO STAY THE STAG'S NEXT RUSH. WHEN SWORD MET HORN . .   277 TWO KINGS   V   15
    OR IF THEY MADE A MOMENT'S STAY . . . .   297 THREE BEGGARS   52
    ARE GONE AWAY, AND SOME THAT STAY . . . .   458 HIS WILDNESS   5
    FROM EVERY QUARTER OF THE WORLD, CAN STAY . . . . . .   471 ALL SOUL NIGHT   12
    NOTHING CAN STAY MY GLANCE . . . .   474 ALL SOUL NIGHT   93
    HESITATE OR STAY? . . . .   505 RESULT THOUGHT   17
    I CANNOT STAY FROM THAT . . . .   533 FIRST CONFESS   8
    OR STAY CONTENT ON THE LOW, ...   589 OLD WICKED MAN   49
    THAT I MAY STAY A SOBER MAN . . . .   591 DRUNK SOBRIETY   3
    SO STAY AT HOME AND DRINK YOUR BEER . . . .   598 STONE CROSS   5
    INFIRM AND AGED I MIGHT STAY . . . .   605 YOU CONTENT   17
    OH STAY, NASCHINA, STAY! . . . .   650 ISLE STAT I 1   153

764

STAY   (CONTINUED)
   OH STAY, NASCHINA, STAY! . . . .   650 ISLE STAT I 1   153
   I BID THEE STAY, RENOUNCING THY MAD QUEST." . . . .   669 ISLE STAT II 3   89
   AND THOU WILT STAY. ALL THOUGHT OF WHAT THEY FIND . . . 670 ISLE STAT II 3   92
   STAY, STAY, OR I WILL HOLD YOUR WHITE ARMS DOWN. . . .   694 MOSADA 1   92
   STAY, STAY, OR I WILL HOLD YOUR WHITE ARMS DOWN. . . .   694 MOSADA 1   92
   OR STAY WITH ME BESIDE THE THAMES. . . . .   741 EARL PAUL   59
   SOME ONE SHOULD STAY AT HER SIDE. . . . .   786 YOUR HEART   V   28
   FLIT TO KILTARTAN CROSS AND STAY . . . .   791 REPRISALS   11
STAYED
   NOR STAYED FOR BITE OR SUP! . . . .   93 FATHER OHART   38
   WITH HEAD BOWED ON HIS KNEES CUCHULAIN STAYED! . . . .   110 CUCHULAIN SEA   71
   THAT IF A DANCER STAYED HIS HUNGRY FOOT . . . .   127 DREAM OF FAERY   22
   I STAGGERED, BUT A BEECH-TREE STAYED MY FALL, ...   286 TWO KINGS   209
   I STAGGERED, BUT A BEECH TREE STAYED MY FALL, ...   286 TWO KINGS   V   209
   HE STAYED FOR A WHILE! AND WE . . . .   341 SHEP GOATHERD   66
   BRED ON THE ATLANTIC, CAN BE STAYED! . . . .   403 FOR DAUGHTER   6
STAYS
   "YET THE WORLD STAYS." "IF THAT BE SO, ...   388 SOLOMON WITCH   33
   ROUND SHE COMES IN STAYS BEFORE THEM! . . . . . .   719 PHANTOM SHIP   17
   "HAS MARRIED AND STAYS . . . .   780 WELL AND TREE   11
STEAD
   THE SPIRITS STOLE, AND GAVE HIM IN ITS STEAD . . . . .   684 SEEKER   55
STEADIED
   AND STEADIED BY A FIN, ...   612 NEWS ORACLE   14
STEADY
   AND COPY THEIR PROUD STEADY GAZE. . . . .   273 GREY ROCK   64
   HER EYES WERE COLD AND STEADY, HER LIPS TIGHT. . . . .   279 TWO KINGS   64
   THEY HAD KEPT A STEADY PACE AS THOUGH THEIR BEDS, . .   372 PHASES OF MOON   5
STEAL
   ROUND US HERDS OF SHADOWS STEAL--- . . . .   737 IN FIRELIGHT   6
STEALTH
   THE MURDEROUS STEALTH OF DAY. . . . .   536 PARTING   8
STEALTHILY
   AND I DREAMED MY LOST LOVE CAME STEALTHILY OUT OF THE WOOD   163 VALLEY LOVERS   3
STEAM
   ROASTING BERRIES STEAM AND SHAKE--- . . . .   727 LOVERS QUARREL   43
STEAMSHIP
   HIDING AMID THE CARGO OF A STEAMSHIP, ...   578 CRAZED GIRL   5
STEED
   A MAIDEN, ON A SLENDER STEED, ...   2 OISIN 1   V   7V
   MOUNT MY WHITE STEED, FOR THE FAIRY STATE . . . . .   9 OISIN 1   V   103
   AND WHEN THE WHITE STEED FELT MY WEIGHT, ...   9 OISIN 1   V   109
   AND NOW A MAID, ON A SWIFT BROWN STEED . . . . . .   12 OISIN 1   V   142
   THE STEED TOWARDS THE MUSIC RACED, ...   13 OISIN 1   V   169
   AMONG THEM 'LIGHTING FROM OUR STEED, ...   14 OISIN 1   V   193
   AND ONCE MORE SADDLED THE WHITE STEED, ...   25 OISIN 1   V   378
   AND WHEN THE WHITE STEED SAW WHAT BLACKNESS GLEAMED, . . 30 OISIN 2   V   24
   WE MOUNTED ON THE STAIR, THE WHITE STEED TYING, . . .   32 OISIN 2   V   46
STEEDS
   OF OUR STRONG STEEDS WAS DARK WITH SWEAT, ...   2 OISIN 1   V   7T
   AND A HUNDRED STEEDS, TUMULTUOUS-FOOTED, ...   8 OISIN 1   V   85A
   NOR TEAR THE FOEMEN FROM THEIR STEEDS. . . . . . .   11 OISIN 1   V   128
   AND THEIR HOUNDS, AND THEIR STEEDS, AND THEIR LOVES, . . . 59 OISIN 3   V   176
STEEL
   LONG WHILE, ARE WHIPS OF STEEL." "IS HE SO DREAD?" . .   35 OISIN 2   V   88
   AGAINST THE STAG. WHEN HORN AND STEEL WERE MET . . .   277 TWO KINGS   15
   FLAMES THAT NO FAGGOT FEEDS, NOR STEEL HAS LIT, . . .   498 BYZANTIUM   26
   OF THOSE STEEL TONGUES! CRASH, SWORDS! WELL THRUST!   665 ISLE STAT II 2   67
      WELL BENT
   THEN FARRELL, STEEL KING, MASTER OF MEN, ...   790 DEDICATION   5
STEEL-BLUE
   STREWING UPON THE ROCKS THEIR STEEL-BLUE HAIR, ...   687 TWO TITANS   30
STEEP
   UNDER THAT COLD AND VAPOUR-TURBANED STEEP, ...   128 DREAM OF FAERY   39
   EVENING AND MORNING, THE STEEP STREET OF URBINO . . .   352 PEOPLE   12
   EVENING AND MORN, THE STEEP STREET OF URBINO . . . .   352 PEOPLE   V   12
   FROM MOUNTAIN STEEP TO STEEP. . . . .   399 BREAK OF DAY   25
   FROM MOUNTAIN STEEP TO STEEP. . . . .   399 BREAK OF DAY   25
   SET ALL YOUR MIND UPON THE STEEP ASCENT, ...   477 SELF AND SOUL   2
   AS WHEN UPON HER CLOUD-O'ER-MUFFLED STEEP . . . . .   645 ISLE STAT I 1   16
STEEPLE
   FROM WHERE THE OLD IVY CRAWLS ROUND THE OLD STEEPLE, . . 728 PRIEST FAIRY   6
STEER
   THAT I MAY DROWN MYSELF? BETTER STEER HOME, ...   222 SHADOW WATER B   12
   AND SO WITH WOLF, AND BOAR, AND STEER. . . . . . .   671 ISLE STAT II 3   122
STEERING
   I HELD A PAINTED STEERING OAR, ...   253 HIS DREAM   V   2
   THE BUTT END OF A STEERING OAR, ...   253 HIS DREAM   V   2
STEERING-OAR
   THE BUTT-END OF A STEERING-OAR, ...   253 HIS DREAM   2
STEERS
   "LIKE THE SPECKLED BIRD THAT STEERS . . . .   341 SHEP GOATHERD   62
STELLA
   BUT MINE SAW STELLA ONCE. WHENCE CAME OUR THOUGHT? . .   486 SEVEN SAGES   6
   MINE SAW STELLA ONCE. WHENCE CAME OUR THOUGHT? . . . .   486 SEVEN SAGES   V   6
   MINE SAW STELLA ONCE. WHEN CAME OUR THOUGHT? . . . .   486 SEVEN SAGES   V   6
STEM   SEE APPLE-STEM
   HIS LONG LAMP-CHIMNEY SHAPED LIKE THE STEM . . . . .   566 LAPIS LAZULI   33
   HIS LONG LAMP CHIMNEY SHAPED LIKE THE STEM . . . . .   566 LAPIS LAZULI   V   33
   AND THEREON GREW A TENDER STEM, ...   743 DANAAN QUICK   14

STEM   (CONTINUED)
PRAISE THE BLOSSOMING APPLE STEM: . . . . 773 SONG DEIRDRE 1 V   21
STEMS   SEE PALM-STEMS
. . . FOR, CUMBROUS WITH STEMS OF THE HAZEL AND OAK, . .   48 OISIN 3   25
FEED A FIRE WITH STEMS OF GRASS: . . . . 727 LOVERS QUARREL   42
STEP   SEE DOOR-STEP
BE STILL: I HEAR THE STEP OF EBREMAR. . . . . 697 MOSADA 2   34
STEPPED
THAT STEPPED OUT OF THEIR CLOTHES, ... 538 LAST CONFESS   14
STEPPING   SEE DELICATE-STEPPING
THE DELICATE STEPPING STAG AND HIS LADY SIGH . . . . 210 RAGGED WOOD   V   2
STEPS
THY WANDERING STEPS ACROSS THE SEA? . . . .   5 OISIN 1   V   51
OF MOONLIT STEPS GLIMMERED: AND LEFT AND RIGHT . . .   31 OISIN 2   35
OF MANY THOUSAND STEPS. SAT EITHER SIDE, ...   31 OISIN 2   V   35
AND CLIMBED SO LONG, I THOUGHT THE LAST STEPS WERE . .   32 OISIN 2   48
WENT WALKING WITH SLOW STEPS ALONG THE GLEANING . . .   68 SAD SHEPHERD   3
PAINTING WITH SHADOW ALL THE MARBLE STEPS: . . . . .   72 ANASHU VIJAYA   30
THE HEAVY STEPS OF THE PLOUGHMAN, SPLASHING THE WINTRY 143 ROSE IN HEART   3
MOULD,
THE HEAVY STEPS OF THE PLOUGHMAN SPLASHING THE WINTER 143 ROSE IN HEART V   3
MOULD,
NOW STEPS DRAW CLOSE, HE HIDES BENEATH A DRUM. . . . 713 FERENCZ RENYI   78
SOME GREAT ONE. NO: I HEAR THE WAVERING STEPS . . . . 720 WITCH VIVIEN   12
STEPT
"A SADDER CREATURE NEVER STEPT . . . .   17 OISIN 1   238
REMEMBERING HOW THE FENIANS STEPT . . . .   24 OISIN 1   370
IN WAR, THE NOBLE FENIANS STEPT. . . . .   24 OISIN 1   V 372
AND WHEN THE SUN ONCE MORE IN SAFFRON STEPT, ...   41 OISIN 2   192
AND WHEN THE SUN IN ALL HIS FLAGRANT SAFFRON STEPT, . .   41 OISIN 2   V 192
BUT WHEN THE SUN ONCE MORE IN SAFFRON STEPT, ...   41 OISIN 2   V 192
OF TWILIGHT AND SLUMBER WERE GONE, AND THAT HOOFS   54 OISIN 3   112
IMPATIENTLY STEPT.
. . . BENEATH ME THE HOOVES IMPATIENTLY STEPT. . . . .   54 OISIN 3   V 112
STERN
THEN, WARRIOR, WHY SO SAD AND STERN, ...   19 OISIN 1   V 286
I SWAYED UPON THE GAUDY STERN . . . . 253 HIS DREAM   1
THERE ON THE HIGH AND PAINTED STERN . . . . . . 253 HIS DREAM   V   1
BEING HIGH AND SOLITARY AND MOST STERN? . . . . . 257 NO SECOND TROY   10
TO THAT STERN COLOUR AND THAT DELICATE LINE . . . . 326 ROBERT GREGORY   67
DOTH STILL THE MAN WHOM EACH STERN ROVER FEARS, . . . 678 ISLE STAT II 3   295
STERNER
YOU KEPT THE MUSES' STERNER LAWS, ... 273 GREY ROCK   59
A STERNER CONSCIENCE AND A FRIENDLIER HOME, ... 321 REED WHISPERER   8
AS THOUGH A STERNER EYE LOOKED THROUGH HER EYE . . . . 619 BRONZE HEAD   23
STERNNESS
ALL THAT STERNNESS AMID CHARM, ... 259 PEACE   8
SO MUCH STERNNESS AND SUCH CHARM." . . . . 259 PEACE   V   8
STERNS
WITH BENDING STERNS AND BENDING BOWS, ...   14 OISIN 1   189
WITH BENDING STERNS AND BENDING BOWS, ...   23 OISIN 1   353
STICK   SEE FIDDLE-STICK
A TATTERED COAT UPON A STICK, UNLESS . . . . . . 407 SAIL BYZANTIUM   10
FINGERED UPON A FIDDLE STICK OR STRING . . . . . . 445 SCHOOL CHILDR   V   46
SOUND OF A STICK UPON THE FLOOR, A SOUND . . . . . 491 COOLE BALLYLEE   25
THAT ON A STICK RELIED . . . . 515 GIRLS SONG B   6
WHO LEANS UPON A STICK, ... 525 DANCING DAYS   20
HIS STOUT STICK UNDER HIS HAND, ... 588 OLD WICKED MAN   20
A STICK OF INCENSE . . . . 619 STICK INCENSE   T
STICKS   SEE BROOM-STICKS
THE ANCIENT HABIT STICKS, ... 431 NINETEEN 19   74
OLD CLOTHES UPON OLD STICKS TO SCARE A BIRD. . . . . 445 SCHOOL CHILDR   48
NOW ALL DRY STICKS UNDER A WINTRY SUN, ... 490 COOLE BALLYLEE   10
STIFF
IN THEIR STIFF, PAINTED CLOTHES, THE PALE UNSATISFIED ONES 318 MAGI   2
"A WOMAN CAN BE PROUD AND STIFF . . . . 513 JANE TALK BISH   13
THOUGH STIFF TO STRIKE A BARGAIN, ... 620 JOHN KINSELLA   13
WITH A STIFF STRAIGHT BACK, ... 627 STATES HOLIDAY   33
STILL   SEE STONY-STILL
WHERE PASSIONATE MAIVE IS STONY STILL: . . . . . .   3 OISIN 1   V   18
YOU ARE STILL WRECKED AMONG HEATHEN DREAMS. . . . .   4 OISIN 1   31
OISIN, THOU ART HALF HEATHEN STILL! . . . . . .   4 OISIN 1   31
AND NOW, STILL SAD; WE CAME TO WHERE . . . . . .   17 OISIN 1   247
AND NOW STILL SAD OUR TROOP DREW NIGH . . . . . .   17 OISIN 1   V 247
UNTIL THE TOSSING ARMS GREW STILL . . . .   21 OISIN 1   322
OF THE THINGS THAT HIS HEART STILL KNOWS WERE SWEET-- .   26 OISIN 1   V 402
WHILE HIS HEART STILL DREAMS OF BATTLE AND LOVE . . .   27 OISIN 1   406
AND HAD DISPORTED IN THE EYES STILL JET . . . . .   31 OISIN 2   V   39
IF THEY STILL SLUMBER, TOUCH THEIR EYELIDS BLUE, . . .   33 OISIN 2   61
BUT FLY WHILE STILL YOU MAY." AND THEREON I: . . .   35 OISIN 2   89
BUT FLEE WHILE YOU STILL MAY." THEN I: . . . . .   35 OISIN 2   V   89
I BURST THE CHAIN: STILL EARLESS, NERVELESS, BLIND, . .   36 OISIN 2   97
STILL EARLESS, NERVELESS, BLIND, THE EAGLES STOOD. . .   36 OISIN 2   100
STILL EARLESS, NERVELESS, BLIND, THE EAGLES DREAMED. . .   36 OISIN 2   V 100
SHOUTED AND HAILED HIM. STILL HE HUNG CONTENT, . . .   36 OISIN 2   107
THE FLOWERS STILL GREW THERE: FAR ON THE SEA'S WASTE . .   39 OISIN 2   163
THE FLOWERS STILL GREW THERE. MOVED BEYOND HIM THE SEA'S   39 OISIN 2   V 163
WASTE:
ON THE ANVIL OF THE WORLD. BE STILL: THE SKIES . . .   42 OISIN 2   204
YET STILL SHE TURNS HER RESTLESS HEAD: . . . . . .   65 HAPPY SHEPHERD   5
AND STILL I DREAM HE TREADS THE LAWN, ...   67 HAPPY SHEPHERD   51

766

STILL   (CONTINUED)

	PAGE	TITLE		LINE
THE SEA SWEPT ON AND CRIED HER OLD CRY STILL,	68	SAD SHEPHERD		10
HAIL! HAIL, MY ANASHUYA. NO! BE STILL.	71	ANASHU VIJAYA		11
HAIL! HAIL, MY ANASHUYA. NAY! BE STILL.	71	ANASHU VIJAYA	V	11
WHO STILL WERE OLD WHEN THE GREAT SEA WAS YOUNG!	74	ANASHU VIJAYA		69
FOR THE KIND WIRES ARE TORN AND STILL,	86	MAD KING GOLL		69
AND STILL, WITH PITYIN', SCORNIN' EYE,	96	MOLL MAGEE		39
COME NEAR, COME NEAR, COME NEAR--AH, LEAVE ME STILL	101	ROSE UPON ROOD		13
AND STILL I FEEL THE CROWN UPON MY HEAD.	103	FERGUS DRUID		20
BUT STILL I FEEL THE CROWN UPON MY HEAD.	103	FERGUS DRUID	V	20
"STILL TREADS THE WORLD AMID HIS ARMED MEN."	107	CUCHULAIN SEA	V	26
STILL SHE GOES WITH FOOTSTEPS WARY,	124	CATHLEEN PARA		11
AND STILL THE STARRY CANDLES FLARE	138	TO IRELAND	V	13
AND STILL THE THOUGHTS OF IRELAND BROOD,	138	TO IRELAND	V	15
WHILE STILL I MAY, I WRITE FOR YOU	139	TO IRELAND		33
WHILE STILL I MAY I WRITE OUT TRUE	139	TO IRELAND	V	33
O SWEET EVERLASTING VOICES, BE STILL!	141	EVERLAST VOICE		1
O SWEET EVERLASTING VOICES, BE STILL.	141	EVERLAST VOICE		8
PALE BROWS, STILL HANDS AND DIM HAIR,	152	LOSS OF LOVE		1
PALE BROW, STILL HANDS, AND DIM HAIR,	152	LOSS OF LOVE	V	1
BE YOU STILL, BE YOU STILL, TREMBLING HEART!	158	TO HIS HEART		1
BE YOU STILL, BE YOU STILL, TREMBLING HEART!	158	TO HIS HEART		1
THE GARDEN HAD FALLEN STILL.	159	CAP AND BELLS		2
AND ONCE, WHEN THE OWLS GREW STILL,	159	CAP AND BELLS	V	2
WE WHO STILL LABOUR BY THE CROMLECH ON THE SHORE,	161	BLACK PIG		5
MASTER OF THE STILL STARS AND OF THE FLAMING DOOR.	161	BLACK PIG		8
AND STILL MURMUR AND LONG;	163	ASKS FORGIVE		18
STILL OVERTHROWN BY A WOMAN'S GAZE,	164	PERFECT BEAUTY	V	4
WITH STILL AND STONY LIMBS AND OPEN EYES.	182	QUEEN MAEVE		46
MORE STILL THAN THEY HAD BEEN FOR A GOOD MONTH,	182	QUEEN MAEVE		54
HAVE SUCH LONG MEMORIES THAT THEY STILL	192	BAILE AILLINN		90
WHO BUT AWAITS HIS HOUR TO SHOUT, STILL HANGS	198	SEVEN WOODS		13
WHETHER HE WILL OR NO! AND BETTER STILL	222	SHADOW WATER B		13
BUT WHY ARE THEY STILL WAITING? WHY ARE THEY	234	SHADOW WATER B		265
BEFORE A HAND CAN TOUCH ME. MY HANDS ARE STILL!	238	SHADOW WATER B		358
WHAT, STILL YOU WOULD HAVE THEIR PRAISE!	259	UNWORTH PRAISE		11
PARDON, OLD FATHERS, IF YOU STILL REMAIN	269	PARDON FATHERS		1
OR ON SOME STILL UNEMPTIED CUP	271	GREY ROCK		21
BUT LET THAT BE--THE GODS WERE STILL.	271	GREY ROCK	V	16
"IF HE BE LIVING STILL THE WHOLE WORLD'S MINE,	280	TWO KINGS	V	85
BUT FINDING HIM STILL SILENT I STOOPED DOWN	281	TWO KINGS		109
OUR SUDDEN PALACES IN THE STILL AIR	284	TWO KINGS		180
THE WIND IS OLD AND STILL AT PLAY	301	RUN PARADISE		22
AND YET STOOD STILL, BECAUSE INSIDE	303	HOUR DAWN		26
POUR WINE AND DANCE IF MANHOOD STILL HAVE PRIDE,	311	MOUNTAIN TOMB		1
IN VAIN, IN VAIN! THE CATARACT STILL CRIES!	311	MOUNTAIN TOMB		9
POUR WINE AND DANCE, IF MANKIND STILL HAVE PRIDE,	311	MOUNTAIN TOMB	V	1
WHAT EAGLE LOOK STILL SHOWS,	316	FRIENDS		25
AND ALL THEIR EYES STILL FIXED, HOPING TO FIND ONCE MORE,	318	MAGI		6
BEN JONSON'S PHRASE--AND STILL MAY TURN MY FEET	321	REED WHISPERER	V	6
MIRRORS A STILL SKY!	322	SWANS AT COOLE		4
UNWEARIED STILL, LOVER BY LOVER,	323	SWANS AT COOLE		19
ATTEND UPON THEM STILL.	323	SWANS AT COOLE		24
BUT NOW THEY DRIFT ON THE STILL WATER,	323	SWANS AT COOLE		25
ALTHOUGH I CAN SEE HIM STILL,	347	FISHERMAN		1
FOR AN EXAMPLE STILL?	365	HER RACE		12
WHILE WONDERING STILL TO BE A SHADE, WITH GRANIA'S SHADE,	366	HER COURAGE	V	4
UNDER YOUR OLD WIND-BEATEN TOWER, WHERE STILL	367	EGO DOMINUS		2
AND, THOUGH YOU HAVE PASSED THE BEST OF LIFE, STILL TRACE,	367	EGO DOMINUS		5
AND SHOULD THEY PAINT OR WRITE, STILL IT IS ACTION?	369	EGO DOMINUS		44
AND SHOULD THEY PAINT OR WRITE STILL IS IT ACTION	369	EGO DOMINUS	V	44
WERE DISTANT STILL. AN OLD MAN COCKED HIS EAR.	372	PHASES OF MOON		7
AND THE LIGHT PROVES THAT HE IS READING STILL.	373	PHASES OF MOON		11
AND THE NEW STILL HIDES HER HORN.	382	VISION ROBART		4
UNDER BLANK EYES AND FINGERS NEVER STILL	382	VISION ROBART		5
YOU SAY THAT WE SHOULD STILL THE LAND	395	SIXTEEN DEAD		7
OR EVERY BELLOWS BURST, BE HAPPY STILL.	405	FOR DAUGHTER		72
SOME FEW REMEMBERED STILL WHEN I WAS YOUNG	410	TOWER		33
OUR SHADOWS ROVE THE GARDEN GRAVEL STILL,	435	NEW FACES		7
A SUDDEN BLOW! THE GREAT WINGS BEATING STILL	441	LEDA AND SWAN		1
A RUSH, A SUDDEN WHEEL, AND HOVERING STILL	441	LEDA AND SWAN	V	1
MUST DRIVE THE ARABIAN HOST. THE VOICE GREW STILL,	467	HARUN RASHID		145
MADE DRIVE THE ARABIAN HOST. THE VOICE GREW STILL,	467	HARUN RASHID	V	145
IS SATO'S ANCIENT BLADE, STILL AS IT WAS,	477	SELF AND SOUL		10
STILL RAZOR-KEEN, STILL LIKE A LOOKING-GLASS	477	SELF AND SOUL		11
STILL RAZOR-KEEN, STILL LIKE A LOOKING-GLASS	477	SELF AND SOUL		11
CAN, TATTERED, STILL PROTECT, FADED ADORN.	477	SELF AND SOUL		16
IS SATO'S ANCIENT SWORD, STILL AS IT WAS.	477	SELF AND SOUL	V	10
STILL RAZOR-KEEN, STILL LIKE A LOOKING GLASS	477	SELF AND SOUL	V	11
STILL RAZOR-KEEN, STILL LIKE A LOOKING GLASS	477	SELF AND SOUL	V	11
MORE BLESSED STILL THIS TOWER!	480	BLOOD AND MOON		2
ALL-DESTROYING SWORD-BLADE STILL.	484	SYMBOLS		3
THAT SO STILL HAD LAIN,	516	MANS SONG		4
WENCHING, DRINKING, STILL REMAIN	529	TOM LUNATIC		9
THAT SAT SO STILL AND PLAYED AT THE CHESS?	550	SEVERED HEAD		12
FROM NEEDLE'S EYE STILL GOAD IT ON.	562	NEEDLES EYE		4
OR LOFTY SLOPE WHERE IT STILL SNOWS	567	LAPIS LAZULI		46
(FOR SINCE THE HORIZON'S BOUGHT STRANGE DOGS ARE STILL)	579	DOR WELLESLEY		7
THAT THE SWORDSMEN AND THE LADIES CAN STILL KEEP COMPANY,	581	CURSE CROMWELL		20
THAT I AM STILL THEIR SERVANT THOUGH ALL ARE UNDERGROUND.	581	CURSE CROMWELL		22
"IRELAND SHALL GET HER FREEDOM AND YOU STILL BREAK STONE."	590	PARNELL		2

	PAGE	TITLE	LINE
STILL (CONTINUED)			
AND KEEP ME DANCING STILL	591	DRUNK SOBRIETY	2
BUT SHE IS STILL ABED,	595	COLONEL MARTIN	31
BUT SHE IS STILL A-BED	595	COLONEL MARTIN V	31
SAID TO THE WOMAN ON HIS KNEES, "LIE STILL.	609	IN TARAS HALLS	2
TO MANY WOMEN I HAVE SAID, "LIE STILL,"	609	IN TARAS HALLS	6
BE STILL, BE STILL, WHAT CAN BE SAID?	613	MARCH SONGS 1	7
BE STILL, BE STILL, WHAT CAN BE SAID?	613	MARCH SONGS 1	7
BE STILL, BE STILL, WHAT CAN BE SAID?	613	MARCH SONGS 1	17
BE STILL, BE STILL, WHAT CAN BE SAID?	613	MARCH SONGS 1	17
BE STILL, BE STILL, WHAT CAN BE SAID?	614	MARCH SONGS 1	27
BE STILL, BE STILL, WHAT CAN BE SAID?	614	MARCH SONGS 1	27
WHILE MAN CAN STILL HIS BODY KEEP	633	MAN AND ECHO	25
CAME CREEPING UP BECAUSE THE MAN WAS STILL.	634	CUCHULAIN COMF	10
WHEN SLEEPERS WAKE AND YET STILL DREAM,	639	BEN BULBEN	59
AND WHEN IT'S VANISHED STILL DECLARE,	639	BEN BULBEN	60
STILL THE INDOMITABLE IRISHRY.	640	BEN BULBEN	83
NO! THOU STANDEST STILL AND STARK,	658	ISLE STAT I 3	90
THE AIR IS STILL ABOVE, AND STILL EACH LEAF,	662	ISLE STAT II 2	7
THE AIR IS STILL ABOVE, AND STILL EACH LEAF,	662	ISLE STAT II 2	7
SO BE THOU STILL, DEAR HEART, A LITTLE WHILE!	677	ISLE STAT II 3	283
DOTH STILL THE WANDERER ROVE? WITH ALL HIS SHIPS	677	ISLE STAT II 3	287
DOTH STILL THE MAN WHOM EACH STERN ROVER FEARS,	678	ISLE STAT II 3	295
DOTH HE STILL DWELL WITHIN THE WOODY SHADE,	678	ISLE STAT II 3	303
ARE STILL THE ACHAIANS' TENTED CHIEFS AT BAY?	679	ISLE STAT II 3	310
STILL STARING AT THEIR FLOWERS,	680	LOVE AND DEATH	25
UNQUENCHABLE STILL GLOWS IN HER DULL STARE,	687	TWO TITANS	17
OR PERCHING ON THE TENTS, A-WEARY STILL.	690	MOSADA 1	8
THE DARK STILL MAN, HAS COME AND SAYS 'TIS SIN.	692	MOSADA 1	47
BE STILL! I HEAR THE STEP OF EBREMAR.	697	MOSADA 2	34
I NEVER KNEW AN EVE SO MARVELLOUS STILL.	702	MOSADA 3	88
STILL WANDER THROUGH THE WORLD. HE'S GONE, HE'S GONE.	703	MOSADA 3	121
TO LOVE EACH OTHER. IN MY PRAYER-BOOK STILL	713	FERENCZ RENYI	94
TO LOVE EACH OTHER. IN MY PRAYER BOOK STILL	713	FERENCZ RENYI V	94
HOW STILL IT IS! I HEAR THE CARP GO SPLASH,	722	WITCH VIVIEN	62
AND EVIL STILL IS ACTION'S CHILD.	728	PRIEST FAIRY	14
THEY GREW SO VERY STILL, I WIS	730	PRIEST FAIRY	66
AND NOW THEY ARE ALL GONE, I FOLLOW STILL.	749	SHADOW WATER A	37
THEY ARE STILL WAITING; AND NOW THE LAGGARD COMES,	754	SHADOW WATER A	150
THEY ARE STILL WAITING; AND A LAGGARD COMES,	754	SHADOW WATER A V	150
OF VOICES AND OF DREAMS. O HEART, BE STILL!	765	SHADOW WATER A	362
RUNS, RUNS AND IS SUDDENLY STILL.	783	GREY ROUND	3
CARRY IT! SUDDENLY IT IS STILL.	783	GREY ROUND	5
O STILL THAT HEART AT LAST.	785	YOUR HEART	8
STILLED			
THE NAMES THAT STILLED YOUR CHILDISH PLAY,	289	SEPTEMBER 1913	10
SOON SHALL OUR WINGS BE STILLED,	643	SONG FAERIES	5
SOON SHALL OUR WINGS BE STILLED,	676	ISLE STAT II 3	252
STILLNESS			
GREAT RULERS OF THE STILLNESS, LET HER NO LONGER BE	175	ELEMENT POWERS V	13
GREAT RULERS OF STILLNESS, LET HER NO LONGER BE	175	ELEMENT POWERS V	13
THE SOUL BEGINS TO TREMBLE INTO STILLNESS,	374	PHASES OF MOON	54
NOTHING BUT STILLNESS CAN REMAIN WHEN HEARTS ARE FULL	426	PHANTOM HATRED	23
THAT STILLNESS FOR A THEME	535	CHOSEN	14
AND CROUCH IN SOME FAR STILLNESS OF THE ISLE, AND DIE.	675	ISLE STAT II 3	246
IN A FAR STILLNESS OF THE ISLAND DIE.	675	ISLE STAT II 3 V	246
STILLY			
AND HAD DISPORTED IN THE STILLY JET,	31	OISIN 2	39
STILT			
FROM COLLAR TO COLLAR, FROM STILT TO STILT, FROM FATHER TO CHILD.	623	HIGH TALK	10
FROM COLLAR TO COLLAR, FROM STILT TO STILT, FROM FATHER TO CHILD.	623	HIGH TALK	10
STILTED			
THE STILTED WATER-HEN	419	MY HOUSE	8
THOSE STILTED BOYS, THAT BURNISHED CHARIOT,	629	CIRCUS ANIMALS	7
STILT-JACK			
MALACHI STILT-JACK AM I, WHATEVER I LEARNED HAS RUN WILD,	623	HIGH TALK	9
STILTS			
PROCESSIONS THAT LACK HIGH STILTS HAVE NOTHING THAT CATCHES THE EYE.	622	HIGH TALK	1
ALL METAPHOR, MALACHI, STILTS AND ALL. A BARNACLE GOOSE	623	HIGH TALK	11
STIR			
OR IN THE WINE-VAT, DWELL BEYOND THE STIR	169	SECRET ROSE	4
OR IN THE WINE VAT, DWELL BEYOND THE STIR	169	SECRET ROSE V	4
UNTIL THE PILLARED DARK BEGAN TO STIR	185	QUEEN MAEVE	110
TO STIR THEIR COVERLET AND THEIR HAIR,	197	BAILE AILLINN	186
THE FORD WHERE DRINKING CATTLE MAKE A STIR	326	ROBERT GREGORY	53
TO STIR THE BOILING POT?	395	SIXTEEN DEAD	6
WHAT STIR RAN THROUGH THE COUNTRYSIDE	488	CRAZED MOON	10
'TIS BUT TO SEE IF ANYTHING WILL STIR	669	ISLE STAT II 3	75
HAD NOT ALL HIS LIMBS A STIR	772	SONG DEIRDRE 1	11
STIRLESS			
OF AWELESS BIRDS, AND ROUND THEIR STIRLESS FEET	16	ANASHU VIJAYA	73
STIRRED			
THEY STIRRED MY SPACIOUS SOUL IN ME NO JOT—	36	OISIN 2 V	94
AND CHAUNTED FOR THREE DAYS. CUCHULAIN STIRRED,	111	CUCHULAIN SEA	83
AND CHANTED FOR THREE DAYS. CUCHULAIN STIRRED,	111	CUCHULAIN SEA V	83
BECAUSE THE DAILY SPECTACLE THAT STIRRED	270	PARDON FATHERS	16
BECAUSE YOU WERE THE SPECTACLE THAT STIRRED	270	PARDON FATHERS V	16
THAT HE, WHEN FRENZY STIRRED HIS THEWS,	271	GREY ROCK	22

768

		PAGE	TITLE		LINE

STIRRED (CONTINUED)
IT MAY BE, AND HAD NOT STIRRED,	381	SONGS FOOL 2		12
NEVER UNTIL THIS NIGHT HAVE I BEEN STIRRED.	389	IMAGE PAST		1
WITH ALL YOUTH'S LONELY WILDNESS STIRRED,	397	POLIT PRISONER		16
THAT STIRRED HER FANTASY AND PLANNED HER CARE,	466	HARUN RASHID	V	114

STIRRING
| . . . A SOUND LIKE THE STIRRING OF FLIES. | 51 | OISIN 3 | | 58 |

STIRS
AND STIRS THE YOUNG KID'S BUDDING HORN,	18	OISIN 1		264
"AN OLD MAN STIRS THE FIRE TO A BLAZE,	26	OISIN 1		400
THE FIRE THAT STIRS ABOUT HER, WHEN SHE STIRS,	200	FOLLY COMFORT		10
THE FIRE THAT STIRS ABOUT HER, WHEN SHE STIRS,	200	FOLLY COMFORT		10
WHEN EVENING STIRS THE JASMINE BOUGH, AND YET	463	HARUN RASHID		53
WHEN EVENING STIRS THE JASMINE, AND YET	463	HARUN RASHID	V	53
LIKE PASSION STIRS THE PEACOCK AND HIS MATE,	465	HARUN RASHID		100
WHERE NOTHING STIRS BUT A MOUSE.	575	ACRE OF GRASS		6
BUT BLESSED HE THAT STIRS THEM NOT	779	ACCURSED WHO		3

STITCHING
| OUR STITCHING AND UNSTITCHING HAS BEEN NAUGHT. | 204 | ADAMS CURSE | | 6 |
| STITCHING AT A PURPLE HOARDED | 440 | WISDOM | | 12 |

STOATS
| OF BITTERNS, AND FISH-EATING STOATS, | 14 | OISIN 1 | | 191 |
| OF BITTERNS AND FISH-EATING STOATS. | 23 | OISIN 1 | | 355 |

STOCK
| MADE LOCK, STOCK AND BARREL | 415 | TOWER | | 150 |
| THE WOMEN TAKE SO LITTLE STOCK | 455 | HIS MEMORIES | | 7 |

STOCKS
| ON GANGLING STOCKS GROWN GREAT, GREAT STOCKS RUN DRY, | 619 | BRONZE HEAD | | 25 |
| ON GANGLING STOCKS GROWN GREAT, GREAT STOCKS RUN DRY, | 619 | BRONZE HEAD | | 25 |

STOLE
AND STOLE THE CRIMSON ROSE,	174	ELEMENT POWERS	V	2
SOME ROGUE OF THE WORLD STOLE THEM TO PATCH UP A FENCE OR A FIRE.	623	HIGH TALK		4
AND WHEN THE FOOL AND BLIND MAN STOLE THE BREAD	630	CIRCUS ANIMALS		25
THE SPIRITS STOLE, AND GAVE HIM IN ITS STEAD	684	SEEKER		55

STOLEN
THE STOLEN CHILD	86	STOLEN CHILD		T
AND OF REDDEST STOLEN CHERRIES.	87	STOLEN CHILD		8
THE STOLEN BRIDE	143	HOST OF AIR	V	T
A LITTLE STOLEN TRESS. I, TOO, AWAIT	170	SECRET ROSE		27

STOLES
| AND OLD MEN WITH CROZIERS AND STOLES. | 167 | BLESSED | | 16 |

STONE   SEE JEWEL-STONE
HUGE FORMS OF STONE: BETWEEN THE LIDS OF ONE	31	OISIN 2	V	37
AND MANANNAN'S DARK TOWER, STONE AFTER STONE,	45	OISIN 2		236
AND MANANNAN'S DARK TOWER, STONE AFTER STONE,	45	OISIN 2		236
LIKE ROTTED FLESH, AND STONE BY STONE MY HALL	45	OISIN 2	V	236
LIKE ROTTED FLESH, AND STONE BY STONE MY HALL	45	OISIN 2	V	236
AND MANANAN'S DARK TOWER, STONE BY STONE,	45	OISIN 2	V	236
AND MANANAN'S DARK TOWER, STONE BY STONE,	45	OISIN 2	V	236
THE MOIL OF MY CENTURIES FILLED ME: AND GONE LIKE A SEA-COVERED STONE	51	OISIN 3		70
IN A LONG IRON SLEEP, AS A FISH IN THE WATER GOES DUMB AS A STONE.	53	OISIN 3		96
A WEASEL MOVING ON FROM STONE TO STONE,	102	FERGUS DRUID		5
A WEASEL MOVING ON FROM STONE TO STONE,	102	FERGUS DRUID		5
MAY SET A STONE UPON ANCESTRAL SORROW!	130	BOOK STORIES		11
UNDER A CAIRN OF SLEEPY STONE	192	BAILE AILLINN		81
ALTHOUGH HE IS CARRYING STONE, BUT TWO	192	BAILE AILLINN		83
CAULDRON AND SPEAR AND STONE AND SWORD,	196	BAILE AILLINN		165
BUT FRUIT THAT IS OF PRECIOUS STONE,	196	BAILE AILLINN		175
HEAVY LIKE STONE, THEIR WISDOM BEING HALF SILENCE.	218	WOODS OF COOLE		26
A BOY OF TWENTY YEARS:—A MOUND AND STONE	276	TWO KINGS	V	F
AND WHERE THE STONE STRUCK FIRE, WHILE IN THE LEAVES	278	TWO KINGS		33
SOME PASSION HAD MADE HER STONE. HEARING A FOOT	279	TWO KINGS		65
AND RAISE HIS PILLAR STONE." KING EOCHAID SAID,	280	TWO KINGS	V	83
THAT MAKE THE HEART AKIN TO THE DUMB STONE.	281	TWO KINGS		94
THAN MOUND AND STONE THAT KEEP ALL VIRTUE IN,	281	TWO KINGS		106
DEARER THAN ANY THAT THE DUMB STONE HIDES,	281	TWO KINGS	V	96
MUST END AT THE DUMB STONE? BUT WHERE WE BUILD	284	TWO KINGS		179
AMID A PLACE OF STONE,	291	TO A FRIEND		13
I'VE STOOD AS I WERE MADE OF STONE	297	THREE BEGGARS		64
ON A WINDY STONE, THE THIRD.	298	THREE HERMITS		5
BUT MIGHT HAVE PUMMELLED AT A STONE	307	HOUR DAWN		114
AND AFTER HEAPED UP STONE ON STONE,	307	HOUR DAWN		116
AND AFTER HEAPED UP STONE ON STONE,	307	HOUR DAWN		116
AND HEAPED UP STONE ON STONE AGAIN,	307	HOUR DAWN		118
AND HEAPED UP STONE ON STONE AGAIN,	307	HOUR DAWN		118
WE SAT AS SILENT AS A STONE,	314	MEMORY YOUTH		15
I SAT AS SILENT AS A STONE	314	MEMORY YOUTH	V	15
IN MOULDED PLASTER OR IN CARVEN STONE?	327	ROBERT GREGORY		77
FROM STONE TO STONE. I AM LOOKING FOR STRAYED SHEEP:	339	SHEP GOATHERD		9
FROM STONE TO STONE. I AM LOOKING FOR STRAYED SHEEP:	339	SHEP GOATHERD		9
THE EXULTATION OF THEIR STONE, THAT CRIED	339	SHEP GOATHERD		25
WHERE STONE IS DARK UNDER FROTH,	348	FISHERMAN		32
WHERE STONE IS DARK WITH FROTH,	348	FISHERMAN	V	32
IN THE GREY STONE TOMB HE MADE.	360	ALF POLLEXFEN		5
HE SET HIS CHISEL TO THE HARDEST STONE.	369	EGO DOMINUS		32
AND AFTER KISSED A STONE,	384	VISION ROBART		64
ENCHANTED TO A STONE	393	EASTER 1916		43
CAN MAKE A STONE OF THE HEART.	394	EASTER 1916		58

	PAGE	TITLE		LINE
STONE (CONTINUED)				
COLD STONE AND WATER. I GREW WILD,	399	BREAK OF DAY		14
WHILE ON THAT OLD GREY STONE I SAT	406	IN TIME OF WAR		2
TO BE CARVED ON A STONE AT THOOR BALLYLEE	406	CARVED STONE		T
TO BE CARVED ON A STONE AT BALLYLEE	406	CARVED STONE	V	T
OF DRIPPING STONE; I DECLARE	414	TOWER		126
BITTER AND VIOLENT MEN, MIGHT REAR IN STONE	418	ANCEST HOUSES		19
A WINDING STAIR, A CHAMBER ARCHED WITH STONE,	419	MY HOUSE		11
A GREY STONE FIREPLACE WITH AN OPEN HEARTH,	419	MY HOUSE		12
A GREY STONE FIRE-PLACE WITH AN OPEN HEARTH,	419	MY HOUSE	V	12
A BARRICADE OF STONE OR OF WOOD;	425	STARES NEST		11
I CLIMB TO THE TOWER-TOP AND LEAN UPON BROKEN STONE,	425	PHANTOM HATRED		1
I CLIMB TO THE TOWER TOP AND LEAN UPON BROKEN STONE,	425	PHANTOM HATRED	V	1
AMID THE ORNAMENTAL BRONZE AND STONE	428	NINETEEN 19		5
MIRACLE-BRED OUT OF THE LIVING STONE;	446	COLONUS PRAISE		13
AND FOUND A HEART OF STONE	451	FIRST LOVE		8
SO LIKE A BIT OF STONE I LIE	452	HUMAN DIGNITY		7
A STONE UPON HER BREAST.	456	FRIENDS YOUTH		6
AND A CLOAK WRAPPED ABOUT THE STONE,	456	FRIENDS YOUTH		7
AND PERCHES ON A STONE;	456	FRIENDS YOUTH		16
BEING ALL ALONE I'D NURSE A STONE	459	HIS WILDNESS		11
BUT WHEN I THINK OF THAT MY TONGUE'S A STONE.	478	SELF AND SOUL		40
LIKE MILK SPILT ON A STONE.	484	SPILT MILK		4
AND SAPLINGS ROOT AMONG THE BROKEN STONE.	489	COOLE PARK 29		28
CROUCH UPON A STONE,	525	DANCING DAYS		4
EVERY DISCOLORATION OF THE STONE,	567	LAPIS LAZULI		43
"IRELAND SHALL GET HER FREEDOM AND YOU STILL BREAK STONE."	590	PARNELL		2
THEY ALWAYS BEAT ON THE SAME SMALL STONE.	591	WHAT WAS LOST		5
THE OLD STONE CROSS	598	STONE CROSS		T
UNDER THE OLD STONE CROSS.	598	STONE CROSS		8
UNDER THE OLD STONE CROSS.	599	STONE CROSS		16
UNDER THE OLD STONE CROSS.	599	STONE CROSS		24
SET UP THE OLD STONE CROSS,	604	YOU CONTENT		10
I KISSED A STONE;	628	JANE MOUNTAIN		20
UNDER BROKEN STONE I HALT	632	MAN AND ECHO		2
AND SHOUT A SECRET TO THE STONE.	632	MAN AND ECHO		5
ARE CHANGED FOR EVER INTO MOON-WHITE STONE.	653	ISLE STAT I 2		43
LONG YEARS AGO, AND UNTO STONE CONGEALED.	656	ISLE STAT I 3		28
AND THEY ARE ALL NOW STONE, AS I SHALL BE,	656	ISLE STAT I 3		35
I PASSED BY MANY CAVES OF DRIPPING STONE.	657	ISLE STAT I 3		47
IS STONE! OLD SLEEPER! THIS SAME AFTERNOON	657	ISLE STAT I 3		74
THE ARCADIANS BRING, AND BID THE STONE BE RAISED	663	ISLE STAT II 2		25
AND HANG O'ER THE HISTORIED STONE!	707	FAIRY PEDANT		6
THE HISTORY HERE IN THE STONE NOW!	707	FAIRY PEDANT		15
THE HISTORY HERE IN THE STONE—	707	FAIRY PEDANT	V	15
AND THIS HARD FLAG OF STONE,	739	EARL PAUL		6
STONE-GREY				
THE WIND-BEATEN, STONE-GREY,	310	PEACOCK		4
STONE'S				
THE STONE'S IN THE MIDST OF ALL.	393	EASTER 1916		56
THINKS THAT THE STONE'S A CHILD.	456	FRIENDS YOUTH		12
STONES SEE THUNDER-STONES				
CRASHED ON THE STONES, UPON THE GLIMMERING STONES,	33	OISIN 2	V	68A
CRASHED ON THE STONES, UPON THE GLIMMERING STONES,	33	OISIN 2	V	68A
GO CAST YOUR BODY ON THE STONES AND PRAY,	42	OISIN 2		207
. . . ON THE BURNING STONES IS THEIR PLACE;	61	OISIN 3		197
. . . ON THE BURNING STONES OF WIDE HELL,	61	OISIN 3		198
WE WILL TEAR OUT THE FLAMING STONES, AND BATTER THE GATEWAY OF BRASS	62	OISIN 3		209
ON THE FLAMING STONES, WITHOUT REFUGE	62	OISIN 3		213
WE WILL TEAR OUT THE RED FLAMING STONES,	62	OISIN 3	V	209
WE WILL TEAR THE RED FLAMING STONES OUT,	62	OISIN 3	V	209
ON THE RED FLAMING STONES WITHOUT REFUGE	62	OISIN 3	V	213
I THROW DOWN THE CHAIN OF SMALL STONES!	63	OISIN 3		222
I WILL PRAY NO MORE WITH THE SMOOTH STONES!	63	OISIN 3	V	221
THERE, DON'T FLING STONES AT ME	94	MOLL MAGEE		2
YE WON'T FLING STONES AT ME!	96	MOLL MAGEE		54
I HAVE BEEN IN THE PATH OF STONES AND THE WOOD OF THORNS,	153	CHANGE BELOVED		3
THEY HAVE HEAPED THE STONES ABOVE HIS GRAVE	193	BAILE AILLINN		115
AND SCRUB A KITCHEN PAVEMENT, OR BREAK STONES	204	ADAMS CURSE		8
AND THROWN THE THUNDER ON THE STONES FOR ALL THAT MAEVE CAN SAY.	207	HANRAHANS SONG		7
AND SHAKE DOWN THUNDER ON THE STONES BECAUSE THE RED WINDS RAVE!	207	HANRAHANS SONG	V	7
AMONG THE STONES AND THORN-TREES, UNDER MORNING LIGHT;	291	PAUDEEN		3
AMONG THE STONES AND THORN TREES, UNDER MORNING LIGHT,	291	PAUDEEN	V	3
OF GREY STONES AND A ROCKY LEDGE	302	HOUR DAWN		12
IF HE BUT SHIFTED A FEW STONES,	302	HOUR DAWN		14
BUT WHILE HE FUMBLED WITH THE STONES	302	HOUR DAWN		16
BEFORE HIS EYES, WHERE STONES HAD BEEN,	302	HOUR DAWN		20
AND THEREON SAW, WHERE STONES HAD BEEN	302	HOUR DAWN	V	20
AND AFTER HEAPED THE STONES AGAIN	307	HOUR DAWN	V	116
WITH ALL THEIR ANCIENT FACES LIKE RAIN-BEATEN STONES,	318	MAGI		4
UPON THE BRIMMING WATER AMONG THE STONES	322	SWANS AT COOLE		5
AND THE PROUD STONES OF GREECE,	415	TOWER		159
THESE STONES REMAIN THEIR MONUMENT AND MINE,	423	MY DESCENDANTS		24
ROUND LOUGH DERG'S HOLY ISLAND I WENT UPON THE STONES,	593	PILGRIM		6
ALL FLAME-LIKE GUSHING FROM THE HOLLOW STONES,	650	ISLE STAT I 1		129
DRY STONES IN A WELL?"	780	WELL AND TREE		8
STONY				
WHERE PASSIONATE MAIVE IS STONY STILL;	3	OISIN 1	V	18

	PAGE	TITLE		LINE
STONY (CONTINUED)				
AND ON THE RUNNEL'S STONY AND BARE EDGE	39	OISIN 2		157
BEFORE EARTH TOOK HIM TO HER STONY CARE:	126	DREAM OF FAERY		4
WITH STILL AND STONY LIMBS AND OPEN EYES.	182	QUEEN MAEVE		46
IN A MOST DESOLATE STONY PLACE,	325	ROBERT GREGORY		30
AN IMAGE THAT MIGHT HAVE BEEN A STONY FACE	368	EGO DOMINUS		28
THAT TWENTY CENTURIES OF STONY SLEEP	402	SECOND COMING		19
THAT THIRTY CENTURIES OF STONY SLEEP	402	SECOND COMING	V	19
AN ACRE OF STONY GROUND,	419	MY HOUSE		3
LEST ON THINE HEART THE STONY SEAL	667	ISLE STAT II 3		41
STONY-HEARTED				
AND STONY-HEARTED: NOW THOU HAST GROWN KIND,	670	ISLE STAT II 3		91
STONY-STILL				
WHERE PASSIONATE MAEVE IS STONY-STILL:	3	OISIN 1		18
STOOD				
AND STOOD BESIDE THE SEA TOGETHER:	9	OISIN 1	V	101B
WHILE ROUND THE SHORE A MILLION STOOD	14	OISIN 1		182
WHEN ONE DAY BY THE TIDE I STOOD,	24	OISIN 1		364
WHEN ONCE BESIDE THE SHORE I STOOD,	24	OISIN 1	V	364
WHEN ONE DAY BY THE SHORE I STOOD,	24	OISIN 1	V	364
AND RODE AND STOOD BESIDE THE SHORE.	25	OISIN 1	V	379A
THAT WITH DIM EYEBALLS STOOD ON EITHER SIDE.	34	OISIN 2		75
STOOD LONELY, WITH DIM EYEBALLS ON EACH SIDE,	34	OISIN 2	V	74
STILL EARLESS, NERVELESS, BLIND, THE EAGLES STOOD.	36	OISIN 2		100
AND STOOD WITHIN: CLOTHED IN A MISTY RAY	36	OISIN 2		104
AND STOOD WITHIN THE HALL. A MISTY RAY	36	OISIN 2	V	104
BUT ONLY EXULTANT FACES. NIAMH STOOD	38	OISIN 2		136
STOOD TIMIDLY. LEST THEY SHOULD SEE SOME SIGHT	38	OISIN 2	V	141
I STOOD UPON THE STAIR: THE SURGES BORE	44	OISIN 2		225
REMEMBERING HOW I HAD STOOD BY WHITE-HAIRED FINN	44	OISIN 2		227
REMEMBERING HOW I STOOD BY WHITE-HAIRED FINN	44	OISIN 2	V	227
HOLDING THAT HORSE LONG SEEN NOT, NIAM STOOD.	44	OISIN 2	V	230
AND WE STOOD ON A SEA'S EDGE WE SAW NOT:	47	OISIN 3		11
. . . WITH BODIES UNGLORIOUS, THEIR CHIEFTAINS STOOD,	58	OISIN 3		166
A WHITEBEARD STOOD HUSHED ON THE PATHWAY.	59	OISIN 3		173
AUTUMN WAS OVER HIM: AND NOW THEY STOOD	80	EPHEMERA		16
I STOOD: KEEN STARS ABOVE ME SHONE,	83	MAD KING GOLL		29
MY HUSBAND STOOD UP PALE,	95	MOLL MAGEE	V	22
IN THREE DAYS' TIME HE STOOD UP WITH A MOAN,	111	CUCHULAIN SEA	V	83
STOOD UP, AND CAME TO THE LONG SANDS ALONE:	111	CUCHULAIN SEA	V	84
WEARY AND KIND ONE STOOD BESIDE HIS SEAT:	112	ROSE OF WORLD	V	13
HE STOOD AMONG A CROWD AT DROMAHAIR:	126	DREAM OF FAERY		1
STOOD UPRIGHT ON THE FLOOR.	133	FR GILLIGAN		24
I DREAMED THAT I STOOD IN A VALLEY, AND AMID SIGHS,	163	VALLEY LOVERS		1
FOR HAPPY LOVERS PASSED TWO BY TWO WHERE I STOOD:	163	VALLEY LOVERS		2
TILL DATHI CAME AND STOOD,	166	BLESSED		2
TILL DATHI CAME AND STOOD,	167	BLESSED	V	48
THE MAINES' CHILDREN DROPPED THEIR SPADES, AND STOOD	185	QUEEN MAEVE		120
TILL IT DIED OUT WHERE AN OLD THORN-TREE STOOD.	186	QUEEN MAEVE		129
FRIEND OF THESE MANY YEARS, YOU TOO HAD STOOD	186	QUEEN MAEVE		130
TILL IT DIED OUT WHERE AN OLD THORN TREE STOOD.	186	QUEEN MAEVE	V	129
FRIEND OF THESE MANY YEARS, YOU TO HAVE STOOD	186	QUEEN MAEVE	V	130
WHO STOOD AMID A SILENCE BY THE THORN	187	QUEEN MAEVE		142
UNTIL YOU STOOD BEFORE ME ON THE DECK--	236	SHADOW WATER B		313
OLD BUTLERS WHEN YOU TOOK TO HORSE AND STOOD	270	PARDON FATHERS	V	10
MAYBE YOUR IMAGES HAVE STOOD,	273	GREY ROCK		50
WHERE BY OLD THORN-TREES THAT MAN STOOD:	274	GREY ROCK		80
WHERE BY OLD THORN TREES THAT MAN STOOD:	274	GREY ROCK	V	80
BUT THEREON EVERY GOD STOOD UP	275	GREY ROCK		116
BECAUSE IT STOOD UPON HIS PATH AND SEEMED	277	TWO KINGS		8
TOWARD PEOPLED TARA, NOR STOOD TO DRAW HIS BREATH	279	TWO KINGS		46
ON PEOPLED TARA, NOR STOOD TO DRAW HIS BREATH	279	TWO KINGS	V	46
TOWARDS PEOPLED TARA, NOR STOOD TO DRAW HIS BREATH	279	TWO KINGS	V	46
BUT WHEN NINE DAYS HAD GONE I STOOD AGAIN	282	TWO KINGS		131
STOOD ON MY PATH. TREMBLING FROM HEAD TO FOOT	283	TWO KINGS		151
STOOD ON MY PATH. TREMBLING FROM HAND TO FOOT	283	TWO KINGS	V	151
AND IN THE MIDST KING EOCHAID'S BROTHER STOOD,	286	TWO KINGS		217
I HAVE STOOD HERE FROM BREAK OF DAY,	294	THREE BEGGARS		2
AND WHEN OLD GUAIRE CAME AND STOOD	297	THREE BEGGARS		54
I'VE STOOD AS I WERE MADE OF STONE	297	THREE BEGGARS		64
AND YET STOOD STILL, BECAUSE INSIDE	303	HOUR DAWN		26
THAT MERELY STOOD, ROCKING THE GLITTERING COACH	344	DAWN		11
THE STATELY MIDNIGHT THROUGH UNTIL THEY STOOD	352	PEOPLE		14
AS IF THE HAIR STOOD UP ON MY HEAD.	358	PRESENCES		2
THEY STOOD IN THE DOOR AND STOOD BETWEEN	358	PRESENCES		9
THEY STOOD IN THE DOOR AND STOOD BETWEEN	358	PRESENCES		9
TO ALL THAT IN YOUR FLESH HAVE STOOD	380	SAINT HUNCH		13
THAT PITCHES COMMON THINGS ABOUT. THERE STOOD	428	NINETEEN 19		4
OR ALL THAT WAYWARD EBB AND FLOW. THERE STOOD	428	NINETEEN 19	V	4
ON ALL THAT WAYWARD EBB AND FLOW. THERE STOOD	428	NINETEEN 19	V	4
THE ROMAN EMPIRE STOOD APPALLED:	437	SONGS PLAY 1		13
AND WONDER IF SHE STOOD SO AT THAT AGE--	444	SCHOOL CHILDR		19
AND ON MY PATHWAY STOOD	451	FIRST LOVE		4
THERE, ON BLOOD-SATURATED GROUND, HAVE STOOD	482	BLOOD AND MOON		35
THERE, ON BLOOD SATURATED GROUND, HAVE STOOD	482	BLOOD AND MOON	V	35
STOOD IN THE CIRCUIT OF A NEEDLE'S EYE.	483	VERONIC NAPKIN		6
SOME FOUND A DIFFERENT POLE, AND WHERE IT STOOD	483	VERONIC NAPKIN		7
AND IN A COPSE OF BEECHES THERE I STOOD,	490	COOLE BALLYLEE		11
BUT A BIRCH-TREE STOOD MY JACK:	508	JANE BISHOP		20
BUT A BIRCH TREE STOOD MY JACK:	508	JANE BISHOP	V	20
THAT FROM CHILDHOOD STOOD	512	JANE ON GOD		14

STOOD (CONTINUED)
```
    CAME WHERE YOU STOOD,                                      518 LOVES LONENESS        4
    AND THEN YOU STOOD AMONG THE DRAGON-RINGS.                 533 HER TRIUMPH           7
    AND THEN YOU STOOD AMONG THE DRAGON RINGS.                 533 HER TRIUMPH      V    7
    TOO OLD FOR A MAN'S LOVE I STOOD IN RAGE                   536 HER VISION            3
    TOO OLD FOR A MAN'S LOVE I STOOD AND RAGED                 536 HER VISION       V    1
    FACE TO FACE WE STOOD:                                     539 MEETING               4
    JUSTIFY ALL THAT HAVE FLED, THAT HAVE STOOD,               546 TO SAME TUNE 2       14
    STOOD OR HAVE MARCHED THE NIGHT LONG                       546 TO SAME TUNE 2       15
    JUSTIFY ALL THAT HAVE FLED OR HAVE STOOD,                  546 TO SAME TUNE 2   V   14
    OF A SLENDER PALM, STOOD BUT A DAY:                        566 LAPIS LAZULI         34
    SHE STOOD IN DESPERATE MUSIC WOUND,                        578 CRAZED GIRL          10
    A PERJURER STOOD READY                                     582 ROGER CASEMENT        9
    JOHN BULL HAS STOOD FOR PARLIAMENT,                        583 GHOST ROG CASE       11
    A MAN WITH A PISTOL STOOD,                                 596 COLONEL MARTIN       56
    WENT TO THE SACRED HOUSE AND STOOD BETWEEN                 609 IN TARAS HALLS       11
    REMEMBER ALL THAT HAVE FLED, THAT HAVE STOOD,              613 MARCH SONGS 1        14
    STOOD, TOOK DEATH LIKE A TUNE                              613 MARCH SONGS 1        15
    A MAN WHO BY A DEAD MAN STOOD.                             671 ISLE STAT II 3      124
    HE SHRANK BEFORE MY VOICE, AND STOOD                       671 ISLE STAT II 3      129
    HE STOOD A MESSENGER.  IN APRIL'S PRIME                    690 MOSADA 1              6
    AND ON TIPTOE THE WINDS A-WHISPERING STOOD.               715 DWELT SYCAMORE        8
    AND ON TIP-TOE THE WINDS A-WHISPERING STOOD.              715 DWELT SYCAMORE V      8
    LISTENING, UPON THEIR SHADOWS STOOD.                      725 LEGEND                8
    THERE STOOD A MAN, OF MEN THE LEAST--                      729 PRIEST FAIRY         24
    AND CAME TO WHERE HIS BRETHREN STOOD.                      730 PRIEST FAIRY         63
    EARL PAUL STOOD ON THE BED OF STRAW,                       740 EARL PAUL            17
    WHEN HUNDREDS STOOD ABOUT TO SEE                           740 EARL PAUL            27
    AND STOOD IN HIS DIM ARMOUR,                               741 EARL PAUL            33
    STOOD THERE THE NORMAN KNIGHT.                             741 EARL PAUL            40
    AND JOHN ROSE UP AND STOOD,                                741 EARL PAUL            54
    AND STOOD IN MY SORROW APART,                              744 GLOVE CLOAK           2
    I STOOD WITH HER CLOAK ON MY ARM                           744 GLOVE CLOAK           5
    I HAVE STOOD SO LONG BY A GAP IN THE WALL                  788 HAWTHORN TREE        15
    BUT NEVER STOOD BEFORE A STAKE                             790 SINGING HEAD         23
```
STOOL
```
    WHEN I HAD LAIN IT ON A STOOL,                             149 WANDER AENGUS V       9
    WHEN I HAD LAID IT ON A STOOL.                             149 WANDER AENGUS V       9
    BUT SOMETHING RUSTLED ON THE STOOL,                        149 WANDER AENGUS V      11
    NO TABLE OR CHAIR OR STOOL NOT SIMPLE ENOUGH               371 ON GOING HOUSE        3
    I SLEPT ON MY THREE-LEGGED STOOL BY THE FIRE,              381 SONGS FOOL 2          1
    THOU HAST FORGOTTEN.  ON THE OAKEN STOOL                   713 FERENCZ RENYI        91
```
STOOP
```
    AND NEVER STOOP TO A MECHANICAL                            417 ANCEST HOUSES         7
    MORE GRIEF IS MINE.  NO MAN SHALL EVER STOOP               661 ISLE STAT II 1       62
```
STOOPED
```
    WHEN I HAD STOOPED AND TENDERLY                             10 OISIN 1         V 112A
    I STOOPED TO BLOW THE FIRE AFLAME.                         149 WANDER AENGUS V      10
    HE HAS STOOPED DOWN AND KISSED HER ON THE LIPS.            232 SHADOW WATER B      230
    BUT THE STAG STOOPED AND RAN AT HIM, AND PASSED,           277 TWO KINGS            12
    BUT THE STAG STOOPED ITS HEAVY BRANCHING HORNS,            277 TWO KINGS       V    12
    BUT FINDING HIM STILL SILENT I STOOPED DOWN                281 TWO KINGS           109
```
STOOPING
```
    AND A SMALL AND A FEEBLE POPULACE STOOPING WITH MATTOCK     58 OISIN 3             164
        AND SPADE,
    AND A SMALL AND A FEEBLE RACE STOOPING WITH MATTOCK AND     58 OISIN 3             164
        SPADE.
    AND A SMALL AND FEEBLE RACE STOOPING WITH MATTOCK           58 OISIN 3         V   164
        AND SPADE.
    THE ANGELS ARE STOOPING                                    118 CRADLE SONG           1
```
STOP
```
    MIND MOVED YET SEEMED TO STOP                              384 VISION ROBART        43
    FOR AIMLESS JOY HAD MADE ME STOP                           400 DEMON BEAST          22
    THIS LOVE THAT MAKES MY HEART'S BLOOD STOP                 499 MOTHER OF GOD        13
    DARED I STOP".                                             559 HE AND SHE            6
    IF HE STOP LOVING ME,                                      569 THREE BUSHES         18
```
STOPPED
```
    BUT I NEVER STOPPED TO QUESTION, WHAT COULD THE BOATMAN SAY 593 PILGRIM             19
    LAY IN THE COFFIN, STOPPED HIS BREATH AND DIED.            609 IN TARAS HALLS       20
    I HAVE STOPPED SO LONG A GAP IN THE WALL                   788 HAWTHORN TREE V      15
```
STOPPING
```
    AND, IN A FAR-OFF, GENTLE VALLEY STOPPING,                  68 SAD SHEPHERD         13
    HE FLED, AND IN A FAR-OFF VALLEY STOPPING,                  68 SAD SHEPHERD V       13
```
STOPS
```
    ABOUT YOUR HEAD TILL THE DUST STOPS YOUR EAR,              293 TO A SHADE           20
    HE HOLDS HIM FROM DESIRE, ALL BUT STOPS HIS BREATHING LEST 559 MAGIC DRUM            1
```
STORE
```
    SOME OLD MISER TELLS HIS STORE:                            647 ISLE STAT I 1        58
    ON NAUGHT HAS SET STORE                                    780 WELL AND TREE        13
```
STORED
```
    "GOD ONLY SEES WHAT DOOM FOR ME LIES STORED."              110 CUCHULAIN SEA V      62
    WHOSE IMAGES, IN THE GREAT MEMORY STORED,                  412 TOWER                85
```
STOREYS
```
    BECAUSE WOMEN IN THE UPPER STOREYS DEMAND A FACE AT THE    623 HIGH TALK             7
        PANE:
```
STORIES
```
    OF STORIES BUILDED BY HIS WORDS                              7 OISIN 1             68
    THE DEDICATION TO A BOOK OF STORIES SELECTED FROM THE IRISH 129 BOOK STORIES         T
        NOVELISTS
    ALL THE LOVE STORIES THAT THEY KNEW.                       197 BAILE AILLINN       197
    YOUR EARS THAN STORIES NOW IN FASHION,                     271 GREY ROCK             5
```

772

	PAGE	TITLE		LINE
STORIES (CONTINUED)				
IS NOT THAT HOW GOOD STORIES RUN?--	271	GREY ROCK		13
CAN KNOW THE STORIES THAT WE KNOW	458	SECRETS OF OLD		11
STORIES OF THE BED OF STRAW	458	SECRETS OF OLD		17
THAT'S HOW ALL NATURAL OR SUPERNATURAL STORIES RUN.	556	RIBH PATRICK		3
BUT STORIES THAT LIVE LONGEST	587	PARNELLITES		29
AND O! BUT SHE HAD STORIES,	620	JOHN KINSELLA		17
STORM				
HE HEARS THE STORM IN THE CHIMNEY ABOVE,	26	OISIN 1		404
A STORM OF BIRDS IN THE ASIAN TREES	27	OISIN 1		416
DRIVEN BY A STORM THAT EVER GRIEVES.	135	TWO TREES	V	28
AND, LIKE A STORM, CRY THE INEFFABLE NAME,	137	TO SOME I TALK		12
WILL HIDE US FROM THE BITTER STORM.	152	HEART OF WOMAN		8
SHALL HIDE US FROM THE BITTER STORM.	152	HEART OF WOMAN	V	8
WOULD THAT THE STORM THAT OVERTHREW MY SHIPS,	235	SHADOW WATER B		286
"WERE NOT ALL HER LIFE BUT STORM,	259	PEACE		4
BECAUSE THERE IS SUCH A STORM AMID MY THOUGHTS	281	TWO KINGS		100
SHE LIVED IN STORM AND STRIFE,	317	NIGHT COME		1
ONCE MORE THE STORM IS HOWLING, AND HALF HID	403	FOR DAUGHTER		1
A PEAR-TREE BROKEN BY THE STORM.	424	ROAD AT DOOR		10
A PEAR TREE BROKEN BY THE STORM.	424	ROAD AT DOOR	V	10
TO BAR THAT FOUL STORM OUT, FOR WE	432	NINETEEN 19		111
NOR STORM DISTURBS, FLAMES BEGOTTEN OF FLAME,	498	BYZANTIUM		27
ALL THAT STORM THAT BLOTS THE DAY	509	JANE REPROVED		3
LOVE STORM! AND STAINED WITH MIST THE NEW MOONS FLARE.	678	ISLE STAT II 3		294
LOVE STORM AND STAINED WITH MIST THE NEW MOON'S FLARE	678	ISLE STAT II 3	V	294
NEVER STORM AROSE SO SWIFTLY! SCARCE THE CHILDREN WERE IN BED,	718	PHANTOM SHIP		4
STORM DARKENED OR STARRY BRIGHT.	739	WHERE BOOKS GO		8
A SUDDEN STORM, AND IT WAS THROWN	784	WOMANS BEAUTY		5
THE STORM AROSE AND SUDDENLY FELL	784	WOMANS BEAUTY		19
STORMBEATEN				
STORMBEATEN COTTAGES.	480	BLOOD AND MOON	V	7
STORM-BEATEN				
WHILE UNDER ITS STORM-BEATEN BREAST	397	POLIT PRISONER		23
STORM-BEATEN COTTAGES--	480	BLOOD AND MOON		7
A STORM-BEATEN OLD WATCH-TOWER,	484	SYMBOLS		1
A STORM-BEATEN OLD WATCH TOWER,	484	SYMBOLS	V	1
STORM-BITTEN				
ON A STORM-BITTEN GREEN.	606	SONGS BURDEN 2		4
STORM-BROKEN				
WERE LOVED BY HIM! THE OLD STORM-BROKEN TREES	326	ROBERT GREGORY		50
STORMS				
AND WANDER IN THE STORMS AND CLINGING SNOWS,	42	OISIN 2		201
I BELLOW TO THE WINDS WHEN STORMS MAKE MOAN,	45	OISIN 2	V	239D
THAT UNIMAGINABLE STORMS OF WIND AND WAVE	236	SHADOW WATER B		317
THAT STORMS ARE SHAKING, HEAR THE ARMED MAN SPEAK.	470	HARUN RASHID	V	193
ALL THOSE STORMS THAT BLOT THE DAY	509	JANE REPROVED	V	3
STORM-SCATTERED				
IN STORM-SCATTERED INTRICACY,	501	VACILLATION		48
STORM-TOSSED				
A WOMAN'S BEAUTY IS A STORM-TOSSED BANNER!	469	HARUN RASHID		188
STORMY				
A STORMY SUNSET ON DOOMED SHIPS!	3	OISIN 1		23
A STORMY SUNSET O'ER DOOMED SHIPS.	3	OISIN 1	V	23
OR STORMY SILVER FRET THE GOLD OF DAY,	128	DREAM OF FAERY		33
THAT THE STORMY NIGHT RECEIVES,	135	TWO TREES		26
ANOTHER EMBLEM THERE! THAT STORMY WHITE	490	COOLE BALLYLEE		17
BUILDING-YARD AND STORMY SHORE,	530	OLD TOM AGAIN		5
BUILDING YARD AND STORMY SHORE,	530	OLD TOM AGAIN	V	5
AT DAYBREAK AFTER STORMY NIGHT	784	WOMANS BEAUTY		3
STORY SEE LOVE-STORY				
OISIN, TELL ME THE FAMOUS STORY	2	OISIN 1	V	1
READING SOME ENTANGLED STORY!	65	HAPPY SHEPHERD	V	16
IN THE VERSE OF ATTIC STORY	65	HAPPY SHEPHERD	V	16
AND TO ITS LIPS THY STORY TELL,	66	HAPPY SHEPHERD		37
CRIED OUT, DIM SEA, HEAR MY MOST PITEOUS STORY!	68	SAD SHEPHERD		9
CRIED ALL HIS STORY TO THE DEWDROPS GLISTENING.	68	SAD SHEPHERD		14
AND THOUGHT, I WILL MY HEAVY STORY TELL	68	SAD SHEPHERD		19
"OH SEA, OLD SEA, HEAR THOU MY PITEOUS STORY!"	68	SAD SHEPHERD	V	9
AND THOUGHT, "TO THIS WILL I MY STORY TELL,	68	SAD SHEPHERD	V	19
SHE DREW FROM ME MY STORY--	96	MOLL MAGEE		37
BALLAD AND STORY, RANN AND SONG!	137	TO IRELAND		4
FOR THERE IS NO HIGH STORY ABOUT QUEENS	186	QUEEN MAEVE		134
EVEN IN AN OLD STORY, IS A BURDEN NOT TO BE BORNE.	210	UNDER THE MOON		20
BECAUSE OF A STORY I HEARD UNDER THE THIN HORN	210	UNDER THE MOON	V	17
BECAUSE OF A STORY I HEARD UNDER A THIN HORN	210	UNDER THE MOON	V	17
IT IS LUCKY THAT THEIR STORY	215	HAPPY TOWNLAND		27
AND THE IMAGES I HAVE WOVEN IN THIS STORY	218	WOODS OF COOLE		21
TO TELL THEM A PLAIN STORY. THAT'S NOT THE STORY!	245	SHADOW WATER B		482
TO TELL THEM A PLAIN STORY. THAT'S NOT THE STORY!	245	SHADOW WATER B		482
HERE'S AN OLD STORY I'VE REMADE,	270	GREY ROCK		3
HERE'S AN OLD STORY I'VE RE-MADE,	270	GREY ROCK	V	3
HAD RAVELLED HER OWN STORY OUT,	272	GREY ROCK		45
THAT TRAGIC STORY MADE,	587	PARNELLITES		26
WHEN HE HEARD THAT STORY TOLD,	596	COLONEL MARTIN		47
WHEN HE HAD HEARD THAT STORY TOLD	596	COLONEL MARTIN	V	47
NO SINGLE STORY WOULD THEY FIND	626	OLD MEN BE MAD		13
THEY HEAR THE STORY OF THE WIND,	655	ISLE STAT I 3		11
AND TELL ME A LOVE STORY WHILE I DRINK.	760	SHADOW WATER A	V	250
AND TELL ITS STORY OVER THEIR BROWN ALE.	767	SHADOW WATER A		393

773

	PAGE	TITLE		LINE

STORY'S
SOMEWHERE IN EAR-SHOT FOR THE STORY'S END, ... 269 PARDON FATHERS 2
AND WHEN THE STORY'S FINISHED, WHAT'S THE NEWS? . . . . 491 COOLE BALLYLEE V 40E
WHEN ALL THAT STORY'S FINISHED, WHAT'S THE NEWS? . . . . 495 CHOICE 5
SAW THE STORY'S END, ... 597 COLONEL MARTIN 69
STOUT
HIS STOUT STICK UNDER HIS HAND, ... 588 OLD WICKED MAN 20
STRADDLE
A STRADDLE ON THE DOLPHIN'S MIRE AND BLOOD . . . . . 498 BYZANTIUM V 33
STRADDLING
STRADDLING EACH A DOLPHIN'S BACK . . . . 612 NEWS ORACLE 13
STRAFFORD
AND EVEN STRAFFORD SMILED AS THOUGH . . . . 400 DEMON BEAST 13
STRAIGHT
IT ROSE IN A STRAIGHT BLUE GARMENT, ... 159 CAP AND BELLS 5
IN A LONG AND STRAIGHT BLUE GARMENT . . . . 159 CAP AND BELLS V 5
AND THOUGHT OF DAYS WHEN HE'D HAD A STRAIGHT BODY, . . 183 QUEEN MAEVE 70
THAT HAD SO STRAIGHT A BACK, ... 458 HIS WILDNESS 4
THOSE TERRIBLE IMPLACABLE STRAIGHT LINES . . . . . 467 HARUN RASHID 142
PALLAS ATHENE IN THAT STRAIGHT BACK AND ARROGANT HEAD! . 578 LOFTY THINGS 11
HOW CAN THE YOUNG GO STRAIGHT? . . . . 607 SONGS BURDEN 2 17
WITH A STIFF STRAIGHT BACK, ... 627 STATES HOLIDAY 33
AND STRAIGHT BEFORE THE SLEEPING PRIEST . . . . . . 729 PRIEST FAIRY 23
STRAIGHTEN
STRAIGHTEN AGED KNEES, ... 505 RESULT THOUGHT 16
STRAIGHTENED
STRAIGHTENED ALL THAT WENT AWRY . . . . 440 WISDOM V 4
BUT I HAVE STRAIGHTENED OUT . . . . 505 RESULT THOUGHT 7
STRAIN
A LITTLE RUNNEL MADE A BUBBLING STRAIN, ... 39 OISIN 2 156
DUSKY AND HERBLESS, WHERE A BUBBLING STRAIN . . . . 39 OISIN 2 V 156
SHIVER UNDER THE LASH, STRAIN, SWEAT AND JOLT . . . . 260 FASC DIFFICULT 7
THAT NEVER KNEW THAT STRAIN WOULD SCARCE SEEM BRIGHT, . 465 HARUN RASHID 88
DID WORDS OF MINE PUT TOO GREAT STRAIN . . . . . . 632 MAN AND ECHO 13
STRAINING
UNDER THE ROOF, AND WITH A STRAINING THROAT . . . . 36 OISIN 2 106
DRIFTING ON HIGH, AND WITH A STRAINING THROAT . . . . 36 OISIN 2 V 106
NOR STRAINING JOY, BUT WHOLE IS JOINED TO WHOLE! . . . 555 RIBH AT TOMB 14
ON STRAINING THIGHS. . . . . 574 LOVERS SONG 6
STRAINS
SO STRAINS TO LOOK BEYOND OUR LIFE, AN EYE . . . . . 465 HARUN RASHID 87
STRAIT
YOUR WEEPING FITS! LOOK YOU, SO VERY STRAIT . . . . 659 ISLE STAT II 1 22
STRAITS
CROSS THE NARROW STRAITS TO LIGHT . . . . 494 AT ALGECIRAS 4
CROSSES THE NARROW STRAITS TO LIGHT . . . . 494 AT ALGECIRAS V 4
CROSS THOSE NARROW STRAITS TO LIGHT . . . . 494 AT ALGECIRAS V 4
STRAND
OR SAT IN DREAMS ON THE PALE STRAND, ... 25 OISIN 1 390
THE OLD BROWN THORN-TREES BREAK IN TWO HIGH OVER CUMMEN 206 HANRAHANS SONG 1
STRAND,
THE OLD BROWN THORN TREES BREAK IN TWO HIGH OVER CUMANN'S 206 HANRAHANS SONG V 1
STRAND,
WEAK AND WORN AND WEARY THE WAVES OF CUMMEN STRAND, . . 207 HANRAHANS SONG V 6
WHAT ARE ALL THOSE FISH THAT LIE GASPING ON THE STRAND? . 485 THREE MOVEMENT 3
FROM THE SEAWEED ON THE STRAND. . . . . 597 COLONEL MARTIN 71
FROM THE SEA-WEED ON THE STRAND. . . . . 597 COLONEL MARTIN V 71
STRANDS
OR WHEN ALONG THE WINTRY STRANDS . . . . 84 MAD KING GOLL 41
OR WHERE ALONG THE WINTRY STRANDS . . . . 84 MAD KING GOLL V 41
STRANGE
OF MANY A FIGURED CREATURE STRANGE, ... 4 OISIN 1 V 27
THAN THIS STRANGE HUMAN BARD," HE CRIED! . . . . . 17 OISIN 1 239
THAN THIS STRANGE BARD," HE CRIED, AND CAUGHT . . . . 17 OISIN 1 V 239
LIAR AND FLATTERER OF THE WEAK, IN WHAT STRANGE CLIME . . 42 OISIN 2 V 198
I AWOKE! THE STRANGE HORSE WITHOUT SUMMONS OUT OF 54 OISIN 3 105
THE DISTANCE RAN,
AND I ON THIS STRANGE ROAD WILL PASS . . . . 97 FOXHUNTER V 11
BUT SEEK ALONE TO HEAR THE STRANGE THINGS SAID . . . 101 ROSE UPON ROOD 19
I DREAMED THAT ONE HAD DIED IN A STRANGE PLACE . . . 123 DREAM OF DEATH 1
STRANGE CREATURES FLUTTER UP BEFORE ONE'S EYES, . . . 222 SHADOW WATER B 18
AND AFTER CIRCLING WITH STRANGE CRIES AWHILE . . . . 223 SHADOW WATER B 26
THROUGH THAT STRANGE ILLNESS THAT HAD FIXED HIM THERE, . 280 TWO KINGS 81
EARNING RESPECT! HAVE NO STRANGE FRIEND! . . . . . 337 SCHOLARS V 9
OF SOME STRANGE WOMAN'S NAME THAT RAN IN HIS HEAD. . . 351 HER PRAISE V 9
THIS NIGHT HAS BEEN SO STRANGE THAT IT SEEMED . . . . 358 PRESENCES 1
THE STRANGE REWARD OF ALL THAT DISCIPLINE. . . . . 374 PHASES OF MOON 57
I SUDDENLY CRIED OUT IN A STRANGE TONGUE . . . . . 387 SOLOMON WITCH 5
STRANGE, BUT THE MAN WHO MADE THE SONG WAS BLIND! . . 411 TOWER 49
THAT NOTHING STRANGE! THE TRAGEDY BEGAN . . . . . 411 TOWER 51
BUT FEEL THE STRANGE HEART BEATING WHERE IT LIES? . . 441 LEDA AND SWAN 8
AND FEELS THE STRANGE HEART BEATING WHERE IT LIES! . . 441 LEDA AND SWAN V 8
A STRANGE THING SURELY THAT MY HEART, WHEN LOVE HAD COME 449 OWEN AHERNE 1
UNSOUGHT
THAT FIRST STRANGE INTEREST IN MY BOOKS AND STUDIES. . . 468 HARUN RASHID V 165
HORTON'S THE FIRST I CALL. HE LOVED STRANGE THOUGHT . 471 ALL SOUL NIGHT 21
AND A MIRACULOUS STRANGE BIRD SHRIEKS AT US. . . . . 534 HER TRIUMPH 12
IF STRANGE MEN COME FROM THE HOUSE . . . . 568 SWEET DANCER 8
STRANGE NIGHT HAS COME! . . . . 574 MAIDS 1ST SONG 6
(FOR SINCE THE HORIZON'S BOUGHT STRANGE DOGS ARE STILL) 579 DOR WELLESLEY 7
THEIR CRIES ARE SWEET AND STRANGE, ... 612 NEWS ORACLE 18

774

		PAGE	TITLE		LINE
STRANGE	(CONTINUED)				
SHEEP-GUIDING, OR THE BRINGING SOME STRANGE BIRD,		650	ISLE STAT I 1		147
STRANGE DRAPERIES DID ALL THE SIDES ADORN,		657	ISLE STAT I 3		55
AND THAT WAS STRANGE; BUT THIS IS MANY A WORLD		664	ISLE STAT II 2		60
BUT WHY THIS WHIM OF THINE? A STRANGE UNREST,		671	ISLE STAT II 3		137
HAVE NOT A MYRIAD SWAYED BELOW STRANGE TREES		724	KANVA ON SELF		11
A STRANGE, UNSERVICEABLE THING,		784	WOMANS BEAUTY		15
ITS STRANGE HEART BEATING FAST		785	YOUR HEART		6
STRANGENESS					
THAT HER OWN STRANGENESS PERPLEXED;		260	UNWORTH PRAISE		14
ESTRANGED AMID THE STRANGENESS OF THEMSELVES,		375	PHASES OF MOON		78
NOR HAD FORGOT THE STRANGENESS OF MY PRESENCE		466	HARUN RASHID	V	119A
STRANGER					
THE STRANGER WATCHED THE SWORD; BUT NIAM FAR,		38	OISIN 2	V	136
STRANGER WITH STRANGER,		574	MAIDS 1ST SONG		3
STRANGER WITH STRANGER,		574	MAIDS 1ST SONG		3
I SAW A STRANGER TAP AND WAIT		696	MOSADA 2		22
A STRANGER NEW ARISEN WAIT		696	MOSADA 2	V	22
THEN THE STRANGER SOFTLY CREW--		697	MOSADA 2		28
THE STRANGER SHOUTED, "OPEN WIDE		697	MOSADA 2	V	24
STRANGER'S					
BEAUTY TO MAKE A STRANGER'S EYE DISTRAUGHT,		403	FOR DAUGHTER		18
BECOME A STRANGER'S LEMAN; AND THAT YOU,		757	SHADOW WATER A		215
STRANGERS					
WHEN STRANGERS MURDERED EMMET, FITZGERALD, TONE,		541	PARN FUNERAL 1		17
STRANGLE					
AS THOUGH TO STRANGLE HER, NO SCREAM		514	JANE GROWN OLD		4
STRAW					
AS THOUGH DRIED STRAW, AND IF WE TURN ABOUT		327	ROBERT GREGORY		83
I WOULD BE--FOR NO KNOWLEDGE IS WORTH A STRAW--		344	DAWN		13
STORIES OF THE BED OF STRAW		458	SECRETS OF OLD		17
"NOT TO DIE ON THE STRAW AT HOME,		587	OLD WICKED MAN		5
"AND HALF FORGET THIS BED OF STRAW		739	EARL PAUL		5
EARL PAUL STOOD ON THE BED OF STRAW,		740	EARL PAUL		17
STRAWBERRY	SEE WILD-STRAWBERRY				
STRAW-DEATH					
AWAITING IN PATIENCE THE STRAW-DEATH,		58	OISIN 3		167
STRAW-PALE					
UNDER THE SHADOW OF STUPID STRAW-PALE LOCKS,		433	NINETEEN 19		127
STRAWS	SEE WINDLE-STRAWS				
THE LITTLE STRAWS WERE TURNIN' ROUND		95	MOLL MAGEE		31
STRAY					
I LET THEM STRAY. I THOUGHT OF RHYME ALONE,		339	SHEP GOATHERD		11
MADE MY ATTENTION STRAY.		507	STREAM AND SUN		5
STRAYED					
THAT WOULD BE HARSH FOR CHILDREN THAT HAVE STRAYED.		201	OLD MEMORY		12
THAT HAD BEEN HARSH FOR CHILDREN THAT HAVE STRAYED.		201	OLD MEMORY	V	12
FROM STONE TO STONE. I AM LOOKING FOR STRAYED SHEEP;		339	SHEP GOATHERD		9
O WHAT A SWEETNESS STRAYED		401	DEMON BEAST		43
STRAYETH					
STRAYING AS THE HERON STRAYETH,		706	DAWN-SONG		27
STRAYING					
STRAYING TOO FAR INTO THE NORTH OR SOUTH,		226	SHADOW WATER B		86
STRAYING AS THE HERON STRAYETH,		706	DAWN-SONG		27
UNTO THE HEART OF THE WOODLAND STRAYING,		728	PRIEST FAIRY		1
STRAYS					
AT LAST CUCHULAIN SPAKE, "A YOUNG MAN STRAYS		109	CUCHULAIN SEA	V	47
O WHAT IF GARDENS WHERE THE PEACOCK STRAYS		418	ANCEST HOUSES		25
STREAM					
THE STREAM CHURNED, CHURNED, AND CHURNED--HIS LIPS APART,		31	OISIN 2		43
THE STREAM CHURNED, CHURNED,		31	OISIN 2	V	43
I SEE MY LIFE GO DRIPPING LIKE A STREAM		104	FERGUS DRUID	V	31
AND RIVER AND STREAM WORK OUT THEIR WILL;		148	INTO TWILIGHT		12
I DROPPED THE BERRY IN A STREAM		149	WANDER AENGUS		7
THE VINEGAR-HEAVY SPONGE, THE FLOWERS BY KEDRON STREAM;		172	TRAV PASSION		5
THE HISSOP-HEAVY SPONGE, THE FLOWERS BY KIDRON STREAM;		172	TRAV PASSION	V	5
DARK AND DULL AND EARTHY THE STREAM OF DRUMAHAIR,		207	HANRAHANS SONG	V	11
OUT OF THE RUNNING STREAM, O MORNING STAR,		251	SHADOW WATER B		610
IN GLENDALOUGH BESIDE THE STREAM,		331	ROUND TOWER		8
WHEN THE FLIES DROP IN THE STREAM;		348	FISHERMAN		34
ON THE GREY SAND BESIDE THE SHALLOW STREAM		367	EGO DOMINUS		1
SHALL WALK THE WET SANDS BY THE EDGE OF THE STREAM		371	EGO DOMINUS		71
SPLASHED, OR AN OTTER SLID INTO THE STREAM.		372	PHASES OF MOON		9
ON THE DARK STREAM		389	IMAGE PAST		3
TO TROUBLE THE LIVING STREAM.		393	EASTER 1916		44
A SHADOW OF CLOUD ON THE STREAM		393	EASTER 1916		49
IN THE ELMS ABOVE THE FLOODED STREAM;		403	FOR DAUGHTER		12
LAST REACH OF GLITTERING STREAM		414	TOWER		143
CROSSING STREAM AGAIN		419	MY HOUSE		9
THAT PLUNGED IN STREAM AGAIN		419	MY HOUSE	V	9
THE MOOR-HEN GUIDES UPON THE STREAM,		424	ROAD AT DOOR		12
STREAM AND SUN AT GLENDALOUGH		506	STREAM AND SUN		T
STREAM AND GLIDING SUN		506	STREAM AND SUN		2
WHAT MOTION OF THE SUN OR STREAM		507	STREAM AND SUN		11
AND BOTH ADRIFT ON THE MIRACULOUS STREAM		535	CHOSEN		16
ALL THE STREAM THAT'S ROARING BY		562	NEEDLES EYE		1
"THAT SOME STREAM OF LIGHTNING		589	OLD WICKED MAN		55
LIKE A LONG-LEGGED FLY UPON THE STREAM		617	LONG-LEG FLY		9
LIKE A LONG-LEGGED FLY UPON THE STREAM		617	LONG-LEG FLY		19
LIKE A LONG-LEGGED FLY UPON THE STREAM		618	LONG-LEG FLY		29
AND SEDGY STREAM, AND IN EACH BABBLING BRAKE		675	ISLE STAT II 3		225

775

		PAGE	TITLE		LINE
STREAM	**(CONTINUED)**				
	I WILL DRINK OUT OF THE STREAM. THE STREAM IS GONE!	761	SHADOW WATER A		273
	I WILL DRINK OUT OF THE STREAM. THE STREAM IS GONE!	761	SHADOW WATER A		273
	THE GRASS AND THE BLUE SHADOW ON THE STREAM	761	SHADOW WATER A		280
	A STREAM HAS TOLD ME THEY ARE BEAUTIFUL.	767	SHADOW WATER A		398
	OUT OF A RUNNING STREAM, O MORNING STAR	769	SHADOW WATER A		426
STREAMING					
	WITH STREAMING HAIR AS WANDERING LIGHTS	667	ISLE STAT II 3		19
STREAM'S					
	THE TOWER SET ON THE STREAM'S EDGE!	326	ROBERT GREGORY		52
	THE TOWER SET BY THE STREAM'S EDGE!	326	ROBERT GREGORY	V	52
STREAMS					
	THAT WAVERED LIKE THE SUMMER STREAMS,	4	OISIN 1		29
	. . . SLOW DROPPING A SOUND IN FAINT STREAMS	51	OISIN 3		67
	AND BY ME, IN SOFT RED RAIMENT, THE FENIANS MOVED IN LOUD STREAMS,	53	OISIN 3		93
	HE RUFFLES WITH HIS BILL THE MINNOWED STREAMS.	73	ANASHU VIJAYA		37
	AND STREAMS, WIDE-WATERING, SALMON-SHOALED,	81	MAD KING GOLL	V	3
	OVER THE YOUNG STREAMS.	88	STOLEN CHILD		37
	OF DEW ON THE YOUNG STREAMS.	88	STOLEN CHILD		37
	FALLS IN SLEEPY STREAMS.	98	FOXHUNTER		16
	POURS ROUND HIS SLEEPY STREAMS.	98	FOXHUNTER	V	16
	POURS ROUND IN SLEEPY STREAMS.	98	FOXHUNTER	V	16
	"I CAN BRING YOU SALMON OUT OF THE STREAMS	167	BLESSED		9
	MIRRORED IN STREAMS THAT NEITHER HAIL NOR RAIN	184	QUEEN MAEVE		89
	THOUGH NOTHING TROUBLES THE GREAT STREAMS	196	BAILE AILLINN		172
	ECHTGE OF STREAMS	203	WITHER BOUGHS	V	T
	AND I FELL ASLEEP UPON LONELY ECHTGE OF STREAMS.	203	WITHER BOUGHS		6
	I KNOW, AND THE CURLEW AND PEEWIT ON ECHTGE OF STREAMS.	204	WITHER BOUGHS		22
	AND THE CURLEW AND PEEWIT KNOW ON ECHTGE OF STREAMS.	204	WITHER BOUGHS	V	22
	LEAPS UPWARD, AS IF ALL THE STREAMS O' THE WORLD	249	SHADOW WATER B		560
	COMPANIONABLE STREAMS OR CLIMB THE AIR;	323	SWANS AT COOLE		21
	AMONG THE STREAMS;	329	MEN IMPROVE		3
	AMONG THE STREAMS.	329	MEN IMPROVE		18
	THAT HER HAIR STREAMS UPON THE WIND,	390	IMAGE PAST		40
	THAT CLIMB THE STREAMS UNTIL	414	TOWER		123
	WHEN ALL STREAMS ARE DRY,	414	TOWER		138
	OUT OF THE OBSCURE DARK OF THE RICH STREAMS,	417	ANCEST HOUSES		14
	THE SUBTERRANEAN STREAMS,	420	MY HOUSE	V	20H
	IRRATIONAL STREAMS OF BLOOD ARE STAINING EARTH!	564	GYRES		5
	AND THE JOY OF THE STREAMS WHERE LONG-LIMBED HERONS WADE!	674	ISLE STAT II 3		217
	AND HEARS THE ROAR OF THE STREAMS WHERE, DRUIDS SAY,	749	SHADOW WATER A		46
	AMONG THOSE STREAMS, OR ON THEIR CLOUDY EDGE.	750	SHADOW WATER A		63
	IN THE COLD STREAMS, AND WAKE TO THEIR DESIRE,	750	SHADOW WATER A		85
	THEY LURE US TO THE STREAMS WHERE THE WORLD ENDS.	764	SHADOW WATER A		334
	ALL DIES AMONG THOSE STREAMS. THE FOOL HAS MADE	764	SHADOW WATER A		335
	WHAT WERE TRUE-LOVE AMONG THE RUSH OF HIS STREAMS?	764	SHADOW WATER A		338
	WHAT WERE TRUE LOVE AMONG THE RUSH OF HIS STREAMS?	764	SHADOW WATER A	V	338
	TO SNATCH ALIVE OUT OF THE STREAMS ALL LOVERS .	765	SHADOW WATER A		347
	THAT HAVE GONE THITHER TO LOOK FOR THE LOUD STREAMS,	765	SHADOW WATER A		348
	TO LEAD US TO THE STREAMS WHERE THE WORLD ENDS.	765	SHADOW WATER A		369
	MY LOVE SHAKES OUT HER HAIR UPON THE STREAMS	768	SHADOW WATER A		416
STREET					
	ALONG THE PEBBLY STREET.	94	MOLL MAGEE		12
	WANDERING FROM BROKEN STREET TO STREET	196	BAILE AILLINN		167
	WANDERING FROM BROKEN STREET TO STREET	196	BAILE AILLINN		167
	ON EVERY CROWDED STREET TO STARE	294	HATED PLAYBOY		3
	WILL GATHER, AND NOT KNOW IT WALKS THE VERY STREET	315	FALLEN MAJESTY		7
	WILL GATHER AND NOT KNOW THAT THROUGH ITS VERY STREET	315	FALLEN MAJESTY	V	7
	EVENING AND MORNING, THE STEEP STREET OF URBINO	352	PEOPLE		12
	EVENING AND MORN, THE STEEP STREET OF URBINO	352	PEOPLE	V	12
	IN THE LONG ECHOING STREET THE LAUGHING DANCERS THRONG,	459	FROM OEDIPUS		7
	AND FOLLOWED THROUGH THE EMPTY STREET, AND SHE,	468	HARUN RASHID	V	154A
	WHILE ON THE SHOP AND STREET I GAZED	501	VACILLATION		40
	SOMEWHERE OFF HENRY STREET!	585	ORAHILLY		31
	AND THERE AT ALL STREET CORNERS	596	COLONEL MARTIN		55
	PICKED UP ON A STREET.	617	LONG-LEG FLY		18
	PICKED UP ON THE STREET.	617	LONG-LEG FLY	V	18
	A MOUND OF REFUSE OR THE SWEEPINGS OF A STREET,	630	CIRCUS ANIMALS		35
	A MOUND OF REFUSE OR THE SWEEPINGS OF THE STREET,	630	CIRCUS ANIMALS	V	35
	AY, AND SHAKES IN SEA-GREEN WAVERINGS ALONG THE FISHERS' STREET!	718	PHANTOM SHIP		2
	AYE AND SHAKES IN SEA GREEN WAVERINGS, ALONG THE FISHERS' STREET.	718	PHANTOM SHIP	V	2
	STREET DANCERS	731	STREET DANCERS		T
	SINGING IN THIS LONDON STREET,	731	STREET DANCERS		1
	WAS CRIED IN STREET AND LANE	740	EARL PAUL		26
STREET-CORNERS					
	AND THERE AT ALL STREET-CORNERS	596	COLONEL MARTIN		55
STREETS					
	UPON THE THRONE AND CRYING ABOUT THE STREETS	198	SEVEN WOODS		7
	OR HURLED THE LITTLE STREETS UPON THE GREAT,	256	NO SECOND TROY		4
	IN THE LONG ECHOING STREETS THE LAUGHING DANCERS THRONG,	459	FROM OEDIPUS	V	7
	LONDON STREETS HAVE HERITAGE.	733	STREET DANCERS		57
STRENGTH					
	AND FLOWING STRENGTH, WITH AGE IS SUBTLE-SOULED.	35	OISIN 2	V	83
	. . . THE STRENGTH OF THE BELL-BRANCH IS NAUGHT,	55	OISIN 3		123
	. . . A SOB FOR THE FENIANS' OLD STRENGTH.	60	OISIN 3		188
	"YOUR STRENGTH, THAT IS SO LOFTY AND FIERCE AND KIND,	201	OLD MEMORY		3
	BECAUSE I HAVE COME INTO MY STRENGTH,	256	WORDS		11
	ALL THAT SWEETNESS AMID STRENGTH?"	259	PEACE		9

776

	PAGE	TITLE		LINE

STRENGTH   (CONTINUED)
TILL THEY HAD CHANGED US TO LIKE STRENGTH?" • • • • • 259 PEACE V 9
SO DID SHE YOUR STRENGTH RENEW, • • • • • • • • 259 UNWORTH PRAISE 6
"YOUR STRENGTH AND NOBLENESS WILL PASS AWAY"? • • • • 285 TWO KINGS 189
OR TILL THE SUN IS IN HIS STRENGTH• • • • • • • • • 305 HOUR DAWN 61
HAD STRENGTH THAT COULD UNBIND • • • • • • • • • 315 FRIENDS 11
I HAVE RAGED AT MY OWN STRENGTH BECAUSE YOU HAVE LOVED IT• 448 HERO GIRL FOOL 9
IF YOU ARE NO MORE STRENGTH THAN I AM BEAUTY • • • • • 448 HERO GIRL FOOL 10
ALL MEN HAVE PRAISED MY STRENGTH BUT NOT MY WORTH• • • 448 HERO GIRL FOOL V 9
THE STRENGTH THAT GIVES OUR BLOOD AND STATE MAGNANIMITY 481 BLOOD AND MOON 29
ALL THEIR WHOLESOME STRENGTH• • • • • • • • • • 505 RESULT THOUGHT 12
NOW STRENGTH OF BODY GOES: • • • • • • • • • • • 575 ACRE OF GRASS 4
BUT HE HAS NEED OF ALL THAT STRENGTH • • • • • • • 624 APPARITIONS 20
STRETCH
HEARING HIM GROAN AND STRETCH • • • • • • • • • 319 DOLLS 13
"STRETCH BONES TILL THE DAYLIGHT COME • • • • • • • 331 ROUND TOWER 5
THAT MADE THEM STRETCH AND YAWN • • • • • • • • • 345 ON WOMAN 21
STRETCH OUT YOUR LIMBS AND SLEEP A LONG SATURNIAN SLEEP: 442 BLACK CENTAUR 13
AND DID AFTER STRETCH AND YAWN"• • • • • • • • • 521 THREE THINGS 17
BUT STRETCH THAT BODY FOR A WHILE • • • • • • • • 534 CONSOLATION 3
STRETCH TOWARDS THE MOONLESS MIDNIGHT OF THE TREES, • • 579 DOR WELLESLEY 1
STRETCH NECK AND CLAP THE WING, • • • • • • • • • 783 GREY ROUND 27
STRETCHED
STRETCHED HIS LONG ARM TO WHERE, A MISTY SMOTHER, • • • 31 OISIN 2 42
• • • AND THE QUIVER OF STRETCHED BOWSTRINGS, • • • • 62 OISIN 3 207
AND STRETCHED OUT SLEEPING ON A PILE OF SKINS • • • • 283 TWO KINGS 141
YOUNG RED-HEAD STRETCHED HIMSELF TO YAWN • • • • • 303 HOUR DAWN V 32A
AND DRANK AND YAWNED AND STRETCHED HIM OUT, • • • • 307 HOUR DAWN 108
HE STRETCHED HIS BONES AND FELL IN A DREAM • • • • • 331 ROUND TOWER 10
STRETCHED UP ON TWO LEGS FROM THE MAT, • • • • • • 381 SONGS FOOL 2 7
UPON A MOMENT, AND SO STRETCHED IT OUT • • • • • • 384 VISION ROBART 46
ALL THE STRETCHED BODY'S LAID ON THE WHITE RUSH • • • 441 LEDA AND SWAN V 7
STRETCHED UNDER A DOORWAY • • • • • • • • • • • 585 ORAHILLY 30
SOME TWENTY FEET FROM TIP TO TIP HAD IT STRETCHED RIGHTLY 593 PILGRIM 17
   OUT,
SOME TWENTY FEET FROM TIP TO TIP HAD ITS WINGS STRETCHED 593 PILGRIM V 17
   RIGHTLY OUT,
AND HAVING STRETCHED AND YAWNED AWHILE • • • • • • 612 NEWS ORACLE 11
I LAY STRETCHED OUT IN THE DIRT • • • • • • • • • 628 JANE MOUNTAIN 21
WHEN WE HALE MEN LIE STRETCHED IN SLUMBER • • • • • 636 BLACK TOWER 23
STRETCHES
FAR UP IN THE STRETCHES OF NIGHT: • • • • • • • • 623 HIGH TALK 12
STRETCHING
AND STRETCHING OUT HER ARMS, RED WITH THE DYE, • • • • 105 CUCHULAIN SEA V 7
AND STRETCHING FORTH HIS ARM AND CUP • • • • • • • 275 GREY ROCK 118
STREW
BUT THE TORN PETALS STREW THE GARDEN PLOT: • • • • • 422 MY DESCENDANTS 7
WHEN THE TORN PETALS STREW THE GARDEN PLOT: • • • • • 422 MY DESCENDANTS V 7
I CAN STREW THE SHEET• • • • • • • • • • • • 572 LADYS 2ND SONG 6
STREWING
STREWING UPON THE ROCKS THEIR STEEL-BLUE HAIR, • • • • 687 TWO TITANS 30
STREWN   SEE SEA-STREWN
LIE STREWN THE YELLOW LEAVES--THE CLOTTED LEAVES. • • • 684 SEEKER 69
LIE STREWN THE CLOTTED LEAVES--THE DEAD OLD LEAVES. • • 684 SEEKER V 69
STRICKEN   SEE TERROR-STRICKEN
AT THE MOST QUIET MIDNIGHT IS TO BE STRICKEN• • • • • 236 SHADOW WATER B 321
STRICKEN WITH PANIC FROM THE ATTACK, • • • • • • • 274 GREY ROCK 75
OUT NAKED ON THE ROADS, AS THE BOOKS SAY, AND STRICKEN 316 COLD HEAVEN 11
THOUGH MARGERY IS STRICKEN DUMB • • • • • • • • 457 SECRETS OF OLD 7
THAT MAN IS STRICKEN DEAF AND DUMB AND BLIND, • • • • 478 SELF AND SOUL 35
A STRICKEN RABBIT IS CRYING OUT— • • • • • • • • 633 MAN AND ECHO 45
STRICKEN ALL THE NIGHT IS PAST— • • • • • • • • 648 ISLE STAT I 1 96
STRIFE
BY KNOWING NOR TUMULT NOR HATE NOR STRIFE, • • • • • 9 OISIN 1 95
AND FLOATING-HAIRED AND PROUD IN STRIFE: • • • • • 9 OISIN 1 V 99
WINGED LOVES BORNE ON IN GENTLE STRIFE, • • • • • • 135 TWO TREES V 14
SHE LIVED IN STORM AND STRIFE, • • • • • • • • • 317 NIGHT COME 1
OF LOVE FROM OUT A DREAMLESS RACE FOR STRIFE, • • • • 684 SEEKER 58
STRIKE
A HUSH: AH, ME: IT HANGS TO STRIKE US DEAD. • • • • 43 OISIN 2 V 208B
I'LL STRIKE A BLOW FOR HIM TO GIVE HIM TIME • • • • • 239 SHADOW WATER B 365
TO HIM THAT STRIKES HIM FIRST: I WILL STRIKE HIM FIRST. 239 SHADOW WATER B 369
TO BURN US TO THE MARROW IF WE STRIKE. • • • • • • 239 SHADOW WATER B 372
I WILL STRIKE AT HIM. AND I: AND I: AND I: • • • • 240 SHADOW WATER B 379
AND STRIKE THE GOLDEN PILLARS WITH MY HANDS. • • • • 246 SHADOW WATER B 502
TO STRIKE YOU DEAD? • • • • • • • • • • • • 359 TO A SQUIRREL 5
"STRIKE ME IF I SHRIEK." • • • • • • • • • • • 455 HIS MEMORIES 18
ARISE AND BID ME STRIKE A MATCH • • • • • • • • 476 EVA GORE-BOOTH 26
AND STRIKE ANOTHER TILL TIME CATCH: • • • • • • • 476 EVA GORE-BOOTH 27
BID ME STRIKE A MATCH AND BLOW. • • • • • • • • 476 EVA GORE-BOOTH 32
DREW A KNIFE TO STRIKE HIM DEAD, • • • • • • • • 514 JANE GROWN OLD 10
SHE HEARS ME STRIKE THE BOARD AND SAY • • • • • • 531 FATHER CHILD 1
I COME TO HEAR IT STRIKE." • • • • • • • • • • 585 ORAHILLY 26
THOUGH STIFF TO STRIKE A BARGAIN, • • • • • • • • 620 JOHN KINSELLA 13
STRIKE QUICKLY: IT WILL FADE OUT WHEN YOU STRIKE. • • 759 SHADOW WATER A 238
STRIKE QUICKLY: IT WILL FADE OUT WHEN YOU STRIKE. • • 759 SHADOW WATER A 238
STRIKES
TO HIM THAT STRIKES HIM FIRST: I WILL STRIKE HIM FIRST. 239 SHADOW WATER B 369
OR STRIKES A SUDDEN CHILL INTO MY BONES • • • • • • 499 MOTHER OF GOD 14

777

```
                                                       PAGE      TITLE            LINE
STRING      SEE HARP-STRING FIDDLE-STRING
    AND TOUCH THE LAUGHING SILVER STRING:   . . . . . .      17 OISIN 1             233
    AND ALL AROUND THE HARP STRING TOLD HIS PRAISE,  . . . .  109 CUCHULAIN SEA  V   44
    I HEAR THE HARP STRING PRAISE THEM OR HEAR THEIR MOURNFUL 210 UNDER THE MOON V   16
        TALK.
    LISTEN TO THAT LOW-LAUGHING STRING OF THE MOON  . . . .  243 SHADOW WATER B    432
    THAT MADE THE BODY SEEM AS IT WERE A STRING  . . . . .   284 TWO KINGS         176
    AND LIKE A LAUGHING STRING  . . . . . . . . . . .       291 TO A FRIEND        11
    A STRING OF SCHOLARS WENT IN FEAR  . . . . . . . . .     381 SONG OF FOOL        7
    FINGERED UPON A FIDDLE STICK OR STRING  . . . . . . .    445 SCHOOL CHILDR  V   46
    OR THE FIDDLE STRING ACCURSED,. . . . . . . . . . .      527 AM OF IRELAND  V   20
    OR SMOTE UPON THE STRING AND TO THE SOUND  . . . . . .   537 HER VISION         15
    A WOMAN, AND AN ARROW ON A STRING:  . . . . . . . .      541 PARN FUNERAL 1     11
    AND ITS OLD SOLE STRING  . . . . . . . . . . . .        627 STATES HOLIDAY     23
    COME THOU, COME, AND TO THIS STRING--  . . . . . . .     646 ISLE STAT I 1      37
    AND A STRING MURMURS AS THOUGH TIME WERE DEAD  . . . .   752 SHADOW WATER A    124
STRINGED
    TO SOME STRINGED INSTRUMENT NONE THERE HAD SEEN,  . . . . 180 QUEEN MAEVE        4
    OF OLD STRINGED INSTRUMENTS, HUNG THERE  . . . . . .     271 GREY ROCK      V   20
    THEIR HAIR MINGLES ON SOME STRINGED INSTRUMENT,  . . .   752 SHADOW WATER A    123
STRING'S     SEE BOW-STRING'S
STRINGS      SEE HARP-STRINGS HEART-STRINGS
    AND, WEEPING OVER THE WHITE STRINGS, HURLED  . . . . .    17 OISIN 1           241
    HEARING AEDH TOUCH THE MOURNFUL STRINGS OF GOLD."  . . .  35 OISIN 2            87
    OF FEVER.  NOW THE STRINGS ARE TORN  . . . . . . . .      86 MAD KING GOLL  V   66
    MY SINGING FADES, THE STRINGS ARE TORN,  . . . . . .      86 MAD KING GOLL  V   66
    WITH HIS OWN FINGERS TOUCHED THE BRAZEN STRINGS. . . . . 109 CUCHULAIN SEA      46
    WITH HIS OWN FINGER TOUCHED THE BRAZEN STRINGS. . . . .  109 CUCHULAIN SEA  V   46
    OR LET ITS MEANING MIX INTO THE STRINGS.  . . . . . .   180 QUEEN MAEVE         8
    AWOKE THE HARP STRINGS LONG AGO.  . . . . . . . . .     190 BAILE AILLINN  V   37
    OR THE TWO STRINGS THAT MADE ONE SOUND  . . . . . .     195 BAILE AILLINN     155
    WERE HOVERING OVER THE HARP STRINGS  . . . . . . .      195 BAILE AILLINN  V  141
    I HEAR THE HARP STRINGS PRAISE THEM, OR HEAR THEIR MOURNFUL 210 UNDER THE MOON V  16
        TALK.
    THE MOUTHS THAT SPEAK, THE NOTES AND STRINGS,  . . . .   212 BLESS PSALTER       2
    AWAKE UNSLEEPING FIRES: AND WOVE SEVEN STRINGS,  . . .   219 HARP OF AENGUS      7
    BY MAGIC STRINGS, I'LL MAKE THIS ANSWER TO IT:  . . .    243 SHADOW WATER B    440
    MY MAGIC STRINGS, I'LL MAKE THIS ANSWER TO IT:  . . .    243 SHADOW WATER B V  440
    FINGERED UPON A FIDDLE-STICK OR STRINGS  . . . . . .     445 SCHOOL CHILDR      46
    AWAKE UNSLEEPING FIRES: AND WOVE SEVEN STRINGS,  . . .   762 SHADOW WATER A    302
STRIP
    THAT STRIP THE BODY BARE."  . . . . . . . . . . .       570 THREE BUSHES       27
STRIPPED
    SLIM ADOLESCENCE THAT A NYMPH HAS STRIPPED,  . . . . .   612 NEWS ORACLE        25
STRIPS
    CUT OUT OUR RHYMES ON STRIPS OF NEW-TORN BARK  . . . .   343 SHEP GOATHERD     115
STRIVE
    IN TRUTH, AN EVIL RACE.  WHY STRIVE FOR HER,  . . . . .  696 MOSADA 2            9
STRIVING
    UNTUNED BY THEIR OWN STRIVING.  IF ONE SUCH  . . . . .   711 FERENCZ RENYI      37
STRODE
    MOST DISTANT STRODE WE.  ON THE FLOOR LAY SLIME,  . . .   37 OISIN 2        V  113
    VIOLENT AND FAMOUS, STRODE AMONG THE DEAD:  . . . . .    634 CUCHULAIN COMF      2
STROKE
    AND YET COULD SING SO FINE A STROKE?"  . . . . . . .     274 GREY ROCK          84
    HEAVEN HAS PUT AWAY THE STROKE OF HER DOOM,  . . . . .   356 BROKEN DREAMS      11
    THE LAST STROKE OF MIDNIGHT DIES.  . . . . . . . .      357 BROKEN DREAMS      37
    THAT I, MIDNIGHT UPON THE STROKE,  . . . . . . . .      507 JANE BISHOP         2
    AT STROKE OF MIDNIGHT SOUL CANNOT ENDURE  . . . . . .   558 RIBH CHRISTIAN     19
    AT STROKE OF MIDNIGHT GOD SHALL WIN.  . . . . . . .     561 FOUR AGES MAN       8
STROKED
    STROKED THE YOUNG WINDS AS THEY ROLLED ON THE PLAIN,  .   27 OISIN 1        V 415C
    NOR CEASED UNTIL WHITE NIAMH STROKED HIS EARS  . . . .    30 OISIN 1            26
STROKES      SEE SWORD-STROKES
    THAT THINK SWORD STROKES WERE BETTER MEANT  . . . . .    276 GREY ROCK      V  129
STRONG
    WE RODE IN SORROW, WITH STRONG HOUNDS THREE,  . . . .      2 OISIN 1        V   7C
    OF OUR STRONG STEEDS WAS DARK WITH SWEAT,  . . . . . .     2 OISIN 1        V   7T
    FOR HE IS STRONG AND CRAFTY AS THE SEAS  . . . . . .      35 OISIN 1            83
    AND ALL THE EXULTANT LABOURS OF THE STRONG.  . . . . .    42 OISIN 2           195
    OF ANCIENT WARRIORS, THE LABOURS OF THE STRONG.  . . . .  42 OISIN 2        V  195
    . . . THE STRONG HOOFS CRUSHING THE SAND AND THE SHELLS.  58 OISIN 3           157
    . . . THE STRONG HOOFS CRUSHING THE SANDS AND THE SHELLS  58 OISIN 3        V  157
    . . . THOUGH SPACIOUS HIS LANDS WERE AND STRONG.  . . .   58 OISIN 3        V  160
    . . . AND NO MAN MAY WAR WITH THE STRONG SPIRITS WAGE:    62 OISIN 3        V  214
    WHO HOLDS THE WORLD BETWEEN HIS BILL AND MADE US STRONG   76 INDIAN ON GOD       6
        OR WEAK
    WHO HOLDS THE WORLD BETWEEN HIS BILL AND MAKES US STRONG  76 INDIAN ON GOD  V    6
        OR WEAK
    FASHIONED TO BE THE MOTHER OF STRONG CHILDREN:  . . .   181 QUEEN MAEVE        26
    THERE'S MANY A STRONG FARMER  . . . . . . . . . .       213 HAPPY TOWNLAND      1
    FOR O, THE STRONG FARMERS  . . . . . . . . . . .        215 HAPPY TOWNLAND     29
    THAN A STRONG BODY AND A READY HAND.  . . . . . . .     232 SHADOW WATER B    236
    THE WEAK LAY HAND ON WHAT THE STRONG HAS DONE,  . . .   265 THESE CLOUDS        3
    KING EOCHAID SEIZED THE HORNS IN HIS STRONG HANDS  . .   278 TWO KINGS          24
    THE STRONG THIGH AND THE AGILE THIGH WERE MET,  . . .   278 TWO KINGS          28
    EOCHAID SEIZED BOTH THE HORNS IN HIS STRONG HANDS  . .   278 TWO KINGS      V   24
    LAID HIS STRONG BONES DOWN IN DEATH  . . . . . . .      360 ALF POLLEXFEN       3
    LAID HIS STRONG BONES IN DEATH  . . . . . . . . .       360 ALF POLLEXFEN  V    3
    MAYBE AN IMAGE IS TOO STRONG  . . . . . . . . . .       388 SOLOMON WITCH      36
    OR MAYBE IS NOT STRONG ENOUGH."  . . . . . . . . .      388 SOLOMON WITCH      37
```

STRONG   (CONTINUED)
    BID A STRONG GHOST STAND AT THE HEAD . . . . 435 FOR MY SON   1
    WHEN MY BLOOD WAS STRONG, ... 457 SECRETS OF OLD   4
    BUT GOOD STRONG BLOWS ARE DELIGHTS TO THE MIND." . . . 544 TO SAME TUNE 1   4
    STRONG DRINK I HAD, AND IT BROUGHT ME TO SORROW. . . . 544 TO SAME TUNE 1   13
    BUT A GOOD STRONG CAUSE AND BLOWS ARE DELIGHT." . . . 545 TO SAME TUNE 1   14
    BUT A GOOD STRONG CAUSE"--THE ROPE GAVE A JERK THERE, . . 545 TO SAME TUNE 1   23
    BUT A GOOD STRONG CAUSE AND THE BLOWS ARE DELIGHT." . . 545 TO SAME TUNE 1 V   14
    WHEN ORDER HAS WEAKENED OR FACTION IS STRONG, ... 548 TO SAME TUNE 3   12
    THAT RULE BECAUSE A STRONG RIGHT ARM . . . . 597 MODEL LAUREATE   11
    CONTACT EVERYTHING ANTAEUS-LIKE GREW STRONG. . . . . 603 GALLERY REVIS   44
    CONTACT ALL THINGS ANTAEUS-LIKE GREW STRONG; . . . . 603 GALLERY REVIS   V 44
    BRACE ME AND MAKE ME STRONG; . . . . 607 SONGS BURDEN 2   24
    BUT GOOD STRONG BLOWS ARE DELIGHTS TO THE MIND." . . . 616 MARCH SONGS 3   4
    STRONG DRINK I HAD, AND IT BROUGHT ME TO SORROW. . . . 616 MARCH SONGS 3   13
    BUT A GOOD STRONG CAUSE AND BLOWS ARE DELIGHT." . . . 616 MARCH SONGS 3   14
    BUT A GOOD STRONG CAUSE"--THE ROPE GAVE A JERK THERE, . . 616 MARCH SONGS 3   23
    SHARP THEIR SPADES, THEIR MUSCLES STRONG, ... 637 BEN BULBEN   22
    SHARP THEIR SPADES, THEIR MUSCLE STRONG, ... 637 BEN BULBEN   V 22
    AND A STRONG GALLEY. I GIVE YOU ALL AS MUCH. . . . . 758 SHADOW WATER A   222
    PRAISE THE BEAUTIFUL AND STRONG; . . . . 773 SONG DEIRDRE 1   19
    THE STRONG MARCH BIRDS A-CROW. . . . . 783 GREY ROUND   26
STRONGER
    ALL MEN, AND STRONGER OF HIS HANDS, ...   7 OISIN 1   V 63
    SITS A YOUNGER AND A STRONGER. . . . . 26 OISIN 1   V 399D
    IT MAKES MY PASSION STRONGER BUT TO THINK . . . . . 465 HARUN RASHID   99
STRONGEST
    THE STRONGEST OF THE WORLD, TO SNATCH MY PREY, ... 45 OISIN 2   V 241
STRONGLY
    . . . WHEN THERE ENTERS THE STRONGLY ARMED GUEST; . . . 62 OISIN 3   210
STROVE
    THAT YOU WERE BEAUTIFUL, AND THAT I STROVE . . . . . 206 ADAMS CURSE   35
STRUCK   SEE FRENZY-STRUCK TERROR-STRUCK MOON-STRUCK CONSCIENCE-STRUCK
    IMAGINED, AS THEY STRUCK THE WAY . . . . 189 BAILE AILLINN   20
    FOR THAT WAS IN THE BARGAIN WHEN WE STRUCK IT. . . . 225 SHADOW WATER B V 68D
    WE SHOULD BE DAZED AND TERROR STRUCK . . . . 272 GREY ROCK   V 37
    AND WHERE THE STONE STRUCK FIRE, WHILE IN THE LEAVES . . 278 TWO KINGS   33
    THAT NONE MIGHT KNOW THAT HE WAS CONSCIENCE STRUCK, . . 462 HARUN RASHID   V 38
    STRUCK DUMB IN THE SIMPLICITY OF FIRE! . . . . . . 502 VACILLATION   75
    SO HARD I STRUCK. . . . . 518 HIS CONFIDENCE   8
    "HIS LIGHT HAD STRUCK ME BLIND . . . . 559 HE AND SHE   5
    HER BARGAIN STRUCK WE LAUGHED AND TALKED . . . . . . 620 JOHN KINSELLA   15
    UP THERE SOME HAWK OR OWL HAS STRUCK, ... 633 MAN AND ECHO   43
STRUCKEN   SEE TERROR-STRUCKEN
    WITH QUAKING JOINTS AND TERROR STRUCKEN FACES, ... 185 QUEEN MAEVE   V 121
STRUGGLE
    THE STRUGGLE OF THE FLY IN MARMALADE. . . . . . . 369 EGO DOMINUS   45
    AND THAT MUST SLEEP, SHRIEK, STRUGGLE TO ESCAPE . . . 444 SCHOOL CHILDR   35
    WILL STRUGGLE. OR HE'LL SEEK ENCHANTER OLD, ... 651 ISLE STAT I 1   162
STRUGGLED
    HORN LOCKED IN SWORD, THEY TUGGED AND STRUGGLED THERE . . 277 TWO KINGS   18
    I STRUGGLED WITH THE HORROR OF DAYBREAK, ... 535 CHOSEN   10
    THEN HE STRUGGLED WITH THE HEART; . . . . 561 FOUR AGES MAN   3
    THEN HE STRUGGLED WITH THE MIND; . . . . 561 FOUR AGES MAN   5
STRUGGLES
    WORN WITH LONG STRUGGLES; AND THE WAVES HAVE SUNG . . . 687 TWO TITANS   23
STRUGGLING
    BUT PRONE ON THE PATHWAY, PRONE STRUGGLING, ... 60 OISIN 3   V 186
    STRUGGLING FOR AN IMAGE ON THE TRACK . . . . 534 CHOSEN   2
    HIS BONDS AWAY, SORE STRUGGLING. NOW AT LAST . . . . 714 FERENCZ RENYI   116
STRUNG
    AND A HUNDRED YOUTHS, WHOSE LIMBS ARE STRUNG . . . . .   9 OISIN 1   V 97
    WHERE THEIR SINEWY MIGHT IS STRUNG . . . . 658 ISLE STAT I 3   88
STRUTS
    THERE STRUTS HAMLET, THERE IS LEAR, ... 565 LAPIS LAZULI   10
STRUTTING
    WITH A STRUTTING TURKEY WALK, ... 627 STATES HOLIDAY   34
STUB
    AND I, THAT I MIGHT FIND AND STUB IT OUT, ... 281 TWO KINGS   V 92
STUBBORN
    THE POET STUBBORN WITH HIS PASSION SANG US . . . . . 356 BROKEN DREAMS   18
STUBBORN-HEARTED
    WOMEN ARE HARD AND PROUD AND STUBBORN-HEARTED, . . . 245 SHADOW WATER B   479
STUCK
    HE HAD KNEES THAT STUCK OUT OF HIS HOSE; . . . . . 190 BAILE AILLINN   27
    ALL KNOW THAT ALL THE DEAD IN THE WORLD ABOUT THAT PLACE 593 PILGRIM   11
      ARE STUCK,
    AND HE STUCK TO HIS THRONE. . . . . 628 JANE MOUNTAIN   10
STUDDED   SEE GEM-STUDDED
STUDENT   SEE FELLOW-STUDENT
    OLD FELLOW STUDENT, WHOSE MOST PATIENT EAR . . . . . 468 HARUN RASHID   V 167
STUDENT'S
    TRUTH FLOURISHES WHERE THE STUDENT'S LAMP HAS SHONE, . . 398 LEADERS CROWD   8
STUDENTS
    ON HEARING THAT THE STUDENTS OF OUR NEW UNIVERSITY . . . 262 STUDENTS AGIT   T
STUDIES
    THAT FIRST STRANGE INTEREST IN MY BOOKS AND STUDIES. . . 468 HARUN RASHID   V 165
STUDIO
    FOR TWENTY MINUTES IN SOME STUDIO. . . . . 602 GALLERY REVIS   16
STUDY
    COMPELLING IT TO STUDY . . . . 416 TOWER   182

	PAGE	TITLE		LINE

STUDY   (CONTINUED)
TO STUDY READING-BOOKS AND HISTORY, ...   443 SCHOOL CHILDR V   4
TO STUDY READING BOOKS AND HISTORY . . . .   443 SCHOOL CHILDR V   4
TO STUDY READING BOOKS AND HISTORIES, ...   443 SCHOOL CHILDR V   4
THAT DAY BY DAY I STUDY AND MARVEL AT, ...   468 HARUN RASHID   157
WHY SHOULD I SEEK FOR LOVE OR STUDY IT? . . . . . .   558 RIBH CHRISTIAN   1
I STUDY HATRED WITH GREAT DILIGENCE, ...   558 RIBH CHRISTIAN   3
STUDYING
NOR IS THERE SINGING SCHOOL BUT STUDYING . . . . .   407 SAIL BYZANTIUM   13
AND THERE'S NO SINGING SCHOOL BUT STUDYING . . . .   407 SAIL BYZANTIUM V 13
STUFF
TO HOLD THE SACRED STUFF HE BREWS . . . .   272 GREY ROCK   24
IN RUSTLE OF LACE OR SILKEN STUFF, ...   358 PRESENCES   5
COAGULATE OF STUFF . . . .   449 HERO GIRL FOOL   26
NOT KNOWING WHAT UNEARTHLY STUFF . . . .   599 STONE CROSS   21
STUFFED
AND STUFFED WITH ALL THAT'S OLD AND BAD: . . . . .   303 HOUR DAWN   V 25
THAT'S STUFFED WITH ALL THAT'S OLD AND BAD: . . . .   303 HOUR DAWN   V 25
STUMBLED
OF OUR OLD PAUDEEN IN HIS SHOP, I STUMBLED BLIND . .   291 PAUDEEN   2
STUMBLED UPON THAT WINDY PLACE . . . .   302 HOUR DAWN   3
STUMBLED ON WINDY CRUACHAN . . . .   302 HOUR DAWN   V 3
BECAUSE HE HAS STUMBLED ON THIS HOLE . . . . . .   304 HOUR DAWN   V 54
HE STUMBLED, TUMBLED, FUMBLED TO AND FRO . . . . .   411 TOWER   61
STUMBLING
. . . THE SOUND OF TWO STUMBLING APART. . . . . . .   60 OISIN 3   V 184
HERDED THE CATTLE CAME WITH STUMBLING FEET, ...   106 CUCHULAIN SEA   19
MERELY FOR STUMBLING ON THIS HOLE . . . .   304 HOUR DAWN   54
STUMBLING UPON THE BLOOD-DARK TRACK ONCE MORE, . . .   622 HOUND VOICE   18
THEN STUMBLING TO THE KILL BESIDE THE SHORE: . . . .   622 HOUND VOICE   19
THAT STUMBLING TO THE KILL BESIDE THE SHORE: . . . .   622 HOUND VOICE   V 19
STUMP
TO BURN THAT STUMP ON THE ACROPOLIS, ...   430 NINETEEN 19   46
STUMPIER
A STUMPIER ON EITHER HAND: . . . .   460 THREE MONUMENT   4
STUMPS
E'EN THOUGH HIS WINGS WERE PLUMELESS STUMPS, ...   670 ISLE STAT II 3   118
STUNTED
BECAUSE WE LOVE BARE HILLS AND STUNTED TREES . . . .   621 HOUND VOICE   1
AND 'MONG THE STUNTED ASH-TREES' DROOPING RINGS, . .   650 ISLE STAT I 1   128
STUPEFIED
OWN NOTHING BUT THEIR BLIND, STUPEFIED HEARTS. . . .   370 EGO DOMINUS   69
STUPID
A STUPID HAPPY CREATURE . . . .   400 DEMON BEAST   31
UNDER THE SHADOW OF STUPID STRAW-PALE LOCKS, ...   433 NINETEEN 19   127
SOME STUPID THING THAT I HAD DONE . . . .   507 STREAM AND SUN   4
STUPIDITY
BUT THE STUPIDITY . . . .   600 SPIRIT MEDIUM   20
HAS BODY AND ITS STUPIDITY, ...   633 MAN AND ECHO   28
STUPOR
MY DAILY THOUGHTS SINCE THE FIRST STUPOR OF YOUTH . .   342 SHEP GOATHERD   83
HIS GOD OF STUPOR AND OF WRATH. . . . .   725 LEGEND   20
STURDIER
MEAN ROOF-TREES WERE THE STURDIER FOR ITS FALL, . . .   264 HOUSE SHAKEN   8
STURDY
AS THE ONE STURDY LEG COULD DO . . . .   302 HOUR DAWN   5
STY
NOT IN SOME FOUL STY." . . . .   513 JANE TALK BISH   6
ANCESTRAL PEARLS ALL PITCHED INTO A STY, ...   619 BRONZE HEAD   26
STYLE
A STYLE IS FOUND BY SEDENTARY TOIL . . . .   370 EGO DOMINUS   65
HE WROTE OF ME IN THAT EXTRAVAGANT STYLE . . . . .   373 PHASES OF MOON   26
SUBMISSIVE
THE FLAGELLANT LASHES THOSE SUBMISSIVE LOINS . . . .   560 WHENCE COME   7
SUBSCRIPTION
TO A WEALTHY MAN WHO PROMISED A SECOND SUBSCRIPTION . . .   287 TO WEALTHY MAN   T
SUBSTANCE
BUT THAT HE FOUND MORE SUBSTANCE THERE THAN DREAMS, . . .   417 ANCEST HOUSES V 10
MORE SUBSTANCE IN OUR ENMITIES . . . .   425 STARES NEST   18
TRANSFIGURED TO PURE SUBSTANCE WHAT HAD ONCE . . . .   555 RIBH AT TOMB   11
YET KEEP HIS SUBSTANCE WHOLE. . . . .   573 LADYS 2ND SONG   13
WHICH OF HER FORMS HAS SHOWN HER SUBSTANCE RIGHT? . .   618 BRONZE HEAD   11
OR MAYBE SUBSTANCE CAN BE COMPOSITE, ...   619 BRONZE HEAD   12
OR MAY BE SUBSTANCE CAN BE COMPOSITE, ...   619 BRONZE HEAD   V 12
SUBSTANTIAL
MUST BE SUBSTANTIAL SOMEWHERE. I HAVE HEARD THE DRUIDS   229 SHADOW WATER B   162
AMONG SUBSTANTIAL THINGS: FOR IT IS DREAMS . . . .   230 SHADOW WATER B   181
I MIGHT HAVE USED THE ONE SUBSTANTIAL RIGHT . . . .   352 PEOPLE   19
HOPING MORE SUBSTANTIAL JOY . . . .   494 AT ALGECIRAS   9
HOPING A MORE SUBSTANTIAL JOY . . . .   494 AT ALGECIRAS   V 9
SUBTERRANEAN
THE SUBTERRANEAN STREAMS, ...   420 MY HOUSE   V 20H
OR FOUND A SUBTERRANEAN REST . . . .   535 CHOSEN   6
SUBTILE
THE SUMMERS FLING THEIR SCENTS? AH, SUBTILE AND SLOW, .   675 ISLE STAT II 3   231
SUBTLE   SEE OVER-SUBTLE
YOUNG SUBTLE CONCHUBAR SAT CLOSE BY ME . . . . . .   102 FERGUS DRUID   10
AND FOUND HER DYEING CLOTH WITH SUBTLE CARE . . . .   105 CUCHULAIN SEA   V 2A
THE DEMONS, WITH THEIR SUBTLE GUILE. . . . . . .   135 TWO TREES   22
COWARDICE, OVER SOME SILLY SUBTLE THOUGHT . . . . .   413 TOWER   V 117
ALONG THE WOOD WITH SUBTLE TREAD AND BENDED BOWS. . .   649 ISLE STAT I 1   111

780

SUBTLE-SOULED
    AND FLOWING STRENGTH, WITH AGE IS SUBTLE-SOULED. . . . .   35 OISIN 2   V   83
SUBTLEST
    THEN CONCHUBAR, THE SUBTLEST OF ALL MEN, ... 110 CUCHULAIN SEA   75
SUCCOUR
    AH ME! TO BE OLD WITHOUT SUCCOUR, A SHOW UNTO CHILDREN,   63 OISIN 3   V 217
    A STAIN,
    UNLESS SOME PITYING GOD SHALL SUCCOUR ME . . . . . . 656 ISLE STAT I 3   36
SUCH
    HOW SUCH A WARRIOR NEVER TURNED HIS GAZE . . . . . .   29 OISIN 2   V   11
    HAVE FACES ALIVE WITH SUCH BEAUTY BEEN KNOWN TO THE SALT   50 OISIN 3   51
    EYE OF MAN,
    ARE FACES ALIVE WITH SUCH BEAUTY MADE KNOWN TO THE SALT   50 OISIN 3   V   51
    EYE OF MAN,
    ARE FACES ALIVE WITH SUCH BEAUTY MADE KNOWN TO THE SOFT   50 OISIN 3   V   51
    EYE OF MAN,
    WHERE SUCH GREY CLOUDS OF INCENSE ROSE . . . . 156 FORGOT BEAUTY   13
    YOU PUT SUCH FOLLY IN OUR HEADS . . . . 190 BAILE AILLINN   32
    HAVE SUCH LONG MEMORIES THAT THEY STILL . . . . . . 192 BAILE AILLINN   90
    MUTTER SUCH THINGS AS THEY AWAKE FROM TRANCE. . . . . 229 SHADOW WATER B 163
    WITH SO RED LIPS, AND RUNNING ON SUCH FEET, ... 231 SHADOW WATER B 199
    AND HAVING SUCH WIDE-OPEN, SHINING EYES. . . . . . . 231 SHADOW WATER B 200
    IF THERE BE SUCH A COUNTRY. NO, NOT THERE, ... 249 SHADOW WATER B 558
    --IT HAD SUCH DIGNITY OF LIMB-- . . . . 254 HIS DREAM   11
    BECAUSE IT HAD SUCH DIGNITY, ... 254 HIS DREAM   19
    TO SUCH A PITCH MY THOUGHT . . . . 255 WOMAN HOMER   11
    OF SUCH NOBLE LINES," I SAID, ... 259 PEACE   6
    "SUCH A DELICATE HIGH HEAD, ... 259 PEACE   7
    SO MUCH STERNNESS AND SUCH CHARM." . . . . 259 PEACE   V   8
    DID NOT THE POET SING IT WITH SUCH AIRS . . . . . . 267 ALL TEMPT ME   7
    BECAUSE THERE IS SUCH A STORM AMID MY THOUGHTS . . . 281 TWO KINGS   100
    GAVE ME SUCH PLEASURE I'D FORGO . . . . 305 HOUR DAWN   69
    HER SOUL HAD SUCH DESIRE . . . . 317 NIGHT COME   2
    BUT SUCH AS I HAVE SEEN UPON HER FACE . . . . 340 SHEP GOATHERD 40
    AND BIRTHDAYS AND HOLIDAYS SUCH PRAISES CAN BE HEARD 353 HIS PHOENIX   2
    TO SUCH A PITCH OF FOLLY I AM BROUGHT, ... 384 VISION ROBART 58
    THEY SAY SUCH DIFFERENT THINGS AT SCHOOL. . . . . . 387 ROBARTES DANCE 52
    OR HERS BEFORE A LOOKING-GLASS, FOR SUCH, ... 403 FOR DAUGHTER   19
    BUT SUCH A FORM AS GRECIAN GOLDSMITHS MAKE . . . . . 408 SAIL BYZANTIUM 27
    HAD SUCH AN ACHING HEART . . . . 422 MY TABLE   28
    BUT O! AMBITIOUS HEART, HAD SUCH A PROOF DRAWN FORTH 427 PHANTOM HATRED 36
    NONE DARED ADMIT, IF SUCH A THOUGHT WERE HIS, . . . 430 NINETEEN 19   44
    THAT HAD SUCH BURDENS ON THE MIND . . . . 432 NINETEEN 19   94
    SUCH DEVILISH THINGS EXIST, ... 436 FOR MY SON   11
    AND DID SUCH PLEASURE TAKE-- . . . . 455 HIS MEMORIES   14
    HOW SUCH A MAN PLEASED WOMEN MOST . . . . 458 SECRETS OF OLD 13
    HOW SUCH A PAIR LOVED MANY YEARS . . . . 458 SECRETS OF OLD 15
    AND SUCH A PAIR BUT ONE, ... 458 SECRETS OF OLD 16
    HOW SUCH A MAN HAD PLEASURED MOST . . . . 458 SECRETS OF OLD V 13
    "BUT SUCH AS YOU AND I DO NOT SEEM OLD . . . . . . 463 HARUN RASHID   55
    ITSELF AND NOT SOME OTHER SOUL. "SUCH LOVE . . . . . 465 HARUN RASHID V 94
    PICK OUT MY FEATURES IN SUCH LIGHT AND SHADE . . . . 466 HARUN RASHID   116
    AND THAT TO SUCH A PITCH OF PASSION WROUGHT . . . . 471 ALL SOUL NIGHT 24
    SUCH THOUGHT--SUCH THOUGHT HAVE I THAT HOLD IT TIGHT 474 ALL SOUL NIGHT 91
    SUCH THOUGHT--SUCH THOUGHT HAVE I THAT HOLD IT TIGHT 474 ALL SOUL NIGHT 91
    SUCH THOUGHT, THAT IN IT BOUND . . . . 474 ALL SOUL NIGHT 97
    AN IMAGE OF SUCH POLITICS. . . . . 475 EVA GORE-BOOTH 13
    SUCH FULLNESS IN THAT QUARTER OVERFLOWS . . . . . . 478 SELF AND SOUL   33
    WHEN SUCH AS I CAST OUT REMORSE . . . . 479 SELF AND SOUL   68
    AND SET SUCH COLOUR THERE, ... 492 ANNE GREGORY   8
    NOT SUCH AS ARE IN NEWTON'S METAPHOR, ... 494 AT ALGECIRAS   11
    THAT SUCH CANNONADE . . . . 496 MOHINI CHATTER 24
    THAT ARE NOT SUITED FOR SUCH MEN AS COME . . . . . 501 VACILLATION   33
    SUCH A DANCE AS THERE WAS DANCED-- . . . . 515 JANE GROWN OLD 20
    SUCH BODY LOVERS HAVE, ... 517 HER ANXIETY   7
    SUCH EXACTING BREATH, ... 517 HER ANXIETY   8
    SLEEP, BELOVED, SUCH A SLEEP . . . . 522 LULLABY   7
    SUCH A SLEEP AND SOUND AS FELL . . . . 522 LULLABY   13
    BELOVED SUCH A SLEEP AS FELL . . . . 522 LULLABY   V 13
    BUFFETED BY SUCH SEAS; . . . . 530 DELPHIC ORACLE   2
    BRINGS SUCH SATISFACTION . . . . 533 FIRST CONFESS 11
    TO THINK HIS PASSION SUCH . . . . 538 LAST CONFESS   8
    "THAT I HAVE MET WITH SUCH," SAID HE, ... 539 MEETING   5
    THAT SUCH AS I HAD SUCH A MAN . . . . 539 MEETING   9
    THAT SUCH AS I HAD SUCH A MAN . . . . 539 MEETING   9
    SUCH A MAN THE MOST." . . . . 539 MEETING   12
    "A LOONY'D BOAST OF SUCH A LOVE," . . . . 539 MEETING   13
    BUT SUCH AS HE FOR SUCH AS ME-- . . . . 539 MEETING   15
    BUT SUCH AS HE FOR SUCH AS ME-- . . . . 539 MEETING   15
    OR LACKING THAT, GOVERNMENT IN SUCH HANDS, ... 543 PARN FUNERAL 2   7
    THE MIRACLE THAT GAVE THEM SUCH A DEATH . . . . . . 555 RIBH AT TOMB   10
    BEEN BONE AND SINEW; WHEN SUCH BODIES JOIN . . . . . 555 RIBH AT TOMB   12
    HOW SOUL MAY WALK WHEN ALL SUCH THINGS ARE PAST, . . 558 RIBH CHRISTIAN 11
    HOW SOUL COULD WALK BEFORE SUCH THINGS BEGAN. . . . 558 RIBH CHRISTIAN 12
    HOW SOUL HAS WALKED BEFORE SUCH THINGS BEGAN. . . . 558 RIBH CHRISTIAN V 12
    DID EVER MEN HEAR SUCH A SONG? . . . . 570 THREE BUSHES   45
    DID EVER MAN RIDE SUCH A RACE? . . . . 570 THREE BUSHES   47
    OR SUCKED SUCH MILK AS HE, ... 584 GHOST ROG CASE 26
    THAT HAD SUCH LITTLE SENSE . . . . 585 ORAHILLY   11
    "AM I SUCH A CRAVEN THAT . . . . 585 ORAHILLY   19
    HE WAS OF SUCH A KIND . . . . 586 PARNELLITES   18

	PAGE	TITLE	LINE
SUCH (CONTINUED)			
THEY WERE NOT SUCH A PLAGUE WHEN I WAS YOUNG;	591	SPUR	3
AND WHAT'S THE ODDS IF SUCH AS THESE	597	MODEL LAUREATE	5
AND SAY MY GLORY WAS I HAD SUCH FRIENDS.	604	GALLERY REVIS	55
HE HAD SUCH CHARACTER.	606	SONGS BURDEN 1	13
SUCH QUESTS AS THESE, I TROW, NEED LITTLE WIT.	650	ISLE STAT I 1	150
SUCH MAY I LOVE. THE SHUDDERING FOREST LIGHTS	651	ISLE STAT I 1	165
SUCH MEN, SUCH HEARTS. BUT, UNCOUTH HUNTER, THOU	651	ISLE STAT I 1	167
SUCH MEN, SUCH HEARTS. BUT, UNCOUTH HUNTER, THOU	651	ISLE STAT I 1	167
IN ALL SUCH THINGS, PRAY LET THINE EARS BE TURNED,	660	ISLE STAT II 1	39
TO US. OH WISE ART THOU IN SUCH A THING,	660	ISLE STAT II 1	46
AND NONE THERE IS; IF SUCH THERE WERE,	668	ISLE STAT II 3	53
FOR SUCH A CALL. LET THE WILD WORD BE CRIED	669	ISLE STAT II 3	76
THE BLESSED GOD WAS GOOD TO SEND US SUCH,	683	SEEKER	40
UNTUNED BY THEIR OWN STRIVING. IF ONE SUCH	711	FERENCZ RENYI	37
GOD! THEY'RE MAD TO FLY SUCH CANVAS!"	718	PHANTOM SHIP	14
I KEEP SUCH THINGS ABOUT ME; THEY ARE FOOD	721	WITCH VIVIEN	37
I MUST BE CAREFUL NOW. I HAVE SUCH PLOTS—	722	WITCH VIVIEN	65
SUCH WAR PLOTS, PEACE PLOTS, LOVE PLOTS—EVERY SIDE;	722	WITCH VIVIEN	66
IMAGINED SUCH A FINE AFFAIR!	791	REPRISALS	14
SUCKED			
AS A HAY-COCK OUT ON THE FLOOD, OR A WOLF SUCKED UNDER A WEIR.	63	OISIN 3	220
AS A GRASS SEED CRUSHED BY A PEBBLE, AS A WOLF SUCKED UNDER A WEIR.	63	OISIN 3	V 220
AND HOOF AND HORN THAT HAD SUCKED IN THEIR SPEED	278	TWO KINGS	30
SUCKED UP THE PASSION OUT OF HIM AGAIN	284	TWO KINGS	160
OR SUCKED SUCH MILK AS HE,	584	GHOST ROG CASE	26
SUCKING			
BY SUCKING AT THE DUGS OF GREECE.	288	TO WEALTHY MAN	28
TO MINE, AND HE IS SLOWLY SUCKING FORTH	684	SEEKER	V 63A
SUCKLE			
AND SUCKLE CHILDREN NOW? ARMED MEN	791	REPRISALS	20
SUDDEN			
AND ONCE A SUDDEN LAUGHTER SPRANG	16	OISIN 1	225
WHERE TREES MADE SUDDEN CAVERN-GLOOMS	16	OISIN 1	V 224B
AND IN A WILD AND SUDDEN DANCE	20	OISIN 1	290
IMMEDIATE, MOURNFUL, WHITE WITH SUDDEN CARES,	44	OISIN 2	V 229A
ONLY A SUDDEN FLAMING WORD,	65	HAPPY SHEPHERD	19
SUDDEN AND LIGHT."	70	CLOAK BOAT	15
AND MAY SOME SUDDEN DREADFUL ILL BEFALL HER!	74	ANASHU VIJAYA	59
PARTED HER LIPS WITH A LOUD SUDDEN CRY.	105	CUCHULAIN SEA	8
HIS SUDDEN VENGEANCE WERE A COUNTRY TALE,	127	DREAM OF FAERY	27
SUDDEN AND LAUGHING. O UNQUIET HEART,	181	QUEEN MAEVE	30
THEIR SUDDEN FRAGRANCES ON THE GREEN AIR;	217	WOODS OF COOLE	10
WOULD RISE A SUDDEN, OR A WAVE SO HUGE	236	SHADOW WATER B	310
HE HAS PUT A SUDDEN DARKNESS OVER THE MOON.	239	SHADOW WATER B	367
BUT IT WAS SUDDEN. YOU ARE IN THE RIGHT!	240	SHADOW WATER B	383
WHY ARE THEY ALL A-FLUTTER OF A SUDDEN?	243	SHADOW WATER B	436
OUR SUDDEN PALACES IN THE STILL AIR	284	TWO KINGS	180
OR THAT OF THE SUDDEN SHOWER	414	TOWER	137
WHERE THROUGH LONG WARS AND SUDDEN NIGHT ALARMS	420	MY HOUSE	24
WHERE THROUGH LONG WARS AND SUDDEN NIGHT ALARUMS	420	MY HOUSE	V 24
A SUDDEN BLAST OF DUSTY WIND AND AFTER	433	NINETEEN 19	119
A SUDDEN BLOW; THE GREAT WINGS BEATING STILL	441	LEDA AND SWAN	1
A RUSH, A SUDDEN WHEEL, AND HOVERING STILL	441	LEDA AND SWAN	V 1
AT SUDDEN THUNDER OF THE MOUNTING SWAN	490	COOLE BALLYLEE	14
OR STRIKES A SUDDEN CHILL INTO MY BONES	499	MOTHER OF GOD	14
MY BODY OF A SUDDEN BLAZED;	501	VACILLATION	41
O WHAT HAS MADE THAT SUDDEN NOISE?	583	GHOST ROG CASE	1
A BLOODY AND A SUDDEN END,	620	JOHN KINSELLA	1
SUDDEN AND LIGHT.	666	ISLE STAT II 3	15
BUT A SUDDEN MELANCHOLY	667	ISLE STAT II 3	30
THE SLEEPER AWOKE WITH A SUDDEN START,	729	PRIEST FAIRY	31
BE FULL OF SUDDEN FEARS,	738	MOURN THEN ON	6
I FELT A SUDDEN TEAR START,	744	GLOVE CLOAK	10
FOR THERE ARE SUDDEN VOICES IN MY EARS.	753	SHADOW WATER A	141
THIS BLADE OUT OF MY HAND AND DIED OF A SUDDEN.	755	SHADOW WATER A	168
I AND THAT MIGHTY KING A SUDDEN BLOW	757	SHADOW WATER A	195
A MAN IS LOST OF A SUDDEN,	783	GREY ROUND	9
A SUDDEN STORM, AND IT WAS THROWN	784	WOMANS BEAUTY	5
SUDDENLY			
WHEN ROUND US SUDDENLY THERE CAME	13	OISIN 1	V 165
HE CHANGED ME SUDDENLY; I WAS LOOKING ANOTHER WAY;	153	CHANGE BELOVED	7
SUDDENLY HURTLE BEFORE MY DREAM-AWAKENED EYES,	161	BLACK PIG	2
SUDDENLY AILELL SPOKE OUT OF HIS SLEEP,	183	QUEEN MAEVE	73
SUDDENLY, AND RAN AT THEM AND HARRIED THEM.	185	QUEEN MAEVE	119
AND NOW THEY ALL WHEEL SUDDENLY AND FLY	234	SHADOW WATER B	258
SUDDENLY DRENCHED HER TO THE SKIN;	275	GREY ROCK	120
MY HANDS WERE PRESSED TO VANISHED SUDDENLY.	286	TWO KINGS	208
A CURLEW ANSWERED; AND SUDDENLY THEREUPON I THOUGHT	291	PAUDEEN	5
SUDDENLY HID LOVE'S MOON AWAY.	313	MEMORY YOUTH	7
SUDDENLY I SAW THE COLD AND ROOK-DELIGHTING HEAVEN	316	COLD HEAVEN	1
SUDDENLY I SAW THE COLD AND ROOK DELIGHTING HEAVEN	316	COLD HEAVEN	V 1
ALL SUDDENLY MOUNT	322	SWANS AT COOLE	10
SUDDENLY I BEGAN,	348	FISHERMAN	26
YOUNG MEN NO LONGER SUDDENLY CATCH THEIR BREATH	355	BROKEN DREAMS	2
SUDDENLY I MEET YOUR FACE.	357	DEEP-SWORN VOW	6
ON THE GREY ROCK OF CASHEL I SUDDENLY SAW	383	VISION ROBART	17
I SUDDENLY CRIED OUT IN A STRANGE TONGUE	387	SOLOMON WITCH	5
WHAT CAN HAVE SUDDENLY ALARMED YOU	389	IMAGE PAST	16

782

	PAGE	TITLE	LINE
SUDDENLY (CONTINUED)			
BUT WHY SHOULD YOU GROW SUDDENLY AFRAID	390	IMAGE PAST	29
THEN SUDDENLY MY HEART IS WRUNG	453	DEATH OF HARE	7
SUDDENLY LIT UP	512	JANE ON GOD	16
TILL SUDDENLY IN GRIEF'S CONTAGION CAUGHT,	537	HER VISION	22
BEFORE A WOMAN'S PORTRAIT SUDDENLY I STAND,	602	GALLERY REVIS	13
AND FLOWERS AND LITTLE CHILDREN. SUDDENLY	688	TWO TITANS	36
SILENCE! THOU SHALT BE DEAD!" NOW SUDDENLY	710	FERENCZ RENYI	16
WITH CRIES AND MURMURS. SUDDENLY HE FLINGS	714	FERENCZ RENYI	101
AND NOW THEY ALL WHEEL SUDDENLY AND FLY	753	SHADOW WATER A	148
RUNS, RUNS AND IS SUDDENLY STILL.	783	GREY ROUND	3
CARRY IT! SUDDENLY IT IS STILL.	783	GREY ROUND	5
THE STORM AROSE AND SUDDENLY FELL	784	WOMANS BEAUTY	19
SUFFER			
SUFFER AS YOUR MOTHER SUFFERED,	313	TWO YEAR LATER	9
THE HEART NEED SUFFER NO DEFEAT! BUT I	464	HARUN RASHID	77
OR MUST SUFFER, IF HE WOOS	479	SELF AND SOUL	63
SUFFERED			
SUFFER AS YOUR MOTHER SUFFERED,	313	TWO YEAR LATER	9
SUFFERING			
A SUFFERING PASSION AND A LABOURING THOUGHT?	420	MY HOUSE V	20J
"ALL MEN LIVE IN SUFFERING,	589	OLD WICKED MAN	46
CAN BURN OUT THAT SUFFERING	589	OLD WICKED MAN	57
SUFFICE			
O WHEN MAY IT SUFFICE?	394	EASTER 1916	59
SUFFICE THE AGEING MAN AS ONCE THE GROWING BOY.	427	PHANTOM HATRED	40
SUFFICIENT			
THAT OUR SUFFICIENT PORTION OF THE WORLD	282	TWO KINGS	119
CONSIDER BEAUTY A SUFFICIENT END,	403	FOR DAUGHTER	21
SUFFICIENT MONEY FOR HIS NEED,	577	WHAT THEN	8
SUGGESTED			
SUGGESTED BY A PICTURE OF A BLACK CENTAUR	442	BLACK CENTAUR V	T
SUIT			
AS WITH AN AUREOLE. MY SUIT TO YOU--	697	MOSADA 2	38
SUITED			
THAT ARE NOT SUITED FOR SUCH MEN AS COME	501	VACILLATION	33
SULLEN			
ON THE LONE BORDER OF THE SULLEN LAKE.	80	EPHEMERA V	17
THE SULLEN WOOD. BUT MANY WOODS I SEE	682	SEEKER	24
THE HEATHEN. YEA, AND SHAKE THE SULLEN KINGS	698	MOSADA 2	55
THIS SULLEN PEASANT SPOILS THE GOOD SUNSHINE,	711	FERENCZ RENYI	42
THIS SULLEN PEASANT SPOILS THE GOOD RED WINE.	711	FERENCZ RENYI	43
THIS SULLEN PEASANT CHILLS THE GOOD SUNSHINE.	711	FERENCZ RENYI V	42
THIS SULLEN PEASANT SOURS THE GOOD RED WINE.	711	FERENCZ RENYI V	43
SULPHUROUS			
HAS NO WORD OF THE SULPHUROUS END.	736	SUMMER EVENING	8
SULTRY			
MY WORKS ARE ALL STAMPED DOWN INTO THE SULTRY MUD.	442	BLACK CENTAUR	3
I SLEPT, 'TWAS SULTRY, AND SCARCE CIRCLING SHOOK	677	ISLE STAT II 3	278
WANDERING IN SULTRY PALACES OF IND,	694	MOSADA 1	102
SUM			
A GOOD ROUND SUM UPON THIS CRUISE, AND TURN--	222	SHADOW WATER B	5
AND 'NEATH IT SIT, AND OF THE WOVEN SUM	663	ISLE STAT II 2	30
SUMMER			
THAT WAVERED LIKE THE SUMMER STREAMS,	4	OISIN 1	29
AND WAVERED LIKE A SUMMER RILL,	4	OISIN 1 V	29
AND THE GENTLE WAVES OF THE SUMMER SEAS,	27	OISIN 1	418
I FELL ON THE PATH, AND THE HORSE WENT AWAY LIKE A SUMMER FLY:	60	OISIN 3	190
WHEN SUMMER GLUTS THE GOLDEN BEES,	84	MAD KING GOLL	38
WHERE SUMMER GLUTS THE GOLDEN BEES,	84	MAD KING GOLL V	38
THAT FROM THOSE FINGERS GLITTERING SUMMER RUNS	128	DREAM OF FAERY	44
UNTIL THE SAP OF SUMMER HAD GROWN WEARY!	130	BOOK STORIES	14
AND WALK AND WALK THROUGH SUMMER GRASS,	150	WANDER AENGUS V	21
WHEN ALL THE WILD SUMMER WAS IN HER GAZE."	200	FOLLY COMFORT	12
THEIR RICHNESS THROUGH THE SUMMER AND THE SPRING:	279	TWO KINGS V	62C
THROUGH SUMMER AND WINTER SEEM	393	EASTER 1916	42
FISH, FLESH, OR FOWL, COMMEND ALL SUMMER LONG	407	SAIL BYZANTIUM	5
AND HAD THE LIVELONG SUMMER DAY TO SPEND.	409	TOWER	10
AND THROUGH THE SPRING ON SUMMER CALL,	434	WHEEL	2
SUMMER AND WINTER, DAY AND NIGHT,	447	COLONUS PRAISE	31
SUMMER AND SPRING	456	SUMMER SPRING	T
WHEN WE HAD ALL THE SUMMER TIME	457	SUMMER SPRING V	15
THAT IN THE EARLY SUMMER OF THE YEAR	462	HARUN RASHID	40
THAT IN THE EARLY SUMMER OF THAT YEAR	462	HARUN RASHID V	40
ALTHOUGH THE SUMMER SUNLIGHT GILD	501	VACILLATION	45
WINTER AND SUMMER TILL OLD AGE BEGAN	629	CIRCUS ANIMALS	5
SING SUMMER WAVES. BUT YONDER SHEPHERD VILE,	649	ISLE STAT I 1	107
DREAMING THE LIVE-LONG SUMMER IN THE SHADE,	650	ISLE STAT I 1	139
THE FEET OF SUMMER DABBLE	680	LOVE AND DEATH	7
WHERE THEY ALL SUMMER FEED THEIR WANDERING FLOCKS,	690	MOSADA 1	5
WHERE SAT OLD SUMMER FADING INTO SONG,	690	MOSADA 1 V	1B
THE WORLD WERE DREAMING IN ITS SUMMER SLEEP:	699	MOSADA 3	11
AS THE SUMMER VOICE OF THE DAYTIME CEASED,	728	PRIEST FAIRY	4
"EVERY SUMMER WILT THOU SEE	730	PRIEST FAIRY	55
A SUMMER EVENING	736	SUMMER EVENING	T
SUMMERED SEE EVER-SUMMERED			
THE EVER SUMMERED SOLITUDES,	21	OISIN 1 V	321
SUMMER'S			
THROUGH SUMMER'S HEAT AND WINTER'S COLD.	86	MAD KING GOLL	71
WE SAT TOGETHER AT ONE SUMMER'S END,	204	ADAMS CURSE	1

		PAGE	TITLE	LINE
SUMMER'S (CONTINUED)				
BLOSSOM FROM THE SUMMER'S WREATH:	• • • • • • • • •	475	EVA GORE-BOOTH	6
AND WHEN THE SUMMER'S DEEP, THEN TO THIS SPOT	• • • •	663	ISLE STAT II 2	24
SUMMERS				
THE SUMMERS FLING THEIR SCENTS? AH, SUBTILE AND SLOW,	• •	675	ISLE STAT II 3	231
WHOSE FOOTFALL I HAVE LONGED FOR, THREE SAD SUMMERS.	• •	692	MOSADA 1	45
SUMMER-TIME				
WHEN WE HAD ALL THE SUMMER-TIME	• • • • • • • •	457	SUMMER SPRING	15
SUMMON				
I CALL TO MY OWN OPPOSITE, SUMMON ALL	• • • • • •	367	EGO DOMINUS	8
I SUMMON TO THE WINDING ANCIENT STAIR:	• • • • • •	477	SELF AND SOUL	1
I SUMMON TO THE WINDY ANCIENT STAIR:	• • • • • •	477	SELF AND SOUL V	1
BREATHLESS MOUTHS MAY SUMMON:	• • • • • • •	497	BYZANTIUM	14
I CAN SUMMON BACK	• • • • • • • •	505	RESULT THOUGHT	11
I COULD SUMMON BACK	• • • • • • • •	505	RESULT THOUGHT V	11
SUMMONED				
SUMMONED THE GENERATIONS OF HIS HOUSE,	• • • • •	609	IN TARAS HALLS	19
WHEN PEARSE SUMMONED CUCHULAIN TO HIS SIDE,	• • • •	611	STATUES	25
LOVER, THE VOICE THAT SUMMONED THEE WAS MINE.	• • • •	685	SEEKER	77
SUMMONS				
I AWOKE: THE STRANGE HORSE WITHOUT SUMMONS OUT OF THE DISTANCE RAN,		54	OISIN 3	105
BUT SUMMONS TO ADVENTURE AND THE MAN	• • • • • • •	373	PHASES OF MOON	37
SUMPTUOUS				
THE HOUR WHEN KAMA, WITH A SUMPTUOUS SMILE,	• • • •	72	ANASHU VIJAYA V	26
SUMS				
AND TOOK THEIR TABLETS AND DID SUMS:	• • • • • •	344	DAWN	9
AND TOOK THEIR TABLETS AND MADE SUMS—	• • • • •	344	DAWN V	9
SUN				
AND WAS BORN WHERE THE SUN DROPS DOWN IN THE TIDE,	• • •	5	OISIN 1 V	49
AND SLEEP DROWN SUN AND MOON AND STAR."	• • • •	5	OISIN 1 V	49
THE RED SUN FALLS AND THE WORLD GROWS DIM."	• • • •	9	OISIN 1	105
OF THE GREAT ROUND SUN, FROM HIS CENTRAL FIRES.	• • •	13	OISIN 1 V	168
AND, AS THE SUN SANK EVER LOWER,	• • • • •	13	OISIN 1	V 170A
UPON THE CENTRE OF THE SUN.	• • • • • • • •	14	OISIN 1	175
WHERE AENGUS DREAMS, FROM SUN TO SUN,	• • • • •	16	OISIN 1	218
WHERE AENGUS DREAMS, FROM SUN TO SUN,	• • • • •	16	OISIN 1	218
AND ROLLS ALONG THE UNWIELDY SUN,	• • • • •	18	OISIN 1	267
ROUND US, AND ROLLS THE UNWIELDY SUN.	• • • • •	18	OISIN 1 V	268
WATCHED WHERE THE SUN IN A SAFFRON BLAZE	• • • •	26	OISIN 1	394
WATCHED THE OLD SUN THAT IN SEA-WAYS .	• • • •	26	OISIN 1 V	394
THE HARE GROWS OLD AS SHE PLAYS IN THE SUN	• • • •	27	OISIN 1	412
"OLD GROWS THE HARE AS SHE PLAYS IN THE SUN,	• • •	28	OISIN 1 V	420
AND EVEN THE SUN, THE DAY CASTLE'S WARDER,	• • •	28	OISIN 1	V 423A
BUT WHEN AT WITHERING OF THE SUN HE KNEW	• • • •	40	OISIN 2 V	173
AND WHEN AT WITHERING OF THE SUN HE KNEW	• • • •	40	OISIN 2	173
AND WHEN THE SUN ONCE MORE IN SAFFRON STEPT,	• • •	41	OISIN 2	192
AND WHEN THE SUN IN ALL HIS FLAGRANT SAFFRON STEPT,	• •	41	OISIN 2 V	192
BUT WHEN THE SUN ONCE MORE IN SAFFRON STEPT,	• • •	41	OISIN 2 V	192
TO LIE UNTIL THE FOURTH MORN SUN EMERGE	• • • •	44	OISIN 2 V	220
• • • THE GLEAMS OF THE WORLD AND THE SUN,	• • •	48	OISIN 3	22
• • • WHEN THE SUN WAS ON SILVER OR GOLD:	• • •	53	OISIN 3	97
THE SUN HAS LAID HIS CHIN ON THE GREY WOOD,	• • •	72	ANASHU VIJAYA	24
THE SUN HATH LAID HIS CHIN ON THE GREY WOOD,	• • •	72	ANASHU VIJAYA V	24
THAT HIDES AWAY THE DYING SUN .	• • • • • •	85	MAD KING GOLL	63
OR FLING MY LAUGHTER TO THE SUN	• • • • •	86	MAD KING GOLL V	69
AND FLING MY LAUGHTER TO THE SUN	• • • • •	86	MAD KING GOLL V	69
THE SUN UPON ALL THINGS THAT GROW	• • • • •	98	FOXHUNTER	15
A MAN CAME SLOWLY FROM THE SETTING SUN,	• • • •	105	CUCHULAIN SEA	1
"YET SOMEWHERE UNDER STARLIGHT OR THE SUN	• • • •	107	CUCHULAIN SEA	28
WHERE THE SUN FALLS INTO THE WESTERN DEEP.	• • • •	108	CUCHULAIN SEA V	34
OR IN THE SUN AND MOON, OR ON THE EARTH,	• • • •	114	ROSE OF BATTLE	17
IT SEEMED THE SUN AND MOON WERE IN THE FRUIT:	• • •	127	DREAM OF FAERY	23
OF SUN AND MOON AND HOLLOW AND WOOD	• • • •	148	INTO TWILIGHT	11
THE GOLDEN APPLES OF THE SUN.	• • • • • •	150	WANDER AENGUS	24
AND HAD ROOTED THE SUN AND MOON AND STARS OUT OF THE SKY		153	CHANGE BELOVED	11
AND ROOTED THE SUN AND MOON AND STARS OUT OF THE SKY,	•	153	CHANGE BELOVED V	11
WHEN WINDS HAVE GATHERED AND SUN AND MOON BURNED DIM	•	175	ELEMENT POWERS	15
ABOUT THE STARS AND MOON AND SUN:	• • • • •	176	BELOVED DEAD	10
ABOVE THE STARS AND MOON AND SUN:	• • • • •	176	BELOVED DEAD V	10
OR APPLES OF THE SUN AND MOON.	• • • • • •	196	BAILE AILLINN	176
WHEN THE SUN LOOKED OUT OF HIS GOLDEN HOOD,	• • •	210	RAGGED WOOD V	3
WHEN THE SUN LOOKED OUT OF HIS GOLDEN HOOD?—	• • •	211	RAGGED WOOD	7
THE SUN WAS LAUGHING SWEETLY,	• • • • •	214	HAPPY TOWNLAND	15
THE SUN WAS LAUGHING SWEETLY,	• • • • •	215	HAPPY TOWNLAND	35
THE SUN WAS LAUGHING SWEETLY,	• • • • •	216	HAPPY TOWNLAND	55
AS A LAMP SHADOW—NO—NO LAMP, THE SUN.	• • • •	229	SHADOW WATER B	160
THAT IS MORE MIGHTY THAN THE SUN AND MOON,	• • •	237	SHADOW WATER B	328
AND I GREW WEARY OF THE SUN .	• • • • • •	256	WORDS	5
I SWAYED MY LEAVES AND FLOWERS IN THE SUN:	• • •	261	COMING WISDOM	3
TO BREED THE LIDLESS EYE THAT LOVES THE SUN?	• • •	264	HOUSE SHAKEN	4
THESE ARE THE CLOUDS ABOUT THE FALLEN SUN,	• • •	265	THESE CLOUDS	1
THESE ARE THE CLOUDS ABOUT THE FALLEN SUN,	• • •	265	THESE CLOUDS	11
"ONLY THE WASTEFUL VIRTUES EARN THE SUN":	• • •	270	PARDON FATHERS	18
AND CAME INTO A WOOD AS THE SUN SET	• • • •	277	TWO KINGS V	3
AND LEFT MERE SLEEP. HE'LL WAKE WHEN THE SUN WAKES,	•	284	TWO KINGS	161
OR TILL THE SUN IS IN HIS STRENGTH.	• • • • •	305	HOUR DAWN	61
OF SUN AND MOON THAT A GOOD HOUR .	• • • •	331	ROUND TOWER	11
YOU HAD BEFORE THE SUN HAD THROWN	• • • • •	333	SOLOMON SHEBA	13
I HAVE NOTHING BUT THE EMBITTERED SUN:	• • • •	344	DEJECTION	8
I MUST ENDURE THE TIMID SUN.	• • • • • • •	344	DEJECTION	11

784

PAGE   TITLE   LINE

SUN (CONTINUED)
AND I HAVE NOTHING BUT HARSH SUN: . . . . 344 DEJECTION   V   8
AND THAT PROUD LOOK AS THOUGH SHE HAD GAZED INTO   354 HIS PHOENIX   29
    THE BURNING SUN,
FROM GOING-DOWN OF THE SUN I HAVE DREAMED . . . . . . 358 PRESENCES   3
FROM GOING DOWN OF THE SUN I HAVE DREAMED . . . . . . 358 PRESENCES   V   3
AND ALL LAUGH IN THE SUN. . . . . 400 DEMON BEAST   8
A GAZE BLANK AND PITILESS AS THE SUN, ... 402 SECOND COMING   15
AYE, SUN AND MOON AND STAR, ALL, ...   415 TOWER   152
THE FINEST PLAY UNDER THE SUN. . . . .   424 ROAD AT DOOR   5
AND NOW BUT GAPE AT THE SUN. . . . .   432 NINETEEN 19   102
WHAT WHOLESOME SUN HAS RIPENED IS WHOLESOME FOOD TO EAT, 442 BLACK CENTAUR   5
UNVISITED BY TEMPEST OR BY SUN, ... 446 COLONUS PRAISE   5
UNTIL IT PLUNGE INTO THE SUN: . . . . 472 ALL SOUL NIGHT   56
UNTIL IT PLUNGED INTO THE SUN: . . . .   472 ALL SOUL NIGHT V   56
BACK TURNED UPON THE BRIGHTNESS OF THE SUN . . . . . 489 COOLE PARK 29   30
NOW ALL DRY STICKS UNDER A WINTRY SUN, ...   490 COOLE BALLYLEE   10
GREATER GLORY IN THE SUN, ... 494 AT ALGECIRAS   13
THE TRIVIAL DAYS AND RAM THEM WITH THE SUN, ... 500 VACILLATION   21
STREAM AND SUN AT GLENDALOUGH . . . . 506 STREAM AND SUN   T
STREAM AND GLIDING SUN . . . .   506 STREAM AND SUN   2
WHAT MOTION OF THE SUN OR STREAM . . . .   507 STREAM AND SUN   11
I CARRY THE SUN IN A GOLDEN CUP, ...   525 DANCING DAYS   7
I CARRY THE SUN IN A GOLDEN CUP, ...   525 DANCING DAYS   15
I CARRY THE SUN IN A GOLDEN CUP, ...   525 DANCING DAYS   23
THERE ALL THE PLANETS DROP IN THE SUN. . . . . . .   557 THERE   4
OF THE BARLEY SHOOTS IN THE SUN. . . . .   643 SONG FAERIES   8
OUT OF THE AIR. AND WHEN? WHEN THE SUN GOES DOWN   652 ISLE STAT I 2   29
THE WIND AT EVENING WHEN THE SUN GOES DOWN . . . .   653 ISLE STAT I 2   50
SEE, YONDER SINKS THE SUN, YONDER A SHADE . . . . . 653 ISLE STAT I 2   52
WHEN LOW THE SUN SANK DOWN IN CLOTTED FLAME . . . . 656 ISLE STAT I 3   30
PIERCED THROUGH, CHATTERING FROM HABIT IN THE SUN,   664 ISLE STAT II 2   53
OH FAMOUS DYING MINION OF THE SUN, ...   673 ISLE STAT II 3   197
AH, WOE IS ME! I GO FROM SUN AND SHADE, ...   674 ISLE STAT II 3   216
OF THE BARLEY SHOOTS IN THE SUN. . . . .   676 ISLE STAT II 3   255
AWAY FROM ALL THE OTHERS. NOW THE SUN . . . . . .   691 MOSADA 1   33
AND ALL THE ELDERS SITTING IN THE SUN . . . . . .   693 MOSADA 1   69
FROM THE WAVES THE SUN HATH REELED. . . . .   705 DAWN-SONG   1
"ON THIS EMBROIDERED CLOUD," THE SUN HATH SAID,   712 FERENCZ RENYI   74
I WILL SWEAR BY SUN AND MOON TO PARDON ALL . . . .   756 SHADOW WATER A   183
BY SUN AND MOON AND A HUNDRED GODS AS WELL, ... 756 SHADOW WATER A   189
AND WILL YOU SWEAR IT BY THE SUN AND MOON? . . . .   758 SHADOW WATER A   229
AND SAID IT WAS MIGHTIER THAN THE SUN AND MOON, . . 762 SHADOW WATER A   289
THE LOVE OF ALL UNDER THE LIGHT OF THE SUN . . . .   765 SHADOW WATER A   353
HAVE FALLEN AND MY SUN AND MOON GONE OUT. . . . .   767 SHADOW WATER A V   405
ONE LIVES IN THE HOUSE OF THE SUN, ...   771 SPINNING SONG   6
"TILL THE SUN GOES DOWN AND AN HOUR OF THE CLOCK"   779 GOING THE ROAD   7
"FOR A YEAR AND A DAY BY THE CLOCK OF THE SUN"   779 GOING THE ROAD   11
THEY DREAM THAT LAUGHED IN THE SUN. . . . .   783 GREY ROUND   13
THEY DREAM AND DARKEN OUR SUN. . . . .   783 GREY ROUND   15
THEY DREAMED THAT LAUGHED IN THE SUN. . . . . . .   783 GREY ROUND   V   13
SUNDAY
WHEN EVERY SUNDAY AFTERNOON . . . .   607 SONGS BURDEN 2   19
SUNDOWN
AND AT THE SUNDOWN THREW HIM IN THE SURGE, ...   44 OISIN 2   219
AND HALF THE KINGS, BEFORE SUNDOWN . . . .   273 GREY ROCK   69
AND HALF HIS KINGS, BEFORE SUNDOWN . . . .   273 GREY ROCK   V   69
KING EOCHAID CAME AT SUNDOWN TO A WOOD . . . . .   276 TWO KINGS   1
SUN-DRY
HE CARVED ON TREES, AND WITH A SUN-DRY WEED . . .   659 ISLE STAT II 1   8
SUNFLOWERS
THE SUNFLOWERS WEAVE A GOLDEN CLIME, ...   736 SUMMER EVENING   9
SUN-FLUSHED
ABOUT A SUN-FLUSHED DOVE-COT, COOING, CLING . . .   710 FERENCZ RENYI   20
SUN-FRECKLED
AND HIS SUN-FRECKLED FACE, ...   348 FISHERMAN   29
SUNG   SEE RE-SUNG
SUNG OF THE BIRDS. OUR TOIL WAS DONE: . . . . . .   14 OISIN 1   V 177
. . . FAR SUNG BY THE SENNACHIES. . . . .   50 OISIN 3   53
. . . FAR SUNG OF THE SENNACHIES. . . . .   50 OISIN 3   V   53
A WOMAN HOMER SUNG . . . .   254 WOMAN HOMER   T
A WOMAN HOMER SUNG. . . . .   255 WOMAN HOMER   19
IN PRAISE OF WHAT ANOTHER'S SAID OR SUNG, ...   262 TO A POET   2
TRUE SONG, THOUGH SPEECH: "MINE AUTHOR SUNG IT ME."   373 PHASES OF MOON   30
WHATEVER HAS BEEN SAID, SIGHED, SUNG, ...   387 SOLOMON WITCH   7
ALL SOUNDS BY BIRD OR ANGEL SUNG . . . .   387 SOLOMON WITCH   V   7
MERE DREAMS, MERE DREAMS! YET HOMER HAD NOT SUNG   417 ANCEST HOUSES   9
HAS PLUCKED A FLOWER AND SUNG HER LOSS: . . . . .   447 COLONUS PRAISE   22
I THIRST FOR ACCUSATION. ALL THAT WAS SUNG, . . .   542 PARN FUNERAL 1   25
ARE SUNG ABOVE THE GLASS, ...   587 PARNELLITES   30
ARE SUNG ABOVE A GLASS: . . . .   587 PARNELLITES   V   30
AS THOUGH SOME BALLAD-SINGER HAD SUNG IT ALL: . . .   602 GALLERY REVIS   24
AS THOUGH SOME BALLAD SINGER HAD SUNG IT ALL. . . .   602 GALLERY REVIS   V   24
ALL CLAMOUR-CLOTHED---WAS'T CLAMOUR WHEN I SUNG, .   649 ISLE STAT I 1   108
WORN WITH LONG STRUGGLES! AND THE WAVES HAVE SUNG   687 TWO TITANS   23
OF THE GREAT WARRIORS WHOSE NAMES HAVE SUNG . . .   698 MOSADA 2   60
AND CRADLED ME HERE WHERE ARE SUNG, ...   708 FAIRY PEDANT   25
SUNK
DARK BALOR, AS OLD AS A FOREST, CAR-BORNE, HIS MIGHTY HEAD   53 OISIN 3   91
    SUNK

785

	PAGE	TITLE		LINE

SUNK   (CONTINUED)

CAME CAR-BORNE BALOR, AS OLD AS A FOREST, HIS VAST FACE SUNK — 53 OISIN 3 — V — 91

CAME BALOR, AS OLD AS A FOREST, CAR BORNE, HIS MIGHTY HEAD SUNK — 53 OISIN 3 — V — 91

AND SHE AND I, BEING SUNK IN HAPPINESS, ... — 463 HARUN RASHID — 51
JUSTIFY ALL THAT HAVE SUNK IN THEIR BLOOD, ... — 546 TO SAME TUNE 2 — 12
NOW SUNK IN REST, ... — 574 MAIDS 1ST SONG — 2
AND NOW LIES SUNK IN SLEEP. WHAT CLIMBS THE STAIR? . . . — 579 DOR WELLESLEY — 11
BUT NOW LIES SUNK IN SLEEP. WHAT CLIMBS THE STAIR? . . . — 579 DOR WELLESLEY — V — 11
REMEMBER ALL THAT HAVE SUNK IN THEIR BLOOD, ... — 613 MARCH SONGS 1 — 12

SUNKEN   SEE DEEP-SUNKEN

DEEP SUNKEN ON THE BLADE'S LENGTH, "MANANAN!" . . . . . — 38 OISIN 2 — V — 128
AND FOUND A DOOR DEEP SUNKEN IN THE WALL, ... — 39 OISIN 2 — 154
AND SUNKEN SHAPE, A NINE DAYS' CORPSE SEA-DASHED— . . . — 40 OISIN 2 — V — 179
AND SUNKEN SHAPE, AGAINST MY FACE AND BREAST, ... — 40 OISIN 2 — V — 179
AND DRIPPING AND SUNKEN SHAPE, TO FACE AND BREAST, . . . — 40 OISIN 2 — V — 179

SUNLESS

MAKE MOAN AND CRY. WITHIN YON SUNLESS VALLEY, ... — 682 SEEKER — 26

SUNLIGHT

O MAY THE MOON AND SUNLIGHT SEEM . . . . — 411 TOWER — 54
ALTHOUGH THE SUMMER SUNLIGHT GILD . . . . — 501 VACILLATION — 45
IN THE SUNLIGHT AND WIND. . . . . — 600 THOSE IMAGES — 4
COURAGEOUS MIRACLES! THE SUNLIGHT SHONE . . . . — 649 ISLE STAT I 1 — 113
THE SUNLIGHT FLICKERING ON THE PEWS, ... — 736 IN CHURCH — 9
THE SUNLIGHT IN THE AIR, ... — 736 IN CHURCH — 10

SUNNIER

SHADY KYLE-DORTHA; SUNNIER KYLE-NA-NO, ... — 217 WOODS OF COOLE — 4

SUNNY

PACING WITH HALF-CLOSED EYELIDS IN A SUNNY SPOT . . . . — 366 HER COURAGE — 7
WHISPERING ALONG THE SUNNY PATH; . . . . — 725 LEGEND — 18

SUN'S

IN THE PALE WEST, AND THE SUN'S RIM SANK, ... — 12 OISIN 1 — 153
NOW IN THE SEA THE SUN'S RIM SANK, ... — 12 OISIN 1 — V — 153
LAND-UNDER-WAVE, WHERE OUT OF THE MOON'S LIGHT AND THE SUN'S — 209 UNDER THE MOON — 6
LOOK UP IN THE SUN'S EYE AND GIVE . . . . — 288 TO WEALTHY MAN — 32
AND THAT IF MEMORY RECUR, THE SUN'S . . . . — 414 TOWER — 119
MELT DOWN, AS IT WERE WAX IN THE SUN'S RAYS; . . . . . — 428 NINETEEN 19 — 12
. . . A LOG-BOOK OF THE SUN'S JOURNEY AND THE MOON'S; . — 480 BLOOD AND MOON — 14
. . . A LOG BOOK OF THE SUN'S JOURNEY AND THE MOON'S, . — 480 BLOOD AND MOON — V — 14

SUNS

WHEN WE ARE DEAD, BEYOND THE SETTING SUNS, ... — 71 ANASHU VIJAYA — 8
OF ALL ON WHOM ARCADIAN SUNS HAVE SHONE . . . . . . — 650 ISLE STAT I 1 — 143

SUNSET

AND LIKE A SUNSET WERE HER LIPS, ... — 3 OISIN 1 — 22
A STORMY SUNSET ON DOOMED SHIPS; . . . . — 3 OISIN 1 — 23
A STORMY SUNSET O'ER DOOMED SHIPS. . . . . — 3 OISIN 1 — V — 23

SUNSHINE

THIS SULLEN PEASANT SPOILS THE GOOD SUNSHINE, ... — 711 FERENCZ RENYI — 42
THIS SULLEN PEASANT CHILLS THE GOOD SUNSHINE. . . . . . — 711 FERENCZ RENYI — V — 42

SUNSICK

THAT DIETH SLOW WITH SUNSICK DOOM. . . . . — 655 ISLE STAT I 3 — 12

SUN-SMITTEN

ON THE SUN-SMITTEN GRASS; . . . . — 99 FOXHUNTER — 42

SUP

NOR STAYED FOR BITE OR SUP; . . . . — 93 FATHER OHART — 38
SHE GIVES ME BITE AND SUP. . . . . — 96 MOLL MAGEE — 40
I'LL NAME THE FRIENDS THAT CANNOT SUP WITH US . . . . — 323 ROBERT GREGORY — 2

SUPERHUMAN

MAN MAKES A SUPERHUMAN . . . . — 415 TOWER — 164
I HAIL THE SUPERHUMAN; . . . . — 497 BYZANTIUM — 15
HUMAN, SUPERHUMAN, A BIRD'S ROUND EYE, ... — 618 BRONZE HEAD — 2
COMPLEXION AND FORM PROVE SUPERHUMAN, ... — 637 BEN BULBEN — 6

SUPER-HUMAN

HUMAN, SUPER-HUMAN, A BIRD'S ROUND EYE, ... — 618 BRONZE HEAD — V — 2

SUPERMAN

MAN MAKES A SUPERMAN, ... — 415 TOWER — V — 164

SUPERNATURAL

CAN RULE BY SUPERNATURAL RIGHT . . . . — 386 ROBARTES DANCE — 36
SUPERNATURAL SONGS . . . . — 554 RIBH AT TOMB — T
THAT'S HOW ALL NATURAL OR SUPERNATURAL STORIES RUN. . . — 556 RIBH PATRICK — 3
NATURAL AND SUPERNATURAL WITH THE SELF-SAME RING ARE WED. — 556 RIBH PATRICK — 4
OR ELSE I THOUGHT HER SUPERNATURAL; . . . . — 619 BRONZE HEAD — 22

SUPERSESSION

SUPERSESSION OF BREATH; . . . . — 476 DEATH — 10

SUPINE

THEY HEALED MY WOUNDS; AND ON THE SKIN SUPINE . . . . — 41 OISIN 2 — V — 187

SUPPER

YON TALL ONE EYES MY SUPPER; CHASE HIM AWAY, ... — 72 ANASHU VIJAYA — 34
YON TALL ONE EYES MY SUPPER; SWIFTLY CHASE HIM . . . . — 72 ANASHU VIJAYA — V — 34
WHEN THE SUPPER HAS BEEN SPREAD. . . . . — 215 HAPPY TOWNLAND — 44

SUPPLER

IF TIME WERE SUPPLER IN THE JOINT, ... — 306 HOUR DAWN — 94

SUPPLIANT

THAT WATCH ME WITH THEIR SUPPLIANT LIGHT— . . . . . . — 723 GIRLS SONG A — 10

SUPPORTING

STANDISH O'GRADY SUPPORTING HIMSELF BETWEEN THE TABLES . . — 577 LOFTY THINGS — 5

SUPPOSE

THOUGH FANTASTIC MEN SUPPOSE . . . . — 530 OLD TOM AGAIN — 4

786

	PAGE	TITLE		LINE

SUPREME
   UPON THE SUPREME THEME OF ART AND SONG! . . . . 523 LONG SILENCE   6
SURE
   AND SOMETIMES I AM SURE SHE KNOWS . . . . 96 MOLL MAGEE   49
   SHE SAYS MY HUSBAND SURE WILL COME . . . . 96 MOLL MAGEE   V   41
   TO SOME SURE COUNTRY, SOME FAMILIAR PLACE. . . . . . . 249 SHADOW WATER B   569
   AND TILL HIS INTELLECT GROWS SURE . . . . 633 MAN AND ECHO   30
SURELY
   I CRIED, "THOU ART SURELY A WARRIOR, FORGETTING HIS FAMOUS   51 OISIN 3   V   61
     LINE.
   A GOOD NAME IS GOODLY TO HEAR OF, AND A GOOD NAME SURELY   51 OISIN 3   V   63
     IS THINE.
   SHE SAYS MY MAN WILL SURELY COME, ... 96 MOLL MAGEE   41
   WHERE TIME WOULD SURELY FORGET US, AND SORROW COME NEAR   122 WHITE BIRDS   10
     US NO MORE!
   WHERE SURELY TIME WOULD FORGET US AND SORROW COME NEAR   122 WHITE BIRDS   V   10
     US NO MORE!
   MAY SURELY BARTER GAZE FOR GAZE. . . . . 139 TO IRELAND   28
   MAY SURELY MEET THEIR ANCIENT GAZE. . . . . 139 TO IRELAND   V   28
   SURELY THINE HOUR HAS COME, THY GREAT WIND BLOWS, . . . 170 SECRET ROSE   31
   YET SURELY THERE ARE MEN WHO HAVE MADE THEIR ART . . . 369 EGO DOMINUS   38
   AND SURELY AFTER TWENTY YEARS IT WAS TIME TO COME." . . . 391 UNDER SATURN   14
   SURELY SOME REVELATION IS AT HAND! . . . . 402 SECOND COMING   9
   SURELY THE SECOND COMING IS AT HAND. . . . . 402 SECOND COMING   10
   SURELY AMONG A RICH MAN'S FLOWERING LAWNS, ... 417 ANCEST HOUSES   1
   A STRANGE THING SURELY THAT MY HEART, WHEN LOVE HAD COME   449 OWEN AHERNE   1
     UNSOUGHT
SURETY
   THE SURETY OF ITS HIDDEN ROOT . . . . 134 TWO TREES   7
SURF
   ROSE IN THE DARKNESS, AND THE WHITE SURF GLEAMED . . . . 30 OISIN 2   23
SURFACE
   ARE NEARER TO THE SURFACE OF THE BODY . . . . 464 HARUN RASHID   67
SURGE
   WHITENED AFAR WITH SURGE, FAN-FORMED AND WIDE, ... 31 OISIN 2   28
   WHITENING THE SURGE AFAR, FAN-FORMED AND WIDE, ... 31 OISIN 2   V   28
   WITH SURGE OF PLUMY FIRE, LUNGING I DRAVE . . . . . . 41 OISIN 2   V   181
   AND AT THE SUNDOWN THREW HIM IN THE SURGE, ... 44 OISIN 2   219
   AND IN THE EVE I THREW HIM IN THE SURGE, ... 44 OISIN 2   V   219
   A GREEN DROP IN THE SURGE, A GLEAM OF LIGHT . . . . . 104 FERGUS DRUID   33
SURGED
   HAD SURGED UP IN A PLUMY FIRE, I DRAVE . . . . 41 OISIN 2   181
   SURGED UP IN PLUMY FIRE, I LUNGED AND DRAVE . . . . . 41 OISIN 2   V   181
SURGES
   WHOSE HOOVES THE TOPS OF THE SURGES GRAZED, ... 12 OISIN 1   V 142A
   I STOOD UPON THE STAIR! THE SURGES BORE . . . . 44 OISIN 2   225
   I RODE AWAY ON THE SURGES, WHERE, HIGH AS THE SADDLE-BOW,   57 OISIN 3   147
   I RODE AWAY ON THE SURGES, WHERE HIGH AS THE SADDLE BOW   57 OISIN 3   V   147
   I RODE AWAY ON THE SURGES, WHERE, HIGH AS THE SADDLEBOW,   57 OISIN 3   V   147
   MAKING WAY FROM THE KINDLING SURGES, I RODE ON A   58 OISIN 3   161
     BRIDLE-PATH
   AND HUMMING SANDS, WHERE WINDY SURGES WEND! . . . . . 68 SAD SHEPHERD   4
   THAT SAW THE SURGES RUNNING BY, ... 338 TOM OROUGHLEY   6
SURGING
   AND SURGING PHOSPHORUS ALONE GAVE LIGHT . . . . 31 OISIN 2   33
   OF SURGING PHOSPHORUS ALONE GAVE LIGHT. . . . . 31 OISIN 2   V   33
SURLY
   SURLY AND DISTANT, MIXED INSEPARABLY . . . . 45 OISIN 2   233
   SURLY AND DISTANT, WITH THE WINDS AND SEA!-- . . . . . 45 OISIN 2   V   234
SURMISE
   BUT INWARDLY, SURMISE COMPANIONS . . . . 320 REED WHISPERER   4
SURMOUNT
   SURMOUNT THEIR BONES! BUT SPEAK WHAT NONE HAVE HEARD. . . 555 RIBH AT TOMB   9
SURMOUNTS
   SURMOUNTS THEIR BONES! BUT SPEAK WHAT NONE HAVE HEARD. . . 555 RIBH AT TOMB   V   9
SURPASSING
   AND THERE'S A SCORE OF DUCHESSES, SURPASSING WOMANKIND,   353 HIS PHOENIX   5
   AND THERE'S A SCORE OF DUCHESSES, SURPASSING WOMAN-KIND,   353 HIS PHOENIX   V   5
SURROUNDED
   . . . AN OLD MAN SURROUNDED WITH DREAMS. . . . . . . 61 OISIN 3   196
SUSTAINS
   THIS FALLEN STAR MY MILK SUSTAINS, ... 499 MOTHER OF GOD   12
   SUSTAINS HIS SOUL IN COURAGE OR IN MIGHT. . . . . . . 650 ISLE STAT I 1   144
SWADDLING
   WINDING-SHEET AND SWADDLING CLOTHES. . . . . 530 OLD TOM AGAIN   V   6
SWADDLING-CLOTHES
   WINDING-SHEET AND SWADDLING-CLOTHES. . . . . 530 OLD TOM AGAIN   6
SWALLOW
   COULD KEEP A SWALLOW TO ITS FIRST INTENT! . . . . . . 489 COOLE PARK 29   19
SWALLOW'S
   I MEDITATE UPON A SWALLOW'S FLIGHT, ... 488 COOLE PARK 29   1
SWALLOWS
   THEY CAME LIKE SWALLOWS AND LIKE SWALLOWS WENT, ... 489 COOLE PARK 29   17
   THEY CAME LIKE SWALLOWS AND LIKE SWALLOWS WENT, ... 489 COOLE PARK 29   17
   (SWALLOWS WERE FLASHING THEIR WHITE BREASTS ABOVE . . . 690 MOSADA 1   7
   OH, SWALLOWS, SWALLOWS, SWALLOWS, WILL YE FLY . . . . 699 MOSADA 3   1
   OH, SWALLOWS, SWALLOWS, SWALLOWS, WILL YE FLY . . . . 699 MOSADA 3   1
   OH, SWALLOWS, SWALLOWS, SWALLOWS, WILL YE FLY . . . . 699 MOSADA 3   1
   HEARKEN, YE SWALLOWS!--I HAVE HOARDED UP . . . . . . 699 MOSADA 3   23
SWAM
   WHEN THE FULL MOON SWAM TO ITS GREATEST HEIGHT . . . . 468 HARUN RASHID   151

787

```
                                                      PAGE      TITLE          LINE
SWAM  (CONTINUED)
     SHAKESPEAREAN FISH SWAM THE SEA, FAR AWAY FROM LAND;  • •   485 THREE MOVEMENT      1
     ROMANTIC FISH SWAM IN NETS COMING TO THE HAND;  • • • •    485 THREE MOVEMENT      2
     AND NOT THE BANKS OF OARS THAT SWAM UPON • • • • • •      610 STATUES            13
SWAN
     WHEN THE SWAN MUST FIX HIS EYE • • • • • • • •            414 TOWER             140
     COMPARES THE SOLITARY SOUL TO A SWAN; • • • • • •         430 NINETEEN 19         60
     THE SWAN HAS LEAPED INTO THE DESOLATE HEAVEN!            431 NINETEEN 19         79
     LEDA AND THE SWAN • • • • • • • • • • •                  441 LEDA AND SWAN        T
     BOOK III  DOVE OR SWAN I.  LEDA • • • • • •              441 LEDA AND SWAN   V    T
     BOOK V:  DOVE OR SWAN  I  LEDA • • • • •                 441 LEDA AND SWAN        T
     FOR EVEN DAUGHTERS OF THE SWAN CAN SHARE • • • •         444 SCHOOL CHILDR       20
     AT SUDDEN THUNDER OF THE MOUNTING SWAN • • • •           490 COOLE BALLYLEE      14
     WHERE THE SWAN DRIFTS UPON A DARKENING FLOOD• • •        492 COOLE BALLYLEE      48
SWAN'S
     THE HORNS AND SHIELDS AND WILD SWAN'S PINIONS; • • •      82 MAD KING GOLL   V    5
SWANS
     AND SWANS WITH THEIR EXULTANT THROATS! • • • • •          14 OISIN 1            192
     TWO SWANS CAME FLYING UP TO HIM, • • • • • •            194 BAILE AILLINN      135
     I KNOW OF THE SLEEPY COUNTRY, WHERE SWANS FLY ROUND • •  204 WITHER BOUGHS       17
     THE WILD SWANS AT COOLE • • • • • • • •                 322 SWANS AT COOLE       T
     ARE NINE-AND-FIFTY SWANS. • • • • • • •                 322 SWANS AT COOLE       6
     ARE NINE AND FIFTY SWANS. • • • • • • •                 322 SWANS AT COOLE  V    6
SWARD
     AND UNTO IT WE'LL DANCE UPON THE SWARD. • • • • •        681 SEEKER              10
SWARM
     BEHOLD, HOW LIKE A SWARM OF FIERY BEES • • • • •         662 ISLE STAT II 2       1
     HIDING THE REBELS SWARM IN YONDER WOOD • • • • •         709 FERENCZ RENYI   V   14
SWARMING
     OR CLUNG THEREON LIKE SWARMING BEES; • • • • • •          14 OISIN 1            181
     LIKE SWARMING BEES, ONE WITH THE DOVE • • • • •           78 INDIAN TO LOVE  V   16
SWARMS
     OR CLUNG AS CLOSE AS SWARMS OF BEES, • • • • • •          14 OISIN 1         V  181
SWAY
     'TIS OVER: FAR WITH MEMORY I SWAY AND ROCK. • • •         43 OISIN 2         V  212
     HIS FINGERS MOVE AND SWAY, • • • • • • •                  98 FOXHUNTER           30
     THOUGH DRUNKEN WITH THE FLAGS THAT SWAY • • • • •        212 BLESS PSALTER        5
SWAYED
     SWAYED, CROONING TO HIMSELF AN UNKNOWN TONGUE! • • •      39 OISIN 2            159
     LAID HANDS ON THE BELL-BRANCH AND SWAYED IT, • • •        51 OISIN 3             56
     THEN HE SWAYED IN HIS FINGERS THE BELL-BRANCH, • • •      51 OISIN 3             67
     IN GRIEF SWAYED TO AND FRO. • • • • • • •               133 FR GILLIGAN         36
     I SWAYED UPON THE GAUDY STERN • • • • • •               253 HIS DREAM            1
     I SWAYED MY LEAVES AND FLOWERS IN THE SUN; • • •        261 COMING WISDOM        3
     O BODY SWAYED TO MUSIC, O BRIGHTENING GLANCE, • • •      446 SCHOOL CHILDR       63
     O BODY SWAYED TO MUSIC BRIGHTENING GLANCE • • •          446 SCHOOL CHILDR   V   63
     HAVE NOT A MYRIAD SWAYED BELOW STRANGE TREES • • •       724 KANVA ON SELF       11
SWAYING
     BENT ALL OUR SWAYING BODIES DOWN, • • • • •              20 OISIN 1            297
     AND KISSED MY EYES, AND, SWAYING HER BRIGHT HEAD • •      29 OISIN 2              6
     AND NOW SANG NIAM, SWAYING HER BRIGHT HEAD • •            29 OISIN 2         V   -6
     SO SANG YOUNG NIAM, SWAYING HER BRIGHT HEAD, • •          30 OISIN 2         V   15
     A PARROT SWAYING ON A TREE • • • • • • •                 77 INDIAN TO LOVE  V    4
     THE DRUIDS CHANTED, SWAYING IN THEIR HANDS • • •        111 CUCHULAIN SEA   V   82
     THE DRUIDS CHAUNTED, SWAYING IN THEIR HANDS • • •       111 CUCHULAIN SEA   V   82
     IN SONG, FROM GOBLIN WATERS SWAYING WHITE, • • •        657 ISLE STAT I 3       51
     ON THEIR SWAYING BLADES OF GRASS, • • • • •             705 DAWN-SONG           14
SWAYS
     A PARROT SWAYS UPON A TREE, • • • • • • •                77 INDIAN TO LOVE       4
SWEAR
     VIJAYA, SWEAR TO HER LOVE NEVER MORE. • • •              74 ANASHU VIJAYA       65
     AY, AY.  SWEAR BY THE PARENTS OF THE GODS, • • •         74 ANASHU VIJAYA       66
     SWEAR!  BY THE PARENTS OF THE GODS, I SWEAR. • • •       75 ANASHU VIJAYA       76
     SWEAR!  BY THE PARENTS OF THE GODS, I SWEAR. • • •       75 ANASHU VIJAYA       76
     PROTECT ME NOW, GODS THAT MY PEOPLE SWEAR BY. • •       241 SHADOW WATER B     396
     I SWEAR BEFORE THE DAWN COMES ROUND AGAIN • •           260 FASC DIFFICULT      12
     ON A FANTASTIC RIDE I SWEAR MY HORSE'S FLANKS WERE SPURRED  391 UNDER SATURN  V    6
     I SWEAR TO GOD I QUESTIONED THEM, AND ALL THEY HAD TO SAY   593 PILGRIM           14
     I SWEAR TO GOD I QUESTIONED THEM ALL AND ALL THEY HAD TO    593 PILGRIM       V   14
       SAY
     AND ALL MEN HEARD THEM SWEAR • • • • • • •              596 COLONEL MARTIN      60
     SWEAR BY WHAT THE SAGES SPOKE • • • • • •               636 BEN BULBEN           1
     SWEAR BY THOSE HORSEMEN, BY THOSE WOMEN • • •            637 BEN BULBEN           5
     GRIEF NEEDS MUCH FEEDING THEN.  OF HIM I SWEAR • •       659 ISLE STAT II 1      20
     BY BOSKY JUNE I SWEAR, AND BY THE BEE, HER MINISTER. •   661 ISLE STAT II 1      74
     I WILL SWEAR BY SUN AND MOON TO PARDON ALL • •           756 SHADOW WATER A     183
     AND WILL YOU SWEAR NEVER TO BE AVENGED • • • •           758 SHADOW WATER A     223
     I SWEAR IT, THOUGH I GLADLY WOULD LIE DOWN • • •         758 SHADOW WATER A     225
     AND WILL YOU SWEAR IT BY THE SUN AND MOON? • • •         758 SHADOW WATER A     229
     I SWEAR IT.  LET EVERY MAN DRAW OUT HIS SWORD. • •       758 SHADOW WATER A     230
SWEARS
     SWEARS THAT HE HEARS THE KING'S GREAT HORN. • •          636 BLACK TOWER         24
SWEAT
     OF OUR STRONG STEEDS WAS DARK WITH SWEAT, • • •            2 OISIN 1         V  7T
     SHIVER UNDER THE LASH, STRAIN, SWEAT AND JOLT • • •      260 FASC DIFFICULT       7
     EVEN LIKE THESE TO RAIL AND SWEAT • • • • •              294 HATED PLAYBOY        5
     AND LIKE THESE TO RAIL AND SWEAT • • • •                 294 HATED PLAYBOY   V    5
     A DEAL I'D SWEAT AND LITTLE EARN • • • • •               331 ROUND TOWER          2
     THE NIGHT CAN SWEAT WITH TERROR AS BEFORE • • •          429 NINETEEN 19         29
SWEATING
     THEY BORE IT WITH STAGGERING AND SWEATING, • • • •        60 OISIN 3            186
```

788

	PAGE	TITLE		LINE
SWEATING (CONTINUED)				
WITH SWEATING, WITH STAGGERING, ...	60	OISIN 3	V	185
SWEEP				
HEARING HELL LOUD WITH A MURMUR, AS SHOUTING AND MOCKING WE SWEEP.	62	OISIN 3		208
AND THEN I MUST SCRUB AND BAKE AND SWEEP	150	OLD MOTHER		3
AND THEN I MUST MEND AND BAKE AND SWEEP	150	OLD MOTHER	V	3
AND THOSE WHITE GLIMMERING FRAGMENTS OF THE MIST SWEEP BY.	426	PHANTOM HATRED		6
WITH PURPLE SANDALS SWEEP THE GRAVE-EYED HOURS--	705	REMEMBRANCE		5
SWEEPING				
CAME NOW THE SLIDING OF TEARS AND SWEEPING OF MIST-COLD HAIR,	47	OISIN 3		7
CAME NOW THE SLIDING OF TEARS AND SWEEPING OF MIST-COLD AIR,	47	OISIN 3	V	7
CAME NOW THE SLIDING OF TEARS AND SWEEPING OF MIST COLD HAIR,	47	OISIN 3	V	7
A MIST THAT IS LIKE BLOWN SNOW IS SWEEPING OVER ALL, . .	425	PHANTOM HATRED		2
SWEEPINGS				
A MOUND OF REFUSE OR THE SWEEPINGS OF A STREET, ...	630	CIRCUS ANIMALS		35
A MOUND OF REFUSE OR THE SWEEPINGS OF THE STREET, . . .	630	CIRCUS ANIMALS	V	35
SWEEPS				
WHAT GREAT TOMB-HAUNTER SWEEPS THE DISTANT SKY	618	BRONZE HEAD		4
NOR TREMBLE TO ITS FALL. THE FIRE SWEEPS ROUND	689	NETTLESHIP		11
SWEET SEE HONEY-SWEET BITTER-SWEET				
THEREON DID SHE LOOK HAUGHTY AND SWEET:	6	OISIN 1		54
WITH LAUGHTER LOW, AND TENDER, AND SWEET!	6	OISIN 1	V	54
SHE SAID, WITH LAUGHTER TENDER AND SWEET!	6	OISIN 1	V	54
AMONG THE WOODLAND GRASSES SWEET, ...	15	OISIN 1	V	199
THUS ON THE WATERS, FAR AND SWEET, ...	26	OISIN 1	V	398A
OF THE THINGS THAT HIS HEART STILL KNOWS WERE SWEET-- . .	26	OISIN 1	V	402
AND NAMED HIM BY SWEET NAMES. A FOAMING TIDE	30	OISIN 2		27
FULL MANY MORE, WHEN PEERED A MAIDEN SWEET	33	OISIN 2	V	68F
AH, SWEET TO ME NOW WERE EVEN BALD CONAN'S SLANDEROUS TONGUE!	55	OISIN 3		116
I SAT AND MUSED AND DRANK SWEET WINE:	82	MAD KING GOLL		13
"WITH HIM IS ONE SWEET THROATED LIKE A BIRD, ...	106	CUCHULAIN SEA	V	16
I HAVE OFTEN HEARD THE SWEET SOUND OF HIS BOW.	109	CUCHULAIN SEA	V	50
I OFTEN HEAR THE SWEET SOUND OF HIS BOW.	109	CUCHULAIN SEA	V	50
THEN CONCOBAR SENT THAT SWEET THROATED MAID	110	CUCHULAIN SEA	V	72
THE BELL THAT CALLS US ON: THE SWEET FAR THING.	115	ROSE OF BATTLE		28
GROW SWEET WITH HIS MOOD.	118	CRADLE SONG	V	8
O SWEET EVERLASTING VOICES, BE STILL:	141	EVERLAST VOICE		1
O SWEET EVERLASTING VOICES, BE STILL.	141	EVERLAST VOICE		8
AND MANY A SWEET THING SAID, ...	144	HOST OF AIR		18
THE TONGUE OF IT SWEET WITH DREAMING	160	CAP AND BELLS	V	17
A CHATTERING WISE AND SWEET, ...	161	CAP AND BELLS		34
"THE ROSE THAT MUST DROP, OUT OF SWEET LEAVES, ...	168	BLESSED	V	37
TILL THE ATTORNEY FOR LOST SOULS CRY HER SWEET CRY, . . .	173	SPEAKS HEARERS		6
TILL MAURYA OF THE WOUNDED HEART CRY A SWEET CRY, . . .	173	SPEAKS HEARERS	V	6
WORTH KNITTING TO A MEASURE OF SWEET SOUND?	181	QUEEN MAEVE		33
OR TWO SWEET BLOSSOMING APPLE-BOUGHS	195	BAILE AILLINN		153
OR TWO SWEET BLOSSOMING APPLE BOUGHS	195	BAILE AILLINN	V	153
WITH ITS SWEET BLOSSOM WHERE HERS WAS:	197	BAILE AILLINN		190
FOR TO ARTICULATE SWEET SOUNDS TOGETHER	205	ADAMS CURSE		10
ON FINDING THAT HER VOICE IS SWEET AND LOW	205	ADAMS CURSE		17
SWEET WITH ALL MUSIC, OUT OF HIS LONG HAIR, ...	219	HARP OF AENGUS		8
BY THE SWEET NAME OF DEATH.	254	HIS DREAM		12
BY THE SWEET NAME OF DEATH.	254	HIS DREAM		20
TO HAVE LIT UPON AS CLEAN AND SWEET A TALE	258	KING NO KING		8
AND THE SWEET LAUGHING EAGLE THOUGHTS THAT GROW	264	HOUSE SHAKEN		5
A SWEET, MIRACULOUS, TERRIFYING SOUND.	277	TWO KINGS		17
A SINGLE SOUL THAT LACKS A SWEET CRYSTALLINE CRY. . . .	291	PAUDEEN		8
THE LINEAMENTS, A HEART THAT LAUGHTER HAS MADE SWEET, . .	315	FALLEN MAJESTY		5
THE LINEAMENTS, THE HEART THAT LAUGHTER HAS MADE SWEET, .	315	FALLEN MAJESTY	V	5
TILL TOES MASTERED A SWEET MEASURE, ...	331	ROUND TOWER		15
MOUTH MASTERED A SWEET SOUND, ...	331	ROUND TOWER		16
AND MAKE THE DAYLIGHT SWEET ONCE MORE: BUT WHEN . . .	339	SHEP GOATHERD		13
OF SORROWFUL, AUSTERE, SWEET, LOFTY PIPE TUNES.	341	SHEP GOATHERD		57
THE HORN'S SWEET NOTE AND THE TOOTH OF THE HOUND. . . .	380	SONGS FOOL 1		12
THE HORN'S SWEET NOTE AND THE TOOTH OF THE HOUND. . . .	381	SONGS FOOL 2		14
SWEET AND HARSH, HARSH AND SWEET, ...	382	SONG OF FOOL		10
SWEET AND HARSH, HARSH AND SWEET, ...	382	SONG OF FOOL		10
WHAT VOICE MORE SWEET THAN HERS	392	EASTER 1916		21
SWEET VOICED AND BEAUTIFUL, ...	392	EASTER 1916	V	22
SO DARING AND SWEET HIS THOUGHT.	393	EASTER 1916		30
SHE SEEMED TO HAVE GROWN CLEAN AND SWEET	397	POLIT PRISONER		17
BUT BECKONED TO SWEET COMPANY.	400	DEMON BEAST		18
AND THAT ITS OWN SWEET WILL IS HEAVEN'S WILL:	405	FOR DAUGHTER		69
AND KNEW THAT SWEET EXTREMITY OF PRIDE	471	ALL SOUL NIGHT		22
BATHED IN MIRACULOUS OIL, SWEET ODOURS FROM IT COME, . .	503	VACILLATION		81
MIND'S BREAD GROW SWEET.	554	CHURCH STATE		6
WITH THAT SWEET CRY.	559	HE AND SHE		12
SWEET DANCER	568	SWEET DANCER		T
AH, DANCER, AH, SWEET DANCER!	568	SWEET DANCER		7
AH, DANCER, AH, SWEET DANCER!	568	SWEET DANCER		14
WASH: MAKE YOUR BODY SWEET:	572	LADYS 2ND SONG		4
THEIR CRIES ARE SWEET AND STRANGE, ...	612	NEWS ORACLE		18
THE WOMEN THAT I PICKED SPOKE SWEET AND LOW	622	HOUND VOICE		8
MAKES ME SWEET MUSIC	627	STATES HOLIDAY		24
TO WELCOME THEE, NASCHINA, WITH SWEET SINGING.	645	ISLE STAT I 1		7
WITH SINGING SWEET AS E'ER ROUND LAKE-LULLED ISLE . . .	649	ISLE STAT I 1		106

789

	PAGE	TITLE		LINE
SWEET (CONTINUED)				
WILD CRIES, GROWN SWEET WITH LULLS AND LINGERINGS LONG.	674	ISLE STAT II 3		222
I NEVER KNEW A NIGHT SO HONEY SWEET.	702	MOSADA 3	V	99
WHITE, RENYI SILENT STANDS; THAT MAIDEN SWEET	713	FERENCZ RENYI	V	84
"I AM LONE LADY QUIETNESS, MY SWEET,	716	DWELT SYCAMORE		13
AND SMILING FROM SWEET THOUGHT,	741	EARL PAUL		42
DARK JOAN CALL THE BERRIES SWEET,	743	DANAAN QUICK		28
SWEET WITH ALL MUSIC, OUT OF HIS LONG HAIR,	762	SHADOW WATER A		303
HATRED MAY BE SWEET TO THE TASTE."	776	AGAINST WITCH		31
HATRED MAY BE SWEET IN THE TASTE."	776	AGAINST WITCH	V	31
IN THAT SWEET WANDERING SNARE.	783	GREY ROUND		10
SWEETEN				
THAT SANG, TO SWEETEN IRELAND'S WRONG,	137	TO IRELAND		3
WHO SANG TO SWEETEN IRELAND'S WRONG,	137	TO IRELAND	V	3
SWEETEN THE LITTLE HALFWAY HOUSE	567	LAPIS LAZULI	V	48
SWEETENED				
SWEETENED BY DEATH, BUT IF I COULD BELIEVE,	285	TWO KINGS		205
SWEETENS				
SWEETENS THE LITTLE HALF-WAY HOUSE	567	LAPIS LAZULI		48
SWEETER				
AND SWEETER OF VOICE THAN THE PLEASANT BIRDS,	9	OISIN 1	V	95
AND FIND THEIR LAUGHTER SWEETER TO THE TASTE	228	SHADOW WATER B		134
SWEETER EMOTION, WORKING IN THEIR VEINS	292	TO A SHADE		13
OF SWEETER IGNORANCE."	343	SHEP GOATHERD		112
HAD FOUND A SWEETER WORD.	539	MEETING		18
"YOUR LIFE CAN GROW MUCH SWEETER IF YOU WILL	634	CUCHULAIN COMF		12
SWEETEST				
AND CALLED HIM SWEETEST NAMES AND SOOTHED HIS FEARS.	30	OISIN 2	V	27
WHOM MEN HAVE NAMED ARCADIA'S SWEETEST TONGUE.	649	ISLE STAT I 1		109
FOR THAT'S THE SWEETEST MUSIC FOR SAD SOULS.	702	MOSADA 3		85
"OR SEEK WHERE SWEETEST WATER BUBBLES,	731	PRIEST FAIRY		79
SWEETHEART				
AND HIS YOUNG SWEETHEART CLOSE BESIDE HIM KNELT,	108	CUCHULAIN SEA		40
SAID, "AENGUS AND HIS SWEETHEART GIVE THEIR THANKS	187	QUEEN MAEVE		146
SWEETHEART, DO NOT LOVE TOO LONG!	211	O DO NOT LOVE		1
A SWEETHEART FROM ANOTHER LIFE FLOATS THERE	390	IMAGE PAST		22
SWEETHEARTS'				
AMONG THOSE MOUTHS THAT SING THEIR SWEETHEARTS' PRAISE,	285	TWO KINGS		185
SWEETLY				
THE SUN WAS LAUGHING SWEETLY,	214	HAPPY TOWNLAND		15
THE SUN WAS LAUGHING SWEETLY,	215	HAPPY TOWNLAND		35
THE SUN WAS LAUGHING SWEETLY,	216	HAPPY TOWNLAND		55
AND TROD SO SWEETLY PROUD	255	WOMAN HOMER		17
SWEETNESS SEE BITTER-SWEETNESS				
WE SHALL MINGLE NO MORE, NOR OUR GAZES EMPTY THEIR	56	OISIN 3		132
SWEETNESS LONE				
AND LIFE IS OVER SAVE THE MURMUR AND THE SWEETNESS.	77	INDIAN TO LOVE	V	5E
AND ALL IS OVER SAVE THE MURMUR AND THE SWEETNESS.	77	INDIAN TO LOVE	V	5E
AND THE SWEETNESS OF DESIRE.	168	BLESSED		38
ALL THAT SWEETNESS AMID STRENGTH?"	259	PEACE		9
THE BITTER SWEETNESS OF FALSE FACES?	275	GREY ROCK		113
SO GREAT A SWEETNESS FLOWS	316	FRIENDS		27
CHILLED BLOOD, THIS SWEETNESS BROUGHT!	401	DEMON BEAST		39
O WHAT A SWEETNESS STRAYED	401	DEMON BEAST		43
THE SWEETNESS THAT ALL LONGED FOR NIGHT AND DAY,	418	ANCEST HOUSES		20
OF THEIR OWN SWEETNESS, BODIES OF THEIR LOVELINESS.	426	PHANTOM HATRED		24
DRUNK WITH THE BITTER SWEETNESS OF HER YOUTH.	469	HARUN RASHID		186
SO GREAT A SWEETNESS FLOWS INTO THE BREAST	479	SELF AND SOUL		69
THE INTELLECTUAL SWEETNESS OF THOSE LINES	489	COOLE PARK 29		23
WHERE HAD HER SWEETNESS GONE?	503	QUARREL IN AGE		1
OVERCOME--O BITTER SWEETNESS,	540	FROM ANTIGONE		1
THE BITTER SWEETNESS OF THE NIGHT	781	HEART FRIGHT		3
SWEETSHOP				
WITH FACE AND NOSE PRESSED TO A SWEETSHOP WINDOW.	370	EGO DOMINUS	V	56
SWEET-SHOP				
WITH FACE AND NOSE PRESSED TO A SWEET-SHOP WINDOW,	370	EGO DOMINUS		56
SWEET-SOUNDING				
BUT THAT SWEET-SOUNDING VOICE RAN ON: "WOMAN,	284	TWO KINGS		165
SWEET-THROATED				
"WITH HIM IS ONE SWEET-THROATED LIKE A BIRD."	106	CUCHULAIN SEA		16
THEN CONCHUBAR SENT THAT SWEET-THROATED MAID,	110	CUCHULAIN SEA		72
SWEET-TONGUED				
IT HAD GROWN SWEET-TONGUED BY DREAMING	160	CAP AND BELLS		17
SWELLING				
AND ALL THEIR SWELLING CANVAS WEAR,	530	OLD TOM AGAIN		2
SWEPT SEE CLEAN-SWEPT				
AND SWEPT OUT OF THE WATTLED HALL	20	OISIN 1		292
SWEPT ON THE DANCE'S LINKED FLOW,	20	OISIN 1	V	291
THE SEA SWEPT ON AND CRIED HER OLD CRY STILL,	68	SAD SHEPHERD		10
BESIDES HER CLEAN SWEPT HEARTH, HER QUIET SHADE:	114	ROSE OF BATTLE	V	11
SWEPT THE SAWDUST FROM THE FLOOR	440	WISDOM		6
AND AFTER, SWEPT FROM THERE,	453	DEATH OF HARE		10
AND SWEPT THE HOUSE AND SANG ABOUT HER WORK	468	HARUN RASHID		148
AND ONCE AGAIN SHE ROSE AND SWEPT THE HOUSE	468	HARUN RASHID		159
WHEN SEA-WIND SWEPT THE CORNER, STANDS:	566	LAPIS LAZULI		32
NO FOX CAN FOUL THE LAIR THE BADGER SWEPT--	603	GALLERY REVIS		39
SWERVED				
LET THE FOOLS RAGE, I SWERVED IN NAUGHT,	577	WHAT THEN		18
SWIFT				
THE SWIFT INNUMERABLE SPEARS,	2	OISIN 1		6
AND NOW A MAID, ON A SWIFT BROWN STEED	12	OISIN 1	V	142

SWIFT   (CONTINUED)
    BUT NIAMH WITH A SWIFT DISTRESS . . . .   15 C''IN 1   211
    WITH A SWIFT AND FRIENDLY GLANCE . . . .   21 OISIN 1   309
    "SWIFT ARE THE YEARS OF A WARRIOR'S PRIDE! . . . .   26 OISIN 1   V 399A
    BEFORE THE SWIFT THINGS THAT SHE DREAMED OF WERE DONE . .   27 OISIN 1   414
    ERE HALF THE SWIFT THINGS THAT SHE DREAMT ON WERE DONE,   28 OISIN 1   V 422
    O SWIFT ON THE SEAS ALL DAY AND NIGHT . . . .   70 CLOAK BOAT   8
    WAS DRIVING CATTLE CAME SHE WITH SWIFT FEET, ...   106 CUCHULAIN SEA V   19
    OF THEIR LONG WINGS, THE FLASH OF THEIR SWIFT FEET. . .   137 TO SOME I TALK V   16
    THE RIDERS UPON THE SWIFT HORSES . . . .   266 GALWAY RACES   V   3
    RIDERS UPON THE SWIFT HORSES, ...   266 GALWAY RACES   V   3
    SWIFT BEATING ON HIS BREAST IN SIBYLLINE FRENZY BLIND . .   481 BLOOD AND MOON   19
    GOLDSMITH AND BURKE, SWIFT AND THE BISHOP OF CLOYNE . .   486 SEVEN SAGES   9
    THE TOMB OF SWIFT WEARS IT AWAY. A VOICE . . . . . .   487 SEVEN SAGES   21
    SWIFT HAS SAILED INTO HIS REST! . . . .   493 SWIFTS EPITAPH   1
    SWIFT HAD SAILED INTO HIS REST! . . . .   493 SWIFTS EPITAPH V   1
    BUT HEAVY FRUIT. HOW SWIFT THE ARGUMENT . . . . . .   665 ISLE STAT II 2   66
    O SWIFT ON THE SEAS ALL DAY AND NIGHT . . . .   666 ISLE STAT II 3   8
    SWIFT LAKE. A VERY LITTLE THING THAT IS, ...   669 ISLE STAT II 3   78
    CHECK. AH! HOW BRIGHT YOUR EYES. HOW SWIFT YOUR MOVES.   722 WITCH VIVIEN   61
SWIFTER
    A SWIFTER CREATURE NEVER WAS BORN, ...   2 OISIN 1   V 7Q
    AND SWIFTER THAN THE SALMON HERDS! . . . .   9 OISIN 1   V 96
SWIFTEST
    "THE SWIFTEST HE TO DANCE OR FLY, ...   729 PRIEST FAIRY   45
SWIFTLY
    YON TALL ONE EYES MY SUPPER! SWIFTLY CHASE HIM . . . .   72 ANASHU VIJAYA V   34
    NEVER STORM AROSE SO SWIFTLY! SCARCE THE CHILDREN WERE   718 PHANTOM SHIP   4
        IN BED,
    TALKING HOURS SWIFTLY PASS! . . . .   727 LOVERS QUARREL   44
SWIFT'S
    SWIFT'S EPITAPH . . . .   493 SWIFTS EPITAPH   T
    "JONATHAN SWIFT'S AT REST! . . . .   493 SWIFTS EPITAPH V   1
    THROUGH JONATHAN SWIFT'S DARK GROVE HE PASSED, AND THERE   543 PARN FUNERAL 2   11
SWIM
    "'TIS JOY MAKES SWIM THE SAPPY TIDE, ...   18 OISIN 1   V 261
    WHAT SHALL I CALL THEM? FISH THAT SWIM, ...   195 BAILE AILLINN   144
    MONSTROUS FAMILIAR IMAGES SWIM TO THE MIND'S EYE. . . .   426 PHANTOM HATRED   8
    ALL THAT COULD RUN OR LEAP OR SWIM . . . .   528 DANCER CRUACH   6
    ALL THAT RUN OR LEAP OR SWIM . . . .   528 DANCER CRUACH V   6
    BEHOLD THAT GREAT PLOTINUS SWIM, ...   530 DELPHIC ORACLE   1
    ALL SWIM WITH TEARS. THE FAERY BOAT'S AT HAND! . . .   663 ISLE STAT II 2   33
SWIMMING
    CAME SWIMMING SADLY DOWN THE MIGHTY STAIR. . . . . .   32 OISIN 2   V 50B
    A MERMAID FOUND A SWIMMING LAD, ...   452 MERMAID   1
    IT SEEMED A GOLD-FISH SWIMMING IN A BOWL. . . . . . .   472 ALL SOUL NIGHT   40
    WHO, SWIMMING, SOUGHT THE ISLAND LONE! . . . .   673 ISLE STAT II 3   181
SWIMS
    THE FAERY SHIP THAT SWIMS ATHWART THE SKY. . . . . .   663 ISLE STAT II 2   16
SWINE
    CRYING, THE PIRATES DROVE HIS SWINE . . . .   82 MAD KING GOLL   15
    WHIPS TO THE SEA THE COWS AND SWINE." . . . .   82 MAD KING GOLL V   16
    TO MIND HIS COWS AND SWINE BY THE RED LAKE. . . . . .   752 SHADOW WATER A   112
SWINEHERD
    AND SAID, "I AM THAT SWINEHERD WHOM YOU BID . . . . .   105 CUCHULAIN SEA   3
    "I AM ALEEL, THE SWINEHERD, WHOM YOU BID . . . . . .   105 CUCHULAIN SEA V   3A
    THAT SWINEHERD STARED UPON HER FACE AND SAID, ...   106 CUCHULAIN SEA   9
    LOOKING ON HER, ALEEL, THE SWINEHERD, SAID! . . . . .   106 CUCHULAIN SEA V   9
    ALEEL, THE SWINEHERD, WEPT AND CAST HIM DOWN . . . .   106 CUCHULAIN SEA V   14
SWING
    SORRY PLACE, WHERE FOR SWING OF THE WAR-AXE IN MY DIM EYES   61 OISIN 3   194
    . . .
    EVEN WHERE HORRIBLE GREEN PARROTS CALL AND SWING. . . .   442 BLACK CENTAUR   2
    EVEN WHERE THE HORRIBLE GREEN PARROTS CALL AND SWING. . .   442 BLACK CENTAUR V   2
SWINGING
    SWINGING, SWINGING ALONG. . . . .   544 TO SAME TUNE 1 V   REF
    SWINGING, SWINGING ALONG. . . . .   544 TO SAME TUNE 1 V   REF
SWIRLED
    SHOUTED. WITH FIRE OF HAIR ABOUT HER SWIRLED, ...   38 OISIN 2   V 134
SWISH
    COME SWISH AROUND, MY PRETTY PUNK, ...   591 DRUNK SOBRIETY   1
SWOLLEN
    O HEAVY SWOLLEN WATERS, BRIM THE FALL OF THE OAK TREES,   207 HANRAHANS SONG V   11
    LIKE HEAVY SWOLLEN WATERS ARE OUR BODIES AND OUR BLOOD!   208 HANRAHANS SONG V   13
SWOON
    HE FELL INTO A DRUID SWOON. . . . .   20 OISIN 1   289
    LOCKE SANK INTO A SWOON! . . . .   439 FRAGMENTS   1
SWOONING
    HURLS THEIR SWOONING LUSTRE UP. . . . .   647 ISLE STAT I 1   49
SWOOPS
    AND DOWN I CAME AS A FALCON SWOOPS . . . .   673 ISLE STAT II 3   178
SWOP
    AGREED THEIR CLOTHES TO SWOP, ...   595 COLONEL MARTIN   20
SWORD
    FROM MACE AND SWORD AND POLE-AXE, LONG AGO . . . . .   31 OISIN 2   30
    BY MACE AND SPEAR AND SWORD OF SEA-GODS, NAILS . . . .   31 OISIN 2   V 30A
    LAID IT AND SIGHED! I HELD A SWORD WHOSE SHINE . . . .   37 OISIN 2   126
    LAID IT AND SIGHED---A SWORD WHOSE WIZARD SHINE . . . .   37 OISIN 2   V 126
    THE STRANGER WATCHED THE SWORD! BUT NIAM FAR, ...   38 OISIN 2   V 136
    OF SWORD AND BRAZEN BATTLE-AXE, WHILE DAY . . . . .   40 OISIN 2   171
    AND WHEN HE KNEW THE SWORD OF MANANNAN . . . . . .   40 OISIN 2   173

		PAGE	TITLE	LINE

SWORD (CONTINUED)

	PAGE	TITLE		LINE
MINGLING OF SWORD AND WAR-AXE, WHILE THE DAY	40	OISIN 2	V	171
THE DRUID SWORD OF MANANAN, HE GREW	40	OISIN 2	V	174
THE DEAD GOD'S SWORD, TO MANY FORMS HE GREW,	40	OISIN 2	V	175
AND ON THESE HANDS THAT MAY NOT LIFT THE SWORD,	103	FERGUS DRUID		24
UPON A SWORD, A FIR-TREE ON A HILL,	104	FERGUS DRUID		34
UPON A SWORD, A FIR TREE ON A HILL,	104	FERGUS DRUID	V	34
AT THE SWORD POINT, AND BADE ME BRING HIM ONE	109	CUCHULAIN SEA	V	53
AT THE SWORD POINT, AND WAITS TILL WE HAVE FOUND	109	CUCHULAIN SEA	V	53
THAT YOU CAME HERE TO MEET THIS ANCIENT SWORD?"	109	CUCHULAIN SEA	V	61
AND WITH THE CLASHING OF THEIR SWORD BLADES MAKE	137	TO SOME I TALK	V	13
A SWORD UPON HIS IRON KNEES,	156	FORGOT BEAUTY	V	23
CAULDRON AND SPEAR AND STONE AND SWORD,	196	BAILE AILLINN		165
A SHADOW DOES NOT CARRY SWORD OR SPEAR.	224	SHADOW WATER B		44
IF YOU WILL DRAW THAT SWORD OUT OF ITS SCABBARD	225	SHADOW WATER B		78
COMES CRYING, "I HAVE RUN UPON THE SWORD.	234	SHADOW WATER B		261
AND SAYS: "A SWORD BLADE PIERCED ME IN MY SLEEP."	234	SHADOW WATER B	V	257
WHERE IS MY SWORD THAT FELL OUT OF MY HAND	241	SHADOW WATER B		397
WHY DO YOU NEED A SWORD? BUT YOU MAY KEEP IT.	241	SHADOW WATER B		400
THIS SWORD IS TO LIE BESIDE HIM IN THE GRAVE.	242	SHADOW WATER B		412
I'LL DO IT FOR HIS SAKE. NO. TAKE THIS SWORD	250	SHADOW WATER B		591
FAREWELL! FAREWELL! THE SWORD IS IN THE ROPE—	251	SHADOW WATER B		595
THAT ONE BELIEVED HE HAD A SWORD UPSTAIRS:	267	ALL TEMPT ME		8
AS THOUGH TO SAY "IT IS THE SWORD ELSEWHERE,"	267	ALL TEMPT ME	V	8
THAT THINK SWORD STROKES WERE BETTER MEANT	276	GREY ROCK	V	129
THEN DREW HIS SWORD TO HOLD ITS LEVELLED POINT	277	TWO KINGS		14
HORN LOCKED IN SWORD, THEY TUGGED AND STRUGGLED THERE	277	TWO KINGS		18
BUT DREW HIS SWORD, AND THOUGHT WITH LEVELLED POINT	277	TWO KINGS	V	14
TO STAY THE STAG'S NEXT RUSH. WHEN SWORD MET HORN	277	TWO KINGS	V	15
THE ENTRAILS OF THE HORSE. DROPPING HIS SWORD	278	TWO KINGS		23
THROUGH THE ENTRAILS OF THE HORSE. DROPPING HIS SWORD	278	TWO KINGS	V	23
SAT UPRIGHT WITH A SWORD BEFORE HER FEET.	279	TWO KINGS		62
AS ON THE BLUE LIGHT OF A SWORD, A MAN	283	TWO KINGS		148
WHERE SATO'S GIFT, A CHANGELESS SWORD,	421	MY TABLE		2
AND SEEMED UNCHANGING LIKE THE SWORD.	421	MY TABLE		21
A GLITTERING SWORD OUT OF THE EAST. A PUFF OF WIND	426	PHANTOM HATRED		5
BID THE GHOST HAVE SWORD IN FIST:	435	FOR MY SON		9
BID THE GHOST HAVE SWORD IN HAND:	435	FOR MY SON	V	9
THE CONSECRATED SWORD UPON MY KNEES	477	SELF AND SOUL	V	9
IS SATO'S ANCIENT SWORD, STILL AS IT WAS,	477	SELF AND SOUL	V	10
GOLD-SOWN SILK ON THE SWORD BLADE:	484	SYMBOLS	V	5
OLD CIVILISATIONS PUT TO THE SWORD.	566	LAPIS LAZULI		27
LONG ERE AN ARROW WHIZZED OR SWORD LEFT SHEATH	650	ISLE STAT I 1		135
THE BROWN WEED BURDEN, SO THE SWORD BRINGS FEAR	660	ISLE STAT II 1		45
HE'LL SNAP HIS SWORD. RAISED IS THE LION'S PAW.	664	ISLE STAT II 2		63
WITHIN HIS CLENCHED TEETH A SWORD,	673	ISLE STAT II 3		182
I FLING AWAY MY SWORD, BLOOD DIM,	743	DANAAN QUICK		20
I DREW MY SWORD TO FLING IT IN A POOL,—	747	SHADOW WATER A		7
NONE SHOULD ESCAPE MY SWORD! I WOULD SEND ALL	752	SHADOW WATER A		111
I PROMISED HIM THAT NONE SHOULD ESCAPE MY SWORD	752	SHADOW WATER A		114
AND SAYS: "A SWORD BLADE PIERCED ME IN MY SLEEP."	753	SHADOW WATER A	V	147
I SWEAR IT. LET EVERY MAN DRAW OUT HIS SWORD.	758	SHADOW WATER A		230
MAY THE SWORD BLADES DRINK THEIR FILL	776	AGAINST WITCH	V	37
A HOUSE, A SWORD, A SHIP, A MASK.	788	BRAVEST ASK		2

SWORD-BLADE

	PAGE	TITLE		LINE
. . . MADE CONCHUBAR'S SWORD-BLADE OF OLD.	52	OISIN 3		80
AND SAYS, "A SWORD-BLADE PIERCED ME IN MY SLEEP."	234	SHADOW WATER B		257
ALL-DESTROYING SWORD-BLADE STILL	484	SYMBOLS		3
GOLD-SEWN SILK ON THE SWORD-BLADE,	484	SYMBOLS		5
AND SAYS, "A SWORD-BLADE PIERCED ME IN MY SLEEP."	753	SHADOW WATER A		147

SWORD-BLADES

	PAGE	TITLE		LINE
AND WITH THE CLASHING OF THEIR SWORD-BLADES MAKE	137	TO SOME I TALK		13
AND WITH THE CLANGING OF THEIR SWORD-BLADES MAKE	137	TO SOME I TALK	V	13
MAY THE SWORD-BLADES DRINK THEIR FILL	776	AGAINST WITCH		37

SWORD-BLUE

	PAGE	TITLE		LINE
OF SWORD-BLUE WAVES OF CALM: WHILE O'ER HEAD BLINK	663	ISLE STAT II 2		42

SWORD-POINT

	PAGE	TITLE		LINE
AT THE SWORD-POINT, AND WAITS TILL WE HAVE FOUND	109	CUCHULAIN SEA		53

SWORD'S

	PAGE	TITLE		LINE
THE SWORD'S A CROSS! THEREON HE DIED:	562	CONJUNCTIONS		3

SWORDS

	PAGE	TITLE		LINE
AND A HUNDRED SWORDS AND A HUNDRED BOWS:	8	OISIN 1	V	91
THEIR SWORDS UPON THEIR IRON KNEES,	156	FORGOT BEAUTY		23
THEY UNHOOK THEIR HEAVY SWORDS	215	HAPPY TOWNLAND		23
NINE SWORDS WITH HANDLES OF RHINOCEROS HORN	239	SHADOW WATER B		368
AND BEAT THE GOLDEN HELMET WITH THEIR SWORDS?	243	SHADOW WATER B		425
HELMETS, AND SWORDS, AND HALF-FORGOTTEN THINGS	257	RECONCILIATION		6
HURL HELMETS, CROWNS, AND SWORDS INTO THE PIT.	257	RECONCILIATION		10
WE MUST GET SWORDS. IS: T THE ONLY WAY? OH, SEE,	660	ISLE STAT II 1		34
THEY GET THEM SWORDS, AND BOTH OR EITHER FALL?	662	ISLE STAT II 1		78
MORE WONDERFUL! AND WE HAVE SWORDS. O NIGHT	664	ISLE STAT II 2		61
OF THOSE STEEL TONGUES! CRASH, SWORDS! WELL THRUST! WELL BENT	665	ISLE STAT II 2		67
A HUNDRED SWORDS, A HUNDRED DRINKING-BOWLS,	756	SHADOW WATER A		186
A HUNDRED SHIELDS OF BRASS, A HUNDRED SWORDS,	756	SHADOW WATER A	V	188
THEY ARE ALWAYS QUARRELLING. GIVE ME YOUR SWORDS.	766	SHADOW WATER A		370
ALE SETS THEM QUARRELLING. GIVE ME YOUR SWORDS.	766	SHADOW WATER A		372
GIVE ME YOUR SWORDS. THEY ARE ALWAYS QUARRELLING.	766	SHADOW WATER A	V	370
IT IS THE BROWN ALE DOES IT. GIVE ME YOUR SWORDS.	766	SHADOW WATER A	V	372

SWORDSMAN

	PAGE	TITLE		LINE
BADE THAT SWORDSMAN TAKE	789	SINGING HEAD		4

```
                                                              PAGE      TITLE          LINE

SWORDSMEN
     AND THE TALL MEN AND THE SWORDSMEN AND THE HORSEMEN, WHERE    580 CURSE CROMWELL       4
       ARE THEY?
     THAT THE SWORDSMEN AND THE LADIES CAN STILL KEEP COMPANY,     581 CURSE CROMWELL      20
SWORD-STROKES
     THAT THINK SWORD-STROKES WERE BETTER MEANT  . . . . . .       276 GREY ROCK          129
SWORE
     I SWORE BUT YESTERDAY IF THE RED GOD  . . . . . . . . .       751 SHADOW WATER A     109
     HE SWORE TO SING MY BEAUTY  . . . . . . . . . . . .           789 SINGING HEAD         7
SWORN      SEE DEEP-SWORN
     WITH SAILORS THAT WERE SWORN TO DO YOUR WILL,  . . . . .      236 SHADOW WATER B     308
     A DEEP SWORN VOW  . . . . . . . . . . . . . . . .             357 DEEP-SWORN VOW V     T
     THAT DEEP SWORN VOW, HAVE BEEN FRIENDS OF MINE,  . . . .      357 DEEP-SWORN VOW V     2
     I AM THINKING OF A CHILD'S VOW SWORN IN VAIN  . . . . .       391 UNDER SATURN        15
     BESIDE A LOCHLANN WHARF, AND THOUGH SHE HAD SWORN  . . .      756 SHADOW WATER A     188
SWUNG
     IN A SAD REVELRY HE SANG AND SWUNG  . . . . . . . .            39 OISIN 2           160
     THAT ON A WILLOW SWUNG.  . . . . . . . . . . . .              308 PLAYER QUEEN         4
SYCAMORE
     A SYCAMORE AND LIME-TREE LOST IN NIGHT  . . . . . . .         488 COOLE PARK 29        3
     A SYCAMORE AND LIME TREE LOST IN NIGHT  . . . . . . .         488 COOLE PARK 29   V    3
     A LITTLE BOY OUTSIDE THE SYCAMORE WOOD  . . . . . . .         715 DWELT SYCAMORE       1
     A LITTLE BOY INSIDE THE SYCAMORE WOOD  . . . . . . .          715 DWELT SYCAMORE       5
SYCAMORES
     SHE WHO DWELT AMONG THE SYCAMORES.  .   . . . . .             715 DWELT SYCAMORE       T
     SHE DWELT AMONG THE SYCAMORES.  . . . . . . . .               715 DWELT SYCAMORE  V    T
SYMBOL
     (I HAVE NO SPEECH BUT SYMBOL, THE PAGAN SPEECH I MADE  . .    365 HER COURAGE          2
     AND NOT A FOUNTAIN, WERE THE SYMBOL WHICH  . . . . .          418 ANCEST HOUSES       15
     I DECLARE THIS TOWER IS MY SYMBOL; I DECLARE  . . . .         480 BLOOD AND MOON      16
     THAT THEY HAD BROUGHT NO FABULOUS SYMBOL THERE  . . . .       537 HER VISION          31
     A SYMBOL OF LONGEVITY;  . . . . . . . . . . . .               566 LAPIS LAZULI        40
SYMBOLIC
     WHERE THE SYMBOLIC ROSE CAN BREAK IN FLOWER,  . . . . .       419 MY HOUSE             4
SYMBOLICAL
     SYMBOLICAL GLORY OF THE EARTH AND AIR!  . . . . . . .         483 VERONIC NAPKIN       3
SYMBOLISE
     AND THAT ALL HEAVENLY GLORY SYMBOLISE--  . . . . . . .        445 SCHOOL CHILDR       55
SYMBOLS
     SYMBOLS OF THE SOUL,  . . . . . . . . . . . . .               420 MY HOUSE        V  20F
     SYMBOLS  . . . . . . . . . . . . . . . . . . .                484 SYMBOLS              T
SYMPATHY
     INTO A SPHERE FROM YOUTHFUL SYMPATHY,  . . . . . . .          443 SCHOOL CHILDR       14
SYNGE
     AND THAT ENQUIRING MAN JOHN SYNGE COMES NEXT,  . . . . .      324 ROBERT GREGORY      25
     THAT MEDITATIVE MAN, JOHN SYNGE, AND THOSE . . . . . .        489 COOLE PARK 29       13
     "GREATEST SINCE REMBRANDT," ACCORDING TO JOHN SYNGE;  .       602 GALLERY REVIS       26
     JOHN SYNGE, I AND AUGUSTA GREGORY, THOUGHT . . . . . .        603 GALLERY REVIS       41
     AND HERE'S JOHN SYNGE HIMSELF, THAT ROOTED MAN,  . . . .      603 GALLERY REVIS       48
     AND HERE'S JOHN SYNGE, A MEDITATIVE MAN,  . . . . . .         603 GALLERY REVIS   V   48
SYSTEM
     HAYNAU, THE MAN OF SYSTEM, LIFTS HIS HAND  . . . . . .        712 FERENCZ RENYI       62
TABLE
     ABOUT MY TABLE TO AND FRO,  . . . . . . . . . .               138 TO IRELAND          24
     FOR ROUND ABOUT MY TABLE GO  . . . . . . . . . .              138 TO IRELAND      V   23
     ABOUT MY TABLE TO AND FRO,  . . . . . . . . . .               139 TO IRELAND          40
     BUT SHE TOOK UP HER FAN FROM THE TABLE  . . . . . . .         160 CAP AND BELLS       19
     BUT SHE TOOK HER FAN FROM THE TABLE,  . . . . . . .           160 CAP AND BELLS   V   19
     SET CARPENTERS TO WORK ON NO WIDE TABLE,  . . . . . .         340 SHEP GOATHERD       50
     NO TABLE OR CHAIR OR STOOL NOT SIMPLE ENOUGH  . . . . .       371 ON GOING HOUSE       3
     ROSE FROM THE TABLE AND DECLARED IT RIGHT  . . . . . .        410 TOWER               43
     MY TABLE  . . . . . . . . . . . . . . . . . .                 421 MY TABLE             T
     BUBBLE UPON THE TABLE.  A GHOST MAY COME!  . . . . . .         470 ALL SOUL NIGHT       5
     THAT TABLE AND THE TALK OF YOUTH,  . . . . . . . .            475 EVA GORE-BOOTH      18
     AUGUSTA GREGORY SEATED AT HER GREAT ORMOLU TABLE,  . . .      577 LOFTY THINGS         7
     I TOLD HIM THAT NIGHTLY FROM SIX TO SEVEN I SAT AT THIS       578 LOFTY THINGS         9
       TABLE,
     AT TABLE OR IN BED.  . . . . . . . . . . . . .                620 JOHN KINSELLA       10
     NO OSCAR RULED THE TABLE,  . . . . . . . . . .                626 STATES HOLIDAY       5
TABLES
     STANDISH O'GRADY SUPPORTING HIMSELF BETWEEN THE TABLES  .     577 LOFTY THINGS         5
     BY TABLES THAT WERE FALLEN INTO DUST  . . . . . . .           724 KANVA ON SELF       13
TABLET
     FOR THINGS BELOW ARE COPIES, THE GREAT SMARAGDINE TABLET      556 RIBH PATRICK         6
       SAID.
TABLE-TOP
     ON THE MARBLE TABLE-TOP.  . . . . . . . . . . .               501 VACILLATION         39
TABLETS
     THEY WROTE ON TABLETS OF THIN BOARD,  . . . . . . .           197 BAILE AILLINN      195
     AND TOOK THEIR TABLETS AND DID SUMS!  . . . . . . .           344 DAWN                 9
     AND TOOK THEIR TABLETS AND MADE SUMS--  . . . . . .           344 DAWN            V    9
TABORS
     FROM MARBLE CITIES LOUD WITH TABORS OF OLD  . . . . .         162 ASKS FORGIVE         9
TAFFRAIL
     AND THE GHASTLY GHOST-FLAMES GLIMMER ALL ALONG THE TAFFRAIL   719 PHANTOM SHIP        21
       RAILS
TAFFREL
     AND THE GHASTLY GHOST FLAMES GLIMMER ALONG THE TAFFREL        719 PHANTOM SHIP    V   21
       RAILS,
TAIL       SEE FISH-TAIL
     HIS LANGUID TAIL ABOVE US, LIT WITH MYRIAD SPOTS OF LIGHT.     77 INDIAN ON GOD       20
```

		PAGE	TITLE	LINE

TAIL   (CONTINUED)

	PAGE	TITLE		LINE
WITH A FISH TAIL, AND TALK	215	HAPPY TOWNLAND	V	46
ONE LASHED HER TAIL: HER EYES LIT BY THE MOON	383	VISION ROBART		29
AS TO A DOG'S TAIL? NEVER HAD I MORE	409	TOWER		4
AS UPON A DOG'S TAIL. NEVER HAD I MORE	409	TOWER	V	4

TAILS   SEE CAT-O'-NINE-TAILS SERPENT-TAILS

TAKE

	PAGE	TITLE		LINE
SHE BID ME TAKE LOVE EASY, AS THE LEAVES GROW ON THE TREE:	90	SALLEY GARDENS		3
SHE BID ME TAKE LIFE EASY, AS THE GRASS GROWS ON THE WEIRS:	90	SALLEY GARDENS		7
SHE BID ME TAKE LOVE EASY, AS THE LEAVES GROW ON THE TREES:	90	SALLEY GARDENS	V	3
THAT CARRIED THE TAKE TO SLIGO TOWN TO BE SOLD, ...	91	OLD FISHERMAN		7
AND NOW AT LAST YOU TAKE ON HUMAN SHAPE--	102	FERGUS DRUID	V	6
TAKE, IF YOU MUST, THIS LITTLE BAG OF DREAMS:	104	FERGUS DRUID		29
TAKE THEN THIS SMALL SLATE-COLOURED BAG OF DREAMS:	104	FERGUS DRUID	V	29
AND NODDING BY THE FIRE, TAKE DOWN THIS BOOK, ...	120	YOU ARE OLD		2
AND KISS HER LIPS AND TAKE HER HANDS:	150	WANDER AENGUS		20
AND KISS HER LIPS AND TAKE HER HAND, ...	150	WANDER AENGUS	V	20
I KNOW OF THE LEAFY PATHS THAT THE WITCHES TAKE	203	WITHER BOUGHS		9
I KNOW OF THE LEAFY PATH THAT THE WITCHES TAKE, ...	203	WITHER BOUGHS	V	9
I SAID: "A LINE WILL TAKE US HOURS MAYBE:	204	ADAMS CURSE		4
TO TAKE HIM WHILE HE SLEEPS AND CARRY HIM	222	SHADOW WATER B		14
AND TAKE THE CAPTAIN'S SHARE OF EVERYTHING	225	SHADOW WATER B		73
THEY TAKE A KISS FOR WHAT A KISS IS WORTH, ...	229	SHADOW WATER B		157
AND PAID YOU ON THE NAIL. TAKE UP THAT ROPE	232	SHADOW WATER B		224
AND DID THOSE WATCHERS BID YOU TAKE ME CAPTIVE?	236	SHADOW WATER B		322
THAT NONE MIGHT TAKE YOU FROM ME. FOR A MOMENT	237	SHADOW WATER B		330
THERE IS NONE TO TAKE HIS SIDE. I AM ON HIS SIDE. . . .	239	SHADOW WATER B		364
I'LL DO IT FOR HIS SAKE. NO. TAKE THIS SWORD	250	SHADOW WATER B		591
WHAT COULD I BUT TAKE UP THE SONG?	254	HIS DREAM		14
BUT THERE IT'S GONE: I WILL NOT TAKE	274	GREY ROCK		92
BUT WHEN HE THOUGHT TO TAKE HER IN HIS ARMS	280	TWO KINGS		67
AND TAKE HER IN THE MIDDLE OF ARMED MEN, ...	282	TWO KINGS		114
BE SECRET AND TAKE DEFEAT	290	TO A FRIEND		2
AND MAYBE I SHALL TAKE A TROUT	297	THREE BEGGARS		67
TO TAKE MY FANCY LIKE THE WIND	301	RUN PARADISE		26
AND SO TAKE THAT AND THAT." THEREON	307	HOUR DAWN		112
O YOU WILL TAKE WHATEVER'S OFFERED	313	TWO YEAR LATER		7
SONG, LET THEM TAKE IT, ...	320	COAT		8
AS OTHERS WILL, WHEN FIRST THEY TAKE POSSESSION, ...	341	SHEP GOATHERD		52
WE TAKE IT FOR THE NORM: YET SHOULD I DREAM	371	ON GOING HOUSE		9
AND WHEN YOU HAVE SPOKEN TAKE THE ROADS AGAIN?	373	PHASES OF MOON		25
THAT IT CAN TAKE WHAT FORM COOK NATURE FANCIES	377	PHASES OF MOON		115
BUT TAKE ME FOR SOME DRUNKEN COUNTRYMAN:	377	PHASES OF MOON		130
THAT IT CAN TAKE WHAT FORM COOK NATURE FANCY	377	PHASES OF MOON	V	115
BUT TAKE ME FOR SOME DRUNKEN COUNTRY MAN:	377	PHASES OF MOON	V	130
TO TAKE THE ROSES FOR HIS MEAT.	382	SONG OF FOOL		12
AND MAY THE DEVIL TAKE THE REST.	386	ROBARTES DANCE		24
BUT WHO CAN TALK OF GIVE AND TAKE, ...	395	SIXTEEN DEAD		3
OR MEDDLE WITH OUR GIVE AND TAKE	395	SIXTEEN DEAD		17
TO WATCH A WHITE GULL TAKE	400	DEMON BEAST		24
FROM A GLAD KINDNESS CANNOT TAKE HIS EYES.	404	FOR DAUGHTER		40
ONCE OUT OF NATURE I SHALL NEVER TAKE	408	SAIL BYZANTIUM		25
BUT TAKE OUR GREATNESS WITH OUR VIOLENCE?	418	ANCEST HOUSES		32
BUT TAKE OUR GREATNESS WITH OUR BITTERNESS?	418	ANCEST HOUSES		40
THE WOMEN TAKE SO LITTLE STOCK	455	HIS MEMORIES		7
AND DID SUCH PLEASURE TAKE--	455	HIS MEMORIES		14
TAKE THIS LIGHT PARCHMENT, PASS THROUGH THE GREAT CHAMBER	461	HARUN RASHID	V	5
HERE, TRAVELLER, SCHOLAR, POET, TAKE YOUR STAND	489	COOLE PARK 29		25
AND IF IT TAKE THE SECOND MUST REFUSE	491	COOLE BALLYLEE	V	40C
AND IF IT TAKE THE SECOND MUST REFUSE	495	CHOICE		3
THAT CANNOT TAKE THE WHOLE	510	JANE JUDGMENT		3
"TAKE THE SOUR	510	JANE JUDGMENT		6
IF YOU TAKE ME, ...	510	JANE JUDGMENT		7
HOWEVER THEY MAY TAKE IT, ...	520	HIS BARGAIN		7
BY SOME NEW-MARRIED BRIDE, I TAKE	535	CHOSEN		13
BY SOME NEW MARRIED BRIDE I TAKE	535	CHOSEN	V	13
AND GIVE HIS OWN AND TAKE HIS OWN	538	LAST CONFESS		19
SOLDIERS TAKE PRIDE IN SALUTING THEIR CAPTAIN, ...	547	TO SAME TUNE 3 V		1
SOME TAKE DELIGHT IN ADORNING A WOMAN.	547	TO SAME TUNE 3 V		3
TAKE TO THE ROADS AND GO MARCHING ALONG.	548	TO SAME TUNE 3		14
SOLDIERS TAKE PRIDE IN SALUTING THEIR CAPTAIN, ...	548	TO SAME TUNE 3		21
WHAT CAN SHE TAKE UNTIL HER MASTER GIVE:	558	RIBH CHRISTIAN		21
HE BADE THEM TAKE AND BURY HER	571	THREE BUSHES		71
WHETHER THEY TAKE THE UPPER ROAD	589	OLD WICKED MAN		48
"TAKE ALL TO YOUR MISTRESS,"	595	COLONEL MARTIN		34
SO WHEN I TAKE ON HALF A SCORE	605	SONGS BURDEN 1		7
THAT PATCHING OLD HEELS THEY MAY SHRIEK, I TAKE TO CHISEL AND PLANE.	623	HIGH TALK		8
THE NIGHEST BLOSSOM WHERE IT FALLS I'LL TAKE.	657	ISLE STAT I 3		65
OH: GRACIOUS PAN, TAKE NOW THY SERVANT'S PART.	657	ISLE STAT I 3		77
DID HER LONELY WATCHING TAKE	658	ISLE STAT I 3		94
NO MORE: TAKE ME INSTEAD OF HER, GREAT SIRS.	695	MOSADA 1		114
BEFORE WE TAKE OUR SEATS ABOVE THE CROWD.	704	MOSADA 1		134
SHE WOULD WEAVE A NET TO TAKE US. SHE MIGHT KEEP FAITH:	756	SHADOW WATER A		190
THE GODS WEAVE NETS, AND TAKE US IN THEIR NETS, ...	764	SHADOW WATER A		339
AND LETS THE KIND WORM TAKE THE LOT:	779	ACCURSED WHO		4
WHY SHOULD THE HEART TAKE FRIGHT?	781	HEART FRIGHT		1
BADE THAT SWORDSMAN TAKE	789	SINGING HEAD		4
NOR LAW NOR PARLIAMENT TAKE HEED.	791	REPRISALS		22

TAKEN

	PAGE	TITLE	LINE
"BUT TILL THE MOON HAS TAKEN ALL, I WAGE	45	OISIN 2	240

TAKEN   (CONTINUED)
     TILL THE MOON HAS TAKEN FLIGHT: . . . .   87 STOLEN CHILD   19
     NOW THAT THE EARTH HAD TAKEN MAN AND ALL: . . . . . .   128 DREAM OF FAERY   40
     NOW THAT OLD EARTH HAD TAKEN MAN AND ALL: . . . . . .   128 DREAM OF FAERY V   40
     YOU HAVE TAKEN PAY AND MADE YOUR BARGAIN FOR IT. . . .   225 SHADOW WATER B   68
     SILENCE! FOR YOU HAVE TAKEN FORGAEL'S PAY. . . . . . .   225 SHADOW WATER B V   68
     BOTH YOU AND I ARE TAKEN IN THE NET. . . . .   237 SHADOW WATER B   323
     IF YOU HAD TAKEN ME BY MAGIC SPELLS. . . . .   245 SHADOW WATER B   490
     BUT NOW THAT THEY HAVE TAKEN TO THE ROAD . . . . . .   247 SHADOW WATER B   526
     O SILVER FISH THAT MY TWO HANDS HAVE TAKEN . . . . .   251 SHADOW WATER B   609
     HAS TAKEN A NEW PHASE. . . . .   379 CAT AND MOON   20
     ROBBERS HAD TAKEN HIS OLD TAMBOURINE, ...   616 MARCH SONGS 3   7
     ROBBERS HAD TAKEN HIS OLD TAMBOURINE. . . . .   616 MARCH SONGS 3   10
     ROBBERS HAD TAKEN HIS OLD TAMBOURINE. . . . .   616 MARCH SONGS 3   17
     ROBBERS HAD TAKEN HIS OLD TAMBOURINE. . . . .   616 MARCH SONGS 3   20
     ROBBERS HAD TAKEN HIS OLD TAMBOURINE. . . . .   616 MARCH SONGS 3   27
     ROBBERS HAD TAKEN HIS OLD TAMBOURINE. . . . .   616 MARCH SONGS 3   30
     TAKEN IN MAGIC, IN THE CHURCH'S NAME . . . .   694 MOSADA 1   104
     BELIEVE THAT GOLD AND WOMEN TAKEN IN WAR . . . . . .   754 SHADOW WATER A   159
     O SILVER FISH THAT MY TWO HANDS HAVE TAKEN . . . . .   769 SHADOW WATER A   425
TAKES
     ATHENE TAKES ACHILLES BY THE HAIR, ...   374 PHASES OF MOON   45
     AMONG TASKS NOT IMPOSSIBLE, IT TAKES . . . .   376 PHASES OF MOON   92
     NO MATTER WHAT HAPPENS AND WHO TAKES THE FALL, . . .   545 TO SAME TUNE 1   22
     NO MATTER WHAT HAPPENS OR WHO TAKES THE FALL, ...   545 TO SAME TUNE 1 V   22
     THE SOLDIER TAKES PRIDE . . . .   547 TO SAME TUNE 3 V   T
     THE SOLDIER TAKES PRIDE IN SALUTING HIS CAPTAIN, . .   547 TO SAME TUNE 3   1
     HE TAKES THE DEVIL'S PAY. . . . .   582 ROGER CASEMENT V   20
     AND TAKES YOU BY THE THROAT! . . . .   598 STONE CROSS   4
     THE SOLDIER TAKES PRIDE IN SALUTING HIS CAPTAIN, . .   614 MARCH SONGS 2   1
     NO MATTER WHAT HAPPENS AND WHO TAKES THE FALL, . . .   616 MARCH SONGS 3   22
     FOR DEATH WHO TAKES WHAT MAN WOULD KEEP, ...   620 JOHN KINSELLA   3
TAKING   SEE LEAVE-TAKING
     TAKING THE MORTAL WARRIORS BY THE HANDS! . . . . . .   29 OISIN 2   V 10B
     HE KNOWS THAT HE IS TAKING YOU TO DEATH! . . . . . .   249 SHADOW WATER B   562
     TAKING DELIGHT THAT HE COULD SPRING! . . . .   317 APPOINTMENT   4
     THERE IS NO LEAVE TAKING. I GO NO MORE. . . . .   702 MOSADA 3   V 100
TALE
     BUT THE TALE, THOUGH WORDS BE LIGHTER THAN AIR, . . .   3 OISIN 1   11
     AND MY OWN TALE AGAIN FOR ME SHALL SING, ...   68 SAD SHEPHERD   22
     AND MINE OWN TALE AGAIN FOR ME SHALL SING, ...   68 SAD SHEPHERD   V 22
     HIS SUDDEN VENGEANCE WERE A COUNTRY TALE. . . . . . .   127 DREAM OF FAERY   27
     THE TALE DROVE HIS FINE ANGRY MOOD AWAY. . . . . . .   128 DREAM OF FAERY   36
     AS IF THERE WERE NO TALE BUT YOUR OWN TALE . . . . . .   181 QUEEN MAEVE   32
     AS IF THERE WERE NO TALE BUT YOUR OWN TALE . . . . . .   181 QUEEN MAEVE   32
     THROUGH WICKED SPELLS. THAT IS NOT ALL THE TALE, . .   242 SHADOW WATER B   408
     TO HAVE LIT UPON AS CLEAN AND SWEET A TALE . . . . . .   258 KING NO KING   8
     BEFORE THE THREE TO END THIS TALE, ...   297 THREE BEGGARS   55
     A WOMAN SPOKE OF SOME NEW TALE SHE HAD READ, ...   350 HER PRAISE   7
     HER SPEECH A WICKED TALE THAT WE MAY VIE WITH HER, .   362 HER COURTESY   6
     HE HAD LEARNT FROM PATER, AND TO ROUND HIS TALE . .   373 PHASES OF MOON   27
     OF A MOCKING TALE OR A GIBE . . . .   392 EASTER 1916   10
     ABOVE A SINKING FIRE, A TALE THAT SHE . . . .   443 SCHOOL CHILDR   10
     ABOVE A SINKING FIRE, SOME TALE THAT SHE . . . . . .   443 SCHOOL CHILDR V   10
     MARK AND DIGEST MY TALE, CARRY IT AFAR . . . .   554 RIBH AT TOMB   3
     ALL KNOW THEIR TALE, ALL KNOW WHAT LEAF AND TWIG, . .   555 RIBH AT TOMB   7
     HAZEL LAVERY LIVING AND DYING, THAT TALE . . . . . .   602 GALLERY REVIS   23
     BY MANY SOUGHT, AND 'TIS A FOREST TALE. . . . .   653 ISLE STAT I 2   40
     AND LET THE TALE BE MOURNFUL EACH ONE TELLS. . . . .   663 ISLE STAT II 2   36
     WILL WONDERING LISTEN, AND THIS TALE SHALL EASE . . .   693 MOSADA 1   70
     THAT SONG I'VE MADE. 'TIS OF AN IRISH TALE. . . . .   696 MOSADA 2   19
     THAT SONG I'VE MADE--IS OF A RUSSIAN TALE . . . . . .   696 MOSADA 2   V   19
     OH, I AM WEARY OF THAT FOOLISH TALE. . . . .   721 WITCH VIVIEN   33
     AND WHEN THEY HEARD THAT TALE OF HIS . . . .   730 PRIEST FAIRY   65
     BELOVED, HEAR MY BITTER TALE!-- . . . .   742 DANAAN QUICK   1
     AND WE GO HOME. COME, AIBRIC! END YOUR TALE . . . .   766 SHADOW WATER A   374
TALE'S
     BUT WHEN, IF THE TALE'S TRUE, ...   346 ON WOMAN   29
TALES   SEE LOVE-TALES
     MOVED ROUND ME, OF SEAMEN OR LANDSMEN, ALL WHO ARE WINTER   53 OISIN 3   86
        TALES!
     DEDICATION OF "IRISH TALES" . . . .   129 BOOK STORIES   V   T
     AND SPOKEN IN THE COUNCIL, AND HEARD TALES . . . . . .   748 SHADOW WATER A   28
TALK
     THAT WE MAY MUSE IN THE STARLIGHT AND TALK OF THE BATTLES   51 OISIN 3   63
        OF OLD!
     I PASSED A LITTLE FURTHER ON AND HEARD A LOTUS TALK! . .   76 INDIAN ON GOD   9
     I PACED A LITTLE FURTHER ON AND HEARD A LOTUS TALK!-- .   76 INDIAN ON GOD V   9
     A THOUSAND YEARS AGO YOU HELD HIGH TALK . . . .   187 QUEEN MAEVE   150
     ALTHOUGH THEY DO NOT TALK OF IT AT SCHOOL-- . . . . .   205 ADAMS CURSE   19
     I HEAR THE HARP-STRING PRAISE THEM, OR HEAR THEIR MOURNFUL 210 UNDER THE MOON   16
        TALK.
     I HEAR THE HARP STRINGS PRAISE THEM, OR HEAR THEIR MOURNFUL 210 UNDER THE MOON V 16
        TALK.
     I HEAR THE HARPSTRING PRAISE THEM OR HEAR THEIR MOURNFUL   210 UNDER THE MOON V 16
        TALK.
     I HEAR THE HARP STRING PRAISE THEM OR HEAR THEIR MOURNFUL 210 UNDER THE MOON V 16
        TALK.
     WITH A FISH-TAIL, AND TALK . . . .   215 HAPPY TOWNLAND   46
     WITH A FISH TAIL, AND TALK . . . .   215 HAPPY TOWNLAND V   46
     AND YET YOU TALK OF LOVE. THE MOVEMENT OF TIME . . .   237 SHADOW WATER B   338

	PAGE	TITLE	LINE

TALK (CONTINUED)

"AND I WILL TALK BEFORE I SLEEP · 304 HOUR DAWN · 44
AND DRINK BEFORE I TALK." AND HE · 304 HOUR DAWN · 45
AND THOUGH I HAVE TURNED THE TALK BY HOOK OR CROOK · 350 HER PRAISE · 5
I WILL TALK NO MORE OF BOOKS OR THE LONG WAR · 351 HER PRAISE · 11
MANAGE THE TALK UNTIL HER NAME COME ROUND. · 351 HER PRAISE · 14
MANAGE TO TALK UNTIL HER NAME COME ROUND. · 351 HER PRAISE V 14
AND WHO CAN SAY BUT SOME YOUNG BELLE MAY WALK AND TALK MEN WILD · 354 HIS PHOENIX · 26
IN RAMBLING TALK WITH AN IMAGE OF AIR: · 357 BROKEN DREAMS · 40
BUT WHO CAN TALK OF GIVE AND TAKE, · 395 SIXTEEN DEAD · 3
THAT HE, ALTHOUGH A COUNTRY'S TALK · 422 MY TABLE · 29
THAT TABLE AND THE TALK OF YOUTH, · 475 EVA GORE-BOOTH · 18
AND GATHER ALL THE TALK? · 499 MOTHER OF GOD · 10
MUCH I TALK, MORE I WALK: · 548 TO SAME TUNE 3 · 9
MUCH I TALK, MORE I WALK: · 548 TO SAME TUNE 3 · 19
MUCH I TALK, MORE I WALK: · 549 TO SAME TUNE 3 · 29
ALL NEIGHBOURLY CONTENT AND EASY TALK ARE GONE, · 580 CURSE CROMWELL · 9
AMONG THE DOGS AND HORSES THAT UNDERSTAND MY TALK. · 581 CURSE CROMWELL · 30
BAWDY TALK FOR THE FISHERMEN: · 588 OLD WICKED MAN · 32
MEMORIES OF THE TALK · 607 SONGS BURDEN 2 · 22
HIGH TALK · 622 HIGH TALK · T
THAT KNOWING BETTER TALK HAD GONE · 627 STATES HOLIDAY · 7
I COULD NOT GO. LET'S TALK, AND LET'S BE SAD, · 651 ISLE STAT I 2 · 7
SHALL SEE A THING TO TALK ON WHEN YOU'RE OLD, · 693 MOSADA 1 · 67
AND HEAVEN, AND HOLINESS. LET'S TALK AND GRIEVE, · 702 MOSADA 3 · 84

TALKED

THAT TALKED OF LOVE OR POLITICS. · 131 OLD PENSIONER · 5
TO SOME I HAVE TALKED WITH BY THE FIRE · 136 TO SOME I TALK · T
AND TALKED OF THE DARK FOLK WHO LIVE IN SOULS · 136 TO SOME I TALK · 4
TO THOSE WITH WHOM I HAVE TALKED MANY TIMES, · 136 TO SOME I TALK V 2
IT TALKED, ERE THE MORN GREW WHITE. · 159 CAP AND BELLS V 6
IT TALKED BEFORE MORN WAS WHITE. · 159 CAP AND BELLS V 6
TALKED OF HIS COUNTRY AND ITS PEOPLE, SANG · 180 QUEEN MAEVE · 3
AND YOU AND I, AND TALKED OF POETRY. · 204 ADAMS CURSE · 3
AND HAVING TALKED TO SOME LATE HOUR · 324 ROBERT GREGORY · 4
WE HAVE TALKED IN THE ONE PLACE, · 332 SOLOMON SHEBA · 4
THAT YOU HAVE TALKED WITH APPARITIONS. INDEED · 342 SHEP GOATHERD · 82
TO WHERE THE DUCHESS AND HER PEOPLE TALKED · 352 PEOPLE · 13
O BUT WE TALKED AT LARGE BEFORE · 395 SIXTEEN DEAD · 1
TALKED OF HONOUR AND OF TRUTH, · 431 NINETEEN 19 · 90
AND TALKED AWAY THE NIGHT, · 456 SUMMER SPRING · 2
AND WHEN WE TALKED OF GROWING UP · 456 SUMMER SPRING · 5
MY GREAT-GRANDFATHER'S FATHER TALKED OF MUSIC, · 486 SEVEN SAGES · 4
MY GREAT-GRANDFATHER'S FATHER TALKED OF MUSIC AND PAINTING, · 486 SEVEN SAGES V 4
HER BARGAIN STRUCK WE LAUGHED AND TALKED · 620 JOHN KINSELLA · 15
I TALKED ABOUT AN APPARITION, · 624 APPARITIONS · 2
TALKED OF ODDS AND ENDS. · 627 STATES HOLIDAY · 8
O'ER MUCH I'VE TALKED: I SHALL BE SILENT SOON, · 657 ISLE STAT I 3 · 75
WE'VE TALKED AND TALKED, AND NOT A WHIT MORE RARE · 659 ISLE STAT II 1 · 21
WE'VE TALKED AND TALKED, AND NOT A WHIT MORE RARE · 659 ISLE STAT II 1 · 21

TALKING

AND I WILL HEAR THEM TALKING IN A MINUTE. · 233 SHADOW WATER B · 250
WHILE TALKING WITH HIS QUEENS, · 345 ON WOMAN · 12
A YOUNG MAN WHEN THE OLD MEN ARE DONE TALKING · 356 BROKEN DREAMS · 16
BY AN OLD HUNTER TALKING WITH GODS· · 605 YOU CONTENT · 23
THE WHOLE WORLD'S SADLY TALKING TO ITSELF. · 652 ISLE STAT I 2 · 12
THE TALKING WINDS HAVE FOUND THEIR HOME, · 686 LIFE · 9
FOR LONG THE BURTHEN OF THEIR TALKING GRIEFS. · 693 MOSADA 1 · 71
HER DREAMS ARE TALKING WITH OLD YEARS. AWAKE, · 702 MOSADA 3 · 89
MURMURS OF HER CHILDREN TALKING— · 705 DAWN-SONG · 6
THERE WAS SOME TALKING OF THE POOR— · 725 LEGEND · 14
THERE WAS SOME TALKING OF MAN'S GOD, · 725 LEGEND · 19
TALKING HOURS SWIFTLY PASS: · 727 LOVERS QUARREL · 44
FOR ALL OUR TALKING. · 785 YOUR HEART · 7

TALKS

CRAZY JANE TALKS WITH THE BISHOP · 513 JANE TALK BISH · T
WHO TALKS OF PLATO'S SPINDLE: · 520 HIS BARGAIN · 1
WHAT HE TALKS ABOUT, · 631 POLITICS · 6

TALL

CAME BLANAID, MAC NESSA, TALL FERGUS WHO FEASTWARD OF OLD TIME SLUNK, · 53 OISIN 3 · 89
YON TALL ONE EYES MY SUPPER: CHASE HIM AWAY, · 72 ANASHU VIJAYA · 34
YON TALL ONE EYES MY SUPPER: SWIFTLY CHASE HIM · 72 ANASHU VIJAYA V 34
TALL WANDS OF ALDER AND WHITE QUICKEN WANDS. · 111 CUCHULAIN SEA V 82A
THE TALL THOUGHT-WOVEN SAILS, THAT FLAP UNFURLED · 113 ROSE OF BATTLE · 2
FROM THE TALL AND THE TUFTED REEDS · 143 HOST OF AIR · 3
TALL, PROUD AND RUDDY, AND LIGHT WINGS · 195 BAILE AILLINN · 140
TALL AND NOBLE BUT WITH FACE AND BOSOM · 199 ARROW · 5
BUT PURER THAN A TALL CANDLE BEFORE THE HOLY ROOD · 208 HANRAHANS SONG · 14
BUT PURE AS A TALL CANDLE BEFORE THE TRINITY · 208 HANRAHANS SONG V 14
BUT PURER THAN A TALL CANDLE BEFORE THE BLESSED ROOD · 208 HANRAHANS SONG V 14
FOR THERE THE TALL DEER AND HIS LEMAN SIGH · 210 RAGGED WOOD V 2
FOR THERE THE TALL DEER AND HIS LEMAN CRY · 211 RAGGED WOOD V 2
AND THE TALL MEN AND THE SWORDSMEN AND THE HORSEMEN, WHERE ARE THEY? · 580 CURSE CROMWELL · 4
TALL PYTHAGORAS. · 611 NEWS ORACLE · 8
TALL DAMES GO WALKING IN GRASS-GREEN AVALON. · 627 STATES HOLIDAY · 13
TALL DAMES GO WALKING IN GRASS-GREEN AVALON. · 627 STATES HOLIDAY · 26
TALL DAMES GO WALKING IN GRASS-GREEN AVALON. · 627 STATES HOLIDAY · 39
TALL DAMES GO WALKING IN GRASS GREEN AVALON. · 627 STATES HOLIDAY V REF

		PAGE	TITLE		LINE

TALL   (CONTINUED)
THAT MAIDEN BRING THEY. WHEN THE TALL RED DEER . . . . . 713 FERENCZ RENYI 79
OF THEIR TALL, NEW-FANGLED QUEEN. . . . . 727 LOVERS QUARREL 48
HIS MEMORY NOW IS A TALL PILLAR, BURNING . . . . . . 738 MOURN THEN ON 15

TALLER
BUT THE TREES GREW TALLER AND CLOSER, ... 48 OISIN 3 17
BUT TALLER THE TREES GREW AND CLOSER, ... 48 OISIN 3 V 17
"BUT YOU HAVE GROWN TO BE THE TALLER MAN." . . . . . 107 CUCHULAIN SEA 27
"NAY, YOU ARE TALLER THAN CUCHULAIN, SON." . . . . . 107 CUCHULAIN SEA V 27
HE WILL BE TALLER NOW——'TWAS LONG AGO. . . . . . . 699 MOSADA 3 15

TALMA
TALMA AND HIS THUNDERBOLT. . . . . 625 NATIVITY 10

TAMBOURINE
ON AN OLD TAMBOURINE. . . . . 613 MARCH SONGS 1 16
ROBBERS HAD TAKEN HIS OLD TAMBOURINE, ... 616 MARCH SONGS 3 7
ROBBERS HAD TAKEN HIS OLD TAMBOURINE. . . . . . . 616 MARCH SONGS 3 10
ROBBERS HAD TAKEN HIS OLD TAMBOURINE. . . . . . . 616 MARCH SONGS 3 17
ROBBERS HAD TAKEN HIS OLD TAMBOURINE, ... 616 MARCH SONGS 3 20
ROBBERS HAD TAKEN HIS OLD TAMBOURINE, ... 616 MARCH SONGS 3 27
ROBBERS HAD TAKEN HIS OLD TAMBOURINE. . . . . . . 616 MARCH SONGS 3 30

TAME
NOR THE TAME WILL, NOR TIMID BRAIN, ... 318 APPOINTMENT 8
A SPECKLED CAT AND A TAME HARE . . . . 380 SONGS FOOL 1 1

TANGLED
AND TANGLED CREEPERS EVERY HOUR . . . . 16 OISIN 1 223
THE TANGLED THOUGHTS OF THE FINISHED DAY . . . . . 728 PRIEST FAIRY 9

TANGLING
WHERE TANGLING CREEPERS EVERY HOUR . . . . 16 OISIN 1 V 223

TAP
I SAW A STRANGER TAP AND WAIT . . . . 696 MOSADA 2 22

TAPER
THE EVERLASTING TAPER LIGHTS THE GLOOM: . . . . . 311 MOUNTAIN TOMB 10

TAPERS
A LADY WITH SOFT EYES LIKE FUNERAL TAPERS. . . . . . 33 OISIN 2 69
DOWN ON US WITH HER EYES LIKE FUNERAL TAPERS. . . . . 33 OISIN 2 V 69
A MAIDEN WITH SOFT EYES LIKE FUNERAL TAPERS, ... 33 OISIN 2 V 69
HAVE LIT LONE TAPERS. NOW THE NIGHT WAS CAST, ... 687 TWO TITANS 27

TAPPING
"CHOOSE!" RESTLESS HAYNAU'S FINGERS TAPPING GO. . . . . 711 FERENCZ RENYI 41

TARA
TARA UPROOTED, AND NEW COMMONNESS . . . . 198 SEVEN WOODS 6
WESTWARD OF TARA. HURRYING TO HIS QUEEN . . . . . 276 TWO KINGS 2
WESTWARD OF TARA. WHERE IN THE MIDDLE WOOD . . . . . 277 TWO KINGS V 4
TOWARD PEOPLED TARA, NOR STOOD TO DRAW HIS BREATH . . . 279 TWO KINGS 46
ON PEOPLED TARA, NOR STOOD TO DRAW HIS BREATH . . . 279 TWO KINGS V 46
TOWARDS PEOPLED TARA, NOR STOOD TO DRAW HIS BREATH . . . 279 TWO KINGS V 46
WESTWARD OF TARA, AMONG THE HAZEL-TREES—— . . . . . 283 TWO KINGS 135
WESTWARD OF TARA, AMONG THE HAZEL-TREES—— . . . . . 283 TWO KINGS V 135
WESTWARD OF TARA, THERE TO AWAIT A FRIEND . . . . . 283 TWO KINGS V 136
CROW UPON TARA." KING EOCHAID BOWED HIS HEAD . . . . 286 TWO KINGS 211
CROW UPON TARA." SHE HAD FIXED HER EYES . . . . . 286 TWO KINGS V 211

TARA'S
IN TARA'S HALLS . . . . 609 IN TARAS HALLS T
A MAN I PRAISE THAT ONCE IN TARA'S HALLS . . . . . 609 IN TARAS HALLS 1

TARAV   SEE PAIRC-NA-TARAV

TARDY
FIERCE THRUST! A TARDY BLOSSOM HAD THE SEED, ... 665 ISLE STAT II 2 65

TARGETED
TARGETED, TROD LIKE SPRING. . . . . 504 QUARREL IN AGE 16

TARN
OF THE TARN WHERE YOUNG WAVES QUICKEN . . . . . . 647 ISLE STAT I 1 48

TARPAULIN
LANDOR'S TARPAULIN ON THE ROOF. . . . . 625 NATIVITY 6

TAR-WATER
DRANK TAR-WATER WITH THE BISHOP OF CLOYNE. . . . . . 486 SEVEN SAGES 5

TASK
FORTH! FORTH! O SPIRITS, YE HAVE HEARD YOUR TASK! . . . 669 ISLE STAT II 3 81

TASK'S
CHOOSING WHATEVER TASK'S MOST DIFFICULT . . . . . . 376 PHASES OF MOON 91

TASKS
AMONG TASKS NOT IMPOSSIBLE, IT TAKES . . . . . . 376 PHASES OF MOON 92

TASTE
AND FIND THEIR LAUGHTER SWEETER TO THE TASTE . . . . 228 SHADOW WATER B 134
THE TIME FOR YOU TO TASTE OF THAT SALT BREATH . . . . 293 TO A SHADE 21
BREAD TASTE SOUR. . . . . 554 CHURCH STATE 12
NO TASTE HAVE I FOR SLUMBER 'NEATH AN OAK. . . . . . 721 WITCH VIVIEN 31
AND TASTE WITH ME THE FAERIES' MEAT. . . . . . . 743 DANAAN QUICK 26
HATRED MAY BE SWEET TO THE TASTE." . . . . 776 AGAINST WITCH 31
HATRED MAY BE SWEET IN THE TASTE." . . . . 776 AGAINST WITCH V 31

TASTING
IS NO MORE THAN A WINE-CUP IN THE TASTING, ... 229 SHADOW WATER B 150
IS NO MORE THAN A WINE CUP IN THE TASTING, ... 229 SHADOW WATER B V 150

TATTER
FOR EVERY TATTER IN ITS MORTAL DRESS, ... 407 SAIL BYZANTIUM 12

TATTERED
O TATTERED CLOUDS OF THE WORLD, CALL FROM THE HIGH CAIRN 207 HANRAHANS SONG V 6
OF MAIVE,
LIKE TATTERED CLOUDS OF THE WORLD, PASSIONS CALL AND OUR 207 HANRAHANS SONG V 8
HEARTS BEAT!
A TATTERED COAT UPON A STICK, UNLESS . . . . . . 407 SAIL BYZANTIUM 10
CAN, TATTERED, STILL PROTECT, FADED ADORN. . . . . 477 SELF AND SOUL 16

	PAGE	TITLE		LINE
TAUGHT SEE STAR-TAUGHT RIGHT-TAUGHT				
HAVE TAUGHT TO IGNORANT MEN MOST VIOLENT WAYS,	256	NO SECOND TROY		3
NO RIGHT TAUGHT MAN DENIES.	590	OLD WICKED MAN	V	58
YET 'TIS NO SIN¡ MY FATHER TAUGHT IT ME.	692	MOSADA 1		50
TAUGHT ME WISE MUSIC, AND GAVE ME THIS OLD HARP¡	750	SHADOW WATER A		76
TAUT				
AND WHAT COULD MAKE THEIR MUSCLES TAUT	295	THREE BEGGARS		17
TAVERN				
SINCE, TAVERN COMRADES, YOU HAVE DIED,	273	GREY ROCK		49
NOW I AM IN THE TAVERN AND LEAN AGAINST THE WALL,	593	PILGRIM	V	21
TAWS				
I LAY ABOUT ME WITH THE TAWS	379	SAINT HUNCH		8
SOLIDER ARISTOTLE PLAYED THE TAWS	445	SCHOOL CHILDR		43
TAYLOR SEE SHAWE-TAYLOR				
FROM CASTLE TAYLOR TO THE ROXBOROUGH SIDE	326	ROBERT GREGORY		58
TE				
AND HAS NOT HEARD ABSOLVO TE.	656	ISLE STAT I 3		19
TEACH				
FROM NOTHING EVERY DAY, AND TEACH	436	FOR MY SON		18
PREFERRED TO TEACH A SCHOOL	472	ALL SOUL NIGHT		46
THOU'LT TEACH ME LAUGHING, AND I'LL TEACH THEE PEACE,	670	ISLE STAT II 3		101
THOU'LT TEACH ME LAUGHING, AND I'LL TEACH THEE PEACE,	670	ISLE STAT II 3		101
WOULD HE TEACH ANY SIN? GAZE IN THE CLOUD	692	MOSADA 1		58
TEACHERS				
INTO THEIR SHINING LIMBS--I'VE HAD GREAT TEACHERS.	231	SHADOW WATER B		195
FOR HOLIEST TEACHERS OF HIS WILL,	736	IN CHURCH		7
TEAR				
AND BID ME STAY, WITH MANY A TEAR¡	10	OISIN 1		113
NOR TEAR THE FOEMEN FROM THEIR STEEDS.	11	OISIN 1		128
WE WILL TEAR OUT THE FLAMING STONES, AND BATTER THE GATEWAY OF BRASS	62	OISIN 3		209
WE WILL TEAR OUT THE RED FLAMING STONES,	62	OISIN 3	V	209
WE WILL TEAR THE RED FLAMING STONES OUT,	62	OISIN 3	V	209
WITH ALL YOUR WHIRLING HAIR, AND DROP MANY AN AZURE TEAR.	73	ANASHU VIJAYA		46
WITH ALL YOUR WHIRLING HAIR, AND DROP THROUGH SPACE AN AZURE TEAR.	73	ANASHU VIJAYA	V	46
WITH ALL YOUR WHIRLING HAIR, AND DROP TEAR UPON AZURE TEAR.	73	ANASHU VIJAYA	V	46
WITH ALL YOUR WHIRLING HAIR, AND DROP TEAR UPON AZURE TEAR.	73	ANASHU VIJAYA	V	46
WITH ALL OUR WHIRLING HAIR, AND DROP MANY AN AZURE TEAR.	73	ANASHU VIJAYA	V	46
WITH A KISS AND A TEAR ON THY DROOPING BROW.	79	FALLING LEAVES		8
FROM FERNS THAT DROP THEIR TEAR	88	STOLEN CHILD	V	36
CAN NEVER TEAR THE LINNET FROM THE LEAF.	405	FOR DAUGHTER		56
AND TEAR THE HEART OUT OF HIS SIDE,	437	SONGS PLAY 1		3
I'D TEAR IT OFF AND THROW IT IN THE FIRE."	462	HARUN RASHID		34
WHAT MATTER? HEAVE NO SIGH, LET NO TEAR DROP,	564	GYRES		11
AND ON THAT CITY DROPPED A TEAR,	725	LEGEND		31
SHE PRAYS FOR EVERY FALLING TEAR	735	IN CHURCH		3
A PRAYER FOR EVERY FALLING TEAR	736	IN CHURCH		15
I FELT A SUDDEN TEAR START,	744	GLOVE CLOAK		10
TEAR-DROP				
BUT SOON A TEAR-DROP STARTED UP,	400	DEMON BEAST		21
TEARDROPS				
AND SHOWED THEIR EYES WITH TEARDROPS DIM,	18	OISIN 1		256
TEARFUL				
UNTIL ONE CAME, A TEARFUL BOY¡	17	OISIN 1		237
AND ONE CAME CLOSE, A TEARFUL BOY.	17	OISIN 1	V	237
TEARING				
THE HORSES OF THE FENIANS--TEARING ASUNDER	43	OISIN 2	V	210
TEARS				
BEFORE THIS DAY¡ FOR NOW THE FALL OF TEARS	30	OISIN 2		18
A HUNDRED SEASONS¡ FOR A SOUND OF TEARS	30	OISIN 2	V	18
AND TELL ME HOW MY KINDRED'S TEARS ARE WELLING,	33	OISIN 2	V	66
CAME NOW THE SLIDING OF TEARS AND SWEEPING OF MIST-COLD HAIR,	47	OISIN 3		7
CAME NOW THE SLIDING OF TEARS AND SWEEPING OF MIST-COLD AIR,	47	OISIN 3	V	7
CAME NOW THE SLIDING OF TEARS AND SWEEPING OF MIST COLD HAIR,	47	OISIN 3	V	7
CAME, AND MY FOREHEAD FELL LOW, AND MY TEARS LIKE BERRIES FELL DOWN¡	57	OISIN 3		154
AND MY TEARS WERE LARGER THAN BERRIES, AND I MURMURED, ˙ ˙ ˙	59	OISIN 3		178
AND MY TEARS WERE LARGE LIKE TO BERRIES, AND I MURMURED, ˙ ˙ ˙	59	OISIN 3	V	178
WHAT KNOW THE PILOTS OF THE STARS OF TEARS?	73	ANASHU VIJAYA		47
THE PHANTOM, BEAUTY, IN A MIST OF TEARS¡	73	ANASHU VIJAYA		55
FROM FERNS THAT DROP THEIR TEARS	88	STOLEN CHILD		36
BUT I WAS YOUNG AND FOOLISH, AND NOW AM FULL OF TEARS.	90	SALLEY GARDENS		8
AND SEEMED THE GREATNESS OF THE WORLD IN TEARS,	120	SORROW OF LOVE		6
AND WITH YOU CAME THE WHOLE OF THE WORLD'S TEARS,	120	SORROW OF LOVE	V	6
UNTIL HE FOUND, WITH LAUGHTER AND WITH TEARS,	170	SECRET ROSE		24
BEFORE HIS EYES, HE HAS TEARS FOR NONE,	192	BAILE AILLINN		82
BUT LAUGHTER AND TEARS--LAUGHTER, LAUGHTER, AND TEARS¡	235	SHADOW WATER B		298
BUT LAUGHTER AND TEARS--LAUGHTER, LAUGHTER, AND TEARS¡	235	SHADOW WATER B		298
AND HAVING SAID IT, BURST IN TEARS.	273	GREY ROCK		48
AND THESE IMMORTAL EYES SHED TEARS--	275	GREY ROCK		100
WE CANNOT PAY ITS TRIBUTE OF WILD TEARS.	334	LIVING BEAUTY		10
FOR ALL THEIR BROOM-STICKS AND THEIR TEARS,	343	DEJECTION		5
THEIR ANGRY TEARS, ARE GONE.	344	DEJECTION		6
AND THEN I LAUGH TILL TEARS RUN DOWN	456	FRIENDS YOUTH		17
LOVE HAS BLINDED HIM WITH TEARS¡	612	NEWS ORACLE		28

798

PAGE   TITLE   LINE

TEARS   (CONTINUED)
WHAT TEARS DOWN A TREE THAT HAS NOTHING WITHIN IT?   . . .   615 MARCH SONGS 2   23
WHAT TEARS DOWN A TREE HAS NOTHING WITHIN IT?   . . . .   615 MARCH SONGS 2   V   23
AND I CRIED TEARS DOWN. . . . .   628 JANE MOUNTAIN   22
WITH TEARS?   I WEARY OF YE.   THERE IS NONE . . .   650 ISLE STAT I 1   142
A WHITE, DUMB THING OF TEARS, HERE LET IT STAND, . .   663 ISLE STAT II 2   21
ALL SWIM WITH TEARS.   THE FAERY BOAT'S AT HAND! . . .   663 ISLE STAT II 2   33
WHOSE INSOLENT EYES UNUSED TO TEARS WOULD WEEP. . . .   678 ISLE STAT II 3   302
NOW WHEREFORE HAST THOU TEARS INNUMEROUS? . . . . .   723 KANVA ON SELF   1
AND TEARS OF FIRE FALL GENTLY IN THE DEW. . . . . .   738 YOU ARE SAD   4
ON TEARS AND LAUGHTER! THEY HAVE LURED YOU HITHER . .   757 SHADOW WATER A   207
I HAVE WET THIS BRAID OF HAIR WITH TEARS WHILE ASLEEP. .   762 SHADOW WATER A   294
TEASE
COME AND TEASE THEM TILL THE DAY. . . . .   727 LOVERS QUARREL   36
TEASING
TEASING EVERY WILFUL MAID. . . . .   727 LOVERS QUARREL   28
TEETH
YOU ARE NOT ITS CORE.   MY TEETH ARE IN THE WORLD, .   235 SHADOW WATER B   279
SANG THROUGH THEIR TEETH FROM NOON TO NOON! . . . .   296 THREE BEGGARS   41
GNASHING OF TEETH, DESPAIR! . . . .   346 ON WOMAN   39
AND CRY IN PLATO'S TEETH, ...   415 TOWER   147
ALL TEETH WERE DRAWN, ALL ANCIENT TRICKS UNLEARNED, . .   429 NINETEEN 19   17
WHERE WE WROUGHT THAT SHALL BREAK THE TEETH OF TIME. .   435 NEW FACES   4
THOSE GREAT SEA-HORSES BARE THEIR TEETH AND LAUGH AT THE   623 HIGH TALK   14
DAWN.
WITHIN HIS CLENCHED TEETH A SWORD. . . . .   673 ISLE STAT II 3   182
TELL
OISIN, TELL ME THE FAMOUS STORY . . . .   2 OISIN 1   V   1
NOW, PLEASANT MAIDEN, TELL TO ME . . . .   5 OISIN 1   V   43
TELL ON, NOR BOW THY HEATHEN CREST . . . .   11 OISIN 1   V 131A
FASTING AND PRAYERS.   TELL ON.   YES, YES, ...   24 OISIN 1   360
FASTING AND PRAYERS.   TELL ON.   AY, AY! . . . . .   24 OISIN 1   V   360
AND TELL ME THAT YOU FOUND A MAN UNBID. . . . . .   33 OISIN 2   67
"AND TELL THEM HOW I WEEP, UNTIL THEY WEEP! . . . .   33 OISIN 2   V   63
AND TELL ME HOW MY KINDRED'S TEARS ARE WELLING, . . .   33 OISIN 2   V   66
AND TELL ME HOW YOU CAME TO ONE UNBID, ...   33 OISIN 2   V   67
AND TELL OF YOUR GOODLY HOUSEHOLD AND THE GOODLY WORKS   51 OISIN 3   62
OF YOUR HANDS,
AND TO ITS LIPS THY STORY TELL, ...   66 HAPPY SHEPHERD   37
AND THOUGHT, I WILL MY HEAVY STORY TELL . . . . . .   68 SAD SHEPHERD   19
AND THOUGHT, "TO THIS WILL I MY STORY TELL, ...   68 SAD SHEPHERD   V   19
"WHO BADE YOU TELL THESE THINGS UPON MY FLOOR?" . . .   106 CUCHULAIN SEA   17
"WHO BADE YOU TELL THESE THINGS?" AND THEN SHE CRIED .   106 CUCHULAIN SEA   V   17
BUT TELL YOUR NAME AND LINEAGE TO HIM . . . . . .   108 CUCHULAIN SEA   36
BUT TELL ALONE YOUR NAME AND HOUSE TO HIM . . . . .   108 CUCHULAIN SEA   V   36
AND WHITE STARS TELL YOUR PRAISE. . . . .   113 ROSE OF PEACE   10
TO THESE OLD NIGHT SHALL ALL HER MYSTERY TELL! . . .   114 ROSE OF BATTLE   22
TELL US IT THEN! . . . .   116 FAERY SONG   12
TELL IT US THEN! . . . .   116 FAERY SONG   V   12
MY RHYMES MORE THAN THEIR RHYMING TELL . . . . . .   138 TO IRELAND   20
HAVE I NOT BID YOU TELL OF THAT GREAT QUEEN . . . .   181 QUEEN MAEVE   34
OUTRUN THE MEASURE.   I'D TELL OF THAT GREAT QUEEN . .   187 QUEEN MAEVE   141
TO TELL HIM HOW THE GIRL AILLINN . . . .   191 BAILE AILLINN   49
THE CRAZY HERDSMAN THAT WILL TELL HIS FELLOWS . . . .   229 SHADOW WATER B   167
AND TELL ME WHO IT IS THAT WE ARE WAKING. . . . .   241 SHADOW WATER B   403
TO TELL THEM A PLAIN STORY.   THAT'S NOT THE STORY! .   245 SHADOW WATER B   482
WILL SAY TO AN OLD MAN, "TELL ME OF THAT LADY . . .   356 BROKEN DREAMS   17
AND HAVING NO DESIRE THEY CANNOT TELL . . . . . .   376 PHASES OF MOON   107
BUT HAVING NO DESIRE THEY CANNOT TELL . . . . . .   376 PHASES OF MOON   V 107
AND SO FORGET THE COMFORT THAT NO WORDS CAN TELL . .   391 UNDER SATURN   V   4
TO TELL YOUR SIMPLEST WANT, AND KNOWN, ...   436 FOR MY SON   21
TO TELL YOUR SIMPLEST WANT, AND KNOW, ...   436 FOR MY SON   V   21
TWO THOUGHTS WERE SO MIXED UP I COULD NOT TELL . . .   471 ALL SOUL NIGHT   31
I HAVE MUMMY TRUTHS TO TELL . . . .   474 ALL SOUL NIGHT   86
YET A MOST GENTLE WOMAN! WHO CAN TELL . . . . . .   618 BRONZE HEAD   10
NOT TO ALLOW HIS LOOKS TO TELL . . . .   624 APPARITIONS   13
AND WHEN THEY KNOW WHAT OLD BOOKS TELL, ...   626 OLD MEN BE MAD   18
SEE, I TELL THY BEAUTIES O'ER, ...   647 ISLE STAT I 1   56
OLD MISER HOARDS OF GRIEF TO TELL AND TELL! . . . .   661 ISLE STAT II 1   55
OLD MISER HOARDS OF GRIEF TO TELL AND TELL! . . . .   661 ISLE STAT II 1   55
AYE, FIGHT WE MUST.   TELL ME, ANTONIO, MIGHT . . . .   662 ISLE STAT II 1   77
AND LET THEM TELL SAD HISTORIES, TILL THEIR EYES . .   663 ISLE STAT II 2   32
AND OF NASCHINA'S NOW THEY TELL--REND! REND! . . .   665 ISLE STAT II 2   69
A LITTLE NEARER THOSE BRIGHT STARS.   TELL ME, . . .   701 MOSADA   59
AND TELL ME A LOVE-STORY WHILE I DRINK. . . . . .   760 SHADOW WATER A   250
AND TELL ME A LOVE STORY WHILE I DRINK. . . . . .   760 SHADOW WATER A V 250
AND TELL HOW MANANAN SACKED MURIAS . . . .   766 SHADOW WATER A   377
AND TELL ITS STORY OVER THEIR BROWN ALE. . . . . .   767 SHADOW WATER A   393
SEEK AIBRIC ON THE LOCHLANN GALLEY, AND TELL HIM . .   767 SHADOW WATER A   401
TELLER   SEE FORTUNE-TELLER
TELLING   SEE A-TELLING
AND ONE WHOM YOU WILL GO TO WITHOUT TELLING, ...   33 OISIN 2   V   67
A PITY BEYOND ALL TELLING . . . .   119 PITY OF LOVE   1
TELLS
THE LOVER TELLS OF THE ROSE IN HIS HEART . . . . .   142 ROSE IN HEART   T
AEDH TELLS OF THE ROSE IN HIS HEART . . . . . .   142 ROSE IN HEART   V   T
THE EAST TELLS ALL HER SECRET JOY BEFORE DAYBREAK, .   154 BELOVED PEACE   V   4
HE TELLS OF A VALLEY FULL OF LOVERS . . . .   163 VALLEY LOVERS   T
AEDH TELLS OF A VALLEY FULL OF LOVERS . . . . . .   163 VALLEY LOVERS   V   T
HE TELLS OF THE PERFECT BEAUTY . . . .   164 PERFECT BEAUTY   T
AEDH TELLS OF THE PERFECT BEAUTY . . . .   164 PERFECT BEAUTY V   T

		PAGE	TITLE	LINE
TELLS (CONTINUED)				
IN ANY ANCIENT BOOK BUT TELLS OF YOU;		186	QUEEN MAEVE	135
MADGE TELLS ME WHAT I DARED NOT THINK		457	SECRETS OF OLD	3
HE TELLS HIS LIES BY ROTE;		598	STONE CROSS	2
SOME OLD MISER TELLS HIS STORE;		647	ISLE STAT I 1	58
TELLS ALL HIS SINNING IN THEIR EARS.		655	ISLE STAT I 3	14
TELLS ALL HER SINNING IN THEIR EARS.		655	ISLE STAT I 3 V	14
YOUNG GUARIMOND HE TELLS THEM O'ER AND O'ER,		661	ISLE STAT II 1	56
AND LET THE TALE BE MOURNFUL EACH ONE TELLS.		663	ISLE STAT II 2	36
TEMPEST				
. . . LOVE-MAKING OR PIERCING THE TEMPEST WITH SAILS.		53	OISIN 3	88
UNVISITED BY TEMPEST OR BY SUN,		446	COLONUS PRAISE	5
IT FEARED TO GIVE ITS LOVE A HURT WITH ALL THE TEMPEST THERE;		450	OWEN AHERNE	7
TEMPESTS				
HAVE BORNE ME WHERE THE TEMPESTS BLIND		6	OISIN 1 V	58
TEMPESTUOUS				
A BUNDLE OF TEMPESTUOUS CLOUD IS BLOWN		541	PARN FUNERAL 1	2
TEMPLE				
I, PRIESTESS OF THIS TEMPLE, OFFER UP		71	ANASHU VIJAYA	12
WITHIN THE TEMPLE, DEVIOUS WALKING, MADE		72	ANASHU VIJAYA	32
I, PRIESTESS OF THIS TEMPLE, OFFER UP		75	ANASHU VIJAYA	84
HIS TEMPLE AND HIS BANQUET HALL;		671	ISLE STAT II 3	134
TEMPT				
ALL THINGS CAN TEMPT ME		267	ALL TEMPT ME	T
ALL THINGS CAN TEMPT ME FROM THIS CRAFT OF VERSE;		267	ALL TEMPT ME	1
TEMPTATION				
MY TEMPTATION IS QUIET.		575	ACRE OF GRASS	7
TEN				
RANKING HIS DRUIDS ROUND HIM TEN BY TEN,		110	CUCHULAIN SEA	76
RANKING HIS DRUIDS ROUND HIM TEN BY TEN,		110	CUCHULAIN SEA	76
SENT FOR HIS DRUIDS TWENTY SCORE AND TEN,		110	CUCHULAIN SEA V	76
AND TEN BY TEN UNDER A QUICKEN TREE,		111	CUCHULAIN SEA V	81A
AND TEN BY TEN UNDER A QUICKEN TREE,		111	CUCHULAIN SEA V	81A
OLD DUBLIN MERCHANT "FREE OF TEN AND FOUR"		269	PARDON FATHERS	3
OLD DUBLIN MERCHANT "FREE OF THE TEN AND FOUR"		269	PARDON FATHERS V	3
FROM NINETEEN HUNDRED NINE OR TEN, PAVLOVA'S HAD THE CRY,		354	HIS PHOENIX	11
AND I ALONE, ONE IN TEN THOUSAND YEARS,		470	HARUN RASHID V	190
OUT OF TEN THOUSAND WINTERS, I ALONE—		470	HARUN RASHID V	190
TENANTS				
ARE MURDERING YOUR TENANTS THERE.		791	REPRISALS	16
TENDER				
WITH LAUGHTER LOW, AND TENDER, AND SWEET;		6	OISIN 1 V	54
SHE SAID, WITH LAUGHTER TENDER AND SWEET;		6	OISIN 1 V	54
AND LIFT YOUR TENDER EYELIDS, MAID,		125	GOES FERGUS	5
THINE EYES GROW FULL OF TENDER CARE;		135	TWO TREES	19
THY TENDER EYES GROW ALL UNKIND;		136	TWO TREES	39
AND YOU WOULD MURMUR TENDER WORDS,		175	BELOVED DEAD	5
I LONG FOR YOUR MERRY AND TENDER AND PITIFUL WORDS,		203	WITHER BOUGHS	3
TENDER AND FEARLESS ON HER FUNERAL PYRE;		688	NETTLESHIP	3
NO TENDER WISDOM FLOODS THE EYES		723	GIRLS SONG A	9
AND THEREON GREW A TENDER ROOT,		743	DANAAN QUICK	13
AND THEREON GREW A TENDER STEM,		743	DANAAN QUICK	14
TENDEREST				
AND THE LONG GREY GRASSES, WHOSE TENDEREST TOUCHES		27	OISIN 1 V	415B
THOUGH TENDEREST ROSES WERE ROUND YOU,		708	FAIRY PEDANT	29
TENDERLY				
WHEN I HAD STOOPED AND TENDERLY		10	OISIN 1 V	112A
TENDERNESS				
OR LOVE'S FIRST TENDERNESS DIE IN OUR GAZE.		27	OISIN 1	411
OR LOVE'S FIRST TENDERNESS DIE IN OUR GAZE.		27	OISIN 1 V	419D
OR LOVE'S FIRST TENDERNESS DIE IN OUR GAZE."		28	OISIN 1 V	427
BUT SHE WHOSE HOURS OF TENDERNESS WERE GONE		38	OISIN 2	138
AND HE HAD KNOWN AT LAST SOME TENDERNESS,		126	DREAM OF FAERY	3
AND BODILY TENDERNESS, AND FINDS THAT EVEN		228	SHADOW WATER B	147
BY TENDERNESS AND CARE,		346	ON WOMAN	37
AND BODILY TENDERNESS TO THE SOFT FIRE		750	SHADOW WATER A	60
AND BODILY TENDERNESS; AND HE WHO LONGS		750	SHADOW WATER A	66
AND BODILY TENDERNESS; BUT LOVE IS MADE		765	SHADOW WATER A	355
TENDING				
THEY WEARY OF TENDING		118	CRADLE SONG V	3
TENDING THE ROSES ROUND HIS LATTICE DOOR.		692	MOSADA 1	53
TENSE				
EVEN THE WISEST MAN GROWS TENSE		638	BEN BULBEN	33
TENT				
TENT POLE OF EDEN; THE TENT'S DRAPERY;		483	VERONIC NAPKIN V	2
LIKE SOME POOR ARAB TRIBESMAN AND HIS TENT.		491	COOLE BALLYLEE	40
OUR MASTER CAESAR IS IN THE TENT		617	LONG-LEG FLY	5
BEFORE HIS TENT THE GENERAL SIPS HIS WINE,		709	FERENCZ RENYI	6
REITERANT. A BIRD GOES BY THE TENT,		711	FERENCZ RENYI	46
REITERANT. A BOY GOES BY THE TENT,		711	FERENCZ RENYI V	46
TENTED				
ARE STILL THE ACHAIANS' TENTED CHIEFS AT BAY?		679	ISLE STAT II 3	310
SINCE 'MONG MY PEOPLE, TENTED ON THE HILLS,		690	MOSADA 1	4
TENTH				
YESTERDAY IN THE TENTH YEAR		361	ALF POLLEXFEN	27
AND ARE WE NOW IN THE TENTH YEAR?		361	ALF POLLEXFEN V	27
TENT-POLE				
TENT-POLE OF EDEN; THE TENT'S DRAPERY;		483	VERONIC NAPKIN	2
TENT'S				
TENT-POLE OF EDEN; THE TENT'S DRAPERY;		483	VERONIC NAPKIN	2

	PAGE	TITLE		LINE
TENT'S (CONTINUED)				
TENT POLE OF EDEN; THE TENT'S DRAPERY;	483	VERONIC NAPKIN	V	2
TENTS				
THOSE WANDERERS THAT WELCOMED IN THEIR TENTS	462	HARUN RASHID		23
THAT THEY HAVE WELCOMED IN THEIR TENTS THE DREAM	462	HARUN RASHID	V	23
OR PERCHING ON THE TENTS, A-WEARY STILL	690	MOSADA 1		8
DOWN THE LONG VALLEYS FROM MY PEOPLE'S TENTS, ...	691	MOSADA 1		30
ALONG THE TENTS, THE FIELDS, THE VILLAGE WALLS.	712	FERENCZ RENYI		71
ALONG THE TENTS, FIELD, THE VILLAGE WALLS.	712	FERENCZ RENYI	V	71
TERESA				
THE BODY OF SAINT TERESA LIES UNDECAYED IN TOMB, . . .	503	VACILLATION		80
TERRACES				
WITH DELICATE FEET UPON OLD TERRACES, ...	418	ANCEST HOUSES		26
TERRIBLE				
HOPELESS AND DEAR, OR TERRIBLE TO THINK ON, ...	281	TWO KINGS		96
A TERRIBLE BEAUTY IS BORN.	392	EASTER 1916		16
A TERRIBLE BEAUTY IS BORN.	393	EASTER 1916		40
A TERRIBLE BEAUTY IS BORN.	394	EASTER 1916		80
THOSE TERRIBLE IMPLACABLE STRAIGHT LINES	467	HARUN RASHID		142
THE POETS HAVE IMAGINED, TERRIBLE AND GAY."	602	GALLERY REVIS		12
I, THROUGH THE TERRIBLE NOVELTY OF LIGHT, STALK ON, STALK ON;	623	HIGH TALK		13
TERRIFIED				
I WAS NO LONGER TERRIFIED--HIS VOICE	284	TWO KINGS		171
FROM TERRIFIED, INVISIBLE BEAST OR BIRD;	389	IMAGE PAST		6
HOW CAN THOSE TERRIFIED VAGUE FINGERS PUSH	441	LEDA AND SWAN		5
TERRIFYING				
A SWEET, MIRACULOUS, TERRIFYING SOUND.	277	TWO KINGS		17
TERROR				
WITH QUAKING JOINTS AND TERROR STRUCKEN FACES, . . .	185	QUEEN MAEVE	V	121
WE SHOULD BE DAZED AND TERROR STRUCK	272	GREY ROCK	V	37
ITS TERROR GROWING WILDER AT EVERY FOOT-FALL, . . .	279	TWO KINGS	V	45D
ITS TERROR GROWING WILDER AT EVERY FOOTFALL . . .	279	TWO KINGS	V	45D
I COWERED BACK UPON THE WALL IN TERROR, ...	284	TWO KINGS		164
IT MUST BE THAT THE TERROR IN THEIR EYES	375	PHASES OF MOON		72
THE NIGHT CAN SWEAT WITH TERROR AS BEFORE	429	NINETEEN 19		29
THE THREEFOLD TERROR OF LOVE; A FALLEN FLARE	499	MOTHER OF GOD		1
THE TERROR OF ALL TERRORS THAT I BORE	499	MOTHER OF GOD		4
THE THREE-FOLD TERROR OF LOVE; A FALLEN FLARE	499	MOTHER OF GOD	V	1
FROM TERROR AND DECEPTION FREED IT CAN	558	RIBH CHRISTIAN		9
AND HE, DESPITE HIS TERROR, CANNOT CEASE	563	MERU		4
AND FINDS THERE NOTHING TO MAKE ITS TERROR LESS . . .	618	BRONZE HEAD		6
A VISION OF TERROR THAT IT MUST LIVE THROUGH	619	BRONZE HEAD		17
WHAT HOUR OF TERROR COMES TO TEST THE SOUL, ...	622	HOUND VOICE		11
IN TERROR FLINGS HER AT HER LOVER'S FEET.	713	FERENCZ RENYI	V	85
TERROR'S				
AND IN THAT TERROR'S NAME OBEYED THE CALL, ...	622	HOUND VOICE		12
TERRORS				
ALL BUT THE TERRORS OF THE WOODLAND FLIGHT FORGOT . .	366	HER COURAGE		5
THE TERROR OF ALL TERRORS THAT I BORE	499	MOTHER OF GOD		4
TERROR-STRICKEN				
WITH QUAKING JOINTS AND TERROR-STRICKEN FACES, . . .	185	QUEEN MAEVE		121
AND THEN, AS TERROR-STRICKEN AS A CHILD	279	TWO KINGS	V	45A
TERROR-STRUCK				
WE SHOULD BE DAZED AND TERROR-STRUCK, ...	272	GREY ROCK		37
WHY IS THE WOMAN TERROR-STRUCK?	625	NATIVITY		11
TERROR-STRUCKEN				
WITH QUAKING JOINTS AND TERROR-STRUCKEN FACES, . . .	185	QUEEN MAEVE	V	121
TEST				
TO TEST THEIR FANCY BY THEIR SIGHT;	410	TOWER		44
TEST EVERY WORK OF INTELLECT OR FAITH, ...	501	VACILLATION		30
EVERYTHING DOWN TO THAT SOLE TEST AGAIN, ...	603	GALLERY REVIS		46
ALL THINGS DOWN TO THAT COMMON TEST AGAIN, ...	603	GALLERY REVIS	V	46
WHAT HOUR OF TERROR COMES TO TEST THE SOUL, ...	622	HOUND VOICE		11
TESTS				
FOR EVERY NERVE, AND TESTS A LOVER	388	SOLOMON WITCH		22
FOR EVERY NERVE; LOVER TESTS LOVER	388	SOLOMON WITCH	V	22
TESTY				
TESTY DELIRIUM	416	TOWER		186
TETHER				
QUIET THE DOG, TETHER THE PONY	617	LONG-LEG FLY		3
A KID, HELD BY ONE SOFT WHITE EAR FOR TETHER, . . .	715	DWELT SYCAMORE		3
TEXT				
BUT HERE'S A HAUGHTIER TEXT, ...	259	UNWORTH PRAISE		12
THAT DYING CHOSE THE LIVING WORLD FOR TEXT	324	ROBERT GREGORY		26
IT FOLLOWS FROM THIS LATIN TEXT	386	ROBARTES DANCE		43
AND ASKED ABOUT THE PICTURES OR THE TEXT; . . .	466	HARUN RASHID		121
THAT HE HAD FOUND A TEXT TO PROVE	492	ANNE GREGORY		15
HE'D FIND FOR THIS SOME HOLY TEXT.	728	PRIEST FAIRY		16
THAMES				
OR STAY WITH ME BESIDE THE THAMES, ...	741	EARL PAUL		59
THAN				
THAN THE HORNLESS DEER WE CHASED THAT MORN, . . .	2	OISIN 1	V	7P
BUT THE TALE, THOUGH WORDS BE LIGHTER THAN AIR, . .	3	OISIN 1		11
THAN DOVES THAT MOANED ROUND EMAN'S HALL . . .	3	OISIN 1	V	7EE
MORE SLEEK THAN ANY GRANARY MOUSE	4	OISIN 1		36
"WERE THERE NO BETTER THAN MY SON	6	OISIN 1		60
WHOSE LONG WOOL WHITER THAN SEA-FROTH FLOWS, . .	8	OISIN 1		90
WHOSE LONG WOOL WHITER THAN SEA FROTH FLOWS, . .	8	OISIN 1	V	90
AND SWEETER OF VOICE THAN THE PLEASANT BIRDS, . .	9	OISIN 1	V	95
AND SWIFTER THAN THE SALMON HERDS;	9	OISIN 1	V	96

		PAGE	TITLE		LINE
THAN	(CONTINUED)				
IN A VIGOUR MORE THAN MORTAL MEASURE,	· · · · · · ·	9	OISIN 1	V	98
WAS NOT MORE LEVEL THAN THE SEA,	· · · · · · ·	13	OISIN 1		157
THAN THIS STRANGE HUMAN BARD," HE CRIED;	· · · · ·	17	OISIN 1		239
THAN THIS STRANGE BARD," HE CRIED, AND CAUGHT	· · · · ·	17	OISIN 1	V	239
BUT FAINTER THAN A YOUNG LAMB'S BLEAT.	· · · · · ·	26	OISIN 1		399
AND FAINTER THAN A YOUNG LAMB'S BLEAT.	· · · · · ·	26	OISIN 1	V	399
· · · FOR WHITER THAN NEW-WASHED FLEECE	· · · · · ·	47	OISIN 3		11
AND MORE COMELY THAN MAN CAN MAKE THEM	· · · · · ·	49	OISIN 3		32
AND EACH OF THE HUGE WHITE CREATURES WAS HUGER THAN		49	OISIN 3		33
FOURSCORE MEN;					
· · · LONG WARLESS, GROWN WHITER THAN CURDS.	· · · ·	49	OISIN 3		36
MORE COMELY THAN MAN MAY MAKE THEM, INLAID WITH SILVER		49	OISIN 3	V	29
AND GOLD,					
AND EACH OF THE HUGE WHITE CREATURES WAS HUGER THAN		49	OISIN 3	V	33
FOUR-SCORE MEN;					
· · · LONG-WARLESS, GROWN WHITER THAN CURDS.	· · · · ·	49	OISIN 3	V	36
IN ONE WAS A BRANCH SOFT-SHINING WITH BELLS MORE MANY THAN		50	OISIN 3		46
SIGHS					
SOFTER THAN SNOW-FLAKES IN APRIL AND PIERCING THE MARROW		51	OISIN 3		68
LIKE FLAME.					
WRAPT IN THE WAVE OF THAT MUSIC, WITH WEARINESS MORE THAN		51	OISIN 3		69
OF EARTH,					
SOFTER THAN SNOWFLAKES IN APRIL, AND PIERCING THE MARROW		51	OISIN 3	V	68
LIKE FLAME.					
WERE THE WINDS LESS SOFT THAN THE BREATH OF A PIGEON	· · ·	56	OISIN 3		134
AND MY TEARS WERE LARGER THAN BERRIES, AND I MURMURED,		59	OISIN 3		178
· · ·					
FOR THE WORLD'S MORE FULL OF WEEPING THAN YOU CAN		87	STOLEN CHILD		12
UNDERSTAND.					
FOR THE WORLD'S MORE FULL OF WEEPING THAN YOU CAN		87	STOLEN CHILD		27
UNDERSTAND.					
FOR THE WORLD'S MORE FULL OF WEEPING THAN YOU CAN		88	STOLEN CHILD		41
UNDERSTAND.					
FROM A WORLD MORE FULL OF WEEPING THAN HE CAN UNDERSTAND.		89	STOLEN CHILD		53
FOR THE WORLD'S MORE FULL OF WEEPING THAN HE CAN UNDERSTAND		89	STOLEN CHILD	V	53
IN THE JUNES THAT WERE WARMER THAN THESE ARE,	· · · · · ·	91	OLD FISHERMAN		3
CAME KEENERS HOARSER THAN ROOKS.	· · · · · · · ·	92	FATHER OHART		22
AND LOVELIER THAN THE MOON UPON THE SEA;	· · · · ·	106	CUCHULAIN SEA	V	16A
"NAY, YOU ARE TALLER THAN CUCHULAIN, SON."	· · · · ·	107	CUCHULAIN SEA	V	27
MORE MOURNFUL THAN THE DEPTH OF STARRY SKIES,	· · · ·	108	CUCHULAIN SEA	V	42
MORE FLEETING THAN THE SEA'S FOAM-FICKLE FACE,	· · · ·	112	ROSE OF WORLD	V	8
MORE FLEETING THAN THE SEA'S FOAM FICKLE FACE,	· · · ·	112	ROSE OF WORLD	V	8
WHO HAVE SOUGHT MORE THAN IS IN RAIN OR DEW	· · · ·	114	ROSE OF BATTLE		16
SHE WAS MORE BEAUTIFUL THAN THY FIRST LOVE,	· · · ·	123	DREAM OF DEATH		11
MY RHYMES MORE THAN THEIR RHYMING TELL	· · · · · ·	138	TO IRELAND		20
IS COMELIER THAN CANDLES AT MOTHER MARY'S FEET,	· · ·	147	UNAPPEAS HOST		12
IS COMELIER THAN CANDLES BEFORE MAURYA'S FEET.	· · · ·	147	UNAPPEAS HOST	V	12
AND LOVE IS LESS KIND THAN THE GREY TWILIGHT,	· · · ·	148	INTO TWILIGHT		15
AND HOPE IS LESS DEAR THAN THE DEW OF THE MORN.	· · · ·	148	INTO TWILIGHT		16
A MORE DREAM-HEAVY HOUR THAN THIS;	· · · · · · ·	156	FORGOT BEAUTY		17
AND WITH HEART MORE OLD THAN THE HORN	· · · · · ·	157	POET BELOVED		5
AND WITH THE HEART MORE OLD THAN THE HORN	· · · · ·	157	POET BELOVED	V	5
WITH WORDS LIGHTER THAN AIR,	· · · · · · · ·	162	ASKS FORGIVE		2
O WINDS, OLDER THAN CHANGING OF NIGHT AND DAY,	· · · ·	162	ASKS FORGIVE		7
O WINDS, ELDER THAN CHANGING OF NIGHT AND DAY,	· · · ·	162	ASKS FORGIVE	V	7
BUT THAT GREAT QUEEN, WHO MORE THAN HALF THE NIGHT		180	QUEEN MAEVE		16
MORE STILL THAN THEY HAD BEEN FOR A GOOD MONTH,	· · ·	182	QUEEN MAEVE		54
THAN ANY WHOSE UNHAPPINESS	· · · · · · · ·	190	BAILE AILLINN		36
AND YOU ARE MORE HEART THAN SHE,	· · · · · · ·	197	BAILE AILLINN		202
IT ALL, AND MORE THAN IT ALL, WOULD COME TO NAUGHT,	· ·	201	OLD MEMORY		8
IT ALL, MORE THAN IT ALL, WOULD COME TO NAUGHT,	· · ·	201	OLD MEMORY	V	8
IS TO WORK HARDER THAN ALL THESE, AND YET	· · · ·	205	ADAMS CURSE		11
BUT PURER THAN A TALL CANDLE BEFORE THE HOLY ROOD	· ·	208	HANRAHANS SONG		14
BUT PURER THAN A TALL CANDLE BEFORE THE BLESSED ROOD	· ·	208	HANRAHANS SONG	V	14
YET DREAMED THAT BEINGS HAPPIER THAN MEN	· · · · ·	218	WOODS OF COOLE		18
THAT HAS LESS UPS AND DOWNS THAN ROBBERY,	· · · · ·	222	SHADOW WATER B		7
AND KISS MORE LIPS THAN LASTING PEACEABLE MEN	· · · ·	225	SHADOW WATER B		71
MORE RICHES THAN THEY EVER HOPED TO FIND?	· · · · ·	226	SHADOW WATER B		94
WHY SHOULD YOU BE MORE FAITHFUL THAN THE REST,	· · ·	227	SHADOW WATER B		109
HOW ARE WE BETTER OFF THAN SEAGHAN THE FOOL,	· · · ·	228	SHADOW WATER B		129
WE HAVE BEEN NO BETTER OFF THAN SEAGHAN THE FOOL,	· ·	228	SHADOW WATER B	V	129
IS NO MORE THAN A WINE-CUP IN THE TASTING,	· · · · ·	229	SHADOW WATER B		150
IS NO MORE THAN A WINE CUP IN THE TASTING,	· · · · ·	229	SHADOW WATER B	V	150
TO MAKE LOW LAUGHTER MORE THAN MEAT AND DRINK,	· · ·	230	SHADOW WATER B		186
THAN A STRONG BODY AND A READY HAND.	· · · · · ·	232	SHADOW WATER B		236
WHAT POWER THAT IS MORE MIGHTY THAN DESIRE	· · · · ·	234	SHADOW WATER B		267
ALTHOUGH YOU ARE MORE BEAUTIFUL THAN ANY,	· · · · ·	236	SHADOW WATER B		305
THAT IS MORE MIGHTY THAN THE SUN AND MOON,	· · · · ·	237	SHADOW WATER B		328
OR THAN THE SHIVERING CASTING-NET OF THE STARS,	· · ·	237	SHADOW WATER B		329
MORE MIGHTY THAN THE STARS HALF TROUBLED ME,	· · · ·	237	SHADOW WATER B		332
BETTER THAN MY OWN HANDS. I HAVE DECEIVED YOU	· · ·	244	SHADOW WATER B		466
AND IF THAT HAPPINESS BE MORE THAN DREAMS,	· · · · ·	248	SHADOW WATER B		554
MORE THAN THE FROTH, THE FEATHER, THE DUST-WHIRL,	· ·	248	SHADOW WATER B		555
MORE THAN THE FROTH, THE FEATHER, THE DUSTWHIRL,	· · ·	248	SHADOW WATER B	V	555
THAT BALANCED WITH A WORD IS MORE THAN NOISE;	· · · ·	258	KING NO KING		4
AYE, AND WORSE WRONG THAN THESE.	· · · · · · ·	260	UNWORTH PRAISE		18
THAN THIS ACCUSTOMED TOIL. WHEN I WAS YOUNG,	· · · ·	267	ALL TEMPT ME		5
COLDER AND DUMBER AND DEAFER THAN A FISH.	· · · · ·	267	ALL TEMPT ME		10
YOUR EARS THAN STORIES NOW IN FASHION,	· · · · · ·	271	GREY ROCK		5
THAT HAS MORE LIFE IN IT THAN DEATH,	· · · · · ·	271	GREY ROCK		8

		PAGE	TITLE	LINE

THAN (CONTINUED)

Text	PAGE	TITLE		LINE
THAN LOVER'S MUSIC--LET THAT BE,	276	GREY ROCK		130
WHITER THAN CURDS, ITS EYES THE TINT OF THE SEA,	277	TWO KINGS		7
MORE HANDS IN HEIGHT THAN ANY STAG IN THE WORLD	277	TWO KINGS		9
THAN MOUND AND STONE THAT KEEP ALL VIRTUE IN,	281	TWO KINGS		106
DEARER THAN ANY THAT THE DUMB STONE HIDES,	281	TWO KINGS	V	96
THAN TRIUMPH, TURN AWAY	291	TO A FRIEND		10
THAT LOVED HIS LEARNING BETTER THAN MANKIND,	324	ROBERT GREGORY		18
OR LEAVE THEM HAPPIER THAN BEFORE.	328	IRISH AIRMAN		8
THAN 'TWERE AN APPARITION. O HEART, WE ARE OLD!	334	LIVING BEAUTY		8
THAN DUMB-BELL AND FOIL	334	SONG		3
THAN DUMB BELL AND FOIL	334	SONG	V	3
MORE THAN ANOTHER	336	YOUNG GIRL		2
YOU ARE MORE BEAUTIFUL THAN ANY ONE,	356	BROKEN DREAMS		27
YOU WERE MORE BEAUTIFUL THAN ANY ONE,	356	BROKEN DREAMS	V	27
YOU ARE MORE BEAUTIFUL THAN ANYONE	356	BROKEN DREAMS	V	27
MORE PLAIN TO THE MIND'S EYE THAN ANY FACE	368	EGO DOMINUS		21
WHAT BETTER THAN CALL A DANCE?	378	CAT AND MOON		13
WHAT VOICE MORE SWEET THAN HERS	392	EASTER 1916		21
THAN THAT I MAY FIND OUT A WAY	401	DEMON BEAST		41
BUT THAT HE FOUND MORE SUBSTANCE THERE THAN DREAMS,	417	ANCEST HOUSES	V	10
THAN IN OUR LOVE! O HONEY-BEES,	425	STARES NEST		19
THAN IN OUR LOVES! OH, HONEY-BEES,	425	STARES NEST	V	19
THE LIVING SEEM MORE SHADOWY THAN THEY.	435	NEW FACES		8
I HAVE LOVED YOU BETTER THAN MY SOUL FOR ALL MY WORDS,	442	BLACK CENTAUR		14
IF YOU ARE NO MORE STRENGTH THAN I AM BEAUTY	448	HERO GIRL FOOL		10
THAN THE HEAVENLY CIRCUIT OF ITS STARS	451	FIRST LOVE		17
THAN HEAVENLY CIRCUIT OF ITS STARS	451	FIRST LOVE	V	17
THAN SOULS THAT START NO GAME AND TURN NO RHYME!	464	HARUN RASHID		68
THAN ALL MY BURSTING SPRINGTIME KNEW. A GIRL	466	HARUN RASHID		105
MORE WOMEN BORN THAN MEN."	485	STATISTICS		4
SEEMED ONCE MORE DEAR THAN LIFE! ANCESTRAL TREES,	491	COOLE BALLYLEE		34
SHADE MORE THAN MAN, MORE IMAGE THAN A SHADE!	497	BYZANTIUM		10
SHADE MORE THAN MAN, MORE IMAGE THAN A SHADE!	497	BYZANTIUM		10
MORE MIRACLE THAN BIRD OR HANDIWORK,	497	BYZANTIUM		18
MORE MIRACLE THAN BIRD OR HANDY-WORK,	497	BYZANTIUM	V	18
SENSE THAN A COMMON MAN?	507	STREAM AND SUN		10
NO BETTER THAN A BEAST	572	LADYS 1ST SONG		11
NO! GREATER THAN PYTHAGORAS, FOR THE MEN	610	STATUES		9
WITH NO MORE SOUND THAN THE MICE MAKE	618	LONG-LEG FLY		27
THAN THE PEEPING PANSY'S FACE,	647	ISLE STAT I 1		52
AND THINE EYES MORE BRIGHT THAN FAERY'S,	647	ISLE STAT I 1		53
BENEATH THE WEIGHT OF GREATER GRIEF THAN I!	661	ISLE STAT II 1		63
IS NOT MORE FAIR AND JOYOUS THAN SHE IS	661	ISLE STAT II 1		71
FAR FLEETER THAN THE MILLION-FOOTED SEA.	670	ISLE STAT II 3		108
TO WATCH THEE PASS? YET DEEPER THAN MEN KNOW	672	ISLE STAT II 3		158
FOR I AM MIGHTIER NOW BY FAR THAN THEE,	673	ISLE STAT II 3		193
DEEPER THAN THE DEEPEST WELL."	697	MOSADA 2		27
YET WHITER BEARD HAVE YOU THAN MERLIN HAD.	721	WITCH VIVIEN		30
THAN OLD MEN'S ANY DAY, AS MERLIN FOUND.	721	WITCH VIVIEN		47
I HOLD HIM DEARER THAN THE GLAD,	723	GIRLS SONG A		3
I HOLD HIM DEARER THAN THE GOOD,	723	GIRLS SONG A		7
I HOLD HIM DEARER THAN THE WISE,	723	GIRLS SONG A		11
THAN IN BRIEF LONGING AND DECEIVING HOPE	750	SHADOW WATER A		65
ARE BETTER THAN THE WOODS WHERE NO LOVE FADES	754	SHADOW WATER A		160
AND SAID IT WAS MIGHTIER THAN THE SUN AND MOON,	762	SHADOW WATER A		289
OR THAN THE SHIVERING CASTING-NET OF THE STARS.	762	SHADOW WATER A		290
OR THAN THE SHIVERING CASTING NET OF THE STARS.	762	SHADOW WATER A	V	290

THANK

Text	PAGE	TITLE		LINE
"I THANK YOU FOR YOUR KINDNESS TO MY BROTHER,	286	TWO KINGS	V	212

THANKED

Text	PAGE	TITLE		LINE
AND THANKED HER FOR HER KINDNESS TO HIS BROTHER,	286	TWO KINGS		212

THANKFUL

Text	PAGE	TITLE		LINE
WITH SPEEDY FEET AND A MOST THANKFUL HEART!	185	QUEEN MAEVE		100
AND BEING THANKFUL MURROUGH FOUND,	274	GREY ROCK		77

THANKS

Text	PAGE	TITLE		LINE
BECAUSE YOU SAVED MY RICE. HAVE YOU NO THANKS?	73	ANASHU VIJAYA		40
SAID, "AENGUS AND HIS SWEETHEART GIVE THEIR THANKS	187	QUEEN MAEVE		146
NOR GAVE GOD THANKS TILL OVERHEAD	307	HOUR DAWN		121
AND GAVE GOD THANKS THAT OVERHEAD	307	HOUR DAWN	V	121
WAKING HE THANKS THE LORD THAT HE	633	MAN AND ECHO		27

THEATRE

Text	PAGE	TITLE		LINE
THEATRE BUSINESS, MANAGEMENT OF MEN.	260	FASC DIFFICULT		11
AT THE ABBEY THEATRE	264	ABBEY THEATRE		T

THEBAID

Text	PAGE	TITLE		LINE
THROUGH BARREN THEBAID,	401	DEMON BEAST		44

THEME

Text	PAGE	TITLE		LINE
IN THE NARROW THEME OF LOVE	333	SOLOMON SHEBA		7
IN THE ONE NARROW THEME OF LOVE	333	SOLOMON SHEBA	V	7
UNTIL HER PRAISE SHOULD BE THE UPPERMOST THEME,	350	HER PRAISE		6
TWO CONTEMPLATING PASSIONS CHOSE ONE THEME	466	HARUN RASHID		117
MUST VANISH ON THE INSTANT IF THE MIND BUT CHANGE ITS THEME!	481	BLOOD AND MOON		27
WE WERE THE LAST ROMANTICS--CHOSE FOR THEME	491	COOLE BALLYLEE		41
WHAT, BE A SINGER BORN AND LACK A THEME?	502	VACILLATION		73
WHAT THEME HAD HOMER BUT ORIGINAL SIN?	502	VACILLATION		77
UPON THE SUPREME THEME OF ART AND SONG!	523	LONG SILENCE		6
THAT STILLNESS FOR A THEME	535	CHOSEN		14
I SOUGHT A THEME AND SOUGHT FOR IT IN VAIN,	629	CIRCUS ANIMALS		1
BUT HUSH, FOR I HAVE LOST THE THEME,	633	MAN AND ECHO		41

803

	PAGE	TITLE	LINE
THEMES			
WHAT CAN I BUT ENUMERATE OLD THEMES?	629	CIRCUS ANIMALS	9
THEMES OF THE EMBITTERED HEART, OR SO IT SEEMS, ...	629	CIRCUS ANIMALS	13
THENCE			
BURIED AND MIGHTY. THENCE I JOURNEYED NOT	39	OISIN 2 V	151
HE WALKED THAT ROOM AND ISSUED THENCE	438	SONGS PLAY 2	2
THENCE HAVE I COME WINGING:	672	ISLE STAT II 3	170
AND NOT COME THENCE: FOR HERE IN THIS SMALL RING-- . . .	699	MOSADA 3	22
THEOLOGY			
RIBH PREFERS AN OLDER THEOLOGY	556	RIBH PATRICK V	T
THEREBY			
AND THESE THINGS CAME, SO MUCH THE MORE THEREBY	265	THESE CLOUDS	8
THEREIN			
THEREIN THE SILVER HARP HE HURLED, ...	17	OISIN 1 V	244
THEREIN ARE MANY QUEENS LIKE BRANWEN AND GUINEVERE: . . .	209	UNDER THE MOON	11
HE IT HAS FOUND SHALL FIND THEREIN	538	LAST CONFESS	17
LIES IN A CIRCLE ON THE GRASS: THEREIN	555	RIBH AT TOMB	26
THEREON			
THEREON DID SHE LOOK HAUGHTY AND SWEET:	6	OISIN 1	54
OR CLUNG THEREON LIKE SWARMING BEES:	14	OISIN 1	181
THEREON YOUNG NIAMH SOFTLY CAME	25	OISIN 1	373
BUT FLY WHILE STILL YOU MAY." AND THEREON I:	35	OISIN 2	89
THEREON IN OGHAM LETTERS, "MANANNAN":	38	OISIN 2	128
THEREON HE SHOOK THE MORE AND CAST HIM DOWN	106	CUCHULAIN SEA	14
THEREON A YOUNG MAN MET HIS EYE, ...	274	GREY ROCK	85
THAT WE MAY HARRY HIM." THEREON	275	GREY ROCK	106
BUT THEREON EVERY GOD STOOD UP	275	GREY ROCK	116
THEREON SHE CAST HERSELF UPON THE GROUND, ...	275	GREY ROCK V	107
FOR MEDICINE." THEREON HE CRIED ALOUD, ...	281	TWO KINGS	98
THEREON HE SEIZED ME IN HIS ARMS, BUT I	285	TWO KINGS	201
THEREON THE BELLOWING OF THE EMPOUNDED HERDS	286	TWO KINGS	214
AND THEREON, MERRY AS A BIRD	296	THREE BEGGARS	25
AND THEREON SAW, WHERE STONES HAD BEEN	302	HOUR DAWN V	20
AND SO TAKE THAT AND THAT." THEREON	307	HOUR DAWN	112
THEREON MY PHOENIX ANSWERED IN REPROOF, ...	352	PEOPLE	22
THEREON I MADE MY MOAN, ...	384	VISION ROBART	63
THEREON REPLIED: "A COCKEREL	387	SOLOMON WITCH	9
THEREON EXPLAINED: "A COCKEREL	387	SOLOMON WITCH V	9
THE GREAT GREY-EYED ATHENE STARES THEREON.	447	COLONUS PRAISE	16
BUT SINCE I LAID A HAND THEREON	451	FIRST LOVE	7
BUT COULD NOT CAST A SINGLE JET THEREON.	482	BLOOD AND MOON	39
I CANNOT LOOK THEREON.	501	VACILLATION	49
THE SWORD'S A CROSS: THEREON HE DIED:	562	CONJUNCTIONS	3
AND DROPPED AND DIED THEREON, FOR SHE	571	THREE BUSHES	54
WHERE MY FRIENDS' PORTRAITS HANG AND LOOK THEREON: . . .	604	GALLERY REVIS	52
I SHALL BE OLD INDEED." THEREON THE MAN	609	IN TARAS HALLS	10
AND THEREON GREW A TENDER ROOT, ...	743	DANAAN QUICK	13
AND THEREON GREW A TENDER STEM, ...	743	DANAAN QUICK	14
AND THEREON GREW THE RUDDY FRUIT	743	DANAAN QUICK	15
THEREUPON			
AND THEREUPON I DREW THE LIVID CHOP	40	OISIN 2	178
"YOU DARE ME TO MY FACE," AND THEREUPON	106	CUCHULAIN SEA	17
THE MARTYRS CALL THE WORLD." AND THEREUPON	205	ADAMS CURSE	14
A CURLEW ANSWERED: AND SUDDENLY THEREUPON I THOUGHT . . .	291	PAUDEEN	5
AND THEREUPON THEIR ANGER GREW, ...	297	THREE BEGGARS V	46
AND THEREUPON IMAGINATION AND HEART WERE DRIVEN	316	COLD HEAVEN	3
AND THEREUPON WITH AGED, HIGH-PITCHED VOICE	375	PHASES OF MOON	84
AND THEREUPON THERE COMES THAT SCREAM	389	IMAGE PAST	5
BUT NOW WIND DROPS, DUST SETTLES: THEREUPON	433	NINETEEN 19	125
AND THEREUPON MY HEART IS DRIVEN WILD:	444	SCHOOL CHILDR	23
AND THEREUPON A COLLOQUY TOOK PLACE	463	HARUN RASHID	45
THAT THEREUPON A COLLOQUY TOOK PLACE	463	HARUN RASHID V	45
AND THEREUPON HIS BOUNTY GAVE WHAT NOW	465	HARUN RASHID	103
AND THEREUPON REPLIES	531	FATHER CHILD	6
THEREUPON, ...	628	JANE MOUNTAIN	18
AND THEREUPON THAT LINEN-CARRIER SAID:	634	CUCHULAIN COMF	11
THERNOT			
NOW, JUDGE, MUST SHEPHERD THERNOT THERE AND I	661	ISLE STAT II 1	65
THERNOT'S			
CEASE! THERNOT'S WOUNDED, CEASE! THEY WILL NOT HEED. . .	665	ISLE STAT II 2	64
THETIS			
PELEUS ON THETIS STARES.	612	NEWS ORACLE	26
THETIS'			
BUT THETIS' BELLY LISTENS.	612	NEWS ORACLE	29
THEWS			
THAT HE, WHEN FRENZY STIRRED HIS THEWS, ...	271	GREY ROCK	22
THICK			
WINE SHALL RUN THICK TO THE END, ...	554	CHURCH STATE	11
AND SEE HOW THICK THE DEW LIES ON MY FACE.	703	MOSADA 3	104
THICKENED SEE HONEY-THICKENED			
AND THICKENED ALL THE WHIRLING AIR. THEN DID	46	OISIN 2	V 245A
THICKENS			
WHO WHEN NIGHT THICKENS ARE AFLOAT	196	BAILE AILLINN	179
THICKER			
THE VAPOUR IS MUCH THICKER. GOD! THE STAKE!	695	MOSADA 1	112
THICKET			
WE DANCED TO WHERE IN THE WINDING THICKET	20	OISIN 1	304
THEN ONWARD IN THE WINDING THICKET	20	OISIN 1 V	304
THIEVE			
AND FREE--'TWILL THIEVE AWAY WITH SLEEPY MOOD	700	MOSADA 3	30

THIEVING
    BUT A THIEVING RASCALLY CUR-- . . . .   552 SONGS REWRIT 2   7
    THEIR THIEVING WINGS THAT WE MIGHT NEVER PART. . . . .   702 MOSADA 3   98

THIGH
    THE STRONG THIGH AND THE AGILE THIGH WERE MET, ...   278 TWO KINGS   28
    THE STRONG THIGH AND THE AGILE THIGH WERE MET, ...   278 TWO KINGS   28
    STARING UPON HIS SINEWY THIGH. . . . .   294 HATED PLAYBOY   6
    MADDENED BY THAT SINEWY THIGH. . . . .   294 HATED PLAYBOY V   6
    STARING ON HIS SINEWY THIGH. . . . .   294 HATED PLAYBOY V   6
    THAT DROPPED UPON MY THIGH." . . . .   309 PLAYER QUEEN   16
    THAT VIGOROUS THIGH, THAT DREAMING EYE? . . . . .   386 ROBARTES DANCE   23
    YOU. SHOULD HAND EXPLORE A THIGH, ...   573 LADYS 3RD SONG   11

THIGHED   SEE GOLDEN-THIGHED
    WORLD-FAMOUS GOLDEN THIGHED PYTHAGORAS . . . . .   445 SCHOOL CHILDR V   45

THIGHS
    "AND THE WORSE DEVIL THAT IS BETWEEN MY THIGHS." . . .   300 BEGGAR CRIED   8
    IS MOVING ITS SLOW THIGHS, WHILE ALL ABOUT IT . . .   402 SECOND COMING   16
    ABOVE THE STAGGERING GIRL, HER THIGHS CARESSED . . .   441 LEDA AND SWAN   2
    THE FEATHERED GLORY FROM HER LOOSENING THIGHS? . .   441 LEDA AND SWAN   6
    THE BIRD DESCENDS, AND HER FRAIL THIGHS ARE PRESSED . .   441 LEDA AND SWAN V   2
    ON STRAINING THIGHS. . . . .   574 LOVERS SONG   6

THIN
    AND THE THIN CRESCENT OF THE MOON, ...   20 OISIN 1   V 288
    UNDER A BEECH AT ALMHUIN AND HEARD THE THIN . . . .   44 OISIN 2   228
    A THIN GREY MAN HALF LOST IN GATHERING NIGHT. . . .   102 FERGUS DRUID   7
    A THIN, GREY MAN, HALF-LOST IN GATHERING NIGHT, . . .   102 FERGUS DRUID V   7
    LOOK ON MY THIN GREY HAIR AND HOLLOW CHEEKS . . . .   103 FERGUS DRUID   23
    THEY WROTE ON TABLETS OF THIN BOARD, ...   197 BAILE AILLINN   195
    BECAUSE OF SOMETHING I HEARD OF UNDER THE THIN HORN . .   210 UNDER THE MOON V   17
    BECAUSE OF A STORY I HEARD UNDER THE THIN HORN . . .   210 UNDER THE MOON V   17
    BECAUSE OF A STORY I HEARD UNDER A THIN HORN . . . .   210 UNDER THE MOON V   17
    IF YOU HAVE REVISITED THE TOWN, THIN SHADE, ...   292 TO A SHADE   1
    WORN THIN BY THE LAPPING OF WATER, ...   330 BONE OF A HARE   11
    THROUGH THE WHITE THIN BONE OF A HARE. . . . . .   330 BONE OF A HARE   16
    THE FIRST THIN CRESCENT IS WHEELED ROUND ONCE MORE. .   377 PHASES OF MOON   116
    MUST RAMBLE, AND THIN OUT . . . .   484 SPILT MILK   3
    THIS IS THE MOON'S HORN! . . . .   519 LOVES LONENESS   8
    NO HAMLET THIN FROM EATING FLIES, A FAT . . . . .   610 STATUES   19
    A WEAK, THIN CHILD, WHEN LAST I SAW HIM THERE. . . .   699 MOSADA 3   14
    TWO WOMEN, WITHERED ONE AND SMALL AND THIN, ...   711 FERENCZ RENYI   51
    UPON THIN BOARDS OF YEW AND APPLE WOOD, ...   764 SHADOW WATER A   343
    UPON THIN BOARDS OF YEW AND APPLE-WOOD, ...   764 SHADOW WATER A V   343

THING
    OF DALLIANCE WITH A DEMON THING. . . . .   2 OISIN 1   4
    TRAPPED OF AN AMOROUS DEMON THING. . . . .   2 OISIN 1   V   4
    FOR BATTLE." "FLY YE FROM A THING SO DREAD. . . . .   35 OISIN 2   V   90
    . . . OF BEST ONES A SAD THING WERE-- . . . . .   63 OISIN 3   V 222
    CONCEIVE A THING SO SAD AND SOFT, A GENTLE THING LIKE ME?   77 INDIAN ON GOD   16
    CONCEIVE A THING SO SAD AND SOFT, A GENTLE THING LIKE ME?   77 INDIAN ON GOD   16
    AND TOADS AND EVERY OUTLAWED THING! . . . . . .   85 MAD KING GOLL V   61
    LAY HIDDEN IN THE SMALL SLATE-COLOURED THING! . . .   104 FERGUS DRUID   40
    THE BELL THAT CALLS US ON! THE SWEET FAR THING. . . .   115 ROSE OF BATTLE   28
    AND MANY A SWEET THING SAID, ...   144 HOST OF AIR   18
    OF THIS OR THAT THING, NOR GREW COLD . . . . . .   189 BAILE AILLINN   9
    OF THIS OR THAT THING, OR GREW COLD . . . . . .   189 BAILE AILLINN V   9
    FOR ANY GENTLE THING SHE SPAKE, ...   191 BAILE AILLINN   63
    SO FULL OF THAT THING AND OF THIS, ...   192 BAILE AILLINN   86
    I SAID! "IT'S CERTAIN THERE IS NO FINE THING . . .   205 ADAMS CURSE   21
    "THERE IS ONE THING THAT ALL WE WOMEN KNOW . . . .   205 ADAMS CURSE V   18
    WHERE PASSION GROWS TO BE A CHANGELESS THING, . . .   231 SHADOW WATER B   213
    CRIED OUT UPON THAT THING BENEATH . . . . . .   254 HIS DREAM   10
    WHAT THING HER BODY WAS." . . . .   255 WOMAN HOMER   14
    WE'LL FIND SO GOOD A THING AS THAT WE HAVE LOST? . .   258 KING NO KING   13
    O LOVE IS THE CROOKED THING, ...   268 BROWN PENNY   9
    NOR HAD THERE BEEN THE NOISE OF LIVING THING . . .   279 TWO KINGS   54
    AND THERE HAD BEEN NO SOUND OF LIVING THING . . . .   279 TWO KINGS V   54
    "ALTHOUGH THE THING THAT YOU HAVE HID WERE EVIL, . .   281 TWO KINGS   103
    BRED TO A HARDER THING . . . .   291 TO A FRIEND   9
    I HAVE NOT FOUND A THING TO EAT, ...   294 THREE BEGGARS   3
    AND EVERY COMFORTABLE THING, ...   307 HOUR DAWN   111
    WHEREON A THING ONCE WALKED THAT SEEMED A BURNING CLOUD.   315 FALLEN MAJESTY   8
    ONCE WALKED A THING THAT SEEMED, AS IT WERE, A BURNING
        CLOUD.   315 FALLEN MAJESTY V   8
    A NOISY AND FILTHY THING." . . . .   319 DOLLS   12
    AND LEARN THAT THE BEST THING IS . . . .   330 BONE OF A HARE   6
    THERE'S NOT A THING BUT LOVE CAN MAKE . . . . .   333 SOLOMON SHEBA   23
    I HAD WISHED A DEAR THING ON THAT DAY . . . . .   341 SHEP GOATHERD V   73
    TO HOPE A THING SO DEAR . . . .   346 ON WOMAN   27
    I MOURN FOR THAT MOST LONELY THING! AND YET GOD'S WILL
        BE DONE!   354 HIS PHOENIX   31
    ALL I HAD RHYMED OF THAT MONSTROUS THING . . . . .   358 PRESENCES   7
    ALL I HAVE RHYMED OF THAT MONSTROUS THING . . . .   358 PRESENCES V   7
    OF THE HOVERING THING NIGHT BROUGHT ME. . . . . .   390 IMAGE PAST   42
    BECAME A BITTER, AN ABSTRACT THING, ...   397 POLIT PRISONER   9
    I COULD NOT FIND A THING SO DEAR." . . . . . .   398 BREAK OF DAY   9
    AN AGED MAN IS BUT A PALTRY THING, ...   407 SAIL BYZANTIUM   9
    MY BODILY FORM FROM ANY NATURAL THING, ...   408 SAIL BYZANTIUM   26
    AND A GREAT ARMY BUT A SHOWY THING! . . . . . .   429 NINETEEN 19   18
    I KNEW THAT HORSE-PLAY, KNEW IT FOR A MURDEROUS THING. .   442 BLACK CENTAUR   4
    I KNEW THAT HORSE PLAY, KNEW IT FOR A MURDEROUS THING. .   442 BLACK CENTAUR V   4

THING (CONTINUED)

	PAGE	TITLE		LINE
A STRANGE THING SURELY THAT MY HEART, WHEN LOVE HAD COME UNSOUGHT	449	OWEN AHERNE		1
AND NOT A THING IS DONE,	451	FIRST LOVE		10
GAME-BIRD, NOR WOMAN DOES THE SAME THING TWICE!	463	HARUN RASHID		60
GAME BIRD, OR WOMAN DOES THE SAME THING TWICE!	463	HARUN RASHID	V	60
GAMEBIRD, NOR WOMAN DOES THE SAME THING TWICE!	463	HARUN RASHID	V	60
BECAUSE I HAVE A MARVELLOUS THING TO SAY.	471	ALL SOUL NIGHT		15
A CERTAIN MARVELLOUS THING	471	ALL SOUL NIGHT		16
I NEED NO OTHER THING,	474	ALL SOUL NIGHT		98
TO THIS AND THAT AND T'OTHER THING,	478	SELF AND SOUL		23
LIVES THAT LONELY THING	504	QUARREL IN AGE		14
EVERY THING THAT HAS LIVED	504	QUARREL IN AGE	V	9
SOME STUPID THING THAT I HAD DONE	507	STREAM AND SUN		4
INTO SOME LESSER THING.	517	HER ANXIETY		5
"THE THIRD THING THAT I THINK OF YET,"	521	THREE THINGS		13
I'D HAVE HIM LOVE THE THING THAT WAS	532	BEFORE WORLD		15
THAT THING ALL BLOOD AND MIRE, THAT BEAST-TORN WRECK,	537	HER VISION		25
WITHOUT A THING IN HIS HEAD	552	SONGS REWRIT 2		10
A MOST ASTONISHING THING—	567	FROM JAPANESE		1
ALL THE OLYMPIANS; A THING NEVER KNOWN AGAIN.	578	LOFTY THINGS		12
A BEAUTIFUL LOFTY THING, OR A THING	578	CRAZED GIRL		7
A BEAUTIFUL LOFTY THING, OR A THING	578	CRAZED GIRL		7
BUT NEVER SAID A THING,	627	STATES HOLIDAY		10
BUT YONDER THING, YON IDLE NOISE, YON CROW,	648	ISLE STAT I 1		104
SOME BARBAROUS, UN-FAERY THING DRAW NEAR.	656	ISLE STAT I 3		21
AND, OH! THE WONDER OF THE THING! EACH CAME	656	ISLE STAT I 3		29
THIS THING WE ASK! MUST WE TWO FIGHT?--JUDGE THOU.	660	ISLE STAT II 1		41
TO US. OH WISE ART THOU IN SUCH A THING,	660	ISLE STAT II 1		46
FOR THIS THING FIGHT--WE LOVE ONE MAID? HER NAME?	661	ISLE STAT II 1		66
DULL-WITTED THING, WITH FACE RED SQUIRREL-BROWN.	661	ISLE STAT II 1		68
A WHITE, DUMB THING OF TEARS. HERE LET IT STAND.	663	ISLE STAT II 2		21
THE FAERY THING FLEW WITH HER O'ER THE GRAY	663	ISLE STAT II 2		38
FROM WHOSE GREEN BANKS NO LIVING THING MAY ROVE,	664	ISLE STAT II 2		57
THE FLOWER, SAVE SOME THING BE FOUND	668	ISLE STAT II 3		51
SWIFT LAKE. A VERY LITTLE THING THAT IS,	669	ISLE STAT II 3		78
I LAUGHED? AND WHY IS THAT A THING SO DEAR?	670	ISLE STAT II 3		97
I CRIED THE THING YOU BADE ME CRY.	670	ISLE STAT II 3		114
A WRIGGLING THING ON THE WHITE LAKE MOVED,	673	ISLE STAT II 3		176
I LIT BY THE THING, 'TWAS A SHEPHERD-BOY,	673	ISLE STAT II 3		180
HIS SLEUTH-HOUNDS FOLLOW EVERY FAERY THING.	675	ISLE STAT II 3		244
SHINE DULL UNMOVING EYES. WHAT THING ART THOU?	685	SEEKER		74
SHALL SEE A THING TO TALK ON WHEN YOU'RE OLD,	693	MOSADA 1		67
BE NOT AFRAID. YOU'LL SEE NO FEARFUL THING.	693	MOSADA 1		74
BECAUSE OF THE THING HIS TONGUE HAD SAID.	730	PRIEST FAIRY		60
"LOVE WOULD BE A THING OF NAUGHT	772	SONG DEIRDRE 1		10
LOVE IS AN IMMODERATE THING	777	SONG DEIRDRE 2		1
HAS MADE IT BUT A LONELY THING.	781	HEART FRIGHT		4
A STRANGE, UNSERVICEABLE THING,	784	WOMANS BEAUTY		15

THINGS   SEE SPIRIT-THINGS

	PAGE	TITLE		LINE
TO ALL THINGS CRIED! "I AM A SLAVE!	19	OISIN 1	V	280
AND THINGS THAT HAVE GROWN SAD ARE WICKED,	20	OISIN 1		301
AND THINGS THAT FEAR THE DAWN OF THE MORROW	20	OISIN 1		302
BUT NOW TWO THINGS DEVOUR MY LIFE!	24	OISIN 1		358
THE THINGS THAT MOST OF ALL I HATE!	24	OISIN 1		359
TWO THINGS THAT 'FORE ALL ELSE I HATE,	24	OISIN 1	V	359
OF THE THINGS THAT HIS HEART STILL KNOWS WERE SWEET—	26	OISIN 1	V	402
BEFORE THE SWIFT THINGS THAT SHE DREAMED OF WERE DONE	27	OISIN 1		414
ERE HALF THE SWIFT THINGS THAT SHE DREAMT ON WERE DONE,	28	OISIN 1	V	422
THINGS DONE ERE GOD FIRST WAS OR MY OLD LINE BEGAN!	29	OISIN 2	V	8
FOR THEIR DIM MINDS WERE WITH THE ANCIENT THINGS.	34	OISIN 2		77
WRAPPED IN THE THINGS OF THE UNHUMAN MIND,	36	OISIN 2		98
ROLLED IN THE THINGS OF THE UNHUMAN MIND,	36	OISIN 2	V	98
"LAST OF MY RACE. THREE THINGS I RULE ALONE—	45	OISIN 2	V	239A
IN A REVERIE FORGETFUL OF ALL THINGS, OVER THE BUBBLING GROUND.	56	OISIN 3		140
IN REVERIE FORGETFUL OF ALL THINGS, OVER THE BUBBLING GROUND.	56	OISIN 3	V	140
OF ALL THE MANY CHANGING THINGS	65	HAPPY SHEPHERD		7
AND, EVER PACING ON THE VERGE OF THINGS.	73	ANASHU VIJAYA		54
THE SUN UPON ALL THINGS THAT GROW	98	FOXHUNTER		15
IN ALL POOR FOOLISH THINGS THAT LIVE A DAY,	101	ROSE UPON ROOD		11
LEST I NO MORE HEAR COMMON THINGS THAT CRAVE!	101	ROSE UPON ROOD		15
BUT SEEK ALONE TO HEAR THE STRANGE THINGS SAID	101	ROSE UPON ROOD		19
BECAUSE I BE NOT OF THE THINGS I DREAM.	103	FERGUS DRUID	V	26A
FROM CHANGE TO CHANGE! I HAVE BEEN MANY THINGS—	104	FERGUS DRUID		32
AND ALL THESE THINGS WERE WONDERFUL AND GREAT!	104	FERGUS DRUID		37
"WHO BADE YOU TELL THESE THINGS UPON MY FLOOR?"	106	CUCHULAIN SEA	V	17
"WHO BADE YOU TELL THESE THINGS?" AND THEN SHE CRIED	106	CUCHULAIN SEA	V	17
SAYING ALL THINGS WERE WELL!	113	ROSE OF PEACE		14
HAD PITY ON THE LEAST OF THINGS	134	FR GILLIGAN		47
FOR ALL THINGS TURN TO BARRENNESS	135	TWO TREES		29
ALL THINGS TURN TO BARRENNESS	135	TWO TREES		29
AND THE WHITE HUSH END ALL THINGS BUT THE BEAT	137	TO SOME I TALK	V	15
OF THINGS DISCOVERED IN THE DEEP,	138	TO IRELAND		21
AND ALL BENIGHTED THINGS THAT GO	139	TO IRELAND		39
AND ALL THE WIZARD THINGS THAT GO	139	TO IRELAND	V	39
ALL THINGS UNCOMELY AND BROKEN, ALL THINGS WORN OUT AND OLD,	142	ROSE IN HEART		1
ALL THINGS UNCOMELY AND BROKEN, ALL THINGS WORN OUT AND OLD,	142	ROSE IN HEART		1

	PAGE	TITLE		LINE
THINGS (CONTINUED)				
ALL THINGS UNCOMELY AND BROKEN, ALL THINGS WORN AND OLD,	142	ROSE IN HEART	V	1
ALL THINGS UNCOMELY AND BROKEN, ALL THINGS WORN AND OLD,	142	ROSE IN HEART	V	1
THE WRONG OF UNSHAPELY THINGS IS A WRONG TOO GREAT TO BE TOLD;	143	ROSE IN HEART		5
THE WRONG OF THE THINGS MISSHAPEN IS WRONG TOO GREAT TO BE TOLD;	143	ROSE IN HEART	V	5
AND TROUBLE WITH A SIGH FOR ALL THINGS LONGING FOR REST	163	ASKS FORGIVE		23
AND WEEP BECAUSE I KNOW ALL THINGS NOW:	177	PAST GREATNESS		2
KNOWING ONE, OUT OF ALL THINGS, ALONE, THAT HIS HEAD	177	PAST GREATNESS		8
THAT ALL THINGS FELL OUT HAPPILY,	189	BAILE AILLINN		22
YET THEY THAT KNOW ALL THINGS BUT KNOW	190	BAILE AILLINN		38
OF THE EBB OF ALL THINGS TO MAKE LOVE	193	BAILE AILLINN	V	109
THEY KNOW UNDYING THINGS, FOR THEY	196	BAILE AILLINN		170
BECAUSE IT IS ALONE OF ALL THINGS HAPPY.	198	SEVEN WOODS		9
MUTTER SUCH THINGS AS THEY AWAKE FROM TRANCE.	229	SHADOW WATER B		163
AMONG SUBSTANTIAL THINGS; FOR IT IS DREAMS	230	SHADOW WATER B		181
HELMETS, AND SWORDS, AND HALF-FORGOTTEN THINGS	257	RECONCILIATION		6
BECAUSE WE HAVE MADE OUR ART OF COMMON THINGS,	265	ABBEY THEATRE		5
AND ALL THINGS AT ONE COMMON LEVEL LIE.	265	THESE CLOUDS		6
AND THESE THINGS CAME, SO MUCH THE MORE THEREBY	265	THESE CLOUDS		8
ALL THINGS CAN TEMPT ME	267	ALL TEMPT ME		T
ALL THINGS CAN TEMPT ME FROM THIS CRAFT OF VERSE:	267	ALL TEMPT ME		1
WEARY OF MANY QUESTIONS: "THERE ARE THINGS	281	TWO KINGS		93
THAT THINGS IT WERE A PRIDE TO GIVE	287	TO WEALTHY MAN		6
BECAUSE OF ALL THINGS KNOWN	291	TO A FRIEND		15
NOTORIOUS, TILL ALL MY PRICELESS THINGS	321	REED WHISPERER		13
FOR ALL THINGS THE DELIGHTED EYE NOW SEES	326	ROBERT GREGORY		49
ON PRETTY THINGS THAT MAY	366	HER CHRIS TREE		7
AND PROVE OF ALL IMAGINABLE THINGS	371	EGO DOMINUS		73
AND PROVE IF ALL IMAGINABLE THINGS	371	EGO DOMINUS	V	73
GAZED UPON ALL THINGS KNOWN, ALL THINGS UNKNOWN,	383	VISION ROBART		30
GAZED UPON ALL THINGS KNOWN, ALL THINGS UNKNOWN,	383	VISION ROBART		30
BEING FIXED ON ALL THINGS LOVED, ALL THINGS UNLOVED,	383	VISION ROBART		34
BEING FIXED ON ALL THINGS LOVED, ALL THINGS UNLOVED,	383	VISION ROBART		34
THEY SAY SUCH DIFFERENT THINGS AT SCHOOL.	387	ROBARTES DANCE		52
YET THE WORLD ENDS WHEN THESE TWO THINGS,	388	SOLOMON WITCH		28
RIGHT MASTERY OF NATURAL THINGS,	401	DEMON BEAST		37
THINGS FALL APART; THE CENTRE CANNOT HOLD;	402	SECOND COMING		3
THINGS FALL APART; THE CENTRE CAN NOT HOLD,	402	SECOND COMING	V	3
IN ABSTRACT THINGS, OR BE DERIDED BY	409	TOWER		15
WITH LEARNED ITALIAN THINGS	415	TOWER		158
ALL THOSE THINGS WHEREOF	415	TOWER		163
WHAT IF THOSE THINGS THE GREATEST OF MANKIND	418	ANCEST HOUSES		38
MANY INGENIOUS LOVELY THINGS ARE GONE	428	NINETEEN 19		1
THAT PITCHES COMMON THINGS ABOUT. THERE STOOD	428	NINETEEN 19		4
MANY INGENUOUS LOVELY THINGS ARE GONE	428	NINETEEN 19	V	1
TO END ALL THINGS, TO END	431	NINETEEN 19	V	81
THERE ARE MALICIOUS THINGS, ALTHOUGH	435	FOR MY SON	V	10
SUCH DEVILISH THINGS EXIST,	436	FOR MY SON		11
UPON A GHOSTLY PARADIGM OF THINGS:	445	SCHOOL CHILDR		42
UPON THE GHOSTLY IMAGES OF THINGS	445	SCHOOL CHILDR	V	42
I HAVE ATTEMPTED MANY THINGS	451	FIRST LOVE		9
OR SAY THE THINGS WE SAY:	458	SECRETS OF OLD		12
COMPANIONSHIP IN THOSE MYSTERIOUS THINGS	465	HARUN RASHID		92
ALL, ALL THOSE GYRES AND CUBES AND MIDNIGHT THINGS	469	HARUN RASHID		184
THOSE CONES AND CUBES AND GYRES, THOSE MIDNIGHT THINGS,	469	HARUN RASHID	V	184
ON GENEROUS THINGS THAT HE DID	473	ALL SOUL NIGHT		69
LONG PAST HIS PRIME REMEMBER THINGS THAT ARE	477	SELF AND SOUL		18
AND GOD-APPOINTED BERKELEY THAT PROVED ALL THINGS A DREAM,	481	BLOOD AND MOON		25
THINGS SAID OR DONE LONG YEARS AGO,	501	VACILLATION		51
OR THINGS I DID NOT DO OR SAY	501	VACILLATION		52
"LET ALL THINGS PASS AWAY."	502	VACILLATION		61
"LET ALL THINGS PASS AWAY."	502	VACILLATION		66
"LET ALL THINGS PASS AWAY."	502	VACILLATION		71
SEEK OUT REALITY, LEAVE THINGS THAT SEEM.	502	VACILLATION		72
ALL THINGS HANG LIKE A DROP OF DEW	505	GRAT INSTRUCT		3
ALL THINGS REMAIN IN GOD.	512	JANE ON GOD		6
ALL THINGS REMAIN IN GOD.	512	JANE ON GOD		12
ALL THINGS REMAIN IN GOD.	512	JANE ON GOD		18
ALL THINGS REMAIN IN GOD.	512	JANE ON GOD		24
THREE THINGS	521	THREE THINGS		T
"O CRUEL DEATH, GIVE THREE THINGS BACK,"	521	THREE THINGS		1
"THREE DEAR THINGS THAT WOMEN KNOW,"	521	THREE THINGS		7
THINGS OUT OF PERFECTION SAIL,	530	OLD TOM AGAIN		1
FOR THINGS BELOW ARE COPIES, THE GREAT SMARAGDINE TABLET SAID.	556	RIBH PATRICK		6
HOW SOUL MAY WALK WHEN ALL SUCH THINGS ARE PAST,	558	RIBH CHRISTIAN		11
HOW SOUL COULD WALK BEFORE SUCH THINGS BEGAN.	558	RIBH CHRISTIAN		12
HOW SOUL HAS WALKED BEFORE SUCH THINGS BEGAN.	558	RIBH CHRISTIAN	V	12
THINGS UNBORN, THINGS THAT ARE GONE,	562	NEEDLES EYE		3
THINGS UNBORN, THINGS THAT ARE GONE,	562	NEEDLES EYE		3
THINGS THOUGHT TOO LONG CAN BE NO LONGER THOUGHT,	564	GYRES		2
EMPEDOCLES HAS THROWN ALL THINGS ABOUT;	564	GYRES		6
THE WORKMAN, NOBLE AND SAINT, AND ALL THINGS RUN	565	GYRES		23
ALL THINGS FALL AND ARE BUILT AGAIN,	566	LAPIS LAZULI		35
BEAUTIFUL LOFTY THINGS	577	LOFTY THINGS		T
BEAUTIFUL LOFTY THINGS: O'LEARY'S NOBLE HEAD;	577	LOFTY THINGS		1
AND WE AND ALL THE MUSES ARE THINGS OF NO ACCOUNT.	580	CURSE CROMWELL		12
BECAUSE IT PROVES THAT THINGS BOTH CAN AND CANNOT BE;	580	CURSE CROMWELL		19
THINGS HID IN THEIR MARROW-BONES	589	OLD WICKED MAN		41

807

		PAGE	TITLE	LINE

THINGS (CONTINUED)

	PAGE	TITLE	LINE
THINGS HID IN THEIR MARROWBONES	589	OLD WICKED MAN V	41
THINGS HID IN THEIR MARROW BONES	589	OLD WICKED MAN V	41
"MY MISTRESS CANNOT SEE THESE THINGS,	595	COLONEL MARTIN	30
FOR THINGS LIKE THESE WHAT DECENT MAN	598	MODEL LAUREATE	22
DEEP-ROOTED THINGS;" BUT NEVER FORESAW ITS END,	603	GALLERY REVIS	37
CONTACT ALL THINGS ANTAEUS-LIKE GREW STRONG;	603	GALLERY REVIS V	44
ALL THINGS DOWN TO THAT COMMON TEST AGAIN,	603	GALLERY REVIS V	46
AND NOT THOSE THINGS THAT THEY WERE EMBLEMS OF.	630	CIRCUS ANIMALS	32
AMONG THOSE BIRD-LIKE THINGS CAME, AND LET FALL	634	CUCHULAIN COMF	8
I FAIN HAD BEEN THE FIRST OF SINGING THINGS	648	ISLE STAT I 1	101
TO PROVE WHAT CAN YE DO? WHAT THINGS ABOVE	650	ISLE STAT I 1	146
IN ALL SUCH THINGS, PRAY LET THINE EARS BE TURNED,	660	ISLE STAT II 1	39
ALL THINGS ARE QUIET IN THE EVE'S WIDE EYE.	662	ISLE STAT II 2	6
AND WHEN THOU HAST THESE THINGS FOR MANY AGES FELT,	674	ISLE STAT II 3	214
AND WHEN THOU HAST THESE THINGS FOR AGES FELT,	674	ISLE STAT II 3 V	214
I KNOW NOT OF THE THINGS YOU SPEAK. BUT WHAT	675	ISLE STAT II 3	239
ARE ALL THINGS WELL WITH YOU AND WITH YOUR SHEEP?	682	SEEKER	13
WITH LITTLE VOICES SONGS OF FEARFUL THINGS.	682	SEEKER	31
TWO SPIRIT THINGS A MAN HATH FOR HIS FRIENDS:	686	DRAWING-ROOM	5
TO LIGHTEST OF LIGHT THINGS ALL SANCTITY.	686	DRAWING-ROOM	8
ABOLISHED BY A MIRE OF LITTLE THINGS.	711	FERENCZ RENYI	36
THE PROUDEST OR MOST COY OF SPIRIT THINGS.	720	WITCH VIVIEN	7
I KEEP SUCH THINGS ABOUT ME: THEY ARE FOOD	721	WITCH VIVIEN	37
THUS PLAY WE FIRST WITH PAWNS, POOR THINGS AND WEAK:	722	WITCH VIVIEN	53
ILL WORDS FOR ALL THINGS SOFT AND FAIR,	723	GIRLS SONG A	6
FOR AS THINGS WERE SO SHALL THINGS EVER BE.	724	KANVA ON SELF	20
FOR AS THINGS WERE SO SHALL THINGS EVER BE.	724	KANVA ON SELF	20
WHAT SHALLOW THOUGHTS ABOUT DEEP THINGS!	725	LEGEND	11
HE THOUGHT WISE THINGS AS HIS GREY HEAD NODDED.	728	PRIEST FAIRY	12
TO LIGHTEST OF ALL LIGHT THINGS SANCTITY.	734	QUATRAIN APHOR	8
TWO SPIRIT THINGS A MAN HATH FOR HIS FRIENDS:	734	QUATRAIN APHOR V	5
TO LIGHTEST OF LIGHT THINGS ALL SANCTITY.	734	QUATRAIN APHOR V	8
TILL ALL THINGS ARE AT REST.	741	EARL PAUL	52
TIME AND THE WORLD AND ALL THINGS DWINDLE OUT.	749	SHADOW WATER A	47
ENDS ALL THINGS. I HAVE SLAIN THE LOCHLANN KING.	754	SHADOW WATER A	163
FOR THE THINGS COME AFTER DEATH?	777	SONG DEIRDRE 2	12
YET ALL THE LOVELY THINGS THAT WERE	788	HAWTHORN TREE	11

THINK

	PAGE	TITLE	LINE
"WE THINK ON OSCAR'S PENCILLED URN,	5	OISIN 1	41
AND THINK THAT YOU WERE HARD AND UNKIND,	146	FISH	7
BUT THINK ABOUT OLD FRIENDS THE MOST:	173	PLEADS FRIEND	5
BUT THINK OF YOUR OLD FRIENDS THE MOST:	173	PLEADS FRIEND V	5
I THINK THAT HE HAS FORGAEL IN HIS NET,	224	SHADOW WATER B	56
AND YET I CANNOT THINK THEY'RE LEADING ME	230	SHADOW WATER B	191
ONE OF THE EVER-LIVING, AS I THINK--	231	SHADOW WATER B	210
AS FOR THIS WOMAN, I THINK SHE IS COMING WITH ME.	248	SHADOW WATER B	545
THE CRAZY NOTHING THAT I THINK IT IS,	248	SHADOW WATER B	556
THOUGH YOU MAY THINK I WASTE MY BREATH	271	GREY ROCK	6
THAT THINK SWORD-STROKES WERE BETTER MEANT	276	GREY ROCK	129
THAT THINK SWORD STROKES WERE BETTER MEANT	276	GREY ROCK V	129
HOPELESS AND DEAR, OR TERRIBLE TO THINK ON,	281	TWO KINGS	96
AND THEN I THINK OF OLD GEORGE POLLEXFEN,	325	ROBERT GREGORY	33
ALL THINK WHAT OTHER PEOPLE THINK:	337	SCHOLARS	9
ALL THINK WHAT OTHER PEOPLE THINK:	337	SCHOLARS	9
I THINK IT BETTER THAT IN TIMES LIKE THESE	359	WAR POEM	1
I THINK IT BETTER THAT AT TIMES LIKE THESE	359	WAR POEM V	1
HE FASHIONED FROM HIS OPPOSITE	368	EGO DOMINUS	27
I SEE A SCHOOLBOY WHEN I THINK OF HIM,	370	EGO DOMINUS	55
I SEE A SCHOOL BOY WHEN I THINK OF HIM	370	EGO DOMINUS V	55
AND THEN HE LAUGHED TO THINK THAT WHAT SEEMED HARD	377	PHASES OF MOON	136
I START OUT OF MY SLEEP TO THINK	380	SONGS FOOL 1	7
EVEN FROM THE FOOT-SOLE THINK IT TOO.	387	ROBARTES DANCE	51
SO LET HER THINK OPINIONS ARE ACCURSED.	405	FOR DAUGHTER	58
WOULD THINK HER SON, DID SHE BUT SEE THAT SHAPE	444	SCHOOL CHILDR	37
I THINK THAT I MAY FIND	449	HERO GIRL FOOL	28
TO THINK OF BURIED HECTOR	455	HIS MEMORIES	5
MADGE TELLS ME WHAT I DARED NOT THINK	457	SECRETS OF OLD	3
CANNOT ENDURE TO THINK YOU TREAD THESE PATHS,	463	HARUN RASHID	52
YOU THINK THAT LOVE HAS SEASONS, AND YOU THINK	464	HARUN RASHID	75
YOU THINK THAT LOVE HAS SEASONS, AND YOU THINK	464	HARUN RASHID	75
THINK WHEN I CHOOSE A BRIDE I CHOOSE FOR EVER:	464	HARUN RASHID	80
IT MAKES MY PASSION STRONGER BUT TO THINK	465	HARUN RASHID	99
BUT THINK THAT HIS MIND'S EYE,	471	ALL SOUL NIGHT	33
MANY A TIME I THINK TO SEEK	475	EVA GORE-BOOTH	14
THINK OF ANCESTRAL NIGHT THAT CAN,	478	SELF AND SOUL	20
BUT WHEN I THINK OF THAT MY TONGUE'S A STONE,	478	SELF AND SOUL	40
SO ARROGANTLY PURE; A CHILD MIGHT THINK	491	COOLE BALLYLEE	23
"THE THIRD THING THAT I THINK OF YET,"	521	THREE THINGS	13
I SHUDDER AND I SIGH TO THINK	524	MAD AS MIST	15
WHY SHOULD HE THINK ME CRUEL	532	BEFORE WORLD	13
WHY SHOULD THEY THINK THAT ARE FOR EVER YOUNG?	537	HER VISION	21
TO THINK HIS PASSION SUCH	538	LAST CONFESS	8
AND LAUGHED UPON HIS BREAST TO THINK	538	LAST CONFESS	11
OH I WOULD THINK THAT I HAD MY FEE,	551	SONGS REWRIT 1 V	7
GOD GUARD ME FROM THOSE THOUGHTS MEN THINK	553	PRAYER OLD AGE	1
I THINK I SHOULD DROP DEAD."	569	THREE BUSHES	13
AND LET HIM THINK ME THERE,	570	THREE BUSHES	23
NOR THINK THAT BODY IS THE WHOLE,	573	LADYS 3RD SONG	4
YOU THINK IT HORRIBLE THAT LUST AND RAGE	591	SPUR	1
"I THINK THAT I SHALL FIND HER	594	COLONEL MARTIN	16

808

			PAGE	TITLE	LINE

THINK   (CONTINUED)
THINK WHERE MAN'S GLORY MOST BEGINS AND ENDS, ...   604 GALLERY REVIS   54
AND THINK IT IS NO SHAME. . . . .   605 SONGS BURDEN 1   4
MY HUNDREDTH YEAR IS AT AN END. I THINK . . . . .   609 IN TARAS HALLS   3
THAT SOMETHING IS ABOUT TO HAPPEN, I THINK . . . .   609 IN TARAS HALLS   4
SOME THINK IT A MATTER OF COURSE THAT CHANCE . . . .   626 OLD MEN BE MAD   9
SOME THINK IT MATTER OF COURSE THAT CHANCE . . . . .   626 OLD MEN BE MAD V   9
BOTH DEAD!--NO TIME TO THINK. I AM SHE, ...   673 ISLE STAT II 3   190
TO SAINTED EBREMAR'S SAD EYES. I THINK . . . . . .   696 MOSADA 2   15
BE ONE?   I THINK ALL'S FINISHED NOW AND SEALED. . . .   701 MOSADA 3   62
FOR AN IMMORTAL WOMAN, AS I THINK. . . . .   755 SHADOW WATER A   173
I THINK HE LIVES IN LOCHLANN. NO, NOT THERE! . . . .   760 SHADOW WATER A V 254A
I THINK THAT THERE IS LOVE IN AIBRIC'S EYES. . . . .   768 SHADOW WATER A   407
THERE'S SO MUCH TO THINK ABOUT . . . .   772 SONG DEIRDRE 1   7
THINKIN'
I'M THINKIN' OF MY BABY . . . .   96 MOLL MAGEE   47
THINKING
IT HAD GROWN WISE-TONGUED BY THINKING . . . . . .   159 CAP AND BELLS   7
IT HAD GROWN MOST WISE WITH THINKING . . . .   159 CAP AND BELLS V   7
AND IT HAD GROWN WISE BY THINKING . . . .   159 CAP AND BELLS V   7
WILL HARDLY SEEM WORTH THINKING OF . . . .   202 NEVER GIVE ALL   2
FOR HE WOULD BE THINKING OF LOVE . . . .   268 BROWN PENNY   12
THINKING OF SAINTS AND OF PETRONIUS ARBITER. . . . .   362 HER COURTESY   8
AHERNE LAUGHED, THINKING OF THE MAN WITHIN, ...   375 PHASES OF MOON   85
IN THINKING OF HIS LOST RENOWN. . . . .   379 SAINT HUNCH   3
I AM THINKING OF A CHILD'S VOW SWORN IN VAIN . . . .   391 UNDER SATURN   15
AND THINKING OF THAT FIT OF GRIEF OR RAGE . . . . .   443 SCHOOL CHILDR   17
THINKING TO SET AT REST . . . .   496 MOHINI CHATTER V   12
NOT WORTH THINKING OF, ...   504 QUARREL IN AGE   5
THINKING TO MEET MY LOVE ONCE MORE . . . .   551 SONGS REWRIT 1 V   15
BOTH DEAD!--NO TIME FOR THINKING. I AM SHE, ...   673 ISLE STAT II 3 V 190
I LEFT HER LIVING, THINKING THAT I HAD FOUND . . . .   755 SHADOW WATER A   174
THINKS
HE THINKS OF THOSE WHO HAVE SPOKEN EVIL OF HIS BELOVED . .   166 EVIL OF BELOV   T
AEDH THINKS OF THOSE WHO HAVE SPOKEN EVIL OF HIS BELOVED   166 EVIL OF BELOV V   T
HE THINKS OF HIS PAST GREATNESS . . . .   177 PAST GREATNESS   T
MONGAN THINKS OF HIS PAST GREATNESS . . . .   177 PAST GREATNESS V   T
THINKS THAT THE STONE'S A CHILD. . . . .   456 FRIENDS YOUTH   12
HE THINKS THAT SHAPE MUST BE HIS SHAPE? . . . . . .   479 SELF AND SOUL   54
THINKS IN A MARROW-BONE! . . . .   553 PRAYER OLD AGE   4
THINKS IN A MARROW BONE! . . . .   553 PRAYER OLD AGE V   4
THE COUNTRY THINKS NO END OF HIM, ...   583 GHOST ROG CASE   13
SHE THINKS, PART WOMAN, THREE PARTS A CHILD, ...   617 LONG-LEG FLY   15
THIRD
OF THE THIRD MOON, THAT HUNG BETWEEN THE NIGHT AND THE DAY,   210 UNDER THE MOON V   18
SLEEP BEFORE THE THIRD NOON SOUNDS." . . . .   295 THREE BEGGARS   24
THE THIRD. "I'LL HURRY TO THE COURSE . . . .   296 THREE BEGGARS   33
BUT THE THIRD CRIED: "I'LL TO THE COURSE . . . . .   296 THREE BEGGARS V   33
ON A WINDY STONE, THE THIRD, ...   298 THREE HERMITS   5
CAUGHT AND CRACKED HIS FLEA, THE THIRD, ...   299 THREE HERMITS   30
MONTASHIGI, THIRD OF HIS FAMILY, FASHIONED IT . . . .   478 SELF AND SOUL   25
"THE THIRD THING THAT I THINK OF YET," . . . . . .   521 THREE THINGS   13
THIRD SONG . . . .   547 TO SAME TUNE 3 V   T
TWO CHINAMEN, BEHIND THEM A THIRD, ...   566 LAPIS LAZULI   37
THE THIRD, DOUBTLESS A SERVING-MAN, ...   566 LAPIS LAZULI   41
THE LADY'S THIRD SONG . . . .   573 LADYS 3RD SONG   T
THIRST
WHEN ALL BUT DEAD OF THIRST, ...   454 EMPTY CUP   2
WHEN ALL BUT DEAD WITH THIRST, ...   454 EMPTY CUP   V   2
YOUR THIRST FOR THOSE OLD CRABBED MYSTERIES, ...   465 HARUN RASHID   86
I THIRST FOR ACCUSATION. ALL THAT WAS SUNG, ...   542 PARN FUNERAL 1   25
TO EASE THEIR WORLD-OLD THIRST ALONG THE BRINK . . . .   663 ISLE STAT II 2   41
NASCHINA'S GONE, DRAWN BY A THIRST OF LOVE, ...   664 ISLE STAT II 2   59
AND HER GIGANTIC LIMBS. THE WEARY THIRST . . . . .   687 TWO TITANS   16
THIRSTING
WHAT THE WORLD'S MILLION LIPS ARE THIRSTING FOR . . . .   229 SHADOW WATER B   161
THIRTEEN   SEE NINETEEN-THIRTEEN
THIRTEENTH
THE THIRTEENTH MOON BUT SETS THE SOUL AT WAR . . . .   374 PHASES OF MOON   50
THIRTY   SEE NINETEEN-THIRTY-TWO NINETEEN-THIRTY-ONE
WHY MUST I LIVE SOME THIRTY, FORTY YEARS, ...   285 TWO KINGS   199
THAT THIRTY CENTURIES OF STONY SLEEP . . . .   402 SECOND COMING V   19
AROUND ME THE IMAGES OF THIRTY YEARS! . . . . . .   601 GALLERY REVIS   1
THITHER
NO LIVE MAN GOES THITHER, ...   62 OISIN 3   V 214
HITHER AND THITHER TO AND FRO THEY TROD . . . . . .   278 TWO KINGS   26
THITHER THY DUST, AND KNEAD IT WITH A CRY, ...   688 TWO TITANS   52
THAT HAVE GONE THITHER TO LOOK FOR THE LOUD STREAMS, . .   765 SHADOW WATER A   348
HITHER AND THITHER AND SAY AT THE HIGH NOON . . . .   767 SHADOW WATER A   404
THONG
BOUND A THONG ABOUT HIS HAND, ...   595 COLONEL MARTIN   25
THONGS
AND CAPTIVES BOUND WITH LEATHERN THONGS . . . . . .   7 OISIN 1   77
MY CAPTIVES, BOUND IN LEATHERN THONGS, ...   8 OISIN 1   V   78
TO THOSE ABOUT, "BEAT HIM WITH THONGS OF HIDE . . . .   106 CUCHULAIN SEA V 17A
WITH THONGS OF LEATHER." AS SHE SPAKE IT WAS! . . . .   106 CUCHULAIN SEA V 17B
THOOR
TO BE CARVED ON A STONE AT THOOR BALLYLEE . . . . .   406 CARVED STONE   T
THORN
OUR HEARTS ENDURE THE PLAITED THORN, THE CROWDED WAY, . .   172 TRAV PASSION   V   3
TILL IT DIED OUT WHERE AN OLD THORN TREE STOOD. . . .   186 QUEEN MAEVE   V 129

	PAGE	TITLE		LINE
THORN (CONTINUED)				
WHO STOOD AMID A SILENCE BY THE THORN	187	QUEEN MAEVE		142
THE OLD BROWN THORN TREES BREAK IN TWO HIGH OVER CUMANN'S STRAND,	206	HANRAHANS SONG	V	1
WERE TWISTED LIKE THE OLD THORN TREES	208	OLD MEN ADMIRE	V	5
WHERE BY OLD THORN TREES THAT MAN STOOD;	274	GREY ROCK	V	80
HE HAD BUT GAZED ON THORN TREES, SPOKE;	274	GREY ROCK	V	82
AMONG THE STONES AND THORN TREES, UNDER MORNING LIGHT, . .	291	PAUDEEN	V	3
TO COLD CLARE ROCK AND GALWAY ROCK AND THORN, ...	326	ROBERT GREGORY		66
THE THORN TREE	350	HER PRAISE	V	T
BUT WALK BY THE DRY THORN UNTIL I HAVE FOUND	351	HER PRAISE		12
AND BODIES BROKEN LIKE A THORN	454	HIS MEMORIES		3
MY ARMS ARE LIKE THE TWISTED THORN	455	HIS MEMORIES		11
UNDER THE RAGGED THORN?	519	LOVES LONENESS		10
THORNS				
UNDER A CROWN OF THORNS AND DARK WITH BLOOD, ...	38	OISIN 2		135
I HAVE BEEN IN THE PATH OF STONES AND THE WOOD OF THORNS,	153	CHANGE BELOVED		3
OUR HEARTS ENDURE THE SCOURGE, THE PLAITED THORNS, THE WAY	172	TRAV PASSION		3
OLD RAGGED ELMS, OLD THORNS INNUMERABLE, ...	419	MY HOUSE		5
THORN-TREE				
TILL IT DIED OUT WHERE AN OLD THORN-TREE STOOD.	186	QUEEN MAEVE		129
WE SAT UNDER AN OLD THORN-TREE	456	SUMMER SPRING		1
THORN-TREES				
THE OLD BROWN THORN-TREES BREAK IN TWO HIGH OVER CUMMEN STRAND,	206	HANRAHANS SONG		1
WERE TWISTED LIKE THE OLD THORN-TREES	208	OLD MEN ADMIRE		5
WHERE BY OLD THORN-TREES THAT MAN STOOD;	274	GREY ROCK		80
HE HAD BUT GAZED ON THORN-TREES, SPOKE, ...	274	GREY ROCK		82
AMONG THE STONES AND THORN-TREES, UNDER MORNING LIGHT; . .	291	PAUDEEN		3
THOROUGHBRED				
SOME BACK A MARE THROWN FROM A THOROUGHBRED, ...	547	TO SAME TUNE 3		3
SOME BACK A MARE THROWN FROM A THOROUGHBRED, ...	614	MARCH SONGS 2		3
THOROUGH-BRED				
SOME BACK A MARE THROWN FROM A THOROUGH-BRED, ...	547	TO SAME TUNE 3	V	3
THOROUGHFARE				
FROM THOROUGHFARE TO THOROUGHFARE, ...	294	HATED PLAYBOY	V	3
FROM THOROUGHFARE TO THOROUGHFARE, ...	294	HATED PLAYBOY	V	3
THOROUGHFARES				
PEDDLED IN THE THOROUGHFARES.	406	FOR DAUGHTER		76
THOUGHT				
WE THOUGHT ON OSCAR'S PENCILLED URN.	2	OISIN 1	V	70
AND NOW I AM DIZZY WITH THE THOUGHT	7	OISIN 1		65
BRINGING ME HONEYED, WANDERING THOUGHT	7	OISIN 1	V	65
NO CREATURE HAD FAMILIAR THOUGHT	17	OISIN 1	V	242
AND CLIMBED SO LONG, I THOUGHT THE LAST STEPS WERE . . .	32	OISIN 2		48
I THOUGHT THE END HAD RESTED, WHEN THESE WORDS	32	OISIN 2	V	49
. . . GROWN MILD WITH MYSTERIOUS THOUGHT	55	OISIN 3		121
AND THOUGHT, I WILL MY HEAVY STORY TELL	68	SAD SHEPHERD		19
AND THOUGHT, "TO THIS WILL I MY STORY TELL, ...	68	SAD SHEPHERD	V	19
A SAD, SAD THOUGHT WENT BY ME SLOWLY!	72	ANASHU VIJAYA		17
THE SAD, SAD THOUGHT HAS GONE FROM ME NOW WHOLLY!	72	ANASHU VIJAYA		19
THE RAVENS OF UNRESTING THOUGHT!	136	TWO TREES		34
AND THOUGHT NOT OF EVIL CHANCE, ...	145	HOST OF AIR		30
DIM POWERS OF DROWSY THOUGHT, LET HER NO LONGER BE . . .	175	ELEMENT POWERS		13
AND THOUGHT OF DAYS WHEN HE'D HAD A STRAIGHT BODY, . . .	183	QUEEN MAEVE		70
HALF CRAZY WITH THE THOUGHT, SHE TOO HAS WEPT!	186	QUEEN MAEVE		140
A MUSIC THAT HAD THOUGHT ENOUGH	193	BAILE AILLINN	V	108
I THOUGHT OF YOUR BEAUTY, AND THIS ARROW.	199	ARROW		1
MADE OUT OF A WILD THOUGHT, IS IN MY MARROW.	199	ARROW		2
O THOUGHT, FLY TO HER WHEN THE END OF DAY	201	OLD MEMORY		1
THROUGH THE LONG YEARS OF YOUTH, AND WHO WOULD HAVE THOUGHT	201	OLD MEMORY		7
I THOUGHT TO FLY TO HER WHEN THE END OF DAY	201	OLD MEMORY	V	1
THOUGHT FLY TO HER WHEN THE END OF DAY	201	OLD MEMORY	V	1
THROUGH THE LONG DAYS OF YOUTH, AND WHO WOULD HAVE THOUGHT	201	OLD MEMORY	V	7
YET IF IT DOES NOT SEEM A MOMENT'S THOUGHT, ...	204	ADAMS CURSE		5
BE THOUGHT AN IDLER BY THE NOISY SET	205	ADAMS CURSE		12
THERE HAVE BEEN LOVERS WHO THOUGHT LOVE SHOULD BE . . .	205	ADAMS CURSE		23
I HAD A THOUGHT FOR NO ONE'S BUT YOUR EARS!	206	ADAMS CURSE		34
I HAD A THOUGHT FOR NO ONE BUT YOUR EARS!	206	ADAMS CURSE		34
THEIR OWN THOUGHT FROM THE OTHER'S, ...	212	O DO NOT LOVE		7
FROM HUMAN THOUGHT, AS HARES AND MICE AND CONEYS	218	WOODS OF COOLE		31
THESE DOZEN WEEKS. AND I HAD THOUGHT TO MAKE	222	SHADOW WATER B		4
I'VE THOUGHT OF THAT. WE MUST HAVE AIBRIC WITH US, . . .	225	SHADOW WATER B		62
I HAVE GOOD REASON FOR THAT THOUGHT. AND NOW	238	SHADOW WATER B		354
I'LL NEVER GIVE ANOTHER THOUGHT TO IT!	245	SHADOW WATER B		477
NO, NO, NOR HALF A THOUGHT; BUT DO NOT SPEAK, ...	245	SHADOW WATER B		478
HOW GREAT A WRONG IT IS TO LET ONE'S THOUGHT	246	SHADOW WATER B		514
I THOUGHT, "HE HOLDS HER DEAR,"	254	WOMAN HOMER		3
TO SUCH A PITCH MY THOUGHT	255	WOMAN HOMER		11
I HAD THIS THOUGHT A WHILE AGO, ...	255	WORDS		1
I HAD THIS THOUGHT AWHILE AGO, ...	255	WORDS	V	1
THOUGH HE'D BUT CANNON--WHEREAS WE THAT HAD THOUGHT . . .	258	KING NO KING		7
THOUGHT, IN THAT SCALE OF HIS!	267	FRIEND ILLNESS		2
HAVING NO THOUGHT BUT FOR HIS QUEEN EDAIN.	276	TWO KINGS	V	1
HE THOUGHT TO HAVE GIVEN HIS HORSE THE SPUR, BUT SAW . .	277	TWO KINGS	V	4B
BUT DREW HIS SWORD, AND THOUGHT WITH LEVELLED POINT . . .	277	TWO KINGS	V	14
BUT WHEN HE THOUGHT TO TAKE HER IN HIS ARMS	280	TWO KINGS		67
THEN HE, DRIVEN BY HIS THOUGHT BEYOND HIS THOUGHT, . . .	282	TWO KINGS		122
THEN HE, DRIVEN BY HIS THOUGHT BEYOND HIS THOUGHT, . . .	282	TWO KINGS		122
THEN HE, DRIVEN BY THIS THOUGHT BEYOND HIS THOUGHT, . . .	282	TWO KINGS	V	122
THEN HE, DRIVEN BY THIS THOUGHT BEYOND HIS THOUGHT, . . .	282	TWO KINGS	V	122

	PAGE	TITLE	LINE

THOUGHT   (CONTINUED)

	PAGE	TITLE		LINE
WHAT TH' ONION-SELLERS THOUGHT OR DID	287	TO WEALTHY MAN		11
WHAT TH' ONION SELLERS THOUGHT OR DID	287	TO WEALTHY MAN	V	11
A CURLEW ANSWERED; AND SUDDENLY THEREUPON I THOUGHT . . .	291	PAUDEEN		5
A CURLEW ANSWERED, AND I WAS STARTLED BY THE THOUGHT . . .	291	PAUDEEN	V	5
HAD GIVEN THEIR CHILDREN'S CHILDREN LOFTIER THOUGHT, . . .	292	TO A SHADE		12
BUT GUAIRE LAUGHED WITH SECRET THOUGHT, ...	295	THREE BEGGARS		19
THE SECOND: "I HAVE THOUGHT AGAIN:	296	THREE BEGGARS		36
"BUT NOW THAT I HAVE THOUGHT AGAIN, ...	296	THREE BEGGARS	V	36
I HAD BEEN HURT," THE OLD BEGGAR THOUGHT	302	HOUR DAWN	V	19
HE GAVE A GASP AND THOUGHT TO HAVE FLED, ...	303	HOUR DAWN		22
HE GAVE A GASP AND THOUGHT TO RUN, ...	303	HOUR DAWN	V	22
I THOUGHT TO WAIT FOR THAT OR THIS:	305	HOUR DAWN		64
MY LIFE OF EVERY PLEASANT THOUGHT	307	HOUR DAWN		110
ONE BECAUSE NO THOUGHT.	315	FRIENDS		4
ONE THAT NO PASSING THOUGHT, ...	315	FRIENDS	V	4
SO WILD THAT EVERY CASUAL THOUGHT OF THAT AND THIS . .	316	COLD HEAVEN		4
A LITTLE NEARER TO HIS THOUGHT	324	ROBERT GREGORY		23
I HAD THOUGHT, SEEING HOW BITTER IS THAT WIND	327	ROBERT GREGORY		89
A FITTER WELCOME: BUT A THOUGHT	328	ROBERT GREGORY		95
I THOUGHT NO MORE WAS NEEDED	334	SONG		1
I THOUGHT 'TWOULD BURN MY BODY	335	SONG		15
WHEN THE WILD THOUGHT, ...	336	YOUNG GIRL		7
I LET THEM STRAY. I THOUGHT OF RHYME ALONE, ...	339	SHEP GOATHERD		11
YOU HAVE PUT THE THOUGHT IN RHYME. I WORKED ALL DAY, .	341	SHEP GOATHERD		58
MAY BE A QUIET THOUGHT TO WIFE AND MOTHER, ...	343	SHEP GOATHERD		118
NOR QUARRELS WITH A THOUGHT	345	ON WOMAN		7
WAS: "YOU, THAT HAVE NOT LIVED IN THOUGHT BUT DEED, . .	353	PEOPLE		30
A THOUGHT FROM PROPERTIUS	355	PROPERTIUS		T
HAPPIER DAYS THOUGHT GOOD:	365	HER RACE		4
WITHOUT AN ANGRY THOUGHT	366	HER CHRIS TREE		2
ALL THOUGHT BECOMES AN IMAGE AND THE SOUL	374	PHASES OF MOON		58
FIXED UPON IMAGES THAT ONCE WERE THOUGHT:	375	PHASES OF MOON		80
AND NEVER WROTE A BOOK, YOUR THOUGHT IS CLEAR.	376	PHASES OF MOON		97
WE NEVER THOUGHT TO ENQUIRE	381	SONGS FOOL 2		3
SO SHE HAD OUTDANCED THOUGHT.	383	VISION ROBART		39
SO THAT SHE DANCED. NO THOUGHT, ...	383	VISION ROBART	V	39
WHO NEVER GAVE THE BURNING TOWN A THOUGHT:	384	VISION ROBART		57
THE COMMONNESS OF THOUGHT AND IMAGES	384	VISION ROBART		61
THE HALF-DEAD DRAGON WAS HER THOUGHT, ...	385	ROBARTES DANCE		6
HER LOVER THOUGHT, UPON THE GLASS	385	ROBARTES DANCE		11
GIVE MAN HIS THOUGHT OR HIS MERE BODY?	386	ROBARTES DANCE		40
WILL BANISH EVERY THOUGHT, UNLESS	387	ROBARTES DANCE		48
AND WOULD NOT NOW BUT THAT HE THOUGHT, ...	388	SOLOMON WITCH		13
THOUGHT TO HAVE CROWED IT IN AGAIN.	388	SOLOMON WITCH		18
ALTHOUGH HE THOUGHT IT WORTH A CROW.	388	SOLOMON WITCH		35
I HAD THOUGHT THAT ALL MY DAYS WERE CAST	389	IMAGE PAST		12
IMAGINE THAT LOST LOVE, INSEPARABLE FROM MY THOUGHT . .	390	UNDER SATURN		2
AND THOUGHT BEFORE I HAD DONE	392	EASTER 1916		9
SO DARING AND SWEET HIS THOUGHT.	393	EASTER 1916		30
HER THOUGHT SOME POPULAR ENMITY:	397	POLIT PRISONER		10
FOR THOUGHT SOME POPULAR ENMITY, ...	397	POLIT PRISONER	V	10
I THOUGHT: "THERE IS A WATERFALL	398	BREAK OF DAY		5
FOR ALL MEN'S THOUGHT GREW CLEAR	400	DEMON BEAST	V	19
YET HAVE NO DEARER THOUGHT	401	DEMON BEAST		40
LOVED AND THOUGHT HIMSELF BELOVED, ...	404	FOR DAUGHTER		39
I THOUGHT IT ALL OUT TWENTY YEARS AGO:	411	TOWER		64
COWARDICE, SOME SILLY OVER-SUBTLE THOUGHT	413	TOWER		117
COWARDICE, OVER SOME SILLY SUBTLE THOUGHT	413	TOWER	V	117
I MOCK PLOTINUS' THOUGHT	415	TOWER		146
A SUFFERING PASSION AND A LABOURING THOUGHT?	420	MY HOUSE	V	20J
TO SILENCE THE ENVY IN MY THOUGHT:	424	ROAD AT DOOR		13
WE THOUGHT IT WOULD OUTLIVE ALL FUTURE DAYS.	428	NINETEEN 19		14
O WHAT FINE THOUGHT WE HAD BECAUSE WE THOUGHT, . . .	428	NINETEEN 19		15
O WHAT FINE THOUGHT WE HAD BECAUSE WE THOUGHT	428	NINETEEN 19		15
O WHAT FINE THOUGHTS WE HAD BECAUSE WE THOUGHT . . .	428	NINETEEN 19	V	15
THOUGHT THAT UNLESS A LITTLE POWDER BURNED	429	NINETEEN 19		21
NONE DARED ADMIT, IF SUCH A THOUGHT WERE HIS, ...	430	NINETEEN 19		44
NOR THOUGHT OF THE LEVELLING WIND.	432	NINETEEN 19		97
THERE LURCHES PAST, HIS GREAT EYES WITHOUT THOUGHT . .	433	NINETEEN 19		126
OF SOME HAUGHTY DEED OR THOUGHT	436	FOR MY SON		13
IN PITY FOR MAN'S DARKENING THOUGHT	438	SONGS PLAY 2		1
PLATO THOUGHT NATURE BUT A SPUME THAT PLAYS	445	SCHOOL CHILDR		41
UNTIL I THOUGHT HER BODY BORE	451	FIRST LOVE		5
EMPTIER OF THOUGHT	451	FIRST LOVE		16
BUT THAT'S A TRAITOR'S THOUGHT. ENOUGH FOR ME . . .	462	HARUN RASHID		39
A MIMICRY OF YOUTH. CAN POET'S THOUGHT	463	HARUN RASHID		62
A MIMICRY OF YOUTH. AN ARTIST'S THOUGHT, ...	463	HARUN RASHID	V	62
LIVED AT MY SIDE: THOUGHT TIME'S DISFIGURING TOUCH . .	466	HARUN RASHID		110
NOR THOUGHT OUT OF HER MIND OR MINE BEGOT, ...	467	HARUN RASHID		140
NOR THOUGHT OUT OF HER MIND OR OUT OF MINE.	467	HARUN RASHID	V	140
HORTON'S THE FIRST I CALL. HE LOVED STRANGE THOUGHT . .	471	ALL SOUL NIGHT		21
WHETHER OF HER OR GOD HE THOUGHT THE MOST, ...	471	ALL SOUL NIGHT		32
I THOUGHT HIM HALF A LUNATIC, HALF KNAVE, ...	473	ALL SOUL NIGHT		64
FOR MEDITATIONS UPON UNKNOWN THOUGHT	473	ALL SOUL NIGHT		74
SUCH THOUGHT--SUCH THOUGHT HAVE I THAT HOLD IT TIGHT .	474	ALL SOUL NIGHT		91
SUCH THOUGHT--SUCH THOUGHT HAVE I THAT HOLD IT TIGHT .	474	ALL SOUL NIGHT		91
SUCH THOUGHT, THAT IN IT BOUND	474	ALL SOUL NIGHT		97
FIX EVERY WANDERING THOUGHT UPON	477	SELF AND SOUL		6
THAT QUARTER WHERE ALL THOUGHT IS DONE:	477	SELF AND SOUL		7
EVERY EVENT IN ACTION OR IN THOUGHT:	479	SELF AND SOUL		66

		PAGE	TITLE		LINE

THOUGHT   (CONTINUED)

```
COUNT EVERY SIN OF ACTION OR OF THOUGHT;  . . . . . .  479 SELF AND SOUL  V   66
WE THAT HAVE DONE AND THOUGHT,  . . . . . . . . .  484 SPILT MILK           1
THAT HAVE THOUGHT AND DONE,  . . . . . . . . . .  484 SPILT MILK           2
BUT MINE SAW STELLA ONCE.  WHENCE CAME OUR THOUGHT?  . .  486 SEVEN SAGES          6
MINE SAW STELLA ONCE.  WHENCE CAME OUR THOUGHT?  . . .  486 SEVEN SAGES    V    6
MINE SAW STELLA ONCE.  WHEN CAME OUR THOUGHT?  . . . .  486 SEVEN SAGES    V    6
THOUGHTS LONG KNITTED INTO A SINGLE THOUGHT,  . . . .  488 COOLE PARK 29        7
AND FROM THE FORTIETH WINTER BY THAT THOUGHT  . . . .  501 VACILLATION         29
BUT THOUGHT THAT I MIGHT SAY OR DO,  . . . . . . .  501 VACILLATION         53
THE RESULTS OF THOUGHT  . . . . . . . . . . . .  504 RESULT THOUGHT       T
CAME TO SO DEEP A THOUGHT  . . . . . . . . . . .  505 RESULT THOUGHT      10
I THOUGHT IT OUT THIS VERY DAY,  . . . . . . . .  525 DANCING DAYS        17
HAD I NEVER THOUGHT  . . . . . . . . . . . . .  534 CONSOLATION          8
A THOUGHTLESS IMAGE OF MANTEGNA'S THOUGHT--  . . . .  537 HER VISION          20
I THOUGHT TO HAVE WHISTLED HER DOWN THAT WAY,  . . . .  551 SONGS REWRIT 1      15
I HAD THOUGHT TO HAVE CALLED HER OUT TO THE DOOR,  . .  551 SONGS REWRIT 1 V    15
FROM EVERY THOUGHT OF GOD MANKIND HAS HAD.  . . . . .  558 RIBH CHRISTIAN      15
THOUGHT IS A GARMENT AND THE SOUL'S A BRIDE  . . . .  558 RIBH CHRISTIAN      16
SENTENCES THAT HE HAS NEVER THOUGHT;  . . . . . . .  560 WHENCE COME          6
BY MANIFOLD ILLUSION! BUT MAN'S LIFE IS THOUGHT,  . . .  563 MERU                 3
THINGS THOUGHT TOO LONG CAN BE NO LONGER THOUGHT,  . .  564 GYRES                2
THINGS THOUGHT TOO LONG CAN BE NO LONGER THOUGHT,  . .  564 GYRES                2
"THAT WAS A LUCKY THOUGHT OF MINE,  . . . . . . .  570 THREE BUSHES        31
THOUGHT FOR I KNOW NOT WHERE,  . . . . . . . . .  574 LOVERS SONG          2
HIS CHOSEN COMRADES THOUGHT AT SCHOOL  . . . . . .  576 WHAT THEN            1
HE THOUGHT THE SAME AND LIVED BY RULE,  . . . . . .  576 WHAT THEN            3
"THE WORK IS DONE," GROWN OLD HE THOUGHT,  . . . . .  577 WHAT THEN           16
"I NEVER THOUGHT OF THAT, SIR."  . . . . . . . .  596 COLONEL MARTIN      66
CHILDLESS I THOUGHT, "MY CHILDREN MAY FIND HERE  . . .  603 GALLERY REVIS       36
JOHN SYNGE, I AND AUGUSTA GREGORY, THOUGHT  . . . .  603 GALLERY REVIS       41
CHILDLESS, I THOUGHT, "MY CHILDREN MAY LEARN HERE  . .  603 GALLERY REVIS  V    36
SOME HAD NO THOUGHT OF VICTORY  . . . . . . . . .  608 SONGS BURDEN 3      19
THE FIRST ADAM IN THEIR THOUGHT,  . . . . . . . .  617 LONG-LEG FLY        22
PROFOUND MCTAGGART THOUGHT SO, AND IN A BREATH  . . .  619 BRONZE HEAD         13
I SAW THE WILDNESS IN HER AND I THOUGHT  . . . . .  619 BRONZE HEAD         16
OR ELSE I THOUGHT HER SUPERNATURAL;  . . . . . . .  619 BRONZE HEAD         22
SAINT JOSEPH THOUGHT THE WORLD WOULD MELT  . . . . .  619 STICK INCENSE        3
I THOUGHT MY DEAR MUST HER OWN SOUL DESTROY,  . . . .  630 CIRCUS ANIMALS      21
THIS DREAM ITSELF HAD ALL MY THOUGHT AND LOVE.  . . .  630 CIRCUS ANIMALS      24
THAT HAS READ AND THOUGHT,  . . . . . . . . . .  631 POLITICS             8
THAT HAS BOTH READ AND THOUGHT,  . . . . . . . .  631 POLITICS       V     8
AND ITS CRY DISTRACTS MY THOUGHT.  . . . . . . . .  633 MAN AND ECHO        46
FORMS A STARK EGYPTIAN THOUGHT,  . . . . . . . .  638 BEN BULBEN          43
CONFUSION FELL UPON OUR THOUGHT.  . . . . . . . .  639 BEN BULBEN          67
AND THOU WILT STAY.  ALL THOUGHT OF WHAT THEY FIND  . .  670 ISLE STAT II 3      92
HE THOUGHT WISE THINGS AS HIS GREY HEAD NODDED.  . . .  728 PRIEST FAIRY        12
AND SMILING FROM SWEET THOUGHT,  . . . . . . . .  741 EARL PAUL           42
AND THOUGHT THAT SHE HAD NO HEART.  . . . . . . .  744 GLOVE CLOAK          4
I THOUGHT SHE LOVED YOU, AND I THOUGHT HER LOVE  . . .  749 SHADOW WATER A      51
I THOUGHT SHE LOVED YOU, AND I THOUGHT HER LOVE  . . .  749 SHADOW WATER A      51
BORN OUT OF IMMODERATE THOUGHT;  . . . . . . . .  772 SONG DEIRDRE 1      12
YOUR OWN THOUGHT WILL HAVE DIED  . . . . . . . .  786 YOUR HEART          30
HER OWN THOUGHT WILL HAVE DIED  . . . . . . . . .  786 YOUR HEART     V    30
HARD-LIVING MEN AND MEN OF THOUGHT  . . . . . . .  787 HUDDON DUDDON       13
IT CHASES OTHER THOUGHT AWAY,  . . . . . . . . .  791 REPRISALS            9
```

THOUGHTED   SEE HAPPIER-THOUGHTED

```
OR HAPPIER THOUGHTED WHEN THE DAY IS SPENT  . . . . .  292 TO A SHADE     V     4
```

THOUGHTLESS

```
A THOUGHTLESS IMAGE OF MANTEGNA'S THOUGHT--  . . . .  537 HER VISION          20
THOUGHTLESS JOY AND SORROW SAGE.  . . . . . . . .  733 STREET DANCERS      47
THOUGHTLESS JOYS AND SORROWS SAGE.  . . . . . . .  733 STREET DANCERS V    47
```

THOUGHT'S

```
. . . THOUGHT'S CROWNED POWERS HE CALLED THEM ONCE.  . . .  480 BLOOD AND MOON      15
```

THOUGHTS

```
AND MAY THE THOUGHTS OF IRELAND BROOD  . . . . . .  138 TO IRELAND          15
AND STILL THE THOUGHTS OF IRELAND BROOD,  . . . . .  138 TO IRELAND     V    15
BEFORE MY THOUGHTS BEGIN TO RUN  . . . . . . . .  189 BAILE AILLINN        3
AND FLYING TOWARDS THEIR PEACE.  PUT BY THESE THOUGHTS,  226 SHADOW WATER B      91
HIS NAME WILL COME INTO OUR THOUGHTS IN A MINUTE.  . .  241 SHADOW WATER B     391
IT WAS THAT HARPER PUT IT IN MY THOUGHTS,  . . . . .  243 SHADOW WATER B     423
BUT NOW IT IS YOUR THOUGHTS THAT WANDER AWAY,  . . .  246 SHADOW WATER B     512
UNTIL MY THOUGHTS CLEARED UP AGAIN,  . . . . . . .  256 WORDS                6
MY BARREN THOUGHTS HAVE CHILLED ME TO THE BONE.  . . .  257 RECONCILIATION      12
MOMENTARY THOUGHTS  . . . . . . . . . . . . .  260 FASC DIFFICULT V     T
AND THE SWEET LAUGHING EAGLE THOUGHTS THAT GROW  . . .  264 HOUSE SHAKEN         5
BECAUSE THERE IS SUCH A STORM AMID MY THOUGHTS  . . .  281 TWO KINGS          100
WITH HIS OLD THOUGHTS, KING GUAIRE WENT  . . . . .  296 THREE BEGGARS       26
WHEN ALL THOUGHTS AND DEEDS ARE RECKONED,  . . . . .  298 THREE HERMITS       15
ALL, ALL ARE IN MY THOUGHTS TO-NIGHT BEING DEAD.  . . .  324 ROBERT GREGORY       8
DISCOVERED THAT MY THOUGHTS, NOT IT,  . . . . . .  333 SOLOMON SHEBA       15
MY DAILY THOUGHTS SINCE THE FIRST STUPOR OF YOUTH  . .  342 SHEP GOATHERD       83
SING, FOR IT MAY BE THAT YOUR THOUGHTS HAVE PLUCKED  . .  342 SHEP GOATHERD       85
FOR ALL MEN'S THOUGHTS GREW CLEAR  . . . . . . .  400 DEMON BEAST         19
THAT ALL HER THOUGHTS MAY LIKE THE LINNET BE,  . . .  404 FOR DAUGHTER        42
THOUGHTS UPON THE PRESENT STATE OF THE WORLD  . . . .  428 NINETEEN 19    V     T
O WHAT FINE THOUGHTS WE HAD BECAUSE WE THOUGHT  . . .  428 NINETEEN 19    V    15
WE PIECED OUR THOUGHTS INTO PHILOSOPHY,  . . . . .  429 NINETEEN 19         30
WHEN THOUGHTS THAT A FOOL  . . . . . . . . . .  449 HERO GIRL FOOL      21
O BUT HER HEART WOULD BREAK TO LEARN MY THOUGHTS ARE FAR  450 OWEN AHERNE         20
   AWAY."
```

	PAGE	TITLE	LINE

THOUGHTS   (CONTINUED)

TWO THOUGHTS WERE SO MIXED UP I COULD NOT TELL • • • • 471 ALL SOUL NIGHT 31
WHEN THOUGHTS RISE UP UNBID • • • • • • • • • • 473 ALL SOUL NIGHT 68
THOUGHTS LONG KNITTED INTO A SINGLE THOUGHT, • • • • • 488 COOLE PARK 29 7
"WHAT CHANGE HAS PUT MY THOUGHTS ASTRAY • • • • • • 529 TOM LUNATIC 3
GOD GUARD ME FROM THOSE THOUGHTS MEN THINK • • • • • 553 PRAYER OLD AGE 1
AN OLD GHOST'S THOUGHTS ARE LIGHTNING, • • • • • • 600 SPIRIT MEDIUM 17
PURSUES THE THOUGHTS THAT I PURSUE, • • • • • • • 633 MAN AND ECHO 32
AND ITS CRY DISTRACTS MY THOUGHTS, • • • • • • 633 MAN AND ECHO V 46
MY DREAMS ROUND THOUGHTS OF PLENTY, AS IN GLOOM • • • 681 SEEKER 3
MY DREAMS O'ER THOUGHTS OF PLENTY, AS THE RED— • • • 681 SEEKER V 3
MY THOUGHTS, AND YONDER BRIGHTENING PATCH OF SKY • • • 700 MOSADA 3 31
WAS EBREMAR, WHOSE THOUGHTS WERE FIXED ON GOD, • • • • 702 MOSADA 3 83
LIKE HAPPY THOUGHTS GROWN SAD IN EVIL DAYS. • • • • 703 MOSADA 3 116
MANSIONS OF MEMORIES AND MELLOW THOUGHTS • • • • • 721 WITCH VIVIEN 21
WHAT SHALLOW THOUGHTS ABOUT DEEP THINGS! • • • • • 725 LEGEND 11
THE TANGLED THOUGHTS OF THE FINISHED DAY • • • • • • 728 PRIEST FAIRY 9
TILL CERTAIN SECOND THOUGHTS HAVE COME • • • • • • 791 REPRISALS 12

THOUGHT-WOVEN

THE TALL THOUGHT-WOVEN SAILS, THAT FLAP UNFURLED • • • 113 ROSE OF BATTLE 2
OUR LONG SHIPS LOOSE THOUGHT-WOVEN SAILS AND WAIT, • • • 115 ROSE OF BATTLE 31

THOUSAND

"AND I WILL MAKE A THOUSAND SONGS, • • • • • • • 7 OISIN 1 75
BELOVED IN A THOUSAND SONGS. • • • • • • • • • 7 OISIN 1 V 76
OF MANY THOUSAND STEPS. SAT EITHER SIDE, • • • • • 31 OISIN 2 V 35
WHO HAS BEEN BURIED SOME TWO THOUSAND YEARS? • • • • 181 QUEEN MAEVE 35
TO MANY THOUSAND EYES, AND TO HER OWN • • • • • • 182 QUEEN MAEVE 65
A THOUSAND YEARS AGO YOU HELD HIGH TALK • • • • • • 187 QUEEN MAEVE 150
I KNOW THAT HE DIED A THOUSAND YEARS AGO, • • • • • 241 SHADOW WATER B 392
AND THAT HE DIED A THOUSAND YEARS AGO. • • • • • • 242 SHADOW WATER B 417
THESE THOUSAND YEARS. WHAT ARE THE BIRDS AT THERE? • • 243 SHADOW WATER B 435
HAVE I NOT LOVED YOU FOR A THOUSAND YEARS? • • • • • 244 SHADOW WATER B 463
THAT YOU WERE BORN A THOUSAND YEARS AGO, • • • • • 245 SHADOW WATER B 468
FOR HE SHALL HAVE A THOUSAND POUNDS • • • • • • • 295 THREE BEGGARS 22
AND TWICE A THOUSAND MORE • • • • • • • • • • 401 DEMON BEAST 47
AND I ALONE, ONE IN TEN THOUSAND YEARS, • • • • • 470 HARUN RASHID V 190
OUT OF TEN THOUSAND WINTERS, I ALONE— • • • • • • 470 HARUN RASHID V 190
UPON A HUNDRED THOUSAND STAGES, • • • • • • • • 566 LAPIS LAZULI 23
COME FORTH, FOR IN A THOUSAND BOWERS • • • • • • • 647 ISLE STAT I 1 64
HAVE I NOT SEEN A THOUSAND SEASONS EBB AND FLOW • • • 675 ISLE STAT II 3 229
THE TIDE OF STARS? HAVE I NOT SEEN A THOUSAND YEARS • • 675 ISLE STAT II 3 230
ERE YONDER PALM COMMENCED HIS THOUSAND YEARS? • • • • 724 KANVA ON SELF 14
UNDER THE WAVES, AND TOOK A THOUSAND WOMEN • • • • • 766 SHADOW WATER A 378

THOUSANDS

THOUSANDS OF YEARS, THOUSANDS OF YEARS, • • • • • • 116 FAERY SONG 3
THOUSANDS OF YEARS, THOUSANDS OF YEARS, • • • • • • 116 FAERY SONG 3
THOUSANDS OF YEARS, THOUSANDS OF YEARS, • • • • • • 116 FAERY SONG 15
THOUSANDS OF YEARS, THOUSANDS OF YEARS, • • • • • • 116 FAERY SONG 15
THOUSANDS OF LEAGUES OVERSEA, • • • • • • • • • 341 SHEP GOATHERD 63
AND FLOWERS AROUND IN CLUSTERING THOUSANDS ARE, • • • 656 ISLE STAT I 3 24

THRALLS

WHO MIGHT HAVE FLOCKS AND HERDS AND MANY THRALLS, • • • 757 SHADOW WATER A 216

THRANEEN

CARED NOT A THRANEEN FOR WHAT CHANCED • • • • • • 514 JANE GROWN OLD 18
CARE NOT A THRANEEN FOR WHAT CHANCED • • • • • • 514 JANE GROWN OLD V 18

THRASH

THAT NIGHT AND MORNING I MAY THRASH • • • • • • • 379 SAINT HUNCH 9

THREAD

AND HOOKED A BERRY TO A THREAD; • • • • • • • • 149 WANDER AENGUS 4
AND PUT A BERRY ON A THREAD; • • • • • • • • • 149 WANDER AENGUS V 4
THE LOVE-TALES WROUGHT WITH SILKEN THREAD • • • • • 155 FORGOT BEAUTY 6
THE LOVE-TALES WOVE WITH SILKEN THREAD • • • • • • 155 FORGOT BEAUTY V 6
"YOUR WELL-BELOVED'S HAIR HAS A THREAD OF GREY, • • • 199 FOLLY COMFORT V 2
THE GOLD AND SILVER THREAD. • • • • • • • • • 308 PLAYER QUEEN 8
SHE PULLED THE THREAD AND BIT THE THREAD • • • • • 308 PLAYER QUEEN 9
SHE PULLED THE THREAD AND BIT THE THREAD • • • • • 308 PLAYER QUEEN 9
ARE BUT LOOSE THREAD, ARE BUT LOOSE THREAD; • • • • 449 HERO GIRL FOOL 23
ARE BUT LOOSE THREAD, ARE BUT LOOSE THREAD; • • • • 449 HERO GIRL FOOL 23
BEFORE THE THREAD BEGAN • • • • • • • • • • 520 HIS BARGAIN 8
WHEN THE LAST THREAD HAS RUN • • • • • • • • • 520 HIS BARGAIN 10
WHEN THE LAZY THREAD HAS RUN— • • • • • • • • 520 HIS BARGAIN V 10
INSTEAD OF THREAD AND NEEDLE • • • • • • • • • 595 COLONEL MARTIN 23
"WE THREAD THE NEEDLES' EYES, AND ALL WE DO • • • • 634 CUCHULAIN COMF 16
THERE ARE SEVEN THAT PULL THE THREAD. • • • • • • 770 SPINNING SONG 1
PUT ALL YOUR POWER ON THE THREAD • • • • • • • 771 SPINNING SONG 12

THREADBARE

• • • SAILS TURNING TO THREADBARE RAGS! • • • • • 55 OISIN 3 118
YOUR HOOD IS THREADBARE—SEE THAT IT BE CHANGED • • • 704 MOSADA 3 133

THREAD-BARE

• • • SAILS TURNING TO THREAD-BARE RAGS! • • • • • 55 OISIN 3 V 118

THREADED

WITH THEIR MUSHROOMS LIGHTLY THREADED • • • • • • 705 DAWN-SONG 13

THREADS   SEE MIST-THREADS

"YOUR WELL-BELOVED'S HAIR HAS THREADS OF GREY, • • • • 199 FOLLY COMFORT 2
"YOUR WELL BELOVED'S HAIR HAS THREADS OF GREY, • • • • 199 FOLLY COMFORT V 2
SEVEN OLD SISTERS WIND THE THREADS OF THE LONG-LIVED ONES, 209 UNDER THE MOON 7
SEVEN OLD SISTERS WIND THE THREADS OF THE LONG LIVED ONES, 209 UNDER THE MOON V 7
HANG THE MIST THREADS FOR A LITTLE WHILE LIKE COBWEBS IN
THE AIR, • • • • • • • • • • • • • • • 719 PHANTOM SHIP V 29
BUT WEAVING IT OUT OF THREADS • • • • • • • • • 743 WISDOM DREAMS 3

		PAGE	TITLE		LINE
THREAT					
	TO BRIBE OR THREAT! HABITS THAT MADE OLD WRONG	428	NINETEEN 19		11
THREATEN					
	THREATEN THE HEAD THAT I LOVE.	119	PITY OF LOVE		8
	ALL THREATEN THE HEAD THAT I LOVE.	119	PITY OF LOVE	V	8
	THOSE BANNERS COME TO BRIBE OR THREATEN, ...	635	BLACK TOWER		11
THREATENED					
	UPON A THREATENED HOUSE	264	HOUSE SHAKEN	V	T
	HER EIGHTIETH WINTER APPROACHING! "YESTERDAY HE THREATENED MY LIFE.	578	LOFTY THINGS		8
THREE					
	HAVE KNOWN THREE CENTURIES, POETS SING, ...	2	OISIN 1		3
	WE RODE IN SORROW, WITH STRONG HOUNDS THREE, ...	2	OISIN 1	V	7C
	HE SHOOK HIMSELF AND NEIGHED THREE TIMES!	10	OISIN 1		110
	AND NEIGHED THREE TIMES. WHEN, WONDERING	10	OISIN 1	V	110A
	AND NIAMH BLEW THREE MERRY NOTES	14	OISIN 1		195
	THAT OLD, SEA-WEEDY, SQUARED, THREE HUNDRED FEET . . .	31	OISIN 2	V	30C
	WE FEASTED FOR THREE DAYS. ON THE FOURTH MORN	43	OISIN 2		214
	THREE DAYS WE FEASTED, WHEN ON THE FOURTH MORN	43	OISIN 2	V	214
	"LAST OF MY RACE, THREE THINGS I RULE ALONE—	45	OISIN 2	V	239A
	AND DEW-BLANCHED HORNS, IN WHOSE HOLLOW A CHILD OF THREE YEARS OLD	49	OISIN 3		30
	AND DEW-BLANCHED HORNS, IN WHOSE HOLLOWS A CHILD OF THREE YEARS OLD	49	OISIN 3	V	31
	AND MY YEARS THREE HUNDRED FELL ON ME, ...	60	OISIN 3		191
	FOR THREE DAYS MORE IN DREADFUL QUIETUDE, ...	110	CUCHULAIN SEA		78
	AND CHAUNTED FOR THREE DAYS. CUCHULAIN STIRRED, . . .	111	CUCHULAIN SEA		83
	IN THREE DAYS' TIME HE STOOD UP WITH A MOAN, ...	111	CUCHULAIN SEA		83
	IN THREE DAYS' TIME, CUCHULAIN WITH A MOAN	111	CUCHULAIN SEA	V	83
	AND CHANTED FOR THREE DAYS. CUCHULAIN STIRRED, . . .	111	CUCHULAIN SEA	V	83
	AND HOW BENEATH THOSE THREE TIMES BLESSED SKIES . . .	127	DREAM OF FAERY	V	21
	AODH TO DECTORA THREE SONGS	152	LOSS OF LOVE	V	T
	HE WILL SMILE ON THE THREE OLD SPIRITS, ...	178	FIDDLER DOONEY		11
	O KINSMEN OF THE THREE IN ONE, ...	213	BLESS PSALTER		14
	AND SAID, "IN TWO OR IN THREE YEARS	272	GREY ROCK		46
	THE THREE BEGGARS	294	THREE BEGGARS		T
	AND THERE TO THREE OLD BEGGARS SAID, ...	295	THREE BEGGARS		10
	ONE OF YOU THREE IS A RICH MAN, ...	295	THREE BEGGARS		21
	BEFORE THE THREE TO END THIS TALE, ...	297	THREE BEGGARS		55
	"TIME'S UP," HE CRIED, AND ALL THE THREE	297	THREE BEGGARS		57
	"TIME'S UP," HE CRIED, AND ALL THE THREE	297	THREE BEGGARS		59
	THE THREE HERMITS	298	THREE HERMITS		T
	THREE OLD HERMITS TOOK THE AIR	298	THREE HERMITS		1
	THREE TIMES IN A SINGLE DAY	298	THREE HERMITS		10
	AND DESOLATE THREE ROCK	310	PEACOCK		5
	NOW MUST I THESE THREE PRAISE—	315	FRIENDS		1
	THREE WOMEN THAT HAVE WROUGHT	315	FRIENDS		2
	AND TWO OR THREE HAD CHARM, ...	350	MEMORY		2
	ANOTHER BOASTS, "I PICK AND CHOOSE AND HAVE BUT TWO OR THREE."	354	HIS PHOENIX		20
	UNDER THE THREE LAST CRESCENTS OF THE MOON, ...	377	PHASES OF MOON		133
	IN CONTEMPLATION HAD THOSE THREE SO WROUGHT	384	VISION ROBART		45
	THREE HUNDRED YEARS BEFORE THE FALL, ...	388	SOLOMON WITCH		11
	WE THREE MAKE UP A SOLITUDE!	457	SECRETS OF OLD		9
	THE THREE MONUMENTS	460	THREE MONUMENT		T
	THE THREE OLD RASCALS LAUGH ALOUD.	460	THREE MONUMENT		12
	THREE MOVEMENTS	485	THREE MOVEMENT		T
	THREE THINGS	521	THREE THINGS		T
	"O CRUEL DEATH, GIVE THREE THINGS BACK,"	521	THREE THINGS		1
	"THREE DEAR THINGS THAT WOMEN KNOW,"	521	THREE THINGS		7
	THREE SONGS TO THE SAME TUNE	543	TO SAME TUNE 1		T
	THREE SONGS TO THE SAME TUNE SECOND SONG	544	TO SAME TUNE 1	V	T
	. . . SHARE GOD THAT IS BUT THREE, ...	556	RIBH PATRICK		11
	THE THREE BUSHES	569	THREE BUSHES		T
	THREE KEGS OF GOLD.	596	COLONEL MARTIN		49
	YOU HAD THREE KEGS" SAID HE.	596	COLONEL MARTIN		65
	WE THREE ALONE IN MODERN TIMES HAD BROUGHT	603	GALLERY REVIS		45
	THREE SONGS TO THE ONE BURDEN	605	SONGS BURDEN 1		T
	THREE MARCHING SONGS	613	MARCH SONGS 1		T
	SHE THINKS, PART WOMAN, THREE PARTS A CHILD, ...	617	LONG-LEG FLY		15
	THROUGH THREE ENCHANTED ISLANDS, ALLEGORICAL DREAMS, .	629	CIRCUS ANIMALS		11
	A BUNDLE OF LINEN. SHROUDS BY TWO AND THREE	634	CUCHULAIN COMF		9
	THREE TIMES THE ROSES HAVE GROWN LESS AND LESS, . . .	690	MOSADA 1		1
	WHOSE FOOTFALL I HAVE LONGED FOR, THREE SAD SUMMERS. .	692	MOSADA 1		45
	WITH THREE BARS CROSSED, AND THESE FOUR WALLS MY WORLD,	700	MOSADA 3		32
	WE THROW THREE TIMES.	721	WITCH VIVIEN		39
	THREE SPANS HIGH AS HE ROSE TO HIS FEET, ...	729	PRIEST FAIRY		25
	THREE MOONS. IT WERE BEST TO KILL HIM, AND CHOOSE OUT	748	SHADOW WATER A		15
	DIMMED AT THREE QUARTER LIGHT	786	YOUR HEART	V	32
	I PUT THREE PERSONS IN THEIR PLACE	787	HUDDON DUDDON		8
THREEFOLD					
	THE THREEFOLD TERROR OF LOVE! A FALLEN FLARE	499	MOTHER OF GOD		1
THREE-FOLD					
	THE THREE-FOLD TERROR OF LOVE! A FALLEN FLARE	499	MOTHER OF GOD	V	1
THREE-LEGGED					
	I SLEPT ON MY THREE-LEGGED STOOL BY THE FIRE, ...	381	SONGS FOOL 2		1
THREE-QUARTER					
	DIMMED AT THREE-QUARTER LIGHT, ...	786	YOUR HEART		32
THREE-ROCK					
	AND DESOLATE THREE-ROCK	310	PEACOCK	V	5

THREES
    CHILDREN SING IN TWOS AND THREES. . . . .   732 STREET DANCERS   17
    THE FLIES THAT DANCE IN THREES, IN TWOS, ...   736 IN CHURCH   11
THREESCORE
    FROM THREESCORE YEARS OF DREAM-LED WANDERING . . . .   682 SEEKER   16
THREE-SIX
    THREE-SIX.   721 WITCH VIVIEN   40
THRESHED
    THAT MEN THRESHED CORN AT MIDNIGHT BY A TRESS, ...   170 SECRET ROSE   26
THRESHING
    FORGOTTEN AT THE THRESHING PLACE: . . . .   195 BAILE AILLINN V 148
THRESHING-PLACE
    FORGOTTEN AT THE THRESHING-PLACE: . . . .   195 BAILE AILLINN   148
THRESHOLD
    ABOUT MY THRESHOLD TO COUNSEL AND TO HELP?" . . . . .   183 QUEEN MAEVE   82
    CAME TO THE THRESHOLD OF THE PAINTED HOUSE . . . . . .   185 QUEEN MAEVE   108
    WHAT ON THE THRESHOLD STANDS? . . . .   583 GHOST ROG CASE   2
    BE DRIVEN FROM THE THRESHOLD . . . .   770 BLOOD BOND   5
    THE THRESHOLD AND THE HEARTHSTONE. . . . .   775 AGAINST WITCH   6
    BUT THE THRESHOLD AND HEARTHSTONE. . . . .   776 AGAINST WITCH   40
THRESHOLDS
    BE DRIVEN FROM THE THRESHOLDS . . . .   770 BLOOD BOND V 4
THREW
    AND AT THE SUNDOWN THREW HIM IN THE SURGE, ...   44 OISIN 2   219
    AND IN THE EVE I THREW HIM IN THE SURGE, ...   44 OISIN 2 V 219
    WHEREFORE I THREW A PENNY . . . .   268 BROWN PENNY   3
    AGAINST A BEECH-BOLE, HE THREW DOWN THE BEAST . . . . .   278 TWO KINGS   36
    AGAINST A BEECH BOLE, HE THREW DOWN THE BEAST . . . . .   278 TWO KINGS V 36
    THEY THREW A HALFPENNY INTO MY CAP, ...   300 RUN PARADISE   2
    THREW UP IN THE AIR HIS MARVELLOUS MOON. . . . . . .   314 MEMORY YOUTH V 21
    AND THREW HIM UP TO LAUGH ON THE BOUGH: . . . .   318 APPOINTMENT   11
    WHETHER SHE THREW THEM UP TO FLOUT ME, ...   390 IMAGE PAST   37
    BUT THEY THREW DOWN THEIR PISTOLS . . . .   596 COLONEL MARTIN   59
    A BERRY THREW FOR ME—OR THEE. . . . .   743 DANAAN QUICK   11
THRICE
    WHEN MAYBE THRICE IN EVERY MOON HER MOUTH . . . . . .   468 HARUN RASHID   162
    AND THRICE THE PEACHES FLUSHED UPON THE WALLS, ...   690 MOSADA 1   2
    AND THRICE THE CORN AROUND THE SICKLES FLAMED, ...   690 MOSADA 1   3
    "SAY AND THRICE ANIGH THY DOOR . . . .   730 PRIEST FAIRY   54
    BUT THE MAN IS THRICE FORLORN, ...   776 AGAINST WITCH   26
THRIVE
    "MY BROTHERS AND MY SISTERS LIVE AND THRIVE, ...   32 OISIN 2 V 50C
    IMAGINES BEST TO MAKE IT THRIVE. . . . .   287 TO WEALTHY MAN   8
    WHAT NONE CAN HAVE AND THRIVE, ...   315 FRIENDS   13
    THE WOMEN NONE CAN KISS AND THRIVE, ...   775 AGAINST WITCH   8
    WOMEN, THAT NONE CAN KISS AND THRIVE, ...   775 AGAINST WITCH V 8
THRIVES
    AND YONDER IN THE GYMNASTS' GARDEN THRIVES . . . . . .   446 COLONUS PRAISE   9
THROAT   SEE CUT-THROAT
    UNDER THE ROOF, AND WITH A STRAINING THROAT . . . . .   36 OISIN 2   106
    DRIFTING ON HIGH, AND WITH A STRAINING THROAT . . . .   36 OISIN 2 V 106
    THROUGH MANY SHAPES: I LUNGED AT THE SMOOTH THROAT . . .   40 OISIN 2   175
    TO MANY SHAPES: I LUNGED AT THE SMOOTH THROAT . . . .   40 OISIN 2 V 175
    . . . AND HEAVING THE PILLAR OF HIS THROAT, ...   51 OISIN 3   59
    CRUEL CLAW AND HUNGRY THROAT, ...   136 TWO TREES   36
    FROM ANY BRAZEN THROAT. . . . .   291 TO A FRIEND   3
    FROM HEEL TO THROAT: . . . .   320 COAT   4
    NO MORE SANG HE, FOR HIS THROAT WAS TOO SMALL: . . . .   545 TO SAME TUNE 1   24
    HE SAID NO MORE FOR HIS THROAT WAS TOO SMALL. . . . .   545 TO SAME TUNE 1 V 24
    AND TAKES YOU BY THE THROAT: . . . .   598 STONE CROSS   4
    NO MORE SANG HE, FOR HIS THROAT WAS TOO SMALL: . . . .   616 MARCH SONGS 3   24
    CURES FOR CALVES WITH 'PLAINING THROAT, ...   717 FAIRY DOCTOR   15
    CURES FOR CALF WITH 'PLAINING THROAT, ...   717 FAIRY DOCTOR V 15
THROATED   SEE REED-THROATED SWEET-THROATED HUNDRED-THROATED
    "WITH HIM IS ONE SWEET THROATED LIKE A BIRD, ...   106 CUCHULAIN SEA V 16
    THEN CONCOBAR SENT THAT SWEET THROATED MAID . . . . .   110 CUCHULAIN SEA V 72
THROATS
    AND SWANS WITH THEIR EXULTANT THROATS: . . . .   14 OISIN 1   192
    THEY HAD CHANGED THEIR THROATS AND HAD THE THROATS   635 CUCHULAIN COMF   25
        OF BIRDS.
    THEY HAD CHANGED THEIR THROATS AND HAD THE THROATS   635 CUCHULAIN COMF   25
        OF BIRDS.
THROB
    FOR ONE THROB OF THE ARTERY, ...   406 IN TIME OF WAR   1
    AND THROB WITHIN THE CIRCLES OF GREEN DAWN. . . . . .   701 MOSADA 3   54
THROBBING   SEE STAR-THROBBING
THRONE
    I PACE REMEMBERING. FROM MY MISTY THRONE . . . . . .   45 OISIN 2 V 239C
    MINE WAS THE THRONE IN EMAN'S HALL, ...   81 MAD KING GOLL V 2
    THRONE OVER THRONE WHERE IN HALF SLEEP, ...   156 FORGOT BEAUTY   22
    THRONE OVER THRONE WHERE IN HALF SLEEP, ...   156 FORGOT BEAUTY   22
    TILL THERE BE NAUGHT BUT THRONE ON THRONE . . . . . .   156 FORGOT BEAUTY V 21
    TILL THERE BE NAUGHT BUT THRONE ON THRONE . . . . . .   156 FORGOT BEAUTY V 21
    UPON THE THRONE AND CRYING ABOUT THE STREETS . . . .   198 SEVEN WOODS   7
    APPLAUD A MODERN THRONE: . . . .   597 MODEL LAUREATE   18
    AND HE STUCK TO HIS THRONE. . . . .   628 JANE MOUNTAIN   10
    AND HEARD EACH UNSEEN ECHO ON HER THRONE, ...   657 ISLE STAT I 3   48
    EACH ONE AT GAZE FOR AYE UPON HIS WHIRLING THRONE. . . .   662 ISLE STAT II 1   81
    AS SLOWLY AUTUMN CLIMBED THE GOLDEN THRONE . . . . .   690 MOSADA 1 V 1A
THRONES
    UPON DARK THRONES. BETWEEN THE LIDS OF ONE . . . . .   31 OISIN 2   37

PAGE   TITLE   LINE

THRONES (CONTINUED)
```
FROM THEIR PALE THRONES AND COMFORT HIM, BUT THEY    . . .    68 SAD SHEPHERD        6
WHAT HAD THE CAESARS BUT THEIR THRONES?  . . . . . . .       401 DEMON BEAST        50
ON THRONES FROM CHINA TO PERU . . . . . . . . . . . .       597 MODEL LAUREATE      1
ABOVE THE ALPUJARRAS ON THEIR THRONES:  . . . . . . .       691 MOSADA 1           27
UPON THEIR THRONES.  THE LIVES OF MEN SHALL FLOW . . . .    698 MOSADA 2           56
```
THRONG
```
AMID THE HOVERING, PITEOUS, PENITENTIAL THRONG."         173 SPEAKS HEARERS      8
A NOBODY IN A GREAT THRONG, . . . . . . . . . . . .      361 ALF POLLEXFEN      29
IN THE LONG ECHOING STREET THE LAUGHING DANCERS THRONG,  459 FROM OEDIPUS        7
IN THE LONG ECHOING STREETS THE LAUGHING DANCERS THRONG, 459 FROM OEDIPUS   V    7
IT SEEMED A QUATTROCENTO PAINTER'S THRONG, . . . . .     537 HER VISION         19
IT SEEMED A QUATTRO-CENTO PAINTER'S THRONG, . . . . .    537 HER VISION     V   19
BRED OUT OF THE CONTAGION OF THE THRONG, . . . . .       542 PARN FUNERAL 1     27
```
THRONGED   SEE LUTE-THRONGED
```
AND MY GAZE WAS THRONGED WITH THE SLEEPERS: . . . . .     50 OISIN 3           49
```
THRONGS
```
. . . DRIVING THE DUST WITH THEIR THRONGS, . . . . .      53 OISIN 3           85
THE THRONGS WITH BLOWN WET HAIR ARE GATHERING NEAR. . .  114 ROSE OF BATTLE V    6
```
THROUGHOUT
```
THROUGHOUT SO MANY VARYING CENTURIES . . . . . . . .     371 ON GOING HOUSE      8
```
THROW
```
I THROW DOWN THE CHAIN OF SMALL STONES! . . . . . .       63 OISIN 3          222
TO THROW ME A BIT OF SALTED FISH. . . . . . . . . .      301 RUN PARADISE        6
I'D TEAR IT OFF AND THROW IT IN THE FIRE." . . . . .     462 HARUN RASHID       34
"UPLIFT THOSE EYES AND THROW . . . . . . . . . . .       516 MANS SONG           7
THROW IT IN EVERY PART." . . . . . . . . . . .           596 COLONEL MARTIN     53
THROW LIKELY COUPLES INTO BED . . . . . . . . . .        606 SONGS BURDEN 1     25
MAYHAP 'TWERE BETTER THAT ASIDE I THROW . . . . .        656 ISLE STAT I 3      38
AND WHO WILL THROW HIS MANSION DOWN . . . . . .          671 ISLE STAT II 3    135
WE THROW THREE TIMES, . . . . . . . . . . . . .          721 WITCH VIVIEN       39
TO THROW THE NORMAN KNIGHT." " . . . . . . . . .         740 EARL PAUL          12
```
THROWN
```
AND HIS LOOSE BULK BE THROWN IN THE LOUD TIDE." . . .     35 OISIN 2           91
NOT EVEN YOUR GOD COULD HAVE THROWN DOWN THAT HALL: . .   36 OISIN 2          109
NOT E'EN THY GOD COULD HAVE THROWN DOWN THAT HALL: . .    36 OISIN 2      V   109
AND THROWN THE THUNDER ON THE STONES FOR ALL THAT MAEVE  207 HANRAHANS SONG      7
  CAN SAY.
NOR ULADH, WHEN NAOISE HAD THROWN A SAIL UPON THE WIND,  209 UNDER THE MOON      4
LAND-OF-THE-TOWER, WHERE AENGUS HAS THROWN THE GATES APART, 209 UNDER THE MOON    8
LAND OF THE TOWER, WHEN AENGUS HAS THROWN THE GATES APART, 209 UNDER THE MOON V   8
I MIGHT HAVE THROWN POOR WORDS AWAY . . . . . . . .      256 WORDS              15
MERE BONE AND MUSCLE THROWN ASIDE . . . . . . . . .      273 GREY ROCK          51
MOANED THE OTHER, "THEY ARE THROWN . . . . . . .         299 THREE HERMITS      22
YOU HAD BEFORE THE SUN HAD THROWN . . . . . . . .        333 SOLOMON SHEBA      13
BROUGHT THE BARE NEWS.  HE HAD THROWN THE CROOK AWAY     339 SHEP GOATHERD      21
WHERE THE SHEEP ARE THROWN IN THE POOL, . . . . . .      341 SHEP GOATHERD  V   71
THE ELABORATE STAR-LIGHT HAS THROWN REFLECTIONS . . .    389 IMAGE PAST     V    2
NOW SHE HAS THROWN HER ARMS ABOVE HER HEAD: . . . .      390 IMAGE PAST         36
A BIT OF BREAD THROWN UP INTO THE AIR: . . . . . .       400 DEMON BEAST        25
IF THROWN IN MADGE'S WAY, . . . . . . . . . . .          457 SECRETS OF OLD      8
THROWN INTO DESPAIR . . . . . . . . . . . . .            492 ANNE GREGORY        2
SOME BACK A MARE THROWN FROM A THOROUGHBRED, . . . .     547 TO SAME TUNE 3      3
SOME BACK A MARE THROWN FROM A THOROUGH-BRED, . . . .    547 TO SAME TUNE 3 V    3
EMPEDOCLES HAS THROWN ALL THINGS ABOUT: . . . . . .      564 GYRES               6
"OF PLASTER SAINTS"; HIS BEAUTIFUL MISCHIEVOUS HEAD THROWN 577 LOFTY THINGS      4
  BACK.
BUT THROWN UPON THIS FILTHY MODERN TIDE . . . . . . .    611 STATUES            29
SOME BACK A MARE THROWN FROM A THOROUGHBRED, . . . .     614 MARCH SONGS 2       3
POOR LOVE AND SORROW, WITH THEIR ARMS THROWN ROUND . .   703 MOSADA 3          119
HE HAS THROWN A DRUID DREAM UPON THE AIR. . . . .        759 SHADOW WATER A    237
I HAD THROWN IT DOWN BEHIND THIS COIL OF ROPE. . . .     759 SHADOW WATER A    245
A SUDDEN STORM, AND IT WAS THROWN . . . . . . . .        784 WOMANS BEAUTY       5
```
THROWS
```
THE ELABORATE STARLIGHT THROWS A REFLECTION . . . . .    389 IMAGE PAST          2
THE MOUNTAIN THROWS A SHADOW, . . . . . . . . .          519 LOVES LONENESS      7
AWAY HER CLINGING HANDS, AND TURNS.  SHE THROWS . . .    714 FERENCZ RENYI     102
HER OFF AND TURNS AWAY.  SHE THROWS . . . . . . .        714 FERENCZ RENYI  V  102
```
THRUST
```
AND THRUST THE TORCH BETWEEN THE SLIMY FLAGS. . . . .     38 OISIN 2          143
TURNING, HE SAW THAT SHE HAD THRUST DEAD LEAVES . . .     80 EPHEMERA          18
THRUST HIM AWAY WITH BOTH MY HANDS AND CRIED, . . .      285 TWO KINGS         202
THE BREAST THRUST OUT IN PRIDE . . . . . . . . .         430 NINETEEN 19        66
THEY BUT THRUST THEIR BURIED MEN . . . . . . . .         637 BEN BULBEN         23
FIERCE THRUST!  A TARDY BLOSSOM HAD THE SEED, . . . .    665 ISLE STAT II 2     65
OF THOSE STEEL TONGUES!  CRASH, SWORDS!  WELL THRUST!    665 ISLE STAT II 2     67
  WELL BENT
AND FLY AMONG THE FOAM.  THRUST DOWN THE HELM, . . . .   750 SHADOW WATER A     88
```
THRUSTING
```
THRUSTING HIS NOSE TO MY SHOULDER: HE KNEW IN HIS BOSOM   54 OISIN 3          106
  DEEP
```
THUMB
```
MACDONAGH'S BONY THUMB? . . . . . . . . . . . .          395 SIXTEEN DEAD       12
HE SO BEWITCHED THE CARDS UNDER HIS THUMB . . . . .      411 TOWER              67
```
THUMBS
```
"THE FIDDLERS ARE ALL THUMBS, . . . . . . . . . .        527 AM OF IRELAND      19
```
THUMPS
```
AND THE HEART THUMPS AT MY SIDE, . . . . . . . . .       456 FRIENDS YOUTH      18
```
THUNDER
```
ARE CHOKED WITH THUNDER, LIGHTNING, AND FIERCE WIND,  . .  42 OISIN 2         205
SAINT, DO YOU WEEP?  I HEAR AMID THE THUNDER . . . . .     43 OISIN 2         209
```

816

	PAGE	TITLE		LINE
THUNDER (CONTINUED)				
SAINT, DOST THOU WEEP? I HEAR AMID THE THUNDER	43	OISIN 2	V	209
MAKE THEIR FAINT THUNDER, AND THE GARDEN BEES	198	SEVEN WOODS		2
AND THROWN THE THUNDER ON THE STONES FOR ALL THAT MAEVE CAN SAY.	207	HANRAHANS SONG		7
AND SHAKE DOWN THUNDER ON THE STONES BECAUSE THE RED WINDS RAVE!	207	HANRAHANS SONG	V	7
THUNDER OF FEET, TUMULT OF IMAGES, ...	433	NINETEEN 19		120
THAT GATHERS VOLUME; NOW A THUNDER CLAP.	487	SEVEN SAGES	V	23
AT SUDDEN THUNDER OF THE MOUNTING SWAN	490	COOLE BALLYLEE		14
MAY THUNDER TIME AWAY, ...	496	MOHINI CHATTER		25
TO HIM WITH THUNDER SHOD, ...	735	IN CHURCH		2
TO HIM WITH THUNDER SHOD, ...	736	IN CHURCH		14
THUNDER-BALL				
FEARFUL OF THE THUNDER-BALL, ...	43	OISIN 2	V	208F
THUNDERBOLT				
TALMA AND HIS THUNDERBOLT.	625	NATIVITY		10
THUNDER-CLAP				
THAT GATHERS VOLUME; NOW A THUNDER-CLAP.	487	SEVEN SAGES		23
THUNDERING				
THUNDERING, AND THE WIDE USELESS WATERS FRAY	45	OISIN 2	V	238
THUNDER-SOUND				
WILL BE THE FAINT FAR THUNDER-SOUND, AS THOUGH	699	MOSADA 3		10
WILL MOVE THE FAINT FAR THUNDER-SOUND, AS THOUGH . . .	699	MOSADA 3	V	10
THUNDERSTONES				
ALL THOSE DREADFUL THUNDERSTONES, ...	509	JANE REPROVED	V	2
THUNDER-STONES				
ALL THOSE DREADFUL THUNDER-STONES, ...	509	JANE REPROVED		2
THURIBLES				
IS IT THESE THAT WITH GOLDEN THURIBLES	167	BLESSED		23
IS IT THOSE THAT WITH GOLDEN THURIBLES	167	BLESSED	V	23
TIDE SEE NOON-TIDE NIGHT-TIDE				
BEYOND THE TUMBLING OF THIS TIDE."	5	OISIN 1		49
THROUGH BITTER TIDE ON FOAM-WET FEET?	5	OISIN 1		51
MY HOME IS FAR FROM WHERE THE TIDE	5	OISIN 1	V	46
IS NIAMH, AND MY LAND WHERE TIDE	5	OISIN 1	V	48
AND WAS BORN WHERE THE SUN DROPS DOWN IN THE TIDE, . . .	5	OISIN 1	V	49
TO SHORES BY THE WASH OF THE TREMULOUS TIDE, ...	8	OISIN 1		81
UPON THEIR SHADOWS IN THE TIDE, ...	14	OISIN 1		185
"'TIS JOY MAKES SWIM THE SAPPY TIDE, ...	18	OISIN 1	V	261
UNCHAINABLE AS THE DIM TIDE, ...	22	OISIN 1		338
WHEN ONE DAY BY THE TIDE I STOOD, ...	24	OISIN 1		364
AND NAMED HIM BY SWEET NAMES. A FOAMING TIDE	30	OISIN 2		27
DARK STATUES GLIMMERED OVER THE PALE TIDE	31	OISIN 2		36
NEARER THE CASTLE CAME WE. A VAST TIDE, ...	31	OISIN 2	V	27A
FOG-DRIPPING, PEDESTALLED ABOVE THE TIDE, ...	31	OISIN 2	V	36
AND HIS LOOSE BULK BE THROWN IN THE LOUD TIDE."	35	OISIN 2		91
FIN, CONAN, OSCAR, MANY MORE, THE TIDE	44	OISIN 2	V	228A
HIGH AS THE SADDLE-GIRTH, COVERING AWAY FROM OUR GLANCES THE TIDE:	47	OISIN 3		2
HIGH AS THE SADDLE GIRTH, COVERING AWAY FROM OUR GLANCES THE TIDE:	47	OISIN 3	V	2
HOW THE SLOW, BLUE-EYED OXEN OF FINN LOW SADLY AT EVENING TIDE.	52	OISIN 3		84
AND SOFTLY COME TO YOUR NIAMH OVER THE TOPS OF THE TIDE:	55	OISIN 3		126
AND SOFTLY COME TO THY NIAM OVER THE TOPS OF THE TIDE:	52	OISIN 3	V	126
FOR I AM IN HIS IMAGE MADE, AND ALL THIS TINKLING TIDE . .	76	INDIAN ON GOD		11
ONE WITH THE TIDE THAT GLEAMS, THE WINGS THAT GLEAM AND DART,	78	INDIAN TO LOVE		15
ONE WITH THE GLIMMERING TIDE, ...	78	INDIAN TO LOVE	V	15
CUCHULAIN BATTLING WITH THE BITTER TIDE:	100	ROSE UPON ROOD		3
GO WATCH THE ROAD BETWEEN THE WOOD AND TIDE, ...	105	CUCHULAIN SEA		4
GO DWELL UPON THE CLIFFS AND WATCH THE TIDE:	105	CUCHULAIN SEA	V	4
AND THE GREY TIDE, THE RED BRANCH MULTITUDE	108	CUCHULAIN SEA	V	38B
AND FOUGHT WITH THE INVULNERABLE TIDE.	111	CUCHULAIN SEA		86
FOR FOUR DAYS WARRED HE WITH THE BITTER TIDE, ...	111	CUCHULAIN SEA	V	85
ABOVE THE TIDE OF HOURS, TROUBLE THE AIR, ...	114	ROSE OF BATTLE		3
ABOVE THE TIDE OF HOURS, RISE ON THE AIR, ...	114	ROSE OF BATTLE	V	3
IN SHAKEN BOUGHS, IN TIDE ON THE SHORE?	141	EVERLAST VOICE		7
AT THE COMING OF NIGHT TIDE, ...	144	HOST OF AIR	V	6
OF THE PALE TIDE WHEN THE MOON HAS SET, ...	146	FISH		2
AS THE TIDE WEARS THE DOVE-GREY SANDS, ...	157	POET BELOVED		4
AS THE TIDE HAS THE DOVE-GREY SANDS, ...	157	POET BELOVED	V	4
ABOVE THE WANDERING TIDE:	162	ASKS FORGIVE		14
AND DRUNK UP THE MURMURING TIDE:	171	MAID QUIET	V	4D
THE GREY WING UPON EVERY TIDE:	290	SEPTEMBER 1913		18
OUT OF THAT RAVING TIDE—IS DRAWN BETWIXT	377	PHASES OF MOON		122
THE BLOOD-DIMMED TIDE IS LOOSED, AND EVERYWHERE	402	SECOND COMING		5
BUT TURN FROM ROSSES' CRAWLING TIDE.	549	SEVERED HEAD		5
BUT THROWN UPON THIS FILTHY MODERN TIDE	611	STATUES		29
THE TIDE OF STARS? HAVE I NOT SEEN A THOUSAND YEARS . .	675	ISLE STAT II 3		230
THE TIDE NARROWS BETWEEN, AND ONE OLD MAN	752	SHADOW WATER A		118
TIDE'S				
DROPPING A VAPOURY FOOTSOLE ON THE TIDE'S DROWSY BLAZE.	78	INDIAN TO LOVE	V	20
TIDES				
THE HERRING ARE NOT IN THE TIDES AS THEY WERE OF OLD: . .	91	OLD FISHERMAN		5
YOU, TOO, HAVE COME WHERE THE DIM TIDES ARE HURLED . . .	115	ROSE OF BATTLE		26
TIED				
WE TIED THE HORSE IN A LEAFY CLUMP, ...	14	OISIN 1		194
AND SHE WITH A WAVE-RUSTED CHAIN WAS TIED	34	OISIN 2		73
WITH CHAIN SEA-ROTTED, ROUND HER MIDDLE TIED, ...	34	OISIN 2	V	75

817

		PAGE	TITLE		LINE
TIED (CONTINUED)					
DECREPIT AGE THAT HAS BEEN TIED TO ME	. . . .	409	TOWER		3
DECREPIT AGE THAT HAS BEEN TIED UPON ME	. . . . . .	409	TOWER	V	3
TIGHT					
HER EYES WERE COLD AND STEADY, HER LIPS TIGHT.	. . . .	279	TWO KINGS		64
HOW SINEW THAT HAS BEEN PULLED TIGHT,	. . . . . .	386	ROBARTES DANCE		34
SUCH THOUGHT--SUCH THOUGHT HAVE I THAT HOLD IT TIGHT	. .	474	ALL SOUL NIGHT		91
CLOSE AND CLING SO TIGHT,	. . . .	538	LAST CONFESS		22
TIGHTEN					
DELIGHTFUL TO THE TOUCH! TIGHTEN THAT HAND	. . . . .	579	DOR WELLESLEY		4
TIGHTENED					
WITH BEAUTY LIKE A TIGHTENED BOW, A KIND	. . . . .	256	NO SECOND TROY		8
HE SAT WITH TIGHTENED REIN AND LOOSENED MOUTH	. . . .	277	TWO KINGS		10
HE SAT WITH TIGHTENED REIN AMAZED, HIS HORSE	. . . .	277	TWO KINGS	V	10
TILL					
YOUR MORTAL SHORES TILL TIME IS DONE!"	. . . . . .	6	OISIN 1	V	59
LOVE, TILL THE DANAAN POETS BROUGHT	. . . .	7	OISIN 1	V	63
I NE'ER LOVED ANY TILL SONG BROUGHT ME	. . . . . .	7	OISIN 1	V	69
SLEEP THERE TILL THE MOON AND THE STARS DIE!"	. . . .	17	OISIN 1		246
TILL ON THE CENTRAL HILL WE HUSHED	. . . .	22	OISIN 1	V	323
BUT THE LOVE-DEW DIMS OUR EYES TILL THE DAY	. . . .	28	OISIN 1		424
ON OUR DARK PATHWAY, TILL A COUNTLESS FLIGHT	. . . .	31	OISIN 2		34
"THIS DEMON SHALL BE BATTERED TILL HE DIE,	. . . . .	35	OISIN 2		90
UNDER THE SHADOWS TILL THE TUMULTS DIED	. . . . . .	38	OISIN 2		140
TILL THE FAR DOORWAY GREW A BURNING BLOT	. . . . .	39	OISIN 2	V	152
"BUT TILL THE MOON HAS TAKEN ALL, I WAGE	. . . . .	45	OISIN 2		240
TILL THE HORSE GAVE A WHINNY!	48	OISIN 3		25
TILL, FATTENING THE WINDS OF THE MORNING, AN ODOUR OF NEW-MOWN HAY		57	OISIN 3		153
TILL I SAW WHERE MAEVE LIES SLEEPING	60	OISIN 3		184
. . . TILL STARLIGHT AND MIDNIGHT PART.	60	OISIN 3		184
AND RODE ON TILL OVER THE WORLD'S RIM FLOATED THE SEA'S OLD SHOUT,		60	OISIN 3	V	183
TILL THEY SHALL SINGING FADE IN RUTH	66	HAPPY SHEPHERD		41
WITH MIRTHFUL SONGS TILL RISE THE DAWN.	67	HAPPY SHEPHERD	V	49
TILL MY OWN WORDS, RE-ECHOING, SHALL SEND	68	SAD SHEPHERD		20
SING, TILL YOU RAISE YOUR HANDS AND SIGH, ...	73	ANASHU VIJAYA		45
SING, TILL YE RAISE YOUR HANDS AND SIGH, ...	73	ANASHU VIJAYA	V	45
TILL THE MOON HAS TAKEN FLIGHT!	87	STOLEN CHILD		19
I MINDED HER TILL MORN.	94	MOLL MAGEE		16
WHOSE BLADE COMPELS, AND WAIT TILL THEY HAVE FOUND .	108	CUCHULAIN SEA		37
AT THE SWORD-POINT, AND WAITS TILL WE HAVE FOUND . .	109	CUCHULAIN SEA		53
AT THE SWORD POINT, AND WAITS TILL WE HAVE FOUND . .	109	CUCHULAIN SEA	V	53
A RAPTUROUS MUSIC, TILL THE MORNING BREAK	137	TO SOME I TALK		14
CONTINUAL MUSIC TILL THE MORNING BREAK, ...	137	TO SOME I TALK	V	14
FLAME UNDER FLAME, TILL TIME BE NO MORE!	141	EVERLAST VOICE		4
AND PLUCK TILL TIME AND TIMES ARE DONE	150	WANDER AENGUS		22
TILL THE SEED OF THE FIRE FLICKER AND GLOW! . . .	150	OLD MOTHER		2
TILL STARS ARE BEGINNING TO BLINK AND PEEP! . . .	150	OLD MOTHER		4
TILL THERE BE NAUGHT BUT THRONE ON THRONE	156	FORGOT BEAUTY	V	21
TILL STARS GREW OUT OF THE AIR.	160	CAP AND BELLS		28
O PITEOUS HEARTS, CHANGING TILL CHANGE BE DEAD . .	163	ASKS FORGIVE		19
TILL ALL THE VALLEYS OF THE WORLD HAVE BEEN WITHERED AWAY.		163	VALLEY LOVERS		8
TILL THE VALLEYS OF THE WORLD HAVE BEEN WITHERED AWAY."		163	VALLEY LOVERS	V	8
AT HUSH OF EVENING TILL GOD BURNS TIME	164	PERFECT BEAUTY	V	7
AT HUSH OF EVENING TILL GOD BURN TIME	164	PERFECT BEAUTY	V	7
TILL DATHI CAME AND STOOD, ...	166	BLESSED		2
TILL DATHI CAME AND STOOD, ...	167	BLESSED	V	4B
TILL VAIN FRENZY AWOKE AND HE DIED! AND HIM . . .	169	SECRET ROSE		12
AND TILL A HUNDRED MORNS HAD FLOWERED RED	170	SECRET ROSE		17
TILL THE ATTORNEY FOR LOST SOULS CRY HER SWEET CRY,	173	SPEAKS HEARERS		6
TILL MAURYA OF THE WOUNDED HEART CRY A SWEET CRY, .	173	SPEAKS HEARERS	V	6
TILL MAEVE CALLED OUT, "THESE ARE BUT COMMON MEN.	186	QUEEN MAEVE		122
TILL IT DIED OUT WHERE AN OLD THORN-TREE STOOD. .	186	QUEEN MAEVE		129
TILL IT DIED OUT WHERE AN OLD THORN TREE STOOD. .	186	QUEEN MAEVE	V	129
THOUGH NOW IT'S HARD, TILL TROUBLE IS AT AN END! . . .	200	FOLLY COMFORT	V	5
WITH WISDOM, THEY WANDER TILL ALL THE YEARS HAVE GONE BY!	204	WITHER BOUGHS		21
TILL HE HAS FALLEN ASLEEP	216	HAPPY TOWNLAND		51
TILL THEY HAD CHANGED US TO LIKE STRENGTH?" . . .	259	PEACE	V	9
TILL THE WILDERNESS CRIED ALOUD, ...	259	UNWORTH PRAISE		8
TILL THAT BE TUMBLED THAT WAS LIFTED HIGH	265	THESE CLOUDS		4
TILL THE STARS HAD RUN AWAY	268	BROWN PENNY		13
TILL YOUR BAD MASTER BLENCHED AND ALL WAS LOST! . .	270	PARDON FATHERS	V	12
TILL ALL THE PLACE WAS BEATEN INTO MIRE.	278	TWO KINGS		27
TILL ALL HAD SEEMED A SHADOW OR A VISION	278	TWO KINGS		43
TILL JUDGMENT HAS BEEN GIVEN, AND IF GUILTY, . . .	280	TWO KINGS		74
AND I BUT ASKED THE MORE, TILL HE CRIED OUT, ...	281	TWO KINGS		92
I WAITED TILL THE NIGHT WAS ON THE TURN, ...	283	TWO KINGS		144
TILL OAK AND HAZEL CEASED AND BEECH BEGAN, ...	283	TWO KINGS	V	139A
BUT FUMBLE IN A GREASY TILL	289	SEPTEMBER 1913		2
ABOUT YOUR HEAD TILL THE DUST STOPS YOUR EAR, . .	293	TO A SHADE		20
ALL SHOUTED TILL THEIR ANGER GREW	297	THREE BEGGARS		46
THEY MAULED AND BIT TILL THE DAY SHONE!	297	THREE BEGGARS		49
AND TILL ANOTHER NIGHT HAD GONE, ...	297	THREE BEGGARS		51
TILL THEY WERE WHIRLING IN A HEAP.	297	THREE BEGGARS	V	47
A SHELTER TILL THE DAYLIGHT BROKE.	302	HOUR DAWN		15
TILL EVEN I SLEEP LIGHT! BUT WHO	303	HOUR DAWN		34
"I'LL HAVE MY SAY, TILL I AM ABLE	304	HOUR DAWN	V	51
"I'D LIKE TO SLEEP TILL WINTER'S GONE	305	HOUR DAWN		60
OR TILL THE SUN IS IN HIS STRENGTH.	305	HOUR DAWN		61
NOR GAVE GOD THANKS TILL OVERHEAD	307	HOUR DAWN		121

	PAGE	TITLE		LINE
TILL (CONTINUED)				
TILL PRIDE HAD MADE HER EYES GROW BRIGHT,	314	MEMORY YOUTH		10
YOUTH'S DREAMY LOAD, TILL SHE	315	FRIENDS		14
ALL TILL MY YOUTH WAS GONE	315	FRIENDS		18
NOTORIOUS, TILL ALL MY PRICELESS THINGS	321	REED WHISPERER		13
TILL ALL HIS GREEK AND LATIN LEARNING SEEMED	324	ROBERT GREGORY		21
"STRETCH BONES TILL THE DAYLIGHT COME	331	ROUND TOWER		5
TILL TOES MASTERED A SWEET MEASURE,	331	ROUND TOWER		15
SANG TILL STARS BEGAN TO FADE,	332	ROUND TOWER		20
TILL WINTER BLASTS WERE GONE, BUT SPEAK OF HER	340	SHEP GOATHERD		33
AND TILL THAT'S DONE CAN NEITHER WORK NOR WAIT.	340	SHEP GOATHERD		45
TILL DAYTIME, PLAYTIME SEEM THE SAME:	343	SHEP GOATHERD		106
TILL, CLAMBERING AT THE CRADLE-SIDE,	343	SHEP GOATHERD		109
TILL THAT IS THEIR LONG SHOUTING PLAYTIME:	343	SHEP GOATHERD	V	106
TILL, CLAMBERING AT THE CRADLE SIDE,	343	SHEP GOATHERD	V	109
TILL THE YELLOW EYE HAS GROWN MILD,	349	HAWK		3
TILL I COULD HEAR THEIR HEARTS BEATING:	358	PRESENCES		11
TILL ALL THE BOUGHS ARE GAY,	366	HER CHRIS TREE		5
THEY RAN FROM CRADLE TO CRADLE TILL AT LAST	375	PHASES OF MOON		69
THE HARE MAY RUN TILL IT'S FOUND	380	SONGS FOOL 1		11
THE PARTICULAR IS POUNDED TILL IT IS MAN.	382	VISION ROBART		6
THERE CAN BE NOTHING SOLIDER TILL I DIE:	383	VISION ROBART		26
AND NEVER CREW AGAIN TILL NOW,	388	SOLOMON WITCH		12
TILL ALL THE EDDIES GLEAM:	389	IMAGE PAST		4
BEWILDERED THEM TILL THEY DIED?	394	EASTER 1916		73
TILL GERMANY'S OVERCOME:	395	SIXTEEN DEAD		8
TILL MAN MADE UP THE WHOLE,	415	TOWER		149
TILL IT WAS BROKEN BY	416	TOWER		179
TILL THE WRECK OF BODY,	416	TOWER		184
TILL HIS MORNING MEAL COME ROUND:	435	FOR MY SON		4
ALL DREAD AFAR TILL MORNING'S BACK,	435	FOR MY SON		6
PROTECTING, TILL THE DANGER PAST,	436	FOR MY SON		31
NOW THAT YOUR TONGUE CANNOT PERSUADE THE CHILD TILL SHE MISTAKE	450	OWEN AHERNE		22
AND THEN I LAUGH TILL TEARS RUN DOWN	456	FRIENDS YOUTH		17
TILL MEDITATION MASTER ALL ITS PARTS,	474	ALL SOUL NIGHT		92
AND STRIKE ANOTHER TILL TIME CATCH:	476	EVA GORE-BOOTH		27
RUN TILL ALL THE SAGES KNOW.	476	EVA GORE-BOOTH		29
TILL THE DAWN BREAK UPON THOSE MINGLED SEAS.	494	AT ALGECIRAS		6
TILL I HAVE TOLD THE SAGES	534	CONSOLATION		5
TILL SUDDENLY IN GRIEF'S CONTAGION CAUGHT,	537	HER VISION		22
HOW CAN SHE LIVE TILL IN HER BLOOD HE LIVE!	558	RIBH CHRISTIAN		24
TILL EITHER NEITHER HAVE ENOUGH,	573	LADYS 3RD SONG		8
TILL I AM TIMON AND LEAR	576	ACRE OF GRASS		15
TILL TRUTH OBEYED HIS CALL:	576	ACRE OF GRASS		18
WINTER AND SUMMER TILL OLD AGE BEGAN	629	CIRCUS ANIMALS		5
WHO KEEPS THE TILL. NOW THAT MY LADDER'S GONE,	630	CIRCUS ANIMALS		38
TURNS INTO A QUESTION TILL	632	MAN AND ECHO		8
AND TILL HIS INTELLECT GROWS SURE,	633	MAN AND ECHO		30
TILL HER BOWELS ARE IN HEAT,	638	BEN BULBEN		49
TILL ALL ELSE IS EMPTY CHAFF,	647	ISLE STAT I 1		60
TILL I LAUGH WHEN OTHERS WEEP,	647	ISLE STAT I 1		61
AND LET THEM TELL SAD HISTORIES, TILL THEIR EYES	663	ISLE STAT II 2		32
TILL HIS LAST WRETCHEDNESS WAS O'ER AND DONE."	664	ISLE STAT II 2		54
TILL THOU REMEMBEREST ONLY HOW THE SEA	670	ISLE STAT II 3		94
AT ARM'S LENGTH, THUS TILL DUMB ETERNITY	671	ISLE STAT II 3		145
GAZE ON TILL RAGGED TIME HIMSELF DECAY.	672	ISLE STAT II 3		148
TILL THEIR FIERCE MISERIES WITHIN HIS EYES	687	TWO TITANS		26
AND ALL WAS DIMNESS, TILL A DYING LEAF	690	MOSADA 1		20
HUSH'D THE FISHERS, TILL A MOTHER CALLS BY NAME HER DROWNED SON:	719	PHANTOM SHIP		23
PRAYED THOSE FORGOTTEN FISHERS, TILL IN THE EASTERN SKIES	719	PHANTOM SHIP		32
ALL THOSE LONG FORGOTTEN FISHERS, TILL IN THE EASTERN SKIES	719	PHANTOM SHIP	V	32
COME AND TEASE THEM TILL THE DAY.	727	LOVERS QUARREL		36
TILL THEY COME WHERE YOUR SAD, SAD HEART IS,	739	WHERE BOOKS GO		5
TILL DAY AND NIGHT TIME END.	741	EARL PAUL		48
TILL ALL THINGS ARE AT REST.	741	EARL PAUL		52
AND NEED NO MORE OF LIFE TILL THE WHITE WINGS	751	SHADOW WATER A		102
TILL HIS EDAINE, NO LONGER A GOLDEN FLY	757	SHADOW WATER A		210
TILL HIS EDAINE, NO MORE A SILVER FLY	757	SHADOW WATER A	V	210
TILL THE SIDE OF HATE COMES UP.	776	AGAINST WITCH		35
TILL IT DIP AN AGEING WING	777	SONG DEIRDRE 2		3
"TILL THE SUN GOES DOWN AND AN HOUR OF THE CLOCK"	779	GOING THE ROAD		7
TILL CERTAIN SECOND THOUGHTS HAVE COME	791	REPRISALS		12
'TILL				
TO LIE THERE 'TILL THE FOURTH DAY SAW EMERGE	44	OISIN 2	V	220
TILLAGE				
AND HIM WHO SOLD TILLAGE, AND HOUSE, AND GOODS,	170	SECRET ROSE		22
AND OVER TILLAGE FIELDS AND PASTURE LANDS	715	FERENCZ RENYI		120
TILLER				
AND OVER THE TILLER AND THE PROW,	197	BAILE AILLINN		183
TIMBER				
DRY TIMBER UNDER THAT RICH FOLIAGE,	536	HER VISION		1
BECAUSE CHILDREN DEMAND DADDY-LONG-LEGS UPON HIS TIMBER TOES,	623	HIGH TALK		6
TIMBERS SEE ROOF-TIMBERS				
TIME SEE WINTER-TIME HARVEST-TIME SUMMER-TIME SPRING-TIME FLOOD-TIME				
YOUR MORTAL SHORES TILL TIME IS DONE!"	6	OISIN 1	V	59
AS THOUGH THEY ALL WERE BEATING TIME,	13	OISIN 1		174
THEN MOCK AT DEATH AND TIME WITH GLANCES	19	OISIN 1		274
WE MOCKED AT TIME AND FATE AND CHANCE	20	OISIN 1		291

819

		PAGE	TITLE	LINE

TIME (CONTINUED)
OF GRIEVOUS TIME ON HIS OLD CRUTCHES, ...		23	OISIN 1	V 341B
KEPT TIME WITH THEIR BRIGHT WINGS AND FEET;		26	OISIN 1	397
BEAT TIME WITH THEIR BRIGHT WINGS AND FEET.		26	OISIN 1	V 397
SINCE GOD MADE TIME AND DEATH AND SLEEP; THE OTHER . . .		31	OISIN 2	41
MADE THE WAY SLIPPERY, AND TIME ON TIME		37	OISIN 2	114
MADE THE WAY SLIPPERY, AND TIME ON TIME		37	OISIN 2	114
GREENISH AND SLIPPERY. TIME AFTER TIME		37	OISIN 2	V 114
GREENISH AND SLIPPERY. TIME AFTER TIME		37	OISIN 2	V 114
SHALL THEY TURN WROTH OR PLUCK THE WINGS OF TIME? . . .		42	OISIN 2	V 199
CAME BLANAID, MAC NESSA, TALL FERGUS WHO FEASTWARD OF OLD TIME SLUNK,		53	OISIN 3	89
CAME BLANID, MAC NESSA, AND FERGUS WHO FEASTWARD OF OLD TIME SLUNK,		53	OISIN 3	V 89
. . . "THE FENIANS A LONG TIME ARE DEAD."		59	OISIN 3	172
. . . HE CRIED, "NO, THE GODS A LONG TIME ARE DEAD." . .		59	OISIN 3	180
. . . HE CRIED, "NAY, THE GODS A LONG TIME ARE DEAD." . .		59	OISIN 3	V 180
THE KINGS OF THE OLD TIME ARE DEAD;		65	HAPPY SHEPHERD	17
THE KINGS OF THE OLD TIME ARE FLED.		65	HAPPY SHEPHERD	V 17
THERE DREAMY TIME LETS FALL HIS SICKLE		77	INDIAN TO LOVE	V 5A
TIME WAS, AS IN A LITTLE TOWN, ...		85	MAD KING GOLL	V 49
TO THE ROSE UPON THE ROOD OF TIME		100	ROSE UPON ROOD	T
COME NEAR; I WOULD, BEFORE MY TIME TO GO, ...		101	ROSE UPON ROOD	22
IN THREE DAYS' TIME HE STOOD UP WITH A MOAN, ...		111	CUCHULAIN SEA	V 83
IN THREE DAYS' TIME, CUCHULAIN WITH A MOAN		111	CUCHULAIN SEA	V 83
WHERE TIME WOULD SURELY FORGET US, AND SORROW COME NEAR US NO MORE;		122	WHITE BIRDS	10
WHERE SURELY TIME WOULD FORGET US AND SORROW COME NEAR US NO MORE!		122	WHITE BIRDS	V 10
THAT TIME CAN NEVER MAR A LOVER'S VOWS		126	DREAM OF FAERY	10
HOW TIME MAY NEVER MAR THEIR FAERY VOWS		126	DREAM OF FAERY	V 10
ERE TIME TRANSFIGURED ME.		131	OLD PENSIONER	6
MY CONTEMPLATIONS ARE OF TIME		131	OLD PENSIONER	11
I SPIT INTO THE FACE OF TIME		132	OLD PENSIONER	17
UPON THE TIME OF SPARROW-CHIRP		133	FR GILLIGAN	21
UPON THE TIME OF SPARROW CHIRP, ...		133	FR GILLIGAN	V 21
WHEN TIME BEGAN TO RANT AND RAGE		138	TO IRELAND	10
AND TIME BADE ALL HIS CANDLES FLARE		138	TO IRELAND	13
WHAT MEASURER TIME HAS LIT ABOVE, ...		139	TO IRELAND	38
FLAME UNDER FLAME, TILL TIME BE NO MORE;		141	EVERLAST VOICE	4
TIME DROPS IN DECAY, ...		142	MOODS	1
OUT-WORN HEART, IN A TIME OUT-WORN, ...		147	INTO TWILIGHT	1
OUTWORN HEART IN A TIME OUTWORN, ...		147	INTO TWILIGHT	V 1
AND TIME AND THE WORLD ARE EVER IN FLIGHT;		148	INTO TWILIGHT	14
AND PLUCK TILL TIME AND TIMES ARE DONE		150	WANDER AENGUS	22
AND TIME AND BIRTH AND CHANGE ARE HURRYING BY.		153	CHANGE BELOVED	9
THE ROSES THAT OF OLD TIME WERE		156	FORGOT BEAUTY	9
THAT IS BRIMMED FROM THE PALE FIRE OF TIME;		157	POET BELOVED	6
IS DROPPING SLEEP, UNTIL GOD BURN TIME, ...		164	PERFECT BEAUTY	7
AT HUSH OF EVENING TILL GOD BURNS TIME		164	PERFECT BEAUTY	V 7
AT HUSH OF EVENING TILL GOD BURN TIME		164	PERFECT BEAUTY	V 7
WHILE TIME AND THE WORLD ARE EBBING AWAY		168	BLESSED	39
UNTIL TIME AND THE WORLD HAVE EBBED AWAY		168	BLESSED	V 39
WHEN WE COME AT THE END OF TIME		178	FIDDLER DOONEY	9
WHEN WE COME AT THE CLOSE OF TIME		178	FIDDLER DOONEY	V 9
IT WAS BEFORE THE TIME OF THE GREAT WAR		182	QUEEN MAEVE	57
AND WITH GLAD VOICE MAEVE ANSWERED "MANY A TIME		183	QUEEN MAEVE	V 79
ABOUT THE TIME WHEN CHRIST WAS BORN, ...		189	BAILE AILLINN	13
A BETTER TIME HAD COME AGAIN		197	BAILE AILLINN	192
TIME CAN BUT MAKE IT EASIER TO BE WISE		200	FOLLY COMFORT	4
TIME CAN BUT MAKE HER BEAUTY OVER AGAIN.		200	FOLLY COMFORT	8
IS EDEN OUT OF TIME AND OUT OF SPACE?		218	WOODS OF COOLE	36
WHERE TIME IS DROWNED IN ODOUR-LADEN WINDS		219	HARP OF AENGUS	3
AND NOW THAT TIME PUTS WATER IN MY BLOOD, ...		222	SHADOW WATER B	V 11A
FLEW WESTWARD; AND MANY A TIME SINCE THEN		223	SHADOW WATER B	27
AND YET YOU TALK OF LOVE. THE MOVEMENT OF TIME . . .		237	SHADOW WATER B	338
I'LL STRIKE A BLOW FOR HIM TO GIVE HIM TIME		239	SHADOW WATER B	365
THAT COMING TIME CAN SAY;		255	WOMAN HOMER	12
AH, THAT TIME COULD TOUCH A FORM		258	PEACE	1
AH, BUT TIME HAS TOUCHED A FORM		258	PEACE	V 1
CAME WHEN TIME HAD TOUCHED HER FORM.		259	PEACE	11
THE COMING OF WISDOM WITH TIME		261	COMING WISDOM	T
TO A CERTAIN COUNTRY HOUSE IN TIME OF CHANGE		264	HOUSE SHAKEN	V T
TIME OUT OF MIND, BECAME TOO RUINOUS		264	HOUSE SHAKEN	3
ONE TIME IT WAS A WOMAN'S FACE, OR WORSE--		267	ALL TEMPT ME	2
NOR CAN TIME WASTE THE CHEEK, NOR IS THERE FOOT . . .		284	TWO KINGS	182
BUT LITTLE TIME HAD THEY TO PRAY		289	SEPTEMBER 1913	12
THE TIME FOR YOU TO TASTE OF THAT SALT BREATH		293	TO A SHADE	21
"TIME TO PUT OFF THE WORLD AND GO SOMEWHERE		299	BEGGAR CRIED	1
I'LL SLEEP AWAY ALL TIME WITHIN IT;		306	HOUR DAWN	74
IF TIME WERE SUPPLER IN THE JOINT, ...		306	HOUR DAWN	94
AND SLEEP AWAY ALL TIME WITHIN IT.		306	HOUR DAWN	V 74
TO BUNDLE TIME AWAY		317	NIGHT COME	11
THE FIRST TIME ON THIS SHORE, ...		323	SWANS AT COOLE	16
SEEING THAT TIME HAS FROZEN UP THE BLOOD		333	LIVING BEAUTY	V 2
BUT LEFT THE HOUSE AS IN HIS FATHER'S TIME		341	SHEP GOATHERD	53
YET NEVER HAVE I, NOW NOR ANY TIME, ...		352	PEOPLE	28
THAT THEY, TIME OVERTHROWN, ...		384	VISION ROBART	47
SHE WOULD HAVE TIME TO TURN HER EYES, ...		385	ROBARTES DANCE	10
BEFORE MY TIME, SEEM LIKE A VIVID MEMORY.		391	UNDER SATURN	10
AND SURELY AFTER TWENTY YEARS IT WAS TIME TO COME." . .		391	UNDER SATURN	14

	PAGE	TITLE	LINE

TIME (CONTINUED)
NOW AND IN TIME TO BE,	394	EASTER 1916	77
A MEDIATION IN TIME OF WAR	406	IN TIME OF WAR	T
A MEDIATION IN TIME OF WAR	406	IN TIME OF WAR V	T
IT IS TIME THAT I WROTE MY WILL,	414	TOWER	121
MEDITATIONS IN TIME OF CIVIL WAR ANCESTRAL HOUSES	417	ANCEST HOUSES V	T
WHERE WE WROUGHT THAT SHALL BREAK THE TEETH OF TIME.	435	NEW FACES	4
LAUGHTER NOT TIME DESTROYED MY VOICE	455	FRIENDS YOUTH	1
WHEN WE HAD ALL THE SUMMER TIME	457	SUMMER SPRING V	15
SO GREAT ITS FAME. WHEN FITTING TIME HAS PASSED	461	HARUN RASHID	19
IN AFTER TIME THEY WILL SPEAK MUCH OF ME	462	HARUN RASHID	29
MANY A TIME I THINK TO SEEK	475	EVA GORE-BOOTH	14
HAVE NO ENEMY BUT TIME,	476	EVA GORE-BOOTH	25
AND STRIKE ANOTHER TILL TIME CATCH,	476	EVA GORE-BOOTH	27
IN MOCKERY OF A TIME	480	BLOOD AND MOON	11
THAT CUT THROUGH TIME OR CROSS IT WITHERSHINS.	489	COOLE PARK 29	24
THAT CAN CROSS TIME AND CUT IT WITHERSHINS.	489	COOLE PARK 29 V	24
THAT CUT THROUGH TIME AND CUT IT WITHERSHINS	489	COOLE PARK 29 V	24
ALL THAT TIME DENIED--	496	MOHINI CHATTER	18
MAY THUNDER TIME AWAY,	496	MOHINI CHATTER	25
IF TIME WERE BUT GONE."	510	JANE JUDGMENT	19
TIME IS UNWOUND,	520	HIS BARGAIN	4
AND TIME RUNS ON," CRIED SHE.	526	AM OF IRELAND	3
AND TIME RUNS ON," HE SAID,	526	AM OF IRELAND	12
AND TIME RUNS ON," CRIED SHE.	527	AM OF IRELAND	16
"BUT TIME RUNS ON, RUNS ON."	527	AM OF IRELAND	26
AND TIME RUNS ON," CRIED SHE.	527	AM OF IRELAND	29
MOUNTED THE MARE OF TIME,	529	TOM CRUACHAN	5
TIME I WERE BURIED," SAID THE OLD, OLD MAN.	548	TO SAME TUNE 3	10
TIME FOR US ALL TO PICK OUT A GOOD TUNE,	548	TO SAME TUNE 3	13
TIME I WERE BURIED," SAID THE OLD, OLD MAN.	548	TO SAME TUNE 3	20
TIME FOR US ALL BOYS, TO HIT ON A TUNE BOYS,	548	TO SAME TUNE 3 V	13
TIME I WERE BURIED," SAID THE OLD, OLD MAN.	549	TO SAME TUNE 3	30
A GREATER, A MORE GRACIOUS TIME HAS GONE,	564	GYRES	12
A YEAR AGO FOR THE FIRST TIME	570	THREE BUSHES	38
AND AT NIGHT TIME WOULD SHE SAY,	570	THREE BUSHES V	30
WHAT CAN THEY KNOW THAT WE KNOW THAT KNOW THE TIME TO DIE?	580	CURSE CROMWELL	14
BEFORE THE BENCH OF TIME,	582	ROGER CASEMENT	6
FROM TIME LONG PASSED AWAY,	589	OLD WICKED MAN	42
AND I AM IN DESPAIR THAT TIME MAY BRING	602	GALLERY REVIS	30
AND RANTING TIME RENEW,	606	SONGS BURDEN 1	20
OF GOD OR WOMAN, THE TIME WERE COME TO DIE."	609	IN TARAS HALLS	15
BUT TIME AMENDS OLD WRONG,	613	MARCH SONGS 1	9
BUT TIME AMENDS OLD WRONG,	613	MARCH SONGS 1	19
BUT TIME AMENDS OLD WRONG,	614	MARCH SONGS 1	29
"SEND WAR IN OUR TIME, O LORD!"	638	BEN BULBEN	26
GAZE ON TILL RAGGED TIME HIMSELF DECAY.	672	ISLE STAT II 3	148
BOTH DEAD!--NO TIME TO THINK. I AM SHE,	673	ISLE STAT II 3	190
BOTH DEAD!--NO TIME FOR THINKING. I AM SHE,	673	ISLE STAT II 3 V	190
THOU SHALT OUTLIVE THINE AMOROUS HAPPY TIME,	674	ISLE STAT II 3	203
TIME GOES. THE FLAKED FIRE OF EVENING CRAWLS	712	FERENCZ RENYI	70
TIME GOES. THE FLICKED FIRE OF EVENING CRAWLS	712	FERENCZ RENYI V	70
I CAME THE FIRST TIME TO THY VILLAGE SCHOOL?	713	FERENCZ RENYI	90
TIME AND THE WITCH VIVIEN.	720	WITCH VIVIEN	T
FIVE-SIX. HA, TIME!	721	WITCH VIVIEN	42
I LOSE! THEY'RE LOADED DICE. TIME ALWAYS PLAYS	721	WITCH VIVIEN	44
UPON MY SOUL, OLD TIME. NO! THUS IT STANDS.	722	WITCH VIVIEN	49
AND NOW WITH FATHER TIME I'M FACE TO FACE.	722	WITCH VIVIEN	57
THEN WHEREFORE FEAR THE USURY OF TIME,	724	KANVA ON SELF	17
AND AS THE TIME TO DARKNESS PLODDED	728	PRIEST FAIRY	11
NOD TO THE IRON SHOES OF TIME,	736	SUMMER EVENING	11
TILL DAY AND NIGHT TIME END.	741	EARL PAUL	48
TIME AND THE WORLD AND ALL THINGS DWINDLE OUT.	749	SHADOW WATER A	47
THAT SHALL BURN TIME WHEN TIMES HAVE EBBED AWAY.	750	SHADOW WATER A	61
AND A STRING MURMURS AS THOUGH TIME WERE DEAD	752	SHADOW WATER A	124
AND I MUST LOSE MORE TIME BECAUSE THESE FOOLS	754	SHADOW WATER A	158
ENDS TIME AND CHANGE.	754	SHADOW WATER A V	163
THE TOPMOST BLOSSOM ON THE BOUGHS OF TIME	756	SHADOW WATER A	178
HAS BLOSSOMED, AND I GROW AS OLD AS TIME.	756	SHADOW WATER A	179
AND I AM OLD AS TIME, BECAUSE I KNOW	756	SHADOW WATER A	179
ALL THAT TIME KNOWS. SPEAK TO ME, QUEEN. O SPEAK!	756	SHADOW WATER A V	180
I GREW AS OLD AS TIME, AND SHE GROWS YOUNG	761	SHADOW WATER A	259
WHERE TIME IS DROWNED IN ODOUR-LADEN WINDS	762	SHADOW WATER A	298

TIME'S
TIME'S BITTER FLOOD WILL RISE,	173	PLEADS FRIEND	6
WASHED BY TIME'S WATERS AS THEY ROSE AND FELL	206	ADAMS CURSE	32
TO GRADUAL TIME'S LAST GIFT, A WRITTEN SPEECH	264	HOUSE SHAKEN	11
"TIME'S UP," HE CRIED, AND ALL THE THREE	297	THREE BEGGARS	57
"TIME'S UP," HE CRIED, AND ALL THE THREE	297	THREE BEGGARS	59
LIVED AT MY SIDE! THOUGHT TIME'S DISFIGURING TOUCH	466	HARUN RASHID	110
LIVED AT MY SIDE! THAT TIME'S DISFIGURING TOUCH	466	HARUN RASHID V	110
OR SHIFT TIME'S FILTHY LOAD,	505	RESULT THOUGHT	15
LEAPS AND TIME'S OLD LANTHORN DIMS.	777	SONG DEIRDRE 2	5

TIMES   SEE MANY-TIMES-TROUBLED
HE SHOOK HIMSELF AND NEIGHED THREE TIMES!	10	OISIN 1	110
AND NEIGHED THREE TIMES. WHEN, WONDERING	10	OISIN 1	V 110A
I LAUGHED AT TIMES UNNUMBERED TREASONS,	23	OISIN 1	V 345D
SAVE ONLY MANY TIMES MY NAME,	25	OISIN 1	375
SHONE MANY TIMES AMONG THE GLIMMERING FLOWERS	30	OISIN 2	21
AT TIMES OUR SLUMBER WAS LIGHTENED.	53	OISIN 3	97
TIMES FROM THE SALTIN' SHED,	94	MOLL MAGEE V	9

821

```
                                                      PAGE    TITLE          LINE
TIMES    (CONTINUED)
    AND HOW BENEATH THOSE THREE TIMES BLESSED SKIES . . . .   127 DREAM OF FAERY V   21
    SPINNING AT ALL TIMES ERI'S GOOD TO-MORROW, . . . . .     129 BOOK STORIES  V   10
    MADE WHEN GOD SLEPT IN TIMES OF OLD. . . . . . . .        135 TWO TREES         32
    MY HEART WOULD BRIM WITH DREAMS ABOUT THE TIMES . . . .   136 TO SOME I TALK     2
    TO THOSE WITH WHOM I HAVE TALKED MANY TIMES, . . . . .    136 TO SOME I TALK V   2
    TO IRELAND IN THE COMING TIMES . . . . . . . . .          137 TO IRELAND        T
    THAT YOU, IN THE DIM COMING TIMES, . . . . . . . .        139 TO IRELAND        46
    AND HOW YOU HAVE LEAPED TIMES OUT OF MIND . . . . . .     146 FISH               5
    AND PLUCK TILL TIME AND TIMES ARE DONE . . . . . .        150 WANDER AENGUS     22
    OUT OF THE BATTLES OF OLD TIMES. . . . . . . . .          158 BELOVED RHYMES     6
    AMONG MY LEAVES IN TIMES OUT OF MIND! . . . . . .         177 PAST GREATNESS     5
    A LATTICED WINDOW.  HIS GLANCE WENT UP AT TIMES . .       180 QUEEN MAEVE        6
    HAD COME AS IN THE OLD TIMES TO COUNSEL HER, . . . .      181 QUEEN MAEVE       42
    HAD COME, AS IN OLD TIMES, TO COUNSEL HER, . . . . .      181 QUEEN MAEVE   V   42
    IN OLD TIMES AMONG THE CLOUDS OF THE AIR. . . . . .       194 BAILE AILLINN    133
    AT ALL TIMES OF THE YEAR! . . . . . . . . . .            214 HAPPY TOWNLAND     6
    AS MEN IN THE OLD TIMES, BEFORE THE HARPS BEGAN, . . .    219 WOODS OF COOLE    43
    AS MEN IN THE OLD TIMES, BEFORE THE HARP BEGAN, . . .     219 WOODS OF COOLE V  43
    THREE TIMES IN A SINGLE DAY . . . . . . . . .            298 THREE HERMITS     10
    MANY TIMES TROUBLED YEARS. . . . . . . . . .            315 FRIENDS       V    7
    NOW AS AT ALL TIMES I CAN SEE IN THE MIND'S EYE, . . .    318 MAGI               1
    I THINK IT BETTER THAT IN TIMES LIKE THESE . . . .        359 WAR POEM           1
    I THINK IT BETTER THAT AT TIMES LIKE THESE . . . . .      359 WAR POEM      V    1
    SO MANY TIMES CHILDISH DELIGHT. . . . . . . . .          399 BREAK OF DAY      11
    OR ELSE BY TOASTING HER A SCORE OF TIMES, . . . . .       410 TOWER             42
    WONDER HOW MANY TIMES I COULD HAVE PROVED MY WORTH . .    427 PHANTOM HATRED    34
    THE EXTRAVAGANCE OF SPRING; OR CERTAIN TIMES . . . .      466 HARUN RASHID  V  125
    MANY TIMES HE DIED, . . . . . . . . . . . .             476 DEATH              5
    MANY TIMES ROSE AGAIN. . . . . . . . . . .              476 DEATH              6
    GOD BE WITH THE TIMES WHEN I . . . . . . . . .           514 JANE GROWN OLD    17
    WE THREE ALONE IN MODERN TIMES HAD BROUGHT . . . . .     603 GALLERY REVIS     45
    MANY TIMES MAN LIVES AND DIES . . . . . . . .            637 BEN BULBEN        13
    THREE TIMES THE ROSES HAVE GROWN LESS AND LESS, . . .     690 MOSADA 1           1
    THEN HAS THIS ONE BEEN SINNED FULL MANY TIMES. . . . .    692 MOSADA 1          49
    WE THROW THREE TIMES. . . . . . . . . . . .             721 WITCH VIVIEN      39
    THAT SHALL BURN TIME WHEN TIMES HAVE EBBED AWAY. . . . .  750 SHADOW WATER A    61
TIMID
    FULL OF EARTH'S OLD TIMID GRACE. . . . . . . . .         124 CATHLEEN PARA     12
    BREATHED ON THE WORLD WITH TIMID BREATH. . . . . . .     266 GALWAY RACES       9
    NOR THE TAME WILL, NOR TIMID BRAIN. . . . . . . .       318 APPOINTMENT        8
    I MUST ENDURE THE TIMID SUN. . . . . . . . . .          344 DEJECTION         11
    THAT WOMEN LAUGHING, OR TIMID OR WILD, . . . . . .       358 PRESENCES          4
    TIMID, ENTANGLED, EMPTY AND ABASHED, . . . . . . .      368 EGO DOMINUS       16
    FOR ALL HIS TIMID HEART, THERE THAT SLOW MAN, . . . .    489 COOLE PARK 29     12
TIMIDLY
    STOOD TIMIDLY.  LEST THEY SHOULD SEE SOME SIGHT . . . .   38 OISIN 2       V  141
TIMON
    TILL I AM TIMON AND LEAR . . . . . . . . . .            576 ACRE OF GRASS     15
TIMOR
    AYE, AND ACHILLES, TIMOR, BABAR, BARHAIM, ALL . . . . .   366 HER COURAGE        9
TINCTURE
    HER HAIR WAS OF A CITRON TINCTURE, . . . . . . . .        3 OISIN 1       V   24
TINKER
    THE ROARING TINKER IF YOU LIKE, . . . . . . . . .       605 SONGS BURDEN 1     1
    PRACTICE A TINKER SHUFFLE . . . . . . . . . . .         617 LONG-LEG FLY      17
TINKLING
    FOR I AM IN HIS IMAGE MADE, AND ALL THIS TINKLING TIDE . .  76 INDIAN ON GOD    11
TINSEL
    THAT CANNOT IN THAT TRASH AND TINSEL HIDE! . . . . . .    558 RIBH CHRISTIAN    17
TINT
    WHITER THAN CURDS, ITS EYES THE TINT OF THE SEA. . . . .  277 TWO KINGS          7
TINTED      SEE LEMON-TINTED
TIP      SEE FINGER-TIP A-TIP-TOE
    AND SIGHING LAID THE PEARLY TIP . . . . . . . . .         12 OISIN 1          150
    SAID NIAM, AS SHE LAID THE TIP . . . . . . . . .          12 OISIN 1       V  150
    SOME TWENTY FEET FROM TIP TO TIP HAD IT STRETCHED RIGHTLY 593 PILGRIM           17
      OUT,
    SOME TWENTY FEET FROM TIP TO TIP HAD IT STRETCHED RIGHTLY 593 PILGRIM           17
      OUT,
    SOME TWENTY FEET FROM TIP TO TIP HAD ITS WINGS STRETCHED  593 PILGRIM       V   17
      RIGHTLY OUT,
    SOME TWENTY FEET FROM TIP TO TIP HAD ITS WINGS STRETCHED  593 PILGRIM       V   17
      RIGHTLY OUT,
    AROUND THE FEATHERY TIP.  UNTO THE SHAFT . . . . . .     657 ISLE STAT I 3     71
    LIES A CHILLY FINGER TIP, . . . . . . . . . . .         732 STREET DANCERS    19
TIPS      SEE FINGER-TIPS
    UPON THE GRASS-BLADES' BENDING TIPS, . . . . . . .        3 OISIN 1       V  7II
TIPTOE      SEE A-TIPTOE
    AND ON TIPTOE THE WINDS A-WHISPERING STOOD. . . . . .    715 DWELT SYCAMORE     8
TIP-TOE
    I PASSED A TIP-TOE UP AND DOWN, . . . . . . . . .        85 MAD KING GOLL V   51
    AND ON TIP-TOE THE WINDS A-WHISPERING STOOD. . . . . .   715 DWELT SYCAMORE V   8
TIRARAGH
    KEENING IN FROM TIRARAGH, . . . . . . . . . . .         93 FATHER OHART      35
TIRE
    WE TIRE OF THE FLAME OF THE METEOR, BEFORE IT CAN FADE   122 WHITE BIRDS        2
      AND FLEE;
    FOR WE TIRE OF THE FLAME OF THE METEOR BEFORE IT CAN PASS 122 WHITE BIRDS   V    2
      BY AND FLEE
```

		PAGE	TITLE		LINE

TIRE   (CONTINUED)
      WE TIRE OF THE FLAME OF THE METEOR, BEFORE IT CAN PASS   122 WHITE BIRDS   V   2
        BY AND FLEE;
      FOR SOULS WHO TIRE AND BLEED, ...   134 FR GILLIGAN   42
      WHOM MAN OR DEVIL CANNOT TIRE, ...   295 THREE BEGGARS   16
      YONDER FOOLISH ONES WILL TIRE . . . .   727 LOVERS QUARREL   47
      BODIES THAT CAN NEVER TIRE . . . .   776 AGAINST WITCH   20
TIRED
      OR TIRED ON ANY DAWNING MORROW, ...   23 OISIN 1   V 341
      WHEN THE POOR TIRED CHILD, PASSION, FALLS ASLEEP. . .   80 EPHEMERA   7
      "THAT WE ARE TIRED, FOR OTHER LOVES AWAIT US; . . . .   80 EPHEMERA   21
      WHERE THE TIRED HORSE-BOYS LAY UPON THE RUSHES, . . .   180 QUEEN MAEVE   13
      I AM SO TIRED OF BEING BACHELOR . . . .   222 SHADOW WATER B   8
      HAS TIRED OF HIS OWN COMPANY? . . . .   303 HOUR DAWN   35
      GROWN TIRED OF HIS OWN COMPANY? . . . .   303 HOUR DAWN   V   37
      TIRED OF THAT COURTLY FASHION, ...   378 CAT AND MOON   15
      TIRED OF HER COURTLY FASHION, ...   378 CAT AND MOON   V   15
      GROWN TIRED OF THEIR SOLITUDE, ...   432 NINETEEN 19   V 105
      I AM TIRED OF CURSING THE BISHOP, ...   628 JANE MOUNTAIN   1
TIRELESS
      "THE RED BRANCH KINGS A TIRELESS BANQUET KEEP, ...   108 CUCHULAIN SEA   V   33
TITAN
      A TITAN, WITH LOUD LAUGHTER, ...   680 LOVE AND DEATH   11
TITANS
      THE TWO TITANS. . . . .   687 TWO TITANS   T
TITTLE
      AND ALL THE SHAPELY BODY NO TITTLE GONE ASTRAY. . . .   354 HIS PHOENIX   30
TOADS
      AND TOADS AND EVERY OUTLAWED THING . . . .   85 MAD KING GOLL   V   61
TOASTING
      OR ELSE BY TOASTING HER A SCORE OF TIMES, ...   410 TOWER   42
TODAY
      FOR NONE ALIVE TODAY . . . .   458 SECRETS OF OLD   V   10
      EVEN TODAY, AFTER SOME SEVEN YEARS . . . .   468 HARUN RASHID   V 161
      WE CALLED IT A GOOD DEATH. TODAY . . . .   791 REPRISALS   3
TO-DAY
      THAT IT WAS YESTERDAY AND NOT TO-DAY . . . .   246 SHADOW WATER B   493
      BECAUSE TO-DAY IS SOME RELIGIOUS FESTIVAL . . . . . .   363 DOLLS FACES   1
      FOR NONE ALIVE TO-DAY . . . .   458 SECRETS OF OLD   10
      EVEN TO-DAY, AFTER SOME SEVEN YEARS . . . .   468 HARUN RASHID   161
      I AM DULL TO-DAY, OR YOU WERE NOW ALL LOST. . . . . .   722 WITCH VIVIEN   59
      "SHIELD BREAKER, BREAK A SHIELD TO-DAY, ...   739 EARL PAUL   1
      SHIELD-BREAKER, BREAK A SHIELD TO-DAY, ...   739 EARL PAUL   V   1
TOE   SEE TIP-TOE A-TIP-TOE
      HEEL UP AND WEIGHT ON TOE, MUST FACE THE WALL . . . .   363 DOLLS FACES   3
      ALL OUT OF SHAPE FROM TOE TO TOP, ...   639 BEN BULBEN   71
TOES
      TO ONE VAST FOOT, FROTH-SPLASHED, WITH CURVED TOES LYING   32 OISIN 2   V 46A
      TILL TOES MASTERED A SWEET MEASURE. . . . .   331 ROUND TOWER   15
      HANDS GRIPPED IN HANDS, TOES CLOSE TOGETHER, ...   332 ROUND TOWER   21
      THE MEDITATIVE CRITIC; ALL ARE ON THEIR TOES, ...   363 DOLLS FACES   8
      BY THE WEBBED TOES, AND THAT ALL-POWERFUL BILL . . .   441 LEDA AND SWAN   V   3
      BY THE WEBBED TOES, AND THAT ALL POWERFUL BILL . . .   441 LEDA AND SWAN   V   3
      BECAUSE CHILDREN DEMAND DADDY-LONG-LEGS UPON HIS TIMBER   623 HIGH TALK   6
        TOES,
      A COCK CAME BY UPON HIS TOES; . . . .   725 LEGEND   26
TOGETHER
      AND STOOD BESIDE THE SEA TOGETHER; . . . .   9 OISIN 1   V 101B
      AND SINGING, SINGING ALL TOGETHER; . . . .   15 OISIN 1   203
      TOGETHER, WHILE THE DARK WOODS RANG, ...   16 OISIN 1   227
      TOGETHER IN THAT HOUR OF GENTLENESS . . . .   80 EPHEMERA   6
      AND CLAP THEIR HANDS TOGETHER, AND HALF CLOSE THEIR EYES,   146 UNAPPEAS HOST   2
      THAT HELD THE LAND TOGETHER THERE, ...   194 BAILE AILLINN   132
      WE SAT TOGETHER AT ONE SUMMER'S END, ...   204 ADAMS CURSE   1
      FOR TO ARTICULATE SWEET SOUNDS TOGETHER . . . .   205 ADAMS CURSE   10
      BUT WE BEND TOGETHER AND KISS THE QUIET FEET . . . .   207 HANRAHANS SONG V   4
      ONE--AND ONE--A COUPLE--FIVE TOGETHER; . . . .   233 SHADOW WATER B   249
      HANDS GRIPPED IN HANDS, TOES CLOSE TOGETHER, ...   332 ROUND TOWER   21
      BEAUTY AND FOOL TOGETHER LAID. . . . .   484 SYMBOLS   6
      CIVILIZATION IS HOOPED TOGETHER, BROUGHT . . . . . .   563 MERU   1
      ALL MUST TOGETHER DO." THAT DONE, THE MAN . . . . . .   634 CUCHULAIN COMF   17
      FILLED THEM AS THEY SAT TOGETHER; . . . .   667 ISLE STAT II 3   31
      IS IN THY FACE, AND LIPS TOGETHER PRESSED; . . . . .   671 ISLE STAT II 3   139
      WHEN HIS SINEWY WINGS TOGETHER CLOSE. . . . .   673 ISLE STAT II 3   179
      NOW FOUR TOGETHER; I SHALL HEAR THEIR WORDS . . . . .   753 SHADOW WATER A   139
      TWO HOVER THERE TOGETHER, AND ONE SAYS, ...   753 SHADOW WATER A   142
      THEY HAVE FLOWN AWAY TOGETHER. WE ARE NEARLY . . . .   754 SHADOW WATER A   154
      AND RULE TOGETHER UNDER A CANOPY. . . . .   767 SHADOW WATER A   385
TOIL   SEE MUCH-TOIL
      SUNG OF THE BIRDS. OUR TOIL WAS DONE; . . . .   14 OISIN 1   V 177
      IN PINCHING WAYS I TOIL AND TURN." . . . .   19 OISIN 1   V 282
      I SANG HOW, WHEN DAY'S TOIL IS DONE, ...   85 MAD KING GOLL   61
      AND HEAVY MORTAL HOPES THAT TOIL AND PASS; . . . . .   101 ROSE UPON ROOD   18
      THAN THIS ACCUSTOMED TOIL. WHEN I WAS YOUNG, ...   267 ALL TEMPT ME   5
      TOIL AND GROW RICH, ...   310 WITCH   1
      A STYLE IS FOUND BY SEDENTARY TOIL . . . .   370 EGO DOMINUS   65
      AN IMAGE OF MYSTERIOUS WISDOM WON BY TOIL; . . . . .   373 PHASES OF MOON   18
      WITH THE GREAT TOIL AND CEREMONY OF STATE, ...   462 HARUN RASHID   V   25
      ENDURE THAT TOIL OF GROWING UP; . . . .   478 SELF AND SOUL   44
      IN LUCK OR OUT THE TOIL HAS LEFT ITS MARK; . . . . .   491 COOLE BALLYLEE V 40F
      IN LUCK OR OUT THE TOIL HAS LEFT ITS MARK; . . . . .   495 CHOICE   6

823

		PAGE	TITLE	LINE
TOIL (CONTINUED)				
FOR ALL MY TOIL HAS HAD FOR ITS HIRE		551	SONGS REWRIT 1 V	3
ALL HIS TWENTIFS CRAMMED WITH TOIL:		576	WHAT THEN	4
THOUGH GRAVE-DIGGERS' TOIL IS LONG,		637	BEN BULBEN	21
BENT LOW WITH TOIL AND HOARIEST YEARS. THE OTHER		711	FERENCZ RENYI	52
IN TOIL OF MEASUREMENT		784	WOMANS BEAUTY V	9
TOILED				
AND UP THE STAIR WE TOILED TO A HIGH DOOR,		36	OISIN 2 V	101
TOILED WITH EMPOUNDED CATTLE THROUGH THE MIRE,		276	TWO KINGS V	2
IL PENSEROSO'S PLATONIST TOILED ON		419	MY HOUSE	14
AND TOILED SO HARD AND LATE		432	NINETEEN 19	95
I TOILED LONG YEARS AND AT LENGTH		505	RESULT THOUGHT	9
TOILED LONG YEARS AND AT LENGTH		505	RESULT THOUGHT V	9
TOILING				
LEST ALL THY TOILING ONLY BREEDS		66	HAPPY SHEPHERD	25
THE SPINNING STARS—THE TOILING SEA—WHIRL ROUND		665	ISLE STAT II 2	72
TOILS				
FROM SOMEBODY THAT TOILS FROM CHAIR TO CHAIR:		491	COOLE BALLYLEE	26
IN TOILS OF MEASUREMENT		784	WOMANS BEAUTY	9
TOKEN				
AS A TOKEN AND A SIGN,		648	ISLE STAT I 1	78
TOLD				
AND TOLD THE PURPLE DEEPS THEIR PRIDE,		14	OISIN 1	186
AS THOUGH HE TOLD HIS NEVER-SLUMBERING HEART		32	OISIN 2	44
AS THOUGH HE TOLD HIS NEVER SLUMBERING HEART		32	OISIN 2 V	44
HE TOLD OF EVERY FROTH-DROP HISSING, FLYING,		32	OISIN 2 V	45
WHEN YOU HAVE TOLD HOW I WEEP ENDLESSLY,		33	OISIN 2	63
AH! THERE HE SNAPS MY RICE. I TOLD YOU SO.		73	ANASHU VIJAYA	38
AND ALL AROUND THE HARP-STRING TOLD HIS PRAISE,		109	CUCHULAIN SEA	44
AND ALL AROUND THE HARPSTRING TOLD HIS PRAISE,		109	CUCHULAIN SEA V	44
AND ALL AROUND THE HARP STRING TOLD HIS PRAISE,		109	CUCHULAIN SEA V	44
IF ALL WERE TOLD:		116	FAERY SONG	4
IF ALL WERE TOLD.		116	FAERY SONG	16
TOLD WHERE—AH, LITTLE, ALL-UNNEEDED VOICE!—		127	DREAM OF FAERY V	30
THE WRONG OF UNSHAPELY THINGS IS A WRONG TOO GREAT TO BE TOLD:		143	ROSE IN HEART	5
THE WRONG OF THE THINGS MISSHAPEN IS WRONG TOO GREAT TO BE TOLD:		143	ROSE IN HEART V	5
SHE TOLD THEM OF THE MANY-CHANGING ONES:		185	QUEEN MAEVE	112
THE BOUGHS HAVE WITHERED BECAUSE I HAVE TOLD THEM MY DREAMS.		203	WITHER BOUGHS	8
THE BOUGHS HAVE WITHERED BECAUSE I HAVE TOLD THEM MY DREAMS.		203	WITHER BOUGHS	16
THE BOUGHS HAVE WITHERED BECAUSE I HAVE TOLD THEM MY DREAMS.		204	WITHER BOUGHS	24
BECAUSE OF SOMETHING TOLD UNDER THE FAMISHED HORN		210	UNDER THE MOON	17
MY MOTHER TOLD ME THAT THERE IS NOT ONE		224	SHADOW WATER B	45
AND YOU HAVE TOLD ME THAT THEIR JOURNEY LIES		231	SHADOW WATER B	205
TOLD HIM, THAT WHEN ORION ROSE, AND ALL		282	TWO KINGS V 132A	
A FRIEND THAT COULD, HE HAD TOLD HER, WORK HIS CURE		283	TWO KINGS	137
THAT COULD, AS HE HAD TOLD HER, WORK HIS CURE,		283	TWO KINGS V	137
AMENDED WHAT WAS TOLD AWRY		440	WISDOM	4
TOLD OF A HARSH REPROOF, OR TRIVIAL EVENT		443	SCHOOL CHILDR	11
TOLD, AND IT SEEMED THAT OUR TWO NATURES BLENT		443	SCHOOL CHILDR	13
TOLD ALL THAT HAD BEEN SAID OR DONE		456	SUMMER SPRING	3
AND TOLD HIM SO, BUT FRIENDSHIP NEVER ENDS:		473	ALL SOUL NIGHT	65
WHEN EVERYTHING IS TOLD.		515	GIRLS SONG B	10
TILL I HAVE TOLD THE SAGES		534	CONSOLATION	5
I TOLD HIM THAT NIGHTLY FROM SIX TO SEVEN I SAT AT THIS TABLE,		578	LOFTY THINGS	9
HE TOLD PEARSE AND CONNOLLY,		585	ORAHILLY	12
WHEN HE HEARD THAT STORY TOLD,		596	COLONEL MARTIN	47
WHEN HE HAD HEARD THAT STORY TOLD		596	COLONEL MARTIN V	47
BUT FIRST YOU MUST BE TOLD OUR CHARACTER:		634	CUCHULAIN COMF	20
ASIDE!—THE WILD HORNS TOLD ALMINTOR'S END,		665	ISLE STAT II 2	68
A VOICE HAS TOLD ME HOW WITHIN THIS LAND		682	SEEKER V	22
FORGIVE! FOR I HAVE TOLD THEM EVERYTHING.		694	MOSADA 1	107
THEY SAID I'D BURN IN HELL UNLESS I TOLD.		694	MOSADA 1	108
HAS TOLD ME THAT THE UNDYING SEND THEIR EAGLES		765	SHADOW WATER A	346
A STREAM HAS TOLD ME THEY ARE BEAUTIFUL.		767	SHADOW WATER A	398
TOLERANCE				
MADE ALL PLATONIC TOLERANCE VAIN		438	SONGS PLAY 2	7
MADE PLATO'S TOLERANCE IN VAIN,		438	SONGS PLAY 2 V	7
TOLLING				
SLOW THE CHAPEL BELL IS TOLLING AS THOUGH THE DEAD PASSED BY.		718	PHANTOM SHIP	16
TOM				
TOM O'ROUGHLEY		337	TOM OROUGHLEY	T
OR SO DID TOM O'ROUGHLEY SAY		338	TOM OROUGHLEY	5
TOM THE LUNATIC		528	TOM LUNATIC	T
SANG OLD TOM THE LUNATIC		528	TOM LUNATIC	1
TOM AT CRUACHAN		529	TOM CRUACHAN	1
OLD TOM AT CRUACHAN		529	TOM CRUACHAN V	T
OLD TOM AGAIN		530	OLD TOM AGAIN	T
COME TOM AND DICK, COME ALL THE TROOP		582	ROGER CASEMENT	17
THE COLONEL SAID TO TOM HIS MAN,		596	COLONEL MARTIN	50
"AND DID YOU KEEP NO GOLD, TOM?		596	COLONEL MARTIN	64
AND TOM MAKE OUT A LIVING		597	COLONEL MARTIN	70
WHEN TOM MADE OUT A LIVING		597	COLONEL MARTIN V	70
TOMB				
AWAY, AWAY! YOU ARE SAFER IN THE TOMB.		293	TO A SHADE	24

TOMB   (CONTINUED)
    THE MOUNTAIN TOMB . . . .   311 MOUNTAIN TOMB   T
    OUR FATHER ROSICROSS IS IN HIS TOMB. . . .   311 MOUNTAIN TOMB   4
    OUR FATHER ROSICROSS IS IN HIS TOMB. . . .   311 MOUNTAIN TOMB   8
    OUR FATHER ROSICROSS SLEEPS IN HIS TOMB. .   311 MOUNTAIN TOMB   12
    AND NEVER COULD HAVE RESTED IN THE TOMB . .   325 ROBERT GREGORY   27
    ON GREAT-GRANDFATHER'S BATTERED TOMB." . .   331 ROUND TOWER   6
    ON GREAT-GRANDFATHER'S BATTERED TOMB." . .   332 ROUND TOWER   30
    ON GREAT-GRANDFATHER'S BATTERED TOMB. . .   332 ROUND TOWER   V   30
    IN THE GREY STONE TOMB HE MADE. . . . . .   360 ALF POLLEXFEN   5
    IN THAT TOMB BY HIM AND HER . . . .   360 ALF POLLEXFEN   7
    AND HEARTIER LOVES! THAT LAMP IS FROM THE TOMB. 398 LEADERS CROWD   12
    IS BUT ITS LONGING FOR THE TOMB. . . . . .   434 WHEEL   8
    THE TOMB OF SWIFT WEARS IT AWAY.   A VOICE . .   487 SEVEN SAGES   21
    PROUD, OPEN-EYED AND LAUGHING TO THE TOMB.   501 VACILLATION   34
    THE BODY OF SAINT TERESA LIES UNDECAYED IN TOMB, 503 VACILLATION   80
    WHAT SEEMS MOST WELCOME IN THE TOMB--PLAY A PREDESTINED 503 VACILLATION 86
        PART.
    (ALL FIND SAFETY IN THE TOMB.) . . . . . .   508 JANE BISHOP   3
    (ALL FIND SAFETY IN THE TOMB.) . . . . . .   508 JANE BISHOP   10
    (ALL FIND SAFETY IN THE TOMB.) . . . . . .   508 JANE BISHOP   17
    (ALL FIND SAFETY IN THE TOMB.) . . . . . .   508 JANE BISHOP   24
    MY BODY IN THE TOMB-- . . . .   511 JANE AND JACK   10
    AND LAID THEM ON LOVE'S LETTERED TOMB! . .   519 HER DREAM   4
    UNDER THE GREAT COMEDIAN'S TOMB THE CROWD.   541 PARN FUNERAL 1   1
    RIBH AT THE TOMB OF BAILE AND AILLINN . .   554 RIBH AT TOMB   T
    AND FOUND HIS FAMILY TOMB . . . .   584 GHOST ROG CASE   32
    FROM EMPTY TOMB OR VIRGIN WOMB? . . . . .   619 STICK INCENSE   2
    THERE IN THE TOMB STAND THE DEAD UPRIGHT, .   635 BLACK TOWER   7
    THERE IN THE TOMB DROPS THE FAINT MOONLIGHT,   636 BLACK TOWER   17
    THERE IN THE TOMB THE DARK GROWS BLACKER,   636 BLACK TOWER   27
    HE GUIDES YE FROM THE TOMB! . . . .   738 MOURN THEN ON   14
    OF MANY A TRAGIC TOMB! . . . .   785 YOUR HEART   10
    OF MANY A TRAGIC TOMB! . . . .   786 YOUR HEART   23
    OF MANY A TRAGIC TOMB! . . . .   786 YOUR HEART   36
    YET RISE FROM YOUR ITALIAN TOMB, ...   791 REPRISALS   10
TOMB-HAUNTER
    WHAT GREAT TOMB-HAUNTER SWEEPS THE DISTANT SKY   618 BRONZE HEAD   4
    NO DARK TOMB-HAUNTER ONCE! HER FORM ALL FULL . . 618 BRONZE HEAD   8
TOMBS
    MADE OF DIM GOLD RAVE OUT IN SECRET TOMBS!   235 SHADOW WATER B   295
    IN TOMBS OF GOLD AND LAPIS LAZULI . . . .   483 OIL AND BLOOD   1
    IN TOMBS OF GOLD AND LAPIS-LAZULI . . . .   483 OIL AND BLOOD V   1
    IN ANCIENT TOMBS I SIGHED, BUT NOT AGAIN!   564 GYRES   14
    MADE OF DIM GOLD, RAVE OUT IN SECRET TOMBS,   765 SHADOW WATER A   345
TOMBSTONE
    UPON A GREY OLD BATTERED TOMBSTONE . . . .   331 ROUND TOWER   7
    UPON THE GREY OLD BATTERED TOMBSTONE . . .   331 ROUND TOWER   V   7
TOMORROW
    TOMORROW NIGHT I WILL BREAK DOWN THE DOOR.   551 SONGS REWRIT 1 V   REF
TO-MORROW
    EVERYTHING THAT FEARS TO-MORROW . . . . .   20 OISIN 1   V   302
    SPINNING AT ALL TIMES ERI'S GOOD TO-MORROW,   129 BOOK STORIES   V   10
    TO-MORROW NIGHT I WILL BREAK DOWN THE DOOR.   551 SONGS REWRIT 1   6
    TO-MORROW NIGHT I WILL BREAK DOWN THE DOOR.   551 SONGS REWRIT 1   12
    TO-MORROW NIGHT I WILL BREAK DOWN THE DOOR.   551 SONGS REWRIT 1   18
    TO-MORROW NIGHT I WILL BREAK IN THE DOOR.   551 SONGS REWRIT 1 V   REF
    THIS EVE, TO-MORROW, OR TO-MORROW NIGHT . .   699 MOSADA 3   2
    THIS EVE, TO-MORROW, OR TO-MORROW NIGHT . .   699 MOSADA 3   2
    FORGAEL CAN DIE TO-MORROW. COME TO THE ALE.   759 SHADOW WATER A   246
    COME TO THE ALE! FOR HE CAN DIE TO-MORROW. .   760 SHADOW WATER A   247
TONE
    AND ROBERT EMMET AND WOLFE TONE, ...   290 SEPTEMBER 1913   21
    LORD EDWARD AND WOLFE TONE, ...   395 SIXTEEN DEAD   16
    WHEN STRANGERS MURDERED EMMET, FITZGERALD, TONE, 541 PARN FUNERAL 1   17
TONES
    OUR TREAD, AS ROSE AND FELL THE LIQUID TONES   33 OISIN 2   V   68B
    TO BLESS THAT ISLE WITH HONEY IN HIS TONES,   128 DREAM OF FAERY V   44
    SAD FAERY TONES. 'TIS THUS THEY EVER SEEM,   654 ISLE STAT I 2   58
TONGUE
    SWAYED, CROONING TO HIMSELF AN UNKNOWN TONGUE!   39 OISIN 2   159
    AH, SWEET TO ME NOW WERE EVEN BALD CONAN'S SLANDEROUS 55 OISIN 3   116
        TONGUE!
    AND NOW MOVES MANY A PLEASANT TONGUE . . .   98 FOXHUNTER   21
    AND MOVES THERE MANY A PLEASANT TONGUE, . .   98 FOXHUNTER   V   23
    AND LEARN TO CHAUNT A TONGUE MEN DO NOT KNOW.   101 ROSE UPON ROOD   21
    AND LEARN TO CHANT A TONGUE MEN DO NOT KNOW.   101 ROSE UPON ROOD V   21
    BURNING IN FIRES OF A SLANDEROUS TONGUE.   148 INTO TWILIGHT   8
    THE TONGUE OF IT SWEET WITH DREAMING . . .   160 CAP AND BELLS V   17
    THE WATERS OF SLEEP CAN MAKE A CHATTERING TONGUE 218 WOODS OF COOLE   25
    YOU SAY, AS I HAVE OFTEN GIVEN TONGUE . . .   262 TO A POET   1
    SO WE SPEAK A DIFFERENT TONGUE. . . . . .   313 TWO YEAR LATER   6
    AND I SPEAK A BARBAROUS TONGUE. . . . . .   313 TWO YEAR LATER   12
    THE EYE OF THE MIND NOR KEEP MY TONGUE FROM SPEECH." 353 PEOPLE   34
    I SUDDENLY CRIED OUT IN A STRANGE TONGUE .   387 SOLOMON WITCH   5
    BUT NOW WITH FLATTERING TONGUE . . . . . .   434 YOUTH AND AGE   3
    NOW THAT YOUR TONGUE CANNOT PERSUADE THE CHILD TILL SHE 450 OWEN AHERNE 22
        MISTAKE
    ON OLD DRY WRITING IN A LEARNED TONGUE, . .   466 HARUN RASHID   123
    . . . MOVE HIS MOUTH AND SINEWY TONGUE. . .   560 MAGIC DRUM   5
    (AN IMAGE OUT OF SPENSER AND THE COMMON TONGUE). 603 GALLERY REVIS   40

	PAGE	TITLE		LINE
TONGUE (CONTINUED)				
GIVE TONGUE, PROCLAIM THEIR HIDDEN NAME--"HOUND VOICE."	622	HOUND VOICE		7
AND YET GAVE TONGUE. "HOUND VOICES" WERE THEY ALL.	622	HOUND VOICE		9
WHOM MEN HAVE NAMED ARCADIA'S SWEETEST TONGUE.	649	ISLE STAT I 1		109
THOU HAST AN OVER-NIMBLE TONGUE. THY GRIEF,	661	ISLE STAT II 1		59
WILD WISDOMS OF SPIRIT AND TONGUE.	708	FAIRY PEDANT		27
WILD SPIRITS OF WISDOM AND TONGUE.	708	FAIRY PEDANT	V	27
BECAUSE OF THE THING HIS TONGUE HAD SAID.	730	PRIEST FAIRY		60
TONGUED SEE SWEET-TONGUED WISE-TONGUED DEWY-TONGUED				
TONGUE'S				
BUT WHEN I THINK OF THAT MY TONGUE'S A STONE.	478	SELF AND SOUL		40
TONGUES				
WERE LOLLING THEIR TONGUES, AND THE SILKEN HAIR	2	OISIN 1	V	7S
AND THE TONGUES OF THE CROWD	172	PLEADS FRIEND	V	2
FOR ALL TONGUES HE KNEW.	594	COLONEL MARTIN		4
OF THOSE STEEL TONGUES! CRASH, SWORDS! WELL THRUST!	665	ISLE STAT II 2		67
WELL BENT				
HAVE CLOTHED THEIR TONGUES WITH SONG OF SONGLESS DAYS?	666	ISLE STAT II 3		17
TO-NIGHT				
ALL, ALL ARE IN MY THOUGHTS TO-NIGHT BEING DEAD.	324	ROBERT GREGORY		8
TONSURED				
CHILDREN AND WOMEN AND TONSURED YOUNG MEN,	167	BLESSED	V	15
TO THOSE THAT NEVER SAW THIS TONSURED HEAD	555	RIBH AT TOMB		4
TOOK				
IN TRUST TOOK HE JOHN'S LANDS;	92	FATHER OHART		5
THE DRUIDS TOOK THEM TO THEIR MYSTERY,	111	CUCHULAIN SEA		82
BEFORE EARTH TOOK HIM TO HER STONY CARE;	126	DREAM OF FAERY		4
BUT SHE TOOK UP HER FAN FROM THE TABLE	160	CAP AND BELLS		19
BUT SHE TOOK HER FAN FROM THE TABLE,	160	CAP AND BELLS	V	19
SHE TOOK THEM INTO HER BOSOM,	160	CAP AND BELLS	V	25
SOME MAY HAVE BLAMED YOU THAT YOU TOOK AWAY	257	RECONCILIATION		1
OLD BUTLERS WHEN YOU TOOK TO HORSE AND STOOD	270	PARDON FATHERS	V	10
ROCK-NURTURED AOIFE TOOK A PIN,	274	GREY ROCK		88
THREE OLD HERMITS TOOK THE AIR	298	THREE HERMITS		1
"I TOOK YOU FOR A BRAWLING GHOST,	304	HOUR DAWN	V	41
AND TOOK THE WOODEN LADLE UP	304	HOUR DAWN	V	46
AND WHAT OF HER THAT TOOK	315	FRIENDS		17
AND I TOOK ALL THE BLAME OUT OF ALL SENSE AND REASON,	316	COLD HEAVEN		7
I TOOK A BROKEN ROOT TO FLING	317	APPOINTMENT		2
OF THAT LATE DEATH TOOK ALL MY HEART FOR SPEECH.	328	ROBERT GREGORY		96
AND TOOK THEIR TABLETS AND DID SUMS;	344	DAWN		9
AND TOOK THEIR TABLETS AND MADE SUMS--	344	DAWN	V	9
MEN AND THEIR BUSINESS TOOK	421	MY TABLE		23
GOD TOOK THE SPINNING-JENNY	439	FRAGMENTS		3
AND TOOK A MESS OF SHADOWS FOR ITS MEAT?	444	SCHOOL CHILDR		28
AND TOOK A MASS OF SHADOWS FOR ITS MEAT,	444	SCHOOL CHILDR	V	28
AND THEREUPON A COLLOQUY TOOK PLACE	463	HARUN RASHID		45
THAT THEREUPON A COLLOQUY TOOK PLACE	463	HARUN RASHID	V	45
THE CHAMBERMAID LIVED LONG, AND TOOK	571	THREE BUSHES		57
STOOD, TOOK DEATH LIKE A TUNE	613	MARCH SONGS 1		15
BUT HE TOOK DOWN THE MOON	616	MARCH SONGS 3		8
BUT HE TOOK DOWN THE MOON	616	MARCH SONGS 3		18
BUT HE TOOK DOWN THE MOON	616	MARCH SONGS 3		28
I TOOK NO TROUBLE TO CONVINCE,	624	APPARITIONS		3
PLAYERS AND PAINTED STAGE TOOK ALL MY LOVE,	630	CIRCUS ANIMALS		31
TOOK UP THE NEAREST AND BEGAN TO SEW.	634	CUCHULAIN COMF		18
AND PASSED THE OUTER HEBRIDES, AND TOOK	749	SHADOW WATER A		42
AND PASSED THE NORTHERN HEBRIDES, AND TOOK	749	SHADOW WATER A	V	42
UNDER THE WAVES, AND TOOK A THOUSAND WOMEN	766	SHADOW WATER A		378
AN ANCIENT LECHER TOOK TO GEESE	792	GEORGE MOORE		3
TOOL				
NOR HAVE HANDS HELD A WEARY TOOL;	19	OISIN 1		283
AND HANDS THAT HOLD NO WEARISOME TOOL,	22	OISIN 1		340
OUR HANDS HAVE KNOWN NO WEARYING TOOL,	22	OISIN 1	V	339
TOOTH				
BRED THAT FIERCE TOOTH AND CLEANLY LIMB	318	APPOINTMENT		10
THE HORN'S SWEET NOTE AND THE TOOTH OF THE HOUND.	380	SONGS FOOL 1		12
THE HORN'S SWEET NOTE AND THE TOOTH OF THE HOUND.	381	SONGS FOOL 2		14
THE WEASEL'S TWIST, THE WEASEL'S TOOTH.	431	NINETEEN 19		92
LOVE IS LIKE THE LION'S TOOTH.	514	JANE GROWN OLD		7
LOVE IS LIKE THE LION'S TOOTH.	514	JANE GROWN OLD		14
LOVE IS LIKE THE LION'S TOOTH.	515	JANE GROWN OLD		21
TOOTHLESS				
HIS TOOTHLESS HOUND AT HIS NERVELESS FEET,	26	OISIN 1	V	400
TOP SEE MOUNTAIN-TOP SPINNING-TOP TOWER-TOP TABLE-TOP				
A FIR-TREE ROARING IN ITS LEAFLESS TOP;	40	OISIN 2		177
A FIR TREE ROARING IN ITS LEAFLESS TOP,	40	OISIN 2	V	177
HAD HAMMERED OUT ON MOUNTAIN TOP	271	GREY ROCK		23
THE GOLDEN TOP OF CARE?	309	PLAYER QUEEN		20
UNTIL THEY PRANCED UPON THE TOP.	331	ROUND TOWER		18
FROM DEATH, AND WOUNDS, OR ON SINAI'S TOP,	375	PHASES OF MOON		67
AND THE MOON SPUN ROUND LIKE A TOP,	378	CAT AND MOON		2
ON THEIR HOLLOW TOP,	415	TOWER		171
I CLIMB TO THE TOWER TOP AND LEAN UPON BROKEN STONE,	425	PHANTOM HATRED	V	1
HALF DEAD AT THE TOP.	480	BLOOD AND MOON		12
HALF DEAD AT THE TOP? NO MATTER WHAT I SAID,	482	BLOOD AND MOON		48
OTTERS BELOW AND MOOR-HENS ON THE TOP,	490	COOLE BALLYLEE		2
OTTERS BELOW AND MOOR HENS ON THE TOP,	490	COOLE BALLYLEE	V	2
FROM DOOR TO TOP!	512	JANE ON GOD		17
ARE SOMEWHERE SLEEPING LIKE A TOP	525	DANCING DAYS		13
DOWN EVERY WITHERED FINGER FROM THE TOP!	537	HER VISION		11

826

	PAGE	TITLE	LINE

TOP   (CONTINUED)
WHEN NATIONS ARE EMPTY UP THERE AT THE TOP,   548 TO SAME TUNE 3   11
WHAT MATTER THOUGH NUMB NIGHTMARE RIDE ON TOP,   564 GYRES   9
AND WHEN THEY CAME TO THE TOP STAIR   595 COLONEL MARTIN   41
WHAT IF THERE'S NOTHING UP THERE AT THE TOP?   615 MARCH SONGS 2   21
ALL OUT OF SHAPE FROM TOE TO TOP,   639 BEN BULBEN   71
LIKE WINE THAT FILLS TO THE TOP   781 MY HEART BEAT   14

TOPERS
WHERE SEVEN EPHESIAN TOPERS SLEPT AND NEVER KNEW   442 BLACK CENTAUR   11

TOPLESS
THOSE TOPLESS TOWERS   293 HELEN LIVED   8
THAT THE TOPLESS TOWERS BE BURNT   617 LONG-LEG FLY   11

TOPMOST
A TREE THERE IS THAT FROM ITS TOPMOST BOUGH   500 VACILLATION   11
THE TOPMOST BLOSSOM ON THE BOUGHS OF TIME   756 SHADOW WATER A   178

TOPPLED
THEY TOPPLED OVER; "WERE IT NOT   302 HOUR DAWN   17

TOPPLES
SOON TOPPLES DOWN THE HILL.   335 YOUNG BEAUTY   6

TOPPLING
I HAD BEEN HURT"; AND TOPPLING BROUGHT   302 HOUR DAWN   19

TOPS
WHOSE HOOVES THE TOPS OF THE SURGES GRAZED,   12 OISIN 1   V 142A
THE TOPS OF THEIR EARS WERE FEATHERED,   49 OISIN 3   34
AND SOFTLY COME TO YOUR NIAMH OVER THE TOPS OF THE TIDE;   55 OISIN 3   126
AND SOFTLY COME TO THY NIAM OVER THE TOPS OF THE TIDE;   52 OISIN 3   V 126
AND PUT HIS PATTERN ROUND THEIR TOPS   272 GREY ROCK   V 24
DEWY-TONGUED, THE DAISY TOPS--   706 DAWN-SONG   22

TORCH
AND IN THE RING A TORCH, AND WITH ITS FLARE   37 OISIN 2   121
WHO BROUGHT US FOUND A TORCH, AND, WITH ITS FLARE   37 OISIN 2   V 122
AND THRUST THE TORCH BETWEEN THE SLIMY FLAGS,   38 OISIN 2   143
ANOINTING, TORCH JAMMED DOWN BETWEEN THE FLAGS,   38 OISIN 2   V 143
FOUND THAT OLD HOUSE, A SPUTTERING TORCH WITHIN,   283 TWO KINGS   140
AND FOUND THE HOUSE, A SPUTTERING TORCH WITHIN,   283 TWO KINGS   V 140
OR DID THE TORCH LIGHT OF THAT MYSTERY   466 HARUN RASHID   V 115
THE PROUD FURIES EACH WITH HER TORCH ON HIGH.   579 DOR WELLESLEY   16
COMPANIONING THE RIVER'S PILGRIM TORCH.   703 MOSADA 3   112

TORCHES
IN DRUID VAPOUR AND MAKE THE TORCHES DIM;   169 SECRET ROSE   11
THE SMOKY TORCHES MADE A GLARE   271 GREY ROCK   18
AND SMOKY TORCHES MADE A GLARE   271 GREY ROCK   V 18
BUT THE DARK CHANGED TO RED, AND TORCHES SHONE,   537 HER VISION   12

TORCHLIGHT
. . . THROUGH TORCHLIGHT AND TUMULTUOUS SONG;   459 FROM OEDIPUS   8
OR DID THE TORCHLIGHT OF THAT MYSTERY   466 HARUN RASHID   115

TORCH-LIGHT
. . . THROUGH TORCH-LIGHT AND TUMULTUOUS SONG;   459 FROM OEDIPUS   V 8
OR DID THE TORCH-LIGHT OF THAT MYSTERY   466 HARUN RASHID   V 115

TORE
WHEN I TORE DOWN THE TREE; BUT WHEN THE WEST   41 OISIN 2   V 180
WHEN I'D TORE DOWN THAT TREE; BUT WHEN THE WEST   41 OISIN 2   V 180
WHEN I TORE DOWN THAT TREE; BUT WHEN THE WEST   41 OISIN 2   V 180
I TORE IT FROM GREEN BOUGHS WINDS TORE AND TOSSED   130 BOOK STORIES   13
I TORE IT FROM GREEN BOUGHS WINDS TORE AND TOSSED   130 BOOK STORIES   13
I TORE IT FROM THE BARREN BOUGHS OF EIRE,   130 BOOK STORIES   15
I TORE IT FROM GREEN BOUGHS WINDS TOSSED AND HURLED,   130 BOOK STORIES   V 13
I TORE IT FROM THE GREEN BOUGHS OF OLD ERI,   130 BOOK STORIES   V 15
TORE FROM THE CLOUDS HIS MARVELLOUS MOON,   314 MEMORY YOUTH   21
I TORE MY BODY THAT ITS WINE MIGHT COVER   537 HER VISION   7
COMMANDING OFFICER THAT TORE   627 STATES HOLIDAY   16

TORMENTED   SEE RAGE-TORMENTED GONG-TORMENTED
THE RAGE DRIVEN, RAGE TORMENTED, AND RAGE HUNGRY TROOP,   426 PHANTOM HATRED V   11

TORN   SEE NEW-TORN DOLPHIN-TORN BEAST-TORN
WHEN I HAD TORN IT DOWN; BUT WHEN THE WEST   41 OISIN 2   V 180
THE FENIAN HORSES; ARMOUR TORN ASUNDER;   43 OISIN 2   210
HAS TORN AND RENT THEIR HEARTS IN TWAIN,   66 HAPPY SHEPHERD V   33
FOR THE KIND WIRES ARE TORN AND STILL,   86 MAD KING GOLL   69
OF FEVER. NOW THE STRINGS ARE TORN   86 MAD KING GOLL   V 66
MY SINGING FADES, THE STRINGS ARE TORN,   86 MAD KING GOLL   V 66
UNTIL AT LAST THE UNLOCKED HORN HAD TORN   278 TWO KINGS   V 21
BUT THE TORN PETALS STREW THE GARDEN PLOT;   422 MY DESCENDANTS   7
WHEN THE TORN PETALS STREW THE GARDEN PLOT;   422 MY DESCENDANTS V   7
THAT FLOWERING, SILKEN, OLD EMBROIDERY, TORN   477 SELF AND SOUL   13
AND OUR HEARTS ARE TORN.   519 LOVES LONENESS   12
NO CIVIL RANCOUR TORN THE LAND APART.   542 PARN FUNERAL 2   4
LIES TORN AND ROTTING. THE FIERCE KESTREL BIRDS,   675 ISLE STAT II 3   234
A WHITE BIRD HAS TORN ME WITH HIS SILVER CLAWS.   759 SHADOW WATER A   234

TORQUE
THESE HANDS WON MANY A TORQUE OF GOLD.   83 MAD KING GOLL   23

TORTOISESHELL
TORTOISESHELL BUTTERFLIES, PEACOCK BUTTERFLIES,   482 BLOOD AND MOON   45

TORTURER
BUT MY HEART'S VICTIM AND ITS TORTURER.   537 HER VISION   32

TOSS   SEE PITCH-AND-TOSS
AND TOSS AND TURN IN NARROW CAVES;   19 OISIN 1   281
LET PAUDEENS PLAY AT PITCH AND TOSS,   288 TO WEALTHY MAN   31
LEAVE PAUDEENS TO THEIR PITCH AND TOSS;   288 TO WEALTHY MAN V   31
THEIR DRINK, THEIR PITCH AND TOSS BY DAY;   607 SONGS BURDEN 2 V   14
AND LITTLE BOYS PLAYED PITCH AND TOSS.   725 LEGEND   4
LIFT THEIR CHINS AND TOSS THEIR CURLS,   726 LOVERS QUARREL   23

PAGE TITLE LINE

TOSS   (CONTINUED)
    MINE WHERE WATERS BROOD AND TOSS: • • • • • • • • • 744 ROSY CROSS 7
TOSSED   SEE STORM-TOSSED
    I TORE IT FROM GREEN BOUGHS WINDS TORE AND TOSSED • • • 130 BOOK STORIES 13
    I TORE IT FROM GREEN BOUGHS WINDS TOSSED AND HURLED, • • 130 BOOK STORIES V 13
    THAT TOSSED A BARE HEEL WHEN AT SCHOOL, • • • • • • 301 RUN PARADISE 19
TOSSING
    WITH AN APPLE OF GOLD IN HER TOSSING HAND: • • • • • 12 OISIN 1 143
    AN APPLE OF GOLD IN HER TOSSING HAND: • • • • • • 12 OISIN 1 V 143
    UNTIL THE TOSSING ARMS GREW STILL • • • • • • • • 21 OISIN 1 322
    GREEN BOUGHS OF TOSSING ALWAYS, WEARY, WEARY, • • • • 130 BOOK STORIES V 14
    TOSSING AND TOSSING TO AND FRO • • • • • • • • • 135 TWO TREES 15
    TOSSING AND TOSSING TO AND FRO • • • • • • • • • 135 TWO TREES V 15
    CAOILTE TOSSING HIS BURNING HAIR, • • • • • • • • 140 HOSTING SIDHE 3
    CAOILTE TOSSING HIS BURNING HAIR, • • • • • • • • 141 HOSTING SIDHE 15
    AND HIDING THEIR TOSSING MANES AND THEIR TUMULTUOUS FEET. 154 BELOVED PEACE 12
    AND HIDE THEIR TOSSING MANES AND THEIR TUMULTUOUS FEET. 154 BELOVED PEACE V 12
    FACE DOWNWARD, TOSSING IN A TROUBLED SLEEP: • • • • 185 QUEEN MAEVE 106
    AND ALL THAT TOSSING OF YOUR WINGS IS JOY, • • • • • 244 SHADOW WATER B 451
    THAT YOUNG MEN, TOSSING ON THEIR BEDS, • • • • • • 337 SCHOLARS 4
    ON DELICATE SENSITIVE EAR OR TOSSING MANE, • • • • • 433 NINETEEN 19 115
    A TOSSING LAUGH BETWEEN THEIR REDNESS 'BIDES— • • • • 685 DRAWING-ROOM 2
    A TOSSING LAUGH BETWEEN THEIR RED ABIDES: • • • • • 735 QUATRAIN APHOR 22
    A TOSSING LAUGH BETWEEN THEIR REDNESS 'BIDES— • • • • 735 QUATRAIN APHOR V 22
TOST   SEE SEA-TOST
    • • • THE LIMBS OF THE FENIANS ARE TOST: • • • • • 62 OISIN 3 213
TOTAL
    HAD THE WORLD'S TOTAL LIFE GATHERED UP, IT SEEMED, • • • 231 SHADOW WATER B 194
TOTTERING
    SO SMALL MAKES ONE GROW WEAK AND TOTTERING: • • • • 700 MOSADA 3 35
TOTTERS
    AND THAT IS WHY THE WORLD TOTTERS ABOUT • • • • • • 233 SHADOW WATER B 238
TOUCH
    AND TOUCH THE LAUGHING SILVER STRING: • • • • • • 17 OISIN 1 233
    AH, TOUCH THEIR BLUE-VEINED EYELIDS IF THEY SLEEP, • • 33 OISIN 2 61
    IF THEY STILL SLUMBER, TOUCH THEIR EYELIDS BLUE, • • • 33 OISIN 2 V 61
    AH, TOUCH THEIR BLUE VEINED EYELIDS IF THEY SLEEP, • • 33 OISIN 2 V 61
    HEARING AEDH TOUCH THE MOURNFUL STRINGS OF GOLD." • • 35 OISIN 2 87
    TO GRASP THE WOMAN. YOU HAVE DARED TO TOUCH HER? • • 223 SHADOW WATER B 39
    BEFORE A HAND CAN TOUCH ME. MY HANDS ARE STILL: • • 238 SHADOW WATER B 358
    AH, THAT TIME COULD TOUCH A FORM • • • • • • • • 258 PEACE 1
    THAT ALL MUST COME TO SIGHT AND TOUCH: • • • • • • 386 ROBARTES DANCE 31
    AND THERE ENDURED HER FINGERS' TOUCH • • • • • • • 397 POLIT PRISONER 5
    AND THERE ENDURED HER FINGER'S TOUCH • • • • • • • 397 POLIT PRISONER V 5
    IS PONDERABLE TO OUR TOUCH. • • • • • • • • • • 399 BREAK OF DAY 18
    OR BY A TOUCH OR A SIGH: • • • • • • • • • • • 413 TOWER 111
    AND SHOULD SOME CRAZY HAND DARE TOUCH A DAUGHTER • • 433 NINETEEN 19 122
    LIVED AT MY SIDE: THOUGHT TIME'S DISFIGURING TOUCH • • 466 HARUN RASHID 110
    LIVED AT MY SIDE: THAT TIME'S DISFIGURING TOUCH • • • 466 HARUN RASHID V 110
    AND THAT SHE DREAMED AWAKE CONTENT TO TOUCH • • • • 466 HARUN RASHID V 125C
    THAT THEY TOUCH OR SIGH. • • • • • • • • • • • 517 HER ANXIETY 9
    EVERY TOUCH THEY GIVE, • • • • • • • • • • • • 517 HER ANXIETY 10
    SCARCE DID HE MY BODY TOUCH, • • • • • • • • • • 535 CHOSEN 4
    DID BUT OUR BODIES TOUCH, • • • • • • • • • • • 538 LAST CONFESS 10
    IF SOUL MAY LOOK AND BODY TOUCH, • • • • • • • • 573 LADYS 2ND SONG 19
    DELIGHTFUL TO THE TOUCH: TIGHTEN THAT HAND • • • • • 579 DOR WELLESLEY 4
    BUT WHAT CAN HE DO BUT TOUCH?" • • • • • • • • 588 OLD WICKED MAN 17
    CAN TOUCH BY MOTHER WIT • • • • • • • • • • • • 589 OLD WICKED MAN 40
    SOME SAY THAT ALL WHO TOUCH THE ISLAND LONE • • • • 653 ISLE STAT I 2 42
    I'M DYING! OH, FORGIVE ME IF I TOUCH • • • • • • 684 SEEKER 70
    TO DEATH. HIS LIPS ARE GLUED, WITH QUIVERING TOUCH, • • 684 SEEKER V 63
    AND ROARS, MAD WITH THE TOUCH OF THE UNKNOWN, • • • • 689 NETTLESHIP 7
    TOUCH NOT THIS BOY, FOR HE IS INNOCENT. • • • • • • 694 MOSADA 1 106
    MY SOUL SHALL TOUCH WITH HIS, AND THE TWO FLAMES • • • 701 MOSADA 3 61
TOUCHED
    AND TOUCHED IT WITH THEIR FINGER-TIPS. • • • • • • 18 OISIN 1 259
    AND TOUCHED IT WITH HIS FINGER-TIPS. • • • • • • 18 OISIN 1 V 259
    LIKE A SMALL RIVER, AND WHERE FEET TOUCHED CAME • • • 37 OISIN 2 117
    WITH HIS OWN FINGERS TOUCHED THE BRAZEN STRINGS. • • • 109 CUCHULAIN SEA 46
    WITH HIS OWN FINGER TOUCHED THE BRAZEN STRINGS. • • • • 109 CUCHULAIN SEA V 46
    AH, BUT TIME HAS TOUCHED A FORM • • • • • • • • 258 PEACE V 1
    CAME WHEN TIME HAD TOUCHED HER FORM. • • • • • • • 259 PEACE 11
    AND TOUCHED HER FOREHEAD WITH HIS LIPS AND SAID: • • • 286 TWO KINGS V 211B
    I WOULD HAVE TOUCHED IT LIKE A CHILD • • • • • • • 399 BREAK OF DAY 12
    BUT KNEW MY FINGER COULD BUT HAVE TOUCHED • • • • • 399 BREAK OF DAY 13
    BUT KNEW MY FINGER WOULD HAVE TOUCHED • • • • • • 399 BREAK OF DAY V 13
    IT HAD NOT TOUCHED OUR LIVES. BUT POPULAR RAGE, • • • 542 PARN FUNERAL 1 20
    SLID CIRCLING DOWN AND SOFTLY TOUCHED MY LIPS • • • • 690 MOSADA 1 21
    JUST NOW MY SOUL ROSE UP AND TOUCHED IT, FAR • • • • 705 REMEMBRANCE 13
TOUCHES
    AND THE LONG GREY GRASSES, WHOSE TENDEREST TOUCHES • • • 27 OISIN 1 V 415B
TOUCHING
    WHOM BRAHMA, TOUCHING WITH HIS FINGER, PRAISES, FOR YOU
        HOLD • • • • • • • • • • • • • • • • • 73 ANASHU VIJAYA 42
    WHOM BRAHMA, TOUCHING WITH HIS FINGER, PRAISES, FOR YE HOLD 73 ANASHU VIJAYA V 42
    DID SHE IN TOUCHING THAT LONE WING • • • • • • • • 397 POLIT PRISONER 7
    THERE IS NO TOUCHING HERE, NOR TOUCHING THERE, • • • • 555 RIBH AT TOMB 13
    THERE IS NO TOUCHING HERE, NOR TOUCHING THERE, • • • • 555 RIBH AT TOMB 13
    AND JOY, THE TOUCHING OF WHOSE FINGER LENDS • • • • • 686 DRAWING-ROOM 7
    AND JOY, THE TOUCHING OF WHOSE FINGER LENDS • • • • • 734 QUATRAIN APHOR 7

		PAGE	TITLE		LINE
TOUT					
	DAN AND JERRY TOUT, ...	520	HIS BARGAIN	V	5
TOWARD					
	TOWARD PEOPLED TARA, NOR STOOD TO DRAW HIS BREATH . . .	279	TWO KINGS		46
TOWARDS					
	THE HORSE TOWARDS THE MUSIC RACED, ...	13	OISIN 1		169
	THE STEED TOWARDS THE MUSIC RACED, ...	13	OISIN 1	V	169
	SAVE DEER TOWARDS NOON THAT WATER SOUGHT.	17	OISIN 1	V	243
	MY PILLARS TOWARDS THEIR FALL.	44	OISIN 2	V	239
	AND FLYING TOWARDS THEIR PEACE. PUT BY THESE THOUGHTS,	226	SHADOW WATER B		91
	TOWARDS THE COUNTRY OF THE DEAD. WHAT MATTER	231	SHADOW WATER B		206
	TOWARDS THE HOUR FOR SPEAKING OF THE DEAD?	276	TWO KINGS	V	D
	HE RAN TOWARDS THE HOUSE HIS FATHERS BUILT	279	TWO KINGS	V	45E
	TOWARDS PEOPLED TARA, NOR STOOD TO DRAW HIS BREATH . .	279	TWO KINGS	V	46
	AND RIDDEN TOWARDS IT, BEING IGNORANT.	286	TWO KINGS	V	218
	TOWARDS NIGHTFALL UPON CERTAIN SET APART	325	ROBERT GREGORY		29
	TOWARDS NIGHTFALL UPON A RACE	325	ROBERT GREGORY		31
	TOWARDS NIGHTFALL UPON A PLACE	325	ROBERT GREGORY	V	31
	BUT WHILE THE MOON IS ROUNDING TOWARDS THE FULL . . .	373	PHASES OF MOON		39
	TOWARDS BREAK OF DAY	398	BREAK OF DAY		T
	I DREAMED TOWARDS BREAK OF DAY, ...	399	BREAK OF DAY		19
	SLOUCHES TOWARDS BETHLEHEM TO BE BORN?	402	SECOND COMING		22
	AND FOLLOWED UP THOSE BAYING CREATURES TOWARDS-- . . .	412	TOWER		72
	O TOWARDS I HAVE FORGOTTEN WHAT--ENOUGH!	412	TOWER		73
	AND TURN TOWARDS MY CHAMBER, CAUGHT	424	ROAD AT DOOR		14
	PLUNGES TOWARDS NOTHING, ARMS AND FINGERS SPREADING WIDE	426	PHANTOM HATRED		13
	AND WHEN I WAKE TOWARDS MORN I DREAD MYSELF, ...	448	HERO GIRL FOOL		5
	THOSE CHINAMEN CLIMB TOWARDS, AND I	567	LAPIS LAZULI		49
	STRETCH TOWARDS THE MOONLESS MIDNIGHT OF THE TREES, . .	579	DOR WELLESLEY		1
	ITS PAVEN LENGTH TOWARDS THE RIVER'S MARGE	702	MOSADA 3		76
	TOWARDS A COUNTRY WHERE THERE ARE NO KINGS.	755	SHADOW WATER A		165
TOWER	SEE LAND-OF-THE-TOWER WATCH-TOWER				
	AND MANANNAN'S DARK TOWER, STONE AFTER STONE, ...	45	OISIN 2		236
	AND MANANAN'S DARK TOWER, STONE BY STONE, ...	45	OISIN 2	V	236
	CAME TO MY TOWER AS AGE DRAGGED AFTER AGE	45	OISIN 2	V	242
	LAND OF THE TOWER, WHEN AENGUS HAS THROWN THE GATES APART,	209	UNDER THE MOON	V	8
	BESIDE YOUNG AENGUS IN HIS TOWER OF GLASS, ...	219	HARP OF AENGUS		2
	AND IN A TOWER OF GLASS, AND FROM THAT DAY	224	SHADOW WATER B		50
	BESIDE A FIRE OF TURF IN TH' ANCIENT TOWER, ...	324	ROBERT GREGORY		3
	THE TOWER SET ON THE STREAM'S EDGE;	326	ROBERT GREGORY		52
	THE TOWER SET BY THE STREAM'S EDGE;	326	ROBERT GREGORY	V	52
	UNDER THE ROUND TOWER	331	ROUND TOWER		T
	BELLOWED AND PRANCED IN THE ROUND TOWER;	331	ROUND TOWER		12
	UNDER YOUR OLD WIND-BEATEN TOWER, WHERE STILL	367	EGO' DOMINUS		2
	GOD GRANT A BLESSING ON THIS TOWER AND COTTAGE . . .	371	ON GOING HOUSE		1
	WE ARE ON THE BRIDGE; THAT SHADOW IS THE TOWER, . . .	372	PHASES OF MOON		10
	FROM THE FAR TOWER WHERE MILTON'S PLATONIST	373	PHASES OF MOON		15
	THE LIGHT IN THE TOWER WINDOW WAS PUT OUT.	377	PHASES OF MOON		139
	AND HEARD THE SEA-WIND SCREAM UPON THE TOWER, ...	403	FOR DAUGHTER		10
	RESTORED THIS TOWER FOR MY WIFE GEORGE;	406	CARVED STONE		4
	THE TOWER	409	TOWER		T
	AN ANCIENT BRIDGE, AND A MORE ANCIENT TOWER, ...	419	MY HOUSE		1
	TOWER WHERE A CANDLE GLEAMS, ...	420	MY HOUSE	V	20I
	MAY THIS LABORIOUS STAIR AND THIS STARK TOWER	423	MY DESCENDANTS		13
	AND FIND A COMFORT IN IT? MAY THIS TOWER	423	MY DESCENDANTS	V	13
	I CLIMB TO THE TOWER TOP AND LEAN UPON BROKEN STONE, .	425	PHANTOM HATRED	V	1
	THE BROKEN WALL, THE BURNING ROOF AND TOWER	441	LEDA AND SWAN		10
	FOR EMBLEMS OF THE DAY AGAINST THE TOWER	478	SELF AND SOUL		29
	MORE BLESSED STILL THIS TOWER;	480	BLOOD AND MOON		2
	ALEXANDRIA'S WAS A BEACON TOWER, AND BABYLON'S . . .	480	BLOOD AND MOON		13
	I DECLARE THIS TOWER IS MY SYMBOL; I DECLARE	480	BLOOD AND MOON		16
	IS EVERY MODERN NATION LIKE THE TOWER, ...	482	BLOOD AND MOON		47
	IS EVERY NATION LIKE THE TOWER	482	BLOOD AND MOON	V	47
	A STORM-BEATEN OLD WATCH TOWER, ...	484	SYMBOLS	V	1
	. . . "THE KING OF THE GREAT CLOCK TOWER"	549	SEVERED HEAD		T
	WHAT SAYS THE CLOCK IN THE GREAT CLOCK TOWER? . . .	549	SEVERED HEAD		3
	WHAT SAYS THE CLOCK IN THE GREAT CLOCK TOWER? . . .	550	SEVERED HEAD		10
	WHAT SAYS THE CLOCK IN THE GREAT CLOCK TOWER? . . .	550	SEVERED HEAD		17
	THE BLACK TOWER	635	BLACK TOWER		T
	SAY THAT THE MEN OF THE OLD BLACK TOWER, ...	635	BLACK TOWER		1
	BESIDE YOUNG AENGUS IN HIS TOWER OF GLASS, ...	762	SHADOW WATER A		297
	TO THE TOWER OVERHEAD, ...	772	SONG DEIRDRE 1		3
	IN THE TOWER OVER HEAD, ...	772	SONG DEIRDRE 1	V	3
	TO THE TOWER OVER HEAD, ...	772	SONG DEIRDRE 1	V	3
TOWER'S					
	THE TOWER'S OLD COOK THAT MUST CLIMB AND CLAMBER . . .	636	BLACK TOWER		21
TOWERS					
	WOVEN INTO HER HAIR, BEFORE DARK TOWERS	30	OISIN 2		22
	IN NIAM'S HAIR--WHEN ROSE A WORLD OF TOWERS	30	OISIN 2	V	22
	WOVE IN HER FLOWER-LIKE HAIR, BEFORE DARK TOWERS . . .	30	OISIN 2	V	22
	FROM THE WHOLE SEVEN SEAS, THOSE TOWERS SET	38	OISIN 2	V	131
	HELD TO THE TOWERS WITH BOASTING SONGS AND GAY. . . .	41	OISIN 2	V	184C
	IT DIED AFAR. GREY SLEET THOSE TOWERS HID	46	OISIN 2	V	245
	OVER THE RAMPARTS AND THE TOWERS, ...	212	BLESS PSALTER		6
	THOSE TOPLESS TOWERS	293	HELEN LIVED		8
	IN STARRY TOWERS OF BABYLON	440	WISDOM		14
	AND SHELLEY HAD HIS TOWERS, ...	480	BLOOD AND MOON		15
	THAT THE TOPLESS TOWERS BE BURNT	617	LONG-LEG FLY		11
TOWER-TOP					
	I CLIMB TO THE TOWER-TOP AND LEAN UPON BROKEN STONE, . .	425	PHANTOM HATRED		1

```
                                                          PAGE    TITLE            LINE
TOWERY
     THE TOWERY GATES OF GORIAS,  . . . . . . . . . . . .  196 BAILE AILLINN       161
TOWN
     I CAME UPON A LITTLE TOWN    . . . . . . . . . . . .   85 MAD KING GOLL        49
     AS ONCE WITHIN A LITTLE TOWN . . . . . . . . . . . .   85 MAD KING GOLL    V   49
     TIME WAS, AS IN A LITTLE TOWN, . . . . . . . . . . .   85 MAD KING GOLL    V   49
     ONCE, WHILE WITHIN A LITTLE TOWN . . . . . . . . . .   85 MAD KING GOLL    V   49
     THAT CARRIED THE TAKE TO SLIGO TOWN TO BE SOLD, . . .  91 OLD FISHERMAN         7
     THAT CARRIED THE FISH FOR THE SALE IN THE FAR-AWAY TOWN, 91 OLD FISHERMAN       7
     WOULD COME AT LAST TO GOD'S GREAT TOWN, . . . . . . .  91 OLD FISHERMAN    V    7
     O MASTERS OF THE GLITTERING TOWN! . . . . . . . . . . 113 ROSE OF PEACE        11
     ARE WHAT THE BLIND AND IGNORANT TOWN . . . . . . . .  212 BLESS PSALTER         3
     IF YOU HAVE REVISITED THE TOWN, THIN SHADE, . . . . . 287 TO WEALTHY MAN        7
     "THOUGH LOGIC-CHOPPERS RULE THE TOWN, . . . . . . . . 292 TO A SHADE            1
     "THOUGH LOGIC CHOPPERS RULE THE TOWN, . . . . . . . . 337 TOM OROUGHLEY         1
     ON THAT OLD QUEEN MEASURING A TOWN . . . . . . . . .  337 TOM OROUGHLEY    V    1
     ON THE OLD QUEEN MEASURING A TOWN . . . . . . . . . . 344 DAWN                  3
     THE DAILY SPITE OF THIS UNMANNERLY TOWN, . . . . . .  344 DAWN             V    3
     WHO NEVER GAVE THE BURNING TOWN A THOUGHT; . . . . .  351 PEOPLE                3
     AND WHEN THROUGH ALL THE TOWN THERE RAN . . . . . . . 384 VISION ROBART        57
     THAT SPEECH WAS ALL THAT THE TOWN KNEW, BUT HE . . .  436 FOR MY SON           25
     IN THIS BLIND BITTER TOWN, . . . . . . . . . . . . .  462 HARUN RASHID         35
     UNTIL THE TOWN LIE BEATEN FLAT. . . . . . . . . . . . 504 QUARREL IN AGE        3
     "SHE MAY BE IN THE TOWN, . . . . . . . . . . . . . .  565 LAPIS LAZULI          8
     CARRY THE GOLD ABOUT THE TOWN, . . . . . . . . . . .  594 COLONEL MARTIN       13
     ON COUNTRY AND ON TOWN, . . . . . . . . . . . . . . . 596 COLONEL MARTIN       52
     LARGER SPARROWS OF THE TOWN, . . . . . . . . . . . .  606 SONGS BURDEN 1       24
     THUS SPAKE THE TOWN JAILOR . . . . . . . . . . . . .  731 STREET DANCERS        5
     WHEN PAUL RODE FROM THE TOWN . . . . . . . . . . . .  740 EARL PAUL            13
                                                           740 EARL PAUL            21
TOWNLAND
     THE HAPPY TOWNLAND . . . . . . . . . . . . . . . . .  213 HAPPY TOWNLAND        T
     IF HE COULD SEE THE TOWNLAND . . . . . . . . . . . .  214 HAPPY TOWNLAND        3
     HE IS RIDING TO THE TOWNLAND . . . . . . . . . . . .  214 HAPPY TOWNLAND       19
     IN THE HIGH HOLLOW TOWNLAND  . . . . . . . . . . . .  214 HAPPY TOWNLAND   V    3
     HE IS RIDING TO THE TOWNLAND . . . . . . . . . . . .  215 HAPPY TOWNLAND       39
     HE IS RIDING TO THE TOWNLAND . . . . . . . . . . . .  216 HAPPY TOWNLAND       59
TOWNS
     AND HARRIED ALBAN TOWNS, AND OVERTHREW . . . . . . .  749 SHADOW WATER A       40
TOY
     GREY TRUTH IS NOW HER PAINTED TOY; . . . . . . . . .   65 HAPPY SHEPHERD        4
     A POISON DROP.  A TOY, A FANCY ONCE, . . . . . . . .  700 MOSADA 3             24
     A POISON DROP.  THE TOY OF FANCY ONCE, . . . . . . .  700 MOSADA 3         V   24
TOYS
     WE HAVE NAUGHT FOR DEATH BUT TOYS. . . . . . . . . .  363 DOLLS DRAWINGS       11
     WE TOO HAD MANY PRETTY TOYS WHEN YOUNG! . . . . . . . 428 NINETEEN 19           9
     FORGET ITS BROKEN TOYS . . . . . . . . . . . . . . .  473 ALL SOUL NIGHT       59
     I WEARY OF YOUR SONGS AND HUNTER'S TOYS. . . . . . .  651 ISLE STAT I 1       157
TRACE
     AND, THOUGH YOU HAVE PASSED THE BEST OF LIFE, STILL TRACE, 367 EGO DOMINUS      5
     AND TRACE THESE CHARACTERS UPON THE SANDS? . . . . .  370 EGO DOMINUS          64
     AND TRACE THESE CHARACTERS UPON THE SAND? . . . . . . 370 EGO DOMINUS      V   64
     CONTENT TO TRACE THAT MISERY TO ITS SOURCE, . . . . . 479 SELF AND SOUL    V   65
     IRELAND'S HISTORY IN THEIR LINEAMENTS TRACE; . . . .  604 GALLERY REVIS        53
     CLIMB TO OUR PROPER DARK, THAT WE MAY TRACE . . . . . 611 STATUES              31
TRACES
     WE AND OUR BITTERNESS HAVE LEFT NO TRACES . . . . .   130 BOOK STORIES         23
TRACK
     ADORNING EVERY SECRET TRACK . . . . . . . . . . . .   509 JANE REPROVED         9
     STRUGGLING FOR AN IMAGE ON THE TRACK . . . . . . . .  534 CHOSEN                2
     STUMBLING UPON THE BLOOD-DARK TRACK ONCE MORE, . . .  622 HOUND VOICE          18
TRADE
     YET NOW IT SEEMS AN IDLE TRADE ENOUGH." . . . . . . . 205 ADAMS CURSE          27
     POETS WITH WHOM I LEARNED MY TRADE, . . . . . . . .   270 GREY ROCK             1
     WHERE WIT AND BEAUTY LEARNED THEIR TRADE . . . . . .  288 TO WEALTHY MAN       16
     THE SECOND: "I SHALL LEARN A TRADE"; . . . . . . . .  296 THREE BEGGARS        32
     ANOTHER SAID: "AND I WILL TRADE . . . . . . . . . . . 296 THREE BEGGARS    V   32
     AS THOUGH HE HAD BUT THAT ONE TRADE ALONE. . . . . .  327 ROBERT GREGORY       80
     MY TRADE ALLOWS! CHOSEN MY COMPANY, . . . . . . . . . 352 PEOPLE               20
     WHERE THE INDIANS TRADE OR JAPANESE? . . . . . . . .  361 ALF POLLEXFEN        20
     THIS SEDENTARY TRADE. . . . . . . . . . . . . . . .   416 TOWER               180
     THE SEDENTARY TRADE. . . . . . . . . . . . . . . . .  416 TOWER            V  180
     WHERE WE SHOULD CAST OFF BODY AND TRADE . . . . . .   431 NINETEEN 19          73
     I KNOW WHAT DEVIL'S TRADE THEY LEARN . . . . . . . .  607 SONGS BURDEN 2       12
     SO I HAVE PICKED A BETTER TRADE . . . . . . . . . .   627 STATES HOLIDAY       11
     IRISH POETS, LEARN YOUR TRADE, . . . . . . . . . . .  639 BEN BULBEN           68
TRADERS
     TRADERS OR SOLDIERS WHO HAVE LEFT ME BLOOD . . . . .  269 PARDON FATHERS   V    7
TRADING
     OR TRADING OUT OF GALWAY INTO SPAIN; . . . . . . . .  269 PARDON FATHERS        4
     A TRADING GALLEY IN HER HELMSMAN'S EYES. . . . . . .  751 SHADOW WATER A       95
TRADITIONAL
     TRADITIONAL SANCTITY AND LOVELINESS; . . . . . . . .  491 COOLE BALLYLEE       42
TRAFFIC
     TOO LONELY FOR THE TRAFFIC OF THE WORLD! . . . . . .  374 PHASES OF MOON       61
     OR TRAFFIC IN THE GRASSHOPPERS OR BEES. . . . . . .   430 NINETEEN 19          48
     OR TRAFFIC IN THE GRASSHOPPERS AND BEES? . . . . . .  430 NINETEEN 19      V   48
     TRAFFIC IN MOCKERY. . . . . . . . . . . . . . . . .   432 NINETEEN 19         112
TRAGEDY
     THAT NOTHING STRANGE! THE TRAGEDY BEGAN . . . . . .   411 TOWER                51
     THAT CHANGED SOME CHILDISH DAY TO TRAGEDY— . . . . .  443 SCHOOL CHILDR        12
     THOSE LOVERS, PURIFIED BY TRAGEDY, . . . . . . . .    555 RIBH AT TOMB         21
```

			PAGE	TITLE	LINE

TRAGEDY   (CONTINUED)
   TRAGEDY WROUGHT TO ITS UTTERMOST. . . . . 566 LAPIS LAZULI   20
TRAGIC
   WHEN HER OWN PEOPLE RULED THIS TRAGIC EIRE! . . . . . 129 BOOK STORIES   2
   OUT OF NO TRAGIC WAR, LOVERS OF LIFE, ... 369 EGO DOMINUS   39
   FOR NATURE'S PULLED HER TRAGIC BUSKIN ON . . . . . . 490 COOLE BALLYLEE   12
   FOR NATURE'S PULLED HER TRAGIC BUCKSKIN ON . . . . . 490 COOLE BALLYLEE V   12
   FOR NATURE'D PULLED HER TRAGIC BUSKIN ON . . . . . . 490 COOLE BALLYLEE V   12
   ALL THOSE TRAGIC CHARACTERS RIDE . . . . 549 SEVERED HEAD   4
   WE THAT LOOK ON BUT LAUGH IN TRAGIC JOY. . . . . . . 564 GYRES   8
   ALL PERFORM THEIR TRAGIC PLAY, ... 565 LAPIS LAZULI   9
   ON ALL THE TRAGIC SCENE THEY STARE. . . . . 567 LAPIS LAZULI   52
   THAT TRAGIC STORY MADE, ... 587 PARNELLITES   26
   OF MANY A TRAGIC TOMB! . . . . 785 YOUR HEART   10
   OF MANY A TRAGIC TOMB! . . . . 786 YOUR HEART   23
   OF MANY A TRAGIC TOMB! . . . . 786 YOUR HEART   36
TRAILING
   AND TRAILING CRIMSON VANS, A MUMBLING BROOD, ... 687 TWO TITANS   20
   TRAILING AND SHINING 'NEATH THE FLICKERING GLARE. . . . 688 TWO TITANS   32
TRAILS
   TRAILS ALL ABOUT THE WRITTEN PAGE. . . . . 138 TO IRELAND   9
TRAIN
   THE BLINDS DRAWN UP"! MAUD GONNE AT HOWTH STATION WAITING 578 LOFTY THINGS   10
    A TRAIN,
TRAITOR
   COOK BARACH, THE TRAITOR! AND WARWARD, ... 53 OISIN 3   90
   OF TRAITOR EVERMORE IS ON OUR NAME." . . . . 712 FERENCZ RENYI   61
   OF TRAITOR EVER MORE IS ON OUR NAME." . . . . 712 FERENCZ RENYI V   61
TRAITOR'S
   BUT THAT'S A TRAITOR'S THOUGHT. ENOUGH FOR ME . . . . 462 HARUN RASHID   39
TRAMPING
   A TRAMPING OF TREMENDOUS FEET, ... 85 MAD KING GOLL   54
   THE TRAMPING OF TREMENDOUS FEET, ... 85 MAD KING GOLL V   54
TRAMPLE
   AND TRAMPLE MY DARK ISLE. . . . . 45 OISIN 2   V 239E
TRAMPLED
   BARKING. WE TRAMPLED UP AND DOWN WITH BLOWS . . . . . 40 OISIN 2   170
   WE TRAMPLED TO AND FRO. WHEN HIS MIND KNEW . . . . . 40 OISIN 2   V 173
   AND DEMONS BE BROKEN IN PIECES, AND TRAMPLED BENEATH THEM 61 OISIN 3   204
    IN DEATH.
   AND DEMONS, ALL BROKEN IN PIECES, BE TRAMPLED BENEATH THEM 61 OISIN 3   V 204
    IN DEATH.
   AND TRAMPLED IN THE BUBBLING MIRE, ... 83 MAD KING GOLL   26
   AND TRAMPLED ON THE BUBBLING MIRE, ... 83 MAD KING GOLL V   26
   AND TRAMPLED THE MOUNTAINS AWAY, ... 171 MAID QUIET V   4C
   AND TRAMPLED THE MOUNTAIN AWAY, ... 171 MAID QUIET V   4C
   BUT UNDER HEAVY LOADS OF TRAMPLED CLAY . . . . 483 OIL AND BLOOD   4
TRANCE
   MUTTER SUCH THINGS AS THEY AWAKE FROM TRANCE. . . . . 229 SHADOW WATER B   163
   ALL KNOWLEDGE LOST IN TRANCE . . . . 343 SHEP GOATHERD   111
   AN AGONY OF TRANCE, ... 498 BYZANTIUM   31
TRANQUILLITY
   O MAY TRANQUILLITY WALK BY HIS ELBOW . . . . 71 ANASHU VIJAYA   2
   OH, MAY TRANQUILLITY BESIDE HIM GO, ... 71 ANASHU VIJAYA V   2
   AND GREAT BOUGHS DROP TRANQUILLITY! . . . . 77 INDIAN TO LOVE   2
TRANSFIGURED
   ERE TIME TRANSFIGURED ME. . . . . 131 OLD PENSIONER   6
   THAT HAS TRANSFIGURED ME. . . . . 131 OLD PENSIONER   12
   THAT HAS TRANSFIGURED ME. . . . . 132 OLD PENSIONER   18
   SHE SMILED AND THAT TRANSFIGURED ME . . . . 451 FIRST LOVE   13
   TRANSFIGURED TO PURE SUBSTANCE WHAT HAD ONCE . . . . 555 RIBH AT TOMB   11
TRANSFIGURING
   GAIETY TRANSFIGURING ALL THAT DREAD. . . . . 565 LAPIS LAZULI   17
TRANSFORM
   TRANSFORM THESE RASCAL BILLOWS INTO WOMEN . . . . . 222 SHADOW WATER B   11
   WOULD TRANSFORM THE PART, ... 506 REMORSE SPEECH   3
TRANSFORMED
   TRANSFORMED UTTERLY! . . . . 393 EASTER 1916   39
TRANSFORMING   SEE WORLD-TRANSFORMING
TRANSLUNAR
   TRANSLUNAR PARADISE. . . . . 415 TOWER   156
TRANSPARENT
   TRANSPARENT LIKE THE WIND, ... 449 HERO GIRL FOOL   27
TRAP
   I TRAP YOU. CHECK. I DO MISCALCULATE. . . . . . . 722 WITCH VIVIEN   58
TRAPPED
   THE WANDERINGS OF OISIN AND HOW A DEMON TRAPPED HIM . . 1 OISIN 1   V   T
   TRAPPED OF AN AMOROUS DEMON THING. . . . . 2 OISIN 1   V   4
TRASH
   THAT CANNOT IN THAT TRASH AND TINSEL HIDE! . . . . . 558 RIBH CHRISTIAN   17
TRAVAIL
   THE TRAVAIL OF PASSION . . . . 172 TRAV PASSION   T
TRAVEL
   WERE I TO TRAVEL FAR AND WIDE . . . . 398 BREAK OF DAY   8
TRAVELLED
   . . . BERKELEY AND BURKE HAVE TRAVELLED THERE. . . . . 481 BLOOD AND MOON   18
   GREAT ROOMS WHERE TRAVELLED MEN AND CHILDREN FOUND . . 491 COOLE BALLYLEE   29
   HAD TRAVELLED HALF THE NIGHT. . . . . 585 ORAHILLY   17
   YET HERE'S A TRAVELLED MAN THAT KNOWS . . . . 631 POLITICS   5
   TRAVELLED TO AND FRO ACROSS THE ATLANTIC, ... 790 DEDICATION   3

		PAGE	TITLE	LINE
TRAVELLER				
HERE, TRAVELLER, SCHOLAR, POET, TAKE YOUR STAND		489	COOLE PARK 29	25
WORLD-BESOTTED TRAVELLER; HE		493	SWIFTS EPITAPH	5
WORLD BESOTTED TRAVELLER; HE		493	SWIFTS EPITAPH V	5
TRAVELLERS				
HAVE DRIVEN TRAVELLERS MAD FOR THEIR OWN SPORT.		227	SHADOW WATER B	105
BENIGHTED TRAVELLERS		419	MY HOUSE	18
TRAVELLING				
HE SHOOK HIMSELF FOR TRAVELLING,		10	OISIN 1 V	110
BUT THAT, LONG TRAVELLING, HE HAD COME		325	ROBERT GREGORY	28
BUT FOR WHAT SOME TRAVELLING MAN		585	ORAHILLY	21
TRAVELLING-MAN				
SAID THE RAMBLING, SHAMBLING TRAVELLING-MAN;		788	HAWTHORN TREE	2
SAID THE RAMBLING, SHAMBLING TRAVELLING-MAN;		788	HAWTHORN TREE	10
TRAVELS				
THAT TRAVELS ON THE MOON.		451	FIRST LOVE	12
WHO TRAVELS WHERE GOD WILLS.		587	OLD WICKED MAN	4
TRAVEL-WEARIED				
CEASE TO REMEMBER THE DELIGHTS OF YOUTH, TRAVEL-WEARIED AGED MAN;		459	FROM OEDIPUS	2
TREACHERY				
ABOVE THE MURDEROUS TREACHERY OF THE MOON,		428	NINETEEN 19 V	3
THIS THEIR WANTON TREACHERY,		727	LOVERS QUARREL	55
TREAD				
OUR TREAD, AS ROSE AND FELL THE LIQUID TONES		33	OISIN 2 V	68B
TREAD SOFTLY BECAUSE YOU TREAD ON MY DREAMS.		176	CLOTHS HEAVEN	8
TREAD SOFTLY BECAUSE YOU TREAD ON MY DREAMS.		176	CLOTHS HEAVEN	8
I BECAME A RUSH THAT HORSES TREAD;		177	PAST GREATNESS	6
TROD WITH A LIGHTER TREAD.		323	SWANS AT COOLE	18
ALL MEN ARE DANCERS AND THEIR TREAD		430	NINETEEN 19	57
SHOULD HEAR MY LIVING FEET, NOR WOULD I TREAD		435	NEW FACES	3
THE HERALD'S CRY, THE SOLDIER'S TREAD		438	SONGS PLAY 2	13
IMMORTAL LADIES TREAD THE GROUND		446	COLONUS PRAISE	6
CANNOT ENDURE TO THINK YOU TREAD THESE PATHS,		463	HARUN RASHID	52
OR ROCKY CISTERN WHERE WE TREAD THE CLOTHES		499	MOTHER OF GOD	9
MEN-AT-ARMS TREAD;		512	JANE ON GOD	8
TREAD AND TREAD THEIR CLOVEN FEET		646	ISLE STAT I 1	24
TREAD AND TREAD THEIR CLOVEN FEET		646	ISLE STAT I 1	24
ALONG THE WOOD WITH SUBTLE TREAD AND BENDED BOWS.		649	ISLE STAT I 1	111
CARVED: HERE, BEYOND THE LAKE'S SLOW-MUFFLED TREAD,		662	ISLE STAT II 2	11
TREADMILL				
THIS WINDING, GYRING, SPIRING TREADMILL OF A STAIR		480	BLOOD AND MOON	17
TREADS				
AND STILL I DREAM HE TREADS THE LAWN		67	HAPPY SHEPHERD	51
BROWN LOLLARD TREADS UPON THE LAWN,		98	FOXHUNTER	17
BROWN DERMOT TREADS UPON THE LAWN,		98	FOXHUNTER V	17
"STILL TREADS THE WORLD AMID HIS ARMED MEN."		107	CUCHULAIN SEA V	26
YET HE WHO TREADS IN MEASURED WAYS		138	TO IRELAND	27
YET HE WHO TREADS IN AUSTERE WAYS		138	TO IRELAND V	27
YOU HAVE MEASURED OUT THE ROAD THAT THE SOUL TREADS		342	SHEP GOATHERD	80
AND NO MAN KNOWS WHAT TREADS THE GRASS.		614	MARCH SONGS 2	10
AND NO MAN KNOWS WHAT TREADS THE GRASS.		615	MARCH SONGS 2	20
AND NO MAN KNOWS WHAT TREADS THE GRASS.		615	MARCH SONGS 2	30
UPON THE MOUNTAIN'S BROW. YONDER HE TREADS		703	MOSADA 3	114
TREASONS				
I LAUGHED AT TIMES UNNUMBERED TREASONS,		23	OISIN 1 V	345D
TREASURE SEE MAY-TREASURE				
THE HOLD IS FULL OF TREASURE. FULL TO THE HATCHES.		247	SHADOW WATER B	532
TREASURE ON TREASURE. BOXES OF PRECIOUS SPICE.		247	SHADOW WATER B	533
TREASURE ON TREASURE. BOXES OF PRECIOUS SPICE.		247	SHADOW WATER B	533
TREASURE AND TREASURE. BOXES OF PRECIOUS SPICE.		247	SHADOW WATER B V	533
TREASURE AND TREASURE. BOXES OF PRECIOUS SPICE.		247	SHADOW WATER B V	533
FOR WE HAVE FOUND A TREASURE THAT'S SO GREAT		248	SHADOW WATER B	540
WHO HAD LOST SOME UNIMAGINABLE TREASURE		278	TWO KINGS	40
THROUGH THE GREAT GALLERY OF THE TREASURE HOUSE		461	HARUN RASHID	5
ALL THE HEALING EARTH MAY TREASURE,		733	STREET DANCERS V	63
TREASURER				
FOR THE GREAT CALIF'S TREASURER AND MY FRIEND,		460	HARUN RASHID V	2
NOW THE GOOD CALIPH'S LEARNED TREASURER,		461	HARUN RASHID	3
TREASURES				
AND DROWNED THE TREASURES OF NINE CONQUERED NATIONS,		235	SHADOW WATER B	287
EVEN FROM THAT DELIGHT MEMORY TREASURES SO,		459	FROM OEDIPUS	4
TREATISE				
PAUSE AT THE TREATISE OF PARMENIDES		461	HARUN RASHID	16
FROM THE GREAT TREATISE OF PARMENIDES;		469	HARUN RASHID	183
TREE SEE OLIVE-TREE CATALPA-TREE THORN-TREE CHESTNUT-TREE CHRISTMAS-TREE PEAR-TREE FIR-TREE YEW-TREE LIME-TREE HAZEL-TREE BEECH-TREE OAK-TREE ROSE-TREE				
LIKE SOOTY FINGERS, MANY A TREE		13	OISIN 1	171
A FIR TREE ROARING IN ITS LEAFLESS TOP,		40	OISIN 2 V	177
WHEN I TORE DOWN THE TREE; BUT WHEN THE WEST		41	OISIN 2 V	180
WHEN I'D TORE DOWN THAT TREE; BUT WHEN THE WEST		41	OISIN 2 V	180
WHEN I TORE DOWN THAT TREE; BUT WHEN THE WEST		41	OISIN 2 V	180
IN THE TREE ROOTS, AND ALL THE SACRED FLOCKS		75	ANASHU VIJAYA	88
IN THE TREE ROOTS, AND ALL THY SACRED FLOCKS		75	ANASHU VIJAYA	88
A PARROT SWAYS UPON A TREE,		77	INDIAN TO LOVE	4
A PARROT SWAYING ON A TREE,		77	INDIAN TO LOVE V	4
FROM POND AND FALLEN TREE—ME SING		85	MAD KING GOLL V	63
SHE BID ME TAKE LOVE EASY, AS THE LEAVES GROW ON THE TREE;		90	SALLEY GARDENS	3
UPON A SWORD, A FIR TREE ON A HILL,		104	FERGUS DRUID V	34
NEAR TO CUCHULLIN, ROUND A QUICKEN TREE,		111	CUCHULAIN SEA V	81A
AND TEN BY TEN UNDER A QUICKEN TREE,		111	CUCHULAIN SEA V	81A

```
                                                      PAGE   TITLE        LINE
TREE   (CONTINUED)
   UNDER A BROKEN TREE  . . . . . . . . . . . . . . .  131 OLD PENSIONER       2
   UPON A BROKEN TREE,  . . . . . . . . . . . . . . .  131 OLD PENSIONER      14
   GREEN OAK AND POPLAR TREE!  . . . . . . . . . . .   132 OLD PENSIONER  V   16
   THE HOLY TREE IS GROWING THERE!  . . . . . . . . .  134 TWO TREES           2
   I HAVE BEEN A HAZEL TREE, AND THEY HUNG  . . . . .  177 PAST GREATNESS V    3
   TILL IT DIED OUT WHERE AN OLD THORN TREE STOOD. . . 186 QUEEN MAEVE    V  129
   A YEW TREE WHERE HIS BODY LAY, . . . . . . . . . .  197 BAILE AILLINN  V  188
   HUM IN THE LIME TREE FLOWERS! AND PUT AWAY . . . .  198 SEVEN WOODS         3
   OUR COURAGE BREAKS LIKE AN OLD TREE IN A BLACK,WIND AND 207 HANRAHANS SONG  3
      DIES,
   LET THE BIRDS SCATTER, FOR THE TREE IS BROKEN,  . . 250 SHADOW WATER B    584
   WHO HAS SEEN A GARDEN IMAGE OR TWISTED TREE  . . .  279 TWO KINGS      V  45B
   I STAGGERED, BUT A BEECH TREE STAYED MY FALL, . . . 286 TWO KINGS      V  209
   AND SO TO THE OTHER TREE AT A BOUND. . . . . . . .  318 APPOINTMENT         7
   THE THORN TREE  . . . . . . . . . . . . . . . . .   350 HER PRAISE     V    T
   THROUGH THE SHAKING TREE . . . . . . . . . . . . .  359 TO A SQUIRREL       3
   HER FRIENDS BRING HER A CHRISTMAS TREE  . . . . . . 366 HER CHRIS TREE      T
   WE'VE CARRIED IN OUR TREE. . . . . . . . . . . . .  366 HER CHRIS TREE      3
   THE ROSE TREE  . . . . . . . . . . . . . . . . . .  396 ROSE TREE           T
   HAS WITHERED OUR ROSE TREE! . . . . . . . . . . .   396 ROSE TREE           4
   CAN MAKE A RIGHT ROSE TREE." . . . . . . . . . . .  396 ROSE TREE          18
   HAVE WITHERED OUR ROSE TREE! . . . . . . . . . . .  396 ROSE TREE      V    4
   MAY SHE BECOME A FLOURISHING HIDDEN TREE . . . . .  404 FOR DAUGHTER       41
   AND CUSTOM FOR THE SPREADING LAUREL TREE. . . . .   406 FOR DAUGHTER       80
   UNDER THE OLD WIND-BROKEN TREE, . . . . . . . . .   406 IN TIME OF WAR      3
   TREE, LIKE A SOOTY FINGER, STARTS FROM THE EARTH!  410 TOWER              19
   A PEAR TREE BROKEN BY THE STORM. . . . . . . . . .  424 ROAD AT DOOR   V   10
   NEITHER CATALPA TREE NOR SCENTED LIME  . . . . . .  435 NEW FACES           2
   O CHESTNUT TREE, GREAT ROOTED BLOSSOMER, . . . . .  446 SCHOOL CHILDR  V   61
   EVEN THE GREY-LEAVED OLIVE TREE  . . . . . . . . .  446 COLONUS PRAISE V   12
   UNDER A BROKEN TREE. . . . . . . . . . . . . . . .  452 HUMAN DIGNITY       8
   UNDER THAT VERY TREE. . . . . . . . . . . . . . .   457 SUMMER SPRING      12
   AND HAUGHTIER-HEADED BURKE THAT PROVED THE STATE A TREE, 481 BLOOD AND MOON 22
   AND HAUGHTIER HEADED BURKE THAT PROVED THE STATE A TREE 481 BLOOD AND MOON V 22
   A SYCAMORE AND LIME TREE LOST IN NIGHT . . . . . .  488 COOLE PARK 29  V    3
   IN THE RICH MIDNIGHT OF THE GARDEN TREE . . . . .   494 AT ALGECIRAS   V    5
   THE BURNING TREE  . . . . . . . . . . . . . . . .   499 VACILLATION    V    T
   A TREE THERE IS THAT FROM ITS TOPMOST BOUGH  . . .  500 VACILLATION        11
   BUT A BIRCH TREE STOOD MY JACK! . . . . . . . . .   508 JANE BISHOP    V   20
   STAMPED BOY AND TREE UPON SICILIAN COIN. . . . . .  541 PARN FUNERAL 1     15
   WHAT HAPPENS A TREE THAT HAS NOTHING WITHIN IT?  .  548 TO SAME TUNE 3     23
   WHAT HAPPENS TO A TREE THAT HAS NOTHING WITHIN IT?  548 TO SAME TUNE 3 V   23
   WHAT TEARS DOWN A TREE THAT HAS NOTHING WITHIN IT?  615 MARCH SONGS 2      23
   WHAT TEARS DOWN A TREE HAS NOTHING WITHIN IT?  . .  615 MARCH SONGS 2  V   23
   CAME AND WERE GONE.  HE LEANT UPON A TREE  . . . .  634 CUCHULAIN COMF      5
   WHEN THE TREE WAS O'ER-APPLED  . . . . . . . . . .  654 ISLE STAT I 2      60
   AND I SANG ROUND THE TREE  . . . . . . . . . . . .  654 ISLE STAT I 2      66
   AND I SANG ROUND THE TREE, . . . . . . . . . . . .  654 ISLE STAT I 2      76
   AND I SANG ROUND THE TREE, . . . . . . . . . . . .  655 ISLE STAT I 2      80
   TWO CAME, HIS NAME AND MINE ON MANY A TREE . . . .  662 ISLE STAT II 2     10
   AN OWL, WHO IN AN ALDER TREE . . . . . . . . . . .  670 ISLE STAT II 3    115
   UNDER A LEMON TREE BESIDE YOUR DOOR! . . . . . . .  693 MOSADA 1           68
   PUFFED LIKE PUFF-BALLS ON A TREE, . . . . . . . .   727 LOVERS QUARREL     37
   THE DANAAN QUICKEN TREE . . . . . . . . . . . . .   742 DANAAN QUICK        T
   (AH, MOURNFUL DANAAN QUICKEN TREE!) . . . . . . .   742 DANAAN QUICK        6
   (AH, MOURNFUL DANAAN QUICKEN TREE!) . . . . . . .   743 DANAAN QUICK       12
   (AH, MOURNFUL DANAAN QUICKEN TREE!) . . . . . . .   743 DANAAN QUICK       18
   (AH, MOURNFUL DANAAN QUICKEN TREE!) . . . . . . .   743 DANAAN QUICK       24
   (AH, MOURNFUL DANAAN QUICKEN TREE!) . . . . . . .   743 DANAAN QUICK       30
   OF THE GOLDEN APPLE TREE! . . . . . . . . . . . .   771 SPINNING SONG       9
   THE WELL AND THE TREE . . . . . . . . . . . . . .   780 WELL AND TREE  V    T
   CRIES OUT THE LEAFLESS TREE, . . . . . . . . . . .  780 WELL AND TREE      10
   A WITHERED TREE?" . . . . . . . . . . . . . . . .   780 WELL AND TREE      16
   THE WICKED HAWTHORN TREE. . . . . . . . . . . . .   788 HAWTHORN TREE  V    T
   SAID THE WICKED, CROOKED, HAWTHORN TREE! . . . . .  788 HAWTHORN TREE       6
   SAID THE WICKED, CROOKED, HAWTHORN TREE. . . . . .  788 HAWTHORN TREE      14
TREES     SEE OLIVE-TREES THORN-TREES BEECH-TREES HAZEL-TREES ROOF-TREES POPLAR-TREES
          ASH-TREES
   THE MIST-DROPS HUNG ON THE FRAGRANT TREES, . . . .    2 OISIN 1        V   7F
   THE REASON OF THE TREMBLING TREES! . . . . . . . .   14 OISIN 1           179
   WHERE TREES MADE SUDDEN CAVERN-GLOOMS  . . . . . .   16 OISIN 1        V 224B
   A STORM OF BIRDS IN THE ASIAN TREES  . . . . . . .   27 OISIN 1           416
   THAT SPRANG UNDER THE SEVEN HAZEL TREES, . . . . .   35 OISIN 2            84
   AT EMAN, 'NEATH THE BEECH TREES, ON EACH SIDE, . .   44 OISIN 2        V  228
   GREY SAND ON THE GREEN OF THE GRASSES AND OVER THE DRIPPING 48 OISIN 3    14
      TREES,
   BUT THE TREES GREW TALLER AND CLOSER, . . . . . .   48 OISIN 3            17
   GREY SANDS ON THE GREEN OF THE GRASSES AND OVER THE 48 OISIN 3        V   14
      DRIPPING TREES,
   BUT TALLER THE TREES GREW AND CLOSER, . . . . . .   48 OISIN 3        V   17
   OF HOLLIES, AND HAZELS, AND OAK TREES, A VALLEY WAS SLOPING 48 OISIN 3 V  26
      AWAY
   GREY SAND ON THE GREEN OF THE GRASSES AND OVER THE DRIPPING 57 OISIN 3   142
      TREES,
   GREY SANDS ON THE GREEN OF THE GRASSES AND OVER THE 57 OISIN 3       V  142
      DRIPPING TREES,
   I PASSED ALONG THE WATER'S EDGE BELOW THE HUMID TREES, . . 76 INDIAN ON GOD 1
   ARISE THE LEOPARD-COLOURED TREES! . . . . . . . .   84 MAD KING GOLL      40
   SHE BID ME TAKE LOVE EASY, AS THE LEAVES GROW ON THE TREES! 90 SALLEY GARDENS V 3
   THIS LADY BY THE TREES"! . . . . . . . . . . . . .  123 DREAM OF DEATH V   10
```

TREES   (CONTINUED)
    THE ROAD-SIDE TREES KEEP MURMURING-- . . . .   131 OLD PENSIONER   V   13
    THE TWO TREES . . . .   134 TWO TREES   T
    OF PASSIONATE MEN, LIKE BATS IN THE DEAD TREES! . . . .   136 TO SOME I TALK   5
    THE OLD BROWN THORN TREES BREAK IN TWO HIGH OVER CUMANN'S   206 HANRAHANS SONG V   1
        STRAND.
    O HEAVY SWOLLEN WATERS, BRIM THE FALL OF THE OAK TREES,   207 HANRAHANS SONG V   11
    WERE TWISTED LIKE THE OLD THORN TREES . . . .   208 OLD MEN ADMIRE V   5
    O HURRY WHERE BY WATER AMONG THE TREES . . . .   210 RAGGED WOOD   1
    O HURRY TO THE WATER AMID THE TREES. . . . .   210 RAGGED WOOD   1
    O HURRY WHERE BY WATER AMONG TREES, ...   210 RAGGED WOOD   V   1
    O HURRY TO THE WATER AMID THE TREES, ...   211 RAGGED WOOD   V   5
    WHERE BY OLD THORN TREES THAT MAN STOOD! . . . .   274 GREY ROCK   V   80
    HE HAD BUT GAZED ON THORN TREES, SPOKE! . . . .   274 GREY ROCK   V   82
    A CLUMP OF BEECH TREES MADE AN EMPTY SPACE . . . . . .   277 TWO KINGS   V   4A
    AND WHERE BEECH TREES HAD MIXED A PALE GREEN LIGHT . .   277 TWO KINGS   V   4
    CLOSE TO A CLUMP OF BEECH TREES IN THE WOOD . . . . .   283 TWO KINGS   V 135
    WESTWARD OF TARA, AMONG THE HAZEL TREES-- . . . . . .   283 TWO KINGS   V 135
    AMONG THE STONES AND THORN TREES, UNDER MORNING LIGHT,   291 PAUDEEN   V   3
    THE TREES ARE IN THEIR AUTUMN BEAUTY, ...   322 SWANS AT COOLE   1
    WERE LOVED BY HIM! THE OLD STORM-BROKEN TREES . . . .   326 ROBERT GREGORY   50
    AND ALIGHT AT THE COMELY TREES AND THE LAWN, ...   330 BONE OF A HARE   4
    IN ONE ANOTHER'S ARMS, BIRDS IN THE TREES . . . . . .   407 SAIL BYZANTIUM   2
    FROM RUIN OR FROM ANCIENT TREES, ...   410 TOWER   23
    GLITTERING AMONG GREY-LEAVED OLIVE TREES, ...   447 COLONUS PRAISE V   21
    SEEMED ONCE MORE DEAR THAN LIFE! ANCESTRAL TREES, . .   491 COOLE BALLYLEE   34
    IN THE RICH MIDNIGHT OF THE GARDEN TREES . . . . . .   494 AT ALGECIRAS   5
    STRETCH TOWARDS THE MOONLESS MIDNIGHT OF THE TREES, .   579 DOR WELLESLEY   1
    THAT PLUCKS THE TREES FOR BREAD? . . . .   621 JOHN KINSELLA   34
    BECAUSE WE LOVE BARE HILLS AND STUNTED TREES . . . .   621 HOUND VOICE   1
    YON WIND GOES SADLY, AND THE GRASS AND TREES . . . .   652 ISLE STAT I 2   10
    WITH ROLLING FIRE, BEYOND THE HIGH TREES TURBANED . .   656 ISLE STAT I 3   32
    HE CARVED ON TREES, AND WITH A SUN-DRY WEED . . . . .   659 ISLE STAT II 1   8
    THE LIGHT IS DANCING O'ER THE KNOTTED TREES, ...   662 ISLE STAT II 2   2
    THIS HEARD I WHERE AMONG THE APPLE TREES, ...   686 LIFE   19
    WHERE SHADOW OF CHERRY, AND SHADOW OF APPLE TREES, . .   710 FERENCZ RENYI   23
    HE NUMBERS. HE, WITH FLOWERING CURRANT TREES, . . .   710 FERENCZ RENYI   V   22
    NOON WRAPT THE TREES IN VEILS OF VIOLET WEATHER, . . .   715 DWELT SYCAMORE   7
    HAVE NOT A MYRIAD SWAYED BELOW STRANGE TREES . . . .   724 KANVA ON SELF   11
    HE'D SLEPT AMONG THE SINGING TREES, ...   728 PRIEST FAIRY   17
    WATCHED OF PLACID POPLAR TREES. . . . .   732 STREET DANCERS V   16
    THIS HEARD I WHERE, AMID THE APPLE TREES, ...   735 QUATRAIN APHOR   17
    THIS HEARD I WHERE AMONG THE APPLE TREES, ...   735 QUATRAIN APHOR   19
    AMONG GREAT TREES, AND IN THE WINGS OF OWLS, ...   762 SHADOW WATER A   285
TREE-WRAPT
    WHOSE DWELLING WAS A TREE-WRAPT ISLAND, LULLED . . . .   693 MOSADA 1   79
TREFOIL
    BUT NEVER SAW THE TREFOIL STAINED WITH BLOOD, ...   487 SEVEN SAGES   19
TREMBLE   SEE A-TREMBLE
    "WHY DO YOU TREMBLE THUS FROM FEET TO CROWN?" . . . .   106 CUCHULAIN SEA   V   13
    AND TREMBLE WITH THEIR LOVE AND KISS. . . . .   196 BAILE AILLINN   169
    THE SOUL BEGINS TO TREMBLE INTO STILLNESS, ...   374 PHASES OF MOON   54
    I TREMBLE TO THE BONE. . . . .   511 JANE AND JACK   2
    NOR TREMBLE TO ITS FALL. THE FIRE SWEEPS ROUND . . .   689 NETTLESHIP   11
    HER EYELIDS TREMBLE AND THE WHITE FOAM FADES! . . . .   761 SHADOW WATER A   264
TREMBLED
    TREMBLED AND GASPED AND SHOULD HAVE RUN . . . .   303 HOUR DAWN   V   22
    UNTIL I CRIED AND TREMBLED AND ROCKED TO AND FRO, . .   316 COLD HEAVEN   8
TREMBLES
    HIM WHO TREMBLES BEFORE THE FLAME AND THE FLOOD, . . .   158 TO HIS HEART   3
    WHO TREMBLES BEFORE THE FLAME AND THE FLOOD, ...   158 TO HIS HEART   V   3
    THAT TREMBLES AND RESOUNDS WITH HYMNS TO THEE, . . .   684 SEEKER   V 69C
    TREMBLES AS A BELL OF GLASS . . . .   705 DAWN-SONG   10
TREMBLING   SEE EVER-TREMBLING
    AND THEY WERE TREMBLING CEASELESSLY, ...   13 OISIN 1   173
    THE REASON OF THE TREMBLING TREES! . . . .   14 OISIN 1   179
    TWO WALLS, A ROOF, A FLOOD! THERE TREMBLING GREEN . .   31 OISIN 2   V   32
    WITH BOWED HEAD, TREMBLING WHEN THE WHITE BLADE SHONE.   38 OISIN 2   137
    TREMBLING, ON THE FLAGS WE FALL. . . . .   43 OISIN 2   V 208E
    ARE BOWED IN SORROW UNDER THEIR TREMBLING LIDS, . . .   79 EPHEMERA   V   2
    THIS BODY TREMBLING LIKE A WIND-BLOWN REED. . . . . .   103 FERGUS DRUID   25
    AND ALL THE TREMBLING FLOWERS THEY BEAR. . . . . . .   134 TWO TREES   4
    BE YOU STILL, BE YOU STILL, TREMBLING HEART! . . . .   158 TO HIS HEART   1
    AND IN THE TREMBLING BLUE-GREEN OF THE SKY . . . . .   206 ADAMS CURSE   30
    TREMBLING IN THE BLUE HEAVENS LIKE A WHITE FAWN . . .   251 SHADOW WATER B   611
    AND TREMBLING WITH HER PASSION SAID, ...   272 GREY ROCK   31
    UPON HIS TREMBLING HORSE, THEN DROVE THE SPUR! . . .   277 TWO KINGS   11
    TREMBLING BENEATH HIM, AND THEN DROVE THE SPUR . . .   277 TWO KINGS   V   11
    STOOD ON MY PATH. TREMBLING FROM HEAD TO FOOT . . .   283 TWO KINGS   151
    STOOD ON MY PATH. TREMBLING FROM HAND TO FOOT . . .   283 TWO KINGS   V 151
    MY BLENCHING AND TREMBLING, ...   532 FIRST CONFESS   4
    THE TREMBLING OF THE APPLE AND THE YEW, ...   555 RIBH AT TOMB   18
    "PRAY FOR THE SOULS IN PURGATORY," THE PALE PRIEST   719 PHANTOM SHIP   31
        TREMBLING CRIES.
    TREMBLING IN THE BLUE HEAVENS LIKE A WHITE FAWN . . .   769 SHADOW WATER A   427
TREMENDOUS
    A TRAMPING OF TREMENDOUS FEET, ...   85 MAD KING GOLL   54
    THE TRAMPING OF TREMENDOUS FEET. . . . .   85 MAD KING GOLL   V   54
TREMULOUS
    TO SHORES BY THE WASH OF THE TREMULOUS TIDE, ...   8 OISIN 1   81
    AND A SAD MOUTH, THAT FEAR MADE TREMULOUS . . . . .   34 OISIN 2   71

TRESS
AND THEY SIGH IF THE WIND BUT LIFT A TRESS! . . . . . 151 OLD MOTHER 8
AND THEY SIGH IF THE WIND BUT LIFT UP A TRESS! . . . . 151 OLD MOTHER V 8
AND BIND UP EVERY WANDERING TRESS! . . . . . . 157 BELOVED RHYMES 2
THAT MEN THRESHED CORN AT MIDNIGHT BY A TRESS, ... 170 SECRET ROSE 26
A LITTLE STOLEN TRESS. I, TOO, AWAIT . . . . . 170 SECRET ROSE 27
HER FEATURES WHEN A TRESS . . . . 363 DOLLS DRAWINGS 5
MERELY TO LOOSEN OUT A TRESS . . . . 390 IMAGE PAST 26
TRESTLES
TWO HEAVY TRESTLES, AND A BOARD . . . . 421 MY TABLE 1
TRIAL
CASEMENT UPON TRIAL, HALF HIDDEN BY THE BARS, ... 601 GALLERY REVIS 3
TRIBE
THE FIRST OF ALL THE TRIBE LAY THERE . . . . . . 455 HIS MEMORIES 13
TRIBES
MINE WERE CLAN MORNA'S TRIBES UNTOLD, ... 81 MAD KING GOLL V 3
TRIBESMAN
LIKE SOME POOR ARAB TRIBESMAN AND HIS TENT. . . . . 491 COOLE BALLYLEE 40
TRIBUTE
WE CANNOT PAY ITS TRIBUTE OF WILD TEARS. . . . . 334 LIVING BEAUTY 10
TRICK
WE'LL KEEP THE SECRET--A NEW TRICK TO PLEASE. . . . . 265 ABBEY THEATRE 10
THEY TURNED A TRICK BY FORGERY . . . . 582 ROGER CASEMENT 7
THEY TURNED A TRICK OF FORGERY . . . . 582 ROGER CASEMENT V 7
TRICKLING
TRICKLING ALONG THE EARTH, I RAVE! . . . . . . 19 OISIN 1 V 281
TRICKS
FOR THEY ARE AT THEIR OLD TRICKS YET. A MAN . . . . 292 TO A SHADE 9
ALL TEETH WERE DRAWN, ALL ANCIENT TRICKS UNLEARNED, . . . 429 NINETEEN 19 17
LET THE NEW FACES PLAY WHAT TRICKS THEY WILL . . . . 435 NEW FACES 5
TRICOLOUR
BLESSING THE TRICOLOUR. "THIS IS NOT," I SAY, ... 601 GALLERY REVIS 10
TRIED
I HAVE KEPT MY FAITH, THOUGH FAITH WAS TRIED, ... 276 GREY ROCK 124
ARDAN, AND THOUGH I CALLED TO HIM AND TRIED . . . 283 TWO KINGS 142
ALL THOSE THAT MANHOOD TRIED, OR CHILDHOOD LOVED . . . 327 ROBERT GREGORY 91
TRIES
UNDER THIS HUMP. GOD TRIES EACH MAN . . . . . . 379 SAINT HUNCH 5
TRIM
WHO WERE NOT BORN TO KEEP IN TRIM . . . . 336 YOUNG BEAUTY 10
TRIMMED
AND TRIMMED WITH MANY A CRIMSON FEATHER! . . . . 15 OISIN 1 206
TRIMMED ROUND WITH MANY A CRIMSON FEATHER! . . . . . 15 OISIN 1 V 206
TRINE
BY OPPOSITION, SQUARE AND TRINE! . . . . 325 ROBERT GREGORY 39
TRINITY
BUT PURE AS A TALL CANDLE BEFORE THE TRINITY . . . . 208 HANRAHANS SONG V 14
RECALL THAT MASCULINE TRINITY. . . . . 556 RIBH PATRICK 2
RECALL HIS TRINITY. A FATHER, MOTHER, CHILD (A DAUGHTER . . 556 RIBH PATRICK V 2
OR A SON),
TRIP
AWAY MUST SHE TRIP! . . . . 559 HE AND SHE 4
TRIPLE
WHO HAS A LIKE VOW FROM THEIR TRIPLE DUN." . . . . 108 CUCHULAIN SEA V 38
WHO HAD A LIKE VOW FROM OUR TRIPLE DUN." . . . . . 109 CUCHULAIN SEA V 54
TRIPS
AS TRIPS THE SCARED MOON . . . . 559 HE AND SHE 3
AS TRIPS THE SACRED MOON . . . . 559 HE AND SHE V 3
FROM THEE I SNATCHED IT! E'EN THE FAY THAT TRIPS . . 670 ISLE STAT II 3 98
TRISTRAM
AS DID THAT WILD TRISTRAM KNOW . . . . 522 LULLABY 8
TRITON
A WEATHER-WORN, MARBLE TRITON . . . . 329 MEN IMPROVE 2
A WEATHER-WORN, MARBLE TRITON . . . . 329 MEN IMPROVE 17
TRIUMPH
IN TRIUMPH WITH HER ARMS AROUND ME, ... 9 OISIN 1 V 107
THAN TRIUMPH, TURN AWAY . . . . 291 TO A FRIEND 10
THE FOOL'S TRIUMPH, NOR YET . . . . 312 CHILD DANCING 7
WHAT'S GOOD OR BAD, OR WHAT IT IS TO TRIUMPH . . . 376 PHASES OF MOON 108
TRIUMPH THAT WE OBEY . . . . 382 VISION ROBART 16
IN TRIUMPH OF INTELLECT . . . . 383 VISION ROBART 31
FOR IF I TRIUMPH I MUST MAKE MEN MAD. . . . . . 411 TOWER 56
HAS BUT ONE COMFORT LEFT! ALL TRIUMPH WOULD . . . 429 NINETEEN 19 39
FOR TRIUMPH CAN BUT MAR OUR SOLITUDE. . . . . . 431 NINETEEN 19 78
HER TRIUMPH . . . . 533 HER TRIUMPH T
WOUND, WOUND, AND SHE MADE IN HER TRIUMPH . . . . 578 CRAZED GIRL 11
AS LIGHT OF TRIUMPH IN THY GOBLIN EYES-- . . . 674 ISLE STAT II 3 199
THEN GIVE ME TRIUMPH IN MY MANY PLOTS. . . . . . 722 WITCH VIVIEN 51
TRIUMPHING
WITH HER TRIUMPHING ARMS AROUND ME, ... 9 OISIN 1 107
"BUT IF YOUR MASTER COMES HOME TRIUMPHING . . . 106 CUCHULAIN SEA 12
TRIVIAL
FOR SOME TRIVIAL AFFAIR . . . . 293 HELEN LIVED 3
TOLD OF A HARSH REPROOF, OR TRIVIAL EVENT . . . . 443 SCHOOL CHILDR 11
THE TRIVIAL DAYS AND RAM THEM WITH THE SUN, ... 500 VACILLATION 21
TROD   SEE STAR-TROD
AND TROD SO SWEETLY PROUD . . . . 255 WOMAN HOMER 17
THAT WITH EMPOUNDED CATTLE TROD THE MIRE, ... 277 TWO KINGS 4
HITHER AND THITHER TO AND FRO THEY TROD . . . . . 278 TWO KINGS 26
TROD WITH A LIGHTER TREAD. . . . . 323 SWANS AT COOLE 18
HAD TROD THE UNEVEN ROAD. THEIR BOOTS WERE SOILED, . . 372 PHASES OF MOON 3

TROD   (CONTINUED)
    WHO TROD UPON THESE ROCKS OR PASSED THIS DOOR,   • • • •   413 TOWER   98
    BUT TROD THE ROAD, OR SPLASHED ABOUT THE SHORE,   • • • •   447 COLONUS PRAISE   27
    BUT TROD THE ROAD, OR PADDLED BY THE SHORE,   • • • • •   447 COLONUS PRAISE V   27
    FIRST TROD ON THE MOUNTAIN'S HEAD • • • • • • • • •   488 CRAZED MOON   9
    TARGETED, TROD LIKE SPRING.   • • • • • • • • • • •   504 QUARREL IN AGE   16
    NO PROUDER TROD THE GROUND, • • • • • • • • • • •   587 PARNELLITES   22
    I WANDERED AND TROD, • • • • • • • • • • • • •   654 ISLE STAT I 2   64
    BEFORE HER I TROD • • • • • •   654 ISLE STAT I 2   74
    WHO CAN HAVE TROD IN THE GRASS? • • • • • • • • • •   781 MY HEART BEAT   4
TRODDEN
    ARE TRODDEN AND BROKEN BY THE HERDS,   • • • • • • • •   190 BAILE AILLINN   43
    BUT FOR THE TRODDEN MIRE, THE POOL OF BLOOD, • • • • •   278 TWO KINGS   44
    THAT SHE MIGHT BE THAT SPRIGHTLY GIRL TRODDEN BY A BIRD;   353 HIS PHOENIX   4
    THAT SHE MIGHT BE THAT SPRIGHTLY GIRL WHO WAS TRODDEN BY   353 HIS PHOENIX   V   4
        A BIRD;
TROIA
    OENONE SAW THE FIRES OF TROIA LEAP,   • • • • • • • •   645 ISLE STAT I 1   17
    HOW HAVE THE YEARS IN TROIA FLOWN AWAY? • • • • • •   679 ISLE STAT II 3   309
TROLLED
    OUR MARRIED VOICES WILDLY TROLLED.   • • • • • • • •   85 MAD KING GOLL   59
    OUR MARRIED VOICE WILDLY TROLLED.   • • • • • • • •   85 MAD KING GOLL V   59
TROMBONE
    AND THE TROMBONE," CRIED HE,   • • • • • • • • • •   527 AM OF IRELAND   23
    "THE TRUMPET AND TROMBONE,"   • • • • • • • • • •   527 AM OF IRELAND   24
TROOP
    AND NOW STILL SAD OUR TROOP DREW NIGH   • • • • • • •   17 OISIN 1   V   247
    IN THEIR LONG LIVES? WILL YOU BE OF OUR TROOP   • • • •   225 SHADOW WATER B   72
    BE OF YOUR TROOP! AIBRIC BE ONE OF YOU • • • • • •   225 SHADOW WATER B   75
    IN THEIR LONG LIVES? IF YOU'LL BE OF OUR TROOP   • • •   225 SHADOW WATER B V   72
    YOU'LL BE AS GOOD A LEADER. BE OF YOUR TROOP! • • • •   225 SHADOW WATER B   73
    WHAT IS THERE BUT A TROOP OF ASH-GREY BIRDS   • • • • •   247 SHADOW WATER B   517
    THAT YOU MIGHT HAVE A TROOP OF FRIENDS, • • • • • •   273 GREY ROCK   58
    TO TROOP WITH THOSE THE WORLD'S FORGOT, • • • • • •   273 GREY ROCK   63
    "THE DANISH TROOP WAS DRIVEN OUT • • • • • • • • •   273 GREY ROCK   65
    OUTRODE HIS TROOP THAT AFTER TWELVE MONTHS' WAR • • • •   276 TWO KINGS   V   1
    THE RAGE-DRIVEN, RAGE-TORMENTED, AND RAGE-HUNGRY TROOP,   426 PHANTOM HATRED   11
    THE RAGE DRIVEN, RAGE TORMENTED, AND RAGE HUNGRY TROOP,   426 PHANTOM HATRED V   11
    AND DEAFENING MUSIC SHOOK THE LEAVES; A TROOP • • • •   537 HER VISION   13
    COME TOM AND DICK, COME ALL THE TROOP   • • • • • • •   582 ROGER CASEMENT   17
    BUT I'D A TROOP OF FRIENDS • • • • • • • • • • •   626 STATES HOLIDAY   6
    A NEW DAY'S TROOP OF WASP AND BEE • • • • • • • • •   646 ISLE STAT I 1   44
    A HORN! SOME TROOP OF ROBBERS WINDING GOES • • • • •   649 ISLE STAT I 1   110
    AND ONLY SHEEP HE LOVED OF ALL THE TROOP. • • • • • •   661 ISLE STAT II 1   61
TROOPER
    TROOPER BELABOURING TROOPER, BITING AT ARM OR AT FACE, • •   426 PHANTOM HATRED   12
    TROOPER BELABOURING TROOPER, BITING AT ARM OR AT FACE, • •   426 PHANTOM HATRED V   12
TROOPING
    THEY WEARY OF TROOPING • • • • • • • • • • • • •   118 CRADLE SONG   3
TROOPS
    HE AND HIS BEST TROOPS BACK TO BACK • • • • • • • • •   274 GREY ROCK   73
    THE OLD TROOPS PARADE, • • • • • • • • • • • •   496 MOHINI CHATTER   22
TROPHIED
    AND MINE WAS EVERY TROPHIED WALL, • • • • • • • • •   82 MAD KING GOLL V   4
TROPIC
    UNDER THE TROPIC SHADE, GREW ROUND AND SLOW, • • • • •   610 STATUES   18
TROTTED
    TROTTED BESIDE HIM IN A PLAYFUL MOOD. • • • • • • • •   715 DWELT SYCAMORE   4
TROTTING   SEE GLOBE-TROTTING
TROUBLE
    WHERE CARE CANNOT TROUBLE THE LEAST OF OUR DAYS, • • • •   27 OISIN 1   409
    TROUBLE HIS SLEEPING; GIVE HIM DREAMS OF ME. • • • • •   75 ANASHU VIJAYA   91
    ABOVE THE TIDE OF HOURS, TROUBLE THE AIR, • • • • • •   114 ROSE OF BATTLE   3
    AND ALL THE TROUBLE OF HER LABOURING SHIPS,   • • • • •   120 SORROW OF LOVE V   7
    AND ALL THE TROUBLE OF HER MYRIAD YEARS. • • • • • •   120 SORROW OF LOVE   8
    AND ALL THEIR TROUBLE DIES INTO ITS PEACE;── • • • • •   128 DREAM OF FAERY V   35
    IF THIS IMPORTUNATE HEART TROUBLE YOUR PEACE • • • • •   162 ASKS FORGIVE   1
    AND TROUBLE WITH A SIGH FOR ALL THINGS LONGING FOR REST   163 ASKS FORGIVE   23
    AND TROUBLE WITH SIGHS FOR ALL HEARTS WITHOUT REST   • • •   163 ASKS FORGIVE V   23
    THOUGH NOW IT'S HARD, TILL TROUBLE IS AT AN END; • • • •   200 FOLLY COMFORT V   5
    "WHAT IS THIS TROUBLE?" HE WOULD ANSWER NOTHING,   • • •   281 TWO KINGS   90
    THOUGH ALWAYS AT MY WORDS HIS TROUBLE GREW;   • • • • •   281 TWO KINGS   91
    SOMETHING HAS TROUBLED ME AND IN MY TROUBLE • • • • •   339 SHEP GOATHERD   10
    FOR RHYME CAN BEAT A MEASURE OUT OF TROUBLE • • • • •   339 SHEP GOATHERD   12
    TO TROUBLE THE LIVING STREAM. • • • • • • • • • •   393 EASTER 1916   44
    AND LATER HAD MUCH TROUBLE FROM A FOOL, • • • • • • •   404 FOR DAUGHTER   26
    ALL THAT GREAT PAST TO A TROUBLE OF FOOLS; • • • • • •   546 TO SAME TUNE 2   22
    ALL THAT GREAT PAST TO A TROUBLE OF FOOLS; • • • • • •   614 MARCH SONGS 1   22
    I TOOK NO TROUBLE TO CONVINCE, • • • • • • • • • •   624 APPARITIONS   3
    IN TROUBLE IS, THE DOE WILL LINGER NEAR. • • • • • •   713 FERENCZ RENYI   80
    AND THEN THE WHOLE WORLD'S TROUBLE WEEPS WITH YOU. • • •   738 YOU ARE SAD   12
    YOUR HEART'S DESIRE AND THE END OF ALL OUR TROUBLE; • •   755 SHADOW WATER A   175
TROUBLED   SEE MANY-TIMES-TROUBLED
    TROUBLED HER SONG. I DO NOT KNOW IF DAYS • • • • • •   30 OISIN 2   19
    TO HIDE FROM THE TROUBLED DAY. • • • • • • • • • •   166 BLESSED   V   4
    HAD TROUBLED HIS SLEEP. BUT ALL HE HAD TO SAY • • • •   182 QUEEN MAEVE   52
    THAT NO GOD TROUBLED NOW, AND, WONDERING • • • • • •   182 QUEEN MAEVE   60
    NOR THE COLD NORTH HAS TROUBLED?" HE REPLIED, • • • •   184 QUEEN MAEVE   90
    FACE DOWNWARD, TOSSING IN A TROUBLED SLEEP; • • • • •   185 QUEEN MAEVE   106
    MORE MIGHTY THAN THE STARS HALF TROUBLED ME, • • • • •   237 SHADOW WATER B   332
    MANY TIMES TROUBLED YEARS, • • • • • • • • • • •   315 FRIENDS   V   7

	PAGE	TITLE		LINE
TROUBLED (CONTINUED)				
SOMETHING HAS TROUBLED ME AND IN MY TROUBLE	339	SHEP GOATHERD		10
TROUBLED HIS ANIMAL BLOOD.	378	CAT AND MOON		8
O HEART, O TROUBLED HEART—THIS CARICATURE,	409	TOWER		2
SATISFIED IF A TROUBLED MIRROR SHOW IT,	430	NINETEEN 19		62
CONTENTED THAT A TROUBLED MIRROR SHOW IT,	430	NINETEEN 19	V	62
AND TROUBLED EYES CAME MORNING'S FIRST-BORN GLOW:	648	ISLE STAT I 1		103
MY EYES ARE TROUBLED BY THE SILVER ARROWS:	761	SHADOW WATER A		269
THAT THE VAST TROUBLED WATERS BRING	784	WOMANS BEAUTY		17
TROUBLES				
WHILE THE WORLD IS FULL OF TROUBLES	87	STOLEN CHILD		22
THOUGH NOTHING TROUBLES THE GREAT STREAMS	196	BAILE AILLINN		172
TROUBLES MY SIGHT: SOMEWHERE IN SANDS OF THE DESERT	402	SECOND COMING		13
TROUBLES MY SIGHT: A WASTE OF DESERT SAND:	402	SECOND COMING	V	13
REMOTE FROM ALL THE HARD EARTH TROUBLES.	731	PRIEST FAIRY		80
TROUBLING SEE WORLD-TROUBLING				
TROUBLING THE ENDLESS REVERIE.	65	HAPPY SHEPHERD		21
TROUP				
COME ALFRED NOYES AND ALL THE TROUP	582	ROGER CASEMENT	V	17
TROUSERS				
EVEN OUR BEAUTY WITH HER TURKISH TROUSERS ON.	364	DOLLS FACES		9
TROUT				
WE SEEK FOR SLUMBERING TROUT	88	STOLEN CHILD		32
AND HIS OWN SNIPE AND TROUT.	92	FATHER OHART		4
WITH HIS SNIPE MARSH AND HIS TROUT.	92	FATHER OHART	V	4
AND CAUGHT A LITTLE SILVER TROUT.	149	WANDER AENGUS		8
AND HOOKED A LITTLE SILVER TROUT.	149	WANDER AENGUS	V	8
IT'S CERTAIN THERE ARE TROUT SOMEWHERE	297	THREE BEGGARS		66
AND MAYBE I SHALL TAKE A TROUT	297	THREE BEGGARS		67
TROW				
SUCH QUESTS AS THESE, I TROW, NEED LITTLE WIT.	650	ISLE STAT I 1		150
OF GREEN ARCADIA DO NOT HIDE, I TROW,	651	ISLE STAT I 1		166
TROY				
TROY PASSED AWAY IN ONE HIGH FUNERAL GLEAM,	111	ROSE OF WORLD		4
NO SECOND TROY	256	NO SECOND TROY		T
WAS THERE ANOTHER TROY FOR HER TO BURN?	257	NO SECOND TROY		12
OF THE MEN AND WOMEN OF TROY,	293	HELEN LIVED		11
ANOTHER TROY MUST RISE AND SET,	437	SONGS PLAY 1		9
AND PUT ALL TROY TO WRECK—	455	HIS MEMORIES		16
AND PUT ALL TROY TO WRACK—	455	HIS MEMORIES	V	16
TROY BACKED ITS HELEN: TROY DIED AND ADORED:	547	TO SAME TUNE 3		4
TROY BACKED ITS HELEN: TROY DIED AND ADORED:	547	TO SAME TUNE 3		4
TROY LOOKED ON HELEN, IT DIED AND ADORED:	547	TO SAME TUNE 3	V	4
HECTOR IS DEAD AND THERE'S A LIGHT IN TROY:	564	GYRES		7
TROY BACKED ITS HELEN: TROY DIED AND ADORED:	614	MARCH SONGS 2		4
TROY BACKED ITS HELEN: TROY DIED AND ADORED:	614	MARCH SONGS 2		4
TRUE				
AND LOVED YOUR BEAUTY WITH LOVE FALSE OR TRUE,	121	YOU ARE OLD		6
AND LOVED YOUR BEAUTY WILL LOVE FALSE OR TRUE:	121	YOU ARE OLD	V	6
TRUE BROTHER OF A COMPANY	137	TO IRELAND		2
TRUE BROTHER OF THAT COMPANY	137	TO IRELAND	V	2
WHILE STILL I MAY I WRITE OUT TRUE	139	TO IRELAND	V	33
THAT IS BAD ENOUGH TO BE TRUE, IS TRUE,	191	BAILE AILLINN		69
THAT IS BAD ENOUGH TO BE TRUE, IS TRUE,	191	BAILE AILLINN		69
BUT IT IS TRUE. WHY DID THEY RUN UPON HIM,	243	SHADOW WATER B		424
OUT OF ALL RECKONING. IS IT NOT TRUE	244	SHADOW WATER B		467
IF SOMETHING THAT'S MOST FABULOUS WERE TRUE—	245	SHADOW WATER B		489
THAT IS NOT TRUE, FOR HE HAS PROMISED ME	248	SHADOW WATER B		552
SPEAK—HE WILL NOT DENY IT. IS THAT TRUE?	249	SHADOW WATER B		563
HE CANNOT CONTRADICT ME. IS THAT TRUE?	249	SHADOW WATER B	V	563
"IF THAT BE TRUE AS IT SEEMS TRUE,	295	THREE BEGGARS		20
"IF THAT BE TRUE AS IT SEEMS TRUE,	295	THREE BEGGARS		20
BUT WHEN, IF THE TALE'S TRUE,	346	ON WOMAN		29
TRUE SONG, THOUGH SPEECH: "MINE AUTHOR SUNG IT ME."	373	PHASES OF MOON		30
THE TRUE FAITH DISCOVERED WAS	440	WISDOM		1
BEING ALL BRIMMED WITH LIFE?" "WERE IT BUT TRUE	465	HARUN RASHID		90
WHAT TRUE LOVE BE?	510	JANE JUDGMENT		17
ALL TRUE LOVE MUST DIE,	517	HER ANXIETY		3
BIDS ALL TRUE LOVERS REST,	536	PARTING		6
WHEN YOU AND MY TRUE LOVER MEET	573	LADYS 3RD SONG		1
ALL HIS HAPPIER DREAMS CAME TRUE—	577	WHAT THEN		11
TO PROVE THEIR FORGERY TRUE:	582	ROGER CASEMENT		10
THOSE WORDS COME TRUE IN THE END	597	COLONEL MARTIN	V	69
AND MAYBE WHAT THEY SAY IS TRUE	631	POLITICS		9
WANDERS AND WAILS BEFORE MY HEART MOST TRUE	738	YOU ARE SAD		8
THAT MY TRUE LOVE WOULD COME IN A SHIP OF PEARL	763	SHADOW WATER A	V	315
WHERE TRUE LOVE WANDERS AMONG THE HOLY WOODS.	764	SHADOW WATER A	V	337
WHAT WERE TRUE LOVE AMONG THE RUSH OF HIS STREAMS?	764	SHADOW WATER A	V	338
TRUE-LOVE				
THAT MY TRUE-LOVE WOULD COME IN A SHIP OF PEARL	763	SHADOW WATER A		315
WHERE TRUE-LOVE WANDERS AMONG THE HOLY WOODS.	764	SHADOW WATER A		337
WHAT WERE TRUE-LOVE AMONG THE RUSH OF HIS STREAMS?	764	SHADOW WATER A		338
TRULY				
AH, YOU WILL KNOW MY LOVED ONE BY HIS HUNTER'S ARROWS	75	ANASHU VIJAYA		80
TRULY,				
TRUMP				
MAID NIAM FROM A LITTLE TRUMP	14	OISIN 1	V	194
OUT OF A LITTLE SILVER TRUMP:	15	OISIN 1		196
TRUMPET				
O: LAY THE SHRILLY TRUMPET DOWN,	212	BLESS PSALTER		4
MICHAEL WILL UNHOOK HIS TRUMPET	215	HAPPY TOWNLAND		41

837

TRUMPET (CONTINUED)
    TO KNOW WHEN MICHAEL'S TRUMPET CRIES . . . . 307 HOUR DAWN   100
    TRUMPET AND KETTLEDRUM, ... 317 NIGHT COME   9
    "THE TRUMPET AND TROMBONE," . . . . 527 AM OF IRELAND   24
    AND LIKE A SILVER TRUMPET RING. . . . . 736 SUMMER EVENING   4
    AND LIKE A SILVER TRUMPET RING. . . . . 737 SUMMER EVENING   20
TRUMPETER
    COULD TRUMPETER MICHAEL BE SO BRAVE?" . . . . 338 TOM OROUGHLEY   13
TRUMPETERS
    THE TRUMPETERS MIGHT BURST WITH TRUMPETING . . . . . 429 NINETEEN 19   22
TRUMPETING
    THE TRUMPETERS MIGHT BURST WITH TRUMPETING . . . . . 429 NINETEEN 19   22
TRUMPETS
    AND THE TRUMPETS ALL ARE BURST, ... 527 AM OF IRELAND   22
TRUMPET-TWISTED
    WHERE MANY A TRUMPET-TWISTED SHELL . . . . 13 OISIN 1   160
TRUNDLED
    LAST NIGHT THEY TRUNDLED DOWN THE ROAD . . . . 425 STARES NEST   13
TRUNK
    FORTH FROM THE HOLLOW ALDER TRUNK . . . . 670 ISLE STAT II 3   120
TRUST
    IN TRUST TOOK HE JOHN'S LANDS! . . . . 92 FATHER OHART   5
    THAT ALL MUST HANG THEIR TRUST . . . . 583 GHOST ROG CASE   16
    FROM POISON! FOR YOU CANNOT TRUST THESE MOORS. . . . 704 MOSADA 3   126
    I ALWAYS SAID YOU COULD NOT TRUST THESE MOORS. . . . 704 MOSADA 3   V 134A
TRUTH   SEE COUNTER-TRUTH
    GREY TRUTH IS NOW HER PAINTED TOY! . . . . 65 HAPPY SHEPHERD   4
    TO HUNGER FIERCELY AFTER TRUTH, ... 66 HAPPY SHEPHERD   24
    NEW DREAMS, NEW DREAMS! THERE IS NO TRUTH . . . . 66 HAPPY SHEPHERD   26
    AND DEAD IS ALL THEIR HUMAN TRUTH. . . . . 66 HAPPY SHEPHERD   34
    WITH THE EVER-LIVING. WHAT IF HE SPEAK THE TRUTH, . . 229 SHADOW WATER B   170
    THAT'S ALL WE SHALL KNOW FOR TRUTH . . . . . . 261 DRINKING SONG   3
    NOW I MAY WITHER INTO THE TRUTH. . . . . 261 COMING WISDOM   4
    WHERE, WHERE BUT HERE HAVE PRIDE AND TRUTH, . . . 262 STUDENTS AGIT   1
    IF BOOKS SPEAK TRUTH, IN SLIEVENAMON-- . . . . . 271 GREY ROCK   V 15
    NOW ALL THE TRUTH IS OUT, ... 290 TO A FRIEND   1
    DISCOVERERS OF FORGOTTEN TRUTH . . . . 324 ROBERT GREGORY   6
    IS THIS MY DREAM, OR THE TRUTH? . . . . 329 MEN IMPROVE   13
    A POET'S MOUTH BE SILENT, FOR IN TRUTH . . . . 359 WAR POEM   2
    WE POETS KEEP OUR MOUTHS SHUT, FOR IN TRUTH . . 359 WAR POEM   V   2
    A POET KEEP HIS MOUTH SHUT, FOR IN TRUTH . . . 359 WAR POEM   V   2
    JUST TRUTH ENOUGH TO SHOW THAT HIS WHOLE LIFE . . 373 PHASES OF MOON   22
    TRUTH FLOURISHES WHERE THE STUDENT'S LAMP HAS SHONE, . . 398 LEADERS CROWD   8
    TALKED OF HONOUR AND OF TRUTH, ... 431 NINETEEN 19   90
    WHERE GOT I THAT TRUTH? . . . . 439 FRAGMENTS   5
    MUST NEEDS NEGLECT! I CANNOT HIDE THE TRUTH . . . 462 HARUN RASHID   26
    MUST NEEDS NEGLECT, BUT CANNOT HIDE THE TRUTH, . . 462 HARUN RASHID   V 26
    "MY FRIENDS ARE GONE, BUT THAT'S A TRUTH . . . . 513 JANE TALK BISH   9
    I SAID THAT SHE HAD DANCED HEART'S TRUTH, . . . 514 JANE GROWN OLD   9
    I LONG FOR TRUTH, AND YET . . . . 533 FIRST CONFESS   7
    CAN MAKE THE TRUTH KNOWN. . . . . 575 ACRE OF GRASS   12
    TILL TRUTH OBEYED HIS CALL! . . . . 576 ACRE OF GRASS   18
    HER LOVE! TO HER WHO WEARS THAT BLOOM COMES TRUTH. . . 653 ISLE STAT I 2   46
    WITH YOU I AM ALL GENTLENESS; IN TRUTH, ... 669 ISLE STAT II 3   70
    SHALL GROW THY BEAUTY AND THY DREAMLESS TRUTH, . . 674 ISLE STAT II 3   207
    SO SHE MUST BURN, YOU SAY? SHE MUST IN TRUTH. . . 696 MOSADA 2   2
    IN TRUTH, AN EVIL RACE. WHY STRIVE FOR HER, . . 696 MOSADA 2   9
    THE BURTHEN OF THY TRUTH. REACH DOWN THY HANDS . . 698 MOSADA 2   53
    AND SAID, "YON BITTERN CRIES, IN TRUTH, ... 731 PRIEST FAIRY   75
TRUTH'S
    IN TRUTH'S CONSUMING ECSTASY, ... 139 TO IRELAND   42
TRUTHS
    OF ALL THOSE TRUTHS THAT ARE YOUR DAILY BREAD! . . 373 PHASES OF MOON   24
    TRUTHS WITHOUT FATHER CAME, TRUTHS THAT NO BOOK . . 467 HARUN RASHID   138
    TRUTHS WITHOUT FATHER CAME, TRUTHS THAT NO BOOK . . 467 HARUN RASHID   138
    SELF-BORN, HIGH-BORN, AND SOLITARY TRUTHS, . . . 467 HARUN RASHID   141
    EVEN THOSE TRUTHS THAT WHEN MY BONES ARE DUST . . 467 HARUN RASHID   144
    TRUTHS THAT WHEN MY VERY BONES ARE DUST . . . . 467 HARUN RASHID   V 144
    I HAVE MUMMY TRUTHS TO TELL . . . . 474 ALL SOUL NIGHT   86
TRY
    I BEAR A BURDEN THAT MIGHT WELL TRY . . . . . 380 SONGS FOOL 1   13
    O! SOLOMON! LET US TRY AGAIN." . . . . 389 SOLOMON WITCH   44
    SO THAT I HAD THE LIMBS TO TRY . . . . 515 JANE GROWN OLD   19
    I TRY TO LIFT MINE ARMS--THEY FALL AGAIN. . . . 701 MOSADA 3   56
TUB
    A LADLE AND A TUB OF BEER, ... 303 HOUR DAWN   29
    INTO THE SLEEPER'S TUB OF BEER . . . . 304 HOUR DAWN   47
    HE DIPPED HIS LADLE IN THE TUB . . . . 307 HOUR DAWN   107
TUCKED
    HAD TUCKED HIMSELF AWAY BESIDE . . . . 303 HOUR DAWN   28
TUFTED
    FROM THE TALL AND THE TUFTED REEDS . . . . . 143 HOST OF AIR   3
    O TUFTED REEDS, BEND LOW AND LOW IN POOLS ON THE GREEN 206 HANRAHANS SONG V   1
      LAND,
    LIKE TUFTED REEDS OUR COURAGE DROOPS IN A BLACK WIND AND 207 HANRAHANS SONG V   3
      DIES!
TUGGED
    HORN LOCKED IN SWORD, THEY TUGGED AND STRUGGLED THERE . . 277 TWO KINGS   18
TULIPS
    LIKE TULIPS IN THE AIR A-WINGING, ... 27 OISIN 1   417

```
                                                    PAGE      TITLE        LINE
TULLY'S
     AND HERE IS TULLY'S OPEN PAGE.  . . . . . . . . .    524 MAD AS MIST         9
TUMBLE
     AND TUMBLE OUT YOUR HAIR . . . . . . . . . . . .     312 CHILD DANCING       4
TUMBLED
     BEING TUMBLED AND BLOWN ABOUT . . . . . . . .        191 BAILE AILLINN      66
     TILL THAT BE TUMBLED THAT WAS LIFTED HIGH . . . . .  265 THESE CLOUDS        4
     HE STUMBLED, TUMBLED, FUMBLED TO AND FRO . . . . .   411 TOWER              61
TUMBLES
     THE NORTH WIND TUMBLES TO AND FRO . . . . . . . .    191 BAILE AILLINN      45
     THAT NORTH WIND TUMBLES TO AND FRO . . . . . . .     191 BAILE AILLINN  V   45
TUMBLING
     BEYOND THE TUMBLING OF THIS TIDE."  . . . . . . .      5 OISIN 1           49
     OR TUMBLING CLOUD."  . . . . . . . . . . . . .       349 HAWK              12
     "WHAT TUMBLING CLOUD DID YOU CLEAVE,  . . . . .      349 HAWK              13
     FROM CLOUD TO TUMBLING CLOUD, . . . . . . . . .      393 EASTER 1916       47
TUMULT
     BY KNOWING NOR TUMULT NOR HATE NOR STRIFE, . . . .     9 OISIN 1           95
     AND DROVE TUMULT AND WAR AWAY . . . . . . . . .       82 MAD KING GOLL      5
     THEIR HOOFS HEAVY WITH TUMULT, THEIR EYES GLIMMERING WHITE!  154 BELOVED PEACE   2
     AND TUMULT OF DEFEATED DREAMS; AND DEEP . . . . . .  169 SECRET ROSE        5
     DROVE TO THIS TUMULT IN THE CLOUDS! . . . . . . .    328 IRISH AIRMAN      12
     BECAUSE OF ALL THAT SENSELESS TUMULT, ALL BUT CRIED . . .  426 PHANTOM HATRED  15
     THUNDER OF FEET, TUMULT OF IMAGES, . . . . . . .     433 NINETEEN 19      120
     IN A GREAT TUMULT OF THE AIR, . . . . . . . . .      519 HER DREAM          6
     IN THE TUMULT OF THE LIMBS . . . . . . . . . .       777 SONG DEIRDRE 2     7
TUMULTS
     UNDER THE SHADOWS TILL THE TUMULTS DIED . . . . .     38 OISIN 2          140
     ON MY POOR BRAIN YOUR BUSY TUMULTS CROWD. . . . . .  648 ISLE STAT I 1    100
TUMULTUOUS
     AND WHEN TUMULTUOUS FEET ENWOUND ME . . . . . . .     83 MAD KING GOLL  V  20
     AND HIDING THEIR TOSSING MANES AND THEIR TUMULTUOUS FEET.  154 BELOVED PEACE    12
     AND HIDE THEIR TOSSING MANES AND THEIR TUMULTUOUS FEET.  154 BELOVED PEACE  V  12
     IN A TUMULTUOUS SONG"! . . . . . . . . . . . .       163 ASKS FORGIVE      20
     IN THIS TUMULTUOUS SPOT, . . . . . . . . . . .       420 MY HOUSE          23
     . . . THROUGH TORCHLIGHT AND TUMULTUOUS SONG! . . . .  459 FROM OEDIPUS      8
     . . . THROUGH TORCH-LIGHT AND TUMULTUOUS SONG! . . . .  459 FROM OEDIPUS  V   8
TUMULTUOUS-FOOTED
     AND A HUNDRED STEEDS, TUMULTUOUS-FOOTED, . . . . . .    8 OISIN 1        V  85A
TUNE
     THOSE MERRY COUPLES DANCING IN TUNE, . . . . . . .     3 OISIN 1           9
     AND FEET OF MAIDENS DANCING IN TUNE, . . . . . . .     3 OISIN 1        V  9
     AND THE DAYS PASS BY LIKE A WAYWARD TUNE. . . . .      8 OISIN 1          83
     WHERE THE VOICE OF CHANGE IS THE VOICE OF A TUNE, . . .   8 OISIN 1          82
     TO THE CRACKED TUNE THAT CHRONOS SINGS, . . . .       65 HAPPY SHEPHERD     9
     TO THE OLD CRACKED TUNE THAT CHRONOS SINGS, . . . .   65 HAPPY SHEPHERD V   9
     MURMURING, TO A FITFUL TUNE, . . . . . . . . .        85 MAD KING GOLL     52
     A MURMURING A MOUNTAIN TUNE, . . . . . . . . .        85 MAD KING GOLL  V  52
     MURMURING A MOUNTAIN TUNE, . . . . . . . . . .        85 MAD KING GOLL  V  52
     A DRUID LAND, A DRUID TUNE! . . . . . . . . .        139 TO IRELAND        32
     IN HER HEART SHE FOUND A TUNE, . . . . . . . .       160 CAP AND BELLS  V  26
     HEARING THE WHOLE EARTH CHANGE ITS TUNE, . . . . .   266 GALWAY RACES      12
     A NEW DANCE TUNE. . . . . . . . . . . . . .          378 CAT AND MOON   V  16
     THREE SONGS TO THE SAME TUNE . . . . . . . . .       543 TO SAME TUNE 1     T
     THREE SONGS TO THE SAME TUNE   SECOND SONG . . . .   544 TO SAME TUNE 1 V   T
     DOWN TO THE TUNE OF O'DONNELL ABU. . . . . . . .     544 TO SAME TUNE 1    10
     ALL THERE CAUGHT UP THE TUNE! . . . . . . . . .      545 TO SAME TUNE 1    15
     DOWN TO THE TUNE OF O'DONNELL ABU. . . . . . . .     545 TO SAME TUNE 1    20
     DOWN TO THE TUNE OF O'DONNELL ABU. . . . . . . .     545 TO SAME TUNE 1    30
     DOWN TO THE TUNE OF O'DONNELL ABU. . . . . . . .     546 TO SAME TUNE 2 V REF
     TIME FOR US ALL TO PICK OUT A GOOD TUNE, . . . . .   548 TO SAME TUNE 3    13
     O ANY OLD WORDS TO A TUNE. . . . . . . . . .         548 TO SAME TUNE 3    16
     DOWN TO THE TUNE OF O'DONNELL ABU. . . . . . . .     548 TO SAME TUNE 3 V REF
     TIME FOR US ALL BOYS, TO HIT ON A TUNE BOYS, . . . . 548 TO SAME TUNE 3 V  13
     LIFT, LIFT, LIFT UP THE TUNE. . . . . . . . . .      548 TO SAME TUNE 3 V  16
     STOOD, TOOK DEATH LIKE A TUNE . . . . . . . . .      613 MARCH SONGS 1     15
     MARCH WIND, AND ANY OLD TUNE, . . . . . . . . .      615 MARCH SONGS 2     25
     AND RATTLED OUT A TUNE! . . . . . . . . . . .        616 MARCH SONGS 3      9
     ALL THERE CAUGHT UP THE TUNE! . . . . . . . . .      616 MARCH SONGS 3     15
     AND RATTLED OUT A TUNE! . . . . . . . . . . .        616 MARCH SONGS 3     19
     AND RATTLED OUT A TUNE! . . . . . . . . . . .        616 MARCH SONGS 3     29
     WITH AN OLD FOUL TUNE. . . . . . . . . . . .         627 STATES HOLIDAY    38
     IN ALL ITS HONEY-THICKENED TUNE . . . . . . . .      736 SUMMER EVENING     7
     AN INTELLECTUAL TUNE, . . . . . . . . . . . .        743 WISDOM DREAMS      2
TUNE'S
     TWO SONGS REWRITTEN FOR THE TUNE'S SAKE . . . . .    550 SONGS REWRIT 1     T
TUNES
     AND AS IT FALLS AWAKENS LEAFY TUNES!-- . . . . . .   127 DREAM OF FAERY V  23
     OF SORROWFUL, AUSTERE, SWEET, LOFTY PIPE TUNES. . .  341 SHEP GOATHERD     57
     AND HE PLAYS TUNES BETWEEN YOUR FEET, . . . . . .    573 LADYS 3RD SONG     2
     THEY SANG, BUT HAD NOR HUMAN TUNES NOR WORDS, . . .  635 CUCHULAIN COMF    23
TUNNELLED
     AND THE ROOF FALLS IN OF HIS TUNNELLED HOUSE. . . .   27 OISIN 1        V 419
     AND THE ROOF FALLS IN OF HIS TUNNELLED HOUSE. . . .   28 OISIN 1          423
TURBANED        SEE VAPOUR-TURBANED
     WITH ROLLING FIRE, BEYOND THE HIGH TREES TURBANED . . .  656 ISLE STAT I 3   32
TURBULENCE
     BEING BY CALVARY'S TURBULENCE UNSATISFIED, . . . . . 318 MAGI               7
     IN GALILEAN TURBULENCE! . . . . . . . . . . .        438 SONGS PLAY 2       3
TURBULENT
     WHENCE TURBULENT ITALY SHOULD DRAW . . . . . . .     288 TO WEALTHY MAN    25
```

	PAGE	TITLE		LINE
TURBULENT (CONTINUED)				
A BOY'S TURBULENT DAYS	496	MOHINI CHATTER		13
TURF				
PILIN' THE WOOD OR PILIN' THE TURF, ...	96	MOLL MAGEE		45
A-PILIN' WOOD OR PILIN' TURF, ...	96	MOLL MAGEE	V	45
BESIDE A FIRE OF TURF IN TH' ANCIENT TOWER, . . .	324	ROBERT GREGORY		3
TURK				
HE SPOKE WITH TURK AND JEW, ...	594	COLONEL MARTIN		2
TURKEY				
WITH A STRUTTING TURKEY WALK, ...	627	STATES HOLIDAY		34
TURKISH				
CUT IN THE TURKISH FASHION, ...	363	DOLLS DRAWINGS		8
EVEN OUR BEAUTY WITH HER TURKISH TROUSERS ON. . . .	364	DOLLS FACES		9
TURN SEE DOWN-TURN				
AND TOSS AND TURN IN NARROW CAVES:	19	OISIN 1		281
IN PINCHING WAYS I TOIL AND TURN."	19	OISIN 1	V	282
AND HOW THOSE LOVERS NEVER TURN THEIR EYES . . .	29	OISIN 2		11
IN WHAT LAND DO THE POWERLESS TURN THE BEAK . . .	42	OISIN 2		198
SHALL THEY TURN WROTH OR PLUCK THE WINGS OF TIME? .	42	OISIN 2	V	199
"O FLAMING LION OF THE WORLD, O WHEN WILL YOU TURN TO YOUR REST?"	56	OISIN 3		129
O FLAMING LION OF THE WORLD, O WHEN WILL YOU TURN TO YOUR REST?"	56	OISIN 3		136
"OH, FLAMING LION OF THE WORLD, OH, WHEN WILT THOU TURN TO THY REST?"	56	OISIN 3	V	129
. . . AND OF OLD WOUNDS, AND TURN TO OUR REST. . . .	62	OISIN 3		212
TURN IF YOU MAY FROM BATTLES NEVER DONE, ...	114	ROSE OF BATTLE		7
"TURN IF YE MAY," I CALL OUT TO EACH ONE, ...	114	ROSE OF BATTLE	V	7
AND NO MORE TURN ASIDE AND BROOD	125	GOES FERGUS		7
FOR ALL THINGS TURN TO BARRENNESS	135	TWO TREES		29
ALL THINGS TURN TO BARRENNESS	135	TWO TREES	V	29
O HEART! O HEART! IF SHE'D BUT TURN HER HEAD, . .	200	FOLLY COMFORT		13
A GOOD ROUND SUM UPON THIS CRUISE, AND TURN-- . .	222	SHADOW WATER B		5
IT WOULD BE BETTER TO TURN HOME AGAIN, ...	222	SHADOW WATER B	V	12
THAT NEVER DID A HAND'S TURN? AIBRIC! AIBRIC! . .	228	SHADOW WATER B		130
WHY DO YOU TURN AWAY AND HIDE YOUR FACE, ...	244	SHADOW WATER B		461
YOU TURN AWAY. WHY DO YOU TURN AWAY?	246	SHADOW WATER B		507
YOU TURN AWAY. WHY DO YOU TURN AWAY?	246	SHADOW WATER B		507
AND SAW WHEREVER I COULD TURN	253	HIS DREAM		3
AND EVERYWHERE THAT I COULD TURN	253	HIS DREAM	V	3
SHADOWS AND SHOWS THAT CAN BUT TURN THE BRAIN." .	281	TWO KINGS		108
I WAITED TILL THE NIGHT WAS ON THE TURN, ...	283	TWO KINGS		144
YET COULD WE TURN THE YEARS AGAIN, ...	290	SEPTEMBER 1913		25
THAN TRIUMPH, TURN AWAY	291	TO A FRIEND		10
BEN JONSON'S PHRASE--AND STILL MAY TURN MY FEET .	321	REED WHISPERER	V	6
AS THOUGH DRIED STRAW, AND IF WE TURN ABOUT . . .	327	ROBERT GREGORY		83
WHEN HER SON'S TURN WAS OVER. SING YOUR SONG. . .	340	SHEP GOATHERD		42
AND THE DOWN TURN OF HIS WRIST	348	FISHERMAN	V	33
DUTIFUL HUSBAND, HONEST WIFE BY TURN, ...	376	PHASES OF MOON		99
A NEW DANCE TURN.	378	CAT AND MOON		16
AND NEW DANCE TURN.	378	CAT AND MOON	V	16
SHE WOULD HAVE TIME TO TURN HER EYES, ...	385	ROBARTES DANCE		10
AND THAT HE WILL TURN GREEN WITH RAGE	385	ROBARTES DANCE		16
HE, TOO, HAS BEEN CHANGED IN HIS TURN, ...	393	EASTER 1916		38
AND WHEN THAT ANCIENT RUFFIAN'S TURN WAS ON . . .	411	TOWER		66
AND TURN TOWARDS MY CHAMBER, CAUGHT	424	ROAD AT DOOR		14
I TURN AWAY AND SHUT THE DOOR, AND ON THE STAIR .	427	PHANTOM HATRED		33
ALL TURN WITH AMOROUS CRIES, OR ANGRY CRIES, . .	433	NINETEEN 19		123
NOR CRY, NOR TURN IN THE BED	435	FOR MY SON		3
I AM JEALOUS OF THE LOOK MEN TURN ON YOU	447	HERO GIRL FOOL	V	A
I HAD BETTER FIND A CONVENT AND TURN NUN:	448	HERO GIRL FOOL		11
"BECAUSE I MADE YOU TURN AWAY AND RUN FROM THAT YOUNG CHILD:	450	OWEN AHERNE		14
THE SECOND BEST'S A GAY GOODNIGHT AND QUICKLY TURN AWAY.	459	FROM OEDIPUS		12
THAN SOULS THAT START NO GAME AND TURN NO RHYME! . . .	464	HARUN RASHID		68
MY HEART COULD NEVER TURN FROM DAILY RUIN, ...	464	HARUN RASHID		83
I HEARD HER VOICE, "TURN THAT I MAY EXPOUND . . .	467	HARUN RASHID		132
THAT TURN DULL-EYED AWAY.	505	RESULT THOUGHT		14
TURN HATRED INTO SPORT, ...	506	REMORSE SPEECH		8
BUT TURN FROM ROSSES' CRAWLING TIDE.	549	SEVERED HEAD		5
I TURN THE PAGES OF MY HOLY BOOK.	555	RIBH AT TOMB		27
A DARKER KNOWLEDGE AND IN HATRED TURN	558	RIBH CHRISTIAN		14
I TURN ROUND	572	LADYS 1ST SONG		1
THEY TURN DOWN THEIR BEDS.	589	OLD WICKED MAN		35
TURN TO A DRUNKEN JOURNALIST!	626	OLD MEN BE MAD		4
I SAW HIM SIGH AND TURN AND PASS AWAY!	690	MOSADA 1		14
WERE HERE, HE WOULD TURN DEATH INTO A CRUTCH! . .	711	FERENCZ RENYI		38
LIFT THEIR CHINS AND TURN AWAY.	726	LOVERS QUARREL		24
ANOTHER LEADER, AND TURN HOME AGAIN.	748	SHADOW WATER A		16
BUT WOULD TURN HOME AGAIN. NO MAN HAD DOUBTS . .	749	SHADOW WATER A		38
AND TURN BRIEF LONGING AND DECEIVING HOPE	750	SHADOW WATER A		59
AND TURN HIS GALLEY ABOUT AND BRING ME HOME. . . .	751	SHADOW WATER A		108
SHE OFFERS GREAT REWARDS IF WE TURN EAST	755	SHADOW WATER A		169
MAY TURN FROM A STATUE	786	YOUR HEART		20
TURNED				
I TURNED IT IN MY HANDS: THE STAINS	24	OISIN 1		368
HOW SUCH A WARRIOR NEVER TURNED HIS GAZE	29	OISIN 2	V	11
HUNG IN THE PASSIONATE DAWN. HE SLOWLY TURNED: . .	40	OISIN 2		167
HUNG THE FRAIL LOFTIER CLOUDLETS. TURNED HE SLOW-- . .	40	OISIN 2	V	167
AND LONELY AND LONGING FOR NIAMH, I SHIVERED AND TURNED ME ABOUT,	60	OISIN 3		181

840

	PAGE	TITLE	LINE

TURNED   (CONTINUED)
I TURNED AND RODE TO THE WESTWARD, AND FOLLOWED THE SEA'S   60 OISIN 3   183
    OLD SHOUT
AND SHIVERING AND LONELY, AND LONGING FOR NIAM, I TURNED   60 OISIN 3   V 181
    ME ABOUT,
AND TURNED THE FARMER'S MEMORY FROM HIS CATTLE, ...   129 BOOK STORIES   6
WHEN NO ONE TURNED TO SEE . . . .   131 OLD PENSIONER V   2
"WHEN YOU WERE GONE, HE TURNED AND DIED . . . . . .   133 FR GILLIGAN   37
SHE TURNED AWAY! HE TURNED AGAIN TO SLEEP . . . . .   182 QUEEN MAEVE   59
SHE TURNED AWAY! HE TURNED AGAIN TO SLEEP . . . . .   182 QUEEN MAEVE   59
THAT HAPPIER BREATH HAD MOVED, HER HUSBAND TURNED . . .   185 QUEEN MAEVE   105
THIS LONG WHILE NOW! WE HAD NOT TURNED AGAINST HIM . .   225 SHADOW WATER B V 68B
THEIR HEADS BEING TURNED WITH PRAISE AND FLATTERY! . .   245 SHADOW WATER B 480
OF A NEW FRIEND HE HAS TURNED A GHOST. . . . . . .   275 GREY ROCK   103
WHAT TURNED SO GOOD A SHEPHERD FROM HIS CHARGE. . . .   339 SHEP GOATHERD   16
AND THOUGH I HAVE TURNED THE TALK BY HOOK OR CROOK . .   350 HER PRAISE   5
IF ON THE LOST, ADMIT YOU TURNED ASIDE . . . . .   413 TOWER   115
WE ARE CLOSED IN, AND THE KEY IS TURNED . . . . .   425 STARES NEST   6
WE ARE CLOSED IN, AND THE KEY TURNED . . . .   425 STARES NEST   V   6
WHAT MATTER THAT NO CANNON HAD BEEN TURNED . . . . .   429 NINETEEN 19   19
WHEN UPWARD TURNED, ON ONE SOLE IMAGE FELL! . . . .   471 ALL SOUL NIGHT   34
WHEN UPWARD TURNED ON ONE SOUL IMAGE FELL . . . .   471 ALL SOUL NIGHT V 34
BACK TURNED UPON THE BRIGHTNESS OF THE SUN . . . . .   489 COOLE PARK 29   30
I TURNED ABOUT AND LOOKED WHERE BRANCHES BREAK . . .   490 COOLE BALLYLEE   15
I TURNED ABOUT AND LOOKED WHERE BRANCHES BROKE . . .   490 COOLE BALLYLEE V 15
WHEN HE TURNED HIS HEAD . . . .   511 JANE AND JACK   16
WHEN YOU TURNED YOUR HEAD . . . .   511 JANE AND JACK V 16
HAD TURNED HIS STATELY HEAD. . . . .   526 AM OF IRELAND   10
WHAT HAS TURNED TO SMOKING WICK . . . .   529 TOM LUNATIC   5
HALF TURNED AND FIXED A GLAZING EYE ON MINE, ...   537 HER VISION   26
THEY TURNED A TRICK BY FORGERY . . . .   582 ROGER CASEMENT   7
THEY TURNED A TRICK OF FORGERY . . . .   582 ROGER CASEMENT V 7
IN ALL SUCH THINGS, PRAY LET THINE EARS BE TURNED, . .   660 ISLE STAT II 1   39
WE TURNED AROUND THE PLACE ALWAY, ...   667 ISLE STAT II 3   40
I AM! ONE SHOULDER TURNED AWRY—WHY THEN . . . . .   692 MOSADA 1   61
THEN TURNED HE FROM THE KING'S COURT. . . . . . .   742 EARL PAUL   65
YOU HAVE DONE WELL, BECAUSE MY BOWS ARE TURNED . . .   755 SHADOW WATER A 164
I HAVE TURNED HOMEWARDS. IN THE EYES OF THE GODS, . .   757 SHADOW WATER A 202
TURNIN'
THE LITTLE STRAWS WERE TURNIN' ROUND . . . . . .   95 MOLL MAGEE   31
TURNING
EVADING, TURNING! ONCE DID I HEW AND HEW . . . . .   40 QISIN 2   V 176
. . . SAILS TURNING TO THREADBARE RAGS! . . . . .   55 OISIN 3   118
. . . SAILS TURNING TO THREAD-BARE RAGS! . . . . .   55 OISIN 3   V 118
. . . TURNING AND TURNING GO, ...   57 OISIN 3   145
. . . TURNING AND TURNING GO, ...   57 OISIN 3   145
SING, TURNING IN YOUR CARS, ...   73 ANASHU VIJAYA   44
TURNING, HE SAW THAT SHE HAD THRUST DEAD LEAVES . . .   80 EPHEMERA   18
AND LAY IN THE DARKNESS, GRUNTING, AND TURNING TO HIS REST. 153 CHANGE BELOVED   12
TURNING AND TURNING IN THE WIDENING GYRE . . . . .   401 SECOND COMING   1
TURNING AND TURNING IN THE WIDENING GYRE . . . . .   401 SECOND COMING   1
TURNS
AND THE KINGFISHER TURNS TO A BALL OF DUST, ...   27 OISIN 1   V 418
AND THE KINGFISHER TURNS TO A BALL OF DUST, ...   28 OISIN 1   422
YET STILL SHE TURNS HER RESTLESS HEAD! . . . . . .   65 HAPPY SHEPHERD   5
THERE'S NOT A WOMAN TURNS HER FACE . . . .   131 OLD PENSIONER   13
THAT TURNS AND CHANGES LIKE HIS DRAUGHTY SEAS? . . .   265 ABBEY THEATRE   12
SHE TURNS THE DOLLS' FACES TO THE WALL . . . . .   363 DOLLS FACES   T
FAIL, AND THAT HISTORY TURNS INTO RUBBISH, ...   546 TO SAME TUNE 2   21
FAIL, AND THAT HISTORY TURNS INTO RUBBISH, ...   614 MARCH SONGS 1   21
TURNS INTO A QUESTION TILL . . . .   632 MAN AND ECHO   8
HE TURNS WHERE, HUNG LIKE DROPS OF DRIPPING GOLD, . .   710 FERENCZ RENYI   18
HE TURNS WHERE, HUNG LIKE DROPS OF LIQUID GOLD, . . .   710 FERENCZ RENYI V 18
AWAY HER CLINGING HANDS, AND TURNS. SHE THROWS . .   714 FERENCZ RENYI   102
HER OFF AND TURNS AWAY. SHE THROWS . . . . . .   714 FERENCZ RENYI V 102
TUUS
EGO DOMINUS TUUS . . . .   367 EGO DOMINUS   T
TWAIN
TO EAGLES TWAIN THAT, FULL OF ANCIENT PRIDE, ...   34 OISIN 2   V   73
HAS CLOVEN AND RENT THEIR HEARTS IN TWAIN, ...   66 HAPPY SHEPHERD   33
HAS TORN AND RENT THEIR HEARTS IN TWAIN, ...   66 HAPPY SHEPHERD V 33
FROM MORN THE TWAIN UNTIL THE EVENING PALES . . .   651 ISLE STAT I 1   161
THOSE TWAIN ARE DUST. WAKE! LIGHT AS A BEE SIPS . . .   678 ISLE STAT II 3 290
TWANGING
AND FEARED ALWAYS THE BOW-STRING'S TWANGING. . . . .   3 OISIN 1   V 7GG
'TWEEN
AND 'TWEEN HIS EARS, ABOVE HIS MANE, ...   2 OISIN 1   V 7AA
SHOUTED A MOMENT 'TWEEN THE EARTH AND SKY. . . . .   675 ISLE STAT II 3 237
TWELFTH
BECAUSE THE HERO'S CRESCENT IS THE TWELFTH. . . . .   374 PHASES OF MOON   47
BECAUSE THE HEROES' CRESCENT IS THE TWELFTH. . . . .   374 PHASES OF MOON V 47
TWELVE
OUTRODE HIS TROOP THAT AFTER TWELVE MONTHS' WAR . . .   276 TWO KINGS   V   1
AND WONDER WHAT HAS AILED HIM THESE TWELVE MONTHS." . .   284 TWO KINGS   163
HAS TWELVE KNIGHTS OVERTHROWN! . . . .   740 EARL PAUL   8
FOR HE HAD OVERTHROWN TWELVE KNIGHTS . . . . . .   741 EARL PAUL   43
OF THE TWELVE KINGS OF THE WORLD TO BE MY KING, . . .   757 SHADOW WATER A 214
AND HAVE BEEN WOOED BY THE TWELVE KINGS OF THE EARTH, . .   757 SHADOW WATER A V 214
I FOUGHT TWELVE BATTLES DRESSED IN GOLDEN ARMOUR. . . .   761 SHADOW WATER A 271
TWELVE-HOURED
I CRIED, "O NIAMH! O WHITE ONE! IF ONLY A TWELVE-HOURED   55 OISIN 3   113
    DAY,

841

		PAGE	TITLE		LINE

TWELVEMONTH
    MAYBE A TWELVEMONTH SINCE . . . . 348 FISHERMAN 25
    MAY BE A TWELVEMONTH SINCE . . . . 348 FISHERMAN V 25
TWELVE-MONTH
    MAYBE A TWELVE-MONTH SINCE . . . . 348 FISHERMAN V 25
TWENTIES
    ALL HIS TWENTIES CRAMMED WITH TOIL: . . . . 576 WHAT THEN 4
TWENTY   SEE SIX-AND-TWENTY FIVE-AND-TWENTY NINETEEN-TWENTY-NINE
    SENT FOR HIS DRUIDS TWENTY SCORE AND TEN, ... 110 CUCHULAIN SEA V 76
    WHEN THEY HAVE TWENTY YEARS: IN MIDDLE LIFE . . . . 229 SHADOW WATER B 156
    A BOY OF TWENTY YEARS:--A MOUND AND STONE . . . . 276 TWO KINGS V F
    AND AFTER TWENTY YEARS THEY LAID . . . . 360 ALF POLLEXFEN 6
    FIVE AND TWENTY YEARS HAVE GONE . . . . 360 ALF POLLEXFEN V 1
    AND SURELY AFTER TWENTY YEARS IT WAS TIME TO COME." . . . 391 UNDER SATURN 14
    THAT TWENTY CENTURIES OF STONY SLEEP . . . . 402 SECOND COMING 19
    I THOUGHT IT ALL OUT TWENTY YEARS AGO: . . . . . . 411 TOWER 64
    AND TWENTY MINUTES MORE OR LESS . . . . 501 VACILLATION 42
    SOME TWENTY FEET FROM TIP TO TIP HAD IT STRETCHED RIGHTLY 593 PILGRIM 17
      OUT,
    SOME TWENTY FEET FROM TIP TO TIP HAD ITS WINGS STRETCHED 593 PILGRIM V 17
      RIGHTLY OUT,
    FOR TWENTY MINUTES IN SOME STUDIO. . . . . 602 GALLERY REVIS 16
    WHAT IF MY GREAT-GRANDDAD HAD A PAIR THAT WERE TWENTY FOOT 622 HIGH TALK 2
      HIGH,
TWENTY-AND-EIGHT
    TWENTY-AND-EIGHT THE PHASES OF THE MOON, ... 373 PHASES OF MOON 31
    TWENTY-AND-EIGHT, AND YET BUT SIX-AND-TWENTY . . . . 373 PHASES OF MOON 33
TWICE
    AND TWICE A HUNDRED WERE THE VASSALS . . . . 23 OISIN 1 V 345E
    AND YET, TWICE BORN, TWICE BURIED, GROW HE MUST, . . . 374 PHASES OF MOON 48
    AND YET, TWICE BORN, TWICE BURIED, GROW HE MUST, . . . 374 PHASES OF MOON 48
    AND TWICE A THOUSAND MORE . . . . 401 DEMON BEAST 47
    GAME-BIRD, NOR WOMAN DOES THE SAME THING TWICE: . . 463 HARUN RASHID 60
    GAME BIRD, OR WOMAN DOES THE SAME THING TWICE: . . 463 HARUN RASHID V 60
    GAMEBIRD, NOR WOMAN DOES THE SAME THING TWICE: . . 463 HARUN RASHID V 60
    AND LOUDLY TWICE THE LIVING WINGS FLAPT WIDE, . . . 659 ISLE STAT II 1 12
    BUT THE MAN IS TWICE FORLORN, ... 776 AGAINST WITCH V 26
TWIG
    ALL KNOW THEIR TALE, ALL KNOW WHAT LEAF AND TWIG, . . 555 RIBH AT TOMB 7
TWIGS
    BUT THE RIGHT TWIGS FOR AN EAGLE'S NEST: . . . . . 288 TO WEALTHY MAN 36
    AND DROP TWIGS LAYER UPON LAYER. . . . . 415 TOWER 168
TWILIGHT
    IN THE POPPY-HUNG HOUSE OF THE TWILIGHT FLUTED: . . . 8 OISIN 1 V 83
    "JOY DROWNS THE TWILIGHT IN THE DEW, ... 18 OISIN 1 261
    OF TWILIGHT WHEN HE'S WEARY. . . . . 32 OISIN 2 V 50H
    OF TWILIGHT AND SLUMBER WERE GONE, AND THAT HOOFS . . 54 OISIN 3 112
      IMPATIENTLY STEPT.
    PIERCING THE TWILIGHT WITH THEIR MURMURING BARBS. . . . 72 ANASHU VIJAYA 28
    AND THE FLAME OF THE BLUE STAR OF TWILIGHT. . . . . 122 WHITE BIRDS 3
    AND SANG HOW DAY A DRUID TWILIGHT SHEDS . . . . . 126 DREAM OF FAERY V 7
    AND OF THE WAYWARD TWILIGHT COMPANIES . . . . . . 136 TO SOME I TALK 6
    AND OF THE WANDERING TWILIGHT COMPANIES . . . . . 136 TO SOME I TALK V 6
    AWAY, COME AWAY, TO THE DIM TWILIGHT. . . . . . . 140 HOSTING SIDHE V 8
    INTO THE TWILIGHT . . . . 147 INTO TWILIGHT T
    THE CELTIC TWILIGHT . . . . 147 INTO TWILIGHT V T.
    LAUGH, HEART, AGAIN IN THE GREY TWILIGHT, ... 147 INTO TWILIGHT 3
    DEW EVER SHINING AND TWILIGHT GREY: . . . . 148 INTO TWILIGHT 6
    AND LOVE IS LESS KIND THAN THE GREY TWILIGHT, ... 148 INTO TWILIGHT 15
    DROWNING LOVE'S LONELY HOUR IN DEEP TWILIGHT OF REST, . 154 BELOVED PEACE 11
    IN TWILIGHT SHAKEN WITH LOW SIGHS: . . . . 156 FORGOT BEAUTY V 10B
    THE TWILIGHT OF FORGIVENESS . . . . 162 ASKS FORGIVE V T
    AND COVER YOUR LIPS WITH ODOROUS TWILIGHT AND SAY: . . 162 ASKS FORGIVE 5
    COVER YOUR LIPS WITH ROSE-HEAVY TWILIGHT, AND SAY: . . 162 ASKS FORGIVE V 5
    THE ODOROUS TWILIGHT THERE. . . . . 163 ASKS FORGIVE 24
    THE ROSE-HEAVY TWILIGHT THERE. . . . . 163 ASKS FORGIVE V 24
    AND WHEN THE SECOND TWILIGHT BROUGHT . . . . . . 296 THREE BEGGARS 42
    UNDER THE OCTOBER TWILIGHT THE WATER . . . . 322 SWANS AT COOLE 3
    ALL'S CHANGED SINCE I, HEARING AT TWILIGHT, ... 322 SWANS AT COOLE 15
    AND MAY DEPARTING TWILIGHT KEEP . . . . 435 FOR MY SON 5
    AH! IT DWELT WITHIN THE TWILIGHT AS THE WORM WITHIN THE 718 PHANTOM SHIP 6
      NUT.
    THAT I WOULD SHED LIKE TWILIGHT OVER YOU. . . . . . 765 SHADOW WATER A 352
TWILIGHTS
    IN TWILIGHTS OF DEW AND OF FIRE." . . . . 168 BLESSED 40
    IN TWILIGHTS OF DEW AND FIRE!" . . . . 168 BLESSED V 40
TWIN-BORN
    WHAT ARE THE TWIN-BORN WATERS, ... 680 LOVE AND DEATH 15
TWINE
    UNMINDFUL OF ITS WOES, WOULD TWINE A WREATH . . . . 650 ISLE STAT I 1 133
TWINED
    THAT JUGGLING NATURE MOUNTS, HER COIL IN THEIR EMBRACES 556 RIBH PATRICK 9
      TWINED.
TWINKLING
    WITH A TWINKLING OF ANCIENT HANDS. . . . . 144 HOST OF AIR 24
    GROWS YOUNG AND A MAN'S HEART GROWS OLD IN A TWINKLING. 761 SHADOW WATER A 263
TWIST
    THE WEASEL'S TWIST, THE WEASEL'S TOOTH. . . . . . . 431 NINETEEN 19 92
TWISTED   SEE TRUMPET-TWISTED
    OUT OF THE MOON'S PALE TWISTED SHELL: . . . . . . 19 OISIN 1 279
    IT FELL, OR FROM THE TWISTED MOON . . . . 19 OISIN 1 V 278

TWISTED   (CONTINUED)
    SOME TWISTED, ECHO-HARBOURING SHELL, ...   66 HAPPY SHEPHERD   36
    WERE TWISTED LIKE THE OLD THORN-TREES . . . .   208 OLD MEN ADMIRE   5
    WERE TWISTED LIKE THE OLD THORN TREES . . . .   208 OLD MEN ADMIRE V   5
    WHO HAS SEEN A GARDEN IMAGE OR TWISTED TREE . . . . . 279 TWO KINGS   V 45B
    MY ARMS ARE LIKE THE TWISTED THORN . . . .   455 HIS MEMORIES   11
    UNTIL MY BEARD IS IN THE TWISTED LEAVES . . . .   683 SEEKER   44
    ONE SHOULDER TWISTED, AND THE CHILDREN CRY . . . . .   695 MOSADA 1   116
TWITTER
    AROUND THE TWITTER OF THE LIPS OF DUST . . . .   685 DRAWING-ROOM   1
    "AROUND, THE TWITTER OF THE LIPS OF DUST . . . . . .   735 QUATRAIN APHOR   21
'TWIXT
    THE HOST IS RUSHING 'TWIXT NIGHT AND DAY, ...   141 HOSTING SIDHE   13
TWO   SEE NINETEEN-THIRTY-TWO
    "WERE THESE TWO BORN IN THE DANAAN LAND, ...   12 OISIN 1   146
    BUT NOW TWO THINGS DEVOUR MY LIFE; . . . .   24 OISIN 1   358
    TWO THINGS THAT 'FORE ALL ELSE I HATE, ...   24 OISIN 1   V 359
    TWO WALLS, A ROOF, A FLOOD: THERE TREMBLING GREEN . . . 31 OISIN 2   V   32
    TO TWO OLD EAGLES, FULL OF ANCIENT PRIDE, ...   34 OISIN 2   74
    THOSE TWO CAME CARRYING WINE AND MEAT AND BREAD, . . .   41 OISIN 2   184
    . . . TWO CARRIED A SACK FULL OF SAND, ...   60 OISIN 3   185
    . . . THE SOUND OF TWO STUMBLING APART. . . . . . .   60 OISIN 3   V 184
    WITH WISDOM HOUR BY HOUR.--MAY WE TWO STAND, ...   71 ANASHU VIJAYA   7
    A CROSS THEY HAD MADE OUT OF TWO BITS OF WOOD, . . .   123 DREAM OF DEATH   7
    THE TWO TREES . . . .   134 TWO TREES   T
    TWO POEMS CONCERNING PEASANT VISIONARIES A CRADLE SONG 146 UNAPPEAS HOST   V   T
    TWO LOVE POEMS THE SHADOWY HORSES . . . .   154 BELOVED PEACE   V   T
    TWO POEMS BY O'SULLIVAN THE RED CONCERNING MARY LAVELL. 157 POET BELOVED   V   T
    FOR HAPPY LOVERS PASSED TWO BY TWO WHERE I STOOD; . . . 163 VALLEY LOVERS   2
    FOR HAPPY LOVERS PASSED TWO BY TWO WHERE I STOOD; . . . 163 VALLEY LOVERS   2
    WHO HAS BEEN BURIED SOME TWO THOUSAND YEARS? . . . .   181 QUEEN MAEVE   35
    UNTIL TWO LOVERS CAME OUT OF THE AIR . . . .   187 QUEEN MAEVE   143
    BAILE'S HEART WAS BROKEN IN TWO; . . . .   192 BAILE AILLINN   70
    ALTHOUGH HE IS CARRYING STONE, BUT TWO . . . . . .   192 BAILE AILLINN   83
    TWO SWANS CAME FLYING UP TO HIM, ...   194 BAILE AILLINN   135
    OR TWO SWEET BLOSSOMING APPLE-BOUGHS . . . .   195 BAILE AILLINN   153
    OR THE TWO STRINGS THAT MADE ONE SOUND . . . . . .   195 BAILE AILLINN   155
    OR TWO SWEET BLOSSOMING APPLE BOUGHS . . . .   195 BAILE AILLINN   V 153
    THOSE OTHER TWO: FOR NEVER YET . . . .   197 BAILE AILLINN   205
    THE OLD BROWN THORN-TREES BREAK IN TWO HIGH OVER CUMMEN 206 HANRAHANS SONG   1
        STRAND
    THE OLD BROWN THORN TREES BREAK IN TWO HIGH OVER CUMANN'S 206 HANRAHANS SONG V   1
        STRAND,
    WHOSE HEART WOULD BREAK IN TWO, ...   213 HAPPY TOWNLAND   2
    YET NEVER HAVE TWO LOVERS KISSED BUT THEY . . . . . .   229 SHADOW WATER B   153
    THE YEW-BOUGH HAS BEEN BROKEN INTO TWO, ...   241 SHADOW WATER B   394
    THE YEW-BOUGH HAS BEEN BROKEN INTO TWO, ...   241 SHADOW WATER B V   394
    THE YEW BOUGH HAS BEEN BROKEN INTO TWO, ...   251 SHADOW WATER B   593
    THE ROPE'S IN TWO--IT FALLS INTO THE SEA, ...   251 SHADOW WATER B   596
    SHALL BE ALONE FOR EVER. WE TWO--THIS CROWN-- . . .   251 SHADOW WATER B   605
    O SILVER FISH THAT MY TWO HANDS HAVE TAKEN . . . . .   251 SHADOW WATER B   609
    THE YEW BOUGH HAS BEEN BROKEN INTO TWO, ...   251 SHADOW WATER B   593
    THE YEW BOUGH HAS BEEN BROKEN IN TWO, ...   251 SHADOW WATER B V   593
    A SECRET BETWEEN YOU TWO, ...   259 UNWORTH PRAISE   9
    AND SAID, "IN TWO OR IN THREE YEARS . . . .   272 GREY ROCK   46
    I'D PROMISED HIM TWO HUNDRED YEARS, ...   275 GREY ROCK   98
    THE TWO KINGS . . . .   276 TWO KINGS   T
    TWO YEARS LATER . . . .   312 TWO YEAR LATER   T
    DARE MATCH IN LEARNING WITH US TWO, ...   333 SOLOMON SHEBA   21
    AND TWO OR THREE HAD CHARM, ...   350 MEMORY   2
    ANOTHER BOASTS, "I PICK AND CHOOSE AND HAVE BUT TWO OR 354 HIS PHOENIX   20
        THREE."
    WHEN TWO CLOSE KINDRED MEET, ...   378 CAT AND MOON   12
    TWO SONGS OF A FOOL . . . .   380 SONGS FOOL 1   T
    STRETCHED UP ON TWO LEGS FROM THE MAT, ...   381 SONGS FOOL 2   7
    AND RIGHT BETWEEN THESE TWO A GIRL AT PLAY . . . . .   383 VISION ROBART   21
    YET THE WORLD ENDS WHEN THESE TWO THINGS. . . . . .   388 SOLOMON WITCH   28
    TWO MEN HAVE FOUNDED HERE. A MAN-AT-ARMS . . . . .   420 MY HOUSE   21
    TWO MEN HAVE FOUND IT HERE. A MAN-AT-ARMS . . . . .   420 MY HOUSE   V   21
    TWO HEAVY TRESTLES, AND A BOARD . . . .   421 MY TABLE   1
    TWO SONGS FROM A PLAY . . . .   437 SONGS PLAY 1   T
    TOLD, AND IT SEEMED THAT OUR TWO NATURES BLENT . . .   443 SCHOOL CHILDR   13
    TWO SONGS FROM THE OLD COUNTRYMAN . . . .   454 EMPTY CUP   V   T
    TWO CONTEMPLATING PASSIONS CHOSE ONE THEME . . . . .   466 HARUN RASHID   117
    AND TWO LONG GLASSES BRIMMED WITH MUSCATEL . . . . .   470 ALL SOUL NIGHT   4
    TWO THOUGHTS WERE SO MIXED UP I COULD NOT TELL . . .   471 ALL SOUL NIGHT   31
    TWO GIRLS IN SILK KIMONOS, BOTH . . . .   475 EVA GORE-BOOTH   3
    TWO GIRLS IN SILK KIMONOS, BOTH . . . .   475 EVA GORE-BOOTH   19
    TO SING A SONG OR TWO, ...   515 GIRLS SONG B   2
    I BROKE MY HEART IN TWO . . . .   518 HIS CONFIDENCE   7
    TWO SONGS REWRITTEN FOR THE TUNE'S SAKE . . . . .   550 SONGS REWRIT 1   T
    BETWEEN TWO BARRELS AT THE INN. . . . .   551 SONGS REWRIT 1   10
    BETWEEN TWO BUSHES UNDER THE RAIN; . . . .   551 SONGS REWRIT 1   14
    TWO CHINAMEN, BEHIND THEM A THIRD, ...   566 LAPIS LAZULI   37
    AND THERE TWO BUSHES PLANTED . . . .   571 THREE BUSHES   59
    LOVE CRAM LOVE'S TWO DIVISIONS . . . .   573 LADYS 2ND SONG   12
    WE'D DRINK A CAN OR TWO; . . . .   606 SONGS BURDEN 1   22
    THAT ON TWO WHEELS RAN . . . .   628 JANE MOUNTAIN   14
    PROPPED UPON MY TWO KNEES, ...   628 JANE MOUNTAIN   19
    THERE IN A TWO HORSED CARRIAGE . . . .   628 JANE MOUNTAIN   V   13
    A BUNDLE OF LINEN. SHROUDS BY TWO AND THREE . . . . . 634 CUCHULAIN COMF   9

		PAGE	TITLE	LINE

TWO (CONTINUED)
- BETWEEN HIS TWO ETERNITIES, • • • • • • • • • • • • 637 BEN BULBEN 14
- SHE SLEEPS WITH OWLETS TWO AND TWO, • • • • • • • • 646 ISLE STAT I 1 34
- SHE SLEEPS WITH OWLETS TWO AND TWO, • • • • • • • • 646 ISLE STAT I 1 34
- I'D BE ALONE. WE TWO, BY THAT PALE FOUNT, • • • • • 650 ISLE STAT I 1 132
- BUT WIDE AWAKE HIS TWO EYES WERE. • • • • • • • • • 655 ISLE STAT I 3 7
- HE PASSED ACROSS THE LAKE. WHEN WE TWO CAME • • • • 658 ISLE STAT II 1 5
- OF HILL TWO SHEPHERDS COME. FAREWELL! I'LL DON • • • 659 ISLE STAT II 1 28
- TWO MEN WHO LOVE ONE MAID HAVE AMPLE CAUSE • • • • • 659 ISLE STAT II 1 30
- OF WAR. OF YORE, TWO SHEPHERDS, WHERE WE PAUSE, • • • 659 ISLE STAT II 1 31
- THIS THING WE ASK! MUST WE TWO FIGHT?--JUDGE THOU. • • • 660 ISLE STAT II 1 41
- TWO CAME, HIS NAME AND MINE ON MANY A TREE • • • • • 662 ISLE STAT II 2 10
- FOR, AH, OUR LIVES WERE BUT TWO STARRY WORDS • • • • 675 ISLE STAT II 3 236
- TWO LONELY SPIRITS WAIT, • • • • • • • • • • 680 LOVE AND DEATH 18
- TWO SPIRIT THINGS A MAN HATH FOR HIS FRIENDS! • • • • 686 DRAWING-ROOM 5
- THE TWO TITANS, • • • • • • • • • • • 687 TWO TITANS T
- TWO FIGURES CROUCHING ON THE BLACK ROCK, BOUND • • • 687 TWO TITANS 5
- WE TWO, BEFORE WE DIE! FOR AZOLAR, • • • • • • 691 MOSADA 1 24
- WE MEET--WE TWO. HOW MERRY ALL THESE ARE • • • 691 MOSADA 1 31
- TWO ONLY NOW THEY ARE, TWO SIDE BY SIDE. • • • • 700 MOSADA 3 49
- TWO ONLY NOW THEY ARE, TWO SIDE BY SIDE. • • • • 700 MOSADA 3 49
- MY SOUL SHALL TOUCH WITH HIS, AND THE TWO FLAMES • • • 701 MOSADA 3 61
- MY COMPANIONS, TWO AND TWO, • • • • • • • • • 705 DAWN-SONG 7
- MY COMPANIONS, TWO AND TWO, • • • • • • • • • 705 DAWN-SONG 7
- LADS AND LASSES, TWO AND TWO, • • • • • • • • 705 DAWN-SONG 15
- LADS AND LASSES, TWO AND TWO, • • • • • • • • 705 DAWN-SONG 15
- A LIZARD CRAWLS--THE TWO MEN GAZE INTENT, • • • 711 FERENCZ RENYI 47
- TWO WOMEN, WITHERED ONE AND SMALL AND THIN, • • • 711 FERENCZ RENYI 51
- BELOVED, HOW TWO LITTLE YEARS AGO • • • • • • • 713 FERENCZ RENYI 89
- THERE FAR AWAY FROM ALL WE TWO WILL GO, • • • • 714 FERENCZ RENYI 99
- FROM HAYNAU'S LIFTED FINGERS--TWO DRAW NIGH • • • • 714 FERENCZ RENYI 104
- ARE TWO RAGGED CHILDREN BRIGHT-- • • • • • • • 731 STREET DANCERS 4
- TWO SPIRIT-THINGS A MAN HATH FOR HIS FRIENDS-- • • • 734 QUATRAIN APHOR 5
- TWO SPIRIT THINGS A MAN HATH FOR HIS FRIENDS! • • • 734 QUATRAIN APHOR V 5
- AMONG THESE MISTY WATERS. TWO! NOW FOUR! • • • • 753 SHADOW WATER A 138
- TWO HOVER THERE TOGETHER, AND ONE SAYS, • • • • • 753 SHADOW WATER A 142
- O SILVER FISH THAT MY TWO HANDS HAVE TAKEN, • • • • 769 SHADOW WATER A 425
- BETWEEN TWO FURROWS UPON THE PLOUGHED LAND! • • • • 784 WOMANS BEAUTY 4

TWO-HORSED
- THERE IN A TWO-HORSED CARRIAGE • • • • • • • • • 628 JANE MOUNTAIN 13

TWOS
- CHILDREN SING IN TWOS AND THREES. • • • • • • • 732 STREET DANCERS 17
- THE FLIES THAT DANCE IN THREES, IN TWOS, • • • • • 736 IN CHURCH 11

TYING
- TYING THE HORSE TO HIS VAST FOOT THAT LAY • • • • 32 OISIN 2 46
- WE MOUNTED ON THE STAIR, THE WHITE STEED TYING, • • • 32 OISIN 2 V 46

TYMPAN
- AND SAW WHERE THIS OLD TYMPAN LAY • • • • • • • • 85 MAD KING GOLL 55

TYRANNY
- AT HUMAN TYRANNY, • • • • • • • • • • • • 131 OLD PENSIONER 10

TYRANT
- AND MADE THE TYRANT BOW. • • • • • • • • • 738 MOURN THEN ON 12

TYRANTS
- NOR TO THE TYRANTS THAT SPAT, • • • • • • • • • 414 TOWER 131

UDDERS
- WITH FAIRY-SMITTEN UDDERS DRY-- • • • • • • • 716 FAIRY DOCTOR 14

UGLINESS
- THEY SAY I AM ALL UGLINESS! LAME-FOOTED • • • • • 692 MOSADA 1 60

ULADH
- ON THE HEIR OF ULADH, BUAN'S SON, • • • • • • 189 BAILE AILLINN 4
- WHERE THE HOUND OF ULADH SAT BEFORE • • • • • 192 BAILE AILLINN 73
- NOR ULADH, WHEN NAOISE HAD THROWN A SAIL UPON THE WIND! 209 UNDER THE MOON 4
- OR ULADH WHEN NAISI HAD HUNG A SAIL UPON THE WIND! • • 209 UNDER THE MOON V 4

ULALU
- BUT LIFT A MOURNFUL ULALU, • • • • • • • • • 86 MAD KING GOLL 68

ULULU
- AND LIFT AN ULULU FORLORN, • • • • • • • • • 86 MAD KING GOLL V 68

UNAFRAID
- THOSE GLANCES UNAFRAID! • • • • • • • • • 516 MANS SONG 8

UNAGEING
- MONUMENTS OF UNAGEING INTELLECT. • • • • • • • • • 407 SAIL BYZANTIUM 8

UNAMBITIOUS
- A HUMOROUS, UNAMBITIOUS MAN, • • • • • • • • 361 ALF POLLEXFEN 25
- BECAUSE THE UNAMBITIOUS THAT HATE THE GODS • • • • • 754 SHADOW WATER A V 158

UNAPPEASABLE
- THE UNAPPEASABLE HOST • • • • • • • • • 146 UNAPPEAS HOST T
- O HEART THE WINDS HAVE SHAKEN, THE UNAPPEASABLE HOST • 147 UNAPPEAS HOST 11
- AND HEART THE WINDS HAVE SHAKEN! THE UNAPPEASABLE HOST • 147 UNAPPEAS HOST V 11
- AND HEAR THE WINDS HAVE SHAKEN, THE UNAPPEASABLE HOST • 147 UNAPPEAS HOST V 11
- THE MOUNTAIN OF THE GODS, THE UNAPPEASABLE GODS • • • 764 SHADOW WATER A 332

UNASSAILABLE
- IMAGINE THAT SOME LOST LOVE, UNASSAILABLE • • • • • 390 UNDER SATURN V 2

UNAVAILING
- THE UNAVAILING OUTCRIES AND THE OLD BITTERNESS • • • • 198 SEVEN WOODS 4

UNBAFFLED
- EACH SHINING CLEAR AS SOME UNBAFFLED STAR! • • • • • 656 ISLE STAT I 3 25

UNBEGOTTEN
- OR THOSE BEGOTTEN OR UNBEGOTTEN • • • • • • • 599 SPIRIT MEDIUM 5
- OR THOSE BEGOTTEN OR UNBEGOTTEN, • • • • • • • 599 SPIRIT MEDIUM 9
- SOME THAT BEING UNBEGOTTEN • • • • • • • • • 600 SPIRIT MEDIUM 11

844

		PAGE	TITLE	LINE

UNBENT
CONSTRAINED, ARRAIGNED, BAFFLED, BENT AND UNBENT • • • • 382 VISION ROBART 9

UNBID
AND TELL ME THAT YOU FOUND A MAN UNBID, • • • • • • • 33 OISIN 2 67
AND TELL ME HOW YOU CAME TO ONE UNBID, • • • • • • • 33 OISIN 2 V 67
WHEN THOUGHTS RISE UP UNBID • • • • • • • • • • • • 473 ALL SOUL NIGHT 68

UNBIND
HAD STRENGTH THAT COULD UNBIND • • • • • • • • • • • 315 FRIENDS 11
WHAT BONDS NO MAN COULD UNBIND, • • • • • • • • • • 785 WOMANS BEAUTY 22

UNBLEMISHED
OF HER UNBLEMISHED LINEAMENTS, A WHITENESS WITH NO STAIN, 353 HIS PHOENIX 3

UNBLESSED
OF ANY UNBLESSED EARTHLY BIRD." • • • • • • • • • 697 MOSADA 2 33

UNBLEST
BUT THOU WOULDST NOT, FOR THEN THOU WERT UNBLEST • • • • 669 ISLE STAT II 3 90

UNBORN
THINGS UNBORN, THINGS THAT ARE GONE, • • • • • • • • 562 NEEDLES EYE 3

UNBOUND
OUR CHEEKS ARE PALE, OUR HAIR IS UNBOUND, • • • • • • 140 HOSTING SIDHE 7
AND THE GIRDLE OF LIGHT IS UNBOUND, • • • • • • • • 165 CRY OF SEDGE 8

UNBROKEN
OF AN UNBROKEN HAPPY MIND, • • • • • • • • • • • • 626 OLD MEN BE MAD 14

UNCEASING
AND ROVE UNCEASING ROUND THEIR DREADFUL BROOD. • • • • 681 SEEKER 5

UNCERTAINTY
ON OUR UNCERTAINTY! SOMEWHERE • • • • • • • • • • 425 STARES NEST 7
OR THE UNCERTAINTY OF HIS SETTING FORTH? • • • • • • 444 SCHOOL CHILDR 40

UNCHAINABLE
UNCHAINABLE AS THE DIM TIDE, • • • • • • • • • • • 22 OISIN 1 338

UNCHANGEABLE
THAT SEEMS UNLIKE ITSELF, THAT SEEMS UNCHANGEABLE, • • • 426 PHANTOM HATRED 4

UNCHANGED
PADDLE AND ARE PERFECT. LEAVE UNCHANGED • • • • • • 357 BROKEN DREAMS 34

UNCHANGING
THE MIND IS MADE UNCHANGING, FOR IT FINDS • • • • • • 227 SHADOW WATER B 101
AND SEEMED UNCHANGING LIKE THE SWORD. • • • • • • • 421 MY TABLE 21
THE SOUL'S UNCHANGING LOOK; • • • • • • • • • • • 422 MY TABLE 24
UNCHANGING AND AT PEACE, AND IT IS RIGHT • • • • • • 465 HARUN RASHID 96
NATURE'S PURE UNCHANGING LIGHT? • • • • • • • • • 529 TOM LUNATIC 6
STANDS IN GOD'S UNCHANGING EYE • • • • • • • • • • 529 TOM LUNATIC 16

UNCHRISTENED
HOMER IS MY EXAMPLE AND HIS UNCHRISTENED HEART. • • • • 503 VACILLATION 87

UNCIVIL
SHE HAS NOT GROWN UNCIVIL • • • • • • • • • • • • 365 HER RACE 1

UNCLES   SEE GREAT-UNCLES
ON UNCLES, AUNTS, GREAT-UNCLES OR GREAT-AUNTS, • • • • 604 YOU CONTENT 3

UNCLOUDED
THE PURITY OF THE UNCLOUDED MOON • • • • • • • • • 482 BLOOD AND MOON 31

UNCOILED
HIS HEAVY RINGS UNCOILED FROM GLIMMERING DEEP TO DEEP! • • 174 ELEMENT POWERS 5

UNCOMELY
ALL THINGS UNCOMELY AND BROKEN, ALL THINGS WORN OUT AND 142 ROSE IN HEART 1
    OLD,
ALL THINGS UNCOMELY AND BROKEN, ALL THINGS WORN AND OLD, 142 ROSE IN HEART V 1

UNCOMPOSITE
LIVE IN UNCOMPOSITE BLESSEDNESS, • • • • • • • • • 387 ROBARTES DANCE 46

UNCONQUERABLE
ENTHRALLED BY THE UNCONQUERABLE DELUSION, • • • • • • 367 EGO DOMINUS 6
THAT THIS UNCONQUERABLE LABYRINTH OF THE BIRDS, • • • • 481 BLOOD AND MOON 23

UNCONTROLLABLE
THE UNCONTROLLABLE MYSTERY ON THE BESTIAL FLOOR. • • • • 318 MAGI 8

UNCOUNTED
OF ALL THE UNCOUNTED BOOKS THAT I HAVE READ, • • • • • 467 HARUN RASHID 139

UNCOUTH
SUCH MEN, SUCH HEARTS. BUT, UNCOUTH HUNTER, THOU • • • 651 ISLE STAT I 1 167
KNOW'ST NAUGHT OF THIS. AND, UNCOUTH HUNTER, NOW-- • • • 651 ISLE STAT I 1 168
AND WHITHER, UNCOUTH HUNTER? WHY SO FAST? • • • • • • 651 ISLE STAT I 2 1

UNDECAYED
THE BODY OF SAINT TERESA LIES UNDECAYED IN TOMB, • • • • 503 VACILLATION 80

UNDER   SEE LAND-UNDER-WAVE
UNDER THE GOLDEN EVENING LIGHT, • • • • • • • • • 25 OISIN 1 385
THAT SPRANG UNDER THE SEVEN HAZEL TREES, • • • • • • 35 OISIN 2 84
UNDER THE ROOF, AND WITH A STRAINING THROAT • • • • • 36 OISIN 2 106
UNDER THE DEEPEST SHADOWS OF THE HALL • • • • • • • 37 OISIN 2 119
PASSED UNDER THE DIM DOORWAY, OUT OF SIGHT, • • • • • 37 OISIN 2 123
PASSED UNDER A DIM DOORWAY, OUT OF SIGHT, • • • • • • 37 OISIN 2 V 123
UNDER A CROWN OF THORNS AND DARK WITH BLOOD, • • • • • 38 OISIN 2 135
UNDER THE SHADOWS TILL THE TUMULTS DIED • • • • • • 38 OISIN 2 140
UNDER A BEECH AT ALMHUIN AND HEARD THE THIN • • • • • 44 OISIN 2 228
WAR ON THE MIGHTIEST MEN UNDER THE SKIES, • • • • • • 45 OISIN 2 241
UNDER THE STARLIGHT AND SHADOW, A MONSTROUS SLUMBERING 48 OISIN 3 27
    FOLK,
AS A HAY-COCK OUT ON THE FLOOD, OR A WOLF SUCKED UNDER 63 OISIN 3 220
    A WEIR.
AS A GRASS SEED CRUSHED BY A PEBBLE, AS A WOLF SUCKED UNDER 63 OISIN 3 V 220
    A WEIR.
BURIED UNDER THE SLEEPY GROUND, • • • • • • • • • 67 HAPPY SHEPHERD 48
THE ISLAND DREAMS UNDER THE DAWN • • • • • • • • • 77 INDIAN TO LOVE 1
HID UNDER QUIET BOUGHS APART, • • • • • • • • • • 78 INDIAN TO LOVE 12
HID UNDER QUIET BOWS APART, • • • • • • • • • • • 78 INDIAN TO LOVE V 12
ARE BOWED IN SORROW UNDER PENDULOUS LIDS, • • • • • • 79 EPHEMERA 2

UNDER (CONTINUED)

	PAGE	TITLE		LINE
LIE NOW HALF HIDDEN UNDER PENDULOUS LIDS,	79	EPHEMERA	V	2
ARE BOWED IN SORROW UNDER THEIR TREMBLING LIDS,	79	EPHEMERA	V	2
AND UNDER THE BLINKING OF THE STARS	83	MAD KING GOLL		20
AND UNDER THE BLINK O' THE MORNING STAR,	83	MAD KING GOLL	V	20
UNDER THE BLESSED MOONLIGHT,	94	MOLL MAGEE		11
I FIND UNDER THE BOUGHS OF LOVE AND HATE,	101	ROSE UPON ROOD		10
YOU HAVE THE HEAVIEST ARM UNDER THE SKY."	107	CUCHULAIN SEA		24
"WHETHER UNDER ITS DAYLIGHT OR ITS STARS	107	CUCHULAIN SEA		25
"YET SOMEWHERE UNDER STARLIGHT OR THE SUN	107	CUCHULAIN SEA		28
"NO, SOMEWHERE UNDER DAYLIGHT OR THE STARS	107	CUCHULAIN SEA	V	25
"WHETHER UNDER ITS DAYLIGHT OR THE STARS	107	CUCHULAIN SEA	V	25
AND TEN BY TEN UNDER A QUICKEN TREE,	111	CUCHULAIN SEA	V	81A
UNDER THE PASSING STARS, FOAM OF THE SKY,	112	ROSE OF WORLD		9
THEY HAVE GONE DOWN UNDER THE SAME WHITE STARS,	115	ROSE OF BATTLE		34
BUT NOW LIES UNDER BOARDS.	123	DREAM OF DEATH		12
UNDER THAT WOVEN CHANGELESS ROOF OF BOUGHS:	126	DREAM OF FAERY		11
UNDER THE WOVEN ROOFS OF QUICKEN BOUGHS:--	126	DREAM OF FAERY	V	11
BEFORE THEY HEAPED HIS GRAVE UNDER THE HILL:	127	DREAM OF FAERY		16
UNDER THE GOLDEN OR THE SILVER SKIES:	127	DREAM OF FAERY		21
HE SLEPT UNDER THE HILL OF LUGNAGALL:	128	DREAM OF FAERY		37
UNDER THAT COLD AND VAPOUR-TURBANED STEEP,	128	DREAM OF FAERY		39
A HONIED RINGING! UNDER THE NEW SKIES	130	BOOK STORIES	V	21
UNDER A BROKEN TREE	131	OLD PENSIONER		2
OR UNDER GREEN SODS LAY.	132	FR GILLIGAN		4
ROOTS HALF HIDDEN UNDER SNOWS,	135	TWO TREES		27
AND ROOTS HALF HIDDEN UNDER SNOWS	135	TWO TREES	V	27
UNDER THE FRUIT OF EVIL AND OF GOOD:	137	TO SOME I TALK		9
AH, FAERIES, DANCING UNDER THE MOON,	139	TO IRELAND		31
FLAME UNDER FLAME, TILL TIME BE NO MORE:	141	EVERLAST VOICE		4
UNDER MY FEET THAT THEY FOLLOW YOU NIGHT AND DAY.	153	CHANGE BELOVED		5
UNDER MY FEET, THAT I FOLLOW YOU, NIGHT AND DAY.	153	CHANGE BELOVED	V	5
BUT FLAME ON FLAME, DEEP UNDER DEEP,	156	FORGOT BEAUTY	V	21
UNDER A CLOUD OF HER HAIR,	160	CAP AND BELLS		26
UNDER HER PURPLE HOOD.	171	MAID QUIET	V	8
UNDER THE DOCK-LEAVES IN THE GROUND,	176	BELOVED DEAD		12
I WOULD SPREAD THE CLOTHS UNDER YOUR FEET:	176	CLOTHS HEAVEN		5
I HAVE SPREAD MY DREAMS UNDER YOUR FEET!	176	CLOTHS HEAVEN		7
AND SET THEM DIGGING UNDER BUAL'S HILL.	184	QUEEN MAEVE		93
UNDER A CAIRN OF SLEEPY STONE	192	BAILE AILLINN		81
BUT THE GREY RUSH UNDER THE WIND	192	BAILE AILLINN		88
FAR OUT UNDER A WINDLESS SKY!	197	BAILE AILLINN		181
UNDER A BITTER BLACK WIND THAT BLOWS FROM THE LEFT HAND!	206	HANRAHANS SONG		2
UNDER THE BITTER BLACK WINDS BLOWING OUT OF THE LEFT HAND!	206	HANRAHANS SONG	V	2
UNDER THE MOON	209	UNDER THE MOON		T
BECAUSE OF SOMETHING TOLD UNDER THE FAMISHED HORN	210	UNDER THE MOON		17
BECAUSE OF SOMETHING I HEARD OF UNDER THE THIN HORN	210	UNDER THE MOON	V	17
BECAUSE OF A STORY I HEARD UNDER THE THIN HORN	210	UNDER THE MOON		17
BECAUSE OF A STORY I HEARD UNDER A THIN HORN	210	UNDER THE MOON	V	17
I HEARD UNDER A RAGGED HOLLOW WOOD,	210	RAGGED WOOD	V	1
THE FLAGSTONE UNDER ALL, THE FIRE OF FIRES,	227	SHADOW WATER B		103
BECAUSE OF THAT OLD DRAUGHT UNDER THE DOOR,	228	SHADOW WATER B		127
IN HAPPY DANCES UNDER A WINDY MOON,	245	SHADOW WATER B		470
SHIVER UNDER THE LASH, STRAIN, SWEAT AND JOLT	260	FASC DIFFICULT		7
"I BID THEM MAKE HIS BED UNDER THIS ROOF	280	TWO KINGS		87
UNDER THE EYELIDS OF ANOTHER, FOR IT WAS MY CRAFT	284	TWO KINGS		156
UNDER A BOW, HE CRIED, "WHAT HAPPINESS	284	TWO KINGS		177
UNDER AN ALIEN EYELID, FOR IT WAS MY CRAFT	284	TWO KINGS	V	156
AMONG THE STONES AND THORN-TREES, UNDER MORNING LIGHT:	291	PAUDEEN		3
AMONG THE STONES AND THORN TREES, UNDER MORNING LIGHT,	291	PAUDEEN	V	3
I CHOSE THIS BURROW UNDER GROUND.	305	HOUR DAWN		73
AT KYLE-NA-NO UNDER THAT ANCIENT ROOF	321	REED WHISPERER		7
UNDER THE OCTOBER TWILIGHT THE WATER	322	SWANS AT COOLE		3
UNDER THE ROUND TOWER	331	ROUND TOWER		T
BORN UNDER THE SKIES	333	SOLOMON SHEBA		20
UNDER HIS FINGERS. I HAD IT FROM HIS MOTHER,	339	SHEP GOATHERD		26
WHERE STONE IS DARK UNDER FROTH,	348	FISHERMAN		32
UNDER YOUR OLD WIND-BEATEN TOWER, WHERE STILL	367	EGO DOMINUS		2
UNDER THE FRENZY OF THE FOURTEENTH MOON,	374	PHASES OF MOON		53
STAND UNDER THE ROUGH ROOF-TIMBERS OF THE HALL	377	PHASES OF MOON		125
UNDER THE THREE LAST CRESCENTS OF THE MOON,	377	PHASES OF MOON		133
UNDER THIS HUMP. GOD TRIES EACH MAN	379	SAINT HUNCH		5
UNDER BLANK EYES AND FINGERS NEVER STILL	382	VISION ROBART		5
"LAST NIGHT, WHERE UNDER THE WILD MOON	387	SOLOMON WITCH		2
UNDER SATURN	390	UNDER SATURN		T
UNDER BEN BULBEN TO THE MEET,	397	POLIT PRISONER		14
WHILE UNDER ITS STORM-BEATEN BREAST	397	POLIT PRISONER		23
UNDER THE FIRST COLD GLEAM OF DAY?	398	BREAK OF DAY		4
UNDER THIS CRADLE-HOOD AND COVERLID	403	FOR DAUGHTER		2
AND UNDER THE ARCHES OF THE BRIDGE, AND SCREAM	403	FOR DAUGHTER		11
UNDER THE OLD WIND-BROKEN TREE,	406	IN TIME OF WAR		3
UNDER THE DAY'S DECLINING BEAM, AND CALL	410	TOWER		21
HE SO BEWITCHED THE CARDS UNDER HIS THUMB	411	TOWER		67
UNDER ECLIPSE AND THE DAY BLOTTED OUT.	414	TOWER		120
THAT UNDER BURSTING DAWN	416	TOWER		176
UNDER ITS ROCKY HOLE.	420	MY HOUSE	V	20C
THE FINEST PLAY UNDER THE SUN.	424	ROAD AT DOOR		5
VALLEY, RIVER, AND ELMS, UNDER THE LIGHT OF A MOON	426	PHANTOM HATRED		3
WHERE EVEN LONGING DROWNS UNDER ITS OWN EXCESS:	426	PHANTOM HATRED		22
VALLEY, RIVER, ELMS, UNDER THE LIGHT OF A MOON	426	PHANTOM HATRED	V	3
AND PLANNED TO BRING THE WORLD UNDER A RULE,	429	NINETEEN 19		31

846

```
                                                    PAGE    TITLE              LINE
UNDER    (CONTINUED)
    UNDER THE SHADOW OF STUPID STRAW-PALE LOCKS,  . . . . .   433 NINETEEN 19          127
    UNDER A BROKEN TREE.  . . . . . . . . . . .              452 HUMAN DIGNITY          8
    WE SAT UNDER AN OLD THORN-TREE . . . . . . . .           456 SUMMER SPRING          1
    UNDER THAT VERY TREE. . . . . . . . .                    457 SUMMER SPRING         12
    AS AIR UNDER A WING, CAN GIVE BIRDS' WIT. . . . . .      462 HARUN RASHID          28
    AS AIR UNDER A WING, CAN GIVE BIRD'S WIT. . . . . . .    462 HARUN RASHID    V     28
    UNDER IT WISDOM STANDS, AND I ALONE--  . . . .          469 HARUN RASHID         189
    UNDER IT ARMED WISDOM STANDS, A SEPARATE WISDOM  . . .   469 HARUN RASHID    V    189
    BUT UNDER HEAVY LOADS OF TRAMPLED CLAY . . . . . .      483 OIL AND BLOOD          4
    UNDER THE RECEDING WAVE. . . . . . . . . .              485 NINETEENTH CEN         4
    UNDER MY WINDOW-LEDGE THE WATERS RACE,  . . . . .       490 COOLE BALLYLEE         1
    NOW ALL DRY STICKS UNDER A WINTRY SUN,  . . . . . .     490 COOLE BALLYLEE        10
    AND THERE IS SHELTER UNDER IT,  . . . . . . . .         509 JANE BISHOP           26
    EYES UNDER EYELIDS DID SO GLEAM;  . . . . . . .         514 JANE GROWN OLD         6
    UNDER THE RAGGED THORN? . . . . . . . . . .             519 LOVES LONENESS        10
    UNDER OAK AND BEECHEN BOUGH,  . . . . . .               522 LULLABY               11
    UNDER OAK AND BEECHES BOUGH,  . . . . . . .             522 LULLABY         V     11
    UNFRIENDLY LAMPLIGHT HID UNDER ITS SHADE,  . . . .      523 LONG SILENCE           3
    UNDER A MARBLE FLAG?  . . . . . . . . .                 525 DANCING DAYS          14
    THAT SLEEPS UNDER THE CANOPY;  . . . . . . . .          528 TOM LUNATIC            2
    THAT SHE IS UNDER BAN . . . . . . .                     531 FATHER CHILD           2
    DRY TIMBER UNDER THAT RICH FOLIAGE,  . . . . .          536 HER VISION             1
    UNDER THE GREAT COMEDIAN'S TOMB THE CROWD.  . . . .     541 PARN FUNERAL 1         1
    GRANDFATHER SANG IT UNDER THE GALLOWS'  . . . . .       544 TO SAME TUNE 1         1
    BETWEEN TWO BUSHES UNDER THE RAIN!  . . . . . .         551 SONGS REWRIT 1        14
    THEIR MOBS PUT UNDER THEIR FEET. . . . . . . .          554 CHURCH STATE           4
    UNDER A RULE, UNDER THE SEMBLANCE OF PEACE . . . .      563 MERU                   2
    UNDER A RULE, UNDER THE SEMBLANCE OF PEACE . . . . .    563 MERU                   2
    CAVERNED IN NIGHT UNDER THE DRIFTED SNOW,  . . . .      563 MERU                  10
    STRETCHED UNDER A DOORWAY  . . . . . . . .             585 ORAHILLY              30
    HIS STOUT STICK UNDER HIS HAND,  . . . . . . .          588 OLD WICKED MAN        20
    AND UNDER EVERY DANCER  . . . . . . . . . .            592 DRUNK SOBRIETY        11
    UNDER THE OLD STONE CROSS.  . . . . . . . .            598 STONE CROSS            8
    UNDER THE OLD STONE CROSS.  . . . . . . . .            599 STONE CROSS           16
    UNDER THE OLD STONE CROSS.  . . . . . . . .            599 STONE CROSS           24
    UNDER THE TROPIC SHADE, GREW ROUND AND SLOW,  . . .     610 STATUES               18
    GRANDFATHER SANG IT UNDER THE GALLOWS!  . . . . .      615 MARCH SONGS 3          1
    A HAND UNDER HIS HEAD. . . . . . . . . . . .           617 LONG-LEG FLY           8
    UNDER BROKEN STONE I HALT  . . . . . . . .             632 MAN AND ECHO           2
    UNDER BEN BULBEN . . . . . . . . . .                   636 BEN BULBEN             T
    UNDER BARE BEN BULBEN'S HEAD . . . . . . . .           640 BEN BULBEN            84
    FLICKERING UNDER THE WHITE MOONSHINE?  . . . . .       646 ISLE STAT I 1         33
    BRIGHT ON A GRASS BLADE'S UNDER SIDE, MIGHT HEAR,  .    689 NETTLESHIP            10
    UNDER A LEMON TREE BESIDE YOUR DOOR;  . . . . . .       693 MOSADA 1              68
    AND WHO WILL MOAN IN THE UNDER PIT,  . . . . . .        716 FAIRY DOCTOR           7
    AND UNDER A SHADY OAK-TREE SAT,  . . . . . .            728 PRIEST FAIRY           7
    AND UNDER HER HOOFS THE MARIGOLDS BEATEN.  . . . .      729 PRIEST FAIRY          36
    MOURNFUL UNDER MOURNFUL STARS.  . . . . . .            737 IN FIRELIGHT           4
    A FRUITFUL LAND UNDER THE AIBHLIN HILLS?  . . . .       748 SHADOW WATER A  V     33
    AND WHEN YOU CAME, THE NORTH UNDER YOUR SAILS,  . .     749 SHADOW WATER A        34
    LOOK! THERE SHE LIES UNDER A FLAPPING SAIL.  . . .     751 SHADOW WATER A        90
    OR A GOD HID THEM UNDER THE SHADOW OF WINGS.  . . .     752 SHADOW WATER A       125
    AMONG THE WINDS, LOOKS UNDER YOUR PALE EYELIDS.  .     757 SHADOW WATER A       211
    AND UNDER LOVERS' EYELIDS.  BEND YOUR HEAD . . . .     762 SHADOW WATER A       286
    UNDER A SILKEN SAIL AND SILVER YARD,  . . . . .        763 SHADOW WATER A       316
    IN HAPPY DANCES, UNDER A WINDY MOON;  . . . . .        763 SHADOW WATER A       318
    THE LOVE OF ALL UNDER THE LIGHT OF THE SUN .  . . .    765 SHADOW WATER A       353
    IMPERISHABLE FIRE UNDER THE BOUGHS  . . . . . .        765 SHADOW WATER A       356
    UNDER THE WAVES, AND TOOK A THOUSAND WOMEN . . . .     766 SHADOW WATER A       378
    AND RULE TOGETHER UNDER A CANOPY.  . . . . . . .       767 SHADOW WATER A       385
    ONE LIVES UNDER THE WAVES,  . . . . . . . . .          770 SPINNING SONG          2
    AND ONE LIVES UNDER THE BOUGHS . . . . . . . .         771 SPINNING SONG          8
UNDERGROUND
    RUN UNDERGROUND, RISE IN A ROCKY PLACE . . . . . .      490 COOLE BALLYLEE         5
    THAT I AM STILL THEIR SERVANT THOUGH ALL ARE UNDERGROUND.  581 CURSE CROMWELL     22
    AND HE IS UNDERGROUND;  . . . . . . . . . . .          586 PARNELLITES            6
UNDERNEATH
    FLED FOAM UNDERNEATH US, AND ROUND US, A WANDERING AND    47 OISIN 3              1
        MILKY SMOKE,
    FLED FOAM UNDERNEATH US, AND ROUND US, A WANDERING AND    47 OISIN 3             12
        MILKY SMOKE.
    FLED FOAM UNDERNEATH US, AND AROUND US, A WANDERING AND   47 OISIN 3        V     1
        MILKY SMOKE,
    FLED FOAM UNDERNEATH ME, AND ROUND ME, A WANDERING AND    57 OISIN 3            148
        MILKY SMOKE.
    INNUMERABLE, SINGING, EXULTANT: THE CLAY UNDERNEATH THEM  61 OISIN 3            203
        SHALL PANT,
    UNDERNEATH THE GRASS AND CLOVER,  . . . . . . . .      124 CATHLEEN PARA          3
    OR ON THE BENCHES UNDERNEATH THE WALLS,  . . . . .     180 QUEEN MAEVE           14
    SAT UNDERNEATH THE MARKET CROSS,  . . . . . . . .      724 LEGEND                 2
    UPON THE ROWERS' BENCHES UNDERNEATH,  . . . . . .      751 SHADOW WATER A        92
UNDERSTAND
    FOR THE WORLD'S MORE FULL OF WEEPING THAN YOU CAN        87 STOLEN CHILD         12
        UNDERSTAND.
    FOR THE WORLD'S MORE FULL OF WEEPING THAN YOU CAN        87 STOLEN CHILD         27
        UNDERSTAND.
    FOR THE WORLD'S MORE FULL OF WEEPING THAN YOU CAN        88 STOLEN CHILD         41
        UNDERSTAND.
    FROM A WORLD MORE FULL OF WEEPING THAN HE CAN UNDERSTAND. 89 STOLEN CHILD        53
    FOR THE WORLD'S MORE FULL OF WEEPING THAN HE CAN UNDERSTAND  89 STOLEN CHILD  V   53
```

847

		PAGE	TITLE	LINE

UNDERSTAND (CONTINUED)
THAT FOLLOWS AFTER. I UNDERSTAND YOU NOW. • • • • • • • • 237 SHADOW WATER B 341
I DO NOT UNDERSTAND. I KNOW YOUR FACE • • • • • • • 244 SHADOW WATER B 465
"MY DARLING CANNOT UNDERSTAND • • • • • • • • • • • 255 WORDS 2
HOPE THAT YOU MAY UNDERSTAND! • • • • • • • • • 309 REALISTS 1
WHAT NONE CAN UNDERSTAND, • • • • • • • • • 315 FRIENDS 12
IN SOMETHING THAT ALL OTHERS UNDERSTAND OR SHARE; • • • 427 PHANTOM HATRED 35
AMONG THE DOGS AND HORSES THAT UNDERSTAND MY TALK. • • 581 CURSE CROMWELL 30
WHO UNDERSTAND THE DARK; • • • • • • • • • • • • 588 OLD WICKED MAN 31
UNDERSTANDS
MY DARLING UNDERSTANDS IT ALL, • • • • • • • • • 256 WORDS 10
NOT A POOR FOOL UNDERSTANDS. • • • • • • • • • 381 SONG OF FOOL 4
UNDERSTOOD
AS HE THAT PRACTISED OR THAT UNDERSTOOD • • • • • • 327 ROBERT GREGORY 75
NOT HIS, NOT MINE." WHO UNDERSTOOD • • • • • • • 387 SOLOMON WITCH 6
I UNDERSTOOD HIS PLAN. • • • • • • • • • • • 400 DEMON BEAST 15
BY QUIET NATURES UNDERSTOOD • • • • • • • • • 405 FOR DAUGHTER 63
THEY UNDERSTOOD THAT WISDOM COMES OF BEGGARY. • • • 487 SEVEN SAGES 26
WHAT MATTER THAT YOU UNDERSTOOD NO WORD! • • • • • 557 RIBH ECSTASY 1
AND UNDERSTOOD HER CASE. • • • • • • • • • 571 THREE BUSHES 69
AND UNDERSTOOD, WHAT NONE HAVE UNDERSTOOD, • • • • 622 HOUND VOICE 13
AND UNDERSTOOD, WHAT NONE HAVE UNDERSTOOD, • • • • 622 HOUND VOICE 13
PLAIN TO BE UNDERSTOOD, • • • • • • • • • • 785 YOUR HEART 2
UNDERTOOK
WHAT THEY UNDERTOOK TO DO • • • • • • • • • 505 GRAT INSTRUCT 1
UNDIMMED
"I COME FROM THE UNDIMMED RIVERS TO BID YOU CALL • • • 184 QUEEN MAEVE V 91
"I AM FROM THE UNDIMMED RIVERS. I BID YOU CALL • • • • 184 QUEEN MAEVE V 91
RUN FOR A MILE UNDIMMED IN HEAVEN'S FACE • • • • 490 COOLE BALLYLEE 3
UNDO
THOSE FANATICS ALL THAT WE DO WOULD UNDO; • • • • • 544 TO SAME TUNE 1 7
THOSE FANATICS ALL THAT WE DO WOULD UNDO; • • • • • 545 TO SAME TUNE 1 17
THOSE FANATICS ALL THAT WE DO WOULD UNDO; • • • • • 545 TO SAME TUNE 1 27
THOSE FANATICS ALL THAT WE DO WOULD UNDO; • • • • • 546 TO SAME TUNE 2 V REF
THOSE FANATICS ALL THAT WE DO WOULD UNDO; • • • • • 548 TO SAME TUNE 3 V REF
UNDONE
AND HAD BEEN SAVAGELY UNDONE • • • • • • • • 314 MEMORY YOUTH 18
AS THOUGH I HAD BEEN UNDONE • • • • • • • • 384 VISION ROBART 55
WHEREBY THE HORN OF PLENTY IS UNDONE. • • • • • 404 FOR DAUGHTER 32
ALL BY THEIR YOUTH UNDONE. • • • • • • • • 504 RESULT THOUGHT 4
OR LEAVE SOME SERVICE ALL UNDONE, • • • • • • • 743 DANAAN QUICK 21
UNDREAMT
THOSE UNDREAMT ACCIDENTS THAT HAVE MADE ME • • • • • • • 321 REED WHISPERER 10
UNDULANT   SEE EVER-UNDULANT
FLASHING AND FLICKERING, WITH EVER UNDULANT WING, • • • 710 FERENCZ RENYI V 19
UNDYING
AMONG UNDYING PEOPLE HAS RUN • • • • • • • • 6 OISIN 1 V 60
IS AN UNDYING MOORFOWL, AND HE LIVES BEYOND THE SKY. • • 76 INDIAN ON GOD 7
THEY KNOW UNDYING THINGS, FOR THEY • • • • • • • 196 BAILE AILLINN 170
UNDYING LOVE TO BUY • • • • • • • • • • • 517 HIS CONFIDENCE 1
FOR UNDYING LOVE? • • • • • • • • • • • • 518 HIS CONFIDENCE 6
FROM THE UNDYING WORM. SHE SLEEPS—MOSADA— • • • • • 701 MOSADA 3 65
HAS TOLD ME THAT THE UNDYING SEND THEIR EAGLES • • • • 765 SHADOW WATER A 346
UNEARTHLY
NOT KNOWING WHAT UNEARTHLY STUFF • • • • • • • • 599 STONE CROSS 21
NOW SADLY, NOW UNEARTHLY GAY, • • • • • • • • 716 FAIRY DOCTOR 3
UNEASY
"NIGHT GROWS UNEASY NEAR THE DAWN • • • • • • • 303 HOUR DAWN 33
THAT'S GROWN UNEASY NEAR THE DAWN • • • • • • • 303 HOUR DAWN V 33
UNEMPTIED
OR ON SOME STILL UNEMPTIED CUP • • • • • • • • 271 GREY ROCK 21
UNENDING
FOR THE ROADS ARE UNENDING, AND THERE IS NO PLACE TO MY   203 WITHER BOUGHS 4
    MIND."
UNEVEN
HAD TROD THE UNEVEN ROAD. THEIR BOOTS WERE SOILED, • • • 372 PHASES OF MOON 3
UNFAERY
I HURL AWAY THESE ALL UNFAERY FEARS. • • • • • • • • 675 ISLE STAT II 3 228
UN-FAERY
SOME BARBAROUS, UN-FAERY THING DRAW NEAR. • • • • • • 656 ISLE STAT I 3 21
UNFALTERING
WITH UNFALTERING PERSISTENCE, • • • • • • • • • 647 ISLE STAT I 1 69
UNFASHIONABLE
ON THAT UNFASHIONABLE GYRE AGAIN. • • • • • • • 565 GYRES 24
UNFELT
WALKED THROUGH THE HOUSE. UNNOTICED AND UNFELT • • • • 468 HARUN RASHID 153
UNFINISHED
THE PLAYER QUEEN SONG FROM AN UNFINISHED PLAY • • • • 308 PLAYER QUEEN V T
THE UNFINISHED MAN AND HIS PAIN • • • • • • • 479 SELF AND SOUL 47
UNFOLD
UNFOLD YOUR FLAMING WINGS AND COVER OUT OF SIGHT • • • • 175 ELEMENT POWERS 11
UNFOLDING
IS FOLDING AND UNFOLDING, AND IN ITS FOLDS • • • • • • 751 SHADOW WATER A 99
UNFOLDS
THE NORTH UNFOLDS ABOVE THEM CLINGING, CREEPING NIGHT, • • 154 BELOVED PEACE 3
UNFOREKNOWN
RECKONED UP EVERY UNFOREKNOWN, UNSEEING • • • • • • 413 TOWER 109
UNFORGIVING
WHO NEVER HEAR THE UNFORGIVING HOUND. • • • • • • • 75 ANASHU VIJAYA 75
WHO NEVER HEARD THE UNFORGIVING HOUND. • • • • • • • 75 ANASHU VIJAYA V 75

848

	PAGE	TITLE	LINE

UNFORGOTTEN
  AND UNFORGOTTEN NAMES, AND THE COLD STARS • • • • • •   757 SHADOW WATER A   204
UNFORMED
  DEFORMED BEYOND DEFORMITY, UNFORMED, • • • • • • • •   376 PHASES OF MOON   111
UNFRIENDLY
  UNFRIENDLY LAMPLIGHT HID UNDER ITS SHADE, • • • • • •   523 LONG SILENCE   3
  THE CURTAINS DRAWN UPON UNFRIENDLY NIGHT, • • • • • •   523 LONG SILENCE   4
UNFURLED
  THE TALL THOUGHT-WOVEN SAILS, THAT FLAP UNFURLED • • • •   113 ROSE OF BATTLE   2
UNGLORIOUS
  • • • WITH BODIES UNGLORIOUS, THEIR CHIEFTAINS STOOD, • •   58 OISIN 3   166
UNGOVERNABLE
  CUCHULAIN FOUGHT THE UNGOVERNABLE SEA: • • • • • • •   630 CIRCUS ANIMALS   26
UNGOVERNED
  OF THE UNGOVERNED UNICORN. • • • • • • • • • • •   776 AGAINST WITCH   25
UNGUENTS
  AND HEALED MY WOUNDS WITH UNGUENTS OUT OF FLOWERS • • •   41 OISIN 2   185
  WITH WITCHERY AND UNGUENTS FROM THE FLOWERS • • • • •   41 OISIN 2   V 185
UNHAPPINESS
  OR FELL INTO UNHAPPINESS, I'VE SAID, • • • • • • • •   186 QUEEN MAEVE   137
  THAN ANY WHOSE UNHAPPINESS • • • • • • • • • • •   190 BAILE AILLINN   36
  FOR HAPPIER LOVE BUT FINDS UNHAPPINESS, • • • • • •   750 SHADOW WATER A   67
UNHAPPY
  UNHAPPY ONE. GO NOT, GO NOT, GO NOT: • • • • • • •   703 MOSADA 3   102
UNHAUNTED
  AND MIGHT HAVE KNOWN AT LAST UNHAUNTED SLEEP • • • •   128 DREAM OF FAERY   38
UNHEARD-OF
  BUT OF A BEAUTIFUL, UNHEARD-OF KIND • • • • • • •   228 SHADOW WATER B   142
UNHOOK
  THEY UNHOOK THEIR HEAVY SWORDS • • • • • • • • •   215 HAPPY TOWNLAND   23
  MICHAEL WILL UNHOOK HIS TRUMPET • • • • • • • •   215 HAPPY TOWNLAND   41
UNHOOKED
  WITH SHOUTING AND THE CLANG OF UNHOOKED ARMS. • • • • •   185 QUEEN MAEVE   111
UNHUMAN
  OF PENSIVE LAUGHTER, UNHUMAN SOUND; • • • • • • •   11 OISIN 1   136
  WRAPPED IN THE THINGS OF THE UNHUMAN MIND, • • • • •   36 OISIN 2   98
  ROLLED IN THE THINGS OF THE UNHUMAN MIND, • • • • •   36 OISIN 2   V 98
  • • • AND FED OF UNHUMAN SLEEP. • • • • • • • •   51 OISIN 3   56
  OF SOME UNHUMAN MISERY • • • • • • • • • • •   85 MAD KING GOLL   V 58
  WITH THEIR UNHUMAN SORROWS. CEASE: NO MORE: • • • •   661 ISLE STAT II 1   58
  THROUGH MISERIES UNHUMAN EVER ON • • • • • • • •   684 SEEKER   59
  TO JOYS UNHUMAN, AND TO THEE--SPEAK: SPEAK: • • • •   684 SEEKER   60
UNICORN
  AS THOUGH A STAG AND UNICORN WERE MET • • • • • •   277 TWO KINGS   19
  OF THE UNGOVERNED UNICORN. • • • • • • • • • •   776 AGAINST WITCH   25
UNICORNS
  MAGICAL UNICORNS BEAR LADIES ON THEIR BACKS. • • • • •   426 PHANTOM HATRED   18
  THE CLOUD-PALE UNICORNS, THE EYES OF AQUAMARINE, • • •   427 PHANTOM HATRED   25
  THE CLOUD PALE UNICORNS, THE EYES OF AQUAMARINE, • • •   427 PHANTOM HATRED V   25
UNIFORM
  HALF DRESSED IN NATIONAL UNIFORM, • • • • • • • •   424 ROAD AT DOOR   7
UNIMAGINABLE
  THAT UNIMAGINABLE STORMS OF WIND AND WAVE • • • • •   236 SHADOW WATER B   317
  TO UNIMAGINABLE HAPPINESS. • • • • • • • • • •   247 SHADOW WATER B   524
  AN UNIMAGINABLE HAPPINESS. • • • • • • • • • •   248 SHADOW WATER B   553
  WHO HAD LOST SOME UNIMAGINABLE TREASURE • • • • • •   278 TWO KINGS   40
UNINHABITED
  UNINHABITED, RUINOUS, • • • • • • • • • • • •   512 JANE ON GOD   15
UNINTELLIGIBLE
  WHEN I AM UNINTELLIGIBLE. • • • • • • • • • •   624 APPARITIONS   14
UNISON
  AND DISCORD FOLLOW UPON UNISON, • • • • • • • •   265 THESE CLOUDS   5
UNIVERSE
  THE UNIVERSE HERSELF WOULD DIE, • • • • • • • •   19 OISIN 1   V 271
UNIVERSE'S
  IN THE UNIVERSE'S REVERIE. • • • • • • • • • •   65 HAPPY SHEPHERD V   21
UNIVERSITY
  ON HEARING THAT THE STUDENTS OF OUR NEW UNIVERSITY • • •   262 STUDENTS AGIT   T
UNJUST
  AND THEY CEASE WITH A SIGH OF "UNJUST: UNJUST:" • • •   27 OISIN 1   V 416
  AND THEY CEASE WITH A SIGH OF "UNJUST: UNJUST:" • • •   27 OISIN 1   V 416
  MUST MURMUR AT LAST, "UNJUST, UNJUST": • • • • • •   28 OISIN 1   420
  MUST MURMUR AT LAST, "UNJUST, UNJUST": • • • • • •   28 OISIN 1   420
UNKIND
  THY TENDER EYES GROW ALL UNKIND: • • • • • • •   136 TWO TREES   39
  AND THINK THAT YOU WERE HARD AND UNKIND, • • • • •   146 FISH   7
  BE NOT UNKIND OR PROUD; • • • • • • • • • •   173 PLEADS FRIEND   4
UNKNOWN
  WAS A BEAUTIFUL YOUTH FROM AN UNKNOWN LAND. • • • •   12 OISIN 1   V 145
  SWAYED, CROONING TO HIMSELF AN UNKNOWN TONGUE: • • •   39 OISIN 2   159
  THE DEWS DROP SLOWLY AND DREAMS GATHER: UNKNOWN SPEARS • •   161 BLACK PIG   1
  OF UNKNOWN PERISHING ARMIES BEAT ABOUT MY EARS. • • •   161 BLACK PIG   4
  THE DEW DROPS SLOWLY: THE DREAMS GATHER: UNKNOWN SPEARS   161 BLACK PIG   V   1
  GAZED UPON ALL THINGS KNOWN, ALL THINGS UNKNOWN, • • •   383 VISION ROBART   30
  HIS VIZIR JAFFER FOR AN UNKNOWN REASON: • • • • •   462 HARUN RASHID   32
  FOR MEDITATIONS UPON UNKNOWN THOUGHT • • • • • •   473 ALL SOUL NIGHT   74
  GRATITUDE TO THE UNKNOWN INSTRUCTORS • • • • • •   505 GRAT INSTRUCT   T
  GRATITUDE TO THE UNKNOWN POWERS • • • • • • •   505 GRAT INSTRUCT   V   T
  AND ROARS, MAD WITH THE TOUCH OF THE UNKNOWN, • • •   689 NETTLESHIP   7
UNLABOURING
  "NEITHER THE LIVING, NOR THE UNLABOURING DEAD, • • • •   34 OISIN 2   79

	PAGE	TITLE		LINE

UNLABOURING   (CONTINUED)
    AND BY THE UNLABOURING BROOD OF THE SKIES: · · · · · ·   164 PERFECT BEAUTY   5
    BEFORE THE UNLABOURING STARS AND YOU. · · · · · · ·   164 PERFECT BEAUTY   8
    BEFORE UNLABOURING STARS AND YOU. · · · · · · · ·   164 PERFECT BEAUTY V   8
UN-LABOURING
    AND BY THE HEAVEN'S UN-LABOURING BROODS: · · · · · ·   164 PERFECT BEAUTY V   5
UNLACE
    DREAMED OF THE HANDS THAT WOULD UNLACE · · · · · · ·   193 BAILE AILLINN   104
UNLANGUID
    UNLANGUID AS THE BIRDS, IN PROUD COMPANIONSHIPS: · · · ·   30 OISIN 2   V 14C
UNLATCHED
    THE MORE I LEAVE THE DOOR UNLATCHED · · · · · · · ·   511 JANE AND JACK   3
UNLAUGHING
    NOR AN UNLAUGHING MOUTH, BUT MINE THAT MOURNS, · · · ·   285 TWO KINGS   184
UNLEARNED
    ALL TEETH WERE DRAWN, ALL ANCIENT TRICKS UNLEARNED, · · ·   429 NINETEEN 19   17
UNLESS
    UNLESS WE DRAIN MORE FLAGONS IN A YEAR · · · · · · ·   225 SHADOW WATER B   70
    UNLESS DESIRE HAD MADE THEM SO?" · · · · · · · ·   295 THREE BEGGARS   18
    WILL BANISH EVERY THOUGHT, UNLESS · · · · · · · ·   387 ROBARTES DANCE   48
    UNLESS A PETAL HIT THE GROUND, · · · · · · · ·   389 SOLOMON WITCH   40
    A TATTERED COAT UPON A STICK, UNLESS · · · · · · ·   407 SAIL BYZANTIUM   10
    THOUGHT THAT UNLESS A LITTLE POWDER BURNED · · · ·   429 NINETEEN 19   21
    UNLESS THE HOLY WRITINGS LIE, · · · · · · · ·   436 FOR MY SON   28
    UNLESS SOME PITYING GOD SHALL SUCCOUR ME · · · ·   656 ISLE STAT I 3   36
    THAT ONE SHALL DIE, UNLESS ONE DIE FOR HER. · · · ·   669 ISLE STAT II 3   74
    THEY SAID I'D BURN IN HELL UNLESS I TOLD. · · · ·   694 MOSADA 1   108
UNLETTERED
    WERE YOU AND I UNLETTERED LADS · · · · · · · ·   524 MAD AS MIST   11
UNLIKE
    THE MOST UNLIKE, BEING MY ANTI-SELF, · · · · · · ·   371 EGO DOMINUS   74
    THAT SEEMS UNLIKE ITSELF, THAT SEEMS UNCHANGEABLE, · · ·   426 PHANTOM HATRED   4
    THAT'S SO UNLIKE MYSELF THAT WHEN YOU PRAISE IT · · ·   447 HERO GIRL FOOL   2
UNLOCKED
    UNTIL AT LAST THE UNLOCKED HORN HAD TORN · · · ·   278 TWO KINGS   V 21
UNLOCKS
    WAS MOVING. BLEEDING NOW, HIS GRASP UNLOCKS, · · · ·   688 TWO TITANS   42
UNLOOSE
    UNLOOSE THE CORD, AND THEY WILL WRAP YOU ROUND. · · · ·   104 FERGUS DRUID   30
UNLOOSED
    STABLING HIS UNLOOSED LIGHTNINGS IN THEIR STALL, · · · ·   36 OISIN 2   110
    HER HEAD CAST BACKWARD IN HER UNLOOSED HAIR. · · · · ·   701 MOSADA 3   67
UNLOVED
    BEING FIXED ON ALL THINGS LOVED, ALL THINGS UNLOVED, · ·   383 VISION ROBART   34
UNMANNED
    HE WHO CAN READ THE SIGNS NOR SINK UNMANNED · · · · ·   429 NINETEEN 19   33
UNMANNERLY
    THE DAILY SPITE OF THIS UNMANNERLY TOWN, · · · · · ·   351 PEOPLE   3
UNMEASURED
    THAT HURRY FROM UNMEASURED MIND · · · · · · · ·   138 TO IRELAND   25
UNMINDFUL
    UNMINDFUL OF ITS WOES, WOULD TWINE A WREATH · · · · ·   650 ISLE STAT I 1   133
UNMIXED
    DRUNK WITH THE UNMIXED WINE. · · · · · · · ·   355 PROPERTIUS   8
UN-MIXED
    DRUNK WITH THE UN-MIXED WINE. · · · · · · · ·   355 PROPERTIUS   V 8
UNMOVED
    AND MY HEART UNMOVED? · · · · · · · · · · ·   532 BEFORE WORLD   12
UNMOVING
    SHINE DULL UNMOVING EYES. WHAT THING ART THOU? · · · ·   685 SEEKER   74
UNNATURAL
    WHO HAD UNNATURAL MAJESTY, AND EYES · · · · · · ·   283 TWO KINGS   149
    BUT WITH A VOICE THAT HAD UNNATURAL MUSIC, · · · · ·   283 TWO KINGS   153
    THAT SEEMS UNNATURAL TO ARABIAN MINDS, · · · · · ·   464 HARUN RASHID   79
    THAT FIRST UNNATURAL INTEREST IN MY BOOKS. · · · ·   468 HARUN RASHID   165
UNNECESSARY
    SANG WHERE--UNNECESSARY CRUEL VOICE-- · · · · · · ·   127 DREAM OF FAERY   30
UNNEEDED   SEE ALL-UNNEEDED
UNNOTICED
    SANG UNNOTICED LIKE A BIRD: · · · · · · · · ·   298 THREE HERMITS   7
    SANG UNNOTICED LIKE A BIRD. · · · · · · · · ·   299 THREE HERMITS   32
    AND LET IT FALL UNNOTICED TO THE FLOOR. · · · · · ·   461 HARUN RASHID   15
    AND IT WOULD FALL UNNOTICED ON THE FLOOR. · · · · ·   461 HARUN RASHID   V 15
    WALKED THROUGH THE HOUSE. UNNOTICED AND UNFELT · · ·   468 HARUN RASHID   153
    HIDDEN FROM EYESIGHT TO THE UNNOTICED END. · · · ·   472 ALL SOUL NIGHT   50
UNNUMBERED
    I LAUGHED AT TIMES UNNUMBERED TREASONS, · · · · · ·   23 OISIN 1   V 345D
    FROM YEAR TO YEAR BY THE UNNUMBERED NESTS · · · · ·   74 ANASHU VIJAYA   72
    SLEEPER, AWAKE! HOW LONG MY SLEEP? UNNUMBERED · · ·   678 ISLE STAT II 3   307
UNPACKS
    HE UNPACKS THE LOADED PERN · · · · · · · · · ·   342 SHEP GOATHERD   97
UNPASSING
    NOR THOSE UNPASSING CARES, · · · · · · · · ·   315 FRIENDS   5
UNPEOPLED
    OR ON THE UNPEOPLED WAVES WITH KINGS TO PULL AT THE OAR,   210 UNDER THE MOON   15
UNPERSUADABLE
    HE FOUND THE UNPERSUADABLE JUSTICE, HE FOUND · · · · ·   369 EGO DOMINUS   36
UNPERTURBED
    THE UNPERTURBED AND COURTLY IMAGES-- · · · · · · ·   352 PEOPLE   11
UNPRUNED
    UNPRUNED IS YOUR BEAUTIFUL PINION · · · · · · · ·   707 FAIRY PEDANT   7

850

		PAGE	TITLE		LINE

UNPUBLISHED
    A LYRIC FROM AN UNPUBLISHED PLAY . . . .   263 MASK   V   T
UNPURGED
    THE UNPURGED IMAGES OF DAY RECEDE; . . . .   497 BYZANTIUM   1
UNQUENCHABLE
    UNQUENCHABLE STILL GLOWS IN HER DULL STARE, ...   687 TWO TITANS   17
UNQUIET
    MURMURING HOW FAR AWAY ARE THE UNQUIET LANDS; . . . . .   78 INDIAN TO LOVE   10
    MURMURING GENTLY HOW FAR OFF ARE THE UNQUIET LANDS; . . .   78 INDIAN TO LOVE V   10
    GIVE THEM UNQUIET DREAMS; . . . .   88 STOLEN CHILD   34
    AND THE LOUD CHANTING OF THE UNQUIET LEAVES, ...   120 SORROW OF LOVE V   11
    AND THE LOUD CHAUNTING OF THE UNQUIET LEAVES, ...   120 SORROW OF LOVE V   11
    SUDDEN AND LAUGHING, O UNQUIET HEART, ...   181 QUEEN MAEVE   30
    THE PACK UPON HIM, GO, UNQUIET WANDERER, ...   292 TO A SHADE   18
    HERDING THE PACK. UNQUIET WANDERER . . . .   292 TO A SHADE   V   18
    QUIET LANDS OR UNQUIET SEAS . . . .   360 ALF POLLEXFEN   19
UNREALITY
    THAT KNOWLEDGE INCREASES UNREALITY, THAT . . . . . .   610 STATUES   21
UNRECKONABLE
    UNRECKONABLE RACE; . . . .   365 HER RACE   8
UNREMEMBERING
    THAT GIRL MY UNREMEMBERING NIGHTS HOLD FAST . . . . .   384 VISION ROBART   50
    THEIR UNREMEMBERING HEARTS AND HEADS . . . .   639 BEN BULBEN   72
UNREPENTING
    AND UNREPENTING FACED YOUR ENDS, ...   273 GREY ROCK   60
UNREPINING
    HATE ON AND LOVE THROUGH UNREPINING HOURS. . . . . .   80 EPHEMERA   22
UNREPROVED
    THE INSOLENT UNREPROVED, ...   347 FISHERMAN   16
UNREQUITED
    RETURNED AND YET UNREQUITED LOVE. . . . .   358 PRESENCES   8
UNREST
    BUT WHY THIS WHIM OF THINE? A STRANGE UNREST, ...   671 ISLE STAT II 3 137
UNRESTING
    THE RAVENS OF UNRESTING THOUGHT; . . . .   136 TWO TREES   34
UNROLLS
    THE NORTH UNROLLS ABOVE THEM CLINGING, CREEPING NIGHT, . .   154 BELOVED PEACE V   3
UNSATISFIED
    IN THEIR STIFF, PAINTED CLOTHES, THE PALE UNSATISFIED ONES   318 MAGI   2
    BEING BY CALVARY'S TURBULENCE UNSATISFIED, ...   318 MAGI   7
    HIS SENSES AND HIS HEART UNSATISFIED, ...   370 EGO DOMINUS   58
    UNSATISFIED . . . .   510 JANE JUDGMENT   2
UNSAY
    THE REST I PASS, ONE SENTENCE I UNSAY. . . . .   542 PARN FUNERAL 2   1
    I PASS THE REST--ONE SENTENCE I UNSAY-- . . . .   542 PARN FUNERAL 2 V 1
UNSEARCHABLE
    SEARCHED THE UNSEARCHABLE--WHY GOOD MEN WEEP; . . . . .   710 FERENCZ RENYI   32
UNSEEING
    RECKONED UP EVERY UNFOREKNOWN, UNSEEING . . . .   413 TOWER   109
UNSEEN
    THEY WALK ON SHORES UNSEEN OF OARING GALLEYS, ...   30 OISIN 2   V 14D
    THE SHOUTING OF AN UNSEEN MAN; . . . .   274 GREY ROCK   76
    AS I WANDERED UNSEEN; . . . .   654 ISLE STAT I 2   71
    AND HEARD EACH UNSEEN ECHO ON HER THRONE, ...   657 ISLE STAT I 3   48
    AND THE CUCKOO UNSEEN IN HIS FESTIVAL MOOD; . . . . .   717 LOVE SONG   7
UNSERVICEABLE
    A STRANGE, UNSERVICEABLE THING, ...   784 WOMANS BEAUTY   15
UNSHAKEN
    BUT WITH THE BURNING, LIVE, UNSHAKEN VOICE . . . . . .   183 QUEEN MAEVE   75
UNSHAPELY
    THE WRONG OF UNSHAPELY THINGS IS A WRONG TOO GREAT TO BE   143 ROSE IN HEART   5
        TOLD;
UNSHELTERED
    HE SAID "QUEEN OF UNSHELTERED CRUACHAN, ...   183 QUEEN MAEVE   V 77
UNSHUT
    OR, THE HOUSE DOOR LEFT UNSHUT, ...   380 SONGS FOOL 1   10
UNSHUTTERED
    SHOWED THEIR FAINT LIGHT THROUGH THE UNSHUTTERED WINDOWS,   279 TWO KINGS   50
UNSLEEPING
    AWAKE UNSLEEPING FIRES; AND WOVE SEVEN STRINGS, ...   219 HARP OF AENGUS   7
    AWAKE UNSLEEPING FIRES; AND WOVE SEVEN STRINGS, ...   762 SHADOW WATER A 302
UNSOUGHT
    A STRANGE THING SURELY THAT MY HEART, WHEN LOVE HAD COME   449 OWEN AHERNE   1
        UNSOUGHT
UNSPOILED
    AND ON MY HEIRS, IF ALL REMAIN UNSPOILED, ...   371 ON GOING HOUSE   2
UNSPOTTED
    UNSPOTTED BY THE CENTURIES; . . . .   477 SELF AND SOUL   12
UNSTEADY
    HAS MADE MY FEET UNSTEADY, AND BLINDED ME. . . . . . .   767 SHADOW WATER A 406
UNSTITCHING
    OUR STITCHING AND UNSTITCHING HAS BEEN NAUGHT. . . .   204 ADAMS CURSE   6
UNSUBDUABLE
    THAT DEMON DULL AND UNSUBDUABLE; . . . .   43 OISIN 2   217
UNTIL
    UNTIL THE DANAAN POETS BROUGHT . . . .   7 OISIN 1   63
    UNTIL THE DANAAN POETS CAME, ...   7 OISIN 1   V 64
    UNTIL ONE CAME, A TEARFUL BOY; . . . .   17 OISIN 1   237
    UNTIL THE TOSSING ARMS GREW STILL . . . .   21 OISIN 1   322
    NOR CEASED UNTIL WHITE NIAMH STROKED HIS EARS . . . . .   30 OISIN 2   26
    "AND TELL THEM HOW I WEEP, UNTIL THEY WEEP; . . . . .   33 OISIN 2   V 63

		PAGE	TITLE	LINE

UNTIL   (CONTINUED)

UNTIL THE GODS AND DEMONS DROP ASLEEP,	• • • • • • •	35 OISIN 2		86
TO LIE UNTIL THE FOURTH MORN SAW EMERGE	• • • • • •	44 OISIN 2		220
TO LIE UNTIL THE FOURTH MORN SUN EMERGE	• • • • • •	44 OISIN 2	V	220
UNTIL I CARVED THESE WORDS!	• • • • •	123 DREAM OF DEATH		10
DREAM, UNTIL GOD BURN NATURE WITH A KISS?	• • • • •	128 DREAM OF FAERY		47
UNTIL HE BURN UP NATURE WITH A KISS!--	• • • • •	128 DREAM OF FAERY	V	47
UNTIL THE SAP OF SUMMER HAD GROWN WEARY!	• • • • •	130 BOOK STORIES		14
FROM OUR BIRTHDAY, UNTIL WE DIE,	• • • • • •	139 TO IRELAND		35
UNTIL ONE BORE BRIDGET HIS BRIDE	• • • • •	145 HOST OF AIR		31
IS DROPPING SLEEP, UNTIL GOD BURN TIME,	• • • • •	164 PERFECT BEAUTY		7
UNTIL THE AXLE BREAK	• • • • • • •	165 CRY OF SEDGE		4
UNTIL TIME AND THE WORLD HAVE EBBED AWAY	• • • • •	168 BLESSED	V	39
UNTIL HE FOUND, WITH LAUGHTER AND WITH TEARS,	• • • •	170 SECRET ROSE		24
OF THE WOMAN THAT HE LOVES, UNTIL HE DIES.	• • • •	177 PAST GREATNESS		10
UNTIL THE PILLARED DARK BEGAN TO STIR	• • • •	185 QUEEN MAEVE		110
UNTIL TWO LOVERS CAME OUT OF THE AIR	• • • • •	187 QUEEN MAEVE		143
HE RAN AND LAUGHED UNTIL HE CAME	• • • • •	194 BAILE AILLINN		128
UNTIL THE MOON HAD SET! AND WHEN I LOOKED	• • • •	223 SHADOW WATER B		22
UNTIL THE OVERBURTHENED MOON IS DEAD.	• • • •	231 SHADOW WATER B		218
UNTIL YOU STOOD BEFORE ME ON THE DECK--	• • • •	236 SHADOW WATER B		313
TO BE HIS BEDFELLOW? UNTIL YOUR LIPS	• • • • •	237 SHADOW WATER B		335
UNTIL MY BODY GIVE YOU KISS FOR KISS.	• • • •	238 SHADOW WATER B		345
UNTIL MY THOUGHTS CLEARED UP AGAIN,	• • • • •	256 WORDS		6
UNTIL AT LAST THE DOUBLE HORNS, DRAWN BACKWARD,	• • •	278 TWO KINGS		21
UNTIL AT LAST THE UNLOCKED HORN HAD TORN	• • • •	278 TWO KINGS	V	21
UNTIL HE CAME BEFORE THE PAINTED WALL.	• • • •	279 TWO KINGS		47
BUT ASKED THE MORE UNTIL HE SPOKE THESE WORDS,	• • •	281 TWO KINGS	V	92A
UNTIL ENOUGH OF PAUDEEN'S PENCE	• • • • •	287 TO WEALTHY MAN		2
AND PRAYER TO SHIVERING PRAYER, UNTIL	• • • •	289 SEPTEMBER 1913		4
UNTIL A CURLEW CRIED AND IN THE LUMINOUS WIND	• • •	291 PAUDEEN		4
AND ARE PLAGUED BY CROWDS, UNTIL	• • • • •	298 THREE HERMITS		20
"I'LL SLEEP UNTIL THE WINTER'S GONE,	• • • • •	305 HOUR DAWN		57
UNTIL I CRIED AND TREMBLED AND ROCKED TO AND FRO,	• •	316 COLD HEAVEN		8
UNTIL IMAGINATION BROUGHT	• • • • • •	328 ROBERT GREGORY		94
UNTIL THEY PRANCED UPON THE TOP.	• • • • •	331 ROUND TOWER		18
NEVER UNTIL THIS MOMENT HAVE WE MET	• • • • •	339 SHEP GOATHERD		7
UNTIL I AM DRIVEN MAD,	• • • • • • •	346 ON WOMAN		35
UNTIL HER PRAISE SHOULD BE THE UPPERMOST THEME,	• • •	350 HER PRAISE		6
BUT WALK BY THE DRY THORN UNTIL I HAVE FOUND	• • •	351 HER PRAISE		12
MANAGE THE TALK UNTIL HER NAME COME ROUND.	• • •	351 HER PRAISE		14
MANAGE TO TALK UNTIL HER NAME COME ROUND.	• • •	351 HER PRAISE	V	14
THE STATELY MIDNIGHT THROUGH UNTIL THEY STOOD	• • •	352 PEOPLE		14
I'D STAND AND MUTTER THERE UNTIL HE CAUGHT	• • •	377 PHASES OF MOON		131
NEVER UNTIL THIS NIGHT HAVE I BEEN STIRRED.	• • •	389 IMAGE PAST		1
UNTIL HER VOICE GREW SHRILL.	• • • • •	392 EASTER 1916		20
UNTIL IMAGINATION, EAR AND EYE,	• • • • •	409 TOWER		13
THAT CLIMB THE STREAMS UNTIL	• • • • •	414 TOWER		123
AND RAINS DOWN LIFE UNTIL THE BASIN SPILLS,	• • •	417 ANCEST HOUSES		4
UNTIL I THOUGHT HER BODY BORE	• • • • •	451 FIRST LOVE		5
UNTIL IT PLUNGE INTO THE SUN!	• • • • •	472 ALL SOUL NIGHT		56
UNTIL IT PLUNGED INTO THE SUN!	• • • • •	472 ALL SOUL NIGHT	V	56
UNTIL THAT GLANCE RUN IN THE WORLD'S DESPITE	• • •	474 ALL SOUL NIGHT		94
CASTS UPON HIS EYES UNTIL AT LAST	• • • • •	479 SELF AND SOUL		53
UNTIL THE MORNING BREAK AS ON A DARK BREAST.	• • •	494 AT ALGECIRAS	V	6
UNTIL IT PARDON ME.	• • • • • • •	516 MANS SONG		18
MAY SING, AND SING UNTIL HE DROP,	• • • • •	525 DANCING DAYS		21
I DID THE DRAGON'S WILL UNTIL YOU CAME!	• • • •	533 HER TRIUMPH		1
WHAT CAN SHE TAKE UNTIL HER MASTER GIVE!	• • •	558 RIBH CHRISTIAN		21
WHERE CAN SHE LOOK UNTIL HE MAKE THE SHOW!	• • •	558 RIBH CHRISTIAN		22
WHAT CAN SHE KNOW UNTIL HE BID HER KNOW!	• • •	558 RIBH CHRISTIAN		23
UNTIL THE TOWN LIE BEATEN FLAT.	• • • • •	565 LAPIS LAZULI		8
NO, NOT UNTIL HE RODE.	• • • • • •	571 THREE BUSHES		48
MY MEDIAEVAL KNEES LACK HEALTH UNTIL THEY BEND,	• •	603 GALLERY REVIS		33
UNTIL, IN SOME CLIFF-SHELTERED BAY	• • • • •	612 NEWS ORACLE		21
AND ALL SEEMS EVIL UNTIL I	• • • • • •	632 MAN AND ECHO		17
UNTIL AFAR APPEAR THE GLEAMING DRAGON-SCALES!	• •	651 ISLE STAT I 1		160
FROM MORN THE TWAIN UNTIL THE EVENING PALES	• •	651 ISLE STAT I 1		161
UNTIL I FIND HIM. WHAT A WEARY WEEK,	• • • •	658 ISLE STAT II 1		2
UNTIL THIS MORN. AS ADDER'S BACK	• • • • •	667 ISLE STAT II 3		22
UNTIL THIS MORN. THE SKY WITH WRACK	• • • •	667 ISLE STAT II 3	V	22
UNTIL WE DIE WITHIN THE CHARMED RING	• • • •	679 ISLE STAT II 3		322
UNTIL MY BEARD IS IN THE TWISTED LEAVES	• • •	683 SEEKER		44
BE PULLERS OF THE OAR UNTIL YOU DIE?	• • • •	757 SHADOW WATER A		217
UNTIL ALL BE RUINOUS.	• • • • • •	775 AGAINST WITCH		4
UNTIL HE HAD DIED OF HIS WOUNDS,	• • • • •	775 AGAINST WITCH		16
OF THE HOME-BREW THERE, UNTIL	• • • • •	776 AGAINST WITCH		38
OF THE HOMEBREW THERE, UNTIL	• • • • •	776 AGAINST WITCH	V	38

UNTIRING

| MUST SPREAD OUT THEIR WINGS UNTIRING, | • • • • • • | 739 WHERE BOOKS GO | | 3 |

UNTO

AND NIGH UNTO HIM EACH ONE DREW,	• • • • •	18 OISIN 1	V	257
AND SANG UNTO THE STARRY BROODS.	• • • • •	22 OISIN 1		326
AS THOUGH UNTO HIS NEVER SLUMBERING HEART	• • •	32 OISIN 2	V	44
FROM SLEEPER UNTO SLEEPER MURMUR YOU.	• • •	33 OISIN 2	V	60
ONCE MORE UNTO YOUR FLOWERS! FOR NONE MAY FIGHT,	• •	34 OISIN 2	V	80
DARKEN! HEAVEN IS ANGRY. CEASE! UNTO MY MIND,	• •	42 OISIN 2	V	205
AND WE ONCE MORE UNTO OUR FIGHTING FELL.	• • •	43 OISIN 2	V	218
• • • FOR BREAST UNTO BREAST	• • • • • •	56 OISIN 3		131
WITHOUT LAUGHTER, A SHOW UNTO CHILDREN,	• • • •	63 OISIN 3		218

		PAGE	TITLE		LINE

UNTO   (CONTINUED)
    AH ME! TO BE OLD WITHOUT SUCCOUR, A SHOW UNTO CHILDREN,   63 OISIN 3   V 217
      A STAIN,
    THAT GOD GIVES UNTO MAN IN SLEEP. • • • • • • •   138 TO IRELAND   V   22
    WHAT ARE THEY? UNTO WHAT COUNTRY DO THEY FLY? • • • •   247 SHADOW WATER B   523
    FROM FATHER UNTO SON • • • • • • • • • • •   421 MY TABLE   19
    UNTO THE WANDERER'S SHIPS, OR AS DAY FILLS • • • •   645 ISLE STAT I 1   10
    UNTO THE DOLOROUS BORDER OF THE FAIRY LAKE. • • • •   655 ISLE STAT I 2   85
    LONG YEARS AGO, AND UNTO STONE CONGEALED. • • • •   656 ISLE STAT I 3   28
    AROUND THE FEATHERY TIP. UNTO THE SHAFT • • • •   657 ISLE STAT I 3   71
    UNTO HER DOOR! FOR THIS, WHERE NOD THE LONG • • •   660 ISLE STAT II 1   43
    FROM THE DEEP EARTH UNTO THE LURID SKY • • • •   662 ISLE STAT II 2   5
    AN OATEN PIPE UNTO A LISTENING FAWN, • • • • •   678 ISLE STAT II 3   301
    AN OATEN PIPE UNTO A LISTENING FAUN, • • • • •   678 ISLE STAT II 3   V 301
    AND UNTO IT WE'LL DANCE UPON THE SWARD. • • • •   681 SEEKER   10
    GOLD UNTO GOLD, A GLEAM IN ITS LONG HAIR, • • • •   720 WITCH VIVIEN   3
    UNTO THE HEART OF THE WOODLAND STRAYING, • • • •   728 PRIEST FAIRY   1
    AND ANSWERED UNTO HIM! • • • • • • • • •   740 EARL PAUL   18
    UNTO THE WHITE SKIES. • • • • • • • • • •   740 EARL PAUL   24
    SHOULD LOOK UPON HIS EYES WITH LOVE UNTO THE END • • •   768 SHADOW WATER A   V 409
UNTOLD
    MINE WERE CLAN MORNA'S TRIBES UNTOLD, • • • • •   81 MAD KING GOLL   V   3
    WHO CAST ROUND FERGUS DREAMS, AND RUIN UNTOLD! • • • •   101 ROSE UPON ROOD   5
UNTOUCHED
    UNTOUCHED OF HUMAN JOY OR HUMAN LOVE? • • • • • •   684 SEEKER   65
UNTROUBLED
    AND LAUGH OVER THE UNTROUBLED WATER • • • • • •   330 BONE OF A HARE   14
    UNTROUBLED BY THE SOUL, • • • • • • • • •   573 LADYS 2ND SONG   11
UNTUNED
    UNTUNED BY THEIR OWN STRIVING. IF ONE SUCH • • • •   711 FERENCZ RENYI   37
UNUSED
    WHOSE INSOLENT EYES UNUSED TO TEARS WOULD WEEP. • • • •   678 ISLE STAT II 3   302
UNVESSELLED
    HALF IN THE UNVESSELLED SEA, WE CLIMBED THE STAIR • • •   32 OISIN 2   47
    HALF IN THE UNVESSELLED SEA, WE'D MOUNTED FAR! • • •   32 OISIN 2   V   47
    HALF IN THE UNVESSELLED SEA, WE CLIMBED THE STAIRS • • •   32 OISIN 2   V   47
UNVISITED
    UNVISITED BY TEMPEST OR BY SUN, • • • • • • •   446 COLONUS PRAISE   5
UNWEARIED
    PROCLAIM WITH THAT UNWEARIED, REEDY CRY • • • • •   128 DREAM OF FAERY   42
    UNWEARIED STILL, LOVER BY LOVER, • • • • • • •   323 SWANS AT COOLE   19
    UNWEARIED EYES UPON THOSE HORRIBLE GREEN BIRDS. • • • •   442 BLACK CENTAUR   16
UNWEARY
    THE MAN IS GONE WHO GUIDED YE, UNWEARY, • • • • •   738 MOURN THEN ON   3
UNWET
    NOR MOUTH FROM KISSING, NOR FROM WINE UNWET! • • • •   311 MOUNTAIN TOMB   7
    NOR MOUTH WITH KISSING NOR WITH WINE UNWET. • • • •   311 MOUNTAIN TOMB   V   7
    NOR MOUTH WITH KISSING NOR WITH THE WINE UNWET. • • • •   311 MOUNTAIN TOMB   V   7
UNWIELDY
    AND ROLLS ALONG THE UNWIELDY SUN. • • • • • •   18 OISIN 1   267
    ROUND US, AND ROLLS THE UNWIELDY SUN. • • • • •   18 OISIN 1   V 268
UNWIND
    WIND AND UNWIND THEIR DANCES WHEN THE LIGHT GROWS COOL • •   203 WITHER BOUGHS   13
    WIND AND UNWIND DANCING WHEN THE LIGHT GROWS COOL • • •   203 WITHER BOUGHS   V   13
    KNOWLEDGE HE SHALL UNWIND • • • • • • • • •   343 SHEP GOATHERD   107
    MAY UNWIND THE WINDING PATH! • • • • • • • •   497 BYZANTIUM   12
UNWITHERING
    HAPPY AS CHILDREN WITH UNWITHERING LIPS, • • • • •   30 OISIN 2   V 14B
    HELP THEM THAT PACE, HAND IN UNWITHERING HAND, • • • •   184 QUEEN MAEVE   V   86
UNWORTHY
    AGAINST UNWORTHY PRAISE • • • • • • • • • •   259 UNWORTH PRAISE   T
UNWOUND
    FOR LOVE IS BUT A SKEIN UNWOUND • • • • • • •   511 JANE AND JACK   5
    TIME IS UNWOUND, • • • • • • • • • • •   520 HIS BARGAIN   4
UNWRAP
    AND MAKES THE INFANT FERNS UNWRAP, • • • • • •   18 OISIN 1   265
UP   SEE PILED-UP HEAPED-UP MAKE-UP
    HE HELD THAT FLASHING SCEPTRE UP. • • • • • •   18 OISIN 1   260
    PASSED A-TIPTOE UP AND DOWN • • • • • • • •   20 OISIN 1   V 294
    AND UP THE STAIR WE TOILED TO A HIGH DOOR, • • •   36 OISIN 2   V 101
    BARKING. WE TRAMPLED UP AND DOWN WITH BLOWS • • •   40 OISIN 2   170
    HAD SURGED UP IN A PLUMY FIRE, I DRAVE • • • •   41 OISIN 2   181
    SURGED UP IN PLUMY FIRE, I LUNGED AND DRAVE • • •   41 OISIN 2   V 181
    • • • SHALL LISTEN AND RISE UP AND WEEP! • • • •   62 OISIN 3   206
    • • • WHO COULD BREAK UP THE WORLD IN THEIR RAGE! • • •   62 OISIN 3   214
    I, PRIESTESS OF THIS TEMPLE, OFFER UP • • • • •   71 ANASHU VIJAYA   12
    I, PRIESTESS OF THIS TEMPLE, OFFER UP • • • • •   75 ANASHU VIJAYA   84
    AND PASSED A-TIPTOE UP AND DOWN, • • • • • •   85 MAD KING GOLL   51
    I PASSED A TIP-TOE UP AND DOWN, • • • • • •   85 MAD KING GOLL   V   51
    I PASSED A-TIPTOE UP AND DOWN, • • • • • • •   85 MAD KING GOLL   V   51
    BUT FATHER JOHN WENT UP, • • • • • • • • •   92 FATHER OHART   9
    AS HE WENT UP AND DOWN! • • • • • • • • •   92 FATHER OHART   18
    WHO DIG OLD CUSTOMS UP. • • • • • • • • •   93 FATHER OHART   40
    MY HUSBAND STOOD UP PALE, • • • • • • • • •   95 MOLL MAGEE   V   22
    MY MONEY'S ALL USED UP, • • • • • • • • •   96 MOLL MAGEE   38
    AND SLOWLY UP AND DOWN. • • • • • • • • •   97 FOXHUNTER   V   8
    AND GENTLY UP AND DOWN. • • • • • • • • •   97 FOXHUNTER   V   8
    IN THREE DAYS' TIME HE STOOD UP WITH A MOAN, • • • •   111 CUCHULAIN SEA   V   83
    STOOD UP, AND CAME TO THE LONG SANDS ALONE! • • • •   111 CUCHULAIN SEA   V   84
    YOUNG MAN, LIFT UP YOUR RUSSET BROW, • • • • •   125 GOES FERGUS   4
    UNTIL HE BURN UP NATURE WITH A KISS!— • • • • •   128 DREAM OF FAERY   V   47

		PAGE	TITLE		LINE
UP	(CONTINUED)				
	LIFT UP BEFORE US WHEN THEY PASS,	135	TWO TREES		23
	LIFT UP BEFORE US AS THEY PASS,	135	TWO TREES	V	23
	BUT HE HEARD HIGH UP IN THE AIR	145	HOST OF AIR		41
	O'DRISCOLL GOT UP FROM THE GRASS,	145	HOST OF AIR	V	37
	AND THEY SIGH IF THE WIND BUT LIFT UP A TRESS;	151	OLD MOTHER	V	8
	THAT WAS BRIMMED UP WITH PRAYER AND REST;	151	HEART OF WOMAN		2
	AND BIND UP EVERY WANDERING TRESS;	157	BELOVED RHYMES		2
	AND BIND UP YOUR LONG HAIR AND SIGH;	158	BELOVED RHYMES		8
	BUT SHE TOOK UP HER FAN FROM THE TABLE	160	CAP AND BELLS		19
	THEY SET UP A NOISE LIKE CRICKETS,	161	CAP AND BELLS		33
	WHEN SHE ROSE UP TO DEPART?	171	MAID QUIET		6
	NOW WORDS THAT CALLED UP THE LIGHTNING	171	MAID QUIET		7
	AND DRUNK UP THE MURMURING TIDE;	171	MAID QUIET	V	4D
	FOR THE WORDS THAT CALLED UP THE LIGHTNING	171	MAID QUIET	V	7
	THEY WILL ALL COME UP TO ME,	179	FIDDLER DOONEY		18
	WILL ALL COME UP TO ME,	179	FIDDLER DOONEY	V	18
	A LATTICED WINDOW. HIS GLANCE WENT UP AT TIMES	180	QUEEN MAEVE		6
	MIGHT BE ACCOMPLISHED. BUNCHING THE CURTAIN UP	183	QUEEN MAEVE		68
	CAME UP OUT OF THE HOLE, AND RED-EARED HOUNDS	185	QUEEN MAEVE		117
	CASTS UP A SHOW AND THE WINDS ANSWER IT	186	QUEEN MAEVE		125
	TWO SWANS CAME FLYING UP TO HIM,	194	BAILE AILLINN		135
	IT MIGHT CALL UP A NEW AGE, CALLING TO MIND	201	OLD MEMORY		4
	HAVE GIVEN THEIR HEARTS UP TO THE PLAY.	202	NEVER GIVE ALL		10
	THE WIND HAS BUNDLED UP THE CLOUDS HIGH OVER KNOCKNAREA,	207	HANRAHANS SONG		6
	THE YELLOW POOL HAS OVERFLOWED HIGH UP ON CLOOTH-NA-BARE,	207	HANRAHANS SONG		11
	THE WINDS HAVE BUNDLED UP THE CLOUDS HIGH OVER KNOCKNAREA	207	HANRAHANS SONG	V	6
	FOR THE GREY WINDS ARE BLOWING UP, OUT OF THE CLINGING SEAS!	207	HANRAHANS SONG	V	12
	ONE GATHERS UP HIS PURPLE GOWN;	212	BLESS PSALTER		9
	AND LIFT UP AN OLD HORN	215	HAPPY TOWNLAND		49
	STRANGE CREATURES FLUTTER UP BEFORE ONE'S EYES,	222	SHADOW WATER B		18
	A BEAUTIFUL YOUNG MAN AND GIRL CAME UP	223	SHADOW WATER B		33
	AND HE MY MASTER FROM MY CHILDHOOD UP!	225	SHADOW WATER B		77
	HAD THE WORLD'S TOTAL LIFE GATHERED UP, IT SEEMED,	231	SHADOW WATER B		194
	AENGUS AND EDAIN RAN OUT OF THE WAVE--	231	SHADOW WATER B		196
	AND PAID YOU ON THE NAIL. TAKE UP THAT ROPE	232	SHADOW WATER B		224
	A MAGIC THAT CAN CALL A DEMON UP,	238	SHADOW WATER B		344
	THAT HE IS HOLDING UP BETWEEN US THERE,	240	SHADOW WATER B		378
	I LOVED HIM; I WOULD COVER UP MY EARS,	246	SHADOW WATER B		494
	BUT I WILL COVER UP YOUR EYES AND EARS,	250	SHADOW WATER B		574
	WHAT COULD I BUT TAKE UP THE SONG?	254	HIS DREAM		14
	UNTIL MY THOUGHTS CLEARED UP AGAIN,	256	WORDS		6
	THAT HAVE TO BE SET UP IN FIFTY WAYS,	260	FASC DIFFICULT		9
	ALL THOSE HAD LIFTED UP THE DIM	272	GREY ROCK		27
	BUT THEREON EVERY GOD STOOD UP	275	GREY ROCK		116
	THE HANDS THAT GATHERED UP THE MIGHT OF THE WORLD,	278	TWO KINGS		29
	SUCKED UP THE PASSION OUT OF HIM AGAIN	284	TWO KINGS		160
	LOOK UP IN THE SUN'S EYE AND GIVE	288	TO WEALTHY MAN		32
	"TIME'S UP," HE CRIED, AND ALL THE THREE	297	THREE BEGGARS		57
	"TIME'S UP," HE CRIED, AND ALL THE THREE	297	THREE BEGGARS		59
	HAD NOT THE SLEEPER STARTED UP,	304	HOUR DAWN		48
	AND TOOK THE WOODEN LADLE UP	304	HOUR DAWN	V	46
	AND AFTER HEAPED UP STONE ON STONE,	307	HOUR DAWN		116
	AND HEAPED UP STONE ON STONE AGAIN,	307	HOUR DAWN		118
	THREW UP IN THE AIR HIS MARVELLOUS MOON.	314	MEMORY YOUTH	V	21
	WHILE UP FROM MY HEART'S ROOT	316	FRIENDS		26
	AND THREW HIM UP TO LAUGH ON THE BOUGH;	318	APPOINTMENT		11
	CLIMB UP THE NARROW WINDING STAIR TO BED!	324	ROBERT GREGORY		5
	AND QUARRELS ARE BLOWN UP UPON THAT HEAD!	324	ROBERT GREGORY		13
	"ALTHOUGH I'D LIE LAPPED UP IN LINEN	331	ROUND TOWER		1
	BELLOWING UP AND BELLOWING ROUND,	331	ROUND TOWER		14
	PRANCING ROUND AND PRANCING UP	331	ROUND TOWER		17
	SEEING THAT TIME HAS FROZEN UP THE BLOOD	333	LIVING BEAUTY	V	2
	THAT HE ALONE HAD GATHERED UP NO GEAR,	340	SHEP GOATHERD		49
	AND CHILDREN WHEN THEY SPRING UP SHOULDER-HIGH,	343	SHEP GOATHERD		119
	AND CHILDREN WHEN THEY SPRING UP SHOULDER HIGH.	343	SHEP GOATHERD	V	119
	THAT GIVES UP ALL HER MIND,	345	ON WOMAN		2
	THAT POUNDS UP ALL ANEW	346	ON WOMAN		31
	TO CALL UP TO THE EYES	347	FISHERMAN		7
	CLIMBING UP TO A PLACE	348	FISHERMAN		31
	I HAVE GONE ABOUT THE HOUSE, GONE UP AND DOWN	350	HER PRAISE		2
	AND THERE'S A PLAYER IN THE STATES WHO GATHERS UP HER CLOAK	354	HIS PHOENIX		12
	AND THERE'S THE PLAYER IN THE STATES WHO GATHERS UP HER CLOAK	354	HIS PHOENIX	V	12
	AS IF THE HAIR STOOD UP ON MY HEAD.	358	PRESENCES		2
	CLIMBED UP MY CREAKING STAIR. THEY HAD READ	358	PRESENCES		6
	HEEL UP AND WEIGHT ON TOE, MUST FACE THE WALL	363	DOLLS FACES		3
	THAT SHADES THE ROAD, OR SETTING UP A COTTAGE	372	ON GOING HOUSE		14
	CAUGHT UP IN CONTEMPLATION, THE MIND'S EYE	375	PHASES OF MOON		79
	WHEN ALL THE DOUGH HAS BEEN SO KNEADED UP	377	PHASES OF MOON		114
	OUT OF THE UP AND DOWN, THE WAGON-WHEEL	377	PHASES OF MOON		120
	OUT OF THE UP AND DOWN, THE WAGON WHEEL	377	PHASES OF MOON	V	120
	THE CREEPING CAT, LOOKED UP.	378	CAT AND MOON		4
	STAND UP AND LIFT YOUR HAND AND BLESS	379	SAINT HUNCH		1
	AND BOTH LOOK UP TO ME ALONE	380	SONGS FOOL 1		4
	AS I LOOK UP TO PROVIDENCE.	380	SONGS FOOL 1		6
	STRETCHED UP ON TWO LEGS FROM THE MAT,	381	SONGS FOOL 2		7
	HAS CALLED UP THE COLD SPIRITS THAT ARE BORN	382	VISION ROBART		2
	HAND LIFTED UP THAT BLEST;	383	VISION ROBART		20
	AN IMAGE UP, OR ANYTHING	390	IMAGE PAST		33

		PAGE	TITLE	LINE

UP   (CONTINUED)

WHETHER SHE THREW THEM UP TO FLOUT ME,   390 IMAGE PAST   37
BUT SOON A TEAR-DROP STARTED UP,   400 DEMON BEAST   21
A BIT OF BREAD THROWN UP INTO THE AIR!   400 DEMON BEAST   25
PROSPER BUT LITTLE, HAS DRIED UP OF LATE,   405 FOR DAUGHTER   51
LIT UP THE DARK MAHOGANY AND THE WINE,   410 TOWER   27
AND FOLLOWED UP THOSE BAYING CREATURES TOWARDS--   412 TOWER   72
BRING UP OUT OF THAT DEEP CONSIDERING MIND   413 TOWER   106
RECKONED UP EVERY UNFOREKNOWN, UNSEEING   413 TOWER   109
TILL MAN MADE UP THE WHOLE,   415 TOWER   149
WHEN THEY HAVE MOUNTED UP,   415 TOWER   169
"VENGEANCE UPON THE MURDERERS," THE CRY GOES UP,   426 PHANTOM HATRED   9
AND AGAMEMNON DEAD. BEING SO CAUGHT UP,   441 LEDA AND SWAN   11
AND WHEN WE TALKED OF GROWING UP   456 SUMMER SPRING   5
WE THREE MAKE UP A SOLITUDE!   457 SECRETS OF OLD   9
O BID ME MOUNT AND SAIL UP THERE   458 HIS WILDNESS   1
THAT PURITY BUILT UP THE STATE   460 THREE MONUMENT   6
AND SPEAK BUT LIES. CALL UP TO MEMORY   462 HARUN RASHID   V 30
THE GARDEN PATHS, NOR COUNTED UP THE ROOMS,   466 HARUN RASHID   119
BUT WOKE AT THE FIRST GLEAM OF DAY, ROSE UP   467 HARUN RASHID   147
TWO THOUGHTS WERE SO MIXED UP I COULD NOT TELL   471 ALL SOUL NIGHT   31
HAD SO LIT UP THE WHOLE   472 ALL SOUL NIGHT   37
AND I CALL UP MACGREGOR FROM THE GRAVE,   473 ALL SOUL NIGHT   61
WHEN THOUGHTS RISE UP UNBID   473 ALL SOUL NIGHT   68
ENDURE THAT TOIL OF GROWING UP!   478 SELF AND SOUL   44
A POWERFUL EMBLEM UP,   480 BLOOD AND MOON   9
THE AVENGING LEAF THOSE FIELDS RAISED UP AGAINST IT.   487 SEVEN SAGES   20
IN COOLE DEMESNE, AND THERE TO FINISH UP   490 COOLE BALLYLEE   6
AND BIDS MY HAIR STAND UP?   499 MOTHER OF GOD   15
AND MAKES MY HAIR STAND UP?   499 MOTHER OF GOD   V 15
SUDDENLY LIT UP   512 JANE ON GOD   16
WRAPPING THAT FOUL BODY UP   525 DANCING DAYS   5
AND AFTER THAT I HELD MY FINGERS UP,   537 HER VISION   9
ALL THERE CAUGHT UP THE TUNE!   545 TO SAME TUNE 1   15
WHEN NATIONS ARE EMPTY UP THERE AT THE TOP,   548 TO SAME TUNE 3   11
LIFT, LIFT, LIFT UP THE TUNE.   548 TO SAME TUNE 3   V 16
MARCH, MARCH, LIFT UP THE SONG!   549 TO SAME TUNE 3   26
LIFT, LIFT, LIFT UP THE SONG.   549 TO SAME TUNE 3   V 26
AS THE MOON SIDLES UP   559 HE AND SHE   1
MUST SHE SIDLE UP,   559 HE AND SHE   2
DO NOT BREAK UP THEIR LINES TO WEEP.   565 LAPIS LAZULI   15
THE BLINDS DRAWN UP! MAUD GONNE AT HOWTH STATION WAITING A TRAIN,   578 LOFTY THINGS   10
HE THAT'S MOUNTING UP MUST ON HIS NEIGHBOUR MOUNT,   580 CURSE CROMWELL   11
COME FILL UP ALL THOSE GLASSES.   586 PARNELLITES   7
AND BOTH CLIMBED UP THE STAIR,   595 COLONEL MARTIN   38
A JOURNALIST MAKES UP HIS LIES   598 STONE CROSS   3
SET UP THE OLD STONE CROSS,   604 YOU CONTENT   10
AND I BEAT UP THE COMMON SORT   605 SONGS BURDEN 1   3
COULD THAT OLD GOD RISE UP AGAIN   606 SONGS BURDEN 1   21
HER HEART MOUNT UP ON HIGH!   608 SONGS BURDEN 3   22
WHAT IF THERE'S NOTHING UP THERE AT THE TOP?   615 MARCH SONGS 2   21
ALL THERE CAUGHT UP THE TUNE!   616 MARCH SONGS 3   15
PICKED UP ON A STREET.   617 LONG-LEG FLY   18
PICKED UP ON THE STREET.   617 LONG-LEG FLY   V 18
SOME DAY WE SHALL GET UP BEFORE THE DAWN   622 HOUND VOICE   15
SOME ROGUE OF THE WORLD STOLE THEM TO PATCH UP A FENCE OR A FIRE.   623 HIGH TALK   4
FAR UP IN THE STRETCHES OF NIGHT!   623 HIGH TALK   12
WHERE I CAN SIT UP HALF THE NIGHT   624 APPARITIONS   11
UP THERE SOME HAWK OR OWL HAS STRUCK,   633 MAN AND ECHO   43
CAME CREEPING UP BECAUSE THE MAN WAS STILL.   634 CUCHULAIN COMF   10
TOOK UP THE NEAREST AND BEGAN TO SEW.   634 CUCHULAIN COMF   18
BUT WINDS COME UP FROM THE SHORE!   635 BLACK TOWER   8
CARES WHAT KING SETS UP HIS RULE.   635 BLACK TOWER   14
BUT WIND COMES UP FROM THE SHORE!   636 BLACK TOWER   18
BUT WIND COMES UP FROM THE SHORE!   636 BLACK TOWER   28
BUT WINDS COME UP FROM THE SHORE!   636 BLACK TOWER   V REF
SCORN THE SORT NOW GROWING UP   639 BEN BULBEN   70
HURLS THEIR SWOONING LUSTRE UP.   647 ISLE STAT I 1   49
GO UP AND DOWN, AND RAISE THEIR HEADS AND SING   682 SEEKER   30
THAT FROM THE FIRE IS EVER POURING UP   683 SEEKER   37
POURS UP AND FLOATS IN FRAGRANCE ROUND MY HEAD   691 MOSADA 1   40
POURS UP AND FLOATS IN FRAGRANCE O'ER MY HEAD   691 MOSADA 1   V 40
HEARKEN, YE SWALLOWS!--I HAVE HOARDED UP   699 MOSADA 3   23
LOOK UP, LOOK UP, THY GOMEZ IS BY THEE.   701 MOSADA 3   68
LOOK UP, LOOK UP, THY GOMEZ IS BY THEE.   701 MOSADA 3   68
LOOK UP, LOOK UP, THY VALLENCE IS BY THEE.   701 MOSADA 3   V 68
LOOK UP, LOOK UP, THY VALLENCE IS BY THEE.   701 MOSADA 3   V 68
I KNEEL BY THEE--NO PARTING NOW--LOOK UP.   702 MOSADA 3   94
OH, WOULD THE BUSY MINUTES MIGHT FOLD UP   702 MOSADA 3   97
JUST NOW MY SOUL ROSE UP AND TOUCHED IT, FAR   705 REMEMBRANCE   13
SO ENDS A BRAIN--A WORLD! THE SMOKE GOES UP,   714 FERENCZ RENYI   111
OF FIRE. SO ENDS A BRAIN--A WORLD! THE SMOKE FLOATS UP,   714 FERENCZ RENYI   V 111
LEAPED UP INTO THE AIR.   741 EARL PAUL   36
AND JOHN ROSE UP AND STOOD,   741 EARL PAUL   54
AND, THOUGH YOU LOVED HER, GAVE HER UP TO ME?   749 SHADOW WATER A   50
AS THOUGH THE WATERS HAD FLOWED UP BETWEEN!   749 SHADOW WATER A   55
WERE THEY BUT LIFTED UP. THE RED HOUND IS FLED.   761 SHADOW WATER A   266
WHEN EARTH AND HEAVEN HAVE BEEN FOLDED UP!   765 SHADOW WATER A   366
TILL THE SIDE OF HATE COMES UP.   776 AGAINST WITCH   35

		PAGE	TITLE		LINE

UP   (CONTINUED)
    UP WITH THE NECK AND CLAP THE WING, ...   782 HEART FRIGHT   6
    UP WITH THE NECK AND CLAP THE WING, ...   782 HEART FRIGHT   13
    UP WITH THE NECK AND CLAP THE WING, ...   782 HEART FRIGHT   20
    BURN THEIR BODIES UP FOR NOUGHT, ...   787 HUDDON DUDDON   14
UPHELD
    ONE HAND UPHELD HIS BEARDLESS CHIN, ...   17 OISIN 1   250
UPHOLSTERIES
    AND THEY BUT FAMOUS OLD UPHOLSTERIES   . . . .   579 DOR WELLESLEY   3
UPLAND
    UPON THE NORMAN UPLAND OR IN THAT POPLAR SHADE, ... 449 OWEN AHERNE   2
    UPON THE NORTHERN UPLAND OR IN THAT POPLAR SHADE,   . . . 449 OWEN AHERNE   V   2
    BUT O! MY HEART COULD BEAR NO MORE WHEN THE UPLAND CAUGHT 450 OWEN AHERNE   11
        THE WIND!
UPLIFT
    "UPLIFT THOSE EYES AND THROW   . . . .   516 MANS SONG   7
UPLIFTED
    UPLIFTED GATEWAY. WITH THE FLASHING BEAT   . . . . . .   31 OISIN 2   V   30D
    AND THE GREEN QUIET, HAVE UPLIFTED THE HEART?   . . . .   219 WOODS OF COOLE   40
UPPER
    WHETHER THEY TAKE THE UPPER ROAD   . . . .   589 OLD WICKED MAN   48
    BECAUSE WOMEN IN THE UPPER STOREYS DEMAND A FACE AT THE   623 HIGH TALK   7
        PANE,
    UPON CLEAR NIGHTS THEY LEAVE THE UPPER AIR   . . . . .   750 SHADOW WATER A   87
UPPERMOST
    UNTIL HER PRAISE SHOULD BE THE UPPERMOST THEME, ... 350 HER PRAISE   6
UPRAISED
    AN ABBOT OR ARCHBISHOP WITH AN UPRAISED HAND   . . . .   601 GALLERY REVIS   9
    UPRAISED HIS VOICE, AND HOOTED ME.   . . . .   670 ISLE STAT II 3 V   117
    UPRAISED THEIR VOICES BITTERLY.   . . . .   730 PRIEST FAIRY   72
UP-RAISED
    UP-RAISED HIS VOICE, AND HOOTED ME.   . . . .   670 ISLE STAT II 3   117
UPRIGHT
    STOOD UPRIGHT ON THE FLOOR.   . . . .   133 FR GILLIGAN   24
    THE PORTER SLEPT, ALTHOUGH HE SAT UPRIGHT   . . . . .   182 QUEEN MAEVE   45
    SAT UPRIGHT WITH A SWORD BEFORE HER FEET.   . . . . .   279 TWO KINGS   62
    I, THOUGH UPRIGHT ON THE SHORE, ...   298 THREE HERMITS   11
    TO KEEP HIM UPRIGHT WHILE HE CURSED.   . . . . . .   302 HOUR DAWN   6
    AND SAW HER SITTING UPRIGHT ON THE BED!   . . . . .   467 HARUN RASHID   134
    I SAW HER SITTING UPRIGHT ON THE BED, ...   467 HARUN RASHID   V   134
    TO HOLD HIMSELF UPRIGHT!   . . . .   515 GIRLS SONG B   7
    BUT BODY WON! IT WALKS UPRIGHT.   . . . .   561 FOUR AGES MAN   2
    STAND UPRIGHT ON YOUR LEGS AWHILE, ...   586 PARNELLITES   3
    STAND UPRIGHT WHILE YOU CAN, ...   586 PARNELLITES   4
    THERE IN THE TOMB STAND THE DEAD UPRIGHT, ...   635 BLACK TOWER   7
UPROAR
    AND WHEN THE UPROAR RAN ALONG THE GRASS   . . . . . .   186 QUEEN MAEVE   127
    NOISE! UPROAR! AND A MOMENTARY BLOT.   . . . .   714 FERENCZ RENYI V   110
    CEASE THE SAILS THEIR FLAPPING UPROAR, AND THE HULL NO   719 PHANTOM SHIP   18
        LONGER ROLLS.
    CEASE THE SAILS, THEIR FLAPPING UPROAR TO THE HULL   719 PHANTOM SHIP   V   18
        NO LONGER ROLLS.
UPROOT
    WE SHADOWS, WHILE THEY UPROOT HIS EARTHY HOUSE,   . . .   184 QUEEN MAEVE   94
    WE SHADOWS, WHILE THEY UPROOT THE EARTHY HOUSE   . . .   184 QUEEN MAEVE   V   94
UPROOTED
    TARA UPROOTED, AND NEW COMMONNESS   . . . .   198 SEVEN WOODS   6
UPROOTING
    RAVENING, RAGING, AND UPROOTING THAT HE MAY COME   . . . 563 MERU   6
UPS
    THAT HAS LESS UPS AND DOWNS THAN ROBBERY.   . . . . . .   222 SHADOW WATER B   7
    NO UPS AND DOWNS, MY PRETTY, ...   592 DRUNK SOBRIETY   13
UPSPRINGING
    WHEN THEY AWAKE UPSPRINGING! WITH LOUD HORN   . . . . .   32 OISIN 2   V   52
UPSTAIRS
    THAT ONE BELIEVED HE HAD A SWORD UPSTAIRS!   . . . . .   267 ALL TEMPT ME   8
    HE ROSE THE LATCH AND WENT UPSTAIRS   . . . .   594 COLONEL MARTIN   7
UPSTANDING
    I CHOOSE UPSTANDING MEN   . . . .   414 TOWER   122
    TO YOUNG UPSTANDING MEN   . . . .   416 TOWER   174
UPTURNED
    FROM DOORED AND WINDOWED CLIFF, OR HALF UPTURNED   . . . 368 EGO DOMINUS   30
UPWARD
    HE BADE HIS SOUL RISE UPWARD   . . . .   159 CAP AND BELLS   3
    HE MADE HIS SOUL GO UPWARD   . . . .   159 CAP AND BELLS V   3
    LEAPS UPWARD, AS IF ALL THE STREAMS O' THE WORLD   . . . 249 SHADOW WATER B   560
    WHEN UPWARD TURNED, ON ONE SOLE IMAGE FELL!   . . . . .   471 ALL SOUL NIGHT   34
    WHEN UPWARD TURNED ON ONE SOUL IMAGE FELL   . . . .   471 ALL SOUL NIGHT V   34
    A GREY BIRD HAS FLOWN BY. HE HAS FLOWN UPWARD.   . . .   753 SHADOW WATER A   134
URBINO
    EVENING AND MORNING, THE STEEP STREET OF URBINO   . . . . 352 PEOPLE   12
    EVENING AND MORN, THE STEEP STREET OF URBINO   . . . . . 352 PEOPLE   V   12
URBINO'S
    UPON URBINO'S WINDY HILL, ...   288 TO WEALTHY MAN   17
URGED
    OF DANAAN HOOVES WE URGED OUR WAY BETWEEN   . . . . . .   31 OISIN 2   V   31
    OUR LEARNED MEN HAVE URGED   . . . .   421 MY TABLE   15
URN
    WE THOUGHT ON OSCAR'S PENCILLED URN.   . . . .   2 OISIN 1   V   70
    "WE THINK ON OSCAR'S PENCILLED URN, ...   5 OISIN 1   41
    AND IN SOME URN FUNEREAL LIE   . . . .   19 OISIN 1   V   272

856

		PAGE	TITLE		LINE
URN	(CONTINUED)				
	OR ELSE ALL JUNO FROM AN URN DISPLAYS • • • • • • •	418	ANCEST HOUSES		27
USE					
	THE WAGES OF SIN IS DEATH. NO USE. NO GOOD• • • • • •	697	MOSADA 2		42
	THE WAGE OF SIN IS DEATH. NO USE. NO USE. • • • • •	697	MOSADA 2	V	42
	THE WAGE OF SIN IS DEATH. NO USE. NO USE. • • • • •	697	MOSADA 2	V	42
	NO USE. AWAY! HEAR, THOU ENDURING GOD, • • • • • •	698	MOSADA 2		50
	NO USE. AWAY! HEAR OH! THOU ENDURING GOD, • • • • •	698	MOSADA 2	V	50
USED					
	MY MONEY'S ALL USED UP, • • • • • • • • • • • • •	96	MOLL MAGEE		38
	I MIGHT HAVE USED THE ONE SUBSTANTIAL RIGHT • • • • •	352	PEOPLE		19
	BUT WHAT THE GREAT AND PASSIONATE HAVE USED • • • • •	371	ON GOING HOUSE		7
	AH! HOW LARGE MICE USED TO BE • • • • • • • • • •	727	LOVERS QUARREL		39
USELESS					
	THUNDERING, AND THE WIDE USELESS WATERS FRAY • • • • •	45	OISIN 2	V	238
	ALONE WITH ALL THIS USELESS HAPPINESS?" • • • • • •	285	TWO KINGS		200
USHEEN					
	FOR LOVE OF USHEEN MY FEET RAN • • • • • • • • • •	6	OISIN 1	V	57
	BY THIS YOUNG MAN, USHEEN MY SON?" • • • • • • • •	6	OISIN 1	V	60
	KNEEL, USHEEN, WEAR OUT THE FLAGS AND PRAY FOR YOUR SOUL	63	OISIN 3	V	215
	THAT IS LOST				
USHEEN'S					
	"RHYME, THAT RHYMED TO USHEEN'S NAME, • • • • • • •	7	OISIN 1	V	64
USNA'S					
	AND USNA'S CHILDREN DIED. • • • • • • • • • • •	111	ROSE OF WORLD		5
USURY					
	THEN WHEREFORE FEAR THE USURY OF TIME, • • • • • • •	724	KANVA ON SELF		17
UTHER'S					
	THE AUSTERE ARTHUR, RULE FROM UTHER'S CHAIR? • • • •	678	ISLE STAT II 3		296
UTMOST					
	AND NOW MY UTMOST MYSTERY IS OUT• • • • • • • • •	469	HARUN RASHID		187
	MY UTMOST PLEASURE WITH A MAN • • • • • • • • • •	535	CHOSEN		12
UTOPIA					
	SOME VAGUE UTOPIA--AND SHE SEEMS, • • • • • • • •	475	EVA GORE-BOOTH		11
UTTERED					
	SO PALE! AND SOUNDS OF WONDER HER LIPS UTTERED, • • •	34	OISIN 2	V	71
UTTERING					
	UTTERING, MASTERING IT, • • • • • • • • • • •	480	BLOOD AND MOON		5
	AND THEN NEW MURMURS CAME NEW UTTERING • • • • • •	657	ISLE STAT I 3		50
UTTERLY					
	I HAVE DECEIVED YOU UTTERLY. HOW CAN THAT BE? • • • •	245	SHADOW WATER B		472
	DANTE ALIGHIERI, SO UTTERLY FOUND HIMSELF • • • • • •	368	EGO DOMINUS		19
	ALL CHANGED, CHANGED UTTERLY! • • • • • • • • • •	392	EASTER 1916		15
	TRANSFORMED UTTERLY! • • • • • • • • • • • • •	393	EASTER 1916		39
	ARE CHANGED, CHANGED UTTERLY! • • • • • • • • • •	394	EASTER 1916		79
UTTERMOST					
	TRAGEDY WROUGHT O ITS UTTERMOST• • • • • • • • •	566	LAPIS LAZULI		20
VACILLATION					
	VACILLATION • • • • • • • • • • • • • • • • •	499	VACILLATION		T
VAGUE					
	A FAR VAGUE SOUND OF FEATHERY CHOIRS. • • • • • • •	13	OISIN 1	V	166
	A MOMENTARY GLIMMER OF VAGUE PHOSPHORUS FLAME. • • • •	37	OISIN 2	V	120
	• • • THE SOUND OF THE SEA'S VAGUE DRUM? • • • • •	56	OISIN 3		135
	VAGUE MEMORIES, NOTHING BUT MEMORIES. • • • • • • •	356	BROKEN DREAMS		15
	VAGUE MEMORIES, NOTHING BUT MEMORIES. • • • • • • •	356	BROKEN DREAMS		20
	VAGUE MEMORIES, NOTHING BUT MEMORIES. • • • • • • •	357	BROKEN DREAMS		41
	FROM VAGUE DISTRESS • • • • • • • • • • • • •	390	IMAGE PAST		24
	HOW CAN THOSE TERRIFIED VAGUE FINGERS PUSH • • • • • •	441	LEDA AND SWAN		5
	SOME VAGUE UTOPIA--AND SHE SEEMS, • • • • • • • •	475	EVA GORE-BOOTH		11
	ALL ASIATIC VAGUE IMMENSITIES, • • • • • • • • •	610	STATUES		12
VAGUELY					
	A MAN--SO VAGUELY THAT HE SEEMED TO DREAM-- • • • • •	351	HER PRAISE	V	8
VAIN					
	AND PONDERED IN A SOFT VAIN MOOD • • • • • • • • •	14	OISIN 1		184
	IN VAIN HER ARMS, IN VAIN HER SOFT WHITE BREAST. • • •	110	CUCHULAIN SEA		74
	IN VAIN HER ARMS, IN VAIN HER SOFT WHITE BREAST. • • •	110	CUCHULAIN SEA		74
	TILL VAIN FRENZY AWOKE AND HE DIED; AND HIM • • • • •	169	SECRET ROSE		12
	IN VAIN, IN VAIN! THE CATARACT STILL CRIES! • • • • •	311	MOUNTAIN TOMB		9
	IN VAIN, IN VAIN! THE CATARACT STILL CRIES! • • • • •	311	MOUNTAIN TOMB		9
	BUT CHARM AND FACE WERE IN VAIN • • • • • • • • •	350	MEMORY		3
	I AM THINKING OF A CHILD'S VOW SWORN IN VAIN • • • • •	391	UNDER SATURN		15
	MADE ALL PLATONIC TOLERANCE VAIN • • • • • • • • •	438	SONGS PLAY 2		7
	AND VAIN ALL DORIC DISCIPLINE. • • • • • • • • •	438	SONGS PLAY 2		8
	MADE PLATO'S TOLERANCE IN VAIN, • • • • • • • • •	438	SONGS PLAY 2	V	7
	AND VAIN THE DORIC DISCIPLINE. • • • • • • • • •	438	SONGS PLAY 2	V	8
	IN VAIN THE DORIC DISCIPLINE. • • • • • • • • •	438	SONGS PLAY 2	V	8
	DELIGHT BECOMES DEATH-LONGING IF ALL LONGING ELSE BE VAIN.	459	FROM OEDIPUS		3
	WE GROPE, AND GROPE IN VAIN, • • • • • • • • • •	487	CRAZED MOON		5
	I WHISTLED AND WHISTLED AND WHISTLED IN VAIN. • • • •	551	SONGS REWRIT 1		16
	I CRIED AND WHISTLED BUT VAIN, ALL VAIN. • • • • • •	551	SONGS REWRIT 1	V	16
	I CRIED AND WHISTLED BUT VAIN, ALL VAIN. • • • • • •	551	SONGS REWRIT 1	V	16
	BUT THERE I LAY AND I WHISTLED IN VAIN. • • • • • •	551	SONGS REWRIT 1	V	16
	A VAIN HOPE • • • • • • • • • • • • • • • • •	553	CHURCH STATE	V	T
	I SOUGHT A THEME AND SOUGHT FOR IT IN VAIN, • • • • •	629	CIRCUS ANIMALS		1
	VAIN GAIETY, VAIN BATTLE, VAIN REPOSE, • • • • • •	629	CIRCUS ANIMALS		12
	VAIN GAIETY, VAIN BATTLE, VAIN REPOSE, • • • • • •	629	CIRCUS ANIMALS		12
	VAIN GAIETY, VAIN BATTLE, VAIN REPOSE, • • • • • •	629	CIRCUS ANIMALS		12
	AND SHIRK IT IN VAIN. THERE IS NO RELEASE • • • • •	632	MAN AND ECHO		21
VAINGLORIOUS					
	A DRUNKEN, VAINGLORIOUS LOUT. • • • • • • • • • •	393	EASTER 1916		32

857

		PAGE	TITLE	LINE

VAIN-GLORIOUS
    A DRUNKEN, VAIN-GLORIOUS LOUT. • • • • • • • • • • • 393 EASTER 1916   V 32
VALE
    WHEN AMBLING DOWN THE VALE WE MET • • • • • • • • • •   2 OISIN 1   V 7U
    FROM ROLLING VALE AND RIVERY GLEN, • • • • • • • • • 83 MAD KING GOLL   19
    'TIS MORN! THY SHEEP ARE WANDERING DOWN THE VALE-- • • 645 ISLE STAT I 1   3
    IN VALE AND DELL SO BLAZE THE DAFFODILLS! • • • • • • 645 ISLE STAT I 1   15
    IF SO I MIGHT, ALONG A DEWY VALE, • • • • • • • • • • 649 ISLE STAT I 1 123
    OF THIS WIDE VALE, EMBOSOMED IN THE AIR, • • • • • • 652 ISLE STAT I 2   19
    ALONG THE VELVET VALE I SAW HIM COME-- • • • • • • • 690 MOSADA 1   10
    WHERE HOMES ONCE WHITENED VALE AND MOUNTAIN CREST! • • 709 FERENCZ RENYI   3
VALERA
    HAD DE VALERA EATEN PARNELL'S HEART • • • • • • • • • 542 PARN FUNERAL 2   2
    OR AM I DE VALERA, • • • • • • • • • • • • • • • • • 627 STATES HOLIDAY   18
VALLENCE
    WHEN MY LOST LOVER LEFT THESE ARMS. MY VALLENCE, • • • 701 MOSADA 3   V 51
    LOOK UP, LOOK UP, THY VALLENCE IS BY THEE. • • • • • 701 MOSADA 3   V 68
    GRIEVE NOT, FOR VALLENCE KNEELS BESIDE THEE--VALLENCE, • 702 MOSADA 3   V 90
    GRIEVE NOT, FOR VALLENCE KNEELS BESIDE THEE--VALLENCE, • 702 MOSADA 3   V 90
    SAFE ON THE BREAST OF VALLENCE IS THY HEAD • • • • • 703 MOSADA 3   101
    GIVE TO THY VALLENCE. VALLENCE--HE HAS GONE • • • • • 703 MOSADA 3   V 110
    GIVE TO THY VALLENCE. VALLENCE--HE HAS GONE • • • • • 703 MOSADA 3   V 110
VALLEY
    A VALLEY FLOWED DOWN FROM HIS HOOFS, AND THERE IN THE LONG 48 OISIN 3   26
        GRASS LAY,
    OF HOLLIES, AND HAZELS, AND OAK TREES, A VALLEY WAS SLOPING 48 OISIN 3   V 26
        AWAY
    AND OVER THE LIMBS AND THE VALLEY THE SLOW OWLS WANDERED 49 OISIN 3   41
        AND CAME,
    AND, IN A FAR-OFF, GENTLE VALLEY STOPPING, • • • • • • 68 SAD SHEPHERD   13
    HE FLED, AND IN A FAR-OFF VALLEY STOPPING, • • • • • • 68 SAD SHEPHERD V 13
    FROM ROLLING VALLEY AND RIVERY GLEN, • • • • • • • • • 83 MAD KING GOLL V 17
    AND SONG THAT DOWN THE VALLEY ROLLED-- • • • • • • • • 84 MAD KING GOLL V 35
    THE VALLEY OF THE BLACK PIG • • • • • • • • • • • • • 161 BLACK PIG   T
    HE TELLS OF A VALLEY FULL OF LOVERS • • • • • • • • • 163 VALLEY LOVERS   T
    THE VALLEY OF LOVERS • • • • • • • • • • • • • • • • 163 VALLEY LOVERS V T
    AEDH TELLS OF A VALLEY FULL OF LOVERS • • • • • • • • 163 VALLEY LOVERS V T
    I DREAMED THAT I STOOD IN A VALLEY, AND AMID SIGHS, • 163 VALLEY LOVERS   1
    TO KNOW THE MOUNTAIN AND THE VALLEY HAVE GRIEVED • • • 343 SHEP GOATHERD 117
    TO KNOW THE MOUNTAIN AND THE VALLEY GRIEVE • • • • • • 343 SHEP GOATHERD V 117
    NEVER TO LEAVE THAT VALLEY HIS FATHERS CALLED THEIR HOME. 391 UNDER SATURN   16
    VALLEY, RIVER, AND ELMS, UNDER THE LIGHT OF A MOON • • 426 PHANTOM HATRED   3
    VALLEY, RIVER, ELMS, UNDER THE LIGHT OF A MOON • • • • 426 PHANTOM HATRED V   3
    THE WOOD AND THE VALLEY AND SEA • • • • • • • • • • • 646 ISLE STAT I 1   42
    MAKE MOAN AND CRY. WITHIN YON SUNLESS VALLEY, • • • • 682 SEEKER   26
    THAT ALL THE VALLEY FILLS • • • • • • • • • • • • • • 781 MY HEART BEAT   10
VALLEY'S
    WATCHED HER THOSE SEAMLESS FACES FROM THE VALLEY'S   55 OISIN 3   122
        GLIMMERING GIRTH!
    WATCHED HER THOSE SEAMLESS FACES FROM THE VALLEY'S MURAL   55 OISIN 3   V 122
        GIRTH
VALLEYS
    O YOU, WITH WHOM, IN SLOPING VALLEYS, • • • • • • • • 10 OISIN 1   119
    OH YE WITH WHOM, IN SLOPING VALLEYS • • • • • • • • • 10 OISIN 1   V 119
    OR WRESTLE WITH THEIR PEERS IN DEWY VALLEYS. • • • • • 30 OISIN 2   V 14E
    A HERDSMAN CAME FROM INLAND VALLEYS • • • • • • • • • 82 MAD KING GOLL   14
    THERE CRIED A HERALD, "TO OUR VALLEYS • • • • • • • • 82 MAD KING GOLL V 14
    CRIED A HERALD, "TO OUR VALLEYS • • • • • • • • • • • 82 MAD KING GOLL V 14
    AND SONG THAT DOWN THE VALLEYS ROLLED-- • • • • • • • 84 MAD KING GOLL V 35
    THAT DOWN THE ECHOING VALLEYS ROLLED. • • • • • • • • 84 MAD KING GOLL V 35
    TILL ALL THE VALLEYS OF THE WORLD HAVE BEEN WITHERED AWAY. 163 VALLEY LOVERS   8
    TILL THE VALLEYS OF THE WORLD HAVE BEEN WITHERED AWAY." 163 VALLEY LOVERS V   8
    FAR OFF IN DROWSY VALLEYS • • • • • • • • • • • • • • 680 LOVE AND DEATH   5
    DOWN THE LONG VALLEYS FROM MY PEOPLE'S TENTS, • • • • 691 MOSADA 1   30
    WE WILL FIND OUT VALLEYS AND WOODS AND MEADOWS • • • • 767 SHADOW WATER A 388
VALOUR
    WITH HER DEAD BROTHER'S VALOUR • • • • • • • • • • • 365 HER RACE   11
VALUE
    TO VALUE BEER! NO HALF-LEGGED FOOL • • • • • • • • • 304 HOUR DAWN   52
    TO VALUE BEER--I WILL HAVE NO FOOL • • • • • • • • • 304 HOUR DAWN   V 52
VAMPIRES
    LIE BODIES OF THE VAMPIRES FULL OF BLOOD! • • • • • • 483 OIL AND BLOOD   5
VAN
    THE VAN OF WANDERING QUIET! ERE YOU BE TOO CALM AND OLD, 73 ANASHU VIJAYA   43
    THE VAN OF WANDERING QUIET! ERE YE BE TOO CALM AND OLD, 73 ANASHU VIJAYA V 43
VANISH
    FOR ALL HIS SPELLS WILL VANISH WHEN HE DIES, • • • • 240 SHADOW WATER B 376
    BUT VANISH WITH OUR BREATH • • • • • • • • • • • • • 431 NINETEEN 19   76
    ALL BREAK AND VANISH, AND EVIL GATHERS HEAD! • • • • 433 NINETEEN 19   117
    MUST VANISH ON THE INSTANT IF THE MIND BUT CHANGE • • 481 BLOOD AND MOON 27
        ITS THEME!
    IN THE FAR WORLD WILL VANISH FROM THY MIND, • • • • • 670 ISLE STAT II 3   93
    HAVE COVERED THEM. WHERE DID THEY VANISH AWAY? • • • 764 SHADOW WATER A 328
VANISHED
    O WHEN WILL YOU GROW WEARY?" THEY HAD VANISHED! • • • 187 QUEEN MAEVE   152
    IT VANISHED LIKE A SHADOW, AND A CRY • • • • • • • • 278 TWO KINGS   38
    MY HANDS WERE PRESSED TO VANISHED SUDDENLY. • • • • • 286 TWO KINGS   208
    VANISHED; AND LEFT BUT MEMORIES, THAT SHOULD BE OUT OF 316 COLD HEAVEN   5
        SEASON
    WHEN HE VANISHED FROM EARS AND EYES. • • • • • • • • 341 SHEP GOATHERD   72
    WHEN IT HAS VANISHED FROM OUR NATURAL EYES! • • • • • 342 SHEP GOATHERD   81

858

VANISHED (CONTINUED)

THE HOLY CENTAURS OF THE HILLS ARE VANISHED; • • • • • • • • 344 DEJECTION   7
BANISHED HEROIC MOTHER MOON AND VANISHED, • • • • • • • 344 DEJECTION   9
HEROIC MOTHER MOON HAS VANISHED, • • • • • • • • 344 DEJECTION   V   9
WHEN THE OLD MOON IS VANISHED FROM THE SKY • • • • • 382 VISION ROBART   3
AND WHEN IT'S VANISHED STILL DECLARE, • • • • • • • 639 BEN BULBEN   60
FADED AND VANISHED; NOTHING NOW IS SEEN, • • • • • 676 ISLE STAT II 3 268
GHOSTS OF HER VANISHED GLORIES, MUSE AND STALK • • • 687 TWO TITANS   21
THE FAIRY VANISHED FROM HIS SIGHT, • • • • • • • 730 PRIEST FAIRY   62

VANISHES

MAN IS IN LOVE AND LOVES WHAT VANISHES, • • • • • • 429 NINETEEN 19   42
TO BE IN LOVE AND LOVE WHAT VANISHES. • • • • • • 429 NINETEEN 19   V 42

VANISHING

WHEN THE OLD MOON IS VANISHING FROM THE SKY • • • • 382 VISION ROBART   V   3

VANITY

O VANITY OF SLEEP, HOPE, DREAM, ENDLESS DESIRE, • • • • 154 BELOVED PEACE   7
AND VANITY HER FOOTFALL LIGHT, • • • • • • • 314 MEMORY YOUTH   12
OR THE DAY'S VANITY, THE NIGHT'S REMORSE. • • • • • 491 COOLE BALLYLEE V 40H
OR THE DAY'S VANITY, THE NIGHT'S REMORSE. • • • • • 495 CHOICE   8
MY CONSCIENCE OR MY VANITY APPALLED. • • • • • • 501 VACILLATION   56

VANITY'S

NO VANITY'S DISPLAYED; • • • • • • • • • • • 532 BEFORE WORLD   6

VANS

AND TRAILING CRIMSON VANS, A MUMBLING BROOD, • • • • 687 TWO TITANS   20

VAPOUR

HALF LOST IN VAPOUR, SHADOWS CALLED OUR NAMES, • • • • 29 OISIN 2   V   3
NOT LOADED CENTURIES MIGHT VAPOUR. RAN • • • • • 38 OISIN 2   V 127
SHAKING AND WAVING, VAPOUR VAPOUR CHASED, • • • • • 39 OISIN 2   164
SHAKING AND WAVING, VAPOUR VAPOUR CHASED, • • • • • 39 OISIN 2   164
GO DWELL UPON THE SEA CLIFFS, VAPOUR HID, • • • • • 105 CUCHULAIN SEA V   4
IN DRUID VAPOUR AND MAKE THE TORCHES DIM; • • • • • 169 SECRET ROSE   11
WHEN IN RAGGED VAPOUR THEY MUTTER NIGHT AND DAY, • • 206 HANRAHANS SONG V   2
DARTING YOU WAVE THEM, DARTING IN THE VAPOUR. • • • 694 MOSADA 1   94
THEM ALL, AND LET THEM FIND YOU IN THE VAPOUR. • • • 694 MOSADA 1   V 108A
FOR YE ARE HID WITH VAPOUR. ROUND THE STAKE • • • 695 MOSADA 1   111
THE VAPOUR IS MUCH THICKER. GOD! THE STAKE! • • • • 695 MOSADA 1   112
BREATHED OUT A DRUID VAPOUR, AND CRUMBLED AWAY • • • 761 SHADOW WATER A 279

VAPOUR-HID

GO DWELL UPON THE SEA CLIFFS, VAPOUR-HID • • • • • 105 CUCHULAIN SEA V   4

VAPOURS

AND FACE THAT SEEMED WROUGHT OUT OF MOONLIT VAPOURS, • • 33 OISIN 2   70
HER FACE SEEMED FASHIONED ALL OF MOONLIT VAPOURS, • • 33 OISIN 2   V 70
SHAKING AND WAVING, VAPOURS VAPOURS CHASED; • • • • 39 OISIN 2   V 164
SHAKING AND WAVING, VAPOURS VAPOURS CHASED; • • • • 39 OISIN 2   V 164
IN ALL HIS EVENING VAPOURS ROLLED-- • • • • • • 86 MAD KING GOLL V 71
WHEN THE WINTRY VAPOURS RISE. • • • • • • • • 643 SONG FAERIES   4
WHEN THE WINTRY VAPOURS RISE. • • • • • • • • 644 SONG FAERIES   16
FAR THE MORNING VAPOURS SHATTER, • • • • • • 648 ISLE STAT I 1   89
OVER THEM CRIMSON VAPOURS WINGING. • • • • • • 648 ISLE STAT I 1   92
WHEN THE WINTRY VAPOURS RISE. • • • • • • • • 676 ISLE STAT II 3 251
WHEN THE WINTRY VAPOURS RISE. • • • • • • • • 676 ISLE STAT II 3 263
FOR YE ARE HID WITH VAPOURS? ROUND THE STAKE • • • 695 MOSADA 1   V 111
ALL HEAVEN'S FLOOR, WITH VAPOURS BEDDED-- • • • • 705 DAWN-SONG   11
DOWN THE VAPOURS FALL AND HIDE THEM FROM THE CHILDREN OF 719 PHANTOM SHIP   27
    A DAY,
AND THE WINDS COME DOWN AND BLOW THEM WITH THE VAPOURS 719 PHANTOM SHIP   28
    FAR AWAY.
NESTED 'MONG THE VAPOURS BROWN. • • • • • • • • 731 STREET DANCERS   6

VAPOUR-TURBANED

UNDER THAT COLD AND VAPOUR-TURBANED STEEP, • • • • • 128 DREAM OF FAERY   39

VAPOURY

WITH VAPOURY FOOTSOLE BY THE WATER'S DROWSY BLAZE. • • • 78 INDIAN TO LOVE   20
A VAPOURY FOOTFALL ON THE OCEAN'S SLEEPY BLAZE. • • • 78 INDIAN TO LOVE V 20
AND DROP A VAPOURY FOOTFALL IN THE WATER'S DROWSY BLAZE. 78 INDIAN TO LOVE V 20
WITH VAPOURY FOOTSOLE AMONG THE WATER'S DROWSY BLAZE. • • 78 INDIAN TO LOVE V 20
DROPPING A VAPOURY FOOTSOLE ON THE TIDE'S DROWSY BLAZE. • 78 INDIAN TO LOVE V 20

VARYING

THROUGHOUT SO MANY VARYING CENTURIES • • • • • • • 371 ON GOING HOUSE   8

VASSALS

AND TWICE A HUNDRED WERE THE VASSALS • • • • • • • 23 OISIN 1   V 345E

VAST

WARS SHADOWY, VAST, EXULTANT; FAERIES OF OLD • • • • • 29 OISIN 2   9
WARS SHADOWY, VAST, EXULTANT; FAIRY KINGS • • • • • 29 OISIN 2   V   9
NEARER THE CASTLE CAME WE. A VAST TIDE, • • • • • 31 OISIN 2   V 27A
TYING THE HORSE TO HIS VAST FOOT THAT LAY • • • • • 32 OISIN 2   46
TO ONE VAST FOOT, FROTH-SPLASHED, WITH CURVED TOES LYING 32 OISIN 2   V 46A
CAME CAR-BORNE BALOR, AS OLD AS A FOREST, HIS VAST FACE 53 OISIN 3   V 91
    SUNK
LONG FLED THE FOAM-FLAKES AROUND ME, THE WINDS FLED OUT 57 OISIN 3   149
    OF THE VAST,
ON THEIR VAST FACES MYSTERY AND DREAMS; • • • • • • 74 ANASHU VIJAYA   70
WHEN A VAST IMAGE OUT OF SPIRITUS MUNDI • • • • • 402 SECOND COMING   12
VAST GREENNESS, WHERE ETERNAL RUMOUR DWELLS, • • • • 657 ISLE STAT I 3   45
OF THOSE VAST WOODS; AND THEN I SAW THE BOAT, • • • 657 ISLE STAT I 3   53
TO SEE THEM DROWNED BY THOSE VAST SOLITUDES, • • • • 661 ISLE STAT II 1   57
AND SOFT, ONE GLIMMERING STAR--WITH POWER VAST; • • • 714 FERENCZ RENYI V 115
THAT THE VAST TROUBLED WATERS BRING • • • • • • 784 WOMANS BEAUTY   17

VASTY

I FOUND, FOAM-OOZY ON THE VASTY STAIR, • • • • • • 43 OISIN 2   V 215

VAT   SEE WINE-VAT

OR IN THE WINE VAT, DWELL BEYOND THE STIR • • • • • 169 SECRET ROSE   V   4

```
                                                          PAGE      TITLE            LINE
VATS
    THERE WE'VE HID OUR FAERY VATS,  . . . . . . . . .     87  STOLEN CHILD           6
VEERING
    VEERING, FLEETING, FICKLE, THE WINDS OF KNOCKNAREA, . .  206  HANRAHANS SONG V     1
    VEERING, FLEETING, FICKLE, OUR LOVES AND ANGERS MEET!  . .  207  HANRAHANS SONG V   3
VEGETATIVE
    DRAWN THROUGH THE WANDERING VEGETATIVE DREAM, . . . . . .  467  HARUN RASHID       143
VEHEMENT
    VEHEMENT AND WITTY SHE HAD SEEMED--: THE VENETIAN LADY . .  363  DOLLS FACES         5
VEILED
    VEILED IN A DREAMY SORROW FOR THEIR LOVE  . . . . . . .  79  EPHEMERA        V    2A
VEILS
    DROPPING FROM THE VEILS OF THE MORNING TO WHERE THE CRICKET  117  ISLE INNISFREE    6
        SINGS!
    NOON WRAPT THE TREES IN VEILS OF VIOLET WEATHER, . . . . .  715  DWELT SYCAMORE      7
    NOON WRAPPED THE WOODS IN VEILS OF VIOLET WEATHER! . . .  715  DWELT SYCAMORE V    7
VEIN
    OR BUT TO FIND IF WITHERED VEIN RAN BLOOD, . . . . . .  537  HER VISION           6
VEINED        SEE BLUE-VEINED
    AH, TOUCH THEIR BLUE VEINED EYELIDS IF THEY SLEEP, . . .  33  OISIN 2         V   61
VEINS
    HAS DRIED THE SAP OUT OF MY VEINS, AND RENT  . . . . .  260  FASC DIFFICULT      2
    SWEETER EMOTION, WORKING IN THEIR VEINS . . . . . . .  292  TO A SHADE          13
    THE FURY AND THE MIRE OF HUMAN VEINS. . . . . . . . .  497  BYZANTIUM            8
    THOSE VEINS MUST SOON BE DRY! . . . . . . . . . . .  513  JANE TALK BISH       4
    AND ALL HIS VEINS HAD NEAR RUN DRY, . . . . . . . .  670  ISLE STAT II 3     119
    THIS DEATH IS HEAVY IN MY VEINS LIKE SLEEP. . . . . .  701  MOSADA 3            57
VELVET
    DROPT DOWN THE VELVET DARKNESS FROM ABOVE, . . . . . .  688  TWO TITANS          37
    ALONG THE VELVET VALE I SAW HIM COME-- . . . . . . .  690  MOSADA 1            10
VENETIAN
    VEHEMENT AND WITTY SHE HAD SEEMED--: THE VENETIAN LADY . .  363  DOLLS FACES         5
    BEAUTIFUL AND GENTLE IN HER VENETIAN WAY. . . . . . .  602  GALLERY REVIS       14
    BEAUTIFUL, GRACIOUS, IN HER VENETIAN WAY. . . . . . .  602  GALLERY REVIS V     14
VENGEANCE
    HIS SUDDEN VENGEANCE WERE A COUNTRY TALE, . . . . . .  127  DREAM OF FAERY      27
    AND I WOULD KNOW IF YOU WILL GIVE ME VENGEANCE. . . . .  235  SHADOW WATER B     301
    IT WAS THIS WOMAN IN HER WOMAN'S VENGEANCE . . . . . .  248  SHADOW WATER B     547
    "VENGEANCE UPON THE MURDERERS," THE CRY GOES UP, . . . .  426  PHANTOM HATRED      9
    "VENGEANCE FOR JACQUES MOLAY."  IN CLOUD-PALE RAGS, OR  426  PHANTOM HATRED     10
        IN LACE,
    FOR VENGEANCE ON THE MURDERERS OF JACQUES MOLAY. . . . .  426  PHANTOM HATRED     16
VENGENCE
    "VENGENCE FOR JACQUES MOLAY."  IN CLOUD PALE RAGS, OR IN  426  PHANTOM HATRED V   10
        LACE,
VERDANT
    IS ROLLED AS VERDANT SMOKE!  O THOU WHOSE FACE . . . .  667  ISLE STAT II 3     35
VERGE
    AND, EVER PACING ON THE VERGE OF THINGS, . . . . . . .  73  ANASHU VIJAYA       54
    THEY ARE CAST BEYOND THE VERGE, AND IN A CLOUD, . . . .  376  PHASES OF MOON     105
VERONESE
    LEARNED LIKE A MAN?  PAUL VERONESE . . . . . . . . .  386  ROBARTES DANCE      26
VERONICA'S
    VERONICA'S NAPKIN . . . . . . . . . . . . . . .  483  VERONIC NAPKIN       T
VERSE
    IN THE VERSE OF ATTIC STORY . . . . . . . . . . .  65  HAPPY SHEPHERD V    16
    ALL THINGS CAN TEMPT ME FROM THIS CRAFT OF VERSE! . . .  267  ALL TEMPT ME        1
    I WRITE IT OUT IN A VERSE-- . . . . . . . . . . .  394  EASTER 1916         74
    CAN PAY THE POET FOR A VERSE AND HEAR THE FIDDLE SOUND,  581  CURSE CROMWELL     21
VERSES
    THE VERSES THAT COULD MOVE THEM ON THE DAY . . . . . .  257  RECONCILIATION      2
    THE VERSES THAT THEY CARED FOR ON THE DAY . . . . . .  257  RECONCILIATION V    2
VERY
    IT SEEMED TO FALL FROM THE VERY FLAME . . . . . . . .  13  OISIN 1         V  167
    THE VERY WORLD ITSELF MAY BE  . . . . . . . . . .  65  HAPPY SHEPHERD V    18
    ALL, ALL, THE VERY BOTTOM OF THE BOWL-- . . . . . . .  227  SHADOW WATER B     118
    WILL GATHER, AND NOT KNOW IT WALKS THE VERY STREET . . .  315  FALLEN MAJESTY      7
    WILL GATHER AND NOT KNOW THAT THROUGH ITS VERY STREET . .  315  FALLEN MAJESTY V    7
    FOR BEAUTY'S VERY SELF, HAS CHARM MADE WISE, . . . . .  404  FOR DAUGHTER       37
    HAS MADE THE VERY OWLS IN CIRCLES MOVE! . . . . . . .  423  MY DESCENDANTS     18
    UNDER THAT VERY TREE. . . . . . . . . . . . . .  457  SUMMER SPRING      12
    AND YET HERSELF CAN SEEM YOUTH'S VERY FOUNTAIN, . . . .  465  HARUN RASHID       89
    TRUTHS THAT WHEN MY VERY BONES ARE DUST . . . . . . .  467  HARUN RASHID V    144
    WHERE VERY FOOT OBEYED HER GLANCE! . . . . . . . . .  488  CRAZED MOON    V   11
    I THOUGHT IT OUT THIS VERY DAY, . . . . . . . . . .  525  DANCING DAYS       17
    O'ER THE LAKE THIS VERY DAY. . . . . . . . . . . .  656  ISLE STAT I 3      17
    YOUR WEEPING FITS!  LOOK YOU, SO VERY STRAIT . . . . .  659  ISLE STAT II 1     22
    AYE, VERY LATELY, SORROW CAME TO WEEP . . . . . . . .  659  ISLE STAT II 1     25
    SWIFT LAKE.  A VERY LITTLE THING THAT IS, . . . . . .  669  ISLE STAT II 3     78
    YES, ALL IS VERY WELL.  WHENCE COMEST THOU? . . . . . .  682  SEEKER             14
    THE VERY SQUIRREL DIES THAT ENTERS THERE. . . . . . .  682  SEEKER             33
    THE VERY SQUIRREL DIES THAT ENTERS IT. . . . . . . .  682  SEEKER         V   33
    I'M WEARY--WEARY, AND 'TIS VERY COLD. . . . . . . .  703  MOSADA 3          122
    AH! IT IS SO VERY BIG, . . . . . . . . . . . . .  726  LOVERS QUARREL     17
    AND WE ARE SO VERY SMALL! . . . . . . . . . . . .  726  LOVERS QUARREL     18
    THEY GREW SO VERY STILL, I WIS . . . . . . . . . .  730  PRIEST FAIRY       66
VESSEL
    SEE THE DARKNESS SLOW DISGORGING A VESSEL BLIND WITH  718  PHANTOM SHIP       12
        SQUALL.
VESTED        SEE NIGHT-VESTED
```

		PAGE	TITLE		LINE

VESTITURE
    O, LADY, THOU WHOSE VESTITURE OF GREEN . . . . 667 ISLE STAT II 3   34

VESTURE
    BUT DOWN TO HER FEET WHITE VESTURE FLOWED, ... 3 OISIN 1   25
    DOWN TO HER FEET WHITE VESTURE FLOWED, ... 3 OISIN 1 V 25
    WALKS IN THE VESTURE OF HER SISTER SORROW. . . . . . 735 QUATRAIN APHOR 28

VEX
    "VEX THEM NO LONGER," NIAMH SAID, ... 12 OISIN 1 148
    "THESE FORMS?" "VEX NOT WITH SPEECH THE PHANTOMS DREAD." 29 OISIN 2 V 5

VEXED
    WERE VEXED TO NIGHTMARE BY A ROCKING CRADLE, ... 402 SECOND COMING 20
    AND KNOWING THAT THE FUTURE WOULD BE VEXED . . . . . 472 ALL SOUL NIGHT 44
    AND BY FOREKNOWLEDGE OF THE FUTURE VEXED: . . . . . 472 ALL SOUL NIGHT V 44
    "WITH ACTION ALL THE WORLD IS VEXED," . . . . . . 728 PRIEST FAIRY 15

VICTIM
    BUT MY HEART'S VICTIM AND ITS TORTURER. . . . . . . 537 HER VISION 32

VICTOR
    FAMOUS, A MAN OF RULES, A VICTOR. STANDS 709 FERENCZ RENYI 9
    THE ARCHANGEL AXEL, VICTOR THE ANGEL . . . . 774 COME RIDE 11

VICTORIES
    THE ISLAND OF VICTORIES . . . . 29 OISIN 2 V T
    THE ISLANDS OF DANCING AND OF VICTORIES . . . . . 46 OISIN 2 247
    ISLES OF THE LIVING AND OF VICTORIES . . . . . . 46 OISIN 2 V 247
    PRAISED THEIR GREAT VICTORIES AND GAVE THEM JOY . . . 286 TWO KINGS V 218B
    THROUGH VICTORIES OF THE MIND, ... 343 SHEP GOATHERD 108

VICTORY
    BUT HAVE NO SHARE IN LOSS OR VICTORY. . . . . . . 104 FERGUS DRUID V 38E
    AND MOCKS RETURNING VICTORY, HE PASSED . . . . . 279 TWO KINGS 58
    THAT EVERY NATURAL VICTORY . . . . 401 DEMON BEAST 34
    SOME HAD NO THOUGHT OF VICTORY . . . . 608 SONGS BURDEN 3 19
    AND CHANTS OF VICTORY AMID THE ENCIRCLING HOUNDS. . . . 622 HOUND VOICE 21

VIE
    HER SPEECH A WICKED TALE THAT WE MAY VIE WITH HER, . . . 362 HER COURTESY 6

VIEW
    DESTROY THE VIEW BY CUTTING DOWN AN ASH . . . . . . 372 ON GOING HOUSE 13
    THE LINEAMENTS THAT PLEASE THEIR VIEW . . . . . 387 ROBARTES DANCE 49
    THAT ALL'S ARRANGED IN ONE CLEAR VIEW, ... 633 MAN AND ECHO 31

VIEWLESS
    THUS, THUS I BECKON FROM HER VIEWLESS FIELDS— . . . . 693 MOSADA 1 75

VIGOROUS
    PUSH OUT HIS VIGOROUS LIMBS AND RUB HIS EYES, ... 284 TWO KINGS 162
    THAT VIGOROUS THIGH, THAT DREAMING EYE? . . . . . 386 ROBARTES DANCE 23
    HAVING INHERITED A VIGOROUS MIND . . . . . . 422 MY DESCENDANTS 1
    AS VIGOROUS OF MIND, AND YET IT SEEMS . . . . . . 422 MY DESCENDANTS 4

VIGOUR
    IN A VIGOUR MORE THAN MORTAL MEASURE, ... 9 OISIN 1 V 98
    IN ALL THE VIGOUR OF ITS BLOOD: . . . . 529 TOM LUNATIC 17

VIJAYA
    ANASHUYA AND VIJAYA . . . . 70 ANASHU VIJAYA T
    VIJAYA, I HAVE BROUGHT MY EVENING RICE: . . . . . 72 ANASHU VIJAYA 23
    VIJAYA, SWEAR TO HER LOVE NEVER MORE. . . . . . 74 ANASHU VIJAYA 65
    FAREWELL, VIJAYA. NAY, NO WORD, NO WORD! . . . . . 75 ANASHU VIJAYA 83
    OF RED FLAMINGOES; AND MY LOVE, VIJAYA: . . . . . 75 ANASHU VIJAYA 89
    OF RED FLAMINGO: AND MY LOVE, VIJAYA, ... 75 ANASHU VIJAYA V 89

VILE
    SING SUMMER WAVES. BUT YONDER SHEPHERD VILE, ... 649 ISLE STAT I 1 107

VILLAGE
    YOU LIVE, AND ON THE VILLAGE BORDER SHE, ... 74 ANASHU VIJAYA 62
    YOU LIVE, AND ON THE BORDER OF THE VILLAGE SHE, ... 74 ANASHU VIJAYA V 62
    THEY BRING YOU MEMORIES OF OLD VILLAGE FACES: . . . . 130 BOOK STORIES V 22
    I POKED ABOUT A VILLAGE CHURCH . . . . 584 GHOST ROG CASE 31
    THY NAME IS?" "RENYI." "OF?" "THIS VILLAGE." "GOOD! 709 FERENCZ RENYI 13
    THY NAME IS?" "FERENCZ RENYI." "OF?" "THIS VILLAGE." 709 FERENCZ RENYI V 13
      "GOOD!
    ALONG THE TENTS, THE FIELDS, THE VILLAGE WALLS. . . . . 712 FERENCZ RENYI 71
    ALONG THE TENTS, FIELD, THE VILLAGE WALLS. . . . . 712 FERENCZ RENYI V 71
    I CAME THE FIRST TIME TO THY VILLAGE SCHOOL? . . . . 713 FERENCZ RENYI 90
    I AM TO BE YOUR WIFE. A VILLAGE HIGH . . . . . . 713 FERENCZ RENYI 97
    I WAS TO BE YOUR WIFE. A VILLAGE HIGH . . . . . . 713 FERENCZ RENYI V 97
    ALL THE DROWNED THAT EVER WERE DROWNED FROM THAT VILLAGE 719 PHANTOM SHIP 20
      BY THE SEA:
    MUSINGLY WANDERED THE VILLAGE PRIEST. . . . . . . 728 PRIEST FAIRY 3

VILLAGES
    LET'S HOME AND SPEND IT IN OUR VILLAGES. . . . . . 248 SHADOW WATER B V 538A

VINCI'
    DA VINCI' FINGER SO HAD FASHIONED IT . . . . . . 444 SCHOOL CHILDR V 26

VINEGAR-HEAVY
    THE VINEGAR-HEAVY SPONGE, THE FLOWERS BY KEDRON STREAM: 172 TRAV PASSION 5

VIOLENCE
    BUT TAKE OUR GREATNESS WITH OUR VIOLENCE? . . . . . 418 ANCEST HOUSES 32
    VIOLENCE UPON THE ROADS: VIOLENCE OF HORSES: . . . . 432 NINETEEN 19 113
    VIOLENCE UPON THE ROADS: VIOLENCE OF HORSES: . . . . 432 NINETEEN 19 113
    WITH SOME SORT OF VIOLENCE . . . . 638 BEN BULBEN 34

VIOLENT
    HAVE TAUGHT TO IGNORANT MEN MOST VIOLENT WAYS, ... 256 NO SECOND TROY 3
    SOME VIOLENT BITTER MAN, SOME POWERFUL MAN . . . . . 418 ANCEST HOUSES 17
    BITTER AND VIOLENT MEN, MIGHT REAR IN STONE . . . . 418 ANCEST HOUSES 19
    TO SHOW HOW VIOLENT GREAT HEARTS CAN LOSE . . . . . 463 HARUN RASHID 47
    HER VIOLENT MAN . . . . 628 JANE MOUNTAIN 16
    VIOLENT AND FAMOUS, STRODE AMONG THE DEAD: . . . . . 634 CUCHULAIN COMF 2

	PAGE	TITLE		LINE

VIOLET
AND SMOKE FROM THIS DEAD HEART DRIFTS THROUGH THE VIOLET 173 SPEAKS HEARERS 3
AIR
MIRACULOUS OIL, ODOUR OF VIOLET. 483 OIL AND BLOOD 3
NOON WRAPT THE TREES IN VEILS OF VIOLET WEATHER. 715 DWELT SYCAMORE 7
NOON WRAPPED THE WOODS IN VEILS OF VIOLET WEATHER: 715 DWELT SYCAMORE V 7
VIOLETS
THE VIOLETS ARE THAT ON THE WOODED HILL 713 FERENCZ RENYI 95
VIRGIN
I SAW A STARING VIRGIN STAND 437 SONGS PLAY 1 1
WHEN THAT FIERCE VIRGIN AND HER STAR 437 SONGS PLAY 1 15
I SAW THAT STARING, VIRGIN STAND 437 SONGS PLAY 1 V 1
WHEN THE FIERCE VIRGIN AND HER STAR 437 SONGS PLAY 1 V 15
THE LION AND THE VIRGIN, 601 THOSE IMAGES 11
FROM EMPTY TOMB OR VIRGIN WOMB? 619 STICK INCENSE 2
VIRGINAL
WHEN SHE IN ALL HER VIRGINAL PRIDE 488 CRAZED MOON 8
VIRGINITY
JACK HAD MY VIRGINITY, 508 JANE BISHOP 22
THAT HAD MY VIRGINITY 508 JANE BISHOP V 23
VIRTUE
THAN MOUND AND STONE THAT KEEP ALL VIRTUE IN, 281 TWO KINGS 106
BUT FAME AND VIRTUE ROT. 584 GHOST ROG CASE 36
VIRTUES
"ONLY THE WASTEFUL VIRTUES EARN THE SUN": 270 PARDON FATHERS 18
BUT I, WHOSE VIRTUES ARE THE DEFINITIONS 353 PEOPLE 32
VISAGE
AND GAZING ON HIS VISAGE WORN, 99 FOXHUNTER V 43
CAN COME UPON THE VISAGE OF THE MOON 482 BLOOD AND MOON 53
OR HAST THOU NEVER SEEN, WITH VISAGE MEEK, 672 ISLE STAT II 3 156
VISAGED SEE LONG-VISAGED
THAT PALE, LONG VISAGED COMPANY 637 BEN BULBEN V 7
VISIBLE
BEYOND THE VISIBLE WORLD. ALL DREAMS OF THE SOUL 374 PHASES OF MOON 63
VISION
TILL ALL HAD SEEMED A SHADOW OR A VISION 278 TWO KINGS 43
IS BUT A VISION OF REALITY. 369 EGO DOMINUS 48
THE DOUBLE VISION OF MICHAEL ROBARTES 382 VISION ROBART T
IN REVERIE, OR IN VISION, SAW 420 MY HOUSE V 20E
HER VISION IN THE WOOD 536 HER VISION T
A VISION OF TERROR THAT IT MUST LIVE THROUGH 619 BRONZE HEAD 17
THE VISION OF A ROCK WHERE LIGHTNINGS WHIRL'D 687 TWO TITANS 1
THE VISION. YOU ARE PALE AND WEEPING. CHILD, 693 MOSADA 1 73
THIS VISION OF PETER AND THE BURNING GATE. 696 MOSADA 2 21
A SAINT OF RUSSIA IN A VISION SAW 696 MOSADA 2 V 21
VISIONARIES
TWO POEMS CONCERNING PEASANT VISIONARIES A CRADLE SONG 146 UNAPPEAS HOST V T
VISIONARY
A VISIONARY WHITE SEA-BIRD 361 ALF POLLEXFEN 37
A VISIONARY WHITE SEA BIRD 361 ALF POLLEXFEN V 37
SAT LATE, OR SHELLEY'S VISIONARY PRINCE: 373 PHASES OF MOON 16
THY GARMENTS' HEM, THOU VISIONARY ONE! 684 SEEKER 71
THY GARMENT'S HEM, THOU VISIONARY ONE! 684 SEEKER V 71
VISIONS
SEER OF VISIONS! NOW EVE FALLS ASLEEP, 691 MOSADA 1 36
VISIT
IF DAYLIGHT EVER VISIT WHERE, 446 COLONUS PRAISE 4
VISITED SEE RE-VISITED
VISITS
MOORE ONCE HAD VISITS FROM THE MUSE 792 GEORGE MOORE 1
VIVID
BEFORE MY TIME, SEEM LIKE A VIVID MEMORY. 391 UNDER SATURN 10
COMING WITH VIVID FACES 391 EASTER 1916 2
VIVIEN
TIME AND THE WITCH VIVIEN. 720 WITCH VIVIEN T
VIZIR
HIS VIZIR JAFFER FOR AN UNKNOWN REASON: 462 HARUN RASHID 32
VOICE
WHERE THE VOICE OF CHANGE IS THE VOICE OF A TUNE, 8 OISIN 1 V 82
WHERE THE VOICE OF CHANGE IS THE VOICE OF A TUNE, 8 OISIN 1 V 82
AND SWEETER OF VOICE THAN THE PLEASANT BIRDS, 9 OISIN 1 95
AND WHEN THEY HEARD HER VOICE THEY RAN 15 OISIN 1 213
WITH A CLEAR VOICE THE YOUNG MAN CRIED, 18 OISIN 1 260
SO SLEEP THEE BY DAYTIME." A VOICE CRIED, 59 OISIN 3 172
SO SLEEP THEY BY DAYTIME." A VOICE CRIED, 59 OISIN 3 V 172
THAT WANES." "AH, WISTFUL VOICE," REPLIED THE OTHER, 79 EPHEMERA V 3
OUR MARRIED VOICE WILDLY TROLLED. 85 MAD KING GOLL V 59
AND CRIED WITH ANGRY VOICE, "IT IS NOT MEET 107 CUCHULAIN SEA 20
SANG WHERE--UNNECESSARY CRUEL VOICE-- 127 DREAM OF FAERY 30
TOLD WHERE--AH, LITTLE, ALL-UNNEEDED VOICE!-- 127 DREAM OF FAERY V 30
AS THOUGH ONE LISTENED THERE, AND HIS VOICE SANK 180 QUEEN MAEVE 7
AND NOT WITH HIS OWN VOICE OR A MAN'S VOICE, 183 QUEEN MAEVE 74
AND NOT WITH HIS OWN VOICE OR A MAN'S VOICE, 183 QUEEN MAEVE 74
BUT WITH THE BURNING, LIVE, UNSHAKEN VOICE 183 QUEEN MAEVE 75
AND WITH GLAD VOICE MAEVE ANSWERED HIM, "WHAT KING 183 QUEEN MAEVE 79
AND WITH GLAD VOICE MAEVE ANSWERED "MANY A TIME 183 QUEEN MAEVE V 79
ON FINDING THAT HER VOICE IS SWEET AND LOW 205 ADAMS CURSE 17
MURMURED WITH HER YOUNG VOICE FOR WHOSE MILD SAKE 205 ADAMS CURSE V 15
HAVE THE BIRDS PASSED US? I COULD HEAR YOUR VOICE, 226 SHADOW WATER B 81
THEY CANNOT HEAR MY VOICE! BUT WHAT'S THE MEANING? 234 SHADOW WATER B 275
AND YOU WILL RECOLLECT MY FACE AND VOICE, 243 SHADOW WATER B 433

VOICE (CONTINUED)
"WOULD IT WERE ANYTHING BUT MERELY VOICE!" . . . . 258 KING NO KING   1
BUT WITH A VOICE THAT HAD UNNATURAL MUSIC, ... 283 TWO KINGS   153
BUT THAT SWEET-SOUNDING VOICE RAN ON: "WOMAN, ... 284 TWO KINGS   165
I WAS NO LONGER TERRIFIED--HIS VOICE . . . . 284 TWO KINGS   171
WOMEN CAN FIND." WITH A MOST MASTERFUL VOICE, ... 284 TWO KINGS   175
WOMEN CAN FIND." WITH A MOST BURNING VOICE . . . . . . 284 TWO KINGS   V 175
AND THEREUPON WITH AGED, HIGH-PITCHED VOICE . . . . . . 375 PHASES OF MOON   84
UNTIL HER VOICE GREW SHRILL. . . . . 392 EASTER 1916   20
WHAT VOICE MORE SWEET THAN HERS . . . . 392 EASTER 1916   21
LAUGHTER NOT TIME DESTROYED MY VOICE . . . . 455 FRIENDS YOUTH   1
I HEARD HER VOICE, "TURN THAT I MAY EXPOUND . . . . . 467 HARUN RASHID   132
MUST DRIVE THE ARABIAN HOST. THE VOICE GREW STILL, . . 467 HARUN RASHID   145
MADE DRIVE THE ARABIAN HOST. THE VOICE GREW STILL, . . 467 HARUN RASHID   V 145
DREAM THAT I LOVE HER ONLY FOR THE VOICE, ... 469 HARUN RASHID   171
IS BUT A PAYMENT FOR THAT MIDNIGHT VOICE . . . . 469 HARUN RASHID   173
ITS FIRST SIMPLICITY, LOVE, VOICE AND ALL, ... 469 HARUN RASHID   177
AND I LEFT SHIVERING. THE VOICE HAS DRAWN . . . . . . 469 HARUN RASHID   179
DREAM THAT I LOVE HER ONLY FOR THAT VOICE, ... 469 HARUN RASHID   V 171
THE TOMB OF SWIFT WEARS IT AWAY. A VOICE . . . . . . 487 SEVEN SAGES   21
NOR HEARD THIS VOICE THAT NINETY YEARS HAVE CRACKED. . 555 RIBH AT TOMB   5
WHAT MATTER? OUT OF CAVERN COMES A VOICE, ... 564 GYRES   15
WHAT MATTER? OUT OF CAVERN COME A VOICE . . . . 564 GYRES   V 15
CARRIAGE AND VOICE HAD HE: . . . . 608 SONGS BURDEN 3   13
HOUND VOICE . . . . 621 HOUND VOICE   T
GIVE TONGUE, PROCLAIM THEIR HIDDEN NAME--"HOUND VOICE." 622 HOUND VOICE   7
INTO THE NIGHT. O ROCKY VOICE, ... 633 MAN AND ECHO   37
WITH FIERY SONG I'LL DROWN YON PUNY VOICE. . . . . . . 648 ISLE STAT I 1   81
I HEAR THE WHOLE SKY'S SORROW IN ONE VOICE. . . . . . 652 ISLE STAT I 2   22
UP-RAISED HIS VOICE, AND HOOTED ME. . . . . 670 ISLE STAT II 3   117
UPRAISED HIS VOICE, AND HOOTED ME. . . . . 670 ISLE STAT II 3 V 117
HE SHRANK BEFORE MY VOICE, AND STOOD . . . . 671 ISLE STAT II 3   129
IT IS THE VOICE OF ALL OUR HEARTS THAT LAUGH. . . . . 681 SEEKER   7
IT IS POSSESSED. A PROPHESYING VOICE. . . . . 681 SEEKER   8
A VOICE CAME CALLING ME TO THIS YOUR LAND, ... 682 SEEKER   22
A VOICE HAS TOLD ME HOW WITHIN THIS LAND . . . . 682 SEEKER   V 22
MY ECHOING HEART. NOW RAISE THY VOICE AND SPEAK! . . . 683 SEEKER   47
LOVER, THE VOICE THAT SUMMONED THEE WAS MINE. . . . . 685 SEEKER   77
FOR ALL I GAVE THE VOICE, FOR ALL MY YOUTH, ... 685 SEEKER   78
AGAIN, THE VOICE! THE VOICE! . . . . 685 SEEKER   81
AGAIN, THE VOICE! THE VOICE! . . . . 685 SEEKER   81
CRIES A VOICE AT ROARING MIDNIGHT BESIDE THE MOONLESS DEEP. 718 PHANTOM SHIP   8
AS THE SUMMER VOICE OF THE DAYTIME CEASED, ... 728 PRIEST FAIRY   4
HEARD THE VOICE OF THEIR DISMAY. . . . . 730 PRIEST FAIRY   74
IF YOU WOULD SERVE ME, AS YOUR WORD AND VOICE . . . . 756 SHADOW WATER A V 183
VOICED
SWEET VOICED AND BEAUTIFUL, ... 392 EASTER 1916   V 22
VOICES
VOICES . . . . 69 CLOAK BOAT   V T
OUR MARRIED VOICES WILDLY TROLLED. . . . . 85 MAD KING GOLL   59
THE EVERLASTING VOICES . . . . 141 EVERLAST VOICE   T
EVERLASTING VOICES . . . . 141 EVERLAST VOICE V T
O SWEET EVERLASTING VOICES, BE STILL! . . . . 141 EVERLAST VOICE   1
O SWEET EVERLASTING VOICES, BE STILL. . . . . 141 EVERLAST VOICE   8
VOICES AMONG THE CROWD . . . . 172 PLEADS FRIEND   2
OUR HEARTS CAN HEAR THE VOICES CHIDE. . . . . 192 BAILE AILLINN   94
OUR HEART CAN HEAR THE VOICES CHIDE. . . . . 192 BAILE AILLINN V 94
MY DREAMS WERE CLOVEN BY VOICES AND BY FIRES: . . . . 218 WOODS OF COOLE   20
MOVED ROUND ME IN THE VOICES AND THE FIRES, ... 218 WOODS OF COOLE   23
YOU SAY THAT ALSO? YOU HAVE HEARD THE VOICES, ... 228 SHADOW WATER B 136
YES, VOICES! BUT I DO NOT CATCH THE WORDS. . . . . . 233 SHADOW WATER B 251
BEING DRIVEN ON BY VOICES AND BY DREAMS . . . . 243 SHADOW WATER B 441
WITH HUMAN VOICES. O I CAN HEAR THEM NOW. . . . . . . 247 SHADOW WATER B 522
OUR VOICES CARRY: AND THOUGH SLUMBER-BOUND, ... 622 HOUND VOICE   5
AND YET GAVE TONGUE. "HOUND VOICES" WERE THEY ALL. . . 622 HOUND VOICE   9
OUR VOICES CARRY: AND THOUGH SLUMBER BOUND, ... 622 HOUND VOICE   V 5
THE FAIRY VOICES . . . . 655 ISLE STAT I 3 V T
WHAT ARE THE VOICES THAT IN FLOWERY WAYS . . . . 666 ISLE STAT II 3   16
WITH LITTLE VOICES SONGS OF FEARFUL THINGS. . . . . . 682 SEEKER   31
UPRAISED THEIR VOICES BITTERLY. . . . . 730 PRIEST FAIRY   72
FOR THERE ARE SUDDEN VOICES IN MY EARS. . . . . 753 SHADOW WATER A 141
OF VOICES AND OF DREAMS. O HEART, BE STILL! . . . . . 765 SHADOW WATER A 362
VOLUME
THAT GATHERS VOLUME: NOW A THUNDER-CLAP. . . . . 487 SEVEN SAGES   23
THAT GATHERS VOLUME: NOW A THUNDER CLAP. . . . . 487 SEVEN SAGES   V 23
VON
VON HUEGEL . . . . 499 VACILLATION   V T
MUST WE PART, VON HUEGEL, THOUGH MUCH ALIKE, FOR WE . . 503 VACILLATION   78
SO GET YOU GONE, VON HUEGEL, THOUGH WITH BLESSINGS ON YOUR 503 VACILLATION   89
   HEAD.
VOTE
AND LET THE NEIGHBOURS VOTE, ... 598 STONE CROSS   6
VOW
WHO HAS A LIKE VOW FROM THEIR TRIPLE DUN." . . . . . . 108 CUCHULAIN SEA V 38
WHO HAD A LIKE VOW FROM OUR TRIPLE DUN." . . . . 109 CUCHULAIN SEA V 54
CUCHULAIN CRIED, "HAVE MADE AND KEEP THAT VOW." . . . . 109 CUCHULAIN SEA V 56
A DEEP-SWORN VOW . . . . 357 DEEP-SWORN VOW   T
A DEEP SWORN VOW . . . . 357 DEEP-SWORN VOW   T
THAT DEEP-SWORN VOW HAVE BEEN FRIENDS OF MINE: . . . . 357 DEEP-SWORN VOW   2
THAT DEEP SWORN VOW, HAVE BEEN FRIENDS OF MINE, ... 357 DEEP-SWORN VOW V 2
I AM THINKING OF A CHILD'S VOW SWORN IN VAIN . . . . . 391 UNDER SATURN   15

		PAGE	TITLE		LINE

VOWED
AS THOUGH THEY'D VOWED TO MEASURE ALL ITS WAYS. . . . . . 711 FERENCZ RENYI 48

VOWS
THAT TIME CAN NEVER MAR A LOVER'S VOWS . . . . 126 DREAM OF FAERY 10
HOW TIME MAY NEVER MAR THEIR FAERY VOWS . . . . 126 DREAM OF FAERY V 10

VOYAGE
MOPING FOR ONE VOYAGE MORE. . . . . 361 ALF POLLEXFEN 22

VOYAGES
I'D GIVE THE PROFIT OF NINE VOYAGES . . . . 222 SHADOW WATER B V 9

WADDING'S
OF OLD LUKE WADDING'S PORTRAIT SAID . . . . 400 DEMON BEAST 10

WADE
WHERE WADE THE CHOIR OF LOVE . . . . 612 NEWS ORACLE V 22
AND THE JOY OF THE STREAMS WHERE LONG-LIMBED HERONS WADE! 674 ISLE STAT II 3 217

WADES
WHERE WADES THE CHOIR OF LOVE . . . . 612 NEWS ORACLE 22

WAGE
"BUT TILL THE MOON HAS TAKEN ALL, I WAGE . . . . . 45 OISIN 2 240
"WITH ALL IN ALL THE WORLD I BATTLE WAGE. . . . . . 45 OISIN 2 V 240
. . . AND NO MAN MAY WAR WITH THE STRONG SPIRITS WAGE! . . 62 OISIN 3 V 214
WAGE AN ETERNAL BATTLE, AND I FEEL . . . . . 104 FERGUS DRUID V 38C
AND WAGE GOD'S BATTLES IN THE LONG GREY SHIPS. . . . 114 ROSE OF BATTLE 20
BRED TO BE A HERO'S WAGE. . . . . 258 PEACE 3
THAT LONG TO GIVE THEMSELVES FOR WAGE, ... 262 STUDENTS AGIT 2
BUT BEAR IN MIND YOUR LOVER'S WAGE . . . . 385 ROBARTES DANCE 14
THE WAGE OF SIN IS DEATH. NO USE. NO USE. . . . . . 697 MOSADA 2 V 42
BLINDER SORROWS, HARDER WAGE— . . . . 733 STREET DANCERS 58

WAGED
HE WITH BODY WAGED A FIGHT, ... 561 FOUR AGES MAN 1

WAGER
YOU'VE NEVER KNOWN, I'D LAY A WAGER ON IT, ... 227 SHADOW WATER B 113

WAGES
I KNOW WHAT WAGES BEAUTY GIVES, ... 336 YOUNG BEAUTY 13
THE WAGES OF SIN IS DEATH. NO USE. NO GOOD. . . . . . 697 MOSADA 2 42

WAGGED
ABOUT WHOSE FACE BIRDS WAGGED THEIR FIERY WINGS, ... 187 QUEEN MAEVE 145

WAGGONS
SEA NYMPHS IN THEIR PEARLY WAGGONS . . . . 309 REALISTS V 5

WAGON
OUT OF THE UP AND DOWN, THE WAGON WHEEL . . . . . . 377 PHASES OF MOON V 120

WAGONETTE
CLIMB ON A WAGONETTE TO SCREAM. . . . . 626 OLD MEN BE MAD 8

WAGONS
SEA-NYMPHS IN THEIR PEARLY WAGONS . . . . 309 REALISTS 5

WAGON-WHEEL
OUT OF THE UP AND DOWN, THE WAGON-WHEEL . . . . . . 377 PHASES OF MOON 120

WAIF
A SEA-WORN WAIF CAME FLOATING BY. . . . . 24 OISIN 1 V 365

WAIL
OH, HADST THOU SEEN BEAUTIFUL NIAM WAIL TO HERSELF AND 54 OISIN 3 V 109
    BLANCH,
O, HAD YOU SEEN BEAUTIFUL NEAVE WAIL TO HERSELF AND BLANCH, 54 OISIN 3 V 109
AND I MUST WAIL BESIDE THE SEA . . . . 86 MAD KING GOLL V 67
THE HOUNDS WAIL FOR THE DEAD. . . . . 99 FOXHUNTER 48
AND WRING MY HANDS, AND WAIL HIM BITTERLY, ... 242 SHADOW WATER B 414
FOR, WANDER AND WAIL AS HE WOULD, ... 378 CAT AND MOON 6
BUT SPEECHLESS, AND THE MAIDEN WITH LONG WAIL . . . . 713 FERENCZ RENYI 85

WAILING
THE WAILING GREW DISTANT! I RODE BY THE WOODS OF 56 OISIN 3 137
    THE WRINKLING BARK,
I KISS MY WAILING CHILD AND PRESS IT TO MY BREAST, . . . 147 UNAPPEAS HOST 5
WAILING UPON A WOMAN'S KNEE, ... 436 FOR MY SON 22

WAILS
WANDERS AND WAILS BEFORE MY HEART MOST TRUE . . . . . 738 YOU ARE SAD 8

WAIT
FOR HIS LAST DAYS TO LIE IN WAIT. . . . . 24 OISIN 1 363
PRAYERS FOR THE LAND. I WILL WAIT HERE, AMRITA. . . . . 71 ANASHU VIJAYA 13
PRAYERS FOR THE LAND. PRAY ON, AND I WILL WAIT YOU, . . 71 ANASHU VIJAYA V 13
WHOSE BLADE COMPELS, AND WAIT TILL THEY HAVE FOUND . . . 108 CUCHULAIN SEA 37
OUR LONG SHIPS LOOSE THOUGHT-WOVEN SAILS AND WAIT, . . . 115 ROSE OF BATTLE 31
TO WAIT THEIR FRIENDS! BUT WHEN THEIR FRIENDS HAVE COME 233 SHADOW WATER B 247
I THOUGHT TO WAIT FOR THAT OR THIS! . . . . 305 HOUR DAWN 64
AND WAIT HIM IN A DRUNKEN SLEEP." . . . . 307 HOUR DAWN 106
AND TILL THAT'S DONE CAN NEITHER WORK NOR WAIT. . . . . 340 SHEP GOATHERD 45
AND WAIT WAR'S MUSIC! PASS THE LITTLE GALLERY! . . . . 461 HARUN RASHID 8
CLIMB YOUR CHAMBER FULL OF BOOKS AND WAIT, ... 579 DOR WELLESLEY 8
I AM NOT DUMB! I'D SOONER SILENT WAIT . . . . . . 646 ISLE STAT I 1 40
BEYOND A MORTAL'S YEARS. I WAIT THE SONG . . . . . 653 ISLE STAT I 2 48
TWO LONELY SPIRITS WAIT, ... 680 LOVE AND DEATH 18
I SAW A STRANGER TAP AND WAIT . . . . 696 MOSADA 2 22
A STRANGER NEW ARISEN WAIT . . . . 696 MOSADA 2 V 22
'TIS LATE, WAIT ONE MORE DAY! BELOW THE HILLS . . . . 702 MOSADA 2 91
GIVE HER TO AIBRIC, IF HE WILL. I WAIT . . . . . 755 SHADOW WATER A 172
I WAIT YOUR WORDS AS THE DEAD WAIT THE LIVING. . . . . 756 SHADOW WATER A 182
I WAIT YOUR WORDS AS THE DEAD WAIT THE LIVING. . . . . 756 SHADOW WATER A V 182

WAITED
WAITED. ABOVE, IN ENDLESS CARVEN JAGS, ... 38 OISIN 2 V 144
I WAITED HOUR BY HOUR, AND THE HIGH DOME, ... 39 OISIN 2 147
OF FACES, WAITED! AND THE LEISURED GAZE . . . . . 39 OISIN 2 149
HOUR AFTER HOUR I WAITED, AND THE DOME . . . . . 39 OISIN 2 V 147
"I HAVE LONG WAITED, MOTHER, FOR THAT WORD! . . . . 107 CUCHULAIN SEA 22

	PAGE	TITLE		LINE

WAITED (CONTINUED)
"LONG HAVE I WAITED, MOTHER, FOR THOSE WORDS, ...   107 CUCHULAIN SEA V 22
"I HAVE LONG WAITED, MOTHER, FOR THOSE WORDS: . . . . .   107 CUCHULAIN SEA V 22
MAEVE WAITED, AND WHEN THAT EAR-PIERCING NOISE . . . . . 182 QUEEN MAEVE 47
ONE THAT THE GENERATIONS HAD LONG WAITED . . . . 182 QUEEN MAEVE 66
I WAITED TILL THE NIGHT WAS ON THE TURN, ... 283 TWO KINGS 144
I WAITED SO FOR THAT OR THIS— . . . . 305 HOUR DAWN V 64
WAITING
WHERE AILLINN RODE WITH WAITING MAIDS . . . . 193 BAILE AILLINN V 102
NO WAITING MAID SHOULD EVER SPREAD . . . . 194 BAILE AILLINN V 120
BUT WHY ARE THEY STILL WAITING? WHY ARE THEY . . . . . 234 SHADOW WATER B 265
ARE LEARNED IN WAITING. YOU CANNOT BUT HAVE SEEN . . . 340 SHEP GOATHERD 48
THE BLINDS DRAWN UP": MAUD GONNE AT HOWTH STATION WAITING 578 LOFTY THINGS 10
  A TRAIN,
SHOULD KEEP THEIR LOVERS WAITING, ... 597 MODEL LAUREATE 7
KEEP THEIR LOVERS WAITING? . . . . 597 MODEL LAUREATE 8
AND KEEP THEIR LOVERS WAITING, ... 597 MODEL LAUREATE 15
KEEP THEIR LOVERS WAITING. . . . . 597 MODEL LAUREATE 16
WOULD KEEP HIS LOVER WAITING, ... 598 MODEL LAUREATE 23
KEEP HIS LOVER WAITING? . . . . 598 MODEL LAUREATE 24
AND MY SOUL IN WAITING DIETH, ... 648 ISLE STAT I 1 87
THEY ARE STILL WAITING: AND NOW THE LAGGARD COMES, . . . 754 SHADOW WATER A 150
THEY ARE STILL WAITING: AND A LAGGARD COMES, ... 754 SHADOW WATER A V 150
SHE WILL ANSWER NOW LIKE ANY WAITING WOMAN . . . . . . 757 SHADOW WATER A 193
I HAVE BEEN WAITING YOU. A MOMENT SINCE . . . . 763 SHADOW WATER A 313
WAITING-MAID
NO WAITING-MAID SHOULD EVER SPREAD . . . . 194 BAILE AILLINN 120
WAITING-MAIDS
WHERE AILLINN RODE WITH WAITING-MAIDS, ... 193 BAILE AILLINN 102
WAITS
AT THE SWORD-POINT, AND WAITS TILL WE HAVE FOUND . . . . 109 CUCHULAIN SEA 53
AT THE SWORD POINT, AND WAITS TILL WE HAVE FOUND . . . . 109 CUCHULAIN SEA V 53
AND WHAT WAITS BEHIND THE DOOR, ... 298 THREE HERMITS 9
THAT WAITS UPON HIS FUTURE DAYS, ... 436 FOR MY SON 14
HE HOVERS ABOVE THE MAST AND WAITS HIS KIND: . . . . . 753 SHADOW WATER A 135
AENGUS LOOKS ON YOU WHEN I LOOK. HE WAITS . . . . . . 757 SHADOW WATER A V 209
WAKE
O'ER MEN WHO SLEEP, AND WAKE, AND DIE, ... 22 OISIN 1 V 340B
WHERE FLAPPING HERONS WAKE . . . . 86 STOLEN CHILD 4
WHEN WILL HE WAKE FROM SLEEP? . . . . 174 ELEMENT POWERS 6
YOU'RE CERTAIN OF IT? I NEVER WAKE FROM SLEEP . . . . . 226 SHADOW WATER B 83
WAKE ALL BELOW! WHY HAVE YOU BROKEN OUR SLEEP? . . . . 233 SHADOW WATER B 242
UPON THAT OTHER SHIP WE ARE TO WAKE. . . . . 240 SHADOW WATER B 381
I HAD FORGOTTEN THAT WE MUST GO WAKE HIM. . . . . . . 240 SHADOW WATER B 384
AND SET YOU DREAMING. HOW CAN WE HAVE A WAKE . . . . . 240 SHADOW WATER B 386
AND LEFT MERE SLEEP. HE'LL WAKE WHEN THE SUN WAKES, . . 284 TWO KINGS 161
"WHAT CARE I IF YOU SLEEP OR WAKE? . . . . 304 HOUR DAWN 40
DO BUT WAKE THE HOPE TO LIVE . . . . 309 REALISTS V 6
AND WHEN I WAKE TOWARDS MORN I DREAD MYSELF, ... 448 HERO GIRL FOOL 5
SOME FEW HALF WAKE AND HALF RENEW THEIR CHOICE, ... 622 HOUND VOICE 6
WHEN SLEEPERS WAKE AND YET STILL DREAM, ... 639 BEN BULBEN 59
AS I MY WATCHING LEST YOU WAKE, ... 658 ISLE STAT I 3 95
I FADE, AND SHALL NOT SEE THE MORNINGS WAKE, ... 674 ISLE STAT II 3 223
THY PEACE. AH, NOW I'LL WAKE THESE SLEEPERS, LOST . . . 677 ISLE STAT II 3 274
O WAKE! WAKE! WAKE! FOR SOFT AS A BEE SIPS . . . . . . 677 ISLE STAT II 3 276
O WAKE! WAKE! WAKE! FOR SOFT AS A BEE SIPS . . . . . . 677 ISLE STAT II 3 276
O WAKE! WAKE! WAKE! FOR SOFT AS A BEE SIPS . . . . . . 677 ISLE STAT II 3 276
OLD WARRIOR, WAKE! FOR SOFT AS A BEE SIPS . . . . . . 677 ISLE STAT II 3 284
THOSE TWAIN ARE DUST. WAKE! LIGHT AS A BEE SIPS . . . . 678 ISLE STAT II 3 290
SEAFARER, WAKE! WAS MY SLEEP LONG? LONG YEARS. . . . . 678 ISLE STAT II 3 292
HE IS LONG DEAD. WAKE! SOFT AS A BEE SIPS . . . . . . 678 ISLE STAT II 3 297
NAY, HE IS GONE. WAKE! WAKE! AS A BEE SIPS . . . . . . 678 ISLE STAT II 3 305
NAY, HE IS GONE. WAKE! WAKE! AS A BEE SIPS . . . . . . 678 ISLE STAT II 3 305
WAKE! MA CUSHLA, SLEEPY-HEADED: . . . . 705 DAWN-SONG 9
WAKE! THE HERON, RISING, HATH . . . . 705 DAWN-SONG 17
WAKE THE LARKS UPON THE GREEN. . . . . 727 LOVERS QUARREL 46
HE CANNOT WAKE THE GOD THAT HIDES IN IT. . . . . 748 SHADOW WATER A 19
WHEN AENGUS AND HIS EDAINE WAKE FROM SLEEP . . . . . . 749 SHADOW WATER A 57
IN THE COLD STREAMS, AND WAKE TO THEIR DESIRE, ... 750 SHADOW WATER A 85
WAKE ALL BELOW. WHY HAVE YOU BROKEN OUR SLEEP? . . . . 753 SHADOW WATER A 132
WAKED
AND HAS NOT YET BEEN WAKED. OHONE! O! O! O! . . . . . 241 SHADOW WATER B 393
I HAD NOT WAKED A SINGLE MINUTE, ... 305 HOUR DAWN 72
IT MAY BE, BEFORE THE WINDS OF BIRTH HAVE WAKED: . . . . 750 SHADOW WATER A 86
WAKEFUL
THE EVER-WINDING WAKEFUL SEA, ... 22 OISIN 1 V 338
BEING WAKEFUL FOR HER SAKE, ... 316 FRIENDS 23
AND AS A SLAVE BEEN WAKEFUL IN THE HALLS . . . . 724 KANVA ON SELF 5
WAKEN
AND "WAKEN, COURTIERS OF THE MORN!" . . . . 18 OISIN 1 V 262
THE NOTES THEY WAKEN SHALL LIVE ON . . . . 213 BLESS PSALTER 16
THOSE IMAGES THAT WAKEN IN THE BLOOD. . . . . 622 HOUND VOICE 14
"WAKEN, WAKEN, SLEEPY FISHERS: NO HOUR IS THIS FOR SLEEP," 718 PHANTOM SHIP 7
"WAKEN, WAKEN, SLEEPY FISHERS: NO HOUR IS THIS FOR SLEEP," 718 PHANTOM SHIP 7
WAKENED
HAD HALF WAKENED SOME OLD MEMORY, ... 284 TWO KINGS V 172
SICK OF HIS GRAVE HAS WAKENED ME? . . . . 303 HOUR DAWN 37
WAKENING   SEE HALF-WAKENING
HALF WAKENING, WE LIFTED OUR EYELIDS, ... 54 OISIN 3 100
WAKENS
AND WHO ARE YOU THAT WAKENS ME? . . . . 303 HOUR DAWN V 35

865

		PAGE	TITLE		LINE

WAKES

AND WAKES THE SLUGGARD SEEDS OF CORN, ... 18 OISIN 1 263
AND LEFT MERE SLEEP. HE'LL WAKE WHEN THE SUN WAKES, . . 284 TWO KINGS 161
SHE HAS BEGUN FORGETTING. WHEN SHE WAKES, ... 760 SHADOW WATER A 255

WAKING

. . . WAKING WHITE AS A SHELL . . . . 54 OISIN 3 103
AND TELL ME WHO IT IS THAT WE ARE WAKING. . . . . . . 241 SHADOW WATER B 403
HAD WAKING WITS; IT SEEMED . . . . 422 MY TABLE 31
WAKING HE THANKS THE LORD THAT HE . . . . 633 MAN AND ECHO 27
FOR EVER ROUND THY WAKING AND THY SLEEP . . . . 688 TWO TITANS 57

WALK

THEY WALK ON SHORES UNSEEN OF OARING GALLEYS, ... 30 OISIN 2 V 14D
O MAY TRANQUILLITY WALK BY HIS ELBOW . . . . 71 ANASHU VIJAYA 2
AND WALK AMONG LONG DAPPLED GRASS, ... 150 WANDER AENGUS 21
AND WALK AND WALK THROUGH SUMMER GRASS, ... 150 WANDER AENGUS V 21
AND WALK AND WALK THROUGH SUMMER GRASS, ... 150 WANDER AENGUS V 21
THE BLESSEDEST SOULS THAT WALK IN THE WORLD . . . . . 167 BLESSED 19
AND WHEN WE WALK WITH KATE OR NAN . . . . 192 BAILE AILLINN 92
ON WET ROADS WHERE MEN WALK. . . . . 215 HAPPY TOWNLAND 48
HAVE SEEN IMMORTAL, MILD, PROUD SHADOWS WALK; . . . . 217 WOODS OF COOLE 12
DID THEIR CATULLUS WALK THAT WAY? . . . . 337 SCHOLARS 12
SHOULD THEIR CATULLUS WALK THAT WAY; . . . . 337 SCHOLARS V 12
BUT WALK BY THE DRY THORN UNTIL I HAVE FOUND . . . . 351 HER PRAISE 12
AND WHO CAN SAY BUT SOME YOUNG BELLE MAY WALK AND TALK 354 HIS PHOENIX 26
    MEN WILD
AND MAY BE THERE'LL BE SOME YOUNG BELLE WALK OUT TO MAKE 354 HIS PHOENIX V 26
    MEN WILD
AND MAYBE THERE'LL BE SOME YOUNG BELLE WALK OUT TO MAKE 354 HIS PHOENIX V 26
    MEN WILD
THAT MICHAEL ROBARTES LEFT, YOU WALK IN THE MOON, . . 367 EGO DOMINUS 4
SHALL WALK THE WET SANDS BY THE EDGE OF THE STREAM . . 371 EGO DOMINUS 71
SHALL WALK THE WET SAND BY THE WATER'S EDGE, ... 371 EGO DOMINUS V 71
FOR SILKEN CLOTHES AND STATELY WALK, ... 422 MY TABLE 30
I WALK THROUGH THE LONG SCHOOLROOM QUESTIONING; . . . 443 SCHOOL CHILDR 1
CHIMNEY CORNER, GARDEN WALK, ... 499 MOTHER OF GOD 8
MINE MUST WALK WHEN DEAD. . . . . 511 JANE AND JACK 18
MINE WOULD WALK, BEING DEAD. . . . . 511 JANE AND JACK V 18
MUCH I TALK, MORE I WALK; . . . . 548 TO SAME TUNE 3 9
MUCH I TALK, MORE I WALK; . . . . 548 TO SAME TUNE 3 19
MUCH I TALK, MORE I WALK; . . . . 549 TO SAME TUNE 3 29
HOW SOUL MAY WALK WHEN ALL SUCH THINGS ARE PAST, . . 558 RIBH CHRISTIAN 11
HOW SOUL COULD WALK BEFORE SUCH THINGS BEGAN. . . . . 558 RIBH CHRISTIAN 12
AND WHEN I PAY ATTENTION I MUST OUT AND WALK . . . . 581 CURSE CROMWELL 29
I WALK IN A BATTLE FOUGHT OVER AGAIN, ... 591 WHAT WAS LOST 2
ON THE GREEN LANDS I WALK . . . . 607 SONGS BURDEN 2 20
BUT FRIENDS WALK BY FRIENDS. . . . . 621 JOHN KINSELLA 32
WITH A STRUTTING TURKEY WALK, ... 627 STATES HOLIDAY 34
THE PHANTOMS OF HER FADED PLEASURES WALK; . . . . . 687 TWO TITANS 19
A BIRD WALK ON THE DOORSTEP. CHECK ONCE MORE. . . . 722 WITCH VIVIEN 64

WALKED

. . . AND I ROSE, AND WALKED ON THE EARTH; . . . . 60 OISIN 3 191
THE LITTLE WAVES THAT WALKED IN EVENING WHITENESS; . 81 EPHEMERA V 24C
THE JESTER WALKED IN THE GARDEN; . . . . 159 CAP AND BELLS 1
MAEVE WALKED, YET WITH SLOW FOOTFALL, BEING OLD, . . 181 QUEEN MAEVE 43
MAEVE WALKED THROUGH THAT GREAT HALL, AND WITH A SIGH 182 QUEEN MAEVE 62
I WALKED AMONG THE SEVEN WOODS OF COOLE; . . . . . . 217 WOODS OF COOLE 1
YET WE, HAD WE WALKED WITHIN . . . . 293 HELEN LIVED 7
WHERE HELEN WALKED WITH HER BOY, ... 293 HELEN LIVED 9
KING GUAIRE WALKED AMID HIS COURT . . . . 295 THREE BEGGARS 8
WHEREON A THING ONCE WALKED THAT SEEMED A BURNING CLOUD. 315 FALLEN MAJESTY 8
ONCE WALKED A THING THAT SEEMED, AS IT WERE, A BURNING 315 FALLEN MAJESTY V 8
    CLOUD.
HAVE WALKED TO THE ALTAR . . . . 355 PROPERTIUS 4
AND FOR AN HOUR I HAVE WALKED AND PRAYED . . . . . . 403 FOR DAUGHTER 7
I HAVE WALKED AND PRAYED FOR THIS YOUNG CHILD AN HOUR 403 FOR DAUGHTER 9
REMEMBERING THAT, IF WALKED SHE THERE, ... 410 TOWER 38
HE WALKED THAT ROOM AND ISSUED THENCE . . . . 438 SONGS PLAY 2 2
SHE WALKED AWHILE AND BLUSHED AWHILE . . . . 451 FIRST LOVE 3
WALKED THROUGH THE HOUSE. UNNOTICED AND UNFELT . . . 468 HARUN RASHID 153
WHAT SCHOOLING HAD THESE FOUR? THEY WALKED THE ROADS 487 SEVEN SAGES 24
HOW SOUL HAS WALKED BEFORE SUCH THINGS BEGAN. . . . 558 RIBH CHRISTIAN V 12
WALKED ON THE WATERS AND BID FORGAEL SEEK . . . . . 747 SHADOW WATER A 12

WALKERS   SEE NIGHT-WALKERS
WALKERS'   SEE NIGHT-WALKERS'

WALKING

AND GRANIA, WALKING AND SMILING, SEWED WITH HER NEEDLE 53 OISIN 3 94
    OF BONE.
WALKING GHOSTLY IN THE DEW, ... 67 HAPPY SHEPHERD 52
WALKING GHOSTLY 'MONG THE DEW, ... 67 HAPPY SHEPHERD V 52
WENT WALKING WITH SLOW STEPS ALONG THE GLEAMING . . . 68 SAD SHEPHERD 3
WITHIN THE TEMPLE, DEVIOUS WALKING, MADE . . . . . . 72 ANASHU VIJAYA 32
WHO MET FAND WALKING AMONG FLAMING DEW . . . . 169 SECRET ROSE 13
IN WALKING NAKED. . . . . 320 COAT 10
BY MERELY WALKING IN A ROOM, ... 356 BROKEN DREAMS 13
LEANING OR STANDING OR WALKING. . . . . 356 BROKEN DREAMS 23
TALL DAMES GO WALKING IN GRASS-GREEN AVALON. . . . . 627 STATES HOLIDAY 13
TALL DAMES GO WALKING IN GRASS-GREEN AVALON. . . . . 627 STATES HOLIDAY 26
TALL DAMES GO WALKING IN GRASS-GREEN AVALON. . . . . 627 STATES HOLIDAY 39
TALL DAMES GO WALKING IN GRASS GREEN AVALON. . . . . 627 STATES HOLIDAY V REF
PROUDLY IN HIS SAFFRON WALKING; . . . . 705 DAWN-SONG 2
AND THE OLD MEN WERE WALKING, WALKING, ... 725 LEGEND 3

866

WALKING   (CONTINUED)
     AND THE OLD MEN WERE WALKING, WALKING, ...   725 LEGEND   3
     FOR GOD IS WALKING IN THE DEW. . . . .   736 SUMMER EVENING   15
     MOVING THERE AND WALKING: . . . .   785 YOUR HEART   5
WALKS
     WILL GATHER, AND NOT KNOW IT WALKS THE VERY STREET . . . 315 FALLEN MAJESTY   7
     LOOK ON THAT FIRE, SALVATION WALKS WITHIN. . . . . . .   502 VACILLATION   76
     BUT BODY WON: IT WALKS UPRIGHT. . . . .   561 FOUR AGES MAN   2
     OBEYS. SOME FIERCE MAGICIAN FLIES OR WALKS . . . . .   720 WITCH VIVIEN   9
     WALKS IN THE VESTURE OF HER SISTER SORROW. . . . . . .   735 QUATRAIN APHOR   28
WALL
     AMONG THE LEAVES OF THE LAUREL WALL, ...   3 OISIN 1   V 7FF
     THAT WOMAN FOUND A RING HUNG ON THE WALL, ...   37 OISIN 2   120
     THAT MAIDEN FOUND A RING HUNG ON THE WALL, ...   37 OISIN 2   V 120
     AND FOUND A DOOR DEEP SUNKEN IN THE WALL, ...   39 OISIN 2   154
     I FOUND A DOOR DEEP-SUNKEN IN THE WALL, ...   39 OISIN 2   V 154
     AND MINE WAS EVERY TROPHIED WALL, ...   82 MAD KING GOLL   V   4
     A WALL BEHIND HIS BACK, OVER HIS HEAD . . . .   180 QUEEN MAEVE   5
     ONE LEANS AND MUTTERS BY THE WALL-- . . . .   212 BLESS PSALTER   10
     UNTIL HE CAME BEFORE THE PAINTED WALL . . . .   279 TWO KINGS   47
     I COWERED BACK UPON THE WALL IN TERROR, ...   284 TWO KINGS   164
     IN THE GREEN SHADOW OF FERRARA WALL: . . . .   352 PEOPLE   9
     IN THE GREEN SHADOW ON FERRARA WALL: . . . .   352 PEOPLE   V   9
     SHE TURNS THE DOLLS' FACES TO THE WALL . . . . . .   363 DOLLS FACES   T
     HEEL UP AND WEIGHT ON TOE, MUST FACE THE WALL . . .   363 DOLLS FACES   3
     NODDED UPON THE WALL, ...   400 DEMON BEAST   12
     AS IN THE GOLD MOSAIC OF A WALL, ...   408 SAIL BYZANTIUM   18
     A FARMHOUSE THAT IS SHELTERED BY ITS WALL, ...   419 MY HOUSE   2
     A FARM-HOUSE THAT IS SHELTERED BY ITS WALL, ...   419 MY HOUSE   V   2
     MY WALL IS LOOSENING; HONEY-BEES, ...   424 STARES NEST   4
     MY WALL IS LOOSENING; HONEY BEES . . . .   424 STARES NEST   V   4
     THE BROKEN WALL, THE BURNING ROOF AND TOWER . . . .   441 LEDA AND SWAN   10
     UPON A PAINTED WALL. . . . .   452 HUMAN DIGNITY   6
     WHO BEAT UPON THE WALL . . . .   576 ACRE OF GRASS   17
     NOW I AM IN THE PUBLIC-HOUSE AND LEAN UPON THE WALL, . 593 PILGRIM   21
     NOW I AM IN THE TAVERN AND LEAN AGAINST THE WALL, . . 593 PILGRIM   V   21
     NOW I AM IN THE PUBLIC HOUSE AND LEAN UPON THE WALL, . 593 PILGRIM   V   21
     HEARD YOU? YOUR LUTE UPON THE WALL HAS SOUNDED! . . . 694 MOSADA 1   V   95
     AND THE FISHER MEN AND WOMEN FROM THE DRIPPING HARBOUR WALL 718 PHANTOM SHIP   11
     I HAVE STOOD SO LONG BY A GAP IN THE WALL . . . . .   788 HAWTHORN TREE   15
     I HAVE STOPPED SO LONG A GAP IN THE WALL . . . . .   788 HAWTHORN TREE   V   15
WALLA   SEE SHAN-WALLA
WALLED
     SPRANG FROM A GATEWAY WALLED AROUND WITH BLACK . . . .   31 OISIN 2   V   29
WALLS
     TWO WALLS, A ROOF, A FLOOD: THERE TREMBLING GREEN . .   31 OISIN 2   V   32
     BETWEEN THE WALLS COVERED WITH BEATEN BRONZE . . . .   180 QUEEN MAEVE   10
     OR ON THE BENCHES UNDERNEATH THE WALLS, ...   180 QUEEN MAEVE   14
     I HELPED YOUR FATHERS WHEN THEY BUILT THESE WALLS, . . 184 QUEEN MAEVE   97
     ROSE ROUND THE WALLS, AND THROUGH THE BRONZE-RINGED DOOR 286 TWO KINGS   215
     ROSE LIKE THESE WALLS FROM THESE . . . .   480 BLOOD AND MOON   6
     A DANCE-LIKE GLORY THAT THOSE WALLS BEGOT. . . . . .   488 COOLE PARK 29   8
     HE NEVER LAY BEHIND FOUR WALLS . . . .   606 SONGS BURDEN 1   12
     DOWN THE MOUNTAIN WALLS . . . .   612 NEWS ORACLE   30
     WHERE RISE THE WALLS MAJESTICAL ABOVE . . . .   679 ISLE STAT II 3   311
     AND THRICE THE PEACHES FLUSHED UPON THE WALLS, . . .   690 MOSADA 3   2
     WITH THREE BARS CROSSED, AND THESE FOUR WALLS MY WORLD, 700 MOSADA 3   32
     ALONG THE TENTS, THE FIELDS, THE VILLAGE WALLS . . .   712 FERENCZ RENYI   71
     ALONG THE TENTS, FIELD, THE VILLAGE WALLS . . . . .   712 FERENCZ RENYI   V   71
     HAST THOU NOT RULED AMONG THE GILDED WALLS? . . . .   724 KANVA ON SELF   7
WAN
     AND THE WAN WAVE THAT LINGERS . . . .   672 ISLE STAT II 3   166
     IN THY WAN FACE? HEAR THOU, O DAUGHTER OF THE DAYS, . 674 ISLE STAT II 3   200
     IN THY WAN FACE? HEAR, DAUGHTER OF THE DAYS: . . . . 674 ISLE STAT II 3 V   200
     BY THOSE WAN STARS THAT SIT IN COMPANY . . . . . .   691 MOSADA 1   26
WAND
     AND CUT AND PEELED A HAZEL WAND; . . . .   149 WANDER AENGUS   3
     A MAN WITH A HAZEL WAND CAME WITHOUT SOUND: . . . .   153 CHANGE BELOVED   6
     A MAN WITH A WAND OF HAZEL CAME WITHOUT SOUND: . . .   153 CHANGE BELOVED V   6
WANDER
     DID YOUR COMPANION WANDER AWAY . . . .   6 OISIN 1   52
     THAT RAISE THEIR HEADS AND WANDER SINGING, ...   27 OISIN 1   419
     AND WANDER IN THE STORMS AND CLINGING SNOWS, ...   42 OISIN 2   201
     TO WANDER BY THEIR MELANCHOLY MINDS. . . . .   72 ANASHU VIJAYA   33
     AND WANDER EVER WITH WOVEN HANDS, ...   78 INDIAN TO LOVE   7
     AND NOW I WANDER IN THE WOODS . . . .   84 MAD KING GOLL   37
     I WANDER ON, AND WAVE MY HANDS, ...   84 MAD KING GOLL   43
     AND I MUST WANDER WOOD AND HILL, ...   86 MAD KING GOLL   70
     AND THEREFORE DO I WANDER ON, ...   131 OLD PENSIONER V   5
     AND THEREFORE DO I WANDER NOW: . . . .   131 OLD PENSIONER V   5
     AND BID THEM WANDER OBEYING YOUR WILL, ...   141 EVERLAST VOICE   3
     I WANDER BY THE EDGE . . . .   165 CRY OF SEDGE   1
     O, WHEN SHALL SORROW WANDER NO MORE IN THE LAND . . . 174 ELEMENT POWERS V   5
     HELP THEM THAT WANDER WITH HAND CLASPING HAND, . . .   184 QUEEN MAEVE   86
     WANDER WHERE EARTH WITHERS AWAY, ...   196 BAILE AILLINN   171
     WITH WISDOM, THEY WANDER TILL ALL THE YEARS HAVE GONE BY: 204 WITHER BOUGHS   21
     IN THE WASTE OF THE HIGH AIR, THAT WE MAY WANDER . .   234 SHADOW WATER B   263
     BUT NOW IT IS YOUR THOUGHTS THAT WANDER AWAY, . . .   246 SHADOW WATER B   512
     WANDER A MOMENT WHEN ONE IS IN LOVE? . . . . . .   246 SHADOW WATER B   515
     PASSION OR CONQUEST, WANDER WHERE THEY WILL, ...   323 SWANS AT COOLE   23
     FOR, WANDER AND WAIL AS HE WOULD, ...   378 CAT AND MOON   6

PAGE   TITLE   LINE

WANDER   (CONTINUED)
    WANDER IN DREAMS NO MORE: . . . .   554 CHURCH STATE   8
    TO WANDER BY THE BUBBLING SHORE. . . . .   668 ISLE STAT II 3   57
    WANDER AWAY FROM MINE? . . . .   686 LIFE   8
    FEET OF DARK GOMEZ, WHERE NOW WANDER YE? . . . . . .   690 MOSADA 1   11
    PICTURED, WHERE WANDER THE BELOVED FEET . . . . . .   692 MOSADA 1   44
    STILL WANDER THROUGH THE WORLD. HE'S GONE, HE'S GONE. . .   703 MOSADA 3   121
    WE WILL WANDER, I AND YOU. . . . .   706 DAWN-SONG   23
    WHO WANDER AND WHISPER ALONE. . . . .   707 FAIRY PEDANT   8
    THEN AWAY AND AWAY WILL I WANDER, ...   707 FAIRY PEDANT   16
    IN THE WASTE AIR. I WILL WANDER BY HIS SIDE . . . . .   754 SHADOW WATER A   152
    THE PALE HOUND AND THE DEER WANDER FOR EVER . . . . .   764 SHADOW WATER A   330
    THE PALE HOUND AND THE DEER WANDER FOREVER . . . . .   764 SHADOW WATER A V   330
    TO WANDER IN: YOU HAVE LOVED MANY WOMEN, ...   767 SHADOW WATER A   389
    AND BID HIM TO YOUR COUNTRY. I SHOULD WANDER . . . . .   767 SHADOW WATER A   403
WANDERED
    SOME WANDERED EVER HAND IN HAND: . . . .   25 OISIN 1   389
    AND OVER THE LIMBS AND THE VALLEY THE SLOW OWLS WANDERED   49 OISIN 3   41
      AND CAME,
    HE WANDERED BY THE SANDS OF LISSADELL: . . . . . .   127 DREAM OF FAERY   13
    WANDERED BETWEEN THE BLUE AND THE GREEN LEAF . . . . .   278 TWO KINGS   41
    "YOU THAT HAVE WANDERED FAR AND WIDE . . . .   295 THREE BEGGARS   11
    "YOU HAVE WANDERED FAR AND WIDE, ...   295 THREE BEGGARS V   11
    AND WANDERED MURMURING EVERYWHERE, "MY CHILD, MY CHILD!"   619 BRONZE HEAD   21
    I WANDERED AND TROD, ...   654 ISLE STAT I 2   64
    AS I WANDERED UNSEEN, ...   654 ISLE STAT I 2   71
    FAIR SHEPHERD, AS WE WANDERED HITHER, ...   669 ISLE STAT II 3   83
    HE HOOTED AS I WANDERED BY. . . . .   670 ISLE STAT II 3   121
    MUSINGLY WANDERED THE VILLAGE PRIEST. . . . .   728 PRIEST FAIRY   3
WANDERER   SEE FELLOW-WANDERER
    OH WANDERER IN THE SOUTHERN WEATHER, ...   77 INDIAN TO LOVE V   1
    THOUGH IT BUT SET US SIGHING. FELLOW WANDERER . . . .   230 SHADOW WATER B V   187
    THE PACK UPON HIM, GO, UNQUIET WANDERER. . . . . . .   292 TO A SHADE   18
    HERDING THE PACK. UNQUIET WANDERER . . . .   292 TO A SHADE   V   18
    WITH CLINGING MIST, EACH STAR-FOUGHT WANDERER CAME . .   656 ISLE STAT I 3   33
    DOTH STILL THE WANDERER ROVE? WITH ALL HIS SHIPS . .   677 ISLE STAT II 3   287
WANDERER'S
    UNTO THE WANDERER'S SHIPS, OR AS DAY FILLS . . . . .   645 ISLE STAT I 1   10
WANDERERS
    DWELT AMONG WINE-STAINED WANDERERS IN DEEP WOODS: . .   170 SECRET ROSE   21
    AENGUS AND EDAIN, THOSE PASSIONATE WANDERERS, ...   228 SHADOW WATER B   138
    THOSE WANDERERS THAT WELCOMED IN THEIR TENTS . . . .   462 HARUN RASHID   23
    THE WAVES, ENORMOUS WANDERERS OF THE WORLD, ...   687 TWO TITANS   3
    GAYEST WANDERERS, I AND YOU, ...   706 DAWN-SONG   31
WANDERING   SEE ROCK-WANDERING FAR-WANDERING NIGHT-WANDERING
    WITH A HEAVY HEART AND A WANDERING MIND, ...   2 OISIN 1   2
    MUST LIVE TO BE OLD LIKE THE WANDERING MOON. . . . . .   3 OISIN 1   12
    THY WANDERING STEPS ACROSS THE SEA? . . . .   5 OISIN 1   V   51
    BRINGING ME HONEYED, WANDERING THOUGHT . . . .   7 OISIN 1   V   65
    BUT NOW A WANDERING LAND BREEZE CAME . . . .   13 OISIN 1   165
    AND, NOW OUR WANDERING HOURS WERE DONE, ...   14 OISIN 1   177
    LIKE TO A MERRY WANDERING ROUT . . . .   18 OISIN 1   253
    AND WAVERING ARMS AND WANDERING DANCES. . . . . . .   19 OISIN 1   275
    AND WAVING ARMS AND WANDERING DANCES. . . . .   19 OISIN 1   V   275
    OR THE GREY WANDERING OSPREY SORROW." . . . .   20 OISIN 1   303
    NOR THE GREY WANDERING OSPREY SORROW." . . . .   21 OISIN 1   319
    ACROSS YOUR WANDERING RUBY CARS . . . .   22 OISIN 1   330
    NOR THE GREY WANDERING OSPREY SORROW." . . . .   23 OISIN 1   342
    FLED FOAM UNDERNEATH US, AND ROUND US, A WANDERING AND   47 OISIN 3   1
      MILKY SMOKE,
    FLED FOAM UNDERNEATH US, AND ROUND US, A WANDERING AND   47 OISIN 3   12
      MILKY SMOKE,
    FLED FOAM UNDERNEATH US, AND AROUND US, A WANDERING AND   47 OISIN 3   V   1
      MILKY SMOKE,
    . . . AND PACING THE SHORES OF THE WANDERING SEAS, . .   50 OISIN 3   55
    AS SHE MURMURED, "O WANDERING OISIN, ...   55 OISIN 3   123
    FLED FOAM UNDERNEATH ME, AND ROUND ME, A WANDERING AND   57 OISIN 3   148
      MILKY SMOKE.
    THE WANDERING EARTH HERSELF MAY BE . . . .   65 HAPPY SHEPHERD   18
    WHEN WANDERING IN THE FOREST, IF HE LOVE . . . . .   71 ANASHU VIJAYA   3
    THE VAN OF WANDERING QUIET: ERE YOU BE TOO CALM AND OLD,   73 ANASHU VIJAYA   43
    THE VAN OF WANDERING QUIET: ERE YE BE TOO CALM AND OLD,   73 ANASHU VIJAYA V   43
    "PASSION HAS OFTEN WORN OUR WANDERING HEARTS." . . . .   80 EPHEMERA   12
    "OFTEN HAS PASSION WORN OUR WANDERING HEARTS, ...   80 EPHEMERA   V   12
    A WHIRLING AND A WANDERING FIRE: . . . .   83 MAD KING GOLL   28
    THE WHIRLING AND THE WANDERING FIRE: . . . .   86 MAD KING GOLL   67
    WHERE THE WANDERING WATER GUSHES . . . .   88 STOLEN CHILD   28
    A GAY WANDERING CRY. . . . .   98 FOXHUNTER   28
    A GAY AND WANDERING CRY. . . . .   98 FOXHUNTER   V   28
    AND WHEN THE WANDERING MUSIC DIES . . . .   99 FOXHUNTER   31
    ETERNAL BEAUTY WANDERING ON HER WAY. . . . .   101 ROSE UPON ROOD   12
    BEFORE HER WANDERING FEET. . . . .   112 ROSE OF WORLD   15
    OR SIGHS AMID THE WANDERING, STARRY MIRTH, ...   114 ROSE OF BATTLE   18
    . . . ON THE WANDERING FOAM! I AND YOU: . . . . .   122 WHITE BIRDS   8
    AND ALL DISHEVELLED WANDERING STARS. . . . .   126 GOES FERGUS   12
    AH, EXILES WANDERING OVER LANDS AND SEAS, ...   129 BOOK STORIES   9
    AH, EXILES, WANDERING OVER MANY SEAS, ...   129 BOOK STORIES   V   9
    AH, EXILES, WANDERING OVER MANY LANDS, ...   130 BOOK STORIES   V   17
    AND OF THE WANDERING TWILIGHT COMPANIES . . . . . .   136 TO SOME I TALK V   6
    DESOLATE WINDS THAT CRY OVER THE WANDERING SEA: . . .   147 UNAPPEAS HOST   7
    THE SONG OF WANDERING AENGUS . . . .   149 WANDER AENGUS   T

WANDERING (CONTINUED)
    THOUGH I AM OLD WITH WANDERING . . . . 150 WANDER AENGUS   17
    AND BIND UP EVERY WANDERING TRESS: . . . . 157 BELOVED RHYMES   2
    ABOVE THE WANDERING TIDE: . . . . 162 ASKS FORGIVE   14
    AND SHE FORGET THE WANDERING AND ALL THE CRIMSON GLOOM . . 175 ELEMENT POWERS V   11
    AND SHE FORGET THE WANDERING AND THE CRIMSON GLOOM . . 175 ELEMENT POWERS V   11
    WHO OF THE WANDERING MANY-CHANGING ONES . . . . . 182 QUEEN MAEVE   51
    OF THE FAR WANDERING SHADOWS HAS COME TO ME, ... 183 QUEEN MAEVE   V   80
    FOR YOU, ALTHOUGH YOU'VE NOT HER WANDERING HEART, . . 186 QUEEN MAEVE   132
    O WANDERING BIRDS AND RUSHY BEDS, ... 190 BAILE AILLINN   31
    WANDERING FROM BROKEN STREET TO STREET . . . . . . 196 BAILE AILLINN   167
    A KING AND A QUEEN ARE WANDERING THERE, AND THE SOUND . 204 WITHER BOUGHS   19
    'TWAS AENGUS AND EDAIN, THE WANDERING LOVERS, ... 224 SHADOW WATER B   42
    AS NOW. DOES WANDERING IN THESE DESOLATE SEAS . . . 236 SHADOW WATER B 314
    SO THAT THE WANDERING FOOT'S CONTENT. . . . . . . 276 GREY ROCK   131
    THAT HAS GROWN WEARY OF THE WANDERING DANCE, ... 285 TWO KINGS   183
    THAT AM A WANDERING WITTED FOOL . . . . 380 SONGS FOOL 1 V 16
    AS THAT OLD WANDERING BEGGAR AND THESE GOD-HATED CHILDREN   459 FROM OEDIPUS   6
      KNOW.
    THAT WANDERING IN A DESERT, FEATURELESS . . . . . . 462 HARUN RASHID   27
    BUT WANDERING ARABS. I COMMEND THE ARABS . . . . . 462 HARUN RASHID V 22
    WANDERING IN A DESERT FEATURELESS . . . . 462 HARUN RASHID V 27
    DRAWN THROUGH THE WANDERING VEGETATIVE DREAM, ... 467 HARUN RASHID   143
    WOUND IN MIND'S WANDERING . . . . 474 ALL SOUL NIGHT   99
    FIX EVERY WANDERING THOUGHT UPON . . . . 477 SELF AND SOUL   6
    AND INTELLECT ITS WANDERING . . . . 478 SELF AND SOUL   22
    CARRIED BY THE WANDERING FOOL. . . . . 484 SYMBOLS   4
    GLANCES OF HER WANDERING EYE . . . . 487 CRAZED MOON   4
    AND THERE IS AN OLD BEGGAR WANDERING IN HIS PRIDE-- . . 580 CURSE CROMWELL   5
    BEST PLEASE A WANDERING MAN. . . . . 606 SONGS BURDEN 1 17
    'TIS MORN: THY SHEEP ARE WANDERING DOWN THE VALE-- . . 645 ISLE STAT I 1   3
    WITH STREAMING HAIR AS WANDERING LIGHTS . . . . . . 667 ISLE STAT II 3 19
    FAIR YOUTH, ALONG A WANDERING WAY . . . . 667 ISLE STAT II 3 38
    MID BUBBLING LEAVES A WANDERING SONG-RAPT BIRD . . . 672 ISLE STAT II 3 154
    MID BABBLING LEAVES A WANDERING SONG-RAPT BIRD . . . 672 ISLE STAT II 3 V 154
    FROM THREESCORE YEARS OF DREAM-LED WANDERING . . . . 682 SEEKER   16
    BUT NOW MY WANDERING SHALL BE DONE, I KNOW. . . . . 682 SEEKER   21
    BUT SOON MY WANDERING SHALL BE DONE I KNOW. . . . . 682 SEEKER   V 21
    WERE ALL MY WANDERING DAYS OF NO AVAIL, ... 684 SEEKER   64
    FORSWEARS HIS WANDERING 'MONG THE PINE, ... 686 LIFE   6
    WHERE THEY ALL SUMMER FEED THEIR WANDERING FLOCKS, . . 690 MOSADA 1   5
    WANDERING IN SULTRY PALACES OF IND, ... 694 MOSADA 1   102
    SHE SMILES--IS HAPPY WITH HER WANDERING GRIEFS. . . . 702 MOSADA 3   95
    OH, HUSH THE WANDERING MUSIC OF THY MIND. . . . . . 703 MOSADA 3   106
    WANDERING OF YORE IN FORESTS RUMOROUS. . . . . . . 723 KANVA ON SELF   3
    THERE THY WANDERING PATHWAY GOES, ... 744 ROSY CROSS   6
    EVEN THE WANDERING ISLANDS OF THE GODS, ... 749 SHADOW WATER A 45
    A WANDERING AIRY MUSIC: . . . . 783 GREY ROUND   7
    IN THAT SWEET WANDERING SNARE. . . . . 783 GREY ROUND   10
    A WANDERING AIRY MUSIC: . . . . 783 GREY ROUND   17
WANDERINGS
    THE WANDERINGS OF OISIN . . . . 1 OISIN 1   T
    THE WANDERINGS OF OISIN AND HOW A DEMON TRAPPED HIM . . 1 OISIN 1   V T
    O'SULLIVAN THE RED UPON HIS WANDERINGS . . . . . . 171 MAID QUIET   V T
    HANRAHAN LAMENTS BECAUSE OF HIS WANDERINGS . . . . . 171 MAID QUIET   V T
    THE LOVER MOURNS BECAUSE OF HIS WANDERINGS . . . . . 171 MAID QUIET   V T
    AWAKEN WANDERINGS OF LIGHT AIR . . . . 197 BAILE AILLINN 185
    FOR ALL HER WANDERINGS OVER-SEA: . . . . 197 BAILE AILLINN 203
    AND AIMLESS WANDERINGS THE WOODLANDS LONE, ... 674 ISLE STAT II 3 209
WANDERING-WITTED
    THAT AM A WANDERING-WITTED FOOL . . . . 380 SONGS FOOL 1   16
WANDERS
    AS IN THE WOODS HE WANDERS, IF HE LOVE . . . . . . 71 ANASHU VIJAYA V   3
    WANDERS LAUGHING AND EATING HER WILD HEART . . . . . 198 SEVEN WOODS   11
    WANDERS OUT INTO THE NIGHT . . . . 508 JANE BISHOP   25
    WANDERS AND WAILS BEFORE MY HEART MOST TRUE . . . . 738 YOU ARE SAD   8
    WHERE TRUE-LOVE WANDERS AMONG THE HOLY WOODS. . . . . 764 SHADOW WATER A 337
    WHERE TRUE LOVE WANDERS AMONG THE HOLY WOODS . . . . 764 SHADOW WATER A V 337
WANDS
    TALL WANDS OF ALDER AND WHITE QUICKEN WANDS. . . . . 111 CUCHULAIN SEA V 82A
    TALL WANDS OF ALDER AND WHITE QUICKEN WANDS. . . . . 111 CUCHULAIN SEA V 82A
WANE
    WHEN THE STARS ARE TO WANE AND THE WORLD BE DONE. . . 16 OISIN 1   220
    "GOD'S FIRE UPON THE WANE, ... 485 STATISTICS   2
    MY WORDS WERE ALL: "HERE NO LOVES WANE AND WITHER, . . 669 ISLE STAT II 3 84
WANES
    THAT WANES." "AH, WISTFUL VOICE," REPLIED THE OTHER, . . 79 EPHEMERA   V 3
WANING
    THE HOUR OF THE WANING OF LOVE HAS BESET US, ... 79 FALLING LEAVES   5
    BECAUSE OUR LOVE IS WANING." AND THEN SHE: . . . . 79 EPHEMERA   3
    "ALTHOUGH OUR LOVE IS WANING, LET US STAND . . . . . 79 EPHEMERA   4
WANT
    TO TELL YOUR SIMPLEST WANT, AND KNOWN, ... 436 FOR MY SON   21
    TO TELL YOUR SIMPLEST WANT, AND KNOW, ... 436 FOR MY SON   21
    "THEN WANT BEFORE YOU DIE." . . . . 596 COLONEL MARTIN 67
    AND WANT HE DID: FOR MY OWN GRAND-DAD . . . . . . 596 COLONEL MARTIN 68
    AND WANT HE DID FOR MY GRAND-DAD SAW . . . . 596 COLONEL MARTIN V 68
WANTED
    . . . THE PEOPLE WANTED PICTURES . . . . 287 TO WEALTHY MAN   T
WANTING
    LONE, AND WANTING THEE, I WEEP: . . . . 647 ISLE STAT I 1   72

	PAGE	TITLE	LINE
WANTON			
IGNORANT AND WANTON AS THE DAWN.	344	DAWN	14
THIS THEIR WANTON TREACHERY.	727	LOVERS QUARREL	55
WANTONNESS			
HOW BUT IN ZIG-ZAG WANTONNESS	338	TOM OROUGHLEY	12
HOW BUT IN ZIGZAG WANTONNESS	338	TOM OROUGHLEY V	12
WHAT BUT HEROIC WANTONNESS?	550	SEVERED HEAD	13
OUT OF MERE WANTONNESS TO LURE A SAIL	750	SHADOW WATER A	79
WAR			
OF WAR WERE ON IT, AND I WEPT.	24	OISIN 1	369
IN WAR, THE NOBLE FENIANS STEPT.	24	OISIN 1 V	372
OF WAR, AND THE CHASE, AND HUNTING, AND PLEASURE. . .	26	OISIN 1 V	403
AN ENDLESS WAR. THE HUNDRED YEARS HAD CEASED. . .	44	OISIN 2	224
AN ENDLESS WAR. THE HUNDREDTH YEAR HAD CEASED. . .	44	OISIN 2 V	224
WAR ON THE MIGHTIEST MEN UNDER THE SKIES.	45	OISIN 2	241
NONE WAR ON THE MASTERS OF HELL.	62	OISIN 3	214
. . . AND NO MAN MAY WAR WITH THE STRONG SPIRITS WAGE.	62	OISIN 3 V	214
AND DROVE TUMULT AND WAR AWAY	82	MAD KING GOLL	5
BUT NOW THE WAR RAGE IN CUCHULAIN WOKE.	110	CUCHULAIN SEA V	65
WHEN THEY FOR WAR ARE MET.	112	ROSE OF PEACE V	2
DANGER NO REFUGE HOLDS, AND WAR NO PEACE.	114	ROSE OF BATTLE	9
IT WAS BEFORE THE TIME OF THE GREAT WAR	182	QUEEN MAEVE	57
FOR LOVE IS WAR, AND THERE IS HATRED IN IT. . . .	244	SHADOW WATER B	459
ON THE DAY'S WAR WITH EVERY KNAVE AND DOLT. . . .	260	FASC DIFFICULT	10
OUTRODE HIS TROOP THAT AFTER TWELVE MONTHS' WAR . .	276	TWO KINGS V	1
AND DIED IN THE GREAT WAR BEYOND THE SEA.	339	SHEP GOATHERD	22
THE OUTRAGEOUS WAR SHALL FADE.	342	SHEP GOATHERD	100
I WILL TALK NO MORE OF BOOKS OR THE LONG WAR . . .	351	HER PRAISE	11
ON BEING ASKED FOR A WAR POEM	359	WAR POEM	T
OUT OF NO TRAGIC WAR, LOVERS OF LIFE.	369	EGO DOMINUS	39
THE THIRTEENTH MOON BUT SETS THE SOUL AT WAR . . .	374	PHASES OF MOON	50
A MEDITATION IN TIME OF WAR	406	IN TIME OF WAR	T
A MEDIATION IN TIME OF WAR	406	IN TIME OF WAR V	T
MEDITATIONS IN TIME OF CIVIL WAR ANCESTRAL HOUSES .	417	ANCEST HOUSES V	T
COMES CRACKING JOKES OF CIVIL WAR	423	ROAD AT DOOR	3
SOME FOURTEEN DAYS OF CIVIL WAR.	425	STARES NEST	12
IT DROPPED THE REINS OF PEACE AND WAR	437	SONGS PLAY 1	14
NOR ACCIDENT OF PEACE NOR WAR	446	COLONUS PRAISE	14
AWAIT THE HOUR OF WAR, ENTER THE SMALL.	461	HARUN RASHID V	8
WITH PERSIAN EMBASSY OR GRECIAN WAR.	462	HARUN RASHID	25
EMBLEMATICAL OF LOVE AND WAR?	477	SELF AND SOUL	19
OF WAR AND WAR'S ALARMS.	631	POLITICS	10
"SEND WAR IN OUR TIME, O LORD!"	638	BEN BULBEN	26
AND THEY WILL WAR, 'MID WONDROUS ELFIN-SIGHTS. . .	651	ISLE STAT I 1	164
OF WAR, OF YORE, TWO SHEPHERDS, WHERE WE PAUSE. . .	659	ISLE STAT II 1	31
SUCH WAR PLOTS, PEACE PLOTS, LOVE PLOTS--EVERY SIDE.	722	WITCH VIVIEN	66
AND PRAISED YOUR WAR AMONG THE ENDLESS SEAS. . . .	749	SHADOW WATER A	35
AND PRAISE A WAR AMONG THE ENDLESS SEAS.	749	SHADOW WATER A V	35
BELIEVE THAT GOLD AND WOMEN TAKEN IN WAR	754	SHADOW WATER A	159
AND MORE, IF YOU WILL WAR AGAINST THE DANES . . .	756	SHADOW WATER A V	190
WAR LADEN GALLEYS, AND ARMIES ON WHITE ROADS. . . .	757	SHADOW WATER A V	203
WAR-AXE			
MINGLING OF SWORD AND WAR-AXE, WHILE THE DAY . . .	40	OISIN 2 V	171
AND BY THEM WERE ARROW AND WAR-AXE, ARROW AND SHIELD AND BLADE.	49	OISIN 3	29
WERE ARROW AND SHIELD AND WAR-AXE, ARROW AND SPEAR AND BLADE.	49	OISIN 3 V	30
SORRY PLACE, WHERE FOR SWING OF THE WAR-AXE IN MY DIM EYES . . .	61	OISIN 3	194
WARDER			
AND EVEN THE SUN, THE DAY CASTLE'S WARDER.	28	OISIN 1	V 423A
WARES			
FOR ARROGANCE AND HATRED ARE THE WARES	406	FOR DAUGHTER	75
TO THOSE YOUR "MELLOW" WARES HAVE WEARIED OUT. . .	721	WITCH VIVIEN	27
WARFARE			
AND GOD WOULD BID HIS WARFARE CEASE.	113	ROSE OF PEACE	13
AND GOD WOULD BID MAN'S WARFARE CEASE.	113	ROSE OF PEACE V	13
WAR-LADEN			
WAR-LADEN GALLEYS, AND ARMIES ON WHITE ROADS. . . .	757	SHADOW WATER A	203
WARLESS SEE LONG-WARLESS			
. . . LONG WARLESS, GROWN WHITER THAN CURDS. . . .	49	OISIN 3	36
WARM			
ROSE EVER OUT OF THE WARM SEA.	13	OISIN 1	172
ROSE EVER FROM THE SEA'S WARM FLOOR.	13	OISIN 1 V	172
AND BLOWS ON HIS HANDS IN THE FIRE'S WARM BLAZE. . .	26	OISIN 1	404
SHALL WARM THEIR LIVES AT MANY A RUSTLING FLAME." .	80	EPHEMERA V	12B
OF THE CALVES ON THE WARM HILLSIDE	88	STOLEN CHILD	45
OF THE CALVES ON THE WARM HILL SIDE.	88	STOLEN CHILD V	45
OF THE CALVES ON THE WARM HILL-SIDE.	88	STOLEN CHILD V	45
THE HOUSE WHERE I WAS SAFE AND WARM.	151	HEART OF WOMAN	6
THE HOME WHERE I WAS SAFE AND WARM?	151	HEART OF WOMAN V	6
MY HEART UPON HIS WARM HEART LIES.	152	HEART OF WOMAN	11
AND SO WARM HER WILD NEST.	415	TOWER	172
BUT NO, IN THIS WARM WEATHER, 'MONG THE HILLS. . .	699	MOSADA 3	9
SITTING ON A WARM SMOOTH MAT	726	LOVERS QUARREL	11
WARMER			
IN THE JUNES THAT WERE WARMER THAN THESE ARE. . . .	91	OLD FISHERMAN	3
WARMS			
"AND YET THE JASMINE SEASON WARMS OUR BLOOD." . . .	464	HARUN RASHID	73
WEASEL WARMS HIM ON THE PATH.	705	DAWN-SONG	19
WAVES OFF THE FLIES, AND WARMS HIM IN THE SHINE. . .	709	FERENCZ RENYI	7

870

WARMTH
AND NOW THE WARMTH OF SIGHS, AND AFTER THE QUIVER OF LIPS. 47 OISIN 3 8
THE WARMTH OF LIFE IS CHILLING, AND THE SHADOWS GROW • • 675 ISLE STAT II 3 232
WARNED
OR WARNED YOU HOW DESPAIRING • • • • • • • • • • 313 TWO YEAR LATER 3
I COULD HAVE WARNED YOU; BUT YOU ARE YOUNG, • • • • • 313 TWO YEAR LATER 5
CRUELTY MUST KEEP; THEREFORE BE WARNED AND GO • • • • 448 HERO GIRL FOOL 7
WAR-RAGE
BUT NOW THE WAR-RAGE IN CUCHULAIN WOKE, • • • • • • 110 CUCHULAIN SEA 65
WARRED
WHEN GODS AND GIANTS WARRED. WE RODE BETWEEN • • • • 31 OISIN 2 31
SO WARRED, SO FEASTED, WITH NOR DREAMS NOR FEARS, • • • 44 OISIN 2 222
SO WARRED, SO FEASTED WE. NO DREAMS, NO FEARS, • • • 44 OISIN 2 V 222
FOR FOUR DAYS WARRED HE WITH THE BITTER TIDE, • • • • 111 CUCHULAIN SEA 85
WARRING
WHERE ARE NOW THE WARRING KINGS, • • • • • • • • 65 HAPPY SHEPHERD 11
WHERE ARE NOW THE WARRING KINGS? • • • • • • • • 65 HAPPY SHEPHERD 13
AND NOW THE SPARROWS WARRING IN THE EAVES, • • • • • 120 SORROW OF LOVE V 9
WARRIOR
BUT, WARRIOR, HERE THERE IS NO LAW; • • • • • • • 19 OISIN 1 283
THEN, WARRIOR, WHY SO SAD AND STERN, • • • • • • • 19 OISIN 1 V 286
THE WARRIOR DREAMS IN AN AGED LEISURE • • • • • • • 26 OISIN 1 V 401
HOW SUCH A WARRIOR NEVER TURNED HIS GAZE • • • • • • 29 OISIN 2 11
YOUNG WARRIOR." "NAY," I ANSWERED; "MY HANDS BURN • • • 35 OISIN 2 V 89B
I CRIED, "THOU ART SURELY A WARRIOR, FORGETTING HIS FAMOUS 51 OISIN 3 V 61
LINE,
AND HE, THE BEST WARRIOR, DEAD • • • • • • • • • 312 CHILD DANCING V 9
OLD WARRIOR, WAKE! FOR SOFT AS A BEE SIPS, • • • • • 677 ISLE STAT II 3 284
WARRIOR'S
FROM SOME DEAD WARRIOR'S BROKEN LANCE; • • • • • • 24 OISIN 1 367
IT WAS OF SOME DEAD WARRIOR'S LANCE. • • • • • • • 24 OISIN 1 V 367
"SWIFT ARE THE YEARS OF A WARRIOR'S PRIDE; • • • • • 26 OISIN 1 V 399A
WARRIORS
THE LONG-HAIRED WARRIORS, THE SPREAD FEAST; • • • • • 2 OISIN 1 V 7
TAKING THE MORTAL WARRIORS BY THE HANDS; • • • • • • 29 OISIN 2 10B
THOSE WARRIORS OF A LONG-FORGOTTEN DAY, • • • • • • 30 OISIN 2 V 14A
OF ANCIENT WARRIORS, THE LABOURS OF THE STRONG. • • • • 42 OISIN 2 195
THESE HANDS SLEW MANY WARRIORS BOLD-- • • • • • • 83 MAD KING GOLL V 23
OF THE GREAT WARRIORS WHOSE NAMES HAVE SUNG • • • • • 698 MOSADA 2 60
WAR'S
IN ITS OWN BEING, AND WHEN THAT WAR'S BEGUN • • • • • 374 PHASES OF MOON 51
AND WAIT WAR'S MUSIC; PASS THE LITTLE GALLERY; • • • • 461 HARUN RASHID 8
OF WAR AND WAR'S ALARMS, • • • • • • • • • • 631 POLITICS 10
WARS
WARS SHADOWY, VAST, EXULTANT; FAERIES OF OLD • • • • 29 OISIN 2 9
WARS SHADOWY, VAST, EXULTANT; FAIRY KINGS • • • • • 29 OISIN 2 V 9
OF WARS WITH THE WIDE WORLD • • • • • • • • • 50 OISIN 3 55
THEN FEAST, MAKING CONVERSE OF WARS, • • • • • • • 62 OISIN 3 212
THEN FEAST, MAKING CONVERSE OF EIRE, OF WARS, • • • • • 62 OISIN 3 V 212
MY FATHER STANDS." "AGED, WORN OUT WITH WARS • • • • 107 CUCHULAIN SEA 29
"NAY, HE IS OLD AND SAD WITH MANY WARS, • • • • • • 107 CUCHULAIN SEA V 29
"BUT HE IS OLD AND SAD WITH MANY WARS." • • • • • • 107 CUCHULAIN SEA 30
BROODING NO MORE UPON GOD'S WARS • • • • • • • • 113 ROSE OF PEACE 5
AND WHEN AT LAST, DEFEATED IN HIS WARS, • • • • • • 115 ROSE OF BATTLE 33
WHEN THE LONG WARS FOR THE WHITE HORN • • • • • • 189 BAILE AILLINN 14
WHERE THROUGH LONG WARS AND SUDDEN NIGHT ALARMS • • • 420 MY HOUSE 24
WHERE THROUGH LONG WARS AND SUDDEN NIGHT ALARUMS • • • 420 MY HOUSE V 24
WITH PERSIAN WARS OR GREEK AMBASSADORS • • • • • • 462 HARUN RASHID V 25
NOW HIS WARS ON GOD BEGIN; • • • • • • • • • 561 FOUR AGES MAN 7
BOWING NATIONS, PLUMED WARS-- • • • • • • • • 737 IN FIRELIGHT 10
AND WHEN YOU CAME TO SCORN OUR LITTLE WARS • • • • • 749 SHADOW WATER A V 34
OR GO BESIDE HIM TO HIS MOUNTAIN WARS. • • • • • • 768 SHADOW WATER A 414
WAR-SONGS
THE WAR-SONGS THAT ROUSED THEM OF OLD; • • • • • • 61 OISIN 3 202
WARTY
HID FROM ALL THOSE WARTY LADS • • • • • • • • • 589 OLD WICKED MAN 43
WARWARD
COOK BARACH, THE TRAITOR; AND WARWARD, • • • • • • 53 OISIN 3 90
WAR-WASTED
HE HAD OUTRIDDEN HIS WAR-WASTED MEN • • • • • • • 277 TWO KINGS 3
HE HAD OUT-RIDDEN HIS WAR-WASTED MEN • • • • • • • 277 TWO KINGS V 3
JOSTLED AND SHOUTED THOSE WAR-WASTED MEN, • • • • • 286 TWO KINGS 216
WAR-WEARY
"I HAVE NOT YET, WAR-WEARY KING, • • • • • • • • 6 OISIN 1 55
WARY
YET SHE GOES WITH FOOTSTEP WARY, • • • • • • • • 124 CATHLEEN PARA 11
STILL SHE GOES WITH FOOTSTEPS WARY, • • • • • • • 124 CATHLEEN PARA V 11
AND GAZE ON THE MEADOW-MICE WARY, • • • • • • • 707 FAIRY PEDANT 18
WASH
TO SHORES BY THE WASH OF THE TREMULOUS TIDE, • • • • 8 OISIN 1 81
WASH! MAKE YOUR BODY SWEET! • • • • • • • • • 572 LADYS 2ND SONG 4
WASHED SEE NEW-WASHED DEW-WASHED
WASHED BY TIME'S WATERS AS THEY ROSE AND FELL • • • • 206 ADAMS CURSE 32
IT HAD WASHED AMONG THE STARS AND PUT THEM OUT, • • • 236 SHADOW WATER B 311
WASHES
WASHES THE SHORES WHERE YE ABIDE, • • • • • • • 5 OISIN 1 V 47
WASP
A NEW DAY'S TROOP OF WASP AND BEE • • • • • • • 646 ISLE STAT I 1 44
WASSAILS
I LOVED AND SANG, AND IN LONG WASSAILS • • • • • • 23 OISIN 1 V 345C

		PAGE	TITLE		LINE
WASTE					
	NEIGHING ALONG THE LIFELESS WASTE;	13	OISIN 1		170
	THE FLOWERS STILL GREW THERE! FAR ON THE SEA'S WASTE	39	OISIN 2		163
	THE FLOWERS STILL GREW THERE. MOVED BEYOND HIM THE SEA'S WASTE;	39	OISIN 2	V	163
	HAS HE NOT LED US INTO THESE WASTE SEAS	221	SHADOW WATER B		1
	WHAT RICHES CAN YOU FIND IN THIS WASTE SEA	226	SHADOW WATER B		97
	IN THE WASTE OF THE HIGH AIR, THAT WE MAY WANDER	234	SHADOW WATER B		263
	THAT WEIGH AND MEASURE ALL IN THESE WASTE SEAS--	235	SHADOW WATER B		292
	THOUGH YOU MAY THINK I WASTE MY BREATH	271	GREY ROCK		6
	FORBID, BESEECH AND WASTE MY BREATH." THEN I!	281	TWO KINGS		102
	AND LOOSEN ON US DREAMS THAT WASTE OUR LIFE,	281	TWO KINGS		107
	NOR CAN TIME WASTE THE CHEEK, NOR IS THERE FOOT	284	TWO KINGS		182
	THE YEARS TO COME SEEMED WASTE OF BREATH,	328	IRISH AIRMAN		14
	A WASTE OF BREATH THE YEARS BEHIND	328	IRISH AIRMAN		15
	ARE MET ON THE WASTE HILLS BY COUNTRYMEN	375	PHASES OF MOON		76
	ARE MET ON THE WASTE HILLS BY COUNTRY MEN	375	PHASES OF MOON	V	76
	TROUBLES MY SIGHT! A WASTE OF DESERT SAND!	402	SECOND COMING	V	13
	AND THROUGH THE FERTILE AND WASTE,	436	FOR MY SON		30
	BY WOOD ANTIQUE, BY WAVE AND WASTE,	670	ISLE STAT II 3		109
	FROM WASTE SEAS CROSS'D, YET EVER GARRULOUS)	690	MOSADA 1		9
	IN THE WASTE AIR. I WILL WANDER BY HIS SIDE	754	SHADOW WATER A		152
	BUT THESE WASTE WATERS AND WIND-BEATEN SAILS	763	SHADOW WATER A		319
	IN WASTE PLACES OF THE SKY,	772	SONG DEIRDRE 1		6
WASTED SEE WAR-WASTED					
	UPON HIS WASTED HANDS,	98	FOXHUNTER		22
	UPON HIS WASTED HANDS,	98	FOXHUNTER	V	24
	WORDS WERE BUT WASTED BREATH!	471	ALL SOUL NIGHT		27
WASTEFUL					
	"ONLY THE WASTEFUL VIRTUES EARN THE SUN";	270	PARDON FATHERS		18
WASTES					
	WHO WASTES HIS BLOOD TO BE ANOTHER'S DREAM.	103	FERGUS DRUID		28
WASTING					
	YOU ARE WASTING AWAY, LITTLE FAIRY.	707	FAIRY PEDANT		12
	YOU ARE WASTING AWAY, LITTLE FAIRY.	707	FAIRY PEDANT		20
	YOU ARE WASTING AWAY, LITTLE FAIRY.	708	FAIRY PEDANT		28
	SHE IS WASTING AWAY, LITTLE FAIRY.	708	FAIRY PEDANT		40
WATCH					
	GO WATCH THE ROAD BETWEEN THE WOOD AND TIDE,	105	CUCHULAIN SEA		4
	BUT NOW I HAVE NO NEED TO WATCH IT MORE."	105	CUCHULAIN SEA		5
	GO DWELL UPON THE CLIFFS AND WATCH THE TIDE;	105	CUCHULAIN SEA	V	4
	TO WATCH A WHITE GULL TAKE	400	DEMON BEAST		24
	AND THERE IS NONE SO FIT TO KEEP A WATCH AND KEEP	442	BLACK CENTAUR		15
	I SAT WHERE I COULD WATCH HER SLEEPING FORM,	467	HARUN RASHID		128
	A STORM-BEATEN OLD WATCH TOWER,	484	SYMBOLS	V	1
	WE LIVED LIKE MEN THAT WATCH A PAINTED STAGE.	542	PARN FUNERAL 1		18
	MAIDEN, COME FORTH! THE WOODS KEEP WATCH FOR THEE!	645	ISLE STAT I 1		1
	THE AGELESS SENTINELS WHO HOLD THEIR WATCH.	664	ISLE STAT II 2		45
	TO WATCH THEE PASS? YET DEEPER THAN MEN KNOW	672	ISLE STAT II 3		158
	NAY HERE, I'LL LAY ME DOWN WHERE I CAN WATCH	700	MOSADA 3		39
	THAT WATCH ME WITH THEIR SUPPLIANT LIGHT--	723	GIRLS SONG A		10
	THE GODS HOLD WATCH ABOUT THE WORDS OF A QUEEN.	756	SHADOW WATER A		191
	O, AENGUS OF THE HERDS, WATCH OVER ME!	762	SHADOW WATER A		291
WATCHED					
	WATCHED WHERE THE SUN IN A SAFFRON BLAZE	26	OISIN 1		394
	WATCHED THE OLD SUN THAT IN SEA-WAYS	26	OISIN 1	V	394
	THE STRANGER WATCHED THE SWORD! BUT NIAM FAR,	38	OISIN 2	V	136
	OF FACES, WATCHED ME, AND THE LEISURED GAZE	39	OISIN 2	V	149
	WATCHED ME WITH MOURNFUL WONDER OUT OF THE WELLS OF HIS EYES,	51	OISIN 3		60
	SO WATCHED I WHEN, MAN OF THE CROZIERS,	54	OISIN 3		101
	WATCHED HER THOSE SEAMLESS FACES FROM THE VALLEY'S GLIMMERING GIRTH!	55	OISIN 3		122
	WATCHED HER THOSE SEAMLESS FACES FROM THE VALLEY'S MURAL GIRTH	55	OISIN 3	V	122
	AMRITA. THIS SAME EVE SHE WATCHED ME PASS.	74	ANASHU VIJAYA	V	64
	AND FROM THAT HOUR HE HAS WATCHED OVER NONE	220	HARP OF AENGUS		13
	HAD WATCHED IN BITTERER SLEEP	399	BREAK OF DAY		22
	HAD WATCHED MY DAILY PASSAGE TO AND FRO;	466	HARUN RASHID		107
	THE DOVES WHOSE GROWING FORMS HE'D WATCHED. NOT THESE	710	FERENCZ RENYI		21
	THE DOVES WHOSE GROWING FORM HE'D WATCHED. NOT THESE	710	FERENCZ RENYI	V	21
	WATCHED OF PLACID POPLAR-TREES,	732	STREET DANCERS		16
	WATCHED OF PLACID POPLAR TREES,	732	STREET DANCERS	V	16
	AND FROM THAT HOUR HE HAS WATCHED OVER NONE	763	SHADOW WATER A		308
WATCHER					
	HE SEEMED THE WATCHER FOR A SIGN. THE OTHER	31	OISIN 2	V	41
	THEY COME WHERE SOME HUGE WATCHER IS,	196	BAILE AILLINN		168
	"WATCHER, WHEREFORE HAVE YE CALLED US?" EYES GO AFTER HIS LEAN HAND,	718	PHANTOM SHIP		10
WATCHERS					
	FROM LASTING WATCHERS, THAT OUTLIVE THE MOON,	236	SHADOW WATER B		320
	AND DID THOSE WATCHERS BID YOU TAKE ME CAPTIVE?	236	SHADOW WATER B		322
WATCHES					
	BENDING HER FACE O'ER HIS, SHE WATCHES MEET	688	TWO TITANS		45
	HE WATCHES OVER NONE BUT FAITHFUL LOVERS.	762	SHADOW WATER A		295
WATCHING					
	OF PLANETS WATCHING, WATCHING THE RACE OF HARES	44	OISIN 2	V	228B
	OF PLANETS WATCHING, WATCHING THE RACE OF HARES	44	OISIN 2	V	228B
	WATCHING THE BLESSED ONES MOVE FAR OFF, AND THE SMILE ON GOD'S FACE,	61	OISIN 3		199
	BUT NOW MY YEARS OF WATCHING ARE NO MORE."	105	CUCHULAIN SEA	V	5

WATCHING   (CONTINUED)
      WATCHING OUR SHEPHERD SPORTS AT HARVEST-TIME . . . . .   340 SHEP GOATHERD   41
      WATCHING O'ER HER AWFUL YOUNG, ...   658 ISLE STAT I 3   87
      DID HER LONELY WATCHING TAKE . . . .   658 ISLE STAT I 3   94
      AS I MY WATCHING LEST YOU WAKE, ...   658 ISLE STAT I 3   95
      WEARY OF WATCHING ROUND THE FIRE AT NIGHT. . . . .   683 SEEKER   42
      THE PREACHER WATCHING FOR THE EVIL HOUR TO PASS, ... 686 LIFE   3
      OF DREAMING AND OF WATCHING BY THE DOOR . . . . . .   700 MOSADA 3   26
      THE PREACHER WATCHING FOR THE ILL HOUR TO PASS-- . . . . 734 QUATRAIN APHOR   3
      THE PREACHER WATCHING FOR THE EVIL HOUR TO PASS, ... 734 QUATRAIN APHOR V   3
WATCH-TOWER
      A STORM-BEATEN OLD WATCH-TOWER, ...   484 SYMBOLS   1
WATER   SEE PUDDLE-WATER TAR-WATER
      SAVE DEER TOWARDS NOON THAT WATER SOUGHT. . . . . . .   17 OISIN 1   V   243
      IN A LONG IRON SLEEP, AS A FISH IN THE WATER GOES DUMB   53 OISIN 3   96
         AS A STONE.
      THE DROWSY WATER RATS! . . . .   87 STOLEN CHILD V   5
      WHERE THE WANDERING WATER GUSHES . . . .   88 STOLEN CHILD   28
      TO AN ISLE IN THE WATER . . . .   89 ISLE IN WATER   T
      TO AN ISLE IN THE WATER . . . .   89 ISLE IN WATER   7
      TO AN ISLE IN THE WATER . . . .   89 ISLE IN WATER   15
      IS HEARD ON THE WATER, AS THEY WERE, THE PROUD AND APART, 91 OLD FISHERMAN   10
      I HEAR LAKE WATER LAPPING WITH LOW SOUNDS BY THE SHORE!   117 ISLE INNISFREE   10
      I HEAR LAKE WATER LAPPING WITH LOW SOUNDS ON THE SHORE!   117 ISLE INNISFREE V   10
      WITH THE EARTH AND THE SKY AND THE WATER, ...   143 ROSE IN HEART   7
      OR ONLY TO THE WATER IN THE WEST! . . . .   155 REPROVE CURLEW   2
      HE HAD PUDDLE WATER IN HIS SHOES! . . . .   190 BAILE AILLINN V   28
      ABOUT THE WINDY WATER SIDE . . . .   192 BAILE AILLINN V   93
      THE OLD MEN ADMIRING THEMSELVES IN THE WATER . . . .   208 OLD MEN ADMIRE   T
      O HURRY WHERE BY WATER AMONG THE TREES . . . . . .   210 RAGGED WOOD   1
      O HURRY TO THE WATER AMID THE TREES, ...   210 RAGGED WOOD   V   1
      O HURRY WHERE BY WATER AMONG TREES, ...   210 RAGGED WOOD   V   1
      O HURRY TO THE WATER AMID THE TREES, ...   211 RAGGED WOOD   V   5
      GABRIEL WILL COME FROM THE WATER . . . .   215 HAPPY TOWNLAND   45
      SHINING ON WATER AND FALLEN AMONG LEAVES, ...   218 WOODS OF COOLE   38
      AND NOW THAT TIME PUTS WATER IN MY BLOOD, ...   222 SHADOW WATER B V   11A
      AND YET YOU SAY THE WATER AND THE WIND . . . . . .   236 SHADOW WATER B V   317
      UNDER THE OCTOBER TWILIGHT THE WATER . . . . . .   322 SWANS AT COOLE   3
      UPON THE BRIMMING WATER AMONG THE STONES . . . . .   322 SWANS AT COOLE   5
      BUT NOW THEY DRIFT ON THE STILL WATER, ...   323 SWANS AT COOLE   25
      WOULD I COULD CAST A SAIL ON THE WATER . . . . . .   330 BONE OF A HARE   1
      I WOULD FIND BY THE EDGE OF THAT WATER . . . . . .   330 BONE OF A HARE   9
      WORN THIN BY THE LAPPING OF WATER, ...   330 BONE OF A HARE   11
      AND LAUGH OVER THE UNTROUBLED WATER . . . .   330 BONE OF A HARE   14
      IT SHUDDERED IN THE WATER! . . . .   345 ON WOMAN   19
      "BUT WHERE CAN WE DRAW WATER," . . . .   396 ROSE TREE   13
      COLD STONE AND WATER. I GREW WILD, ...   399 BREAK OF DAY   14
      SHOOK OFF THE WATER FROM HIS BACK! . . . .   400 DEMON BEAST   29
      AND BEAUTY-DRUNKEN BY THE WATER . . . .   447 COLONUS PRAISE   20
      WHAT'S WATER BUT THE GENERATED SOUL? . . . . . .   490 DANCER CRUACH   8
      WHETHER IN WOOD, WATER OR CLOUD, ...   528 DANCER CRUACH   7
      DROWN, DROWN IN THE WATER BUTT, ...   546 TO SAME TUNE 2 V   REF
      BY WATER, HERB AND SOLITARY PRAYER . . . .   555 RIBH AT TOMB   23
      WHEN DARK HANGS UPON THE WATER . . . .   589 OLD WICKED MAN   34
      AN AMBUSH! PILGRIMS AT THE WATER SIDE! . . . . . .   601 GALLERY REVIS V   2
      AND THE GREAT WATER SIGHED FOR LOVE, ...   611 NEWS ORACLE   3
      AS LIES DARK WATER IN A MURMUROUS GLADE, ...   650 ISLE STAT I 1   138
      OF LILAC O'ER THE PULSING WATER GLEAMS, ...   664 ISLE STAT II 2   48
      OF THINE CRY OVER WOLD AND WATER WHITE, ...   669 ISLE STAT II 3   73
      FAR OUT UPON THE WATER WORLD AND RINGED . . . . .   693 MOSADA 1   80
      "OR SEEK WHERE SWEETEST WATER BUBBLES, ...   731 PRIEST FAIRY   79
      THERE'S BARLEY THERE, AND WATER THERE, ...   774 COME RIDE   7
WATER-BUTT
      DROWN, DROWN IN THE WATER-BUTT, ...   546 TO SAME TUNE 2   9
      DROWN, DROWN IN THE WATER-BUTT, ...   546 TO SAME TUNE 2   19
      DROWN, DROWN IN THE WATER-BUTT, ...   547 TO SAME TUNE 2   29
WATER-COURSE
      SEEMS A WATER-COURSE OR AN AVALANCHE, ...   567 LAPIS LAZULI   45
WATERED
      "IT NEEDS TO BE BUT WATERED," . . . .   396 ROSE TREE   7
WATERFALL
      I THOUGHT! "THERE IS A WATERFALL . . . .   398 BREAK OF DAY   5
      THAT WAS BESIDE THE WATERFALL, THY WORDS . . . . .   683 SEEKER   49
      "BEHOLD THE KNIGHT OF THE WATERFALL, WHOSE HEART . . . . 684 SEEKER   54
WATER-FLOWERS
      OVER THE LAKE THE WATER-FLOWERS . . . .   647 ISLE STAT I 1   66
WATER-FOWLS
      OF THE DREAMING WATER-FOWLS, ...   644 SONG FAERIES   12
      OF THE DREAMING WATER-FOWLS, ...   676 ISLE STAT II 3   259
WATERHEN
      THE WATERHEN MUST CHANGE HER GROUND! . . . . . .   326 ROBERT GREGORY V   55
WATER-HEN
      THE WATER-HEN MUST CHANGE HER GROUND! . . . . . .   326 ROBERT GREGORY   55
      WHAT MADE THAT SOUND? A RAT OR WATER-HEN . . . . .   372 PHASES OF MOON   8
      THE STILTED WATER-HEN . . . .   419 MY HOUSE   8
WATERING   SEE WIDE-WATERING
WATER-LILY
      BY A BROAD WATER-LILY LEAF! . . . .   195 BAILE AILLINN   146
WATERPROOF
      WHAT MADE THE CEILING WATERPROOF? . . . .   625 NATIVITY   5

| | PAGE | TITLE | LINE |

WATER-RATS
    THE DROWSY WATER-RATS: . . . .   87 STOLEN CHILD   5
WATER'S
    I PASSED ALONG THE WATER'S EDGE BELOW THE HUMID TREES, . .   76 INDIAN ON GOD   1
    WITH VAPOURY FOOTSOLE BY THE WATER'S DROWSY BLAZE. . . . .   78 INDIAN TO LOVE   20
    AND DROP A VAPOURY FOOTFALL IN THE WATER'S DROWSY BLAZE. . .   78 INDIAN TO LOVE V 20
    WITH VAPOURY FOOTSOLE AMONG THE WATER'S DROWSY BLAZE. . . . 78 INDIAN TO LOVE V 20
    AND GOD'S BELL BUOYED TO BE THE WATER'S CARE: . . . . .   114 ROSE OF BATTLE   4
    FOR WIND OR WATER'S ROAR? . . . .   312 CHILD DANCING   3
    SHALL WALK THE WET SAND BY THE WATER'S EDGE, ...   371 EGO DOMINUS   V 71
    I RIDE WITH FALCON TO THE WATER'S EDGE . . . .   463 HARUN RASHID   V 57
WATERS
    AND WHERE THE WOOD AND WATERS MEET . . . .   14 OISIN 1   193
    ON THEIR OWN SELVES IN THE WATERS WHITE, ...   14 OISIN 1   V 185
    AND WHERE THE WOODS AND WATERS MEET . . . .   14 OISIN 1   V 193
    THAT KEPT DIM WATERS FROM THE SKY: . . . .   17 OISIN 1   243
    THUS ON THE WATERS, FAR AND SWEET, ...   26 OISIN 1   V 398A
    AND THE MOON GOAD THE WATERS NIGHT AND DAY, ...   45 OISIN 2   238
    THUNDERING, AND THE WIDE USELESS WATERS FRAY . . . . . .   45 OISIN 2   238
    O HAD YOU SEEN BEAUTIFUL NIAMH GROW WHITE AS THE WATERS   54 OISIN 3   109
      ARE WHITE,
    AND RUSHES WAVED AND WATERS ROLLED. . . . .   84 MAD KING GOLL   35
    TO THE WATERS AND THE WILD . . . .   87 STOLEN CHILD   10
    TO THE WATERS AND THE WILD . . . .   87 STOLEN CHILD   25
    TO THE WOODS AND WATERS WILD . . . .   87 STOLEN CHILD   V REF
    TO THE WATERS AND THE WILD . . . .   88 STOLEN CHILD   39
    TO THE WATERS AND THE WILD . . . .   88 STOLEN CHILD   51
    LIKE THE PALE WATERS IN THEIR WINTRY RACE, ...   112 ROSE OF WORLD   8
    WHERE MOUSE-GREY WATERS ARE FLOWING, ...   119 PITY OF LOVE   7
    THE MOUSE-GREY WATERS ON FLOWING, ...   119 PITY OF LOVE   V   5
    WHATEVER RAVELLED WATERS RISE AND FALL . . . .   127 DREAM OF FAERY   32
    OR ONLY TO WATERS IN THE WEST: . . . .   155 REPROVE CURLEW V   2
    OR ONLY TO THE WATERS IN THE WEST: . . . .   155 REPROVE CURLEW V   2
    MIRRORED IN WATERS THAT NOR HAIL NOR RAIN . . . .   184 QUEEN MAEVE   V 89
    WASHED BY TIME'S WATERS AS THEY ROSE AND FELL . . . . . .   206 ADAMS CURSE   32
    O HEAVY SWOLLEN WATERS, BRIM THE FALL OF THE OAK TREES, . .   207 HANRAHANS SONG V 11
    LIKE HEAVY FLOODED WATERS OUR BODIES AND OUR BLOOD: . . .   208 HANRAHANS SONG   13
    LIKE HEAVY SWOLLEN WATERS ARE OUR BODIES AND OUR BLOOD: . .   208 HANRAHANS SONG V 13
    BY THE WATERS. . . . .   208 OLD MEN ADMIRE   6
    LIKE THE WATERS." . . . .   208 OLD MEN ADMIRE   9
    DEDICATION TO THE "SHADOWY WATERS" . . . .   217 WOODS OF COOLE V   T
    OF FORGAEL AND DECTORA AND THE EMPTY WATERS . . . . . .   218 WOODS OF COOLE   22
    THE WATERS OF SLEEP CAN MAKE A CHATTERING TONGUE . . . . .   218 WOODS OF COOLE   25
    THE SHADOWY WATERS . . . .   221 SHADOW WATER B   T
    THAT NOTHING CAN AMEND IT BUT THESE WATERS, ...   227 SHADOW WATER B   120
    BUT DESOLATE WATERS AND A BATTERED SHIP. . . . .   246 SHADOW WATER B   497
    BESIDE THE BRACKISH WATERS OF THE BOYNE . . . .   270 PARDON FATHERS   11
    AND THOUGH THEY HAVE TO CROSS THE LOUGHLAN WATERS . . . . .   282 TWO KINGS   113
    UNDER MY WINDOW-LEDGE THE WATERS RACE. . . . .   490 COOLE BALLYLEE   1
    THE ECSTATIC WATERS LAUGH BECAUSE . . . .   612 NEWS ORACLE   17
    THE POPLARS GAZE ACROSS THE WATERS GREY, ...   653 ISLE STAT I 2   34
    IN SONG, FROM GOBLIN WATERS SWAYING WHITE, ...   657 ISLE STAT I 3   51
    LIVING, WIDE WINGED, ON THE WATERS FLOAT. . . . .   657 ISLE STAT I 3   54
    SLOW WATERS, AND THE BOAT AND MAIDEN SINK . . . .   663 ISLE STAT II 2   39
    PIERCING THE QUIVERING WATERS THROUGH AND THROUGH, ...   664 ISLE STAT II 2   44
    BEHOLD THE FLASHING WATERS. . . . .   680 LOVE AND DEATH   1
    WHAT ARE THE TWIN-BORN WATERS, ...   680 LOVE AND DEATH   15
    AND WHERE THE POLAR WINDS AND WATERS WRESTLE . . . . . .   682 SEEKER   18
    BEYOND WHERE THE WATERS ARE MOVING, ...   739 WHERE BOOKS GO   7
    MINE WHERE WATERS BROOD AND TOSS: . . . .   744 ROSY CROSS   7
    THE SHADOWY WATERS . . . .   745 SHADOW WATER A   T
    WALKED ON THE WATERS AND BID FORGAEL SEEK . . . .   747 SHADOW WATER A   12
    AS THOUGH THE WATERS HAD FLOWED UP BETWEEN: . . . . . .   749 SHADOW WATER A   55
    AMONG THE WATERS THAT NO PILOT KNOWS. . . . .   750 SHADOW WATER A   80
    AMONG THESE MISTY WATERS. TWO! NOW FOUR! . . . .   753 SHADOW WATER A   138
    HAVE THE WINDS BLOWN YOU AMONG THESE EMPTY WATERS? . . . .   756 SHADOW WATER A   192
    BECAUSE THESE WATERS MAKE ALL WOMEN ONE. . . . .   757 SHADOW WATER A   194
    I HAVE FOUND NOTHING BUT THESE EMPTY WATERS: . . . . . .   757 SHADOW WATER A   201
    THE WINDS AND WATERS TO BE YOUR HOME FOR EVER: . . . . .   762 SHADOW WATER A   282
    THE WINDS AND WATERS TO BE YOUR HOME FOREVER: . . . . .   762 SHADOW WATER A V 282
    BUT THESE WASTE WATERS AND WIND-BEATEN SAILS . . . . . .   763 SHADOW WATER A   319
    THE CLOUDY WATERS AND THE GLIMMERING WINDS . . . .   764 SHADOW WATER A   327
    AMONG THE WINDS AND WATERS: AND WHEN THEY PASS . . . . .   764 SHADOW WATER A   331
    THAT THE VAST TROUBLED WATERS BRING . . . .   784 WOMANS BEAUTY   17
WATERS'
    BY THE SINGING WATERS' EDGE, ...   646 ISLE STAT I 1   23
WATER-SERPENT
    THE WATER-SERPENT SINGS HIS HEART . . . .   673 ISLE STAT II 3   184
WATER-SIDE
    ABOUT THE WINDY WATER-SIDE, ...   192 BAILE AILLINN   93
    AN AMBUSH: PILGRIMS AT THE WATER-SIDE: . . . .   601 GALLERY REVIS   2
WATTLE
    IN THE FENIANS' DWELLINGS OF WATTLE LEAN ON THE CHESSBOARDS   55 OISIN 3   115
      AND PLAY,
WATTLED
    AND SWEPT OUT OF THE WATTLED HALL . . . .   20 OISIN 1   292
WATTLES
    A HOUSE OF WATTLES, CLAY, AND SKIN: . . . .   17 OISIN 1   249
    MUCH WONDERING TO SEE UPON ALL HANDS, OF WATTLES . . . . .   58 OISIN 3   162
      AND WOODWORK MADE,

WATTLES (CONTINUED)
 MUCH WONDERING TO SEE UPON ALL HANDS, OF WATTLES 58 OISIN 3 V 162
  AND WOOD-WORK MADE,
 AND A SMALL CABIN BUILD THERE, OF CLAY AND WATTLES MADE: 117 ISLE INNISFREE 2
 AND A SMALL CABIN BUILT THERE, OF CLAY AND WATTLES MADE: 117 ISLE INNISFREE V 2
WAVE   SEE LAND-UNDER-WAVE
 THROUGH HEART AND SPINE: AND CAST HIM IN THE WAVE 41 OISIN 2 182
 THROUGH HEART AND DEMON SPINE, AND IN THE WAVE 41 OISIN 2 V 182
 WRAPT IN THE WAVE OF THAT MUSIC, WITH WEARINESS MORE THAN 51 OISIN 3 69
  OF EARTH,
 WHERE DAFFODIL AND LILY WAVE, 67 HAPPY SHEPHERD 46
 I WANDER ON, AND WAVE MY HANDS, 84 MAD KING GOLL 43
 WHERE THE WAVE OF MOONLIGHT GLOSSES 87 STOLEN CHILD 13
 UPON THE DANCER BY THE DREAMLESS WAVE. 128 DREAM OF FAERY 45
 THAT NONE MAY FEEL THE POWER OF SQUALL AND WAVE, 128 DREAM OF FAERY V 45
 GREAT POWERS OF FALLING WAVE AND WIND AND WINDY FIRE, 174 ELEMENT POWERS 7
 YOU GREAT ANGELIC POWERS OF WIND, AND WAVE, AND FIRE, 174 ELEMENT POWERS V 7
 GREAT ELEMENTAL POWERS OF WIND, AND WAVE, AND FIRE, 174 ELEMENT POWERS V 7
 FOLK DANCE LIKE A WAVE OF THE SEA: 178 FIDDLER DOONEY 2
 AND DANCE LIKE A WAVE OF THE SEA. 179 FIDDLER DOONEY 20
 "FROM HEAT AND COLD AND WIND AND WAVE: 193 BAILE AILLINN 114
 "HE IS WELL OUT OF WIND AND WAVE, 193 BAILE AILLINN V 114
 IN A WHITE BREAKING WAVE: THEY HAD THE LOOK 223 SHADOW WATER B 34
 AENGUS AND EDAIN RAN UP OUT OF THE WAVE-- 231 SHADOW WATER B 196
 WOULD RISE OF A SUDDEN, OR A WAVE SO HUGE 236 SHADOW WATER B 310
 AND LISTENING TO THE CRY OF WIND AND WAVE 236 SHADOW WATER B 315
 THAT UNIMAGINABLE STORMS OF WIND AND WAVE 236 SHADOW WATER B 317
 AND LISTENING TO THE CRY OF THE WIND AND WAVE 236 SHADOW WATER B V 315
 OR WAVE TO DROWN. BUT I HAVE DONE WITH WORDS, 238 SHADOW WATER B 348
 AND BARREN AS A BREAKING WAVE 456 FRIENDS YOUTH 11
 UNDER THE RECEDING WAVE. 485 NINETEENTH CEN 4
 WHEN NETTLES WAVE UPON A SHAPELESS MOUND 489 COOLE PARK 29 27
 KEEP DANCING LIKE A WAVE, 592 DRUNK SOBRIETY 10
 DREAMING OF FLASHING FLIGHT AND OF THE PLUMED WAVE. 650 ISLE STAT I 1 140
 BEYOND THE LAKE, WHOSE SMALLEST WAVE WAS BURDENED 656 ISLE STAT I 3 31
 BY WOOD ANTIQUE, BY WAVE AND WASTE, 670 ISLE STAT II 3 109
 AND THE WAN WAVE THAT LINGERS 672 ISLE STAT II 3 166
 BEFORE A DEATH. O'ER WAVE AND BANK 673 ISLE STAT II 3 185
 BUT NOW I WAVE HER HITHER TO MY SIDE. 694 MOSADA 1 91
 DARTING YOU WAVE THEM, DARTING IN THE VAPOUR. 694 MOSADA 1 94
 I WAVE THEM HITHER, MY BREAST HEAVES WITH JOY. 694 MOSADA 1 98
 AT LAST. BUT NOW I WAVE HER TO MY SIDE. 694 MOSADA 1 V 91
 HIDE WHERE HE WILL, IN WAVE OR WRINKLED MOON, 720 WITCH VIVIEN 8
 THE MOTHER OF THE WAVE SIGHS TOO, 738 YOU ARE SAD 10
 AND HER DIM WAVE BIDS MAN BE NO MORE GLAD, 738 YOU ARE SAD 11
 PLANTED IN THE RUNNING WAVE: 775 AGAINST WITCH 13
WAVED
 AS LIKE A RUDDY MOTH THEY WAVED AND FLUTTERED. 34 OISIN 2 V 72
 AND RUSHES WAVED AND WATERS ROLLED. 84 MAD KING GOLL 35
 AND WAVED IT OFF ON THE AIR. 160 CAP AND BELLS 20
 AND WAVED IT OUT ON THE AIR. 160 CAP AND BELLS V 20
WAVER
 AMID MEN'S SOULS, THAT WAVER AND GIVE PLACE 112 ROSE OF WORLD 7
WAVERED
 THAT WAVERED LIKE THE SUMMER STREAMS, 4 OISIN 1 29
 AND WAVERED LIKE A SUMMER RILL, 4 OISIN 1 V 29
WAVERING
 AND WAVERING ARMS AND WANDERING DANCES. 19 OISIN 1 275
 THE ROUND GREEN EYES AND THE LONG WAVERING BODIES 343 DEJECTION 2
 SOME GREAT ONE. NO: I HEAR THE WAVERING STEPS 720 WITCH VIVIEN 12
WAVERINGS
 AY, AND SHAKES IN SEA-GREEN WAVERINGS ALONG THE FISHERS' 718 PHANTOM SHIP 2
  STREET:
 AYE AND SHAKES IN SEA GREEN WAVERINGS, ALONG THE FISHERS' 718 PHANTOM SHIP V 2
  STREET.
WAVE-RUSTED
 AND SHE WITH A WAVE-RUSTED CHAIN WAS TIED 34 OISIN 2 73
WAVES
 AND TO THE WAVES THAT GLIMMER BY 20 OISIN 1 298
 HEAPED BESIDE THE GLIMMERING WAVES, 21 OISIN 1 314
 HEAVED BESIDE THE GLIMMERING WAVES, 21 OISIN 1 V 314
 AND THE GENTLE WAVES OF THE SUMMER SEAS, 27 OISIN 1 418
 ONE WITH THE WAVES THAT SOFTLY ROUND US LAUGH AND DART. 78 INDIAN TO LOVE V 15
 THE LITTLE WAVES THAT WALKED IN EVENING WHITENESS, 81 EPHEMERA V 24C
 YOU WAVES, THOUGH YOU DANCE BY MY FEET LIKE CHILDREN AT 90 OLD FISHERMAN 1
  PLAY,
 YE WAVES, THOUGH YE DANCE 'FORE MY FEET LIKE CHILDREN AT 90 OLD FISHERMAN V 1
  PLAY,
 . . . THE WAVES WERE MORE GAY, 91 OLD FISHERMAN 3
 THAT HE MAY FIGHT THE WAVES OF THE LOUD SEA." 111 CUCHULAIN SEA V 81
 THAT HE MIGHT FIGHT THE WAVES OF THE LOUD SEA." 111 CUCHULAIN SEA V 81
 AND THE WAVES FLOWED ABOVE HIM AND HE DIED. 111 CUCHULAIN SEA V 86
 HAS GIVEN THE WAVES THEIR MELODY, 134 TWO TREES 10
 WEAK AND WORN AND WEARY THE WAVES OF CUMMEN STRAND, 207 HANRAHANS SONG V 6
 OR ON THE UNPEOPLED WAVES WITH KINGS TO PULL AT THE OAR, 210 UNDER THE MOON 15
 AM I TO FEAR THE WAVES, OR IS THE MOON 246 SHADOW WATER B 508
 SO LET US DANCE ON FRINGED WAVES, 644 SONG FAERIES 9
 AND THE WAVES ARE LEAPING WHITE, 646 ISLE STAT I 1 27
 OF THE TARN WHERE YOUNG WAVES QUICKEN 647 ISLE STAT I 1 48
 SING SUMMER WAVES, BUT YONDER SHEPHERD VILE, 649 ISLE STAT I 1 107
 THE WAVES IN YONDER LAKE WHERE POINTS MY HAND 652 ISLE STAT I 2 13

	PAGE	TITLE		LINE
WAVES (CONTINUED)				
AND THE WAVES BOWED BEFORE IT LIKE MOWN CORN, ...	657	ISLE STAT I 3		56
AND SHOREWARD WAVES, WE NIGH HAVE FOUGHT! WAVES BRING . .	660	ISLE STAT II 1		44
AND SHOREWARD WAVES, WE NIGH HAVE FOUGHT! WAVES BRING . .	660	ISLE STAT II 1		44
THE WHITE WAVES WRAP IT IN A SHEET OF FLAME, ...	662	ISLE STAT II 2		14
HERE WHERE THE ROUND WAVES COME, HERE LET THEM BUILD, . .	663	ISLE STAT II 2		19
OF SWORD-BLUE WAVES OF CALM! WHILE O'ER HEAD BLINK . . .	663	ISLE STAT II 2		42
OH, HEART! HER DIRGE! WITH RUSHING ARMS THE WAVES . . .	665	ISLE STAT II 2		70
AT THEIR FEET THE WAVES IN RINGS	667	ISLE STAT II 3		25
SO LET US DANCE ON THE FRINGED WAVES, ...	676	ISLE STAT II 3		256
THE WAVES, ENORMOUS WANDERERS OF THE WORLD, ...	687	TWO TITANS		3
WORN WITH LONG STRUGGLES! AND THE WAVES HAVE SUNG . . .	687	TWO TITANS		23
FROM THE WAVES THE SUN HATH REELED, ...	705	DAWN-SONG		1
WAVES OFF THE FLIES, AND WARMS HIM IN THE SHINE.	709	FERENCZ RENYI		7
YE BY THE WAVES THAT CLOSE IN OUR SAD NATION, ...	738	MOURN THEN ON		5
A PATH AMONG THESE WAVES AND WEIGH THE WIND?	748	SHADOW WATER A		21
AND NOW THE WAVES ARE CRYING IN MY EARS, ...	761	SHADOW WATER A		276
UNDER THE WAVES, AND TOOK A THOUSAND WOMEN	766	SHADOW WATER A		378
ONE LIVES UNDER THE WAVES, ...	770	SPINNING SONG		2
WAVES'				
ENAMOURED OF THE WAVES' IMPETUOUS LIPS.	677	ISLE STAT II 3		289
WAVETH				
HE IS A MONSTROUS PEACOCK, AND HE WAVETH ALL THE NIGHT . .	77	INDIAN ON GOD		19
WAVE-WHITENED				
A BONE WAVE-WHITENED AND DRIED IN THE WIND.	521	THREE THINGS		6
A BONE WAVE-WHITENED AND DRIED IN THE WIND.	521	THREE THINGS		12
A BONE WAVE-WHITENED AND DRIED IN THE WIND.	521	THREE THINGS		18
WAVE-WORN				
WHEN HER OWN PEOPLE RULED IN WAVE-WORN ERI, ...	129	BOOK STORIES	V	2
WAVING SEE A-WAVING				
AMONG THE FIELDS OF WAVING FERN.	2	OISIN 1	V	7N
AMONG THE WAVING FIELDS OF FERN!	4	OISIN 1		38
AND WAVING ARMS AND WANDERING DANCES.	19	OISIN 1	V	275
WE FLUNG ON HIGH EACH WAVING HAND, ...	22	OISIN 1		325
FLUNG ON HIGH EACH WAVING HAND, ...	22	OISIN 1	V	325
SHAKING AND WAVING, VAPOUR VAPOUR CHASED, ...	39	OISIN 2		164
SHAKING AND WAVING, VAPOURS VAPOURS CHASED!	39	OISIN 2	V	164
OUR ARMS ARE WAVING, OUR LIPS ARE APART!	140	HOSTING SIDHE		9
AND WAVING WHITE WINGS TO AND FRO	197	BAILE AILLINN		184
AND WITH THE WAVING OF YOUR WINGS, ...	212	BLESS PSALTER		7
AND HIS HAIR WAS AS YELLOW AS WAVING WHEAT.	729	PRIEST FAIRY		26
WAX				
MELT DOWN, AS IT WERE WAX IN THE SUN'S RAYS!	428	NINETEEN 19		12
WAXEN				
THAT WAXEN SEAL, THAT SIGNATURE, ...	598	MODEL LAUREATE		21
WAXING				
WITH A SOB FOR MEN WAXING SO WEAKLY, ...	60	OISIN 3		188
WAY SEE HALF-WAY				
OF DANAAN HOOVES WE URGED OUR WAY BETWEEN	31	OISIN 2	V	31
OF EVERY FOAMDROP ON ITS MISTY WAY.	32	OISIN 2		45
BENEATH HAD PACED CONTENT! WE HELD OUR WAY	36	OISIN 2		103
BASALTIC, MIGHT HAVE PACED. WE HELD OUR WAY	36	OISIN 2	V	103
MADE THE WAY SLIPPERY, AND TIME ON TIME	37	OISIN 2		114
GAVE TO HIGH NOON AND NOON TO NIGHT GAVE WAY!	40	OISIN 2		172
GAVE TO THE NOON, AND NOON TO EVE GAVE WAY, ...	40	OISIN 2	V	172
THE SEASHINE ON OUR FACES, WE OUR WAY	41	OISIN 2	V	184B
GATHER SEA-SLIME AND FALL THE SEAWARD WAY, ...	45	OISIN 2		237
GATHERS SEA-SLIME AND GOES THE SEAWARD WAY, ...	45	OISIN 2	V	237
GATHER SEA SLIME AND FALL THE SEAWARD WAY, ...	45	OISIN 2	V	237
THEIR NAKED AND GLEAMING BODIES POURED OUT AND HEAPED IN THE WAY.	48	OISIN 3		28
MAKING WAY FROM THE KINDLING SURGES, I RODE ON A BRIDLE-PATH	58	OISIN 3		161
A LITTLE WAY WITHIN THE GLOOM A ROEBUCK RAISED HIS EYES	76	INDIAN ON GOD		13
AND HE WENT HIS WAY WITH A FROWN.	92	FATHER OHART		20
AND WENT ON HIS WAY WITH A FROWN.	92	FATHER OHART	V	20
AND WENT HIS WAY WITH A FROWN.	92	FATHER OHART	V	20
THIS WAY WERE ALL REPROVED	93	FATHER OHART		39
ETERNAL BEAUTY WANDERING ON HER WAY.	101	ROSE UPON ROOD		12
"I ONLY ASK WHAT WAY MY JOURNEY LIES, ...	108	CUCHULAIN SEA		31
HE CHANGED ME SUDDENLY! I WAS LOOKING ANOTHER WAY! . . .	153	CHANGE BELOVED		7
CAME BY THE WOODY WAY	166	BLESSED	V	2
"I HAVE COME BY THE WINDY WAY	167	BLESSED		6
"I COME BY THE WINDY WAY	167	BLESSED	V	6
AND FOLLOW THE WAY OF THE WIND!	168	BLESSED		28
OUR HEARTS ENDURE THE SCOURGE, THE PLAITED THORNS, THE WAY	172	TRAV PASSION		3
OUR HEARTS ENDURE THE PLAITED THORN, THE CROWDED WAY, . .	172	TRAV PASSION	V	3
SHE HAD BEEN BEAUTIFUL IN THAT OLD WAY	180	QUEEN MAEVE		19
IMAGINED, AS THEY STRUCK THE WAY	189	BAILE AILLINN		20
WHEN THEY HAD RIDDEN A LITTLE WAY	191	BAILE AILLINN		56
WHO KNOW THE WAY THAT NAOISE WENT?	193	BAILE AILLINN		96
TO LOVE YOU IN THE OLD HIGH WAY OF LOVE!	206	ADAMS CURSE		36
MAYBE THEY LINGER BY THE WAY.	212	BLESS PSALTER		8
WHAT GOOD IS THERE IN THIS HARD WAY OF LIVING, ...	225	SHADOW WATER B		69
HAVE LOVED THAT WAY—THERE IS NO OTHER WAY.	229	SHADOW WATER B		152
HAVE LOVED THAT WAY—THERE IS NO OTHER WAY.	229	SHADOW WATER B		152
THEY'LL FLY UPON THAT SECRET WAY OF THEIRS.	233	SHADOW WATER B		248
FOOT AFTER FOOT WAS GIVING WAY, ...	274	GREY ROCK		72
I GROPED MY WAY FROM BEECH TO HAZEL WOOD, ...	283	TWO KINGS		139
THEN FEARING THAT SOME LABOURER, ON HIS WAY	283	TWO KINGS		145
I GROPED MY WAY THROUGH BOUGHS, AND OVER ROOTS, ...	283	TWO KINGS	V	139

```
                                                    PAGE     TITLE            LINE
WAY   (CONTINUED)
      FOR ONLY RUBBISH COMES MY WAY.  .   .   .   .   .   .   .   .   295 THREE BEGGARS          4
      WHILE I MUST HURRY UPON MY WAY,  .   .   .   .   .   .   .   .   301 RUN PARADISE          23
      DID THEIR CATULLUS WALK THAT WAY?  .   .   .   .   .   .   .   337 SCHOLARS              12
      SHOULD THEIR CATULLUS WALK THAT WAY!   .   .   .   .   .   .   337 SCHOLARS        V     12
      WITH ALL A WOMAN'S PASSION, A CHILD'S IMPERIOUS WAY,   .   .   354 HIS PHOENIX           14
      THAN THAT I MAY FIND OUT A WAY .   .   .   .   .   .   .   .   401 DEMON BEAST           41
      BEING FATHERLESS COULD HAVE HER WAY  .   .   .   .   .   .   .   404 FOR DAUGHTER          28
      IN THE BEST MODERN WAY--THE CHILDREN'S EYES  .   .   .   .   .   443 SCHOOL CHILDR          6
      IF THROWN IN MADGE'S WAY,  .   .   .   .   .   .   .   .   .   457 SECRETS OF OLD         8
      "THAT IS A LONG WAY OFF,  .   .   .   .   .   .   .   .   .   526 AM OF IRELAND         11
      BEFORE I HAD MARKED HIM ON HIS NORTHERN WAY,   .   .   .   .   535 CHOSEN                 8
      I THOUGHT TO HAVE WHISTLED HER DOWN THAT WAY,  .   .   .   .   551 SONGS REWRIT 1        15
      BEAUTIFUL AND GENTLE IN HER VENETIAN WAY.  .   .   .   .   .   602 GALLERY REVIS         14
      BEAUTIFUL, GRACIOUS, IN HER VENETIAN WAY,  .   .   .   .   .   602 GALLERY REVIS   V     14
      BUT LIKED THE WAY HIS FINGER SMELT .   .   .   .   .   .   .   619 STICK INCENSE          4
      JOY'S BROTHER, FEAR, LURKS IN EACH LEAFY WAY.  .   .   .   .   651 ISLE STAT I 1        156
      AND FOUND.  'TIS WELL!--ANOTHER MILE OF WAY  .   .   .   .   651 ISLE STAT I 2          6
      WE MUST GET SWORDS.  IS'T THE ONLY WAY?  OH, SEE,  .   .   .   660 ISLE STAT II 1        34
      THERE IS NO WAY BUT THAT YE FIGHT I WIS,   .   .   .   .   .   662 ISLE STAT II 1        75
      FAIR YOUTH, ALONG A WANDERING WAY  .   .   .   .   .   .   .   667 ISLE STAT II 3        38
      DEAR HEART, THERE IS A SECRET WAY THAT LEADS   .   .   .   .   702 MOSADA 3              75
      THE FOOT-WORN WAY IS LONG, AND IT GROWS DARK.  .   .   .   .   702 MOSADA 3              92
      THE FOOTWORN WAY IS LONG, AND IT GROWS DARK.   .   .   .   .   702 MOSADA 3        V     92
      FROM HERE, ALONG THE SHADOWY WAY THAT WINDS  .   .   .   .   703 MOSADA 3             111
      THE FAIRY DOCTOR COMES OUR WAY .   .   .   .   .   .   .   .   716 FAIRY DOCTOR           1
      AND SENT THE OLD MEN ON THEIR WAY, .   .   .   .   .   .   .   725 LEGEND                23
      A WOODMAN ON HIS HOMEWARD WAY  .   .   .   .   .   .   .   .   730 PRIEST FAIRY          73
      THROUGH THE LONG BITTER WAY. .   .   .   .   .   .   .   .   .   738 MOURN THEN ON          4
      IT MAY BE NOW THAT I CAN GO MY WAY .   .   .   .   .   .   .   751 SHADOW WATER A        96
      WHEN ALL GATHER THEY WILL FLY UPON THEIR WAY.  .   .   .   .   753 SHADOW WATER A       136
      I SHALL FIND OUT IF I HAVE LOST MY WAY   .   .   .   .   .   753 SHADOW WATER A       137
      I SHALL FIND OUT IF I HAVE LOST THE WAY  .   .   .   .   .   753 SHADOW WATER A  V    137
      A QUARTER OF THE HEAVENS FROM OUR RIGHT WAY.   .   .   .   .   754 SHADOW WATER A       155
      MY WAY IS WEST.  SHE SEEMS BOTH YOUNG AND SHAPELY!   .   .   755 SHADOW WATER A       171
      I SPARED HER HANDMAID, TOO!  BUT HALF WAY HITHER   .   .   .   755 SHADOW WATER A  V    167
WAYS      SEE CAST-A-WAYS SEA-WAYS
      THEY LED US BY LONG AND SHADOWY WAYS .   .   .   .   .   .   16 OISIN 1              221
      THEY LEAD US BY LONG AND SHADOWY WAYS  .   .   .   .   .   .   16 OISIN 1         V    221
      IN PINCHING WAYS I TOIL AND TURN."   .   .   .   .   .   .   19 OISIN 1         V    282
      WAS SLUMBERING HALF IN THE SEA WAYS! .   .   .   .   .   .   26 OISIN 1         V    395
      THE WHIRLING WAYS OF STARS THAT PASS--   .   .   .   .   .   66 HAPPY SHEPHERD        30
      WHEN EVE HAS HUSHED THE FEATHERED WAYS,  .   .   .   .   .   78 INDIAN TO LOVE        19
      WHERE EVE HAS HUSHED THE FEATHERED WAYS,   .   .   .   .   78 INDIAN TO LOVE  V     19
      COME NEAR ME, WHILE I SING THE ANCIENT WAYS!   .   .   .   100 ROSE UPON ROOD         2
      SING OF OLD EIRE AND THE ANCIENT WAYS!   .   .   .   .   .   101 ROSE UPON ROOD        23
      DRIVING THE DEER ALONG THE WOODY WAYS.   .   .   .   .   .   109 CUCHULAIN SEA   V     48
      LED ON BY GENTLE WAYS!   .   .   .   .   .   .   .   .   .   113 ROSE OF PEACE         12
      IN THOSE GREAT IGNORANT LEAFY WAYS!  .   .   .   .   .   .   135 TWO TREES             16
      YET HE WHO TREADS IN MEASURED WAYS   .   .   .   .   .   .   138 TO IRELAND            27
      YET HE WHO TREADS IN AUSTERE WAYS  .   .   .   .   .   .   .   138 TO IRELAND      V     27
      AND THE WINDS THAT BLOW THROUGH THE STARRY WAYS,   .   .   158 TO HIS HEART           4
      AND THE WINDS BLOWING THROUGH THE STARRY WAYS, .   .   .   158 TO HIS HEART    V      4
      BURNS BUT MORE CLEARLY.  O SHE HAD NOT THESE WAYS  .   .   200 FOLLY COMFORT         11
      HAVE TAUGHT TO IGNORANT MEN MOST VIOLENT WAYS, .   .   .   256 NO SECOND TROY         3
      THAT HAVE TO BE SET UP IN FIFTY WAYS.  .   .   .   .   .   .   260 FASC DIFFICULT         9
      O WHAT IF LEVELLED LAWNS AND GRAVELLED WAYS  .   .   .   .   418 ANCEST HOUSES         29
      "GO YOUR WAYS, O GO YOUR WAYS, .   .   .   .   .   .   .   .   588 OLD WICKED MAN        28
      "GO YOUR WAYS, O GO YOUR WAYS, .   .   .   .   .   .   .   .   588 OLD WICKED MAN        28
      FROM THE WOOD'S WAYS, THEN, LIKE A SILVER FLAME,   .   .   658 ISLE STAT II 1         6
      AND MEASURE OUT THE WAYS OF CHIVALRY.  .   .   .   .   .   .   660 ISLE STAT II 1        37
      WHAT ARE THE VOICES THAT IN FLOWERY WAYS   .   .   .   .   666 ISLE STAT II 3        16
      BEHOLD THE LOVING LOVELESS FLOWER OF LONE WAYS,  .   .   .   674 ISLE STAT II 3       201
      AS THOUGH THEY'D VOWED TO MEASURE ALL ITS WAYS.  .   .   .   711 FERENCZ RENYI         48
      OF SOME MILD WOMAN, OR IN CHILDREN'S WAYS. .   .   .   .   .   750 SHADOW WATER A        74
WAYWARD
      AND THE DAYS PASS BY LIKE A WAYWARD TUNE,  .   .   .   .   .   8 OISIN 1               83
      AND OF THE WAYWARD TWILIGHT COMPANIES  .   .   .   .   .   .   136 TO SOME I TALK         6
      WHERE THE PROUD, WAYWARD SQUIRREL WENT,  .   .   .   .   .   317 APPOINTMENT            3
      OR ALL THAT WAYWARD EBB AND FLOW.  THERE STOOD   .   .   .   428 NINETEEN 19     V      4
      ON ALL THAT WAYWARD EBB AND FLOW.  THERE STOOD   .   .   .   428 NINETEEN 19     V      4
WEAK
      WITH BARREN WORDS AND FLATTERIES OF THE WEAK.  .   .   .   .   42 OISIN 2              197
      FOR HE IS WEAK AND POOR AND BLIND, AND LIES  .   .   .   .   42 OISIN 2              203
      LIAR AND FLATTERER OF THE WEAK, IN WHAT STRANGE CLIME  .   42 OISIN 2         V    198
      AY, OISIN KNOWS, FOR HE IS OF THE WEAK,  .   .   .   .   .   42 OISIN 2         V    202
      WEAK, IN THE MIDST OF THE MEADOW,  .   .   .   .   .   .   .   54 OISIN 3              102
      WHO HOLDS THE WORLD BETWEEN HIS BILL AND MADE US STRONG
          OR WEAK                                                   76 INDIAN ON GOD          6
      WHO HOLDS THE WORLD BETWEEN HIS BILL AND MAKES US STRONG
          OR WEAK                                                   76 INDIAN ON GOD   V      6
      THE WEAK WORM HIDING DOWN IN ITS SMALL CAVE,   .   .   .   .   101 ROSE UPON ROOD        16
      WEAK AND WORN AND WEARY THE WAVES OF CUMMEN STRAND,  .   .   207 HANRAHANS SONG V       6
      WEAK AND WORN AND WEARY OUR COURAGE DROOPS AND DIES  .   .   207 HANRAHANS SONG V       8
      THE WEAK LAY HAND ON WHAT THE STRONG HAS DONE, .   .   .   265 THESE CLOUDS           3
      WHO HAVE FAILED, BEING WEAK OF WILL.   .   .   .   .   .   298 THREE HERMITS         18
      WEAK AS A WORM.  .   .   .   .   .   .   .   .   .   .   .   .   574 MAIDS 1ST SONG        10
      SOON WILT THOU SMILE, FOR HERE THE WINDS ARE WEAK  .   .   671 ISLE STAT II 3       141
      GOING THE FOREST THROUGH, WITH FLUTINGS WEAK!  .   .   .   672 ISLE STAT II 3       155
      BEFORE I AM TOO WEAK, FIERCE MORTAL, LET ME FLY,   .   .   .   675 ISLE STAT II 3       245
      BEFORE I AM TOO WEAK, OH LET ME FLY,   .   .   .   .   .   .   675 ISLE STAT II 3 V     245
```

WEAK   (CONTINUED)
    A WEAK, THIN CHILD, WHEN LAST I SAW HIM THERE. . . . . . 699 MOSADA 3   14
    SO SMALL MAKES ONE GROW WEAK AND TOTTERING! . . . . . . 700 MOSADA 3   35
    IF THESE BE PRECIOUS." "I AM OLD AND WEAK," . . . . . . 711 FERENCZ RENYI   55
    I'M WEAK, AND BY THE HANDS SHALL HOLD EACH ONE . . . . . 712 FERENCZ RENYI   57
    FOR I AM OLD AND WEAK." AND AT HER SIDE . . . . 712 FERENCZ RENYI   59
    I'M WEAK, AND BY THE HAND SHALL HOLD EACH ONE . . . . . 712 FERENCZ RENYI V 57
    THUS PLAY WE FIRST WITH PAWNS, POOR THINGS AND WEAK! . . 722 WITCH VIVIEN   53
WEAKENED
    WHEN ORDER HAS WEAKENED OR FACTION IS STRONG, ... 548 TO SAME TUNE 3 12
WEAKLY
    WITH A SOB FOR MEN WAXING SO WEAKLY, ... 60 OISIN 3   188
    I'D ALWAYS BEEN BUT WEAKLY. . . . . 94 MOLL MAGEE   13
WEALTH
    ARE DRIVEN BY WEALTH AS BEGGARS BY THE ITCH;" . . . . . 300 BEGGAR CRIED   14
    WHETHER HEALTH, WEALTH OR PEACE OF MIND WERE SPENT . . . 429 NINETEEN 19   36
    AND PEACE BE WITH YOU, PEACE AND WEALTH OF DAYS. . . . . 682 SEEKER   28
    THE WRINKLED SQUANDERER OF HUMAN WEALTH. . . . . 720 WITCH VIVIEN   16
    AND TO GIVE WEALTH OF OXEN AND SHEEP TO ALL; . . . . . . 756 SHADOW WATER A 184
    SO MUCH OF WEALTH AS MAY BEFIT THEIR RANK! . . . . . . 756 SHADOW WATER A V 186
WEALTHY
    TO A WEALTHY MAN WHO PROMISED A SECOND SUBSCRIPTION . . . 287 TO WEALTHY MAN   T
WEAR
    BUT KNEEL AND WEAR OUT THE FLAGS AND PRAY FOR YOUR SOUL . 63 OISIN 3   215
        THAT IS LOST
    BUT WEEP THOU, AND WEAR THOU THE FLAGS WITH THY KNEES, . 63 OISIN 3   V 215
    BUT WEEP YOU, AND WEAR YOU THE FLAGS WITH YOUR KNEES, . . 63 OISIN 3   V 215
    BUT WEEP YOU AND KNEEL! WEAR OUT THE FLAGS! . . . . . . 63 OISIN 3   V 215
    KNEEL, USHEEN, WEAR OUT THE FLAGS AND PRAY FOR YOUR SOUL 63 OISIN 3   V 215
        THAT IS LOST
    THEY PINE AWAY AND YELLOW AND WEAR OUT, ... 81 EPHEMERA   V 24H
    AND NOW AT LAST YOU WEAR A HUMAN SHAPE, ... 102 FERGUS DRUID   6
    WAS BORN TO WEAR A CROWN. . . . . 308 PLAYER QUEEN   12
    ALL WEAR THE CARPET WITH THEIR SHOES! . . . . 337 SCHOLARS   8
    WEAR OUT THE CARPET WITH THEIR SHOES. . . . . 337 SCHOLARS   V   8
    PERMIT FOUL YEARS TO WEAR . . . . 472 ALL SOUL NIGHT 49
    AND ALL THEIR SWELLING CANVAS WEAR, ... 530 OLD TOM AGAIN   2
    AND ALL THEIR YELLOW CANVAS WEAR, ... 530 OLD TOM AGAIN V 2
    NO MATTER WHAT THE NAMES THEY WEAR! . . . . 582 ROGER CASEMENT V 17
    AND WEAR A COAT IN FASHION, ... 607 SONGS BURDEN 2 21
WEARIED   SEE TRAVEL-WEARIED
    BEING WEARIED OUT, I LOVE IN MAN THE CHILD? . . . . . . 285 TWO KINGS   192
    BUT WEARIED RUNNING ROUND AND ROUND IN THEIR COURSES . . 433 NINETEEN 19   116
    TO THOSE YOUR "MELLOW" WARES HAVE WEARIED OUT. . . . . . 721 WITCH VIVIEN   27
WEARINESS
    LULLED WEARINESS, AND SOFTLY ROUND . . . . 11 OISIN 1   137
    LULLED WEARINESS! AND CLOSELY ROUND . . . . 11 OISIN 1   V 137
    BY AGE'S WEARINESS ARE SLAIN, ... 27 OISIN 1   V 415A
    AND "A WEARINESS SOON IS MY SPEED," SAYS THE MOUSE, . . . 27 OISIN 1   V 417
    AND "MY SPEED IS A WEARINESS," FALTERS THE MOUSE, ... 28 OISIN 1   V 421
    WRAPT IN THE WAVE OF THAT MUSIC, WITH WEARINESS MORE THAN 51 OISIN 3   69
        OF EARTH,
    A WEARINESS COMES FROM THOSE DREAMERS . . . . 122 WHITE BIRDS   5
    AND A WEARINESS COMES FROM THOSE DREAMERS . . . . 122 WHITE BIRDS V   5
    THE GLASS OF OUTER WEARINESS, ... 135 TWO TREES   31
    PLEASURE ITSELF CAN BRING NO WEARINESS, ... 284 TWO KINGS   181
WEARISOME
    AND HANDS THAT HOLD NO WEARISOME TOOL, ... 22 OISIN 1   340
WEARS
    AS THE TIDE WEARS THE DOVE-GREY SANDS, ... 157 POET BELOVED   4
    THE TOMB OF SWIFT WEARS IT AWAY. A VOICE . . . . 487 SEVEN SAGES   21
    KEVIN O'HIGGINS' COUNTENANCE THAT WEARS . . . . 601 GALLERY REVIS   5
    KEVIN O'HIGGINS, AND THAT LOOK HE WEARS, ... 601 GALLERY REVIS V 5
    HER LOVE! TO HER WHO WEARS THAT BLOOM COMES TRUTH. . . . 653 ISLE STAT I 2   46
WEARY   SEE WAR-WEARY A-WEARY BATTLE-WEARY
    NOR HAVE HANDS HELD A WEARY TOOL! . . . . 19 OISIN 1   283
    OF TWILIGHT WHEN HE'S WEARY. . . . . 32 OISIN 2   V 50H
    RETURN WHEN YOU ARE WEARY. . . . . 33 OISIN 2   V 65
    YET WEARY WITH PASSIONS THAT FADED . . . . 50 OISIN 3   52
    I SAW HOW THOSE SLUMBERERS, GROWN WEARY. . . . . 50 OISIN 3   54
    HELPLESS, MEN LIFTING THE LIDS OF HIS WEARY . . . . . . 53 OISIN 3   92
        AND DEATH-MAKING EYE.
    HELPLESS, MEN LIFTING THE LIDS OF HIS WEARY . . . . . . 53 OISIN 3   V 92
        AND DEATH-POURING EYE.
    WEARY, WITH ALL HIS POPPIES GATHERED ROUND HIM. . . . . 72 ANASHU VIJAYA   25
    AND WEARY AND WORN ARE OUR SAD SOULS NOW! . . . . 79 FALLING LEAVES   6
    "YOUR EYES THAT ONCE WERE NEVER WEARY OF MINE . . . . . 79 EPHEMERA   1
    A WEARY WOMAN SLEEPS SO HARD! . . . . 95 MOLL MAGEE   21
    AND WEARY OF THE CRASH OF BATTLE CARS." . . . . 107 CUCHULAIN SEA V 30
    WEARY AND KIND ONE LINGERED BY HIS SEAT! . . . . 112 ROSE OF WORLD   13
    WEARY AND KIND ONE STOOD BESIDE HIS SEAT! . . . . 112 ROSE OF WORLD V 13
    THEY WEARY OF TROOPING . . . . 118 CRADLE SONG   3
    THEY WEARY OF TENDING . . . . 118 CRADLE SONG V   3
    HAD HID AWAY EARTH'S OLD AND WEARY CRY. . . . . 120 SORROW OF LOVE V 4
    ARE SHAKEN WITH EARTH'S OLD AND WEARY CRY. . . . . 120 SORROW OF LOVE V 12
    UNTIL THE SAP OF SUMMER HAD GROWN WEARY! . . . . 130 BOOK STORIES   14
    GREEN BOUGHS OF TOSSING ALWAYS, WEARY, WEARY, ... 130 BOOK STORIES V 14
    GREEN BOUGHS OF TOSSING ALWAYS, WEARY, WEARY, ... 130 BOOK STORIES V 14
    WAS WEARY NIGHT AND DAY! . . . . 132 FR GILLIGAN   2
    BEING WEARY OF THE WORLD'S EMPIRES, BOW DOWN TO YOU, . . 161 BLACK PIG   7

	PAGE	TITLE	LINE
WEARY (CONTINUED)			
O WHEN WILL YOU GROW WEARY?" THEY HAD VANISHED;	187	QUEEN MAEVE	152
AS WEARY HEARTED AS THAT HOLLOW MOON.	206	ADAMS CURSE V	38
WEAK AND WORN AND WEARY THE WAVES OF CUMMEN STRAND,	207	HANRAHANS SONG V	6
WEAK AND WORN AND WEARY OUR COURAGE DROOPS AND DIES	207	HANRAHANS SONG V	8
AND KEEP TO THE ONE WEARY MARRIAGE-BED,	224	SHADOW WATER B	55
AND KEEP TO THE ONE WEARY MARRIAGE BED,	224	SHADOW WATER B V	55
AND I GREW WEARY OF THE SUN	256	WORDS	5
WEARY OF MANY QUESTIONS. "THERE ARE THINGS	281	TWO KINGS	93
"A WEARY WOOING AND A LONG," HE SAID.	283	TWO KINGS	154
THAT HAS GROWN WEARY OF THE WANDERING DANCE,	285	TWO KINGS	183
THAT HAS GROWN WEARY OF THE WHIRLING DANCE,	285	TWO KINGS V	183
AND THEN, GROWN WEARY, PRAYED AND CURSED ,	307	HOUR DAWN	117
BUT, WEARY RUNNING ROUND AND ROUND IN THEIR COURSES,	433	NINETEEN 19 V	116
SOMETHING MADE THESE EYEBALLS WEARY	529	TOM LUNATIC	11
WEARY OF REAPING THE BARREN NIGHT	648	ISLE STAT I 1	84
WITH TEARS? I WEARY OF YE. THERE IS NONE	650	ISLE STAT I 1	142
I WEARY OF YOUR SONGS AND HUNTER'S TOYS.	651	ISLE STAT I 1	157
UNTIL I FIND HIM. WHAT A WEARY WEEK,	658	ISLE STAT II 1	2
WEARY OF WATCHING ROUND THE FIRE AT NIGHT.	683	SEEKER	42
AND HER GIGANTIC LIMBS. THE WEARY THIRST	687	TWO TITANS	16
I'M WEARY--WEARY, AND 'TIS VERY COLD.	703	MOSADA 3	122
I'M WEARY--WEARY, AND 'TIS VERY COLD.	703	MOSADA 3	122
"A LITTLE WILL I LAY MY WEARY HEAD,	712	FERENCZ RENYI	75
OH, I AM WEARY OF THAT FOOLISH TALE.	721	WITCH VIVIEN	33
AT THE HOUSE OF WEARY MEN	727	LOVERS QUARREL	51
BUT YOU GREW WEARY OF HER. WHEN I HOLD	749	SHADOW WATER A	53
SHE BIDS US FOLLOW HER. I HAVE GROWN WEARY	758	SHADOW WATER A	218
IT MAY BE, AND HAVE GROWN WEARY OF LOVE.	767	SHADOW WATER A	390
WEARY-HEARTED			
AS WEARY-HEARTED AS THAT HOLLOW MOON.	206	ADAMS CURSE	38
WEARYING			
OUR HANDS HAVE KNOWN NO WEARYING TOOL,	22	OISIN 1 V	339
WEASEL			
A WEASEL MOVING ON FROM STONE TO STONE,	102	FERGUS DRUID	5
WEASEL WARMS HIM ON THE PATH.	705	DAWN-SONG	19
WEASEL'S			
THE WEASEL'S TWIST, THE WEASEL'S TOOTH.	431	NINETEEN 19	92
THE WEASEL'S TWIST, THE WEASEL'S TOOTH.	431	NINETEEN 19	92
WEASELS			
FOR NO LIVE CREATURES LIVED THERE, NO WEASELS MOVED IN THE DARK	48	OISIN 3	19
FOR NO LIVE CREATURES LIVE THERE, NO WEASELS MOVE IN THE DARK;	56	OISIN 3	139
WHO ARE BUT WEASELS FIGHTING IN A HOLE.	429	NINETEEN 19	32
WEATHER			
OH WANDERER IN THE SOUTHERN WEATHER,	77	INDIAN TO LOVE V	1
LIKE AN OLD PAUPER, IN ALL KINDS OF WEATHER;	205	ADAMS CURSE	9
MAYBE THE WEATHER WAS ACCURSED	305	HOUR DAWN	65
BECAUSE THE WEATHER WAS A-CURSED	305	HOUR DAWN V	65
OF THE FOUL WEATHER, HAIL AND RAIN,	424	ROAD AT DOOR	9
HOW GOES THE WEATHER?	585	ORAHILLY	9
HOW GOES THE WEATHER?	585	ORAHILLY	18
HOW GOES THE WEATHER?	585	ORAHILLY	27
HOW GOES THE WEATHER?	585	ORAHILLY	36
BUT NO, IN THIS WARM WEATHER, 'MONG THE HILLS,	699	MOSADA 3	9
NOON WRAPT THE TREES IN VEILS OF VIOLET WEATHER,	715	DWELT SYCAMORE	7
NOON WRAPPED THE WOODS IN VEILS OF VIOLET WEATHER;	715	DWELT SYCAMORE V	7
WEATHER-WORN			
A WEATHER-WORN, MARBLE TRITON	329	MEN IMPROVE	2
A WEATHER-WORN, MARBLE TRITON	329	MEN IMPROVE	17
WEAVE			
"WHAT DO YOU WEAVE SO SOFT AND BRIGHT?"	69	CLOAK BOAT V	1
"WHAT DO YOU WEAVE SO FAIR AND BRIGHT?"	69	CLOAK BOAT V	1
THE CLOAK I WEAVE OF SORROW:	69	CLOAK BOAT V	2
"WHAT DO YOU WEAVE WITH WOOL SO WHITE?"	70	CLOAK BOAT	11
"I WEAVE THE SHOES OF SORROW:	70	CLOAK BOAT	12
HE WOULD GO WEAVE OUT OF THE STARS	113	ROSE OF PEACE	7
WHAT DO YOU WEAVE SO FAIR AND BRIGHT?	666	ISLE STAT II 3	1
THE CLOAK I WEAVE OF SORROW:	666	ISLE STAT II 3	2
WHAT DO YOU WEAVE WITH WOOL SO WHITE?	666	ISLE STAT II 3	11
AND ON THIS LOOM I WEAVE THY DESTINY."	716	DWELT SYCAMORE	14
THE SUNFLOWERS WEAVE A GOLDEN CLIME,	736	SUMMER EVENING	9
SHE WOULD WEAVE A NET TO TAKE US. SHE MIGHT KEEP FAITH!	756	SHADOW WATER A	190
THE GODS WEAVE NETS, AND TAKE US IN THEIR NETS,	764	SHADOW WATER A	339
THE GODS HATE HAPPINESS, AND WEAVE THEIR NETS	767	SHADOW WATER A	399
WEAVER			
OR WEAVER BENT AT HIS LOOM,	589	OLD WICKED MAN	51
WEAVES			
NOT THERE, FOR THERE A SPIDER WEAVES HER WEB.	700	MOSADA 3	38
WEAVING SEE A-WEAVING			
WEAVING OLDEN DANCES,	87	STOLEN CHILD	17
OUR ARMS ARE WEAVING, OUR LIPS ARE APART;	140	HOSTING SIDHE V	9
OF MOSS, A MAIDEN WEAVING. SINGETH SHE:	716	DWELT SYCAMORE	12
I PRAY THAT I EVER BE WEAVING	743	WISDOM DREAMS	1
BUT WEAVING IT OUT OF THREADS	743	WISDOM DREAMS	3
WEB			
THEN EMER CAST THE WEB UPON THE FLOOR,	105	CUCHULAIN SEA	6
A SHINING WEB, A FLOATING RIBBON OF CLOTH,	430	NINETEEN 19	50
NOT THERE, FOR THERE A SPIDER WEAVES HER WEB.	700	MOSADA 3	38

879

	PAGE	TITLE		LINE
WEBBED				
BY THE WEBBED TOES, AND THAT ALL-POWERFUL BILL	441	LEDA AND SWAN	V	3
BY THE WEBBED TOES, AND THAT ALL POWERFUL BILL	441	LEDA AND SWAN	V	3
WEB-HEAPED				
UPON THE WEB-HEAPED FLOOR, AND CRIED HIS WORD!	106	CUCHULAIN SEA		15
UPON THE WEB-HEAPED FLOOR, AND THUS HIS WORD, ...	106	CUCHULAIN SEA	V	15
WEBS				
AH! DRUID, DRUID, HOW GREAT WEBS OF SORROW	104	FERGUS DRUID		39
BY THE DARK WEBS, HER NAPE CAUGHT IN HIS BILL, ...	441	LEDA AND SWAN		3
WED				
"YOU ONLY WILL I WED," I CRIED, ...	7	OISIN 1		74
IN LOVE. I CRIED, "THEE WILL I WED, ...	7	OISIN 1	V	74
AND MADE MY LIPS AND MUSIC WED, ...	134	TWO TREES		11
BAILE AND AILLINN WOULD BE WED.	190	BAILE AILLINN		24
WITH: "YOU MUST HOME AGAIN, AND WED	191	BAILE AILLINN		58
"O LADY, WED WITH ONE OF US";	191	BAILE AILLINN		61
NATURAL AND SUPERNATURAL WITH THE SELF-SAME RING ARE WED.	556	RIBH PATRICK		4
WEDDED				
WHO WEDDED MEN WITH RINGS OF DRUID GOLD;	29	OISIN 2		10
WEDDING				
WEDDING THE QUEENS OF EARTHLY LANDS WITH RINGS	29	OISIN 2		10
WEDDING THE QUEENS OF EARTHLY LANDS WITH RINGS	29	OISIN 2	V	10
WEED SEE SEA-WEED				
HE CARVED ON TREES, AND WITH A SUN-DRY WEED	659	ISLE STAT II 1		8
THE BROWN WEED BURDEN, SO THE SWORD BRINGS FEAR	660	ISLE STAT II 1		45
WEEDING				
OR WEEDING OR PLOUGHING WITH FACES A-SHINING WITH MUCH-TOIL WET;	58	OISIN 3		165
WEEDS SEE SHORE-WEEDS				
HOW THE FALCONER FOLLOWS THE FALCON IN THE WEEDS OF THE HERON'S PLOT,	52	OISIN 3		79
WEEDY SEE SEA-WEEDY				
IN ENDLESS DARK, AND BY THE WEEDY MARGE	682	SEEKER		19
WEEK				
UNTIL I FIND HIM. WHAT A WEARY WEEK, ...	658	ISLE STAT II 1		2
WEEKS				
THESE DOZEN WEEKS. AND I HAD THOUGHT TO MAKE	222	SHADOW WATER B		4
AND SO THE WEEKS PASSED BY. BUT WHEN I SAID, ...	280	TWO KINGS		89
I SOUGHT IT DAILY FOR SIX WEEKS OR SO.	629	CIRCUS ANIMALS		2
WEEP				
IN BROODING MEMORY, NOR WEEP.	11	OISIN 1	V	131B
AND STAY A LITTLE WHILE, AND BID THEM WEEP;	33	OISIN 2		60
WHEN YOU HAVE TOLD HOW I WEEP ENDLESSLY, ...	33	OISIN 2		63
"AND TELL THEM HOW I WEEP, UNTIL THEY WEEP;	33	OISIN 2		63
"AND TELL THEM HOW I WEEP, UNTIL THEY WEEP;	33	OISIN 2	V	63
AND I MUST NEEDS ENDURE AND HATE AND WEEP, ...	35	OISIN 2		85
SAINT, DO YOU WEEP? I HEAR AMID THE THUNDER	43	OISIN 2		209
SAINT, DOST THOU WEEP? I HEAR AMID THE THUNDER	43	OISIN 2	V	209
BUT WEEP FOR YOUR NIAMH, O OISIN, WEEP; FOR IF ONLY YOUR SHOE	55	OISIN 3		127
BUT WEEP FOR YOUR NIAMH, O OISIN, WEEP; FOR IF ONLY YOUR SHOE	55	OISIN 3		127
BUT WEEP FOR THY NIAM, OH OISIN, WEEP; FOR IF ONLY THY SHOE	55	OISIN 3	V	127
BUT WEEP FOR THY NIAM, OH OISIN, WEEP; FOR IF ONLY THY SHOE	55	OISIN 3	V	127
. . . SHALL LISTEN AND RISE UP AND WEEP;	62	OISIN 3		206
BUT WEEP THOU, AND WEAR THOU THE FLAGS WITH THY KNEES, . . .	63	OISIN 3	V	215
BUT WEEP YOU, AND WEAR YOU THE FLAGS WITH YOUR KNEES, . . .	63	OISIN 3	V	215
BUT WEEP YOU AND KNEEL; WEAR OUT THE FLAGS!	63	OISIN 3	V	215
OR PACE AND WEEP IN WOODS FORLORN, ...	86	MAD KING GOLL	V	68
I CAN BUT WEEP AND SIGH."	99	FOXHUNTER		36
AND WEEP BECAUSE I KNOW ALL THINGS NOW:	177	PAST GREATNESS		2
HIS FACE BOWED LOW TO WEEP THE END	192	BAILE AILLINN		75
I COULD WEEP THAT THE OLD IS OUT OF SEASON.	199	ARROW		8
AS I AM DOING NOW. WHY DO YOU WEEP?	246	SHADOW WATER B		495
I WEEP BECAUSE I'VE NOTHING FOR YOUR EYES	246	SHADOW WATER B		496
I WEEP--I WEEP BECAUSE BARE NIGHT'S ABOVE, ...	246	SHADOW WATER B		499
I WEEP--I WEEP BECAUSE BARE NIGHT'S ABOVE, ...	246	SHADOW WATER B		499
SHOULD LAUGH AND WEEP AN HOUR UPON THE CLOCK.	471	ALL SOUL NIGHT		20
SHOULD LAUGH AND WEEP AN HOUR UPON THE CLOCK.	474	ALL SOUL NIGHT		90
SHOULD WEEP AND LAUGH AN HOUR UPON THE CLOCK.	474	ALL SOUL NIGHT	V	90
AND YET I WEEP--OEDIPUS' CHILD	540	FROM ANTIGONE		15
DO NOT BREAK UP THEIR LINES TO WEEP.	565	LAPIS LAZULI		15
TILL I LAUGH WHEN OTHERS WEEP, ...	647	ISLE STAT I 1		61
LONE, AND WANTING THEE, I WEEP;	647	ISLE STAT I 1		72
WHERE ALL NIGHT LONG THE HEAVENS WEEP AND WEEP, ...	649	ISLE STAT I 1		124
WHERE ALL NIGHT LONG THE HEAVENS WEEP AND WEEP, ...	649	ISLE STAT I 1		124
AYE, VERY LATELY, SORROW CAME TO WEEP	659	ISLE STAT II 1		25
WHOSE INSOLENT EYES UNUSED TO TEARS WOULD WEEP	678	ISLE STAT II 3		302
SEARCHED THE UNSEARCHABLE--WHY GOOD MEN WEEP:	710	FERENCZ RENYI		32
FOR MERRY MEN THAT WEEP, ...	736	IN CHURCH		6
COVER THEIR FACES WITH THEIR HAIR AND WEEP.	764	SHADOW WATER A		333
WEEPING				
AND, WEEPING OVER THE WHITE STRINGS, HURLED	17	OISIN 1		241
"FLEE FROM HIM," PEARL-PALE NIAMH WEEPING CRIED, ...	35	OISIN 2		92
TO FLY A SPIRIT," NIAM WEEPING SAID.	35	OISIN 2	V	92
AND ON MY BOSOM LAID HER WEEPING HEAD.	46	OISIN 2		250
FOR THE WORLD'S MORE FULL OF WEEPING THAN YOU CAN UNDERSTAND.	87	STOLEN CHILD		12
FOR THE WORLD'S MORE FULL OF WEEPING THAN YOU CAN UNDERSTAND.	87	STOLEN CHILD		27

880

		PAGE	TITLE		LINE
WEEPING	(CONTINUED)				
	FOR THE WORLD'S MORE FULL OF WEEPING THAN YOU CAN UNDERSTAND.	88	STOLEN CHILD		41
	FROM A WORLD MORE FULL OF WEEPING THAN HE CAN UNDERSTAND.	89	STOLEN CHILD		53
	FOR THE WORLD'S MORE FULL OF WEEPING THAN HE CAN UNDERSTAND	89	STOLEN CHILD	V	53
	WHEN, WEEPING SCORE BY SCORE,	93	FATHER OHART		26
	HE CAUGHT HIS BREATH AND CAST HIM WEEPING DOWN	106	CUCHULAIN SEA	V	14
	SHE HAS GONE WEEPING AWAY.	152	LOSS OF LOVE		7
	THAT YOU ARE WEEPING FOR. NO, FOR HE IS DEAD.	243	SHADOW WATER B		427
	AND WHILE WE'RE IN OUR LAUGHING, WEEPING FIT,	257	RECONCILIATION		9
	WEEPING WHEN ALL OTHERS LAUGH.	647	ISLE STAT I 1		62
	YOUR WEEPING FITS! LOOK YOU, SO VERY STRAIT	659	ISLE STAT II 1		22
	AH! YOU ARE WEEPING! HERE SHOULD ALL GRIEF CEASE.	672	ISLE STAT II 3		149
	THE VISION. YOU ARE PALE AND WEEPING. CHILD,	693	MOSADA 1		73
	I HAVE ROUSED THEE! FOR THE WEEPING	729	PRIEST FAIRY		40
	PITY THESE WEEPING EYES! I WILL FOLLOW YOU.	768	SHADOW WATER A		420
WEEPS					
	SAY HOW HE WEEPS IN ERI."	33	OISIN 2	V	68
	THE WEST WEEPS IN PALE DEW AND SIGHS PASSING AWAY,	154	BELOVED PEACE		5
	THE MOTHER OF THE STARS WEEPS TOO,	738	YOU ARE SAD		2
	AND THEN THE WHOLE WORLD'S TROUBLE WEEPS WITH YOU.	738	YOU ARE SAD		12
WEIGH					
	BUT WEIGH THIS SONG WITH THE GREAT AND THEIR PRIDE!	166	EVIL OF BELOV		4
	THAT WEIGH AND MEASURE ALL IN THESE WASTE SEAS—	235	SHADOW WATER B		292
	PARDON, AND YOU THAT DID NOT WEIGH THE COST,	269	PARDON FATHERS	V	9
	WEIGH ME DOWN, AND NOT A DAY	501	VACILLATION		54
	WEIGH THEM IN AN HOUR OF DREAMING,	737	IN FIRELIGHT		11
	A PATH AMONG THESE WAVES AND WEIGH THE WIND?	748	SHADOW WATER A		21
	AND WERE ALL DREAMS, IT WOULD NOT WEIGH IN THE HAND.	750	SHADOW WATER A		77
WEIGHED					
	NOW I HAVE SEEN IT WEIGHED	267	FRIEND ILLNESS		6
	THEY WEIGHED SO LIGHTLY WHAT THEY GAVE.	290	SEPTEMBER 1913		30
WEIGHS					
	AND THE WHOLE WORLD WEIGHS DOWN UPON MY HEART—	104	FERGUS DRUID	V	38A
	RESPONSIBILITY SO WEIGHS ME DOWN.	501	VACILLATION		50
WEIGHT					
	BUT WHEN THE HORSE HAD FELT MY WEIGHT,	9	OISIN 1		109
	AND WHEN THE WHITE STEED FELT MY WEIGHT,	9	OISIN 1	V	109
	THE ODOROUS WEIGHT OF HIS CURLS OF LIGHT,	28	OISIN 1	V	423D
	HE DREADS THE WEIGHT OF MORTAL HOURS.	212	BLESS PSALTER		11
	HEEL UP AND WEIGHT ON TOE, MUST FACE THE WALL	363	DOLLS FACES		3
	BENEATH THE WEIGHT OF GREATER GRIEF THAN I;	661	ISLE STAT II 1		63
WEIGHTY					
	AND IMPORTUNE WITH WEIGHTY WORDS THIS MOOR,	698	MOSADA 2		45
	A WEIGHTY QUESTION, FOR IT IS THE LAST.	700	MOSADA 3		37
WEIR					
	AS A HAY-COCK OUT ON THE FLOOD, OR A WOLF SUCKED UNDER A WEIR.	63	OISIN 3		220
	AS A GRASS SEED CRUSHED BY A PEBBLE, AS A WOLF SUCKED UNDER A WEIR.	63	OISIN 3	V	220
WEIRS					
	SHE BID ME TAKE LIFE EASY, AS THE GRASS GROWS ON THE WEIRS;	90	SALLEY GARDENS		7
WELCOME					
	HE HAS OVER-LINGERED HIS WELCOME; THE DAYS,	26	OISIN 1		402
	HE HATH OVER LINGERED HIS WELCOME; THE DAYS,	27	OISIN 1	V	406
	AND BADE ALL WELCOME, BEING IGNORANT.	286	TWO KINGS		218
	AND RIDDEN OUT TO WELCOME THEM, AND NOW,	286	TWO KINGS	V	218
	A FITTER WELCOME; BUT A THOUGHT	328	ROBERT GREGORY		95
	NEW WELCOME AND OLD WISDOM AT HER FIRE	340	SHEP GOATHERD		32
	WELCOME, AND THE ORMONDES ALL	400	DEMON BEAST		11
	WHAT SEEMS MOST WELCOME IN THE TOMB—PLAY A PREDESTINED PART.	503	VACILLATION		86
	AND ALL MY FRIENDS WERE THERE AND MADE ME WELCOME TOO;	581	CURSE CROMWELL		27
	TO WELCOME THEE, NASCHINA, WITH SWEET SINGING.	645	ISLE STAT I 1		7
	TO WELCOME THEE, WHEN O'ER THE OWLET'S WINGS	648	ISLE STAT I 1		102
	THOU'RT WELCOME. LIE THERE CLOSE AGAINST MY FINGERS.	700	MOSADA 3		44
WELCOMED					
	THOSE WANDERERS THAT WELCOMED IN THEIR TENTS	462	HARUN RASHID		23
	THAT THEY HAVE WELCOMED IN THEIR TENTS THE DREAM	462	HARUN RASHID	V	23
WELCOMER					
	HE MIGHT HAVE BEEN YOUR HEARTIEST WELCOMER.	326	ROBERT GREGORY		56
WELCOMING					
	EACH CAME ONE MORN, WITH WELCOMING OF SONG,	660	ISLE STAT II 1		42
WELFARE					
	A HELEN OF SOCIAL WELFARE DREAM,	626	OLD MEN BE MAD		7
WELL					
	FOR WE KNEW WELL THE OLD WAS OVER.	25	OISIN 1		379
	FOR WELL WE KNEW THE OLD WAS OVER,	25	OISIN 1	V	379
	OR GOIN' TO THE WELL,	96	MOLL MAGEE		46
	SAYING ALL THINGS WERE WELL;	113	ROSE OF PEACE		14
	HE MUSED BESIDE THE WELL OF SCANAVIN,	127	DREAM OF FAERY		25
	BECAUSE, TO HIM WHO PONDERS WELL,	138	TO IRELAND		19
	AH! WISE, MY HEART KNOWS WELL HOW WISE.	193	BAILE AILLINN		99
	"HE IS WELL OUT OF WIND AND WAVE,	193	BAILE AILLINN	V	114
	"YOUR WELL BELOVED'S HAIR HAS THREADS OF GREY,	199	FOLLY COMFORT	V	2
	AND WHO COULD PLAY IT WELL ENOUGH	202	NEVER GIVE ALL		11
	AND WHO CAN PLAY IT WELL ENOUGH	202	NEVER GIVE ALL	V	11
	I SAW THEM ON THAT NIGHT AS WELL AS YOU.	223	SHADOW WATER B		29
	AND DRAGS HIM THROUGH THE SEA. WELL, NET OR NONE,	224	SHADOW WATER B		57
	FOR HE CAN JUDGE THE STARS AS WELL AS FORGAEL.	225	SHADOW WATER B		63
	NO, NO, DO NOT SAY THAT. YOU KNOW RIGHT WELL	227	SHADOW WATER B		107

881

WELL (CONTINUED)

THAT SET HIM TO THE FANCY. ALL WOULD BE WELL . . . . 230 SHADOW WATER B 177
I KNEW HIM WELL, AND WHILE I HEARD HIM LAUGHING . . . . . 242 SHADOW WATER B 419
FROM WELL SIDE OR FROM PLOUGH LAND, WAS THEIR NOISE; . . . 279 TWO KINGS V 53
I SAW, BEFORE I HAD WELL FINISHED. . . . . 322 SWANS AT COOLE 9
IN MUSCULAR YOUTH WELL KNOWN TO MAYO MEN . . . . 325 ROBERT GREGORY 34
WELL KNOWN FOR HORSEMANSHIP TO CONNACHT MEN . . . . . . 325 ROBERT GREGORY V 34
WHAT OTHER COULD SO WELL HAVE COUNSELLED US . . . . . . 327 ROBERT GREGORY 73
THE SHEEP HAD GONE FROM THEIRS. I KNOW RIGHT WELL . . . . 339 SHEP GOATHERD 15
AND BE WELL PLEASED REMEMBERING IT, FOR IN THE OLD DAYS, . 351 HER PRAISE 16
AND YOU KNOW WELL HOW GREAT THE LONGING HAS BEEN, ... 352 PEOPLE 7
WHEN AGE MIGHT WELL HAVE CHILLED HIS BLOOD." . . . . . . 356 BROKEN DREAMS 19
I BEAR A BURDEN THAT MIGHT WELL TRY . . . . 380 SONGS FOOL 1 13
THAT IS HOW HE LEARNT SO WELL . . . . 382 SONG OF FOOL 11
SHE HAD RIDDEN WELL TO HOUNDS. . . . . 392 EASTER 1916 V 23
MAY WELL BE OF ALL EVIL CHANCES CHIEF. . . . . 405 FOR DAUGHTER 53
A SCENE WELL SET AND EXCELLENT COMPANY. . . . . 489 COOLE PARK 29 16
AND THE RICH MAN HAD PAID THEM WELL . . . . 596 COLONEL MARTIN 57
OBSERVANT OLD MEN KNOW IT WELL; . . . . 626 OLD MEN BE MAD 17
SING WHATEVER IS WELL MADE, ... 639 BEN BULBEN 69
AND FOUND.   'TIS WELL!--ANOTHER MILE OF WAY . . . . . . 651 ISLE STAT I 2 6
NO OTHER BIRD MAY ENTER IN. WELL? LATE-- . . . . . . 659 ISLE STAT II 1 24
IT IS THE SHEPHERD GUARIMOND, WHO LOVETH WELL . . . . . . 661 ISLE STAT II 1 53
NASCHINA. OH, I KNOW HER WELL--A LAME, ... 661 ISLE STAT II 1 67
OF THOSE STEEL TONGUES! CRASH, SWORDS! WELL THRUST! . . 665 ISLE STAT II 2 67
   WELL BENT
OF THOSE STEEL TONGUES! CRASH, SWORDS! WELL THRUST! . . 665 ISLE STAT II 2 67
   WELL BENT
WELL NIGH IMMORTAL IN THIS CHARMED CLIME, ... 674 ISLE STAT II 3 202
ARE ALL THINGS WELL WITH YOU AND WITH YOUR SHEEP? . . . 682 SEEKER 13
YES, ALL IS VERY WELL. WHENCE COMEST THOU? . . . . . . 682 SEEKER 14
DEEPER THAN THE DEEPEST WELL." . . . . 697 MOSADA 2 27
AND POUR UPON THE WORLD! AH! WELL A DAY! . . . . 703 MOSADA 3 V 118
HAS FLICKERED AND GONE OUT. I AM NOT WELL. . . . . . . 704 MOSADA 3 129
BEFORE HIM ONE WELL GUARDED, WITH BOUND HANDS: . . . . . 709 FERENCZ RENYI 10
WELL THEN, TO BUSINESS; WHAT IS IN YOUR BAG? . . . . . . 720 WITCH VIVIEN 19
A FAIRY WHOM WE LOVED FULL WELL; . . . . 729 PRIEST FAIRY 44
YOU HAVE DONE WELL, BECAUSE MY BOWS ARE TURNED . . . . . 755 SHADOW WATER A 164
BY SUN AND MOON AND A HUNDRED GODS AS WELL. . . . . . . 756 SHADOW WATER A 189
WELL SHELTERED FROM THE WINDS, AND FRUITFUL FIELDS, . . . 758 SHADOW WATER A 221
AH, WELL! THEY ARE CALLING ME--THEY ARE CALLING ME. . . 760 SHADOW WATER A 251
WE WILL NOT QUARREL, NOW THAT ALL IS WELL, ... 766 SHADOW WATER A 373
THE WELL AND THE TREE . . . . 780 WELL AND TREE V T
CRIES OUT THE EMPTY WELL, ... 780 WELL AND TREE 2
DRY STONES IN A WELL?" . . . . 780 WELL AND TREE 8
AND ALL SEEM WELL ENOUGH, ... 786 YOUR HEART 15
THE HEART WELL WORN UPON THE SLEEVE MAY BE THE BEST OF . 790 HEART SLEEVE 1
   SIGHTS,

WELL-A-DAY

AND POUR UPON THE WORLD! AH! WELL-A-DAY! . . . . 703 MOSADA 3 118

WELL-BELOVED

THROUGH ALL THE WELL-BELOVED GLADE. . . . . 67 HAPPY SHEPHERD V 46C
UPON A DIM, GREEN, WELL-BELOVED ISLE, ... 126 DREAM OF FAERY V 8
HIS WELL-BELOVED THROUGH A MORTAL'S EYES! . . . . 763 SHADOW WATER A 322

WELL-BELOVED'S

"YOUR WELL-BELOVED'S HAIR HAS THREADS OF GREY, ... 199 FOLLY COMFORT 2
"YOUR WELL-BELOVED'S HAIR HAS A THREAD OF GREY, ... 199 FOLLY COMFORT V 2

WELLESLEY

TO DOROTHY WELLESLEY . . . . 579 DOR WELLESLEY T

WELL-GROOMED

AND PEARLY WHITE HIS WELL-GROOMED HAIR. . . . . 3 OISIN 1 V 7CC

WELLING

AND TELL ME HOW MY KINDRED'S TEARS ARE WELLING, ... 33 OISIN 2 V 66

WELLKNOWN

IN MUSCULAR YOUTH WELLKNOWN TO MAYO MEN . . . . 324 ROBERT GREGORY V 34

WELL-KNOWN

THE WELL-KNOWN FACES ARE ALL GONE, ... 132 OLD PENSIONER V 17

WELL-NIGH

WELL-NIGH IMMORTAL IN THIS CHARMED CLIME! . . . . 674 ISLE STAT II 3 V 202
AND THEN HIS HEART GREW WELL-NIGH DEAD . . . . 730 PRIEST FAIRY 59

WELLS

WATCHED ME WITH MOURNFUL WONDER OUT OF THE WELLS OF HIS . 51 OISIN 3 60
   EYES.
"WHEN ALL THE WELLS ARE PARCHED AWAY? . . . . 396 ROSE TREE 15

WELLSIDE

FROM WELLSIDE OR FROM PLOUGHLAND, WAS THERE NOISE! . . . 279 TWO KINGS V 53

WELL-SIDE

FROM WELL-SIDE OR FROM PLOUGH-LAND, WAS THERE NOISE! . . 279 TWO KINGS 53

WELL-SIDES

CABINS GONE NOW, OLD WELL-SIDES, OLD DEAR PLACES, . . . 130 BOOK STORIES V 23

WENCH

WHEN MOCKING MUSES CHOSE THE COUNTRY WENCH. . . . . . . 413 TOWER 96
AND LOVE WENCH WISDOM'S CRUEL FACE. . . . . 787 HUDDON DUDDON 10

WENCHING

WENCHING, DRINKING, STILL REMAIN . . . . 529 TOM LUNATIC 9
THAT SEEMED BUT A WILD WENCHING MAN; . . . . 550 SEVERED HEAD 16

WENCH-WISDOM'S

AND LOVE WENCH-WISDOM'S CRUEL FACE. . . . . 787 HUDDON DUDDON 10

WEND

AND HUMMING SANDS, WHERE WINDY SURGES WEND! . . . . . . 68 SAD SHEPHERD 4

		PAGE	TITLE		LINE
WENT					
WENT WE TO FIND THEIR PRINCE'S HALL-- • • • • • • •		16	OISIN 1	V	217
WE WENT A-FISHING IN LONG BOATS • • • • • • • • •		23	OISIN 1		352
AND THE EARS OF THE HORSE WENT SINKING AWAY IN THE HOLLOW NIGHT,		48	OISIN 3		21
WENT THE LAUGHTER OF SCORN FROM MY MOUTH • • • • • • •		58	OISIN 3		168
AND BECAUSE I WENT BY THEM SO HUGH AND SO SPEEDY WITH EYES SO BRIGHT,		59	OISIN 3		169
AND BEFORE I WENT BY THEM SO HUGE AND SO SPEEDY WITH EYES SO BRIGHT,		59	OISIN 3	V	169
AND THE DREAMS OF THE ISLANDS WENT OUT OF ME, • • • • •		59	OISIN 3	V	175
I FELL ON THE PATH, AND THE HORSE WENT AWAY LIKE A SUMMER FLY,		60	OISIN 3		190
WENT WALKING WITH SLOW STEPS ALONG THE GLEAMING • • • •		68	SAD SHEPHERD		3
A SAD, SAD THOUGHT WENT BY ME SLOWLY, • • • • • • •		72	ANASHU VIJAYA		17
BUT FATHER JOHN WENT UP, • • • • • • • • • • • •		92	FATHER OHART		9
AND FATHER JOHN WENT DOWN, • • • • • • • • • • •		92	FATHER OHART		10
AS HE WENT UP AND DOWN, • • • • • • • • • • • •		92	FATHER OHART		18
AND HE WENT HIS WAY WITH A FROWN. • • • • • • • •		92	FATHER OHART		20
AND WENT ON HIS WAY WITH A FROWN. • • • • • • • •		92	FATHER OHART	V	20
AND WENT HIS WAY WITH A FROWN. • • • • • • • • •		92	FATHER OHART	V	20
I WENT AWAY IN SILENCE, • • • • • • • • • • • •		95	MOLL MAGEE		27
I WENT AWAY IN SILENCE, • • • • • • • • • • • •		95	MOLL MAGEE		33
SEEK OUT WHAT MAN HE IS." ONE WENT AND CAME. • • • • •		109	CUCHULAIN SEA		51
AND WENT DOWN TO THE LONG SANDS ALONE, • • • • • • •		111	CUCHULAIN SEA	V	84
AND HE WENT DOWN TO THE LONG SANDS ALONE, • • • • • •		111	CUCHULAIN SEA	V	84
THEY WENT FORTH TO THE BATTLE, BUT THEY ALWAYS FELL • • •		113	ROSE OF BATTLE	V	T
AS HE WENT BY THE SANDS OF LISADILL • • • • • • • •		127	DREAM OF FAERY	V	13
AND THE MOTH-HOUR WENT FROM THE FIELDS, • • • • • • •		133	FR GILLIGAN		15
MAY KNOW HOW MY HEART WENT WITH THEM • • • • • • • •		139	TO IRELAND		47
I WENT OUT TO THE HAZEL WOOD, • • • • • • • • • •		149	WANDER AENGUS		1
I WENT TO BLOW THE FIRE AFLAME, • • • • • • • • •		149	WANDER AENGUS		10
I WENT TO BLOW THE FIRE A-FLAME, • • • • • • • • •		149	WANDER AENGUS	V	10
HE LEFT THEM WHERE SHE WENT BY. • • • • • • • • •		160	CAP AND BELLS		24
A LATTICED WINDOW. HIS GLANCE WENT UP AT TIMES • • • •		180	QUEEN MAEVE		6
WHO KNOW THE WAY THAT NAOISE WENT? • • • • • • • •		193	BAILE AILLINN		96
WITH LIGHTNING, YOU WENT FROM ME, AND I COULD FIND • • •		257	RECONCILIATION		4
WHEN CUPS WENT ROUND AT CLOSE OF DAY-- • • • • • • •		271	GREY ROCK		12
AND AT THOSE WORDS I ROSE AND I WENT OUT • • • • • • •		282	TWO KINGS		125
AND FOR NINE DAYS MY MIND WENT WHIRLING ROUND • • • • •		282	TWO KINGS		127
WENT OUT. AMONG THE IVY-COVERED ROCKS, • • • • • • •		283	TWO KINGS		147
WITH HIS OLD THOUGHTS, KING GUAIRE WENT • • • • • • •		296	THREE BEGGARS		26
WENT DOWN UPON A HAND AND KNEE • • • • • • • • • •		304	HOUR DAWN	V	45
"HE WENT AWAY," MY MOTHER SANG, • • • • • • • • •		308	PLAYER QUEEN		5
WHERE THE PROUD, WAYWARD SQUIRREL WENT, • • • • • • •		317	APPOINTMENT		3
THE CAT WENT HERE AND THERE • • • • • • • • • • •		378	CAT AND MOON		1
A STRING OF SCHOLARS WENT IN FEAR • • • • • • • • •		381	SONG OF FOOL		7
IN PAINTING OR IN POTTERY, WENT • • • • • • • • •		421	MY TABLE		18
STRAIGHTENED ALL THAT WENT AWRY • • • • • • • • •		440	WISDOM	V	4
IT COULD NOT BEAR THAT BURDEN AND THEREFORE IT WENT MAD. •		449	OWEN AHERNE		4
IT FEARED THE HURT THAT SHE COULD GIVE AND THEREFORE IT WENT MAD.		450	OWEN AHERNE		8
I RAN, I RAN, FROM MY LOVE'S SIDE BECAUSE MY HEART WENT MAD.		450	OWEN AHERNE		12
THEY CAME LIKE SWALLOWS AND LIKE SWALLOWS WENT, • • • •		489	COOLE PARK 29		17
WENT IN THE DAWNING LIGHT • • • • • • • • • • • •		512	JANE ON GOD		3
I WENT OUT ALONE • • • • • • • • • • • • • • •		515	GIRLS SONG B		1
MONEY I HAD, AND IT WENT IN THE NIGHT, • • • • • • •		544	TO SAME TUNE 1		12
THEN THEY AND THEIR WISDOM WENT TO RACK, • • • • • • •		566	LAPIS LAZULI		28
ROUND LOUGH DERG'S HOLY ISLAND I WENT UPON THE STONES, • •		593	PILGRIM		6
THE COLONEL WENT OUT SAILING. • • • • • • • • • •		594	COLONEL MARTIN		1
HE ROSE THE LATCH AND WENT UPSTAIRS • • • • • • • •		594	COLONEL MARTIN		7
THE COLONEL WENT OUT SAILING. • • • • • • • • • •		594	COLONEL MARTIN		9
THE COLONEL WENT OUT SAILING. • • • • • • • • • •		594	COLONEL MARTIN		18
THE COLONEL WENT OUT SAILING. • • • • • • • • • •		595	COLONEL MARTIN		27
THE COLONEL WENT OUT SAILING. • • • • • • • • • •		595	COLONEL MARTIN		36
AND HE WENT IN AND SHE WENT ON • • • • • • • • • •		595	COLONEL MARTIN		37
AND HE WENT IN AND SHE WENT ON • • • • • • • • • •		595	COLONEL MARTIN		37
THE COLONEL WENT OUT SAILING. • • • • • • • • • •		596	COLONEL MARTIN		45
THE COLONEL WENT OUT SAILING. • • • • • • • • • •		596	COLONEL MARTIN		54
THE COLONEL WENT OUT SAILING. • • • • • • • • • •		596	COLONEL MARTIN		63
THE COLONEL WENT OUT SAILING. • • • • • • • • • •		597	COLONEL MARTIN		72
WENT TO THE SACRED HOUSE AND STOOD BETWEEN • • • • • •		609	IN TARAS HALLS		11
MONEY I HAD, AND IT WENT IN THE NIGHT, • • • • • • •		616	MARCH SONGS 3		12
THE GHOSTS WENT BY ME WITH THEIR LIPS APART • • • • • •		734	QUATRAIN APHOR		13
HE, THOUGH BUT A LANDSMAN, WENT TO THE MAST-HEAD, • • •		790	DEDICATION		4
WEPT					
AND WEPT, AND RAISED THEIR LAMENTING HANDS, • • • • • •		10	OISIN 1		112
THEY WEPT, AND RAISED LAMENTING HANDS. • • • • • • •		10	OISIN 1	V	112
AND THE FENIANS ALL HAD WEPT WITH ME, • • • • • • • •		10	OISIN 1	V	113
AND, PATRICK! BY YOUR BEARD, THEY WEPT, • • • • • • •		17	OISIN 1		236
OH, PATRICK, BY THY BEARD, THEY WEPT, • • • • • • • •		17	OISIN 1	V	236
OF WAR WERE ON IT, AND I WEPT, • • • • • • • • • •		24	OISIN 1		369
LORD OF THE CROZIERS, YOU EVEN HAD LIFTED YOUR HANDS AND WEPT,		54	OISIN 3		110
LORD OF THE CROSIERS, THOU EVEN HADST LIFTED THY HANDS AND WEPT,		54	OISIN 3	V	110
ALEEL, THE SWINEHERD, WEPT AND CAST HIM DOWN • • • • •		106	CUCHULAIN SEA	V	14
FEASTED, AND WEPT THE BARROWS OF HIS DEAD, • • • • • •		170	SECRET ROSE		18
AND THOUGH THE SEVEN LIGHTS BOWED IN THEIR DANCE AND WEPT,		174	ELEMENT POWERS		3
"SHE WILL GROW OLD AND DIE, AND SHE HAS WEPT!" • • • •		186	QUEEN MAEVE		138

WEPT (CONTINUED)

	PAGE	TITLE		LINE
HALF CRAZY WITH THE THOUGHT, SHE TOO HAS WEPT!	186	QUEEN MAEVE		140
HE ALWAYS WEPT THEM ON THAT DAY,	192	BAILE AILLINN		78
THAT SHE AMONG HER WINDS MIGHT KNOW HE WEPT;	220	HARP OF AENGUS		12
THAT SHE AMONG HER WOODS MIGHT KNOW HE WEPT!	220	HARP OF AENGUS	V	12
AND ALMOST WEPT BECAUSE THEY COULD NOT FIND IT.	229	SHADOW WATER B		155
AND WEPT BECAUSE SHE HAD DREAMT THAT I	308	PLAYER QUEEN		11
AND NOW THAT END HAS COME I HAVE NOT WEPT;	603	GALLERY REVIS		38
BUT NOW THAT END HAS COME I HAVE NOT WEPT;	603	GALLERY REVIS	V	38
THAT SHE AMONG HER WINDS MIGHT KNOW HE WEPT;	763	SHADOW WATER A		307

WEST

	PAGE	TITLE		LINE
IN THE PALE WEST, AND THE SUN'S RIM SANK,	12	OISIN 1		153
HORROR FROM HORROR GREW; BUT WHEN THE WEST	41	OISIN 2		180
FORMS WITHOUT NUMBER! WHEN THE LIVE WEST FLASHED	41	OISIN 2	V	180
WHEN I HAD TORN IT DOWN; BUT WHEN THE WEST	41	OISIN 2	V	180
WHEN I TORE DOWN THE TREE; BUT WHEN THE WEST	41	OISIN 2	V	180
WHEN I'D TORE DOWN THAT TREE; BUT WHEN THE WEST	41	OISIN 2	V	180
WHEN I TORE DOWN THAT TREE; BUT WHEN THE WEST	41	OISIN 2	V	180
SANG THAT SOMEWHERE TO NORTH OR WEST OR SOUTH	127	DREAM OF FAERY		19
SANG HOW SOMEWHERE TO NORTH OR WEST OR SOUTH	127	DREAM OF FAERY		19
DESOLATE WINDS THAT HOVER IN THE FLAMING WEST!	147	UNAPPEAS HOST		8
I WOULD THAT THE BOAR WITHOUT BRISTLES HAD COME FROM THE WEST	153	CHANGE BELOVED		10
THE WEST WEEPS IN PALE DEW AND SIGHS PASSING AWAY,	154	BELOVED PEACE		5
OR ONLY TO THE WATER IN THE WEST;	155	REPROVE CURLEW		2
OR ONLY TO WATERS IN THE WEST;	155	REPROVE CURLEW	V	2
OR ONLY TO THE WATERS IN THE WEST;	155	REPROVE CURLEW	V	2
THE BANNERS OF EAST AND WEST,	165	CRY OF SEDGE		7
AND LIGHTS WERE PALING OUT OF THE WEST,	175	BELOVED DEAD		2
AND LIGHT WERE PALING OUT OF THE WEST,	175	BELOVED DEAD	V	2
AND SET THEM DIGGING IN THE WEST OF THE HILL.	184	QUEEN MAEVE	V	93
THAT FLY INTO THE WEST? BUT LISTEN, LISTEN!	247	SHADOW WATER B		518
WHAT IS THERE BUT THE SLOWLY FADING WEST?	390	IMAGE PAST		19
THE WEST WIND MADE IT PITIFUL, AND THE NORTH WIND AFRAID.	449	OWEN AHERNE		6
SCARCE SANK HE FROM THE WEST	535	CHOSEN		5
LIBATIONS, FROM THE HUNGARY OF THE WEST.	709	FERENCZ RENYI		5
MY WAY IS WEST. SHE SEEMS BOTH YOUNG AND SHAPELY;	755	SHADOW WATER A		171

WESTERN

	PAGE	TITLE		LINE
AT EVENING IN MY WESTERN DUN."	8	OISIN 1		79
AND PRAISE THEE IN MY WESTERN HALL."	8	OISIN 1	V	79
WHERE THE SUN FALLS INTO THE WESTERN DEEP.	108	CUCHULAIN SEA	V	34
. . . OF THE WESTERN WORLD", [NINETEEN-SEVEN]	294	HATED PLAYBOY		T
THE ATTACK ON "THE PLAYBOY OF THE WESTERN WORLD"	294	HATED PLAYBOY		T
THAT HAVE THE FRENZY OF OUR WESTERN SEAS,	384	VISION ROBART		62
ALTHOUGH THAT WESTERN CLOUD IS LUMINOUS,	488	COOLE PARK 29		4

WESTWARD

	PAGE	TITLE		LINE
I TURNED AND RODE TO THE WESTWARD, AND FOLLOWED THE SEA'S OLD SHOUT	60	OISIN 3		183
FLEW WESTWARD; AND MANY A TIME SINCE THEN	223	SHADOW WATER B		27
WESTWARD OF TARA. HURRYING TO HIS QUEEN	276	TWO KINGS		2
WESTWARD OF TARA. WHERE IN THE MIDDLE WOOD	277	TWO KINGS	V	4
WESTWARD OF TARA, AMONG THE HAZEL-TREES—	283	TWO KINGS		135
WESTWARD OF TARA, AMONG THE HAZEL TREES—	283	TWO KINGS	V	135
WESTWARD OF TARA, THERE TO AWAIT A FRIEND	283	TWO KINGS	V	136

WET SEE FOAM-WET

	PAGE	TITLE		LINE
TO THIS DIM SHORE ON FOAM WET FEET?	5	OISIN 1	V	51
FOR LOVE OF OISIN FOAM WET FEET	6	OISIN 1	V	57
AND SHORES THE FROTH LIPS WET!	33	OISIN 2		59
OR WEEDING OR PLOUGHING WITH FACES A-SHINING WITH MUCH-TOIL WET;	58	OISIN 3		165
AND YELLOW THE WET WILD-STRAWBERRY LEAVES.	79	FALLING LEAVES		4
THE THRONGS WITH BLOWN WET HAIR ARE GATHERING NEAR.	114	ROSE OF BATTLE	V	6
THE COLD WET WINDS EVER BLOWING,	119	PITY OF LOVE		5
AND THE COLD WET WINDS EVER BLOWING,	119	PITY OF LOVE	V	7
FOR THE WET WINDS ARE BLOWING OUT OF THE CLINGING AIR;	207	HANRAHANS SONG		12
ON WET ROADS WHERE MEN WALK,	215	HAPPY TOWNLAND		48
"THOUGH TO MY FEATHERS IN THE WET,	294	THREE BEGGARS		1
"THOUGH TO MY FEATHERS IN THE WET	297	THREE BEGGARS		63
AMID WET ROCKS AND HEATHER,	311	PEACOCK		8
BETWEEN ROCK AND WET HEATHER,	311	PEACOCK	V	8
THAT THE SALT DROPS HAVE WET!	312	CHILD DANCING		5
SHALL WALK THE WET SANDS BY THE EDGE OF THE STREAM	371	EGO DOMINUS		71
SHALL WALK THE WET SAND BY THE WATER'S EDGE,	371	EGO DOMINUS	V	71
HARDLY DARED TO WET HIS MOUTH	454	EMPTY CUP		3
THEIR SHROUDS ARE BLOODY AND THEIR LIPS ARE WET.	483	OIL AND BLOOD		6
I HAVE WET THIS BRAID OF HAIR WITH TEARS WHILE ASLEEP.	762	SHADOW WATER A		294

WHARF

	PAGE	TITLE		LINE
BESIDE A LOCHLANN WHARF, AND THOUGH SHE HAD SWORN	756	SHADOW WATER A		188

WHARVES

	PAGE	TITLE		LINE
UPON THE WHARVES OF SORROW, AND HEARD RING	115	ROSE OF BATTLE		27

WHEAT

	PAGE	TITLE		LINE
WAS ROBBED BEFORE EARTH GAVE THE WHEAT;	196	BAILE AILLINN		166
BECAUSE OF SOME GREEN WING, GATHERED OLD MUMMY WHEAT	442	BLACK CENTAUR		7
WHAT A CROP OF MUMMY WHEAT!	562	CONJUNCTIONS		2
AND HIS HAIR WAS AS YELLOW AS WAVING WHEAT.	729	PRIEST FAIRY		26
AND WHEAT IN THE WHEAT-EAR WITHERED,	783	GREY ROUND		19

WHEAT-EAR

	PAGE	TITLE		LINE
AND WHEAT IN THE WHEAT-EAR WITHERED,	783	GREY ROUND		19

WHEATEN

	PAGE	TITLE		LINE
OR MICE IN THE ONE WHEATEN SHEAF	195	BAILE AILLINN		147

```
                                                      PAGE     TITLE          LINE
WHEEL     SEE WAGON-WHEEL
    ROLLING HIS FLAGRANT WHEEL OUT OF THE DEEP,   . . . . .  42 OISIN 2          193
    ROLLING HIS WHEEL, WE SANG BESIDE THE DEEP    . . . . .  42 OISIN 2        V 193
    AND NOW THEY ALL WHEEL SUDDENLY AND FLY . . . . . . . . 234 SHADOW WATER B   258
    . . . I.   THE WHEEL AND THE PHASES OF THE MOON . . . . 372 PHASES OF MOON V   T
    OUT OF THE UP AND DOWN, THE WAGON WHEEL . . . . . . . . 377 PHASES OF MOON V 120
    THE WHEEL . . . . . . . . . . . . . . . . . . . . . . . 434 WHEEL              T
    A RUSH, A SUDDEN WHEEL, AND HOVERING STILL . . . . . . 441 LEDA AND SWAN  V   1
    I'VE LED THEE HERE, AND AS A WHEEL . . . . . . . . . . 667 ISLE STAT II 3    39
    FLIETH FORTUNE'S FURIOUS WHEEL. . . . . . . . . . . . . 737 IN FIRELIGHT       8
    AND NOW THEY ALL WHEEL SUDDENLY AND FLY . . . . . . . . 753 SHADOW WATER A   148
    AT THE BURNING WHEEL OF LOVE . . . . . . . . . . . . . 776 AGAINST WITCH     34
    TO GARRET OR CELLAR A WHEEL I SEND, . . . . . . . . . . 787 GARRET CELLAR      1
WHEELED
    THE FIRST THIN CRESCENT IS WHEELED ROUND ONCE MORE. . . 377 PHASES OF MOON   116
WHEELING
    AND SCATTER WHEELING IN GREAT BROKEN RINGS . . . . . . 322 SWANS AT COOLE    11
WHEELS    SEE CHARIOT-WHEELS
    AND PACE THE WOODS, AND DRIVE MY CHARIOT WHEELS . . . . 103 FERGUS DRUID   V  18
    WHEELS BY MILK-WHITE ASSES DRAWN . . . . . . . . . . . 502 VACILLATION       62
    THAT ON TWO WHEELS RAN . . . . . . . . . . . . . . . . 628 JANE MOUNTAIN     14
WHENCE
    WHENCE TURBULENT ITALY SHOULD DRAW . . . . . . . . . . 288 TO WEALTHY MAN    25
    BUT MINE SAW STELLA ONCE.  WHENCE CAME OUR THOUGHT? . . 486 SEVEN SAGES        6
    MINE SAW STELLA ONCE.  WHENCE CAME OUR THOUGHT? . . . . 486 SEVEN SAGES    V   6
    WHENCE HAD THEY COME? . . . . . . . . . . . . . . . . . 560 WHENCE COME        T
    WHAT MASTER MADE THE LASH.  WHENCE HAD THEY COME, . . . 560 WHENCE COME        9
    WHENCE DID ALL THAT FURY COME? . . . . . . . . . . . . 619 STICK INCENSE      1
    BUT WHENCE, AND WHEN? OVER THE WILLOWS SERE . . . . . . 652 ISLE STAT I 2     28
    YES, ALL IS VERY WELL.  WHENCE COMEST THOU? . . . . . . 682 SEEKER            14
WHEREAS
    THOUGH HE'D BUT CANNON--WHEREAS WE THAT HAD THOUGHT . . 258 KING NO KING       7
WHEREAT
    WHEREAT THE LIVING MOCK, . . . . . . . . . . . . . . . 474 ALL SOUL NIGHT    87
WHEREBY
    WHEREBY THE HAYSTACK- AND ROOF-LEVELLING WIND, . . . . 403 FOR DAUGHTER       5
    WHEREBY THE HORN OF PLENTY IS UNDONE. . . . . . . . . . 404 FOR DAUGHTER      32
    THAT WHEREBY A HOUSE LAY WRECKED? . . . . . . . . . . . 632 MAN AND ECHO      16
    THAT WHEREBY A HOUSE WAS WRECKED? . . . . . . . . . . . 632 MAN AND ECHO   V  16
    NAMES WHEREBY A MAN HAS KNOWN . . . . . . . . . . . . . 775 AGAINST WITCH      5
WHEREFORE
    BUT WHEREFORE NOW?"  "THERE IS A MAN TO DIE; . . . . . 107 CUCHULAIN SEA     23
    AH, WHEREFORE MURMUR YE . . . . . . . . . . . . . . . . 131 OLD PENSIONER  V  14
    WHEREFORE I THREW A PENNY . . . . . . . . . . . . . . . 268 BROWN PENNY        3
    NASCHINA, WHEREFORE ARE YOUR EYES SO BRIGHT . . . . . . 650 ISLE STAT I 1    141
    AND WHEREFORE HAVE WE COME? A SONG TO HEAR. . . . . . . 652 ISLE STAT I 2     27
    AND WHEREFORE, THEN, SHOULD THY GREY EYES . . . . . . . 686 LIFE               7
    AND WHEREFORE SHOULD THY BRIGHT BROW ROAM . . . . . . . 686 LIFE              11
    "WATCHER, WHEREFORE HAVE YE CALLED US?" EYES GO AFTER . 718 PHANTOM SHIP      10
        HIS LEAN HAND,
    NOW WHEREFORE HAST THOU TEARS INNUMEROUS? . . . . . . . 723 KANVA ON SELF      1
    THEN WHEREFORE FEAR THE USURY OF TIME, . . . . . . . . 724 KANVA ON SELF     17
    I HAVE FORGOTTEN WHEREFORE.  THE RED HOUND . . . . . . 747 SHADOW WATER A     8
    AND NONE KNOWS WHEREFORE; BUT THE HEART'S DESIRE . . . 764 SHADOW WATER A   340
WHEREIN
    WHEREIN THE GAZING HEART DOUBLES HER MIGHT. . . . . . . 326 ROBERT GREGORY    69
WHEREOF
    AND THINE OWN SADNESS, WHEREOF STARS, GROWN OLD . . . . 101 ROSE UPON ROOD     6
    ALL THOSE THINGS WHEREOF . . . . . . . . . . . . . . . 415 TOWER            163
    YONDER'S THE ISLE IN SEARCH WHEREOF WE CAME; . . . . . 662 ISLE STAT II 2    13
WHEREON
    WHEREON I WROTE AND WROUGHT, . . . . . . . . . . . . . 255 WOMAN HOMER        8
    WHEREON MAD FINGERS PLAY . . . . . . . . . . . . . . . 291 TO A FRIEND       12
    WHEREON A THING ONCE WALKED THAT SEEMED A BURNING CLOUD. 315 FALLEN MAJESTY    8
    WHEREON 'TWERE BEST . . . . . . . . . . . . . . . . . . 389 IMAGE PAST        17
    WITH ALL THOSE CALENDARS WHEREON . . . . . . . . . . . 432 NINETEEN 19       99
    WHEREON THE BLEAK NORTH BLOWS, . . . . . . . . . . . . 454 HIS MEMORIES       4
    A SPOT WHEREON THE FOUNDERS LIVED AND DIED . . . . . . 491 COOLE BALLYLEE    33
WHERETHROUGH
    WHERETHROUGH A HUNDRED HORSEMEN ON THE FLOOR . . . . . . 36 OISIN 2        V 102
WHIG
    BURKE WAS A WHIG.  WHETHER THEY KNEW OR NOT, . . . . . 486 SEVEN SAGES        8
WHIGGERY
    FROM FOUR GREAT MINDS THAT HATED WHIGGERY. . . . . . . 486 SEVEN SAGES        7
    ALL HATED WHIGGERY; BUT WHAT IS WHIGGERY? . . . . . . . 486 SEVEN SAGES       10
    ALL HATED WHIGGERY; BUT WHAT IS WHIGGERY? . . . . . . . 486 SEVEN SAGES       10
    OR OUT OF DRUNKARD'S EYE.  ALL'S WHIGGERY NOW, . . . . 486 SEVEN SAGES       13
    OR DRUNKARD'S EYE.  ALL'S WHIGGERY NOW, . . . . . . . . 486 SEVEN SAGES    V  13
    OR OUT OF A DRUNKARD'S EYE.  ALL'S WHIGGERY NOW, . . . 486 SEVEN SAGES    V  13
WHILE
    WHILE A HUNDRED YOUTHS, MIGHTY OF LIMB, . . . . . . . . . 8 OISIN 1           94
    WHILE ROUND THE SHORE A MILLION STOOD . . . . . . . . . 14 OISIN 1          182
    TOGETHER, WHILE THE DARK WOODS RANG, . . . . . . . . . . 16 OISIN 1          227
    AND WHILE THEY SANG, A SINGER LAID . . . . . . . . . . . 16 OISIN 1        V 231
    WHILE HIS HEART STILL DREAMS OF BATTLE AND LOVE . . . . 27 OISIN 1          406
    AND STAY A LITTLE WHILE, AND BID THEM WEEP; . . . . . . 33 OISIN 2           60
    BUT FLY WHILE STILL YOU MAY."  AND THEREON I; . . . . . 35 OISIN 2           89
    LONG WHILE, ARE WHIPS OF STEEL."  "IS HE SO DREAD?" . . 35 OISIN 2        V  88
    BUT FLEE WHILE YOU STILL MAY."  THEN I; . . . . . . . . 35 OISIN 2        V  89
    BUT FLEE WHILE YOU MAY FLEE FROM HIM."  THEN I; . . . . 35 OISIN 2        V  89
    SHOWED PRINTS OF SEA-BORN SCALES, WHILE DOWN THROUGH IT  37 OISIN 2          115
```

WHILE (CONTINUED)

	PAGE	TITLE	LINE
WHILE HIGH FRAIL CLOUDLETS, FED WITH A GREEN LIGHT,	40	OISIN 2	165
OF SWORD AND BRAZEN BATTLE-AXE, WHILE DAY	40	OISIN 2	171
MINGLING OF SWORD AND WAR-AXE, WHILE THE DAY	40	OISIN 2 V	171
WHILE THE WOOD-PECKER MADE A MERRY DIN,	44	OISIN 2	228
AND DRIFTING GREYNESS, WHILE THIS MONOTONE,	45	OISIN 2	232
WHILE IN THIS PLACE AND THAT PLACE,	58	OISIN 3	166
THY FRETFUL WORDS A LITTLE WHILE,	66	HAPPY SHEPHERD	40
WHILE WE ALONE HAVE ROUND US WOVEN WOODS,	73	ANASHU VIJAYA	56
AMRITA, WHILE--AH ME! YOU LOVE ANOTHER,	74	ANASHU VIJAYA	58
WHILE OUR LOVE GROWS AN INDIAN STAR,	78	INDIAN TO LOVE	13
WHILE GROWS OUR LOVE AN INDIAN STAR,	78	INDIAN TO LOVE V	13
WHILE SLOWLY HE WHOSE HAND HELD HERS REPLIED:	80	EPHEMERA	11
WHILE SLOWLY ANSWERED HE WHOSE HAND HELD HERS--	80	EPHEMERA V	11
WHILE HE BENT DOWN HIS FADING HEAD,	82	MAD KING GOLL	10
ONCE, WHILE WITHIN A LITTLE TOWN	85	MAD KING GOLL V	49
WHILE THE WORLD IS FULL OF TROUBLES	87	STOLEN CHILD	22
COME NEAR ME, WHILE I SING THE ANCIENT WAYS!	100	ROSE UPON ROOD	2
"YOUR HEAD A WHILE SEEMED LIKE A WOMAN'S HEAD	110	CUCHULAIN SEA	63
WHILE DAY ITS BURDEN ON TO EVENING BORE,	110	CUCHULAIN SEA	70
WHILE HUSHED FROM FEAR, OR LOUD WITH HOPE, A BAND	114	ROSE OF BATTLE	5
WHILE I STAND ON THE ROADWAY, OR ON THE PAVEMENTS GREY,	117	ISLE INNISFREE	11
WHILE I STAND ON THE ROADWAY, OR ON THE PAVEMENT GREY,	117	ISLE INNISFREE V	11
WHILE YOUNG STARS ABOUT HER DANCE.	125	CATHLEEN PARA V	16
BUT WHILE HE PASSED BEFORE A PLASHY PLACE,	127	DREAM OF FAERY	17
AND ALL GREW FRIENDLY FOR A LITTLE WHILE.	129	BOOK STORIES	8
FOR ALL WHO HEARD IT DREAMED A LITTLE WHILE.	129	BOOK STORIES TV	8
AND ALL WHO HEARD GREW FRIENDLY FOR A WHILE.	129	BOOK STORIES V	8
ONCE, WHILE HE NODDED ON A CHAIR,	132	FR GILLIGAN	5
WHILE I SLEPT ON THE CHAIR"!	133	FR GILLIGAN	26
OR ONLY GAZE A LITTLE WHILE:	135	TWO TREES	24
WHILE I WROUGHT OUT THESE FITFUL DANAAN RHYMES,	136	TO SOME I TALK	1
WHILE THE NIGHT GREW, ABOVE THE FADING COALS,	136	TO SOME I TALK V	3
WHILE STILL I MAY, I WRITE FOR YOU	139	TO IRELAND	33
WHILE STILL I MAY I WRITE OUT TRUE	139	TO IRELAND V	33
HE HEARD WHILE HE SANG AND DREAMED	144	HOST OF AIR	9
WHILE THE YOUNG LIE LONG AND DREAM IN THEIR BED	150	OLD MOTHER	5
WHILE I MUST WORK BECAUSE I AM OLD,	151	OLD MOTHER	9
WHILE TIME AND THE WORLD ARE EBBING AWAY	168	BLESSED	39
WHILE LIGHTS WERE PALING ONE BY ONE.	176	BELOVED DEAD	13
WHILE BIRDS GREW SILENT ONE BY ONE.	176	BELOVED DEAD V	13
WE SHADOWS, WHILE THEY UPROOT HIS EARTHY HOUSE,	184	QUEEN MAEVE	94
WE SHADOWS, WHILE THEY UPROOT THE EARTHY HOUSE	184	QUEEN MAEVE V	94
WHILE OVER THEM BIRDS OF AENGUS FLY,	197	BAILE AILLINN	182
AMONG PIGEONS AND BEES, WHILE THAT GREAT ARCHER,	198	SEVEN WOODS	12
WHERE ONE FOUND LANCELOT CRAZED AND HID HIM FOR A WHILE:	209	UNDER THE MOON	3
TO TAKE HIM WHILE HE SLEEPS AND CARRY HIM	222	SHADOW WATER B	14
TO MAKE AN END WHILE HE IS SLEEPING THERE.	222	SHADOW WATER B V	14
WHILE I WAS LOOKING THEY ROSE HURRIEDLY,	223	SHADOW WATER B	25
THE OTHER NIGHT, WHILE HE WAS PLAYING IT,	223	SHADOW WATER B	32
I'D DROWN HIM WHILE WE HAVE THE CHANCE TO DO IT.	224	SHADOW WATER B	58
I'D KILL HIM WHILE WE HAVE THE CHANCE TO DO IT.	224	SHADOW WATER B V	58
TO MAKE AN END OF FORGAEL WHILE HE SLEEPS.	225	SHADOW WATER B	65
THIS LONG WHILE NOW: WE HAD NOT TURNED AGAINST HIM	225	SHADOW WATER B V	68B
AND LISTEN TO ME FOR A WHILE. THE SAILORS	226	SHADOW WATER B	92
AND NOW THEY WILL NOT FOLLOW, WHILE I SEEK	226	SHADOW WATER B	95
NOT IN ITS IMAGE ON THE MIRROR! WHILE	230	SHADOW WATER B	189
TO MAKE HER FAST WHILE WE ARE PLUNDERING HER.	232	SHADOW WATER B	225
AND OVERPOWER THE CREW WHILE YET ASLEEP!	233	SHADOW WATER B	240
WHILE THERE'S A ROPE TO RUN INTO A NOOSE	238	SHADOW WATER B	347
I KNEW HIM WELL, AND WHILE I HEARD HIM LAUGHING	242	SHADOW WATER B	419
I HAD THIS THOUGHT A WHILE AGO,	255	WORDS	1
AND WHILE WE'RE IN OUR LAUGHING, WEEPING FIT,	257	RECONCILIATION	9
WHILE THOSE SAME HUNDREDS MOCK ANOTHER DAY	265	ABBEY THEATRE	4
AND WHERE THE STONE STRUCK FIRE, WHILE IN THE LEAVES	278	TWO KINGS	33
"WHILE I HAVE HIM AND YOU IT MATTERS LITTLE	280	TWO KINGS	85
WHILE THAT GREAT JUAN GALLOPED BY:	294	HATED PLAYBOY V	4
WHILE HE'D RUMMAGED RAGS AND HAIR,	299	THREE HERMITS	29
WHILE I MUST HURRY UPON MY WAY,	301	RUN PARADISE	23
WHILE I AM RUNNING TO PARADISE.	301	RUN PARADISE V	REF
TO KEEP HIM UPRIGHT WHILE HE CURSED.	302	HOUR DAWN	6
BUT WHILE HE FUMBLED AT THE STONES	302	HOUR DAWN	16
AND ALL THE WHILE HER NEEDLE PULLED	308	PLAYER QUEEN	7
WHILE UP FROM MY HEART'S ROOT	316	FRIENDS	26
WHILE I, FROM THAT REED-THROATED WHISPERER	320	REED WHISPERER	1
--SEEING THAT FAME HAS PERISHED THIS LONG WHILE,	321	REED WHISPERER	11
TO CHANGE MY LOVES WHILE DANCING	330	BONE OF A HARE	7
AND RUNS OR A WHILE HALF-FLIES	341	SHEP GOATHERD	64
HE STAYED FOR A WHILE: AND WE	341	SHEP GOATHERD	66
AND RUNS FOR A WHILE OR A WHILE HALF-FLIES	341	SHEP GOATHERD V	64
AND RUNS FOR A WHILE OR A WHILE HALF-FLIES	341	SHEP GOATHERD V	64
WHILE TALKING WITH HIS QUEENS,	345	ON WOMAN	12
WHILE WONDERING STILL TO BE A SHADE, WITH GRANIA'S SHADE,	366	HER COURAGE V	4
THE SENTIMENTALIST HIMSELF: WHILE ART	369	EGO DOMINUS	47
BUT WHILE THE MOON IS ROUNDING TOWARDS THE FULL	373	PHASES OF MOON	39
WHILE MICHAEL ANGELO'S SISTINE ROOF,	386	ROBARTES DANCE	32
THAT WOMAN A WHILE WOULD BE SHRILL	392	EASTER 1916 V	17
WHILE THOSE DEAD MEN ARE LOITERING THERE	395	SIXTEEN DEAD	5
WHILE UNDER ITS STORM-BEATEN BREAST	397	POLIT PRISONER	23
THE BEST LACK ALL CONVICTION, WHILE THE WORST	402	SECOND COMING	7
IS MOVING ITS SLOW THIGHS, WHILE ALL ABOUT IT	402	SECOND COMING	16

		PAGE	TITLE	LINE

WHILE   (CONTINUED)

THE BEST LACK CONVICTION, WHILE THE WORST . . . . . . 402 SECOND COMING V 7
WHILE THAT GREAT QUEEN, THAT ROSE OUT OF THE SPRAY, . . . 404 FOR DAUGHTER 27
WHILE ON THAT OLD GREY STONE I SAT . . . . 406 IN TIME OF WAR 2
WHILE THEIR GREAT WOODEN DICE BEAT ON THE BOARD. . . . . 412 TOWER 88
SEEMED FOR A WHILE TO HAVE GROWN YOUNG AGAIN! . . . . . 462 HARUN RASHID 36
WHILE OUR GROSS PALATES DRINK FROM THE WHOLE WINE, ... 471 ALL SOUL NIGHT 10
WHILE ON THE SHOP AND STREET I GAZED . . . . 501 VACILLATION 40
AND MY BLOOD BE COLD THE WHILE . . . . 532 BEFORE WORLD 11
BUT STRETCH THAT BODY FOR A WHILE . . . . 534 CONSOLATION 3
WHILE NIGHT SHUTS THE EYES . . . . 535 PARTING 2
WHILE HIS LOUD SONG REPROVES . . . . 536 PARTING 7
STAND UPRIGHT WHILE YOU CAN, ... 586 PARNELLITES 4
WHILE MAN CAN STILL HIS BODY KEEP . . . . 633 MAN AND ECHO 25
WHILE THE WORLD IS ROLL'D IN LIGHT. . . . . 646 ISLE STAT I 1 29
OF SWORD-BLUE WAVES OF CALM! WHILE O'ER HEAD BLINK . . . 663 ISLE STAT II 2 42
SO BE THOU STILL, DEAR HEART, A LITTLE WHILE! . . . . . 677 ISLE STAT II 3 283
THE YEARS OF GOBLIN SLEEP. AH! WHILE I SLUMBERED, ... 679 ISLE STAT II 3 308
A LITTLE WHILE AND--RED EVE DIES-- . . . . 686 LIFE 13
AND, WHILE THEY GATHER ROUND MY BECKONING ARMS, ... 694 MOSADA 1 100
WHILE O'ER THE BUDS, AND O'ER THE GRASS-BLADES, BRIGHT . . 704 REMEMBRANCE 3
REMEMBERING THEE, I MUSE, WHILE FADES IN FLIGHT . . . . 705 REMEMBRANCE 6
WHILE THE MORNING STAR DECAYETH . . . . 706 DAWN-SONG 29
COME AWAY WHILE THE MOON'S IN THE WOODLAND, ... 707 FAIRY PEDANT 9
WHILE I MURMUR A LITTLE AND PONDER . . . . 707 FAIRY PEDANT 14
COME AWAY WHILE THE MOON'S IN THE WOODLAND, ... 708 FAIRY PEDANT 37
HANG THE MIST-THREADS FOR A LITTLE WHILE LIKE COBWEBS IN 719 PHANTOM SHIP 29
    THE AIR!
HANG THE MIST THREADS FOR A LITTLE WHILE LIKE COBWEBS IN 719 PHANTOM SHIP V 29
    THE AIR,
WHILE WE SHAKE OUR HEADS AND SCOLD . . . . 727 LOVERS QUARREL 54
FOR WHILE I BLAMED THEM I COULD HEAR . . . . 743 DANAAN QUICK 27
BE PATIENT YET A WHILE! FOR THIS NINTH MOON, ... 748 SHADOW WATER A 23
SO THESE WOULD HAVE KILLED FORGAEL WHILE ASLEEP . . . . 748 SHADOW WATER A 25
BUT WILL IT HOLD WHILE WE ARE EMPTYING HER? . . . . . 754 SHADOW WATER A 156
WHILE THE WIND IS LIGHT. THE OAR CAN HARDLY MOVE HER, . . 754 SHADOW WATER A 157
I LINGER WHILE THE BIRDS ARE ON THE WING, ... 754 SHADOW WATER A V 157
I SHALL BE HOME NOW IN A LITTLE WHILE, ... 759 SHADOW WATER A 240
SHE WILL SAY SOMETHING IN A LITTLE WHILE. . . . . . . 760 SHADOW WATER A 248
AND TELL ME A LOVE-STORY WHILE I DRINK. . . . . . . 760 SHADOW WATER A 250
AND TELL ME A LOVE STORY WHILE I DRINK. . . . . . . 760 SHADOW WATER A V 250
I HAVE WET THIS BRAID OF HAIR WITH TEARS WHILE ASLEEP. . . 762 SHADOW WATER A 294
AND WHILE SHE FADES AND LIFE WITHERS AWAY, ... 768 SHADOW WATER A 422
WHILE THEY MURMUR, "AFTER THIS . . . . 776 AGAINST WITCH 30

WHIM

SHALL FOLLOW YOUR HORN AND OBEY YOUR WHIM, ... 9 OISIN 1 99
WOULD NOURISH HIS WHIM. . . . . 310 PEACOCK 6
IT IS MY WHIM! BID SOME ATTENDANT SPRITE . . . . . . 669 ISLE STAT II 3 72
BUT WHY THIS WHIM OF THINE? A STRANGE UNREST, ... 671 ISLE STAT II 3 137
BELOVED, BLAME THE DANAAN WHIM, ... 743 DANAAN QUICK 22
THOUGH THE CHANGE WERE BUT A WHIM! . . . . 775 AGAINST WITCH 17
THOUGH THEIR CHANGE WERE BUT A WHIM! . . . . 775 AGAINST WITCH V 17

WHIMPERING

AND LIONESS, WITH ALL THEIR WHIMPERING CUBS! . . . . . 73 ANASHU VIJAYA 53
WITH THE WHIMPERING DEAD. . . . . 118 CRADLE SONG 4
THE DOORS OF HELL AND BLOW THERE MANY A WHIMPERING GHOST! 147 UNAPPEAS HOST 10
AMONG THE WHIMPERING GHOSTS. MATE THUS. ALREADY? . . . 722 WITCH VIVIEN 68

WHIM'S

HE FOLLOWS WHATEVER WHIM'S MOST DIFFICULT . . . . . . 374 PHASES OF MOON 40

WHIMS

AMONG WHIMS NOT IMPOSSIBLE, AND THOUGH SCARRED, ... 374 PHASES OF MOON 41

WHIMSEY

AND LAUGH OUT THEIR WHIMSEY AND WORK OUT THEIR WILL. . . . 148 INTO TWILIGHT V 12
LAUGH OUT THEIR WHIMSEY AND WORK OUT THEIR WILL. . . . . 148 INTO TWILIGHT V 12

WHINNIED

A SQUIRREL WHINNIED AND A BIRD SCREAMED OUT! . . . . . 278 TWO KINGS 34

WHINNY

TILL THE HORSE GAVE A WHINNY! . . . . 48 OISIN 3 25

WHINNYING

AND HE, WITH THAT LOW WHINNYING SOUND . . . . 318 APPOINTMENT 5

WHIP

WHERE THE DEMONS WHIP THEM WITH WIRES . . . . 61 OISIN 3 198
OR FROM SOME BLOODY WHIP IN THEIR OWN HANDS. . . . . . 375 PHASES OF MOON 68

WHIPS

LONG WHILE, ARE WHIPS OF STEEL." "IS HE SO DREAD?" . . . 35 OISIN 2 V 88
WHIPS TO THE SEA THE COWS AND SWINE." . . . . 82 MAD KING GOLL V 16

WHIRL   SEE DUST-WHIRL

THE WINDS AWAKEN, THE LEAVES WHIRL ROUND, ... 140 HOSTING SIDHE 6
THAT SEEMED TO WHIRL UPON A COMPASS-POINT, ... 489 COOLE PARK 29 21
THAT SEEMED TO WHIRL UPON A COMPASS POINT, ... 489 COOLE PARK 29 V 21
THE SPINNING STARS--THE TOILING SEA--WHIRL ROUND . . . . 665 ISLE STAT II 2 72

WHIRL'D

THE VISION OF A ROCK WHERE LIGHTNINGS WHIRL'D . . . . . 687 TWO TITANS 1

WHIRLED

IN DREARY DANCING PAST US WHIRLED, ... 65 HAPPY SHEPHERD 8
HAD FALLEN AMONG DANCERS, HAD WHIRLED THEM ROUND . . . . 430 NINETEEN 19 52
ON THE SOUL'S JOURNEY. HOW IT IS WHIRLED ABOUT, ... 472 ALL SOUL NIGHT 54

WHIRLING

AND THEN AWAY, AWAY, LIKE WHIRLING FLAMES! . . . . . . 29 OISIN 2 2
AND THICKENED ALL THE WHIRLING AIR. THEN DID . . . . . 46 OISIN 2 V 245A
THE WHIRLING WAYS OF STARS THAT PASS-- . . . . 66 HAPPY SHEPHERD 30

887

WHIRLING   (CONTINUED)
   WITH ALL YOUR WHIRLING HAIR, AND DROP MANY AN AZURE TEAR.   73 ANASHU VIJAYA   46
   WITH ALL YOUR WHIRLING HAIR, AND DROP THROUGH SPACE AN   73 ANASHU VIJAYA V   46
     AZURE TEAR.
   WITH ALL YOUR WHIRLING HAIR, AND DROP TEAR UPON AZURE TEAR.   73 ANASHU VIJAYA V   46
   WITH ALL OUR WHIRLING HAIR, AND DROP MANY AN AZURE TEAR.   73 ANASHU VIJAYA V   46
   A WHIRLING AND A WANDERING FIRE!   83 MAD KING GOLL   28
   A FEVER AND A WHIRLING FIRE!   83 MAD KING GOLL V   28
   THE WHIRLING AND THE WANDERING FIRE!   86 MAD KING GOLL   67
   OUT OF THEIR WHIRLING CARS,   175 ELEMENT POWERS V   16
   WITH EQUAL COURAGE IN THAT WHIRLING ROUT!   186 QUEEN MAEVE   131
   AND FOR NINE DAYS MY MIND WENT WHIRLING ROUND   282 TWO KINGS   127
   DANCED IN THE WHIRLING FOAM AND IN THE DUST,   284 TWO KINGS   167
   THAT HAS GROWN WEARY OF THE WHIRLING DANCE,   285 TWO KINGS V   183
   AND THEY WERE WHIRLING IN A HEAP.   297 THREE BEGGARS   47
   TILL THEY WERE WHIRLING IN A HEAP.   297 THREE BEGGARS V   47
   WHAT SET IT WHIRLING ROUND?   520 HIS BARGAIN   2
   OF THE WHIRLING ZODIAC.   535 CHOSEN   3
   EACH ONE AT GAZE FOR AYE UPON HIS WHIRLING THRONE.   662 ISLE STAT II 1   81
   FOR THEY ARE BUT WHIRLING WIND,   775 AGAINST WITCH   9
WHIRLS
   AMONG HER WILDERING WHIRLS, FORGETTING HIM.   69 SAD SHEPHERD   28
   WITHIN HER WILDERING WHIRLS—FORGETTING HIM.   69 SAD SHEPHERD V   28
   IT WHIRLS INTO THE FOAM. O ANCIENT WORM,   251 SHADOW WATER B   597
   WHIRLS OUT NEW RIGHT AND WRONG,   430 NINETEEN 19   55
   WHIRLS IN THE OLD INSTEAD!   430 NINETEEN 19   56
WHIRLWIND
   THE DARKNESS OF THE WHIRLWIND SHATTERED DEEP.   688 TWO TITANS   58
WHIRR
   AND WINDS BLOWING FROM FLOWERS, AND WHIRR OF FEATHERS   219 WOODS OF COOLE   39
WHISPER
   A WHISPER OF IMPETUOUS FEET,   15 OISIN 1   199
   ERE LONG AN ANSWERING WHISPER FLEW,   15 OISIN 1 V   197
   AND THEN AN ANSWERING WHISPER FLEW   15 OISIN 1 V   197
   GROWN DESOLATE, WHISPER AND SIGH TO EACH OTHER!   26 OISIN 1   403
   GROWN DESOLATE, WHISPER AND SIGH TO EACH OTHER.   27 OISIN 1 V   407
   AND WHISPER, "THE INNUMERABLE REEDS   81 EPHEMERA V   24E
   ALL THAT I SEEK! AND WHISPER IT AS THOUGH   371 EGO DOMINUS   76
   FOR SPRING RICE HAD TO WHISPER IT,   582 ROGER CASEMENT   13
   OR WHISPER THAT A MAN'S A FOOL   635 BLACK TOWER   12
   WHO WANDER AND WHISPER ALONE.   707 FAIRY PEDANT   8
   WHISPER LEST WE TOO MAY SADDEN,   737 IN FIRELIGHT   5
   THE HANDMAIDS LAUGH AND WHISPER IN THE DOOR.   759 SHADOW WATER A   242
WHISPERED
   WHISPERED TO THE SEA WHOSE FLOW   20 OISIN 1 V   298
   AND WHISPERED TO MANKIND.   133 FR GILLIGAN   20
   I WHISPERED, "I AM TOO YOUNG."   268 BROWN PENNY   1
WHISPERER
   WHILE I, FROM THAT REED-THROATED WHISPERER   320 REED WHISPERER   1
WHISPERING   SEE A-WHISPERING
   AND WHISPERING TO HERSELF ENWOUND ME!   9 OISIN 1   108
   AND THEN AN ANSWERING WHISPERING FLEW   15 OISIN 1   197
   HE HAD GONE WHISPERING FORTH WITH CUMBERED HEART,   37 OISIN 2 V   111
   AND HUNG WITH SLIME, AND WHISPERING IN HIS HAIR,   43 OISIN 2   216
   HUNG ROUND WITH SLIME, AND WHISPERING IN HIS HAIR,   43 OISIN 2 V   216
   AND MY OWN WHISPERING WORDS BE COMFORTING,   68 SAD SHEPHERD   23
   AND MINE OWN WHISPERING WORDS BE COMFORTING,   68 SAD SHEPHERD V   23
   AND EVERY WHISPERING DRUID SAID,   82 MAD KING GOLL V   9
   AND EVERY WHISPERING OLD MAN SAID,   82 MAD KING GOLL V   9
   AND WHISPERING IN THEIR EARS   88 STOLEN CHILD   33
   THE COZENING FORTUNE-TELLER THAT COMES WHISPERING,   228 SHADOW WATER B   123
   AND WHISPERING THAT NONE BUT HE SHOULD HEAR.   281 TWO KINGS   110
   SOFT AS THE WHISPERING OF A LONG-LOST FOOTSTEP   699 MOSADA 3   5
   SOFT AS A LONG DEAD FOOTSTEP WHISPERING THROUGH   699 MOSADA 3 V   5
   SOFT AS THE WHISPERING OF A LOST FOOTSTEP   699 MOSADA 3 V   5
   EACH OTHER'S NECKS, AND WHISPERING AS THEY GO,   703 MOSADA 3   120
   WHISPERING ALONG THE SUNNY PATH!   725 LEGEND   18
   THEY ARE GONE, THEY ARE GONE. WHISPERING WERE ENOUGH.   778 SONG DEIRDRE 3   3
WHISPERS
   ALONE WITH OUR OWN WHISPERS AND REPLIES—   702 MOSADA 3   80
   HE WHISPERS TO A SOLDIER, WHO GOES OUT—   711 FERENCZ RENYI   44
WHISTLE
   IS WHAT I CAN WHISTLE ALONE AND ALONE.   551 SONGS REWRIT 1   4
WHISTLED
   I THOUGHT TO HAVE WHISTLED HER DOWN THAT WAY.   551 SONGS REWRIT 1   15
   I WHISTLED AND WHISTLED AND WHISTLED IN VAIN.   551 SONGS REWRIT 1   16
   I WHISTLED AND WHISTLED AND WHISTLED IN VAIN.   551 SONGS REWRIT 1   16
   I WHISTLED AND WHISTLED AND WHISTLED IN VAIN.   551 SONGS REWRIT 1   16
   I CRIED AND WHISTLED BUT VAIN, ALL VAIN.   551 SONGS REWRIT 1 V   16
   BUT THERE I LAY AND I WHISTLED IN VAIN.   551 SONGS REWRIT 1 V   16
WHISTLING
   THAT NESTLES ALONE IN THE WHISTLING WIND,   657 ISLE STAT I 3   68
WHIT
   WE'VE TALKED AND TALKED, AND NOT A WHIT MORE RARE   659 ISLE STAT II 1   21
   SHE CARES NO WHIT FOR EITHER, BUT HAS BLEST   660 ISLE STAT II 1   49
WHITE   SEE FOAM-WHITE SNOW-WHITE MILK-WHITE MOON-WHITE
   AND THE WHITE BODY THAT LAY BY MINE!   3 OISIN 1   10
   BUT DOWN TO HER FEET WHITE VESTURE FLOWED,   3 OISIN 1   25
   AND PEARLY WHITE HIS WELL-GROOMED HAIR.   3 OISIN 1 V 7CC
   DOWN TO HER FEET WHITE VESTURE FLOWED,   3 OISIN 1 V   25
   WHERE I WOULD BE WHEN THE WHITE MOON CLIMBS,   9 OISIN 1   104

WHITE   (CONTINUED)

	PAGE	TITLE		LINE
MOUNT MY WHITE STEED, FOR THE FAIRY STATE	9	OISIN 1	V	103
AND WHEN THE WHITE STEED FELT MY WEIGHT,	9	OISIN 1	V	109
OR ARE YOU PHANTOMS WHITE AS SNOW,	10	OISIN 1		117
OR ARE YE PHANTOMS WHITE AS SNOW,	10	OISIN 1	V	117
MY HUMAN SORROW HER WHITE ARMS WOUND.	11	OISIN 1		138
ALL PEARLY WHITE, SAVE ONE RED EAR;	12	OISIN 1		141
BUT NOW THE MOON LIKE A WHITE ROSE SHONE	12	OISIN 1		152
ON THEIR OWN SELVES IN THE WATERS WHITE;	14	OISIN 1	V	185
THEIR BROWS WERE WHITE AS FRAGRANT MILK,	15	OISIN 1		204
THEIR BROWS WERE WHITE AS THE FRAGRANT MILK	15	OISIN 1	V	204
WHERE WHITE DEWDROPS IN MILLIONS FALL;	16	OISIN 1	V	222
AND, WEEPING OVER THE WHITE STRINGS, HURLED	17	OISIN 1		241
WHITE FLOWERS OF THE FOAM A STAFF OF WOOD	24	OISIN 1	V	366
AND ONCE MORE SADDLED THE WHITE STEED,	25	OISIN 1	V	378
WITH ME IN HER WHITE ARMS A HUNDRED YEARS	30	OISIN 2		17
ROSE IN THE DARKNESS, AND THE WHITE SURF GLEAMED	30	OISIN 2		23
NOR CEASED UNTIL WHITE NIAMH STROKED HIS EARS	30	OISIN 2		26
AND WHEN THE WHITE STEED SAW WHAT BLACKNESS GLEAMED,	30	OISIN 2	V	24
WE MOUNTED ON THE STAIR; THE WHITE STEED TYING,	32	OISIN 2	V	46
WITH BOWED HEAD, TREMBLING WHEN THE WHITE BLADE SHONE,	38	OISIN 2		137
A DEMON'S LEISURE; EYES, FIRST WHITE, NOW BURNED	40	OISIN 2		168
A DEMON'S LEISURE. EYES FIRST WHITE AS SNOW,	40	OISIN 2	V	168
THAT FEED WHITE MOTHS BY SOME DE DANAAN SHRINE;	41	OISIN 2		186
FEEDING WHITE MOTHS AROUND SOME EASTERN SHRINE;	41	OISIN 2	V	186
IMMEDIATE, MOURNFUL, WHITE WITH SUDDEN CARES,	44	OISIN 2	V	229A
AND EACH OF THE HUGE WHITE CREATURES WAS HUGER THAN FOURSCORE MEN;	49	OISIN 3		33
AND EACH OF THE HUGE WHITE CREATURES WAS HUGER THAN FOUR-SCORE MEN;	49	OISIN 3	V	33
AND THE CHIEF OF THE HUGE WHITE CREATURES,	50	OISIN 3		43
AND, MAN OF THE MANY WHITE CROZIERS, A CENTURY THERE I FORGOT	52	OISIN 3		77
AND, MAN OF THE MANY WHITE CROZIERS, A CENTURY THERE I FORGOT	52	OISIN 3		81
. . . WAKING WHITE AS A SHELL	54	OISIN 3		103
O HAD YOU SEEN BEAUTIFUL NIAMH GROW WHITE AS THE WATERS ARE WHITE,	54	OISIN 3		109
O HAD YOU SEEN BEAUTIFUL NIAMH GROW WHITE AS THE WATERS ARE WHITE,	54	OISIN 3		109
I CRIED, "O NIAMH! O WHITE ONE! IF ONLY A TWELVE-HOURED DAY,	55	OISIN 3		113
. . . "WHERE WHITE CLOUDS LIE SPREAD	59	OISIN 3		178
"WHAT DO YOU WEAVE WITH WOOL SO WHITE?"	70	CLOAK BOAT		11
TO THE BIRDS IN THE WHITE OF THE AIR.	92	FATHER OHART		16
IN THE WHITE BORDER OF THE MURMURING SEA;	103	FERGUS DRUID		19
WHO LOVES YOU, NO WHITE ARMS TO WRAP YOU ROUND,	109	CUCHULAIN SEA		59
IN VAIN HER ARMS, IN VAIN HER SOFT WHITE BREAST.	110	CUCHULAIN SEA		74
TALL WANDS OF ALDER AND WHITE QUICKEN WANDS.	111	CUCHULAIN SEA	V	82A
AND WHITE STARS TELL YOUR PRAISE,	113	ROSE OF PEACE		10
THEY HAVE GONE DOWN UNDER THE SAME WHITE STARS,	115	ROSE OF BATTLE		34
ABOVE YOUR WHITE BED,	118	CRADLE SONG	V	2
THE CRUMBLING MOON, THE WHITE STARS IN THE SKY,	120	SORROW OF LOVE	V	10
THE CURD-PALE MOON, THE WHITE STARS IN THE SKY,	120	SORROW OF LOVE	V	10
THE WHITE BIRDS	121	WHITE BIRDS		T
I WOULD THAT WE WERE, MY BELOVED, WHITE BIRDS ON THE FOAM OF THE SEA!	121	WHITE BIRDS		1
O WOULD THAT WE WERE, MY BELOVED, WHITE BIRDS ON THE FOAM OF THE SEA,	121	WHITE BIRDS	V	1
FOR I WOULD WE WERE CHANGED TO WHITE BIRDS	122	WHITE BIRDS		8
WERE WE ONLY WHITE BIRDS, MY BELOVED,	122	WHITE BIRDS		12
WITH WHITE FEET OF ANGELS SEVEN	125	CATHLEEN PARA	V	13
HER WHITE FEET GO GLIMMERING;	125	CATHLEEN PARA	V	14
AND THE WHITE BREAST OF THE DIM SEA	126	GOES FERGUS		11
AND THE WHITE HUSH END ALL BUT THE LOUD BEAT	137	TO SOME I TALK		15
OF THEIR LONG WINGS, THE FLASH OF THEIR WHITE FEET.	137	TO SOME I TALK		16
AND THE WHITE HUSH END ALL THINGS BUT THE BEAT	137	TO SOME I TALK	V	15
FOR GOD GOES BY WITH WHITE FOOTFALL.	139	TO IRELAND		44
FOR GOD GOES BY WITH WHITE FOOT-FALL.	139	TO IRELAND	V	44
AND A YOUNG GIRL WHITE BREAD.	144	HOST OF AIR		20
AND WHEN WHITE MOTHS WERE ON THE WING,	149	WANDER AENGUS		5
AND MY WHITE BREAST ON HIS HE LAID.	151	HEART OF WOMAN	V	4
DO YOU NOT HEAR ME CALLING, WHITE DEER WITH NO HORNS?	153	CHANGE BELOVED		1
THEIR HOOFS HEAVY WITH TUMULT, THEIR EYES GLIMMERING WHITE!	154	BELOVED PEACE		2
I HEAR WHITE BEAUTY SIGHING, TOO,	156	FORGOT BEAUTY		19
WHITE WOMAN THAT PASSION HAS WORN	157	POET BELOVED		3
WHITE WOMAN WITH NUMBERLESS DREAMS,	157	POET BELOVED		7
IT TALKED, ERE THE MORN GREW WHITE,	159	CAP AND BELLS	V	6
IT TALKED BEFORE MORN WAS WHITE,	159	CAP AND BELLS	V	6
AND HURLED IT FROM ITS PLACE BEFORE HIS FOOTSTOOL WHITE,	174	ELEMENT POWERS	V	3
WITH LONG WHITE BODIES CAME OUT OF THE AIR	185	QUEEN MAEVE		118
WHEN THE LONG WARS FOR THE WHITE HORN	189	BAILE AILLINN		14
AND WAVING WHITE WINGS TO AND FRO	197	BAILE AILLINN		184
IN A WHITE BREAKING WAVE; THEY HAD THE LOOK	223	SHADOW WATER B		34
TREMBLING IN THE BLUE HEAVENS LIKE A WHITE FAWN	251	SHADOW WATER B		611
THROUGH THE WHITE THIN BONE OF A HARE	330	BONE OF A HARE		16
A VISIONARY WHITE SEA-BIRD	361	ALF POLLEXFEN		37
A VISIONARY WHITE SEA BIRD	361	ALF POLLEXFEN	V	37
NO RED AND WHITE OF A FACE,	365	HER RACE		6
THAT LOFTY WHITE STAG, LEAP	399	BREAK OF DAY		24
TO WATCH A WHITE GULL TAKE	400	DEMON BEAST		24

889

		PAGE	TITLE	LINE

WHITE   (CONTINUED)
AND THOSE WHITE GLIMMERING FRAGMENTS OF THE MIST SWEEP BY.		426 PHANTOM HATRED		6
AND HOW CAN BODY, LAID IN THAT WHITE RUSH,		441 LEDA AND SWAN		7
ALL THE STRETCHED BODY'S LAID ON THE WHITE RUSH		441 LEDA AND SWAN	V	7
A KIND OLD NUN IN A WHITE HOOD REPLIES:		443 SCHOOL CHILDR		2
INTO THE YOLK AND WHITE OF THE ONE SHELL.		443 SCHOOL CHILDR		16
OF HORSES AND HORSES OF THE SEA, WHITE HORSES.		447 COLONUS PRAISE		32
WITH HER WHITE FINGER. I LED HER HOME ASLEEP		468 HARUN RASHID		158
ANOTHER EMBLEM THERE! THAT STORMY WHITE		490 COOLE BALLYLEE		17
OF RASCALS BLACK AND WHITE		597 MODEL LAUREATE		10
AND THE WAVES ARE LEAPING WHITE,		646 ISLE STAT I 1		27
FLICKERING UNDER THE WHITE MOONSHINE?		646 ISLE STAT I 1		33
WHERE ALL NIGHT LONG THE LONELY MOON, THE WHITE		650 ISLE STAT I 1		126
IN SONG, FROM GOBLIN WATERS SWAYING WHITE,		657 ISLE STAT I 3		51
HE SAT, AND THEN I HEARD THE WHITE LAKE SING,		659 ISLE STAT II 1		15
THE WHITE WAVES WRAP IT IN A SHEET OF FLAME,		662 ISLE STAT II 2		14
A WHITE, DUMB THING OF TEARS; HERE LET IT STAND,		663 ISLE STAT II 2		21
AND ONE ARM POINTING THUS, IN MARBLE WHITE.		663 ISLE STAT II 2		28
WHAT DO YOU WEAVE WITH WOOL SO WHITE?		666 ISLE STAT II 3		11
OF THINE CRY OVER WOLD AND WATER WHITE,		669 ISLE STAT II 3		73
WHERE IN WHITE EXULTATION		672 ISLE STAT II 3		164
A WRIGGLING THING ON THE WHITE LAKE MOVED,		673 ISLE STAT II 3		176
(SWALLOWS WERE FLASHING THEIR WHITE BREASTS ABOVE		690 MOSADA 1		7
AND CALM, ROBED ALL IN RAIMENT MOONY WHITE.		693 MOSADA 1		77
WITH WONDERFUL WHITE SANDS, WHERE NEVER YET		693 MOSADA 1		81
WHITE LILIES, AND HER SONG FLEW FORTH AFAR		693 MOSADA 1		85
WITH WONDERFUL WHITE SAND, WHERE NEVER YET		693 MOSADA 1	V	81
STAY, STAY, OR I WILL HOLD YOUR WHITE ARMS DOWN.		694 MOSADA 1		92
AFAR ALONG THE FLEET WHITE RIVER'S FACE--		702 MOSADA 3		79
WHITE, RENYI SILENT STANDS; THAT MAIDEN SWEET		713 FERENCZ RENYI	V	84
A KID, HELD BY ONE SOFT WHITE EAR FOR TETHER,		715 DWELT SYCAMORE		3
GONE THE STARS AND GONE THE WHITE MOON,		718 PHANTOM SHIP		3
NOW THY GREAT WHITE DOLL TO HOLD--		726 LOVERS QUARREL		15
ROLLS ALONG THE SEA SANDS WHITE.		732 STREET DANCERS		34
ROLLS ALONG THE SEA-SANDS WHITE.		732 STREET DANCERS	V	34
ROUND US THE WHITE ROADS ARE ENDLESS,		737 IN FIRELIGHT		3
UNTO THE WHITE SKIES.		740 EARL PAUL		24
AND NEED NO MORE OF LIFE TILL THE WHITE WINGS		751 SHADOW WATER A		102
WAR-LADEN GALLEYS, AND ARMIES ON WHITE ROADS,		757 SHADOW WATER A		203
WAR LADEN GALLEYS, AND ARMIES ON WHITE ROADS,		757 SHADOW WATER A	V	203
THE HAND THAT WOUNDS. A WHITE BIRD BEATS HIS WINGS		758 SHADOW WATER A	V	232
A WHITE BIRD BEATS HIS WINGS UPON MY FACE.		759 SHADOW WATER A		233
A WHITE BIRD HAS TORN ME WITH HIS SILVER CLAWS,		759 SHADOW WATER A		234
I AM BLIND AND DEAF BECAUSE OF THE WHITE WINGS.		759 SHADOW WATER A		235
THE WHITE FOOL MAKES AT MORNING OUT OF FOAM!		761 SHADOW WATER A		261
HER EYELIDS TREMBLE AND THE WHITE FOAM FADES:		761 SHADOW WATER A		264
TREMBLING IN THE BLUE HEAVENS LIKE A WHITE FAWN		769 SHADOW WATER A		427
A WOMAN'S BEAUTY IS LIKE A WHITE		784 WOMANS BEAUTY		1
FRAIL BIRD, LIKE A WHITE SEA-BIRD ALONE		784 WOMANS BEAUTY		2

WHITEBEARD
| A WHITEBEARD STOOD HUSHED ON THE PATHWAY, | | 59 OISIN 3 | | 173 |

WHITE-HAIRED
| REMEMBERING HOW I HAD STOOD BY WHITE-HAIRED FINN | | 44 OISIN 2 | | 227 |
| REMEMBERING HOW I STOOD BY WHITE-HAIRED FINN | | 44 OISIN 2 | V | 227 |

WHITE-HORNED
| OVER THE WHITE-HORNED BULL AND THE BROWN BULL. | | 182 QUEEN MAEVE | | 58 |

WHITENED   SEE WAVE-WHITENED
WHITENED AFAR WITH SURGE, FAN-FORMED AND WIDE,		31 OISIN 2		28
AND WHEN THE MORNING WHITENED		160 CAP AND BELLS		23
AND AS SOON AS THE MORN HAD WHITENED,		160 CAP AND BELLS	V	23
WHERE HOMES ONCE WHITENED VALE AND MOUNTAIN CREST:		709 FERENCZ RENYI		3

WHITENESS
SHE LIMPS ALONG IN AN AGED WHITENESS:		27 OISIN 1		415
SHE LIMPS ALONG IN AN AGED WHITENESS,		28 OISIN 1	V	423
THE LITTLE WAVES THAT WALKED IN EVENING WHITENESS,		81 EPHEMERA	V	24C
OF HER UNBLEMISHED LINEAMENTS, A WHITENESS WITH NO STAIN,		353 HIS PHOENIX		3

WHITENING
WHITENING THE SURGE AFAR, FAN-FORMED AND WIDE,		31 OISIN 2	V	28
SCARCE LEFT A WHITENING FEATHER, GREY AND SERE:		34 OISIN 2	V	76A
WITH HEAVY WHITENING WINGS, AND A HEART FALLEN COLD!		147 UNAPPEAS HOST		4
BOWS THE BEDOUIN'S WHITENING HAIR--		733 STREET DANCERS		45

WHITER
WHOSE LONG WOOL WHITER THAN SEA-FROTH FLOWS,		8 OISIN 1		90
WHOSE LONG WOOL WHITER THAN SEA FROTH FLOWS,		8 OISIN 1	V	90
. . . FOR WHITER THAN NEW-WASHED FLEECE		47 OISIN 3		11
. . . LONG WARLESS, GROWN WHITER THAN CURDS.		49 OISIN 3		36
. . . LONG-WARLESS, GROWN WHITER THAN CURDS.		49 OISIN 3	V	36
WHITER THAN CURDS, ITS EYES THE TINT OF THE SEA.		277 TWO KINGS		7
YET WHITER BEARD HAVE YOU THAN MERLIN HAD.		721 WITCH VIVIEN		30

WHITES
| WILD FLAMES OF RED AND CREAMY WHITES, | | 18 OISIN 1 | V | 255 |

WHITEST
| I WONDER WHICH IS WHITEST, THEY OR THOU. | | 700 MOSADA 3 | | 45 |

WHITETHORN
| AT SOME OLD WINDING WHITETHORN ROOT | | 342 SHEP GOATHERD | | 101 |

WHITHER
AND WHITHER THE WISE HEART KNOWS!		168 BLESSED		34
WHITHER HER FOOTSTEPS GO.		175 ELEMENT POWERS		18
AND WHITHER, UNCOUTH HUNTER? WHY SO FAST?		651 ISLE STAT I 2		1
MY WORDS WERE ALL: "O WHITHER, WHITHER, WHITHER		669 ISLE STAT II 3		87
MY WORDS WERE ALL: "O WHITHER, WHITHER, WHITHER		669 ISLE STAT II 3		87

WHITHER   (CONTINUED)
    MY WORDS WERE ALL; "O WHITHER, WHITHER, WHITHER . . . .   669 ISLE STAT II 3   87
    BUT FAITHFUL LOVERS. WHITHER HAVE YOU COME, ...   763 SHADOW WATER A V 309
WHIZZED
    LONG ERE AN ARROW WHIZZED OR SWORD LEFT SHEATH . . . .   650 ISLE STAT I 1   135
WHOLE
    MAY SLEEP IN THE END WITH THE WHOLE OF HIS FATE DONE, . .   28 OISIN 1   V 423F
    FROM THE WHOLE SEVEN SEAS, THOSE TOWERS SET . . . . .   38 OISIN 2   V 131
    . . . AND THE WHOLE OF THE WORLD WAS ONE. . . . . . .   48 OISIN 3   24
    WERE THE MEMORIES OF THE WHOLE OF MY SORROW . . . . .   52 OISIN 3   71
    . . . AND THE MEMORIES OF THE WHOLE OF MY MIRTH, ...   52 OISIN 3   71
    THE WHOLE OF THE LONG DAY. . . . .   94 MOLL MAGEE   8
    THIS WHOLE DAY HAVE I FOLLOWED IN THE ROCKS, ...   102 FERGUS DRUID   1
    THE WHOLE DAY HAVE I FOLLOWED IN THE ROCKS, ...   102 FERGUS DRUID V 1
    AND THE WHOLE WORLD WEIGHS DOWN UPON MY HEART-- . . . .   104 FERGUS DRUID V 38A
    AND WITH YOU CAME THE WHOLE OF THE WORLD'S TEARS, . . .   120 SORROW OF LOVE V 6
    DRAGONS WITH EYES OF RUBY. THE WHOLE SHIP . . . . .   248 SHADOW WATER B   535
    CRIED OUT THE WHOLE NIGHT LONG, ...   254 HIS DREAM   16
    HEARING THE WHOLE EARTH CHANGE ITS TUNE, ...   266 GALWAY RACES   12
    THOUGH FLAME HAD BURNED THE WHOLE . . . .   267 FRIEND ILLNESS   4
    "IF HE BE LIVING STILL THE WHOLE WORLD'S MINE, ...   280 TWO KINGS   V 85
    THEY MAULED AND BIT THE WHOLE NIGHT THROUGH; . . . . .   297 THREE BEGGARS   48
    OUT-SCREAMS THE WHOLE SHELF! "ALTHOUGH . . . . . .   319 DOLLS   7
    JUST TRUTH ENOUGH TO SHOW THAT HIS WHOLE LIFE . . . .   373 PHASES OF MOON 22
    COULD ROUSE MY WHOLE NATURE. . . . .   400 DEMON BEAST   32
    TILL MAN MADE UP THE WHOLE, ...   415 TOWER   149
    THAT WE MIGHT MAKE IT WHOLE; . . . .   457 SUMMER SPRING   8
    WHILE OUR GROSS PALATES DRINK FROM THE WHOLE WINE, . . .   471 ALL SOUL NIGHT 10
    HAD SO LIT UP THE WHOLE . . . .   472 ALL SOUL NIGHT 37
    NO LIVING MAN CAN DRINK FROM THE WHOLE WINE. . . . .   474 ALL SOUL NIGHT 85
    THAT CANNOT TAKE THE WHOLE . . . .   510 JANE JUDGMENT   3
    FOR NOTHING CAN BE SOLE OR WHOLE . . . .   513 JANE TALK BISH 17
    NOR STRAINING JOY, BUT WHOLE IS JOINED TO WHOLE; . . .   555 RIBH AT TOMB   14
    NOR STRAINING JOY, BUT WHOLE IS JOINED TO WHOLE; . . .   555 RIBH AT TOMB   14
    YET KEEP HIS SUBSTANCE WHOLE. . . . .   573 LADYS 2ND SONG 13
    NOR THINK THAT BODY IS THE WHOLE, ...   573 LADYS 3RD SONG   4
    FOR I CAN PUT THE WHOLE LOT DOWN, AND ALL I HAVE TO SAY   593 PILGRIM   24
    THE WHOLE WORLD'S SADLY TALKING TO ITSELF. . . . . .   652 ISLE STAT I 2   12
    YON EAGER LARK, THAT FILLS WITH SONG THE WHOLE . . . .   652 ISLE STAT I 2   18
    I HEAR THE WHOLE SKY'S SORROW IN ONE VOICE. . . . .   652 ISLE STAT I 2   22
    "AND CUT NO WOOD THE WHOLE DAY LONG, ...   731 PRIEST FAIRY   81
    AND THEN THE WHOLE WORLD'S TROUBLE WEEPS WITH YOU. . . .   738 YOU ARE SAD   12
    I'D LET THE WHOLE WORLD GO; . . . .   782 HEART FRIGHT   9
WHOLE-MAD
    HALF-DRUNK OR WHOLE-MAD SOLDIERY . . . .   791 REPRISALS   15
WHOLESOME
    OLD WHOLESOME GOBAN HAD NO SAY; . . . .   271 GREY ROCK   10
    WHAT WHOLESOME SUN HAS RIPENED IS WHOLESOME FOOD TO EAT,   442 BLACK CENTAUR   5
    WHAT WHOLESOME SUN HAS RIPENED IS WHOLESOME FOOD TO EAT,   442 BLACK CENTAUR   5
    ALL THEIR WHOLESOME STRENGTH. . . . .   505 RESULT THOUGHT 12
WHOLLY
    THE SAD, SAD THOUGHT HAS GONE FROM ME NOW WHOLLY; . . .   72 ANASHU VIJAYA   19
    COULD WE BUT GIVE US WHOLLY TO THE DREAMS, ...   230 SHADOW WATER B 178
    NOW THEIR SONGS ARE MOURNFUL WHOLLY . . . . . .   667 ISLE STAT II 3   32
WHORL
    TO ROUND THAT SHELL'S ELABORATE WHORL, ...   509 JANE REPROVED   8
WICK
    AND LEAVE NO SMOKING WICK BEHIND, ...   306 HOUR DAWN   97
    I BADE, BECAUSE THE WICK AND OIL ARE SPENT . . . . .   333 LIVING BEAUTY   1
    THE WICK OF YOUTH BEING BURNED AND THE OIL SPENT, . . .   334 LIVING BEAUTY V 3
    WHEN OIL AND WICK ARE BURNED IN ONE; . . . . . .   388 SOLOMON WITCH   30
    WHAT HAS TURNED TO SMOKING WICK . . . .   529 TOM LUNATIC   5
WICKED
    AND THINGS THAT HAVE GROWN SAD ARE WICKED, ...   20 OISIN 1   301
    EVERYTHING THAT'S SAD IS WICKED-- . . . .   20 OISIN 1   V 301
    WISE BIDDY EARLY CALLED THE WICKED WOOD; . . . . .   218 WOODS OF COOLE 15
    YOU HAVE A DRUID CRAFT OF WICKED SOUND . . . . . .   237 SHADOW WATER B 342
    YOU HAVE A DRUID CRAFT, WICKED SOUND . . . .   237 SHADOW WATER B V 342
    THROUGH WICKED SPELLS. THAT IS NOT ALL THE TALE, . . .   242 SHADOW WATER B 408
    TO SHAKE THEIR WICKED SIDES AT YOUTH . . . . . .   262 STUDENTS AGIT   3
    HER SPEECH A WICKED TALE THAT WE MAY VIE WITH HER, . . .   362 HER COURTESY   6
    THE WILD OLD WICKED MAN . . . .   587 OLD WICKED MAN   T
    SAID THAT WILD OLD WICKED MAN . . . .   587 OLD WICKED MAN   3
    HOW SINFULLY THE WICKED SCOFF!" . . . .   725 LEGEND   22
    THE WICKED HAWTHORN TREE . . . .   788 HAWTHORN TREE V T
    SAID THE WICKED, CROOKED, HAWTHORN TREE; . . . . .   788 HAWTHORN TREE   6
    SAID THE WICKED, CROOKED, HAWTHORN TREE. . . . . .   788 HAWTHORN TREE   14
WICKS
    THAT SAW THE WICKS GROW YELLOW IN THE DAWN; . . . .   352 PEOPLE   18
WIDE   SEE WORLD-WIDE
    WHITENED AFAR WITH SURGE, FAN-FORMED AND WIDE, ...   31 OISIN 2   28
    WHITENING THE SURGE AFAR, FAN-FORMED AND WIDE, ...   31 OISIN 2   V 28
    I FOUND, DROPPING SEA-FOAM ON THE WIDE STAIR, ...   43 OISIN 2   215
    I FOUND, DROPPING SEA FOAM ON THE WIDE STAIR, ...   43 OISIN 2   V 215
    THUNDERING, AND THE WIDE USELESS WATERS FRAY . . . .   45 OISIN 2   V 238
    NOW IN A PLACE OF STAR-FIRE, AND NOW IN A SHADOW-PLACE   49 OISIN 3   42
        WIDE;
    NOW IN A PLACE OF STAR-FIRE, AND NOW IN A SHADOW PLACE   49 OISIN 3   V 42
        WIDE;
    OF WARS WITH THE WIDE WORLD . . . .   50 OISIN 3   55
    . . . ON THE BURNING STONES OF WIDE HELL, ...   61 OISIN 3   198

WIDE   (CONTINUED)
```
    IS BUT A SLIDING DROP OF RAIN BETWEEN HIS PETALS WIDE. . .      76 INDIAN ON GOD       12
    IS BUT A SLIDING DROP OF RAIN WITHIN HIS PETALS WIDE."  . .     76 INDIAN ON GOD   V   12
    WHEN, OPENIN' WIDE HIS DOOR,  . . . . . . . . . . .            96 MOLL MAGEE          50
    WHEN THE FLAMING LUTE-THRONGED ANGELIC DOOR IS WIDE:   . .     172 TRAV PASSION         1
    AND SHOOK HIM WIDE AWAKE, AND BID HIM SAY  . . . . . .        182 QUEEN MAEVE         50
    SPEAK IT, THAT I MAY SEND THROUGH THE WIDE WORLD . . . .      281 TWO KINGS           97
    "YOU THAT HAVE WANDERED FAR AND WIDE . . . . . . . .         295 THREE BEGGARS       11
    "YOU HAVE WANDERED FAR AND WIDE,  . . . . . . . . .          295 THREE BEGGARS   V   11
    AND THEN AT LAST BEING WIDE AWAKE  . . . . . . . . .         304 HOUR DAWN       V   40
    SET CARPENTERS TO WORK ON NO WIDE TABLE,  . . . . . .        340 SHEP GOATHERD       50
    WERE I TO TRAVEL FAR AND WIDE  . . . . . . . . . . .         398 BREAK OF DAY         8
    PLUNGES TOWARDS NOTHING, ARMS AND FINGERS SPREADING WIDE     426 PHANTOM HATRED      13
    THEY ARE SPREAD WIDE THAT EACH . . . . . . . . . .          488 CRAZED MOON         17
    THEY ATE SPREAD WIDE THAT EACH . . . . . . . . . .          488 CRAZED MOON     V   17
    YOU ASK WHAT I HAVE FOUND, AND FAR AND WIDE I GO:  . . .     580 CURSE CROMWELL       1
    THAT CRIED IT FAR AND WIDE,  . . . . . . . . . . .          582 ROGER CASEMENT      18
    AND WIDE AWAKE KNOW THAT THE HUNT IS ON:  . . . . . .        622 HOUND VOICE         17
    OF THIS WIDE VALE, EMBOSOMED IN THE AIR,  . . . . . .        652 ISLE STAT I 2       19
    BUT WIDE AWAKE HIS TWO EYES WERE.  . . . . . . . .          655 ISLE STAT I 3        7
    LIVING, WIDE WINGED, ON THE WATERS FLOAT.  . . . . .         657 ISLE STAT I 3       54
    AND LOUDLY TWICE THE LIVING WINGS FLAPT WIDE,  . . . . .     659 ISLE STAT II 1      12
    OF THE WIDE WOODS.  AND THE DEEP EARTH GATHERED THEM.  .     660 ISLE STAT II 1      33
    ALL THINGS ARE QUIET IN THE EVE'S WIDE EYE.  . . . . .       662 ISLE STAT II 2       6
    AS THOUGH SHE WHOM YOU FEAR HAD CROSSED THE WIDE . .        669 ISLE STAT II 3      77
    THEN HE SHOUTED, "OPEN WIDE . . . . . . . . . . .           697 MOSADA 2            24
    AND HE SHOUTED OPEN WIDE . . . . . . . . . . . .            697 MOSADA 2        V   24
    THE STRANGER SHOUTED, "OPEN WIDE . . . . . . . . .          697 MOSADA 2        V   24
    OF A WIDE WOOD'S LEAFY LEISURE,  . . . . . . . . .          731 STREET DANCERS      11
    ALTHOUGH WIDE WORLD HOLD NOT . . . . . . . . . .            786 YOUR HEART          16
WIDE-EYED
    AND NEVER ANY MORE THE WIDE-EYED BANDS . . . . . .          674 ISLE STAT II 3     218
WIDENING
    TURNING AND TURNING IN THE WIDENING GYRE  . . . . .         401 SECOND COMING        1
WIDE-OPEN
    AND HAVING SUCH WIDE-OPEN, SHINING EYES.  . . . . .         231 SHADOW WATER B     200
WIDE-WATERING
    AND STREAMS, WIDE-WATERING, SALMON-SHOALED,  . . . .         81 MAD KING GOLL   V    3
WIDTH
    AND SHAKES O'ER THE WIDTH OF THE SEA-WORLD BORDER  . . .     28 OISIN 1         V 423C
WIFE
    AND NIAMH BE WITH YOU FOR A WIFE."  . . . . . . . .           9 OISIN 1            101
    AND I BE WITH THEE AS THY WIFE."  . . . . . . . .            9 OISIN 1         V  101
    THE GENTLE NIAMH WAS MY WIFE:  . . . . . . . . .            24 OISIN 1            357
    THE SICK MAN'S WIFE OPENED THE DOOR:  . . . . . .          133 FR GILLIGAN         31
    THAT EDAIN, MIDHIR'S WIFE, HAD WOVE  . . . . . . .         195 BAILE AILLINN      142
    WHEN MIDHIR'S WIFE HAD CHANGED HER TO A FLY,  . . .        220 HARP OF AENGUS      10
    OF THAT MORE POWERFUL LIFE?  HIS WIFE KNOWS BETTER.  .     230 SHADOW WATER B     172
    RAYMOND LULLY AND HIS WIFE PERNELLA  . . . . . . .         253 HIS DREAM       V    T
    PALE-FACED, ALONE UPON A BENCH, HIS WIFE  . . . . .        279 TWO KINGS       V   61
    THAT I MAY CLAIM YOU AS MY WIFE AGAIN."  . . . . .         284 TWO KINGS          170
    YET ANSWERED HIM, "I AM KING EOCHAID'S WIFE  . . . .       284 TWO KINGS          173
    "AND GET A COMFORTABLE WIFE AND HOUSE  . . . . . .         299 BEGGAR CRIED         5
    THE DOLL-MAKER'S WIFE IS AWARE . . . . . . . . .           319 DOLLS               14
    EVEN BEFORE HIS CHILDREN AND HIS WIFE?  . . . . . .        340 SHEP GOATHERD       34
    MAY BE A QUIET THOUGHT TO WIFE AND MOTHER,  . . . .        343 SHEP GOATHERD      118
    BY HIS WIFE ELIZABETH  . . . . . . . . . . . .             360 ALF POLLEXFEN        4
    DUTIFUL HUSBAND, HONEST WIFE BY TURN,  . . . . . .         376 PHASES OF MOON      99
    RESTORED THIS TOWER FOR MY WIFE GEORGE:  . . . . .         406 CARVED STONE         4
    A SMALL OLD HOUSE, WIFE, DAUGHTER, SON,  . . . . .         577 WHAT THEN           12
    A HUSBAND THAT HAD SOLD HIS WIFE . . . . . . . .           587 PARNELLITES         27
    A HUSBAND WHO HAD SOLD HIS WIFE  . . . . . . . .           587 PARNELLITES     V   27
    HIS WIFE HE FOUND AND THE RICH MAN . . . . . . .           595 COLONEL MARTIN      43
    I AM TO BE YOUR WIFE.  A VILLAGE HIGH  . . . . . .         713 FERENCZ RENYI       97
    I WAS TO BE YOUR WIFE.  A VILLAGE HIGH  . . . . . .        713 FERENCZ RENYI   V   97
    THEN EACH WIFE AND MAID AND MOTHER CALLS BY NAME           719 PHANTOM SHIP        24
        SOME DROWNED ONE.
    WHEN MIDHER'S WIFE HAD CHANGED HER TO A FLY  . . . .       763 SHADOW WATER A     305
    "GIVE ME YOUR WIFE," SAID HE,  . . . . . . . . .           779 GOING THE ROAD       5
WIFELESS
    "O WHAT'S A WIFELESS MAN?" SAID HE,  . . . . . . .         594 COLONEL MARTIN       5
WIGHT
    TO THE GREEN ISLE OF WIGHT . . . . . . . . . .             740 EARL PAUL           10
WILD
    ACROSS THE GLOSSY SEA."  "OH, WILD . . . . . . .             6 OISIN 1         V   58
    OVER THE GLOSSY SEA."  "O, WILD  . . . . . . . .             6 OISIN 1         V   58
    WILD FLAMES OF RED AND GOLD AND BLUE,  . . . . . .          18 OISIN 1            252
    WILD FLAMES OF RED AND CREAMY WHITES,  . . . . . .          18 OISIN 1         V  255
    AND IN A WILD AND SUDDEN DANCE . . . . . . . . .            20 OISIN 1            290
    OR THE WILD GREY OSPREY SORROW."  . . . . . . . .           20 OISIN 1         V  303
    OR THE WILD GREY OSPREY SORROW."  . . . . . . . .           21 OISIN 1         V  319
    OR FEAR THE WILD GREY OSPREY SORROW."  . . . . . .          23 OISIN 1         V  342
    "BUT NEVER WITH US WHERE THE WILD FOWL CHASES  . . .        27 OISIN 1         V  408
    AND CHASE THE WILD BEE HOMEWARD TO HIS HIVE  . . . .        32 OISIN 2         V  50D
    THE WILD FOWL OF THE AIR INCREASED:  . . . . . . .          82 MAD KING GOLL        8
    THE HORNS AND SHIELDS AND WILD SWAN'S PINIONS:  . . .       82 MAD KING GOLL   V    5
    THE WILD BOAR KNOWS ME, BY ONE EAR . . . . . . .           84 MAD KING GOLL   V   45
    TO THE WATERS AND THE WILD . . . . . . . . . .             87 STOLEN CHILD        10
    TO THE WATERS AND THE WILD . . . . . . . . . .             87 STOLEN CHILD        25
    TO THE WOODS AND WATERS WILD . . . . . . . . .             87 STOLEN CHILD    V  REF
    TO THE WATERS AND THE WILD . . . . . . . . . .             88 STOLEN CHILD        39
```

892

WILD (CONTINUED)
   TO THE WATERS AND THE WILD . . . .   88 STOLEN CHILD   51
   A WILD AND FOOLISH LABOURER IS A KING . . . . .   103 FERGUS DRUID   V   27
   THE WILD DUCK AND THE DRAKE . . . .   143 HOST OF AIR   2
   THOUGH YOU HAVE THE WILL OF THE WILD BIRDS, . . 176 BELOVED DEAD   8
   WHEN NIGHT WAS AT ITS DEEPEST, A WILD GOOSE . . 181 QUEEN MAEVE   36
   WHERE WILD BEES HIVE ON THE GREAT PLAIN. . . . . 194 BAILE AILLINN   123
   QUIET'S WILD HEART, LIKE DAILY MEAT; . . . . . . 196 BAILE AILLINN   178
   BUT A WILD APPLE HID THE GRASS . . . .   197 BAILE AILLINN   189
   WANDERS LAUGHING AND EATING HER WILD HEART . . . 198 SEVEN WOODS   11
   MADE OUT OF A WILD THOUGHT, IS IN MY MARROW. . . 199 ARROW   2
   WHEN ALL THE WILD SUMMER WAS IN HER GAZE." . .   200 FOLLY COMFORT   12
   GATHERS THE WILD DUCK FROM THE WINTER DAWN; . . 217 WOODS OF COOLE   3
   DIM PAIRC-NA-CARRAIG, WHERE THE WILD BEES FLING   217 WOODS OF COOLE   9
   BECAUSE HER HANDS HAD BEEN MADE WILD BY LOVE. . . 219 HARP OF AENGUS   9
   AS THAT WILD AENGUS. LONG BEFORE HER DAY . . .   224 SHADOW WATER B   47
   AND IF SHE HEAR HIM MUTTER OF WILD RIDERS, . . . 230 SHADOW WATER B   175
   SHE WILL BE LIKE A WILD CAT; FOR THESE QUEENS .   232 SHADOW WATER B   233
   UPON HIS SHOULDERS. YOU'VE NOTHING BUT WILD WORDS, 235 SHADOW WATER B   300
   BUT WHERE'S THE WILD DOG THAT HAS PRAISED HIS FLEAS? 262 TO A POET   V   4
   TO FIND IF HEARTS BE WILD AND WISE, ...   263 MASK   4
   ITS FLESH BEING WILD, AND IT AGAIN . . . . . .   266 GALWAY RACES   13
   FLESH WILD AGAIN, AND IT AGAIN . . . .   266 GALWAY RACES   V   13
   AND AFTER, WHEN HER BLOOD RAN WILD, ...   272 GREY ROCK   44
   WAS IT FOR THIS THE WILD GEESE SPREAD . . . . .   290 SEPTEMBER 1913   17
   SO WILD THAT EVERY CASUAL THOUGHT OF THAT AND THIS . 316 COLD HEAVEN   4
   THE WILD SWANS AT COOLE . . . .   322 SWANS AT COOLE   T
   THAT GOLDEN KING AND THAT WILD LADY . . . . . .   332 ROUND TOWER   19
   WE CANNOT PAY ITS TRIBUTE OF WILD TEARS, ... 334 LIVING BEAUTY   10
   WHEN THE WILD THOUGHT, ...   336 YOUNG GIRL   7
   SEED-PODS AND FLOWERS THAT ARE NOT ALL WILD POPPY. . 342 SHEP GOATHERD   88
   SEED PODS AND FLOWERS THAT ARE NOT ALL WILD POPPY. . 342 SHEP GOATHERD V   88
   ALL THE WILD WITCHES, THOSE MOST NOBLE LADIES, . . 343 DEJECTION   4
   THE SCULLION GONE WILD." . . . .   349 HAWK   6
   AND WHO CAN SAY BUT SOME YOUNG BELLE MAY WALK AND TALK 354 HIS PHOENIX   26
      MEN WILD
   THERE'LL BE THAT CROWD TO MAKE MEN WILD THROUGH ALL THE 354 HIS PHOENIX V 25
      CENTURIES,
   AND MAY BE THERE'LL BE SOME YOUNG BELLE WALK OUT TO MAKE 354 HIS PHOENIX V 26
      MEN WILD
   AND MAYBE THERE'LL BE SOME YOUNG BELLE WALK OUT TO MAKE 354 HIS PHOENIX V 26
      MEN WILD
   THAT WOMEN LAUGHING, OR TIMID OR WILD, ... 358 PRESENCES   4
   FANTASTICAL AND WILD . . . .   364 END OF DAY   3
   "LAST NIGHT, WHERE UNDER THE WILD MOON . . . . . 387 SOLOMON WITCH   2
   ON LIMBS THAT HAD RUN WILD. . . . .   394 EASTER 1916   64
   COLD STONE AND WATER. I GREW WILD, ...   399 BREAK OF DAY   14
   AND SO WARM HER WILD NEST. . . . .   415 TOWER   172
   CONSIDERING WHAT WILD INFANCY . . . .   440 WISDOM   19
   AND THEREUPON MY HEART IS DRIVEN WILD; . . . .   444 SCHOOL CHILDR   23
   . . . AND THE WILD BIRD MATE IN THE WILD." . .   450 OWEN AHERNE   16
   . . . AND THE WILD BIRD MATE IN THE WILD." . .   450 OWEN AHERNE   16
   O LET HER CHOOSE A YOUNG MAN NOW AND ALL FOR HIS 450 OWEN AHERNE   24
      WILD SAKE."
   SHE THAT HAS BEEN WILD . . . .   456 FRIENDS YOUTH   10
   BUT THE WILD BEDOUIN. THOUGH I APPROVE . . . .   462 HARUN RASHID   22
   THE WILD STAG AND THE DOE; THAT MOUTH TO MOUTH   465 HARUN RASHID   101
   WILD WITH DIVINITY, ...   472 ALL SOUL NIGHT   36
   I HAD WILD JACK FOR A LOVER; . . . .   512 JANE ON GOD   19
   AS DID THAT WILD TRISTRAM KNOW . . . .   522 LULLABY   8
   BY THAT GREAT GLORY DRIVEN WILD. . . . .   540 FROM ANTIGONE   13
   MARINERS, WILD HARVESTERS; . . . .   540 FROM ANTIGONE   V   5
   THAT SEEMED BUT A WILD WENCHING MAN; . . . . . . 550 SEVERED HEAD   16
   THE WILD OLD WICKED MAN . . . .   587 OLD WICKED MAN   T
   SAID THAT WILD OLD WICKED MAN . . . .   587 OLD WICKED MAN   3
   THEN SAID SHE TO THAT WILD OLD MAN, ...   588 OLD WICKED MAN   19
   BUT A WILD OLD MAN IN THE LIGHT, ...   589 OLD WICKED MAN   38
   THAT CONSTITUTE THE WILD, ...   601 THOSE IMAGES   10
   ALL THAT IS NOT ITSELF! I HAD GROWN WILD . . .   619 BRONZE HEAD   20
   MALACHI STILT-JACK AM I, WHATEVER I LEARNED HAS RUN WILD, 623 HIGH TALK   9
   OH, CEASE YOUR SINGING! WILD AND SHRILL AND LOUD, . . 648 ISLE STAT I 1   99
   CURVING BENEATH THE PROW; AS SOME WILD DRAKE . . 659 ISLE STAT II 1   16
   ASIDE!--THE WILD HORNS TOLD ALMINTOR'S END, . .   665 ISLE STAT II 2   68
   FOR SUCH A CALL. LET THE WILD WORD BE CRIED . .   669 ISLE STAT II 3   76
   WILD CRIES, GROWN SWEET WITH LULLS AND LINGERINGS LONG. 674 ISLE STAT II 3 222
   WILD INDOLENCE AND MUSIC HAVE NO DATE. . . . . . 686 LIFE   20
   WILD WISDOMS OF SPIRIT AND TONGUE. . . . . . .   708 FAIRY PEDANT   27
   WILD SPIRITS OF WISDOM AND TONGUE. . . . . . .   708 FAIRY PEDANT   V   27
   WILD BEES' HONEY LAID FOR THEE." . . . .   730 PRIEST FAIRY   56
   WILD INDOLENCE AND MUSIC HAVE NO DATE, ... 735 QUATRAIN APHOR   18
   BECAUSE HER HANDS HAD BEEN MADE WILD BY LOVE; . . 762 SHADOW WATER A   304
   THOSE WILD HANDS THAT HAVE EMBRACED . . . . . .   776 AGAINST WITCH   32
   MY HEART RAN WILD WHEN IT HEARD . . . .   783 GREY ROUND   21
WILDER
   ITS TERROR GROWING WILDER AT EVERY FOOT-FALL, . . 279 TWO KINGS   V   45D
   ITS TERROR GROWING WILDER AT EVERY FOOTFALL, . . 279 TWO KINGS   V   45D
   AND THE MOON IS WILDER EVERY MINUTE. . . . . .   389 SOLOMON WITCH   43
WILDERING
   AMONG HER WILDERING WHIRLS, FORGETTING HIM. . .   69 SAD SHEPHERD   28
   WITHIN HER WILDERING WHIRLS--FORGETTING HIM. . .   69 SAD SHEPHERD   V   28

893

	PAGE	TITLE	LINE

WILDERNESS
O BEAST OF THE WILDERNESS, BIRD OF THE AIR, ... 177 PAST GREATNESS 11
TILL THE WILDERNESS CRIED ALOUD, ... 259 UNWORTH PRAISE 8
AMID THE ELABORATE WILDERNESS OF THE AIR. . . . . . . 278 TWO KINGS 31
INTO THE SECRET WILDERNESS OF THEIR LOVE. . . . . . . 778 SONG DEIRDRE 3 4
HE HAD FAMISHED IN A WILDERNESS. . . . . 789 SINGING HEAD 1

WILDEST
LAUGHING GOES IN WILDEST MOOD, ... 732 STREET DANCERS 41

WILDLY
OUR MARRIED VOICES WILDLY TROLLED. . . . . 85 MAD KING GOLL 59
OUR MARRIED VOICE WILDLY TROLLED. . . . . 85 MAD KING GOLL V 59
HOW COULD SHE MATE WITH FIFTY YEARS THAT WAS SO WILDLY 450 OWEN AHERNE 15
   BRED?

WILDNESS
WITH ALL YOUTH'S LONELY WILDNESS STIRRED, ... 397 POLIT PRISONER 16
THAT IMAGE CAN BRING WILDNESS, BRING A RAGE . . . . . 431 NINETEEN 19 80
AND I REMEMBER WILDNESS LOST . . . . 453 DEATH OF HARE 9
HIS WILDNESS . . . . 458 HIS WILDNESS T
I SAW THE WILDNESS IN HER AND I THOUGHT . . . . . . 619 BRONZE HEAD 16

WILDS
THE DEMONS OF THE WILDS AND WINDS FOR FRIGHT . . . . . 34 OISIN 2 V 81B

WILD-STRAWBERRY
AND YELLOW THE WET WILD-STRAWBERRY LEAVES. . . . . . 79 FALLING LEAVES 4

WILFUL
TEASING EVERY WILFUL MAID. . . . . 727 LOVERS QUARREL 28

WILL   SEE GOOD-WILL
AND BID THEM WANDER OBEYING YOUR WILL, ... 141 EVERLAST VOICE 3
AND RIVER AND STREAM WORK OUT THEIR WILL. . . . . . 148 INTO TWILIGHT 12
AND LAUGH OUT THEIR WHIMSEY AND WORK OUT THEIR WILL. . . 148 INTO TWILIGHT V 12
LAUGH OUT THEIR WHIMSEY AND WORK OUT THEIR WILL. . . . 148 INTO TWILIGHT V 12
AND THE CHANGING MOON WORK OUT THEIR WILL. . . . . . 148 INTO TWILIGHT V 12
THOUGH YOU HAVE THE WILL OF THE WILD BIRDS, ... 176 BELOVED DEAD 8
QUEEN OF HIGH CRUACHAN." "I OBEY YOUR WILL . . . . . 184 QUEEN MAEVE 99
WITH SAILORS THAT WERE SWORN TO DO YOUR WILL, ... 236 SHADOW WATER B 308
I'D DO YOUR WILL, BUT THEY ARE TOO HIGH--TOO HIGH. . . . 250 SHADOW WATER B 577
AND WHEN I HAD GOT MY WILL AND DRAWN YOU HERE, ... 284 TWO KINGS 158
THAT HE MIGHT LEARN THE SHEPHERDS' WILL. . . . . . . 288 TO WEALTHY MAN 19
WHO HAVE FAILED, BEING WEAK OF WILL, ... 298 THREE HERMITS 18
NOR THE TAME WILL, NOR TIMID BRAIN, ... 318 APPOINTMENT 8
I MOURN FOR THAT MOST LONELY THING; AND YET GOD'S WILL 354 HIS PHOENIX 31
   BE DONE!
OR SICKNESS BREAK HER WILL . . . . 365 HER RACE 10
WHEN HAD I MY OWN WILL? . . . . 382 VISION ROBART 7
IN IGNORANT GOOD WILL, ... 392 EASTER 1916 V 18
HAD IGNORANT GOOD WILL; . . . . 392 EASTER 1916 V 19
AND THAT ITS OWN SWEET WILL IS HEAVEN'S WILL; . . . . 405 FOR DAUGHTER 69
AND THAT ITS OWN SWEET WILL IS HEAVEN'S WILL; . . . . 405 FOR DAUGHTER 69
IT IS TIME THAT I WROTE MY WILL; . . . . 414 TOWER 121
ACCOMPLISHED HIS PREDESTINED WILL. . . . . 522 LULLABY 16
I DID THE DRAGON'S WILL UNTIL YOU CAME . . . . . . 533 HER TRIUMPH 1
GIVES FORTH. HE, THE ETERNAL, WORKS HIS WILL. . . . . 689 NETTLESHIP 16
I HERE ARREST THEE. IT WAS ALLAH'S WILL. . . . . . 694 MOSADA 1 105
I HERE ARREST THEE. IT IS ALLAH'S WILL. . . . . . . 694 MOSADA 1 V 105
FORGIVE ME! IT WAS ALLAH'S WILL. THE CORDS. . . . . 695 MOSADA 1 109
FORGIVE ME! OR I WILL DIE. 'TWAS ALLAH'S WILL. . . . 695 MOSADA 1 118
FORGIVE ME! IT WAS ALLAH'S WILL. NOW CORDS. . . . . 695 MOSADA 1 V 109
FOR HOLIEST TEACHERS OF HIS WILL, ... 736 IN CHURCH 7
IS IT YOUR WILL THAT I, WHO AM A QUEEN . . . . . . 757 SHADOW WATER A 212
COME RIDE AND RIDE WITH A WILL! . . . . 773 COME RIDE 2

WILLED
FOR SO SHE WILLED--THOU HEARD'ST? UPON THE BREAST . . 653 ISLE STAT I 2 32

WILLIAM
SINCE OLD WILLIAM POLLEXFEN . . . . 360 ALF POLLEXFEN 2
I, THE POET WILLIAM YEATS, ... 406 CARVED STONE 1
OR THAT WILLIAM BLAKE . . . . 576 ACRE OF GRASS 16
OLD WILLIAM POLLEXFEN, ... 604 YOU CONTENT 14

WILLINGLY
AND IF YOU SAY THAT SHE CAME WILLINGLY-- . . . . . 244 SHADOW WATER B 460
AND YOU SAY THAT SHE CAME WILLINGLY-- . . . . . . 244 SHADOW WATER B V 460

WILLOW
THE WILLOW OF THE MANY-SORROWED WORLD. . . . . . . 130 BOOK STORIES V 16
SHANWALLA, WHERE A WILLOW BORDERED POND . . . . . . 217 WOODS OF COOLE V 2
THAT ON A WILLOW SWUNG. . . . . 308 PLAYER QUEEN 4
AND HANGING O'ER THE HUSH OF WILLOW BOWERS, ... 705 REMEMBRANCE 8
A SCORE OF YARDS OFF 'NEATH A WILLOW, SHOT. . . . . 712 FERENCZ RENYI 65
AND SHE IS DRAGGED TO WHERE THE WILLOW BANDS . . . . 714 FERENCZ RENYI 108
BESIDE THE WILLOW. NAY, TO YONDER STAR, ... 715 FERENCZ RENYI 118
BENEATH THE WILLOW--NAY, TO YONDER STAR, ... 715 FERENCZ RENYI V 118

WILLOW-BORDERED
SHAN-WALLA, WHERE A WILLOW-BORDERED POND . . . . . 217 WOODS OF COOLE 2

WILLOW-GLADE
SO! MID THE WILLOW-GLADE YOU PAUSE AT LAST. . . . . 651 ISLE STAT I 2 2

WILLOWS
BUT WHENCE, AND WHEN? OVER THE WILLOWS SERE . . . . 652 ISLE STAT I 2 28
OVER THE CROWN OF THE WILLOWS BROWN. . . . . . . 653 ISLE STAT I 2 30
OVER THE CROWN OF THE WILLOWS BROWN. . . . . . . 653 ISLE STAT I 2 51
BY THE WILLOWS IN THE GLADE, ... 726 LOVERS QUARREL 3

WILLS
AS THOUGH TO CHOOSE WHATEVER SHAPE IT WILLS . . . . 417 ANCEST HOUSES 6
WHO TRAVELS WHERE GOD WILLS. . . . . 587 OLD WICKED MAN 4

894

	PAGE	TITLE		LINE
WILSON				
CALVERT AND WILSON, BLAKE AND CLAUDE, ...	639	BEN BULBEN		64
AND WILSON, BLAKE AND CALVERT, CLAUDE, ...	639	BEN BULBEN	V	64
WIN				
AND SHE, TO WIN HIM, HIS GREY HAIR CARESSED;	110	CUCHULAIN SEA		73
TO WIN A WOMAN IN HER OWN DESPITE, ...	244	SHADOW WATER B		458
TO WIN A WOMAN IS IN HER OWN DESPITE, ...	244	SHADOW WATER B	V	458
"AND IF I WIN," ONE BEGGAR SAID, ...	296	THREE BEGGARS		29
AT STROKE OF MIDNIGHT GOD SHALL WIN.	561	FOUR AGES MAN		8
THAT MURMURS WITH HOLY WOODS, AND WIN THEIR HELP	757	SHADOW WATER A		199
WIND SEE SEA-WIND				
"WHY DO YOU WIND NO HORN?" SHE SAID, ...	4	OISIN 1		32
WHY DO YOU WIND NO HORN?" SHE SAID.	4	OISIN 1	V	33
AND NOW A LADY RODE LIKE THE WIND	12	OISIN 1		142
AND NOW A MAIDEN RODE LIKE THE WIND	12	OISIN 1	V	142
ARE CHOKED WITH THUNDER, LIGHTNING, AND FIERCE WIND, . .	42	OISIN 2		205
OLD AND REMEMBERING, WHAT AVAILS THE WIND	42	OISIN 2	V	206
INTO THE CLANGOUR OF THE WIND AND SEA.	45	OISIN 2		234
. . . LIKE THE ROARING OF WIND IN A WOOD.	58	OISIN 3		168
AND LEAVES SHOOK IN THE WIND;	133	FR GILLIGAN		18
OR ELSE THEY STAND AND SNIFF THE WIND, ...	136	TWO TREES		37
WHEN THEY ARE HEARD UPON THE WIND, ...	136	TWO TREES	V	37
TO RANT AND RAGE IN FLOOD AND WIND;	138	TO IRELAND		26
IN FLOOD AND FIRE AND CLAY AND WIND, ...	138	TO IRELAND	V	25
THAT YOU CALL IN BIRDS, IN WIND ON THE HILL, ...	141	EVERLAST VOICE		6
AND THEY SIGH IF THE WIND BUT LIFT A TRESS:	151	OLD MOTHER		8
AND THEY SIGH IF THE WIND BUT LIFT UP A TRESS;	151	OLD MOTHER	V	8
THERE IS ENOUGH EVIL IN THE CRYING OF WIND.	155	REPROVE CURLEW		6
WHERE WIND CRIES IN THE SEDGE:	165	CRY OF SEDGE		3
BETWEEN THE WIND AND THE WOOD.	166	BLESSED		4
BETWEEN THE WIND AND THE WOOD.	167	BLESSED	V	4D
BUT I CAN SEE WHERE THE WIND GOES	168	BLESSED		27
AND FOLLOW THE WAY OF THE WIND;	168	BLESSED		28
"AND BLESSEDNESS GOES WHERE THE WIND GOES, ...	168	BLESSED		29
BUT I HAVE FOUND WHERE THE WIND GOES	168	BLESSED	V	27
BY A GREY SHORE WHERE THE WIND NEVER BLEW, ...	170	SECRET ROSE		14
THE HOUR OF THY GREAT WIND OF LOVE AND HATE.	170	SECRET ROSE		28
SURELY THINE HOUR HAS COME, THY GREAT WIND BLOWS, ...	170	SECRET ROSE		31
GREAT POWERS OF FALLING WAVE AND WIND AND WINDY FIRE, . .	174	ELEMENT POWERS		7
YOU GREAT ANGELIC POWERS OF WIND, AND WAVE, AND FIRE, . .	174	ELEMENT POWERS	V	7
GREAT ELEMENTAL POWERS OF WIND, AND WAVE, AND FIRE, . . .	174	ELEMENT POWERS	V	7
I BECAME A MAN, A HATER OF THE WIND, ...	177	PAST GREATNESS		7
NOR THE GREY RUSH WHEN THE WIND IS HIGH, ...	189	BAILE AILLINN		2
NOR THE GREY RUSH WHEN WIND IS HIGH	189	BAILE AILLINN	V	2
WITH ALL THIS CRYING IN THE WIND, ...	190	BAILE AILLINN		33
THE NORTH WIND TUMBLES TO AND FRO	191	BAILE AILLINN		45
THAT NORTH WIND TUMBLES TO AND FRO	191	BAILE AILLINN	V	45
BUT THE GREY RUSH UNDER THE WIND	192	BAILE AILLINN		88
"FROM HEAT AND COLD AND WIND AND WAVE;	193	BAILE AILLINN		114
"HE IS WELL OUT OF WIND AND WAVE, ...	193	BAILE AILLINN	V	114
FOR WHEN WE HAVE BLAMED THE WIND WE CAN BLAME LOVE; . . .	201	OLD MEMORY		10
NO BOUGHS HAVE WITHERED BECAUSE OF THE WINTRY WIND; . . .	203	WITHER BOUGHS		7
WIND AND UNWIND THEIR DANCES WHEN THE LIGHT GROWS COOL . .	203	WITHER BOUGHS		13
NO BOUGHS HAVE WITHERED BECAUSE OF THE WINTRY WIND; . . .	203	WITHER BOUGHS		15
WIND AND UNWIND DANCING WHEN THE LIGHT GROWS COOL . . .	203	WITHER BOUGHS	V	13
NO BOUGHS HAVE WITHERED BECAUSE OF THE WINTRY WIND; . . .	204	WITHER BOUGHS		23
UNDER A BITTER BLACK WIND THAT BLOWS FROM THE LEFT HAND;	206	HANRAHANS SONG		2
OUR COURAGE BREAKS LIKE AN OLD TREE IN A BLACK WIND AND DIES,	207	HANRAHANS SONG		3
THE WIND HAS BUNDLED UP THE CLOUDS HIGH OVER KNOCKNAREA,	207	HANRAHANS SONG		6
LIKE TUFTED REEDS OUR COURAGE DROOPS IN A BLACK WIND AND DIES:	207	HANRAHANS SONG	V	3
WHEN THE WIND COMES BLOWING ACROSS THE HILLY LAND;	207	HANRAHANS SONG	V	7
NOR ULADH, WHEN NAOISE HAD THROWN A SAIL UPON THE WIND;	209	UNDER THE MOON		4
SEVEN OLD SISTERS WIND THE THREADS OF THE LONG-LIVED ONES,	209	UNDER THE MOON		7
OR ULADH WHEN NAISI HAD HUNG A SAIL UPON THE WIND;	209	UNDER THE MOON	V	4
SEVEN OLD SISTERS WIND THE THREADS OF THE LONG LIVED ONES,	209	UNDER THE MOON	V	7
I'VE HEARD A RUSTLING OVERHEAD IN THE WIND.	223	SHADOW WATER B		28
PEACEABLE MEN THAT SHUT THE WIND AWAY, ...	224	SHADOW WATER B		54
AND YOU HAD SPREAD A SAIL FOR HOME, A WIND	236	SHADOW WATER B		309
AND LISTENING TO THE CRY OF WIND AND WAVE	236	SHADOW WATER B		315
THAT UNIMAGINABLE STORMS OF WIND AND WAVE	236	SHADOW WATER B		317
AND LISTENING TO THE CRY OF THE WIND AND WAVE	236	SHADOW WATER B	V	315
AND YET YOU SAY THE WATER AND THE WIND	236	SHADOW WATER B	V	317
IN ISLANDS WHERE THE CHILDREN OF AENGUS WIND	245	SHADOW WATER B		469
THEY HAVE GONE ABOUT THE WORLD LIKE WIND, ...	289	SEPTEMBER 1913		11
UNTIL A CURLEW CRIED AND IN THE LUMINOUS WIND	291	PAUDEEN		4
THE WIND IS OLD AND STILL AT PLAY	301	RUN PARADISE		22
TO TAKE MY FANCY LIKE THE WIND	301	RUN PARADISE		26
CURSING THE WIND. IT WAS AS MUCH	302	HOUR DAWN	V	4
AND THE SHEEP BLEATING AT THE WIND	306	HOUR DAWN		78
IF A GOOD EASTER WIND WERE BLOWING, ...	306	HOUR DAWN		86
AND THOUGH THE WINTER WIND IS BAD	306	HOUR DAWN		87
IF BUT THIS WIND WERE IN THE SOUTH."	306	HOUR DAWN		90
OR THAT THE WIND WOULD SHIFT A POINT, ...	306	HOUR DAWN		92
NEITHER THE SPRING NOR THE SOUTH WIND	306	HOUR DAWN		95
TO A CHILD DANCING IN THE WIND	312	CHILD DANCING		T
FOR WIND OR WATER'S ROAR?	312	CHILD DANCING		3
THE MONSTROUS CRYING OF WIND?	312	CHILD DANCING		12
I HAD THOUGHT, SEEING HOW BITTER IS THAT WIND	327	ROBERT GREGORY		89
HAIR SPREAD ON THE WIND THEY MADE;	332	ROUND TOWER		22

	PAGE	TITLE		LINE

WIND (CONTINUED)

HAIRS SPREAD ON THE WIND THEY MADE:	332	ROUND TOWER	V	22
WHAT'S DYING BUT A SECOND WIND?	338	TOM OROUGHLEY		11
SOME BEGGAR SHELTERING FROM THE WIND, AND THERE	351	HER PRAISE		13
THAT BELLIES AND DRAGS IN THE WIND	358	BALLOON MIND		3
WHO KNOWS HOW SHE DRANK THE WIND	381	SONGS FOOL 2		6
THAT HER HAIR STREAMS UPON THE WIND,	390	IMAGE PAST		40
OR MAYBE BUT A WIND THAT BLOWS	396	ROSE TREE		5
WIND SHADOWS OF THE INDIGNANT DESERT BIRDS.	402	SECOND COMING	V	17
WHEREBY THE HAYSTACK- AND ROOF-LEVELLING WIND,	403	FOR DAUGHTER		5
ASSAULT AND BATTERY OF THE WIND	405	FOR DAUGHTER		55
FOR AN OLD BELLOWS FULL OF ANGRY WIND?	405	FOR DAUGHTER		64
OLD LECHER WITH A LOVE ON EVERY WIND,	413	TOWER		105
OF EVERY WIND THAT BLOWS:	419	MY HOUSE		7
LIFE SCARCE CAN CAST A FRAGRANCE ON THE WIND,	422	MY DESCENDANTS		5
A GLITTERING SWORD OUT OF THE EAST. A PUFF OF WIND	426	PHANTOM HATRED		5
NOR THOUGHT OF THE LEVELLING WIND.	432	NINETEEN 19		97
WIND SHRIEKED--AND WHERE ARE THEY?	432	NINETEEN 19		107
A SUDDEN BLAST OF DUSTY WIND AND AFTER	433	NINETEEN 19		119
THEIR PURPOSE IN THE LABYRINTH OF THE WIND:	433	NINETEEN 19		121
ACCORDING TO THE WIND, FOR ALL ARE BLIND.	433	NINETEEN 19		124
BUT NOW WIND DROPS, DUST SETTLES: THEREUPON	433	NINETEEN 19		125
HOLLOW OF CHEEK AS THOUGH IT DRANK THE WIND	444	SCHOOL CHILDR		27
TRANSPARENT LIKE THE WIND,	449	HERO GIRL FOOL		27
THE SOUTH WIND BROUGHT IT LONGING, AND THE EAST WIND DESPAIR,	449	OWEN AHERNE		5
THE SOUTH WIND BROUGHT IT LONGING, AND THE EAST WIND DESPAIR,	449	OWEN AHERNE		5
THE WEST WIND MADE IT PITIFUL, AND THE NORTH WIND AFRAID.	449	OWEN AHERNE		6
THE WEST WIND MADE IT PITIFUL, AND THE NORTH WIND AFRAID.	449	OWEN AHERNE		6
THE SOUTH WIND BROUGHT IT LONGING, AND THE EAST BROUGHT IN DESPAIR,	449	OWEN AHERNE	V	5
THE SOUTH WIND BROUGHT IT LONGING, AND THE EAST BROUGHT IT DESPAIR,	449	OWEN AHERNE	V	5
BUT O: MY HEART COULD BEAR NO MORE WHEN THE UPLAND CAUGHT THE WIND:	450	OWEN AHERNE		11
A BONE WAVE-WHITENED AND DRIED IN THE WIND.	521	THREE THINGS		6
A BONE WAVE-WHITENED AND DRIED IN THE WIND.	521	THREE THINGS		12
A BONE WAVE-WHITENED AND DRIED IN THE WIND.	521	THREE THINGS		18
COLD AS THE MARCH WIND HIS EYES.	531	FATHER CHILD		8
O MARCHING WIND, O A BLAST OF THE WIND,	548	TO SAME TUNE 3		24
O MARCHING WIND, O A BLAST OF THE WIND,	548	TO SAME TUNE 3		24
"BECAUSE I HELPED TO WIND THE CLOCK	585	ORAHILLY		25
IN THE SUNLIGHT AND WIND.	600	THOSE IMAGES		4
AND THE WIND SIGHED TOO.	611	NEWS ORACLE		4
A BLAST OF THE WIND, O A MARCHING WIND,	615	MARCH SONGS 2		24
A BLAST OF THE WIND, O A MARCHING WIND,	615	MARCH SONGS 2		24
MARCH WIND, AND ANY OLD TUNE,	615	MARCH SONGS 2		25
A BLAST OF WIND, O A MARCHING WIND,	615	MARCH SONGS 2	V	24
A BLAST OF WIND, O A MARCHING WIND,	615	MARCH SONGS 2	V	24
BUT WIND COMES UP FROM THE SHORE:	636	BLACK TOWER		18
BUT WIND COMES UP FROM THE SHORE:	636	BLACK TOWER		28
YON WIND GOES SADLY, AND THE GRASS AND TREES	652	ISLE STAT I 2		10
THE WIND AT EVENING WHEN THE SUN GOES DOWN	653	ISLE STAT I 2		50
THEY HEAR THE STORY OF THE WIND,	655	ISLE STAT I 3		11
UPON THE WIND, AND GUIDE MINE ARROW'S COURSE.	657	ISLE STAT I 3		62
THAT NESTLES ALONE IN THE WHISTLING WIND,	657	ISLE STAT I 3		68
BEFORE THE WIND. SAW YOU HIS EYES A-GLITTER?	683	SEEKER		35
THE MOTHER OF THE WIND MOURNS TOO,	738	YOU ARE SAD		6
AND HER OLD WIND THAT NO MIRTH EVER HAD,	738	YOU ARE SAD		7
BUT THAT THE WIND CHANGED: FOR I FOLLOWED HIM	747	SHADOW WATER A		4
AND HEARD THE MUSIC IN THE WIND, AND SAW	747	SHADOW WATER A		5
A PATH AMONG THESE WAVES AND WEIGH THE WIND?	748	SHADOW WATER A		21
AND I HAVE HEARD THEM CALL FROM WIND TO WIND	750	SHADOW WATER A		83
AND I HAVE HEARD THEM CALL FROM WIND TO WIND	750	SHADOW WATER A		83
AND NO MAN KILL ME: FOR SOME WIND HAS BLOWN	751	SHADOW WATER A		97
MAKE GALLEYS OUT OF WIND THAT CHANGE TO WIND	751	SHADOW WATER A		105
MAKE GALLEYS OUT OF WIND THAT CHANGE TO WIND	751	SHADOW WATER A		105
WHILE THE WIND IS LIGHT. THE OAR CAN HARDLY MOVE HER,	754	SHADOW WATER A		157
OF FOLLOWING FORGAEL'S DREAM FROM WIND TO WIND.	758	SHADOW WATER A		219
OF FOLLOWING FORGAEL'S DREAM FROM WIND TO WIND.	758	SHADOW WATER A		219
AND A COLD WIND IS BLOWING IN MY HAIR.	761	SHADOW WATER A		277
AND BRING ME WHERE THE CHILDREN OF AENGUS WIND	763	SHADOW WATER A		317
WHERE THE WORLD ENDS, OR RUNS FROM WIND TO WIND	768	SHADOW WATER A		417
WHERE THE WORLD ENDS, OR RUNS FROM WIND TO WIND	768	SHADOW WATER A		417
HAD WOVEN HER OF WIND. LIFE WITHERS OUT	768	SHADOW WATER A	V	423
LET THE WIND BEAR WITNESS,	770	BLOOD BOND		8
COME RIDE LIKE THE MARCH WIND:	774	COME RIDE		6
RUN LIKE THE MARCH WIND:	774	COME RIDE	V	6
GATHER ON THE WIND AND DRIVE	775	AGAINST WITCH		7
FOR THEY ARE BUT WHIRLING WIND,	775	AGAINST WITCH		9
AND THE WIND BLOWS IT AWAY.	783	GREY ROUND		20

WIND-BEATEN

THE WIND-BEATEN, STONE-GREY,	310	PEACOCK		4
UNDER YOUR OLD WIND-BEATEN TOWER, WHERE STILL	367	EGO DOMINUS		2
BUT THESE WASTE WATERS AND WIND-BEATEN SAILS	763	SHADOW WATER A		319

WIND-BLOWN

THIS BODY TREMBLING LIKE A WIND-BLOWN REED.	103	FERGUS DRUID		25
"O HEARTS OF WIND-BLOWN FLAME!	162	ASKS FORGIVE		6
"THE WIND-BLOWN CLAMOUR OF THE BARNACLE-GEESE."	300	BEGGAR CRIED		20
AS A WREATH OF SMOKE IN WIND-BLOWN FLIGHT	730	PRIEST FAIRY		61

		PAGE	TITLE		LINE

WIND-BROKEN
UNDER THE OLD WIND-BROKEN TREE, • • • • • • • • • 406 IN TIME OF WAR 3
WINDING   SEE EVER-WINDING
WE DANCED TO WHERE IN THE WINDING THICKET • • • • • • 20 OISIN 1 304
THEN ONWARD IN THE WINDING THICKET • • • • • • • • 20 OISIN 1 V 304
AND GOD STANDS WINDING HIS LONELY HORN, • • • • • • • 148 INTO TWILIGHT 13
CLIMB UP THE NARROW WINDING STAIR TO BED! • • • • • • 324 ROBERT GREGORY 5
AT SOME OLD WINDING WHITETHORN ROOT • • • • • • • • 342 SHEP GOATHERD 101
A WINDING STAIR, A CHAMBER ARCHED WITH STONE, • • • • • 419 MY HOUSE 11
I SUMMON TO THE WINDING ANCIENT STAIR! • • • • • • • 477 SELF AND SOUL 1
THIS WINDING, GYRING, SPIRING TREADMILL OF A STAIR • • • 480 BLOOD AND MOON 17
MAY UNWIND THE WINDING PATH! • • • • • • • • • • 497 BYZANTIUM 12
OR WINDING THROUGH THE GROVE • • • • • • • • • • 530 DELPHIC ORACLE 7
A HORN! SOME TROOP OF ROBBERS WINDING GOES • • • • • • 649 ISLE STAT I 1 110
WINDINGS
AND ALL THE WINDINGS THERE. • • • • • • • • • • • 520 HIS BARGAIN 12
WINDING-SHEET
WINDING-SHEET AND SWADDLING-CLOTHES. • • • • • • • • 530 OLD TOM AGAIN 6
WINDING-SHEET AND SWADDLING CLOTHES. • • • • • • • • 530 OLD TOM AGAIN V 6
WINDLESS
THE DANCE WOUND THROUGH THE WINDLESS WOODS! • • • • • 21 OISIN 1 320
THEN ON AMONG THE WINDLESS WOODS, • • • • • • • • • 21 OISIN 1 V 320
FAR OUT UNDER A WINDLESS SKY! • • • • • • • • • • 197 BAILE AILLINN 181
WINDLE-STRAWS
WINDLE-STRAWS I. O'SULLIVAN RUA TO THE CURLEW • • • • 155 REPROVE CURLEW V T
WINDOW
AND STAND ON HER WINDOW SILL. • • • • • • • • • • 159 CAP AND BELLS V 4
SHE OPENED HER DOOR AND HER WINDOW, • • • • • • • • 160 CAP AND BELLS 29
A LATTICED WINDOW. HIS GLANCE WENT UP AT TIMES • • • • 180 QUEEN MAEVE 6
IN THEIR GREAT WINDOW LOOKING AT THE DAWN! • • • • • • 352 PEOPLE 15
WITH FACE AND NOSE PRESSED TO A SWEET-SHOP WINDOW, • • • 370 EGO DOMINUS 56
WITH FACE AND NOSE PRESSED TO A SWEETSHOP WINDOW. • • • 370 EGO DOMINUS V 56
THE LIGHT IN THE TOWER WINDOW WAS PUT OUT. • • • • • • 377 PHASES OF MOON 139
THE STARE'S NEST BY MY WINDOW • • • • • • • • • • 424 STARES NEST T
THE JAY'S NEST BY MY WINDOW • • • • • • • • • • • 424 STARES NEST V T
PERCHED IN SOME WINDOW OF HER MOTHER'S HOUSE • • • • • 466 HARUN RASHID 106
HEARD YOU? YOUR LUTE HUNG IN THE WINDOW SOUNDED! • • • 694 MOSADA 1 95
FROM THE GREAT PAINTED WINDOW WRAPS HIS BROW, • • • • • 697 MOSADA 2 37
FLOATING FROM YON BARRED WINDOW. SMALL NEW-COMER, • • • 700 MOSADA 3 43
FLOATING FROM YON BARRED WINDOW. NEW COMER, • • • • • 700 MOSADA 3 V 43
WINDOWED
FROM DOORED AND WINDOWED CLIFF, OR HALF UPTURNED • • • • 368 EGO DOMINUS 30
WINDOW-GLASS
GLASS-MOSAIC, WINDOW-GLASS, • • • • • • • • • • • 440 WISDOM 3
WINDOW-LEDGE
UNDER MY WINDOW-LEDGE THE WATERS RACE, • • • • • • • 490 COOLE BALLYLEE 1
WINDOWLESS
WINDOWLESS, PILLARLESS, MULTITUDINOUS HOME • • • • • • 39 OISIN 2 148
WINDOW'S
BY A WINDOW'S FEEBLE LIGHT • • • • • • • • • • • 731 STREET DANCERS 3
WINDOWS
THE WINDOWS AND THE DOORS WERE SHUT, • • • • • • • • 95 MOLL MAGEE 29
SHOWED THEIR FAINT LIGHT THROUGH THE UNSHUTTERED WINDOWS, 279 TWO KINGS 50
GREAT WINDOWS OPEN TO THE SOUTH, • • • • • • • • • 475 EVA GORE-BOOTH 2
UPON THE DUSTY, GLITTERING WINDOWS CLING, • • • • • • 482 BLOOD AND MOON 43
ITS OPEN LIGHTED DOORWAY AND ITS WINDOWS ALL ALIGHT, • • 581 CURSE CROMWELL 26
SCARCE THE OLD AND WIZEN HOUSES HAD THEIR DOORS AND WINDOWS 718 PHANTOM SHIP 5
   SHUT.
SCARCE THE OLD AND WIZENED HOUSES HAD THEIR DOORS 718 PHANTOM SHIP V 5
   AND WINDOWS SHUT.
WINDOW-SILL
AND STAND ON HER WINDOW-SILL. • • • • • • • • • • 159 CAP AND BELLS 4
WINDS
STROKED THE YOUNG WINDS AS THEY ROLLED ON THE PLAIN, • • 27 OISIN 1 V 415C
THE DEMONS OF THE WILDS AND WINDS FOR FRIGHT • • • • • 34 OISIN 2 V 81B
SURLY AND DISTANT, WITH THE WINDS AND SEA!— • • • • • 45 OISIN 2 V 234
I BELLOW TO THE WINDS WHEN STORMS MAKE MOAN, • • • • • 45 OISIN 2 V 239D
WERE THE WINDS LESS SOFT THAN THE BREATH OF A PIGEON • • 56 OISIN 3 134
AND THE WINDS MADE THE SANDS ON THE SEA'S EDGE • • • • 57 OISIN 3 145
LONG FLED THE FOAM-FLAKES AROUND ME, THE WINDS FLED OUT 57 OISIN 3 149
   OF THE VAST,
TILL, FATTENING THE WINDS OF THE MORNING, AN ODOUR 57 OISIN 3 153
   OF NEW-MOWN HAY
THE COLD WET WINDS EVER BLOWING, • • • • • • • • • 119 PITY OF LOVE 5
AND THE COLD WET WINDS EVER BLOWING, • • • • • • • • 119 PITY OF LOVE V 7
I TORE IT FROM GREEN BOUGHS WINDS TORE AND TOSSED • • • 130 BOOK STORIES 13
I TORE IT FROM GREEN BOUGHS WINDS TOSSED AND HURLED, • • 130 BOOK STORIES V 13
THE WINDS AWAKEN, THE LEAVES WHIRL ROUND, • • • • • • 140 HOSTING SIDHE 6
FOR WINDS WILL BEAR THEM GENTLY WHEN THE EAGLE FLIES, • • 146 UNAPPEAS HOST V 3
FOR THEY WILL RIDE THE WINDS WHEN THE GIER-EAGLE FLIES • 146 UNAPPEAS HOST V 3
DESOLATE WINDS THAT CRY OVER THE WANDERING SEA! • • • • 147 UNAPPEAS HOST 7
DESOLATE WINDS THAT HOVER IN THE FLAMING WEST! • • • • 147 UNAPPEAS HOST 8
DESOLATE WINDS THAT BEAT THE DOORS OF HEAVEN, AND BEAT • 147 UNAPPEAS HOST 9
O HEART THE WINDS HAVE SHAKEN, THE UNAPPEASABLE HOST • • 147 UNAPPEAS HOST 11
AND HEART THE WINDS HAVE SHAKEN! THE UNAPPEASABLE HOST • 147 UNAPPEAS HOST V 11
AND HEAR THE WINDS HAVE SHAKEN, THE UNAPPEASABLE HOST • 147 UNAPPEAS HOST V 11
AND THE WINDS THAT BLOW THROUGH THE STARRY WAYS, • • • 158 TO HIS HEART 4
LET THE STARRY WINDS AND THE FLAME AND THE FLOOD • • • 158 TO HIS HEART 5
AND THE WINDS BLOWING THROUGH THE STARRY WAYS, • • • • 158 TO HIS HEART V 4
O WINDS, OLDER THAN CHANGING OF NIGHT AND DAY, • • • • 162 ASKS FORGIVE 7
O WINDS, ELDER THAN CHANGING OF NIGHT AND DAY, • • • • 162 ASKS FORGIVE V 7

897

		PAGE	TITLE		LINE

WINDS (CONTINUED)

THE WINDS THAT AWAKENED THE STARS	171 MAID QUIET		3
FOR THE WINDS THAT AWAKENED THE STAR, ...	171 MAID QUIET	V	3
FOR THE WINDS THAT AWAKENED THE STARS	171 MAID QUIET	V	3
WHEN WINDS HAVE GATHERED AND SUN AND MOON BURNED DIM . . .	175 ELEMENT POWERS		15
CASTS UP A SHOW AND THE WINDS ANSWER IT	186 QUEEN MAEVE		125
VEERING, FLEETING, FICKLE, THE WINDS OF KNOCKNAREA, . . .	206 HANRAHANS SONG	V	1
UNDER THE BITTER BLACK WINDS BLOWING OUT OF THE LEFT HAND!	206 HANRAHANS SONG	V	2
FOR THE WET WINDS ARE BLOWING OUT OF THE CLINGING AIR! . .	207 HANRAHANS SONG		12
THE WINDS HAVE BUNDLED UP THE CLOUDS HIGH OVER KNOCKNAREA	207 HANRAHANS SONG	V	6
AND SHAKE DOWN THUNDER ON THE STONES BECAUSE THE RED WINDS RAVE!	207 HANRAHANS SONG	V	7
FOR THE GREY WINDS ARE BLOWING UP, OUT OF THE CLINGING SEAS!	207 HANRAHANS SONG	V	12
AND WINDS AND PONDS COVER MORE QUIET WOODS, ...	218 WOODS OF COOLE		34
MORE SHINING WINDS, MORE STAR-GLIMMERING PONDS?	218 WOODS OF COOLE		35
AND WINDS BLOWING FROM FLOWERS, AND WHIRR OF FEATHERS . .	219 WOODS OF COOLE		39
WHERE TIME IS DROWNED IN ODOUR-LADEN WINDS	219 HARP OF AENGUS		3
THAT SHE AMONG HER WINDS MIGHT KNOW HE WEPT!	220 HARP OF AENGUS		12
IT WAS THEIR HANDS THAT PLUCKED THE WINDS AWAKE	237 SHADOW WATER B		324
THOSE WINDS THAT CLAMOUR OF APPROACHING NIGHT.	431 NINETEEN 19		68
THAT WINDS OF WINTER BLOW	431 NINETEEN 19		87
FOR THE FOUL WINDS BLOW!	523 MAD AS MIST		2
BUT I WOKE IN AN OLD RUIN THAT THE WINDS HOWLED THROUGH!	581 CURSE CROMWELL		28
BUT WINDS COME UP FROM THE SHORE!	635 BLACK TOWER		8
THEY SHAKE WHEN THE WINDS ROAR, ...	635 BLACK TOWER		9
THEY SHAKE WHEN THE WINDS ROAR, ...	636 BLACK TOWER		19
THEY SHAKE WHEN THE WINDS ROAR, ...	636 BLACK TOWER		29
BUT WINDS COME UP FROM THE SHORE!	636 BLACK TOWER	V	REF
AS BLOSSOMS, WHEN THE WINDS OF MARCH	671 ISLE STAT II 3		127
SOON WILT THOU SMILE, FOR HERE THE WINDS ARE WEAK . . .	671 ISLE STAT II 3		141
AND HOLLOW LULLING THE YOUNG WINDS WITH SONG.	675 ISLE STAT II 3		226
AND WHERE THE POLAR WINDS AND WATERS WRESTLE	682 SEEKER		18
THE TALKING WINDS HAVE FOUND THEIR HOME.	686 LIFE		9
FROM HERE, ALONG THE SHADOWY WAY THAT WINDS	703 MOSADA 3		111
AND ON TIPTOE THE WINDS A-WHISPERING STOOD.	715 DWELT SYCAMORE		8
AND ON TIP-TOE THE WINDS A-WHISPERING STOOD.	715 DWELT SYCAMORE	V	8
. . . CEASE THE WINDS, AND ON THEIR POLES	719 PHANTOM SHIP		17
AND THE WINDS COME DOWN AND BLOW THEM WITH THE VAPOURS FAR AWAY.	719 PHANTOM SHIP		28
IT MAY BE, BEFORE THE WINDS OF BIRTH HAVE WAKED! . . .	750 SHADOW WATER A		86
HAVE THE WINDS BLOWN YOU AMONG THESE EMPTY WATERS? . . .	756 SHADOW WATER A		192
AMONG THE WINDS, LOOKS UNDER YOUR PALE EYELIDS.	757 SHADOW WATER A		211
WELL SHELTERED FROM THE WINDS, AND FRUITFUL FIELDS, . . .	758 SHADOW WATER A		221
THE WINDS AND WATERS TO BE YOUR HOME FOR EVER!	762 SHADOW WATER A		282
WHERE TIME IS DROWNED IN ODOUR-LADEN WINDS	762 SHADOW WATER A		298
THE WINDS AND WATERS TO BE YOUR HOME FOREVER!	762 SHADOW WATER A	V	282
THAT SHE AMONG HER WINDS MIGHT KNOW HE WEPT!	763 SHADOW WATER A		307
AND SHE, NO LONGER BLOWN AMONG THE WINDS, ...	763 SHADOW WATER A		323
THE CLOUDY WATERS AND THE GLIMMERING WINDS	764 SHADOW WATER A		327
AMONG THE WINDS AND WATERS! AND WHEN THEY PASS	764 SHADOW WATER A		331
ALL THAT KNOW LOVE AMONG THE WINDS OF THE WORLD	767 SHADOW WATER A		386
THAT HAVE KNOWN LOVE AMONG THE WINDS OF THE WORLD . . .	767 SHADOW WATER A		392
LOVE WAS NOT MADE FOR DARKNESS AND THE WINDS	767 SHADOW WATER A		394
WHETHER AMONG THE COLD WINDS OF THE DEAD.	768 SHADOW WATER A	V	413
OR AMONG WINDS THAT MOVE IN THE MEADOWS AND WOODS. . . .	768 SHADOW WATER A	V	413
AND ONE WHERE THE WINDS ARE WOVE, ...	771 SPINNING SONG		3
WHEN THE WINDS ARE CALLING THERE, ...	772 SONG DEIRDRE 1		4
BECAUSE THE NIGHT WINDS BLOW	782 HEART FRIGHT		16
THE WINDS OUT OF CLARE-GALWAY	783 GREY ROUND		4

WINDWARD

| IF I GO NEARER TO THE WINDWARD SIDE, ... | 753 SHADOW WATER A | | 140 |

WINDY

AND HUMMING SANDS, WHERE WINDY SURGES WEND!	68 SAD SHEPHERD		4
"I HAVE COME BY THE WINDY WAY	167 BLESSED		6
"I COME BY THE WINDY WAY	167 BLESSED	V	6
GREAT POWERS OF FALLING WAVE AND WIND AND WINDY FIRE, . .	174 ELEMENT POWERS		7
ABOUT THE WINDY WATER-SIDE, ...	192 BAILE AILLINN		93
ABOUT THE WINDY WATER SIDE	192 BAILE AILLINN	V	93
ALIGHTED ON THE WINDY GRASS.	195 BAILE AILLINN		138
AMONG THE WINDY MEADOWS OF THE DAWN."	234 SHADOW WATER B		264
IN HAPPY DANCES UNDER A WINDY MOON.	245 SHADOW WATER B		470
THE GREY ROCK AND THE WINDY LIGHT?	275 GREY ROCK		111
ABOVE A WINDY PRECIPICE?" THEN HE!	285 TWO KINGS		195
UPON URBINO'S WINDY HILL, ...	288 TO WEALTHY MAN		17
ON A WINDY STONE, THE THIRD, ...	298 THREE HERMITS		5
AS I CAME OVER WINDY GAP	300 RUN PARADISE		1
STUMBLED UPON THAT WINDY PLACE	302 HOUR DAWN		3
STUMBLED ON WINDY CRUACHAN	302 HOUR DAWN	V	3
AND EVERY WINDY QUARTER HOWL	405 FOR DAUGHTER		71
I SUMMON TO THE WINDY ANCIENT STAIR!	477 SELF AND SOUL	V	1
DANCED ON CRUACHAN'S WINDY PLAIN, ...	528 DANCER CRUACH		4
DANCED IT ON CRUACHAN'S WINDY PLAIN, ...	528 DANCER CRUACH	V	4
AMONG THE WINDY MEADOWS OF THE DAWN."	754 SHADOW WATER A		153
IN HAPPY DANCES, UNDER A WINDY MOON!	763 SHADOW WATER A		318

WINE

AND BOWLS OF BARLEY, HONEY, AND WINE, ...	3 OISIN 1		8
AND OIL AND WINE AND HONEY AND MILK, ...	8 OISIN 1		92
AND HONEY, AND OIL, AND WINE, AND MILK, ...	8 OISIN 1	V	92
THOSE TWO CAME CARRYING WINE AND MEAT AND BREAD, . . .	41 OISIN 2		184
WE LAY ON SKINS OF OTTERS, AND DRANK WINE, ...	41 OISIN 2		188

898

WINE   (CONTINUED)

HOPING AND FEARING, BROUGHT ME WINE AND BREAD.   41 OISIN 2   V 184A
OF WOLVES, OF BOREAL BEARS, WE QUAFFED THE WINE   41 OISIN 2   V 188
I SAT AND MUSED AND DRANK SWEET WINE: 82 MAD KING GOLL   13
AND A YOUNG MAN BROUGHT HIM RED WINE   144 HOST OF AIR   19
THE BREAD AND THE WINE HAD A DOOM,   144 HOST OF AIR   25
AND ONE HAS SEEN IN THE REDNESS OF WINE   168 BLESSED   35
OR IN THE WINE VAT, DWELL BEYOND THE STIR   169 SECRET ROSE   V 4
POURED OUT WINE FOR THE HIGH INVISIBLE ONES.   219 WOODS OF COOLE   44
A MELANCHOLY THAT A CUP OF WINE,   227 SHADOW WATER B 114
IS NO MORE THAN A WINE CUP IN THE TASTING,   229 SHADOW WATER B V 150
THAT HAS THE HEADY FLAVOUR OF NEW WINE,   240 SHADOW WATER B 374
WINE COMES IN AT THE MOUTH   261 DRINKING SONG   1
AND THOUGH AT BOTTLING OF YOUR WINE   271 GREY ROCK   9
FOR ALL WERE FULL OF WINE AND MEAT.   271 GREY ROCK   17
THOUGH AT THE BOTTLING OF YOUR WINE   271 GREY ROCK   V 9
TO HOLD THE WINE THEY BUY OF HIM.   272 GREY ROCK   V 25
'TWAS WINE OR WOMEN, OR SOME CURSE--   273 GREY ROCK   54
AND SHE WITH GOBAN'S WINE ADRIP,   276 GREY ROCK   121
POUR WINE AND DANCE IF MANHOOD STILL HAVE PRIDE,   311 MOUNTAIN TOMB   1
NOR MOUTH FROM KISSING, NOR FROM WINE UNWET: 311 MOUNTAIN TOMB   7
POUR WINE AND DANCE, IF MANKIND STILL HAVE PRIDE,   311 MOUNTAIN TOMB V 1
NOR MOUTH WITH KISSING NOR WITH WINE UNWET.   311 MOUNTAIN TOMB V 7
NOR MOUTH WITH KISSING NOR WITH THE WINE UNWET.   311 MOUNTAIN TOMB V 7
DRUNK WITH THE UNMIXED WINE.   355 PROPERTIUS   8
DRUNK WITH THE UN-MIXED WINE.   355 PROPERTIUS   V 8
OR WHEN I GROW EXCITED WITH WINE,   357 DEEP-SWORN VOW   5
DID GOD IN PORTIONING WINE AND BREAD   386 ROBARTES DANCE   39
LIT UP THE DARK MAHOGANY AND THE WINE,   410 TOWER   27
I BRING FULL-FLAVOURED WINE OUT OF A BARREL FOUND   442 BLACK CENTAUR   10
I BRING FULL FLAVOURED WINE OUT OF A BARREL FOUND   442 BLACK CENTAUR V 10
THE WINE DARK OF THE WOOD'S INTRICACIES,   446 COLONUS PRAISE V 2
WHILE OUR GROSS PALATES DRINK FROM THE WHOLE WINE,   471 ALL SOUL NIGHT   10
NO LIVING MAN CAN DRINK FROM THE WHOLE WINE.   474 ALL SOUL NIGHT   85
I TORE MY BODY THAT ITS WINE MIGHT COVER   537 HER VISION   7
NOR KNEW, DRUNKEN WITH SINGING AS WITH WINE,   537 HER VISION   30
O BUT HEART'S WINE SHALL RUN PURE,   554 CHURCH STATE   5
WINE SHALL RUN THICK TO THE END,   554 CHURCH STATE   11
WINE OR LOVE DRUG HIM TO SLEEP,   633 MAN AND ECHO   26
WINE OR LOVE DRUGS HIM TO SLEEP,   633 MAN AND ECHO   V 26
THEIR MONEY SPENT, THEIR WINE GONE SOUR,   635 BLACK TOWER   3
BEFORE HIS TENT THE GENERAL SIPS HIS WINE,   709 FERENCZ RENYI   6
THIS SULLEN PEASANT SPOILS THE GOOD RED WINE.   711 FERENCZ RENYI   43
THIS SULLEN PEASANT SOURS THE GOOD RED WINE.   711 FERENCZ RENYI V 43
IN OTHER LIVES? HAST THOU NOT QUAFFED OLD WINE   724 KANVA ON SELF   12
LIKE WINE THAT FILLS TO THE TOP   781 MY HEART BEAT   14
WINE-BREATH
TO DRINK FROM THE WINE-BREATH   471 ALL SOUL NIGHT   9
WINE-CUP
BY A SPILLED WINE-CUP LIE.   168 BLESSED   V 32
IS NO MORE THAN A WINE-CUP IN THE TASTING,   229 SHADOW WATER B 150
WINE-DARK
THE WINE-DARK OF THE WOOD'S INTRICACIES.   446 COLONUS PRAISE   2
AT WINE-DARK MIDNIGHT IN THE SACRED WOOD,   536 HER VISION   2
STARED AT THE WINE-DARK NAIL, OR DARK THAT RAN   537 HER VISION   10
WINE-DRENCHED
THOSE WINE-DRENCHED EYES, AND CURSE OUR LUCK   272 GREY ROCK   39
WINE-STAINED
DWELT AMONG WINE-STAINED WANDERERS IN DEEP WOODS: 170 SECRET ROSE   21
WINE-VAT
OR IN THE WINE-VAT, DWELL BEYOND THE STIR   169 SECRET ROSE   4
WING
FROM WHERE THE BIRDS OF AENGUS WING?"   6 OISIN 1   53
THE RAINS ARE FROM HIS DRIPPING WING, THE MOONBEAMS FROM 76 INDIAN ON GOD   8
   HIS EYE.
FLAME TO FLAME AND WING TO WING.   125 CATHLEEN PARA   16
FLAME TO FLAME AND WING TO WING.   125 CATHLEEN PARA   16
FLAME ON FLAME AND WING ON WING.   125 CATHLEEN PARA V 16
FLAME ON FLAME AND WING ON WING.   125 CATHLEEN PARA V 16
WHO RISE, WING ABOVE WING, FLAME ABOVE FLAME,   137 TO SOME I TALK   11
WHO RISE, WING ABOVE WING, FLAME ABOVE FLAME,   137 TO SOME I TALK   11
AND WHEN WHITE MOTHS WERE ON THE WING,   149 WANDER AENGUS   5
ARE DUST ON THE MOTH'S WING: THAT NOTHING MATTERS   235 SHADOW WATER B 297
THE GREY WING UPON EVERY TIDE: 290 SEPTEMBER 1913   18
DID SHE IN TOUCHING THAT LONE WING   397 POLIT PRISONER   7
BECAUSE OF SOME GREEN WING, GATHERED OLD MUMMY WHEAT 442 BLACK CENTAUR   7
AS AIR UNDER A WING, CAN GIVE BIRDS' WIT.   462 HARUN RASHID   28
AS AIR UNDER A WING, CAN GIVE BIRD'S WIT.   462 HARUN RASHID   V 28
A COUPLE OF NIGHT-MOTHS ARE ON THE WING.   482 BLOOD AND MOON   46
A COUPLE OF NIGHT MOTHS ARE ON THE WING,   482 BLOOD AND MOON V 46
AN EAGLE ON THE WING,   601 THOSE IMAGES   14
EACH OTHER ANSWERING. THEN BETWEEN EACH WING   659 ISLE STAT II 1   14
YON ARCHER, HE WHO HATH THE HALCYON'S WING   679 ISLE STAT II 3 316
AMONG THE BOUGHS, BLUE AS THE HALCYON'S WING,   683 SEEKER   38
WITHIN THE WOODWAYS, BLUE AS THE HALCYON'S WING,   683 SEEKER   V 38
THY WITHERED FOE, AND WITH THE PURPLE WING   688 TWO TITANS   55
FLASHING AND FLICKERING WITH EVER-UNDULANT WING   710 FERENCZ RENYI   19
FLASHING AND FLICKERING WITH EVER UNDULANT WING,   710 FERENCZ RENYI V 19
THEIR DREAD OF AUTUMN'S MORTAL WING,   736 SUMMER EVENING   2
AND DREAD NO MORE FOUL AUTUMN'S WING,   737 SUMMER EVENING   18
I LINGER WHILE THE BIRDS ARE ON THE WING,   754 SHADOW WATER A V 157

	PAGE	TITLE	LINE

WING   (CONTINUED)
THAT HAVE BUILT ALL ARE DUST ON A MOTH'S WING.	757	SHADOW WATER A	205
TILL IT DIP AN AGEING WING	777	SONG DEIRDRE 2	3
UP WITH THE NECK AND CLAP THE WING,	782	HEART FRIGHT	6
UP WITH THE NECK AND CLAP THE WING,	782	HEART FRIGHT	13
UP WITH THE NECK AND CLAP THE WING,	782	HEART FRIGHT	20
STRETCH NECK AND CLAP THE WING,	783	GREY ROUND	27

WINGED
AND HOW THE WINGED SANDALS DART,	135	TWO TREES	18
WINGED LOVES BORNE ON IN GENTLE STRIFE,	135	TWO TREES V	14
WITH THE LONELY, PROUD, WINGED MULTITUDE.	158	TO HIS HEART V	7
ARE YOU NOT HAPPY WINGED BODIES NOW?	234	SHADOW WATER B	273
NOW THAT YOU HAVE HAPPY WINGED BODIES?	234	SHADOW WATER B V	273
ALONE AND WINGED. OUR LOVE SHALL BE LIKE THEIRS	250	SHADOW WATER B	581
AND RODE OUR WINGED HORSE!	392	EASTER 1916	25
AND OUR WINGED METTLESOME HORSE.	392	EASTER 1916 V	25
LIVING, WIDE WINGED, ON THE WATERS FLOAT.	657	ISLE STAT I 3	54
THE WINGED WONDER OF ALL FAERY LAND.	657	ISLE STAT I 3	57
AND THE HAPPY WINGED DAY,	668	ISLE STAT II 3	64

WINGING   SEE A-WINGING
AND THRO' THE ODOROUS AIR LOVE-DREAMS ARE WINGING--	645	ISLE STAT I 1	5
OVER THEM CRIMSON VAPOURS WINGING.	648	ISLE STAT I 1	92
THENCE HAVE I COME WINGING!	672	ISLE STAT II 3	170
NOW HERE I COME WINGING!	672	ISLE STAT II 3 V	170

WINGS
KEPT TIME WITH THEIR BRIGHT WINGS AND FEET!	26	OISIN 1	397
BEAT TIME WITH THEIR BRIGHT WINGS AND FEET.	26	OISIN 1 V	397
FANNED THE DELIGHTED AIR LIKE WINGS OF BIRDS!	32	OISIN 2	50
FEW FEATHERS WERE ON THEIR DISHEVELLED WINGS.	34	OISIN 2	76
CHAINED WAS SHE. ON THEIR WINGS THE HUNDREDTH YEAR	34	OISIN 2 V	76
LIKE WINGS OF KINGFISHERS! AND HE AROSE	40	OISIN 2	169
SHALL THEY TURN WROTH OR PLUCK THE WINGS OF TIME?	42	OISIN 2 V	199
WHEN BRUSHED WITH THE WINGS OF THE OWLS;	53	OISIN 3	98
. . . DEEP HORROR OF EYES AND OF WINGS,	62	OISIN 3	205
ONE WITH THE TIDE THAT GLEAMS, THE WINGS THAT GLEAM AND DART.	78	INDIAN TO LOVE	15
. . . THE WINGS THAT GLIMMER AND GLEAM AND DART!	78	INDIAN TO LOVE V	15
. . . AND WINGS, THAT GLIMMER AND GLEAM AND DART,	78	INDIAN TO LOVE V	15
FIRST AS A RAVEN ON WHOSE ANCIENT WINGS	102	FERGUS DRUID	3
AND EVENING FULL OF THE LINNET'S WINGS.	117	ISLE INNISFREE	8
AND EVENING FULL OF THE LINNETS' WINGS.	117	ISLE INNISFREE V	8
AND SHAKE THEIR RAGGED WINGS! ALAS!	136	TWO TREES	38
AND WHEN THEY SHAKE THEIR WINGS--ALAS!	136	TWO TREES V	38
OF THEIR LONG WINGS, THE FLASH OF THEIR WHITE FEET.	137	TO SOME I TALK	16
OF THEIR LONG WINGS; THE FLASH OF THEIR SWIFT FEET.	137	TO SOME I TALK V	16
WITH HEAVY WHITENING WINGS, AND A HEART FALLEN COLD!	147	UNAPPEAS HOST	4
UNFOLD YOUR FLAMING WINGS AND COVER OUT OF SIGHT	175	ELEMENT POWERS	11
ABOUT WHOSE FACE BIRDS WAGGED THEIR FIERY WINGS,	187	QUEEN MAEVE	145
TALL, PROUD AND RUDDY, AND LIGHT WINGS	195	BAILE AILLINN	140
AND WAVING WHITE WINGS TO AND FRO	197	BAILE AILLINN	184
AND WITH THE WAVING OF YOUR WINGS.	212	BLESS PSALTER	7
AND ALL THAT TOSSING OF YOUR WINGS IS JOY,	244	SHADOW WATER B	451
WHERE WINGS HAVE MEMORY OF WINGS, AND ALL	264	HOUSE SHAKEN	6
WHERE WINGS HAVE MEMORY OF WINGS, AND ALL	264	HOUSE SHAKEN	6
ALL THEIR LIVES THROUGH INTO SOME DRIFT OF WINGS.	265	ABBEY THEATRE	7
UPON THEIR CLAMOROUS WINGS.	322	SWANS AT COOLE	12
THE BELL-BEAT OF THEIR WINGS ABOVE MY HEAD,	323	SWANS AT COOLE	17
THE INNUMERABLE CLANGING WINGS THAT HAVE PUT OUT THE MOON.	427	PHANTOM HATRED	32
THE WINGS HALF SPREAD FOR FLIGHT,	430	NINETEEN 19	65
A SUDDEN BLOW! THE GREAT WINGS BEATING STILL	441	LEDA AND SWAN	1
WINGS BEATING ABOUT THE ROOM!	499	MOTHER OF GOD	3
THOSE DEEDS WERE BEST THAT GAVE THE MINUTE WINGS	533	HER TRIUMPH	5
SOME TWENTY FEET FROM TIP TO TIP HAD ITS WINGS STRETCHED RIGHTLY OUT,	593	PILGRIM V	17
SOON SHALL OUR WINGS BE STILLED,	643	SONG FAERIES	5
TO WELCOME THEE, WHEN O'ER THE OWLET'S WINGS	648	ISLE STAT I 1	102
UPON HIS WINGS. THRO' YONDER GREEN ABYSS	649	ISLE STAT I 1	114
SOME GOBLIN, MY SERVANT, ON WINGS THAT ARE FLEET,	657	ISLE STAT II 1	67
AND LOUDLY TWICE THE LIVING WINGS FLAPT WIDE,	659	ISLE STAT II 1	12
HALF LIT, SO FLAPT THE WINGS ACROSS THE LAKE--	659	ISLE STAT II 1	17
GENTLY SHOOK THEIR MOTH-LIKE WINGS!	667	ISLE STAT II 3	26
E'EN THOUGH HIS WINGS WERE PLUMELESS STUMPS,	670	ISLE STAT II 3	118
AS MOTHS WITH BROKEN WINGS, AND AS WE SIT	671	ISLE STAT II 3	142
WHEN HIS SINEWY WINGS TOGETHER CLOSE.	673	ISLE STAT II 3	179
SOON SHALL OUR WINGS BE STILLED,	676	ISLE STAT II 3	252
WERE FURLED THE WINGS OF SHIPS. THERE IN A DELL,	693	MOSADA 1	82
THEIR THIEVING WINGS THAT WE MIGHT NEVER PART.	702	MOSADA 3	98
AH! WOE FOR YOUR WINGS AND YOUR HEAD--	708	FAIRY PEDANT	34
MUST SPREAD OUT THEIR WINGS UNTIRING.	739	WHERE BOOKS GO	3
OR BE HIS FOOD, I FOLLOW THE GREY WINGS,	751	SHADOW WATER A	101
AND NEED NO MORE OF LIFE TILL THE WHITE WINGS	751	SHADOW WATER A	102
OR A GOD HID THEM UNDER THE SHADOW OF WINGS.	752	SHADOW WATER A	125
THE HAND THAT WOUNDS. A WHITE BIRD BEATS HIS WINGS	758	SHADOW WATER A V	232
A WHITE BIRD BEATS HIS WINGS UPON MY FACE.	759	SHADOW WATER A	233
I AM BLIND AND DEAF BECAUSE OF THE WHITE WINGS,	759	SHADOW WATER A	235
I AM AFRAID OF THE HARP. O! WINGS ON WINGS!	759	SHADOW WATER A	236
I AM AFRAID OF THE HARP. O! WINGS ON WINGS!	759	SHADOW WATER A	236
AMONG GREAT TREES, AND IN THE WINGS OF OWLS,	762	SHADOW WATER A	285

WINKING
| IS BUT THE WINKING OF AN EYE! | 139 | TO IRELAND | 36 |

WINNING
    FOR MOTHER EVE'S WINNING • • • • • • • • • • • •   654 ISLE STAT I 2   61
WINS
    FOR THE HEART CRIES THAT WHAT DECEPTION WINS • • • • •   448 HERO GIRL FOOL   6
WINTER
    MOVED ROUND ME, OF SEAMEN OR LANDSMEN, ALL WHO ARE WINTER   53 OISIN 3   86
        TALES,
    THE HEAVY STEPS OF THE PLOUGHMAN SPLASHING THE WINTER   143 ROSE IN HEART V   3
        MOULD,
    GATHERS THE WILD DUCK FROM THE WINTER DAWN, • • • • •   217 WOODS OF COOLE   3
    AND THOUGH THE WINTER WIND IS BAD • • • • • • • •   306 HOUR DAWN   87
    TILL WINTER BLASTS WERE GONE, BUT SPEAK OF HER • • • •   340 SHEP GOATHERD   33
    THROUGH SUMMER AND WINTER SEEM • • • • • • • •   393 EASTER 1916   42
    THAT WINDS OF WINTER BLOW • • • • • • • • • •   431 NINETEEN 19   87
    SUMMER AND WINTER, DAY AND NIGHT, • • • • • • •   447 COLONUS PRAISE   31
    OF THAT OR THE NEXT WINTER WOULD BE DEATH. • • • • •   471 ALL SOUL NIGHT   30
    AND FROM THE FORTIETH WINTER BY THAT THOUGHT • • • • • •   501 VACILLATION   29
    HER EIGHTIETH WINTER APPROACHING, "YESTERDAY HE THREATENED   578 LOFTY THINGS   8
        MY LIFE,
    WINTER AND SUMMER TILL OLD AGE BEGAN • • • • • • •   629 CIRCUS ANIMALS   5
WINTER'S
    THROUGH SUMMER'S HEAT AND WINTER'S COLD. • • • • •   86 MAD KING GOLL   71
    "I'LL SLEEP UNTIL THE WINTER'S GONE, • • • • • •   305 HOUR DAWN   57
    "I'D LIKE TO SLEEP TILL WINTER'S GONE • • • • •   305 HOUR DAWN   60
    OR AN OLD MAN UPON A WINTER'S NIGHT. • • • • • •   359 WAR POEM   6
    DECLARE THAT WINTER'S BEST OF ALL, • • • • •   434 WHEEL   4
    OR WHERE THAT SNOW AND WINTER'S DREADFUL BLAST • • • •   563 MERU   11
WINTERS
    YET PRAISE THE WINTERS GONE, • • • • • • • •   336 YOUNG BEAUTY   15
    WITH SIXTY OR MORE WINTERS ON ITS HEAD, • • • • •   444 SCHOOL CHILDR   38
    OUT OF TEN THOUSAND WINTERS, I ALONE-- • • • •   470 HARUN RASHID V   190
WINTER-TIME
    THROUGH WINTER-TIME WE CALL ON SPRING, • • • • • •   434 WHEEL   1
WINTRY
    OR WHEN ALONG THE WINTRY STRANDS • • • • • • •   84 MAD KING GOLL   41
    OR WHERE ALONG THE WINTRY STRANDS • • • • • •   84 MAD KING GOLL V   41
    LIFTS SLOW HIS WINTRY HEAD, • • • • • • • •   99 FOXHUNTER   46
    LIKE THE PALE WATERS IN THEIR WINTRY RACE, • • • • • •   112 ROSE OF WORLD   8
    THE HEAVY STEPS OF THE PLOUGHMAN, SPLASHING THE WINTRY   143 ROSE IN HEART   3
        MOULD,
    NO BOUGHS HAVE WITHERED BECAUSE OF THE WINTRY WIND, • • •   203 WITHER BOUGHS   7
    NO BOUGHS HAVE WITHERED BECAUSE OF THE WINTRY WIND, • • •   203 WITHER BOUGHS   15
    NO BOUGHS HAVE WITHERED BECAUSE OF THE WINTRY WIND, • • •   204 WITHER BOUGHS   23
    WHEN THE RAIN IS PELTING OUT OF THE WINTRY AIR, • • •   207 HANRAHANS SONG V   12
    IF HONOUR FIND HIM IN THE WINTRY BLAST? • • • • •   479 SELF AND SOUL   56
    NOW ALL DRY STICKS UNDER A WINTRY SUN, • • • • •   490 COOLE BALLYLEE   10
    OR WINTRY MOONLIGHT SINK THE FIELD • • • • • •   501 VACILLATION   47
    NOW THEY RIDE THE WINTRY DAWN • • • • • • •   637 BEN BULBEN   10
    WHEN THE WINTRY VAPOURS RISE. • • • • • • •   643 SONG FAERIES   4
    WHEN THE WINTRY VAPOURS RISE. • • • • • • •   644 SONG FAERIES   16
    WHEN THE WINTRY VAPOURS RISE. • • • • • • •   676 ISLE STAT II 3   251
    WHEN THE WINTRY VAPOURS RISE. • • • • • • •   676 ISLE STAT II 3   263
    THE FOOL THAT CAME OUT OF THE WINTRY WOOD • • • • • •   750 SHADOW WATER A   75
WIRE
    WHEN MY HAND PASSED FROM WIRE TO WIRE • • • • • •   86 MAD KING GOLL   65
    WHEN MY HAND PASSED FROM WIRE TO WIRE • • • • • •   86 MAD KING GOLL   65
WIRE-JOINTED
    BY THESE WIRE-JOINTED JAWS AND LIMBS OF WOOD, • • • • •   382 VISION ROBART   10
WIRES
    WHERE THE DEMONS WHIP THEM WITH WIRES • • •   61 OISIN 3   198
    FOR THE KIND WIRES ARE TORN AND STILL, • • • • • •   86 MAD KING GOLL   69
WIS   SEE I-WIS
    AND FAR AWAY THE HERON SAILS, I WIS. • • • • •   649 ISLE STAT I 1   116
    THERE IS NO WAY BUT THAT YE FIGHT I WIS, • • • •   662 ISLE STAT II 1   75
    THEY GREW SO VERY STILL, I WIS • • • • • •   730 PRIEST FAIRY   66
WISDOM
    OF ALL THAT WISDOM AND THE FAME • • • • • •   7 OISIN 1   66
    WITH WISDOM HOUR BY HOUR.--MAY WE TWO STAND, • • • •   71 ANASHU VIJAYA   7
    WITH WISDOM HOUR BY HOUR.--MAY WE TOO STAND, • • • •   71 ANASHU VIJAYA V   7
    BUT LEARN THE DREAMING WISDOM THAT IS YOURS. • • • •   103 FERGUS DRUID   22
    AND GAZED UPON THE WISDOM OF HIS EYES. • • • • •   108 CUCHULAIN SEA V   41
    REMEMBER THE WISDOM OUT OF THE OLD DAYS, • • • • •   158 TO HIS HEART   2
    AND WISDOM THAT CAUGHT FIRE LIKE THE DRIED FLAX, • • •   181 QUEEN MAEVE   28
    WITH WISDOM, THEY WANDER TILL ALL THE YEARS HAVE GONE BY,   204 WITHER BOUGHS   21
    HEAVY LIKE STONE, THEIR WISDOM BEING HALF SILENCE. • • •   218 WOODS OF COOLE   26
    THEY THAT HAVE ALL THE WISDOM THAT'S IN LIFE, • • • •   235 SHADOW WATER B   293
    THE COMING OF WISDOM WITH TIME • • • • • • •   261 COMING WISDOM   T
    ALL WISDOM SHUT INTO HIS ONYX EYES, • • • • • •   311 MOUNTAIN TOMB   11
    ALL WISDOM SHUT INTO ITS ONYX EYES, • • • • • •   311 MOUNTAIN TOMB V   11
    I HAD THE WISDOM LOVE BRINGS FORTH, • • • • • •   313 MEMORY YOUTH   2
    I HAD THE WISDOM LOVE CAN BRING, • • • • • •   313 MEMORY YOUTH V   2
    "AND WISDOM IS A BUTTERFLY • • • • • • •   338 TOM OROUGHLEY   7
    NEW WELCOME AND OLD WISDOM AT HER FIRE • • • •   340 SHEP GOATHERD   32
    AN IMAGE OF MYSTERIOUS WISDOM WON BY TOIL, • • • • •   373 PHASES OF MOON   18
    AUSTERITY, A PLACE SET OUT FOR WISDOM • • • • •   377 PHASES OF MOON   127
    FOR HOW SHOULD I FORGET THE WISDOM THAT YOU BROUGHT, • •   391 UNDER SATURN   4
    THE HALF-READ WISDOM OF DAEMONIC IMAGES, • • • • •   427 PHANTOM HATRED   39
    THE HALF-READ WISDOM OF DEMONIC IMAGES, • • • • •   427 PHANTOM HATRED V   39
    THE HALF READ WISDOM OF DAEMONIC IMAGES, • • • • •   427 PHANTOM HATRED V   39
    WISDOM • • • • • • • • • • • • • •   440 WISDOM   T
    INNOCENCE, AND WISDOM HE. • • • • • • • •   440 WISDOM   17

	PAGE	TITLE		LINE
WISDOM (CONTINUED)				
NOR BLEAR-EYED WISDOM OUT OF MIDNIGHT OIL.	446	SCHOOL CHILDR		60
MURMURED THE WISDOM OF THE DESERT DJINNS,	468	HARUN RASHID		163
HAS SPOKEN THE WISDOM OF THE DESERT DJINNS,	468	HARUN RASHID	V	163
HAS MURMURED WISDOM OF THE DESERT DJINNS,	468	HARUN RASHID	V	163
A QUALITY OF WISDOM FROM HER LOVE'S	469	HARUN RASHID		180
UNDER IT WISDOM STANDS, AND I ALONE--	469	HARUN RASHID		189
QUALITY OF WISDOM FROM LOVE'S QUALITY,	469	HARUN RASHID	V	180
UNDER IT ARMED WISDOM STANDS, A SEPARATE WISDOM	469	HARUN RASHID	V	189
UNDER IT ARMED WISDOM STANDS, A SEPARATE WISDOM	469	HARUN RASHID	V	189
FOR WISDOM IS THE PROPERTY OF THE DEAD,	482	BLOOD AND MOON		49
THEY UNDERSTOOD THAT WISDOM COMES OF BEGGARY.	487	SEVEN SAGES		26
ALL NIGHT'S FATHOMLESS WISDOM COME,	519	HER DREAM		2
BODILY DECREPITUDE IS WISDOM; YOUNG	523	LONG SILENCE		7
O BUT THERE IS WISDOM	534	CONSOLATION		1
PLUCKED BITTER WISDOM THAT ENRICHED HIS BLOOD.	543	PARN FUNERAL 2		12
THEN THEY AND THEIR WISDOM WENT TO RACK!	566	LAPIS LAZULI		28
THE WISDOM OF THE PEOPLE'S GONE,	607	SONGS BURDEN 2		16
AND ELVISH WISDOM, AND LONG YEARS OF YOUTH	653	ISLE STAT I 2		47
AND FULL OF WISDOM IS EACH BLOOM,	655	ISLE STAT I 3		9
WILD SPIRITS OF WISDOM AND TONGUE.	708	FAIRY PEDANT	V	27
NO TENDER WISDOM FLOODS THE EYES	723	GIRLS SONG A		9
"MAN OF WISDOM, FROM THY SLEEPING	729	PRIEST FAIRY		39
"MAN OF WISDOM, DOST THOU KNOW	729	PRIEST FAIRY		47
WISDOM AND DREAMS	743	WISDOM DREAMS		T
WISDOM AND DREAMS ARE ONE,	743	WISDOM DREAMS		5
AND WISDOM THE FRUIT OF THE GARDEN.	743	WISDOM DREAMS		7
I DOUBT YOUR WISDOM, BUT DO NOT DOUBT MY LOVE.	748	SHADOW WATER A		31
ALTHOUGH I DOUBT YOUR WISDOM, DO NOT DOUBT .	748	SHADOW WATER A	V	31
FOR I HAVE ALL HIS GARDEN WISDOM. O SPEAK!	756	SHADOW WATER A		180
THE FOOL, WHO HAS MADE THE WISDOM THAT MEN WRITE	764	SHADOW WATER A		342
AND ALL THE WISDOM THAT OLD IMAGES,	764	SHADOW WATER A		344
WISDOM'S SEE WENCH-WISDOM'S				
OF BEAUTY'S CRUELTY AND WISDOM'S CHATTER--	377	PHASES OF MOON		121
AND LOVE WENCH WISDOM'S CRUEL FACE.	787	HUDDON DUDDON		10
WISDOMS				
OF THE DIM WISDOMS OLD AND DEEP,	138	TO IRELAND	V	21
WILD WISDOMS OF SPIRIT AND TONGUE.	708	FAIRY PEDANT		27
WISE				
AND A HUNDRED MAIDENS WISE AND YOUNG,	8	OISIN 1	V	94
THEN NO WISE WORSHIP DUSTY DEEDS,	65	HAPPY SHEPHERD	V	22
AGED AND WISE, THEY SEEK THEIR WONTED PERCHES	72	ANASHU VIJAYA		31
I WAS A WISE YOUNG KING OF OLD!	81	MAD KING GOLL	V	1
FIELDS FATTENING SLOW, MEN WISE IN JOY,	82	MAD KING GOLL	V	6
THIS WOULD I SAY, MOST WISE OF LIVING SOULS!	102	FERGUS DRUID		9
WHEN I GAVE JUDGMENT, AND HIS WORDS WERE WISE,	102	FERGUS DRUID		11
FOR HE WHO MADE YOU BITTER MADE YOU WISE."	108	CUCHULAIN SEA		32
FOR GOD WHO MADE YOU BITTER MADE YOU WISE."	108	CUCHULAIN SEA	V	32
AND AT THAT SINGING HE WAS NO MORE WISE.	127	DREAM OF FAERY		24
IT HAD GROWN MOST WISE WITH THINKING	159	CAP AND BELLS	V	7
AND IT HAD GROWN WISE BY THINKING	159	CAP AND BELLS	V	7
A CHATTERING WISE AND SWEET,	161	CAP AND BELLS		34
AND WHITHER THE WISE HEART KNOWS!	168	BLESSED		34
WHO BEING LOVELY WAS SO WISE--	193	BAILE AILLINN		98
AH! WISE, MY HEART KNOWS WELL HOW WISE.	193	BAILE AILLINN		99
AH! WISE, MY HEART KNOWS WELL HOW WISE.	193	BAILE AILLINN		99
WHERE THAT WISE HARPER'S FINGER RAN.	195	BAILE AILLINN		156
WHERE THAT WISE HARPER'S FINGERS RAN.	195	BAILE AILLINN	V	156
TIME CAN BUT MAKE IT EASIER TO BE WISE	200	FOLLY COMFORT		4
AND SO BE PATIENT; BE WISE AND PATIENT FRIEND."	200	FOLLY COMFORT	V	6
WISE BIDDY EARLY CALLED THE WICKED WOOD!	218	WOODS OF COOLE		15
TO FIND IF HEARTS BE WILD AND WISE,	263	MASK		4
THERE IS NOBODY WISE ENOUGH	268	BROWN PENNY		10
NOW FROM THAT JUICE THAT MADE THEM WISE	272	GREY ROCK		26
BUT FROM THE JUICE THAT MADE THEM WISE	272	GREY ROCK	V	26
DELIGHTED TO BE BUT WISE,	329	MEN IMPROVE		10
THAT SOLOMON GREW WISE	345	ON WOMAN		11
THIS WISE AND SIMPLE MAN.	347	FISHERMAN		8
THE BEATING DOWN OF THE WISE	348	FISHERMAN		23
THOSE MEN THAT IN THEIR WRITINGS ARE MOST WISE	370	EGO DOMINUS		68
ALONE, IMPORTANT AND WISE,	379	CAT AND MOON		26
AND ON THE INSTANT WOULD GROW WISE.	385	ROBARTES DANCE		12
FOR BEAUTY'S VERY SELF, HAS CHARM MADE WISE,	404	FOR DAUGHTER		37
COME LET US MOCK AT THE WISE!	432	NINETEEN 19		98
TO HELP GOOD, WISE OR GREAT	432	NINETEEN 19		110
FROM ALL THAT MAKES A WISE OLD MAN	553	PRAYER OLD AGE		5
TO US. OH WISE ART THOU IN SUCH A THING,	660	ISLE STAT II 1		46
THE SQUIRREL YONDER, HUSHED AND WISE,	686	LIFE		5
I HOLD HIM DEARER THAN THE WISE,	723	GIRLS SONG A		11
AND FOR HIM MAKE ME WISE AND BRIGHT.	723	GIRLS SONG A		12
HE THOUGHT WISE THINGS AS HIS GREY HEAD NODDED.	728	PRIEST FAIRY		12
BECAUSE A GOD HAS MADE HIM WISE WITH DREAMS!	748	SHADOW WATER A		26
TAUGHT ME WISE MUSIC, AND GAVE ME THIS OLD HARP!	750	SHADOW WATER A		76
BUT OUR SILENCE HAD BEEN WISE.	773	SONG DEIRDRE 1		22
YET OUR SILENCE HAD BEEN WISE;	773	SONG DEIRDRE 1	V	22
WISER				
SHE IS NOT WISER NOR LOVELIER,	197	BAILE AILLINN		201
ARE WISER WITCHCRAFT, FOR OUR PEACE AWAKES	763	SHADOW WATER A		320
WISEST				
EVEN THE WISEST MAN GROWS TENSE	638	BEN BULBEN		33
AND SHOUT AT THE WISEST OWLS	644	SONG FAERIES		10

902

		PAGE	TITLE		LINE

WISEST (CONTINUED)
AND SHOUT AT THE WISEST OWLS . . . . 676 ISLE STAT II 3 257
WISE-TONGUED
IT HAD GROWN WISE-TONGUED BY THINKING . . . . 159 CAP AND BELLS 7
WISH
YET WOULD BE NOW, COULD I BUT HAVE MY WISH, ... 267 ALL TEMPT ME 9
I WOULD BE NOW, COULD I BUT HAVE MY WISH, ... 267 ALL TEMPT ME V 9
AND ALL THAT I NEED DO IS TO WISH . . . . 300 RUN PARADISE 4
COULD MAKE ME WISH FOR ANYTHING THIS DAY, ... 338 SHEP GOATHERD 3
LET THE YOUNG WISH. BUT WHAT HAS BROUGHT YOU HERE? . . . 339 SHEP GOATHERD 6
THAT MOST RESPECTED LADY'S EVERY WISH. . . . . . . 410 TOWER 29
THEY SAY THE WISH ITSELF IS HALF THE SIN! . . . . . 692 MOSADA 1 48
WISHED
"YOU WILL HAVE ALL YOU HAVE WISHED FOR WHEN YOU HAVE EARNED 228 SHADOW WATER B 124
I WISHED BEFORE IT CEASED. NOR BIRD NOR BEAST . . . . 338 SHEP GOATHERD 2
YEAR. I WISHED BEFORE IT CEASED. NOR BIRD NOR BEAST . . 338 SHEP GOATHERD V 2
I MIGHT HAVE WISHED ON THE DAY . . . . 341 SHEP GOATHERD 73
I HAD WISHED A DEAR THING ON THAT DAY . . . . 341 SHEP GOATHERD V 73
WISHES
HE WISHES HIS BELOVED WERE DEAD . . . . 175 BELOVED DEAD T
AEDH WISHES HIS BELOVED WERE DEAD . . . . 175 BELOVED DEAD V T
HE WISHES FOR THE CLOTHS OF HEAVEN . . . . 176 CLOTHS HEAVEN T
AEDH WISHES FOR THE CLOTHS OF HEAVEN . . . . 176 CLOTHS HEAVEN V T
WISTFUL
THAT WANES." "AH, WISTFUL VOICE," REPLIED THE OTHER, . . 79 EPHEMERA V 3
SINGS THE YOUNG WISTFUL SPIRIT OF A STAR . . . . . 705 REMEMBRANCE 10
WIT   SEE MOTHER-WIT
WHERE WIT AND BEAUTY LEARNED THEIR TRADE . . . . . 288 TO WEALTHY MAN 16
I HAD MY SHARE OF MOTHER WIT! . . . . 313 MEMORY YOUTH V 3
A PRETENCE OF WIT." . . . . 349 HAWK 18
MATCHING OUR BROKEN-HEARTED WIT AGAINST HER WIT, . . . 362 HER COURTESY 7
MATCHING OUR BROKEN-HEARTED WIT AGAINST HER WIT, . . . 362 HER COURTESY 7
AS AIR UNDER A WING, CAN GIVE BIRDS' WIT. . . . . . 462 HARUN RASHID 28
AS AIR UNDER A WING, CAN GIVE BIRD'S WIT. . . . . . 462 HARUN RASHID V 28
AND HEAVENLY MUSIC IF THEY GAVE IT WIT! . . . . . . 533 HER TRIUMPH 6
IT IS OF GOD AND PASSES HUMAN WIT. . . . . 558 RIBH CHRISTIAN 2
CAN TOUCH BY MOTHER WIT . . . . 589 OLD WICKED MAN 40
WITH SOME FRIEND THAT HAS THE WIT . . . . 624 APPARITIONS 12
WITH SOME FRIEND WHO HAS THE WIT . . . . 624 APPARITIONS V 12
SUCH QUESTS AS THESE, I TROW, NEED LITTLE WIT. . . . . 650 ISLE STAT I 1 150
HE KNOWS BY SIGNS OF SECRET WIT . . . . 716 FAIRY DOCTOR 5
WITCH
THE WITCH. . . . . 310 WITCH T
WITH A FOUL WITCH . . . . 310 WITCH 3
SOLOMON AND THE WITCH . . . . 387 SOLOMON WITCH T
THAT THE WITCH OF ATLAS KNEW. . . . . 637 BEN BULBEN 3
A BEARDED WITCH, HER SLUGGISH HEAD LOW BENT . . . . 685 SEEKER 72
TIME AND THE WITCH VIVIEN. . . . . 720 WITCH VIVIEN T
WITCHCRAFT
ARE WISER WITCHCRAFT, FOR OUR PEACE AWAKES . . . . 763 SHADOW WATER A 320
AGAINST WITCHCRAFT . . . . 775 AGAINST WITCH V T
WITCHERY
WITH WITCHERY AND UNGUENTS FROM THE FLOWERS . . . . 41 OISIN 2 V 185
WITCHES
I KNOW OF THE LEAFY PATHS THAT THE WITCHES TAKE . . . 203 WITHER BOUGHS 9
I KNOW OF THE LEAFY PATH THAT THE WITCHES TAKE, . . . 203 WITHER BOUGHS V 9
ALL THE WILD WITCHES, THOSE MOST NOBLE LADIES, . . . 343 DEJECTION 4
WITHER
AND THE MOON LIKE A PALE ROSE WITHER AWAY." . . . . 28 OISIN 1 427
THEIR HAUGHTY IMAGES THAT CANNOT WITHER, ... 184 QUEEN MAEVE 87
NOW I MAY WITHER INTO THE TRUTH. . . . . 261 COMING WISDOM 4
SHALL WITHER THAT OLD MARVEL, FOR . . . . 447 COLONUS PRAISE 15
MY WORDS WERE ALL, "HERE NO LOVES WANE AND WITHER, . . 669 ISLE STAT II 3 84
WITHERED
THESE NOW OUTWORN AND WITHERED HANDS . . . . . . 23 OISIN 1 349
THESE NOW O'ERWORN AND WITHERED HANDS, ... 23 OISIN 1 V 348
A DUSKY DEMON DRY AS A WITHERED SEDGE . . . . . . 39 OISIN 2 158
A DUSK DEMON, DRY AS A WITHERED SEDGE, ... 39 OISIN 2 V 158
A HUSKY DEMON, DRY AS A WITHERED SEDGE . . . . . . 39 OISIN 2 V 158
BLIND AND NIGH DEAF, WITH WITHERED ARMS HE LIES . . . 42 OISIN 2 V 203
"I WOULD DIE LIKE A SMALL WITHERED LEAF IN THE AUTUMN, . 56 OISIN 3 131
     . . .
TILL ALL THE VALLEYS OF THE WORLD HAVE BEEN WITHERED AWAY. 163 VALLEY LOVERS 8
TILL THE VALLEYS OF THE WORLD HAVE BEEN WITHERED AWAY." . 163 VALLEY LOVERS V 8
NO BOUGHS HAVE WITHERED BECAUSE OF THE WINTRY WIND! . . 203 WITHER BOUGHS 7
THE BOUGHS HAVE WITHERED BECAUSE I HAVE TOLD THEM 203 WITHER BOUGHS 8
  MY DREAMS.
NO BOUGHS HAVE WITHERED BECAUSE OF THE WINTRY WIND! . . 203 WITHER BOUGHS 15
THE BOUGHS HAVE WITHERED BECAUSE I HAVE TOLD THEM 203 WITHER BOUGHS 16
  MY DREAMS.
NO BOUGHS HAVE WITHERED BECAUSE OF THE WINTRY WIND! . . 204 WITHER BOUGHS 23
THE BOUGHS HAVE WITHERED BECAUSE I HAVE TOLD THEM 204 WITHER BOUGHS 24
  MY DREAMS.
OR ON THE WITHERED MEN THAT SAW . . . . 344 DAWN 5
HAS WITHERED OUR ROSE TREE! . . . . 396 ROSE TREE 4
HAVE WITHERED OUR ROSE TREE! . . . . 396 ROSE TREE V 4
AND WITHERED TO A BAG OF BONES! . . . . 401 DEMON BEAST 49
WHEN WITHERED OLD AND SKELETON-GAUNT, ... 475 EVA GORE-BOOTH 12
"INTO A WITHERED CRONE." . . . . 516 MANS SONG 2
NO WITHERED CRONE I SAW . . . . 516 MANS SONG 11
OR BUT TO FIND IF WITHERED VEIN RAN BLOOD, ... 537 HER VISION 6

903

		PAGE	TITLE		LINE
WITHERED	**(CONTINUED)**				
DOWN EVERY WITHERED FINGER FROM THE TOP:		537	HER VISION		11
EVERYTHING ELSE WITHERED AND MUMMY-DEAD.		618	BRONZE HEAD		3
AS A LEAF THAT IS OLD, AND WITHERED, AND COLD,		643	SONG FAERIES		3
AS A LEAF THAT IS OLD, AND WITHERED, AND COLD,		644	SONG FAERIES		15
AS A LEAF THAT IS OLD, AND WITHERED, AND COLD,		676	ISLE STAT II 3		250
AS A LEAF THAT IS OLD, AND WITHERED, AND COLD,		676	ISLE STAT II 3		262
WITH WREATHS OF WITHERED FLOWERS		680	LOVE AND DEATH		17
WITH WREATHS OF WITHERED FLOWERS		680	LOVE AND DEATH		19
ON HER BROAD BREAST! BENEATH HER WITHERED BROWS		685	SEEKER		73
THY WITHERED FOE, AND WITH THE PURPLE WING		688	TWO TITANS		55
TWO WOMEN, WITHERED ONE AND SMALL AND THIN,		711	FERENCZ RENYI		51
A LITTLE WITHERED MAN, AND OLD.		716	FAIRY DOCTOR		4
THE LITTLE WITHERED MAN, AND OLD.		717	FAIRY DOCTOR		24
A WITHERED TREE?"		780	WELL AND TREE		16
OUR LUCK IS WITHERED AWAY,		783	GREY ROUND		18
AND WHEAT IN THE WHEAT-EAR WITHERED,		783	GREY ROUND		19
WITHERING					
BUT WHEN AT WITHERING OF THE SUN HE KNEW		40	OISIN 2	V	173
AND WHEN AT WITHERING OF THE SUN HE KNEW		40	OISIN 2	V	173
THE WITHERING OF THE BOUGHS		203	WITHER BOUGHS		T
LOVE'S MOON WAS WITHERING AWAY.		313	MEMORY YOUTH	V	7
THAT BLOW WHEN HEAVEN AND EARTH ARE WITHERING,		767	SHADOW WATER A		395
WITHERS					
WANDER WHERE EARTH WITHERS AWAY.		196	BAILE AILLINN		171
AND WHILE SHE FADES AND LIFE WITHERS AWAY,		768	SHADOW WATER A		422
HAD WOVEN HER OF WIND. LIFE WITHERS OUT		768	SHADOW WATER A	V	423
WITHERSHINS					
THAT CUT THROUGH TIME OR CROSS IT WITHERSHINS.		489	COOLE PARK 29		24
THAT CAN CROSS TIME AND CUT IT WITHERSHINS.		489	COOLE PARK 29		24
THAT CUT THROUGH TIME AND CUT IT WITHERSHINS		489	COOLE PARK 29	V	24
WITHHOLD					
DO NOT THE REST WITHHOLD.		588	OLD WICKED MAN		11
"LOVE TO GIVE OR TO WITHHOLD		588	OLD WICKED MAN		21
WITHHOLDS					
WITHHOLDS THEM NOW? HAVE THE EVER-LIVING ONES		234	SHADOW WATER B		269
WITHIN					
A BEAUTIFUL YOUNG MAN DREAMED WITHIN		17	OISIN 1		248
WE PASSED THE PORTALS, AND WITHIN,		17	OISIN 1	V	250
WITHIN HIS OTHER HAND WERE FLITTING		18	OISIN 1		253
WE DANCED TO WHERE WITHIN THE GLOOM		21	OISIN 1	V	305
I HEARD ONE SAY, "WITHIN HIS EYES		25	OISIN 1	V	380
AND STOOD WITHIN: CLOTHED IN A MISTY RAY		36	OISIN 2		104
AND STOOD WITHIN THE HALL. A MISTY RAY		36	OISIN 2	V	104
WITHIN HER WILDERING WHIRLS—FORGETTING HIM.		69	SAD SHEPHERD	V	28
WITHIN THE TEMPLE, DEVIOUS WALKING, MADE		72	ANASHU VIJAYA		32
A LITTLE WAY WITHIN THE GLOOM A ROEBUCK RAISED HIS EYES		76	INDIAN ON GOD		13
IS BUT A SLIDING DROP OF RAIN WITHIN HIS PETALS WIDE."		76	INDIAN ON GOD		12
I RULED AND RULED MY LIFE WITHIN—		82	MAD KING GOLL	V	7
AS ONCE WITHIN A LITTLE TOWN		85	MAD KING GOLL	V	49
ONCE, WHILE WITHIN A LITTLE TOWN		85	MAD KING GOLL	V	49
WITHOUT DOORS OR WITHIN,		96	MOLL MAGEE		44
SOMEWHERE WITHIN SOME HOLLOW HILL,		271	GREY ROCK	V	14
SHE'LL NOT BE PROUD, KNOWING WITHIN HER HEART		282	TWO KINGS		118
FOUND THAT OLD HOUSE, A SPUTTERING TORCH WITHIN,		283	TWO KINGS		140
AND FOUND THE HOUSE, A SPUTTERING TORCH WITHIN,		283	TWO KINGS	V	140
THAT WHEN HE HAS FALLEN ASLEEP WITHIN MY ARMS,		285	TWO KINGS		191
YET WE, HAD WE WALKED WITHIN		293	HELEN LIVED		7
I'LL SLEEP AWAY ALL TIME WITHIN IT:		306	HOUR DAWN		74
AND SLEEP AWAY ALL TIME WITHIN IT.		306	HOUR DAWN	V	74
HIS BODY MOULDED FROM WITHIN HIS BODY		374	PHASES OF MOON		43
AHERNE LAUGHED, THINKING OF THE MAN WITHIN,		375	PHASES OF MOON		85
WITHIN MY ARMS GREAT SOLOMON,		387	SOLOMON WITCH		4
NOR ANY HUMAN SIGHT WITHIN IT		389	SOLOMON WITCH		41
AND A HORSE PLASHES WITHIN IT:		393	EASTER 1916		52
THOUGH BUT A FEW LEARNED MEN SHALL LOOK WITHIN,		461	HARUN RASHID	V	18A
LOOK ON THAT FIRE, SALVATION WALKS WITHIN.		502	VACILLATION		76
WHAT HAPPENS A TREE THAT HAS NOTHING WITHIN IT?		548	TO SAME TUNE 3		23
WHAT HAPPENS TO A TREE THAT HAS NOTHING WITHIN IT?		548	TO SAME TUNE 3	V	23
WHAT TEARS DOWN A TREE THAT HAS NOTHING WITHIN IT?		615	MARCH SONGS 2		23
WHAT TEARS DOWN A TREE HAS NOTHING WITHIN IT?		615	MARCH SONGS 2	V	23
AND I THERE WITHIN.		621	JOHN KINSELLA		28
WITHIN THE DROWSY BLOSSOM HANGS THE BEE:		645	ISLE STAT I 1		2
WITHIN THE FOLD TO HEAR THE CREAKING GATE—		646	ISLE STAT I 1		41
AS WITHIN A CELLAR CHILLY		647	ISLE STAT I 1		57
BINDS, AS WITHIN A GIRDLE OR A RING,		657	ISLE STAT I 3		59
WITHIN MINE HEART: AND NAUGHT BUT SORROW NOW		659	ISLE STAT II 1		26
FOR EACH WITHIN HIMSELF HATH ALL		671	ISLE STAT II 3		132
THE WORLD, WITHIN HIS FOLDED HEART,		671	ISLE STAT II 3		133
WITHIN HIS CLENCHED TEETH A SWORD.		673	ISLE STAT II 3		182
I SEE WITHIN A CLOVEN ROCK DISPART		673	ISLE STAT II 3		195
DOTH HE STILL DWELL WITHIN THE WOODY SHADE,		678	ISLE STAT II 3		303
UNTIL WE DIE WITHIN THE CHARMED RING		679	ISLE STAT II 3		322
MAKE MOAN AND CRY. WITHIN YON SUNLESS VALLEY,		682	SEEKER		26
A VOICE HAS TOLD ME HOW WITHIN THIS LAND		682	SEEKER	V	22
WITHIN THE WOODWAYS, BLUE AS THE HALCYON'S WING,		683	SEEKER	V	38
TILL THEIR FIERCE MISERIES WITHIN HIS EYES		687	TWO TITANS		26
AND THROB WITHIN THE CIRCLES OF GREEN DAWN.		701	MOSADA 3		54
THE FLAME THAT SHONE WITHIN HIS EYES BUT NOW		704	MOSADA 3		128
AH! IT DWELT WITHIN THE TWILIGHT AS THE WORM WITHIN THE NUT.		718	PHANTOM SHIP		6

PAGE   TITLE   LINE

WITHIN   (CONTINUED)
    AH! IT DWELT WITHIN THE TWILIGHT AS THE WORM WITHIN THE   718 PHANTOM SHIP   6
        NUT.
    HE HAD DREAMED THE COW HAD GOT WITHIN   729 PRIEST FAIRY   33
    ON BRAHMA'S GATEWAY, "THEY WITHIN HAVE FED   735 QUATRAIN APHOR   15
    BEING IMAGINED WITHIN   785 WOMANS BEAUTY   23
WITHOUT
    AND NOW FLED BY, MIST-COVERED, WITHOUT SOUND,   29 OISIN 2   3
    AND ONE WHOM YOU WILL GO TO WITHOUT TELLING,   33 OISIN 2   V 67
    FORMS WITHOUT NUMBER! WHEN THE LIVE WEST FLASHED   41 OISIN 2   V 180
    WE SANG THE LOVES AND ANGERS WITHOUT SLEEP,   42 OISIN 2   194
    THE SPACIOUS LOVES, THE ANGER WITHOUT SLEEP   42 OISIN 2   V 194
    I AWOKE! THE STRANGE HORSE WITHOUT SUMMONS OUT OF   54 OISIN 3   105
        THE DISTANCE RAN,
    . . . HE SAD AS A CHILD WITHOUT MILK!   59 OISIN 3   174
    ON THE FLAMING STONES, WITHOUT REFUGE,   62 OISIN 3   213
    ON THE RED FLAMING STONES WITHOUT REFUGE   62 OISIN 3   V 213
    WITHOUT LAUGHTER, A SHOW UNTO CHILDREN,   63 OISIN 3   218
    FOR THY YOUTH WITHOUT PEACE, AND THY YEARS WITH THE DEMONS,   63 OISIN 3   V 216
    . . .
    AH ME! TO BE OLD WITHOUT SUCCOUR, A SHOW UNTO CHILDREN,   63 OISIN 3   V 217
        A STAIN,
    WITHOUT LAUGHTER, A COUGHING, ALONE WITH REMEMBRANCE AND   63 OISIN 3   V 218
        FEAR!
    WITHOUT DOORS OR WITHIN,   96 MOLL MAGEE   44
    AND WHAT TO ME WAS BURDEN WITHOUT END,   102 FERGUS DRUID   12
    HE MUSED UPON HIS MOCKERS! WITHOUT FAIL   127 DREAM OF FAERY   26
    A MAN WITH A HAZEL WAND CAME WITHOUT SOUND   153 CHANGE BELOVED   6
    I WOULD THAT THE BOAR WITHOUT BRISTLES HAD COME FROM THE   153 CHANGE BELOVED   10
        WEST
    A MAN WITH A WAND OF HAZEL CAME WITHOUT SOUND!   153 CHANGE BELOVED V 6
    AND TROUBLE WITH SIGHS FOR ALL HEARTS WITHOUT REST   163 ASKS FORGIVE   V 23
    GROW GENTLE WITHOUT SORROWING,   193 BAILE AILLINN   110
    GROW GENTLE WITHOUT SORROWINGS!   193 BAILE AILLINN   V 110
    HAVE HAPPINESS WITHOUT AN END,   195 BAILE AILLINN   158
    WITH A SLOW SMILE AND WITHOUT SOUND,   275 GREY ROCK   117
    HE RODE A RACE WITHOUT A BIT?   326 ROBERT GREGORY   63
    WITHOUT AN ANGRY THOUGHT   366 HER CHRIS TREE   2
    LIFE OVERFLOWS WITHOUT AMBITIOUS PAINS!   417 ANCEST HOUSES   3
    THERE LURCHES PAST, HIS GREAT EYES WITHOUT THOUGHT   433 NINETEEN 19   126
    TRUTHS WITHOUT FATHER CAME, TRUTHS THAT NO BOOK   467 HARUN RASHID   138
    WITHOUT A FRIEND ON THE EARTH   552 SONGS REWRIT 2   6
    WITHOUT A THING IN HIS HEAD   552 SONGS REWRIT 2   10
    WITHOUT A FRIEND ON THIS EARTH   552 SONGS REWRIT 2 V 6
    WITHOUT THERE OF A LITTLE, LIGHT OLD MAN!   720 WITCH VIVIEN   13
    WITHOUT MY GLASS I'D BE A SORRY CLOWN.   721 WITCH VIVIEN   29
WITHSTOOD
    A BUTLER OR AN ARMSTRONG THAT WITHSTOOD   270 PARDON FATHERS   10
WITNESS
    LET THE SEA BEAR WITNESS,   770 BLOOD BOND   7
    LET THE WIND BEAR WITNESS,   770 BLOOD BOND   8
    LET THE EARTH BEAR WITNESS,   770 BLOOD BOND   9
    LET THE FIRE BEAR WITNESS,   770 BLOOD BOND   10
    LET THE DEW BEAR WITNESS,   770 BLOOD BOND   11
    LET THE STARS BEAR WITNESS!   770 BLOOD BOND   12
WITNESSED
    HAVE WITNESSED THE BINDING.   770 BLOOD BOND   15
WIT'S
    AND MANY A DARLING WIT'S GROWN DULL   301 RUN PARADISE   18
WITS
    INDIGNANT AT THE FUMBLING WITS, THE OBSCURE SPITE   291 PAUDEEN   1
    AND THEN I'D STAGGER OUT. HE'D CRACK HIS WITS   377 PHASES OF MOON   134
    THE COMFORT THAT YOU MADE? ALTHOUGH MY WITS HAVE GONE   391 UNDER SATURN   5
    MUSIC HAD DRIVEN THEIR WITS ASTRAY--   411 TOWER   47
    HAD WAKING WITS! IT SEEMED   422 MY TABLE   31
    FOR THE EMBRACE OF NOTHING! AND I, MY WITS ASTRAY   426 PHANTOM HATRED   14
    FROM SHALLOW WITS! WHO KNOWS NO WORK CAN STAND,   429 NINETEEN 19   35
    POETS AND WITS ABOUT HIM DREW!   577 WHAT THEN   14
    IN COUNTRY SHAWL OR PARIS CLOAK, HAD PUT MY WITS ASTRAY,   592 PILGRIM   3
    THE HARE HATH LAID ASLEEP HER FROLIC WITS,   712 FERENCZ RENYI   72
    COME TO THE CHESS, FOR YOUNG GIRLS' WITS ARE BETTER   721 WITCH VIVIEN   46
    NIGH OF HIS WITS BY FEAR BEREFT.   730 PRIEST FAIRY   50
WITTED   SEE WANDERING-WITTED DULL-WITTED
    THAT AM A WANDERING WITTED FOOL   380 SONGS FOOL 1   V 16
WITTY
    OR A WITTY LOVELY LADY."   299 THREE HERMITS   28
    THE WITTY MAN AND HIS JOKE   347 FISHERMAN   19
    VEHEMENT AND WITTY SHE HAD SEEMED--! THE VENETIAN LADY   363 DOLLS FACES   5
WIVE
    HAS LOVER LIVED, BUT LONGED TO WIVE   197 BAILE AILLINN   206
    WHAT CAN BOOKS OF MEN THAT WIVE   309 REALISTS   2
WIVES
    FROM THE WIVES, AND THE CATS, AND THE CHILDREN,   92 FATHER OHART   15
    FROM THEIR WIVES, AND THEIR CATS, AND THEIR CHILDREN,   92 FATHER OHART   V 15
    OF HEN WIVES AND OF QUEER OLD MEN   607 SONGS BURDEN 2 V 23
WIZARD
    IN EVERY BRAIN A WIZARD GLOW,   20 OISIN 1   V 291A
    LAID IT AND SIGHED--A SWORD WHOSE WIZARD SHINE   37 OISIN 2   V 126
    MURMURING A WIZARD SONG FOR THEE.   134 TWO TREES   12
    AND ALL THE WIZARD THINGS THAT GO   139 TO IRELAND   V 39
    FROM MY WIZARD ISLAND LAIR,   668 ISLE STAT II 3   63

905

WIZARDRY
    IN SILENCE, THAT FAMED FLOWER OF WIZARDRY, ... 673 ISLE STAT II 3 192
WIZEN
    SCARCE THE OLD AND WIZEN HOUSES HAD THEIR DOORS AND WINDOWS 718 PHANTOM SHIP 5
      SHUT.
WIZENED
    SCARCE THE OLD AND WIZENED HOUSES HAD THEIR DOORS 718 PHANTOM SHIP V 5
      AND WINDOWS SHUT.
WOE
    WHO IS AMRITA? WOE! AH, WOE IS ME! . . . . 71 ANASHU VIJAYA V 15
    WHO IS AMRITA? WOE! AH, WOE IS ME! . . . . 71 ANASHU VIJAYA V 15
    AH WOE! FULL MANY A CREAK GAVE THE CREEL IN THE CART . 91 OLD FISHERMAN V 6
    AH, WOE IS ME! I GO FROM SUN AND SHADE, ... 674 ISLE STAT II 3 216
    SHE IS LONG AGES DUST. AH, WOE IS ME! . . . . 679 ISLE STAT II 3 313
    FOR ALL MY JOY--AH, WOE! . . . . 685 SEEKER 79
    AH! WOE FOR THE LOSS OF YOUR FACE, ... 708 FAIRY PEDANT 32
    AH! WOE FOR YOUR WINGS AND YOUR HEAD-- . . . . . . 708 FAIRY PEDANT 34
    AH! WOE FOR YOUR EYES AND THEIR BRIGHTNESS-- . . . . 708 FAIRY PEDANT 35
    AH! WOE FOR YOUR SLIPPERS OF RED. . . . . 708 FAIRY PEDANT 36
WOE-BEGONE
    AND WOE-BEGONE. FOR THEM NO EVIL DAY! . . . . 677 ISLE STAT II 3 275
WOES
    UNMINDFUL OF ITS WOES, WOULD TWINE A WREATH . . . . . 650 ISLE STAT I 1 133
WOKE
    BUT NOW THE WAR-RAGE IN CUCHULAIN WOKE, ... 110 CUCHULAIN SEA 65
    BUT NOW THE WAR RAGE IN CUCHULAIN WOKE, ... 110 CUCHULAIN SEA V 65
    BUT WOKE AT THE FIRST GLEAM OF DAY, ROSE UP . . . . . 467 HARUN RASHID 147
    BUT I WOKE IN AN OLD RUIN THAT THE WINDS HOWLED THROUGH: 581 CURSE CROMWELL 28
    AND THE PALE BLOSSOM: BUT I WOKE INSTEAD . . . . . . 761 SHADOW WATER A 281
WOLD
    OF THINE CRY OVER WOLD AND WATER WHITE, ... 669 ISLE STAT II 3 73
    OVER THE SORREL-COVERED WOLD-- . . . . 716 FAIRY DOCTOR 2
WOLF
    AS A HAY-COCK OUT ON THE FLOOD, OR A WOLF SUCKED UNDER 63 OISIN 3 220
      A WEIR.
    AS A GRASS SEED CRUSHED BY A PEBBLE, AS A WOLF SUCKED UNDER 63 OISIN 3 V 220
      A WEIR.
    THE GREY WOLF KNOWS ME: BY ONE EAR . . . . 84 MAD KING GOLL 45
    AND SO WITH WOLF, AND BOAR, AND STEER. . . . . 671 ISLE STAT II 3 122
WOLF-BREEDING
    WOLF-BREEDING MOUNTAINS, GALLERIED EMAN, ... 81 MAD KING GOLL V 2
WOLFE
    AND ROBERT EMMET AND WOLFE TONE, ... 290 SEPTEMBER 1913 21
    LORD EDWARD AND WOLFE TONE, ... 395 SIXTEEN DEAD 16
WOLVES
    OF WOLVES, OF BOREAL BEARS, WE QUAFFED THE WINE . . . 41 OISIN 2 V 188
    AND ON THE SKINS OF WOLVES AND BEARS WE SLEPT! . . . 41 OISIN 2 V 191
    . . . "THE FENIANS HUNT WOLVES IN THE NIGHT, ... 59 OISIN 3 171
    THEY LEFT THEIR BODIES TO FATTEN THE WOLVES, ... 545 TO SAME TUNE 2 2
    THEY LEFT THEIR BODIES TO FATTEN THE WOLVES, ... 613 MARCH SONGS 1 2
WOMAN   SEE WOOD-WOMAN QUEEN-WOMAN
    "O PLEASANT WOMAN," ANSWERED FINN, ... 5 OISIN 1 40
    THAT WOMAN FOUND A RING HUNG ON THE WALL, ... 37 OISIN 2 120
    A WEARY WOMAN SLEEPS SO HARD! . . . . 95 MOLL MAGEE 21
    NO WOMAN LOVES ME, NO MAN SEEKS MY HELP, ... 103 FERGUS DRUID V 26
    THERE'S NOT A WOMAN TURNS HER FACE . . . . 131 OLD PENSIONER 13
    THE HEART OF THE WOMAN . . . . 151 HEART OF WOMAN T
    THE DESIRE OF MAN AND OF WOMAN . . . . 153 CHANGE BELOVED V T
    WHITE WOMAN THAT PASSION HAS WORN . . . . 157 POET BELOVED 3
    WHITE WOMAN WITH NUMBERLESS DREAMS, ... 157 POET BELOVED 7
    A WOMAN OF SO SHINING LOVELINESS . . . . 170 SECRET ROSE 25
    OF THE WOMAN THAT HE LOVES, UNTIL HE DIES. . . . . 177 PAST GREATNESS 10
    AND THAT MILD WOMAN OF THE SOUTH, ... 189 BAILE AILLINN 6
    AS WHEN NEWLY GROWN TO BE A WOMAN, ... 199 ARROW 4
    THAT BEAUTIFUL MILD WOMAN, YOUR CLOSE FRIEND, . . 204 ADAMS CURSE 2
    THAT BEAUTIFUL MILD WOMAN FOR WHOSE SAKE . . . . 205 ADAMS CURSE 15
    REPLIED: "TO BE BORN WOMAN IS TO KNOW-- . . . . . 205 ADAMS CURSE 18
    THE MARTYRS CALL THE WORLD." THAT WOMAN THEN . . 205 ADAMS CURSE V 14
    AND THE WOOD WOMAN, WHOSE LOVER WAS CHANGED TO A BLUE-EYED 209 UNDER THE MOON V 13
      HAWK:
    TO GRASP THE WOMAN. YOU HAVE DARED TO TOUCH HER? . . 223 SHADOW WATER B 39
    FOR THAT BRIEF SIGHING. IF YOU HAD LOVED SOME WOMAN-- . 228 SHADOW WATER B 135
    THAT MUCH IS CERTAIN. I SHALL FIND A WOMAN, ... 231 SHADOW WATER B 209
    AND WHERE THERE IS ONE WOMAN THERE'LL BE OTHERS. . . 232 SHADOW WATER B 227
    TO WIN A WOMAN IN HER OWN DESPITE, ... 244 SHADOW WATER B 458
    TO WIN A WOMAN IS IN HER OWN DESPITE, ... 244 SHADOW WATER B V 458
    SOME OTHER WOMAN HAS A CLAIM ON YOU. . . . . . . 245 SHADOW WATER B 474
    LET'S HOME: I'D GIVE SOME RUBIES TO A WOMAN. . . . 248 SHADOW WATER B 537
    AND HAVING LIT UPON THIS WOMAN THERE, ... 248 SHADOW WATER B 542
    AS FOR THIS WOMAN, I THINK SHE IS COMING WITH ME. . 248 SHADOW WATER B 545
    IT WAS THIS WOMAN IN HER WOMAN'S VENGEANCE . . . . 248 SHADOW WATER B 547
    AND HAVING LIT UPON THIS WOMAN HERE, ... 248 SHADOW WATER B V 542
    I AM A WOMAN, I DIE AT EVERY BREATH. . . . . . . 250 SHADOW WATER B 583
    A WOMAN HOMER SUNG . . . . 254 WOMAN HOMER T
    A WOMAN HOMER SUNG, ... 255 WOMAN HOMER 19
    FOR ONE THAT WAS LIKE WOMAN MADE . . . . 272 GREY ROCK 29
    I KNEW A WOMAN NONE COULD PLEASE, ... 272 GREY ROCK 41
    I KNOW A WOMAN NONE COULD PLEASE, ... 272 GREY ROCK V 41
    A KIND MILD WOMAN HAD SHE BEEN, WHO POURED . . . 279 TWO KINGS V 62A
    SAID, "IF A WOMAN HAS PUT THIS ON YOU, ... 281 TWO KINGS 111
    BUT THAT SWEET-SOUNDING VOICE RAN ON: "WOMAN, . . 284 TWO KINGS 165

WOMAN   (CONTINUED)
    OR I HAD NO WOMAN THERE TO KISS! . . . .   305 HOUR DAWN   66
    THE MAN AND THE WOMAN BRING . . . .   319 DOLLS   10
    "THERE'S NOT A MAN OR WOMAN . . . .   333 SOLOMON SHEBA   19
    ON WOMAN . . . .   345 ON WOMAN   T
    MAY GOD BE PRAISED FOR WOMAN . . . .   345 ON WOMAN   1
    A WOMAN SPOKE OF SOME NEW TALE SHE HAD READ, . . .   350 HER PRAISE   7
    SHE KNOWS HERSELF A WOMAN. . . . .   365 HER RACE   5
    A SPHINX WITH WOMAN BREAST AND LION PAW, ...   383 VISION ROBART   18
    AND MUST NO BEAUTIFUL WOMAN BE . . . .   386 ROBARTES DANCE   25
    THAT WOMAN A WHILE WOULD BE SHRILL . . . .   392 EASTER 1916   V 17
    THE WOMAN THAT BY ME LAY . . . .   398 BREAK OF DAY   2
    HAVE I NOT SEEN THE LOVELIEST WOMAN BORN . . . . .   405 FOR DAUGHTER   59
    UPON A WOMAN WON OR WOMAN LOST? . . . .   413 TOWER   114
    UPON A WOMAN WON OR WOMAN LOST? . . . .   413 TOWER   114
    AND LEAVE A WOMAN AND A MAN BEHIND . . . .   422 MY DESCENDANTS   3
    TO LEAVE A WOMAN AND A MAN BEHIND . . . .   422 MY DESCENDANTS   V 3
    A WOMAN AND A MAN, ...   436 FOR MY SON   27
    IF YOU HAVE SEEN THAT IMAGE AND NOT THE WOMAN. . .   448 HERO GIRL FOOL   8
    I DID NOT FIND IN ANY CAGE THE WOMAN AT MY SIDE. . .   450 OWEN AHERNE   19
    OR COURT A WOMAN! NEITHER ENEMY, ...   463 HARUN RASHID   59
    GAME-BIRD, NOR WOMAN DOES THE SAME THING TWICE! . .   463 HARUN RASHID   60
    GAME BIRD, OR WOMAN DOES THE SAME THING TWICE! . .   463 HARUN RASHID   V 60
    GAMEBIRD, NOR WOMAN DOES THE SAME THING TWICE! . .   463 HARUN RASHID   V 60
    HAVE LIT UPON A WOMAN WHO SO SHARES . . . .   465 HARUN RASHID   85
    A PROUD WOMAN NOT KINDRED OF HIS SOUL. . . . . . .   479 SELF AND SOUL   64
    UPON AN AGED WOMAN AND HER HOUSE, ...   488 COOLE PARK 29   2
    EVERY COMMON WOMAN KNOWS, ...   499 MOTHER OF GOD   7
    ONE DEAR BRILLIANT WOMAN! . . . .   504 RESULT THOUGHT   2
    "A WOMAN CAN BE PROUD AND STIFF . . . .   513 JANE TALK BISH   13
    A WOMAN YOUNG AND OLD I FATHER AND CHILD . . . .   531 FATHER CHILD   V T
    A WOMAN, AND AN ARROW ON A STRING! . . . .   541 PARN FUNERAL 1   11
    THAT WOMAN, THE GREAT MOTHER IMAGING, ...   541 PARN FUNERAL 1   13
    "DROWN ALL THE DOGS," SAID THE FIERCE YOUNG WOMAN, . 546 TO SAME TUNE 2   7
    DROWN ALL THE DOGS," SAID THE FIERCE YOUNG WOMAN. .   546 TO SAME TUNE 2   10
    "DROWN ALL THE DOGS," SAID THE FIERCE YOUNG WOMAN. . 546 TO SAME TUNE 2   17
    DROWN ALL THE DOGS," SAID THE FIERCE YOUNG WOMAN. .   546 TO SAME TUNE 2   20
    "DROWN ALL THE DOGS," SAID THE FIERCE YOUNG WOMAN. . 547 TO SAME TUNE 2   27
    DROWN ALL THE DOGS," SAID THE FIERCE YOUNG WOMAN. .   547 TO SAME TUNE 2   30
    SOME TAKE DELIGHT IN ADORNING A WOMAN. . . . . . .   547 TO SAME TUNE 3   V 3
    . . . MAN, WOMAN, CHILD (A DAUGHTER OR A SON), . .   556 RIBH PATRICK   2
    WHY DO I HATE MAN, WOMAN OR EVENT? . . . .   558 RIBH CHRISTIAN   7
    BUT IN THAT WOMAN, IN THAT HOUSEHOLD WHERE . . . .   603 GALLERY REVIS   34
    SAID TO THE WOMAN ON HIS KNEES, "LIE STILL. . . .   609 IN TARAS HALLS   2
    AND GIVEN EVERYTHING A WOMAN NEEDS, ...   609 IN TARAS HALLS   7
    OF GOD OR WOMAN, THE TIME WERE COME TO DIE." . . .   609 IN TARAS HALLS   15
    SHE THINKS, PART WOMAN, THREE PARTS A CHILD, . . .   617 LONG-LEG FLY   15
    YET A MOST GENTLE WOMAN! WHO CAN TELL . . . . . .   618 BRONZE HEAD   10
    WHAT WOMAN HUGS HER INFANT THERE? . . . .   625 NATIVITY   1
    WHY IS THE WOMAN TERROR-STRUCK? . . . .   625 NATIVITY   11
    LION AND WOMAN AND THE LORD KNOWS WHAT. . . . . . .   629 CIRCUS ANIMALS   8
    A CAPTIVE WOMAN FROM THE NARROW BRIDGE, ...   749 SHADOW WATER A   49
    A WOMAN IN MY ARMS, SHE SINKS AWAY . . . .   749 SHADOW WATER A   54
    NO MAN NOR WOMAN HAS LOVED OTHERWISE . . . .   750 SHADOW WATER A   64
    OF SOME MILD WOMAN, OR IN CHILDREN'S WAYS. . . . .   750 SHADOW WATER A   74
    NO MAN NOR WOMAN HAS LOVED OTHERWISE . . . .   750 SHADOW WATER A   V 64
    A WOMAN LIES AMONG EMBROIDERIES. . . . .   752 SHADOW WATER A   120
    FOR AN IMMORTAL WOMAN, AS I THINK. . . . .   755 SHADOW WATER A   173
    SHE WILL ANSWER NOW LIKE ANY WAITING WOMAN . . . .   757 SHADOW WATER A   193
    I CEASED TO BE A WOMAN, BEING A QUEEN. . . . . . .   758 SHADOW WATER A   228
WOMANHOOD
    IN THE FIRST LOVELINESS OF WOMANHOOD, ...   356 BROKEN DREAMS   24
WOMANKIND
    AND THERE'S A SCORE OF DUCHESSES, SURPASSING WOMANKIND,   353 HIS PHOENIX   5
WOMAN-KIND
    AND THERE'S A SCORE OF DUCHESSES, SURPASSING WOMAN-KIND, 353 HIS PHOENIX   V 5
WOMAN'S
    NO WOMAN'S LOVED ME, NO MAN SOUGHT MY HELP. . . .   103 FERGUS DRUID   26
    "YOUR HEAD A WHILE SEEMED LIKE A WOMAN'S HEAD . . .   110 CUCHULAIN SEA   63
    ARE OVERTHROWN BY A WOMAN'S GAZE . . . .   164 PERFECT BEAUTY   4
    STILL OVERTHROWN BY A WOMAN'S GAZE, ...   164 PERFECT BEAUTY   V 4
    WHATEVER WOMAN'S LOVER HAD HIT HER FANCY, ...   181 QUEEN MAEVE   24
    A CHILD'S LAUGHTER, A WOMAN'S KISS. . . . .   190 BAILE AILLINN   40
    A LUCKY BATTLE, OR A WOMAN'S KISS . . . .   227 SHADOW WATER B   115
    BUT WITH A MAN'S HEAD, OR A FAIR WOMAN'S, ...   233 SHADOW WATER B   245
    AND NOW A LAGGARD WITH A WOMAN'S HEAD . . . . . .   234 SHADOW WATER B   260
    IT WAS THIS WOMAN IN HER WOMAN'S VENGEANCE . . . .   248 SHADOW WATER B   547
    BEING FOR A WOMAN'S SAKE. . . . .   259 UNWORTH PRAISE   4
    ONE TIME IT WAS A WOMAN'S FACE, OR WORSE— . . . .   267 ALL TEMPT ME   2
    YOU'D CRY, "SOME WOMAN'S YELLOW HAIR . . . .   290 SEPTEMBER 1913   28
    WHAT WOMAN'S SATISFIED, ...   334 SONG   8
    OF SOME STRANGE WOMAN'S NAME THAT RAN IN HIS HEAD. . 351 HER PRAISE   V 9
    WITH ALL A WOMAN'S PASSION, A CHILD'S IMPERIOUS WAY,   354 HIS PHOENIX   14
    END IN A BEAUTIFUL MAN'S OR WOMAN'S BODY. . . . .   374 PHASES OF MOON   64
    THAT WOMAN'S DAYS WERE SPENT . . . .   392 EASTER 1916   17
    WAILING UPON A WOMAN'S KNEE, ...   436 FOR MY SON   22
    THAT MAKE A MAN'S SOUL OR A WOMAN'S SOUL . . . . .   465 HARUN RASHID   93
    GAVE BUT MORE REASON FOR A WOMAN'S CARE. . . . . .   466 HARUN RASHID   111
    A WOMAN'S BEAUTY IS A STORM-TOSSED BANNER! . . . .   469 HARUN RASHID   188
    THE BEAUTY OF A WOMAN'S MIND OR BODY . . . .   469 HARUN RASHID   V 187
    AND YET A WOMAN'S POWERFUL CHARACTER . . . .   489 COOLE PARK 29   18

907

	PAGE	TITLE	LINE
WOMAN'S (CONTINUED)			
OF CHILDREN'S GRATITUDE OR WOMAN'S LOVE.	500	VACILLATION	26
REMEMBERING A WOMAN'S BEAUTY.	552	SONGS REWRIT 2 V	11
UPON A WOMAN'S BREAST."	590	OLD WICKED MAN	62
BEFORE A WOMAN'S PORTRAIT SUDDENLY I STAND,	602	GALLERY REVIS	13
ON THAT WOMAN'S REELING BRAIN?	632	MAN AND ECHO	14
FOR LOVE IS A-WEAVING WHEN A WOMAN'S HEART	761	SHADOW WATER A	262
A WOMAN'S BEAUTY IS LIKE A WHITE	784	WOMANS BEAUTY	1
OR IN MERE WOMAN'S CRUELTY	789	SINGING HEAD	11
WOMB			
THE HEAVENS IN MY WOMB.	499	MOTHER OF GOD	5
I CARRY FROM MY MOTHER'S WOMB	506	REMORSE SPEECH	14
IN MY MOTHER'S WOMB.	511	JANE AND JACK	12
FOR THE WOMB THE SEED SIGHS.	574	LOVERS SONG	3
OR CHILD HID IN THE WOMB.	589	OLD WICKED MAN	53
FROM EMPTY TOMB OR VIRGIN WOMB?	619	STICK INCENSE	2
WOMEN			
OLD WOMEN WERE KEENING THE DEAD:	145	HOST OF AIR V	40D
I CRIED IN MY DREAM, O WOMEN, BID THE YOUNG MEN LAY	163	VALLEY LOVERS	5
AND I CRIED IN MY DREAM "O WOMEN, BID THE YOUNG MEN LAY	163	VALLEY LOVERS V	5
WOMEN AND CHILDREN, YOUNG MEN WITH BOOKS,	167	BLESSED	15
CHILDREN AND WOMEN AND TONSURED YOUNG MEN,	167	BLESSED V	15
O WOMEN, KNEELING BY YOUR ALTAR-RAILS LONG HENCE,	173	SPEAKS HEARERS	1
O, WOMEN, KNEELING BY YOUR ALTAR RAILS LONG HENCE,	173	SPEAKS HEARERS V	1
TO PASSIONATE WOMEN IF IT SEEM	202	NEVER GIVE ALL	3
"THERE IS ONE THING THAT ALL WE WOMEN KNOW	205	ADAMS CURSE V	18
TO DREAM OF WOMEN WHOSE BEAUTY WAS FOLDED IN DISMAY,	210	UNDER THE MOON	19
TRANSFORM THESE RASCAL BILLOWS INTO WOMEN	222	SHADOW WATER B	11
HAS BEAUTIFUL WOMEN TO PLEASE EVERY MAN,	228	SHADOW WATER B	144
WRUNG FROM THE COLD WOMEN OF THE SEA—	237	SHADOW WATER B	343
WOMEN ARE HARD AND PROUD AND STUBBORN-HEARTED,	245	SHADOW WATER B	479
OF MEN AND WOMEN MADE LIKE THESE:	272	GREY ROCK	43
'TWAS WINE OR WOMEN, OR SOME CURSE—	273	GREY ROCK	54
THE WOMEN OF HIS HOUSEHOLD WERE ASLEEP,	282	TWO KINGS V	133
WOMEN CAN FIND." WITH A MOST MASTERFUL VOICE,	284	TWO KINGS	175
WOMEN CAN FIND." WITH A MOST BURNING VOICE	284	TWO KINGS V	175
OF THE MEN AND WOMEN OF TROY,	293	HELEN LIVED	11
THREE WOMEN THAT HAVE WROUGHT	315	FRIENDS	2
THAT WOMEN LAUGHING, OR TIMID OR WILD,	358	PRESENCES	4
AT ALL THESE DEATH-BEDS WOMEN HEARD	361	ALF POLLEXFEN	36
AT ALL THESE DEATHBEDS WOMEN HEARD	361	ALF POLLEXFEN V	36
AND THAT ALL BEAUTIFUL WOMEN MAY	387	ROBARTES DANCE	45
IT'S CERTAIN THAT FINE WOMEN EAT	404	FOR DAUGHTER	30
DID ALL OLD MEN AND WOMEN, RICH AND POOR,	413	TOWER	97
MEMORIES OF THE WORDS OF WOMEN.	415	TOWER	162
THE WOMEN TAKE SO LITTLE STOCK	455	HIS MEMORIES	7
HOW SUCH A MAN PLEASED WOMEN MOST	458	SECRETS OF OLD	13
BODIES OF HOLY MEN AND WOMEN EXUDE	483	OIL AND BLOOD	2
MORE WOMEN BORN THAN MEN."	485	STATISTICS	4
ALL WOMEN DOTE UPON AN IDLE MAN	500	VACILLATION	23
"THREE DEAR THINGS THAT WOMEN KNOW,"	521	THREE THINGS	7
OF ALL GOOD MEN AND WOMEN.	531	FATHER CHILD	3
ALL STATELY WOMEN MOVING TO A SONG	537	HER VISION	17
I GAVE WHAT OTHER WOMEN GAVE	538	LAST CONFESS	13
LOVERS OF HORSES AND OF WOMEN, SHALL,	564	GYRES	19
I HAVE HEARD THAT HYSTERICAL WOMEN SAY	565	LAPIS LAZULI	1
WHAT MATTER, WE ARE BUT WOMEN,	572	LADYS 2ND SONG	3
NOTHING THAT COMMON WOMEN PONDER ON	579	DOR WELLESLEY	12
"BECAUSE I AM MAD ABOUT WOMEN	587	OLD WICKED MAN	1
AND WHAT'S THE GOOD OF WOMEN, FOR ALL THAT THEY CAN SAY	592	PILGRIM	4
THAT MEN AND WOMEN OF ALL SORTS	597	MODEL LAUREATE	3
APPROVED PATTERNS OF WOMEN OR OF MEN	602	GALLERY REVIS	31
TO MANY WOMEN I HAVE SAID, "LIE STILL,"	609	IN TARAS HALLS	6
GAVE WOMEN DREAMS AND DREAMS THEIR LOOKING-GLASS.	610	STATUES	16
GAVE WOMEN DREAMS AND DREAMS THEIR LOOKING GLASS.	610	STATUES V	16
THE WOMEN THAT I PICKED SPOKE SWEET AND LOW	622	HOUND VOICE	8
BECAUSE WOMEN IN THE UPPER STOREYS DEMAND A FACE AT THE PANE,	623	HIGH TALK	7
SWEAR BY THOSE HORSEMEN, BY THOSE WOMEN	637	BEN BULBEN	5
TWO WOMEN, WITHERED ONE AND SMALL AND THIN,	711	FERENCZ RENYI	51
AND THE FISHER MEN AND WOMEN FROM THE DRIPPING HARBOUR WALL	718	PHANTOM SHIP	11
THE BOYS, THE WOMEN, AND OLD MEN,	725	LEGEND	7
AND DROVE THE BOYS AND WOMEN OFF.	725	LEGEND	24
THE WOMEN SLINGERS ON THE NARROW BRIDGE,	749	SHADOW WATER A V	41
BUT WOMEN AND JUGGLERS AND PLAYERS ON THE HARP.	752	SHADOW WATER A	115
BELIEVE THAT GOLD AND WOMEN TAKEN IN WAR	754	SHADOW WATER A	159
BECAUSE THESE WATERS MAKE ALL WOMEN ONE.	757	SHADOW WATER A	194
UNDER THE WAVES, AND TOOK A THOUSAND WOMEN	766	SHADOW WATER A	378
TO WANDER IN: YOU HAVE LOVED MANY WOMEN,	767	SHADOW WATER A	389
THE WOMEN NONE CAN KISS AND THRIVE,	775	AGAINST WITCH	8
WOMEN, THAT NONE CAN KISS AND THRIVE,	775	AGAINST WITCH V	8
GAVE ALL THE LOVE THAT WOMEN KNOW!	789	SINGING HEAD	21
WHERE MAY NEW-MARRIED WOMEN SIT	791	REPRISALS	19
WOMEN'S			
I HAVE OLD WOMEN'S SECRETS NOW	457	SECRETS OF OLD	1
WOMEN-SLINGERS			
THE WOMEN-SLINGERS ON THE NARROW BRIDGE,	749	SHADOW WATER A	41
WON			
THESE HANDS WON MANY A TORQUE OF GOLD.	83	MAD KING GOLL	23
HAS WON THE GOLD HIS CARS OF BATTLE BRING."	106	CUCHULAIN SEA	11
NOR WON THE GOLD THAT NOW CUCHULAIN BRINGS."	106	CUCHULAIN SEA V	11

WON   (CONTINUED)
"FROM THE GREY SHIPS AND BATTLES NEVER WON.   114 ROSE OF BATTLE V   8
BEAUTY THAT WE HAVE WON   293 HELEN LIVED   5
LOVE LOST AS SOON AS WON,   312 CHILD DANCING   8
WHO HAS WON A DRUNKEN CHEER,   347 FISHERMAN   18
AN IMAGE OF MYSTERIOUS WISDOM WON BY TOIL!   373 PHASES OF MOON   18
HE MIGHT HAVE WON FAME IN THE END,   392 EASTER 1916   28
I SAW MY FREEDOM WON   400 DEMON BEAST   7
UPON A WOMAN WON OR WOMAN LOST?   413 TOWER   114
WHAT NO DECEPTION WON. I HAVE HEARD THEM SAY   448 HERO GIRL FOOL V   13
NO LOOSE-LIPPED DEMAGOGUE HAD WON THE DAY,   542 PARN FUNERAL 2   3
NO LOOSE LIPPED DEMAGOGUE HAD WON THE DAY,   542 PARN FUNERAL 2 V   3
BUT BODY WON! IT WALKS UPRIGHT.   561 FOUR AGES MAN   2
AFTER CERTAIN YEARS HE WON   577 WHAT THEN   7
I SING WHAT WAS LOST AND DREAD WHAT WAS WON,   591 WHAT WAS LOST   1
COMPLETENESS OF THEIR PASSIONS WON!   637 BEN BULBEN   9
IF WHEN THE BATTLE IS HALF WON,   743 DANAAN QUICK   19
WONDER
SO PALE! AND SOUNDS OF WONDER HER LIPS UTTERED,   34 OISIN 2   V   71
WATCHED ME WITH MOURNFUL WONDER OUT OF THE WELLS OF HIS   51 OISIN 3   60
EYES.
STARED ON THE MOURNFUL WONDER OF HIS EYES,   108 CUCHULAIN SEA   41
UPON THE MOURNFUL WONDER OF HIS EYES,   108 CUCHULAIN SEA V   42
AND PONDERED ON THE WONDER OF HIS DAYS,   108 CUCHULAIN SEA V   43
MOURNFUL THAT NO NEW WONDER MAY BETIDE,   111 ROSE OF WORLD   3
WHY, IT'S A WONDER OUT OF RECKONING   243 SHADOW WATER B   445
AND WONDER WHAT HAS AILED HIM THESE TWELVE MONTHS." 284 TWO KINGS   163
(I WONDER IF THE BUILDER HAS BEEN PAID)   292 TO A SHADE   3
WONDER HOW MANY TIMES I COULD HAVE PROVED MY WORTH   427 PHANTOM HATRED   34
IN MOMENTARY WONDER STARE UPON   443 SCHOOL CHILDR   7
AND WONDER IF SHE STOOD SO AT THAT AGE--   444 SCHOOL CHILDR   19
AND, OH! THE WONDER OF THE THING! EACH CAME   656 ISLE STAT I 3   29
THE WINGED WONDER OF ALL FAERY LAND,   657 ISLE STAT I 3   57
TO MAKE US GLAD WITH WONDER AS WE SAT   683 SEEKER   41
I WONDER WHICH IS WHITEST, THEY OR THOU.   700 MOSADA 3   45
WONDERED
AND WONDERED WHAT WAS LEFT FOR MASSACRE TO SAVE.   619 BRONZE HEAD   28
WONDERFUL
AND ALL THESE THINGS WERE WONDERFUL AND GREAT!   104 FERGUS DRUID   37
MORE WONDERFUL! AND WE HAVE SWORDS. O NIGHT   664 ISLE STAT II 2   61
WITH WONDERFUL WHITE SANDS, WHERE NEVER YET   693 MOSADA 1   81
WITH WONDERFUL WHITE SAND, WHERE NEVER YET   693 MOSADA 1   V   81
WONDERFULLY
OR SOME SMALL BEAST MOST WONDERFULLY FURR'D,   650 ISLE STAT I 1   148
WONDERING
AND NEIGHED THREE TIMES. WHEN, WONDERING   10 OISIN 1   V 110A
MUCH WONDERING TO SEE UPON ALL HANDS, OF WATTLES   58 OISIN 3   162
AND WOODWORK MADE,
MUCH WONDERING TO SEE UPON ALL HANDS, OF WATTLES   58 OISIN 3   V 162
AND WOOD-WORK MADE,
WONDERING TO LAY HER IN THAT SOLITUDE,   123 DREAM OF DEATH   5
AND WONDERING PLANTED BY HER SOLITUDE   123 DREAM OF DEATH V   5
AND WONDERING WHO OF THE MANY-CHANGING SIDHE   181 QUEEN MAEVE   41
AND WONDERING WHO OF THE MANY CHANGING SIDHE   181 QUEEN MAEVE   V 41
THAT NO GOD TROUBLED NOW, AND WONDERING   182 QUEEN MAEVE   60
WHILE WONDERING STILL TO BE A SHADE, WITH GRANIA'S SHADE,   366 HER COURAGE   V   4
WILL WONDERING LISTEN, AND THIS TALE SHALL EASE   693 MOSADA 1   70
WONDERS   SEE WOOD-OF-WONDERS
THEY KNOW ALL WONDERS, FOR THEY PASS   196 BAILE AILLINN   160
OF WONDERS THAT HAVE HAPPENED   215 HAPPY TOWNLAND   47
OF WONDERS! EVE OF PRODIGIES! DRAW! DRAW!   664 ISLE STAT II 2   62
WONDROUS
THERE WAS A WONDROUS YOUNG MAN SITTING.   18 OISIN 1   V 252
AND THEY WILL WAR, 'MID WONDROUS ELFIN-SIGHTS!   651 ISLE STAT I 1   164
AND FADED NOW IS ALL THY WONDROUS ART.   673 ISLE STAT II 3   194
WHO, DREAMING TO A WONDROUS AGE, LIVED ON,   692 MOSADA 1   52
WONTED
AGED AND WISE, THEY SEEK THEIR WONTED PERCHES   72 ANASHU VIJAYA   31
WOOD   SEE LARCH-WOOD ASH-WOOD APPLE-WOOD PINE-WOOD
AND WHERE THE WOOD AND WATERS MEET   14 OISIN 1   193
OF DREAMY FOAM A STAFF OF WOOD   24 OISIN 1   366
I DREW IT FORTH! THE STAFF OF WOOD,   24 OISIN 1   V 366
WHITE FLOWERS OF THE FOAM A STAFF OF WOOD   24 OISIN 1   V 366
THE WOOD WAS SO SPACIOUS ABOVE THEM,   49 OISIN 3   37
SO SPACIOUS THE WOOD WAS ABOVE THEM,   49 OISIN 3   V   37
. . . LIKE THE ROARING OF WIND IN A WOOD.   58 OISIN 3   168
THE SUN HAS LAID HIS CHIN ON THE GREY WOOD,   72 ANASHU VIJAYA   24
THE SUN HATH LAID HIS CHIN ON THE GREY WOOD,   72 ANASHU VIJAYA V   24
AND I MUST WANDER WOOD AND HILL   86 MAD KING GOLL   70
I MUST AWAY BY WOOD AND SEA   86 MAD KING GOLL V 67
OF SLEUTH WOOD IN THE LAKE,   86 STOLEN CHILD   2
BEYOND OLD MARTIN'S WOOD,   95 MOLL MAGEE   V   34
PILIN' THE WOOD OR PILIN' THE TURF,   96 MOLL MAGEE   45
A-PILIN' WOOD OR PILIN' TURF,   96 MOLL MAGEE   V   45
THE DRUID, GREY, WOOD NURTURED, QUIET EYED,   101 ROSE UPON ROOD V   4
GO WATCH THE ROAD BETWEEN THE WOOD AND TIDE,   105 CUCHULAIN SEA   4
BETWEEN THE LAVISH SHELTER OF A WOOD   108 CUCHULAIN SEA V 38A
A CROSS THEY HAD MADE OUT OF TWO BITS OF WOOD,   123 DREAM OF DEATH   7
I CAME AND WROTE UPON A CROSS OF WOOD--   123 DREAM OF DEATH V   7
AND RULES THE SHADOWS OF THE WOOD,   126 GOES FERGUS   10
OF SUN AND MOON AND HOLLOW AND WOOD   148 INTO TWILIGHT   11

909

WOOD (CONTINUED)

	PAGE	TITLE		LINE
OF THE FLOOD AND FLAME, OF THE HEIGHT AND WOOD,	148	INTO TWILIGHT	V	11
OF HOLLOW WOOD AND THE HILLY WOOD	148	INTO TWILIGHT	V	11
OF HOLLOW WOOD AND THE HILLY WOOD	148	INTO TWILIGHT	V	11
I WENT OUT TO THE HAZEL WOOD,	149	WANDER AENGUS		1
I HAVE BEEN IN THE PATH OF STONES AND THE WOOD OF THORNS,	153	CHANGE BELOVED		3
AND I DREAMED MY LOST LOVE CAME STEALTHILY OUT OF THE WOOD	163	VALLEY LOVERS		3
BETWEEN THE WIND AND THE WOOD,	166	BLESSED		4
ARE SINGING ABOUT THE WOOD?"	167	BLESSED		24
BETWEEN THE WIND AND THE WOOD,	167	BLESSED	V	4D
AND THE WOOD WOMAN, WHOSE LOVER WAS CHANGED TO A BLUE-EYED HAWK;	209	UNDER THE MOON	V	13
THE RAGGED WOOD	210	RAGGED WOOD		T
THE HOLLOW WOOD	210	RAGGED WOOD		T
I HEARD UNDER A RAGGED HOLLOW WOOD,	210	RAGGED WOOD	V	1
O HURRY TO THE RAGGED WOOD, FOR THERE	211	RAGGED WOOD		9
O HURRY TO THE HOLLOW WOOD, FOR THERE	211	RAGGED WOOD	V	9
IN A GOLDEN AND SILVER WOOD;	214	HAPPY TOWNLAND		10
IN A GOLD AND SILVER WOOD;	214	HAPPY TOWNLAND	V	10
DIM INCHY WOOD, THAT HIDES BADGER AND FOX	218	WOODS OF COOLE		13
AND MARTEN-CAT, AND BORDERS THAT OLD WOOD	218	WOODS OF COOLE		14
WISE BIDDY EARLY CALLED THE WICKED WOOD;	218	WOODS OF COOLE		15
AND MARTIN CAT, AND BORDERS THAT OLD WOOD	218	WOODS OF COOLE	V	14
HE MADE A HARP WITH DRUID APPLE WOOD	220	HARP OF AENGUS	V	11
UPON THE MISTY BORDER OF THE WOOD,	251	SHADOW WATER B		612
KING EOCHAID CAME AT SUNDOWN TO A WOOD	276	TWO KINGS		1
BETWEEN THE WOOD OF DURAS AND MAGAI	276	TWO KINGS	V	G
AND CAME INTO A WOOD AS THE SUN SET	277	TWO KINGS	V	3
WESTWARD OF TARA. WHERE IN THE MIDDLE WOOD	277	TWO KINGS	V	4
I GROPED MY WAY FROM BEECH TO HAZEL WOOD,	283	TWO KINGS		139
CLOSE TO A CLUMP OF BEECH TREES IN THE WOOD	283	TWO KINGS	V	135
ALL WORK IN METAL OR IN WOOD,	327	ROBERT GREGORY		76
HOVERING OVER THE WOOD	349	HAWK		10
MY GREAT WOOD LECTERN AND THE FIRE	358	PRESENCES		10
BY THESE WIRE-JOINTED JAWS AND LIMBS OF WOOD,	382	VISION ROBART		10
BUT GREGORY'S WOOD AND ONE BARE HILL	403	FOR DAUGHTER		4
A BARRICADE OF STONE OR OF WOOD;	425	STARES NEST		11
AN ANCIENT IMAGE MADE OF OLIVE WOOD--	428	NINETEEN 19		6
YOUR HOOVES HAVE STAMPED AT THE BLACK MARGIN OF THE WOOD,	442	BLACK CENTAUR		1
THE HARE LEAP TO THE WOOD,	453	DEATH OF HARE		2
AM SET DOWN STANDING IN THE WOOD	453	DEATH OF HARE		11
UPON THE BORDER OF THAT LAKE'S A WOOD	490	COOLE BALLYLEE		9
WHETHER IN WOOD, WATER OR CLOUD,	528	DANCER CRUACH		7
HER VISION IN THE WOOD	536	HER VISION		T
AT WINE-DARK MIDNIGHT IN THE SACRED WOOD,	536	HER VISION		2
'TIS MORN, AND FROM THE DEW-DRENCH'D WOOD I'VE SPED	645	ISLE STAT I 1		6
THE WOOD AND THE VALLEY AND SEA	646	ISLE STAT I 1		42
ALONG THE WOOD WITH SUBTLE TREAD AND BENDED BOWS.	649	ISLE STAT I 1		111
HERE IS THE PLACE, THE CLIFF-ENCIRCLED WOOD;	651	ISLE STAT I 2		3
BY WOOD ANTIQUE, BY WAVE AND WASTE,	670	ISLE STAT II 3		109
THE SULLEN WOOD. BUT MANY WOODS I SEE	682	SEEKER		24
SEEK NOT THAT WOOD, FOR THERE THE GOBLIN SNAKES	682	SEEKER		29
HIDING THE REBELS WORM IN YONDER WOOD	709	FERENCZ RENYI		14
HIDING THE REBELS SWARM IN YONDER WOOD	709	FERENCZ RENYI	V	14
HIDING THE REBEL WORMS IN YONDER WOOD,	709	FERENCZ RENYI	V	14
A LITTLE BOY OUTSIDE THE SYCAMORE WOOD	715	DWELT SYCAMORE		1
A LITTLE BOY INSIDE THE SYCAMORE WOOD	715	DWELT SYCAMORE		5
IN THE BOSOM AFAR OF THE FRAGRANT WOOD.	717	LOVE SONG		9
AWAY IN THE HEART OF THE ANTIQUE WOOD;	730	PRIEST FAIRY		64
"AND CUT NO WOOD THE WHOLE DAY LONG,	731	PRIEST FAIRY		81
FROM PLAYING HURLEY IN THE WOOD	743	DANAAN QUICK		9
IN A WOOD OF DEW AND MOSS,	744	ROSY CROSS		5
OUT OF THAT ISLAND WHERE THE FOOL OF THE WOOD	747	SHADOW WATER A		2
THAT DRUIDS WRITE ON YEW AND APPLE WOOD,	748	SHADOW WATER A		29
THE FOOL THAT CAME OUT OF THE WINTRY WOOD	750	SHADOW WATER A		75
HEARING THE HARPERS PLAY, THE PINE WOOD CRACKLE,	759	SHADOW WATER A	V	241
HE MADE A HARP WITH DRUID APPLE WOOD	763	SHADOW WATER A		306
UPON THIN BOARDS OF YEW AND APPLE WOOD,	764	SHADOW WATER A		343
UPON THE MISTY BORDER OF THE WOOD,--	769	SHADOW WATER A		428

WOOD-CUTTER

	PAGE	TITLE		LINE
WITH HER OLD FATHER THE BLIND WOOD-CUTTER;	74	ANASHU VIJAYA		63
THE DAUGHTER OF THE GREY OLD WOOD-CUTTER,	74	ANASHU VIJAYA	V	63

WOODED

	PAGE	TITLE	LINE
THE VIOLETS ARE THAT ON THE WOODED HILL	713	FERENCZ RENYI	95
HANGS O'ER ALL THE WOODED EARTH.	731	STREET DANCERS	8

WOODEN

	PAGE	TITLE		LINE
I HAVE A LUCKY WOODEN SHIN	302	HOUR DAWN		18
HAD DIPPED THE WOODEN LADLE DEEP	304	HOUR DAWN		46
AND TOOK THE WOODEN LADLE UP	304	HOUR DAWN	V	46
WHILE THEIR GREAT WOODEN DICE BEAT ON THE BOARD.	412	TOWER		88
COVERS ITS WOODEN SHEATH.	421	MY TABLE		7
THE WOODEN SCABBARD BOUND AND WOUND,	477	SELF AND SOUL		15

WOODLAND

	PAGE	TITLE		LINE
TO THAT LOW LAUGHING WOODLAND RHYME.	14	OISIN 1		176
AMONG THE WOODLAND GRASSES SWEET;	15	OISIN 1	V	199
I LEAD ALONG THE WOODLAND DEER;	84	MAD KING GOLL		46
AND WHETHER I GO IN MY DREAMS BY WOODLAND, OR DUN, OR SHORE,	210	UNDER THE MOON		14
THE WOODLAND PATHS ARE DRY,	322	SWANS AT COOLE		2
ALL BUT THE TERRORS OF THE WOODLAND FLIGHT FORGOT	366	HER COURAGE		5
ALL BUT THE PERILS OF THE WOODLAND FLIGHT FORGOT,	366	HER COURAGE	V	5

WOODLAND   (CONTINUED)
   HERE, WHERE MEN KNOW THE GRACIOUS WOODLAND JOYS, ... 651 ISLE STAT I 1   154
   AND SEE AGAIN THE HAPPY WOODLAND LIGHT, ... 664 ISLE STAT II 2   58
   AGAIN THE WOODLAND LAUGHTER, AND THE CLEAR . . . . . . 674 ISLE STAT II 3   221
   COME AWAY WHILE THE MOON'S IN THE WOODLAND, ... 707 FAIRY PEDANT   9
   COME AWAY WHILE THE MOON'S IN THE WOODLAND, ... 708 FAIRY PEDANT   37
   DEEP IN THE WOODLAND PAUSED THEY, THE SIX FEET . . . . 716 DWELT SYCAMORE   9
   DEEP IN THE WOODLAND PASSED THEY. THE SIX FEET . . . . 716 DWELT SYCAMORE V   9
   UNTO THE HEART OF THE WOODLAND STRAYING, ... 728 PRIEST FAIRY   1
WOODLANDS
   AND AIMLESS WANDERINGS THE WOODLANDS LONE, ... 674 ISLE STAT II 3   209
   THE HOLLOW WOODLANDS FEEL HIM THERE. . . . . 737 SUMMER EVENING   17
WOODMAN
   A WOODMAN ON HIS HOMEWARD WAY . . . . 730 PRIEST FAIRY   73
WOODMAN'S
   TO AN OLD EMPTY WOODMAN'S HOUSE THAT'S HIDDEN . . . . 282 TWO KINGS   134
WOOD-NURTURED
   THE DRUID, GREY, WOOD-NURTURED, QUIET-EYED, ... 101 ROSE UPON ROOD   4
WOOD-OF-WONDERS
   AND WOOD-OF-WONDERS, WHERE ONE KILLS AN OX AT DAWN. . . 209 UNDER THE MOON   9
WOOD-PECKER
   WHILE THE WOOD-PECKER MADE A MERRY DIN, ...   44 OISIN 2   V 228
WOODPECKER'S
   THE BARRED WOODPECKER'S MANSION IS AND DEEP, ... 659 ISLE STAT II 1   23
WOOD-RHAPSODISTS
   POOR SAD WOOD-RHAPSODISTS. NOT SO; THEY'RE GLAD. . . . 652 ISLE STAT I 2   16
WOOD'S
   THE RIVERS, AND THE WOOD'S OLD NIGHT. . . . . . .   25 OISIN 1   V 387
   BETWEEN WOOD'S RIM AND THE HORSES OF THE SEA. . . . . 108 CUCHULAIN SEA   34
   GO THERE, AND LIGHT A CAMP-FIRE AT WOOD'S RIM, ... 108 CUCHULAIN SEA   35
   GO THERE, AND LIGHT A CAMP FIRE AT WOOD'S RIM, ... 108 CUCHULAIN SEA   V 35
   AND PIERCE THE DEEP WOOD'S WOVEN SHADE, ... 125 GOES FERGUS   2
   BY THE WOOD'S EDGE WHERE ONLY EQUALS MEET, ... 321 REED WHISPERER V   8
   THE WINE-DARK OF THE WOOD'S INTRICACIES, ... 446 COLONUS PRAISE   2
   THE WINE DARK OF THE WOOD'S INTRICACIES, ... 446 COLONUS PRAISE V   2
   FROM THE WOOD'S WAYS, THEN, LIKE A SILVER FLAME, . . . 658 ISLE STAT I 1   6
   FROM THE DIM WOOD'S FOUNDATION-- . . . . 672 ISLE STAT II 3   162
   SAW ON THE WOOD'S EDGE GLEAM AN ASH-GREY FEATHER; . . . 715 DWELT SYCAMORE   2
   OF A WIDE WOOD'S LEAFY LEISURE, ... 731 STREET DANCERS   11
WOODS
   AND WHERE THE WOODS AND WATERS MEET . . . . . .   14 OISIN 1   V 193
   AND FROM THE WOODS RUSHED OUT A BAND . . . . . .   15 OISIN 1   201
   AND FROM THE WOODS THERE RUSHED A BAND . . . . . .   15 OISIN 1   V 201
   TOGETHER, WHILE THE DARK WOODS RANG, ...   16 OISIN 1   227
   NOW IN THE WOODS, AWAY WITH THEM . . . .   16 OISIN 1   V 216A
   ON IN THE WOODS, AWAY WITH THEM, ...   16 OISIN 1   V 222A
   THE DANCE WOUND THROUGH THE WINDLESS WOODS; . . . .   21 OISIN 1   320
   THEN ON AMONG THE WINDLESS WOODS . . . .   21 OISIN 1   V 320
   WE PASSED BY WOODS, AND LAWNS OF CLOVER, ...   25 OISIN 1   377
   BY WOODS OF MOSS, BY LAWNS OF CLOVER, ...   25 OISIN 1   V 377
   THE WAILING GREW DISTANT; I RODE BY THE WOODS OF   56 OISIN 3   137
     THE WRINKLING BARK,
   THE WOODS OF ARCADY ARE DEAD, ...   64 HAPPY SHEPHERD   1
   AS IN THE WOODS HE WANDERS, IF HE LOVE . . . . .   71 ANASHU VIJAYA V   3
   WHILE WE ALONE HAVE ROUND US WOVEN WOODS, ...   73 ANASHU VIJAYA   56
   AMONG THE MOULDERING OF ANCIENT WOODS . . . . .   74 ANASHU VIJAYA   61
   THE WOODS WERE ROUND THEM, AND THE YELLOW LEAVES . .   80 EPHEMERA   13
   AND NOW I WANDER IN THE WOODS . . . .   84 MAD KING GOLL   37
   AND BORE IT TO THE WOODS WITH ME; . . . . . .   85 MAD KING GOLL   57
   OR PACE AND WEEP IN WOODS FORLORN, ...   86 MAD KING GOLL V   68
   TO THE WOODS AND WATERS WILD . . . .   87 STOLEN CHILD V   REF
   AND PACE THE WOODS, AND DRIVE MY CHARIOT-WHEELS . . 103 FERGUS DRUID   18
   AND PACE THE WOODS, AND DRIVE MY CHARIOT WHEELS . . 103 FERGUS DRUID V   18
   AND THE MOUNTAINS AND WOODS . . . . 142 MOODS   3
   THE MOUNTAINS AND WOODS . . . . 142 MOODS   V   3
   O DAUGHTER OF THE ISLAND OF WOODS; . . . . . . 164 PERFECT BEAUTY V   1
   DWELT AMONG WINE-STAINED WANDERERS IN DEEP WOODS; . . 170 SECRET ROSE   21
   IN THE SEVEN WOODS . . . . 198 SEVEN WOODS   T
   I HAVE HEARD THE PIGEONS IN THE SEVEN WOODS . . . . 198 SEVEN WOODS   1
   I WALKED AMONG THE SEVEN WOODS OF COOLE; . . . . 217 WOODS OF COOLE   1
   SEVEN ODOURS, SEVEN MURMURS, SEVEN WOODS. . . . . 218 WOODS OF COOLE   16
   IN THE LAST RIDGE OF THE BARLEY? DO OUR WOODS . . 218 WOODS OF COOLE   33
   AND WINDS AND PONDS COVER MORE QUIET WOODS. . . . . 218 WOODS OF COOLE   34
   THAT SHE AMONG HER WOODS MIGHT KNOW HE WEPT; . . . 220 HARP OF AENGUS V   12
   "I HAVE SENT AMONG THE FIELDS OR TO THE WOODS . . . 280 TWO KINGS   69
   "I HAVE SENT OUT INTO THE FIELDS AND WOODS . . . . 280 TWO KINGS   V   69
   LIKE THE EYES OF SOME GREAT KITE SCOURING THE WOODS, . . 283 TWO KINGS   150
   INTO THE FOLD, WE'LL TO THE WOODS AND THERE . . . . 343 SHEP GOATHERD   114
   BUT GREGORY'S WOODS AND ONE BARE HILL . . . . 403 FOR DAUGHTER V   4
   MAIDEN, COME FORTH; THE WOODS KEEP WATCH FOR THEE; . . 645 ISLE STAT I 1   1
   WITH THAT SONG LEADING WHERE HARMONIC WOODS . . . 657 ISLE STAT I 3   43
   LONE REGENT OF THE WOODS, DEEP MUTTERING, ... 657 ISLE STAT I 3   49
   OF THOSE VAST WOODS; AND THEN I SAW THE BOAT, . . . 657 ISLE STAT I 3   53
   OF THE WIDE WOODS. AND THE DEEP EARTH GATHERED THEM. . 660 ISLE STAT II 1   33
   IN THE DEEP CENTRES OF THE SECRET WOODS. . . . . . 661 ISLE STAT II 1   54
   WHAT IS IT, FRIEND? HE LOST I' THE WOODS THE CHIEF . . 661 ISLE STAT II 1   60
   OF THE DREAD WOODS; ALONG THEIR RUSSET FLOOR . . . 675 ISLE STAT II 3   243
   THE SULLEN WOOD. BUT MANY WOODS I SEE . . . . 682 SEEKER   24
   ABOVE, THE WOODS WHERE WITH THE SOFT MILD EYE . . . 710 FERENCZ RENYI   26
   WHERE IN THE WOODS OR HILLS THE REBELS BE?" . . . . 713 FERENCZ RENYI   V 83A
   NOON WRAPPED THE WOODS IN VEILS OF VIOLET WEATHER; . . 715 DWELT SYCAMORE V   7

911

		PAGE	TITLE		LINE
WOODS (CONTINUED)					
	AND AWAY IN THE WOODS WE WILL SCATTER THE DEW!	717	LOVE SONG		2
	THE LIVING WOODS FOREGO THEIR CARE,	736	SUMMER EVENING		1
	ARE BETTER THAN THE WOODS WHERE NO LOVE FADES	754	SHADOW WATER A		160
	THAT MURMURS WITH HOLY WOODS, AND WIN THEIR HELP	757	SHADOW WATER A		199
	WHERE TRUE-LOVE WANDERS AMONG THE HOLY WOODS.	764	SHADOW WATER A		337
	WHERE TRUE LOVE WANDERS AMONG THE HOLY WOODS.	764	SHADOW WATER A	V	337
	WHERE ARE THESE BOUGHS? WHERE ARE THE HOLY WOODS	765	SHADOW WATER A		359
	THAT LIVES AMONG THE WOODS OF THE DARK HOUNDS.	766	SHADOW WATER A		376
	WE WILL FIND OUT VALLEYS AND WOODS AND MEADOWS	767	SHADOW WATER A		388
	OR AMONG WINDS THAT MOVE IN THE MEADOWS AND WOODS.	768	SHADOW WATER A	V	413
WOODS'					
	BY RIVERS AND THE WOODS' OLD NIGHT!	25	OISIN 1		387
WOODWAYS					
	WITHIN THE WOODWAYS, BLUE AS THE HALCYON'S WING,	683	SEEKER	V	38
WOOD-WOMAN					
	AND THE WOOD-WOMAN, WHOSE LOVER WAS CHANGED TO A BLUE-EYED HAWK!	209	UNDER THE MOON		13
WOODWORK					
	MUCH WONDERING TO SEE UPON ALL HANDS, OF WATTLES AND WOODWORK MADE,	58	OISIN 3		162
WOOD-WORK					
	MUCH WONDERING TO SEE UPON ALL HANDS, OF WATTLES AND WOOD-WORK MADE,	58	OISIN 3	V	162
WOODY					
	OVER THE BARE AND WOODY LAND,	15	OISIN 1		198
	UPON THE WOODY CENTRAL HILL!	22	OISIN 1		323
	I CHASED UPON THAT WOODY SHORE	23	OISIN 1		344
	OH, PATRICK, ON THAT WOODY SHORE	23	OISIN 1	V	343
	DRIVING THE DEER ALONG THE WOODY WAYS.	109	CUCHULAIN SEA	V	48
	CAME BY THE WOODY WAY	166	BLESSED	V	2
	DOTH HE STILL DWELL WITHIN THE WOODY SHADE,	678	ISLE STAT II 3		303
	I HURRIED FROM THE WOODY SHORE,	742	DANAAN QUICK		4
WOOED					
	AND HAVE BEEN WOOED BY THE TWELVE KINGS OF THE EARTH,	757	SHADOW WATER A	V	214
WOOING					
	"A WEARY WOOING AND A LONG," HE SAID,	283	TWO KINGS		154
WOOL					
	WHOSE LONG WOOL WHITER THAN SEA-FROTH FLOWS,	8	OISIN 1		90
	WHOSE LONG WOOL WHITER THAN SEA FROTH FLOWS,	8	OISIN 1	V	90
	THEN MUSE THEY ON THE HOUSEHOLD WOOL INTENT,	32	OISIN 1	V	55
	"WHAT DO YOU WEAVE WITH WOOL SO WHITE?"	70	CLOAK BOAT		11
	WHO COME WITH THEIR CROWNS OF PEARL AND THEIR SPINDLES OF WOOL,	203	WITHER BOUGHS		10
	WHAT DO YOU WEAVE WITH WOOL SO WHITE?	666	ISLE STAT II 3		11
	HEAVY WITH WOOL THE SHEEP ARE GATHERED IN,	681	SEEKER		1
WOOLLY					
	NASCHINA, HAIL! I'D DRIVE THY WOOLLY SHEEP,	649	ISLE STAT I 1		122
WOOS					
	OR MUST SUFFER, IF HE WOOS	479	SELF AND SOUL		63
WORD SEE MINSTREL-WORD					
	AND CAUGHT MY HANDS, BUT SPAKE NO WORD	25	OISIN 1		374
	AND CAUGHT MY HANDS AND SPAKE NO WORD	25	OISIN 1	V	374
	NO CENTURIES COULD DIM, AND A WORD RAN	38	OISIN 2		127
	WORD BE-MOCKERS?--BY THE ROOD,	65	HAPPY SHEPHERD		12
	AN IDLE WORD IS NOW THEIR GLORY,	65	HAPPY SHEPHERD		14
	ONLY A SUDDEN FLAMING WORD,	65	HAPPY SHEPHERD		19
	WORD BEMOCKERS?--BY THE ROOD	65	HAPPY SHEPHERD	V	12
	NO WORD OF THEIRS--THE COLD STAR-BANE	66	HAPPY SHEPHERD		32
	FAREWELL, VIJAYA. NAY, NO WORD, NO WORD!	75	ANASHU VIJAYA		83
	FAREWELL, VIJAYA. NAY, NO WORD, NO WORD!	75	ANASHU VIJAYA		83
	THAT WORD OF THE SOUL'S PEACE--"ETERNITY."	81	EPHEMERA	V	24B
	I KNOW THE WORD THEY CRY, "ETERNITY!"	81	EPHEMERA	V	24F
	MY WORD WAS LAW FROM ITH TO EMAIN,	81	MAD KING GOLL		2
	UPON THE WEB-HEAPED FLOOR, AND CRIED HIS WORD!	106	CUCHULAIN SEA		15
	UPON THE WEB-HEAPED FLOOR, AND THUS HIS WORD,	106	CUCHULAIN SEA	V	15
	"I HAVE LONG WAITED, MOTHER, FOR THAT WORD!	107	CUCHULAIN SEA		22
	HE KNELT HIM AT THAT WORD.	133	FR GILLIGAN		40
	THAT BALANCED WITH A WORD IS MORE THAN NOISE!	258	KING NO KING		4
	A WORD AND A JEST.	293	HELEN LIVED		12
	BELIEVING EVERY WORD I SAID,	314	MEMORY YOUTH		8
	WE KNEW, THOUGH SHE'D NOT SAID A WORD,	314	MEMORY YOUTH		16
	AND KNEW, THOUGH SHE'D NOT SAID A WORD,	314	MEMORY YOUTH	V	16
	THEY CHANGE THEIR BODIES AT A WORD. AND THEN?	376	PHASES OF MOON		113
	THAT EVERY GIFT AND EVERY WORD OF PRAISE	469	HARUN RASHID		172
	HAD FOUND A SWEETER WORD.	539	MEETING		18
	I PRAY--FOR FASHION'S WORD IS OUT	553	PRAYER OLD AGE		9
	WHAT MATTER THAT YOU UNDERSTOOD NO WORD!	557	RIBH ECSTASY		1
	AND ALL IT KNOWS IS THAT ONE WORD "REJOICE!"	564	GYRES		16
	HE WROTE OUT THAT WORD HIMSELF,	585	ORAHILLY		7
	I SHOULD NOT GET THE WORD	585	ORAHILLY		20
	FOR SUCH A CALL. LET THE WILD WORD BE CRIED	669	ISLE STAT II 3		76
	A FOOLISH WORD THOU GAVEST ME!	671	ISLE STAT II 3		131
	KNOWING THAT THOU HADST SINGLED ME WITH WORD	684	SEEKER		57
	EVER MORE TO SPEAK A WORD	697	MOSADA 2		32
	HAS NO WORD OF THE SULPHUROUS END.	736	SUMMER EVENING		8
	IF YOU WOULD SERVE ME, AS YOUR WORD AND VOICE	756	SHADOW WATER A	V	183
	OR GIVE BUT A SIGH AND A WORD,	786	YOUR HEART		12
	A PASSING WORD.	786	YOUR HEART		13
	OR GIVE BUT A SIGH AND A WORD,	786	YOUR HEART		25
	A PASSING WORD.	786	YOUR HEART		26

912

		PAGE	TITLE	LINE
WORD (CONTINUED)				
OR GIVE BUT A SIGH AND A WORD, ...		786	YOUR HEART	38
A PASSING WORD.		786	YOUR HEART	39
WORDINESS				
YOU'RE FULL OF WORDINESS. COME, HEAR MY SONG.		696	MOSADA 2	8
WORDLESS				
WITH NO RETURNING GLANCE, IN WORDLESS MOOD		44	OISIN 2	V 230A
WORDS				
BUT THE TALE, THOUGH WORDS BE LIGHTER THAN AIR, ...		3	OISIN 1	11
OF STORIES BUILDED BY HIS WORDS		7	OISIN 1	68
AND DROPS OF HONEY ARE HIS WORDS, ...		7	OISIN 1	V 64
LIKE DROPS OF HONEY CAME THEIR WORDS, ...		26	OISIN 1	398
HUNG FROM THE MORNING STAR: WHEN THESE MILD WORDS . .		32	OISIN 2	49
I THOUGHT THE END HAD RESTED, WHEN THESE WORDS		32	OISIN 2	V 49
WITH BARREN WORDS AND FLATTERIES OF THE WEAK.		42	OISIN 2	197
WORDS ALONE ARE CERTAIN GOOD.		65	HAPPY SHEPHERD	10
THY FRETFUL WORDS A LITTLE WHILE, ...		66	HAPPY SHEPHERD	40
FOR WORDS ALONE ARE CERTAIN GOOD:		66	HAPPY SHEPHERD	43
AND WORDS ALONE ARE CERTAIN GOOD, ...		66	HAPPY SHEPHERD	V 43
TILL MY OWN WORDS, RE-ECHOING, SHALL SEND		68	SAD SHEPHERD	20
AND MY OWN WHISPERING WORDS BE COMFORTING, ...		68	SAD SHEPHERD	23
AND MINE OWN WORDS RE-ECHOING SHALL SEND		68	SAD SHEPHERD	V 20
AND MINE OWN WHISPERING WORDS BE COMFORTING, ...		68	SAD SHEPHERD	V 23
CHANGED ALL HIS WORDS TO INARTICULATE MOAN		69	SAD SHEPHERD	V 27
WHEN I GAVE JUDGMENT, AND HIS WORDS WERE WISE, ...		102	FERGUS DRUID	11
"LONG HAVE I WAITED, MOTHER: FOR THOSE WORDS, ...		107	CUCHULAIN SEA	V 22
"I HAVE LONG WAITED, MOTHER, FOR THOSE WORDS:		107	CUCHULAIN SEA	V 22
UNTIL I CARVED THESE WORDS:		123	DREAM OF DEATH	10
AND BLAME YOU WITH MANY BITTER WORDS.		146	FISH	8
WITH WORDS LIGHTER THAN AIR, ...		162	ASKS FORGIVE	2
NOW WORDS THAT CALLED UP THE LIGHTNING		171	MAID QUIET	7
FOR THE WORDS THAT CALLED UP THE LIGHTNING		171	MAID QUIET	V 7
AND YOU WOULD MURMUR TENDER WORDS, ...		175	BELOVED DEAD	5
AND WHEN I'D WRITE IT OUT ANEW, THE WORDS, ...		186	QUEEN MAEVE	139
A MURMUR OF SOFT WORDS AND MEETING LIPS.		187	QUEEN MAEVE	154
AND THAT DEAR WORDS MEANT NOTHING?" BUT ENOUGH, . .		201	OLD MEMORY	9
I LONG FOR YOUR MERRY AND TENDER AND PITIFUL WORDS, .		203	WITHER BOUGHS	3
YES, VOICES! BUT I DO NOT CATCH THE WORDS.		233	SHADOW WATER B	251
UPON HIS SHOULDERS. YOU'VE NOTHING BUT WILD WORDS, .		235	SHADOW WATER B	300
OR WAVE TO DROWN. BUT I HAVE DONE WITH WORDS, . . .		238	SHADOW WATER B	348
THEY'RE CRYING OUT, COULD YOU BUT HEAR THEIR WORDS, .		247	SHADOW WATER B	529
AND THERE'S NO HELP IN WORDS. TO THE OTHER SHIP, . .		250	SHADOW WATER B	585
WORDS		255	WORDS	T
AND WORDS OBEY MY CALL":		256	WORDS	12
I MIGHT HAVE THROWN POOR WORDS AWAY		256	WORDS	15
AND AT THESE WORDS HE PALED; AS SHE HAD PALED, . . .		280	TWO KINGS	76
THOUGH ALWAYS AT MY WORDS HIS TROUBLE GREW:		281	TWO KINGS	91
BUT ASKED THE MORE UNTIL HE SPOKE THESE WORDS, . . .		281	TWO KINGS	V 92A
AND AT THOSE WORDS I ROSE AND I WENT OUT		282	TWO KINGS	125
THOUGH I HAVE MANY WORDS, ...		334	SONG	7
AND YET, BECAUSE MY HEART LEAPED AT HER WORDS, . . .		353	PEOPLE	35
AND SO FORGET THE COMFORT THAT NO WORDS CAN TELL . .		391	UNDER SATURN	V 4
OR POLITE MEANINGLESS WORDS.		392	EASTER 1916	6
POLITE MEANINGLESS WORDS, ...		392	EASTER 1916	8
"O WORDS ARE LIGHTLY SPOKEN."		396	ROSE TREE	1
"MAYBE A BREATH OF POLITIC WORDS		396	ROSE TREE	3
"SOME POLITICIANS IDLE WORDS		396	ROSE TREE	V 3
THE SECOND COMING! HARDLY ARE THOSE WORDS OUT . . .		402	SECOND COMING	11
MEMORIES OF THE WORDS OF WOMEN, ...		415	TOWER	162
I HAVE LOVED YOU BETTER THAN MY SOUL FOR ALL MY WORDS,		442	BLACK CENTAUR	14
WORDS WERE BUT WASTED BREATH:		471	ALL SOUL NIGHT	27
SPOKE THESE, OR WORDS LIKE THESE.		496	MOHINI CHATTER	15
WORDS FOR MUSIC PERHAPS		507	JANE BISHOP	V T
O ANY OLD WORDS TO A TUNE.		548	TO SAME TUNE 3	16
SPEAKING TO A DRUNKEN AUDIENCE HIGH NONSENSICAL WORDS:		577	LOFTY THINGS	6
"KIND ARE ALL YOUR WORDS, MY DEAR, ...		588	OLD WICKED MAN	10
WORDS I HAVE THAT CAN PIERCE THE HEART, ...		588	OLD WICKED MAN	16
THOSE WORDS COME TRUE IN THE END		597	COLONEL MARTIN	V 69
"FORGETTING HUMAN WORDS," A GRAVE DEEP FACE.		603	GALLERY REVIS	49
HAVE I, THAT PUT IT INTO WORDS, ...		604	YOU CONTENT	5
DID WORDS OF MINE PUT TOO GREAT STRAIN		632	MAN AND ECHO	13
COULD MY SPOKEN WORDS HAVE CHECKED		632	MAN AND ECHO	15
THEY SANG, BUT HAD NOR HUMAN TUNES NOR WORDS, ...		635	CUCHULAIN COMF	23
KNOW THAT WHEN ALL WORDS ARE SAID		638	BEN BULBEN	27
BY HIS COMMAND THESE WORDS ARE CUT:		640	BEN BULBEN	91
MY WORDS WERE ALL: "HERE NO LOVES WANE AND WITHER, .		669	ISLE STAT II 3	84
MY WORDS WERE ALL: "O WHITHER, WHITHER, WHITHER . .		669	ISLE STAT II 3	87
I CRIED THE WORDS YOU BID ME CRY.		673	ISLE STAT II 3	186
FOR, AH! OUR LIVES WERE BUT TWO STARRY WORDS		675	ISLE STAT II 3	236
AS WORDS OF THINE THROUGH FOURSCORE YEARS HAVE FILLED		683	SEEKER	46
THAT WAS BESIDE THE WATERFALL, THY WORDS		683	SEEKER	49
AND IMPORTUNE WITH WEIGHTY WORDS THIS MOOR, ...		698	MOSADA 2	45
ILL WORDS FOR ALL THINGS SOFT AND FAIR, ...		723	GIRLS SONG A	6
ALL THE WORDS THAT I GATHER, ...		739	WHERE BOOKS GO	1
AND ALL THE WORDS THAT I WRITE, ...		739	WHERE BOOKS GO	2
NOW FOUR TOGETHER! I SHALL HEAR THEIR WORDS		753	SHADOW WATER A	139
I AWAIT YOUR WORDS AS THE BLIND GRASS AWAITS		756	SHADOW WATER A	181
THE GODS HOLD WATCH ABOUT THE WORDS OF A QUEEN. . . .		756	SHADOW WATER A	191
I WAIT YOUR WORDS AS THE DEAD WAIT THE LIVING. . . .		756	SHADOW WATER A	V 182
WORDY				
THEY WERE OF NO WORDY MOOD:		65	HAPPY SHEPHERD	V 13A

	PAGE	TITLE		LINE
WORDY (CONTINUED)				
I' FAITH THOU EVER WAST A WORDY SPIRIT!	673	ISLE STAT II 3		175
WORE				
AND WHEN THEY SAW THE CLOAK I WORE	15	OISIN 1		207
AND WHEN THEY SAW THAT THE BRATTA I WORE	15	OISIN 1	V	207
AND HE WORE SMALL HOLES IN HIS SHOES, ...	92	FATHER OHART		11
AND HE WORE LARGE HOLES IN HIS GOWN.	92	FATHER OHART		12
WORE IT IN THE WORLD'S EYES	320	COAT		6
WORE IT IN THE WORLD'S EYE	320	COAT	V	6
FOR HE HIS SLIPPERS WORE.	595	COLONEL MARTIN		40
WORK SEE MASTER-WORK WOOD-WORK FARM-WORK HANDY-WORK				
MY WORK WAS SALTIN' HERRINGS	94	MOLL MAGEE		7
AND RIVER AND STREAM WORK OUT THEIR WILL!	148	INTO TWILIGHT		12
AND LAUGH OUT THEIR WHIMSEY AND WORK OUT THEIR WILL. .	148	INTO TWILIGHT	V	12
LAUGH OUT THEIR WHIMSEY AND WORK OUT THEIR WILL. . .	148	INTO TWILIGHT	V	12
AND THE CHANGING MOON WORK OUT THEIR WILL.	148	INTO TWILIGHT	V	12
WHILE I MUST WORK BECAUSE I AM OLD, ...	151	OLD MOTHER		9
AND I MUST WORK BECAUSE I AM OLD.	151	OLD MOTHER	V	10
THAT WORK TOO DIFFICULT FOR MORTAL HANDS	182	QUEEN MAEVE		67
IS TO WORK HARDER THAN ALL THESE, AND YET	205	ADAMS CURSE		11
ENOUGH IF THE WORK HAS SEEMED, ...	259	UNWORTH PRAISE		5
HEARERS AND HEARTENERS OF THE WORK!	266	GALWAY RACES		6
HEARERS, HEARTENERS OF THE WORK, ...	266	GALWAY RACES	V	6
SIGHED, "YOU, EVEN YOU YOURSELF, COULD WORK THE CURE!" .	282	TWO KINGS		124
A FRIEND THAT COULD, HE HAD TOLD HER, WORK HIS CURE .	283	TWO KINGS		137
THAT COULD, AS HE HAD TOLD HER, WORK HIS CURE, . . .	283	TWO KINGS	V	137
TO A FRIEND WHOSE WORK HAS COME TO NOTHING	290	TO A FRIEND		T
ALL WORK IN METAL OR IN WOOD, ...	327	ROBERT GREGORY		76
BECAUSE THE WORK HAD FINISHED IN THAT FLARE.	327	ROBERT GREGORY		85
AND TILL THAT'S DONE CAN NEITHER WORK NOR WAIT. . . .	340	SHEP GOATHERD		45
SET CARPENTERS TO WORK ON NO WIDE TABLE.	340	SHEP GOATHERD		50
"WHAT HAVE I EARNED FOR ALL THAT WORK," I SAID, . . .	351	PEOPLE		1
AND SMITHY WORK FROM THE GORT FORGE, ...	406	CARVED STONE		3
CONCEIVES A CHANGELESS WORK OF ART.	421	MY TABLE		14
FROM SHALLOW WITS; WHO KNOWS NO WORK CAN STAND, . . .	429	NINETEEN 19		35
ON MASTER WORK OF INTELLECT OR HAND, ...	429	NINETEEN 19	V	37
AND SWEPT THE HOUSE AND SANG ABOUT HER WORK	468	HARUN RASHID		148
PERFECTION OF THE LIFE, OR OF THE WORK, ...	491	COOLE BALLYLEE	V	40B
PERFECTION OF THE LIFE, OR OF THE WORK, ...	495	CHOICE		2
TEST EVERY WORK OF INTELLECT OR FAITH, ...	501	VACILLATION		30
WHEN, THE POTION'S WORK BEING DONE, ...	522	LULLABY		9
CONDUCT AND WORK GROW COARSE, AND COARSE THE SOUL, . .	564	GYRES		17
"THE WORK IS DONE," GROWN OLD HE THOUGHT, ...	577	WHAT THEN		16
I WHO HAVE ALWAYS HATED WORK, ...	605	YOU CONTENT		19
THE SPIRITUAL INTELLECT'S GREAT WORK, ...	632	MAN AND ECHO		20
NOR CAN THERE BE WORK SO GREAT	632	MAN AND ECHO		23
NOR CAN THERE BE A WORK SO GREAT	632	MAN AND ECHO	V	23
AND, ALL WORK DONE, DISMISSES ALL	633	MAN AND ECHO		34
KNOW HIS WORK OR CHOOSE HIS MATE.	638	BEN BULBEN		36
POET AND SCULPTOR, DO THE WORK, ...	638	BEN BULBEN		37
TO THEIR FARM WORK! HOW SILENT ALL WILL BE!	699	MOSADA 3		8
WORK AT THE CIDER PRESS.	774	COME RIDE		12
WORKED				
IT WORKED AT THEM, DAY OUT, DAY IN, ...	158	BELOVED RHYMES		4
YOU HAVE PUT THE THOUGHT IN RHYME. I WORKED ALL DAY, .	341	SHEP GOATHERD		58
WORKING SEE MIRACLE-WORKING				
SWEETER EMOTION, WORKING IN THEIR VEINS	292	TO A SHADE		13
BEFORE THE SECRET WORKING MIND!	639	BEN BULBEN		51
WORKING-CARPENTER				
OF THAT WORKING-CARPENTER.	440	WISDOM		7
OF A WORKING-CARPENTER.	440	WISDOM	V	7
WORKMAN				
THE WORKMAN, NOBLE AND SAINT, AND ALL THINGS RUN . . .	565	GYRES		23
WORKS				
AND TELL OF YOUR GOODLY HOUSEHOLD AND THE GOODLY WORKS	51	OISIN 3		62
OF YOUR HANDS,				
AND EVEN THE NAMES OF HIS FATHERS, AND EVEN THE WORKS OF	51	OISIN 3	V	62
HIS HANDS?				
AND THESE WERE THE WORKS OF JOHN, ...	93	FATHER OHART		25
AND THAT IF OUR WORKS COULD	431	NINETEEN 19		75
MY WORKS ARE ALL STAMPED DOWN INTO THE SULTRY MUD. . .	442	BLACK CENTAUR		3
WHEN ALL WORKS THAT HAVE	449	HERO GIRL FOOL		18
GREAT WORKS CONSTRUCTED THERE IN NATURE'S SPITE . . .	488	COOLE PARK 29		5
AND CALL THOSE WORKS EXTRAVAGANCE OF BREATH	501	VACILLATION		32
GIVES FORTH. HE, THE ETERNAL, WORKS HIS WILL. . . .	689	NETTLESHIP		16
WORLD SEE SEA-WORLD				
THE RED SUN FALLS AND THE WORLD GROWS DIM."	9	OISIN 1		105
WHEN THE STARS ARE TO WANE AND THE WORLD BE DONE. . .	16	OISIN 1		220
"O SADDEST HARP IN ALL THE WORLD, ...	17	OISIN 1		245
"THE SADDEST HARP IN ALL THE WORLD!"	17	OISIN 1	V	246
IN NIAM'S HAIR--WHEN ROSE A WORLD OF TOWERS	30	OISIN 2	V	22
MAKING A WORLD ABOUT HER IN THE AIR, ...	37	OISIN 2		122
MAKING A WORLD ABOUT HER, PASSED FROM SIGHT	37	OISIN 2	V	123
TO RULE MORE MIGHTY MEN, AND TO THE WORLD	38	OISIN 2	V	133
ON THE ANVIL OF THE WORLD. BE STILL! THE SKIES . . .	42	OISIN 2		204
UPON THE ANVIL OF THE WORLD. THE SKIES	42	OISIN 2	V	204
GOD SHAKES THE WORLD WITH RESTLESS HANDS. MORE NEAR .	43	OISIN 2	V	208
"WITH ALL IN ALL THE WORLD I BATTLE WAGE.	45	OISIN 2	V	240
THE STRONGEST OF THE WORLD, TO SNATCH MY PREY, . . .	45	OISIN 2	V	241
. . . THE GLEAMS OF THE WORLD AND THE SUN, ...	48	OISIN 3		22
. . . AND THE WHOLE OF THE WORLD WAS ONE.	48	OISIN 3		24

	PAGE	TITLE	LINE

WORLD   (CONTINUED)

```
• • • NO• NOT SINCE THE WORLD BEGAN, • • • • • • • •      50 OISIN 3            49
OF WARS WITH THE WIDE WORLD • • • • • • • • • • •         50 OISIN 3            55
"O FLAMING LION OF THE WORLD, O WHEN WILL YOU TURN TO YOUR 56 OISIN 3          129
   REST?"
O FLAMING LION OF THE WORLD, O WHEN WILL YOU TURN TO YOUR  56 OISIN 3          136
   REST?"
"OH, FLAMING LION OF THE WORLD, OH, WHEN WILT THOU TURN    56 OISIN 3        V 129
   TO THY REST?"
• • • WHO COULD BREAK UP THE WORLD IN THEIR RAGE: • • •    62 OISIN 3          214
OF OLD THE WORLD ON DREAMING FED: • • • • • • • • •        64 HAPPY SHEPHERD     3
BUT O, SICK CHILDREN OF THE WORLD, • • • • • • • •         65 HAPPY SHEPHERD     6
THE VERY WORLD ITSELF MAY BE • • • • • • • • • •           65 HAPPY SHEPHERD V  18
WHO HOLDS THE WORLD BETWEEN HIS BILL AND MADE US STRONG     76 INDIAN ON GOD     6
   OR WEAK
WHO MADE THE WORLD AND RULETH IT, HE HANGETH ON A STALK,    76 INDIAN ON GOD    10
WHO HOLDS THE WORLD BETWEEN HIS BILL AND MAKES US STRONG    76 INDIAN ON GOD  V  6
   OR WEAK
WHILE THE WORLD IS FULL OF TROUBLES • • • • • • •          87 STOLEN CHILD      22
FROM A WORLD MORE FULL OF WEEPING THAN HE CAN UNDERSTAND•   89 STOLEN CHILD      53
AND THE WORLD ROUND KNOCKNASHEE • • • • • • • • •          93 FATHER OHART      31
TO SEE THE WORLD ONCE MORE• • • • • • • • • • • •          97 FOXHUNTER          4
THE SORROWS OF THE WORLD BOW DOWN MY HEAD, • • • • •       104 FERGUS DRUID   V 38A
AND THE WHOLE WORLD WEIGHS DOWN UPON MY HEART-- • • •      104 FERGUS DRUID   V 38A
"STILL TREADS THE WORLD AMID HIS ARMED MEN•" • • • •       107 CUCHULAIN SEA  V  26
THE ROSE OF THE WORLD • • • • • • • • • • • •              111 ROSE OF WORLD      T
WE AND THE LABOURING WORLD ARE PASSING BY: • • • •         112 ROSE OF WORLD      6
HE MADE THE WORLD TO BE A GRASSY ROAD • • • • • •          112 ROSE OF WORLD     14
ROSE OF ALL ROSES, ROSE OF ALL THE WORLD: • • • •          113 ROSE OF BATTLE     1
ROSE OF ALL ROSES, ROSE OF ALL THE WORLD: • • • •          115 ROSE OF BATTLE    25
GIVE TO THESE CHILDREN, NEW FROM THE WORLD, • • • •        116 FAERY SONG         5
GIVE TO THESE CHILDREN, NEW FROM THE WORLD, • • • •        116 FAERY SONG         9
AND SEEMED THE GREATNESS OF THE WORLD IN TEARS, • • •      120 SORROW OF LOVE     6
THE WILLOW OF THE MANY-SORROWED WORLD• • • • • • •         130 BOOK STORIES   V  16
AND GOD COVERED THE WORLD WITH SHADE, • • • • • •          133 FR GILLIGAN       19
AND TIME AND THE WORLD ARE EVER IN FLIGHT: • • • • •       148 INTO TWILIGHT     14
• • • AND HIS BELOVED, AND LONGS FOR THE END OF THE WORLD  153 CHANGE BELOVED     T
THAT HAS LONG FADED FROM THE WORLD: • • • • • • •          155 FORGOT BEAUTY      3
THAT HAS LONG FADED IN THE WORLD: • • • • • • •            155 FORGOT BEAUTY  V   3
TILL ALL THE VALLEYS OF THE WORLD HAVE BEEN WITHERED AWAY•  163 VALLEY LOVERS      8
TILL THE VALLEYS OF THE WORLD HAVE BEEN WITHERED AWAY•"     163 VALLEY LOVERS  V   8
THE BLESSEDEST SOULS THAT WALK IN THE WORLD • • • • •      167 BLESSED           19
I SEE THE BLESSEDEST SOUL IN THE WORLD • • • • • •         168 BLESSED           31
WHILE TIME AND THE WORLD ARE EBBING AWAY • • • • • •       168 BLESSED           39
AND HAVE SEEN THE BLESSEDEST SOUL IN THE WORLD, • • • •    168 BLESSED        V  31
UNTIL TIME AND THE WORLD HAVE EBBED AWAY • • • • •         168 BLESSED        V  39
AND LOST THE WORLD AND EMER FOR A KISS: • • • • • •        170 SECRET ROSE       15
SHE COULD HAVE CALLED OVER THE RIM OF THE WORLD • • •      181 QUEEN MAEVE       23
THE MARTYRS CALL THE WORLD•" AND THEREUPON • • • • •       205 ADAMS CURSE       14
THE MARTYRS CALL THE WORLD•"  THAT WOMAN THEN • • • • •    205 ADAMS CURSE    V  14
O TATTERED CLOUDS OF THE WORLD, CALL FROM THE HIGH CAIRN   207 HANRAHANS SONG V   6
   OF MAIVE•
LIKE TATTERED CLOUDS OF THE WORLD, PASSIONS CALL AND OUR   207 HANRAHANS SONG V   8
   HEARTS BEAT:
O MY SHARE OF THE WORLD, O YELLOW HAIR: • • • • • •        211 RAGGED WOOD       11
DYING AT EVERY MOMENT IN THE WORLD, • • • • • • •          226 SHADOW WATER B    90
KNOWING IT FOR THE WORLD'S END?  WHERE THE WORLD ENDS      226 SHADOW WATER B   100
THE ROOTS OF THE WORLD•  SHADOWS BEFORE NOW • • • •        227 SHADOW WATER B   104
WHERE I AM RID OF LIFE—THE EVENTS OF THE WORLD-- • •       227 SHADOW WATER B   121
THE ROOTS OF THE WORLD•  WHO KNOWS THAT SHADOWS • • •      227 SHADOW WATER B V 104
BREATHE ON THE BURNISHED MIRROR OF THE WORLD • • • •       228 SHADOW WATER B   132
THAT IS NOT IN THE WORLD•  AND YET THE WORLD • • • •       228 SHADOW WATER B   143
THAT IS NOT IN THE WORLD•  AND YET THE WORLD • • • •       228 SHADOW WATER B   143
AND GET INTO THEIR WORLD THAT TO THE SENSE • • • •         230 SHADOW WATER B   179
THAT LIFT US TO THE FLOWING, CHANGING WORLD • • • •        230 SHADOW WATER B   182
BUT DREAMS THAT HURRY FROM BEYOND THE WORLD • • • •        230 SHADOW WATER B   185
AND THAT IS WHY THE WORLD TOTTERS ABOUT • • • • •          233 SHADOW WATER B   238
YOU ARE NOT ITS CORE•  MY TEETH ARE IN THE WORLD,          235 SHADOW WATER B   279
THERE'S NOTHING IN THE WORLD THAT'S WORTH A FEAR• • •      238 SHADOW WATER B   353
I WOULD THAT THERE WAS NOTHING IN THE WORLD • • • •        246 SHADOW WATER B   503
"THERE IS A COUNTRY AT THE END OF THE WORLD • • • •        247 SHADOW WATER B   530
BUT IN SOME ISLAND WHERE THE LIFE OF THE WORLD • • •       249 SHADOW WATER B   559
LEAPS UPWARD, AS IF ALL THE STREAMS O' THE WORLD • • •     249 SHADOW WATER B   560
DRAGON THAT LOVED THE WORLD AND HELD US TO IT, • • •       251 SHADOW WATER B   598
YOU ARE BROKEN, YOU ARE BROKEN•  THE WORLD DRIFTS AWAY,    251 SHADOW WATER B   599
FOR WE WILL GAZE UPON THIS WORLD NO LONGER• • • • •        251 SHADOW WATER B   614
FOR HE WILL GAZE UPON THIS WORLD NO LONGER• • • • •        251 SHADOW WATER B V 614
FOR WE WILL GAZE UPON THE WORLD NO LONGER• • • • •         251 SHADOW WATER B V 614
WE'LL OUT, FOR THE WORLD LIVES AS LONG AGO: • • • •        257 RECONCILIATION     8
HOW SHOULD THE WORLD BE LUCKIER IF THIS HOUSE, • • • •     264 HOUSE SHAKEN       1
BREATHED ON THE WORLD WITH TIMID BREATH• • • • • •         266 GALWAY RACES       9
WORLD, AS IT WERE A COAL, • • • • • • • • • •              267 FRIEND ILLNESS     5
MORE HANDS IN HEIGHT THAN ANY STAG IN THE WORLD • • •      277 TWO KINGS          9
THE HANDS THAT GATHERED UP THE MIGHT OF THE WORLD, • •     278 TWO KINGS         29
BUT IF NOT LIVING, HALF THE WORLD IS LOST•" • • • •        280 TWO KINGS      V  86
SPEAK IT, THAT I MAY SEND THROUGH THE WIDE WORLD • •       281 TWO KINGS         97
THAT OUR SUFFICIENT PORTION OF THE WORLD • • • • •         282 TWO KINGS        119
THEY HAVE GONE ABOUT THE WORLD LIKE WIND, • • • •          289 SEPTEMBER 1913    11
• • • OF THE WESTERN WORLD", [NINETEEN—SEVEN] • • •        294 HATED PLAYBOY      T
THE ATTACK ON "THE PLAYBOY OF THE WESTERN WORLD" • • •     294 HATED PLAYBOY  V   T
"TIME TO PUT OFF THE WORLD AND GO SOMEWHERE • • • •        299 BEGGAR CRIED       1
```

915

	PAGE	TITLE	LINE
WORLD (CONTINUED)			
THAT DYING CHOSE THE LIVING WORLD FOR TEXT • • • • •	324	ROBERT GREGORY	26
THE ENTIRE COMBUSTIBLE WORLD IN ONE SMALL ROOM • • • • •	327	ROBERT GREGORY	82
ALL THE COMBUSTIBLE WORLD IN ONE SMALL ROOM • • • • •	327	ROBERT GREGORY V	82
AT THE OLD BITTER WORLD WHERE THEY MARRY IN CHURCHES, • • •	330	BONE OF A HARE	13
THE WORLD A NARROW POUND." • • • • • • • • • •	333	SOLOMON SHEBA	24
WE HAVE GIVEN THE WORLD OUR PASSION, • • • • • • •	363	DOLLS DRAWINGS	10
WE AND OUR DOLLS BEING BUT THE WORLD WERE BEST AWAY. • •	364	DOLLS FACES	12
FOR THOSE THAT LOVE THE WORLD SERVE IT IN ACTION, • • •	369	EGO DOMINUS	42
WHAT PORTION IN THE WORLD CAN THE ARTIST HAVE • • • •	369	EGO DOMINUS	49
NO ONE DENIES TO KEATS LOVE OF THE WORLD: • • • • •	370	EGO DOMINUS	52
SHUT OUT FROM ALL THE LUXURY OF THE WORLD, • • • • •	370	EGO DOMINUS	60
TOO LONELY FOR THE TRAFFIC OF THE WORLD: • • • • • •	374	PHASES OF MOON	61
BEYOND THE VISIBLE WORLD. ALL DREAMS OF THE SOUL • • •	374	PHASES OF MOON	63
IT SOUGHT ITSELF AND AFTERWARDS THE WORLD. • • • • • •	376	PHASES OF MOON	95
AND THIS FOUL WORLD WERE DEAD AT LAST. • • • • • • •	388	SOLOMON WITCH	16
YET THE WORLD ENDS WHEN THESE TWO THINGS, • • • • • •	388	SOLOMON WITCH	28
"YET THE WORLD STAYS." "IF THAT BE SO, • • • • • •	388	SOLOMON WITCH	33
MERE ANARCHY IS LOOSED UPON THE WORLD, • • • • • • •	402	SECOND COMING	4
THOUGHTS UPON THE PRESENT STATE OF THE WORLD • • • • •	428	NINETEEN 19 V	T
AND PLANNED TO BRING THE WORLD UNDER A RULE, • • • • •	429	NINETEEN 19	31
BEING BY THE WORLD OPPRESSED, • • • • • • • • •	434	YOUTH AND AGE	2
THE MIGHTIEST OF THE PRINCES OF THE WORLD • • • • • •	462	HARUN RASHID	41
FROM EVERY QUARTER OF THE WORLD, CAN STAY • • • • • •	471	ALL SOUL NIGHT	12
THAT THIS PRAGMATICAL, PREPOSTEROUS PIG OF A WORLD, • • •	481	BLOOD AND MOON	26
BUT WE OLD MEN ARE MASSED AGAINST THE WORLD. • • • • •	486	SEVEN SAGES	14
BUT WE OLD MEN ARE OUT AGAINST THE WORLD. • • • • • •	486	SEVEN SAGES V	14
WORLD BESOTTED TRAVELLER: HE • • • • • • • • •	493	SWIFTS EPITAPH V	5
BEFORE THE WORLD WAS MADE." • • • • • • • • • •	516	MANS SONG	12
'GAT THE FOAL OF THE WORLD." • • • • • • • • •	529	TOM CRUACHAN	6
BEFORE THE WORLD WAS MADE • • • • • • • • • • •	531	BEFORE WORLD	T
BEFORE THE WORLD WAS MADE. • • • • • • • • • •	532	BEFORE WORLD	8
BEFORE THE WORLD WAS MADE. • • • • • • • • • •	532	BEFORE WORLD	16
THEY GAVE IT OUT TO ALL THE WORLD, • • • • • • • •	582	ROGER CASEMENT	11
ALL KNOW THAT ALL THE DEAD IN THE WORLD ABOUT THAT PLACE ARE STUCK,	593	PILGRIM	11
ON THIS FOUL WORLD IN ITS DECLINE AND FALL: • • • • •	619	BRONZE HEAD	24
SAINT JOSEPH THOUGHT THE WORLD WOULD MELT • • • • • •	619	STICK INCENSE	3
SOME ROGUE OF THE WORLD STOLE THEM TO PATCH UP A FENCE OR A FIRE.	623	HIGH TALK	4
SOME KNEW WHAT AILED THE WORLD • • • • • • • • •	627	STATES HOLIDAY	9
WHILE THE WORLD IS ROLL'D IN LIGHT. • • • • • • • •	646	ISLE STAT I 1	29
ALL THE WORLD IS RINGING, RINGING: • • • • • • • •	648	ISLE STAT I 1	93
ALL THE WORLD IS SINGING, SINGING. • • • • • • • •	648	ISLE STAT I 1	94
WILL CIRCLE ROUND THE WORLD UPON A QUEST, • • • • • •	651	ISLE STAT I 1	159
O'ER GRIEF. THE WORLD DRINKS SORROW FROM THE BEAMS • •	664	ISLE STAT II 2	46
AND THAT WAS STRANGE: BUT THIS IS MANY A WORLD • • • •	664	ISLE STAT II 2	60
IN THE FAR WORLD WILL VANISH FROM THY MIND, • • • • •	670	ISLE STAT II 3	93
THE WORLD, WITHIN HIS FOLDED HEART, • • • • • • • •	671	ISLE STAT II 3	133
THE WAVES, ENORMOUS WANDERERS OF THE WORLD, • • • • •	687	TWO TITANS	3
YET SOMEWHERE IN THE FOOTSORE WORLD WE MEET, • • • • •	691	MOSADA 1	23
FAR OUT UPON THE WATER WORLD AND RINGED • • • • • •	693	MOSADA 1	80
AND—MERCY IS THE MANNA OF THE WORLD. • • • • • • •	697	MOSADA 2	41
THE WORLD TO ITS FIERCE INFANCY AGAIN. • • • • • • •	698	MOSADA 2	61
THE WORLD WERE DREAMING IN ITS SUMMER SLEEP: • • • • •	699	MOSADA 3	11
FOR IT ALONE OF ALL THE WORLD WILL DO • • • • • • •	700	MOSADA 3	28
WITH THREE BARS CROSSED, AND THESE FOUR WALLS MY WORLD, •	700	MOSADA 3	32
THE NOISY WORLD DIVIDES. HOW SOON A DEED • • • • •	700	MOSADA 3	34
AND POUR UPON THE WORLD: AH: WELL-A-DAY: • • • • •	703	MOSADA 3	118
AND POUR UPON THE WORLD: AH: WELL A DAY! • • • • •	703	MOSADA 3 V	118
STILL WANDER THROUGH THE WORLD. HE'S GONE, HE'S GONE. • •	703	MOSADA 3	121
SO ENDS A BRAIN—A WORLD: THE SMOKE GOES UP, • • •	714	FERENCZ RENYI	111
OF FIRE. SO ENDS A BRAIN—A WORLD: THE SMOKE FLOATS UP,	714	FERENCZ RENYI V	111
THE WORLD GROWS OLD AND PLAYS THE FOOL." • • • • • •	725	LEGEND	12
"WITH ACTION ALL THE WORLD IS VEXED," • • • • • •	728	PRIEST FAIRY	15
HIS HEART'S DESIRE WHERE THE WORLD DWINDLES OUT? • • •	747	SHADOW WATER A	13
TIME AND THE WORLD AND ALL THINGS DWINDLE OUT. • • • •	749	SHADOW WATER A	47
BREATHE ON THE BURNISHED MIRROR OF THE WORLD • • • • •	750	SHADOW WATER A	69
HOW ALL THAT DIE ARE BORNE ABOUT THE WORLD • • • • •	750	SHADOW WATER A	84
OF THE TWELVE KINGS OF THE WORLD TO BE MY KING, • • •	757	SHADOW WATER A	214
THEY LURE US TO THE STREAMS WHERE THE WORLD ENDS. • • •	764	SHADOW WATER A	334
TO LEAD US TO THE STREAMS WHERE THE WORLD ENDS. • • • •	765	SHADOW WATER A	369
ALL THAT KNOW LOVE AMONG THE WINDS OF THE WORLD • • •	767	SHADOW WATER A	386
THAT HAVE KNOWN LOVE AMONG THE WINDS OF THE WORLD • • •	767	SHADOW WATER A	392
WHERE THE WORLD ENDS, OR RUNS FROM WIND TO WIND • • • •	768	SHADOW WATER A	417
FOR WE WILL GAZE UPON THIS WORLD NO LONGER. • • • • •	769	SHADOW WATER A	430
UPON THIS WORLD NO LONGER. THE HARP CRIES OUT. • • •	769	SHADOW WATER A V	430
I'D LET THE WHOLE WORLD GO: • • • • • • • • •	782	HEART FRIGHT	9
ALTHOUGH WIDE WORLD HOLD NOT • • • • • • • • •	786	YOUR HEART	16
WORLD-BESOTTED			
WORLD-BESOTTED TRAVELLER: HE • • • • • • • • •	493	SWIFTS EPITAPH	5
WORLD-FAMOUS			
WORLD-FAMOUS GOLDEN-THIGHED PYTHAGORAS • • • • • • •	445	SCHOOL CHILDR	45
WORLD-FAMOUS GOLDEN THIGHED PYTHAGORAS • • • • • • •	445	SCHOOL CHILDR V	45
WORLD-FORGOTTEN			
UPON A WOVEN WORLD-FORGOTTEN ISLE • • • • • • • •	126	DREAM OF FAERY	8
WORLD-OLD			
TO EASE THEIR WORLD-OLD THIRST ALONG THE BRINK • • • •	663	ISLE STAT II 2	41
WORLD'S			
AND RODE ON TILL OVER THE WORLD'S RIM FLOATED THE SEA'S OLD SHOUT,	60	OISIN 3 V	183

916

		PAGE	TITLE		LINE
WORLD'S (CONTINUED)					
FOR THE WORLD'S MORE FULL OF WEEPING THAN YOU CAN UNDERSTAND.		87	STOLEN CHILD		12
FOR THE WORLD'S MORE FULL OF WEEPING THAN YOU CAN UNDERSTAND.		87	STOLEN CHILD		27
FOR THE WORLD'S MORE FULL OF WEEPING THAN YOU CAN UNDERSTAND.		88	STOLEN CHILD		41
FOR THE WORLD'S MORE FULL OF WEEPING THAN HE CAN UNDERSTAND		89	STOLEN CHILD	V	53
AND WITH YOU CAME THE WHOLE OF THE WORLD'S TEARS,		120	SORROW OF LOVE	V	6
FOR IN THE WORLD'S FIRST BLOSSOMING AGE		138	TO IRELAND	V	10
BEING WEARY OF THE WORLD'S EMPIRES, BOW DOWN TO YOU,		161	BLACK PIG		7
"O WHAT OF THE WORLD'S BANE?"		214	HAPPY TOWNLAND		14
THAT IS THE WORLD'S BANE."		214	HAPPY TOWNLAND		20
O WHAT IS THE WORLD'S BANE?,		214	HAPPY TOWNLAND	V	REF
"O WHAT OF THE WORLD'S BANE?"		215	HAPPY TOWNLAND		34
THAT IS THE WORLD'S BANE."		215	HAPPY TOWNLAND		40
"O WHAT OF THE WORLD'S BANE?"		216	HAPPY TOWNLAND		54
THAT IS THE WORLD'S BANE."		216	HAPPY TOWNLAND		60
KNOWING IT FOR THE WORLD'S END? WHERE THE WORLD ENDS		226	SHADOW WATER B		100
WHAT THE WORLD'S MILLION LIPS ARE THIRSTING FOR		229	SHADOW WATER B		161
HAD THE WORLD'S TOTAL LIFE GATHERED UP, IT SEEMED,		231	SHADOW WATER B		194
SHALL LIGHT UPON A PLACE IN THE WORLD'S CORE,		231	SHADOW WATER B		212
YOU ARE NOT THE WORLD'S CORE. O NO, NO, NO!		234	SHADOW WATER B		277
TO TROOP WITH THOSE THE WORLD'S FORGOT,		273	GREY ROCK		63
AND THE WORLD'S ALTERED SINCE YOU DIED,		276	GREY ROCK		126
"IF HE BE LIVING STILL THE WHOLE WORLD'S MINE,		280	TWO KINGS	V	85
AND DREAM THAT ALL THE WORLD'S A FRIEND,		313	TWO YEAR LATER		8
WORE IT IN THE WORLD'S EYES		320	COAT		6
WORE IT IN THE WORLD'S EYE		320	COAT	V	6
TO HAVE PUBLISHED ALL TO BE A WORLD'S DELIGHT.		327	ROBERT GREGORY		72
THEY'LL COUGH IN THE INK TO THE WORLD'S END;		337	SCHOLARS	V	7
IT WOULD BE THE WORLD'S SERVANT, AND AS IT SERVES,		376	PHASES OF MOON		90
AND HIDE IT THERE, FOR CALIPHS TO WORLD'S END		461	HARUN RASHID		17
UNTIL THAT GLANCE RUN IN THE WORLD'S DESPITE		474	ALL SOUL NIGHT		94
WHAT WERE ALL THE WORLD'S ALARMS		522	LULLABY		3
WHAT ARE ALL THE WORLD'S ALARMS?		522	LULLABY	V	3
THE WHOLE WORLD'S SADLY TALKING TO ITSELF.		652	ISLE STAT I 2		12
THE LION, THE WORLD'S GREAT SOLITARY, BENDS		689	NETTLESHIP		5
AND THEN THE WHOLE WORLD'S TROUBLE WEEPS WITH YOU.		738	YOU ARE SAD		12
WORLDS					
THE MAKER OF THE STARS AND WORLDS		724	LEGEND		1
"THE PROPS," SAID HE, "OF STARS AND WORLDS		725	LEGEND		5
THE MAKER OF THE STARS AND WORLDS		725	LEGEND		29
WORLD-TRANSFORMING					
WHEN WORLD-TRANSFORMING CHARLEMAGNE WAS CONCEIVED?		560	WHENCE COME		12
WORLD-TROUBLING					
THE HEARTS OF THE WORLD-TROUBLING SEAMEN,		82	MAD KING GOLL		4
WORLDWIDE					
AH, WORLDWIDE NATION, ALWAYS GROWING SORROW!		130	BOOK STORIES	V	11
WORLD-WIDE					
AH, WORLD-WIDE NATION, ALWAYS GROWING SORROW,		130	BOOK STORIES	V	11
WORM SEE LUG-WORM GLOW-WORM CANKER-WORM					
THE WEAK WORM HIDING DOWN IN ITS SMALL CAVE,		101	ROSE UPON ROOD		16
IT WHIRLS INTO THE FOAM. O ANCIENT WORM,		251	SHADOW WATER B		597
BEFORE THE FULL MOON, HELPLESS AS A WORM.		374	PHASES OF MOON		49
OR THE HUMBLER WORM, I CLIMBED BEN BULBEN'S BACK		409	TOWER		9
WEAK AS A WORM,		574	MAIDS 1ST SONG		10
DULL AS A WORM,		575	MAIDS 2ND SONG		2
LIMP AS A WORM,		575	MAIDS 2ND SONG		4
BLIND AS A WORM.		575	MAIDS 2ND SONG		6
ARISE, WORM, AND FOLLOW!		655	ISLE STAT I 2		83
FROM THE UNDYING WORM. SHE SLEEPS--MOSADA--		701	MOSADA 3		65
HIDING THE REBELS WORM IN YONDER WOOD		709	FERENCZ RENYI		14
WHERE WORM THE REBELS, OR MY BULLETS LAY		713	FERENCZ RENYI		83
AH! IT DWELT WITHIN THE TWILIGHT AS THE WORM WITHIN THE NUT.		718	PHANTOM SHIP		6
AND LETS THE KIND WORM TAKE THE LOT!		779	ACCURSED WHO		4
WORMS					
WHO MADE THE GRASS AND MADE THE WORMS AND MADE MY FEATHERS GAY,		77	INDIAN ON GOD		18
DID NOT THE WORMS THAT SPIRED ABOUT HIS BONES		128	DREAM OF FAERY		41
WERE NOT THE WORMS THAT SPIRED ABOUT HIS BONES		128	DREAM OF FAERY	V	41
HIDING THE REBEL WORMS IN YONDER WOOD,		709	FERENCZ RENYI		14
WORN SEE WEATHER-WORN WAVE-WORN SEA-WORN OUT-WORN LOVE-WORN FOOT-WORN SORROW-WORN					
YE WORN DEED-DOERS, AND MY NAME		5	OISIN 1	V	48
O WORN DEED-DOER." "WHAT MAY BRING		5	OISIN 1	V	50
THAT LACKEY THE WORN MOON IN MIDNIGHT HOURS,		41	OISIN 2	V	185A
THEIR FACES ARE ALL WORN, AND IN THEIR EYES		73	ANASHU VIJAYA		48
AND WEARY AND WORN ARE OUR SAD SOULS NOW:		79	FALLING LEAVES		6
"PASSION HAS OFTEN WORN OUR WANDERING HEARTS."		80	EPHEMERA		12
"OFTEN HAS PASSION WORN OUR WANDERING HEARTS,		80	EPHEMERA	V	12
AND GAZING ON HIS VISAGE WORN,		99	FOXHUNTER	V	43
MY FATHER STANDS." "AGED, WORN OUT WITH WARS		107	CUCHULAIN SEA		29
ALL THINGS UNCOMELY AND BROKEN, ALL THINGS WORN OUT AND OLD,		142	ROSE IN HEART		1
ALL THINGS UNCOMELY AND BROKEN, ALL THINGS WORN AND OLD,		142	ROSE IN HEART	V	1
WHITE WOMAN THAT PASSION HAS WORN		157	POET BELOVED		3
BECAUSE A LOVER'S HEART'S WORN OUT,		191	BAILE AILLINN		65
A MOON, WORN AS IF IT HAD BEEN A SHELL		206	ADAMS CURSE		31
A MOON--MOON WORN AS IF IT HAD BEEN A SHELL		206	ADAMS CURSE	V	31
WEAK AND WORN AND WEARY THE WAVES OF CUMMEN STRAND,		207	HANRAHANS SONG	V	6

	PAGE	TITLE		LINE
WORN (CONTINUED)				
WEAK AND WORN AND WEARY OUR COURAGE DROOPS AND DIES	207	HANRAHANS SONG	V	8
SHE MAY HAVE WORN SILK CLOTHES, OR WORN A CROWN, ...	282	TWO KINGS		117
SHE MAY HAVE WORN SILK CLOTHES, OR WORN A CROWN, ...	282	TWO KINGS		117
MY BROTHER MOURTEEN IS WORN OUT	301	RUN PARADISE		8
I AM WORN OUT WITH DREAMS;	329	MEN IMPROVE		1
WORN THIN BY THE LAPPING OF WATER.	330	BONE OF A HARE		11
THEIR CONNEMARA CLOTH WORN OUT OF SHAPE;	372	PHASES OF MOON		4
BUT LIVED WHERE MOTLEY IS WORN;	392	EASTER 1916		14
WHEREVER GREEN IS WORN.	394	EASTER 1916		78
SHOULD FIND NO BURDEN BUT ITSELF AND YET SHOULD BE WORN OUT.	449	OWEN AHERNE		3
IS WORN AS THOUGH WITH FIRE. OH, GOBLIN QUEEN, ...	667	ISLE STAT II 3		36
THE BANKS ARE WORN FOR EVER	680	LOVE AND DEATH		9
WORN WITH LONG STRUGGLES; AND THE WAVES HAVE SUNG	687	TWO TITANS		23
WORN BY THE SOLSTICE FIERCE, AND MADE IT PURE.	692	MOSADA 1		57
THE HEART WELL WORN UPON THE SLEEVE MAY BE THE BEST OF SIGHTS,	790	HEART SLEEVE		1
WORSE				
AYE, AND WORSE WRONG THAN THESE.	260	UNWORTH PRAISE		18
ONE TIME IT WAS A WOMAN'S FACE, OR WORSE--	267	ALL TEMPT ME		2
AND EVIL MUST IT BE, IF DONE 'TWERE WORSE	281	TWO KINGS		105
"AND THE WORSE DEVIL THAT IS BETWEEN MY THIGHS."	300	BEGGAR CRIED		8
OR WHAT WORSE EVIL COME--	416	TOWER		188
KNOW WORSE EVIL OF THE BODY;	573	LADYS 3RD SONG		6
I HAVE FOUND SOMETHING WORSE	628	JANE MOUNTAIN		5
MOSADA, IT IS THEN SO MUCH THE WORSE;	692	MOSADA 1	V	41A
WORSHIP				
THEN NOWISE WORSHIP DUSTY DEEDS, ...	65	HAPPY SHEPHERD		22
THEN NO WISE WORSHIP DUSTY DEEDS, ...	65	HAPPY SHEPHERD	V	22
BOTH NUNS AND MOTHERS WORSHIP IMAGES, ...	445	SCHOOL CHILDR		49
WORST				
FOR HE IS THE WORST OF ALL DEAD MEN."	272	GREY ROCK		36
THOUGH COURTEOUS TO THE WORST; MUCH FALLING HE	324	ROBERT GREGORY		19
THE BEST LACK ALL CONVICTION, WHILE THE WORST	402	SECOND COMING		7
THE BEST LACK CONVICTION, WHILE THE WORST	402	SECOND COMING	V	7
AN INTELLECTUAL HATRED IS THE WORST, ...	405	FOR DAUGHTER		57
THAT THE WORST ROGUES AND RASCALS HAD DIED OUT.	428	NINETEEN 19		16
ALL OF THAT WORST IGNOMINY	436	FOR MY SON		23
THAT HAS THE WORST OF ALL BAD NAMES;	531	FATHER CHILD		5
THE WORST A COAT UPON A COAT-HANGER.	624	APPARITIONS		8
THE WORST A COAT UPON A COAT-HANGER.	624	APPARITIONS		16
THE WORST A COAT UPON A COAT-HANGER.	624	APPARITIONS		24
IS THE WORST MAN HAS TO FEAR.	637	BEN BULBEN		20
WORTH				
WORTH KNITTING TO A MEASURE OF SWEET SOUND?	181	QUEEN MAEVE		33
WILL HARDLY SEEM WORTH THINKING OF	202	NEVER GIVE ALL		2
THEY TAKE A KISS FOR WHAT A KISS IS WORTH, ...	229	SHADOW WATER B		157
THERE'S NOTHING IN THE WORLD THAT'S WORTH A FEAR. . . .	238	SHADOW WATER B		353
OR HOW SHOULD LOVE BE WORTH ITS PAINS WERE IT NOT . . .	285	TWO KINGS		190
AS IF IT WERE NOT WORTH THE DOING.	306	HOUR DAWN		84
I WOULD BE--FOR NO KNOWLEDGE IS WORTH A STRAW--	344	DAWN		13
OPINION IS NOT WORTH A RUSH;	385	ROBARTES DANCE		1
ALTHOUGH HE THOUGHT IT WORTH A CROW.	388	SOLOMON WITCH		35
WONDER HOW MANY TIMES I COULD HAVE PROVED MY WORTH . . .	427	PHANTOM HATRED		34
FOR ALL MEN LOVE YOUR WORTH; AND I MUST RAGE	447	HERO GIRL FOOL	V	8
IF YOU HAVE SEEN THAT IMAGE AND NOT MY WORTH.	448	HERO GIRL FOOL	V	8
ALL MEN HAVE PRAISED MY STRENGTH BUT NOT MY WORTH. . . .	448	HERO GIRL FOOL	V	9
AND NOT THEIR WORTH. GOD LOVES US FOR OUR WORTH; . . .	448	HERO GIRL FOOL	V	15
AND NOT THEIR WORTH. GOD LOVES US FOR OUR WORTH; . . .	448	HERO GIRL FOOL	V	15
NOT WORTH THINKING OF, ...	504	QUARREL IN AGE		5
FOR BEAUTY DIES OF BEAUTY, WORTH OF WORTH, ...	564	GYRES		3
FOR BEAUTY DIES OF BEAUTY, WORTH OF WORTH, ...	564	GYRES		3
IF YOU ARE WORTH MY HOPE! NEITHER CONTENT	579	DOR WELLESLEY		13
A LITTLE MOORISH GIRL? SMALL WORTH. MY SONG--	696	MOSADA 2		10
BUT IS EDAIN WORTH A SONG	773	SONG DEIRDRE 1		17
WORTHY				
SCARCE WORTHY OF A HOOF GOLD-SHOD.	2	OISIN 1	V	7Y
YOUR QUESTIONER, OISIN, IS WORTHY, HE COMES FROM THE FENIAN LANDS."	51	OISIN 3		64
IF WORTHY THEIR PROMINENT PART IN THE PLAY, ...	565	LAPIS LAZULI		14
A FINISH WORTHY OF THE START.	626	OLD MEN BE MAD		15
SO WORTHY AMONG MEN. I FOLLOW YOU, ...	768	SHADOW WATER A	V	412
WORTHY'S				
WORTHY'S THY QUESTIONER, OISIN, HE FROM THE FENIAN LANDS."	51	OISIN 3	V	64
WOUND				
MY HUMAN SORROW HER WHITE ARMS WOUND.	11	OISIN 1		138
MY HUMAN SADNESS FAY ARMS WOUND.	11	OISIN 1	V	138
THE DANCE WOUND THROUGH THE WINDLESS WOODS;	21	OISIN 1		320
BUT KNOW YOUR HAIR WAS BOUND AND WOUND	176	BELOVED DEAD		9
NOR ON THE ANCIENT BEATEN PATHS, THAT WOUND	279	TWO KINGS		52
AND OTHER COMFORT WERE A BITTER WOUND;	429	NINETEEN 19	V	41
HAS WOUND UPON A SPOOL	449	HERO GIRL FOOL		22
WOUND IN MIND'S PONDERING	471	ALL SOUL NIGHT		13
AS MUMMIES IN THE MUMMY-CLOTH ARE WOUND;	471	ALL SOUL NIGHT		14
AS MUMMIES IN THE MUMMY CLOTH ARE WOUND;	471	ALL SOUL NIGHT	V	14
WOUND IN MIND'S WANDERING	474	ALL SOUL NIGHT		99
AS MUMMIES IN THE MUMMY-CLOTH ARE WOUND.	474	ALL SOUL NIGHT		100
AS MUMMIES IN THE MUMMY CLOTH ARE WOUND.	474	ALL SOUL NIGHT	V	100
THE WOODEN SCABBARD BOUND AND WOUND, ...	477	SELF AND SOUL		15
BUT WHEN HE WOUND HER COAL-BLACK HAIR	514	JANE GROWN OLD		3

918

WOUND   (CONTINUED)
    SANG OF THE BEAST THAT GAVE THE FATAL WOUND. . . . . .   537 HER VISION   16
    SHE STOOD IN DESPERATE MUSIC WOUND, ...   578 CRAZED GIRL   10
    WOUND, WOUND, AND SHE MADE IN HER TRIUMPH . . . .   578 CRAZED GIRL   11
    WOUND, WOUND, AND SHE MADE IN HER TRIUMPH . . . .   578 CRAZED GIRL   11
WOUNDED
    THE KNOTTED SCOURGE, THE NAIL-PIERCED HANDS, THE WOUNDED   172 TRAV PASSION   V   4
    SIDE,
    TILL MAURYA OF THE WOUNDED HEART CRY A SWEET CRY, . . .   173 SPEAKS HEARERS V   6
    SHOULDERED A LITTER WITH A WOUNDED MAN, ...   537 HER VISION   14
    CEASE! THERNOT'S WOUNDED, CEASE! THEY WILL NOT HEED. . .   665 ISLE STAT II 2   64
WOUND'S
    THAT THE IMMEDICABLE WOUND'S BEYOND . . . .   282 TWO KINGS   V   129
WOUNDS
    AND HEALED MY WOUNDS WITH UNGUENTS OUT OF FLOWERS . . .   41 OISIN 2   185
    THEY HEALED MY WOUNDS; AND ON THE SKIN SUPINE . . . . .   41 OISIN 2   V   187
    . . . AND OF OLD WOUNDS, AND TURN TO OUR REST. . . . .   62 OISIN 3   212
    . . . AND OF OLD WOUNDS AND REST. . . . .   62 OISIN 3   V   212
    THE PAIN OF WOUNDS, THE LABOUR OF THE SPEAR, ...   104 FERGUS DRUID   V 38D
    CROWDED WITH BITTER FACES, THE WOUNDS IN PALM AND SIDE,   172 TRAV PASSION   4
    TO HIM THAT WOUNDS HIM TO THE DEATH. I'LL DO IT. . . .   240 SHADOW WATER B   375
    SEEING, KING'S SON, WHAT WOUNDS YOU HAVE." . . . . .   275 GREY ROCK   94
    FROM DEATH, AND WOUNDS, OR ON SINAI'S TOP, ...   375 PHASES OF MOON   67
    THEIR WOUNDS OPEN AGAIN. . . . .   612 NEWS ORACLE   16
    THEN CLEANING OUT AND BANDAGING OF WOUNDS, ...   622 HOUND VOICE   20
    A MAN THAT HAD SIX MORTAL WOUNDS, A MAN . . . . . .   634 CUCHULAIN COMF   1
    AS THOUGH TO MEDITATE ON WOUNDS AND BLOOD. . . . . .   634 CUCHULAIN COMF   6
    THE HAND THAT WOUNDS HIM, BECAUSE THE GODS ARE HIS FRIENDS.   758 SHADOW WATER A   232
    THE HAND THAT WOUNDS. A WHITE BIRD BEATS HIS WINGS . . .   758 SHADOW WATER A V   232
    UNTIL HE HAD DIED OF HIS WOUNDS, ...   775 AGAINST WITCH   16
    WHAT WOUNDS, WHAT BLOODY PRESS, ...   785 WOMANS BEAUTY   26
WOVE
    WOVE IN HER FLOWER-LIKE HAIR, BEFORE DARK TOWERS . . . .   30 OISIN 2   V   22
    THE LOVE-TALES WOVE WITH SILKEN THREAD . . . .   155 FORGOT BEAUTY   V   6
    WHEN SONGS I WOVE FOR MY BELOVED HIDE THE PRAYER, . . .   173 SPEAKS HEARERS   2
    BEND DOWN AND PRAY FOR ALL THAT SIN I WOVE IN SONG, . . .   173 SPEAKS HEARERS   5
    WHEN SONG I WOVE FOR MY BELOVED HIDES THE PRAYER, . . .   173 SPEAKS HEARERS V   2
    BEND DOWN AND PRAY FOR THE GREAT SIN I WOVE IN SONG, . . .   173 SPEAKS HEARERS V   5
    THAT EDAIN, MIDHIR'S WIFE, HAD WOVE . . . .   195 BAILE AILLINN   142
    AWAKE UNSLEEPING FIRES! AND WOVE SEVEN STRINGS, ...   219 HARP OF AENGUS   7
    AND IN HER SINGING WOVE AROUND HER HEAD . . . . . .   693 MOSADA 1   84
    AWAKE UNSLEEPING FIRES! AND WOVE SEVEN STRINGS, ...   762 SHADOW WATER A   302
    AND ONE WHERE THE WINDS ARE WOVE, ...   771 SPINNING SONG   3
WOVEN   SEE THOUGHT-WOVEN
    AND WITH THE WOVEN CRIMSON GLOWED . . . .   3 OISIN 1   V   26
    EACH ONE WOVEN TO THE OTHER, ...   22 OISIN 1   334
    EACH ONE WOVEN TO HIS BROTHER . . . .   22 OISIN 1   335
    WOVEN INTO HER HAIR, BEFORE DARK TOWERS . . . . . .   30 OISIN 2   22
    WHILE WE ALONE HAVE ROUND US WOVEN WOODS, ...   73 ANASHU VIJAYA   56
    AND WANDER EVER WITH WOVEN HANDS, ...   78 INDIAN TO LOVE   7
    A WOVEN SILENCE, OR BUT CAME TO CAST . . . .   114 ROSE OF BATTLE   13
    AND PIERCE THE DEEP WOOD'S WOVEN SHADE, ...   125 GOES FERGUS   2
    UPON A WOVEN WORLD-FORGOTTEN ISLE . . . .   126 DREAM OF FAERY   8
    UNDER THAT WOVEN CHANGELESS ROOF OF BOUGHS! . . . . .   126 DREAM OF FAERY   11
    UNDER THE WOVEN ROOFS OF QUICKEN BOUGHS!-- . . . . .   126 DREAM OF FAERY V   11
    WOVEN BY LADIES IN THEIR HAIR, ...   156 FORGOT BEAUTY   10
    AND THE IMAGES I WOVEN IN THIS STORY . . . .   218 WOODS OF COOLE   21
    AND 'NEATH IT SIT, AND OF THE WOVEN SUM . . . . . .   663 ISLE STAT II 2   30
    I HAD WOVEN OF THE SLEEP THAT IS IN POOLS . . . . .   762 SHADOW WATER A   284
    I AM CAUGHT IN WOVEN NETS OF ENCHANTMENT. LOOK! . . .   762 SHADOW WATER A   293
    O! I WOULD BREAK THIS NET THE GODS HAVE WOVEN . . . .   765 SHADOW WATER A   361
    THE NETS THE GODS HAVE WOVEN AND OUR OWN HEARTS, . . .   766 SHADOW WATER A   383
    HAD WOVEN HER OF WIND. LIFE WITHERS OUT . . . . . .   768 SHADOW WATER A V   423
WRACK
    AND PUT ALL TROY TO WRACK-- . . . .   455 HIS MEMORIES   V   16
    AMID THE CLOUDY WRACK, ...   458 HIS WILDNESS   2
    RUIN, WRECK AND WRACK! . . . .   505 RESULT THOUGHT   8
    ALL THE WRECK AND WRACK! . . . .   505 RESULT THOUGHT V   8
    THE SKY WAS BANDED O'ER WITH WRACK. . . . .   667 ISLE STAT II 3   23
    UNTIL THIS MORN. THE SKY WITH WRACK . . . .   667 ISLE STAT II 3 V   22
WRACKED
    EMPTIED, RUINED, WRACKED, AND LOST, ...   776 AGAINST WITCH   27
WRAP
    UNLOOSE THE CORD, AND THEY WILL WRAP YOU ROUND. . . . .   104 FERGUS DRUID   30
    WHO LOVES YOU, NO WHITE ARMS TO WRAP YOU ROUND, ...   109 CUCHULAIN SEA   59
    WHEN MY ARMS WRAP YOU ROUND I PRESS . . . .   155 FORGOT BEAUTY   1
    THE WHITE WAVES WRAP IT IN A SHEET OF FLAME, ...   662 ISLE STAT II 2   14
    THEY WILL WRAP THEM IN THE SHROUD, ...   733 STREET DANCERS   55
WRAPPED
    A SORROW WRAPPED EACH MERRY FACE, ...   17 OISIN 1   235
    AND WRAPPED IN DREAMS RODE OUT AGAIN . . . .   25 OISIN 1   382
    WRAPPED IN THE THINGS OF THE UNHUMAN MIND, ...   36 OISIN 2   98
    "HE WHO IS WRAPPED IN PURPLE ROBES, ...   134 FR GILLIGAN   45
    AND WRAPPED THE FLAMES ABOVE HIS HOLY HEAD! . . . . .   162 ASKS FORGIVE   17
    AND A CLOAK WRAPPED ABOUT THE STONE, ...   456 FRIENDS YOUTH   7
    I WRAPPED HER IN A HOODED CLOAK, AND SHE, ...   468 HARUN RASHID   154
    I WRAPPED HER IN A HEAVY HOODED CLOAK, ...   468 HARUN RASHID   V   154
    I WRAPPED HER IN A HEAVY HOODED CLOAK, AND SHE . . . .   468 HARUN RASHID   V   154
    NOON WRAPPED THE WOODS IN VEILS OF VIOLET WEATHER! . . .   715 DWELT SYCAMORE V   7
WRAPPING
    AND WRAPPING MY FACE IN MY HAIR, ...   59 OISIN 3   177

	PAGE	TITLE	LINE

WRAPPING (CONTINUED)
WRAPPING THAT FOUL BODY UP . . . . 525 DANCING DAYS   5
WRAPS
A GENTLE FEELING WRAPS THEM LIKE A FLEECE, ... 128 DREAM OF FAERY V   34
FROM THE GREAT PAINTED WINDOW WRAPS HIS BROW, ... 697 MOSADA 2   37
WRAPT   SEE TREE-WRAPT
WRAPT ROUND IN SOME DIM MEMORY, IT SEEMED-- . . . . . 36 OISIN 2   V   99
WRAPT IN THE WAVE OF THAT MUSIC, WITH WEARINESS MORE THAN
OF EARTH,   51 OISIN 3   69
NOON WRAPT THE TREES IN VEILS OF VIOLET WEATHER, ... 715 DWELT SYCAMORE   7
WRATH
OF RAVENING SORROW, OR THE HAND OF WRATH? . . . . . . 42 OISIN 2   199
HIS GOD OF STUPOR AND OF WRATH. . . . . 725 LEGEND   20
WREATH
BLOSSOM FROM THE SUMMER'S WREATH; . . . . . . 475 EVA GORE-BOOTH   6
UNMINDFUL OF ITS WOES, WOULD TWINE A WREATH . . . . . 650 ISLE STAT I 1   133
AS A WREATH OF SMOKE IN WIND-BLOWN FLIGHT . . . . . 730 PRIEST FAIRY   61
WREATHS
WITH WREATHS OF WITHERED FLOWERS . . . . 680 LOVE AND DEATH   17
WITH WREATHS OF WITHERED FLOWERS, ... 680 LOVE AND DEATH   19
WRECK
TILL THE WRECK OF BODY, ... 416 TOWER   184
AND PUT ALL TROY TO WRECK-- . . . . 455 HIS MEMORIES   16
RUIN, WRECK AND WRACK; . . . . 505 RESULT THOUGHT   8
ALL THE WRECK AND WRACK; . . . . 505 RESULT THOUGHT V   8
THAT THING ALL BLOOD AND MIRE, THAT BEAST-TORN WRECK, . . 537 HER VISION   25
WRECKED
YOU ARE STILL WRECKED AMONG HEATHEN DREAMS. . . . . . 4 OISIN 1   31
BITTER GLORY WRECKED. . . . . 504 RESULT THOUGHT   6
AND BY ITS FORMLESS SPAWNING FURY WRECKED, ... 611 STATUES   30
THAT WHEREBY A HOUSE LAY WRECKED? . . . . 632 MAN AND ECHO   16
THAT WHEREBY A HOUSE WAS WRECKED? . . . . 632 MAN AND ECHO   V 16
WREN
WHO GIVETH TO THE GOLDEN-CRESTED WREN . . . . . . 698 MOSADA 2   51
WRESTLE
OR WRESTLE WITH THEIR PEERS IN DEWY VALLEYS. . . . . 30 OISIN 2   V 14E
AND WHERE THE POLAR WINDS AND WATERS WRESTLE . . . . . 682 SEEKER   18
WRESTLED
WRESTLED AMONG THE ISLAND BANDS. . . . . 23 OISIN 1   350
WRETCH
HER HUSBAND HAS HEARD THE WRETCH, ... 319 DOLLS   15
FROM ANY PASSING WRETCH; . . . . 598 STONE CROSS   12
WRETCHED
MY WRETCHED DRAGON IS PERPLEXED. . . . . 386 ROBARTES DANCE   41
WRETCHEDLY
IS SHADOW, AND NOT LINGER WRETCHEDLY . . . . . . 230 SHADOW WATER B   180
WRETCHEDNESS
TILL HIS LAST WRETCHEDNESS WAS O'ER AND DONE." . . . . 664 ISLE STAT II 2   54
WRETCHES
"AND ALL THOSE LIES HAVE BUT ONE END, POOR WRETCHES TO
BETRAY;   450 OWEN AHERNE   18
WRIGGLING
A WRIGGLING THING ON THE WHITE LAKE MOVED, ... 673 ISLE STAT II 3   176
WRING
AND WRING MY HANDS, AND WAIL HIM BITTERLY, ... 242 SHADOW WATER B   414
WRINKLED
WRINKLED LIKE THE FOOT OF A GOOSE, ... 508 JANE BISHOP   16
HIDE WHERE HE WILL, IN WAVE OR WRINKLED MOON, ... 720 WITCH VIVIEN   8
THE WRINKLED SQUANDERER OF HUMAN WEALTH. . . . . . 720 WITCH VIVIEN   16
WRINKLES
WHO FINDING THE FIRST WRINKLES ON A FACE . . . . . 472 ALL SOUL NIGHT   42
THEIR EYES MID MANY WRINKLES, THEIR EYES, ... 567 LAPIS LAZULI   55
AND--NO; I'LL NONE OF THESE, OLD FATHER WRINKLES. . . . 721 WITCH VIVIEN   23
WRINKLING
. . . IMMENSE IN THEIR WRINKLING BARK; . . . . . . 48 OISIN 3   17
THE WAILING GREW DISTANT; I RODE BY THE WOODS OF
THE WRINKLING BARK,   56 OISIN 3   137
WRIST
AND THE DOWN-TURN OF HIS WRIST . . . . 348 FISHERMAN   33
AND THE DOWN TURN OF HIS WRIST . . . . 348 FISHERMAN   V 33
NOR A CAGE, NOR ALIGHT UPON WRIST, ... 349 HAWK   8
AND PADDLE TO THE WRIST . . . . 356 BROKEN DREAMS   31
THAT HAD A SOUND FLY-FISHER'S WRIST . . . . 625 OLD MEN BE MAD   3
THAT HAD A SOUND FLY FISHER'S WRIST . . . . 625 OLD MEN BE MAD V   3
WRIT
THE CAPTIVE'S JOURNEYS TO AND FRO WERE WRIT . . . . . 37 OISIN 2   116
THE CAPTIVES' JOURNEYS TO AND FRO WERE WRIT . . . . . 37 OISIN 2   V 116
IN CHANGELESS OGHAM LETTERS WRIT-- . . . . 194 BAILE AILLINN   117
R.I.P." WRIT IN BLOOD. . . . . 585 ORAHILLY   35
WRITE
WHILE STILL I MAY, I WRITE FOR YOU . . . . 139 TO IRELAND   33
WHILE STILL I MAY I WRITE OUT TRUE . . . . 139 TO IRELAND   V 33
AND WHEN I'D WRITE IT OUT ANEW, THE WORDS, ... 186 QUEEN MAEVE   139
AND MORE I MAY NOT WRITE OF, FOR THEY THAT CLEAVE . . . 218 WOODS OF COOLE   24
AND MORE I MAY NOT WRITE OF, FOR THEM THAT CLEAVE . . . 218 WOODS OF COOLE V 24
TO WRITE FOR MY OWN RACE . . . . 347 FISHERMAN   11
AND SHOULD THEY PAINT OR WRITE, STILL IT IS ACTION; . . . 369 EGO DOMINUS   44
AND SHOULD THEY PAINT OR WRITE STILL IS IT ACTION, . . . 369 EGO DOMINUS   V 44
I WRITE IT OUT IN A VERSE-- . . . . 394 EASTER 1916   74
KUSTA BEN LUKA IS MY NAME, I WRITE . . . . 460 HARUN RASHID   1
AND ALL THE WORDS THAT I WRITE, ... 739 WHERE BOOKS GO   2

WRITE (CONTINUED)

THAT DRUIDS WRITE ON YEW AND APPLE WOOD, ... 748 SHADOW WATER A 29
THE FOOL, WHO HAS MADE THE WISDOM THAT MEN WRITE . . . . 764 SHADOW WATER A 342

WRITERS

AND POETS FOUND, OLD WRITERS SAY, ... 197 BAILE AILLINN 187
NEVER TO HAVE LIVED IS BEST, ANCIENT WRITERS SAY! . . . 459 FROM OEDIPUS 10
AND WRITERS BY THE SCORE . . . . 582 ROGER CASEMENT 16
HAVE NOT OLD WRITERS SAID . . . . 781 MY HEART BEAT 6

WRITING

ON OLD DRY WRITING IN A LEARNED TONGUE, ... 466 HARUN RASHID 123
AS IF THAT WRITING OR THE FIGURED PAGE . . . . . . 466 HARUN RASHID 126

WRITINGS

THOSE MEN THAT IN THEIR WRITINGS ARE MOST WISE . . . . 370 EGO DOMINUS 68
UNLESS THE HOLY WRITINGS LIE, ... 436 FOR MY SON 28
THE WRITINGS I HAVE CAST AWAY! . . . . 779 ACCURSED WHO 2

WRITTEN   SEE HALF-WRITTEN RE-WRITTEN

THE CAPTIVES' FOOTSTEPS WRITTEN TO AND FRO: . . . . . 37 OISIN 2 V 118
TRAILS ALL ABOUT THE WRITTEN PAGE. . . . . 138 TO IRELAND 9
TO GRADUAL TIME'S LAST GIFT, A WRITTEN SPEECH . . . . 264 HOUSE SHAKEN 11
LINES WRITTEN IN DEJECTION . . . . 343 DEJECTION T
I SHALL HAVE WRITTEN HIM ONE . . . . 348 FISHERMAN 38
A CANDLE AND WRITTEN PAGE. . . . . 419 MY HOUSE 13
THE HALF IMAGINED, THE HALF WRITTEN PAGE. . . . . . . 431 NINETEEN 19 V 83
WRITTEN IN GOLD UPON A PURPLE STAIN, ... 461 HARUN RASHID 10
AS THOUGH THE WRITTEN OR THE PICTURED PAGE . . . . . 466 HARUN RASHID V 126
WHATEVER'S WRITTEN IN WHAT POETS NAME . . . . 492 COOLE BALLYLEE 43
ALL THAT IS WRITTEN IN WHAT POETS NAME . . . . 492 COOLE BALLYLEE V 43
A MEDITATION WRITTEN DURING SICKNESS AT ALGECIRAS . . . 493 AT ALGECIRAS V T

WRONG

THAT SANG, TO SWEETEN IRELAND'S WRONG, ... 137 TO IRELAND 3
WHO SANG TO SWEETEN IRELAND'S WRONG, ... 137 TO IRELAND V 3
THE WRONG OF UNSHAPELY THINGS IS A WRONG TOO GREAT TO BE 143 ROSE IN HEART 5
    TOLD:
THE WRONG OF UNSHAPELY THINGS IS A WRONG TOO GREAT TO BE 143 ROSE IN HEART 5
    TOLD:
THE WRONG OF THE THINGS MISSHAPEN IS WRONG TOO GREAT TO 143 ROSE IN HEART V 5
    BE TOLD:
THE WRONG OF THE THINGS MISSHAPEN IS WRONG TOO GREAT TO 143 ROSE IN HEART V 5
    BE TOLD:
COME CLEAR OF THE NETS OF WRONG AND RIGHT: . . . . . 147 INTO TWILIGHT 2
COME CLEAR OFF THE NETS OF WRONG AND RIGHT: . . . . . 147 INTO TWILIGHT V 2
BUT I HAVE DONE SO GREAT A WRONG AGAINST YOU, ... 245 SHADOW WATER B 483
HOW GREAT A WRONG IT IS TO LET ONE'S THOUGHT . . . . . 246 SHADOW WATER B 514
BUT O: 'TWAS BITTER WRONG . . . . 255 WOMAN HOMER 5
AYE, AND WORSE WRONG THAN THESE. . . . . 260 UNWORTH PRAISE 18
THE SPEAKING OF IT COULD BE NO GREAT WRONG, ... 281 TWO KINGS 104
I CAN FORGIVE EVEN THAT WRONG OF WRONGS, ... 321 REED WHISPERER 9
YOUR COCKEREL FOUND US IN THE WRONG . . . . 388 SOLOMON WITCH 34
HE HAD DONE MOST BITTER WRONG . . . . 393 EASTER 1916 33
TO BRIBE OR THREAT: HABITS THAT MADE OLD WRONG . . . . 428 NINETEEN 19 11
WHIRLS OUT NEW RIGHT AND WRONG, ... 430 NINETEEN 19 55
HAVE WRONG TO BROOD UPON—ENOUGH OF THAT, ... 444 SCHOOL CHILDR V 30
WITH A COMMON WRONG OR RIGHT. . . . . 476 EVA GORE-BOOTH 23
BUT TIME AMENDS OLD WRONG, ... 613 MARCH SONGS 1 9
BUT TIME AMENDS OLD WRONG, ... 613 MARCH SONGS 1 19
BUT TIME AMENDS OLD WRONG, ... 614 MARCH SONGS 1 29
IF WRONG MY CHOICE, AS SILENT AS THOU ART. . . . . . 657 ISLE STAT I 3 76
THE FRIENDS THAT HAVE IT I DO WRONG . . . . 778 FRIENDS WRONG 1

WRONGED

HOW HAVE I WRONGED HER NOW THAT SHE IS MERRY? . . . . 244 SHADOW WATER B 448

WRONGING

ARE WRONGING YOUR IMAGE THAT BLOSSOMS A ROSE . . . . . 143 ROSE IN HEART 4

WRONGS

I CAN FORGIVE EVEN THAT WRONG OF WRONGS, ... 321 REED WHISPERER 9
ALL WRONGS DONE. . . . . 518 HIS CONFIDENCE 4

WROTE

I CAME AND WROTE UPON A CROSS OF WOOD— . . . . . . 123 DREAM OF DEATH V 7
THEY WROTE ON TABLETS OF THIN BOARD, ... 197 BAILE AILLINN 195
WHEREON I WROTE AND WROUGHT, ... 255 WOMAN HOMER 8
HE WROTE OF ME IN THAT EXTRAVAGANT STYLE . . . . . . 373 PHASES OF MOON 26
AND NEVER WROTE A BOOK, YOUR THOUGHT IS CLEAR. . . . . 376 PHASES OF MOON 97
IT IS TIME THAT I WROTE MY WILL . . . . 414 TOWER 121
AND WROTE BY CANDLE-LIGHT: BUT HER FORM MOVED, ... 467 HARUN RASHID 129
AND WROTE BY CANDLE LIGHT: BUT HER FORM MOVED . . . . 467 HARUN RASHID V 129
I WROTE UPON . . . . 517 HIS CONFIDENCE 2
WHERE—WROTE A LEARNED ASTROLOGER— . . . . 535 CHOSEN 17
EVERYTHING HE WROTE WAS READ, ... 577 WHAT THEN 6
HE WROTE OUT THAT WORD HIMSELF, ... 585 ORAHILLY 7
HE WROTE IT ON THE SANDS (THE OWLS MAY READ . . . . . 659 ISLE STAT II 1 9

WROTH

SHALL THEY TURN WROTH OR PLUCK THE WINGS OF TIME? . . . 42 OISIN 2 V 199
. . . AND PRAYING, AND WROTH WITH THE BELLS, ... 58 OISIN 3 159

WROUGHT

AND FACE THAT SEEMED WROUGHT OUT OF MOONLIT VAPOURS, . . 33 OISIN 2 70
FOR HE HAS WROUGHT MIDNIGHT AND DAWN AND DAY. . . . . 43 OISIN 2 208
SO LIVED I AND LIVED NOT, SO WROUGHT I AND WROUGHT NOT, 53 OISIN 3 95
    . . .
SO LIVED I AND LIVED NOT, SO WROUGHT I AND WROUGHT NOT, 53 OISIN 3 95
    . . .
WHILE I WROUGHT OUT THESE FITFUL DANAAN RHYMES, ... 136 TO SOME I TALK 1
THE DANAAN CHILDREN LAUGH, IN CRADLES OF WROUGHT GOLD, . 146 UNAPPEAS HOST 1

		PAGE	TITLE		LINE

WROUGHT   (CONTINUED)
THE FAERY CHILDREN LAUGH IN CRADLES OF WROUGHT GOLD, • • • 146 UNAPPEAS HOST V   1
THE LOVE-TALES WROUGHT WITH SILKEN THREAD • • • • • 155 FORGOT BEAUTY   6
QUEENS WROUGHT WITH GLIMMERING HANDS; • • • • • • 162 ASKS FORGIVE   12
BUT LET A GENTLE SILENCE WROUGHT WITH MUSIC FLOW • • • • 175 ELEMENT POWERS   17
WHEREON I WROTE AND WROUGHT. • • • • • • • • 255 WOMAN HOMER   8
WROUGHT OF HIGH LAUGHTER, LOVELINESS AND EASE? • • • • 264 HOUSE SHAKEN   12
OLD GOBAN HAMMERED THEM AND WROUGHT THEM, • • • • • 271 GREY ROCK   V   23
THREE WOMEN THAT HAVE WROUGHT • • • • • • • • 315 FRIENDS   2
AS THOUGH THEY'D WROUGHT IT. • • • • • • • • 320 COAT   7
WHEN SHE THE IRON WROUGHT, OR • • • • • • • • 345 ON WOMAN   17
IN CONTEMPLATION HAD THOSE THREE SO WROUGHT • • • • • 384 VISION ROBART   45
WHERE WE WROUGHT THAT SHALL BREAK THE TEETH OF TIME. • • • 435 NEW FACES   4
AND THAT TO SUCH A PITCH OF PASSION WROUGHT • • • • • 471 ALL SOUL NIGHT   24
AND EVERYTHING THAT YOUR OWN HANDS HAVE WROUGHT, • • • • 501 VACILLATION   31
TRAGEDY WROUGHT TO ITS UTTERMOST. • • • • • • • 566 LAPIS LAZULI   20
FORMS THAT GENTLER PHIDIAS WROUGHT. • • • • • • 638 BEN BULBEN   44
WITH SHIELD AND ARMOUR WROUGHT WITH GOLD, • • • • • 741 EARL PAUL   37

WRUNG
ARE WITH NEW SORROW WRUNG; • • • • • • • • 99 FOXHUNTER   38
WRUNG FROM THE COLD WOMEN OF THE SEA-- • • • • • 237 SHADOW WATER B   343
THEN SUDDENLY MY HEART IS WRUNG • • • • • • • 453 DEATH OF HARE   7

YARD   SEE PALACE-YARD BUILDING-YARD
BUILDING YARD AND STORMY SHORE, • • • • • • • 530 OLD TOM AGAIN V   5
WHAT'S EQUALITY?--MUCK IN THE YARD; • • • • • • 547 TO SAME TUNE 3 V   4
UNDER A SILKEN SAIL AND SILVER YARD. • • • • • • 763 SHADOW WATER A   316

YARDS
• • • I FLUNG IT FIVE YARDS WITH MY HAND, • • • • 60 OISIN 3   187
A SCORE OF YARDS OFF 'NEATH A WILLOW, SHOT. • • • • 712 FERENCZ RENYI   65

YAWN
YOUNG RED-HEAD STRETCHED HIMSELF TO YAWN • • • • • 303 HOUR DAWN   V 32A
THAT MADE THEM STRETCH AND YAWN, • • • • • • • 345 ON WOMAN   21
AND DID AFTER STRETCH AND YAWN"; • • • • • • • 521 THREE THINGS   17

YAWNED
AND DRANK AND YAWNED AND STRETCHED HIM OUT, • • • • 307 HOUR DAWN   108
AND HAVING STRETCHED AND YAWNED AWHILE • • • • • 612 NEWS ORACLE   11

YAWNS
CAN BUT SHOW THAT HEAVEN YAWNS; • • • • • • 509 JANE REPROVED   4

YEA
YEA, NOBLE AND MOST KNIGHTLY HATH IT BEEN. • • • • 679 ISLE STAT II 3   320
THE HEATHEN. YEA, AND SHAKE THE SULLEN KINGS • • • • 698 MOSADA 2   55

YEAR   SEE SIXTY-YEAR-OLD HUNDRED-YEAR-OLD A-YEAR
CHAINED WAS SHE. ON THEIR WINGS THE HUNDREDTH YEAR • • • 34 OISIN 2   V   76
AN ENDLESS WAR. THE HUNDREDTH YEAR HAD CEASED. • • • • 44 OISIN 2   V 224
FROM YEAR TO YEAR BY THE UNNUMBERED NESTS • • • • • 74 ANASHU VIJAYA   72
FROM YEAR TO YEAR BY THE UNNUMBERED NESTS • • • • • 74 ANASHU VIJAYA   72
AND SING FROM SHORE TO SHORE, AND EVERY YEAR • • • • 81 EPHEMERA   V 24G
AT ALL TIMES OF THE YEAR; • • • • • • • • 214 HAPPY TOWNLAND   6
UNLESS WE DRAIN MORE FLAGONS IN A YEAR • • • • • 225 SHADOW WATER B   70
THAT EVERY YEAR I HAVE CRIED, "AT LENGTH • • • • • 256 WORDS   9
GIDDY WITH HIS HUNDREDTH YEAR, • • • • • • • 298 THREE HERMITS   6
GIDDY WITH HIS HUNDREDTH YEAR, • • • • • • • 299 THREE HERMITS   31
SO SLEPT FOR HALF A YEAR OR SO; • • • • • • • 305 HOUR DAWN   67
BUT YEAR BY YEAR I FOUND THAT LESS • • • • • • 305 HOUR DAWN   68
BUT YEAR BY YEAR I FOUND THAT LESS • • • • • • 305 HOUR DAWN   68
AND SLEPT FOR HALF A YEAR OR SO; • • • • • • 305 HOUR DAWN   V 67
THEY WERE MY CLOSE COMPANIONS MANY A YEAR, • • • • 325 ROBERT GREGORY   41
THAT CRY'S FROM THE FIRST CUCKOO OF THE YEAR. • • • • 338 SHEP GOATHERD   1
YEAR. I WISHED BEFORE IT CEASED. NOR BIRD NOR BEAST • • 338 SHEP GOATHERD V   2
YESTERDAY IN THE TENTH YEAR • • • • • • • • 361 ALF POLLEXFEN   27
NOW THAT HIS FIFTIETH YEAR HAD COME, • • • • • • 361 ALF POLLEXFEN   31
AND WE ARE NOW IN THE TENTH YEAR? • • • • • • 361 ALF POLLEXFEN V   27
THAT I MYSELF FOR PORTIONS OF THE YEAR • • • • • 371 ON GOING HOUSE   5
SO THE PLATONIC YEAR • • • • • • • • • 430 NINETEEN 19   54
A SIXTY YEAR OLD SMILING PUBLIC MAN. • • • • • • 443 SCHOOL CHILDR V   8
AND SPEAK BUT FANTASY. RECALL THE YEAR • • • • • 462 HARUN RASHID   30
AND SPEAK BUT PHANTASY. RECALL THE YEAR • • • • • 462 HARUN RASHID   V   30
THAT IN THE EARLY SUMMER OF THE YEAR • • • • • 462 HARUN RASHID   40
THAT YEAR WHEN GREAT HAROUN EL RASHID KILLED • • • • 462 HARUN RASHID   V   31
THAT IN THE EARLY SUMMER OF THAT YEAR • • • • • 462 HARUN RASHID   V   40
MY FIFTIETH YEAR HAD COME AND GONE, • • • • • • 501 VACILLATION   35
A YEAR AGO FOR THE FIRST TIME • • • • • • • 570 THREE BUSHES   38
WHO CAN KNOW THE YEAR, MY DEAR, • • • • • • 588 OLD WICKED MAN   12
MY HUNDREDTH YEAR IS AT AN END. I THINK • • • • • 609 IN TARAS HALLS   3
HE BADE, HIS HUNDRED AND FIRST YEAR AT END, • • • • 609 IN TARAS HALLS   16
"FOR A YEAR AND A DAY BY THE CLOCK OF THE SUN" • • • 779 GOING THE ROAD   11
ALTHOUGH YOUR LAST EXCITING YEAR • • • • • • 791 REPRISALS   5

YEAR'S
AND WHEN AT ONE YEAR'S END I FOUND • • • • • 305 HOUR DAWN   71

YEARS
SAD TO REMEMBER, SICK WITH YEARS, • • • • • • 2 OISIN 1   5
'TIS SAD REMEMBERING, SICK WITH YEARS, • • • • • 2 OISIN 1   V   5
IN OTHER YEARS FROM SOME OLD STAR • • • • • • 19 OISIN 1   V 277
AFAR FROM WHERE THE YEARS ARE FLYING • • • • • 22 OISIN 1   V 340A
O PATRICK! FOR A HUNDRED YEARS • • • • • • 23 OISIN 1   343
O PATRICK! FOR A HUNDRED YEARS • • • • • • 23 OISIN 1   346
O PATRICK! FOR A HUNDRED YEARS • • • • • • 23 OISIN 1   351
O PATRICK! FOR A HUNDRED YEARS • • • • • • 23 OISIN 1   356
A HUNDRED YEARS I CHASED THE BOAR, • • • • • 23 OISIN 1   V 344
OH, PATRICK, THERE A HUNDRED YEARS, • • • • • 23 OISIN 1   V 346
"SWIFT ARE THE YEARS OF A WARRIOR'S PRIDE! • • • • 26 OISIN 1   V 399A

922

	PAGE	TITLE		LINE

YEARS   (CONTINUED)

"BUT NEVER THE YEARS IN THE ISLE'S SOFT PLACES	27	OISIN 1	V	419A
"BUT NEVER THE YEARS IN OUR ISLE'S SOFT PLACES	28	OISIN 1	V	424
WITH ME IN HER WHITE ARMS A HUNDRED YEARS	30	OISIN 2		17
TO JOIN HIS BROTHERS IN THE HOME OF YEARS	30	OISIN 2	V	17
HIS NEW-HEALED SHAPE; AND FOR A HUNDRED YEARS	44	OISIN 2		221
AN ENDLESS WAR. THE HUNDRED YEARS HAD CEASED;	44	OISIN 2		224
HIS HEALED SHAPE; AND FOR A HUNDRED YEARS	44	OISIN 2		221
HIS NEW HEALED SHAPE; AND FOR A HUNDRED YEARS	44	OISIN 2	V	221
AND DEW-BLANCHED HORNS, IN WHOSE HOLLOW A CHILD OF THREE YEARS OLD	49	OISIN 3		30
AND DEW-BLANCHED HORNS, IN WHOSE HOLLOWS A CHILD OF THREE YEARS OLD	49	OISIN 3	V	31
. . . AND YEARS AFTER YEARS 'GAN FLOW;	52	OISIN 3		75
. . . AND YEARS AFTER YEARS 'GAN FLOW;	52	OISIN 3		75
. . . AND YEARS AFTER YEARS 'GAN THEIR FLOW;	52	OISIN 3		75
. . . AND YEARS AFTER YEARS 'GAN THEIR FLOW;	52	OISIN 3	V	75
AND MY YEARS THREE HUNDRED FELL ON ME,	60	OISIN 3		191
FOR THY YOUTH WITHOUT PEACE, AND THY YEARS WITH THE DEMONS, . . .	63	OISIN 3	V	216
BUT NOW MY YEARS OF WATCHING ARE NO MORE."	105	CUCHULAIN SEA	V	5
THOUSANDS OF YEARS, THOUSANDS OF YEARS,	116	FAERY SONG		3
THOUSANDS OF YEARS, THOUSANDS OF YEARS,	116	FAERY SONG		3
THOUSANDS OF YEARS, THOUSANDS OF YEARS,	116	FAERY SONG		15
THOUSANDS OF YEARS, THOUSANDS OF YEARS,	116	FAERY SONG		15
AND ALL THE BURDEN OF HER MYRIAD YEARS.	120	SORROW OF LOVE	V	8
AND ALL THE TROUBLE OF HER MYRIAD YEARS.	120	SORROW OF LOVE	V	8
AND HE HAD KNOWN AT LAST SOME PRUDENT YEARS	127	DREAM OF FAERY		15
AND SOUGHT THROUGH LANDS AND ISLANDS NUMBERLESS YEARS,	170	SECRET ROSE		23
WHO HAS BEEN BURIED SOME TWO THOUSAND YEARS?	181	QUEEN MAEVE		35
FRIEND OF THESE MANY YEARS, YOU TOO HAD STOOD	186	QUEEN MAEVE		130
FRIEND OF THESE MANY YEARS, YOU TO HAVE STOOD	186	QUEEN MAEVE	V	130
A THOUSAND YEARS AGO YOU HELD HIGH TALK	187	QUEEN MAEVE		150
FOR ALTHOUGH YEARS HAD PASSED AWAY	192	BAILE AILLINN		77
THROUGH THE LONG YEARS OF YOUTH: AND WHO WOULD HAVE THOUGHT	201	OLD MEMORY		7
WITH WISDOM, THEY WANDER TILL ALL THE YEARS HAVE GONE BY;	204	WITHER BOUGHS		21
ABOUT THE STARS AND BROKE IN DAYS AND YEARS.	206	ADAMS CURSE		33
ABOUT THE STARN AND BROKE IN DAYS AND YEARS.	206	ADAMS CURSE	V	33
ALL THROUGH THE YEARS OF OUR YOUTH	211	O DO NOT LOVE		5
TOO MANY YEARS TO LIFT A HAND AGAINST YOU.	227	SHADOW WATER B		111
WHEN THEY HAVE TWENTY YEARS; IN MIDDLE LIFE	229	SHADOW WATER B		156
I KNOW THAT HE DIED A THOUSAND YEARS AGO,	241	SHADOW WATER B		392
AND THAT HE DIED A THOUSAND YEARS AGO.	242	SHADOW WATER B		417
THESE THOUSAND YEARS. WHAT ARE THE BIRDS AT THERE?	243	SHADOW WATER B		435
HAVE I NOT LOVED YOU FOR A THOUSAND YEARS?	244	SHADOW WATER B		463
THAT YOU WERE BORN A THOUSAND YEARS AGO,	245	SHADOW WATER B		468
AND SAID, "IN TWO OR IN THREE YEARS	272	GREY ROCK		46
I'D PROMISED HIM TWO HUNDRED YEARS,	275	GREY ROCK		98
A BOY OF TWENTY YEARS;—A MOUND AND STONE	276	TWO KINGS	V	F
WHY MUST I LIVE SOME THIRTY, FORTY YEARS,	285	TWO KINGS		199
YET COULD WE TURN THE YEARS AGAIN,	290	SEPTEMBER 1913		25
HE HAD COUNTED, WHERE LONG YEARS AGO	302	HOUR DAWN		7
HE COUNTED, WHERE LONG YEARS AGO	302	HOUR DAWN	V	7
TWO YEARS LATER	312	TWO YEAR LATER		T
MANY-TIMES-TROUBLED YEARS,	315	FRIENDS		7
MANY TIMES TROUBLED YEARS,	315	FRIENDS	V	7
THE YEARS TO COME SEEMED WASTE OF BREATH,	328	IRISH AIRMAN		14
A WASTE OF BREATH THE YEARS BEHIND	328	IRISH AIRMAN		15
MEN IMPROVE WITH THE YEARS	329	MEN IMPROVE		T
FOR MEN IMPROVE WITH THE YEARS;	329	MEN IMPROVE		11
AND NOW THAT I HAVE COME TO FIFTY YEARS	344	DEJECTION		10
AFTER NINE YEARS, I SINK MY HEAD ABASHED.	353	PEOPLE		37
FIVE-AND-TWENTY YEARS HAVE GONE	360	ALF POLLEXFEN		1
AND AFTER TWENTY YEARS THEY LAID	360	ALF POLLEXFEN		6
FIVE AND TWENTY YEARS HAVE GONE	360	ALF POLLEXFEN	V	1
HE WOULD NEVER KNOW ME AFTER ALL THESE YEARS	377	PHASES OF MOON		129
THREE HUNDRED YEARS BEFORE THE FALL,	388	SOLOMON WITCH		11
AND SURELY AFTER TWENTY YEARS IT WAS TIME TO COME."	391	UNDER SATURN		14
RECALL THE YEARS BEFORE HER MIND	397	POLIT PRISONER		8
THAT THE FUTURE YEARS HAD COME,	403	FOR DAUGHTER		14
I THOUGHT IT ALL OUT TWENTY YEARS AGO;	411	TOWER		64
IT LAY FIVE HUNDRED YEARS.	421	MY TABLE		11
WE, WHO SEVEN YEARS AGO	431	NINETEEN 19		89
HOW COULD SHE MATE WITH FIFTY YEARS THAT WAS SO WILDLY BRED?	450	OWEN AHERNE		15
HER CHILDISH GRATITUDE FOR LOVE AND MATCH YOUR FIFTY YEARS?	450	OWEN AHERNE		23
HOW SUCH A PAIR LOVED MANY YEARS	458	SECRETS OF OLD		15
ARE BRIDELESS." "I AM FALLING INTO YEARS."	463	HARUN RASHID		54
EVEN TO-DAY, AFTER SOME SEVEN YEARS	468	HARUN RASHID		161
EVEN TODAY, AFTER SOME SEVEN YEARS	468	HARUN RASHID	V	161
AND I ALONE, ONE IN TEN THOUSAND YEARS,	470	HARUN RASHID	V	190
PERMIT FOUL YEARS TO WEAR	472	ALL SOUL NIGHT		49
PARDONED, DRAGS OUT LONELY YEARS	475	EVA GORE-BOOTH		8
FIVE HUNDRED YEARS AGO, ABOUT IT LIE	478	SELF AND SOUL		26
THINGS SAID OR DONE LONG YEARS AGO,	501	VACILLATION		51
I TOILED LONG YEARS AND AT LENGTH	505	RESULT THOUGHT		9
TOILED LONG YEARS AND AT LENGTH	505	RESULT THOUGHT	V	9
HOW MANY YEARS AGO	524	MAD AS MIST		10
FORTY YEARS LATER	542	PARN FUNERAL 2	V	T
NOR HEARD THIS VOICE THAT NINETY YEARS HAVE CRACKED.	555	RIBH AT TOMB		5
SEVENTY YEARS HAVE I LIVED;	567	FROM JAPANESE		2

	PAGE	TITLE	LINE

YEARS   (CONTINUED)

SEVENTY YEARS HAVE I LIVED	567	FROM JAPANESE	5
SEVENTY YEARS HAVE I LIVED, ...	567	FROM JAPANESE	7
SEVENTY YEARS MAN AND BOY, ...	567	FROM JAPANESE	8
AFTER CERTAIN YEARS HE WON	577	WHAT THEN	7
AROUND ME THE IMAGES OF THIRTY YEARS!	601	GALLERY REVIS	1
I MET HER ALL BUT FIFTY YEARS AGO	602	GALLERY REVIS	15
HE LACKED THOSE YEARS THAT GO WITH SKILL, ...	608	SONGS BURDEN 3	14
SO MANY YEARS COMPANIONED BY A HOUND.	621	HOUND VOICE	4
LONG YEARS AGO, A CHURCH STANDS NEAR, ...	640	BEN BULBEN	87
AND ELVISH WISDOM, AND LONG YEARS OF YOUTH . . .	653	ISLE STAT I 2	47
BEYOND A MORTAL'S YEARS. I WAIT THE SONG	653	ISLE STAT I 2	48
LONG YEARS AGO, AND UNTO STONE CONGEALED.	656	ISLE STAT I 3	28
A SHEPHERDESS LONG YEARS FORETOLD!	668	ISLE STAT II 3	49
HAD HOOTED FOR AN HUNDRED YEARS, ...	670	ISLE STAT II 3	116
IN THOSE FAR YEARS, O DAUGHTER OF THE DAYS. . . .	674	ISLE STAT II 3	213
IN THOSE FAIR YEARS, O DAUGHTER OF THE DAYS. . . .	674	ISLE STAT II 3 V	213
THE TIDE OF STARS? HAVE I NOT SEEN A THOUSAND YEARS	675	ISLE STAT II 3	230
HAVE I SLEPT LONG? LONG YEARS. WITH HUNGRY HEART	677	ISLE STAT II 3	286
SEAFARER, WAKE! WAS MY SLEEP LONG? LONG YEARS. . .	678	ISLE STAT II 3	292
THE YEARS OF GOBLIN SLEEP. AH! WHILE I SLUMBERED, .	679	ISLE STAT II 3	308
HOW HAVE THE YEARS IN TROIA FLOWN AWAY?	679	ISLE STAT II 3	309
FROM THREESCORE YEARS OF DREAM-LED WANDERING . . .	682	SEEKER	16
AS WORDS OF THINE THROUGH FOURSCORE YEARS HAVE FILLED	683	SEEKER	46
FOR YEARS HIS DAYS HAD DAWNED AND FADED THUS . . .	692	MOSADA 1	54
HER DREAMS ARE TALKING WITH OLD YEARS. AWAKE, . .	702	MOSADA 3	89
BENT LOW WITH TOIL AND HOARIEST YEARS. THE OTHER .	711	FERENCZ RENYI	52
BELOVED, HOW TWO LITTLE YEARS AGO	713	FERENCZ RENYI	89
ERE YONDER PALM COMMENCED HIS THOUSAND YEARS? . . .	724	KANVA ON SELF	14
HAS MOULDED THE HARD YEARS.	738	MOURN THEN ON	8
THE YEARS THAT HAVE GONE OVER HER FROM THE HOUR .	760	SHADOW WATER A	256
FOR THESE NINE YEARS? O ARROW UPON ARROW!	761	SHADOW WATER A	268
OUTWEIGHED ALL OTHER YEARS, YOU SAID, ...	791	REPRISALS	6

YEATS

AND OF A RED-HAIRED YEATS WHOSE LOOKS, ALTHOUGH HE DIED	391	UNDER SATURN	9
I, THE POET WILLIAM YEATS, ...	406	CARVED STONE	1
IN DRUMCLIFF CHURCHYARD YEATS IS LAID.	640	BEN BULBEN	85

YELLED

| HOWLED, MIAU-D, BARKED, BRAYED, BELLED, YELLED, CRIED, CROWED, | 387 | SOLOMON WITCH | 8 |

YELLING

| I HAVE POINTED OUT THE YELLING PACK, ... | 453 | DEATH OF HARE | 1 |

YELLOW   SEE GRASS-YELLOW

THEIR CLOAKS MADE OUT OF YELLOW SILK, ...	15	OISIN 1	205
THEIR ROBES WERE ALL OF YELLOW SILK	15	OISIN 1 V	205
THEIR BRATTAS MADE OUT OF YELLOW SILK, ...	15	OISIN 1 V	205
YELLOW THE LEAVES OF THE ROWAN ABOVE US, ...	79	FALLING LEAVES	3
AND YELLOW THE WET WILD-STRAWBERRY LEAVES. . . .	79	FALLING LEAVES	4
THE WOODS WERE ROUND THEM, AND THE YELLOW LEAVES .	80	EPHEMERA	13
THEY PINE AWAY AND YELLOW AND WEAR OUT, ...	81	EPHEMERA V	24H
THE YELLOW POOL HAS OVERFLOWED HIGH UP ON CLOOTH-NA-BARE,	207	HANRAHANS SONG	11
THE YELLOW POOL HAS OVERFLOWED HIGH UPON CLOOTH-NA-BARE,	207	HANRAHANS SONG V	11
O MY SHARE OF THE WORLD, O YELLOW HAIR!	211	RAGGED WOOD	11
WHEN WE HAVE NEITHER BROWN NOR YELLOW ALE? . . .	240	SHADOW WATER B	387
YOU'D CRY, "SOME WOMAN'S YELLOW HAIR	290	SEPTEMBER 1913	28
AND SAW A FLAKE OF THE YELLOW FOAM	309	PLAYER QUEEN	15
I SAW A FLAKE OF YELLOW FOAM	309	PLAYER QUEEN V	15
ON HIS YELLOW LEGS THROUGH OUR MEADOWS, ...	341	SHEP GOATHERD	65
UPON HIS YELLOW LEGS THROUGH OUR MEADOWS, ...	341	SHEP GOATHERD V	65
TILL THE YELLOW EYE HAS GROWN MILD, ...	349	HAWK	3
THAT SAW THE WICKS GROW YELLOW IN THE DAWN! . . .	352	PEOPLE	18
AND NOT YOUR YELLOW HAIR."	492	ANNE GREGORY	6
AND NOT MY YELLOW HAIR."	492	ANNE GREGORY	12
AND NOT YOUR YELLOW HAIR."	492	ANNE GREGORY	18
AND ALL THEIR YELLOW CANVAS WEAR, ...	530	OLD TOM AGAIN V	2
SO LET US DANCE WHERE THE YELLOW LANCE	643	SONG FAERIES	7
THE PANTHER WITH HER YELLOW HIDE, ...	658	ISLE STAT I 3	83
SO LET US DANCE WHERE THE YELLOW LANCE	676	ISLE STAT II 3	254
LIE STREWN THE YELLOW LEAVES--THE CLOTTED LEAVES. .	684	SEEKER	69
WHERE LIES A SHALLOP IN THE YELLOW REEDS.	702	MOSADA 3	77
AND HIS HAIR WAS AS YELLOW AS WAVING WHEAT. . . .	729	PRIEST FAIRY	26
BRUSHING BACK HIS YELLOW HAIR!	729	PRIEST FAIRY	38
WHO SAID WE HAD A SKIN OF YELLOW ALE?	759	SHADOW WATER A	243
(O THE BROWN AND THE YELLOW BEER!)	779	GOING THE ROAD	2
(O THE BROWN AND THE YELLOW BEER!)	779	GOING THE ROAD	6
(O THE BROWN AND THE YELLOW BEER!)	779	GOING THE ROAD	10

YELLOW-EYED

| YELLOW-EYED HAWK OF THE MIND, ... | 349 | HAWK | 14 |

YELPING

| HIDING AWAY THE OCEAN'S YELPING FLOCKS. . . . . . | 688 | TWO TITANS | 38 |

YES

FASTING AND PRAYERS. TELL ON. YES, YES, ...	24	OISIN 1	360
FASTING AND PRAYERS. TELL ON. YES, YES, ...	24	OISIN 1	360
NO MORTAL CAN. YES! IF THEY GIVE US HELP. . . .	229	SHADOW WATER B	165
YES, VOICES! BUT I DO NOT CATCH THE WORDS. . . .	233	SHADOW WATER B	251
YES, ALL IS VERY WELL. WHENCE COMEST THOU? . . .	682	SEEKER	14

YESTERDAY

ONE THAT IS EVER KIND SAID YESTERDAY!	199	FOLLY COMFORT	1
THAT IT WAS YESTERDAY AND NOT TO-DAY.	246	SHADOW WATER B	493
AND YESTERDAY THE YOUNGEST SON, ...	361	ALF POLLEXFEN	24
YESTERDAY IN THE TENTH YEAR	361	ALF POLLEXFEN	27

		PAGE	TITLE		LINE
YESTERDAY (CONTINUED)					
HER EIGHTIETH WINTER APPROACHING: "YESTERDAY HE THREATENED MY LIFE.		578	LOFTY THINGS		8
OUR LOVE SHALL BE OF YESTERDAY, ...		686	LIFE		14
I SWORE BUT YESTERDAY IF THE RED GOD		751	SHADOW WATER A		109
YESTERNIGHT					
BUT YESTERNIGHT DECLARE		492	ANNE GREGORY		14
YET					
YET WILL I MAKE ALL PLAIN FOR THEE.		2	OISIN 1	V	7B
AND YET, OF YORE, MUCH PEACE HE HAD		2	OISIN 1	V	7K
AND YET, OF YORE, MUCH PEACE HE HAD, ...		4	OISIN 1		36
"I HAVE NOT YET, WAR-WEARY KING, ...		6	OISIN 1		55
YET NOW I CHOOSE, FOR THESE FOUR FEET		6	OISIN 1		57
YET LOVE AND KISS ON DIM SHORES FAR AWAY		29	OISIN 2		13
YET SANG NO MORE AS WHEN, LIKE A BROWN BEE		30	OISIN 2		15
OR HOURS PASSED BY, YET HOLD THE MORNING RAYS . . .		30	OISIN 2		20
YET DIMLY DEEM I THAT THE MORNING RAYS		30	OISIN 2	V	20
JABBER AND SCREAM. YET HE, FOR ALL HIS BOLD . . .		34	OISIN 2	V	82
YET DO WITH US WHATE'ER THOU WILT, ...		43	OISIN 2	V	208G
YET WEARY WITH PASSIONS THAT FADED		50	OISIN 3		52
YET STILL SHE TURNS HER RESTLESS HEAD:		65	HAPPY SHEPHERD		5
"THOUGH OUR SAD LOVE IS FADING, LET US YET		79	EPHEMERA	V	4
A GENTLE YET A KINGLY CHILD:		82	MAD KING GOLL	V	8
"YET SOMEWHERE UNDER STARLIGHT OR THE SUN		107	CUCHULAIN SEA		28
YET SHE GOES WITH FOOTSTEP WARY, ...		124	CATHLEEN PARA		11
AND YET THE SADDEST CHIMES ARE BEST ENJOYED. . . .		130	BOOK STORIES		20
AND YET THE BEAUTIES THAT I LOVED		131	OLD PENSIONER		15
YET HE WHO TREADS IN MEASURED WAYS		138	TO IRELAND		27
YET HE WHO TREADS IN AUSTERE WAYS		138	TO IRELAND	V	27
AND YET HAD BEEN GREAT-BODIED AND GREAT-LIMBED, .		181	QUEEN MAEVE		25
MAEVE WALKED, YET WITH SLOW FOOTFALL, BEING OLD, .		181	QUEEN MAEVE		43
AND YET HAD BEEN GREAT BODIED AND GREAT LIMBED, .		181	QUEEN MAEVE	V	25
AND THE BROWN BULL HAD NOT YET COME, ...		189	BAILE AILLINN		15
YET THEY THAT KNOW ALL THINGS BUT KNOW		190	BAILE AILLINN		38
THOSE OTHER TWO: FOR NEVER YET		197	BAILE AILLINN		205
THIS BEAUTY'S KINDER, YET FOR A REASON		199	ARROW		7
YET IF IT DOES NOT SEEM A MOMENT'S THOUGHT, . . .		204	ADAMS CURSE		5
IS TO WORK HARDER THAN ALL THESE, AND YET		205	ADAMS CURSE		11
YET NOW IT SEEMS AN IDLE TRADE ENOUGH."		205	ADAMS CURSE		27
THAT IT HAD ALL SEEMED HAPPY, AND YET WE'D GROWN .		206	ADAMS CURSE		37
YET DREAMED THAT BEINGS HAPPIER THAN MEN		218	WOODS OF COOLE		18
THESE MANY DAYS: AND YET THERE MUST BE MANY . . .		226	SHADOW WATER B		89
THAT IS NOT IN THE WORLD. AND YET THE WORLD . . .		228	SHADOW WATER B		143
YET NEVER HAVE TWO LOVERS KISSED BUT THEY		229	SHADOW WATER B		153
AND YET I CANNOT THINK THEY'RE LEADING ME		230	SHADOW WATER B		191
AND OVERPOWER THE CREW WHILE YET ASLEEP:		233	SHADOW WATER B		240
BUT HAVE NOT BITTEN YET. I AM A QUEEN, ...		235	SHADOW WATER B		280
HAD DROWNED ME ALSO. BUT, BEING YET ALIVE, . . .		235	SHADOW WATER B		289
BRING MADNESS? QUEEN, I AM NOT MAD. YET SAY . . .		236	SHADOW WATER B		316
AND YET YOU SAY THE WATER AND THE WIND		236	SHADOW WATER B	V	317
AND YET YOU TALK OF LOVE. THE MOVEMENT OF TIME .		237	SHADOW WATER B		338
AND HAS NOT YET BEEN WAKED. OHONE: O: O: O: . . .		241	SHADOW WATER B		393
AND YET YOU MAKE A CLAMOUR OF REPROACH, ...		243	SHADOW WATER B		444
YET OLD ROMANCE BEING KIND, LET HIM PREVAIL . . .		258	KING NO KING		5
YET SHE, SINGING UPON HER ROAD, ...		260	UNWORTH PRAISE		19
AND YET NOT COLD."		263	MASK		5
YET WOULD BE NOW: COULD I BUT HAVE MY WISH, . . .		267	ALL TEMPT ME		9
AND THEREFORE EARNED THE RIGHT—AND YET		273	GREY ROCK		61
AND YET COULD GIVE SO FINE A STROKE?"		274	GREY ROCK		84
I'D SAVED HIS LIFE, YET FOR THE SAKE		275	GREY ROCK		102
I'D SAVE HIS LIFE, YET FOR THE SAKE		275	GREY ROCK	V	102
YET ANSWERED HIM, "I AM KING EOCHAID'S WIFE . . .		284	TWO KINGS		173
YET THEY WERE OF A DIFFERENT KIND, ...		289	SEPTEMBER 1913		9
YET COULD WE TURN THE YEARS AGAIN, ...		290	SEPTEMBER 1913		25
FOR THEY ARE AT THEIR OLD TRICKS YET. A MAN . . .		292	TO A SHADE		9
YET WE, HAD WE WALKED WITHIN		293	HELEN LIVED		7
"MAYBE I SHALL BE LUCKY YET, ...		297	THREE BEGGARS		61
YET NEVER HAVE I LIT ON A FRIEND		301	RUN PARADISE		25
AND YET STOOD STILL, BECAUSE INSIDE		303	HOUR DAWN		26
BRING ROSES IF THE ROSE BE YET IN BLOOM:		311	MOUNTAIN TOMB		2
THE FOOL'S TRIUMPH, NOR YET		312	CHILD DANCING		7
AND YET FOR ALL THAT I COULD SAY, ...		313	MEMORY YOUTH		4
YET WE, FOR ALL THAT PRAISE, COULD FIND		314	MEMORY YOUTH		13
AND YET HIS MIND OUTRAN THE HORSES' FEET.		326	ROBERT GREGORY		64
AND YET HE HAD THE INTENSITY		327	ROBERT GREGORY		71
AND YET, AND YET, ...		329	MEN IMPROVE		12
AND YET, AND YET, ...		329	MEN IMPROVE		12
YET PRAISE THE WINTERS GONE:		336	YOUNG BEAUTY		15
YET DID BUT LOOK, ROCKING THE GLITTERING COACH .		344	DAWN	V	11
YET NEVER COULD, ALTHOUGH		345	ON WOMAN		13
YET NEVER HAVE I, NOW NOR ANY TIME, ...		352	PEOPLE		28
AND YET, BECAUSE MY HEART LEAPED AT HER WORDS, .		353	PEOPLE		35
I MOURN FOR THAT MOST LONELY THING: AND YET GOD'S WILL BE DONE:		354	HIS PHOENIX		31
AND YET YOUR BODY HAD A FLAW:		356	BROKEN DREAMS		28
AND YET YOUR BEAUTY HAD A FLAW:		356	BROKEN DREAMS	V	28
YET ALWAYS WHEN I LOOK DEATH IN THE FACE, ...		357	DEEP-SWORN VOW		3
RETURNED AND YET UNREQUITED LOVE.		358	PRESENCES		8
LACKING THE COUNTENANCE OF OUR FRIENDS. AND YET .		368	EGO DOMINUS		17
YET SURELY THERE ARE MEN WHO HAVE MADE THEIR ART .		369	EGO DOMINUS		38
BUT DISSIPATION AND DESPAIR? AND YET		369	EGO DOMINUS		51

925

	PAGE	TITLE	LINE
YET (CONTINUED)			
I CALL TO THE MYSTERIOUS ONE WHO YET	371	EGO DOMINUS	70
WE TAKE IT FOR THE NORM! YET SHOULD I DREAM	371	ON GOING HOUSE	9
TWENTY-AND-EIGHT, AND YET BUT SIX-AND-TWENTY	373	PHASES OF MOON	33
AND YET, TWICE BORN, TWICE BURIED, GROW HE MUST,	374	PHASES OF MOON	48
AND YET THEY SPEAK WHAT'S BLOWN INTO THE MIND!	376	PHASES OF MOON	110
BUT THE ESCAPE! THE SONG'S NOT FINISHED YET.	377	PHASES OF MOON	117
DAY AFTER DAY, YET NEVER FIND THE MEANING.	377	PHASES OF MOON	135
YET LITTLE PEACE HE HAD.	383	VISION ROBART	35
MIND MOVED YET SEEMED TO STOP	384	VISION ROBART	43
WERE DEAD YET FLESH AND BONE.	384	VISION ROBART	48
AND YET IN FLYING FLING INTO MY MEAT	384	VISION ROBART	53
YET BE BUT SINEW. I HAVE HEARD SAID	386	ROBARTES DANCE	37
YET THE WORLD ENDS WHEN THESE TWO THINGS,	388	SOLOMON WITCH	28
"YET THE WORLD STAYS." "IF THAT BE SO,	388	SOLOMON WITCH	33
YET I NUMBER HIM IN THE SONG!	393	EASTER 1916	35
YET I AM CERTAIN AS CAN BE	401	DEMON BEAST	33
THAT NEVER YET HAD FREEMAN	401	DEMON BEAST	36
YET HAVE NO DEARER THOUGHT	401	DEMON BEAST	40
MAY SHE BE GRANTED BEAUTY AND YET NOT	403	FOR DAUGHTER	17
YET CHOSE A BANDY-LEGGED SMITH FOR MAN.	404	FOR DAUGHTER	29
YET MANY, THAT HAVE PLAYED THE FOOL	404	FOR DAUGHTER	36
YET KNOWS THAT TO BE CHOKED WITH HATE	405	FOR DAUGHTER	52
YET, NOW I HAVE CONSIDERED IT, I FIND	411	TOWER	50
MERE DREAMS, MERE DREAMS! YET HOMER HAD NOT SUNG	417	ANCEST HOUSES	9
YET IF NO CHANGE APPEARS	421	MY TABLE	12
AS VIGOROUS OF MIND, AND YET IT SEEMS	422	MY DESCENDANTS	4
YET NO CLEAR FACT TO BE DISCERNED!	425	STARES NEST	9
AND YET IT LACK ALL GLORY! AND PERCHANCE	429	NINETEEN 19	23
DRIVE TO A FLASHIER BAUBLE YET.	437	SONGS PLAY 1	12
AND THAT ALONE! YET I, BEING DRIVEN HALF INSANE	442	BLACK CENTAUR	6
AND YET THEY TOO BREAK HEARTS--O PRESENCES	445	SCHOOL CHILDR	53
SHOULD FIND NO BURDEN BUT ITSELF AND YET SHOULD BE WORN OUT.	449	OWEN AHERNE	3
AND YET THERE BEAUTY LAY!	455	HIS MEMORIES	12
WHEN EVENING STIRS THE JASMINE BOUGH, AND YET	463	HARUN RASHID	53
WHEN EVENING STIRS THE JASMINE, AND YET	463	HARUN RASHID V	53
"AND YET THE JASMINE SEASON WARMS OUR BLOOD."	464	HARUN RASHID	73
AND YET HERSELF CAN SEEM YOUTH'S VERY FOUNTAIN.	465	HARUN RASHID	89
YET WAS IT LOVE OF ME, OR WAS IT LOVE	466	HARUN RASHID	112
IT SEEMS ENOUGH THAT I AM THERE! AND YET,	468	HARUN RASHID	166
AND THERE, FREE AND YET FAST,	472	ALL SOUL NIGHT	57
AND YET AGAIN, IF IT BE LIFE TO PITCH	479	SELF AND SOUL	58
AND YET A WOMAN'S POWERFUL CHARACTER	489	COOLE PARK 29	18
AND YET UPON MY BREAST	496	MOHINI CHATTER	10
"OLD LOVERS YET MAY HAVE	496	MOHINI CHATTER	17
OLD LOVERS YET SHALL HAVE	496	MOHINI CHATTER V	17
THOSE IMAGES THAT YET	498	BYZANTIUM	38
AND HALF IS HALF AND YET IS ALL THE SCENE!	500	VACILLATION	14
AND YET UPON THESE MAXIMS MEDITATE!	500	VACILLATION	22
YET HE, AN OLD BOOK IN HIS FIST!	508	JANE BISHOP	12
"THE THIRD THING THAT I THINK OF YET,"	521	THREE THINGS	13
THAT WE DESCANT AND YET AGAIN DESCANT	523	LONG SILENCE	5
I LONG FOR TRUTH, AND YET	533	FIRST CONFESS	7
AND YET I WEEP--OEDIPUS' CHILD	540	FROM ANTIGONE	15
YET I AM SHRUNKEN TO SKIN AND BONE	550	SONGS REWRIT 1 V	2
YET AM I SHRUNKEN TO SKIN AND BONE,	550	SONGS REWRIT 1 V	2
YET ALL MUST COPY COPIES, ALL INCREASE THEIR KIND!	556	RIBH PATRICK	7
YET THEY, SHOULD THE LAST SCENE BE THERE,	565	LAPIS LAZULI	12
YET WHAT COULD I BUT DROP DOWN DEAD	569	THREE BUSHES	19
YET KEEP HIS SUBSTANCE WHOLE.	573	LADYS 2ND SONG	13
AS THOUGH TO DRAW THEM CLOSER YET. RAMMED FULL	579	DOR WELLESLEY	5
POETRY, MUSIC, I HAVE LOVED, AND YET	599	SPIRIT MEDIUM	1
AND YET WHO KNOWS WHAT'S YET TO COME?	608	SONGS BURDEN 3	23
AND YET WHO KNOWS WHAT'S YET TO COME?	608	SONGS BURDEN 3	23
NO, NO, MY SON, NOT YET!	614	MARCH SONGS 2	8
NO, NO, MY SON, NOT YET!	615	MARCH SONGS 2	18
NO, NO, MY SON, NOT YET!	615	MARCH SONGS 2	28
YET A MOST GENTLE WOMAN! WHO CAN TELL	618	BRONZE HEAD	10
AND YET GAVE TONGUE. "HOUND VOICES" WERE THEY ALL.	622	HOUND VOICE	9
HEART-MYSTERIES THERE, AND YET WHEN ALL IS SAID	630	CIRCUS ANIMALS	27
HEART MYSTERIES THERE, AND YET WHEN ALL IS SAID	630	CIRCUS ANIMALS V	27
YET HERE'S A TRAVELLED MAN THAT KNOWS	631	POLITICS	5
WHEN SLEEPERS WAKE AND YET STILL DREAM,	639	BEN BULBEN	59
TO WATCH THEE PASS? YET DEEPER THAN MEN KNOW	672	ISLE STAT II 3	158
YET EVER MORE, THROUGH ALL THY DAYS OF RUTH,	674	ISLE STAT II 3	206
IT IS, YET SHALL IT FAIL THEE DAY AND NIGHT	674	ISLE STAT II 3	211
YET EVERMORE, THROUGH ALL THY DAYS OF RUTH,	674	ISLE STAT II 3 V	206
A PEERING HARE'S! AND YET I MURMURED NOT,	684	SEEKER	56
THOU WILT NOT SPEAK, OH CRUEL ART THOU YET!	684	SEEKER V	69A
FROM WASTE SEAS CROSS'D, YET EVER GARRULOUS)	690	MOSADA 1	9
YET SOMEWHERE IN THE FOOTSORE WORLD WE MEET!	691	MOSADA 1	23
YET 'TIS NO SIN! MY FATHER TAUGHT IT ME.	692	MOSADA 1	50
WITH WONDERFUL WHITE SANDS, WHERE NEVER YET	693	MOSADA 1	81
WITH WONDERFUL WHITE SAND, WHERE NEVER YET	693	MOSADA 1 V	81
AND DYING MEN--AND YET--BUT NO, FAREWELL.	698	MOSADA 2	49
YET WHITER BEARD HAVE YOU THAN MERLIN HAD.	721	WITCH VIVIEN	30
SORROW-WORN, YET PLACID-BROWED.	733	STREET DANCERS	56
SORROW-WORN, YET PLACID BROWED.	733	STREET DANCERS V	56
YET ONE JOY HAVE I, HID CLOSE,	744	ROSY CROSS	8
BE PATIENT YET A WHILE! FOR THIS NINTH MOON,	748	SHADOW WATER A	23

926

YET   (CONTINUED)
   BE PATIENT YET AWHILE! FOR THIS NINTH MOON, ... 748 SHADOW WATER A V 23
   AND YET, THERE IS A LOVE THAT THE GODS GIVE, ... 749 SHADOW WATER A   56
   YET OUR SILENCE HAD BEEN WISE: . . . . 773 SONG DEIRDRE 1 V 22
   YET ALL THE LOVELY THINGS THAT WERE . . . . 788 HAWTHORN TREE   11
   YET RISE FROM YOUR ITALIAN TOMB, ... 791 REPRISALS   10
   MEN THAT REVERE YOUR FATHER YET . . . . 791 REPRISALS   17
YEW
   A CYPRESS AND A YEW. . . . . 123 DREAM OF DEATH V   6
   MADE OF THE APPLE AND THE YEW, ... 197 BAILE AILLINN   196
   A YEW TREE WHERE HIS BODY LAY, ... 197 BAILE AILLINN V 188
   THE YEW BOUGH HAS BEEN BROKEN INTO TWO, ... 241 SHADOW WATER B V 394
   THE YEW BOUGH HAS BEEN BROKEN INTO TWO, ... 251 SHADOW WATER B V 593
   THE YEW BOUGH HAS BEEN BROKEN IN TWO, ... 251 SHADOW WATER B V 593
   THE POSTS OF POLISHED YEW, CIRCLED WITH BRONZE, ... 279 TWO KINGS   48
   WHAT JUNCTURE OF THE APPLE AND THE YEW, ... 555 RIBH AT TOMB   8
   THE TREMBLING OF THE APPLE AND THE YEW, ... 555 RIBH AT TOMB   18
   THAT DRUIDS WRITE ON YEW AND APPLE WOOD, ... 748 SHADOW WATER A   29
   UPON THIN BOARDS OF YEW AND APPLE WOOD, ... 764 SHADOW WATER A 343
   UPON THIN BOARDS OF YEW AND APPLE-WOOD, ... 764 SHADOW WATER A V 343
   PRAISE THE REDNESS OF THE YEW: . . . . 773 SONG DEIRDRE 1   20
YEW-BOUGH
   THE YEW-BOUGH HAS BEEN BROKEN INTO TWO, ... 241 SHADOW WATER B 394
   THE YEW-BOUGH HAS BEEN BROKEN INTO TWO, ... 251 SHADOW WATER B 593
YEW-TREE
   A YEW-TREE WHERE HIS BODY LAY: . . . . 197 BAILE AILLINN   188
YOLK
   INTO THE YOLK AND WHITE OF THE ONE SHELL. . . . . . 443 SCHOOL CHILDR   16
YON
   AMRITA. DRAW YOU NEAR, AND 'NEATH YON PILLAR . . . . 71 ANASHU VIJAYA V 13A
   YON TALL ONE EYES MY SUPPER! CHASE HIM AWAY, ... 72 ANASHU VIJAYA   34
   YON TALL ONE EYES MY SUPPER! SWIFTLY CHASE HIM . . . . 72 ANASHU VIJAYA V 34
   WITH FIERY SONG I'LL DROWN YON PUNY VOICE. . . . . . 648 ISLE STAT I 1   81
   BUT YONDER THING, YON IDLE NOISE, YON CROW, ... 648 ISLE STAT I 1   104
   BUT YONDER THING, YON IDLE NOISE, YON CROW, ... 648 ISLE STAT I 1   104
   YON SHEPHERD--CAME YOUR SPIRIT TO BEGUILE . . . . . 648 ISLE STAT I 1   105
   YON WIND GOES SADLY, AND THE GRASS AND TREES . . . . 652 ISLE STAT I 2   10
   YON EAGER LARK, THAT FILLS WITH SONG THE WHOLE . . . . 652 ISLE STAT I 2   18
   DOTH NOT YON BIRD, YON QUIVERING BIRD, REJOICE? . . . 652 ISLE STAT I 2   21
   DOTH NOT YON BIRD, YON QUIVERING BIRD, REJOICE? . . . 652 ISLE STAT I 2   21
   CAN ENTER THERE. SEE! SEE! ABOVE YON BROW . . . . . 659 ISLE STAT II 1   27
   YON IS THE HUNTER'S, SIR ALMINTOR'S, PAGE! . . . . . 660 ISLE STAT II 1   35
   OF BEAMS A-FLICKER ON YON LONELY FIR. . . . . . . 661 ISLE STAT II 1   72
   MY SINKING BRAIN!--CEASE!--CEASE! HEARD YE YON SOUND? . 665 ISLE STAT II 2   73
   MORE DARK BENEATH THE POPLARS, WHERE YON OWL . . . . 675 ISLE STAT II 3 233
   YON ARCHER, HE WHO HATH THE HALCYON'S WING . . . . . 679 ISLE STAT II 3 316
   MAKE MOAN AND CRY. WITHIN YON SUNLESS VALLEY, ... 682 SEEKER   26
   HIS BODY SHAKE? AY, QUIVERING AS YON SMOKE . . . . . 683 SEEKER   36
   AMONG THE FRUIT. BUT YON, LAME COLA CROUCHES . . . . 691 MOSADA 3   V 32
   AND YON FEW STARS GROWN DIM, LIKE EYES OF LOVERS . . . 700 MOSADA 3   33
   FLOATING FROM YON BARRED WINDOW. SMALL NEW-COMER, . . 700 MOSADA 3   43
   FLOATING FROM YON BARRED WINDOW. NEW COMER, ... 700 MOSADA 3   V 43
   YON BAUBLE OF THE HEAVENS, HE LIFTS HIS HANDS, ... 715 FERENCZ RENYI   119
   HUGS AND PETS AND PATS YON NEWT, ... 727 LOVERS QUARREL   27
   AND SAID, "YON BITTERN CRIES, IN TRUTH, ... 731 PRIEST FAIRY   75
YONDER
   OUT YONDER, WHERE THE RACE COURSE IS, ... 266 GALWAY RACES V   1
   AND YONDER IN THE GYMNASTS' GARDEN THRIVES . . . . . 446 COLONUS PRAISE   9
   BUT YONDER THING, YON IDLE NOISE, YON CROW, ... 648 ISLE STAT I 1   104
   SING SUMMER WAVES. BUT YONDER SHEPHERD VILE, ... 649 ISLE STAT I 1   107
   UPON HIS WINGS. THRO' YONDER GREEN ABYSS . . . . . 649 ISLE STAT I 1   114
   THE WAVES IN YONDER LAKE WHERE POINTS MY HAND . . . . 652 ISLE STAT I 2   13
   NAY, NAY, ALMINTOR, YONDER SONG IS GLAD. . . . . . 652 ISLE STAT I 2   23
   OF YONDER LAKE, FROM WHOSE GREEN BANKS ALWAY . . . . 653 ISLE STAT I 2   33
   SEE, YONDER SINKS THE SUN, YONDER A SHADE . . . . . 653 ISLE STAT I 2   52
   SEE, YONDER SINKS THE SUN, YONDER A SHADE . . . . . 653 ISLE STAT I 2   52
   THERE WHERE YONDER SQUIRREL CRUNCHES . . . . 655 ISLE STAT I 3   4
   FROM YONDER PINNACLE ABOVE THE LAKE . . . . 657 ISLE STAT I 3   63
   AND YONDER HUDDLING BLACKNESS DRAWETH NIGH-- . . . . 663 ISLE STAT II 2   15
   AND PENETRATION OF THEIR EYES. WHERE YONDER BLOTCH . . 664 ISLE STAT II 2   47
   TO YONDER ISLE, WHERE NEVER SAIL WAS FURLED, ... 664 ISLE STAT II 2   56
   OF HIM ON YONDER BRAZEN-GATED SPOT, ... 675 ISLE STAT II 3 240
   WITH PATIENT BEAUTY YONDER ATTIC BUST . . . . 685 DRAWING-ROOM   3
   THE SQUIRREL YONDER, HUSHED AND WISE, ... 686 LIFE   5
   YONDER THE SICKLE OF THE MOON SAILS ON, ... 688 NETTLESHIP   1
   SINKS DOWN AT LAST WITH YONDER MINARET, ... 691 MOSADA 1   V 36
   THAT YOU SHALL SEE ON YONDER GLOWING CLOUD . . . . . 692 MOSADA 1   V 43
   YONDER HE COMES! BRIGHT-EYED, AND HOLLOW-CHEEKED . . . 697 MOSADA 2   35
   MY THOUGHTS, AND YONDER BRIGHTENING PATCH OF SKY . . . 700 MOSADA 3   31
   YONDER A LEAF . . . . 700 MOSADA 3   41
   UPON THE MOUNTAIN'S BROW. YONDER HE TREADS . . . . . 703 MOSADA 3   114
   HIDING THE REBELS WORM IN YONDER WOOD . . . . 709 FERENCZ RENYI   14
   HIDING THE REBELS SWARM IN YONDER WOOD . . . . . . 709 FERENCZ RENYI V 14
   HIDING THE REBEL WORMS IN YONDER WOOD, ... 709 FERENCZ RENYI V 14
   OR YONDER MOUNTAINS. WHERE? THOU SHALT BE FREE-- . . 710 FERENCZ RENYI   15
   OR YONDER MOUNTAIN. WHERE? THOU SHALT BE FREE-- . . 710 FERENCZ RENYI V 15
   AND LOST AND FAR IN YONDER HILLS I KNOW: . . . . . 713 FERENCZ RENYI   98
   BESIDE THE WILLOW. NAY, TO YONDER STAR, ... 715 FERENCZ RENYI   118
   BENEATH THE WILLOW--NAY, TO YONDER STAR, ... 715 FERENCZ RENYI V 118
   MY IMAGE YONDER? AH, MY BEAUTIFUL, ... 720 WITCH VIVIEN   4
   ERE YONDER PALM COMMENCED HIS THOUSAND YEARS? . . . . 724 KANVA ON SELF   14

		PAGE	TITLE	LINE

YONDER (CONTINUED)

YONDER SEE THE FAIRY GIRLS • • • • • • • • • • • • • 726 LOVERS QUARREL   21
YONDER FOOLISH ONES WILL TIRE • • • • • • • • • • • 727 LOVERS QUARREL   47
WITH PATIENT BEAUTY YONDER ATTIC BUST • • • • • • • 735 QUATRAIN APHOR   23

YONDER'S

YONDER'S THE ISLE IN SEARCH WHEREOF WE CAME: • • • • • 662 ISLE STAT II 2   13

YORE

AND YET, OF YORE, MUCH PEACE HE HAD • • • • • • • •   2 OISIN 1   V   7K
AND YET, OF YORE, MUCH PEACE HE HAD, • • • • • • • •   4 OISIN 1   V   36
LOVE FROM HEAVEN CAME OF YORE • • • • • • • • • • •   648 ISLE STAT I 1   77
OF WAR. OF YORE, TWO SHEPHERDS, WHERE WE PAUSE, • • • 659 ISLE STAT II 1   31
SHE WAS A GREAT ENCHANTRESS ONCE OF YORE. • • • • • • 693 MOSADA 1   78
WANDERING OF YORE IN FORESTS RUMOROUS. • • • • • • • 723 KANVA ON SELF   3
HAST THOU NOT SAT OF YORE UPON THE KNEES • • • • • • 724 KANVA ON SELF   9

YOUNG

OF THE YOUNG. "YOUNG MAIDEN, WHAT MAY BRING • • • • •   5 OISIN 1   V   50
OF THE YOUNG. "YOUNG MAIDEN, WHAT MAY BRING • • • • •   5 OISIN 1   V   50
YOUNG PRINCESS, WHY WERT THOU BEGUILED • • • • • • •   6 OISIN 1   V   59
YOUNG PRINCESS, WHEN WERE YOU BEGUILED • • • • • • •   6 OISIN 1   V   59
OF OISIN: THE YOUNG MAN, MY SON? • • • • • • • • •   6 OISIN 1   V   60
BY THIS YOUNG MAN, USHEEN MY SON?" • • • • • • • •   6 OISIN 1   V   60
PRINCESS, BY THIS YOUNG MAN, MY SON?" • • • • • • •   6 OISIN 1   V   61
ON THIS YOUNG MAN, OISIN, MY SON?" • • • • • • • •   6 OISIN 1   V   61
YOUNG NIAM, AND THOU SHALT BE CALLEN • • • • • • • •   7 OISIN 1   V   75
AND A HUNDRED MAIDENS WISE AND YOUNG, • • • • • • •   8 OISIN 1   V   94
AND A BEAUTIFUL YOUNG MAN FOLLOWED BEHIND • • • • • • 12 OISIN 1   144
A BEAUTIFUL YOUNG MAN FOLLOWED BEHIND. • • • • • • • 12 OISIN 1   V   145
A BEAUTIFUL YOUNG MAN DREAMED WITHIN • • • • • • • • 17 OISIN 1   248
AND STIRS THE YOUNG KID'S BUDDING HORN. • • • • • • • 18 OISIN 1   264
THERE WAS A WONDROUS YOUNG MAN SITTING. • • • • • • • 18 OISIN 1   V   252
WITH A CLEAR VOICE THE YOUNG MAN CRIED. • • • • • • • 18 OISIN 1   V   260
THEREON YOUNG NIAMH SOFTLY CAME • • • • • • • •   25 OISIN 1   373
BUT FAINTER THAN A YOUNG LAMB'S BLEAT. • • • • • • • 26 OISIN 1   399
AND FAINTER THAN A YOUNG LAMB'S BLEAT. • • • • • • • 26 OISIN 1   V   399
STROKED THE YOUNG WINDS AS THEY ROLLED ON THE PLAIN, • • 27 OISIN 1   V   415C
SO SANG YOUNG NIAM, SWAYING HER BRIGHT HEAD, • • • • 30 OISIN 2   V   15
A-MURMUR LIKE YOUNG PARTRIDGE: WITH LOUD HORN • • • • 32 OISIN 2   52
FROM HIGH ABOVE, LIKE FEATHERS OF YOUNG BIRDS • • • • 32 OISIN 2   V   50
"THEY MURMUR LIKE YOUNG PARTRIDGE IN THE MORN, • • • 32 OISIN 2   V   51
YOUNG WARRIOR." "NAY," I ANSWERED: "MY HANDS BURN • • 35 OISIN 2   V   89B
WE SAW, SOME NEW, SOME PRINTED WHEN THE PLACE WAS YOUNG, • 37 OISIN 2   V   116
OUTCRY OF BATS. AND THEN YOUNG NIAMH CAME • • • • • 44 OISIN 2   229
THE HARE LEAPED IN THE GRASS. YOUNG NIAMH CAME • • • 44 OISIN 2   V   229
• • • WHEN THE SEVENFOLD SEAS WERE YOUNG. • • • • •   50 OISIN 3   52
• • • WHEN THE SEVEN-FOLD SEAS WERE YOUNG: • • • • • 50 OISIN 3   V   52
• • • AND MOVE WHERE THE OLD MEN AND YOUNG • • • • • 55 OISIN 3   114
• • • AND MARCH ON AS OXEN MOVE OVER YOUNG GRASS: • • 62 OISIN 3   211
WHO STILL WERE OLD WHEN THE GREAT SEA WAS YOUNG: • • 74 ANASHU VIJAYA   69
THE FLIES BELOW THE LEAVES, AND THE YOUNG MICE • • • 75 ANASHU VIJAYA   87
AND SLEEK YOUNG JOY IS NO MORE FICKLE. • • • • • • • 77 INDIAN TO LOVE V   5C
I WAS A WISE YOUNG KING OF OLD: • • • • • • • • • •   81 MAD KING GOLL V   1
"THIS YOUNG MAN BRINGS THE AGE OF GOLD." • • • • • • 82 MAD KING GOLL V   11
AND YOUNG HARES BROOK MY HARMLESS HOLD-- • • • • • • 84 MAD KING GOLL V   47
OVER THE YOUNG STREAMS. • • • • • • • • • • • • •   88 STOLEN CHILD   37
OF DEW ON THE YOUNG STREAMS. • • • • • • • • • • •   88 STOLEN CHILD   V   37
BUT I, BEING YOUNG AND FOOLISH, WITH HER WOULD NOT AGREE. • 90 SALLEY GARDENS   4
BUT I WAS YOUNG AND FOOLISH, AND NOW AM FULL OF TEARS. • • 90 SALLEY GARDENS   8
THE YOUNG BIRDS AND OLD BIRDS • • • • • • • • • • • 93 FATHER OHART   33
FOR LEADING AGED HOUNDS AND YOUNG • • • • • • • • • 98 FOXHUNTER   23
AND NOW WITH AGED HOUNDS AND YOUNG • • • • • • • •   98 FOXHUNTER   V   21
AGED HOUNDS AND YOUNG. • • • • • • • • • • • • • •   99 FOXHUNTER   40
THE OLD HOUNDS AND THE YOUNG. • • • • • • • • • • • 99 FOXHUNTER   V   40
BOTH AGED HOUNDS AND YOUNG. • • • • • • • • • • • • 99 FOXHUNTER   V   40
YOUNG SUBTLE CONCHUBAR SAT CLOSE BY ME • • • • • • 102 FERGUS DRUID   10
AND HIS YOUNG SWEETHEART CLOSE BESIDE HIM KNELT, • • 108 CUCHULAIN SEA   40
AND HIS YOUNG DEAR ONE CLOSE BESIDE HIM KNELT, • • • 108 CUCHULAIN SEA V   40
HE SPAKE TO THE YOUNG MAN, "IS THERE NO MAID • • • • 109 CUCHULAIN SEA   58
AT LAST CUCHULAIN SPAKE, "A YOUNG MAN STRAYS • • • • 109 CUCHULAIN SEA V   47
WHILE YOUNG STARS ABOUT HER DANCE. • • • • • • • • 125 CATHLEEN PARA V   16
YOUNG MAN, LIFT UP YOUR RUSSET BROW, • • • • • • • 125 GOES FERGUS   4
AND HE SAW YOUNG MEN AND YOUNG GIRLS • • • • • • • 144 HOST OF AIR   13
AND HE SAW YOUNG MEN AND YOUNG GIRLS • • • • • • • 144 HOST OF AIR   13
AND A YOUNG MAN BROUGHT HIM RED WINE • • • • • • • 144 HOST OF AIR   19
AND A YOUNG GIRL WHITE BREAD. • • • • • • • • • •   144 HOST OF AIR   20
THE HANDSOMEST YOUNG MAN THERE, • • • • • • • • •   145 HOST OF AIR   34
OLD MEN AND YOUNG MEN AND YOUNG GIRLS • • • • • •   145 HOST OF AIR   39
OLD MEN AND YOUNG MEN AND YOUNG GIRLS • • • • • •   145 HOST OF AIR   39
YOUR MOTHER EIRE IS ALWAYS YOUNG, • • • • • • • •   148 INTO TWILIGHT   5
THY MOTHER ERI IS ALWAYS YOUNG, • • • • • • • • •   148 INTO TWILIGHT V   5
AND THE YOUNG LIE LONG AND DREAM IN THEIR BED • • • 150 OLD MOTHER   5
WHILE THE YOUNG LIE LONG AND DREAM IN THEIR BED • • 150 OLD MOTHER   V   5
BUT THE YOUNG LIE LONG AND DREAM IN THEIR BED • • • 150 OLD MOTHER   V   5
BUT THE YOUNG QUEEN WOULD NOT LISTEN: • • • • • •   159 CAP AND BELLS   9
THAT SAW YOUNG NIAMH HOVER WITH LOVE-LORN FACE • • 162 ASKS FORGIVE   13
I CRIED IN MY DREAM, O WOMEN, BID THE YOUNG MEN LAY • • 163 VALLEY LOVERS   5
AND I CRIED IN MY DREAM "O WOMEN, BID THE YOUNG MEN LAY 163 VALLEY LOVERS V   5
WOMEN AND CHILDREN, YOUNG MEN WITH BOOKS, • • • •   167 BLESSED   15
CHILDREN AND WOMEN AND TONSURED YOUNG MEN. • • •   167 BLESSED   V   15
I HAVE DRUNK ALE FROM THE COUNTRY OF THE YOUNG • • 177 PAST GREATNESS   1
THOUGH NOW IN HER OLD AGE, IN HER YOUNG AGE • • •   180 QUEEN MAEVE   18
YOUNG BAILE HONEY-MOUTH, WHOM SOME • • • • • • •   189 BAILE AILLINN   16

		PAGE	TITLE		LINE
YOUNG (CONTINUED)					
OF HARPERS AND YOUNG MEN: AND THEY		189	BAILE AILLINN		19
YOUNG BAILE HONEY MOUTH, WHOM SOME		189	BAILE AILLINN	V	16
AND OLD AND YOUNG MEN RODE WITH HER:		191	BAILE AILLINN		51
A YOUNG MAN CRIED AND KISSED HER HAND,		191	BAILE AILLINN		60
FOR THIS YOUNG GIRL AND THIS YOUNG MAN		195	BAILE AILLINN		157
FOR THIS YOUNG GIRL AND THIS YOUNG MAN		195	BAILE AILLINN		157
MURMURED WITH HER YOUNG VOICE FOR WHOSE MILD SAKE		205	ADAMS CURSE	V	15
IN FINDING THAT IT'S YOUNG AND MILD AND LOW,		205	ADAMS CURSE	V	17
BESIDE YOUNG AENGUS IN HIS TOWER OF GLASS,		219	HARP OF AENGUS		2
A BEAUTIFUL YOUNG MAN AND GIRL CAME UP		223	SHADOW WATER B		33
WHEN I WAS YOUNG,		254	WOMAN HOMER		2
WHEN I WAS YOUNG,		255	WOMAN HOMER		16
THAN THIS ACCUSTOMED TOIL. WHEN I WAS YOUNG,		267	ALL TEMPT ME		5
THE YOUNG MAN'S SONG		268	BROWN PENNY	V	T
I WHISPERED, "I AM TOO YOUNG."		268	BROWN PENNY		1
"GO AND LOVE, GO AND LOVE, YOUNG MAN,		268	BROWN PENNY		5
IF THE LADY BE YOUNG AND FAIR."		268	BROWN PENNY		6
YOU HAD TO FACE YOUR ENDS WHEN YOUNG—		273	GREY ROCK		53
THEREON A YOUNG MAN MET HIS EYE,		274	GREY ROCK		85
YOUNG RED-HEAD STRETCHED HIMSELF TO YAWN		303	HOUR DAWN	V	32A
"HOW YOUNG IT IS, HOW YOUNG!"		308	PLAYER QUEEN		2
"HOW YOUNG IT IS, HOW YOUNG!"		308	PLAYER QUEEN		2
BEING YOUNG YOU HAVE NOT KNOWN		312	CHILD DANCING		6
I COULD HAVE WARNED YOU: BUT YOU ARE YOUNG,		313	TWO YEAR LATER		5
BUT I AM OLD AND YOU ARE YOUNG,		313	TWO YEAR LATER		11
TO KEEP THE BODY YOUNG.		334	SONG		4
TO A YOUNG BEAUTY		335	YOUNG BEAUTY		T
TO A YOUNG GIRL		336	YOUNG GIRL		T
THAT YOUNG MEN, TOSSING ON THEIR BEDS,		337	SCHOLARS		4
LET THE YOUNG WISH. BUT WHAT HAS BROUGHT YOU HERE?		339	SHEP GOATHERD		6
HEARING IT NOW HAVE SIGHED FOR THAT YOUNG MAN		342	SHEP GOATHERD		77
OR A YOUNG GIRL DRESSED OUT IN HER NEW GOWN,		350	HER PRAISE		4
THOUGH SHE HAD YOUNG MEN'S PRAISE AND OLD MEN'S BLAME,		351	HER PRAISE		17
AMONG THE POOR BOTH OLD AND YOUNG GAVE HER PRAISE.		351	HER PRAISE		18
THE YOUNG MEN EVERY NIGHT APPLAUD THEIR GABY'S LAUGHING EYE,		353	HIS PHOENIX		9
AND WHO CAN SAY BUT SOME YOUNG BELLE MAY WALK AND TALK MEN WILD		354	HIS PHOENIX		26
AND MAY BE THERE'LL BE SOME YOUNG BELLE WALK OUT TO MAKE MEN WILD		354	HIS PHOENIX	V	26
AND MAYBE THERE'LL BE SOME YOUNG BELLE WALK OUT TO MAKE MEN WILD		354	HIS PHOENIX	V	26
YOUNG MEN NO LONGER SUDDENLY CATCH THEIR BREATH		355	BROKEN DREAMS		2
A YOUNG MAN WHEN THE OLD MEN ARE DONE TALKING		356	BROKEN DREAMS		16
A YOUNG GIRL IN THE INDOLENCE OF HER YOUTH,		359	WAR POEM		5
WHEN, YOUNG AND BEAUTIFUL,		392	EASTER 1916		22
I HAVE WALKED AND PRAYED FOR THIS YOUNG CHILD AN HOUR		403	FOR DAUGHTER		9
THAT IS NO COUNTRY FOR OLD MEN. THE YOUNG		407	SAIL BYZANTIUM		1
SOME FEW REMEMBERED STILL WHEN I WAS YOUNG		410	TOWER		33
TO YOUNG UPSTANDING MEN		416	TOWER		174
THAT DEAD YOUNG SOLDIER IN HIS BLOOD:		425	STARES NEST		14
WE TOO HAD MANY PRETTY TOYS WHEN YOUNG:		428	NINETEEN 19		9
MUCH DID I RAGE WHEN YOUNG,		434	YOUTH AND AGE		1
"BECAUSE I MADE YOU TURN AWAY AND RUN FROM THAT YOUNG CHILD:		450	OWEN AHERNE		14
O LET HER CHOOSE A YOUNG MAN NOW AND ALL FOR HIS WILD SAKE."		450	OWEN AHERNE		24
FOUR SONGS FROM THE YOUNG COUNTRYMAN		451	FIRST LOVE	V	T
THE YOUNG COUNTRYMAN		451	FIRST LOVE	V	T
A MAN YOUNG AND OLD FIRST LOVE		451	FIRST LOVE	V	T
THAT HAD THOSE OF THE YOUNG:		457	SECRETS OF OLD		2
SEEMED FOR A WHILE TO HAVE GROWN YOUNG AGAIN:		462	HARUN RASHID		36
"NEVER SHALL A YOUNG MAN,		492	ANNE GREGORY		1
THAT YOUNG MEN IN DESPAIR		492	ANNE GREGORY		10
SAW I AN OLD MAN YOUNG		515	GIRLS SONG B		11
OR YOUNG MAN OLD?		515	GIRLS SONG B		12
OR A YOUNG MAN OLD?		515	GIRLS SONG B	V	12
YOUNG MAN'S SONG		516	MANS SONG		T
BODILY DECREPITUDE IS WISDOM: YOUNG		523	LONG SILENCE		7
A WOMAN YOUNG AND OLD I FATHER AND CHILD		531	FATHER CHILD	V	T
WHY SHOULD THEY THINK THAT ARE FOR EVER YOUNG?		537	HER VISION		21
"DROWN ALL THE DOGS," SAID THE FIERCE YOUNG WOMAN,		546	TO SAME TUNE 2		7
DROWN ALL THE DOGS," SAID THE FIERCE YOUNG WOMAN.		546	TO SAME TUNE 2		10
"DROWN ALL THE DOGS," SAID THE FIERCE YOUNG WOMAN,		546	TO SAME TUNE 2		17
DROWN ALL THE DOGS," SAID THE FIERCE YOUNG WOMAN.		546	TO SAME TUNE 2		20
"DROWN ALL THE DOGS," SAID THE FIERCE YOUNG WOMAN,		547	TO SAME TUNE 2		27
DROWN ALL THE DOGS," SAID THE FIERCE YOUNG WOMAN.		547	TO SAME TUNE 2		30
WHAT FROM THE FOREST CAME? WHAT BEAST HAS LICKED ITS YOUNG?		560	MAGIC DRUM		6
I SHOULD BE BLAMED, YOUNG MAN.		569	THREE BUSHES		6
I HAVE WHAT NO YOUNG MAN CAN HAVE		588	OLD WICKED MAN		14
"A YOUNG MAN IN THE DARK AM I,		589	OLD WICKED MAN		37
THEY WERE NOT SUCH A PLAGUE WHEN I WAS YOUNG:		591	SPUR		3
IN A YOUNG MAN'S BED."		594	COLONEL MARTIN		17
I PITY ALL THE YOUNG,		607	SONGS BURDEN 2		11
HOW CAN THE YOUNG GO STRAIGHT?		607	SONGS BURDEN 2		17
YOUNG MEN KNOW NOTHING OF THIS SORT,		626	OLD MEN BE MAD		16
BUT O THAT I WERE YOUNG AGAIN		631	POLITICS		11
OF THE TARN WHERE YOUNG WAVES QUICKEN		647	ISLE STAT I 1		48
WATCHING O'ER HER AWFUL YOUNG,		658	ISLE STAT I 3		87

929

		PAGE	TITLE	LINE

YOUNG (CONTINUED)

O'ER HER YOUNG SO EAGERLY	658	ISLE STAT I 3	93
YOUNG GUARIMOND HE TELLS THEM O'ER AND O'ER, ...	661	ISLE STAT II 1	56
THE RED SQUIRREL SHALL REAR HER YOUNG WHERE THOU HAST DWELT—	674	ISLE STAT II 3	215
AND HOLLOW LULLING THE YOUNG WINDS WITH SONG.	675	ISLE STAT II 3	226
THROUGH HIS SAD SOUL FOR EVER OLD AND YOUNG, ...	687	TWO TITANS	25
A LOTUS IN THEIR HANDS—YOUNG MOORISH GIRL	694	MOSADA 1	103
YOUNG MOORISH GIRL, THY FINAL HOUR IS HERE!	701	MOSADA 3	63
SINGS THE YOUNG WISTFUL SPIRIT OF A STAR	705	REMEMBRANCE	10
THE SPIRIT OF YOUNG RENYI HAS GROWN OLD.	710	FERENCZ RENYI	17
THE YOUNG ONE WITH THE OTHERS." RENYI'S PALE	713	FERENCZ RENYI	84
I AM SO YOUNG. DOST THOU NO LONGER KNOW, ...	713	FERENCZ RENYI	88
A PEASANT YOUNG AND FAIR, HER EYES FOR FEAR	713	FERENCZ RENYI V	81
YOUNG FERENCZ RENYI BURSTS HIS BONDS—AT LAST, ...	714	FERENCZ RENYI V	116
COME TO THE CHESS, FOR YOUNG GIRLS' WITS ARE BETTER .	721	WITCH VIVIEN	46
MY WAY IS WEST. SHE SEEMS BOTH YOUNG AND SHAPELY!	755	SHADOW WATER A	171
I GREW AS OLD AS TIME, AND SHE GROWS YOUNG	761	SHADOW WATER A	259
GROWS YOUNG AND A MAN'S HEART GROWS OLD IN A TWINKLING.	761	SHADOW WATER A	263
BESIDE YOUNG AENGUS IN HIS TOWER OF GLASS, ...	762	SHADOW WATER A	297

YOUNGER

SITS A YOUNGER AND A STRONGER.	26	OISIN 1	V 399D
THE LIVING BEAUTY IS FOR YOUNGER MEN!	334	LIVING BEAUTY	9
"HE GROWS YOUNGER EVERY SECOND	342	SHEP GOATHERD	89
OR BRIGHTEN ONLY FOR SOME YOUNGER EYE, ...	464	HARUN RASHID	82
I KNOW NOT WHAT THE YOUNGER DREAMS—	475	EVA GORE-BOOTH	10

YOUNGEST

AND YESTERDAY THE YOUNGEST SON, ...	361	ALF POLLEXFEN	24
GO ASK THE YOUNGEST ANGEL, ...	680	LOVE AND DEATH	29
THOUGH YOUNGEST OF ALL IN OUR GOOD BAND, ...	707	FAIRY PEDANT	11
THOUGH YOUNGEST OF ALL IN OUR GOOD BAND, ...	708	FAIRY PEDANT	39

YOUTH

AND LOVE, IN THE HOURS WHEN YOUTH HAS CEASED! . . .	2	OISIN 1	V 7A
WAS A BEAUTIFUL YOUTH FROM AN UNKNOWN LAND. . . .	12	OISIN 1	V 145
OR THE SOFTNESS OF YOUTH BE GONE FROM OUR FACES, . .	27	OISIN 1	410
WILL THE SOFTNESS OF YOUTH BE GONE FROM OUR FACES, . .	27	OISIN 1	V 410
OR THE SOFTNESS OF YOUTH BE GONE FROM OUR FACES, . .	27	OISIN 1	V 419C
OR THE SOFTNESS OF YOUTH BE GONE FROM OUR FACES, . .	28	OISIN 1	V 426
THE YOUTH AND LADY AND THE DEER AND HOUND! . . .	29	OISIN 2	4
ONCE MORE—THE YOUTH AND LADY, DEER AND HOUND! . .	29	OISIN 2	V 2
WHICH IS THE ISLE OF YOUTH?" "NONE KNOW," SHE SAID, .	46	OISIN 2	V 249
THE DEER AND THE HOUND, AND THE LADY AND YOUTH, . .	47	OISIN 3	V 3
CAME AFTER THE HARD GAZE OF YOUTH, OR AN OLD MAN LIFTED HIS HEAD!	59	OISIN 3	170
. . . AND THEIR YOUTH, AND THEIR EYES SOFT AS SILK. . .	59	OISIN 3	V 176
THROUGH THE DEMON LOVE OF ITS YOUTH	63	OISIN 3	216
FOR THY YOUTH WITHOUT PEACE, AND THY YEARS WITH THE DEMONS, . .	63	OISIN 3	V 216
MY SONGS OF OLD EARTH'S DREAMY YOUTH!	67	HAPPY SHEPHERD	54
THROUGH THE LONG YEARS OF YOUTH, AND WHO WOULD HAVE THOUGHT	201	OLD MEMORY	7
THROUGH THE LONG DAYS OF YOUTH, AND WHO WOULD HAVE THOUGHT	201	OLD MEMORY	V 7
ALL THROUGH THE YEARS OF OUR YOUTH	211	O DO NOT LOVE	5
YOUTH AND AGE	261	COMING WISDOM	V T
THROUGH ALL THE LYING DAYS OF MY YOUTH	261	COMING WISDOM	2
TO SHAKE THEIR WICKED SIDES AT YOUTH	262	STUDENTS AGIT	3
A MEMORY OF YOUTH	313	MEMORY YOUTH	T
ALL TILL MY YOUTH WAS GONE	315	FRIENDS	18
WITH THE HOT BLOOD OF YOUTH, OF LOVE CROSSED LONG AGO! . .	316	COLD HEAVEN	6
OR MERE COMPANIONS OF MY YOUTH, ...	324	ROBERT GREGORY	7
IN MUSCULAR YOUTH WELL KNOWN TO MAYO MEN	325	ROBERT GREGORY	34
IN MUSCULAR YOUTH WELLKNOWN TO MAYO MEN	325	ROBERT GREGORY V	34
IN MUSCULAR YOUTH, AT MEETS OR AT RACECOURSES, . . .	325	ROBERT GREGORY V	35
WHEN I HAD MY BURNING YOUTH!	329	MEN IMPROVE	15
THE WICK OF YOUTH BEING BURNED AND THE OIL SPENT, . .	334	LIVING BEAUTY V	3
YOUTH TO PROLONG	334	SONG	2
MOST COURTEOUS TO SLOW AGE AND HASTY YOUTH, . . .	339	SHEP GOATHERD	19
I TOO HAVE RHYMED MY REVERIES, BUT YOUTH	340	SHEP GOATHERD	43
YOUTH CAN EXCEL THEM IN ACCOMPLISHMENT, ...	340	SHEP GOATHERD	47
AND I THAT MADE LIKE MUSIC IN MY YOUTH	342	SHEP GOATHERD	76
MY DAILY THOUGHTS SINCE THE FIRST STUPOR OF YOUTH . .	342	SHEP GOATHERD	83
I KNEW A PHOENIX IN MY YOUTH, SO LET THEM HAVE THEIR DAY.	353	HIS PHOENIX	8
I KNEW A PHOENIX IN MY YOUTH, SO LET THEM HAVE THEIR DAY.	354	HIS PHOENIX	16
I KNEW A PHOENIX IN MY YOUTH, SO LET THEM HAVE THEIR DAY.	354	HIS PHOENIX	24
I KNEW A PHOENIX IN MY YOUTH, SO LET THEM HAVE THEIR DAY.	354	HIS PHOENIX	32
A YOUNG GIRL IN THE INDOLENCE OF HER YOUTH, ...	359	WAR POEM	5
AMID THE DREAMS OF YOUTH) LET HER COME FACE TO FACE, . .	366	HER COURAGE	3
BECAUSE I HAVE NO OTHER YOUTH, CAN MAKE ME PINE! . .	391	UNDER SATURN	3
BEING A PORTION OF MY YOUTH, CAN MAKE ME PINE . . .	391	UNDER SATURN V	3
YOUTH AND AGE	434	YOUTH AND AGE	T
THE FRIENDS OF HIS YOUTH	455	FRIENDS YOUTH	T
CEASE TO REMEMBER THE DELIGHTS OF YOUTH, TRAVEL-WEARIED AGED MAN!	459	FROM OEDIPUS	2
A MIMICRY OF YOUTH. CAN POET'S THOUGHT	463	HARUN RASHID	62
A MIMICRY OF YOUTH. AN ARTIST'S THOUGHT	463	HARUN RASHID V	62
THE SOUL'S OWN YOUTH AND NOT THE BODY'S YOUTH . . .	464	HARUN RASHID	69
THE SOUL'S OWN YOUTH AND NOT THE BODY'S YOUTH . . .	464	HARUN RASHID	69
HEARD ALL THE ANXIETY OF MY PASSIONATE YOUTH, . . .	468	HARUN RASHID	168
DRUNK WITH THE BITTER SWEETNESS OF HER YOUTH. . . .	469	HARUN RASHID	186
DRUNK WITH THE BITTER-SWEETNESS OF HER YOUTH. . . .	469	HARUN RASHID V	186
THAT TABLE AND THE TALK OF YOUTH, ...	475	EVA GORE-BOOTH	18
ALL BY THEIR YOUTH UNDONE, ...	504	RESULT THOUGHT	4

930

		PAGE	TITLE	LINE
YOUTH (CONTINUED)				
DANCING WITH HER CHOSEN YOUTH,	• • • • • • • • • •	514	JANE GROWN OLD	2
ESCAPED FROM BITTER YOUTH,	• • • • • • • • •	568	SWEET DANCER	4
"THE DEAD IRELAND OF MY YOUTH, BUT AN IRELAND	• • • • •	602	GALLERY REVIS	11
AND ELVISH WISDOM, AND LONG YEARS OF YOUTH	• • • • • •	653	ISLE STAT I 2	47
FAIR YOUTH, ALONG A WANDERING WAY	• • • • • • •	667	ISLE STAT II 3	38
THERE'S LITTLE I'D REFUSE THEE, DEAREST YOUTH.	• • • •	669	ISLE STAT II 3	71
MY LIPS, FAIR YOUTH. IT SHALL BE AS YOU ASK.	• • • •	669	ISLE STAT II 3	80
BUT ART THOU HAPPY? YOUTH, I AM AT PEACE.	• • • • •	672	ISLE STAT II 3	150
SHALL BE THE HUNTER-LOVER OF THY YOUTH.	• • • • •	674	ISLE STAT II 3	205
WAS MY SLEEP LONG, OH, YOUTH? LONG, LONG AND DEEP.	• • •	678	ISLE STAT II 3	299
YOUTH, HERE WILL WE ABIDE, AND BE THOU KING	• • • •	679	ISLE STAT II 3	314
FOR ALL I GAVE THE VOICE, FOR ALL MY YOUTH,	• • • • •	685	SEEKER	78
A GREY-HAIRED YOUTH, WHOSE CHEEKS HAD NEVER FOUND,	• • •	687	TWO TITANS	7
CRAMM'D ALL HER YOUTH; AND HATES HAVE BOUGHT AND SOLD	• •	687	TWO TITANS	13
ABOUT THE SEA. BEFORE HER LIES THAT YOUTH,	• • • •	687	TWO TITANS	22
THE YOUTH HAD FLUNG HIS ARMS AROUND THE ROCKS,	• • •	688	TWO TITANS	40
GATHERED ON HER OWN LIPS, OH YOUTH, AND FLING	• • • •	688	TWO TITANS	53
PEACE OF YOUTH AND PEACE OF AGE,	• • • • • • • •	733	STREET DANCERS	46
YOUTHFUL				
AND WITH THE FERVOUR OF MY YOUTHFUL EYES,	• • • • • •	356	BROKEN DREAMS	25
INTO A SPHERE FROM YOUTHFUL SYMPATHY,	• • • • • •	443	SCHOOL CHILDR	14
WHAT YOUTHFUL MOTHER, A SHAPE UPON HER LAP	• • • • •	444	SCHOOL CHILDR	33
IN THEIR DAYS OF YOUTHFUL MIRTH!	• • • • • • • •	727	LOVERS QUARREL	40
YOUTH'S				
YOUTH'S DREAMY LOAD, TILL SHE	• • • • • • • •	315	FRIENDS	14
YOUTH'S BITTERNESS BEING PAST,	• • • • • • • • •	389	IMAGE PAST	11
WITH ALL YOUTH'S LONELY WILDNESS STIRRED,	• • • • •	397	POLIT PRISONER	16
AND YET HERSELF CAN SEEM YOUTH'S VERY FOUNTAIN,	• • •	465	HARUN RASHID	89
YOUTHS				
WHILE A HUNDRED YOUTHS, MIGHTY OF LIMB,	• • • • • •	8	OISIN 1	94
AND A HUNDRED YOUTHS, WHOSE LIMBS ARE STRUNG	• • • •	9	OISIN 1	V 97
OF YOUTHS AND MAIDENS HAND IN HAND,	• • • • • •	15	OISIN 1	V 202
ZAG SEE ZIG-ZAG				
ZEPPELIN				
AEROPLANE AND ZEPPELIN WILL COME OUT,	• • • • • •	565	LAPIS LAZULI	6
ZIGZAG				
HOW BUT IN ZIGZAG WANTONNESS	• • • • • • • •	338	TOM OROUGHLEY	V 12
ZIG-ZAG				
HOW BUT IN ZIG-ZAG WANTONNESS	• • • • • • • •	338	TOM OROUGHLEY	12
ZODIAC				
THE ONE DISASTROUS ZODIAC, MUTTERING	• • • • • • •	282	TWO KINGS	128
FROM THE ZODIAC,	• • • • • • • • • • • •	533	FIRST CONFESS	14
OF THE WHIRLING ZODIAC.	• • • • • • • • • •	535	CHOSEN	3
THE ZODIAC IS CHANGED INTO A SPHERE.	• • • • • • •	535	CHOSEN	18

931

APPENDIX

APPENDIX

Index Words in Order of Frequency

1019 ALL

575 OLD

556 AS

483 OUT

456 MAN

353 LOVE

336 ONE

289 COME

281 LIKE

272 HEART

263 MEN

260 SOME

244 EYES MORE

242 LONG

240 DOWN

221 GREAT

213 AWAY

208 MADE

204 UP

197 NIGHT

196 THOUGHT

194 DAY

187 SAID

184 BEFORE

182 KNOW

177 YET YOUNG

176 MOON

174 WORLD

170 NEVER UNDER

167 CAME

166 ROUND

163 AMONG

162 TIME

161 THINGS

156 LIGHT

154 STILL WIND

150 DEAD

148 MANY

145 THAN TILL

144 GONE

142 SONG WHILE

138 HAIR

137 HEAD

136 GO

135 HANDS

134 WHITE

131 FACE SAY

130 LITTLE

129 YEARS

128 GOD MIND

126 SEA

125 OVER

124 SLEEP

123 EVERY

122 OWN SOUL

121 HAND

116 HEARD

115 FOUND

114 BEING

113 STARS

111 ABOUT SUN TWO

110 STOOD

109 AIR CRIED HALF LET

108 FEET

106 ONCE

105 HEAR

104 BODY LIFE

103 DREAMS HOUSE

102 DEATH FAR GREY SAW

101
DAYS
GOOD

100
DREAM
FIND

99
CRY
RED

98
SUCH
WOMAN

97
SANG

94
MAKE
PLACE
WILD

93
KING
MOST
SING

92
ALONE
HIGH
THING

91
DEAR
DIE
EVER
GIVE
STONE

90
WANDERING

89
WOOD

88
ABOVE
AFTER
LIPS

86
EYE
SAD

85
LOOK

84
FULL

83
FIRE
UNTIL

82
BRING

NOTHING
WINDS

81
DIM
FIRST
TAKE
WORDS

80
BIRDS
END
SEE

79
BEAUTY
DARK
DOOR
LAY
TREE

78
BIRD
BLOOD

77
NAME
SORROW

76
BREAST
GAVE
LAST
LOST
SWEET
WAY

75
GREEN
LEAVES

74
PALE
YOUTH

73
NONE

72
LOVED

69
PASS
RUN
WENT

68
DEEP
KNEW
SEEMED

67
CALL
DONE
PEACE
SET
VOICE

66
BETWEEN
GRASS
JOY
SIDE
THREE
TURN

65
ANCIENT
CHILD
GOLD
HOUR
PUT
THINK
WOMEN

64
BROUGHT
GOLDEN
PRAISE
SOUND

63
DIED
NEW
PASSED

62
GROWN
LIE

61
DANCE
GREW
KEEP
LIVE
WATERS
WINGS

60
BROKEN
COMES
EVEN
SWORD
WOODS

59
FRIEND
HUNDRED
TREES
WELL

58
ARMS
BESIDE
CHILDREN
KNOWS
MOTHER
REST
SHORE

57
MOUNTAIN
SPEAK
WITHIN

56
ALONG
ANY
DAWN
HEARTS
MUSIC
SINGING
WISDOM

55
BEAUTIFUL
LAID
MINE

54
COLD
IMAGE
MAN'S
ONLY
SKY

53
AGE
EARTH
ROSE (Noun)
SILVER

52
BED
BLIND
LOW
PLAY

51
FLY
GROW
LEFT
MUCH
SAT
TELL
WEARY

50
BELOVED
GAZE
LIES
WINE

49
AMID
GOES
KISS
LAND
NEAR
QUEEN

48
BID
FALL
FOOL
LOVERS
PROUD
WATER

47
BEYOND
CHANGED

FELL
GIRL
HEAVY
RAN
RIGHT

46
BITTER
FATHER
O'ER
ROSE (Verb)
SEAS
SIGH
TIDE
WISE

45
BOUGHS
COUNTRY
EVENING
FEAR
FLAME
HOLY
HORN
LIVING
PRIDE
SON

44
BETTER
BREAK
CALLED
CARE
CAST
HUMAN
MAYBE
MORNING
SHADOWS
SMALL
STRONG

43
BREATH
BRIGHT
DROP
HOME
KNOWN
LADY
LOOKED
RIDE
TIMES

42
BOOK
CERTAIN
CHANGE
ENOUGH
LIVED
RODE
SEEM
SEEN
SOFT
THOUGHTS
TOLD
TOWER
WAR
WORD

41	TALK	RISE	SOULS	LONGING
BROWN	TOOK	WILL	SPRING	MOCK
HILL	WORLD'S	WOMAN'S	TALE	MORTAL
LAKE			THROWN	NINE
LAUGHTER	**35**	**31**	TWILIGHT	PASSING
LONELY	AROUND	BACK	WAYS	STAIR
MEMORY	BONE	CAUGHT		VAIN
OFF	BORN	CRIES	**27**	WEST
STAR	DREAMED	DRIVEN	AENGUS	WRONG
WORK	FOAM	EVIL	BEND	
	HAPPY	FOLLOW	BLOW	**24**
40	PEOPLE	GATHER	DELIGHT	BEES
DESIRE	SEVEN	HUNG	DRINK	BONES
DEW	STRANGE	KNEES	DRUID	COMING
GODS	TOMB	LIFT	EDGE	DANAAN
HOLLOW	WALK	MERRY	FOUL	EYELIDS
IMAGES	WANDER	SHADE	GHOST	FLAMING
KINGS	YEAR	SUDDENLY	HELD	GENTLE
LEAVE		SUMMER	HIDDEN	MEASURE
LOVER	**34**	THEREON	HIDE	MEMORIES
POOR	BEAT	TOUCH	HORSES	OPEN
TURNED	BODIES	TRUE	LAUGHED	PART
	BOY	WORN	LONGER	ROAD
39	BURNING		NIAM	RUNNING
CLOSE	DANCING	**30**	SANDS	SPIRIT
FRIENDS	EAR	APPLE	SINCE	STAY
HORSE	EMPTY	EARS	UNTO	TALKED
MOUTH	FOOT	FAERY	WIFE	VOICES
STREAMS	FORTH	GARDEN		WEAK
WAVE	HOUND	LEARNED	**26**	
WAVES	STONES	LIVES	BATTLE	**23**
WEEP	TUNE	MAD	BROTHER	ASK
WITHERED	WING	MAKES	CLOUDS	BEAR
	WITHOUT	RAGE	DAUGHTER	BOW
38		SHAPE	DRY	CROSS
BEST	**33**	SKIES	FINGER	DARKNESS
GROWS	BLOSSOM	WALL	GLAD	DREAD
HOPE	CEASE		HOURS	DROWN
LAUGH	CONTENT	**29**	IRELAND	DUST
MOURNFUL	DEER	COMMON	ISLAND	DYING
NEED	FINGERS	DREAMING	LIT	FOLLOWED
PASSION	GAY	EVERYTHING	MAID	LOVES
SILENCE	GRAVE	FALLEN	MIGHTY	MEN'S
WIDE	LANDS	FLOWERS	SLEPT	RULE
YONDER	LAUGHING	HILLS	SOMETHING	SAME
	LOUD	MEET	SPREAD	SECOND
37	MATTER	MET	TONGUE	SEEMS
FAIR	MIDNIGHT	MURMURING	TOWARDS	SHIP
GROUND	SECRET	PLAIN	TOWN	SHOW
HARP	SLOW	RICH	YON	SILENT
HEAVEN	TRUTH	SEEK		SOMEWHERE
HOLD	WAKE	SIGHT	**25**	SOUGHT
KIND	YELLOW	STORY	APART	STANDS
QUIET			ASLEEP	VERY
SHAKE	**32**	**28**	AWAKE	WROUGHT
STREAM	AGAINST	BADE	BEAST	
SUDDEN	ALWAYS	BEGAN	BLACK	**22**
TEARS	BOUND	BLUE	CARRY	BEHIND
WHOLE	CLOUD	CRAZY	CLEAR	BENEATH
	CROWD	GLORY	CLOAK	CHAIR
36	FIERCE	HALL	CROWN	ELSE
AGO	FLED	HOUNDS	CUCHULAIN	FIGHT
BEGGAR	FLOOR	HUSH	DIES	FLOWER
FACES	FRO	ISLE	FAIRY	FREE
SHADOW	HID	PRAY	GLASS	HAPPINESS
SONGS	MORN	RACE	GLIMMERING	HEART'S
STAND	NIAMH	RHYME	GOD'S	MILD
	REMEMBERING	SOON		

22 (cont.)
MOVED
NAY
PAINTED
SHEPHERD
SHONE
STORM
STREET
TALL
TOP
TROUBLE
WASTE
WINDY

21
AFAR
AFRAID
BELL
BLESSED
BOOKS
BUILD
CRYING
CUP
DREW
DROPS
FOREST
HATE
HELP
LIMBS
MERE
MOVE
OISIN
ONES
PAST
PRAYER
SAIL
SAND
SCHOOL
SHADOWY
SLEEPY
SLOWLY
SOUTH
SPEECH
SWIFT
THOUSAND
TOGETHER
WALKED
WEPT
WHIRLING
WORTH

20
BEATING
BENT
BRINGS
CHOOSE
DRAW
DRIPPING
DUMB
FORGAEL
GATHERED
GLEAM
HAZEL
LEAF
LEARN
LONE
LORD

LOVELY
LOVE'S
MAIDEN
MURMURED
NAMES
PASSIONATE
PURPLE
ROSES
SACRED
SAVE
SPOKE
SUNG
TAKEN
TEAR
THIN
TREMBLING
VALLEY
WAIT
WEEPING
WET

19
BLOWS
BOUGH
BRANCH
CHANCE
COMPANY
DROPPING
DROWNED
FENIANS
FILL
GRIEF
GROWING
HATRED
HAVING
HEADS
HONEY
HURRY
IGNORANT
MANKIND
PLEASURE
READ
REMEMBER
ROOM
SAKE
SHUT
SILK
SOFTLY
SPEAR
SWEAR
WON
WOUND
WOVEN

18
ACROSS
BARE
BOSOM
BURN
CALLING
CENTURIES
DESOLATE
DRAWN
DROVE
DULL
EVE
FISH

FLAMES
FLESH
GLOOM
JOHN
MASTER
MOMENT
MURMUR
NARROW
NOON
NORTH
PLEASE
POETS
PRIEST
ROCK
RUNS
SIN
STRENGTH
TROOP
WALKING
WARS
WHISPERING
WINTRY

17
ALOUD
ARROW
BEECH
BENDING
BLADE
BROOD
CRIMSON
DANCED
DEMON
DESPAIR
DRUNK
FADE
FALLS
FAMOUS
FEARS
FEATHER
FIELDS
FLIES
FLIGHT
FORGOTTEN
FOUR
GET
GIVES
GLITTERING
HARE
HEARING
HITHER
HORSEMEN
HOST
HUSBAND
IMMORTAL
KISSED
LATE
LEAFY
LEAP
LOOSE
MARBLE
MARCH
MIST
MOAN
MOOD
NATURAL
NOBLE

PATH
ROOF
SAILS
SEA'S
SENT
SHEEP
SHOOK
SIGHED
SLEEPING
STARE
STRIKE
STRINGS
SWEETNESS
SWORDS
THREAD
TOIL
TOSSING
WATCHED
WOUNDS

16
ALE
ALIVE
ANSWER
ANSWERED
ANYTHING
AWHILE
BEER
BEHOLD
BLOWN
BROKE
BURIED
CLAY
CLOCK
CUT
DEMONS
DRUNKEN
ENDS
FEEL
FLUNG
FOOTFALL
FORGOT
HEAPED
IMAGINATION
INTELLECT
KNOWING
LADIES
LESS
MICHAEL
MIRE
MIRROR
NEEDS
OAK
PIERCED
PLAYED
POET
POWER
RAGGED
RING
RUIN
SCARCE
SHINING
SOLITUDE
SPOT
STAG
TERROR
THEREUPON

TREAD
TROUBLED
VAPOURS
WAITING
WONDER

15
AGED
AYE
BEE
BELOW
BIT
BRIDE
BROW
COLONEL
COVER
CRADLE
CREATURES
DANCERS
DROWSY
FAINT
FEW
FLYING
FORM
GAZED
GIRLS
GIVEN
GLANCE
HARD
HELL
HUSHED
JANE
KEPT
KILLED
KNEE
LEAST
LEST
LIFTED
MAEVE
MINUTE
NAUGHT
PATRICK
PROMISED
RAIN
RAISE
RAISED
REASON
ROLLED
RUSH
SADNESS
SAYS
SCORE
SEND
SHELL
SHIELD
SHIPS
SIGHS
SKIN
SMOKE
SPIRITS
STARRY
STATE
STRETCHED
TABLE
TELLS
THINKING
WALLS

10 (cont.)

AUTUMN
BATTERED
BEARD
BEGIN
BEN
BLOOM
BOAT
BRAN
BRAZEN
BUBBLING
BUILT
BURNED
CALM
CANDLES
CAP
CASEMENT
CHASED
CLOTH
COURAGE
COVERED
CRUEL
DAILY
DECLARE
DELIGHTED
DRAGGED
EARTH'S
EAST
ENDURE
ESCAPE
FADES
FAME
FAST
FATE
FEATHERS
FERGUS
FLASHING
FORMS
GENTLY
GLIMMER
HONOUR
HORNS
HURLED
IMAGINING
IMPOSSIBLE
ISLANDS
KIN
KINDNESS
LEAN
LOMAIR
LOSS
LOVELINESS
LOVER'S
LYING
MOUSE
NASCHINA
NOTE
OVERHEAD
PAGE
PARADISE
PARNELL
PAY
PERFECT
PHANTOM
PHANTOMS
PINE
PLANNED

PLANTED
PLAYS
REIN
ROBBERS
ROPE
ROUGH
ROVE
SADDLE
SCREAM
SHED
SHOULDER
SHOUTED
SHOWS
SIGHING
SINK
SOLITARY
SORROWS
STAIN
STEPS
STIRRED
STONY
STORIES
STRUCK
SWEPT
TEN
TENDERNESS
THINKS
THROW
TO-MORROW
TURNING
UNDERSTOOD
UNLESS
VAGUE
VISION
WAGE
WEARINESS
WOE
WONDERING
WRAPPED

9

AROSE
BAG
BALLAD
BATTLES
BEAUTY'S
BLEW
BRANCHES
BROWS
BURST
BUSY
CATTLE
CAVERN
CENTURY
CHAIN
CHILDHOOD
CHOICE
CLINGING
COAT
DARE
DARED
DAY'S
DEAF
DECAY
DOUBT
ENEMY
EXULTANT

FEATHERS
FIELD
FINN
FLARE
FLOWED
FOL DE ROL
FOX
FROTH
GAZING
GIFT
GLEAMS
GOMEZ
GREATER
HANGS
HAPPIER
HEAVENLY
HELEN
HIDING
HOLDS
HOMER
HOOD
HOOVES
INSTEAD
JOURNEY
KEEN
LABYRINTH
LAD
LILY
LINGER
LOCHLANN
LOSE
LOUT
MAKING
MANSION
MARROW
MASTERS
MERCHANT
MINDS
MODERN
'MONG
MONSTROUS
MOURN
MOVING
MULTITUDE
MURDEROUS
NAKED
NATION
NEARER
NOSE
OIL
PACING
PARDON
PEARL-PALE
PENNY
PLACES
PRESSED
REACH
REEDS
RENYI
REVERIE
RINGS
ROCKS
SADLY
SEAT
SENSE
SERVANTS
SHADES

SILKEN
SINGLE
SINKS
SLEEPER
SPACE
SPADE
START
STEED
STIR
STIRS
STRAIGHT
SUNK
SWAN
SWAYED
SWAYING
TIME'S
TORCH
TRAMPLED
TREASURE
TUMULT
TWICE
TWISTED
UNDERNEATH
UNQUIET
WORKS

8

AILLINN
ANGELS
ASIDE
AWAKENED
AZURE
BANNERS
BECOME
BELLS
BERRIES
BETRAYED
BLAME
BLAST
BLOSSOMS
BOYS
BRIDGE
BRIGHTNESS
BUY
CARS
CHAMBER
CHANGELESS
CHEEK
CHILDISH
CLOSED
COLOUR
COOLE
CRACKED
CRAFT
CROZIERS
CUSHIONED
DART
DIMNESS
DOG
DOORWAY
DRAGON
DREAMY
DRINKING
DRUIDS
DUN
EAGLES
EQUAL

EVERYWHERE
FAIL
FANATIC
FANTASY
FASHIONED
FLEE
FLOATS
FOLDED
FOOD
FRET
GATHERS
GOING
GRASSY
GREATNESS
HA
HANRAHAN
HAWK
HEARS
HOOFS
HOUSEHOLD
HUNTER
HUNTING
HUNTSMAN
HURT
IDLE
INDIAN
INNOCENCE
IRISH
JACK
KILL
KING'S
KNEEL
LAIN
LAMP
LASS
LATER
LEANING
LEVEL
LIMB
LINE
LINEAMENTS
LISTENING
LONELINESS
LOWER
MARVELLOUS
MEANING
MICE
MIRACLE
MIXED
MOMENTARY
MOONLIT
NEIGHBOUR
NEWS
NIGHT'S
NIGHTS
OBEY
O'DONNELL
O'LEARY
OSPREY
PAUL
PEARSE
PHOENIX
PILLARS
PLANETS
PLAYING
PLEASANT
POINT

8 (cont.)
PULL
PULLED
PURPOSE
ROAR
RUTH
SAGES
SALT
SEED
SHEBA
SHEPHERDS
SHIVERING
SHOOT
SHOT
SHOUT
SHOWN
SHY
SICK
SISTER
SIT
SLAVE
SLUMBER
SOLE
SOMEBODY
SOUNDS
SQUIRREL
STARING
STEPT
STORMY
STRETCH
SUN'S
SURGES
TEETH
THIGH
THRUST
TIP
TOES
UNHUMAN
VALE
VOW
WANDERINGS
WARRIOR
WATER'S
WHENCE
WILLOW
WOODY
WORSE

7
ABSTRACT
ACTION
A-FLUTTER
ALL'S
APPLES
ASKED
AWAIT
BANE
BARGAIN
BEGINS
BENCH
BILL
BOARD
BORNE
BOUGHT
BRED
BRILLIANT
BROAD

BULL
BURKE
CANDLE-END
CART
CARVEN
CHRIST
CIRCLE
CIRCLES
CITY
CLAMOUR
CLAP
CONNOLLY
CONSCIENCE
CRACK
CREATURE
CREEPING
CREW
CUMHAL
DARLING
DESPITE
DIPPED
DOUBLE
DOVE
DRANK
EARTHLY
EAT
EBB
EMER
ENCHANTED
ERI
EYEBALLS
FAITHFUL
FAR-OFF
FAY
FEED
FERENCZ
FIFTY
FIGHTING
FIVE
FLASH
FLEET
FLOCK
FLOWING
FLOWN
FLUTTER
FOLIAGE
FORETOLD
FUNERAL
FURTHER
GALLERY
GALLEYS
GARDENS
GATES
GATEWAY
GREGORY
GUILE
GYRES
HARSH
HATED
HEARTH
HOPING
HOUSES
HOVERING
HURL
HURRIED
KEENING
LADLE

LADS
LANE
LAWN
LEADER
LEARNING
LEISURE
LIDS
LIGHTLY
LIP
LONG-LEGGED
LOOKING-GLASS
LOT
LUCKY
MAIDENS
MARCHING
MARKED
MARRIAGE
MARRIED
MEADOWS
MEDITATION
MIGHTIER
MINGLING
MOCKERY
MOONLIGHT
MOONS
MOUND
MUMMY
MUSE
MUSES
NAILS
NEXT
NOBODY
ONE'S
OVERTHROWN
OWL
PACK
PERFECTION
PLAINS
PLATO'S
POEMS
POPULAR
POST
PRAYERS
RANK
REFUSE
REPLY
RINGING
ROBERT
ROGER
ROOTED
RUDDY
RULED
SAFFRON
SCALE
SCHOLAR
SCORN
SEDGE
SELF-SAME
SERVED
SHAPES
SHIELDS
SHINE
SHOUTING
SHRIEK
SINEWY
SKINS
SLUMBERING

SOFTNESS
SOLDIERS
SOLID
SOOTH
SOUL'S
SPEARS
SPRANG
STARK
STAYED
STEEP
STICK
STILLNESS
STRAND
STRANGER
STRICKEN
STUDY
SUBSTANCE
SULLEN
SWALLOWS
SWIM
TAMBOURINE
TASTE
TERRIBLE
THIRST
THRONG
TIMID
TIRE
TO-DAY
TOOTH
TOSS
TOUCHING
TRESS
TROUT
TRUMPET
TRUTHS
TUMULTUOUS
TWELVE
UNDYING
VALLENCE
WAIL
WED
WEIGH
WESTERN
WESTWARD
WHEREON
WHIM
WHITER
WHITHER
WINDOWS
WISH
WOOL
WORE
YESTERDAY
YORE

6
ABOUNDING
ACCURSED
ACCUSTOMED
AIRY
AMRITA
ANIMAL
ARCADY
ARMIES
ASTRAY
A-TIPTOE
AWAITS

AWAKEN
AWOKE
BARLEY
BEGOTTEN
BEGUN
BIND
BITTERNESS
BLESSEDEST
BLEST
BLOT
BOAST
BRAHMA
BRASS
BRIGHTENING
BROTHERS
BURNISHED
CALLS
CANNON
CAOILTE
CAPTAIN
CARDS
CARES
CARVED
CASTS
CERTAINLY
CHARACTER
CHARM
CHARMED
CHILL
CHURNED
CLING
CLOTHS
CLOVEN
COCKS
COIL
COMELY
COMPANION
CONAN
COOK
CORN
COUNT
COUNTED
COUNTRYMAN
COURT
COWS
CREST
CROWDS
CROWNS
CRUELTY
CUCKOO
CURSED
DANCES
DATHI
DEED
DEEDS
DENIES
DEPART
DEVIL
DIFFERENT
DIFFICULT
DIGNITY
DISCIPLINE
DISTRESS
DIZZY
DOME
DRESSED
DRIFTING

6 (cont.)

DRUM
EAGLE
EARL
EARNED
EASY
EATEN
ECSTASY
EMBROIDERED
ENTER
ETERNAL
FABULOUS
FALCON
FAMILY
FANATICS
FEARFUL
FEASTED
FELT
FENIAN
FIDDLE
FIERY
FIN
FIT
FLAPPING
FOLDS
FOLLOWS
FOOLS
FOOTSOLE
FORGETTING
FRIGHT
FROZEN
FURY
GALWAY
GILLIGAN
GLADE
GLANCES
GOLDEN-ARMED
GOLDSMITH
GOOSE
GOVERNMENT
HAMMER
HANGING
HAUGHTY
HEAVING
HEEL
HEROIC
HOPELESS
HOPES
HORRIBLE
HORROR
HUNGER
HUNGRY
HURRYING
ILL
INNUMERABLE
INSTANT
IVORY
JET
JOINED
JOYOUS
JUSTIFY
KINGDOM
KNIGHT
KNOCKNAREA
LADY'S
LAME
LANCE

LAWNS
LEGS
LET'S
LIFE'S
LIFTS
LINGERING
LONGS
MAGICAL
MAJESTY
MARRY
MASTERFUL
MATE
MEETS
METEOR
MILKY
MINNALOUSHE
MIRACULOUS
MISERY
MISS
MOCKED
MORROW
MOSADA
MOUTHS
MYSTERIOUS
NATIONS
NECK
NOD
NODDING
NOISY
ODOUR
ORO
O'SULLIVAN
OTTERS
OUTLIVE
PASSIONS
PATHS
PAUSE
PAUSED
PEARL
PICKED
PICTURE
PIERCING
PILOTS
PIPING
PITEOUS
PLAYER
PLOT
PLOTS
PLUCK
POEM
PORTRAIT
PROVED
PYTHAGORAS
QUARTER
QUEST
RAGING
RAVING
REJOICE
REMORSE
RENOWNED
RESTLESS
RHYMED
RIDERS
RIDGE
ROBARTES
ROLLS
ROOD

RUBY
RUSTLING
SAFE
SANCTITY
SCATTER
SCEOLAN
SETS
SETTING
SETTLED
SHELTER
SHELTERED
SHOP
SHOWED
SHUDDER
SIGN
SIMPLE
SIPS
SLAVES
SLEW
SLIDING
SMILING
SOLD
SOLITUDES
SORE
SPACIOUS
SPEAKS
SPECKLED
SPEED
SPELLS
STAFF
STAGE
STAKE
STATUES
STERN
STOOL
STOOPED
STRAW
STROKE
STUMBLING
SUMMON
SUNLIGHT
SURGE
SWANS
SWEAT
SWEETER
SYNGE
TENT
TENTS
TEXT
THIGHS
THOUSANDS
THREADS
THRESHOLD
THRONES
TOILED
TOPS
TOWNLAND
TRACE
TREMBLE
UNCHANGING
UNNOTICED
UPWARD
VANISH
VEINS
VENGEANCE
VIJAYA
VIOLENT

VIRGIN
WAITS
WANDERER
WANDERS
WARRIORS
WEALTH
WEIGHT
WHIGGERY
WHISTLED
WIN
WINTER'S
WITCH
WITNESS
WOMB
WOODEN
WRACK
WRIST

5

ABU
AGES
ALLAH'S
ALMOST
AMOROUS
ANSWERING
APPARITIONS
ARGUMENT
ARMY
ASKS
ASTONISHED
ATTENTION
AVALON
AWRY
BALLYLEE
BANDS
BARBAROUS
BARS
BATS
BAY
BEAMS
BECAME
BEGGARS
BEGOT
BELL-BRANCH
BLACKENED
BLESSING
BLINDED
BLINK
BLOODY
BLOTTED
BLUE-EYED
BOAR
BOARDS
BOTTOM
BOY'S
BRAWLING
BREAKS
BREASTS
BREEZE
BRIM
BRIMMED
BRUSH
BULBEN
BURTHEN
BUSINESS
BYZANTIUM
CAIRN

CALVES
CARED
CARRIES
CASE
CASUAL
CATCH
CATHLEEN
CENTRAL
CHARACTERS
CHEER
CHILDREN'S
CHOIR
CHRYSOLITE
CLAWS
CLIMBING
CLOUD-PALE
COARSE
COCK
COMFORTABLE
CONFUSION
CONNEMARA
CONTENTED
COOL
COUNSEL
COXCOMB
CRADLES
CRAWLS
CROOKED
CROWDED
CROWNED
CUPS
CURTAIN
DAWNING
DAYTIME
DEARER
DEDICATION
DEEPS
DEWDROPS
DIETH
DIG
DIRTY
DISTANCE
DOE
DOOM
DOZEN
DRIFT
DROOPING
DWELLS
EARTHY
EDAINE
EDEN
EIRE
ELEMENTAL
EMBLEMS
EMBROIDERY
EMPTIED
ENFOLD
EVERLASTING
FANCIED
FANTASTIC
FARM
FAWN
FEATHERED
FEEDS
FELLOW
FICKLE
FIFTEEN

5 (cont.)

FISHER
FISHERS
FLICKER
FLINGS
FLOAT
FLOATING
FLOWERING
FLOWS
FLUTTERING
FOOTING
FOREHEAD
FOUNTAIN
FOURTH
FRAGRANT
FRENZY-STRUCK
FROWN
FUTURE
GAME
GARMENT
GAUDY
GEORGE
GHOSTLY
GIRL'S
GLEAMING
GODHEAD
GOWN
GRACIOUS
GRANT
GRASS-GREEN
GRATITUDE
GRAVES
GREECE
GREEK
GRIEVE
GROPE
GUARD
HAMMERED
HAPPENS
HARDLY
HARES
HARPERS
HARRIED
HEALTH
HEAP
HEARERS
HEATHEN
HELPLESS
HENCE
HERALD
HERON
HIGHER
HILLY
HIRE
HOLDING
HOMEWARD
HOOF
HORNLESS
HORSEMAN
HORSE'S
HUNDREDTH
IGNORANCE
INNOCENT
INSOLENT
INTENT
IOLLAN
JUDGMENT

KEEPS
KINSALE
KNEELING
LABOUR
LAIR
LANGUID
LARGE
LASH
LASTING
LAUREL
LEANT
LINGERED
LOADED
LUTE
MARE
MERCY
MERELY
MESH
METAL
METEORS
MILE
MIX
MOLL
MOODS
MOONLESS
MOOR
MOORISH
MOTH
MOULD
MOURNS
MOUTHFUL
MUSHROOMS
MUTTER
MUTTERING
MYRIAD
NEIGHBOURS
NIGHTFALL
NINETEEN
NUMBER
NUMBERLESS
OATH
OBEYED
ODOROUS
OLDER
OLIVE
OPPOSITE
OTTER
OVERCOME
PAID
PAINS
PAINT
PAIR
PATHWAY
PEOPLE'S
PICTURES
PITILESS
PLAN
PLAYERS
PLOUGH
PLUNGE
POLITICS
POLLEXFEN
PONDERED
POOLS
POPPIES
PORTION
POUR

POURS
POWERFUL
PRECIOUS
PRESS
PROOF
PROW
QUALITY
QUARREL
QUARRELLING
QUESTIONED
RABBIT
RAG
RAIL
RAMBLING
RANTING
REALITY
RENT
REPLIES
RIBH
RICHES
RIDDEN
ROCKED
RODY
ROLLY
ROMANTIC
ROUT
ROVER
RUBBISH
RUSHED
SAFETY
SAILED
SAILORS
SALMON
SANDALS
SCARCELY
SCATTERED
SCEPTRE
SEASON
SEASONS
SEES
SERVANT
SERVING
SHALLOW
SHAME
SHELLS
SHROUD
SHRUNKEN
SITS
SLEEK
SLEEPERS
SLENDER
SLIME
SLOPING
SMILES
SMOTE
SNOWS
SOBER
SOD
SOLEMN
SORRY
SPEAKING
SPORT
SPUR
SQUARE
STAGGERING
STATELY
STEEL

STOP
STORMS
STRAIN
STRIFE
STUMBLED
SUBSTANTIAL
SUBTLE
SUCKED
SUNKEN
SUPERNATURAL
SWEEP
SWINEHERD
SWORD-BLADE
SWORN
SYMBOL
TAIL
TALLER
TEACH
TEST
THANKS
THITHER
THORN-TREES
THRICE
THRIVE
TIED
TOMBS
TONGUES
TRANSFIGURED
TRAVELLED
TROUBLES
TWAIN
UNAPPEASABLE
UNDO
UNDONE
UNSEEN
USE
UTTERLY
VANITY
VAPOURY
VICTORIES
VICTORY
VISIONARY
WAKEN
WAKING
WALKS
WANDERERS
WANT
WATTLES
WAYWARD
WEARS
WEAVING
WHEAT
WHEREBY
WHIRLS
WICK
WILDERNESS
WILDNESS
WISHED
WITHER
WITHERING
WIZARD
WOKE
WOLVES
WORTHY
WRAP
WRECK
WRECKED

YES
YOUNGER

4

ABASHED
ACCOMPLISHED
ACCORDING
ACHING
ADORED
AIMLESS
ALARMS
ALEEL
ALMINTOR
ALMINTOR'S
ALREADY
AMBITION
AMENDS
ANGELIC
ANGER
ANGERS
ANIMATE
ANSWERS
ANTONIO
APPEAR
APPEARS
APPROPRIATE
ARCADIAN
ARROGANT
ARTHUR
ASH
ASH-GREY
ASIAN
ATHENE
AUGUSTA
AWAKENS
BABY
BABYLONIAN
BADGER
BALD
BALL
BANISHED
BANKS
BANQUET
BARD
BASE
BEAM
BELIEVE
BELLY
BERRY
BESEECHING
BIRD'S
BITTERLY
BLAMED
BLESSEDNESS
BODY'S
BORDERED
BOTTLE
BOYHOOD
BRAHMA'S
BREAKER
BREASTPLATE
BREATHING
BREATHLESS
BREWED
BRIDGET
BROODING
BROODS

3 (cont.)

CLOYNE
COAL
COAT-HANGER
COFFIN
COMELIER
COMMAND
COMPLACENT
COMPLEXITIES
COMPOSITE
CONFESSION
CONFIDENCE
CONSIDERING
CONSUME
CONTACT
CONTEMPLA-
   TION
CONTINUALLY
CONVERSE
COPY
CORNERS
CORPSE
COTTAGES
COUNTESS
COUNTRIES
COUPLE
COUPLES
COURSES
COVERING
COVERS
CRAFTY
CRANE
CRAWL
CREEL
CREEPS
CRESCENTS
CREVICE
CRICKET
CROWED
CROZIERED
CRUACHAN'S
CRUTCHES
CUCHULAIN'S
CUCHULLIN
CURDS
CURE
CURES
CURSING
CURVED
CYPRESS
DAEMONIC
DARKENING
DATE
DAUGHTERS
DAWNED
DAYS'
DEATH-BED
DEATH'S
DECEIT
DECEPTION
DECK
DECLARED
DEEPER
DEFEAT
DEFEATED
DEFORMITY
DELIGHTS

DELL
DEMAND
DEPTHS
DERIDED
DESK
DESPAIRING
DESTROY
DESTROYED
DICE
DIGGING
DISAPPEAR
DISASTER
DISCLOSE
DISPLAY
DOG'S
DOLL
DOLOROUS
DOLPHIN'S
DOONEY
DORIC
DOUBTLESS
DOUGH
DOVES
DOWNY
DRAGS
DRAPERY
DRAVE
DRAWS
DREAMER
DROOP
DRUMS
DRUNKARD'S
DUBLIN
DUTY
EARLESS
EARLY
EARN
EASTERN
ECHO
ELEGANCE
EMAN'S
EMBITTERED
EMERGE
EMOTION
EMPEROR'S
EMPOUNDED
ENAMELLED
ENTANGLED
ENTERS
ENWOUND
EOCHAID'S
EQUALITY
ERECT
ESTABLISHED
ESTRANGED
EXCITED
EXIST
EXTRAVAGANCE
EYELID
FALCONER
FALSE
FAMILIAR
FAND
FARMER'S
FARM-HOUSE
FAT
FATHER'S

FATIGUE
FAUN
FEARED
FEASTWARD
FEATHERY
FEEDING
FELLOWS
FERN
FERNS
FESTIVAL
FEVER
FIDDLER
FIDGET
FIGURE
FILLING
FILTHY
FINAL
FINDRINNY
FINGER-TIPS
FIR
FIST
FITTING
FLAG
FLAGRANT
FLAT
FLAW
FLEAS
FLIT
FLOODED
FLOORS
FLOWER-LIKE
FLOWERY
FLUTTERED
FOAM-WET
FOLLOWING
'FORE
FORGERY
FORGETFUL
FORGETFULNESS
FORGIVENESS
FORTY
FOSTER
FOXES
FRAGMENTS
FREEDOM
FRIENDLY
FRIEND'S
FURROWS
GAIN
GALLANT
GALLOWS
'GAN
GAP
GAZES
GEAR
GHOSTS
GIDDY
GIVING
GLAMOUR
GLEAMED
GLEN
GLIMMERED
GLOSSY
GOVERN
GRANDFATHER
GRASSHOPPER
GREATEST

GREENNESS
GREET
GREGORY'S
GROAN
GUERDON
GUIDES
GUIDING
GYRING
HAIRS
HALCYON'S
HAMMERS
HAPLESS
HARDER
HARMONIOUS
HARP-STRINGS
HARRY
HARUN
HASTEN
HAUGHTIER
HAY
HEARTHSTONE
HEAT
HEATH
HEAVED
HEBRIDES
HEELS
HELM
HERB
HERDSMAN
HERMITS
HERON-BILLED
HERON'S
HEW
HIGH-BORN
HO
HOARY
HOLIEST
HOMESTEADS
HONEY-BEES
HONEY-MOUTH
HORSEMANSHIP
HOT
HOULIHAN
HOWLED
HUEGEL
HUGH
HUNCHBACK
HUNDREDS
HUNT
IMMORTALITY
IMMORTALS
IMPERISHABLE
IMPETUOUS
INCENSE
INDIGNANT
INDOLENCE
INK
INLAID
INNISFREE
INSTRUMENT
INTRICACIES
INVENT
ITALIAN
IVORIES
JACQUES
JAPANESE
JASMINE

JEALOUS
JESTER
JEWELRY
JOIN
JOINT
JOSTLED
JOURNEYMAN
JOURNEYS
JUAN
JUST
KEEPING
KEGS
KETTLE
KINDLY
KINE
KINGDOMS
KINGLY
KISSING
KNITTED
KNITTING
KNOCK
KYLE-NA-NO
LABORIOUS
LAGGARD
LAKE'S
LAMBS
LAMENTS
LAPIS
LAVELL
LAWS
LAZULI
LEAFAGE
LEAFLESS
LEAPS
LEMAN
LETTER
LETTERED
LETTERS
LEVELLED
LIBERTY
LIGHTED
LIGHTNINGS
LIKELY
LILIES
LINEN
LINKED
LIQUID
LIZARDS
LO
LOAD
LOGIC
LOINS
LONG-LOST
LOTUS
LOVELESS
LOVE-LORN
LOVING
LULLED
LUMINOUS
LUNGED
LURE
MAC
MADDENED
MAGEE
MAGNIFICENCE
MAIDS
MAIL

3 (cont.)

	NUN	PUSHED	SEIZED	STEADY
MAJESTICAL	OBSCURE	PUTS	SEPARATE	STELLA
MANANAN	ODOUR-LADEN	QUAKING	SEPULCHRE	STERNER
MANANNAN	O'DRISCOLL	QUATTROCENTO	SERPENT	STICKS
MANES	OFFER	QUENCHLESS	SERVING-MAN	STILLED
MAN-HEADED	OGHAM	QUESTIONER	SEXUAL	STOPPED
MANHOOD	O'HART	QUICKLY	SHADY	STRAITS
MANNER	OISIN'S	QUIETNESS	SHAPELY	STRANGENESS
MANY-CHANGING	ONWARD	QUIETUDE	SHARED	STRAYING
MARCHES	OPINION	QUIVER	SHARPENED	STREW
MARINERS	ORDER	RAFTER	SHAWL	STRINGED
MARRIAGE-BED	OUTLANDISH	RAIMENT	SHEPHERDESS	STRONGER
MARROW-BONES	OUTRAGEOUS	RAINS	SHIFT	STRUGGLE
MARSH	OUTWORN	RANGE	SHIRK	STRUGGLING
MAST	OVERBOARD	RAPTUROUS	SHIRT	STUCK
MASTER'S	PADDLE	RARE	SHOD	STUPID
MATCHING	PAINTER	RATTLED	SHONEEN	SUFFER
MATTERS	PAINTER'S	RAVENING	SHOOTS	SUFFERING
MATTOCK	PAINTING	READY	SHOULDERED	SUFFICIENT
MEASURED	PALING	RECKONED	SHOULDERS	SULTRY
MEASURES	PALM	RED-ROSE-	SHRIEKED	SUMMONED
MEDITATIONS	PAN	BORDERED	SHRIEKS	SUNSET
MEDITATIVE	PARCHMENT	REED	SHRILL	SUP
MEN-AT-ARMS	PARLIAMENT	REELED	SHUFFLE	SUPPER
MERMAID	PARTED	REFUGE	SHUTS	SWAY
MIDDLETON	PASSES	RELIGIOUS	SICKLE	SWEETEN
MIDHIR'S	PAVEMENT	REMEMBERS	SICKNESS	SWIFTLY
MILK-WHITE	PEAK	REND	SIGNS	SWIFT'S
MISTRESS	PEASANT'S	RENOWN	SINEW	SWINE
MOLAY	PEBBLES	REPOSE	SINNING	SWING
MOMENT'S	PEN	REPROACH	SISTERS	SWORD-BLADES
MONGAN	PERISHED	REPROVED	SIXTEEN	TABLETS
MONOTONE	PERSIAN	REPROVES	SKEIN	TALES
MOORFOWL	PHASES	REVERENCE	SKILL	TALKS
MOOR-HENS	PILE	REVERIES	SKIPPER	TEMPEST
MORNIN'	PILGRIM	RISES	SLATE-COLOURED	TERRIFIED
MORNING'S	PILIN'	RIVERY	SLEEVE	THIRTY
MORTAL'S	PIN	ROADWAY	SLUNK	THOUGHTLESS
MOULDED	PINING	ROBE	SMITHY	THREATEN
MOULDERING	PINIONS	ROCKING	SMITTEN	THROATS
MOVEMENT	PIOUS	ROMAN	SNARE	TIGHTENED
MRS	PIPE	ROME	SOMBRE	TODAY
MUIRTHEMNE	PIRATES	ROSICROSS	SOMEONE	TONE
MUMMY-CLOTH	PITIFUL	ROUSED	SOMETIMES	TONES
MUNICIPAL	PLATONIC	ROW	SOONER	TOOL
MUNSTER	PLATONIST	RUA	SOULS'	TOSSED
MURDER	PLAYBOY	RUINOUS	SOUR	TOY
MURIAS	PLAYTIME	RUSHING	SOURCE	TRACK
MURMUROUS	PLEASURES	RUSHY	SPAIN	TRAITOR
MUSCLE	PLUMED	RUSSET	SPARROWS	TRANCE
MUSCULAR	PLUMY	RUSTLE	SPECTACLE	TRANQUILLITY
MUSICAL	POET'S	SALLEY	SPEEDY	TRAVELLER
NAN	POINTED	SALTIN'	SPICE	TRAVELLING
NATIVITY	PONDER	SAND-SACK	SPINNING	TRICK
NATURES	POUND	SAVAGE	SPIT	TRICKS
NEAREST	PREACHER	SAVED	SPITE	TRIED
NEEDLE	PREDESTINED	SCARLET	SPRIGHTLY	TRINITY
NE'ER	PRESENT	SCENTED	SPRITE	TRIPS
NEGLECT	PRINCES	SCHOLARS	SPY	TRIVIAL
NESSA	PROCLAIM	SCHOOLING	STAINED	TRUE-LOVE
NEW-MOWN	PROCLAIMING	SCOFF	STAIRS	TUB
NIGHTLY	PROPER	SCREEN	STAMPED	TUFTED
NOBLENESS	PROPHESYING	SCRUB	STARLIT	TUMBLED
NODDED	PURITY	SEA-KING	STARTED	TURF
NORMAN	PURSE	SEAWARD	STARVED	UNBEGOTTEN
NOURISH	PURSUING	SEA-WAYS	STATION	UNBID
NUMBERS	PUSH	SEEKS	STAYS	UNCOUTH

3 (cont.)

UNDERGROUND
UNDIMMED
UNHAPPINESS
UNICORNS
UNKIND
UNLIKE
UNNUMBERED
UNVESSELLED
UNWEARIED
UNWET
UPLAND
UPPER
UPRAISED
USHEEN
VEILS
VENETIAN
VESTURE
VIEW
VISAGE
VON
WAILING
WAKED
WAKEFUL
WAKES
WAND
WANE
WANING
WARMS
WARNED
WARRING
WARRIOR'S
WAR'S
WAR-WASTED
WARY
WASTED
WATCHER
WATER-BUTT
WATERFALL
WATER-HEN
WAVERING
WAVE-WHITENED
WEARIED
WEASELS
WEB
WEEKS
WELL-BELOVED
WHEELS
WHEREOF
WHIRLED
WHISPERED
WHOLLY
WILDER
WILDLY
WIND-BEATEN
WINDLESS
WINE-DARK
WINTERS
WIS
WISEST
WITCHES
WITHERS
WITHERSHINS
WITTY
WIVES
WONDERS
WORLDS

WORSHIP
WRAPT
WREATH
WRINKLED
WRINKLES
WRITINGS
WRUNG
YARD
YAWN
YEATS
YOUTHS

2
ABEAT
ABED
A-BED
ABODE
ABSURDITY
ABUNDANCE
ACCIDENT
ACCOMPLISHMENT
ACCUSING
ACHILLES
A-CROW
ADAM
ADDER'S
ADVENTURE
AENGUS'
AFFAIR
AFFAIRS
AFTERNOON
AGEING
AGELESS
A-GLEAM
AHERNE
AILED
AILELL
AILLINN'S
AILS
AIMED
ALCIBIADES
ALCOVES
ALEXANDER'S
ALIT
ALLEYS
ALLOW
AL-RASHID
ALTER
ALTERED
AMBITIOUS
AMBUSH
AMEND
AMETHYST
ANNE
ANNIVERSARY
ANOINT
ANTAEUS-LIKE
ANXIETY
APPALLED
APPAREL
APPARITION
APPEARED
APPLAUD
APPLAUSE
APPOINTMENT
APPROACHING
APRIL

ARABS
ARCADIANS
ARCHANGELS
ARCHER
ARCHERY
ARDAN
ARRANGED
ARRAYED
ARREST
ARROW'S
ARROWY
ARTICULATE
ASHES
A-SHINING
ASHWOOD
ASSURANCE
ASUNDER
ATHWART
ATLANTIC
ATMOSPHERE
A-TREMBLE
ATTEND
ATTENDANCE
AUTUMN'S
AWAKES
A-WHISPERING
BACKED
BACKWARD
BAKE
BAKED
BALLOON
BAN
BANISH
BANK
BANNER
BAR
BARKING
BARRENNESS
BARTER
BASALTIC
BASIN
BATED
BATHED
BATHING
BATTER
BAUBLE
BAYS
BEADS
BEAK
BEARDED
BEARDLESS
BEATS
BECKON
BEDDED
BEGET
BEGGAR'S
BEGGARY
BEGINNING
BEGUILE
BEINGS
BELFRY
BELIEVED
BELL-MOUNTED
BELLOWED
BELLOWS
BENCHES
BENDS

BENIGHTED
BERENICE'S
BERKELEY
BESIDES
BETIDE
BETWIXT
BIBLE
BIDDY'S
'BIDES
BIG
BINDING
BIRCH
BIRTHDAYS
BITE
BITS
BITTEN
BITTERNS
BLANCH
BLANID
BLANK
BLAZING
BLEEDING
BLENCHING
BLINDING
BLINDS
BLOOD-DARK
BLOOD-SODDEN
BLOSSOMED
BLOSSOMER
BLUES
BOAT'S
BOATS
BOBBIN
BOLE
BONY
BOOM
BORDERS
BOTTLING
BOUNTY
BOWERS
BOWL
BOWLS
BRACE
BRAID
BRAVEST
BRAZEN-GATED
BREAKING
BREATHE
BREEDS
BRIBE
BRIDE-BED
BRIDLE
BRIGHTENED
BRIMMING
BRINGING
BRINK
BROKEN-HEARTED
BROOCH
BROOK
BROWSING
BRUTE
BRYCELINDE
BUBBLE
BUCKLERS
BUILDED
BUILDING
BULBEN'S

BULK
BULOO
BUOYED
BURDENSOME
BURIAL-MOUNDS
BURNT
BUSKIN
BUST
BUTLERS
BUTT
CABIN
CAER
CAGED
CALF
CALIF'S
CALIPHS
CALVERT
CAMPING
CANDLE-LIGHT
CANN
CANNS
CAPS
CAPTAIN'S
CAPTAINS
CAPTIVES
CAPTIVES'
CAR
CAR-BORNE
CARDINAL
CAROL
CARP
CARPET
CARRYING
CARVE
CASHEL
CASKET
CASTING-NET
CATULLUS
CAVES
CEASELESSLY
CENTAURS
CEREMONIOUS
CHAIRED
CHAMBERMAID'S
CHANCED
CHANCES
CHANT
CHANTED
CHARIOT
CHATTER
CHATTERJEE
CHAUNTED
CHESS
CHESTNUTS
CHIDE
CHILDLESS
CHILLY
CHIME
CHIMED
CHINAMEN
CHINS
CHIVALRY
CHOKED
CHRISTENED
CHRONOS
CHRYSELEPHANTINE
CHRYSOPRASE

2 (cont.)

CIRCLED
CLAIMED
CLAMBER
CLAMBERING
CLAMOROUS
CLAN
CLANG
CLASH
CLAUDE
CLEANS
CLEAR-BROWED
CLEFT
CLERIC
CLEVER
CLINGETH
CLIP
CLIPPED
CLOSES
CLOSING
CLOUDLETS
CLUNG
CLUTCHES
COACH
COALS
COBWEBS
COILING
COIN
COLLAR
COLLAR-BONE
COLLOQUY
COLONUS
COLONUS'
COLOURED
COLOURS
COMBUSTIBLE
COMFORTING
COMMENTARY
COMMONNESS
COMMONPLACE
COMPANIES
COMPANIONABLE
COMPELS
COMPLAIN
COMPLETE
COMPREHENSION
CONCERNING
CONDUCT
CONFLAGRATION
CONFUSEDLY
CONSECRATED
CONSIDER
CONSIDERED
CONSOLATION
CONSTELLATIONS
CONSUMED
CONSUMING
CONTAGION
CONTINUAL
CONVICTED
CONVICTION
COOKING
COPIED
COPIES
CORNER
CORNFIELD
COST

COT
COTTAGE
COUCH
COUGH
COUNTENANCE
COUNTRYMEN
COUNTRY'S
COURTESIES
COURTIER
COURTIERS
COUSINS
COWARDICE
COWER
CRACKLE
CRASH
CRAVEN
CRAWLED
CRAWLING
CREAKING
CREATE
CREATED
CREEPERS
CREVROE
CROMLECH
CROMWELL'S
CRONE
CROOK
CRO-PATRICK
CROSIERED
CROSIERS
CROSS-GARTERED
CROUCH
CROUCHED
CROUCHES
CROUCHING
CROZIER
CRUCIFIX
CRUMB
CRUSHED
CRUTCH
CRY'S
CUBES
CUMBERED
CUMMEN
CURLS
CURRANT
CUSHIONS
CUSTOM
DAIRY
DAN
DANCE'S
DANDLED
DANES
DANGEROUS
DANTE
DAPPLED
DARING
DARKEN
DARTING
DAY-BREAK
DAZZLED
DEAFENING
DEAREST
DEATHLESS
DEATH-PALE
DECIDED
DECLINE

DECLINING
DECREED
DECREPIT
DECREPITUDE
DEDICATE
DEEP-ROOTED
DEEP-SWORN
DEFENDING
DEFORMED
DELIBERATELY
DELIRIUM
DELPHIC
DELUSIONS
DELVES
DEMAGOGUE
DEMESNE
DEMONIC
DEMON'S
DENIED
DENY
DEPTH
DERISION
DERMOT
DESCANT
DESCENDANTS
DESCENDS
DESERTED
DESERTION
DESOLATION
DESPERATE
DEVIL'S
DEVOTEE
DEW-BLANCHED
DEW-DROPPING
DEW-DROWNED
DEWS
DIALOGUE
DIMINISHED
DIMS
DINE
DIP
DIRGE
DIRT
DISCERNED
DISEMBOWELLED
DISFIGURING
DISGRACE
DISH
DISHEVELLED
DISMAY
DISPORTED
DISTRACTED
DISTRACTS
DISTRAUGHT
DISTURBS
DIVE
DIVISION
DJINN
DJINNS
DOCTOR
DOING
DOLL-MAKER'S
DOOMS
DOROTHY
DOUBLING
DOUBLY
DOUBTFUL

DOWNS
DRAGONS
DRAKE
DRAPERIES
DRASTIC
DRAWING-ROOM
DREAM-DIMMED
DREAMERS
DREAM-HEAVY
DREARY
DRIFTED
DRINKS
DRIVES
DROPT
DROWNING
DROWNS
DRUG
DRUMCLIFF
DRUNKARDS
DUCHESSES
DUCK
DUG
DUSK
DWELLER
DWINDLE
DYE
EAGER
EARLIEST
EASIER
EASTER
EATING
EBBED
EBULLIENT
ECHOES
ECSTATIC
EDDIES
EDDY
EDEN-SOD
EDMUND
EDWARD
EL
ELDER
ELDEST
ELECT
ELEMENT
ELEMENTS
EMAIN
EMAN
EMBATTLED
EMBLEM
EMBLEMATICAL
EMBOSOMED
EMBRACE
EMBROIDERIES
EMMET'S
EMPEROR
ENCHANTRESS
ENDURED
ENEMY'S
ENGLAND
ENMITY
ENORMOUS
ENQUIRE
ENTERPRISE
ENTRAILS
ENTRANCE
ENWROUGHT

EPITAPH
ESCAPED
ESERKELLY
EVER-RUSTLING
EVE'S
EXAMPLE
EXCELLENCE
EXCESS
EXERCISE
EXISTENCE
EXTREME
EXULTATION
EYED
EZEKIEL'S
FAERIES'
FAGGOTS
FAILURE
FAINTER
FAIR-HAIRED
FAMILIES
FAMISHED
FAN-FORMED
FANTASIES
FANTASTICAL
FARE
FARMER
FARMERS
FASCINATION
FASHION'S
FASTENED
FATAL
FATTENING
FEARLESS
FEATING
FEATURELESS
FEEBLER
FEELING
FENCE
FENIANS'
FERRARA
FETCH
FIELD-MOUSE
FIEND
FIFTIETH
FINGERETH
FINMOLE
FIRBOLGS'
FIRELIGHT
FIR-TREE
FISH-EATING
FISHERS'
FITZGERALD
FLAKE
FLAKED
FLAKES
FLAMINGOES
FLAPT
FLASHES
FLATTER
FLATTERY
FLEA
FLEETNESS
FLINGING
FLOATED
FLOPPING
FLUTE
FLUTED

2 (cont.)

FOAMING
FOIL
FONDLE
FONDLED
FOOT-SOLE
FOOTSTOOL
FORBID
FORCE
FORD
FOREHEADS
FOREKNOWLEDGE
FOREMOST
FORESAW
FOREVER
FORGED
FORMLESS
FORTUNE
FOSTER-MOTHER
FOUNTAINS
FOURSCORE
FOXHUNTER
FRANCE
FRENCH
FRENZIED
FRESH
FRINGED
FROSTY
FRUITFUL
FRUITS
FULLNESS
FUMBLED
FUMBLING
FURIES
FURIOUS
FURLED
GABRIEL
GAIETY
GALLOPING
GARDEN'S
GARMENTS'
GASP
GAUNT
GAZELLE
GEESE
GEM-STUDDED
GENERATION
GHASTLY
GHOST'S
GILD
GILDED
GIRDLE
GIVER
GLAMOURS
GLASNEVIN
GLASSES
GLENDALOUGH
GLITTERED
GLOOMY
GLOVE
GLOWED
GLOWING
GLOW-WORM
GLUTS
GOAD
GOATHERD
GOATS

GOBAN'S
GODLESS
GODS'
GOLD-EMBROIDERED
GOLDS
GORT
GOSPELLER
GRAINS
GRAMMAR
GRANDCHILDREN
GRAND-DAD
GRANDDAUGHTER
GRANDSON
GRANIA'S
GRASP
GRAY
GRAZE
GRAZING
GREAT-GRANDFATHER
GREAT-GRANDSON
GRECIAN
GREYNESS
GRIEF'S
GRIEFS
GRIEVOUS
GRIPPED
GROANED
GROPED
GUARDED
GUARIMOND
GUEST
GUIDO
GUINEAS
GULLS
GULPH
GUN
GUNSHOT
GYPSY
HADES'
HAILED
HALE
HALF-CLOSED
HALF-FLIES
HALF-FORGOTTEN
HALFPENNIES
HALF-PENNIES
HALF-READ
HANDLED
HANDMAID
HANDY-WORK
HANGETH
HAPPIEST
HARBOUR
HARK
HARLOT
HAROUN
HARPSTRING
HARP-STRING
HARVEST
HARVESTERS
HASSAN
HASTE
HAT
HATES
HATING

HAYNAU'S
HAZELS
HEADLONG
HEADY
HEALTHY
HEARTS'
HEAVENS'
HEAVILY
HEAVINESS
HEDGES
HEIR
HEIRS
HELEN'S
HELMETS
HELMS
HELPED
HEN
HENRY
HENS
HERBLESS
HERBS
HERD
HERESIES
HERITAGE
HERO
HEROICALLY
HERONS
HERO'S
HERRINGS
HIVES
HOARD
HOARDED
HOLES
HOLIDAY
HOLLO
HOMER'S
HONEYCOMB
HOOK
HOOKS
HORIZON
HORIZON'S
HORN'S
HORSE-BOYS
HOWL
HUES
HUGER
HUGS
HULL
HUM
HUMBLY
HUMILITY
HUMMING
HUMOROUS
HURLEY
HURTING
HURTS
HYSTERICA
HYSTERICAL
IDIOT
IDLENESS
IDLING
IGNOBLE
IGNOMINY
ILL-BRED
ILLNESS
IMAGED
IMAGINABLE

IMAGING
IMITATORS
IMMEDICABLE
IMMENSE
IMMODERATE
IMMORAL
IMPATIENTLY
IMPORTUNE
IMPROVE
IMPURE
INANIMATE
INARTICULATE
INDIA
INDOLENT
INFANCY
INFANT
INFERIOR
INFINITE
INHERIT
INHERITED
INHERITOR
INHUMAN
INNER
INNOCENTS
INSEPARABLY
INSIDE
INSULT
INTENSITY
INTERCOURSE
INTEREST
INVISIBLE
INWROUGHT
ISLE'S
IVY
JABBER
JAGS
JAMES
JAWS
JEALOUSY
JERK
JERRY
JEW
JOHNSON
JONATHAN
JONSON'S
JOURNALIST
JOURNEYED
JOURNEY'S
JOY'S
JUGGLERIES
JUGGLING
JULIET
KAMA
KANVA
KATE
KATHLEEN-NY-HOOLIHAN
KEEPER
KEVIN
KEY
KICKED
KILTARTAN
KILVARNET
KIMONOS
KINSMEN
KITE
KITH

KNEAD
KNEADED
KNEELS
KNIFE
KNIGHTS
KNIT
KNOCKED
KNOCKFEFIN
KNOT-GRASS
KNOTTED
LABAN
LABOURS
LACKS
LAMB'S
LAMENTATION
LANCELOT
LANDSMAN
LANDWARD
LAPPED
LARGER
LATELY
LATEST
LATIN
LAUGHS
LAYER
LEAF-SOWN
LEATHERN
LEBEEN-LONE
LECHER
LECHEROUS
LEDAEAN
LEDGE
LEGEND
LEISURED
LEMON
LENDS
LEOPARD
LETS
LEVELLING
LIME-TREE
LIMPS
LINEAGE
LINGERS
LINNET
LIONESS
LIONS
LISSADELL
LISTENED
LITERATURE
LIVELONG
LIVE-LONG
LIVERY
LOCKED
LOFTIER
LOG
LONG-FORGOTTEN
LOOM
LOOPHOLE
LORDS
LORE
LOUDER
LOUDLY
LOUGH
LOUGHLAN
LOVELIER
LOVELIEST
LOVERS'

951

2 (cont.)

TARA'S
TASTING
TAVERN
TAWS
TEACHERS
TEARFUL
TELLING
TEMPT
TENDEREST
TENDING
TENTED
TENTH
TENT'S
TERRORS
TERROR-
  STRICKEN
TERROR-STRUCK
TESTS
TETHER
THANKFUL
THEATRE
THEMES
THICK
THICKET
THIEVING
THORN-TREE
THOROUGHBRED
THOROUGHFARE
THOUGHT-
  WOVEN
THRANEEN
THREADBARE
THREATENED
THREES
THROATED
THROB
THRONGS
THUMB
THUNDER-
  SOUND
THURIBLES
TIDES
TILLAGE
TIMBER
TINKER
TIP-TOE
TOE
TOILING
TOILS
TOLERANCE
TOMB-HAUNTER
TOMBSTONE
TONSURED
TOPLESS
TOPMOST
TORCHLIGHT
TORCH-LIGHT
TRADING
TRAILING
TRAMPING
TRANSFORM
TRAPPED
TRAVELLERS
TRAVELLING-
  MAN
TRAVELS

TREACHERY
TREASURER
TREASURES
TREATISE
TREMBLED
TREMENDOUS
TREMULOUS
TRIMMED
TRIPLE
TRITON
TRIUMPHING
TROIA
TROLLED
TROMBONE
TROOPER
TROOPS
TROW
TRUMP
TUMBLES
TUMULTS
TUNNELLED
TURBULENCE
TURBULENT
TURKISH
'TWEEN
TWELFTH
TWELVEMONTH
TWENTY-AND-
  EIGHT
TWIGS
TWILIGHTS
TWINKLING
TWITTER
TWOS
TYING
UNAMBITIOUS
UNBIND
UNBOUND
UNCERTAINTY
UNCOMELY
UNCONQUER-
  ABLE
UNDERSTANDS
UNEARTHLY
UNEASY
UNFINISHED
UNFORGIVING
UNFRIENDLY
UNGUENTS
UNHOOK
UNICORN
UNLOOSED
UNREMEMBERING
UNSAY
UNSLEEPING
UNTOLD
UNTROUBLED
UNWIELDY
UNWITHERING
UNWOUND
UPLIFTED
UPROOT
UPS
UPSTAIRS
UPSTANDING
URBINO
URGED

USELESS
UTMOST
UTTERING
VALERA
VALLEY'S
VALUE
VAN
VANISHES
VEERING
VELVET
VERGE
VERSES
VEX
VICTOR
VIGOUR
VIRGINITY
VIRTUE
VIRTUES
VIVID
VOLUME
VOWS
WADE
WAGES
WAKENED
WANDS
WANTON
W'ARES
WARFARE
WARMTH
WASH
WASHED
WATCHERS
WATCHES
WATER-FOWLS
WATER-SIDE
WAVERED
WAVERINGS
WEAKLY
WEASEL
WEASEL'S
WEATHER-WORN
WEBBED
WEB-HEAPED
WEBS
WEED
WEIGHED
WEIGHS
WEIGHTY
WEIR
WELCOMED
WELL-BELOVED'S
WELL-NIGH
WELLS
WENCH
WENCHING
WHIMSEY
WHIP
WHIPS
WHISPERS
WHIT
WHITE-HAIRED
WILDERING
WILLINGLY
WILLS
WILSON
WINDING-SHEET
WINE-CUP

WIRE
WIRES
WISDOM'S
WISDOMS
WISER
WISTFUL
WITCHCRAFT
WITHHOLD
WIVE
WOLD
WOLFE
WOOD-CUTTER
WOODED
WOODLANDS
WORDY
WORKED
WORKING
WORKING-
  CARPENTER
WORLD-FAMOUS
WRAPPING
WRAPS
WRATH
WREATHS
WRESTLE
WRETCH
WRINKLING
WRITING
WRONGS
WROTH
YARDS
YAWNED
YEA
YEW-BOUGH

1

ABBOT
ABD
ABD-AL-RABBAN
ABIDES
ABLOW
A-BLOWIN'
ABOLISHED
ABROAD
ABSENT
ABSOLVO
ABSTINENCE
ABSURD
ABYSS
ACACIA
ACADEMY
ACCEPT
ACCEPTED
ACCIDENTAL
ACCIDENTS
ACCLAIMING
ACCOMPLISH
ACCOUNT
ACCOUNTED
ACCUSATION
ACCUSE
ACH
ACHAIANS'
ACKNOWLEDGE
ACORNS
ACQUAINTANCE
ACROPOLIS

ACTION'S
ACTOR
ACTORS
ACTUAL
A-CURSED
ADDERS
ADDING
ADDRESSED
ADMIRED
ADMIRING
ADMONISH
ADOLESCENCE
ADORE
ADORES
ADRIFT
ADRIP
ADVANCE
ADVERSITY
AEROPLANE
AERY
AFFABLE
AFFECTION
AFFECTIONS
AFFIRMS
AFFLICT
A-FISHING
A-FLAME
AFLASH
A-FLASH
A-FLICKER
AFLOAT
A-FLUTTERING
AFOOT
AFORETIME
AFRICA
AFRICAN
AFTERWARDS
AGAMEMNON
AGATE
AGE'S
AGHAST
AGILE
AGIN
AGLEAM
A-GLITTER
AGREE
AGREED
A-HAWKING
AHEAD
AI
AIBHLIN
AIBRIC'S
AID
AILING
AIMLESSNESS
AIR-BREATH
AIRMAN
AKIN
ALARM
ALARMED
ALARUMS
ALBAN
ALCOVE'S
ALE-HORNS
ALEXANDER
ALEXANDRIA'S
ALHAMBRA

1 (cont.)
ALIENS
ALIGHIERI
ALIGHTED
ALIKE
A-LIT
ALLAH
ALL-DESTROYING
ALLEGORICAL
ALLEN'S
ALLIANCES
ALL-LABOURING
ALLOWS
ALL-POWERFUL
ALL-UNNEEDED
ALMANACS
ALMHUIN
ALMHUIN'S
ALPUJARRAS
AL-RABBAN
AL-RASCHID
ALT
ALTAR-PIECE
ALTAR-RAILS
ALTERNATIVE
ALTERS
ALTOGETHER
AMAZED
AMBASSADOR
AMBASSADORS
AMBERGRIS
AMBERS
AMBITIONS
AMBLING
AMBUSCADE
AMENDED
AMERGIN
AMERICAN
AMPLE
A-MURMUR
ANALYTIC
ANARCHY
ANBUAL'S
ANCESTOR
ANCESTORS
ANEMONES
ANGELO'S
ANIGH
ANIMAL'S
ANIMALS
ANIMALS'
ANKLES
ANNOTATE
ANNOUNCES
ANNUS
ANODYNE
ANOINTING
ANON
ANTELOPE
ANTELOPES
ANTHONY
ANTIGONE
ANTINOMIES
ANTIQUARIAN
ANTI-SELF
ANTLERS
ANXIOUS

ANYBODY
ANYWHERE
AOIBHIN
AOIFE
AOLAN
APHORISMS
A-PILIN'
APOLOGIA
APPLE-BOUGHS
APPLE-STEM
APPOINTED
APPROVE
APRIL'S
A-QUAKE
AQUILINE
ARABIA'S
ARBITER
ARCADIA
ARCADIA'S
ARCHANGEL
ARCHBISHOP
ARCHED
ARCHES
ARCHIMEDES'
ARCHITECT
ARGIVE
ARGO'S
ARGOSY
ARGUE
ARGUED
ARISEN
ARISTOTLE
ARMCHAIR
ARMIES'
ARMLETS
ARMOURED
ARM'S
ARMSTRONG
A-ROVING
ARRAIGNED
ARROGANCE
ARROGANTLY
ARTERY
ARTICULATION
ARTIFICE
ARTISSON
ARTIST'S
ARTISTS
ASCENDS
ASCENT
A-SHAKE
ASHEN
ASHORE
ASH-TREES'
ASH-WOOD
ASIATIC
ASLAUGA
ASS
ASSAILS
ASSAULT
ASS-BACK
ASSES
ASSIZE
ASS'S
ASSUAGE
ASTONISHING
ASTONISHMENT

ASTRADDLE
A-TELLING
ATHEIST
ATHENE'S
ATHENIAN
ATLAS
ATTEMPTED
ATTENDANT
ATTENDANTS
ATTIS'
ATTORNEY
AUGHT
AUGUSTUS
AUNTS
AUREOLE
AUSTERITY
AUSTRIAN
AUTHOR
AUTHORITY
AUTHORS
AVAIL
AVAILS
AVALANCHE
AVALLON
AVE
AVENGED
AVENGING
AVOW
AWAITING
AWARDED
AWARE
A-WAVING
A-WEARY
A-WEAVING
AWELESS
AWFUL
A-WINGING
AXEL
AXES
AXLE
A-YEAR
AZOLAR
AZURES
BABAR
BABYLON'S
BACCHANT
BACHELOR
BACKGROUNDS
BACKS
BACKWARDS
BADGERED
BAFFLED
BAGPIPES
BAILE'S
BALANCE
BALES
BALLAD-SINGER
BALLINAFAD
BALLS
BANDAGING
BANDIT
BANDY
BANDY-LEGGED
BANKERS
BANKRUPT
BANNERET
BANSHEE

BARACH
BARB
BARBS
BARCELONA
BARHAIM
BARNACLE
BARNACLE-GEESE
BARREL-HOOPS
BARRELS
BARRICADE
BARROW
BARROWS
BARTERED
BASALT
BASE-BORN
BASKETS
BAT
BATHE
BATTERING
BATTERY
BATTLE-AXE
BATTLE-AXES
BATTLE-BANNERS
BATTLE-
  BREAKING
BATTLE-HOST
BATTLEMENT
BATTLEMENTS
BATTLE-WEARY
BATTLING
BAWDY
BAWLS
BAWN
BEACON
BEAN
BEANFEAST
BEANFEST
BEAN-ROWS
BEARDS
BEASTS
BEAST-TORN
BEAUJOLET
BEAUTY-
  DRUNKEN
BEAUVARLET
BECK
BECKONED
BECKONING
BECKONS
BEDFELLOW
BEDOUIN
BEDSTEAD
BEECH-BOLE
BEECH-BOUGH
BEECHEN
BEECH-LEAVES
BEECH-TREE
BEECH-TREES
BEE-LOUD
BEERY
BEE'S
BEES'
BEETLES
BEFIT
BEFITTING
BEG
BEGETTER

BEGGAR-KINGS
BEGGARLY
BEGGARMAN
BEGGARS'
BEGONE
BELABOURING
BELIEF
BELIEVING
BELL-BEAT
BELLED
BELLIES
BELL-NOTES
BELLOW
BELLYFUL
BELONG
BELONGS
BELOVED'S
BELOVEDS
BELT
BEMOCKERS
BE-MOCKERS
BENDED
BERA
BEREFT
BESEECH
BESET
BESOM
BESOT
BESOTTED
BESOTTING
BEST-ENDOWED
BESTIAL
BESTIR
BEST'S
BETAKE
BETHLEHEM
BETRAY
BETTERS
BEWILDER
BEWILDERMENT
BEWITCHED
BEWITCHMENT
BIDDEN
BIDDY
BIER
BIGOT
BILLOWS
BINDS
BIRCH-TREE
BIRD-CLAWS
BIRD-LIKE
BIRDLY
BIRDS'
BIRTHDAY
BIRTH-HOUR
BISCAY
BISHOPS
BITING
BITTERER
BITTEREST
BITTERN
BITTER-SWEET
BITTER-
  SWEETNESS
BLACKBIRDS
BLACKENS
BLACKER

1 (cont.)
BLADDERED
BLANAID
BLANCHED
BLAND
BLASPHEMOUS
BLASTED
BLASTS
BLAZED
BLEAK
BLEAR-EYED
BLEATING
BLEED
BLEMISH
BLENCH
BLENDING
BLENT
BLESSINGS
BLINDER
BLITHER
BLOCKS
BLONDE
BLOOD-BEGOTTEN
BLOOD-DIMMED
BLOODLESS
BLOOD-RED
BLOOD-
 SATURATED
BLOTCH
BLOTS
BLOWIN'
BLUE-GREEN
BLUER
BLUE-VEINED
BLUSHED
BLUSHES
BOARDED
BOASTING
BOASTS
BOATMAN
BOB
BODES
BODICES
BODIED
BODKIN
BOG
BOG'S
BOILED
BOILING
BOISTEROUS
BOLTS
BOMB-BALLS
BOOTS
BORDA
BOREAL
BOREDOM
BOREEN
BORROW
BOSKY
BOTTLES
BOUNTIFUL
BOWELS
BOW-LEGGED
BOW-STRING'S
BOWSTRINGS
BOX-BORDERED
BOYNE

BRACKISH
BRAHMIN
BRAINS
BRAKE
BRANCHING
BRAND
BRAND-NEW
BRANWEN
BRATTA
BRATTAS
BRAVED
BRAVELY
BRAY
BRAYED
BREAKERS
BREATHES
BREECHED
BREEZES
BRESSEL
BRETHREN
BREWS
BRIAR
BRIDEGROOM
BRIDE-GROOM
BRIDEGROOM'S
BRIDELESS
BRIDE'S
BRIDLED
BRIDLE-PATH
BRIGAND
BRIGHTEN
BRIGHTER
BRIGHT-EYED
BRIMFUL
BRISTLES
BRITAIN
BRITISH
BRITTLE
BROACHED
BROKENHEARTED
BRONZED
BRONZE-RINGED
BROODED
BROOM
BROOM-STICKS
BROTHER'S
BROWED
BROWNING
BROWSE
BROW-SHADING
BRUISE
BRUISED
BRUISING
BRUSHED
BRUSHES
BRUSHING
BUAL'S
BUAN'S
BUBBLED
BUCKET
BUCKLED
BUCKSKIN
BUD
BUDDHA
BUDDHA'S
BUDDING
BUDS

BUFFETED
BUGLE
BUILDER
BUILDINGS
BUILDING-YARD
BUILDS
BULLETS
BULLO
BUM
BUNCH
BUNCHES
BUNCHING
BURDENED
BURGHERS
BURIAL-MOUND
BURKE'S
BURROW
BURROWING
BURSTS
BURY
BUSH
BUSTLE
BUTLER
BUTTED
BUTT-END
BUTTERMILK
BUTTING
BUYING
BYRE
BYRNE
BYRNES
CABBAGE
CABBAGES
CABINS
CAESARS
CAGES
CAIRN-HEAPED
CAIRN'S
CAKE
CALCULATION
CALCULATIONS
CALENDARS
CALIPH'S
CALLED'ST
CALLEN
CALLIMACHUS
CALUMNY
CALVARY'S
CAMEL
CAMEL-BACK
CAMEL-DUNG
CAMEL'S
CAMP-FIRE
CAMPING-PLACE
CAMP'S
CANDLE-LIKE
CANDLE'S
CANDLESTICK
CANKER-WORM
CANNONADE
CANNON-SHOT
CANTERED
CAPTIVE'S
CARD
CARGO
CARHEADS
CARICATURE

CARROT
CART-HORSE
CASTAWAYS
CAST-A-WAYS
CASTLE'S
CATALPA
CATALPA-TREE
CATCH-CRIES
CATCHES
CATCHING
CAT-HEADED
CATHEDRAL
CAT-O'-NINE-
 TAILS
CATTLE-BIRDS
CAULDRON
CAVE-MOUTH
CAVERNED
CAVERN-GLOOMS
CAVERNS
CAVE'S
CEDAR
CEDAR-BOARDED
CEILING
CELEBRANT
CELEBRATE
CELL
CELTIC
CENTRES
CEPHISUS
CEREMONIAL
CEREMONY'S
CHAFF
CHAINED
CHAINS
CHAMBERS
CHANCELLOR
CHANGERS
CHANNELS
CHANTING
CHANTS
CHARGERS
CHARIOT-WHEELS
CHARLEMAGNE
CHARTER
CHASTITY
CHAT
CHAUCER
CHAUNTING
CHEATED
CHECKED
CHEERS
CHEESE
CHERRIES
CHERRY
CHERRY-BRANCH
CHERUBIM
CHESHIRE
CHESSBOARDS
CHESTNUT
CHESTNUT-TREE
CHIEFLY
CHIEFS
CHIEFTAINS
CHILD-BEARING
CHILLING
CHILLS

CHIMAERAS
CHIMES
CHINESE
CHIRP
CHOIRS
CHOKE
CHOOSES
CHOOSING
CHOPPERS
CHORUS
CHOU
CHRISTENDOM
CHRISTMAS
CHRISTMAS-TREE
CHRONICLER
CHRONICLERS
CHRONICLING
CHUBBY
CHURCHMEN
CHURCH'S
CHURCHYARD
CICERO
CIDER
CINCTURE
CINNAMON
CIPHER
CISTERN
CIVILISATION
CIVILISATIONS
CIVILIZATION
CLAMOUR-
 CLOTHED
CLANKING
CLANN
CLAPPED
CLARE
CLARE-GALWAY
CLARIONET
CLASPING
CLATTER
CLAY-COLD
CLAY-PILED
CLEANING
CLEANLY
CLEAN-SWEPT
CLEARED
CLEARLY
CLEAR-SHINING
CLENCHED
CLERGYMEN
CLERICS
CLERK
CLIFF-ENCIRCLED
CLIFF-SHELTERED
CLOAKS
CLOGGED
CLOONE
CLOSE-CROPPED
CLOTHING
CLOUDLESS
CLOUD-O'ER-
 MUFFLED
CLUB
CLUMSINESS
CLUSTERING
CLUSTERS
CLYTEMNESTRA

1 (cont.)

COAGULATE
COAL-BLACK
COARSE-BRED
COARSENESS
COAST
COCK-A-DOODLE-
  DOODLE-DO
COCK'S
CODGERS
COGENT
COGNOMEN
COILS
COLA'S
COLDER
COLIN
COLLEENS
COLLEGE
COLONIES
COLOONEY
COLOONY
COLT
COLTSFOOT
COMB
COMBS
COMEDIAN'S
COMEDIES
COMEDY
COMER
COMEST
COMETH
COMFORTERS
COMMANDED
COMMANDING
COMMENCED
COMMENDED
COMMINGLING
COMMIT
COMMITTED
COMMONEST
COMMUNE
COMMUNIST
COMPANIONED
COMPANIONING
COMPANIONSHIP
COMPANION-
  SHIPS
COMPARES
COMPASS
COMPASS-POINT
COMPEL
COMPELLING
COMPENSATION
COMPETE
COMPLACENCY
COMPLAINED
COMPLAINING
COMPLETED
COMPLETENESS
COMPLETES
COMPLEXION
COMPLEXITY
COMPLIMENT
COMPOSE
COMPOUNDED
COMRADE
CON

CONAN'S
CONCEIVE
CONCEIVED
CONCEIVES
CONCENTRATION
CONCH
CONCHUBAR'S
CONCOBAR
CONDEMNED
CONES
CONEYS
CONFER
CONFESS
CONFRONTING
CONGEALED
CONHOR
CONJUNCTIONS
CONNACHT
CONOR
CONQUER
CONQUERED
CONQUEROR
CONQUERORS
CONQUEST
CONSCIENCE-
  STRUCK
CONSIDERATION
CONSIDERS
CONSPIRACY
CONSPIRING
CONSTITUTE
CONSTRAINED
CONSTRUCTED
CONSUMES
CONSUMMATION
CONTEMPLATING
CONTEMPLATIONS
CONTEMPLATIVE
CONTEND
CONTEST
CONTRADICT
CONTRAPUNTAL
CONTROL
CONVENT
CONVENTIONAL
CONVERGE
CONVINCE
COOING
COPSE
COPULATE
COQUETRY
CORAL
CORBETS
CORD
CORDELIA
CORMAC'S
CORMORANTS
CORRIDOR
COSGRAVE
COSIMO
COSSETING
COUNCIL
COUNCILS
COUNSELLED
COUNSELS
COUNTENANCES
COUNTER

COUNTER-TRUTH
COUNTING-HOUSE
COUNTLESS
COUNTRYSIDE
COUNTRY-SIDE
COUNTY
COUPLED
COURAGEOUS
COURT-LADIES'
COURT-LADY'S
COVERLET'S
COVERLID
COWARD
COWARDLY
COWARDS
COWERED
COY
COZENING
CRABBED
CRACKING
CRACKLING
CRACK-PATED
CRADLED
CRADLE-HOOD
CRADLE-SIDE
CRAM
CRAMM'D
CRAMMED
CRANBERRY
CRAOIBHIN
CRASHED
CRASHING
CRAVE
CRAVING
CREAKY
CREAMY
CREASES
CREATION
CRESTED
CRETAN
CREVICED
CREVICES
CRICKETS
CRIETH
CRIME'S
CRITIC
CRITICS
CROACH
CROCUS
CROMWELL
CROON
CROONING
CROP
CROPS
CROSS'D
CROSSES
CROSSING
CROWNLESS
CRUCIFIED
CRUELTIES
CRUISE
CRUMBLED
CRUMPLE
CRUMPLED
CRUNCHES
CRUSH
CRUST

CRYSTALLINE
CU
CUB
CUBS
CUCHULIN
CUFF
CUMANN'S
CUMBROUS
CUPBOARDS
CUR
CURD-PALE
CURED
CURRANT-BUSHES
CURSES
CURTAINED
CURTAINS
CURVING
CUSHLA
CUSTOMARY
CUSTOMS
CUT-THROAT
CUTTING
DA
DABBLE
DABBLED
DADDY-LONG-
  LEGS
DAEMONS
DAFFODIL
DAISY
DALLIANCE
DAMAGES
DAMNED
DAMP
DAMPED
DAMS
DANCE-LIKE
DANCING-PLACE
DANE
DANGLING
DANISH
DAPHNE
DARGAN'S
DARK-BEAKED
DARKENED
DARKER
DARKEST
DASHED
DATELESS
DAVIS
DAWNS
DAWN-SONG
DAWS
DAYLIGHT-
  DARKENING
DAY-LONG
DAYSPRING
DAZZLING
DEADLY
DEAFENED
DEAFENS
DEAFER
DEAN
DEARTH
DEATHBED
DEATHBEDS
DEATH-BEDS

DEATHFUL
DEATH-HOUR
DEATH-IN-LIFE
DEATH-LONGING
DEATH-MAKING
DEATH-POURING
DEATHS
DECAYETH
DECEITLESS
DECEIVE
DECENT
DECIDE
DECKED
DECLAIMING
DECLENSION
DECLIVITIES
DECREES
DEED-DOER
DEED-DOERS
DEEM
DEEPENED
DEEPENING
DEEP-EYED
DEEP-SUNKEN
DEER-HOUNDS
DEFAMED
DEFENCE
DEFILE
DEFILED
DEFILING
DEFINITIONS
DEGREES
DEIGN
DEIRDRE'S
DEITIES
DEJECTION
DELACROIX
DELIBERATE
DELICATE-
  STEPPING
DELIGHTFUL
DELIGHTING
DELIVER
DELIVERANCE
DELIVERED
DELIVERER
DELLS
DELUSION
DEMONIAC
DEMONSTRATE
DENIS
DENOUNCES
DENT
DENYING
DEPARTING
DERG'S
DERIDING
DERMUID
DESCEND
DESERT-CAVES
DESIGN
DESIGNED
DESISTED
DESTINY
DESTROYS
DEVILISH
DEVILS

956

1 (cont.)

EYE'S
EYES'
EYESIGHT
EYNE
FABLE
FABRIC
FACED
FACING
FACT
FACTION
FADETH
FAERYLAND
FAERY'S
FAGGOT
FAILED
FAILS
FAIN
FAIRIES'
FAIRS
FAIRY-HAUNTED
FAIRYLAND
FAIRY'S
FAIRY-SMITTEN
FAITHFULLEST
FAITHLESS
FALIAS
FALSTAFFAN
FALSTAFFIAN
FALTER
FALTERS
FAMED
FAMISH
FANATICISM
FANCIES
FANCY-MAN
FANNED
FAR-AWAY
FARISTAH
FARMHOUSE
FARM-WORK
FARRELL
FARROW
FARTHEST
FAR-WANDERING
FASTED
FASTEN
FATED
FATHERLESS
FATHOMLESS
FATNESS
FATTER
FAVOURED
FAVOURITE
FEACRA
FEATHER-BED
FECUND
FEE
FEEBLY
FEELS
FELLOW-ARTIST
FELLOW-
  ROYSTERER
FELLOW-STUDENT
FELLOW-
  WANDERER

FENCED
FERGUSON
FERTILE
FERVOUR
FETLOCKS
FEVER-FREE
FEVERISH
FIBROUS
FIDDLE-BOW
FIDDLERS
FIDDLE'S
FIDDLES
FIDDLE-STICK
FIDDLE-STRING
FIELDS'
FIERCELY
FIFTEENTH
FIGHTING-MEN
FIGURATIVE
FINDRIAS
FINEST
FINGER'S
FINGERS'
FINGER-TIP
FINVARRA
FIRE-BORN
FIRED
FIRELIT
FIREPLACE
FIRE-PLACE
FIRE'S
FIRM
FIRST-BORN
FIRWOOD
FISHER-LADS
FISHERMEN
FISHER'S
FISHES
FISHES'
FISHING-LINES
FISHLIKE
FISH'S
FISH-TAIL
FITS
FITTER
FIVE-AND-TWENTY
FIVE-SIX
FLAGELLANT
FLAGON
FLAGONS
FLAGSTONE
FLAME-
  BEWILDERED
FLAMED
FLAME-LIKE
FLAMINGO
FLANK
FLAP
FLASHIER
FLATTERER
FLATTERIES
FLATTERING
FLAVOUR
FLAVOURED
FLAX
FLEEING

FLEETER
FLICKED
FLICKERED
FLICKERS
FLIETH
FLITTING
FLOATING-HAIRED
FLOODS
FLOOD-TIME
FLORENCE
FLOURISH
FLOURISHES
FLOURISHING
FLOUT
FLOWERED
FLOWERS'
FLUSH
FLUSHED
FLUSHES
FLUTES
FLUTINGS
FLUTTERS
FLY-CATCHERS
FLY-FISHER'S
FOAL
FOAMDROP
FOAMDROPS
FOAM-FICKLE
FOAM-FLAKES
FOAM-GLOBES
FOAM-OOZY
FOAM-PALE
FOAM-WHITE
FOE
FOEMAN'S
FOEMEN
FOEMEN'S
FOG
FOG-DRIPPING
FOILED
FOLKS
FOLKS'
FOLLOWERS
FOND
FONDER
FOOL-DRIVEN
FOOLED
FOOL'S
FOOT'S
FOOTSORE
FOOTWORN
FOOT-WORN
FORAY
FORBADE
FORBIDDEN
FOREBEAR
FOREFATHERS
FOREGATHER
FOREGO
FORESEES
FOREST'S
FORGAIL'S
FORGATHERED
FORGE
FORGER
FORGIVING

FORGO
FORMATION
FORSAKE
FORSAKEN
FORSWEAR
FORSWEARS
FORTIETH
FORTUNE'S
FORTUNE-TELLER
FORTY-NINE
FOSTER-MOTHER'S
FOUNDATION
FOUNDATIONS
FOUNDED
FOUNDERS
FOUNT
FOUNTAIN'S
FOUNTS
FOURS
FOUR-SCORE
FOUR-SIX
FOURTEEN
FOURTEENTH
FOXGLOVE
FOX-GLOVE
FOXHOUNDS
FOX-HUNTER
FRAGILE
FRAGMENT
FRAGRANCES
FRANKINCENSE
FRAY
FRECKLED
FREED
FREELANDS
FREEMAN
FRENZIES
FRESHET
FRETFUL
FRIENDLIER
FRIENDS'
FRIGHTED
FRIGID
FROG
FROG-SPAWN
FROLIC
FROTH-DROP
FROTH-LIPS
FROTH-SPLASHED
FROTHY
FROZE
FRUITAGE
FULLER'S
FULL-FLAVOURED
FUMBLE
FUME
FUNDS
FUNEREAL
FURNITURE
FURR'D
FURTHEST
FURZE
GABHRA'S
GABY'S
GAFFER
GAINSAY

GALILEAN
GALILEE
GALLERIED
GALLERIES
GALLIVANTING
GAMBLER
GAMEBIRD
GAME-BIRD
GANGLING
GANNET
GANNETS
GAPE
GARDEN-BOY
GARLANDED
GARMENT'S
GARMENTS
GARNERED
GARRET
GARRULOUS
GASPED
GASPING
'GAT
GAUGE
GAVEST
GAVRA
GAVRA'S
GAYEST
GAZEBO
GENERAL
GENERATED
GENEROSITY
GENEROUS
GENII
GENTLEMAN
GENTLER
GEOMETRY
GEORGIAN
GER-EAGLE
GERMAN
GERMANY'S
GETTING
GHOST-FLAMES
GHOST-LOVER
GIANT
GIANTS
GIBE
GIER-EAGLE
GIFTED
GIFTS
GIGANTIC
GILLYFLOWER
GIMLET
GIORGIONE
GIRLHOOD'S
GIRLS'
GIST
GIVETH
GLADDENED
GLADLY
GLAMOURED
GLANCED
GLASS-MOSAIC
GLAZING
GLEN-CAR
GLIDE
GLIDING

1 (cont.)

GLISTEN
GLISTENING
GLITTER
GLITTERS
GLOBE-TROTTING
GLOOMED
GLORIES
GLORIFIED
GLORIOUS
GLOSSES
GLOWS
GLUED
GNASHING
GOAT-HEAD
GOATHERDS
GOAT'S
GOATS'
GOBAN'D
GOBLINS
GOD-APPOINTED
GODDESS
GOD-FORSAKEN
GOD-HATED
GOD-KIND
GOIN'
GOING-DOWN
GOLDEN-CRESTED
GOLDEN-THIGHED
GOLDFISH
GOLD-FISH
GOLD-SEWN
GOLD-SHOD
GOLDSMITHS
GOLD-SOWN
GOLL
GONG-
  TORMENTED
GONNE
GOODMAN
GOODNESS
GOODNIGHT
GOODS
GOOD-WILL
GORE-BOOTH
GORIAS
GORSE
GOSPELLERS'
GOVERNED
GRADUAL
GRAND
GRANDAM
GRAND-CHILDREN
GRANDEST
GRANDFATHER'S
GRANDFATHERS
GRANIA
GRANTED
GRAPE-CLUSTER
GRAPES
GRASS-BARNACLE
GRASS-BLADES
GRASS-BLADES'
GRASS-COLOURED
GRASS-LEAF
GRASS-YELLOW
GRATED

GRATTAN
GRATTAN'S
GRAVE-DIGGERS
GRAVE-DIGGERS'
GRAVE-EYED
GRAVEL
GRAVELLED
GRAVITY
GRAZED
GREASE
GREASY
GREAT-AUNTS
GREAT-
  BLADDERED
GREAT-BODIED
GREAT-
  GRANDCHILDREN
GREAT-
  GRANDDAD
GREAT-
  GRANDFATHERS
GREAT-LIMBED
GREAT-ROOTED
GREAT-UNCLES
GREEDY
GREEKS
GREENISH
GREEN-PATED
GREY-EYED
GREY-GREEN
GREY-HAIRED
GRIDDLE
GRIDDLE-CAKE
GRIEF-
  DISTRAUGHT
GRIEVED
GRIEVES
GRIEVING
GRIFFITH
GRIMALKIN
GRINDING
GRIP
GRIPS
GRISLY
GROSS
GROUND-IVY'S
GROUNDS
GROUSE
GROWETH
GRUBS
GRUMBLE
GRUNT
GRUNTING
GUARD-HOUSE
GUARDIAN
GUARDLESS
GUARDS
GUARDSMEN'S
GUESS
GUIDE
GUIDED
GUIDOBALDO
GUILTY
GUINEVERE
GULLEON'S
GUNNEL
GUSHES

GUSHING
GUST
GUTTER
GUTTERS
GYMNASTS'
HABILIMENT
HABITS
HABITUAL
HACK
HADES
HAG
HAIR-DYE
HALF-AWAKENED
HALF-DEAD
HALF-DECEIT
HALF-DONE
HALF-DRUNK
HALF-HOUR'S
HALF-IMAGINED
HALF-LEGENDARY
HALF-LEGGED
HALF-LIGHT
HALF-LOST
HALF-LYING
HALF-MOUNTED
HALFPENCE
HALFPENNY
HALF-WAKENING
HALFWAY
HALF-WAY
HALF-WRITTEN
HALLOWED
HALT
HALVE
HALVED
HANDLE
HANDLES
HANDMAIDS
HAND'S
HANDSOMEST
HANGMAN'S
HANRAHAN'S
HAPPEN
HAPPENED
HAPPIER-
  THOUGHTED
HAPPILY
HARDEST
HARDIHOOD
HARD-LIVING
HARD-RIDING
HARE'S
HARM
HARMLESS
HARMONIC
HARMONY
HARNESS
HARPER
HARPING
HARPS
HARRIERS
HARROW
HARSHNESS
HART
HARVEST'S
HARVEST-TIME
HASTY

HATCHES
HATER
HATS
HAUGHTIER-
  HEADED
HAUNTED
HAUNTS
HAWKS
HAY-COCK
HAYMOUSE
HAYSTACK
HAZEL-TREE
HAZEL-TREES
HEADED
HEAPED-UP
HEARD'ST
HEARKEN
HEARTACHE
HEART-BREAK
HEARTBURN
HEARTED
HEARTIER
HEARTIEST
HEART-MYSTERIES
HEART-REVEALING
HEART-SMITTEN
HEART-STRINGS
HEARTY
HEAVE
HEAVES
HEAVIER
HEAVIEST
HEAVILY-BUILT
HEBER'S
HEEDS
HEIGHTS
HELICON
HELL'S
HELMET
HELMSMAN'S
HELPER
HELPFUL
HENWIVES
HERALD'S
HERDED
HERDING
HERDSMEN
HERESY
HERMIT
HERODIAS'
HEROES'
HERRING
HESITATE
HIBERNIAN
HIBERNIANS
HIERARCHY
HIGHEST
HIGH-HORSE
HIGHLAND
HIGH-PITCHED
HIGHWAY
HILL-HEADS
HILL'S
HILLSIDE
HILL-SIDE
HIMALAY
HISS

HISSING
HISSOP-HEAVY
HISTORIANS
HISTORIC
HISTORIED
HISTORY'S
HITCHED
HOARDS
HOARIEST
HOARSER
HOB
HOISTING
HOLIDAYS
HOLLIES
HOLLOW-CHEEKED
HOMEBREW
HOME-BREW
HOMES
HOMESTEAD
HOMEWARDS
HONEST
HONESTY
HONEY-BEE
HONEY-
  COLOURED
HONEY-COMB
HONEYED
HONEY-HEART
HONEY-HEARTED
HONEY-MARTS
HONEY-PALE
HONEY-POT
HONEY-SWEET
HONEY-
  THICKENED
HONIED
HONOURED
HOOPED
HORACE
HORDE
HORNED
HORSE-BACK
HORSED
HORSEHAIR
HORSE-HAIR
HORSE-HOOF
HORSE-PLAY
HORSES'
HORTON'S
HOSE
HOSTED
HOSTS
HOUR-GLASS
HOURLY
HOUR'S
HOVERS
HOWEVER
HOWLING
HOWLS
HOWTH
HUCKSTER'S
HUDDLE
HUDDLING
HUMBLER
HUMID
HUMMING-SEA
HUMP

HUNCH
HUNDRED-
   THROATED
HUNDRED-YEAR-
   OLD
HUNGARY
HUNKERS
HUNTER-FRIEND
HUNTER-LOVER
HUNTING-CALL
HUNTING-SPEAR
HUNTING-SPEARS
HURLS
HURRIEDLY
HURRIES
HURTLE
HURTLING
HUSH-A-BYE
HUSH'D
HUSKY
HYDE
HYMNS
HYSTERICO-
   PASSIO
ICICLES
IDA'S
IDLER
IL
ILLUSION
ILLUSIONS
IMAGINATIONS
IMAGINES
IMAGININGS
IMITATE
IMITATED
IMITATION
IMMEDIATE
IMMENSITIES
IMMORTALS'
IMPART
IMPASSIONED
IMPATIENT
IMPERIOUS
IMPERMANENT
IMPLACABLE
IMPORTANT
IMPORTUNATE
IMPRISONED
IMPROVISATION
IMPROVISING
IMPULSE
IMPULSIVE
IMPURITIES
IMPURITY
INCANTATION
INCAPABLE
INCENDIARY
INCH
INCHY
INCIDENT
INCLEMENCY
INCLINE
INCOMPATIBLE
INCORRUPTIBLE
INCREASE
INCREASED

INCREASES
INCREASING
IND
INDIANS
INDIA'S
INDIGNATIO
INDIGNATION
INDIVIDUAL
INDOMITABLE
INDUSTRY
INEFFABLE
INEXTRICABLE
INFAMY
INFANTINE
INFIDEL
INFIRM
INFLUENCE
INGENIOUS
INGENUOUS
INGRATITUDE
INHABITANT
INHERITANCE
INISHMURRAY
INJURE
INJUSTICE
INLAND
INMOST
INN
INNKEEPER'S
INNUMEROUS
INSANE
INSATIABLE
INSEPARABLE
INSIPID
INSPIRED
INSTEP'S
INSTRUCTORS
INSTRUMENTS
INSUFFICIENT
INTELLECT'S
INTELLIGIBLE
INTEMPERANCE
INTEMPERATE
INTERMINABLE
INTERVENED
INTIMACY
INTOLERABLE
INTOXICANT
INTRICACY
INTRICATE
INTRIGUE
INTRODUCTION
INVER
INVULNERABLE
INWARDLY
IOLAN
IRISHRY
IRRATIONAL
IRREGULAR
IRVING
ISAIAH'S
ISOLATED
ISSUE
ISSUED
ITALY
ITCH
ITERATION

ITH
IVIED
IVY-COVERED
IVY'S
I-WIS
JACKASS
JADE
JAFFER
JAFFER'S
JAILBIRD
JAILOR
JAMMED
JAUNTING
JAY'S
JESSAMINE
JEST
JEWEL
JEWELLED
JEWELS
JEWEL-STONE
JIG
JILL
JINN
JOAN
JOE
JOHN'S
JOKE
JOKES
JOLLY
JOLT
JOSEPH
JOSEPH'S
JOURNEY-DULL
JOURNEYING
JOURNEY-MAN
JOVIAL
JUBILANT
JUGGLER
JUGGLERS
JUNCTURE
JUNES
JUNO
JUNO'S
JUPITER
JUSTICE
KATHLEEN
KAURI
KEATS
KEDRON
KEENED
KEENERS
KEENIN'
KENNEL
KERCHIEF
KERRY
KESTREL
KETTLEDRUM
KETTLEDRUMS
KETTLES
KEYS
KHAKI
KID
KIDRON
KID'S
KILBARNET
KILLS
KILTARTAN'S

KINDER
KINDLING
KINDRED'S
KINDS
KINGFISHERS
KING-
   REMEMBERING
KINSELLA'S
KINSMAN
KISSES
KITCHEN
KNEE-CAP
KNIGHTLY
KNOCKNASHEE
KNOCKS
KNOLL
KNOWER
KNOWEST
KNOWETH
KNOW'ST
KUSTA
KYLE-DORTHA
KYLE-NA-INO
KYTELER
LABOURED
LABOURER'S
LABURNUM
LACERATE
LACKEY
LADDER'S
LADDERS
LADEN
LADIES'
LAEN
LAGOON
LAIGHEN
LAKE-
   ENBOSOMED
LAKE-LULLED
LAKE-NURTURED
LAKES
LAMB
LAME-FOOTED
LAMENT
LAMP-CHIMNEY
LAMPLIGHT
LAMPS
LAND-OF-THE-
   TOWER
LANDOR
LANDOR'S
LAND'S
LANDSMEN
LAND-UNDER-
   WAVE
LANGUAGE
LANGUORS
LANTERN
LANTHORN
LAP
LAPIS-LAZULI
LAPO
LAPWING
LAPWINGS
LARCH-WOOD
LARDER
LARGELY

LARK
LARKS
LASHED
LASSES
LATCH
LATCHES
LATE-LOST
LATE-RISEN
LATTICE
LATTICED
LAUGH'D
LAUGHTER-LIPPED
LAUGHTER-LIT
LAUNCH
LAUREATE
LAURELLED
LAVERY
LAVISH
LAYS
LAZY
LEA
LEADERS
LEADERSHIP
LEADS
LEAF-CROWNED
LEAF-HID
LEAGUES
LEANED
LEANNESS
LEAPT
LEARN'D
LEARNS
LEATHER
LEATHER-COATED
LEAVE-TAKING
LECHING
LECTERN
LEG
LEGENDARY
LEMON-TINTED
LEND
LENGTHEN
LENGTHENING
LEOPARD-
   COLOURED
LEOPARDS
LESSON
LETHEAN
LET'ST
LEVEE
LEV'RET'S
LIAR
LIBATIONS
LIBERAL
LIBRARY
LICE
LICKED
LICKS
LIDLESS
LIED
LIETH
LIEUTENANT
LIFE-IN-DEATH
LIFE-KEY
LIFELESS
LIFETIME
'LIGHTED

1 (cont.)

LIGHT-
  ENDAPPLED
LIGHTENED
'LIGHTING
LIGHTLESS
LIGHTNESS
LIGHT-
  OBLITERATING
LIKED
LIKELIHOOD
LIKENESS
LILAC
LILY-BLANCHED
LIMBED
LIMESTONE
LIMP
LIMPED
LINED
LINEN-CARRIER
LINEN-CHEST
LINGERETH
LINGERINGS
LINK
LINKS
LINNET'S
LINNETS'
LIONEL
LIPPED
LIQUORICE
LISADILL
LISS
LISTENS
LISTLESS
LIST'NING
LITTER
LITTLE-LAND
LIVELY
LIVER
LIVERPOOL
LIVERY-STABLE
LIZARD
LOADS
LOADSTONE
LOAM
LOCK
LOCKE
LODGE
LOG-BOOK
LOGIC-
  CHOPPERS
LOIE
LOIN
LOITERING
LOLLING
LONG-ARMED
LONGEST
LONGEVITY
LONG-HAIRED
LONGHI
LONGINGS
LONG-LIMBED
LONG-LIVED
LONG-OARED
LONG-PLANNED
LONG-VISAGED
LONG-WARLESS

LOOMED
LOONY'D
LOOPED
LOOPS
LOOSE-LIPPED
LOOSELY
LOOSENS
LORD'S
LOUD-CRASHING
LOUNGING
LOUR
LOVE-DEW
LOVE-DREAMS
LOVE-LONGING
LOVELORN
LOVE-MAKING
LOVE-PLAY
LOVE-SICK
LOVE-STORY
LOVETH
LOVE-WORN
LOWERED
LOWING
LOWLIER
LOWLINESS
LOWLY
LOYAL
LUCKIER
LUGAIDH'S
LUGNAGALL
LUG-WORM
LUKA
LUKE
LULLING
LULLS
LULLY
LUMBERING
LUNGING
LURCHES
LURES
LURID
LURKS
LUSH
LUST
LUTE-THRONGED
LUXURIANT
LUXURY
LYNX'S
LYRIC
LYRICS
MA
MACBRIDE
MACCARTAN
MACDONAGH
MACDONAGH'S
MADAM
MADEST
MADGE'S
MADMAN'S
MADONNA
MAGAI
MAGH
MAGICIAN
MAGNANIMITIES
MAGNIFIED
MAGNIFY
MAGNITUDE

MAGNUS
MAHOGANY
MAHRAJAS
MAIDEN'S
MAIL'D
MAIMED
MAINLY
MAJESTIC
MAJOR
MAKE-UP
MALEDICTION
MALIGN
MALL
MALLET
MANACLE
MANAGED
MANAGEMENT
MANANAN'S
MANANNAN'S
MANCINI'S
MANGAN
MANIFOLD
MAN-KIND
MANLY
MANNA
MANNED
MANNERS
MANNION
MANNIONS
MAN-PICKER
MANSIONS
MANTEGNA'S
MANUSCRIPT
MANY-
  COLOURED
MANY-FOLDED
MANY-MINDED
MANY-
  PASTURED
MANY-PILLARED
MANY-
  SORROWED
MANY-TIMES-
  TROUBLED
MAPS
MARBLES
MARCO
MARGARET
MARGIN
MARIE
MARIGOLDS
MARJORIE
MARKET-PLACE
MARKETS
MARKIEWICZ
MARMALADE
MARRIAGE-DAY
MARRIAGES
MARRIAGE-SONG
MARROW-BONE
MARROWBONES
MARS
MARSHY
MART
MARTEN-CAT
MASCULINE
MASKER'S

MASONS
MASSACRE
MASSED
MASTERING
MASTER-WORK
MAST-HEAD
MATERNAL
MATHERS
MATTRESS
MAUD
MAURYA
MAURYA'S
MAXIMS
MAYOR
MAY-TREASURE
MCTAGGART
MEADOW-MICE
MEADOW-
  SAFFRONS
MEAGRE
MEASURELESS
MEASURER
MECHANICAL
MEDDLE
MEDDLING
MEDIAEVAL
MEDIAN
MEDIATION
MEDICABLE
MEDICINE
MEDIUM
MEDIUM'S
MEEK
MEETINGS
MEG
MELODIES
MEMORIAM
MENTAL
MENTIONED
MERCHANTS
MERGE
MERIDIAN
MESS
MESSENGER
METHINKS
METTLESOME
MIAU-D
MICHAELANGELO
MICHAEL'S
MICHELOZZO'S
MIDDAY
MID-DAY
MIDDLE-AGE
MIDDLE-AGES
MIDHIR
MIDNIGHT'S
MIDSUMMER
MIEN
MILCH
MILCH-COWS
MILKING
MILKING-PLACE
MILKING-SHED
MILK-PALE
MILLION-FOOTED
MILTON'S
MIMIC

MIMICKING
MINARET
MINDFUL
MINGLE
MINGLES
MINION
MINIONS
'MINISHED
MINISTER
MINISTERING
MINNOWED
MINOS
MINSTREL-WORD
MIRACLE-BRED
MIRACLE-
  WORKING
MIRROR-
  RESEMBLING
MIRRORS
MIRROR-SCALED
MISCALCULATE
MISCHIEVOUS
MISERABLE
MISERRIMUS
MISREPRESENT
MISS'D
MISSHAPEN
MISTAKE
MIST-COVERED
MIST-DROPS
MISTOOK
MIST-THREADS
MITCHEL'S
MOANING
MOB
MOBILE
MOCHARABUIEE
MOCKS
MODEL
MODISH
MOIDERED
MOIL
MOISTENED
MOISTURE
MOLE
MONK
MONKEY
MONK'S-HOOD
MONK'S-HOOD'S
MONTENEGRIN
MONTH
MONTH'S
MOODY
MOON-
  ACCURSED
MOONBEAMS
MOONEEN
MOON-
  LUMINOUS
MOONSHINE
MOON-STRUCK
MOON-WHITE
MOOR-COCKS
MOORED
MOOR-HEN
MOPING
MORALISE

1 (cont.)

MORALIST
MORALIZE
MORAL'S
MORNA'S
MORN-
  BEWILDERED
MORNS
MOSAIC
MOSCOW
MOTHERHOOD
MOTHER-OF-
  PEARL
MOTHER-WIT
MOTION
MOTIONED
MOTIONS
MOTLEY
MOTORS
MOULDING
MOUND'S
MOUNTAINOUS
MOUNTAIN-TOP
MOURNING
MOURTEEN
MOUSELIKE
MOUSE-LIKE
MOUSETAIL
MOVEMENTS
MOVIN'
MUCH-TOIL
MUCK
MUD
MUDDY
MUFFLED
MULE-BACK
MULTITUDINOUS
MUMMY-DEAD
MURDERER
MURDER'S
MURMURING'S
MUSES'
MUSINGLY
MYRRH
MYSTIC
MYTHOLOGICAL
MYTHOLOGIES
NAIL-PIERCED
NAISI
NAMING
NAPE
NARCISSUS
NARROWS
NATIONAL
NATURE'D
NEARLY
NEAT
NECESSITOUS
NECKLACE
NECK'S
NECKS
NEEDED
NEEDLES
NEEDLES'
NEEDLESS
NEIGH
NEIGHBOURLY

NEIGHBOUR'S
NEIGHBOURS'
NEIGHING
NESSA'S
NESTED
NESTLES
NETTED
NETTLES
NETTLESHIP'S
NEVER-ANXIOUS
NEVER-LIFTING
NEVER-
  SLUMBERING
NEW-BORN
NEW-COMER
NEW-FANGLED
NEW-HEALED
NEWT
NEWTON'S
NEW-TORN
NEW-WASHED
NIAM'S
NIETZSCHE
NIGHEST
NIGHT-
  COLOURED
NIGHT-DARK
NIGHT-GOWN
NIGHTINGALE
NIGHTINGALE'S
NIGHTJAR
NIGHT-MOTHS
NIGHT-TIDE
NIGHT-VESTED
NIGHT-WALKERS
NIGHT-WALKERS'
NIGHT-
  WANDERING
NINE-AND-FIFTY
NINETEEN-SEVEN
NINETEEN-
  THIRTEEN
NINETEEN-
  THIRTY-TWO
NINETEEN-
  TWENTY-NINE
NINETY
NINETY-FOUR
NOAH'S
NOBLY
NONCHALANCE
NONSENSICAL
NOOK
NO-ONE
NOONTIDE
NOON-TIDE
NORMANDY
NORTHUMBER-
  LAND
NOSTERS
NOSTRIL
NOSTRILS
NOTHINGS
NOTORIETY
NOTORIOUS
NOVELIST
NOVELS

NOVELTY
NOWISE
NOYES
NUNS
NURSE
NURSED
NUT
NYMPH
OAK-TREE
OARING
OATMEAL
OATMEAL-CHEST
OBEDIENCE
OBEYING
OBEYS
OBSCURITY
OBSERVANT
OBSTACLE
O'BYRNES
OCCURRED
O'DUFFY
ODYSSEUS
OEDIPUS
OEDIPUS'
O'ER-APPLED
O'ER-MUFFLED
O'ERWORN
OFFENDED
OFFERED
OFFERS
OFFICER
O'GRADY
O'HIGGINS'
OHONE
OILY
O'LEARY'S
OLDEN
OLIVE-TREE
OLIVE-TREES
OLLAVE
OLYMPIANS
ONE-ARMED
ONE-EYED
ONE-LEGGED
ONION
ONION-SELLERS
ONLIE
OOZY
OPEN-EYED
OPEN-
  HANDEDNESS
OPENIN'
OPENS
OPHELIA
OPINIONATED
OPINIONS
OPOPONAX
OPPOSITION
OPPRESSED
OPTIC
ORB
ORBIT
ORCHARD-
  CIRCLED
ORCHARDS
ORCHIL
ORIGINAL

ORION
ORMOLU
ORMONDES
ORNAMENTAL
OSAFUME
OSIER
OUGHT
OUNCE
OUSEL
OUTBALANCE
OUT-BURN
OUTCRIES
OUTCRY
OUTDANCED
OUTGREW
OUTLAWED
OUTLAWS
OUTLIVEST
OUT-LIVING
OUTRAN
OUTRIDDEN
OUT-RIDDEN
OUTRIGHT
OUTRODE
OUTRUN
OUT-SCREAMS
OUT-SPREAD
OUTWEIGH
OUTWEIGHED
OVEN
OVER-BOLD
OVERBURTHENED
OVERFLOW
OVER-LINGERED
OVERLOOKS
OVERMUCH
OVER-MUCH
OVER-NIMBLE
OVERPOWER
OVERSEA
OVER-SEA
OVER-SUBTLE
OVERTHROW
OVERTURNED
OWEN
OWLET'S
OWLETS
OX
PACES
PADDLED
PADDLER'S
PAGES
PAINTERS
PAINTS
PAIRC-NA-
  CARRAIG
PAIRC-NA-TARAV
PALATES
PALES
PALETTE
PALLOR
PALMER
PALMER'S
PALM-STEMS
PALTRY
PANE
PANEL

PANNIERED
PAN'S
PANSY'S
PANT
PANTHER-KITTENS
PARABLE
PARADE
PARADIGM
PARADISE'S
PARAGON
PARCHED
PARE
PARIS'
PARISH
PARNASSUS
PARNELLITE
PARTIAL
PARTICULARS
PARTLY
PARTY
PASSAGE
PASSAGES
PASSION-
  DIMMED
PASSION-DRIVEN
PASSIONED
PASTERN
PASTURED
PATCHED
PATCHING
PATE
PATRIOTS
PATS
PAUDEEN'S
PAUPER
PAVEMENTS
PAVEN
PAVLOVA'S
PAWNS
PAYMENTS
PEACE-MAKING
PEACHES
PEACOCKS
PEAHENS
PEA-HENS
PEALED
PEAR
PEAR-TREE
PEASANTRY
PEASANTS
PEBBLE
PEDANTIC
PEDANTRY
PEDDLED
PEDESTALLED
PEDLAR
PEEPING
PEG
PELEUS
PELTING
PENAL
PENETRATION
PENITENCE
PENITENTIAL
PENNIES
PENNON
PENSEROSO'S

1 (cont.)

PENSIVELY
PERCH
PERCHED
PERCHING
PERFECTED
PERFECTLY
PERFORM
PERFUME
PERILOUS
PERILS
PERISHING
PERJURER
PERJURER'S
PERMANENT
PERMIT
PERN
PERNE
PERNED
PERNELLA
PERPETUAL
PERSEUS
PERSONAE
PERSONS
PERTURB
PERU
PERVERSE
PESTLE
PETRONIUS
PETS
PEWS
PHARAOH'S
PHASE
PHILOSOPHER
PHILOSOPHERS
PHRASING
PICTURE-BOOK
PIEBALD
PIECE
PIECED
PIED
PIETY
PIKES
PILFERERS
PILLARLESS
PILLOWS
PINCHES
PINCHING
PINE-WOOD
PINION
PINNACLE
PIN'S
PISTOL
PISTOLS
PITCH-AND-TOSS
PITCHES
PITRI'S
PITTANCE
PITY-CRAZED
PITYIN'
PLACID-BROWED
PLAGUED
PLAINLY
PLAIN'S
PLANE
PLANES
PLANNING

PLANS
PLANTS
PLASHES
PLASHY
PLATE
PLATONISTS
PLAUSIBLE
PLAUTUS
PLAY-BOY
PLAYFUL
PLEASES
PLEASING
PLEDGE
PLENTIFUL
PLENTY'S
PLODDED
PLOTINUS'
PLOUGHING
PLOUGHLAND
PLOUGHSHARE
PLOVER'S
PLOVERS
PLUCKS
PLUMAGE
PLUME
PLUMELESS
PLUNDERING
PLUNGES
PLUNGING
PLUTARCH
PLUTO
POCKET
PODS
POIGNANT
POINTING
POINTS
POISED
POISONOUS
POKED
POLE-AXE
POLECAT
POLES
POLE-STAR
POLITICAL
POLITICIAN
POLITICIANS
POMP
PONDERABLE
PONDERS
PONIES
PONY
POORER
POPE'S
POPLAR-TREES
POPPY-HUNG
POPULOUS
PORTAL
PORTALS
PORTER
PORTER-
 DRINKERS'
PORTER'S
PORTIONING
PORTIONS
PORTLY
POSE
POSEIDON

POSSESSED
POSSESSION
POSSIBLE
POSTS
POT-BELLIED
POT-HOUSE
POTION'S
POTTERY
POUNDED
POWDER
POWERLESS
PRACTICE
PRACTISE
PRACTISED
PRAGMATICAL
PRANCE
PRAYER-BOOK
PRAYETH
PRAYING
PRECEDENTS
PRECIPICE
PRECISION
PREFERRED
PREFERS
PRELUDE
PREPARATION
PREPOSTEROUS
PRESSING
PRETENDING
PREVAIL
PRIAM
PRICELESS
PRIEST'S
PRIESTS
PRIMORDIAL
PRIMUM
PRINCE'S
PRINCIPLES
PRINTED
PRISONER
PRISONERS
PRISONS
PRIVACY
PRIVET
PROCESSIONS
PRODIGIES
PRODUCTS
PROFANE
PROFESSOR
PROFFERING
PROFIT
PROLONG
PROMINENT
PROMISE-
 BREAKER
PROPERTIUS
PROPINQUITY
PROPS
PROSAIC
PROSPER
PROTECTED
PROTEST
PROTEUS
PROUDER
PROUDEST
PROUDLY
PRUDENT

PUBERTY
PUBLIC-HOUSE
PUDDLE
PUDDLE-WATER
PUFF
PUFF-BALLS
PULSE
PULSING
PUMMELLED
PUMMELLING
PUNY
PUPILS
PUPPY
PURCHASED
PUREBRED
PURE-BRED
PURIFIED
PURSES
PURSUE
PURSUES
PUTTING
QUARRIED
QUARRY
QUATRAINS
QUAY
QUENCHED
QUERN
QUESTIONS
QUESTS
QUICKLIME
QUICK-LIME
QUIET-EYED
QUIET'S
QUINTO-CENTO
QUIRE
QUIRES
QUITE
QUOTE
RABBIT-HOLE
RACE-COURSE
RACE-COURSES
RACHLIN
RACK
RADDLING
RADICAL
RAFTERY'S
RAG-AND-BONE
RAGE-DRIVEN
RAGE-HUNGRY
RAGE-TORMENTED
RAILING
RAIN-BEATEN
RAISEST
RAISING
RAJA'S
RAJAS
RAMBLE
RAMBLED
RAMBLES
RAMMED
RANCOROUS
RANDY
RANG
RANGED
RANGER
RANKED
RANKING

RANN
RANTED
RANT'S
RAPHAEL
RAPIER
RASCALLY
RAT
RATIONAL
RAVEL
RAVEN-COVERED
RAYLESS
RAYMOND
REACHED
REACHES
READIER
READING-BOOKS
REAL
REALISTS
REALM
REAP
REAPING-HOOK
REBEL
REBELLION
RECALLED
RECEDE
RECEDING
RECEIVES
RECENT
RECKLESS
RECKON
RECLINES
RECOGNIZE
RECOLLECT
RECONCILIATION
RECORD
RECORDS
RECOVERED
RECOVERING
RECOVERS
RECUR
REDDENS
REDDEST
RED-HEAD
RED-HEADED
REED-THROATED
REEL
REELING
REFLECTION
REFLECTIONS
REFORM
REFORMER
REGARDLESS
REGENT
REGRET
REIGN
REIGNED
RELEASE
RELIED
RELIEF
RELIVE
RE-LIVE
RELY
REMAINED
REMBRANDT
REMEMBEREST
REMINDED
RENDS

RENOUNCE	R.I.P.	RUFFLED	SCHOOLMASTERS	SEMELE'S
RENOUNCING	RIPENED	RUFFLES	SCHOOLROOM	SENSELESS
RENYI'S	RIPENING	RULETH	SCONCE	SENSES
REPENTANCE	RIPPED	RUMBLE	SCOOPED	SENSUAL
REPINING	RISEN	RUMOROUS	SCORES	SENSUALITY
REPRISALS	RITES	RUNABOUT	SCORNIN'	SENSUOUS
REPUTATION	RIVETED	RUNNERS	SCOT-FREE	SENTIMENTALIST
REPUTE	RIVULET'S	RURY'S	SCOURING	SENTINELS
RESEMBLE	RIVULETS	RUSSIA	SCOWL	SENTRIES
RESEMBLING	ROAD-METAL	RUSTLES	SCRATCH	SEPTEMBER
RESERVED	ROADSIDE	RUTHLESS	SCULLION	SERAPHS
RESIGNED	ROAD-SIDE	SACKED	SCULPTOR	SERPENT-TAILS
RESINOUS	ROARER	SADDEN	SCYTHE	SERVANT'S
RESOUNDED	ROARS	SADDLEBOW	SEA-BORN	SERVES
RESOUNDING	ROASTING	SADDLE-BOW	SEA-COVERED	SERVING-MAID
RESOUNDS	ROBBED	SADDLED	SEA-DASHED	SETTLES
RESOURCE	ROBBER	SADDLE-GIRTH	SEAFARER	SEVERAL
RESPECT	ROBED	SAD'S	SEAFARERS	SEWED
RESPECTABLE	ROCK-BORN	SAEVA	SEA-FOAM	SHADED
RESPONSIBILITIES	ROCK-BRED	SAFER	SEA-FROTH	SHADOWED
RESPONSIBILITY	ROCK-NURTURED	SAILOR'S	SEA-GOD	SHADOWING
RESTLESS-FOOTED	ROCK'S	SAINTED	SEA-GOD'S	SHADOWLESS
RESTLESSNESS	ROCK-	SAINT'S	SEA-HORSES	SHADOW-PLACE
RESTORED	WANDERING	SAKE'S	SEALING	SHAGGY
RESTRAINING	ROGUES	SALAD	SEAMEW	SHAKESPEAREAN
RESULTS	ROLL'D	SALAMIS	SEA-MEW	SHALLOP
RESUME	ROMANTICS	SALE	SEA-NYMPHS	SHALLOWING
RE-SUNG	ROMP	SALIVA	SEARCHED	SHAMED
RETIRING	ROOFLESS	SALMON-FALLS	SEA-RIDER	SHAMELESS
RETURNS	ROOF-LEVELLING	SALMON-	SEA-ROTTED	SHAMMING
REVELATION	ROOFS	SHOALED	SEAS'	SHANWALLA
REVERBERATED	ROOF-TIMBERS	SALTED	SEA-SANDS	SHAN-WALLA
REVERE	ROOF-TREES	SALT-FLAKES	SEA-SHELLS	SHAPELESS
REVERENT	ROOK	SALVATION	SEASHINE	SHARES
REVERSAL	ROOK-	SAMUEL	SEA-SHINE	SHATTER
RE-VISITED	DELIGHTING	SAN	SEA-STARVED	SHAUL
REWARDED	ROOKS	SANDALLED	SEA-STREWN	SHAVINGS
REWARDING	ROOMFUL	SANDALWOOD	SEA-TOST	SHAWE-TAYLOR
REWARDS	ROPE'S	SANDED	SEAWAYS	SHEAF
REWORDING	ROPES	SANDY	SEAWEED	SHEEN
REWRITTEN	ROSA	SANDYMOUNT	SEA-WEED	SHEEP-GUIDING
RE-WRITTEN	ROSE-BREATH	SAPLINGS	SEAWEED-	SHEETS
RHADAMANTHUS	ROSE'S	SAPPHO'S	COVERED	SHELF
RHAPSODY	ROSE-TREE	SAPPING	SEA-WEEDY	SHELLEY
RHETORICIAN	ROSSES	SAPPY	SEA-WORLD	SHELLEY'S
RHINOCEROS	ROT	SARDONYX	SECOND-BEST	SHELL'S
RHYMER	ROTE	SATIN	SECRET'S	SHEPHERD-BOY
RHYMER'S	ROTS	SATURATED	SECT	SHEPHERD'S
RHYTHM	ROTTED	SATURNIAN	SECTION	SHIFTED
RIB	ROUGE	SATURNINE	SEDGY	SHIFTS
RIBBON	ROUNDING	SATYRS	SEED-PODS	SHININ'
RICHNESS	ROUNDLY	SAVAGELY	SEEKING	SHIPBOARD
RICK	ROVED	SAVES	SEEMING	SHIVERS
RIDDLED	ROWAN	SAWDUST	SEER	SHOREWARD
RIDES	ROWBOAT	SCAFFOLDING	SEIZE	SHORE-WEEDS
RIDICULOUS	ROW-BOAT	SCALED	SELDOM	SHORN
RIGHTFUL	ROWED	SCANAVIN	SELECTED	SHORTEN
RIGHT-TAUGHT	ROWERS'	SCARE	SELF-ACCUSED	SHOULDER-HIGH
RILL	ROWS	SCARECROW	SELF-	SHOVE
RILLS	ROXBOROUGH	SCARES	AFFRIGHTING	SHOWERED
RIME	ROYAL	SCARRED	SELF-APPEASING	SHOWY
RINGDOVE'S	ROYSTERER	SCENERY	SELF-DELIGHT	SHUDDERED
RING-DOVE'S	RUBBED	SCENES	SELFSAME	SHUFFLED
RINGER	RUBBING	SCENT	SELF-SOWN	SHUFFLING
RINSING	RUBIES	SCENTS	SELLERS	SHUN
RINSING-POOL	RUEFUL	SCHOLARLY	SELLING	SHUTTLE
	RUFFIAN'S	SCHOOLCHILDREN	SEMBLANCE	SIBYLLINE

1 (cont.)

SIBYL'S
SICILIAN
SICKEN
SICKENING
SIDLE
SIDLED
SIDLES
SIDNEY
SIEVE
SIGNATURE
SILL
SILVER-PROUD
SILVER-
SANDALLED
SILVER-SHOED
SINAI'S
SINBAD
SINFULLY
SINGE
SINGETH
SINGING-
MASTERS
SINGLED
SINS
SISTERHOOD
SISTER'S
SIX-AND-TWENTY
SIXES
SIXTY-YEAR-OLD
SKELETON-GAUNT
SKELPING
SKIRT
SKY'S
SLAB
SLANDER
SLANDERED
SLATE
SLATES
SLAUGHTERED
SLAY
SLEEPILY
SLEEPING-ROOM
SLEEP'S
SLEEPY-HEADED
SLEIVEENS
SLEUTH
SLEUTH-HOUNDS
SLIDES
SLIGHT
SLIM
SLIMY
SLINGERS
SLINGS
SLIPPED
SLIPPER
SLIPPERED
SLOPES
SLOUCHES
SLOW-FOOTING
SLOW-MUFFLED
SLUMBER-BOUND
SLUMBERERS
SLUT
SLY
SMARAGDINE
SMART

SMELLED
SMELT
SMITH
SMOOTHS
SMOTHER
SMOULDERING
SMUGGLER
SNAKES
SNAP
SNAPS
SNATCHED
SNATCHES
SNICKED
SNIFF
SNORE
SNOWFLAKES
SNOW-FLAKES
SOBS
SOCIAL
SOCK
SOCKS
SODS
SOFTENING
SOFTEST
SOFT-SHINING
SOILED
SOLDERED
SOLEMN-EYED
SOLSTICE
SOMEHOW
SOMETIME
SOMEWHAT
SON'S
SOOT
SOOTHE
SOOTHED
SORACA
SORDID
SORREL-COVERED
SORRELS
SORROWING
SORROWINGS
SOURS
SOUTHWARD
SPAN
SPANISH
SPANS
SPARKLING
SPARKS
SPARROW-CHIRP
SPARS
SPARTAN
SPASM
SPAWNING
SPEAKERS
SPEAR-GRASS
SPEARHEAD'S
SPEAR-HEAD'S
SPEARSHAFT
SPEAR-SHAFT
SPECTRAL
SPEECHLESS
SPEEDS
SPELL-BOUND
SPENSER
SPHINX
SPICE-ISLES

SPIDER
SPIDERS
SPIES
SPILLED
SPILLS
SPINDLE
SPINDLES
SPINNER
SPINNING-JENNY
SPINNING-TOP
SPIRAL
SPIRIT-THINGS
SPIRITUAL
SPIRITUALISED
SPIRITUS
SPLASH
SPLEEN
SPLIT
SPLITS
SPOIL
SPOILT
SPONTANEOUS
SPORTS
SPOTS
SPOTTED
SPRAY-DABBLED
SPRIGHTS
SPRINGING
SPRINGS
SPRITES
SPUME
SPYING
SQUANDERER
SQUARED
SQUEAKY
SQUIRREL-BROWN
SQUIRREL'S
SQUIRRELS
STABLE-KEEPER
STABLES
STAFFORD
STAGES
STAG'S
STAID
STAINING
STAINS
STAKES
STALKED
STALKS
STALL
STAMMERING
STAMP
STAMPER
STANDEST
STANDISH
STAR-BANE
STAR-ENVIOUS
STARE'S
STAR-FIRES
STAR-FLAME
STAR-FOUGHT
STAR-
GLIMMERING
STARLING
STARN
STARRED
STAR-

SHUDDERING
STAR-TAUGHT
STARTING-POST
STAR-TROD
STARTS
STARVE
STATESMAN'S
STATESMEN
STATISTICS
STATUARY
STATUED
STAVE
STEAD
STEADIED
STEAL
STEALTH
STEALTHILY
STEAM
STEAMSHIP
STEEL-BLUE
STEEPLE
STEERING-OAR
STEERS
STEP
STEPPED
STEPPING
STILLY
STILT-JACK
STIRLESS
STIRRING
STOLES
STONE-GREY
STONY-HEARTED
STONY-STILL
STOREYS
STORMBEATEN
STORM-BITTEN
STORM-BROKEN
STORM-
SCATTERED
STORM-TOSSED
STOUT
STRADDLE
STRADDLING
STRAFFORD
STRAIGHTEN
STRAINS
STRAIT
STRANGERS
STRANGLE
STRAW-DEATH
STRAW-PALE
STRAWS
STRAYETH
STREAMING
STREET-CORNERS
STRETCHES
STREWING
STRIP
STRIPPED
STRIPS
STRIVE
STRIVING
STROKES
STRONGEST
STRONGLY
STROVE

STRUCKEN
STRUGGLES
STRUTS
STRUTTING
STUB
STUBBORN
STUBBORN-
HEARTED
STUDENT
STUDENT'S
STUDENTS
STUDIES
STUDIO
STUMP
STUMPIER
STUMPS
STUPEFIED
STURDIER
STURDY
SUBMISSIVE
SUBSCRIPTION
SUBTILE
SUBTLE-SOULED
SUBTLEST
SUCKLE
SUFFERED
SUGGESTED
SUIT
SUITED
SULPHUROUS
SUMMERED
SUMMER-TIME
SUMPTUOUS
SUNDAY
SUN-DRY
SUNFLOWERS
SUN-FLUSHED
SUN-FRECKLED
SUNLESS
SUNNIER
SUNSICK
SUN-SMITTEN
SUPER-HUMAN
SUPERMAN
SUPERSESSION
SUPINE
SUPPLER
SUPPLIANT
SUPPORTING
SUPPOSE
SUPREME
SURETY
SURF
SURFACE
SURMISE
SURMOUNT
SURMOUNTS
SURROUNDED
SWADDLING
SWADDLING-
CLOTHES
SWALLOW
SWALLOW'S
SWAN'S
SWARD
SWARMS
SWAYS

1 (cont.)
SWEARS
SWEETENED
SWEETENS
SWEETHEARTS'
SWEETSHOP
SWEET-SHOP
SWEET-
  SOUNDING
SWEET-TONGUED
SWELLING
SWERVED
SWIFTEST
SWIMS
SWIRLED
SWISH
SWOONING
SWOOPS
SWOP
SWORD-BLUE
SWORD-POINT
SWORD'S
SWORDSMAN
SWORD-STROKES
SYMBOLIC
SYMBOLICAL
SYMBOLISE
SYMPATHY
SYSTEM
TABLET
TABLE-TOP
TABORS
TAFFRAIL
TAFFREL
TALE'S
TALMA
TANGLING
TAP
TAPER
TAPPING
TARDY
TARGETED
TARN
TARPAULIN
TAR-WATER
TASK
TASK'S
TASKS
TATTER
TAUT
TAYLOR
TE
TEAR-DROP
TEARDROPS
TEARING
TEASE
TEASING
TEMPESTS
TEMPESTUOUS
TEMPTATION
TENANTS
TENDERLY
TENSE
TENT-POLE
TERESA
TERRACES
TERRIFYING

TERROR'S
TERROR-
  STRUCKEN
TESTY
THAMES
THANK
THANKED
THEBAID
THEOLOGY
THEREBY
THERNOT
THERNOT'S
THETIS
THETIS'
THEWS
THICKENED
THICKENS
THICKER
THIEVE
THIGHED
THINKIN'
THIRSTING
THIRTEENTH
THONG
THOOR
THOROUGH-BRED
THOROUGHFARES
THOUGHTED
THOUGHT'S
THRALLS
THRASH
THREAD-BARE
THREADED
THREAT
THREEFOLD
THREE-FOLD
THREE-LEGGED
THREE-QUARTER
THREE-ROCK
THREESCORE
THREE-SIX
THRESHED
THRESHING
THRESHING-PLACE
THRESHOLDS
THRIVES
THRONGED
THROUGHOUT
THRUSTING
THUMBS
THUMPS
THUNDER-BALL
THUNDERBOLT
THUNDER-CLAP
THUNDERING
THUNDERSTONES
THUNDER-STONES
TIDE'S
TIGHTEN
'TILL
TILLER
TIMIDLY
TIMON
TIMOR
TINCTURE
TINKLING
TINSEL

TINT
TIPS
TIPTOE
TIRARAGH
TIRELESS
TITAN
TITANS
TITTLE
TOADS
TOASTING
TOKEN
TOLLING
TOMORROW
TONGUE'S
TO-NIGHT
TOOTHLESS
TOPERS
TOPPLED
TOPPLES
TOPPLING
TORMENTED
TORQUE
TORTOISESHELL
TORTURER
TOST
TOTAL
TOTTERING
TOTTERS
TOUCHES
TOUT
TOWARD
TOWER'S
TOWER-TOP
TOWERY
TOWNS
TRACES
TRADERS
TRADITIONAL
TRAILS
TRAIN
TRAITOR'S
TRAMPLE
TRANSFIGURING
TRANSFORMED
TRANSLUNAR
TRANSPARENT
TRAP
TRASH
TRAVAIL
TRAVEL
TRAVEL-WEARIED
TREADMILL
TREASONS
TREE-WRAPT
TREFOIL
TRESTLES
TRIAL
TRIBE
TRIBES
TRIBESMAN
TRIBUTE
TRICKLING
TRICOLOUR
TRIES
TRIM
TRINE
TRIP

TRISTRAM
TROOPING
TROPHIED
TROPIC
TROTTED
TROUBLING
TROUP
TROUSERS
TRULY
TRUMPETER
TRUMPETERS
TRUMPETING
TRUMPETS
TRUMPET-
  TWISTED
TRUNDLED
TRUNK
TRUTH'S
TUCKED
TUGGED
TULIPS
TULLY'S
TUMBLE
TUMULTUOUS-
  FOOTED
TUNE'S
TURBANED
TURK
TURKEY
TURNIN'
TUUS
TWANGING
TWELVE-HOURED
TWELVE-MONTH
TWENTIES
TWIG
TWIN-BORN
TWINE
TWINED
TWIST
'TWIST
TWO-HORSED
TYMPAN
TYRANNY
TYRANT
TYRANTS
UDDERS
UGLINESS
ULALU
ULULU
UNAFRAID
UNAGEING
UNASSAILABLE
UNAVAILING
UNBAFFLED
UNBENT
UNBLEMISHED
UNBLESSED
UNBLEST
UNBORN
UNBROKEN
UNCEASING
UNCHAINABLE
UNCHANGEABLE
UNCHANGED
UNCHRISTENED
UNCIVIL

UNCLES
UNCLOUDED
UNCOILED
UNCOMPOSITE
UNCONTROLLABLE
UNCOUNTED
UNDECAYED
UNDERTOOK
UNDREAMT
UNDULANT
UNEMPTIED
UNENDING
UNEVEN
UNFAERY
UN-FAERY
UNFALTERING
UNFASHIONABLE
UNFELT
UNFOLD
UNFOLDING
UNFOLDS
UNFOREKNOWN
UNFORGOTTEN
UNFORMED
UNFURLED
UNGLORIOUS
UNGOVERNABLE
UNGOVERNED
UNHAPPY
UNHAUNTED
UNHEARD-OF
UNHOOKED
UNIFORM
UNINHABITED
UNINTELLIGIBLE
UNISON
UNIVERSE
UNIVERSE'S
UNIVERSITY
UN-LABOURING
UNLACE
UNLANGUID
UNLATCHED
UNLAUGHING
UNLEARNED
UNLETTERED
UNLOCKED
UNLOCKS
UNLOOSE
UNLOVED
UNMANNED
UNMANNERLY
UNMEASURED
UNMINDFUL
UNMIXED
UN-MIXED
UNMOVED
UNMOVING
UNNECESSARY
UNPACKS
UNPASSING
UNPEOPLED
UNPERSUADABLE
UNPERTURBED
UNPRUNED
UNPUBLISHED
UNPURGED

UNQUENCHABLE
UNREALITY
UNRECKONABLE
UNREPENTING
UNREPINING
UNREPROVED
UNREQUITED
UNREST
UNRESTING
UNROLLS
UNSEARCHABLE
UNSEEING
UNSERVICEABLE
UNSHAKEN
UNSHAPELY
UNSHELTERED
UNSHUT
UNSHUTTERED
UNSOUGHT
UNSPOILED
UNSPOTTED
UNSTEADY
UNSTITCHING
UNSUBDUABLE
UNTIRING
UNTOUCHED
UNTUNED
UNUSED
UNVISITED
UNWEARY
UNWORTHY
UNWRAP
UPHELD
UPHOLSTERIES
UPLIFT
UPPERMOST
UP-RAISED
UPROOTED
UPROOTING
UPSPRINGING
UPTURNED
URBINO'S
USHEEN'S
USNA'S
USURY
UTHER'S
UTOPIA
UTTERED
UTTERMOST
VACILLATION
VAGUELY
VAINGLORIOUS
VAIN-GLORIOUS
VALOUR
VAMPIRES
VANISHING
VANITY'S
VANS
VAPOUR-HID
VAPOUR-
  TURBANED
VARYING
VASSALS
VASTY
VAT
VATS

VEGETATIVE
VEHEMENT
VEILED
VEIN
VEINED
VENGENCE
VERDANT
VERONESE
VERONICA'S
VESSEL
VESTITURE
VICTIM
VIE
VIEWLESS
VILE
VILLAGES
VINCI'S
VINEGAR-HEAVY
VIOLETS
VIRGINAL
VISAGED
VISIBLE
VISIONARIES
VISIONS
VISIT
VISITS
VIVIEN
VIZIR
VOICED
VOTE
VOWED
VOYAGE
VOYAGES
WADDING'S
WADES
WAGED
WAGER
WAGGED
WAGGONS
WAGON
WAGONETTE
WAGONS
WAGON-WHEEL
WAIF
WAILS
WAITING-MAID
WAITING-MAIDS
WAKENING
WAKENS
WALLED
WANDERER'S
WANDERING-
  WITTED
WANES
WANTED
WANTING
WARDER
WAR-LADEN
WARLESS
WARMER
WAR-RAGE
WAR-SONGS
WARTY
WARWARD
WAR-WEARY
WASHES
WASP

WASSAILS
WASTEFUL
WASTES
WATCH-TOWER
WATER-COURSE
WATERED
WATER-FLOWERS
WATERHEN
WATER-LILY
WATERPROOF
WATER-RATS
WATERS'
WATER-SERPENT
WATTLE
WATTLED
WAVER
WAVE-RUSTED
WAVES'
WAVETH
WAVE-WORN
WAX
WAXEN
WAXING
WEAKENED
WEALTHY
WEARISOME
WEARY-
  HEARTED
WEARYING
WEAVER
WEAVES
WEDDED
WEDDING
WEEDING
WEEDS
WEEDY
WEEK
WEIRS
WELCOMER
WELCOMING
WELFARE
WELL-A-DAY
WELLESLEY
WELL-GROOMED
WELLING
WELLKNOWN
WELL-KNOWN
WELLSIDE
WELL-SIDE
WELL-SIDES
WENCH-
  WISDOM'S
WEND
WHARF
WHARVES
WHEAT-EAR
WHEATEN
WHEELED
WHEELING
WHEREAS
WHEREAT
WHEREIN
WHERETHROUGH
WHIG
WHIM'S
WHIMS
WHINNIED

WHINNY
WHINNYING
WHIRL'D
WHIRLWIND
WHIRR
WHISPERER
WHISTLE
WHISTLING
WHITEBEARD
WHITE-HORNED
WHITES
WHITEST
WHITETHORN
WHIZZED
WHOLE-MAD
WHORL
WICKS
WIDE-EYED
WIDENING
WIDE-OPEN
WIDE-WATERING
WIDTH
WIFELESS
WIGHT
WILDEST
WILDS
WILD-
  STRAWBERRY
WILFUL
WILLED
WILLOW-
  BORDERED
WILLOW-GLADE
WIND-BROKEN
WINDINGS
WINDLE-STRAWS
WINDOWED
WINDOW-GLASS
WINDOW-LEDGE
WINDOWLESS
WINDOW'S
WINDOW-SILL
WINDWARD
WINE-BREATH
WINE-
  DRENCHED
WINE-STAINED
WINE-VAT
WINKING
WINNING
WINS
WINTER-TIME
WIRE-JOINTED
WISE-TONGUED
WITCHERY
WITHHOLDS
WITHSTOOD
WITNESSED
WIT'S
WITTED
WIZARDRY
WIZEN
WIZENED
WOE-BEGONE
WOES
WOLF-BREEDING
WOMANHOOD

WOMANKIND
WOMAN-KIND
WOMEN'S
WOMEN-
  SLINGERS
WONDERED
WONDERFULLY
WONTED
WOODMAN
WOODMAN'S
WOOD-
  NURTURED
WOOD-OF-
  WONDERS
WOOD-PECKER
WOODPECKER'S
WOOD-
  RHAPSODISTS
WOODS'
WOODWAYS
WOOD-WOMAN
WOODWORK
WOOD-WORK
WOOED
WOOING
WOOLLY
WOOS
WORDINESS
WORDLESS
WORKMAN
WORLD-
  BESOTTED
WORLD-
  FORGOTTEN
WORLD-OLD
WORLD-
  TRANSFORMING
WORLD-
  TROUBLING
WORLDWIDE
WORLD-WIDE
WORTHY'S
WOUND'S
WRACKED
WREN
WRESTLED
WRETCHED
WRETCHEDLY
WRETCHEDNESS
WRETCHES
WRIGGLING
WRING
WRONGED
WRONGING
YAWNS
YEAR'S
YELLED
YELLING
YELLOW-EYED
YELPING
YESTERNIGHT
YEW-TREE
YOLK
YONDER'S
ZEPPELIN
ZIGZAG
ZIG-ZAG